Mergent's

HANDBOOK OF
COMMON STOCKS

2013 Spring

MERGENT

INTRODUCTION

Mergent's Handbook of Common Stocks provides quick and easy access to basic financial and business information on more than 900 stocks that are included in the Russell 1000, S&P 500, S&P 400 and Mergent's Dividend Achievers. The Tab Section provides one-line information on New York Stock Exchange companies.

The price charts, statistics, and analyses are presented in a format that provides the investor with the necessary perspective for acting on investment advice or suggestions. It also affords investors the opportunity to make investment decisions on their own.

Statistics and analyses are revised quarterly. Every effort is made to secure the most current operating results and dividend information available. In the case of year-end results, preliminary results are shown and analyzed as they are received. Full statistical presentations of annual report information are shown in the following edition. The schedule below describes the publication dates and company reporting periods usually covered in each edition.

The Winter Edition (published in January) covers quarterly reports and preliminary annual reports through September 30.

The Spring Edition (published in April) covers quarterly reports and preliminary annual reports through December 31.

The Summer Edition (published in July) covers quarterly reports and preliminary annual reports through March 31.

The Fall Edition (published in October) covers quarterly reports and preliminary annual reports through June 30.

Note: For various reasons, some companies may not report in time to meet our publication deadlines. Company reports received close to press time are shown in the Addenda. The remainder of late reports are published and analyzed in the next edition of the Handbook.

The special section on these opening pages contains a number of features, including a guide on how to use this book, a classification of companies by their major line of business based on their NAIC code, outstanding stock price movements by company, plus long-term charts on popular stock market averages. The Addenda provide the latest developments available just prior to publication but after the company reports have been completed.

TABLE OF CONTENTS

Page

HOW TO USE THIS BOOK... 4a

SPECIAL FEATURES

CHARTS

ADDENDA

COMPANY REPORTS

3a

HOW TO USE THIS BOOK

The presentation of historical data and analytical comments provides the answers to four basic questions for each company:

1. What does the company do? (See G.)
2. How has it done in the past? (See B, J.)
3. How is it doing now? (See C, D, H.)
4. How will it fare in the future? (See I.)

A. CAPSULE STOCK INFORMATION shows where the stock is traded and its symbol, a recent price and price/earnings ratio, plus the yield afforded by the indicated dividend based on a recent price. The indicated dividend is the current annualized dividend based on the most recent price. Some companies are designated as Dividend Achievers. Dividend Achievers have, by *Mergent's* criteria, increased their cash dividend payments for at least ten consecutive years, adjusting for splits. The number of years of consecutive increases is given for each Dividend Achiever.

B. LONG-TERM PRICE CHART illustrates the pattern of monthly stock price movements, fully adjusted for stock dividends and splits. The chart points out the degree of volatility in the price movement of the company's stock and what its long-term trend has been. It also shows how it has performed long-term relative to an initial investment in the S&P 500 Index equal to the price of the company's stock at the beginning of the period shown in the price chart. It indicates areas of price support and resistance, plus other technical points to be considered by the investor. The bars at the base of the long-term price chart indicate the monthly trading volume. Monthly trading volume offers the individual an opportunity to recognize at what periods stock accumulation occurs and what percent of a company's outstanding shares are traded.

PRICE SCORES – Above each company's price/volume chart are its *Mergent's Price Scores*. These are basic measures of the stock's performance. Each stock is measured against the New York Stock Exchange Composite Index.

A score of 100 indicates that the stock did as well as the New York Stock Exchange Composite Index during the time period. A score of less than 100 means that the stock did not do as well; a score of more than 100 means that the stock outperformed the NYSE Composite Index. All stock prices are adjusted for splits and stock dividends. The time periods measured for each company conclude with the date of the recent price shown in the top line of each company's profile.

The *7 YEAR PRICE SCORE* mirrors the common stock's price growth over the previous seven years. The higher the price score, the better the relative performance. It is based on the ratio of the latest 12-month average price to the current seven-year average. This ratio is then indexed against the same ratio for the market as a whole (the New York Stock Exchange Composite Index), which is taken as 100.

The *12 MONTH PRICE SCORE* is a similar measurement but for a shorter period of time. It is based on the ratio of the latest two-month average price to the current 12-month average. As was done for the Long-Term Price Score, this ratio is also indexed to the same ratio for the market as a whole.

C. INTERIM EARNINGS (Per Share) – Figures are reported after the effect of extraordinary items, discontinued operations and cumulative effects of accounting changes. Each figure is for the quarterly period indicated. These figures are essentially as reported by the company, although all figures are adjusted for all stock dividends and splits.

ILLUSTRATIVE INC.

Exchange	**A**	Symbol	Price	52Wk Range	Yield	P/E	Div Achiever
NYS		ABBB	$35.32 (3/28/2013)	35.32-28.47	1.59	9.49	40 Years

*7 Year Price Score 109.61 *NYSE Composite Index=100   *12 Month Price Score 99.85

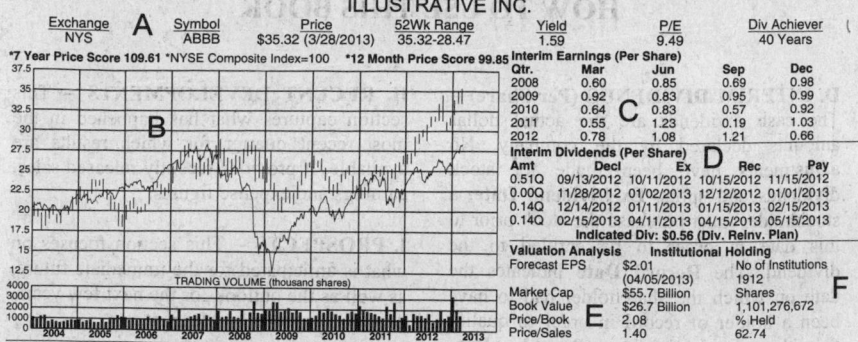

Interim Earnings (Per Share)

Qtr.	Mar	Jun	Sep	Dec
2008	0.60	0.85	0.69	0.98
2009	0.92	0.83	0.95	0.99
2010	0.64	0.83	0.57	0.92
2011	0.55	1.23	0.19	1.03
2012	0.78	1.08	1.21	0.66

C

Interim Dividends (Per Share) **D**

Amt	Decl	Ex	Rec	Pay
0.51Q	09/13/2012	10/11/2012	10/15/2012	11/15/2012
0.00Q	11/28/2012	01/02/2013	12/12/2012	01/01/2013
0.14Q	12/14/2012	01/11/2013	01/15/2013	02/15/2013
0.14Q	02/15/2013	04/11/2013	04/15/2013	05/15/2013

Indicated Div: $0.56 (Div. Reinv. Plan)

Valuation Analysis   Institutional Holding **F**

Forecast EPS	$2.01	No of Institutions
	(04/05/2013)	1912
Market Cap	$55.7 Billion	Shares
Book Value	$26.7 Billion	1,101,276,672
Price/Book	2.08	% Held
Price/Sales	1.40	62.74

E

TRADING VOLUME (thousand shares)

B

Business Summary: Medical Instruments & Equipment (MIC: 4.3.1 SIC: 3841 NAIC: 339112) **G**

illustrative Inc. is engaged in the discovery, development, manufacture, and sale of health care products. Co.'s reportable segments include: Established Pharmaceutical Products, which includes a line of branded generic pharmaceutical products; Nutritional Products, which includes a line of adult and pediatric nutritional products; Diagnostic Products, which includes diagnostic systems and tests for blood banks, hospitals, commercial laboratories and alternate-care testing sites; and Vascular Products, which includes coronary, endovascular, structural heart, vessel closure and other medical device products. Non-reportable segments include the Diabetes Care and Medical Optics segments.

Recent Developments: For the year ended Dec 31 2012, net income increased 26.1% to US$5.96 billion from US$4.73 billion in the prior year. Revenues were US$39.87 billion, up 2.6% from US$38.85 billion the year before. Operating income was US$8.08 billion versus US$5.75 billion in the prior year, an increase of 40.6%. Direct operating expenses declined 2.7% to US$15.12 billion from US$15.54 billion in the comparable period the year before. Indirect operating expenses decreased 5.1% to US$16.67 billion from US$17.56 billion in the equivalent prior-year period. **H**

Prospects: Our evaluation of Illustrative Inc. as of Apr. 7, 2013 is the result of our systematic analysis on three basic characteristics: earnings strength, relative valuation, and recent stock price movement. The company has generated a negative trend in earnings per share over the past 5 quarters and while recent estimates for the company have remained steady, AB has posted better than expected results. Based on operating earnings yield, the company is undervalued when compared to all of the companies in our coverage universe. Share price changes over the past year indicates that AB will perform in line with the market over the near term. **I**

Financial Data
(US$ in Thousands)

		12/31/2012	12/31/2011	12/31/2010	12/31/2009	12/31/2008	12/31/2007	12/31/2006	12/31/2005
Earnings Per Share		3.72	3.01	2.96	3.69	3.12	2.31	1.12	2.16
Cash Flow Per Share		5.90	5.76	5.65	4.70	4.51	3.36	3.44	3.25
Tang Book Value Per Share	**J**	1.50	N.M.	N.M.	2.17	1.51	1.24	N.M.	2.89
Dividends Per Share		2.010	1.880	1.720	1.560	1.405	1.270	1.160	1.085
Dividend Payout %		54.03	62.46	58.11	42.28	45.03	54.98	103.57	50.23
Income Statement									
Total Revenue		39,873,910	38,851,259	35,166,721	30,764,707	29,527,552	25,914,238	22,476,322	22,337,808
EBITDA		9,674,326	8,855,110	9,243,371	9,515,184	7,861,635	6,175,053	3,364,171	5,322,325
Depn & Amortn		2,898,534	3,211,523	3,082,855	1,939,533	1,797,101	1,747,031	1,271,265	990,131
Income Before Taxes		6,262,614	5,198,642	5,712,834	7,193,774	5,737,289	3,971,632	1,800,559	4,178,532
Income Taxes		299,694	470,193	1,086,662	1,447,936	1,122,070	863,334	559,615	1,247,855
Net Income		5,962,920	4,728,449	4,626,172	5,745,838	4,880,719	3,606,314	1,716,755	3,372,065
Average Shares		1,591,838	1,567,389	1,556,022	1,555,126	1,560,753	1,560,057	1,536,724	1,564,103
Balance Sheet									
Current Assets		31,322,583	23,768,774	22,317,529	23,313,891	17,042,559	14,042,733	11,281,883	11,386,028
Total Assets		67,234,944	60,276,893	59,462,266	52,416,623	42,419,204	39,713,924	36,178,172	29,141,203
Current Liabilities		13,280,176	15,480,228	17,262,434	13,049,489	11,591,908	9,103,278	11,951,195	7,415,514
Long-Term Obligations		18,085,302	12,039,822	12,523,517	11,266,294	8,713,327	9,487,789	7,009,664	4,571,504
Total Liabilities		40,513,983	35,837,060	37,074,131	29,560,885	24,939,235	21,935,384	22,123,986	14,725,932
Stockholders' Equity		26,720,961	24,439,833	22,388,135	22,855,627	17,479,551	17,778,540	14,054,186	14,415,271
Shares Outstanding		1,576,667	1,570,378	1,546,983	1,551,167	1,552,432	1,549,910	1,537,243	1,539,234
Statistical Record									
Return on Assets %		9.33	7.90	8.27	12.12	11.85	9.50	5.26	11.65
Return on Equity %		23.25	20.19	20.45	28.49	27.61	22.66	12.06	23.47
EBITDA Margin %		24.26	22.79	26.28	30.93	26.62	23.83	14.97	23.83
Net Margin %		14.95	12.17	13.15	18.68	16.53	13.92	7.64	15.10
Asset Turnover		0.62	0.65	0.63	0.65	0.72	0.68	0.69	0.77
Current Ratio		2.36	1.54	1.29	1.79	1.47	1.54	0.94	1.54
Debt to Equity		0.68	0.49	0.56	0.49	0.50	0.53	0.50	0.32
Price Range		34.51-25.91	26.95-21.61	26.91-21.94	27.39-19.87	28.95-23.66	28.44-23.43	23.67-18.92	23.92-18.00
P/E Ratio		9.28-6.96	8.95-7.18	9.09-7.41	7.42-5.38	9.28-7.58	12.31-10.14	21.14-16.90	11.07-8.34
Average Yield %		6.66	7.70	7.08	6.73	5.32	4.88	5.38	5.00

Address: 100 AAAA Park Road, Abbott Park, IL 60064-6400
Telephone: 847-222-2222 **K**

Web Site: www.illustrative.com
Officers: Miles Smith - Chairman, Chief Executive Officer Richard Jonesy - Executive Vice President

Auditors: Ernst & Young LLP
Investor Contact: 847-222-2222
Transfer Agents: Computershare Trust Company, NA, Providence, RI

5a

HOW TO USE THIS BOOK

D. INTERIM DIVIDENDS (Per Share) –
The cash dividends are the actual dollar
amounts declared by the company. No
adjustments have been made for stock
dividends and splits. **Ex-Dividend Date**: a
stockholder must purchase the stock prior to
this date in order to be entitled to the
dividend. The **Record Date** indicates the
date on which the shareholder had to have
been a holder of record in order to qualify
for the dividend. The **Payable Date**
indicates the date the company paid or
intends to pay the dividend. The cash
amount shown in the first column is
followed by a letter (example "Q" for
quarterly) to indicate the frequency of the
dividend. A notation of "Dividend payment
suspended" indicates that dividend payments
have been suspended within the most recent
ten years.
Indicated Dividend This is the annualized
amount (fully adjusted for splits) of the latest
regular cash dividend. Companies with
Dividend Reinvestment Plans are indicated
here.

E. VALUATION ANALYSIS is a tool for
evaluating a company's stock. Included are:
Forecast Earnings Per Share (EPS), Market
Capitalization, Book Value, Price/Book and
Price/Sales.

F. INSTITUTIONAL HOLDINGS –
indicates the number of investment
companies, insurance companies, mutual
funds, bank trust and college endowment
funds holding the stock and the total number
of shares held as last reported.

G. BUSINESS SUMMARY explains what
a company does in terms of the products or
services it sells, its markets, and the position
the company occupies in its industry. For a
quick reference, included are the Company's
Standard Industrial Classification (SIC),
North American Industry Classification
(NAIC) and Mergent's Industry
Classification (MIC).

H. RECENT DEVELOPMENTS – This
section captures what has happened in the
most recent quarter for which results are
available. It provides recently released sales,
earnings and expense figures.

I. PROSPECTS – This section focuses on
what is anticipated for the immediate future,
as well as the outlook for the next few years,
based on analysis by Mergent.

J. FINANCIAL DATA (fully adjusted for
stock dividends and splits) is provided for at
least the past seven fiscal years preceded by
the most recent three-, six- and nine-month
results if available.
Fiscal Years are the annual financial
reporting periods as determined by each
company. Annual prices and dividends are
displayed based on the Company's fiscal
year.

Per Share Data:
The Earnings Per Share figure is based on
a trailing 12-month period. Earnings per
share, and all per share figures, are adjusted
for subsequent stock dividends and splits.
Cash Flow Per Share represents the
annualized cash flow from operating
activities (or for quarters, TTM cash flow
from operating activities) divided by the
average shares outstanding.
Tangible Book Value Per Share is
calculated as stockholders equity (the value
of common shares, paid-in capital and
retained earnings) minus preferred stock and
intangibles such as goodwill, patents and
excess acquisition costs, divided by shares
outstanding. It demonstrates the underlying
cash value of each common share if the
company were to be liquidated as of that
date.

Dividends Per Share is the total of cash
payments made per share to shareholders for
the trailing 12-month period.

HOW TO USE THIS BOOK

Dividend Payout % is the proportion of earnings available for common stock that is paid to common shareholders in the form of cash dividends. It is significant because it indicates what percentage of earnings is being reinvested in the business for internal growth.

EDITOR'S NOTE: TTM net income is net income for the last 365 days (normally four reported quarters) ended on the quarterly balance sheet date. Where that last 365 days does not exactly equate to the last four reported quarters the net income for any included partial quarter is adjusted on a pro-rata basis.

INCOME STATEMENT, BALANCE SHEET AND STATISTICAL RECORD

Includes pertinent earnings and balance sheet information essential to analyzing a corporation's performance. The comparisons provide the necessary historical perspective to intelligently review the various operating and financial trends. Generic definitions follow.

Income Statement:

Total Revenues consists of all revenues from operations.

EBITDA represents earnings before, interest, taxes, depreciation and amortization, and special items.

Depreciation and Amortization includes all non-cash charges such as depletion and amortization as well as depreciation.

Income Before Taxes is the remaining income *after* deducting all costs, expenses, property charges, interest etc. but *before* deducting income taxes.

Income Taxes includes the amount charged against earnings to provide for current and deferred income taxes.

Net Income consists of all revenues less all expenses (operating and non-operating), and is presented before preference and common dividends.

Average Shares Outstanding is the weighted average number of shares including common equivalent shares outstanding during the year, as reported by the corporation and fully adjusted for all stock dividends and splits. The use of *average shares* minimizes the distortion in *earnings per share* which could result from issuance of a large amount of stock or the company's purchase of a large amount of its own stock during the year.

Balance Sheet:

Current Assets includes the short-term assets expected to be realized or consumed within one year. Normally includes cash and cash equivalents, short term investments, receivables, prepayments and inventories.

Total Assets represents all of the assets of the company, including tangible and intangible, and current and non-current.

Current Liabilities are all of the obligations of the company normally expected to be paid within one year. Includes bank overdrafts, short-term debt, payables and accruals.

Long-Term Obligations are the total long-term debts (due beyond one year) reported by the company, including bonds, capital lease obligations, notes, mortgages, debentures, etc.

Total Liabilities represents all liabilities of the company, whether current or non-current.

Stockholders' Equity is the sum of all capital stock accounts – paid in capital (including additional premium), retained earnings, and all other capital balances.

Shares Outstanding is the number of shares outstanding as of the date of the company's quarterly/annual report, exclusive of treasury stock and adjusted for subsequent stock dividends and splits.

Statistical Record:

Return on Assets % represents the ratio of annualized net income (or for Mos, TTM net income) to average total assets. This ratio

HOW TO USE THIS BOOK

represents how effectively assets are being used to produce a profit.

Return on Equity % is the ratio of annualized net income (or for Mos, TTM net income) to average stockholders' equity, expressed as a percentage. This ratio illustrates how effectively the investment of the stockholders is being utilized to earn a profit.

EBITDA Margin % represents earnings before interest, taxes, depreciation and amortization as a percentage of total revenue.

Net Margin % is net income expressed as a percentage of total revenues.

Asset Turnover is annualized total revenue (or for Mos, TTM total revenue) divided by average total assets. A measure of efficiency for the use of assets.

Current Ratio represents current assets divided by current liabilities. The higher the figure the better the company is able to meet its current liabilities out of its current assets. A key measure of liquidity for industrial companies.

Debt to Equity is the ratio of long-term obligations to stockholders' equity.

Price Ranges are based on each Company's fiscal year. Where actual stock sales did not take place, a range of lowest bid and highest asked prices is shown.

Price/Earnings Ratio is shown as a range. The figures are calculated by dividing the stock's highest price for the year and its lowest price by the year's earnings per share. Growth stocks tend to command higher P/Es than cyclical stocks.

Average Yield % is the ratio of annual dividends to the real average of the prices over the fiscal year.

EDITOR'S NOTE: In order to preserve the historical relationships between prices, earnings and dividends, figures are not restated to reflect subsequent events. Figures are presented in U.S. dollars unless otherwise indicated.

K. ADDITIONAL INFORMATION on each stock includes the officers of the company, investor relations contact, address, telephone number, web site and transfer agents.

OTHER DEFINITIONS

Factors Pertaining Especially to Real Estate Investment Trusts

Property Income is income from property rental and other associated activities.

Non-Property Income includes interest income and other income not from property activities.

Factors Pertaining Especially to Utilities

PPE Turnover represents annualized total revenue (or for Mos, TTM total revenue) divided by average net property, plant and equipment.

Factors Pertaining Especially to Banks

Interest Income is all interest income, including income from loans and leases, securities and deposits.

Interest Expense is all interest expense, including from loans and leases, securities and deposits.

Net Interest Income is interest income less interest expense. This figure is presented before provision for losses.

Provision for Losses represents the amount charged against earnings to increase the provision made for losses on loans and leases.

Non-Interest Income is any income that is not interest-related. Such income could include trading revenue and gains on the sale of assets.

Non-Interest Expense is all expenses that are not interest-related, including employment costs, office costs, marketing costs, etc.

Net Loans & Leases includes all loans and leases net of provisions for losses. May include commercial, agricultural, real estate, consumer and foreign loans.

Total Deposits are all time and demand deposits entrusted to a bank.

Net Interest Margin % is net interest income before provisions expressed as a

HOW TO USE THIS BOOK

percentage of total interest income. A key measure of bank profitability.

Efficiency Ratio % is non-interest expense expressed as a percentage of total revenue.

Loans to Deposits are net loans and leases divided by total deposits. A key measure of bank liquidity.

Factors Pertaining Especially to Insurance Companies

Premium Income is the amount of insurance premiums received from policyholders. This is the primary revenue source for insurance companies.

Benefits and Claims represents the payments made to policyholders under the terms of insurance contracts.

Loss Ratio % is benefits and claims expressed as a percentage of premium income. A key ratio of insurance company profitability.

ABBREVIATIONS AND SYMBOLS

A..Annual
ASE.................American Stock Exchange
()..Deficit
(Div. Reinv. Plan)..Dividend Reinvest Plan offered
E..Extra
M..Monthly
N/A.......................................Not Applicable
N.M.............................Not Meaningful
NMS..................National Market Systems
NYS................New York Stock Exchange
Q..Quarterly
S.................................Semi-Annual
Sp..............................Special Dividend
U..........................Frequency Unknown

ANALYSIS OF STOCK PRICE MOVEMENTS BY COMPANY

For the three-month period beginning Jan. 1, 2013 and ending Mar. 31, 2013, the Dow Jones Industrial Average advanced 11.25%, while the broader New York Stock Exchange Composite climbed 6.25%. The Dow and NYSE began the period at 13,104.30 and 8,571.53, respectively. The Dow posted its period high of 14,585.10 on Mar. 28, 2013, while the NYSE reported its respective three-month high of 9,128.89 on Mar. 14, 2013. The Dow and NYSE's highs were supported by continued modest U.S. economic growth, as well as the Federal Reserve's determination to lower long-term interest rates to boost spending, borrowing and economic growth. The Federal Reserve's program, initiated in September 2012, includes purchasing $85 billion of mortgage-backed securities and Treasuries each month. Notably, the Federal Reserve has stated that it will continue to buy bonds until it observes a substantial improvement in the labor market outlook, and will hold short-term borrowing costs near zero until unemployment falls to at least 6.5%, provided that inflation remains within its guidelines. Conversely, both the Dow and NYSE would both post their respective lows of 13,104.30 and 8,571.08 on Jan. 2, 2013. The indices' period lows were influenced in part by concerns of a slowdown in U.S. economic growth and the uncertain outlook of corporate profits The Dow would close the three-month period at 14,578.54, while the NYSE would finish at 9,107.04.

Over the last twelve months, the best performing stock was **MEMC Electronic Materials.** Co.'s solar energy segment has benefited from higher solar project sales.

The second-best price performer was **OfficeMax Inc.** On Feb. 20, 2013, Co. and Office Depot, Inc. announced the signing of a definitive merger agreement under which the companies would combine

Tenet Healthcare Corp. was the third-best performing stock. Co.'s top line has benefited from strong volume increases and continued pricing strength.

The fourth-best performing stock was **Marathon Petroleum Corp.** Co.'s operating results are being fueled by gains in Refining & Marketing segment income, due to refining and marketing gross margin gains.

Tesoro Corporation was the fifth-best performing stock. Co. has experienced higher gross refining margins driven by feedstock advantages from crude oil discounts relative to industry benchmarks during 2012.

The sixth-best performing stock was **Office Depot, Inc.** On Feb. 20, 2013, Co. and OfficeMax, Inc. announced the signing of a definitive merger agreement under which the companies would combine.

ITT Educational Services, Inc. was the worst performing stock over the last twelve months. Co. continues to experience a decrease in new student enrollment.

The second-worst performer was **Quicksilver Resources, Inc.** Co. is focused on improving its liquidity through asset sales, joint ventures and other measures, further reducing its overall cost structure, and on matching its capital spending to operational cash flow.

The third-worst price performer was **Advanced Micro Devices, Inc.** Co.'s operating results have been hurt by declines in both unit shipments and average selling prices at its Computing Solutions segment.

The fourth-worst performing stock was **Cliffs Natural Resources, Inc.** Co. expects pricing for the commodities it sells, which includes iron ore and metallurgical coal, to remain volatile.

VeriFone Systems Inc. was the fifth-worst performing stock. Co. anticipates that weak macroeconomic conditions, particularly in Europe, will continue to have an unfavorable affect on revenue growth.

AK Steel Holding Corp. was the sixth-worst price performer. Co.'s operating results have been affected by lower global demand and selling prices for steel.

SHORT-TERM PRICE SCORES: COMPANY RANKINGS

25 HIGHEST	SHORT-TERM PRICE SCORE♦	LONG-TERM PRICE SCORE♦	PRICE RANGE (52 Wks.)	RECENT PRICE
MEMC Electronic Materials	144.6	10.6	5.66 - 1.54	4.40
OfficeMax Inc.	143.6	36.8	13.00 - 4.17	11.61
Tenet Healthcare Corp.	140.9	108.6	47.58 - 17.56	47.58
Marathon Petroleum Corp.	137.8	...	91.13 - 34.28	89.60
Tesoro Corporation	135.8	119.2	58.97 - 21.55	58.55
Office Depot, Inc.	135.0	21.5	5.02 - 1.51	3.93
KB HOME	134.2	55.7	22.10 - 6.53	21.77
Louisiana-Pacific Corp.	133.8	110.6	22.18 - 8.04	21.60
Valero Energy Corp.	133.0	78.6	48.51 - 20.37	45.49
CVR Energy Inc.	132.6	...	61.40 - 23.95	51.62
Community Health Systems	130.9	85.9	47.39 - 20.98	47.39
Oshkosh Corp.	129.5	74.5	42.49 - 18.70	42.49
Genworth Financial, Inc.	128.7	36.3	10.51 - 4.12	10.00
Computer Sciences Corp.	128.3	68.2	50.50 - 22.50	49.23
Terex Corp.	128.1	60.1	36.66 - 14.11	34.42
Vanguard Health Systems, Inc.	128.1	...	17.45 - 7.35	14.87
Eagle Materials Inc.	127.6	125.9	71.57 - 29.84	66.63
Block (H&R), Inc.	127.4	87.1	29.42 - 14.47	29.42
LinkedIn Corp.	127.2	...	181.48 - 91.09	176.06
Aecom Technology Corp.	126.3	...	32.95 - 14.91	32.80
Western Refining Inc.	125.4	126.1	38.82 - 17.51	35.41
Health Management Associates	125.3	80.8	12.91 - 5.99	12.87
Cabot Oil & Gas Corp.	124.6	167.4	68.26 - 29.54	67.61
Delta Air Lines, Inc.	123.9	...	17.07 - 8.55	16.51
PulteGroup, Inc.	123.8	89.2	21.67 - 7.69	20.24

25 LOWEST

ITT Educational Services, Inc.	39.6	39.7	68.83 - 12.36	13.78
Quicksilver Resources, Inc.	54.9	22.1	5.75 - 1.67	2.25
Advanced Micro Devices, Inc.	60.0	39.2	8.20 - 1.86	2.55
Cliffs Natural Resources, Inc.	60.0	73.5	71.16 - 18.46	19.01
VeriFone Systems Inc.	65.0	105.6	54.45 - 18.24	20.68
AK Steel Holding Corp.	67.6	22.9	7.66 - 3.31	3.31
Monster Worldwide Inc.	70.1	29.6	9.83 - 4.97	5.07
Penney (J.C.) Co., Inc.	71.0	52.4	36.72 - 14.43	15.11
Forest Oil Corp.	73.1	32.8	13.32 - 5.26	5.26
Herbalife Ltd.	74.7	143.5	72.69 - 26.06	37.45
Arch Coal, Inc.	75.0	23.6	10.63 - 4.90	5.43
Walter Energy, Inc.	76.2	63.4	68.30 - 28.03	28.50
Weight Watchers International	77.0	106.1	78.61 - 40.33	42.11
Coach, Inc.	77.4	119.8	78.46 - 46.50	49.99
WMWARE, Inc.	78.0	...	114.62 - 70.37	78.88
Newfield Exporation Co.	78.8	57.6	36.23 - 22.38	22.42
Spirit AeroSystems Holdings	79.0	...	25.85 - 14.04	18.99
Aeropostale Inc.	79.2	73.8	23.05 - 11.95	13.60
Wiley (John) & Sons Inc.	80.3	94.2	51.32 - 36.09	38.96
Ultra Petroleum Corp.	80.3	39.0	24.07 - 16.00	20.10
Newmont Mining Corp.	80.6	84.8	57.20 - 38.60	41.89
Diebold, Inc.	81.1	85.1	40.68 - 27.61	30.32
Barrett (Bill) Corp.	81.4	55.2	26.58 - 15.65	20.27
Sandridge Energy, Inc.	81.7	...	8.14 - 5.19	5.27
Booz Allen Hamilton Holding Corp.	81.8	...	19.06 - 11.90	13.44

♦For definition see page 4a.

Ranking by Total Revenues

Based on most recent fiscal year-end figures.

Rank	Company Name	Revenues ($Mill)	Rank	Company Name	Revenues ($Mill)
1.	Exxon Mobil Corp.	482,295.0	26.	Boeing Co.	81,698.0
2.	Wal-Mart Stores, Inc.	469,162.0	27.	AmerisourceBergen Corp.	79,489.6
3.	Chevron Corporation	241,909.0	28.	Philip Morris International	77,393.0
4.	Phillips 66	182,922.0	29.	Home Depot Inc	74,754.0
5.	Berkshire Hathaway Inc.	162,463.0	30.	Target Corp	73,301.0
6.	General Motors Co.	152,256.0	31.	Walgreen Co.	71,633.0
7.	General Electric Co	147,359.0	32.	MetLife Inc	68,150.0
8.	Valero Energy Corp.	139,250.0	33.	Johnson & Johnson	67,224.0
9.	Ford Motor Co.	134,252.0	34.	Caterpillar Inc.	65,875.0
10.	AT&T Inc	127,434.0	35.	American Intl. Group Inc	65,656.0
11.	CVS Caremark Corporation	123,133.0	36.	PepsiCo Inc.	65,492.0
12.	McKesson Corp.	122,734.0	37.	ConocoPhillips	62,004.0
13.	Hewlett-Packard Co	120,357.0	38.	WellPoint Inc	61,711.7
14.	Verizon Communications	115,846.0	39.	Bunge Ltd.	60,991.0
15.	UnitedHealth Group Inc	110,618.0	40.	Pfizer Inc	58,986.0
16.	JPMorgan Chase & Co.	108,184.0	41.	United Technologies Corp.	57,708.0
17.	Cardinal Health, Inc.	107,552.0	42.	Dow Chemical Co.	56,786.0
18.	Intl. Bus. Machines Corp.	104,507.0	43.	United Parcel Service Inc	54,127.0
19.	Bank of America Corp.	100,078.0	44.	Lowe's Companies Inc	50,521.0
20.	Kroger Co.	96,751.0	45.	Coca-Cola Co	48,017.0
21.	Wells Fargo & Co.	91,247.0	46.	Merck & Co., Inc	47,267.0
22.	Citigroup Inc	90,708.0	47.	Lockheed Martin Corp.	47,182.0
23.	Prudential Financial, Inc.	84,815.0	48.	Archer Daniels Midland Co.	46,729.0
24.	Procter & Gamble Co.	83,680.0	49.	Best Buy Inc	45,085.0
25.	Marathon Petroleum Corp.	82,492.0	50.	Safeway Inc.	44,206.5

Ranking by Net Income

Based on most recent fiscal year-end figures.

Rank	Company Name	Net Income ($Mill)	Rank	Company Name	Net Income ($Mill)
1.	Exxon Mobil Corp.	44,880.0	26.	Schlumberger Ltd.	5,490.0
2.	Chevron Corporation	26,179.0	27.	McDonald's Corp	5,464.8
3.	JPMorgan Chase & Co.	21,284.0	28.	United Technologies Corp.	5,130.0
4.	Wells Fargo & Co.	18,897.0	29.	Occidental Petroleum Corp	4,598.0
5.	Wal-Mart Stores, Inc.	16,999.0	30.	Home Depot Inc	4,535.0
6.	Intl. Bus. Machines Corp.	16,604.0	31.	American Express Co.	4,482.0
7.	Berkshire Hathaway Inc.	14,824.0	32.	3M Co	4,444.0
8.	Pfizer Inc	14,570.0	33.	Bank of America Corp.	4,188.0
9.	General Electric Co	13,641.0	34.	Altria Group Inc	4,180.0
10.	Johnson & Johnson	10,853.0	35.	Phillips 66	4,124.0
11.	Procter & Gamble Co.	10,756.0	36.	Lilly (Eli) & Co.	4,088.6
12.	Coca-Cola Co	9,019.0	37.	Freeport-McMoRan Copper	3,980.0
13.	Philip Morris International	8,800.0	38.	Union Pacific Corp	3,943.0
14.	ConocoPhillips	8,428.0	39.	Boeing Co.	3,900.0
15.	Citigroup Inc	7,541.0	40.	CVS Caremark Corporation	3,877.0
16.	AT&T Inc	7,264.0	41.	Medtronic, Inc.	3,617.0
17.	General Motors Co.	6,188.0	42.	Capital One Financial Corp	3,517.0
18.	PepsiCo Inc.	6,178.0	43.	American Intl. Group Inc	3,438.0
19.	Merck & Co., Inc	6,168.0	44.	Marathon Petroleum Corp.	3,389.0
20.	Abbott Laboratories	5,962.9	45.	Deere & Co.	3,064.7
21.	Disney (Walt) Co.	5,682.0	46.	Time Warner Inc	3,019.0
22.	Caterpillar Inc.	5,681.0	47.	PNC Financial Services Grp	3,001.0
23.	Ford Motor Co.	5,665.0	48.	Target Corp	2,999.0
24.	U.S. Bancorp	5,647.0	49.	Honeywell International	2,926.0
25.	UnitedHealth Group Inc	5,526.0	50.	Illinois Tool Works, Inc.	2,870.0

Ranking by Total Assets

Based on most recent fiscal year-end figures.

Rank	Company Name	Assets ($Mill)	Rank	Company Name	Assets ($Mill)
1.	JPMorgan Chase & Co.	2,359,141.0	26.	BB&T Corp.	183,872.0
2.	Bank of America Corp.	2,209,974.0	27.	SunTrust Banks, Inc.	173,442.0
3.	Citigroup Inc	1,864,660.0	28.	Principal Financial Group	161,926.5
4.	Wells Fargo & Co.	1,422,968.0	29.	American Express Co.	153,140.0
5.	MetLife Inc	836,781.0	30.	General Motors Co.	149,422.0
6.	Morgan Stanley	780,960.0	31.	Ameriprise Financial Inc	134,729.0
7.	Prudential Financial, Inc.	709,298.0	32.	Schwab (Charles) Corp.	133,637.0
8.	General Electric Co	685,328.0	33.	Annaly Capital Management	133,452.3
9.	American Intl Group Inc	548,633.0	34.	Procter & Gamble Co.	132,244.0
10.	Berkshire Hathaway Inc.	427,452.0	35.	AFLAC Inc.	131,094.0
11.	Bank of New York Mellon	358,990.0	36.	Allstate Corp.	126,947.0
12.	U.S. Bancorp	353,855.0	37.	Johnson & Johnson	121,347.0
13.	Exxon Mobil Corp.	333,795.0	38.	Regions Financial Corp	121,347.0
14.	Capital One Financial Corp	312,918.0	39.	Intl. Bus. Machines Corp.	119,213.0
15.	PNC Financial Services Grp	305,107.0	40.	ConocoPhillips	117,144.0
16.	Hartford Financial Services	298,513.0	41.	Duke Energy Corp	113,856.0
17.	AT&T Inc	272,315.0	42.	Genworth Financial, Inc.	113,312.0
18.	Chevron Corporation	232,982.0	43.	Hewlett-Packard Co	108,768.0
19.	Verizon Communications	225,222.0	44.	Merck & Co., Inc	106,132.0
20.	State Street Corp.	222,582.0	45.	Travelers Companies Inc	104,938.0
21.	Lincoln National Corp.	218,869.0	46.	ACE, Ltd.	92,545.0
22.	Wal-Mart Stores, Inc.	203,105.0	47.	United Technologies Corp.	89,409.0
23.	BlackRock, Inc.	200,451.0	48.	Caterpillar Inc.	89,356.0
24.	Ford Motor Co.	190,554.0	49.	KeyCorp	89,236.0
25.	Pfizer Inc	185,798.0	50.	Boeing Co.	88,896.0

Ranking by Market Capitalization

Based on most recent fiscal year-end figures and closing prices at 03/28/2013

Rank	Company Name	Market Cap ($Mill)	Rank	Company Name	Market Cap ($Mill)
1.	Covidien Plc	3,350,265.3	26.	American Express Co.	74,519.8
2.	Exxon Mobil Corp.	403,733.3	27.	ConocoPhillips	73,381.7
3.	Wal-Mart Stores, Inc.	246,373.5	28.	3M Co	73,352.9
4.	General Electric Co	240,408.0	29.	Altria Group Inc	69,118.9
5.	Intl. Bus. Machines Corp.	237,724.9	30.	Time Warner Inc	68,909.6
6.	Chevron Corporation	230,831.4	31.	CVS Caremark Corporation	67,703.4
7.	Johnson & Johnson	227,902.4	32.	Bristol-Myers Squibb Co.	67,442.6
8.	Procter & Gamble Co.	210,501.0	33.	Union Pacific Corp	66,832.8
9.	Pfizer Inc	207,476.3	34.	Boeing Co.	64,916.8
10.	AT&T Inc	201,487.2	35.	Lilly (Eli) & Co.	64,423.2
11.	Wells Fargo & Co.	194,969.9	36.	MasterCard Inc	63,832.7
12.	JPMorgan Chase & Co.	180,414.5	37.	U.S. Bancorp	63,224.6
13.	Coca-Cola Co	180,229.7	38.	Occidental Petroleum Corp	63,128.2
14.	Philip Morris International	152,766.5	39.	United Parcel Service Inc	62,155.2
15.	Verizon Communications	140,484.2	40.	Honeywell International, Inc.	59,058.4
16.	Merck & Co., Inc	133,588.6	41.	UnitedHealth Group Inc	58,636.0
17.	Bank of America Corp.	131,790.9	42.	Accenture plc	58,213.1
18.	Citigroup Inc	128,543.9	43.	Caterpillar Inc.	56,969.6
19.	PepsiCo Inc.	122,049.5	44.	Monsanto Co.	56,389.6
20.	Home Depot Inc	103,659.4	45.	Colgate-Palmolive Co.	55,202.2
21.	Disney (Walt) Co.	102,548.8	46.	Enterprise Products Partners	54,189.1
22.	McDonald's Corp	99,968.3	47.	Abbott Laboratories	53,692.0
23.	Schlumberger Ltd.	99,473.1	48.	Duke Energy Corp	51,150.8
24.	Visa Inc	89,910.6	49.	EMC Corp.	50,274.8
25.	United Technologies Corp.	85,641.7	50.	Simon Property Group, Inc.	49,734.7

Ranking by Current Yield
Based on closing prices at 03/28/2013

Rank	Company Name	Yield %	Rank	Company Name	Yield %
1.	Annaly Capital Management	12.27	26.	Lorillard, Inc.	5.45
2.	Dolby Laboratories Inc	11.92	27.	Reynolds American Inc	5.30
3.	Hatteras Financial Corp	11.30	28.	Entergy Corp.	5.25
4.	Chimera Investment Corp	11.29	29.	FirstEnergy Corp.	5.21
5.	Pitney Bowes Inc	10.09	30.	Altria Group Inc	5.12
6.	Southern Copper Corp	10.01	31.	Pepco Holdings Inc.	5.05
7.	Vector Group Ltd	9.93	32.	Regal Entertainment Group	5.04
8.	NuStar Energy L.P.	8.21	33.	TECO Energy Inc.	4.94
9.	Suburban Propane Partners	7.71	34.	AT&T Inc	4.91
10.	Enbridge Energy Partners	7.18	35.	Realty Income Corp.	4.80
11.	N.Y. Community Bancorp	6.97	36.	Liberty Property Trust	4.78
12.	Hospitality Properties Trust	6.85	37.	Lockheed Martin Corp.	4.77
13.	Buckeye Partners, L.P.	6.79	38.	PPL Corp	4.69
14.	Inergy L.P.	6.51	39.	Integrys Energy Group Inc	4.68
15.	Mercury General Corp.	6.46	40.	Digital Realty Trust, Inc.	4.66
16.	TC PipeLines, LP	6.41	41.	Urstadt Biddle Properties	4.60
17.	Valley National Bancorp	6.35	42.	Ameren Corp.	4.57
18.	Mack Cali Realty Corp	6.29	43.	Lexmark International, Inc.	4.55
19.	CenturyLink, Inc.	6.15	44.	Health Care REIT Inc.	4.51
20.	Exelon Corp.	6.09	45.	AGL Resources Inc.	4.48
21.	Global Partners LP	5.93	46.	Hawaiian Electric Industries	4.47
22.	Omega Healthcare Investors	5.93	47.	CommonWealth REIT	4.46
23.	Senior Housing Properties	5.81	48.	Avista Corp.	4.45
24.	Old Republic International	5.66	49.	Home Properties Inc	4.42
25.	Kinder Morgan Energy Partn	5.55	50.	ConocoPhillips	4.39

Ranking by Return on Equity
Based on most recent fiscal year-end figures.

Rank	Company Name	Return on Equity %	Rank	Company Name	Return on Equity %
1.	Pitney Bowes Inc	1,239.30	26.	Polaris Industries Inc.	52.32
2.	Moody's Corp.	636.55	27.	OfficeMax Inc	52.13
3.	Lockheed Martin Corp.	526.44	28.	MBIA Inc.	50.51
4.	Energy Transfer Equity	420.65	29.	Michael Kors Holdings Ltd.	50.24
5.	Tempur-Pedic International	401.23	30.	Bally Technologies Inc	49.32
6.	Tenneco Inc	222.97	31.	AOL Inc.	48.51
7.	US Airways Group Inc	135.16	32.	WABCO Holdings Inc	47.67
8.	Dean Foods Co.	124.66	33.	Allison Transmission Hldgs	47.08
9.	Altria Group Inc	121.75	34.	Deluxe Corp.	46.23
10.	Alliance Data Systems	119.55	35.	Kellogg Co	46.12
11.	Western Union Co.	111.48	36.	Western Refining Inc	46.02
12.	Colgate-Palmolive Co.	108.03	37.	Deere & Co.	44.81
13.	Herbalife Ltd.	97.03	38.	Toro Co.	44.61
14.	ITT Educational Services	94.73	39.	Southern Copper Corp	43.95
15.	Brunswick Corp.	91.83	40.	Rockwell Collins, Inc.	43.66
16.	Intl. Bus. Machines Corp.	84.92	41.	Lear Corp.	43.19
17.	Boeing Co.	82.91	42.	MasterCard Inc	43.04
18.	Yum! Brands, Inc.	80.53	43.	Rockwell Automation, Inc.	40.84
19.	Campbell Soup Co.	78.16	44.	Brinker International, Inc.	40.51
20.	Hillshire Brands Co	77.74	45.	Grace (W.R.) Co.	40.12
21.	Hershey Company	69.91	46.	The Gap, Inc.	39.53
22.	Gartner, Inc.	67.74	47.	Tupperware Brands Corp	39.50
23.	Accenture plc	63.47	48.	Celanese Corp	39.29
24.	Coach, Inc.	57.79	49.	Scripps Networks Interactive	38.84
25.	TJX Companies, Inc.	54.57	50.	Graco Inc.	38.50

Ranking by High P/E Ratio
Based on closing prices at 03/28/2013

Rank	Company Name	P/E Ratio	Rank	Company Name	P/E Ratio
1.	Barrett (Bill) Corp	2,027.00	26.	Pioneer Natural Resources	82.83
2.	Centene Corp	1,468.00	27.	Hyatt Hotels Corp	81.57
3.	Range Resources Corp	1,013.00	28.	Urstadt Biddle Properties	80.59
4.	LinkedIn Corp	926.63	29.	Wash. Real Estate Invest.	79.54
5.	Forest City Enterprises	888.50	30.	Spirit AeroSystems Holdings	79.13
6.	General Cable Corp.	457.88	31.	Targa Resources Corp	74.68
7.	Royal Caribbean Cruises	415.25	32.	Fairchild Semiconductor Intl.	74.42
8.	Bunge Ltd.	388.58	33.	Amer. Campus Communities	69.75
9.	St. Joe Co.	303.57	34.	United Rentals, Inc.	69.58
10.	Host Hotels & Resorts Inc	218.63	35.	Health Care REIT Inc.	69.30
11.	Verizon Communications	158.55	36.	Red Hat Inc	68.32
12.	Douglas Emmett Inc	155.81	37.	Rackspace Hosting Inc	67.31
13.	Hospira Inc	121.59	38.	Alexandria Real Estate Eq.	65.12
14.	Actavis, Inc	121.20	39.	Tanger Factory Outlet Ctrs	63.47
15.	IDEX Corporation	118.71	40.	Brunswick Corp.	63.37
16.	Kinder Morgan Inc.	110.51	41.	Grace (W.R.) Co.	63.02
17.	Dominion Resources Inc	109.77	42.	Prudential Financial, Inc.	62.76
18.	Cabot Oil & Gas Corp.	109.05	43.	Mack Cali Realty Corp	60.87
19.	Crown Castle International	108.81	44.	EOG Resources, Inc.	60.70
20.	Louisiana-Pacific Corp.	108.00	45.	Ventas, Inc.	59.51
21.	United Parcel Service Inc	103.49	46.	Sunoco Logistics Partners	59.45
22.	Suburban Propane Partners	101.14	47.	Equity Lifestyle Properties	58.18
23.	Unit Corp.	94.90	48.	Taubman Centers, Inc.	56.69
24.	Ashland Inc	90.61	49.	Martin Marietta Materials	55.75
25.	Forest Laboratories, Inc.	88.47	50.	EQT Corp.	55.53

Ranking by Low P/E Ratio
Based on closing prices at 03/28/2013

Rank	Company Name	P/E Ratio	Rank	Company Name	P/E Ratio
1.	Berkshire Hathaway Inc.	0.01	26.	SunTrust Banks, Inc.	8.03
2.	MBIA Inc.	1.62	27.	WellPoint Inc	8.10
3.	ITT Educational Services	2.36	28.	RenaissanceRe Holdings	8.19
4.	OfficeMax Inc	2.45	29.	Everest Re Group Ltd	8.22
5.	NACCO Industries Inc.	2.56	30.	Horace Mann Educators	8.31
6.	Synovus Financial Corp.	3.26	31.	Joy Global Inc	8.35
7.	AOL Inc.	3.43	32.	AFLAC Inc.	8.51
8.	Lear Corp.	4.27	33.	Horton (D.R.) Inc.	8.53
9.	CapitalSource Inc	4.52	34.	Meritor Inc	8.60
10.	Inergy L.P.	4.80	35.	Allison Transmission Hldgs	8.70
11.	US Airways Group Inc	5.17	36.	Alleghany Corp.	8.71
12.	Hillshire Brands Co	5.87	37.	Tenneco Inc	8.74
13.	Cabot Corp.	6.12	38.	SAIC Inc	8.80
14.	HollyFrontier Corp.	6.14	39.	Western Union Co.	8.90
15.	CF Industries Holdings Inc	6.66	40.	Arrow Electronics, Inc.	8.91
16.	Pitney Bowes Inc	6.72	41.	Unum Group	8.91
17.	Allied World Assur. Co.Hldg	6.97	42.	Capital One Financial	8.92
18.	Reinsurance Grp of America	7.00	43.	Chevron Corporation	8.92
19.	TRW Automotive Holdings	7.02	44.	ConocoPhillips	8.94
20.	Lincoln National Corp.	7.15	45.	Northrop Grumman Corp.	8.98
21.	Hatteras Financial Corp	7.47	46.	Marathon Petroleum Corp.	9.06
22.	Booz Allen Hamilton Hldg.	7.72	47.	Alliant Techsystems Inc.	9.10
23.	Assurant Inc	7.94	48.	JPMorgan Chase & Co.	9.13
24.	Leucadia National Corp.	7.97	49.	Herbalife Ltd.	9.25
25.	Unisys Corp.	8.01	50.	Humana Inc.	9.25

CLASSIFICATION BY INDUSTRY

Accommodation and Food Services
Accommodation
Choice Hotels International, Inc.
Host Hotels & Resorts Inc.
Hyatt Hotels Corp
*Marriott International, Inc.
Park Place Entertainment Corp.
Wyndham Worldwide Corp.

Food Services and Drinking Places
Brinker International, Inc.
Chipotle Mexican Grill Inc
*Darden Restaurants, Inc.
*McDonald's Corporation
Ruby Tuesday, Inc.
Tim Hortons, Inc.
*Yum! Brands, Inc.

Administrative & Support and Waste
Management & Remediation Services
Administrative and Support Services
*Equifax Inc.
*ManpowerGroup
Mid Atlantic Medical Services
Robert Half International, Inc.
*Rollins, Inc.

Waste Management and Remediation Services
Clean Harbors, Inc.
*Johnson Controls, Inc.
Republic Services, Inc.
Waste Connections, Inc.
*Waste Management, Inc.

Arts, Entertainment, and Recreation
Bally Technologies Inc.
Boyd Gaming Corp.
*Carnival Corp.
*Disney (Walt) Company (The)
GTECH Holdings Corp.
International Game Technology
Las Vegas Sands Corp.
Life Time Fitness Inc.
Live Nation Entertainment, Inc.
MGM Resorts International
Royal Caribbean Cruises Ltd.
WMS Industries Inc.

Construction
ABM Industries Incorporated
*Boston Properties, Inc.
Chicago Bridge & Iron Co., N.V.
Eagle Materials Inc.
EMCOR Group, Inc.
*Forest City Enterprises, Inc.
Fortune Brands Home & Security, Inc.
*Granite Construction Inc.
Horton (D.R.) Inc.
Jacobs Engineering Group Inc.
KB Home
KBR Inc.
Lennar Corporation

M.D.C. Holdings, Inc.
Martin Marietta Materials, Inc.
*MDU Resources Group, Inc.
NVR Inc.
Owens Corning
Pulte Homes, Inc.
Quanta Services, Inc.
Toll Brothers, Inc.
Tutor Perini Corp.
URS Corp.

Educational Services
DeVry Inc.
ITT Educational Services, Inc.

Electric Power Generation
Calpine Corp.
Covanta Holding Corp.
NRG Energy, Inc.
Ormat Technologies Inc

Finance and Insurance
Commercial Banking
*BancorpSouth, Inc.
*Bank of America Corporation
*Bank of Hawaii Corporation
*Bank of New York Mellon Corp.
BankUnited Inc.
*BB&T Corporation
City National Corporation
*Comerica, Inc.
*Community Bank System, Inc.
Cullen/Frost Bankers, Inc.
*First Horizon National Corporation
*Hudson United Bancorp
*J.P. Morgan Chase & Co.
*KeyCorp
*M&T Bank Corporation
*North Fork Bancorporation, Inc.
*PNC Financial Services Group
Prosperity Bancshares Inc.
*Regions Financial Corp.
*State Street Corporation
*SunTrust Banks, Inc.
*Synovus Financial Corporation
*TCF Financial Corp.
*U.S. Bancorp
*Valley National Bancorp
*Wells Fargo & Company
*Wilmington Trust Corporation

Direct Health and Medical Insurance Carriers
*AFLAC Incorporated
Cigna Corp.
Humana Inc.
Pacificare Health Systems, Inc.
Reinsurance Group of America
UnitedHealth Group Inc.
Universal American Corp.
*UnumProvident Corporation
WellCare Health Plans Inc.

Direct Life Insurance Carriers
Assurant Inc.
*Genworth Financial Inc. (Holding Co)
*Lincoln National Corporation
Principal Financial Group, Inc.
*Protective Life Corporation
Prudential Financial, Inc.
Stancorp Financial Group, Inc.
*Torchmark Corporation

Direct Property and Casualty Insurance Carriers
Allied World Assurance Company Holdings AG
Allmerica Financial Corporation
*Allstate Corporation (The)
*American Financial Group, Inc.
American International Group
Aspen Insurance Holdings Ltd
Berkley (W.R.) Corporation
Berkshire Hathaway Inc.
*Chubb Corporation (The)
CNA Financial Corporation
Endurance Specialty Holdings Ltd
Everest Re Group Ltd
Hanover Insurance Group Inc.
HCC Insurance Holdings, Inc.
Horace Mann Educators Corp.
*Kemper Corp.
Leucadia National Corporation
Loews Corporation
Markel Corporation
Mercury General Corporation
Progressive Corporation (The)
RenaissanceRe Holdings Ltd
*RLI Corp.
*The St Paul Travelers Companies Inc.
White Mountains Insurance Group, Ltd
XL Capital Plc

Direct Title Insurance Carriers
Alleghany Corporation
*CoreLogic Inc.
Fidelity National Financial Inc.

Insurance Agencies and Brokerages
Aetna, Inc.
Anthem, Inc.
Brown & Brown, Inc.
Centene Corp
Gallagher (Arthur J.) & Company
*Hartford Financial Services Group
Metlife, Inc.
WellPoint Inc.

Mortgage and Nonmortgage Loan Brokers
CapitalSource Inc.
*New York Community Bancorp, Inc.

Nondepository Credit Intermediation
*American Express Company
Ameriprise Financial Inc.
*Capital One Financial Corp.

Discover Financial Services
Greenhill & Co. Inc.
Invesco Ltd
Lazard Ltd
*Morgan Stanley

Real Estate Investment Trusts
Alexandria Real Estate Equities, Inc.
American Campus Communities Inc.
American Tower Corp
AMB Property Corporation
*Annaly Capital Management Inc.
Apartment Investment & Mngmnt
AvalonBay Communities, Inc.
*Brandywine Realty Trust
*BRE Properties, Inc.
Camden Property Trust
*Chimera Investment Corp.
*Commonwealth REIT
Corporate Office Properties Trust
*DDR Corp
Digital Realty Trust Inc.
Douglas Emmett Inc.
*Duke Realty Corporation
Equity Lifestyle Properties Inc
*Equity One, Inc.
*Equity Residential Prop. Trust
*Essex Property Trust, Inc.
Extra Space Storage Inc
*Federal Realty Investment Trust
General Growth Properties Inc.
Hatteras Financial Corp
*HCP, Inc.
*Health Care REIT Inc.
*Highwoods Properties, Inc.
*Home Properties, Inc.
*Hospitality Properties Trust
*Kilroy Realty Corp.
*Kimco Realty Corp.
*Liberty Property Trust
*Macerich Company (The)
*Mack-Cali Realty Corporation
*Mid-America Apartment Communities Inc
National Health Investors, Inc.
*National Retail Properties Inc.
*Omega Healthcare Investors, Inc.
Piedmont Office Realty Trust Inc
Plum Creek Timber Company
*ProLogis
Public Storage, Inc.
Realty Income Corp.
*Regency Centers Corporation
*Shurgard Storage Centers, Inc.
*Simon Property Group, Inc.
SL Green Realty Corp.
*Senior Housing Properties Trust
Starwood Hotels & Resorts
*Tanger Factory Outlet Centers, Inc.
*Taubman Centers, Inc.
*UDR Inc.
*Universal Health Realty Inc. Trust

Management of Companies & Enterprises
*AT&T Inc.
*Universal Corporation

Manufacturing
Beverage and Tobacco Product Manufacturing
*Altria Group, Inc.
*Beam Inc.
*Brown-Forman Corporation
*Coca-Cola Company (The)
*Coca-Cola Enterprises Inc.
 Constellation Brands, Inc.
 Dr Pepper Snapple Group Inc
 Lorillard, Inc.
 Molson Coors Brewing Company
*PepsiCo Inc.
*Philip Morris International Inc.
*Reynolds American Inc.
*Vector Group Inc.

Chemical Manufacturing
*3M Company
*Air Products & Chemicals, Inc.
*Albemarle Corporation
 Alberto-Culver Company
*Avon Products, Inc.
*Ashland, Inc.
*Cabot Corporation
 Celanese Corp.
 CF Industries Holdings Inc.
 Charles River Laboratories Int.
 Chemtura Corp.
*Church & Dwight Company, Inc.
*Clorox Company (The)
*Colgate-Palmolive Company
 Compass Minerals International Inc.
 Cytec Industries, Inc.
*Dow Chemical Company
*du Pont (E.I.) de Nemours & Co.
*Eastman Chemical Company
*Ecolab, Inc.
*Estee Lauder Companies, Inc.
*Fuller (H.B.) Company
 Grace (W.R.) Co.
 Huntsman Corp.
 IMC Global, Inc.
*International Flavors & Fragrances
 Intrepid Potash Inc.
 Monsanto Co.
*Olin Corporation
*PPG Industries, Inc.
*Praxair, Inc.
*Procter & Gamble Company
 Rockwood Holdings Inc.
*Rohm & Haas Company
*RPM International Inc.
 Scotts Company (The)
*Sherwin-Williams Company
 Stepan Co.
 Westlake Chemical Corp.
*Valspar Corporation (The)

Computer and Electronic Product Manufacturing
 Advanced Micro Devices, Inc.
 Agilent Technologies, Inc.
*Allegheny Technologies Inc.
*Ametek, Inc.
*AVX Corporation
*Corning Incorporated
 EMC Corporation
*Emerson Electric Co.
 Esterline Technologies Corp
 Fairchild Semiconductor Int'l.
 Freescale Semiconductor Ltd
 Global Payments Inc.
 Harman International Industries
 Juniper Networks Inc.
*Harris Corporation
*Hewlett-Packard Company
*International Business Machines
 International Rectifier Corp.
 Jabil Circuit, Inc.
 L-3 Communications Holdings
 Lexmark International, Inc.
*Medtronic, Inc.
 MEMC Electronic Materials, Inc.
 Mettler-Toledo International Inc.
 Micron Technology, Inc.
*Motorola Solutions Inc.
 Plantronics, Inc.
*Raytheon Company
*Rockwell Collins, Inc.
 Teradyne, Inc.
 Teradata Corp.
 Thermo Fisher Scientific Inc.
 TE Connectivity Ltd
 Unisys Corporation
 Vishay Intertechnology, Inc.
 Waters Corporation

Electrical Equipment, Appliance, and Component Manufacturing
 Acuity Brands Inc.
 Amphenol Corp
 Anixter International Inc.
*Eaton Corporation
 Energizer Holdings, Inc.
 General Cable Corp.
*General Electric Company
*Hubbell, Inc.
 Jarden Corp.
 Regal-Beloit Corp.
*Rockwell Automation
*Smith (A.O.) Corporation
 Tyco International Ltd
*Whirlpool Corporation

Fabricated Metal Product Manufacturing
 Alliant Techsystems Inc.
*Badger Meter, Inc.
*Ball Corporation

*Crane Co.
Crown Holdings, Inc.
Danaher Corporation
Greif Inc.
*Harsco Corporation
McDermott International, Inc.
*Parker-Hannifin Corp.
Shaw Group Inc. (The)
*Snap-On Incorporated
*Stanley Works
*Timken Company (The)
Valmont Industries, Inc.

Food Manufacturing
*Archer Daniels Midland Co.
Bunge Ltd
*Campbell Soup Company
*ConAgra Foods, Inc.
Corn Products International Inc.
Dean Foods Company
*Flowers Foods, Inc.
*General Mills, Inc.
*Heinz (H.J.) Company
*Hershey Foods Corporation
Hillshire Brands Co
*Hormel Foods Corporation
*Kellogg Company
*McCormick & Company, Inc.
Mead Johnson Nutrition Co.
Ralcorp Holdings Inc.
*Sensient Technologies Corp.
Smithfield Foods, Inc.
*Smucker (J.M.) Company
Tootsie Roll Industries, Inc.
*Tyson Foods, Inc.

Furniture and Related Product Manufacturing
HNI Corporation
Leggett & Platt, Incorporated
*Masco Corporation
Tempur-Pedic International Inc.
Steelcase Inc.

Machinery Manufacturing
AGCO Corporation
Babcock & Wilcox Co. (The)
*Brunswick Corporation
*Caterpillar Inc.
*Cummins Inc.
*Deere & Company
*Diebold, Inc.
*Donaldson Company, Inc.
*Dover Corporation
Dresser-Rand Group Inc.
Flowserve Corporation
FMC Corporation
FMC Technologies, Inc.
Gardner Denver, Inc.
*Graco Inc.
*IDEX Corporation
Ingersoll-Rand Plc
*ITT Industries Inc.
Joy Global Inc.

*Kennametal Inc.
Lindsay Corp
*Manitowoc Company, Inc. (The)
Lennox International Inc.
NACCO Industries, Inc.
*Pall Corporation
Roper Industries, Inc.
SPX Corporation
Terex Corporation
*Tennant Company
*Toro Co. (The)
Varian Medical Systems, Inc.
Watsco Inc.
*Xerox Corporation
Xylem Inc.
*York International Corporation

Medical Equipment and Supplies Manufacturing
Advanced Medical Optics Inc.
Alere Inc.
*Bard (C.R.), Inc.
*Baxter International Inc.
*Becton, Dickinson and Company
Bio-Rad Laboratories, Inc.
Boston Scientific Corporation
CareFusion Corp
Cooper Companies, Inc.
Covidien Plc
*Hill-Rom Holdings, Inc.
Mine Safety Appliances Company
ResMed Inc.
St. Jude Medical, Inc.
Steris Corporation
Stryker Corporation
*Teleflex Inc.
Zimmer Holdings, Inc.

Nonmetallic Mineral Product Manufacturing
Brink's Company (The)
Carbo Ceramics Inc.
Minerals Technologies Inc.
Oil-Dri Corp. of America
Owens-Illinois, Inc.
USG Corporation

Paper and Wood Product Manufacturing
*Avery Dennison Corporation
*Bemis Company, Inc.
*Boise Cascade Corporation
Domtar Corp.
*International Paper Company
*Kimberly-Clark Corporation
*Louisiana-Pacific Corporation
*MeadWestvaco Corporation
Packaging Corp. of America
*Rayonier Inc.
Rock-Tenn Co.
*Sonoco Products Company
St. Joe Company (The)
Tenneco Inc.

Petroleum and Coal Products Manufacturing
*Chevron Corp.
Cobalt International Energy Inc.
*ConocoPhillips
CVR Energy Inc.
*Exxon Mobil Corporation
*Hess Corp.
HollyFrontier Corp
*Marathon Petroleum Corp
Murphy Oil Corporation
Phillips 66
Tesoro Corporation
Valero Energy Corporation
Western Refining Inc.

Pharmaceutical Preparation Manufacturing
*Abbott Laboratories
*Allergan, Inc.
AmerisourceBergen Corporation
*Bristol-Myers Squibb Company
Edwards Lifesciences Corp.
Forest Laboratories, Inc.
Genentech, Inc.
Hospira Inc.
*Johnson & Johnson
*Lilly (Eli) & Company
*Merck & Co., Inc.
*Pfizer Inc.
Teva Pharmaceutical Industries

Plastics and Rubber Products Manufacturing
AptarGroup Inc.
Armstrong World Industry Inc.
*Carlisle Companies Incorporated
*Illinois Tool Works, Incorporated
*Myers Industries, Inc.
*Newell Rubbermaid Inc.
Sealed Air Corporation
Tupperware Brands Corporation
*West Pharmaceutical Services

Primary Metal Manufacturing
*AK Steel Holding Corporation
*Alcoa, Inc.
Carpenter Technology Corp.
Commercial Metals Co.
*Nucor Corporation
Precision Castparts Corp.
*United States Steel Corporation
*Worthington Industries, Inc.

Printing and Related Support Activities
Deluxe Corporation

Textiles, Apparel, and Leather Manufacturing
Coach, Inc.
GUESS ?, Inc.
Michael Kors Holdings Ltd
Mohawk Industries, Inc.
*NIKE, Inc.
PVH Corp.
Ralph Lauren Corp
Under Armour Inc.

*VF Corporation

Transportation Equipment Manufacturing
Allison Transmission Holdings Inc
Autoliv, Inc.
*Boeing Company (The)
*BorgWarner Inc.
*Clarcor Inc.
Dana Holding Corp
*Ford Motor Company
General Dynamics Corporation
General Motors Co.
*Harley-Davidson, Inc.
*Honeywell International Inc.
Lear Corp.
*Lockheed Martin Corporation
*Meritor Inc.
*Modine Manufacturing Company
Navistar International Inc.
*Oshkosh Corp.
*Polaris Industries Inc.
Sequa Corporation
Spirit AeroSystems Holdings Inc.
*Textron Inc.
Thor Industries, Inc.
Transdigm Group Inc.
Trinity Industries, Inc.
TRW Automotive Holdings Corp.
*United Technologies Corp.
*Visteon Corporation
WABCO Holdings Inc.
Wabtec Corp.

Other Manufacturing
*Brady Corporation

Mining
Activities Support for Mining
*Baker Hughes Inc.
Cameron International Corp.
Diamond Offshore Drilling, Inc.
Dril-Quip, Inc.
EOG Resources, Inc.
Halliburton Company
Helix Energy Solutions Group Inc.
Helmerich & Payne, Inc.
*Marathon Oil Corporation
Noble Corp
Oceaneering International, Inc.
Oil States International, Inc.
Pride International, Inc.
Rowan Companies Plc
RPC, Inc.
Schlumberger Ltd.
SEACOR Holdings Inc.
Superior Energy Services, Inc.

Mining (except Oil and Gas)
*Arch Coal, Inc.
Alpha Natural Resources Inc.
Cliffs Natural Resources, Inc.
CONSOL Energy Inc.
Freeport-McMoRan Copper & Gold

*Massey Energy Co.
Mosaic Co. (The)
Newmont Mining Corporation
Peabody Energy Corp.
*Southern Copper Corp.
*Vulcan Materials Company
Walter Energy, Inc.

Oil and Gas Extraction
*Anadarko Petroleum Corp.
*Apache Corporation
Atwood Oceanics, Inc.
Barrett (Bill) Corp.
Cabot Oil & Gas Corp.
Chesapeake Energy Corp.
Cimarex Energy Co.
Comstock Resources, Inc.
Concho Resources Inc
Continental Resources Inc.
Denbury Resources, Inc.
Devon Energy Corporation
Exco Resources
Forest Oil Corporation
*Kerr-McGee Corporation
Nabors Industries Ltd.
Newfield Exploration Co.
Noble Corp.
Noble Energy, Inc.
*Occidental Petroleum Corp.
Pioneer Natural Resources Co.
Plains Exploration & Production Co. L.P.
QEP Resources Inc
Quicksilver Resources, Inc.
Range Resources Corp.
SandRidge Energy Inc.
St. Mary Land & Exploration Co.
Southwestern Energy Company
Ultra Petroleum Corp
Unit Corp.
Whiting Petroleum Corp.
WPX Energy, Inc.

Other Services
ARAMARK Corporation
Clear Channel Outdoor Holdings
Corrections Corporation of America
Genpact Ltd
Hillenbrand Inc.
ITC Holdings Corp.
*Regis Corporation
Reliance Steel & Aluminum Co.
SAIC Inc.
Service Corporation International
*Suburban Propane Partners L.P.
Towers Watson & Co.
Valassis Communications, Inc.
Weight Watchers International
Wex Inc.

Professional, Scientific, and Technical Services
Accenture Ltd
Aecom Technology Corp.

Agere Systems Inc.
AOL Inc.
*Block (H & R), Inc.
Booz Allen Hamilton Holding Corp.
Computer Sciences Corporation
Convergys Corporation
Corporate Executive Board Co.
Covance Inc.
Fluor Corporation
FTI Consulting Inc.
Gartner Group, Inc.
*Interpublic Group of Companies
Korn/Ferry International
LinkedIn Corp
Moody's Corporation
*Omnicom Group, Inc.
*PerkinElmer, Inc.
Quest Diagnostics, Incorporated
Synnex Corp.

Real Estate and Rental and Leasing
Real Estate
Alexander & Baldwin Inc.
CBRE Group Inc.
Howard Hughes Corp
Jones Lang LaSalle Inc.
*W.P. Carey & Co. LLC

Rental and Leasing Services
Air Lease Corp
Hertz Global Holdings Inc.
United Rentals, Inc.

Retail Trade
Building Material and Garden Equipment and Supplies Dealers
*Home Depot (The), Inc.
*Lowe's Companies, Inc.
Wesco International, Inc.

Clothing and Clothing Accessories Stores
Abercrombie & Fitch Co.
Aeropostale Inc.
American Eagle Outfitters, Inc.
ANN INC
Carter's Inc
Chico's FAS, Inc.
DSW Inc.
*Foot Locker, Inc.
Gap, Inc. (The)
Nordstrom, Inc.
Payless ShoeSource Inc.
*Tiffany & Co.
TJX Companies, Inc. (The)

Furniture and Consumer Electronics
Aaron's, Inc.
Best Buy Co., Inc.
GameStop Corp.
*Pier 1 Imports, Inc.
*RadioShack Corporation
Williams-Sonoma, Inc.

General Merchandise Stores
Big Lots, Inc.
Dillard's, Inc.
Dollar General Corp.
Family Dollar Stores, Inc.
Kohl's Corporation
Macys Inc.
Penney (J.C.) Company, Inc.
Saks Incorporated
*Target Corporation
*Wal-Mart Stores, Inc.

Grocery Stores
Kroger Company (The)
*Ruddick Corporation
Safeway Inc.

Health and Personal Care Stores
*CVS/Caremark Corporation
*Omnicare, Inc.
*Rite Aid Corporation
*Walgreen Co.

Motor Vehicle and Parts Dealers
Advance Auto Parts, Inc.
Asbury Automotive Group, Inc.
AutoNation, Inc.
AutoZone, Inc.
Carmax Inc.
Group 1 Automotive, Inc.
KAR Auction Services Inc.
Penske Automotive Group Inc.
Sonic Automotive, Inc.

Sporting Goods, Hobby, Book, and Music Stores and other
Barnes & Noble, Inc.
Dick's Sporting Goods, Inc.
*Office Depot, Inc.
*OfficeMax Inc.
Sally Beauty Holdings Inc.
Signet Jewelers Ltd.
*Sotheby's Holdings, Inc.

Transportation and Warehousing
AirTran Holdings, Inc.
Alaska Air Group, Inc.
*Atmos Energy Corporation
*Buckeye Partners, L.P.
Con-Way Inc.
*CSX Corporation
Delta Air Lines, Inc.
Enbridge Energy Partners, L.P.
*Energy Transfer Equity L P
*Enterprise Products Partners L.P.
*FedEx Corporation
*GATX Corporation
Global Partners LP
Inergy L.P.
Iron Mountain Incorporated
Kansas City Southern
Kinder Morgan Inc.
Kirby Corp.

Magellan Midstream Partners LP
*Norfolk Southern Corporation
NuStar Energy L.P.
*OGE Energy Corp.
Plains All American Pipeline, L.P.
*Ryder System, Inc.
Southwest Airlines Co.
*Spectra Energy Corp.
Targa Resources Corp
TC PipeLines, LP
Teekay Corp
*Tidewater Inc.
*Union Pacific Corp.
United Parcel Service, Inc.
US Airways Group Inc.
Western Gas Resources, Inc.
Williams Companies, Inc. (The)

Utilities
Utilities - Electric
AES Corporation (The)
*Alliant Energy Corporation
*Ameren Corporation
*American Electric Power Co.
*Avista Corp.
*Black Hills Corporation
*CenterPoint Energy, Inc.
*Cleco Corp.
*CMS Energy Corporation
*Consolidated Edison, Inc.
*Dominion Resources, Inc.
*DTE Energy Co.
*Duke Energy Corporation
*Edison International
*Entergy Corporation
*Exelon Corporation
*FirstEnergy Corporation
*Great Plains Energy Incorporated
*Hawaiian Electric Industries, Inc.
*Idacorp, Inc.
*Integrys Energy Group Inc.
*NextEra Energy Inc.
New Jersey Resources Corp.
*NiSource, Inc.
*Northeast Utilities
*NV Energy, Inc.
*Pepco Holdings, Inc.
*PG&E Corporation
*Pinnacle West Capital Corp.
*PNM Resources, Inc.
*PPL Corporation
*Puget Energy, Inc.
RRI Energy, Inc.
*SCANA Corporation
*Southern Company (The)
*TECO Energy, Inc.
*Westar Energy, Inc.
*Wisconsin Energy Corporation
*Xcel Energy, Inc.

Utilities - Natural Gas
*AGL Resources Inc.

Airgas Inc.
*Energen Corporation
*Equitable Resources, Inc.
Kinder Morgan Energy Partner, L.P.
*National Fuel Gas Company
Northwest Natural Gas Co.
*Oneok Inc.
*Piedmont Natural Gas Company
*Questar Corporation
*Sempra Energy
South Jersey Industries, Inc.
*UGI Corporation
*Vectren Corporation
*WGL Holdings, Inc.

Utilities - Water
*American States Water Co.
American Water Works Co., Inc.
*Aqua America, Inc.
*California Water Service Group
SJW Corp.

Wholesale Trade
Wholesale Trade, Durable Goods
Arrow Electronics, Inc.
*Avnet, Inc.
Ceridian Corporation
*Genuine Parts Company
Grainger (W.W.), Inc.
Hughes Supply, Inc.
Ingram Micro Inc.
MSC Industrial Direct Co., Inc.
National-Oilwell, Inc.
*Owens & Minor, Inc.
*Pitney Bowes Inc.
*Weyerhaeuser Company
World Fuel Services Corp.

Wholesale Trade, Nondurable Goods
Cardinal Health, Inc.
*Crompton Corporation
Herbalife Ltd.
*McKesson Corporation
Nu Skin Enterprises, Inc.
*Supervalu Inc.
*Sysco Corporation

* **Designates companies offering dividend reinvestment plans.**

DOW JONES INDUSTRIAL AVERAGE
PRICES - EARNINGS - DIVIDENDS

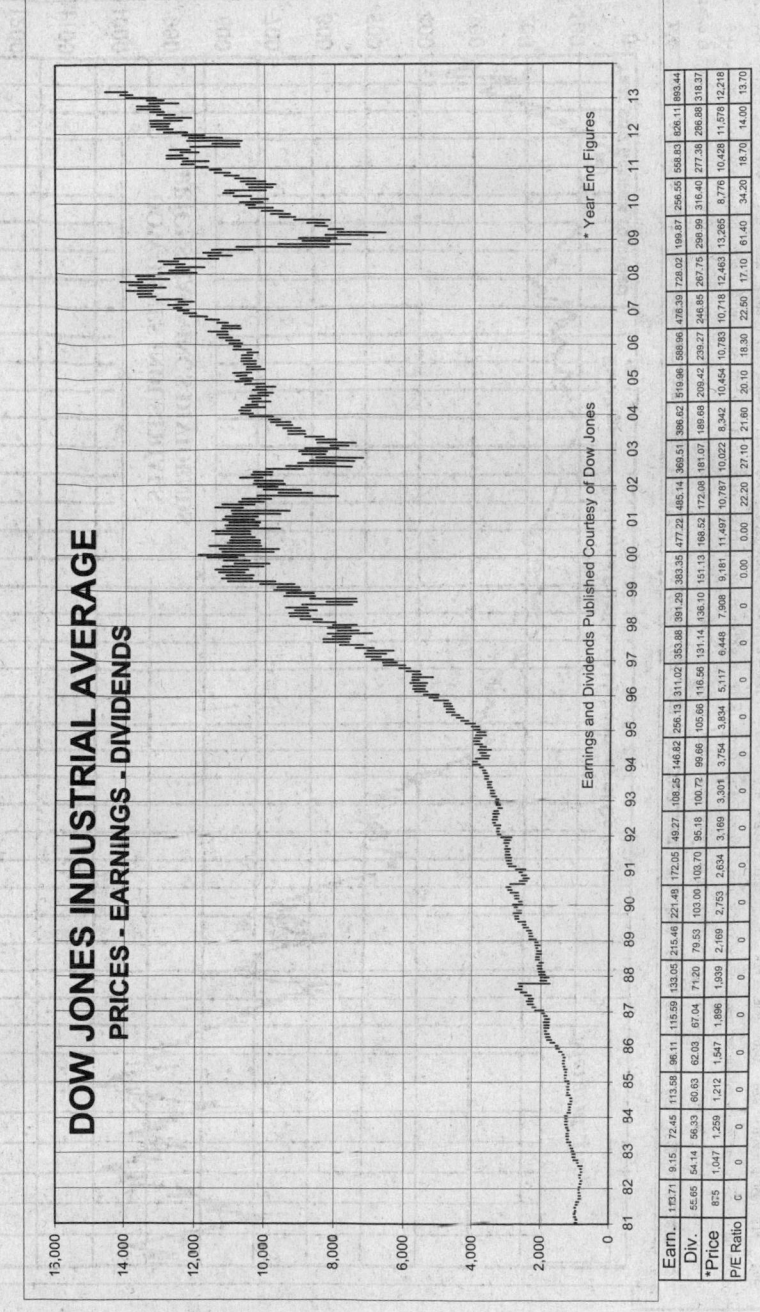

* Year End Figures

Earnings and Dividends Published Courtesy of Dow Jones

(y-axis: 15,000 · 14,000 · 12,000 · 10,000 · 8,000 · 6,000 · 4,000 · 2,000 · 0)

	81	82	83	84	85	86	87	88	89	90	91	92	93	94	95	96	97	98	99	00	01	02	03	04	05	06	07	08	09	10	11	12	13
Earn.	113.71	9.15	72.45	113.58	96.11	115.59	133.05	215.46	221.48	172.05	49.27	108.25	148.82	256.13	311.02	353.88	391.29	383.35	477.22	485.14	369.51	386.62	519.96	588.96	476.39	729.02	199.87	256.55	558.83	826.11	893.44		
Div.	55.65	54.14	56.33	60.63	62.03	67.04	71.20	79.53	103.00	103.70	95.18	100.72	99.66	105.66	118.56	131.14	136.10	151.13	168.52	172.08	181.07	189.68	209.42	239.27	246.85	267.75	298.99	316.40	277.38	286.88	318.37		
*Price	875	1,047	1,259	1,212	1,547	1,896	1,939	2,169	2,753	2,634	3,169	3,301	3,754	3,834	5,117	6,448	7,908	9,181	11,497	10,787	10,022	8,342	10,454	10,783	10,718	12,463	13,265	8,776	10,428	11,578	12,218	13,104	16,576
P/E Ratio	c	0	0	0	0	0	0	0	0	0	0	0	0	0	0	0	0	0	0.00	0.00	0.00	22.20	27.10	21.60	20.10	18.30	22.50	17.10	61.40	34.20	18.70	14.00	13.70

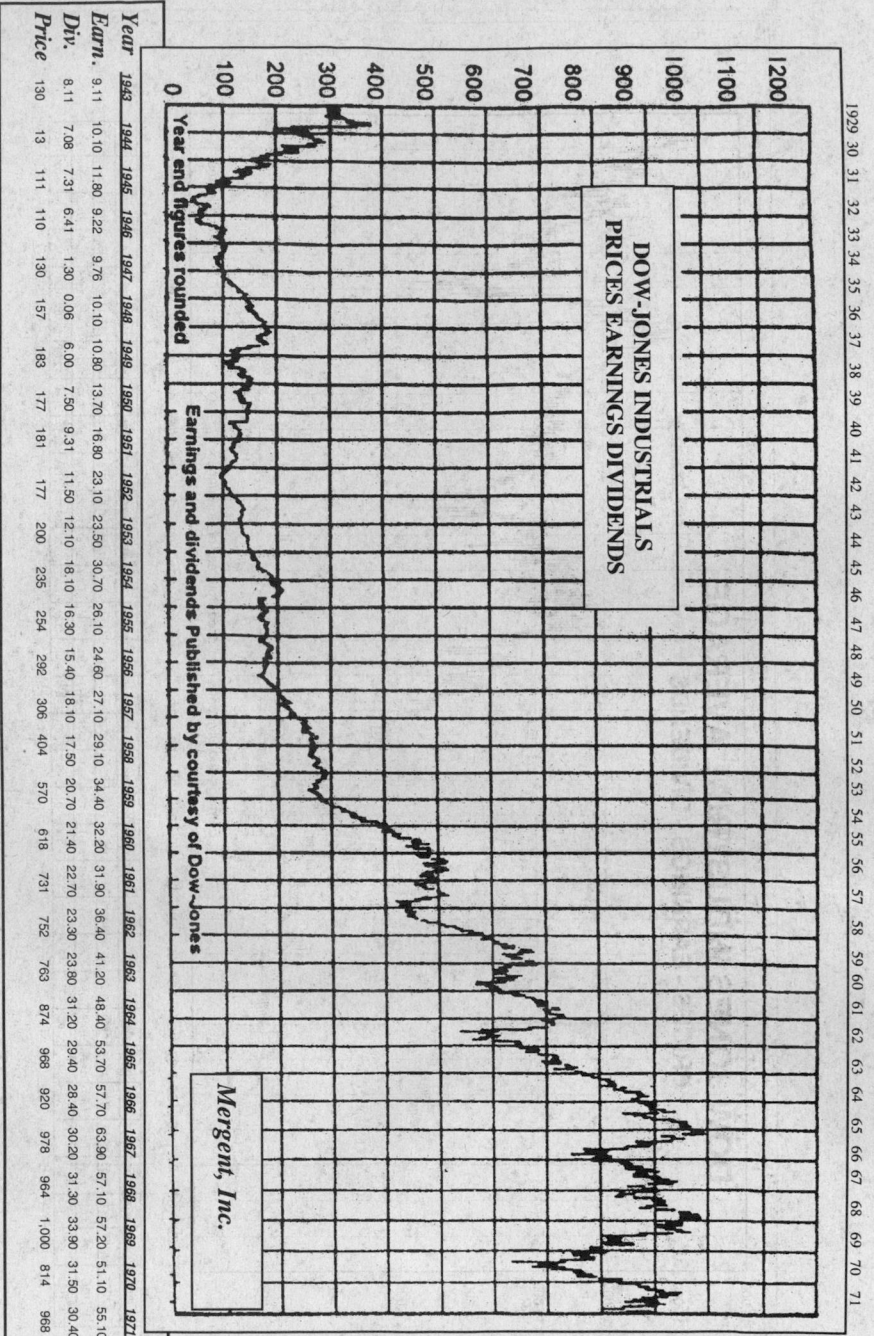

DOW-JONES INDUSTRIALS PRICES EARNINGS DIVIDENDS

Year end figures rounded

Earnings and dividends Published by courtesy of Dow-Jones

Mergent, Inc.

Year	1943	1944	1945	1946	1947	1948	1949	1950	1951	1952	1953	1954	1955	1956	1957	1958	1959	1960	1961	1962	1963	1964	1965	1966	1967	1968	1969	1970	1971
Earn.	9.11	10.10	11.80	9.76	10.10	10.10	10.80	13.70	16.80	23.10	23.50	30.70	26.10	24.60	27.10	29.10	34.40	32.20	31.90	36.40	41.20	48.40	53.70	57.70	63.90	57.10	57.20	51.10	55.10
Div.	8.11	7.08	7.31	6.41	1.30	0.06	6.00	7.50	9.31	11.50	12.10	18.10	16.30	15.40	18.10	17.50	20.70	21.40	22.70	23.30	23.80	31.20	29.40	28.40	30.20	31.30	33.90	31.50	30.40
Price	130	13	111	110	130	157	183	177	181	177	200	235	254	292	306	404	570	618	731	752	763	874	968	920	978	964	1,000	814	968

26a

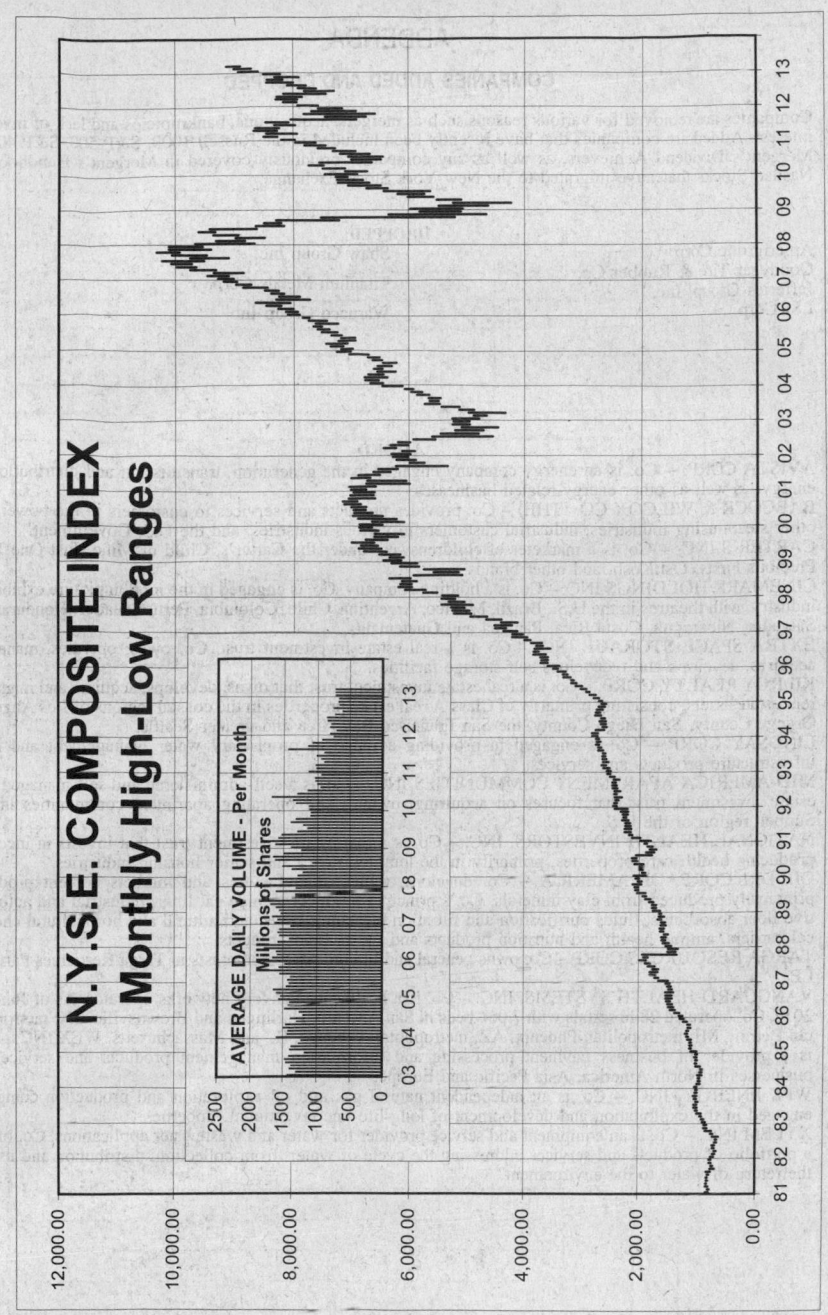

N.Y.S.E. COMPOSITE INDEX
Monthly High-Low Ranges

AVERAGE DAILY VOLUME - Per Month
Millions of Shares

27a

ADDENDA

COMPANIES ADDED AND DROPPED

Companies are removed for various reasons such as mergers, acquisitions, bankruptcies and lack of investor interest. Added are companies that have recently been included in the Russell 1000, S&P 500, S&P 400 or Mergent's Dividend Achievers, as well as any companies previously covered in Mergent's Handbook of Nasdaq Stocks that have migrated to the New York Stock Exchange.

Amerigroup Corp
Goodyear Tire & Rubber Co.
Jefferies Group, Inc.
LSI Corp

DROPPED

Shaw Group Inc.

Titanium Metals Corp.

Warnaco Group Inc

ADDED

AVISTA CORP. – Co. is an energy company engaged in the generation, transmission and distribution of energy, as well as other energy-related businesses.

BABCOCK & WILCOX CO. (THE) – Co. provides products and services to customers in the power and other steam-using industries, industrial customers in various industries, and the U.S. Government.

CARTER'S INC. – Co. is a marketer of childrenswear under the Carter's, Child of Mine, Just One You, Precious Firsts, OshKosh, and other brands.

CINEMARK HOLDINGS INC. – Co. is a holding company. Co. is engaged in the motion picture exhibition industry, with theatres in the U.S., Brazil, Mexico, Argentina, Chile, Colombia, Peru, Ecuador, Honduras, El Salvador, Nicaragua, Costa Rica, Panama and Guatemala.

EXTRA SPACE STORAGE INC. – Co. is a real estate investment trust. Co. owns, operates, manages, acquires, develops and redevelops self-storage facilities.

KILROY REALTY CORP. – Co. is a real estate investment trust that owns, develops, acquires and manages real estate assets, consisting primarily of Class A real estate properties in the coastal regions of Los Angeles, Orange County, San Diego County, the San Francisco Bay Area and greater Seattle.

LINDSAY CORP – Co. is engaged in providing a range of proprietary water management and road infrastructure products and services.

MID-AMERICA APARTMENT COMMUNITIES INC. – Co. is a self-administered and self-managed real estate investment trust that focuses on acquiring, owning and operating apartment communities in the Sunbelt region of the U.S.

NATIONAL HEALTH INVESTORS, INC. – Co. is a real estate investment trust that invests in income-producing health care properties, primarily in the long-term care and senior housing industries.

OIL-DRI CORP. OF AMERICA – Co. develops, mines, manufactures and markets sorbent products principally produced from clay minerals. Co.'s principal products include cat litter, industrial and automotive floor absorbents, fluids purification and filtration bleaching clays, agricultural and horticultural chemical carriers, animal health and nutrition products and sports field products.

TARGA RESOURCES CORP – Co. owns general and limited partner interests in Targa Resources Partners LP.

VANGUARD HEALTH SYSTEMS, INC. – Co. is a healthcare delivery networks operator. As of June 30 2012, Co. operated 28 hospitals with 7,064 beds in San Antonio, Harlingen and Brownsville, TX; metropolitan Detroit, MI; metropolitan Phoenix, AZ; metropolitan Chicago, IL; and Massachusetts. WEX INC. – Co. is a provider of business payment processing and information management products and services to businesses in North America, Asia Pacific and Europe.

WPX ENERGY, INC. – Co. is an independent natural gas and oil exploration and production company engaged in the exploitation and development of long-life unconventional properties.

XYLEM INC. – Co. is an equipment and service provider for water and wastewater applications. Co. offers a portfolio of products and services addressing the cycle of water, from collection, distribution and use to the return of water to the environment.

ADDENDA (Continued)

RECENT AND PENDING STOCK DIVIDENDS AND SPLITS

Company	Amount	Ex-Div. Date	Date of Record	Payable Date
Colgate-Palmolive Co.	100%	5/16/2013	4/23/2013	5/15/2013
Jarden Corp.	3-for-2	3/19/2013	2/25/2012	3/18/2013
Lorillard, Inc.	3-for-1	1/16/2013	12/14/2012	1/15/2013
Salesforce.Com Inc.	4-for-1	4/18/2013	4/3/2013	4/17/2013
Tootsie Roll Industries Inc.	3%	3/1/2013	3/5/2013	4/5/2013

RECENT DIVIDEND CHANGES

Company	Latest Dividend Amount	Payable	Company	Latest Dividend Amount	Payable
Increased			**Increased**		
Agilent Technologies, Inc.	0.12 Q	3/28/13	NV Energy, Inc.	0.19 Q	3/1/13
Air Products & Chemicals, Inc.	0.71 Q	3/27/13	Occidental Petroleum Corp.	0.64 Q	3/6/13
Albermarle Corp.	0.24 Q	3/13/13	Old Republic International Corp.	0.18 Q	3/7/13
Alexandria Real Estate Equities	0.60 Q	3/26/13	Omnicom Group, Inc.	0.40 Q	3/1/13
AvalonBay Communities, Inc.	1.07 Q	3/26/13	Owens & Minor, Inc.	0.24 Q	3/13/13
BlackRock, Inc.	1.68 Q	3/5/13	Packaging Corp of America	0.31 Q	3/13/13
BRE Properties, Inc.	0.40 Q	3/13/13	Piedmont Natural Gas Co., Inc.	0.31 Q	3/21/13
Camden Property Trust	0.63 Q	3/26/13	PPL Corp.	0.37 Q	3/6/13
Chico's FAS Inc.	0.06 Q	3/14/13	Praxair, Inc.	0.60 Q	3/5/13
Chubb Corp.	0.44 Q	3/13/13	Principal Financial Group, Inc.	0.23 Q	3/7/13
Coca-Cola Co	0.28 Q	3/13/13	Public Serive Enterprise Group	0.36 Q	3/6/13
Coca-Cola Enterprises, Inc.	0.20 Q	3/6/13	Realtiy Income Corp.	0.18 Q	3/27/13
Comerica, Inc.	0.17 Q	3/13/13	Reliance Steel & Aluminum Co.	0.30 Q	3/6/13
Convergys Corp.	0.06 Q	3/20/13	RenaissanceRe Holdings Ltd.	0.28 Q	3/13/13
Corporate Executive Board Co.	0.23 Q	3/13/13	Rockwood Holdings, Inc.	0.40 Q	3/5/13
Covanta Holding Corp.	0.17 Q	3/26/13	SCANA Corp.	0.51 Q	3/7/13
DDR Corp.	0.14 Q	3/12/13	Sempra Energy	0.63 Q	3/26/13
Deere & Co.	0.51 Q	3/26/13	St. Jude Medical, Inc.	0.25 Q	3/26/13
Digital Realty Trust, Inc.	0.78 Q	3/13/13	State Street Corp.	0.26 Q	3/27/13
Dr. Pepper Snapple Group Inc.	0.38 Q	3/13/13	Taubman Centers, Inc.	0.50 Q	3/14/13
Endurance Specialty Holdings Ltd.	0.32 Q	3/13/13	Telephone & Data Systems	0.13 Q	3/13/13
Equity Lifestyle Properties Inc.	0.50 Q	3/26/13	Tupperware Brands Corp.	0.62 Q	3/18/13
Essex Property Trust, Inc.	1.21 Q	3/26/13	URS Corp.	0.21 Q	3/13/13
Exco Resources Inc.	0.05 Q	3/13/13	Ventas, Inc.	0.67 Q	3/6/13
Family Dollar Stores, Inc.	0.26 Q	3/13/13	W.P. Carey, Inc.	0.82 Q	3/26/13
Fidelity National Info. Svcs	0.22 Q	3/13/13	Wal-Mart Stores, Inc.	0.47 Q	3/8/13
First Horizon National Corp.	0.05 Q	3/13/13	Waste Management, Inc.	0.37 Q	3/7/13
Flowserve Corp.	0.42 Q	3/26/13	Weingarten Realty Investors	0.31 Q	3/5/13
GameStop Corp.	0.28 Q	3/1/13	WellPoint, Inc.	0.38 Q	3/6/13
Genuine Parts Co.	0.54 Q	3/6/13	Westar Energy, Inc.	0.34 Q	3/7/13
Halliburton Co.	0.13 Q	3/4/13	Williams Cos, Inc.	0.34 Q	3/6/13
Home Depot, Inc.	0.39 Q	3/12/13	Wyndham Worldwide Corp.	0.29 Q	3/12/13
Horace Mann Educators Corp.	0.20 Q	3/14/13	Xerox Corp.	0.06 Q	3/26/13
Host Hotels & Resorts, Inc.	0.10 Q	3/26/13	XL Group Plc	0.14 Q	3/13/13
Huntsman Corp.	0.13 Q	3/13/13	Zimmer Holdings	0.20 Q	3/26/13
Ingersoll-Rand Plc	0.21 Q	3/8/13			
Ingredion Inc.	0.38 Q	3/27/12	**Decreased**		
International Game Technology	0.08 Q	3/19/13	Berkley (W.R.) Corp.	0.09 Q	3/27/13
Interpublic Group of Companies	0.08 Q	3/7/13	Brown-Forman Corp.	0.26 Q	3/6/13
Kansas City Southern	0.22 Q	3/7/13	CapitalSource Inc.	0.01 Q	3/12/13
KBR, Inc.	0.08 Q	3/13/13	CenturyLink, Inc.	0.54 Q	3/7/13
Kimberly-Clark Corp.	0.81 Q	3/6/13	Dick's Sporting Goods, Inc.	0.13 Q	3/6/13
Kohl's Corp.	0.35 Q	3/11/13	Dillard's, Inc.	0.05 Q	3/26/13
Mead Johnson Nutrition Co.	0.34 Q	3/11/13	Equity Residential	0.40 Q	3/20/13
Myers Industries, Inc.	0.09 Q	3/7/13	HollyFrontier Corp.	0.30 Q	3/13/13
National Health Investors, Inc.	0.70 Q	3/26/13	Las Vegas Sands Corp.	0.35 Q	3/19/13
Newmont Mining Corp.	0.43 Q	3/11/13	Regal Entertainment Group	0.21 Q	3/1/13
Nordstrom, Inc.	0.30 Q	3//7/13			

RECENT AND PENDING NAME CHANGES

Old	New
Genworth Financial Inc.	Genworth Financial Inc. (Holding Co)
Limited Brands Inc.	L Brands, Inc.
Watson Pharmaceuticals, Inc.	Actavis, Inc.

LATEST DEVELOPMENTS

AMERICAN GRETINGS CORP. – On April 1, 2013, Co. announced that it has signed a definitive agreement under which a newly organized entity owned by the Weiss Family will acquire Co. Under the agreement, American Greetings class A and class B shareholders, excluding the Weiss Family and related entities, will receive $18.20, and, if declared by the Board of Directors, one regular quarterly dividend of $0.15 per share declared and payable in a manner consistent with Co.'s past practice. The total value of the transaction, which is targeted to close in July 2013, is approximately $878.0 million.

GENERAL ELECTRIC CO. – On April 8, 2013, Co. and Lufkin Industries Inc. announced a joint agreement whereby Co. will acquire Lufkin Industries Inc., a provider of artificial lift technologies for the oil and gas industry and a manufacturer of industrial gears, for approximately $3.30 billion. Lufkin shareholders will receive $88.50 per share in cash for each of their Lufkin shares.

PENNEY (J.C.) & CO., INC. – On April 15, 2013, Co. announced it has drawn $850.0 million out of its $1.85 billion committed revolving credit facility. Proceeds will be used to fund working capital requirements and capital expenditures, including the replenishment of inventory levels in anticipation of the completion of its newly renovated home departments.

THERMO FISHER SCIENTIFIC INC. – On April 15, 2013, Co. and Life Technologies Corporation announced a definitive agreement under which Co. will acquire Life Technologies for $76.00 in cash per fully diluted common share, or approximately $13.60 billion, plus the assumption of net debt at close ($2.20 billion as of year end 2012). The transaction, which is expected to close early in 2014, is subject to a Life shareholder vote and satisfying customary closing conditions, including regulatory approvals.

The 2013 Common Dividend Achievers

Companies listed below qualified for the 2013 Spring Edition of Mergent's Dividend Achievers. Also shown are total numbers of consecutive years of dividend growth.

Company Name	Years of Growth	Company Name	Years of Growth
3M Co	54	Diebold, Inc.	59
Abbott Laboratories	40	Donaldson Co. Inc.	17
ABM Industries, Inc.	48	Dover Corp	57
AFLAC Inc.	30	Eaton Vance Corp	31
AGL Resources Inc.	10	Ecolab, Inc.	20
Air Products & Chemicals, Inc.	30	Emerson Electric Co.	56
Albemarle Corp.	18	Energen Corp.	30
Altria Group Inc	47	Enterprise Products Partners L.P.	14
American States Water Co.	59	EOG Resources, Inc.	13
AptarGroup Inc.	19	Essex Property Trust, Inc.	18
Aqua America Inc	21	Exxon Mobil Corp.	30
Archer Daniels Midland Co.	38	FactSet Research Systems Inc.	13
AT&T Inc	28	Family Dollar Stores, Inc.	36
Atmos Energy Corp.	25	Federal Realty Investment Trust (MD)	45
Avista Corp.	10	Franklin Resources, Inc.	23
Badger Meter, Inc.	20	Fuller (H.B.) Company	45
Bard (C.R.), Inc.	41	General Dynamics Corp.	21
Becton, Dickinson and Co.	40	Genuine Parts Co.	56
Bemis Co Inc	29	Graco Inc.	13
Berkley (W. R.) Corp.	11	Grainger (W.W.) Inc.	41
Black Hills Corporation	41	Harris Corp.	11
Brady Corp.	28	HCC Insurance Holdings, Inc.	16
Brown & Brown, Inc.	19	HCP, Inc.	27
Brown-Forman Corp.	28	Helmerich & Payne, Inc.	36
Buckeye Partners, L.P.	17	Hormel Foods Corp.	46
California Water Service Group	45	Illinois Tool Works, Inc.	50
Carbo Ceramics Inc.	12	International Business Machines Corp.	17
Cardinal Health, Inc.	16	International Flavors & Fragrances Inc.	10
Carlisle Companies Inc.	36	Johnson & Johnson	50
Caterpillar Inc.	19	Kimberly-Clark Corp.	38
Chevron Corporation	25	Kinder Morgan Energy Partners, L.P.	16
Chubb Corp.	48	Leggett & Platt, Inc.	41
Church & Dwight Co., Inc.	16	Lindsay Corp	10
Clarcor Inc.	32	Lockheed Martin Corp.	10
Clorox Co.	36	Lowe's Companies Inc	51
Coca-Cola Co (The)	50	Magellan Midstream Partners LP	11
Colgate-Palmolive Co.	50	McCormick & Co., Inc.	26
Community Bank System, Inc.	21	McDonald's Corp	36
ConocoPhillips	12	McGraw-Hill Cos., Inc. (The)	39
Consolidated Edison, Inc.	38	MDU Resources Group Inc.	22
Cullen/Frost Bankers, Inc.	19	Medtronic, Inc.	35

The 2013 Common Dividend Achievers (Cont.)

Company Name	Years of Growth	Company Name	Years of Growth
Mercury General Corp.	26	Senior Housing Properties Trust	11
Meredith Corp.	19	Sherwin-Williams Co.	33
Mine Safety Appliances Co	42	SJW Corp.	45
Monsanto Co.	11	Smith (A.O.) Corp	20
Murphy Oil Corp	13	Smucker (J.M.) Co.	15
NACCO Industries Inc.	29	Sonoco Products Co.	29
National Fuel Gas Co. (NJ)	41	South Jersey Industries, Inc.	13
National Health Investors, Inc.	10	Southern Company (The)	11
National Retail Properties Inc	23	Stancorp Financial Group Inc	13
New Jersey Resources Corp	17	Stanley Black & Decker, Inc.	45
NextEra Energy Inc	17	Stepan Co.	45
NIKE, Inc	11	Stryker Corp.	20
Norfolk Southern Corp.	11	Sunoco Logistics Partners L.P.	10
Northeast Utilities	13	Sysco Corp.	36
Northwest Natural Gas Co.	57	Tanger Factory Outlet Centers, Inc.	19
NU Skin Enterprises, Inc.	11	Target Corp	41
Nucor Corp.	40	TC PipeLines, LP	13
NuStar Energy L.P.	11	Telephone & Data Systems, Inc	38
Occidental Petroleum Corp	10	Tennant Co.	40
Oil-Dri Corp. of America	10	Tiffany & Co.	10
Old Republic International Corp.	31	TJX Companies, Inc.	16
Oneok Inc.	10	Tootsie Roll Industries Inc	49
Owens & Minor, Inc.	15	UGI Corp.	25
Parker Hannifin Corp.	56	UniSource Energy Corp.	12
PepsiCo Inc.	41	United Technologies Corp.	19
Piedmont Natural Gas Co., Inc.	33	Universal Corp.	42
Pitney Bowes Inc	29	Universal Health Realty Income Trust	25
Plains All American Pipeline, L.P.	13	Urstadt Biddle Properties Inc	14
Polaris Industries Inc.	17	Valmont Industries, Inc.	11
PPG Industries, Inc.	41	Valspar Corp.	34
PPL Corp	13	Vector Group Ltd	14
Praxair, Inc.	20	Vectren Corp	37
Procter & Gamble Co.	59	VF Corp.	40
Prosperity Bancshares Inc.	13	W.P. Carey & Co. LLC	14
Questar Corp.	33	Walgreen Co.	37
Realty Income Corp.	18	Wal-Mart Stores, Inc.	37
RLI Corp.	36	Watsco Inc.	11
Rollins, Inc.	10	West Pharmaceutical Services, Inc.	20
Roper Industries, Inc	20	Westwood Holdings Group Inc	10
RPM International Inc (DE)	39	WGL Holdings, Inc.	36
SCANA Corp	12	Wiley (John) & Sons Inc.	19

AARON'S, INC.

Exchange	Symbol	Price	52Wk Range	Yield	P/E
NYS	AAN	$28.68 (3/28/2013)	31.16-24.83	0.24	12.75

*7 Year Price Score 132.60 *NYSE Composite Index=100   *12 Month Price Score 91.97

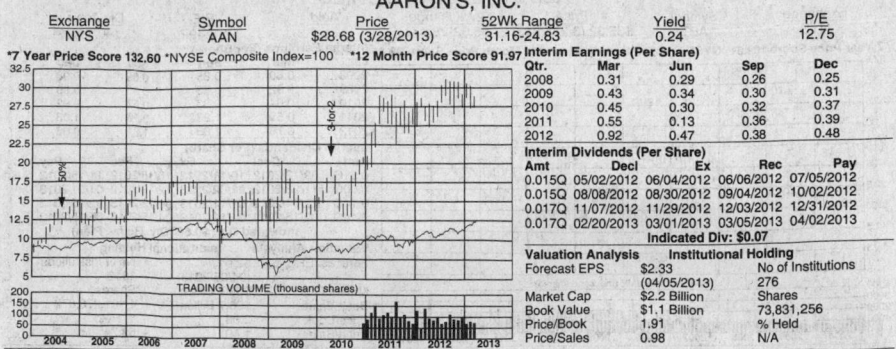

Interim Earnings (Per Share)

Qtr.	Mar	Jun	Sep	Dec
2008	0.31	0.29	0.26	0.25
2009	0.43	0.34	0.30	0.31
2010	0.45	0.30	0.32	0.37
2011	0.55	0.13	0.36	0.39
2012	0.92	0.47	0.38	0.48

Interim Dividends (Per Share)

Amt	Decl	Ex	Rec	Pay
0.015Q	05/02/2012	06/04/2012	06/06/2012	07/05/2012
0.015Q	08/08/2012	08/30/2012	09/04/2012	10/02/2012
0.017Q	11/07/2012	11/29/2012	12/03/2012	12/31/2012
0.017Q	02/20/2013	03/01/2013	03/05/2013	04/02/2013

Indicated Div: $0.07

Valuation Analysis		Institutional Holding	
Forecast EPS	$2.33	No of Institutions	
	(04/05/2013)	276	
Market Cap	$2.2 Billion	Shares	
Book Value	$1.1 Billion	73,831,256	
Price/Book	1.91	% Held	
Price/Sales	0.98	N/A	

TRADING VOLUME (thousand shares)

Business Summary: Retail - Furniture & Home Furnishings (MIC: 2.1.6 SIC: 7359 NAIC: 532299)

Aaron's is a retailer of consumer electronics, computers, residential furniture, household appliances and accessories. Co. engages in the lease ownership, lease and retail sale of products such as widescreen televisions, computers, living room, dining room and bedroom furniture, washers, dryers and refrigerators. Co. operates four reportable segments: Sales and Lease Ownership, Franchise, HomeSmart and Manufacturing. As of Dec 31 2012, Co. had 2,073 stores, comprised of 1,324 Company-operated stores in 29 states and 749 independently-owned franchised stores in 48 states and Canada.

Recent Developments: For the year ended Dec 31 2012, net income increased 52.1% to US$173.0 million from US$113.8 million in the prior year. Revenues were US$2.22 billion, up 9.9% from US$2.02 billion the year before. Operating income was US$279.7 million versus US$186.4 million in the prior year, an increase of 50.1%. Direct operating expenses rose 9.2% to US$411.1 million from US$376.5 million in the comparable period the year before. Indirect operating expenses increased 5.0% to US$1.53 billion from US$1.46 billion in the equivalent prior-year period.

Prospects: Our evaluation of Aaron's Inc as of Apr. 7, 2013 is the result of our systematic analysis on three basic characteristics: earnings strength, relative valuation, and recent stock price movement. The company has managed to produce a neutral trend in earnings per share over the past 5 quarters and while recent estimates for the company have remained steady, AAN has posted results that fell short of analysts expectations. Based on operating earnings yield, the company is undervalued when compared to all of the companies in our coverage universe. Share price changes over the past year indicates that AAN will perform well over the near term.

Financial Data
(US$ in Thousands)

	12/31/2012	12/31/2011	12/31/2010	12/31/2009	12/31/2008	12/31/2007	12/31/2006	12/31/2005
Earnings Per Share	2.25	1.43	1.44	1.37	1.11	0.97	0.98	0.76
Cash Flow Per Share	0.79	...	0.61	2.39	0.99	1.34	0.95	(0.09)
Tang Book Value Per Share	11.83	9.93	9.65	8.45	7.06	6.53	6.05	4.44
Dividends Per Share	0.620	0.054	0.049	0.092	0.087	0.081	0.076	0.072
Dividend Payout %	27.56	3.78	3.40	6.70	7.83	8.36	7.76	9.47
Income Statement								
Total Revenue	2,222,588	2,024,049	1,876,847	1,752,787	1,592,608	1,494,911	1,326,592	1,125,505
EBITDA	332,806	233,286	235,282	221,438	185,798	172,424	163,539	126,456
Depn & Amortn	53,100	45,200	41,400	40,700	38,400	35,100	29,100	25,600
Income Before Taxes	276,855	183,377	190,786	176,439	139,580	128,845	124,710	92,337
Income Taxes	103,812	69,610	72,410	63,561	53,811	48,570	46,075	34,344
Net Income	173,043	113,767	118,376	112,601	90,189	80,275	78,635	57,993
Average Shares	76,826	...	82,102	81,951	81,283	82,623	80,065	76,207
Balance Sheet								
Current Assets	1,342,110	1,283,122	1,090,949	894,264	815,378	718,042	693,876	623,671
Total Assets	1,812,929	1,735,149	1,502,072	1,321,456	1,233,270	1,113,176	979,606	858,515
Current Liabilities	271,554	317,844	253,352	215,482	208,271	171,671	148,930	136,974
Long-Term Obligations	141,528	153,789	41,790	55,044	114,817	185,832	129,974	211,873
Total Liabilities	676,803	758,595	522,655	434,196	471,726	439,796	372,591	424,044
Stockholders' Equity	1,136,126	976,554	979,417	887,260	761,544	673,380	607,015	434,471
Shares Outstanding	75,720	75,640	80,087	81,357	80,475	80,410	81,208	75,040
Statistical Record								
Return on Assets %	9.73	7.03	8.38	8.82	7.67	7.67	8.56	7.44
Return on Equity %	16.34	11.63	12.68	13.66	12.54	12.54	15.10	14.33
EBITDA Margin %	14.97	11.53	12.54	12.63	11.67	11.53	12.33	11.24
Net Margin %	7.79	5.62	6.31	6.42	5.66	5.37	5.93	5.15
Asset Turnover	1.25	1.25	1.33	1.37	1.35	1.43	1.44	1.44
Current Ratio	4.94	4.04	4.31	4.15	3.91	4.18	4.66	4.55
Debt to Equity	0.12	0.16	0.04	0.06	0.15	0.28	0.21	0.49
Price Range	31.16-24.83	29.16-19.19	20.79-13.00	20.30-11.47	16.69-9.51	18.35-11.05	17.59-13.07	15 60-10.46
P/E Ratio	13.85-11.04	20.39-13.42	14.44-9.03	14.82-8.37	15.03-8.57	18.91-11.40	17.95-13.33	20.53-13.76
Average Yield %	2.24	0.21	0.29	0.62	0.64	0.52	0.49	0.55

Address: 309 E. Paces Ferry Road, N.E., Atlanta, GA 30305-2377 Telephone: 404-231-0011	Web Site: www.aaronsinc.com Officers: R. Charles Loudermilk - Chairman Emeritus, Chairman, Chief Executive Officer Ronald W. Allen - President, Interim President, Chief Executive Officer	Auditors: Ernst & Young LLP Investor Contact: 678-402-3116 Transfer Agents: Computershare Investor Services, Canton, MA

ABBOTT LABORATORIES

Exchange	Symbol	Price	52Wk Range	Yield	P/E	Div Achiever
NYS	ABT	$35.32 (3/28/2013)	35.32-28.47	1.59	9.49	40 Years

*7 Year Price Score 109.61 *NYSE Composite Index=100 *12 Month Price Score 99.85

Interim Earnings (Per Share)

Qtr.	Mar	Jun	Sep	Dec
2008	0.60	0.85	0.69	0.98
2009	0.92	0.83	0.95	0.99
2010	0.64	0.83	0.57	0.92
2011	0.55	1.23	0.19	1.03
2012	0.78	1.08	1.21	0.66

Interim Dividends (Per Share)

Amt	Decl	Ex	Rec	Pay
0.51Q	09/13/2012	10/11/2012	10/15/2012	11/15/2012
0.00Q	11/28/2012	01/02/2013	12/12/2012	01/01/2013
0.14Q	12/14/2012	01/11/2013	01/15/2013	02/15/2013
0.14Q	02/15/2013	04/11/2013	04/15/2013	05/15/2013

Indicated Div: $0.56 (Div. Reinv. Plan)

Valuation Analysis

		Institutional Holding	
Forecast EPS	$2.01	No of Institutions	
	(04/05/2013)	1912	
Market Cap	$55.7 Billion	Shares	
Book Value	$26.7 Billion	1,101,276,672	
Price/Book	2.08	% Held	
Price/Sales	1.40	62.74	

Business Summary: Medical Instruments & Equipment (MIC: 4.3.1 SIC: 3841 NAIC: 339112)

Abbott Laboratories is engaged in the discovery, development, manufacture, and sale of health care products. Co.'s reportable segments include: Established Pharmaceutical Products, which includes a line of branded generic pharmaceutical products; Nutritional Products, which includes a line of adult and pediatric nutritional products; Diagnostic Products, which includes diagnostic systems and tests for blood banks, hospitals, commercial laboratories and alternate-care testing sites; and Vascular Products, which includes coronary, endovascular, structural heart, vessel closure and other medical device products. Non-reportable segments include the Diabetes Care and Medical Optics segments.

Recent Developments: For the year ended Dec 31 2012, net income increased 26.1% to US$5.96 billion from US$4.73 billion in the prior year. Revenues were US$39.87 billion, up 2.6% from US$38.85 billion the year before. Operating income was US$8.08 billion versus US$5.75 billion in the prior year, an increase of 40.6%. Direct operating expenses declined 2.7% to US$15.12 billion from US$15.54 billion in the comparable period the year before. Indirect operating expenses decreased 5.1% to US$16.67 billion from US$17.56 billion in the equivalent prior-year period.

Prospects: Our evaluation of Abbott Laboratories as of Apr. 7, 2013 is the result of our systematic analysis on three basic characteristics: earnings strength, relative valuation, and recent stock price movement. The company has generated a negative trend in earnings per share over the past 5 quarters and while recent estimates for the company have remained steady, ABT has posted better than expected results. Based on operating earnings yield, the company is undervalued when compared to all of the companies in our coverage universe. Share price changes over the past year indicates that ABT will perform in line with the market over the near term.

Financial Data

(US$ in Thousands)	12/31/2012	12/31/2011	12/31/2010	12/31/2009	12/31/2008	12/31/2007	12/31/2006	12/31/2005
Earnings Per Share	3.72	3.01	2.96	3.69	3.12	2.31	1.12	2.16
Cash Flow Per Share	5.90	5.76	5.65	4.70	4.51	3.36	3.44	3.25
Tang Book Value Per Share	1.50	N.M.	N.M.	2.17	1.51	1.24	N.M.	2.89
Dividends Per Share	2.010	1.880	1.720	1.560	1.405	1.270	1.160	1.085
Dividend Payout %	54.03	62.46	58.11	42.28	45.03	54.98	103.57	50.23
Income Statement								
Total Revenue	39,873,910	38,851,259	35,166,721	30,764,707	29,527,552	25,914,238	22,476,322	22,337,808
EBITDA	9,674,326	8,855,110	9,243,371	9,515,184	7,861,635	6,175,053	3,364,171	5,322,325
Depn & Amortn	2,898,534	3,211,523	3,082,855	1,939,533	1,797,101	1,747,031	1,271,265	990,131
Income Before Taxes	6,262,614	5,198,642	5,712,834	7,193,774	5,737,289	3,971,632	1,800,559	4,178,532
Income Taxes	299,694	470,193	1,086,662	1,447,936	1,122,070	863,334	559,615	1,247,855
Net Income	5,962,920	4,728,449	4,626,172	5,745,838	4,880,719	3,606,314	1,716,755	3,372,065
Average Shares	1,591,838	1,567,389	1,556,022	1,555,126	1,560,753	1,560,657	1,536,724	1,564,103
Balance Sheet								
Current Assets	31,322,583	23,768,774	22,317,529	23,313,891	17,042,559	14,042,733	11,281,883	11,386,028
Total Assets	67,234,944	60,276,893	59,462,266	52,416,623	42,419,204	39,713,924	36,178,172	29,141,203
Current Liabilities	13,280,176	15,480,228	17,262,434	13,049,489	11,591,908	9,103,278	11,951,195	7,415,514
Long-Term Obligations	18,085,302	12,039,822	12,523,517	11,266,294	8,713,327	9,487,789	7,009,664	4,571,504
Total Liabilities	40,513,983	35,837,060	37,074,131	29,560,885	24,939,235	21,935,384	22,123,986	14,725,932
Stockholders' Equity	26,720,961	24,439,833	22,388,135	22,855,627	17,479,551	17,778,540	14,054,186	14,415,271
Shares Outstanding	1,576,667	1,570,378	1,546,983	1,551,167	1,552,432	1,549,910	1,537,243	1,539,234
Statistical Record								
Return on Assets %	9.33	7.90	8.27	12.12	11.85	9.50	5.26	11.65
Return on Equity %	23.25	20.19	20.45	28.49	27.61	22.66	12.06	23.47
EBITDA Margin %	24.26	22.79	26.28	30.93	26.62	23.83	14.97	23.83
Net Margin %	14.95	12.17	13.15	18.68	16.53	13.92	7.64	15.10
Asset Turnover	0.62	0.65	0.63	0.65	0.72	0.68	0.69	0.77
Current Ratio	2.36	1.54	1.29	1.79	1.47	1.54	0.94	1.54
Debt to Equity	0.68	0.49	0.56	0.49	0.50	0.53	0.50	0.32
Price Range	34.51-25.91	26.95-21.61	26.91-21.94	27.39-19.87	28.95-23.66	28.44-23.43	23.67-18.92	23.92-18.00
P/E Ratio	9.28-6.96	8.95-7.18	9.09-7.41	7.42-5.38	9.28-7.58	12.31-10.14	21.14-16.90	11.07-8.34
Average Yield %	6.66	7.70	7.08	6.73	5.32	4.88	5.38	5.00

Address: 100 Abbott Park Road, Abbott Park, IL 60064-6400 Telephone: 847-937-6100	Web Site: www.abbott.com Officers: Miles D. White - Chairman, Chief Executive Officer Richard W. Ashley - Executive Vice President	Auditors: Ernst & Young LLP Investor Contact: 847-937-7300 Transfer Agents: Computershare Trust Company, NA, Providence, RI

ABERCROMBIE & FITCH CO.

Exchange	Symbol	Price	52Wk Range	Yield	P/E
NYS	ANF	$46.20 (3/28/2013)	53.29-29.06	1.73	16.21

*7 Year Price Score 69.64   *NYSE Composite Index=100   *12 Month Price Score 108.27

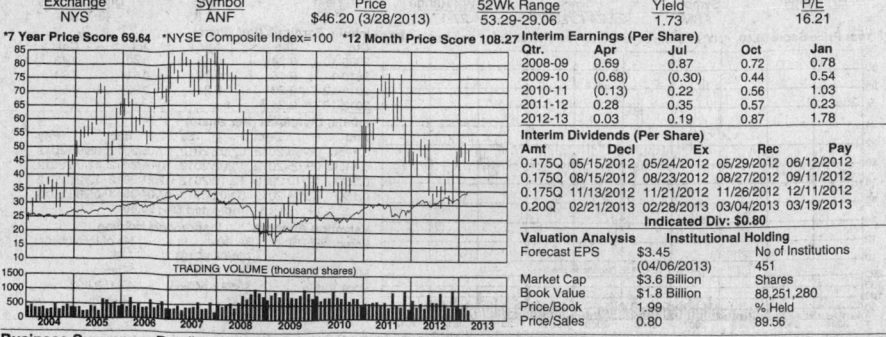

Interim Earnings (Per Share)

Qtr.	Apr	Jul	Oct	Jan
2008-09	0.69	0.87	0.72	0.78
2009-10	(0.68)	(0.30)	0.44	0.54
2010-11	(0.13)	0.22	0.56	1.03
2011-12	0.28	0.35	0.57	0.23
2012-13	0.03	0.19	0.87	1.78

Interim Dividends (Per Share)

Amt	Decl	Ex	Rec	Pay
0.175Q	05/15/2012	05/24/2012	05/29/2012	06/12/2012
0.175Q	08/15/2012	08/23/2012	08/27/2012	09/11/2012
0.175Q	11/13/2012	11/21/2012	11/26/2012	12/11/2012
0.20Q	02/21/2013	02/28/2013	03/04/2013	03/19/2013

Indicated Div: $0.80

Valuation Analysis

		Institutional Holding	
Forecast EPS	$3.45	No of Institutions	
	(04/06/2013)	451	
Market Cap	$3.6 Billion	Shares	
Book Value	$1.8 Billion	88,251,280	
Price/Book	1.99	% Held	
Price/Sales	0.80	89.56	

Business Summary: Retail - Apparel and Accessories (MIC: 2.1.5 SIC: 5651 NAIC: 448140)

Abercrombie & Fitch, through its subsidiaries, is a specialty retailer that operates stores and direct-to-consumer operations. Through these channels, Co. sells an array of products, including: casual sportswear apparel, including knit and woven shirts, graphic t-shirts, fleece, jeans and woven pants, shorts, sweaters, and outerwear; personal care products; and accessories for men, women and kids. Co. also operates stores and direct-to-consumer operations offering bras, underwear, personal care products, sleepwear and at-home products for girls. As of Jan 28 2012, Co. operated 946 stores in the U.S. and 99 stores outside of the U.S.

Recent Developments: For the year ended Feb 2 2013, income from continuing operations increased 65.6% to US$237.0 million from US$143.1 million a year earlier. Net income increased 64.7% to US$237.0 million from US$143.9 million in the prior year. Revenues were US$4.51 billion, up 8.5% from US$4.16 billion the year before. Operating income was US$374.2 million versus US$221.4 million in the prior year, an increase of 69.0%. Direct operating expenses rose 5.4% to US$1.69 billion from US$1.61 billion in the comparable period the year before. Indirect operating expenses increased 4.9% to US$2.44 billion from US$2.33 billion in the equivalent prior-year period.

Prospects: Our evaluation of Abercrombie & Fitch Co. as of Apr. 7, 2013 is the result of our systematic analysis on three basic characteristics: earnings strength, relative valuation, and recent stock price movement. The company has produced a positive trend in earnings per share over the past 5 quarters and while recent estimates for the company have remained steady, ANF has posted better than expected results. Based on operating earnings yield, the company is undervalued when compared to all of the companies in our coverage universe. Share price changes over the past year indicates that ANF will perform poorly over the near term.

Financial Data

(US$ in Thousands)	02/02/2013	01/28/2012	01/29/2011	01/30/2010	01/31/2009	02/02/2008	02/03/2007	01/28/2006
Earnings Per Share	2.85	1.43	1.67	...	3.05	5.20	4.59	3.66
Cash Flow Per Share	8.21	4.22	4.46	4.59	5.67	9.40	6.50	5.22
Tang Book Value Per Share	23.18	21.75	21.67	20.78	21.06	18.78	15.92	11.34
Dividends Per Share	0.700	0.700	0.700	0.700	0.700	0.700	0.700	0.600
Dividend Payout %	24.56	48.95	41.92	...	22.95	13.46	15.25	16.39
Income Statement								
Total Revenue	4,510,805	4,158,058	3,468,777	2,928,626	3,540,276	3,749,847	3,318,158	2,784,711
EBITDA	552,536	374,728	412,712	309,482	621,526	886,795	769,761	634,417
Depn & Amortn	178,303	184,698	180,780	191,570	182,140	146,298	111,671	91,679
Income Before Taxes	366,945	186,453	228,570	119,510	450,768	759,325	671,986	549,412
Income Taxes	129,934	59,591	78,287	40,557	178,513	283,628	249,800	215,426
Net Income	237,011	127,658	150,283	254	272,255	475,697	422,186	333,986
Average Shares	83,175	89,537	89,851	88,609	89,291	91,523	92,010	91,221
Balance Sheet								
Current Assets	1,307,824	1,488,775	1,433,268	1,235,846	1,084,825	1,140,255	1,092,078	947,084
Total Assets	2,987,401	3,048,153	2,947,902	2,821,866	2,848,181	2,567,598	2,248,067	1,789,718
Current Liabilities	690,801	705,353	558,851	449,372	449,797	543,113	510,627	491,554
Long-Term Obligations	63,942	57,851	68,566	71,213	100,000	...	...	...
Total Liabilities	1,169,133	1,185,697	1,057,118	993,949	1,002,603	949,285	842,770	794,601
Stockholders' Equity	1,818,268	1,862,456	1,890,784	1,827,917	1,845,578	1,618,313	1,405,297	995,117
Shares Outstanding	78,445	85,638	87,246	87,985	87,635	86,158	88,300	87,726
Statistical Record								
Return on Assets %	7.73	4.27	5.22	0.01	10.08	19.81	20.57	21.35
Return on Equity %	12.67	6.82	8.10	0.01	15.76	31.55	34.61	40.24
EBITDA Margin %	12.25	9.01	11.90	10.57	17.56	23.65	23.20	22.78
Net Margin %	5.25	3.07	4.33	0.01	7.69	12.69	12.72	11.99
Asset Turnover	1.47	1.39	1.21	1.04	1.31	1.56	1.62	1.78
Current Ratio	1.89	2.11	2.56	2.75	2.41	2.10	2.14	1.93
Debt to Equity	0.04	0.03	0.04	0.04	0.05	...	...	...
Price Range	53.53-29.06	77.14-44.23	58.14-30.39	41.84-17.11	81.96-14.15	84.51-68.15	81.51-50.95	73.14-44.36
P/E Ratio	18.78-10.20	53.94-30.93	34.81-18.20	N.M.	26.87-4.64	16.25-13.11	17.76-11.10	19.98-12.12
Average Yield %	1.71	1.13	1.67	2.38	1.36	0.90	1.08	1.01

Address: 6301 Fitch Path, New Albany, OH 43054
Telephone: 614-283-6500

Web Site: www.abercrombie.com
Officers: Michael S. Jeffries - Chairman, President (frmr), Chief Executive Officer Jonathan E. Ramsden - Executive Vice President, Chief Financial Officer

Auditors: PricewaterhouseCoopers LLP
Investor Contact: 614-283-6751
Transfer Agents: American Stock Transfer & Trust Company, Brooklyn, NY

3

ABM INDUSTRIES, INC.

Exchange	Symbol	Price	52Wk Range	Yield	P/E	Div Achiever
NYS	ABM	$22.24 (3/28/2013)	24.27-17.95	2.70	18.85	48 Years

*7 Year Price Score 86.40   *NYSE Composite Index=100   *12 Month Price Score 100.31

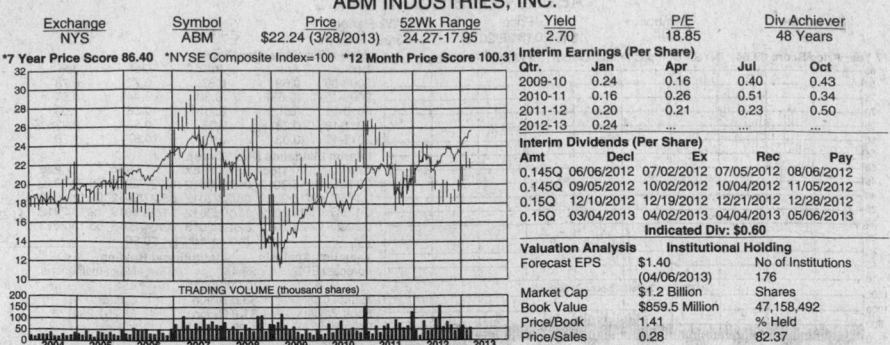

Interim Earnings (Per Share)

Qtr.	Jan	Apr	Jul	Oct
2009-10	0.24	0.16	0.40	0.43
2010-11	0.16	0.26	0.51	0.34
2011-12	0.20	0.21	0.23	0.50
2012-13	0.24	...	...	...

Interim Dividends (Per Share)

Amt	Decl	Ex	Rec	Pay
0.145Q	06/06/2012	07/02/2012	07/05/2012	08/06/2012
0.145Q	09/05/2012	10/02/2012	10/04/2012	11/05/2012
0.15Q	12/10/2012	12/19/2012	12/21/2012	12/28/2012
0.15Q	03/04/2013	04/02/2013	04/04/2013	05/06/2013

Indicated Div: $0.60

Valuation Analysis

		Institutional Holding	
Forecast EPS	$1.40	No of Institutions	
	(04/06/2013)	176	
Market Cap	$1.2 Billion	Shares	
Book Value	$859.5 Million	47,158,492	
Price/Book	1.41	% Held	
Price/Sales	0.28	82.37	

Business Summary: Sanitation Services (MIC: 7.5.3 SIC: 7349 NAIC: 561720)

ABM Industries is a provider of facilities management services. Co. has four reportable operating segments: Janitorial, which provides janitorial services, including floor cleaning and finishing, window washing, furniture polishing, carpet cleaning and dusting, and other building cleaning services; Facility Solutions, which provides end-to-end integrated facility applications services; Parking, which operates parking lots and garages; and Security, which provides security services including staffing of security officers; mobile patrol services; investigative services; electronic monitoring of fire, life safety systems, and access control devices; and security consulting services.

Recent Developments: For the quarter ended Jan 31 2013, income from continuing operations increased 25.8% to US$13.4 million from US$10.6 million in the year-earlier quarter. Net income increased 25.9% to US$13.4 million from US$10.6 million in the year-earlier quarter. Revenues were US$1.18 billion, up 10.1% from US$1.07 billion the year before. Operating income was US$19.3 million versus US$17.8 million in the prior-year quarter, an increase of 8.5%. Direct operating expenses rose 10.5% to US$1.07 billion from US$966.4 million in the comparable period the year before. Indirect operating expenses increased 6.0% to US$94.9 million from US$89.6 million in the equivalent prior-year period.

Prospects: Our evaluation of ABM Industries Inc. as of Apr. 7, 2013 is the result of our systematic analysis on three basic characteristics: earnings strength, relative valuation, and recent stock price movement. The company has managed to produce a neutral trend in earnings per share over the past 5 quarters and while recent estimates for the company have been mixed, ABM has posted better than expected results. Based on operating earnings yield, the company is undervalued when compared to all of the companies in our coverage universe. Share price changes over the past year indicates that ABM will perform poorly over the near term.

Financial Data

(US$ in Thousands)	3 Mos	10/31/2012	10/31/2011	10/31/2010	10/31/2009	10/31/2008	10/31/2007	10/31/2006
Earnings Per Share	1.18	1.14	1.27	1.23	1.05	0.88	1.04	1.88
Cash Flow Per Share	2.33	2.78	3.01	2.88	2.74	1.35	1.10	2.66
Tang Book Value Per Share	N.M.	N.M.	N.M.	1.51	1.54	0.90	6.58	5.54
Dividends Per Share	0.585	0.580	0.560	0.540	0.520	0.500	0.480	0.440
Dividend Payout %	49.58	50.88	44.09	43.90	49.52	56.82	46.15	23.40
Income Statement								
Total Revenue	1,182,123	4,300,265	4,246,842	3,495,747	3,481,823	3,623,590	2,842,811	2,792,668
EBITDA	26,495	147,117	170,216	144,976	123,825	127,544	99,019	179,000
Depn & Amortn	7,189	50,864	52,648	36,264	33,284	28,035	18,765	20,764
Income Before Taxes	15,996	86,254	101,763	104,073	84,660	84,316	79,787	157,741
Income Taxes	3,809	29,931	36,980	40,203	29,170	31,585	27,347	64,536
Net Income	13,382	62,582	68,504	64,121	54,293	45,434	52,440	93,205
Average Shares	55,497	54,914	54,103	52,908	51,845	51,386	50,629	49,678
Balance Sheet								
Current Assets	820,478	767,427	733,757	608,756	620,997	635,069	642,890	631,741
Total Assets	2,088,148	1,869,251	1,879,598	1,548,670	1,521,153	1,549,913	1,120,673	1,016,274
Current Liabilities	459,154	473,910	443,196	333,851	342,694	361,089	289,744	319,285
Long-Term Obligations	423,000	215,000	300,000	140,500	172,500	230,000	...	...
Total Liabilities	1,228,685	1,018,853	1,083,712	809,645	834,103	905,862	514,915	475,027
Stockholders' Equity	859,463	850,398	795,886	739,025	687,050	644,051	605,758	541,247
Shares Outstanding	54,627	54,393	53,333	52,635	51,688	50,963	50,019	48,634
Statistical Record								
Return on Assets %	3.29	3.33	4.00	4.18	3.54	3.39	4.91	9.71
Return on Equity %	7.85	7.58	8.93	8.99	8.16	7.25	9.14	18.33
EBITDA Margin %	2.24	3.42	4.01	4.15	3.56	3.52	3.48	6.41
Net Margin %	1.13	1.46	1.61	1.83	1.56	1.25	1.84	3.34
Asset Turnover	2.22	2.29	2.48	2.28	2.27	2.71	2.66	2.91
Current Ratio	1.79	1.62	1.66	1.82	1.81	1.76	2.22	1.98
Debt to Equity	0.49	0.25	0.38	0.19	0.25	0.36	...	...
Price Range	24.50-17.95	24.50-17.95	27.00-17.29	22.77-18.35	22.98-11.79	27.39-13.28	30.43-19.59	21.65-16.22
P/E Ratio	20.76-15.21	21.49-15.75	21.26-13.61	18.51-14.92	21.89-11.23	31.13-15.09	29.26-18.84	11.52-8.63
Average Yield %	2.84	2.79	2.41	2.59	2.93	2.37	1.96	2.38

Address: 551 Fifth Avenue, Suite 300, New York, NY 10176 Telephone: 212-297-0200	Web Site: www.abm.com Officers: Maryellen C. Herringer - Chairman Henrik C. Slipsager - President, Chief Executive Officer	Auditors: KPMG LLP Transfer Agents: BNY Mellon Shareowner Services, Inc., Pittsburgh, PA

ACCENTURE PLC

Exchange	Symbol	Price	52Wk Range	Yield	P/E
NYS	ACN	$75.97 (3/28/2013)	78.35-55.28	2.13	16.44

*7 Year Price Score 132.30 *NYSE Composite Index=100 ***12 Month Price Score 104.55**

TRADING VOLUME (thousand shares)

Interim Earnings (Per Share)

Qtr.	Nov	Feb	May	Aug
2009-10	0.67	0.60	0.73	0.66
2010-11	0.81	0.75	0.93	0.91
2011-12	0.96	0.97	1.03	0.88
2012-13	1.06	1.65	...	...

Interim Dividends (Per Share)

Amt	Decl	Ex	Rec	Pay
0.675S	09/27/2011	10/12/2011	10/14/2011	11/15/2011
0.675S	03/22/2012	04/11/2012	04/13/2012	05/15/2012
0.81S	09/27/2012	10/10/2012	10/12/2012	11/15/2012
0.81S	03/27/2013	04/10/2013	04/12/2013	05/15/2013

Indicated Div: $1.62

Valuation Analysis		Institutional Holding	
Forecast EPS	$4.28	No of Institutions	
	(04/05/2013)	N/A	
Market Cap	$51.8 Billion	Shares	
Book Value	$5.5 Billion	N/A	
Price/Book	9.50	% Held	
Price/Sales	1.72	N/A	

Business Summary: IT Services (MIC: 6.3.1 SIC: 7389 NAIC: 561499)

Accenture is a holding company engaged in providing management consulting, technology and outsourcing services. Co. has five operating groups: Communications, Media & Technology, which serves the communications, electronics, high technology, media and entertainment industries; Financial Service, which serves the banking, capital markets and insurance industries; Health & Public Service, which serves healthcare payers and providers, as well as government agencies and public service organizations; Products, which serves interconnected consumer-relevant industries; and Resources, which serves the chemicals, energy, forest products, metals and mining, utilities and related industries.

Recent Developments: For the quarter ended Feb 28 2013, net income increased 66.2% to US$1.19 billion from US$714.2 million in the year-earlier quarter. Revenues were US$7.49 billion, up 3.2% from US$7.26 billion the year before. Operating income was US$1.16 billion versus US$889.3 million in the prior-year quarter, an increase of 30.9%. Direct operating expenses rose 2.3% to US$5.26 billion from US$5.14 billion in the comparable period the year before. Indirect operating expenses decreased 13.1% to US$1.07 billion from US$1.23 billion in the equivalent prior-year period.

Prospects: Our evaluation of Accenture PLC as of Apr. 7, 2013 is the result of our systematic analysis on three basic characteristics: earnings strength, relative valuation, and recent stock price movement. The company has produced a positive trend in earnings per share over the past 5 quarters and while recent estimates for the company have been mixed, ACN has posted better than expected results. Based on operating earnings yield, the company is undervalued when compared to all of the companies in our coverage universe. Share price changes over the past year indicates that ACN will perform in line with the market over the near term.

Financial Data

(US$ in Thousands)	6 Mos	3 Mos	08/31/2012	08/31/2011	08/31/2010	08/31/2009	08/31/2008	08/31/2007
Earnings Per Share	4.62	3.94	3.84	3.40	2.66	2.44	2.65	1.97
Cash Flow Per Share	5.31	5.74	6.60	5.33	4.85	5.07	4.58	4.35
Tang Book Value Per Share	5.89	4.58	4.33	3.98	2.89	2.89	2.33	1.87
Dividends Per Share	1.485	1.485	1.350	0.900	1.125	0.500	0.420	0.350
Dividend Payout %	32.14	37.69	35.16	26.47	42.29	20.49	15.85	17.77
Income Statement								
Total Revenue	15,161,356	7,668,036	29,777,985	27,352,914	23,094,078	23,170,968	25,313,826	21,452,747
EBITDA	2,514,559	1,182,162	4,194,677	3,783,488	3,168,187	2,920,775	3,334,708	2,749,878
Depn & Amortn	297,190	139,924	317,992	297,549	269,072	278,840	318,863	260,490
Income Before Taxes	2,227,805	1,046,456	3,904,174	3,512,022	2,914,369	2,677,736	3,107,762	2,618,918
Income Taxes	274,676	280,425	1,079,241	958,782	853,910	739,590	910,574	895,861
Net Income	1,800,619	698,817	2,553,510	2,277,677	1,780,656	1,589,963	1,691,751	1,243,148
Average Shares	714,807	716,368	726,416	742,184	766,047	785,374	822,371	861,923
Balance Sheet								
Current Assets	12,016,949	12,013,526	12,587,931	11,471,183	9,563,625	8,990,514	9,159,128	7,971,178
Total Assets	16,358,730	16,408,020	16,665,415	15,731,510	12,835,253	12,255,734	12,398,525	10,747,162
Current Liabilities	7,365,474	7,977,359	8,109,205	7,906,589	6,567,604	6,151,381	6,847,878	6,962,616
Long-Term Obligations	16	19	22	...	1,445	361	1,708	2,565
Total Liabilities	10,906,381	11,901,387	12,519,582	11,852,559	9,999,507	9,369,141	9,858,019	8,683,830
Stockholders' Equity	5,452,349	4,506,633	4,145,833	3,878,951	2,835,746	2,886,593	2,540,506	2,063,332
Shares Outstanding	681,678	681,362	676,750	690,799	690,063	712,875	731,213	758,550
Statistical Record								
Return on Assets %	19.08	16.47	15.72	15.95	14.19	12.90	14.58	12.33
Return on Equity %	61.85	63.10	63.47	67.84	62.24	58.59	73.29	62.82
EBITDA Margin %	16.59	15.42	14.09	13.83	13.72	12.61	13.17	12.82
Net Margin %	11.88	9.11	8.58	8.33	7.71	6.86	6.68	5.79
Asset Turnover	1.87	1.88	1.83	1.92	1.84	1.88	2.18	2.13
Current Ratio	1.63	1.51	1.55	1.45	1.45	1.46	1.34	1.14
Price Range	75.40-55.28	71.39-51.74	65.89-49.82	63.44-36.60	44.67-33.00	41.96-26.67	42.21-32.79	43.81-28.38
P/E Ratio	16.32-11.97	18.12-13.13	17.16-12.97	18.66-10.76	16.79-12.41	17.20-10.93	15.93-12.37	22.24-14.41
Average Yield %	2.27	2.41	2.32	1.76	2.82	1.57	1.12	0.95

Address: 1 Grand Canal Square, Grand Canal Harbour, Dublin, 2	Web Site: www.accenture.com	Auditors: KPMG LLP
Telephone: 164-620-00	Officers: William D. Green - Chairman, Chief Executive Officer Pierre Nanterme - Chief Executive Officer	Investor Contact: 353-140-78203 Transfer Agents: Computershare, Canton, MA

ACE, LTD.

Exchange	Symbol	Price	52Wk Range	Yield	P/E
NYS	ACE	$88.97 (3/28/2013)	89.06-69.17	2.20	11.28

*7 Year Price Score 115.99 *NYSE Composite Index=100 *12 Month Price Score 102.29

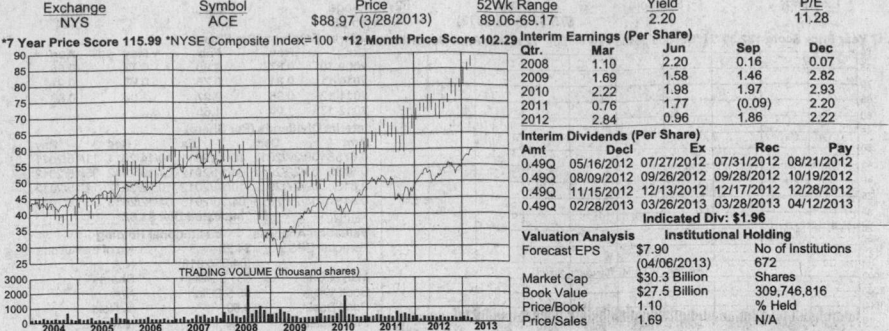

TRADING VOLUME (thousand shares)

Interim Earnings (Per Share)

Qtr.	Mar	Jun	Sep	Dec
2008	1.10	2.20	0.16	0.07
2009	1.69	1.58	1.46	2.82
2010	2.22	1.98	1.97	2.93
2011	0.76	1.77	(0.09)	2.20
2012	2.84	0.96	1.86	2.22

Interim Dividends (Per Share)

Amt	Decl	Ex	Rec	Pay
0.49Q	05/16/2012	07/27/2012	07/31/2012	08/21/2012
0.49Q	08/09/2012	09/26/2012	09/28/2012	10/19/2012
0.49Q	11/15/2012	12/13/2012	12/17/2012	12/28/2012
0.49Q	02/28/2013	03/26/2013	03/28/2013	04/12/2013

Indicated Div: $1.96

Valuation Analysis

		Institutional Holding	
Forecast EPS	$7.90	No of Institutions	
	(04/06/2013)	672	
Market Cap	$30.3 Billion	Shares	
Book Value	$27.5 Billion	309,746,816	
Price/Book	1.10	% Held	
Price/Sales	1.69	N/A	

Business Summary: General Insurance (MIC: 5.2.1 SIC: 6331 NAIC: 524130)

ACE is a holding company. Through its direct and indirect subsidiaries, Co. is an insurance and reinsurance organization, serving commercial and individual customers in more than 170 countries. Co. serves the property and casualty insurance and reinsurance needs of businesses in a range of industries. Co. also provides insurance products such as personal accident, supplemental health, and life insurance to individuals in select countries. As of Dec 31 2011, Co. had four segments: Insurance - North American; Insurance - Overseas General; Global Reinsurance; and Life.

Recent Developments: For the year ended Dec 31 2012, net income increased 75.7% to US$2.71 billion from US$1.54 billion in the prior year. Revenues were US$17.94 billion, up 6.5% from US$16.83 billion the year before. Net premiums earned were US$15.68 billion versus US$15.39 billion in the prior year, an increase of 1.9%. Net investment income fell 2.7% to US$2.18 billion from US$2.24 billion a year ago.

Prospects: Our evaluation of ACE Ltd. as of Apr. 7, 2013 is the result of our systematic analysis on three basic characteristics: earnings strength, relative valuation, and recent stock price movement. The company has generated a negative trend in earnings per share over the past 5 quarters and while recent estimates for the company have remained steady, ACE has posted results that fell short of analysts expectations. Based on operating earnings yield, the company is undervalued when compared to all of the companies in our coverage universe. Share price changes over the past year indicates that ACE will perform in line with the market over the near term.

Financial Data
(US$ in Thousands)

	12/31/2012	12/31/2011	12/31/2010	12/31/2009	12/31/2008	12/31/2007	12/31/2006	12/31/2005
Earnings Per Share	7.89	4.65	9.11	7.55	3.53	7.66	6.91	3.31
Cash Flow Per Share	11.72	10.26	10.44	9.90	12.45	14.47	12.76	14.73
Tang Book Value Per Share	66.28	58.43	54.67	46.76	32.07	42.29	35.36	28.17
Dividends Per Share	2.060	1.150	1.300	1.190	1.090	1.060	0.980	...
Dividend Payout %	26.11	32.25	14.27	15.76	30.88	13.84	14.18	...
Income Statement								
Premium Income	15,677,000	15,387,000	13,504,000	13,240,000	13,203,000	12,297,000	11,825,000	11,748,000
Total Revenue	17,936,000	16,834,000	16,006,000	15,075,000	13,632,000	14,154,000	13,328,000	13,088,000
Benefits & Claims	10,174,000	9,921,000	7,936,000	7,747,000	8,002,000	7,519,000	7,193,000	8,714,000
Income Before Taxes	2,896,000	2,053,000	3,600,000	3,119,000	1,526,000	3,199,000	2,771,000	1,301,000
Income Taxes	270,000	506,000	559,000	528,000	370,000	575,000	522,000	273,000
Net Income	2,706,000	1,585,000	3,108,000	2,549,000	1,197,000	2,578,000	2,305,000	1,028,000
Average Shares	342,746	340,780	341,246	337,539	332,481	330,447	327,232	297,299
Balance Sheet								
Total Assets	92,545,000	87,505,000	83,355,000	77,980,000	72,057,000	72,090,000	67,135,000	62,440,000
Total Liabilities	65,014,000	62,989,000	60,381,000	58,313,000	57,611,000	55,413,000	52,857,000	50,628,000
Stockholders' Equity	27,531,000	24,516,000	22,974,000	19,667,000	14,446,000	16,677,000	14,278,000	11,812,000
Shares Outstanding	340,321	336,927	334,942	336,524	333,645	329,704	326,455	323,322
Statistical Record								
Return on Assets %	3.00	1.86	3.85	3.40	1.66	3.70	3.56	1.73
Return on Equity %	10.37	6.68	14.58	14.94	7.67	16.66	17.67	9.50
Loss Ratio %	64.90	64.48	58.77	58.51	60.61	61.14	60.83	74.17
Net Margin %	15.09	9.42	19.42	16.91	8.78	18.21	17.29	7.85
Price Range	81.70-68.98	73.33-58.98	62.37-47.50	55.14-31.84	66.00-37.97	63.97-53.22	61.16-48.18	56.57-38.70
P/E Ratio	10.35-8.74	15.77-12.68	6.85-5.21	7.30-4.22	18.70-10.76	8.35-6.95	8.85-6.97	17.09-11.69
Average Yield %	2.76	2.27	2.40	2.55	1.99	1.79	1.81	...

Address: Baerengasse 32, Zurich, CH-8001 **Telephone:** 434-567-600	**Web Site:** www.acegroup.com **Officers:** Evan G. Greenberg - Chairman, President, Chief Executive Officer John W. Keogh - Vice-Chairman, Chief Executive Officer	**Auditors:** PricewaterhouseCoopers LLP **Investor Contact:** 441-299-9283 **Transfer Agents:** Mellon Investor Services LLC, Ridgefield Park, NJ

ACTAVIS, INC

Exchange	Symbol	Price	52Wk Range	Yield	P/E
NYS	ACT	$92.11 (3/28/2013)	92.11-65.85	N/A	121.20

*7 Year Price Score 162.16 *NYSE Composite Index=100   *12 Month Price Score 98.64

Interim Earnings (Per Share)

Qtr.	Mar	Jun	Sep	Dec
2008	0.45	0.53	0.62	0.49
2009	0.43	0.46	0.55	0.51
2010	0.57	0.57	0.21	0.14
2011	0.36	0.42	0.54	0.75
2012	0.43	(0.49)	0.60	0.22

Interim Dividends (Per Share)

No Dividends Paid

Valuation Analysis

		Institutional Holding	
Forecast EPS	$8.05	No of Institutions	
	(04/05/2013)	623	
Market Cap	$11.8 Billion	Shares	
Book Value	$3.8 Billion	116,486,256	
Price/Book	3.07	% Held	
Price/Sales	1.99	N/A	

Business Summary: Pharmaceuticals (MIC: 4.1.1 SIC: 2834 NAIC: 325412)

Actavis is a pharmaceutical company engaged in the development, manufacturing, marketing, sale and distribution of generic and brand pharmaceutical products. Co. operates its business in the following operating segments: Global Generics, which is engaged in the development, manufacturing and sale of generic pharmaceutical products; Global Brands, which markets a number of products, including Androderm®, Gelnique®, and INFeD®, among others; and Distribution, which distributes generic and selected brand pharmaceutical products, vaccines, injectables and over-the-counter medicines to independent pharmacies, alternate care providers, pharmacy chains and physicians' offices.

Recent Developments: For the year ended Dec 31 2012, net income decreased 62.1% to US$98.3 million from US$259.1 million in the prior year. Revenues were US$5.91 billion, up 29.0% from US$4.58 billion the year before. Operating income was US$320.8 million versus US$536.2 million in the prior year, a decrease of 40.2%. Direct operating expenses rose 32.2% to US$3.39 billion from US$2.56 billion in the comparable period the year before. Indirect operating expenses increased 48.6% to US$2.20 billion from US$1.48 billion in the equivalent prior-year period.

Prospects: Our evaluation of Actavis, Inc. as of Apr. 7, 2013 is the result of our systematic analysis on three basic characteristics: earnings strength, relative valuation, and recent stock price movement. The company has generated a negative trend in earnings per share over the past 5 quarters and while recent estimates for the company have been raised by analysts, ACT has posted better than expected results. Based on operating earnings yield, the company is undervalued when compared to all of the companies in our coverage universe. Share price changes over the past year indicates that ACT will perform poorly over the near term.

Financial Data

(US$ in Thousands)	12/31/2012	12/31/2011	12/31/2010	12/31/2009	12/31/2008	12/31/2007	12/31/2006	12/31/2005
Earnings Per Share	0.76	2.06	1.48	1.96	2.09	1.27	(4.37)	1.21
Cash Flow Per Share	5.28	5.08	4.67	3.59	4.04	4.18	4.63	3.10
Tang Book Value Per Share	N.M.	1.90	0.97	N.M.	6.51	3.56	0.10	8.81
Income Statement								
Total Revenue	5,914,900	4,584,400	3,566,900	2,793,000	2,535,501	2,496,651	1,979,244	1,646,203
EBITDA	455,500	633,800	433,400	477,400	456,866	329,510	(364,713)	257,406
Depn & Amortn	97,500	93,600	101,900	96,400	90,047	77,150	54,636	42,787
Income Before Taxes	243,800	460,500	249,000	351,800	347,690	216,773	(413,015)	219,416
Income Taxes	146,800	196,900	67,300	140,600	119,934	83,254	34,056	81,183
Net Income	97,300	260,900	184,400	222,000	238,379	141,030	(445,005)	138,233
Average Shares	128,400	126,500	124,200	116,400	117,723	117,039	101,761	120,021
Balance Sheet								
Current Assets	3,879,700	2,569,700	1,799,400	1,771,000	1,458,417	1,173,776	1,261,676	1,360,430
Total Assets	14,103,500	6,698,300	5,827,300	5,992,200	3,677,887	3,472,027	3,760,577	3,080,033
Current Liabilities	2,710,600	1,839,500	820,700	1,052,400	481,995	444,927	689,929	245,670
Long-Term Obligations	6,257,100	665,300	849,700	999,000	824,678	899,408	1,124,145	587,935
Total Liabilities	10,269,700	3,134,700	2,545,600	2,969,100	1,569,302	1,622,562	2,080,189	975,792
Stockholders' Equity	3,833,800	3,563,600	3,281,700	3,023,100	2,108,585	1,849,465	1,680,388	2,104,241
Shares Outstanding	127,700	127,200	125,800	123,400	104,608	103,658	102,467	101,805
Statistical Record								
Return on Assets %	0.93	4.17	3.12	4.59	6.65	3.90	N.M.	4.37
Return on Equity %	2.62	7.62	5.85	8.65	12.01	7.99	N.M.	6.36
EBITDA Margin %	7.70	13.83	12.15	17.09	18.02	13.20	N.M.	15.64
Net Margin %	1.64	5.69	5.17	7.95	9.40	5.65	N.M.	8.40
Asset Turnover	0.57	0.73	0.60	0.58	0.71	0.69	0.58	0.52
Current Ratio	1.43	1.40	2.19	1.68	3.03	2.64	1.83	5.54
Debt to Equity	1.63	0.19	0.26	0.33	0.39	0.49	0.67	0.28
Price Range	90.85-55.89	72.10-50.59	51.95-37.69	40.12-23.74	31.14-20.76	33.69-25.28	34.76-21.42	36.61-28.11
P/E Ratio	119.54-73.54	35.00-24.56	35.10-25.47	20.47-12.11	14.90-9.93	26.53-19.91	...	30.26-23.23

Address: Morris Corporate Center III, 400 Interpace Parkway, Parsippany, NJ 07054 **Telephone:** 862-261-7000 **Fax:** 909-270-1096	Web Site: www.watsonpharm.com Officers: Andrew L. Turner - Chairman Paul M. Bisaro - President, Chief Executive Officer	Auditors: PricewaterhouseCoopers LLP Investor Contact: 862-261-7488 Transfer Agents: American Stock Transfer and Trust Company, New York, NY

7

ACUITY BRANDS INC (HOLDING COMPANY)

Exchange	Symbol	Price	52Wk Range	Yield	P/E
NYS	AYI	$69.35 (3/28/2013)	72.93-48.90	0.75	25.31

*7 Year Price Score 122.25 *NYSE Composite Index=100 *12 Month Price Score 103.18

Interim Earnings (Per Share)

Qtr.	Nov	Feb	May	Aug
2009-10	0.53	0.17	0.48	0.62
2010-11	0.56	0.45	0.62	0.79
2011-12	0.70	0.46	0.79	0.77
2012-13	0.61	0.57	...	...

Interim Dividends (Per Share)

Amt	Decl	Ex	Rec	Pay
0.13Q	06/29/2012	07/16/2012	07/18/2012	08/01/2012
0.13Q	09/28/2012	10/16/2012	10/18/2012	11/01/2012
0.13Q	01/04/2013	01/16/2013	01/18/2013	02/01/2013
0.13Q	03/29/2013	04/15/2013	04/17/2013	05/01/2013

Indicated Div: $0.52

Valuation Analysis

		Institutional Holding	
Forecast EPS	$3.25 (04/05/2013)	No of Institutions	282
Market Cap	$2.9 Billion	Shares	42,562,448
Book Value	$890.7 Million	% Held	92.61
Price/Book	3.29		
Price/Sales	1.49		

TRADING VOLUME (thousand shares)

Business Summary: Electrical Equipment (MIC: 7.3.1 SIC: 3648 NAIC: 335129)

Acuity Brands is a provider of lighting products for commercial, institutional, industrial, infrastructure, and residential applications. Co.'s lighting products include devices such as luminaires, lighting controls, power supplies, prismatic skylights, light-emitting diode lamps, and integrated lighting systems for indoor and outdoor applications utilizing a combination of light sources, including daylight, and other devices controlled by software that monitors and manages light levels. Co. manufactures or procures lighting devices primarily in North America, Europe and Asia.

Recent Developments: For the quarter ended Feb 28 2013, net income increased 26.7% to US$24.7 million from US$19.5 million in the year-earlier quarter. Revenues were US$486.7 million, up 6.3% from US$457.7 million the year before. Operating income was US$45.1 million versus US$39.0 million in the prior-year quarter, an increase of 15.6%. Direct operating expenses rose 7.7% to US$297.0 million from US$275.8 million in the comparable period the year before. Indirect operating expenses increased 1.2% to US$144.6 million from US$142.9 million in the equivalent prior-year period.

Prospects: Our evaluation of Acuity Brands Inc. as of Apr. 7, 2013 is the result of our systematic analysis on three basic characteristics: earnings strength, relative valuation, and recent stock price movement. The company has managed to produce a neutral trend in earnings per share over the past 5 quarters. However, while recent estimates for the company have been mixed, AYI has posted results that were in line with analysts expectations. Based on operating earnings yield, the company is about fairly valued when compared to all of the companies in our coverage universe. Share price changes over the past year indicates that AYI will perform well over the near term.

Financial Data

(US$ in Thousands)	6 Mos	3 Mos	08/31/2012	08/31/2011	08/31/2010	08/31/2009	08/31/2008	08/31/2007
Earnings Per Share	2.74	2.63	2.72	2.42	1.80	2.04	3.56	3.37
Cash Flow Per Share	3.19	3.11	4.15	3.82	3.78	2.27	5.44	5.66
Tang Book Value Per Share	2.55	1.96	1.06	N.M.	N.M.	N.M.	2.56	3.82
Dividends Per Share	0.520	0.520	0.520	0.520	0.520	0.520	0.520	0.600
Dividend Payout %	18.98	19.77	19.12	21.49	28.89	25.49	14.61	17.80
Income Statement								
Total Revenue	967,800	481,100	1,933,700	1,795,700	1,626,900	1,657,404	2,026,644	2,530,668
EBITDA	113,000	58,100	237,200	216,300	176,700	185,465	288,665	296,432
Depn & Amortn	19,900	10,000	27,500	28,800	28,500	29,600	29,700	38,405
Income Before Taxes	77,600	40,400	179,000	157,600	118,800	127,323	230,550	227,887
Income Taxes	26,800	14,300	62,700	52,100	39,800	42,126	81,918	79,833
Net Income	50,800	26,100	116,300	105,500	79,600	84,909	148,255	148,054
Average Shares	42,500	42,300	41,900	42,800	43,300	41,557	41,609	43,897
Balance Sheet								
Current Assets	783,700	773,300	779,000	630,500	626,300	422,900	756,147	867,985
Total Assets	1,742,400	1,731,700	1,736,900	1,597,400	1,503,600	1,290,603	1,408,691	1,612,508
Current Liabilities	312,500	321,300	364,800	331,400	321,300	476,089	522,566	470,396
Long-Term Obligations	353,500	353,500	353,500	353,400	353,300	22,047	203,953	371,027
Total Liabilities	851,700	865,600	902,900	840,400	809,200	618,463	833,145	940,542
Stockholders' Equity	890,700	866,100	834,000	757,000	694,400	672,140	575,546	671,966
Shares Outstanding	42,280	42,242	41,789	41,488	42,116	42,433	40,201	43,314
Statistical Record								
Return on Assets %	7.04	6.76	6.96	6.80	5.70	6.29	9.79	9.69
Return on Equity %	13.95	13.78	14.58	14.54	11.65	13.61	23.70	24.39
EBITDA Margin %	11.68	12.08	12.27	12.05	10.86	11.19	14.24	11.71
Net Margin %	5.25	5.43	6.01	5.88	4.89	5.12	7.32	5.85
Asset Turnover	1.18	1.17	1.16	1.16	1.16	1.23	1.34	1.66
Current Ratio	2.51	2.41	2.14	1.90	1.95	0.89	1.45	1.85
Debt to Equity	0.40	0.41	0.42	0.47	0.51	0.03	0.35	0.55
Price Range	72.93-48.90	68.95-47.98	64.98-33.97	60.96-38.74	47.56-30.98	45.12-20.23	53.50-34.55	54.15-35.58
P/E Ratio	26.62-17.85	26.22-18.24	23.89-12.49	25.19-16.01	26.42-17.21	22.12-9.92	15.03-9.70	16.07-10.56
Average Yield %	0.84	0.88	0.97	0.98	1.36	1.74	1.19	1.31

Address: 1170 Peachtree Street, N.E., Suite 2400, Atlanta, GA 30309-7676 Telephone: 404-853-1400 Fax: 404-853-1300	Web Site: www.acuitybrands.com Officers: Vernon J. Nagel - Chairman, President, Chief Executive Officer Richard K. Reece - Executive Vice President, Chief Financial Officer	Auditors: Ernst & Young LLP Investor Contact: 404-853-1400 Transfer Agents: Computershare Shareowner Services, Pittsburgh, PA

ADVANCE AUTO PARTS INC

Exchange	Symbol	Price	52Wk Range	Yield	P/E
NYS	AAP	$82.65 (3/28/2013)	92.37-65.59	0.29	15.83

*7 Year Price Score 132.68 *NYSE Composite Index=100   *12 Month Price Score 96.06

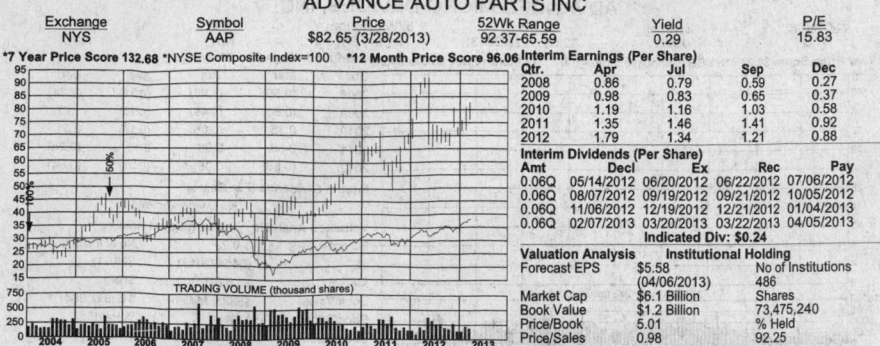

Interim Earnings (Per Share)

Qtr.	Apr	Jul	Sep	Dec
2008	0.86	0.79	0.59	0.27
2009	0.98	0.83	0.65	0.37
2010	1.19	1.16	1.03	0.58
2011	1.35	1.46	1.41	0.92
2012	1.79	1.34	1.21	0.88

Interim Dividends (Per Share)

Amt	Decl	Ex	Rec	Pay
0.06Q	05/14/2012	06/20/2012	06/22/2012	07/06/2012
0.06Q	08/07/2012	09/19/2012	09/21/2012	10/05/2012
0.06Q	11/06/2012	12/19/2012	12/21/2012	01/04/2013
0.06Q	02/07/2013	03/20/2013	03/22/2013	04/05/2013
		Indicated Div: $0.24		

Valuation Analysis		Institutional Holding	
Forecast EPS	$5.58	No of Institutions	
	(04/06/2013)	486	
Market Cap	$6.1 Billion	Shares	73,475,240
Book Value	$1.2 Billion	% Held	92.25
Price/Book	5.01		
Price/Sales	0.98		

Business Summary: Retail - Automotive (MIC: 2.1.4 SIC: 5531 NAIC: 441310)

Advance Auto Parts is a retailer of automotive aftermarket parts, accessories, batteries and maintenance items for cars, vans, sport utility vehicles and light trucks. Co. serves both do-it-yourself and do-it-for-me customers. Co. operates in two reportable segments: Advance Auto Parts, comprised of its store operations which operate under the trade names Advance Auto Parts and Advance Discount Auto Parts; and Autopart International, which consists solely of the operations of Autopart International, Inc. which operates under the Autopart International trade name. Co. operated 3,794 stores as of Dec 29 2012.

Recent Developments: For the year ended Dec 29 2012, net income decreased 1.8% to US$387.7 million from US$394.7 million in the prior year. Revenues were US$6.21 billion, up 0.6% from US$6.17 billion the year before. Operating income was US$657.3 million versus US$664.6 million in the prior year, a decrease of 1.1%. Direct operating expenses rose 0.2% to US$3.11 billion from US$3.10 billion in the comparable period the year before. Indirect operating expenses increased 1.5% to US$2.44 billion from US$2.40 billion in the equivalent prior-year period.

Prospects: Our evaluation of Advance Auto Parts Inc. as of Apr. 7, 2013 is the result of our systematic analysis on three basic characteristics: earnings strength, relative valuation, and recent stock price movement. The company has produced a positive trend in earnings per share over the past 5 quarters. However, while recent estimates for the company have been mixed, AAP has posted better than expected results. Based on operating earnings yield, the company is undervalued when compared to all of the companies in our coverage universe. Share price changes over the past year indicates that AAP will perform very poorly over the near term.

Financial Data

(US$ in Thousands)	12/29/2012	12/31/2011	01/01/2011	01/02/2010	01/03/2009	12/29/2007	12/30/2006	12/31/2005
Earnings Per Share	5.22	5.11	3.95	2.83	2.50	2.28	2.16	2.13
Cash Flow Per Share	9.40	10.99	7.76	7.43	4.98	3.96	3.15	3.01
Tang Book Value Per Share	15.06	10.17	11.95	13.05	10.68	9.72	9.20	7.88
Dividends Per Share	0.240	0.240	0.240	0.240	0.240	0.240	0.240	...
Dividend Payout %	4.60	4.70	6.08	8.48	9.60	10.53	11.11	...
Income Statement								
Total Revenue	6,205,003	6,170,462	5,925,203	5,412,623	5,142,255	4,844,404	4,616,503	4,264,971
EBITDA	843,824	838,404	747,294	604,761	559,774	563,625	543,971	531,245
Depn & Amortn	185,909	174,219	163,378	149,769	145,353	146,182	138,064	119,938
Income Before Taxes	624,074	633,236	557,055	431,655	380,692	382,634	369,915	378,923
Income Taxes	236,404	238,554	211,002	161,282	142,654	144,317	138,597	144,198
Net Income	387,670	394,682	346,053	270,373	238,038	238,317	231,318	234,725
Average Shares	74,062	77,071	87,155	95,113	95,305	104,654	107,124	109,987
Balance Sheet								
Current Assets	3,184,200	2,293,820	2,124,271	1,887,618	1,807,626	1,682,825	1,611,973	1,547,940
Total Assets	4,613,814	3,655,754	3,354,217	3,072,963	2,964,065	2,805,566	2,682,681	2,542,149
Current Liabilities	2,559,638	2,187,875	1,848,049	1,466,027	1,364,994	1,225,928	1,113,420	1,141,464
Long-Term Obligations	604,461	415,136	300,851	202,927	455,161	505,062	477,173	406,040
Total Liabilities	3,403,120	2,807,840	2,314,843	1,790,598	1,888,899	1,781,771	1,651,827	1,622,378
Stockholders' Equity	1,210,694	847,914	1,039,374	1,282,365	1,075,166	1,023,795	1,030,854	919,771
Shares Outstanding	73,383	72,799	81,956	93,623	94,852	99,060	105,351	108,198
Statistical Record								
Return on Assets %	9.40	11.29	10.80	8.98	8.12	8.71	8.88	9.92
Return on Equity %	37.77	41.94	29.89	23.00	22.31	23.26	23.78	28.67
EBITDA Margin %	13.60	13.59	12.61	11.17	10.89	11.63	11.78	12.46
Net Margin %	6.25	6.40	5.84	5.00	4.63	4.92	5.01	5.50
Asset Turnover	1.50	1.77	1.85	1.80	1.75	1.77	1.77	1.80
Current Ratio	1.24	1.05	1.15	1.29	1.32	1.37	1.45	1.36
Debt to Equity	0.50	0.49	0.29	0.16	0.42	0.49	0.46	0.44
Price Range	92.37-65.59	72.16-50.04	68.54-39.16	47.06-30.13	44.61-74.17	42.26-30.31	44.61-28.70	47.29-28.17
P/E Ratio	17.70-12.57	14.12-9.79	17.35-9.91	16.63-10.65	17.84-9.67	18.54-13.29	20.65-13.29	22.20-13.22
Average Yield %	0.32	0.38	0.46	0.60	0.68	0.64	0.65	...

Address: 5008 Airport Road, Roanoke, VA 24012	Web Site: www.advanceautoparts.com	Auditors: Deloitte & Touche LLP
Telephone: 540-362-4911	Officers: George E. Sherman - President Darren R. Jackson - President, Chief Executive Officer	Investor Contact: 540-561-6444 Transfer Agents: BNY Mellon Shareowner Services, Pittsburgh, PA

ADVANCED MICRO DEVICES, INC.

Exchange	Symbol	Price	52Wk Range	Yield	P/E
NYS	AMD	$2.55 (3/28/2013)	8.20-1.86	N/A	N/A

*7 Year Price Score 39.23   *NYSE Composite Index=100   *12 Month Price Score 60.05

TRADING VOLUME (thousand shares)

Interim Earnings (Per Share)

Qtr.	Mar	Jun	Sep	Dec
2008	(0.59)	(1.96)	(0.21)	(2.34)
2009	(0.66)	(0.49)	(0.18)	1.77
2010	0.35	(0.06)	(0.17)	0.51
2011	0.68	0.08	0.13	(0.24)
2012	(0.80)	0.05	(0.21)	(0.64)

Interim Dividends (Per Share)

No Dividends Paid

Valuation Analysis   **Institutional Holding**

Forecast EPS	$-0.29	No of Institutions
	(04/06/2013)	395
Market Cap	$1.8 Billion	Shares
Book Value	$538.0 Million	312,912,864
Price/Book	3.38	% Held
Price/Sales	0.34	42.03

Business Summary: Semiconductors (MIC: 6.2.4 SIC: 3674 NAIC: 334413)

Advanced Micro Devices is a semiconductor company. Co. provides x86 microprocessors, as standalone devices or as incorporated as an accelerated processing unit, for the commercial and consumer markets, embedded microprocessors for commercial, commercial client and consumer markets and chipsets for desktop and mobile devices, including mobile personal computers (PCs), and tablets, workstations and servers; as well as graphics, video and multimedia products for desktop and mobile devices, including mobile PCs and tablets, home media PCs and professional workstations, servers and technology for game consoles. Co. has two segments: Computing Solutions and Graphics.

Recent Developments: For the year ended Dec 29 2012, loss from continuing operations was US$1.18 billion compared with income of US$495.0 million a year earlier. Net loss amounted to US$1.18 billion versus net income of US$491.0 million in the prior year. Revenues were US$5.42 billion, down 17.4% from US$6.57 billion the year before. Operating loss was US$1.06 billion versus an income of US$368.0 million in the prior year. Direct operating expenses rose 15.4% to US$4.19 billion from US$3.63 billion in the comparable period the year before. Indirect operating expenses decreased 10.9% to US$2.29 billion from US$2.57 billion in the equivalent prior-year period.

Prospects: Our evaluation of Advanced Micro Devices Inc. as of Apr. 7, 2013 is the result of our systematic analysis on three basic characteristics: earnings strength, relative valuation, and recent stock price movement. The company has suffered a very negative trend in earnings per share over the past 5 quarters. Because the company lacks sufficient analyst estimate data, we place greater weight on the historical EPS trend as the measure of earnings strength. Based on operating earnings yield, the company is overvalued when compared to all of the companies in our coverage universe. Share price changes over the past year indicates that AMD will perform very poorly over the near term.

Financial Data
(US$ in Thousands)

	12/29/2012	12/31/2011	12/25/2010	12/26/2009	12/27/2008	12/29/2007	12/31/2006	12/25/2005
Earnings Per Share	(1.60)	0.66	0.64	0.45	(5.10)	(6.06)	(0.34)	0.40
Cash Flow Per Share	(0.46)	0.52	(0.58)	0.70	(1.14)	(0.56)	2.57	3.72
Tang Book Value Per Share	N.M.	1.82	0.96	0.34	...	0.82	2.49	7.70
Income Statement								
Total Revenue	5,422,000	6,568,000	6,494,000	5,403,000	5,808,000	6,013,000	5,649,000	5,847,577
EBITDA	(857,000)	415,000	1,476,000	1,778,000	(817,000)	(1,734,000)	777,000	1,371,953
Depn & Amortn	193,000	246,000	317,000	948,000	1,116,000	1,138,000	837,000	1,163,937
Income Before Taxes	(1,217,000)	(1,000)	971,000	408,000	(2,260,000)	(3,166,000)	(70,000)	140,266
Income Taxes	(34,000)	(4,000)	38,000	112,000	68,000	23,000	23,000	(6,642)
Net Income	(1,183,000)	491,000	471,000	293,000	(3,098,000)	(3,379,000)	(166,000)	165,483
Average Shares	741,000	742,000	733,000	678,000	607,000	558,000	492,000	440,776
Balance Sheet								
Current Assets	2,265,000	3,229,000	3,594,000	4,275,000	2,379,000	3,816,000	3,963,000	3,558,836
Total Assets	4,000,000	4,954,000	4,964,000	9,078,000	7,675,000	11,550,000	13,147,000	7,287,779
Current Liabilities	1,397,000	1,774,000	1,674,000	2,210,000	2,226,000	2,625,000	2,852,000	1,821,961
Long-Term Obligations	2,037,000	1,527,000	2,188,000	4,252,000	4,702,000	5,031,000	3,672,000	1,327,065
Total Liabilities	3,462,000	3,364,000	3,951,000	8,430,000	7,757,000	8,560,000	7,362,000	3,935,942
Stockholders' Equity	538,000	1,590,000	1,013,000	648,000	(82,000)	2,990,000	5,785,000	3,351,837
Shares Outstanding	713,000	698,000	683,000	671,000	609,000	606,000	547,000	435,526
Statistical Record								
Return on Assets %	N.M.	9.74	6.73	3.51	N.M.	N.M.	N.M.	2.19
Return on Equity %	N.M.	37.12	56.87	103.82	N.M.	N.M.	N.M.	5.22
EBITDA Margin %	N.M.	6.32	22.73	32.91	N.M.	N.M.	13.75	23.46
Net Margin %	N.M.	7.48	7.25	5.42	N.M.	N.M.	N.M.	2.83
Asset Turnover	1.21	1.30	0.93	0.65	0.61	0.49	0.54	0.77
Current Ratio	1.62	1.82	2.15	1.93	1.07	1.45	1.39	1.95
Debt to Equity	3.79	0.96	2.16	6.56	...	1.68	0.63	0.40
Price Range	8.25-1.86	9.44-4.53	10.16-5.61	9.91-2.00	8.00-1.80	20.18-7.32	42.10-17.39	30.50-14.16
P/E Ratio	...	14.30-6.86	15.88-8.77	22.02-4.44	...	...	...	76.25-35.40

Address: One AMD Place, Sunnyvale, CA 94088	Web Site: www.amd.com	Auditors: Ernst & Young LLP
Telephone: 408-749-4000	Officers: Bruce L. Claflin - Chairman, Chairman (frmr), Executive Chairman Rory P. Read - President, Chief Executive Officer	Investor Contact: 408-749-3124 Transfer Agents: ComputerShare Investor Services, Providence, RI

10

AECOM TECHNOLOGY CORP (DE)

Exchange	Symbol	Price	52Wk Range	Yield	P/E
NYS	ACM	$32.80 (3/28/2013)	32.95-14.91	N/A	N/A

*7 Year Price Score N/A   *NYSE Composite Index=100   *12 Month Price Score 126.32

Interim Earnings (Per Share)

Qtr.	Dec	Mar	Jun	Sep
2009-10	0.40	0.51	0.56	0.58
2010-11	0.48	0.49	0.62	0.74
2011-12	0.42	0.43	0.63	(1.99)
2012-13	0.36	...	...	...

Interim Dividends (Per Share)

No Dividends Paid

Valuation Analysis		Institutional Holding	
Forecast EPS	$2.50	No of Institutions	
	(04/05/2013)	285	
Market Cap	$3.3 Billion	Shares	
Book Value	$2.0 Billion	70,198,016	
Price/Book	1.62	% Held	
Price/Sales	0.40	56.53	

Business Summary: Construction Services (MIC: 7.5.4 SIC: 8711 NAIC: 541330)

Aecom Technology is a provider of technical and management support services for public and private clients. Co. provides its services through two business segments: Professional Technical Services, which delivers planning, consulting, architectural and engineering design, and program and construction management services to commercial and government clients in end markets such as transportation, facilities, environmental, energy, water and government markets; and Management Support Services, which provides program and facilities management and maintenance, training, logistics, consulting, technical assistance and systems integration services, primarily for agencies of the U.S. government.

Recent Developments: For the quarter ended Dec 31 2012, net income decreased 19.5% to US$39.0 million from US$48.4 million in the year-earlier quarter. Revenues were US$2.02 billion, down 0.6% from US$2.03 billion the year before. Operating income was US$61.9 million versus US$76.7 million in the prior-year quarter, a decrease of 19.3%. Direct operating expenses was unchanged at US$1.94 billion versus the comparable period the year before. Indirect operating expenses increased 18.6% to US$16.2 million from US$13.6 million in the equivalent prior-year period.

Prospects: Our evaluation of AECOM Technology Corp. as of Apr. 7, 2013 is the result of our systematic analysis on three basic characteristics: earnings strength, relative valuation, and recent stock price movement. The company has managed to produce a neutral trend in earnings per share over the past 5 quarters. However, while recent estimates for the company have been mixed, ACM has posted better than expected results. Based on operating earnings yield, the company is undervalued when compared to all of the companies in our coverage universe. Share price changes over the past year indicates that ACM will perform well over the near term.

Financial Data
(US$ in Thousands)

	3 Mos	09/30/2012	09/30/2011	09/30/2010	09/30/2009	09/30/2008	09/30/2007	09/30/2006
Earnings Per Share	(0.57)	(0.52)	2.33	2.05	1.73	1.41	1.15	0.74
Cash Flow Per Share	4.84	3.86	1.12	1.39	2.02	1.53	1.88	2.21
Tang Book Value Per Share	1.31	2.78	1.19	2.52	5.43	4.58	6.88	...
Income Statement								
Total Revenue	2,017,272	8,218,180	8,037,374	6,545,791	6,119,465	5,194,482	4,237,270	3,421,492
EBITDA	80,219	91,029	452,972	389,358	323,522	257,777	176,611	124,955
Depn & Amortn	23,902	77,100	73,200	59,300	57,500	44,600	32,500	28,100
Income Before Taxes	45,766	(31,167)	339,361	320,130	255,331	213,913	140,790	86,279
Income Taxes	12,703	74,416	100,090	91,696	77,002	76,321	47,203	25,223
Net Income	38,109	(58,567)	275,800	236,887	189,696	147,226	100,297	53,686
Average Shares	105,538	111,875	118,345	115,463	109,706	104,215	87,537	72,658
Balance Sheet								
Current Assets	3,258,532	3,147,293	2,990,066	2,946,499	2,214,535	2,105,250	1,576,463	1,093,875
Total Assets	5,808,025	5,664,568	5,789,328	5,242,909	3,789,881	3,596,190	2,491,821	1,825,774
Current Liabilities	2,233,124	2,078,402	1,814,446	1,852,260	1,556,739	1,474,079	978,808	892,552
Long-Term Obligations	1,021,772	907,141	1,144,723	914,686	142,102	365,974	39,186	122,790
Total Liabilities	3,758,557	3,495,104	3,449,617	3,152,897	2,060,163	2,173,197	1,213,336	1,147,013
Stockholders' Equity	2,049,468	2,169,464	2,339,711	2,090,012	1,729,718	1,422,993	1,278,485	678,761
Shares Outstanding	100,935	107,041	113,248	115,316	110,890	102,983	99,061	...
Statistical Record								
Return on Assets %	N.M.	N.M.	5.00	5.25	5.14	4.82	4.65	3.30
Return on Equity %	N.M.	N.M.	12.45	12.40	12.03	10.87	10.25	9.76
EBITDA Margin %	3.98	1.11	5.64	5.95	5.29	4.96	4.17	3.65
Net Margin %	1.89	N.M.	3.43	3.62	3.10	2.83	2.37	1.57
Asset Turnover	1.39	1.43	1.46	1.45	1.66	1.70	1.96	2.11
Current Ratio	1.46	1.51	1.65	1.59	1.42	1.43	1.61	1.23
Debt to Equity	0.50	0.42	0.49	0.44	0.08	0.26	0.03	0.18
Price Range	24.37-14.91	24.06-14.91	29.93-17.67	30.73-22.02	32.99-15.22	37.25-23.01	35.94-21.00	...
P/E Ratio	...	...	12.85-7.58	14.99-10.74	19.07-8.80	26.42-16.32	31.25-18.26	...

Address: 555 South Flower Street, Suite 3700, Los Angeles, CA 90071 Telephone: 213-593-8000	Web Site: www.aecom.com Officers: Richard G. Newman - Chairman Emeritus John M. Dionisio - Chairman, Chief Executive Officer	Auditors: Ernst & Young LLP Investor Contact: 212-973-2982 Transfer Agents: Computershare Investor Services, LLC, Canton, MA

AEROPOSTALE INC

Exchange	Symbol	Price	52Wk Range	Yield	P/E
NYS	ARO	$13.60 (3/28/2013)	23.05-11.95	N/A	31.63

*7 Year Price Score 73.80   *NYSE Composite Index=100   *12 Month Price Score 79.16

TRADING VOLUME (thousand shares)

Interim Earnings (Per Share)

Qtr.	Apr	Jul	Oct	Jan
2008-09	0.17	0.21	0.42	0.67
2009-10	0.31	0.38	0.61	0.97
2010-11	0.48	0.46	0.63	0.92
2011-12	0.20	0.04	0.30	0.32
2012-13	0.13	0.00	0.31	(0.01)

Interim Dividends (Per Share)

Amt	Decl	Ex	Rec	Pay
50%	07/11/2007	08/22/2007	08/06/2007	08/21/2007
50%	02/03/2010	03/05/2010	02/24/2010	03/04/2010

Valuation Analysis   **Institutional Holding**

Forecast EPS	$0.55	No of Institutions
	(04/06/2013)	323
Market Cap	$1.1 Billion	Shares
Book Value	$410.4 Million	79,913,912
Price/Book	2.59	% Held
Price/Sales	0.45	90.49

Business Summary: Retail - Apparel and Accessories (MIC: 2.1.5 SIC: 5621 NAIC: 448120)

Aéropostale is a mall-based retailer of casual apparel and accessories, principally targeting 14 to 17 year-old young women and men through its Aéropostale stores and four to 12 year-old kids through its P.S. from Aéropostale stores. Aéropostale products can only be purchased in Aéropostale stores and online at www.aeropostale.com. P.S. from Aéropostale products can be purchased in P.S. from Aéropostale stores, in certain Aéropostale stores and online at www.ps4u.com and www.aeropostale.com. As of Jan 28 2012, Co. operated 986 Aéropostale stores, consisting of 918 stores in 50 states and Puerto Rico, 68 stores in Canada, and 71 P.S. from Aéropostale stores in 20 states.

Recent Developments: For the year ended Feb 2 2013, net income decreased 49.8% to US$34.9 million from US$69.5 million in the prior year. Revenues were US$2.39 billion, up 1.9% from US$2.34 billion the year before. Operating income was US$59.5 million versus US$113.5 million in the prior year, a decrease of 47.6%. Direct operating expenses rose 3.6% to US$1.80 billion from US$1.73 billion in the comparable period the year before. Indirect operating expenses increased 7.1% to US$529.8 million from US$494.8 million in the equivalent prior-year period.

Prospects: Our evaluation of Aeropostale Inc. as of Apr. 7, 2013 is the result of our systematic analysis on three basic characteristics: earnings strength, relative valuation, and recent stock price movement. The company has generated a negative trend in earnings per share over the past 5 quarters. However, while recent estimates for the company have been lowered by analysts, ARO has posted better than expected results. Based on operating earnings yield, the company is overvalued when compared to all of the companies in our coverage universe. Share price changes over the past year indicates that ARO will perform very poorly over the near term.

Financial Data
(US$ in Thousands)

	02/02/2013	01/28/2012	01/29/2011	01/30/2010	01/31/2009	02/02/2008	02/03/2007	01/28/2006
Earnings Per Share	0.43	0.85	2.49	2.27	1.47	1.15	0.88	0.67
Cash Flow Per Share	1.78	1.60	2.88	3.37	2.02	1.54	1.46	1.17
Tang Book Value Per Share	4.87	5.07	5.12	4.62	3.54	1.97	2.67	2.32
Income Statement								
Total Revenue	2,386,178	2,342,260	2,400,434	2,230,105	1,885,531	1,590,883	1,413,208	1,204,347
EBITDA	125,298	178,615	445,494	435,585	294,099	239,253	197,766	157,731
Depn & Amortn	65,787	65,100	58,700	52,900	45,800	36,800	30,000	22,300
Income Before Taxes	59,026	113,098	386,676	382,806	248,809	209,003	174,830	139,101
Income Taxes	24,103	43,583	155,337	153,349	99,387	79,806	68,183	55,147
Net Income	34,923	69,515	231,339	229,457	149,422	129,197	106,647	83,954
Average Shares	80,494	81,811	92,762	101,025	101,364	112,269	120,955	125,858
Balance Sheet								
Current Assets	439,940	441,799	469,565	530,017	393,881	284,687	398,793	339,339
Total Assets	740,844	735,233	773,197	792,309	657,919	514,169	581,164	503,951
Current Liabilities	203,506	193,211	216,102	241,840	175,437	197,387	164,798	126,353
Total Liabilities	330,480	325,799	340,560	357,820	302,859	316,893	269,048	219,161
Stockholders' Equity	410,364	409,434	432,637	434,489	355,060	197,276	312,116	284,790
Shares Outstanding	78,279	80,830	84,580	93,995	100,395	100,026	116,201	121,612
Statistical Record								
Return on Assets %	4.66	9.24	29.64	31.73	25.57	23.66	19.34	18.51
Return on Equity %	8.38	16.56	53.50	58.28	54.25	50.87	35.16	32.19
EBITDA Margin %	5.25	7.63	18.56	19.53	15.60	15.04	13.99	13.10
Net Margin %	1.46	2.97	9.64	10.29	7.92	8.12	7.55	6.97
Asset Turnover	3.18	3.11	3.08	3.08	3.23	2.91	2.56	2.65
Current Ratio	2.16	2.29	2.17	2.19	2.25	1.44	2.42	2.69
Price Range	23.05-11.95	26.64-9.31	32.08-21.30	29.47-13.78	24.53-8.50	21.10-12.25	16.34-9.52	15.54-8.14
P/E Ratio	53.60-27.79	31.34-10.95	12.88-8.55	12.98-6.07	16.68-5.78	18.35-10.65	18.57-10.82	23.20-12.15

Address: 112 W. 34th Street, 22nd Floor, New York, NY 10120 Telephone: 646-485-5410	Web Site: www.aeropostale.com; www.ps4u.com Officers: Thomas P. Johnson - Chief Executive Officer Mary Jo Pile - Executive Vice President, Chief Stores Officer	Auditors: Deloitte and Touche LLP Investor Contact: 646-452-1876 Transfer Agents: American Stock Transfer & Trust Company, New York, NY

AES CORP.

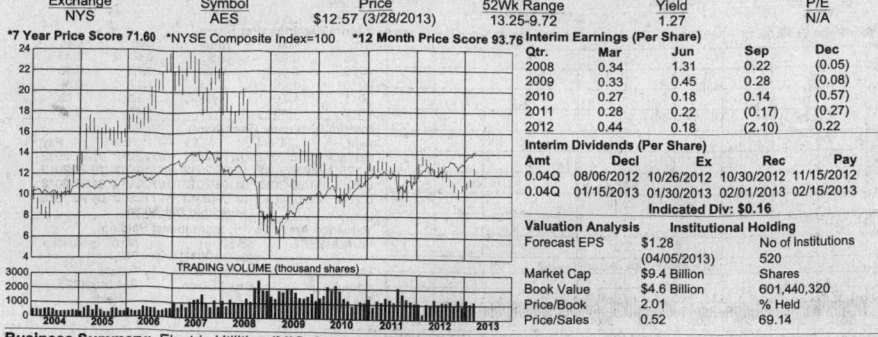

Exchange	Symbol	Price	52Wk Range	Yield	P/E
NYS	AES	$12.57 (3/28/2013)	13.25-9.72	1.27	N/A

7 Year Price Score 71.60   *NYSE Composite Index=100   *12 Month Price Score 93.76

Interim Earnings (Per Share)

Qtr.	Mar	Jun	Sep	Dec
2008	0.34	1.31	0.22	(0.05)
2009	0.33	0.45	0.28	(0.08)
2010	0.27	0.18	0.14	(0.57)
2011	0.28	0.22	(0.17)	(0.27)
2012	0.44	0.18	(2.10)	0.22

Interim Dividends (Per Share)

Amt	Decl	Ex	Rec	Pay
0.04Q	08/06/2012	10/26/2012	10/30/2012	11/15/2012
0.04Q	01/15/2013	01/30/2013	02/01/2013	02/15/2013

Indicated Div: $0.16

Valuation Analysis   **Institutional Holding**

Forecast EPS	$1.28	No of Institutions
	(04/05/2013)	520
Market Cap	$9.4 Billion	Shares
Book Value	$4.6 Billion	601,440,320
Price/Book	2.01	% Held
Price/Sales	0.52	69.14

Business Summary: Electric Utilities (MIC: 3.1.1 SIC: 4911 NAIC: 221121)

AES Corporation is a holding company. Through its subsidiaries and affiliates, Co. operates a portfolio of electricity generation and distribution businesses. Co. owns and/or operates power plants to generate and sell power to customers, such as utilities, industrial users, and other intermediaries. Also, Co. owns and/or operates utilities to generate or purchase, distribute, transmit and sell electricity to end-user customers in the residential, commercial, industrial and governmental sectors within a defined service area. In certain circumstances, Co.'s utilities also generate and sell electricity on the wholesale market. As of Dec 31 2012, Co. served about 12.2 million utility customers.

Recent Developments: For the year ended Dec 31 2012, loss from continuing operations was US$360.0 million compared with income of US$1.58 billion a year earlier. Net loss amounted to US$357.0 million versus net income of US$1.53 billion in the prior year. Revenues were US$18.14 billion, up 7.2% from US$16.92 billion the year before. Direct operating expenses rose 12.2% to US$14.43 billion from US$12.86 billion in the comparable period the year before. Indirect operating expenses increased 277.1% to US$2.19 billion from US$581.0 million in the equivalent prior-year period.

Prospects: Our evaluation of AES Corp. as of Apr. 7, 2013 is the result of our systematic analysis on three basic characteristics: earnings strength, relative valuation, and recent stock price movement. The company has managed to produce a neutral trend in earnings per share over the past 5 quarters and while recent estimates for the company have been mixed, AES has posted better than expected results. Based on operating earnings yield, the company is undervalued when compared to all of the companies in our coverage universe. Share price changes over the past year indicates that AES will perform very poorly over the near term.

Financial Data
(US$ in Millions)

	12/31/2012	12/31/2011	12/31/2010	12/31/2009	12/31/2008	12/31/2007	12/31/2006	12/31/2005
Earnings Per Share	(1.21)	0.07	0.01	0.98	1.82	(0.14)	0.39	0.95
Cash Flow Per Share	3.83	3.71	4.56	3.32	3.23	3.53	3.65	3.31
Tang Book Value Per Share	2.98	2.25	6.03	4.38	2.64	1.85	1.97	0.34
Dividends Per Share	0.040	...	...	...	...	...	...	...
Income Statement								
Total Revenue	18,141	17,274	16,647	14,119	16,070	13,588	12,299	11,086
EBITDA	2,788	4,536	3,259	4,515	5,028	3,711	3,474	3,776
Depn & Amortn	1,251	1,154	1,100	1,005	973	885	888	889
Income Before Taxes	314	2,179	1,044	2,343	2,751	1,538	1,227	1,382
Income Taxes	708	636	307	599	774	685	403	465
Net Income	(912)	58	9	658	1,234	(95)	261	630
Average Shares	755	783	769	670	689	678	672	664
Balance Sheet								
Current Assets	8,465	9,228	9,446	8,787	7,326	8,336	6,565	5,232
Total Assets	41,830	45,333	40,511	39,535	34,806	34,453	31,163	29,432
Current Liabilities	8,319	8,446	8,065	6,621	5,182	5,482	5,029	5,406
Long-Term Obligations	18,519	20,116	16,693	17,943	16,863	16,629	14,892	15,908
Total Liabilities	37,183	39,309	33,978	34,800	31,137	31,289	28,127	27,783
Stockholders' Equity	4,647	6,024	6,533	4,735	3,669	3,164	3,036	1,649
Shares Outstanding	744	765	787	667	662	670	665	655
Statistical Record								
Return on Assets %	N.M.	0.14	0.02	1.77	3.55	N.M.	0.86	2.13
Return on Equity %	N.M.	0.92	0.16	15.66	36.02	N.M.	11.14	38.25
EBITDA Margin %	15.37	26.26	19.58	31.98	31.29	27.31	28.25	34.06
Net Margin %	N.M.	0.34	0.05	4.66	7.68	N.M.	2.12	5.68
Asset Turnover	0.42	0.40	0.42	0.38	0.46	0.41	0.41	0.37
Current Ratio	1.02	1.09	1.17	1.33	1.41	1.52	1.31	0.97
Debt to Equity	3.99	3.34	2.56	3.79	4.60	5.26	4.91	9.65
Price Range	13.80-9.72	13.38-9.44	14.13-8.90	15.24-4.91	21.99-6.40	23.90-17.76	23.72-16.20	17.65-12.84
P/E Ratio	...	191.14-134.86	N.M.	15.55-5.01	12.08-3.52	...	60.82-41.54	18.58-13.52
Average Yield %	0.34	...	...	...	...	...	...	...

Address: 4300 Wilson Boulevard, Arlington, VA 22203 Telephone: 703-522-1315 Fax: 703-528-4510	Web Site: www.aes.com Officers: Philip A. Odeen - Chairman Andres R. Gluski - President, Chief Executive Officer, Executive Vice President, Chief Operating Officer	Auditors: Ernst & Young LLP Investor Contact: 703-682-6399 Transfer Agents: Computershare, Providence, RI

13

AETNA INC.

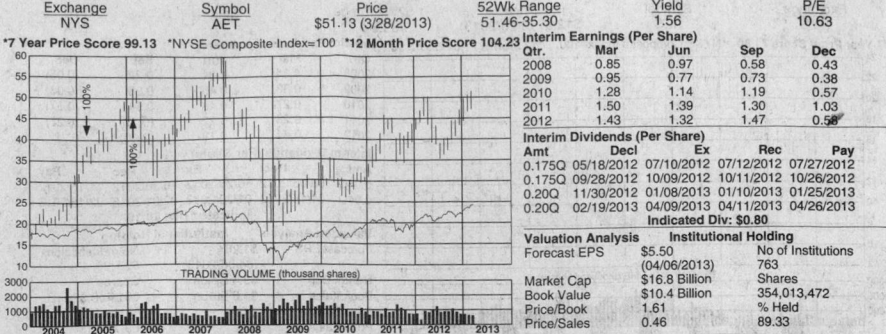

Exchange	Symbol	Price	52Wk Range	Yield	P/E
NYS	AET	$51.13 (3/28/2013)	51.46-35.30	1.56	10.63

*7 Year Price Score 99.13 *NYSE Composite Index=100 *12 Month Price Score 104.23

Interim Earnings (Per Share)

Qtr.	Mar	Jun	Sep	Dec
2008	0.85	0.97	0.58	0.43
2009	0.95	0.77	0.73	0.38
2010	1.28	1.14	1.19	0.57
2011	1.50	1.39	1.30	1.03
2012	1.43	1.32	1.47	0.58

Interim Dividends (Per Share)

Amt	Decl	Ex	Rec	Pay
0.175Q	05/18/2012	07/10/2012	07/12/2012	07/27/2012
0.175Q	09/28/2012	10/09/2012	10/11/2012	10/26/2012
0.20Q	11/30/2012	01/08/2013	01/10/2013	01/25/2013
0.20Q	02/19/2013	04/09/2013	04/11/2013	04/26/2013

Indicated Div: $0.80

Valuation Analysis / Institutional Holding

Forecast EPS	$5.50	No of Institutions
	(04/06/2013)	763
Market Cap	$16.8 Billion	Shares
Book Value	$10.4 Billion	354,013,472
Price/Book	1.61	% Held
Price/Sales	0.46	89.33

Business Summary: Life & Health (MIC: 5.2.2 SIC: 6324 NAIC: 524114)

Aetna is a health care benefits company. Co. has three segments: Health Care, which provides medical, pharmacy benefit management services, dental, behavioral health and vision plans, and emerging businesses products and services such as Accountable Care Solutions; Group Insurance, which provides life, disability, and long-term care insurance products to employers; and Large Case Pensions, which manages a range of retirement products including pension and annuity products for tax-qualified pension plans. Co.'s customers include employer groups, individuals, college students, health plans, health care providers, governmental units, government-sponsored plans, labor groups and expatriates.

Recent Developments: For the year ended Dec 31 2012, net income decreased 16.5% to US$1.66 billion from US$1.99 billion in the prior year. Revenues were US$36.60 billion, up 8.3% from US$33.78 billion the year before. Net premiums earned were US$31.72 billion versus US$28.97 billion in the prior year, an increase of 9.5%. Net investment income fell 1.3% to US$918.3 million from US$930.8 million a year ago.

Prospects: Our evaluation of Aetna Inc. as of Apr. 7, 2013 is the result of our systematic analysis on three basic characteristics: earnings strength, relative valuation, and recent stock price movement. The company has managed to produce a neutral trend in earnings per share over the past 5 quarters and while recent estimates for the company have been mixed, AET has posted results that fell short of analysts expectations. Based on operating earnings yield, the company is undervalued when compared to all of the companies in our coverage universe. Share price changes over the past year indicates that AET will perform very poorly over the near term.

Financial Data
(US$ in Thousands)

	12/31/2012	12/31/2011	12/31/2010	12/31/2009	12/31/2008	12/31/2007	12/31/2006	12/31/2005
Earnings Per Share	4.81	5.22	4.18	2.84	2.83	3.47	2.99	2.70
Cash Flow Per Share	5.34	6.73	3.40	5.64	4.63	4.06	3.09	3.27
Tang Book Value Per Share	10.30	8.46	11.05	8.74	5.33	8.46	7.46	8.57
Dividends Per Share	0.700	0.450	0.040	0.040	0.040	0.040	0.040	0.020
Dividend Payout %	14.55	8.62	0.96	1.41	1.41	1.15	1.34	0.74
Income Statement								
Premium Income	31,715,400	28,965,000	29,432,700	30,136,200	27,384,100	23,479,400	21,109,500	18,927,700
Total Revenue	36,595,900	33,779,800	34,246,000	34,764,100	30,950,700	27,599,600	25,145,700	22,491,900
Benefits & Claims	2,949,500	1,876,500	2,013,400	2,078,100	1,938,700	2,248,100	2,319,000	2,364,500
Income Before Taxes	2,545,400	3,077,800	2,644,200	1,901,200	2,174,200	2,796,400	2,586,600	2,547,400
Income Taxes	887,500	1,092,100	877,400	624,700	790,100	965,400	901,000	912,900
Net Income	1,657,900	1,985,700	1,766,800	1,276,500	1,384,100	1,831,000	1,701,700	1,634,500
Average Shares	345,000	380,200	422,900	449,500	488,300	527,000	569,100	604,900
Balance Sheet								
Total Assets	41,494,500	38,593,100	37,739,400	38,550,400	35,852,500	50,724,700	47,626,400	44,364,600
Total Liabilities	31,088,700	28,472,900	27,848,600	29,046,600	27,666,100	40,686,300	38,481,300	34,259,700
Stockholders' Equity	10,405,800	10,120,200	9,890,800	9,503,800	8,186,400	10,038,400	9,145,100	10,104,900
Shares Outstanding	327,600	349,700	384,400	430,800	456,300	496,300	516,000	566,500
Statistical Record								
Return on Assets %	4.13	5.20	4.63	3.43	3.19	3.72	3.70	3.78
Return on Equity %	16.11	19.85	18.22	14.43	15.15	19.09	17.68	17.04
Loss Ratio %	9.30	6.48	6.84	6.90	7.08	9.57	10.99	12.49
Net Margin %	4.53	5.88	5.16	3.67	4.47	6.63	6.77	7.27
Price Range	50.23-35.30	45.90-30.51	35.38-25.99	34.52-18.99	59.19-17.68	59.76-40.89	52.32-30.99	49.34-30.16
P/E Ratio	10.44-7.34	8.79-5.84	8.46-6.22	12.15-6.69	20.92-6.25	17.22-11.78	17.50-10.36	18.27-11.17
Average Yield %	1.65	1.15	0.13	0.15	0.10	0.08	0.09	0.05

Address: 151 Farmington Avenue, Hartford, CT 06156 Telephone: 860-273-0123	Web Site: www.aetna.com Officers: Mark T. Bertolini - Chairman, President, Chief Executive Officer Joseph M. Zubretsky - Senior Executive Vice President, Chief Financial Officer, Chief Enterprise Risk Officer	Auditors: KPMG LLP Investor Contact: 860-273-2402 Transfer Agents: Computershare Trust Company, N.A, Providence, RI

14

AFFILIATED MANAGERS GROUP INC.

Exchange	Symbol	Price	52Wk Range	Yield	P/E
NYS	AMG	$153.57 (3/28/2013)	155.18-96.00	N/A	46.82

*7 Year Price Score 117.54 *NYSE Composite Index=100 ***12 Month Price Score 110.48**

Interim Earnings (Per Share)

Qtr.	Mar	Jun	Sep	Dec
2008	0.90	0.89	0.59	(1.69)
2009	0.15	0.26	0.40	0.56
2010	0.38	0.53	0.65	1.24
2011	0.74	0.85	0.76	0.77
2012	0.71	0.12	1.04	1.41

Interim Dividends (Per Share)

No Dividends Paid

Valuation Analysis		Institutional Holding	
Forecast EPS	$9.25	No of Institutions	
	(04/06/2013)	479	
Market Cap	$8.3 Billion	Shares	
Book Value	$2.1 Billion	55,940,248	
Price/Book	3.97	% Held	
Price/Sales	4.58	93.82	

Business Summary: Wealth Management (MIC: 5.5.2 SIC: 6282 NAIC: 523920)

Affiliated Managers Group is an asset management company with equity investments in a group of investment management firms (Affiliates). Co.'s Affiliates provide investment management services to institutional clients, mutual funds and individuals. As of Dec 31 2012, Co. managed $431.80 billion in assets through its Affiliates in three principal distribution channels: Institutional, which manages assets for large institutional investors world-wide; Mutual Fund, which provides advisory or sub-advisory services to mutual funds and other retail-oriented products; and High Net Worth, which provides advisory services to ultra-high net worth individuals, families and charitable foundations.

Recent Developments: For the year ended Dec 31 2012, net income increased 14.4% to US$411.4 million from US$359.6 million in the prior year. Revenues were US$1.81 billion, up 5.9% from US$1.70 billion the year before. Operating income was US$400.4 million versus US$486.1 million in the prior year, a decrease of 17.6%. Indirect operating expenses increased 15.3% to US$1.41 billion from US$1.22 billion in the equivalent prior-year period.

Prospects: Our evaluation of Affiliated Managers Group Inc. as of Apr. 7, 2013 is the result of our systematic analysis on three basic characteristics: earnings strength, relative valuation, and recent stock price movement. The company has enjoyed a very positive trend in earnings per share over the past 5 quarters and while recent estimates for the company have been raised by analysts, AMG has posted better than expected results. Based on operating earnings yield, the company is about fairly valued when compared to all of the companies in our coverage universe. Share price changes over the past year indicates that AMG will perform well over the near term.

Financial Data
(US$ in Thousands)

	12/31/2012	12/31/2011	12/31/2010	12/31/2009	12/31/2008	12/31/2007	12/31/2006	12/31/2005
Earnings Per Share	3.28	3.11	2.81	1.38	0.57	4.58	3.74	2.81
Cash Flow Per Share	12.21	13.68	10.14	5.88	6.67	11.09	9.62	6.06
Income Statement								
Total Revenue	1,805,500	1,704,800	1,358,242	841,840	1,158,217	1,369,866	1,170,353	916,492
EBITDA	644,700	578,800	457,003	292,930	445,626	580,401	498,234	369,243
Depn & Amortn	222,300	97,700	60,066	32,939	33,854	31,653	27,378	24,873
Income Before Taxes	365,500	380,000	305,800	181,862	337,881	471,829	412,056	306,944
Income Taxes	83,800	93,100	91,523	28,003	20,935	106,866	86,610	70,583
Net Income	411,400	359,600	291,713	186,237	23,170	181,961	151,277	119,069
Average Shares	53,000	53,000	49,398	43,333	40,872	44,921	45,159	44,689
Balance Sheet								
Current Assets	912,300	876,400	769,430	585,582	641,321	649,757	554,279	337,802
Total Assets	6,187,100	5,218,900	5,291,215	3,390,906	3,246,370	3,395,705	2,665,920	2,321,636
Current Liabilities	375,800	417,600	407,457	227,115	212,572	316,352	287,813	256,588
Long-Term Obligations	1,630,600	1,198,200	1,391,990	964,334	1,471,480	1,997,583	1,378,858	899,732
Total Liabilities	4,102,900	3,352,900	3,491,252	2,281,216	2,153,810	2,926,503	2,166,698	1,504,255
Stockholders' Equity	2,084,200	1,866,000	1,799,963	1,109,690	1,092,560	469,202	499,222	817,381
Shares Outstanding	53,900	53,900	53,944	45,795	45,795	28,158	29,595	33,598
Statistical Record								
Return on Assets %	7.19	6.84	6.72	5.61	0.70	6.00	6.07	5.60
Return on Equity %	20.77	19.62	20.05	16.91	2.96	37.58	22.98	15.61
EBITDA Margin %	35.71	33.95	33.65	34.80	38.48	42.37	42.57	40.29
Net Margin %	22.79	21.09	21.48	22.12	2.00	13.28	12.93	12.99
Asset Turnover	0.32	0.32	0.31	0.25	0.35	0.45	0.47	0.43
Current Ratio	2.43	2.10	1.89	2.58	3.02	2.05	1.93	1.32
Debt to Equity	0.78	0.64	0.77	0.87	1.35	4.26	2.76	1.10
Price Range	132.30-96.00	112.20-72.88	101.86-59.70	73.28-29.19	117.46-18.99	134.92-103.89	106.71-82.38	82.76-57.08
P/E Ratio	40.34-29.27	36.08-23.43	36.25-21.25	53.10-21.15	206.07-33.32	29.46-22.68	28.53-22.03	29.45-20.31

Address: 600 Hale Street, Prides Crossing, MA 01965 Telephone: 617-747-3300	Web Site: www.amg.com Officers: Sean M. Healey - Chairman, Chief Executive Officer John Kingston - Vice-Chairman, Secretary, General Counsel	Auditors: PricewaterhouseCoopers LLP Transfer Agents: American Stock Transfer & Trust Company, New York, NY

15

AFLAC INC.

Exchange	Symbol	Price	52Wk Range	Yield	P/E	Div Achiever
NYS	AFL	$52.02 (3/28/2013)	54.70-38.45	2.69	8.51	30 Years

*7 Year Price Score 87.84   *NYSE Composite Index=100   *12 Month Price Score 99.01

Interim Earnings (Per Share)

Qtr.	Mar	Jun	Sep	Dec
2008	0.98	1.00	0.21	0.43
2009	1.22	0.67	0.77	0.53
2010	1.35	1.23	1.46	0.92
2011	0.84	0.60	1.59	1.16
2012	1.68	1.03	2.16	1.24

Interim Dividends (Per Share)

Amt	Decl	Ex	Rec	Pay
0.33Q	04/24/2012	05/14/2012	05/16/2012	06/01/2012
0.33Q	07/24/2012	08/13/2012	08/15/2012	09/04/2012
0.35Q	10/23/2012	11/09/2012	11/14/2012	12/03/2012
0.35Q	02/05/2013	02/13/2013	02/15/2013	03/01/2013

Indicated Div: $1.40 (Div. Reinv. Plan)

Valuation Analysis

Forecast EPS	$6.36 (04/06/2013)
Market Cap	$24.3 Billion
Book Value	$16.0 Billion
Price/Book	1.52
Price/Sales	0.96

Institutional Holding

No of Institutions	949
Shares	309,349,312
% Held	58.47

Business Summary: Life & Health (MIC: 5.2.2 SIC: 6321 NAIC: 524114)

AFLAC is a holding company. Through its subsidiary, American Family Life Assurance Company of Columbus, which operates in the U.S. (Aflac U.S.) and as a branch in Japan (Aflac Japan), Co. provides supplemental health and life insurance. Aflac Japan sells voluntary supplemental insurance products, including cancer plans, general medical indemnity plans, medical/sickness riders, care plans, living benefit life plans, life insurance plans and annuities. Aflac U.S. sells voluntary supplemental insurance products including accident, cancer, critical illness/ critical care, hospital intensive care, hospital indemnity, dental, and vision care plans, as well as life and short-term disability plans.

Recent Developments: For the year ended Dec 31 2012, net income increased 48.0% to US$2.87 billion from US$1.94 billion in the prior year. Revenues were US$25.36 billion, up 14.4% from US$22.17 billion the year before. Net premiums earned were US$22.15 billion versus US$20.36 billion in the prior year, an increase of 8.8%. Net investment income rose 5.9% to US$3.47 billion from US$3.28 billion a year ago.

Prospects: Our evaluation of AFLAC Inc. as of Apr. 7, 2013 is the result of our systematic analysis on three basic characteristics: earnings strength, relative valuation, and recent stock price movement. The company has managed to produce a neutral trend in earnings per share over the past 5 quarters. However, while recent estimates for the company have been lowered by analysts, AFL has posted better than expected results. Based on operating earnings yield, the company is undervalued when compared to all of the companies in our coverage universe. Share price changes over the past year indicates that AFL will perform well over the near term.

Financial Data
(US$ in Thousands)

	12/31/2012	12/31/2011	12/31/2010	12/31/2009	12/31/2008	12/31/2007	12/31/2006	12/31/2005
Earnings Per Share	6.11	4.18	4.95	3.19	2.62	3.31	2.95	2.92
Cash Flow Per Share	31.94	23.24	14.90	13.21	10.46	9.54	8.87	8.85
Tang Book Value Per Share	34.16	28.96	23.54	17.96	14.23	18.08	16.93	15.89
Dividends Per Share	1.340	1.230	1.140	1.120	0.960	0.800	0.550	0.440
Dividend Payout %	21.93	29.43	23.03	35.11	36.64	24.17	18.64	15.07
Income Statement								
Premium Income	22,148,000	20,362,000	18,073,000	16,621,000	14,947,000	12,973,000	12,314,000	11,990,000
Total Revenue	25,364,000	22,171,000	20,732,000	18,254,000	16,554,000	15,393,000	14,616,000	14,363,000
Benefits & Claims	15,330,000	13,749,000	12,106,000	11,308,000	10,499,000	9,285,000	9,016,000	8,890,000
Income Before Taxes	4,302,000	2,992,000	3,585,000	2,235,000	1,914,000	2,499,000	2,264,000	2,226,000
Income Taxes	1,436,000	1,028,000	1,241,000	738,000	660,000	865,000	781,000	743,000
Net Income	2,866,000	1,964,000	2,344,000	1,497,000	1,254,000	1,634,000	1,483,000	1,483,000
Average Shares	469,287	469,370	473,085	469,063	478,815	493,971	501,827	507,704
Balance Sheet								
Total Assets	131,094,000	117,102,000	101,039,000	84,106,000	79,331,000	65,805,000	59,805,000	56,361,000
Total Liabilities	115,116,000	103,596,000	89,983,000	75,689,000	72,692,000	57,010,000	51,464,000	48,434,000
Stockholders' Equity	15,978,000	13,506,000	11,056,000	8,417,000	6,639,000	8,795,000	8,341,000	7,927,000
Shares Outstanding	467,786	466,310	469,661	468,568	466,615	486,530	492,550	498,894
Statistical Record								
Return on Assets %	2.30	1.80	2.53	1.83	1.72	2.60	2.55	2.56
Return on Equity %	19.39	15.99	24.07	19.89	16.21	19.07	18.23	19.14
Loss Ratio %	69.22	67.52	66.98	68.03	70.24	71.57	73.22	74.15
Net Margin %	11.30	8.86	11.31	8.20	7.58	10.62	10.15	10.33
Price Range	54.70-38.45	59.28-31.46	57.85-40.48	47.14-11.49	68.22-30.38	62.90-45.64	49.30-42.46	49.60-35.70
P/E Ratio	8.95-6.29	14.18-7.53	11.69-8.18	14.78-3.60	26.04-11.60	19.00-13.79	16.71-14.39	16.99-12.23
Average Yield %	2.90	2.62	2.25	3.25	1.67	1.50	1.20	1.03

Address: 1932 Wynnton Road, Columbus, GA 31999 **Telephone:** 706-323-3431 **Fax:** 706-596-3488	**Web Site:** www.aflac.com **Officers:** Daniel P. Amos - Chairman, Chief Executive Officer Kriss Cloninger - President, Chief Financial Officer, Treasurer	**Auditors:** KPMG LLP **Investor Contact:** 706-596-3264 **Transfer Agents:** AFLAC Incorporated, Columbus, GA

AGCO CORP.

Exchange	Symbol	Price	52Wk Range	Yield	P/E
NYS	AGCO	$52.12 (3/28/2013)	55.12-38.56	N/A	9.83

*7 Year Price Score 101.49 *NYSE Composite Index=100 *12 Month Price Score 103.27

TRADING VOLUME (thousand shares)

Interim Earnings (Per Share)

Qtr.	Mar	Jun	Sep	Dec
2008	0.63	1.34	1.04	1.08
2009	0.36	0.61	0.12	0.35
2010	0.10	0.66	0.65	0.88
2011	0.81	1.36	0.87	2.91
2012	1.21	2.08	0.96	1.05

Interim Dividends (Per Share)

No Dividends Paid

Valuation Analysis		Institutional Holding	
Forecast EPS	$5.29	No of Institutions	
	(04/05/2013)	472	
Market Cap	$5.0 Billion	Shares	
Book Value	$3.5 Billion	94,330,112	
Price/Book	1.46	% Held	
Price/Sales	0.51	86.35	

Business Summary: Construction Services (MIC: 7.5.4 SIC: 3523 NAIC: 333111)

AGCO is a manufacturer and distributor of agricultural equipment and related replacement parts. Co. sells a range of agricultural equipment, including tractors, combines, self-propelled sprayers, hay tools, forage equipment, tillage, implements and grain storage and protein production systems. Co.'s products are marketed under a number of brands including: Challenger®, Fendt®, Massey Ferguson®, Valtra® and GSI®. Co. also provides retail financing through its AGCO Finance retail financing joint ventures with Cooperatieve Centrale Raiffeisen-Boerenleenbank B.A. In addition, Co. provides a wholesale financing to its dealers primarily in the U.S. and Canada.

Recent Developments: For the year ended Dec 31 2012, net income decreased 11.8% to US$516.4 million from US$585.3 million in the prior year. Revenues were US$9.96 billion, up 13.6% from US$8.77 billion the year before. Operating income was US$693.2 million versus US$610.3 million in the prior year, an increase of 13.6%. Direct operating expenses rose 12.0% to US$7.84 billion from US$7.00 billion in the comparable period the year before. Indirect operating expenses increased 22.7% to US$1.43 billion from US$1.17 billion in the equivalent prior-year period.

Prospects: Our evaluation of AGCO Corp. as of Apr. 7, 2013 is the result of our systematic analysis on three basic characteristics: earnings strength, relative valuation, and recent stock price movement. The company has generated a negative trend in earnings per share over the past 5 quarters. However, while recent estimates for the company have been mixed, AGCO has posted better than expected results. Based on operating earnings yield, the company is undervalued when compared to all of the companies in our coverage universe. Share price changes over the past year indicates that AGCO will perform well over the near term.

Financial Data

(US$ in Thousands)	12/31/2012	12/31/2011	12/31/2010	12/31/2009	12/31/2008	12/31/2007	12/31/2006	12/31/2005
Earnings Per Share	5.30	5.95	2.29	1.44	4.09	2.55	(0.71)	0.35
Cash Flow Per Share	6.84	7.59	4.73	3.81	3.17	5.51	4.87	2.72
Tang Book Value Per Share	17.20	11.67	19.91	17.31	12.99	12.79	7.61	5.61
Income Statement								
Total Revenue	9,962,200	8,773,200	6,896,600	6,630,400	8,424,600	6,828,100	5,435,000	5,449,700
EBITDA	888,300	764,700	462,500	344,700	691,400	484,900	151,500	346,000
Depn & Amortn	229,900	173,500	154,300	147,600	146,500	133,500	115,500	105,900
Income Before Taxes	600,800	561,000	274,900	153,800	525,800	327,300	(19,200)	160,100
Income Taxes	137,900	24,600	104,400	56,500	164,600	111,400	73,500	151,100
Net Income	516,400	585,300	220,200	135,700	400,000	246,300	(64,900)	31,600
Average Shares	98,600	98,100	96,400	94,100	97,700	96,600	90,800	90,700
Balance Sheet								
Current Assets	3,954,700	3,662,800	3,121,000	2,788,900	3,005,200	2,721,700	2,309,000	2,086,200
Total Assets	7,721,800	7,257,200	5,436,900	5,062,200	4,954,800	4,787,600	4,114,500	3,861,200
Current Liabilities	2,464,800	2,205,500	1,912,900	1,718,100	1,978,500	2,083,300	1,623,600	1,260,400
Long-Term Obligations	1,035,600	1,409,700	443,000	454,000	682,000	294,100	577,400	841,800
Total Liabilities	4,257,100	4,262,000	2,778,500	2,660,700	2,997,800	2,744,600	2,620,900	2,445,200
Stockholders' Equity	3,464,700	2,995,200	2,658,400	2,401,500	1,957,000	2,043,000	1,493,600	1,416,000
Shares Outstanding	96,815	97,194	93,143	92,453	91,844	91,609	91,177	90,508
Statistical Record								
Return on Assets %	6.88	9.22	4.19	2.71	8.19	5.53	N.M.	0.77
Return on Equity %	15.94	20.71	8.70	6.23	19.95	13.93	N.M.	2.23
EBITDA Margin %	8.92	8.72	6.71	5.20	8.21	7.10	2.79	6.35
Net Margin %	5.18	6.67	3.19	2.05	4.75	3.61	N.M.	0.58
Asset Turnover	1.33	1.38	1.31	1.32	1.72	1.53	1.36	1.34
Current Ratio	1.60	1.66	1.63	1.62	1.52	1.31	1.42	1.66
Debt to Equity	0.30	0.47	0.17	0.19	0.35	0.14	0.39	0.59
Price Range	52.94-38.56	58.13-32.39	50.94-25.86	33.50-15.10	70.51-19.35	70.78-29.18	32.93-16.31	21.89-14.74
P/E Ratio	9.99-7.28	9.77-5.44	22.24-11.29	23.26-10.49	17.24-4.73	27.76-11.44	...	62.54-42.11

Address: 4205 River Green Parkway, Duluth, GA 30096	Web Site: www.agcocorp.com	Auditors: KPMG LLP
Telephone: 770-813-9200	Officers: Martin H. Richenhagen - Chairman, President, Chief Executive Officer Andrew H. Beck - Senior Vice President, Chief Financial Officer	Transfer Agents: Computershare Trust Company, N.A., Clanton, MA

AGILENT TECHNOLOGIES, INC.

Exchange	Symbol	Price	52Wk Range	Yield	P/E
NYS	A	$41.97 (3/28/2013)	45.29-35.51	1.00	13.41

*7 Year Price Score 104.84 *NYSE Composite Index=100   *12 Month Price Score 98.26

Interim Earnings (Per Share)

Qtr.	Jan	Apr	Jul	Oct
2009-10	0.22	0.31	0.58	0.83
2010-11	0.54	0.56	0.92	0.81
2011-12	0.65	0.72	0.69	1.21
2012-13	0.51	...	...	...

Interim Dividends (Per Share)

Amt	Decl	Ex	Rec	Pay
0.10Q	05/16/2012	06/29/2012	07/03/2012	07/25/2012
0.10Q	09/20/2012	09/28/2012	10/02/2012	10/24/2012
0.10Q	11/16/2012	12/27/2012	12/31/2012	01/23/2013
0.12Q	01/17/2013	03/28/2013	04/02/2013	04/24/2013

Indicated Div: $0.42

Valuation Analysis		Institutional Holding	
Forecast EPS	$2.90 (04/06/2013)	No of Institutions	706
Market Cap	$14.6 Billion	Shares	324,827,232
Book Value	$5.3 Billion	% Held	81.50
Price/Book	2.72		
Price/Sales	2.11		

Business Summary: Biotechnology (MIC: 4.1.2 SIC: 3825 NAIC: 334515)

Agilent Technologies is a measurement company, providing bio-analytical and electronic measurement applications. Co. has four segments: life sciences, which includes liquid chromatography mass spectrometry systems, and laboratory software and informatics systems; chemical analysis, which includes gas chromatography mass spectrometry systems, and inductively coupled plasma mass spectrometry instruments; diagnostics and genomics, which includes immunohistochemistry, and deoxyribonucleic acid mutation detection; and electronic measurement, which includes electronic measurement instruments and systems, software design tools and related services for electronics equipment and microscopy products.

Recent Developments: For the quarter ended Jan 31 2013, net income decreased 22.2% to US$179.0 million from US$230.0 million in the year-earlier quarter. Revenues were US$1.68 billion, up 2.8% from US$1.64 billion the year before. Operating income was US$217.0 million versus US$271.0 million in the prior-year quarter, a decrease of 19.9%. Direct operating expenses rose 5.1% to US$800.0 million from US$761.0 million in the comparable period the year before. Indirect operating expenses increased 10.0% to US$663.0 million from US$603.0 million in the equivalent prior-year period.

Prospects: Our evaluation of Agilent Technologies Inc. as of Apr. 7, 2013 is the result of our systematic analysis on three basic characteristics: earnings strength, relative valuation, and recent stock price movement. The company has managed to produce a neutral trend in earnings per share over the past 5 quarters and while recent estimates for the company have remained steady, A has posted results that fell short of analysts expectations. Based on operating earnings yield, the company is undervalued when compared to all of the companies in our coverage universe. Share price changes over the past year indicates that A will perform in line with the market over the near term.

Financial Data

(US$ in Millions)	3 Mos	10/31/2012	10/31/2011	10/31/2010	10/31/2009	10/31/2008	10/31/2007	10/31/2006
Earnings Per Share	3.13	3.27	2.85	1.94	(0.09)	1.87	1.57	7.50
Cash Flow Per Share	3.81	3.52	3.63	2.07	1.18	2.08	2.46	1.47
Tang Book Value Per Share	3.48	3.09	6.67	3.69	4.86	4.82	6.75	7.79
Dividends Per Share	0.400	0.300	...	...	...	...	...	...
Dividend Payout %	12.78	9.17	...	...	...	...	...	...
Income Statement								
Total Revenue	1,680	6,858	6,615	5,444	4,481	5,774	5,420	4,973
EBITDA	312	1,306	1,246	892	178	951	731	664
Depn & Amortn	94	171	142	124	112	126	142	141
Income Before Taxes	195	1,043	1,032	692	7	815	670	632
Income Taxes	16	(110)	20	8	38	122	32	91
Net Income	179	1,153	1,012	684	(31)	693	638	3,307
Average Shares	352	353	355	353	346	371	406	441
Balance Sheet								
Current Assets	4,712	4,629	5,569	6,169	3,961	3,208	3,671	3,958
Total Assets	10,653	10,536	9,057	9,696	7,612	7,437	7,554	7,369
Current Liabilities	1,846	1,893	1,837	3,083	1,123	1,325	1,663	1,538
Long-Term Obligations	2,111	2,112	1,932	2,190	2,904	2,125	2,087	1,500
Total Liabilities	5,305	5,354	4,749	6,468	5,106	4,878	4,320	3,721
Stockholders' Equity	5,348	5,182	4,308	3,228	2,506	2,559	3,234	3,648
Shares Outstanding	347	346	346	346	346	349	370	408
Statistical Record								
Return on Assets %	11.16	11.74	10.79	7.90	N.M.	9.22	8.55	46.84
Return on Equity %	22.39	24.23	26.86	23.86	N.M.	23.86	18.54	85.57
EBITDA Margin %	18.57	19.04	18.84	16.39	3.97	16.47	13.49	13.35
Net Margin %	10.65	16.81	15.30	12.56	N.M.	12.00	11.77	66.50
Asset Turnover	0.70	0.70	0.71	0.63	0.60	0.77	0.73	0.70
Current Ratio	2.55	2.45	3.03	2.00	3.53	2.42	2.21	2.57
Debt to Equity	0.39	0.41	0.45	0.68	1.16	0.83	0.65	0.41
Price Range	45.86-35.51	45.86-32.93	52.58-29.40	37.23-25.03	28.81-12.44	38.01-18.92	40.40-30.69	36.90-25.53
P/E Ratio	14.65-11.35	14.02-10.07	18.45-10.32	19.19-12.90	...	20.33-10.12	25.73-19.55	4.92-3.40
Average Yield %	1.00	0.76	...	...	...	...	...	...

Address: 5301 Stevens Creek Blvd., Santa Clara, CA 95051 Telephone: 408-345-8886	Web Site: www.investor.agilent.com Officers: Ronald S. Nersesian - President, Executive Vice President, Senior Vice President, Chief Operating Officer, Division Officer William P. Sullivan - Chief Executive Officer, President	Auditors: PricewaterhouseCoopers LLP Investor Contact: 877-942-4200 Transfer Agents: Computershare Investor Services, Canton, MA

18

AGL RESOURCES INC.

Exchange	Symbol	Price	52Wk Range	Yield	P/E	Div Achiever
NYS	GAS	$41.95 (3/28/2013)	42.28-36.85	4.48	18.16	10 Years

*7 Year Price Score 94.57   *NYSE Composite Index=100   *12 Month Price Score 94.80

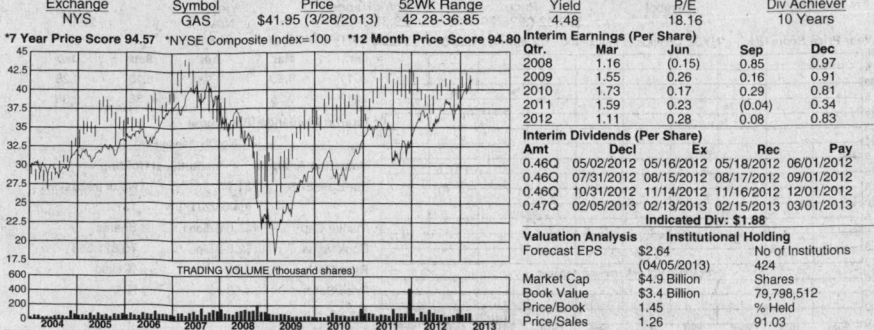

Interim Earnings (Per Share)

Qtr.	Mar	Jun	Sep	Dec
2008	1.16	(0.15)	0.85	0.97
2009	1.55	0.26	0.16	0.91
2010	1.73	0.17	0.29	0.81
2011	1.59	0.23	(0.04)	0.34
2012	1.11	0.28	0.08	0.83

Interim Dividends (Per Share)

Amt	Decl	Ex	Rec	Pay
0.46Q	05/02/2012	05/16/2012	05/18/2012	06/01/2012
0.46Q	07/31/2012	08/15/2012	08/17/2012	09/01/2012
0.46Q	10/31/2012	11/14/2012	11/16/2012	12/01/2012
0.47Q	02/05/2013	02/13/2013	02/15/2013	03/01/2013

Indicated Div: $1.88

Valuation Analysis   **Institutional Holding**

Forecast EPS	$2.64	No of Institutions
	(04/05/2013)	424
Market Cap	$4.9 Billion	Shares
Book Value	$3.4 Billion	79,798,512
Price/Book	1.45	% Held
Price/Sales	1.26	91.03

TRADING VOLUME (thousand shares)

Business Summary: Gas Utilities (MIC: 3.3.1 SIC: 4924 NAIC: 221210)

AGL Resources is an energy services holding company. Co.'s operating segments includes: distribution operations, which includes natural gas local distribution utilities; retail operations, which markets natural gas and related home services; wholesale services, is involved in asset management and optimization, storage, transportation, producer and peaking services, natural gas supply, natural gas services and wholesale marketing; midstream operations, which operates non-utility storage and pipeline facilities; and cargo shipping, which transports containerized freight in the Bahamas and the Caribbean.

Recent Developments: For the year ended Dec 31 2012, net income increased 53.8% to US$286.0 million from US$186.0 million in the prior year. Revenues were US$3.92 billion, up 67.8% from US$2.34 billion the year before. Operating income was US$610.0 million versus US$440.0 million in the prior year, an increase of 38.6%. Direct operating expenses rose 63.3% to US$1.79 billion from US$1.10 billion in the comparable period the year before. Indirect operating expenses increased 89.9% to US$1.52 billion from US$801.0 million in the equivalent prior-year period.

Prospects: Our evaluation of AGL Resources Inc. as of Apr. 7, 2013 is the result of our systematic analysis on three basic characteristics: earnings strength, relative valuation, and recent stock price movement. The company has enjoyed a very positive trend in earnings per share over the past 5 quarters. However, while recent estimates for the company have been mixed, GAS has posted results that fell short of analysts expectations. Based on operating earnings yield, the company is undervalued when compared to all of the companies in our coverage universe. Share price changes over the past year indicates that GAS will perform poorly over the near term.

Financial Data
(US$ in Thousands)

	12/31/2012	12/31/2011	12/31/2010	12/31/2009	12/31/2008	12/31/2007	12/31/2006	12/31/2005
Earnings Per Share	2.31	2.12	3.00	2.88	2.84	2.72	2.72	2.48
Cash Flow Per Share	8.55	5.61	6.80	7.71	2.97	4.88	4.56	1.01
Tang Book Value Per Share	12.56	11.97	17.88	17.57	16.05	16.24	15.30	13.86
Dividends Per Share	1.741	1.899	1.760	1.720	1.680	1.640	1.480	1.300
Dividend Payout %	75.37	89.57	58.67	59.72	59.15	60.29	54.41	52.42
Income Statement								
Total Revenue	3,922,000	2,338,000	2,373,000	2,317,000	2,800,000	2,494,000	2,621,000	2,718,000
EBITDA	1,049,000	633,000	659,000	643,000	636,000	637,000	625,000	574,000
Depn & Amortn	415,000	186,000	160,000	158,000	152,000	144,000	138,000	133,000
Income Before Taxes	450,000	311,000	390,000	384,000	369,000	368,000	364,000	332,000
Income Taxes	164,000	125,000	140,000	135,000	132,000	127,000	129,000	117,000
Net Income	271,000	172,000	234,000	222,000	217,000	211,000	212,000	193,000
Average Shares	117,500	80,900	77,800	77,100	76,600	77,400	78,000	77,800
Balance Sheet								
Current Assets	2,668,000	2,746,000	2,162,000	2,000,000	2,042,000	1,811,000	1,822,000	2,032,000
Total Assets	14,141,000	13,913,000	7,518,000	7,074,000	6,710,000	6,268,000	6,147,000	6,251,000
Current Liabilities	3,338,000	3,084,000	2,428,000	1,772,000	1,983,000	1,645,000	1,627,000	1,939,000
Long-Term Obligations	3,327,000	3,561,000	1,673,000	1,974,000	1,675,000	1,674,000	1,622,000	1,615,000
Total Liabilities	10,728,000	10,595,000	5,705,000	5,294,000	5,058,000	4,607,000	4,538,000	4,752,000
Stockholders' Equity	3,413,000	3,318,000	1,813,000	1,780,000	1,652,000	1,661,000	1,609,000	1,499,000
Shares Outstanding	117,855	117,000	78,000	77,500	76,900	76,400	77,700	77,700
Statistical Record								
Return on Assets %	1.93	1.61	3.21	3.22	3.33	3.40	3.42	3.25
Return on Equity %	8.03	6.70	13.03	12.94	13.06	12.91	13.64	13.38
EBITDA Margin %	26.75	27.07	27.77	27.75	22.71	25.54	23.85	21.12
Net Margin %	6.91	7.36	9.86	9.58	7.75	8.46	8.09	7.10
Asset Turnover	0.28	0.22	0.33	0.34	0.43	0.40	0.42	0.46
Current Ratio	0.80	0.89	0.89	1.13	1.03	1.10	1.12	1.05
Debt to Equity	0.97	1.07	0.92	1.11	1.01	1.01	1.01	1.08
Price Range	42.28-36.85	43.50-34.98	39.98-34.62	37.48-24.18	39.03-25.63	44.12-35.81	39.70-34.41	39.10-32.25
P/E Ratio	18.30-15.95	20.52-16.50	13.33-11.54	13.01-8.40	13.74-9.02	16.22-13.17	14.60-12.65	15.77-13.00
Average Yield %	4.40	4.77	4.70	5.36	5.05	4.09	4.04	3.65

Address: Ten Peachtree Place N.E., Atlanta, GA 30309 Telephone: 404-584-4000	Web Site: www.aglresources.com Officers: Andrew W. Evans - Executive Vice President, Chief Financial Officer Ralph Cleveland - Executive Vice President	Auditors: PricewaterhouseCoopers LLP Investor Contact: 404-584-4577 Transfer Agents: Wells Fargo Shareowner Services, St. Paul, MN

AIR LEASE CORP

Exchange	Symbol	Price	52Wk Range	Yield	P/E
NYS	AL	$29.32 (3/28/2013)	29.36-18.62	N/A	22.91

*7 Year Price Score N/A   *NYSE Composite Index=100   *12 Month Price Score 112.23

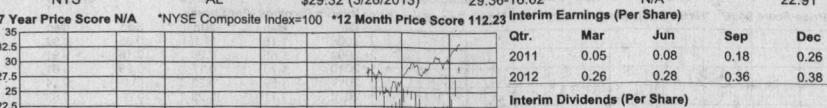

Interim Earnings (Per Share)

Qtr.	Mar	Jun	Sep	Dec
2011	0.05	0.08	0.18	0.26
2012	0.26	0.28	0.36	0.38

Interim Dividends (Per Share)

No Dividends Paid

Valuation Analysis   **Institutional Holding**

Forecast EPS	$1.77	No of Institutions
	(04/05/2013)	137
Market Cap	$3.0 Billion	Shares
Book Value	$2.3 Billion	75,821,368
Price/Book	1.27	% Held
Price/Sales	4.53	N/A

Business Summary: Miscellaneous Transportation Services (MIC: 7.4.5 SIC: 7359 NAIC: 532411)

Air Lease is an aircraft leasing company. Co. is primarily engaged in purchasing commercial aircraft which, it in turn, leases to airlines around the world. Co.'s fleet is comprised of narrowbody (single-aisle) aircraft; select widebody (twin-aisle) aircraft; and turboprop aircraft. In addition, Co. also provides fleet management services to third parties for a fee. These services are similar to those Co. performs with its fleet, including leasing, re-leasing, lease management and sales services. As of Dec 31 2011, Co.'s fleet consisted of 102 aircraft, comprised of 81 single-aisle jet aircraft, 19 twin-aisle widebody aircraft and two turboprop aircraft.

Recent Developments: For the year ended Dec 31 2012, net income increased 147.8% to US$131.9 million from US$53.2 million in the prior year. Revenues were US$655.7 million, up 94.7% from US$336.7 million the year before. Indirect operating expenses increased 77.9% to US$451.8 million from US$253.9 million in the equivalent prior-year period.

Prospects: Our evaluation of Air Lease Corp as of Apr. 7, 2013 is the result of our systematic analysis on three basic characteristics: earnings strength, relative valuation, and recent stock price movement. The company has managed to produce a neutral trend in earnings per share over the past 5 quarters and while recent estimates for the company have been raised by analysts, AL has posted better than expected results. Based on operating earnings yield, the company is about fairly valued when compared to all of the companies in our coverage universe. Share price changes over the past year indicates that AL will perform in line with the market over the near term.

Financial Data
(US$ in Thousands)

	12/31/2012	12/31/2011	12/31/2010
Earnings Per Share	1.28	0.59	(1.32)
Cash Flow Per Share	4.85	2.98	...
Tang Book Value Per Share	23.04	21.61	18.73
Income Statement			
Total Revenue	655,746	336,741	58,366
EBITDA	550,611	240,010	(30,591)
Depn & Amortn	216,219	112,307	19,262
Income Before Taxes	203,973	82,841	(60,915)
Income Taxes	72,054	29,609	(8,875)
Net Income	131,919	53,232	(52,040)
Average Shares	107,656	90,416	39,511
Balance Sheet			
Current Assets	901,114	783,511	569,739
Total Assets	7,353,624	5,164,593	2,276,282
Current Liabilities	502,392	338,802	131,328
Long-Term Obligations	4,384,732	2,602,799	911,981
Total Liabilities	5,021,003	2,988,310	1,051,347
Stockholders' Equity	2,332,621	2,176,283	1,224,935
Shares Outstanding	101,247	100,714	65,393
Statistical Record			
Return on Assets %	2.10	1.43	...
Return on Equity %	5.84	3.13	...
EBITDA Margin %	83.97	71.27	N.M.
Net Margin %	20.12	15.81	N.M.
Asset Turnover	0.10	0.09	...
Current Ratio	1.79	2.31	4.34
Debt to Equity	1.88	1.20	0.74
Price Range	25.58-18.62	29.70-17.83	...
P/E Ratio	19.98-14.55	50.34-30.22	...

Address: 2000 Avenue of the Stars, Suite 1000N, Los Angeles, CA 90067 Telephone: 310-553-0555	Web Site: www.airleasecorp.com Officers: Steven F. Udvar-Hazy - Chairman, Chief Executive Officer John L. Plueger - President, Chief Operating Officer	Auditors: KPMG LLP Investor Contact: 310-553-0555 Transfer Agents: American Stock Transfer and Trust Company

AIR PRODUCTS & CHEMICALS, INC.

Exchange	Symbol	Price	52Wk Range	Yield	P/E	Div Achiever
NYS	APD	$87.12 (3/28/2013)	92.68-76.88	3.26	15.56	30 Years

*7 Year Price Score 93.29 *NYSE Composite Index=100 *12 Month Price Score 96.23

Interim Earnings (Per Share)

Qtr.	Dec	Mar	Jun	Sep
2009-10	1.16	1.16	1.17	1.25
2010-11	1.23	1.39	1.50	1.51
2011-12	1.16	1.38	2.26	0.65
2012-13	1.31	...	...	...

Interim Dividends (Per Share)

Amt	Decl	Ex	Rec	Pay
0.64Q	05/17/2012	06/28/2012	07/02/2012	08/13/2012
0.64Q	09/20/2012	09/27/2012	10/01/2012	11/13/2012
0.64Q	11/15/2012	12/28/2012	01/02/2013	02/11/2013
0.71Q	03/21/2013	03/27/2013	04/01/2013	05/13/2013

Indicated Div: $2.84 (Div. Reinv. Plan)

Valuation Analysis / **Institutional Holding**

Forecast EPS	$5.79	No of Institutions	
	(04/05/2013)	858	
Market Cap	$18.1 Billion	Shares	
Book Value	$6.3 Billion	213,634,432	
Price/Book	2.87	% Held	
Price/Sales	1.84	83.78	

TRADING VOLUME (thousand shares)

Business Summary: Specialty Chemicals (MIC: 8.3.2 SIC: 2813 NAIC: 325120)

Air Products and Chemicals is engaged in providing atmospheric gases, process and specialty gases, performance materials, equipment, and services. Co.'s segments are: Merchant Gases, which sells atmospheric gases, process gases, specialty gases, and certain services and equipment; Tonnage Gases, which provides hydrogen, carbon monoxide, nitrogen, oxygen, and synthesis gas; Electronics and Performance Materials, which provides specialty gases, as well as tonnage gases, chemical mechanical planarization slurries, specialty chemicals, services, and equipment; and Equipment and Energy, which designs and manufactures cryogenic equipment.

Recent Developments: For the quarter ended Dec 31 2012, income from continuing operations increased 22.1% to US$285.8 million from US$234.1 million in the year-earlier quarter. Net income increased 12.1% to US$287.2 million from US$256.3 million in the year-earlier quarter. Revenues were US$2.56 billion, up 10.4% from US$2.32 billion the year before. Operating income was US$372.4 million versus US$353.8 million in the prior-year quarter, an increase of 5.3%. Direct operating expenses rose 10.3% to US$1.90 billion from US$1.72 billion in the comparable period the year before. Indirect operating expenses increased 18.1% to US$289.9 million from US$245.4 million in the equivalent prior-year period.

Prospects: Our evaluation of Air Products & Chemicals Inc. as of Apr. 7, 2013 is the result of our systematic analysis on three basic characteristics: earnings strength, relative valuation, and recent stock price movement. The company has produced a positive trend in earnings per share over the past 5 quarters. However, while recent estimates for the company have been mixed, APD has posted better than expected results. Based on operating earnings yield, the company is undervalued when compared to all of the companies in our coverage universe. Share price changes over the past year indicates that APD will perform in line with the market over the near term.

Financial Data

(US$ in Thousands)	3 Mos	09/30/2012	09/30/2011	09/30/2010	09/30/2009	09/30/2008	09/30/2007	09/30/2006
Earnings Per Share	5.60	5.44	5.63	4.74	2.96	4.15	4.64	3.18
Cash Flow Per Share	7.68	8.33	8.23	7.17	6.30	7.89	6.86	5.96
Tang Book Value Per Share	18.95	19.38	22.09	20.33	17.10	18.21	18.53	17.44
Dividends Per Share	2.560	2.500	2.230	1.920	1.790	1.700	1.480	1.340
Dividend Payout %	45.71	45.96	39.61	40.51	60.47	40.96	31.90	42.14
Income Statement								
Total Revenue	2,562,400	9,611,700	10,082,000	9,026,000	8,256,200	10,414,500	10,037,800	8,850,400
EBITDA	590,900	2,094,200	2,473,000	2,231,700	1,664,900	2,345,400	2,230,300	1,813,600
Depn & Amortn	218,500	817,200	856,500	846,100	826,000	857,800	831,400	761,700
Income Before Taxes	336,600	1,158,700	1,506,700	1,267,100	724,400	1,333,800	1,244,500	941,600
Income Taxes	92,200	287,300	408,400	339,500	185,300	365,300	301,200	271,200
Net Income	278,300	1,167,300	1,224,200	1,029,100	631,300	909,700	1,035,600	723,400
Average Shares	212,600	214,700	217,600	217,100	213,500	219,200	223,200	227,500
Balance Sheet								
Current Assets	3,563,100	3,415,800	3,189,800	3,033,800	2,997,800	2,848,100	2,858,400	2,612,600
Total Assets	17,393,100	16,941,800	14,290,700	13,505,900	13,029,100	12,571,300	12,659,500	11,180,700
Current Liabilities	2,966,900	2,689,900	2,342,000	2,244,100	2,503,600	2,212,000	2,422,700	2,323,400
Long-Term Obligations	5,107,300	4,584,200	3,927,500	3,659,800	3,715,600	3,515,400	2,976,500	2,280,200
Total Liabilities	11,093,800	10,464,600	8,494,900	7,959,000	8,237,200	7,540,600	7,163,900	6,256,700
Stockholders' Equity	6,299,300	6,477,200	5,795,800	5,546,900	4,791,900	5,030,700	5,495,600	4,924,000
Shares Outstanding	207,624	212,475	210,185	213,802	211,260	209,334	215,355	217,250
Statistical Record								
Return on Assets %	7.54	7.45	8.81	7.76	4.93	7.19	8.69	6.70
Return on Equity %	19.62	18.97	21.59	19.91	12.85	17.24	19.88	15.23
EBITDA Margin %	23.06	21.79	24.53	24.73	20.17	22.52	22.22	20.49
Net Margin %	10.86	12.14	12.14	11.40	7.65	8.73	10.32	8.17
Asset Turnover	0.62	0.61	0.73	0.68	0.65	0.82	0.84	0.82
Current Ratio	1.20	1.27	1.36	1.35	1.20	1.29	1.18	1.12
Debt to Equity	0.81	0.71	0.68	0.66	0.78	0.70	0.54	0.46
Price Range	92.68-76.88	92.68-73.87	97.79-74.80	84.71-64.81	80.20-41.65	106.03-66.41	97.82-66.59	69.23-53.33
P/E Ratio	16.55-13.73	17.04-13.58	17.37-13.29	17.87-13.67	27.09-14.07	25.55-16.00	21.08-14.37	21.77-16.77
Average Yield %	3.05	2.97	2.54	2.53	2.95	1.79	1.91	2.14

Address: 7201 Hamilton Boulevard, Allentown, PA 18195-1501 **Telephone:** 610-481-4911 **Fax:** 610-481-5900	Web Site: www.airproducts.com **Officers:** John E. McGlade - Chairman, President, Chief Executive Officer M. Scott Crocco - Senior Vice President, Chief Financial Officer, Vice President, Controller, Principal Accounting Officer	**Auditors:** KPMG LLP **Investor Contact:** 610-481-7461 **Transfer Agents:** American Stock Transfer & Trust Company, Brooklyn, NY

AIRGAS INC.

<table>
<tr><td>Exchange
NYS</td><td>Symbol
ARG</td><td>Price
$99.16 (3/28/2013)</td><td>52Wk Range
103.52-78.13</td><td>Yield
1.61</td><td>P/E
22.74</td></tr>
</table>

*7 Year Price Score 136.06 *NYSE Composite Index=100 *12 Month Price Score 103.34

Interim Earnings (Per Share)

Qtr.	Jun	Sep	Dec	Mar
2009-10	0.66	0.65	0.56	0.47
2010-11	0.76	0.78	0.65	0.74
2011-12	0.93	1.01	0.93	1.13
2012-13	1.15	1.03	1.05	...

Interim Dividends (Per Share)

Amt	Decl	Ex	Rec	Pay
0.40Q	05/03/2012	06/13/2012	06/15/2012	06/29/2012
0.40Q	08/14/2012	09/12/2012	09/14/2012	09/28/2012
0.40Q	11/20/2012	12/12/2012	12/14/2012	12/28/2012
0.40Q	01/29/2013	03/12/2013	03/14/2013	03/28/2013

Indicated Div: $1.60

Valuation Analysis | **Institutional Holding**

Forecast EPS	$4.34 (04/05/2013)	No of Institutions 469
Market Cap	$7.6 Billion	Shares 71,076,112
Book Value	$1.8 Billion	% Held
Price/Book	4.13	80.65
Price/Sales	1.54	

Business Summary: Industrial Machinery & Equipment (MIC: 7.2.1 SIC: 5084 NAIC: 325120)

Airgas is a distributor of industrial, medical and specialty gases, and hardgoods, such as welding equipment and supplies. Co. is a producer of atmospheric gases, carbon dioxide, dry ice and nitrous oxide, and a distributor of refrigerants, ammonia products and process chemicals. Co. also provides supply chain management services, and product and process technical support. Co. has two segments: Distribution, which engages in the distribution of industrial and medical gases and hardgoods, and in the production of gases; and All Other Operations, which consists of six business units which manufacture and/or distribute carbon dioxide, dry ice, nitrous oxide, ammonia and refrigerant gases.

Recent Developments: For the quarter ended Dec 31 2012, net income increased 14.3% to US$82.9 million from US$72.6 million in the year-earlier quarter. Revenues were US$1.21 billion, up 4.7% from US$1.15 billion the year before. Operating income was US$147.3 million versus US$131.0 million in the prior-year quarter, an increase of 12.4%. Direct operating expenses rose 1.4% to US$527.5 million from US$520.4 million in the comparable period the year before. Indirect operating expenses increased 6.1% to US$533.0 million from US$502.3 million in the equivalent prior-year period.

Prospects: Our evaluation of Airgas Inc. as of Apr. 7, 2013 is the result of our systematic analysis on three basic characteristics: earnings strength, relative valuation, and recent stock price movement. The company has managed to produce a neutral trend in earnings per share over the past 5 quarters. However, while recent estimates for the company have been lowered by analysts, ARG has posted results that fell short of analysts expectations. Based on operating earnings yield, the company is about fairly valued when compared to all of the companies in our coverage universe. Share price changes over the past year indicates that ARG will perform well over the near term.

Financial Data
(US$ in Thousands)

	9 Mos	6 Mos	3 Mos	03/31/2012	03/31/2011	03/31/2010	03/31/2009	03/31/2008
Earnings Per Share	4.36	4.24	4.22	4.00	2.93	2.34	3.12	2.66
Cash Flow Per Share	7.37	7.38	7.08	6.59	3.30	7.31	7.11	6.74
Tang Book Value Per Share	5.34	6.94	5.48	4.86	5.28	5.69	3.59	3.59
Dividends Per Share	1.520	1.440	1.360	1.250	1.010	0.760	0.560	0.390
Dividend Payout %	34.86	33.96	32.23	31.25	34.47	32.48	17.95	14.66
Income Statement								
Total Revenue	3,694,574	2,486,866	1,257,256	4,746,283	4,251,467	3,864,005	4,349,455	4,017,024
EBITDA	669,254	448,752	231,038	803,579	716,695	612,359	734,543	650,397
Depn & Amortn	214,770	142,352	70,985	245,076	250,518	234,949	220,795	189,775
Income Before Taxes	406,382	274,770	144,303	492,166	406,123	314,100	429,353	370,762
Income Taxes	151,649	102,952	53,505	178,792	156,357	117,800	168,265	144,184
Net Income	254,733	171,818	90,798	313,374	249,766	196,300	261,088	223,348
Average Shares	78,944	78,892	78,799	78,324	85,252	83,787	83,816	84,235
Balance Sheet								
Current Assets	1,388,957	1,341,810	1,331,795	1,274,206	1,120,645	711,335	717,970	638,714
Total Assets	5,539,061	5,408,978	5,373,406	5,320,585	4,935,881	4,495,932	4,399,537	3,979,261
Current Liabilities	1,094,755	866,422	898,483	930,049	564,503	475,643	432,460	506,391
Long-Term Obligations	1,706,926	1,752,515	1,751,155	1,761,902	1,842,994	1,499,384	1,750,308	1,539,648
Total Liabilities	3,701,315	3,502,386	3,537,336	3,570,327	3,200,999	2,700,388	2,827,782	2,565,925
Stockholders' Equity	1,837,746	1,906,592	1,836,070	1,750,258	1,734,882	1,795,544	1,571,755	1,413,336
Shares Outstanding	76,560	77,166	85,954	76,667	79,596	83,226	81,403	82,288
Statistical Record								
Return on Assets %	6.42	6.33	6.30	6.09	5.30	4.41	6.23	6.09
Return on Equity %	19.69	19.11	19.66	17.93	14.15	11.66	17.49	17.55
EBITDA Margin %	18.11	18.04	18.38	16.93	16.86	15.85	16.89	16.19
Net Margin %	6.89	6.91	7.22	6.60	5.87	5.08	6.00	5.56
Asset Turnover	0.92	0.93	0.93	0.92	0.90	0.87	1.04	1.10
Current Ratio	1.27	1.55	1.48	1.37	1.99	1.50	1.66	1.26
Debt to Equity	0.93	0.92	0.95	1.01	1.06	0.84	1.11	1.09
Price Range	92.49-77.02	92.49-62.47	92.49-58.50	89.43-58.50	71.00-59.79	65.71-33.81	64.72-27.09	55.27-40.24
P/E Ratio	21.21-17.67	21.81-14.73	21.92-13.86	22.36-14.63	24.23-20.41	28.08-14.45	20.74-8.68	20.78-15.13
Average Yield %	1.79	1.78	1.78	1.76	1.56	1.42	1.22	0.83

<table>
<tr><td>Address: 259 North Radnor-Chester Road, Suite 100, Radnor, PA 19087-5283
Telephone: 610-687-5253
Fax: 610-687-1052</td><td>Web Site: www.airgas.com
Officers: John C. van Roden - Chairman Peter McCausland - Executive Chairman, Chairman, President, Chief Executive Officer</td><td>Auditors: KPMG LLP
Investor Contact: 180-025-52165
Transfer Agents: Wells Fargo Shareowner Services, Mendota Heights, MN</td></tr>
</table>

AK STEEL HOLDING CORP.

Exchange	Symbol	Price	52Wk Range	Yield	P/E
NYS	AKS	$3.31 (3/28/2013)	7.66-3.31	N/A	N/A

*7 Year Price Score 22.91 *NYSE Composite Index=100 *12 Month Price Score 67.60

TRADING VOLUME (thousand shares)

Interim Earnings (Per Share)

Qtr.	Mar	Jun	Sep	Dec
2008	0.90	1.29	1.67	(3.82)
2009	(0.67)	(0.43)	0.06	0.37
2010	0.02	0.24	(0.54)	(0.89)
2011	0.08	0.30	(0.03)	(1.76)
2012	(0.11)	(6.55)	(0.55)	(1.85)

Interim Dividends (Per Share)

Amt	Decl	Ex	Rec	Pay
0.05Q	07/26/2011	08/11/2011	08/15/2011	09/09/2011
0.05Q	10/25/2011	11/10/2011	11/15/2011	12/09/2011
0.05Q	01/24/2012	02/08/2012	02/10/2012	03/09/2012
0.05Q	04/24/2012	05/11/2012	05/15/2012	06/08/2012

Valuation Analysis | **Institutional Holding**

Forecast EPS	$-0.03	No of Institutions
	(04/05/2013)	279
Market Cap	$450.0 Million	Shares
Book Value	N/A	86,903,472
Price/Book	N/A	% Held
Price/Sales	0.08	73.67

Business Summary: Non-Precious Metals (MIC: 8.2.2 SIC: 3312 NAIC: 331111)

AK Steel Holding is a producer of flat-rolled carbon steels, including coated, cold-rolled and hot-rolled products, and stainless and electrical steels that are sold in sheet and strip form. These products are sold to the automotive, infrastructure and manufacturing, and distributors and converters markets. Co.'s operations also include AK Tube LLC, which finishes flat-rolled carbon and stainless steel into welded steel tubing; European trading companies that buy and sell steel and steel products and other materials, a 49.9% equity interest in Magnetation LLC, which produces iron ore concentrate; and AK Coal Resources, Inc., which controls metallurgical coal reserves in Pennsylvannia.

Recent Developments: For the year ended Dec 31 2012, net loss amounted to US$998.6 million versus a net loss of US$160.1 million in the prior year. Revenues were US$5.93 billion, down 8.3% from US$6.47 billion the year before. Operating loss was US$128.1 million versus a loss of US$201.3 million in the prior year. Direct operating expenses declined 8.2% to US$5.54 billion from US$6.04 billion in the comparable period the year before. Indirect operating expenses decreased 17.4% to US$522.7 million from US$632.5 million in the equivalent prior-year period.

Prospects: Our evaluation of AK Steel Holding Corp. as of Apr. 7, 2013 is the result of our systematic analysis on three basic characteristics: earnings strength, relative valuation, and recent stock price movement. The company has produced a positive trend in earnings per share over the past 5 quarters. Because the company lacks sufficient analyst estimate data, we place greater weight on the historical EPS trend as the measure of earnings strength. Based on operating earnings yield, the company is overvalued when compared to all of the companies in our coverage universe. Share price changes over the past year indicates that AKS will perform well over the near term.

Financial Data

(US$ in Thousands)	12/31/2012	12/31/2011	12/31/2010	12/31/2009	12/31/2008	12/31/2007	12/31/2006	12/31/2005
Earnings Per Share	(9.06)	(1.41)	(1.17)	(0.68)	0.04	3.46	0.11	(0.02)
Cash Flow Per Share	(2.39)	(1.64)	(1.21)	0.54	0.74	6.34	0.62	2.55
Tang Book Value Per Share	...	3.19	5.52	7.71	8.43	7.51	3.44	1.30
Dividends Per Share	0.100	0.200	0.200	0.200	0.200	...	...	...
Dividend Payout %	...	...	...	...	500.00	...	...	...
Income Statement								
Total Revenue	5,933,700	6,468,000	5,968,300	4,076,800	7,644,300	7,003,000	6,069,000	5,647,400
EBITDA	70,100	(21,600)	54,000	140,900	231,200	823,700	280,000	321,200
Depn & Amortn	192,000	185,000	197,100	204,600	202,100	196,300	194,000	196,400
Income Before Taxes	(208,600)	(254,100)	(174,500)	(98,000)	(6,900)	591,300	(3,100)	38,000
Income Taxes	790,000	(94,000)	(43,800)	(20,000)	(10,900)	203,600	(15,100)	38,800
Net Income	(1,027,300)	(155,600)	(128,900)	(74,600)	4,000	387,700	12,000	(2,300)
Average Shares	113,000	109,800	109,600	109,000	111,900	111,900	110,500	109,700
Balance Sheet								
Current Assets	1,442,700	1,274,400	1,404,100	1,630,100	2,002,800	2,426,800	2,547,500	2,246,400
Total Assets	3,903,100	4,449,900	4,188,600	4,274,700	4,682,000	5,197,400	5,517,600	5,487,900
Current Liabilities	812,400	1,137,100	844,500	740,700	734,200	972,900	931,500	903,400
Long-Term Obligations	1,411,200	650,000	650,600	605,800	632,600	652,700	1,115,200	1,114,900
Total Liabilities	4,408,400	4,061,400	3,543,900	3,393,900	3,714,000	4,322,700	5,100,600	5,267,400
Stockholders' Equity	(505,300)	388,500	644,700	880,800	968,000	874,700	417,000	220,500
Shares Outstanding	135,944	110,284	109,986	109,394	110,394	111,497	110,324	109,806
Statistical Record								
Return on Assets %	N.M.	N.M.	N.M.	N.M.	0.08	7.24	0.22	N.M.
Return on Equity %	...	N.M.	N.M.	N.M.	0.43	60.03	3.76	N.M.
EBITDA Margin %	1.18	N.M.	0.90	3.46	3.02	11.76	4.61	5.69
Net Margin %	N.M.	N.M.	N.M.	N.M.	0.05	5.54	0.20	N.M.
Asset Turnover	1.42	1.50	1.41	0.91	1.54	1.31	1.10	1.03
Current Ratio	1.78	1.12	1.66	2.20	2.73	2.49	2.73	2.49
Debt to Equity	...	1.67	1.01	0.69	0.65	0.75	2.67	5.06
Price Range	10.04-3.57	17.61-5.77	25.77-11.52	23.39-5.45	72.89-5.22	53.21-16.39	17.03-7.74	17.94-6.30
P/E Ratio	...	...	...	...	N.M.	15.38-4.74	154.82-70.36	...
Average Yield %	1.60	1.62	1.20	1.29	0.46	...	...	...

Address: 9227 Centre Pointe Drive, West Chester, OH 45069 Telephone: 513-425-5000 Fax: 513-425-5220	Web Site: www.aksteel.com Officers: James L. Wainscott - Chairman, President, Chief Executive Officer David C. Horn - Executive Vice President, Secretary, General Counsel	Auditors: Ernst & Young LLP Investor Contact: 513-425-2888 Transfer Agents: Computershare Investor Services, LLC, Canton, MA

ALASKA AIR GROUP, INC.

Exchange	Symbol	Price	52Wk Range	Yield	P/E
NYS	ALK	$63.96 (3/28/2013)	63.96-32.20	N/A	14.54

*7 Year Price Score 160.07 *NYSE Composite Index=100 *12 Month Price Score 123.01

Interim Earnings (Per Share)

Qtr.	Mar	Jun	Sep	Dec
2008	(0.48)	0.87	(1.20)	(1.03)
2009	(0.27)	0.40	1.23	0.34
2010	0.07	0.80	1.66	0.88
2011	1.00	0.39	1.06	0.88
2012	0.56	0.93	2.27	0.63

Interim Dividends (Per Share)

Amt	Decl	Ex	Rec	Pay
100%	02/16/2012	03/19/2012	03/02/2012	03/16/2012

Valuation Analysis   Institutional Holding

Forecast EPS	$5.50	No of Institutions
	(04/06/2013)	308
Market Cap	$4.5 Billion	Shares
Book Value	$1.4 Billion	69,320,848
Price/Book	3.17	% Held
Price/Sales	0.97	94.70

Business Summary: Airlines/Air Freight (MIC: 7.4.4 SIC: 4512 NAIC: 481111)

Alaska Air Group is engaged in providing air transportation services through its two main operating subsidiaries, Alaska Airlines, Inc. (Alaska) and Horizon Air Industries, Inc. (Horizon). Alaska operates a fleet of passenger jets (mainline operations) and contracts with Horizon, SkyWest Airlines, Inc. and Peninsula Airways, Inc. for regional capacity. Horizon operates a fleet of turboprop aircraft and sells all of its capacity to Alaska pursuant to a capacity purchase arrangement. As of Dec 31 2012, Co.'s operating fleet consisted of a total of 172 aircrafts.

Recent Developments: For the year ended Dec 31 2012, net income increased 29.0% to US$316.0 million from US$245.0 million in the prior year. Revenues were US$4.66 billion, up 7.9% from US$4.32 billion the year before. Operating income was US$532.0 million versus US$449.0 million in the prior year, an increase of 18.5%. Direct operating expenses rose 9.9% to US$2.32 billion from US$2.11 billion in the comparable period the year before. Indirect operating expenses increased 2.7% to US$1.81 billion from US$1.76 billion in the equivalent prior-year period.

Prospects: Our evaluation of Alaska Air Group Inc. as of Apr. 7, 2013 is the result of our systematic analysis on three basic characteristics: earnings strength, relative valuation, and recent stock price movement. The company has managed to produce a neutral trend in earnings per share over the past 5 quarters and while recent estimates for the company have been raised by analysts, ALK has posted results that fell short of analysts expectations. Based on operating earnings yield, the company is undervalued when compared to all of the companies in our coverage universe. Share price changes over the past year indicates that ALK will perform well over the near term.

Financial Data
(US$ in Thousands)

	12/31/2012	12/31/2011	12/31/2010	12/31/2009	12/31/2008	12/31/2007	12/31/2006	12/31/2005
Earnings Per Share	4.40	3.33	3.42	1.68	(1.87)	1.54	(0.69)	(0.01)
Cash Flow Per Share	10.62	9.70	7.73	4.26	2.25	6.01	5.93	4.92
Tang Book Value Per Share	20.19	16.54	15.39	12.25	9.12	13.46	10.99	11.87
Income Statement								
Total Revenue	4,657,000	4,317,800	3,832,300	3,399,800	3,662,600	3,506,000	3,334,400	2,975,300
EBITDA	805,000	693,500	709,100	482,400	28,100	385,300	68,700	305,900
Depn & Amortn	264,000	246,900	230,500	219,200	204,600	177,400	157,500	145,500
Income Before Taxes	514,000	393,700	405,900	202,900	(213,200)	201,600	(87,800)	137,200
Income Taxes	198,000	149,200	154,800	81,300	(77,300)	76,600	(35,200)	52,700
Net Income	316,000	244,500	251,100	121,600	(135,900)	125,000	(52,600)	(5,900)
Average Shares	71,784	73,420	73,572	72,308	72,686	80,848	75,878	67,834
Balance Sheet								
Current Assets	1,737,000	1,595,500	1,662,000	1,634,300	1,508,900	1,390,300	1,572,300	1,540,300
Total Assets	5,505,000	5,195,000	5,016,600	4,985,000	4,835,600	4,490,900	4,077,100	3,792,000
Current Liabilities	1,501,000	1,509,600	1,424,700	1,258,300	1,360,600	1,388,000	1,236,700	1,165,600
Long-Term Obligations	871,000	1,099,000	1,313,000	1,699,200	1,596,300	1,124,600	1,031,700	969,100
Total Liabilities	4,084,000	4,021,800	3,911,200	4,112,900	4,173,700	3,466,900	3,191,600	2,964,400
Stockholders' Equity	1,421,000	1,173,200	1,105,400	872,100	661,900	1,024,000	885,500	827,600
Shares Outstanding	70,376	70,949	71,847	71,182	72,549	76,101	80,587	66,908
Statistical Record								
Return on Assets %	5.89	4.79	5.02	2.48	N.M.	2.92	N.M.	N.M.
Return on Equity %	24.30	21.46	25.40	15.85	N.M.	13.09	N.M.	N.M.
EBITDA Margin %	17.29	16.06	18.50	14.19	0.77	10.99	2.06	10.28
Net Margin %	6.79	5.66	6.55	3.58	N.M.	3.57	N.M.	N.M.
Asset Turnover	0.87	0.85	0.77	0.69	0.78	0.82	0.85	0.83
Current Ratio	1.16	1.06	1.17	1.30	1.11	1.00	1.27	1.32
Debt to Equity	0.61	0.94	1.19	1.95	2.41	1.10	1.17	1.17
Price Range	44.92-32.20	38.26-25.66	29.53-15.67	18.07-6.97	14.63-5.40	22.23-10.90	22.28-15.03	18.68-13.29
P/E Ratio	10.21-7.32	11.49-7.71	8.63-4.58	10.76-4.15	...	14.44-7.08	...	...

Address: 19300 International Boulevard, Seattle, WA 98188 Telephone: 206-392-5040	Web Site: www.alaskaair.com Officers: William S. Ayer - Chairman, President, Chief Executive Officer Bradley D. Tilden - Chief Executive Officer	Auditors: KPMG LLP Transfer Agents: Computershare Trust Company, N.A, Providence, RI

24

ALBEMARLE CORP.

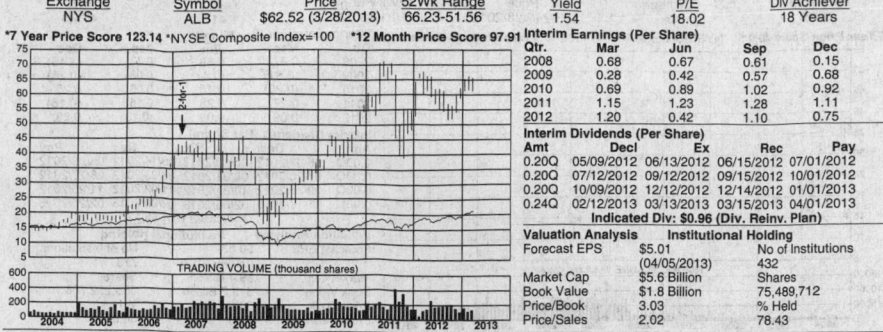

Exchange	Symbol	Price	52Wk Range	Yield	P/E	Div Achiever
NYS	ALB	$62.52 (3/28/2013)	66.23-51.56	1.54	18.02	18 Years

*7 Year Price Score 123.14 *NYSE Composite Index=100   *12 Month Price Score 97.91

Interim Earnings (Per Share)

Qtr.	Mar	Jun	Sep	Dec
2008	0.68	0.67	0.61	0.15
2009	0.28	0.42	0.57	0.68
2010	0.69	0.89	1.02	0.92
2011	1.15	1.23	1.28	1.11
2012	1.20	0.42	1.10	0.75

Interim Dividends (Per Share)

Amt	Decl	Ex	Rec	Pay
0.20Q	05/09/2012	06/13/2012	06/15/2012	07/01/2012
0.20Q	07/12/2012	09/12/2012	09/15/2012	10/01/2012
0.20Q	10/09/2012	12/12/2012	12/14/2012	01/01/2013
0.24Q	02/12/2013	03/13/2013	03/15/2013	04/01/2013

Indicated Div: $0.96 (Div. Reinv. Plan)

Valuation Analysis / **Institutional Holding**

Forecast EPS	$5.01	No of Institutions
	(04/05/2013)	432
Market Cap	$5.6 Billion	Shares
Book Value	$1.8 Billion	75,489,712
Price/Book	3.03	% Held
Price/Sales	2.02	78.43

TRADING VOLUME (thousand shares)

Business Summary: Specialty Chemicals (MIC: 8.3.2 SIC: 2821 NAIC: 325211)

Albemarle is a developer, manufacturer and marketer of chemicals for petroleum refining, consumer electronics, plastics/packaging, construction, automotive, lubricants, pharmaceuticals, crop protection, food-safety and custom chemistry services markets. As of Dec 31 2012, Co. conducted its business through three operating segments: Polymer Solutions, which consists of two product market categories: flame retardants and stabilizers and curatives; Catalysts, which includes Co.'s refinery catalysts and performance catalyst solutions businesses; as well as Fine Chemistry, which consists of two categories: performance chemicals and fine chemistry services and intermediates.

Recent Developments: For the year ended Dec 31 2012, net income decreased 21.4% to US$330.1 million from US$420.2 million in the prior year. Revenues were US$2.75 billion, down 4.3% from US$2.87 billion the year before. Operating income was US$406.2 million versus US$517.8 million in the prior year, a decrease of 21.6%. Direct operating expenses declined 4.1% to US$1.84 billion from US$1.91 billion in the comparable period the year before. Indirect operating expenses increased 15.3% to US$503.8 million from US$437.2 million in the equivalent prior-year period.

Prospects: Our evaluation of Albemarle Corp. as of Apr. 7, 2013 is the result of our systematic analysis on three basic characteristics: earnings strength, relative valuation, and recent stock price movement. The company has managed to produce a neutral trend in earnings per share over the past 5 quarters. However, while recent estimates for the company have been mixed, ALB has posted better than expected results. Based on operating earnings yield, the company is undervalued when compared to all of the companies in our coverage universe. Share price changes over the past year indicates that ALB will perform in line with the market over the near term.

Financial Data
(US$ in Thousands)

	12/31/2012	12/31/2011	12/31/2010	12/31/2009	12/31/2008	12/31/2007	12/31/2006	12/31/2005
Earnings Per Share	3.47	4.77	3.51	1.94	2.10	2.36	1.47	1.21
Cash Flow Per Share	5.47	5.38	3.63	3.92	3.45	2.55	3.98	1.82
Tang Book Value Per Share	16.45	13.37	11.02	8.33	6.81	8.83	6.59	5.73
Dividends Per Share	0.800	0.670	0.560	0.500	0.480	0.420	0.345	0.310
Dividend Payout %	23.05	14.05	15.95	25.77	22.86	17.80	23.47	25.73
Income Statement								
Total Revenue	2,745,420	2,869,005	2,362,764	2,005,394	2,467,115	2,336,187	2,368,306	2,107,499
EBITDA	495,693	671,797	500,136	272,157	318,918	409,151	276,250	179,334
Depn & Amortn	88,300	83,600	82,500	87,300	97,400	93,000	98,900	13,925
Income Before Taxes	374,593	550,623	392,103	160,273	183,343	277,819	133,386	123,438
Income Taxes	82,533	130,014	92,719	(7,028)	(6,539)	55,078	2,192	27,593
Net Income	311,536	436,280	323,720	178,368	194,202	229,690	142,969	114,867
Average Shares	89,884	91,522	92,184	92,046	92,530	97,216	97,136	95,496
Balance Sheet								
Current Assets	1,407,313	1,355,620	1,348,198	1,032,087	1,178,923	1,053,438	960,854	873,663
Total Assets	3,437,291	3,203,824	3,068,081	2,771,557	2,872,717	2,830,450	2,530,368	2,547,243
Current Liabilities	385,009	401,178	364,177	353,264	438,367	402,917	482,949	421,917
Long-Term Obligations	686,588	749,257	851,927	776,403	906,062	707,311	681,859	775,589
Total Liabilities	1,603,693	1,612,547	1,652,007	1,565,861	1,806,946	1,552,145	1,502,270	1,616,968
Stockholders' Equity	1,833,598	1,591,277	1,416,074	1,205,696	1,065,771	1,278,305	1,028,098	930,275
Shares Outstanding	88,899	88,841	91,593	91,509	90,980	94,734	94,860	93,499
Statistical Record								
Return on Assets %	9.36	13.91	11.09	6.32	6.79	8.57	5.63	4.60
Return on Equity %	18.14	29.01	24.69	15.71	16.52	19.92	14.60	13.99
EBITDA Margin %	18.06	23.42	21.17	13.57	12.93	17.51	11.66	8.51
Net Margin %	11.35	15.21	13.70	8.89	7.87	9.83	6.04	5.45
Asset Turnover	0.82	0.91	0.81	0.71	0.86	0.87	0.93	0.84
Current Ratio	3.66	3.38	3.70	2.92	2.69	2.61	1.99	2.07
Debt to Equity	0.37	0.47	0.60	0.64	0.85	0.55	0.66	0.83
Price Range	67.70-51.56	71.11-39.00	56.73-34.86	37.27-15.81	45.79-16.46	47.76-35.03	36.65-19.41	19.45-16.23
P/E Ratio	19.51-14.86	14.91-8.18	16.16-9.93	19.21-8.15	21.80-7.84	20.24-14.84	24.93-13.21	16.08-13.41
Average Yield %	1.35	1.17	1.27	1.77	1.40	1.02	1.34	1.70

Address: 451 Florida Street, Baton Rouge, LA 70801 Telephone: 225-388-8011	Web Site: www.albemarle.com Officers: Mark C. Rohr - Chairman William M. Gottwald - Vice-Chairman	Auditors: PricewaterhouseCoopers LLP Investor Contact: 225-388-7322 Transfer Agents: Wells Fargo Bank, N.A., Shareowner Services, St. Paul, MN

25

ALCOA, INC.

Exchange	Symbol	Price	52Wk Range	Yield	P/E
NYS	AA	$8.52 (3/28/2013)	10.17-8.02	1.41	47.33

*7 Year Price Score 40.01 *NYSE Composite Index=100 *12 Month Price Score 90.52

Interim Earnings (Per Share)

Qtr.	Mar	Jun	Sep	Dec
2008	0.37	0.66	0.33	(1.45)
2009	(0.61)	(0.47)	0.08	(0.28)
2010	(0.20)	0.13	0.06	0.25
2011	0.27	0.28	0.15	(0.16)
2012	0.09	0.00	(0.13)	0.23

Interim Dividends (Per Share)

Amt	Decl	Ex	Rec	Pay
0.03Q	05/03/2012	05/10/2012	05/14/2012	05/25/2012
0.03Q	07/20/2012	08/01/2012	08/03/2012	08/27/2012
0.03Q	09/27/2012	10/31/2012	11/02/2012	11/25/2012
0.03Q	01/17/2013	02/06/2013	02/08/2013	02/25/2013

Indicated Div: $0.12

Valuation Analysis

		Institutional Holding	
Forecast EPS	$0.53 (04/06/2013)	No of Institutions	773
Market Cap	$9.1 Billion	Shares	655,272,768
Book Value	$13.2 Billion	% Held	56.67
Price/Book	0.69		
Price/Sales	0.38		

Business Summary: Non-Precious Metals (MIC: 8.2.2 SIC: 3356 NAIC: 331491)

Alcoa is engaged in the production and management of primary aluminum, fabricated aluminum, and alumina combined, through its participation in various aspects of the industry: technology, mining, refining, smelting, fabricating, and recycling. Non-aluminum products include precision castings and aerospace and industrial fasteners. Co.'s operations consist of four reportable segments: Alumina; Primary Metals; Global Rolled Products; and Engineered Products and Solutions. Co.'s products are used in aircraft, automobiles, commercial transportation, packaging, building and construction, oil and gas, defense, consumer electronics, and industrial applications.

Recent Developments: For the year ended Dec 31 2012, income from continuing operations decreased 80.0% to US$162.0 million from US$808.0 million a year earlier. Net income decreased 79.9% to US$162.0 million from US$805.0 million in the prior year. Revenues were US$23.70 billion, down 5.0% from US$24.95 billion the year before. Direct operating expenses rose 0.0% to US$20.49 billion from US$20.48 billion in the comparable period the year before. Indirect operating expenses decreased 7.6% to US$3.23 billion from US$3.50 billion in the equivalent prior-year period.

Prospects: Our evaluation of Alcoa Inc. as of Apr. 7, 2013 is the result of our systematic analysis on three basic characteristics: earnings strength, relative valuation, and recent stock price movement. The company has enjoyed a very positive trend in earnings per share over the past 5 quarters. However, while recent estimates for the company have been lowered by analysts, AA has posted better than expected results. Based on operating earnings yield, the company is overvalued when compared to all of the companies in our coverage universe. Share price changes over the past year indicates that AA will perform in line with the market over the near term.

Financial Data

(US$ in Thousands)	12/31/2012	12/31/2011	12/31/2010	12/31/2009	12/31/2008	12/31/2007	12/31/2006	12/31/2005
Earnings Per Share	0.18	0.55	0.24	(1.23)	(0.09)	2.95	2.57	1.40
Cash Flow Per Share	1.40	2.07	2.22	1.46	1.52	3.61	2.95	1.92
Tang Book Value Per Share	7.09	7.56	7.75	6.94	7.61	12.75	8.53	6.96
Dividends Per Share	0.120	0.120	0.120	0.260	0.680	0.680	0.600	0.600
Dividend Payout %	66.67	21.82	50.00	...	...	23.05	23.35	42.86
Income Statement								
Total Revenue	23,700,000	24,951,000	21,013,000	18,439,000	26,901,000	30,748,000	30,379,000	26,159,000
EBITDA	2,273,000	3,033,000	2,460,000	279,000	2,257,000	5,959,000	4,872,000	2,182,216
Depn & Amortn	1,462,000	1,481,000	1,451,000	1,311,000	1,152,000	1,200,000	1,217,000	1,216
Income Before Taxes	352,000	1,048,000	534,000	(1,484,000)	751,000	4,420,000	3,360,000	1,907,000
Income Taxes	162,000	255,000	148,000	(574,000)	342,000	1,555,000	835,000	441,000
Net Income	191,000	611,000	254,000	(1,151,000)	(74,000)	2,564,000	2,248,000	1,233,000
Average Shares	1,076,000	1,161,000	1,025,000	935,000	818,000	869,000	875,000	876,900
Balance Sheet								
Current Assets	7,700,000	7,713,000	6,869,000	7,022,000	8,150,000	8,086,000	9,157,000	8,790,000
Total Assets	40,179,000	40,120,000	39,293,000	38,472,000	37,822,000	38,803,000	37,183,000	33,696,000
Current Liabilities	5,942,000	6,013,000	5,236,000	5,414,000	7,279,000	7,166,000	7,281,000	7,368,000
Long-Term Obligations	8,311,000	8,640,000	8,842,000	8,974,000	8,509,000	6,371,000	5,910,000	5,279,000
Total Liabilities	26,980,000	26,276,000	25,682,000	26,012,000	26,087,000	22,787,000	22,552,000	20,323,000
Stockholders' Equity	13,199,000	13,844,000	13,611,000	12,460,000	11,735,000	16,016,000	14,631,000	13,373,000
Shares Outstanding	1,067,211	1,064,412	1,022,025	974,378	800,317	827,401	867,739	870,268
Statistical Record								
Return on Assets %	0.47	1.54	0.65	N.M.	N.M.	6.75	6.34	3.72
Return on Equity %	1.41	4.45	1.95	N.M.	N.M.	16.73	16.05	9.25
EBITDA Margin %	9.59	12.16	11.71	1.51	8.39	19.38	16.04	8.34
Net Margin %	0.81	2.45	1.21	N.M.	N.M.	8.34	7.40	4.71
Asset Turnover	0.59	0.63	0.54	0.48	0.70	0.81	0.86	0.79
Current Ratio	1.30	1.28	1.31	1.30	1.12	1.13	1.26	1.19
Debt to Equity	0.63	0.62	0.65	0.72	0.73	0.40	0.40	0.39
Price Range	10.76-8.02	18.13-8.52	17.45-10.00	16.34-5.22	44.59-6.85	47.35-28.48	36.59-26.60	32.12-22.54
P/E Ratio	59.78-44.56	32.96-15.49	72.71-41.67	...	...	16.05-9.65	14.24-10.35	22.94-16.10
Average Yield %	1.32	0.86	0.86	2.40	2.37	1.86	1.99	2.14

Address: 390 Park Avenue, New York, NY 10022-4608 Telephone: 212-836-2732	Web Site: www.alcoa.com Officers: Klaus Kleinfeld - Chairman, President, Chief Executive Officer, Chief Operating Officer Christopher L. Ayers - Executive Vice President, Division Officer	Auditors: PricewaterhouseCoopers LLP Investor Contact: 212-836-2674 Transfer Agents: Computershare

ALERE INC.

Exchange	Symbol	Price	52Wk Range	Yield	P/E
NYS	ALR	$25.53 (3/28/2013)	25.89-17.40	N/A	N/A

*7 Year Price Score 54.80 *NYSE Composite Index=100 *12 Month Price Score 104.76

TRADING VOLUME (thousand shares)

Interim Earnings (Per Share)

Qtr.	Mar	Jun	Sep	Dec
2008	(0.05)	(0.43)	(0.12)	0.14
2009	0.01	(0.02)	0.17	(0.04)
2010	0.11	(0.10)	(0.03)	(12.24)
2011	0.09	(0.05)	2.48	(4.14)
2012	(0.05)	(0.23)	(0.11)	(0.84)

Interim Dividends (Per Share)

No Dividends Paid

Valuation Analysis

Forecast EPS	$2.27
	(04/05/2013)
Market Cap	$2.1 Billion
Book Value	$2.2 Billion
Price/Book	0.95
Price/Sales	0.73

Institutional Holding

No of Institutions	256
Shares	74,886,768
% Held	N/A

Business Summary: Medical Instruments & Equipment (MIC: 4.3.1 SIC: 2835 NAIC: 325413)

Alere is focused on near-patient diagnosis, monitoring and health management. Co.'s professional diagnostics segment includes an array of diagnostic test products and other in vitro diagnostic tests marketed to medical personnel and laboratories for detection of diseases and conditions within its areas of focus. Co.'s health management segment provides programs and services focused on wellness, disease and condition management, productivity enhancement and informatics. Co.'s consumer diagnostics segment consists of manufacturing operations related to to its role as the manufacturer of products for SPD Swiss Precision Diagnostics, Co.'s 50/50 joint venture with The Procter & Gamble Company.

Recent Developments: For the year ended Dec 31 2012, loss from continuing operations was US$77.9 million compared with a loss of US$133.3 million a year earlier. Net loss amounted to US$77.9 million versus a net loss of US$133.3 million in the prior year. Revenues were US$2.82 billion, up 18.1% from US$2.39 billion the year before. Operating income was US$109.1 million versus a loss of US$252.9 million in the prior year. Direct operating expenses rose 21.9% to US$1.39 billion from US$1.14 billion in the comparable period the year before. Indirect operating expenses decreased 12.0% to US$1.32 billion from US$1.50 billion in the equivalent prior-year period.

Prospects: Our evaluation of Alere Inc. as of Apr. 7, 2013 is the result of our systematic analysis on three basic characteristics: earnings strength, relative valuation, and recent stock price movement. The company has produced a positive trend in earnings per share over the past 5 quarters. However, while recent estimates for the company have been lowered by analysts, ALR has posted results that fell short of analysts expectations. Based on operating earnings yield, the company is undervalued when compared to all of the companies in our coverage universe. Share price changes over the past year indicates that ALR will perform very poorly over the near term.

Financial Data
(US$ in Thousands)

	12/31/2012	12/31/2011	12/31/2010	12/31/2009	12/31/2008	12/31/2007	12/31/2006	12/31/2005
Earnings Per Share	(1.23)	(1.58)	(12.33)	0.13	(0.46)	(4.69)	(0.49)	(0.79)
Cash Flow Per Share	3.96	3.26	3.26	3.57	1.90	1.72	1.00	1.09
Tang Book Value Per Share	N.M.	N.M.	N.M.	N.M.	N.M.	N.M.	0.90	N.M.
Income Statement								
Total Revenue	2,818,825	2,386,527	2,155,347	1,922,641	1,671,426	839,540	569,454	421,850
EBITDA	228,789	121,624	(860,651)	201,346	113,440	(136,337)	33,055	24,305
Depn & Amortn	109,700	83,700	67,700	54,300	51,800	28,300	17,600	14,900
Income Before Taxes	(121,471)	(166,047)	(1,067,786)	40,248	(39,504)	(247,662)	(11,115)	(12,390)
Income Taxes	(30,319)	(24,214)	(29,931)	15,627	(16,686)	(1,799)	5,727	6,819
Net Income	(78,182)	(133,542)	(1,017,310)	33,716	(21,768)	(241,491)	(16,842)	(19,209)
Average Shares	80,587	83,128	84,445	81,967	77,778	51,510	34,109	24,358
Balance Sheet								
Current Assets	1,406,737	1,293,727	1,194,257	1,266,958	822,543	952,974	275,544	194,333
Total Assets	7,067,928	6,672,701	6,330,374	6,943,992	5,955,360	4,883,201	1,085,771	791,166
Current Liabilities	648,809	624,452	782,858	438,014	365,345	278,908	142,231	109,810
Long-Term Obligations	3,641,592	3,280,080	2,379,968	2,129,455	1,501,025	1,366,753	194,888	259,595
Total Liabilities	4,887,506	4,443,467	3,755,336	3,416,437	2,676,522	2,293,272	371,633	393,858
Stockholders' Equity	2,180,422	2,229,234	2,575,038	3,527,555	3,278,838	2,589,929	714,138	397,308
Shares Outstanding	80,897	79,968	84,928	83,567	78,431	76,784	39,215	27,497
Statistical Record								
Return on Assets %	N.M.	N.M.	N.M.	0.52	N.M.	N.M.	N.M.	N.M.
Return on Equity %	N.M.	N.M.	N.M.	0.99	N.M.	N.M.	N.M.	N.M.
EBITDA Margin %	8.12	5.10	N.M.	10.47	6.79	N.M.	5.80	5.76
Net Margin %	N.M.	N.M.	N.M.	1.75	N.M.	N.M.	N.M.	N.M.
Asset Turnover	0.41	0.37	0.32	0.30	0.31	0.28	0.61	0.62
Current Ratio	2.17	2.07	1.53	2.89	2.25	3.42	1.94	1.77
Debt to Equity	1.67	1.47	0.92	0.60	0.46	0.53	0.27	0.65
Price Range	26.01-17.40	41.00-18.51	44.85-25.80	43.73-18.91	62.35-13.88	64.65-37.65	40.58-23.74	29.60-20.81
P/E Ratio	...	...	...	336.38-145.46	...	...	...	...

Address: 51 Sawyer Road, Suite 200, Waltham, MA 02453	Web Site: www.alere.com	Auditors: PricewaterhouseCoopers LLP
Telephone: 781-647-3900	Officers: Ron Zwanziger - Chairman, President, Chief Executive Officer Paul T. Hempel - Senior Vice President, Secretary, General Counsel	Transfer Agents: Computershare, Providence, RI
Fax: 781-647-3939		

27

ALEXANDER & BALDWIN INC.

Exchange	Symbol	Price	52Wk Range	Yield	P/E
NYS	ALEX	$35.75 (3/28/2013)	36.52-25.30	N/A	N/A

*7 Year Price Score N/A   *NYSE Composite Index=100   *12 Month Price Score N/A

Interim Earnings (Per Share)

Qtr.	Mar	Jun	Sep	Dec
2012	0.07	(0.10)	0.31	0.20

Interim Dividends (Per Share)

No Dividends Paid

Valuation Analysis		Institutional Holding	
Forecast EPS	$0.45	No of Institutions	
	(04/05/2013)	N/A	
Market Cap	$1.5 Billion	Shares	
Book Value	$914.4 Million	N/A	
Price/Book	1.68	% Held	
Price/Sales	N/A	N/A	

Business Summary: Property, Real Estate & Development (MIC: 5.3.2 SIC: 6512 NAIC: 531120)

Alexander & Baldwin is a Hawaii-focused land company with interests in real estate development, real estate leasing and agribusiness. Its assets include nearly 88,000 acres of land in Hawaii; 7.9 million square feet of retail, office and industrial properties in Hawaii and on the Mainland; and a real estate development portfolio encompassing residential and commercial projects across Hawaii. Co. has 36,000 acres in productive agriculture. Co. also plays a role as a provider of renewable energy on Maui and Kauai, supplying approximately six percent of the power consumed on each island. Co.'s segments consist of Real Estate Sales, Real Estate Leasing and Agribusiness.

Recent Developments: For the year ended Dec 31 2012, income from continuing operations increased 105.8% to US$17.7 million from US$8.6 million a year earlier. Net income decreased 12.8% to US$20.5 million from US$23.5 million in the prior year. Revenues were US$296.7 million, up 10.8% from US$267.7 million the year before. Revenues from property income rose 3.8% to US$114.4 million from US$110.2 million in the corresponding earlier year.

Prospects: Our evaluation of Alexander & Baldwin Inc. as of Apr. 7, 2013 is the result of our systematic analysis on three basic characteristics: earnings strength, relative valuation, and recent stock price movement. The company has enjoyed a very positive trend in earnings per share over the past 5 quarters. However, while recent estimates for the company have been lowered by analysts, ALEX has posted better than expected results. Based on operating earnings yield, the company is overvalued when compared to all of the companies in our coverage universe. Share price changes over the past year indicates that ALEX will perform very poorly over the near term.

Financial Data
(US$ in Thousands)

	12/31/2012	12/31/2011	12/31/2010	12/31/2009
Earnings Per Share	0.48	0.56	...	...
Cash Flow Per Share	...	0.25	...	...
Tang Book Value Per Share	21.31	...	...	...
Income Statement				
Total Revenue	296,700	268,700	263,000	190,800
EBITDA	66,400	67,200	46,200	8,300
Depn & Amortn	35,100	34,800	35,200	34,800
Income Before Taxes	16,500	15,600	(3,600)	(42,900)
Income Taxes	(1,200)	6,800	(2,200)	(18,100)
Net Income	20,500	23,500	33,100	10,900
Average Shares	42,900	42,100	...	...
Balance Sheet				
Current Assets	63,400	68,800	70,300	...
Total Assets	1,437,300	1,386,600	1,341,500	...
Current Liabilities	69,600	90,000	175,600	...
Long-Term Obligations	220,000	327,200	249,600	...
Total Liabilities	522,900	660,800	652,900	...
Stockholders' Equity	914,400	725,800	688,600	...
Shares Outstanding	42,900	...	...	...
Statistical Record				
Return on Assets %	...	1.72	...	...
Return on Equity %	...	3.32	...	...
EBITDA Margin %	22.38	25.01	17.57	4.35
Net Margin %	6.91	8.75	12.59	5.71
Asset Turnover	...	0.20	...	...
Current Ratio	0.91	0.76	0.40	...
Debt to Equity	0.24	0.45	0.36	...
Price Range	34.25-25.30	...	...	...
P/E Ratio	71.35-52.71	...	...	...

Address: 822 Bishop Street, Honolulu, HI 96813 Telephone: 808-525-6611	Web Site: www.alexanderbaldwin.com Officers: Walter A. Dods - Chairman Stanley M. Kuriyama - President, Chief Executive Officer	Auditors: Deloitte & Touche LLP Transfer Agents: Computershare Shareowner Services LLC

ALEXANDRIA REAL ESTATE EQUITIES, INC.

Exchange	Symbol	Price	52Wk Range	Yield	P/E
NYS	ARE	$70.98 (3/28/2013)	76.65-64.75	3.10	65.12

*7 Year Price Score 82.11 *NYSE Composite Index=100 *12 Month Price Score 92.18

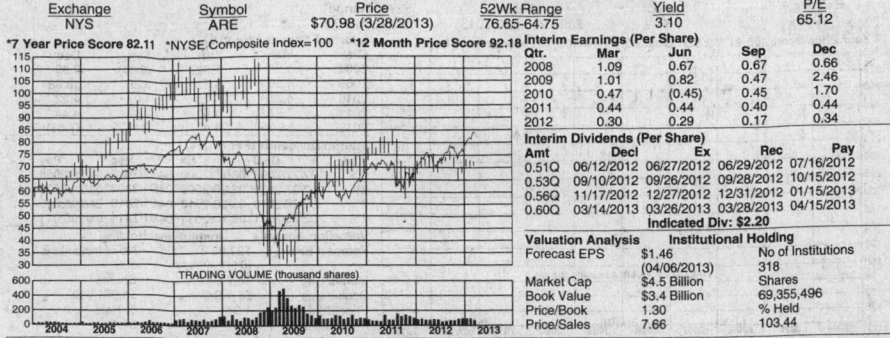

Interim Earnings (Per Share)

Qtr.	Mar	Jun	Sep	Dec
2008	1.09	0.67	0.67	0.66
2009	1.01	0.82	0.47	2.46
2010	0.47	(0.45)	0.45	1.70
2011	0.44	0.44	0.40	0.44
2012	0.30	0.29	0.17	0.34

Interim Dividends (Per Share)

Amt	Decl	Ex	Rec	Pay
0.51Q	06/12/2012	06/27/2012	06/29/2012	07/16/2012
0.53Q	09/10/2012	09/26/2012	09/28/2012	10/15/2012
0.56Q	11/17/2012	12/27/2012	12/31/2012	01/15/2013
0.60Q	03/14/2013	03/26/2013	03/28/2013	04/15/2013

Indicated Div: $2.20

Valuation Analysis

		Institutional Holding	
Forecast EPS	$1.46	No of Institutions	
	(04/06/2013)	318	
Market Cap	$4.5 Billion	Shares	
Book Value	$3.4 Billion	69,355,496	
Price/Book	1.30	% Held	
Price/Sales	7.66	103.44	

Business Summary: REITs (MIC: 5.3.1 SIC: 6798 NAIC: 525930)

Alexandria Real Estate Equities is a self-administered and self-managed real estate investment trust focused principally on owning, operating, developing, redeveloping, and acquiring real estate for the life science industry. Co.'s client tenants span the life science industry, including academic and medical institutions, multinational pharmaceutical companies, public and private biotechnology entities, U.S. government research agencies, medical device companies, industrial biotech companies, venture capital firms, and life science product and service companies. As of Dec. 31 2012 Co. had 178 properties aggregating approximately 17.1 million rentable sq. ft.

Recent Developments: For the year ended Dec 31 2012, income from continuing operations decreased 18.6% to US$101.4 million from US$124.6 million a year earlier. Net income decreased 22.1% to US$105.5 million from US$135.4 million in the prior year. Revenues were US$586.1 million, up 6.9% from US$548.2 million the year before. Revenues from property income rose 4.6% to US$567.6 million from US$542.5 million in the corresponding earlier year.

Prospects: Our evaluation of Alexandria Real Estate Equities Inc. as of Apr. 7, 2013 is the result of our systematic analysis on three basic characteristics: earnings strength, relative valuation, and recent stock price movement. The company has managed to produce a neutral trend in earnings per share over the past 5 quarters. Because the company lacks sufficient analyst estimate data, we place greater weight on the historical EPS trend as the measure of earnings strength. Based on operating earnings yield, the company is overvalued versus all of the companies in our coverage universe. Share price changes over the past year indicates that ARE will perform in line with the market over the near term.

Financial Data

(US$ in Thousands)	12/31/2012	12/31/2011	12/31/2010	12/31/2009	12/31/2008	12/31/2007	12/31/2006	12/31/2005
Earnings Per Share	1.09	1.73	2.19	2.72	3.09	2.63	2.25	2.22
Cash Flow Per Share	4.90	4.18	4.53	5.34	7.33	6.25	5.11	5.76
Tang Book Value Per Share	48.41	48.65	46.38	44.33	40.46	43.48	40.14	28.64
Dividends Per Share	2.090	1.860	1.500	1.850	3.180	3.040	2.860	2.720
Dividend Payout %	191.74	107.51	68.49	68.01	102.91	115.59	127.11	122.52
Income Statement								
Total Revenue	586,073	573,443	487,303	480,140	460,668	405,360	316,821	244,084
EBITDA	369,778	361,455	285,591	345,507	295,642	272,490	223,308	174,044
Depn & Amortn	199,148	161,813	136,663	127,806	105,797	95,272	77,680	60,993
Income Before Taxes	101,446	136,235	79,286	136,430	111,054	88,831	74,257	63,935
Net Income	105,528	135,393	139,022	141,648	122,869	93,724	73,416	63,433
Average Shares	62,160	59,077	48,405	38,600	31,907	30,004	25,524	21,316
Balance Sheet								
Current Assets	189,367	109,351	125,078	121,821	145,396	66,700	43,638	29,688
Total Assets	7,150,116	6,574,129	5,905,861	5,457,227	5,131,096	4,642,094	3,617,477	2,362,450
Current Liabilities	465,109	361,972	335,371	304,202	418,916	274,864	183,482	105,869
Long-Term Obligations	3,181,949	2,779,264	2,584,162	2,746,946	2,966,963	2,787,904	2,024,866	1,406,666
Total Liabilities	3,708,265	3,199,828	2,977,036	3,133,819	3,460,900	3,138,274	2,265,825	1,532,650
Stockholders' Equity	3,441,851	3,374,301	2,928,825	2,323,408	1,670,196	1,503,820	1,351,652	829,800
Shares Outstanding	63,244	61,560	54,966	43,846	31,899	31,603	29,012	22,441
Statistical Record								
Return on Assets %	1.53	2.17	2.45	2.68	2.51	2.27	2.46	3.00
Return on Equity %	3.09	4.30	5.29	7.09	7.72	6.56	6.73	8.75
EBITDA Margin %	63.09	63.03	58.61	71.96	64.18	67.22	70.48	71.30
Net Margin %	18.01	23.61	28.53	29.50	26.67	23.12	23.17	25.99
Asset Turnover	0.09	0.09	0.09	0.09	0.09	0.10	0.11	0.12
Current Ratio	0.41	0.30	0.37	0.40	0.35	0.24	0.24	0.28
Debt to Equity	0.92	0.82	0.88	1.18	1.78	1.85	1.50	1.70
Price Range	76.65-64.75	84.93-57.19	75.07-56.89	66.98-30.71	114.05-33.59	113.41-86.13	104.79-82.36	85.70-62.87
P/E Ratio	70.32-59.40	49.09-33.06	34.28-25.98	24.63-11.29	36.91-10.87	43.12-32.75	46.57-36.60	38.60-28.32
Average Yield %	2.91	2.53	2.20	3.90	3.49	3.03	3.08	3.63

Address: 385 East Colorado Boulevard, Suite 299, Pasadena, CA 91101 **Telephone:** 626-578-0777	**Web Site:** www.are.com **Officers:** Joel S. Marcus - Chairman, President, Chief Executive Officer Dean A. Shigenaga - Senior Vice President, Chief Financial Officer, Treasurer	**Auditors:** Ernst & Young LLP **Investor Contact:** 626-396-4828 **Transfer Agents:** American Stock Transfer & Trust Company, New York, NY

29

ALLEGHANY CORP.

Exchange	Symbol	Price	52Wk Range	Yield	P/E
NYS	Y	$395.92 (3/28/2013)	395.92-320.78	N/A	8.71

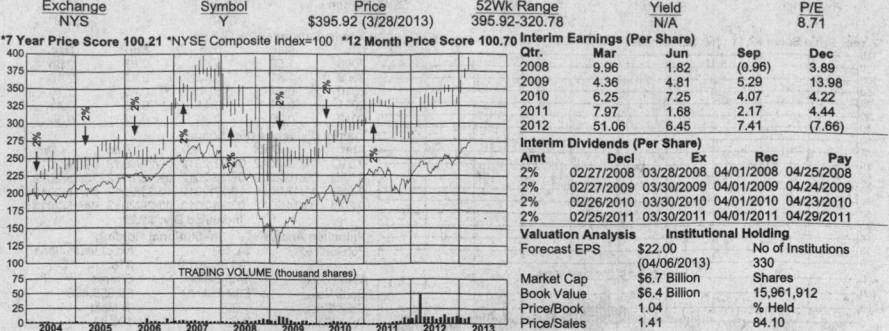

*7 Year Price Score 100.21 *NYSE Composite Index=100 *12 Month Price Score 100.70

Interim Earnings (Per Share)

Qtr.	Mar	Jun	Sep	Dec
2008	9.96	1.82	(0.96)	3.89
2009	4.36	4.81	5.29	13.98
2010	6.25	7.25	4.07	4.22
2011	7.97	1.68	2.17	4.44
2012	51.06	6.45	7.41	(7.66)

Interim Dividends (Per Share)

Amt	Decl	Ex	Rec	Pay
2%	02/27/2008	03/28/2008	04/01/2008	04/25/2008
2%	02/27/2009	03/30/2009	04/01/2009	04/24/2009
2%	02/26/2010	03/30/2010	04/01/2010	04/23/2010
2%	02/25/2011	03/30/2011	04/01/2011	04/29/2011

Valuation Analysis / **Institutional Holding**

Forecast EPS	$22.00 (04/06/2013)	No of Institutions	330
Market Cap	$6.7 Billion	Shares	15,961,912
Book Value	$6.4 Billion	% Held	84.10
Price/Book	1.04		
Price/Sales	1.41		

Business Summary: General Insurance (MIC: 5.2.1 SIC: 6331 NAIC: 524127)

Alleghany is engaged in the property and casualty reinsurance and insurance business. Reinsurance business is conducted through certain subsidiaries of Co.'s wholly-owned subsidiary Transatlantic Holdings, Inc. Insurance business is conducted through certain subsidiaries of Alleghany Insurance Holdings LLC. Co. operates two reportable segments: the reinsurance segment and the insurance segment.

Recent Developments: For the year ended Dec 31 2012, net income increased 390.2% to US$702.2 million from US$143.3 million in the prior year. Revenues were US$4.75 billion, up 384.1% from US$981.8 million the year before. Net premiums earned were US$3.73 billion versus US$747.6 million in the prior year, an increase of 399.3%.

Prospects: Our evaluation of Alleghany Corp. as of Apr. 7, 2013 is the result of our systematic analysis on three basic characteristics: earnings strength, relative valuation, and recent stock price movement. The company has suffered a very negative trend in earnings per share over the past 5 quarters and while recent estimates for the company have remained steady, Y has posted better than expected results. Based on operating earnings yield, the company is about fairly valued when compared to all of the companies in our coverage universe. Share price changes over the past year indicates that Y will perform in line with the market over the near term.

Financial Data
(US$ in Thousands)

	12/31/2012	12/31/2011	12/31/2010	12/31/2009	12/31/2008	12/31/2007	12/31/2006	12/31/2005
Earnings Per Share	45.48	16.20	21.85	28.51	14.82	30.86	27.45	5.90
Cash Flow Per Share	32.02	10.63	6.70	15.84	37.36	54.34	62.91	42.75
Tang Book Value Per Share	366.57	325.87	309.39	278.99	250.14	258.09	223.49	191.06
Income Statement								
Premium Income	3,733,005	747,639	768,134	845,015	948,652	1,155,221	1,010,129	849,653
Total Revenue	4,753,212	981,837	985,352	1,184,392	989,100	1,432,041	1,209,165	1,095,956
Benefits & Claims	2,630,170	429,986	377,937	442,104	570,019	550,329	498,954	747,967
Income Before Taxes	719,276	190,837	277,371	395,380	61,052	477,780	362,930	59,819
Income Taxes	17,032	47,586	78,869	124,381	20,485	157,901	106,109	13,842
Net Income	702,244	143,251	198,502	270,999	147,971	305,277	251,244	52,334
Average Shares	15,441	8,811	9,081	9,518	8,822	9,902	9,169	8,880
Balance Sheet								
Total Assets	22,807,967	6,478,089	6,431,699	6,192,770	6,181,828	6,733,046	6,178,740	5,913,731
Total Liabilities	16,404,180	3,552,412	3,522,831	3,475,249	3,535,139	3,939,171	3,755,494	4,045,404
Stockholders' Equity	6,403,787	2,925,677	2,908,868	2,717,521	2,646,689	2,793,875	2,423,246	1,868,327
Shares Outstanding	16,890	8,551	8,941	9,218	8,779	8,831	8,787	8,902
Statistical Record								
Return on Assets %	4.78	2.22	3.14	4.38	2.29	4.73	4.16	1.01
Return on Equity %	15.01	4.91	7.06	10.10	5.42	11.70	11.71	2.89
Loss Ratio %	70.46	57.51	49.20	52.32	60.09	47.64	49.40	88.03
Net Margin %	14.77	14.59	20.15	22.88	14.96	21.32	20.78	4.78
Price Range	355.46-284.25	338.90-277.26	304.90-248.75	287.82-214.73	395.78-178.57	397.72-321.13	329.69-239.11	284.15-231.96
P/E Ratio	7.82-6.25	20.92-17.11	13.95-11.38	10.10-7.53	26.71-12.05	12.89-10.41	12.01-8.71	48.16-39.32

Address: 7 Times Square Tower, 17th Floor, New York, NY 10036 Telephone: 212-752-1356 Fax: 212-759-8149	Web Site: www.alleghany.com Officers: John J. Burns - Chairman Weston M. Hicks - President, Chief Executive Officer	Auditors: Ernst & Young LLP Transfer Agents: Computershare Trust Company, N.A, Providence, RI

ALLEGHENY TECHNOLOGIES, INC

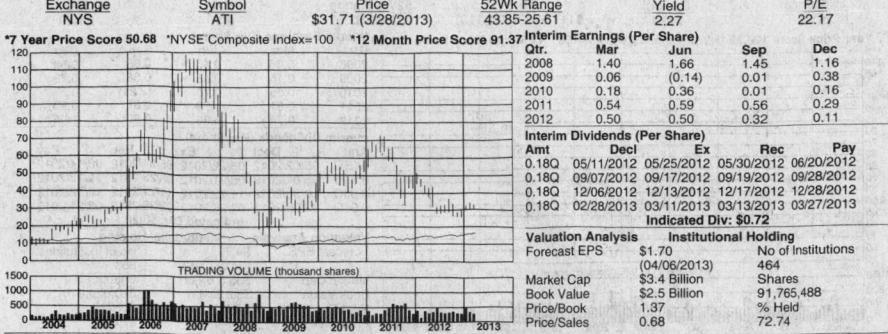

Exchange	Symbol	Price	52Wk Range	Yield	P/E
NYS	ATI	$31.71 (3/28/2013)	43.85-25.61	2.27	22.17

*7 Year Price Score 50.68 *NYSE Composite Index=100 *12 Month Price Score 91.37

Interim Earnings (Per Share)

Qtr.	Mar	Jun	Sep	Dec
2008	1.40	1.66	1.45	1.16
2009	0.06	(0.14)	0.01	0.38
2010	0.18	0.36	0.01	0.16
2011	0.54	0.59	0.56	0.29
2012	0.50	0.50	0.32	0.11

Interim Dividends (Per Share)

Amt	Decl	Ex	Rec	Pay
0.18Q	05/11/2012	05/25/2012	05/30/2012	06/20/2012
0.18Q	09/07/2012	09/17/2012	09/19/2012	09/28/2012
0.18Q	12/06/2012	12/13/2012	12/17/2012	12/28/2012
0.18Q	02/28/2013	03/11/2013	03/13/2013	03/27/2013
		Indicated Div: $0.72		

Valuation Analysis / **Institutional Holding**

Valuation Analysis		Institutional Holding	
Forecast EPS	$1.70	No of Institutions	
	(04/06/2013)	464	
Market Cap	$3.4 Billion	Shares	
Book Value	$2.5 Billion	91,765,488	
Price/Book	1.37	% Held	
Price/Sales	0.68	72.74	

TRADING VOLUME (thousand shares)

Business Summary: Non-Precious Metals (MIC: 8.2.2 SIC: 3317 NAIC: 331210)

Allegheny Technologies is a metals producer. Co. operates in three business segments: High Performance Metals, which produces, converts and distributes a range of alloys primarily in long product forms such as ingot, billet, bar, shapes and rectangles, rod, wire, tube, and castings; Flat-Rolled Products, which produces, converts and distributes stainless steel and alloys in a range of product forms, including plate, sheet, engineered strip, and Precision Rolled Strip® products, as well as grain-oriented electrical steel sheet; and Engineered Products, which includes the production of tungsten powder, tungsten heavy alloys, tungsten carbide materials, and tungsten carbide cutting tools.

Recent Developments: For the year ended Dec 31 2012, net income decreased 24.8%.to US$167.8 million from US$223.1 million in the prior year. Revenues were US$5.03 billion, down 2.9% from US$5.18 billion the year before. Operating income was US$315.4 million versus US$431.1 million in the prior year, a decrease of 26.8%. Direct operating expenses declined 0.7% to US$4.34 billion from US$4.37 billion in the comparable period the year before. Indirect operating expenses decreased 1.1% to US$377.8 million from US$382.1 million in the equivalent prior-year period.

Prospects: Our evaluation of Allegheny Technologies Inc. as of Apr. 7, 2013 is the result of our systematic analysis on three basic characteristics: earnings strength, relative valuation, and recent stock price movement. The company has managed to produce a neutral trend in earnings per share over the past 5 quarters and while recent estimates for the company have been mixed, ATI has posted better than expected results. Based on operating earnings yield, the company is about fairly valued when compared to all of the companies in our coverage universe. Share price changes over the past year indicates that ATI will perform poorly over the near term.

Financial Data
(US$ in Thousands)

	12/31/2012	12/31/2011	12/31/2010	12/31/2009	12/31/2008	12/31/2007	12/31/2006	12/31/2005
Earnings Per Share	1.43	1.97	0.72	0.32	5.67	7.26	5.59	3.57
Cash Flow Per Share	4.02	2.90	0.28	2.25	7.59	6.98	3.18	2.31
Tang Book Value Per Share	16.20	16.34	18.61	18.40	18.19	19.82	12.71	6.11
Dividends Per Share	0.720	0.720	0.720	0.720	0.720	0.570	0.430	0.280
Dividend Payout %	50.35	36.55	100.00	225.00	12.70	7.85	7.69	7.84
Income Statement								
Total Revenue	5,031,500	5,183,000	4,047,800	3,054,900	5,309,700	5,452,500	4,936,600	3,539,900
EBITDA	509,600	606,100	329,900	216,800	990,000	1,261,800	984,800	428,500
Depn & Amortn	194,000	174,400	141,500	132,600	118,800	102,900	84,200	77,300
Income Before Taxes	244,000	339,400	125,700	64,900	867,700	1,154,100	877,300	312,600
Income Taxes	76,200	116,300	47,000	26,900	294,200	400,200	297,300	(54,700)
Net Income	158,400	214,300	70,700	31,700	565,900	747,100	571,900	359,800
Average Shares	116,600	113,900	98,720	98,130	99,840	102,960	102,380	100,800
Balance Sheet								
Current Assets	2,510,600	2,569,500	2,115,100	1,997,600	1,929,400	2,248,700	1,987,900	1,484,000
Total Assets	6,247,800	6,046,900	4,493,600	4,346,000	4,170,400	4,095,600	3,282,200	2,731,600
Current Liabilities	871,500	861,800	791,000	624,600	693,900	704,000	645,500	560,900
Long-Term Obligations	1,463,000	1,482,000	921,900	1,037,600	494,600	507,300	529,900	547,000
Total Liabilities	3,768,200	3,571,600	2,452,800	2,333,800	2,209,100	1,872,100	1,789,600	1,931,700
Stockholders' Equity	2,479,600	2,475,300	2,040,800	2,012,200	1,961,300	2,223,500	1,492,600	799,900
Shares Outstanding	107,398	106,354	98,542	98,070	97,330	101,586	101,201	98,200
Statistical Record								
Return on Assets %	2.57	4.07	1.60	0.74	13.65	20.25	19.02	14.26
Return on Equity %	6.38	9.49	3.49	1.60	26.97	40.21	49.89	58.70
EBITDA Margin %	10.13	11.69	8.15	7.10	18.65	23.14	19.95	12.10
Net Margin %	3.15	4.13	1.75	1.04	10.66	13.70	11.58	10.16
Asset Turnover	0.82	0.98	0.92	0.72	1.28	1.48	1.64	1.40
Current Ratio	2.88	2.98	2.67	3.20	2.78	3.19	3.08	2.65
Debt to Equity	0.59	0.60	0.45	0.52	0.25	0.23	0.36	0.68
Price Range	51.62-25.61	72.74-32.78	58.97-39.73	45.73-17.49	86.40-15.24	118.78-83.22	98.20-36.05	36.53-18.03
P/E Ratio	36.10-17.91	36.92-16.64	81.90-55.18	142.91-54.66	15.24-2.69	16.36-11.46	17.57-6.45	10.23-5.05
Average Yield %	2.06	1.28	1.46	2.32	1.33	0.56	0.66	1.08

Address: 1000 Six PPG Place,	Web Site: www.atimetals.com	Auditors: Ernst & Young LLP
Pittsburgh, PA 15222-5479	Officers: Richard J. Harshman - Chairman, President,	Investor Contact: 412-394-3004
Telephone: 412-394-2800	Chief Executive Officer L. Patrick Hassey - Chairman,	Transfer Agents: Computershare,
	Outgoing Chief Executive Officer	Pittsburgh, PA

ALLERGAN, INC

Exchange	Symbol	Price	52Wk Range	Yield	P/E
NYS	AGN	$111.63 (3/28/2013)	111.89-82.07	0.18	31.18

*7 Year Price Score 126.36 *NYSE Composite Index=100 *12 Month Price Score 105.90

Interim Earnings (Per Share)

Qtr.	Mar	Jun	Sep	Dec
2008	0.36	0.48	0.55	0.50
2009	0.15	0.58	0.58	0.72
2010	0.55	0.78	(2.21)	0.87
2011	0.51	0.79	0.81	0.90
2012	0.74	0.96	0.82	1.06

Interim Dividends (Per Share)

Amt	Decl	Ex	Rec	Pay
0.05Q	05/02/2012	05/22/2012	05/24/2012	06/14/2012
0.05Q	08/01/2012	08/21/2012	08/23/2012	09/13/2012
0.05Q	10/30/2012	11/19/2012	11/21/2012	12/12/2012
0.05Q	02/05/2013	02/26/2013	02/28/2013	03/21/2013

Indicated Div: $0.20

Valuation Analysis / **Institutional Holding**

Forecast EPS	$4.77
	(04/05/2013)
Market Cap	$33.5 Billion
Book Value	$5.8 Billion
Price/Book	5.74
Price/Sales	5.77

No of Institutions	853
Shares	310,020,416
% Held	87.86

Business Summary: Pharmaceuticals (MIC: 4.1.1 SIC: 2834 NAIC: 325412)

Allergan is a health care company that develops and commercializes pharmaceuticals, biologics, medical devices and over-the-counter products. Co. produces pharmaceutical products, including: ophthalmic products for dry eye, glaucoma, inflammation, infection, allergy and retinal disease; Botox® for certain therapeutic and aesthetic indications; skin care products for acne, psoriasis, eyelash growth and other prescription and over-the-counter skin care products; and urologics products. Also, Co. produces medical devices, including: breast implants for augmentation, revision and reconstructive surgery and tissue expanders; obesity intervention products; and facial aesthetics products.

Recent Developments: For the year ended Dec 31 2012, net income increased 17.5% to US$1.10 billion from US$938.1 million in the prior year. Revenues were US$5.81 billion, up 7.1% from US$5.42 billion the year before. Operating income was US$1.61 billion versus US$1.37 billion in the prior year, an increase of 18.2%. Direct operating expenses rose 3.6% to US$775.5 million from US$748.7 million in the comparable period the year before. Indirect operating expenses increased 3.4% to US$3.42 billion from US$3.31 billion in the equivalent prior-year period.

Prospects: Our evaluation of Allergan Inc. as of Apr. 7, 2013 is the result of our systematic analysis on three basic characteristics: earnings strength, relative valuation, and recent stock price movement. The company has managed to produce a neutral trend in earnings per share over the past 5 quarters and while recent estimates for the company have remained steady, AGN has posted results that fell short of analysts expectations. Based on operating earnings yield, the company is about fairly valued when compared to all of the companies in our coverage universe. Share price changes over the past year indicates that AGN will perform in line with the market over the near term.

Financial Data

(US$ in Thousands)	12/31/2012	12/31/2011	12/31/2010	12/31/2009	12/31/2008	12/31/2007	12/31/2006	12/31/2005
Earnings Per Share	3.58	3.01	...	2.03	1.89	1.62	(0.44)	1.50
Cash Flow Per Share	5.29	3.55	1.53	3.67	2.24	2.60	2.54	1.62
Tang Book Value Per Share	7.73	6.55	5.39	4.53	1.48	0.54	0.76	5.24
Dividends Per Share	0.200	0.200	0.200	0.200	0.200	0.200	0.200	0.200
Dividend Payout %	5.59	6.64	...	9.85	10.58	12.35	...	13.29
Income Statement								
Total Revenue	5,806,100	5,419,100	4,919,400	4,503,600	4,403,400	3,938,900	3,063,300	2,319,200
EBITDA	1,721,500	1,492,200	380,200	1,064,700	965,200	815,100	71,400	664,900
Depn & Amortn	131,300	127,600	138,000	146,300	150,900	121,300	79,600	88,700
Income Before Taxes	1,533,300	1,299,700	170,800	848,500	787,200	687,700	(19,500)	599,200
Income Taxes	430,800	361,600	165,900	224,700	207,000	186,200	107,500	192,400
Net Income	1,098,800	934,500	600	621,300	578,600	499,300	(127,400)	403,900
Average Shares	307,100	310,200	308,000	305,800	306,400	308,700	293,800	268,000
Balance Sheet								
Current Assets	4,458,800	4,048,300	3,993,700	3,106,300	2,270,600	2,124,200	2,130,300	1,825,600
Total Assets	9,179,300	8,508,600	8,308,100	7,536,600	6,791,300	6,579,300	5,767,100	2,850,500
Current Liabilities	1,095,200	955,000	1,528,400	811,600	697,000	715,700	658,100	1,044,000
Long-Term Obligations	1,512,400	1,515,400	1,534,200	1,491,300	1,635,300	1,590,200	1,606,400	57,500
Total Liabilities	3,342,200	3,199,000	3,550,400	2,713,800	2,781,000	2,840,700	2,624,000	1,283,600
Stockholders' Equity	5,837,100	5,309,600	4,757,700	4,822,800	4,010,300	3,738,600	3,143,100	1,566,900
Shares Outstanding	300,324	305,272	305,525	304,433	304,088	305,907	304,538	265,648
Statistical Record								
Return on Assets %	12.39	11.11	0.01	8.67	8.63	8.09	N.M.	15.82
Return on Equity %	19.66	18.57	0.01	14.07	14.89	14.51	N.M.	30.11
EBITDA Margin %	29.65	27.54	7.73	23.64	21.92	20.69	2.33	28.67
Net Margin %	18.92	17.24	0.01	13.80	13.14	12.68	N.M.	17.42
Asset Turnover	0.65	0.64	0.62	0.63	0.66	0.64	0.71	0.91
Current Ratio	4.07	4.24	2.61	3.83	3.26	2.97	3.24	1.75
Debt to Equity	0.26	0.29	0.32	0.31	0.41	0.43	0.51	0.04
Price Range	96.59-82.07	89.01-68.61	74.53-56.77	63.61-35.88	68.69-29.65	68.45-52.91	61.51-46.81	54.97-34.53
P/E Ratio	26.98-22.92	29.57-22.79	N.M.	31.33-17.67	36.34-15.69	42.25-32.66	...	36.65-23.02
Average Yield %	0.22	0.25	0.31	0.40	0.38	0.33	0.36	0.47

Address: 2525 Dupont Drive, Irvine, CA 92612 Telephone: 714-246-4500	Web Site: www.allergan.com Officers: David E.I. Pyott - Chairman, President, Chief Executive Officer Jeffrey L. Edwards - Executive Vice President, Chief Financial Officer	Auditors: Ernst & Young LLP Investor Contact: 714-246-4636 Transfer Agents: Wells Fargo Shareowner Services, St. Paul, MN

ALLIANCE DATA SYSTEMS CORP.

Exchange	Symbol	Price	52Wk Range	Yield	P/E
NYS	ADS	$161.89 (3/28/2013)	161.89-121.25	N/A	24.60

7 Year Price Score 161.08 *NYSE Composite Index=100   *12 Month Price Score 103.24

TRADING VOLUME (thousand shares)

Interim Earnings (Per Share)

Qtr.	Mar	Jun	Sep	Dec
2008	0.61	0.60	0.99	0.78
2009	0.45	0.51	0.83	0.71
2010	0.84	0.83	0.96	0.85
2011	1.56	1.19	1.60	1.10
2012	1.86	1.63	1.84	1.25

Interim Dividends (Per Share)

No Dividends Paid

Valuation Analysis   Institutional Holding

Forecast EPS	$9.90	No of Institutions
	(04/06/2013)	493
Market Cap	$8.0 Billion	Shares
Book Value	$528.5 Million	72,709,792
Price/Book	15.19	% Held
Price/Sales	2.21	129.01

Business Summary: Business Services (MIC: 7.5.2 SIC: 7389 NAIC: 522320)

Alliance Data Systems is a provider of marketing and customer loyalty services. Co. provides a portfolio of integrated outsourced marketing services, including customer loyalty programs, database marketing services, marketing strategy consulting, analytics and creative services, direct marketing services and private label and co-brand retail credit card programs. Co. facilitates and manages interactions between its clients and their customers through consumer marketing channels that include in-store, on-line, catalog, mail, telephone and email, and mobile and social media. Co. has three segments: LoyaltyOne, Epsilon, and Private Label Services and Credit.

Recent Developments: For the year ended Dec 31 2012, income from continuing operations increased 33.9% to US$422.3 million from US$315.3 million a year earlier. Net income increased 33.9% to US$422.3 million from US$315.3 million in the prior year. Revenues were US$3.64 billion, up 14.8% from US$3.17 billion the year before. Operating income was US$974.4 million versus US$812.7 million in the prior year, an increase of 19.9%. Direct operating expenses rose 16.3% to US$2.11 billion from US$1.81 billion in the comparable period the year before. Indirect operating expenses increased 2.1% to US$560.4 million from US$548.7 million in the equivalent prior-year period.

Prospects: Our evaluation of Alliance Data Systems Corp. as of Apr. 7, 2013 is the result of our systematic analysis on three basic characteristics: earnings strength, relative valuation, and recent stock price movement. The company has managed to produce a neutral trend in earnings per share over the past 5 quarters and while recent estimates for the company have been raised by analysts, ADS has posted better than expected results. Based on operating earnings yield, the company is about fairly valued when compared to all of the companies in our coverage universe. Share price changes over the past year indicates that ADS will perform well over the near term.

Financial Data

(US$ in Thousands)	12/31/2012	12/31/2011	12/31/2010	12/31/2009	12/31/2008	12/31/2007	12/31/2006	12/31/2005
Earnings Per Share	6.58	5.45	3.48	2.49	2.95	2.03	2.32	1.64
Cash Flow Per Share	22.62	19.95	17.18	6.43	6.29	7.29	5.88	1.33
Income Statement								
Total Revenue	3,641,390	3,173,287	2,791,421	1,964,341	2,025,267	2,291,189	1,998,742	1,552,437
EBITDA	1,114,038	940,206	747,140	512,747	585,992	488,269	457,064	318,967
Depn & Amortn	139,674	127,526	117,920	104,990	125,491	143,994	109,797	82,359
Income Before Taxes	682,904	514,095	310,890	262,946	396,853	274,752	306,269	222,126
Income Taxes	260,648	198,809	115,252	86,227	153,454	110,691	116,664	83,381
Net Income	422,256	315,286	193,737	143,734	217,393	164,061	189,605	138,745
Average Shares	64,143	57,804	55,710	57,706	73,640	80,811	81,686	84,637
Balance Sheet								
Current Assets	9,132,143	6,606,967	6,129,535	2,359,505	1,939,060	1,453,041	1,309,975	1,042,453
Total Assets	12,000,139	8,980,249	8,272,152	5,225,667	4,357,039	4,103,594	3,404,015	2,926,082
Current Liabilities	5,032,777	3,855,171	3,862,188	2,130,012	1,949,352	1,325,724	877,720	1,048,571
Long-Term Obligations	2,051,570	2,874,848	2,030,593	2,422,889	1,706,626	644,375	741,675	258,501
Total Liabilities	11,471,652	8,804,283	8,249,058	4,952,891	3,962,919	2,906,628	2,332,482	2,004,975
Stockholders' Equity	528,487	175,966	23,094	272,776	394,120	1,196,966	1,071,533	921,107
Shares Outstanding	49,603	49,830	51,371	52,199	62,807	78,762	79,654	80,405
Statistical Record								
Return on Assets %	4.01	3.65	2.87	3.00	5.12	4.37	5.99	5.37
Return on Equity %	119.55	316.77	130.96	43.11	27.25	14.46	19.03	15.49
EBITDA Margin %	30.59	29.63	26.77	26.10	28.93	21.31	22.87	20.55
Net Margin %	11.60	9.94	6.94	7.32	10.73	7.16	9.49	8.94
Asset Turnover	0.35	0.37	0.41	0.41	0.48	0.61	0.63	0.60
Current Ratio	1.81	1.71	1.59	1.11	0.99	1.10	1.49	0.99
Debt to Equity	3.88	16.34	87.93	8.88	4.33	0.54	0.69	0.28
Price Range	148.02-103.04	105.74-70.68	77.98-53.05	68.52-23.79	74.99-37.00	80.72-57.14	66.00-36.96	47.48-32.79
P/E Ratio	22.50-15.34	19.40-12.97	22.41-15.24	27.52-9.55	25.42-12.54	39.76-28.15	28.45-15.93	28.95-19.99

Address: 7500 Dallas Parkway, Suite 700, Plano, TX 75024 **Telephone:** 214-494-3000	**Web Site:** www.alliancedata.com **Officers:** Edward J. Heffernan - President, Chief Executive Officer Bryan J. Kennedy - Executive Vice President, Division Officer	**Auditors:** Deloitte & Touche LLP **Investor Contact:** 212-850-5721 **Transfer Agents:** ComputerShare Investor Services, Providence, RI

ALLIANT ENERGY CORP.

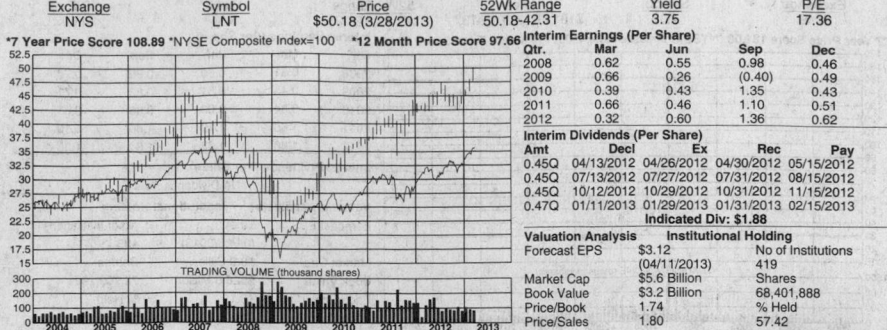

Exchange	Symbol	Price	52Wk Range	Yield	P/E
NYS	LNT	$50.18 (3/28/2013)	50.18-42.31	3.75	17.36

*7 Year Price Score 108.89 *NYSE Composite Index=100   *12 Month Price Score 97.66

Interim Earnings (Per Share)

Qtr.	Mar	Jun	Sep	Dec
2008	0.62	0.55	0.98	0.46
2009	0.66	0.26	(0.40)	0.49
2010	0.39	0.43	1.35	0.43
2011	0.66	0.46	1.10	0.51
2012	0.32	0.60	1.36	0.62

Interim Dividends (Per Share)

Amt	Decl	Ex	Rec	Pay
0.45Q	04/13/2012	04/26/2012	04/30/2012	05/15/2012
0.45Q	07/13/2012	07/27/2012	07/31/2012	08/15/2012
0.45Q	10/12/2012	10/29/2012	10/31/2012	11/15/2012
0.47Q	01/11/2013	01/29/2013	01/31/2013	02/15/2013

Indicated Div: $1.88

Valuation Analysis

	Institutional Holding	
Forecast EPS	$3.12 (04/11/2013)	No of Institutions 419
Market Cap	$5.6 Billion	Shares
Book Value	$3.2 Billion	68,401,888
Price/Book	1.74	% Held
Price/Sales	1.80	57.42

Business Summary: Electric Utilities (MIC: 3.1.1 SIC: 4931 NAIC: 221122)

Alliant Energy is a public utility holding company. As of Dec 31 2012, Co. provided regulated electricity and natural gas service to approximately 1.0 million electric and approximately 415,000 natural gas customers in the Midwest. The primary subsidiaries of Co. are: Interstate Power and Light Company and Wisconsin Power and Light Company, which are public utilities engaged principally in the generation and distribution of electricity and the distribution and transportation of natural gas; Alliant Energy Resources, LLC, which manages a portfolio of subsidiaries and investments; and Alliant Energy Corporate Services, Inc., which provides administrative services.

Recent Developments: For the year ended Dec 31 2012, net income increased 4.3% to US$335.7 million from US$321.9 million in the prior year. Revenues were US$3.09 billion, down 3.9% from US$3.22 billion the year before. Operating income was US$519.7 million versus US$513.3 million in the prior year, an increase of 1.2%. Direct operating expenses declined 6.3% to US$2.14 billion from US$2.29 billion in the comparable period the year before. Indirect operating expenses increased 2.7% to US$430.6 million from US$419.2 million in the equivalent prior-year period.

Prospects: Our evaluation of Alliant Energy Corp. as of Apr. 7, 2013 is the result of our systematic analysis on three basic characteristics: earnings strength, relative valuation, and recent stock price movement. The company has generated a negative trend in earnings per share over the past 5 quarters and while recent estimates for the company have remained steady, LNT has posted better than expected results. Based on operating earnings yield, the company is undervalued when compared to all of the companies in our coverage universe. Share price changes over the past year indicates that LNT will perform poorly over the near term.

Financial Data

(US$ in Thousands)	12/31/2012	12/31/2011	12/31/2010	12/31/2009	12/31/2008	12/31/2007	12/31/2006	12/31/2005
Earnings Per Share	2.89	2.74	2.60	1.01	2.61	3.78	2.69	(0.07)
Cash Flow Per Share	7.57	6.35	8.92	5.96	2.89	5.24	3.60	5.15
Tang Book Value Per Share	28.79	27.68	26.63	25.60	27.77	26.50	24.93	22.94
Dividends Per Share	1.800	1.700	1.580	1.500	1.400	1.270	1.150	1.050
Dividend Payout %	62.28	62.04	60.77	148.51	53.64	33.60	42.75	...
Income Statement								
Total Revenue	3,094,500	3,665,300	3,416,100	3,432,800	3,681,700	3,437,600	3,359,400	3,279,600
EBITDA	929,500	870,500	918,900	552,000	780,200	1,066,000	925,800	464,300
Depn & Amortn	387,900	380,100	344,100	317,700	286,400	310,000	305,400	380,400
Income Before Taxes	388,900	336,400	415,100	83,600	387,000	651,200	495,800	(56,100)
Income Taxes	89,400	55,100	145,200	(9,200)	140,200	255,800	203,000	(52,900)
Net Income	335,700	321,900	306,300	129,700	288,000	425,300	315,700	(7,700)
Average Shares	110,768	110,678	110,521	110,352	110,308	112,521	117,190	116,793
Balance Sheet								
Current Assets	994,300	866,500	1,092,700	1,377,300	1,445,600	1,472,300	1,173,800	1,783,400
Total Assets	10,785,500	9,687,900	9,282,900	9,036,000	8,201,500	7,189,700	7,084,100	7,733,100
Current Liabilities	1,020,000	855,000	866,700	1,074,100	1,038,200	937,000	1,102,100	1,580,300
Long-Term Obligations	3,136,600	2,703,100	2,703,400	2,404,500	1,748,300	1,404,500	1,323,300	1,914,800
Total Liabilities	7,590,600	6,614,900	6,329,300	6,203,400	5,134,200	4,264,700	4,189,000	5,048,800
Stockholders' Equity	3,194,900	3,073,000	2,953,600	2,832,600	3,067,300	2,925,000	2,895,100	2,684,300
Shares Outstanding	110,987	111,018	110,893	110,656	110,449	110,359	116,126	117,035
Statistical Record								
Return on Assets %	3.27	3.39	3.34	1.50	3.73	5.96	4.26	N.M.
Return on Equity %	10.68	10.68	10.59	4.40	9.59	14.61	11.32	N.M.
EBITDA Margin %	30.04	23.75	26.90	16.08	21.19	31.01	27.56	14.16
Net Margin %	10.85	8.78	8.97	3.78	7.82	12.37	9.40	N.M.
Asset Turnover	0.30	0.39	0.37	0.40	0.48	0.48	0.45	0.41
Current Ratio	0.97	1.01	1.26	1.28	1.39	1.57	1.07	1.13
Debt to Equity	0.98	0.88	0.92	0.85	0.57	0.48	0.46	0.71
Price Range	47.50-42.10	44.32-34.30	37.63-30.26	31.19-20.46	42.12-24.29	45.74-35.81	39.70-28.50	30.39-25.88
P/E Ratio	16.44-14.57	16.18-12.52	14.47-11.64	30.88-20.26	16.14-9.31	12.10-9.47	14.76-10.59	...
Average Yield %	4.07	4.28	4.61	5.72	4.10	3.13	3.32	3.77

Address: 4902 N. Biltmore Lane, Madison, WI 53718	Web Site: www.alliantenergy.com	Auditors: Deloitte & Touche LLP
Telephone: 608-458-3311	Officers: Patricia L. Kampling - President, Chief Executive Officer, Chief Operating Officer Thomas L. Aller - Senior Vice President	Investor Contact: 608-458-3956
Fax: 608-458-4824		Transfer Agents: Wells Fargo Shareowner Services, St. Paul, MN

ALLIANT TECHSYSTEMS INC.

Exchange	Symbol	Price	52Wk Range	Yield	P/E
NYS	ATK	$72.43 (3/28/2013)	72.43-44.00	1.44	9.10

*7 Year Price Score 63.16 *NYSE Composite Index=100 *12 Month Price Score 110.12

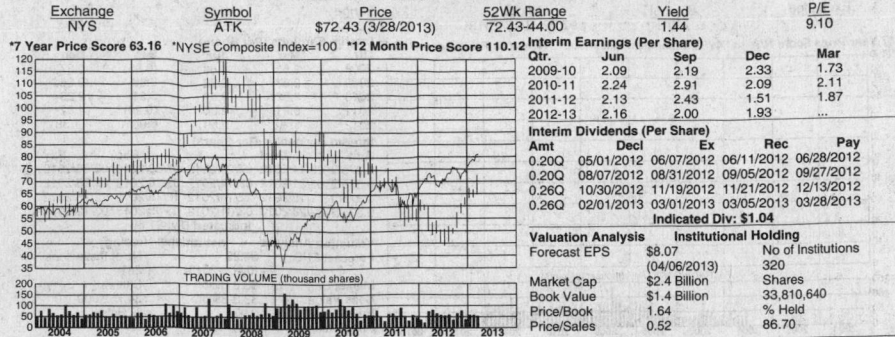

Interim Earnings (Per Share)

Qtr.	Jun	Sep	Dec	Mar
2009-10	2.09	2.19	2.33	1.73
2010-11	2.24	2.91	2.09	2.11
2011-12	2.13	2.43	1.51	1.87
2012-13	2.16	2.00	1.93	...

Interim Dividends (Per Share)

Amt	Decl	Ex	Rec	Pay
0.20Q	05/01/2012	06/07/2012	06/11/2012	06/28/2012
0.20Q	08/07/2012	08/31/2012	09/05/2012	09/27/2012
0.26Q	10/30/2012	11/19/2012	11/21/2012	12/13/2012
0.26Q	02/01/2013	03/01/2013	03/05/2013	03/28/2013

Indicated Div: $1.04

Valuation Analysis / Institutional Holding

Forecast EPS	$8.07
	(04/06/2013)
Market Cap	$2.4 Billion
Book Value	$1.4 Billion
Price/Book	1.64
Price/Sales	0.52

No of Institutions	320
Shares	33,810,640
% Held	86.70

TRADING VOLUME (thousand shares)

Business Summary: Defense (MIC: 7.1.2 SIC: 3483 NAIC: 332993)

Alliant Techsystems is an aerospace, defense, and commercial products company and supplier of products to the U.S. Government, allied nations, and prime contractors. Co. has four segments: Aerospace Systems, which provides rocket motor systems and engineering and technical services; Armament Systems, which develops and produces military ammunition, gun systems, propellant and energetic materials; Missile Products, which includes missile defense interceptor capabilities, airborne missile warning systems, fuzes, and defense electronics; and Security and Sporting, which produces ammunition and accessories sold to sporting, law enforcement, U.S. Government, and international markets.

Recent Developments: For the quarter ended Dec 30 2012, net income increased 27.1% to US$63.2 million from US$49.8 million in the year-earlier quarter. Revenues were US$1.06 billion, down 5.5% from US$1.12 billion the year before. Operating income was US$106.9 million versus US$105.4 million in the prior-year quarter, an increase of 1.4%. Direct operating expenses declined 4.0% to US$836.6 million from US$871.7 million in the comparable period the year before. Indirect operating expenses decreased 19.7% to US$112.8 million from US$140.4 million in the equivalent prior-year period.

Prospects: Our evaluation of Alliant Techsystems Inc. as of Apr. 7, 2013 is the result of our systematic analysis on three basic characteristics: earnings strength, relative valuation, and recent stock price movement. The company has managed to produce a neutral trend in earnings per share over the past 5 quarters. However, while recent estimates for the company have been mixed, ATK has posted better than expected results. Based on operating earnings yield, the company is undervalued when compared to all of the companies in our coverage universe. Share price changes over the past year indicates that ATK will perform well over the near term.

Financial Data

(US$ in Thousands)	9 Mos	6 Mos	3 Mos	03/31/2012	03/31/2011	03/31/2010	03/31/2009	03/31/2008
Earnings Per Share	7.96	7.54	7.97	7.93	9.32	8.33	4.56	6.32
Cash Flow Per Share	11.28	10.30	6.98	11.29	12.65	5.90	12.98	11.59
Tang Book Value Per Share	2.55	3.58	N.M.	N.M.	N.M.	N.M.	N.M.	N.M.
Dividends Per Share	0.860	0.800	0.800	0.800	0.200	...	...	...
Dividend Payout %	10.80	10.61	10.04	10.09	2.15	...	...	...
Income Statement								
Total Revenue	3,208,271	2,152,089	1,082,301	4,613,399	4,842,264	4,807,666	4,583,224	4,171,725
EBITDA	426,373	293,082	162,744	604,471	636,912	612,167	470,210	508,014
Depn & Amortn	90,042	63,610	32,056	108,885	111,186	99,830	85,753	77,486
Income Before Taxes	284,671	191,746	110,938	406,966	438,674	435,417	321,970	350,381
Income Taxes	85,330	55,637	39,997	143,762	124,963	156,473	166,664	127,658
Net Income	199,065	135,889	70,829	262,612	313,175	278,714	155,119	222,347
Average Shares	32,652	32,591	32,741	33,112	33,615	33,462	34,013	35,208
Balance Sheet								
Current Assets	2,098,296	1,748,387	1,794,512	2,009,695	2,059,233	1,718,978	1,580,272	1,247,916
Total Assets	4,259,928	4,151,423	4,313,415	4,541,746	4,443,845	3,869,624	3,593,163	3,196,194
Current Liabilities	760,576	739,712	762,404	919,780	1,063,486	787,815	1,009,130	630,887
Long-Term Obligations	1,047,118	1,045,380	1,263,681	1,272,002	1,289,709	1,379,804	1,160,703	1,455,000
Total Liabilities	2,812,363	2,782,978	3,027,868	3,314,951	3,287,087	3,071,030	2,978,153	2,455,086
Stockholders' Equity	1,447,565	1,368,445	1,285,547	1,226,795	1,156,758	798,594	615,010	741,108
Shares Outstanding	32,742	32,667	32,654	33,142	33,519	33,047	32,783	32,795
Statistical Record								
Return on Assets %	6.12	5.91	6.09	5.83	7.53	7.47	4.57	7.31
Return on Equity %	18.89	18.91	21.22	21.98	32.03	39.43	22.88	34.14
EBITDA Margin %	13.29	13.62	15.04	13.10	13.15	12.73	10.26	12.18
Net Margin %	6.20	6.31	6.54	5.69	6.47	5.80	3.38	5.33
Asset Turnover	1.06	1.10	1.07	1.02	1.16	1.29	1.35	1.37
Current Ratio	2.76	2.36	2.35	2.18	1.94	2.18	1.57	1.98
Debt to Equity	0.72	0.76	0.98	1.04	1.11	1.73	1.89	1.96
Price Range	63.52-44.00	63.09-44.00	72.36-45.47	75.97-50.12	83.40-60.32	90.67-66.98	113.69-62.12	119.85-88.50
P/E Ratio	7.98-5.53	8.37-5.84	9.08-5.71	9.58-6.32	8.95-6.47	10.88-8.04	24.93-13.62	18.96-14.00
Average Yield %	1.61	1.50	1.41	1.29	0.28	...	...	...

Address: 1300 Wilson Boulevard, Suite 400, Arlington, VA 22209-2307 **Telephone:** 703-412-5960	**Web Site:** www.atk.com **Officers:** Ronald R. Fogleman - Chairman Mark W. DeYoung - President, Chief Executive Officer	**Auditors:** Deloitte & Touche, LLP **Investor Contact:** 952-351-3056 **Transfer Agents:** Computershare Shareowner Services, Jersey City, NJ

ALLIED WORLD ASSURANCE COMPANY HOLDINGS AG

Exchange	Symbol	Price	52Wk Range	Yield	P/E
NYS	AWH	$92.72 (3/28/2013)	92.72-68.90	1.62	6.97

*7 Year Price Score N/A   *NYSE Composite Index=100   *12 Month Price Score 102.17

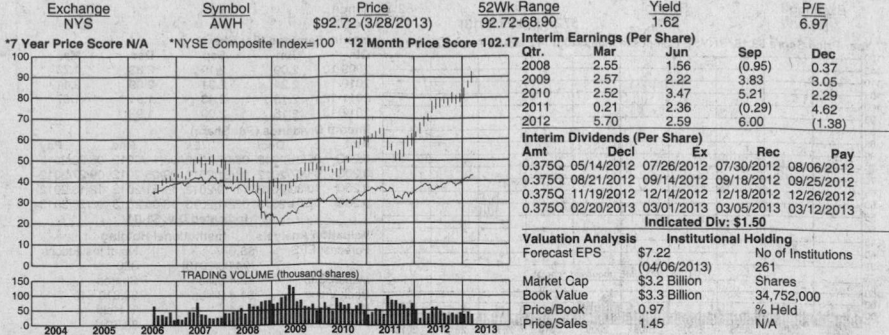

Interim Earnings (Per Share)

Qtr.	Mar	Jun	Sep	Dec
2008	2.55	1.56	(0.95)	0.37
2009	2.57	2.22	3.83	3.05
2010	2.52	3.47	5.21	2.29
2011	0.21	2.36	(0.29)	4.62
2012	5.70	2.59	6.00	(1.38)

Interim Dividends (Per Share)

Amt	Decl	Ex	Rec	Pay
0.375Q	05/14/2012	07/26/2012	07/30/2012	08/06/2012
0.375Q	08/21/2012	09/14/2012	09/18/2012	09/25/2012
0.375Q	11/19/2012	12/14/2012	12/18/2012	12/26/2012
0.375Q	02/20/2013	03/01/2013	03/05/2013	03/12/2013

Indicated Div: $1.50

Valuation Analysis / **Institutional Holding**

Forecast EPS	$7.22 (04/06/2013)	No of Institutions	261
Market Cap	$3.2 Billion	Shares	34,752,000
Book Value	$3.3 Billion	% Held	
Price/Book	0.97	N/A	
Price/Sales	1.45		

Business Summary: General Insurance (MIC: 5.2.1 SIC: 6331 NAIC: 524126)

Allied World Assurance Company Holdings is a holding company that underwrites a portfolio of property and casualty lines of business through offices in Bermuda, Hong Kong, Ireland, Singapore, Switzerland, the U.K. and the U.S. Co. operates in three business segments: U.S. insurance, which provides a range of specialty liability products, with a focus on coverages for healthcare and professional liability risks; international insurance, which includes its direct insurance operations outside of the U.S.; and reinsurance, which includes the reinsurance of property, general casualty, professional liability, specialty lines and property catastrophe coverages written by other insurance companies.

Recent Developments: For the year ended Dec 31 2012, net income increased 79.6% to US$493.0 million from US$274.5 million in the prior year. Revenues were US$2.22 billion, up 25.9% from US$1.76 billion the year before. Net premiums earned were US$1.75 billion versus US$1.46 billion in the prior year, an increase of 20.0%. Net investment income rose 129.9% to US$473.6 million from US$206.0 million a year ago.

Prospects: Our evaluation of Allied World Assurance Company Holdings AG as of Apr. 7, 2013 is the result of our systematic analysis on three basic characteristics: earnings strength, relative valuation, and recent stock price movement. The company has suffered a very negative trend in earnings per share over the past 5 quarters and while recent estimates for the company have been mixed, AWH has posted better than expected results. Based on operating earnings yield, the company is about fairly valued when compared to all of the companies in our coverage universe. Share price changes over the past year indicates that AWH will perform in line with the market over the near term.

Financial Data
(US$ in Thousands)

	12/31/2012	12/31/2011	12/31/2010	12/31/2009	12/31/2008	12/31/2007	12/31/2006	12/31/2005
Earnings Per Share	13.30	6.92	13.32	11.67	3.59	7.53	7.75	(3.19)
Cash Flow Per Share	17.41	14.39	9.71	13.50	13.39	12.72	14.46	14.55
Tang Book Value Per Share	86.40	74.90	72.21	58.00	42.35	45.87	36.76	28.23
Dividends Per Share	1.875	0.750	1.050	0.740	0.750	...	...	...
Dividend Payout %	14.10	10.84	7.88	6.34	20.89	...	...	...
Income Statement								
Premium Income	1,748,898	1,456,992	1,359,548	1,316,892	1,116,905	1,159,942	1,252,010	1,271,511
Total Revenue	2,222,475	1,764,761	1,890,048	1,695,848	1,153,575	1,450,257	1,467,692	1,439,848
Benefits & Claims	1,139,264	959,156	707,883	604,060	641,122	682,340	739,133	1,344,600
Income Before Taxes	511,447	305,528	691,950	643,531	176,002	470,286	447,829	(160,220)
Income Taxes	18,440	30,980	26,945	36,644	(7,633)	1,104	4,991	(444)
Net Income	493,007	274,548	665,005	606,887	183,635	469,182	442,838	(159,776)
Average Shares	37,069	39,667	49,913	51,992	51,147	62,331	57,115	50,162
Balance Sheet								
Total Assets	12,029,946	11,122,158	10,427,631	9,653,153	9,072,079	7,899,108	7,620,580	6,610,492
Total Liabilities	8,703,611	7,973,136	7,351,811	6,439,858	6,655,217	5,659,266	5,400,496	5,190,226
Stockholders' Equity	3,326,335	3,149,022	3,075,820	3,213,295	2,416,862	2,239,842	2,220,084	1,420,266
Shares Outstanding	34,797	37,742	38,089	49,734	49,036	48,741	60,287	50,162
Statistical Record								
Return on Assets %	4.25	2.55	6.62	6.48	2.16	6.05	6.22	N.M.
Return on Equity %	15.19	8.82	21.15	21.56	7.87	21.04	24.33	N.M.
Loss Ratio %	65.14	65.83	52.07	45.87	57.40	58.83	59.04	105.75
Net Margin %	22.18	15.56	35.18	35.79	15.92	32.35	30.17	(11.10)
Price Range	82.63-61.00	65.02-49.53	61.17-41.51	48.74-33.00	50.17-22.46	53.00-41.15	44.12-34.10	...
P/E Ratio	6.21-4.59	9.40-7.16	4.59-3.12	4.18-2.83	13.97-6.26	7.04-5.46	5.69-4.40	...
Average Yield %	2.50	1.28	2.10	1.77	1.90	...	...	...

Address: Lindenstrasse 8, Zug, 6340 Baar	Web Site: www.awac.com	Auditors: Deloitte & Touche Ltd.
Telephone: 417-681-080	Officers: Bart Friedman - Deputy Chairman Scott A. Carmilani - President, Chief Executive Officer	Transfer Agents: Continental Stock Transfer & Trust Company

ALLISON TRANSMISSION HOLDINGS INC

Exchange	Symbol	Price	52Wk Range	Yield	P/E
NYS	ALSN	$24.01 (3/28/2013)	25.02-16.21	1.00	8.70

*7 Year Price Score N/A   *NYSE Composite Index=100   *12 Month Price Score 105.84

Interim Earnings (Per Share)

Qtr.	Mar	Jun	Sep	Dec
2011	0.20	(0.09)	0.21	0.24
2012	0.31	2.21	0.17	0.06

Interim Dividends (Per Share)

Amt	Decl	Ex	Rec	Pay
0.06Q	05/08/2012	05/16/2012	05/18/2012	05/31/2012
0.06Q	08/09/2012	08/13/2012	08/15/2012	08/31/2012
0.06Q	11/06/2012	11/14/2012	11/16/2012	11/30/2012
0.06Q	02/14/2013	02/21/2013	02/25/2013	03/11/2013

Indicated Div: $0.24

Valuation Analysis

		Institutional Holding	
Forecast EPS	$0.91	No of Institutions	
	(04/06/2013)	106	
Market Cap	$4.4 Billion	Shares	
Book Value	$1.4 Billion	190,578,656	
Price/Book	3.26	% Held	
Price/Sales	2.06	N/A	

TRADING VOLUME (thousand shares)

Business Summary: Auto Parts (MIC: 1.8.2 SIC: 3714 NAIC: 336350)

Allison Transmission Holdings is engaged in manufacturing fully-automatic transmissions for medium- and heavy-duty commercial vehicles, medium- and heavy-tactical U.S. military vehicles and hybrid-propulsion systems for transit buses. Co.'s 12 different transmissions are used in a wide variety of applications, including on-highway trucks (distribution, refuse, construction, fire and emergency), buses (primarily school and transit), motorhomes, off-highway vehicles and equipment (primarily energy and mining) and military vehicles (wheeled and tracked). Co. also sells support equipment and Allison-branded replacement parts for use in the vehicle aftermarket.

Recent Developments: For the year ended Dec 31 2012, net income increased 399.2% to US$514.2 million from US$103.0 million in the prior year. Revenues were US$2.14 billion, down 1.0% from US$2.16 billion the year before. Operating income was US$420.2 million versus US$429.0 million in the prior year, a decrease of 2.1%. Direct operating expenses declined 1.7% to US$1.19 billion from US$1.21 billion in the comparable period the year before. Indirect operating expenses increased 1.6% to US$534.1 million from US$525.5 million in the equivalent prior-year period.

Prospects: Our evaluation of Allison Transmission Holding as of Apr. 7, 2013 is the result of our systematic analysis on three basic characteristics: earnings strength, relative valuation, and recent stock price movement. The company has generated a negative trend in earnings per share over the past 5 quarters. However, while recent estimates for the company have been lowered by analysts, ALSN has posted results that fell short of analysts expectations. Based on operating earnings yield, the company is about fairly valued when compared to all of the companies in our coverage universe. Share price changes over the past year indicates that ALSN will perform poorly over the near term.

Financial Data

(US$ in Thousands)	12/31/2012	12/31/2011	12/31/2010	12/31/2009
Earnings Per Share	2.76	0.56	0.16	(1.79)
Cash Flow Per Share	2.73	2.59	2.14	...
Dividends Per Share	0.180	...	...	...
Dividend Payout %	6.52	...	...	...
Income Statement				
Total Revenue	2,141,800	2,162,800	1,926,300	1,766,700
EBITDA	619,900	623,600	614,600	213,500
Depn & Amortn	252,500	255,700	253,800	261,800
Income Before Taxes	216,200	150,600	83,300	(282,500)
Income Taxes	(298,000)	47,600	53,700	41,400
Net Income	514,200	103,000	29,600	(323,900)
Average Shares	186,200	183,275	181,367	181,322
Balance Sheet				
Current Assets	490,300	702,700	645,500	...
Total Assets	4,866,000	5,192,600	5,310,400	...
Current Liabilities	377,800	449,900	417,500	...
Long-Term Obligations	2,801,300	3,345,000	3,637,700	...
Total Liabilities	3,509,100	4,370,900	4,568,700	...
Stockholders' Equity	1,356,900	821,700	741,700	...
Shares Outstanding	184,084	181,375	181,375	...
Statistical Record				
Return on Assets %	10.20	1.96	...	...
Return on Equity %	47.08	13.18	...	...
EBITDA Margin %	28.94	28.83	31.91	12.08
Net Margin %	24.01	4.76	1.54	N.M.
Asset Turnover	0.42	0.41	...	...
Current Ratio	1.30	1.56	1.55	...
Debt to Equity	2.06	4.07	4.90	...
Price Range	25.02-16.21	...	...	...
P/E Ratio	9.07-5.87	...	...	...
Average Yield %	0.91	...	...	...

Address: One Allison Way, Indianapolis, IN 46222 Telephone: 317-242-5000	Web Site: www.allisontransmission.com Officers: Lawrence E. Dewey - Chairman, President, Chief Executive Officer David S. Graziosi - Executive Vice President, Chief Financial Officer, Treasurer	Auditors: PricewaterhouseCoopers LLP Investor Contact: 317-242-3078 Transfer Agents: American Stock Transfer & Trust Company, LLC, Brooklyn, NY

ALLSTATE CORP.

Exchange	Symbol	Price	52Wk Range	Yield	P/E
NYS	ALL	$49.07 (3/28/2013)	49.07-31.97	2.04	10.49

*7 Year Price Score 87.41   *NYSE Composite Index=100   *12 Month Price Score 109.74

Interim Earnings (Per Share)

Qtr.	Mar	Jun	Sep	Dec
2008	0.62	0.05	(1.71)	(2.07)
2009	(0.51)	0.72	0.41	0.96
2010	0.22	0.27	0.68	0.55
2011	0.97	(1.19)	0.32	1.39
2012	1.53	0.86	1.48	0.82

Interim Dividends (Per Share)

Amt	Decl	Ex	Rec	Pay
0.22Q	05/21/2012	05/30/2012	06/01/2012	07/02/2012
0.22Q	07/24/2012	08/29/2012	08/31/2012	10/01/2012
0.22Q	11/06/2012	11/28/2012	11/30/2012	12/31/2012
0.25Q	02/06/2013	02/26/2013	02/28/2013	04/01/2013

Indicated Div: $1.00 (Div. Reinv. Plan)

Valuation Analysis

Forecast EPS	$4.70 (04/06/2013)
Market Cap	$23.5 Billion
Book Value	$20.6 Billion
Price/Book	1.14
Price/Sales	0.71

Institutional Holding

No of Institutions	904
Shares	418,243,936
% Held	73.66

TRADING VOLUME (thousand shares)

Business Summary: General Insurance (MIC: 5.2.1 SIC: 6331 NAIC: 524126)

Allstate is a holding company. Through its subsidiaries, Co. is engaged in the personal property and casualty insurance business and the life insurance, retirement and investment products business. Co. has four business segments: Allstate Protection, which sells private passenger auto and homeowners insurance; Allstate Financial, which provides life insurance, voluntary accident and health insurance products, and retirement and investment products; Discontinued Lines and Coverages, which includes results from insurance coverage that Co. no longer writes and results for certain commercial and other businesses in run-off; and Corporate and Other.

Recent Developments: For the year ended Dec 31 2012, net income increased 193.0% to US$2.31 billion from US$787.0 million in the prior year. Revenues were US$33.32 billion, up 2.0% from US$32.65 billion the year before. Net premiums earned were US$28.98 billion versus US$28.18 billion in the prior year, an increase of 2.8%. Net investment income rose 1.0% to US$4.01 billion from US$3.97 billion a year ago.

Prospects: Our evaluation of Allstate Corp. as of Apr. 7, 2013 is the result of our systematic analysis on three basic characteristics: earnings strength, relative valuation, and recent stock price movement. The company has suffered a very negative trend in earnings per share over the past 5 quarters and while recent estimates for the company have been raised by analysts, ALL has posted better than expected results. Based on operating earnings yield, the company is undervalued when compared to all of the companies in our coverage universe. Share price changes over the past year indicates that ALL will perform well over the near term.

Financial Data

(US$ in Millions)	12/31/2012	12/31/2011	12/31/2010	12/31/2009	12/31/2008	12/31/2007	12/31/2006	12/31/2005
Earnings Per Share	4.68	1.51	1.71	1.58	(3.07)	7.77	7.84	2.64
Cash Flow Per Share	6.22	3.70	6.83	7.97	7.14	9.17	7.99	8.47
Tang Book Value Per Share	40.38	34.79	34.04	29.45	21.95	37.35	33.80	29.97
Dividends Per Share	0.880	0.840	0.800	0.800	1.640	1.520	1.400	1.280
Dividend Payout %	18.80	55.63	46.78	50.63	...	19.56	17.86	48.48
Income Statement								
Premium Income	28,978	28,180	28,125	28,152	28,862	29,099	29,333	29,088
Total Revenue	33,315	32,654	31,400	32,013	29,394	36,769	35,796	35,383
Benefits & Claims	20,302	21,922	20,766	20,363	21,676	19,256	17,587	22,790
Income Before Taxes	3,306	960	1,126	1,248	(3,025)	6,653	7,178	2,088
Income Taxes	1,000	172	198	394	(1,346)	2,017	2,185	323
Net Income	2,306	788	928	854	(1,679)	4,636	4,993	1,765
Average Shares	493	523	542	540	546	596	637	667
Balance Sheet								
Total Assets	126,947	125,563	130,874	132,652	134,798	156,408	157,554	156,072
Total Liabilities	106,367	106,889	111,858	115,960	122,157	134,557	135,708	135,886
Stockholders' Equity	20,580	18,674	19,016	16,692	12,641	21,851	21,846	20,186
Shares Outstanding	479	501	533	537	536	563	622	646
Statistical Record								
Return on Assets %	1.82	0.61	0.70	0.64	N.M.	2.95	3.18	1.15
Return on Equity %	11.72	4.18	5.20	5.82	N.M.	21.22	23.76	8.40
Loss Ratio %	70.06	77.79	73.83	72.33	75.10	66.17	59.96	78.35
Net Margin %	6.92	2.41	2.96	2.67	(5.71)	12.61	13.95	4.99
Price Range	42.62-27.56	34.31-22.68	35.43-27.26	33.26-14.12	52.67-18.10	65.36-49.22	65.92-50.42	62.33-49.67
P/E Ratio	9.11-5.89	22.72-15.02	20.72-15.94	21.05-8.94	...	8.41-6.33	8.41-6.43	23.61-18.81
Average Yield %	2.47	2.92	2.61	3.09	3.82	2.44	2.23	2.30

Address: 2775 Sanders Road, Northbrook, IL 60062 Telephone: 847-402-5000	Web Site: www.allstate.com Officers: Thomas J. Wilson - Chairman, President, Chief Executive Officer Steven E. Shebik - Executive Vice President, Chief Financial Officer	Auditors: Deloitte & Touche LLP Investor Contact: 180-041-68803 Transfer Agents: Wells Fargo Bank, N.A., Shareowner Services, St. Paul, MN

ALPHA NATURAL RESOURCES INC

Exchange	Symbol	Price	52Wk Range	Yield	P/E
NYS	ANR	$8.21 (3/28/2013)	16.82-5.53	N/A	N/A

*7 Year Price Score 26.35 *NYSE Composite Index=100 ***12 Month Price Score 84.68**

Interim Earnings (Per Share)

Qtr.	Mar	Jun	Sep	Dec
2008	0.39	1.04	0.97	(0.07)
2009	0.58	0.22	(0.16)	0.14
2010	0.12	0.32	0.27	0.09
2011	0.41	(0.36)	0.29	(4.13)
2012	(0.13)	(10.14)	(0.21)	(0.58)

Interim Dividends (Per Share)

No Dividends Paid

Valuation Analysis		Institutional Holding	
Forecast EPS	$-2.00 (04/05/2013)	No of Institutions	33
Market Cap	$1.8 Billion	Shares	9,443,582
Book Value	$5.0 Billion	% Held	
Price/Book	0.36	N/A	
Price/Sales	0.26		

Business Summary: Mining (MIC: 8.2.4 SIC: 1221 NAIC: 212111)

Alpha Natural Resources supplies and exports metallurgical coal for use in the steel-making process and supplies thermal coal to electric utilities and manufacturing industries. Co. has two reportable segments: Eastern Coal Operations, which consists of the mines in Northern and Central Appalachia, Co.'s coal brokerage activities and its road construction business; and Western Coal Operations, which consists of two Powder River Basin mines in Wyoming. Co.'s other category includes equipment sales and repair operations; terminal services; the leasing of mineral rights, among others. As of Dec 31 2012, Co. controlled approx. 4.60 billion tons of proven and probable coal reserves.

Recent Developments: For the year ended Dec 31 2012, loss from continuing operations was US$2.44 billion compared with a loss of US$677.4 million a year earlier. Net loss amounted to US$2.44 billion versus a net loss of US$677.4 million in the prior year. Revenues were US$6.97 billion, down 1.9% from US$7.11 billion the year before. Operating loss was US$2.80 billion versus a loss of US$569.0 million in the prior year. Direct operating expenses rose 0.4% to US$5.77 billion from US$5.74 billion in the comparable period the year before. Indirect operating expenses increased 107.0% to US$4.00 billion from US$1.93 billion in the equivalent prior-year period.

Prospects: Our evaluation of Alpha Natural Resources inc. as of Apr. 7, 2013 is the result of our systematic analysis on three basic characteristics: earnings strength, relative valuation, and recent stock price movement. The company has enjoyed a very positive trend in earnings per share over the past 5 quarters. Because the company lacks sufficient analyst estimate data, we place greater weight on the historical EPS trend as the measure of earnings strength. Based on operating earnings yield, the company is overvalued when compared to all of the companies in our coverage universe. Share price changes over the past year indicates that ANR will perform poorly over the near term.

Financial Data

(US$ in Thousands)	12/31/2012	12/31/2011	12/31/2010	12/31/2009	12/31/2008	12/31/2007	12/31/2006	12/31/2005
Earnings Per Share	(11.06)	(3.76)	0.79	0.63	2.36	0.43	2.00	0.38
Cash Flow Per Share	2.35	3.81	5.79	3.93	6.67	3.49	3.28	2.69
Tang Book Value Per Share	18.91	21.95	17.52	15.25	9.95	5.34	4.80	2.84
Income Statement								
Total Revenue	6,974,884	7,109,186	3,917,156	2,495,507	2,554,124	1,877,574	1,910,662	1,627,335
EBITDA	(2,151,131)	(150,075)	429,090	297,456	409,470	238,543	280,032	132,672
Depn & Amortn	641,239	428,306	257,649	182,616	175,940	164,484	141,448	60,502
Income Before Taxes	(2,987,144)	(716,317)	101,436	33,784	200,484	36,184	97,649	43,297
Income Taxes	(549,996)	(38,927)	4,218	(33,023)	39,139	8,629	(30,519)	18,953
Net Income	(2,437,148)	(677,390)	95,551	58,005	165,537	27,734	128,168	21,213
Average Shares	220,261	180,126	121,757	91,702	70,259	65,009	64,150	56,049
Balance Sheet								
Current Assets	2,333,222	2,480,493	1,375,837	1,051,825	991,783	380,209	338,654	318,915
Total Assets	13,089,806	16,510,814	5,179,283	5,122,771	1,728,292	1,210,914	1,145,793	1,013,658
Current Liabilities	1,222,608	1,766,049	447,146	435,193	262,593	223,062	222,190	283,841
Long-Term Obligations	3,291,037	2,922,052	742,312	756,753	520,625	425,451	421,456	423,547
Total Liabilities	8,121,991	9,082,616	2,523,247	2,531,482	1,002,615	830,078	801,744	800,893
Stockholders' Equity	4,967,815	7,428,198	2,656,036	2,591,289	725,677	380,836	344,049	212,765
Shares Outstanding	220,600	219,800	120,500	120,453	70,513	65,769	64,964	64,420
Statistical Record								
Return on Assets %	N.M.	N.M.	1.85	1.69	11.23	2.35	11.87	2.85
Return on Equity %	N.M.	N.M.	3.64	3.50	29.84	7.65	46.04	16.72
EBITDA Margin %	N.M.	N.M.	10.95	11.92	16.03	12.70	14.66	8.15
Net Margin %	N.M.	N.M.	2.44	2.32	6.48	1.48	6.71	1.30
Asset Turnover	0.47	0.66	0.76	0.73	1.73	1.59	1.77	2.18
Current Ratio	1.91	1.40	3.08	2.42	3.78	1.70	1.52	1.12
Debt to Equity	0.66	0.39	0.28	0.29	0.72	1.12	1.22	1.99
Price Range	22.78-5.53	67.38-16.04	60.16-32.07	46.07-14.73	104.93-14.68	33.84-12.45	26.58-14.23	32.08-18.82
P/E Ratio	...	...	76.15-40.59	73.13-23.38	44.46-6.22	78.70-28.95	13.29-7.12	84.42-49.53

Address: One Alpha Place, P.O. Box 16429, Abingdon, VA 24209	Web Site: www.alphanr.com	Auditors: KPMG LLP
Telephone: 276-619-4410	Officers: Kevin S. Crutchfield - Chairman, Chief Executive Officer Paul H. Vining - President, Chief Commercial Officer, Executive Vice President	Transfer Agents: Computershare Trust Company, N.A.

ALTRIA GROUP INC

Exchange	Symbol	Price	52Wk Range	Yield	P/E	Div Achiever
NYS	MO	$34.39 (3/28/2013)	36.16-30.49	5.12	16.69	47 Years

*7 Year Price Score 127.48 *NYSE Composite Index=100 *12 Month Price Score 94.62

Interim Earnings (Per Share)

Qtr.	Mar	Jun	Sep	Dec
2008	1.16	0.45	0.42	0.33
2009	0.28	0.49	0.42	0.35
2010	0.39	0.50	0.54	0.44
2011	0.45	0.21	0.57	0.41
2012	0.48	0.60	0.32	0.55

Interim Dividends (Per Share)

Amt	Decl	Ex	Rec	Pay
0.41Q	05/17/2012	06/13/2012	06/15/2012	07/10/2012
0.44Q	08/24/2012	09/12/2012	09/14/2012	10/10/2012
0.44Q	12/12/2012	12/21/2012	12/26/2012	01/10/2013
0.44Q	02/27/2013	03/13/2013	03/15/2013	04/10/2013

Indicated Div: $1.76 (Div. Reinv. Plan)

Valuation Analysis	Institutional Holding	
Forecast EPS	$2.39	No of Institutions
	(04/06/2013)	1399
Market Cap	$69.1 Billion	Shares
Book Value	$3.2 Billion	1,348,291,072
Price/Book	21.82	% Held
Price/Sales	2.81	58.26

TRADING VOLUME (thousand shares)

Business Summary: Tobacco Products (MIC: 1.3.1 SIC: 2111 NAIC: 312221).

Altria Group is a holding company. Co.'s subsidiaries include: Philip Morris USA Inc. (PM USA), which is engaged in the manufacture and sale of cigarettes and certain smokeless products in the U.S.; John Middleton Co., which is engaged in the manufacture and sale of machine-made cigars and pipe tobacco, and is a wholly-owned subsidiary of PM USA; and UST LLC, which through its direct and indirect wholly-owned subsidiaries, including U.S. Smokeless Tobacco Company LLC and Ste. Michelle Wine Estates Ltd., is engaged in the manufacture and sale of smokeless products and wine. Co.'s reportable segments are smokeable products, smokeless products and wine.

Recent Developments: For the year ended Dec 31 2012, net income increased 23.3% to US$4.18 billion from US$3.39 billion in the prior year. Revenues were US$24.62 billion, up 3.4% from US$23.80 billion the year before. Operating income was US$7.25 billion versus US$6.07 billion in the prior year, an increase of 19.5%. Direct operating expenses rose 1.3% to US$15.06 billion from US$14.86 billion in the comparable period the year before. Indirect operating expenses decreased 19.5% to US$2.31 billion from US$2.87 billion in the equivalent prior-year period.

Prospects: Our evaluation of Altria Group Inc. as of Apr. 7, 2013 is the result of our systematic analysis on three basic characteristics: earnings strength, relative valuation, and recent stock price movement. The company has managed to produce a neutral trend in earnings per share over the past 5 quarters. However, while recent estimates for the company have been mixed, MO has posted better than expected results. Based on operating earnings yield, the company is undervalued when compared to all of the companies in our coverage universe. Share price changes over the past year indicates that MO will perform poorly over the near term.

Financial Data
(US$ in Thousands)

	12/31/2012	12/31/2011	12/31/2010	12/31/2009	12/31/2008	12/31/2007	12/31/2006	12/31/2005
Earnings Per Share	2.06	1.64	1.87	1.54	2.36	4.62	5.71	4.99
Cash Flow Per Share	1.92	1.75	1.33	1.67	2.35	4.91	6.51	5.34
Tang Book Value Per Share	N.M.	N.M.	N.M.	N.M.	N.M.	2.66	N.M.	N.M.
Dividends Per Share	1.700	1.580	1.460	1.320	1.680	3.050	3.320	3.060
Dividend Payout %	82.52	96.34	78.07	85.71	71.19	66.02	58.14	61.32
Income Statement								
Total Revenue	24,618,000	23,800,000	24,363,000	23,556,000	19,356,000	73,801,000	101,407,000	97,854,000
EBITDA	6,604,000	6,321,000	6,504,000	5,753,000	4,704,000	14,215,000	19,217,000	18,267,000
Depn & Amortn	225,000	253,000	276,000	291,000	215,000	980,000	1,804,000	1,675,000
Income Before Taxes	5,253,000	4,852,000	5,095,000	4,277,000	4,322,000	13,020,000	16,536,000	15,435,000
Income Taxes	2,294,000	2,189,000	1,816,000	1,669,000	1,699,000	4,096,000	4,351,000	4,618,000
Net Income	4,180,000	3,390,000	3,905,000	3,206,000	4,930,000	9,786,000	12,022,000	10,435,000
Average Shares	2,024,000	2,064,000	2,079,000	2,071,000	2,087,000	2,116,000	2,105,000	2,090,000
Balance Sheet								
Current Assets	6,315,000	7,131,000	5,981,000	5,773,000	11,076,000	22,890,000	26,152,000	25,781,000
Total Assets	35,329,000	36,962,000	37,402,000	36,677,000	27,215,000	57,211,000	104,270,000	107,949,000
Current Liabilities	8,251,000	7,643,000	6,840,000	7,992,000	7,142,000	18,782,000	25,427,000	26,158,000
Long-Term Obligations	12,419,000	13,089,000	12,194,000	11,185,000	7,339,000	7,963,000	14,498,000	17,868,000
Total Liabilities	32,161,000	33,282,000	32,210,000	32,608,000	24,387,000	38,657,000	64,651,000	72,242,000
Stockholders' Equity	3,168,000	3,680,000	5,192,000	4,069,000	2,828,000	18,554,000	39,619,000	35,707,000
Shares Outstanding	2,009,740	2,044,419	2,088,739	2,076,028	2,061,371	2,107,676	2,097,080	2,084,264
Statistical Record								
Return on Assets %	11.53	9.12	10.54	10.04	11.65	12.12	11.33	9.96
Return on Equity %	121.75	76.42	84.33	92.97	45.99	33.64	31.92	31.42
EBITDA Margin %	26.83	26.56	26.70	24.42	24.30	19.26	18.95	18.67
Net Margin %	16.98	14.24	16.03	13.61	13.61	13.26	11.86	10.66
Asset Turnover	0.68	0.64	0.66	0.74	0.46	0.91	0.96	0.93
Current Ratio	0.77	0.93	0.87	0.72	1.55	1.22	1.03	0.99
Debt to Equity	3.92	3.56	2.35	2.75	2.60	0.43	0.37	0.50
Price Range	36.16-28.14	30.31-23.51	26.15-19.37	20.37-14.62	24.43-14.45	24.12-19.03	19.96-15.90	17.90-14.01
P/E Ratio	17.55-13.66	18.48-14.34	13.98-10.36	13.23-9.49	10.35-6.12	5.22-4.12	3.50-2.78	3.59-2.81
Average Yield %	5.24	5.99	6.62	7.60	8.17	14.28	18.65	19.38

Address: 6601 West Broad Street, Richmond, VA 23230 Telephone: 804-274-2200	Web Site: www.altria.com Officers: Martin J. Barrington - Chairman, Chief Executive Officer, Vice-Chairman David R. Beran - Vice-Chairman	Auditors: PricewaterhouseCoopers LLP Investor Contact: 804-484-8222 Transfer Agents: Computershare Trust Company, N.A., Providence, RI

AMDOCS LTD.

Exchange	Symbol	Price	52Wk Range	Yield	P/E
NYS	DOX	$36.25 (3/28/2013)	36.56-28.37	N/A	15.17

*7 Year Price Score 95.29   ***NYSE Composite Index=100**   ***12 Month Price Score 101.72**

TRADING VOLUME (thousand shares)

Interim Earnings (Per Share)

Qtr.	Dec	Mar	Jun	Sep
2009-10	0.43	0.33	0.45	0.48
2010-11	0.38	0.50	0.50	0.49
2011-12	0.53	0.60	0.59	0.59
2012-13	0.61	...	...	...

Interim Dividends (Per Share)

No Dividends Paid

Valuation Analysis | **Institutional Holding**

Forecast EPS	$2.92	No of Institutions
	(04/10/2013)	316
Market Cap	$5.9 Billion	Shares
Book Value	$3.1 Billion	178,272,160
Price/Book	1.90	% Held
Price/Sales	1.80	86.78

Business Summary: IT Services (MIC: 6.3.1 SIC: 7371 NAIC: 511210)

Amdocs is a sofware and services solutions group based in the United Kingdom. Co. provides software and services for communications, media and entertainment industry service providers. Co. operates in one segment, providing integrated products and services. Co. designs, develops, markets, supports and operates customer experience systems primarily for wireless, wireline, cable and satellite service providers throughout the world. Co. also offers a full range of advertising and media solutions for local marketing service providers and search and directory publishers. Co.'s production and operating facilities are located in Brazil, Canada, Cyprus, India, Ireland, Israel and the United States.

Recent Developments: For the quarter ended Dec 31 2012, net income increased 6.8% to US$99.0 million from US$92.7 million in the year-earlier quarter. Revenues were US$826.4 million, up 2.4% from US$807.0 million the year before. Operating income was US$112.7 million versus US$109.0 million in the prior-year quarter, an increase of 3.3%. Direct operating expenses rose 3.6% to US$535.6 million from US$517.1 million in the comparable period the year before. Indirect operating expenses decreased 1.5% to US$178.1 million from US$180.9 million in the equivalent prior-year period.

Prospects: Our evaluation of Amdocs Ltd. as of Apr. 7, 2013 is the result of our systematic analysis on three basic characteristics: earnings strength, relative valuation, and recent stock price movement. The company has managed to produce a neutral trend in earnings per share over the past 5 quarters and while recent estimates for the company have remained steady, DOX has posted better than expected results. Based on operating earnings yield, the company is undervalued when compared to all of the companies in our coverage universe. Share price changes over the past year indicates that DOX will perform well over the near term.

Financial Data

(US$ in Thousands)	3 Mos	09/30/2012	09/30/2011	09/30/2010	09/30/2009	09/30/2008	09/30/2007	09/30/2006
Earnings Per Share	2.39	2.31	1.86	1.69	1.58	1.74	1.65	1.48
Cash Flow Per Share	3.14	3.05	2.89	3.38	2.56	2.33	2.04	2.11
Tang Book Value Per Share	7.56	7.08	6.24	7.11	7.05	4.94	3.85	1.67
Income Statement								
Total Revenue	826,359	3,246,903	3,177,728	2,984,223	2,862,607	3,162,096	2,836,173	2,480,050
EBITDA	123,890	549,942	590,920	609,102	562,837	492,283	432,392	369,742
Depn & Amortn	11,233	107,470	186,556	198,669	195,518	86,687	74,959	37,610
Income Before Taxes	112,549	441,524	395,707	385,298	366,154	417,551	407,999	373,873
Income Taxes	13,534	50,153	49,042	41,392	39,978	38,645	43,062	55,237
Net Income	99,015	391,371	346,665	343,906	326,176	378,906	364,937	318,636
Average Shares	163,587	169,437	186,559	204,076	207,606	219,606	223,256	218,534
Balance Sheet								
Current Assets	1,920,073	2,041,070	1,979,320	2,251,799	1,872,558	2,005,587	1,889,067	1,638,706
Total Assets	4,497,599	4,645,223	4,636,572	4,820,604	4,328,417	4,579,063	4,344,599	3,962,828
Current Liabilities	843,821	1,065,558	1,011,206	1,024,147	610,867	830,024	974,727	1,031,687
Long-Term Obligations	...	...	...	...	1,020	450,000	450,000	450,000
Total Liabilities	1,403,145	1,612,021	1,613,271	1,591,224	1,115,364	1,773,872	1,744,356	1,808,663
Stockholders' Equity	3,094,454	3,033,202	3,023,301	3,229,380	3,213,053	2,805,191	2,600,243	2,154,165
Shares Outstanding	161,776	162,454	174,692	193,049	205,079	203,916	209,762	206,793
Statistical Record								
Return on Assets %	8.93	8.41	7.33	7.52	7.32	8.47	8.79	8.89
Return on Equity %	13.07	12.89	11.09	10.68	10.84	13.98	15.35	16.72
EBITDA Margin %	14.99	16.94	18.60	20.41	19.66	15.57	15.25	14.91
Net Margin %	11.98	12.05	10.91	11.52	11.39	11.98	12.87	12.85
Asset Turnover	0.73	0.70	0.67	0.65	0.64	0.71	0.68	0.69
Current Ratio	2.28	1.92	1.96	2.20	3.07	2.42	1.94	1.59
Debt to Equity	...	...	...	...	N.M.	0.16	0.17	0.21
Price Range	34.94-28.37	33.55-26.01	31.77-25.97	32.23-24.39	27.38-15.83	37.87-25.23	40.46-33.12	40.70-25.48
P/E Ratio	14.62-11.87	14.52-11.26	17.08-13.96	19.07-14.43	17.33-10.02	21.76-14.50	24.52-20.07	27.50-17.22

Address: Suite 5, Tower Hill House Le Bordage, St. Peter Port, GY1 3QT Telephone: 148-172-8444	Web Site: www.amdocs.com Officers: Bruce K. Anderson - Chairman Thomas G. O'Brien - Treasurer, Secretary	Auditors: Ernst & Young LLP Investor Contact: 314-212-8328 Transfer Agents: American Stock Transfer & Trust Company, Brookly, NY

AMEREN CORP.

Exchange	Symbol	Price	52Wk Range	Yield	P/E
NYS	AEE	$35.02 (3/28/2013)	35.02-28.55	4.57	N/A

*7 Year Price Score 79.25 *NYSE Composite Index=100 *12 Month Price Score 95.58

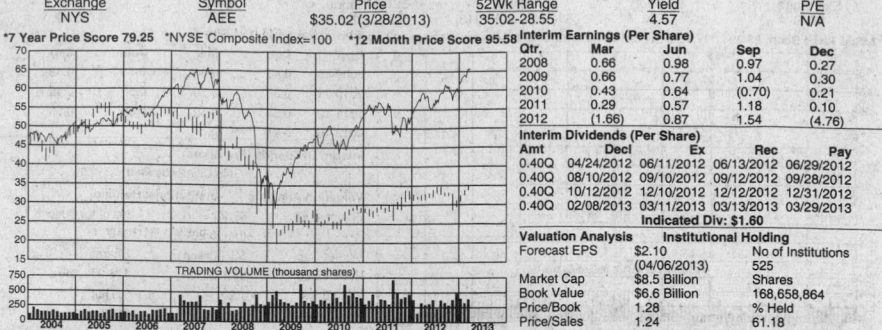

Interim Earnings (Per Share)

Qtr.	Mar	Jun	Sep	Dec
2008	0.66	0.98	0.97	0.27
2009	0.66	0.77	1.04	0.30
2010	0.43	0.64	(0.70)	0.21
2011	0.29	0.57	1.18	0.10
2012	(1.66)	0.87	1.54	(4.76)

Interim Dividends (Per Share)

Amt	Decl	Ex	Rec	Pay
0.40Q	04/24/2012	06/11/2012	06/13/2012	06/29/2012
0.40Q	08/10/2012	09/10/2012	09/12/2012	09/28/2012
0.40Q	10/12/2012	12/10/2012	12/12/2012	12/31/2012
0.40Q	02/08/2013	03/11/2013	03/13/2013	03/29/2013

Indicated Div: $1.60

Valuation Analysis

		Institutional Holding	
Forecast EPS	$2.10	No of Institutions	
	(04/06/2013)	525	
Market Cap	$8.5 Billion	Shares	
Book Value	$6.6 Billion	168,658,864	
Price/Book	1.28	% Held	
Price/Sales	1.24	61.18	

Business Summary: Electric Utilities (MIC: 3.1.1 SIC: 4931 NAIC: 221111)

Ameren is a public utility holding company. Through its subsidiaries, Co. operates electric generation, transmission, and distribution businesses, natural gas transmission and distribution businesses, and merchant generation businesses in Missouri and Illinois. Co. has three reportable segments: Ameren Missouri, consisting of Union Electric Company (UE); Ameren Illinois, which consists of Ameren Illinois Company (AIC); and Merchant Generation, consisting of Ameren Energy Generating Company. At Dec 31 2011, UE supplied electric to 1.2 million customers and natural gas to 127,000 customers, and AIC supplied electric to 1.2 million customers and natural gas to 809,000 customers.

Recent Developments: For the year ended Dec 31 2012, net loss amounted to US$974.0 million versus net income of US$526.0 million in the prior year. Revenues were US$6.83 billion, down 9.3% from US$7.53 billion the year before. Operating loss was unchanged at US$1.24 billion versus the prior year. Direct operating expenses declined 13.7% to US$4.25 billion from US$4.92 billion in the comparable period the year before. Indirect operating expenses increased 179.5% to US$3.82 billion from US$1.37 billion in the equivalent prior-year period.

Prospects: Our evaluation of Ameren Corp. as of Apr. 7, 2013 is the result of our systematic analysis on three basic characteristics: earnings strength, relative valuation, and recent stock price movement. The company has managed to produce a neutral trend in earnings per share over the past 5 quarters and while recent estimates for the company have been raised by analysts, AEE has posted results that fell short of analysts expectations. Based on operating earnings yield, the company is undervalued when compared to all of the companies in our coverage universe. Share price changes over the past year indicates that AEE will perform poorly over the near term.

Financial Data

(US$ in Thousands)	12/31/2012	12/31/2011	12/31/2010	12/31/2009	12/31/2008	12/31/2007	12/31/2006	12/31/2005
Earnings Per Share	(4.01)	2.15	0.58	2.78	2.88	2.98	2.66	3.02
Cash Flow Per Share	6.95	7.78	7.71	8.97	7.28	5.31	6.22	5.83
Tang Book Value Per Share	25.51	30.92	30.42	29.04	29.02	28.41	27.74	26.07
Dividends Per Share	1.600	1.555	1.540	1.540	2.540	2.540	2.540	2.540
Dividend Payout %	...	72.33	265.52	55.40	88.19	85.23	95.49	84.11
Income Statement								
Total Revenue	6,828,000	7,531,000	7,638,000	7,090,000	7,839,000	7,546,000	6,880,000	6,780,000
EBITDA	(397,000)	2,084,000	1,800,000	2,260,000	2,130,000	2,145,000	1,888,000	1,919,000
Depn & Amortn	842,000	829,000	860,000	826,000	762,000	791,000	707,000	631,000
Income Before Taxes	(1,654,000)	836,000	476,000	956,000	971,000	986,000	869,000	1,000,000
Income Taxes	(680,000)	310,000	325,000	332,000	327,000	330,000	284,000	356,000
Net Income	(974,000)	519,000	139,000	612,000	605,000	618,000	547,000	606,000
Average Shares	242,600	241,500	238,800	220,400	210,100	207,400	205,600	200,800
Balance Sheet								
Current Assets	2,369,000	2,295,000	2,894,000	2,842,000	2,515,000	2,480,000	1,874,000	1,818,000
Total Assets	21,835,000	23,645,000	23,515,000	23,790,000	22,657,000	20,728,000	19,578,000	18,162,000
Current Liabilities	1,698,000	1,785,000	1,888,000	1,711,000	3,063,000	2,902,000	2,202,000	1,487,000
Long-Term Obligations	6,626,000	6,677,000	7,313,000	7,943,000	6,554,000	5,691,000	5,285,000	5,354,000
Total Liabilities	15,219,000	15,726,000	15,785,000	15,937,000	15,499,000	13,781,000	12,800,000	11,603,000
Stockholders' Equity	6,616,000	7,919,000	7,730,000	7,853,000	7,158,000	6,947,000	6,778,000	6,559,000
Shares Outstanding	242,600	242,600	240,400	237,400	212,300	208,300	206,600	204,700
Statistical Record								
Return on Assets %	N.M.	2.20	0.59	2.64	2.78	3.07	2.90	3.40
Return on Equity %	N.M.	6.63	1.78	8.15	8.56	9.01	8.20	9.65
EBITDA Margin %	N.M.	27.67	23.57	31.88	27.17	28.43	27.44	28.30
Net Margin %	N.M.	6.89	1.82	8.63	7.72	8.19	7.95	8.94
Asset Turnover	0.30	0.32	0.32	0.31	0.36	0.37	0.36	0.38
Current Ratio	1.40	1.29	1.53	1.66	0.82	0.85	0.85	1.22
Debt to Equity	1.00	0.84	0.95	1.01	0.92	0.82	0.78	0.82
Price Range	34.71-28.55	33.81-25.97	29.83-23.59	34.92-19.76	54.21-27.54	54.93-47.54	55.12-48.04	56.29-47.72
P/E Ratio	...	15.73-12.08	51.43-40.67	12.56-7.11	18.82-9.56	18.43-15.95	20.72-18.06	18.64-15.80
Average Yield %	4.96	5.28	5.77	5.97	6.21	4.88	4.93	4.85

Address: 1901 Chouteau Avenue, St. Louis, MO 63103	Web Site: www.ameren.com	Auditors: PricewaterhouseCoopers LLP
Telephone: 314-621-3222	Officers: Thomas R. Voss - Chairman, President, Chief Executive Officer Martin J. Lyons - Senior Vice President, Chief Financial Officer	Investor Contact: 314-554-3502
Fax: 314-621-2888		Transfer Agents: Ameren Services Company, St. Louis, MO

AMERICAN CAMPUS COMMUNITIES INC

Exchange	Symbol	Price	52Wk Range	Yield	P/E
NYS	ACC	$45.34 (3/28/2013)	47.88-42.51	2.98	69.75

*7 Year Price Score 127.99 *NYSE Composite Index=100 *12 Month Price Score 92.86

Interim Earnings (Per Share)

Qtr.	Mar	Jun	Sep	Dec
2008	0.18	(0.04)	(0.31)	(0.08)
2009	0.01	(0.11)	(0.11)	(0.05)
2010	(0.05)	0.01	0.06	0.23
2011	0.25	0.31	0.02	0.22
2012	0.26	0.16	0.00	0.25

Interim Dividends (Per Share)

Amt	Decl	Ex	Rec	Pay
0.338Q	05/02/2012	05/11/2012	05/15/2012	05/29/2012
0.338Q	08/01/2012	08/10/2012	08/14/2012	08/28/2012
0.338Q	11/01/2012	11/08/2012	11/13/2012	11/27/2012
0.338Q	01/29/2013	02/06/2013	02/08/2013	02/22/2013

Indicated Div: $1.35

Valuation Analysis		Institutional Holding	
Forecast EPS	$0.92	No of Institutions	
	(04/06/2013)	335	
Market Cap	$4.7 Billion	Shares	
Book Value	$2.6 Billion	110,903,992	
Price/Book	1.79	% Held	
Price/Sales	9.66	101.29	

Business Summary: REITs (MIC: 5.3.1 SIC: 6798 NAIC: 525930)

American Campus Communities is a real estate investment trust that owns, manages and develops student housing properties. Co. focuses on the acquisition, design, financing, development, construction management, leasing and management of student housing properties. Co. also provides construction management and development services, primarily for student housing properties owned by colleges and universities, charitable foundations, and others. At Dec 31 2011, Co.'s property portfolio contained 116 properties, with 101 owned off-campus student housing properties, 10 American Campus Equity properties, four on-campus participating properties, and one property containing a retail shopping center.

Recent Developments: For the year ended Dec 31 2012, income from continuing operations increased 36.5% to US$56.7 million from US$41.6 million a year earlier. Net income increased 3.9% to US$60.2 million from US$58.0 million in the prior year. Revenues were US$491.3 million, up 27.0% from US$386.8 million the year before. Revenues from property income rose 27.9% to US$474.2 million from US$370.7 million in the corresponding earlier year.

Prospects: Our evaluation of American Campus Communities Inc. as of Apr. 7, 2013 is the result of our systematic analysis on three basic characteristics: earnings strength, relative valuation, and recent stock price movement. The company has suffered a very negative trend in earnings per share over the past 5 quarters. Because the company lacks sufficient analyst estimate data, we place greater weight on the historical EPS trend as the measure of earnings strength. Based on operating earnings yield, the company is overvalued when compared to all of the companies in our coverage universe. Share price changes over the past year indicates that ACC will perform poorly over the near term.

Financial Data

(US$ in Thousands)	12/31/2012	12/31/2011	12/31/2010	12/31/2009	12/31/2008	12/31/2007	12/31/2006	12/31/2005
Earnings Per Share	0.65	0.80	0.26	(0.28)	(0.34)	(0.07)	1.17	0.65
Cash Flow Per Share	2.39	1.89	2.05	1.63	0.89	1.20	1.86	1.37
Tang Book Value Per Share	25.30	18.90	18.15	17.22	18.60	16.29	16.13	12.99
Dividends Per Share	1.350	1.350	1.350	1.350	1.350	1.350	1.350	1.350
Dividend Payout %	207.69	168.75	519.23				115.38	207.69
Income Statement								
Total Revenue	491,290	390,317	344,991	309,590	235,413	147,135	118,953	87,474
EBITDA	118,644	98,873	89,951	73,048	47,542	55,933	53,960	37,145
Depn & Amortn	6,800	4,100	1,800	10,200	9,400	30,106	25,525	16,471
Income Before Taxes	57,027	43,143	27,684	221	(10,765)	(567)	3,728	4,131
Income Taxes	725	433	570	540	388	756	28	186
Net Income	56,636	56,629	16,210	(12,840)	(13,055)	(1,686)	22,597	9,662
Average Shares	85,309	69,807	59,338	48,706	38,316	26,099	20,967	15,047
Balance Sheet								
Current Assets	72,366	50,679	146,007	101,373	63,343	29,585	93,496	36,753
Total Assets	5,118,962	3,008,582	2,693,484	2,234,981	2,183,909	1,076,296	884,381	550,862
Current Liabilities	56,046	36,884	34,771	26,543	35,440	14,360	13,616	7,983
Long-Term Obligations	2,221,105	1,447,530	1,345,103	1,223,455	1,276,921	543,030	432,294	291,646
Total Liabilities	2,470,581	1,633,366	1,479,522	1,335,951	1,395,925	631,919	514,907	327,635
Stockholders' Equity	2,648,381	1,375,216	1,213,962	899,030	787,984	444,377	369,474	223,227
Shares Outstanding	104,665	72,759	66,875	52,203	42,354	27,275	22,903	17,190
Statistical Record								
Return on Assets %	1.39	1.99	0.66	N.M.	N.M.	N.M.	3.15	2.10
Return on Equity %	2.81	4.37	1.53	N.M.	N.M.	N.M.	7.63	5.35
EBITDA Margin %	24.15	25.33	26.07	23.60	20.20	38.01	45.36	42.46
Net Margin %	11.53	14.51	4.70	N.M.	N.M.	N.M.	19.00	11.05
Asset Turnover	0.12	0.14	0.14	0.14	0.14	0.15	0.17	0.19
Current Ratio	1.29	1.37	4.20	3.82	1.79	2.06	6.87	4.60
Debt to Equity	0.84	1.05	1.11	1.36	1.62	1.22	1.17	1.31
Price Range	47.69-40.86	42.39-30.78	33.39-24.62	28.68-15.61	33.88-16.61	32.39-24.30	29.75-22.71	26.35-19.10
P/E Ratio	73.37-62.86	52.99-38.48	128.42-94.69	...	...	...	25.43-19.41	40.54-29.38
Average Yield %	3.04	3.79	4.68	5.84	4.89	4.70	5.26	5.95

Address: 12700 Hill Country Blvd., Suite T-200, Austin, TX 78738 **Telephone:** 512-732-1000 **Fax:** 512-732-2450	**Web Site:** www.americancampus.com **Officers:** R. D. Burck - Chairman William C. Bayless - President, Chief Executive Officer	**Auditors:** Ernst & Young LLP **Investor Contact:** 512-732-1041 **Transfer Agents:** Wells Fargo Bank, N.A., Shareowner Services, South St. Paul, MN

AMERICAN EAGLE OUTFITTERS, INC.

Exchange	Symbol	Price	52Wk Range	Yield	P/E
NYS	AEO	$18.70 (3/28/2013)	23.80-16.27	2.35	16.12

*7 Year Price Score 97.69   *NYSE Composite Index=100   *12 Month Price Score 93.05

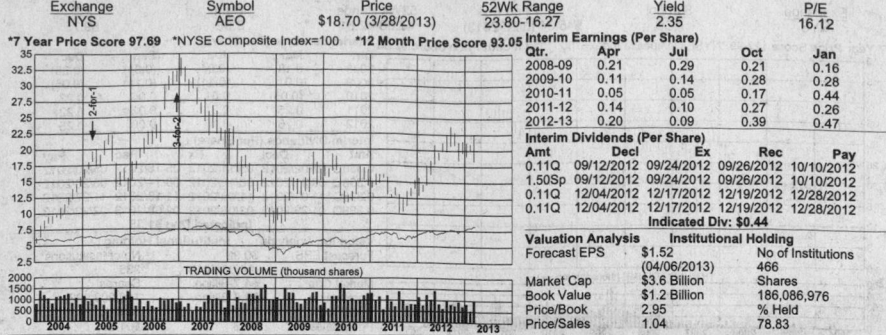

Interim Earnings (Per Share)

Qtr.	Apr	Jul	Oct	Jan
2008-09	0.21	0.29	0.21	0.16
2009-10	0.11	0.14	0.28	0.28
2010-11	0.05	0.05	0.17	0.44
2011-12	0.14	0.10	0.27	0.26
2012-13	0.20	0.09	0.39	0.47

Interim Dividends (Per Share)

Amt	Decl	Ex	Rec	Pay
0.11Q	09/12/2012	09/24/2012	09/26/2012	10/10/2012
1.50Sp	09/12/2012	09/24/2012	09/26/2012	10/10/2012
0.11Q	12/04/2012	12/17/2012	12/19/2012	12/28/2012
0.11Q	12/04/2012	12/17/2012	12/19/2012	12/28/2012

Indicated Div: $0.44

Valuation Analysis

		Institutional Holding	
Forecast EPS	$1.52 (04/06/2013)	No of Institutions	466
Market Cap	$3.6 Billion	Shares	186,086,976
Book Value	$1.2 Billion	% Held	78.83
Price/Book	2.95		
Price/Sales	1.04		

Business Summary: Retail - Apparel and Accessories (MIC: 2.1.5 SIC: 5651 NAIC: 448140)

American Eagle Outfitters is a retailer that operates stores in the U.S. and Canada and online at ae.com®. Through its family of brands, Co. provides clothing, accessories and personal care products. Co.'s brands include the American Eagle Outfitters® (AE), aerie® by American Eagle® (aerie), and 77kids by american eagle® (77kids). Co.'s online business, AEO Direct, consists of its e-commerce operations, ae.com®, aerie.com and 77kids.com, and ships to 77 countries worldwide. As of Jan 28 2012, Co. operated 911 American Eagle Outfitters stores, 158 aerie stand-alone stores and 21 77kids stores. Co. also had 21 franchised stores operated by its franchise partners in 10 countries.

Recent Developments: For the year ended Feb 2 2013, income from continuing operations increased 50.7% to US$264.1 million from US$175.3 million a year earlier. Net income increased 53.0% to US$232.1 million from US$151.7 million in the prior year. Revenues were US$3.48 billion, up 11.4% from US$3.12 billion the year before. Operating income was US$394.6 million versus US$269.3 million in the prior year, an increase of 46.5%. Direct operating expenses rose 5.6% to US$2.09 billion from US$1.98 billion in the comparable period the year before. Indirect operating expenses increased 13.8% to US$995.7 million from US$875.3 million in the equivalent prior-year period.

Prospects: Our evaluation of American Eagle Outfitters Inc. as of Apr. 7, 2013 is the result of our systematic analysis on three basic characteristics: earnings strength, relative valuation, and recent stock price movement. The company has generated a negative trend in earnings per share over the past 5 quarters. However, while recent estimates for the company have been lowered by analysts, AEO has posted results that fell short of analysts expectations. Based on operating earnings yield, the company is undervalued when compared to all of the companies in our coverage universe. Share price changes over the past year indicates that AEO will perform very well over the near term.

Financial Data

(US$ in Thousands)	02/02/2013	01/28/2012	01/29/2011	01/30/2010	01/31/2009	02/02/2008	02/03/2007	01/28/2006
Earnings Per Share	1.16	0.77	0.70	0.81	0.86	1.82	1.70	1.26
Cash Flow Per Share	2.51	1.23	2.02	1.88	1.48	2.15	3.31	2.12
Tang Book Value Per Share	6.08	7.04	6.89	7.58	6.81	6.50	6.36	5.16
Dividends Per Share	2.050	0.440	0.930	0.400	0.400	0.375	0.275	0.183
Dividend Payout %	176.72	57.14	132.86	49.38	46.51	20.60	16.18	14.55
Income Statement								
Total Revenue	3,475,802	3,159,818	2,967,559	2,990,520	2,988,866	3,055,419	2,794,409	2,309,371
EBITDA	524,794	374,944	434,253	377,274	427,843	745,200	716,936	551,023
Depn & Amortn	122,756	137,934	139,169	144,883	130,802	108,819	87,869	74,056
Income Before Taxes	402,038	237,010	295,084	232,391	297,041	636,381	629,067	476,967
Income Taxes	137,940	85,305	113,150	63,369	117,980	236,362	241,708	183,256
Net Income	232,108	151,705	140,647	169,022	179,061	400,019	387,359	294,153
Average Shares	200,665	196,314	201,818	209,512	207,582	220,280	228,384	233,031
Balance Sheet								
Current Assets	1,141,800	1,287,488	1,174,410	1,167,030	925,359	1,020,834	1,198,254	1,080,672
Total Assets	1,756,053	1,950,802	1,879,998	2,138,148	1,963,676	1,867,680	1,987,484	1,605,649
Current Liabilities	435,902	405,401	387,837	408,955	401,763	376,178	460,464	361,623
Total Liabilities	534,866	533,951	528,927	559,631	554,645	527,216	570,172	450,097
Stockholders' Equity	1,221,187	1,416,851	1,351,071	1,578,517	1,409,031	1,340,464	1,417,312	1,155,552
Shares Outstanding	192,604	193,848	194,366	206,832	205,281	204,480	221,284	221,896
Statistical Record								
Return on Assets %	12.32	7.94	7.02	8.26	9.37	20.81	21.21	20.35
Return on Equity %	17.31	10.99	9.63	11.35	13.06	29.09	29.62	27.84
EBITDA Margin %	15.10	11.87	14.63	12.62	14.31	24.39	25.66	23.86
Net Margin %	6.68	4.80	4.74	5.65	5.99	13.09	13.86	12.74
Asset Turnover	1.85	1.65	1.48	1.46	1.56	1.59	1.53	1.60
Current Ratio	2.62	3.18	3.03	2.85	2.30	2.71	2.60	2.99
Price Range	23.80-13.58	16.18-10.17	19.34-11.60	19.62-8.44	23.45-7.11	32.67-17.70	34.34-16.80	22.32-13.33
P/E Ratio	20.52-11.71	21.01-13.21	27.63-16.57	24.22-10.42	27.27-8.27	17.95-9.73	20.20-9.88	17.71-10.58
Average Yield %	10.55	3.21	6.13	2.75	2.75	1.46	1.10	1.03

Address: 77 Hot Metal Street, Pittsburgh, PA 15203-2329 Telephone: 412-432-3300	Web Site: www.ae.com Officers: Jay L. Schottenstein - Chairman Roger S. Markfield - Vice-Chairman, Executive Creative Director; Chief Design Officer	Auditors: Ernst & Young LLP Transfer Agents: National City Bank, Cleveland, OH

AMERICAN ELECTRIC POWER COMPANY, INC.

Exchange	Symbol	Price	52Wk Range	Yield	P/E
NYS	AEP	$48.63 (3/28/2013)	48.63-37.22	3.87	18.70

*7 Year Price Score 98.65 *NYSE Composite Index=100 ***12 Month Price Score 100.91**

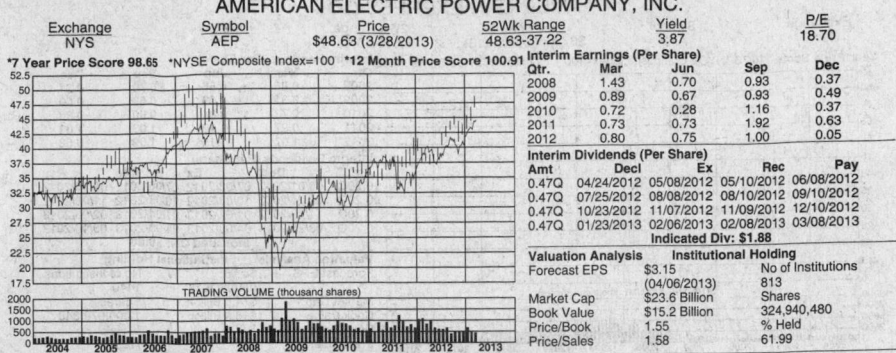

Interim Earnings (Per Share)

Qtr.	Mar	Jun	Sep	Dec
2008	1.43	0.70	0.93	0.37
2009	0.89	0.67	0.93	0.49
2010	0.72	0.28	1.16	0.37
2011	0.73	0.73	1.92	0.63
2012	0.80	0.75	1.00	0.05

Interim Dividends (Per Share)

Amt	Decl	Ex	Rec	Pay
0.47Q	04/24/2012	05/08/2012	05/10/2012	06/08/2012
0.47Q	07/25/2012	08/08/2012	08/10/2012	09/10/2012
0.47Q	10/23/2012	11/07/2012	11/09/2012	12/10/2012
0.47Q	01/23/2013	02/06/2013	02/08/2013	03/08/2013

Indicated Div: $1.88

Valuation Analysis / **Institutional Holding**

Forecast EPS	$3.15	No of Institutions
	(04/06/2013)	813
Market Cap	$23.6 Billion	Shares
Book Value	$15.2 Billion	324,940,480
Price/Book	1.55	% Held
Price/Sales	1.58	61.99

TRADING VOLUME (thousand shares)

Business Summary: Electric Utilities (MIC: 3.1.1 SIC: 4911 NAIC: 221122)

American Electric Power Company is a public utility holding company. Through its subsidiaries, Co. provides electric service, consisting of generation, transmission and distribution, on an integrated basis to its retail customers. The service areas of Co.'s public utility subsidiaries cover portions of the states of Arkansas, Indiana, Kentucky, Louisiana, Michigan, Ohio, Oklahoma, Tennessee, Texas, Virginia and West Virginia. The generating and transmission facilities of Co.'s public utility subsidiaries are interconnected and their operations are coordinated. Transmission networks are interconnected with distribution facilities in the territories served.

Recent Developments: For the year ended Dec 31 2012, net income decreased 35.2% to US$1.26 billion from US$1.95 billion in the prior year. Revenues were US$14.95 billion, down 1.1% from US$15.12 billion the year before. Operating income was US$2.66 billion versus US$2.78 billion in the prior year, a decrease of 4.5%. Direct operating expenses declined 3.7% to US$9.36 billion from US$9.72 billion in the comparable period the year before. Indirect operating expenses increased 12.0% to US$2.93 billion from US$2.62 billion in the equivalent prior-year period.

Prospects: Our evaluation of American Electric Power Company Inc. as of Apr. 7, 2013 is the result of our systematic analysis on three basic characteristics: earnings strength, relative valuation, and recent stock price movement. The company has managed to produce a neutral trend in earnings per share over the past 5 quarters and while recent estimates for the company have been raised by analysts, AEP has posted better than expected results. Based on operating earnings yield, the company is undervalued when compared to all of the companies in our coverage universe. Share price changes over the past year indicates that AEP will perform in line with the market over the near term.

Financial Data
(US$ in Thousands)

	12/31/2012	12/31/2011	12/31/2010	12/31/2009	12/31/2008	12/31/2007	12/31/2006	12/31/2005
Earnings Per Share	2.60	4.02	2.53	2.96	3.42	2.72	2.53	2.08
Cash Flow Per Share	7.83	7.86	5.55	5.40	6.39	5.99	6.93	4.81
Tang Book Value Per Share	31.19	30.18	28.30	27.46	26.30	25.13	23.69	23.04
Dividends Per Share	1.880	1.850	1.710	1.640	1.640	1.580	1.500	1.420
Dividend Payout %	72.31	46.02	67.59	55.41	47.95	58.09	59.29	68.27
Income Statement								
Total Revenue	14,945,000	15,116,000	14,427,000	13,489,000	14,440,000	13,380,000	12,622,000	12,111,000
EBITDA	4,728,000	5,092,000	4,628,000	4,571,000	4,540,000	4,076,000	3,726,000	3,514,000
Depn & Amortn	1,918,000	1,792,000	1,780,000	1,660,000	1,571,000	1,578,000	1,517,000	1,364,000
Income Before Taxes	1,822,000	2,367,000	1,849,000	1,938,000	2,011,000	1,657,000	1,477,000	1,453,000
Income Taxes	604,000	818,000	643,000	575,000	642,000	516,000	485,000	430,000
Net Income	1,259,000	1,946,000	1,214,000	1,360,000	1,380,000	1,089,000	1,002,000	814,000
Average Shares	485,084	482,460	479,601	458,982	403,640	400,198	396,483	391,000
Balance Sheet								
Current Assets	4,589,000	4,182,000	5,016,000	4,756,000	3,775,000	3,052,000	3,588,000	3,945,000
Total Assets	54,367,000	52,223,000	50,455,000	48,348,000	45,155,000	40,366,000	37,987,000	36,172,000
Current Liabilities	6,823,000	6,611,000	6,518,000	5,327,000	6,297,000	5,207,000	5,456,000	5,460,000
Long-Term Obligations	15,586,000	15,083,000	15,502,000	15,757,000	15,536,000	14,202,000	12,429,000	11,073,000
Total Liabilities	39,130,000	37,559,000	36,773,000	35,147,000	34,401,000	30,226,000	28,514,000	27,023,000
Stockholders' Equity	15,237,000	14,664,000	13,682,000	13,201,000	10,754,000	10,140,000	9,473,000	9,149,000
Shares Outstanding	485,668	483,422	480,807	478,054	406,071	400,426	396,674	393,718
Statistical Record								
Return on Assets %	2.36	3.79	2.46	2.91	3.22	2.78	2.70	2.30
Return on Equity %	8.40	13.73	9.03	11.35	13.17	11.10	10.76	9.18
EBITDA Margin %	31.64	33.69	32.08	33.89	31.44	30.46	29.52	29.01
Net Margin %	8.42	12.87	8.41	10.08	9.56	8.14	7.94	6.72
Asset Turnover	0.28	0.29	0.29	0.29	0.34	0.34	0.34	0.34
Current Ratio	0.67	0.63	0.77	0.89	0.60	0.59	0.66	0.72
Debt to Equity	1.02	1.03	1.13	1.19	1.44	1.40	1.31	1.21
Price Range	45.27-37.22	41.65-33.60	37.70-30.97	35.58-24.28	48.52-27.85	50.95-41.86	42.93-32.31	40.25-32.50
P/E Ratio	17.41-14.32	10.36-8.36	14.90-12.24	12.02-8.20	14.19-8.14	18.73-15.39	16.97-12.77	19.35-15.62
Average Yield %	4.59	4.96	4.94	5.49	4.20	3.40	4.08	3.92

Address: 1 Riverside Plaza, Columbus, OH 43215	Web Site: www.aep.com	Auditors: Deloitte & Touche LLP
Telephone: 614-716-1000	Officers: Nicholas K. Akins - President, Chief Executive Officer Robert P. Powers - Executive Vice President, Chief Operating Officer, Division Officer	Investor Contact: 614-716-2819
Fax: 614-223-1823		Transfer Agents: Computershare Trust Company, N.A., Providence, RI

AMERICAN EXPRESS CO.

Exchange	Symbol	Price	52Wk Range	Yield	P/E
NYS	AXP	$67.46 (3/28/2013)	67.46-53.43	1.19	17.34

*7 Year Price Score 110.78 *NYSE Composite Index=100 *12 Month Price Score 99.42

TRADING VOLUME (thousand shares)

Interim Earnings (Per Share)

Qtr.	Mar	Jun	Sep	Dec
2008	0.85	0.56	0.70	0.21
2009	0.31	0.09	0.53	0.60
2010	0.73	0.84	0.90	0.88
2011	0.97	1.10	1.03	1.01
2012	1.07	1.15	1.09	0.58

Interim Dividends (Per Share)

Amt	Decl	Ex	Rec	Pay
0.20Q	05/01/2012	07/03/2012	07/06/2012	08/10/2012
0.20Q	09/24/2012	10/03/2012	10/05/2012	11/09/2012
0.20Q	11/20/2012	01/02/2013	01/04/2013	02/08/2013
0.20Q	03/25/2013	04/03/2013	04/05/2013	05/10/2013

Indicated Div: $0.80

Valuation Analysis

		Institutional Holding	
Forecast EPS	$4.76	No of Institutions	
	(04/06/2013)	1440	
Market Cap	$74.5 Billion	Shares	
Book Value	$18.9 Billion	1,000,979,840	
Price/Book	3.95	% Held	
Price/Sales	2.20	79.58	

Business Summary: Credit & Lending (MIC: 5.4.1 SIC: 6141 NAIC: 522210)

American Express is a bank holding company. Through its subsidiaries, Co. is a global services company. Co.'s range of products and services includes: charge and credit card products; expense management products and services; consumer and business travel services; stored value products such as Travelers Cheques and other prepaid products; network services; merchant acquisition and processing, servicing and settlement, and point-of-sale, marketing and information products and services for merchants; and fee services, including fraud prevention services and the design of customer loyalty and rewards programs.

Recent Developments: For the year ended Dec 31 2012, income from continuing operations decreased 8.5% to US$4.48 billion from US$4.90 billion a year earlier. Net income decreased 9.2% to US$4.48 billion from US$4.94 billion in the prior year. Net interest income increased 5.8% to US$4.63 billion from US$4.38 billion in the prior year. Provision for loan losses was US$1.99 billion versus US$1.11 billion in the prior year, an increase of 79.0%. Non-interest income rose 5.3% to US$26.95 billion from US$25.59 billion, while non-interest expense advanced 5.7% to US$23.14 billion.

Prospects: Our evaluation of American Express Co. as of Apr. 7, 2013 is the result of our systematic analysis on three basic characteristics: earnings strength, relative valuation, and recent stock price movement. The company has managed to produce a neutral trend in earnings per share over the past 5 quarters and while recent estimates for the company have been mixed, AXP has posted better than expected results. Based on operating earnings yield, the company is undervalued when compared to all of the companies in our coverage universe. Share price changes over the past year indicates that AXP will perform poorly over the near term.

Financial Data

(US$ in Thousands)	12/31/2012	12/31/2011	12/31/2010	12/31/2009	12/31/2008	12/31/2007	12/31/2006	12/31/2005
Earnings Per Share	3.89	4.12	3.35	1.54	2.33	3.36	2.99	2.97
Cash Flow Per Share	6.22	8.89	7.82	5.47	7.49	7.23	7.43	6.52
Tang Book Value Per Share	13.31	12.43	10.54	9.53	7.61	9.52	8.77	8.50
Dividends Per Share	0.780	0.720	0.720	0.720	0.720	0.600	0.540	0.480
Dividend Payout %	20.05	17.48	21.49	46.75	30.90	17.86	18.06	16.16
Income Statement								
Total Revenue	33,808,000	32,282,000	30,242,000	26,730,000	31,920,000	31,557,000	27,136,000	24,267,000
EBITDA	7,442,000	7,874,000	6,881,000	3,911,000	4,293,000	6,214,000	7,209,000	5,770,000
Depn & Amortn	991,000	918,000	917,000	1,070,000	712,000	648,000	645,000	602,000
Income Before Taxes	6,451,000	6,956,000	5,964,000	2,841,000	3,581,000	5,566,000	5,328,000	4,248,000
Income Taxes	1,969,000	2,057,000	1,907,000	704,000	710,000	1,518,000	1,599,000	1,027,000
Net Income	4,482,000	4,935,000	4,057,000	2,130,000	2,699,000	4,012,000	3,707,000	3,734,000
Average Shares	1,141,000	1,184,000	1,195,000	1,171,000	1,157,000	1,196,000	1,238,000	1,258,000
Balance Sheet								
Current Assets	68,164,000	69,002,000	57,143,000	53,746,000	57,118,000	53,742,000	46,807,000	42,623,000
Total Assets	153,140,000	153,337,000	147,042,000	124,088,000	126,074,000	149,830,000	127,853,000	113,960,000
Current Liabilities	57,724,000	56,903,000	48,450,000	43,534,000	39,340,000	48,030,000	55,797,000	55,211,000
Long-Term Obligations	58,973,000	59,570,000	66,416,000	52,338,000	60,041,000	55,285,000	42,747,000	30,781,000
Total Liabilities	134,254,000	134,543,000	130,812,000	109,682,000	114,233,000	138,801,000	117,342,000	103,411,000
Stockholders' Equity	18,886,000	18,794,000	16,230,000	14,406,000	11,841,000	11,029,000	10,511,000	10,549,000
Shares Outstanding	1,105,000	1,164,000	1,197,000	1,192,000	1,160,000	1,158,000	1,199,000	1,241,000
Statistical Record								
Return on Assets %	2.92	3.29	2.99	1.70	1.95	2.89	3.07	2.44
Return on Equity %	23.72	28.18	26.49	16.23	23.54	37.25	35.20	28.11
EBITDA Margin %	22.01	24.39	22.75	14.63	13.45	19.69	26.57	23.78
Net Margin %	13.26	15.29	13.42	7.97	8.46	12.71	13.66	15.39
Asset Turnover	0.22	0.21	0.22	0.21	0.23	0.23	0.22	0.16
Current Ratio	1.18	1.21	1.18	1.23	1.45	1.12	0.84	0.77
Debt to Equity	3.12	3.17	4.09	3.63	5.07	5.01	4.07	2.92
Price Range	61.05-48.24	53.59-42.36	48.05-36.79	41.83-10.26	52.02-17.23	65.55-50.84	61.90-50.62	52.84-43.60
P/E Ratio	15.69-12.40	13.01-10.28	14.34-10.98	27.16-6.66	22.33-7.39	19.51-15.13	20.70-16.93	17.79-14.68
Average Yield %	1.39	1.52	1.73	2.67	1.90	1.01	0.99	1.00

Address: World Financial Center, 200 Vesey Street, New York, NY 10285 Telephone: 212-640-2000	Web Site: www.americanexpress.com Officers: Kenneth I. Chenault - Chairman, Chief Executive Officer Edward P. Gilligan - Vice-Chairman, Division Officer	Auditors: PricewaterhouseCoopers LLP Investor Contact: 212-640-2000 Transfer Agents: BNY Mellon Shareowner Services, Pittsburg, PA

AMERICAN FINANCIAL GROUP, INC (HOLDING CO.)

Exchange	Symbol	Price	52Wk Range	Yield	P/E
NYS	AFG	$47.38 (3/28/2013)	47.38-36.58	1.65	9.31

*7 Year Price Score 114.65 *NYSE Composite Index=100 *12 Month Price Score 103.36

Interim Earnings (Per Share)

Qtr.	Mar	Jun	Sep	Dec
2008	0.64	0.52	0.18	0.33
2009	0.88	1.09	1.09	1.38
2010	0.93	0.97	1.21	1.22
2011	0.79	0.52	0.94	1.09
2012	1.14	1.01	2.39	0.59

Interim Dividends (Per Share)

Amt	Decl	Ex	Rec	Pay
0.195Q	10/01/2012	10/11/2012	10/15/2012	10/25/2012
0.25Q	12/06/2012	12/13/2012	12/17/2012	12/24/2012
0.195Q	01/02/2013	01/11/2013	01/15/2013	01/25/2013
0.195Q	04/01/2013	04/11/2013	04/15/2013	04/25/2013

Indicated Div: $0.78

Valuation Analysis

		Institutional Holding	
Forecast EPS	$3.83	No of Institutions	
	(04/06/2013)	302	
Market Cap	$4.2 Billion	Shares	
Book Value	$4.6 Billion	65,564,168	
Price/Book	0.92	% Held	
Price/Sales	0.83	53.63	

Business Summary: General Insurance (MIC: 5.2.1 SIC: 6331 NAIC: 524126)

American Financial Group is a holding company. Through its subsidiaries, Co. is engaged in property and casualty insurance. Co. operates in four segments: Property and Casualty Insurance, which covers property and transportation (inland and ocean marine, agricultural-related and commercial automobile), specialty casualty (executive and professional liability, umbrella and excess liability, general liability, targeted programs and worker's compensation) and specialty financial (fidelity and surety, and lease and loan services); Annuity, which sells fixed and fixed-indexed annuities in the related markets; Run-off long-term care and life; and Other, which includes commercial real estate.

Recent Developments: For the year ended Dec 31 2012, net income increased 26.0% to US$402.0 million from US$319.0 million in the prior year. Revenues were US$5.06 billion, up 6.6% from US$4.75 billion the year before. Net premiums earned were US$3.17 billion versus US$3.19 billion in the prior year, a decrease of 0.8%.

Prospects: Our evaluation of American Financial Group Inc. as of Apr. 7, 2013 is the result of our systematic analysis on three basic characteristics: earnings strength, relative valuation, and recent stock price movement. The company has generated a negative trend in earnings per share over the past 5 quarters. However, while recent estimates for the company have been lowered by analysts, AFG has posted better than expected results. Based on operating earnings yield, the company is undervalued when compared to all of the companies in our coverage universe. Share price changes over the past year indicates that AFG will perform poorly over the near term.

Financial Data
(US$ in Thousands)

	12/31/2012	12/31/2011	12/31/2010	12/31/2009	12/31/2008	12/31/2007	12/31/2006	12/31/2005
Earnings Per Share	5.09	3.33	4.33	4.45	1.67	3.10	3.75	1.75
Cash Flow Per Share	8.65	6.58	7.91	7.90	8.48	6.70	8.20	8.83
Tang Book Value Per Share	49.37	44.55	40.73	31.52	19.72	25.04	23.14	19.56
Dividends Per Share	0.970	0.662	0.575	0.520	0.500	0.400	0.367	0.333
Dividend Payout %	19.06	19.89	13.28	11.69	29.94	12.90	9.78	19.08
Income Statement								
Premium Income	3,165,000	3,189,000	3,001,000	2,855,900	3,301,800	3,126,400	2,917,800	2,737,503
Total Revenue	5,062,000	4,750,000	4,497,000	4,320,600	4,292,700	4,404,700	4,250,100	4,038,283
Benefits & Claims	2,779,000	2,623,000	2,269,000	1,982,800	2,377,100	2,149,500	2,109,600	2,317,225
Income Before Taxes	537,000	560,000	689,000	812,900	315,900	638,900	697,600	356,814
Income Taxes	135,000	240,000	266,000	282,200	115,900	225,800	235,700	115,843
Net Income	488,000	343,000	479,000	519,300	195,800	383,200	453,400	206,580
Average Shares	95,900	102,900	110,500	116,800	116,700	123,200	120,500	117,769
Balance Sheet								
Total Assets	39,171,000	36,042,000	32,454,000	27,683,300	26,427,500	25,807,500	25,101,100	22,815,992
Total Liabilities	34,593,000	31,497,000	27,984,000	23,902,200	23,937,500	22,761,400	22,172,200	20,358,450
Stockholders' Equity	4,578,000	4,545,000	4,470,000	3,781,100	2,490,000	3,046,100	2,928,900	2,457,542
Shares Outstanding	88,979	97,846	105,168	113,386	115,599	113,499	119,303	117,101
Statistical Record								
Return on Assets %	1.29	1.00	1.59	1.92	0.75	1.51	1.89	0.91
Return on Equity %	10.67	7.61	11.61	16.56	7.05	12.83	16.83	8.45
Loss Ratio %	87.80	82.25	75.61	69.43	71.99	68.75	72.30	84.65
Net Margin %	9.64	7.22	10.65	12.02	4.56	8.70	10.67	5.12
Price Range	40.25-36.58	37.30-30.09	32.61-24.30	26.42-13.04	32.00-15.41	36.50-25.57	36.35-24.83	25.92-18.68
P/E Ratio	7.91-7.19	11.20-9.04	7.53-5.61	5.94-2.93	19.16-9.23	11.77-8.25	9.69-6.62	14.81-10.67
Average Yield %	2.54	1.94	1.97	2.38	1.92	1.24	1.24	1.52

Address: 301 East Fourth Street, Cincinnati, OH 45202 Telephone: 513-579-2121 Fax: 513-579-0108	Web Site: www.AFGinc.com Officers: Carl H. Lindner - Chairman Carl H. Lindner - Co-President, Co-Chief Executive Officer	Auditors: Ernst & Young LLP Investor Contact: 513-579-6739 Transfer Agents: American Stock Transfer & Trust Company, New York, NY

AMERICAN GREETINGS CORP.

Exchange	Symbol	Price	52Wk Range	Yield	P/E
NYS	AM	$16.10 (3/28/2013)	17.38-12.66	3.73	N/A

*7 Year Price Score 73.70   *NYSE Composite Index=100   *12 Month Price Score 96.20

Interim Earnings (Per Share)

Qtr.	May	Aug	Nov	Feb
2009-10	0.25	0.59	0.75	0.44
2010-11	0.75	0.21	0.78	0.36
2011-12	0.78	0.35	0.50	(0.21)
2012-13	0.20	(0.13)	(0.03)	...

Interim Dividends (Per Share)

Amt	Decl	Ex	Rec	Pay
0.15Q	06/15/2012	07/02/2012	07/05/2012	07/16/2012
0.15Q	09/10/2012	09/27/2012	10/01/2012	10/11/2012
0.15Q	12/07/2012	12/17/2012	12/19/2012	12/28/2012
0.15Q	03/08/2013	03/25/2013	03/27/2013	04/08/2013

Indicated Div: $0.60

Valuation Analysis / **Institutional Holding**

Forecast EPS	$0.80
	(04/05/2013)
Market Cap	$509.4 Million
Book Value	$643.2 Million
Price/Book	0.79
Price/Sales	0.29

No of Institutions	210
Shares	35,569,512
% Held	
	95.07

Business Summary: Printing (MIC: 7.5.5 SIC: 2771 NAIC: 511191)

American Greetings is engaged in the design, manufacture and sale of everyday and seasonal greeting cards and other social expression products. Co. manufactures or sells greeting cards, gift packaging, party goods, stationery and giftware in North America, primarily in the U.S. and Canada, and throughout the world, primarily in the U.K., Australia and New Zealand. Co. also engages in design and character licensing and manufacture custom display fixtures for its products and products of others. At Feb 29 2012, Co. operated in four business segments: North American Social Expression Products, International Social Expression Products, AG Interactive and non-reportable operating segments.

Recent Developments: For the quarter ended Nov 23 2012, net loss amounted to US$809,000 versus net income of US$20.2 million in the year-earlier quarter. Revenues were US$506.8 million, up 9.0% from US$465.0 million the year before. Operating income was US$436,000 versus US$33.2 million in the prior-year quarter, a decrease of 98.7%. Direct operating expenses rose 5.9% to US$244.1 million from US$230.6 million in the comparable period the year before. Indirect operating expenses increased 30.4% to US$262.3 million from US$201.2 million in the equivalent prior-year period.

Prospects: Our evaluation of American Greetings Corp. as of Apr. 7, 2013 is the result of our systematic analysis on three basic characteristics: earnings strength, relative valuation, and recent stock price movement. The company has generated a negative trend in earnings per share over the past 5 quarters. However, while recent estimates for the company have been mixed, AM has posted results that fell short of analysts expectations. Based on operating earnings yield, the company is undervalued when compared to all of the companies in our coverage universe. Share price changes over the past year indicates that AM will perform poorly over the near term.

Financial Data

(US$ in Thousands)	9 Mos	6 Mos	3 Mos	02/29/2012	02/28/2011	02/28/2010	02/28/2009	02/29/2008
Earnings Per Share	(0.17)	0.36	0.84	1.42	2.11	2.03	(4.89)	1.52
Cash Flow Per Share	5.67	3.83	4.35	2.93	4.50	5.00	1.57	4.48
Tang Book Value Per Share	20.33	20.84	20.10	19.74	17.82	15.32	12.39	13.50
Dividends Per Share	0.600	0.600	0.600	0.600	0.560	0.480	0.480	0.400
Dividend Payout %	...	166.67	71.43	42.25	26.54	23.65	...	26.32
Income Statement								
Total Revenue	1,293,756	786,942	393,106	1,695,144	1,592,568	1,635,858	1,690,738	1,776,451
EBITDA	51,362	36,237	26,127	184,116	217,008	185,229	(212,518)	180,119
Depn & Amortn	36,095	23,310	11,469	34,210	36,465	39,640	42,843	43,903
Income Before Taxes	2,250	4,349	10,420	97,815	156,007	120,954	(274,933)	123,968
Income Taxes	63	1,353	3,170	40,617	68,989	39,380	(47,174)	40,648
Net Income	2,187	2,996	7,250	57,198	87,018	81,574	(227,759)	83,003
Average Shares	31,877	33,753	36,154	40,288	41,244	40,159	46,543	54,506
Balance Sheet								
Current Assets	761,510	648,112	546,817	640,959	700,924	677,424	561,395	669,370
Total Assets	1,704,719	1,572,402	1,488,471	1,549,464	1,532,402	1,529,651	1,433,788	1,804,428
Current Liabilities	423,872	348,535	296,817	305,081	342,545	372,043	343,405	452,421
Long-Term Obligations	356,832	280,181	225,181	225,181	232,688	328,723	389,473	200,518
Total Liabilities	1,061,499	913,647	809,037	822,006	783,491	893,587	904,599	861,017
Stockholders' Equity	643,220	658,755	679,434	727,458	748,911	636,064	529,189	943,411
Shares Outstanding	31,637	31,614	33,805	36,853	40,407	39,480	40,542	48,757
Statistical Record								
Return on Assets %	N.M.	0.84	2.09	3.70	5.68	5.51	N.M.	4.62
Return on Equity %	N.M.	1.82	4.35	7.73	12.57	14.00	N.M.	8.46
EBITDA Margin %	3.97	4.60	6.65	10.86	13.63	11.32	N.M.	10.14
Net Margin %	0.17	0.38	1.84	3.37	5.46	4.99	N.M.	4.67
Asset Turnover	1.08	1.09	1.11	1.10	1.04	1.10	1.04	0.99
Current Ratio	1.80	1.86	1.84	2.10	2.05	1.82	1.63	1.48
Debt to Equity	0.55	0.43	0.33	0.31	0.31	0.52	0.74	0.21
Price Range	17.59-12.50	21.29-12.50	24.55-12.50	24.60-12.50	25.92-18.36	24.00-3.24	19.72-3.73	28.98-17.93
P/E Ratio	...	59.14-34.72	29.23-14.88	17.32-8.80	12.28-8.70	11.82-1.60	...	19.07-11.80
Average Yield %	3.98	3.86	3.38	3.04	2.63	3.30	3.57	1.65

Address: One American Road, Cleveland, OH 44144	Web Site: www.americangreetings.com	Auditors: Ernst & Young LLP
Telephone: 216-252-7300	Officers: Morry Weiss - Chairman Zev Weiss - Chief Executive Officer	Investor Contact: 216-252-4864
Fax: 216-255-6777		Transfer Agents: Wells Fargo Shareowner Services, St. Paul, MN

AMERICAN INTERNATIONAL GROUP INC

Exchange	Symbol	Price	52Wk Range	Yield	P/E
NYS	AIG	$38.82 (3/28/2013)	39.58-27.21	N/A	19.03

*7 Year Price Score 7.02   *NYSE Composite Index=100   *12 Month Price Score 104.28

Interim Earnings (Per Share)

Qtr.	Mar	Jun	Sep	Dec
2008	(61.80)	(41.20)	(181.00)	(468.80)
2009	(39.60)	2.30	0.68	(65.56)
2010	2.16	(3.96)	(17.62)	16.48
2011	(0.35)	1.00	(2.16)	11.03
2012	1.71	1.33	1.13	(2.17)

Interim Dividends (Per Share)

Amt	Decl	Ex	Rec	Pay
0.20Q	11/14/2007	03/05/2008	03/07/2008	03/21/2008
0.20Q	03/12/2008	06/04/2008	06/06/2008	06/20/2008
0.22Q	05/08/2008	09/03/2008	09/05/2008	09/19/2008
1-for-20	...	06/30/2009	...	...

Valuation Analysis   **Institutional Holding**

Forecast EPS	$3.38	No of Institutions
	(04/06/2013)	1151
Market Cap	$57.3 Billion	Shares
Book Value	$98.0 Billion	1,345,265,408
Price/Book	0.58	% Held
Price/Sales	0.87	N/A

Business Summary: General Insurance (MIC: 5.2.1 SIC: 6331 NAIC: 524126)

American International Group is a holding company. Co. is an insurance company that provides property casualty insurance, life insurance, retirement products, mortgage insurance and other financial services serving commercial, institutional and individual customers. Co. has two reportable segments, AIG Property Casualty, which provides commercial insurance and consumer insurance products for commercial, institutional and individual customers; and AIG Life and Retirement, which provides life insurance and retirement services products. Co.'s other operations include its mortgage guaranty business operated by United Guaranty Corp., a provider of private residential mortgage guaranty insurance.

Recent Developments: For the year ended Dec 31 2012, income from continuing operations decreased 60.3% to US$7.75 billion from US$19.54 billion a year earlier. Net income decreased 82.7% to US$3.70 billion from US$21.33 billion in the prior year. Revenues were US$65.66 billion, up 9.8% from US$59.81 billion the year before. Net premiums earned were US$38.01 billion versus US$38.99 billion in the prior year, a decrease of 2.5%. Net investment income rose 37.9% to US$20.34 billion from US$14.76 billion a year ago.

Prospects: Our evaluation of American International Group Inc. as of Apr. 7, 2013 is the result of our systematic analysis on three basic characteristics: earnings strength, relative valuation, and recent stock price movement. The company has suffered a very negative trend in earnings per share over the past 5 quarters and while recent estimates for the company have been raised by analysts, AIG has posted better than expected results. Based on operating earnings yield, the company is undervalued when compared to all of the companies in our coverage universe. Share price changes over the past year indicates that AIG will perform in line with the market over the near term.

Financial Data
(US$ in Thousands)

	12/31/2012	12/31/2011	12/31/2010	12/31/2009	12/31/2008	12/31/2007	12/31/2006	12/31/2005
Earnings Per Share	2.04	9.44	11.60	(90.48)	(756.80)	47.80	107.20	79.80
Cash Flow Per Share	2.17	0.02	123.80	137.33	5.72	272.12	52.37	193.59
Tang Book Value Per Share	66.38	55.33	85.45	N.M.	340.10	683.80	716.90	603.93
Dividends Per Share	...	...	...	...	12.400	14.600	12.600	12.600
Dividend Payout %	...	...	...	...	...	11.75	19.79	15.79
Income Statement								
Premium Income	38,011,000	38,990,000	48,029,000	64,702,000	83,505,000	79,302,000	74,083,000	70,209,000
Total Revenue	65,656,000	64,237,000	77,301,000	96,004,000	11,104,000	110,064,000	113,194,000	108,905,000
Benefits & Claims	31,977,000	33,449,000	45,874,000	61,436,000	63,299,000	66,115,000	59,706,000	63,711,000
Income Before Taxes	9,322,000	(1,065,000)	17,936,000	(13,648,000)	(108,761,000)	8,943,000	21,687,000	15,213,000
Income Taxes	1,570,000	(18,036,000)	5,859,000	(1,878,000)	(8,374,000)	1,455,000	6,537,000	4,258,000
Net Income	3,438,000	17,798,000	7,786,000	(10,949,000)	(99,289,000)	6,200,000	14,048,000	10,477,000
Average Shares	1,687,226	1,799,458	136,649	135,324	131,700	129,900	131,150	131,350
Balance Sheet								
Total Assets	548,633,000	555,773,000	683,443,000	847,585,000	860,418,000	1,060,505,000	979,414,000	853,370,000
Total Liabilities	450,631,000	450,822,000	598,124,000	777,761,000	807,708,000	964,604,000	877,546,000	766,867,000
Stockholders' Equity	98,002,000	104,951,000	85,319,000	69,824,000	52,710,000	95,901,000	101,868,000	86,503,000
Shares Outstanding	1,476,321	1,896,821	140,463	135,070	134,483	126,479	130,059	129,832
Statistical Record								
Return on Assets %	0.62	2.87	1.02	N.M.	N.M.	0.61	1.53	1.27
Return on Equity %	3.38	18.71	10.04	N.M.	N.M.	6.27	14.92	12.52
Loss Ratio %	84.13	85.79	95.51	94.95	75.80	83.37	80.59	90.74
Net Margin %	5.24	27.71	10.07	(11.40)	(894.17)	5.63	12.41	9.62
Price Range	37.21-23.54	61.18-20.10	59.38-22.16	50.23-7.00	1186.40-27.00	1453.00-1026.60	1456.20-1155.20	1462.40-1007.00
P/E Ratio	18.24-11.54	6.48-2.13	5.12-1.91	...	...	30.40-21.48	13.58-10.78	18.33-12.62
Average Yield %	...	...	...	...	2.04	1.18	0.96	1.03

Address: 180 Maiden Lane, New York, NY 10038	Web Site: www.aigcorporate.com	Auditors: PricewaterhouseCoopers LLP
Telephone: 212-770-7000	Officers: Robert S. Miller - Chairman Robert Herman Benmosche - President, Chief Executive Officer	Transfer Agents: Wells Fargo Bank, N.A., Shareowner Services, St. Paul, MN
Fax: 212-785-2175		

AMERICAN STATES WATER CO.

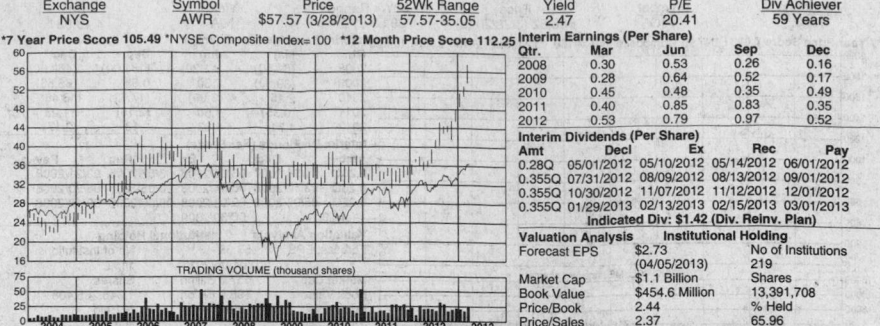

Exchange	Symbol	Price	52Wk Range	Yield	P/E	Div Achiever
NYS	AWR	$57.57 (3/28/2013)	57.57-35.05	2.47	20.41	59 Years

*7 Year Price Score 105.49 *NYSE Composite Index=100 *12 Month Price Score 112.25

Interim Earnings (Per Share)

Qtr.	Mar	Jun	Sep	Dec
2008	0.30	0.53	0.26	0.16
2009	0.28	0.64	0.52	0.17
2010	0.45	0.48	0.35	0.49
2011	0.40	0.85	0.83	0.35
2012	0.53	0.79	0.97	0.52

Interim Dividends (Per Share)

Amt	Decl	Ex	Rec	Pay
0.28Q	05/01/2012	05/10/2012	05/14/2012	06/01/2012
0.355Q	07/31/2012	08/09/2012	08/13/2012	09/01/2012
0.355Q	10/30/2012	11/07/2012	11/12/2012	12/01/2012
0.355Q	01/29/2013	02/13/2013	02/15/2013	03/01/2013

Indicated Div: $1.42 (Div. Reinv. Plan)

Valuation Analysis | **Institutional Holding**

Forecast EPS	$2.73	No of Institutions
	(04/05/2013)	219
Market Cap	$1.1 Billion	Shares
Book Value	$454.6 Million	13,391,708
Price/Book	2.44	% Held
Price/Sales	2.37	65.96

TRADING VOLUME (thousand shares)

Business Summary: Water Utilities (MIC: 3.2.1 SIC: 4941 NAIC: 221310)

American States Water is a holding company. Co. is the parent company of Golden State Water Company (GSWC) and American States Utility Services, Inc. (ASUS) and its subsidiaries. Co. has three reportable segments: water, electric and contracted services. Within the segments, Co. has three principal business units: water and electric service utility operations conducted through GSWC; and contracted services conducted through ASUS and its subsidiaries. As of Dec 31 2011, GSWC served 255,935 water customers and 23,508 electric customers.

Recent Developments: For the year ended Dec 31 2012, income from continuing operations increased 28.9% to US$54.1 million from US$42.0 million a year earlier. Net income increased 18.1% to US$54.1 million from US$45.9 million in the prior year. Revenues were US$466.9 million, up 11.2% from US$419.9 million the year before. Operating income was US$111.1 million versus US$95.1 million in the prior year, an increase of 16.8%. Indirect operating expenses increased 9.5% to US$355.8 million from US$324.8 million in the equivalent prior-year period.

Prospects: Our evaluation of American States Water Co. as of Apr. 7, 2013 is the result of our systematic analysis on three basic characteristics: earnings strength, relative valuation, and recent stock price movement. The company has generated a negative trend in earnings per share over the past 5 quarters and while recent estimates for the company have been raised by analysts, AWR has posted better than expected results. Based on operating earnings yield, the company is about fairly valued when compared to all of the companies in our coverage universe. Share price changes over the past year indicates that AWR will perform very well over the near term.

Financial Data
(US$ in Thousands)

	12/31/2012	12/31/2011	12/31/2010	12/31/2009	12/31/2008	12/31/2007	12/31/2006	12/31/2005
Earnings Per Share	2.82	2.43	1.77	1.62	1.26	1.61	1.33	1.57
Cash Flow Per Share	5.33	4.29	2.89	4.02	3.59	2.98	3.04	3.25
Tang Book Value Per Share	23.57	21.69	20.20	19.16	17.68	16.88	15.96	15.02
Dividends Per Share	1.270	1.100	1.040	1.010	1.000	0.955	0.910	0.900
Dividend Payout %	45.04	45.27	58.76	62.35	79.37	59.32	68.42	57.32
Income Statement								
Total Revenue	466,908	419,274	398,942	360,973	318,718	301,370	268,629	236,197
EBITDA	154,759	133,257	111,523	103,272	86,439	96,972	83,337	82,094
Depn & Amortn	43,234	38,349	38,167	33,557	31,562	28,941	26,272	21,846
Income Before Taxes	90,093	72,086	54,126	48,356	35,384	48,820	38,762	46,649
Income Taxes	35,945	30,076	23,035	18,825	13,379	20,790	15,681	21,945
Net Income	54,148	45,859	33,197	29,531	22,005	28,030	23,081	26,766
Average Shares	19,131	18,837	18,736	18,188	17,394	17,177	17,101	16,809
Balance Sheet								
Current Assets	184,033	165,601	204,984	96,015	90,614	63,015	64,436	68,866
Total Assets	1,280,943	1,238,362	1,192,035	1,113,293	1,061,287	963,898	936,955	876,777
Current Liabilities	93,697	104,370	178,842	99,706	137,397	94,251	85,903	77,585
Long-Term Obligations	332,463	340,395	299,839	305,866	266,536	267,226	267,833	268,405
Total Liabilities	826,364	829,696	814,494	753,863	750,784	661,769	653,221	612,683
Stockholders' Equity	454,579	408,666	377,541	359,430	310,503	302,129	283,734	264,094
Shares Outstanding	19,237	18,788	18,630	18,532	17,301	17,231	17,049	16,797
Statistical Record								
Return on Assets %	4.29	3.77	2.88	2.72	2.17	2.95	2.55	3.17
Return on Equity %	12.51	11.67	9.01	8.82	7.16	9.57	8.43	10.38
EBITDA Margin %	33.15	31.78	27.95	28.61	27.12	32.18	31.02	34.76
Net Margin %	11.60	10.94	8.32	8.18	6.90	9.30	8.59	11.33
Asset Turnover	0.37	0.35	0.35	0.33	0.31	0.32	0.30	0.28
Current Ratio	1.96	1.59	1.15	0.96	0.66	0.67	0.75	0.89
Debt to Equity	0.73	0.83	0.79	0.85	0.86	0.88	0.94	1.02
Price Range	47.98-34.29	36.32-31.27	39.06-31.60	38.54-29.78	41.91-27.70	45.45-33.82	42.39-30.68	34.06-24.64
P/E Ratio	17.01-12.16	14.95-12.87	22.07-17.85	23.79-18.38	33.26-21.98	28.23-21.01	31.87-23.07	21.69-15.69
Average Yield %	3.15	3.20	2.98	2.94	2.86	2.46	2.47	3.12

Address: 630 East Foothill Boulevard, San Dimas, CA 91773-1212 Telephone: 909-394-3600 Fax: 909-394-1382	Web Site: www.aswater.com Officers: Lloyd E. Ross - Chairman Robert J. Sprowls - President, Chief Executive Officer	Auditors: PricewaterhouseCoopers LLP Investor Contact: 909-394-3600 Transfer Agents: Mellon Investor Services LLC, Jersey City, NJ

AMERICAN TOWER CORP

Exchange	Symbol	Price	52Wk Range	Yield	P/E
NYS	AMT	$76.92 (3/28/2013)	79.90-61.62	1.35	48.07

*7 Year Price Score 137.51 *NYSE Composite Index=100   ***12 Month Price Score 97.49**

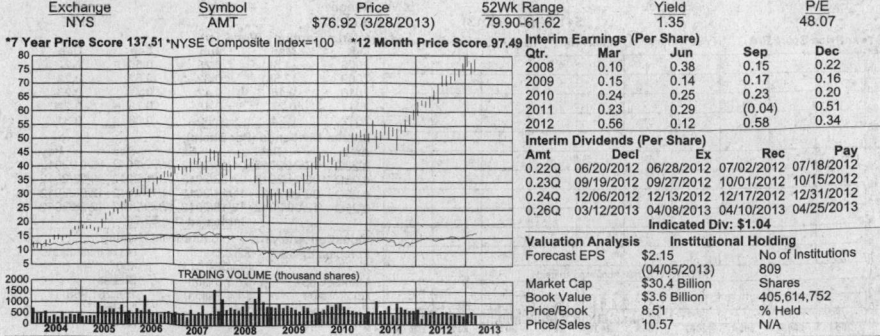

Interim Earnings (Per Share)

Qtr.	Mar	Jun	Sep	Dec
2008	0.10	0.38	0.15	0.22
2009	0.15	0.14	0.17	0.16
2010	0.24	0.25	0.23	0.20
2011	0.23	0.29	(0.04)	0.51
2012	0.56	0.12	0.58	0.34

Interim Dividends (Per Share)

Amt	Decl	Ex	Rec	Pay
0.22Q	06/20/2012	06/28/2012	07/02/2012	07/18/2012
0.23Q	09/19/2012	09/27/2012	10/01/2012	10/15/2012
0.24Q	12/06/2012	12/13/2012	12/17/2012	12/31/2012
0.26Q	03/12/2013	04/08/2013	04/10/2013	04/25/2013

Indicated Div: $1.04

Valuation Analysis | **Institutional Holding**

Forecast EPS	$2.15 (04/05/2013)	No of Institutions 809
Market Cap	$30.4 Billion	Shares 405,614,752
Book Value	$3.6 Billion	% Held N/A
Price/Book	8.51	
Price/Sales	10.57	

Business Summary: Services (MIC: 6.1.2 SIC: 4899 NAIC: 517212)

American Tower is a holding company. Co. operates as a wireless and broadcast communications infrastructure that owns, operates and develops communications sites. Co.'s primary business is leasing antenna space on multi-tenant communications sites to wireless service providers, radio and television broadcast companies, wireless data providers, government agencies, municipalities and tenants in a range of other industries. Co. also provides tower-related services domestically, including site acquisition, zoning and permitting services and structural analysis services. Co.'s segments include: domestic rental and management; international rental and management; and network development services.

Recent Developments: For the year ended Dec 31 2012, income from continuing operations increased 55.6% to US$594.0 million from US$381.8 million a year earlier. Net income increased 55.6% to US$594.0 million from US$381.8 million in the prior year. Revenues were US$2.88 billion, up 17.7% from US$2.44 billion the year before. Operating income was US$1.12 billion versus US$920.1 million in the prior year, an increase of 21.7%. Direct operating expenses rose 16.3% to US$722.5 million from US$621.0 million in the comparable period the year before. Indirect operating expenses increased 14.6% to US$1.03 billion from US$902.4 million in the equivalent prior-year period.

Prospects: Our evaluation of Americann Tower REIT, Inc. as of Apr. 7, 2013 is the result of our systematic analysis on three basic characteristics: earnings strength, relative valuation, and recent stock price movement. The company has suffered a very negative trend in earnings per share over the past 5 quarters. However, while recent estimates for the company have been lowered by analysts, AMT has posted results that fell short of analysts expectations. Based on operating earnings yield, the company is overvalued when compared to all of the companies in our coverage universe. Share price changes over the past year indicates that AMT will perform well over the near term.

Financial Data

(US$ in Thousands)	12/31/2012	12/31/2011	12/31/2010	12/31/2009	12/31/2008	12/31/2007	12/31/2006	12/31/2005
Earnings Per Share	1.60	0.99	0.92	0.61	0.84	0.13	0.06	(0.57)
Cash Flow Per Share	3.57	2.95	2.55	2.11	1.95	1.68	1.46	1.31
Tang Book Value Per Share	N.M.	N.M.	N.M.	N.M.	N.M.	N.M.	0.88	0.74
Dividends Per Share	0.900	0.350	...	...	...	...	...	...
Dividend Payout %	56.25	35.35	...	...	...	...	...	...
Income Statement								
Total Revenue	2,875,960	2,443,532	1,985,335	1,724,114	1,593,504	1,456,594	1,317,385	944,786
EBITDA	1,492,921	1,150,557	1,068,807	1,079,815	1,022,596	894,326	801,067	535,143
Depn & Amortn	411,900	353,400	286,000	424,457	414,758	530,717	537,770	458,832
Income Before Taxes	701,294	506,895	556,025	421,487	371,920	152,840	70,864	(127,474)
Income Taxes	107,304	125,080	182,489	182,565	135,509	59,809	41,768	4,003
Net Income	637,283	396,462	372,936	246,595	347,246	56,316	27,484	(171,590)
Average Shares	399,287	400,195	404,072	406,948	418,357	426,079	436,217	302,510
Balance Sheet								
Current Assets	829,528	842,771	1,404,174	651,356	473,680	245,674	486,022	225,878
Total Assets	14,089,129	12,232,430	10,368,014	8,512,668	8,211,665	8,130,457	8,613,219	8,768,220
Current Liabilities	632,178	779,591	542,195	391,244	302,645	317,378	569,629	453,216
Long-Term Obligations	8,693,345	7,134,492	5,512,492	4,141,060	4,331,309	4,283,467	3,289,109	3,451,276
Total Liabilities	10,516,028	8,945,210	6,866,570	5,197,586	5,220,343	5,108,365	4,228,303	4,241,640
Stockholders' Equity	3,573,101	3,287,220	3,501,444	3,315,082	2,991,322	3,022,092	4,384,916	4,526,580
Shares Outstanding	395,091	393,642	398,677	401,596	396,976	399,518	424,672	412,654
Statistical Record								
Return on Assets %	4.83	3.51	3.95	2.95	4.24	0.67	0.32	N.M.
Return on Equity %	18.53	11.68	10.94	7.82	11.52	1.52	0.62	N.M.
EBITDA Margin %	51.91	47.09	53.84	62.63	64.17	61.40	60.81	56.64
Net Margin %	22.16	16.22	18.78	14.30	21.79	3.87	2.09	N.M.
Asset Turnover	0.22	0.22	0.21	0.21	0.19	0.17	0.15	0.14
Current Ratio	1.31	1.08	2.59	1.66	1.57	0.77	0.85	0.50
Debt to Equity	2.43	2.17	1.57	1.25	1.45	1.42	0.75	0.76
Price Range	77.27-58.81	60.70-46.35	53.14-38.86	43.47-25.69	45.72-20.14	46.34-37.18	38.27-27.30	28.09-16.46
P/E Ratio	48.29-36.76	61.31-46.82	57.76-42.24	71.26-42.11	54.43-23.98	356.46-286.00	637.83-455.00	...
Average Yield %	1.31	0.66	...	...	...	...	...	...

Address: 116 Huntington Avenue, Boston, MA 02116
Telephone: 617-375-7500

Web Site: www.americantower.com
Officers: James D. Taiclet - Chairman, President, Chief Executive Officer Thomas A. Bartlett - Executive Vice President, Chief Financial Officer, Treasurer

Auditors: Deloitte & Touche LLP
Investor Contact: 617-375-7500
Transfer Agents: Computershare, Jersey City, NJ

AMERICAN WATER WORKS CO, INC.

Exchange	Symbol	Price	52Wk Range	Yield	P/E
NYS	AWK	$41.44 (3/28/2013)	41.44-33.01	2.41	20.62

*7 Year Price Score N/A *NYSE Composite Index=100 ***12 Month Price Score 99.74**

Interim Earnings (Per Share)

Qtr.	Mar	Jun	Sep	Dec
2008	(4.58)	0.28	0.55	0.22
2009	(2.58)	0.32	0.52	0.23
2010	0.18	0.42	0.71	0.23
2011	0.27	0.48	0.78	0.22
2012	0.24	0.60	0.86	0.31

Interim Dividends (Per Share)

Amt	Decl	Ex	Rec	Pay
0.23Q	02/24/2012	04/18/2012	04/20/2012	06/01/2012
0.25Q	05/11/2012	07/03/2012	07/06/2012	09/03/2012
0.25Q	09/20/2012	11/14/2012	11/16/2012	12/03/2012
0.25Q	12/06/2012	12/18/2012	12/20/2012	12/28/2012
		Indicated Div: $1.00		

Valuation Analysis

		Institutional Holding	
Forecast EPS	$2.22	No of Institutions	
	(04/06/2013)	450	
Market Cap	$7.3 Billion	Shares	
Book Value	$4.4 Billion	156,261,968	
Price/Book	1.65	% Held	
Price/Sales	2.55	N/A	

TRADING VOLUME (thousand shares)

Business Summary: Water Utilities (MIC: 3.2.1 SIC: 4941 NAIC: 221310)
American Water Works Company is a holding company. Co. conducts substantially all of its business operations through its subsidiaries. As of Dec 31 2011, Co. provided an estimated 15.0 million people with drinking water, wastewater and other water-related services in over 30 states and two Canadian provinces. Co. has two operating segments: Regulated Businesses, which involves the ownership of subsidiaries that provide water and wastewater utility services to residential, commercial, industrial and other customers, including sale for resale and public authority customers; and Market-Based Operations, which provides services that are not subject to economic regulation.

Recent Developments: For the year ended Dec 31 2012, income from continuing operations increased 22.7% to US$374.3 million from US$304.9 million a year earlier. Net income increased 15.7% to US$358.1 million from US$309.6 million in the prior year. Revenues were US$2.88 billion, up 7.9% from US$2.67 billion the year before. Operating income was US$925.0 million versus US$803.1 million in the prior year, an increase of 15.2%. Indirect operating expenses increased 4.8% to US$1.95 billion from US$1.86 billion in the equivalent prior-year period.

Prospects: Our evaluation of American Water Works Co. Inc. as of Apr. 7, 2013 is the result of our systematic analysis on three basic characteristics: earnings strength, relative valuation, and recent stock price movement. The company has generated a negative trend in earnings per share over the past 5 quarters and while recent estimates for the company have been mixed, AWK has posted results that fell short of analysts expectations. Based on operating earnings yield, the company is about fairly valued when compared to all of the companies in our coverage universe. Share price changes over the past year indicates that AWK will perform in line with the market over the near term.

Financial Data

(US$ in Thousands)	12/31/2012	12/31/2011	12/31/2010	12/31/2009	12/31/2008	12/31/2007	12/31/2006
Earnings Per Share	2.01	1.75	1.53	(1.39)	(3.52)	(2.14)	(1.01)
Cash Flow Per Share	5.40	4.61	4.43	3.55	3.44	2.96	...
Tang Book Value Per Share	18.28	17.31	16.44	15.75	15.02	13.03	...
Dividends Per Share	1.210	0.900	0.860	0.820	0.400	...	...
Dividend Payout %	60.20	51.43	56.21	...	...	...	...
Income Statement							
Total Revenue	2,876,889	2,666,236	2,710,677	2,440,703	2,336,928	2,214,215	2,093,067
EBITDA	1,233,328	1,066,028	1,024,036	428,995	79,656	280,175	497,755
Depn & Amortn	314,639	268,987	275,844	262,825	267,763	263,737	249,355
Income Before Taxes	631,258	503,680	449,436	(111,665)	(450,594)	(255,519)	(108,938)
Income Taxes	257,008	198,751	181,609	121,418	111,827	86,756	46,912
Net Income	358,070	309,613	267,827	(233,083)	(562,421)	(342,826)	(162,243)
Average Shares	177,671	176,531	175,124	168,164	159,967	160,000	160,000
Balance Sheet							
Current Assets	499,447	1,397,659	534,307	499,127	417,675	430,354	...
Total Assets	14,718,976	14,776,391	14,079,773	13,452,651	13,231,818	12,951,327	...
Current Liabilities	994,832	1,489,105	774,506	607,392	1,104,760	774,489	...
Long-Term Obligations	5,190,509	5,339,947	5,410,271	5,288,180	4,624,063	4,674,837	...
Total Liabilities	10,273,988	10,536,007	9,947,501	9,447,235	9,125,260	8,404,713	...
Stockholders' Equity	4,444,988	4,240,384	4,132,272	4,005,416	4,106,558	4,546,614	...
Shares Outstanding	176,988	175,664	174,996	174,630	160,000	160,000	160,000
Statistical Record							
Return on Assets %	2.42	2.15	1.95	N.M.	N.M.	...	...
Return on Equity %	8.22	7.40	6.58	N.M.	N.M.	...	...
EBITDA Margin %	42.87	39.98	37.78	17.58	3.41	12.65	23.78
Net Margin %	12.45	11.61	9.88	N.M.	N.M.	N.M.	N.M.
Asset Turnover	0.19	0.18	0.20	0.18	0.18	...	...
Current Ratio	0.50	0.94	0.69	0.82	0.38	0.56	...
Debt to Equity	1.17	1.26	1.31	1.32	1.13	1.03	...
Price Range	38.35-31.38	32.55-25.23	25.73-19.92	22.68-16.53	23.37-17.16	...	...
P/E Ratio	19.08-15.61	18.60-14.42	16.82-13.02	...	...	...	...
Average Yield %	3.43	3.12	3.84	4.20	1.93	...	...

Address: 1025 Laurel Oak Road, Voorhees, NJ 08043 Telephone: 856-346-8200	Web Site: www.amwater.com Officers: George MacKenzie - Chairman Jeffry E. Sterba - President, Chief Executive Officer	Auditors: PricewaterhouseCoopers LLP Investor Contact: 856-566-4005 Transfer Agents: American Stock Transfer & Trust Company, Brooklyn, N Y

52

AMERIPRISE FINANCIAL INC

Exchange	Symbol	Price	52Wk Range	Yield	P/E
NYS	AMP	$73.65 (3/28/2013)	74.88-45.46	2.44	15.94

*7 Year Price Score 107.58 *NYSE Composite Index=100 *12 Month Price Score 109.80

Interim Earnings (Per Share)

Qtr.	Mar	Jun	Sep	Dec
2008	0.82	0.93	(0.32)	(1.63)
2009	0.58	0.41	1.00	0.91
2010	0.81	0.98	1.32	1.08
2011	0.94	1.23	1.13	1.08
2012	1.05	0.99	0.79	1.78

Interim Dividends (Per Share)

Amt	Decl	Ex	Rec	Pay
0.35Q	04/23/2012	05/02/2012	05/04/2012	05/18/2012
0.35Q	07/25/2012	08/01/2012	08/03/2012	08/17/2012
0.45Q	10/24/2012	11/01/2012	11/05/2012	11/16/2012
0.45Q	01/30/2013	02/07/2013	02/11/2013	02/22/2013

Indicated Div: $1.80

Valuation Analysis

	Institutional Holding	
Forecast EPS	$6.54 (04/06/2013)	No of Institutions 649
Market Cap	$15.0 Billion	Shares 202,791,600
Book Value	$9.1 Billion	% Held 82.71
Price/Book	1.65	
Price/Sales	1.47	

TRADING VOLUME (thousand shares)

Business Summary: Wealth Management (MIC: 5.5.2 SIC: 6282 NAIC: 523930)

Ameriprise Financial is a holding company. Through its subsidiaries, Co. is engaged in providing financial planning, products and services for its clients. Co.'s operating segments include: Advice & Wealth Management, which provides financial planning and advice, as well as brokerage and banking services to retail clients through Co.'s affiliated advisors; Asset Management, which provides investment advice and investment products to retail and institutional clients; Annuities, which provides variable and fixed annuity products of RiverSource Life companies; Protection, which provides protection products including life, disability income and property-casualty insurance; and Corporate & Other.

Recent Developments: For the year ended Dec 31 2012, income from continuing operations decreased 15.6% to US$903.0 million from US$1.07 billion a year earlier. Net income decreased 10.8% to US$901.0 million from US$1.01 billion in the prior year. Revenues were US$10.22 billion, up 0.2% from US$10.19 billion the year before. Direct operating expenses rose 5.4% to US$5.66 billion from US$5.37 billion in the comparable period the year before. Indirect operating expenses decreased 1.7% to US$3.32 billion from US$3.38 billion in the equivalent prior-year period.

Prospects: Our evaluation of Ameriprise Financial Inc. as of Apr. 7, 2013 is the result of our systematic analysis on three basic characteristics: earnings strength, relative valuation, and recent stock price movement. The company has managed to produce a neutral trend in earnings per share over the past 5 quarters and while recent estimates for the company have been raised by analysts, AMP has posted better than expected results. Based on operating earnings yield, the company is undervalued when compared to all of the companies in our coverage universe. Share price changes over the past year indicates that AMP will perform well over the near term.

Financial Data

(US$ in Millions)	12/31/2012	12/31/2011	12/31/2010	12/31/2009	12/31/2008	12/31/2007	12/31/2006	12/31/2005
Earnings Per Share	4.62	4.37	4.18	2.95	(0.17)	3.39	2.54	2.32
Cash Flow Per Share	6.86	9.02	7.91	(5.19)	8.98	3.58	2.51	3.82
Tang Book Value Per Share	44.58	46.21	43.47	36.35	28.53	34.29	32.83	30.76
Dividends Per Share	1.430	0.870	0.710	0.680	0.640	0.560	0.440	0.110
Dividend Payout %	30.95	19.91	16.99	23.05	...	16.52	17.32	4.74
Income Statement								
Total Revenue	10,217	10,192	9,976	7,805	6,970	8,654	8,140	7,484
EBITDA	1,666	1,845	2,051	1,229	(93)	1,274	1,106	962
Depn & Amortn	152	143	167	182	169	146	128	144
Income Before Taxes	1,238	1,385	1,594	920	(371)	1,016	862	745
Income Taxes	335	355	334	183	(333)	202	166	187
Net Income	1,029	1,076	1,097	722	(38)	814	631	574
Average Shares	222	246	262	244	224	239	248	247
Balance Sheet								
Current Assets	7,265	8,869	9,946	9,165	11,998	8,609	6,913	5,713
Total Assets	134,729	133,986	131,192	113,774	95,676	109,230	104,172	93,121
Current Liabilities	8,351	11,419	10,335	9,472	9,116	7,388	8,509	2,780
Long-Term Obligations	7,384	7,571	7,852	2,249	2,027	2,018	2,225	1,833
Total Liabilities	125,637	123,731	120,467	104,501	89,498	101,420	96,247	85,434
Stockholders' Equity	9,092	10,255	10,725	9,273	6,178	7,810	7,925	7,687
Shares Outstanding	203	221	246	255	216	227	241	249
Statistical Record								
Return on Assets %	0.76	0.81	0.90	0.69	N.M.	0.76	0.64	0.62
Return on Equity %	10.61	10.26	10.97	9.35	N.M.	10.35	8.08	7.98
EBITDA Margin %	16.31	18.10	20.56	15.75	N.M.	14.72	13.59	12.85
Net Margin %	10.07	10.56	11.00	9.25	N.M.	9.41	7.75	7.67
Asset Turnover	0.08	0.08	0.08	0.07	0.07	0.08	0.08	0.08
Current Ratio	0.87	0.78	0.96	0.97	1.32	1.17	0.81	2.06
Debt to Equity	0.81	0.74	0.73	0.24	0.33	0.26	0.28	0.24
Price Range	63.52-45.46	64.73-37.34	57.97-35.83	39.52-13.80	57.12-12.37	66.95-54.10	55.30-40.69	43.90-32.39
P/E Ratio	13.75-9.84	14.81-8.54	13.87-8.57	13.40-4.68	...	19.75-15.96	21.77-16.02	18.92-13.96
Average Yield %	2.61	1.63	1.57	2.44	1.57	0.93	0.95	0.29

Address: 1099 Ameriprise Financial Center, Minneapolis, MN 55474 **Telephone:** 612-671-3131	**Web Site:** www.ameriprise.com **Officers:** James M. Cracchiolo - Chairman, Chief Executive Officer Kim Michelle Sharan - Executive Vice President, Chief Marketing Officer	**Auditors:** PricewaterhouseCoopers LLP **Investor Contact:** 612-671-2080 **Transfer Agents:** Computershare Trust Company, N.A, Providence, RI

AMERISOURCEBERGEN CORP.

Exchange	Symbol	Price	52Wk Range	Yield	P/E
NYS	ABC	$51.45 (3/28/2013)	51.45-35.95	1.63	17.74

*7 Year Price Score 127.93 *NYSE Composite Index=100 *12 Month Price Score 107.93

Interim Earnings (Per Share)

Qtr.	Dec	Mar	Jun	Sep
2009-10	0.52	0.63	0.57	0.50
2010-11	0.57	0.77	0.66	0.54
2011-12	0.62	0.81	0.71	0.67
2012-13	0.71	...	...	...

Interim Dividends (Per Share)

Amt	Decl	Ex	Rec	Pay
0.13Q	05/10/2012	05/17/2012	05/21/2012	06/04/2012
0.13Q	08/09/2012	08/17/2012	08/21/2012	09/04/2012
0.21Q	11/01/2012	11/15/2012	11/19/2012	12/03/2012
0.21Q	02/04/2013	02/13/2013	02/15/2013	03/04/2013

Indicated Div: $0.84

Valuation Analysis / **Institutional Holding**

Forecast EPS	$3.05	No of Institutions
	(04/06/2013)	627
Market Cap	$11.8 Billion	Shares
Book Value	$2.3 Billion	234,322,720
Price/Book	5.06	% Held
Price/Sales	0.15	81.19

Business Summary: Pharmaceuticals (MIC: 4.1.1 SIC: 5122 NAIC: 424210)

AmerisourceBergen is a pharmaceutical services company. Co. distributes a range of brand-name pharmaceuticals, generic pharmaceuticals, over-the-counter healthcare products, home healthcare supplies and equipment, and related services to healthcare providers including acute care hospitals and health systems, independent and chain retail pharmacies, mail order pharmacies, medical and dialysis clinics, physicians and physician group practices, long-term care and other alternate site pharmacies, and other customers. Co. also provides pharmacy services to certain drug patients, and furnishes healthcare providers and pharmaceutical manufacturers with related services such as pharmacy automation.

Recent Developments: For the quarter ended Dec 31 2012, net income increased 4.0% to US$168.6 million from US$162.1 million in the year-earlier quarter. Revenues were US$21.47 billion, up 5.7% from US$20.31 billion the year before. Operating income was US$287.3 million versus US$281.4 million in the prior-year quarter, an increase of 2.1%. Direct operating expenses rose 5.4% to US$20.79 billion from US$19.73 billion in the comparable period the year before. Indirect operating expenses increased 27.2% to US$384.7 million from US$302.5 million in the equivalent prior-year period.

Prospects: Our evaluation of AmerisourceBergen Corp. as of Apr. 7, 2013 is the result of our systematic analysis on three basic characteristics: earnings strength, relative valuation, and recent stock price movement. The company has managed to produce a neutral trend in earnings per share over the past 5 quarters. However, while recent estimates for the company have been mixed, ABC has posted better than expected results. Based on operating earnings yield, the company is undervalued when compared to all of the companies in our coverage universe. Share price changes over the past year indicates that ABC will perform poorly over the near term.

Financial Data

(US$ in Thousands)	3 Mos	09/30/2012	09/30/2011	09/30/2010	09/30/2009	09/30/2008	09/30/2007	09/30/2006
Earnings Per Share	2.90	2.80	2.54	2.22	1.66	0.77	1.25	1.13
Cash Flow Per Share	2.72	5.15	4.29	3.93	2.61	2.29	3.26	1.97
Tang Book Value Per Share	N.M.	N.M.	0.01	0.39	N.M.	N.M.	1.44	3.95
Dividends Per Share	0.600	0.520	0.430	0.320	0.210	0.150	0.100	0.050
Dividend Payout %	20.69	18.57	16.93	14.41	12.65	19.48	8.00	4.44
Income Statement								
Total Revenue	21,466,314	79,489,596	80,217,558	77,953,979	71,759,990	70,189,733	66,074,312	61,203,145
EBITDA	330,678	1,377,084	1,312,105	1,183,016	956,993	901,073	898,952	833,224
Depn & Amortn	43,396	118,529	104,743	82,753	74,612	75,239	81,614	80,131
Income Before Taxes	268,584	1,163,131	1,130,641	1,027,769	824,074	761,338	785,050	740,629
Income Taxes	106,359	454,945	424,017	391,021	312,222	292,274	291,282	272,617
Net Income	168,611	718,986	706,624	636,748	503,397	250,559	469,167	467,714
Average Shares	235,992	256,903	277,417	287,246	302,754	324,920	375,772	414,892
Balance Sheet								
Current Assets	11,022,199	10,987,151	11,217,623	10,748,350	9,953,753	8,669,761	8,714,300	9,210,407
Total Assets	15,495,532	15,444,126	14,982,671	14,434,843	13,572,740	12,217,786	12,310,064	12,783,920
Current Liabilities	11,435,737	11,214,482	10,855,120	9,906,344	9,479,610	8,167,589	7,857,036	7,459,188
Long-Term Obligations	1,396,107	1,446,770	972,863	1,343,158	1,176,933	1,187,412	1,227,298	1,093,931
Total Liabilities	13,158,297	12,987,414	12,115,813	11,480,546	10,856,271	9,507,741	9,210,344	8,642,763
Stockholders' Equity	2,337,235	2,456,712	2,866,858	2,954,297	2,716,469	2,710,045	3,099,720	4,141,157
Shares Outstanding	229,920	235,394	260,991	277,521	287,922	312,430	338,952	392,701
Statistical Record								
Return on Assets %	4.61	4.71	4.80	4.55	3.90	2.04	3.74	3.87
Return on Equity %	27.68	26.94	24.28	22.46	18.55	8.60	12.96	11.11
EBITDA Margin %	1.54	1.73	1.64	1.52	1.33	1.28	1.36	1.36
Net Margin %	0.79	0.90	0.88	0.82	0.70	0.36	0.71	0.76
Asset Turnover	5.12	5.21	5.45	5.57	5.56	5.71	5.27	5.07
Current Ratio	0.96	0.98	1.03	1.08	1.05	1.06	1.11	1.23
Debt to Equity	0.60	0.59	0.34	0.45	0.43	0.44	0.40	0.26
Price Range	43.91-35.95	42.08-35.57	43.09-30.66	32.88-21.62	22.38-13.74	23.86-18.82	27.34-21.58	23.57-17.80
P/E Ratio	15.14-12.40	15.03-12.70	16.96-12.07	14.81-9.74	13.48-8.28	30.99-24.45	21.88-17.26	20.86-15.76
Average Yield %	1.54	1.37	1.16	1.14	1.18	0.71	0.42	0.24

Address: 1300 Morris Drive, Chesterbrook, PA 19087-5594	**Web Site:** www.amerisourcebergen.com	**Auditors:** Ernst & Young LLP
Telephone: 610-727-7000	**Officers:** Richard C. Gozon - Chairman Steven H. Collis - President, Chief Executive Officer	**Investor Contact:** 610-727-7199
Fax: 610-647-0141		**Transfer Agents:** ComputerShare Fund Company, N.A., Providence, RI

AMETEK, INC.

Exchange	Symbol	Price	52Wk Range	Yield	P/E
NYS	AME	$43.36 (3/28/2013)	43.36-30.40	0.55	23.06

*7 Year Price Score 146.17 *NYSE Composite Index=100 *12 Month Price Score 107.55

Interim Earnings (Per Share)

Qtr.	Mar	Jun	Sep	Dec
2008	0.28	0.27	0.29	0.18
2009	0.24	0.21	0.18	0.21
2010	0.24	0.28	0.32	0.33
2011	0.37	0.39	0.40	0.42
2012	0.45	0.47	0.47	0.49

Interim Dividends (Per Share)

Amt	Decl	Ex	Rec	Pay
3-for-2	05/01/2012	07/02/2012	06/15/2012	06/29/2012
0.06Q	07/27/2012	09/12/2012	09/14/2012	09/28/2012
0.06Q	10/26/2012	12/05/2012	12/07/2012	12/21/2012
0.06Q	02/07/2013	03/12/2013	03/14/2013	03/28/2013

Indicated Div: $0.24

Valuation Analysis

		Institutional Holding	
Forecast EPS	$2.12	No of Institutions	
	(04/05/2013)	492	
Market Cap	$10.6 Billion	Shares	
Book Value	$2.5 Billion	219,701,184	
Price/Book	4.16	% Held	
Price/Sales	3.17	85.65	

TRADING VOLUME (thousand shares)

Business Summary: Electrical Equipment (MIC: 7.3.1 SIC: 3621 NAIC: 335312)

Ametek is a manufacturer of electronic instruments and electromechanical devices with operations in North America, Europe, Asia and South America. Co. markets its products through two groups: the Electronic Instruments Group, which provides monitoring, testing, calibration and display devices for the process, aerospace, power and industrial markets; and the Electromechanical Group, which produces engineered electrical connectors for electronic applications, motion control solutions, metals and alloys and electric motors, blowers and heat exchangers. End markets include aerospace and defense, medical devices, office equipment, factory automation, mass transit and other industrial markets.

Recent Developments: For the year ended Dec 31 2012, net income increased 19.4% to US$459.1 million from US$384.5 million in the prior year. Revenues were US$3.33 billion, up 11.5% from US$2.99 billion the year before. Operating income was US$745.9 million versus US$635.9 million in the prior year, an increase of 17.3%. Direct operating expenses rose 10.1% to US$2.15 billion from US$1.96 billion in the comparable period the year before. Indirect operating expenses increased 9.0% to US$434.2 million from US$398.2 million in the equivalent prior-year period.

Prospects: Our evaluation of Ametek Inc. as of Apr. 7, 2013 is the result of our systematic analysis on three basic characteristics: earnings strength, relative valuation, and recent stock price movement. The company has managed to produce a neutral trend in earnings per share over the past 5 quarters and while recent estimates for the company have remained steady, AME has posted better than expected results. Based on operating earnings yield, the company is about fairly valued when compared to all of the companies in our coverage universe. Share price changes over the past year indicates that AME will perform well over the near term.

Financial Data

(US$ in Thousands)	12/31/2012	12/31/2011	12/31/2010	12/31/2009	12/31/2008	12/31/2007	12/31/2006	12/31/2005
Earnings Per Share	1.88	1.58	1.17	0.85	1.02	0.94	0.76	0.59
Cash Flow Per Share	2.53	2.12	1.77	1.52	1.03	1.17	0.96	0.71
Dividends Per Share	0.220	0.160	0.120	0.107	0.107	0.107	0.080	0.071
Dividend Payout %	11.70	10.13	10.23	12.57	10.44	11.32	10.53	12.06
Income Statement								
Total Revenue	3,334,213	2,989,914	2,470,952	2,098,355	2,531,135	2,136,850	1,819,290	1,434,457
EBITDA	791,624	675,244	519,192	405,592	475,711	425,600	344,775	272,084
Depn & Amortn	53,677	48,873	45,420	42,209	45,843	42,290	38,922	34,963
Income Before Taxes	662,475	556,642	406,250	294,633	366,216	336,444	263,686	204,208
Income Taxes	203,343	172,178	122,318	88,863	119,264	108,424	81,752	63,565
Net Income	459,132	384,464	283,932	205,770	246,952	228,020	181,934	140,643
Average Shares	243,986	243,162	241,326	242,662	241,746	242,055	239,868	238,649
Balance Sheet								
Current Assets	1,164,743	1,059,119	974,492	969,430	954,586	952,204	684,063	556,307
Total Assets	5,190,056	4,319,490	3,818,915	3,246,032	3,055,542	2,745,700	2,130,876	1,780,600
Current Liabilities	879,969	628,875	550,859	424,802	447,513	640,750	480,900	405,792
Long-Term Obligations	1,133,121	1,123,416	1,071,360	955,880	1,093,243	666,953	518,267	475,309
Total Liabilities	2,654,905	2,266,685	2,043,711	1,679,008	1,767,770	1,504,993	1,164,204	975,048
Stockholders' Equity	2,535,151	2,052,805	1,775,204	1,567,024	1,287,772	1,240,707	966,672	805,552
Shares Outstanding	243,395	240,557	241,064	242,738	240,136	241,578	238,632	237,857
Statistical Record								
Return on Assets %	9.63	9.45	8.04	6.53	8.49	9.35	9.30	8.79
Return on Equity %	19.96	20.09	16.99	14.42	19.48	20.66	20.53	19.20
EBITDA Margin %	23.74	22.58	21.01	19.33	18.79	19.92	18.95	18.97
Net Margin %	13.77	12.86	11.49	9.81	9.76	10.67	10.00	9.80
Asset Turnover	0.70	0.73	0.70	0.67	0.87	0.88	0.93	0.90
Current Ratio	1.32	1.68	1.77	2.28	2.13	1.49	1.42	1.37
Debt to Equity	0.45	0.55	0.60	0.61	0.85	0.54	0.54	0.59
Price Range	38.02-28.17	31.18-20.95	27.47-16.07	17.49-10.96	23.58-12.50	21.29-13.75	14.97-11.91	13.17-10.07
P/E Ratio	20.22-14.98	19.73-13.26	23.48-13.74	20.58-12.89	23.12-12.25	22.65-14.63	19.70-15.66	22.33-17.07
Average Yield %	0.65	0.59	0.60	0.72	0.56	0.61	0.60	0.60

Address: 1100 Cassatt Road, P.O. Box 1764, Berwyn, PA 19312-1177 Telephone: 610-647-2121 Fax: 610-647-0211	Web Site: www.ametek.com Officers: Frank S. Hermance - Chairman, Chief Executive Officer Robert R. Mandos - Executive Vice President, Senior Vice President, Chief Financial Officer, Comptroller	Auditors: Ernst & Young LLP Investor Contact: 610-647-2121 Transfer Agents: American Stock Transfer and Trust Co., New York, NY

AMPHENOL CORP.

Exchange	Symbol	Price	52Wk Range	Yield	P/E
NYS	APH	$74.65 (3/28/2013)	74.65-51.19	0.56	22.02

*7 Year Price Score 125.87 *NYSE Composite Index=100 *12 Month Price Score 106.64

Interim Earnings (Per Share)

Qtr.	Mar	Jun	Sep	Dec
2008	0.54	0.61	0.63	0.56
2009	0.43	0.43	0.47	0.50
2010	0.56	0.74	0.78	0.74
2011	0.72	0.85	0.79	0.69
2012	0.77	0.86	0.90	0.86

Interim Dividends (Per Share)

Amt	Decl	Ex	Rec	Pay
0.105Q	04/24/2012	06/11/2012	06/13/2012	07/05/2012
0.105Q	07/25/2012	09/10/2012	09/12/2012	10/03/2012
0.105Q	10/24/2012	12/10/2012	12/12/2012	01/02/2013
0.105Q	01/24/2013	03/11/2013	03/13/2013	04/03/2013

Indicated Div: $0.42

Valuation Analysis | **Institutional Holding**

Forecast EPS	$3.82 (04/05/2013)	No of Institutions 557
Market Cap	$11.9 Billion	Shares
Book Value	$2.4 Billion	178,451,808
Price/Book	4.91	% Held
Price/Sales	2.78	97.18

TRADING VOLUME (thousand shares)

Business Summary: Electrical Equipment (MIC: 7.3.1 SIC: 3678 NAIC: 334417)

Amphenol is engaged in designing, manufacturing and marketing electrical, electronic and fiber optic connectors, interconnect systems, antennas and coaxial and high-speed specialty cable. Co. has two reportable business segments. The Interconnect Products and Assemblies segment produces connectors and connector assemblies primarily for the communications, aerospace, industrial and automotive markets. The Cable Products segment produces coaxial and flat ribbon cable and related products primarily for communication markets, including cable television.

Recent Developments: For the year ended Dec 31 2012, net income increased 5.8% to US$559.5 million from US$528.8 million in the prior year. Revenues were US$4.29 billion, up 8.9% from US$3.94 billion the year before. Operating income was US$828.3 million versus US$751.7 million in the prior year, an increase of 10.2%. Direct operating expenses rose 9.4% to US$2.95 billion from US$2.70 billion in the comparable period the year before. Indirect operating expenses increased 4.7% to US$514.9 million from US$492.0 million in the equivalent prior-year period.

Prospects: Our evaluation of Amphenol Corp. as of Apr. 7, 2013 is the result of our systematic analysis on three basic characteristics: earnings strength, relative valuation, and recent stock price movement. The company has produced a positive trend in earnings per share over the past 5 quarters and while recent estimates for the company have been mixed, APH has posted better than expected results. Based on operating earnings yield, the company is about fairly valued when compared to all of the companies in our coverage universe. Share price changes over the past year indicates that APH will perform well over the near term.

Financial Data
(US$ in Thousands)

	12/31/2012	12/31/2011	12/31/2010	12/31/2009	12/31/2008	12/31/2007	12/31/2006	12/31/2005
Earnings Per Share	3.39	3.05	2.82	1.83	2.34	1.94	1.40	1.14
Cash Flow Per Share	4.17	3.33	2.44	3.39	2.73	2.17	1.62	1.30
Tang Book Value Per Share	3.11	2.61	4.49	2.18	0.68	0.97	N.M.	N.M.
Dividends Per Share	0.420	0.060	0.060	0.060	0.060	0.060	0.060	0.060
Dividend Payout %	12.39	1.97	2.13	3.28	2.56	3.09	4.30	5.26
Income Statement								
Total Revenue	4,292,065	3,939,786	3,554,101	2,820,065	3,236,471	2,851,041	2,471,430	1,808,147
EBITDA	948,721	868,975	802,229	579,483	718,852	627,982	491,196	387,784
Depn & Amortn	121,779	119,439	102,846	98,524	91,302	82,348	73,124	51,642
Income Before Taxes	778,841	716,752	663,688	446,527	592,580	511,502	379,273	312,052
Income Taxes	219,333	187,910	161,275	119,311	163,003	147,790	117,581	101,629
Net Income	555,317	524,191	496,405	317,834	419,151	353,194	255,691	206,339
Average Shares	163,947	171,825	176,325	173,941	178,813	182,503	183,347	180,943
Balance Sheet								
Current Assets	2,706,915	2,181,237	1,992,130	1,420,395	1,335,864	1,223,808	934,605	709,814
Total Assets	5,215,463	4,445,225	4,015,857	3,219,184	2,994,159	2,675,733	2,195,397	1,932,540
Current Liabilities	888,514	642,415	654,990	503,159	634,832	520,481	447,659	335,930
Long-Term Obligations	1,606,204	1,376,831	799,640	753,050	786,020	721,561	677,173	765,970
Total Liabilities	2,785,504	2,273,456	1,695,002	1,473,107	1,644,734	1,410,819	1,292,403	1,243,305
Stockholders' Equity	2,429,959	2,171,769	2,320,855	1,746,077	1,349,425	1,264,914	902,994	689,235
Shares Outstanding	159,857	163,122	175,550	173,209	171,186	178,840	178,265	178,623
Statistical Record								
Return on Assets %	11.47	12.39	13.72	10.23	14.74	14.50	12.39	12.74
Return on Equity %	24.07	23.34	24.41	20.54	31.98	32.58	32.12	35.25
EBITDA Margin %	22.10	22.06	22.57	20.55	22.21	22.03	19.87	21.45
Net Margin %	12.94	13.31	13.97	11.27	12.95	12.39	10.35	11.41
Asset Turnover	0.89	0.93	0.98	0.91	1.14	1.17	1.20	1.12
Current Ratio	3.05	3.40	3.04	2.82	2.10	2.35	2.09	2.11
Debt to Equity	0.66	0.63	0.34	0.43	0.58	0.57	0.75	1.11
Price Range	65.01-45.82	58.60-39.80	53.30-38.52	46.97-21.90	51.95-19.00	47.16-30.80	34.63-22.23	22.74-16.98
P/E Ratio	19.18-13.52	19.21-13.05	18.90-13.66	25.67-11.97	22.20-8.12	24.31-15.87	24.73-15.88	19.95-14.89
Average Yield %	0.73	0.12	0.13	0.18	0.15	0.16	0.21	0.24

Address: 358 Hall Avenue, Wallingford, CT 06492 **Telephone:** 203-265-8900 **Fax:** 203-265-8746	**Web Site:** www.amphenol.com **Officers:** Richard Adam Norwitt - President, Chief Executive Officer Gary A. Anderson - Senior Vice President, Division Officer	**Auditors:** Deloitte & Touche LLP **Transfer Agents:** Computershare Trust Company, N.A., Providence, RI

ANADARKO PETROLEUM CORP

Exchange	Symbol	Price	52Wk Range	Yield	P/E
NYS	APC	$87.45 (3/28/2013)	88.88-57.12	0.41	18.45

*7 Year Price Score 107.09 *NYSE Composite Index=100 *12 Month Price Score 104.88

Interim Earnings (Per Share)

Qtr.	Mar	Jun	Sep	Dec
2008	0.61	0.05	4.62	1.71
2009	(0.73)	(0.48)	0.40	0.49
2010	1.43	(0.08)	(0.05)	0.22
2011	0.43	1.08	(6.12)	(0.72)
2012	4.28	(0.18)	0.24	0.40

Interim Dividends (Per Share)

Amt	Decl	Ex	Rec	Pay
0.09Q	05/15/2012	06/11/2012	06/13/2012	06/27/2012
0.09Q	08/07/2012	09/10/2012	09/12/2012	09/26/2012
0.09Q	11/06/2012	12/10/2012	12/12/2012	12/26/2012
0.09Q	02/14/2013	03/11/2013	03/13/2013	03/27/2013

Indicated Div: $0.36

Valuation Analysis   **Institutional Holding**

Forecast EPS	$4.14	No of Institutions
	(04/06/2013)	1088
Market Cap	$43.8 Billion	Shares
Book Value	$20.6 Billion	505,238,656
Price/Book	2.12	% Held
Price/Sales	3.26	81.75

Business Summary: Production & Extraction (MIC: 9.1.1 SIC: 1311 NAIC: 211111)

Anadarko Petroleum is an independent exploration and production company. Co. has three segments: oil and gas exploration and production, which explores for and produces natural gas, crude oil, condensate, and natural gas liquids (NGLs); midstream, which engages in gathering, processing, treating, and transporting Co. and third-party oil, natural-gas, and NGLs production; and marketing, which sells much of its production, as well as third-party purchased volumes. At Dec 31 2012, Co.'s proved reserves consisted of 2.56 billion barrels of oil equivalent, of which 8.33 trillion cubic feet were natural gas, 767.00 billion barrels were oil and condensate and 405.0 million barrels were NGLs.

Recent Developments: For the year ended Dec 31 2012, net income amounted to US$2.45 billion versus a net loss of US$2.57 billion in the prior year. Revenues were US$13.41 billion, down 4.0% from US$13.97 billion the year before. Operating income was US$3.73 billion versus a loss of US$1.87 billion in the prior year. Direct operating expenses rose 23.7% to US$4.64 billion from US$3.75 billion in the comparable period the year before. Indirect operating expenses decreased 58.3% to US$5.04 billion from US$12.09 billion in the equivalent prior-year period.

Prospects: Our evaluation of Anadarko Petroleum Corp. as of Apr. 7, 2013 is the result of our systematic analysis on three basic characteristics: earnings strength, relative valuation, and recent stock price movement. The company has enjoyed a very positive trend in earnings per share over the past 5 quarters. However, while recent estimates for the company have been lowered by analysts, APC has posted better than expected results. Based on operating earnings yield, the company is overvalued when compared to all of the companies in our coverage universe. Share price changes over the past year indicates that APC will perform poorly over the near term.

Financial Data
(US$ in Thousands)

	12/31/2012	12/31/2011	12/31/2010	12/31/2009	12/31/2008	12/31/2007	12/31/2006	12/31/2005
Earnings Per Share	4.74	(5.32)	1.52	(0.28)	6.97	8.08	10.46	5.20
Cash Flow Per Share	16.63	5.03	10.60	8.18	13.82	6.24	10.64	8.82
Tang Book Value Per Share	29.87	24.63	30.98	29.65	29.10	23.83	21.95	21.06
Dividends Per Share	0.360	0.360	0.360	0.360	0.360	0.360	0.360	0.360
Dividend Payout %	7.59	...	23.68	...	5.16	4.46	3.44	6.93
Income Statement								
Total Revenue	13,411,000	13,967,000	10,984,000	9,000,000	15,723,000	15,892,000	10,187,000	7,100,000
EBITDA	8,271,000	1,245,000	6,210,000	4,126,000	9,305,000	10,261,000	6,869,000	5,439,000
Depn & Amortn	3,964,000	3,830,000	3,714,000	3,532,000	3,194,000	2,840,000	1,976,000	1,343,000
Income Before Taxes	3,565,000	(3,424,000)	1,641,000	(108,000)	5,369,000	6,329,000	4,238,000	3,895,000
Income Taxes	1,120,000	(856,000)	820,000	(5,000)	2,148,000	2,559,000	1,442,000	1,424,000
Net Income	2,391,000	(2,649,000)	761,000	(135,000)	3,261,000	3,781,000	4,854,000	2,466,000
Average Shares	502,000	498,000	497,000	480,000	468,000	468,000	464,000	474,000
Balance Sheet								
Current Assets	6,795,000	6,931,000	6,675,000	6,083,000	5,375,000	4,516,000	4,614,000	2,916,000
Total Assets	52,589,000	51,779,000	51,559,000	50,123,000	48,923,000	48,481,000	58,844,000	22,588,000
Current Liabilities	3,994,000	4,899,000	4,114,000	3,824,000	5,536,000	5,257,000	16,758,000	2,403,000
Long-Term Obligations	13,269,000	15,060,000	12,722,000	11,149,000	9,128,000	11,151,000	11,520,000	3,555,000
Total Liabilities	31,960,000	33,674,000	30,875,000	30,195,000	30,128,000	32,117,000	43,931,000	11,537,000
Stockholders' Equity	20,629,000	18,105,000	20,684,000	19,928,000	18,795,000	16,364,000	14,913,000	11,051,000
Shares Outstanding	500,500	498,400	496,200	492,600	459,900	468,000	467,000	463,800
Statistical Record								
Return on Assets %	4.57	N.M.	1.50	N.M.	6.68	7.05	11.92	11.53
Return on Equity %	12.31	N.M.	3.75	N.M.	18.50	24.18	37.39	24.25
EBITDA Margin %	61.67	8.91	56.54	45.84	59.18	64.57	67.43	76.61
Net Margin %	17.83	N.M.	6.93	N.M.	20.74	23.79	47.65	34.73
Asset Turnover	0.26	0.27	0.22	0.18	0.32	0.30	0.25	0.33
Current Ratio	1.70	1.41	1.62	1.59	0.97	0.86	0.28	1.21
Debt to Equity	0.64	0.83	0.62	0.56	0.49	0.68	0.77	0.32
Price Range	87.50-57.12	84.71-60.53	76.16-34.83	69.36-31.15	79.86-27.17	67.05-38.63	56.70-41.09	50.38-30.20
P/E Ratio	18.46-12.05	...	50.11-22.91	...	11.46-3.90	8.30-4.78	5.42-3.93	9.69-5.81
Average Yield %	0.50	0.47	0.60	0.72	0.63	0.72	0.75	0.88

Address: 1201 Lake Robbins Drive, The Woodlands, TX 77380-1046 Telephone: 832-636-1000	Web Site: www.anadarko.com Officers: James T. Hackett - Executive Chairman, Chairman, Chief Executive Officer R. A. Walker - President, Chief Executive Officer, Chief Operating Officer	Auditors: KPMG LLP Investor Contact: 832-636-2306 Transfer Agents: Computershare, Pittsburgh, PA

ANIXTER INTERNATIONAL INC

Exchange	Symbol	Price	52Wk Range	Yield	P/E
NYS	AXE	$69.92 (3/28/2013)	73.06-49.76	N/A	18.95

*7 Year Price Score 97.43   *NYSE Composite Index=100   *12 Month Price Score 103.47

Interim Earnings (Per Share)

Qtr.	Mar	Jun	Sep	Dec
2008	1.45	1.71	1.58	0.34
2009	0.72	(2.53)	0.61	0.36
2010	0.16	0.98	1.03	0.88
2011	1.23	1.43	1.26	1.44
2012	1.61	1.28	0.61	0.17

Interim Dividends (Per Share)

Amt	Decl	Ex	Rec	Pay
3.25Sp	09/23/2010	10/13/2010	10/15/2010	10/28/2010
4.50Sp	04/24/2012	05/14/2012	05/16/2012	05/31/2012

Valuation Analysis | **Institutional Holding**

Forecast EPS	$6.34	No of Institutions
	(04/05/2013)	252
Market Cap	$2.3 Billion	Shares
Book Value	$969.9 Million	35,312,028
Price/Book	2.35	% Held
Price/Sales	0.36	83.76

TRADING VOLUME (thousand shares)

Business Summary: Electrical Equipment (MIC: 7.3.1 SIC: 5063 NAIC: 423610)

Anixter International is engaged in the distribution of communication and security products, electrical wire and cable products and fasteners and other small parts (C Class inventory components) through Anixter Inc. and its subsidiaries. Co. operates three segments: Enterprise Cabling and Security Solutions, Electrical and Electronic Wire and Cable, and OEM Supply.

Recent Developments: For the year ended Dec 28 2012, income from continuing operations decreased 37.9% to US$124.6 million from US$200.7 million a year earlier. Net income decreased 33.7% to US$124.8 million from US$188.2 million in the prior year. Revenues were US$6.25 billion, up 1.7% from US$6.15 billion the year before. Operating income was US$282.5 million versus US$362.8 million in the prior year, a decrease of 22.1%. Direct operating expenses rose 2.2% to US$4.84 billion from US$4.74 billion in the comparable period the year before. Indirect operating expenses increased 7.8% to US$1.13 billion from US$1.04 billion in the equivalent prior-year period.

Prospects: Our evaluation of Anixter International Inc. as of Apr. 7, 2013 is the result of our systematic analysis on three basic characteristics: earnings strength, relative valuation, and recent stock price movement. The company has generated a negative trend in earnings per share over the past 5 quarters. However, while recent estimates for the company have been lowered by analysts, AXE has posted better than expected results. Based on generating earnings yield, the company is undervalued when compared to all of the companies in our coverage universe. Share price changes over the past year indicates that AXE will perform in line with the market over the near term.

Financial Data

(US$ in Thousands)	12/28/2012	12/31/2011	12/31/2010	01/01/2010	01/02/2009	12/28/2007	12/29/2006	12/30/2005
Earnings Per Share	3.69	5.36	3.05	(0.83)	5.07	6.00	4.86	2.22
Cash Flow Per Share	4.30	4.22	5.74	12.60	3.47	3.72	(1.03)	0.01
Tang Book Value Per Share	19.30	19.55	18.54	19.20	16.34	17.74	15.12	10.06
Dividends Per Share	4.500	...	3.250	...	...	...	...	4.000
Dividend Payout %	121.95	...	106.56	...	...	...	...	180.18
Income Statement								
Total Revenue	6,253,100	6,146,900	5,472,100	4,982,400	6,136,600	5,852,900	4,938,600	3,847,400
EBITDA	301,400	387,100	339,900	120,400	400,700	473,500	360,100	206,100
Depn & Amortn	32,500	33,500	107,000	37,100	34,600	30,800	24,000	21,500
Income Before Taxes	209,200	303,500	179,300	17,200	318,100	397,500	303,000	157,400
Income Taxes	84,600	102,800	70,800	46,500	122,400	144,000	93,700	67,400
Net Income	124,800	188,200	108,500	(29,300)	195,700	253,500	209,300	90,000
Average Shares	33,800	35,100	35,500	35,100	38,600	42,200	43,100	40,800
Balance Sheet								
Current Assets	2,450,100	2,402,900	2,281,200	2,051,000	2,344,400	2,378,900	2,020,300	1,536,700
Total Assets	3,089,600	3,034,000	2,933,300	2,671,700	3,091,700	3,016,200	2,566,200	2,012,100
Current Liabilities	967,300	1,026,900	1,071,200	670,000	993,500	939,900	922,500	604,100
Long-Term Obligations	982,200	806,800	688,800	821,400	917,500	937,200	597,000	625,100
Total Liabilities	2,119,700	2,032,800	1,922,500	1,647,600	2,055,900	1,968,400	1,604,200	1,305,700
Stockholders' Equity	969,900	1,001,200	1,010,800	1,024,100	1,035,800	1,047,800	962,000	706,400
Shares Outstanding	32,537	33,228	34,323	34,700	35,322	36,335	39,500	38,378
Statistical Record								
Return on Assets %	4.10	6.31	3.88	N.M.	6.30	9.11	9.17	4.85
Return on Equity %	12.73	18.71	10.69	N.M.	18.48	25.30	25.16	12.28
EBITDA Margin %	4.82	6.30	6.21	2.42	6.53	8.09	7.29	5.36
Net Margin %	2.00	3.06	1.98	N.M.	3.19	4.33	4.24	2.34
Asset Turnover	2.05	2.06	1.96	1.73	1.98	2.10	2.16	2.07
Current Ratio	2.53	2.34	2.13	3.06	2.36	2.53	2.19	2.54
Debt to Equity	1.01	0.81	0.68	0.80	0.89	0.89	0.62	0.88
Price Range	73.37-49.76	75.58-45.10	60.80-38.74	47.95-24.60	73.81-22.63	86.11-50.32	61.10-39.12	42.01-31.31
P/E Ratio	19.88-13.49	14.10-8.41	19.93-12.70	...	14.56-4.46	14.35-8.39	12.57-8.05	18.92-14.10
Average Yield %	7.30	...	6.58	...	...	...	...	10.75

Address: 2301 Patriot Blvd., Glenview, IL 60026	Web Site: www.anixter.com	Auditors: Ernst & Young LLP
Telephone: 224-521-8000	Officers: Samuel Zell - Chairman Robert J. Eck - President, Chief Executive Officer	Investor Contact: 224-521-8895
		Transfer Agents: Wells Fargo Shareowner Services, St. Paul, MN

ANNALY CAPITAL MANAGEMENT INC

Exchange	Symbol	Price	52Wk Range	Yield	P/E
NYS	NLY	$15.89 (3/28/2013)	17.75-14.01	12.27	9.29

*7 Year Price Score 88.38 *NYSE Composite Index=100   ***12 Month Price Score 88.77**

Interim Earnings (Per Share)

Qtr.	Mar	Jun	Sep	Dec
2008	0.53	0.59	0.54	(1.03)
2009	0.63	1.08	0.51	1.30
2010	0.49	(0.40)	(0.03)	1.98
2011	0.89	0.14	(0.98)	0.51
2012	0.89	(0.10)	0.22	0.71

Interim Dividends (Per Share)

Amt	Decl	Ex	Rec	Pay
0.55Q	06/19/2012	06/27/2012	06/29/2012	07/26/2012
0.50Q	09/19/2012	09/27/2012	10/01/2012	10/29/2012
0.45Q	12/18/2012	12/26/2012	12/28/2012	01/29/2013
0.45Q	03/20/2013	03/27/2013	04/01/2013	04/29/2013

Indicated Div: $1.95

Valuation Analysis   **Institutional Holding**

Forecast EPS	$1.35	No of Institutions
	(04/05/2013)	763
Market Cap	$15.1 Billion	Shares
Book Value	$15.9 Billion	476,983,808
Price/Book	0.95	% Held
Price/Sales	5.63	50.76

TRADING VOLUME (thousand shares)

Business Summary: REITs (MIC: 5.3.1 SIC: 6798 NAIC: 525930)

Annaly Capital Management is a self-advised and self-managed real estate investment trust. Co. owns, manages, and finances a portfolio of real estate related investments, including mortgage pass-through certificates, collateralized mortgage obligations, Agency callable debentures, and other securities representing interests in or obligations backed by pools of mortgage loans. Co.'s wholly-owned subsidiaries provide real estate, asset management and other financial services. Co. also owns subsidiaries engaged in corporate middle market lending transactions, providing warehouse financing to residential mortgage originators, and advice on commercial real estate transactions, among others.

Recent Developments: For the year ended Dec 31 2012, net income increased 403.9% to US$1.74 billion from US$344.5 million in the prior year. Revenues were US$2.67 billion, up 138.8% from US$1.12 billion the year before.

Prospects: Our evaluation of Annaly Capital Management Inc. as of Apr. 7, 2013 is the result of our systematic analysis on three basic characteristics: earnings strength, relative valuation, and recent stock price movement. The company has generated a negative trend in earnings per share over the past 5 quarters and while recent estimates for the company have been raised by analysts, NLY has posted results that fell short of analysts expectations. Based on operating earnings yield, the company is undervalued when compared to all of the companies in our coverage universe. Share price changes over the past year indicates that NLY will perform poorly over the near term.

Financial Data
(US$ in Thousands)

	12/31/2012	12/31/2011	12/31/2010	12/31/2009	12/31/2008	12/31/2007	12/31/2006	12/31/2005
Earnings Per Share	1.71	0.37	2.04	3.52	0.64	1.31	0.44	(0.19)
Cash Flow Per Share	7.83	2.77	18.47	19.78	2.18	1.77	1.32	2.30
Tang Book Value Per Share	15.78	16.04	15.32	17.00	13.04	12.71	11.90	10.42
Dividends Per Share	1.969	1.969	1.969	1.969	1.969	1.969	1.969	1.969
Dividend Payout %	115.13	532.10	96.51	55.93	307.62	150.29	447.44	...
Income Statement								
Interest Income	3,259,145	3,579,618	2,683,134	2,922,602	3,115,428	2,355,538	1,221,882	705,046
Interest Expense	667,172	480,326	1,163,332	1,295,762	1,888,912	1,926,465	1,055,013	568,560
Net Interest Income	2,591,973	3,099,292	1,519,802	1,626,840	1,226,516	429,073	166,869	136,486
Non-Interest Income	(584,602)	(2,459,576)	(79,224)	483,988	(751,803)	61,144	(19,191)	(100,711)
Non-Interest Expense	235,559	237,344	171,847	131,908	105,211	66,313	43,507	34,278
Income Before Taxes	1,771,812	402,372	1,299,769	1,996,104	372,215	423,904	101,678	1,497
Income Taxes	35,912	59,051	35,434	34,381	25,977	8,870	7,538	10,744
Net Income	1,735,900	344,461	1,267,280	1,961,471	346,180	414,384	93,816	(9,247)
Average Shares	1,005,755	874,518	625,307	553,130	507,024	306,263	167,746	122,475
Balance Sheet								
Total Assets	133,452,295	109,630,002	83,026,590	69,376,190	57,597,615	53,903,514	30,715,980	16,063,422
Total Liabilities	117,527,851	93,837,088	73,121,658	59,758,650	50,318,301	48,587,110	28,061,473	14,559,399
Stockholders' Equity	15,924,444	15,792,914	9,904,932	9,617,540	7,279,314	5,316,404	2,654,507	1,504,023
Shares Outstanding	947,213	970,161	631,594	553,134	541,475	401,822	205,345	123,684
Statistical Record								
Return on Assets %	1.42	0.36	1.66	3.09	0.62	0.98	0.40	N.M.
Return on Equity %	10.92	2.68	12.98	23.22	5.48	10.40	4.51	N.M.
Net Interest Margin %	79.53	86.58	56.64	55.66	39.37	18.22	13.66	19.36
Efficiency Ratio %	8.81	21.19	6.60	3.87	4.45	2.74	3.62	5.67
Price Range	17.75-14.01	18.72-15.48	18.70-15.34	19.67-12.50	21.00-11.21	18.18-13.03	14.42-11.34	20.00-10.94
P/E Ratio	10.38-8.19	50.59-41.84	9.17-7.52	5.59-3.55	32.81-17.52	13.88-9.95	32.77-25.77	...
Average Yield %	12.07	11.30	11.20	12.30	12.34	12.91	15.39	12.12

Address: 1211 Avenue of the Americas, Suite 2902, New York, NY 10036 Telephone: 212-696-0100 Fax: 212-696-9809	Web Site: www.annaly.com Officers: Wellington J. Denahan-Norris - Chairman, Vice-Chairman, Chief Executive Officer, Co-Chief Executive Officer, Chief Operating Officer Kevin Keyes - President, Chief Strategy Officer, Managing Director	Auditors: Ernst & Young LLP Investor Contact: 888-826-6259 Transfer Agents: Computershare Shareowner Services LLC, Jersey City, NJ

ANN INC

Exchange	Symbol	Price	52Wk Range	Yield	P/E
NYS	ANN	$29.02 (3/28/2013)	39.34-24.13	N/A	13.82

*7 Year Price Score 108.83 *NYSE Composite Index=100 *12 Month Price Score 89.13

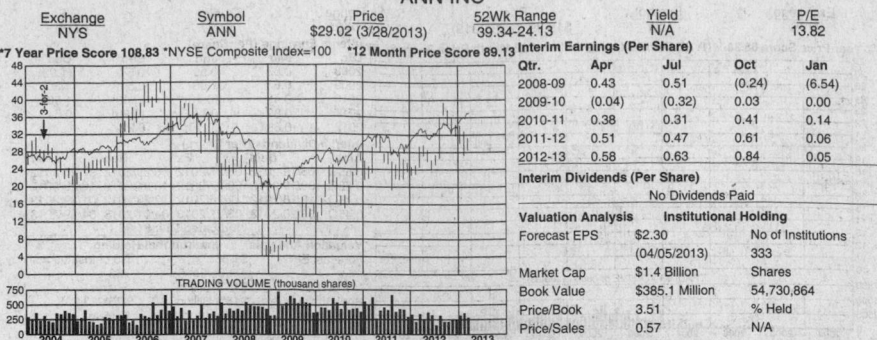

Interim Earnings (Per Share)

Qtr.	Apr	Jul	Oct	Jan
2008-09	0.43	0.51	(0.24)	(6.54)
2009-10	(0.04)	(0.32)	0.03	0.00
2010-11	0.38	0.31	0.41	0.14
2011-12	0.51	0.47	0.61	0.06
2012-13	0.58	0.63	0.84	0.05

Interim Dividends (Per Share)

No Dividends Paid

Valuation Analysis   **Institutional Holding**

Forecast EPS	$2.30	No of Institutions
	(04/05/2013)	333
Market Cap	$1.4 Billion	Shares
Book Value	$385.1 Million	54,730,864
Price/Book	3.51	% Held
Price/Sales	0.57	N/A

Business Summary: Retail - Apparel and Accessories (MIC: 2.1.5 SIC: 5621 NAIC: 448120)

Ann is a holding company. Through its wholly-owned subsidiaries, Co. is a retailer of women's apparel including career and casual separates, dresses, tops and weekend wear, as well as shoes and accessories, sold primarily under the Ann Taylor and LOFT brands. As of Jan 28 2012, Co. operated 953 retail stores in 46 states, the District of Columbia and Puerto Rico, of which 280 were Ann Taylor stores, 500 were LOFT stores, 99 were Ann Taylor Factory stores and 74 were LOFT Outlet stores. In addition, Co. sells its products online at www.anntaylor.com and www.LOFT.com, or by phone at 1-800-DIAL-ANN and 1-888-LOFT-444. Co.'s trademarks include AnnTaylor®, LOFT® and AnnTaylor Loft®.

Recent Developments: For the year ended Feb 2 2013, net income increased 18.5% to US$102.6 million from US$86.6 million in the prior year. Revenues were US$2.38 billion, up 7.4% from US$2.21 billion the year before. Operating income was US$166.8 million versus US$145.5 million in the prior year, an increase of 14.6%. Direct operating expenses rose 6.9% to US$1.07 billion from US$1.00 billion in the comparable period the year before. Indirect operating expenses increased 6.9% to US$1.14 billion from US$1.06 billion in the equivalent prior-year period.

Prospects: Our evaluation of ANN Inc as of Apr. 7, 2013 is the result of our systematic analysis on three sample characteristics: earnings strength, relative valuation, and recent stock price movement. The company has generated a negative trend in earnings per share over the past 5 quarters. However, while recent estimates for the company have been lowered by analysts, ANN has posted better than expected results. Based on operating earnings yield, the company is undervalued when compared to all of the companies in our coverage universe. Share price changes over the past year indicates that ANN will perform well over the near term.

Financial Data
(US$ in Thousands)

	02/02/2013	01/28/2012	01/29/2011	01/30/2010	01/31/2009	02/02/2008	02/03/2007	01/28/2006
Earnings Per Share	2.10	1.64	1.24	(0.32)	(5.82)	1.53	1.98	1.13
Cash Flow Per Share	5.36	4.07	2.88	2.36	3.02	4.11	4.10	4.36
Tang Book Value Per Share	8.26	7.38	7.65	7.10	7.27	9.08	11.00	10.32
Income Statement								
Total Revenue	2,375,509	2,212,493	1,980,195	1,828,523	2,194,559	2,396,510	2,342,907	2,073,146
EBITDA	264,402	239,699	215,290	80,446	(249,437)	272,186	329,737	224,826
Depn & Amortn	97,800	94,200	95,500	104,400	122,200	116,800	105,900	93,800
Income Before Taxes	167,653	144,447	119,122	(26,110)	(371,422)	161,040	238,781	138,261
Income Taxes	65,068	57,881	45,725	(7,902)	(37,516)	63,805	95,799	56,389
Net Income	102,585	86,566	73,397	(18,208)	(333,906)	97,235	142,982	81,872
Average Shares	48,094	52,029	58,110	56,782	57,366	63,452	72,107	72,270
Balance Sheet								
Current Assets	506,029	475,317	549,913	504,895	423,596	507,891	690,605	676,212
Total Assets	942,205	887,681	926,820	902,141	960,439	1,393,755	1,568,503	1,492,906
Current Liabilities	336,754	285,897	281,908	275,374	305,583	312,876	299,418	257,586
Total Liabilities	557,095	523,804	503,375	484,955	543,927	554,271	518,592	458,424
Stockholders' Equity	385,110	363,877	423,445	417,186	416,512	839,484	1,049,911	1,034,482
Shares Outstanding	46,605	49,278	55,348	58,774	57,255	60,879	69,373	72,491
Statistical Record								
Return on Assets %	11.03	9.57	8.05	N.M.	N.M.	6.58	9.19	5.82
Return on Equity %	26.95	22.05	17.51	N.M.	N.M.	10.32	13.50	8.37
EBITDA Margin %	11.13	10.83	10.87	4.40	N.M.	11.36	14.07	10.84
Net Margin %	4.32	3.91	3.71	N.M.	N.M.	4.06	6.10	3.95
Asset Turnover	2.55	2.45	2.17	1.97	1.87	1.62	1.51	1.47
Current Ratio	1.50	1.66	1.95	1.83	1.39	1.62	2.31	2.63
Price Range	39.34-22.91	32.00-19.27	28.03-13.39	17.40-2.82	28.81-3.90	39.67-19.28	44.56-32.32	35.13-21.31
P/E Ratio	18.73-10.91	19.51-11.75	22.60-10.80	...	...	25.93-12.60	22.51-16.32	31.09-18.86

Address: 7 Times Square, New York, NY 10036 Telephone: 212-541-3300	Web Site: www.anntaylor.com Officers: Kay Krill - President, Chief Executive Officer Michael J. Nicholson - Executive Vice President, Chief Financial Officer, Chief Operating Officer, Treasurer	Auditors: Deloitte & Touche LLP Transfer Agents: Computershare, Pittsburgh, PA

AOL INC.

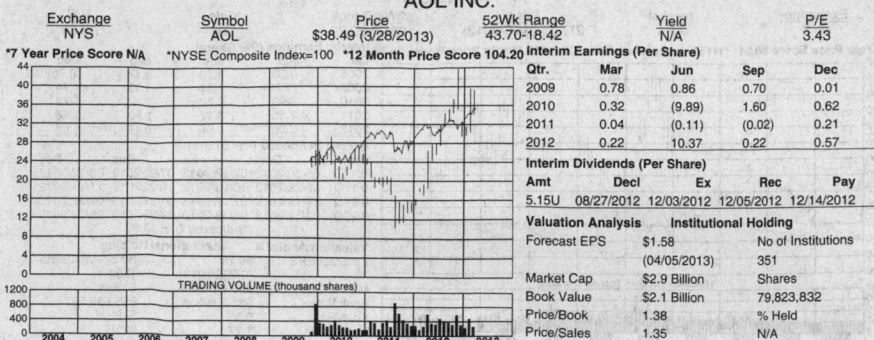

Exchange	Symbol	Price	52Wk Range	Yield	P/E
NYS	AOL	$38.49 (3/28/2013)	43.70-18.42	N/A	3.43

*7 Year Price Score N/A   *NYSE Composite Index=100   *12 Month Price Score 104.20

Interim Earnings (Per Share)

Qtr.	Mar	Jun	Sep	Dec
2009	0.78	0.86	0.70	0.01
2010	0.32	(9.89)	1.60	0.62
2011	0.04	(0.11)	(0.02)	0.21
2012	0.22	10.37	0.22	0.57

Interim Dividends (Per Share)

Amt	Decl	Ex	Rec	Pay
5.15U	08/27/2012	12/03/2012	12/05/2012	12/14/2012

Valuation Analysis   **Institutional Holding**

Forecast EPS	$1.58	No of Institutions	
	(04/05/2013)	351	
Market Cap	$2.9 Billion	Shares	
Book Value	$2.1 Billion	79,823,832	
Price/Book	1.38	% Held	
Price/Sales	1.35	N/A	

Business Summary: Internet & Software (MIC: 6.3.2 SIC: 7311 NAIC: 541810)

AOL is a web services company. Co.'s business operations are focused on the following: AOL Properties, which include its owned and operated content, products and services in The Huffington Post Media Group, AOL Services and Local and Mapping strategy areas, and its AOL Ventures, as well as co-branded websites owned or operated by third parties; and advertising, which focuses on the sale of advertising on third party websites. Co. markets its products to advertisers on AOL Properties and the third party network under the brand AOL Advertising. Co. markets its products to publishers on the third party network under the brand Advertising.com. and also markets offerings as video advertisements.

Recent Developments: For the year ended Dec 31 2012, income from continuing operations increased to US$1.05 billion from US$13.1 million a year earlier. Net income increased to US$1.05 billion from US$13.1 million in the prior year. Revenues were US$2.19 billion, down 0.5% from US$2.20 billion the year before. Operating income was US$1.20 billion versus US$45.8 million in the prior year, an increase of. Direct operating expenses rose 0.2% to US$1.59 billion from US$1.58 billion in the comparable period the year before. Indirect operating income amounted to US$597.4 million compared with an expense of US$571.9 million in the equivalent prior-year period.

Prospects: Our evaluation of AOL Inc. as of Apr. 7, 2013 is the result of our systematic analysis on three basic characteristics: earnings strength, relative valuation, and recent stock price movement. The company has generated a negative trend in earnings per share over the past 5 quarters and while recent estimates for the company have been raised by analysts, AOL has posted better than expected results. Based on operating earnings yield, the company is overvalued when compared to all of the companies in our coverage universe. Share price changes over the past year indicates that AOL will perform very well over the near term.

Financial Data
(US$ in Thousands)	12/31/2012	12/31/2011	12/31/2010	12/31/2009	12/31/2008	12/31/2007	12/31/2006
Earnings Per Share	11.21	0.12	(7.34)	2.35	(14.44)	13.21	7.09
Cash Flow Per Share	4.00	2.84	5.56	8.58	8.81	9.62	...
Tang Book Value Per Share	12.02	10.32	12.90	6.16	...	...	...
Dividends Per Share	5.150	...	...	...	...	...	...
Dividend Payout %	45.94	...	...	...	...	...	...
Income Statement							
Total Revenue	2,191,700	2,202,100	2,416,700	3,257,400	4,165,800	5,180,700	7,786,700
EBITDA	1,387,000	295,200	(627,600)	599,900	(1,005,300)	1,950,900	1,330,700
Depn & Amortn	176,900	252,900	341,600	144,700	166,200	95,900	133,500
Income Before Taxes	1,210,100	42,300	(969,200)	455,200	(1,171,500)	1,855,000	1,197,200
Income Taxes	162,400	29,200	(178,500)	206,700	355,100	641,700	480,700
Net Income	1,048,400	13,100	(782,500)	248,800	(1,525,800)	1,396,100	749,700
Average Shares	93,500	106,000	106,600	105,800	105,700	105,700	105,700
Balance Sheet							
Current Assets	887,600	809,600	1,239,200	687,400	740,400	1,275,900	...
Total Assets	2,797,300	2,825,000	2,962,300	3,963,100	4,861,300	6,863,100	...
Current Liabilities	510,200	514,800	558,600	751,400	629,600	1,169,400	...
Long-Term Obligations	56,300	66,200	50,900	41,500	410,700	351,900	...
Total Liabilities	659,200	652,400	675,400	902,000	1,125,100	1,595,900	...
Stockholders' Equity	2,138,100	2,172,600	2,286,900	3,061,100	3,736,200	5,267,200	...
Shares Outstanding	76,600	94,278	106,700	105,800	...	...	...
Statistical Record							
Return on Assets %	37.19	0.45	N.M.	5.64	N.M.	...	...
Return on Equity %	48.51	0.59	N.M.	7.32	N.M.	...	...
EBITDA Margin %	63.28	13.41	N.M.	18.42	N.M.	37.66	17.09
Net Margin %	47.84	0.59	N.M.	7.64	N.M.	26.95	9.63
Asset Turnover	0.78	0.76	0.70	0.74	0.71	...	...
Current Ratio	1.74	1.57	2.22	0.91	1.18	1.09	...
Debt to Equity	0.03	0.03	0.02	0.01	0.11	0.07	...
Price Range	43.70-14.93	24.73-10.24	29.18-20.07	26.35-22.75	...	...	...
P/E Ratio	3.90-1.33	206.08-85.33	...	11.21-9.68	...	...	...
Average Yield %	18.46	...	...	...	...	...	...

Address: 770 Broadway, New York, NY 10003
Telephone: 212-652-6400

Web Site: www.corp.aol.com
Officers: Timothy M. Armstrong - Chairman, Chief Executive Officer Julie Jacobs - Executive Vice President, Corporate Secretary, General Counsel

Auditors: Ernst & Young LLP
Investor Contact: 877-265-1010
Transfer Agents: Computershare Trust Company, N.A., Canton, MA

APACHE CORP.

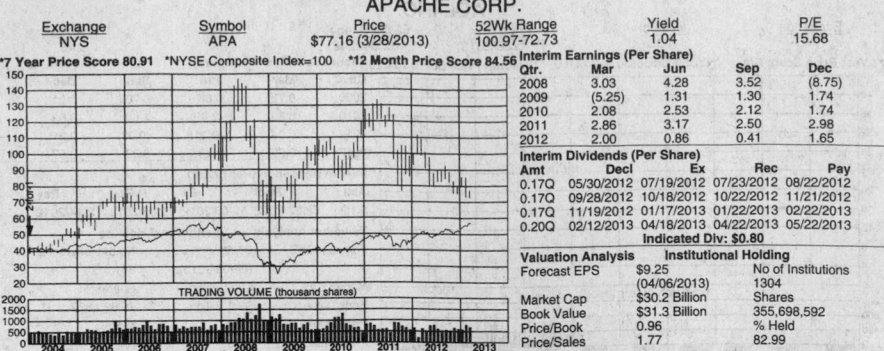

Exchange	Symbol	Price	52Wk Range	Yield	P/E
NYS	APA	$77.16 (3/28/2013)	100.97-72.73	1.04	15.68

*7 Year Price Score 80.91   *NYSE Composite Index=100   *12 Month Price Score 84.56

Interim Earnings (Per Share)

Qtr.	Mar	Jun	Sep	Dec
2008	3.03	4.28	3.52	(8.75)
2009	(5.25)	1.31	1.30	1.74
2010	2.08	2.53	2.12	1.74
2011	2.86	3.17	2.50	2.98
2012	2.00	0.86	0.41	1.65

Interim Dividends (Per Share)

Amt	Decl	Ex	Rec	Pay
0.17Q	05/30/2012	07/19/2012	07/23/2012	08/22/2012
0.17Q	09/28/2012	10/18/2012	10/22/2012	11/21/2012
0.17Q	11/19/2012	01/17/2013	01/22/2013	02/22/2013
0.20Q	02/12/2013	04/18/2013	04/22/2013	05/22/2013

Indicated Div: $0.80

Valuation Analysis

		Institutional Holding	
Forecast EPS	$9.25 (04/06/2013)	No of Institutions	1304
Market Cap	$30.2 Billion	Shares	355,698,592
Book Value	$31.3 Billion	% Held	82.99
Price/Book	0.96		
Price/Sales	1.77		

Business Summary: Production & Extraction (MIC: 9.1.1 SIC: 1311 NAIC: 211111)

Apache is an independent energy company that is engaged in exploring for, developing, and producing natural gas, crude oil, and natural gas liquids. As of Dec 31 2012, Co. had exploration and production interests in six countries: the U.S., Canada, Egypt, Australia, the U.K. in the North Sea, and Argentina. Co. also pursues exploration interests in other countries. As of Dec 31 2012, Co. had total estimated proved reserves of 1.44 billion barrels of oil of crude oil, condensate, and natural gas liquids and 8.50 trillion cubic feet of natural gas.

Recent Developments: For the year ended Dec 31 2012, net income decreased 56.3% to US$2.00 billion from US$4.58 billion in the prior year. Revenues were US$17.08 billion, up 1.1% from US$16.89 billion the year before. Direct operating expenses rose 12.8% to US$3.27 billion from US$2.90 billion in the comparable period the year before. Indirect operating expenses increased 52.8% to US$8.77 billion from US$5.74 billion in the equivalent prior-year period.

Prospects: Our evaluation of Apache Corp. as of Apr. 7, 2013 is the result of our systematic analysis on three basic characteristics: earnings strength, relative valuation, and recent stock price movement. The company has enjoyed a very positive trend in earnings per share over the past 5 quarters. However, while recent estimates for the company have been lowered by analysts, APA has posted results that fell short of analysts expectations. Based on operating earnings yield, the company is undervalued when compared to all of the companies in our coverage universe. Share price changes over the past year indicates that APA will perform poorly over the near term.

Financial Data

(US$ in Thousands)	12/31/2012	12/31/2011	12/31/2010	12/31/2009	12/31/2008	12/31/2007	12/31/2006	12/31/2005
Earnings Per Share	4.92	11.47	8.46	(0.87)	2.09	8.39	7.64	7.84
Cash Flow Per Share	21.80	25.92	19.11	12.58	21.07	17.09	13.07	13.17
Tang Book Value Per Share	73.58	69.38	57.84	46.34	48.46	45.33	39.01	31.06
Dividends Per Share	0.660	0.600	0.600	0.600	0.700	0.600	0.450	0.340
Dividend Payout %	13.41	5.23	7.09	...	33.49	7.15	5.89	4.34
Income Statement								
Total Revenue	17,078,000	16,888,000	12,092,000	8,614,826	12,389,750	9,977,858	8,288,779	7,584,244
EBITDA	12,151,000	12,455,000	8,518,000	5,781,853	8,948,685	7,240,340	5,967,840	5,742,007
Depn & Amortn	7,109,000	4,204,000	3,083,000	5,213,224	7,850,258	2,347,791	1,816,359	1,419,430
Income Before Taxes	4,877,000	8,093,000	5,206,000	326,391	932,392	4,672,612	4,009,595	4,206,254
Income Taxes	2,876,000	3,509,000	2,174,000	610,789	220,438	1,860,254	1,457,144	1,582,524
Net Income	2,001,000	4,584,000	3,032,000	(284,398)	711,954	2,812,358	2,552,451	2,623,730
Average Shares	391,000	400,000	359,000	335,852	337,191	334,596	333,211	333,749
Balance Sheet								
Current Assets	4,962,000	4,803,000	3,480,000	4,585,849	4,450,974	2,752,251	2,490,271	2,162,077
Total Assets	60,737,000	52,051,000	43,425,000	28,185,743	29,186,485	28,634,651	24,308,175	19,271,796
Current Liabilities	5,536,000	4,963,000	3,524,000	2,392,558	2,615,228	2,665,016	3,811,612	2,186,564
Long-Term Obligations	11,355,000	6,785,000	8,095,000	4,950,390	4,808,975	4,011,605	2,019,831	2,191,954
Total Liabilities	29,406,000	23,058,000	19,048,000	12,407,122	12,677,764	13,256,672	11,117,122	8,730,581
Stockholders' Equity	31,331,000	28,993,000	24,377,000	15,778,621	16,508,721	15,377,979	13,191,053	10,541,215
Shares Outstanding	391,640	384,117	382,391	336,436	334,710	332,927	330,737	330,121
Statistical Record								
Return on Assets %	3.54	9.60	8.47	N.M.	2.46	10.62	11.71	15.09
Return on Equity %	6.62	17.18	15.10	N.M.	4.45	19.69	21.51	27.99
EBITDA Margin %	71.15	73.75	70.44	67.12	72.23	72.56	72.00	75.71
Net Margin %	11.72	27.14	25.07	N.M.	5.75	28.19	30.79	34.59
Asset Turnover	0.30	0.35	0.34	0.30	0.43	0.38	0.38	0.44
Current Ratio	0.90	0.97	0.99	1.92	1.70	1.03	0.65	0.99
Debt to Equity	0.36	0.23	0.33	0.31	0.29	0.26	0.15	0.21
Price Range	111.57-75.07	133.37-76.50	119.92-82.75	105.13-51.38	146.80-61.55	108.45-63.16	75.53-57.23	77.26-47.73
P/E Ratio	22.68-15.26	11.63-6.67	14.17-9.78	...	70.24-29.45	12.93-7.53	9.89-7.49	9.85-6.09
Average Yield %	0.74	0.54	0.60	0.73	0.65	0.73	0.67	0.53

Address: One Post Oak Central, 2000 Post Oak Boulevard, Suite 100, Houston, TX 77056-4400 Telephone: 713-296-6000 Fax: 713-296-6490	Web Site: www.apachecorp.com Officers: G. Steven Farris - Chairman, Chief Executive Officer Roger B. Plank - President, Chief Corporate Officer	Auditors: Ernst & Young LLP Investor Contact: 713-296-6472 Transfer Agents: Wells Fargo Bank N.A., South St. Paul, MN

APARTMENT INVESTMENT & MANAGEMENT CO.

Exchange	Symbol	Price	52Wk Range	Yield	P/E
NYS	AIV	$30.66 (3/28/2013)	30.85-24.30	3.13	50.26

*7 Year Price Score 80.67 *NYSE Composite Index=100 *12 Month Price Score 100.05

TRADING VOLUME (thousand shares)

Interim Earnings (Per Share)

Qtr.	Mar	Jun	Sep	Dec
2008	(0.43)	2.76	1.81	(0.95)
2009	(0.33)	(0.26)	(0.35)	(0.06)
2010	(0.35)	(0.15)	(0.25)	(0.33)
2011	(0.27)	(0.28)	(0.12)	(0.19)
2012	(0.09)	0.00	0.17	0.50

Interim Dividends (Per Share)

Amt	Decl	Ex	Rec	Pay
0.18Q	05/03/2012	05/16/2012	05/18/2012	05/31/2012
0.20Q	08/01/2012	08/15/2012	08/17/2012	08/31/2012
0.20Q	10/30/2012	11/14/2012	11/16/2012	11/30/2012
0.24Q	01/31/2013	02/13/2013	02/15/2013	02/28/2013

Indicated Div: $0.96

Valuation Analysis   **Institutional Holding**

Forecast EPS	$-0.10
	(04/06/2013)
Market Cap	$4.5 Billion
Book Value	$915.4 Million
Price/Book	4.88
Price/Sales	4.32

No of Institutions	349
Shares	152,925,888
% Held	101.60

Business Summary: REITs (MIC: 5.3.1 SIC: 6798 NAIC: 525930)

Apartment Investment & Management is a real estate investment trust engaged in the ownership and operation of a portfolio of apartment properties. Co.'s business is organized in two core activities: Property Operations, which involves market-rate apartments with rents paid by the resident as well as apartments with rents that are generally paid, in whole or part, by a government agency; and Portfolio Management, which involves portfolio and capital allocation decisions such as transactions to buy or sell properties, or modify its ownership interest in properties. At Dec 31 2011 , Co.'s portfolio of owned and/or managed properties consisted of 518 properties with 93,694 apartment units.

Recent Developments: For the year ended Dec 31 2012, loss from continuing operations was US$14.9 million compared with a loss of US$135.6 million a year earlier. Net income amounted to US$195.4 million versus a net loss of US$58.2 million in the prior year. Revenues were US$1.03 billion, up 5.2% from US$981.9 million the year before. Revenues from property income rose 5.1% to US$991.4 million from US$943.3 million in the corresponding earlier year.

Prospects: Our evaluation of Apartment Investment & Management Co. as of Apr. 7, 2013 is the result of our systematic analysis on three basic characteristics: earnings strength, relative valuation, and recent stock price movement. The company has enjoyed a very positive trend in earnings per share over the past 5 quarters. Because the company lacks sufficient analyst estimate data, we place greater weight on the historical EPS trend as the measure of earnings strength. Based on operating earnings yield, the company is overvalued when compared to all of the companies in our coverage universe. Share price changes over the past year indicates that AIV will perform poorly over the near term.

Financial Data
(US$ in Thousands)

	12/31/2012	12/31/2011	12/31/2010	12/31/2009	12/31/2008	12/31/2007	12/31/2006	12/31/2005
Earnings Per Share	0.61	(0.86)	(1.08)	(1.00)	2.98	(0.36)	1.00	(0.18)
Cash Flow Per Share	2.35	2.17	2.21	2.05	3.47	4.67	5.56	3.79
Tang Book Value Per Share	5.82	2.08	3.47	5.23	6.21	10.68	15.66	17.82
Dividends Per Share	0.760	0.480	0.300	0.400	7.480	4.310	2.400	3.000
Dividend Payout %	124.59	...	...	...	251.01	...	240.00	...
Income Statement								
Total Revenue	1,033,197	1,079,584	1,144,934	1,195,763	1,457,918	1,721,184	1,690,994	1,521,523
EBITDA	576,113	554,385	576,037	566,394	656,403	1,268,164	1,225,055	1,064,716
Depn & Amortn	350,692	385,191	435,802	455,258	469,289	501,888	489,068	413,775
Income Before Taxes	(11,427)	(131,545)	(161,210)	(203,683)	(164,465)	386,685	360,227	314,532
Income Taxes	(929)	(7,166)	(18,433)	(18,671)	(53,371)	...	...	...
Net Income	132,456	(57,087)	(71,728)	(64,274)	415,463	29,911	176,787	70,982
Average Shares	134,479	119,312	116,369	114,301	121,213	99,629	95,758	93,894
Balance Sheet								
Current Assets	368,189	430,784	508,600	524,427	839,847	814,081	863,858	748,091
Total Assets	6,401,380	6,871,862	7,378,566	7,906,468	9,403,157	10,606,532	10,289,775	10,016,751
Current Liabilities	30,747	66,091	109,662	118,640	203,499	181,318	167,060	73,170
Long-Term Obligations	4,688,447	5,172,320	5,457,783	5,637,253	6,681,140	7,456,725	6,805,093	6,284,243
Total Liabilities	5,485,955	5,963,533	6,312,524	6,636,750	7,984,723	8,856,828	7,949,883	7,300,648
Stockholders' Equity	915,425	908,329	1,066,042	1,269,718	1,418,434	1,749,704	2,339,892	2,716,103
Shares Outstanding	145,563	120,916	117,642	116,479	116,180	96,130	96,820	95,732
Statistical Record								
Return on Assets %	1.99	N.M.	N.M.	N.M.	4.14	0.29	1.74	0.71
Return on Equity %	14.49	N.M.	N.M.	N.M.	26.16	1.46	6.99	2.48
EBITDA Margin %	55.76	51.35	50.31	47.37	45.02	73.68	72.45	69.98
Net Margin %	12.82	N.M.	N.M.	N.M.	28.50	1.74	10.45	4.67
Asset Turnover	0.16	0.15	0.15	0.14	0.15	0.16	0.17	0.15
Current Ratio	11.97	6.52	4.64	4.42	4.13	4.49	5.17	10.22
Debt to Equity	5.12	5.69	5.12	4.44	4.71	4.26	2.91	2.31
Price Range	28.27-22.40	27.97-20.29	25.93-15.21	16.73-4.94	40.69-7.92	64.35-34.62	58.88-38.72	44.01-35.15
P/E Ratio	46.34-36.72	...	...	...	13.65-2.66	...	58.88-38.72	...
Average Yield %	2.92	1.94	1.44	3.87	24.15	8.66	4.95	7.80

Address: 4582 South Ulster Street, Suite 1100, Denver, CO 80237 **Telephone:** 303-757-8101 **Fax:** 303-759-3226	**Web Site:** www.aimco.com **Officers:** Terry Considine - Chairman, Chief Executive Officer Daniel S. Matula - Executive Vice President	**Auditors:** Ernst & Young LLP **Investor Contact:** 303-691-4350 **Transfer Agents:** Computershare Trust Company, N.A., Providence, RI

APTARGROUP INC.

Exchange	Symbol	Price	52Wk Range	Yield	P/E	Div Achiever
NYS	ATR	$57.35 (3/28/2013)	57.35-45.80	1.74	24.10	19 Years

*7 Year Price Score 112.32 *NYSE Composite Index=100   *12 Month Price Score 96.93

Interim Earnings (Per Share)

Qtr.	Mar	Jun	Sep	Dec
2008	0.52	0.64	0.57	0.46
2009	0.38	0.41	0.48	0.52
2010	0.56	0.67	0.68	0.58
2011	0.64	0.74	0.72	0.57
2012	0.64	0.61	0.62	0.52

Interim Dividends (Per Share)

Amt	Decl	Ex	Rec	Pay
0.22Q	04/12/2012	04/24/2012	04/26/2012	05/17/2012
0.22Q	07/17/2012	08/07/2012	08/09/2012	08/30/2012
0.22Q	10/25/2012	11/05/2012	11/07/2012	11/28/2012
0.25Q	01/17/2013	01/28/2013	01/30/2013	02/20/2013

Indicated Div: $1.00

Valuation Analysis | **Institutional Holding**

Forecast EPS $2.78 (04/06/2013)	No of Institutions 323
Market Cap $3.8 Billion	Shares
Book Value $1.4 Billion	76,433,800
Price/Book 2.74	% Held
Price/Sales 1.62	88.17

Business Summary: Plastics (MIC: 8.4.2 SIC: 3089 NAIC: 326199)

AptarGroup is a provider of a range of packaging delivery systems. Co. operates in the packaging components industry, which includes the development, manufacture and sale of consumer product dispensing systems. Co.'s dispensing systems include pumps, closures and aerosol valves. Co. is organized into three segments. Operations that sell dispensing systems primarily to the beauty, personal care and house care markets form the Beauty and Home segment. Operations that sell dispensing systems to the prescription drug and consumer healthcare markets form the Pharma segment. Operations that sell dispensing systems primarily to the food and beverage markets form the Food and Beverage segment.

Recent Developments: For the year ended Dec 31 2012, net income decreased 11.6% to US$162.4 million from US$183.6 million in the prior year. Revenues were US$2.33 billion, down 0.3% from US$2.34 billion the year before. Operating income was US$258.9 million versus US$287.1 million in the prior year, a decrease of 9.8%. Direct operating expenses rose 1.4% to US$1.59 billion from US$1.57 billion in the comparable period the year before. Indirect operating expenses were unchanged at US$481.8 million versus the equivalent prior-year period.

Prospects: Our evaluation of AptarGroup Inc. as of Apr. 7, 2013 is the result of our systematic analysis on three basic characteristics: earnings strength, relative valuation, and recent stock price movement. The company has enjoyed a very positive trend in earnings per share over the past 5 quarters and while recent estimates for the company have remained steady, ATR has posted results that fell short of analysts expectations. Based on operating earnings yield, the company is about fairly valued when compared to all of the companies in our coverage universe. Share price changes over the past year indicates that ATR will perform very poorly over the near term.

Financial Data

(US$ in Thousands)	12/31/2012	12/31/2011	12/31/2010	12/31/2009	12/31/2008	12/31/2007	12/31/2006	12/31/2005
Earnings Per Share	2.38	2.65	2.48	1.79	2.18	1.98	1.44	1.39
Cash Flow Per Share	4.71	3.92	3.89	4.34	3.97	3.98	2.83	2.76
Tang Book Value Per Share	14.81	15.96	15.67	15.05	13.16	12.88	10.39	8.71
Dividends Per Share	0.880	0.800	0.660	0.600	0.560	0.500	0.420	0.350
Dividend Payout %	36.97	30.19	26.61	33.52	25.69	25.25	29.27	25.27
Income Statement								
Total Revenue	2,331,036	2,337,183	2,076,719	1,841,616	2,071,685	1,892,167	1,601,385	1,380,009
EBITDA	391,629	418,585	394,832	324,755	351,115	328,999	269,688	245,798
Depn & Amortn	133,845	132,048	129,339	127,709	124,884	118,946	109,037	96,693
Income Before Taxes	241,830	274,959	254,370	183,894	220,664	199,479	147,880	139,965
Income Taxes	78,953	91,312	80,796	59,461	67,473	60,488	45,410	41,919
Net Income	162,612	183,683	173,481	124,623	153,495	141,739	102,896	100,034
Average Shares	68,395	69,274	69,815	69,785	70,518	71,523	71,744	72,354
Balance Sheet								
Current Assets	1,038,933	1,143,950	1,063,983	943,491	859,749	1,003,445	762,820	605,291
Total Assets	2,324,412	2,159,295	2,032,718	1,956,193	1,831,822	1,911,950	1,592,012	1,357,319
Current Liabilities	455,323	518,849	423,322	417,315	375,027	565,189	400,185	320,762
Long-Term Obligations	352,860	254,910	258,773	209,616	226,888	146,711	168,877	144,541
Total Liabilities	944,522	869,519	753,795	703,348	700,792	792,932	645,612	547,931
Stockholders' Equity	1,379,890	1,289,776	1,278,923	1,252,845	1,131,030	1,119,018	946,400	809,388
Shares Outstanding	65,928	65,900	66,800	67,300	67,600	68,200	69,200	69,800
Statistical Record								
Return on Assets %	7.23	8.76	8.70	6.58	8.18	8.09	6.98	7.32
Return on Equity %	12.15	14.30	13.70	10.46	13.61	13.72	11.72	11.89
EBITDA Margin %	16.80	17.91	19.01	17.63	16.95	17.39	16.84	17.81
Net Margin %	6.98	7.86	8.35	6.77	7.41	7.49	6.43	7.25
Asset Turnover	1.04	1.12	1.04	0.97	1.10	1.08	1.09	1.01
Current Ratio	2.28	2.20	2.51	2.26	2.29	1.78	1.91	1.89
Debt to Equity	0.26	0.20	0.20	0.17	0.20	0.13	0.18	0.18
Price Range	55.26-45.80	54.34-42.79	48.22-35.03	38.89-25.30	46.16-26.49	44.70-29.10	30.88-23.65	27.50-23.72
P/E Ratio	23.22-19.24	20.51-16.15	19.44-14.13	21.73-14.13	21.17-12.15	22.58-14.70	21.44-16.42	19.78-17.06
Average Yield %	1.71	1.61	1.58	1.80	1.47	1.36	1.56	1.38

Address: 475 West Terra Cotta Avenue, Suite E, Crystal Lake, IL 60014 Telephone: 815-477-0424 Fax: 815-477-0481	Web Site: www.aptar.com Officers: King W. Harris - Chairman Peter H. Pfeiffer - President, Chief Executive Officer	Auditors: PricewaterhouseCoopers LLP Investor Contact: 815-477-0424 Transfer Agents: Wells Fargo Shareowner Services, South St. Paul, MN

AQUA AMERICA INC

Exchange	Symbol	Price	52Wk Range	Yield	P/E	Div Achiever
NYS	WTR	$31.44 (3/28/2013)	31.44-21.52	2.23	22.46	21 Years

*7 Year Price Score 106.60 *NYSE Composite Index=100 *12 Month Price Score 105.83

Interim Earnings (Per Share)

Qtr.	Mar	Jun	Sep	Dec
2008	0.11	0.17	0.26	0.19
2009	0.14	0.19	0.25	0.20
2010	0.16	0.22	0.32	0.21
2011	0.22	0.27	0.30	0.24
2012	0.27	0.30	0.36	0.47

Interim Dividends (Per Share)

Amt	Decl	Ex	Rec	Pay
0.165Q	05/01/2012	05/15/2012	05/17/2012	06/01/2012
0.165Q	08/02/2012	08/15/2012	08/17/2012	09/01/2012
0.175Q	08/02/2012	11/14/2012	11/16/2012	12/01/2012
0.175Q	02/01/2013	02/13/2013	02/15/2013	03/01/2013

Indicated Div: $0.70 (Div. Reinv. Plan)

Valuation Analysis — **Institutional Holding**

Forecast EPS	$1.40	No of Institutions
	(04/06/2013)	364
Market Cap	$4.4 Billion	Shares
Book Value	$1.4 Billion	72,479,304
Price/Book	3.18	% Held
Price/Sales	5.82	48.24

Business Summary: Water Utilities (MIC: 3.2.1 SIC: 4941 NAIC: 221310)

Aqua America is the holding company for regulated utilities providing water or wastewater services in Pennsylvania, Texas, North Carolina, Ohio, Illinois, New Jersey, New York, Florida, Indiana, Virginia, Maine, and Georgia. Co.'s subsidiary, Aqua Pennsylvania, Inc., provides water or wastewater services in the suburban areas in counties north and west of the City of Philadelphia and in 25 other counties in Pennsylvania. Co. provides water and wastewater services through operating and maintenance contracts with municipal authorities and other parties as well as sludge hauling, septage and grease services, backflow prevention services, and other non-regulated water and wastewater services.

Recent Developments: For the year ended Dec 31 2012, income from continuing operations increased 29.9% to US$184.1 million from US$141.7 million a year earlier. Net income increased 37.4% to US$196.6 million from US$143.1 million in the prior year. Revenues were US$757.8 million, up 10.3% from US$687.3 million the year before. Operating income was US$321.5 million versus US$280.8 million in the prior year, an increase of 14.5%. Direct operating expenses rose 5.9% to US$271.8 million from US$256.7 million in the comparable period the year before. Indirect operating expenses increased 9.8% to US$164.4 million from US$149.7 million in the equivalent prior-year period.

Prospects: Our evaluation of Aqua America Inc. as of Apr. 7, 2013 is the result of our systematic analysis on three basic characteristics: earnings strength, relative valuation, and recent stock price movement. The company has managed to produce a neutral trend in earnings per share over the past 5 quarters. However, while recent estimates for the company have been lowered by analysts, WTR has posted results that fell short of analysts expectations. Based on operating earnings yield, the company is about fairly valued when compared to all of the companies in our coverage universe. Share price changes over the past year indicates that WTR will perform in line with the market over the near term.

Financial Data

(US$ in Thousands)	12/31/2012	12/31/2011	12/31/2010	12/31/2009	12/31/2008	12/31/2007	12/31/2006	12/31/2005
Earnings Per Share	1.40	1.03	0.90	0.77	0.73	0.71	0.70	0.71
Cash Flow Per Share	2.64	2.65	1.93	1.90	1.64	1.46	1.31	1.57
Tang Book Value Per Share	9.69	8.82	8.23	7.81	7.52	7.04	6.79	6.14
Dividends Per Share	0.670	0.630	0.590	0.550	0.510	0.480	0.444	0.399
Dividend Payout %	47.86	61.17	65.56	71.43	69.86	67.61	63.40	56.25
Income Statement								
Total Revenue	757,760	711,956	726,072	670,539	626,972	602,499	533,491	496,779
EBITDA	438,516	405,597	400,788	355,741	325,374	305,641	285,723	265,619
Depn & Amortn	111,767	111,942	121,067	114,939	94,300	83,178	75,041	65,488
Income Before Taxes	248,992	215,853	204,069	172,195	162,502	155,542	152,250	148,069
Income Taxes	66,881	71,091	80,094	67,842	64,584	60,528	60,246	56,913
Net Income	196,563	143,069	123,975	104,353	97,918	95,014	92,004	91,156
Average Shares	139,934	138,689	137,296	136,129	134,705	133,602	131,774	129,206
Balance Sheet								
Current Assets	260,894	320,453	145,419	121,571	121,041	115,511	134,700	89,956
Total Assets	4,858,517	4,348,420	4,072,466	3,762,597	3,485,022	3,226,912	2,877,903	2,626,725
Current Liabilities	274,164	425,673	223,715	201,007	193,171	183,212	255,611	263,339
Long-Term Obligations	1,543,954	1,395,457	1,531,976	1,386,557	1,248,104	1,215,053	951,660	878,438
Total Liabilities	3,472,813	3,097,107	2,898,212	2,653,693	2,426,576	2,250,614	1,956,273	1,814,802
Stockholders' Equity	1,385,704	1,251,313	1,174,254	1,108,904	1,058,446	976,298	921,630	811,923
Shares Outstanding	140,167	138,815	137,775	136,486	135,369	133,400	132,325	128,970
Statistical Record								
Return on Assets %	4.26	3.40	3.16	2.88	2.91	3.11	3.34	3.67
Return on Equity %	14.87	11.80	10.86	9.63	9.60	10.01	10.61	11.69
EBITDA Margin %	57.87	56.97	55.20	53.05	51.90	50.73	53.56	53.47
Net Margin %	25.94	20.10	17.07	15.56	15.62	15.77	17.25	18.35
Asset Turnover	0.16	0.17	0.19	0.19	0.19	0.20	0.19	0.20
Current Ratio	0.95	0.75	0.65	0.60	0.63	0.63	0.53	0.34
Debt to Equity	1.11	1.12	1.30	1.25	1.18	1.24	1.03	1.08
Price Range	26.85-21.18	23.65-19.28	22.89-16.59	21.19-15.45	21.93-14.06	26.44-21.20	29.59-20.61	28.97-17.61
P/E Ratio	19.18-15.13	22.96-18.72	25.43-18.43	27.52-20.06	30.04-20.08	37.24-29.86	42.27-29.44	40.80-24.80
Average Yield %	2.81	2.85	3.10	3.10	2.81	2.11	1.82	1.77

Address: 762 W. Lancaster Avenue, Bryn Mawr, PA 19010-3489	Web Site: www.aquaamerica.com	Auditors: PricewaterhouseCoopers LLP
Telephone: 610-527-8000	Officers: Nicholas DeBenedictis - Chairman, President, Chief Executive Officer Christopher H. Franklin - Executive Vice President, Senior Vice President, Region Officer	Investor Contact: 610-645-1191 Transfer Agents: Computershare Trust Company, N.A., Providence, RI

ARCH COAL, INC.

Exchange	Symbol	Price	52Wk Range	Yield	P/E
NYS	ACI	$5.43 (3/28/2013)	10.63-4.90	2.21	N/A

*7 Year Price Score 23.57   *NYSE Composite Index=100   *12 Month Price Score 75.05

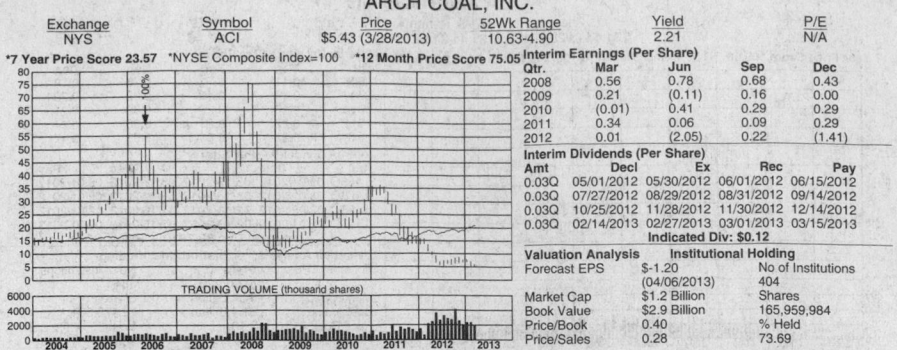

Interim Earnings (Per Share)

Qtr.	Mar	Jun	Sep	Dec
2008	0.56	0.78	0.68	0.43
2009	0.21	(0.11)	0.16	0.00
2010	(0.01)	0.41	0.29	0.29
2011	0.34	0.06	0.09	0.29
2012	0.01	(2.05)	0.22	(1.41)

Interim Dividends (Per Share)

Amt	Decl	Ex	Rec	Pay
0.03Q	05/01/2012	05/30/2012	06/01/2012	06/15/2012
0.03Q	07/27/2012	08/29/2012	08/31/2012	09/14/2012
0.03Q	10/25/2012	11/28/2012	11/30/2012	12/14/2012
0.03Q	02/14/2013	02/27/2013	03/01/2013	03/15/2013

Indicated Div: $0.12

Valuation Analysis / **Institutional Holding**

Forecast EPS	$-1.20 (04/06/2013)	No of Institutions 404
Market Cap	$1.2 Billion	Shares
Book Value	$2.9 Billion	165,959,984
Price/Book	0.40	% Held
Price/Sales	0.28	73.69

TRADING VOLUME (thousand shares)

Business Summary: Mining (MIC: 8.2.4 SIC: 1221 NAIC: 212111)

Arch Coal is a coal producer. Co. produces coal from surface and underground mines for sale to domestic and international customers as steam coal to power plants and industrial facilities and metallurgical coal used in steel production. At Dec 31 2011, Co. operated, or contracted out the operation of, 46 active mines located in each of the coal-producing regions of the U.S. In addition, Co. owns a 99% membership interest in a joint venture named Arch Western Resources, LLC (Arch Western), which operates coal mines in Wyoming, Colorado and Utah. Co. also acts as the managing member of Arch Western. Co.'s reportable segments are: Powder River Basis; Western Bituminous; Appalachia; and Other.

Recent Developments: For the year ended Dec 31 2012, net loss amounted to US$683.7 million versus net income of US$142.8 million in the prior year. Revenues were US$4.16 billion, down 3.0% from US$4.29 billion the year before. Operating loss was US$681.6 million versus an income of US$413.6 million in the prior year. Direct operating expenses rose 5.2% to US$3.44 billion from US$3.27 billion in the comparable period the year before. Indirect operating expenses increased 132.1% to US$1.40 billion from US$604.4 million in the equivalent prior-year period.

Prospects: Our evaluation of Arch Coal Inc. as of Apr. 7, 2013 is the result of our systematic analysis on three basic characteristics: earnings strength, relative valuation, and recent stock price movement. The company has suffered a very negative trend in earnings per share over the past 5 quarters. Because the company lacks sufficient analyst estimate data, we place greater weight on the historical EPS trend as the measure of earnings strength. Based on operating earnings yield, the company is overvalued when compared to all of the companies in our coverage universe. Share price changes over the past year indicates that ACI will perform very poorly over the near term.

Financial Data
(US$ in Thousands)

	12/31/2012	12/31/2011	12/31/2010	12/31/2009	12/31/2008	12/31/2007	12/31/2006	12/31/2005
Earnings Per Share	(3.24)	0.74	0.97	0.28	2.45	1.21	1.80	0.17
Cash Flow Per Share	1.57	3.38	4.29	2.54	4.72	2.32	2.16	2.00
Tang Book Value Per Share	12.20	14.09	13.05	12.32	11.78	10.42	9.32	8.03
Dividends Per Share	0.200	0.430	0.390	0.360	0.340	0.270	0.220	0.160
Dividend Payout %	...	58.11	40.21	128.57	13.88	22.31	12.22	91.43
Income Statement								
Total Revenue	4,159,038	4,285,895	3,186,268	2,576,081	2,983,806	2,413,644	2,500,431	2,508,773
EBITDA	(184,699)	820,713	727,719	444,945	753,237	469,406	537,574	278,894
Depn & Amortn	520,557	458,585	410,511	321,231	292,848	242,062	208,354	212,301
Income Before Taxes	(1,017,404)	135,251	177,108	25,404	396,104	155,079	268,581	3,473
Income Taxes	(333,717)	(7,589)	17,714	(16,775)	41,774	(19,850)	7,650	(34,650)
Net Income	(683,955)	141,683	158,857	42,169	354,330	174,929	260,931	38,123
Average Shares	211,381	190,905	163,210	151,272	144,416	144,019	144,812	129,940
Balance Sheet								
Current Assets	1,914,104	1,182,774	734,914	686,782	706,378	521,145	487,277	729,564
Total Assets	10,006,777	10,213,959	4,880,769	4,840,596	3,978,964	3,594,599	3,320,814	3,051,440
Current Liabilities	577,069	1,020,668	527,346	631,727	659,747	556,515	440,806	513,188
Long-Term Obligations	5,085,879	3,762,297	1,538,744	1,540,223	1,098,948	1,085,579	1,122,595	971,755
Total Liabilities	7,152,210	6,635,919	2,643,262	2,725,490	2,250,231	2,062,913	1,955,220	1,867,199
Stockholders' Equity	2,854,567	3,578,040	2,237,507	2,115,106	1,728,733	1,531,686	1,365,594	1,184,241
Shares Outstanding	212,247	211,671	162,605	162,441	142,833	143,158	142,179	142,572
Statistical Record								
Return on Assets %	N.M.	1.88	3.27	0.96	9.33	5.06	8.19	1.21
Return on Equity %	N.M.	4.87	7.30	2.19	21.68	12.08	20.47	3.37
EBITDA Margin %	N.M.	19.15	22.84	17.27	25.24	19.45	21.50	11.12
Net Margin %	N.M.	3.31	4.99	1.64	11.88	7.25	10.44	1.52
Asset Turnover	0.41	0.57	0.66	0.58	0.79	0.70	0.78	0.80
Current Ratio	3.32	1.16	1.39	1.09	1.07	0.94	1.11	1.42
Debt to Equity	1.78	1.05	0.69	0.73	0.64	0.71	0.82	0.82
Price Range	15.70-5.26	36.04-13.22	35.26-19.32	25.08-12.01	75.44-10.46	44.93-27.42	54.94-26.45	40.34-16.82
P/E Ratio	...	48.70-17.86	36.35-19.92	89.57-42.89	30.79-4.27	37.13-22.66	30.52-14.69	237.26-98.91
Average Yield %	2.34	1.70	1.56	2.00	0.77	0.78	0.58	0.57

Address: One CityPlace Drive, Ste. 300, St. Louis, MO 63141 Telephone: 314-994-2700	Web Site: www.archcoal.com Officers: Steven F. Leer - Chairman, Chief Executive Officer John W. Eaves - President, Chief Executive Officer, Chief Operating Officer	Auditors: Ernst & Young LLP Transfer Agents: American Stock Transfer & Trust Company, New York, NY

ARCHER DANIELS MIDLAND CO.

Exchange	Symbol	Price	52Wk Range	Yield	P/E	Div Achiever
NYS	ADM	$33.73 (3/28/2013)	33.73-24.48	2.25	26.15	38 Years

*7 Year Price Score 80.48 ***NYSE Composite Index=100** ***12 Month Price Score 100.90**

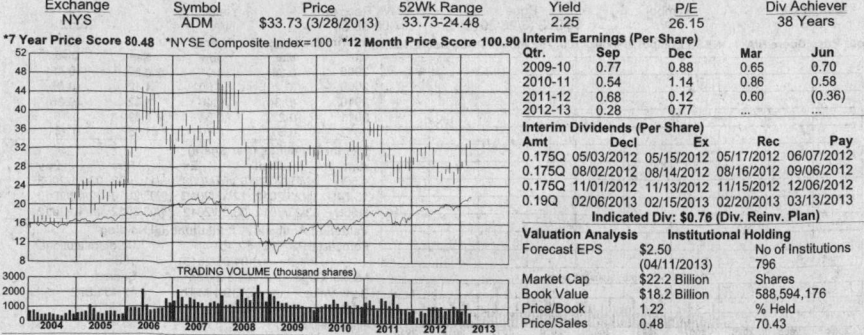

Interim Earnings (Per Share)

Qtr.	Sep	Dec	Mar	Jun
2009-10	0.77	0.88	0.65	0.70
2010-11	0.54	1.14	0.86	0.58
2011-12	0.68	0.12	0.60	(0.36)
2012-13	0.28	0.77	...	...

Interim Dividends (Per Share)

Amt	Decl	Ex	Rec	Pay
0.175Q	05/03/2012	05/15/2012	05/17/2012	06/07/2012
0.175Q	08/02/2012	08/14/2012	08/16/2012	09/06/2012
0.175Q	11/01/2012	11/13/2012	11/15/2012	12/06/2012
0.19Q	02/06/2013	02/15/2013	02/20/2013	03/13/2013

Indicated Div: $0.76 (Div. Reinv. Plan)

Valuation Analysis   **Institutional Holding**

Forecast EPS	$2.50	No of Institutions
	(04/11/2013)	796
Market Cap	$22.2 Billion	Shares
Book Value	$18.2 Billion	588,594,176
Price/Book	1.22	% Held
Price/Sales	0.48	70.43

Business Summary: Food (MIC: 1.2.1 SIC: 2041 NAIC: 311211)

Archer-Daniels-Midland is a processor of oilseeds, corn, wheat, cocoa, and other agricultural commodities and is a manufacturer of protein meal, vegetable oil, corn sweeteners, flour, biodiesel, ethanol, and other food and feed ingredients. Co. also has a grain elevator and transportation network to procure, store, clean, and transport agricultural commodities. Co. has three segments: Oilseeds Processing, which is involved in the origination, merchandising, crushing, and further processing of oilseeds; Corn Processing, which is engaged in corn wet milling and dry milling activities; and Agricultural Services, which buys, stores, cleans, and transports agricultural commodities.

Recent Developments: For the quarter ended Dec 31 2012, net income advanced to US$510.0 million from US$80.0 million in the year-earlier quarter. Revenues were US$24.92 billion, an increase of 6.9% from US$23.31 billion the year before. Direct operating expenses rose 6.4% to US$23.93 billion from US$22.49 billion in the comparable period the year before.

Prospects: Our evaluation of Archer Daniels Midland Co. as of Apr. 7, 2013 is the result of our systematic analysis on three basic characteristics: earnings strength, relative valuation, and recent stock price movement. The company has produced a positive trend in earnings per share over the past 5 quarters. However, while recent estimates for the company have been mixed, ADM has posted better than expected results. Based on operating earnings yield, the company is undervalued when compared to all of the companies in our coverage universe. Share price changes over the past year indicates that ADM will perform poorly over the near term.

Financial Data
(US$ in Thousands)

	12/31/2012	06/30/2012	06/30/2011	06/30/2010	06/30/2009	06/30/2008	06/30/2007	06/30/2006
Earnings Per Share	1.05	1.84	3.13	3.00	2.65	2.79	3.30	2.00
Cash Flow Per Share	2.49	4.34	(3.64)	4.17	8.31	(4.96)	0.47	2.11
Tang Book Value Per Share	27.87	26.35	26.93	22.04	20.20	20.16	17.80	14.47
Dividends Per Share	0.700	0.685	0.620	0.580	0.540	0.490	0.430	0.370
Dividend Payout %	66.67	37.23	19.81	19.33	20.38	17.56	13.03	18.50
Income Statement								
Total Revenue	46,729,000	89,038,000	80,676,000	61,682,000	69,207,000	69,816,000	44,018,000	36,596,111
EBITDA	1,331,000	2,470,000	3,696,000	3,358,000	3,549,000	3,407,000	3,995,000	2,702,805
Depn & Amortn	435,000	848,000	877,000	912,000	730,000	721,000	701,000	656,714
Income Before Taxes	742,000	1,293,000	2,473,000	2,024,000	2,389,000	2,209,000	2,860,000	1,680,911
Income Taxes	303,000	523,000	997,000	666,000	827,000	822,000	992,000	543,180
Net Income	692,000	1,223,000	2,036,000	1,930,000	1,707,000	1,802,000	2,162,000	1,312,070
Average Shares	661,000	666,000	654,000	644,000	644,000	646,000	656,000	656,287
Balance Sheet								
Current Assets	29,762,000	26,954,000	27,504,000	18,134,000	19,408,000	25,455,000	15,122,000	11,826,277
Total Assets	45,136,000	41,553,000	42,193,000	31,548,000	31,585,000	37,056,000	25,118,000	21,269,030
Current Liabilities	16,993,000	14,626,000	13,218,000	8,573,000	8,885,000	14,621,000	7,868,000	6,164,767
Long-Term Obligations	6,456,000	6,535,000	8,266,000	6,830,000	7,800,000	7,690,000	4,752,000	4,050,323
Total Liabilities	26,216,000	23,584,000	23,385,000	16,939,000	18,086,000	23,566,000	13,865,000	11,462,150
Stockholders' Equity	18,920,000	17,969,000	18,808,000	14,609,000	13,499,000	13,490,000	11,253,000	9,806,880
Shares Outstanding	659,000	659,000	676,000	639,000	642,000	644,000	614,400	655,685
Statistical Record								
Return on Assets %	1.05	2.91	5.52	6.11	4.97	5.78	9.32	6.58
Return on Equity %	2.43	6.63	12.19	13.73	12.65	14.53	20.53	14.39
EBITDA Margin %	2.85	2.77	4.58	5.44	5.13	4.88	9.08	7.39
Net Margin %	1.48	1.37	2.52	3.13	2.47	2.58	4.91	3.59
Asset Turnover	0.71	2.12	2.19	1.95	2.02	2.24	1.90	1.84
Current Ratio	1.75	1.84	2.08	2.12	2.18	1.74	1.92	1.92
Debt to Equity	0.34	0.36	0.44	0.47	0.58	0.57	0.42	0.41
Price Range	29.10-24.48	33.50-24.16	37.65-25.50	32.61-24.51	33.75-15.29	48.18-32.09	44.00-30.70	45.25-20.56
P/E Ratio	27.71-23.31	18.21-13.13	12.03-8.15	10.87-8.17	12.74-5.77	17.27-11.50	13.33-9.30	22.63-10.28
Average Yield %	2.59	2.31	1.93	2.00	2.08	1.26	1.18	1.27

Address: 4666 Faries Parkway, P.O. Box 1470, Decatur, IL 62525
Telephone: 217-424-5200
Fax: 217-424-5381

Web Site: www.adm.com
Officers: Patricia A. Woertz - Chairman, President, Chief Executive Officer Steven Richard Mills - Senior Executive Vice President

Auditors: Ernst & Young LLP
Investor Contact: 217-424-5656
Transfer Agents: Hickory Point Bank & Trust, fsb, Decatur, IL

ARMSTRONG WORLD INDUSTRY INC

Exchange	Symbol	Price	52Wk Range	Yield	P/E
NYS	AWI	$55.89 (3/28/2013)	57.00-38.65	N/A	25.52

*7 Year Price Score N/A   *NYSE Composite Index=100   *12 Month Price Score 102.28

Interim Earnings (Per Share)

Qtr.	Mar	Jun	Sep	Dec
2008	0.26	0.91	0.69	(0.45)
2009	(0.20)	0.50	1.12	(0.07)
2010	(0.34)	0.46	0.42	(0.36)
2011	0.23	0.64	0.89	0.15
2012	0.31	0.70	1.05	0.14

Interim Dividends (Per Share)

Amt	Decl	Ex	Rec	Pay
4.50U	02/29/2008	03/07/2008	03/11/2008	03/31/2008
13.74U	11/23/2010	12/13/2010	12/03/2010	12/10/2010
8.55U	03/23/2012	03/30/2012	04/03/2012	04/10/2012

Valuation Analysis   **Institutional Holding**

Forecast EPS	$2.45 (04/05/2013)	No of Institutions 166
Market Cap	$3.3 Billion	Shares
Book Value	$719.1 Million	42,431,872
Price/Book	4.58	% Held
Price/Sales	1.26	58.42

Business Summary: Metal Products (MIC: 8.2.3 SIC: 3089 NAIC: 326199)

Armstrong World Industries is a producer of flooring products and ceiling systems for use in the construction and renovation of residential, commercial and institutional buildings. Co.'s segments include: Building Products, which produces suspended mineral fiber, soft fiber and metal ceiling systems; Resilient Flooring, which produces floor coverings, and sells laminate flooring and vinyl tile products, adhesives, installation and maintenance materials and accessories; Wood Flooring, which sells wood flooring products such as pre-finished solid and engineered wood floors, and related accessories; and Cabinets, which produces kitchen and bathroom cabinetry and related products.

Recent Developments: For the year ended Dec 31 2012, net income increased 16.8% to US$131.3 million from US$112.4 million in the prior year. Revenues were US$2.62 billion, down 3.8% from US$2.72 billion the year before. Operating income was US$271.2 million versus US$239.8 million in the prior year, an increase of 13.1%. Direct operating expenses declined 4.3% to US$1.99 billion from US$2.08 billion in the comparable period the year before. Indirect operating expenses decreased 11.3% to US$362.0 million from US$408.1 million in the equivalent prior-year period.

Prospects: Our evaluation of Armstrong World Industries Inc. as of Apr. 7, 2013 is the result of our systematic analysis on three basic characteristics: earnings strength, relative valuation, and recent stock price movement. The company has generated a negative trend in earnings per share over the past 5 quarters. However, while recent estimates for the company have been mixed, AWI has posted better than expected results. Based on operating earnings yield, the company is about fairly valued when compared to all of the companies in our coverage universe. Share price changes over the past year indicates that AWI will perform well over the near term.

Financial Data
(US$ in Thousands)

	12/31/2012	12/31/2011	12/31/2010	12/31/2009	12/31/2008	12/31/2007	12/31/2006	09/30/2006
Earnings Per Share	2.19	1.90	0.19	1.36	1.43	2.56	0.04	...
Cash Flow Per Share	3.72	3.64	3.30	4.58	3.79	10.27	1.27	...
Tang Book Value Per Share	3.25	10.01	9.21	22.75	19.60	30.81	26.65	...
Dividends Per Share	8.550	...	13.740	...	4.500	...	...	...
Dividend Payout %	390.41	...	7,231.58	...	314.69	...	...	...
Income Statement								
Total Revenue	2,618,900	2,859,500	2,766,400	2,780,000	3,393,000	3,549,700	817,300	2,608,600
EBITDA	327,900	297,700	185,500	199,600	314,000	406,000	47,400	2,215,800
Depn & Amortn	112,700	113,800	143,300	146,800	149,800	137,800	32,200	101,200
Income Before Taxes	164,600	138,200	21,700	35,200	133,400	213,200	1,800	2,109,400
Income Taxes	76,100	80,700	55,700	(2,500)	109,000	106,400	3,800	726,600
Net Income	131,300	112,400	11,000	77,700	81,000	145,300	2,200	1,355,800
Average Shares	59,500	58,800	58,200	57,000	56,600	56,700	55,300	...
Balance Sheet								
Current Assets	1,019,900	1,209,300	1,020,700	1,331,600	1,261,500	1,501,000	1,371,400	...
Total Assets	2,854,300	2,994,700	2,922,400	3,302,600	3,351,800	4,649,900	4,170,700	...
Current Liabilities	384,700	386,100	382,900	357,300	385,400	497,300	516,600	...
Long-Term Obligations	1,038,000	822,900	839,600	432,500	454,800	485,800	801,500	...
Total Liabilities	2,135,200	1,864,500	1,831,600	1,403,300	1,607,500	2,212,700	2,006,000	...
Stockholders' Equity	719,100	1,130,200	1,090,800	1,899,300	1,744,300	2,437,200	2,164,700	...
Shares Outstanding	58,934	58,424	58,070	57,433	57,049	56,828	56,091	...
Statistical Record								
Return on Assets %	4.48	3.80	0.35	2.34	2.02	3.29	0.05	...
Return on Equity %	14.16	10.12	0.74	4.27	3.86	6.31	0.52	...
EBITDA Margin %	12.52	10.41	6.71	7.18	9.25	11.44	5.80	84.94
Net Margin %	5.01	3.93	0.40	2.79	2.39	4.09	0.27	51.97
Asset Turnover	0.89	0.97	0.89	0.84	0.85	0.80	0.19	...
Current Ratio	2.65	3.13	2.67	3.73	3.27	3.02	2.65	...
Debt to Equity	1.44	0.73	0.77	0.23	0.26	0.20	0.37	...
Price Range	58.13-38.65	48.01-32.80	53.55-28.59	44.69-9.45	40.69-14.54	56.99-35.97	42.40-35.41	...
P/E Ratio	26.54-17.65	25.27-17.26	281.84-150.47	32.86-6.95	28.45-10.17	22.26-14.05	N.M.	...
Average Yield %	18.02	...	35.14	...	14.71	...	...	...

Address: 2500 Columbia Avenue, Lancaster, PA 17603	Web Site: www.armstrong.com	Auditors: KPMG LLP
Telephone: 717-397-0611	Officers: James J. O'Connor - Chairman Matthew J. Espe - President, Chief Executive Officer	Investor Contact: 717-396-6354
		Transfer Agents: American Stock Transfer & Trust Company, New York, NY

ARROW ELECTRONICS, INC.

Exchange	Symbol	Price	52Wk Range	Yield	P/E
NYS	ARW	$40.62 (3/28/2013)	42.61-31.02	N/A	8.91

*7 Year Price Score 101.28 *NYSE Composite Index=100 *12 Month Price Score 100.94

TRADING VOLUME (thousand shares)

Interim Earnings (Per Share)

Qtr.	Mar	Jun	Sep	Dec
2008	0.69	0.79	0.63	(7.19)
2009	0.22	0.18	0.10	0.53
2010	0.71	0.96	1.00	1.33
2011	1.16	1.33	1.15	1.53
2012	1.00	1.02	0.94	1.60

Interim Dividends (Per Share)

No Dividends Paid

Valuation Analysis		Institutional Holding	
Forecast EPS	$4.35	No of Institutions	
	(04/05/2013)	380	
Market Cap	$4.3 Billion	Shares	
Book Value	$4.0 Billion	117,723,152	
Price/Book	1.08	% Held	
Price/Sales	0.21	86.65	

Business Summary: Electrical Equipment (MIC: 7.3.1 SIC: 5045 NAIC: 334419)

Arrow Electronics is a provider of products, services, and solutions to industrial and commercial users of electronic components and enterprise computing solutions. Co. offers a spectrum of products on behalf of electronic components and enterprise computing solutions suppliers, including materials planning, new product design services, programming and assembly services, inventory management, reverse logistics, electronics asset disposition, training and education, and a managed services including cloud computing, security, and networking services. Co. also provides an online supply chain tools. Co. has two business segments: Global Components and Global Enterprise Computing Solutions.

Recent Developments: For the year ended Dec 31 2012, net income decreased 15.5% to US$506.7 million from US$599.3 million in the prior year. Revenues were US$20.41 billion, down 4.6% from US$21.39 billion the year before. Operating income was US$804.1 million versus US$908.8 million in the prior year, a decrease of 11.5%. Direct operating expenses declined 4.2% to US$17.67 billion from US$18.44 billion in the comparable period the year before. Indirect operating expenses decreased 5.2% to US$1.93 billion from US$2.04 billion in the equivalent prior-year period.

Prospects: Our evaluation of Arrow Electronics Inc. as of Apr. 7, 2013 is the result of our systematic analysis on three basic characteristics: earnings strength, relative valuation, and recent stock price movement. The company has enjoyed a very positive trend in earnings per share over the past 5 quarters and while recent estimates for the company have been raised by analysts, ARW has posted better than expected results. Based on operating earnings yield, the company is undervalued when compared to all of the companies in our coverage universe. Share price changes over the past year indicates that ARW will perform in line with the market over the near term.

Financial Data

(US$ in Thousands)	12/31/2012	12/31/2011	12/31/2010	12/31/2009	12/31/2008	12/31/2007	12/31/2006	12/31/2005
Earnings Per Share	4.56	5.17	4.01	1.03	(5.08)	3.28	3.16	2.09
Cash Flow Per Share	6.16	1.06	1.87	7.09	5.12	6.91	0.99	3.42
Tang Book Value Per Share	17.52	16.12	16.70	16.61	14.84	14.43	14.42	11.00
Income Statement								
Total Revenue	20,405,128	21,390,264	18,744,676	14,684,101	16,761,009	15,984,992	13,577,112	11,164,196
EBITDA	954,019	1,051,743	863,508	369,832	(414,059)	777,157	674,600	530,971
Depn & Amortn	149,896	142,707	114,303	102,357	89,540	90,252	70,980	58,024
Income Before Taxes	702,247	803,065	672,634	184,190	(603,462)	585,277	513,056	381,069
Income Taxes	203,642	210,485	199,378	65,416	16,722	180,697	128,457	131,248
Net Income	506,332	598,810	479,630	123,512	(613,739)	407,792	388,331	253,609
Average Shares	111,077	115,932	119,577	120,489	120,773	124,429	123,181	124,080
Balance Sheet								
Current Assets	7,715,301	7,024,591	7,085,834	5,839,628	5,345,768	5,589,395	4,895,621	4,517,474
Total Assets	10,785,687	9,829,079	9,600,538	7,762,366	7,118,285	8,059,860	6,669,572	6,044,917
Current Liabilities	4,910,211	3,958,927	4,343,243	3,332,246	2,968,362	2,987,374	2,504,110	2,331,878
Long-Term Obligations	1,587,478	1,927,823	1,761,203	1,276,138	1,223,985	1,223,337	976,774	1,138,981
Total Liabilities	6,802,465	6,160,267	6,349,343	4,845,406	4,441,587	4,508,000	3,673,013	3,672,031
Stockholders' Equity	3,983,222	3,668,812	3,251,195	2,916,960	2,676,698	3,551,860	2,996,559	2,372,886
Shares Outstanding	106,001	111,814	114,647	119,828	119,308	122,827	122,419	120,014
Statistical Record								
Return on Assets %	4.90	6.16	5.52	1.66	N.M.	5.54	6.11	4.39
Return on Equity %	13.20	17.31	15.55	4.42	N.M.	12.45	14.46	11.11
EBITDA Margin %	4.68	4.92	4.61	2.52	N.M.	4.86	4.97	4.76
Net Margin %	2.48	2.80	2.56	0.84	N.M.	2.55	2.86	2.27
Asset Turnover	1.97	2.20	2.16	1.97	2.20	2.17	2.14	1.93
Current Ratio	1.57	1.77	1.63	1.75	1.80	1.87	1.96	1.94
Debt to Equity	0.40	0.53	0.54	0.44	0.46	0.34	0.33	0.48
Price Range	42.63-31.02	46.53-25.98	34.39-22.01	29.98-15.17	39.28-11.82	44.33-32.70	36.65-26.00	33.25-21.71
P/E Ratio	9.35-6.80	9.00-5.03	8.58-5.49	29.11-14.73	...	13.52-9.97	11.60-8.23	15.91-10.39

Address: 7459 S. Lima Street, Englewood, CO 80112 Telephone: 303-824-4000	Web Site: www.arrow.com Officers: William E. Mitchell - Chairman John C. Waddell - Vice-Chairman	Auditors: Ernst & Young LLP Transfer Agents: Wells Fargo Shareowner Services, South St. Paul, MN

ASBURY AUTOMOTIVE GROUP, INC

Exchange	Symbol	Price	52Wk Range	Yield	P/E
NYS	ABG	$36.69 (3/28/2013)	38.04-22.18	N/A	14.06

*7 Year Price Score 143.17 *NYSE Composite Index=100 ***12 Month Price Score 109.98**

Interim Earnings (Per Share)

Qtr.	Mar	Jun	Sep	Dec
2008	0.33	0.34	0.19	(11.51)
2009	0.01	0.17	0.22	0.01
2010	0.22	0.39	0.38	0.16
2011	0.59	0.43	0.38	0.67
2012	0.56	0.67	0.66	0.73

Interim Dividends (Per Share)

Dividend Payment Suspended

Valuation Analysis   **Institutional Holding**

Forecast EPS	$3.00	No of Institutions	
	(04/05/2013)	172	
Market Cap	$1.1 Billion	Shares	
Book Value	$402.8 Million	33,488,376	
Price/Book	2.85	% Held	
Price/Sales	0.25	91.51	

Business Summary: Retail - Automotive (MIC: 2.1.4 SIC: 5599 NAIC: 441229)

Asbury Automotive Group is an automotive retailer, which operated 99 franchises (79 dealership locations) as of Dec 31 2011. Co. provides automotive products and services, including new and used vehicles, vehicle maintenance, replacement parts and collision repair services, new and used vehicle financing; and aftermarket products such as insurance, warranty and service contracts. Co.'s retail network is made of up dealerships operating primarily under eight locally-branded dealership groups: Nalley Automotive Group, Courtesy Autogroup, Coggin Automotive Group, Crown Automotive Company, David McDavid Auto Group, North Point Auto Group, Gray-Daniels Auto Family, and Plaza Motor Company.

Recent Developments: For the year ended Dec 31 2012, income from continuing operations increased 79.1% to US$83.3 million from US$46.5 million a year earlier. Net income increased 21.1% to US$82.2 million from US$67.9 million in the prior year. Revenues were US$4.64 billion, up 12.1% from US$4.14 billion the year before. Operating income was US$185.9 million versus US$131.2 million in the prior year, an increase of 41.7%. Direct operating expenses rose 12.7% to US$3.88 billion from US$3.44 billion in the comparable period the year before. Indirect operating expenses increased 1.7% to US$577.7 million from US$567.8 million in the equivalent prior-year period.

Prospects: Our evaluation of Asbury Automotive Group Inc. as of Apr. 7, 2013 is the result of our systematic analysis on three basic characteristics: earnings strength, relative valuation, and recent stock price movement. The company has generated a negative trend in earnings per share over the past 5 quarters and while recent estimates for the company have been mixed, ABG has posted better than expected results. Based on operating earnings yield, the company is undervalued when compared to all of the companies in our coverage universe. Share price changes over the past year indicates that ABG will perform well over the near term.

Financial Data
(US$ in Thousands)

	12/31/2012	12/31/2011	12/31/2010	12/31/2009	12/31/2008	12/31/2007	12/31/2006	12/31/2005
Earnings Per Share	2.61	2.08	1.14	0.41	(10.66)	1.53	1.78	1.86
Cash Flow Per Share	(0.66)	(5.69)	0.31	3.47	16.65	2.14	3.87	(1.24)
Tang Book Value Per Share	10.84	8.76	7.07	6.94	6.48	1.51	3.71	1.45
Dividends Per Share	...	...	...	...	0.675	0.850	0.400	...
Dividend Payout %	...	...	...	...	...	55.56	22.47	...
Income Statement								
Total Revenue	4,640,300	4,276,700	3,936,000	3,650,600	4,619,500	5,712,967	5,748,331	5,540,663
EBITDA	208,100	155,000	133,800	118,100	(364,100)	184,339	208,027	184,387
Depn & Amortn	22,600	22,700	21,100	23,500	23,400	21,500	20,200	19,700
Income Before Taxes	133,300	77,600	60,500	38,600	(456,900)	84,823	107,700	95,758
Income Taxes	50,000	29,600	23,200	14,400	(133,800)	30,537	40,546	35,854
Net Income	82,200	67,900	38,100	13,400	(338,000)	50,955	60,749	61,081
Average Shares	31,500	32,600	33,300	32,900	31,700	33,340	34,067	32,896
Balance Sheet								
Current Assets	986,400	792,500	877,300	815,600	1,019,700	1,192,422	1,293,064	1,185,180
Total Assets	1,661,400	1,419,400	1,486,300	1,400,900	1,654,300	2,016,300	2,030,837	1,930,800
Current Liabilities	779,800	636,300	635,800	598,800	854,500	871,667	881,055	838,226
Long-Term Obligations	461,400	439,100	534,900	528,800	548,300	473,851	454,010	472,427
Total Liabilities	1,258,600	1,092,800	1,199,200	1,157,300	1,431,600	1,432,075	1,419,004	1,383,034
Stockholders' Equity	402,800	326,600	287,100	243,600	222,700	584,225	611,833	547,766
Shares Outstanding	31,316	31,320	32,798	32,430	31,951	31,581	33,534	32,848
Statistical Record								
Return on Assets %	5.32	4.67	2.64	0.88	N.M.	2.52	3.07	3.19
Return on Equity %	22.48	22.13	14.36	5.75	N.M.	8.52	10.48	11.89
EBITDA Margin %	4.48	3.62	3.40	3.24	N.M.	3.23	3.62	3.33
Net Margin %	1.77	1.59	0.97	0.37	N.M.	0.89	1.06	1.10
Asset Turnover	3.00	2.94	2.73	2.39	2.51	2.82	2.90	2.89
Current Ratio	1.26	1.25	1.38	1.36	1.19	1.37	1.47	1.41
Debt to Equity	1.15	1.34	1.86	2.17	2.46	0.81	0.74	0.86
Price Range	32.35-21.50	21.66-15.04	18.80-9.82	14.86-2.01	17.39-2.00	29.82-14.84	25.98-16.33	18.00-13.71
P/E Ratio	12.39-8.24	10.41-7.23	16.49-8.61	36.24-4.90	...	19.49-9.70	14.60-9.17	9.68-7.37
Average Yield %	...	...	...	...	5.91	3.69	1.94	...

Address: 2905 Premiere Parkway NW, Suite 300, Duluth, GA 30097 Telephone: 770-418-8200	Web Site: www.asburyauto.com Officers: Charles R. Oglesby - Executive Chairman Craig T. Monaghan - President, Chief Executive Officer	Auditors: Ernst & Young LLP Investor Contact: 770-418-8210 Transfer Agents: Computershare Trust Company, N. A., Providence, RI

ASHLAND INC

Exchange	Symbol	Price	52Wk Range	Yield	P/E
NYS	ASH	$74.30 (3/28/2013)	86.37-58.77	1.21	90.61

*7 Year Price Score 120.59 *NYSE Composite Index=100   ***12 Month Price Score 99.47**

(Stock price chart 2004–2013 with TRADING VOLUME (thousand shares))

Interim Earnings (Per Share)

Qtr.	Dec	Mar	Jun	Sep
2009-10	1.10	0.27	1.85	0.95
2010-11	1.09	4.39	1.09	(1.40)
2011-12	0.77	1.10	1.90	(3.44)
2012-13	1.26	...	...	...

Interim Dividends (Per Share)

Amt	Decl	Ex	Rec	Pay
0.225Q	05/17/2012	05/30/2012	06/01/2012	06/15/2012
0.225Q	07/18/2012	08/15/2012	08/17/2012	09/15/2012
0.225Q	11/15/2012	11/29/2012	12/03/2012	12/15/2012
0.225Q	01/30/2013	02/13/2013	02/15/2013	03/15/2013

Indicated Div: $0.90

Valuation Analysis

		Institutional Holding	
Forecast EPS	$6.67	No of Institutions	
	(04/05/2013)	448	
Market Cap	$5.9 Billion	Shares	
Book Value	$4.2 Billion	73,422,784	
Price/Book	1.41	% Held	
Price/Sales	0.72	91.16	

Business Summary: Specialty Chemicals (MIC: 8.3.2 SIC: 5169 NAIC: 325199)

Ashland is a chemical company. Co. operates in four reportable segments: Ashland Specialty Ingredients, which provides products, technologies and resources for the personal care, pharmaceutical, food and beverage, coatings, construction and energy markets; Ashland Water Technologies, a chemicals supplier of process, utility and functional chemistries; Ashland Performance Materials, which provides unsaturated polyester resins and epoxy vinyl ester resins, gelcoats, adhesives, coatings and elastomers, as well as metal casting consumables and design services; and Ashland Consumer Markets, which produces and distributes automotive, commercial and industrial lubricants and car-care products.

Recent Developments: For the quarter ended Dec 31 2012, income from continuing operations increased 70.0% to US$102.0 million from US$60.0 million in the year-earlier quarter. Net income increased 65.6% to US$101.0 million from US$61.0 million in the year-earlier quarter. Revenues were US$1.87 billion, down 3.2% from US$1.93 billion the year before. Operating income was US$176.0 million versus US$144.0 million in the prior-year quarter, an increase of 22.2%. Direct operating expenses declined 5.4% to US$1.33 billion from US$1.41 billion in the comparable period the year before. Indirect operating expenses decreased 4.5% to US$361.0 million from US$378.0 million in the equivalent prior-year period.

Prospects: Our evaluation of Ashland Inc. as of Apr. 7, 2013 is the result of our systematic analysis on three basic characteristics: earnings strength, relative valuation, and recent stock price movement. The company has generated a negative trend in earnings per share over the past 5 quarters. However, while recent estimates for the company have been lowered by analysts, ASH has posted results that fell short of analysts expectations. Based on operating earnings yield, the company is undervalued when compared to all of the companies in our coverage universe. Share price changes over the past year indicates that ASH will perform very well over the near term.

Financial Data

(US$ in Thousands)	3 Mos	09/30/2012	09/30/2011	09/30/2010	09/30/2009	09/30/2008	09/30/2007	09/30/2006
Earnings Per Share	0.82	0.33	5.17	4.18	0.96	2.63	3.60	5.64
Cash Flow Per Share	8.19	4.92	3.12	6.63	14.26	7.57	3.14	2.08
Tang Book Value Per Share	N.M.	N.M.	N.M.	5.85	2.13	44.35	44.08	41.58
Dividends Per Share	0.850	0.800	0.650	0.450	0.300	1.100	11.300	1.100
Dividend Payout %	103.66	242.42	12.57	10.77	31.25	41.83	313.89	19.50
Income Statement								
Total Revenue	1,869,000	8,206,000	6,502,000	9,012,000	8,106,000	8,381,000	7,834,000	7,277,000
EBITDA	181,000	726,000	443,000	963,000	743,000	375,000	343,000	272,000
Depn & Amortn	5,000	497,000	325,000	385,000	391,000	145,000	133,000	111,000
Income Before Taxes	132,000	(14,000)	3,000	392,000	158,000	261,000	259,000	212,000
Income Taxes	30,000	(52,000)	(53,000)	91,000	80,000	86,000	58,000	29,000
Net Income	101,000	26,000	414,000	332,000	71,000	167,000	230,000	407,000
Average Shares	80,000	80,000	80,000	79,000	73,000	64,000	64,000	72,000
Balance Sheet								
Current Assets	3,077,000	3,209,000	3,387,000	2,833,000	2,473,000	3,032,000	3,276,000	4,250,000
Total Assets	12,376,000	12,524,000	12,966,000	9,531,000	9,447,000	5,771,000	5,686,000	6,590,000
Current Liabilities	1,770,000	1,913,000	1,739,000	1,687,000	1,566,000	1,230,000	1,152,000	2,041,000
Long-Term Obligations	3,090,000	3,131,000	3,648,000	1,108,000	1,537,000	45,000	64,000	70,000
Total Liabilities	8,224,000	8,495,000	8,831,000	5,728,000	5,863,000	2,569,000	2,532,000	3,494,000
Stockholders' Equity	4,152,000	4,029,000	4,135,000	3,803,000	3,584,000	3,202,000	3,154,000	3,096,000
Shares Outstanding	78,979	79,000	78,000	79,000	75,000	63,000	63,000	67,000
Statistical Record								
Return on Assets %	0.53	0.20	3.68	3.50	0.93	2.91	3.75	6.07
Return on Equity %	1.61	0.64	10.43	8.99	2.09	5.24	7.36	11.91
EBITDA Margin %	9.68	8.85	6.81	10.69	9.17	4.47	4.38	3.74
Net Margin %	5.40	0.32	6.37	3.68	0.88	1.99	2.94	5.59
Asset Turnover	0.65	0.64	0.58	0.95	1.07	1.46	1.28	1.09
Current Ratio	1.74	1.68	1.95	1.68	1.58	2.47	2.84	2.08
Debt to Equity	0.74	0.78	0.88	0.29	0.43	0.01	0.02	0.02
Price Range	80.79-57.89	76.73-42.79	68.34-44.14	63.28-34.14	44.62-5.60	67.41-27.51	70.81-50.94	74.55-51.23
P/E Ratio	98.52-70.60	232.52-129.67	13.22-8.54	15.14-8.17	46.48-5.83	25.63-10.46	19.67-14.15	13.22-9.08
Average Yield %	1.25	1.28	1.06	0.95	1.44	2.24	17.76	1.76

Address: 50 E. RiverCenter Boulevard, P.O. Box 391, Covington, KY 41012-0391
Telephone: 859-815-3333

Web Site: www.ashland.com
Officers: James J. O'Brien - Chairman, Chief Executive Officer Peter J. Ganz - Senior Vice President, General Counsel, Secretary

Auditors: PricewaterhouseCoopers LLP
Investor Contact: 859-815-3527
Transfer Agents: Wells Fargo Shareowner Services, South Saint Paul, MN

ASPEN INSURANCE HOLDINGS LTD

Exchange	Symbol	Price	52Wk Range	Yield	P/E
NYS	AHL	$38.58 (3/28/2013)	38.58-27.01	1.76	11.41

*7 Year Price Score 103.26 *NYSE Composite Index=100 ***12 Month Price Score 107.26**

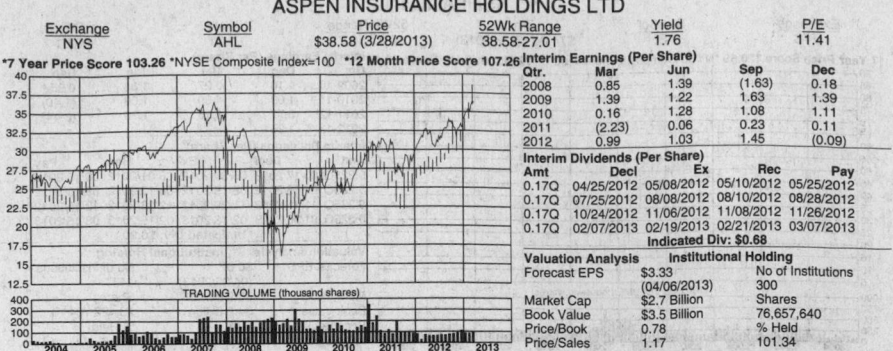

Interim Earnings (Per Share)

Qtr.	Mar	Jun	Sep	Dec
2008	0.85	1.39	(1.63)	0.18
2009	1.39	1.22	1.63	1.39
2010	0.16	1.28	1.08	1.11
2011	(2.23)	0.06	0.23	0.11
2012	0.99	1.03	1.45	(0.09)

Interim Dividends (Per Share)

Amt	Decl	Ex	Rec	Pay
0.17Q	04/25/2012	05/08/2012	05/10/2012	05/25/2012
0.17Q	07/25/2012	08/08/2012	08/10/2012	08/28/2012
0.17Q	10/24/2012	11/06/2012	11/08/2012	11/26/2012
0.17Q	02/07/2013	02/19/2013	02/21/2013	03/07/2013

Indicated Div: $0.68

Valuation Analysis

		Institutional Holding	
Forecast EPS	$3.33	No of Institutions	
	(04/06/2013)	300	
Market Cap	$2.7 Billion	Shares	
Book Value	$3.5 Billion	76,657,640	
Price/Book	0.78	% Held	
Price/Sales	1.17	101.34	

Business Summary: General Insurance (MIC: 5.2.1 SIC: 6331 NAIC: 524126)

Aspen Insurance Holdings is a holding company. Through its subsidiaries in three main jurisdictions, the U.K., Bermuda, and the U.S., Co. conducts insurance and reinsurance business. Co. operates in the global markets for property and casualty insurance and reinsurance. Co. manages its insurance and reinsurance businesses as two underwriting segments, Aspen Insurance and Aspen Reinsurance. Co.'s insurance segment is comprised of property, casualty, marine, energy and transportation insurance and financial and professional lines insurance. Co.'s reinsurance segment is comprised of property reinsurance (catastrophe and other), casualty reinsurance and specialty reinsurance.

Recent Developments: For the year ended Dec 31 2012, net income amounted to US$280.4 million versus a net loss of US$110.1 million in the prior year. Revenues were US$2.33 billion, up 7.3% from US$2.17 billion the year before. Net premiums earned were US$2.08 billion versus US$1.89 billion in the prior year, an increase of 10.3%. Net investment income fell 9.2% to US$204.9 million from US$225.6 million a year ago.

Prospects: Our evaluation of Aspen Insurance Holdings Ltd. as of Apr. 7, 2013 is the result of our systematic analysis on three basic characteristics: earnings strength, relative valuation, and recent stock price movement. The company has suffered a very negative trend in earnings per share over the past 5 quarters and while recent estimates for the company have been raised by analysts, AHL has posted better than expected results. Based on operating earnings yield, the company is undervalued when compared to all of the companies in our coverage universe. Share price changes over the past year indicates that AHL will perform in line with the market over the near term.

Financial Data
(US$ in Thousands)

	12/31/2012	12/31/2011	12/31/2010	12/31/2009	12/31/2008	12/31/2007	12/31/2006	12/31/2005
Earnings Per Share	3.38	(1.82)	3.62	5.64	0.89	5.11	3.75	(2.40)
Cash Flow Per Share	6.96	4.86	8.18	7.82	6.38	8.81	7.54	10.66
Tang Book Value Per Share	49.03	44.61	42.18	39.57	34.00	32.85	27.12	19.30
Dividends Per Share	...	0.600	0.600	0.600	0.600	...	...	...
Dividend Payout %	...	...	16.57	10.64	67.42	...	...	...
Income Statement								
Premium Income	2,083,500	1,888,500	1,898,900	1,823,000	1,701,700	1,733,600	1,676,200	1,508,400
Total Revenue	2,329,400	2,077,700	2,190,400	2,074,900	1,785,200	2,008,100	1,859,500	1,649,100
Benefits & Claims	...	...	...	...	...	919,800	889,900	1,358,500
Income Before Taxes	295,400	(143,000)	340,300	534,700	140,200	574,000	470,400	(160,400)
Income Taxes	15,000	(37,200)	27,600	60,800	36,400	85,000	92,300	17,400
Net Income	280,400	(105,800)	312,700	473,900	103,800	489,000	378,100	(177,800)
Average Shares	73,689	70,665	80,014	85,327	85,532	90,355	96,734	74,020
Balance Sheet								
Total Assets	10,310,600	9,476,500	8,832,100	8,257,200	7,288,800	7,201,300	6,640,100	6,537,800
Total Liabilities	6,822,400	6,304,900	5,590,700	4,951,800	4,509,700	4,383,700	4,250,800	4,498,000
Stockholders' Equity	3,488,200	3,171,600	3,241,400	3,305,400	2,779,100	2,817,600	2,389,300	2,039,800
Shares Outstanding	70,753	70,655	76,342	83,327	81,506	85,510	87,788	95,209
Statistical Record								
Return on Assets %	2.83	N.M.	3.66	6.10	1.43	7.07	5.74	N.M.
Return on Equity %	8.40	N.M.	9.55	15.58	3.70	18.78	17.07	N.M.
Loss Ratio %	...	...	...	...	...	53.06	53.09	90.06
Net Margin %	12.04	(5.09)	14.28	22.84	5.81	24.35	20.33	(10.78)
Price Range	33.58-26.17	30.74-22.16	31.50-24.31	28.25-18.60	29.90-14.33	30.34-22.63	27.05-21.53	30.15-22.34
P/E Ratio	9.93-7.74	...	8.70-6.72	5.01-3.30	33.60-16.10	5.94-4.43	7.21-5.74	...
Average Yield %	...	2.26	2.15	2.47	2.41	...	...	...

Address: 141 Front Street, Hamilton, HM 19	Web Site: www.aspen.bm	Auditors: KPMG Audit Plc
Telephone: 441-295-8201	Officers: Glyn Jones - Chairman Christopher O'Kane - Chief Executive Officer	Investor Contact: 646-502-1076
		Transfer Agents: Computershare Investor Services, Jersey City, NJ

ASSURANT INC

Exchange	Symbol	Price	52Wk Range	Yield	P/E
NYS	AIZ	$45.01 (3/28/2013)	45.01-32.57	1.87	7.94

*7 Year Price Score 77.80 *NYSE Composite Index=100 ***12 Month Price Score 103.36**

TRADING VOLUME (thousand shares)

Interim Earnings (Per Share)

Qtr.	Mar	Jun	Sep	Dec
2008	1.57	1.59	(0.95)	1.54
2009	0.68	1.63	1.22	0.09
2010	1.34	1.46	1.30	(1.61)
2011	1.39	1.68	0.79	1.70
2012	1.81	1.94	1.52	0.37

Interim Dividends (Per Share)

Amt	Decl	Ex	Rec	Pay
0.21Q	05/11/2012	05/24/2012	05/29/2012	06/12/2012
0.21Q	07/12/2012	08/23/2012	08/27/2012	09/11/2012
0.21Q	11/09/2012	11/21/2012	11/26/2012	12/10/2012
0.21Q	01/11/2013	02/21/2013	02/25/2013	03/11/2013

Indicated Div: $0.84

Valuation Analysis / Institutional Holding

Forecast EPS	$5.65	No of Institutions
	(04/06/2013)	409
Market Cap	$3.5 Billion	Shares
Book Value	$5.2 Billion	81,327,552
Price/Book	0.68	% Held
Price/Sales	0.42	85.40

Business Summary: Life & Health (MIC: 5.2.2 SIC: 6321 NAIC: 524113)

Assurant is a holding company. Through its subsidiaries, Co. is a provider of insurance products and related services. Co. has four operating segments: Assurant Solutions, which provides debt protection administration, credit-related insurance, warranties and service contracts, and pre-funded funeral insurance; Assurant Specialty Property, which provides lender-placed homeowners insurance and manufactured housing homeowners insurance; Assurant Health, which provides individual health and small employer group health insurance; and Assurant Employee Benefits, which provides group dental insurance, group disability insurance, and group life insurance.

Recent Developments: For the year ended Dec 31 2012, net income decreased 10.3% to US$483.7 million from US$539.0 million in the prior year. Revenues were US$8.51 billion, up 2.8% from US$8.27 billion the year before. Net premiums earned were US$7.24 billion versus US$7.13 billion in the prior year, an increase of 1.6%. Net investment income rose 3.4% to US$713.1 million from US$689.5 million a year ago.

Prospects: Our evaluation of Assurant Inc. as of Apr. 7, 2013 is the result of our systematic analysis on three basic characteristics: earnings strength, relative valuation, and recent stock price movement. The company has suffered a very negative trend in earnings per share over the past 5 quarters. However, while recent estimates for the company have been mixed, AIZ has posted better than expected results. Based on operating earnings yield, the company is undervalued when compared to all of the companies in our coverage universe. Share price changes over the past year indicates that AIZ will perform very poorly over the near term.

Financial Data
(US$ in Thousands)

	12/31/2012	12/31/2011	12/31/2010	12/31/2009	12/31/2008	12/31/2007	12/31/2006	12/31/2005
Earnings Per Share	5.67	5.58	2.50	3.63	3.77	5.38	5.57	3.50
Cash Flow Per Share	8.04	8.85	4.89	2.29	8.46	10.05	7.28	7.51
Tang Book Value Per Share	54.43	46.13	40.79	33.66	23.07	27.64	24.81	22.17
Dividends Per Share	0.810	0.700	0.630	0.590	0.540	0.460	0.380	0.310
Dividend Payout %	14.29	12.54	25.20	16.25	14.32	8.55	6.82	8.86
Income Statement								
Total Revenue	8,508,270	8,272,804	8,527,722	8,700,501	8,601,228	8,453,515	8,070,584	7,497,675
EBITDA	867,652	830,508	726,107	832,047	683,927	1,127,344	1,205,614	766,767
Depn & Amortn	49,595	55,193	59,017	61,772	59,696	55,126	48,629	49,901
Income Before Taxes	757,751	714,955	606,444	709,606	563,278	1,011,040	1,095,742	655,608
Income Taxes	274,046	169,116	327,267	279,032	115,482	357,294	379,871	176,253
Net Income	483,705	545,839	279,177	430,574	447,796	653,746	717,418	479,355
Average Shares	85,307	97,795	111,473	118,495	118,836	121,436	128,812	136,945
Balance Sheet								
Current Assets	8,363,865	7,822,065	7,196,530	6,648,574	6,456,272	5,875,746	5,966,572	6,317,660
Total Assets	28,946,607	27,115,445	26,397,018	25,841,796	24,514,586	26,750,316	25,165,148	25,365,453
Current Liabilities	504,901	485,010	487,338	393,016	360,026	422,138	475,743	509,334
Long-Term Obligations	972,399	972,278	972,164	972,592	971,957	971,863	971,774	971,690
Total Liabilities	23,761,241	22,088,509	21,616,481	20,988,547	20,805,081	22,661,413	21,332,551	21,665,894
Stockholders' Equity	5,185,366	5,026,936	4,780,537	4,853,249	3,709,505	4,088,903	3,832,597	3,699,559
Shares Outstanding	78,664	88,524	102,000	116,648	117,368	117,808	122,618	130,591
Statistical Record								
Return on Assets %	1.72	2.04	1.07	1.71	1.74	2.52	2.84	1.92
Return on Equity %	9.45	11.13	5.80	10.06	11.45	16.51	19.05	13.07
EBITDA Margin %	10.20	10.04	8.51	9.56	7.95	13.34	14.94	10.23
Net Margin %	5.69	6.60	3.27	4.95	5.21	7.73	8.89	6.39
Asset Turnover	0.30	0.31	0.33	0.35	0.33	0.33	0.32	0.30
Current Ratio	16.57	16.13	14.77	16.92	17.93	13.92	12.54	12.40
Debt to Equity	0.19	0.19	0.20	0.20	0.26	0.24	0.25	0.26
Price Range	43.35-32.57	41.71-31.23	41.68-29.48	33.04-16.95	70.28-12.77	69.74-47.50	56.47-43.23	44.50-29.85
P/E Ratio	7.65-5.74	7.47-5.60	16.67-11.79	9.10-4.67	18.64-3.39	12.96-8.83	10.14-7.76	12.71-8.53
Average Yield %	2.18	1.88	1.76	2.20	0.99	0.81	0.76	0.85

Address: One Chase Manhattan Plaza, 41st Floor, New York, NY 10005
Telephone: 212-859-7000

Web Site: www.assurant.com
Officers: Robert Brian Pollock - President, Chief Executive Officer Michael J. Peninger - Executive Vice President, Chief Financial Officer

Auditors: PricewaterhouseCoopers LLP
Transfer Agents: Computershare Shareowner Services, Pittsburgh, PA

ASSURED GUARANTY LTD

Exchange	Symbol	Price	52Wk Range	Yield	P/E
NYS	AGO	$20.61 (3/28/2013)	20.95-11.26	1.94	36.16

*7 Year Price Score 70.96 ***NYSE Composite Index=100** ***12 Month Price Score 120.07**

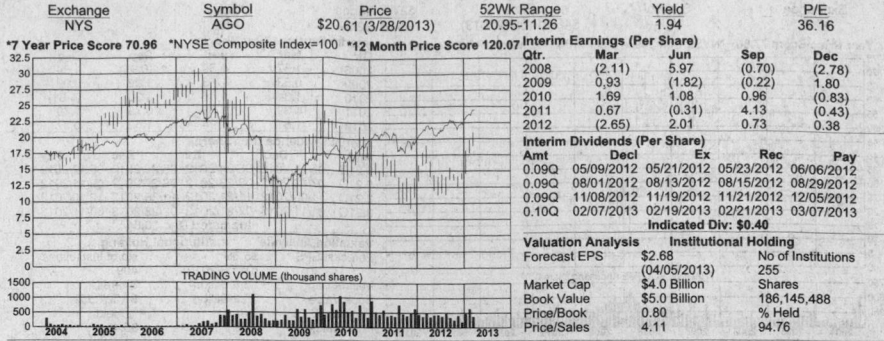

Interim Earnings (Per Share)

Qtr.	Mar	Jun	Sep	Dec
2008	(2.11)	5.97	(0.70)	(2.78)
2009	0.93	(1.82)	(0.22)	1.80
2010	1.69	1.08	0.96	(0.83)
2011	0.67	(0.31)	4.13	(0.43)
2012	(2.65)	2.01	0.73	0.38

Interim Dividends (Per Share)

Amt	Decl	Ex	Rec	Pay
0.09Q	05/09/2012	05/21/2012	05/23/2012	06/06/2012
0.09Q	08/01/2012	08/13/2012	08/15/2012	08/29/2012
0.09Q	11/08/2012	11/19/2012	11/21/2012	12/05/2012
0.10Q	02/07/2013	02/19/2013	02/21/2013	03/07/2013

Indicated Div: $0.40

Valuation Analysis

	Institutional Holding
Forecast EPS $2.68 (04/05/2013)	No of Institutions 255
Market Cap $4.0 Billion	Shares 186,145,488
Book Value $5.0 Billion	% Held 94.76
Price/Book 0.80	
Price/Sales 4.11	

Business Summary: General Insurance (MIC: 5.2.1 SIC: 6351 NAIC: 561450)

Assured Guaranty is a holding company that provides, through its subsidiaries, credit protection products to the U.S. and international public finance, infrastructure and structured finance markets. The securities insured by Co. include taxable and tax-exempt obligations issued by U.S. state or municipal governmental authorities, utility districts or facilities; notes or bonds issued to finance international infrastructure projects; and asset-backed securities issued by special purpose entities. Co. markets its credit protection products directly to issuers and underwriters of public finance, infrastructure and structured finance securities as well as to investors in such debt obligations.

Recent Developments: For the year ended Dec 31 2012, net income decreased 85.8% to US$110.0 million from US$773.0 million in the prior year. Revenues were US$973.0 million, down 46.5% from US$1.82 billion the year before. Net premiums earned were US$853.0 million versus US$920.0 million in the prior year, a decrease of 7.3%. Net investment income rose 2.0% to US$404.0 million from US$396.0 million a year ago.

Prospects: Our evaluation of Assured Guaranty Ltd. as of Apr. 7, 2013 is the result of our systematic analysis on three basic characteristics: earnings strength, relative valuation, and recent stock price movement. The company has managed to produce a neutral trend in earnings per share over the past 5 quarters. However, while recent estimates for the company have been mixed, AGO has posted better than expected results. Based on operating earnings yield, the company is undervalued when compared to all of the companies in our coverage universe. Share price changes over the past year indicates that AGO will perform in line with the market over the near term.

Financial Data

(US$ in Thousands)	12/31/2012	12/31/2011	12/31/2010	12/31/2009	12/31/2008	12/31/2007	12/31/2006	12/31/2005
Earnings Per Share	0.57	4.18	2.90	0.75	0.77	(4.46)	2.15	2.53
Cash Flow Per Share	(0.87)	3.68	0.57	2.21	4.84	5.67	3.57	2.38
Tang Book Value Per Share	25.74	25.89	20.67	19.12	20.24	19.78	23.18	21.08
Dividends Per Share	0.360	0.180	0.180	0.180	0.180	0.160	0.140	0.120
Dividend Payout %	63.16	4.31	6.21	24.00	23.38	...	6.51	4.74
Income Statement								
Total Revenue	973,000	1,819,313	1,401,301	929,587	553,188	(299,322)	322,058	294,534
EBITDA	228,000	1,151,830	781,481	227,448	138,011	(436,847)	209,821	250,167
Depn & Amortn	4,000	18,256	46,338	21,997	2,397	2,649	6,075	7,026
Income Before Taxes	132,000	1,034,462	635,522	142,668	112,331	(463,025)	189,974	229,621
Income Taxes	22,000	258,842	86,609	36,862	43,448	(159,753)	30,240	41,173
Net Income	110,000	775,620	548,913	97,186	68,883	(303,272)	159,734	188,448
Average Shares	190,700	185,500	188,900	129,128	88,946	68,029	74,248	74,487
Balance Sheet								
Current Assets	3,036,000	3,173,762	4,182,787	4,196,737	584,902	671,301	222,998	205,536
Total Assets	17,242,000	18,091,531	20,471,512	16,593,436	4,555,707	3,800,359	2,935,340	2,676,471
Current Liabilities	219,000	170,982	367,451	186,744	26,541	27,103	50,389	56,717
Long-Term Obligations	836,000	1,038,302	1,052,936	1,066,413	347,210	347,146	347,083	197,344
Total Liabilities	12,248,000	13,373,095	16,672,748	13,072,928	2,629,485	2,133,789	1,284,579	1,014,958
Stockholders' Equity	4,994,000	4,718,436	3,798,764	3,520,508	1,926,222	1,666,570	1,650,761	1,661,513
Shares Outstanding	194,003	182,235	183,744	184,162	90,955	79,948	67,534	74,761
Statistical Record								
Return on Assets %	0.62	4.02	2.96	0.92	1.64	N.M.	5.69	7.02
Return on Equity %	2.26	18.21	15.00	3.57	3.82	N.M.	9.64	11.82
EBITDA Margin %	23.43	63.31	55.77	24.47	24.95	...	65.15	84.94
Net Margin %	11.31	42.63	39.17	10.45	12.45	...	49.60	63.98
Asset Turnover	0.05	0.09	0.08	0.09	0.13	...	0.11	0.11
Current Ratio	13.86	18.56	11.38	22.47	22.04	24.77	4.43	3.62
Debt to Equity	0.17	0.22	0.28	0.30	0.18	0.21	0.21	0.12
Price Range	18.98-11.26	19.75-9.19	24.62-13.13	25.91-2.95	27.05-6.12	30.74-15.37	27.39-24.08	26.55-17.36
P/E Ratio	33.30-19.75	4.72-2.20	8.49-4.53	34.55-3.93	35.13-7.95	...	12.74-11.20	10.49-6.86
Average Yield %	2.53	1.27	0.96	1.28	0.98	0.60	0.55	0.56

Address: 30 Woodbourne Avenue, Hamilton, HM 08 **Telephone:** 441-279-5700	**Web Site:** www.assuredguaranty.com **Officers:** Dominic J. Frederico - Deputy Chairman, President, Chief Executive Officer Robert B. Mills - Chief Operating Officer	**Auditors:** PricewaterhouseCoopers LLP **Transfer Agents:** Mellon Investor Services LLC

ASTORIA FINANCIAL CORP.

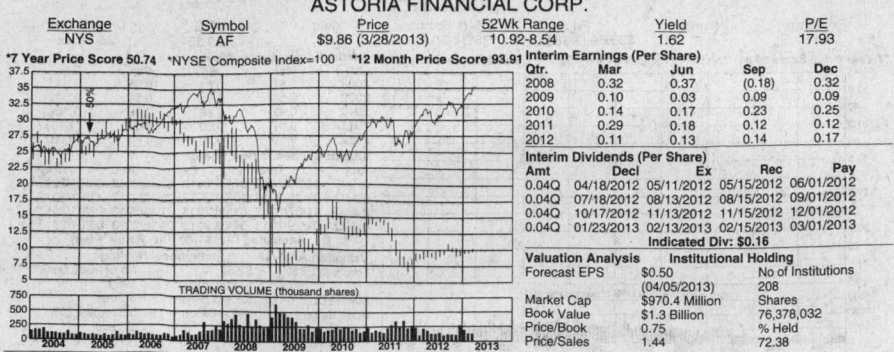

Exchange	Symbol	Price	52Wk Range	Yield	P/E
NYS	AF	$9.86 (3/28/2013)	10.92-8.54	1.62	17.93

*7 Year Price Score 50.74 *NYSE Composite Index=100 *12 Month Price Score 93.91

Interim Earnings (Per Share)

Qtr.	Mar	Jun	Sep	Dec
2008	0.32	0.37	(0.18)	0.32
2009	0.10	0.03	0.09	0.09
2010	0.14	0.17	0.23	0.25
2011	0.29	0.18	0.12	0.12
2012	0.11	0.13	0.14	0.17

Interim Dividends (Per Share)

Amt	Decl	Ex	Rec	Pay
0.04Q	04/18/2012	05/11/2012	05/15/2012	06/01/2012
0.04Q	07/18/2012	08/13/2012	08/15/2012	09/01/2012
0.04Q	10/17/2012	11/13/2012	11/15/2012	12/01/2012
0.04Q	01/23/2013	02/13/2013	02/15/2013	03/01/2013

Indicated Div: $0.16

Valuation Analysis / **Institutional Holding**

Forecast EPS	$0.50	No of Institutions
	(04/05/2013)	208
Market Cap	$970.4 Million	Shares
Book Value	$1.3 Billion	76,378,032
Price/Book	0.75	% Held
Price/Sales	1.44	72.38

TRADING VOLUME (thousand shares)

Business Summary: Credit & Lending (MIC: 5.4.1 SIC: 6035 NAIC: 522120)

Astoria Financial is a unitary savings and loan association holding company of Astoria Federal Savings and Loan Association and its consolidated subsidiaries (Astoria Federal). Astoria Federal's primary business is accepting retail deposits from the general public and investing those deposits, together with funds generated from operations, principal repayments on loans and securities and borrowings, primarily in one-to-four family mortgage loans, multi-family mortgage loans, commercial real estate loans and mortgage-backed securities. Astoria Federal also invests in consumer and other loans. At Dec 31 2011, Co. had total assets of $17.02 billion and total deposits of $11.25 billion.

Recent Developments: For the year ended Dec 31 2012, net income decreased 21.0% to US$53.1 million from US$67.2 million in the prior year. Net interest income decreased 7.2% to US$348.3 million from US$375.4 million in the prior year. Provision for loan losses was US$40.4 million versus US$37.0 million in the prior year, an increase of 9.2%. Non-interest income rose 6.3% to US$73.2 million from US$68.9 million, while non-interest expense declined 0.4% to US$300.1 million.

Prospects: Our evaluation of Astoria Financial Corp. as of Apr. 7, 2013 is the result of our systematic analysis on three basic characteristics: earnings strength, relative valuation, and recent stock price movement. The company has produced a positive trend in earnings per share over the past 5 quarters. However, while recent estimates for the company have been lowered by analysts, AF has posted better than expected results. Based on operating earnings yield, the company is undervalued when compared to all of the companies in our coverage universe. Share price changes over the past year indicates that AF will perform well over the near term.

Financial Data
(US$ in Thousands)

	12/31/2012	12/31/2011	12/31/2010	12/31/2009	12/31/2008	12/31/2007	12/31/2006	12/31/2005
Earnings Per Share	0.55	0.70	0.78	0.30	0.83	1.36	1.80	2.26
Cash Flow Per Share	1.96	2.44	2.89	1.86	2.63	2.30	2.29	2.68
Tang Book Value Per Share	11.20	10.74	10.70	10.45	10.31	10.58	10.33	10.94
Dividends Per Share	0.250	0.520	0.520	0.520	1.040	1.040	0.960	0.800
Dividend Payout %	45.45	74.29	66.67	173.33	125.30	76.47	53.33	35.40
Income Statement								
Interest Income	600,509	695,248	855,299	997,541	1,089,711	1,105,322	1,086,814	1,082,987
Interest Expense	252,240	319,822	421,732	568,772	694,327	771,794	696,429	604,207
Net Interest Income	348,269	375,426	433,567	428,769	395,384	333,528	390,385	478,780
Provision for Losses	40,400	37,000	115,000	200,000	69,000	2,500	...	...
Non-Interest Income	73,235	68,915	81,188	79,801	11,180	75,790	91,350	102,199
Non-Interest Expense	300,133	301,417	284,918	270,056	233,260	231,273	221,803	228,734
Income Before Taxes	80,971	105,924	114,837	38,514	104,304	175,545	259,932	352,245
Income Taxes	27,880	38,715	41,103	10,830	28,962	50,723	85,035	118,442
Net Income	53,091	67,209	73,734	27,684	75,342	124,822	174,897	233,803
Average Shares	95,455	93,253	91,776	90,602	90,687	92,092	97,280	103,408
Balance Sheet								
Net Loans & Leases	13,154,777	13,149,813	14,066,418	15,620,947	16,598,687	16,082,374	14,908,291	14,334,785
Total Assets	16,496,642	17,022,055	18,089,269	20,252,179	21,982,111	21,719,368	21,554,519	22,380,271
Total Deposits	10,443,958	11,245,614	11,599,000	12,812,238	13,479,924	13,049,438	13,224,024	12,810,455
Total Liabilities	15,202,653	15,770,857	16,847,489	19,043,565	20,800,342	20,508,024	20,338,765	21,030,044
Stockholders' Equity	1,293,989	1,251,198	1,241,780	1,208,614	1,181,769	1,211,344	1,215,754	1,350,227
Shares Outstanding	98,419	98,537	97,877	97,083	95,881	95,728	98,211	104,967
Statistical Record								
Return on Assets %	0.32	0.38	0.38	0.13	0.34	0.58	0.80	1.02
Return on Equity %	4.16	5.39	6.02	2.32	6.28	10.29	13.63	17.19
Net Interest Margin %	58.00	54.00	50.69	42.98	36.28	30.17	35.92	44.21
Efficiency Ratio %	44.55	39.44	30.42	25.07	21.19	19.58	18.83	19.30
Loans to Deposits	1.26	1.17	1.21	1.22	1.23	1.23	1.13	1.12
Price Range	10.92-8.33	15.06-6.64	17.46-11.65	16.84-6.10	28.87-14.44	30.29-23.00	31.79-27.32	30.21-24.11
P/E Ratio	19.85-15.15	21.51-9.49	22.38-14.94	56.13-20.03	34.78-17.40	22.27-16.91	17.66-15.18	13.37-10.67
Average Yield %	2.63	4.44	3.80	5.31	4.76	3.94	3.19	2.96

Address: One Astoria Federal Plaza, Lake Success, NY 11042-1085 Telephone: 516-327-3000 Fax: 516-327-7860	Web Site: www.astoriafederal.com Officers: Ralph F. Palleschi - Non-Executive Chairman Gerard C. Keegan - Vice-Chairman, Chief Executive Officer, Chief Administrative Officer, Chief Operating Officer	Auditors: KPMG LLP Investor Contact: 516-327-3000 Transfer Agents: Computershare, South Hackensack, NJ

AT&T INC

Exchange	Symbol	Price	52Wk Range	Yield	P/E	Div Achiever
NYS	T	$36.69 (3/28/2013)	38.34-30.13	4.91	29.35	28 Years

*7 Year Price Score 99.01   *NYSE Composite Index=100   *12 Month Price Score 94.41

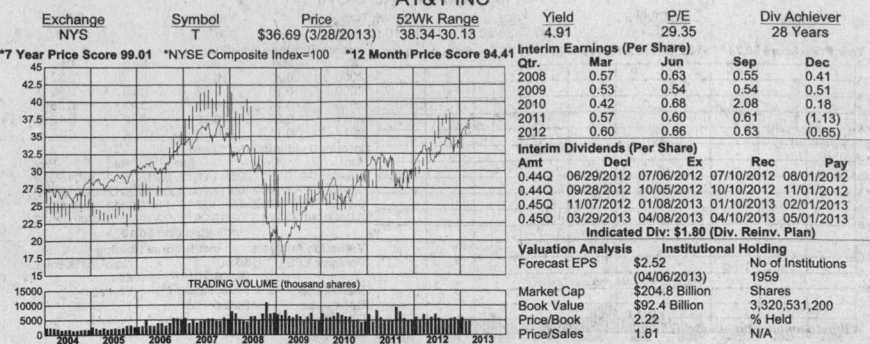

Interim Earnings (Per Share)

Qtr.	Mar	Jun	Sep	Dec
2008	0.57	0.63	0.55	0.41
2009	0.53	0.54	0.54	0.51
2010	0.42	0.68	2.08	0.18
2011	0.57	0.60	0.61	(1.13)
2012	0.60	0.66	0.63	(0.65)

Interim Dividends (Per Share)

Amt	Decl	Ex	Rec	Pay
0.44Q	06/29/2012	07/06/2012	07/10/2012	08/01/2012
0.44Q	09/28/2012	10/05/2012	10/10/2012	11/01/2012
0.45Q	11/07/2012	01/08/2013	01/10/2013	02/01/2013
0.45Q	03/29/2013	04/08/2013	04/10/2013	05/01/2013

Indicated Div: $1.80 (Div. Reinv. Plan)

Valuation Analysis

		Institutional Holding	
Forecast EPS	$2.52	No of Institutions	
	(04/06/2013)	1959	
Market Cap	$204.8 Billion	Shares	
Book Value	$92.4 Billion	3,320,531,200	
Price/Book	2.22	% Held	
Price/Sales	1.61	N/A	

Business Summary: Services (MIC: 6.1.2 SIC: 4813 NAIC: 511140)

AT&T is a provider of telecommunications services in the U.S. and globally. The services and products that Co. provides include: wireless communications, local exchange services, long-distance services, data/broadband and Internet services, video services, telecommunications equipment, managed networking, and wholesale services. Co. groups its subsidiaries as follows: wireless subsidiaries provide both wireless voice and data communications services across the U.S. and in foreign countries; and wireline subsidiaries provide primarily landline voice and data communication services, AT&T U-verse® high-speed broadband, video, and voice services and managed networking to business customers.

Recent Developments: For the year ended Dec 31 2012, income from continuing operations increased 80.2% to US$7.54 billion from US$4.18 billion a year earlier. Net income increased 80.2% to US$7.54 billion from US$4.18 billion in the prior year. Revenues were US$127.43 billion, up 0.6% from US$126.72 billion the year before. Operating income was US$13.00 billion versus US$9.22 billion in the prior year, an increase of 41.0%. Direct operating expenses rose 0.7% to US$55.22 billion from US$54.84 billion in the comparable period the year before. Indirect operating expenses decreased 5.5% to US$59.22 billion from US$62.67 billion in the equivalent prior-year period.

Prospects: Our evaluation of AT&T Inc. as of Apr. 7, 2013 is the result of our systematic analysis on three basic characteristics: earnings strength, relative valuation, and recent stock price movement. The company has managed to produce a neutral trend in earnings per share over the past 5 quarters. However, while recent estimates for the company have been mixed, T has posted results that fell short of analysts expectations. Based on operating earnings yield, the company is undervalued when compared to all of the companies in our coverage universe. Share price changes over the past year indicates that T will perform in line with the market over the near term.

Financial Data

(US$ in Thousands)	12/31/2012	12/31/2011	12/31/2010	12/31/2009	12/31/2008	12/31/2007	12/31/2006	12/31/2005
Earnings Per Share	1.25	0.66	3.35	2.12	2.16	1.94	1.89	1.42
Cash Flow Per Share	6.73	5.84	5.92	5.84	5.66	5.56	4.02	3.85
Tang Book Value Per Share	N.M.	N.M.	N.M.	N.M.	N.M.	N.M.	N.M.	8.29
Dividends Per Share	1.760	1.720	1.680	1.640	1.600	1.420	1.330	1.290
Dividend Payout %	140.80	260.61	50.15	77.36	74.07	73.20	70.37	90.85
Income Statement								
Total Revenue	127,434,000	126,723,000	124,280,000	123,018,000	124,028,000	118,928,000	63,055,000	43,862,000
EBITDA	30,064,000	25,835,000	36,872,000	37,603,000	37,787,000	36,644,000	19,178,000	13,554,000
Depn & Amortn	16,933,000	16,368,000	16,402,000	15,959,000	15,313,000	15,625,000	8,874,000	7,372,000
Income Before Taxes	9,687,000	5,932,000	17,476,000	18,265,000	19,084,000	17,512,000	8,838,000	5,109,000
Income Taxes	2,900,000	2,532,000	(1,162,000)	6,156,000	7,036,000	6,253,000	3,525,000	932,000
Net Income	7,264,000	3,944,000	19,864,000	12,535,000	12,867,000	11,951,000	7,356,000	4,786,000
Average Shares	5,820,999	5,949,999	5,937,999	5,923,999	5,957,999	6,169,999	3,902,000	3,379,000
Balance Sheet								
Current Assets	22,706,000	23,027,000	19,951,000	24,334,000	22,556,000	24,686,000	25,553,000	14,654,000
Total Assets	272,315,000	270,344,000	268,488,000	268,752,000	265,245,000	275,644,000	270,634,000	145,632,000
Current Liabilities	31,787,000	30,794,000	33,951,000	36,705,000	42,290,000	39,274,000	40,482,000	25,418,000
Long-Term Obligations	66,358,000	61,300,000	58,971,000	64,720,000	60,872,000	57,255,000	50,063,000	26,115,000
Total Liabilities	179,953,000	164,810,000	156,841,000	166,852,000	168,898,000	160,277,000	155,094,000	90,942,000
Stockholders' Equity	92,362,000	105,534,000	111,647,000	101,900,000	96,347,000	115,367,000	115,540,000	54,690,000
Shares Outstanding	5,581,394	5,926,511	5,911,086	5,901,930	5,893,008	6,043,544	6,238,745	3,876,884
Statistical Record								
Return on Assets %	2.67	1.46	7.39	4.69	4.74	4.38	3.53	3.76
Return on Equity %	7.32	3.63	18.60	12.65	12.12	10.35	8.64	10.06
EBITDA Margin %	23.59	20.39	29.67	30.57	30.47	30.81	30.41	30.90
Net Margin %	5.70	3.11	15.98	10.19	10.37	10.05	11.67	10.91
Asset Turnover	0.47	0.47	0.46	0.46	0.46	0.44	0.30	0.34
Current Ratio	0.71	0.75	0.59	0.66	0.53	0.63	0.63	0.58
Debt to Equity	0.72	0.58	0.53	0.64	0.63	0.50	0.43	0.48
Price Range	38.34-29.16	31.86-27.33	29.44-24.13	29.42-21.72	41.56-22.42	42.83-33.81	35.75-24.45	25.77-22.10
P/E Ratio	30.67-23.33	48.27-41.41	8.79-7.20	13.88-10.25	19.24-10.38	22.08-17.43	18.92-12.94	18.15-15.56
Average Yield %	5.20	5.86	6.30	6.40	4.81	3.62	4.54	5.38

Address: 208 S. Akard St., Dallas, TX 75202
Telephone: 210-821-4105

Web Site: www.att.com
Officers: Randall L. Stephenson - Chairman, President, Chief Executive Officer, Senior Executive Vice President, Chief Financial Officer, Chief Operating Officer William A. Blase - Senior Executive Vice President

Auditors: Ernst & Young LLP
Investor Contact: 210-351-2058
Transfer Agents: Computershare Trust Company, N.A, Providence, RI

ATMOS ENERGY CORP.

Exchange	Symbol	Price	52Wk Range	Yield	P/E	Div Achiever
NYS	ATO	$42.69 (3/28/2013)	42.69-30.91	3.28	17.01	25 Years

*7 Year Price Score 105.46 *NYSE Composite Index=100 *12 Month Price Score 101.74

TRADING VOLUME (thousand shares)

Interim Earnings (Per Share)

Qtr.	Dec	Mar	Jun	Sep
2009-10	1.00	1.22	(0.03)	0.02
2010-11	0.81	1.45	(0.01)	0.02
2011-12	0.75	1.20	0.34	0.09
2012-13	0.88	...	...	...

Interim Dividends (Per Share)

Amt	Decl	Ex	Rec	Pay
0.345Q	05/02/2012	05/23/2012	05/25/2012	06/11/2012
0.345Q	08/08/2012	08/23/2012	08/27/2012	09/10/2012
0.35Q	11/07/2012	11/21/2012	11/26/2012	12/10/2012
0.35Q	02/06/2013	02/28/2013	03/04/2013	03/18/2013

Indicated Div: $1.40 (Div. Reinv. Plan)

Valuation Analysis / **Institutional Holding**

Forecast EPS	$2.47 (04/05/2013)	No of Institutions 363
Market Cap	$3.9 Billion	Shares
Book Value	$2.4 Billion	61,869,960
Price/Book	1.59	% Held
Price/Sales	1.15	59.15

Business Summary: Gas Utilities (MIC: 3.3.1 SIC: 4924 NAIC: 486210)

Atmos Energy is engaged in the regulated natural gas distribution and transmission and storage businesses as well as other nonregulated natural gas businesses. Co. has three segments: natural gas distribution, which includes regulated natural gas distribution and related sales operations; regulated transmission and storage, which includes the regulated pipeline and storage operations of Co.'s Atmos Pipeline - Texas Division; and nonregulated, which includes its nonregulated natural gas management, nonregulated natural gas transmission, storage and other services. At Sep 30 2012, Co. delivered natural gas to residential, commercial, public authority and industrial customers in nine states.

Recent Developments: For the quarter ended Dec 31 2012, income from continuing operations increased 24.0% to US$77.3 million from US$62.4 million in the year-earlier quarter. Net income increased 17.5% to US$80.5 million from US$68.5 million in the year-earlier quarter. Revenues were US$1.03 billion, down 4.6% from US$1.08 billion the year before. Operating income was US$154.9 million versus US$139.5 million in the prior-year quarter, an increase of 11.1%. Direct operating expenses declined 7.8% to US$671.8 million from US$728.6 million in the comparable period the year before. Indirect operating expenses decreased 3.9% to US$207.4 million from US$215.9 million in the equivalent prior-year period.

Prospects: Our evaluation of Atmos Energy Corp. as of Apr. 7, 2013 is the result of our systematic analysis on three basic characteristics: earnings strength, relative valuation, and recent stock price movement. The company has generated a negative trend in earnings per share over the past 5 quarters and while recent estimates for the company have been raised by analysts, ATO has posted results that fell short of analysts expectations. Based on operating earnings yield, the company is undervalued when compared to all of the companies in our coverage universe. Share price changes over the past year indicates that ATO will perform in line with the market over the near term.

Financial Data

(US$ in Thousands)	3 Mos	09/30/2012	09/30/2011	09/30/2010	09/30/2009	09/30/2008	09/30/2007	09/30/2006
Earnings Per Share	2.51	2.37	2.27	2.20	2.08	2.00	1.92	1.82
Cash Flow Per Share	7.00	6.49	6.46	7.91	10.09	4.14	6.29	3.86
Tang Book Value Per Share	18.60	17.93	16.78	15.95	15.52	14.46	13.75	11.13
Dividends Per Share	1.385	1.380	1.360	1.340	1.320	1.300	1.280	1.260
Dividend Payout %	55.18	58.23	59.91	60.91	63.46	65.00	66.67	69.23
Income Statement								
Total Revenue	1,034,155	3,438,483	4,347,634	4,789,690	4,969,080	7,221,305	5,898,431	6,152,363
EBITDA	216,248	678,173	696,781	706,230	661,401	631,215	606,875	569,464
Depn & Amortn	60,628	246,577	233,383	217,133	217,302	200,589	199,055	185,967
Income Before Taxes	125,098	290,422	312,573	334,626	291,269	292,704	262,584	236,890
Income Taxes	47,750	98,226	113,689	128,787	100,291	112,373	94,092	89,153
Net Income	80,465	216,717	207,601	205,839	190,978	180,331	168,492	147,737
Average Shares	91,309	91,172	90,652	92,422	92,024	90,272	87,745	81,390
Balance Sheet								
Current Assets	1,164,634	827,962	1,010,953	875,192	828,940	1,285,104	1,068,895	1,117,545
Total Assets	7,964,218	7,495,675	7,282,871	6,763,791	6,343,766	6,386,699	5,896,917	5,719,547
Current Liabilities	1,645,051	1,275,954	867,598	1,166,079	737,421	1,207,087	919,678	1,119,161
Long-Term Obligations	1,956,376	1,956,305	2,206,117	1,809,551	2,169,400	2,119,792	2,126,315	2,180,362
Total Liabilities	5,540,213	5,136,432	5,027,450	4,585,443	4,167,005	4,334,207	3,931,163	4,071,449
Stockholders' Equity	2,424,005	2,359,243	2,255,421	2,178,348	2,176,761	2,052,492	1,965,754	1,648,098
Shares Outstanding	90,516	90,239	90,296	90,164	92,551	90,814	89,326	81,739
Statistical Record								
Return on Assets %	2.93	2.92	2.96	3.14	3.00	2.93	2.90	2.60
Return on Equity %	9.75	9.37	9.36	9.45	9.03	8.95	9.32	9.09
EBITDA Margin %	20.91	19.72	16.03	14.74	13.31	8.74	10.29	9.26
Net Margin %	7.78	6.30	4.78	4.30	3.84	2.50	2.86	2.40
Asset Turnover	0.43	0.46	0.62	0.73	0.78	1.17	1.02	1.08
Current Ratio	0.71	0.65	1.17	0.75	1.12	1.06	1.16	1.00
Debt to Equity	0.81	0.83	0.98	0.83	1.00	1.03	1.08	1.32
Price Range	36.94-30.60	36.94-30.60	34.98-28.87	30.06-26.41	28.80-20.20	29.46-25.09	33.11-26.47	29.11-25.79
P/E Ratio	14.72-12.19	15.59-12.91	15.41-12.72	13.66-12.00	13.85-9.71	14.73-12.55	17.24-13.79	15.99-14.17
Average Yield %	4.07	4.11	4.20	4.70	5.35	4.79	4.16	4.66

Address: Three Lincoln Centre, Suite 1800, 5430 LBJ Freeway, Dallas, TX 75240 **Telephone:** 972-934-9227 **Fax:** 972-855-3075	**Web Site:** www.atmosenergy.com **Officers:** Kim R. Cocklin - President, Chief Executive Officer Louis P. Gregory - Senior Vice President, General Counsel, Secretary	**Auditors:** Ernst & Young LLP **Investor Contact:** 972-855-3729 **Transfer Agents:** American Stock Transfer & Trust Company, New York, NY

ATWOOD OCEANICS, INC.

Exchange	Symbol	Price	52Wk Range	Yield	P/E
NYS	ATW	$52.54 (3/28/2013)	55.44-35.50	N/A	12.39

*7 Year Price Score 113.50 *NYSE Composite Index=100 *12 Month Price Score 104.60

TRADING VOLUME (thousand shares)

Interim Earnings (Per Share)

Qtr.	Dec	Mar	Jun	Sep
2009-10	1.03	1.03	0.91	0.99
2010-11	0.81	1.08	1.15	1.11
2011-12	1.00	0.90	0.79	1.45
2012-13	1.10	...	...	...

Interim Dividends (Per Share)

Amt	Decl	Ex	Rec	Pay
100%	06/11/2008	07/14/2008	06/27/2008	07/11/2008

Valuation Analysis | **Institutional Holding**

Forecast EPS	$4.99	No of Institutions
	(04/06/2013)	377
Market Cap	$3.4 Billion	Shares
Book Value	$2.0 Billion	58,825,216
Price/Book	1.71	% Held
Price/Sales	4.07	86.44

Business Summary: Equipment & Services (MIC: 9.1.3 SIC: 1382 NAIC: 213112)

Atwood Oceanics and its subsidiaries is a global offshore drilling contractor engaged in the drilling and completion of exploratory and developmental oil and gas wells. As of Sep 30 2012, Co. owned a fleet of 11 mobile offshore drilling units, which consisted of six semisubmersible rigs, four jackup rigs, and one semisubmersible tender assist rig, located in the U.S. Gulf of Mexico, the Mediterranean Sea, offshore West Africa, offshore Southeast Asia and offshore Australia. In addition, Co. is constructing three drillships and two jackups. Co.'s customers consist primarily of integrated oil and natural gas companies and independent oil and natural gas companies.

Recent Developments: For the quarter ended Dec 31 2012, net income increased 11.2% to US$72.8 million in the year-earlier quarter. Revenues were US$245.1 million, up 32.7% from US$184.7 million the year before. Operating income was US$88.4 million versus US$76.9 million in the prior-year quarter, an increase of 15.0%. Direct operating expenses rose 42.9% to US$111.9 million from US$78.3 million in the comparable period the year before. Indirect operating expenses increased 52.1% to US$44.8 million from US$29.5 million in the equivalent prior-year period.

Prospects: Our evaluation of Atwood Oceanics Inc. as of Apr. 7, 2013 is the result of our systematic analysis on three basic characteristics: earnings strength, relative valuation, and recent stock price movement. The company has produced a positive trend in earnings per share over the past 5 quarters. However, while recent estimates for the company have been mixed, ATW has posted better than expected results. Based on operating earnings yield, the company is undervalued when compared to all of the companies in our coverage universe. Share price changes over the past year indicates that ATW will perform in line with the market over the near term.

Financial Data
(US$ in Thousands)

	3 Mos	09/30/2012	09/30/2011	09/30/2010	09/30/2009	09/30/2008	09/30/2007	09/30/2006
Earnings Per Share	4.24	4.14	4.15	3.95	3.89	3.34	2.19	1.37
Cash Flow Per Share	4.80	3.91	5.25	4.76	4.75	3.00	3.04	1.38
Tang Book Value Per Share	30.72	29.63	25.44	21.26	17.16	13.18	9.72	7.39
Income Statement								
Total Revenue	245,093	787,421	645,076	650,562	586,507	526,604	403,037	276,625
EBITDA	116,953	390,009	372,257	359,370	333,561	279,389	192,573	123,403
Depn & Amortn	28,582	70,599	43,597	37,030	35,119	34,783	33,366	26,401
Income Before Taxes	84,087	313,304	324,847	319,979	296,431	244,775	159,959	91,836
Income Taxes	11,256	41,133	53,173	62,983	45,686	29,337	20,935	5,714
Net Income	72,831	272,171	271,674	256,996	250,745	215,438	139,024	86,122
Average Shares	66,092	65,781	65,403	65,028	64,493	64,556	63,628	62,884
Balance Sheet								
Current Assets	368,368	370,534	460,931	359,994	304,604	308,264	216,179	147,673
Total Assets	3,258,946	2,943,762	2,375,391	1,724,440	1,509,402	1,099,958	717,724	593,829
Current Liabilities	136,090	136,667	159,323	93,460	112,918	60,212	57,630	61,365
Long-Term Obligations	1,070,000	830,000	520,000	230,000	275,000	170,000	...	28,000
Total Liabilities	1,242,620	1,004,340	722,604	354,306	407,109	256,268	101,869	134,935
Stockholders' Equity	2,016,326	1,939,422	1,652,787	1,370,134	1,102,293	843,690	615,855	458,894
Shares Outstanding	65,632	65,452	64,960	64,443	64,236	64,031	63,350	62,092
Statistical Record								
Return on Assets %	9.96	10.21	13.25	15.89	19.22	23.64	21.20	15.81
Return on Equity %	14.96	15.11	17.97	20.79	25.77	29.44	25.87	20.98
EBITDA Margin %	47.72	49.53	57.71	55.24	56.87	53.05	47.78	44.61
Net Margin %	29.72	34.56	42.12	39.50	42.75	40.91	34.49	31.13
Asset Turnover	0.30	0.30	0.31	0.40	0.45	0.58	0.61	0.51
Current Ratio	2.71	2.71	2.89	3.85	2.70	5.12	3.75	2.41
Debt to Equity	0.53	0.43	0.31	0.17	0.25	0.20	...	0.06
Price Range	50.03-35.50	49.34-31.98	48.33-29.73	40.09-24.21	36.40-13.49	62.17-33.31	40.28-21.01	29.04-16.65
P/E Ratio	11.80-8.37	11.92-7.72	11.65-7.16	10.15-6.13	9.36-3.47	18.61-9.97	18.39-9.59	21.20-12.15

Address: 15835 Park Ten Place Drive, Houston, TX 77084 **Telephone:** 281-749-7800	**Web Site:** www.atwd.com **Officers:** Robert J. Saltiel - President, Chief Executive Officer Mark-Anthony Lovell Mey - Senior Vice President, Chief Financial Officer	**Auditors:** PricewaterhouseCoopers LLP **Investor Contact:** 281-749-7902 **Transfer Agents:** Continental Stock Transfer & Trust Company, New York, NY

AUTOLIV INC.

Exchange	Symbol	Price	52Wk Range	Yield	P/E
NYS	ALV	$69.14 (3/28/2013)	69.58-51.89	2.89	13.61

*7 Year Price Score 102.66 *NYSE Composite Index=100 *12 Month Price Score 100.52

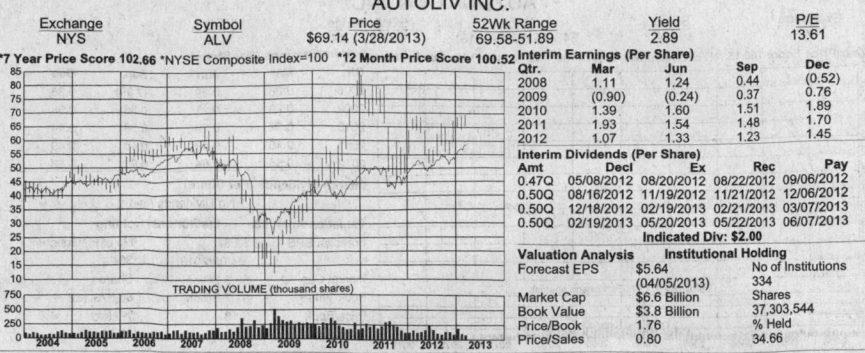

Interim Earnings (Per Share)

Qtr.	Mar	Jun	Sep	Dec
2008	1.11	1.24	0.44	(0.52)
2009	(0.90)	(0.24)	0.37	0.76
2010	1.39	1.60	1.51	1.89
2011	1.93	1.54	1.48	1.70
2012	1.07	1.33	1.23	1.45

Interim Dividends (Per Share)

Amt	Decl	Ex	Rec	Pay
0.47Q	05/08/2012	08/20/2012	08/22/2012	09/06/2012
0.50Q	08/16/2012	11/19/2012	11/21/2012	12/06/2012
0.50Q	12/18/2012	02/19/2013	02/21/2013	03/07/2013
0.50Q	02/19/2013	05/20/2013	05/22/2013	06/07/2013

Indicated Div: $2.00

Valuation Analysis | **Institutional Holding**

Forecast EPS	$5.64	No of Institutions
	(04/05/2013)	334
Market Cap	$6.6 Billion	Shares
Book Value	$3.8 Billion	37,303,544
Price/Book	1.76	% Held
Price/Sales	0.80	34.66

TRADING VOLUME (thousand shares)

Business Summary: Auto Parts (MIC: 1.8.2 SIC: 3714 NAIC: 336399)

Autoliv functions as a holding corporation. Through its two principal subsidiaries, Autoliv AB and Autoliv ASP, Inc., Co. is engaged as a developer, manufacturer and supplier to the automotive industry of automotive safety systems with a range of products, including modules and components for passenger and driver-side airbags, airbag protection systems, seatbelts, steering wheels, safety electronics, whiplash protection systems and child seats, as well as night vision systems, radar and other safety systems. Co.'s geographical regions are in Europe, the Americas, China, Japan and the Rest of Asia.

Recent Developments: For the year ended Dec 31 2012, net income decreased 22.6% to US$485.6 million from US$627.0 million in the prior year. Revenues were US$8.27 billion, up 0.4% from US$8.23 billion the year before. Operating income was US$705.4 million versus US$889.2 million in the prior year, a decrease of 20.7%. Direct operating expenses rose 1.8% to US$6.62 billion from US$6.50 billion in the comparable period the year before. Indirect operating expenses increased 12.2% to US$940.8 million from US$838.7 million in the equivalent prior-year period.

Prospects: Our evaluation of Autoliv Inc. as of Apr. 7, 2013 is the result of our systematic analysis on three basic characteristics: earnings strength, relative valuation, and recent stock price movement. The company has managed to produce a neutral trend in earnings per share over the past 5 quarters and while recent estimates for the company have been raised by analysts, ALV has posted better than expected results. Based on operating earnings yield, the company is undervalued when compared to all of the companies in our coverage universe. Share price changes over the past year indicates that ALV will perform poorly over the near term.

Financial Data
(US$ in Thousands)

	12/31/2012	12/31/2011	12/31/2010	12/31/2009	12/31/2008	12/31/2007	12/31/2006	12/31/2005
Earnings Per Share	5.08	6.65	6.39	0.12	2.28	3.68	4.88	3.26
Cash Flow Per Share	7.34	8.50	10.59	6.04	8.52	10.02	6.82	5.37
Tang Book Value Per Share	21.48	18.11	13.55	7.75	5.28	7.99	9.07	7.61
Dividends Per Share	1.890	1.730	0.650	0.210	1.600	1.540	1.360	1.170
Dividend Payout %	37.20	26.02	10.17	175.00	70.18	41.85	27.87	35.89
Income Statement								
Total Revenue	8,266,700	8,232,400	7,170,600	5,120,700	6,473,200	6,769,000	6,118,000	6,204,900
EBITDA	972,000	1,146,900	1,132,600	378,300	651,800	814,100	813,300	821,200
Depn & Amortn	273,200	268,300	281,700	314,300	346,900	320,800	298,800	308,900
Income Before Taxes	660,500	821,500	800,000	1,700	244,800	439,800	476,200	474,900
Income Taxes	183,000	201,300	210,000	(7,100)	76,300	150,300	58,900	173,200
Net Income	483,100	623,400	590,600	10,000	164,700	287,900	402,300	292,600
Average Shares	95,100	93,700	92,400	84,500	72,100	78,300	82,500	89,700
Balance Sheet								
Current Assets	3,289,200	3,000,300	2,688,600	2,179,600	2,086,300	2,095,200	2,098,400	2,162,500
Total Assets	6,570,300	6,117,300	5,664,500	5,185,600	5,205,600	5,305,400	5,110,800	5,065,200
Current Liabilities	1,849,800	2,085,900	1,834,500	1,693,500	1,380,700	1,663,300	1,531,600	1,764,300
Long-Term Obligations	562,900	363,500	637,700	820,700	1,401,100	1,040,300	887,700	757,100
Total Liabilities	2,811,700	2,783,900	2,737,200	2,797,400	3,089,100	2,956,300	2,707,900	2,749,100
Stockholders' Equity	3,758,600	3,333,400	2,927,300	2,388,200	2,116,500	2,349,100	2,402,900	2,316,100
Shares Outstanding	95,500	89,293	88,963	85,100	70,300	73,800	80,100	83,700
Statistical Record								
Return on Assets %	7.59	10.58	10.89	0.19	3.13	5.53	7.91	5.62
Return on Equity %	13.59	19.91	22.22	0.44	7.36	12.12	17.05	11.82
EBITDA Margin %	11.76	13.93	15.80	7.39	10.07	12.03	13.29	13.23
Net Margin %	5.84	7.57	8.24	0.20	2.54	4.25	6.58	4.72
Asset Turnover	1.30	1.40	1.32	0.99	1.23	1.30	1.20	1.19
Current Ratio	1.78	1.44	1.47	1.29	1.51	1.26	1.37	1.23
Debt to Equity	0.15	0.11	0.22	0.34	0.66	0.44	0.37	0.33
Price Range	69.05-51.89	83.53-46.14	81.49-40.91	44.35-12.33	61.72-15.12	64.65-52.67	60.72-47.53	51.80-41.10
P/E Ratio	13.59-10.21	12.56-6.94	12.75-6.40	369.58-102.75	27.07-6.63	17.57-14.31	12.44-9.74	15.89-12.61
Average Yield %	3.10	2.63	1.14	0.73	3.87	2.63	2.47	2.57

Address: Vasagatan 11, 7th Floor, SE-111 20, Box 70381, Stockholm, SE-107 24 **Telephone:** 858-720-600	**Web Site:** www.autoliv.com **Officers:** Lars Nyberg - Chairman Jan Carlson - President, Chief Executive Officer	**Auditors:** Ernst & Young AB **Investor Contact:** 248-475-0427 **Transfer Agents:** Computershare Trust Company N.A

AUTONATION, INC.

Exchange	Symbol	Price	52Wk Range	Yield	P/E
NYS	AN	$43.75 (3/28/2013)	48.60-32.54	N/A	17.36

*7 Year Price Score 148.15 *NYSE Composite Index=100 *12 Month Price Score 102.16

TRADING VOLUME (thousand shares)

Interim Earnings (Per Share)

Qtr.	Mar	Jun	Sep	Dec
2008	0.28	0.29	(7.99)	0.36
2009	0.20	0.21	0.36	0.36
2010	0.32	0.29	0.38	0.44
2011	0.46	0.49	0.48	0.49
2012	0.55	0.64	0.66	0.68

Interim Dividends (Per Share)

No Dividends Paid

Valuation Analysis		Institutional Holding	
Forecast EPS	$2.87	No of Institutions	
	(04/05/2013)	304	
Market Cap	$5.3 Billion	Shares	
Book Value	$1.7 Billion	86,573,152	
Price/Book	3.13	% Held	
Price/Sales	0.34	48.20	

Business Summary: Retail - Automotive (MIC: 2.1.4 SIC: 5511 NAIC: 441110)

AutoNation, through its subsidiaries, is an automotive retailer. Co. provides a range of automotive products and services, including new vehicles, used vehicles, parts and service, which includes automotive repair and maintenance services as well as wholesale parts and collision businesses, and automotive finance and insurance products, which includes the arranging of financing for vehicle purchases through third-party finance sources. As of Dec 31 2012, Co. owned and operated 265 new vehicle franchises from 221 stores located in the U.S., predominantly in metropolitan markets in the Sunbelt region. As of Dec 31 2012, Co. had three operating segments: Domestic, Import, and Premium Luxury.

Recent Developments: For the year ended Dec 31 2012, income from continuing operations increased 11.6% to US$317.3 million from US$284.2 million a year earlier. Net income increased 12.4% to US$316.4 million from US$281.4 million in the prior year. Revenues were US$15.67 billion, up 13.3% from US$13.83 billion the year before. Operating income was US$645.3 million versus US$572.0 million in the prior year, an increase of 12.8%. Direct operating expenses rose 14.3% to US$13.18 billion from US$11.53 billion in the comparable period the year before. Indirect operating expenses increased 6.3% to US$1.84 billion from US$1.73 billion in the equivalent prior-year period.

Prospects: Our evaluation of AutoNation Inc. as of Apr. 7, 2013 is the result of our systematic analysis on three basic characteristics: earnings strength, relative valuation, and recent stock price movement. The company has managed to produce a neutral trend in earnings per share over the past 5 quarters. However, while recent estimates for the company have been mixed, AN has posted better than expected results. Based on operating earnings yield, the company is undervalued when compared to all of the companies in our coverage universe. Share price changes over the past year indicates that AN will perform very well over the near term.

Financial Data

(US$ in Thousands)	12/31/2012	12/31/2011	12/31/2010	12/31/2009	12/31/2008	12/31/2007	12/31/2006	12/31/2005
Earnings Per Share	2.52	1.91	1.43	1.12	(6.99)	1.39	1.38	1.85
Cash Flow Per Share	2.55	2.60	1.60	2.09	3.84	1.04	1.33	2.21
Tang Book Value Per Share	1.32	3.72	4.95	5.84	-4.93	2.20	2.88	6.53
Income Statement								
Total Revenue	15,668,800	13,832,300	12,461,000	10,757,800	14,131,900	17,691,500	18,988,600	19,253,400
EBITDA	741,800	657,300	558,800	509,300	(1,152,000)	799,300	887,800	895,200
Depn & Amortn	92,900	88,000	80,300	80,700	96,100	96,000	86,600	88,400
Income Before Taxes	516,800	461,300	381,300	351,000	(1,422,700)	459,300	542,100	622,900
Income Taxes	199,500	177,100	146,000	116,800	(197,300)	171,300	210,700	227,400
Net Income	316,400	281,400	226,600	198,000	(1,243,100)	278,700	316,900	496,500
Average Shares	125,800	147,300	158,600	177,300	177,800	200,000	229,300	268,000
Balance Sheet								
Current Assets	3,361,100	2,676,200	2,629,100	2,250,600	2,554,100	3,238,400	3,385,800	3,880,400
Total Assets	7,203,000	6,198,800	5,974,200	5,407,300	6,014,100	8,479,600	8,607,000	8,824,500
Current Liabilities	3,201,700	2,462,600	2,399,400	1,863,400	2,455,800	2,901,800	3,030,500	3,412,100
Long-Term Obligations	2,066,300	1,634,400	1,340,600	1,105,000	1,225,600	1,751,900	1,557,900	484,400
Total Liabilities	5,514,500	4,304,200	3,895,300	3,104,100	3,816,000	5,006,100	4,894,300	4,155,000
Stockholders' Equity	1,688,500	1,894,600	2,078,900	2,303,200	2,198,100	3,473,500	3,712,700	4,669,500
Shares Outstanding	120,856	135,784	148,364	171,731	176,853	180,356	206,752	262,232
Statistical Record								
Return on Assets %	4.71	4.62	3.98	3.47	N.M.	3.26	3.64	5.67
Return on Equity %	17.61	14.16	10.34	8.80	N.M.	7.76	7.56	11.12
EBITDA Margin %	4.73	4.75	4.48	4.73	N.M.	4.52	4.68	4.65
Net Margin %	2.02	2.03	1.82	1.84	N.M.	1.58	1.67	2.58
Asset Turnover	2.33	2.27	2.19	1.88	1.94	2.07	2.18	2.20
Current Ratio	1.05	1.09	1.10	1.21	1.04	1.12	1.12	1.14
Debt to Equity	1.22	0.86	0.64	0.48	0.56	0.50	0.42	0.10
Price Range	48.45-32.54	40.93-27.53	28.46-17.59	21.17-7.91	17.00-4.21	23.08-14.94	22.85-18.99	22.60-17.92
P/E Ratio	19.23-12.91	21.43-14.41	19.90-12.30	18.90-7.06	...	16.60-10.75	16.56-13.76	12.22-9.69

Address: 200 SW 1st Avenue, Fort Lauderdale, FL 33301 Telephone: 954-769-6000 Fax: 954-779-3884	Web Site: www.autonation.com Officers: Michael J. Jackson - Chairman, Chief Executive Officer Michael E. Maroone - President, Chief Operating Officer	Auditors: KPMG LLP Investor Contact: 954-769-7342 Transfer Agents: Computershare Investor Services LLC, Canton, MA

AUTOZONE, INC.

Exchange	Symbol	Price	52Wk Range	Yield	P/E
NYS	AZO	$396.77 (3/28/2013)	397.13-344.99	N/A	15.95

*7 Year Price Score 161.84 *NYSE Composite Index=100   *12 Month Price Score 94.36

Interim Earnings (Per Share)

Qtr.	Nov	Feb	Apr	Aug
2009-10	2.82	2.46	4.12	5.60
2010-11	3.77	3.34	5.29	7.12
2011-12	4.68	4.15	6.28	8.40
2012-13	5.41	4.78	...	...

Interim Dividends (Per Share)

No Dividends Paid

Valuation Analysis   **Institutional Holding**

Forecast EPS	$27.64	No of Institutions
	(04/05/2013)	601
Market Cap	$14.3 Billion	Shares
Book Value	N/A	35,478,004
Price/Book	N/A	% Held
Price/Sales	1.64	80.14

Business Summary: Retail - Automotive (MIC: 2.1.4 SIC: 5531 NAIC: 441310)

AutoZone is a retailer and a distributor of automotive replacement parts and accessories. At Aug 25 2012, Co. operated 4,685 stores in the U.S., including Puerto Rico, and 321 in Mexico. Each of Co.'s stores carries products for cars, sport utility vehicles, vans and light trucks, including new and remanufactured automotive hard parts, maintenance items, accessories and non-automotive products. Co. also has a commercial sales program that provides commercial credit and delivery of parts and other products to local, regional and national repair garages, dealers, service stations and public sector accounts. Co. also sells the ALLDATA brand automotive diagnostic and repairs software.

Recent Developments: For the quarter ended Feb 9 2013, net income increased 5.6% to US$176.2 million from US$166.9 million in the year-earlier quarter. Revenues were US$1.86 billion, up 2.8% from US$1.80 billion the year before. Operating income was US$317.6 million versus US$300.7 million in the prior-year quarter, an increase of 5.6%. Direct operating expenses rose 1.8% to US$893.2 million from US$877.9 million in the comparable period the year before. Indirect operating expenses increased 3.0% to US$644.4 million from US$625.6 million in the equivalent prior-year period.

Prospects: Our evaluation of AutoZone Inc. as of Apr. 7, 2013 is the result of our systematic analysis on three basic characteristics: earnings strength, relative valuation, and recent stock price movement. The company has managed to produce a neutral trend in earnings per share over the past 5 quarters and while recent estimates for the company have remained steady, AZO has posted better than expected results. Based on operating earnings yield, the company is undervalued when compared to all of the companies in our coverage universe. Share price changes over the past year indicates that AZO will perform poorly over the near term.

Financial Data

(US$ in Thousands)	6 Mos	3 Mos	08/25/2012	08/27/2011	08/28/2010	08/29/2009	08/30/2008	08/25/2007
Earnings Per Share	24.87	24.24	23.48	19.47	14.97	11.73	10.04	8.53
Cash Flow Per Share	35.13	32.57	31.72	30.38	24.74	16.76	14.32	12.26
Tang Book Value Per Share	...	...	...	...	...	...	N.M.	1.52
Income Statement								
Total Revenue	3,846,238	1,991,040	8,603,863	8,072,973	7,362,618	6,816,824	6,522,706	6,169,804
EBITDA	684,753	365,217	1,848,788	1,699,974	1,517,993	1,360,139	1,295,480	1,216,396
Depn & Amortn	3,905	1,941	219,897	205,171	198,579	184,077	171,346	161,130
Income Before Taxes	598,420	322,172	1,452,986	1,324,246	1,160,505	1,033,746	1,007,389	936,150
Income Taxes	218,722	118,720	522,613	475,272	422,194	376,697	365,783	340,478
Net Income	379,698	203,452	930,373	848,974	738,311	657,049	641,606	595,672
Average Shares	36,904	37,586	39,625	43,603	49,304	55,992	63,875	69,844
Balance Sheet								
Current Assets	3,123,368	3,062,291	2,978,946	2,792,425	2,611,821	2,561,730	2,586,301	2,270,455
Total Assets	6,662,188	6,398,039	6,265,639	5,869,602	5,571,594	5,318,405	5,257,112	4,804,709
Current Liabilities	4,231,808	3,744,492	3,655,592	3,430,896	3,063,960	2,706,752	2,519,320	2,285,895
Long-Term Obligations	3,513,273	3,802,705	3,718,302	3,317,600	2,882,300	2,726,900	2,250,000	1,935,618
Total Liabilities	8,212,297	7,989,408	7,813,664	7,123,834	6,310,359	5,751,479	5,027,425	4,401,509
Stockholders' Equity	(1,550,109)	(1,591,369)	(1,548,025)	(1,254,232)	(738,765)	(433,074)	229,687	403,200
Shares Outstanding	36,079	36,473	37,028	40,109	45,107	50,801	59,608	65,960
Statistical Record								
Return on Assets %	14.97	15.29	15.38	14.88	13.60	12.46	12.55	12.80
Return on Equity %	...	...	...	...	...	...	199.48	136.88
EBITDA Margin %	17.80	18.34	21.49	21.06	20.62	19.95	19.86	19.72
Net Margin %	9.87	10.22	10.81	10.52	10.03	9.64	9.84	9.65
Asset Turnover	1.37	1.41	1.42	1.42	1.36	1.29	1.28	1.33
Current Ratio	0.74	0.82	0.81	0.81	0.85	0.95	1.03	0.99
Debt to Equity	...	...	...	...	...	...	9.80	4.80
Price Range	397.13-344.99	397.13-318.06	397.13-307.00	304.10-209.78	214.65-135.31	166.82-89.09	138.96-103.43	140.10-87.21
P/E Ratio	15.97-13.87	16.38-13.12	16.91-13.07	15.62-10.77	14.34-9.04	14.22-7.60	13.84-10.30	16.42-10.22

Address: 123 South Front Street, Memphis, TN 38103 Telephone: 901-495-6500 Fax: 901-495-8300	Web Site: www.autozone.com Officers: William C. Rhodes - Chairman, President, Chief Executive Officer, Customer Satisfaction William T. Giles - Executive Vice President, Chief Financial Officer, Treasurer, Customer Satisfaction	Auditors: Ernst & Young LLP Investor Contact: 901-495-7185 Transfer Agents: ComputerShare Investor Services, Providence, RI

AVALONBAY COMMUNITIES, INC.

Exchange	Symbol	Price	52Wk Range	Yield	P/E
NYS	AVB	$126.67 (3/28/2013)	151.00-124.02	3.38	29.32

*7 Year Price Score 112.75 ***NYSE Composite Index=100** ***12 Month Price Score 85.71**

TRADING VOLUME (thousand shares)

Interim Earnings (Per Share)

Qtr.	Mar	Jun	Sep	Dec
2008	0.60	1.61	2.98	(0.03)
2009	0.59	0.22	0.72	0.39
2010	0.88	0.61	0.29	0.31
2011	0.35	0.49	0.49	3.54
2012	0.60	1.63	0.89	1.19

Interim Dividends (Per Share)

Amt	Decl	Ex	Rec	Pay
0.97Q	05/23/2012	06/27/2012	06/29/2012	07/16/2012
0.97Q	09/07/2012	09/26/2012	09/28/2012	10/15/2012
0.97Q	11/08/2012	12/27/2012	12/31/2012	01/15/2013
1.07Q	01/30/2013	03/26/2013	03/28/2013	04/15/2013

Indicated Div: $4.28

Valuation Analysis

		Institutional Holding	
Forecast EPS	$2.18 (04/06/2013)	No of Institutions	519
Market Cap	$14.5 Billion	Shares	126,439,088
Book Value	$6.8 Billion	% Held	
Price/Book	2.12		118.04
Price/Sales	13.95		

Business Summary: REITs (MIC: 5.3.1 SIC: 6798 NAIC: 525930)

AvalonBay Communities is a real estate investment trust. Co. is engaged in the development, redevelopment, acquisition, ownership and operation of multifamily communities in the U.S. Co.'s markets are located in the following regions of the U.S.: New England, the New York/New Jersey Metro area, the Washington DC Metro area, the Pacific Northwest, Northern and Southern California and the Midwest. At Jan 31 2012, Co. owned or held a direct or indirect ownership interest in 180 operating apartment communities containing 53,090 apartment homes in 10 states and the District of Columbia.

Recent Developments: For the year ended Dec 31 2012, income from continuing operations increased 73.7% to US$264.8 million from US$152.4 million a year earlier. Net income decreased 4.0% to US$423.6 million from US$441.4 million in the prior year. Revenues were US$1.04 billion, up 11.0% from US$936.1 million the year before.

Prospects: Our evaluation of AvalonBay Communities Inc. as of Apr. 7, 2013 is the result of our systematic analysis on three basic characteristics: earnings strength, relative valuation, and recent stock price movement. The company has suffered a very negative trend in earnings per share over the past 5 quarters. Because the company lacks sufficient analyst estimate data, we place greater weight on the historical EPS trend as the measure of earnings strength. Based on operating earnings yield, the company is overvalued when compared to all of the companies in our coverage universe. Share price changes over the past year indicates that AVB will perform poorly over the near term.

Financial Data

(US$ in Thousands)	12/31/2012	12/31/2011	12/31/2010	12/31/2009	12/31/2008	12/31/2007	12/31/2006	12/31/2005
Earnings Per Share	4.32	4.87	2.07	1.93	5.17	4.38	3.57	4.21
Cash Flow Per Share	5.54	4.78	3.96	4.74	5.02	5.79	4.75	4.20
Tang Book Value Per Share	59.76	46.18	38.54	37.41	37.82	39.14	35.24	34.50
Dividends Per Share	3.880	3.570	3.570	3.570	5.378	3.400	3.120	2.840
Dividend Payout %	89.81	73.31	172.46	184.97	104.01	77.63	87.39	67.46
Income Statement								
Total Revenue	1,038,660	968,711	895,266	851,582	854,208	812,741	737,300	670,680
EBITDA	605,468	560,430	504,695	437,310	418,094	411,225	426,499	385,398
Depn & Amortn	260,094	250,269	232,942	218,286	199,452	181,725	162,896	162,063
Income Before Taxes	208,454	141,982	96,544	68,701	103,764	131,955	152,557	96,236
Net Income	423,869	441,622	175,331	155,647	411,487	358,160	278,399	322,378
Average Shares	98,025	90,777	84,632	80,599	77,578	79,856	75,586	74,759
Balance Sheet								
Current Assets	2,808,399	713,926	502,058	340,013	289,240	239,935	172,130	80,662
Total Assets	11,160,078	8,482,390	7,821,488	7,457,605	7,173,374	6,736,484	5,813,186	5,165,060
Current Liabilities	182,648	156,473	142,954	141,488	281,463	148,964	136,456	124,765
Long-Term Obligations	3,851,033	3,632,296	4,067,657	3,974,872	3,674,457	3,208,202	2,825,586	2,366,564
Total Liabilities	4,322,863	4,087,649	4,510,870	4,407,478	4,256,978	3,709,830	3,181,748	2,623,397
Stockholders' Equity	6,837,215	4,394,741	3,310,618	3,050,127	2,916,396	3,026,654	2,631,438	2,541,663
Shares Outstanding	114,403	95,175	85,899	81,528	77,119	77,318	74,668	73,663
Statistical Record								
Return on Assets %	4.30	5.42	2.30	2.13	5.90	5.71	5.07	6.30
Return on Equity %	7.53	11.46	5.51	5.22	13.81	12.66	10.76	13.09
EBITDA Margin %	58.29	57.85	56.37	51.35	48.95	50.60	57.85	57.46
Net Margin %	40.81	45.59	19.58	18.28	48.17	44.07	37.76	48.07
Asset Turnover	0.11	0.12	0.12	0.12	0.12	0.13	0.13	0.13
Current Ratio	15.38	4.56	3.51	2.40	1.03	1.61	1.26	0.65
Debt to Equity	0.56	0.83	1.23	1.30	1.26	1.06	1.07	0.93
Price Range	151.01-124.26	139.51-109.16	114.80-73.21	86.59-40.11	107.70-42.80	148.52-91.56	134.00-91.44	92.65-66.05
P/E Ratio	34.95-28.76	28.65-22.41	55.46-35.37	44.87-20.78	20.83-8.28	33.91-20.90	37.54-25.61	22.01-15.69
Average Yield %	2.81	2.88	3.63	5.84	6.06	2.81	2.72	3.61

Address: Ballston Tower, 671 N. Glebe Road, Suite 800, Arlington, VA 22203 Telephone: 703-329-6300	Web Site: www.avalonbay.com Officers: Timothy J. Naughton - Chairman, President, Chief Executive Officer Thomas J. Sargeant - Executive Vice President, Chief Financial Officer	Auditors: Ernst & Young LLP Investor Contact: 703-317-4681 Transfer Agents: Computershare Shareowner Services, LLC, Pittsburgh, PA

AVERY DENNISON CORP.

Exchange	Symbol	Price	52Wk Range	Yield	P/E
NYS	AVY	$43.07 (3/28/2013)	43.58-26.38	2.51	20.71

*7 Year Price Score 70.02 *NYSE Composite Index=100 *12 Month Price Score 114.06

Interim Earnings (Per Share)

Qtr.	Mar	Jun	Sep	Dec
2008	0.69	0.93	0.63	0.44
2009	(8.99)	0.38	0.59	0.52
2010	0.51	0.78	0.60	1.07
2011	0.42	0.69	0.47	0.21
2012	0.41	0.62	0.57	0.48

Interim Dividends (Per Share)

Amt	Decl	Ex	Rec	Pay
0.27Q	04/26/2012	06/04/2012	06/06/2012	06/20/2012
0.27Q	07/26/2012	08/31/2012	09/05/2012	09/19/2012
0.27Q	10/25/2012	12/03/2012	12/05/2012	12/19/2012
0.27Q	01/23/2013	03/04/2013	03/06/2013	03/20/2013

Indicated Div: $1.08 (Div. Reinv. Plan)

Valuation Analysis | **Institutional Holding**

Forecast EPS	$2.58	No of Institutions
	(04/06/2013)	459
Market Cap	$4.3 Billion	Shares
Book Value	$1.6 Billion	104,645,432
Price/Book	2.72	% Held
Price/Sales	0.71	86.09

Business Summary: Office Equipment & Furniture (MIC: 7.5.1 SIC: 2672 NAIC: 322222)

Avery Dennison operates in two reportable segments: Pressure-sensitive Materials, which manufactures and sells Fasson®-, JAC®-, and Avery Dennison®-brand pressure-sensitive label and packaging materials, Avery®- and Avery Dennison®-brand graphics and graphic films, Avery Dennison®-brand reflective products, Avery Dennison®-brand tapes and performance polymers (used to manufacture pressure-sensitive materials); and Retail Branding and Information Solutions, which designs, manufactures and sells a range of brand identification and information management products to retailers, brand owners, apparel manufacturers, distributors and industrial customers.

Recent Developments: For the year ended Dec 29 2012, income from continuing operations increased 9.5% to US$169.1 million from US$154.4 million a year earlier. Net income increased 13.3% to US$215.4 million from US$190.1 million in the prior year. Revenues were US$6.04 billion, up 0.2% from US$6.03 billion the year before. Direct operating expenses declined 1.0% to US$4.46 billion from US$4.50 billion in the comparable period the year before. Indirect operating expenses increased 2.6% to US$1.32 billion from US$1.29 billion in the equivalent prior-year period.

Prospects: Our evaluation of Avery Dennison Corp. as of Apr. 7, 2013 is the result of our systematic analysis on three basic characteristics: earnings strength, relative valuation, and recent stock price movement. The company has enjoyed a very positive trend in earnings per share over the past 5 quarters and while recent estimates for the company have been mixed, AVY has posted better than expected results. Based on operating earnings yield, the company is about fairly valued when compared to all of the companies in our coverage universe. Share price changes over the past year indicates that AVY will perform well over the near term.

Financial Data
(US$ in Thousands)

	12/29/2012	12/31/2011	01/01/2011	01/02/2010	12/27/2008	12/29/2007	12/30/2006	12/31/2005
Earnings Per Share	2.08	1.78	2.97	(7.21)	2.70	3.07	3.66	2.25
Cash Flow Per Share	5.02	4.01	4.61	5.40	5.50	5.10	5.13	4.42
Tang Book Value Per Share	6.92	6.94	4.52	1.42	N.M.	N.M.	8.84	7.42
Dividends Per Share	1.080	1.000	0.800	1.220	1.640	1.610	1.570	1.530
Dividend Payout %	51.92	56.18	26.94	...	60.74	52.44	42.90	68.00
Income Statement								
Total Revenue	6,035,600	6,026,300	6,512,700	5,952,700	6,710,400	6,307,800	5,575,900	5,473,500
EBITDA	478,400	471,900	600,800	(518,000)	591,100	664,600	635,400	580,400
Depn & Amortn	150,100	168,000	172,900	187,600	204,600	184,100	154,300	155,700
Income Before Taxes	255,500	232,900	351,300	(790,900)	270,600	375,300	425,600	366,800
Income Taxes	86,400	78,500	34,400	(44,200)	4,500	71,800	73,100	75,000
Net Income	215,400	190,100	316,900	(746,700)	266,100	303,500	367,200	226,400
Average Shares	103,500	106,800	106,800	103,600	98,700	98,900	100,400	100,500
Balance Sheet								
Current Assets	2,411,700	2,218,800	1,951,900	1,733,200	1,930,400	2,058,300	1,655,400	1,558,300
Total Assets	5,105,300	4,972,700	5,099,400	5,002,800	6,035,700	6,244,800	4,293,600	4,203,900
Current Liabilities	2,074,500	1,647,100	1,831,800	1,867,700	2,058,000	2,477,600	1,698,800	1,525,600
Long-Term Obligations	702,200	954,200	956,200	1,088,700	1,544,800	1,145,000	501,600	723,000
Total Liabilities	3,524,400	3,314,200	3,453,700	3,640,200	4,285,700	4,255,400	2,613,100	2,692,000
Stockholders' Equity	1,580,900	1,658,500	1,645,700	1,362,600	1,750,000	1,989,400	1,680,500	1,511,900
Shares Outstanding	99,915	106,269	105,391	105,298	98,366	98,386	98,313	99,727
Statistical Record								
Return on Assets %	4.29	3.79	6.29	N.M.	4.35	5.78	8.67	5.28
Return on Equity %	13.34	11.54	21.13	N.M.	14.27	16.59	23.07	14.84
EBITDA Margin %	7.93	7.83	9.23	N.M.	8.81	10.54	11.40	10.60
Net Margin %	3.57	3.15	4.87	N.M.	3.97	4.81	6.59	4.14
Asset Turnover	1.20	1.20	1.29	1.06	1.10	1.20	1.32	1.28
Current Ratio	1.16	1.35	1.07	0.93	0.94	0.83	0.97	1.02
Debt to Equity	0.44	0.58	0.58	0.80	0.88	0.58	0.30	0.48
Price Range	34.97-26.38	43.11-23.97	42.49-30.79	40.02-17.26	53.14-25.02	69.67-49.69	69.11-55.09	62.53-50.30
P/E Ratio	16.81-12.68	24.22-13.47	14.31-10.37	...	19.68-9.27	22.69-16.19	18.88-15.05	27.79-22.36
Average Yield %	3.54	2.90	2.15	4.12	3.70	2.61	2.58	2.73

Address: Miller Corporate Center, 150 North Orange Grove Boulevard, Pasadena, CA 91103
Telephone: 626-304-2000
Fax: 626-792-7312

Web Site: www.averydennison.com
Officers: Dean A. Scarborough - Chairman, President, Chief Executive Officer Daniel R. O'Bryant - Executive Vice President

Auditors: PricewaterhouseCoopers LLP
Investor Contact: 626-304-2000
Transfer Agents: Computershare Trust Co., N.A., Providence, RI

AVISTA CORP.

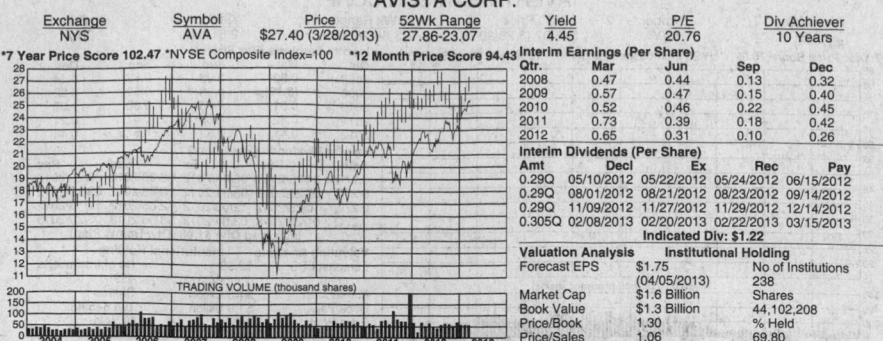

Exchange	Symbol	Price	52Wk Range	Yield	P/E	Div Achiever
NYS	AVA	$27.40 (3/28/2013)	27.86-23.07	4.45	20.76	10 Years

*7 Year Price Score 102.47 *NYSE Composite Index=100   *12 Month Price Score 94.43

Interim Earnings (Per Share)

Qtr.	Mar	Jun	Sep	Dec
2008	0.47	0.44	0.13	0.32
2009	0.57	0.47	0.15	0.40
2010	0.52	0.46	0.22	0.45
2011	0.73	0.39	0.18	0.42
2012	0.65	0.31	0.10	0.26

Interim Dividends (Per Share)

Amt	Decl	Ex	Rec	Pay
0.29Q	05/10/2012	05/22/2012	05/24/2012	06/15/2012
0.29Q	08/01/2012	08/21/2012	08/23/2012	09/14/2012
0.29Q	11/09/2012	11/27/2012	11/29/2012	12/14/2012
0.305Q	02/08/2013	02/20/2013	02/22/2013	03/15/2013

Indicated Div: $1.22

Valuation Analysis / **Institutional Holding**

Forecast EPS	$1.75 (04/05/2013)	No of Institutions 238
Market Cap	$1.6 Billion	Shares 44,102,208
Book Value	$1.3 Billion	% Held 69.80
Price/Book	1.30	
Price/Sales	1.06	

Business Summary: Electric Utilities (MIC: 3.1.1 SIC: 4931 NAIC: 221121)

Avista is an energy company engaged in the generation, transmission and distribution of energy, as well as other energy-related businesses. Co. has two segments: Avista Utilities and Ecova. Through Avista Utilities, Co. generates, transmits and distributes electricity and natural gas. The utility also engages in wholesale purchases and sales of electricity and natural gas. Co.'s Ecova segment provides energy and management programs and services throughout North America. Ecova's primary product lines include expense management services as well as energy management services that include procurement, conservation, performance reporting, and financial planning.

Recent Developments: For the year ended Dec 31 2012, net income decreased 23.9% to US$78.8 million from US$103.5 million in the prior year. Revenues were US$1.55 billion, down 4.5% from US$1.62 billion the year before. Operating income was US$190.1 million versus US$228.0 million in the prior year, a decrease of 16.6%. Direct operating expenses declined 6.5% to US$1.08 billion from US$1.16 billion in the comparable period the year before. Indirect operating expenses increased 17.4% to US$274.9 million from US$234.2 million in the equivalent prior-year period.

Prospects: Our evaluation of Avista Corp. as of Apr. 7, 2013 is the result of our systematic analysis on three basic characteristics: earnings strength, relative valuation, and recent stock price movement. The company has produced a positive trend in earnings per share over the past 5 quarters. However, while recent estimates for the company have been lowered by analysts, AVA has posted results that fell short of analysts expectations. Based on operating earnings yield, the company is undervalued when compared to all of the companies in our coverage universe. Share price changes over the past year indicates that AVA will perform poorly over the near term.

Financial Data
(US$ in Thousands)

	12/31/2012	12/31/2011	12/31/2010	12/31/2009	12/31/2008	12/31/2007	12/31/2006	12/31/2005
Earnings Per Share	1.32	1.72	1.65	1.58	1.36	0.72	1.47	0.92
Cash Flow Per Share	5.35	4.66	4.11	4.73	2.15	4.77	4.10	2.65
Tang Book Value Per Share	19.01	19.63	19.26	18.72	18.30	17.27	17.46	15.87
Dividends Per Share	1.160	1.100	1.000	0.810	0.690	0.595	0.570	0.545
Dividend Payout %	87.88	63.95	60.61	51.27	50.74	82.64	38.78	59.24
Income Statement								
Total Revenue	1,547,002	1,619,780	1,558,740	1,512,565	1,676,763	1,417,757	1,506,311	1,359,607
EBITDA	343,932	372,558	325,519	353,718	324,679	249,829	343,744	252,954
Depn & Amortn	149,849	142,537	104,695	156,807	143,141	116,625	151,151	104,303
Income Before Taxes	120,061	160,171	146,105	134,971	119,245	62,809	115,223	71,029
Income Taxes	41,261	56,632	51,157	46,323	45,625	24,334	42,090	25,861
Net Income	78,210	100,224	92,425	87,071	73,620	38,475	73,133	45,168
Average Shares	59,201	58,092	55,824	54,942	54,028	53,263	49,897	48,979
Balance Sheet								
Current Assets	505,794	614,556	579,565	418,923	482,227	332,185	1,032,274	1,770,368
Total Assets	4,313,179	4,214,531	3,940,095	3,606,599	3,630,747	3,189,797	4,056,508	4,948,494
Current Liabilities	576,149	627,174	579,175	503,417	688,544	763,649	945,209	1,729,888
Long-Term Obligations	1,301,752	1,254,176	1,199,517	1,087,696	922,661	634,892	1,063,257	1,103,393
Total Liabilities	3,053,702	3,028,830	2,814,311	2,555,672	2,633,864	2,275,831	3,139,662	4,177,366
Stockholders' Equity	1,259,477	1,185,701	1,125,784	1,051,287	996,883	913,966	916,846	771,128
Shares Outstanding	59,812	58,422	57,119	54,836	54,487	52,909	52,514	48,593
Statistical Record								
Return on Assets %	1.83	2.46	2.45	2.41	2.15	1.06	1.62	1.04
Return on Equity %	6.38	8.67	8.49	8.50	7.68	4.20	8.67	5.93
EBITDA Margin %	22.23	23.00	20.88	23.39	19.36	17.62	22.82	18.60
Net Margin %	5.06	6.19	5.93	5.76	4.39	2.71	4.86	3.32
Asset Turnover	0.36	0.40	0.41	0.42	0.49	0.39	0.33	0.31
Current Ratio	0.88	0.98	1.00	0.83	0.70	0.43	1.09	1.02
Debt to Equity	1.03	1.06	1.07	1.03	0.93	0.69	1.16	1.43
Price Range	27.86-23.07	26.41-21.39	22.72-18.79	22.28-12.77	23.30-16.58	25.71-18.77	27.27-17.88	19.97-16.56
P/E Ratio	21.11-17.48	15.35-12.44	13.77-11.39	14.10-8.08	17.13-12.19	35.71-26.07	18.55-12.16	21.71-18.00
Average Yield %	4.55	4.55	4.76	4.49	3.39	2.68	2.52	3.04

Address: 1411 East Mission Avenue, Spokane, WA 99202-2600	**Web Site:** www.avistacorp.com	**Auditors:** Doloitte & Touche LLP
Telephone: 509-489-0500	**Officers:** Scott L. Morris - Chairman, President, Chief Executive Officer Mark T. Thies - Senior Vice President, Chief Financial Officer	**Investor Contact:** 509-489-0500
Fax: 509-482-4361		**Transfer Agents:** Computershare, Pittsburgh, PA

AVNET INC

Exchange	Symbol	Price	52Wk Range	Yield	P/E
NYS	AVT	$36.20 (3/28/2013)	36.86-27.01	N/A	10.06

*7 Year Price Score 97.41   *NYSE Composite Index=100   *12 Month Price Score 101.70

Interim Earnings (Per Share)

Qtr.	Sep	Dec	Mar	Jun
2009-10	0.33	0.68	0.75	0.92
2010-11	0.90	0.91	0.98	1.55
2011-12	0.90	0.98	1.00	0.91
2012-13	0.70	0.99	...	...

Interim Dividends (Per Share)

No Dividends Paid

Valuation Analysis

	Institutional Holding	
Forecast EPS	$3.46	No of Institutions
	(04/05/2013)	453
Market Cap	$4.9 Billion	Shares
Book Value	$4.1 Billion	152,374,848
Price/Book	1.20	% Held
Price/Sales	0.20	86.26

Business Summary: Electrical Equipment (MIC: 7.3.1 SIC: 5065 NAIC: 423690)

Avnet is a distributor of electronic components, enterprise computer and storage products and embedded subsystems as received from its suppliers or with assembly or other services added by Co. Also, Co. provides engineering design, materials management and logistics services, system integration and configuration, and supply chain services that can be customized. Co.'s Electronics Marketing group markets and sells semiconductors and interconnect, passive and electromechanical devices and embedded products. Co.'s Technology Solutions group focuses on the distribution of enterprise computing servers and systems, software, storage, services and applications from technology manufacturers.

Recent Developments: For the quarter ended Dec 29 2012, net income decreased 6.5% to US$137.5 million from US$147.0 million in the year-earlier quarter. Revenues were US$6.70 billion, up 0.1% from US$6.69 billion the year before. Operating income was US$195.6 million versus US$230.9 million in the prior-year quarter, a decrease of 15.3%. Direct operating expenses rose 0.4% to US$5.93 billion from US$5.91 billion in the comparable period the year before. Indirect operating expenses increased 3.6% to US$572.9 million from US$553.2 million in the equivalent prior-year period.

Prospects: Our evaluation of Avnet Inc. as of Apr. 7, 2013 is the result of our systematic analysis on three basic characteristics: earnings strength, relative valuation, and recent stock price movement. The company has enjoyed a very positive trend in earnings per share over the past 5 quarters and while recent estimates for the company have been raised by analysts, AVT has posted better than expected results. Based on operating earnings yield, the company is undervalued when compared to all of the companies in our coverage universe. Share price changes over the past year indicates that AVT will perform in line with the market over the near term.

Financial Data

(US$ in Thousands)	6 Mos	3 Mos	06/30/2012	07/02/2011	07/03/2010	06/27/2009	06/28/2008	06/30/2007
Earnings Per Share	3.60	3.59	3.79	4.34	2.68	(7.44)	3.27	2.63
Cash Flow Per Share	5.05	5.78	3.60	1.83	(0.20)	7.43	3.03	4.91
Tang Book Value Per Share	20.95	20.37	19.68	20.75	16.09	14.63	16.00	13.34
Income Statement								
Total Revenue	12,569,522	5,870,057	25,707,522	26,534,413	19,160,172	16,229,896	17,952,707	15,681,087
EBITDA	387,279	160,955	952,286	1,020,934	696,523	(965,940)	830,411	707,525
Depn & Amortn	57,840	28,208	70,645	57,516	49,692	50,653	49,171	43,734
Income Before Taxes	277,751	108,857	790,782	870,966	585,083	(1,083,074)	708,955	586,619
Income Taxes	39,965	8,552	223,763	201,897	174,713	39,388	209,874	193,552
Net Income	237,786	100,305	567,019	669,069	410,370	(1,122,462)	499,081	393,067
Average Shares	138,575	143,359	149,553	154,337	153,093	150,898	152,420	149,613
Balance Sheet								
Current Assets	8,449,779	8,118,800	8,254,439	8,227,207	6,630,168	5,144,252	5,971,146	5,488,845
Total Assets	10,549,530	10,103,124	10,167,866	9,905,569	7,782,382	6,273,516	8,200,130	7,355,119
Current Liabilities	4,769,995	4,545,402	4,798,652	4,477,728	3,439,615	2,455,860	2,779,592	2,776,985
Long-Term Obligations	1,508,196	1,399,832	1,271,985	1,273,509	1,243,681	946,573	1,181,498	1,155,990
Total Liabilities	6,443,633	6,123,341	6,262,134	5,849,499	4,773,265	3,512,659	4,065,439	3,954,474
Stockholders' Equity	4,105,897	3,979,783	3,905,732	4,056,070	3,009,117	2,760,857	4,134,691	3,400,645
Shares Outstanding	136,347	138,663	142,548	152,797	151,836	151,066	150,398	149,805
Statistical Record								
Return on Assets %	5.01	5.31	5.66	7.59	5.74	N.M.	6.43	5.81
Return on Equity %	13.03	13.36	14.28	18.99	13.99	N.M.	13.28	12.65
EBITDA Margin %	3.08	2.74	3.70	3.85	3.64	N.M.	4.63	4.51
Net Margin %	1.89	1.71	2.21	2.52	2.14	N.M.	2.78	2.51
Asset Turnover	2.43	2.53	2.57	3.01	2.68	2.25	2.31	2.32
Current Ratio	1.77	1.79	1.72	1.84	1.93	2.09	2.15	1.98
Debt to Equity	0.37	0.35	0.33	0.31	0.41	0.34	0.29	0.34
Price Range	36.83-27.01	36.83-24.77	36.83-24.19	37.81-22.86	33.49-20.31	31.00-12.10	44.33-26.19	43.62-16.77
P/E Ratio	10.23-7.50	10.26-6.90	9.72-6.38	8.71-5.27	12.50-7.58	...	13.56-8.01	16.59-6.38

Address: 2211 South 47th Street, Phoenix, AZ 85034	Web Site: www.avnet.com	Auditors: KPMG LLP
Telephone: 480-643-2000	Officers: Richard P. Hamada - President, Executive Officer, Chief Operating Officer Steven C. Church - Senior Vice President, Chief Business Development and Process Officer	Investor Contact: 480-643-7053 Transfer Agents: American Stock Transfer & Trust Company, Brooklyn, NY

AVON PRODUCTS, INC.

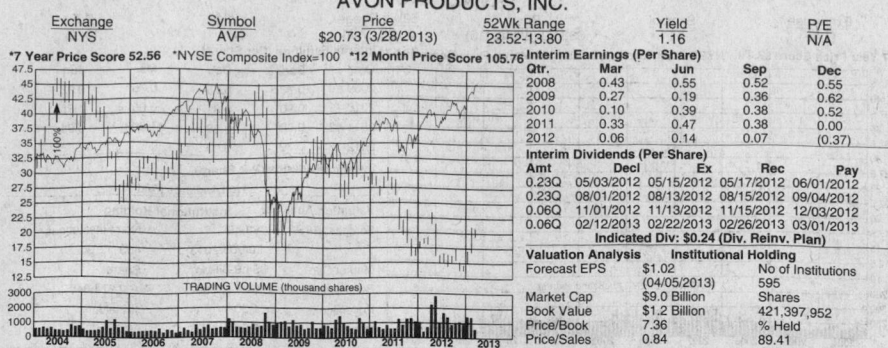

Exchange	Symbol	Price	52Wk Range	Yield	P/E
NYS	AVP	$20.73 (3/28/2013)	23.52-13.80	1.16	N/A

*7 Year Price Score 52.56   *NYSE Composite Index=100   *12 Month Price Score 105.76

Interim Earnings (Per Share)

Qtr.	Mar	Jun	Sep	Dec
2008	0.43	0.55	0.52	0.55
2009	0.27	0.19	0.36	0.62
2010	0.10	0.39	0.38	0.52
2011	0.33	0.47	0.38	0.00
2012	0.06	0.14	0.07	(0.37)

Interim Dividends (Per Share)

Amt	Decl	Ex	Rec	Pay
0.23Q	05/03/2012	05/15/2012	05/17/2012	06/01/2012
0.23Q	08/01/2012	08/13/2012	08/15/2012	09/04/2012
0.06Q	11/01/2012	11/13/2012	11/15/2012	12/03/2012
0.06Q	02/12/2013	02/22/2013	02/26/2013	03/01/2013

Indicated Div: $0.24 (Div. Reinv. Plan)

Valuation Analysis

Institutional Holding	
Forecast EPS	$1.02	No of Institutions
	(04/05/2013)	595
Market Cap	$9.0 Billion	Shares
Book Value	$1.2 Billion	421,397,952
Price/Book	7.36	% Held
Price/Sales	0.84	89.41

TRADING VOLUME (thousand shares)

Business Summary: Household & Personal Products (MIC: 1.7.1 SIC: 5122 NAIC: 446120)

Avon Products is a manufacturer and marketer of beauty and related products. Co.'s product categories are Beauty, which includes color cosmetics, fragrances, skin care and personal care; Fashion, which includes fashion jewelry, watches, apparel, footwear, accessories and children's products; and Home, which includes gift and decorative products, housewares, entertainment and leisure products, children's and nutritional products. Co.'s business is conducted primarily in one channel, direct selling. Co.'s reportable segments are based on geographic operations and include commercial business units in Latin America; Europe; Middle East & Africa; North America; and Asia Pacific.

Recent Developments: For the year ended Dec 31 2012, loss from continuing operations was US$38.2 million compared with income of US$526.4 million a year earlier. Net loss amounted to US$38.2 million versus net income of US$517.8 million in the prior year. Revenues were US$10.72 billion, down 5.1% from US$11.29 billion the year before. Operating income was US$314.8 million versus US$854.6 million in the prior year, a decrease of 63.2%. Direct operating expenses rose 0.5% to US$4.17 billion from US$4.15 billion in the comparable period the year before. Indirect operating expenses decreased 0.9% to US$6.23 billion from US$6.29 billion in the equivalent prior-year period.

Prospects: Our evaluation of Avon Products Inc. as of Apr. 7, 2013 is the result of our systematic analysis on three basic characteristics: earnings strength, relative valuation, and recent stock price movement. The company has enjoyed a very positive trend in earnings per share over the past 5 quarters and while recent estimates for the company have been mixed, AVP has posted better than expected results. Based on operating earnings yield, the company is overvalued when compared to all of the companies in our coverage universe. Share price changes over the past year indicates that AVP will perform very poorly over the near term.

Financial Data

(US$ in Thousands)	12/31/2012	12/31/2011	12/31/2010	12/31/2009	12/31/2008	12/31/2007	12/31/2006	12/31/2005
Earnings Per Share	(0.10)	1.18	1.39	1.45	2.04	1.21	1.06	1.81
Cash Flow Per Share	1.28	1.52	1.61	1.83	1.75	1.36	1.78	1.92
Tang Book Value Per Share	1.13	1.49	1.10	2.16	0.76	1.66	1.79	1.76
Dividends Per Share	0.750	0.920	0.880	0.840	0.800	0.740	0.700	0.660
Dividend Payout %	...	77.97	63.31	57.93	39.22	61.16	66.04	36.46
Income Statement								
Total Revenue	10,717,100	11,291,600	10,862,800	10,382,800	10,690,100	9,938,700	8,763,900	8,149,600
EBITDA	470,200	993,000	1,163,700	1,144,100	1,443,500	1,007,300	873,000	1,256,400
Depn & Amortn	162,400	174,000	145,200	133,000	141,900	128,900	115,600	106,500
Income Before Taxes	218,600	742,600	945,400	926,500	1,238,300	796,100	703,500	1,124,200
Income Taxes	256,800	216,200	350,200	298,300	362,700	262,800	223,400	269,700
Net Income	(42,500)	513,600	606,300	625,800	875,300	530,700	477,600	847,600
Average Shares	431,900	432,100	431,350	428,540	429,530	436,890	449,160	469,470
Balance Sheet								
Current Assets	3,928,900	4,098,800	4,184,300	4,189,300	3,556,900	3,515,400	3,334,400	2,920,900
Total Assets	7,382,500	7,735,000	7,873,700	6,832,700	6,074,000	5,716,200	5,238,200	4,763,300
Current Liabilities	2,704,600	2,891,000	2,956,300	2,274,800	2,912,200	3,053,400	2,550,100	2,501,600
Long-Term Obligations	2,623,900	2,459,100	2,408,600	2,307,800	1,456,200	1,167,900	1,170,700	766,500
Total Liabilities	6,165,400	6,164,600	6,217,200	5,560,100	5,399,100	5,004,600	4,447,800	3,969,100
Stockholders' Equity	1,217,100	1,570,400	1,656,500	1,272,600	674,900	711,600	790,400	794,200
Shares Outstanding	432,200	430,800	429,500	427,480	426,300	427,700	441,300	451,480
Statistical Record								
Return on Assets %	N.M.	6.58	8.25	9.70	14.81	9.69	9.55	19.02
Return on Equity %	N.M.	31.83	41.40	64.27	125.92	70.67	60.28	97.18
EBITDA Margin %	4.39	8.79	10.71	11.02	13.50	10.14	9.96	15.42
Net Margin %	N.M.	4.55	5.58	6.03	8.19	5.34	5.45	10.40
Asset Turnover	1.41	1.45	1.48	1.61	1.81	1.81	1.75	1.83
Current Ratio	1.45	1.42	1.42	1.84	1.22	1.15	1.31	1.17
Debt to Equity	2.16	1.57	1.45	1.81	2.16	1.64	1.48	0.97
Price Range	23.52-13.80	30.91-16.09	35.49-25.73	36.12-15.20	45.25-18.38	41.66-31.97	33.88-27.01	45.07-24.71
P/E Ratio	...	26.19-13.64	25.53-18.51	24.91-10.48	22.18-9.01	34.43-26.42	31.96-25.48	24.90-13.65
Average Yield %	4.42	3.70	2.90	3.09	2.24	1.97	2.30	1.87

Address: 777 Third Avenue, New York, NY 10017-1307
Telephone: 212-282-5000
Fax: 212-282-6035

Web Site: www.avon.com
Officers: Sherilyn S. McCoy - Chief Executive Officer Kimberly A. Ross - Executive Vice President, Chief Financial Officer

Auditors: PricewaterhouseCoopers LLP
Investor Contact: 212-282-5320
Transfer Agents: Computer Investors Services, Canton, MA

AVX CORP.

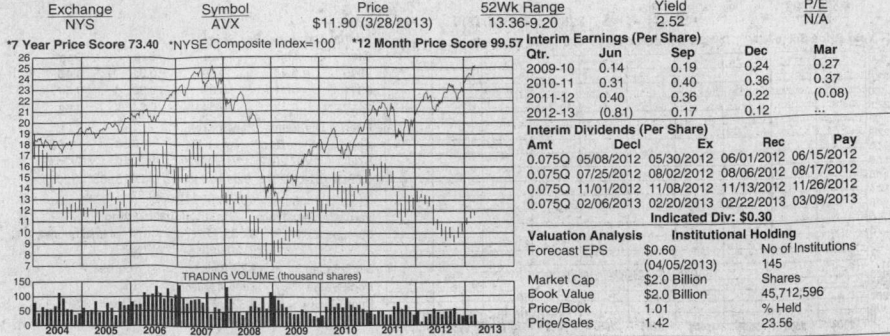

Exchange	Symbol	Price	52Wk Range	Yield	P/E
NYS	AVX	$11.90 (3/28/2013)	13.36-9.20	2.52	N/A

*7 Year Price Score 73.40   *NYSE Composite Index=100   *12 Month Price Score 99.57

Interim Earnings (Per Share)

Qtr.	Jun	Sep	Dec	Mar
2009-10	0.14	0.19	0.24	0.27
2010-11	0.31	0.40	0.36	0.37
2011-12	0.40	0.36	0.22	(0.08)
2012-13	(0.81)	0.17	0.12	...

Interim Dividends (Per Share)

Amt	Decl	Ex	Rec	Pay
0.075Q	05/08/2012	05/30/2012	06/01/2012	06/15/2012
0.075Q	07/25/2012	08/02/2012	08/06/2012	08/17/2012
0.075Q	11/01/2012	11/08/2012	11/13/2012	11/26/2012
0.075Q	02/06/2013	02/20/2013	02/22/2013	03/09/2013

Indicated Div: $0.30

Valuation Analysis / **Institutional Holding**

Forecast EPS	$0.60	No of Institutions
	(04/05/2013)	145
Market Cap	$2.0 Billion	Shares
Book Value	$2.0 Billion	45,712,596
Price/Book	1.01	% Held
Price/Sales	1.42	23.56

TRADING VOLUME (thousand shares)

Business Summary: Electrical Equipment (MIC: 7.3.1 SIC: 3675 NAIC: 334414)

AVX is a manufacturer and supplier of passive electronic components and interconnect products. Co.'s product groups, Ceramic Components, Tantalum Components, Advanced Components, Interconnect Products and Kyocera Electronic Devices (KED) are organized into three segments: Passive Components, which manufacture multi-layered ceramic and solid tantalum capacitors, film capacitors, high power capacitors and varistors; Interconnect, which manufactures and sells electronic connectors and interconnect systems; and KED Resale, which distributes and sells certain Kyocera Corporation of Japan electronic component and connector products to certain customers and in certain territories outside of Japan.

Recent Developments: For the quarter ended Dec 31 2012, net income decreased 46.1% to US$19.9 million from US$36.9 million in the year-earlier quarter. Revenues were US$339.9 million, down 0.3% from US$340.9 million the year before. Operating income was US$33.2 million versus US$50.2 million in the prior-year quarter, a decrease of 33.8%. Direct operating expenses rose 5.7% to US$277.5 million from US$262.5 million in the comparable period the year before. Indirect operating expenses increased 3.8% to US$29.2 million from US$28.1 million in the equivalent prior-year period.

Prospects: Our evaluation of AVX Corp. as of Apr. 7, 2013 is the result of our systematic analysis on three basic characteristics: earnings strength, relative valuation, and recent stock price movement. The company has enjoyed a very positive trend in earnings per share over the past 5 quarters and while recent estimates for the company have remained steady, AVX has posted results that fell short of analysts expectations. Based on operating earnings yield, the company is about fairly valued when compared to all of the companies in our coverage universe. Share price changes over the past year indicates that AVX will perform poorly over the near term.

Financial Data

(US$ in Thousands)	9 Mos	6 Mos	3 Mos	03/31/2012	03/31/2011	03/31/2010	03/31/2009	03/31/2008
Earnings Per Share	(0.60)	(0.50)	(0.31)	0.90	1.43	0.84	0.47	0.87
Cash Flow Per Share	1.04	1.03	1.06	0.87	0.89	1.18	0.38	1.06
Tang Book Value Per Share	10.36	10.27	10.10	11.08	10.55	9.12	8.32	9.21
Dividends Per Share	0.300	0.300	0.280	0.260	0.190	0.160	0.160	0.160
Dividend Payout %	...	...	...	28.89	13.29	19.05	34.04	18.39
Income Statement								
Total Revenue	1,053,852	713,977	353,154	1,545,254	1,653,176	1,304,966	1,389,613	1,619,275
EBITDA	(121,545)	(166,601)	(216,424)	216,313	370,910	223,146	137,904	214,137
Depn & Amortn	33,700	21,430	10,554	42,499	43,220	53,798	61,738	53,542
Income Before Taxes	(149,689)	(184,317)	(225,108)	179,905	334,259	176,357	97,139	203,365
Income Taxes	(60,807)	(75,570)	(88,324)	27,100	90,256	33,499	16,293	53,892
Net Income	(88,882)	(108,747)	(136,784)	152,805	244,003	142,858	80,846	149,473
Average Shares	168,994	169,248	169,528	170,134	170,390	170,274	170,689	172,065
Balance Sheet								
Current Assets	1,906,795	1,785,515	1,718,731	1,727,145	1,602,115	1,316,358	1,132,504	1,377,205
Total Assets	2,579,623	2,574,748	2,558,207	2,468,012	2,319,482	2,051,492	1,872,529	2,109,078
Current Liabilities	315,861	317,269	312,197	297,073	235,665	193,273	149,402	220,516
Total Liabilities	593,044	598,859	606,394	347,259	280,065	250,485	202,776	279,727
Stockholders' Equity	1,986,579	1,975,889	1,951,813	2,120,753	2,039,417	1,801,007	1,669,753	1,829,351
Shares Outstanding	168,897	169,071	169,431	169,601	170,142	170,074	170,384	171,066
Statistical Record								
Return on Assets %	N.M.	N.M.	N.M.	6.37	11.16	7.28	4.06	7.44
Return on Equity %	N.M.	N.M.	N.M.	7.33	12.71	8.23	4.62	8.60
EBITDA Margin %	N.M.	N.M.	N.M.	14.00	22.44	17.10	9.92	13.22
Net Margin %	N.M.	N.M.	N.M.	9.89	14.76	10.95	5.82	9.23
Asset Turnover	0.57	0.57	0.59	0.64	0.76	0.67	0.70	0.81
Current Ratio	6.04	5.63	5.51	5.81	6.80	6.81	7.58	6.25
Price Range	13.85-9.20	13.95-9.32	15.66-10.32	16.48-11.10	16.24-12.16	14.34-9.08	13.72-7.38	18.24-11.86
P/E Ratio	...	...	...	18.31-12.33	11.36-8.50	17.07-10.81	29.19-15.70	20.97-13.63
Average Yield %	2.68	2.52	2.21	1.91	1.32	1.40	1.57	1.05

Address: 1 AVX Boulevard, Fountain Inn, SC 29644
Telephone: 864-967-2150

Web Site: www.avx.com
Officers: John S. Gilbertson - Chairman, President, Chief Executive Officer John Lawing - President, Chief Operating Officer, Division Officer

Auditors: PricewaterhouseCoopers LLP
Investor Contact: 843-448-9411
Transfer Agents: The American Stock Transfer and Trust Company, New York, NY

BABCOCK & WILCOX CO. (THE)

Exchange	Symbol	Price	52Wk Range	Yield	P/E
NYS	BWC	$28.41 (3/28/2013)	28.41-23.02	1.13	14.87

*7 Year Price Score N/A ***NYSE Composite Index=100** ***12 Month Price Score 97.92**

TRADING VOLUME (thousand shares)

Interim Earnings (Per Share)

Qtr.	Mar	Jun	Sep	Dec
2010	0.14	0.00	0.31	0.45
2011	0.11	0.39	0.39	0.54
2012	0.39	0.54	0.34	0.64

Interim Dividends (Per Share)

Amt	Decl	Ex	Rec	Pay
0.08Q	11/07/2012	11/15/2012	11/19/2012	12/17/2012
0.08Q	02/08/2013	02/14/2013	02/19/2013	03/12/2013

Indicated Div: $0.32

Valuation Analysis   **Institutional Holding**

Forecast EPS	$2.33	No of Institutions	
	(04/05/2013)	N/A	
Market Cap	$3.3 Billion	Shares	
Book Value	$986.4 Million	N/A	
Price/Book	3.32	% Held	
Price/Sales	0.99	N/A	

Business Summary: Electric Utilities (MIC: 3.1.1 SIC: 3621 NAIC: 335312)

Babcock & Wilcox provides products and services to customers in the power and other steam-using industries, industrial customers in various industries, and the U.S. Government. Co. has four business segments: Power Generation, which supplies boilers fired, environmental components, and related services to customers; Nuclear Operations, which engineers, designs and manufactures naval nuclear reactor components; Technical Services, which provides services such as uranium processing and environmental site restoration; and Nuclear Energy, which supplies nuclear steam generators and components.

Recent Developments: For the year ended Dec 31 2012, net income increased 208.1% to US$217.6 million from US$70.6 million in the prior year. Revenues were US$3.29 billion, up 11.5% from US$2.95 billion the year before. Operating income was US$346.0 million versus US$95.7 million in the prior year, an increase of 262.3%. Indirect operating expenses increased 3.1% to US$2.94 billion from US$2.86 billion in the equivalent prior-year period.

Prospects: Our evaluation of The Babcock & Wilcox Co. as of Apr. 7, 2013 is the result of our systematic analysis on three basic characteristics: earnings strength, relative valuation, and recent stock price movement. The company has generated a negative trend in earnings per share over the past 5 quarters and while recent estimates for the company have been raised by analysts, BWC has posted better than expected results. Based on operating earnings yield, the company is undervalued when compared to all of the companies in our coverage universe. Share price changes over the past year indicates that BWC will perform in line with the market over the near term.

Financial Data

(US$ in Thousands)	12/31/2012	12/31/2011	12/31/2010	12/31/2009	12/31/2008	12/31/2007
Earnings Per Share	1.91	1.43	1.30	...	...	...
Cash Flow Per Share	1.56	1.48	1.65	...	...	...
Tang Book Value Per Share	6.12	4.65	3.79	...	...	...
Dividends Per Share	0.080	...	...	...	...	...
Dividend Payout %	4.19	...	...	...	...	...
Income Statement						
Total Revenue	3,291,359	2,952,040	2,688,811	2,854,632	3,398,574	3,199,944
EBITDA	314,353	221,281	234,590	260,958	429,701	320,375
Depn & Amortn	59,400	61,800	61,100	62,600	41,300	38,800
Income Before Taxes	252,709	156,280	161,738	177,207	380,947	268,701
Income Taxes	101,861	72,982	82,294	84,381	108,885	99,018
Net Income	227,695	169,654	153,262	147,764	323,766	215,250
Average Shares	119,021	118,404	117,626	...	...	...
Balance Sheet						
Current Assets	1,521,086	1,487,076	1,209,116	1,306,715	1,222,834	...
Total Assets	2,840,355	2,789,111	2,500,510	2,603,859	2,506,841	...
Current Liabilities	1,079,288	1,154,807	981,827	1,235,176	1,312,874	...
Long-Term Obligations	430	633	855	324,790	324,309	...
Total Liabilities	1,853,920	1,963,317	1,787,651	2,483,153	2,576,389	...
Stockholders' Equity	986,435	825,794	712,859	120,706	(69,548)	...
Shares Outstanding	115,235	118,107	116,862	...	...	...
Statistical Record						
Return on Assets %	8.07	6.41	6.01	5.78	...	...
Return on Equity %	25.06	22.05	36.77	577.68	...	...
EBITDA Margin %	9.55	7.50	8.72	9.14	12.64	10.01
Net Margin %	6.92	5.75	5.70	5.18	9.53	6.73
Asset Turnover	1.17	1.12	1.05	1.12	...	...
Current Ratio	1.41	1.29	1.23	1.06	0.93	...
Debt to Equity	N.M.	N.M.	N.M.	2.69	...	...
Price Range	27.72-23.02	35.57-18.54	25.97-21.25	...	...	...
P/E Ratio	14.51-12.05	24.87-12.97	19.98-16.35	...	...	...
Average Yield %	0.32	...	...	...	...	...

Address: The Harris Building, 13024 Ballantyne Corporate Place, Suite 700, Charlotte, NC 28277 **Telephone:** 704-625-4900	**Web Site:** www.babcock.com **Officers:** John A. Fees - Chairman E. James Ferland - President, Chief Executive Officer	**Auditors:** Deloitte & Touche LLP **Investor Contact:** 704-625-4937 **Transfer Agents:** Computershare Trust Company, N.A., Providence, RI

BADGER METER, INC.

Exchange	Symbol	Price	52Wk Range	Yield	P/E	Div Achiever
NYS	BMI	$53.52 (3/28/2013)	53.75-32.75	1.27	27.45	20 Years

*7 Year Price Score 100.61 *NYSE Composite Index=100 *12 Month Price Score 113.03

Interim Earnings (Per Share)

Qtr.	Mar	Jun	Sep	Dec
2008	0.41	0.48	0.39	0.42
2009	0.47	0.52	0.96	0.33
2010	0.36	0.53	0.60	0.42
2011	0.22	0.52	0.46	0.08
2012	0.42	0.52	0.62	0.39

Interim Dividends (Per Share)

Amt	Decl	Ex	Rec	Pay
0.16Q	04/27/2012	05/29/2012	05/31/2012	06/15/2012
0.17Q	08/10/2012	08/29/2012	08/31/2012	09/14/2012
0.17Q	11/09/2012	11/28/2012	11/30/2012	12/14/2012
0.17Q	02/15/2013	02/26/2013	02/28/2013	03/15/2013

Indicated Div: $0.68 (Div. Reinv. Plan)

Valuation Analysis   **Institutional Holding**

Forecast EPS	$2.33	No of Institutions
	(04/05/2013)	164
Market Cap	$766.1 Million	Shares
Book Value	$171.2 Million	11,516,016
Price/Book	4.47	% Held
Price/Sales	2.40	69.63

TRADING VOLUME (thousand shares)

Business Summary: Electronic Instruments & Related Products (MIC: 6.2.3 SIC: 3824 NAIC: 334514)

Badger Meter manufactures and sells products incorporating flow measurement and control technologies. Co.'s product lines fall into two categories: water applications, which sells water meters and related technologies and services used by water utilities, and products for other water-based purposes such as irrigation, water reclamation and industrial process applications; and specialty applications, which sells meters and related technologies and services for measuring fluids in industries such as food and beverage, pharmaceutical production, heating, ventilating and air conditioning, and measuring and dispensing automotive fluids, as well as radio technology to natural gas utilities.

Recent Developments: For the year ended Dec 31 2012, net income increased 46.3% to US$28.0 million from US$19.2 million in the prior year. Revenues were US$319.7 million, up 21.6% from US$262.9 million the year before. Operating income was US$44.5 million versus US$27.5 million in the prior year, an increase of 61.5%. Direct operating expenses rose 14.0% to US$197.4 million from US$173.1 million in the comparable period the year before. Indirect operating expenses increased 24.9% to US$77.8 million from US$62.3 million in the equivalent prior-year period.

Prospects: Our evaluation of Badger Meter Inc. as of Apr. 7, 2013 is the result of our systematic analysis on three basic characteristics: earnings strength, relative valuation, and recent stock price movement. The company has managed to produce a neutral trend in earnings per share over the past 5 quarters and while recent estimates for the company have remained steady, BMI has posted results that fell short of analysts expectations. Based on operating earnings yield, the company is about fairly valued when compared to all of the companies in our coverage universe. Share price changes over the past year indicates that BMI will perform very well over the near term.

Financial Data

(US$ in Thousands)	12/31/2012	12/31/2011	12/31/2010	12/31/2009	12/31/2008	12/31/2007	12/31/2006	12/31/2005
Earnings Per Share	1.95	1.27	1.91	2.28	1.69	1.13	0.52	0.94
Cash Flow Per Share	2.42	2.09	1.23	2.47	1.85	1.99	1.21	1.36
Tang Book Value Per Share	5.38	9.01	8.31	7.61	5.34	5.82	4.54	4.80
Dividends Per Share	0.660	0.600	0.520	0.460	0.400	0.340	0.310	0.290
Dividend Payout %	33.85	47.24	27.23	20.18	23.67	30.09	59.62	30.69
Income Statement								
Total Revenue	319,660	262,915	276,634	250,337	279,552	234,816	229,754	216,654
EBITDA	52,056	34,678	51,527	48,974	46,856	36,924	35,377	30,570
Depn & Amortn	7,587	7,144	6,704	6,731	5,954	6,308	6,589	6,164
Income Before Taxes	43,471	27,349	44,438	42,333	39,555	29,325	27,489	22,798
Income Taxes	15,439	8,188	15,776	15,553	14,471	10,939	10,921	9,545
Net Income	28,032	19,161	28,662	34,170	25,084	16,457	7,548	13,253
Average Shares	14,399	15,049	15,006	14,948	14,837	14,617	14,389	14,022
Balance Sheet								
Current Assets	121,374	101,195	97,337	86,680	86,529	79,934	79,359	72,564
Total Assets	290,453	218,910	215,864	191,016	195,358	150,301	139,383	145,867
Current Liabilities	94,080	22,413	32,679	26,261	50,789	41,209	45,711	39,586
Long-Term Obligations	...	...	...	...	5,504	3,129	5,928	15,360
Total Liabilities	119,206	39,629	47,481	46,555	84,335	58,332	67,564	72,451
Stockholders' Equity	171,247	179,281	168,383	144,461	111,023	91,969	71,819	73,416
Shares Outstanding	14,314	15,122	15,048	14,972	14,808	14,518	14,154	13,696
Statistical Record								
Return on Assets %	10.98	8.81	14.09	17.69	14.47	11.36	5.29	9.18
Return on Equity %	15.95	11.02	18.32	26.75	24.65	20.10	10.39	19.28
EBITDA Margin %	16.28	13.19	18.63	19.56	16.76	15.72	15.40	14.11
Net Margin %	8.77	7.29	10.36	13.65	8.97	7.01	3.29	6.12
Asset Turnover	1.25	1.21	1.36	1.30	1.61	1.62	1.61	1.50
Current Ratio	1.29	4.52	2.98	3.30	1.70	1.94	1.74	1.83
Debt to Equity	...	...	...	...	0.05	0.03	0.08	0.21
Price Range	48.27-29.68	45.19-27.06	45.05-35.22	43.84-23.10	60.47-19.17	46.05-23.53	32.50-19.81	25.52-13.06
P/E Ratio	24.75-15.22	35.58-21.31	23.59-18.44	19.23-10.13	35.78-11.34	40.75-20.82	62.50-38.10	27.14-13.89
Average Yield %	1.78	1.69	1.30	1.30	0.95	1.09	1.21	1.57

Address: 4545 W. Brown Deer Road, Milwaukee, WI 53223 **Telephone:** 414-355-0400 **Fax:** 414-355-7499	**Web Site:** www.badgermeter.com **Officers:** Richard A. Meeusen - Chairman, President, Chief Executive Officer Richard E. Johnson - Senior Vice President, Chief Financial Officer, Treasurer	**Auditors:** Ernst & Young LLP **Investor Contact:** 414-371-5702 **Transfer Agents:** American Stock Transfer & Trust Company, LLC, New York, NY

BAKER HUGHES INC.

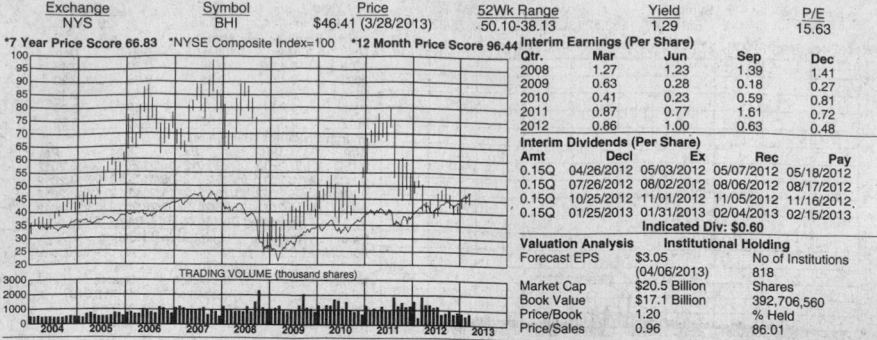

Exchange	Symbol	Price	52Wk Range	Yield	P/E
NYS	BHI	$46.41 (3/28/2013)	50.10-38.13	1.29	15.63

*7 Year Price Score 66.83 *NYSE Composite Index=100 *12 Month Price Score 96.44

Interim Earnings (Per Share)

Qtr.	Mar	Jun	Sep	Dec
2008	1.27	1.23	1.39	1.41
2009	0.63	0.28	0.18	0.27
2010	0.41	0.23	0.59	0.81
2011	0.87	0.77	1.61	0.72
2012	0.86	1.00	0.63	0.48

Interim Dividends (Per Share)

Amt	Decl	Ex	Rec	Pay
0.15Q	04/26/2012	05/03/2012	05/07/2012	05/18/2012
0.15Q	07/26/2012	08/02/2012	08/06/2012	08/17/2012
0.15Q	10/25/2012	11/01/2012	11/05/2012	11/16/2012
0.15Q	01/25/2013	01/31/2013	02/04/2013	02/15/2013

Indicated Div: $0.60

Valuation Analysis

Forecast EPS	$3.05 (04/06/2013)
Market Cap	$20.5 Billion
Book Value	$17.1 Billion
Price/Book	1.20
Price/Sales	0.96

Institutional Holding

No of Institutions	818
Shares	392,706,560
% Held	86.01

TRADING VOLUME (thousand shares)

Business Summary: Equipment & Services (MIC: 9.1.3 SIC: 3533 NAIC: 333132)

Baker Hughes is a supplier of oilfield services, products, technology and systems to the oil and natural gas industry. Co. provides products and services for: drilling and evaluation of oil and natural gas wells; completion and production of oil and natural gas wells; and other businesses, including downstream refining, and process and pipeline services. Co. has five segments. Four of these segments represent its oilfield operations and their geographic organization: North America; Latin America; Europe/Africa/Russia Caspian; and Middle East/Asia Pacific. In addition, Co.'s Industrial Services and Other segment include its downstream refining, and process and pipeline services businesses.

Recent Developments: For the year ended Dec 31 2012, net income decreased 24.4% to US$1.32 billion from US$1.74 billion in the prior year. Revenues were US$21.36 billion, up 7.7% from US$19.83 billion the year before. Operating income was US$2.19 billion versus US$2.60 billion in the prior year, a decrease of 15.7%. Direct operating expenses rose 13.7% to US$17.36 billion from US$15.26 billion in the comparable period the year before. Indirect operating expenses decreased 7.8% to US$1.81 billion from US$1.97 billion in the equivalent prior-year period.

Prospects: Our evaluation of Baker Hughes Inc. as of Apr. 7, 2013 is the result of our systematic analysis on three basic characteristics: earnings strength, relative valuation, and recent stock price movement. The company has generated a negative trend in earnings per share over the past 5 quarters. However, while recent estimates for the company have been lowered by analysts, BHI has posted better than expected results. Based on operating earnings yield, the company is undervalued when compared to all of the companies in our coverage universe. Share price changes over the past year indicates that BHI will perform in line with the market over the near term.

Financial Data

(US$ in Thousands)	12/31/2012	12/31/2011	12/31/2010	12/31/2009	12/31/2008	12/31/2007	12/31/2006	12/31/2005
Earnings Per Share	2.97	3.97	2.06	1.36	5.30	4.73	7.27	2.57
Cash Flow Per Share	4.16	3.46	2.17	4.00	5.24	4.64	1.78	2.81
Tang Book Value Per Share	22.94	19.79	15.42	18.18	16.89	15.14	11.58	9.42
Dividends Per Share	0.600	0.600	0.600	0.600	0.560	0.520	0.520	0.475
Dividend Payout %	20.20	15.11	29.13	44.12	10.57	10.99	7.15	18.48
Income Statement								
Total Revenue	21,361,000	19,831,000	14,414,000	9,664,000	11,864,000	10,428,200	9,027,400	7,185,500
EBITDA	3,619,000	3,781,000	2,492,000	1,447,000	3,011,000	2,793,900	4,106,400	1,617,200
Depn & Amortn	1,427,000	1,221,000	1,069,000	711,000	632,000	516,100	428,600	383,800
Income Before Taxes	1,982,000	2,339,000	1,282,000	611,000	2,317,000	2,255,500	3,676,400	1,179,100
Income Taxes	665,000	596,000	463,000	190,000	684,000	742,800	1,338,200	404,800
Net Income	1,311,000	1,739,000	812,000	421,000	1,635,000	1,513,900	2,419,000	878,400
Average Shares	441,000	438,000	395,000	311,000	309,000	320,100	332,600	341,500
Balance Sheet								
Current Assets	10,417,000	9,797,000	8,707,000	6,225,000	7,145,000	5,455,600	4,967,800	3,840,100
Total Assets	26,689,000	24,847,000	22,986,000	11,439,000	11,861,000	9,856,600	8,705,700	7,807,400
Current Liabilities	4,124,000	3,502,000	3,139,000	1,613,000	2,511,000	1,617,900	1,621,900	1,360,700
Long-Term Obligations	3,837,000	3,845,000	3,554,000	1,785,000	1,775,000	1,069,400	1,073,800	1,078,000
Total Liabilities	9,620,000	9,101,000	8,886,000	4,155,000	5,054,000	3,551,000	3,462,800	3,109,600
Stockholders' Equity	17,069,000	15,746,000	14,100,000	7,284,000	6,807,000	6,305,600	5,242,900	4,697,800
Shares Outstanding	441,000	437,000	432,000	312,000	309,000	315,400	319,900	341,500
Statistical Record								
Return on Assets %	5.07	7.27	4.72	3.61	15.02	16.31	29.30	12.01
Return on Equity %	7.97	11.65	7.59	5.98	24.87	26.22	48.67	20.44
EBITDA Margin %	16.94	19.07	17.29	14.97	25.38	26.79	45.49	22.51
Net Margin %	6.14	8.77	5.63	4.36	13.78	14.52	26.80	12.22
Asset Turnover	0.83	0.83	0.84	0.83	1.09	1.12	1.09	0.98
Current Ratio	2.53	2.80	2.77	3.86	2.85	3.37	3.06	2.82
Debt to Equity	0.22	0.24	0.25	0.25	0.26	0.17	0.20	0.23
Price Range	52.40-38.13	79.94-44.47	57.17-35.87	47.67-26.58	89.56-26.02	98.67-62.74	88.60-62.17	62.76-41.20
P/E Ratio	17.64-12.84	20.14-11.20	27.75-17.41	35.05-19.54	16.90-4.91	20.86-13.26	12.19-8.55	24.42-16.03
Average Yield %	1.36	0.94	1.30	1.61	0.86	0.66	0.71	0.93

Address: 2929 Allen Parkway, Suite 2100, Houston, TX 77019-2118	**Web Site:** www.bakerhughes.com	**Auditors:** Deloitte & Touche LLP
Telephone: 713-439-8600	**Officers:** Martin S. Craighead - Chairman, President, Chief Executive Officer Peter A. Ragauss - Senior Vice President, Chief Financial Officer	**Investor Contact:** 713-439-8039
Fax: 713-439-8699		**Transfer Agents:** BNY Mellon Shareowner Services LLC, Jersey City, NJ

BALL CORP

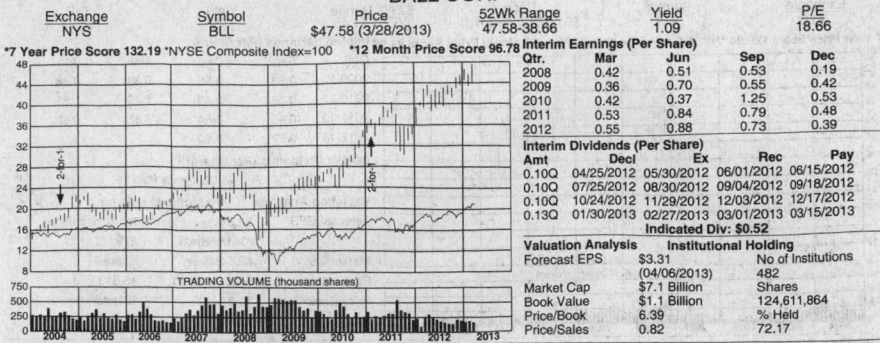

Exchange	Symbol	Price	52Wk Range	Yield	P/E
NYS	BLL	$47.58 (3/28/2013)	47.58-38.66	1.09	18.66

*7 Year Price Score 132.19 *NYSE Composite Index=100 *12 Month Price Score 96.78

Interim Earnings (Per Share)

Qtr.	Mar	Jun	Sep	Dec
2008	0.42	0.51	0.53	0.19
2009	0.36	0.70	0.55	0.42
2010	0.42	0.37	1.25	0.53
2011	0.53	0.84	0.79	0.48
2012	0.55	0.88	0.73	0.39

Interim Dividends (Per Share)

Amt	Decl	Ex	Rec	Pay
0.10Q	04/25/2012	05/30/2012	06/01/2012	06/15/2012
0.10Q	07/25/2012	08/30/2012	09/04/2012	09/18/2012
0.10Q	10/24/2012	11/29/2012	12/03/2012	12/17/2012
0.13Q	01/30/2013	02/27/2013	03/01/2013	03/15/2013

Indicated Div: $0.52

Valuation Analysis

		Institutional Holding	
Forecast EPS	$3.31	No of Institutions	
	(04/06/2013)	482	
Market Cap	$7.1 Billion	Shares	
Book Value	$1.1 Billion	124,611,864	
Price/Book	6.39	% Held	
Price/Sales	0.82	72.17	

Business Summary: Metal Products (MIC: 8.2.3 SIC: 3411 NAIC: 332431)

Ball is a supplier of metal packaging. Co. produces steel food containers and steel and aluminum containers for beverages, food, personal care and household products, as well as steel paint cans, decorative steel tins and aluminum slugs. Co. sells its packaging products mainly to beverage, food, personal care and household products companies. Also, Co.'s aerospace business designs, develops and manufactures aerospace systems for civil, commercial and national security aerospace markets. Co. produces spacecraft, instruments and sensors, radio frequency systems and components, data exploitation applications and a variety of aerospace technologies and products that enable deep space missions.

Recent Developments: For the year ended Dec 31 2012, income from continuing operations decreased 8.4% to US$429.3 million from US$468.6 million a year earlier. Net income decreased 8.5% to US$426.5 million from US$466.3 million in the prior year. Revenues were US$8.74 billion, up 1.2% from US$8.63 billion the year before. Operating income was US$790.5 million versus US$836.9 million in the prior year, a decrease of 5.5%. Direct operating expenses rose 1.3% to US$7.17 billion from US$7.08 billion in the comparable period the year before. Indirect operating expenses increased 8.2% to US$771.2 million from US$712.8 million in the equivalent prior-year period.

Prospects: Our evaluation of Ball Corp. as of Apr. 7, 2013 is the result of our systematic analysis on three basic characteristics: earnings strength, relative valuation, and recent stock price movement. The company has managed to produce a neutral trend in earnings per share over the past 5 quarters and while recent estimates for the company have remained steady, BLL has posted results that fell short of analysts' expectations. Based on operating earnings yield, the company is undervalued when compared to all of the companies in our coverage universe. Share price changes over the past year indicates that BLL will perform poorly over the near term.

Financial Data

(US$ in Thousands)	12/31/2012	12/31/2011	12/31/2010	12/31/2009	12/31/2008	12/31/2007	12/31/2006	12/31/2005
Earnings Per Share	2.55	2.63	2.55	2.04	1.65	1.37	1.57	1.19
Cash Flow Per Share	5.50	5.74	2.85	2.98	3.26	3.33	1.94	2.59
Dividends Per Share	0.400	0.280	0.200	0.200	0.200	0.200	0.200	0.200
Dividend Payout %	15.69	10.65	7.84	9.80	12.16	14.60	12.74	16.81
Income Statement								
Total Revenue	8,735,700	8,630,900	7,630,000	7,345,300	7,561,500	7,389,700	6,621,500	5,751,200
EBITDA	1,038,800	1,116,500	1,016,800	922,400	870,300	777,700	819,300	664,600
Depn & Amortn	248,300	279,600	252,200	267,800	279,800	263,800	238,000	202,100
Income Before Taxes	595,600	659,800	606,400	537,400	452,800	364,500	446,900	346,100
Income Taxes	165,000	201,300	175,800	162,800	147,400	95,700	131,600	99,300
Net Income	403,500	444,000	468,000	387,900	319,500	281,300	329,600	261,500
Average Shares	158,084	168,590	183,538	189,978	194,038	205,520	209,902	219,464
Balance Sheet								
Current Assets	2,339,400	2,321,900	2,305,700	1,923,300	2,165,300	1,842,900	1,761,300	1,225,800
Total Assets	7,507,100	7,284,600	6,927,700	6,488,300	6,368,700	6,020,600	5,840,900	4,343,400
Current Liabilities	1,685,800	1,856,100	1,383,300	1,428,600	1,862,400	1,513,100	1,454,300	1,176,000
Long-Term Obligations	3,085,300	2,696,700	2,701,600	2,283,900	2,107,100	2,181,800	2,270,400	1,473,300
Total Liabilities	6,392,500	6,065,500	5,409,700	4,907,000	5,282,900	4,678,100	4,675,500	3,508,100
Stockholders' Equity	1,114,600	1,219,100	1,518,000	1,581,300	1,085,800	1,342,500	1,165,400	835,300
Shares Outstanding	149,729	160,315	172,158	188,041	187,463	200,448	208,273	208,400
Statistical Record								
Return on Assets %	5.44	6.25	6.98	6.03	5.14	4.74	6.47	5.93
Return on Equity %	34.49	32.44	30.20	29.09	26.24	22.43	32.95	27.21
EBITDA Margin %	11.89	12.94	13.33	12.56	11.51	10.52	12.37	11.56
Net Margin %	4.62	5.14	6.13	5.28	4.23	3.81	4.98	4.55
Asset Turnover	1.18	1.21	1.14	1.14	1.22	1.25	1.30	1.30
Current Ratio	1.39	1.25	1.67	1.35	1.16	1.22	1.21	1.04
Debt to Equity	2.77	2.21	1.78	1.44	1.94	1.63	1.95	1.76
Price Range	45.46-36.25	40.36-30.22	34.83-24.13	26.13-18.45	27.92-14.07	27.88-21.95	22.40-17.36	22.93-17.78
P/E Ratio	17.83-14.22	15.35-11.49	13.66-9.46	12.81-9.04	16.92-8.52	20.35-16.03	14.26-11.05	19.27-14.94
Average Yield %	0.96	0.78	0.70	0.88	0.91	0.80	0.87	1.01

Address: 10 Longs Peak Drive, P.O. Box 5000, Broomfield, CO 80021-2510
Telephone: 303-469-3131
Fax: 303-460-2127

Web Site: www.ball.com
Officers: R. David Hoover - Chairman, President John A. Hayes - President, Chief Executive Officer

Auditors: PricewaterhouseCoopers LLP
Investor Contact: 303-460-3537
Transfer Agents: Computershare, Providence, RI

BALLY TECHNOLOGIES INC

Exchange	Symbol	Price	52Wk Range	Yield	P/E
NYS	BYI	$51.97 (3/28/2013)	52.45-41.89	N/A	18.11

*7 Year Price Score 120.94 *NYSE Composite Index=100 *12 Month Price Score 97.05

Interim Earnings (Per Share)

Qtr.	Sep	Dec	Mar	Jun
2009-10	0.53	0.58	0.39	0.88
2010-11	0.39	0.49	0.43	0.51
2011-12	0.45	0.54	0.67	0.63
2012-13	0.77	0.80	...	...

Interim Dividends (Per Share)

No Dividends Paid

Valuation Analysis		Institutional Holding	
Forecast EPS	$3.34	No of Institutions	
	(04/05/2013)	279	
Market Cap	$2.1 Billion	Shares	
Book Value	$196.4 Million	45,313,200	
Price/Book	10.90	% Held	
Price/Sales	2.26	N/A	

Business Summary: Internet & Software (MIC: 6.3.2 SIC: 7372 NAIC: 511210)

Bally Technologies is a gaming company that designs, manufactures, operates, and distributes technology-based gaming devices, systems, server-based applications, custom mobile applications, and other applications. Co. is engaged in three businesses: gaming equipment, which includes the sale of gaming devices and related equipment, parts and conversion kits; gaming operations, which includes the operation of linked progressive systems, video lottery and centrally determined systems, and the rental of gaming devices and content; and systems, which includes the sale and support of systems-based software and hardware products and related recurring maintenance.

Recent Developments: For the quarter ended Dec 31 2012, net income increased 36.2% to US$33.1 million from US$24.3 million in the year-earlier quarter. Revenues were US$238.3 million, up 13.2% from US$210.5 million the year before. Operating income was US$56.7 million versus US$43.0 million in the prior-year quarter, an increase of 31.7%. Direct operating expenses rose 4.6% to US$81.5 million from US$77.9 million in the comparable period the year before. Indirect operating expenses increased 11.9% to US$100.1 million from US$89.5 million in the equivalent prior-year period.

Prospects: Our evaluation of Bally Technologies Inc. as of Apr. 7, 2013 is the result of our systematic analysis on three basic characteristics: earnings strength, relative valuation, and recent stock price movement. The company has managed to produce a neutral trend in earnings per share over the past 5 quarters and while recent estimates for the company have been mixed, BYI has posted better than expected results. Based on operating earnings yield, the company is undervalued when compared to all of the companies in our coverage universe. Share price changes over the past year indicates that BYI will perform in line with the market over the near term.

Financial Data

(US$ in Thousands)	6 Mos	3 Mos	06/30/2012	06/30/2011	06/30/2010	06/30/2009	06/30/2008	06/30/2007
Earnings Per Share	2.87	2.61	2.28	1.81	2.38	2.22	1.85	0.40
Cash Flow Per Share	3.39	3.00	3.04	1.09	2.37	3.03	1.25	0.48
Tang Book Value Per Share	N.M.	N.M.	N.M.	0.36	6.37	4.46	2.25	0.25
Income Statement								
Total Revenue	473,490	235,151	879,759	758,155	778,191	883,429	899,691	682,318
EBITDA	109,336	53,286	259,876	228,801	256,973	284,548	263,400	128,218
Depn & Amortn	888	440	83,260	78,384	76,884	72,109	61,733	59,528
Income Before Taxes	101,840	49,373	164,459	143,393	170,818	196,717	178,616	38,106
Income Taxes	37,818	18,429	63,549	45,182	60,721	68,481	66,793	10,975
Net Income	65,658	32,532	101,148	98,263	137,477	126,309	107,207	22,328
Average Shares	41,494	42,115	44,420	54,420	57,675	57,058	58,157	55,543
Balance Sheet								
Current Assets	532,345	509,696	480,459	473,677	476,409	423,639	547,687	421,883
Total Assets	997,721	989,390	970,467	927,394	913,176	880,882	995,124	824,895
Current Liabilities	208,320	214,111	214,037	160,616	174,553	178,050	294,398	256,938
Long-Term Obligations	538,125	538,750	494,375	500,250	131,250	173,750	291,341	321,583
Total Liabilities	801,272	816,382	774,359	714,489	371,365	444,576	671,799	625,441
Stockholders' Equity	196,449	173,008	196,108	212,905	541,811	436,306	323,325	199,454
Shares Outstanding	41,201	40,894	42,102	44,397	54,392	54,312	55,144	54,025
Statistical Record								
Return on Assets %	12.77	11.88	10.63	10.68	15.33	13.47	11.75	2.95
Return on Equity %	58.44	60.30	49.32	26.04	28.11	33.26	40.90	13.00
EBITDA Margin %	23.09	22.66	29.54	30.18	33.02	32.21	29.28	18.79
Net Margin %	13.87	13.83	11.50	12.96	17.67	14.30	11.92	3.27
Asset Turnover	0.99	0.96	0.92	0.82	0.87	0.94	0.99	0.90
Current Ratio	2.56	2.38	2.24	2.95	2.73	2.38	1.86	1.64
Debt to Equity	2.74	3.11	2.52	2.35	0.24	0.40	0.90	1.61
Price Range	50.48-39.37	49.39-25.15	48.55-25.15	43.59-30.75	46.85-27.79	35.47-13.33	51.98-24.37	27.82-14.83
P/E Ratio	17.59-13.72	18.92-9.64	21.29-11.03	24.08-16.99	19.68-11.68	15.98-6.00	28.10-13.17	69.55-37.08

Address: 6601 S. Bermuda Rd., Las Vegas, NV 89119	Web Site: www.ballytech.com	Auditors: Deloitte & Touche LLP
Telephone: 702-584-7700	**Officers:** Kevin Verner - Chairman Ramesh Srinivasan - President, Chief Executive Officer, Chief Operating Officer	**Transfer Agents:** American Stock Transfer & Trust Company, New York, NY
Fax: 702-263-5636		

BANCORPSOUTH INC.

Exchange	Symbol	Price	52Wk Range	Yield	P/E
NYS	BXS	$16.30 (3/28/2013)	16.40-12.47	0.25	18.11

*7 Year Price Score 64.84 *NYSE Composite Index=100 *12 Month Price Score 98.47

Interim Earnings (Per Share)

Qtr.	Mar	Jun	Sep	Dec
2008	0.43	0.49	0.34	0.20
2009	0.35	0.41	0.26	(0.03)
2010	0.10	(0.15)	0.13	0.19
2011	(0.01)	0.15	0.14	0.16
2012	0.25	0.22	0.25	0.18

Interim Dividends (Per Share)

Amt	Decl	Ex	Rec	Pay
0.01Q	04/25/2012	06/13/2012	06/15/2012	07/02/2012
0.01Q	07/18/2012	09/12/2012	09/14/2012	10/01/2012
0.01Q	10/24/2012	12/12/2012	12/14/2012	01/02/2013
0.01Q	01/23/2013	03/13/2013	03/15/2013	04/01/2013

Indicated Div: $0.04 (Div. Reinv. Plan)

Valuation Analysis

Forecast EPS $0.90 (04/06/2013)
Market Cap $1.5 Billion
Book Value $1.4 Billion
Price/Book 1.06
Price/Sales 2.01

Institutional Holding

No of Institutions 217
Shares 59,851,472
% Held 66.61

TRADING VOLUME (thousand shares)

Business Summary: Banking (MIC: 5.1.1 SIC: 6022 NAIC: 522110)

BancorpSouth is a financial holding company. Through its principal bank subsidiary, BancorpSouth Bank (the Bank), Co. is engaged in providing a range of financial services to individuals and small-to-medium size businesses, investment brokerage services and sales of other insurance products, personal trust and estate services, certain employee benefit accounts and plans, including individual retirement accounts, and limited corporate trust functions. Co. operates three segments: Community Banking, Insurance Agencies, and General Corporate and Other. At Dec 31 2012, Co. had total assets of $13.4 billion and total deposits of $11.1 billion.

Recent Developments: For the year ended Dec 31 2012, net income increased 124.4% to US$84.3 million from US$37.6 million in the prior year. Net interest income decreased 4.7% to US$414.6 million from US$434.9 million in the prior year. Provision for loan losses was US$28.0 million versus US$130.1 million in the prior year, a decrease of 78.5%. Non-interest income rose 3.4% to US$280.1 million from US$270.8 million, while non-interest expense advanced 2.9% to US$549.2 million.

Prospects: Our evaluation of BancorpSouth Inc. as of Apr. 7, 2013 is the result of our systematic analysis on three basic characteristics: earnings strength, relative valuation, and recent stock price movement. The company has generated a negative trend in earnings per share over the past 5 quarters and while recent estimates for the company have been mixed, BXS has posted results that fell short of analysts expectations. Based on operating earnings yield, the company is about fairly valued when compared to all of the companies in our coverage universe. Share price changes over the past year indicates that BXS will perform in line with the market over the near term.

Financial Data
(US$ in Thousands)

	12/31/2012	12/31/2011	12/31/2010	12/31/2009	12/31/2008	12/31/2007	12/31/2006	12/31/2005
Earnings Per Share	0.90	0.45	0.27	0.99	1.45	1.69	1.57	1.47
Cash Flow Per Share	1.42	3.07	2.69	3.36	1.49	1.39	1.57	2.40
Tang Book Value Per Share	12.43	11.88	11.41	12.06	11.69	11.44	11.16	10.58
Dividends Per Share	0.040	0.140	0.880	0.880	0.870	0.830	0.790	0.760
Dividend Payout %	4.44	31.11	325.93	88.89	60.00	49.11	50.32	51.70
Income Statement								
Interest Income	486,424	537,853	582,762	615,414	705,413	801,242	681,891	559,936
Interest Expense	71,833	102,940	141,620	170,515	264,577	378,343	296,092	204,379
Net Interest Income	414,591	434,913	441,142	444,899	440,836	422,899	385,799	355,557
Provision for Losses	28,000	130,081	204,016	117,324	56,176	22,696	8,577	24,467
Non-Interest Income	280,149	270,845	264,144	275,276	242,380	231,799	206,094	198,812
Non-Interest Expense	549,193	533,633	487,033	490,017	452,686	428,058	393,154	362,010
Income Before Taxes	117,547	42,044	14,237	112,834	174,354	203,944	190,162	167,800
Income Taxes	33,252	4,475	(8,705)	30,105	53,943	66,001	64,968	52,601
Net Income	84,295	37,569	22,942	82,729	120,411	137,943	125,194	115,199
Average Shares	93,864	83,509	83,515	83,430	82,793	81,845	79,542	78,597
Balance Sheet								
Net Loans & Leases	8,601,661	8,758,651	9,229,891	9,679,436	9,747,726	9,193,019	7,861,960	7,338,326
Total Assets	13,397,198	12,995,851	13,615,010	13,167,867	13,480,218	13,189,841	12,040,521	11,768,674
Total Deposits	11,088,146	10,955,189	11,490,021	10,677,702	9,711,872	10,064,099	9,710,578	9,607,258
Total Liabilities	11,948,146	11,732,939	12,392,766	11,891,571	12,239,958	11,993,215	11,013,936	10,791,508
Stockholders' Equity	1,449,052	1,262,912	1,222,244	1,276,296	1,240,260	1,196,626	1,026,585	977,166
Shares Outstanding	94,437	83,483	83,481	83,450	83,105	82,299	79,109	79,237
Statistical Record								
Return on Assets %	0.64	0.28	0.17	0.62	0.90	1.09	1.05	1.02
Return on Equity %	6.20	3.02	1.84	6.57	9.86	12.41	12.50	12.17
Net Interest Margin %	85.23	80.86	75.70	72.29	62.49	52.78	56.58	63.50
Efficiency Ratio %	71.64	65.99	57.51	55.02	47.76	41.44	44.27	47.72
Loans to Deposits	0.78	0.80	0.80	0.91	1.00	0.91	0.81	0.76
Price Range	15.57-10.89	16.67-8.34	24.49-12.56	25.13-16.55	29.95-15.81	27.51-21.60	28.50-22.08	24.99-20.01
P/E Ratio	17.30-12.10	37.04-18.53	90.70-46.52	25.38-16.72	20.66-10.90	16.28-12.78	18.15-14.06	17.00-13.61
Average Yield %	0.29	1.12	4.97	4.01	3.83	3.38	3.06	3.42

Address: One Mississippi Plaza, 201 South Spring Street, Tupelo, MS 38804 **Telephone:** 662-680-2000	**Web Site:** www.bancorpsouth.com **Officers:** Aubrey B. Patterson - Chairman, Chief Executive Officer James V. Kelley - President, Chief Operating Officer	**Auditors:** KPMG LLP **Investor Contact:** 662-680-2000 **Transfer Agents:** Registrar and Transfer Company, Cranford, NJ

BANK OF AMERICA CORP.

Exchange	Symbol	Price	52Wk Range	Yield	P/E
NYS	BAC	$12.18 (3/28/2013)	12.78-6.83	0.33	48.72

*7 Year Price Score 34.70 *NYSE Composite Index=100 *12 Month Price Score 116.18

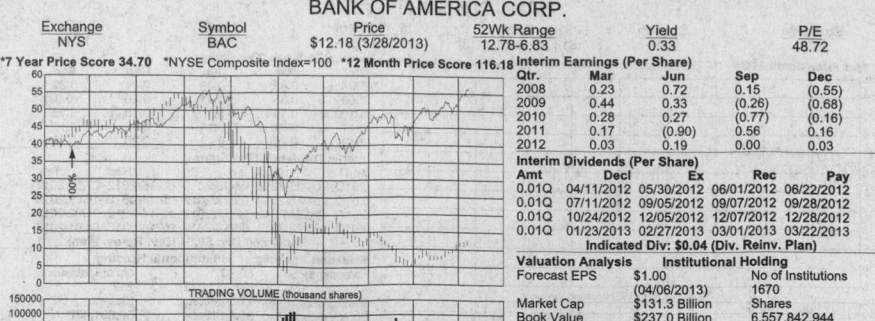

Interim Earnings (Per Share)

Qtr.	Mar	Jun	Sep	Dec
2008	0.23	0.72	0.15	(0.55)
2009	0.44	0.33	(0.26)	(0.68)
2010	0.28	0.27	(0.77)	(0.16)
2011	0.17	(0.90)	0.56	0.16
2012	0.03	0.19	0.00	0.03

Interim Dividends (Per Share)

Amt	Decl	Ex	Rec	Pay
0.01Q	04/11/2012	05/30/2012	06/01/2012	06/22/2012
0.01Q	07/11/2012	09/05/2012	09/07/2012	09/28/2012
0.01Q	10/24/2012	12/05/2012	12/07/2012	12/28/2012
0.01Q	01/23/2013	02/27/2013	03/01/2013	03/22/2013

Indicated Div: $0.04 (Div. Reinv. Plan)

Valuation Analysis | **Institutional Holding**

Forecast EPS	$1.00 (04/06/2013)	No of Institutions	1670
Market Cap	$131.3 Billion	Shares	6,557,842,944
Book Value	$237.0 Billion	% Held	
Price/Book	0.55		57.73
Price/Sales	1.31		

Business Summary: Banking (MIC: 5.1.1 SIC: 6021 NAIC: 522110)

Bank of America is a bank and financial holding company. Through its banking and various nonbanking subsidiaries throughout the U.S. and in international markets, Co. provides a range of banking and nonbanking financial services and products through five business segments: Consumer & Business Banking, Consumer Real Estate Services, Global Banking, Global Markets and Global Wealth & Investment Management, as well as All Other. Co. operates its banking activities primarily under two charters: Bank of America, National Association, and FIA Card Services, National Association. As of Dec 31 2012, Co. had total assets of $2.21 trillion and deposits of $1.10 trillion.

Recent Developments: For the year ended Dec 31 2012, net income increased 189.6% to US$4.19 billion from US$1.45 billion in the prior year. Net interest income decreased 8.9% to US$40.66 billion from US$44.62 billion in the prior year. Provision for loan losses was US$8.17 billion versus US$13.41 billion in the prior year, a decrease of 39.1%. Non-interest income fell 12.6% to US$42.68 billion from US$48.84 billion, while non-interest expense declined 10.2% to US$72.09 billion.

Prospects: Our evaluation of Bank of America Corp. as of Apr. 7, 2013 is the result of our systematic analysis on three basic characteristics: earnings strength, relative valuation, and recent stock price movement. The company has generated a negative trend in earnings per share over the past 5 quarters. However, while recent estimates for the company have been mixed, BAC has posted better than expected results. Based on operating earnings yield, the company is undervalued when compared to all of the companies in our coverage universe. Share price changes over the past year indicates that BAC will perform well over the near term.

Financial Data

(US$ in Millions)	12/31/2012	12/31/2011	12/31/2010	12/31/2009	12/31/2008	12/31/2007	12/31/2006	12/31/2005
Earnings Per Share	0.25	0.01	(0.37)	(0.29)	0.55	3.30	4.59	4.04
Cash Flow Per Share	(1.29)	6.36	8.44	16.79	0.88	2.49	3.21	(3.05)
Tang Book Value Per Share	12.59	11.98	11.18	8.80	7.14	11.54	12.18	12.48
Dividends Per Share	0.040	0.040	0.040	0.040	2.240	2.400	2.120	1.900
Dividend Payout %	16.00	400.00	...	...	407.27	72.73	46.19	47.03
Income Statement								
Interest Income	57,400	66,236	75,497	77,916	85,684	87,304	78,585	58,626
Interest Expense	16,744	21,620	23,974	30,807	40,324	52,871	43,994	27,889
Net Interest Income	40,656	44,616	51,523	47,109	45,360	34,433	34,591	30,737
Provision for Losses	8,169	13,410	28,435	48,570	26,825	8,385	5,010	4,014
Non-Interest Income	42,678	48,838	58,697	72,534	27,422	31,886	37,989	26,438
Non-Interest Expense	72,093	80,274	83,108	66,713	41,529	37,010	35,597	28,681
Income Before Taxes	3,072	(230)	(1,323)	4,360	4,428	20,924	31,973	24,480
Income Taxes	(1,116)	(1,676)	915	(1,916)	420	5,942	10,840	8,015
Net Income	4,188	1,446	(2,238)	6,276	4,008	14,982	21,133	16,465
Average Shares	10,841	10,254	9,790	7,729	4,612	4,480	4,595	4,069
Balance Sheet								
Net Loans & Leases	903,053	906,179	933,613	906,802	939,829	864,756	697,474	565,746
Total Assets	2,209,974	2,129,046	2,264,909	2,223,299	1,817,943	1,715,746	1,459,737	1,291,803
Total Deposits	1,105,261	1,033,041	1,010,430	991,611	882,997	805,177	693,497	634,670
Total Liabilities	1,973,018	1,898,945	2,036,661	1,991,855	1,640,891	1,568,943	1,324,465	1,190,270
Stockholders' Equity	236,956	230,101	228,248	231,444	177,052	146,803	135,272	101,533
Shares Outstanding	10,779	10,536	10,085	8,650	5,017	4,437	4,458	4,000
Statistical Record								
Return on Assets %	0.19	0.07	N.M.	0.31	0.23	0.94	1.54	1.37
Return on Equity %	1.79	0.63	N.M.	3.07	2.47	10.62	17.85	16.37
Net Interest Margin %	70.83	67.36	68.25	60.46	52.94	39.44	44.02	52.43
Efficiency Ratio %	72.04	69.76	61.93	44.34	36.72	31.05	30.54	33.72
Loans to Deposits	0.82	0.88	0.92	0.91	1.06	1.07	1.01	0.89
Price Range	11.61-5.80	15.25-4.99	19.48-10.95	18.59-3.14	45.03-11.25	54.05-41.10	54.90-43.09	47.08-41.57
P/E Ratio	46.44-23.20	N.M.	...	...	81.87-20.45	16.38-12.45	11.96-9.39	11.65-10.29
Average Yield %	0.47	0.40	0.27	0.32	7.27	4.84	4.27	4.23

Address: Bank of America Corporate Center, 100 North Tryon Street, Charlotte, NC 28255	Web Site: www.bankofamerica.com	Auditors: PricewaterhouseCoopers LLP
Telephone: 704-386-5681	Officers: Charles O. Holliday - Chairman Charles K. Gifford - Chairman Emeritus, Chairman	Investor Contact: 800-521-3984
Fax: 704-388-9278		Transfer Agents: Computershare Trust Company, N.A., Providence, RI

BANK OF HAWAII CORP

Exchange	Symbol	Price	52Wk Range	Yield	P/E
NYS	BOH	$50.81 (3/28/2013)	50.81-42.04	3.54	13.84

*7 Year Price Score 87.91   *NYSE Composite Index=100   *12 Month Price Score 97.08

Interim Earnings (Per Share)

Qtr.	Mar	Jun	Sep	Dec
2008	1.18	1.00	0.99	0.82
2009	0.75	0.65	0.76	0.84
2010	1.09	0.96	0.91	0.84
2011	0.88	0.74	0.92	0.85
2012	0.95	0.90	0.92	0.90

Interim Dividends (Per Share)

Amt	Decl	Ex	Rec	Pay
0.45Q	04/23/2012	05/29/2012	05/31/2012	06/14/2012
0.45Q	07/23/2012	08/29/2012	08/31/2012	09/17/2012
0.45Q	10/22/2012	11/28/2012	11/30/2012	12/14/2012
0.45Q	01/30/2013	02/26/2013	02/28/2013	03/14/2013

Indicated Div: $1.80 (Div. Reinv. Plan)

Valuation Analysis   **Institutional Holding**

Forecast EPS	$3.50	No of Institutions
(04/06/2013)		304
Market Cap	$2.3 Billion	Shares
Book Value	$1.0 Billion	39,502,200
Price/Book	2.23	% Held
Price/Sales	3.66	71.82

TRADING VOLUME (thousand shares)

Business Summary: Banking (MIC: 5.1.1 SIC: 6022 NAIC: 522110)

Bank of Hawaii is a bank holding company. Through its principal subsidiary, Bank of Hawaii, Co. provides financial services and products in Hawaii, Guam, and other Pacific Islands. Co.'s segments include: Retail Banking, which provides loan and lease, deposit, and retail life insurance products to consumers and small businesses; Commercial Banking, which provides corporate banking and commercial real estate loans, among others; Investment Services, which includes trust services and investment management, among others; and Treasury, which consists of corporate asset and liability management activities. As of Dec 31 2011, Co. had total assets of $13.85 billion and deposits of $10.59 billion.

Recent Developments: For the year ended Dec 31 2012, net income increased 3.8% to US$166.1 million from US$160.0 million in the prior year. Net interest income decreased 3.3% to US$377.3 million from US$390.2 million in the prior year. Provision for loan losses was US$979,000 versus US$12.7 million in the prior year, a decrease of 92.3%. Non-interest income rose 1.3% to US$200.3 million from US$197.7 million, while non-interest expense declined 4.0% to US$334.3 million.

Prospects: Our evaluation of Bank of Hawaii Corp. as of Apr. 7, 2013 is the result of our systematic analysis on three basic characteristics: earnings strength, relative valuation, and recent stock price movement. The company has managed to produce a neutral trend in earnings per share over the past 5 quarters and while recent estimates for the company have been raised by analysts, BOH has posted better than expected results. Based on operating earnings yield, the company is undervalued when compared to all of the companies in our coverage universe. Share price changes over the past year indicates that BOH will perform poorly over the near term.

Financial Data

(US$ in Thousands)	12/31/2012	12/31/2011	12/31/2010	12/31/2009	12/31/2008	12/31/2007	12/31/2006	12/31/2005
Earnings Per Share	3.67	3.39	3.80	3.00	3.99	3.69	3.52	3.41
Cash Flow Per Share	4.92	4.88	4.17	6.29	3.87	4.77	4.16	4.44
Tang Book Value Per Share	21.56	20.61	19.84	17.46	15.39	14.15	11.70	12.49
Dividends Per Share	1.800	1.800	1.800	1.800	1.770	1.670	1.520	1.360
Dividend Payout %	49.05	53.10	47.37	60.00	44.36	45.26	43.18	39.88
Income Statement								
Interest Income	420,489	439,693	465,251	497,794	550,101	601,875	572,672	506,442
Interest Expense	43,218	49,485	58,771	85,460	131,324	206,857	170,059	99,329
Net Interest Income	377,271	390,208	406,480	412,334	418,777	395,018	402,613	407,113
Provision for Losses	979	12,690	55,287	107,878	60,515	15,507	10,758	4,588
Non-Interest Income	200,286	197,655	255,258	267,808	258,113	240,487	216,176	209,314
Non-Interest Expense	334,288	348,193	347,579	350,024	346,774	335,407	320,962	327,642
Income Before Taxes	242,290	226,980	260,215	222,240	269,601	284,591	287,069	284,197
Income Taxes	76,214	66,937	76,273	78,207	77,388	100,888	106,710	102,636
Net Income	166,076	160,043	183,942	144,033	192,213	183,703	180,359	181,561
Average Shares	45,249	47,224	48,355	48,009	48,200	49,833	51,178	53,310
Balance Sheet								
Net Loans & Leases	5,747,038	5,418,655	5,205,998	5,632,671	6,428,275	6,502,204	6,544,111	6,095,361
Total Assets	13,728,372	13,846,391	13,126,787	12,414,827	10,763,475	10,472,942	10,571,815	10,187,038
Total Deposits	11,529,482	10,592,623	9,888,995	9,409,676	8,292,098	7,942,372	8,023,394	7,907,468
Total Liabilities	12,706,707	12,843,724	12,115,654	11,518,854	9,972,771	9,722,687	9,852,395	9,493,686
Stockholders' Equity	1,021,665	1,002,667	1,011,133	895,973	790,704	750,255	719,420	693,352
Shares Outstanding	44,754	45,947	48,097	48,018	47,753	48,589	56,827	51,276
Statistical Record								
Return on Assets %	1.20	1.19	1.44	1.24	1.81	1.75	1.74	1.82
Return on Equity %	16.36	15.89	19.29	17.08	24.88	25.00	25.53	24.08
Net Interest Margin %	89.72	88.75	87.37	82.83	76.13	65.63	70.30	80.39
Efficiency Ratio %	53.85	54.63	48.24	45.72	42.91	39.82	40.69	45.78
Loans to Deposits	0.50	0.51	0.53	0.60	0.78	0.82	0.82	0.77
Price Range	49.60-42.04	49.11-35.03	53.53-42.21	47.92-25.70	70.00-37.36	54.85-46.78	54.87-47.33	54.14-44.05
P/E Ratio	13.51-11.46	14.49-10.33	14.09-11.11	15.97-8.57	17.54-9.36	14.86-12.68	15.59-13.45	15.88-12.92
Average Yield %	3.90	4.07	3.84	4.65	3.58	3.21	2.96	2.76

Address: 130 Merchant Street,	Web Site: www.boh.com	Auditors: Ernst & Young LLP
Honolulu, HI 96813	Officers: Peter S. Ho - Chairman, President, Chief	Investor Contact: 808-694-8430
Telephone: 808-538-4727	Executive Officer, Chief Banking Officer Wayne Y.	Transfer Agents: Computershare
	Hamano - Vice-Chairman, Chief Commercial Officer	Investor Services, LLC, Canton, MA

BANK OF NEW YORK MELLON CORP

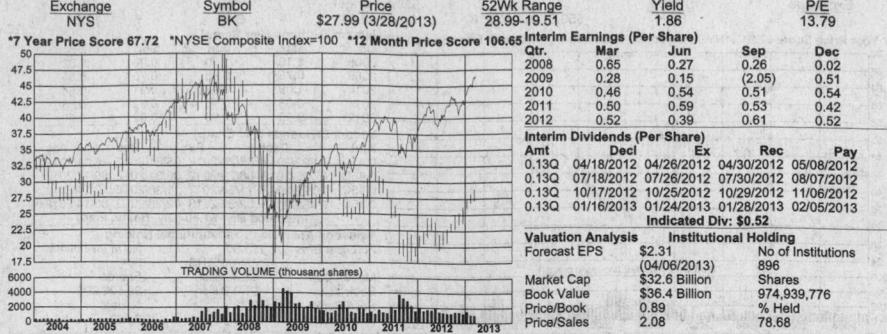

Exchange	Symbol	Price	52Wk Range	Yield	P/E
NYS	BK	$27.99 (3/28/2013)	28.99-19.51	1.86	13.79

*7 Year Price Score 67.72   *NYSE Composite Index=100   *12 Month Price Score 106.65

Interim Earnings (Per Share)

Qtr.	Mar	Jun	Sep	Dec
2008	0.65	0.27	0.26	0.02
2009	0.28	0.15	(2.05)	0.51
2010	0.46	0.54	0.51	0.54
2011	0.50	0.59	0.53	0.42
2012	0.52	0.39	0.61	0.52

Interim Dividends (Per Share)

Amt	Decl	Ex	Rec	Pay
0.13Q	04/18/2012	04/26/2012	04/30/2012	05/08/2012
0.13Q	07/18/2012	07/26/2012	07/30/2012	08/07/2012
0.13Q	10/17/2012	10/25/2012	10/29/2012	11/06/2012
0.13Q	01/16/2013	01/24/2013	01/28/2013	02/05/2013

Indicated Div: $0.52

Valuation Analysis

		Institutional Holding	
Forecast EPS	$2.31	No of Institutions	
	(04/06/2013)	896	
Market Cap	$32.6 Billion	Shares	
Book Value	$36.4 Billion	974,939,776	
Price/Book	0.89	% Held	
Price/Sales	2.08	78.68	

Business Summary: Banking (MIC: 5.1.1 SIC: 6022 NAIC: 522110)

Bank of New York Mellon is a bank holding company. Through its subsidiaries, Co. provides financial products and services in domestic and international markets. Co.'s principal segments are: Investment Management, comprised of its affiliated investment management boutiques, wealth management business and global distribution companies; and Investment Services, which provides global custody and related services, broker-dealer services, collateral services, alternative investment services, corporate trust and depositary receipt services, and clearing services and global payment/working capital services. As of Dec 31 2012, Co. had total assets of $358.99 billion and deposits of $246.10 billion.

Recent Developments: For the year ended Dec 31 2012, income from continuing operations decreased 1.8% to US$2.52 billion from US$2.57 billion a year earlier. Net income decreased 1.8% to US$2.52 billion from US$2.57 billion in the prior year. Net interest income increased 2.2% to US$2.57 billion from US$2.51 billion in the prior year. Provision for loan losses was US$80.0 million versus US$1.0 million in the prior year, an increase of. Non-interest income fell 0.6% to US$12.15 billion from US$12.22 billion, while non-interest expense advanced 2.0% to US$11.33 billion.

Prospects: Our evaluation of Bank of New York Mellon Corp. as of Apr. 7, 2013 is the result of our systematic analysis on three basic characteristics: earnings strength, relative valuation, and recent stock price movement. The company has managed to produce a neutral trend in earnings per share over the past 5 quarters. However, while recent estimates for the company have been mixed, BK has posted results that fell short of analysts expectations. Based on operating earnings yield, the company is undervalued when compared to all of the companies in our coverage universe. Share price changes over the past year indicates that BK will perform well over the near term.

Financial Data

(US$ in Thousands)	12/31/2012	12/31/2011	12/31/2010	12/31/2009	12/31/2008	12/31/2007
Earnings Per Share	2.03	2.03	2.05	(1.16)	1.20	2.18
Cash Flow Per Share	1.38	1.81	3.34	3.21	2.54	...
Tang Book Value Per Share	9.77	7.75	6.22	5.42	2.53	5.37
Dividends Per Share	0.520	0.480	0.360	0.510	0.960	0.480
Dividend Payout %	25.62	23.65	17.56	...	80.00	22.02
Income Statement						
Total Revenue	15,653,000	15,804,000	14,920,000	8,279,000	16,339,000	14,782,000
Income Before Taxes	3,302,000	3,617,000	3,694,000	(2,208,000)	1,939,000	3,225,000
Income Taxes	779,000	1,048,000	1,047,000	(1,395,000)	497,000	998,000
Net Income	2,445,000	2,569,000	2,581,000	(1,083,000)	1,419,000	2,039,000
Average Shares	1,178,430	1,223,026	1,216,214	1,178,907	1,152,621	934,704
Balance Sheet						
Total Assets	358,990,000	325,266,000	247,259,000	212,224,000	237,512,000	197,656,000
Total Liabilities	322,559,000	291,849,000	214,905,000	183,247,000	209,462,000	168,253,000
Stockholders' Equity	36,431,000	33,417,000	32,354,000	28,977,000	28,050,000	29,403,000
Shares Outstanding	1,163,490	1,209,674	1,241,530	1,207,834	1,148,467	1,145,983
Statistical Record						
Return on Assets %	0.71	0.90	1.12	N.M.	0.65	...
Return on Equity %	6.98	7.81	8.42	N.M.	4.93	...
Net Margin %	15.62	16.26	17.30	N.M.	8.68	13.79
Asset Turnover	0.05	0.06	0.06	0.04	0.07	...
Price Range	26.20-19.51	32.37-17.71	32.54-24.16	32.56-18.02	49.17-22.66	49.82-39.52
P/E Ratio	12.91-9.61	15.95-8.72	15.87-11.79	...	40.98-18.88	22.85-18.13
Average Yield %	2.30	1.92	1.30	1.87	2.52	1.09

Address: One Wall Street, New York, NY 10286 **Telephone:** 212-495-1784	**Web Site:** www.bnymellon.com **Officers:** Gerald L. Hassell - Chairman, President, Chief Executive Officer Karen B. Peetz - President, Senior Executive Vice President	**Auditors:** KPMG LLP **Investor Contact:** 412-234-4633 **Transfer Agents:** Computershare Shareowner Services LLC, Jersey City, NJ

BANKUNITED INC.

Exchange	Symbol	Price	52Wk Range	Yield	P/E
NYS	BKU	$25.62 (3/28/2013)	28.57-22.16	3.28	12.50

*7 Year Price Score N/A *NYSE Composite Index=100 *12 Month Price Score 101.08

Interim Earnings (Per Share)

Qtr.	Mar	Jun	Sep	Dec
2010	0.65	0.55	0.48	0.30
2011	(0.72)	0.44	0.45	0.42
2012	0.49	0.48	0.48	0.61

Interim Dividends (Per Share)

Amt	Decl	Ex	Rec	Pay
0.17Q	06/19/2012	06/28/2012	07/02/2012	07/16/2012
0.17Q	09/14/2012	09/27/2012	10/01/2012	10/15/2012
0.21Q	11/26/2012	12/11/2012	12/13/2012	12/27/2012
0.21Q	03/14/2013	03/27/2013	04/01/2013	04/15/2013

Indicated Div: $0.84

Valuation Analysis

		Institutional Holding	
Forecast EPS	$1.73 (04/05/2013)	No of Institutions	141
Market Cap	$2.4 Billion	Shares	103,413,112
Book Value	$1.8 Billion	% Held	N/A
Price/Book	1.35		
Price/Sales	3.00		

TRADING VOLUME (thousand shares)

Business Summary: Banking (MIC: 5.1.1 SIC: 6035 NAIC: 522190)

BankUnited is a savings and loan holding company with two wholly-owned subsidiaries: BankUnited, a federally-chartered, federally-insured savings association, and BankUnited Investment Services, Inc., a Florida insurance agency which provides wealth management products and financial planning services. BankUnited provides a range of banking and related services to individual and corporate customers through 95 branch offices located in 15 Florida counties. As of Dec 31 2011, Co. had total assets of $11.32 billion and total deposits of $7.36 billion.

Recent Developments: For the year ended Dec 31 2012, net income increased 234.4% to US$211.3 million from US$63.2 million in the prior year. Net interest income increased 19.7% to US$597.6 million from US$499.2 million in the prior year. Provision for loan losses was US$8.9 million versus US$13.8 million in the prior year, a decrease of 36.7%. Non-interest income fell 45.3% to US$89.2 million from US$163.2 million, while non-interest expense declined 29.1% to US$323.1 million.

Prospects: Our evaluation of BankUnited Inc as of Apr. 7, 2013 is the result of our systematic analysis on three basic characteristics: earnings strength, relative valuation, and recent stock price movement. The company has managed to produce a neutral trend in earnings per share over the past 5 quarters. However, while recent estimates for the company have been mixed, BKU has posted better than expected results. Based on operating earnings yield, the company is undervalued when compared to all of the companies in our coverage universe. Share price changes over the past year indicates that BKU will perform very well over the near term.

Financial Data
(US$ in Thousands)

	12/31/2012	12/31/2011	12/31/2010	12/31/2009
Earnings Per Share	2.05	0.62	1.99	1.29
Cash Flow Per Share	(3.74)	(2.60)	(4.82)	...
Tang Book Value Per Share	18.28	15.01	12.74	11.14
Dividends Per Share	0.720	0.560	...	...
Dividend Payout %	35.12	90.32	...	...
Income Statement				
Total Revenue	810,103	801,314	855,467	588,352
EBITDA	358,865	200,344	315,640	200,621
Depn & Amortn	14,000	7,600	3,100	1,200
Income Before Taxes	344,865	192,744	312,540	199,421
Income Taxes	133,605	129,576	127,805	80,375
Net Income	211,260	63,168	184,735	119,046
Average Shares	93,828	95,605	92,950	92,664
Balance Sheet				
Current Assets	4,667,765	4,632,774	3,708,784	2,842,692
Total Assets	12,375,953	11,322,038	10,869,560	11,129,961
Current Liabilities	8,546,248	7,418,091	7,168,838	7,866,454
Long-Term Obligations	1,916,919	2,236,131	2,255,200	2,079,051
Total Liabilities	10,569,273	9,786,758	9,616,052	10,035,701
Stockholders' Equity	1,806,680	1,535,280	1,253,508	1,094,260
Shares Outstanding	95,006	97,700	92,971	92,767
Statistical Record				
Return on Assets %	1.78	0.57	1.68	...
Return on Equity %	12.61	4.53	15.74	...
EBITDA Margin %	44.30	25.00	36.90	34.10
Net Margin %	26.08	7.88	21.59	20.23
Asset Turnover	0.07	0.07	0.08	...
Current Ratio	0.55	0.62	0.52	0.36
Debt to Equity	1.06	1.46	1.80	1.90
Price Range	26.15-22.04	29.72-19.39	...	...
P/E Ratio	12.76-10.75	47.94-31.27	...	...
Average Yield %	3.00	2.23	...	...

Address: 14817 Oak Lane, Miami Lakes, FL 33016
Telephone: 305-569-2000

Web Site: www.bankunited.com
Officers: John Adam Kanas - Chairman, President, Chief Executive Officer John Bohlsen - Vice-Chairman, Chief Lending Officer

Auditors: KPMG LLP
Transfer Agents: Registrar and Transfer Company

BARD (C.R.), INC.

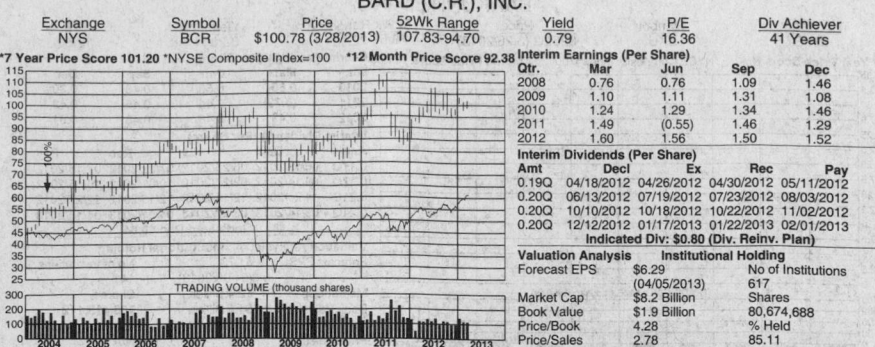

Exchange	Symbol	Price	52Wk Range	Yield	P/E	Div Achiever
NYS	BCR	$100.78 (3/28/2013)	107.83-94.70	0.79	16.36	41 Years

*7 Year Price Score 101.20 *NYSE Composite Index=100 *12 Month Price Score 92.38

Interim Earnings (Per Share)

Qtr.	Mar	Jun	Sep	Dec
2008	0.76	0.76	1.09	1.46
2009	1.10	1.11	1.31	1.08
2010	1.24	1.29	1.34	1.46
2011	1.49	(0.55)	1.46	1.29
2012	1.60	1.56	1.50	1.52

Interim Dividends (Per Share)

Amt	Decl	Ex	Rec	Pay
0.19Q	04/18/2012	04/26/2012	04/30/2012	05/11/2012
0.20Q	06/13/2012	07/19/2012	07/23/2012	08/03/2012
0.20Q	10/10/2012	10/18/2012	10/22/2012	11/02/2012
0.20Q	12/12/2012	01/17/2013	01/22/2013	02/01/2013

Indicated Div: $0.80 (Div. Reinv. Plan)

Valuation Analysis

		Institutional Holding	
Forecast EPS	$6.29	No of Institutions	
	(04/05/2013)	617	
Market Cap	$8.2 Billion	Shares	
Book Value	$1.9 Billion	80,674,688	
Price/Book	4.28	% Held	
Price/Sales	2.78	85.11	

Business Summary: Medical Instruments & Equipment (MIC: 4.3.1 SIC: 3841 NAIC: 339112)

Bard (C. R.) designs, manufactures, packages, distributes and sells medical, surgical, diagnostic and patient care devices. Co. has four main product group categories: vascular, which covers a range of minimally invasive devices for the treatment of peripheral vascular disease and heart arrhythmias; urology, which includes basic drainage products, continence products and urological specialty products; oncology, which covers a range of devices used in the treatment and management of various cancers and other diseases and disorders; as well as surgical specialties, which includes implanted grafts and fixation devices for hernia and soft tissue repairs.

Recent Developments: For the year ended Dec 31 2012, net income increased 61.6% to US$530.1 million from US$328.0 million in the prior year. Revenues were US$2.96 billion, up 2.1% from US$2.90 billion the year before. Direct operating expenses rose 2.6% to US$1.13 billion from US$1.10 billion in the comparable period the year before. Indirect operating expenses increased 4.3% to US$1.06 billion from US$1.02 billion in the equivalent prior-year period.

Prospects: Our evaluation of Bard (C.R.) Inc. as of Apr. 7, 2013 is the result of our systematic analysis on three basic characteristics: earnings strength, relative valuation, and recent stock price movement. The company has managed to produce a neutral trend in earnings per share over the past 5 quarters and while recent estimates for the company have remained steady, BCR has posted better than expected results. Based on operating earnings yield, the company is undervalued when compared to all of the companies in our coverage universe. Share price changes over the past year indicates that BCR will perform in line with the market over the near term.

Financial Data

(US$ in Thousands)	12/31/2012	12/31/2011	12/31/2010	12/31/2009	12/31/2008	12/31/2007	12/31/2006	12/31/2005
Earnings Per Share	6.16	3.69	5.32	4.60	4.06	3.84	2.55	3.12
Cash Flow Per Share	7.92	8.41	6.83	6.34	5.17	5.33	3.22	3.83
Tang Book Value Per Share	1.10	0.17	5.69	13.34	11.62	10.73	9.46	9.08
Dividends Per Share	0.780	0.740	0.700	0.660	0.620	0.580	0.540	0.500
Dividend Payout %	12.66	20.05	13.16	14.35	15.27	15.10	21.18	16.03
Income Statement								
Total Revenue	2,958,100	2,896,400	2,720,200	2,534,900	2,452,100	2,202,000	1,985,500	1,771,300
EBITDA	813,500	586,900	778,500	730,700	596,800	607,100	381,200	482,300
Depn & Amortn	47,000	43,200	51,800	51,000	51,300	48,600	44,600	39,000
Income Before Taxes	732,400	510,800	717,700	671,500	549,900	577,300	347,600	449,600
Income Taxes	202,300	182,800	208,100	210,100	133,400	170,900	75,500	112,500
Net Income	530,100	328,000	509,200	460,100	416,500	406,400	272,100	337,100
Average Shares	84,400	87,300	94,600	99,000	102,500	105,900	106,900	108,000
Balance Sheet								
Current Assets	1,847,200	1,685,900	1,529,300	1,491,800	1,354,200	1,242,000	1,133,900	1,264,100
Total Assets	4,151,300	3,931,100	3,171,500	2,906,900	2,665,700	2,475,500	2,277,200	2,265,600
Current Liabilities	447,600	904,100	397,700	281,700	273,100	281,700	295,900	640,600
Long-Term Obligations	1,409,600	908,700	896,900	149,800	149,800	149,800	150,600	800
Total Liabilities	2,225,600	2,148,900	1,540,000	713,300	688,500	627,500	579,200	729,500
Stockholders' Equity	1,925,700	1,782,200	1,631,500	2,193,600	1,977,200	1,848,000	1,698,000	1,536,100
Shares Outstanding	81,697	84,543	84,973	95,917	99,393	100,191	103,155	104,012
Statistical Record								
Return on Assets %	13.08	9.24	16.75	16.51	16.16	17.10	11.98	15.77
Return on Equity %	28.51	19.22	26.62	22.06	21.72	22.92	16.83	23.28
EBITDA Margin %	27.50	20.26	28.62	28.83	24.34	27.57	19.20	27.23
Net Margin %	17.92	11.32	18.72	18.15	16.99	18.46	13.70	19.03
Asset Turnover	0.73	0.82	0.90	0.91	0.95	0.93	0.87	0.83
Current Ratio	4.13	1.86	3.85	5.30	4.96	4.41	3.83	1.97
Debt to Equity	0.73	0.51	0.55	0.07	0.08	0.08	0.09	N.M.
Price Range	107.83-85.45	113.32-82.39	95.72-76.18	88.41-70.39	99.66-75.99	95.05-77.25	85.43-60.25	72.79-61.36
P/E Ratio	17.50-13.87	30.71-22.33	17.99-14.32	19.22-15.30	24.55-18.72	24.75-20.12	33.50-23.63	23.33-19.67
Average Yield %	0.79	0.77	0.85	0.85	0.68	0.70	0.74	0.75

Address: 730 Central Avenue, Murray Hill, NJ 07974	**Web Site:** www.crbard.com	**Auditors:** KPMG LLP
Telephone: 908-277-8000	**Officers:** Timothy M. Ring - Chairman, Chief Executive Officer John H. Weiland - President, Chief Operating Officer	**Investor Contact:** 908-277-8065
Fax: 908-277-8278		**Transfer Agents:** Computershare Trust Company, N.A., Canton, MA

BARNES & NOBLE INC

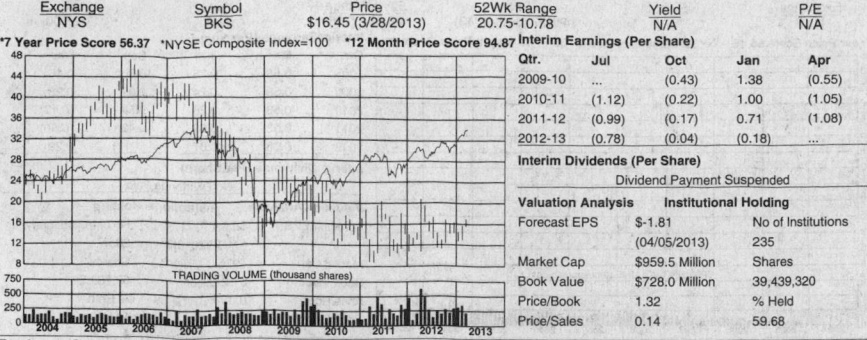

Exchange	Symbol	Price	52Wk Range	Yield	P/E
NYS	BKS	$16.45 (3/28/2013)	20.75-10.78	N/A	N/A

*7 Year Price Score 56.37 *NYSE Composite Index=100 *12 Month Price Score 94.87

Interim Earnings (Per Share)

Qtr.	Jul	Oct	Jan	Apr
2009-10	...	(0.43)	1.38	(0.55)
2010-11	(1.12)	(0.22)	1.00	(1.05)
2011-12	(0.99)	(0.17)	0.71	(1.08)
2012-13	(0.78)	(0.04)	(0.18)	...

Interim Dividends (Per Share)

Dividend Payment Suspended

Valuation Analysis   **Institutional Holding**

Forecast EPS	$-1.81	No of Institutions	
	(04/05/2013)	235	
Market Cap	$959.5 Million	Shares	
Book Value	$728.0 Million	39,439,320	
Price/Book	1.32	% Held	
Price/Sales	0.14	59.68	

Business Summary: Retail - Specialty (MIC: 2.1.3 SIC: 5942 NAIC: 451211)

Barnes & Noble is engaged in the sale of trade books, mass market paperbacks, children's books, eBooks and other digital content, NOOK® and related accessories, bargain books, magazines, gifts, cafe products and services, educational toys and games, music and movies direct to customers through its bookstores or on barnesandnoble.com. As of Apr 28 2012, Co. operated 1,338 bookstores in 50 states, including 647 bookstores on college campuses, operated an eCommerce site and developed digital content products and software. Co.'s three segments were B&N Retail, which included 691 bookstores; B&N College, which operated 647 stores; and NOOK, which included Co.'s digital business.

Recent Developments: For the quarter ended Jan 26 2013, net loss amounted to US$6.1 million versus net income of US$52.0 million in the year-earlier quarter. Revenues were US$2.22 billion, down 8.8% from US$2.44 billion the year before. Operating loss was US$294,000 versus an income of US$89.7 million in the prior-year quarter. Direct operating expenses declined 6.3% to US$1.67 billion from US$1.79 billion in the comparable period the year before. Indirect operating expenses decreased 2.4% to US$549.9 million from US$563.1 million in the equivalent prior-year period.

Prospects: Our evaluation of Barnes & Noble Inc. as of Apr. 7, 2013 is the result of our systematic analysis on three basic characteristics: earnings strength, relative valuation, and recent stock price movement. The company has suffered a very negative trend in earnings per share over the past 5 quarters. Because the company lacks sufficient analyst estimate data, we place greater weight on the historical EPS trend as the measure of earnings strength. Based on operating earnings yield, the company is overvalued when compared to all of the companies in our coverage universe. Share price changes over the past year indicates that BKS will perform in line with the market over the near term.

Financial Data

(US$ in Thousands)	9 Mos	6 Mos	3 Mos	04/28/2012	04/30/2011	05/01/2010	05/02/2009	01/31/2009
Earnings Per Share	(2.08)	(1.19)	(1.32)	(1.41)	(1.31)	0.63	(0.05)	1.32
Cash Flow Per Share	1.08	4.35	3.42	(0.42)	3.53	2.32	(2.15)	6.83
Tang Book Value Per Share	N.M.	N.M.	N.M.	N.M.	N.M.	N.M.	10.40	10.95
Dividends Per Share	...	...	...	...	0.750	1.000	1.000	0.900
Dividend Payout %	...	...	...	...	...	158.73	...	68.18
Income Statement								
Total Revenue	5,561,984	3,338,039	1,453,507	7,129,199	6,998,565	5,810,564	1,105,152	5,121,804
EBITDA	124,051	71,275	3,833	141,441	122,125	259,473	47,983	315,091
Depn & Amortn	171,409	118,339	58,035	238,048	244,734	214,464	46,426	174,104
Income Before Taxes	(73,193)	(64,128)	(63,143)	(96,607)	(122,609)	45,009	(3,443)	140,987
Income Taxes	(25,580)	(22,573)	(22,163)	(27,740)	(48,652)	8,365	(1,374)	55,591
Net Income	(47,613)	(38,747)	(40,980)	(68,867)	(73,920)	36,676	(2,693)	75,920
Average Shares	58,316	58,168	58,021	57,337	56,588	56,153	54,759	57,327
Balance Sheet								
Current Assets	2,572,375	2,715,072	2,304,256	1,997,793	1,747,021	1,719,477	1,518,561	1,723,304
Total Assets	4,276,261	4,431,025	4,044,684	3,765,249	3,596,466	3,705,686	2,780,105	2,993,888
Current Liabilities	2,310,345	2,216,563	2,174,326	1,827,280	1,734,677	1,724,408	1,291,696	1,475,675
Long-Term Obligations	127,250	465,650	452,800	324,200	313,100	260,400	...	...
Total Liabilities	3,548,249	3,694,766	3,335,540	3,017,592	2,776,556	2,803,868	1,869,864	2,072,274
Stockholders' Equity	728,012	736,259	709,144	747,657	819,910	901,818	910,241	921,614
Shares Outstanding	58,329	58,236	58,090	57,654	57,055	55,708	55,077	54,615
Statistical Record								
Return on Assets %	N.M.	N.M.	N.M.	N.M.	N.M.	1.13	N.M.	2.44
Return on Equity %	N.M.	N.M.	N.M.	N.M.	N.M.	4.06	N.M.	7.63
EBITDA Margin %	2.23	2.14	0.26	1.98	1.75	4.47	3.89	6.15
Net Margin %	N.M.	N.M.	N.M.	N.M.	N.M.	0.63	N.M.	1.48
Asset Turnover	1.64	1.68	1.79	1.94	1.92	1.80	0.29	1.65
Current Ratio	1.11	1.22	1.06	1.09	1.01	1.00	1.18	1.17
Debt to Equity	0.17	0.63	0.64	0.43	0.38	0.29	...	...
Price Range	20.75-10.78	20.75-10.78	20.75-9.98	20.41-9.98	22.60-8.77	26.78-16.51	26.13-15.68	34.03-12.25
P/E Ratio	...	...	...	...	...	42.51-26.21	...	25.78-9.28
Average Yield %	...	...	...	...	5.04	4.70	4.95	3.65

Address: 122 Fifth Avenue, New York, NY 10011	**Web Site:** www.barnesandnobleinc.com	**Auditors:** Ernst & Young LLP
Telephone: 212-633-3300	**Officers:** Leonard Riggio - Chairman Stephen Riggio - Vice-Chairman	**Investor Contact:** 212-633-3489
Fax: 212-366-5186		**Transfer Agents:** BNY Mellon Shareowner Services, Jersey City, NJ

BARRETT (BILL) CORP

Exchange	Symbol	Price	52Wk Range	Yield	P/E
NYS	BBG	$20.27 (3/28/2013)	26.58-15.65	N/A	2027.00

*7 Year Price Score 55.18   *NYSE Composite Index=100   *12 Month Price Score 81.41

Interim Earnings (Per Share)

Qtr.	Mar	Jun	Sep	Dec
2008	0.68	0.75	0.80	0.16
2009	0.59	0.24	0.02	0.28
2010	0.53	0.86	0.54	(0.17)
2011	0.33	0.69	0.43	(0.80)
2012	0.76	0.07	(1.11)	0.29

Interim Dividends (Per Share)

No Dividends Paid

Valuation Analysis   **Institutional Holding**

Forecast EPS	$0.53	No of Institutions
	(04/06/2013)	235
Market Cap	$976.0 Million	Shares
Book Value	$1.2 Billion	62,787,224
Price/Book	0.83	% Held
Price/Sales	1.39	114.25

Business Summary: Production & Extraction (MIC: 9.1.1 SIC: 1311 NAIC: 211111)

Bill Barrett and its subsidiaries explores for and develops oil and natural gas in the Rocky Mountain region. Co.'s portfolio of exploration and development properties consist of: Piceance Basin in northwestern Colorado; Uinta Basin in northeastern Utah; Denver-Julesburg Basin in Colorado's eastern plains and parts of southern Wyoming, western Kansas and western Nebraska; Powder River Basin in northeastern Wyoming; Wind River Basin in central Wyoming; and Paradox Basin in southwestern Colorado and southeastern Utah. At Dec 31 2011, Co.'s total proved reserves were 1.36 trillion cubic feet equivalent, which consisted of 30.6 million barrels of oil and 1.18 trillion cubic feet of natural gas.

Recent Developments: For the year ended Dec 31 2012, net income decreased 98.1% to US$582,000 from US$30.7 million in the prior year. Revenues were US$700.2 million, down 10.9% from US$785.6 million the year before. Operating income was US$23.2 million versus US$121.7 million in the prior year, a decrease of 80.9%. Direct operating expenses rose 9.2% to US$204.8 million from US$187.5 million in the comparable period the year before. Indirect operating expenses decreased 0.9% to US$472.2 million from US$476.4 million in the equivalent prior-year period.

Prospects: Our evaluation of Barrett (Bill) Corp. as of Apr. 7, 2013 is the result of our systematic analysis on three basic characteristics: earnings strength, relative valuation, and recent stock price movement. The company has enjoyed a very positive trend in earnings per share over the past 5 quarters. However, while recent estimates for the company have been mixed, BBG has posted better than expected results. Based on operating earnings yield, the company is overvalued when compared to all of the companies in our coverage universe. Share price changes over the past year indicates that BBG will perform very poorly over the near term.

Financial Data
(US$ in Thousands)

	12/31/2012	12/31/2011	12/31/2010	12/31/2009	12/31/2008	12/31/2007	12/31/2006	12/31/2005
Earnings Per Share	0.01	0.65	1.75	1.12	2.39	0.60	1.40	0.55
Cash Flow Per Share	8.21	10.30	9.89	10.75	9.04	5.71	5.42	4.26
Tang Book Value Per Share	24.56	25.49	24.37	22.62	24.10	17.28	17.14	14.48
Income Statement								
Total Revenue	700,195	771,361	698,464	598,163	617,911	390,270	375,329	288,759
EBITDA	432,836	409,699	445,051	380,366	394,167	226,897	248,053	130,899
Depn & Amortn	335,267	302,307	272,696	261,983	208,052	172,536	139,105	90,674
Income Before Taxes	2,218	48,379	128,455	88,174	172,317	43,998	101,136	39,027
Income Taxes	1,636	17,672	47,953	37,956	64,670	17,244	39,125	15,222
Net Income	582	30,707	80,502	50,218	107,647	26,754	62,011	23,805
Average Shares	47,353	47,236	45,887	45,035	45,036	44,677	44,269	43,439
Balance Sheet								
Current Assets	228,339	246,343	207,648	180,039	313,374	131,427	138,507	141,318
Total Assets	2,869,449	2,687,930	2,038,500	1,866,123	1,995,063	1,329,687	1,187,401	888,945
Current Liabilities	213,133	233,198	165,957	153,292	225,794	139,568	119,795	132,798
Long-Term Obligations	1,156,654	882,240	404,399	402,250	426,500	274,000	188,000	86,000
Total Liabilities	1,686,674	1,469,092	897,538	837,568	907,265	556,176	431,004	258,162
Stockholders' Equity	1,182,775	1,218,838	1,140,962	1,028,555	1,087,798	773,511	756,397	630,783
Shares Outstanding	48,150	47,809	46,813	45,475	45,128	44,760	44,141	43,571
Statistical Record								
Return on Assets %	0.02	1.30	4.12	2.60	6.46	2.13	5.97	3.00
Return on Equity %	0.05	2.60	7.42	4.75	11.54	3.50	8.94	3.81
EBITDA Margin %	61.82	53.11	63.72	63.59	63.79	58.14	66.09	45.33
Net Margin %	0.08	3.98	11.53	8.40	17.42	6.86	16.52	8.24
Asset Turnover	0.25	0.33	0.36	0.31	0.37	0.31	0.36	0.36
Current Ratio	1.07	1.06	1.25	1.17	1.39	0.94	1.16	1.06
Debt to Equity	0.98	0.72	0.35	0.39	0.39	0.35	0.25	0.14
Price Range	36.42-15.65	51.54-32.13	41.13-29.16	37.36-17.40	60.29-16.04	46.80-25.54	40.50-23.00	42.20-26.28
P/E Ratio	N.M.	79.29-49.43	23.50-16.66	33.36-15.54	25.23-6.71	78.00-42.57	28.93-16.43	76.73-47.78

Address: 1099 18th Street, Suite 2300, Denver, CO 80202 **Telephone:** 303-293-9100	**Web Site:** www.billbarrettcorp.com **Officers:** Jim W. Mogg - Chairman R. Scot Woodall - Interim President, Interim Chief Executive Officer, Executive Vice President, Chief Operating Officer	**Auditors:** Deloitte & Touche LLP **Investor Contact:** 303-312-8155 **Transfer Agents:** Computershare, Jersey City, NJ

BAXTER INTERNATIONAL INC.

Exchange	Symbol	Price	52Wk Range	Yield	P/E
NYS	BAX	$72.64 (3/28/2013)	72.64-49.03	2.48	17.38

*7 Year Price Score 99.84   *NYSE Composite Index=100   *12 Month Price Score 104.03

TRADING VOLUME (thousand shares)

Interim Earnings (Per Share)

Qtr.	Mar	Jun	Sep	Dec
2008	0.67	0.85	0.74	0.90
2009	0.83	0.96	0.87	0.93
2010	(0.11)	0.90	0.89	0.72
2011	0.98	1.07	1.01	0.82
2012	1.04	1.19	1.06	0.89

Interim Dividends (Per Share)

Amt	Decl	Ex	Rec	Pay
0.335Q	05/07/2012	06/06/2012	06/08/2012	07/02/2012
0.45Q	07/25/2012	09/05/2012	09/07/2012	10/01/2012
0.45Q	11/13/2012	12/05/2012	12/07/2012	01/03/2013
0.45Q	02/19/2013	03/06/2013	03/08/2013	04/01/2013

Indicated Div: $1.80

Valuation Analysis

		Institutional Holding	
Forecast EPS	$4.66	No of Institutions	
	(04/06/2013)	1149	
Market Cap	$39.7 Billion	Shares	
Book Value	$6.9 Billion	530,517,632	
Price/Book	5.72	% Held	
Price/Sales	2.80	81.60	

Business Summary: Medical Instruments & Equipment (MIC: 4.3.1 SIC: 3841 NAIC: 339112)

Baxter International develops, manufactures and markets products for people with hemophilia, immune disorders, infectious diseases, kidney disease, trauma, and other chronic and acute medical conditions. Co. applies a combination of knowledge in medical devices, pharmaceuticals and biotechnology to create products that are used by hospitals, kidney dialysis centers, nursing homes, rehabilitation centers, doctors' offices, clinical and medical research laboratories, and by patients at home under physician supervision. Co. manufactures products in 27 countries and sells them in more than 100 countries. Co.'s operations are comprised of the BioScience and Medical Products segments.

Recent Developments: For the year ended Dec 31 2012, net income increased 3.1% to US$2.33 billion from US$2.26 billion in the prior year. Revenues were US$14.19 billion, up 2.1% from US$13.89 billion the year before. Direct operating expenses rose 0.6% to US$6.89 billion from US$6.85 billion in the comparable period the year before. Indirect operating expenses increased 9.3% to US$4.48 billion from US$4.10 billion in the equivalent prior-year period.

Prospects: Our evaluation of Baxter International Inc. as of Apr. 7, 2013 is the result of our systematic analysis on three basic characteristics: earnings strength, relative valuation, and recent stock price movement. The company has managed to produce a neutral trend in earnings per share over the past 5 quarters. However, while recent estimates for the company have been mixed, BAX has posted better than expected results. Based on operating earnings yield, the company is undervalued when compared to all of the companies in our coverage universe. Share price changes over the past year indicates that BAX will perform well over the near term.

Financial Data

(US$ in Millions)	12/31/2012	12/31/2011	12/31/2010	12/31/2009	12/31/2008	12/31/2007	12/31/2006	12/31/2005
Earnings Per Share	4.18	3.88	2.39	3.59	3.16	2.61	2.13	1.52
Cash Flow Per Share	5.62	4.95	5.09	4.79	4.01	3.58	3.35	2.49
Tang Book Value Per Share	6.63	6.14	6.98	8.08	6.79	7.53	6.42	3.61
Dividends Per Share	1.570	1.265	1.180	1.070	0.912	0.720	0.582	0.582
Dividend Payout %	37.56	32.60	49.37	29.81	28.88	27.59	27.32	38.29
Income Statement								
Total Revenue	14,190	13,893	12,843	12,562	12,348	11,263	10,378	9,849
EBITDA	3,661	3,537	2,674	3,482	3,105	2,664	2,291	2,059
Depn & Amortn	712	670	685	638	553	501	488	482
Income Before Taxes	2,862	2,813	1,902	2,746	2,476	2,141	1,769	1,459
Income Taxes	563	553	463	519	437	407	348	486
Net Income	2,326	2,224	1,420	2,205	2,014	1,707	1,397	956
Average Shares	556	573	594	614	637	654	656	629
Balance Sheet								
Current Assets	9,260	8,650	7,989	8,271	7,148	7,555	6,970	5,116
Total Assets	20,390	19,073	17,489	17,354	15,405	15,294	14,686	12,727
Current Liabilities	4,759	4,857	4,041	4,464	3,635	3,812	3,610	4,165
Long-Term Obligations	5,580	4,749	4,363	3,440	3,362	2,664	2,567	2,414
Total Liabilities	13,452	12,488	10,922	10,163	9,176	8,378	8,414	8,428
Stockholders' Equity	6,938	6,585	6,567	7,191	6,229	6,916	6,272	4,299
Shares Outstanding	546	560	580	600	615	633	650	624
Statistical Record								
Return on Assets %	11.76	12.17	8.15	13.46	13.09	11.39	10.19	7.11
Return on Equity %	34.31	33.82	20.64	32.86	30.56	25.89	26.43	23.89
EBITDA Margin %	25.80	25.46	20.82	27.72	25.15	23.65	22.08	20.91
Net Margin %	16.39	16.01	11.06	17.55	16.31	15.16	13.46	9.71
Asset Turnover	0.72	0.76	0.74	0.77	0.80	0.75	0.76	0.73
Current Ratio	1.95	1.78	1.98	1.85	1.97	1.98	1.93	1.23
Debt to Equity	0.80	0.72	0.66	0.48	0.54	0.39	0.41	0.56
Price Range	68.81-49.03	62.41-47.65	61.71-40.47	60.50-46.41	71.15-48.50	61.09-46.33	47.21-35.45	40.95-33.37
P/E Ratio	16.46-11.73	16.09-12.28	25.82-16.93	16.85-12.93	22.52-15.35	23.41-17.75	22.16-16.64	26.94-21.95
Average Yield %	2.70	2.33	2.36	1.98	1.49	1.42	1.42	1.56

Address: One Baxter Parkway, Deerfield, IL 60015 Telephone: 224-948-2000 Fax: 847-948-2964	Web Site: www.baxter.com Officers: Robert L. Parkinson - Chairman, President, Chief Executive Officer Phillip L. Batchelor - Corporate Vice-President	Auditors: PricewaterhouseCoopers LLP Investor Contact: 224-948-3371 Transfer Agents: Computershare Trust Company, N.A., Providence, RI

BB&T CORP.

Exchange	Symbol	Price	52Wk Range	Yield	P/E
NYS	BBT	$31.39 (3/28/2013)	33.99-27.09	2.93	11.63

*7 Year Price Score 87.86 *NYSE Composite Index=100 *12 Month Price Score 92.63

Interim Earnings (Per Share)

Qtr.	Mar	Jun	Sep	Dec
2008	0.78	0.78	0.65	0.51
2009	0.48	0.20	0.23	0.27
2010	0.27	0.30	0.30	0.29
2011	0.32	0.44	0.52	0.56
2012	0.61	0.72	0.66	0.71

Interim Dividends (Per Share)

Amt	Decl	Ex	Rec	Pay
0.20Q	06/26/2012	07/03/2012	07/06/2012	08/01/2012
0.20Q	08/28/2012	10/03/2012	10/05/2012	11/01/2012
0.20Q	12/18/2012	01/02/2013	01/04/2013	02/01/2013
0.23Q	01/22/2013	02/06/2013	02/08/2013	03/01/2013

Indicated Div: $0.92 (Div. Reinv. Plan)

Valuation Analysis

		Institutional Holding	
Forecast EPS	$2.88 (04/06/2013)	No of Institutions	796
Market Cap	$22.0 Billion	Shares	
Book Value	$21.2 Billion	405,279,136	
Price/Book	1.04	% Held	
Price/Sales	2.05	55.29	

TRADING VOLUME (thousand shares)

Business Summary: Banking (MIC: 5.1.1 SIC: 6021 NAIC: 522110)

BB&T is a financial holding company. Through its Branch Banking and Trust Company (Branch Bank) subsidiary, Co. provides a range of banking services to individuals and businesses, and provides a range of loans to businesses and consumers. Branch Bank also markets a range of deposit services to individuals, businesses and public entities. Branch Bank provides, either directly, or through its subsidiaries, lease financing to businesses and municipal governments; factoring; discount brokerage services, annuities and mutual funds; life insurance, and property and casualty insurance, among others. As of Dec 31 2011, Co. had total assets of $174.58 billion and total deposits of $124.94 billion.

Recent Developments: For the year ended Dec 31 2012, net income increased 52.3% to US$2.03 billion from US$1.33 billion in the prior year. Net interest income increased 6.4% to US$5.86 billion from US$5.51 billion in the prior year. Provision for loan losses was US$1.06 billion versus US$1.19 billion in the prior year, a decrease of 11.2%. Non-interest income rose 22.7% to US$3.82 billion from US$3.11 billion, while non-interest expense advanced 0.4% to US$5.83 billion.

Prospects: Our evaluation of BB&T Corp. as of Apr. 7, 2013 is the result of our systematic analysis on three basic characteristics: earnings strength, relative valuation, and recent stock price movement. The company has managed to produce a neutral trend in earnings per share over the past 5 quarters. However, while recent estimates for the company have been lowered by analysts, BBT has posted better than expected results. Based on operating earnings yield, the company is undervalued when compared to all of the companies in our coverage universe. Share price changes over the past year indicates that BBT will perform in line with the market over the near term.

Financial Data

(US$ in Thousands)	12/31/2012	12/31/2011	12/31/2010	12/31/2009	12/31/2008	12/31/2007	12/31/2006	12/31/2005
Earnings Per Share	2.70	1.83	1.16	1.15	2.71	3.14	2.81	3.00
Cash Flow Per Share	5.28	6.55	4.18	(0.78)	9.73	1.92	1.44	3.22
Tang Book Value Per Share	15.63	14.82	13.09	12.56	11.73	11.86	11.04	11.76
Dividends Per Share	0.760	0.640	0.600	1.240	1.860	1.760	1.600	1.460
Dividend Payout %	28.15	34.97	51.72	107.83	68.63	56.05	56.94	48.67
Income Statement								
Interest Income	6,917,000	6,885,000	7,115,000	6,884,000	7,207,000	7,894,000	6,893,000	5,505,842
Interest Expense	1,060,000	1,378,000	1,795,000	2,040,000	2,969,000	4,014,000	3,185,000	1,980,969
Net Interest Income	5,857,000	5,507,000	5,320,000	4,844,000	4,238,000	3,880,000	3,708,000	3,524,873
Provision for Losses	1,057,000	1,190,000	2,638,000	2,811,000	1,445,000	448,000	240,000	217,263
Non-Interest Income	3,820,000	3,113,000	3,957,000	3,934,000	3,197,000	2,774,000	2,521,000	2,325,622
Non-Interest Expense	5,828,000	5,802,000	5,670,000	4,931,000	3,921,000	3,636,000	3,516,000	3,166,501
Income Before Taxes	2,792,000	1,628,000	969,000	1,036,000	2,069,000	2,570,000	2,473,000	2,466,731
Income Taxes	764,000	296,000	115,000	159,000	550,000	836,000	945,000	812,962
Net Income	2,028,000	1,332,000	854,000	877,000	1,519,000	1,734,000	1,528,000	1,653,769
Average Shares	708,877	705,168	701,039	635,619	552,498	551,755	543,890	551,379
Balance Sheet								
Net Loans & Leases	116,346,000	108,949,000	104,556,000	103,607,000	97,095,000	90,682,000	82,703,000	74,198,188
Total Assets	183,872,000	174,579,000	157,081,000	165,764,000	152,015,000	132,618,000	121,351,000	109,169,759
Total Deposits	133,075,000	124,939,000	107,213,000	114,965,000	98,613,000	86,766,000	80,971,000	74,281,799
Total Liabilities	162,714,000	157,161,000	140,645,000	149,573,000	135,978,000	119,986,000	109,606,000	98,040,645
Stockholders' Equity	21,158,000	17,418,000	16,436,000	16,191,000	16,037,000	12,632,000	11,745,000	11,129,114
Shares Outstanding	699,728	697,143	694,381	689,750	559,248	545,955	541,475	543,102
Statistical Record								
Return on Assets %	1.13	0.80	0.53	0.55	1.06	1.37	1.33	1.58
Return on Equity %	10.49	7.87	5.23	5.44	10.57	14.23	13.36	15.03
Net Interest Margin %	84.68	79.99	74.77	70.37	58.80	49.15	53.79	64.02
Efficiency Ratio %	54.28	58.03	51.21	45.58	37.69	34.08	37.35	40.43
Loans to Deposits	0.87	0.87	0.98	0.90	0.98	1.05	1.02	1.00
Price Range	33.99-25.79	29.17-19.17	35.61-21.87	29.53-13.32	41.14-19.82	44.15-30.67	44.63-38.37	43.77-37.08
P/E Ratio	12.59-9.55	15.94-10.48	30.70-18.85	25.68-11.58	15.18-7.31	14.06-9.77	15.88-13.65	14.59-12.36
Average Yield %	2.51	2.56	2.19	5.42	6.02	4.41	3.81	3.60

Address: 200 West Second Street, Winston-Salem, NC 27101 Telephone: 336-733-2000 Fax: 336-671-2399	Web Site: www.BBT.com Officers: Kelly S. King - Chairman, President, Chief Executive Officer Christopher L. Henson - Senior Executive Vice President, Chief Operating Officer	Auditors: PricewaterhouseCoopers LLP Investor Contact: 336-733-3021 Transfer Agents: Computershare, Inc., Providence, RI

BEAM INC

Exchange	Symbol	Price	52Wk Range	Yield	P/E
NYS	BEAM	$63.54 (3/28/2013)	63.54-53.16	1.42	26.70

*7 Year Price Score 108.93 *NYSE Composite Index=100 *12 Month Price Score 95.56

Interim Earnings (Per Share)

Qtr.	Mar	Jun	Sep	Dec
2008	0.77	0.88	2.21	(1.81)
2009	0.05	0.66	0.82	0.07
2010	0.47	1.48	0.66	0.55
2011	0.52	2.09	2.67	0.54
2012	0.49	0.62	0.47	0.79

Interim Dividends (Per Share)

Amt	Decl	Ex	Rec	Pay
0.205Q	04/25/2012	05/07/2012	05/09/2012	06/01/2012
0.205Q	07/24/2012	08/06/2012	08/08/2012	09/04/2012
0.205Q	10/04/2012	11/05/2012	11/07/2012	12/03/2012
0.225Q	01/25/2013	02/04/2013	02/06/2013	03/01/2013

Indicated Div: $0.90 (Div. Reinv. Plan)

Valuation Analysis — **Institutional Holding**

Forecast EPS	$2.63 (04/11/2013)	No of Institutions 641
Market Cap	$10.2 Billion	Shares 137,837,600
Book Value	$4.6 Billion	% Held
Price/Book	2.21	N/A
Price/Sales	4.13	

Business Summary: Beverages (MIC: 1.2.2 SIC: 2084 NAIC: 312130)

Beam and its subsidiaries operate in the beverage alcohol industry. Co. makes and sells branded distilled spirits products. Co.'s principal products include bourbon whiskey, tequila, Scotch whisky, Canadian whisky, vodka, cognac, rum, cordials, and pre-mixed cocktails. Co.'s brands include: Jim Beam Bourbon, Maker's Mark Bourbon, Sauza Tequila, Courvoisier Cognac, Canadian Club Whisky, Teacher's Scotch, Pinnacle Vodka, Laphroaig Scotch, Knob Creek Bourbon, Basil Hayden's Bourbon, Kilbeggan Irish Whiskey, Cruzan Rum, Hornitos Tequila, Skinnygirl Cocktails, and Sourz Liqueurs. The principal markets for Co.'s spirits products are the U.S., Australia, Germany, Spain, the U.K., and Canada.

Recent Developments: For the year ended Dec 31 2012, income from continuing operations increased 198.7% to US$398.2 million from US$133.3 million a year earlier. Net income decreased 58.2% to US$382.4 million from US$915.5 million in the prior year. Revenues were US$2.47 billion, up 6.7% from US$2.31 billion the year before. Operating income was US$575.9 million versus US$395.5 million in the prior year, an increase of 45.6%. Direct operating expenses rose 4.0% to US$1.03 billion from US$987.8 million in the comparable period the year before. Indirect operating expenses decreased 7.0% to US$862.5 million from US$927.8 million in the equivalent prior-year period.

Prospects: Our evaluation of Beam Inc. as of Apr. 7, 2013 is the result of our systematic analysis on three basic characteristics: earnings strength, relative valuation, and recent stock price movement. The company has suffered a very negative trend in earnings per share over the past 5 quarters. However, while recent estimates for the company have been mixed, BEAM has posted better than expected results. Based on operating earnings yield, the company is about fairly valued when compared to all of the companies in our coverage universe. Share price changes over the past year indicates that BEAM will perform in line with the market over the near term.

Financial Data
(US$ in Thousands)

	12/31/2012	12/31/2011	12/31/2010	12/31/2009	12/31/2008	12/31/2007	12/31/2006	12/31/2005
Earnings Per Share	2.38	5.78	3.16	1.60	2.02	4.87	5.42	4.13
Cash Flow Per Share	2.38	2.94	5.06	5.76	5.37	6.31	6.59	5.51
Dividends Per Share	0.820	0.760	0.760	1.010	1.720	1.620	1.500	1.380
Dividend Payout %	34.45	13.15	24.05	63.13	85.15	33.26	27.68	33.41
Income Statement								
Total Revenue	2,465,900	2,311,100	7,141,500	6,694,700	7,608,900	8,563,100	8,769,000	7,061,200
EBITDA	728,000	471,900	1,043,800	751,200	688,300	1,693,700	1,795,200	1,307,100
Depr & Amortn	119,100	188,100	242,400	252,000	262,800	279,900	254,700	222,100
Income Before Taxes	502,000	169,300	587,600	283,400	188,400	1,120,200	1,209,100	926,100
Income Taxes	103,800	36,000	91,600	36,300	95,600	346,300	311,100	324,500
Net Income	382,400	911,400	487,600	242,800	311,100	762,600	830,100	621,100
Average Shares	160,800	157,800	154,300	151,800	153,700	156,500	153,000	150,500
Balance Sheet								
Current Assets	2,863,400	2,434,400	4,343,000	3,871,700	3,468,100	3,780,900	3,930,100	3,192,700
Total Assets	8,636,900	7,491,800	12,675,300	12,370,600	12,091,900	13,956,900	14,668,300	13,201,500
Current Liabilities	1,208,600	758,700	2,106,900	1,463,600	1,190,100	2,093,900	2,515,400	2,817,900
Long-Term Obligations	2,024,900	1,902,100	3,637,400	4,413,300	4,688,600	3,942,700	5,034,900	4,889,900
Total Liabilities	4,024,800	3,392,100	7,004,200	7,278,200	7,405,900	8,271,400	9,940,300	9,555,900
Stockholders' Equity	4,612,100	4,099,700	5,671,100	5,092,400	4,686,000	5,685,500	4,728,000	3,645,600
Shares Outstanding	160,120	155,939	153,212	150,452	150,101	153,913	151,909	146,290
Statistical Record								
Return on Assets %	4.73	9.04	3.89	1.99	2.38	5.33	5.96	5.89
Return on Equity %	8.75	18.66	9.06	4.97	5.98	14.65	19.83	18.12
EBITDA Margin %	29.52	20.42	14.62	11.22	9.05	19.78	20.47	18.51
Net Margin %	15.51	39.44	6.83	3.63	4.09	8.91	9.47	8.80
Asset Turnover	0.30	0.23	0.57	0.55	0.58	0.60	0.63	0.67
Current Ratio	2.37	3.21	2.06	2.65	2.91	1.81	1.56	1.13
Debt to Equity	0.44	0.46	0.64	0.87	1.00	0.69	1.06	1.34
Price Range	63.51-50.58	52.52-39.79	48.71-29.77	35.39-13.81	57.14-24.24	69.03-55.94	66.01-53.25	69.57-54.64
P/E Ratio	26.68-21.25	9.09-6.88	15.41-9.42	22.12-8.63	28.29-12.00	14.18-11.49	12.18-9.82	16.85-13.23
Average Yield %	1.42	1.59	2.01	3.57	3.82	2.59	2.53	2.22

Address: 510 Lake Cook Road, Deerfield, IL 60015	Web Site: www.beamglobal.com	Auditors: PricewaterhouseCoopers LLP
Telephone: 847-948-8888	Officers: Matthew J. Shattock - President, Chief Executive Officer Robert F. Probst - Senior Vice President, Chief Financial Officer	Investor Contact: 847-484-4410 Transfer Agents: Wells Fargo Shareowner Services, St. Paul, MN

BECTON, DICKINSON AND CO.

Exchange	Symbol	Price	52Wk Range	Yield	P/E	Div Achiever
NYS	BDX	$95.61 (3/28/2013)	95.61-72.18	2.07	12.71	40 Years

*7 Year Price Score 91.86 *NYSE Composite Index=100 *12 Month Price Score 104.43

Interim Earnings (Per Share)

Qtr.	Dec	Mar	Jun	Sep
2009-10	1.30	1.24	1.29	1.68
2010-11	1.36	1.38	1.53	1.36
2011-12	1.21	1.38	1.59	1.42
2012-13	3.13	...	...	...

Interim Dividends (Per Share)

Amt	Decl	Ex	Rec	Pay
0.45Q	05/22/2012	06/06/2012	06/08/2012	06/29/2012
0.45Q	07/24/2012	09/05/2012	09/07/2012	09/28/2012
0.495Q	11/20/2012	12/06/2012	12/10/2012	12/31/2012
0.495Q	01/29/2013	03/06/2013	03/08/2013	03/29/2013

Indicated Div: $1.98 (Div. Reinv. Plan)

Valuation Analysis / **Institutional Holding**

Forecast EPS	$5.71 (04/05/2013)	No of Institutions	1012
Market Cap	$18.5 Billion	Shares	180,213,120
Book Value	$4.5 Billion	% Held	76.68
Price/Book	4.15		
Price/Sales	2.37		

Business Summary: Medical Instruments & Equipment (MIC: 4.3.1 SIC: 3841 NAIC: 339112)

Becton, Dickinson and Company is a medical technology company engaged principally in the development, manufacture and sale of medical devices, instrument systems and reagents. Co.'s operations consist of three business segments: BD Medical, which produces an array of medical devices that are used in a range of healthcare settings; BD Diagnostics, which provides products for the collection and transport of diagnostics specimens, as well as instruments and reagent systems to detect a range of infectious diseases, healthcare-associated infections and cancers; and BD Biosciences, which produces research and clinical tools that facilitate the study of cells, and the components of cells.

Recent Developments: For the quarter ended Dec 31 2012, income from continuing operations increased 8.7% to US$270.2 million from US$248.5 million in the year-earlier quarter. Net income increased 137.8% to US$625.4 million from US$263.0 million in the year-earlier quarter. Revenues were US$1.90 billion, up 3.7% from US$1.83 billion the year before. Operating income was US$392.1 million versus US$336.8 million in the prior-year quarter, an increase of 16.4%. Direct operating expenses declined 0.7% to US$894.1 million from US$900.5 million in the comparable period the year before. Indirect operating expenses increased 3.3% to US$614.0 million from US$594.5 million in the equivalent prior-year period.

Prospects: Our evaluation of Becton, Dickinson and Co. as of Apr. 7, 2013 is the result of our systematic analysis on three basic characteristics: earnings strength, relative valuation, and recent stock price movement. The company has produced a positive trend in earnings per share over the past 5 quarters. However, while recent estimates for the company have been mixed, BDX has posted better than expected results. Based on operating earnings yield, the company is undervalued when compared to all of the companies in our coverage universe. Share price changes over the past year indicates that BDX will perform poorly over the near term.

Financial Data

(US$ in Thousands)	3 Mos	09/30/2012	09/30/2011	09/30/2010	09/30/2009	09/30/2008	09/30/2007	09/30/2006
Earnings Per Share	7.52	5.59	5.62	5.49	4.99	4.46	3.49	2.93
Cash Flow Per Share	8.18	8.22	7.74	7.08	7.03	6.89	5.05	4.36
Tang Book Value Per Share	11.07	9.65	12.67	16.87	16.52	15.38	12.82	11.18
Dividends Per Share	1.845	1.800	1.640	1.480	1.320	1.140	0.980	0.860
Dividend Payout %	24.53	32.20	29.18	26.96	26.45	25.56	28.08	29.35
Income Statement								
Total Revenue	1,900,192	7,708,382	7,828,904	7,372,333	7,160,874	7,155,910	6,359,708	5,834,827
EBITDA	521,636	2,067,671	2,261,162	2,179,407	2,116,696	1,856,092	1,484,501	1,306,169
Depn & Amortn	128,833	510,938	504,089	502,113	470,193	305,510	280,357	264,462
Income Before Taxes	365,696	1,472,408	1,716,263	1,661,160	1,639,262	1,553,607	1,203,945	1,034,957
Income Taxes	95,447	362,880	451,411	484,820	426,208	425,689	347,778	279,366
Net Income	625,436	1,169,927	1,270,994	1,317,610	1,231,603	1,126,996	890,033	752,280
Average Shares	199,570	209,181	226,280	240,136	246,798	252,681	254,810	256,554
Balance Sheet								
Current Assets	5,477,472	5,322,071	4,668,331	4,505,250	4,646,954	3,614,675	3,130,566	3,185,253
Total Assets	11,629,437	11,360,909	10,430,428	9,650,694	9,304,624	7,912,943	7,329,365	6,824,525
Current Liabilities	2,003,782	1,978,055	1,823,228	1,671,673	1,777,093	1,416,579	1,478,809	1,576,329
Long-Term Obligations	3,761,592	3,761,112	2,484,665	1,495,357	1,488,460	953,226	955,713	956,971
Total Liabilities	7,159,968	7,225,020	5,602,253	4,216,114	4,161,912	2,977,375	2,967,408	2,988,321
Stockholders' Equity	4,469,469	4,135,889	4,828,175	5,434,580	5,142,712	4,935,568	4,361,957	3,836,204
Shares Outstanding	193,961	196,911	214,818	229,816	237,082	243,077	243,837	245,468
Statistical Record								
Return on Assets %	13.30	10.71	12.66	13.90	14.31	14.75	12.58	11.67
Return on Equity %	33.32	26.03	24.77	24.91	24.44	24.18	21.71	21.13
EBITDA Margin %	27.45	26.82	28.88	29.56	29.56	25.94	23.34	22.39
Net Margin %	32.91	15.18	16.23	17.87	17.20	15.75	13.99	12.89
Asset Turnover	0.68	0.71	0.78	0.78	0.83	0.94	0.90	0.90
Current Ratio	2.73	2.69	2.56	2.70	2.61	2.55	2.12	2.02
Debt to Equity	0.84	0.91	0.51	0.28	0.29	0.19	0.22	0.25
Price Range	79.91-72.18	79.91-70.65	89.74-73.25	80.14-66.60	80.26-60.26	92.34-77.93	82.61-68.81	70.67-50.07
P/E Ratio	10.63-9.60	14.30-12.64	15.97-13.03	14.60-12.13	16.08-12.08	20.70-17.47	23.67-19.72	24.12-17.09
Average Yield %	2.42	2.39	2.01	2.01	1.94	1.34	1.30	1.40

Address: 1 Becton Drive, Franklin Lakes, NJ 07417-1880
Telephone: 201-847-6800

Web Site: www.bd.com
Officers: Vincent A. Forlenza - Chairman, President, Chief Executive Officer, Chief Operating Officer Gary M. Cohen - Executive Vice President

Auditors: Ernst & Young LLP
Investor Contact: 180-028-46845
Transfer Agents: Computershare Trust Company, N.A., Canton, MA

BEMIS CO INC

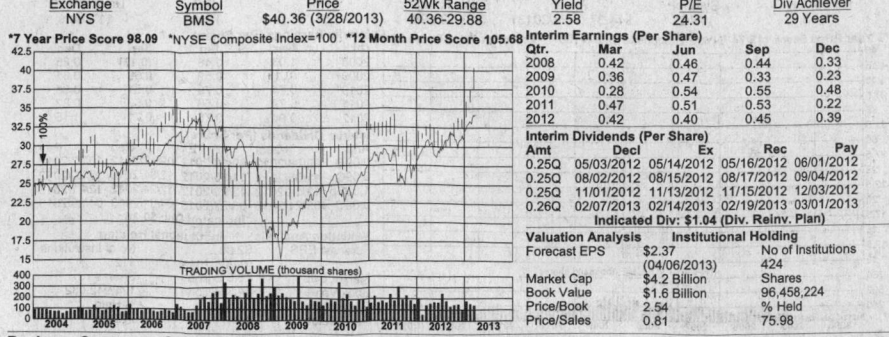

Exchange	Symbol	Price	52Wk Range	Yield	P/E	Div Achiever
NYS	BMS	$40.36 (3/28/2013)	40.36-29.88	2.58	24.31	29 Years

*7 Year Price Score 98.09 *NYSE Composite Index=100 *12 Month Price Score 105.68

Interim Earnings (Per Share)

Qtr.	Mar	Jun	Sep	Dec
2008	0.42	0.46	0.44	0.33
2009	0.36	0.47	0.33	0.23
2010	0.28	0.54	0.55	0.48
2011	0.47	0.51	0.53	0.22
2012	0.42	0.42	0.45	0.39

Interim Dividends (Per Share)

Amt	Decl	Ex	Rec	Pay
0.25Q	05/03/2012	05/14/2012	05/16/2012	06/01/2012
0.25Q	08/02/2012	08/15/2012	08/17/2012	09/04/2012
0.25Q	11/01/2012	11/13/2012	11/15/2012	12/03/2012
0.26Q	02/07/2013	02/14/2013	02/19/2013	03/01/2013

Indicated Div: $1.04 (Div. Reinv. Plan)

Valuation Analysis / **Institutional Holding**

Forecast EPS	$2.37 (04/06/2013)	No of Institutions	424
Market Cap	$4.2 Billion	Shares	
Book Value	$1.6 Billion		96,458,224
Price/Book	2.54	% Held	
Price/Sales	0.81		75.98

TRADING VOLUME (thousand shares)

Business Summary: Containers & Packaging (MIC: 8.1.3 SIC: 2671 NAIC: 322221)

Bemis is engaged in manufacturing packaging products and pressure sensitive materials. Co. has three segments, U.S. Packaging, Global Packaging and Pressure Sensitive Materials. Products within the U.S. and Global Packaging business segments service packaging applications for markets such as food, medical devices, personal care, agribusiness, chemicals, pet food, and consumer products. Products produced within the Pressure Sensitive Materials business segment include film, paper, and metalized plastic film printing stocks used for primary package labeling, promotional decoration, bar code inventory control labels, and laser printing for administrative office and promotional applications.

Recent Developments: For the year ended Dec 31 2012, income from continuing operations decreased 7.2% to US$173.8 million from US$187.3 million a year earlier. Net income decreased 7.2% to US$173.8 million from US$187.3 million in the prior year. Revenues were US$5.14 billion, down 3.4% from US$5.32 billion the year before. Operating income was US$345.5 million versus US$367.4 million in the prior year, a decrease of 6.0%. Direct operating expenses declined 5.0% to US$4.19 billion from US$4.41 billion in the comparable period the year before. Indirect operating expenses increased 10.9% to US$602.0 million from US$542.8 million in the equivalent prior-year period.

Prospects: Our evaluation of Bemis Co Inc. as of Apr. 7, 2013 is the result of our systematic analysis on three basic characteristics: earnings strength, relative valuation, and recent stock price movement. The company has enjoyed a very positive trend in earnings per share over the past 5 quarters and while recent estimates for the company have been mixed, BMS has posted better than expected results. Based on operating earnings yield, the company is about fairly valued when compared to all of the companies in our coverage universe. Share price changes over the past year indicates that BMS will perform poorly over the near term.

Financial Data
(US$ in Thousands)

	12/31/2012	12/31/2011	12/31/2010	12/31/2009	12/31/2008	12/31/2007	12/31/2006	12/31/2005
Earnings Per Share	1.66	1.73	1.85	1.38	1.65	1.74	1.65	1.51
Cash Flow Per Share	4.07	4.02	3.39	4.60	2.93	3.94	3.33	2.63
Tang Book Value Per Share	3.93	3.02	6.18	9.90	6.72	8.12	7.31	6.29
Dividends Per Share	1.000	0.960	0.920	0.900	0.880	0.840	0.760	0.720
Dividend Payout %	60.24	55.49	49.73	65.22	53.33	48.28	46.06	47.68
Income Statement								
Total Revenue	5,139,200	5,322,670	4,835,042	3,514,586	3,779,373	3,649,281	3,639,363	3,473,950
EBITDA	555,200	590,232	611,272	442,470	470,600	499,325	491,846	472,602
Depn & Amortn	205,700	221,200	210,500	160,108	162,662	159,452	153,258	151,499
Income Before Taxes	278,600	292,223	327,284	240,310	268,525	289,605	289,336	282,366
Income Taxes	104,800	104,900	117,600	87,800	96,300	104,300	109,500	113,900
Net Income	173,800	184,081	205,111	147,221	166,214	181,554	176,296	162,529
Average Shares	103,900	105,072	108,750	103,601	100,969	104,114	106,767	107,819
Balance Sheet								
Current Assets	1,525,000	1,549,011	1,466,919	2,005,348	982,658	1,136,943	1,093,712	987,810
Total Assets	4,185,700	4,320,444	4,285,831	3,928,705	2,822,314	3,191,396	3,039,009	2,964,600
Current Liabilities	643,000	681,965	675,259	524,855	421,781	534,550	555,455	474,320
Long-Term Obligations	1,417,600	1,554,750	1,283,525	1,227,514	659,984	775,456	722,211	790,107
Total Liabilities	2,544,800	2,738,341	2,406,208	2,124,973	1,475,783	1,629,064	1,566,993	1,615,245
Stockholders' Equity	1,640,900	1,582,103	1,879,623	1,803,732	1,346,531	1,562,332	1,472,016	1,349,355
Shares Outstanding	103,200	102,983	107,673	108,223	99,708	100,518	104,841	105,305
Statistical Record								
Return on Assets %	4.08	4.28	4.99	4.36	5.51	5.83	5.87	5.96
Return on Equity %	10.76	10.64	11.14	9.35	11.40	11.97	12.50	12.23
EBITDA Margin %	10.80	11.09	12.64	12.59	12.45	13.68	13.51	13.60
Net Margin %	3.38	3.46	4.24	4.19	4.40	4.98	4.84	4.68
Asset Turnover	1.21	1.24	1.18	1.04	1.25	1.17	1.21	1.27
Current Ratio	2.37	2.27	2.17	3.82	2.33	2.13	1.97	2.08
Debt to Equity	0.86	0.98	0.68	0.68	0.49	0.50	0.49	0.59
Price Range	33.79-29.78	34.25-27.53	33.90-26.72	30.90-17.09	29.31-21.57	36.23-25.85	34.82-28.49	31.36-23.44
P/E Ratio	20.36-17.94	19.80-15.91	18.32-14.44	22.39-12.38	17.76-13.07	20.82-14.86	21.10-17.27	20.77-15.52
Average Yield %	3.17	3.07	3.04	3.06	3.60	3.43	2.67	2.62

Address: One Neenah Center, 4th Floor, P.O. Box 669, Neenah, WI 54957-0669 Telephone: 920-727-4100	Web Site: www.bemis.com Officers: Jeffrey H. Curler - Chairman Emeritus, Chairman Henry J. Theisen - President, Chief Executive Officer	Auditors: PricewaterhouseCoopers LLP Investor Contact: 920-727-4100 Transfer Agents: Wells Fargo Bank, N.A., South St. Paul, MN

105

BERKLEY (W. R.) CORP.

Exchange	Symbol	Price	52Wk Range	Yield	P/E	Div Achiever
NYS	WRB	$44.37 (3/28/2013)	44.37-35.98	0.81	12.46	11 Years

*7 Year Price Score 112.74 *NYSE Composite Index=100 *12 Month Price Score 99.98

Interim Earnings (Per Share)

Qtr.	Mar	Jun	Sep	Dec
2008	1.03	0.46	(0.17)	0.25
2009	(0.13)	0.59	0.59	0.81
2010	0.74	0.70	0.61	0.85
2011	0.79	0.56	0.53	0.82
2012	0.94	0.76	0.71	1.15

Interim Dividends (Per Share)

Amt	Decl	Ex	Rec	Pay
0.09Q	08/08/2012	09/10/2012	09/12/2012	10/02/2012
0.09Q	11/08/2012	11/30/2012	12/04/2012	12/20/2012
1.00Sp	12/14/2012	12/20/2012	12/24/2012	12/31/2012
0.09Q	03/21/2013	03/27/2013	04/01/2013	04/09/2013

Indicated Div: $0.36

Valuation Analysis

		Institutional Holding	
Forecast EPS	$2.98 (04/06/2013)	No of Institutions	412
Market Cap	$6.0 Billion	Shares	124,942,032
Book Value	$4.3 Billion	% Held	
Price/Book	1.40		72.24
Price/Sales	1.04		

Business Summary: General Insurance (MIC: 5.2.1 SIC: 6331 NAIC: 524126)

W. R. Berkley is an insurance holding company. Co. operates in the following segments: specialty, which underwrite risks within the excess and surplus lines market and on an admitted basis; regional, which provide insurance products and services that meet the needs of each regionally differentiated customer base; alternative markets, which provides insurance products, analytical tools and risk management services; reinsurance, which provides other insurance companies and self-insureds with assistance in managing their net risk through reinsurance; and international, which writes business in almost 40 countries worldwide, with branches or offices in 15 locations outside the U.S.

Recent Developments: For the year ended Dec 31 2012, net income increased 30.6% to US$510.6 million from US$391.1 million in the prior year. Revenues were US$5.82 billion, up 12.9% from US$5.16 billion the year before. Net premiums earned were US$4.67 billion versus US$4.16 billion in the prior year, an increase of 12.3%. Net investment income rose 11.5% to US$586.8 million from US$526.4 million a year ago.

Prospects: Our evaluation of Berkley (W. R.) Corp. as of Apr. 7, 2013 is the result of our systematic analysis on three basic characteristics: earnings strength, relative valuation, and recent stock price movement. The company has generated a negative trend in earnings per share over the past 5 quarters and while recent estimates for the company have been raised by analysts, WRB has posted better than expected results. Based on operating earnings yield, the company is undervalued when compared to all of the companies in our coverage universe. Share price changes over the past year indicates that WRB will perform poorly over the near term.

Financial Data
(US$ in Thousands)

	12/31/2012	12/31/2011	12/31/2010	12/31/2009	12/31/2008	12/31/2007	12/31/2006	12/31/2005
Earnings Per Share	3.56	2.71	2.90	1.86	1.62	3.78	3.46	2.72
Cash Flow Per Share	4.91	4.80	3.03	1.97	9.28	7.83	8.15	9.03
Tang Book Value Per Share	31.01	28.49	25.62	22.29	18.20	19.23	16.95	13.08
Dividends Per Share	1.350	0.310	0.270	0.240	0.230	0.200	0.160	0.133
Dividend Payout %	37.92	11.44	9.31	12.90	14.20	5.29	4.62	4.90
Income Statement								
Premium Income	4,673,516	4,160,867	3,835,582	3,805,849	4,289,580	4,663,701	4,692,622	4,460,935
Total Revenue	5,823,554	5,155,984	4,724,069	4,431,178	4,708,808	5,553,639	5,394,831	4,996,839
Benefits & Claims	2,948,479	2,658,365	2,309,867	2,336,707	2,688,661	2,779,578	2,864,498	2,781,802
Income Before Taxes	701,928	518,283	603,305	382,230	326,322	1,057,634	988,645	770,537
Income Taxes	191,285	123,550	153,739	73,150	44,919	310,905	286,398	222,521
Net Income	510,643	394,733	449,566	309,080	281,141	743,646	699,518	544,892
Average Shares	143,314	145,672	155,081	166,574	173,454	196,698	201,961	200,425
Balance Sheet								
Total Assets	20,155,896	18,487,731	17,528,547	17,328,596	16,121,158	16,832,170	15,656,489	13,896,287
Total Liabilities	15,849,679	14,479,305	13,825,671	13,732,529	13,074,839	13,262,395	12,321,330	11,329,210
Stockholders' Equity	4,306,217	4,008,426	3,702,876	3,596,067	3,046,319	3,569,775	3,335,159	2,567,077
Shares Outstanding	136,017	137,520	141,009	156,552	161,467	180,320	192,771	191,264
Statistical Record								
Return on Assets %	2.64	2.19	2.58	1.85	1.70	4.58	4.73	4.30
Return on Equity %	12.25	10.24	12.32	9.31	8.48	21.54	23.70	23.30
Loss Ratio %	63.09	63.89	60.22	61.40	62.68	59.60	61.04	62.36
Net Margin %	8.77	7.66	9.52	6.98	5.97	13.39	12.97	10.90
Price Range	40.21-33.85	35.68-26.71	28.55-24.11	31.00-18.86	31.00-18.30	34.68-26.36	40.80-30.91	32.45-20.66
P/E Ratio	11.29-9.51	13.17-9.86	9.84-8.31	16.67-10.14	19.14-11.30	9.17-6.97	11.79-8.93	11.93-7.60
Average Yield %	3.60	1.00	1.01	1.00	0.87	0.64	0.45	0.54

Address: 475 Steamboat Road, Greenwich, CT 06830 **Telephone:** 203-629-3000 **Fax:** 203-629-3492	**Web Site:** www.wrberkley.com **Officers:** William R. Berkley - Chairman, Chief Executive Officer W. Robert Berkley - President, Chief Operating Officer	**Auditors:** KPMG LLP **Investor Contact:** 203-629-3040 **Transfer Agents:** Wells Fargo Bank, N.A., South St. Paul, MN

BERKSHIRE HATHAWAY INC.

Exchange	Symbol	Price	52Wk Range	Yield	P/E
NYS	BRK A	$104.20 (3/28/2013)	104.20-78.70	N/A	0.01

*7 Year Price Score 102.64 ***NYSE Composite Index=100** ***12 Month Price Score 105.56**

Interim Earnings (Per Share)

Qtr.	Mar	Jun	Sep	Dec
2008	607.00	1859.00	682.00	75.00
2009	(990.00)	2123.00	2087.00	1970.00
2010	2272.00	1195.00	1814.00	2663.00
2011	917.00	2072.00	1380.00	1847.00
2012	1966.00	1882.00	2373.00	2757.00

Interim Dividends (Per Share)

No Dividends Paid

Valuation Analysis — **Institutional Holding**

Forecast EPS	$5.50	No of Institutions
	(04/06/2013)	1563
Market Cap	$171.2 Million	Shares
Book Value	$187.6 Billion	741,194,432
Price/Book	0.00	% Held
Price/Sales	0.00	13.53

TRADING VOLUME (thousand shares)

Business Summary: General Insurance (MIC: 5.2.1 SIC: 6331 NAIC: 524126)

Berkshire Hathaway is a holding company. Through its subsidiaries, Co. engages in a number of business activities, including: property and casualty insurance and reinsurance; railroad, which operate railroad systems in North America through BNSF Railway Company; utilities and energy, particularly regulated electric and gas utility, including power generation and distribution activities; manufacturing, service and retailing businesses including wholesale distribution and logistics services, and manufacturers of clothing and footwear; and finance, which include proprietary investing, manufactured housing and related consumer financing, transportation equipment leasing and furniture leasing.

Recent Developments: For the year ended Dec 31 2012, net income increased 42.5% to US$15.31 billion from US$10.75 billion in the prior year. Revenues were US$162.46 billion, up 13.1% from US$143.69 billion the year before. Net premiums earned were US$34.55 billion versus US$32.08 billion in the prior year, an increase of 7.7%.

Prospects: Our evaluation of Berkshire Hathaway Inc. as of Apr. 7, 2013 is the result of our systematic analysis on three basic characteristics: earnings strength, relative valuation, and recent stock price movement. The company has generated a negative trend in earnings per share over the past 5 quarters and while recent estimates for the company have remained steady, BRK.B has posted results that fell short of analysts expectations. Based on operating earnings yield, the company is about fairly valued when compared to all of the companies in our coverage universe. Share price changes over the past year indicates that BRK.B will perform well over the near term.

Financial Data
(US$ in Thousands)

	12/31/2012	12/31/2011	12/31/2010	12/31/2009	12/31/2008	12/31/2007	12/31/2006	12/31/2005
Earnings Per Share	8,977.00	6,215.00	7,928.00	5,193.00	3,224.00	8,548.00	7,144.00	5,538.00
Cash Flow Per Share	12,652.36	12,410.52	10,940.53	10,215.49	7,244.38	8,119.03	6,612.37	6,134.66
Tang Book Value Per Share	81,027.67	67,625.75	65,718.52	62,593.93	48,724.72	56,775.47	49,383.24	44,031.30
Income Statement								
Premium Income	34,545,000	32,075,000	30,749,000	27,884,000	25,525,000	31,783,000	23,964,000	21,997,000
Total Revenue	162,463,000	143,688,000	136,185,000	112,493,000	107,786,000	118,245,000	98,539,000	81,663,000
Benefits & Claims	25,227,000	25,708,000	22,540,000	20,089,000	18,099,000	22,796,000	14,686,000	17,116,000
Income Before Taxes	22,236,000	15,314,000	19,051,000	11,552,000	7,574,000	20,161,000	16,778,000	12,268,000
Income Taxes	6,924,000	4,568,000	5,607,000	3,538,000	1,978,000	6,594,000	5,505,000	4,159,000
Net Income	14,824,000	10,254,000	12,967,000	8,055,000	4,994,000	13,213,000	11,015,000	8,528,000
Average Shares	1,651	1,649	1,635	1,551	1,548	1,545	1,541	1,539
Balance Sheet								
Total Assets	427,452,000	392,647,000	372,229,000	297,119,000	267,399,000	273,160,000	248,437,000	198,325,000
Total Liabilities	239,805,000	227,797,000	214,911,000	166,017,000	158,132,000	152,427,000	140,018,000	106,841,000
Stockholders' Equity	187,647,000	164,850,000	157,318,000	131,102,000	109,267,000	120,733,000	108,419,000	91,484,000
Shares Outstanding	1,642	1,650	1,648	1,551	1,549	1,547	1,542	1,540
Statistical Record								
Return on Assets %	3.61	2.68	3.87	2.85	1.84	5.07	4.93	4.40
Return on Equity %	8.39	6.37	8.99	6.70	4.33	11.53	11.02	9.62
Loss Ratio %	73.03	80.15	73.30	72.04	70.91	71.72	61.28	77.81
Net Margin %	9.12	7.14	9.52	7.16	4.63	11.17	11.18	10.44
Price Range	90.69-76.29	87.28-66.00	83.72-64.94	70.80-46.00	95.90-52.40	99.70-69.58	76.00-57.00	61.16-53.50
P/E Ratio	0.01-0.01	0.01-0.01	0.01-0.01	0.01-0.01	0.03-0.02	0.01-0.01	0.01-0.01	0.01-0.01

Address: 3555 Farnam Street, Omaha, NE 68131 **Telephone:** 402-346-1400	**Web Site:** www.berkshirehathaway.com **Officers:** Warren Edward Buffett - Chairman, Chief Executive Officer Charles T. Munger - Vice-Chairman	**Auditors:** Deloitte & Touche LLP **Transfer Agents:** Wells Fargo Bank, N.A., St. Paul, MN

BEST BUY INC

Exchange	Symbol	Price	52Wk Range	Yield	P/E
NYS	BBY	$22.15 (3/28/2013)	23.64-11.29	3.07	N/A

*7 Year Price Score 43.10   *NYSE Composite Index=100   *12 Month Price Score 94.97

Interim Earnings (Per Share)

Qtr.	May	Aug	Nov	Feb
2009-10	0.36	0.37	0.53	1.83
2010-11	0.36	0.60	0.54	1.58
2011-12	0.35	0.47	0.42	(4.59)
2012-13	0.46	0.04	(0.03)	(1.77)

Interim Dividends (Per Share)

Amt	Decl	Ex	Rec	Pay
0.16Q	05/23/2012	06/08/2012	06/12/2012	07/03/2012
0.17Q	06/21/2012	09/07/2012	09/11/2012	10/02/2012
0.17Q	11/21/2012	12/07/2012	12/11/2012	12/31/2012
0.17Q	03/04/2013	03/19/2013	03/21/2013	04/11/2013

Indicated Div: $0.68

Valuation Analysis

		Institutional Holding	
Forecast EPS	$2.19 (04/06/2013)	No of Institutions	657
Market Cap	$7.5 Billion	Shares	243,683,424
Book Value	$3.1 Billion	% Held	60.95
Price/Book	2.45		
Price/Sales	N/A		

TRADING VOLUME (thousand shares)

Business Summary: Retail - Appliances and Electronics (MIC: 2.1.7 SIC: 5731 NAIC: 443112)

Best Buy is a retailer of consumer electronics, computing and mobile phone products, entertainment products, appliances and related services. Co. operates retail stores and call centers and conducts online retail operations under a range of brand names such as Best Buy (BestBuy.com, BestBuy.ca), Best Buy Mobile (BestBuyMobile.com), The Carphone Warehouse (CarphoneWarehouse.com), Five Star, Future Shop (FutureShop.ca), Geek Squad, Magnolia Audio Video, Pacific Sales and The Phone House (PhoneHouse.com). Co. operates two reportable segments: Domestic, which is comprised of its operations in the U.S.; and International, which is comprised of its operations in Canada, Europe, China and Mexico.

Recent Developments: For the quarter ended Nov 3 2012, loss from continuing operations was US$5.0 million compared with income of nil in the year-earlier quarter. Net income decreased 99.2% to US$1.0 million from US$131.0 million in the year-earlier quarter. Revenues were US$10.75 billion, down 11.1% from US$12.10 billion the year before. Operating income was US$12.0 million versus US$178.0 million in the prior-year quarter, a decrease of 93.3%. Direct operating expenses declined 10.9% to US$8.17 billion from US$9.17 billion in the comparable period the year before. Indirect operating expenses decreased 6.5% to US$2.57 billion from US$2.75 billion in the equivalent prior-year period.

Prospects: Our evaluation of Best Buy Inc. as of Apr. 7, 2013 is the result of our systematic analysis on three basic characteristics: earnings strength, relative valuation, and recent stock price movement. The company has managed to produce a neutral trend in earnings per share over the past 5 quarters and while recent estimates for the company have been raised by analysts, BBY has posted better than expected results. Based on operating earnings yield, the company is undervalued when compared to all of the companies in our coverage universe. Share price changes over the past year indicates that BBY will perform very poorly over the near term.

Financial Data
(US$ in Thousands)

	02/02/2013	03/03/2012	02/26/2011	02/27/2010	02/28/2009	03/01/2008	03/03/2007	02/25/2006
Earnings Per Share	(1.30)	(3.36)	3.08	3.10	2.39	3.12	2.79	2.27
Cash Flow Per Share	4.66	8.84	2.94	5.31	4.56	4.62	3.60	3.47
Tang Book Value Per Share	6.50	6.01	9.71	8.19	4.70	8.04	10.82	9.60
Dividends Per Share	0.660	0.620	0.580	0.560	0.540	0.460	0.360	0.307
Dividend Payout %	...	...	18.83	18.06	22.59	14.74	12.90	13.51
Income Statement								
Total Revenue	45,085,000	50,705,000	50,272,000	49,694,000	45,015,000	40,023,000	35,934,000	30,848,000
EBITDA	758,000	2,122,000	3,143,000	3,215,000	2,587,000	2,870,000	2,528,000	2,104,000
Depn & Amortn	832,000	945,000	978,000	926,000	793,000	580,000	509,000	456,000
Income Before Taxes	(186,000)	1,043,000	2,078,000	2,195,000	1,700,000	2,228,000	2,130,000	1,721,000
Income Taxes	231,000	709,000	714,000	802,000	674,000	815,000	752,000	581,000
Net Income	(441,000)	(1,231,000)	1,277,000	1,317,000	1,003,000	1,407,000	1,377,000	1,140,000
Average Shares	338,600	366,300	416,500	427,500	422,900	452,900	496,200	504,800
Balance Sheet								
Current Assets	12,047,000	10,297,000	10,473,000	10,566,000	8,192,000	7,342,000	9,081,000	7,985,000
Total Assets	16,787,000	16,005,000	17,849,000	18,302,000	15,826,000	12,758,000	13,570,000	11,864,000
Current Liabilities	10,810,000	8,855,000	8,663,000	8,978,000	8,435,000	6,769,000	6,301,000	6,056,000
Long-Term Obligations	1,153,000	1,685,000	711,000	1,104,000	1,126,000	627,000	590,000	178,000
Total Liabilities	13,726,000	12,260,000	11,247,000	11,982,000	11,183,000	8,274,000	7,369,000	6,607,000
Stockholders' Equity	3,061,000	3,745,000	6,602,000	6,320,000	4,643,000	4,484,000	6,201,000	5,257,000
Shares Outstanding	338,276	341,400	392,590	418,815	413,684	410,578	480,655	485,098
Statistical Record								
Return on Assets %	N.M.	N.M.	7.08	7.74	7.04	10.72	10.65	10.32
Return on Equity %	N.M.	N.M.	19.82	24.09	22.04	26.41	23.65	23.56
EBITDA Margin %	1.68	4.18	6.25	6.47	5.75	7.17	7.04	6.82
Net Margin %	N.M.	N.M.	2.54	2.65	2.23	3.52	3.83	3.70
Asset Turnover	2.99	2.95	2.79	2.92	3.16	3.05	2.78	2.79
Current Ratio	1.11	1.16	1.21	1.18	0.97	1.08	1.44	1.32
Debt to Equity	0.38	0.45	0.11	0.17	0.24	0.14	0.10	0.03
Price Range	27.51-11.29	33.03-22.12	48.58-31.39	45.37-24.71	47.52-17.42	53.38-42.69	58.72-43.96	55.11-32.31
P/E Ratio	...	...	15.77-10.19	14.64-7.97	19.88-7.29	17.11-13.68	21.05-15.76	24.28-14.23
Average Yield %	3.62	2.25	1.50	1.49	1.51	0.98	0.69	0.74

Address: 7601 Penn Avenue South, Richfield, MN 55423 **Telephone:** 612-291-1000	**Web Site:** www.bestbuy.com **Officers:** Hatim A. Tyabji - Chairman Richard M. Schulze - Chairman Emeritus, Chairman	**Auditors:** Deloitte & Touche LLP **Investor Contact:** 866-758-1457 **Transfer Agents:** Computershare Trust Company, N.A., Providence, RI

BIG LOTS, INC.

Exchange	Symbol	Price	52Wk Range	Yield	P/E
NYS	BIG	$35.27 (3/28/2013)	45.87-26.86	N/A	12.04

*7 Year Price Score 104.76 *NYSE Composite Index=100 *12 Month Price Score 92.07

Interim Earnings (Per Share)

Qtr.	Apr	Jul	Oct	Jan
2008-09	0.42	0.32	0.15	0.96
2009-10	0.44	0.34	0.37	1.27
2010-11	0.68	0.48	0.23	1.42
2011-12	0.70	0.50	0.06	1.69
2012-13	0.63	0.36	(0.10)	2.01

Interim Dividends (Per Share)

No Dividends Paid

Valuation Analysis / Institutional Holding

Forecast EPS	$3.17	No of Institutions
	(04/05/2013)	376
Market Cap	$2.0 Billion	Shares
Book Value	$758.1 Million	70,694,488
Price/Book	2.66	% Held
Price/Sales	0.37	93.24

Business Summary: Retail - General Merchandise/Department Stores (MIC: 2.1.1 SIC: 5331 NAIC: 452990)

Big Lots is a broadline closeout retailer. Co.'s merchandising categories consist of: Consumables, which includes food, health and beauty, plastics, paper, chemical, and pet departments; Furniture, which includes upholstery, mattresses, ready-to-assemble, and case goods departments; Home, which includes domestics, stationery, and home decorative departments; Seasonal, which includes lawn and garden, and other holiday departments; Play n' Wear, which includes electronics, toys, jewelry, infant accessories, and apparel departments; and Hardlines and Other, which includes paint, and home maintenance departments. At Jan 28 2012, Co. operated a total of 1,533 stores in the U.S. and Canada.

Recent Developments: For the year ended Feb 2 2013, income from continuing operations decreased 14.5% to US$177.2 million from US$207.2 million a year earlier. Net income decreased 14.5% to US$177.1 million from US$207.1 million in the prior year. Revenues were US$5.40 billion, up 3.8% from US$5.20 billion the year before. Operating income was US$298.5 million versus US$345.6 million in the prior year, a decrease of 13.6%. Direct operating expenses rose 4.8% to US$3.28 billion from US$3.13 billion in the comparable period the year before. Indirect operating expenses increased 5.5% to US$1.82 billion from US$1.72 billion in the equivalent prior-year period.

Prospects: Our evaluation of Big Lots Inc. as of Apr. 7, 2013 is the result of our systematic analysis on three basic characteristics: earnings strength, relative valuation, and recent stock price movement. The company has produced a positive trend in earnings per share over the past 5 quarters. However, while recent estimates for the company have been lowered by analysts, BIG has posted better than expected results. Based on operating earnings yield, the company is undervalued when compared to all of the companies in our coverage universe. Share price changes over the past year indicates that BIG will perform very poorly over the near term.

Financial Data

(US$ in Thousands)	02/02/2013	01/28/2012	01/29/2011	01/30/2010	01/31/2009	02/02/2008	02/03/2007	01/28/2006
Earnings Per Share	2.93	2.99	2.83	2.42	1.85	1.55	1.11	(0.09)
Cash Flow Per Share	4.62	4.67	4.07	4.82	2.61	3.05	3.40	1.89
Tang Book Value Per Share	13.00	12.75	12.81	12.22	9.53	7.72	10.30	9.47
Income Statement								
Total Revenue	5,400,119	5,202,269	4,952,244	4,726,772	4,645,283	4,656,302	4,743,048	4,429,905
EBITDA	404,805	435,702	435,951	399,914	333,547	324,964	269,093	135,530
Depn & Amortn	106,300	90,280	78,606	74,904	78,624	88,484	101,279	108,657
Income Before Taxes	294,313	341,892	355,384	323,345	249,706	239,203	170,490	20,914
Income Taxes	117,148	134,657	132,837	121,975	94,908	88,023	57,872	5,189
Net Income	177,121	207,064	222,524	200,369	151,547	158,461	124,045	(10,088)
Average Shares	60,476	69,419	78,581	82,681	82,076	102,542	111,930	113,677
Balance Sheet								
Current Assets	1,090,630	1,006,656	1,051,719	1,122,966	870,871	891,110	1,149,047	993,754
Total Assets	1,753,626	1,641,310	1,619,599	1,669,493	1,432,458	1,443,815	1,720,526	1,625,497
Current Liabilities	629,634	584,820	541,931	542,520	515,095	500,344	474,232	436,523
Long-Term Obligations	171,200	65,900	...	...	...	163,700	...	5,500
Total Liabilities	995,484	818,077	672,806	668,081	657,613	805,329	590,823	546,773
Stockholders' Equity	758,142	823,233	946,793	1,001,412	774,845	638,486	1,129,703	1,078,724
Shares Outstanding	57,269	63,609	73,894	81,922	81,315	82,682	109,633	113,932
Statistical Record								
Return on Assets %	10.27	12.73	13.57	12.95	10.57	10.04	7.29	N.M.
Return on Equity %	22.04	23.46	22.91	22.62	21.50	17.97	11.05	N.M.
EBITDA Margin %	7.50	8.38	8.80	8.46	7.18	6.98	5.67	3.06
Net Margin %	3.28	3.98	4.49	4.24	3.26	3.40	2.62	N.M.
Asset Turnover	3.13	3.20	3.02	3.06	3.24	2.95	2.79	2.64
Current Ratio	1.73	1.72	1.94	2.07	1.69	1.78	2.42	2.28
Debt to Equity	0.23	0.08	...	...	...	0.26	...	0.01
Price Range	46.81-26.86	44.04-29.02	41.14-27.91	31.17-12.99	34.71-13.33	35.60-12.62	26.10-12.71	14.11-10.08
P/E Ratio	15.98-9.17	14.73-9.71	14.54-9.86	12.88-5.37	18.76-7.21	22.97-8.14	23.51-11.45	...

Address: 300 Phillipi Road, P.O. Box 28512, Columbus, OH 43228-5311 **Telephone:** 614-278-6800 **Fax:** 614-278-6666	**Web Site:** www.biglots.com **Officers:** John Charles Martin - Executive Vice President, Executive Vice President, Chief Merchandising Officer Charles W. Haubiel - Executive Vice President, Executive Vice President, Secretary, General Counsel, Chief Administrative Officer	**Auditors:** Deloitte & Touche LLP **Investor Contact:** 614-278-6622 **Transfer Agents:** Computershare Investor Services, Canton, MA	

BIO-RAD LABORATORIES, INC.

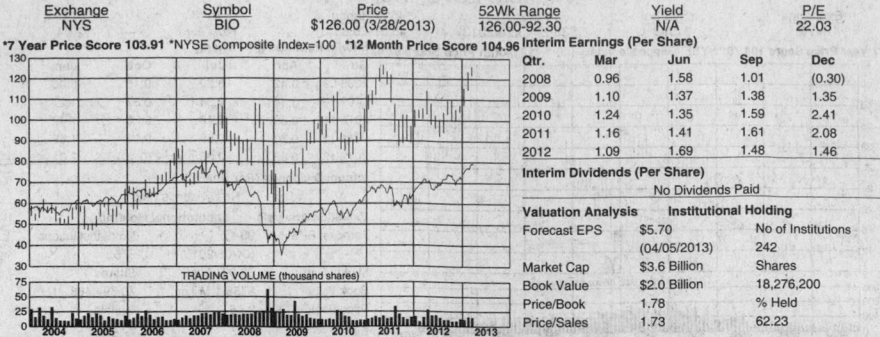

Exchange	Symbol	Price	52Wk Range	Yield	P/E
NYS	BIO	$126.00 (3/28/2013)	126.00-92.30	N/A	22.03

*7 Year Price Score 103.91 *NYSE Composite Index=100 *12 Month Price Score 104.96

Interim Earnings (Per Share)

Qtr.	Mar	Jun	Sep	Dec
2008	0.96	1.58	1.01	(0.30)
2009	1.10	1.37	1.38	1.35
2010	1.24	1.35	1.59	2.41
2011	1.16	1.41	1.61	2.08
2012	1.09	1.69	1.48	1.46

Interim Dividends (Per Share)
No Dividends Paid

Valuation Analysis

		Institutional Holding	
Forecast EPS	$5.70	No of Institutions	
	(04/05/2013)	242	
Market Cap	$3.6 Billion	Shares	
Book Value	$2.0 Billion	18,276,200	
Price/Book	1.78	% Held	
Price/Sales	1.73	62.23	

Business Summary: Biotechnology (MIC: 4.1.2 SIC: 3826 NAIC: 334516)

Bio-Rad Laboratories manufactures and supplies the life science research, healthcare, analytical chemistry and other markets with a range of products and systems used to separate chemical and biological materials to identify, analyze and purify their components. Co. has two reportable segments: Life Science, which develops, manufactures and sells and services reagents, apparatus and instruments used for biological research; and Clinical Diagnostics, which designs, manufactures, sells and supports test and informatics systems, test kits and quality controls that serve clinical laboratories in the diagnostics market. Both segments operate worldwide.

Recent Developments: For the year ended Dec 31 2012, net income decreased 8.0% to US$163.8 million from US$178.0 million in the prior year. Revenues were US$2.07 billion, unchanged from the year before. Operating income was US$257.2 million versus US$295.2 million in the prior year, a decrease of 12.9%. Direct operating expenses rose 2.2% to US$915.1 million from US$895.6 million in the comparable period the year before. Indirect operating expenses increased 1.6% to US$896.9 million from US$882.7 million in the equivalent prior-year period.

Prospects: Our evaluation of Bio-Rad Laboratories Inc. as of Apr. 7, 2013 is the result of our systematic analysis on three basic characteristics: earnings strength, relative valuation, and recent stock price movement. The company has generated a negative trend in earnings per share over the past 5 quarters and while recent estimates for the company have been raised by analysts, BIO has posted better than expected results. Based on operating earnings yield, the company is about fairly valued when compared to all of the companies in our coverage universe. Share price changes over the past year indicates that BIO will perform poorly over the near term.

Financial Data

(US$ in Thousands)	12/31/2012	12/31/2011	12/31/2010	12/31/2009	12/31/2008	12/31/2007	12/31/2006	12/31/2005
Earnings Per Share	5.72	6.26	6.59	5.20	3.25	3.41	3.83	3.06
Cash Flow Per Share	9.83	9.27	8.17	11.86	7.07	7.18	4.48	4.16
Tang Book Value Per Share	44.04	36.03	34.78	26.42	17.95	16.10	24.73	19.68
Income Statement								
Total Revenue	2,069,235	2,073,529	1,927,118	1,784,244	1,764,365	1,461,052	1,273,930	1,180,985
EBITDA	393,043	401,697	353,300	296,656	230,656	183,949	222,749	175,114
Depn & Amortn	130,400	121,000	74,500	69,500	66,300	53,500	48,700	49,100
Income Before Taxes	222,931	235,762	220,283	185,832	142,843	120,843	142,027	93,371
Income Taxes	59,084	57,739	33,348	36,667	44,579	26,548	38,764	15,792
Net Income	163,778	178,223	185,490	144,620	89,510	92,994	103,263	81,553
Average Shares	28,642	28,468	28,151	27,828	27,527	27,260	26,949	26,662
Balance Sheet								
Current Assets	1,929,932	1,798,155	1,975,346	1,562,674	1,093,941	1,028,974	1,129,777	1,008,211
Total Assets	3,436,753	3,096,803	3,062,764	2,535,853	2,037,264	1,971,594	1,596,168	1,426,582
Current Liabilities	469,920	459,115	666,627	419,972	418,034	414,168	319,533	319,243
Long-Term Obligations	732,414	731,698	731,100	737,919	445,979	441,805	425,625	425,687
Total Liabilities	1,426,018	1,352,866	1,526,068	1,276,127	996,533	999,904	776,630	768,608
Stockholders' Equity	2,010,735	1,743,937	1,536,696	1,259,726	1,040,731	971,690	819,538	657,974
Shares Outstanding	28,481	28,184	27,852	27,526	27,319	26,884	26,504	26,226
Statistical Record								
Return on Assets %	5.00	5.79	6.63	6.32	4.45	5.21	6.83	5.79
Return on Equity %	8.70	10.87	13.27	12.57	8.87	10.38	13.98	13.00
EBITDA Margin %	18.99	19.37	18.33	16.63	13.07	12.59	17.49	14.83
Net Margin %	7.91	8.60	9.63	8.11	5.07	6.36	8.11	6.91
Asset Turnover	0.63	0.67	0.69	0.78	0.88	0.82	0.84	0.84
Current Ratio	4.11	3.92	2.96	3.72	2.62	2.48	3.54	3.16
Debt to Equity	0.36	0.42	0.48	0.59	0.43	0.45	0.52	0.65
Price Range	114.25-92.30	126.34-87.54	113.63-81.50	100.46-53.10	108.10-61.52	107.57-67.67	84.01-57.25	66.90-47.06
P/E Ratio	19.97-16.14	20.18-13.98	17.24-12.37	19.32-10.21	33.26-18.93	31.55-19.84	21.93-14.95	21.86-15.38

Address: 1000 Alfred Nobel Drive, Hercules, CA 94547	Web Site: www.bio-rad.com	Auditors: Ernst & Young LLP
Telephone: 510-724-7000	Officers: David Schwartz - Chairman Norman D. Schwartz - President, Chief Executive Officer	Investor Contact: 510-741-6104
Fax: 510-741-5817		Transfer Agents: Computershare, Canton, MA

BLACK HILLS CORPORATION

Exchange	Symbol	Price	52Wk Range	Yield	P/E	Div Achiever
NYS	BKH	$44.04 (3/28/2013)	44.08-30.67	3.45	23.81	41 Years

*7 Year Price Score 96.66 ***NYSE Composite Index=100** ***12 Month Price Score 108.44**

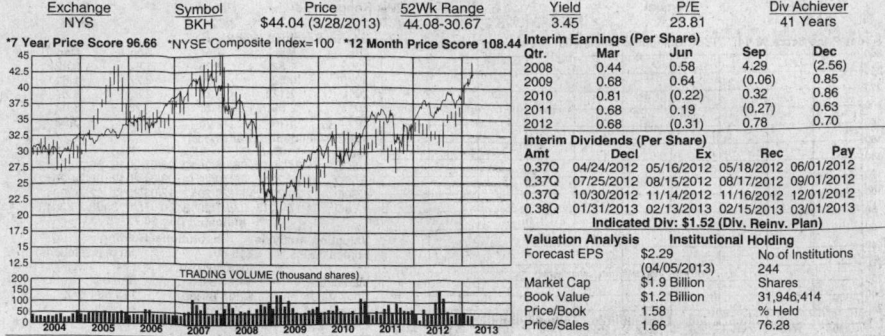

Interim Earnings (Per Share)

Qtr.	Mar	Jun	Sep	Dec
2008	0.44	0.58	4.29	(2.56)
2009	0.68	0.64	(0.06)	0.85
2010	0.81	(0.22)	0.32	0.86
2011	0.68	0.19	(0.27)	0.63
2012	0.68	(0.31)	0.78	0.70

Interim Dividends (Per Share)

Amt	Decl	Ex	Rec	Pay
0.37Q	04/24/2012	05/16/2012	05/18/2012	06/01/2012
0.37Q	07/25/2012	08/15/2012	08/17/2012	09/01/2012
0.37Q	10/30/2012	11/14/2012	11/16/2012	12/01/2012
0.38Q	01/31/2013	02/13/2013	02/15/2013	03/01/2013

Indicated Div: $1.52 (Div. Reinv. Plan)

Valuation Analysis / **Institutional Holding**

Forecast EPS	$2.29	No of Institutions	
	(04/05/2013)	244	
Market Cap	$1.9 Billion	Shares	
Book Value	$1.2 Billion	31,946,414	
Price/Book	1.58	% Held	
Price/Sales	1.66	76.28	

Business Summary: Electric Utilities (MIC: 3.1.1 SIC: 4911 NAIC: 221121)

Black Hills is a holding company. Through its subsidiaries, Co. operates primarily in the U.S. with two business groups: Utilities, which comprised of its regulated Electric Utilities and regulated Gas Utilities segments; and Non-regulated Energy, which comprised of its Oil and Gas, Power Generation, and Coal Mining segments. As of Dec 31 2012, Co. generated, transmitted and distributed electricity to approximately 202,000 customers in South Dakota, Wyoming, Colorado and Montana; and distributed natural gas to about 532,000 customers in Colorado, Iowa, Kansas and Nebraska. As of the same date, Co. had total oil and gas reserves of about 80.68 billion cubic feet equivalent.

Recent Developments: For the year ended Dec 31 2012, income from continuing operations increased 119.3% to US$88.5 million from US$40.4 million a year earlier. Net income increased 63.9% to US$81.5 million from US$49.7 million in the prior year. Revenues were US$1.17 billion, down 7.7% from US$1.27 billion the year before. Operating income was US$243.7 million versus US$186.2 million in the prior year, an increase of 30.9%. Direct operating expenses declined 19.7% to US$735.3 million from US$915.9 million in the comparable period the year before. Indirect operating expenses increased 14.6% to US$194.9 million from US$170.0 million in the equivalent prior-year period.

Prospects: Our evaluation of Black Hills Corp. as of Apr. 7, 2013 is the result of our systematic analysis on three basic characteristics: earnings strength, relative valuation, and recent stock price movement. The company has produced a positive trend in earnings per share over the past 5 quarters and while recent estimates for the company have remained steady, BKH has posted better than expected results. Based on operating earnings yield, the company is about fairly valued when compared to all of the companies in our coverage universe. Share price changes over the past year indicates that BKH will perform in line with the market over the near term.

Financial Data

(US$ in Thousands)	12/31/2012	12/31/2011	12/31/2010	12/31/2009	12/31/2008	12/31/2007	12/31/2006	12/31/2005
Earnings Per Share	1.85	1.24	1.76	2.11	2.75	2.64	2.42	1.00
Cash Flow Per Share	7.21	5.61	3.80	7.01	3.80	6.81	7.83	5.34
Tang Book Value Per Share	19.80	19.40	18.88	18.65	17.76	24.32	22.03	20.49
Dividends Per Share	1.480	1.460	1.440	1.420	1.400	1.370	1.320	1.280
Dividend Payout %	80.00	117.74	81.82	67.30	50.91	51.89	54.55	128.00
Income Statement								
Total Revenue	1,173,884	1,272,188	1,307,251	1,269,578	1,005,790	695,914	656,882	1,391,644
EBITDA	408,195	281,493	308,348	309,212	69,577	279,614	247,386	176,095
Depn & Amortn	160,181	135,591	126,894	121,297	107,263	99,700	94,083	89,306
Income Before Taxes	136,895	57,468	92,424	110,728	(85,798)	147,373	106,705	40,011
Income Taxes	48,040	18,224	25,298	33,315	(29,395)	45,641	33,802	18,299
Net Income	81,528	49,730	68,685	81,555	105,080	98,772	81,019	33,420
Average Shares	44,073	40,081	39,091	38,684	38,193	37,414	33,549	33,288
Balance Sheet								
Current Assets	405,106	758,921	670,871	624,870	799,513	530,901	474,501	541,968
Total Assets	3,729,471	4,127,083	3,711,509	3,317,698	3,379,889	2,472,866	2,244,676	2,119,960
Current Liabilities	734,889	878,067	787,440	644,859	1,253,673	580,957	528,978	470,623
Long-Term Obligations	938,877	1,280,409	1,186,050	1,015,912	501,252	564,372	628,340	670,193
Total Liabilities	2,496,962	2,917,747	2,611,239	2,232,861	2,329,353	1,503,011	1,454,635	1,381,081
Stockholders' Equity	1,232,509	1,209,336	1,100,270	1,084,837	1,050,536	969,855	790,041	738,879
Shares Outstanding	44,206	43,924	39,269	38,968	38,635	37,796	33,369	33,155
Statistical Record								
Return on Assets %	2.07	1.27	1.95	2.44	3.58	4.19	3.71	1.60
Return on Equity %	6.66	4.31	6.29	7.64	10.37	11.22	10.60	4.53
EBITDA Margin %	34.77	22.13	23.59	24.36	6.92	40.18	37.66	12.65
Net Margin %	6.95	3.91	5.25	6.42	10.45	14.19	12.33	2.40
Asset Turnover	0.30	0.32	0.37	0.38	0.34	0.30	0.30	0.67
Current Ratio	0.55	0.86	0.85	0.97	0.64	0.91	0.90	1.15
Debt to Equity	0.76	1.06	1.08	0.94	0.48	0.58	0.80	0.91
Price Range	36.95-30.67	34.80-26.61	34.11-25.86	27.82-14.59	44.10-21.99	44.90-35.76	37.93-32.75	43.54-29.42
P/E Ratio	19.97-16.58	28.06-21.46	19.38-14.69	13.18-6.91	16.04-8.00	17.01-13.55	15.67-13.53	43.54-29.42
Average Yield %	4.40	4.65	4.79	6.15	4.21	3.40	3.79	3.51

Address: 625 Ninth Street, Rapid City, SD 57701 **Telephone:** 605-721-1700	**Web Site:** www.blackhillscorp.com **Officers:** David R. Emery - Chairman, President, Chief Executive Officer Anthony S. Cleberg - Executive Vice President, Chief Financial Officer	**Auditors:** Deloitte & Touche LLP **Investor Contact:** 605-721-1171 **Transfer Agents:** Wells Fargo Shareowner Services, St. Paul, MN

BLACKROCK, INC.

Exchange	Symbol	Price	52Wk Range	Yield	P/E
NYS	BLK	$256.88 (3/28/2013)	258.70-163.37	2.62	18.63

*7 Year Price Score 98.14 *NYSE Composite Index=100 *12 Month Price Score 114.39

Interim Earnings (Per Share)

Qtr.	Mar	Jun	Sep	Dec
2008	1.82	2.05	1.62	0.42
2009	0.62	1.59	2.27	1.61
2010	2.17	2.21	2.83	3.34
2011	2.89	3.21	3.23	3.04
2012	3.14	3.08	3.65	3.92

Interim Dividends (Per Share)

Amt	Decl	Ex	Rec	Pay
1.50Q	05/24/2012	06/05/2012	06/07/2012	06/25/2012
1.50Q	07/26/2012	08/30/2012	09/04/2012	09/24/2012
1.50Q	11/20/2012	11/29/2012	12/03/2012	12/24/2012
1.68Q	01/17/2013	03/05/2013	03/07/2013	03/25/2013

Indicated Div: $6.72

Valuation Analysis

		Institutional Holding	
Forecast EPS	$15.60	No of Institutions	
	(04/06/2013)	774	
Market Cap	$43.4 Billion	Shares	
Book Value	$25.4 Billion	143,304,672	
Price/Book	1.71	% Held	
Price/Sales	4.65	75.03	

TRADING VOLUME (thousand shares)

Business Summary: Finance Intermediaries & Services (MIC: 5.5.1 SIC: 6211 NAIC: 523999)

BlackRock is an investment management firm. Investment management services primarily consist of the management of equity, fixed income, multi-asset class, alternative investment and cash management products. Co. provides its investment products in a variety of vehicles, including open-end and closed-end mutual funds, iShares® exchange-traded funds, collective investment trusts and separate accounts. In addition, Co. provides market risk management, financial markets advisory and enterprise investment system services. As of Dec 31 2011, Co. managed $3.51 trillion of assets under management on behalf of institutional and individual investors worldwide.

Recent Developments: For the year ended Dec 31 2012, net income increased 4.3% to US$2.44 billion from US$2.34 billion in the prior year. Revenues were US$9.34 billion, up 2.8% from US$9.08 billion the year before. Operating income was US$3.52 billion versus US$3.25 billion in the prior year, an increase of 8.5%. Indirect operating expenses decreased 0.3% to US$5.81 billion from US$5.83 billion in the equivalent prior-year period.

Prospects: Our evaluation of BlackRock Inc. as of Apr. 7, 2013 is the result of our systematic analysis on three basic characteristics: earnings strength, relative valuation, and recent stock price movement. The company has produced a positive trend in earnings per share over the past 5 quarters and while recent estimates for the company have been raised by analysts, BLK has posted better than expected results. Based on operating earnings yield, the company is undervalued when compared to all of the companies in our coverage universe. Share price changes over the past year indicates that BLK will perform in line with the market over the near term.

Financial Data

(US$ in Thousands)	12/31/2012	12/31/2011	12/31/2010	12/31/2009	12/31/2008	12/31/2007	12/31/2006	12/31/2005
Earnings Per Share	13.79	12.37	10.55	6.11	5.91	7.53	3.87	3.50
Cash Flow Per Share	12.77	15.34	13.06	10.24	14.75	4.57	8.94	3.97
Tang Book Value Per Share	N.M.	N.M.	N.M.	N.M.	0.78	N.M.	N.M.	6.85
Dividends Per Share	6.000	5.500	4.000	3.120	3.120	2.680	1.680	1.200
Dividend Payout %	43.51	44.46	37.91	51.06	52.79	35.59	43.41	34.29
Income Statement								
Total Revenue	9,337,000	9,081,000	8,612,000	4,700,000	5,064,000	4,844,655	2,097,976	1,191,386
EBITDA	3,971,000	3,605,000	3,476,000	1,572,000	1,315,000	2,069,609	610,955	414,581
Depn & Amortn	286,000	294,000	305,000	232,000	230,000	197,478	72,806	30,902
Income Before Taxes	3,470,000	3,135,000	3,021,000	1,272,000	1,019,000	1,822,719	528,233	375,755
Income Taxes	1,030,000	796,000	971,000	375,000	388,000	463,832	189,463	138,558
Net Income	2,458,000	2,337,000	2,063,000	875,000	786,000	995,272	322,602	233,908
Average Shares	178,017	187,116	192,692	139,481	132,996	132,088	83,358	66,875
Balance Sheet								
Current Assets	6,856,000	5,466,000	5,462,000	6,438,000	2,933,000	2,892,140	2,124,670	794,646
Total Assets	200,451,000	179,896,000	178,459,000	177,994,000	19,924,000	22,561,515	20,469,492	1,848,000
Current Liabilities	2,716,000	2,428,000	2,745,000	5,000,000	1,674,000	2,289,905	2,048,948	637,879
Long-Term Obligations	5,687,000	4,690,000	3,259,000	3,434,000	946,000	947,021	253,167	253,791
Total Liabilities	175,048,000	154,848,000	152,365,000	153,665,000	7,858,000	10,964,560	9,687,612	925,757
Stockholders' Equity	25,403,000	25,048,000	26,094,000	24,329,000	12,066,000	11,596,955	10,781,880	922,243
Shares Outstanding	168,875	138,463	131,216	61,896	117,291	116,059	116,408	64,000
Statistical Record								
Return on Assets %	1.29	1.30	1.16	0.88	3.69	4.63	2.89	15.63
Return on Equity %	9.72	9.14	8.18	4.81	6.63	8.89	5.51	27.67
EBITDA Margin %	42.53	39.70	40.36	33.45	25.97	42.72	29.12	34.80
Net Margin %	26.33	25.74	23.95	18.62	15.52	20.54	15.38	19.63
Asset Turnover	0.05	0.05	0.05	0.05	0.24	0.23	0.19	0.80
Current Ratio	2.52	2.25	1.99	1.29	1.75	1.26	1.04	1.25
Debt to Equity	0.22	0.19	0.12	0.14	0.08	0.08	0.02	0.28
Price Range	209.29-163.37	207.06-141.77	242.81-139.44	240.80-90.57	230.75-98.88	222.03-144.70	156.31-108.00	113.45-70.00
P/E Ratio	15.18-11.85	16.74-11.46	23.02-13.22	39.41-14.82	39.04-16.73	29.49-19.22	40.39-27.91	32.41-20.00
Average Yield %	3.24	3.07	2.21	1.81	1.67	1.59	1.21	1.41

Address: 55 East 52nd Street, New York, NY 10055 Telephone: 212-810-5300	Web Site: www.blackrock.com Officers: Laurence D. Fink - Chairman, Chief Executive Officer Robert W. Fairbairn - Vice-Chairman, Division Officer	Auditors: Deloitte & Touche LLP Transfer Agents: Computershare

BLOCK (H & R), INC.

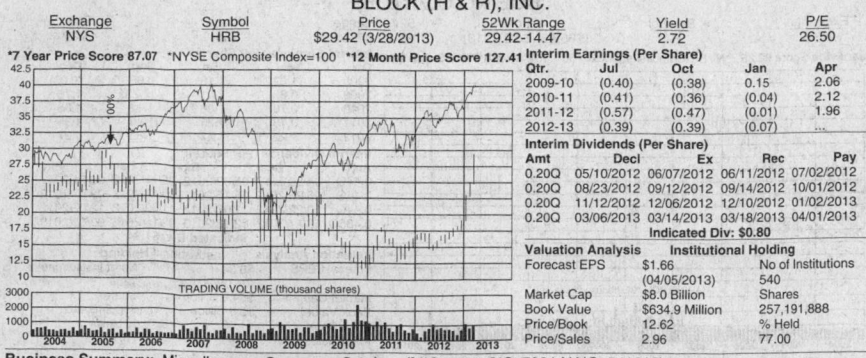

Exchange	Symbol	Price	52Wk Range	Yield	P/E
NYS	HRB	$29.42 (3/28/2013)	29.42-14.47	2.72	26.50

*7 Year Price Score 87.07   *NYSE Composite Index=100   *12 Month Price Score 127.41

Interim Earnings (Per Share)

Qtr.	Jul	Oct	Jan	Apr
2009-10	(0.40)	(0.38)	0.15	2.06
2010-11	(0.41)	(0.36)	(0.04)	2.12
2011-12	(0.57)	(0.47)	(0.01)	1.96
2012-13	(0.39)	(0.39)	(0.07)	...

Interim Dividends (Per Share)

Amt	Decl	Ex	Rec	Pay
0.20Q	05/10/2012	06/07/2012	06/11/2012	07/02/2012
0.20Q	08/23/2012	09/12/2012	09/14/2012	10/01/2012
0.20Q	11/12/2012	12/06/2012	12/10/2012	01/02/2013
0.20Q	03/06/2013	03/14/2013	03/18/2013	04/01/2013

Indicated Div: $0.80

Valuation Analysis | **Institutional Holding**

Forecast EPS	$1.66	No of Institutions
	(04/05/2013)	540
Market Cap	$8.0 Billion	Shares
Book Value	$634.9 Million	257,191,888
Price/Book	12.62	% Held
Price/Sales	2.96	77.00

TRADING VOLUME (thousand shares)

Business Summary: Miscellaneous Consumer Services (MIC: 2.2.3 SIC: 7291 NAIC: 541213)

H&R Block and its subsidiaries are engaged in providing tax preparation and banking services. Co.'s Tax Services segment provides assisted income tax return preparation, digital tax services and other services and products related to income tax return preparation to the general public primarily in the U.S., and also in Canada and Australia. This segment also provides financial services including the H&R Block Prepaid Emerald MasterCard® and Emerald Advance lines of credit through Co.'s H&R Block Bank subsidiary, along with other retail banking services, including checking and savings accounts, individual retirement accounts and certificates of deposit.

Recent Developments: For the quarter ended Jan 31 2013, loss from continuing operations was US$16.9 million compared with a loss of US$3.6 million in the year-earlier quarter. Net loss amounted to US$17.7 million versus a net loss of US$3.3 million in the year-earlier quarter. Revenues were US$472.0 million, down 28.8% from US$663.3 million the year before. Operating loss was US$92.6 million versus a loss of US$3.7 million in the prior-year quarter. Direct operating expenses declined 17.1% to US$377.6 million from US$455.2 million in the comparable period the year before. Indirect operating expenses decreased 11.7% to US$187.0 million from US$211.7 million in the equivalent prior-year period.

Prospects: Our evaluation of Block (H & R) Inc. as of Apr. 7, 2013 is the result of our systematic analysis on three basic characteristics: earnings strength, relative valuation, and recent stock price movement. The company has produced a positive trend in earnings per share over the past 5 quarters and while recent estimates for the company have been mixed, HRB has posted results that fell short of analysts expectations. Based on operating earnings yield, the company is undervalued when compared to all of the companies in our coverage universe. Share price changes over the past year indicates that HRB will perform poorly over the near term.

Financial Data

(US$ in Thousands)	9 Mos	6 Mos	3 Mos	04/30/2012	04/30/2011	04/30/2010	04/30/2009	04/30/2008
Earnings Per Share	1.11	1.17	1.09	0.89	1.31	1.43	1.45	(0.94)
Cash Flow Per Share	1.59	1.39	1.38	1.21	1.66	1.77	3.08	0.66
Tang Book Value Per Share	N.M.	N.M.	0.49	2.17	0.77	0.72	0.51	N.M.
Dividends Per Share	0.800	0.800	0.750	0.700	0.600	0.600	0.593	0.563
Dividend Payout %	72.07	68.38	68.81	78.65	45.80	41.96	40.86	...
Income Statement								
Total Revenue	705,731	233,752	96,489	2,893,771	3,774,296	3,874,332	4,083,577	4,403,877
EBITDA	(373,526)	(297,325)	(152,964)	645,370	769,225	881,035	935,970	842,440
Depn & Amortn	54,299	34,232	16,305	69,300	92,200	96,900	96,600	95,200
Income Before Taxes	(427,825)	(331,557)	(169,269)	576,070	677,025	784,135	839,370	745,221
Income Taxes	(204,061)	(124,708)	(63,619)	230,102	257,620	295,189	326,315	290,745
Net Income	(230,392)	(212,684)	(107,441)	265,932	406,110	479,242	485,673	(308,647)
Average Shares	271,542	271,145	277,155	298,601	309,777	333,236	334,539	327,468
Balance Sheet								
Current Assets	1,736,549	1,706,953	1,417,599	2,500,994	2,477,731	2,649,036	2,571,080	2,381,580
Total Assets	3,932,496	3,896,730	3,594,277	4,649,567	5,207,961	5,234,318	5,359,722	5,623,425
Current Liabilities	2,063,194	1,931,902	1,977,397	2,526,428	2,214,675	2,321,491	2,398,280	3,096,376
Long-Term Obligations	906,012	906,125	408,992	409,115	1,049,754	1,060,144	1,107,122	1,031,784
Total Liabilities	3,297,608	3,203,797	2,748,604	3,323,675	3,758,387	3,793,688	3,953,863	4,635,607
Stockholders' Equity	634,888	692,933	845,673	1,325,892	1,449,574	1,440,630	1,405,859	987,818
Shares Outstanding	272,319	316,628	316,628	292,119	305,366	323,306	334,101	326,010
Statistical Record								
Return on Assets %	8.10	9.40	8.44	5.38	7.78	9.05	8.84	N.M.
Return on Equity %	49.36	47.57	32.08	19.11	28.10	33.67	40.58	N.M.
EBITDA Margin %	N.M.	N.M.	N.M.	22.30	20.38	22.74	22.92	19.13
Net Margin %	N.M.	N.M.	N.M.	9.19	10.76	12.37	11.89	N.M.
Asset Turnover	0.62	0.74	0.73	0.59	0.72	0.73	0.74	0.67
Current Ratio	0.84	0.88	0.72	0.99	1.12	1.14	1.07	0.77
Debt to Equity	1.43	1.31	0.48	0.31	0.72	0.74	0.79	1.04
Price Range	23.07-14.47	17.96-14.42	17.20-12.73	17.48-12.73	18.92-10.62	23.07-13.94	26.50-14.78	23.89-17.00
P/E Ratio	20.78-13.04	15.35-12.32	15.78-11.68	19.64-14.30	14.44-8.11	16.13-9.75	18.28-10.19	...
Average Yield %	4.71	4.96	4.87	4.52	4.18	3.29	2.82	2.74

Address: One H&R Block Way, Kansas City, MO 64105 Telephone: 816-854-3000	Web Site: www.hrblock.com Officers: Robert A. Gerard - Chairman William C. Cobb - President, Chief Executive Officer	Auditors: Deloitte & Touche LLP Investor Contact: 816-854-4199 Transfer Agents: Wells Fargo Shareowner Services, St. Paul, MN

BOEING CO. (THE)

Exchange	Symbol	Price	52Wk Range	Yield	P/E
NYS	BA	$85.85 (3/28/2013)	86.62-67.24	2.26	16.80

*7 Year Price Score 92.25   *NYSE Composite Index=100   *12 Month Price Score 98.30

Interim Earnings (Per Share)

Qtr.	Mar	Jun	Sep	Dec
2008	1.62	1.16	0.96	(0.09)
2009	0.86	1.41	(2.23)	1.78
2010	0.70	1.06	1.12	1.56
2011	0.78	1.25	1.46	1.85
2012	1.22	1.27	1.35	1.27

Interim Dividends (Per Share)

Amt	Decl	Ex	Rec	Pay
0.44Q	04/30/2012	05/09/2012	05/11/2012	06/01/2012
0.44Q	06/25/2012	08/15/2012	08/17/2012	09/07/2012
0.44Q	10/29/2012	11/07/2012	11/09/2012	12/07/2012
0.485Q	12/17/2012	02/13/2013	02/15/2013	03/08/2013

Indicated Div: $1.94

Valuation Analysis   **Institutional Holding**

Forecast EPS	$6.34	No of Institutions
	(04/06/2013)	1259
Market Cap	$64.9 Billion	Shares
Book Value	$5.9 Billion	596,240,448
Price/Book	11.06	% Held
Price/Sales	0.79	75.19

Business Summary: Aerospace (MIC: 7.1.1 SIC: 3721 NAIC: 336411)

Boeing, together with its subsidiaries, is an aerospace firm engaged in the design, development, manufacture, sale, service and support of commercial jetliners, military aircraft, satellites, missile defense, human space flight and launch systems and services. Co. provides assistance and services to facilitate aircraft operation to the operators of its commercial airplane models. These activities and services include flight and maintenance training, field service support, engineering services, and technical data and documents. While its main operations are in the U.S., Co. conducts operations in many countries and has a network of international partners, key suppliers and subcontractors.

Recent Developments: For the year ended Dec 31 2012, income from continuing operations decreased 2.7% to US$3.90 billion from US$4.01 billion a year earlier. Net income decreased 2.9% to US$3.90 billion from US$4.02 billion in the prior year. Revenues were US$81.70 billion, up 18.9% from US$68.74 billion the year before. Operating income was US$6.31 billion versus US$5.84 billion in the prior year, an increase of 8.0%. Direct operating expenses rose 22.9% to US$68.64 billion from US$55.87 billion in the comparable period the year before. Indirect operating expenses decreased 4.0% to US$6.74 billion from US$7.02 billion in the equivalent prior-year period.

Prospects: Our evaluation of Boeing Co. as of Apr. 7, 2013 is the result of our systematic analysis on three basic characteristics: earnings strength, relative valuation, and recent stock price movement. The company has produced a positive trend in earnings per share over the past 5 quarters. However, while recent estimates for the company have been mixed, BA has posted better than expected results. Based on operating earnings yield, the company is undervalued when compared to all of the companies in our coverage universe. Share price changes over the past year indicates that BA will perform very poorly over the near term.

Financial Data
(US$ in Millions)

	12/31/2012	12/31/2011	12/31/2010	12/31/2009	12/31/2008	12/31/2007	12/31/2006	12/31/2005
Earnings Per Share	5.11	5.34	4.45	1.84	3.67	5.28	2.85	3.20
Cash Flow Per Share	9.88	5.39	4.00	7.90	(0.55)	12.62	9.73	8.88
Tang Book Value Per Share	N.M.	N.M.	N.M.	N.M.	...	4.99	N.M.	10.32
Dividends Per Share	1.760	1.680	1.680	1.680	1.600	1.400	1.200	1.000
Dividend Payout %	34.44	31.46	37.75	91.30	43.60	26.52	42.11	31.25
Income Statement								
Total Revenue	81,698	68,735	64,306	68,281	60,909	66,387	61,530	54,845
EBITDA	7,621	7,213	6,336	3,343	5,376	7,444	4,592	4,205
Depn & Amortn	1,248	1,322	1,313	1,273	1,179	1,130	1,158	1,092
Income Before Taxes	5,910	5,393	4,507	1,731	3,995	6,118	3,194	2,819
Income Taxes	2,007	1,382	1,196	396	1,341	2,060	988	257
Net Income	3,900	4,018	3,307	1,312	2,672	4,074	2,215	2,572
Average Shares	763	753	744	713	729	772	787	802
Balance Sheet								
Current Assets	57,309	49,810	40,572	35,275	25,964	27,280	22,983	21,968
Total Assets	88,896	79,986	68,565	62,053	53,779	58,986	51,794	60,058
Current Liabilities	44,982	41,274	35,395	32,883	30,925	31,538	29,701	28,188
Long-Term Obligations	8,973	10,018	11,473	12,217	6,952	7,455	8,157	9,538
Total Liabilities	83,029	76,471	65,799	59,925	55,073	49,982	47,055	48,999
Stockholders' Equity	5,867	3,515	2,766	2,128	(1,294)	9,004	4,739	11,059
Shares Outstanding	755	744	735	755	726	768	788	800
Statistical Record								
Return on Assets %	4.61	5.41	5.06	2.27	4.73	7.36	3.96	4.51
Return on Equity %	82.91	127.94	135.15	314.63	69.12	59.29	28.04	23.02
EBITDA Margin %	9.33	10.49	9.85	4.90	8.83	11.21	7.46	7.67
Net Margin %	4.77	5.85	5.14	1.92	4.39	6.14	3.60	4.69
Asset Turnover	0.96	0.93	0.98	1.18	1.08	1.20	1.10	0.96
Current Ratio	1.27	1.21	1.15	1.07	0.84	0.86	0.77	0.78
Debt to Equity	1.53	2.85	4.15	5.74	...	0.83	1.72	0.86
Price Range	77.27-67.24	79.95-57.41	75.59-54.13	56.05-29.36	87.46-37.11	107.23-85.43	91.10-66.50	71.49-49.64
P/E Ratio	15.12-13.16	14.97-10.75	16.99-12.16	30.46-15.96	23.83-10.11	20.31-16.18	31.96-23.33	22.34-15.51
Average Yield %	2.41	2.41	2.54	3.72	2.41	1.48	1.50	1.61

Address: 100 N. Riverside Plaza, Chicago, IL 60606-1596 **Telephone:** 312-544-2000	**Web Site:** www.boeing.com **Officers:** W. James McNerney - Chairman, President, Chief Executive Officer J. Michael Luttig - Executive Vice President, General Counsel	**Auditors:** Deloitte & Touche LLP **Transfer Agents:** Computershare Trust Company, N.A., Providence, RI

114

BOOZ ALLEN HAMILTON HOLDING CORP.

Exchange	Symbol	Price	52Wk Range	Yield	P/E
NYS	BAH	$13.44 (3/28/2013)	19.06-11.90	2.68	7.72

*7 Year Price Score N/A   *NYSE Composite Index=100   *12 Month Price Score 81.85

Interim Earnings (Per Share)

Qtr.	Jun	Sep	Dec	Mar
2010-11	0.23	0.12	0.18	0.12
2011-12	0.37	0.53	0.44	0.36
2012-13	0.43	0.27	0.68	...

Interim Dividends (Per Share)

Amt	Decl	Ex	Rec	Pay
6.50Sp	07/30/2012	09/04/2012	08/15/2012	08/31/2012
0.09Q	07/30/2012	08/10/2012	08/14/2012	08/31/2012
0.09Q	10/29/2012	11/08/2012	11/13/2012	11/30/2012
0.09Q	01/30/2013	02/07/2013	02/11/2013	02/28/2013

Indicated Div: $0.36

Valuation Analysis / Institutional Holding

Forecast EPS	$1.63 (04/05/2013)	No of Institutions	134
Market Cap	$2.0 Billion	Shares	214,411,440
Book Value	$184.5 Million	% Held	N/A
Price/Book	10.62		
Price/Sales	0.34		

Business Summary: IT Services (MIC: 6.3.1 SIC: 8742 NAIC: 541611)

Booz Allen Hamilton Holding is a holding company. Through its subsidiaries, Co. is engaged in providing management and technology consulting services to the U.S. government in the defense, intelligence and civil markets. Additionally, Co. provides management and technology consulting services to major corporations. Co.'s major clients include the Department of Defense, all branches of the U.S. military, the U.S. Intelligence Community, and civil agencies such as the Department of Homeland Security, the Department of Energy, the Department of Health and Human Services, the Department of the Treasury, and the Environmental Protection Agency.

Recent Developments: For the quarter ended Dec 31 2012, net income decreased 10.6% to US$56.2 million from US$62.9 million in the year-earlier quarter. Revenues were US$1.39 billion, down 3.5% from US$1.44 billion the year before. Operating income was US$116.6 million versus US$98.2 million in the prior-year quarter, an increase of 18.7%. Direct operating expenses declined 5.1% to US$692.9 million from US$730.0 million in the comparable period the year before. Indirect operating expenses decreased 5.1% to US$583.2 million from US$614.6 million in the equivalent prior-year period.

Prospects: Our evaluation of Booz Allen Hamilton Holding as of Apr. 7, 2013 is the result of our systematic analysis on three basic characteristics: earnings strength, relative valuation, and recent stock price movement. The company has generated a negative trend in earnings per share over the past 5 quarters and while recent estimates for the company have remained steady, BAH has posted better than expected results. Based on operating earnings yield, the company is undervalued when compared to all of the companies in our coverage universe. Share price changes over the past year indicates that BAH will perform very well over the near term.

Financial Data
(US$ in Thousands)

	9 Mos	6 Mos	3 Mos	03/31/2012	03/31/2011	03/31/2010	03/31/2009	07/31/2008
Earnings Per Share	1.74	1.50	1.76	1.70	0.66	0.22	(0.37)	(568.13)
Cash Flow Per Share	3.75	4.29	2.89	2.76	2.59	2.54	2.57	...
Dividends Per Share	8.360	8.270	1.680	0.090	...	...	...	...
Dividend Payout %	480.46	551.33	95.45	5.29	...	...	...	...
Income Statement								
Total Revenue	4,212,769	2,820,074	1,432,424	5,859,218	5,591,296	5,122,633	2,941,275	1,409,943
EBITDA	331,086	212,257	115,729	450,752	311,956	253,462	67,860	(441,443)
Depn & Amortn	5,417	3,318	1,476	58,800	52,000	55,200	35,300	11,900
Income Before Taxes	274,881	179,882	103,007	343,874	128,064	48,994	(60,930)	(453,653)
Income Taxes	110,636	71,821	41,062	103,919	43,370	23,575	(22,147)	(56,109)
Net Income	164,245	108,061	61,945	239,955	84,694	25,419	(38,783)	(1,245,915)
Average Shares	145,063	144,249	142,677	140,812	127,448	116,228	105,695	2,193
Balance Sheet								
Current Assets	1,396,652	1,442,662	1,473,145	1,657,663	1,365,649	1,370,168	1,432,893	...
Total Assets	3,150,906	3,090,078	3,109,022	3,314,791	3,024,023	3,062,223	3,182,249	...
Current Liabilities	976,297	969,054	878,252	914,446	866,135	785,920	643,585	...
Long-Term Obligations	1,675,364	1,691,088	909,453	922,925	964,328	1,546,782	1,220,502	...
Total Liabilities	2,966,384	2,970,544	2,089,174	2,129,606	2,116,773	2,552,640	2,121,906	...
Stockholders' Equity	184,522	119,534	1,019,848	1,185,185	907,250	509,583	1,060,343	...
Shares Outstanding	145,749	144,565	143,510	142,552	140,215	120,647	120,498	...
Statistical Record								
Return on Assets %	6.76	7.12	8.17	7.55	2.78	0.81	...	...
Return on Equity %	32.39	37.23	25.15	22.87	11.96	3.24	...	...
EBITDA Margin %	7.86	7.53	8.08	7.69	5.58	4.95	2.31	N.M.
Net Margin %	3.90	3.83	4.32	4.10	1.51	0.50	N.M.	N.M.
Asset Turnover	1.81	1.86	1.90	1.84	1.84	1.64	...	...
Current Ratio	1.43	1.49	1.68	1.81	1.58	1.74	2.23	...
Debt to Equity	9.08	14.15	0.89	0.78	1.06	3.04	1.15	...
Price Range	19.06-11.90	19.06-11.90	19.87-13.52	19.87-13.52	20.00-18.00	...	...	...
P/E Ratio	10.95-6.84	12.71-7.93	11.29-7.68	11.69-7.95	30.30-27.27	...	...	...
Average Yield %	53.02	50.61	10.20	0.52	...	...	...	...

Address: 8283 Greensboro Drive, McLean, VA 22102 Telephone: 703-902-5000	Web Site: www.boozallen.com Officers: Ralph W. Shrader - Chairman, President, Chief Executive Officer Samuel R. Strickland - Executive Vice President, Chief Financial Officer, Chief Administrative Officer	Auditors: Ernst & Young LLP Investor Contact: 703-377-5332 Transfer Agents: Computershare, Jersey City, NJ

BORG WARNER INC

Exchange	Symbol	Price	52Wk Range	Yield	P/E
NYS	BWA	$77.34 (3/28/2013)	85.46-60.54	N/A	18.55

*7 Year Price Score 130.50 *NYSE Composite Index=100   *12 Month Price Score 97.96

Interim Earnings (Per Share)

Qtr.	Mar	Jun	Sep	Dec
2008	0.75	0.74	(1.12)	(0.70)
2009	(0.06)	(0.31)	0.15	0.45
2010	0.63	0.68	0.87	0.89
2011	1.00	1.31	1.15	1.00
2012	1.28	1.00	0.85	1.02

Interim Dividends (Per Share)

Dividend Payment Suspended

Valuation Analysis	Institutional Holding	
Forecast EPS	$5.30	No of Institutions
	(04/05/2013)	539
Market Cap	$8.9 Billion	Shares
Book Value	$3.1 Billion	119,660,912
Price/Book	2.90	% Held
Price/Sales	1.24	95.10

Business Summary: Auto Parts (MIC: 1.8.2 SIC: 3714 NAIC: 336350)

BorgWarner is a supplier of automotive systems and components for powertrain applications. Co. has two segments: engine, which develops and manufactures turbochargers, emissions systems, timing devices and chain products, thermal systems, diesel cold start, gasoline ignition application, and cabin heaters; and drivetrain, which designs and manufactures automatic transmission components and modules, and all-wheel drive torque management systems. Co.'s products are sold to original equipment manufacturers of light vehicles, commercial vehicles, off-highway vehicles, and to certain Tier One vehicle systems suppliers and into the aftermarket for light, commercial and off-highway vehicles.

Recent Developments: For the year ended Dec 31 2012, net income decreased 8.4% to US$522.4 million from US$570.6 million in the prior year. Revenues were US$7.18 billion, up 1.0% from US$7.11 billion the year before. Operating income was US$752.9 million versus US$797.5 million in the prior year, a decrease of 5.6%. Direct operating expenses rose 0.2% to US$5.72 billion from US$5.70 billion in the comparable period the year before. Indirect operating expenses increased 16.5% to US$714.0 million from US$612.9 million in the equivalent prior-year period.

Prospects: Our evaluation of Borg Warner Inc. as of Apr. 7, 2013 is the result of our systematic analysis on three basic characteristics: earnings strength, relative valuation, and recent stock price movement. The company has generated a negative trend in earnings per share over the past 5 quarters. However, while recent estimates for the company have been mixed, BWA has posted better than expected results. Based on operating earnings yield, the company is undervalued when compared to all of the companies in our coverage universe. Share price changes over the past year indicates that BWA will perform poorly over the near term.

Financial Data

(US$ in Thousands)	12/31/2012	12/31/2011	12/31/2010	12/31/2009	12/31/2008	12/31/2007	12/31/2006	12/31/2005
Earnings Per Share	4.17	4.45	3.07	0.23	(0.31)	2.45	1.83	2.09
Cash Flow Per Share	7.78	6.48	4.72	3.01	3.45	5.20	3.85	3.50
Tang Book Value Per Share	14.67	8.83	8.69	8.35	6.97	8.73	5.79	4.50
Dividends Per Share	...	...	...	0.120	0.440	0.340	0.320	0.280
Dividend Payout %	...	...	...	52.17	...	13.88	17.53	13.43
Income Statement								
Total Revenue	7,183,200	7,114,700	5,652,800	3,961,800	5,263,900	5,328,600	4,585,400	4,293,800
EBITDA	1,046,800	1,100,800	775,500	324,400	294,100	682,700	528,000	504,500
Depn & Amortn	293,900	303,300	271,200	273,600	286,800	264,600	256,600	185,600
Income Before Taxes	718,200	727,700	438,300	(3,900)	(24,400)	390,100	234,400	286,000
Income Taxes	238,600	195,300	81,700	(18,500)	33,300	113,900	32,400	55,100
Net Income	500,900	550,100	377,400	27,000	(35,600)	288,500	211,600	239,600
Average Shares	121,377	128,468	129,575	116,939	116,007	117,840	115,942	114,796
Balance Sheet								
Current Assets	2,472,800	2,137,800	2,059,900	1,551,800	1,308,200	1,580,300	1,437,500	1,168,700
Total Assets	6,400,800	5,958,600	5,555,000	4,811,400	4,644,000	4,958,500	4,584,000	4,089,400
Current Liabilities	1,603,100	1,905,400	1,392,300	1,046,200	1,250,000	1,083,900	1,034,800	1,122,100
Long-Term Obligations	823,800	751,300	1,051,900	773,200	459,600	572,600	569,400	440,600
Total Liabilities	3,318,200	3,570,700	3,296,400	2,626,100	2,638,000	2,637,400	2,708,600	2,445,200
Stockholders' Equity	3,082,600	2,387,900	2,258,600	2,185,300	2,006,000	2,321,100	1,875,400	1,644,200
Shares Outstanding	115,572	108,514	112,316	116,837	115,532	116,128	115,386	114,268
Statistical Record								
Return on Assets %	8.08	9.56	7.28	0.57	N.M.	6.05	4.88	6.29
Return on Equity %	18.26	23.68	16.99	1.29	N.M.	13.75	12.02	15.08
EBITDA Margin %	14.57	15.47	13.72	8.19	5.59	12.81	11.51	11.75
Net Margin %	6.97	7.73	6.68	0.68	N.M.	5.41	4.61	5.58
Asset Turnover	1.16	1.24	1.09	0.84	1.09	1.12	1.06	1.13
Current Ratio	1.54	1.12	1.48	1.48	1.05	1.46	1.39	1.04
Debt to Equity	0.27	0.31	0.47	0.35	0.23	0.25	0.30	0.27
Price Range	87.05-60.54	81.66-56.14	73.14-33.22	35.85-15.18	55.28-16.11	52.85-29.30	33.65-26.75	30.81-22.63
P/E Ratio	20.88-14.52	18.35-12.62	23.82-10.82	155.87-66.00	...	21.57-11.96	18.39-14.61	14.74-10.83
Average Yield %	...	...	...	0.43	1.13	0.81	1.04	1.02

Address: 3850 Hamlin Road, Auburn Hills, MI 48326	**Web Site:** www.borgwarner.com	**Auditors:** PricewaterhouseCoopers LLP
Telephone: 248-754-9200	**Officers:** Timothy M. Manganello - Chairman, Chief Executive Officer James R. Verrier - President, Chief Executive Officer, Vice President, Chief Operating Officer	**Investor Contact:** 248-754-0881 **Transfer Agents:** BNY Mellon Shareowner Services, Jersey City, NJ

BOSTON PROPERTIES, INC.

Exchange	Symbol	Price	52Wk Range	Yield	P/E
NYS	BXP	$101.06 (3/28/2013)	116.07-99.03	2.57	52.64

*7 Year Price Score 105.00 *NYSE Composite Index=100 ***12 Month Price Score 89.97**

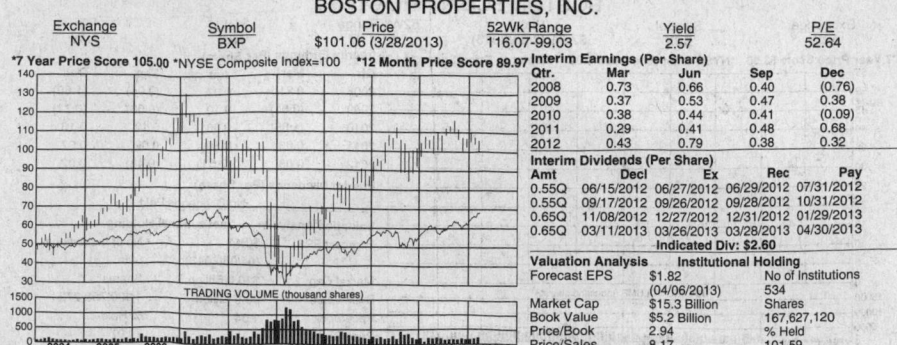

Interim Earnings (Per Share)

Qtr.	Mar	Jun	Sep	Dec
2008	0.73	0.66	0.40	(0.76)
2009	0.37	0.53	0.47	0.38
2010	0.38	0.44	0.41	(0.09)
2011	0.29	0.41	0.48	0.68
2012	0.43	0.79	0.38	0.32

Interim Dividends (Per Share)

Amt	Decl	Ex	Rec	Pay
0.55Q	06/15/2012	06/27/2012	06/29/2012	07/31/2012
0.55Q	09/17/2012	09/26/2012	09/28/2012	10/31/2012
0.65Q	11/08/2012	12/27/2012	12/31/2012	01/29/2013
0.65Q	03/11/2013	03/26/2013	03/28/2013	04/30/2013

Indicated Div: $2.60

Valuation Analysis **Institutional Holding**

Forecast EPS	$1.82
	(04/06/2013)
Market Cap	$15.3 Billion
Book Value	$5.2 Billion
Price/Book	2.94
Price/Sales	8.17

No of Institutions	534
Shares	167,627,120
% Held	101.59

Business Summary: REITs (MIC: 5.3.1 SIC: 6798 NAIC: 525930)

Boston Properties is a real estate investment trust. Co. owns and develops office properties in the U.S. At Dec 31 2010, Co. owned or had interests in 153 properties, totaling approximately 42.2 million net rentable square feet, consisting of: 146 office properties including 128 Class A office properties (including six properties under construction) and 18 Office/Technical properties; one hotel; three retail properties; and three residential properties, with one under construction. Co.'s segments by geographic area are Boston, New York, Princeton, San Francisco and Washington, DC. Segments by property type include: Class A Office, Office/Technical, Residential and Hotel.

Recent Developments: For the year ended Dec 31 2012, income from continuing operations decreased 5.7% to US$294.2 million from US$311.9 million a year earlier. Net income increased 5.8% to US$332.1 million from US$313.8 million in the prior year. Revenues were US$1.88 billion, up 7.1% from US$1.75 billion the year before. Revenues from property income rose 7.2% to US$1.80 billion from US$1.68 billion in the corresponding earlier year.

Prospects: Our evaluation of Boston Properties Inc. as of Apr. 7, 2013 is the result of our systematic analysis on three basic characteristics: earnings strength, relative valuation, and recent stock price movement. The company has generated a negative trend in earnings per share over the past 5 quarters. Because the company lacks sufficient analyst estimate data, we place greater weight on the historical EPS trend as the measure of earnings strength. Based on operating earnings yield, the company is overvalued when compared to all of the companies in our coverage universe. Share price changes over the past year indicates that BXP will perform in line with the market over the near term.

Financial Data

(US$ in Thousands)	12/31/2012	12/31/2011	12/31/2010	12/31/2009	12/31/2008	12/31/2007	12/31/2006	12/31/2005
Earnings Per Share	1.92	1.86	1.14	1.76	1.03	10.94	7.46	3.86
Cash Flow Per Share	4.27	4.16	2.70	4.71	4.66	5.30	4.60	4.24
Tang Book Value Per Share	34.35	33.23	31.59	32.41	29.14	30.70	27.43	25.92
Dividends Per Share	2.300	2.050	2.000	2.180	2.720	8.700	8.120	5.190
Dividend Payout %	119.79	110.22	175.44	123.86	264.08	79.52	108.85	134.46
Income Statement								
Total Revenue	1,876,267	1,759,526	1,550,804	1,522,249	1,488,400	1,482,289	1,477,586	1,437,635
EBITDA	1,470,211	1,366,059	1,290,190	881,213	1,067,489	911,406	894,339	882,106
Depn & Amortn	454,044	439,184	338,371	321,681	304,147	288,978	276,759	267,641
Income Before Taxes	602,603	532,744	573,740	236,699	491,370	336,541	319,320	306,374
Net Income	289,650	272,679	159,072	231,014	125,232	1,324,690	873,635	438,292
Average Shares	150,711	146,218	140,057	131,512	121,299	120,780	117,077	113,559
Balance Sheet								
Current Assets	2,152,220	2,836,349	1,629,480	2,197,161	918,934	2,052,428	1,135,961	642,138
Total Assets	15,462,321	14,782,966	13,348,263	12,348,703	10,911,645	11,192,637	9,695,022	8,902,368
Current Liabilities	382,051	316,145	329,417	376,683	336,085	1,145,049	1,008,267	265,377
Long-Term Obligations	8,912,369	8,704,138	7,786,001	6,719,771	6,271,916	5,492,166	4,600,937	4,826,254
Total Liabilities	10,254,380	9,861,316	8,919,968	7,847,049	7,380,378	7,523,812	6,471,796	5,985,022
Stockholders' Equity	5,207,941	4,921,650	4,428,295	4,501,654	3,531,267	3,668,825	3,223,226	2,917,346
Shares Outstanding	151,601	148,107	140,199	138,880	121,180	119,502	117,503	112,542
Statistical Record								
Return on Assets %	1.91	1.94	1.24	1.99	1.13	12.68	9.40	4.88
Return on Equity %	5.70	5.83	3.56	5.75	3.47	38.44	28.45	14.98
EBITDA Margin %	78.36	77.64	83.19	57.89	71.72	61.49	60.53	61.36
Net Margin %	15.44	15.50	10.26	15.18	8.41	89.37	59.13	30.49
Asset Turnover	0.12	0.13	0.12	0.13	0.13	0.14	0.16	0.16
Current Ratio	5.63	8.97	4.95	5.83	2.73	1.79	1.13	2.42
Debt to Equity	1.71	1.77	1.76	1.49	1.78	1.50	1.43	1.65
Price Range	116.07-97.49	112.36-84.66	90.73-62.49	70.80-31.49	105.04-43.28	130.75-88.71	118.00-75.36	76.25-56.93
P/E Ratio	60.45-50.78	60.41-45.52	79.59-54.82	40.23-17.89	101.98-42.02	11.95-8.11	15.82-10.10	19.75-14.75
Average Yield %	2.16	2.10	2.54	4.13	3.16	8.03	8.56	7.69

Address: Prudential Center, 800 Boylston Street, Suite 1900, Boston, MA 02199-8103 **Telephone:** 617-236-3300 **Fax:** 617-536-3128	**Web Site:** www.bostonproperties.com **Officers:** Mortimer B. Zuckerman - Chairman, Executive Chairman, Chief Executive Officer Douglas T. Linde - President, Chief Merchandising Officer, Principal Operating Officer	**Auditors:** PricewaterhouseCoopers LLP **Investor Contact:** 617-236-3343 **Transfer Agents:** Computershare Trust Company, N.A., Providence, RI

BOSTON SCIENTIFIC CORP.

Exchange	Symbol	Price	52Wk Range	Yield	P/E
NYS	BSX	$7.81 (3/28/2013)	7.81-4.97	N/A	N/A

*7 Year Price Score 53.50 ***NYSE Composite Index=100** ***12 Month Price Score 114.86**

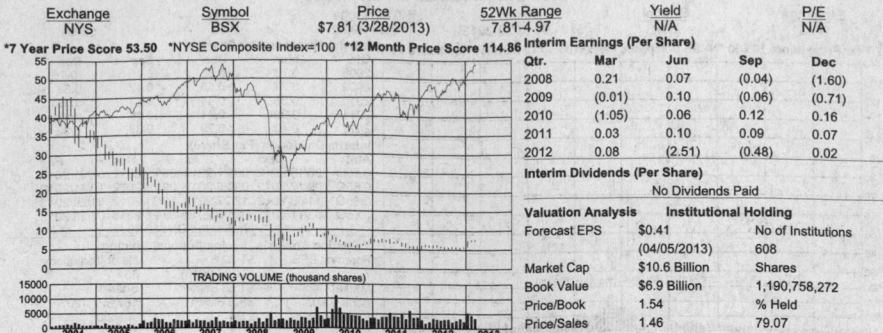

Interim Earnings (Per Share)

Qtr.	Mar	Jun	Sep	Dec
2008	0.21	0.07	(0.04)	(1.60)
2009	(0.01)	0.10	(0.06)	(0.71)
2010	(1.05)	0.06	0.12	0.16
2011	0.03	0.10	0.09	0.07
2012	0.08	(2.51)	(0.48)	0.02

Interim Dividends (Per Share)

No Dividends Paid

Valuation Analysis   **Institutional Holding**

Forecast EPS	$0.41	No of Institutions
	(04/05/2013)	608
Market Cap	$10.6 Billion	Shares
Book Value	$6.9 Billion	1,190,758,272
Price/Book	1.54	% Held
Price/Sales	1.46	79.07

Business Summary: Medical Instruments & Equipment (MIC: 4.3.1 SIC: 3841 NAIC: 339112)

Boston Scientific is a developer, manufacturer and marketer of medical devices that are used in a range of interventional medical field. As of Dec 31 2012, Co. sold its products by seven core businesses, Interventional Cardiology, Cardiac Rhythm Management, Endoscopy, Peripheral Interventions, Urology/Women's Health, Neuromodulation, and Electrophysiology. Co. sells its products in the following geographic regions: the U.S.; Europe, the Middle East and Africa; Japan; and Inter-Continental, consisting of Asia Pacific and the Americas, which include the emerging markets of Brazil, China and India. Co. markets its products to hospitals, clinics, outpatient facilities and medical offices.

Recent Developments: For the year ended Dec 31 2012, net loss amounted to US$4.07 billion versus net income of US$441.0 million in the prior year. Revenues were US$7.25 billion, down 4.9% from US$7.62 billion the year before. Operating loss was US$3.87 billion versus an income of US$904.0 million in the prior year. Direct operating expenses declined 11.7% to US$2.35 billion from US$2.66 billion in the comparable period the year before. Indirect operating expenses increased 116.0% to US$8.77 billion from US$4.06 billion in the equivalent prior-year period.

Prospects: Our evaluation of Boston Scientific Corp. as of Apr. 7, 2013 is the result of our systematic analysis on three basic characteristics: earnings strength, relative valuation, and recent stock price movement. The company has produced a positive trend in earnings per share over the past 5 quarters. However, while recent estimates for the company have been mixed, BSX has posted results that were in line with analysts expectations. Based on operating earnings yield, the company is about fairly valued when compared to all of the companies in our coverage universe. Share price changes over the past year indicates that BSX will perform poorly over the near term.

Financial Data

(US$ in Thousands)	12/31/2012	12/31/2011	12/31/2010	12/31/2009	12/31/2008	12/31/2007	12/31/2006	12/31/2005
Earnings Per Share	(2.89)	0.29	(0.70)	(0.68)	(1.36)	(0.33)	(2.81)	0.75
Cash Flow Per Share	0.89	0.67	0.21	0.55	0.81	0.63	1.45	1.09
Tang Book Value Per Share	N.M.	N.M.	N.M.	N.M.	N.M.	N.M.	N.M.	0.67
Income Statement								
Total Revenue	7,249,000	7,622,000	7,806,000	8,188,000	8,050,000	8,357,000	7,821,000	6,283,000
EBITDA	(3,563,000)	1,219,000	(367,000)	(578,000)	(1,242,000)	299,000	(2,849,000)	1,143,000
Depn & Amortn	288,000	296,000	303,000	323,000	321,000	298,000	251,000	162,000
Income Before Taxes	(4,107,000)	642,000	(1,063,000)	(1,308,000)	(2,031,000)	(569,000)	(3,535,000)	891,000
Income Taxes	(39,000)	201,000	2,000	(283,000)	5,000	(74,000)	42,000	263,000
Net Income	(4,068,000)	441,000	(1,065,000)	(1,025,000)	(2,036,000)	(495,000)	(3,577,000)	628,000
Average Shares	1,406,700	1,519,000	1,517,800	1,507,900	1,498,500	1,486,900	1,273,700	837,600
Balance Sheet								
Current Assets	3,022,000	3,105,000	3,615,000	4,061,000	5,452,000	5,921,000	4,901,000	2,631,000
Total Assets	17,154,000	21,290,000	22,128,000	25,177,000	27,139,000	31,197,000	31,096,000	8,196,000
Current Liabilities	1,772,000	1,807,000	2,609,000	3,022,000	3,233,000	3,250,000	2,630,000	1,479,000
Long-Term Obligations	4,252,000	4,257,000	4,934,000	5,915,000	6,743,000	7,933,000	8,895,000	1,864,000
Total Liabilities	10,284,000	9,937,000	10,832,000	12,876,000	13,965,000	16,100,000	15,798,000	3,914,000
Stockholders' Equity	6,870,000	11,353,000	11,296,000	12,301,000	13,174,000	15,097,000	15,298,000	4,282,000
Shares Outstanding	1,355,711	1,449,055	1,520,780	1,510,753	1,501,635	1,491,234	1,474,674	820,349
Statistical Record								
Return on Assets %	N.M.	2.03	N.M.	N.M.	N.M.	N.M.	N.M.	7.67
Return on Equity %	N.M.	3.89	N.M.	N.M.	N.M.	N.M.	N.M.	15.12
EBITDA Margin %	N.M.	15.99	N.M.	N.M.	N.M.	3.58	N.M.	18.19
Net Margin %	N.M.	5.79	N.M.	N.M.	N.M.	N.M.	N.M.	10.00
Asset Turnover	0.38	0.35	0.33	0.31	0.28	0.27	0.40	0.77
Current Ratio	1.71	1.72	1.39	1.34	1.69	1.82	1.86	1.78
Debt to Equity	0.62	0.37	0.44	0.48	0.51	0.53	0.58	0.44
Price Range	6.36-4.97	7.79-5.09	9.62-5.13	11.75-6.14	14.11-5.48	18.59-11.47	26.48-14.65	35.55-22.95
P/E Ratio	...	26.86-17.55	...	...	...	...	...	47.40-30.60

Address: One Boston Scientific Place, Natick, MA 01760-1537 Telephone: 508-650-8000 Fax: 508-647-2200	Web Site: www.bostonscientific.com Officers: Peter M. Nicholas - Chairman Michael F. Mahoney - President, Chief Executive Officer	Auditors: Ernst & Young LLP Investor Contact: 508-650-8023 Transfer Agents: Computershare Shareowner Services

BOYD GAMING CORP.

Exchange	Symbol	Price	52Wk Range	Yield	P/E
NYS	BYD	$8.27 (3/28/2013)	8.66-4.76	N/A	N/A

*7 Year Price Score 33.40   *NYSE Composite Index=100   *12 Month Price Score 100.07

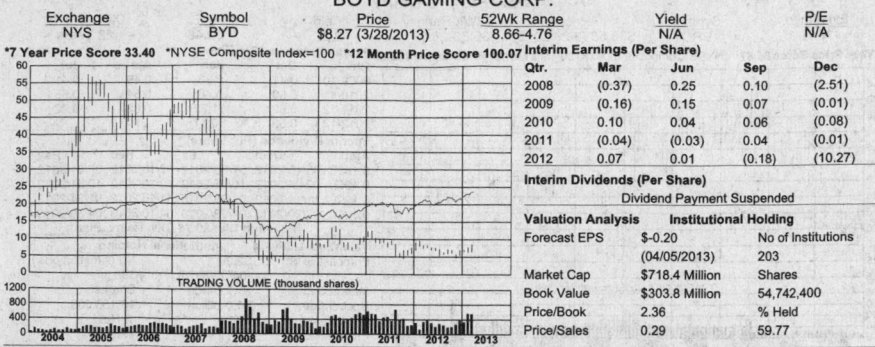

Interim Earnings (Per Share)

Qtr.	Mar	Jun	Sep	Dec
2008	(0.37)	0.25	0.10	(2.51)
2009	(0.16)	0.15	0.07	(0.01)
2010	0.10	0.04	0.06	(0.08)
2011	(0.04)	(0.03)	0.04	(0.01)
2012	0.07	0.01	(0.18)	(10.27)

Interim Dividends (Per Share)

Dividend Payment Suspended

Valuation Analysis	Institutional Holding
Forecast EPS $-0.20	No of Institutions
(04/05/2013)	203
Market Cap $718.4 Million	Shares
Book Value $303.8 Million	54,742,400
Price/Book 2.36	% Held
Price/Sales 0.29	59.77

TRADING VOLUME (thousand shares)

Business Summary: Hotels, Restaurants & Travel (MIC: 2.2.1 SIC: 7011 NAIC: 721120)

Boyd Gaming is a gaming company. As of Dec 31 2011, Co. had gaming operations in Nevada, Illinois, Louisiana, Mississippi, Indiana and New Jersey. Co. also owned and operated Dania Jai-Alai, which is a pari-mutuel jai-alai facility located in Dania Beach, FL; a travel agency in Hawaii; and an insurance company that underwrites travel-related insurance in Hawaii; and owned 87 acres of land on the Las Vegas Strip, where its Echelon development project is located. As of the same date, Co. had four reportable segments: Las Vegas Locals; Downtown Las Vegas; Midwest and South; and Atlantic City.

Recent Developments: For the year ended Dec 31 2012, net loss amounted to US$923.1 million versus a net loss of US$8.0 million in the prior year. Revenues were US$2.49 billion, up 6.5% from US$2.34 billion the year before. Operating loss was US$854.9 million versus an income of US$233.1 million in the prior year. Direct operating expenses rose 8.4% to US$1.40 billion from US$1.29 billion in the comparable period the year before. Indirect operating expenses increased 139.1% to US$1.94 billion from US$813.5 million in the equivalent prior-year period.

Prospects: Our evaluation of Boyd Gaming Corp. as of Apr. 7, 2013 is the result of our systematic analysis on three basic characteristics: earnings strength, relative valuation, and recent stock price movement. The company has suffered a very negative trend in earnings per share over the past 5 quarters. Because the company lacks sufficient analyst estimate data, we place greater weight on the historical EPS trend as the measure of earnings strength. Based on operating earnings yield, the company is overvalued when compared to all of the companies in our coverage universe. Share price changes over the past year indicates that BYD will perform very poorly over the near term.

Financial Data
(US$ in Thousands)

	12/31/2012	12/31/2011	12/31/2010	12/31/2009	12/31/2008	12/31/2007	12/31/2006	12/31/2005
Earnings Per Share	(10.37)	(0.04)	0.12	0.05	(2.54)	3.42	1.30	1.60
Cash Flow Per Share	1.62	2.91	3.29	2.79	2.50	3.24	4.75	4.74
Tang Book Value Per Share	N.M.	4.79	5.97	6.05	5.78	5.05	2.28	2.09
Dividends Per Share	...	...	...	...	0.300	0.585	0.530	0.460
Dividend Payout %	...	...	...	...	...	17.11	40.77	28.75
Income Statement								
Total Revenue	2,487,426	2,336,238	2,140,899	1,640,986	1,780,967	1,997,119	2,192,634	2,223,020
EBITDA	(655,512)	435,007	383,937	245,740	(23,082)	410,392	518,749	457,607
Depn & Amortn	199,500	190,600	199,000	165,725	173,734	171,139	212,673	179,723
Income Before Taxes	(1,143,847)	(6,278)	16,243	(66,809)	(305,892)	101,799	160,643	149,085
Income Taxes	(220,772)	1,721	8,236	1,076	(26,531)	64,027	85,491	84,050
Net Income	(908,865)	(3,854)	10,310	4,241	(223,005)	303,035	116,778	144,610
Average Shares	87,652	87,263	86,831	86,517	87,854	88,608	89,593	90,507
Balance Sheet								
Current Assets	355,593	342,894	279,876	192,737	214,448	339,128	374,678	288,161
Total Assets	6,332,193	5,883,054	5,702,546	4,459,957	4,605,427	4,487,596	3,901,299	4,424,971
Current Liabilities	750,564	472,020	612,215	295,359	353,323	380,132	331,990	439,826
Long-Term Obligations	4,827,853	3,347,226	3,193,065	2,576,911	2,647,058	2,265,929	2,133,016	2,552,795
Total Liabilities	6,028,402	4,680,962	4,513,341	3,303,588	3,461,905	3,102,190	2,791,347	3,326,967
Stockholders' Equity	303,791	1,202,092	1,189,205	1,156,369	1,143,522	1,385,406	1,109,952	1,098,004
Shares Outstanding	86,871	86,572	86,244	86,130	87,814	87,747	87,105	89,286
Statistical Record								
Return on Assets %	N.M.	N.M.	0.20	0.09	N.M.	7.22	2.81	3.47
Return on Equity %	N.M.	N.M.	0.88	0.37	N.M.	24.29	10.58	14.17
EBITDA Margin %	N.M.	18.62	17.93	14.98	N.M.	20.55	23.66	20.58
Net Margin %	N.M.	N.M.	0.48	0.26	N.M.	15.17	5.33	6.51
Asset Turnover	0.41	0.40	0.42	0.36	0.39	0.48	0.53	0.53
Current Ratio	0.47	0.73	0.46	0.65	0.61	0.89	1.13	0.66
Debt to Equity	15.89	2.78	2.69	2.23	2.31	1.64	1.92	2.32
Price Range	9.61-4.76	12.42-4.48	13.78-6.80	12.61-3.08	34.07-3.02	53.15-34.07	54.01-33.54	57.50-37.87
P/E Ratio	...	...	114.83-56.67	252.20-61.60	...	15.54-9.96	41.55-25.80	35.94-23.67
Average Yield %	...	...	...	...	2.09	1.31	1.24	0.95

Address: 3883 Howard Hughes Parkway, Ninth Floor, Las Vegas, NV 89169
Telephone: 702-792-7200

Web Site: www.boydgaming.com
Officers: William S. Boyd - Executive Chairman, Chief Executive Officer Marianne Boyd Johnson - Vice-Chairman, Executive Vice President

Auditors: Deloitte & Touche LLP
Investor Contact: 702-792-7234
Transfer Agents: Wells Fargo Shareowner Services, South St. Paul, MN

BRADY CORP.

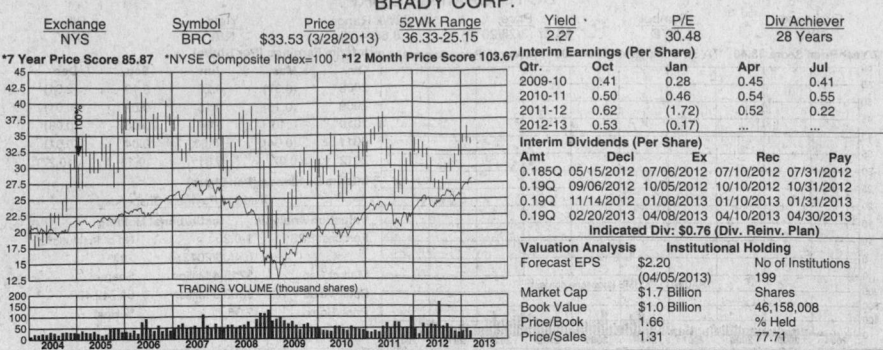

Exchange	Symbol	Price	52Wk Range	Yield ·	P/E	Div Achiever
NYS	BRC	$33.53 (3/28/2013)	36.33-25.15	2.27	30.48	28 Years

*7 Year Price Score 85.87   *NYSE Composite Index=100   *12 Month Price Score 103.67

Interim Earnings (Per Share)

Qtr.	Oct	Jan	Apr	Jul
2009-10	0.41	0.28	0.45	0.41
2010-11	0.50	0.46	0.54	0.55
2011-12	0.62	(1.72)	0.52	0.22
2012-13	0.53	(0.17)	...	...

Interim Dividends (Per Share)

Amt	Decl	Ex	Rec	Pay
0.185Q	05/15/2012	07/06/2012	07/10/2012	07/31/2012
0.19Q	09/06/2012	10/05/2012	10/10/2012	10/31/2012
0.19Q	11/14/2012	01/08/2013	01/10/2013	01/31/2013
0.19Q	02/20/2013	04/08/2013	04/10/2013	04/30/2013

Indicated Div: $0.76 (Div. Reinv. Plan)

Valuation Analysis   **Institutional Holding**

Forecast EPS	$2.20 (04/05/2013)	No of Institutions 199
Market Cap	$1.7 Billion	Shares
Book Value	$1.0 Billion	46,158,008
Price/Book	1.66	% Held
Price/Sales	1.31	77.71

Business Summary: Electrical Equipment (MIC: 7.3.1 SIC: 3999 NAIC: 339950)

Brady is a manufacturer and marketer of identification applications and other products. Co. operates three business platforms: Identification Solution, which includes products such as facility identification, labeling systems, spill control, lockout/tagout, materials and printing systems for product identification, handheld printers, wire markets, self-expiring name tags, badges, and access control software and products; Direct Marketing, which includes products such as informational signs, tags, security and traffic related products, first aid supplies, material handling, asset identification, and regulatory products; and Die-Cut, which includes customized precision die-cut products.

Recent Developments: For the quarter ended Jan 31 2013, net loss amounted to US$8.7 million versus a net loss of US$90.0 million in the year-earlier quarter. Revenues were US$324.2 million, up 1.1% from US$320.6 million the year before. Operating income was US$25.5 million versus a loss of US$77.2 million in the prior-year quarter. Direct operating expenses rose 4.1% to US$174.1 million from US$167.3 million in the comparable period the year before. Indirect operating expenses decreased 45.9% to US$124.6 million from US$230.5 million in the equivalent prior-year period.

Prospects: Our evaluation of Brady Corp. as of Apr. 7, 2013 is the result of our systematic analysis on three basic characteristics: earnings strength, relative valuation, and recent stock price movement. The company has produced a positive trend in earnings per share over the past 5 quarters. However, while recent estimates for the company have been lowered by analysts, BRC has posted results that fell short of analysts expectations. Based on operating earnings yield, the company is undervalued when compared to all of the companies in our coverage universe. Share price changes over the past year indicates that BRC will perform well over the near term.

Financial Data

(US$ in Thousands)	6 Mos	3 Mos	07/31/2012	07/31/2011	07/31/2010	07/31/2009	07/31/2008	07/31/2007
Earnings Per Share	1.10	(0.45)	(0.35)	2.04	1.55	1.33	2.41	2.00
Cash Flow Per Share	2.84	2.93	2.75	3.18	3.15	2.41	4.15	2.52
Tang Book Value Per Share	N.M.	5.47	4.82	5.00	2.53	1.60	1.64	0.07
Dividends Per Share	0.750	0.745	0.740	0.720	0.700	0.680	0.600	0.560
Dividend Payout %	68.18	...	...	35.29	45.16	51.13	24.90	28.00
Income Statement								
Total Revenue	661,828	337,646	1,324,269	1,339,597	1,259,096	1,208,702	1,523,016	1,362,631
EBITDA	93,226	55,508	85,827	215,009	183,646	177,024	273,159	228,718
Depn & Amortn	22,046	10,675	43,987	48,827	53,022	54,851	60,587	53,856
Income Before Taxes	62,611	40,670	22,750	144,058	109,402	97,272	186,187	151,928
Income Taxes	44,107	13,482	40,661	35,406	27,446	27,150	53,999	42,540
Net Income	18,504	27,188	(17,911)	108,652	81,956	70,122	132,188	109,388
Average Shares	51,177	51,312	52,453	53,133	52,946	52,866	54,873	54,741
Balance Sheet								
Current Assets	543,017	692,482	650,854	758,287	668,972	509,427	699,085	583,413
Total Assets	1,785,969	1,651,424	1,607,719	1,861,505	1,746,531	1,583,267	1,850,513	1,698,857
Current Liabilities	381,477	272,191	267,018	301,881	293,788	222,472	308,561	280,054
Long-Term Obligations	264,417	259,729	254,944	331,914	382,940	346,457	457,143	478,575
Total Liabilities	748,119	610,458	598,366	705,313	741,504	632,175	828,705	807,845
Stockholders' Equity	1,037,850	1,040,966	1,009,353	1,156,192	1,005,027	951,092	1,021,808	891,012
Shares Outstanding	51,250	51,102	51,554	53,132	52,624	52,529	53,753	54,125
Statistical Record								
Return on Assets %	3.32	N.M.	N.M.	6.02	4.92	4.08	7.43	7.14
Return on Equity %	5.55	N.M.	N.M.	10.05	8.38	7.11	13.78	13.36
EBITDA Margin %	14.09	16.44	6.48	16.05	14.59	14.65	17.94	16.79
Net Margin %	2.80	8.05	N.M.	8.11	6.51	5.80	8.68	8.03
Asset Turnover	0.76	0.75	0.76	0.74	0.76	0.70	0.86	0.89
Current Ratio	1.42	2.54	2.44	2.51	2.28	2.29	2.27	2.08
Debt to Equity	0.25	0.25	0.25	0.29	0.38	0.36	0.45	0.54
Price Range	35.00-25.15	34.40-25.15	34.40-24.73	38.49-25.35	35.28-24.37	39.68-14.61	43.78-28.58	40.52-30.91
P/E Ratio	31.82-22.86	...	...	18.87-12.43	22.76-15.72	29.83-10.98	18.17-11.86	20.26-15.46
Average Yield %	2.48	2.49	2.51	2.23	2.37	2.69	1.71	1.58

Address: 6555 West Good Hope Road, Milwaukee, WI 53223 Telephone: 414-358-6600	Web Site: www.bradycorp.com Officers: Frank M. Jaehnert - President; Chief Executive Officer Thomas J. Felmer - Senior Vice President, Chief Financial Officer, Division Officer	Auditors: Deloitte & Touche LLP Investor Contact: 414-438-6895 Transfer Agents: Wells Fargo Bank Minnesota, N.A., St. Paul, MN

BRANDYWINE REALTY TRUST

Exchange	Symbol	Price	52Wk Range	Yield	P/E
NYS	BDN	$14.85 (3/28/2013)	14.85-10.66	4.04	N/A

*7 Year Price Score 67.54 ***NYSE Composite Index=100** ***12 Month Price Score 104.23**

Interim Earnings (Per Share)

Qtr.	Mar	Jun	Sep	Dec
2008	0.15	0.08	0.01	0.17
2009	(0.03)	0.03	0.04	0.00
2010	(0.02)	(0.06)	(0.06)	(0.05)
2011	(0.02)	(0.06)	0.03	(0.05)
2012	0.05	0.01	0.10	(0.22)

Interim Dividends (Per Share)

Amt	Decl	Ex	Rec	Pay
0.15Q	05/31/2012	07/02/2012	07/05/2012	07/19/2012
0.15Q	09/11/2012	10/03/2012	10/05/2012	10/19/2012
0.15Q	12/11/2012	01/02/2013	01/04/2013	01/18/2013
0.15Q	03/13/2013	04/03/2013	04/05/2013	04/19/2013

Indicated Div: $0.60

Valuation Analysis

		Institutional Holding	
Forecast EPS	$-0.02	No of Institutions	
	(04/06/2013)	299	
Market Cap	$2.1 Billion	Shares	
Book Value	$1.8 Billion	154,885,344	
Price/Book	1.22	% Held	
Price/Sales	3.81	101.36	

TRADING VOLUME (thousand shares)

Business Summary: REITs (MIC: 5.3.1 SIC: 6798 NAIC: 525930)

Brandywine Realty Trust is a real estate investment trust. Co. provides leasing, property management, development, redevelopment, acquisition and other tenant-related services for a portfolio of office and industrial properties. Co. owns its assets and conducts its operations through Brandywine Operating Partnership, L.P. and its subsidiaries. As of Dec 31 2011, Co. owned and consolidated 232 properties. Co. also owned interests in 18 unconsolidated real estate ventures. Co. manages its portfolio within seven segments: Pennsylvania Suburbs, Philadelphia Central Business District, Metropolitan Washington D.C, New Jersey/Delaware, Richmond, VA, Austin, TX and California.

Recent Developments: For the year ended Dec 31 2012, loss from continuing operations was US$30.2 million compared with a loss of US$19.0 million a year earlier. Net income amounted to US$6.5 million versus a net loss of US$4.7 million in the prior year. Revenues were US$559.8 million, down 0.3% from US$561.8 million the year before. Revenues from property income fell 0.6% to US$541.7 million from US$544.8 million in the corresponding earlier year.

Prospects: Our evaluation of Brandywine Realty Trust as of Apr. 7, 2013 is the result of our systematic analysis on three basic characteristics: earnings strength, relative valuation, and recent stock price movement. The company has managed to produce a neutral trend in earnings per share over the past 5 quarters. Because the company lacks sufficient analyst estimate data, we place greater weight on the historical EPS trend as the measure of earnings strength. Based on operating earnings yield, the company is overvalued when compared to all of the companies in our coverage universe. Share price changes over the past year indicates that BDN will perform poorly over the near term.

Financial Data
(US$ in Thousands)

	12/31/2012	12/31/2011	12/31/2010	12/31/2009	12/31/2008	12/31/2007	12/31/2006	12/31/2005
Earnings Per Share	(0.06)	(0.10)	(0.19)	...	0.41	0.55	0.03	0.62
Cash Flow Per Share	1.09	1.32	1.41	1.97	2.63	2.52	2.70	2.24
Tang Book Value Per Share	11.72	12.52	13.03	13.83	17.14	17.53	18.30	18.28
Dividends Per Share	0.600	0.600	0.600	0.600	1.760	1.760	1.300	1.780
Dividend Payout %	...	...	...	...	429.27	320.00	4,333.33	287.10
Income Statement								
Total Revenue	559,833	581,805	566,897	582,219	608,111	683,972	662,801	391,460
EBITDA	458,579	456,804	421,498	445,884	468,099	536,661	548,317	280,254
Depn & Amortn	206,148	220,284	193,260	192,426	198,897	231,393	252,771	103,134
Income Before Taxes	115,446	101,937	95,050	114,354	122,821	142,137	129,275	104,133
Net Income	6,595	(4,499)	(17,074)	8,026	43,480	56,453	10,482	42,767
Average Shares	143,257	135,444	131,743	113,251	87,583	87,321	90,070	56,104
Balance Sheet								
Current Assets	139,213	125,595	130,729	102,472	133,433	105,755	139,482	85,580
Total Assets	4,506,709	4,557,718	4,690,378	4,663,750	4,737,690	5,214,099	5,508,263	2,805,745
Current Liabilities	178,178	193,393	216,410	110,398	104,112	123,100	151,160	81,515
Long-Term Obligations	2,465,330	2,393,995	2,430,446	2,454,577	2,753,672	3,100,969	3,152,230	1,521,384
Total Liabilities	2,754,431	2,701,127	2,840,876	2,780,318	3,080,846	3,470,864	3,610,337	1,700,881
Stockholders' Equity	1,752,278	1,856,591	1,849,502	1,883,432	1,656,844	1,743,235	1,897,926	1,104,864
Shares Outstanding	143,538	142,690	134,485	128,582	88,158	87,015	88,327	56,179
Statistical Record								
Return on Assets %	0.15	N.M.	N.M.	0.17	0.87	1.05	0.25	1.57
Return on Equity %	0.36	N.M.	N.M.	0.45	2.55	3.10	0.70	3.80
EBITDA Margin %	81.91	78.51	74.35	76.58	76.98	78.46	82.73	71.59
Net Margin %	1.18	N.M.	N.M.	1.38	7.15	8.25	1.58	10.92
Asset Turnover	0.12	0.13	0.12	0.12	0.12	0.13	0.16	0.14
Current Ratio	0.78	0.65	0.60	0.93	1.28	0.86	0.92	1.05
Debt to Equity	1.41	1.29	1.31	1.30	1.66	1.78	1.66	1.38
Price Range	12.88-9.40	12.76-7.09	13.36-10.00	11.85-2.52	19.86-3.73	36.14-17.78	35.37-27.65	32.71-26.30
P/E Ratio	...	...	...	...	48.44-9.10	65.71-32.33	N.M.	52.76-42.42
Average Yield %	5.17	5.65	5.17	7.68	11.92	6.19	4.14	6.11

Address: 555 East Lancaster Avenue, Radnor, PA 19087 Telephone: 610-325-5600	Web Site: www.brandywinerealty.com Officers: Gerard H. Sweeney - President, Chief Executive Officer Howard M. Sipzner - Executive Vice President, Chief Financial Officer	Auditors: PricewaterhouseCoopers LLP Investor Contact: 610-832-7702 Transfer Agents: Computershare, Providence, RI

BRE PROPERTIES, INC.

Exchange	Symbol	Price	52Wk Range	Yield	P/E
NYS	BRE	$48.68 (3/28/2013)	53.26-46.46	3.25	27.98

*7 Year Price Score 96.47 *NYSE Composite Index=100 *12 Month Price Score 90.64

Interim Earnings (Per Share)

Qtr.	Mar	Jun	Sep	Dec
2008	0.28	0.31	0.80	1.12
2009	0.25	0.54	0.31	(0.15)
2010	0.10	0.26	0.30	(0.01)
2011	0.15	0.09	0.23	0.46
2012	0.24	0.37	0.17	0.96

Interim Dividends (Per Share)

Amt	Decl	Ex	Rec	Pay
0.385Q	05/01/2012	06/13/2012	06/15/2012	06/29/2012
0.385Q	07/31/2012	09/12/2012	09/14/2012	09/28/2012
0.385Q	10/30/2012	12/12/2012	12/14/2012	12/31/2012
0.395Q	02/04/2013	03/13/2013	03/15/2013	03/29/2013

Indicated Div: $1.58

Valuation Analysis / **Institutional Holding**

Forecast EPS	$1.06 (04/05/2013)	No of Institutions 304
Market Cap	$3.7 Billion	Shares
Book Value	$1.7 Billion	76,130,640
Price/Book	2.22	% Held
Price/Sales	9.60	95.62

Business Summary: REITs (MIC: 5.3.1 SIC: 6798 NAIC: 525930)

BRE Properties is a self-administered equity real estate investment trust focused on the ownership, operation, development, and acquisition of apartment communities. Co.'s operating and investment activities are primarily focused on the major markets within the state of California, and in the Seattle, WA region. Co. also owns and operates apartment communities in the Phoenix, AZ market and in the Denver, CO market. Co.'s portfolio had real estate assets that included wholly or majority owned completed apartment communities, multifamily communities owned in joint ventures, and apartment communities in various stages of construction and development.

Recent Developments: For the year ended Dec 31 2012, income from continuing operations increased 23.8% to US$71.5 million from US$57.8 million a year earlier. Net income increased 74.0% to US$137.6 million from US$79.1 million in the prior year. Revenues were US$390.1 million, up 7.5% from US$363.1 million the year before. Revenues from property income rose 7.2% to US$375.0 million from US$349.7 million in the corresponding earlier year.

Prospects: Our evaluation of BRE Properties Inc. as of Apr. 7, 2013 is the result of our systematic analysis on three basic characteristics: earnings strength, relative valuation, and recent stock price movement. The company has enjoyed a very positive trend in earnings per share over the past 5 quarters. Because the company lacks sufficient analyst estimate data, we place greater weight on the historical EPS trend as the measure of earnings strength. Based on operating earnings yield, the company is overvalued when compared to all of the companies in our coverage universe. Share price changes over the past year indicates that BRE will perform poorly over the near term.

Financial Data

(US$ in Thousands)	12/31/2012	12/31/2011	12/31/2010	12/31/2009	12/31/2008	12/31/2007	12/31/2006	12/31/2005
Earnings Per Share	1.74	0.93	0.67	0.95	2.50	2.11	1.96	1.22
Cash Flow Per Share	2.63	2.42	2.29	2.48	3.26	3.11	3.37	2.48
Tang Book Value Per Share	21.92	21.31	19.73	18.55	18.47	18.11	19.35	20.00
Dividends Per Share	1.540	1.500	1.500	1.875	2.250	2.150	2.050	2.000
Dividend Payout %	88.51	161.29	223.88	197.37	90.00	101.90	104.59	163.93
Income Statement								
Total Revenue	390,138	371,381	341,973	344,604	350,919	345,163	329,968	298,133
EBITDA	232,547	233,532	186,251	209,294	231,388	230,066	235,237	191,572
Depn & Amortn	101,618	103,940	94,384	88,419	81,459	79,949	74,834	74,276
Income Before Taxes	62,839	54,997	7,528	38,141	64,130	67,365	80,204	40,743
Net Income	137,144	77,887	53,389	62,455	140,811	128,081	120,195	80,948
Average Shares	76,920	71,670	61,420	52,761	51,700	51,780	52,150	51,790
Balance Sheet								
Current Assets	73,672	23,217	19,618	32,771	43,367	43,923	38,953	37,242
Total Assets	3,498,982	3,352,621	3,156,247	2,980,008	2,991,329	2,953,660	2,823,491	2,704,390
Current Liabilities	75,789	63,273	52,070	56,409	91,039	80,406	77,192	55,999
Long-Term Obligations	1,731,960	1,662,671	1,792,918	1,867,075	1,926,096	1,919,082	1,668,910	1,560,574
Total Liabilities	1,812,500	1,742,172	1,879,854	1,957,089	2,046,403	2,030,468	1,846,646	1,678,248
Stockholders' Equity	1,686,482	1,610,449	1,276,393	1,022,919	944,926	923,192	976,845	1,026,142
Shares Outstanding	76,925	75,556	64,675	55,136	51,149	50,968	50,484	51,312
Statistical Record								
Return on Assets %	3.99	2.39	1.74	2.09	4.72	4.43	4.35	3.10
Return on Equity %	8.30	5.40	4.64	6.35	15.03	13.48	12.00	7.81
EBITDA Margin %	59.61	62.88	54.46	60.73	65.94	66.65	71.29	64.26
Net Margin %	35.15	20.97	15.61	18.12	40.13	37.11	36.43	27.15
Asset Turnover	0.11	0.11	0.11	0.12	0.12	0.12	0.12	0.11
Current Ratio	0.97	0.37	0.38	0.58	0.48	0.55	0.50	0.67
Debt to Equity	1.03	1.03	1.40	1.83	2.04	2.08	1.71	1.52
Price Range	53.26-46.46	54.25-40.66	45.91-30.79	34.41-17.81	52.16-19.31	71.77-39.97	66.30-47.21	47.47-34.90
P/E Ratio	30.61-26.70	58.33-43.72	68.52-45.96	36.22-18.75	20.86-7.72	34.01-18.94	33.83-24.09	38.91-28.61
Average Yield %	3.10	3.16	3.81	7.23	5.31	3.74	3.63	4.88

Address: 525 Market Street, 4th Floor, San Francisco, CA 94105-2712
Telephone: 415-445-6530

Web Site: www.breproperties.com
Officers: Irving F. Lyons - Chairman Constance B. Moore - President, Chief Executive Officer, Chief Operating Officer

Auditors: Ernst & Young LLP
Investor Contact: 415-445-6500
Transfer Agents: Wells Fargo Shareowner Services, Minneapolis, MN

BRINKER INTERNATIONAL, INC.

Exchange	Symbol	Price	52Wk Range	Yield	P/E
NYS	EAT	$37.65 (3/28/2013)	37.65-26.65	2.12	18.73

*7 Year Price Score 124.04 *NYSE Composite Index=100   *12 Month Price Score 97.44

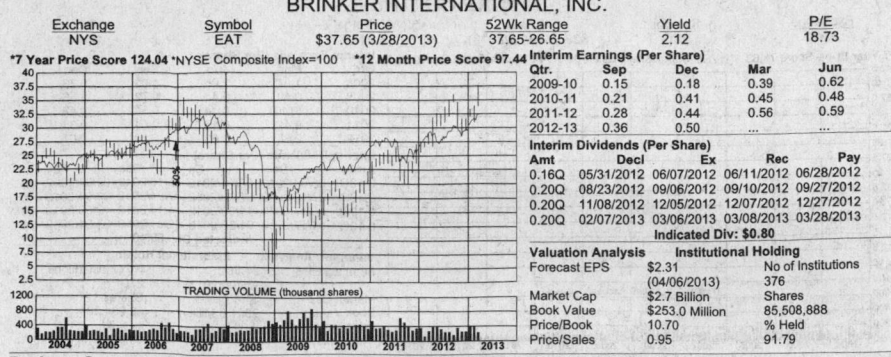

Interim Earnings (Per Share)

Qtr.	Sep	Dec	Mar	Jun
2009-10	0.15	0.18	0.39	0.62
2010-11	0.21	0.41	0.45	0.48
2011-12	0.28	0.44	0.56	0.59
2012-13	0.36	0.50	...	...

Interim Dividends (Per Share)

Amt	Decl	Ex	Rec	Pay
0.16Q	05/31/2012	06/07/2012	06/11/2012	06/28/2012
0.20Q	08/23/2012	09/06/2012	09/10/2012	09/27/2012
0.20Q	11/08/2012	12/05/2012	12/07/2012	12/27/2012
0.20Q	02/07/2013	03/06/2013	03/08/2013	03/28/2013

Indicated Div: $0.80

Valuation Analysis | **Institutional Holding**

Forecast EPS	$2.31 (04/06/2013)	No of Institutions 376
Market Cap	$2.7 Billion	Shares 85,508,888
Book Value	$253.0 Million	% Held 91.79
Price/Book	10.70	
Price/Sales	0.95	

Business Summary: Hotels, Restaurants & Travel (MIC: 2.2.1 SIC: 5812 NAIC: 722110)

Brinker International owns, develops, operates and franchises the Chili's Grill & Bar (Chili's) and Maggiano's Little Italy (Maggiano's) restaurant brands. Co.'s Chili's restaurants menu includes Baby Back Ribs, Big Mouth Burgers, Sizzling Fajitas, Chicken Crispers and Chips and Salsa, as well as a range of appetizers, entrees and desserts. Co.'s Maggiano's Italian-American restaurants serve appetizers, entrees with pasta, chicken, seafood, veal and steaks, and desserts, as well as alcoholic beverages. At June 27 2012, Co.'s system of company-owned and franchised restaurants included 1,581 restaurants located in 50 states and Washington, D.C. Co. also has restaurants in other countries.

Recent Developments: For the quarter ended Dec 26 2012, net income increased 4.2% to US$37.2 million from US$35.7 million in the year-earlier quarter. Revenues were US$689.8 million, up 1.2% from US$681.9 million the year before. Operating income was US$61.6 million versus US$55.9 million in the prior-year quarter, an increase of 10.1%. Direct operating expenses rose 0.8% to US$564.0 million from US$559.6 million in the comparable period the year before. Indirect operating expenses decreased 3.3% to US$64.2 million from US$66.4 million in the equivalent prior-year period.

Prospects: Our evaluation of Brinker International Inc. as of Apr. 7, 2013 is the result of our systematic analysis on three basic characteristics: earnings strength, relative valuation, and recent stock price movement. The company has generated a negative trend in earnings per share over the past 5 quarters. However, while recent estimates for the company have been mixed, EAT has posted better than expected results. Based on operating earnings yield, the company is undervalued when compared to all of the companies in our coverage universe. Share price changes over the past year indicates that EAT will perform poorly over the near term.

Financial Data
(US$ in Thousands)

	6 Mos	3 Mos	06/27/2012	06/29/2011	06/30/2010	06/24/2009	06/25/2008	06/27/2007
Earnings Per Share	2.01	1.95	1.87	1.53	1.34	0.77	0.49	1.85
Cash Flow Per Share	4.42	4.13	3.87	2.87	2.86	2.70	3.52	4.02
Tang Book Value Per Share	1.77	1.95	2.48	3.80	5.95	5.05	4.49	6.05
Dividends Per Share	0.720	0.680	0.640	0.560	0.470	0.440	0.420	0.337
Dividend Payout %	35.82	34.87	34.22	36.60	35.07	57.14	85.71	18.20
Income Statement								
Total Revenue	1,373,271	683,507	2,820,722	2,761,386	2,858,498	3,620,580	4,235,223	4,376,904
EBITDA	175,241	79,970	360,663	340,087	296,333	281,045	266,228	538,431
Depn & Amortn	65,608	32,629	125,054	128,447	135,832	160,977	165,512	189,032
Income Before Taxes	95,678	40,452	208,809	183,329	131,986	86,738	54,854	318,470
Income Taxes	30,637	12,588	57,577	42,269	28,264	7,572	3,132	88,421
Net Income	65,041	27,864	151,232	141,060	137,704	79,166	51,722	230,049
Average Shares	74,720	76,558	80,664	92,320	103,044	102,713	104,897	124,116
Balance Sheet								
Current Assets	262,604	190,639	194,846	221,360	501,067	369,215	454,721	364,181
Total Assets	1,501,206	1,431,856	1,436,072	1,484,568	1,852,104	1,948,947	2,193,122	2,318,021
Current Liabilities	431,384	356,636	401,749	405,601	449,877	408,882	526,169	525,082
Long-Term Obligations	684,171	671,031	587,890	502,572	524,511	727,447	901,604	826,918
Total Liabilities	1,248,223	1,163,767	1,126,199	1,045,658	1,123,356	1,302,023	1,598,033	1,512,932
Stockholders' Equity	252,983	268,089	309,873	438,910	728,748	646,924	595,089	805,089
Shares Outstanding	71,893	73,117	74,342	82,938	101,571	102,124	101,316	110,127
Statistical Record								
Return on Assets %	10.50	10.84	10.38	8.48	7.13	3.83	2.30	10.16
Return on Equity %	50.50	48.07	40.51	24.23	19.70	12.78	7.41	24.53
EBITDA Margin %	12.76	11.70	12.79	12.32	10.37	7.76	6.29	12.30
Net Margin %	4.74	4.08	5.36	5.11	4.82	2.19	1.22	5.26
Asset Turnover	1.90	1.98	1.94	1.66	1.48	1.75	1.88	1.93
Current Ratio	0.61	0.53	0.48	0.55	1.11	0.90	0.86	0.69
Debt to Equity	2.70	2.50	1.90	1.15	0.72	1.12	1.52	1.03
Price Range	35.98-25.66	35.98-20.07	32.69-20.01	26.03-14.12	20.71-12.60	20.84-3.99	30.14-15.32	35.50-21.15
P/E Ratio	17.90-12.77	18.45-10.29	17.48-10.70	17.01-9.23	15.46-9.40	27.06-5.18	61.51-31.27	19.19-11.43
Average Yield %	2.33	2.38	2.46	2.67	2.87	3.09	1.84	1.14

Address: 6820 LBJ Freeway, Dallas, TX 75240	**Web Site:** www.brinker.com	**Auditors:** KPMG LLP
Telephone: 972-980-9917	**Officers:** Douglas H. Brooks - Chairman, President, Chief Executive Officer Wyman T. Roberts - President, Chief Executive Officer, Division Officer	**Investor Contact:** 972-980-9917 **Transfer Agents:** BNY Mellon Share Owner Services, Jersey City, NJ

BRINKS CO (THE)

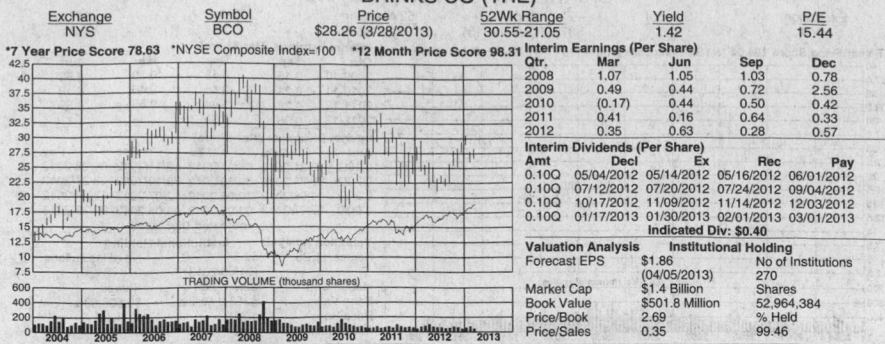

Exchange	Symbol	Price	52Wk Range	Yield	P/E
NYS	BCO	$28.26 (3/28/2013)	30.55-21.05	1.42	15.44

*7 Year Price Score 78.63   *NYSE Composite Index=100   *12 Month Price Score 98.31

Interim Earnings (Per Share)

Qtr.	Mar	Jun	Sep	Dec
2008	1.07	1.05	1.03	0.78
2009	0.49	0.44	0.72	2.56
2010	(0.17)	0.44	0.50	0.42
2011	0.41	0.16	0.64	0.33
2012	0.35	0.63	0.28	0.57

Interim Dividends (Per Share)

Amt	Decl	Ex	Rec	Pay
0.10Q	05/04/2012	05/14/2012	05/16/2012	06/01/2012
0.10Q	07/12/2012	07/20/2012	07/24/2012	09/04/2012
0.10Q	10/17/2012	11/09/2012	11/14/2012	12/03/2012
0.10Q	01/17/2013	01/30/2013	02/01/2013	03/01/2013

Indicated Div: $0.40

Valuation Analysis

Forecast EPS	$1.86 (04/05/2013)
Market Cap	$1.4 Billion
Book Value	$501.8 Million
Price/Book	2.69
Price/Sales	0.35

Institutional Holding

No of Institutions	270
Shares	52,964,384
% Held	99.46

Business Summary: Business Services (MIC: 7.5.2 SIC: 4731 NAIC: 488510)

Brink's is a provider of logistics and security applications. Other services provided are armored transportation, automated teller machine replenishment and servicing; network infrastructure services; secure global transportation of valuables; currency deposit processing and cash management services. Cash management services include cash logistics services; deploying and servicing safes and safe control devices; coin sorting and wrapping, integrated check and cash processing services; providing bill payment acceptance and processing services to utility companies and other billers; and guarding services (including airport security or Aviation Security).

Recent Developments: For the year ended Dec 31 2012, income from continuing operations increased 5.9% to US$127.6 million from US$120.5 million a year earlier. Net income increased 11.4% to US$109.7 million from US$98.5 million in the prior year. Revenues were US$3.84 billion, up 2.0% from US$3.77 billion the year before. Operating income was US$171.2 million versus US$199.5 million in the prior year, a decrease of 14.2%. Direct operating expenses rose 2.0% to US$3.12 billion from US$3.06 billion in the comparable period the year before. Indirect operating expenses increased 8.5% to US$552.4 million from US$509.0 million in the equivalent prior-year period.

Prospects: Our evaluation of Brink's Co as of Apr. 7, 2013 is the result of our systematic analysis on three basic characteristics: earnings strength, relative valuation, and recent stock price movement. The company has generated a negative trend in earnings per share over the past 5 quarters and while recent estimates for the company have remained steady, BCO has posted results that fell short of analysts expectations. Based on operating earnings yield, the company is undervalued when compared to all of the companies in our coverage universe. Share price changes over the past year indicates that BCO will perform very well over the near term.

Financial Data
(US$ in Thousands)

	12/31/2012	12/31/2011	12/31/2010	12/31/2009	12/31/2008	12/31/2007	12/31/2006	12/31/2005
Earnings Per Share	1.83	1.55	1.18	4.21	3.93	2.92	11.64	2.50
Cash Flow Per Share	5.16	5.17	4.88	4.14	9.20	9.76	0.65	5.58
Tang Book Value Per Share	4.22	2.41	4.07	5.26	1.17	18.17	12.49	12.22
Dividends Per Share	0.400	0.400	0.400	0.400	0.400	0.362	0.212	0.100
Dividend Payout %	21.86	25.81	33.90	9.50	10.18	12.41	1.83	4.00
Income Statement								
Total Revenue	3,842,100	3,885,500	3,121,500	3,135,000	3,163,500	3,219,000	2,837,600	2,549,000
EBITDA	342,000	332,100	283,000	282,500	338,900	426,000	333,400	231,800
Depn & Amortn	174,600	162,400	136,600	135,100	122,300	153,500	133,100	119,800
Income Before Taxes	148,500	151,600	135,700	146,900	219,600	270,300	201,000	102,700
Income Taxes	26,900	59,400	67,100	(61,100)	53,000	102,200	82,700	49,500
Net Income	88,900	74,500	57,100	200,200	183,300	137,300	587,200	142,400
Average Shares	48,600	48,100	48,400	47,500	46,700	47,000	50,500	57,000
Balance Sheet								
Current Assets	995,500	933,900	877,400	690,100	832,400	845,700	750,800	1,701,800
Total Assets	2,553,900	2,406,200	2,270,500	1,879,800	1,815,800	2,394,300	2,188,000	3,036,900
Current Liabilities	743,000	702,100	676,000	520,300	535,100	639,900	606,700	1,125,800
Long-Term Obligations	335,600	335,300	323,700	172,300	173,000	89,200	126,300	251,900
Total Liabilities	2,052,100	1,998,200	1,754,300	1,344,900	1,601,800	1,348,000	1,434,200	2,199,400
Stockholders' Equity	501,800	408,000	516,200	534,900	214,000	1,046,300	753,800	837,500
Shares Outstanding	47,800	46,900	46,400	47,900	45,700	48,400	48,500	58,700
Statistical Record								
Return on Assets %	3.57	3.19	2.75	10.83	8.68	5.99	22.48	4.98
Return on Equity %	19.49	16.12	10.86	53.47	29.01	15.25	73.80	18.84
EBITDA Margin %	8.90	8.55	9.07	9.01	10.71	13.23	11.75	9.09
Net Margin %	2.31	1.92	1.83	6.39	5.79	4.27	20.69	5.59
Asset Turnover	1.54	1.66	1.50	1.70	1.50	1.40	1.09	0.89
Current Ratio	1.34	1.33	1.30	1.33	1.56	1.32	1.24	1.51
Debt to Equity	0.67	0.82	0.63	0.32	0.81	0.09	0.17	0.30
Price Range	29.62-21.05	34.28-21.85	29.29-18.39	31.07-21.38	40.53-18.90	37.62-29.81	35.90-26.47	26.89-16.81
P/E Ratio	16.19-11.50	22.12-14.10	24.82-15.58	7.38-5.08	10.31-4.81	12.88-10.21	3.08-2.27	10.76-6.73
Average Yield %	1.61	1.43	1.66	1.50	1.20	1.07	0.72	0.48

Address: 1801 Bayberry Court, Richmond, VA 23226-8100	Web Site: www.brinks.com	Auditors: KPMG LLP
Telephone: 804-289-9600	Officers: Thomas C. Schievelbein - Chairman, President, Chief Executive Officer, interim Executive Chairman, Interim President, Interim Chief Executive Officer Holly R. Tyson - Vice President	Investor Contact: 804-289-9708
Fax: 804-289-9770		Transfer Agents: American Stock Transfer & Trust Company, New York, NY

BRISTOL-MYERS SQUIBB CO.

Exchange	Symbol	Price	52Wk Range	Yield	P/E
NYS	BMY	$41.19 (3/28/2013)	41.19-30.81	3.40	35.51

*7 Year Price Score 113.51 *NYSE Composite Index=100 *12 Month Price Score 101.48

Interim Earnings (Per Share)

Qtr.	Mar	Jun	Sep	Dec
2008	0.33	0.38	1.29	0.63
2009	0.32	0.49	0.48	4.04
2010	0.43	0.53	0.55	0.28
2011	0.57	0.52	0.56	0.50
2012	0.64	0.38	(0.43)	0.55

Interim Dividends (Per Share)

Amt	Decl	Ex	Rec	Pay
0.34Q	06/26/2012	07/03/2012	07/06/2012	08/01/2012
0.34Q	09/18/2012	10/03/2012	10/05/2012	11/01/2012
0.35Q	12/04/2012	01/02/2013	01/04/2013	02/01/2013
0.35Q	03/07/2013	04/03/2013	04/05/2013	05/01/2013

Indicated Div: $1.40

Valuation Analysis | **Institutional Holding**

Forecast EPS	$1.84 (04/05/2013)	No of Institutions 1541
Market Cap	$67.1 Billion	Shares
Book Value	$13.6 Billion	1,194,670,464
Price/Book	4.93	% Held
Price/Sales	3.81	63.09

Business Summary: Pharmaceuticals (MIC: 4.1.1 SIC: 2834 NAIC: 325412)

Bristol-Myers Squibb is engaged in the discovery, development, licensing, manufacturing, marketing, distribution and sale of biopharmaceutical products. Co. has products in the following therapeutic classes, among others: cardiovascular; virology, including human immunodeficiency virus infection; oncology; neuroscience; immunoscience; and metabolics. Co.'s key products include: Abilify, an atypical antipsychotic agent for adult patients with schizophrenia, bipolar mania disorder and major depressive disorder; and Plavix, for protection against fatal or non-fatal heart attack or stroke in patients with a history of heart attack, stroke, peripheral arterial disease or acute coronary syndrome.

Recent Developments: For the year ended Dec 31 2012, net income decreased 52.5% to US$2.50 billion from US$5.26 billion in the prior year. Revenues were US$17.62 billion, down 17.1% from US$21.24 billion the year before. Direct operating expenses declined 17.6% to US$4.61 billion from US$5.60 billion in the comparable period the year before. Indirect operating expenses increased 19.5% to US$10.75 billion from US$9.00 billion in the equivalent prior-year period.

Prospects: Our evaluation of Bristol-Myers Squibb Co. as of Apr. 7, 2013 is the result of our systematic analysis on three basic characteristics: earnings strength, relative valuation, and recent stock price movement. The company has generated a negative trend in earnings per share over the past 5 quarters. However, while recent estimates for the company have been mixed, BMY has posted better than expected results. Based on operating earnings yield, the company is about fairly valued when compared to all of the companies in our coverage universe. Share price changes over the past year indicates that BMY will perform very poorly over the near term.

Financial Data

(US$ in Millions)	12/31/2012	12/31/2011	12/31/2010	12/31/2009	12/31/2008	12/31/2007	12/31/2006	12/31/2005
Earnings Per Share	1.16	2.16	1.79	5.34	2.63	1.09	0.81	1.52
Cash Flow Per Share	4.14	2.85	2.62	2.06	1.87	1.60	1.06	0.94
Tang Book Value Per Share	N.M.	4.29	4.17	3.94	3.16	2.14	1.68	2.28
Dividends Per Share	1.360	1.320	0.960	1.250	1.550	1.120	1.120	1.120
Dividend Payout %	117.24	61.11	53.63	23.41	58.94	102.75	138.27	73.68
Income Statement								
Total Revenue	17,621	21,244	19,484	18,808	20,597	19,348	17,914	19,207
EBITDA	2,798	7,202	6,301	5,651	5,596	3,733	2,949	4,960
Depn & Amortn	382	448	473	469	562	542	564	577
Income Before Taxes	2,340	6,700	5,758	5,052	4,854	3,010	2,161	4,182
Income Taxes	(161)	1,721	1,558	1,182	1,320	803	610	932
Net Income	1,960	3,709	3,102	10,612	5,247	2,165	1,585	3,000
Average Shares	1,688	1,717	1,727	1,978	2,001	1,980	1,963	1,983
Balance Sheet								
Current Assets	9,521	15,318	13,273	13,958	14,763	10,348	10,302	12,283
Total Assets	35,897	32,970	31,076	31,008	29,552	26,172	25,575	28,138
Current Liabilities	8,279	7,780	6,739	6,313	6,710	8,644	6,496	6,890
Long-Term Obligations	6,568	5,376	5,328	6,130	6,585	4,381	7,248	8,364
Total Liabilities	22,274	17,014	15,363	16,165	17,311	15,610	15,584	16,930
Stockholders' Equity	13,623	15,956	15,713	14,843	12,241	10,562	9,991	11,208
Shares Outstanding	1,630	1,690	1,704	1,714	1,979	1,979	1,967	1,957
Statistical Record								
Return on Assets %	5.68	11.58	9.99	35.05	18.78	8.37	5.90	10.24
Return on Equity %	13.22	23.42	20.30	78.36	45.89	21.07	14.95	28.02
EBITDA Margin %	15.88	33.90	32.34	30.05	27.17	19.29	16.46	25.82
Net Margin %	11.12	17.46	15.92	56.42	25.47	11.19	8.85	15.62
Asset Turnover	0.51	0.66	0.63	0.62	0.74	0.75	0.67	0.66
Current Ratio	1.15	1.97	1.97	2.21	2.20	1.20	1.59	1.78
Debt to Equity	0.48	0.34	0.34	0.41	0.54	0.41	0.73	0.75
Price Range	36.15-30.81	35.29-24.97	27.93-22.44	25.96-17.51	27.08-17.26	32.14-26.10	26.32-20.24	26.48-21.03
P/E Ratio	31.16-26.56	16.34-11.56	15.60-12.54	4.86-3.28	10.30-6.56	29.49-23.94	32.49-24.99	17.42-13.84
Average Yield %	4.08	4.56	3.74	5.75	7.15	3.89	4.64	4.62

Address: 345 Park Avenue, New York, NY 10154
Telephone: 212-546-4000
Fax: 212-546-4020

Web Site: www.bms.com
Officers: Lamberto Andreotti - President, Chief Executive Officer Charles A. Bancroft - Executive Vice President, Chief Financial Officer, Acting Chief Financial Officer

Auditors: Deloitte & Touche LLP
Investor Contact: 609-252-4611
Transfer Agents: BNY Mellon Shareowner Services, Jersey City, NJ

BROADRIDGE FINANCIAL SOLUTIONS INC

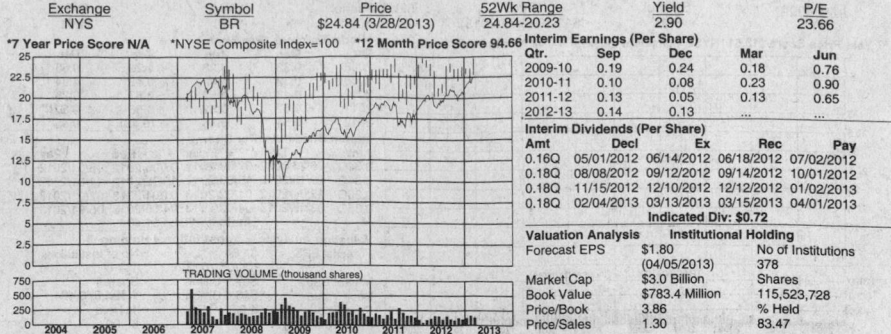

Exchange	Symbol	Price	52Wk Range	Yield	P/E
NYS	BR	$24.84 (3/28/2013)	24.84-20.23	2.90	23.66

*7 Year Price Score N/A   *NYSE Composite Index=100   *12 Month Price Score 94.66

Interim Earnings (Per Share)

Qtr.	Sep	Dec	Mar	Jun
2009-10	0.19	0.24	0.18	0.76
2010-11	0.10	0.08	0.23	0.90
2011-12	0.13	0.05	0.13	0.65
2012-13	0.14	0.13	...	...

Interim Dividends (Per Share)

Amt	Decl	Ex	Rec	Pay
0.16Q	05/01/2012	06/14/2012	06/18/2012	07/02/2012
0.18Q	08/08/2012	09/12/2012	09/14/2012	10/01/2012
0.18Q	11/15/2012	12/10/2012	12/12/2012	01/02/2013
0.18Q	02/04/2013	03/13/2013	03/15/2013	04/01/2013

Indicated Div: $0.72

Valuation Analysis   Institutional Holding

Forecast EPS	$1.80	No of Institutions
	(04/05/2013)	378
Market Cap	$3.0 Billion	Shares
Book Value	$783.4 Million	115,523,728
Price/Book	3.86	% Held
Price/Sales	1.30	83.47

TRADING VOLUME (thousand shares)

Business Summary: Finance Intermediaries & Services (MIC: 5.5.1 SIC: 7389 NAIC: 523999)

Broadridge Financial Solutions is a provider of investor communications and services to banks/broker-dealers, mutual funds and corporate issuers. Co.'s systems and services include investor communication services, securities processing and operations outsourcing services. Co.'s services help its clients serve their customers across the investment lifecycle, including pre-trade, trade, and post-trade processing. Co. has four businesses, Bank/Broker-Dealer Communications, Mutual Fund and Retirement Solutions, Corporate Issuer Solutions, and Bank/Broker-Dealer Technology and Operations, which operate in two segments: Investor Communication Solutions and Securities Processing Solutions.

Recent Developments: For the quarter ended Dec 31 2012, income from continuing operations increased 132.4% to US$15.8 million from US$6.8 million in the year-earlier quarter. Net income increased 132.4% to US$15.8 million from US$6.8 million in the year-earlier quarter. Revenues were US$493.2 million, up 2.8% from US$479.8 million the year before. Direct operating expenses rose 1.3% to US$387.6 million from US$382.6 million in the comparable period the year before. Indirect operating expenses decreased 6.6% to US$80.9 million from US$86.6 million in the equivalent prior-year period.

Prospects: Our evaluation of Broadridge Financial Solutions Inc. as of Apr. 7, 2013 is the result of our systematic analysis on three basic characteristics: earnings strength, relative valuation, and recent stock price movement. The company has managed to produce a neutral trend in earnings per share over the past 5 quarters. However, while recent estimates for the company have been lowered by analysts, BR has posted results that fell short of analysts expectations. Based on operating earnings yield, the company is undervalued when compared to all of the companies in our coverage universe. Share price changes over the past year indicates that BR will perform poorly over the near term.

Financial Data

(US$ in Thousands)	6 Mos	3 Mos	06/30/2012	06/30/2011	06/30/2010	06/30/2009	06/30/2008	06/30/2007
Earnings Per Share	1.05	0.97	0.97	1.32	1.37	1.58	1.36	1.42
Cash Flow Per Share	2.26	2.03	2.34	1.53	2.65	2.56	3.44	1.16
Tang Book Value Per Share	N.M.	N.M.	N.M.	N.M.	1.95	2.56	1.65	0.14
Dividends Per Share	0.680	0.660	0.640	0.600	0.560	0.280	0.240	0.060
Dividend Payout %	64.76	68.04	65.98	45.45	40.88	17.72	17.65	4.23
Income Statement								
Total Revenue	989,000	495,800	2,303,500	2,166,900	2,209,200	2,149,300	2,207,500	2,137,900
EBITDA	81,600	42,600	270,900	313,500	383,500	392,800	388,300	395,000
Depn & Amortn	22,300	11,000	58,500	36,100	32,300	33,000	33,100	62,500
Income Before Taxes	53,300	28,600	200,900	269,700	342,100	346,300	325,900	320,800
Income Taxes	19,200	10,300	75,900	97,900	117,000	123,000	133,700	123,700
Net Income	34,100	18,300	123,600	169,600	190,000	223,300	192,200	197,100
Average Shares	125,500	127,100	127,500	128,300	139,100	141,600	141,000	139,000
Balance Sheet								
Current Assets	653,600	620,900	777,400	751,400	992,400	2,003,600	2,079,200	1,960,000
Total Assets	1,856,200	1,830,500	1,987,600	1,904,000	1,794,400	2,774,700	2,833,600	2,678,200
Current Liabilities	344,400	313,600	410,300	782,700	486,400	1,420,700	1,525,400	1,428,600
Long-Term Obligations	524,400	524,400	524,400	124,300	324,100	324,100	447,900	617,700
Total Liabilities	1,072,800	1,041,000	1,137,100	1,106,700	987,300	1,865,700	2,087,800	2,147,100
Stockholders' Equity	783,400	789,500	850,500	797,300	807,100	909,000	745,800	531,100
Shares Outstanding	121,800	122,100	124,800	123,700	129,200	139,300	140,400	139,300
Statistical Record								
Return on Assets %	7.15	6.66	6.33	9.17	8.32	7.96	6.96	8.19
Return on Equity %	17.13	15.83	14.96	21.14	22.14	26.99	30.02	25.04
EBITDA Margin %	8.25	8.59	11.76	14.47	17.36	18.28	17.59	18.48
Net Margin %	3.45	3.69	5.37	7.83	8.60	10.39	8.71	9.22
Asset Turnover	1.24	1.24	1.18	1.17	0.97	0.77	0.80	0.89
Current Ratio	1.90	1.98	1.89	0.96	2.04	1.41	1.36	1.37
Debt to Equity	0.67	0.66	0.62	0.16	0.40	0.36	0.60	1.16
Price Range	24.85-20.23	24.85-19.18	24.85-19.18	24.07-18.96	24.00-15.47	21.44-9.72	23.96-16.29	21.43-18.91
P/E Ratio	23.67-19.27	25.62-19.77	25.62-19.77	18.23-14.36	17.52-11.29	13.57-6.15	17.62-11.98	15.09-13.32
Average Yield %	2.99	2.95	2.88	2.72	2.68	1.72	1.19	0.30

Address: 1981 Marcus Avenue, Lake Success, NY 11042 Telephone: 516-472-5400	Web Site: www.broadridge.com Officers: John E. Hogan - President, Chief Operating Officer Timothy C. Gokey - Senior Vice President, Chief Operating Officer, Chief Development Officer	Auditors: Deloitte & Touche LLP Transfer Agents: Broadridge Corporate Issuer Solutions, Inc.

BROOKDALE SENIOR LIVING INC

Exchange	Symbol	Price	52Wk Range	Yield	P/E
NYS	BKD	$27.88 (3/28/2013)	29.65-15.19	N/A	N/A

*7 Year Price Score 80.15 *NYSE Composite Index=100 *12 Month Price Score 116.10

Interim Earnings (Per Share)

Qtr.	Mar	Jun	Sep	Dec
2008	(0.54)	(0.03)	(0.36)	(2.74)
2009	(0.13)	(0.10)	(0.18)	(0.18)
2010	(0.12)	(0.08)	(0.14)	(0.07)
2011	(0.10)	(0.28)	(0.06)	(0.12)
2012	(0.09)	(0.15)	(0.10)	(0.20)

Interim Dividends (Per Share)

Dividend Payment Suspended

Valuation Analysis   **Institutional Holding**

Forecast EPS	$-0.05	No of Institutions
	(04/05/2013)	242
Market Cap	$3.5 Billion	Shares
Book Value	$1.0 Billion	121,298,440
Price/Book	3.52	% Held
Price/Sales	1.28	95.31

Business Summary: Hospitals & Health Care Facilities (MIC: 4.2.1 SIC: 8052 NAIC: 623311)

Brookdale Senior Living is a holding company. Through its operating subsidiaries, Co. is an operator of senior living communities, with 647 communities in 36 states at Dec 31 2012. Co. owns, leases and operates retirement centers, assisted living and dementia-care communities and continuing care retirement centers ("CCRCs"). As of Dec 31 2012, Co. operated 76 retirement center communities with 14,528 units, 433 assisted living communities with 21,594 units, 27 rental CCRC communities with 6,748 units, 14 entry fee CCRC communities with 5,866 units and 97 communities with 17,998 units.

Recent Developments: For the year ended Dec 31 2012, net loss amounted to US$65.6 million versus a net loss of US$68.2 million in the prior year. Revenues were US$2.77 billion, up 12.7% from US$2.46 billion the year before. Operating income was US$82.3 million versus US$90.2 million in the prior year, a decrease of 8.8%. Indirect operating expenses increased 13.5% to US$2.69 billion from US$2.37 billion in the equivalent prior-year period.

Prospects: Our evaluation of Brookdale Senior Living Inc. as of Apr. 7, 2013 is the result of our systematic analysis on three basic characteristics: earnings strength, relative valuation, and recent stock price movement. The company has suffered a very negative trend in earnings per share over the past 5 quarters. Because the company lacks sufficient analyst estimate data, we place greater weight on the historical EPS trend as the measure of earnings strength. Based on operating earnings yield, the company is overvalued when compared to all of the companies in our coverage universe. Share price changes over the past year indicates that BKD will perform very well over the near term.

Financial Data
(US$ in Thousands)

	12/31/2012	12/31/2011	12/31/2010	12/31/2009	12/31/2008	12/31/2007	12/31/2006	12/31/2005
Earnings Per Share	(0.54)	(0.56)	(0.41)	(0.60)	(3.67)	(1.60)	(1.34)	(0.41)
Cash Flow Per Share	2.38	2.22	1.90	2.13	1.34	1.97	1.06	0.15
Tang Book Value Per Share	5.79	6.19	6.27	6.32	5.88	7.94	10.97	8.69
Dividends Per Share	...	...	...	...	0.750	1.950	1.550	0.250
Income Statement								
Total Revenue	2,770,085	2,457,918	2,213,264	2,023,068	1,928,054	1,839,296	1,309,913	213,047
EBITDA	331,158	318,473	320,983	266,534	1,313	207,712	134,515	5,055
Depn & Amortn	248,500	247,100	258,000	233,900	242,800	251,200	180,734	17,855
Income Before Taxes	(60,113)	(67,267)	(80,501)	(99,621)	(459,111)	(260,246)	(142,202)	(24,109)
Income Taxes	2,044	2,340	(31,432)	(32,926)	(86,731)	(101,260)	(38,491)	150
Net Income	(65,645)	(68,175)	(48,901)	(66,255)	(373,241)	(161,979)	(108,087)	(24,456)
Average Shares	121,991	121,161	120,010	111,288	101,667	101,511	80,842	59,710
Balance Sheet								
Current Assets	309,038	280,875	328,109	317,421	280,785	291,835	270,232	145,877
Total Assets	4,665,978	4,466,061	4,530,470	4,645,943	4,449,258	4,811,622	4,742,455	1,697,811
Current Liabilities	1,121,503	620,950	606,358	689,309	646,012	549,767	508,905	171,443
Long-Term Obligations	2,169,826	2,415,971	2,498,620	2,459,341	2,390,000	2,317,217	1,852,474	754,169
Total Liabilities	3,663,261	3,425,853	3,470,473	3,559,361	3,488,657	3,392,084	2,978,443	1,067,408
Stockholders' Equity	1,002,717	1,040,208	1,059,997	1,086,582	960,601	1,419,538	1,764,012	630,403
Shares Outstanding	126,689	125,354	124,316	123,206	105,256	104,962	104,542	65,006
Statistical Record								
EBITDA Margin %	11.95	12.96	14.50	13.17	0.07	11.29	10.27	2.37
Asset Turnover	0.61	0.55	0.48	0.44	0.42	0.39	0.41	0.17
Current Ratio	0.28	0.45	0.54	0.46	0.43	0.53	0.53	0.85
Debt to Equity	2.16	2.32	2.36	2.26	2.49	1.63	1.05	1.20
Price Range	25.72-15.19	28.05-11.54	22.07-12.77	20.54-2.55	28.41-3.15	49.70-27.93	52.57-29.36	31.15-25.30
Average Yield %	...	...	...	...	3.96	4.69	3.66	0.88

Address: 111 Westwood Place, Suite 400, Brentwood, TN 37027 Telephone: 615-221-2250	Web Site: www.brookdaleliving.com Officers: Wesley R. Edens - Chairman William B. Doniger - Vice-Chairman	Auditors: Ernst & Young LLP Investor Contact: 615-221-2250 Transfer Agents: American Stock Transfer & Trust Company, New York, NY

BROWN & BROWN, INC.

Exchange	Symbol	Price	52Wk Range	Yield	P/E	Div Achiever
NYS	BRO	$32.04 (3/28/2013)	32.04-23.48	1.12	25.43	19 Years

*7 Year Price Score 101.66 *NYSE Composite Index=100 *12 Month Price Score 102.81

Interim Earnings (Per Share)

Qtr.	Mar	Jun	Sep	Dec
2008	0.37	0.29	0.29	0.23
2009	0.34	0.29	0.29	0.17
2010	0.31	0.29	0.31	0.22
2011	0.32	0.26	0.30	0.25
2012	0.34	0.29	0.34	0.29

Interim Dividends (Per Share)

Amt	Decl	Ex	Rec	Pay
0.085Q	04/24/2012	05/02/2012	05/04/2012	05/16/2012
0.085Q	07/18/2012	08/06/2012	08/08/2012	08/15/2012
0.09Q	10/23/2012	11/05/2012	11/07/2012	11/14/2012
0.09Q	01/16/2013	01/28/2013	01/30/2013	02/13/2013

Indicated Div: $0.36

Valuation Analysis

		Institutional Holding	
Forecast EPS	$1.46 (04/06/2013)	No of Institutions	301
Market Cap	$4.6 Billion	Shares	119,007,680
Book Value	$1.8 Billion	% Held	70.91
Price/Book	2.55		
Price/Sales	3.84		

Business Summary: Brokers & Intermediaries (MIC: 5.2.3 SIC: 6411 NAIC: 524210)

Brown & Brown is an insurance agency, wholesale brokerage, insurance programs and service organization. Co. has four segments: Retail Division, which provides insurance products and services; National Programs Division including Professional Programs, which provides professional liability and related package products, and Special Programs, which markets targeted products and services for specific industries, trade groups, public entities, and market niches; Wholesale Brokerage Division, which markets and sells excess and surplus commercial insurance products and services and reinsurance products and services; and Services Division, which provides insurance-related services, among others.

Recent Developments: For the year ended Dec 31 2012, net income increased 12.2% to US$184.0 million from US$164.0 million in the prior year. Revenues were US$1.20 billion, up 18.4% from US$1.01 billion the year before.

Prospects: Our evaluation of Brown & Brown Inc. as of Apr. 7, 2013 is the result of our systematic analysis on three basic characteristics: earnings strength, relative valuation, and recent stock price movement. The company has enjoyed a very positive trend in earnings per share over the past 5 quarters. However, while recent estimates for the company have been mixed, BRO has posted better than expected results. Based on operating earnings yield, the company is about fairly valued when compared to all of the companies in our coverage universe. Share price changes over the past year indicates that BRO will perform in line with the market over the near term.

Financial Data

(US$ in Thousands)	12/31/2012	12/31/2011	12/31/2010	12/31/2009	12/31/2008	12/31/2007	12/31/2006	12/31/2005
Earnings Per Share	1.26	1.13	1.12	1.08	1.17	1.35	1.22	1.08
Cash Flow Per Share	1.58	1.71	2.15	1.62	2.42	1.53	1.61	1.55
Dividends Per Share	0.345	0.325	0.313	0.302	0.285	0.250	0.210	0.170
Dividend Payout %	27.38	28.76	27.90	28.01	24.36	18.52	17.21	15.74
Income Statement								
Total Revenue	1,200,032	1,013,542	973,492	967,877	977,554	959,667	878,004	785,807
EBITDA	336,281	297,045	293,208	282,593	300,474	338,092	304,707	268,660
Depn & Amortn	15,373	12,392	12,639	13,240	13,286	12,763	11,309	10,061
Income Before Taxes	304,811	270,521	266,098	254,754	272,498	311,527	280,041	244,130
Income Taxes	120,766	106,526	104,346	101,460	106,374	120,568	107,691	93,579
Net Income	184,045	163,995	161,752	153,294	166,124	190,959	172,350	150,551
Average Shares	142,010	140,264	139,318	137,507	141,558	141,257	141,020	139,776
Balance Sheet								
Current Assets	759,512	708,127	652,809	613,699	523,032	587,382	648,206	619,767
Total Assets	3,128,058	2,607,011	2,400,814	2,224,226	2,119,580	1,960,659	1,807,952	1,608,660
Current Liabilities	567,781	481,620	470,157	478,953	522,643	556,123	590,667	582,818
Long-Term Obligations	450,000	250,033	250,067	250,209	253,616	227,707	226,252	214,179
Total Liabilities	1,320,725	963,048	894,470	854,352	877,839	863,201	878,607	844,316
Stockholders' Equity	1,807,333	1,643,963	1,506,344	1,369,874	1,241,741	1,097,458	929,345	764,344
Shares Outstanding	143,878	143,352	142,795	142,076	141,544	140,673	140,016	139,383
Statistical Record								
Return on Assets %	6.40	6.55	6.99	7.06	8.12	10.13	10.09	10.53
Return on Equity %	10.64	10.41	11.25	11.74	14.16	18.84	20.35	21.68
EBITDA Margin %	28.02	29.31	30.12	29.20	30.74	35.23	34.70	34.19
Net Margin %	15.34	16.18	16.62	15.84	16.99	19.90	19.63	19.16
Asset Turnover	0.42	0.40	0.42	0.45	0.48	0.51	0.51	0.55
Current Ratio	1.34	1.47	1.39	1.28	1.00	1.06	1.10	1.06
Debt to Equity	0.25	0.15	0.17	0.18	0.20	0.21	0.24	0.28
Price Range	27.64-22.29	26.91-17.00	24.20-16.50	21.39-15.65	23.96-16.59	28.96-23.10	35.23-27.42	31.24-21.30
P/E Ratio	21.94-17.69	23.81-15.04	21.61-14.73	19.81-14.49	20.48-14.18	21.45-17.11	28.88-22.48	28.93-19.72
Average Yield %	1.36	1.49	1.58	1.61	1.46	0.95	0.69	0.71

Address: 220 South Ridgewood Avenue, Daytona Beach, FL 32114 **Telephone:** 386-252-9601	**Web Site:** www.bbinsurance.com **Officers:** J. Hyatt Brown - Chairman Jim W. Henderson - Vice-Chairman, Chief Operating Officer	**Auditors:** Deloitte & Touche LLP **Investor Contact:** 386-252-9601 **Transfer Agents:** American Stock Transfer & Trust Company, New York, NY

BROWN-FORMAN CORP.

Exchange	Symbol	Price	52Wk Range	Yield	P/E	Div Achiever
NYS	BF B	$71.40 (3/28/2013)	71.40-54.73	1.43	26.35	28 Years

*7 Year Price Score 132.39 *NYSE Composite Index=100   *12 Month Price Score 97.27

Interim Earnings (Per Share)

Qtr.	Jul	Oct	Jan	Apr
2009-10	0.54	0.66	0.49	0.33
2010-11	0.51	0.70	0.64	0.75
2011-12	0.54	0.73	0.62	0.49
2012-13	0.69	0.80	0.73	...

Interim Dividends (Per Share)

Amt	Decl	Ex	Rec	Pay
0.233Q	07/26/2012	09/05/2012	09/07/2012	10/01/2012
0.255Q	11/15/2012	12/03/2012	12/05/2012	12/26/2012
4.00Sp	11/27/2012	12/10/2012	12/12/2012	12/27/2012
0.255Q	01/22/2013	03/06/2013	03/08/2013	04/01/2013

Indicated Div: $1.02

Valuation Analysis

Forecast EPS	$2.68 (04/06/2013)
Market Cap	$15.3 Billion
Book Value	$1.5 Billion
Price/Book	10.04
Price/Sales	5.46

Institutional Holding

No of Institutions	96
Shares	48,095,472
% Held	33.85

Business Summary: Beverages (MIC: 1.2.2 SIC: 2084 NAIC: 312130)

Brown-Forman is primarily engaged in the manufacturing, bottling, importing, exporting, and marketing of a variety of alcoholic beverage brands. Co.'s principal beverage brands are: Jack Daniel's Tennessee Whiskey; Chambord Vodka; Jack Daniel's Single Barrel; Don Eduardo Tequila; Jack Daniel's Ready-to-Drinks; Early Times Bourbon; Jack Daniel's Tennessee Honey; Early Times Kentucky Whisky; Gentleman Jack; el Jimador Tequilas; Southern Comfort; Herradura Tequilas; Southern Comfort Ready-to-Drinks; Korbel California Champagnes; Southern Comfort Ready-to-Pours; Maximus Vodka; Southern Comfort Lime; New Mix Ready-to-Drinks; Southern Comfort Fiery Pepper; and Old Forester Bourbon.

Recent Developments: For the quarter ended Jan 31 2013, net income increased 18.4% to US$157.6 million from US$133.1 million in the year-earlier quarter. Revenues were US$746.9 million, up 6.5% from US$701.6 million the year before. Operating income was US$237.0 million versus US$206.2 million in the prior-year quarter, an increase of 14.9%. Direct operating expenses declined 4.2% to US$240.2 million from US$250.7 million in the comparable period the year before. Indirect operating expenses increased 10.2% to US$269.7 million from US$244.7 million in the equivalent prior-year period.

Prospects: Our evaluation of Brown-Forman Corp. as of Apr. 7, 2013 is the result of our systematic analysis on three basic characteristics: earnings strength, relative valuation, and recent stock price movement. The company has managed to produce a neutral trend in earnings per share over the past 5 quarters. However, while recent estimates for the company have been mixed, BF.B has posted better than expected results. Based on operating earnings yield, the company is about fairly valued when compared to all of the companies in our coverage universe. Share price changes over the past year indicates that BF.B will perform well over the near term.

Financial Data

(US$ in Thousands)	9 Mos	6 Mos	3 Mos	04/30/2012	04/30/2011	04/30/2010	04/30/2009	04/30/2008
Earnings Per Share	2.71	2.60	2.52	2.37	2.60	2.01	1.91	1.90
Cash Flow Per Share	2.54	2.46	2.53	2.40	2.41	2.46	2.18	2.32
Tang Book Value Per Share	1.08	5.12	4.24	3.68	3.52	2.54	2.02	1.49
Dividends Per Share	4.955	0.933	0.913	0.893	1.493	0.783	0.746	0.685
Dividend Payout %	183.07	35.94	36.20	37.64	57.44	38.91	38.99	36.09
Income Statement								
Total Revenue	2,189,400	1,442,500	665,800	2,723,000	2,586,000	2,469,000	2,481,000	2,582,000
EBITDA	757,200	507,600	233,200	837,000	911,000	769,000	716,000	737,000
Depn & Amortn	36,100	23,600	11,500	49,000	56,000	59,000	55,000	52,000
Income Before Taxes	704,000	474,600	217,100	760,000	829,000	682,000	630,000	644,000
Income Taxes	226,000	154,100	69,600	247,000	257,000	233,000	195,000	204,000
Net Income	478,000	320,500	147,500	513,000	572,000	449,000	435,000	440,000
Average Shares	215,051	214,891	214,798	216,150	219,769	222,862	227,283	231,766
Balance Sheet								
Current Assets	2,046,400	2,055,000	1,849,500	1,749,000	1,976,000	1,527,000	1,574,000	1,456,000
Total Assets	3,832,300	3,803,900	3,583,000	3,477,000	3,712,000	3,383,000	3,475,000	3,405,000
Current Liabilities	807,300	505,900	476,300	404,000	707,000	546,000	836,000	984,000
Long-Term Obligations	996,600	501,400	502,100	503,000	504,000	508,000	509,000	417,000
Total Liabilities	2,313,500	1,499,100	1,461,000	1,408,000	1,652,000	1,488,000	1,659,000	1,680,000
Stockholders' Equity	1,518,800	2,304,800	2,122,000	2,069,000	2,060,000	1,895,000	1,816,000	1,725,000
Shares Outstanding	213,615	199,568	199,286	213,111	217,485	220,444	225,190	226,108
Statistical Record								
Return on Assets %	15.51	14.92	14.80	14.23	16.12	13.09	12.65	12.62
Return on Equity %	32.78	25.88	25.88	24.78	28.93	24.20	24.57	26.61
EBITDA Margin %	34.58	35.19	35.03	30.74	35.23	31.15	28.86	28.54
Net Margin %	21.83	22.22	22.15	18.84	22.12	18.19	17.53	17.04
Asset Turnover	0.74	0.73	0.75	0.76	0.73	0.72	0.72	0.74
Current Ratio	2.53	4.06	3.88	4.33	2.79	2.80	1.88	1.48
Debt to Equity	0.66	0.22	0.24	0.24	0.24	0.27	0.28	0.24
Price Range	70.18-53.17	67.17-48.53	64.63-41.49	57.71-41.49	48.68-36.30	40.12-27.83	41.85-24.67	40.31-33.16
P/E Ratio	25.90-19.62	25.83-18.67	25.65-16.47	24.35-17.51	18.72-13.96	19.96-13.85	21.91-12.91	21.22-17.45
Average Yield %	8.11	1.61	1.70	1.76	3.51	2.36	2.19	1.84

Address: 850 Dixie Highway, Louisville, KY 40210 **Telephone:** 502-585-1100 **Fax:** 502-774-7876	**Web Site:** www.brown-forman.com **Officers:** Paul C. Varga - Chairman, Chief Executive Officer James S. Welch - Vice-Chairman, Executive Director	**Auditors:** PricewaterhouseCoopers LLP **Transfer Agents:** Computershare Inc., Providence, RI

BRUNSWICK CORP.

Exchange	Symbol	Price	52Wk Range	Yield	P/E
NYS	BC	$34.22 (3/28/2013)	37.23-19.83	0.15	63.37

*7 Year Price Score 117.47 *NYSE Composite Index=100 *12 Month Price Score 123.37

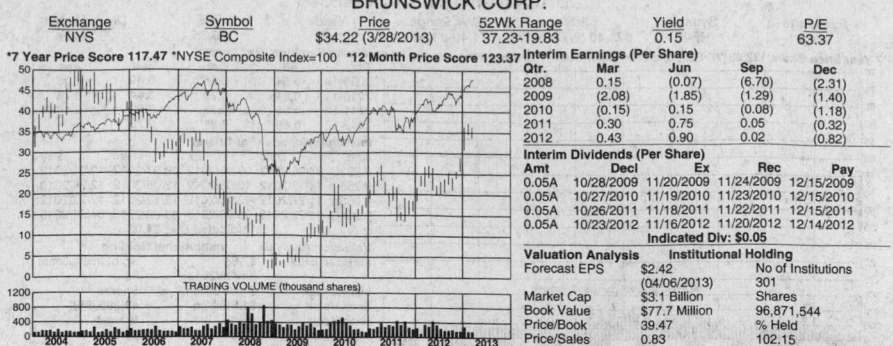

Interim Earnings (Per Share)

Qtr.	Mar	Jun	Sep	Dec
2008	0.15	(0.07)	(6.70)	(2.31)
2009	(2.08)	(1.85)	(1.29)	(1.40)
2010	(0.15)	0.15	(0.08)	(1.18)
2011	0.30	0.75	0.05	(0.32)
2012	0.43	0.90	0.02	(0.82)

Interim Dividends (Per Share)

Amt	Decl	Ex	Rec	Pay
0.05A	10/28/2009	11/20/2009	11/24/2009	12/15/2009
0.05A	10/27/2010	11/19/2010	11/23/2010	12/15/2010
0.05A	10/26/2011	11/18/2011	11/22/2011	12/15/2011
0.05A	10/23/2012	11/16/2012	11/20/2012	12/14/2012

Indicated Div: $0.05

Valuation Analysis   **Institutional Holding**

Forecast EPS	$2.42 (04/06/2013)	No of Institutions 301
Market Cap	$3.1 Billion	Shares
Book Value	$77.7 Million	96,871,544
Price/Book	39.47	% Held
Price/Sales	0.83	102.15

Business Summary: Leisure Equipment (MIC: 1.6.1 SIC: 3511 NAIC: 333611)

Brunswick is a designer, manufacturer and marketer of recreation products. Co. operates in four reportable segments: marine engine, which provides a range of sterndrive propulsion systems, inboard engines and outboard engines; boat, which provides fiberglass pleasure boats, offshore fishing boats, aluminum fishing boats, pontoon and deck boats; fitness, which provides fitness equipment such as treadmills, total body cross-trainers, stair climbers, and strength-training equipment; and bowling and billiards, which provides a line of consumer billiards tables, Air Hockey table games, foosball tables, other gaming tables and related accessories, as well as operates retail bowling centers.

Recent Developments: For the year ended Dec 31 2012, income from continuing operations increased 62.7% to US$147.4 million from US$90.6 million a year earlier. Net income decreased 30.5% to US$50.0 million from US$71.9 million in the prior year. Revenues were US$3.72 billion, up 1.3% from US$3.67 billion the year before. Operating income was US$264.1 million versus US$213.7 million in the prior year, an increase of 23.6%. Direct operating expenses declined 0.7% to US$2.77 billion from US$2.79 billion in the comparable period the year before. Indirect operating expenses increased 2.4% to US$679.9 million from US$663.7 million in the equivalent prior-year period.

Prospects: Our evaluation of Brunswick Corp. as of Apr. 7, 2013 is the result of our systematic analysis on three basic characteristics: earnings strength, relative valuation, and recent stock price movement. The company has generated a negative trend in earnings per share over the past 5 quarters. However, while recent estimates for the company have been mixed, BC has posted better than expected results. Based on operating earnings yield, the company is undervalued when compared to all of the companies in our coverage universe. Share price changes over the past year indicates that BC will perform very well over the near term.

Financial Data

(US$ in Thousands)	12/31/2012	12/31/2011	12/31/2010	12/31/2009	12/31/2008	12/31/2007	12/31/2006	12/31/2005
Earnings Per Share	0.54	0.78	(1.25)	(6.63)	(8.93)	1.24	1.41	3.90
Cash Flow Per Share	1.78	1.00	2.32	1.42	(0.14)	3.50	3.35	4.44
Tang Book Value Per Share	N.M.	N.M.	N.M.	N.M.	4.02	11.07	9.75	9.99
Dividends Per Share	0.050	0.050	0.050	0.050	0.050	0.600	0.600	0.600
Dividend Payout %	9.26	6.41	...	...	...	48.39	42.55	15.38
Income Statement								
Total Revenue	3,717,600	3,748,000	3,403,300	2,776,100	4,708,700	5,671,200	5,665,000	5,923,800
EBITDA	335,900	269,100	128,600	(440,000)	(426,400)	295,100	506,600	678,100
Depn & Amortn	85,900	97,200	119,500	146,100	164,800	180,100	167,300	162,200
Income Before Taxes	184,800	94,000	(81,700)	(669,000)	(638,700)	71,400	294,800	477,700
Income Taxes	33,600	17,400	25,900	(98,500)	155,900	13,100	46,500	110,400
Net Income	50,000	71,900	(110,600)	(586,200)	(788,100)	111,600	133,900	385,400
Average Shares	92,400	92,200	88,700	88,400	88,300	90,200	94,700	98,800
Balance Sheet								
Current Assets	1,360,100	1,356,100	1,535,800	1,458,700	1,736,900	2,114,300	2,078,400	2,235,000
Total Assets	2,424,200	2,494,000	2,678,000	2,709,400	3,223,900	4,365,600	4,450,300	4,621,500
Current Liabilities	937,200	908,100	951,600	906,600	1,001,200	1,296,200	1,293,200	1,305,200
Long-Term Obligations	563,600	690,400	828,400	839,400	728,500	727,400	725,700	723,700
Total Liabilities	2,346,500	2,463,100	2,607,600	2,499,100	2,494,000	2,472,700	2,578,500	2,642,700
Stockholders' Equity	77,700	30,900	70,400	210,300	729,900	1,892,900	1,871,800	1,978,800
Shares Outstanding	89,631	89,104	88,661	88,263	87,745	87,446	90,867	95,657
Statistical Record								
Return on Assets %	2.03	2.78	N.M.	N.M.	N.M.	2.53	2.95	8.60
Return on Equity %	91.83	141.95	N.M.	N.M.	N.M.	5.93	6.95	20.88
EBITDA Margin %	9.04	7.18	3.78	N.M.	N.M.	5.20	8.94	11.45
Net Margin %	1.34	1.92	N.M.	N.M.	N.M.	1.97	2.36	6.51
Asset Turnover	1.51	1.45	1.26	0.94	1.24	1.29	1.25	1.32
Current Ratio	1.45	1.49	1.61	1.61	1.73	1.63	1.61	1.71
Debt to Equity	7.25	22.34	11.77	3.99	1.00	0.38	0.39	0.37
Price Range	29.09-18.49	27.01-13.50	22.69-10.37	13.11-2.18	19.28-2.01	34.80-17.05	42.30-27.56	49.50-35.09
P/E Ratio	53.87-34.24	34.63-17.31	...	...	...	28.06-13.75	30.00-19.55	12.69-9.00
Average Yield %	0.21	0.26	0.32	0.73	0.41	2.13	1.74	1.39

Address: 1 N. Field Court, Lake Forest, IL 60045-4811 **Telephone:** 847-735-4700 **Fax:** 847-735-4765	**Web Site:** www.brunswick.com **Officers:** Dustan E. McCoy - Chairman, Chief Executive Officer William L. Metzger - Senior Vice President, Chief Financial Officer, Vice President, Treasurer	**Auditors:** Ernst & Young LLP **Investor Contact:** 847-735-4612 **Transfer Agents:** ComputerShare Investor Services, Providence, RI

BUCKEYE PARTNERS, L.P.

Exchange	Symbol	Price	52Wk Range	Yield	P/E	Div Achiever
NYS	BPL	$61.16 (3/28/2013)	61.16-44.65	6.79	26.36	17 Years

*7 Year Price Score 88.59 *NYSE Composite Index=100 *12 Month Price Score 100.44

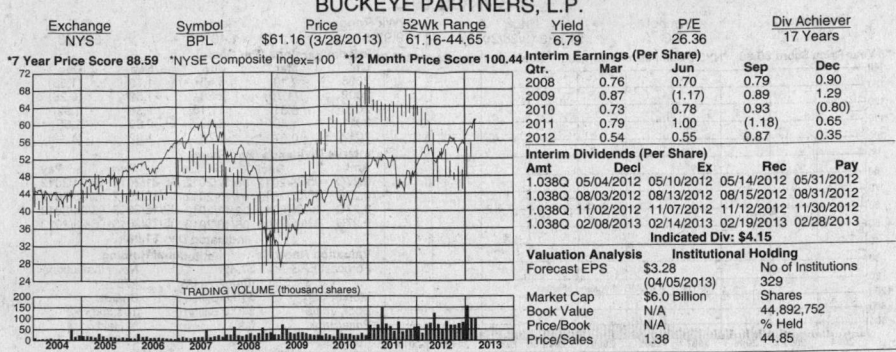

Interim Earnings (Per Share)

Qtr.	Mar	Jun	Sep	Dec
2008	0.76	0.70	0.79	0.90
2009	0.87	(1.17)	0.89	1.29
2010	0.73	0.78	0.93	(0.80)
2011	0.79	1.00	(1.18)	0.65
2012	0.54	0.55	0.87	0.35

Interim Dividends (Per Share)

Amt	Decl	Ex	Rec	Pay
1.038Q	05/04/2012	05/10/2012	05/14/2012	05/31/2012
1.038Q	08/03/2012	08/13/2012	08/15/2012	08/31/2012
1.038Q	11/02/2012	11/07/2012	11/12/2012	11/30/2012
1.038Q	02/08/2013	02/14/2013	02/19/2013	02/28/2013

Indicated Div: $4.15

Valuation Analysis / **Institutional Holding**

Forecast EPS	$3.28 (04/05/2013)	No of Institutions 329
Market Cap	$6.0 Billion	Shares 44,892,752
Book Value	N/A	% Held 44.85
Price/Book	N/A	
Price/Sales	1.38	

Business Summary: Equipment & Services (MIC: 9.1.3 SIC: 4613 NAIC: 486910)

Buckeye Partners is a holding company. Through its subsidiaries, Co. operates in five segments, which include: Pipelines & Terminals, which owns and operates pipeline located primarily in the northeastern and upper midwestern portions of the U.S. and services delivery locations; International Operations, which includes marine terminals that provide bulk storage and throughput services to crude oil and petroleum products; Natural Gas Storage, which operates a natural gas facility in Northern California; Energy Services, which is a wholesale distributor of refined petroleum products in the U.S. in areas; and Development & Logistics, which operates and maintains third-party pipelines.

Recent Developments: For the year ended Dec 31 2012, net income increased 101.1% to US$230.6 million from US$114.7 million in the prior year. Revenues were US$4.36 billion, down 8.5% from US$4.76 billion the year before. Operating income was US$339.2 million versus US$188.7 million in the prior year, an increase of 79.8%. Direct operating expenses declined 11.3% to US$3.74 billion from US$4.22 billion in the comparable period the year before. Indirect operating expenses decreased 21.8% to US$276.2 million from US$353.2 million in the equivalent prior-year period.

Prospects: Our evaluation of Buckeye Partners, L.P. as of Apr. 7, 2013 is the result of our systematic analysis on three basic characteristics: earnings strength, relative valuation, and recent stock price movement. The company has produced a positive trend in earnings per share over the past 5 quarters. However, while recent estimates for the company have been lowered by analysts, BPL has posted better than expected results. Based on operating earnings yield, the company is about fairly valued when compared to all of the companies in our coverage universe. Share price changes over the past year indicates that BPL will perform very poorly over the near term.

Financial Data
(US$ in Thousands)

	12/31/2012	12/31/2011	12/31/2010	12/31/2009	12/31/2008	12/31/2007	12/31/2006	12/31/2005
Earnings Per Share	2.32	1.20	1.65	1.84	3.15	3.03	2.64	2.69
Cash Flow Per Share	4.53	4.47	11.24	1.11	4.50	4.70	3.80	3.84
Dividends Per Share	4.150	4.025	3.825	3.625	3.425	3.225	3.025	2.825
Dividend Payout %	178.88	335.42	231.82	197.01	108.73	106.44	114.58	105.02
Income Statement								
Total Revenue	4,357,242	4,759,610	3,151,268	1,770,372	1,896,652	519,347	461,760	408,446
EBITDA	458,956	329,291	333,514	259,920	304,746	245,134	201,053	175,137
Depn & Amortn	120,200	105,500	54,700	50,700	47,200	39,400	38,700	31,822
Income Before Taxes	223,776	104,230	189,645	134,369	183,159	155,356	110,240	99,958
Income Taxes	(675)	...	...	...	...	...	...	...
Net Income	226,417	108,501	43,080	140,982	184,389	155,356	110,240	99,958
Average Shares	97,635	90,772	26,086	50,663	47,763	42,101	39,202	37,145
Balance Sheet								
Current Assets	634,322	626,036	626,631	613,723	414,028	200,338	129,427	98,368
Total Assets	5,981,009	5,570,376	3,574,216	3,255,649	3,034,410	2,133,652	1,995,470	1,816,867
Current Liabilities	594,366	554,979	516,520	417,733	291,714	92,494	89,549	62,153
Long-Term Obligations	2,735,244	2,393,574	1,519,393	1,498,970	1,445,722	849,177	994,127	899,077
Total Liabilities	3,608,696	3,267,207	2,181,811	2,040,511	1,858,913	1,043,480	1,185,588	1,058,290
Shares Outstanding	98,345	93,273	71,436	51,682	48,616	45,962	39,697	38,162
Statistical Record								
Return on Assets %	3.91	2.37	1.26	4.48	7.12	7.52	5.78	5.97
EBITDA Margin %	10.53	6.92	10.58	14.68	16.07	47.20	43.54	42.88
Net Margin %	5.20	2.28	1.37	7.96	9.72	29.91	23.87	24.47
Asset Turnover	0.75	1.04	0.92	0.56	0.73	0.25	0.24	0.24
Current Ratio	1.07	1.13	1.21	1.47	1.42	2.17	1.45	1.58
Price Range	64.17-44.65	68.52-57.61	69.80-52.33	55.59-32.25	50.29-25.69	55.49-46.00	46.78-40.71	50.21-41.92
P/E Ratio	27.66-19.25	57.10-48.01	42.30-31.72	30.21-17.53	15.97-8.16	18.31-15.18	17.72-15.42	18.67-15.58
Average Yield %	7.84	6.30	6.26	8.27	8.06	6.35	6.93	6.22

Address: One Greenway Plaza, Suite 600, Houston, TX 77046 **Telephone:** 832-615-8600	**Web Site:** www.buckeye.com **Officers:** Clark C. Smith - President, Chief Executive Officer, Chief Operating Officer, Associate/Affiliate Company Officer Keith E. St. Clair - Senior Vice President, Chief Financial Officer, Associate/Affiliate Company Officer	**Auditors:** Deloitte & Touche LLP **Investor Contact:** 800-422-2825 **Transfer Agents:** First Chicago Trust Company a Division of Equiserv, Jersey City, NJ

BUNGE LTD.

Exchange	Symbol	Price	52Wk Range	Yield	P/E
NYS	BG	$73.83 (3/28/2013)	79.92-57.83	1.46	388.58

*7 Year Price Score 86.80   *NYSE Composite Index=100   *12 Month Price Score 100.96

Interim Earnings (Per Share)

Qtr.	Mar	Jun	Sep	Dec
2008	2.10	5.45	1.70	(1.53)
2009	(1.76)	2.28	1.62	(0.26)
2010	0.31	11.15	1.36	1.97
2011	1.49	2.02	0.89	1.65
2012	0.57	1.78	1.92	(4.10)

Interim Dividends (Per Share)

Amt	Decl	Ex	Rec	Pay
0.27Q	05/24/2012	08/17/2012	08/21/2012	09/04/2012
0.27Q	08/02/2012	11/15/2012	11/19/2012	12/03/2012
0.27Q	12/05/2012	02/13/2013	02/15/2013	03/04/2013
0.27Q	03/05/2013	05/16/2013	05/20/2013	06/03/2013

Indicated Div: $1.08

Valuation Analysis   **Institutional Holding**

Forecast EPS	$7.42	No of Institutions
	(04/06/2013)	478
Market Cap	$10.8 Billion	Shares
Book Value	$10.9 Billion	105,398,712
Price/Book	0.99	% Held
Price/Sales	0.18	63.99

Business Summary: Food (MIC: 1.2.1 SIC: 2079 NAIC: 311225)

Bunge is a holding company. Through its subsidiaries, Co. is an agribusiness and food company operating in the farm-to-consumer food chain. Co. conducts its operations in four divisions: agribusiness, which is involved in the purchase, storage, transport, processing and sale of agricultural commodities and commodity products; sugar and bioenergy, which produces and sells sugar and ethanol derived from sugarcane, as well as energy derived from their production process; food and ingredients, which consists of two segments: edible oil products and milling products; and fertilizer, which is involved in producing, blending and distributing fertilizer products for the agricultural industry.

Recent Developments: For the year ended Dec 31 2012, income from continuing operations decreased 60.8% to US$378.0 million from US$965.0 million a year earlier. Net income decreased 96.2% to US$36.0 million from US$940.0 million in the prior year. Revenues were US$60.99 billion, up 8.7% from US$56.10 billion the year before. Direct operating expenses rose 9.3% to US$58.42 billion from US$53.47 billion in the comparable period the year before. Indirect operating expenses increased 37.0% to US$2.20 billion from US$1.61 billion in the equivalent prior-year period.

Prospects: Our evaluation of Bunge Ltd. as of Apr. 7, 2013 is the result of our systematic analysis on three basic characteristics: earnings strength, relative valuation, and recent stock price movement. The company has generated a negative trend in earnings per share over the past 5 quarters and while recent estimates for the company have been mixed, BG has posted results that fell short of analysts expectations. Based on operating earnings yield, the company is undervalued when compared to all of the companies in our coverage universe. Share price changes over the past year indicates that BG will perform well over the near term.

Financial Data

(US$ in Millions)	12/31/2012	12/31/2011	12/31/2010	12/31/2009	12/31/2008	12/31/2007	12/31/2006	12/31/2005
Earnings Per Share	0.19	6.07	15.06	2.22	7.73	5.95	4.28	4.43
Cash Flow Per Share	(3.12)	17.83	(17.25)	(2.91)	20.87	(3.40)	(2.42)	3.41
Tang Book Value Per Share	65.09	68.93	70.99	54.77	44.82	48.66	38.71	32.87
Dividends Per Share	1.040	0.960	0.900	0.820	...	...	...	...
Dividend Payout %	547.37	15.82	5.98	36.94	...	...	...	...
Income Statement								
Total Revenue	60,991	58,743	45,707	41,926	52,574	37,842	26,274	24,275
EBITDA	1,117	1,637	3,699	733	2,112	1,014	1,007	924
Depn & Amortn	504	497	420	427	428	(374)	324	278
Income Before Taxes	372	940	3,050	145	1,537	1,201	522	519
Income Taxes	(6)	44	689	(110)	245	310	(36)	(82)
Net Income	64	942	2,354	361	1,064	778	521	530
Average Shares	147	155	156	127	137	130	120	120
Balance Sheet								
Current Assets	17,264	13,128	15,815	11,783	13,176	14,518	8,393	6,564
Total Assets	27,280	23,275	26,001	21,286	20,230	21,991	14,347	11,446
Current Liabilities	11,561	6,947	10,004	6,207	8,074	8,834	4,515	3,617
Long-Term Obligations	3,532	3,348	2,551	3,618	3,032	3,435	2,874	2,557
Total Liabilities	16,418	11,568	13,781	11,792	12,794	14,046	8,679	7,220
Stockholders' Equity	10,862	11,707	12,220	9,494	7,436	7,945	5,668	4,226
Shares Outstanding	146	143	146	134	121	121	119	119
Statistical Record								
Return on Assets %	0.25	3.82	9.96	1.74	5.03	4.28	4.04	4.74
Return on Equity %	0.57	7.87	21.68	4.26	13.80	11.43	10.53	13.95
EBITDA Margin %	1.83	2.79	8.09	1.75	4.02	2.68	3.83	3.81
Net Margin %	0.10	1.60	5.15	0.86	2.02	2.06	1.98	2.18
Asset Turnover	2.41	2.38	1.93	2.02	2.48	2.08	2.04	2.17
Current Ratio	1.49	1.89	1.58	1.90	1.63	1.64	1.86	1.81
Debt to Equity	0.33	0.29	0.21	0.38	0.41	0.43	0.51	0.61
Price Range	73.82-57.22	75.44-55.51	71.29-46.29	72.41-41.61	133.00-29.99	124.23-70.13	73.17-48.23	67.31-48.30
P/E Ratio	388.53-301.16	12.43-9.14	4.73-3.07	32.62-18.74	17.21-3.88	20.88-11.79	17.10-11.27	15.19-10.90
Average Yield %	1.59	1.47	1.55	1.39	...	...	...	...

Address: 50 Main Street, White Plains, NY 10606	Web Site: www.bunge.com	Auditors: Deloitte & Touche LLP
Telephone: 914-684-2800	Officers: Alberto Weisser - Chairman, Chief Executive Officer Soren Schröder - Chief Executive Officer, Region Officer	Investor Contact: 914-684-3476 Transfer Agents: Computershare Shareowner Services LLC, Jersey City, NJ

CABLEVISION SYSTEMS CORP.

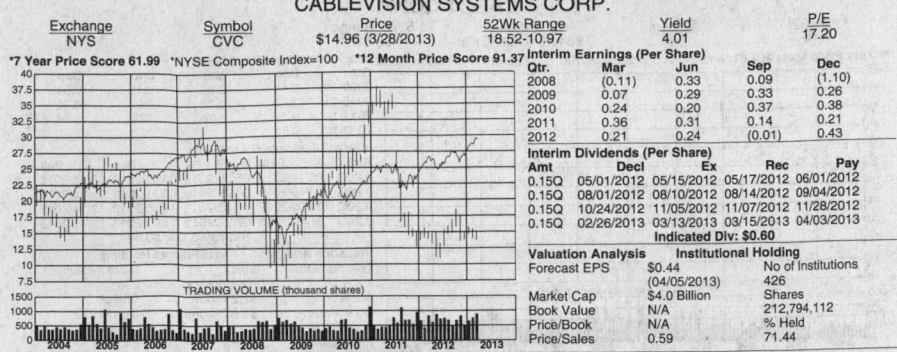

Exchange	Symbol	Price	52Wk Range	Yield	P/E
NYS	CVC	$14.96 (3/28/2013)	18.52-10.97	4.01	17.20

*7 Year Price Score 61.99 *NYSE Composite Index=100 *12 Month Price Score 91.37

Interim Earnings (Per Share)

Qtr.	Mar	Jun	Sep	Dec
2008	(0.11)	0.33	0.09	(1.10)
2009	0.07	0.29	0.33	0.26
2010	0.24	0.20	0.37	0.38
2011	0.36	0.31	0.14	0.21
2012	0.21	0.24	(0.01)	0.43

Interim Dividends (Per Share)

Amt	Decl	Ex	Rec	Pay
0.15Q	05/01/2012	05/15/2012	05/17/2012	06/01/2012
0.15Q	08/01/2012	08/10/2012	08/14/2012	09/04/2012
0.15Q	10/24/2012	11/05/2012	11/07/2012	11/28/2012
0.15Q	02/26/2013	03/13/2013	03/15/2013	04/03/2013

Indicated Div: $0.60

Valuation Analysis

Forecast EPS	$0.44 (04/05/2013)
Market Cap	$4.0 Billion
Book Value	N/A
Price/Book	N/A
Price/Sales	0.59

Institutional Holding

No of Institutions	426
Shares	212,794,112
% Held	71.44

Business Summary: Radio & Television (MIC: 2.3.1 SIC: 4841 NAIC: 515210)

Cablevision Systems, through its CSC Holdings, LLC subsidiary, is a cable operator serving video customers in and around the New York metropolitan area and in Montana, Wyoming, Colorado and Utah. Co. also provides data and Voice over Internet Protocol services using its cable television broadband network. Through its Cablevision Lightpath, Inc. subsidiary, Co. provides telephone services and Internet access to the business market. In addition, Co. owns approximately 97.2% of Newsday LLC, which operates a newspaper publishing business. Co. also owns regional news and high school sports programming services, a motion picture theatre business and a cable television advertising sales business.

Recent Developments: For the year ended Dec 31 2012, income from continuing operations decreased 86.0% to US$33.4 million from US$238.7 million a year earlier. Net income decreased 20.1% to US$233.6 million from US$292.3 million in the prior year. Revenues were US$6.71 billion, up 0.1% from US$6.70 billion the year before. Operating income was US$759.5 million versus US$1.23 billion in the prior year, a decrease of 38.2%. Indirect operating expenses increased 8.7% to US$5.95 billion from US$5.47 billion in the equivalent prior-year period.

Prospects: Our evaluation of Cablevision Systems Corp. as of Apr. 7, 2013 is the result of our systematic analysis on three basic characteristics: earnings strength, relative valuation, and recent stock price movement. The company has suffered a very negative trend in earnings per share over the past 5 quarters. However, while recent estimates for the company have been lowered by analysts, CVC has posted results that fell short of analysts expectations. Based on operating earnings yield, the company is overvalued when compared to all of the companies in our coverage universe. Share price changes over the past year indicates that CVC will perform poorly over the near term.

Financial Data

(US$ in Thousands)	12/31/2012	12/31/2011	12/31/2010	12/31/2009	12/31/2008	12/31/2007	12/31/2006	12/31/2005
Earnings Per Share	0.87	1.02	1.20	0.96	(0.78)	0.74	(0.45)	0.33
Cash Flow Per Share	4.38	5.06	5.78	5.61	4.87	3.26	3.39	3.28
Dividends Per Share	0.600	0.575	0.475	0.400	0.200	...	10.000	...
Dividend Payout %	68.97	56.37	39.58	41.67	...	...	...	...
Income Statement								
Total Revenue	6,705,461	6,700,848	7,231,249	7,773,276	7,230,116	6,484,481	5,927,462	5,175,911
EBITDA	1,842,812	2,172,774	2,361,179	2,349,905	1,572,377	2,117,353	1,753,859	1,627,705
Depn & Amortn	1,065,957	1,003,974	985,747	1,082,248	1,106,929	1,118,508	1,127,914	1,078,780
Income Before Taxes	57,184	423,094	591,269	521,019	(317,426)	98,147	(265,070)	(198,586)
Income Taxes	23,821	184,436	225,550	235,702	(82,688)	79,181	(134,217)	(79,401)
Net Income	233,523	291,857	360,948	285,572	(227,576)	218,456	(126,465)	94,300
Average Shares	267,330	284,904	301,880	298,444	290,286	294,604	283,627	281,936
Balance Sheet								
Current Assets	1,373,487	1,354,952	1,639,875	2,055,365	1,858,869	1,744,287	1,667,447	2,130,502
Total Assets	7,246,224	7,143,325	8,840,685	9,325,725	9,383,208	9,140,577	9,844,857	9,844,509
Current Liabilities	1,692,948	1,595,428	2,162,113	2,070,240	2,297,158	2,351,538	2,430,698	2,558,263
Long-Term Obligations	10,578,202	10,792,752	12,126,732	10,839,677	11,285,730	10,785,346	11,764,477	8,953,341
Total Liabilities	12,885,388	12,719,180	15,137,603	14,481,680	14,745,455	14,239,367	15,184,110	12,313,275
Stockholders' Equity	(5,639,164)	(5,575,855)	(6,296,918)	(5,155,955)	(5,362,247)	(5,098,790)	(5,339,253)	(2,468,766)
Shares Outstanding	264,698	274,307	295,203	302,022	297,131	294,272	292,380	289,428
Statistical Record								
Return on Assets %	3.24	3.65	3.97	3.05	N.M.	2.30	N.M.	0.89
EBITDA Margin %	27.48	32.43	32.65	30.23	21.75	32.65	29.59	31.45
Net Margin %	3.48	4.36	4.99	3.67	N.M.	3.37	N.M.	1.82
Asset Turnover	0.93	0.84	0.80	0.83	0.78	0.68	0.60	0.49
Current Ratio	0.81	0.85	0.76	0.99	0.81	0.74	0.69	0.83
Price Range	18.52-10.97	37.72-12.75	34.72-20.76	21.60-7.82	26.90-9.58	31.80-19.77	23.59-15.64	26.94-18.99
P/E Ratio	21.29-12.61	36.98-12.50	28.93-17.30	22.50-8.14	...	42.97-26.72	...	81.63-57.54
Average Yield %	4.15	2.18	1.83	2.47	1.07	...	49.64	...

Address: 1111 Stewart Avenue, Bethpage, NY 11714
Telephone: 516-803-2300
Fax: 516-803-2273

Web Site: www.cablevision.com
Officers: Charles F. Dolan - Chairman David G. Ellen - Executive Vice President, General Counsel

Auditors: KPMG LLP
Transfer Agents: Wells Fargo Shareowner Services, St. Paul, MN

CABOT CORP.

Exchange	Symbol	Price	52Wk Range	Yield	P/E
NYS	CBT	$34.20 (3/28/2013)	44.66-33.72	2.34	6.12

*7 Year Price Score 102.87 *NYSE Composite Index=100   *12 Month Price Score 88.12

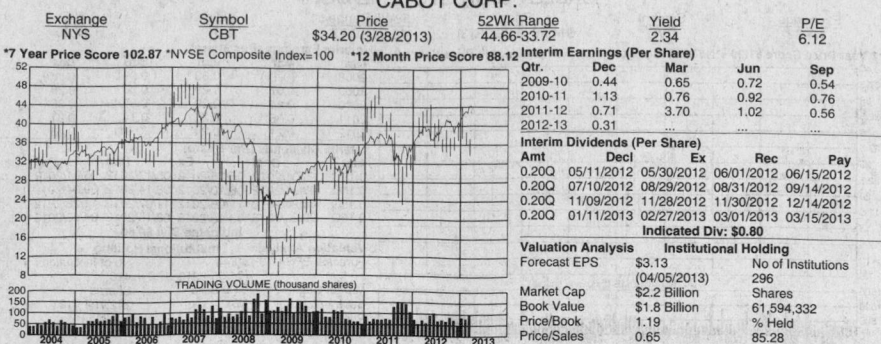

Interim Earnings (Per Share)

Qtr.	Dec	Mar	Jun	Sep
2009-10	0.44	0.65	0.72	0.54
2010-11	1.13	0.76	0.92	0.76
2011-12	0.71	3.70	1.02	0.56
2012-13	0.31	...	...	...

Interim Dividends (Per Share)

Amt	Decl	Ex	Rec	Pay
0.20Q	05/11/2012	05/30/2012	06/01/2012	06/15/2012
0.20Q	07/10/2012	08/29/2012	08/31/2012	09/14/2012
0.20Q	11/09/2012	11/28/2012	11/30/2012	12/14/2012
0.20Q	01/11/2013	02/27/2013	03/01/2013	03/15/2013

Indicated Div: $0.80

Valuation Analysis

		Institutional Holding	
Forecast EPS	$3.13 (04/05/2013)	No of Institutions	296
Market Cap	$2.2 Billion	Shares	61,594,332
Book Value	$1.8 Billion	% Held	85.28
Price/Book	1.19		
Price/Sales	0.65		

Business Summary: Specialty Chemicals (MIC: 8.3.2 SIC: 2895 NAIC: 325182)

Cabot is a chemicals and performance materials company. Co. has four business segments: Reinforcement Materials, which includes rubber blacks products used in tires and industrial products; Performance Materials, which is comprised of carbon black and thermoplastic concentrates and compounds, as well as fumed silica, fumed alumina and dispersions; Advanced Technologies, which is comprised of the Inkjet Colorants, Aerogel, Security Materials, Elastomer Composites and Specialty Fluids Businesses; and Purification Solutions, which consist of activated carbon products used for the purification of water, air, food and beverages, pharmaceuticals and other liquids and gases.

Recent Developments: For the quarter ended Dec 31 2012, income from continuing operations decreased 37.5% to US$25.0 million from US$40.0 million in the year-earlier quarter. Net income decreased 52.9% to US$24.0 million from US$51.0 million in the year-earlier quarter. Revenues were US$820.0 million, up 7.6% from US$762.0 million the year before. Operating income was US$55.0 million versus US$61.0 million in the prior-year quarter, a decrease of 9.8%. Direct operating expenses rose 8.7% to US$673.0 million from US$619.0 million in the comparable period the year before. Indirect operating expenses increased 12.2% to US$92.0 million from US$82.0 million in the equivalent prior-year period.

Prospects: Our evaluation of Cabot Corp. as of Apr. 7, 2013 is the result of our systematic analysis on three basic characteristics: earnings strength, relative valuation, and recent stock price movement. The company has generated a negative trend in earnings per share over the past 5 quarters. However, while recent estimates for the company have been lowered by analysts, CBT has posted results that fell short of analysts expectations. Based on operating earnings yield, the company is undervalued when compared to all of the companies in our coverage universe. Share price changes over the past year indicates that CBT will perform well over the near term.

Financial Data

(US$ in Thousands)	3 Mos	09/30/2012	09/30/2011	09/30/2010	09/30/2009	09/30/2008	09/30/2007	09/30/2006
Earnings Per Share	5.59	5.99	3.57	2.35	(1.23)	1.34	1.90	1.28
Cash Flow Per Share	5.42	6.53	3.02	3.89	6.33	1.96	4.98	4.20
Tang Book Value Per Share	16.03	15.83	22.66	19.26	16.77	18.57	17.71	17.44
Dividends Per Share	0.780	0.760	0.720	0.720	0.720	0.720	0.720	0.640
Dividend Payout %	13.95	12.69	20.17	30.64	...	53.73	37.89	50.00
Income Statement								
Total Revenue	820,000	3,300,000	3,102,000	2,893,000	2,243,000	3,191,000	2,616,000	2,543,000
EBITDA	105,000	440,000	378,000	388,000	94,000	308,000	340,000	249,000
Depn & Amortn	49,000	153,000	138,000	142,000	169,000	162,000	148,000	130,000
Income Before Taxes	41,000	245,000	203,000	208,000	(102,000)	112,000	168,000	97,000
Income Taxes	19,000	55,000	6,000	46,000	(22,000)	14,000	38,000	9,000
Net Income	20,000	388,000	236,000	154,000	(77,000)	86,000	129,000	88,000
Average Shares	64,100	64,200	65,400	64,000	63,000	64,000	68,000	68,000
Balance Sheet								
Current Assets	1,415,000	1,443,000	1,555,000	1,438,000	1,200,000	1,408,000	1,275,000	1,255,000
Total Assets	4,376,000	4,399,000	3,141,000	2,886,000	2,676,000	2,858,000	2,636,000	2,534,000
Current Liabilities	797,000	919,000	656,000	539,000	477,000	601,000	547,000	505,000
Long-Term Obligations	1,241,000	1,172,000	556,000	600,000	623,000	586,000	503,000	459,000
Total Liabilities	2,538,000	2,586,000	1,654,000	1,584,000	1,542,000	1,609,000	1,442,000	1,338,000
Stockholders' Equity	1,838,000	1,813,000	1,487,000	1,302,000	1,134,000	1,249,000	1,194,000	1,196,000
Shares Outstanding	63,994	63,347	63,860	65,370	65,309	65,277	65,279	63,286
Statistical Record								
Return on Assets %	9.70	10.26	7.83	5.54	N.M.	3.12	4.99	3.59
Return on Equity %	21.78	23.45	16.92	12.64	N.M.	7.02	10.79	7.67
EBITDA Margin %	12.80	13.33	12.19	13.41	4.19	9.65	13.00	9.79
Net Margin %	2.44	11.76	7.61	5.32	N.M.	2.70	4.93	3.46
Asset Turnover	0.90	0.87	1.03	1.04	0.81	1.16	1.01	1.04
Current Ratio	1.78	1.57	2.37	2.67	2.52	2.34	2.33	2.49
Debt to Equity	0.68	0.65	0.37	0.46	0.55	0.47	0.42	0.38
Price Range	44.66-32.73	44.66-23.27	47.83-24.78	33.65-21.04	31.78-8.04	38.11-22.71	49.77-35.53	39.22-30.77
P/E Ratio	7.99-5.86	7.46-3.88	13.40-6.94	14.32-8.95	...	28.44-16.95	26.19-18.70	30.64-24.04
Average Yield %	2.03	2.08	1.86	2.59	4.28	2.37	1.64	1.86

Address: Two Seaport Lane, Boston, MA 02210-2019 **Telephone:** 617-345-0100 **Fax:** 617-242-6103	**Web Site:** www.cabot-corp.com **Officers:** Patrick M. Prevost - President, Chief Executive Officer Dirk L. Blevi - Executive Vice President, Region Officer	**Auditors:** Deloitte & Touche LLP **Investor Contact:** 617-342-6090 **Transfer Agents:** Computershare Trust Company, N.A., Providence, RI

CABOT OIL & GAS CORP.

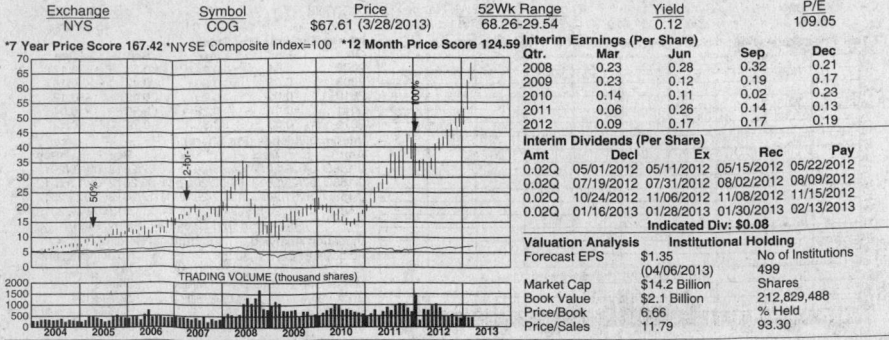

Exchange	Symbol	Price	52Wk Range	Yield	P/E
NYS	COG	$67.61 (3/28/2013)	68.26-29.54	0.12	109.05

*7 Year Price Score 167.42 *NYSE Composite Index=100 *12 Month Price Score 124.59

Interim Earnings (Per Share)

Qtr.	Mar	Jun	Sep	Dec
2008	0.23	0.28	0.32	0.21
2009	0.23	0.12	0.19	0.17
2010	0.14	0.11	0.02	0.23
2011	0.06	0.26	0.14	0.13
2012	0.09	0.17	0.17	0.19

Interim Dividends (Per Share)

Amt	Decl	Ex	Rec	Pay
0.02Q	05/01/2012	05/11/2012	05/15/2012	05/22/2012
0.02Q	07/19/2012	07/31/2012	08/02/2012	08/09/2012
0.02Q	10/24/2012	11/06/2012	11/08/2012	11/15/2012
0.02Q	01/16/2013	01/28/2013	01/30/2013	02/13/2013
			Indicated Div: $0.08	

Valuation Analysis / **Institutional Holding**

Forecast EPS	$1.35 (04/06/2013)	No of Institutions 499
Market Cap	$14.2 Billion	Shares 212,829,488
Book Value	$2.1 Billion	% Held 93.30
Price/Book	6.66	
Price/Sales	11.79	

TRADING VOLUME (thousand shares)

Business Summary: Production & Extraction (MIC: 9.1.1 SIC: 1311 NAIC: 211111)

Cabot Oil & Gas is an oil and gas company engaged in the development, exploitation, exploration, production and marketing of natural gas, crude oil and, to a lesser extent, natural gas liquids. Co. also transports, stores, gathers and produces natural gas for resale. Co.'s primary areas of operation include Appalachia, east and south Texas, and Oklahoma. As of Dec 31 2011, Co. had proved reserves totaling approximately 3.03 trillion cubic feet of natural gas equivalents, of which 96.0% were natural gas.

Recent Developments: For the year ended Dec 31 2012, net income increased 7.6% to US$131.7 million from US$122.4 million in the prior year. Revenues were US$1.20 billion, up 22.9% from US$979.9 million the year before. Operating income was US$306.1 million versus US$306.9 million in the prior year, a decrease of 0.2%. Direct operating expenses rose 29.2% to US$290.1 million from US$224.6 million in the comparable period the year before. Indirect operating expenses increased 35.7% to US$608.4 million from US$448.4 million in the equivalent prior-year period.

Prospects: Our evaluation of Cabot Oil & Gas Corp. as of Apr. 7, 2013 is the result of our systematic analysis on three basic characteristics: earnings strength, relative valuation, and recent stock price movement. The company has enjoyed a very positive trend in earnings per share over the past 5 quarters and while recent estimates for the company have been mixed, COG has posted better than expected results. Based on operating earnings yield, the company is overvalued when compared to all of the companies in our coverage universe. Share price changes over the past year indicates that COG will perform very well over the near term.

Financial Data

(US$ in Thousands)	12/31/2012	12/31/2011	12/31/2010	12/31/2009	12/31/2008	12/31/2007	12/31/2006	12/31/2005
Earnings Per Share	0.62	0.58	0.49	0.71	1.04	0.85	1.63	0.75
Cash Flow Per Share	3.10	2.41	2.33	2.96	3.14	2.38	1.84	1.87
Tang Book Value Per Share	10.15	10.09	9.00	8.74	8.66	5.49	4.91	3.09
Dividends Per Share	0.080	0.060	0.060	0.060	0.060	0.055	0.040	0.037
Dividend Payout %	12.90	10.34	12.24	8.45	5.77	6.43	2.46	4.91
Income Statement								
Total Revenue	1,204,546	979,864	844,035	879,276	945,791	732,170	761,988	682,797
EBITDA	762,803	654,372	596,903	503,539	557,415	418,644	657,921	367,189
Depn & Amortn	456,670	347,522	330,464	221,270	185,403	143,951	128,975	108,458
Income Before Taxes	237,840	235,187	198,498	223,290	335,623	257,332	510,505	236,234
Income Taxes	106,110	112,779	95,112	74,947	124,333	90,109	189,330	87,789
Net Income	131,730	122,408	103,386	148,343	211,290	167,423	321,175	148,445
Average Shares	210,993	210,761	210,390	209,365	203,452	196,260	197,201	198,901
Balance Sheet								
Current Assets	270,310	345,800	203,008	281,502	460,551	221,413	315,682	230,312
Total Assets	4,616,313	4,331,493	4,005,031	3,683,401	3,701,664	2,208,594	1,834,491	1,495,370
Current Liabilities	444,139	343,344	303,835	308,741	378,913	252,266	251,027	218,584
Long-Term Obligations	1,012,000	950,000	975,000	805,000	831,143	330,000	220,000	320,000
Total Liabilities	2,484,866	2,226,725	2,132,331	1,870,887	1,911,102	1,138,337	889,293	895,159
Stockholders' Equity	2,131,447	2,104,768	1,872,700	1,812,514	1,790,562	1,070,257	945,198	600,211
Shares Outstanding	210,025	208,615	208,015	207,308	206,718	194,953	192,427	194,272
Statistical Record								
Return on Assets %	2.94	2.94	2.69	4.02	7.13	8.28	19.29	10.97
Return on Equity %	6.20	6.16	5.61	8.23	14.73	16.61	41.57	28.12
EBITDA Margin %	63.33	66.78	70.72	57.27	58.94	57.18	86.34	53.78
Net Margin %	10.94	12.49	12.25	16.87	22.34	22.87	42.15	21.74
Asset Turnover	0.27	0.24	0.22	0.24	0.32	0.36	0.46	0.50
Current Ratio	0.61	1.01	0.67	0.91	1.22	0.88	1.26	1.05
Debt to Equity	0.47	0.45	0.52	0.44	0.46	0.31	0.23	0.53
Price Range	51.07-29.54	44.30-18.72	23.11-13.49	22.86-9.07	35.56-10.65	20.94-14.03	16.43-9.61	12.89-6.95
P/E Ratio	82.37-47.65	76.37-32.27	47.17-27.54	32.20-12.77	34.19-10.25	24.64-16.50	10.08-5.89	17.18-9.26
Average Yield %	0.20	0.21	0.34	0.40	0.27	0.31	0.32	0.38

Address: Three Memorial City Plaza, 840 Gessner Road, Suite 1400, Houston, TX 77024	Web Site: www.cabotog.com	Auditors: PricewaterhouseCoopers LLP
Telephone: 281-589-4600	Officers: Dan O. Dinges - Chairman, President, Chief Executive Officer Scott C. Schroeder - Vice President, Chief Financial Officer	Investor Contact: 281-589-4993
Fax: 281-589-4653		Transfer Agents: Wells Fargo Bank, N.A., Shareowner Services, South St. Paul, MN

CALIFORNIA WATER SERVICE GROUP (DE)

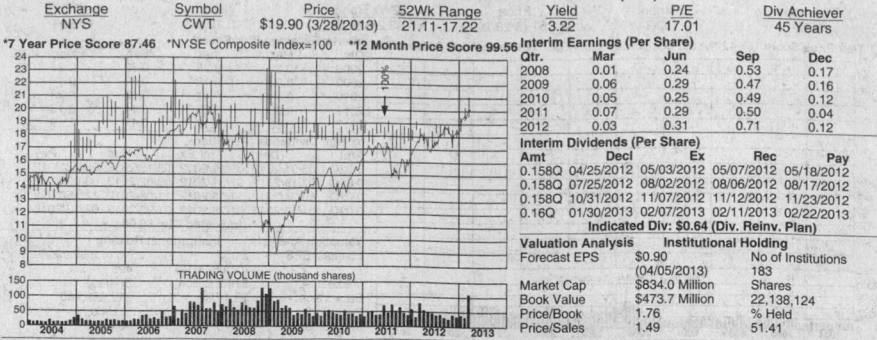

Exchange	Symbol	Price	52Wk Range	Yield	P/E	Div Achiever
NYS	CWT	$19.90 (3/28/2013)	21.11-17.22	3.22	17.01	45 Years

*7 Year Price Score 87.46   *NYSE Composite Index=100   *12 Month Price Score 99.56

Interim Earnings (Per Share)

Qtr.	Mar	Jun	Sep	Dec
2008	0.01	0.24	0.53	0.17
2009	0.06	0.29	0.47	0.16
2010	0.05	0.25	0.49	0.12
2011	0.07	0.29	0.50	0.04
2012	0.03	0.31	0.71	0.12

Interim Dividends (Per Share)

Amt	Decl	Ex	Rec	Pay
0.158Q	04/25/2012	05/03/2012	05/07/2012	05/18/2012
0.158Q	07/25/2012	08/02/2012	08/06/2012	08/17/2012
0.158Q	10/31/2012	11/07/2012	11/12/2012	11/23/2012
0.16Q	01/30/2013	02/07/2013	02/11/2013	02/22/2013

Indicated Div: $0.64 (Div. Reinv. Plan)

Valuation Analysis		Institutional Holding	
Forecast EPS	$0.90	No of Institutions	
	(04/05/2013)	183	
Market Cap	$834.0 Million	Shares	
Book Value	$473.7 Million	22,138,124	
Price/Book	1.76	% Held	
Price/Sales	1.49	51.41	

Business Summary: Water Utilities (MIC: 3.2.1 SIC: 4941 NAIC: 221310)

California Water Service Group is a holding company. Through its subsidiaries, Co. is engaged in the production, purchase, storage, treatment, testing, distribution and sale of water for domestic, industrial, public and irrigation uses, and for fire protection. Co. also provides non-regulated water-related services under agreements, including water system operation, and billing and meter reading services. As of Dec 31 2011, Co. provided its services to approximately 471,900 customers in 83 California communities; 4,200 customers on the islands of Maui and Hawaii, HI; 15,700 customers in the Tacoma and Olympia, WA; and 7,700 customers in the Belen, Los Lunas and Elephant Butte areas, NM.

Recent Developments: For the year ended Dec 31 2012, net income increased 29.5% to US$48.8 million from US$37.7 million in the prior year. Revenues were US$560.0 million, up 11.6% from US$501.8 million the year before. Operating income was US$73.8 million versus US$67.2 million in the prior year, an increase of 9.9%. Direct operating expenses rose 16.4% to US$288.6 million from US$248.0 million in the comparable period the year before. Indirect operating expenses increased 5.8% to US$197.5 million from US$186.6 million in the equivalent prior-year period.

Prospects: Our evaluation of California Water Service Group as of Apr. 7, 2013 is the result of our systematic analysis on three basic characteristics: earnings strength, relative valuation, and recent stock price movement. The company has generated a negative trend in earnings per share over the past 5 quarters. However, while recent estimates for the company have been lowered by analysts, CWT has posted better than expected results. Based on operating earnings yield, the company is undervalued when compared to all of the companies in our coverage universe. Share price changes over the past year indicates that CWT will perform well over the near term.

Financial Data

(US$ in Thousands)	12/31/2012	12/31/2011	12/31/2010	12/31/2009	12/31/2008	12/31/2007	12/31/2006	12/31/2005
Earnings Per Share	1.17	0.90	0.91	0.97	0.95	0.75	0.67	0.73
Cash Flow Per Share	3.14	2.66	1.81	1.75	2.30	1.21	1.61	2.35
Tang Book Value Per Share	11.24	10.69	10.39	10.07	9.63	9.33	9.16	7.99
Dividends Per Share	0.630	0.615	0.595	0.590	0.585	0.580	0.575	0.570
Dividend Payout %	53.85	68.33	65.75	60.51	61.58	77.33	85.82	77.55
Income Statement								
Total Revenue	559,966	501,814	460,399	449,372	410,312	367,082	334,717	320,728
EBITDA	154,252	143,439	133,314	129,186	121,227	98,981	89,163	93,660
Depn & Amortn	57,973	53,063	46,244	42,613	40,158	34,236	31,317	28,731
Income Before Taxes	68,184	60,737	60,725	65,366	64,312	49,046	40,877	47,229
Income Taxes	19,356	23,025	23,069	24,812	24,507	17,887	15,297	20,006
Net Income	48,828	37,712	37,656	40,554	39,805	31,159	25,580	27,223
Average Shares	41,892	41,772	41,638	41,532	41,468	41,378	37,850	36,804
Balance Sheet								
Current Assets	146,564	113,888	126,210	92,241	79,798	59,975	109,624	52,224
Total Assets	1,995,924	1,854,587	1,692,066	1,525,581	1,418,107	1,184,499	1,165,019	996,945
Current Liabilities	243,067	151,875	107,348	110,358	123,196	69,653	70,225	76,816
Long-Term Obligations	434,467	481,632	479,181	374,269	287,498	289,220	291,814	274,142
Total Liabilities	1,522,212	1,404,758	1,256,540	1,104,947	1,015,158	795,315	783,242	699,529
Stockholders' Equity	473,712	449,829	435,526	420,634	402,949	389,184	381,777	297,416
Shares Outstanding	41,908	41,817	41,666	41,530	41,446	41,332	41,314	36,780
Statistical Record								
Return on Assets %	2.53	2.13	2.34	2.76	3.05	2.65	2.37	2.81
Return on Equity %	10.55	8.52	8.80	9.85	10.02	8.08	7.53	9.25
EBITDA Margin %	27.55	28.58	28.96	28.75	29.55	26.96	26.64	29.20
Net Margin %	8.72	7.52	8.18	9.02	9.70	8.49	7.64	8.49
Asset Turnover	0.29	0.28	0.29	0.31	0.31	0.31	0.31	0.33
Current Ratio	0.60	0.75	1.18	0.84	0.65	0.86	1.56	0.68
Debt to Equity	0.92	1.07	1.10	0.89	0.71	0.74	0.76	0.92
Price Range	19.21-17.22	19.21-16.89	19.77-16.98	23.22-16.77	23.22-14.87	22.27-17.23	22.68-16.86	20.95-16.06
P/E Ratio	16.42-14.72	21.34-18.77	21.73-18.66	23.93-17.29	24.44-15.65	29.69-22.97	33.85-25.16	28.70-22.00
Average Yield %	3.46	3.37	3.24	3.07	3.12	2.97	2.94	3.12

Address: 1720 North First Street, San Jose, CA 95112
Telephone: 408-367-8200

Web Site: www.calwatergroup.com
Officers: Peter C. Nelson - Chairman, President, Chief Executive Officer Martin A. Kropelnicki - Vice President, Chief Financial Officer, Treasurer, Acting Principal Accounting Officer, President, Chief Operating Officer

Auditors: Deloitte & Touche LLP
Investor Contact: 408-367-8200
Transfer Agents: AST Stockholder Services, Brooklyn, NY

CALPINE CORP

Exchange	Symbol	Price	52Wk Range	Yield	P/E
NYS	CPN	$20.60 (3/28/2013)	20.60-15.97	N/A	49.05

*7 Year Price Score N/A   *NYSE Composite Index=100   *12 Month Price Score 99.60

TRADING VOLUME (thousand shares)

Interim Earnings (Per Share)

Qtr.	Mar	Jun	Sep	Dec
2008	(0.44)	0.41	0.28	(0.23)
2009	0.07	(0.16)	0.49	(0.08)
2010	(0.10)	(0.24)	0.45	(0.05)
2011	(0.61)	(0.14)	0.39	(0.03)
2012	(0.02)	(0.69)	0.94	0.21

Interim Dividends (Per Share)

No Dividends Paid

Valuation Analysis   **Institutional Holding**

Forecast EPS	$0.53	No of Institutions
	(04/05/2013)	344
Market Cap	$9.4 Billion	Shares
Book Value	$4.0 Billion	422,490,912
Price/Book	2.36	% Held
Price/Sales	1.72	N/A

Business Summary: Electric Utilities (MIC: 3.1.1 SIC: 4911 NAIC: 221122)

Calpine is a wholesale power producer with operations throughout the U.S. Co. owns and operates primarily natural gas-fired and geothermal power plants in North America and has a presence in wholesale power markets in California, Texas and the Mid-Atlantic region of the U.S. Co.'s portfolio is primarily comprised natural gas-fired combustion turbines and geothermal steam turbines. As of Dec 31 2012, Co.'s portfolio consisted of 92 power plants located throughout 20 states in the U.S. and Canada, with an aggregate generation capacity of 27,321 Megawatts. Co. sells wholesale power, steam, capacity, renewable energy credits and ancillary services to its customers.

Recent Developments: For the year ended Dec 31 2012, income from continuing operations was US$199.0 million compared with a loss of US$189.0 million a year earlier. Net income amounted to US$199.0 million versus a net loss of US$189.0 million in the prior year. Revenues were US$5.48 billion, down 19.4% from US$6.80 billion the year before. Operating income was US$1.00 billion versus US$800.0 million in the prior year, an increase of 25.3%. Direct operating expenses declined 22.4% to US$4.51 billion from US$5.81 billion in the comparable period the year before. Indirect operating income amounted to US$32.0 million compared with an expense of US$187.0 million in the equivalent prior-year period.

Prospects: Our evaluation of Calpine Corp. as of Apr. 7, 2013 is the result of our systematic analysis on three basic characteristics: earnings strength, relative valuation, and recent stock price movement. The company has suffered a very negative trend in earnings per share over the past 5 quarters. However, while recent estimates for the company have been mixed, CPN has posted results that fell short of analysts expectations. Based on operating earnings yield, the company is overvalued when compared to all of the companies in our coverage universe. Share price changes over the past year indicates that CPN will perform poorly over the near term.

Financial Data

(US$ in Thousands)	12/31/2012	12/31/2011	12/31/2010	12/31/2009	12/31/2008	12/31/2007	12/31/2006	12/31/2005
Earnings Per Share	0.42	(0.39)	0.06	0.31	0.02	5.62	(3.68)	(21.44)
Cash Flow Per Share	1.39	1.60	1.91	1.57	1.02	0.38	0.33	(1.53)
Tang Book Value Per Share	8.74	8.93	10.45	9.87	10.19	...	...	...
Income Statement								
Total Revenue	5,478,000	6,800,000	6,545,000	6,564,000	9,937,000	7,970,000	6,705,760	10,112,658
EBITDA	1,472,000	1,079,000	1,100,000	1,392,000	1,629,000	4,574,000	(29,253)	(8,752,955)
Depn & Amortn	557,000	560,000	568,000	469,000	437,000	472,000	484,200	526,000
Income Before Taxes	190,000	(232,000)	(246,000)	110,000	168,000	2,147,000	(1,696,528)	(10,592,017)
Income Taxes	19,000	(22,000)	(68,000)	15,000	(47,000)	(546,000)	64,158	(741,398)
Net Income	199,000	(190,000)	31,000	149,000	10,000	2,693,000	(1,764,907)	(9,939,208)
Average Shares	471,743	485,381	487,294	486,319	485,546	479,478	479,136	463,567
Balance Sheet								
Current Assets	2,832,000	3,562,000	3,429,000	4,099,000	7,500,000	4,531,000	3,168,329	3,428,037
Total Assets	16,549,000	17,371,000	17,256,000	16,650,000	20,738,000	18,482,000	18,590,265	20,544,797
Current Liabilities	1,318,000	2,162,000	1,789,000	2,749,000	5,616,000	3,604,000	6,057,947	7,142,412
Long-Term Obligations	10,635,000	10,321,000	10,104,000	8,996,000	9,756,000	9,946,000	3,351,627	2,462,462
Total Liabilities	12,555,000	13,067,000	12,613,000	12,202,000	16,368,000	23,134,000	25,743,165	26,052,882
Stockholders' Equity	3,994,000	4,304,000	4,643,000	4,448,000	4,370,000	(4,652,000)	(7,152,900)	(5,508,085)
Shares Outstanding	457,048	481,743	444,435	442,998	428,960	479,314	529,764	569,081
Statistical Record								
Return on Assets %	1.17	N.M.	0.18	0.80	0.05	14.53	N.M.	N.M.
Return on Equity %	4.78	N.M.	0.68	3.38	...	...	...	...
EBITDA Margin %	26.87	15.87	16.81	21.21	16.39	57.39	N.M.	N.M.
Net Margin %	3.63	N.M.	0.47	2.27	0.10	33.79	N.M.	N.M.
Asset Turnover	0.32	0.39	0.39	0.35	0.51	0.43	0.34	0.42
Current Ratio	2.15	1.65	1.92	1.49	1.34	1.26	0.52	0.48
Debt to Equity	2.66	2.40	2.18	2.02	2.23	...	...	...
Price Range	18.90-14.51	16.88-12.93	14.02-10.80	14.68-4.78	23.00-6.52	...	...	...
P/E Ratio	45.00-34.55	...	233.67-180.00	47.35-15.42	N.M.	...	...	...

Address: 717 Texas Avenue, Suite 1000, Houston, TX 77002 **Telephone:** 713-830-2000	**Web Site:** www.calpine.com **Officers:** J. Stuart Ryan - Chairman Jack A. Fusco - President, Chief Executive Officer	**Auditors:** PricewaterhouseCoooers LLP **Investor Contact:** 713-830-8775 **Transfer Agents:** ComputerShare Investor Services, Providence, RI

CAMDEN PROPERTY TRUST

Exchange	Symbol	Price	52Wk Range	Yield	P/E
NYS	CPT	$68.68 (3/28/2013)	71.59-62.70	3.67	20.81

*7 Year Price Score 108.45 *NYSE Composite Index=100   *12 Month Price Score 95.16

Interim Earnings (Per Share)

Qtr.	Mar	Jun	Sep	Dec
2008	0.27	0.31	1.32	(0.61)
2009	0.11	0.30	0.06	(1.26)
2010	0.03	0.03	0.02	0.24
2011	0.10	(0.23)	0.16	0.63
2012	1.07	0.26	0.35	1.64

Interim Dividends (Per Share)

Amt	Decl	Ex	Rec	Pay
0.56Q	06/15/2012	06/27/2012	06/29/2012	07/17/2012
0.56Q	09/14/2012	09/26/2012	09/28/2012	10/17/2012
0.56Q	12/03/2012	12/13/2012	12/17/2012	01/17/2013
0.63Q	01/31/2013	03/26/2013	03/28/2013	04/17/2013

Indicated Div: $2.52

Valuation Analysis

		Institutional Holding	
Forecast EPS	$1.60	No of Institutions	
	(04/06/2013)	362	
Market Cap	$6.6 Billion	Shares	
Book Value	$2.6 Billion	87,933,632	
Price/Book	2.58	% Held	
Price/Sales	8.88	98.36	

Business Summary: REITs (MIC: 5.3.1 SIC: 6798 NAIC: 525930)

Camden Property Trust is a real estate investment trust primarily engaged in the ownership, management, development, acquisition, and construction of multifamily apartment communities. Co.'s properties typically consist of mid-rise buildings or two and three story buildings in a landscaped setting and provide residents with a variety of amenities, such as swimming pools and clubhouse, among others. As of Dec 31 2012, Co. owned interests in, operated, or were developing 202 multifamily properties comprising 68,620 apartment homes across the U.S. Of these 202 properties, nine properties were under development. Co. also owns land parcels it may develop into multifamily apartment communities.

Recent Developments: For the year ended Dec 31 2012, income from continuing operations increased 616.8% to US$169.3 million from US$23.6 million a year earlier. Net income increased 390.2% to US$293.9 million from US$60.0 million in the prior year. Revenues were US$744.3 million, up 15.9% from US$642.5 million the year before. Revenues from property income rose 17.2% to US$727.9 million from US$621.1 million in the corresponding earlier year.

Prospects: Our evaluation of Camden Property Trust as of Apr. 7, 2013 is the result of our systematic analysis on three basic characteristics: earnings strength, relative valuation, and recent stock price movement. The company has generated a negative trend in earnings per share over the past 5 quarters. Because the company lacks sufficient analyst estimate data, we place greater weight on the historical EPS trend as the measure of earnings strength. Based on operating earnings yield, the company is overvalued when compared to all of the companies in our coverage universe. Share price changes over the past year indicates that CPT will perform poorly over the near term.

Financial Data

(US$ in Thousands)	12/31/2012	12/31/2011	12/31/2010	12/31/2009	12/31/2008	12/31/2007	12/31/2006	12/31/2005
Earnings Per Share	3.30	0.66	0.33	(0.80)	1.28	2.51	3.96	3.58
Cash Flow Per Share	3.86	3.37	3.27	3.49	3.91	3.84	4.09	3.86
Tang Book Value Per Share	26.64	21.97	21.66	21.15	21.38	23.40	26.68	22.56
Dividends Per Share	2.240	1.960	1.800	2.050	2.800	2.760	2.640	2.540
Dividend Payout %	67.88	296.97	545.45	...	218.75	109.96	66.67	70.95
Income Statement								
Total Revenue	744,315	677,263	638,741	649,369	604,476	634,082	634,960	568,581
EBITDA	468,132	329,751	324,927	242,477	303,980	337,440	361,166	319,696
Depn & Amortn	213,480	187,668	178,567	176,340	172,126	160,826	175,292	184,542
Income Before Taxes	150,370	29,669	20,467	(62,159)	(545)	60,333	67,530	23,606
Income Taxes	1,208	2,220	1,581	967	843	3,052	...	...
Net Income	293,900	59,961	31,142	(44,203)	70,973	148,457	232,846	199,086
Average Shares	85,556	73,701	68,957	62,359	55,272	59,125	59,524	56,313
Balance Sheet								
Current Assets	66,285	91,270	211,177	149,773	116,785	104,435	85,258	65,926
Total Assets	5,385,172	4,622,075	4,699,737	4,607,999	4,730,342	4,890,760	4,586,050	4,487,799
Current Liabilities	180,317	154,994	139,189	130,686	149,111	175,035	191,208	173,971
Long-Term Obligations	2,510,468	2,432,112	2,563,754	2,625,199	2,832,396	2,828,095	2,330,976	2,633,091
Total Liabilities	2,822,073	2,765,433	2,915,393	2,979,663	3,318,848	3,359,447	2,851,694	3,116,896
Stockholders' Equity	2,563,099	1,856,642	1,784,344	1,628,336	1,411,494	1,531,313	1,734,356	1,370,903
Shares Outstanding	96,201	84,517	82,386	76,996	66,028	65,434	65,006	60,763
Statistical Record								
Return on Assets %	5.86	1.29	0.67	N.M.	1.47	3.13	5.13	5.59
Return on Equity %	13.26	3.29	1.83	N.M.	4.81	9.09	15.00	18.88
EBITDA Margin %	62.89	48.69	50.87	37.34	50.29	53.22	56.88	56.23
Net Margin %	39.49	8.85	4.88	N.M.	11.74	23.41	36.67	35.01
Asset Turnover	0.15	0.15	0.14	0.14	0.13	0.13	0.14	0.16
Current Ratio	0.37	0.59	1.52	1.15	0.78	0.60	0.45	0.38
Debt to Equity	0.98	1.31	1.44	1.61	2.01	1.85	1.34	1.92
Price Range	71.59-59.61	69.32-53.09	54.13-36.77	44.01-17.56	55.35-18.96	79.26-45.78	80.97-58.40	60.18-45.31
P/E Ratio	21.69-18.06	105.03-80.44	164.03-111.42	...	43.24-14.81	31.58-18.24	20.45-14.75	16.81-12.66
Average Yield %	3.39	3.27	3.93	6.59	6.32	4.22	3.42	4.85

Address: 3 Greenway Plaza, Suite 1300, Houston, TX 77046 Telephone: 713-354-2500	Web Site: www.camdenliving.com Officers: Richard J. Campo - Chairman, Chief Executive Officer D. Keith Oden - President	Auditors: Deloitte & Touche LLP Investor Contact: 713-354-2549 Transfer Agents: American Stock Transfer and Trust Company, New York, NY

CAMERON INTERNATIONAL CORP

Exchange	Symbol	Price	52Wk Range	Yield	P/E
NYS	CAM	$65.20 (3/28/2013)	66.66-38.91	N/A	21.59

*7 Year Price Score 116.55 *NYSE Composite Index=100 ***12 Month Price Score 109.85**

Interim Earnings (Per Share)

Qtr.	Mar	Jun	Sep	Dec
2008	0.55	0.65	0.73	0.67
2009	0.52	0.62	0.56	0.40
2010	0.48	0.52	0.61	0.66
2011	0.43	0.59	0.67	0.40
2012	0.54	0.70	0.90	0.87

Interim Dividends (Per Share)

No Dividends Paid

Valuation Analysis

		Institutional Holding	
Forecast EPS	$3.85	No of Institutions	
	(04/06/2013)	641	
Market Cap	$16.1 Billion	Shares	
Book Value	$5.6 Billion	259,789,472	
Price/Book	2.89	% Held	
Price/Sales	1.89	N/A	

Business Summary: Equipment & Services (MIC: 9.1.3 SIC: 3533 NAIC: 333132)

Cameron International provides flow equipment products, systems and services to oil, gas and process industries. Co. has three segments: Drilling and Production Systems, which provides systems and equipment used to control pressures and direct flows of oil and gas wells; Valves and Measurement, which provide valves and measurement systems used to control, direct and measure the flow of oil and gas as they are moved from individual wellheads to refineries, petrochemical plants and industrial centers for processing; and Process and Compression Systems, which provides oil and gas separation equipment, heaters, dehydration and desalting units, and membrane separation systems, among others.

Recent Developments: For the year ended Dec 31 2012, net income increased 43.8% to US$750.5 million from US$521.9 million in the prior year. Revenues were US$8.50 billion, up 22.2% from US$6.96 billion the year before. Direct operating expenses rose 24.5% to US$6.02 billion from US$4.84 billion in the comparable period the year before. Indirect operating expenses increased 4.8% to US$1.54 billion from US$1.47 billion in the equivalent prior-year period.

Prospects: Our evaluation of Cameron International Corp. as of Apr. 7, 2013 is the result of our systematic analysis on three basic characteristics: earnings strength, relative valuation, and recent stock price movement. The company has enjoyed a very positive trend in earnings per share over the past 5 quarters and while recent estimates for the company have been mixed, CAM has posted results that fell short of analysts expectations. Based on operating earnings yield, the company is about fairly valued when compared to all of the companies in our coverage universe. Share price changes over the past year indicates that CAM will perform well over the near term.

Financial Data

(US$ in Thousands)	12/31/2012	12/31/2011	12/31/2010	12/31/2009	12/31/2008	12/31/2007	12/31/2006	12/31/2005
Earnings Per Share	3.02	2.09	2.27	2.11	2.60	2.16	1.36	0.76
Cash Flow Per Share	2.76	0.85	1.21	2.77	4.53	2.06	2.41	1.59
Tang Book Value Per Share	13.40	11.33	10.91	9.04	6.88	6.23	4.74	4.18
Income Statement								
Total Revenue	8,502,100	6,959,000	6,134,800	5,223,245	5,848,877	4,666,368	3,742,907	2,517,847
EBITDA	1,240,200	895,300	953,900	844,031	993,103	782,501	558,248	340,305
Depn & Amortn	211,800	160,200	142,600	114,683	98,728	81,458	75,909	78,400
Income Before Taxes	938,000	651,100	733,300	642,829	872,058	708,475	488,601	263,012
Income Taxes	187,500	129,200	170,400	167,310	278,332	207,615	170,785	91,882
Net Income	750,500	521,900	562,900	475,519	593,726	500,860	317,816	171,130
Average Shares	248,100	249,200	247,500	225,026	228,647	231,387	233,984	225,216
Balance Sheet								
Current Assets	6,910,600	5,828,600	4,932,900	4,714,159	4,056,443	3,071,931	2,907,652	1,728,056
Total Assets	11,158,200	9,361,700	8,005,100	7,725,373	5,902,371	4,730,819	4,350,750	3,098,562
Current Liabilities	3,169,000	2,680,300	2,573,900	2,296,213	2,111,761	1,692,876	1,628,212	921,861
Long-Term Obligations	2,047,000	1,574,200	772,900	1,232,302	1,256,385	745,128	745,408	444,435
Total Liabilities	5,592,100	4,654,300	3,612,700	3,805,613	3,582,815	2,635,855	2,609,311	1,503,799
Stockholders' Equity	5,566,100	4,707,400	4,392,400	3,919,760	2,319,556	2,094,964	1,741,439	1,594,763
Shares Outstanding	246,696	245,532	243,913	244,657	216,892	218,008	224,579	231,258
Statistical Record								
Return on Assets %	7.29	6.01	7.16	6.98	11.14	11.03	8.53	6.27
Return on Equity %	14.57	11.47	13.54	15.24	26.83	26.11	19.05	12.12
EBITDA Margin %	14.59	12.87	15.55	16.16	16.98	16.77	14.91	13.52
Net Margin %	8.83	7.50	9.18	9.10	10.15	10.73	8.49	6.80
Asset Turnover	0.83	0.80	0.78	0.77	1.10	1.03	1.00	0.92
Current Ratio	2.18	2.17	1.92	2.05	1.92	1.81	1.79	1.87
Debt to Equity	0.37	0.33	0.18	0.31	0.54	0.36	0.43	0.28
Price Range	58.99-38.91	62.07-40.12	51.36-31.89	42.31-17.32	57.67-16.68	52.51-24.93	28.75-19.28	21.25-12.88
P/E Ratio	19.53-12.88	29.70-19.20	22.63-14.05	20.05-8.21	22.18-6.42	24.31-11.54	21.14-14.18	27.96-16.95

Address: 1333 West Loop South, Suite 1700, Houston, TX 77027 **Telephone:** 713-513-3300 **Fax:** 713-513-3320	**Web Site:** www.c-a-m.com **Officers:** Jack B. Moore - Chairman, President, Chief Executive Officer John D. Carne - Executive Vice President, Senior Vice President, Chief Operating Officer, Division Officer, Joint Venture Officer	**Auditors:** Ernst & Young LLP **Investor Contact:** 713-513-3300 **Transfer Agents:** Computershare Trust Company, N.A., Providence, RI

CAMPBELL SOUP CO.

Exchange	Symbol	Price	52Wk Range	Yield	P/E
NYS	CPB	$45.36 (3/28/2013)	45.36-31.33	2.56	19.47

*7 Year Price Score 90.86 *NYSE Composite Index=100 *12 Month Price Score 106.79

Interim Earnings (Per Share)

Qtr.	Oct	Jan	Apr	Jul
2009-10	0.87	0.74	0.49	0.33
2010-11	0.82	0.71	0.57	0.31
2011-12	0.82	0.64	0.55	0.40
2012-13	0.78	0.60	...	...

Interim Dividends (Per Share)

Amt	Decl	Ex	Rec	Pay
0.29Q	06/27/2012	07/05/2012	07/09/2012	07/30/2012
0.29Q	09/24/2012	10/04/2012	10/09/2012	10/29/2012
0.29Q	11/14/2012	12/12/2012	12/14/2012	12/28/2012
0.29Q	12/04/2012	12/12/2012	12/14/2012	12/28/2012

Indicated Div: $1.16

Valuation Analysis

		Institutional Holding	
Forecast EPS	$2.56 (04/05/2013)	No of Institutions	625
Market Cap	$14.2 Billion	Shares	163,599,424
Book Value	$1.2 Billion	% Held	42.04
Price/Book	12.24		
Price/Sales	1.75		

Business Summary: Food (MIC: 1.2.1 SIC: 2032 NAIC: 311422)

Campbell Soup is a manufacturer and marketer of convenience food products. Co. operates in five segments: U.S. Simple Meals, which includes Campbell's soups, Prego pasta sauce, and Pace Mexican sauce; Global Baking and Snacking, which includes Pepperidge Farm products and Arnott's biscuits; International Simple Meals and Beverages, which includes Erasco and Heisse Tasse soups, Liebig and Royco soups, and Devos Lemmens mayonnaise and cold sauces; U.S. Beverages, which consist of the U.S. retail beverages business and includes V8 juices and beverages and Campbell's tomato juice; and North America Foodservice, which distributes soup and beverage products in the U.S. and Canada.

Recent Developments: For the quarter ended Jan 27 2013, net income decreased 7.0% to US$187.0 million from US$201.0 million in the year-earlier quarter. Revenues were US$2.33 billion, up 10.5% from US$2.11 billion the year before. Operating income was US$301.0 million versus US$329.0 million in the prior-year quarter, a decrease of 8.5%. Direct operating expenses rose 16.4% to US$1.51 billion from US$1.30 billion in the comparable period the year before. Indirect operating expenses increased 7.5% to US$518.0 million from US$482.0 million in the equivalent prior-year period.

Prospects: Our evaluation of Campbell Soup Co. as of Apr. 7, 2013 is the result of our systematic analysis on three basic characteristics: earnings strength, relative valuation, and recent stock price movement. The company has managed to produce a neutral trend in earnings per share over the past 5 quarters and while recent estimates for the company have remained steady, CPB has posted better than expected results. Based on operating earnings yield, the company is undervalued when compared to all of the companies in our coverage universe. Share price changes over the past year indicates that CPB will perform poorly over the near term.

Financial Data
(US$ in Thousands)

	6 Mos	3 Mos	07/29/2012	07/31/2011	08/01/2010	08/02/2009	08/03/2008	07/29/2007
Earnings Per Share	2.33	2.37	2.41	2.42	2.42	2.06	3.06	2.16
Cash Flow Per Share	3.63	3.59	3.54	3.51	3.12	3.32	2.02	1.75
Dividends Per Share	1.450	1.160	1.160	1.145	1.075	1.000	0.880	0.800
Dividend Payout %	62.23	48.95	48.13	47.31	44.42	48.54	28.76	37.04
Income Statement								
Total Revenue	4,669,000	2,336,000	7,707,000	7,719,000	7,676,000	7,586,000	7,998,000	7,867,000
EBITDA	905,000	483,000	1,470,000	1,544,000	1,599,000	1,449,000	1,386,000	1,576,000
Depn & Amortn	219,000	98,000	258,000	265,000	251,000	264,000	288,000	283,000
Income Before Taxes	622,000	352,000	1,106,000	1,168,000	1,242,000	1,079,000	939,000	1,149,000
Income Taxes	192,000	109,000	342,000	366,000	398,000	347,000	268,000	326,000
Net Income	435,000	245,000	774,000	805,000	844,000	736,000	1,165,000	854,000
Average Shares	316,000	316,000	319,000	329,000	343,000	358,000	381,000	396,000
Balance Sheet								
Current Assets	2,264,000	2,401,000	1,771,000	1,963,000	1,687,000	1,551,000	1,693,000	1,578,000
Total Assets	8,593,000	8,747,000	6,530,000	6,862,000	6,276,000	6,056,000	6,474,000	6,445,000
Current Liabilities	2,891,000	3,092,000	2,070,000	1,989,000	2,065,000	1,628,000	2,403,000	2,030,000
Long-Term Obligations	2,940,000	2,940,000	2,004,000	2,427,000	1,945,000	2,246,000	1,633,000	2,074,000
Total Liabilities	7,433,000	7,648,000	5,632,000	5,774,000	5,350,000	5,328,000	5,156,000	5,150,000
Stockholders' Equity	1,160,000	1,099,000	898,000	1,088,000	926,000	728,000	1,318,000	1,295,000
Shares Outstanding	313,000	313,000	312,000	320,000	336,000	343,000	356,000	379,000
Statistical Record								
Return on Assets %	9.69	9.61	11.59	12.29	13.73	11.78	17.74	11.96
Return on Equity %	62.76	66.73	78.16	80.16	102.34	72.14	87.73	55.92
EBITDA Margin %	19.38	20.68	19.07	20.00	20.83	19.10	17.33	20.03
Net Margin %	9.32	10.49	10.04	10.43	11.00	9.70	14.57	10.86
Asset Turnover	1.06	1.00	1.15	1.18	1.25	1.21	1.22	1.10
Current Ratio	0.78	0.78	0.86	0.99	0.82	0.95	0.70	0.78
Debt to Equity	2.53	2.68	2.23	2.23	2.10	3.09	1.24	1.60
Price Range	36.95-31.33	35.48-31.25	34.44-29.77	37.47-32.77	37.49-30.03	40.15-24.87	38.32-31.00	42.39-35.92
P/E Ratio	15.86-13.45	14.97-13.19	14.29-12.35	15.48-13.54	15.49-12.41	19.49-12.07	12.52-10.13	19.62-16.63
Average Yield %	4.25	3.48	3.56	3.30	3.16	3.19	2.53	2.08

Address: 1 Campbell Place, Camden, NJ 08103-1799
Telephone: 856-342-4800
Fax: 856-342-3878

Web Site: www.campbellsoupcompany.com
Officers: Denise M. Morrison - President, Chief Executive Officer Mark R. Alexander - Senior Vice President, Region Officer

Auditors: PricewaterhouseCoopers LLP
Investor Contact: 856-342-6081
Transfer Agents: Computershare Trust Company, N.A., Providence, RI

CAPITAL ONE FINANCIAL CORP

Exchange	Symbol	Price	52Wk Range	Yield	P/E
NYS	COF	$54.95 (3/28/2013)	62.88-48.40	0.36	8.92

*7 Year Price Score 96.76   *NYSE Composite Index=100   *12 Month Price Score 88.77

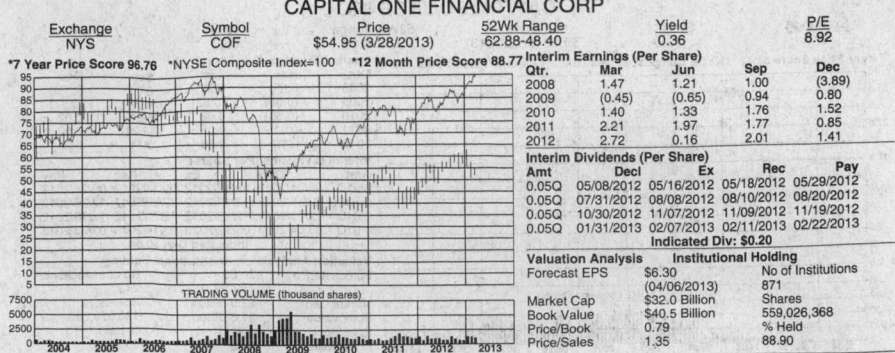

Interim Earnings (Per Share)

Qtr.	Mar	Jun	Sep	Dec
2008	1.47	1.21	1.00	(3.89)
2009	(0.45)	(0.65)	0.94	0.80
2010	1.40	1.33	1.76	1.52
2011	2.21	1.97	1.77	0.85
2012	2.72	0.16	2.01	1.41

Interim Dividends (Per Share)

Amt	Decl	Ex	Rec	Pay
0.05Q	05/08/2012	05/16/2012	05/18/2012	05/29/2012
0.05Q	07/31/2012	08/08/2012	08/10/2012	08/20/2012
0.05Q	10/30/2012	11/07/2012	11/09/2012	11/19/2012
0.05Q	01/31/2013	02/07/2013	02/11/2013	02/22/2013

Indicated Div: $0.20

Valuation Analysis

		Institutional Holding	
Forecast EPS	$6.30 (04/06/2013)	No of Institutions	871
Market Cap	$32.0 Billion	Shares	559,026,368
Book Value	$40.5 Billion	% Held	88.90
Price/Book	0.79		
Price/Sales	1.35		

Business Summary: Credit & Lending (MIC: 5.4.1 SIC: 6022 NAIC: 522110)

Capital One Financial is a financial services holding company. Through its subsidiaries, Co. provides an array of financial products and services to consumers, small businesses and commercial clients. Co.'s Capital One Bank (USA), National Association subsidiary provides credit and debit card products, other lending products and deposit products. Co.'s Capital One, National Association subsidiary provides a range of banking products and financial services to consumers, small businesses and commercial clients. As of Dec 31 2012, Co. had total assets of $312.92 billion and deposits of $212.49 billion.

Recent Developments: For the year ended Dec 31 2012, net income increased 11.8% to US$3.52 billion from US$3.15 billion in the prior year. Net interest income increased 30.2% to US$16.59 billion from US$12.74 billion in the prior year. Provision for loan losses was US$4.42 billion versus US$2.36 billion in the prior year, an increase of 87.1%. Non-interest income rose 35.9% to US$4.81 billion from US$3.54 billion, while non-interest expense advanced 28.0% to US$11.95 billion.

Prospects: Our evaluation of Capital One Financial Corp. as of Apr. 7, 2013 is the result of our systematic analysis on three basic characteristics: earnings strength, relative valuation, and recent stock price movement. The company has produced a positive trend in earnings per share over the past 5 quarters. However, while recent estimates for the company have been lowered by analysts, COF has posted results that fell short of analysts expectations. Based on operating earnings yield, the company is undervalued when compared to all of the companies in our coverage universe. Share price changes over the past year indicates that COF will perform in line with the market over the near term.

Financial Data

(US$ in Thousands)	12/31/2012	12/31/2011	12/31/2010	12/31/2009	12/31/2008	12/31/2007	12/31/2006	12/31/2005
Earnings Per Share	6.16	6.80	6.01	0.74	(0.21)	3.97	7.62	6.73
Cash Flow Per Share	16.11	16.35	18.01	6.53	9.23	33.34	10.91	14.01
Tang Book Value Per Share	45.68	34.95	28.34	28.55	29.48	30.74	28.30	33.99
Dividends Per Share	0.200	0.200	0.200	0.525	1.500	0.107	0.107	0.107
Dividend Payout %	3.25	2.94	3.33	70.95	...	2.69	1.40	1.58
Income Statement								
Interest Income	18,964,000	14,987,000	15,353,000	10,664,585	11,111,999	11,078,156	8,194,229	5,726,881
Interest Expense	2,375,000	2,246,000	2,896,000	2,967,470	3,963,284	4,548,311	3,094,599	2,046,639
Net Interest Income	16,589,000	12,741,000	12,457,000	7,697,115	7,148,715	6,529,845	5,099,630	3,680,242
Provision for Losses	4,415,000	2,360,000	3,907,000	4,230,111	5,101,040	2,636,502	1,476,438	1,491,072
Non-Interest Income	4,807,000	3,538,000	3,714,000	5,286,152	6,743,971	8,054,223	6,996,732	6,358,105
Non-Interest Expense	11,946,000	9,332,000	7,934,000	7,417,054	8,210,027	8,078,010	6,967,193	5,718,273
Income Before Taxes	5,035,000	4,587,000	4,330,000	1,336,102	581,619	3,869,556	3,652,731	2,829,002
Income Taxes	1,301,000	1,334,000	1,280,000	349,485	497,102	1,277,837	1,238,238	1,019,855
Net Income	3,517,000	3,147,000	2,743,000	883,781	(45,998)	1,570,332	2,414,493	1,809,147
Average Shares	566,000	459,000	456,000	431,415	377,667	395,545	317,023	268,908
Balance Sheet								
Net Loans & Leases	200,934,000	131,843,000	120,547,000	86,759,911	96,493,811	98,842,027	94,332,139	58,057,681
Total Assets	312,918,000	206,019,000	197,503,000	169,646,363	165,913,452	150,590,369	149,739,285	88,701,411
Total Deposits	212,485,000	128,226,000	122,210,000	115,809,096	108,620,789	82,990,462	85,770,892	47,933,267
Total Liabilities	272,419,000	176,353,000	170,962,000	143,056,953	139,301,019	126,296,257	124,504,079	74,572,497
Stockholders' Equity	40,499,000	29,666,000	26,541,000	26,589,410	26,612,433	24,294,112	25,235,206	14,128,914
Shares Outstanding	582,207	459,947	457,013	455,170	391,796	372,854	409,925	300,761
Statistical Record								
Return on Assets %	1.35	1.56	1.49	0.53	N.M.	1.05	2.03	2.54
Return on Equity %	10.00	11.20	10.33	3.32	N.M.	6.34	12.27	16.07
Net Interest Margin %	87.48	85.01	81.14	72.17	64.33	58.94	62.23	64.26
Efficiency Ratio %	50.25	50.38	41.61	46.50	45.98	42.22	45.86	47.32
Loans to Deposits	0.95	1.03	0.99	0.75	0.89	1.19	1.10	1.21
Price Range	61.40-43.75	56.21-37.63	46.73-34.63	41.05-8.31	56.97-25.19	83.61-45.66	89.92-69.88	88.01-70.65
P/E Ratio	9.97-7.10	8.27-5.53	7.78-5.76	55.47-11.23	...	21.06-11.50	11.80-9.17	13.08-10.50
Average Yield %	0.37	0.42	0.50	1.94	3.46	0.15	0.13	0.14

Address: 1680 Capital One Drive, McLean, VA 22102 Telephone: 703-720-1000	Web Site: www.capitalone.com Officers: Richard D. Fairbank - Chairman, President, Chief Executive Officer Richard Scott Blackley - Senior Vice President, Principal Accounting Officer, Controller	Auditors: Ernst & Young LLP Investor Contact: 703-720-2455 Transfer Agents: Computershare Trust Company, N.A., Providence, RI

CAPITALSOURCE INC

Exchange	Symbol	Price	52Wk Range	Yield	P/E
NYS	CSE	$9.62 (3/28/2013)	9.78-6.02	0.42	4.52

*7 Year Price Score 59.72   *NYSE Composite Index=100   *12 Month Price Score 110.71

Interim Earnings (Per Share)

Qtr.	Mar	Jun	Sep	Dec
2008	0.03	0.25	0.03	(1.20)
2009	(0.36)	(0.82)	(0.87)	(0.77)
2010	(0.66)	0.06	0.24	0.02
2011	0.01	0.05	(0.26)	0.02
2012	0.10	1.66	0.14	0.25

Interim Dividends (Per Share)

Amt	Decl	Ex	Rec	Pay
0.01Q	09/04/2012	09/12/2012	09/14/2012	09/28/2012
0.50Sp	12/10/2012	12/18/2012	12/20/2012	12/26/2012
0.01Q	12/10/2012	12/18/2012	12/20/2012	12/26/2012
0.01Q	03/04/2013	03/12/2013	03/14/2013	03/28/2013

Indicated Div: $0.04

Valuation Analysis

		Institutional Holding	
Forecast EPS	$0.63 (04/06/2013)	No of Institutions	243
Market Cap	$2.0 Billion	Shares	190,973,680
Book Value	$1.6 Billion	% Held	53.76
Price/Book	1.24		
Price/Sales	3.83		

Business Summary: Banking (MIC: 5.1.1 SIC: 6029 NAIC: 522110)

CapitalSource is a commercial lender that, through its subsidiary, CapitalSource Bank, provides financial products to small and middle market businesses nationwide and provides depository products to customers and, to a lesser extent, borrowers in southern and central California. Co.'s primary commercial lending products include senior secured, asset-backed, real estate loans, which have a first priority lien in the collateral securing the loan. Co.'s primary depository products and services include savings and money market accounts, individual retirement account products and certificates of deposit. As of Dec 31 2011, Co. had total assets of $8.30 billion and deposits of $5.12 billion.

Recent Developments: For the year ended Dec 31 2012, income from continuing operations was US$490.6 million compared with a loss of US$52.0 million a year earlier. Net income amounted to US$490.6 million versus a net loss of US$52.0 million in the prior year. Net interest income increased 7.9% to US$388.8 million from US$360.4 million in the prior year. Provision for loan losses was US$39.4 million versus US$93.0 million in the prior year, a decrease of 57.6%. Non-interest income fell 46.2% to US$49.8 million from US$92.7 million, while non-interest expense declined 48.4% to US$193.7 million.

Prospects: Our evaluation of CapitalSource Inc. as of Apr. 7, 2013 is the result of our systematic analysis on three basic characteristics: earnings strength, relative valuation, and recent stock price movement. The company has suffered a very negative trend in earnings per share over the past 5 quarters and while recent estimates for the company have been mixed, CSE has posted better than expected results. Based on operating earnings yield, the company is undervalued when compared to all of the companies in our coverage universe. Share price changes over the past year indicates that CSE will perform well over the near term.

Financial Data

(US$ in Thousands)	12/31/2012	12/31/2011	12/31/2010	12/31/2009	12/31/2008	12/31/2007	12/31/2006	12/31/2005
Earnings Per Share	2.13	(0.17)	(0.34)	(2.84)	(0.89)	0.91	1.65	1.33
Cash Flow Per Share	1.21	1.30	0.94	6.23	11.53	(3.93)	(0.00)	(2.46)
Tang Book Value Per Share	6.93	5.47	5.82	6.22	9.43	11.70	11.53	8.55
Dividends Per Share	0.540	0.040	0.040	0.040	1.300	2.380	2.020	2.500
Dividend Payout %	25.35	...	...	...	...	261.54	122.42	187.97
Income Statement								
Interest Income	468,214	510,390	639,641	885,470	1,241,707	1,440,298	1,187,018	645,290
Interest Expense	79,407	150,010	232,096	437,713	712,110	847,241	606,725	185,935
Net Interest Income	388,807	360,380	407,545	447,757	529,597	593,057	580,293	459,355
Provision for Losses	39,442	92,985	307,080	845,986	593,046	78,641	81,562	65,680
Non-Interest Income	57,905	(26,313)	...	33,985	107,748	97,013	30,742	...
Non-Interest Expense	201,741	256,163	228,554	287,868	291,195	267,991	216,052	143,836
Income Before Taxes	205,529	(15,081)	(161,324)	(757,997)	(420,979)	268,788	350,749	269,072
Income Taxes	(285,081)	36,942	(20,802)	136,314	(199,781)	87,563	67,132	104,400
Net Income	490,610	(52,023)	(109,254)	(869,019)	(222,624)	176,287	279,276	164,672
Average Shares	230,154	302,998	320,836	306,417	251,213	193,282	169,220	123,433
Balance Sheet								
Net Loans & Leases	6,044,676	5,729,537	5,922,650	7,588,805	8,807,133	9,581,718	7,547,339	5,779,966
Total Assets	8,549,005	8,300,068	9,445,407	12,246,942	18,414,901	18,040,349	15,210,574	6,987,068
Total Deposits	5,579,270	5,124,995	4,621,273	4,483,879	5,043,695	...	...	...
Total Liabilities	6,923,833	6,724,922	7,391,465	10,063,809	15,575,780	15,458,078	13,117,534	5,787,130
Stockholders' Equity	1,625,172	1,575,146	2,053,942	2,183,133	2,839,121	2,582,271	2,093,040	1,199,938
Shares Outstanding	209,551	256,112	323,225	323,042	282,804	220,704	181,452	140,405
Statistical Record								
Return on Assets %	5.81	N.M.	N.M.	N.M.	N.M.	1.06	2.52	2.81
Return on Equity %	30.58	N.M.	N.M.	N.M.	N.M.	7.54	16.96	15.34
Net Interest Margin %	83.04	70.61	63.71	50.57	42.65	41.18	48.89	71.19
Efficiency Ratio %	38.35	52.92	...	31.31	21.58	17.43	17.74	...
Loans to Deposits	1.08	1.12	1.28	1.69	1.75	...	...	...
Price Range	8.05-6.02	8.17-5.15	7.10-3.93	4.93-0.90	17.85-3.16	28.25-14.05	28.45-21.64	25.72-18.27
P/E Ratio	3.78-2.83	...	...	...	...	31.04-15.44	17.24-13.12	19.34-13.74
Average Yield %	7.69	0.61	0.73	1.12	11.18	10.73	8.28	11.38

Address: 633 West 5th Street, 33rd Floor, Los Angeles, CA 90071	Web Site: www.capitalsource.com	Auditors: Ernst & Young LLP
Telephone: 213-443-7700	Officers: William G. Byrnes - Chairman Dean C. Graham - President, Chief Operating Officer	Investor Contact: 212-321-7212 Transfer Agents: American Stock Transfer & Trust Company, New York, NY

CARBO CERAMICS INC.

Exchange	Symbol	Price	52Wk Range	Yield	P/E	Div Achiever
NYS	CRR	$91.07 (3/28/2013)	104.39-61.00	1.19	19.84	12 Years

*7 Year Price Score 101.60 *NYSE Composite Index=100 *12 Month Price Score 105.68

Interim Earnings (Per Share)

Qtr.	Mar	Jun	Sep	Dec
2008	0.58	0.55	0.75	2.63
2009	0.70	0.41	0.62	0.54
2010	0.82	0.81	0.87	0.90
2011	1.30	1.29	1.59	1.43
2012	1.31	1.38	1.04	0.86

Interim Dividends (Per Share)

Amt	Decl	Ex	Rec	Pay
0.27Q	07/17/2012	07/30/2012	08/01/2012	08/15/2012
0.27Q	09/18/2012	10/31/2012	11/01/2012	11/15/2012
0.27Q	01/22/2013	01/30/2013	02/01/2013	02/15/2013
0.27Q	03/19/2013	04/29/2013	05/01/2013	05/15/2013

Indicated Div: $1.08

Valuation Analysis

Institutional Holding	
Forecast EPS	$4.23	No of Institutions
	(04/06/2013)	286
Market Cap	$2.1 Billion	Shares
Book Value	$713.1 Million	26,395,892
Price/Book	2.95	% Held
Price/Sales	3.26	93.64

TRADING VOLUME (thousand shares)

Business Summary: Equipment & Services (MIC: 9.1.3 SIC: 3299 NAIC: 327999)

CARBO Ceramics is a supplier of ceramic proppant. Co. also sells resin-coated sand. Co. provides fracture simulation software, fracture design and consulting services, and a range of technologies for spill prevention, containment and countermeasures. Co. sells the majority of its products and services to operators of oil and natural gas wells and to oilfield service companies. Co.'s products and services are used in the hydraulic fracturing of natural gas and oil wells. Co. primarily manufactures five distinct ceramic proppants. CARBOHSP® and CARBOPROP® are proppants used in deep oil and gas wells. CARBOLITE®, CARBOECONOPROP® and CARBOHYDROPROP® are lightweight ceramic proppants.

Recent Developments: For the year ended Dec 31 2012, net income decreased 18.6% to US$105.9 million from US$130.1 million in the prior year. Revenues were US$645.5 million, up 3.2% from US$625.7 million the year before. Operating income was US$158.9 million versus US$197.6 million in the prior year, a decrease of 19.6%. Direct operating expenses rose 15.9% to US$422.0 million from US$364.0 million in the comparable period the year before. Indirect operating expenses increased 0.8% to US$64.6 million from US$64.1 million in the equivalent prior-year period.

Prospects: Our evaluation of Carbo Ceramics Inc. as of Apr. 7, 2013 is the result of our systematic analysis on three basic characteristics: earnings strength, relative valuation, and recent stock price movement. The company has generated a negative trend in earnings per share over the past 5 quarters. However, while recent estimates for the company have been mixed, CRR has posted results that fell short of analysts expectations. Based on operating earnings yield, the company is about fairly valued when compared to all of the companies in our coverage universe. Share price changes over the past year indicates that CRR will perform poorly over the near term.

Financial Data

(US$ in Thousands)	12/31/2012	12/31/2011	12/31/2010	12/31/2009	12/31/2008	12/31/2007	12/31/2006	12/31/2005
Earnings Per Share	4.59	5.62	3.40	2.27	4.51	2.20	2.22	1.93
Cash Flow Per Share	6.79	4.84	4.00	0.95	3.11	2.45	2.09	2.20
Tang Book Value Per Share	30.35	26.75	22.02	19.22	18.52	14.94	13.16	11.18
Dividends Per Share	1.020	0.880	0.760	0.700	0.620	0.520	0.440	0.360
Dividend Payout %	22.22	15.66	22.35	30.84	13.75	23.64	19.82	18.65
Income Statement								
Total Revenue	645,536	625,705	473,082	341,872	387,828	340,351	312,126	252,673
EBITDA	203,419	233,268	146,899	104,248	112,496	104,570	100,936	83,068
Depn & Amortn	44,893	36,015	27,728	24,905	24,638	23,589	18,712	12,949
Income Before Taxes	158,590	197,450	119,349	79,794	88,349	81,400	83,814	71,875
Income Taxes	52,657	67,314	40,633	26,984	27,944	27,530	29,561	25,463
Net Income	105,933	130,136	78,716	52,810	110,316	53,870	54,253	46,620
Average Shares	22,969	23,012	22,977	23,111	24,460	24,483	24,400	24,177
Balance Sheet								
Current Assets	349,917	302,565	237,655	218,870	295,712	144,272	143,925	148,287
Total Assets	808,838	740,865	599,571	513,412	549,279	453,123	404,665	355,796
Current Liabilities	50,830	79,066	51,247	32,458	83,848	33,264	34,246	36,309
Total Liabilities	95,800	110,707	77,592	56,096	106,745	63,684	61,806	62,430
Stockholders' Equity	713,078	630,158	521,979	457,316	442,534	389,439	342,859	293,366
Shares Outstanding	23,092	23,106	23,108	23,077	23,637	24,516	24,391	24,286
Statistical Record								
Return on Assets %	13.63	19.42	14.15	9.94	21.95	12.56	14.27	14.27
Return on Equity %	15.73	22.59	16.08	11.74	26.45	14.71	17.05	17.34
EBITDA Margin %	31.51	37.28	31.05	30.49	29.01	30.72	32.34	32.88
Net Margin %	16.41	20.80	16.64	15.45	28.44	15.83	17.38	18.45
Asset Turnover	0.83	0.93	0.85	0.64	0.77	0.79	0.82	0.77
Current Ratio	6.88	3.83	4.64	6.74	3.53	4.34	4.20	4.08
Price Range	133.99-61.00	180.25-94.18	103.81-59.27	70.77-27.43	61.83-31.50	51.94-34.34	67.37-32.90	67.57-41.77
P/E Ratio	29.19-13.29	32.07-16.76	30.53-17.43	31.18-12.08	13.71-6.98	23.61-15.61	30.35-14.82	35.01-21.64
Average Yield %	1.23	0.65	0.99	1.63	1.38	1.18	0.94	0.68

Address: 575 North Dairy Ashford, Suite 300, Houston, TX 77079 Telephone: 281-921-6400	Web Site: www.carboceramics.com Officers: William C. Morris - Chairman Gary A. Kolstad - President, Chief Executive Officer	Auditors: Ernst & Young LLP Investor Contact: 281-921-6400 Transfer Agents: BNY Mellon Shareholder Services, Jersey City, NJ

143

CARDINAL HEALTH, INC.

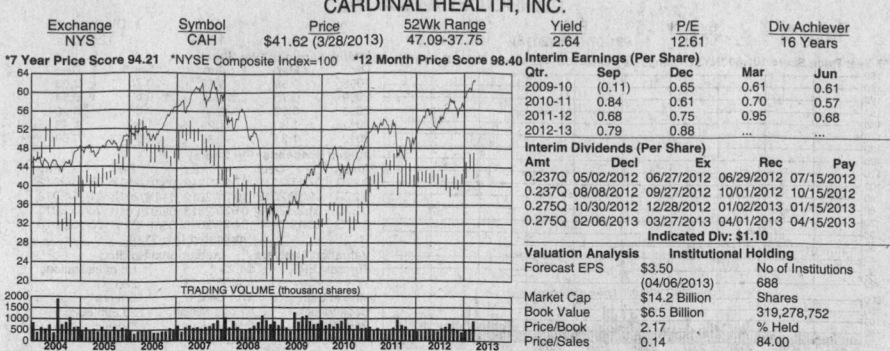

Exchange	Symbol	Price	52Wk Range	Yield	P/E	Div Achiever
NYS	CAH	$41.62 (3/28/2013)	47.09-37.75	2.64	12.61	16 Years

*7 Year Price Score 94.21   *NYSE Composite Index=100   *12 Month Price Score 98.40

Interim Earnings (Per Share)

Qtr.	Sep	Dec	Mar	Jun
2009-10	(0.11)	0.65	0.61	0.61
2010-11	0.84	0.61	0.70	0.57
2011-12	0.68	0.75	0.95	0.68
2012-13	0.79	0.88	...	...

Interim Dividends (Per Share)

Amt	Decl	Ex	Rec	Pay
0.237Q	05/02/2012	06/27/2012	06/29/2012	07/15/2012
0.237Q	08/08/2012	09/27/2012	10/01/2012	10/15/2012
0.275Q	10/30/2012	12/28/2012	01/02/2013	01/15/2013
0.275Q	02/06/2013	03/27/2013	04/01/2013	04/15/2013

Indicated Div: $1.10

Valuation Analysis

Forecast EPS	$3.50 (04/06/2013)
Market Cap	$14.2 Billion
Book Value	$6.5 Billion
Price/Book	2.17
Price/Sales	0.14

Institutional Holding

No of Institutions	688
Shares	319,278,752
% Held	84.00

Business Summary: Pharmaceuticals (MIC: 4.1.1 SIC: 5122 NAIC: 424210)

Cardinal Health is a healthcare services company providing pharmaceutical and medical products and services. Co. operates in two segments: Pharmaceutical and Medical. The Pharmaceutical segment, among others, distributes branded and generic pharmaceutical, over-the-counter healthcare and consumer products; operates nuclear pharmacies and cyclotron facilities; franchises retail pharmacies; and provides pharmacy services to hospitals and other healthcare facilities. The Medical segment, among others, distributes a range of medical, surgical and laboratory products, including single-use surgical drapes, gowns and apparel; exam and surgical gloves; and fluid suction and collection systems.

Recent Developments: For the quarter ended Dec 31 2012, income from continuing operations increased 14.6% to US$303.0 million from US$264.4 million in the year-earlier quarter. Net income increased 15.6% to US$303.0 million from US$262.0 million in the year-earlier quarter. Revenues were US$25.23 billion, down 6.8% from US$27.08 billion the year before. Operating income was US$506.0 million versus US$449.3 million in the prior-year quarter, an increase of 12.6%. Direct operating expenses declined 7.5% to US$24.01 billion from US$25.96 billion in the comparable period the year before. Indirect operating expenses increased 8.0% to US$718.0 million from US$664.6 million in the equivalent prior-year period.

Prospects: Our evaluation of Cardinal Health Inc. as of Apr. 7, 2013 is the result of our systematic analysis on three basic characteristics: earnings strength, relative valuation, and recent stock price movement. The company has managed to produce a neutral trend in earnings per share over the past 5 quarters. However, while recent estimates for the company have been mixed, CAH has posted better than expected results. Based on operating earnings yield, the company is undervalued when compared to all of the companies in our coverage universe. Share price changes over the past year indicates that CAH will perform well over the near term.

Financial Data

(US$ in Thousands)	6 Mos	3 Mos	06/30/2012	06/30/2011	06/30/2010	06/30/2009	06/30/2008	06/30/2007
Earnings Per Share	3.30	3.17	3.06	2.72	1.77	3.18	3.57	4.77
Cash Flow Per Share	3.60	3.64	3.40	4.00	5.95	4.38	4.21	3.10
Tang Book Value Per Share	6.20	5.41	5.40	4.53	8.48	7.30	4.26	4.12
Dividends Per Share	0.965	0.905	0.882	0.800	0.720	0.595	0.500	0.390
Dividend Payout %	29.24	28.55	28.84	29.41	40.68	18.71	14.01	8.18
Income Statement								
Total Revenue	51,121,000	25,889,000	107,552,000	102,644,200	98,502,800	99,512,400	91,091,400	86,852,000
EBITDA	1,151,000	553,000	2,034,000	1,854,100	1,558,500	2,192,000	2,410,900	1,625,900
Depn & Amortn	176,000	88,000	241,000	243,000	233,400	306,300	289,700	252,200
Income Before Taxes	922,000	439,000	1,698,000	1,518,300	1,211,600	1,667,000	1,949,800	1,252,300
Income Taxes	347,000	167,000	628,000	552,100	624,600	524,200	633,900	412,600
Net Income	575,000	271,000	1,069,000	959,000	642,200	1,151,600	1,300,600	1,931,100
Average Shares	343,000	344,000	349,000	352,500	361,400	361,500	364,000	404,700
Balance Sheet								
Current Assets	17,861,000	18,007,000	17,510,000	16,315,900	14,918,900	15,799,000	14,184,200	14,544,500
Total Assets	24,642,000	24,820,000	24,260,000	22,845,900	19,990,200	25,118,800	23,448,200	23,153,800
Current Liabilities	14,202,000	14,669,000	14,174,000	13,369,500	11,537,600	11,399,800	10,375,900	11,459,700
Long-Term Obligations	2,423,000	2,408,000	2,418,000	2,175,300	1,896,100	3,280,000	3,687,400	3,457,300
Total Liabilities	18,100,000	18,539,000	18,016,000	16,997,300	14,714,100	16,394,100	15,700,700	15,776,900
Stockholders' Equity	6,542,000	6,281,000	6,244,000	5,848,600	5,276,100	8,724,700	7,747,500	7,376,900
Shares Outstanding	341,000	340,000	343,000	351,100	356,400	360,000	357,100	368,100
Statistical Record								
Return on Assets %	4.68	4.60	4.53	4.48	2.85	4.74	5.57	8.30
Return on Equity %	18.35	18.39	17.63	17.24	9.17	13.98	17.15	24.34
EBITDA Margin %	2.25	2.14	1.89	1.81	1.58	2.20	2.65	1.87
Net Margin %	1.12	1.05	0.99	0.93	0.65	1.16	1.43	2.22
Asset Turnover	4.29	4.44	4.55	4.79	4.37	4.10	3.90	3.73
Current Ratio	1.26	1.23	1.24	1.22	1.29	1.39	1.37	1.27
Debt to Equity	0.37	0.38	0.39	0.37	0.36	0.38	0.48	0.47
Price Range	43.50-37.75	45.49-37.75	46.83-37.99	45.54-29.96	36.45-21.06	40.45-20.38	51.18-35.76	54.05-44.40
P/E Ratio	13.18-11.44	14.35-11.91	15.30-12.42	16.74-11.01	20.59-11.90	12.72-6.41	14.34-10.02	11.33-9.31
Average Yield %	2.34	2.18	2.10	2.10	2.34	2.10	1.16	0.80

Address: 7000 Cardinal Place, Dublin, OH 43017 Telephone: 614-757-5000	Web Site: www.cardinalhealth.com Officers: George S. Barrett - Chairman, Chief Executive Officer Mark R. Blake - Executive Vice President	Auditors: Ernst & Young LLP Investor Contact: 614-757-7115 Transfer Agents: Computershare, Providence, RI

CAREFUSION CORP

Exchange	Symbol	Price	52Wk Range	Yield	P/E
NYS	CFN	$34.99 (3/28/2013)	34.99-23.98	N/A	24.30

*7 Year Price Score N/A   *NYSE Composite Index=100   *12 Month Price Score 109.15

Interim Earnings (Per Share)

Qtr.	Sep	Dec	Mar	Jun
2009-10	0.37	0.32	(0.04)	0.23
2010-11	0.17	0.34	0.20	0.37
2011-12	0.30	0.42	0.13	0.45
2012-13	0.38	0.48	...	...

Interim Dividends (Per Share)

No Dividends Paid

Valuation Analysis   Institutional Holding

Forecast EPS	$2.15	No of Institutions
	(04/05/2013)	437
Market Cap	$7.8 Billion	Shares
Book Value	$5.5 Billion	208,837,488
Price/Book	1.42	% Held
Price/Sales	2.15	91.22

Business Summary: Medical Instruments & Equipment (MIC: 4.3.1 SIC: 5047 NAIC: 423450)

CareFusion is a medical technology company. Co. has two segments. In its Medical Systems segment, Co. develops, manufactures and markets capital equipment and related supplies for medication management, which includes its infusion and medication dispensing technologies, supplies dispensing technologies and respiratory technologies. In its Procedural Solutions segment, Co. develops, manufactures and markets single-use skin antiseptic and other patient-preparation products, non-dedicated intravenous infusion administration sets and accessories, reusable surgical instruments and non-dedicated ventilator circuits and other disposables used for providing respiratory therapy.

Recent Developments: For the quarter ended Dec 31 2012, income from continuing operations increased 14.9% to US$108.0 million from US$94.0 million in the year-earlier quarter. Net income increased 13.7% to US$108.0 million from US$95.0 million in the year-earlier quarter. Revenues were US$909.0 million, up 2.1% from US$890.0 million the year before. Operating income was US$171.0 million versus US$143.0 million in the prior-year quarter, an increase of 19.6%. Direct operating expenses declined 1.1% to US$438.0 million from US$443.0 million in the comparable period the year before. Indirect operating expenses decreased 1.3% to US$300.0 million from US$304.0 million in the equivalent prior-year period.

Prospects: Our evaluation of Carefusion Corp. as of Apr. 7, 2013 is the result of our systematic analysis on three basic characteristics: earnings strength, relative valuation, and recent stock price movement. The company has produced a positive trend in earnings per share over the past 5 quarters and while recent estimates for the company have remained steady, CFN has posted better than expected results. Based on operating earnings yield, the company is about fairly valued when compared to all of the companies in our coverage universe. Share price changes over the past year indicates that CFN will perform in line with the market over the near term.

Financial Data

(US$ in Millions)	6 Mos	3 Mos	06/30/2012	06/30/2011	06/30/2010	06/30/2009	06/30/2008	06/30/2007
Earnings Per Share	1.44	1.38	1.30	1.08	0.87	...	...	...
Cash Flow Per Share	3.24	3.30	2.92	1.45	3.18	...	...	...
Tang Book Value Per Share	7.10	6.64	6.15	5.60	3.43	4.73	...	...
Income Statement								
Total Revenue	1,746	837	3,598	3,528	3,929	4,501	4,518	3,478
EBITDA	405	188	683	601	568	942	1,015	749
Depn & Amortn	91	45	109	105	96	120	101	76
Income Before Taxes	276	124	487	413	357	719	847	618
Income Taxes	81	37	126	124	186	151	184	116
Net Income	192	84	293	244	194	568	663	502
Average Shares	224	224	226	225	223	...	...	...
Balance Sheet								
Current Assets	3,013	2,885	3,118	2,868	2,508	2,390	2,322	...
Total Assets	8,412	8,253	8,488	8,221	7,943	8,349	8,329	...
Current Liabilities	595	565	933	619	753	762	800	...
Long-Term Obligations	1,151	1,151	1,151	1,387	1,386	1,159	1,539	...
Total Liabilities	2,939	2,911	3,257	3,128	3,239	2,898	3,281	...
Stockholders' Equity	5,473	5,342	5,231	5,093	4,704	5,451	5,048	...
Shares Outstanding	222	222	221	223	222	221	...	...
Statistical Record								
Return on Assets %	3.85	3.75	3.50	3.02	2.38	6.81	...	...
Return on Equity %	6.04	5.92	5.66	4.98	3.82	10.82	...	...
EBITDA Margin %	23.20	22.46	18.98	17.04	14.46	20.93	22.47	21.54
Net Margin %	11.00	10.04	8.14	6.92	4.94	12.62	14.67	14.43
Asset Turnover	0.43	0.44	0.43	0.44	0.48	0.54	...	...
Current Ratio	5.06	5.11	3.34	4.63	3.33	3.14	2.90	...
Debt to Equity	0.21	0.22	0.22	0.27	0.29	0.21	0.30	...
Price Range	29.05-22.82	28.63-22.82	28.14-22.26	29.89-20.68	28.94-17.73	...	...	...
P/E Ratio	20.17-15.85	20.75-16.54	21.65-17.12	27.68-19.15	33.26-20.38	...	...	...

Address: 3750 Torrey View Court, San Diego, CA 92130 Telephone: 858-617-2000	Web Site: www.carefusion.com Officers: Kieran T. Gallahue - Chairman, Chief Executive Officer Joan Stafslien - Executive Vice President, Chief Compliance Officer, General Counsel, Secretary	Auditors: Ernst & Young LLP Investor Contact: 858-617-4621 Transfer Agents: Computershare Trust Company, N.A., Canton, MA

CARLISLE COMPANIES INC.

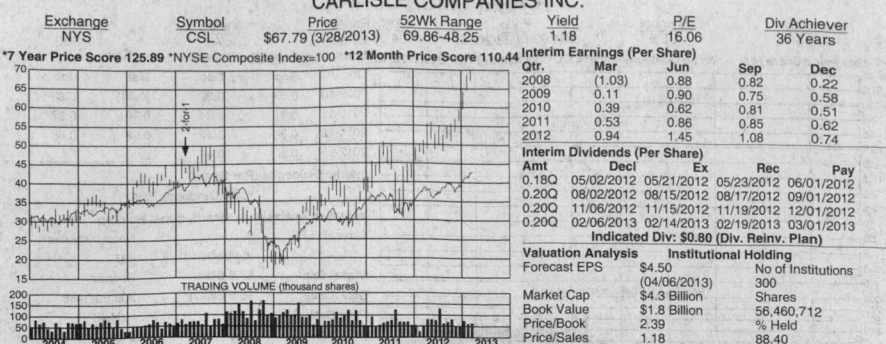

Exchange	Symbol	Price	52Wk Range	Yield	P/E	Div Achiever
NYS	CSL	$67.79 (3/28/2013)	69.86-48.25	1.18	16.06	36 Years

*7 Year Price Score 125.89 *NYSE Composite Index=100 ***12 Month Price Score 110.44**

Interim Earnings (Per Share)

Qtr.	Mar	Jun	Sep	Dec
2008	(1.03)	0.88	0.82	0.22
2009	0.11	0.90	0.75	0.58
2010	0.39	0.62	0.81	0.51
2011	0.53	0.86	0.85	0.62
2012	0.94	1.45	1.08	0.74

Interim Dividends (Per Share)

Amt	Decl	Ex	Rec	Pay
0.18Q	05/02/2012	05/21/2012	05/23/2012	06/01/2012
0.20Q	08/02/2012	08/15/2012	08/17/2012	09/01/2012
0.20Q	11/06/2012	11/15/2012	11/19/2012	12/01/2012
0.20Q	02/06/2013	02/14/2013	02/19/2013	03/01/2013

Indicated Div: $0.80 (Div. Reinv. Plan)

Valuation Analysis **Institutional Holding**

Forecast EPS	$4.50 (04/06/2013)	No of Institutions 300
Market Cap	$4.3 Billion	Shares
Book Value	$1.8 Billion	56,460,712
Price/Book	2.39	% Held
Price/Sales	1.18	88.40

Business Summary: Rubber Products (MIC: 8.4.1 SIC: 3069 NAIC: 326299)

Carlisle Companies is a holding company. Through its subsidiaries, Co. is a manufacturing company. Co. has five segments: construction materials, which provide rubber and thermoplastic polyolefin roofing membranes, and other roofing accessories; transportation products, comprised of the tire and wheel and power transmission belt product lines; brake and friction, which consists of off-highway braking systems and friction products; interconnect technologies, which provides wire, cable, connectors and cable assemblies; and foodservice products, which include foodservice permanentware, table coverings, cookware, catering equipment, fiberglass and composite material trays and dishes.

Recent Developments: For the year ended Dec 31 2012, income from continuing operations increased 46.9% to US$267.3 million from US$181.9 million a year earlier. Net income increased 49.9% to US$270.2 million from US$180.3 million in the prior year. Revenues were US$3.63 billion, up 12.6% from US$3.22 billion the year before. Direct operating expenses rose 7.2% to US$2.73 billion from US$2.55 billion in the comparable period the year before. Indirect operating expenses increased 17.8% to US$473.4 million from US$402.0 million in the equivalent prior-year period.

Prospects: Our evaluation of Carlisle Companies Inc. as of Apr. 7, 2013 is the result of our systematic analysis on three basic characteristics: earnings strength, relative valuation, and recent stock price movement. The company has generated a negative trend in earnings per share over the past 5 quarters and while recent estimates for the company have been raised by analysts, CSL has posted better than expected results. Based on operating earnings yield, the company is undervalued when compared to all of the companies in our coverage universe. Share price changes over the past year indicates that CSL will perform well over the near term.

Financial Data

(US$ in Thousands)	12/31/2012	12/31/2011	12/31/2010	12/31/2009	12/31/2008	12/31/2007	12/31/2006	12/31/2005
Earnings Per Share	4.22	2.86	2.34	2.34	0.91	3.44	3.46	1.71
Cash Flow Per Share	7.75	3.11	1.76	7.38	4.52	4.20	0.32	3.47
Tang Book Value Per Share	3.36	2.85	6.16	9.79	8.46	11.79	9.98	6.57
Dividends Per Share	0.760	0.700	0.660	0.630	0.600	0.560	0.520	0.480
Dividend Payout %	18.01	24.48	28.21	26.92	65.93	16.28	15.01	28.07
Income Statement								
Total Revenue	3,629,400	3,224,500	2,527,700	2,379,500	2,971,400	2,876,383	2,572,510	2,209,610
EBITDA	498,900	343,200	254,900	263,500	304,800	390,699	331,245	261,440
Depn & Amortn	74,600	68,100	58,800	56,600	59,400	61,313	55,614	51,974
Income Before Taxes	398,800	253,900	187,800	197,900	217,800	319,342	255,317	193,558
Income Taxes	131,500	72,000	57,200	46,100	68,300	106,321	78,031	60,224
Net Income	270,200	180,300	145,600	144,600	55,800	215,637	215,689	106,365
Average Shares	63,610	62,495	61,592	61,234	61,332	62,630	62,236	62,156
Balance Sheet								
Current Assets	1,205,300	1,214,100	1,016,900	799,800	968,100	1,023,192	978,241	661,172
Total Assets	3,457,300	3,137,900	2,529,500	1,914,100	2,075,900	1,988,794	1,877,817	1,563,257
Current Liabilities	470,600	613,500	456,400	301,100	442,500	388,187	466,686	372,711
Long-Term Obligations	752,500	604,300	405,100	156,100	273,300	262,809	274,658	282,426
Total Liabilities	1,669,200	1,637,800	1,188,800	695,500	981,800	869,899	935,608	833,018
Stockholders' Equity	1,788,100	1,500,100	1,340,700	1,218,600	1,094,100	1,118,895	942,209	730,239
Shares Outstanding	63,127	61,664	61,024	60,645	60,532	60,603	61,450	60,714
Statistical Record								
Return on Assets %	8.17	6.36	6.55	7.25	2.74	11.15	12.54	6.94
Return on Equity %	16.39	12.69	11.38	12.50	5.03	20.92	25.79	14.89
EBITDA Margin %	13.75	10.64	10.08	11.07	10.26	13.58	12.88	11.83
Net Margin %	7.44	5.59	5.76	6.08	1.88	7.50	8.38	4.81
Asset Turnover	1.10	1.14	1.14	1.19	1.46	1.49	1.50	1.44
Current Ratio	2.56	1.98	2.23	2.66	2.19	2.64	2.10	1.77
Debt to Equity	0.42	0.40	0.30	0.13	0.25	0.23	0.29	0.39
Price Range	59.36-45.56	50.55-30.52	41.63-28.05	36.28-18.11	39.67-17.26	50.00-36.80	45.04-33.84	37.31-29.78
P/E Ratio	14.07-10.80	17.67-10.67	17.79-11.99	15.50-7.74	43.59-18.97	14.53-10.70	13.02-9.78	21.82-17.42
Average Yield %	1.45	1.65	1.84	2.34	2.03	1.28	1.30	1.43

Address: 11605 North Community House Road, Suite 600, Charlotte, NC 28277	Web Site: www.carlisle.com	Auditors: Ernst & Young LLP
Telephone: 704-501-1100	Officers: David A. Roberts - Chairman, President, Chief Executive Officer Steven J. Ford - Vice President, Chief Financial Officer, Secretary, General Counsel	Investor Contact: 704-501-1100
Fax: 704-501-1190		Transfer Agents: Computershare Investor Services LLC, Chicago, IL

CARMAX INC.

Exchange	Symbol	Price	52Wk Range	Yield	P/E
NYS	KMX	$41.70 (3/28/2013)	41.70-25.22	N/A	23.04

*7 Year Price Score 123.19 *NYSE Composite Index=100 *12 Month Price Score 110.55

TRADING VOLUME (thousand shares)

Interim Earnings (Per Share)

Qtr.	May	Aug	Nov	Feb
2009-10	0.13	0.46	0.33	0.34
2010-11	0.44	0.48	0.36	0.39
2011-12	0.55	0.49	0.36	0.40
2012-13	0.52	0.48	0.41	...

Interim Dividends (Per Share)

No Dividends Paid

Valuation Analysis		Institutional Holding	
Forecast EPS	$1.87	No of Institutions	
	(04/05/2013)	457	
Market Cap	$9.5 Billion	Shares	
Book Value	$3.0 Billion	250,485,792	
Price/Book	3.15	% Held	
Price/Sales	0.90	97.23	

Business Summary: Retail - Automotive (MIC: 2.1.4 SIC: 5521 NAIC: 441120)

CarMax is holding company. Through its subsidiaries, Co. is engaged as a retailer of used cars. In addition, Co. sells new vehicles at four locations under franchise agreements with three new car manufacturers. Co. provides customers with a range of other related products and services, including the appraisal and purchase of vehicles directly from consumers; the sale of service plans, guaranteed asset protection and accessories; and vehicle repair service. As of Feb 29 2012, Co. operated 108 used car superstores in 53 metropolitan markets, of which 58 of the 108 used car superstores were leased and the remaining 50 stores were owned.

Recent Developments: For the quarter ended Nov 30 2012, net income increased 15.3% to US$94.7 million from US$82.1 million in the year-earlier quarter. Revenues were US$2.60 billion, up 15.1% from US$2.26 billion the year before. Direct operating expenses rose 15.3% to US$2.26 billion from US$1.96 billion in the comparable period the year before. Indirect operating expenses increased 12.3% to US$192.8 million from US$171.6 million in the equivalent prior-year period.

Prospects: Our evaluation of Carmax Inc. as of Apr. 7, 2013 is the result of our systematic analysis on three basic characteristics: earnings strength, relative valuation, and recent stock price movement. The company has enjoyed a very positive trend in earnings per share over the past 5 quarters and while recent estimates for the company have been mixed, KMX has posted better than expected results. Based on operating earnings yield, the company is about fairly valued when compared to all of the companies in our coverage universe. Share price changes over the past year indicates that KMX will perform in line with the market over the near term.

Financial Data
(US$ in Thousands)

	9 Mos	6 Mos	3 Mos	02/29/2012	02/28/2011	02/28/2010	02/28/2009	02/29/2008
Earnings Per Share	1.81	1.76	1.77	1.79	1.67	1.26	0.27	0.83
Cash Flow Per Share	(2.44)	(1.17)	(0.88)	(0.27)	(0.08)	0.23	1.22	0.37
Tang Book Value Per Share	13.25	12.91	12.35	11.77	10.15	8.67	7.23	6.81
Income Statement								
Total Revenue	8,134,870	5,532,424	2,774,420	10,003,599	8,975,554	7,470,193	6,973,966	8,199,571
EBITDA	624,281	439,472	226,758	783,436	675,541	513,724	155,839	347,273
Depn & Amortn	70,721	46,442	22,982	82,812	59,421	58,328	54,741	46,615
Income Before Taxes	529,200	376,735	195,633	666,910	613,490	452,496	96,798	297,069
Income Taxes	202,137	144,353	74,887	253,115	232,612	170,828	37,585	115,044
Net Income	327,063	232,382	120,746	413,795	380,878	281,668	59,213	182,025
Average Shares	232,656	231,696	231,802	230,721	227,601	222,234	220,513	220,522
Balance Sheet								
Current Assets	2,085,364	1,961,548	1,931,007	1,853,448	1,410,098	1,556,412	1,287,752	1,356,925
Total Assets	9,297,683	8,871,440	8,598,163	8,331,543	6,839,909	2,556,191	2,379,187	2,333,161
Current Liabilities	575,692	525,839	618,516	646,313	508,217	477,351	490,770	490,024
Long-Term Obligations	5,552,488	5,255,330	5,022,569	4,863,318	3,909,492	27,371	178,062	227,153
Total Liabilities	6,274,014	5,921,853	5,777,815	5,658,431	4,548,279	622,609	786,120	844,235
Stockholders' Equity	3,023,669	2,949,587	2,820,348	2,673,112	2,291,630	1,933,582	1,593,067	1,488,926
Shares Outstanding	228,216	228,444	228,305	227,118	225,885	223,065	220,392	218,616
Statistical Record								
Return on Assets %	4.96	5.03	5.18	5.44	8.11	11.41	2.51	8.61
Return on Equity %	14.84	14.83	15.55	16.62	18.03	15.97	3.84	13.27
EBITDA Margin %	7.67	7.94	8.17	7.83	7.53	6.88	2.23	4.24
Net Margin %	4.02	4.20	4.35	4.14	4.24	3.77	0.85	2.22
Asset Turnover	1.25	1.27	1.28	1.32	1.91	3.03	2.96	3.88
Current Ratio	3.62	3.73	3.12	2.87	2.77	3.26	2.62	2.77
Debt to Equity	1.84	1.78	1.78	1.82	1.71	0.01	0.11	0.15
Price Range	36.26-25.22	34.98-23.41	34.98-23.41	35.38-23.41	36.83-18.67	24.50-8.68	21.73-6.23	27.40-16.63
P/E Ratio	20.03-13.93	19.88-13.30	19.76-13.23	19.77-13.08	22.05-11.18	19.44-6.89	80.48-23.07	33.01-20.04

Address: 12800 Tuckahoe Creek Parkway, Richmond, VA 23238 Telephone: 804-747-0422	Web Site: www.carmax.com Officers: William R. Tiefel - Chairman Thomas J. Folliard - President, Chief Executive Officer	Auditors: KPMG LLP Investor Contact: 804-747-0422 Transfer Agents: Wells Fargo Bank, N.A., South St. Paul, MN

CARNIVAL CORP.

Exchange	Symbol	Price	52Wk Range	Yield	P/E
NYS	CCL	$34.30 (3/28/2013)	39.32-30.49	2.92	18.05

*7 Year Price Score 83.93   *NYSE Composite Index=100   *12 Month Price Score 93.39

TRADING VOLUME (thousand shares)

Interim Earnings (Per Share)

Qtr.	Feb	May	Aug	Nov
2009-10	0.22	0.32	1.62	0.31
2010-11	0.19	0.26	1.69	0.28
2011-12	(0.18)	0.02	1.71	0.12
2012-13	0.05	...	...	...

Interim Dividends (Per Share)

Amt	Deci	Ex	Rec	Pay
0.25Q	07/11/2012	08/22/2012	08/24/2012	09/14/2012
0.25Q	10/08/2012	11/20/2012	11/23/2012	12/14/2012
0.50Sp	11/16/2012	12/05/2012	12/07/2012	12/28/2012
0.25Q	01/17/2013	02/20/2013	02/22/2013	03/15/2013

Indicated Div: $1.00

Valuation Analysis | **Institutional Holding**

Forecast EPS	$2.00 (04/06/2013)	No of Institutions 623
Market Cap	$26.6 Billion	Shares
Book Value	$23.5 Billion	437,182,048
Price/Book	1.13	% Held
Price/Sales	1.73	51.71

Business Summary: Hotels, Restaurants & Travel (MIC: 2.2.1 SIC: 4489 NAIC: 483212)

Carnival is a cruise and leisure travel company. Co. has a portfolio of several cruise brands that are sold to several vacation markets. Each of Co.'s cruise brands is an operating segment that it aggregated into either the North America or Europe, Australia & Asia (EAA) reportable cruise segments. Co.'s North America segment cruise brands include Carnival Cruise Lines, Princess Cruises, Holland America Line, and Seabourn. Co.'s EAA segment cruise brands include Costa Cruises', AIDA Cruises, P&O Cruises (U.K.), Cunard, P&O Cruises (Australia), and Ibero Cruises.

Recent Developments: For the quarter ended Feb 28 2013, net income amounted to US$37.0 million versus a net loss of US$139.0 million in the year-earlier quarter. Revenues were US$3.59 billion, up 0.3% from US$3.58 billion the year before. Operating income was US$145.0 million versus a loss of US$82.0 million in the prior-year quarter. Direct operating expenses declined 3.5% to US$2.60 billion from US$2.69 billion in the comparable period the year before. Indirect operating expenses decreased 12.5% to US$849.0 million from US$970.0 million in the equivalent prior-year period.

Prospects: Our evaluation of Carnival Corp. as of Apr. 7, 2013 is the result of our systematic analysis on three basic characteristics: earnings strength, relative valuation, and recent stock price movement. The company has produced a positive trend in earnings per share over the past 5 quarters. However, while recent estimates for the company have been lowered by analysts, CCL has posted better than expected results. Based on operating earnings yield, the company is about fairly valued when compared to all of the companies in our coverage universe. Share price changes over the past year indicates that CCL will perform very well over the near term.

Financial Data

(US$ in Thousands)	3 Mos	11/30/2012	11/30/2011	11/30/2010	11/30/2009	11/30/2008	11/30/2007	11/30/2006
Earnings Per Share	1.90	1.67	2.42	2.47	2.24	2.90	2.95	2.77
Cash Flow Per Share	3.96	3.84	4.79	4.85	4.25	4.30	5.13	4.54
Tang Book Value Per Share	24.62	25.05	24.68	23.28	21.90	18.52	19.01	17.10
Dividends Per Share	1.500	1.000	1.000	0.400	...	1.600	1.375	1.025
Dividend Payout %	78.95	59.88	41.32	16.19	...	55.17	46.61	37.00
Income Statement								
Total Revenue	3,593,000	15,382,000	15,793,000	14,469,000	13,157,000	14,646,000	13,033,000	11,839,000
EBITDA	509,000	3,155,000	3,788,000	3,761,000	3,481,000	4,005,000	3,825,000	3,593,000
Depn & Amortn	389,000	1,527,000	1,522,000	1,416,000	1,309,000	1,249,000	1,101,000	988,000
Income Before Taxes	39,000	1,302,000	1,912,000	1,979,000	1,806,000	2,377,000	2,424,000	2,318,000
Income Taxes	2,000	4,000	...	1,000	16,000	47,000	16,000	39,000
Net Income	37,000	1,298,000	1,912,000	1,978,000	1,790,000	2,330,000	2,408,000	2,279,000
Average Shares	778,000	779,000	789,000	805,000	804,000	816,000	828,000	836,000
Balance Sheet								
Current Assets	1,792,000	1,821,000	1,312,000	1,244,000	1,518,000	1,650,000	1,976,000	1,995,000
Total Assets	38,675,000	39,161,000	38,637,000	37,490,000	36,835,000	33,400,000	34,181,000	30,552,000
Current Liabilities	6,782,000	7,340,000	6,105,000	5,755,000	4,967,000	5,781,000	7,260,000	5,415,000
Long-Term Obligations	7,622,000	7,168,000	8,053,000	8,011,000	9,097,000	7,735,000	6,313,000	6,355,000
Total Liabilities	15,152,000	15,232,000	14,805,000	14,459,000	14,800,000	14,302,000	14,218,000	12,342,000
Stockholders' Equity	23,523,000	23,929,000	23,832,000	23,031,000	22,035,000	19,098,000	19,963,000	18,210,000
Shares Outstanding	775,000	776,000	777,000	790,000	787,000	785,000	787,000	794,000
Statistical Record								
Return on Assets %	3.80	3.33	5.02	5.32	5.10	6.88	7.44	7.73
Return on Equity %	6.25	5.42	8.16	8.78	8.70	11.90	12.62	12.96
EBITDA Margin %	14.17	20.51	23.99	25.99	26.46	27.35	29.35	30.35
Net Margin %	1.03	8.44	12.11	13.67	13.60	15.91	18.48	19.25
Asset Turnover	0.40	0.39	0.41	0.39	0.37	0.43	0.40	0.40
Current Ratio	0.26	0.25	0.21	0.22	0.31	0.29	0.27	0.37
Debt to Equity	0.32	0.30	0.34	0.35	0.41	0.41	0.32	0.35
Price Range	39.32-29.48	39.16-29.48	47.85-29.42	44.70-30.14	33.95-16.98	45.80-15.02	52.39-42.23	56.00-36.41
P/E Ratio	20.69-15.52	23.45-17.65	19.77-12.16	18.10-12.20	15.16-7.58	15.79-5.18	17.76-14.32	20.22-13.14
Average Yield %	4.29	2.96	2.64	1.10	...	4.32	2.89	2.19

Address: 3655 N.W. 87th Avenue, Miami, FL 33178-2428 Telephone: 305-599-2600	Web Site: www.carnivalcorporation.com Officers: Micky Meir Arison - Chairman, Chief Executive Officer Howard S. Frank - Vice-Chairman, Chief Operating Officer	Auditors: PricewaterhouseCoopers LLP Investor Contact: 305-406-5559 Transfer Agents: ComputerShare Investor Services, Providence, RI

CARPENTER TECHNOLOGY CORP.

Exchange	Symbol	Price	52Wk Range	Yield	P/E
NYS	CRS	$49.29 (3/28/2013)	56.81-42.27	1.46	17.42

*7 Year Price Score 97.88   *NYSE Composite Index=100   *12 Month Price Score 90.11

TRADING VOLUME (thousand shares)

Interim Earnings (Per Share)

Qtr.	Sep	Dec	Mar	Jun
2009-10	(0.21)	0.08	0.05	0.13
2010-11	0.17	0.21	0.64	0.57
2011-12	0.53	0.52	0.69	0.78
2012-13	0.74	0.62	...	...

Interim Dividends (Per Share)

Amt	Decl	Ex	Rec	Pay
0.18Q	04/17/2012	04/27/2012	05/01/2012	06/07/2012
0.18Q	08/14/2012	08/24/2012	08/28/2012	09/07/2012
0.18Q	10/08/2012	10/19/2012	10/23/2012	12/06/2012
0.18Q	01/30/2013	02/08/2013	02/12/2013	03/07/2013

Indicated Div: $0.72

Valuation Analysis

		Institutional Holding	
Forecast EPS	$3.04 (04/06/2013)	No of Institutions	305
Market Cap	$2.6 Billion	Shares	45,644,208
Book Value	$1.2 Billion	% Held	96.83
Price/Book	2.19		
Price/Sales	1.15		

Business Summary: Non-Precious Metals (MIC: 8.2.2 SIC: 3312 NAIC: 331111)

Carpenter Technology manufactures, fabricates and distributes metals. Co. has three reportable segments: Specialty Alloys Operations, which consists of alloy and stainless steel manufacturing operations; Latrobe, which consists of the manufacturing and distribution operations of the Latrobe Specialty Metals, Inc. business and Co.'s distribution business in Mexico; and Performance Engineered Products, which consists of the operations of Dynamet titanium business, Carpenter Powder Products business, and the Amega West Services, LLC business. Co.'s primary classes of products are: alloys, stainless steels, titanium products, powder metals and alloy and tools steels.

Recent Developments: For the quarter ended Dec 31 2012, net income increased 39.5% to US$33.2 million from US$23.8 million in the year-earlier quarter. Revenues were US$533.5 million, up 23.8% from US$431.1 million the year before. Operating income was US$52.7 million versus US$43.9 million in the prior-year quarter, an increase of 20.0%. Direct operating expenses rose 24.3% to US$430.9 million from US$346.8 million in the comparable period the year before. Indirect operating expenses increased 23.5% to US$49.9 million from US$40.4 million in the equivalent prior-year period.

Prospects: Our evaluation of Carpenter Technology Corp. as of Apr. 7, 2013 is the result of our systematic analysis on three basic characteristics: earnings strength, relative valuation, and recent stock price movement. The company has managed to produce a neutral trend in earnings per share over the past 5 quarters. However, while recent estimates for the company have been mixed, CRS has posted better than expected results. Based on operating earnings yield, the company is undervalued when compared to all of the companies in our coverage universe. Share price changes over the past year indicates that CRS will perform in line with the market over the near term.

Financial Data

(US$ in Thousands)	6 Mos	3 Mos	06/30/2012	06/30/2011	06/30/2010	06/30/2009	06/30/2008	06/30/2007
Earnings Per Share	2.83	2.73	2.53	1.59	0.04	1.08	5.70	4.32
Cash Flow Per Share	3.60	3.74	3.39	1.46	2.62	3.31	4.49	5.35
Tang Book Value Per Share	15.73	15.16	13.99	15.66	11.84	12.79	17.31	19.18
Dividends Per Share	0.720	0.720	0.720	0.720	0.720	0.720	0.630	0.487
Dividend Payout %	25.44	26.37	28.46	45.28	1,800.00	66.67	11.05	11.30
Income Statement								
Total Revenue	1,078,500	544,900	2,028,700	1,675,100	1,198,600	1,362,300	1,953,500	1,944,800
EBITDA	167,800	90,300	282,400	160,400	74,500	123,900	347,000	377,700
Depn & Amortn	51,100	25,500	71,500	59,200	53,600	49,500	46,800	47,100
Income Before Taxes	107,300	59,700	188,000	85,200	4,700	63,000	296,200	329,800
Income Taxes	35,900	19,600	67,000	16,100	2,600	15,100	96,800	103,800
Net Income	72,200	39,200	121,200	71,000	2,100	47,900	277,700	227,200
Average Shares	53,500	53,400	47,800	44,700	44,400	44,200	48,700	52,600
Balance Sheet								
Current Assets	1,127,900	1,191,900	1,249,700	1,157,600	820,200	749,700	966,700	1,255,700
Total Assets	2,582,200	2,603,100	2,627,800	1,991,900	1,583,200	1,497,400	1,712,200	2,025,700
Current Liabilities	476,000	518,900	554,200	395,400	218,100	198,500	325,600	366,200
Long-Term Obligations	305,200	305,600	305,900	407,800	259,600	258,600	276,700	299,500
Total Liabilities	1,394,900	1,437,500	1,524,000	1,226,200	1,009,800	880,400	873,000	958,000
Stockholders' Equity	1,187,300	1,165,600	1,103,800	765,700	573,400	617,000	839,200	1,067,700
Shares Outstanding	52,675	52,632	52,412	44,107	43,967	44,029	45,295	52,243
Statistical Record								
Return on Assets %	6.56	6.10	5.23	3.97	0.14	2.98	14.82	11.61
Return on Equity %	14.95	14.33	12.93	10.60	0.35	6.58	29.05	22.56
EBITDA Margin %	15.56	16.57	13.92	9.58	6.22	9.09	17.76	19.42
Net Margin %	6.69	7.19	5.97	4.24	0.18	3.52	14.22	11.68
Asset Turnover	1.01	0.96	0.88	0.94	0.78	0.85	1.04	0.99
Current Ratio	2.37	2.30	2.25	2.93	3.76	3.78	2.97	3.43
Debt to Equity	0.26	0.26	0.28	0.53	0.45	0.42	0.33	0.28
Price Range	56.81-42.27	59.53-41.32	59.53-41.32	57.68-30.58	42.52-16.87	43.65-11.93	79.40-43.30	68.27-45.34
P/E Ratio	20.07-14.94	21.81-15.14	23.53-16.33	36.28-19.23	N.M.	40.42-11.05	13.93-7.60	15.80-10.49
Average Yield %	1.43	1.42	1.41	1.78	2.54	3.13	1.02	0.86

Address: P.O. Box 14662, Reading, PA 19610	**Web Site:** www.cartech.com	**Auditors:** PricewaterhouseCoopers LLP
Telephone: 610-208-2000	**Officers:** Gregory A. Pratt - Chairman, Interim President, Chief Executive Officer William A. Wulfsohn - President, Chief Executive Officer	**Investor Contact:** 610-208-3476
Fax: 610-208-2361		**Transfer Agents:** American Stock Transfer & Trust Company

CARTER'S INC

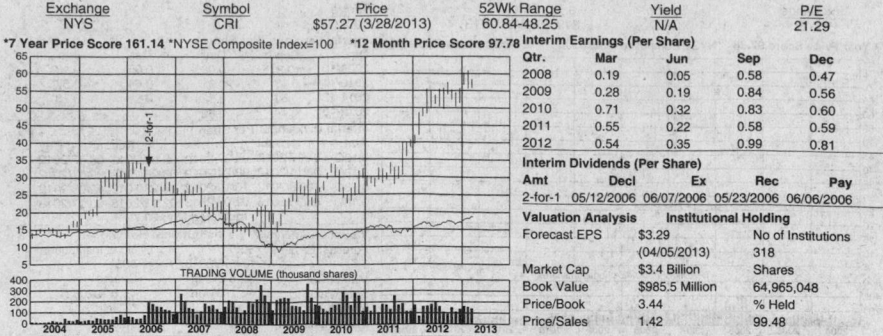

Exchange	Symbol	Price	52Wk Range	Yield	P/E
NYS	CRI	$57.27 (3/28/2013)	60.84-48.25	N/A	21.29

*7 Year Price Score 161.14 *NYSE Composite Index=100   *12 Month Price Score 97.78

Interim Earnings (Per Share)

Qtr.	Mar	Jun	Sep	Dec
2008	0.19	0.05	0.58	0.47
2009	0.28	0.19	0.84	0.56
2010	0.71	0.32	0.83	0.60
2011	0.55	0.22	0.58	0.59
2012	0.54	0.35	0.99	0.81

Interim Dividends (Per Share)

Amt	Decl	Ex	Rec	Pay
2-for-1	05/12/2006	06/07/2006	05/23/2006	06/06/2006

Valuation Analysis

		Institutional Holding	
Forecast EPS	$3.29 (04/05/2013)	No of Institutions	318
Market Cap	$3.4 Billion	Shares	64,965,048
Book Value	$985.5 Million	% Held	99.48
Price/Book	3.44		
Price/Sales	1.42		

Business Summary: Apparel, Footwear & Accessories (MIC: 1.4.2 SIC: 2341 NAIC: 315291)

Carter's is a marketer of childrenswear under the Carter's, Child of Mine, Just One You, Precious Firsts, OshKosh, and other brands. Under its Carter's brand, Co. designs, sources, and markets a range of products, mainly for sizes newborn to seven. Under its OshKosh brand, Co. designs, sources, and markets a range of young children's apparel, mainly for children in sizes newborn to 12. Co.'s international segment includes its Canadian retail and wholesale operations, existing international wholesale sales, and royalty income from its international licensees. At Dec 31 2011, Co. operated 359 Carter's and 170 OshKosh outlet and brand retail stores in the U.S. and 65 retail stores in Canada.

Recent Developments: For the year ended Dec 29 2012, net income increased 41.3% to US$161.2 million from US$114.0 million in the prior year. Revenues were US$2.38 billion, up 12.9% from US$2.11 billion the year before. Operating income was US$262.0 million versus US$187.5 million in the prior year, an increase of 39.8%. Direct operating expenses rose 1.9% to US$1.44 billion from US$1.42 billion in the comparable period the year before. Indirect operating expenses increased 33.9% to US$676.0 million from US$504.8 million in the equivalent prior-year period.

Prospects: Our evaluation of Carter Holdings Inc. as of Apr. 7, 2013 is the result of our systematic analysis on three basic characteristics: earnings strength, relative valuation, and recent stock price movement. The company has generated a negative trend in earnings per share over the past 5 quarters and while recent estimates for the company have been mixed, CRI has posted better than expected results. Based on operating earnings yield, the company is about fairly valued when compared to all of the companies in our coverage universe. Share price changes over the past year indicates that CRI will perform in line with the market over the near term.

Financial Data

(US$ in Thousands)	12/29/2012	12/31/2011	01/01/2011	01/02/2010	01/03/2009	12/29/2007	12/30/2006	12/31/2005
Earnings Per Share	2.69	1.94	2.46	1.97	1.29	(1.22)	1.42	0.78
Cash Flow Per Share	4.80	1.41	1.48	3.33	3.21	0.90	1.53	2.40
Tang Book Value Per Share	8.28	5.30	4.13	1.93	N.M.	N.M.	N.M.	N.M.
Income Statement								
Total Revenue	2,381,734	2,109,734	1,749,256	1,589,677	1,490,016	1,412,246	1,343,467	1,121,358
EBITDA	301,631	220,536	273,206	224,170	138,099	19,462	186,878	120,857
Depn & Amortn	39,500	32,500	29,950	28,557	2,605	25,471	21,767	19,748
Income Before Taxes	255,391	180,888	233,386	183,828	117,407	(29,088)	138,188	77,867
Income Taxes	94,241	66,872	86,914	68,188	42,349	41,530	50,968	30,665
Net Income	161,150	114,016	146,472	115,640	75,058	(70,618)	87,220	47,202
Average Shares	59,069	58,214	59,016	58,347	58,276	57,871	61,247	60,753
Balance Sheet								
Current Assets	957,703	782,147	716,263	675,668	513,091	433,649	402,421	399,045
Total Assets	1,630,109	1,402,709	1,257,182	1,208,599	1,051,057	974,668	1,123,191	1,116,727
Current Liabilities	244,235	152,753	183,372	170,617	140,127	106,758	136,517	156,603
Long-Term Obligations	186,000	236,000	236,000	331,020	334,523	338,026	342,405	426,791
Total Liabilities	644,630	597,000	577,246	652,575	624,461	592,539	627,700	730,083
Stockholders' Equity	985,479	805,709	679,936	556,024	426,596	382,129	495,491	386,644
Shares Outstanding	59,126	58,595	57,493	58,081	56,352	57,663	58,927	57,819
Statistical Record								
Return on Assets %	10.66	8.60	11.91	10.26	7.29	N.M.	7.81	5.29
Return on Equity %	18.04	15.39	23.77	23.60	18.26	N.M.	19.83	13.25
EBITDA Margin %	12.66	10.45	15.62	14.10	9.27	1.38	13.91	10.78
Net Margin %	6.77	5.40	8.37	7.27	5.04	N.M.	6.49	4.21
Asset Turnover	1.57	1.59	1.42	1.41	1.45	1.35	1.20	1.26
Current Ratio	3.92	5.12	3.91	3.96	3.66	4.06	2.95	2.55
Debt to Equity	0.19	0.29	0.35	0.60	0.78	0.88	0.69	1.10
Price Range	57.44-39.49	40.62-27.04	33.63-22.34	29.13-14.13	22.21-12.65	27.73-18.53	35.11-21.33	32.30-16.36
P/E Ratio	21.35-14.68	20.94-13.94	13.67-9.08	14.79-7.17	17.22-9.81	...	24.73-15.02	41.40-20.97

Address: The Proscenium, 1170 Peachtree Street N.E., Suite 900, Atlanta, GA 30309 Telephone: 404-745-2700	Web Site: www.carters.com Officers: Michael Dennis Casey - Chairman, President, Chief Executive Officer Brian J. Lynch - President, Executive Vice President	Auditors: PricewaterhouseCoopers LLP Transfer Agents: American Stock Transfer & Trust Company, New York, NY

CATERPILLAR INC.

Exchange	Symbol	Price	52Wk Range	Yield	P/E	Div Achiever
NYS	CAT	$86.97 (3/28/2013)	109.21-79.64	2.39	10.26	19 Years

*7 Year Price Score 108.41 *NYSE Composite Index=100   *12 Month Price Score 93.85

Interim Earnings (Per Share)

Qtr.	Mar	Jun	Sep	Dec
2008	1.45	1.74	1.39	1.09
2009	(0.19)	0.60	0.64	0.36
2010	0.36	1.09	1.22	1.47
2011	1.84	1.52	1.71	2.32
2012	2.37	2.54	2.54	1.04

Interim Dividends (Per Share)

Amt	Decl	Ex	Rec	Pay
0.46Q	04/11/2012	04/19/2012	04/23/2012	05/19/2012
0.52Q	06/13/2012	07/18/2012	07/20/2012	08/20/2012
0.52Q	10/08/2012	10/18/2012	10/22/2012	11/20/2012
0.52Q	12/12/2012	12/20/2012	12/24/2012	12/31/2012

Indicated Div: $2.08 (Div. Reinv. Plan)

Valuation Analysis

		Institutional Holding	
Forecast EPS	$7.93	No of Institutions	
	(04/06/2013)	1478	
Market Cap	$57.0 Billion	Shares	
Book Value	$17.5 Billion	458,040,064	
Price/Book	3.25	% Held	
Price/Sales	0.86	62.02	

Business Summary: Construction Services (MIC: 7.5.4 SIC: 3531 NAIC: 333120)

Caterpillar is engaged in manufacturing construction and mining equipment, diesel and natural gas engines, industrial gas turbines and diesel-electric locomotives. Co.'s segments include: Construction Industries, which supports customers using machinery in infrastructure and building construction applications; Resource Industries, which supports customers using machinery in mine and quarry applications; Power Systems, which supports customers using reciprocating engines, turbines and related parts across industries serving electric power, industrial, petroleum and marine applications, among others; and Financial Products, which provides retail and wholesale financing for Co.'s products.

Recent Developments: For the year ended Dec 31 2012, net income increased 14.9% to US$5.72 billion from US$4.98 billion in the prior year. Revenues were US$65.88 billion, up 9.5% from US$60.14 billion the year before. Operating income was US$8.57 billion versus US$7.15 billion in the prior year, an increase of 19.9%. Direct operating expenses rose 8.0% to US$47.06 billion from US$43.58 billion in the comparable period the year before. Indirect operating expenses increased 8.9% to US$10.25 billion from US$9.41 billion in the equivalent prior-year period.

Prospects: Our evaluation of Caterpillar Inc. as of Apr. 7, 2013 is the result of our systematic analysis on three basic characteristics: earnings strength, relative valuation, and recent stock price movement. The company has generated a negative trend in earnings per share over the past 5 quarters. However, while recent estimates for the company have been lowered by analysts, CAT has posted results that fell short of analysts expectations. Based on operating earnings yield, the company is undervalued when compared to all of the companies in our coverage universe. Share price changes over the past year indicates that CAT will perform in line with the market over the near term.

Financial Data

(US$ in Thousands)	12/31/2012	12/31/2011	12/31/2010	12/31/2009	12/31/2008	12/31/2007	12/31/2006	12/31/2005
Earnings Per Share	8.48	7.40	4.15	1.43	5.66	5.37	5.17	4.04
Cash Flow Per Share	8.01	10.87	7.93	10.31	7.82	12.43	8.80	4.59
Tang Book Value Per Share	10.04	2.22	11.59	9.61	5.51	10.33	7.07	9.77
Dividends Per Share	2.480	1.800	1.720	1.680	1.560	1.320	1.100	0.910
Dividend Payout %	29.25	24.32	41.45	117.48	27.56	24.58	21.28	22.52
Income Statement								
Total Revenue	65,875,000	60,138,000	42,588,000	32,396,000	51,324,000	44,958,000	41,517,000	36,339,000
EBITDA	11,921,000	10,158,000	7,209,000	4,257,000	7,807,000	8,098,000	7,712,000	6,373,000
Depn & Amortn	2,421,000	2,211,000	2,202,000	2,254,000	1,907,000	1,725,000	1,554,000	1,444,000
Income Before Taxes	8,236,000	6,725,000	3,750,000	569,000	4,473,000	4,953,000	4,861,000	3,901,000
Income Taxes	2,528,000	1,720,000	968,000	(270,000)	953,000	1,485,000	1,405,000	1,120,000
Net Income	5,681,000	4,928,000	2,700,000	895,000	3,557,000	3,541,000	3,537,000	2,854,000
Average Shares	669,600	666,100	650,400	626,000	627,900	659,500	683,800	705,800
Balance Sheet								
Current Assets	42,524,000	38,128,000	31,810,000	26,789,000	31,633,000	25,477,000	23,093,000	22,790,000
Total Assets	89,356,000	81,446,000	64,020,000	60,038,000	67,782,000	56,132,000	50,879,000	47,069,000
Current Liabilities	29,755,000	28,561,000	22,020,000	19,292,000	26,069,000	22,245,000	19,252,000	19,092,000
Long-Term Obligations	27,752,000	24,944,000	20,437,000	21,847,000	22,834,000	17,829,000	17,680,000	15,677,000
Total Liabilities	71,824,000	68,563,000	53,196,000	51,298,000	61,695,000	47,249,000	44,020,000	38,637,000
Stockholders' Equity	17,532,000	12,883,000	10,824,000	8,740,000	6,087,000	8,883,000	6,859,000	8,432,000
Shares Outstanding	655,048	647,533	638,822	624,722	601,526	623,986	645,808	670,867
Statistical Record								
Return on Assets %	6.63	6.78	4.35	1.40	5.73	6.62	7.22	6.33
Return on Equity %	37.25	41.57	27.60	12.07	47.39	44.99	46.26	35.90
EBITDA Margin %	18.10	16.89	16.93	13.14	15.21	18.01	18.58	17.54
Net Margin %	8.62	8.19	6.34	2.76	6.93	7.88	8.52	7.85
Asset Turnover	0.77	0.83	0.69	0.51	0.83	0.84	0.85	0.81
Current Ratio	1.43	1.33	1.44	1.39	1.21	1.15	1.20	1.19
Debt to Equity	1.58	1.94	1.89	2.50	3.75	2.01	2.58	1.86
Price Range	116.20-79.64	115.41-70.55	94.63-50.78	60.40-22.17	85.28-32.78	86.98-58.17	81.14-57.80	59.64-41.73
P/E Ratio	13.70-9.39	15.60-9.53	22.80-12.24	42.24-15.50	15.07-5.79	16.20-10.83	15.69-11.18	14.76-10.33
Average Yield %	2.67	1.86	2.49	4.00	2.40	1.82	1.60	1.79

Address: 100 NE Adams Street, Peoria, IL 61629 **Telephone:** 309-675-1000 **Fax:** 309-675-4332	**Web Site:** www.caterpillar.com **Officers:** Douglas R. Oberhelman - Chairman, Vice-Chairman, Chief Executive Officer James B. Buda - Senior Vice President, Vice President, Chief Legal Officer, Secretary, General Counsel	**Auditors:** PricewaterhouseCoopers LLP **Investor Contact:** 309-675-4549 **Transfer Agents:** Computershare Shareowner Services LLC, Providence, RI

CBRE GROUP INC

Exchange	Symbol	Price	52Wk Range	Yield	P/E
NYS	CBG	$25.25 (3/28/2013)	25.36-15.10	N/A	26.03

*7 Year Price Score 86.50   *NYSE Composite Index=100   *12 Month Price Score 115.56

TRADING VOLUME (thousand shares)

Interim Earnings (Per Share)

Qtr.	Mar	Jun	Sep	Dec
2008	0.10	0.08	0.19	(5.18)
2009	(0.14)	(0.02)	0.04	0.23
2010	(0.02)	0.17	0.18	0.30
2011	0.11	0.19	0.20	0.25
2012	0.08	0.23	0.12	0.53

Interim Dividends (Per Share)
No Dividends Paid

Valuation Analysis | Institutional Holding

Forecast EPS	$1.42	No of Institutions
	(04/05/2013)	431
Market Cap	$8.3 Billion	Shares
Book Value	$1.5 Billion	338,020,352
Price/Book	5.41	% Held
Price/Sales	1.28	N/A

Business Summary: Property, Real Estate & Development (MIC: 5.3.2 SIC: 6531 NAIC: 531210)

CBRE Group is a holding company. Through its subsidiaries, Co. provides commercial real estate services under the CBRE brand name, investment management services under the CBRE Global Investors brand name and development services under the Trammell Crow brand name. Co. has five segments: Americas, which provides occupier/tenant and investor/owner services, including real estate services, capital markets and valuation; Europe, Middle East and Africa; Asia Pacific; Global Investment Management, which provides investment management services; and Development Services, which provides development services to users of and investors in commercial real estate, as well as for its own account

Recent Developments: For the year ended Dec 31 2012, income from continuing operations increased 26.5% to US$304.2 million from US$240.4 million a year earlier. Net income increased 5.0% to US$304.8 million from US$290.3 million in the prior year. Revenues were US$6.51 billion, up 10.3% from US$5.91 billion the year before.

Prospects: Our evaluation of CBRE Group Inc. as of Apr. 7, 2013 is the result of our systematic analysis on three basic characteristics: earnings strength, relative valuation, and recent stock price movement. The company has managed to produce a neutral trend in earnings per share over the past 5 quarters and while recent estimates for the company have been mixed, CBG has posted better than expected results. Based on operating earnings yield, the company is about fairly valued when compared to all of the companies in our coverage universe. Share price changes over the past year indicates that CBG will perform well over the near term.

Financial Data
(US$ in Thousands)

	12/31/2012	12/31/2011	12/31/2010	12/31/2009	12/31/2008	12/31/2007	12/31/2006	12/31/2005
Earnings Per Share	0.97	0.74	0.63	0.12	(4.81)	1.66	1.35	0.95
Cash Flow Per Share	0.90	1.13	1.96	0.77	(0.62)	2.84	1.63	1.62
Income Statement								
Total Revenue	6,514,099	5,905,411	5,115,316	4,165,820	5,128,817	6,034,249	4,032,027	2,910,641
EBITDA	672,374	519,768	486,931	275,867	(732,255)	715,337	568,602	401,620
Depn & Amortn	76,200	54,200	58,700	59,400	63,900	53,900	43,700	36,600
Income Before Taxes	428,749	324,762	245,496	33,450	(945,549)	527,450	489,717	319,960
Income Taxes	185,322	189,103	130,368	26,993	50,810	192,643	198,326	138,881
Net Income	315,555	239,162	200,345	33,341	(1,012,066)	390,505	318,571	217,341
Average Shares	327,044	323,723	319,016	279,995	210,539	234,978	235,118	229,855
Balance Sheet								
Current Assets	4,084,550	3,550,047	2,260,870	2,266,725	1,915,533	2,360,830	2,212,013	1,292,947
Total Assets	7,809,542	7,219,143	5,121,568	5,039,406	4,726,414	6,242,573	5,944,631	2,815,672
Current Liabilities	2,972,293	2,680,648	1,956,768	1,629,041	1,872,845	2,428,361	1,906,013	1,137,803
Long-Term Obligations	2,543,707	2,611,187	1,851,901	2,372,302	2,287,001	1,991,852	2,232,857	549,156
Total Liabilities	6,270,331	6,067,662	4,213,353	4,410,284	4,611,728	5,254,030	4,762,990	2,021,987
Stockholders' Equity	1,539,211	1,151,481	908,215	629,122	114,686	988,543	1,181,641	793,685
Shares Outstanding	330,082	327,972	323,594	321,767	262,336	201,594	227,474	221,353
Statistical Record								
Return on Assets %	4.19	3.88	3.94	0.68	N.M.	6.41	7.27	8.54
Return on Equity %	23.39	23.22	26.06	8.96	N.M.	35.99	32.26	32.11
EBITDA Margin %	10.32	8.80	9.52	6.62	N.M.	11.85	14.10	13.80
Net Margin %	4.84	4.05	3.92	0.80	N.M.	6.47	7.90	7.47
Asset Turnover	0.86	0.96	1.01	0.85	0.93	0.99	0.92	1.14
Current Ratio	1.37	1.32	1.16	1.39	1.02	0.97	1.16	1.14
Debt to Equity	1.65	2.27	2.04	3.77	19.94	2.01	1.89	0.69
Price Range	20.86-15.10	29.70-12.78	21.31-12.16	14.04-2.36	24.01-3.22	41.44-18.38	33.83-20.10	19.82-10.61
P/E Ratio	21.51-15.57	40.14-17.27	33.83-19.30	117.00-19.67	...	24.96-11.07	25.06-14.89	20.86-11.16

Address: 11150 Santa Monica Boulevard, Suite 1600, Los Angeles, CA 90025 Telephone: 310-405-8900	Web Site: www.cbre.com Officers: Richard C. Blum - Chairman Raymond E. Wirta - Vice-Chairman	Auditors: KPMG LLP Investor Contact: 949-809-4308 Transfer Agents: Broadbridge Corporate Issuer Solutions, Inc., Philadelphia, PA

CBS CORP

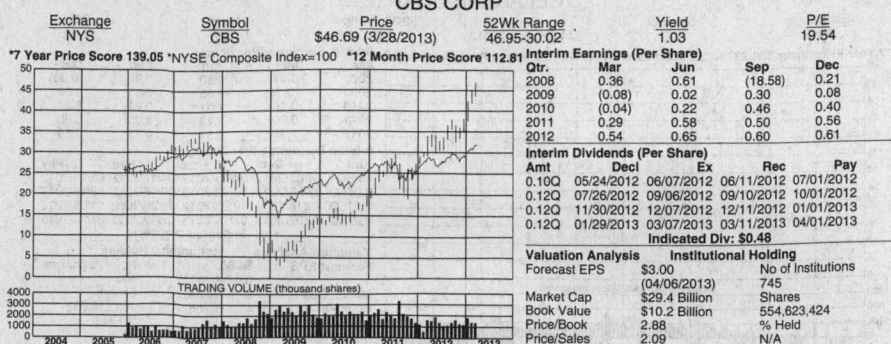

Exchange	Symbol	Price	52Wk Range	Yield	P/E
NYS	CBS	$46.69 (3/28/2013)	46.95-30.02	1.03	19.54

*7 Year Price Score 139.05 *NYSE Composite Index=100 *12 Month Price Score 112.81

Interim Earnings (Per Share)

Qtr.	Mar	Jun	Sep	Dec
2008	0.36	0.61	(18.58)	0.21
2009	(0.08)	0.02	0.30	0.08
2010	(0.04)	0.22	0.46	0.40
2011	0.29	0.58	0.50	0.56
2012	0.54	0.65	0.60	0.61

Interim Dividends (Per Share)

Amt	Decl	Ex	Rec	Pay
0.10Q	05/24/2012	06/07/2012	06/11/2012	07/01/2012
0.12Q	07/26/2012	09/06/2012	09/10/2012	10/01/2012
0.12Q	11/30/2012	12/07/2012	12/11/2012	01/01/2013
0.12Q	01/29/2013	03/07/2013	03/11/2013	04/01/2013

Indicated Div: $0.48

Valuation Analysis   **Institutional Holding**

Forecast EPS	$3.00	No of Institutions
	(04/06/2013)	745
Market Cap	$29.4 Billion	Shares
Book Value	$10.2 Billion	554,623,424
Price/Book	2.88	% Held
Price/Sales	2.09	N/A

Business Summary: Radio & Television (MIC: 2.3.1 SIC: 4833 NAIC: 515120)

CBS is a mass media company. Co. operates in the following segments: entertainment segment consists of the CBS Television Network, CBS Television Studios and CBS Global Distribution Group, CBS Films, and CBS Interactive; Cable Networks, which is composed of Showtime Networks, CBS Sports Network, and Smithsonian Networks; Publishing, which consists of Simon & Schuster; Local Broadcasting, which is composed of CBS Television Stations and CBS Radio; and Outdoor Americas, which provides advertising space on various structures, including billboards, transit shelters and benches, buses, rail systems, mall kiosks, stadium signage, and in retail stores.

Recent Developments: For the year ended Dec 31 2012, income from continuing operations increased 17.5% to US$1.63 billion from US$1.39 billion a year earlier. Net income increased 20.6% to US$1.57 billion from US$1.31 billion in the prior year. Revenues were US$14.09 billion, up 3.3% from US$13.64 billion the year before. Operating income was US$2.98 billion versus US$2.62 billion in the prior year, an increase of 13.9%. Direct operating expenses rose 1.1% to US$7.97 billion from US$7.88 billion in the comparable period the year before. Indirect operating expenses were unchanged at US$3.14 billion versus the equivalent prior-year period.

Prospects: Our evaluation of CBS Corp. as of Apr. 7, 2013 is the result of our systematic analysis on three basic characteristics: earnings strength, relative valuation, and recent stock price movement. The company has produced a positive trend in earnings per share over the past 5 quarters and while recent estimates for the company have remained steady, CBS has posted results that fell short of analysts expectations. Based on operating earnings yield, the company is undervalued when compared to all of the companies in our coverage universe. Share price changes over the past year indicates that CBS will perform well over the near term.

Financial Data
(US$ in Thousands)

	12/31/2012	12/31/2011	12/31/2010	12/31/2009	12/31/2008	12/31/2007	12/31/2006	12/31/2005
Earnings Per Share	2.39	1.92	1.04	0.33	(17.43)	1.73	2.15	(8.98)
Cash Flow Per Share	2.82	2.63	2.56	1.39	3.20	3.06	2.47	4.48
Dividends Per Share	0.440	0.350	0.200	0.200	1.060	0.940	0.740	0.280
Dividend Payout %	18.41	18.23	19.23	60.61	...	54.34	34.42	...
Income Statement								
Total Revenue	14,089,000	14,245,000	14,059,800	13,014,600	13,950,400	14,072,900	14,320,200	14,536,400
EBITDA	3,326,000	2,938,000	2,177,200	1,427,700	(11,657,700)	2,947,396	3,025,600	(6,313,900)
Depn & Amortn	369,000	426,000	432,400	448,700	413,000	359,596	439,500	498,700
Income Before Taxes	2,561,000	2,083,000	1,221,500	443,000	(12,575,100)	2,133,000	2,132,700	(7,511,700)
Income Taxes	892,000	755,000	462,700	182,800	(919,300)	821,500	652,200	808,100
Net Income	1,574,000	1,305,000	724,200	226,500	(11,673,400)	1,247,000	1,660,500	(7,089,100)
Average Shares	659,000	681,000	694,500	682,900	669,800	721,900	771,800	789,700
Balance Sheet								
Current Assets	5,720,000	5,543,000	5,334,700	5,636,900	5,192,800	6,030,900	8,144,100	6,795,500
Total Assets	26,466,000	26,197,000	26,142,600	26,962,000	26,889,300	40,430,200	43,508,800	43,029,600
Current Liabilities	3,941,000	3,933,000	4,025,500	4,746,500	4,800,900	4,404,600	4,399,500	5,378,600
Long-Term Obligations	5,904,000	5,958,000	5,973,500	6,553,300	6,974,800	7,068,600	7,027,300	7,153,200
Total Liabilities	16,253,000	16,289,000	16,322,000	17,942,600	18,292,000	18,957,800	19,986,300	21,292,600
Stockholders' Equity	10,213,000	9,908,000	9,820,600	9,019,400	8,597,300	21,472,400	23,522,500	21,737,000
Shares Outstanding	630,000	651,000	680,200	674,800	670,800	671,900	768,400	751,700
Statistical Record								
Return on Assets %	5.96	4.99	2.73	0.84	N.M.	2.97	3.84	N.M.
Return on Equity %	15.60	13.23	7.69	2.57	N.M.	5.54	7.34	N.M.
EBITDA Margin %	23.61	20.62	15.49	10.97	N.M.	20.94	21.13	N.M.
Net Margin %	11.17	9.16	5.15	1.74	N.M.	8.86	11.60	N.M.
Asset Turnover	0.53	0.54	0.53	0.48	0.41	0.34	0.33	0.26
Current Ratio	1.45	1.41	1.33	1.19	1.08	1.37	1.85	1.26
Debt to Equity	0.58	0.60	0.61	0.73	0.81	0.33	0.30	0.33
Price Range	38.05-27.27	29.54-18.95	19.59-12.67	14.35-3.09	27.25-4.51	35.00-25.84	31.99-23.95	26.70-25.00
P/E Ratio	15.92-11.41	15.39-9.87	18.84-12.18	43.48-9.36	...	20.23-14.94	14.88-11.14	...
Average Yield %	1.33	1.43	1.32	2.26	5.98	3.05	2.73	1.10

Address: 51 W. 52nd Street, New York, NY 10019
Telephone: 212-975-4321

Web Site: www.cbscorporation.com
Officers: Sumner M. Redstone - Chairman Shari Redstone - Vice-Chairwoman

Auditors: PricewaterhouseCoopers LLP
Investor Contact: 187-722-70787
Transfer Agents: Wells Fargo Shareowner Services, St. Paul, MN

CELANESE CORP (DE)

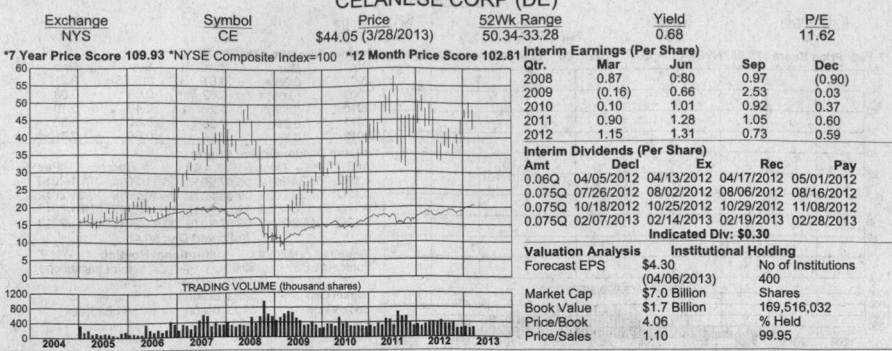

<table>
<thead>
<tr><th>Exchange</th><th>Symbol</th><th>Price</th><th>52Wk Range</th><th>Yield</th><th>P/E</th></tr>
</thead>
<tbody>
<tr><td>NYS</td><td>CE</td><td>$44.05 (3/28/2013)</td><td>50.34-33.28</td><td>0.68</td><td>11.62</td></tr>
</tbody>
</table>

*7 Year Price Score 109.93 *NYSE Composite Index=100 *12 Month Price Score 102.81

Interim Earnings (Per Share)

Qtr.	Mar	Jun	Sep	Dec
2008	0.87	0:80	0.97	(0.90)
2009	(0.16)	0.66	2.53	0.03
2010	0.10	1.01	0.92	0.37
2011	0.90	1.28	1.05	0.60
2012	1.15	1.31	0.73	0.59

Interim Dividends (Per Share)

Amt	Decl	Ex	Rec	Pay
0.06Q	04/05/2012	04/13/2012	04/17/2012	05/01/2012
0.075Q	07/26/2012	08/02/2012	08/06/2012	08/16/2012
0.075Q	10/18/2012	10/25/2012	10/29/2012	11/08/2012
0.075Q	02/07/2013	02/14/2013	02/19/2013	02/28/2013

Indicated Div: $0.30

Valuation Analysis / **Institutional Holding**

Forecast EPS	$4.30 (04/06/2013)	No of Institutions 400
Market Cap	$7.0 Billion	Shares
Book Value	$1.7 Billion	169,516,032
Price/Book	4.06	% Held
Price/Sales	1.10	99.95

Business Summary: Specialty Chemicals (MIC: 8.3.2 SIC: 5169 NAIC: 424690)

Celanese is a technology and specialty materials company. Co.'s business involves processing chemical raw materials, such as methanol, carbon monoxide and ethylene, and natural products, including wood pulp, into value-added chemicals, thermoplastic polymers and other chemical-based products. Co. operates four business segments: Advanced Engineered Materials, Consumer Specialties, Industrial Specialties and Acetyl Intermediates.

Recent Developments: For the year ended Dec 31 2012, income from continuing operations increased 0.5% to US$609.0 million from US$606.0 million a year earlier. Net income decreased 0.3% to US$605.0 million from US$607.0 million in the prior year. Revenues were US$6.42 billion, down 5.1% from US$6.76 billion the year before. Operating income was US$511.0 million versus US$690.0 million in the prior year, a decrease of 25.9%. Direct operating expenses declined 1.9% to US$5.23 billion from US$5.33 billion in the comparable period the year before. Indirect operating expenses decreased 8.5% to US$681.0 million from US$744.0 million in the equivalent prior-year period.

Prospects: Our evaluation of Celanese Corp. as of Apr. 7, 2013 is the result of our systematic analysis on three basic characteristics: earnings strength, relative valuation, and recent stock price movement. The company has produced a positive trend in earnings per share over the past 5 quarters. However, while recent estimates for the company have been lowered by analysts, CE has posted better than expected results. Based on operating earnings yield, the company is undervalued when compared to all of the companies in our coverage universe. Share price changes over the past year indicates that CE will perform well over the near term.

Financial Data

(US$ in Thousands)	12/31/2012	12/31/2011	12/31/2010	12/31/2009	12/31/2008	12/31/2007	12/31/2006	12/31/2005
Earnings Per Share	3.79	3.82	2.38	3.11	1.73	2.49	2.36	1.67
Cash Flow Per Share	4.55	4.08	2.92	4.15	3.94	3.66	4.74	4.62
Tang Book Value Per Share	4.94	2.45	N.M.	N.M.	N.M.	N.M.	N.M.	N.M.
Dividends Per Share	0.270	0.220	0.180	0.160	0.160	0.160	0.160	0.080
Dividend Payout %	7.12	5.76	7.56	5.14	9.25	6.43	6.78	4.79
Income Statement								
Total Revenue	6,418,000	6,763,000	5,918,000	5,082,000	6,823,000	6,444,000	6,656,000	6,070,000
EBITDA	910,000	1,075,000	823,000	682,000	941,000	864,000	1,103,000	779,000
Depn & Amortn	312,000	294,000	256,000	290,000	331,000	281,000	268,000	218,000
Income Before Taxes	415,000	563,000	370,000	193,000	380,000	365,000	578,000	301,000
Income Taxes	48,000	149,000	112,000	(243,000)	63,000	110,000	253,000	57,000
Net Income	605,000	607,000	377,000	488,000	282,000	426,000	406,000	277,000
Average Shares	159,796	158,947	158,372	157,115	163,471	171,227	171,807	166,200
Balance Sheet								
Current Assets	2,839,000	2,703,000	2,668,000	2,856,000	2,284,000	3,063,000	3,111,000	2,579,000
Total Assets	9,000,000	8,518,000	8,281,000	8,410,000	7,166,000	8,058,000	7,895,000	7,445,000
Current Liabilities	1,355,000	1,385,000	1,542,000	1,607,000	1,369,000	2,031,000	2,216,000	2,013,000
Long-Term Obligations	2,930,000	2,873,000	2,990,000	3,259,000	3,300,000	3,284,000	3,189,000	3,282,000
Total Liabilities	7,270,000	7,177,000	7,355,000	7,826,000	6,984,000	6,996,000	7,108,000	7,210,000
Stockholders' Equity	1,730,000	1,341,000	926,000	584,000	182,000	1,062,000	787,000	235,000
Shares Outstanding	159,642	156,463	155,759	144,394	143,505	152,102	158,668	158,562
Statistical Record								
Return on Assets %	6.89	7.23	4.52	6.27	3.69	5.34	5.29	3.73
Return on Equity %	39.29	53.55	49.93	127.42	45.21	46.08	79.45	450.41
EBITDA Margin %	14.18	15.90	13.91	13.42	13.79	13.41	16.57	12.83
Net Margin %	9.43	8.98	6.37	9.60	4.13	6.61	6.10	4.56
Asset Turnover	0.73	0.81	0.71	0.65	0.89	0.81	0.87	0.82
Current Ratio	2.10	1.95	1.73	1.78	1.67	1.51	1.40	1.28
Debt to Equity	1.69	2.14	3.23	5.58	18.13	3.09	4.05	13.97
Price Range	52.22-33.28	57.66-31.49	41.17-23.84	33.08-7.52	50.00-7.60	44.33-24.76	25.88-17.25	20.06-14.06
P/E Ratio	13.78-8.78	15.09-8.24	17.30-10.02	10.64-2.42	28.90-4.39	17.80-9.94	10.97-7.31	12.01-8.42
Average Yield %	0.64	0.49	0.57	0.74	0.47	0.45	0.79	0.47

<table>
<tbody>
<tr><td>Address: 222 West Las Colinas Blvd., Suite 900N, Irving, TX 75039-5421
Telephone: 972-443-4000</td><td>Web Site: www.celanese.com
Officers: Mark C. Rohr - Chairman, Chief Executive Officer Curtis S. Shaw - Executive Vice President, Corporate Secretary, General Counsel</td><td>Auditors: KPMG LLP
Investor Contact: 972-443-4965
Transfer Agents: ComputerShare Investor Services, Providence, RI</td></tr>
</tbody>
</table>

CENTENE CORP

Exchange	Symbol	Price	52Wk Range	Yield	P/E
NYS	CNC	$44.04 (3/28/2013)	50.80-26.84	N/A	1468.00

*7 Year Price Score 134.70 *NYSE Composite Index=100 *12 Month Price Score 103.69

TRADING VOLUME (thousand shares)

Interim Earnings (Per Share)

Qtr.	Mar	Jun	Sep	Dec
2008	0.57	0.41	0.41	0.49
2009	0.42	0.46	0.48	0.53
2010	0.49	0.45	0.44	0.50
2011	0.46	0.54	0.55	0.57
2012	0.45	(0.68)	0.07	0.17

Interim Dividends (Per Share)

No Dividends Paid

Valuation Analysis		Institutional Holding	
Forecast EPS	$2.65	No of Institutions	
	(04/06/2013)	307	
Market Cap	$2.3 Billion	Shares	
Book Value	$953.1 Million	58,008,592	
Price/Book	2.42	% Held	
Price/Sales	0.27	101.40	

Business Summary: Hospitals & Health Care Facilities (MIC: 4.2.1 SIC: 6324 NAIC: 524114)

Centene is a multi-line healthcare enterprise operating in two segments: Medicaid Managed Care, which provides Medicaid and Medicaid-related health plan coverage to individuals through government subsidized programs; and Specialty Services segment, which provides products for behavioral health, care management software, health insurance exchanges, individual health insurance, life and health management, long-term care programs, managed vision, telehealth services, and pharmacy benefits management to state programs, healthcare organizations, employer groups and other commercial organizations, as well as to its own subsidiaries.

Recent Developments: For the year ended Dec 31 2012, loss from continuing operations was US$11.3 million compared with income of US$108.4 million a year earlier. Net loss amounted to US$11.3 million versus net income of US$108.4 million in the prior year. Revenues were US$8.67 billion, up 62.3% from US$5.34 billion the year before.

Prospects: Our evaluation of Centene Corp. as of Apr. 7, 2013 is the result of our systematic analysis on three basic characteristics: earnings strength, relative valuation, and recent stock price movement. The company has produced a positive trend in earnings per share over the past 5 quarters. However, while recent estimates for the company have been lowered by analysts, CNC has posted results that fell short of analysts expectations. Based on operating earnings yield, the company is overvalued when compared to all of the companies in our coverage universe. Share price changes over the past year indicates that CNC will perform in line with the market over the near term.

Financial Data
(US$ in Thousands)

	12/31/2012	12/31/2011	12/31/2010	12/31/2009	12/31/2008	12/31/2007	12/31/2006	12/31/2005
Earnings Per Share	0.03	2.12	1.88	1.89	1.88	1.64	(1.01)	1.24
Cash Flow Per Share	5.40	5.21	3.46	5.77	5.12	4.64	4.52	1.75
Tang Book Value Per Share	12.93	12.31	9.81	8.19	7.45	5.97	4.02	4.13
Income Statement								
Total Revenue	8,667,612	5,340,582	4,448,323	4,102,864	3,364,515	2,919,292	2,279,020	1,505,864
EBITDA	58,948	237,454	209,405	186,929	181,742	102,486	5,003	97,980
Depn & Amortn	50,112	42,249	37,131	33,103	28,453	23,224	16,019	8,134
Income Before Taxes	(11,624)	174,885	154,282	137,508	136,616	63,636	(21,652)	85,856
Income Taxes	(329)	66,522	59,900	48,841	52,435	22,367	21,977	30,224
Net Income	1,859	111,218	94,836	83,671	83,497	73,402	(43,629)	55,632
Average Shares	53,714	52,474	50,447	44,316	44,398	44,823	43,160	45,027
Balance Sheet								
Current Assets	1,373,602	940,010	656,821	616,134	666,343	446,339	451,821	272,605
Total Assets	2,741,682	2,190,336	1,943,882	1,702,364	1,451,152	1,119,122	894,980	668,030
Current Liabilities	1,197,090	837,613	765,246	715,908	640,978	486,800	387,951	214,651
Long-Term Obligations	535,481	348,344	327,824	307,085	264,637	206,406	174,646	92,448
Total Liabilities	1,788,626	1,254,702	1,149,943	1,101,519	949,880	704,075	568,557	315,982
Stockholders' Equity	953,056	935,634	793,939	600,845	501,272	415,047	326,423	352,048
Shares Outstanding	52,329	50,864	49,616	43,179	42,987	43,667	43,369	42,988
Statistical Record								
Return on Assets %	0.08	5.38	5.20	5.31	6.48	7.29	N.M.	9.30
Return on Equity %	0.20	12.86	13.60	15.18	18.17	19.80	N.M.	17.85
EBITDA Margin %	0.68	4.45	4.71	4.56	5.40	3.51	0.22	6.51
Net Margin %	0.02	2.08	2.13	2.04	2.48	2.51	N.M.	3.69
Asset Turnover	3.51	2.58	2.44	2.60	2.61	2.90	2.92	2.52
Current Ratio	1.15	1.12	0.86	0.86	1.04	0.92	1.16	1.27
Debt to Equity	0.56	0.37	0.41	0.51	0.53	0.50	0.54	0.26
Price Range	50.80-26.84	40.54-25.34	26.31-17.87	22.27-15.04	28.40-13.30	27.56-18.27	29.31-13.60	37.38-18.00
P/E Ratio	N.M.	19.12-11.95	13.99-9.51	11.78-7.96	15.11-7.07	16.80-11.14	...	30.15-14.52

Address: 7700 Forsyth Boulevard, St. Louis, MO 63105	Web Site: www.centene.com	Auditors: KPMG LLP
Telephone: 314-725-4477	Officers: Michael F. Neidorff - Chairman, President, Chief Executive Officer Mark W. Eggert - Executive Vice President	Transfer Agents: Broadridge Corporate Issuer Solutions, Inc., Philadelphia, PA
Fax: 314-725-5180		

155

CENTERPOINT ENERGY, INC

Exchange	Symbol	Price	52Wk Range	Yield	P/E
NYS	CNP	$23.96 (3/28/2013)	23.96-19.00	3.46	24.70

*7 Year Price Score 112.99 *NYSE Composite Index=100 *12 Month Price Score 97.54

Interim Earnings (Per Share)

Qtr.	Mar	Jun	Sep	Dec
2008	0.36	0.30	0.39	0.25
2009	0.19	0.24	0.31	0.27
2010	0.29	0.20	0.29	0.29
2011	0.35	0.28	2.27	0.28
2012	0.34	0.29	0.02	0.31

Interim Dividends (Per Share)

Amt	Decl	Ex	Rec	Pay
0.203Q	04/26/2012	05/14/2012	05/16/2012	06/08/2012
0.203Q	07/26/2012	08/14/2012	08/16/2012	09/10/2012
0.203Q	10/24/2012	11/14/2012	11/16/2012	12/10/2012
0.207Q	01/25/2013	02/13/2013	02/15/2013	03/08/2013

Indicated Div: $0.83

Valuation Analysis

		Institutional Holding	
Forecast EPS	$1.26 (04/05/2013)	No of Institutions	546
Market Cap	$10.3 Billion	Shares	337,668,416
Book Value	$4.3 Billion		
Price/Book	2.38	% Held	72.92
Price/Sales	1.38		

TRADING VOLUME (thousand shares)

Business Summary: Electric Utilities (MIC: 3.1.1 SIC: 4911 NAIC: 221111)

CenterPoint Energy is a public utility holding company. Through its operating subsidiaries, Co. owns and operates electric transmission and distribution facilities, natural gas distribution facilities, interstate pipelines and natural gas gathering, processing and treating facilities. As of Dec 31 2011, Co.'s subsidiary, CenterPoint Energy Houston Electric, LLC, provided electric transmission and distribution services to 86 retail electric providers in the Texas Gulf Coast; while CenterPoint Energy Resources Corp., another subsidiary, engaged in regulated natural gas sales and transportation for about 3.3 million customers in Arkansas, Louisiana, Minnesota, Mississippi, Oklahoma and Texas.

Recent Developments: For the year ended Dec 31 2012, net income decreased 69.3% to US$417.0 million from US$1.36 billion in the prior year. Revenues were US$7.45 billion, down 11.8% from US$8.45 billion the year before. Operating income was US$1.04 billion versus US$1.30 billion in the prior year, a decrease of 20.0%. Indirect operating expenses decreased 10.3% to US$6.41 billion from US$7.15 billion in the equivalent prior-year period.

Prospects: Our evaluation of Centerpoint Energy Inc. as of Apr. 7, 2013 is the result of our systematic analysis on three basic characteristics: earnings strength, relative valuation, and recent stock price movement. The company has produced a positive trend in earnings per share over the past 5 quarters. However, while recent estimates for the company have been lowered by analysts, CNP has posted better than expected results. Based on operating earnings yield, the company is about fairly valued when compared to all of the companies in our coverage universe. Share price changes over the past year indicates that CNP will perform very poorly over the near term.

Financial Data

(US$ in Thousands)	12/31/2012	12/31/2011	12/31/2010	12/31/2009	12/31/2008	12/31/2007	12/31/2006	12/31/2005
Earnings Per Share	0.97	3.17	1.07	1.01	1.30	1.17	1.33	0.75
Cash Flow Per Share	4.34	4.44	3.38	5.04	2.52	2.42	3.18	0.20
Tang Book Value Per Share	6.62	5.93	3.53	2.41	0.99	0.35	N.M.	N.M.
Dividends Per Share	0.810	0.790	0.780	0.760	0.730	0.680	0.600	0.400
Dividend Payout %	83.51	24.92	72.90	75.25	56.15	58.12	45.11	53.33
Income Statement								
Total Revenue	7,452,000	8,450,000	8,785,000	8,281,000	11,322,000	9,623,000	9,319,000	9,722,000
EBITDA	1,435,000	1,800,000	1,347,000	1,160,000	1,288,000	1,172,000	1,064,000	810,000
Depn & Amortn	562,000	529,000	531,000	496,000	478,000	455,000	440,000	432,000
Income Before Taxes	726,000	1,144,000	676,000	533,000	674,000	594,000	494,000	378,000
Income Taxes	340,000	404,000	263,000	176,000	278,000	195,000	62,000	153,000
Net Income	417,000	1,357,000	442,000	372,000	447,000	399,000	432,000	252,000
Average Shares	429,794	428,724	413,000	367,681	343,555	342,507	324,778	346,028
Balance Sheet								
Current Assets	2,874,000	2,337,000	2,582,000	2,904,000	3,035,000	2,788,000	2,995,000	2,891,000
Total Assets	22,871,000	21,703,000	20,111,000	19,773,000	19,676,000	17,872,000	17,633,000	17,116,000
Current Liabilities	3,575,000	2,593,000	2,620,000	3,038,000	2,848,000	3,791,000	4,221,000	3,014,000
Long-Term Obligations	8,357,000	8,641,000	9,001,000	9,119,000	10,181,000	8,364,000	7,802,000	8,568,000
Total Liabilities	18,570,000	17,481,000	16,913,000	17,134,000	17,639,000	16,062,000	16,077,000	15,820,000
Stockholders' Equity	4,301,000	4,222,000	3,198,000	2,639,000	2,037,000	1,810,000	1,556,000	1,296,000
Shares Outstanding	428,000	426,000	425,000	391,000	346,000	323,000	314,000	310,000
Statistical Record								
Return on Assets %	1.87	6.49	2.22	1.89	2.37	2.25	2.49	1.43
Return on Equity %	9.76	36.58	15.14	15.91	23.18	23.71	30.29	20.99
EBITDA Margin %	19.26	21.30	15.33	14.01	11.38	12.18	11.42	8.33
Net Margin %	5.60	16.06	5.03	4.49	3.95	4.15	4.64	2.59
Asset Turnover	0.33	0.40	0.44	0.42	0.60	0.54	0.54	0.55
Current Ratio	0.80	0.90	0.99	0.96	1.07	0.74	0.71	0.96
Debt to Equity	1.94	2.05	2.81	3.46	5.00	4.62	5.01	6.61
Price Range	21.75-18.23	21.29-15.20	16.92-12.90	14.81-8.88	17.16-9.08	20.02-15.15	16.80-11.73	15.13-10.65
P/E Ratio	22.42-18.79	6.72-4.79	15.81-12.06	14.66-8.79	13.20-6.98	17.11-12.95	12.63-8.82	20.17-14.20
Average Yield %	4.03	4.27	5.30	6.38	4.98	3.88	4.41	3.13

Address: 1111 Louisiana Street, Houston, TX 77002 **Telephone:** 713-207-1111	**Web Site:** www.centerpointenergy.com **Officers:** Milton Carroll - Chairman David M. McClanahan - President, Chief Executive Officer	**Auditors:** Deloitte & Touche LLP **Investor Contact:** 713-207-6500 **Transfer Agents:** CenterPoint Energy Investor Services

CENTURYLINK, INC.

Exchange	Symbol	Price	52Wk Range	Yield	P/E
NYS	CTL	$35.13 (3/28/2013)	42.95-32.27	6.15	28.10

*7 Year Price Score 91.81 *NYSE Composite Index=100 *12 Month Price Score 84.88

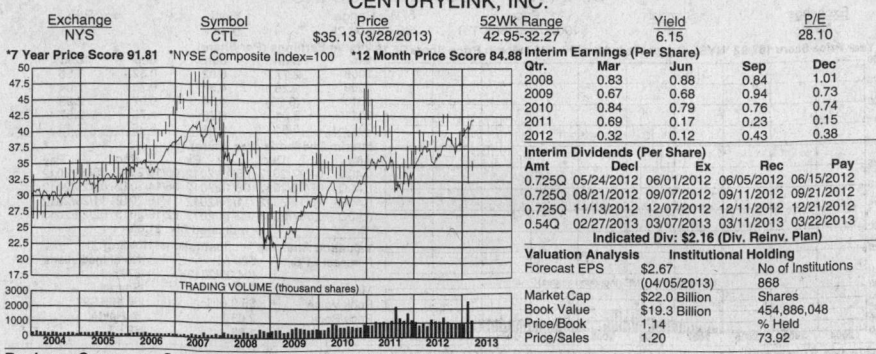

Interim Earnings (Per Share)

Qtr.	Mar	Jun	Sep	Dec
2008	0.83	0.88	0.84	1.01
2009	0.67	0.68	0.94	0.73
2010	0.84	0.79	0.76	0.74
2011	0.69	0.17	0.23	0.15
2012	0.32	0.12	0.43	0.38

Interim Dividends (Per Share)

Amt	Decl	Ex	Rec	Pay
0.725Q	05/24/2012	06/01/2012	06/05/2012	06/15/2012
0.725Q	08/21/2012	09/07/2012	09/11/2012	09/21/2012
0.725Q	11/13/2012	12/07/2012	12/11/2012	12/21/2012
0.54Q	02/27/2013	03/07/2013	03/11/2013	03/22/2013

Indicated Div: $2.16 (Div. Reinv. Plan)

Valuation Analysis

		Institutional Holding	
Forecast EPS	$2.67	No of Institutions	
	(04/05/2013)	868	
Market Cap	$22.0 Billion	Shares	
Book Value	$19.3 Billion	454,886,048	
Price/Book	1.14	% Held	
Price/Sales	1.20	73.92	

Business Summary: Services (MIC: 6.1.2 SIC: 4813 NAIC: 517110)

CenturyLink is a holding company. Through its subsidiaries, Co. is a communications company engaged primarily in providing a range of communications services to its residential, business, governmental and wholesale customers. Co.'s communications services include local and long-distance, network access, private line, public access, broadband, data, managed hosting, colocation, wireless and video services. In certain local and regional markets, Co. also provides local access and fiber transport services to competitive local exchange carriers and security monitoring. Co. has four operating segments: regional markets, business markets, wholesale markets, and Savvis operations.

Recent Developments: For the year ended Dec 31 2012, net income increased 35.6% to US$777.0 million from US$573.0 million in the prior year. Revenues were US$18.38 billion, up 19.7% from US$15.35 billion the year before. Operating income was US$2.71 billion versus US$2.03 billion in the prior year, an increase of 34.0%. Direct operating expenses rose 20.8% to US$7.64 billion from US$6.33 billion in the comparable period the year before. Indirect operating expenses increased 14.6% to US$8.02 billion from US$7.00 billion in the equivalent prior-year period.

Prospects: Our evaluation of CenturyLink, Inc. as of Apr. 7, 2013 is the result of our systematic analysis on three basic characteristics: earnings strength, relative valuation, and recent stock price movement. The company has enjoyed a very positive trend in earnings per share over the past 5 quarters and while recent estimates for the company have been raised by analysts, CTL has posted results that fell short of analysts expectations. Based on operating earnings yield, the company is about fairly valued when compared to all of the companies in our coverage universe. Share price changes over the past year indicates that CTL will perform poorly over the near term.

Financial Data
(US$ in Thousands)

	12/31/2012	12/31/2011	12/31/2010	12/31/2009	12/31/2008	12/31/2007	12/31/2006	12/31/2005
Earnings Per Share	1.25	1.07	3.13	3.23	3.56	3.72	3.07	2.49
Cash Flow Per Share	9.75	7.89	6.80	7.92	8.32	9.42	7.21	7.37
Tang Book Value Per Share	N.M.	N.M.	N.M.	N.M.	N.M.	N.M.	N.M.	0.90
Dividends Per Share	2.900	2.900	2.900	2.800	2.168	0.260	0.250	0.240
Dividend Payout %	232.00	271.03	92.65	86.69	60.88	6.99	8.14	9.64
Income Statement								
Total Revenue	18,376,000	15,351,000	7,041,534	4,974,239	2,599,747	2,656,241	2,447,730	2,479,252
EBITDA	5,667,000	4,621,000	3,316,563	2,023,726	1,269,206	1,355,948	1,307,506	1,263,561
Depn & Amortn	3,098,000	2,601,000	1,227,000	838,800	506,900	524,100	520,400	528,900
Income Before Taxes	1,250,000	948,000	1,532,085	814,512	560,089	618,942	591,149	532,860
Income Taxes	473,000	375,000	582,951	301,881	194,357	200,572	221,122	203,291
Net Income	777,000	573,000	947,705	647,211	365,732	418,370	370,027	334,479
Average Shares	622,285	534,121	301,297	199,057	102,871	113,094	122,229	136,087
Balance Sheet								
Current Assets	3,613,000	3,523,000	1,143,129	1,123,591	555,407	292,399	290,117	423,016
Total Assets	54,020,000	56,139,000	22,038,098	22,562,729	8,254,195	8,184,553	7,441,007	7,762,707
Current Liabilities	4,595,000	4,019,000	1,011,042	1,707,195	458,390	736,535	617,565	746,230
Long-Term Obligations	19,400,000	21,356,000	7,316,004	7,253,653	3,294,119	2,734,357	2,412,852	2,376,070
Total Liabilities	34,731,000	35,312,000	12,396,857	13,101,790	5,090,955	4,775,348	4,250,056	4,145,434
Stockholders' Equity	19,289,000	20,827,000	9,641,241	9,460,939	3,163,240	3,409,205	3,190,951	3,617,273
Shares Outstanding	625,658	618,514	304,947	299,189	100,277	108,491	113,253	131,074
Statistical Record								
Return on Assets %	1.41	1.47	4.25	4.20	4.44	5.35	4.87	4.30
Return on Equity %	3.86	3.76	9.92	10.25	11.10	12.68	10.87	9.52
EBITDA Margin %	30.84	30.10	47.10	40.68	48.82	51.05	53.42	50.97
Net Margin %	4.23	3.73	13.46	13.01	14.07	15.75	15.12	13.49
Asset Turnover	0.33	0.39	0.32	0.32	0.32	0.34	0.32	0.32
Current Ratio	0.79	0.88	1.13	0.66	1.21	0.40	0.47	0.57
Debt to Equity	1.01	1.03	0.76	0.77	1.04	0.80	0.76	0.66
Price Range	42.95-36.59	46.73-31.82	46.80-32.93	36.82-23.56	41.58-21.81	49.52-40.30	43.79-32.84	36.28-30.26
P/E Ratio	34.36-29.27	43.67-29.74	14.95-10.52	11.40-7.29	11.68-6.13	13.31-10.83	14.26-10.70	14.57-12.15
Average Yield %	7.37	7.50	7.81	9.14	6.42	0.57	0.65	0.72

Address: 100 CenturyLink Drive, Monroe, LA 71203	**Web Site:** www.centurylink.com	**Auditors:** KPMG LLP
Telephone: 318-388-9000	**Officers:** Glen F. Post - President, Chief Executive Officer R. Stewart Ewing - Executive Vice President, Chief Financial Officer	**Investor Contact:** 318-340-5627
Fax: 318-789-8656		**Transfer Agents:** ComputershareTrust Company, Providence, RI

157

CF INDUSTRIES HOLDINGS INC

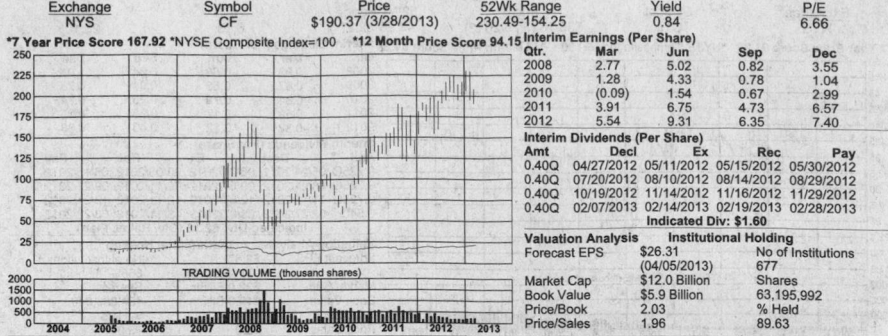

Exchange	Symbol	Price	52Wk Range	Yield	P/E
NYS	CF	$190.37 (3/28/2013)	230.49-154.25	0.84	6.66

*7 Year Price Score 167.92 *NYSE Composite Index=100 *12 Month Price Score 94.15

Interim Earnings (Per Share)

Qtr.	Mar	Jun	Sep	Dec
2008	2.77	5.02	0.82	3.55
2009	1.28	4.33	0.78	1.04
2010	(0.09)	1.54	0.67	2.99
2011	3.91	6.75	4.73	6.57
2012	5.54	9.31	6.35	7.40

Interim Dividends (Per Share)

Amt	Decl	Ex	Rec	Pay
0.40Q	04/27/2012	05/11/2012	05/15/2012	05/30/2012
0.40Q	07/20/2012	08/10/2012	08/14/2012	08/29/2012
0.40Q	10/19/2012	11/14/2012	11/16/2012	11/29/2012
0.40Q	02/07/2013	02/14/2013	02/19/2013	02/28/2013
			Indicated Div: $1.60	

Valuation Analysis / **Institutional Holding**

Forecast EPS	$26.31 (04/05/2013)	No of Institutions	677
Market Cap	$12.0 Billion	Shares	
Book Value	$5.9 Billion		63,195,992
Price/Book	2.03	% Held	
Price/Sales	1.96		89.63

TRADING VOLUME (thousand shares)

Business Summary: Agricultural Chemicals (MIC: 8.3.3 SIC: 2875 NAIC: 325314)

CF Industries Holdings is engaged in manufacturing and distributing nitrogen and phosphate fertilizer products. Co.'s operations are organized into two business segments: the nitrogen segment and the phosphate segment. Co.'s principal fertilizer products in the nitrogen segment are ammonia, granular urea, urea ammonium nitrate solution, and ammonium nitrate. Co.'s other nitrogen products include urea liquor, diesel exhaust fluid, and aqua ammonia. Co.'s principal fertilizer products in the phosphate segment are diammonium phosphate and monoammonium phosphate. Co.'s principal customers are cooperatives and independent fertilizer distributors.

Recent Developments: For the year ended Dec 31 2012, net income increased 9.2% to US$1.92 billion from US$1.76 billion in the prior year. Revenues were US$6.10 billion, unchanged from the year before. Operating income was US$2.96 billion versus US$2.79 billion in the prior year, an increase of 6.1%. Direct operating expenses declined 6.6% to US$2.99 billion from US$3.20 billion in the comparable period the year before. Indirect operating expenses increased 46.4% to US$153.9 million from US$105.1 million in the equivalent prior-year period.

Prospects: Our evaluation of CF Industries Holdings Inc. as of Apr. 7, 2013 is the result of our systematic analysis on three basic characteristics: earnings strength, relative valuation, and recent stock price movement. The company has managed to produce a neutral trend in earnings per share over the past 5 quarters and while recent estimates for the company have been raised by analysts, CF has posted better than expected results. Based on operating earnings yield, the company is undervalued when compared to all of the companies in our coverage universe. Share price changes over the past year indicates that CF will perform well over the near term.

Financial Data

(US$ in Thousands)	12/31/2012	12/31/2011	12/31/2010	12/31/2009	12/31/2008	12/31/2007	12/31/2006	12/31/2005
Earnings Per Share	28.59	21.98	5.34	7.42	12.15	6.57	0.60	(2.04)
Cash Flow Per Share	37.08	29.96	18.46	14.06	11.52	12.43	3.70	2.49
Tang Book Value Per Share	60.18	37.13	26.77	35.58	27.63	21.09	13.89	13.72
Dividends Per Share	1.600	1.000	0.400	0.400	0.400	0.080	0.080	0.020
Dividend Payout %	5.60	4.55	7.49	5.39	3.29	1.22	13.33	...
Income Statement								
Total Revenue	6,104,000	6,097,900	3,965,000	2,608,400	3,921,100	2,756,700	1,949,500	1,908,400
EBITDA	3,333,300	3,157,100	1,291,700	793,600	1,251,700	687,700	166,800	207,200
Depn & Amortn	419,800	416,200	394,800	101,000	100,800	84,500	94,600	97,500
Income Before Taxes	2,782,500	2,595,400	677,100	695,600	1,175,400	625,900	81,800	110,300
Income Taxes	964,200	926,500	273,700	246,000	378,100	199,500	19,700	128,700
Net Income	1,848,700	1,539,200	349,200	365,600	684,600	372,700	33,300	(39,000)
Average Shares	64,700	70,000	65,400	49,200	56,400	56,700	55,100	54,999
Balance Sheet								
Current Assets	2,807,600	1,798,600	1,341,400	1,283,100	1,433,200	1,279,100	633,100	576,100
Total Assets	10,166,900	8,974,500	8,758,500	2,494,900	2,387,600	2,012,500	1,290,400	1,228,100
Current Liabilities	950,200	1,031,200	946,600	479,800	818,100	629,300	353,400	341,100
Long-Term Obligations	1,600,000	1,617,800	1,954,100	4,700	...	4,900	4,200	4,200
Total Liabilities	4,264,700	4,427,500	4,708,100	766,000	1,049,500	825,500	523,400	472,200
Stockholders' Equity	5,902,200	4,547,000	4,050,400	1,728,900	1,338,100	1,187,000	767,000	755,900
Shares Outstanding	62,950	65,420	71,267	48,569	48,391	56,245	55,172	55,027
Statistical Record								
Return on Assets %	19.26	17.36	6.21	14.98	31.03	22.57	2.64	N.M.
Return on Equity %	35.29	35.81	12.08	23.84	54.08	38.15	4.37	N.M.
EBITDA Margin %	54.61	51.77	32.58	30.42	31.92	24.95	8.56	10.86
Net Margin %	30.29	25.24	8.81	14.02	17.46	13.52	1.71	N.M.
Asset Turnover	0.64	0.69	0.70	1.07	1.78	1.67	1.55	1.38
Current Ratio	2.95	1.74	1.42	2.67	1.75	2.03	1.79	1.69
Debt to Equity	0.27	0.36	0.48	N.M.	...	N.M.	0.01	0.01
Price Range	224.51-153.81	189.78-120.98	136.67-58.56	94.95-44.25	169.62-39.38	116.56-26.42	26.39-13.04	17.93-11.30
P/E Ratio	7.85-5.38	8.63-5.50	25.59-10.97	12.80-5.96	13.96-3.24	17.74-4.02	43.98-21.73	...
Average Yield %	0.83	...	0.68	0.42	0.53	0.36	0.14	0.13

Address: 4 Parkway North, Suite 400, Deerfield, IL 60015 Telephone: 847-405-2400	Web Site: www.cfindustries.com Officers: Stephen R. Wilson - Chairman, President, Chief Executive Officer Dennis P. Kelleher - Senior Vice President, Chief Financial Officer, Principal Financial Officer	Auditors: KPMG LLP Investor Contact: 847-405-2550 Transfer Agents: Computershare Trust Company, N.A., Providence, RI

CHARLES RIVER LABORATORIES INTERNATIONAL INC.

Exchange	Symbol	Price	52Wk Range	Yield	P/E
NYS	CRL	$44.27 (3/28/2013)	45.79-31.82	N/A	22.02

*7 Year Price Score 81.82   *NYSE Composite Index=100   *12 Month Price Score 102.75

Interim Earnings (Per Share)

Qtr.	Mar	Jun	Sep	Dec
2008	0.64	0.71	0.63	(9.74)
2009	0.38	0.52	0.57	0.27
2010	0.26	0.22	(0.40)	(5.49)
2011	0.57	0.63	0.37	0.56
2012	0.54	0.63	0.46	0.38

Interim Dividends (Per Share)

No Dividends Paid

Valuation Analysis

	Institutional Holding	
Forecast EPS	$2.85	No of Institutions
	(04/05/2013)	315
Market Cap	$2.1 Billion	Shares
Book Value	$600.8 Million	55,604,240
Price/Book	3.55	% Held
Price/Sales	1.89	92.85

Business Summary: Biotechnology (MIC: 4.1.2 SIC: 8731 NAIC: 541710)

Charles River Laboratories International, together with its subsidiaries, provides services that aid the drug discovery and development process to pharmaceutical and biotechnology companies, as well as government agencies, hospitals and academic institutions. Co. has two business segments: Research Models and Services, which include sales of research models, genetically engineered models and services, insourcing services, research animal diagnostic services, discovery services, in vitro products and services, and avian vaccine products and services; and Preclinical Services, which includes preclinical services such as discovery support, safety assessment and biopharmaceutical services.

Recent Developments: For the year ended Dec 29 2012, income from continuing operations decreased 11.6% to US$102.1 million from US$115.5 million a year earlier. Net income decreased 11.0% to US$97.9 million from US$110.0 million in the prior year. Revenues were US$1.13 billion, down 1.1% from US$1.14 billion the year before. Operating income was US$165.8 million versus US$174.3 million in the prior year, a decrease of 4.9%. Direct operating expenses declined 0.9% to US$733.9 million from US$740.4 million in the comparable period the year before. Indirect operating expenses increased 0.8% to US$229.9 million from US$227.9 million in the equivalent prior-year period.

Prospects: Our evaluation of Charles River Laboratories International Inc. as of Apr. 7, 2013 is the result of our systematic analysis on three basic characteristics: earnings strength, relative valuation, and recent stock price movement. The company has managed to produce a neutral trend in earnings per share over the past 5 quarters. However, while recent estimates for the company have been lowered by analysts, CRL has posted better than expected results. Based on operating earnings yield, the company is undervalued when compared to all of the companies in our coverage universe. Share price changes over the past year indicates that CRL will perform in line with the market over the near term.

Financial Data
(US$ in Thousands)

	12/29/2012	12/31/2011	12/25/2010	12/26/2009	12/27/2008	12/29/2007	12/30/2006	12/31/2005
Earnings Per Share	2.01	2.14	(5.38)	1.74	(7.76)	2.25	(0.80)	1.96
Cash Flow Per Share	4.35	4.00	2.70	3.34	4.17	4.32	2.56	3.34
Tang Book Value Per Share	6.37	4.80	6.52	10.73	9.03	8.67	4.72	2.92
Income Statement								
Total Revenue	1,129,530	1,142,647	1,133,416	1,202,551	1,343,493	1,230,626	1,058,385	1,122,228
EBITDA	243,774	259,126	(206,340)	262,565	(364,509)	312,122	271,740	283,300
Depn & Amortn	81,275	85,231	93,649	93,553	91,183	86,379	82,586	102,455
Income Before Taxes	129,746	132,662	(334,082)	149,107	(461,010)	217,422	176,564	160,413
Income Taxes	27,628	17,140	23	39,725	61,944	59,400	49,738	16,576
Net Income	97,295	109,566	(336,669)	114,441	(521,843)	154,406	(55,783)	141,999
Average Shares	48,406	51,318	62,561	65,635	67,273	68,735	69,948	72,902
Balance Sheet								
Current Assets	485,252	425,843	552,894	595,601	618,139	607,864	501,093	419,322
Total Assets	1,586,344	1,558,320	1,733,373	2,204,093	2,159,918	2,805,537	2,557,544	2,538,209
Current Liabilities	342,247	216,797	259,780	249,773	300,998	302,528	259,331	311,412
Long-Term Obligations	527,075	703,170	670,270	457,419	540,646	484,998	547,084	260,217
Total Liabilities	985,539	1,032,737	1,045,950	828,850	960,893	945,070	962,333	711,196
Stockholders' Equity	600,805	525,583	687,423	1,375,243	1,199,025	1,860,467	1,595,211	1,827,013
Shares Outstanding	48,220	48,875	56,441	65,877	67,052	68,135	66,919	71,955
Statistical Record								
Return on Assets %	6.20	6.55	N.M.	5.26	N.M.	5.77	N.M.	5.41
Return on Equity %	17.32	17.77	N.M.	8.92	N.M.	8.96	N.M.	8.47
EBITDA Margin %	21.58	22.68	N.M.	21.83	N.M.	25.36	25.67	25.24
Net Margin %	8.61	9.59	N.M.	9.52	N.M.	12.55	N.M.	12.65
Asset Turnover	0.72	0.68	0.58	0.55	0.54	0.46	0.42	0.43
Current Ratio	1.42	1.96	2.13	2.38	2.05	2.01	1.93	1.35
Debt to Equity	0.88	1.34	0.98	0.33	0.45	0.26	0.34	0.14
Price Range	41.24-27.39	42.47-25.95	41.56-28.25	40.09-23.15	68.82-20.78	67.35-43.24	50.56-33.92	52.71-41.76
P/E Ratio	20.52-13.63	19.85-12.13	...	23.04-13.30	...	29.93-19.22	...	26.89-21.31

Address: 251 Ballardvale Street, Wilmington, MA 01887	Web Site: www.criver.com	Auditors: PricewaterhouseCoopers LLP
Telephone: 781-222-6000	Officers: James C. Foster - Chairman, President, Chief Executive Officer Thomas F. Ackerman - Corporate Executive Vice President, Chief Financial Officer	Investor Contact: 978-658-6000 Transfer Agents: ComputerShare Investor Services, Providence, RI

159

CHESAPEAKE ENERGY CORP.

Exchange	Symbol	Price	52Wk Range	Yield	P/E
NYS	CHK	$20.41 (3/28/2013)	23.31-13.55	1.71	N/A

*7 Year Price Score 58.92   *NYSE Composite Index=100   *12 Month Price Score 99.81

TRADING VOLUME (thousand shares)

Interim Earnings (Per Share)

Qtr.	Mar	Jun	Sep	Dec
2008	(0.29)	(3.17)	5.61	(1.59)
2009	(9.63)	0.39	0.30	(0.79)
2010	0.92	0.37	0.75	0.27
2011	(0.32)	0.68	1.23	0.63
2012	(0.11)	1.29	(3.19)	0.40

Interim Dividends (Per Share)

Amt	Decl	Ex	Rec	Pay
0.087Q	06/12/2012	07/12/2012	07/16/2012	07/31/2012
0.087Q	09/24/2012	10/11/2012	10/15/2012	10/31/2012
0.087Q	12/17/2012	01/11/2013	01/15/2013	01/31/2013
0.087Q	04/08/2013	04/11/2013	04/15/2013	04/30/2013

Indicated Div: $0.35

Valuation Analysis

		Institutional Holding	
Forecast EPS	$1.25 (04/06/2013)	No of Institutions	771
Market Cap	$13.6 Billion	Shares	562,657,344
Book Value	$15.6 Billion	% Held	79.62
Price/Book	0.87		
Price/Sales	1.10		

Business Summary: Production & Extraction (MIC: 9.1.1 SIC: 1311 NAIC: 211111)

Chesapeake Energy is a holding company. Through its subsidiaries, Co. is engaged in the exploration, development and acquisition of properties for the production of natural gas, oil and natural gas liquids (NGL) from underground reservoirs. Additionally, Co. provides marketing, midstream, drilling and other oilfield services. Co.'s operations are located onshore and in the continental U.S. As of Dec 31 2012, Co. had estimated total proved reserves of 10.93 billion cubic feet of gas, 495.5 million barrels of oil and 297.3 million barrels of NGL.

Recent Developments: For the year ended Dec 31 2012, net loss amounted to US$594.0 million versus net income of US$1.76 billion in the prior year. Revenues were US$12.32 billion, up 5.9% from US$11.64 billion the year before. Operating loss was US$1.69 billion versus an income of US$2.92 billion in the prior year. Direct operating expenses rose 9.6% to US$7.27 billion from US$6.63 billion in the comparable period the year before. Indirect operating expenses increased 224.1% to US$6.74 billion from US$2.08 billion in the equivalent prior-year period.

Prospects: Our evaluation of Chesapeake Energy Corp. as of Apr. 7, 2013 is the result of our systematic analysis on three basic characteristics: earnings strength, relative valuation, and recent stock price movement. The company has enjoyed a very positive trend in earnings per share over the past 5 quarters and while recent estimates for the company have been raised by analysts, CHK has posted better than expected results. Based on operating earnings yield, the company is about fairly valued when compared to all of the companies in our coverage universe. Share price changes over the past year indicates that CHK will perform very poorly over the near term.

Financial Data

(US$ in Thousands)	12/31/2012	12/31/2011	12/31/2010	12/31/2009	12/31/2008	12/31/2007	12/31/2006	12/31/2005
Earnings Per Share	(1.46)	2.32	2.51	(9.57)	1.14	2.62	4.35	2.51
Cash Flow Per Share	4.40	9.27	8.11	7.12	9.74	10.82	12.15	7.47
Tang Book Value Per Share	18.83	20.57	18.65	16.95	26.00	21.85	20.32	12.42
Dividends Per Share	0.350	0.250	0.300	0.300	0.292	0.263	0.230	0.195
Dividend Payout %	...	10.78	11.95	...	25.66	10.02	5.29	7.77
Income Statement								
Total Revenue	12,316,000	11,635,000	9,366,000	7,702,000	11,629,000	7,800,000	7,325,595	4,665,290
EBITDA	1,914,000	4,847,000	4,368,000	(7,481,000)	3,658,000	4,729,000	5,000,689	2,653,490
Depn & Amortn	2,811,000	1,923,000	1,692,000	1,694,000	2,147,000	1,997,000	1,470,071	950,749
Income Before Taxes	(974,000)	2,880,000	2,657,000	(9,288,000)	1,186,000	2,341,000	3,255,359	1,493,393
Income Taxes	(380,000)	1,123,000	1,110,000	(3,483,000)	463,000	890,000	1,252,036	545,091
Net Income	(769,000)	1,742,000	1,774,000	(5,830,000)	723,000	1,451,000	2,003,323	948,302
Average Shares	643,000	752,000	706,000	612,000	545,000	487,000	458,603	366,683
Balance Sheet								
Current Assets	2,948,000	3,177,000	3,266,000	2,446,000	4,292,000	1,396,000	1,153,869	1,183,397
Total Assets	41,611,000	41,835,000	37,179,000	29,914,000	38,444,000	30,734,000	24,417,167	16,118,462
Current Liabilities	6,266,000	7,082,000	4,490,000	2,688,000	3,621,000	2,761,000	1,889,809	1,964,088
Long-Term Obligations	12,819,000	10,824,000	12,640,000	12,295,000	14,184,000	10,950,000	7,375,548	5,489,742
Total Liabilities	26,042,000	25,211,000	21,915,000	18,470,000	22,147,000	18,604,000	13,165,696	9,944,139
Stockholders' Equity	15,569,000	16,624,000	15,264,000	11,444,000	16,297,000	12,130,000	11,251,471	6,174,323
Shares Outstanding	664,319	659,335	654,029	647,671	607,296	511,147	457,433	370,189
Statistical Record								
Return on Assets %	N.M.	4.41	5.29	N.M.	2.08	5.26	9.88	7.78
Return on Equity %	N.M.	10.93	13.28	N.M.	5.07	12.41	22.99	20.31
EBITDA Margin %	15.54	41.66	46.64	N.M.	31.46	60.63	68.26	56.88
Net Margin %	N.M.	14.97	18.94	N.M.	6.22	18.60	27.35	20.33
Asset Turnover	0.29	0.29	0.28	0.23	0.34	0.28	0.36	0.38
Current Ratio	0.47	0.45	0.73	0.91	1.19	0.51	0.61	0.60
Debt to Equity	0.82	0.65	0.83	1.07	0.87	0.90	0.66	0.89
Price Range	25.58-13.55	35.61-22.06	28.97-20.04	29.46-13.50	69.40-11.32	41.06-27.30	35.04-27.02	38.86-15.22
P/E Ratio	...	15.35-9.51	11.54-7.98	...	60.88-9.93	15.67-10.42	8.06-6.21	15.48-6.06
Average Yield %	1.80	0.85	1.28	1.39	0.71	0.77	0.74	0.77

Address: 6100 North Western Avenue, Oklahoma City, OK 73118	Web Site: www.chk.com	Auditors: PricewaterhouseCoopers LLP
Telephone: 405-848-8000	Officers: Steven C. Dixon - Acting Chief Executive Officer, Executive Vice President, Chief Operating Officer Douglas J. Jacobson - Executive Vice President	Investor Contact: 405-935-4763
Fax: 405-483-0573		Transfer Agents: Computershare Trust Company, N.A., Canton, MA

CHEVRON CORPORATION

Exchange	Symbol	Price	52Wk Range	Yield	P/E	Div Achiever
NYS	CVX	$118.82 (3/28/2013)	121.18-96.41	3.03	8.92	25 Years

*7 Year Price Score 112.99 *NYSE Composite Index=100 *12 Month Price Score 98.44

Interim Earnings (Per Share)

Qtr.	Mar	Jun	Sep	Dec
2008	2.48	2.90	3.85	2.44
2009	0.92	0.87	1.92	1.53
2010	2.27	2.70	1.87	2.64
2011	3.09	3.85	3.92	2.58
2012	3.27	3.66	2.69	3.70

Interim Dividends (Per Share)

Amt	Decl	Ex	Rec	Pay
0.90Q	04/25/2012	05/16/2012	05/18/2012	06/11/2012
0.90Q	07/25/2012	08/15/2012	08/17/2012	09/10/2012
0.90Q	10/31/2012	11/14/2012	11/16/2012	12/10/2012
0.90Q	01/30/2013	02/13/2013	02/15/2013	03/11/2013

Indicated Div: $3.60 (Div. Reinv. Plan)

Valuation Analysis / **Institutional Holding**

Forecast EPS	$12.41 (04/06/2013)	No of Institutions	2106
Market Cap	$231.3 Billion	Shares	1,381,181,952
Book Value	$136.5 Billion	% Held	61.94
Price/Book	1.69		
Price/Sales	0.96		

Business Summary: Refining & Marketing (MIC: 9.1.2 SIC: 2911 NAIC: 324110)

Chevron is engaged in petroleum operations, chemicals operations, mining activities, power generation and energy services. Co.'s upstream operations include exploring, developing and producing crude oil and natural gas, and processing, liquefaction, transportation and regasification associated with liquefied natural gas. Co.'s downstream operations include refining crude oil into petroleum products, and manufactures and markets commodity petrochemicals, plastics for industrial uses and fuel and lubricant additives. At Dec 31 2012, Co. had net proved reserves of 6.48 billion barrels of crude oil, condensate, natural gas liquids and synthetic oil, and 29.20 trillion cubic feet of natural gas.

Recent Developments: For the year ended Dec 31 2012, net income decreased 2.5% to US$26.34 billion from US$27.01 billion in the prior year. Revenues were US$241.91 billion, down 4.6% from US$253.71 billion the year before. Direct operating expenses declined 6.1% to US$140.77 billion from US$149.92 billion in the comparable period the year before. Indirect operating expenses decreased 2.4% to US$54.81 billion from US$56.15 billion in the equivalent prior-year period.

Prospects: Our evaluation of Chevron Corporation as of Apr. 7, 2013 is the result of our systematic analysis on three basic characteristics: earnings strength, relative valuation, and recent stock price movement. The company has produced a positive trend in earnings per share over the past 5 quarters. However, while recent estimates for the company have been mixed, CVX has posted better than expected results. Based on operating earnings yield, the company is undervalued when compared to all of the companies in our coverage universe. Share price changes over the past year indicates that CVX will perform in line with the market over the near term.

Financial Data

(US$ in Millions)	12/31/2012	12/31/2011	12/31/2010	12/31/2009	12/31/2008	12/31/2007	12/31/2006	12/31/2005
Earnings Per Share	13.32	13.44	9.48	5.24	11.67	8.77	7.80	6.54
Cash Flow Per Share	19.85	20.69	15.70	9.73	14.51	11.79	11.13	9.38
Tang Book Value Per Share	67.75	58.92	50.04	43.48	40.93	34.66	29.71	26.00
Dividends Per Share	3.510	3.090	2.840	2.660	2.530	2.260	2.010	1.750
Dividend Payout %	26.35	22.99	29.96	50.76	21.68	25.77	25.77	26.76
Income Statement								
Total Revenue	241,909	253,706	204,928	171,636	273,005	220,904	210,118	198,200
EBITDA	59,745	60,545	45,168	30,666	52,585	41,148	40,003	31,688
Depn & Amortn	13,413	12,911	13,063	12,110	9,528	8,708	7,506	5,913
Income Before Taxes	46,332	47,634	32,055	18,528	43,057	32,274	32,046	25,293
Income Taxes	19,996	20,626	12,919	7,965	19,026	13,479	14,838	11,098
Net Income	26,179	26,895	19,024	10,483	23,931	18,688	17,138	14,099
Average Shares	1,965	2,001	2,007	2,001	2,038	2,132	2,198	2,156
Balance Sheet								
Current Assets	55,720	53,234	48,841	37,216	36,470	39,377	36,304	34,336
Total Assets	232,982	209,474	184,769	164,621	161,165	148,786	132,628	125,833
Current Liabilities	34,212	33,600	29,012	26,211	32,023	33,798	28,409	25,011
Long-Term Obligations	12,065	9,812	11,289	10,130	6,083	6,070	7,679	12,131
Total Liabilities	96,458	88,092	79,688	72,707	74,517	71,698	63,693	63,157
Stockholders' Equity	136,524	121,382	105,081	91,914	86,648	77,088	68,935	62,676
Shares Outstanding	1,946	1,981	2,007	2,007	2,004	2,090	2,165	2,233
Statistical Record								
Return on Assets %	11.80	13.64	10.89	6.44	15.40	13.28	13.26	12.87
Return on Equity %	20.25	23.75	19.31	11.74	29.15	25.60	26.04	26.13
EBITDA Margin %	24.70	23.86	22.04	17.87	19.26	18.63	19.04	15.99
Net Margin %	10.82	10.60	9.28	6.11	8.77	8.46	8.16	7.11
Asset Turnover	1.09	1.29	1.17	1.05	1.76	1.57	1.63	1.81
Current Ratio	1.63	1.58	1.68	1.42	1.14	1.17	1.28	1.37
Debt to Equity	0.09	0.08	0.11	0.11	0.07	0.08	0.11	0.19
Price Range	117.96-96.41	109.66-89.88	91.60-67.31	79.64-56.46	103.09-57.83	94.86-66.43	75.97-54.08	65.77-50.51
P/E Ratio	8.86-7.24	8.16-6.69	9.66-7.10	15.20-10.77	8.83-4.96	10.82-7.57	9.74-6.93	10.06-7.72
Average Yield %	3.26	3.07	3.63	3.79	2.98	2.74	3.19	3.04

Address: 6001 Bollinger Canyon Road, San Ramon, CA 94583-2324	Web Site: www.chevron.com	Auditors: PricewaterhouseCoopers LLP
Telephone: 925-842-1000	Officers: John S. Watson - Chairman, Vice-Chairman, Chief Executive Officer George L. Kirkland - Vice-Chairman, Division Officer	Investor Contact: 925-842-5690
Fax: 925-894-6017		Transfer Agents: Computershare Shareowner Services LLC, Pittsburgh, PA

CHICAGO BRIDGE & IRON CO., N.V. (NETHERLANDS)

Exchange	Symbol	Price	52Wk Range	Yield	P/E
NYS	CBI	$62.10 (3/28/2013)	62.10-33.47	0.32	20.23

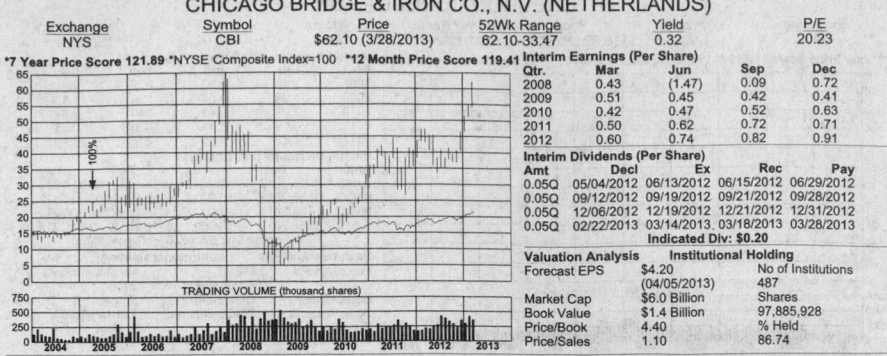

*7 Year Price Score 121.89 *NYSE Composite Index=100 *12 Month Price Score 119.41

Interim Earnings (Per Share)

Qtr.	Mar	Jun	Sep	Dec
2008	0.43	(1.47)	0.09	0.72
2009	0.51	0.45	0.42	0.41
2010	0.42	0.47	0.52	0.63
2011	0.50	0.62	0.72	0.71
2012	0.60	0.74	0.82	0.91

Interim Dividends (Per Share)

Amt	Decl	Ex	Rec	Pay
0.05Q	05/04/2012	06/13/2012	06/15/2012	06/29/2012
0.05Q	09/12/2012	09/19/2012	09/21/2012	09/28/2012
0.05Q	12/06/2012	12/19/2012	12/21/2012	12/31/2012
0.05Q	02/22/2013	03/14/2013	03/18/2013	03/28/2013

Indicated Div: $0.20

Valuation Analysis

		Institutional Holding	
Forecast EPS	$4.20 (04/05/2013)	No of Institutions	487
Market Cap	$6.0 Billion	Shares	97,885,928
Book Value	$1.4 Billion	% Held	86.74
Price/Book	4.40		
Price/Sales	1.10		

Business Summary: Construction Services (MIC: 7.5.4 SIC: 1799 NAIC: 238990)

Chicago Bridge & Iron is an engineering, procurement and construction service provider and a process technology licensor. Co. has three business sectors: Steel Plate Structures, which provides engineering, procurement, fabrication and construction, including mechanical erection services, for the hydrocarbon, water and nuclear industries; Project Engineering and Construction, which provides engineering, procurement, fabrication and construction services for upstream and downstream energy infrastructure facilities; and Lummus Technology, which provides licenses, services, catalysts and equipment to companies in the hydrocarbon refining, petrochemicals, and gas processing industries.

Recent Developments: For the year ended Dec 31 2012, net income increased 24.2% to US$317.1 million from US$255.2 million in the prior year. Revenues were US$5.49 billion, up 20.5% from US$4.55 billion the year before. Operating income was US$455.6 million versus US$355.2 million in the prior year, an increase of 28.3%. Direct operating expenses rose 20.3% to US$4.79 billion from US$3.98 billion in the comparable period the year before. Indirect operating expenses increased 13.0% to US$243.1 million from US$215.0 million in the equivalent prior-year period.

Prospects: Our evaluation of Chicago Bridge & Iron Co., N.V. as of Apr. 7, 2013 is the result of our systematic analysis on three basic characteristics: earnings strength, relative valuation, and recent stock price movement. The company has enjoyed a very positive trend in earnings per share over the past 5 quarters and while recent estimates for the company have been raised by analysts, CBI has posted better than expected results. Based on operating earnings yield, the company is about fairly valued when compared to all of the companies in our coverage universe. Share price changes over the past year indicates that CBI will perform poorly over the near term.

Financial Data

(US$ in Thousands)	12/31/2012	12/31/2011	12/31/2010	12/31/2009	12/31/2008	12/31/2007	12/31/2006	12/31/2005
Earnings Per Share	3.07	2.55	2.04	1.79	(0.22)	1.71	1.19	0.16
Cash Flow Per Share	2.09	4.21	2.93	2.58	0.28	4.67	4.92	1.69
Tang Book Value Per Share	2.84	0.65	N.M.	N.M.	N.M.	N.M.	2.99	2.30
Dividends Per Share	0.200	0.200	...	...	0.160	0.160	0.120	0.105
Dividend Payout %	6.51	7.84	...	...		9.36	10.08	65.63
Income Statement								
Total Revenue	5,485,206	4,550,542	3,642,318	4,556,503	5,944,981	4,363,492	3,125,307	2,257,517
EBITDA	504,133	408,494	356,681	358,690	72,362	204,456	147,211	51,734
Depn & Amortn	66,421	70,184	72,885	79,531	78,244	3,996	1,572	1,499
Income Before Taxes	426,135	335,076	272,065	259,593	(18,565)	224,312	161,308	47,888
Income Taxes	127,003	96,765	79,966	114,917	37,470	57,354	38,127	28,379
Net Income	301,665	255,032	204,559	174,289	(21,146)	165,640	116,968	15,977
Average Shares	98,230	100,204	100,458	97,244	95,401	96,808	98,509	99,766
Balance Sheet								
Current Assets	2,721,555	1,661,321	1,202,486	1,195,578	1,191,115	1,674,033	1,346,388	950,603
Total Assets	4,329,675	3,291,983	2,909,534	3,016,767	3,000,718	3,330,923	1,835,010	1,377,819
Current Liabilities	1,772,522	1,743,424	1,440,633	1,679,875	1,988,125	2,169,783	1,187,758	758,643
Long-Term Obligations	800,000		40,000	80,000	120,000	160,000		25,000
Total Liabilities	2,961,922	2,114,249	1,854,072	2,142,947	2,444,893	2,604,204	1,292,575	894,151
Stockholders' Equity	1,367,753	1,177,734	1,055,462	873,820	555,825	726,719	542,435	483,668
Shares Outstanding	96,835	97,595	99,342	100,203	95,277	96,690	95,967	98,133
Statistical Record								
Return on Assets %	7.89	8.22	6.90	5.79	N.M.	6.41	7.28	1.29
Return on Equity %	23.64	22.84	21.21	24.38	N.M.	26.10	22.80	3.35
EBITDA Margin %	9.19	8.98	9.79	7.87	1.22	4.69	4.71	2.29
Net Margin %	5.50	5.60	5.62	3.83	N.M.	3.80	3.74	0.71
Asset Turnover	1.44	1.47	1.23	1.51	1.87	1.69	1.95	1.82
Current Ratio	1.54	0.95	0.83	0.71	0.60	0.77	1.13	1.25
Debt to Equity	0.58	...	0.04	0.09	0.22	0.22		0.05
Price Range	47.40-33.47	44.51-26.68	33.20-16.94	20.88-4.87	63.10-5.51	62.13-26.18	31.20-21.60	32.50-18.30
P/E Ratio	15.44-10.90	17.45-10.46	16.27-8.30	11.66-2.72	...	36.33-15.31	26.22-18.15	203.13-114.38
Average Yield %	0.50	0.55	...	...	0.49	0.41	0.48	0.43

Address: Oostduinlaan 75, The Hague, 2596 JJ	**Web Site:** www.cbi.com	**Auditors:** Ernst & Young LLP
Telephone: 703-732-010	**Officers:** Philip K. Asherman - President, Chief Executive Officer, Managing Director Beth A. Bailey - Executive Vice President, Chief Administrative Officer	**Transfer Agents:** The Bank of New York

162

CHICO'S FAS INC

Exchange	Symbol	Price	52Wk Range	Yield	P/E
NYS	CHS	$16.80 (3/28/2013)	19.64-13.68	1.31	15.56

*7 Year Price Score 105.13 *NYSE Composite Index=100 *12 Month Price Score 93.97

Interim Earnings (Per Share)

Qtr.	Apr	Jul	Oct	Jan
2008-09	0.07	0.04	0.01	(0.23)
2009-10	0.08	0.08	0.13	0.10
2010-11	0.20	0.17	0.16	0.11
2011-12	0.26	0.25	0.16	0.16
2012-13	0.32	0.32	0.25	0.19

Interim Dividends (Per Share)

Amt	Decl	Ex	Rec	Pay
0.052Q	04/12/2012	06/07/2012	06/11/2012	06/25/2012
0.052Q	06/25/2012	09/06/2012	09/10/2012	09/24/2012
0.052Q	11/20/2012	11/29/2012	12/03/2012	12/17/2012
0.055Q	02/20/2013	03/14/2013	03/18/2013	04/01/2013

Indicated Div: $0.22

Valuation Analysis / Institutional Holding

Forecast EPS	$1.23 (04/05/2013)	No of Institutions 407
Market Cap	$2.7 Billion	Shares 157,125,584
Book Value	$1.1 Billion	% Held 86.24
Price/Book	2.50	
Price/Sales	1.06	

TRADING VOLUME (thousand shares)

Business Summary: Retail - Apparel and Accessories (MIC: 2.1.5 SIC: 5621 NAIC: 448120)

Chico's FAS is a specialty retailer of private label women's clothing, intimates, complementary accessories, as well as other non-clothing items. Co.'s portfolio of brands consists of four brands: Chico's, White House | Black Market, Soma Intimates, and Boston Proper. Co. sells its products through retail stores, catalog, and via the Internet at www.chicos.com, www.whbm.com, www.soma.com, and www.bostonproper.com. As of Jan 28 2012, Co. had 1,256 stores located throughout the U.S., the U.S. Virgin Islands and Puerto Rico.

Recent Developments: For the year ended Feb 2 2013, net income increased 27.9% to US$180.2 million from US$140.9 million in the prior year. Revenues were US$2.58 billion, up 17.5% from US$2.20 billion the year before. Operating income was US$287.5 million versus US$222.4 million in the prior year, an increase of 29.3%. Direct operating expenses rose 16.4% to US$1.13 billion from US$970.0 million in the comparable period the year before. Indirect operating expenses increased 16.0% to US$1.16 billion from US$1.00 billion in the equivalent prior-year period.

Prospects: Our evaluation of Chico's FAS Inc. as of Apr. 7, 2013 is the result of our systematic analysis on three basic characteristics: earnings strength, relative valuation, and recent stock price movement. The company has managed to produce a neutral trend in earnings per share over the past 5 quarters. However, while recent estimates for the company have been mixed, CHS has posted better than expected results. Based on operating earnings yield, the company is undervalued when compared to all of the companies in our coverage universe. Share price changes over the past year indicates that CHS will perform in line with the market over the near term.

Financial Data
(US$ in Thousands)

	02/02/2013	01/28/2012	01/29/2011	01/30/2010	01/31/2009	02/02/2008	02/03/2007	01/28/2006
Earnings Per Share	1.08	0.82	0.64	0.39	(0.11)	0.50	0.93	1.06
Cash Flow Per Share	2.22	1.51	1.36	1.22	0.57	1.19	1.60	1.49
Tang Book Value Per Share	4.46	3.85	5.22	4.75	4.33	4.41	4.02	3.91
Dividends Per Share	0.210	0.200	0.160	...	...	...	...	...
Dividend Payout %	19.44	24.39	25.00	...	...	...	...	...
Income Statement								
Total Revenue	2,581,057	2,196,360	1,904,954	1,713,150	1,582,405	1,714,326	1,646,482	1,404,575
EBITDA	396,009	321,807	271,195	204,525	57,978	220,270	320,457	347,165
Depn & Amortn	108,471	99,430	94,113	96,372	97,572	91,979	69,404	48,852
Income Before Taxes	288,419	223,974	178,794	109,846	(31,837)	139,160	261,679	306,549
Income Taxes	108,200	83,100	63,400	40,200	(12,700)	48,012	95,043	112,568
Net Income	180,219	140,874	115,394	69,646	(19,137)	88,875	166,636	193,981
Average Shares	164,119	170,250	178,033	178,857	175,861	176,355	178,452	182,407
Balance Sheet								
Current Assets	597,993	497,426	756,765	599,980	486,375	486,733	471,856	537,978
Total Assets	1,580,628	1,425,152	1,416,021	1,318,803	1,226,183	1,250,126	1,058;134	999,413
Current Liabilities	302,411	238,109	221,277	194,706	146,736	181,193	144,232	122,668
Total Liabilities	487,429	415,924	351,114	336,885	323,987	337,610	254,203	192,986
Stockholders' Equity	1,093,199	1,009,228	1,064,907	981,918	902,196	912,516	803,931	806,427
Shares Outstanding	162,774	165,736	177,899	178,126	177,130	176,245	175,749	181,726
Statistical Record								
Return on Assets %	11.80	9.94	8.46	5.49	N.M.	7.72	15.94	22.68
Return on Equity %	16.87	13.62	11.31	7.41	N.M.	10.38	20.36	28.45
EBITDA Margin %	15.34	14.65	14.24	11.94	3.66	12.85	19.46	24.72
Net Margin %	6.98	6.41	6.06	4.07	N.M.	5.18	10.12	13.81
Asset Turnover	1.69	1.55	1.40	1.35	1.28	1.49	1.57	1.64
Current Ratio	1.98	2.09	3.42	3.08	3.31	2.69	3.27	4.39
Price Range	19.64-11.41	16.26-9.94	16.42-8.26	14.74-3.42	10.60-1.74	27.24-6.71	48.90-17.80	45.85-24.81
P/E Ratio	18.19-10.56	19.83-12.12	25.66-12.91	37.79-8.77	...	54.48-13.42	52.58-19.14	43.25-23.41
Average Yield %	1.27	1.52	1.36	...	...	...	...	...

Address: 11215 Metro Parkway, Fort Myers, FL 33966 **Telephone:** 239-277-6200	**Web Site:** www.chicosfas.com **Officers:** Ross E. Roeder - Chairman David F. Dyer - President, Chief Executive Officer	**Auditors:** Ernst & Young LLP **Transfer Agents:** The Registrar and Transfer Company, Cransford, NJ

CHIMERA INVESTMENT CORP

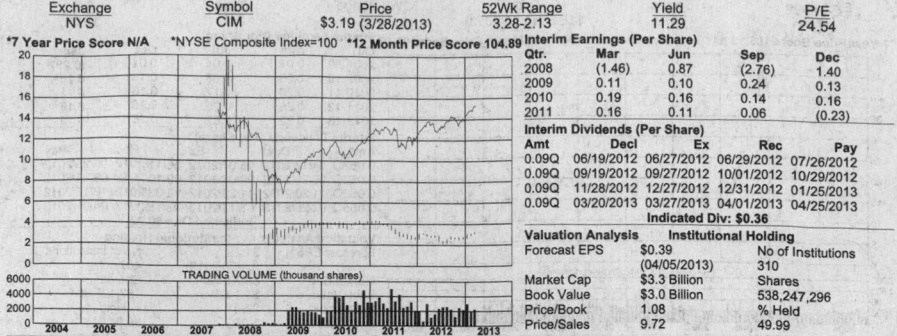

Exchange	Symbol	Price	52Wk Range	Yield	P/E
NYS	CIM	$3.19 (3/28/2013)	3.28-2.13	11.29	24.54

*7 Year Price Score N/A *NYSE Composite Index=100 *12 Month Price Score 104.89

Interim Earnings (Per Share)

Qtr.	Mar	Jun	Sep	Dec
2008	(1.46)	0.87	(2.76)	1.40
2009	0.11	0.10	0.24	0.13
2010	0.19	0.16	0.14	0.16
2011	0.16	0.11	0.06	(0.23)

Interim Dividends (Per Share)

Amt	Decl	Ex	Rec	Pay
0.09Q	06/19/2012	06/27/2012	06/29/2012	07/26/2012
0.09Q	09/19/2012	09/27/2012	10/01/2012	10/29/2012
0.09Q	11/28/2012	12/27/2012	12/31/2012	01/25/2013
0.09Q	03/20/2013	03/27/2013	04/01/2013	04/25/2013

Indicated Div: $0.36

Valuation Analysis   **Institutional Holding**

Forecast EPS	$0.39 (04/05/2013)	No of Institutions 310
Market Cap	$3.3 Billion	Shares
Book Value	$3.0 Billion	538,247,296
Price/Book	1.08	% Held
Price/Sales	9.72	49.99

Business Summary: Finance Intermediaries & Services (MIC: 5.5.1 SIC: 6111 NAIC: 522294)

Chimera Investment is a specialty finance company that invests, either directly or indirectly through its subsidiaries, in residential mortgage-backed securities, residential mortgage loans, commercial mortgage loans, real estate-related securities and various other asset classes. Co. is externally managed by Fixed Income Discount Advisory Company, an investment advisor.

Recent Developments: For the year ended Dec 31 2011, net income decreased 44.7% to US$137.3 million from US$248.4 million in the prior year. Net interest income increased 32.7% to US$570.2 million from US$429.7 million in the prior year. Non-interest loss was US$367.7 million versus a non-interest loss of US$126.4 million., while non-interest expense advanced 19.4% to US$64.5 million.

Prospects: On Sept 14, 2012, Co. announced that it has received a four-month extension for continued listing and trading of its stock on the New York Stock Exchange (NYSE). The extension granted by the NYSE, which is subject to review by the NYSE on an ongoing basis, provides Co. until Jan. 15, 2013 to file its 2011 Annual Report on Form 10-K with the Securities and Exchange Commission. Co. previously announced that it would delay the filing of its Form 10-K for the year ended Dec. 31, 2011, and its Form 10-Q for the quarters ended March 31 and June 30, 2012, due to the evaluation of its non-Agency residential mortgage-backed securities portfolio to determine the appropriate treatment under GAAP.

Financial Data

(US$ in Thousands)	12/31/2011	12/31/2010	12/31/2009	12/31/2008	12/31/2007
Earnings Per Share	0.13	0.65	0.64	(1.90)	(0.08)
Cash Flow Per Share	0.44	0.37	0.33	...	...
Tang Book Value Per Share	2.97	3.59	3.17	2.34	14.29
Dividends Per Share	0.510	0.690	0.430	0.620	0.025
Dividend Payout %	392.31	106.15	67.19	...	...
Income Statement					
Total Revenue	337,320	735,471	391,934	(45,226)	(664)
EBITDA	89,781	286,172	274,735	(119,503)	(2,999)
Depn & Amortn	(48,154)	(247,435)	(49,249)	294	(98)
Income Before Taxes	137,935	533,607	323,984	(119,797)	(2,901)
Income Taxes	606	756	1,000.00	12	5
Net Income	137,329	532,851	323,983	(119,809)	(2,906)
Average Shares	1,027,171	822,617	507,042	63,155	37,401
Balance Sheet					
Current Assets	255,624	56,261	57,407	37,431	13,412
Total Assets	7,747,135	8,073,700	4,618,328	1,477,501	1,565,636
Current Liabilities	2,789,220	2,122,576	2,092,425	571,624	1,020,862
Long-Term Obligations	...	2,245,315	390,350	488,743	...
Total Liabilities	4,699,516	4,390,694	2,491,766	1,063,046	1,026,747
Stockholders' Equity	3,047,619	3,683,006	2,126,562	414,455	538,889
Shares Outstanding	1,027,467	1,027,034	670,371	177,198	37,705
Statistical Record					
Return on Assets %	1.74	8.40	10.63	...	...
Return on Equity %	4.08	18.34	25.50	...	...
EBITDA Margin %	26.62	38.91	70.10	...	...
Net Margin %	40.71	72.45	82.66	...	...
Asset Turnover	0.04	0.12	0.13	...	...
Current Ratio	0.09	0.03	0.03	0.07	0.01
Debt to Equity	...	0.61	0.18	1.18	...
Price Range	4.31-2.51	4.30-3.51	4.30-2.49	19.59-1.90	17.88-14.10
P/E Ratio	33.15-19.31	6.62-5.40	6.72-3.89	...	...
Average Yield %	14.75	17.39	12.13	6.36	0.16

Address: 1211 Avenue of the Americas, Suite 2902, New York, NY 10036 Telephone: 646-454-3759	Web Site: www.chimerareit.com Officers: Matthew Lambiase - President, Chief Executive Officer William B. Dyer - Head of Underwriting	Auditors: Ernst & Young LLP Investor Contact: 866-315-9930 Transfer Agents: Computershare Shareowner Services LLC, Jersey City, NJ

CHIPOTLE MEXICAN GRILL INC

Exchange	Symbol	Price	52Wk Range	Yield	P/E
NYS	CMG	$325.87 (3/28/2013)	440.40-236.24	N/A	37.24

*7 Year Price Score 175.26 *NYSE Composite Index=100 *12 Month Price Score 89.39

Interim Earnings (Per Share)

Qtr.	Mar	Jun	Sep	Dec
2008	0.52	0.74	0.59	0.52
2009	0.78	1.10	1.08	0.99
2010	1.19	1.46	1.52	1.46
2011	1.46	1.59	1.90	1.80
2012	1.97	2.56	2.27	1.95

Interim Dividends (Per Share)

No Dividends Paid

Valuation Analysis | **Institutional Holding**

Forecast EPS	$10.29	No of Institutions
	(04/06/2013)	519
Market Cap	$10.1 Billion	Shares
Book Value	$1.2 Billion	33,062,128
Price/Book	8.13	% Held
Price/Sales	3.71	101.15

TRADING VOLUME (thousand shares)

Business Summary: Hotels, Restaurants & Travel (MIC: 2.2.1 SIC: 5812 NAIC: 722110)

Chipotle Mexican Grill and its subsidiaries operate Chipotle Mexican Grill restaurants, which serve a menu of burritos, tacos, burrito bowls (a burrito without the tortilla) and salads. In addition to sodas, fruit drinks and organic milk, the majority of Co.'s restaurants provide a range of beer and margaritas. As of Dec 31 2012, Co. operated 1,410 restaurants, including Chipotle restaurants throughout the U.S., as well as five in Canada, five in London, England, and one in Paris, France, and also one ShopHouse Southeast Asian Kitchen, which serves main dishes consist of rice or noodle bowls made with steak, chicken, meatballs made with pork and chicken, or tofu.

Recent Developments: For the year ended Dec 31 2012, net income increased 29.3% to US$278.0 million from US$214.9 million in the prior year. Revenues were US$2.73 billion, up 20.3% from US$2.27 billion the year before. Operating income was US$455.9 million versus US$350.6 million in the prior year, an increase of 30.0%. Direct operating expenses rose 18.5% to US$1.99 billion from US$1.68 billion in the comparable period the year before. Indirect operating expenses increased 19.2% to US$284.5 million from US$238.7 million in the equivalent prior-year period.

Prospects: Our evaluation of Chipotle Mexican Grill Inc. as of Apr. 7, 2013 is the result of our systematic analysis on three basic characteristics: earnings strength, relative valuation, and recent stock price movement. The company has generated a negative trend in earnings per share over the past 5 quarters and while recent estimates for the company have been raised by analysts, CMG has posted results that fell short of analysts expectations. Based on operating earnings yield, the company is overvalued when compared to all of the companies in our coverage universe. Share price changes over the past year indicates that CMG will perform very poorly over the near term.

Financial Data
(US$ in Thousands)

	12/31/2012	12/31/2011	12/31/2010	12/31/2009	12/31/2008	12/31/2007	12/31/2006	12/31/2005
Earnings Per Share	8.75	6.76	5.64	3.95	2.36	2.13	1.28	1.43
Cash Flow Per Share	13.29	13.17	9.26	8.21	6.04	4.50	3.23	2.95
Tang Book Value Per Share	39.37	32.71	25.39	21.65	18.66	16.47	14.02	11.10
Income Statement								
Total Revenue	2,731,224	2,269,548	1,835,922	1,518,417	1,331,968	1,085,782	822,930	627,695
EBITDA	541,815	425,500	356,752	265,013	176,809	151,778	96,205	59,020
Depn & Amortn	84,130	74,938	68,921	61,308	52,770	43,595	34,253	28,026
Income Before Taxes	457,685	349,705	289,061	204,225	127,206	114,002	68,255	30,240
Income Taxes	179,685	134,760	110,080	77,380	49,004	43,439	26,832	(7,456)
Net Income	278,000	214,945	178,981	126,845	78,202	70,563	41,423	37,696
Average Shares	31,783	31,775	31,735	32,102	33,146	33,146	32,465	26,374
Balance Sheet								
Current Assets	546,607	501,192	406,221	297,454	211,072	201,844	178,837	17,824
Total Assets	1,668,667	1,425,308	1,121,605	961,505	824,985	722,115	604,208	392,495
Current Liabilities	186,852	157,453	123,054	102,153	76,788	73,301	61,201	41,982
Long-Term Obligations	3,386	3,529	3,661	3,782	3,878	3,960	4,036	3,476
Total Liabilities	422,741	381,082	310,732	258,044	202,395	160,005	130,251	83,141
Stockholders' Equity	1,245,926	1,044,226	810,873	703,461	622,590	562,110	473,957	309,354
Shares Outstanding	31,093	31,252	31,074	31,483	32,186	32,805	32,544	26,281
Statistical Record								
Return on Assets %	17.92	16.88	17.18	14.20	10.08	10.64	8.31	10.44
Return on Equity %	24.21	23.17	23.64	19.13	13.17	13.62	10.58	13.18
EBITDA Margin %	19.84	18.75	19.43	17.45	13.27	13.98	11.69	9.40
Net Margin %	10.18	9.47	9.75	8.35	5.87	6.50	5.03	6.01
Asset Turnover	1.76	1.78	1.76	1.70	1.72	1.64	1.65	1.74
Current Ratio	2.93	3.18	3.30	2.91	2.75	2.75	2.92	0.42
Debt to Equity	N.M.	N.M.	N.M.	0.01	0.01	0.01	0.01	0.01
Price Range	440.40-236.24	343.37-212.66	258.82-86.43	97.05-47.42	147.07-38.69	152.36-55.00	67.05-41.46	...
P/E Ratio	50.33-27.00	50.79-31.46	45.89-15.32	24.57-12.01	62.32-16.39	71.53-25.82	52.38-32.39	...

Address: 1401 Wynkoop Street, Suite 500, Denver, CO 80202 Telephone: 303-595-4000	Web Site: www.chipotle.com Officers: Steve Ells - Chairman, Co-Chief Executive Officer Montgomery F. Moran - Co-Chief Executive Officer, Corporate Secretary	Auditors: Ernst & Young LLP Transfer Agents: Wells Fargo Shareowner Services, Mendota Heights, MN

CHOICE HOTELS INTERNATIONAL, INC.

Exchange	Symbol	Price	52Wk Range	Yield	P/E
NYS	CHH	$42.31 (3/28/2013)	44.21-30.80	1.75	20.44

*7 Year Price Score 90.14   *NYSE Composite Index=100   *12 Month Price Score 99.25

Interim Earnings (Per Share)

Qtr.	Mar	Jun	Sep	Dec
2008	0.30	0.43	0.57	0.30
2009	0.27	0.42	0.55	0.39
2010	0.26	0.45	0.68	0.40
2011	0.26	0.46	0.71	0.42
2012	0.34	0.55	0.76	0.42

Interim Dividends (Per Share)

Amt	Decl	Ex	Rec	Pay
10.41Sp	07/26/2012	08/24/2012	08/20/2012	08/23/2012
0.185Q	09/14/2012	09/28/2012	10/02/2012	10/12/2012
0.185Q	12/05/2012	12/14/2012	12/18/2012	12/27/2012
0.185Q	02/13/2013	03/28/2013	04/02/2013	04/16/2013

Indicated Div: $0.74

Valuation Analysis

		Institutional Holding	
Forecast EPS	$1.97 (04/05/2013)	No of Institutions	145
Market Cap	$2.5 Billion	Shares	26,216,180
Book Value	N/A	% Held	N/A
Price/Book	N/A		
Price/Sales	3.56		

Business Summary: Hotels, Restaurants & Travel (MIC: 2.2.1 SIC: 7011 NAIC: 721110)

Choice Hotels International is a hotel franchisor with 6,178 hotels open and 490 hotels under construction, awaiting conversion or approved for development as of Dec 31, 2011 representing 497,205 rooms open and 39,675 rooms under construction, awaiting conversion or approved for development in 49 states, the District of Columbia and over 35 countries and territories outside the U.S. Co. franchises lodging properties under the following proprietary brand names: Comfort Inn®, Comfort Suites®, Quality®, Clarion®, Sleep Inn®, Econo Lodge®, Rodeway Inn®, MainStay Suites®, Suburban Extended Stay Hotel®, Cambria Suites® and Ascend Collection®.

Recent Developments: For the year ended Dec 31 2012, net income increased 9.3% to US$120.7 million from US$110.4 million in the prior year. Revenues were US$691.5 million, up 8.3% from US$638.8 million the year before. Operating income was US$193.1 million versus US$171.9 million in the prior year, an increase of 12.4%. Direct operating expenses rose 10.2% to US$388.3 million from US$352.5 million in the comparable period the year before. Indirect operating expenses decreased 3.8% to US$110.1 million from US$114.4 million in the equivalent prior-year period.

Prospects: Our evaluation of Choice Hotels International Inc. as of Apr. 7, 2013 is the result of our systematic analysis on three basic characteristics: earnings strength, relative valuation, and recent stock price movement. The company has managed to produce a neutral trend in earnings per share over the past 5 quarters. However, while recent estimates for the company have been mixed, CHH has posted better than expected results. Based on operating earnings yield, the company is about fairly valued when compared to all of the companies in our coverage universe. Share price changes over the past year indicates that CHH will perform in line with the market over the near term.

Financial Data

(US$ in Thousands)	12/31/2012	12/31/2011	12/31/2010	12/31/2009	12/31/2008	12/31/2007	12/31/2006	12/31/2005
Earnings Per Share	2.07	1.85	1.80	1.63	1.60	1.70	1.68	1.32
Cash Flow Per Share	2.79	2.29	2.46	1.87	1.68	2.28	2.35	2.06
Dividends Per Share	11.150	0.740	0.740	0.740	0.880	0.620	0.540	0.468
Dividend Payout %	538.65	40.00	41.11	45.40	55.00	36.47	32.14	35.42
Income Statement								
Total Revenue	691,509	638,793	596,076	564,178	641,680	615,494	544,662	477,399
EBITDA	197,005	172,021	163,162	150,873	177,396	188,199	170,383	148,170
Depn & Amortn	2,400	2,600	2,400	2,800	2,800	3,000	4,100	4,000
Income Before Taxes	168,956	157,788	156,985	149,521	155,904	172,656	154,226	129,939
Income Taxes	48,481	47,661	50,770	52,384	57,107	62,585	42,491	43,177
Net Income	120,687	110,396	107,441	98,250	100,211	111,301	112,787	87,565
Average Shares	57,653	58,934	59,041	60,224	62,521	65,331	67,050	66,336
Balance Sheet								
Current Assets	233,470	194,796	163,582	127,862	120,216	105,951	87,082	63,000
Total Assets	510,772	447,689	411,722	340,037	328,219	328,384	303,309	265,100
Current Liabilities	176,137	184,565	165,258	131,806	135,067	147,516	139,791	120,145
Long-Term Obligations	847,150	252,032	251,554	277,700	284,400	272,378	172,390	273,972
Total Liabilities	1,059,676	473,250	469,793	454,249	465,889	485,445	365,689	432,276
Stockholders' Equity	(548,904)	(25,561)	(58,071)	(114,212)	(137,670)	(157,061)	(62,380)	(167,176)
Shares Outstanding	58,171	58,277	59,583	59,541	60,704	62,091	66,355	65,219
Statistical Record								
Return on Assets %	25.11	25.69	28.58	29.40	30.44	35.24	39.69	33.20
EBITDA Margin %	28.49	26.93	27.37	26.74	27.65	30.58	31.28	31.04
Net Margin %	17.45	17.28	18.02	17.41	15.62	18.08	20.71	18.34
Asset Turnover	1.44	1.49	1.59	1.69	1.95	1.95	1.92	1.81
Current Ratio	1.33	1.06	0.99	0.97	0.89	0.72	0.62	0.52
Price Range	44.21-30.80	41.25-26.54	39.55-29.57	32.94-23.25	35.62-20.14	44.28-33.20	61.62-35.62	42.14-28.20
P/E Ratio	21.36-14.88	22.30-14.35	21.97-16.43	20.21-14.26	22.26-12.59	26.05-19.53	36.68-21.20	31.92-21.37
Average Yield %	31.06	2.11	2.12	2.59	3.00	1.63	1.16	1.45

Address: 10750 Columbia Pike, Silver Spring, MD 20901
Telephone: 301-592-5000

Web Site: www.choicehotels.com
Officers: Stewart Bainum - Chairman Charles A. Ledsinger - Vice-Chairman

Auditors: PricewaterhouseCoopers LLP
Investor Contact: 301-592-5026
Transfer Agents: Computershare Investor Services, Canton, MA

CHUBB CORP.

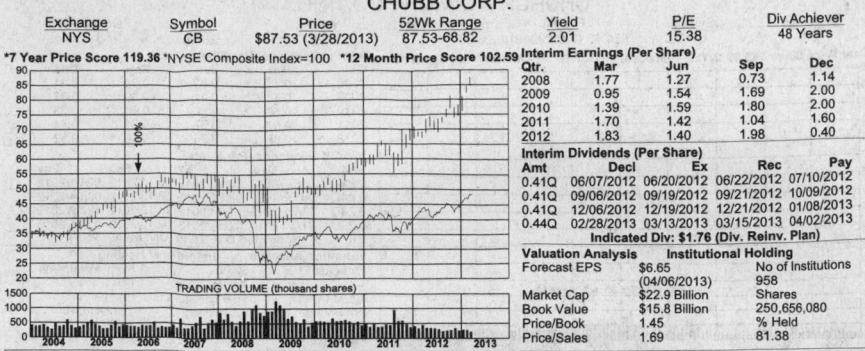

Exchange	Symbol	Price	52Wk Range	Yield	P/E	Div Achiever
NYS	CB	$87.53 (3/28/2013)	87.53-68.82	2.01	15.38	48 Years

*7 Year Price Score 119.36 *NYSE Composite Index=100 *12 Month Price Score 102.59

Interim Earnings (Per Share)

Qtr.	Mar	Jun	Sep	Dec
2008	1.77	1.27	0.73	1.14
2009	0.95	1.54	1.69	2.00
2010	1.39	1.59	1.80	2.00
2011	1.70	1.42	1.04	1.60
2012	1.83	1.40	1.98	0.40

Interim Dividends (Per Share)

Amt	Decl	Ex	Rec	Pay
0.41Q	06/07/2012	06/20/2012	06/22/2012	07/10/2012
0.41Q	09/06/2012	09/19/2012	09/21/2012	10/09/2012
0.41Q	12/06/2012	12/19/2012	12/21/2012	01/08/2013
0.44Q	02/28/2013	03/13/2013	03/15/2013	04/02/2013

Indicated Div: $1.76 (Div. Reinv. Plan)

Valuation Analysis

		Institutional Holding	
Forecast EPS	$6.65 (04/06/2013)	No of Institutions	958
Market Cap	$22.9 Billion	Shares	250,656,080
Book Value	$15.8 Billion	% Held	81.38
Price/Book	1.45		
Price/Sales	1.69		

TRADING VOLUME (thousand shares)

Business Summary: General Insurance (MIC: 5.2.1 SIC: 6331 NAIC: 524126)

Chubb is a holding company. Through its subsidiaries, Co. is principally engaged in the property and casualty insurance business. Co.'s Chubb Personal Insurance business unit provides coverage of homes, automobiles and other personal possessions. Chubb Personal Insurance also provides supplemental accident and health insurance. Co.'s Chubb Commercial Insurance business unit provides a range of commercial insurance products. Co.'s Chubb Specialty Insurance business unit provides a variety of liability products for privately and publicly owned companies, financial institutions, firms and healthcare organizations. Chubb Specialty Insurance also includes Co.'s surety business.

Recent Developments: For the year ended Dec 31 2012, net income decreased 7.9% to US$1.55 billion from US$1.68 billion in the prior year. Revenues were US$13.60 billion, up 0.1% from US$13.59 billion the year before. Net premiums earned were US$11.84 billion versus US$11.64 billion in the prior year, an increase of 1.7%. Net investment income fell 5.4% to US$1.56 billion from US$1.64 billion a year ago.

Prospects: Our evaluation of Chubb Corp. as of Apr. 7, 2013 is the result of our systematic analysis on three basic characteristics: earnings strength, relative valuation, and recent stock price movement. The company has suffered a very negative trend in earnings per share over the past 5 quarters and while recent estimates for the company have been raised by analysts, CB has posted better than expected results. Based on operating earnings yield, the company is undervalued when compared to all of the companies in our coverage universe. Share price changes over the past year indicates that CB will perform in line with the market over the near term.

Financial Data
(US$ in Thousands)

	12/31/2012	12/31/2011	12/31/2010	12/31/2009	12/31/2008	12/31/2007	12/31/2006	12/31/2005
Earnings Per Share	5.69	5.76	6.76	6.18	4.92	7.01	5.98	4.47
Cash Flow Per Share	8.51	6.49	7.37	6.96	7.03	8.11	8.10	9.47
Tang Book Value Per Share	58.68	55.45	50.67	45.68	36.81	37.31	32.57	28.56
Dividends Per Share	1.640	1.560	1.480	1.400	1.320	1.160	1.000	0.860
Dividend Payout %	28.82	27.08	21.89	22.65	26.83	16.55	16.72	19.24
Income Statement								
Premium Income	11,838,000	11,644,000	11,215,000	11,331,000	11,828,000	11,946,000	11,958,000	12,176,000
Total Revenue	13,595,000	13,585,000	13,319,000	13,016,000	13,221,000	14,107,000	14,003,000	14,082,300
Benefits & Claims	7,507,000	7,407,000	6,499,000	6,268,000	6,898,000	6,299,000	6,574,000	7,813,500
Income Before Taxes	1,996,000	2,199,000	2,988,000	2,962,000	2,407,000	3,937,000	3,525,000	2,447,000
Income Taxes	451,000	521,000	814,000	779,000	603,000	1,130,000	997,000	621,100
Net Income	1,545,000	1,678,000	2,174,000	2,183,000	1,804,000	2,807,000	2,528,000	1,825,900
Average Shares	271,400	291,400	321,600	353,000	366,800	400,300	422,400	408,400
Balance Sheet								
Total Assets	52,184,000	50,865,000	50,249,000	50,449,000	48,429,000	50,574,000	50,277,000	48,060,700
Total Liabilities	36,357,000	35,291,000	34,719,000	34,815,000	34,997,000	36,129,000	36,414,000	35,653,700
Stockholders' Equity	15,827,000	15,574,000	15,530,000	15,634,000	13,432,000	14,445,000	13,863,000	12,407,000
Shares Outstanding	261,763	272,460	297,272	332,007	352,254	374,649	411,276	418,076
Statistical Record								
Return on Assets %	2.99	3.32	4.32	4.42	3.63	5.57	5.14	3.96
Return on Equity %	9.81	10.79	13.95	15.02	12.91	19.83	19.25	16.21
Loss Ratio %	63.41	63.61	57.95	55.32	58.32	52.73	54.98	64.17
Net Margin %	11.36	12.35	16.32	16.77	13.64	19.90	18.05	12.97
Price Range	81.19-66.90	70.31-55.43	60.23-47.66	53.79-35.00	64.50-38.75	55.91-47.36	54.65-46.80	49.06-36.67
P/E Ratio	14.27-11.76	12.21-9.62	8.91-7.05	8.70-5.66	13.11-7.88	7.98-6.76	9.14-7.83	10.98-8.20
Average Yield %	2.26	2.50	2.76	3.14	2.64	2.20	1.99	2.02

Address: 15 Mountain View Road, Warren, NJ 07059	**Web Site:** www.chubb.com	**Auditors:** Ernst & Young LLP
Telephone: 908-903-2000	**Officers:** John D. Finnegan - Chairman, President, Chief Executive Officer John J. Degnan - Vice-Chairman, Chief Operating Officer	**Investor Contact:** 908-903-2365
Fax: 908-903-2003		**Transfer Agents:** Computershare Shareholder Services LLC, Jersey City, NJ

CHURCH & DWIGHT CO., INC.

Exchange	Symbol	Price	52Wk Range	Yield	P/E	Div Achiever
NYS	CHD	$64.63 (3/28/2013)	64.63-49.21	1.73	26.38	16 Years

*7 Year Price Score 145.39 *NYSE Composite Index=100 ***12 Month Price Score 102.88**

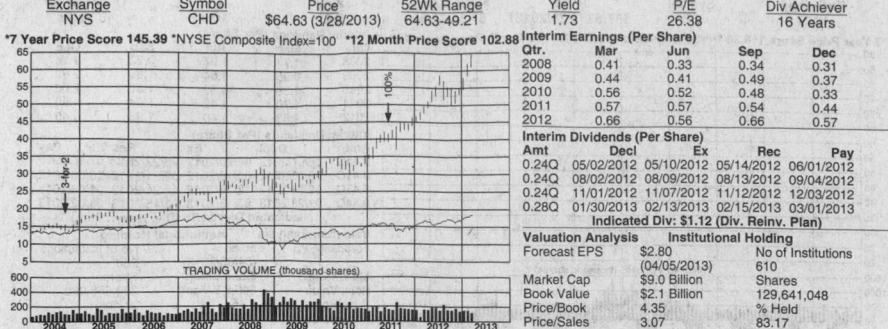

Interim Earnings (Per Share)

Qtr.	Mar	Jun	Sep	Dec
2008	0.41	0.33	0.34	0.31
2009	0.44	0.41	0.49	0.37
2010	0.56	0.52	0.48	0.33
2011	0.57	0.57	0.54	0.44
2012	0.66	0.56	0.66	0.57

Interim Dividends (Per Share)

Amt	Decl	Ex	Rec	Pay
0.24Q	05/02/2012	05/10/2012	05/14/2012	06/01/2012
0.24Q	08/02/2012	08/09/2012	08/13/2012	09/04/2012
0.24Q	11/01/2012	11/07/2012	11/12/2012	12/03/2012
0.28Q	01/30/2013	02/13/2013	02/15/2013	03/01/2013

Indicated Div: $1.12 (Div. Reinv. Plan)

Valuation Analysis   **Institutional Holding**

Forecast EPS	$2.80 (04/05/2013)	No of Institutions 610
Market Cap	$9.0 Billion	Shares
Book Value	$2.1 Billion	129,641,048
Price/Book	4.35	% Held
Price/Sales	3.07	83.17

Business Summary: Household & Personal Products (MIC: 1.7.1 SIC: 2841 NAIC: 325611)

Church & Dwight Co. develops, manufactures and markets a range of household, personal care and specialty products. Co. sells its consumer products under a variety of brands through a distribution platform that includes supermarkets, mass merchandisers, wholesale clubs, drugstores, convenience stores, dollar, pet and other specialty stores and websites, all of which sell the products to consumers. Co. also sells specialty products to industrial customers and distributors. Co. operates three segments: consumer domestic, consumer international, and specialty products.

Recent Developments: For the year ended Dec 31 2012, net income increased 13.0% to US$349.8 million from US$309.6 million in the prior year. Revenues were US$2.92 billion, up 6.3% from US$2.75 billion the year before. Operating income was US$545.1 million versus US$492.6 million in the prior year, an increase of 10.7%. Direct operating expenses rose 6.2% to US$1.63 billion from US$1.53 billion in the comparable period the year before. Indirect operating expenses increased 3.4% to US$746.3 million from US$721.9 million in the equivalent prior-year period.

Prospects: Our evaluation of Church & Dwight Co. Inc. as of Apr. 7, 2013 is the result of our systematic analysis on three basic characteristics: earnings strength, relative valuation, and recent stock price movement. The company has managed to produce a neutral trend in earnings per share over the past 5 quarters and while recent estimates for the company have remained steady, CHD has posted better than expected results. Based on operating earnings yield, the company is about fairly valued when compared to all of the companies in our coverage universe. Share price changes over the past year indicates that CHD will perform in line with the market over the near term.

Financial Data
(US$ in Thousands)

	12/31/2012	12/31/2011	12/31/2010	12/31/2009	12/31/2008	12/31/2007	12/31/2006	12/31/2005
Earnings Per Share	2.45	2.12	1.88	1.71	1.39	1.23	1.03	0.92
Cash Flow Per Share	3.73	3.06	3.02	2.85	2.47	1.89	1.44	1.49
Tang Book Value Per Share	N.M.	1.88	0.99	N.M.	N.M.	N.M.	N.M.	N.M.
Dividends Per Share	0.960	0.680	0.310	0.230	0.170	0.150	0.130	0.120
Dividend Payout %	39.18	32.08	16.53	13.49	12.23	12.20	12.56	13.11
Income Statement								
Total Revenue	2,921,900	2,749,300	2,589,220	2,520,922	2,422,398	2,220,940	1,945,661	1,736,506
EBITDA	603,600	543,100	485,109	472,675	389,471	351,387	295,587	247,191
Depn & Amortn	56,000	49,800	44,113	56,921	45,600	35,800	35,600	33,000
Income Before Taxes	533,600	484,600	413,219	380,186	296,926	256,695	205,959	170,093
Income Taxes	192,700	185,000	147,562	148,715	113,078	95,900	74,171	52,068
Net Income	349,800	309,600	270,717	243,533	195,174	169,025	138,927	122,906
Average Shares	142,700	145,800	144,402	142,954	142,232	140,624	137,892	138,578
Balance Sheet								
Current Assets	933,800	755,200	649,481	928,265	665,121	735,353	556,070	494,438
Total Assets	4,098,100	3,117,600	2,945,194	3,118,446	2,801,438	2,532,490	2,334,154	1,962,117
Current Liabilities	725,600	383,600	447,092	567,032	387,121	457,789	444,404	409,710
Long-Term Obligations	649,400	249,700	249,673	597,347	781,402	707,311	792,925	635,261
Total Liabilities	2,037,200	1,077,000	1,074,505	1,516,863	1,469,925	1,452,225	1,470,317	1,265,239
Stockholders' Equity	2,060,900	2,040,600	1,870,689	1,601,583	1,331,513	1,080,265	863,837	696,878
Shares Outstanding	138,781	142,287	142,409	141,098	140,145	132,487	130,722	128,777
Statistical Record								
Return on Assets %	9.67	10.21	8.93	8.23	7.30	6.95	6.47	6.40
Return on Equity %	17.01	15.83	15.59	16.61	16.14	17.39	17.80	19.56
EBITDA Margin %	20.66	19.75	18.74	18.75	16.08	15.82	15.19	14.23
Net Margin %	11.97	11.26	10.46	9.66	8.06	7.61	7.14	7.08
Asset Turnover	0.81	0.91	0.85	0.85	0.91	0.91	0.91	0.90
Current Ratio	1.29	1.97	1.45	1.64	1.72	1.61	1.25	1.21
Debt to Equity	0.32	0.12	0.13	0.37	0.59	0.65	0.92	0.91
Price Range	58.76-44.80	46.34-34.28	35.33-29.86	30.97-23.14	32.19-24.85	28.47-21.63	21.69-16.48	19.52-16.15
P/E Ratio	23.98-18.29	21.86-16.17	18.79-15.89	18.11-13.53	23.15-17.88	23.14-17.58	21.06-16.00	21.22-17.55
Average Yield %	1.84	1.67	0.94	0.84	0.60	0.61	0.69	0.68

Address: 500 Charles Ewing Boulevard, Ewing, NJ 08628
Telephone: 609-806-1200
Fax: 609-497-7269

Web Site: www.churchdwight.com
Officers: James R. Craigie - Chairman, Chief Executive Officer Susan E. Goldy - Executive Vice President, Secretary, General Counsel

Auditors: Deloitte & Touche LLP
Investor Contact: 609-497-7111
Transfer Agents: Computershare Investor Services, LLC, Canton, MA

CIGNA CORP

Exchange	Symbol	Price	52Wk Range	Yield	P/E
NYS	CI	$62.37 (3/28/2013)	62.63-39.66	0.06	11.12

*7 Year Price Score 110.87 *NYSE Composite Index=100 *12 Month Price Score 110.95

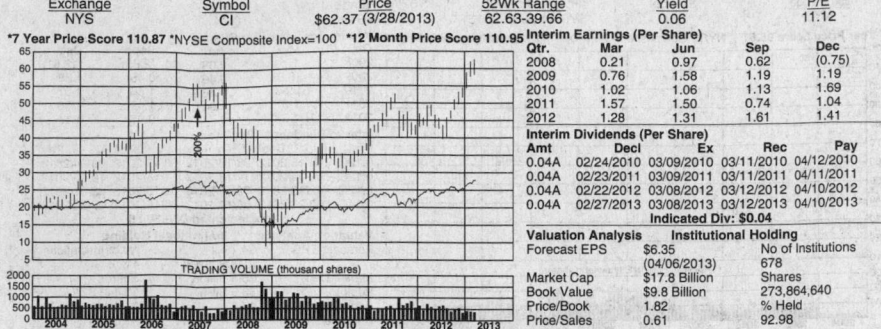

Interim Earnings (Per Share)

Qtr.	Mar	Jun	Sep	Dec
2008	0.21	0.97	0.62	(0.75)
2009	0.76	1.58	1.19	1.19
2010	1.02	1.06	1.13	1.69
2011	1.57	1.50	0.74	1.04
2012	1.28	1.31	1.61	1.41

Interim Dividends (Per Share)

Amt	Decl	Ex	Rec	Pay
0.04A	02/24/2010	03/09/2010	03/11/2010	04/12/2010
0.04A	02/23/2011	03/09/2011	03/11/2011	04/11/2011
0.04A	02/22/2012	03/08/2012	03/12/2012	04/10/2012
0.04A	02/27/2013	03/08/2013	03/12/2013	04/10/2013

Indicated Div: $0.04

Valuation Analysis

		Institutional Holding	
Forecast EPS	$6.35 (04/06/2013)	No of Institutions	678
Market Cap	$17.8 Billion	Shares	273,864,640
Book Value	$9.8 Billion	% Held	92.98
Price/Book	1.82		
Price/Sales	0.61		

TRADING VOLUME (thousand shares)

Business Summary: Life & Health (MIC: 5.2.2 SIC: 6324 NAIC: 524114)

Cigna is a holding company. Through its subsidiaries, Co. operates as a global health services organization. Co.'s businesses are reported in five segments: HealthCare, which includes medical, dental, behavioral health, and prescription drug plans; Disability and Life, which provides disability insurance, life insurance, accident, and specialty insurance; International, which includes supplemental health, life and accident insurance products, and international health care products; Run-off Reinsurance, which provides guaranteed minimum death benefits and guaranteed minimum income benefits reinsurance businesses; and Other Operations, which includes corporate-owned life insurance.

Recent Developments: For the year ended Dec 31 2012, net income increased 28.8% to US$1.62 billion from US$1.26 billion in the prior year. Revenues were US$29.12 billion, up 33.2% from US$21.87 billion the year before. Net premiums earned were US$26.19 billion versus US$18.97 billion in the prior year, an increase of 38.1%. Net investment income fell 0.2% to US$1.14 billion from US$1.15 billion a year ago.

Prospects: Our evaluation of Cigna Corp. as of Apr. 7, 2013 is the result of our systematic analysis on three basic characteristics: earnings strength, relative valuation, and recent stock price movement. The company has managed to produce a neutral trend in earnings per share over the past 5 quarters. However, while recent estimates for the company have been mixed, CI has posted better than expected results. Based on operating earnings yield, the company is undervalued when compared to all of the companies in our coverage universe. Share price changes over the past year indicates that CI will perform poorly over the near term.

Financial Data
(US$ in Millions)

	12/31/2012	12/31/2011	12/31/2010	12/31/2009	12/31/2008	12/31/2007	12/31/2006	12/31/2005
Earnings Per Share	5.61	4.84	4.89	4.73	1.05	3.87	3.43	4.17
Cash Flow Per Share	8.23	5.51	6.39	2.72	6.01	4.74	1.94	1.88
Tang Book Value Per Share	13.18	18.14	12.97	9.27	2.63	10.60	8.87	10.28
Dividends Per Share	0.040	0.040	0.040	0.040	0.040	0.038	0.033	0.033
Dividend Payout %	0.71		0.83	0.82	0.85	3.81	0.99	0.97	0.80
Income Statement								
Premium Income	26,187	19,089	18,393	16,041	16,203	15,008	13,641	13,695
Total Revenue	29,119	21,998	21,253	18,414	19,101	17,623	16,547	16,684
Benefits & Claims	17,859	12,724	12,288	10,030	12,227	10,199	9,264	9,646
Income Before Taxes	2,477	1,968	1,870	1,898	378	1,631	1,731	1,793
Income Taxes	853	640	521	594	90	511	572	517
Net Income	1,623	1,327	1,345	1,302	292	1,115	1,155	1,625
Average Shares	289	274	275	275	276	288	336	389
Balance Sheet								
Total Assets	53,734	51,047	45,682	43,013	41,406	40,065	42,399	44,863
Total Liabilities	43,965	42,703	39,037	37,596	37,814	35,317	38,069	39,503
Stockholders' Equity	9,769	8,344	6,645	5,417	3,592	4,748	4,330	5,360
Shares Outstanding	285	285	271	274	271	279	292	363
Statistical Record								
Return on Assets %	3.09	2.74	3.03	3.08	0.71	2.70	2.65	2.58
Return on Equity %	17.87	17.71	22.30	28.90	6.98	24.56	23.84	30.77
Loss Ratio %	68.20	66.66	66.81	62.53	75.46	67.96	67.91	70.43
Net Margin %	5.57	6.03	6.33	7.07	1.53	6.33	6.98	9.74
Price Range	54.49-39.66	52.62-36.66	38.26-29.77	37.19-12.87	56.36-8.82	56.33-42.65	44.42-29.58	39.77-26.20
P/E Ratio	9.71-7.07	10.87-7.57	7.82-6.09	7.86-2.72	53.68-8.40	14.56-11.02	12.95-8.62	9.54-6.28
Average Yield %	0.09	0.09	0.12	0.16	0.11	0.08	0.09	0.10

Address: 900 Cottage Grove Road, Bloomfield, CT 06002 **Telephone:** 860-226-6000 **Fax:** 860-226-6741	**Web Site:** www.cigna.com **Officers:** Isaiah Harris - Chairman David M. Cordani - President, Chief Executive Officer	**Auditors:** PricewaterhouseCoopers LLP **Investor Contact:** 215-.76-1.1414 **Transfer Agents:** BNY Mellon Shareowner Services, Pittsburgh, PA

CIMAREX ENERGY CO

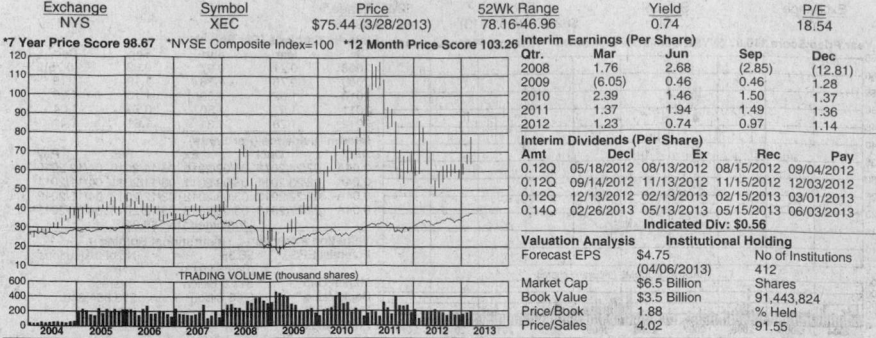

Exchange	Symbol	Price	52Wk Range	Yield	P/E
NYS	XEC	$75.44 (3/28/2013)	78.16-46.96	0.74	18.54

*7 Year Price Score 98.67 *NYSE Composite Index=100 *12 Month Price Score 103.26

Interim Earnings (Per Share)

Qtr.	Mar	Jun	Sep	Dec
2008	1.76	2.68	(2.85)	(12.81)
2009	(6.05)	0.46	0.46	1.28
2010	2.39	1.46	1.50	1.37
2011	1.37	1.94	1.49	1.36
2012	1.23	0.74	0.97	1.14

Interim Dividends (Per Share)

Amt	Decl	Ex	Rec	Pay
0.12Q	05/18/2012	08/13/2012	08/15/2012	09/04/2012
0.12Q	09/14/2012	11/13/2012	11/15/2012	12/03/2012
0.12Q	12/13/2012	02/13/2013	02/15/2013	03/01/2013
0.14Q	02/26/2013	05/13/2013	05/15/2013	06/03/2013

Indicated Div: $0.56

Valuation Analysis

Forecast EPS	$4.75
	(04/06/2013)
Market Cap	$6.5 Billion
Book Value	$3.5 Billion
Price/Book	1.88
Price/Sales	4.02

Institutional Holding

No of Institutions	412
Shares	91,443,824
% Held	91.55

Business Summary: Production & Extraction (MIC: 9.1.1 SIC: 1311 NAIC: 211111)

Cimarex Energy is an independent oil and gas exploration and production company. Co. operations are mainly located in Texas, Oklahoma, New Mexico and Kansas. Co.'s exploration and production activities are conducted primarily in two main areas: the Permian Basin, which encompasses west Texas and southeast New Mexico; and the Mid-Continent region, which consists of Oklahoma, the Texas Panhandle and southwest Kansas. Co.'s Gulf Coast operations are conducted in southeast Texas. As of Dec 31 2012, Co.'s proved oil and gas reserves totaled 2.3 trillion cubic feet of natural gas equivalent, consisted of 1.3 trillion cubic feet of gas, 168 million barrels of oil and natural gas liquids.

Recent Developments: For the year ended Dec 31 2012, net income decreased 33.2% to US$353.8 million from US$529.9 million in the prior year. Revenues were US$1.62 billion, down 7.6% from US$1.76 billion the prior year. Operating income was US$571.0 million versus US$838.3 million in the prior year, a decrease of 31.9%. Direct operating expenses rose 4.0% to US$315.9 million from US$303.8 million in the comparable period the year before. Indirect operating expenses increased 19.7% to US$737.0 million from US$615.9 million in the equivalent prior-year period.

Prospects: Our evaluation of Cimarex Energy Co as of Apr. 7, 2013 is the result of our systematic analysis on three basic characteristics: earnings strength, relative valuation, and recent stock price movement. The company has enjoyed a very positive trend in earnings per share over the past 5 quarters. However, while recent estimates for the company have been mixed, XEC has posted better than expected results. Based on operating earnings yield, the company is undervalued when compared to all of the companies in our coverage universe. Share price changes over the past year indicates that XEC will perform very poorly over the near term.

Financial Data

(US$ in Thousands)	12/31/2012	12/31/2011	12/31/2010	12/31/2009	12/31/2008	12/31/2007	12/31/2006	12/31/2005
Earnings Per Share	4.07	6.15	6.70	(3.82)	(11.07)	4.09	4.11	4.90
Cash Flow Per Share	14.03	15.06	13.25	8.02	16.74	12.16	10.70	10.88
Tang Book Value Per Share	32.96	28.44	22.51	16.12	19.91	31.11	27.57	22.80
Dividends Per Share	0.460	0.380	0.300	0.240	0.240	0.160	0.160	...
Dividend Payout %	11.30	6.18	4.48	...	...	3.91	3.89	...
Income Statement								
Total Revenue	1,623,938	1,757,889	1,613,683	1,009,794	1,970,347	1,431,166	1,267,144	1,118,622
EBITDA	1,088,609	1,238,496	1,225,351	(206,413)	(873,647)	1,022,794	942,626	785,490
Depn & Amortn	513,916	390,461	304,222	265,699	547,404	461,791	396,394	263,246
Income Before Taxes	560,550	841,481	913,731	(488,481)	(1,430,298)	544,625	544,324	516,455
Income Taxes	206,727	311,549	338,949	(176,538)	(528,613)	198,156	198,605	188,130
Net Income	353,823	529,932	574,782	(311,943)	(901,685)	346,469	345,719	328,325
Average Shares	85,034	86,232	85,782	84,192	81,478	84,632	84,090	67,000
Balance Sheet								
Current Assets	470,137	457,895	561,767	407,258	514,944	564,577	416,757	429,028
Total Assets	6,305,152	5,428,577	4,358,247	3,444,537	4,164,933	5,362,794	4,829,750	4,180,335
Current Liabilities	645,862	616,339	512,313	388,763	469,589	424,571	354,588	397,418
Long-Term Obligations	750,000	405,000	350,000	392,793	591,223	487,159	443,667	352,451
Total Liabilities	2,830,416	2,297,964	1,748,415	1,406,431	1,815,568	2,103,507	1,853,607	1,584,882
Stockholders' Equity	3,474,736	3,130,613	2,609,832	2,038,106	2,349,365	3,259,287	2,976,143	2,595,453
Shares Outstanding	86,595	85,774	85,234	83,541	83,258	82,541	82,883	82,377
Statistical Record								
Return on Assets %	6.01	10.83	14.73	N.M.	N.M.	6.80	7.67	12.42
Return on Equity %	10.68	18.46	24.73	N.M.	N.M.	11.11	12.41	19.92
EBITDA Margin %	67.04	70.45	75.94	N.M.	N.M.	71.47	74.39	70.22
Net Margin %	21.79	30.15	35.62	N.M.	N.M.	24.21	27.28	29.35
Asset Turnover	0.28	0.36	0.41	0.27	0.41	0.28	0.28	0.42
Current Ratio	0.73	0.74	1.10	1.05	1.10	1.33	1.18	1.08
Debt to Equity	0.22	0.13	0.13	0.19	0.25	0.15	0.15	0.14
Price Range	86.41-46.96	117.56-53.37	89.85-49.21	53.95-15.92	73.70-22.68	42.86-34.12	47.31-33.43	45.93-34.58
P/E Ratio	21.23-11.54	19.12-8.68	13.41-7.34	...	...	10.48-8.34	11.51-8.13	9.37-7.06
Average Yield %	0.75		0.45	0.43	0.71	0.48	0.42	0.40	...

Address: 1700 Lincoln Street, Suite 1800, Denver, CO 80203-4518 **Telephone:** 303-295-3995	**Web Site:** www.cimarex.com **Officers:** Thomas E. Jorden - Executive Vice President, President, Chief Executive Officer Joseph R. Albi - Executive Vice President, Chief Operating Officer	**Auditors:** KPMG LLP **Investor Contact:** 303-295-3995 **Transfer Agents:** Continental Stock Transfer & Trust Company, New York, NY

CINEMARK HOLDINGS INC

Exchange	Symbol	Price	52Wk Range	Yield	P/E
NYS	CNK	$29.44 (3/28/2013)	29.49-21.37	2.85	20.03

*7 Year Price Score N/A   *NYSE Composite Index=100   *12 Month Price Score 105.33

Interim Earnings (Per Share)

Qtr.	Mar	Jun	Sep	Dec
2008	0.05	0.14	0.19	(0.83)
2009	0.16	0.17	0.19	0.35
2010	0.31	0.35	0.29	0.33
2011	0.22	0.35	0.41	0.16
2012	0.37	0.45	0.41	0.24

Interim Dividends (Per Share)

Amt	Decl	Ex	Rec	Pay
0.21Q	05/11/2012	06/04/2012	06/06/2012	06/19/2012
0.21Q	08/08/2012	08/17/2012	08/21/2012	09/05/2012
0.21Q	11/06/2012	11/19/2012	11/21/2012	12/07/2012
0.21Q	02/14/2013	02/28/2013	03/04/2013	03/15/2013

Indicated Div: $0.84

Valuation Analysis / **Institutional Holding**

Forecast EPS	$1.80	No of Institutions
	(04/06/2013)	307
Market Cap	$3.4 Billion	Shares
Book Value	$1.1 Billion	102,552,464
Price/Book	3.12	% Held
Price/Sales	1.37	83.95

Business Summary: Entertainment (MIC: 2.3.2 SIC: 7832 NAIC: 512131)

Cinemark Holdings is a holding company. Co. is engaged in the motion picture exhibition industry, with theatres in the U.S., Brazil, Mexico, Argentina, Chile, Colombia, Peru, Ecuador, Honduras, El Salvador, Nicaragua, Costa Rica, Panama and Guatemala. Co. has two reportable segments: the U.S. markets and international markets. In its domestic markets, Co.'s theatres are part of the in-theatre digital network operated by National CineMedia, LLC. In certain of its international markets, Co. outsources its screen advertising to local companies who have established relationships with local advertisers. As of Dec 31 2011, Co. operated 456 theatres and 5,152 screens in the U.S. and Latin America.

Recent Developments: For the year ended Dec 31 2012, net income increased 29.3% to US$171.4 million from US$132.6 million in the prior year. Revenues were US$2.47 billion, up 8.5% from US$2.28 billion the year before. Operating income was US$383.7 million versus US$308.5 million in the prior year, an increase of 24.4%. Direct operating expenses rose 6.4% to US$968.6 million from US$910.7 million in the comparable period the year before. Indirect operating expenses increased 5.7% to US$1.12 billion from US$1.06 billion in the equivalent prior-year period.

Prospects: Our evaluation of Cinemark Holdings Inc. as of Apr. 7, 2013 is the result of our systematic analysis on three basic characteristics: earnings strength, relative valuation, and recent stock price movement. The company has generated a negative trend in earnings per share over the past 5 quarters. However, while recent estimates for the company have been lowered by analysts, CNK has posted results that fell short of analysts expectations. Based on operating earnings yield, the company is about fairly valued when compared to all of the companies in our coverage universe. Share price changes over the past year indicates that CNK will perform in line with the market over the near term.

Financial Data

(US$ in Thousands)	12/31/2012	12/31/2011	12/31/2010	12/31/2009	12/31/2008	12/31/2007	12/31/2006	12/31/2005
Earnings Per Share	1.47	1.14	1.29	0.87	(0.45)	0.85	0.01	(0.31)
Cash Flow Per Share	3.48	3.47	2.37	1.63	2.39	2.70	1.83	2.01
Dividends Per Share	0.840	0.840	0.750	0.720	0.720	0.310	...	...
Dividend Payout %	57.14	73.68	58.14	82.76	...	36.47	...	...
Income Statement								
Total Revenue	2,473,531	2,279,613	2,141,144	1,976,500	1,742,287	1,682,841	1,220,594	1,020,597
EBITDA	544,395	465,124	455,915	388,159	233,216	476,098	205,668	131,309
Depn & Amortn	143,394	150,149	138,637	144,055	151,425	144,629	90,081	71,870
Income Before Taxes	283,709	199,981	210,939	146,508	(21,002)	204,136	16,641	(15,303)
Income Taxes	125,398	73,050	57,838	44,845	21,055	111,962	12,685	9,408
Net Income	168,949	130,557	146,120	97,108	(48,325)	88,920	841	(25,408)
Average Shares	113,824	113,224	112,151	110,255	107,341	104,720	86,618	82,199
Balance Sheet								
Current Assets	845,161	627,118	577,053	507,297	403,381	414,035	206,353	206,688
Total Assets	3,863,226	3,522,408	3,421,478	3,276,448	3,065,708	3,296,892	3,171,582	1,864,852
Current Liabilities	338,204	305,027	271,940	280,832	231,170	218,322	230,822	160,067
Long-Term Obligations	1,893,571	1,691,633	1,654,417	1,664,506	1,614,192	1,631,065	2,009,572	1,048,224
Total Liabilities	2,779,161	2,509,531	2,399,931	2,376,616	2,254,452	2,277,689	2,482,285	1,345,503
Stockholders' Equity	1,084,065	1,012,877	1,021,547	899,832	811,256	1,019,203	689,297	519,349
Shares Outstanding	114,949	114,201	113,750	110,917	108,835	106,983	92,560	82,531
Statistical Record								
Return on Assets %	4.56	3.76	4.36	3.06	N.M.	2.75	0.03	...
Return on Equity %	16.07	12.83	15.21	11.35	N.M.	10.41	0.14	...
EBITDA Margin %	22.01	20.40	21.29	19.64	13.39	28.29	16.85	12.87
Net Margin %	6.83	5.73	6.82	4.91	N.M.	5.28	0.07	N.M.
Asset Turnover	0.67	0.66	0.64	0.62	0.55	0.52	0.48	...
Current Ratio	2.50	2.06	2.12	1.81	1.74	1.90	0.89	1.29
Debt to Equity	1.75	1.67	1.62	1.85	1.99	1.60	2.92	2.02
Price Range	27.20-18.04	21.75-16.82	19.35-12.95	14.53-6.83	17.00-6.88	19.70-15.70	...	...
P/E Ratio	18.50-12.27	19.08-14.75	15.00-10.04	16.70-7.85	...	23.18-18.47	...	...
Average Yield %	3.64	4.31	4.59	6.98	5.63	1.74	...	...

Address: 3900 Dallas Parkway, Suite 500, Plano, TX 75093 **Telephone:** 972-665-1000	**Web Site:** www.cinemark.com **Officers:** Lee Roy Mitchell - Chairman Timothy Warner - President, Chief Executive Officer, Chief Operating Officer	**Auditors:** Deloitte & Touche LLP **Investor Contact:** 972-665-1500 **Transfer Agents:** Wells Fargo Shareholder Services

CITIGROUP INC

Exchange	Symbol	Price	52Wk Range	Yield	P/E
NYS	C	$44.24 (3/28/2013)	47.60-24.82	N/A	18.13

*7 Year Price Score 18.00 *NYSE Composite Index=100 *12 Month Price Score 116.02

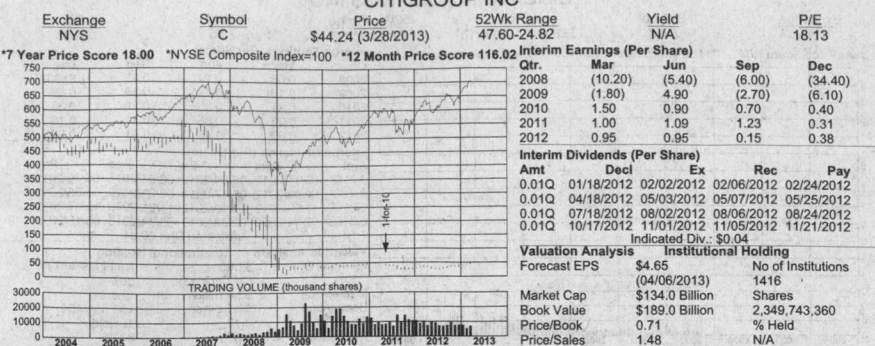

Interim Earnings (Per Share)

Qtr.	Mar	Jun	Sep	Dec
2008	(10.20)	(5.40)	(6.00)	(34.40)
2009	(1.80)	4.90	(2.70)	(6.10)
2010	1.50	0.90	0.70	0.40
2011	1.00	1.09	1.23	0.31
2012	0.95	0.95	0.15	0.38

Interim Dividends (Per Share)

Amt	Decl	Ex	Rec	Pay
0.01Q	01/18/2012	02/02/2012	02/06/2012	02/24/2012
0.01Q	04/18/2012	05/03/2012	05/07/2012	05/25/2012
0.01Q	07/18/2012	08/02/2012	08/06/2012	08/24/2012
0.01Q	10/17/2012	11/01/2012	11/05/2012	11/21/2012

Indicated Div.: $0.04

Valuation Analysis | **Institutional Holding**

Forecast EPS	$4.65 (04/06/2013)	No of Institutions 1416
Market Cap	$134.0 Billion	Shares
Book Value	$189.0 Billion	2,349,743,360
Price/Book	0.71	% Held
Price/Sales	1.48	N/A

Business Summary: Banking (MIC: 5.1.1 SIC: 6021 NAIC: 522110)

Citigroup is a financial services holding company whose businesses provide consumers, corporations, governments and institutions with a range of financial products and services. Co. operates in two primary business segments: Citicorp, consisting of Co.'s Global Consumer Banking businesses and Institutional Clients Group; and Citi Holdings, consisting of its Brokerage and Asset Management, Local Consumer Lending businesses, and Special Asset Pool. Co. operates in North America, Europe, Middle East and Africa, Latin America and Asia. As of Dec 31 2012, Co. had total assets of $1.86 trillion and total deposits of $930.56 billion.

Recent Developments: For the year ended Dec 31 2012, income from continuing operations decreased 28.8% to US$7.91 billion from US$11.10 billion a year earlier. Net income decreased 30.8% to US$7.76 billion from US$11.22 billion in the prior year. Net interest income decreased 1.7% to US$47.60 billion from US$48.45 billion in the prior year. Provision for loan losses was US$10.85 billion versus US$11.77 billion in the prior year, a decrease of 7.9%. Non-interest income fell 24.5% to US$22.57 billion from US$29.91 billion, while non-interest expense declined 1.1% to US$51.39 billion.

Prospects: Our evaluation of Citigroup Inc. as of Apr. 7, 2013 is the result of our systematic analysis on three basic characteristics: earnings strength, relative valuation, and recent stock price movement. The company has generated a negative trend in earnings per share over the past 5 quarters. However, while recent estimates for the company have been mixed, C has posted results that fell short of analysts expectations. Based on operating earnings yield, the company is undervalued when compared to all of the companies in our coverage universe. Share price changes over the past year indicates that C will perform well over the near term.

Financial Data

(US$ in Thousands)	12/31/2012	12/31/2011	12/31/2010	12/31/2009	12/31/2008	12/31/2007	12/31/2006	12/31/2005
Earnings Per Share	2.44	3.63	3.50	(8.00)	(55.90)	7.20	43.10	47.50
Cash Flow Per Share	4.86	15.38	12.40	(48.17)	182.85	(145.60)	(0.20)	62.84
Tang Book Value Per Share	50.57	48.88	43.00	39.23	44.07	99.52	141.42	127.57
Dividends Per Share	0.040	0.030	...	0.100	11.200	21.600	19.600	17.600
Dividend Payout %	1.64	0.83	...	...	...	300.00	45.48	37.05
Income Statement								
Interest Income	68,138,000	72,681,000	79,516,000	76,635,000	106,655,000	124,467,000	96,431,000	76,021,000
Interest Expense	20,535,000	24,234,000	24,864,000	27,721,000	52,963,000	77,531,000	56,943,000	36,676,000
Net Interest Income	47,603,000	48,447,000	54,652,000	48,914,000	53,692,000	46,936,000	39,488,000	39,345,000
Provision for Losses	10,848,000	11,773,000	25,194,000	38,760,000	33,674,000	17,424,000	6,738,000	7,929,000
Non-Interest Income	22,570,000	29,906,000	31,949,000	31,371,000	(899,000)	34,762,000	50,127,000	44,297,000
Non-Interest Expense	51,389,000	51,956,000	48,223,000	49,324,000	72,174,000	62,573,000	53,238,000	46,280,000
Income Before Taxes	7,936,000	14,624,000	13,184,000	(7,799,000)	(53,055,000)	1,701,000	29,639,000	29,433,000
Income Taxes	27,000	3,521,000	2,233,000	(6,733,000)	(20,612,000)	(2,201,000)	8,101,000	9,078,000
Net Income	7,541,000	11,067,000	10,602,000	(1,606,000)	(27,684,000)	3,617,000	21,538,000	24,589,000
Average Shares	3,015,500	2,998,800	2,967,810	1,209,900	579,510	499,530	498,610	516,040
Balance Sheet								
Net Loans & Leases	630,009,000	617,127,000	608,139,000	555,471,000	664,600,000	761,876,000	670,252,000	573,721,000
Total Assets	1,864,660,000	1,873,878,000	1,913,902,000	1,856,646,000	1,938,470,000	2,187,631,000	1,884,318,000	1,494,037,000
Total Deposits	930,560,000	865,936,000	844,968,000	835,903,000	774,185,000	826,230,000	712,041,000	592,595,000
Total Liabilities	1,675,611,000	1,696,072,000	1,750,434,000	1,703,946,000	1,796,840,000	2,074,033,000	1,764,535,000	1,381,500,000
Stockholders' Equity	189,049,000	177,806,000	163,468,000	152,700,000	141,630,000	113,598,000	119,783,000	112,537,000
Shares Outstanding	3,028,884	2,923,878	2,905,836	2,848,327	545,006	499,458	491,199	498,022
Statistical Record								
Return on Assets %	0.40	0.58	0.56	N.M.	N.M.	0.18	1.28	1.65
Return on Equity %	4.10	6.49	6.71	N.M.	N.M.	3.10	18.54	22.17
Net Interest Margin %	69.86	66.66	68.73	63.83	50.34	37.71	40.95	51.76
Efficiency Ratio %	56.65	50.65	43.26	45.67	68.25	39.30	36.33	38.46
Loans to Deposits	0.68	0.71	0.72	0.66	0.86	0.92	0.94	0.97
Price Range	40.17-24.82	51.30-23.11	49.70-31.50	74.60-10.20	296.90-37.70	552.50-292.90	564.10-450.50	497.80-430.50
P/E Ratio	16.46-10.17	14.13-6.37	14.20-9.00	...	...	76.74-40.68	13.09-10.45	10.48-9.06
Average Yield %	0.12	0.08	...	0.27	5.87	4.52	4.01	3.77

Address: 399 Park Avenue, New York, NY 10022	Web Site: www.citigroup.com	Auditors: KPMG LLP
Telephone: 212-559-1000	Officers: Michael E. O'Neill - Chairman Lewis B. Kaden - Vice-Chairman	Investor Contact: 212-559-2718
Fax: 212-816-8913		Transfer Agents: Computershare Trust Company, N.A., Providence, RI

CITY NATIONAL CORP. (BEVERLY HILLS, CA)

Exchange	Symbol	Price	52Wk Range	Yield	P/E
NYS	CYN	$58.91 (3/28/2013)	59.61-46.39	1.70	15.38

*7 Year Price Score 84.40 *NYSE Composite Index=100 *12 Month Price Score 100.88

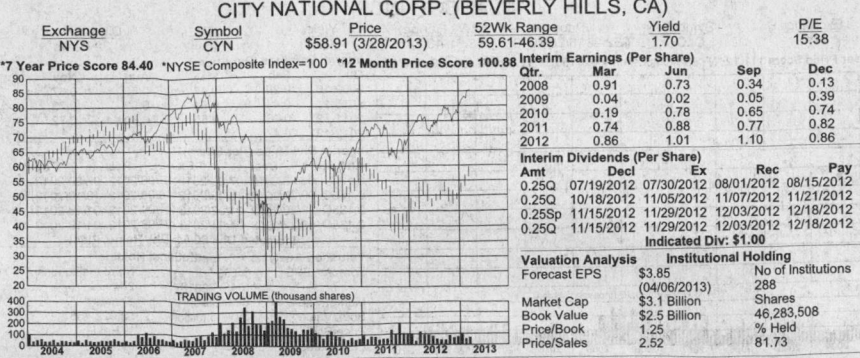

Interim Earnings (Per Share)

Qtr.	Mar	Jun	Sep	Dec
2008	0.91	0.73	0.34	0.13
2009	0.04	0.02	0.05	0.39
2010	0.19	0.78	0.65	0.74
2011	0.74	0.88	0.77	0.82
2012	0.86	1.01	1.10	0.86

Interim Dividends (Per Share)

Amt	Decl	Ex	Rec	Pay
0.25Q	07/19/2012	07/30/2012	08/01/2012	08/15/2012
0.25Q	10/18/2012	11/05/2012	11/07/2012	11/21/2012
0.25Sp	11/15/2012	11/29/2012	12/03/2012	12/18/2012
0.25Q	11/15/2012	11/29/2012	12/03/2012	12/18/2012

Indicated Div: $1.00

Valuation Analysis

Forecast EPS	$3.85
	(04/06/2013)
Market Cap	$3.1 Billion
Book Value	$2.5 Billion
Price/Book	1.25
Price/Sales	2.52

Institutional Holding

No of Institutions	288
Shares	46,283,508
% Held	81.73

TRADING VOLUME (thousand shares)

Business Summary: Banking (MIC: 5.1.1 SIC: 6021 NAIC: 522110)

City National is a bank holding and financial holding company. Co. provides banking, investing and trust services via its subsidiary, City National Bank (the Bank). Co. has three segments: Commercial and Private Banking, which provides banking services, including commercial and mortgage loans, lines of credit, deposits, cash management services, international trade finance and letters of credit to businesses, entrepreneurs and individuals; Wealth Management, which includes its investment advisory affiliates and the Bank's Wealth Management Services; and Other, which includes other subsidiaries of Co. At Dec 31 2011, Co. had total assets of $23.67 billion and deposits of $20.39 billion.

Recent Developments: For the year ended Dec 31 2012, net income increased 18.8% to US$209.1 million from US$176.1 million in the prior year. Net interest income increased 7.5% to US$830.8 million from US$773.0 million in the prior year. Provision for loan losses was US$55.3 million versus US$56.1 million in the prior year, a decrease of 1.4%. Non-interest income rose 4.6% to US$357.6 million from US$341.9 million, while non-interest expense advanced 2.5% to US$825.1 million.

Prospects: Our evaluation of City National Corp. as of Apr. 7, 2013 is the result of our systematic analysis on three basic characteristics: earnings strength, relative valuation, and recent stock price movement. The company has generated a negative trend in earnings per share over the past 5 quarters and while recent estimates for the company have been raised by analysts, CYN has posted results that fell short of analysts expectations. Based on operating earnings yield, the company is undervalued when compared to all of the companies in our coverage universe. Share price changes over the past year indicates that CYN will perform in line with the market over the near term.

Financial Data
(US$ in Thousands)

	12/31/2012	12/31/2011	12/31/2010	12/31/2009	12/31/2008	12/31/2007	12/31/2006	12/31/2005
Earnings Per Share	3.83	3.21	2.36	0.50	2.11	4.52	4.66	4.60
Cash Flow Per Share	4.92	11.59	11.16	5.49	6.49	2.75	2.99	5.83
Tang Book Value Per Share	30.90	30.90	27.39	24.54	23.77	23.54	25.13	23.61
Dividends Per Share	1.500	0.800	0.400	0.550	1.920	1.840	1.640	1.440
Dividend Payout %	39.16	24.92	16.95	110.00	91.00	40.71	35.19	31.30
Income Statement								
Interest Income	886,551	843,090	830,196	709,800	784,688	894,101	826,294	718,552
Interest Expense	55,715	70,100	99,871	85,024	184,792	285,829	220,405	106,125
Net Interest Income	830,836	772,990	730,325	624,776	599,896	608,272	605,889	612,427
Provision for Losses	55,346	56,146	179,218	285,000	127,000	20,000	(610)	...
Non-Interest Income	357,603	341,867	361,375	290,515	266,984	303,202	242,564	208,189
Non-Interest Expense	825,138	805,095	751,330	580,128	582,141	529,245	476,219	438,385
Income Before Taxes	307,955	253,616	161,152	50,163	157,739	362,229	372,844	382,231
Income Taxes	98,822	77,561	26,055	(1,886)	47,405	130,660	133,363	141,821
Net Income	208,049	172,421	131,177	51,339	104,956	222,713	233,523	234,735
Average Shares	53,475	52,849	52,455	50,421	48,570	49,290	50,063	51,062
Balance Sheet								
Net Loans & Leases	15,526,630	13,464,117	12,919,754	13,710,236	12,220,213	11,462,115	10,230,663	9,111,619
Total Assets	28,618,492	23,666,291	21,353,118	21,078,757	16,455,515	15,889,290	14,884,381	14,581,860
Total Deposits	23,502,355	20,387,582	18,176,862	17,379,448	12,652,124	11,822,505	12,172,816	12,138,472
Total Liabilities	26,113,174	21,521,442	19,393,539	19,092,434	14,411,501	14,233,683	13,393,466	13,123,852
Stockholders' Equity	2,505,318	2,144,849	1,959,579	1,986,323	2,044,014	1,655,607	1,490,915	1,458,008
Shares Outstanding	53,216	52,499	52,246	51,536	48,548	48,235	47,882	49,713
Statistical Record								
Return on Assets %	0.79	0.77	0.62	0.27	0.65	1.45	1.59	1.63
Return on Equity %	8.92	8.40	6.65	2.55	5.66	14.16	15.84	16.73
Net Interest Margin %	93.72	91.69	87.97	88.02	76.45	68.03	73.33	85.23
Efficiency Ratio %	66.32	67.94	63.05	57.99	55.35	44.20	44.55	47.30
Loans to Deposits	0.66	0.66	0.71	0.79	0.97	0.97	0.84	0.75
Price Range	54.63-45.39	62.90-36.01	64.13-45.60	48.70-22.83	65.35-34.97	78.39-59.10	78.00-63.69	75.60-66.88
P/E Ratio	14.26-11.85	19.60-11.22	27.17-19.32	97.40-45.66	30.97-16.57	17.34-13.08	16.74-13.67	16.43-14.54
Average Yield %	3.00	1.58	0.74	1.48	3.89	2.59	2.33	2.02

Address: City National Plaza, 555 South Flower Street, Los Angeles, CA 90071 **Telephone:** 213-673-7700	**Web Site:** www.cnb.com **Officers:** Bram Goldsmith - Chairman Russell D. Goldsmith - President, Chief Executive Officer	**Auditors:** KPMG LLP **Investor Contact:** 213-673-7615 **Transfer Agents:** Computershare Investor Services, Canton, MA

CLARCOR INC.

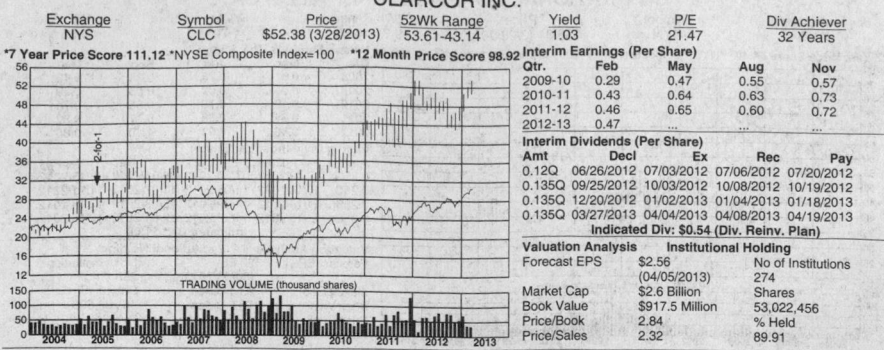

Exchange	Symbol	Price	52Wk Range	Yield	P/E	Div Achiever
NYS	CLC	$52.38 (3/28/2013)	53.61-43.14	1.03	21.47	32 Years

*7 Year Price Score 111.12 *NYSE Composite Index=100 *12 Month Price Score 98.92

Interim Earnings (Per Share)

Qtr.	Feb	May	Aug	Nov
2009-10	0.29	0.47	0.55	0.57
2010-11	0.43	0.64	0.63	0.73
2011-12	0.46	0.65	0.60	0.72
2012-13	0.47	...	...	...

Interim Dividends (Per Share)

Amt	Decl	Ex	Rec	Pay
0.12Q	06/26/2012	07/03/2012	07/06/2012	07/20/2012
0.135Q	09/25/2012	10/03/2012	10/08/2012	10/19/2012
0.135Q	12/20/2012	01/02/2013	01/04/2013	01/18/2013
0.135Q	03/27/2013	04/04/2013	04/08/2013	04/19/2013

Indicated Div: $0.54 (Div. Reinv. Plan)

Valuation Analysis | **Institutional Holding**

Forecast EPS	$2.56 (04/05/2013)	No of Institutions	274
Market Cap	$2.6 Billion	Shares	53,022,456
Book Value	$917.5 Million	% Held	89.91
Price/Book	2.84		
Price/Sales	2.32		

Business Summary: Industrial Machinery & Equipment (MIC: 7.2.1 SIC: 3714 NAIC: 336399)

Clarcor is a global provider of filtration products, filtration systems and services, and consumer and industrial packaging products. Co. has three reportable segments: Engine/Mobile Filtration, which manufactures and markets a line of filters used in the filtration of oils, air, fuel, coolant, hydraulic and transmission fluids; the Industrial/Environmental Filtration segment, which manufactures and markets a line of filters, cartridges, dust collectors, filtration systems, engineered filtration products and technologies used in the filtration of air and industrial fluid processes; and the Packaging segment, which manufactures and markets consumer and industrial packaging products.

Recent Developments: For the quarter ended Mar 2 2013, net income was unchanged at US$23.5 million versus US$23.5 million the year-earlier quarter. Revenues were US$256.3 million, down 0.4% from US$257.3 million the year before. Operating income was US$33.8 million versus US$34.3 million in the prior-year quarter, a decrease of 1.4%. Direct operating expenses rose 2.2% to US$174.8 million from US$171.0 million in the comparable period the year before. Indirect operating expenses decreased 8.2% to US$47.7 million from US$51.9 million in the equivalent prior-year period.

Prospects: Our evaluation of Clarcor Inc. as of Apr. 7, 2013 is the result of our systematic analysis on three basic characteristics: earnings strength, relative valuation, and recent stock price movement. The company has enjoyed a very positive trend in earnings per share over the past 5 quarters. However, while recent estimates for the company have been lowered by analysts, CLC has posted better than expected results. Based on operating earnings yield, the company is about fairly valued when compared to all of the companies in our coverage universe. Share price changes over the past year indicates that CLC will perform in line with the market over the near term.

Financial Data

(US$ in Thousands)	3 Mos	11/30/2012	12/03/2011	11/27/2010	11/28/2009	11/29/2008	12/01/2007	12/02/2006
Earnings Per Share	2.44	2.42	2.42	1.88	1.40	1.86	1.78	1.59
Cash Flow Per Share	2.83	2.72	2.33	2.82	2.24	2.12	2.74	1.23
Tang Book Value Per Share	11.72	11.34	9.98	8.69	7.19	6.55	7.68	7.21
Dividends Per Share	0.510	0.495	0.435	0.398	0.367	0.330	0.297	0.275
Dividend Payout %	20.90	20.45	17.98	21.14	26.25	17.74	16.71	17.30
Income Statement								
Total Revenue	256,271	1,121,765	1,126,601	1,011,429	907,748	1,059,601	921,191	904,347
EBITDA	41,896	208,849	207,954	169,800	133,496	175,761	150,758	146,919
Depn & Amortn	8,081	25,925	26,826	26,119	26,005	25,231	20,858	20,891
Income Before Taxes	33,804	182,997	181,308	143,423	105,649	145,371	130,509	126,941
Income Taxes	10,276	59,657	56,947	47,072	33,819	49,310	39,675	43,795
Net Income	23,462	122,986	124,003	96,081	71,543	95,654	90,659	82,710
Average Shares	50,409	50,882	51,191	51,156	51,045	51,410	50,885	52,176
Balance Sheet								
Current Assets	636,167	654,594	600,899	526,273	448,528	432,571	371,920	380,340
Total Assets	1,186,170	1,205,502	1,134,933	1,042,411	973,890	957,882	739,135	727,516
Current Liabilities	139,214	174,891	160,050	163,457	131,942	143,503	114,171	118,428
Long-Term Obligations	16,407	16,391	15,981	17,331	52,096	83,822	17,329	15,946
Total Liabilities	268,648	304,658	300,206	285,941	287,271	306,123	183,405	190,007
Stockholders' Equity	917,522	900,844	834,727	756,470	686,619	651,759	555,730	537,509
Shares Outstanding	49,684	49,652	50,144	50,334	50,392	50,794	49,218	51,082
Statistical Record								
Return on Assets %	10.64	10.57	11.21	9.56	7.43	11.30	12.40	11.73
Return on Equity %	13.84	14.25	15.33	13.35	10.72	15.89	16.63	16.12
EBITDA Margin %	16.35	18.62	18.46	16.79	14.71	16.59	16.37	16.25
Net Margin %	9.16	10.96	11.01	9.50	7.88	9.03	9.84	9.15
Asset Turnover	0.97	0.96	1.02	1.01	0.94	1.25	1.26	1.28
Current Ratio	4.57	3.74	3.75	3.22	3.40	3.01	3.26	3.21
Debt to Equity	0.02	0.02	0.02	0.02	0.08	0.13	0.03	0.03
Price Range	52.22-43.14	53.47-43.14	49.23-39.17	42.01-30.72	34.19-23.41	44.25-25.62	41.88-30.07	36.27-26.97
P/E Ratio	21.40-17.68	22.10-17.83	20.34-16.19	22.35-16.34	24.42-16.72	23.79-13.77	23.53-16.89	22.81-16.96
Average Yield %	1.06	1.02	0.99	1.11	1.21	0.88	0.86	0.87

Address: 840 Crescent Centre Drive, Suite 600, Franklin, TN 37067
Telephone: 615-771-3100

Web Site: www.clarcor.com
Officers: Christopher L. Conway - President, Chief Executive Officer, Chief Operating Officer David J. Lindsay - Vice President, Chief Administrative Officer

Auditors: PricewaterhouseCoopers LLP
Investor Contact: 615-771-3100
Transfer Agents: Computershare Investor Services, Canton, MA

CLEAN HARBORS, INC

Exchange	Symbol	Price	52Wk Range	Yield	P/E
NYS	CLH	$58.09 (3/28/2013)	68.49-47.16	N/A	24.20

*7 Year Price Score 137.73 *NYSE Composite Index=100   *12 Month Price Score 87.30

Interim Earnings (Per Share)

Qtr.	Mar	Jun	Sep	Dec
2008	0.22	0.35	0.30	0.38
2009	0.11	0.18	0.18	0.27
2010	0.20	1.10	0.73	0.44
2011	0.43	0.55	0.70	0.72
2012	0.60	0.44	0.23	1.13

Interim Dividends (Per Share)

Amt	Decl	Ex	Rec	Pay
100%	06/08/2011	07/27/2011	07/06/2011	07/26/2011

Valuation Analysis

		Institutional Holding	
Forecast EPS	$2.68 (04/05/2013)	No of Institutions	322
Market Cap	$3.5 Billion	Shares	57,047,168
Book Value	$1.4 Billion	% Held	98.12
Price/Book	2.45		
Price/Sales	1.60		

Business Summary: Sanitation Services (MIC: 7.5.3 SIC: 4953 NAIC: 562112)

Clean Harbors is a provider of environmental, energy and industrial services throughout North America. Co. has four operating segments: Technical Services, which provides a range of hazardous material management services; Field Services, which provides a variety of environmental cleanup services on customer sites or other locations; Industrial Services, which provides industrial and specialty services to refineries, chemical plants, oil sands facilities, pulp and paper mills, and other industrial facilities; and Oil and Gas Field Services, which provides fluid handling, fluid hauling, downhole servicing, surface rentals, exploration, mapping and directional boring services.

Recent Developments: For the year ended Dec 31 2012, income from continuing operations increased 1.9% to US$129.7 million from US$127.3 million a year earlier. Net income increased 1.9% to US$129.7 million from US$127.3 million in the prior year. Revenues were US$2.19 billion, up 10.3% from US$1.98 billion the year before. Operating income was US$202.2 million versus US$217.7 million in the prior year, a decrease of 7.1%. Direct operating expenses rose 11.6% to US$1.54 billion from US$1.38 billion in the comparable period the year before. Indirect operating expenses increased 15.2% to US$445.1 million from US$386.5 million in the equivalent prior-year period.

Prospects: Our evaluation of Clean Harbors Inc. as of Apr. 7, 2013 is the result of our systematic analysis on three basic characteristics: earnings strength, relative valuation, and recent stock price movement. The company has generated a negative trend in earnings per share over the past 5 quarters and while recent estimates for the company have been raised by analysts, CLH has posted results that fell short of analysts expectations. Based on operating earnings yield, the company is overvalued when compared to all of the companies in our coverage universe. Share price changes over the past year indicates that CLH will perform very poorly over the near term.

Financial Data

(US$ in Thousands)	12/31/2012	12/31/2011	12/31/2010	12/31/2009	12/31/2008	12/31/2007	12/31/2006	12/31/2005
Earnings Per Share	2.40	2.39	2.46	0.73	1.25	1.07	1.13	0.72
Cash Flow Per Share	6.00	3.39	4.26	1.88	2.43	2.02	1.57	0.95
Tang Book Value Per Share	4.40	12.01	11.49	8.45	7.01	2.62	2.25	0.49
Income Statement								
Total Revenue	2,187,908	1,984,136	1,731,244	1,074,220	1,030,713	946,917	829,809	711,170
EBITDA	338,456	348,302	307,807	144,366	148,766	124,925	102,355	82,172
Depn & Amortn	163,439	124,235	95,394	66,895	46,386	39,530	36,955	30,302
Income Before Taxes	127,730	184,678	184,477	61,472	93,977	72,238	52,953	29,116
Income Taxes	(1,944)	57,426	56,756	26,225	36,491	28,040	6,339	3,495
Net Income	129,674	127,252	130,515	36,686	57,486	44,198	46,675	25,621
Average Shares	54,079	53,324	52,934	49,866	45,732	41,260	41,314	35,434
Balance Sheet								
Current Assets	1,086,793	891,868	752,537	620,250	489,052	380,438	322,819	324,048
Total Assets	3,825,806	2,085,803	1,602,475	1,401,068	898,336	769,888	670,808	614,364
Current Liabilities	569,052	381,742	306,284	233,320	181,373	210,853	198,354	223,694
Long-Term Obligations	1,402,879	530,578	270,846	299,348	53,230	122,232	123,170	99,898
Total Liabilities	2,393,734	1,184,816	821,648	787,243	469,291	566,991	497,622	498,706
Stockholders' Equity	1,432,072	900,987	780,827	613,825	429,045	202,897	173,186	115,658
Shares Outstanding	60,385	53,182	52,772	52,461	47,466	40,655	39,370	38,705
Statistical Record								
Return on Assets %	4.38	6.90	8.69	3.19	6.87	6.14	7.26	4.58
Return on Equity %	11.09	15.13	18.72	7.04	18.14	23.50	32.32	40.44
EBITDA Margin %	15.47	17.55	17.78	13.44	14.43	13.19	12.33	11.55
Net Margin %	5.93	6.41	7.54	3.42	5.58	4.67	5.62	3.60
Asset Turnover	0.74	1.08	1.15	0.93	1.23	1.31	1.29	1.27
Current Ratio	1.91	2.34	2.46	2.66	2.70	1.80	1.63	1.45
Debt to Equity	0.98	0.59	0.35	0.49	0.12	0.60	0.71	0.86
Price Range	70.30-47.16	64.17-40.58	42.09-26.75	31.84-20.54	41.40-24.76	27.57-21.52	24.20-12.40	17.77-6.96
P/E Ratio	29.29-19.65	26.85-16.98	17.11-10.87	43.61-28.14	33.12-19.81	25.76-20.11	21.42-10.98	24.68-9.67

Address: 42 Longwater Drive, Norwell, MA 02061-9149
Telephone: 781-792-5000

Web Site: www.cleanharbors.com
Officers: Alan S. McKim - Chairman, President, Chief Executive Officer James M. Rutledge - Vice-Chairman, President, Chief Financial Officer, Executive Vice President, Chief Operating Officer, Treasurer

Auditors: Deloitte & Touche LLP
Investor Contact: 617-542-5300
Transfer Agents: American Stock Transfer & Trust Company, New York, NY

CLEAR CHANNEL OUTDOOR HOLDINGS INC

Exchange	Symbol	Price	52Wk Range	Yield	P/E
NYS	CCO	$7.49 (3/28/2013)	8.23-4.69	N/A	N/A

*7 Year Price Score 41.00 *NYSE Composite Index=100 *12 Month Price Score 105.80

Interim Earnings (Per Share)

Qtr.	Mar	Jun	Sep	Dec
2008	...	...	0.03	(8.53)
2009	(0.25)	(1.94)	(0.10)	(0.17)
2010	(0.14)	(0.03)	(0.10)	0.01
2011	(0.03)	0.07	0.01	0.06
2012	(0.14)	(0.04)	0.05	(0.42)

Interim Dividends (Per Share)

Amt	Decl	Ex	Rec	Pay
6.083Sp	02/29/2012	03/16/2012	03/12/2012	03/15/2012

Valuation Analysis | Institutional Holding

Forecast EPS	$-0.10	No of Institutions
	(04/05/2013)	133
Market Cap	$2.7 Billion	Shares
Book Value	$198.2 Million	45,047,560
Price/Book	13.50	% Held
Price/Sales	0.91	104.65

TRADING VOLUME (thousand shares)

Business Summary: Advertising (MIC: 2.3.4 SIC: 7312 NAIC: 541850)

Clear Channel Outdoor Holdings is a holding company. Co. provides clients with advertising opportunities through billboards, street furniture displays, transit displays and other out-of-home advertising displays, such as wallscapes, spectaculars and mall displays, which Co. owns or operates in key markets worldwide. Co. has two segments: Americas outdoor advertising ("Americas") and International outdoor advertising ("International"). The Americas segment primarily includes operations in the U.S., Canada and Latin America. The International segment primarily includes operations in Europe, Asia and Australia. As of Dec 31 2012, Co. owned or operated more than 750,000 advertising displays.

Recent Developments: For the year ended Dec 31 2012, net loss amounted to US$159.2 million versus net income of US$63.2 million in the prior year. Revenues were US$2.95 billion, down 1.9% from US$3.00 billion the year before. Operating income was US$267.0 million versus US$302.9 million in the prior year, a decrease of 11.9%. Direct operating expenses declined 1.7% to US$1.61 billion from US$1.64 billion in the comparable period the year before. Indirect operating expenses increased 0.6% to US$1.07 billion from US$1.06 billion in the equivalent prior-year period.

Prospects: Our evaluation of Clear Channel Outdoor Holdings Inc. as of Apr. 7, 2013 is the result of our systematic analysis on three basic characteristics: earnings strength, relative valuation, and recent stock price movement. The company has managed to produce a neutral trend in earnings per share over the past 5 quarters. Because the company lacks sufficient analyst estimate data, we place greater weight on the historical EPS trend as the measure of earnings strength. Based on operating earnings yield, the company is overvalued when compared to all of the companies in our coverage universe. Share price changes over the past year indicates that CCO will perform poorly over the near term.

Financial Data

(US$ in Thousands)	12/31/2012	12/31/2011	12/31/2010	12/31/2009	12/31/2008	07/30/2008	12/31/2007	12/31/2006
Earnings Per Share	(0.54)	0.11	(0.26)	(2.46)	(8.50)	0.47	0.69	0.43
Cash Flow Per Share	0.99	1.45	1.48	1.24	0.76	1.61	1.96	1.53
Tang Book Value Per Share	N.M.	N.M.	N.M.	N.M.	N.M.	...	0.88	N.M.
Dividends Per Share	6.083	...	...	...	...	...	...	...
Income Statement								
Total Revenue	2,946,944	3,003,874	2,797,994	2,698,024	1,327,224	1,962,063	3,281,836	2,897,721
EBITDA	453,200	729,497	588,699	(497,552)	(3,052,896)	452,121	911,669	767,998
Depn & Amortn	410,227	432,035	413,588	338,456	161,009	216,994	346,298	322,208
Income Before Taxes	(267,142)	100,486	(44,882)	(990,203)	(3,286,768)	146,340	407,490	283,207
Income Taxes	(107,089)	43,296	21,599	(149,110)	(271,895)	51,576	146,641	122,080
Net Income	(183,112)	42,946	(87,523)	(868,189)	(3,018,637)	167,554	245,990	153,072
Average Shares	356,915	356,528	355,568	355,377	355,308	355,741	355,806	352,262
Balance Sheet								
Current Assets	1,515,400	1,453,728	1,569,978	1,640,545	1,554,652	...	1,607,107	1,189,915
Total Assets	7,105,782	7,088,185	7,096,050	7,192,422	8,050,761	...	5,935,604	5,421,891
Current Liabilities	811,405	720,983	785,421	771,093	791,865	...	921,292	841,509
Long-Term Obligations	4,935,388	2,522,103	2,522,133	2,561,805	2,532,332	...	2,594,922	2,597,883
Total Liabilities	6,907,627	4,579,488	4,597,789	4,624,775	4,718,751	...	3,952,874	3,835,513
Stockholders' Equity	198,155	2,508,697	2,498,261	2,567,647	3,332,010	...	1,982,730	1,586,378
Shares Outstanding	357,247	356,028	355,802	355,798	355,681	...	355,493	354,565
Statistical Record								
Return on Assets %	N.M.	0.61	N.M.	N.M.	N.M.	...	4.33	2.96
Return on Equity %	N.M.	1.72	N.M.	N.M.	N.M.	...	13.78	10.95
EBITDA Margin %	15.38	24.29	21.04	N.M.	N.M.	23.04	27.78	26.50
Net Margin %	N.M.	1.43	N.M.	N.M.	N.M.	8.54	7.50	5.28
Asset Turnover	0.41	0.42	0.39	0.35	0.19	...	0.58	0.56
Current Ratio	1.87	2.02	2.00	2.13	1.96	...	1.74	1.41
Debt to Equity	24.91	1.01	1.01	1.00	0.76	...	1.31	1.64
Price Range	14.36-4.69	15.36-8.81	14.25-8.37	11.12-2.43	17.75-3.57	27.66-12.28	29.78-23.50	27.94-18.92
P/E Ratio	...	139.64-80.09	...	...	...	58.85-26.13	43.16-34.06	64.98-44.00
Average Yield %	79.37	...	...	...	...	...	...	...

Address: 200 East Basse Road, San Antonio, TX 78209 **Telephone:** 210-832-3700	**Web Site:** www.clearchanneloutdoor.com **Officers:** Robert W. Pittman - Executive Chairman, Holding/Parent Company Officer Randall T. Mays - President, Holding/Parent Company Officer, Sister Company Officer	**Auditors:** Ernst & Young LLP **Transfer Agents:** The Bank of New York, New York, NY

CLECO CORP.

Exchange	Symbol	Price	52Wk Range	Yield	P/E
NYS	CNL	$47.03 (3/28/2013)	47.03-38.46	2.87	17.42

*7 Year Price Score 126.55 *NYSE Composite Index=100   *12 Month Price Score 97.81

Interim Earnings (Per Share)

Qtr.	Mar	Jun	Sep	Dec
2008	0.37	0.49	0.62	0.23
2009	0.11	0.45	0.99	0.21
2010	2.48	0.58	0.82	0.33
2011	0.48	1.15	1.08	0.51
2012	0.50	0.77	1.05	0.38

Interim Dividends (Per Share)

Amt	Decl	Ex	Rec	Pay
0.313Q	04/27/2012	05/03/2012	05/07/2012	05/15/2012
0.338Q	07/26/2012	08/03/2012	08/07/2012	08/15/2012
0.338Q	10/25/2012	11/05/2012	11/07/2012	11/15/2012
0.338Q	01/24/2013	02/01/2013	02/05/2013	02/15/2013

Indicated Div: $1.35

Valuation Analysis / Institutional Holding

Forecast EPS	$2.52 (04/05/2013)	No of Institutions	282
Market Cap	$2.8 Billion	Shares	48,020,680
Book Value	$1.5 Billion	% Held	70.64
Price/Book	1.89		
Price/Sales	2.86		

TRADING VOLUME (thousand shares)

Business Summary: Electric Utilities (MIC: 3.1.1 SIC: 4911 NAIC: 221121)

Cleco is a public utility holding company which holds investments in several subsidiaries, including Cleco Power LLC (Cleco Power) and Cleco Midstream Resources LLC (Midstream), which are its operating business segments. Cleco Power is an electric utility engaged principally in the generation, transmission, distribution and sale of electricity. Midstream is a merchant energy subsidiary that owns and operates a merchant power plant. As of Dec 31 2012, Cleco Power served approximately 283,000 customers in Louisiana through its retail business and 10 communities across Louisiana and Mississippi. Midstream is a merchant energy subsidiary that owns and operates the Coughlin merchant power plant.

Recent Developments: For the year ended Dec 31 2012, net income decreased 16.4% to US$163.6 million from US$195.8 million in the prior year. Revenues were US$993.7 million, down 11.1% from US$1.12 billion the year before. Operating income was US$281.7 million versus US$298.2 million in the prior year, a decrease of 5.6%. Direct operating expenses declined 18.0% to US$541.1 million from US$659.6 million in the comparable period the year before. Indirect operating expenses increased 7.2% to US$171.0 million from US$159.4 million in the equivalent prior-year period.

Prospects: Our evaluation of Cleco Corp. as of Apr. 7, 2013 is the result of our systematic analysis on three basic characteristics: earnings strength, relative valuation, and recent stock price movement. The company has enjoyed a very positive trend in earnings per share over the past 5 quarters and while recent estimates for the company have remained steady, CNL has posted better than expected results. Based on operating earnings yield, the company is undervalued when compared to all of the companies in our coverage universe. Share price changes over the past year indicates that CNL will perform poorly over the near term.

Financial Data

(US$ in Thousands)	12/31/2012	12/31/2011	12/31/2010	12/31/2009	12/31/2008	12/31/2007	12/31/2006	12/31/2005
Earnings Per Share	2.70	3.22	4.20	1.76	1.70	2.54	1.36	3.53
Cash Flow Per Share	4.35	5.09	3.20	2.25	1.49	4.46	1.73	5.05
Tang Book Value Per Share	22.84	21.33	19.36	15.90	14.86	16.85	15.23	13.73
Dividends Per Share	1.300	1.123	0.975	0.900	0.900	0.900	0.900	0.900
Dividend Payout %	48.15	34.86	23.21	51.14	52.94	35.43	66.18	25.50
Income Statement								
Total Revenue	993,697	1,117,313	1,148,666	853,758	1,080,198	1,030,616	1,000,675	920,154
EBITDA	445,192	426,252	566,610	261,056	250,999	235,529	201,061	176,043
Depn & Amortn	132,407	119,790	112,203	78,204	77,876	79,904	74,975	60,330
Income Before Taxes	228,975	236,695	359,040	133,309	126,140	129,413	92,267	80,488
Income Taxes	65,327	102,897	142,498	9,579	18,457	70,772	42,049	115,951
Net Income	163,648	195,848	255,391	106,307	102,141	151,789	74,591	182,644
Average Shares	60,628	60,833	60,754	60,498	60,214	59,717	55,028	51,760
Balance Sheet								
Current Assets	447,338	456,785	608,850	493,925	466,379	408,677	537,308	434,468
Total Assets	4,147,349	4,050,202	4,161,410	3,694,847	3,341,204	2,710,735	2,461,104	2,149,488
Current Liabilities	294,630	321,002	477,681	241,804	360,833	361,579	388,511	294,104
Long-Term Obligations	1,257,258	1,337,056	1,399,709	1,320,299	1,106,819	769,103	619,341	609,643
Total Liabilities	2,648,136	2,630,345	2,843,203	2,578,775	2,280,339	1,699,366	1,564,883	1,443,225
Stockholders' Equity	1,499,213	1,419,857	1,318,207	1,116,072	1,060,865	1,011,369	896,221	706,263
Shares Outstanding	60,355	60,291	60,526	60,259	60,042	59,943	57,524	49,993
Statistical Record								
Return on Assets %	3.98	4.77	6.50	3.02	3.37	5.87	3.24	9.16
Return on Equity %	11.18	14.31	20.98	9.77	9.83	15.91	9.31	28.82
EBITDA Margin %	44.80	38.15	49.33	30.58	23.24	22.85	20.09	19.13
Net Margin %	16.47	17.53	22.23	12.45	9.46	14.73	7.45	19.85
Asset Turnover	0.24	0.27	0.29	0.24	0.36	0.40	0.43	0.46
Current Ratio	1.52	1.42	1.27	2.04	1.29	1.13	1.38	1.48
Debt to Equity	0.84	0.94	1.06	1.18	1.04	0.76	0.69	0.86
Price Range	44.27-36.24	38.18-30.36	31.71-24.62	27.99-19.06	28.22-20.24	29.01-22.48	26.09-21.05	24.05-19.05
P/E Ratio	16.40-13.42	11.86-9.43	7.55-5.86	15.90-10.83	16.60-11.91	11.42-8.85	19.18-15.48	6.81-5.40
Average Yield %	3.20	3.27	3.47	3.87	3.75	3.48	3.82	4.21

Address: 2030 Donahue Ferry Road, Pineville, LA 71360-5226 Telephone: 318-484-7400	Web Site: www.cleco.com Officers: J. Patrick Garrett - Chairman Bruce A. Williamson - President, Chief Executive Officer	Auditors: Deloitte and Touche LLP Transfer Agents: Computershare Trust Company, N.A, Providence, RI

177

CLIFFS NATURAL RESOURCES, INC.

Exchange	Symbol	Price	52Wk Range	Yield	P/E
NYS	CLF	$19.01 (3/28/2013)	71.16-18.46	3.16	N/A

*7 Year Price Score 73.54 *NYSE Composite Index=100 *12 Month Price Score 60.05

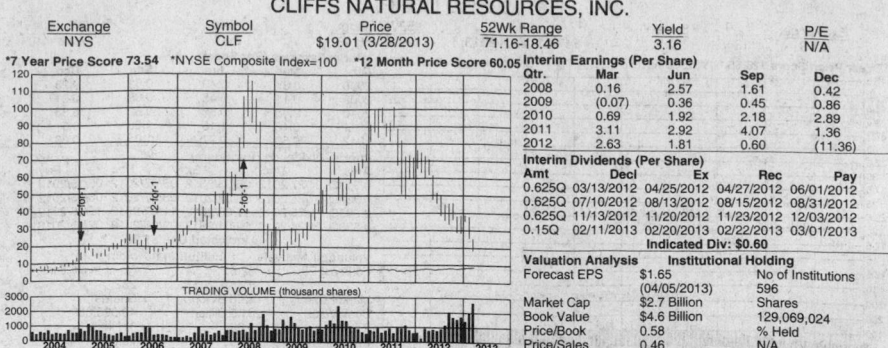

Interim Earnings (Per Share)

Qtr.	Mar	Jun	Sep	Dec
2008	0.16	2.57	1.61	0.42
2009	(0.07)	0.36	0.45	0.86
2010	0.69	1.92	2.18	2.89
2011	3.11	2.92	4.07	1.36
2012	2.63	1.81	0.60	(11.36)

Interim Dividends (Per Share)

Amt	Decl	Ex	Rec	Pay
0.625Q	03/13/2012	04/25/2012	04/27/2012	06/01/2012
0.625Q	07/10/2012	08/13/2012	08/15/2012	08/31/2012
0.625Q	11/13/2012	11/20/2012	11/23/2012	12/03/2012
0.15Q	02/11/2013	02/20/2013	02/22/2013	03/01/2013

Indicated Div: $0.60

Valuation Analysis | **Institutional Holding**

Forecast EPS	$1.65	No of Institutions
	(04/05/2013)	596
Market Cap	$2.7 Billion	Shares
Book Value	$4.6 Billion	129,069,024
Price/Book	0.58	% Held
Price/Sales	0.46	N/A

TRADING VOLUME (thousand shares)

Business Summary: Non-Precious Metals (MIC: 8.2.2 SIC: 1099 NAIC: 212299)

Cliffs Natural Resources is an international mining and natural resources company, a iron ore producer and a producer of metallurgical coal. In the U.S., Co. operates five iron ore mines in Michigan and Minnesota, six metallurgical coal mines located in West Virginia and Alabama and one thermal coal mine located in West Virginia. Co. also operates two iron ore mines in Eastern Canada. As of Dec 31 2012, Co.'s Asia Pacific operations consist of its Koolyanobbing iron ore mining complex in Western Australia. Co.'s operations are: U.S. Iron Ore, Eastern Canadian Iron Ore, Asia Pacific Iron Ore, North American Coal, Latin American Iron Ore, Ferroalloys and its Global Exploration Group.

Recent Developments: For the year ended Dec 31 2012, loss from continuing operations was US$1.16 billion compared with income of US$1.79 billion a year earlier. Net loss amounted to US$1.13 billion versus net income of US$1.81 billion in the prior year. Revenues were US$5.87 billion, down 10.5% from US$6.56 billion the year before. Operating loss was US$308.8 million versus an income of US$2.30 billion in the prior year. Direct operating expenses rose 18.9% to US$4.70 billion from US$3.95 billion in the comparable period the year before. Indirect operating expenses increased 371.5% to US$1.48 billion from US$314.1 million in the equivalent prior-year period.

Prospects: Our evaluation of Cliffs Natural Resources, Inc. as of Apr. 7, 2013 is the result of our systematic analysis on three basic characteristics: earnings strength, relative valuation, and recent stock price movement. The company has produced a positive trend in earnings per share over the past 5 quarters. However, while recent estimates for the company have been lowered by analysts, CLF has posted results that fell short of analysts expectations. Based on operating earnings yield, the company is undervalued when compared to all of the companies in our coverage universe. Share price changes over the past year indicates that CLF will perform very well over the near term.

Financial Data

(US$ in Thousands)	12/31/2012	12/31/2011	12/31/2010	12/31/2009	12/31/2008	12/31/2007	12/31/2006	12/31/2005
Earnings Per Share	(6.32)	11.48	7.49	1.64	4.76	2.57	2.60	2.49
Cash Flow Per Share	3.60	16.32	9.76	1.49	8.39	3.48	5.09	5.92
Tang Book Value Per Share	30.43	31.59	25.64	17.97	14.46	14.56	11.22	9.24
Dividends Per Share	2.155	0.840	0.507	0.255	0.350	0.250	0.237	0.150
Dividend Payout %	...	7.32	6.78	15.55	7.35	9.73	9.13	6.02
Income Statement								
Total Revenue	5,872,700	6,794,300	4,682,200	2,342,000	3,609,100	2,275,200	1,921,700	1,739,500
EBITDA	(12,700)	2,686,300	1,523,400	439,400	843,400	452,600	416,900	411,500
Depn & Amortn	293,500	237,800	165,400	120,600	113,500	69,300	42,700	52,800
Income Before Taxes	(501,800)	2,241,500	1,298,200	290,600	716,300	380,700	387,800	368,100
Income Taxes	255,900	420,100	292,000	20,800	144,200	84,100	90,900	84,800
Net Income	(899,400)	1,619,100	1,019,900	205,100	515,800	270,000	280,100	277,600
Average Shares	142,351	141,012	136,138	125,751	108,288	105,026	107,654	111,344
Balance Sheet								
Current Assets	1,650,000	1,790,700	2,583,700	1,161,200	861,700	754,600	782,300	636,000
Total Assets	13,574,900	14,541,700	7,778,200	4,639,300	4,111,100	3,075,800	1,939,700	1,746,700
Current Liabilities	1,381,500	1,493,300	1,028,700	570,400	844,900	399,600	374,900	362,700
Long-Term Obligations	3,960,700	3,608,700	1,713,100	525,000	525,000	440,000	...	...
Total Liabilities	8,942,200	8,756,700	3,932,300	2,096,500	2,360,400	1,777,400	1,021,600	922,600
Stockholders' Equity	4,632,700	5,785,000	3,845,900	2,542,800	1,750,700	1,298,400	918,100	824,100
Shares Outstanding	142,495	142,021	135,456	130,971	113,508	89,167	81,810	87,661
Statistical Record								
Return on Assets %	N.M.	14.51	16.43	4.69	14.31	10.77	15.20	19.09
Return on Equity %	N.M.	33.62	31.93	9.55	33.74	24.36	32.15	39.08
EBITDA Margin %	N.M.	39.54	32.54	18.76	23.37	19.89	21.69	23.66
Net Margin %	N.M.	23.83	21.78	8.76	14.29	11.87	14.58	15.96
Asset Turnover	0.42	0.61	0.75	0.54	1.00	0.91	1.04	1.20
Current Ratio	1.19	1.20	2.51	2.04	1.02	1.89	2.09	1.75
Debt to Equity	0.85	0.62	0.45	0.21	0.30	0.34	...	...
Price Range	76.55-28.40	101.43-48.30	79.98-39.95	47.41-12.01	119.19-14.11	52.38-23.20	27.06-15.86	24.38-11.97
P/E Ratio	...	8.84-4.21	10.68-5.33	28.91-7.32	25.04-2.96	20.38-9.03	10.41-6.10	9.79-4.81
Average Yield %	4.31	1.03	0.84	0.90	0.53	0.67	1.13	0.84

Address: 200 Public Square, Cleveland, OH 44114-2315	**Web Site:** www.cliffsnaturalresources.com	**Auditors:** Deloitte & Touche LLP
Telephone: 216-694-5700	**Officers:** Joseph A. Carrabba - Chairman Laurie Brlas - Executive Vice President, Chief Financial Officer, Division Officer	**Investor Contact:** 216-694-6532
Fax: 216-694-4880		**Transfer Agents:** Wells Fargo Shareowner Services, St. Paul, MN

CLOROX CO.

Exchange	Symbol	Price	52Wk Range	Yield	P/E	Div Achiever
NYS	CLX	$88.53 (3/28/2013)	88.53-67.03	2.89	20.73	36 Years

*7 Year Price Score 103.19 *NYSE Composite Index=100 *12 Month Price Score 103.93

Interim Earnings (Per Share)

Qtr.	Sep	Dec	Mar	Jun
2009-10	1.11	0.77	1.16	1.20
2010-11	1.52	0.15	1.09	1.25
2011-12	0.98	0.79	1.01	1.32
2012-13	1.01	0.93	...	...

Interim Dividends (Per Share)

Amt	Decl	Ex	Rec	Pay
0.64Q	05/14/2012	07/23/2012	07/25/2012	08/10/2012
0.64Q	09/12/2012	10/22/2012	10/24/2012	11/16/2012
0.64Q	11/13/2012	01/18/2013	01/23/2013	02/15/2013
0.64Q	02/13/2013	04/22/2013	04/24/2013	05/10/2013

Indicated Div: $2.56 (Div. Reinv. Plan)

Valuation Analysis

		Institutional Holding	
Forecast EPS	$4.35 (04/05/2013)	No of Institutions	765
Market Cap	$11.6 Billion	Shares	104,144,656
Book Value	$56.0 Million	% Held	69.93
Price/Book	206.88		
Price/Sales	2.07		

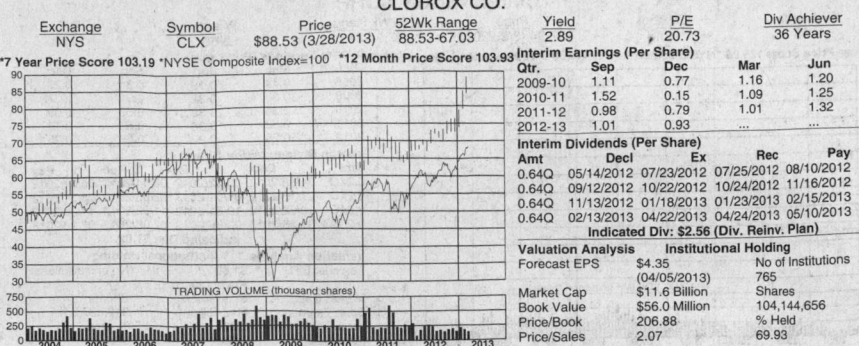

TRADING VOLUME (thousand shares)

Business Summary: Household & Personal Products (MIC: 1.7.1 SIC: 2842 NAIC: 325612)

Clorox principally produces, markets and sells consumer products through mass merchandisers, grocery stores, other retail outlets, distributors and medical supply providers. Co. markets brand names including its bleach and cleaning products, Clorox Healthcare®, HealthLink®, Aplicare® and Dispatch® products, Green Works® home care products, Pine-Sol® cleaners, Poett® home care products, Fresh Step® cat litter, Glad® bags, wraps and containers, Kingsford® charcoal, Hidden Valley® and K C Masterpiece® dressings and sauces, Brita® water-filtration products, and Burt's Bees® and gud® personal care products. Co. has four segments: Cleaning; Household; Lifestyle; and International.

Recent Developments: For the quarter ended Dec 31 2012, net income increased 17.1% to US$123.0 million from US$105.0 million in the year-earlier quarter. Revenues were US$1.33 billion, up 8.5% from US$1.22 billion the year before. Direct operating expenses rose 6.7% to US$762.0 million from US$714.0 million in the comparable period the year before. Indirect operating expenses increased 6.5% to US$375.0 million from US$352.0 million in the equivalent prior-year period.

Prospects: Our evaluation of Clorox Co. as of Apr. 7, 2013 is the result of our systematic analysis on three basic characteristics: earnings strength, relative valuation, and recent stock price movement. The company has managed to produce a neutral trend in earnings per share over the past 5 quarters and while recent estimates for the company have been mixed, CLX has posted better than expected results. Based on operating earnings yield, the company is about fairly valued when compared to all of the companies in our coverage universe. Share price changes over the past year indicates that CLX will perform in line with the market over the near term.

Financial Data
(US$ in Thousands)

	6 Mos	3 Mos	06/30/2012	06/30/2011	06/30/2010	06/30/2009	06/30/2008	06/30/2007
Earnings Per Share	4.27	4.13	4.09	4.02	4.24	3.81	3.24	3.26
Cash Flow Per Share	5.87	5.29	4.66	5.11	5.84	5.31	5.21	4.68
Dividends Per Share	2.480	2.440	2.400	2.200	2.000	1.840	1.600	1.200
Dividend Payout %	58.08	59.08	58.68	54.73	47.17	48.29	49.38	36.81
Income Statement								
Total Revenue	2,663,000	1,338,000	5,468,000	5,231,000	5,534,000	5,450,000	5,273,000	4,847,000
EBITDA	538,000	271,000	1,064,000	815,000	1,227,000	1,143,000	1,041,000	1,024,000
Depn & Amortn	90,000	44,000	167,000	162,000	174,000	180,000	193,000	180,000
Income Before Taxes	382,000	194,000	772,000	533,000	917,000	806,000	692,000	739,000
Income Taxes	126,000	61,000	248,000	276,000	322,000	274,000	232,000	247,000
Net Income	256,000	133,000	541,000	557,000	603,000	537,000	461,000	501,000
Average Shares	132,444	131,702	132,310	138,101	141,534	141,063	142,004	153,935
Balance Sheet								
Current Assets	1,552,000	1,745,000	1,376,000	1,279,000	1,124,000	1,180,000	1,249,000	1,032,000
Total Assets	4,502,000	4,747,000	4,355,000	4,163,000	4,555,000	4,576,000	4,708,000	3,666,000
Current Liabilities	1,373,000	1,725,000	2,061,000	1,365,000	1,647,000	1,937,000	1,661,000	1,427,000
Long-Term Obligations	2,169,000	2,169,000	1,571,000	2,125,000	2,124,000	2,151,000	2,720,000	1,462,000
Total Liabilities	4,446,000	4,767,000	4,490,000	4,249,000	4,472,000	4,751,000	5,078,000	3,495,000
Stockholders' Equity	56,000	(20,000)	(135,000)	(86,000)	83,000	(175,000)	(370,000)	171,000
Shares Outstanding	130,862	130,318	129,562	131,066	138,764	139,157	138,038	151,256
Statistical Record								
Return on Assets %	12.78	12.33	12.67	12.78	13.21	11.57	10.98	13.76
Return on Equity %	...	...	...	...	...	...	...	6,680.00
EBITDA Margin %	20.20	20.25	19.46	15.58	22.17	20.97	19.74	21.13
Net Margin %	9.61	9.94	9.89	10.65	10.90	9.85	8.74	10.34
Asset Turnover	1.28	1.25	1.28	1.20	1.21	1.17	1.26	1.33
Current Ratio	1.13	1.01	0.67	0.94	0.68	0.61	0.75	0.72
Debt to Equity	38.73	...	...	...	25.59	...	...	8.55
Price Range	76.47-67.03	73.44-63.71	74.55-63.71	71.26-61.57	65.32-55.83	63.95-45.90	66.74-51.82	68.50-58.35
P/E Ratio	17.91-15.70	17.78-15.43	18.23-15.58	17.73-15.32	15.41-13.17	16.78-12.05	20.60-15.99	21.01-17.90
Average Yield %	3.48	3.53	3.52	3.33	3.28	3.34	2.68	1.88

Address: 1221 Broadway, Oakland, CA 94612-1888
Telephone: 510-271-7000
Fax: 510-832-1463

Web Site: www.thecloroxcompany.com
Officers: Donald R. Knauss - Chairman, Chief Executive Officer Lawrence S. Peiros - Executive Vice President, Chief Operating Officer

Auditors: Ernst & Young LLP
Transfer Agents: Computershare, Providence, RI

CMS ENERGY CORP

Exchange	Symbol	Price	52Wk Range	Yield	P/E
NYS	CMS	$27.94 (3/28/2013)	27.94-21.52	3.65	19.68

*7 Year Price Score 125.08 *NYSE Composite Index=100 *12 Month Price Score 101.67

Interim Earnings (Per Share)

Qtr.	Mar	Jun	Sep	Dec
2008	0.44	0.19	0.34	0.27
2009	0.30	0.32	0.31	(0.01)
2010	0.34	0.32	0.53	0.09
2011	0.52	0.38	0.53	0.15
2012	0.25	0.37	0.55	0.25

Interim Dividends (Per Share)

Amt	Decl	Ex	Rec	Pay
0.24Q	04/16/2012	05/02/2012	05/04/2012	05/31/2012
0.24Q	07/16/2012	08/01/2012	08/03/2012	08/31/2012
0.24Q	10/22/2012	10/31/2012	11/02/2012	11/30/2012
0.255Q	01/25/2013	02/06/2013	02/08/2013	02/28/2013

Indicated Div: $1.02

Valuation Analysis

		Institutional Holding	
Forecast EPS	$1.65	No of Institutions	
	(04/05/2013)	471	
Market Cap	$7.4 Billion	Shares	
Book Value	$3.2 Billion	242,887,264	
Price/Book	2.31	% Held	
Price/Sales	1.18	87.49	

Business Summary: Electric Utilities (MIC: 3.1.1 SIC: 4931 NAIC: 221119)

CMS Energy is an energy company. Co. has several subsidiaries, including Consumers Energy Company (Consumers), an electric and gas utility, and CMS Enterprises Company (CMS Enterprises), primarily a domestic independent power producer. Consumers serves individuals and businesses operating in the alternative energy, automotive, chemical, metal, and food products industries, and a group of other industries. CMS Enterprises, through its subsidiaries and equity investments, is engaged primarily in independent power production. Co. has three business segments: electric utility, gas utility, and enterprises, its non-utility operations and investments.

Recent Developments: For the year ended Dec 31 2012, income from continuing operations decreased 9.2% to US$377.0 million from US$415.0 million a year earlier. Net income decreased 7.9% to US$384.0 million from US$417.0 million in the prior year. Revenues were US$6.25 billion, down 3.8% from US$6.50 billion the year before. Operating income was unchanged at US$1.00 billion versus the prior year. Direct operating expenses declined 8.9% to US$3.20 billion from US$3.51 billion in the comparable period the year before. Indirect operating expenses increased 3.2% to US$2.05 billion from US$1.99 billion in the equivalent prior-year period.

Prospects: Our evaluation of CMS Energy Corp. as of Apr. 7, 2013 is the result of our systematic analysis on three basic characteristics: earnings strength, relative valuation, and recent stock price movement. The company has managed to produce a neutral trend in earnings per share over the past 5 quarters and while recent estimates for the company have remained steady, CMS has posted better than expected results. Based on operating earnings yield, the company is undervalued when compared to all of the companies in our coverage universe. Share price changes over the past year indicates that CMS will perform in line with the market over the near term.

Financial Data
(US$ in Millions)

	12/31/2012	12/31/2011	12/31/2010	12/31/2009	12/31/2008	12/31/2007	12/31/2006	12/31/2005
Earnings Per Share	1.42	1.58	1.28	0.91	1.23	(1.02)	(0.41)	(0.44)
Cash Flow Per Share	4.75	4.66	4.14	3.73	2.49	0.12	3.13	3.05
Tang Book Value Per Share	12.09	11.92	11.19	11.42	10.88	9.46	9.91	10.41
Dividends Per Share	0.960	0.840	0.660	0.500	0.360	0.200	...	...
Dividend Payout %	67.61	53.16	51.56	54.95	29.27	...	...	...
Income Statement								
Total Revenue	6,253	6,503	6,432	6,205	6,821	6,464	6,810	6,288
EBITDA	1,604	1,558	1,618	1,360	1,431	592	608	152
Depn & Amortn	598	546	616	612	625	600	620	565
Income Before Taxes	622	606	590	337	444	(350)	(432)	(831)
Income Taxes	245	191	224	115	142	(195)	(158)	(168)
Net Income	382	415	340	229	300	(215)	(79)	(84)
Average Shares	268	263	252	237	234	222	219	211
Balance Sheet								
Current Assets	2,422	2,565	2,759	2,742	2,827	2,884	3,143	3,899
Total Assets	17,131	16,452	15,616	15,256	14,901	14,196	15,371	16,020
Current Liabilities	1,797	2,338	2,021	1,954	1,863	2,477	2,156	2,113
Long-Term Obligations	6,863	6,207	6,636	6,092	6,243	5,788	6,422	7,286
Total Liabilities	13,937	13,424	12,823	12,415	12,151	11,772	12,832	13,393
Stockholders' Equity	3,194	3,028	2,793	2,841	2,750	2,424	2,539	2,627
Shares Outstanding	264	254	249	227	226	225	222	220
Statistical Record								
Return on Assets %	2.27	2.59	2.20	1.52	2.06	N.M.	N.M.	N.M.
Return on Equity %	12.25	14.26	12.07	8.19	11.56	N.M.	N.M.	N.M.
EBITDA Margin %	25.65	23.96	25.16	21.92	20.98	9.16	8.93	2.42
Net Margin %	6.11	6.38	5.29	3.69	4.40	N.M.	N.M.	N.M.
Asset Turnover	0.37	0.41	0.42	0.41	0.47	0.44	0.43	0.39
Current Ratio	1.35	1.10	1.37	1.40	1.52	1.16	1.46	1.85
Debt to Equity	2.15	2.05	2.38	2.14	2.27	2.39	2.53	2.77
Price Range	24.81-21.33	22.35-17.16	19.16-14.26	16.04-10.09	17.38-8.81	18.93-15.48	16.95-12.46	16.71-9.81
P/E Ratio	17.47-15.02	14.15-10.86	14.97-11.14	17.63-11.09	14.13-7.16	...	...	...
Average Yield %	4.16	4.26	3.98	3.97	2.69	1.16	...	...

Address: One Energy Plaza, Jackson, MI 49201 **Telephone:** 517-788-0550	**Web Site:** www.cmsenergy.com **Officers:** John G. Russell - President, Chief Executive Officer Thomas J. Webb - Executive Vice President, Chief Financial Officer	**Auditors:** PricewaterhouseCoopers LLP **Investor Contact:** 517-788-1868 **Transfer Agents:** Investor Services Department, Jackson, MI

CNA FINANCIAL CORP.

Exchange	Symbol	Price	52Wk Range	Yield	P/E
NYS	CNA	$32.69 (3/28/2013)	32.69-25.91	2.45	14.03

*7 Year Price Score 89.55 *NYSE Composite Index=100 *12 Month Price Score 101.89

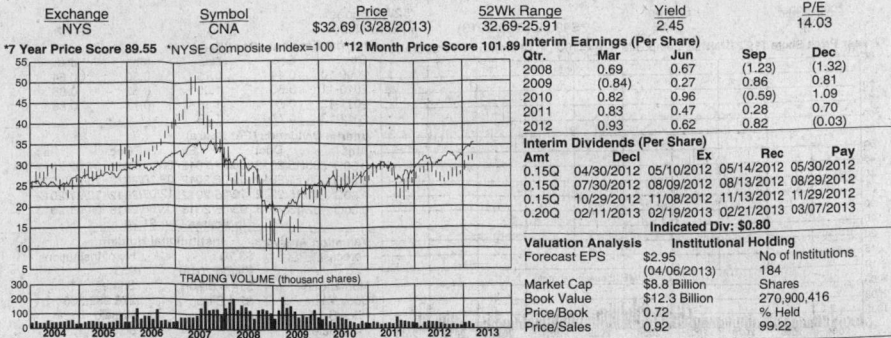

Interim Earnings (Per Share)

Qtr.	Mar	Jun	Sep	Dec
2008	0.69	0.67	(1.23)	(1.32)
2009	(0.84)	0.27	0.86	0.81
2010	0.82	0.96	(0.59)	1.09
2011	0.83	0.47	0.28	0.70
2012	0.93	0.62	0.82	(0.03)

Interim Dividends (Per Share)

Amt	Decl	Ex	Rec	Pay
0.15Q	04/30/2012	05/10/2012	05/14/2012	05/30/2012
0.15Q	07/30/2012	08/09/2012	08/13/2012	08/29/2012
0.15Q	10/29/2012	11/08/2012	11/13/2012	11/29/2012
0.20Q	02/11/2013	02/19/2013	02/21/2013	03/07/2013

Indicated Div: $0.80

Valuation Analysis		Institutional Holding	
Forecast EPS	$2.95	No of Institutions	
	(04/06/2013)	184	
Market Cap	$8.8 Billion	Shares	
Book Value	$12.3 Billion	270,900,416	
Price/Book	0.72	% Held	
Price/Sales	0.92	99.22	

Business Summary: General Insurance (MIC: 5.2.1 SIC: 6331 NAIC: 524126)

CNA Financial is an insurance holding company. Co.'s insurance products primarily include commercial property and casualty coverages, including surety. Co.'s services include risk management, information services, warranty and claims administration. Co.'s products and services are primarily marketed through independent agents, brokers and managing general underwriters to a variety of customers. Co.'s core property and casualty commercial insurance operations are reported in three business segments: CNA Specialty, CNA Commercial and Hardy. Co.'s non-core operations are managed in two segments: Life & Group Non-Core and Corporate & Other Non-Core.

Recent Developments: For the year ended Dec 31 2012, income from continuing operations decreased 0.2% to US$628.0 million from US$629.0 million a year earlier. Net income was unchanged at US$628.0 million versus US$628.0 million the prior year. Revenues were US$9.55 billion, up 6.7% from US$8.95 billion the year before. Net premiums earned were US$6.88 billion versus US$6.60 billion in the prior year, an increase of 4.2%. Net investment income rose 11.1% to US$2.28 billion from US$2.05 billion a year ago.

Prospects: Our evaluation of CNA Financial Corp. as of Apr. 7, 2013 is the result of our systematic analysis on three basic characteristics: earnings strength, relative valuation, and recent stock price movement. The company has suffered a very negative trend in earnings per share over the past 5 quarters and while recent estimates for the company have remained steady, CNA has posted results that fell short of analysts expectations. Based on operating earnings yield, the company is undervalued when compared to all of the companies in our coverage universe. Share price changes over the past year indicates that CNA will perform poorly over the near term.

Financial Data
(US$ in Thousands)

	12/31/2012	12/31/2011	12/31/2010	12/31/2009	12/31/2008	12/31/2007	12/31/2006	12/31/2005
Earnings Per Share	2.33	2.28	2.28	1.10	(1.18)	3.13	4.05	0.76
Cash Flow Per Share	4.63	6.32	(0.33)	4.68	5.77	4.56	8.58	8.47
Tang Book Value Per Share	45.14	42.40	40.18	35.38	20.39	36.84	35.51	31.46
Dividends Per Share	0.600	0.400	...	...	0.450	0.350	...	...
Dividend Payout %	25.75	17.54	...	...	...	11.18	...	...
Income Statement								
Premium Income	6,882,000	6,603,000	6,515,000	6,721,000	7,151,000	7,484,000	7,603,000	7,569,000
Total Revenue	9,547,000	8,947,000	9,209,000	8,472,000	7,799,000	9,885,000	10,376,000	9,862,000
Income Before Taxes	872,000	877,000	1,112,000	540,000	(562,000)	1,222,000	1,650,000	162,000
Income Taxes	244,000	246,000	333,000	57,000	(311,000)	317,000	469,000	(105,000)
Net Income	628,000	614,000	690,000	419,000	(299,000)	851,000	1,108,000	264,000
Average Shares	269,800	269,600	269,500	269,100	269,400	271,800	262,300	256,000
Balance Sheet								
Total Assets	58,522,000	55,179,000	55,331,000	55,298,000	51,688,000	56,732,000	60,283,000	58,786,000
Total Liabilities	46,208,000	43,622,000	44,377,000	44,638,000	44,811,000	46,582,000	50,515,000	49,836,000
Stockholders' Equity	12,314,000	11,557,000	10,954,000	10,660,000	6,877,000	10,150,000	9,768,000	8,950,000
Shares Outstanding	269,399	269,274	269,139	269,026	269,024	271,662	271,108	256,001
Statistical Record								
Return on Assets %	1.10	1.11	1.25	0.78	N.M.	1.45	1.86	0.44
Return on Equity %	5.25	5.46	6.38	4.78	N.M.	8.55	11.84	2.91
Net Margin %	6.58	6.86	7.49	4.95	(3.83)	8.61	10.68	2.68
Price Range	30.67-25.91	31.04-21.58	28.99-22.15	25.99-6.49	34.23-9.36	51.81-32.70	40.32-29.88	34.91-25.84
P/E Ratio	13.16-11.12	13.61-9.46	12.71-9.71	23.63-5.90	...	16.55-10.45	9.96-7.38	45.93-34.00
Average Yield %	2.14	1.48	...	...	1.82	0.83	...	...

Address: 333 S. Wabash, Chicago, IL 60604	Web Site: www.cna.com	Auditors: Deloitte & Touche LLP
Telephone: 312-822-5000	Officers: Thomas F. Motamed - Chairman, Chief Executive Officer D. Craig Mense - Executive Vice President, Chief Financial Officer	Investor Contact: 312-822-4278
Fax: 312-822-6419		Transfer Agents: Wells Fargo Bank, N.A., St. Paul, MN

COACH, INC.

Exchange	Symbol	Price	52Wk Range	Yield	P/E
NYS	COH	$49.99 (3/28/2013)	78.46-46.50	2.40	13.77

*7 Year Price Score 119.77 *NYSE Composite Index=100   *12 Month Price Score 77.43

Interim Earnings (Per Share)

Qtr.	Sep	Dec	Mar	Jun
2009-10	0.44	0.75	0.50	0.64
2010-11	0.63	1.00	0.62	0.68
2011-12	0.73	1.18	0.77	0.86
2012-13	0.77	1.23	...	...

Interim Dividends (Per Share)

Amt	Decl	Ex	Rec	Pay
0.30Q	05/15/2012	05/31/2012	06/04/2012	07/02/2012
0.30Q	08/21/2012	09/06/2012	09/10/2012	10/01/2012
0.30Q	11/15/2012	12/05/2012	12/07/2012	12/27/2012
0.30Q	02/13/2013	03/06/2013	03/08/2013	04/01/2013

Indicated Div: $1.20

Valuation Analysis

Forecast EPS	$3.70
	(04/06/2013)
Market Cap	$14.0 Billion
Book Value	$2.1 Billion
Price/Book	6.74
Price/Sales	2.85

Institutional Holding

No of Institutions	953
Shares	278,982,336
% Held	86.78

Business Summary: Apparel, Footwear & Accessories (MIC: 1.4.2 SIC: 3171 NAIC: 316992)

Coach is a marketer of accessories and gifts for women and men. Co.'s product offerings include women's and men's bags, accessories, business cases, footwear, wearables, jewelry, sunwear, travel bags, watches and fragrance. Co. operates in two business segments: Direct-to-Consumer and Indirect. Direct-to-Consumer, which includes sales to consumers through Co.-operated stores in North America; Japan; Hong Kong, Macau and mainland China; Taiwan; Singapore and the Internet; and Indirect, which includes sales to wholesale customers and distributors in over 20 countries, including the U.S., and royalties earned on licensed product.

Recent Developments: For the quarter ended Dec 29 2012, net income increased 1.5% to US$352.8 million from US$347.5 million in the year-earlier quarter. Revenues were US$1.50 billion, up 3.8% from US$1.45 billion the year before. Operating income was US$526.6 million versus US$500.9 million in the prior-year quarter, an increase of 5.1%. Direct operating expenses rose 3.7% to US$418.4 million from US$403.4 million in the comparable period the year before. Indirect operating expenses increased 2.7% to US$558.8 million from US$544.3 million in the equivalent prior-year period.

Prospects: Our evaluation of Coach Inc. as of Apr. 7, 2013 is the result of our systematic analysis on three basic characteristics: earnings strength, relative valuation, and recent stock price movement. The company has managed to produce a neutral trend in earnings per share over the past 5 quarters. However, while recent estimates for the company have been lowered by analysts, COH has posted results that fell short of analysts expectations. Based on operating earnings yield, the company is undervalued when compared to all of the companies in our coverage universe. Share price changes over the past year indicates that COH will perform very poorly over the near term.

Financial Data

(US$ in Thousands)	6 Mos	3 Mos	06/30/2012	07/02/2011	07/03/2010	06/27/2009	06/28/2008	06/30/2007
Earnings Per Share	3.63	3.58	3.53	2.92	2.33	1.91	2.17	1.76
Cash Flow Per Share	4.30	4.21	4.25	3.51	3.13	2.51	2.60	2.11
Tang Book Value Per Share	6.04	5.56	5.64	4.41	4.01	4.41	3.73	4.52
Dividends Per Share	1.125	1.050	0.975	0.675	0.375	0.075	...	...
Dividend Payout %	30.99	29.33	27.62	23.12	16.09	3.93	...	...
Income Statement								
Total Revenue	2,665,124	1,161,350	4,763,180	4,158,507	3,607,636	3,230,468	3,180,757	2,612,456
EBITDA	931,598	365,749	1,637,852	1,425,294	1,276,915	1,094,927	1,247,833	1,074,284
Depn & Amortn	76,881	36,104	132,909	125,106	126,744	123,014	100,704	80,887
Income Before Taxes	855,019	329,681	1,505,663	1,301,219	1,151,928	977,081	1,194,949	1,034,670
Income Taxes	280,874	108,300	466,753	420,419	416,988	353,712	411,910	398,141
Net Income	574,145	221,381	1,038,910	880,800	734,940	623,369	783,055	663,665
Average Shares	286,223	288,497	294,129	301,558	315,848	325,620	360,332	377,356
Balance Sheet								
Current Assets	1,848,367	1,768,587	1,804,528	1,452,388	1,302,641	1,396,409	1,385,709	1,740,196
Total Assets	3,279,429	3,151,378	3,104,321	2,635,116	2,467,115	2,564,336	2,273,844	2,449,512
Current Liabilities	768,936	730,903	718,160	593,017	529,036	459,652	450,941	407,996
Long-Term Obligations	485	985	985	23,360	24,159	25,072	2,580	2,865
Total Liabilities	1,197,097	1,157,285	1,111,390	1,022,547	961,822	868,294	758,024	539,158
Stockholders' Equity	2,082,332	1,994,093	1,992,931	1,612,569	1,505,293	1,696,042	1,515,820	1,910,354
Shares Outstanding	280,630	283,641	285,118	288,514	296,867	318,006	336,728	372,521
Statistical Record								
Return on Assets %	32.93	34.67	36.30	34.62	28.74	25.84	33.25	32.65
Return on Equity %	53.18	54.86	57.79	56.66	45.17	38.92	45.84	42.95
EBITDA Margin %	34.96	31.49	34.39	34.27	35.39	33.89	39.23	41.12
Net Margin %	21.54	19.06	21.81	21.18	20.37	19.30	24.62	25.40
Asset Turnover	1.55	1.62	1.66	1.63	1.41	1.34	1.35	1.29
Current Ratio	2.40	2.42	2.51	2.45	2.46	3.04	3.07	4.27
Debt to Equity	N.M.	N.M.	N.M.	0.01	0.02	0.01	N.M.	N.M.
Price Range	79.03-49.33	79.03-49.33	79.03-45.96	65.99-34.37	44.32-23.56	31.19-11.73	50.70-24.62	53.79-25.58
P/E Ratio	21.77-13.59	22.08-13.78	22.39-13.02	22.60-11.77	19.02-10.11	16.33-6.14	23.36-11.35	30.56-14.53
Average Yield %	1.79	1.64	1.51	1.33	1.06	0.35	...	...

Address: 516 West 34th Street, New York, NY 10001 **Telephone:** 212-594-1850 **Fax:** 212-594-1682	**Web Site:** www.coach.com **Officers:** Lew Frankfort - Chairman, Chief Executive Officer Jerry Stritzke - President, Chief Operating Officer	**Auditors:** Deloitte & Touche LLP **Transfer Agents:** Mellon Investor Services, Jersey City, NJ

COBALT INTERNATIONAL ENERGY INC.

Exchange	Symbol	Price	52Wk Range	Yield	P/E
NYS	CIE	$28.20 (3/28/2013)	31.36-20.11	N/A	N/A

*7 Year Price Score N/A   *NYSE Composite Index=100   *12 Month Price Score 96.41

Interim Earnings (Per Share)

Qtr.	Mar	Jun	Sep	Dec
2010	(0.09)	(0.12)	(0.10)	(0.08)
2011	(0.05)	(0.05)	(0.12)	(0.13)
2012	(0.09)	(0.35)	(0.10)	(0.16)

Interim Dividends (Per Share)

No Dividends Paid

Valuation Analysis   **Institutional Holding**

Forecast EPS	$-0.57	No of Institutions
	(04/06/2013)	265
Market Cap	$11.5 Billion	Shares
Book Value	$2.7 Billion	563,047,296
Price/Book	4.26	% Held
Price/Sales	N/A	N/A

Business Summary: Production & Extraction (MIC: 9.1.1 SIC: 1311 NAIC: 211111)

Cobalt International Energy is a holding company. Through its subsidiaries, Co. is engaged as an oil-focused exploration and production company with prospect inventory in the deepwater of the U.S. Gulf of Mexico and offshore Angola and Gabon in West Africa. Co. has two geographic operating segments: the Deepwater U.S. Gulf of Mexico, where Co. primarily targets subsalt Miocene and Lower Tertiary horizons and owned working interests in 231 blocks within the deepwater as of Dec 31 2011; and West Africa Deepwater, where Co. has licenses with pre-salt and above salt exploration potential offshore Angola and Gabon.

Recent Developments: For the year ended Dec 31 2012, net loss amounted to US$283.0 million versus a net loss of US$133.6 million in the prior year. Operating loss was US$284.8 million versus a loss of US$137.8 million in the prior year. Direct operating expenses rose 91.0% to US$61.6 million from US$32.2 million in the comparable period the year before. Indirect operating expenses increased 111.4% to US$223.2 million from US$105.6 million in the equivalent prior-year period.

Prospects: Our evaluation of Cobalt International Energy Inc. as of Apr. 7, 2013 is the result of our systematic analysis on three basic characteristics: earnings strength, relative valuation, and recent stock price movement. The company has generated a negative trend in earnings per share over the past 5 quarters. Because the company lacks sufficient analyst estimate data, we place greater weight on the historical EPS trend as the measure of earnings strength. Based on operating earnings yield, the company is overvalued when compared to all of the companies in our coverage universe. Share price changes over the past year indicates that CIE will perform very poorly over the near term.

Financial Data
(US$ in Thousands)

	12/31/2012	12/31/2011	12/31/2010	12/31/2009	12/31/2008	12/31/2007	12/31/2006
Earnings Per Share	(0.70)	(0.35)	(0.39)	...	...	...	...
Cash Flow Per Share	(0.35)	(0.15)	(0.38)	...	...	...	...
Tang Book Value Per Share	6.61	5.36	4.90	5.11	...	...	...
Income Statement							
EBITDA	(283,628)	(137,136)	(137,258)	(81,070)	(72,545)	(109,902)	(111,857)
Depn & Amortn	1,200	700	800	700	683	436	292
Income Before Taxes	(282,999)	(133,637)	(136,476)	(81,257)	(71,596)	(108,954)	(111,527)
Net Income	(282,999)	(133,637)	(136,476)	(81,257)	(71,596)	(108,954)	(111,527)
Average Shares	403,356	376,603	349,342	...	...	...	...
Balance Sheet							
Current Assets	2,456,742	1,335,094	889,632	1,154,487	23,819	99,371	...
Total Assets	4,011,459	2,527,944	1,746,443	1,812,105	784,604	254,658	...
Current Liabilities	160,956	238,069	24,559	70,523	44,133	10,785	...
Long-Term Obligations	991,191	...	...	...	...	...	...
Total Liabilities	1,322,241	449,030	27,409	70,523	44,133	10,785	...
Stockholders' Equity	2,689,218	2,078,914	1,719,034	1,741,582	740,471	(221,870)	...
Shares Outstanding	406,596	387,531	350,733	340,517	...	...	...
Statistical Record							
Current Ratio	15.26	5.61	36.22	16.37	0.54	9.21	...
Debt to Equity	0.37	...	...	...	...	...	...
Price Range	33.03-15.86	16.81-7.06	15.72-6.52	13.88-13.34	...	...	...

Address: Cobalt Center, 920 Memorial City Way, Suite 100, Houston, TX 77024 **Telephone:** 713-579-9100	**Web Site:** www.cobaltintl.com **Officers:** Joseph H. Bryant - Chairman, Chief Executive Officer John P. Wilkirson - Executive Vice President, Chief Financial Officer	**Auditors:** Ernst & Young LLP **Investor Contact:** 713-452-2322 **Transfer Agents:** Continental Stock Transfer & Trust Company

COCA-COLA CO (THE)

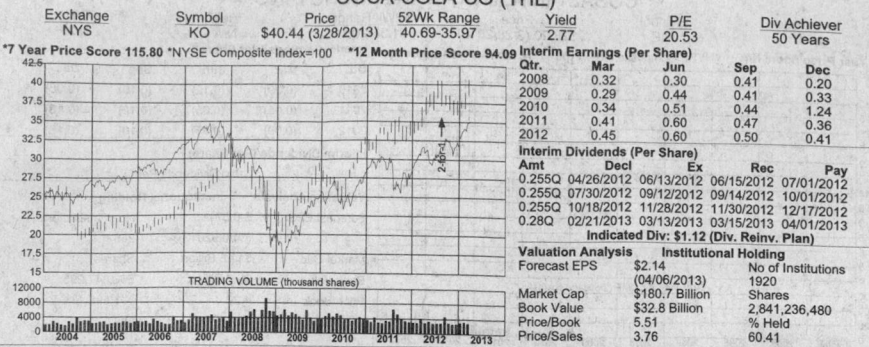

Exchange	Symbol	Price	52Wk Range	Yield	P/E	Div Achiever
NYS	KO	$40.44 (3/28/2013)	40.69-35.97	2.77	20.53	50 Years

*7 Year Price Score 115.80 *NYSE Composite Index=100   *12 Month Price Score 94.09

Interim Earnings (Per Share)

Qtr.	Mar	Jun	Sep	Dec
2008	0.32	0.30	0.41	0.20
2009	0.29	0.44	0.41	0.33
2010	0.34	0.51	0.44	1.24
2011	0.41	0.60	0.47	0.36
2012	0.45	0.60	0.50	0.41

Interim Dividends (Per Share)

Amt	Decl	Ex	Rec	Pay
0.255Q	04/26/2012	06/13/2012	06/15/2012	07/01/2012
0.255Q	07/30/2012	09/12/2012	09/14/2012	10/01/2012
0.255Q	10/18/2012	11/28/2012	11/30/2012	12/17/2012
0.28Q	02/21/2013	03/13/2013	03/15/2013	04/01/2013

Indicated Div: $1.12 (Div. Reinv. Plan)

Valuation Analysis   **Institutional Holding**

Forecast EPS	$2.14 (04/06/2013)	No of Institutions 1920
Market Cap	$180.7 Billion	Shares
Book Value	$32.8 Billion	2,841,236,480
Price/Book	5.51	% Held
Price/Sales	3.76	60.41

Business Summary: Beverages (MIC: 1.2.2 SIC: 2086 NAIC: 312111)

Coca-Cola is a beverage company. Co. owns or licenses and markets nonalcoholic beverage brands, primarily sparkling beverages and a range of still beverages such as waters, enhanced waters, juices and juice drinks, ready-to-drink teas and coffees, and energy and sports drinks. Co.'s primary nonalcoholic sparkling beverage brands include Coca-Cola, Diet Coke, Fanta, and Sprite. Co. markets, manufactures and sells beverage concentrates and syrups, including fountain syrups, and finished sparkling and still beverages. Co. also distributes certain Monster brands, primarily Monster Energy beverages, and certain Dr Pepper Snapple Group, Inc. brands, in certain territories in the U.S. and Canada.

Recent Developments: For the year ended Dec 31 2012, net income increased 5.1% to US$9.09 billion from US$8.65 billion in the prior year. Revenues were US$48.02 billion, up 3.2% from US$46.54 billion the year before. Operating income was US$10.78 billion versus US$10.17 billion in the prior year, an increase of 6.0%. Direct operating expenses rose 4.6% to US$19.05 billion from US$18.22 billion in the comparable period the year before. Indirect operating expenses increased 0.2% to US$18.19 billion from US$18.15 billion in the equivalent prior-year period.

Prospects: Our evaluation of Coca-Cola Co as of Apr. 7, 2013 is the result of our systematic analysis on three basic characteristics: earnings strength, relative valuation, and recent stock price movement. The company has managed to produce a neutral trend in earnings per share over the past 5 quarters and while recent estimates for the company have remained steady, KO has posted better than expected results. Based on operating earnings yield, the company is about fairly valued when compared to all of the companies in our coverage universe. Share price changes over the past year indicates that KO will perform poorly over the near term.

Financial Data

(US$ in Thousands)	12/31/2012	12/31/2011	12/31/2010	12/31/2009	12/31/2008	12/31/2007	12/31/2006	12/31/2005
Earnings Per Share	1.97	1.85	2.53	1.47	1.25	1.28	1.08	1.02
Cash Flow Per Share	2.36	2.07	2.06	1.77	1.63	1.55	1.27	1.34
Tang Book Value Per Share	1.22	0.88	0.89	2.60	1.72	2.05	2.54	2.65
Dividends Per Share	1.020	0.940	0.880	0.820	0.760	0.680	0.620	0.560
Dividend Payout %	51.78	50.95	34.78	55.97	61.04	52.92	57.41	54.90
Income Statement								
Total Revenue	48,017,000	46,542,000	35,119,000	30,990,000	31,944,000	28,857,000	24,088,000	23,104,000
EBITDA	12,639,000	12,355,000	14,838,000	9,294,000	9,430,000	8,404,000	7,266,000	6,767,000
Depn & Amortn	1,723,000	1,672,000	1,204,000	1,023,000	1,012,000	979,000	763,000	752,000
Income Before Taxes	10,990,000	10,749,000	13,218,000	8,165,000	8,313,000	7,205,000	6,476,000	6,010,000
Income Taxes	2,723,000	2,805,000	2,384,000	2,040,000	1,632,000	1,892,000	1,498,000	1,818,000
Net Income	9,019,000	8,572,000	11,809,000	6,824,000	5,807,000	5,981,000	5,080,000	4,872,000
Average Shares	4,583,999	4,645,999	4,665,999	4,657,999	4,671,999	4,661,999	4,699,999	4,785,999
Balance Sheet								
Current Assets	30,328,000	25,497,000	21,579,000	17,551,000	12,176,000	12,105,000	8,441,000	10,250,000
Total Assets	86,174,000	79,974,000	72,921,000	48,671,000	40,519,000	43,269,000	29,963,000	29,427,000
Current Liabilities	27,821,000	24,283,000	18,508,000	13,721,000	12,988,000	13,225,000	8,890,000	9,836,000
Long-Term Obligations	14,736,000	13,656,000	14,041,000	5,059,000	2,781,000	3,277,000	1,314,000	1,154,000
Total Liabilities	53,384,000	48,339,000	41,918,000	23,872,000	20,047,000	21,525,000	13,043,000	13,072,000
Stockholders' Equity	32,790,000	31,635,000	31,003,000	24,799,000	20,472,000	21,744,000	16,920,000	16,355,000
Shares Outstanding	4,468,999	4,525,999	4,583,999	4,605,999	4,623,999	4,635,999	4,635,999	4,737,999
Statistical Record								
Return on Assets %	10.83	11.21	19.42	15.30	13.82	16.33	17.11	16.04
Return on Equity %	27.92	27.37	42.32	30.15	27.44	30.94	30.53	30.18
EBITDA Margin %	26.32	26.55	42.25	29.99	29.52	29.12	30.16	29.29
Net Margin %	18.78	18.42	33.63	22.02	18.18	20.73	21.09	21.09
Asset Turnover	0.58	0.61	0.58	0.69	0.76	0.79	0.81	0.76
Current Ratio	1.09	1.05	1.17	1.28	0.94	0.92	0.95	1.04
Debt to Equity	0.45	0.43	0.45	0.20	0.14	0.15	0.08	0.07
Price Range	40.56-33.49	35.62-30.80	32.88-25.02	29.56-18.93	32.78-20.50	32.05-22.95	24.50-20.05	22.63-20.16
P/E Ratio	20.59-17.00	19.25-16.65	13.00-9.89	20.11-12.87	26.22-16.40	25.04-17.93	22.69-18.56	22.18-19.76
Average Yield %	2.75	2.82	3.11	3.36	2.82	2.53	2.83	2.62

Address: One Coca-Cola Plaza, Atlanta, GA 30313
Telephone: 404-676-2121
Fax: 404-676-6792

Web Site: www.thecoca-colacompany.com
Officers: Ahmet Muhtar Kent - Chairman, President, Chief Executive Officer Alexander B. Cummings - Executive Vice President, Chief Administrative Officer

Auditors: Ernst & Young LLP
Investor Contact: 404-676-2777
Transfer Agents: Computershare Trust Company N.A

COCA-COLA ENTERPRISES INC

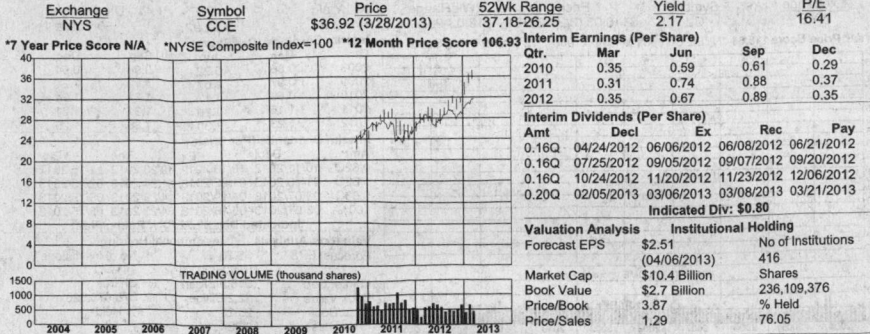

Exchange	Symbol	Price	52Wk Range	Yield	P/E
NYS	CCE	$36.92 (3/28/2013)	37.18-26.25	2.17	16.41

*7 Year Price Score N/A   *NYSE Composite Index=100   *12 Month Price Score 106.93

Interim Earnings (Per Share)

Qtr.	Mar	Jun	Sep	Dec
2010	0.35	0.59	0.61	0.29
2011	0.31	0.74	0.88	0.37
2012	0.35	0.67	0.89	0.35

Interim Dividends (Per Share)

Amt	Decl	Ex	Rec	Pay
0.16Q	04/24/2012	06/06/2012	06/08/2012	06/21/2012
0.16Q	07/25/2012	09/05/2012	09/07/2012	09/20/2012
0.16Q	10/24/2012	11/20/2012	11/23/2012	12/06/2012
0.20Q	02/05/2013	03/06/2013	03/08/2013	03/21/2013

Indicated Div: $0.80

Valuation Analysis

		Institutional Holding	
Forecast EPS	$2.51	No of Institutions	
	(04/06/2013)	416	
Market Cap	$10.4 Billion	Shares	
Book Value	$2.7 Billion	236,109,376	
Price/Book	3.87	% Held	
Price/Sales	1.29	76.05	

Business Summary: Beverages (MIC: 1.2.2 SIC: 2086 NAIC: 312111)

Coca-Cola Enterprises is engaged in marketing, producing, and distributing nonalcoholic beverages. Co. conducts its business primarily under agreements with The Coca-Cola Company (TCCC). These agreements give Co. the exclusive right to market, produce, and distribute beverage products of TCCC in specified territories. Co.'s bottling territories consist of Belgium, continental France, Great Britain, Luxembourg, Monaco, the Netherlands, Norway, and Sweden. Co. has bottling rights within its territories for various beverages, including products with the name Coca-Cola. Other primary brands in Co.'s beverage portfolio include Diet Coke/Coca-Cola light, Coca-Cola Zero, Fanta, and Capri-Sun.

Recent Developments: For the year ended Dec 31 2012, net income decreased 9.6% to US$677.0 million from US$749.0 million in the prior year. Revenues were US$8.06 billion, down 2.7% from US$8.28 billion the year before. Operating income was US$928.0 million versus US$1.03 billion in the prior year, a decrease of 10.2%. Direct operating expenses declined 1.8% to US$5.16 billion from US$5.25 billion in the comparable period the year before. Indirect operating expenses decreased 1.3% to US$1.97 billion from US$2.00 billion in the equivalent prior-year period.

Prospects: Our evaluation of Coca-Cola Enterprises Inc. as of Apr. 7, 2013 is the result of our systematic analysis on three basic characteristics: earnings strength, relative valuation, and recent stock price movement. The company has managed to produce a neutral trend in earnings per share over the past 5 quarters. However, while recent estimates for the company have been lowered by analysts, CCE has posted better than expected results. Based on operating earnings yield, the company is undervalued when compared to all of the companies in our coverage universe. Share price changes over the past year indicates that CCE will perform well over the near term.

Financial Data
(US$ in Millions)

	12/31/2012	12/31/2011	12/31/2010	12/31/2009	12/31/2008	12/31/2007
Earnings Per Share	2.25	2.29	1.83	...	...	...
Cash Flow Per Share	3.21	2.70	...	...	...	...
Dividends Per Share	0.640	0.510	0.120	...	...	...
Dividend Payout %	28.44	22.27	6.56	...	...	...
Income Statement						
Total Revenue	8,062	8,284	6,714	6,517	6,619	6,246
EBITDA	1,266	1,351	1,073	1,090	1,042	1,012
Depn & Amortn	335	321	264	280	294	297
Income Before Taxes	837	945	746	727	629	568
Income Taxes	160	196	122	151	115	44
Net Income	677	749	624	576	514	524
Average Shares	301	327	340	...	...	...
Balance Sheet						
Current Assets	2,762	2,686	2,230	2,356	1,985	...
Total Assets	9,510	9,094	8,596	7,972	7,071	...
Current Liabilities	2,579	1,848	1,942	2,192	1,946	...
Long-Term Obligations	2,834	2,996	2,124	235	500	...
Total Liabilities	6,817	6,195	5,453	4,793	4,645	...
Stockholders' Equity	2,693	2,899	3,143	3,179	2,426	...
Shares Outstanding	282	304	332	...	...	...
Statistical Record						
Return on Assets %	7.26	8.47	...	7.66	...	...
Return on Equity %	24.15	24.79	...	20.55	...	...
EBITDA Margin %	15.70	16.31	15.98	16.73	15.74	16.20
Net Margin %	8.40	9.04	9.29	8.84	7.77	8.39
Asset Turnover	0.86	0.94	...	0.87	...	...
Current Ratio	1.07	1.45	1.15	1.07	1.02	...
Debt to Equity	1.05	1.03	0.68	0.07	0.21	...
Price Range	32.24-25.46	29.82-23.61	25.93-22.01	...	...	...
P/E Ratio	14.33-11.32	13.02-10.31	14.17-12.03	...	...	...
Average Yield %	2.20	1.91	0.49	...	...	...

Address: 2500 Windy Ridge Parkway, Atlanta, GA 30339
Telephone: 678-260-3000

Web Site: www.cokecce.com
Officers: John F. Brock - Chairman, Chief Executive Officer William W. Douglas - Executive Vice President, Chief Financial Officer

Auditors: Ernst & Young LLP
Transfer Agents: Computershare Trust Company, N.A., Providence, RI

COLGATE-PALMOLIVE CO.

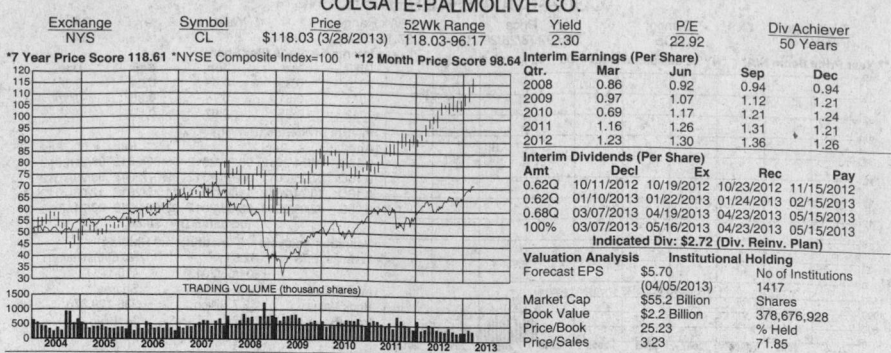

Exchange	Symbol	Price	52Wk Range	Yield	P/E	Div Achiever
NYS	CL	$118.03 (3/28/2013)	118.03-96.17	2.30	22.92	50 Years

*7 Year Price Score 118.61 *NYSE Composite Index=100   *12 Month Price Score 98.64

Interim Earnings (Per Share)

Qtr.	Mar	Jun	Sep	Dec
2008	0.86	0.92	0.94	0.94
2009	0.97	1.07	1.12	1.21
2010	0.69	1.17	1.21	1.24
2011	1.16	1.26	1.31	1.21
2012	1.23	1.30	1.36	1.26

Interim Dividends (Per Share)

Amt	Decl	Ex	Rec	Pay
0.62Q	10/11/2012	10/19/2012	10/23/2012	11/15/2012
0.62Q	01/10/2013	01/22/2013	01/24/2013	02/15/2013
0.68Q	03/07/2013	04/19/2013	04/23/2013	05/15/2013
100%	03/07/2013	05/16/2013	04/23/2013	05/15/2013

Indicated Div: $2.72 (Div. Reinv. Plan)

Valuation Analysis

	Institutional Holding
Forecast EPS $5.70 (04/05/2013)	No of Institutions 1417
Market Cap $55.2 Billion	Shares 378,676,928
Book Value $2.2 Billion	% Held 71.85
Price/Book 25.23	
Price/Sales 3.23	

Business Summary: Household & Personal Products (MIC: 1.7.1 SIC: 2844 NAIC: 325611)

Colgate-Palmolive is a consumer products company. Co. manages its business in two product segments: Oral, Personal and Home Care; and Pet Nutrition. Co.'s Oral Care products include Colgate Total, Colgate Sensitive Pro-Relief, Colgate Max Fresh, Colgate Optic White and Colgate Luminous White toothpastes, Colgate 360° manual toothbrushes and Colgate and Colgate Plax mouth rinses. Co.'s Personal Care products include the Palmolive, Protex and Softsoap brands. Co. manufactures and markets a range of products for Home Care, including Palmolive and Ajax dishwashing liquids, Fabuloso and Ajax household cleaners and Murphy's Oil Soap. Pet Nutrition sells pet nutrition products for dogs and cats.

Recent Developments: For the year ended Dec 31 2012, net income increased 3.0% to US$2.63 billion from US$2.55 billion in the prior year. Revenues were US$17.09 billion, up 2.1% from US$16.73 billion the year before. Operating income was US$3.89 billion versus US$3.84 billion in the prior year, an increase of 1.2%. Direct operating expenses rose 0.1% to US$7.15 billion from US$7.14 billion in the comparable period the year before. Indirect operating expenses increased 5.1% to US$6.04 billion from US$5.75 billion in the equivalent prior-year period.

Prospects: Our evaluation of Colgate-Palmolive Co. as of Apr. 7, 2013 is the result of our systematic analysis on three basic characteristics: earnings strength, relative valuation, and recent stock price movement. The company has produced a positive trend in earnings per share over the past 5 quarters and while recent estimates for the company have remained steady, CL has posted better than expected results. Based on operating earnings yield, the company is about fairly valued when compared to all of the companies in our coverage universe. Share price changes over the past year indicates that CL will perform in line with the market over the near term.

Financial Data

(US$ in Thousands)	12/31/2012	12/31/2011	12/31/2010	12/31/2009	12/31/2008	12/31/2007	12/31/2006	12/31/2005
Earnings Per Share	5.15	4.94	4.31	4.37	3.66	3.20	2.46	2.43
Cash Flow Per Share	6.69	5.93	6.58	6.56	4.41	4.31	3.54	3.43
Dividends Per Share	2.440	2.270	2.030	1.720	1.560	1.400	1.250	1.110
Dividend Payout %	47.38	45.95	47.10	39.36	42.62	43.75	50.81	45.68
Income Statement								
Total Revenue	17,085,000	16,734,000	15,564,000	15,327,000	15,329,900	13,789,700	12,237,700	11,396,900
EBITDA	3,913,000	3,863,000	3,506,000	3,632,000	3,116,000	2,734,700	2,230,900	2,283,900
Depn & Amortn	31,000	28,000	22,000	22,000	18,800	18,200	16,300	15,600
Income Before Taxes	3,867,000	3,783,000	3,425,000	3,533,000	3,001,600	2,559,900	2,055,900	2,132,300
Income Taxes	1,243,000	1,235,000	1,117,000	1,141,000	967,900	759,100	648,400	727,600
Net Income	2,472,000	2,431,000	2,203,000	2,291,000	1,957,200	1,737,400	1,353,400	1,351,400
Average Shares	480,100	492,000	510,900	524,600	535,000	543,700	550,500	556,500
Balance Sheet								
Current Assets	4,556,000	4,402,000	3,730,000	3,810,000	3,710,000	3,618,500	3,301,000	2,757,100
Total Assets	13,394,000	12,724,000	11,172,000	11,134,000	9,979,300	10,112,000	9,138,000	8,507,100
Current Liabilities	3,736,000	3,716,000	3,728,000	3,599,000	2,953,300	3,162,700	3,469,100	2,743,000
Long-Term Obligations	4,926,000	4,430,000	2,815,000	2,821,000	3,585,300	3,221,900	2,720,400	2,918,000
Total Liabilities	11,205,000	10,349,000	8,497,000	8,018,000	8,057,200	7,825,800	7,727,100	7,157,000
Stockholders' Equity	2,189,000	2,375,000	2,675,000	3,116,000	1,922,100	2,286,200	1,410,900	1,350,100
Shares Outstanding	467,864	480,018	494,850	494,165	501,412	509,034	512,658	516,170
Statistical Record								
Return on Assets %	18.88	20.35	19.75	21.70	19.43	18.05	15.34	15.73
Return on Equity %	108.03	96.28	76.08	90.95	92.76	93.99	98.04	104.13
EBITDA Margin %	22.90	23.08	22.53	23.70	20.33	19.83	18.23	20.04
Net Margin %	14.47	14.53	14.15	14.95	12.77	12.60	11.06	11.86
Asset Turnover	1.30	1.40	1.40	1.45	1.52	1.43	1.39	1.33
Current Ratio	1.22	1.18	1.00	1.06	1.26	1.14	0.95	1.01
Debt to Equity	2.25	1.87	1.05	0.91	1.87	1.41	1.93	2.16
Price Range	110.62-88.25	93.96-75.93	85.81-73.75	86.32-55.05	80.98-54.77	80.64-64.44	66.83-53.70	56.39-48.55
P/E Ratio	21.48-17.14	19.02-15.37	19.91-17.11	19.75-12.60	22.13-14.96	25.20-20.14	27.17-21.83	23.21-19.98
Average Yield %	2.42	2.66	2.54	2.45	2.16	2.02	2.09	2.13

Address: 300 Park Avenue, New York, NY 10022	Web Site: www.colgate.com	Auditors: PricewaterhouseCoopers LLP
Telephone: 212-310-2000	Officers: Ian M. Cook - Chairman, President, Chief Executive Officer Andrew D. Hendry - Senior Vice President, General Counsel, Secretary, Chief Legal Officer	Investor Contact: 212-310-2575
Fax: 212-310-3284		Transfer Agents: Computershare, Inc. Pittsburgh, PA

COMERICA, INC.

Exchange	Symbol	Price	52Wk Range	Yield	P/E
NYS	CMA	$35.95 (3/28/2013)	36.78-27.87	1.89	13.46

*7 Year Price Score 74.39 *NYSE Composite Index=100 *12 Month Price Score 102.69

Interim Earnings (Per Share)

Qtr.	Mar	Jun	Sep	Dec
2008	0.73	0.37	0.19	0.01
2009	(0.16)	(0.10)	(0.10)	(0.43)
2010	(0.46)	0.39	0.33	0.54
2011	0.57	0.53	0.51	0.48
2012	0.66	0.73	0.61	0.67

Interim Dividends (Per Share)

Amt	Decl	Ex	Rec	Pay
0.15Q	04/24/2012	06/13/2012	06/15/2012	07/01/2012
0.15Q	07/24/2012	09/12/2012	09/14/2012	10/01/2012
0.15Q	11/13/2012	12/12/2012	12/14/2012	01/01/2013
0.17Q	01/22/2013	03/13/2013	03/15/2013	04/01/2013

Indicated Div: $0.68 (Div. Reinv. Plan)

Valuation Analysis

		Institutional Holding	
Forecast EPS	$2.78	No of Institutions	
	(04/06/2013)	518	
Market Cap	$6.8 Billion	Shares	
Book Value	$6.9 Billion	176,544,320	
Price/Book	0.98	% Held	
Price/Sales	2.52	81.54	

TRADING VOLUME (thousand shares)

Business Summary: Banking (MIC: 5.1.1 SIC: 6021 NAIC: 522110)

Comerica is a financial holding company. Co.'s principal activity is lending to and accepting deposits from businesses and individuals. Co.'s principal business segments are: Business Bank, which provides products and services to middle market businesses, multinational corporations and governmental entities; Retail Bank, which provides small business banking and personal financial services, as well as consumer products; and Wealth Management, which provides products and services such as fiduciary services and private banking, and sells annuity products, disability and long-term care insurance products. As of Dec 31 2012, Co. had total assets of $65.36 billion and deposits of $52.20 billion.

Recent Developments: For the year ended Dec 31 2012, income from continuing operations increased 32.6% to US$521.0 million from US$393.0 million a year earlier. Net income increased 32.6% to US$521.0 million from US$393.0 million in the prior year. Net interest income increased 4.5% to US$1.73 billion from US$1.65 billion in the prior year. Provision for loan losses was US$79.0 million versus US$144.0 million in the prior year, a decrease of 45.1%. Non-interest income rose 3.3% to US$818.0 million from US$792.0 million, while non-interest expense declined 0.8% to US$1.76 billion.

Prospects: Our evaluation of Comerica Inc. as of Apr. 7, 2013 is the result of our systematic analysis on three basic characteristics: earnings strength, relative valuation, and recent stock price movement. The company has managed to produce a neutral trend in earnings per share over the past 5 quarters and while recent estimates for the company have remained steady, CMA has posted better than expected results. Based on operating earnings yield, the company is undervalued when compared to all of the companies in our coverage universe. Share price changes over the past year indicates that CMA will perform in line with the market over the near term.

Financial Data

(US$ in Thousands)	12/31/2012	12/31/2011	12/31/2010	12/31/2009	12/31/2008	12/31/2007	12/31/2006	12/31/2005
Earnings Per Share	2.67	2.09	0.88	(0.79)	1.29	4.43	5.49	5.11
Cash Flow Per Share	3.94	4.88	7.56	0.61	5.77	6.63	6.09	4.16
Tang Book Value Per Share	36.87	34.80	32.81	32.27	33.38	34.12	32.70	31.11
Dividends Per Share	0.550	0.400	0.250	0.200	2.310	2.560	2.360	2.200
Dividend Payout %	20.60	19.14	28.41	...	179.07	57.79	42.99	43.05
Income Statement								
Interest Income	1,863,000	1,809,000	1,853,000	2,105,000	3,051,000	3,730,000	3,422,000	2,726,000
Interest Expense	135,000	156,000	207,000	538,000	1,236,000	1,727,000	1,439,000	770,000
Net Interest Income	1,728,000	1,653,000	1,646,000	1,567,000	1,815,000	2,003,000	1,983,000	1,956,000
Provision for Losses	79,000	153,000	480,000	1,082,000	686,000	212,000	37,000	(47,000)
Non-Interest Income	818,000	792,000	789,000	1,050,000	893,000	888,000	855,000	942,000
Non-Interest Expense	1,757,000	1,762,000	1,640,000	1,650,000	1,751,000	1,691,000	1,674,000	1,666,000
Income Before Taxes	710,000	530,000	315,000	(115,000)	271,000	988,000	1,127,000	1,279,000
Income Taxes	189,000	137,000	55,000	(131,000)	59,000	306,000	345,000	418,000
Net Income	521,000	393,000	277,000	17,000	213,000	686,000	893,000	861,000
Average Shares	192,000	186,000	173,000	149,000	151,000	155,000	162,000	169,000
Balance Sheet								
Net Loans & Leases	45,428,000	41,953,000	39,335,000	41,176,000	49,735,000	50,186,000	46,938,000	42,731,000
Total Assets	65,359,000	61,008,000	53,667,000	59,249,000	67,548,000	62,331,000	58,001,000	53,013,000
Total Deposits	52,202,000	47,755,000	40,471,000	39,665,000	41,955,000	44,278,000	44,927,000	42,431,000
Total Liabilities	58,417,000	54,140,000	47,874,000	52,220,000	60,396,000	57,214,000	52,848,000	47,945,000
Stockholders' Equity	6,942,000	6,868,000	5,793,000	7,029,000	7,152,000	5,117,000	5,153,000	5,068,000
Shares Outstanding	188,275	197,333	176,535	151,179	150,490	149,988	157,574	162,900
Statistical Record								
Return on Assets %	0.82	0.69	0.49	0.03	0.33	1.14	1.61	1.64
Return on Equity %	7.52	6.21	4.32	0.24	3.46	13.36	17.47	16.93
Net Interest Margin %	92.75	91.38	88.83	74.44	59.49	53.70	57.95	71.75
Efficiency Ratio %	65.54	67.74	62.07	52.30	44.40	36.62	39.14	45.42
Loans to Deposits	0.87	0.88	0.97	1.04	1.19	1.13	1.04	1.01
Price Range	33.57-26.72	43.36-21.98	44.60-29.57	31.70-12.36	45.14-16.75	63.72-40.89	60.07-50.70	63.21-53.46
P/E Ratio	12.57-10.01	20.75-10.52	50.68-33.60	...	34.99-12.98	14.38-9.23	10.94-9.23	12.37-10.46
Average Yield %	1.81	1.25	0.66	0.86	7.28	4.59	4.16	3.79

Address: Comerica Bank Tower, 1717 Main Street, MC 6404, Dallas, TX 75201
Telephone: 214-462-6831

Web Site: www.comerica.com
Officers: Ralph W. Babb - Chairman, President, Chief Executive Officer Karen L. Parkhill - Vice-Chairwoman, Chief Financial Officer

Auditors: Ernst & Young LLP
Investor Contact: 214-462-6831
Transfer Agents: Wells Fargo Shareowner Services, South St. Paul, MN

COMMERCIAL METALS CO.

Exchange	Symbol	Price	52Wk Range	Yield	P/E
NYS	CMC	$15.85 (3/28/2013)	17.41-11.47	3.03	14.81

*7 Year Price Score 64.48   *NYSE Composite Index=100   *12 Month Price Score 106.79

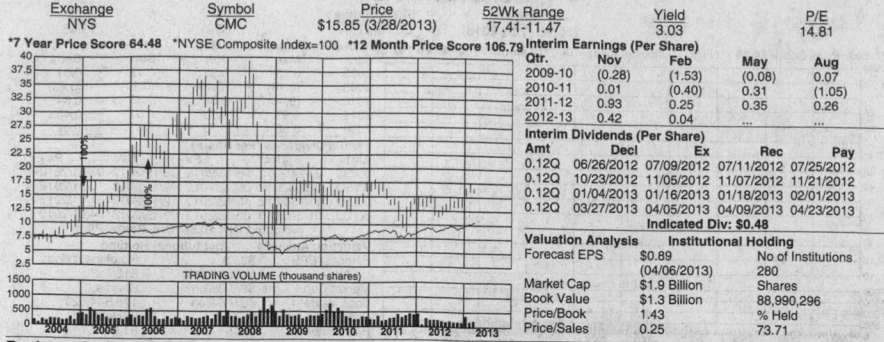

Interim Earnings (Per Share)

Qtr.	Nov	Feb	May	Aug
2009-10	(0.28)	(1.53)	(0.08)	0.07
2010-11	0.01	(0.40)	0.31	(1.05)
2011-12	0.93	0.25	0.35	0.26
2012-13	0.42	0.04	...	...

Interim Dividends (Per Share)

Amt	Decl	Ex	Rec	Pay
0.12Q	06/26/2012	07/09/2012	07/11/2012	07/25/2012
0.12Q	10/23/2012	11/05/2012	11/07/2012	11/21/2012
0.12Q	01/04/2013	01/16/2013	01/18/2013	02/01/2013
0.12Q	03/27/2013	04/05/2013	04/09/2013	04/23/2013

Indicated Div: $0.48

Valuation Analysis

		Institutional Holding	
Forecast EPS	$0.89 (04/06/2013)	No of Institutions	280
Market Cap	$1.9 Billion	Shares	88,990,296
Book Value	$1.3 Billion	% Held	73.71
Price/Book	1.43		
Price/Sales	0.25		

Business Summary: Non-Precious Metals (MIC: 8.2.2 SIC: 3312 NAIC: 331111)

Commercial Metals produces, recycles and markets steel and metal products, related materials and services. The Americas Recycling segment consists of the scrap metal processing and sales operations. The Americas Mills segment includes the domestic steel mills. The Americas Fabrication segment includes the rebar fabrication operations, and fence post manufacturing and other products facilities. The International Mills segment includes the minimill and recycling business in Poland and fabrication business in Europe; and International Marketing and Distribution segment includes global operations for the sales, distribution and processing of steel products, metals and other industrial products.

Recent Developments: For the quarter ended Feb 28 2013, income from continuing operations decreased 83.4% to US$4.6 million from US$27.8 million in the year-earlier quarter. Net income decreased 84.1% to US$4.6 million from US$28.9 million in the year-earlier quarter. Revenues were US$1.73 billion, down 11.6% from US$1.96 billion the year before. Direct operating expenses declined 10.5% to US$1.59 billion from US$1.77 billion in the comparable period the year before. Indirect operating expenses decreased 5.4% to US$132.3 million from US$139.9 million in the equivalent prior-year period.

Prospects: Our evaluation of Commercial Metals Co. as of Apr. 7, 2013 is the result of our systematic analysis on three basic characteristics: earnings strength, relative valuation, and recent stock price movement. The company has generated a negative trend in earnings per share over the past 5 quarters. However, while recent estimates for the company have been lowered by analysts, CMC has posted results that fell short of analysts expectations. Based on operating earnings yield, the company is about fairly valued when compared to all of the companies in our coverage universe. Share price changes over the past year indicates that CMC will perform very well over the near term.

Financial Data

(US$ in Thousands)	6 Mos	3 Mos	08/31/2012	08/31/2011	08/31/2010	08/31/2009	08/31/2008	08/30/2007
Earnings Per Share	1.07	1.28	1.78	(1.13)	(1.81)	0.18	1.97	2.92
Cash Flow Per Share	0.69	1.06	1.69	0.24	0.40	7.18	(0.38)	3.92
Tang Book Value Per Share	10.44	10.57	10.05	9.37	10.31	12.93	13.65	12.74
Dividends Per Share	0.480	0.480	0.480	0.480	0.480	0.480	0.450	0.330
Dividend Payout %	44.86	37.50	26.97	...	...	266.67	22.84	11.30
Income Statement								
Total Revenue	3,518,900	1,789,226	7,828,440	7,918,430	6,306,102	6,793,396	10,427,378	8,329,016
EBITDA	109,005	86,098	363,784	120,283	39,836	263,538	528,937	684,522
Depn & Amortn	(5,815)	(2,908)	131,495	159,576	168,934	154,679	135,069	107,305
Income Before Taxes	81,306	71,982	162,793	(110,099)	(204,606)	31,861	335,605	540,883
Income Taxes	27,232	22,515	(46,190)	19,328	(38,118)	12,734	103,886	172,769
Net Income	54,294	49,717	207,484	(129,617)	(205,344)	20,802	231,966	355,431
Average Shares	117,573	117,093	116,783	114,995	113,524	113,880	117,685	121,681
Balance Sheet								
Current Assets	2,223,496	2,303,925	2,239,831	2,326,253	2,175,206	1,997,552	3,217,443	2,458,852
Total Assets	3,409,465	3,497,569	3,441,246	3,683,131	3,706,153	3,687,556	4,746,371	3,472,663
Current Liabilities	1,023,724	1,099,574	901,134	1,198,854	1,102,959	815,338	1,732,481	1,072,589
Long-Term Obligations	950,407	953,530	1,157,073	1,167,497	1,197,282	1,181,740	1,197,533	706,817
Total Liabilities	2,112,738	2,189,368	2,194,878	2,522,706	2,455,417	2,157,863	3,107,988	1,924,096
Stockholders' Equity	1,296,727	1,308,201	1,246,368	1,160,425	1,250,736	1,529,693	1,638,383	1,548,567
Shares Outstanding	116,878	116,448	116,351	115,533	114,325	112,573	113,777	118,566
Statistical Record								
Return on Assets %	3.61	4.27	5.81	N.M.	N.M.	0.49	5.61	11.19
Return on Equity %	9.86	12.00	17.19	N.M.	N.M.	1.31	14.48	25.75
EBITDA Margin %	3.10	4.81	4.65	1.52	0.63	3.88	5.07	8.22
Net Margin %	1.54	2.78	2.65	N.M.	N.M.	0.31	2.22	4.27
Asset Turnover	2.14	2.18	2.19	2.14	1.71	1.61	2.52	2.62
Current Ratio	2.17	2.10	2.49	1.94	1.97	2.45	1.86	2.29
Debt to Equity	0.73	0.73	0.93	1.01	0.96	0.77	0.73	0.46
Price Range	17.41-11.47	15.30-11.47	15.30-8.69	18.09-10.72	21.11-12.39	24.59-6.33	39.41-23.57	36.59-19.09
P/E Ratio	16.27-10.72	11.95-8.96	8.60-4.88	...	...	136.61-35.17	20.01-11.96	12.53-6.54
Average Yield %	3.45	3.56	3.71	3.17	3.06	3.45	1.46	1.14

Address: 6565 N. MacArthur Blvd., Irving, TX 75039	**Web Site:** www.cmc.com	**Auditors:** Deloitte & Touche LLP
Telephone: 214-689-4300	**Officers:** Anthony A. Massaro - Chairman Joseph A. Alvarado - President, Chief Executive Officer	**Investor Contact:** 972-308-5349
Fax: 214-689-5886		**Transfer Agents:** StockTrans?, a Broadridge Company

COMMONWEALTH REIT

Exchange	Symbol	Price	52Wk Range	Yield	P/E
NYS	CWH	$22.44 (3/28/2013)	25.25-13.58	4.46	N/A

*7 Year Price Score 55.37 ***NYSE Composite Index=100** ***12 Month Price Score 114.35**

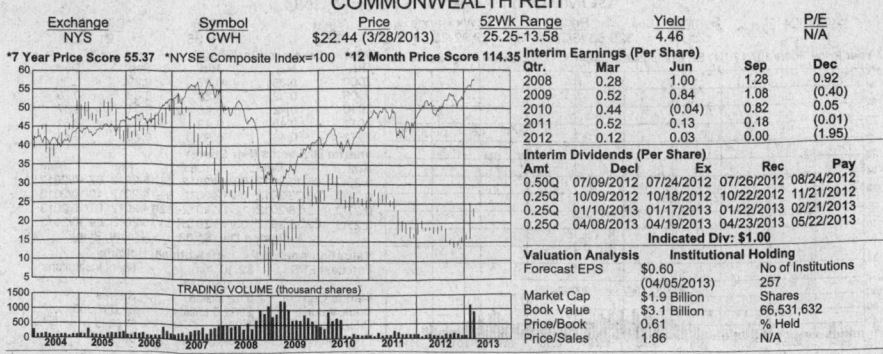

Interim Earnings (Per Share)
Qtr.	Mar	Jun	Sep	Dec
2008	0.28	1.00	1.28	0.92
2009	0.52	0.84	1.08	(0.40)
2010	0.44	(0.04)	0.82	0.05
2011	0.52	0.13	0.18	(0.01)
2012	0.12	0.03	0.00	(1.95)

Interim Dividends (Per Share)
Amt	Decl	Ex	Rec	Pay
0.50Q	07/09/2012	07/24/2012	07/26/2012	08/24/2012
0.25Q	10/09/2012	10/18/2012	10/22/2012	11/21/2012
0.25Q	01/10/2013	01/17/2013	01/22/2013	02/21/2013
0.25Q	04/08/2013	04/19/2013	04/23/2013	05/22/2013

Indicated Div: $1.00

Valuation Analysis
Forecast EPS	$0.60
	(04/05/2013)
Market Cap	$1.9 Billion
Book Value	$3.1 Billion
Price/Book	0.61
Price/Sales	1.86

Institutional Holding
No of Institutions	257
Shares	66,531,632
% Held	N/A

TRADING VOLUME (thousand shares)

Business Summary: REITs (MIC: 5.3.1 SIC: 6798 NAIC: 525930)

Commonwealth REIT is a real estate investment trust. Co.'s primary business is the ownership and operation of real estate, including office and industrial buildings and leased industrial land. As of Dec 31 2011, Co. owned 516 properties. Co.'s portfolio includes 317 office properties and 199 industrial & other properties, which include industrial and commercial lands in Oahu, HI. Also, 11 of Co.'s total are located in Australia. Co.'s properties are located in both central business district areas and suburban areas. Co. has concentrations of properties in six major geographic segments: Metro Philadelphia, PA; Oahu, HI; Metro Chicago, IL; Metro Denver, CO; Australia and Metro Washington, DC.

Recent Developments: For the year ended Dec 31 2012, income from continuing operations increased 34.6% to US$101.1 million from US$75.1 million a year earlier. Net loss amounted to US$79.8 million versus net income of US$110.0 million in the prior year. Revenues were US$1.01 billion, up 15.9% from US$874.2 million the year before.

Prospects: Our evaluation of Commonwealth REIT as of Apr. 7, 2013 is the result of our systematic analysis on three basic characteristics: earnings strength, relative valuation, and recent stock price movement. The company has enjoyed a very positive trend in earnings per share over the past 5 quarters. Because the company lacks sufficient analyst estimate data, we place greater weight on the historical EPS trend as the measure of earnings strength. Based on operating earnings yield, the company is overvalued when compared to all of the companies in our coverage universe. Share price changes over the past year indicates that CWH will perform poorly over the near term.

Financial Data
(US$ in Thousands)	12/31/2012	12/31/2011	12/31/2010	12/31/2009	12/31/2008	12/31/2007	12/31/2006	12/31/2005
Earnings Per Share	(1.81)	0.81	1.26	2.04	3.44	1.12	3.76	2.40
Cash Flow Per Share	3.30	3.40	3.90	5.30	5.26	5.07	5.46	4.57
Tang Book Value Per Share	29.49	33.32	36.30	39.43	39.32	39.40	40.90	41.22
Dividends Per Share	1.750	2.000	1.000	2.040	3.360	3.360	...	...
Dividend Payout %	...	246.91	79.37	100.00	97.67	300.00	...	...
Income Statement								
Total Revenue	1,013,092	911,948	793,370	849,722	835,540	840,010	795,821	710,758
EBITDA	476,565	400,352	394,131	398,460	417,856	329,032	581,940	507,228
Depn & Amortn	188,123	166,444	180,619	155,341	155,026	147,550	128,768	111,951
Income Before Taxes	85,626	40,602	37,029	70,855	84,079	12,206	290,014	253,104
Income Taxes	3,207	1,347	550	735	773	395	...	...
Net Income	(79,845)	109,984	135,409	164,674	244,645	124,255	250,580	164,984
Average Shares	83,750	84,726	72,001	63,353	63,915	60,888	54,131	49,457
Balance Sheet								
Current Assets	372,239	418,224	390,359	224,224	223,194	235,873	211,984	183,178
Total Assets	8,189,634	7,447,026	6,588,520	6,121,321	6,016,099	5,859,332	5,575,949	5,327,167
Current Liabilities	231,002	193,346	155,344	161,877	127,293	115,903	166,525	104,680
Long-Term Obligations	4,349,821	3,577,331	3,206,066	2,992,650	2,889,918	2,774,160	2,397,231	2,520,156
Total Liabilities	5,084,206	3,878,509	3,456,830	3,232,255	3,094,987	2,956,449	2,625,181	2,681,681
Stockholders' Equity	3,105,428	3,568,517	3,131,690	2,889,066	2,921,112	2,902,883	2,950,768	2,645,486
Shares Outstanding	83,804	83,721	72,138	55,965	56,932	56,361	52,512	52,465
Statistical Record								
Return on Assets %	N.M.	1.57	2.13	2.71	4.11	2.17	4.60	3.25
Return on Equity %	N.M.	3.28	4.50	5.67	8.38	4.25	8.96	6.66
EBITDA Margin %	47.04	43.90	49.68	46.89	50.01	39.17	73.12	71.36
Net Margin %	N.M.	12.06	17.07	19.38	29.28	14.79	31.49	23.21
Asset Turnover	0.13	0.13	0.12	0.14	0.14	0.15	0.15	0.14
Current Ratio	1.61	2.16	2.51	1.39	1.75	2.04	1.27	1.75
Debt to Equity	1.40	1.00	1.02	1.04	0.99	0.96	0.81	0.95
Price Range	20.61-13.58	28.71-15.95	32.80-23.27	32.28-10.72	33.56-6.28	54.16-29.92	50.96-41.76	52.64-40.80
P/E Ratio	...	35.44-19.69	26.03-18.47	15.82-5.25	9.76-1.83	48.36-26.71	13.55-11.11	21.93-17.00
Average Yield %	10.25	8.77	3.71	10.07	13.28	7.99	...	...

Address: Two Newton Place, 255 Washington Street, Suite 300, Newton, MA 02458-1634
Telephone: 617-332-3990
Fax: 617-332-2261

Web Site: www.cwhreit.com
Officers: Adam D. Portnoy - President John C. Popeo - Chief Financial Officer, Treasurer, Assistant Secretary

Auditors: Ernst & Young LLP
Investor Contact: 617-796-8222
Transfer Agents: Wells Fargo Bank, National Association, St. Paul, MN

COMMUNITY BANK SYSTEM, INC.

Exchange	Symbol	Price	52Wk Range	Yield	P/E	Div Achiever
NYS	CBU	$29.63 (3/28/2013)	29.92-25.55	3.64	15.35	21 Years

*7 Year Price Score 107.17 *NYSE Composite Index=100 *12 Month Price Score 96.39

Interim Earnings (Per Share)

Qtr.	Mar	Jun	Sep	Dec
2008	0.36	0.37	0.39	0.36
2009	0.32	0.28	0.38	0.29
2010	0.42	0.48	0.51	0.47
2011	0.48	0.49	0.54	0.51
2012	0.48	0.53	0.46	0.47

Interim Dividends (Per Share)

Amt	Decl	Ex	Rec	Pay
0.26Q	05/10/2012	06/13/2012	06/15/2012	07/10/2012
0.27Q	08/23/2012	09/12/2012	09/14/2012	10/10/2012
0.27Q	11/28/2012	12/12/2012	12/14/2012	01/10/2013
0.27Q	02/25/2013	03/13/2013	03/15/2013	04/10/2013

Indicated Div: $1.08 (Div. Reinv. Plan)

Valuation Analysis | **Institutional Holding**

Forecast EPS	$2.10 (04/05/2013)	No of Institutions 174
Market Cap	$1.2 Billion	Shares 26,067,308
Book Value	$902.8 Million	% Held 67.80
Price/Book	1.30	
Price/Sales	3.08	

TRADING VOLUME (thousand shares)

Business Summary: Banking (MIC: 5.1.1 SIC: 6021 NAIC: 522110)

Community Bank System is a single bank holding company. Through its subsidiary, Community Bank, N.A. (the Bank), Co. operates as a community bank providing a range of banking and financial services to retail, commercial, and municipal customers. The Bank operates 168 customer facilities throughout 35 counties of Upstate New York, where it operates as Community Bank, N.A. and five counties of Northeastern Pennsylvania, where it is known as First Liberty Bank & Trust, offering a range of commercial and retail banking services. As of Dec 31 2011, Co. had total assets of $6.49 billion and total deposits of $4.80 billion.

Recent Developments: For the year ended Dec 31 2012, net income increased 5.4% to US$77.1 million from US$73.1 million in the prior year. Net interest income increased 10.0% to US$230.4 million from US$209.4 million in the prior year. Provision for loan losses was US$9.1 million versus US$4.7 million in the prior year, an increase of 92.3%. Non-interest income rose 11.2% to US$99.2 million from US$89.2 million, while non-interest expense advanced 11.2% to US$211.8 million.

Prospects: Our evaluation of Community Bank System Inc. as of Apr. 7, 2013 is the result of our systematic analysis on three basic characteristics: earnings strength, relative valuation, and recent stock price movement. The company has enjoyed a very positive trend in earnings per share over the past 5 quarters. However, while recent estimates for the company have been mixed, CBU has posted results that fell short of analysts expectations. Based on operating earnings yield, the company is undervalued when compared to all of the companies in our coverage universe. Share price changes over the past year indicates that CBU will perform in line with the market over the near term.

Financial Data

(US$ in Thousands)	12/31/2012	12/31/2011	12/31/2010	12/31/2009	12/31/2008	12/31/2007	12/31/2006	12/31/2005
Earnings Per Share	1.93	2.01	1.89	1.26	1.49	1.42	1.26	1.65
Cash Flow Per Share	2.76	2.73	2.95	1.33	1.80	1.69	2.44	2.39
Tang Book Value Per Share	13.01	11.19	8.87	7.56	6.62	7.51	7.17	7.77
Dividends Per Share	1.060	1.000	0.940	0.880	0.860	0.820	0.780	0.740
Dividend Payout %	54.92	49.75	49.74	69.84	57.72	57.75	61.90	44.85
Income Statement								
Interest Income	281,400	270,969	248,281	248,782	250,859	256,237	231,901	219,194
Interest Expense	50,976	61,556	66,597	83,282	102,352	120,263	97,092	75,572
Net Interest Income	230,424	209,413	181,684	165,500	148,507	135,974	134,809	143,622
Provision for Losses	9,108	4,736	7,205	9,790	6,730	2,004	6,585	8,534
Non-Interest Income	99,246	89,222	88,792	83,535	73,474	53,286	49,276	60,846
Non-Interest Expense	211,757	190,372	176,886	186,178	158,562	142,074	127,203	127,389
Income Before Taxes	108,805	103,527	86,385	53,067	56,689	45,182	50,297	68,545
Income Taxes	31,737	30,385	23,065	11,622	10,749	2,291	11,920	17,740
Net Income	77,068	73,142	63,320	41,445	45,940	42,891	38,377	50,805
Average Shares	39,671	36,182	33,269	32,821	30,826	30,232	30,392	30,838
Balance Sheet								
Net Loans & Leases	3,822,688	3,429,344	2,987,805	3,059,354	3,096,565	2,784,628	2,665,245	2,379,236
Total Assets	7,496,800	6,488,275	5,444,506	5,402,813	5,174,552	4,697,502	4,497,797	4,152,734
Total Deposits	5,628,039	4,795,245	3,934,045	3,924,486	3,700,812	3,228,464	3,168,299	2,984,768
Total Liabilities	6,594,022	5,713,692	4,837,248	4,837,116	4,629,901	4,218,718	4,036,269	3,695,139
Stockholders' Equity	902,778	774,583	607,258	565,697	544,651	478,784	461,528	457,595
Shares Outstanding	39,625	36,986	33,318	32,800	32,633	29,634	30,020	29,956
Statistical Record								
Return on Assets %	1.10	1.23	1.17	0.78	0.93	0.93	0.89	1.19
Return on Equity %	9.16	10.59	10.80	7.47	8.95	9.12	8.35	10.90
Net Interest Margin %	81.88	77.28	73.18	66.52	59.20	53.07	58.13	65.52
Efficiency Ratio %	55.63	52.85	52.48	56.02	48.89	45.90	45.24	45.49
Loans to Deposits	0.68	0.72	0.76	0.78	0.84	0.86	0.84	0.80
Price Range	29.38-25.55	28.34-21.81	28.58-17.87	24.39-13.74	29.80-18.09	23.61-17.09	24.85-18.90	28.25-21.42
P/E Ratio	15.22-13.24	14.10-10.85	15.12-9.46	19.36-10.90	20.00-12.14	16.63-12.04	19.72-15.00	17.12-12.98
Average Yield %	3.84	4.03	4.03	4.98	3.74	4.02	3.52	3.13

Address: 5790 Widewaters Parkway, DeWitt, NY 13214-1883 Telephone: 315-445-2282	Web Site: www.communitybankna.com Officers: Nicholas A. DiCerbo - Chairman Mark E. Tryniski - President, Chief Executive Officer	Auditors: PricewaterhouseCoopers LLP Investor Contact: 315-445-3121 Transfer Agents: American Stock Transfer & Trust Company, New York, NY

COMMUNITY HEALTH SYSTEMS, INC.

Exchange	Symbol	Price	52Wk Range	Yield	P/E
NYS	CYH	$47.39 (3/28/2013)	47.39-20.98	N/A	16.01

*7 Year Price Score 85.94   *NYSE Composite Index=100   *12 Month Price Score 130.91

Interim Earnings (Per Share)

Qtr.	Mar	Jun	Sep	Dec
2008	0.63	0.50	0.53	0.65
2009	0.65	0.65	0.65	0.71
2010	0.75	0.74	0.76	0.75
2011	0.67	0.39	0.83	0.36
2012	0.85	0.93	0.49	0.69

Interim Dividends (Per Share)

Amt	Decl	Ex	Rec	Pay
0.25U	12/07/2012	12/13/2012	12/17/2012	12/28/2012

Valuation Analysis

		Institutional Holding	
Forecast EPS	$3.77	No of Institutions	
	(04/06/2013)	348	
Market Cap	$4.4 Billion	Shares	
Book Value	$2.7 Billion	93,736,224	
Price/Book	1.60	% Held	
Price/Sales	0.33	93.26	

Business Summary: Hospitals & Health Care Facilities (MIC: 4.2.1 SIC: 8062 NAIC: 622110)

Community Health Systems is an operator of hospitals in non-urban and certain urban markets. Services provided by Co.'s hospitals include general acute care, emergency room, general and specialty surgery, critical care, internal medicine, obstetrics, diagnostic, psychiatric and rehabilitation services. Co. also provides additional outpatient services at urgent care centers, occupational medicine clinics, imaging, cancer and ambulatory surgery centers and home health and hospice agencies. Through its Quorum Health Resources, LLC subsidiary, Co. provides management and consulting services to non-affiliated general acute care hospitals. As of Dec 31 2012, Co. owned or leased 135 hospitals.

Recent Developments: For the year ended Dec 31 2012, income from continuing operations increased 3.1% to US$346.3 million from US$335.9 million a year earlier. Net income increased 24.6% to US$345.8 million from US$277.6 million in the prior year. Revenues were US$13.03 billion, up 9.4% from US$11.91 billion the year before. Operating income was US$1.21 billion versus US$1.13 billion in the prior year, an increase of 6.7%. Indirect operating expenses increased 9.7% to US$11.82 billion from US$10.77 billion in the equivalent prior-year period.

Prospects: Our evaluation of Community Health Systems Inc. as of Apr. 7, 2013 is the result of our systematic analysis on three basic characteristics: earnings strength, relative valuation, and recent stock price movement. The company has generated a negative trend in earnings per share over the past 5 quarters. However, while recent estimates for the company have been mixed, CYH has posted results that fell short of analysts expectations. Based on operating earnings yield, the company is undervalued when compared to all of the companies in our coverage universe. Share price changes over the past year indicates that CYH will perform very well over the near term.

Financial Data
(US$ in Thousands)

	12/31/2012	12/31/2011	12/31/2010	12/31/2009	12/31/2008	12/31/2007	12/31/2006	12/31/2005
Earnings Per Share	2.96	2.23	3.01	2.66	2.32	0.32	1.75	1.79
Cash Flow Per Share	14.31	14.03	12.96	11.88	11.29	7.35	3.69	4.64
Tang Book Value Per Share	N.M.	N.M.	N.M.	N.M.	N.M.	N.M.	4.12	3.26
Dividends Per Share	0.250	...	...	...	...	...	...	...
Dividend Payout %	8.45	...	...	...	...	...	...	...
Income Statement								
Total Revenue	13,028,985	13,626,168	12,986,500	12,107,613	10,840,098	7,127,494	4,365,576	3,738,320
EBITDA	1,810,229	1,726,131	1,724,767	1,625,116	2,140,230	790,877	572,026	574,799
Depn & Amortn	725,558	657,665	609,839	566,543	506,694	332,580	188,771	166,162
Income Before Taxes	461,738	424,056	463,002	409,609	981,611	93,764	280,956	314,024
Income Taxes	157,502	137,653	159,993	141,325	129,479	43,003	106,682	120,782
Net Income	265,640	201,948	279,983	243,150	218,304	30,289	168,263	167,544
Average Shares	89,806	90,666	92,946	91,517	94,288	94,642	96,232	98,579
Balance Sheet								
Current Assets	3,419,142	2,846,089	2,871,193	2,674,995	2,605,050	2,552,898	1,021,384	914,209
Total Assets	16,606,335	15,208,840	14,698,123	14,021,472	13,818,254	13,493,643	4,506,579	3,934,218
Current Liabilities	2,143,220	1,911,139	1,642,040	1,457,796	1,533,970	1,447,935	575,283	437,403
Long-Term Obligations	9,451,394	8,782,798	8,808,382	8,844,638	8,937,984	9,077,367	1,905,781	1,648,500
Total Liabilities	13,875,128	12,811,744	12,508,659	12,070,837	12,145,389	11,782,839	2,782,906	2,369,641
Stockholders' Equity	2,731,207	2,397,096	2,189,464	1,950,635	1,672,865	1,710,804	1,723,673	1,564,577
Shares Outstanding	91,950	90,571	92,669	93,037	91,507	95,635	94,050	93,564
Statistical Record								
Return on Assets %	1.67	1.35	1.95	1.75	1.59	0.34	3.99	4.43
Return on Equity %	10.33	8.81	13.53	13.42	12.87	1.76	10.23	11.95
EBITDA Margin %	13.89	12.67	13.28	13.42	19.74	11.10	13.10	15.38
Net Margin %	2.04	1.48	2.16	2.01	2.01	0.42	3.85	4.48
Asset Turnover	0.82	0.91	0.90	0.87	0.79	0.79	1.03	0.99
Current Ratio	1.60	1.49	1.75	1.83	1.70	1.76	1.78	2.09
Debt to Equity	3.46	3.66	4.02	4.53	5.34	5.31	1.11	1.05
Price Range	31.66-16.69	42.10-15.29	41.77-26.07	37.59-13.12	39.17-11.35	43.04-27.86	39.65-32.36	40.69-27.01
P/E Ratio	10.70-5.64	18.88-6.86	13.88-8.66	14.13-4.93	16.88-4.89	134.50-87.06	22.66-18.49	22.73-15.09
Average Yield %	0.99	...	...	...	...	...	...	...

Address: 4000 Meridian Boulevard, Franklin, TN 37067 Telephone: 615-465-7000	Web Site: www.chs.net Officers: Wayne T. Smith - Chairman, President, Chief Executive Officer W. Larry Cash - Executive Vice President, Chief Financial Officer	Auditors: Deloitte & Touche LLP Investor Contact: 615-465-7000 Transfer Agents: Registrar and Transfer Company, Cranford, NJ

COMPASS MINERALS INTERNATIONAL INC

Exchange	Symbol	Price	52Wk Range	Yield	P/E
NYS	CMP	$78.90 (3/28/2013)	80.65-68.84	2.76	29.77

*7 Year Price Score 109.18 *NYSE Composite Index=100   *12 Month Price Score 92.45

TRADING VOLUME (thousand shares)

Interim Earnings (Per Share)

Qtr.	Mar	Jun	Sep	Dec
2008	1.48	0.05	0.87	2.42
2009	1.85	0.42	0.77	1.87
2010	1.77	0.34	0.58	1.83
2011	1.69	0.42	1.03	1.31
2012	1.19	0.28	0.28	0.90

Interim Dividends (Per Share)

Amt	Decl	Ex	Rec	Pay
0.495Q	05/10/2012	05/30/2012	06/01/2012	06/15/2012
0.495Q	08/09/2012	08/29/2012	08/31/2012	09/14/2012
0.495Q	11/08/2012	11/28/2012	11/30/2012	12/14/2012
0.545Q	02/11/2013	02/27/2013	03/01/2013	03/15/2013

Indicated Div: $2.18

Valuation Analysis / **Institutional Holding**

Forecast EPS	$3.85 (04/05/2013)	No of Institutions 281
Market Cap	$2.6 Billion	Shares 41,051,552
Book Value	$503.5 Million	% Held 98.81
Price/Book	5.21	
Price/Sales	2.79	

Business Summary: Mining (MIC: 8.2.4 SIC: 1499 NAIC: 212399)

Compass Minerals International, through its subsidiaries, is a producer of minerals, including salt, sulfate of potash specialty fertilizer and magnesium chloride. Co. provides highway deicing salt to customers in North America and the U.K. and specialty fertilizer to growers and fertilizer distributors worldwide. Co. also produces and markets consumer deicing and water conditioning products, ingredients used in consumer and commercial food preparation, and other mineral-based products for consumer, agricultural and industrial applications. In the U.K., Co. operates a records management business utilizing excavated areas of its Winsford salt mine with two other locations in London, England.

Recent Developments: For the year ended Dec 31 2012, net income decreased 40.3% to US$88.9 million from US$149.0 million in the prior year. Revenues were US$941.9 million, down 14.8% from US$1.11 billion the year before. Operating income was US$133.2 million versus US$215.3 million in the prior year, a decrease of 38.1%. Direct operating expenses declined 10.2% to US$714.8 million from US$795.9 million in the comparable period the year before. Indirect operating expenses decreased 0.6% to US$93.9 million from US$94.5 million in the equivalent prior-year period.

Prospects: Our evaluation of Compass Minerals International Inc. as of Apr. 7, 2013 is the result of our systematic analysis on three basic characteristics: earnings strength, relative valuation, and recent stock price movement. The company has managed to produce a neutral trend in earnings per share over the past 5 quarters. However, while recent estimates for the company have been mixed, CMP has posted better than expected results. Based on operating earnings yield, the company is overvalued when compared to all of the companies in our coverage universe. Share price changes over the past year indicates that CMP will perform in line with the market over the near term.

Financial Data

(US$ in Thousands)	12/31/2012	12/31/2011	12/31/2010	12/31/2009	12/31/2008	12/31/2007	12/31/2006	12/31/2005
Earnings Per Share	2.65	4.45	4.51	4.92	4.81	2.43	1.69	0.97
Cash Flow Per Share	4.57	7.67	7.37	3.65	7.66	3.61	2.96	2.79
Tang Book Value Per Share	12.89	11.78	10.04	6.23	1.36	...	...	...
Dividends Per Share	1.980	1.800	1.560	1.420	1.340	1.280	1.220	1.100
Dividend Payout %	74.72	40.45	34.59	28.86	27.86	52.67	72.19	113.40
Income Statement								
Total Revenue	941,900	1,105,700	1,068,900	963,100	1,167,700	857,300	660,700	742,300
EBITDA	195,300	284,500	271,200	307,800	311,200	176,000	165,400	150,100
Depn & Amortn	65,800	66,200	53,300	44,900	42,600	41,300	41,900	45,900
Income Before Taxes	111,300	197,300	195,300	237,100	227,000	80,100	69,800	42,600
Income Taxes	22,400	48,300	44,600	73,200	67,500	100	14,800	15,800
Net Income	88,900	149,000	150,600	163,900	159,500	80,000	55,000	30,900
Average Shares	33,135	32,934	32,763	32,596	33,166	32,931	32,592	32,049
Balance Sheet								
Current Assets	506,900	515,800	521,400	483,400	390,500	365,700	283,800	334,400
Total Assets	1,300,600	1,205,500	1,114,300	1,003,800	822,600	820,000	706,300	750,300
Current Liabilities	199,300	326,800	182,600	184,600	215,500	165,100	119,000	139,400
Long-Term Obligations	478,400	326,700	482,500	486,600	491,600	602,700	582,400	612,400
Total Liabilities	797,100	758,900	766,500	780,700	758,100	824,600	771,400	829,400
Stockholders' Equity	503,500	446,600	347,800	223,100	64,500	(4,600)	(65,100)	(79,100)
Shares Outstanding	33,272	33,023	32,809	32,643	32,437	32,341	32,097	31,834
Statistical Record								
Return on Assets %	7.08	12.85	14.22	17.95	19.37	10.48	7.55	4.19
Return on Equity %	18.66	37.51	52.76	113.98	531.10	...	...	...
EBITDA Margin %	20.73	25.73	25.37	31.96	26.65	20.53	25.03	20.22
Net Margin %	9.44	13.48	14.09	17.02	13.66	9.33	8.32	4.16
Asset Turnover	0.75	0.95	1.01	1.05	1.42	1.12	0.91	1.01
Current Ratio	2.54	1.58	2.86	2.62	1.81	2.22	2.38	2.40
Debt to Equity	0.95	0.73	1.39	2.18	7.62	...	...	...
Price Range	80.65-68.38	97.61-64.80	89.66-63.04	69.87-46.51	85.61-37.11	43.30-30.50	34.27-22.13	26.50-21.66
P/E Ratio	30.43-25.80	21.93-14.56	19.88-13.98	14.20-9.45	17.80-7.72	17.82-12.55	20.28-13.09	27.32-22.33
Average Yield %	2.68	2.17	2.03	2.48	2.23	3.72	4.50	4.57

Address: 9900 West 109th Street, Suite 100, Overland Park, KS 66210 **Telephone:** 913-344-9200	**Web Site:** www.compassminerals.com **Officers:** Francis J. Malecha - President, Chief Executive Officer Richard S. Grant - Interim Chief Executive Officer	**Auditors:** Ernst & Young LLP **Investor Contact:** 913-344-9200 **Transfer Agents:** Computershare Trust Company, N.A., Providence, RI

COMPUTER SCIENCES CORP.

Exchange	Symbol	Price	52Wk Range	Yield	P/E
NYS	CSC	$49.23 (3/28/2013)	50.50-22.50	1.63	14.74

*7 Year Price Score 68.20 *NYSE Composite Index=100 *12 Month Price Score 128.27

TRADING VOLUME (thousand shares)

Interim Earnings (Per Share)

Qtr.	Jun	Sep	Dec	Mar
2009-10	0.85	1.40	1.36	1.66
2010-11	0.91	1.18	1.54	1.09
2011-12	1.17	(18.56)	(8.96)	(1.02)
2012-13	0.26	0.83	3.27	

Interim Dividends (Per Share)

Amt	Decl	Ex	Rec	Pay
0.20Q	05/21/2012	06/12/2012	06/14/2012	07/12/2012
0.20Q	08/08/2012	08/31/2012	09/05/2012	10/04/2012
0.20Q	12/18/2012	12/26/2012	12/28/2012	01/18/2013
0.20Q	03/07/2013	03/14/2013	03/18/2013	04/15/2013

Indicated Div: $0.80

Valuation Analysis / Institutional Holding

Forecast EPS	$2.67 (04/05/2013)	No of Institutions	469
Market Cap	$7.6 Billion	Shares	147,029,680
Book Value	$3.3 Billion	% Held	87.10
Price/Book	2.29		
Price/Sales	0.48		

Business Summary: IT Services (MIC: 6.3.1 SIC: 7373 NAIC: 541512)

Computer Sciences operates in the information technology (IT) and professional services industry. Co.'s clients comprise governments and commercial enterprises that engage in the development, deployment, and ongoing operation of IT services and IT-enabled business operations. Co.'s service offerings include IT and business process outsourcing, emerging services such as cloud computing and cybersecurity protection, and other IT and professional services. Co. also licenses software systems including Software as a Service for the financial services, healthcare and other markets and provides a range of end-to-end business services that meet the needs of commercial and government clients.

Recent Developments: For the quarter ended Dec 28 2012, income from continuing operations was US$123.0 million compared with a loss of US$1.42 billion in the year-earlier quarter. Net income amounted to US$513.0 million versus a net loss of US$1.39 billion in the year-earlier quarter. Revenues were US$3.78 billion, up 2.5% from US$3.69 billion the year before. Direct operating expenses declined 33.0% to US$3.00 billion from US$4.47 billion in the comparable period the year before. Indirect operating expenses decreased 9.3% to US$574.0 million from US$633.0 million in the equivalent prior-year period.

Prospects: Our evaluation of Computer Sciences Corp. as of Apr. 7, 2013 is the result of our systematic analysis on three basic characteristics: earnings strength, relative valuation, and recent stock price movement. The company has enjoyed a very positive trend in earnings per share over the past 5 quarters. However, while recent estimates for the company have been lowered by analysts, CSC has posted better than expected results. Based on operating earnings yield, the company is undervalued when compared to all of the companies in our coverage universe. Share price changes over the past year indicates that CSC will perform very well over the near term.

Financial Data

(US$ in Thousands)	9 Mos	6 Mos	3 Mos	03/30/2012	04/01/2011	04/02/2010	04/03/2009	03/28/2008
Earnings Per Share	3.34	(8.89)	(28.28)	(27.37)	4.73	5.28	7.31	3.20
Cash Flow Per Share	10.15	12.11	9.30	7.61	10.15	10.81	12.91	8.05
Tang Book Value Per Share	4.00	N.M.	N.M.	N.M.	14.61	9.27	3.74	0.22
Dividends Per Share	0.800	0.800	0.800	0.800	0.700	...	...	...
Dividend Payout %	23.95	...	...	...	14.80	...	...	...
Income Statement								
Total Revenue	11,434,000	7,811,000	3,957,000	15,877,000	16,042,000	16,128,000	16,739,900	16,499,500
EBITDA	1,051,000	916,000	292,000	(3,456,000)	2,228,000	2,405,000	2,438,600	2,352,600
Depn & Amortn	538,000	560,000	178,000	763,000	1,140,000	1,156,000	1,270,000	1,286,400
Income Before Taxes	380,000	276,000	74,000	(4,357,000)	957,000	1,024,000	949,100	917,900
Income Taxes	106,000	96,000	32,000	(121,000)	243,000	204,000	(166,100)	373,300
Net Income	680,000	170,000	40,000	(4,242,000)	740,000	817,000	1,115,200	544,600
Average Shares	156,084	155,754	155,647	155,012	156,605	154,754	152,614	170,168
Balance Sheet								
Current Assets	5,618,000	5,468,000	4,799,000	4,883,000	7,557,000	8,422,000	7,707,200	6,923,200
Total Assets	11,260,000	11,649,000	10,926,000	11,189,000	16,120,000	16,455,000	15,618,700	15,774,800
Current Liabilities	3,287,000	4,015,000	4,409,000	4,536,000	4,178,000	4,122,000	4,016,200	5,590,300
Long-Term Obligations	2,398,000	2,399,000	1,461,000	1,486,000	2,409,000	3,669,000	4,172,600	2,635,300
Total Liabilities	7,963,000	8,786,000	8,248,000	8,410,000	8,616,000	10,009,000	10,108,800	10,313,000
Stockholders' Equity	3,297,000	2,863,000	2,678,000	2,779,000	7,504,000	6,446,000	5,509,900	5,461,800
Shares Outstanding	153,551	158,362	155,330	155,200	154,480	153,949	151,498	151,116
Statistical Record								
Return on Assets %	4.67	N.M.	N.M.	N.M.	4.56	5.11	6.99	3.70
Return on Equity %	16.09	N.M.	N.M.	N.M.	10.64	13.70	20.00	9.63
EBITDA Margin %	9.19	11.73	7.38	N.M.	13.89	14.91	14.57	14.26
Net Margin %	5.95	2.18	1.01	N.M.	4.61	5.07	6.66	3.30
Asset Turnover	1.40	1.26	1.16	1.17	0.99	1.01	1.05	1.12
Current Ratio	1.71	1.36	1.09	1.08	1.81	2.04	1.92	1.24
Debt to Equity	0.73	0.84	0.55	0.53	0.32	0.57	0.76	0.48
Price Range	40.58-22.50	34.68-22.50	38.36-22.91	50.98-22.91	56.54-39.81	58.13-36.15	49.15-24.41	61.79-38.49
P/E Ratio	12.15-6.74	...	...	...	11.95-8.42	11.01-6.85	6.72-3.34	19.31-12.03
Average Yield %	2.68	2.88	2.80	2.42	1.45	...	...	...

Address: 3170 Fairview Park Drive, Falls Church, VA 22042	Web Site: www.csc.com	Auditors: Deloitte & Touche LLP
Telephone: 703-876-1000	Officers: Michael W. Laphen - Chairman, President, Chief Executive Officer John Michael Lawrie - President, Chief Executive Officer	Investor Contact: 800-.54-2.3070 Transfer Agents: Computershare, Pittsburgh, PA

COMSTOCK RESOURCES, INC.

Exchange	Symbol	Price	52Wk Range	Yield	P/E
NYS	CRK	$16.25 (3/28/2013)	20.37-13.07	N/A	N/A

*7 Year Price Score 47.55   *NYSE Composite Index=100   *12 Month Price Score 84.81

Interim Earnings (Per Share)

Qtr.	Mar	Jun	Sep	Dec
2008	0.91	1.81	4.91	(2.12)
2009	(0.12)	(0.26)	(0.28)	(0.15)
2010	0.16	(0.04)	(0.10)	(0.45)
2011	0.05	0.08	0.03	(0.89)
2012	0.14	(0.22)	(0.56)	(1.53)

Interim Dividends (Per Share)
No Dividends Paid

Valuation Analysis

		Institutional Holding	
Forecast EPS	$-0.91	No of Institutions	
	(04/06/2013)	240	
Market Cap	$786.6 Million	Shares	
Book Value	$933.5 Million	61,470,016	
Price/Book	0.84	% Held	
Price/Sales	1.72	105.19	

TRADING VOLUME (thousand shares)

Business Summary: Production & Extraction (MIC: 9.1.1 SIC: 1311 NAIC: 211111)

Comstock Resources is engaged in the acquisition, development, production and exploration of oil and natural gas. Co.'s oil and gas operations are concentrated in the East Texas/North Louisiana region, which consists of Logansport, Toledo Bend, Beckville, Waskom, Blocker, Mansfield, Hico-Knowles, Darco, Douglass, Longwood, Drew and other fields; and South Texas region, which includes Eagle Ford, Fandango, Double A Wells, Rosita, Javelina, Las Hermanitas, Segno and other fields. As of Dec 31 2011, Co. had total proved reserves of 1.31 trillion cubic feet of gas equivalent, which consisted of 32.1 million barrels of oil and 1.12 trillion cubic feet of natural gas.

Recent Developments: For the year ended Dec 31 2012, net loss amounted to US$100.1 million versus a net loss of US$33.5 million in the prior year. Revenues were US$456.2 million, up 5.0% from US$434.4 million the year before. Operating loss was US$131.7 million versus a loss of US$41.3 million in the prior year. Direct operating expenses rose 29.5% to US$102.0 million from US$78.7 million in the comparable period the year before. Indirect operating expenses increased 22.4% to US$485.9 million from US$397.0 million in the equivalent prior-year period.

Prospects: Our evaluation of Comstock Resources Inc. as of Apr. 7, 2013 is the result of our systematic analysis on three basic characteristics: earnings strength, relative valuation, and recent stock price movement. The company has generated a negative trend in earnings per share over the past 5 quarters. Because the company lacks sufficient analyst estimate data, we place greater weight on the historical EPS trend as the measure of earnings strength. Based on operating earnings yield, the company is overvalued when compared to all of the companies in our coverage universe. Share price changes over the past year indicates that CRK will perform very poorly over the near term.

Financial Data

(US$ in Thousands)	12/31/2012	12/31/2011	12/31/2010	12/31/2009	12/31/2008	12/31/2007	12/31/2006	12/31/2005
Earnings Per Share	(2.16)	(0.73)	(0.43)	(0.81)	5.53	1.54	1.61	1.47
Cash Flow Per Share	5.63	6.19	6.84	3.92	10.09	10.28	8.64	5.56
Tang Book Value Per Share	19.28	21.56	22.40	22.63	22.87	16.99	15.37	13.56
Income Statement								
Total Revenue	456,194	434,367	349,141	291,076	590,309	687,073	511,928	303,336
EBITDA	287,724	288,878	221,006	182,998	303,616	478,697	355,426	229,104
Depn & Amortn	370,563	295,076	216,245	214,400	182,989	244,777	155,571	64,280
Income Before Taxes	(147,414)	(48,096)	(24,432)	(47,243)	96,828	193,983	173,438	146,156
Income Taxes	(47,354)	(14,624)	(4,846)	(10,772)	38,611	85,177	74,339	35,815
Net Income	(100,060)	(33,472)	(19,586)	(36,471)	251,962	68,901	70,665	60,479
Average Shares	46,422	45,997	45,561	45,004	45,440	44,405	43,556	41,154
Balance Sheet								
Current Assets	77,146	113,090	135,731	273,386	130,028	124,505	98,828	52,770
Total Assets	2,567,143	2,639,884	1,964,214	1,858,961	1,577,890	2,354,387	1,878,125	1,016,663
Current Liabilities	139,058	187,207	155,064	94,771	114,455	130,800	151,861	68,117
Long-Term Obligations	1,324,383	1,196,908	513,372	470,836	210,000	760,000	455,000	243,000
Total Liabilities	1,633,609	1,602,259	895,683	792,850	515,805	1,582,743	1,195,562	433,804
Stockholders' Equity	933,534	1,037,625	1,068,531	1,066,111	1,062,085	771,644	682,563	582,859
Shares Outstanding	48,408	48,125	47,706	47,103	46,442	45,428	44,395	42,969
Statistical Record								
Return on Assets %	N.M.	N.M.	N.M.	N.M.	12.78	3.26	4.88	6.18
Return on Equity %	N.M.	N.M.	N.M.	N.M.	27.41	9.48	11.17	12.89
EBITDA Margin %	63.07	66.51	63.30	62.87	51.43	69.67	69.43	75.53
Net Margin %	N.M.	N.M.	N.M.	N.M.	42.68	10.03	13.80	19.94
Asset Turnover	0.17	0.19	0.18	0.17	0.30	0.32	0.35	0.31
Current Ratio	0.55	0.60	0.88	2.88	1.14	0.95	0.65	0.77
Debt to Equity	1.42	1.15	0.48	0.44	0.20	0.98	0.67	0.42
Price Range	20.37-11.61	32.74-14.14	44.00-19.88	49.82-27.00	86.70-28.12	38.97-25.29	33.99-25.07	33.20-19.90
P/E Ratio	...	...	...	...	15.68-5.08	25.31-16.42	21.11-15.57	22.59-13.54

Address: 5300 Town and Country Blvd., Suite 500, Frisco, TX 75034 Telephone: 972-668-8800	Web Site: www.comstockresources.com Officers: M. Jay Allison - Chairman, President, Chief Executive Officer Roland O. Burns - Senior Vice President, Chief Financial Officer, Treasurer, Secretary	Auditors: Ernst & Young LLP Investor Contact: 800-877-1322 Transfer Agents: American Stock Transfer & Trust Company, New York, NY

CON-WAY INC

Exchange	Symbol	Price	52Wk Range	Yield	P/E
NYS	CNW	$35.21 (3/28/2013)	38.12-26.48	1.14	19.03

*7 Year Price Score 74.12 *NYSE Composite Index=100 *12 Month Price Score 101.18

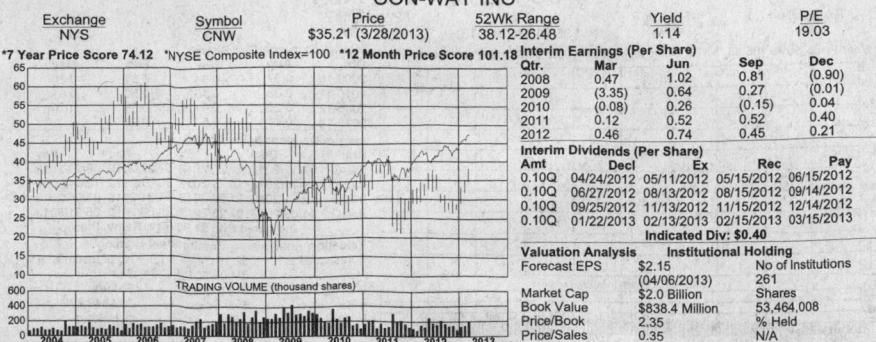

Interim Earnings (Per Share)

Qtr.	Mar	Jun	Sep	Dec
2008	0.47	1.02	0.81	(0.90)
2009	(3.35)	0.64	0.27	(0.01)
2010	(0.08)	0.26	(0.15)	0.04
2011	0.12	0.52	0.52	0.40
2012	0.46	0.74	0.45	0.21

Interim Dividends (Per Share)

Amt	Decl	Ex	Rec	Pay
0.10Q	04/24/2012	05/11/2012	05/15/2012	06/15/2012
0.10Q	06/27/2012	08/13/2012	08/15/2012	09/14/2012
0.10Q	09/25/2012	11/13/2012	11/15/2012	12/14/2012
0.10Q	01/22/2013	02/13/2013	02/15/2013	03/15/2013

Indicated Div: $0.40

Valuation Analysis

	Institutional Holding	
Forecast EPS	$2.15 (04/06/2013)	No of Institutions 261
Market Cap	$2.0 Billion	Shares 53,464,008
Book Value	$838.4 Million	% Held
Price/Book	2.35	N/A
Price/Sales	0.35	

Business Summary: Trucking (MIC: 7.4.1 SIC: 4213 NAIC: 484122)

Con-way provides transportation, logistics and supply-chain management services for a range of manufacturing, industrial and retail customers. Co. has four reporting segments: freight, which provides regional, inter-regional and transcontinental less-than-truckload freight services throughout North America; logistics, which develops contract-logistics solutions, including the management of distribution networks and supply-chain engineering and consulting; truckload, which provides asset-based full-truckload freight services throughout North America; and other, which consists of Road Systems, a trailer manufacturer, and certain corporate activities.

Recent Developments: For the year ended Dec 31 2012, net income increased 18.2% to US$104.5 million from US$88.4 million in the prior year. Revenues were US$5.58 billion, up 5.5% from US$5.29 billion the year before. Operating income was US$228.8 million versus US$207.9 million in the prior year, an increase of 10.1%. Direct operating expenses rose 9.1% to US$1.77 billion from US$1.63 billion in the comparable period the year before. Indirect operating expenses increased 3.5% to US$3.58 billion from US$3.46 billion in the equivalent prior-year period.

Prospects: Our evaluation of Con-way Inc. as of Apr. 7, 2013 is the result of our systematic analysis on three basic characteristics: earnings strength, relative valuation, and recent stock price movement. The company has generated a negative trend in earnings per share over the past 5 quarters. However, while recent estimates for the company have been lowered by analysts, CNW has posted results that fell short of analysts expectations. Based on operating earnings yield, the company is about fairly valued when compared to all of the companies in our coverage universe. Share price changes over the past year indicates that CNW will perform in line with the market over the near term.

Financial Data

(US$ in Thousands)	12/31/2012	12/31/2011	12/31/2010	12/31/2009	12/31/2008	12/31/2007	12/31/2006	12/31/2005
Earnings Per Share	1.85	1.57	0.07	(2.33)	1.40	3.04	4.98	3.85
Cash Flow Per Share	5.56	6.22	3.52	5.82	6.68	8.25	8.86	4.17
Tang Book Value Per Share	8.38	6.97	8.12	5.85	0.03	5.36	13.22	14.71
Dividends Per Share	0.400	0.400	0.400	0.400	0.400	0.400	0.400	0.400
Dividend Payout %	21.62	25.48	571.43	...	28.57	13.16	8.03	10.39
Income Statement								
Total Revenue	5,580,247	5,289,953	4,952,000	4,269,239	5,036,817	4,387,363	4,221,478	4,169,590
EBITDA	430,631	395,061	254,472	149,271	410,672	461,129	556,021	501,827
Depn & Amortn	204,900	191,400	178,900	175,100	212,819	172,979	129,506	113,205
Income Before Taxes	170,954	148,072	16,557	(90,269)	134,917	245,345	392,309	351,121
Income Taxes	66,408	59,629	12,572	17,478	69,494	88,871	119,978	121,873
Net Income	104,546	88,443	3,985	(107,747)	73,749	152,912	266,132	223,029
Average Shares	56,485	56,101	53,169	47,525	48,619	48,327	52,280	56,213
Balance Sheet								
Current Assets	1,151,374	1,190,390	1,120,077	1,076,894	951,082	855,478	1,090,484	1,444,047
Total Assets	3,141,464	3,100,016	2,943,732	2,896,217	3,071,707	3,017,680	2,301,889	2,480,572
Current Liabilities	707,692	723,470	651,890	791,484	658,077	681,492	559,802	631,496
Long-Term Obligations	749,371	770,238	793,950	760,789	926,224	955,722	557,723	581,469
Total Liabilities	2,303,079	2,340,762	2,124,200	2,209,488	2,446,115	2,108,584	1,561,110	1,569,654
Stockholders' Equity	838,385	759,254	819,532	686,729	625,592	909,096	740,779	910,918
Shares Outstanding	55,981	55,597	54,866	49,224	45,857	45,215	46,448	52,276
Statistical Record								
Return on Assets %	3.34	2.93	0.14	N.M.	2.42	5.75	11.13	8.96
Return on Equity %	13.05	11.20	0.53	N.M.	9.58	18.54	32.23	26.42
EBITDA Margin %	7.72	7.47	5.14	3.50	8.15	10.51	13.17	12.04
Net Margin %	1.87	1.67	0.08	N.M.	1.46	3.49	6.30	5.35
Asset Turnover	1.78	1.75	1.70	1.43	1.65	1.65	1.77	1.68
Current Ratio	1.63	1.65	1.72	1.36	1.45	1.26	1.95	2.29
Debt to Equity	0.89	1.01	0.97	1.11	1.48	1.05	0.75	0.64
Price Range	37.74-26.48	41.87-21.13	40.05-26.21	47.56-13.20	54.03-20.61	56.96-38.14	61.06-42.89	59.73-41.74
P/E Ratio	20.40-14.31	26.67-13.46	572.14-374.43	...	38.59-14.72	18.74-12.55	12.26-8.61	15.51-10.84
Average Yield %	1.28	1.24	1.22	1.29	0.93	0.82	0.78	0.81

Address: 2211 Old Earhart Road, Suite 100, Ann Arbor, MI 48105
Telephone: 734-994-6600

Web Site: www.con-way.com
Officers: W. Keith Kennedy - Chairman W. G. Lehmkuhl - President, Executive Vice President

Auditors: KPMG LLP
Investor Contact: 650-378-5353
Transfer Agents: Computershare Shareowner Services LLC

CONAGRA FOODS, INC.

Exchange	Symbol	Price	52Wk Range	Yield	P/E
NYS	CAG	$35.81 (3/28/2013)	35.81-23.81	2.79	28.20

*7 Year Price Score 105.85 *NYSE Composite Index=100 *12 Month Price Score 111.49

Interim Earnings (Per Share)

Qtr.	Aug	Nov	Feb	May
2009-10	0.37	0.54	0.51	0.20
2010-11	0.33	0.45	0.50	0.61
2011-12	0.20	0.41	0.65	(0.14)
2012-13	0.61	0.51	0.29	...

Interim Dividends (Per Share)

Amt	Decl	Ex	Rec	Pay
0.24Q	07/17/2012	07/25/2012	07/27/2012	08/29/2012
0.25Q	09/20/2012	10/29/2012	10/31/2012	12/04/2012
0.25Q	12/11/2012	01/29/2013	01/31/2013	03/05/2013
0.25Q	04/03/2013	04/26/2013	04/30/2013	05/31/2013

Indicated Div: $1.00 (Div. Reinv. Plan)

Valuation Analysis		Institutional Holding	
Forecast EPS	$2.15 (04/06/2013)	No of Institutions	749
Market Cap	$14.9 Billion	Shares	337,543,872
Book Value	$5.0 Billion	% Held	68.73
Price/Book	2.97		
Price/Sales	1.04		

TRADING VOLUME (thousand shares)

Business Summary: Food (MIC: 1.2.1 SIC: 2024 NAIC: 311520)

ConAgra Foods is a food company. Co. has two segments: Consumer Foods and Commercial Foods. The Consumer Foods reporting segment includes food products which are sold in various retail and foodservice channels, principally in North America. The products include a variety of categories across frozen, refrigerated, and shelf-stable temperature classes. The Commercial Foods reporting segment includes commercially branded foods and ingredients, which are sold principally to foodservice, food manufacturing, and industrial customers. The segment's primary products include: specialty potato products, milled grain ingredients, a variety of vegetable products, seasonings, blends, and flavors.

Recent Developments: For the quarter ended Feb 24 2013, income from continuing operations decreased 56.0% to US$123.4 million from US$280.7 million in the year-earlier quarter. Net income decreased 56.0% to US$123.4 million from US$280.7 million in the year-earlier quarter. Revenues were US$3.85 billion, up 13.4% from US$3.40 billion the year before. Direct operating expenses rose 14.1% to US$2.98 billion from US$2.61 billion in the comparable period the year before. Indirect operating expenses increased 68.5% to US$684.6 million from US$406.4 million in the equivalent prior-year period.

Prospects: Our evaluation of ConAgra Foods Inc. as of Apr. 7, 2013 is the result of our systematic analysis on three basic characteristics: earnings strength, relative valuation, and recent stock price movement. The company has generated a negative trend in earnings per share over the past 5 quarters and while recent estimates for the company have been mixed, CAG has posted results that fell short of analysts expectations. Based on operating earnings yield, the company is undervalued when compared to all of the companies in our coverage universe. Share price changes over the past year indicates that CAG will perform well over the near term.

Financial Data
(US$ in Thousands)

	9 Mos	6 Mos	3 Mos	05/27/2011	05/29/2011	05/30/2010	05/31/2009	05/25/2008
Earnings Per Share	1.27	1.63	1.53	1.12	1.88	1.62	2.15	1.90
Cash Flow Per Share	2.57	2.56	2.61	2.55	3.16	3.33	0.27	0.21
Tang Book Value Per Share	N.M.	N.M.	N.M.	N.M.	0.38	1.12	0.89	2.14
Dividends Per Share	0.980	0.970	0.960	0.950	0.890	0.790	0.760	0.750
Dividend Payout %	77.17	59.51	62.75	84.82	47.34	48.77	35.35	39.47
Income Statement								
Total Revenue	10,897,900	7,047,400	3,311,900	13,262,600	12,303,100	12,079,400	12,731,200	11,605,700
EBITDA	1,342,800	969,400	508,800	850,300	1,420,200	1,253,000	1,152,400	952,100
Depn & Amortn	299,200	185,800	91,400	21,100	17,800	7,800	6,600	2,600
Income Before Taxes	870,300	680,900	368,100	625,200	1,224,900	1,084,800	959,600	696,200
Income Taxes	310,600	232,600	123,500	195,800	421,000	362,100	337,200	227,200
Net Income	581,700	461,700	250,100	467,900	817,000	725,800	978,400	930,600
Average Shares	417,800	411,700	412,000	418,300	434,300	447,100	455,400	490,900
Balance Sheet								
Current Assets	5,146,000	4,065,000	3,475,900	3,218,800	3,899,300	3,960,100	3,336,600	6,082,000
Total Assets	21,107,500	12,524,500	11,928,600	11,441,900	11,408,700	11,738,000	11,073,300	13,682,500
Current Liabilities	3,422,500	2,388,300	2,594,300	2,225,200	2,125,600	2,036,200	1,574,700	3,651,300
Long-Term Obligations	9,845,300	3,609,300	2,859,700	2,858,600	2,870,300	3,226,400	3,461,300	3,386,900
Total Liabilities	16,084,300	7,922,200	7,375,100	7,002,400	6,707,200	6,814,100	6,352,400	8,345,100
Stockholders' Equity	5,023,200	4,602,300	4,553,500	4,439,500	4,701,500	4,923,900	4,720,900	5,337,400
Shares Outstanding	416,616	403,648	405,830	407,612	410,494	442,269	441,657	484,371
Statistical Record								
Return on Assets %	3.17	5.60	5.38	4.11	7.08	6.38	7.78	7.31
Return on Equity %	10.37	14.49	13.64	10.27	17.02	15.09	19.14	18.81
EBITDA Margin %	12.32	13.76	15.36	6.41	11.54	10.37	9.05	8.20
Net Margin %	5.34	6.55	7.55	3.53	6.64	6.01	7.69	8.02
Asset Turnover	0.87	1.15	1.15	1.16	1.07	1.06	1.01	0.91
Current Ratio	1.50	1.70	1.34	1.45	1.83	1.94	2.12	1.67
Debt to Equity	1.96	0.78	0.63	0.64	0.61	0.66	0.73	0.63
Price Range	33.92-23.81	28.76-23.81	27.18-22.99	27.18-22.72	25.58-21.14	26.28-18.51	24.00-13.80	27.43-21.00
P/E Ratio	26.71-18.75	17.64-14.61	17.76-15.03	24.27-20.29	13.61-11.24	16.22-11.43	11.16-6.42	14.44-11.05
Average Yield %	3.59	3.72	3.78	3.74	3.86	3.55	4.15	3.09

Address: One ConAgra Drive, Omaha, NE 68102-5001 Telephone: 402-240-4000	Web Site: www.conagrafoods.com Officers: Gary M. Rodkin - President, Chief Executive Officer Colleen R. Batcheler - Executive Vice President, General Counsel, Corporate Secretary	Auditors: KPMG LLP Investor Contact: 402-240-4154 Transfer Agents: Wells Fargo Shareowner Services, St. Paul, MN

CONCHO RESOURCES INC

Exchange	Symbol	Price	52Wk Range	Yield	P/E
NYS	CXO	$97.43 (3/28/2013)	108.20-77.80	N/A	23.48

*7 Year Price Score N/A   ***NYSE Composite Index=100**   ***12 Month Price Score 94.99**

TRADING VOLUME (thousand shares)

Interim Earnings (Per Share)

Qtr.	Mar	Jun	Sep	Dec
2008	0.29	(0.19)	1.72	1.56
2009	(0.16)	(0.39)	0.23	0.19
2010	0.75	1.35	0.22	(0.14)
2011	0.42	2.24	3.44	(0.81)
2012	0.30	3.07	0.06	0.72

Interim Dividends (Per Share)
No Dividends Paid

Valuation Analysis		Institutional Holding	
Forecast EPS	$4.39	No of Institutions	
	(04/06/2013)	385	
Market Cap	$10.2 Billion	Shares	
Book Value	$3.5 Billion	101,244,688	
Price/Book	2.94	% Held	
Price/Sales	5.60	N/A	

Business Summary: Production & Extraction (MIC: 9.1.1 SIC: 1311 NAIC: 211111)

Concho Resources is an oil and natural gas company engaged in the acquisition, development and exploration of oil and natural gas properties. Co. refers to its three core operating areas as the New Mexico Shelf, where it primarily targets the Yeso and Lower Abo formations; the Delaware Basin, where it primarily targets the Bone Spring formation (including the Avalon shale and the Bone Spring sands) and the Wolfcamp shale; and the Texas Permian, where it primarily targets the Wolfberry, a term applied to the combined Wolfcamp and Spraberry horizons. As of Dec 31 2011, Co. had total proved reserves of 238.3 million barrels of oil and 889.35 billion cubic feet of natural gas.

Recent Developments: For the year ended Dec 31 2012, income from continuing operations decreased 2.7% to US$408.2 million from US$419.5 million a year earlier. Net income decreased 21.2% to US$431.7 million from US$548.1 million in the prior year. Revenues were US$1.82 billion, up 12.5% from US$1.62 billion the year before. Operating income was US$850.6 million versus US$803.7 million in the prior year, an increase of 5.8%. Direct operating expenses rose 23.7% to US$343.7 million from US$277.9 million in the comparable period the year before. Indirect operating expenses increased 16.7% to US$625.5 million from US$536.2 million in the equivalent prior-year period.

Prospects: Our evaluation of Concho Resources Inc. as of Apr. 7, 2013 is the result of our systematic analysis on three basic characteristics: earnings strength, relative valuation, and recent stock price movement. The company has managed to produce a neutral trend in earnings per share over the past 5 quarters. However, while recent estimates for the company have been mixed, CXO has posted results that fell short of analysts expectations. Based on operating earnings yield, the company is about fairly valued when compared to all of the companies in our coverage universe. Share price changes over the past year indicates that CXO will perform poorly over the near term.

Financial Data
(US$ in Thousands)

	12/31/2012	12/31/2011	12/31/2010	12/31/2009	12/31/2008	12/31/2007	12/31/2006	12/31/2005
Earnings Per Share	4.15	5.28	2.18	(0.12)	3.46	0.38	0.59	(0.70)
Cash Flow Per Share	11.96	11.69	7.04	4.23	4.93	2.64	2.37	6.18
Tang Book Value Per Share	32.95	28.54	22.91	15.14	15.18	10.23	9.73	13.45
Income Statement								
Total Revenue	1,819,814	1,739,967	972,576	544,447	533,789	294,333	198,290	54,936
EBITDA	1,417,104	1,293,188	615,620	203,901	593,738	158,267	126,830	18,708
Depn & Amortn	575,128	428,377	249,850	206,143	123,912	80,846	62,216	11,619
Income Before Taxes	659,271	746,451	305,683	(30,534)	440,787	41,379	34,047	3,993
Income Taxes	251,041	285,848	122,649	(20,732)	162,085	16,019	14,379	2,039
Net Income	431,689	548,137	204,370	(9,802)	278,702	25,360	19,668	1,954
Average Shares	103,972	103,653	93,837	84,912	80,587	66,309	50,729	4,059
Balance Sheet								
Current Assets	458,882	411,023	330,633	217,258	278,783	109,442	63,765	59,192
Total Assets	8,589,437	6,849,576	5,368,494	3,171,085	2,815,203	1,508,229	1,390,072	232,385
Current Liabilities	740,086	701,477	506,989	337,014	270,818	128,642	70,501	40,346
Long-Term Obligations	3,101,103	2,080,141	1,668,521	845,836	630,000	325,404	495,100	72,000
Total Liabilities	5,123,241	3,868,837	2,984,620	1,835,657	1,490,049	732,831	814,916	122,715
Stockholders' Equity	3,466,196	2,980,739	2,383,874	1,335,428	1,325,154	775,398	575,156	109,670
Shares Outstanding	104,581	103,756	102,810	85,803	84,825	75,832	59,092	8,141
Statistical Record								
Return on Assets %	5.58	8.97	4.79	N.M.	12.86	1.75	2.42	...
Return on Equity %	13.36	20.44	10.99	N.M.	26.46	3.76	5.74	...
EBITDA Margin %	77.87	74.32	63.30	37.45	111.23	53.77	63.96	34.05
Net Margin %	23.72	31.50	21.01	N.M.	52.21	8.62	9.92	3.56
Asset Turnover	0.24	0.28	0.23	0.18	0.25	0.20	0.24	...
Current Ratio	0.62	0.59	0.65	0.64	1.03	0.85	0.90	1.47
Debt to Equity	0.89	0.70	0.70	0.63	0.48	0.42	0.86	0.66
Price Range	113.43-77.80	109.79-67.25	88.43-42.86	46.17-17.38	40.18-15.18	21.99-12.54	...	...
P/E Ratio	27.33-18.75	20.79-12.74	40.56-19.66	...	11.61-4.39	57.87-33.00	...	...

Address: One Concho Center, 600 West Illinois Avenue, Midland, TX 79701 Telephone: 432-683-7443	Web Site: www.conchoresources.com Officers: Timothy A. Leach - Chairman, President, Chief Executive Officer Darin G. Holderness - Senior Vice President, Chief Financial Officer, Principal Accounting Officer, Treasurer	Auditors: Grant Thornton LLP Investor Contact: 432-683-7443 Transfer Agents: American Stock Transfer & Trust Company, New York, NY

CONOCOPHILLIPS

Exchange	Symbol	Price	52Wk Range	Yield	P/E	Div Achiever
NYS	COP	$60.10 (3/28/2013)	61.66-50.82	4.39	8.94	12 Years

*7 Year Price Score 98.94   *NYSE Composite Index=100   *12 Month Price Score 95.24

Interim Earnings (Per Share)

Qtr.	Mar	Jun	Sep	Dec
2008	2.62	3.50	3.39	(20.66)
2009	0.56	0.87	1.00	0.81
2010	1.40	2.77	2.05	1.41
2011	2.09	2.41	1.91	2.55
2012	2.27	1.80	1.46	1.17

Interim Dividends (Per Share)

Amt	Decl	Ex	Rec	Pay
0.66Q	05/09/2012	05/17/2012	05/21/2012	06/01/2012
0.66Q	07/10/2012	07/19/2012	07/23/2012	09/04/2012
0.66Q	10/04/2012	10/11/2012	10/15/2012	12/03/2012
0.66Q	02/06/2013	02/14/2013	02/19/2013	03/01/2013

Indicated Div: $2.64 (Div. Reinv. Plan)

Valuation Analysis | **Institutional Holding**

Forecast EPS	$5.42 (04/06/2013)	No of Institutions 1767
Market Cap	$73.3 Billion	Shares
Book Value	$48.0 Billion	928,010,688
Price/Book	1.53	% Held
Price/Sales	1.18	64.23

TRADING VOLUME (thousand shares)

Business Summary: Production & Extraction (MIC: 9.1.1 SIC: 2911 NAIC: 324110)

ConocoPhillips is engaged in exploring for, producing, transporting and marketing crude oil, bitumen, natural gas, liquefied natural gas (LNG) and natural gas liquids. Co. manages its operations through six operating segments, which are defined by geographic region: Alaska, Lower 48 and Latin America, Canada, Europe, Asia Pacific and Middle East, and Other International. At Dec 31 2012, Co.'s continuing operations were producing in the U.S., Norway, the U.K., Canada, Australia, offshore Timor-Leste in the Timor Sea, Indonesia, China, Malaysia, Qatar, Libya and Russia. Also, as of Dec 31 2012, Co. had total net proved reserves of 8.64 billion barrels of oil equivalent.

Recent Developments: For the year ended Dec 31 2012, income from continuing operations increased 4.1% to US$7.48 billion from US$7.19 billion a year earlier. Net income decreased 32.0% to US$8.50 billion from US$12.50 billion in the prior year. Revenues were US$62.00 billion, down 6.2% from US$66.07 billion the year before. Direct operating expenses declined 11.6% to US$32.03 billion from US$36.22 billion in the comparable period the year before. Indirect operating expenses increased 0.7% to US$14.56 billion from US$14.45 billion in the equivalent prior-year period.

Prospects: Our evaluation of ConocoPhillips as of Apr. 7, 2013 is the result of our systematic analysis on three basic characteristics: earnings strength, relative valuation, and recent stock price movement. The company has managed to produce a neutral trend in earnings per share over the past 5 quarters. However, while recent estimates for the company have been lowered by analysts, COP has posted better than expected results. Based on operating earnings yield, the company is undervalued when compared to all of the companies in our coverage universe. Share price changes over the past year indicates that COP will perform in line with the market over the near term.

Financial Data
(US$ in Thousands)

	12/31/2012	12/31/2011	12/31/2010	12/31/2009	12/31/2008	12/31/2007	12/31/2006	12/31/2005
Earnings Per Share	6.72	8.97	7.62	3.24	(11.16)	7.22	9.66	9.55
Cash Flow Per Share	11.16	14.29	11.52	8.39	14.83	15.12	13.57	12.65
Tang Book Value Per Share	39.33	47.56	43.69	38.04	33.23	36.40	30.50	26.34
Dividends Per Share	2.640	2.640	2.150	1.910	1.880	1.640	1.440	1.180
Dividend Payout %	39.29	29.43	28.22	58.95	...	22.71	14.91	12.36
Income Statement								
Total Revenue	62,004,000	251,226,000	198,655,000	152,840,000	246,182,000	194,495,000	188,523,000	183,364,000
EBITDA	22,712,000	31,907,000	29,997,000	20,616,000	6,424,000	32,910,000	36,780,000	28,330,000
Depn & Amortn	6,580,000	7,934,000	9,060,000	9,295,000	9,012,000	8,298,000	7,284,000	4,253,000
Income Before Taxes	15,423,000	23,001,000	19,750,000	10,032,000	(3,523,000)	23,359,000	28,409,000	23,580,000
Income Taxes	7,942,000	10,499,000	8,333,000	5,096,000	13,405,000	11,381,000	12,783,000	9,907,000
Net Income	8,428,000	12,436,000	11,358,000	4,858,000	(16,998,000)	11,891,000	15,550,000	13,529,000
Average Shares	1,253,093	1,387,100	1,491,067	1,497,608	1,523,432	1,645,919	1,609,530	1,417,028
Balance Sheet								
Current Assets	23,989,000	30,218,000	34,660,000	21,167,000	20,843,000	24,735,000	25,066,000	19,612,000
Total Assets	117,144,000	153,230,000	156,314,000	152,588,000	142,865,000	177,757,000	164,781,000	106,999,000
Current Liabilities	17,443,000	28,068,000	27,419,000	23,695,000	21,780,000	26,882,000	26,431,000	21,359,000
Long-Term Obligations	20,770,000	21,610,000	22,656,000	26,925,000	27,085,000	20,289,000	23,091,000	10,758,000
Total Liabilities	69,157,000	88,006,000	87,752,000	90,121,000	87,700,000	88,774,000	82,135,000	54,268,000
Stockholders' Equity	47,987,000	65,224,000	68,562,000	62,467,000	55,165,000	88,983,000	82,646,000	52,731,000
Shares Outstanding	1,220,017	1,285,669	1,467,655	1,524,998	1,520,918	1,613,841	1,646,082	1,377,849
Statistical Record								
Return on Assets %	6.22	8.04	7.35	3.29	N.M.	6.94	11.44	13.54
Return on Equity %	14.85	18.59	17.34	8.26	N.M.	13.86	22.97	28.35
EBITDA Margin %	36.63	12.70	15.10	13.49	2.61	16.92	19.51	15.45
Net Margin %	13.59	4.95	5.72	3.18	N.M.	6.11	8.25	7.38
Asset Turnover	0.46	1.62	1.29	1.03	1.53	1.14	1.39	1.83
Current Ratio	1.38	1.08	1.26	0.89	0.96	0.92	0.95	0.92
Debt to Equity	0.43	0.33	0.33	0.43	0.49	0.23	0.28	0.20
Price Range	59.63-50.82	61.91-46.49	51.91-36.11	42.45-26.78	73.02-31.86	68.74-47.13	55.70-42.71	54.06-31.85
P/E Ratio	8.87-7.56	6.90-5.18	6.81-4.74	13.10-8.27	...	9.52-6.53	5.77-4.42	5.66-3.34
Average Yield %	4.71	4.83	5.09	5.50	3.29	2.80	2.96	2.68

Address: 600 North Dairy Ashford, Houston, TX 77079 Telephone: 281-293-1000 Fax: 281-661-7636	Web Site: www.conocophillips.com Officers: Ryan M. Lance - Chairman, President, Chief Executive Officer, Region Officer, Division Officer John A. Carrig - President, Chief Operating Officer	Auditors: Ernst & Young LLP Transfer Agents: BNY Mellon Shareowner Services, Jersey City, NJ

CONSOL ENERGY INC

Exchange	Symbol	Price	52Wk Range	Yield	P/E
NYS	CNX	$33.65 (3/28/2013)	36.60-26.80	1.49	19.79

*7 Year Price Score 64.54   *NYSE Composite Index=100   *12 Month Price Score 94.12

Interim Earnings (Per Share)

Qtr.	Mar	Jun	Sep	Dec
2008	0.41	0.54	0.49	0.96
2009	1.08	0.62	0.48	0.78
2010	0.54	0.29	0.33	0.47
2011	0.84	0.34	0.73	0.85
2012	0.42	0.67	(0.05)	0.66

Interim Dividends (Per Share)

Amt	Decl	Ex	Rec	Pay
0.125Q	04/27/2012	05/09/2012	05/11/2012	05/25/2012
0.125Q	07/27/2012	08/08/2012	08/10/2012	08/24/2012
0.125Q	10/26/2012	11/07/2012	11/09/2012	11/23/2012
0.125Q	12/10/2012	12/19/2012	12/21/2012	12/28/2012

Indicated Div: $0.50

Valuation Analysis | **Institutional Holding**

Forecast EPS	$1.00	No of Institutions
	(04/06/2013)	457
Market Cap	$7.7 Billion	Shares
Book Value	$4.0 Billion	243,643,296
Price/Book	1.94	% Held
Price/Sales	1.41	98.87

Business Summary: Mining (MIC: 8.2.4 SIC: 1221 NAIC: 212111)

CONSOL Energy is engaged in producing coal and natural gas for energy and raw material markets, which include the electric power generation industry and the steelmaking industry. Additionally, Co. provides energy services, including river and dock services, terminal services, industrial supply services, water services and land resource management services. Co. has two principal business divisions: Coal and Gas. Co. is engaged in developing unconventional gas resources including the early development of coalbed methane production. At Dec 31 2012, Co.'s estimated net proved gas reserves consisted of 4.0 trillion cubic feet.

Recent Developments: For the year ended Dec 31 2012, net income decreased 38.6% to US$388.1 million from US$632.5 million in the prior year. Revenues were US$5.43 billion, down 11.2% from US$6.12 billion the year before. Direct operating expenses declined 5.0% to US$3.61 billion from US$3.80 billion in the comparable period the year before. Indirect operating expenses decreased 13.4% to US$1.33 billion from US$1.53 billion in the equivalent prior-year period.

Prospects: Our evaluation of Consol Energy Inc. as of Apr. 7, 2013 is the result of our systematic analysis on three basic characteristics: earnings strength, relative valuation, and recent stock price movement. The company has enjoyed a very positive trend in earnings per share over the past 5 quarters. However, while recent estimates for the company have been lowered by analysts, CNX has posted better than expected results. Based on operating earnings yield, the company is overvalued when compared to all of the companies in our coverage universe. Share price changes over the past year indicates that CNX will perform very poorly over the near term.

Financial Data

(US$ in Thousands)	12/31/2012	12/31/2011	12/31/2010	12/31/2009	12/31/2008	12/31/2007	12/31/2006	12/31/2005
Earnings Per Share	1.70	2.76	1.60	2.95	2.40	1.45	2.20	3.13
Cash Flow Per Share	3.19	6.74	5.26	5.23	5.63	3.76	3.62	2.23
Tang Book Value Per Share	17.33	15.90	13.02	9.86	8.10	6.66	5.84	5.54
Dividends Per Share	0.625	0.425	0.400	0.400	0.400	0.310	0.280	0.280
Dividend Payout %	36.76	15.40	25.00	13.56	16.67	21.38	12.73	8.95
Income Statement								
Total Revenue	5,430,307	6,117,242	5,236,021	4,621,875	4,652,445	3,762,197	3,715,171	3,810,449
EBITDA	1,344,772	1,662,302	1,244,768	1,261,151	1,156,270	789,042	875,996	943,852
Depn & Amortn	627,438	626,005	571,823	441,387	394,492	379,231	300,010	261,851
Income Before Taxes	497,274	787,953	467,913	788,345	725,595	428,957	550,920	654,684
Income Taxes	109,701	155,456	109,287	221,203	239,934	136,137	112,430	64,339
Net Income	388,410	632,497	346,781	539,717	442,470	267,782	408,882	580,861
Average Shares	229,141	229,003	217,037	182,821	184,679	184,149	185,638	185,534
Balance Sheet								
Current Assets	1,539,094	1,897,977	1,115,006	941,036	983,814	683,155	914,496	998,500
Total Assets	12,670,909	12,525,700	12,070,610	7,725,401	7,370,458	6,208,090	5,663,332	5,087,652
Current Liabilities	1,387,099	1,388,397	1,664,785	1,428,586	1,511,740	1,016,397	740,124	803,922
Long-Term Obligations	3,174,586	3,177,423	3,186,138	422,908	468,351	488,925	492,745	438,367
Total Liabilities	8,717,117	8,914,815	9,126,133	5,939,853	5,908,271	4,993,671	4,597,181	4,062,296
Stockholders' Equity	3,953,792	3,610,885	2,944,477	1,785,548	1,462,187	1,214,419	1,066,151	1,025,356
Shares Outstanding	228,094	227,056	226,162	181,086	180,549	182,291	182,654	185,050
Statistical Record								
Return on Assets %	3.08	5.14	3.50	7.15	6.50	4.51	7.61	12.51
Return on Equity %	10.24	19.30	14.66	33.24	32.97	23.48	39.10	77.74
EBITDA Margin %	24.76	27.17	23.77	27.29	24.85	20.97	23.58	24.77
Net Margin %	7.15	10.34	6.62	11.68	9.51	7.12	11.01	15.24
Asset Turnover	0.43	0.50	0.53	0.61	0.68	0.63	0.69	0.82
Current Ratio	1.11	1.37	0.67	0.66	0.65	0.67	1.24	1.24
Debt to Equity	0.80	0.88	1.08	0.24	0.32	0.40	0.46	0.43
Price Range	39.37-26.80	55.49-31.70	56.34-31.21	52.87-22.58	117.34-18.83	73.58-29.19	48.13-29.06	39.52-18.95
P/E Ratio	23.16-15.76	20.11-11.49	35.21-19.51	17.92-7.65	48.89-7.85	50.74-20.13	21.88-13.21	12.62-6.05
Average Yield %	1.93	0.92	0.96	1.08	0.61	0.69	0.75	1.00

Address: 1000 Consol Energy Drive, Canonsburg, PA 15317-6506	Web Site: www.consolenergy.com	Auditors: PricewaterhouseCoopers LLP
Telephone: 724-485-4000	Officers: J. Brett Harvey - Chairman, Chief Executive Officer John L. Whitmire - Chairman, Vice-Chairman	Investor Contact: 724-485-4169 Transfer Agents: Computershare Trust Company, Providence, RI

CONSOLIDATED EDISON, INC.

Exchange	Symbol	Price	52Wk Range	Yield	P/E	Div Achiever
NYS	ED	$61.03 (3/28/2013)	64.94-54.10	4.03	15.81	38 Years

*7 Year Price Score 109.23 *NYSE Composite Index=100   *12 Month Price Score 91.16

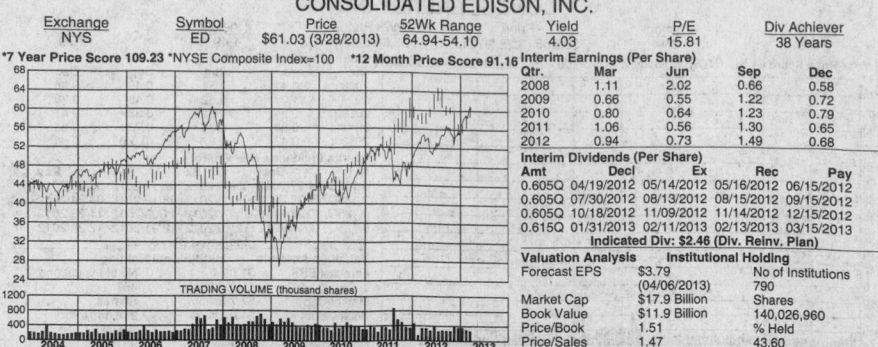

Interim Earnings (Per Share)

Qtr.	Mar	Jun	Sep	Dec
2008	1.11	2.02	0.66	0.58
2009	0.66	0.55	1.22	0.72
2010	0.80	0.64	1.23	0.79
2011	1.06	0.56	1.30	0.65
2012	0.94	0.73	1.49	0.68

Interim Dividends (Per Share)

Amt	Decl	Ex	Rec	Pay
0.605Q	04/19/2012	05/14/2012	05/16/2012	06/15/2012
0.605Q	07/30/2012	08/13/2012	08/15/2012	09/15/2012
0.605Q	10/18/2012	11/09/2012	11/14/2012	12/15/2012
0.615Q	01/31/2013	02/11/2013	02/13/2013	03/15/2013

Indicated Div: $2.46 (Div. Reinv. Plan)

Valuation Analysis

	Institutional Holding	
Forecast EPS	$3.79	No of Institutions
	(04/06/2013)	790
Market Cap	$17.9 Billion	Shares
Book Value	$11.9 Billion	140,026,960
Price/Book	1.51	% Held
Price/Sales	1.47	43.60

Business Summary: Electric Utilities (MIC: 3.1.1 SIC: 4931 NAIC: 221121)

Consolidated Edison is a holding company. Co. owns Consolidated Edison Company of New York, Inc., which delivers electricity, natural gas and steam to customers in New York City and Westchester County; and Orange and Rockland Utilities, Inc., which delivers electricity and natural gas to customers in southeastern New York, northern New Jersey and northeastern Pennsylvania. Co. also has the following competitive energy businesses: Consolidated Edison Solutions, Inc., a retail energy services company; Consolidated Edison Energy, Inc., a wholesale energy supply and services company; and Consolidated Edison Development, Inc., a company that develops and participates in infrastructure projects.

Recent Developments: For the year ended Dec 31 2012, net income increased 7.4% to US$1.14 billion from US$1.06 billion in the prior year. Revenues were US$12.19 billion, down 5.4% from US$12.89 billion the year before. Operating income was US$2.34 billion versus US$2.24 billion in the prior year, an increase of 4.5%. Direct operating expenses declined 11.3% to US$7.07 billion from US$7.97 billion in the comparable period the year before. Indirect operating expenses increased 3.8% to US$2.78 billion from US$2.68 billion in the equivalent prior-year period.

Prospects: Our evaluation of Consolidated Edison Inc. as of Apr. 7, 2013 is the result of our systematic analysis on three basic characteristics; earnings strength, relative valuation, and recent stock price movement. The company has managed to produce a neutral trend in earnings per share over the past 5 quarters. However, while recent estimates for the company have been lowered by analysts, ED has posted results that fell short of analysts expectations. Based on operating earnings yield, the company is undervalued when compared to all of the companies in our coverage universe. Share price changes over the past year indicates that ED will perform poorly over the near term.

Financial Data
(US$ in Thousands)

	12/31/2012	12/31/2011	12/31/2010	12/31/2009	12/31/2008	12/31/2007	12/31/2006	12/31/2005
Earnings Per Share	3.86	3.57	3.47	3.14	4.37	3.47	2.95	2.94
Cash Flow Per Share	8.85	10.72	8.37	8.96	2.30	5.84	5.43	3.25
Tang Book Value Per Share	39.05	38.30	37.18	35.72	34.69	32.64	30.03	28.65
Dividends Per Share	2.420	2.400	2.380	2.360	2.340	2.320	2.300	2.280
Dividend Payout %	62.69	67.23	68.59	75.16	53.55	66.86	77.97	77.55
Income Statement								
Total Revenue	12,188,000	12,938,000	13,325,000	13,032,000	13,583,000	13,120,000	12,137,000	11,690,000
EBITDA	3,342,000	3,189,000	3,013,000	2,658,000	3,005,000	1,903,000	1,705,000	1,570,000
Depn & Amortn	997,000	933,000	853,000	728,000	541,000	9,000	10,000	10,000
Income Before Taxes	1,741,000	1,662,000	1,551,000	1,319,000	1,920,000	1,377,000	1,145,000	1,096,000
Income Taxes	600,000	600,000	548,000	440,000	524,000	437,000	390,000	341,000
Net Income	1,141,000	1,062,000	1,003,000	879,000	1,196,000	929,000	737,000	719,000
Average Shares	294,500	294,400	285,900	276,300	273,600	267,300	250,300	244,700
Balance Sheet								
Current Assets	3,451,000	3,638,000	3,507,000	3,243,000	3,319,000	2,605,000	2,937,000	3,153,000
Total Assets	41,209,000	39,214,000	36,146,000	33,873,000	33,498,000	28,343,000	26,699,000	24,850,000
Current Liabilities	3,945,000	2,987,000	2,366,000	2,952,000	3,205,000	3,895,000	2,917,000	3,323,000
Long-Term Obligations	10,064,000	10,145,000	10,678,000	9,868,000	9,249,000	7,633,000	8,324,000	7,428,000
Total Liabilities	29,340,000	27,565,000	24,872,000	23,411,000	23,587,000	19,054,000	18,482,000	17,327,000
Stockholders' Equity	11,869,000	11,649,000	11,274,000	10,462,000	9,911,000	9,289,000	8,217,000	7,523,000
Shares Outstanding	292,871	292,888	291,616	281,123	273,721	272,024	257,456	245,286
Statistical Record								
Return on Assets %	2.83	2.82	2.86	2.61	3.86	3.38	2.86	3.03
Return on Equity %	9.68	9.27	9.23	8.63	12.42	10.61	9.36	9.72
EBITDA Margin %	27.42	24.65	22.61	20.40	22.12	14.50	14.05	13.43
Net Margin %	9.36	8.21	7.53	6.74	8.81	7.08	6.07	6.15
Asset Turnover	0.30	0.34	0.38	0.39	0.44	0.48	0.47	0.49
Current Ratio	0.87	1.22	1.48	1.10	1.04	0.67	1.01	0.95
Debt to Equity	0.85	0.87	0.95	0.94	0.93	0.82	1.01	0.99
Price Range	64.94-54.10	62.59-48.85	51.00-41.66	46.13-32.70	48.85-37.53	52.63-43.65	49.13-41.40	49.24-41.41
P/E Ratio	16.82-14.02	17.53-13.68	14.70-12.01	14.69-10.41	11.18-8.59	15.17-12.58	16.65-14.03	16.75-14.09
Average Yield %	4.07	4.46	5.16	5.99	5.67	4.84	5.04	5.24

Address: 4 Irving Place, New York, NY 10003	Web Site: www.conedison.com	Auditors: PricewaterhouseCoopers LLP
Telephone: 212-460-4600	Officers: Kevin Burke - Chairman, President, Chief Executive Officer John D. McMahon - Executive Vice President	Investor Contact: 212-460-6611
Fax: 212-475-0734		Transfer Agents: Computershare, Pittsburgh, PA

200

CONSTELLATION BRANDS INC

Exchange	Symbol	Price	52Wk Range	Yield	P/E
NYS	STZ	$47.64 (3/28/2013)	47.64-18.69	N/A	22.26

*7 Year Price Score 130.38 *NYSE Composite Index=100 *12 Month Price Score 120.24

TRADING VOLUME (thousand shares)

Interim Earnings (Per Share)

Qtr.	May	Aug	Nov	Feb
2009-10	0.03	0.45	0.20	(0.23)
2010-11	0.22	0.43	0.65	1.32
2011-12	0.35	0.76	0.52	0.51
2012-13	0.38	0.67	0.58	...

Interim Dividends (Per Share)

No Dividends Paid

Valuation Analysis / Institutional Holding

Valuation Analysis		Institutional Holding	
Forecast EPS	$2.85	No of Institutions	
	(04/11/2013)	491	
Market Cap	$8.7 Billion	Shares	
Book Value	$2.8 Billion	161,451,536	
Price/Book	3.15	% Held	
Price/Sales	3.21	72.52	

Business Summary: Beverages (MIC: 1.2.2 SIC: 2084 NAIC: 312130)

Constellation Brands is a producer and marketer of beverage alcohol with a portfolio of wine brands, spirits, imported beer and other select beverage alcohol products. Co. has two business segments: Constellation Wines North America (CWNA), which sells a number of wine brands across categories such as, table wine, sparkling wine and dessert wine, as well as spirits brands; and Crown Imports LLC, which has the exclusive right to import, market and sell primarily the Modelo Brands, which include Corona Extra, Corona Light, Modelo Especial, Pacifico, Negra Modelo and Victoria. CWNA wine brands include among others, Robert Mondavi Brands, Clos du Bois, Blackstone, Estancia, Arbor Mist and Simi.

Recent Developments: For the quarter ended Nov 30 2012, net income increased 4.5% to US$109.5 million from US$104.8 million in the year-earlier quarter. Revenues were US$766.9 million, up 9.4% from US$700.7 million the year before. Operating income was US$158.8 million versus US$160.3 million in the prior-year quarter, a decrease of 0.9%. Direct operating expenses rose 9.2% to US$456.1 million from US$417.8 million in the comparable period the year before. Indirect operating expenses increased 24.0% to US$152.0 million from US$122.6 million in the equivalent prior-year period.

Prospects: Our evaluation of Constellation Brands Inc. as of Apr. 7, 2013 is the result of our systematic analysis on three basic characteristics: earnings strength, relative valuation, and recent stock price movement. The company has generated a negative trend in earnings per share over the past 5 quarters. However, while recent estimates for the company have been mixed, STZ has posted better than expected results. Based on operating earnings yield, the company is about fairly valued when compared to all of the companies in our coverage universe. Share price changes over the past year indicates that STZ will perform very well over the near term.

Financial Data
(US$ in Thousands)

	9 Mos	6 Mos	3 Mos	02/29/2012	02/28/2011	02/28/2010	02/28/2009	02/29/2008
Earnings Per Share	2.14	2.08	2.17	2.13	2.62	0.45	(1.40)	(2.83)
Cash Flow Per Share	2.93	3.56	3.44	3.83	2.94	1.83	2.33	2.37
Income Statement								
Total Revenue	2,100,200	1,333,300	634,800	2,654,300	3,332,000	3,364,800	3,654,600	3,773,000
EBITDA	489,700	291,100	132,800	584,900	621,700	454,600	166,600	(202,000)
Depn & Amortn	97,000	57,200	29,500	98,400	119,200	143,800	143,600	154,700
Income Before Taxes	226,000	128,600	52,600	305,500	307,200	45,700	(293,400)	(698,500)
Income Taxes	103,500	63,100	41,200	89,000	(8,500)	160,000	194,600	172,700
Net Income	306,100	196,600	72,000	445,000	559,500	99,300	(301,400)	(613,300)
Average Shares	189,696	184,640	190,261	208,655	213,765	221,210	193,906	195,135
Balance Sheet								
Current Assets	2,480,600	2,177,900	1,971,400	2,034,300	2,083,000	2,589,100	2,534,500	3,199,000
Total Assets	8,322,700	8,040,500	7,008,200	7,109,900	7,167,600	8,094,300	8,036,500	10,052,800
Current Liabilities	787,800	656,000	587,900	1,199,600	662,900	1,372,600	1,326,400	1,718,300
Long-Term Obligations	3,928,900	3,928,700	3,285,400	2,421,400	3,136,700	3,277,100	3,971,100	4,648,700
Total Liabilities	5,547,400	5,422,400	4,708,400	4,433,900	4,615,700	5,518,000	6,128,200	7,286,900
Stockholders' Equity	2,775,300	2,618,100	2,299,800	2,676,000	2,551,900	2,576,300	1,908,300	2,765,900
Shares Outstanding	183,567	182,313	176,999	214,601	211,162	222,241	219,144	216,053
Statistical Record								
Return on Assets %	5.26	5.37	6.28	6.22	7.33	1.23	N.M.	N.M.
Return on Equity %	15.11	15.21	17.65	16.98	21.82	4.43	N.M.	N.M.
EBITDA Margin %	23.32	21.83	20.92	22.04	18.66	13.51	4.56	N.M.
Net Margin %	14.57	14.75	11.34	16.77	16.79	2.95	N.M.	N.M.
Asset Turnover	0.35	0.35	0.38	0.37	0.44	0.42	0.40	0.39
Current Ratio	3.15	3.32	3.35	1.70	3.14	1.89	1.91	1.86
Debt to Equity	1.42	1.50	1.43	0.90	1.23	1.27	2.08	1.68
Price Range	36.92-18.69	32.94-17.54	24.69-16.63	22.97-16.63	22.40-15.26	17.42-10.75	22.98-10.80	25.99-18.96
P/E Ratio	17.25-8.73	15.84-8.43	11.38-7.66	10.78-7.81	8.55-5.82	38.71-24.33	...	...

Address: 207 High Point Drive, Building 100, Victor, NY 14564 Telephone: 585-678-7100	Web Site: www.cbrands.com Officers: Richard Sands - Chairman Robert Sands - President, Chief Executive Officer	Auditors: KPMG LLP Investor Contact: 585-678-7483 Transfer Agents: BNY Mellon Shareowner Services, Jersey City, NJ

CONTINENTAL RESOURCES INC.

Exchange	Symbol	Price	52Wk Range	Yield	P/E
NYS	CLR	$86.93 (3/28/2013)	92.70-62.58	N/A	21.36

*7 Year Price Score N/A *NYSE Composite Index=100 *12 Month Price Score 103.82

TRADING VOLUME (thousand shares)

Interim Earnings (Per Share)

Qtr.	Mar	Jun	Sep	Dec
2008	0.52	0.75	0.62	0.00
2009	(0.16)	0.08	0.21	0.29
2010	0.43	0.60	0.23	(0.27)
2011	(0.80)	1.33	2.44	(0.64)
2012	0.38	2.25	0.24	1.21

Interim Dividends (Per Share)
No Dividends Paid

Valuation Analysis

		Institutional Holding	
Forecast EPS	$5.01	No of Institutions	
	(04/05/2013)	352	
Market Cap	$16.1 Billion	Shares	
Book Value	$3.2 Billion	41,953,168	
Price/Book	5.10	% Held	
Price/Sales	6.27	21.38	

Business Summary: Production & Extraction (MIC: 9.1.1 SIC: 1311 NAIC: 211111)

Continental Resources is engaged in crude oil and natural gas exploration, development and production activities in the North, South, and East regions of the U.S. As of Dec 31 2011, Co.'s estimated proved reserves were 508.4 million barrels of oil equivalent (MMBoe), with estimated proved developed reserves of 205.2 MMBoe. Crude oil comprised 64.0% of Co.'s total estimated proved reserves.

Recent Developments: For the year ended Dec 31 2012, net income increased 72.3% to US$739.4 million from US$429.1 million in the prior year. Revenues were US$2.57 billion, up 55.9% from US$1.65 billion the year before. Operating income was US$1.29 billion versus US$760.8 million in the prior year, an increase of 69.9%. Indirect operating expenses increased 43.9% to US$1.28 billion from US$889.0 million in the equivalent prior-year period.

Prospects: Our evaluation of Continental Resources Inc. as of Apr. 7, 2013 is the result of our systematic analysis on three basic characteristics: earnings strength, relative valuation, and recent stock price movement. The company has enjoyed a very positive trend in earnings per share over the past 5 quarters and while recent estimates for the company have been mixed, CLR has posted better than expected results. Based on operating earnings yield, the company is about fairly valued when compared to all of the companies in our coverage universe. Share price changes over the past year indicates that CLR will perform in line with the market over the near term.

Financial Data
(US$ in Thousands)

	12/31/2012	12/31/2011	12/31/2010	12/31/2009	12/31/2008	12/31/2007	12/31/2006	12/31/2005
Earnings Per Share	4.07	2.41	0.99	0.42	1.89	0.17	1.59	1.22
Cash Flow Per Share	8.98	6.01	3.87	2.23	4.27	2.38	2.64	1.68
Tang Book Value Per Share	17.05	12.76	7.09	6.06	5.60	3.69	3.08	2.04
Dividends Per Share	...	...	...	...	...	0.330	0.551	0.013
Dividend Payout %	...	...	...	...	...	194.12	34.75	1.04
Income Statement								
Total Revenue	2,572,520	1,649,789	839,065	626,211	960,490	582,215	483,652	375,764
EBITDA	1,990,602	1,156,011	554,362	342,125	679,291	405,977	329,026	259,534
Depn & Amortn	694,698	391,844	242,748	208,885	148,573	96,261	64,760	49,868
Income Before Taxes	1,155,196	687,445	258,467	110,008	518,530	296,777	252,956	195,446
Income Taxes	415,811	258,373	90,212	38,670	197,580	268,197	(132)	1,139
Net Income	739,385	429,072	168,255	71,338	320,950	28,580	253,088	194,307
Average Shares	181,846	178,230	169,779	169,529	169,392	165,422	159,665	159,302
Balance Sheet								
Current Assets	946,783	936,373	582,326	236,028	277,695	205,564	104,981	88,847
Total Assets	9,140,009	5,646,086	3,591,785	2,314,927	2,215,879	1,365,173	858,929	600,234
Current Liabilities	1,125,865	1,111,801	702,222	219,710	403,594	266,106	188,637	99,289
Long-Term Obligations	3,537,771	1,254,301	925,991	523,524	376,400	165,000	140,000	143,000
Total Liabilities	5,976,310	3,337,960	2,383,630	1,284,648	1,267,171	742,041	368,468	275,504
Stockholders' Equity	3,163,699	2,308,126	1,208,155	1,030,279	948,708	623,132	490,461	324,730
Shares Outstanding	185,604	180,871	170,408	169,968	169,558	168,864	159,106	159,048
Statistical Record								
Return on Assets %	9.97	9.29	5.70	3.15	17.88	2.57	34.69	...
Return on Equity %	26.95	24.40	15.03	7.21	40.73	5.13	62.09	...
EBITDA Margin %	77.38	70.07	66.07	54.63	70.72	69.73	68.03	69.07
Net Margin %	28.74	26.01	20.05	11.39	33.42	4.91	52.33	51.71
Asset Turnover	0.35	0.36	0.28	0.28	0.53	0.52	0.66	...
Current Ratio	0.84	0.84	0.83	1.07	0.69	0.77	0.56	0.89
Debt to Equity	1.12	0.54	0.77	0.51	0.40	0.26	0.29	0.44
Price Range	94.93-62.58	72.12-45.43	59.11-37.35	45.47-14.28	81.60-13.54	27.03-14.10		
P/E Ratio	23.32-15.38	29.93-18.85	59.71-37.73	108.26-34.00	43.17-7.16	159.00-82.94	...	...
Average Yield %	...	...	...	...	...	1.77	...	...

Address: 20 N. Broadway, Oklahoma City, OK 73102 Telephone: 405-234-9000	Web Site: www.contres.com Officers: Harold G. Hamm - Chairman, Chief Executive Officer Jeffrey B. Hume - Vice-Chairman, President, Chief Operating Officer	Auditors: Grant Thornton LLP Investor Contact: 405-234-9127 Transfer Agents: American Stock Transfer & Trust Company, New York

CONVERGYS CORP.

Exchange	Symbol	Price	52Wk Range	Yield	P/E
NYS	CVG	$17.03 (3/28/2013)	17.23-12.52	1.41	19.80

*7 Year Price Score 93.46   *NYSE Composite Index=100   *12 Month Price Score 99.54

Interim Earnings (Per Share)

Qtr.	Mar	Jun	Sep	Dec
2008	0.28	0.32	(1.15)	(0.24)
2009	0.23	(0.50)	(0.70)	0.34
2010	0.28	0.22	0.23	(1.16)
2011	0.28	0.26	1.75	0.44
2012	0.22	0.13	0.24	0.26

Interim Dividends (Per Share)

Amt	Decl	Ex	Rec	Pay
0.05Q	05/08/2012	06/20/2012	06/22/2012	07/06/2012
0.05Q	07/26/2012	09/19/2012	09/21/2012	10/05/2012
0.05Q	10/23/2012	12/19/2012	12/21/2012	01/04/2013
0.06Q	02/07/2013	03/20/2013	03/22/2013	04/05/2013

Indicated Div: $0.24

Valuation Analysis   **Institutional Holding**

Forecast EPS	$1.02	No of Institutions
	(04/06/2013)	281
Market Cap	$1.8 Billion	Shares
Book Value	$1.4 Billion	109,784,280
Price/Book	1.31	% Held
Price/Sales	0.90	87.17

TRADING VOLUME (thousand shares)

Business Summary: Miscellaneous Consumer Services (MIC: 2.2.3 SIC: 8742 NAIC: 541613)

Convergys is engaged in providing customer management services, focusing on bringing value to its clients through every customer interaction. Co.'s customer and relationship management provides solutions across the customer lifecycle, including: Customer Service; Customer Retention; Technical Support; Business-to-Consumer Sales; Complex Device Support; Business-to-Business Sales and Account Management; Back Office; Collections; Quality Assurance; Direct Response; and Home Agent.

Recent Developments: For the year ended Dec 31 2012, income from continuing operations decreased 90.0% to US$28.2 million from US$282.5 million a year earlier. Net income decreased 70.0% to US$100.6 million from US$334.8 million in the prior year. Revenues were US$2.01 billion, up 3.7% from US$1.93 billion the year before. Operating income was US$38.6 million versus US$110.1 million in the prior year, a decrease of 64.9%. Direct operating expenses rose 4.0% to US$1.29 billion from US$1.24 billion in the comparable period the year before. Indirect operating expenses increased 16.2% to US$676.9 million from US$582.7 million in the equivalent prior-year period.

Prospects: Our evaluation of Convergys Corp. as of Apr. 7, 2013 is the result of our systematic analysis on three basic characteristics: earnings strength, relative valuation, and recent stock price movement. The company has managed to produce a neutral trend in earnings per share over the past 5 quarters and while recent estimates for the company have remained steady, CVG has posted better than expected results. Based on operating earnings yield, the company is undervalued when compared to all of the companies in our coverage universe. Share price changes over the past year indicates that CVG will perform very well over the near term.

Financial Data

(US$ in Thousands)	12/31/2012	12/31/2011	12/31/2010	12/31/2009	12/31/2008	12/31/2007	12/31/2006	12/31/2005
Earnings Per Share	0.86	2.72	(0.43)	(0.63)	(0.75)	1.23	1.17	0.86
Cash Flow Per Share	1.00	1.64	1.58	2.16	1.55	1.57	2.55	1.66
Tang Book Value Per Share	7.32	4.88	2.65	0.87	0.38	4.57	3.85	3.13
Dividends Per Share	0.150	...	...	...	...	...	...	...
Dividend Payout %	17.44	...	...	...	...	...	...	...
Income Statement								
Total Revenue	2,005,000	2,262,000	2,203,400	2,827,200	2,785,800	2,844,300	2,789,800	2,582,100
EBITDA	125,300	265,000	11,600	(10,800)	(58,000)	364,200	385,700	348,300
Depn & Amortn	82,400	86,900	97,300	118,900	119,000	115,400	130,100	126,100
Income Before Taxes	29,300	162,000	(105,200)	(158,600)	(199,600)	231,300	232,800	201,000
Income Taxes	1,100	118,900	16,700	(40,300)	(71,000)	76,100	78,400	90,800
Net Income	100,600	334,800	(53,200)	(77,300)	(92,900)	169,500	166,200	122,600
Average Shares	117,100	122,900	123,100	122,800	123,500	137,700	141,700	142,900
Balance Sheet								
Current Assets	1,100,600	951,100	705,500	961,100	978,000	861,600	930,200	849,000
Total Assets	2,037,900	2,325,900	2,125,300	2,613,600	2,841,400	2,564,200	2,540,300	2,411,400
Current Liabilities	286,500	382,200	471,200	889,100	798,200	426,900	595,900	617,800
Long-Term Obligations	59,900	121,000	119,300	64,400	406,400	259,300	259,600	297,500
Total Liabilities	666,000	914,400	941,200	1,407,200	1,691,300	1,042,500	1,085,200	1,056,300
Stockholders' Equity	1,371,900	1,411,500	1,184,100	1,206,400	1,150,100	1,521,700	1,455,100	1,355,100
Shares Outstanding	105,900	115,400	122,100	123,100	122,100	128,200	136,500	139,900
Statistical Record								
Return on Assets %	4.60	15.04	N.M.	N.M.	N.M.	6.64	6.71	5.31
Return on Equity %	7.21	25.80	N.M.	N.M.	N.M.	11.39	11.83	9.29
EBITDA Margin %	6.25	11.72	0.53	N.M.	N.M.	12.80	13.83	13.49
Net Margin %	5.02	14.80	N.M.	N.M.	N.M.	5.96	5.96	4.75
Asset Turnover	0.92	1.02	0.93	1.04	1.03	1.11	1.13	1.12
Current Ratio	3.84	2.49	1.50	1.08	1.23	2.02	1.56	1.37
Debt to Equity	0.04	0.09	0.10	0.05	0.35	0.17	0.18	0.22
Price Range	17.23-12.19	14.72-8.61	13.72-9.52	11.93-5.56	16.65-4.06	27.24-15.49	24.54-15.55	17.78-12.58
P/E Ratio	20.03-14.17	5.41-3.17	...	...	...	22.15-12.59	20.97-13.29	20.67-14.63
Average Yield %	1.03	...	...	...	...	...	...	...

Address: 201 East Fourth Street, Cincinnati, OH 45202 Telephone: 513-723-7000	Web Site: www.convergys.com Officers: Jeffrey H. Fox - Executive Chairman, President, Chief Executive Officer Andrea J. Ayers - President, Chief Executive Officer, Division Officer	Auditors: Ernst & Young LLP Investor Contact: 888-284-9900 Transfer Agents: Computershare Investor Services, LLC, Canton, MA

COOPER COMPANIES, INC. (THE)

Exchange	Symbol	Price	52Wk Range	Yield	P/E
NYS	COO	$107.88 (3/28/2013)	108.23-72.29	0.06	19.87

*7 Year Price Score 153.27 *NYSE Composite Index=100 *12 Month Price Score 106.23

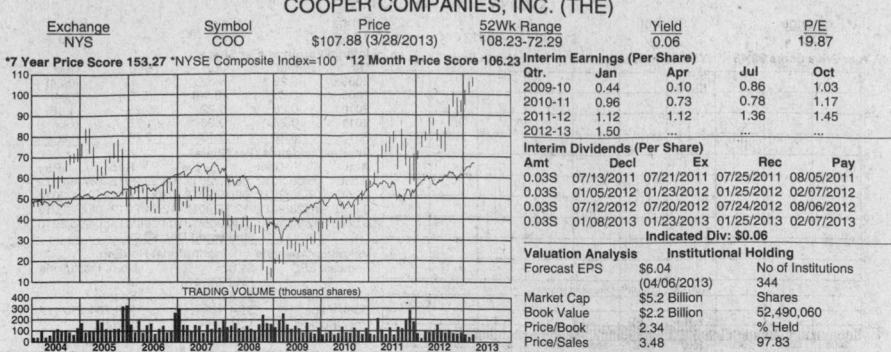

Interim Earnings (Per Share)

Qtr.	Jan	Apr	Jul	Oct
2009-10	0.44	0.10	0.86	1.03
2010-11	0.96	0.73	0.78	1.17
2011-12	1.12	1.12	1.36	1.45
2012-13	1.50	...	...	...

Interim Dividends (Per Share)

Amt	Decl	Ex	Rec	Pay
0.03S	07/13/2011	07/21/2011	07/25/2011	08/05/2011
0.03S	01/05/2012	01/23/2012	01/25/2012	02/07/2012
0.03S	07/12/2012	07/20/2012	07/24/2012	08/06/2012
0.03S	01/08/2013	01/23/2013	01/25/2013	02/07/2013

Indicated Div: $0.06

Valuation Analysis / **Institutional Holding**

Forecast EPS	$6.04 (04/06/2013)	No of Institutions 344
Market Cap	$5.2 Billion	Shares
Book Value	$2.2 Billion	52,490,060
Price/Book	2.34	% Held
Price/Sales	3.48	97.83

Business Summary: Medical Instruments & Equipment (MIC: 4.3.1 SIC: 3851 NAIC: 339115)

The Cooper Companies is a medical device company. Co. operates through two business units, CooperVision, Inc. (CooperVision) and CooperSurgical, Inc. (CooperSurgical). CooperVision is a manufacturer providing products for contact lens wearers. CooperVision develops, manufactures and markets a range of monthly, two-week and single-use contact lenses. CooperSurgical focuses on supplying women's health clinicians with products and treatment options to improve the delivery of healthcare to women. CooperSurgical products support the point of healthcare delivery in the hospital, clinicians office and fertility clinics.

Recent Developments: For the quarter ended Jan 31 2013, net income increased 37.2% to US$74.9 million from US$54.6 million in the year-earlier quarter. Revenues were US$379.8 million, up 16.5% from US$326.1 million the year before. Operating income was US$68.8 million versus US$61.7 million in the prior-year quarter, an increase of 11.5%. Direct operating expenses rose 20.5% to US$139.3 million from US$115.6 million in the comparable period the year before. Indirect operating expenses increased 15.4% to US$171.7 million from US$148.7 million in the equivalent prior-year period.

Prospects: Our evaluation of Cooper Companies Inc. as of Apr. 7, 2013 is the result of our systematic analysis on three basic characteristics: earnings strength, relative valuation, and recent stock price movement. The company has generated a negative trend in earnings per share over the past 5 quarters. However, while recent estimates for the company have been mixed, COO has posted better than expected results. Based on operating earnings yield, the company is about fairly valued when compared to all of the companies in our coverage universe. Share price changes over the past year indicates that COO will perform well over the near term.

Financial Data

(US$ in Thousands)	3 Mos	10/31/2012	10/31/2011	10/31/2010	10/31/2009	10/31/2008	10/31/2007	10/31/2006
Earnings Per Share	5.43	5.05	3.63	2.43	2.21	1.43	(0.25)	1.44
Cash Flow Per Share	6.63	6.56	7.17	5.88	4.94	2.14	3.00	3.65
Tang Book Value Per Share	13.31	12.55	11.13	6.34	3.73	0.77	0.54	0.32
Dividends Per Share	0.060	0.060	0.060	0.060	0.060	0.060	0.060	0.060
Dividend Payout %	1.10	1.19	1.65	2.47	2.71	4.20	...	4.17
Income Statement								
Total Revenue	379,839	1,445,136	1,330,835	1,158,517	1,080,421	1,063,176	950,641	858,960
EBITDA	90,914	398,437	308,255	255,095	251,573	209,176	127,866	168,230
Depn & Amortn	7,371	111,214	98,149	94,001	92,602	82,185	84,511	61,647
Income Before Taxes	80,976	275,452	192,764	124,426	114,828	76,207	672	73,337
Income Taxes	6,041	26,808	17,334	11,623	14,280	10,731	11,864	7,103
Net Income	74,667	248,339	175,430	112,803	100,548	65,476	(11,192)	66,234
Average Shares	49,633	49,152	48,309	46,505	45,478	46,844	44,707	47,569
Balance Sheet								
Current Assets	680,848	657,860	540,347	491,340	503,878	526,032	517,522	456,951
Total Assets	2,969,544	2,941,384	2,624,518	2,525,018	2,551,907	2,587,616	2,560,271	2,352,601
Current Liabilities	226,132	262,552	267,206	199,520	175,414	255,407	286,480	276,630
Long-Term Obligations	377,512	348,422	327,453	591,977	771,630	861,781	830,116	681,286
Total Liabilities	737,482	748,633	687,030	858,242	1,011,565	1,170,540	1,136,682	974,092
Stockholders' Equity	2,232,062	2,192,751	1,937,488	1,666,776	1,540,342	1,417,076	1,423,589	1,378,509
Shares Outstanding	48,316	48,440	47,846	45,827	45,244	45,129	44,869	44,548
Statistical Record								
Return on Assets %	9.65	8.90	6.81	4.44	3.91	2.54	N.M.	2.92
Return on Equity %	12.89	11.99	9.73	7.03	6.80	4.60	N.M.	5.00
EBITDA Margin %	23.93	27.57	23.16	22.02	23.28	19.67	13.45	19.59
Net Margin %	19.66	17.18	13.18	9.74	9.31	6.16	N.M.	7.71
Asset Turnover	0.54	0.52	0.52	0.46	0.42	0.41	0.39	0.38
Current Ratio	3.01	2.51	2.02	2.46	2.87	2.06	1.81	1.65
Debt to Equity	0.17	0.16	0.17	0.36	0.50	0.61	0.58	0.49
Price Range	102.08-72.14	100.67-56.64	83.00-48.98	50.82-28.45	31.35-10.94	44.58-15.48	57.63-42.00	73.80-42.57
P/E Ratio	18.80-13.29	19.93-11.22	22.87-13.49	20.91-11.71	14.19-4.95	31.17-10.83	...	51.25-29.56
Average Yield %	0.07	0.08	0.09	0.15	0.25	0.17	0.12	0.11

Address: 6140 Stoneridge Mall Road, Suite 590, Pleasanton, CA 94588	Web Site: www.coopercos.com	Auditors: KPMG LLP
Telephone: 925-460-3600	Officers: A. Thomas Bender - Chairman Allan E. Rubenstein - Vice-Chairman	Investor Contact: 925-460-3663
Fax: 925-460-3648		Transfer Agents: American Stock Transfer & Trust Company, New York, NY

CORELOGIC INC.

Exchange	Symbol	Price	52Wk Range	Yield	P/E
NYS	CLGX	$25.86 (3/28/2013)	28.78-15.08	N/A	23.72

*7 Year Price Score 108.78 ***NYSE Composite Index=100** ***12 Month Price Score 105.10**

Interim Earnings (Per Share)

Qtr.	Mar	Jun	Sep	Dec
2008	0.32	0.21	(0.09)	(0.72)
2009	0.38	0.75	0.59	0.37
2010	0.28	0.22	(0.80)	(0.24)
2011	0.20	0.29	(1.01)	(0.20)
2012	0.16	0.40	0.37	0.16

Interim Dividends (Per Share)

No Dividends Paid

Valuation Analysis		Institutional Holding	
Forecast EPS	$1.70	No of Institutions	
	(04/05/2013)	326	
Market Cap	$2.5 Billion	Shares	
Book Value	$1.2 Billion	90,917,872	
Price/Book	2.16	% Held	
Price/Sales	1.61	N/A	

Business Summary: Business Services (MIC: 7.5.2 SIC: 7374 NAIC: 519190)

CoreLogic is a property information, analytics and services provider in the U.S. and Australia. The markets Co. serves include real estate and mortgage finance, insurance, capital markets and government. Co. has three segments: data and analytics, which provides access to data assets including real estate information, mortgage-backed, employment verification and under-banked credit information; mortgage origination services, which provides loan origination and closing-related services to mortgage originators; and asset management and processing solutions, which provides analytical and outsourcing services primarily relating to defaulting and foreclosed mortgage loans to mortgage servicers.

Recent Developments: For the year ended Dec 31 2012, income from continuing operations increased 129.7% to US$122.9 million from US$53.5 million a year earlier. Net income amounted to US$111.6 million versus a net loss of US$73.6 million in the prior year. Revenues were US$1.57 billion, up 17.1% from US$1.34 billion the year before. Operating income was US$222.3 million versus US$88.7 million in the prior year, an increase of 150.6%. Direct operating expenses rose 12.1% to US$839.6 million from US$749.1 million in the comparable period the year before. Indirect operating expenses increased 1.0% to US$505.8 million from US$500.8 million in the equivalent prior-year period.

Prospects: Our evaluation of CoreLogic Inc. as of Apr. 7, 2013 is the result of our systematic analysis on three basic characteristics: earnings strength, relative valuation, and recent stock price movement. The company has generated a negative trend in earnings per share over the past 5 quarters and while recent estimates for the company have been mixed, CLGX has posted better than expected results. Based on operating earnings yield, the company is about fairly valued when compared to all of the companies in our coverage universe. Share price changes over the past year indicates that CLGX will perform very well over the near term.

Financial Data
(US$ in Thousands)

	12/31/2012	12/31/2011	12/31/2010	12/31/2009	12/31/2008	12/31/2007	12/31/2006	12/31/2005
Earnings Per Share	1.09	(0.68)	(0.60)	2.09	(0.28)	(0.03)	2.92	4.97
Cash Flow Per Share	3.52	1.47	1.85	5.16	0.83	6.97	6.36	9.77
Tang Book Value Per Share	N.M.	N.M.	N.M.	2.70	N.M.	0.78	6.41	6.96
Dividends Per Share	...	...	...	0.880	0.880	0.880	0.720	...
Dividend Payout %	...	...	...	42.11	...	...	24.66	...
Income Statement								
Total Revenue	1,567,633	1,338,547	1,623,272	5,972,777	6,213,758	8,195,605	8,499,066	8,061,758
EBITDA	297,044	212,390	174,763	700,481	378,280	463,042	875,167	1,114,377
Depn & Amortn	77,300	63,700	59,300	219,922	262,945	232,339	206,925	157,439
Income Before Taxes	167,276	90,400	85,050	423,797	44,211	152,063	596,903	903,628
Income Taxes	80,396	67,175	35,313	154,621	15,846	43,689	220,100	324,500
Net Income	112,293	(74,609)	(67,330)	199,651	(26,320)	(3,119)	287,676	485,266
Average Shares	104,050	109,712	112,363	95,478	92,516	94,649	98,653	97,795
Balance Sheet								
Current Assets	589,924	655,979	855,777	1,696,529	1,737,686	1,959,807	2,074,716	2,138,460
Total Assets	3,029,827	3,110,071	3,219,832	8,723,097	8,730,055	8,647,921	8,224,285	7,598,641
Current Liabilities	517,091	527,252	729,634	2,238,605	2,292,314	1,867,309	1,871,737	1,732,115
Long-Term Obligations	792,324	846,027	487,437	791,083	868,274	906,046	847,991	848,569
Total Liabilities	1,860,526	1,867,550	1,675,492	5,568,802	6,038,179	5,663,096	5,022,232	4,592,094
Stockholders' Equity	1,169,301	1,242,521	1,544,340	3,154,295	2,691,876	2,984,825	3,202,053	3,006,547
Shares Outstanding	97,698	106,544	115,499	103,283	92,963	91,830	96,484	95,860
Statistical Record								
Return on Assets %	3.65	N.M.	N.M.	2.29	N.M.	N.M.	3.64	7.03
Return on Equity %	9.29	N.M.	N.M.	6.83	N.M.	N.M.	9.27	17.74
EBITDA Margin %	18.95	15.87	10.77	11.73	6.09	5.65	10.30	13.82
Net Margin %	7.16	N.M.	N.M.	3.34	N.M.	N.M.	3.38	6.02
Asset Turnover	0.51	0.42	0.27	0.68	0.71	0.97	1.07	1.17
Current Ratio	1.14	1.24	1.17	0.76	0.76	1.05	1.11	1.23
Debt to Equity	0.68	0.68	0.32	0.25	0.32	0.30	0.26	0.28
Price Range	28.00-12.55	20.91-7.80	20.34-16.02	18.35-10.61	23.61-8.19	29.85-16.29	25.43-19.56	26.55-16.96
P/E Ratio	25.69-11.51			8.78-5.08			8.71-6.70	5.34-3.41
Average Yield %	...	...	...	5.75	5.48	3.72	3.25	...

Address: 40 Pacifica, Irvine, CA 92618-7471 **Telephone:** 949-214-1013	**Web Site:** www.corelogic.com **Officers:** Anand K. Nallathambi - President, Chief Executive Officer George S. Livermore - Executive Vice President, Division Officer	**Auditors:** Pricewaterhouse Coopers LLP **Investor Contact:** 703-610-5410 **Transfer Agents:** Wells Fargo Shareowner Services, South Saint Paul, MN

CORNING, INC.

Exchange	Symbol	Price	52Wk Range	Yield	P/E
NYS	GLW	$13.33 (3/28/2013)	14.45-10.88	2.70	11.59

*7 Year Price Score 61.52 *NYSE Composite Index=100 *12 Month Price Score 92.33

Interim Earnings (Per Share)

Qtr.	Mar	Jun	Sep	Dec
2008	0.64	2.01	0.49	0.17
2009	0.01	0.39	0.41	0.47
2010	0.52	0.58	0.50`	0.66
2011	0.47	0.47	0.51	0.31
2012	0.30	0.30	0.35	0.20

Interim Dividends (Per Share)

Amt	Decl	Ex	Rec	Pay
0.075Q	04/26/2012	05/29/2012	05/31/2012	06/29/2012
0.075Q	07/18/2012	08/29/2012	08/31/2012	09/28/2012
0.09Q	10/03/2012	11/14/2012	11/16/2012	12/14/2012
0.09Q	02/06/2013	02/26/2013	02/28/2013	03/28/2013

Indicated Div: $0.36

Valuation Analysis		Institutional Holding	
Forecast EPS	$1.17 (04/05/2013)	No of Institutions	1091
Market Cap	$19.6 Billion	Shares	
Book Value	$21.5 Billion		1,171,612,032
Price/Book	0.91	% Held	
Price/Sales	2.45		70.11

Business Summary: Electrical Equipment (MIC: 7.3.1 SIC: 3211 NAIC: 327211)

Corning is a manufacturer of glass and ceramics. Co. operates in five segments: Display Technologies, which manufactures glass substrates for flat panel liquid crystal displays; Telecommunications, which manufactures optical fiber and cable and hardware and equipment components for the telecommunications industry; Environmental Technologies, which manufactures ceramic substrates and filters for automotive and diesel applications; Specialty Materials, which manufactures products that provide material formulations for glass, glass ceramics and fluoride crystals; and Life Sciences, which manufactures glass and plastic labware, equipment, media and reagents for scientific applications.

Recent Developments: For the year ended Dec 31 2012, net income decreased 38.4% to US$1.73 billion from US$2.81 billion in the prior year. Revenues were US$8.01 billion, up 1.5% from US$7.89 billion the year before. Operating income was US$1.32 billion versus US$1.69 billion in the prior year, a decrease of 22.0%. Direct operating expenses rose 6.7% to US$4.62 billion from US$4.32 billion in the comparable period the year before. Indirect operating expenses increased 10.9% to US$2.08 billion from US$1.87 billion in the equivalent prior-year period.

Prospects: Our evaluation of Corning Inc. as of Apr. 7, 2013 is the result of our systematic analysis on three basic characteristics: earnings strength, relative valuation, and recent stock price movement. The company has enjoyed a very positive trend in earnings per share over the past 5 quarters and while recent estimates for the company have remained steady, GLW has posted better than expected results. Based on operating earnings yield, the company is undervalued when compared to all of the companies in our coverage universe. Share price changes over the past year indicates that GLW will perform very poorly over the near term.

Financial Data

(US$ in Thousands)	12/31/2012	12/31/2011	12/31/2010	12/31/2009	12/31/2008	12/31/2007	12/31/2006	12/31/2005
Earnings Per Share	1.15	1.77	2.25	1.28	3.32	1.34	1.16	0.38
Cash Flow Per Share	2.14	2.04	2.46	1.34	1.36	1.33	1.16	1.32
Tang Book Value Per Share	13.60	13.30	11.95	9.57	8.49	5.86	4.43	3.43
Dividends Per Share	0.315	0.225	0.200	0.200	0.200	0.100	...	...
Dividend Payout %	27.39	12.71	8.89	15.63	6.02	7.46	...	...
Income Statement								
Total Revenue	8,012,000	7,890,000	6,632,000	5,395,000	5,948,000	5,860,000	5,174,000	4,579,000
EBITDA	2,396,000	2,766,000	2,837,000	1,354,000	2,192,000	1,478,200	1,510,000	1,139,000
Depn & Amortn	997,000	957,000	854,000	792,000	695,000	250,200	591,000	512,000
Income Before Taxes	1,302,000	1,739,000	1,885,000	499,000	1,523,000	1,291,000	961,000	572,000
Income Taxes	389,000	408,000	287,000	(74,000)	(2,405,000)	80,000	55,000	578,000
Net Income	1,728,000	2,805,000	3,558,000	2,008,000	5,257,000	2,150,000	1,855,000	585,000
Average Shares	1,506,000	1,583,000	1,581,000	1,568,000	1,584,000	1,603,000	1,594,000	1,535,000
Balance Sheet								
Current Assets	9,695,000	8,677,000	8,859,000	5,521,000	4,619,000	5,294,000	4,798,000	3,860,000
Total Assets	29,375,000	27,848,000	25,833,000	21,295,000	19,256,000	15,215,000	13,065,000	11,175,000
Current Liabilities	1,956,000	2,097,000	1,986,000	1,539,000	2,052,000	2,512,000	2,319,000	2,216,000
Long-Term Obligations	3,382,000	2,364,000	2,262,000	1,930,000	1,527,000	1,514,000	1,696,000	1,789,000
Total Liabilities	7,889,000	6,770,000	6,458,000	5,752,000	5,813,000	5,719,000	5,819,000	5,566,000
Stockholders' Equity	21,486,000	21,078,000	19,375,000	15,543,000	13,443,000	9,496,000	7,246,000	5,609,000
Shares Outstanding	1,470,000	1,515,000	1,561,000	1,553,000	1,548,000	1,568,000	1,565,000	1,536,000
Statistical Record								
Return on Assets %	6.02	10.45	15.10	9.90	30.42	15.21	15.31	5.60
Return on Equity %	8.10	13.87	20.38	13.85	45.71	25.68	28.86	12.41
EBITDA Margin %	29.91	35.06	42.78	25.10	36.85	25.23	29.18	24.87
Net Margin %	21.57	35.55	53.65	37.22	88.38	36.69	35.85	12.78
Asset Turnover	0.28	0.29	0.28	0.27	0.34	0.41	0.43	0.44
Current Ratio	4.96	4.14	4.46	3.59	2.25	2.11	2.07	1.74
Debt to Equity	0.16	0.11	0.12	0.12	0.11	0.16	0.23	0.32
Price Range	14.62-10.88	23.37-11.88	20.92-15.68	19.34-9.13	27.77-7.82	27.22-18.46	29.09-17.82	21.74-10.74
P/E Ratio	12.71-9.46	13.20-6.71	9.30-6.97	15.11-7.13	8.36-2.36	20.31-13.78	25.08-15.36	57.21-28.26
Average Yield %	2.46	1.29	1.10	1.36	1.01	0.42	...	...

Address: One Riverfront Plaza, Corning, NY 14831 Telephone: 607-974-9000	Web Site: www.corning.com Officers: Wendell P. Weeks - Chairman, President, Chief Executive Officer James B. Flaws - Vice-Chairman, Chief Financial Officer	Auditors: PricewaterhouseCoopers LLP Transfer Agents: Computershare Investor Services LLC, Chicago, IL

CORPORATE EXECUTIVE BOARD CO.

Exchange	Symbol	Price	52Wk Range	Yield	P/E
NYS	CEB	$58.16 (3/28/2013)	58.82-34.86	1.55	52.87

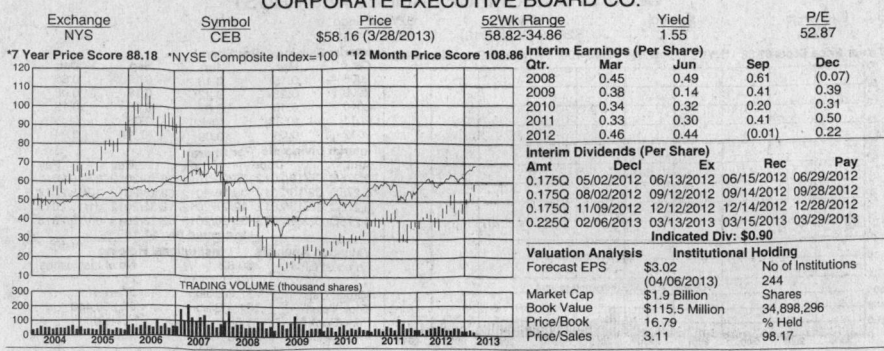

*7 Year Price Score 88.18 ***NYSE Composite Index=100** ***12 Month Price Score 108.86**

Interim Earnings (Per Share)

Qtr.	Mar	Jun	Sep	Dec
2008	0.45	0.49	0.61	(0.07)
2009	0.38	0.14	0.41	0.39
2010	0.34	0.32	0.20	0.31
2011	0.33	0.30	0.41	0.50
2012	0.46	0.44	(0.01)	0.22

Interim Dividends (Per Share)

Amt	Decl	Ex	Rec	Pay
0.175Q	05/02/2012	06/13/2012	06/15/2012	06/29/2012
0.175Q	08/02/2012	09/12/2012	09/14/2012	09/28/2012
0.175Q	11/09/2012	12/12/2012	12/14/2012	12/28/2012
0.225Q	02/06/2013	03/13/2013	03/15/2013	03/29/2013

Indicated Div: $0.90

Valuation Analysis **Institutional Holding**

Forecast EPS	$3.02	No of Institutions
	(04/06/2013)	244
Market Cap	$1.9 Billion	Shares
Book Value	$115.5 Million	34,898,296
Price/Book	16.79	% Held
Price/Sales	3.11	98.17

Business Summary: Business Services (MIC: 7.5.2 SIC: 8742 NAIC: 541611)

Corporate Executive Board provides products and services such as best practices studies, executive education, analysis, proprietary databases and decision support tools to drive corporate performance. Co.'s products and services focus on five corporate functions: finance, corporate services, and corporate strategy; human resources; information technology; legal, risk, and compliance; and sales, marketing, and communications. In addition, Co. serves businesses in the financial services industry and government agencies through insights, tools, and peer collaboration. Co. primarily delivers its products and services to a global client base through annual, fixed-fee membership subscriptions.

Recent Developments: For the year ended Dec 31 2012, net income decreased 29.6% to US$37.1 million from US$52.7 million in the prior year. Revenues were US$622.7 million, up 28.5% from US$484.7 million the year before. Operating income was US$84.7 million versus US$96.5 million in the prior year, a decrease of 12.2%. Direct operating expenses rose 33.8% to US$223.8 million from US$167.3 million in the comparable period the year before. Indirect operating expenses increased 42.2% to US$314.2 million from US$220.9 million in the equivalent prior-year period.

Prospects: Our evaluation of Corporate Executive Board Co. as of Apr. 7, 2013 is the result of our systematic analysis on three basic characteristics: earnings strength, relative valuation, and recent stock price movement. The company has generated a negative trend in earnings per share over the past 5 quarters and while recent estimates for the company have been mixed, CEB has posted better than expected results. Based on operating earnings yield, the company is about fairly valued when compared to all of the companies in our coverage universe. Share price changes over the past year indicates that CEB will perform well over the near term.

Financial Data
(US$ in Thousands)

	12/31/2012	12/31/2011	12/31/2010	12/31/2009	12/31/2008	12/31/2007	12/31/2006	12/31/2005
Earnings Per Share	1.10	1.53	1.17	1.33	1.48	2.17	1.94	1.83
Cash Flow Per Share	3.64	2.94	2.48	0.84	2.48	3.00	3.43	4.59
Tang Book Value Per Share	N.M.	1.10	1.16	0.32	N.M.	0.08	7.96	9.55
Dividends Per Share	0.700	0.600	0.440	0.740	1.760	1.600	1.200	0.400
Dividend Payout %	63.64	39.22	37.61	55.64	118.92	73.73	61.86	21.86
Income Statement								
Total Revenue	622,654	484,663	438,907	442,906	558,352	532,716	460,623	362,226
EBITDA	105,019	109,807	83,010	90,918	103,548	141,188	138,432	170,910
Depn & Amortn	19,600	13,500	14,600	17,300	15,800	13,100	9,700	7,300
Income Before Taxes	74,620	96,307	68,410	73,618	87,748	128,088	128,732	113,610
Income Taxes	37,569	38,860	28,047	27,989	36,957	47,501	49,561	38,550
Net Income	37,051	52,655	40,363	45,629	50,791	80,587	79,171	75,060
Average Shares	33,821	34,419	34,553	34,293	34,329	37,159	40,721	41,092
Balance Sheet								
Current Assets	367,019	348,276	298,759	203,436	190,986	271,966	482,158	579,095
Total Assets	1,322,249	533,692	510,149	423,195	446,465	544,772	736,055	726,995
Current Liabilities	520,053	368,886	344,358	298,792	355,765	417,431	400,506	332,012
Long-Term Obligations	528,280	...	...	...	...	...	...	...
Total Liabilities	1,206,747	454,128	427,333	372,918	417,862	477,225	418,190	341,581
Stockholders' Equity	115,502	79,564	82,816	50,277	28,603	67,547	317,865	385,414
Shares Outstanding	33,337	33,302	34,322	34,147	34,043	34,993	38,947	39,482
Statistical Record								
Return on Assets %	3.98	10.09	8.65	10.49	10.22	12.58	10.82	11.50
Return on Equity %	37.88	64.85	60.65	115.69	105.36	41.82	22.51	21.06
EBITDA Margin %	16.87	22.66	18.91	20.53	18.55	26.50	30.05	33.38
Net Margin %	5.95	10.86	9.20	10.30	9.10	15.13	17.19	20.72
Asset Turnover	0.67	0.93	0.94	1.02	1.12	0.83	0.63	0.55
Current Ratio	0.71	0.94	0.87	0.68	0.54	0.65	1.20	1.74
Debt to Equity	4.57	...	...	...	...	...	...	...
Price Range	53.86-34.86	45.45-28.21	38.92-21.29	26.51-12.93	60.10-19.78	95.42-60.06	112.43-81.57	91.47-62.00
P/E Ratio	48.96-31.69	29.71-18.44	33.26-18.20	19.93-9.72	40.61-13.36	43.97-27.68	57.95-42.05	49.98-33.88
Average Yield %	1.62	1.59	1.51	3.67	4.65	2.24	1.26	0.54

Address: 1919 North Lynn Street, Arlington, VA 22209 **Telephone:** 571-303-3000	**Web Site:** www.executiveboard.com **Officers:** Thomas L. Monahan - Chairman, Chief Executive Officer Richard S. Lindahl - Chief Financial Officer	**Auditors:** Ernst & Young LLP **Investor Contact:** 571-303-6956 **Transfer Agents:** Computershare, Jersey City, NJ

CORPORATE OFFICE PROPERTIES TRUST

Exchange	Symbol	Price	52Wk Range	Yield	P/E
NYS	OFC	$26.68 (3/28/2013)	27.42-21.31	4.12	N/A

*7 Year Price Score 62.53 *NYSE Composite Index=100 *12 Month Price Score 100.27

Interim Earnings (Per Share)

Qtr.	Mar	Jun	Sep	Dec
2008	0.15	0.18	0.19	0.35
2009	0.23	0.22	0.18	0.08
2010	0.10	0.07	0.08	0.19
2011	(0.33)	(0.42)	0.03	(1.24)
2012	0.04	0.09	(0.39)	0.24

Interim Dividends (Per Share)

Amt	Decl	Ex	Rec	Pay
0.275Q	05/10/2012	06/27/2012	06/29/2012	07/16/2012
0.275Q	09/13/2012	09/26/2012	09/28/2012	10/15/2012
0.275Q	12/13/2012	12/27/2012	12/31/2012	01/15/2013
0.275Q	02/28/2013	03/26/2013	03/28/2013	04/15/2013

Indicated Div: $1.10

Valuation Analysis

		Institutional Holding	
Forecast EPS	$0.82 (04/05/2013)	No of Institutions	257
Market Cap	$2.2 Billion	Shares	87,256,440
Book Value	$1.4 Billion	% Held	102.87
Price/Book	1.58		
Price/Sales	4.09		

Business Summary: REITs (MIC: 5.3.1 SIC: 6798 NAIC: 525930)

Corporate Office Properties Trust is an office real estate investment trust that focuses on serving the specialized requirements of the U.S. Government and defense information technology sectors. As of Dec 31 2012, Co.'s investments in real estate included the following: 208 operating office properties totaling 18.8 million square feet that were 88.0% occupied; 13 office properties under construction or redevelopment; land held or under pre-construction totaling 1,694 acres (including 561 acres controlled but not owned); and a partially operational, wholesale data center.

Recent Developments: For the year ended Dec 31 2012, income from continuing operations was US$6.6 million compared with a loss of US$81.9 million a year earlier. Net income amounted to US$20.3 million versus a net loss of US$127.6 million in the prior year. Revenues were US$528.0 million, up 3.0% from US$512.8 million the year before. Revenues from property income rose 6.0% to US$454.2 million from US$428.5 million in the corresponding earlier year.

Prospects: Our evaluation of Corporate Office Properties Trust as of Apr. 7, 2013 is the result of our systematic analysis on three basic characteristics: earnings strength, relative valuation, and recent stock price movement. The company has generated a negative trend in earnings per share over the past 5 quarters and while recent estimates for the company have remained steady, OFC has posted results that fell short of analysts expectations. Based on operating earnings yield, the company is overvalued when compared to all of the companies in our coverage universe. Share price changes over the past year indicates that OFC will perform in line with the market over the near term.

Financial Data
(US$ in Thousands)

	12/31/2012	12/31/2011	12/31/2010	12/31/2009	12/31/2008	12/31/2007	12/31/2006	12/31/2005
Earnings Per Share	(0.03)	(1.94)	0.43	0.70	0.87	0.39	0.69	0.63
Cash Flow Per Share	2.60	2.19	2.62	3.48	3.77	2.96	2.73	2.57
Tang Book Value Per Share	11.81	14.53	16.63	15.88	16.25	15.07	13.68	12.31
Dividends Per Share	1.100	1.650	1.610	1.530	1.425	1.300	1.180	1.070
Dividend Payout %	...	...	374.42	218.57	163.79	333.33	171.01	169.84
Income Statement								
Total Revenue	528,007	556,841	564,475	767,519	588,018	410,174	361,403	329,145
EBITDA	297,443	248,861	357,687	333,434	323,270	315,493	269,374	224,355
Depn & Amortn	113,480	148,730	135,453	117,311	106,859	109,316	81,151	65,369
Income Before Taxes	96,511	4,453	129,937	139,079	134,835	120,469	113,998	100,091
Income Taxes	381	(10,679)	108	196	201	569	887	668
Net Income	20,977	(117,675)	42,760	56,329	58,668	34,784	49,227	39,031
Average Shares	73,454	69,382	59,944	56,407	48,865	47,630	43,262	38,997
Balance Sheet								
Current Assets	51,398	69,917	60,994	74,599	85,518	84,015	105,470	47,866
Total Assets	3,653,759	3,867,524	3,844,517	3,380,022	3,112,867	2,931,853	2,419,601	2,130,376
Current Liabilities	154,252	161,011	164,288	177,072	149,883	128,782	107,591	73,170
Long-Term Obligations	2,019,168	2,426,303	2,323,681	2,053,841	1,866,623	1,825,842	1,498,537	1,348,351
Total Liabilities	2,288,335	2,732,099	2,617,880	2,352,502	2,179,553	2,109,211	1,745,298	1,547,863
Stockholders' Equity	1,365,424	1,135,425	1,226,637	1,027,520	933,314	822,642	674,303	582,513
Shares Outstanding	80,952	72,011	66,931	58,342	51,790	47,366	42,897	39,927
Statistical Record								
Return on Assets %	0.56	N.M.	1.18	1.74	1.94	1.30	2.16	2.02
Return on Equity %	1.67	N.M.	3.79	5.75	6.66	4.65	7.83	7.07
EBITDA Margin %	56.33	44.69	63.37	43.44	54.98	76.92	74.54	68.16
Net Margin %	3.97	N.M.	7.58	7.34	9.98	8.48	13.62	11.86
Asset Turnover	0.14	0.14	0.16	0.24	0.19	0.15	0.16	0.17
Current Ratio	0.33	0.43	0.37	0.42	0.57	0.65	0.98	0.65
Debt to Equity	1.48	2.14	1.89	2.00	2.00	2.22	2.22	2.31
Price Range	26.12-20.96	36.74-19.37	43.19-33.16	39.34-21.36	42.60-21.39	56.00-30.97	51.20-36.24	36.90-25.35
P/E Ratio	...	...	100.44-77.12	56.20-30.51	48.97-24.59	143.59-79.41	74.20-52.52	58.57-40.24
Average Yield %	4.69	5.56	4.28	4.88	4.24	3.00	2.69	3.50

Address: 6711 Columbia Gateway Drive, Suite 300, Columbia, MD 21046
Telephone: 443-285-5400

Web Site: www.copt.com
Officers: Jay H. Shidler - Chairman Clay W. Hamlin - Vice-Chairman

Auditors: PricewaterhouseCoopers LLP
Investor Contact: 443-285-5400
Transfer Agents: Wells Fargo Shareowner Services

CORRECTIONS CORPORATION OF AMERICA

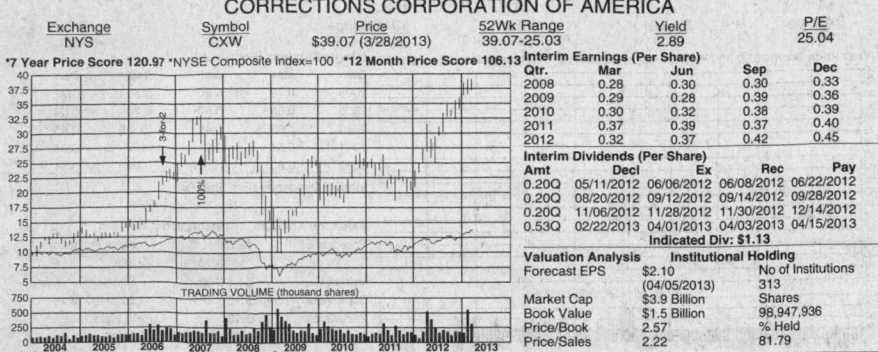

Exchange	Symbol	Price	52Wk Range	Yield	P/E
NYS	CXW	$39.07 (3/28/2013)	39.07-25.03	2.89	25.04

*7 Year Price Score 120.97 *NYSE Composite Index=100 *12 Month Price Score 106.13

Interim Earnings (Per Share)

Qtr.	Mar	Jun	Sep	Dec
2008	0.28	0.30	0.30	0.33
2009	0.29	0.28	0.39	0.36
2010	0.30	0.32	0.38	0.39
2011	0.37	0.39	0.37	0.40
2012	0.32	0.37	0.42	0.45

Interim Dividends (Per Share)

Amt	Decl	Ex	Rec	Pay
0.20Q	05/11/2012	06/06/2012	06/08/2012	06/22/2012
0.20Q	08/20/2012	09/12/2012	09/14/2012	09/28/2012
0.20Q	11/06/2012	11/28/2012	11/30/2012	12/14/2012
0.53Q	02/22/2013	04/01/2013	04/03/2013	04/15/2013

Indicated Div: $1.13

Valuation Analysis / **Institutional Holding**

Forecast EPS	$2.10	No of Institutions
	(04/05/2013)	313
Market Cap	$3.9 Billion	Shares
Book Value	$1.5 Billion	98,947,936
Price/Book	2.57	% Held
Price/Sales	2.22	81.79

Business Summary: REITs (MIC: 5.3.1 SIC: 6798 NAIC: 525930)

Corrections Corporation of America is an owner and operator of privatized correctional and detention facilities and a prison operators. Co. focuses on owning, operating, and managing prisons and other correctional facilities and providing inmate residential and prisoner transportation services for governmental agencies. Co.'s facilities provide a variety of rehabilitation and educational programs, including basic education, religious services, life skills and employment training and substance abuse treatment. Co. also provides health care (including medical, dental and psychiatric services), food services, and work and recreational programs.

Recent Developments: For the year ended Dec 31 2012, income from continuing operations decreased 4.1% to US$157.1 million from US$163.8 million a year earlier. Net income decreased 3.5% to US$156.8 million from US$162.5 million in the prior year. Revenues were US$1.76 billion, up 2.1% from US$1.72 billion the year before. Revenues from property income rose 20.9% to US$2.7 million from US$2.2 million in the corresponding earlier year.

Prospects: Our evaluation of Corrections Corporation of America as of Apr. 7, 2013 is the result of our systematic analysis on three basic characteristics: earnings strength, relative valuation, and recent stock price movement. The company has enjoyed a very positive trend in earnings per share over the past 5 quarters and while recent estimates for the company have remained steady, CXW has posted better than expected results. Based on operating earnings yield, the company is about fairly valued when compared to all of the companies in our coverage universe. Share price changes over the past year indicates that CXW will perform well over the near term.

Financial Data
(US$ in Thousands)

	12/31/2012	12/31/2011	12/31/2010	12/31/2009	12/31/2008	12/31/2007	12/31/2006	12/31/2005
Earnings Per Share	1.56	1.54	1.39	1.32	1.20	1.06	0.85	0.42
Cash Flow Per Share	2.84	3.35	2.28	2.71	2.19	2.05	1.44	1.33
Tang Book Value Per Share	15.08	14.02	13.29	12.32	10.96	9.71	8.47	7.57
Dividends Per Share	0.600	...	...	...	...	...	...	...
Dividend Payout %	38.46	...	...	...	...	...	...	...
Income Statement								
Total Revenue	1,759,885	1,735,613	1,675,031	1,669,963	1,598,906	1,478,837	1,331,088	1,192,640
EBITDA	417,172	440,851	429,421	414,068	398,995	349,403	297,371	205,280
Depn & Amortn	114,100	109,100	106,400	103,800	95,500	82,800	72,200	63,900
Income Before Taxes	244,709	258,811	251,894	237,488	244,091	212,827	166,388	77,452
Income Taxes	87,586	96,301	94,297	81,745	92,127	80,312	61,149	26,888
Net Income	156,761	162,510	157,193	154,954	150,941	133,373	105,239	50,122
Average Shares	100,623	105,535	112,977	117,290	126,250	125,381	123,058	120,843
Balance Sheet								
Current Assets	350,742	359,429	378,293	325,255	338,299	340,663	391,242	320,131
Total Assets	2,974,742	3,019,631	2,983,228	2,905,743	2,871,374	2,485,740	2,250,860	2,086,313
Current Liabilities	166,458	198,362	205,855	194,583	191,823	214,731	164,382	173,312
Long-Term Obligations	1,111,545	1,245,014	1,156,568	1,149,099	1,192,632	975,677	975,968	963,800
Total Liabilities	1,453,122	1,611,609	1,512,357	1,463,197	1,491,015	1,263,765	1,201,179	1,169,682
Stockholders' Equity	1,521,620	1,408,022	1,470,871	1,442,546	1,380,359	1,221,975	1,049,681	916,631
Shares Outstanding	100,105	99,528	109,754	115,962	124,673	124,472	122,084	119,082
Statistical Record								
Return on Assets %	5.22	5.41	5.34	5.36	5.62	5.63	4.85	2.44
Return on Equity %	10.67	11.29	10.79	10.98	11.57	11.74	10.70	5.79
EBITDA Margin %	23.70	25.40	25.64	24.80	24.95	23.63	22.34	17.21
Net Margin %	8.91	9.36	9.38	9.28	9.44	9.02	7.91	4.20
Asset Turnover	0.59	0.58	0.57	0.58	0.60	0.62	0.61	0.58
Current Ratio	2.11	1.81	1.84	1.67	1.76	1.59	2.38	1.85
Debt to Equity	0.73	0.88	0.79	0.80	0.86	0.80	0.93	1.05
Price Range	35.87-20.96	26.35-18.64	26.71-17.83	26.20-9.82	29.64-12.23	33.01-21.80	23.98-13.56	14.99-11.83
P/E Ratio	22.99-13.44	17.11-12.10	19.22-12.83	19.85-7.44	24.70-10.19	31.14-20.57	28.21-15.95	35.69-28.17
Average Yield %	2.02	...	...	...	...	...	...	...

Address: 10 Burton Hills Blvd., Nashville, TN 37215 **Telephone:** 615-263-3000	**Web Site:** www.cca.com **Officers:** John D. Ferguson - Chairman Damon T. Hininger - President, Chief Executive Officer	**Auditors:** Ernst & Young LLP **Investor Contact:** 615-263-3005 **Transfer Agents:** American Stock Transfer and Trust Company, New York, NY

209

COVANCE INC.

Exchange	Symbol	Price	52Wk Range	Yield	P/E
NYS	CVD	$74.32 (3/28/2013)	74.32-44.60	N/A	44.24

*7 Year Price Score 80.92   *NYSE Composite Index=100   *12 Month Price Score 118.42

Interim Earnings (Per Share)

Qtr.	Mar	Jun	Sep	Dec
2008	0.76	0.80	0.80	0.72
2009	0.63	0.67	0.79	0.64
2010	0.60	0.49	(0.49)	0.45
2011	0.54	0.61	0.67	0.34
2012	0.60	(0.23)	0.69	0.61

Interim Dividends (Per Share)

No Dividends Paid

Valuation Analysis

		Institutional Holding	
Forecast EPS	$3.04	No of Institutions	
	(04/05/2013)	389	
Market Cap	$4.1 Billion	Shares	
Book Value	$1.3 Billion	58,358,016	
Price/Book	3.13	% Held	
Price/Sales	1.73	90.79	

Business Summary: Biotechnology (MIC: 4.1.2 SIC: 8731 NAIC: 541710)

Covance is a drug development services company providing a range of early-stage and late-stage product development services primarily to the pharmaceutical, biotechnology and medical device industries. Co. also provides laboratory testing services to the chemical, agrochemical and food industries. The services Co. provides constitute two segments: early development services, which include discovery support services, preclinical services and clinical pharmacology services; and late-stage development services, which include central laboratory, Phase II-IV clinical development, and market access services. Co.'s operations are principally focused in the U.S. and Europe.

Recent Developments: For the year ended Dec 31 2012, net income decreased 28.3% to US$94.7 million from US$132.2 million in the prior year. Revenues were US$2.37 billion, up 5.8% from US$2.24 billion the year before. Operating income was US$115.9 million versus US$180.6 million in the prior year, a decrease of 35.8%. Direct operating expenses rose 9.2% to US$1.76 billion from US$1.61 billion in the comparable period the year before. Indirect operating expenses increased 10.3% to US$494.5 million from US$448.3 million in the equivalent prior-year period.

Prospects: Our evaluation of Covance Inc. as of Apr. 7, 2013 is the result of our systematic analysis on three basic characteristics: earnings strength, relative valuation, and recent stock price movement. The company has enjoyed a very positive trend in earnings per share over the past 5 quarters and while recent estimates for the company have remained steady, CVD has posted better than expected results. Based on operating earnings yield, the company is about fairly valued when compared to all of the companies in our coverage universe. Share price changes over the past year indicates that CVD will perform well over the near term.

Financial Data

(US$ in Thousands)	12/31/2012	12/31/2011	12/31/2010	12/31/2009	12/31/2008	12/31/2007	12/31/2006	12/31/2005
Earnings Per Share	1.68	2.16	1.06	2.73	3.08	2.71	2.24	1.88
Cash Flow Per Share	4.73	4.08	5.30	4.06	4.52	4.60	4.00	2.91
Tang Book Value Per Share	21.78	21.86	19.12	20.02	17.21	15.69	12.57	10.68
Income Statement								
Total Revenue	2,365,759	2,236,446	2,038,473	1,962,626	1,827,067	1,631,516	1,406,058	1,250,454
EBITDA	223,920	270,662	145,644	328,346	338,462	301,611	249,625	221,834
Depn & Amortn	115,600	103,400	101,800	90,300	70,600	65,000	56,600	47,800
Income Before Taxes	104,814	165,283	43,792	237,845	274,323	246,412	200,589	177,671
Income Taxes	10,099	33,574	(23,655)	62,870	79,415	72,934	57,179	58,786
Net Income	94,732	132,189	68,254	175,882	196,760	175,929	144,998	119,619
Average Shares	56,290	61,091	64,472	64,341	63,981	64,820	64,782	63,773
Balance Sheet								
Current Assets	1,234,704	1,086,910	945,811	877,672	737,690	770,057	639,566	546,710
Total Assets	2,288,342	2,108,008	1,965,542	1,974,944	1,753,088	1,560,185	1,297,678	1,056,603
Current Liabilities	882,573	537,029	499,174	402,744	459,795	358,160	289,704	252,728
Long-Term Obligations	...	...	87,500	...	...	...	...	...
Total Liabilities	981,150	650,213	685,721	563,940	558,239	449,997	374,383	324,832
Stockholders' Equity	1,307,192	1,457,795	1,279,821	1,411,004	1,194,849	1,110,188	923,295	731,771
Shares Outstanding	54,985	60,843	60,265	64,105	63,297	64,041	63,941	62,810
Statistical Record								
Return on Assets %	4.30	6.49	3.46	9.44	11.84	12.31	12.32	12.07
Return on Equity %	6.83	9.66	5.07	13.50	17.03	17.30	17.52	17.47
EBITDA Margin %	9.47	12.10	7.14	16.73	18.52	18.49	17.75	17.74
Net Margin %	4.00	5.91	3.35	8.96	10.77	10.78	10.31	9.57
Asset Turnover	1.07	1.10	1.03	1.05	1.10	1.14	1.19	1.26
Current Ratio	1.40	2.02	1.89	2.18	1.60	2.15	2.21	2.16
Debt to Equity	...	...	0.07	...	...	...	...	...
Price Range	59.03-43.31	63.23-43.43	63.25-37.93	58.56-32.99	97.61-32.84	90.17-58.49	68.00-49.15	52.96-35.86
P/E Ratio	35.14-25.78	29.27-20.11	59.67-35.78	21.45-12.08	31.69-10.66	33.27-21.58	30.36-21.94	28.17-19.07

Address: 210 Carnegie Center, Princeton, NJ 08540	Web Site: www.covance.com	Auditors: Ernst & Young LLP
Telephone: 609-452-4440	Officers: Joseph L. Herring - Chairman, Chief Executive Officer William E. Klitgaard - Corporate Senior Vice President, Chief Financial Officer, Chief Information Officer, Treasurer, Principal Accounting Officer	Investor Contact: 609-452-4953 Transfer Agents: ComputerShare Investor Services, Chicago, IL

COVANTA HOLDING CORP

Exchange	Symbol	Price	52Wk Range	Yield	P/E
NYS	CVA	$20.15 (3/28/2013)	20.15-15.42	3.28	23.43

*7 Year Price Score 81.22   *NYSE Composite Index=100   *12 Month Price Score 101.97

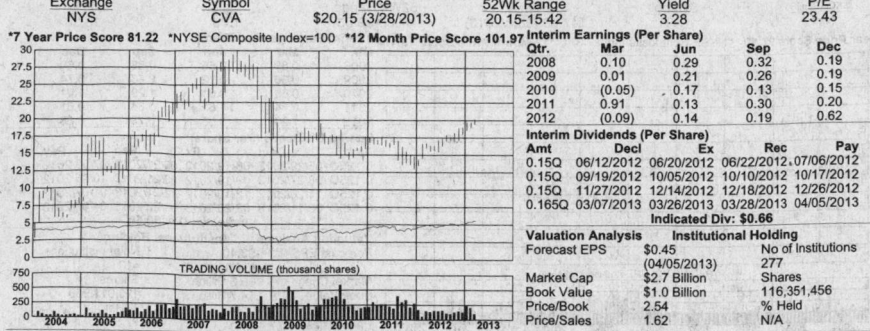

Interim Earnings (Per Share)

Qtr.	Mar	Jun	Sep	Dec
2008	0.10	0.29	0.32	0.19
2009	0.01	0.21	0.26	0.19
2010	(0.05)	0.17	0.13	0.15
2011	0.91	0.13	0.30	0.20
2012	(0.09)	0.14	0.19	0.62

Interim Dividends (Per Share)

Amt	Decl	Ex	Rec	Pay
0.15Q	06/12/2012	06/20/2012	06/22/2012	07/06/2012
0.15Q	09/19/2012	10/05/2012	10/10/2012	10/17/2012
0.15Q	11/27/2012	12/14/2012	12/18/2012	12/26/2012
0.165Q	03/07/2013	03/26/2013	03/28/2013	04/05/2013

Indicated Div: $0.66

Valuation Analysis

		Institutional Holding	
Forecast EPS	$0.45 (04/05/2013)	No of Institutions	277
Market Cap	$2.7 Billion	Shares	116,351,456
Book Value	$1.0 Billion	% Held	N/A
Price/Book	2.54		
Price/Sales	1.62		

Business Summary: Electric Utilities (MIC: 3.1.1 SIC: 4911 NAIC: 221111)

Covanta Holding is a holding company. Co. is an operator of infrastructure for the conversion of waste to energy, as well as other waste disposal and renewable energy production businesses. Co. conducts all of its operations through subsidiaries which are engaged predominantly in the businesses of waste and energy services. Co. has one reportable segment which is Americas and is comprised of waste and energy services operations primarily in the U.S. and Canada. Co. holds equity interests in energy-from-waste facilities in China and Italy. Co. also has investments in subsidiaries engaged in insurance operations in California, primarily in property and casualty insurance.

Recent Developments: For the year ended Dec 31 2012, income from continuing operations increased 40.5% to US$118.0 million from US$84.0 million a year earlier. Net income decreased 48.9% to US$116.0 million from US$227.0 million in the prior year. Revenues were US$1.64 billion, down 0.4% from US$1.65 billion the year before. Operating income was US$252.0 million versus US$218.0 million in the prior year, an increase of 15.6%. Direct operating expenses rose 0.1% to US$963.0 million from US$962.0 million in the comparable period the year before. Indirect operating expenses decreased 8.7% to US$429.0 million from US$470.0 million in the equivalent prior-year period.

Prospects: Our evaluation of Covanta Holding Corp. as of Apr. 7, 2013 is the result of our systematic analysis on three basic characteristics: earnings strength, relative valuation, and recent stock price movement. The company has generated a negative trend in earnings per share over the past 5 quarters and while recent estimates for the company have been mixed, CVA has posted results that fell short of analysts expectations. Based on operating earnings yield, the company is overvalued when compared to all of the companies in our coverage universe. Share price changes over the past year indicates that CVA will perform well over the near term.

Financial Data
(US$ in Thousands)

	12/31/2012	12/31/2011	12/31/2010	12/31/2009	12/31/2008	12/31/2007	12/31/2006	12/31/2005
Earnings Per Share	0.86	1.54	0.40	0.66	0.90	0.85	0.72	0.46
Cash Flow Per Share	2.58	2.56	2.82	2.58	2.62	2.35	2.12	1.70
Tang Book Value Per Share	2.86	2.49	2.31	4.62	4.21	3.52	1.79	N.M.
Dividends Per Share	0.600	0.300	1.500	...	...	...	...	...
Dividend Payout %	69.77	19.48	375.00	...	...	...	...	...
Income Statement								
Total Revenue	1,644,000	1,650,000	1,582,301	1,550,467	1,664,253	1,433,087	1,268,536	978,763
Income Before Taxes	134,000	107,000	56,501	137,436	214,878	148,013	122,228	77,565
Income Taxes	26,000	28,000	23,355	50,044	92,227	31,040	38,465	34,651
Net Income	114,000	219,000	61,654	101,645	139,273	130,513	105,789	59,326
Average Shares	133,000	142,000	153,928	154,994	154,732	153,997	147,030	127,910
Balance Sheet								
Total Assets	4,526,000	4,385,000	4,676,302	4,934,282	4,279,989	4,368,499	4,437,820	4,702,165
Total Liabilities	3,478,000	3,302,000	3,548,616	3,551,276	3,127,870	3,342,437	3,698,668	4,102,924
Stockholders' Equity	1,048,000	1,083,000	1,127,686	1,383,006	1,152,119	1,026,062	739,152	599,241
Shares Outstanding	132,000	136,000	149,891	154,936	154,279	153,921	147,499	141,165
Statistical Record								
Return on Assets %	2.55	4.83	1.28	2.21	3.21	2.96	2.31	1.79
Return on Equity %	10.67	19.81	4.91	8.02	12.75	14.79	15.81	16.16
Net Margin %	6.93	13.27	3.90	6.56	8.37	9.11	8.34	6.06
Price Range	18.96-13.49	17.59-13.02	19.54-14.30	22.68-12.92	29.96-17.35	28.34-21.48	22.75-14.45	17.51-8.00
P/E Ratio	22.05-15.69	11.42-8.45	48.85-35.75	34.36-19.58	33.29-19.28	33.34-25.27	31.60-20.07	38.07-17.39
Average Yield %	3.59	1.88	9.16	...	...	...	...	...

Address: 445 South Street, Morristown, NJ 07960 **Telephone:** 862-345-5000	**Web Site:** www.covantaholding.com **Officers:** Samuel Zell - Chairman Anthony J. Orlando - President, Chief Executive Officer	**Auditors:** Ernst & Young LLP **Investor Contact:** 862-345-5456 **Transfer Agents:** American Stock Transfer and Trust Company, New York, NY

COVENTRY HEALTH CARE INC.

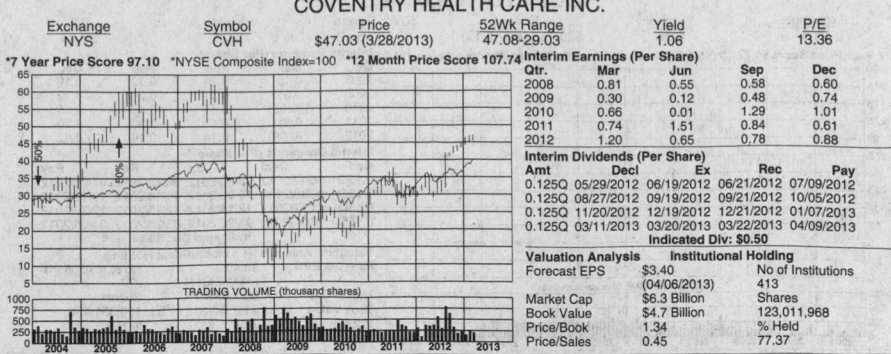

Exchange	Symbol	Price	52Wk Range	Yield	P/E
NYS	CVH	$47.03 (3/28/2013)	47.08-29.03	1.06	13.36

*7 Year Price Score 97.10 *NYSE Composite Index=100 *12 Month Price Score 107.74

Interim Earnings (Per Share)

Qtr.	Mar	Jun	Sep	Dec
2008	0.81	0.55	0.58	0.60
2009	0.30	0.12	0.48	0.74
2010	0.66	0.01	1.29	1.01
2011	0.74	1.51	0.84	0.61
2012	1.20	0.65	0.78	0.88

Interim Dividends (Per Share)

Amt	Decl	Ex	Rec	Pay
0.125Q	05/29/2012	06/19/2012	06/21/2012	07/09/2012
0.125Q	08/27/2012	09/19/2012	09/21/2012	10/05/2012
0.125Q	11/20/2012	12/19/2012	12/21/2012	01/07/2013
0.125Q	03/11/2013	03/20/2013	03/22/2013	04/09/2013

Indicated Div: $0.50

Valuation Analysis

		Institutional Holding	
Forecast EPS	$3.40 (04/06/2013)	No of Institutions	413
Market Cap	$6.3 Billion	Shares	123,011,968
Book Value	$4.7 Billion	% Held	77.37
Price/Book	1.34		
Price/Sales	0.45		

Business Summary: Life & Health (MIC: 5.2.2 SIC: 6324 NAIC: 524114)

Coventry Health Care is a managed healthcare company operating health plans, insurance companies, network rental and workers' compensation services companies. Co. operates through three segments: Health Plan and Medical Services, comprising its health plan commercial risk, commercial management services, Medicare Advantage Coordinated Care Plans and Medicaid products; Specialized Managed Care, which includes Medicare Part D, network rental and its behavioral health benefits businesses; and Workers' Compensation, comprised of its workers' compensation services businesses such as provider network access, bill review, care management services and pharmacy benefit management, among others.

Recent Developments: For the year ended Dec 31 2012, net income decreased 10.3% to US$487.1 million from US$543.1 million in the prior year. Revenues were US$14.11 billion, up 15.8% from US$12.19 billion the year before. Net premiums earned were US$12.93 billion versus US$11.01 billion in the prior year, an increase of 17.4%.

Prospects: Our evaluation of Coventry Health Care Inc. as of Apr. 7, 2013 is the result of our systematic analysis on three basic characteristics: earnings strength, relative valuation, and recent stock price movement. The company has enjoyed a very positive trend in earnings per share over the past 5 quarters and while recent estimates for the company have been raised by analysts, CVH has posted better than expected results. Based on operating earnings yield, the company is undervalued when compared to all of the companies in our coverage universe. Share price changes over the past year indicates that CVH will perform well over the near term.

Financial Data
(US$ in Thousands)

	12/31/2012	12/31/2011³	12/31/2010	12/31/2009	12/31/2008	12/31/2007	12/31/2006	12/31/2005
Earnings Per Share	3.52	3.70	2.97	1.64	2.54	3.98	3.47	3.10
Cash Flow Per Share	3.45	2.77	1.86	6.01	4.20	3.74	6.72	5.09
Tang Book Value Per Share	13.47	11.30	8.14	4.81	1.28	0.89	5.92	3.21
Dividends Per Share	0.500	...	...	...	...	...	...	...
Dividend Payout %	14.20	...	...	...	...	...	...	...
Income Statement								
Total Revenue	14,113,363	12,186,683	11,587,916	13,903,526	11,913,646	9,879,531	7,733,756	6,611,246
EBITDA	891,603	1,029,663	843,552	670,229	786,762	1,171,487	1,026,694	912,939
Depn & Amortn	78,700	72,500	76,600	80,800	84,600	94,400	77,900	55,100
Income Before Taxes	784,535	858,101	686,534	504,554	605,776	994,870	896,348	799,425
Income Taxes	297,472	314,996	247,918	189,220	223,881	368,776	336,303	297,786
Net Income	487,063	543,105	438,616	242,301	381,895	626,094	560,045	501,639
Average Shares	136,778	146,741	147,579	147,395	150,208	157,357	161,434	161,716
Balance Sheet								
Current Assets	2,882,119	2,969,508	3,034,941	2,850,158	2,410,490	1,846,701	2,134,382	1,325,702
Total Assets	8,750,988	8,813,532	8,495,585	8,166,532	7,727,398	7,158,791	5,665,107	4,895,172
Current Liabilities	2,045,070	2,352,155	2,282,998	2,398,433	2,025,775	1,749,821	1,651,989	1,270,227
Long-Term Obligations	1,585,190	1,584,700	1,599,396	1,902,472	1,902,472	1,662,021	750,500	760,500
Total Liabilities	4,028,073	4,302,541	4,296,419	4,453,978	4,296,729	3,857,312	2,712,105	2,340,469
Stockholders' Equity	4,722,915	4,510,991	4,199,166	3,712,554	3,430,669	3,301,479	2,953,002	2,554,703
Shares Outstanding	134,573	141,172	149,427	147,990	148,288	154,636	159,441	162,717
Statistical Record								
Return on Assets %	5.53	6.28	5.26	3.05	5.12	9.76	10.61	13.87
Return on Equity %	10.52	12.47	11.09	6.78	11.31	20.02	20.34	26.63
EBITDA Margin %	6.32	8.45	7.28	4.82	6.60	11.86	13.28	13.81
Net Margin %	3.45	4.46	3.79	1.74	3.21	6.34	7.24	7.59
Asset Turnover	1.60	1.41	1.39	1.75	1.60	1.54	1.46	1.83
Current Ratio	1.41	1.26	1.33	1.19	1.19	1.06	1.29	1.04
Debt to Equity	0.34	0.35	0.38	0.43	0.55	0.50	0.25	0.30
Price Range	44.92-29.03	37.72-26.40	26.93-17.19	25.24-8.02	61.70-10.01	62.36-49.44	61.24-44.78	60.20-34.54
P/E Ratio	12.76-8.25	10.19-7.14	9.07-5.79	15.39-4.89	24.29-3.94	15.67-12.42	17.65-12.90	19.42-11.14
Average Yield %	1.38	...	...	...	...	...	...	...

Address: 6720-B Rockledge Drive, Suite 700, Bethesda, MD 20817 **Telephone:** 301-581-0600 **Fax:** 301-493-0742	**Web Site:** www.coventryhealth.com **Officers:** Allen F. Wise - Chairman, Chief Executive Officer Randy P. Giles - Executive Vice President, Chief Financial Officer, Treasurer	**Auditors:** Ernst & Young LLP **Investor Contact:** 301-581-5717 **Transfer Agents:** Computershare

COVIDIEN PLC

Exchange	Symbol	Price	52Wk Range	Yield	P/E
NYS	COV	$67.84 (3/28/2013)	67.84-50.61	N/A	17.26

*7 Year Price Score N/A   *NYSE Composite Index=100   *12 Month Price Score 103.20

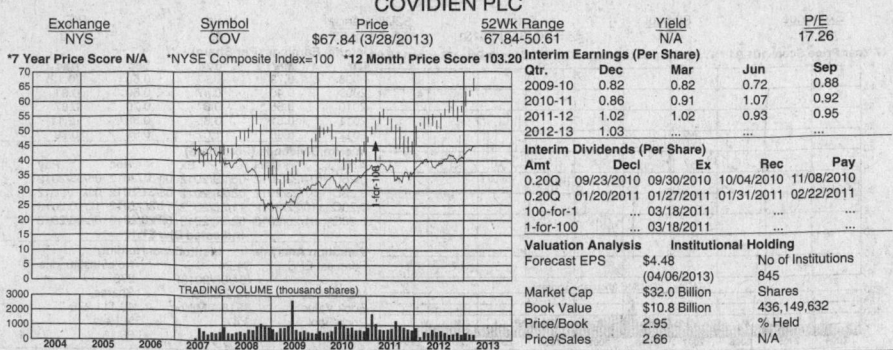

Interim Earnings (Per Share)

Qtr.	Dec	Mar	Jun	Sep
2009-10	0.82	0.82	0.72	0.88
2010-11	0.86	0.91	1.07	0.92
2011-12	1.02	1.02	0.93	0.95
2012-13	1.03	...	...	...

Interim Dividends (Per Share)

Amt	Decl	Ex	Rec	Pay
0.20Q	09/23/2010	09/30/2010	10/04/2010	11/08/2010
0.20Q	01/20/2011	01/27/2011	01/31/2011	02/22/2011
100-for-1	...	03/18/2011	...	...
1-for-100	...	03/18/2011	...	...

Valuation Analysis   **Institutional Holding**

Forecast EPS	$4.48	No of Institutions
	(04/06/2013)	845
Market Cap	$32.0 Billion	Shares
Book Value	$10.8 Billion	436,149,632
Price/Book	2.95	% Held
Price/Sales	2.66	N/A

Business Summary: Medical Instruments & Equipment (MIC: 4.3.1 SIC: 3841 NAIC: 339112)

Covidien is engaged in the development, manufacture and sale of healthcare products for use in clinical and home settings. Co. operates its businesses through three segments: Medical Devices, which includes endomechanical instruments, energy devices, soft tissue repair products, vascular products, oximetry and monitoring products, airway and ventilation products and other medical products; Pharmaceuticals, which includes specialty pharmaceuticals, active pharmaceutical ingredients, contrast products and radiopharmaceuticals; and Medical Supplies, which includes nursing care products, medical surgical products, SharpSafety products and original equipment manufacturer products.

Recent Developments: For the quarter ended Dec 28 2012, net income decreased 0.2% to US$493.0 million from US$494.0 million in the year-earlier quarter. Revenues were US$3.06 billion, up 5.5% from US$2.90 billion the year before. Operating income was US$658.0 million versus US$636.0 million in the prior-year quarter, an increase of 3.5%. Direct operating expenses rose 8.6% to US$1.30 billion from US$1.20 billion in the comparable period the year before. Indirect operating expenses increased 3.1% to US$1.10 billion from US$1.07 billion in the equivalent prior-year period.

Prospects: Our evaluation of Covidien PLC as of Apr. 7, 2013 is the result of our systematic analysis on three basic characteristics: earnings strength, relative valuation, and recent stock price movement. The company has enjoyed a very positive trend in earnings per share over the past 5 quarters and while recent estimates for the company have been raised by analysts, COV has posted better than expected results. Based on operating earnings yield, the company is undervalued when compared to all of the companies in our coverage universe. Share price changes over the past year indicates that COV will perform poorly over the near term.

Financial Data
(US$ in Thousands)

	3 Mos	09/28/2012	09/30/2011	09/24/2010	09/25/2009	09/26/2008	09/28/2007	09/29/2006
Earnings Per Share	3.93	3.92	3.76	3.24	1.79	2.70	(0.69)	2.33
Cash Flow Per Share	4.83	5.06	4.35	4.38	3.74	1.32	4.46	2.43
Tang Book Value Per Share	N.M.	N.M.	N.M.	N.M.	0.79	1.41	N.M.	...
Income Statement								
Total Revenue	3,056,000	11,852,000	11,574,000	10,429,000	10,677,000	9,910,000	10,170,000	9,647,000
EBITDA	823,000	2,848,000	2,794,000	2,463,000	2,354,000	2,467,000	588,000	2,382,000
Depn & Amortn	164,000	409,000	397,000	360,000	353,000	322,000	285,000	269,000
Income Before Taxes	610,000	2,249,000	2,216,000	1,926,000	1,851,000	1,979,000	151,000	1,974,000
Income Taxes	117,000	347,000	333,000	363,000	949,000	536,000	488,000	504,000
Net Income	493,000	1,905,000	1,868,000	1,632,000	907,000	1,361,000	(342,000)	1,155,000
Average Shares	477,000	486,000	497,000	504,000	505,000	505,000	497,000	497,000
Balance Sheet								
Current Assets	5,995,000	6,272,000	5,773,000	5,740,000	5,462,000	5,289,000	7,556,000	3,643,000
Total Assets	22,049,000	22,257,000	20,374,000	20,387,000	17,139,000	16,003,000	18,328,000	14,108,000
Current Liabilities	2,483,000	2,912,000	2,400,000	3,126,000	2,239,000	2,098,000	5,367,000	1,647,000
Long-Term Obligations	4,569,000	4,531,000	4,197,000	4,451,000	2,961,000	2,986,000	3,565,000	2,248,000
Total Liabilities	11,217,000	11,692,000	10,557,000	11,413,000	9,138,000	8,256,000	11,586,000	5,487,000
Stockholders' Equity	10,832,000	10,565,000	9,817,000	8,974,000	8,001,000	7,747,000	6,742,000	8,621,000
Shares Outstanding	471,329	472,168	513,786	495,081	499,049	503,162	497,530	...
Statistical Record								
Return on Assets %	8.93	8.96	9.02	8.72	5.49	7.95	N.M.	...
Return on Equity %	18.07	18.74	19.56	19.28	11.55	18.84	N.M.	...
EBITDA Margin %	26.93	24.03	24.14	23.62	22.05	24.89	5.78	24.69
Net Margin %	16.13	16.07	16.14	15.65	8.49	13.73	N.M.	11.97
Asset Turnover	0.56	0.56	0.56	0.56	0.65	0.58	0.63	...
Current Ratio	2.41	2.15	2.41	1.84	2.44	2.52	1.41	2.21
Debt to Equity	0.42	0.43	0.43	0.50	0.37	0.39	0.53	0.26
Price Range	60.44-44.86	60.33-42.16	57.48-39.48	52.28-35.34	54.91-27.90	56.68-38.00	46.50-37.98	...
P/E Ratio	15.38-11.41	15.39-10.76	15.29-10.50	16.14-10.91	30.68-15.59	20.99-14.07	...	...

Address: 20 on Hatch, Lower Hatch Street, Dublin 2
Telephone: 143-817-00

Web Site: www.covidien.com
Officers: Jose E. Almeida - Chairman, President, Chief Executive Officer, Senior Vice President, Division Officer Charles J. Dockendorff - Executive Vice President, Chief Financial Officer

Auditors: Deloitte & Touche LLP
Investor Contact: 508-452-4343
Transfer Agents: Computershare Shareowner Services LLC, Jersey City, NJ

CRANE CO.

Exchange	Symbol	Price	52Wk Range	Yield	P/E
NYS	CR	$55.86 (3/28/2013)	56.77-35.53	2.01	15.02

*7 Year Price Score 101.94 *NYSE Composite Index=100 *12 Month Price Score 113.03

Interim Earnings (Per Share)

Qtr.	Mar	Jun	Sep	Dec
2008	0.79	0.97	0.60	(0.12)
2009	0.40	0.47	0.60	0.81
2010	0.56	0.67	0.70	0.67
2011	0.81	0.85	0.89	(2.11)
2012	0.88	1.07	0.99	0.79

Interim Dividends (Per Share)

Amt	Decl	Ex	Rec	Pay
0.26Q	04/23/2012	05/29/2012	05/31/2012	06/08/2012
0.28Q	07/23/2012	08/29/2012	08/31/2012	09/11/2012
0.28Q	10/22/2012	11/28/2012	11/30/2012	12/10/2012
0.28Q	01/28/2013	02/26/2013	02/28/2013	03/08/2013

Indicated Div: $1.12

Valuation Analysis — **Institutional Holding**

Forecast EPS	$4.24 (04/05/2013)	No of Institutions 275
Market Cap	$3.2 Billion	Shares
Book Value	$918.4 Million	43,111,276
Price/Book	3.47	% Held
Price/Sales	1.24	66.15

Business Summary: Industrial Machinery & Equipment (MIC: 7.2.1 SIC: 3499 NAIC: 332999)

Crane is a manufacturer of industrial products. Co.'s business consists of five segments: Aerospace & Electronics, which supplies components and systems, including original equipment and aftermarket parts, for both the commercial and military aerospace industries; Engineered Materials, which manufactures fiberglass-reinforced plastic panels; Merchandising Systems, which includes the Vending Solutions and Payment Solutions businesses; Fluid Handling, which is a provider of fluid handling equipment, such as valves, lined pipe and pumps; and Controls, which provides sensing and control applications and is engaged in control applications for certain environments.

Recent Developments: For the year ended Dec 31 2012, income from continuing operations increased 759.9% to US$196.2 million from US$22.8 million a year earlier. Net income increased 721.5% to US$217.8 million from US$26.5 million in the prior year. Revenues were US$2.58 billion, up 3.1% from US$2.50 billion the year before. Operating income was US$310.4 million versus US$36.6 million in the prior year, an increase of 748.9%. Direct operating expenses rose 3.4% to US$1.71 billion from US$1.65 billion in the comparable period the year before. Indirect operating expenses decreased 31.1% to US$558.7 million from US$810.6 million in the equivalent prior-year period.

Prospects: Our evaluation of Crane Co. as of Apr. 7, 2013 is the result of our systematic analysis on three basic characteristics: earnings strength, relative valuation, and recent stock price movement. The company has managed to produce a neutral trend in earnings per share over the past 5 quarters and while recent estimates for the company have been raised by analysts, CR has posted results that fell short of analysts expectations. Based on operating earnings yield, the company is undervalued when compared to all of the companies in our coverage universe. Share price changes over the past year indicates that CR will perform in line with the market over the near term.

Financial Data
(US$ in Thousands)

	12/31/2012	12/31/2011	12/31/2010	12/31/2009	12/31/2008	12/31/2007	12/31/2006	12/31/2005
Earnings Per Share	3.72	0.44	2.59	2.28	2.24	(1.04)	2.67	2.25
Cash Flow Per Share	4.08	2.58	2.28	3.23	3.20	3.88	2.98	3.04
Tang Book Value Per Share	N.M.	N.M.	0.21	0.09	N.M.	N.M.	1.51	2.06
Dividends Per Share	1.080	0.980	0.860	0.800	0.760	0.660	0.550	0.450
Dividend Payout %	29.03	222.73	33.20	35.09	33.93	...	20.60	20.00
Income Statement								
Total Revenue	2,579,068	2,545,867	2,217,825	2,196,343	2,604,307	2,619,171	2,256,889	2,061,249
EBITDA	349,957	84,974	277,586	223,312	214,056	(85,183)	265,655	266,317
Depn & Amortn	40,400	39,900	41,000	14,067	14,668	17,889	13,886	55,715
Income Before Taxes	284,605	20,454	210,929	184,926	183,852	(124,217)	233,693	190,558
Income Taxes	88,416	(6,062)	56,739	50,846	48,694	(56,553)	73,447	60,486
Net Income	216,993	26,315	154,170	133,856	135,158	(62,342)	165,887	136,037
Average Shares	58,293	59,204	59,562	58,812	60,298	60,037	62,103	60,413
Balance Sheet								
Current Assets	1,180,521	1,032,232	988,661	1,046,346	1,021,240	1,037,622	880,409	798,395
Total Assets	2,889,878	2,843,531	2,706,697	2,712,898	2,774,488	2,877,292	2,430,484	2,139,486
Current Liabilities	511,888	533,095	498,554	466,782	538,664	493,552	461,926	398,589
Long-Term Obligations	399,092	398,914	398,736	398,557	398,479	398,301	391,760	293,248
Total Liabilities	1,971,495	2,029,978	1,721,753	1,827,136	2,036,426	1,992,489	1,511,881	1,386,192
Stockholders' Equity	918,383	813,553	984,944	885,762	738,062	884,803	918,603	753,294
Shares Outstanding	57,106	57,614	58,160	58,526	58,489	60,161	60,472	60,408
Statistical Record								
Return on Assets %	7.55	0.95	5.69	4.88	4.77	N.M.	7.26	6.39
Return on Equity %	24.99	2.93	16.48	16.49	16.61	N.M.	19.84	19.20
EBITDA Margin %	13.57	3.34	12.52	10.17	8.22	N.M.	11.77	12.92
Net Margin %	8.41	1.03	6.95	6.09	5.19	N.M.	7.35	6.60
Asset Turnover	0.90	0.92	0.82	0.80	0.92	0.99	0.99	0.97
Current Ratio	2.31	1.94	1.98	2.24	1.90	2.10	1.91	2.00
Debt to Equity	0.43	0.49	0.40	0.45	0.54	0.45	0.43	0.39
Price Range	51.07-35.53	51.06-34.03	41.30-28.97	32.21-12.85	45.74-11.03	49.52-35.79	45.34-35.60	37.15-25.48
P/E Ratio	13.73-9.55	116.05-77.34	15.95-11.19	14.13-5.64	20.42-4.92	...	16.98-13.33	16.51-11.32
Average Yield %	2.54	2.18	2.43	3.50	2.27	1.53	1.40	1.55

Address: 100 First Stamford Place, Stamford, CT 06902 Telephone: 203-363-7300	Web Site: www.craneco.com Officers: R. S. Evans - Chairman Max H. Mitchell - President, Executive Vice President, Chief Operating Officer	Auditors: Deloitte & Touche LLP Investor Contact: 203-363-7352 Transfer Agents: Equiserve Trust Company N.A.

CROWN CASTLE INTERNATIONAL CORP

Exchange	Symbol	Price	52Wk Range	Yield	P/E
NYS	CCI	$69.64 (3/28/2013)	75.13-52.60	N/A	108.81

*7 Year Price Score 142.33 *NYSE Composite Index=100 *12 Month Price Score 101.02

Interim Earnings (Per Share)

Qtr.	Mar	Jun	Sep	Dec
2008	(0.07)	0.19	(0.13)	(0.25)
2009	0.02	(0.41)	(0.13)	0.05
2010	(0.43)	(0.36)	(0.49)	0.12
2011	0.12	0.09	0.15	0.16
2012	0.17	0.40	0.14	(0.07)

Interim Dividends (Per Share)

No Dividends Paid

Valuation Analysis   Institutional Holding

Forecast EPS	$0.42	No of Institutions
	(04/05/2013)	516
Market Cap	$20.4 Billion	Shares
Book Value	$2.9 Billion	291,390,016
Price/Book	6.95	% Held
Price/Sales	8.39	96.66

Business Summary: Services (MIC: 6.1.2 SIC: 4899 NAIC: 517212)

Crown Castle International owns, operates and leases shared wireless infrastructure including: towers and other structures such as rooftops; distributed antenna systems, a type of small cell network (small cells); and interests in land under third party towers in several forms (collectively, third party land interests). Co.'s core business is providing access, including space or capacity, to its approximately 31,500 towers, and to a lesser extent, to its small cells, and third party land interests to wireless communications companies. Co. also provides certain network services, mainly consisting of antenna installations and subsequent augmentations, and additional site development services.

Recent Developments: For the year ended Dec 31 2012, net income increased 17.2% to US$200.9 million from US$171.5 million in the prior year. Revenues were US$2.43 billion, up 19.7% from US$2.03 billion the year before. Operating income was US$834.7 million versus US$692.3 million in the prior year, an increase of 20.6%. Direct operating expenses rose 23.9% to US$729.0 million from US$588.4 million in the comparable period the year before. Indirect operating expenses increased 15.6% to US$869.0 million from US$752.0 million in the equivalent prior-year period.

Prospects: Our evaluation of Crown Castle International Corp. as of Apr. 7, 2013 is the result of our systematic analysis on three basic characteristics: earnings strength, relative valuation, and recent stock price movement. The company has suffered a very negative trend in earnings per share over the past 5 quarters and while recent estimates for the company have been mixed, CCI has posted results that fell short of analysts expectations. Based on operating earnings yield, the company is overvalued when compared to all of the companies in our coverage universe. Share price changes over the past year indicates that CCI will perform very well over the near term.

Financial Data

(US$ in Thousands)	12/31/2012	12/31/2011	12/31/2010	12/31/2009	12/31/2008	12/31/2007	12/31/2006	12/31/2005
Earnings Per Share	0.64	0.52	(1.16)	(0.47)	(0.25)	(0.87)	(0.30)	(2.07)
Cash Flow Per Share	2.66	2.27	2.10	1.99	1.81	1.25	1.33	0.94
Tang Book Value Per Share	N.M.	N.M.	N.M.	N.M.	N.M.	N.M.	2.24	5.37
Income Statement								
Total Revenue	2,432,680	2,032,729	1,878,658	1,685,407	1,526,504	1,385,486	788,221	676,759
EBITDA	1,136,215	1,074,528	529,863	629,546	579,294	424,205	386,614	294,825
Depn & Amortn	438,900	387,800	379,300	379,600	380,500	400,300	271,030	272,230
Income Before Taxes	100,827	179,807	(338,105)	(190,523)	(153,219)	(317,003)	(48,373)	(393,654)
Income Taxes	(100,061)	8,347	(26,846)	(76,400)	(104,361)	(94,039)	843	3,225
Net Income	188,584	171,077	(310,940)	(114,332)	(48,858)	(222,813)	(41,893)	(401,537)
Average Shares	291,270	285,947	286,764	286,622	282,007	279,937	207,245	217,759
Balance Sheet								
Current Assets	1,581,324	599,152	545,145	1,196,033	485,168	497,255	800,027	221,295
Total Assets	16,088,709	10,545,096	10,469,529	10,956,606	10,361,722	10,488,133	5,006,168	4,131,317
Current Liabilities	1,237,858	402,106	440,885	754,105	834,358	371,987	200,795	464,214
Long-Term Obligations	10,923,186	6,853,182	6,750,207	6,361,954	5,630,527	5,987,695	3,513,890	1,975,686
Total Liabilities	13,149,963	7,853,819	7,707,575	7,704,711	7,331,131	7,007,424	3,937,016	2,640,998
Stockholders' Equity	2,938,746	2,691,277	2,761,954	3,251,895	3,030,591	3,480,709	1,069,152	1,490,319
Shares Outstanding	293,164	284,449	290,826	292,729	288,464	282,507	202,080	214,188
Statistical Record								
Return on Assets %	1.41	1.63	N.M.	N.M.	N.M.	N.M.	N.M.	N.M.
Return on Equity %	6.68	6.27	N.M.	N.M.	N.M.	N.M.	N.M.	N.M.
EBITDA Margin %	46.71	52.86	28.20	37.35	37.95	30.62	49.05	43.56
Net Margin %	7.75	8.42	N.M.	N.M.	N.M.	N.M.	N.M.	N.M.
Asset Turnover	0.18	0.19	0.18	0.16	0.15	0.18	0.17	0.16
Current Ratio	1.28	1.49	1.24	1.59	0.58	1.34	3.98	0.48
Debt to Equity	3.72	2.55	2.44	1.96	1.86	1.72	3.29	1.33
Price Range	72.16-44.92	46.17-37.37	44.15-34.82	39.79-15.84	42.70-10.19	42.75-30.66	35.45-26.90	28.25-15.53
P/E Ratio	112.75-70.19	88.79-71.87	...	...	...	...	...	...

Address: 1220 Augusta Drive, Suite 500, Houston, TX 77057-2261	Web Site: www.crowncastle.com	Auditors: PricewaterhouseCoopers LLP
Telephone: 713-570-3000	Officers: J. Landis Martin - Chairman Patrick Slowey - Senior Vice President	Investor Contact: 713-570-3050
		Transfer Agents: BNY Mellon Shareowner Services

CROWN HOLDINGS INC

Exchange	Symbol	Price	52Wk Range	Yield	P/E
NYS	CCK	$41.61 (3/28/2013)	41.61-32.69	N/A	11.10

*7 Year Price Score 117.80 *NYSE Composite Index=100 *12 Month Price Score 98.25

Interim Earnings (Per Share)

Qtr.	Mar	Jun	Sep	Dec
2008	0.17	0.61	0.70	(0.08)
2009	0.25	0.65	0.67	0.50
2010	0.25	0.69	0.78	0.29
2011	0.10	0.83	0.84	0.06
2012	0.46	0.89	2.20	0.22

Interim Dividends (Per Share)

No Dividends Paid

Valuation Analysis | **Institutional Holding**

Forecast EPS	$3.29	No of Institutions
	(04/06/2013)	414
Market Cap	$6.0 Billion	Shares
Book Value	N/A	144,612,896
Price/Book	N/A	% Held
Price/Sales	0.70	84.52

TRADING VOLUME (thousand shares)

Business Summary: Metal Products (MIC: 8.2.3 SIC: 3411 NAIC: 332431)

Crown Holdings is engaged in the design, manufacture and sale of packaging products for consumer goods. Co.'s primary products include steel and aluminum cans for food, beverage, household and other consumer products and metal vacuum closures and caps. These products are sold through Co.'s sales organization to the soft drink, food, citrus, brewing, household products, personal care and various other industries. Co.'s business is organized geographically within three divisions: Americas, which include Americas Beverage and North America Food; European, which includes European Beverage, European Food and European Specialty Packaging; and Asia-Pacific.

Recent Developments: For the year ended Dec 31 2012, net income increased 66.2% to US$658.0 million from US$396.0 million in the prior year. Revenues were US$8.47 billion, down 2.0% from US$8.64 billion the year before. Direct operating expenses declined 1.4% to US$7.19 billion from US$7.30 billion in the comparable period the year before. Indirect operating expenses decreased 15.8% to US$641.0 million from US$761.0 million in the equivalent prior-year period.

Prospects: Our evaluation of Crown Holdings Inc. as of Apr. 7, 2013 is the result of our systematic analysis on three basic characteristics: earnings strength, relative valuation, and recent stock price movement. The company has enjoyed a very positive trend in earnings per share over the past 5 quarters. However, while recent estimates for the company has been mixed, CCK has posted results that fell short of analysts expectations. Based on operating earnings yield, the company is undervalued when compared to all of the companies in our coverage universe. Share price changes over the past year indicates that CCK will perform poorly over the near term.

Financial Data
(US$ in Millions)

	12/31/2012	12/31/2011	12/31/2010	12/31/2009	12/31/2008	12/31/2007	12/31/2006	12/31/2005
Earnings Per Share	3.75	1.83	2.00	2.06	1.39	3.19	1.82	(2.18)
Cash Flow Per Share	4.22	2.50	3.70	4.75	2.64	3.16	2.15	(0.74)
Income Statement								
Total Revenue	8,470	8,644	7,941	7,938	8,305	7,727	6,982	6,908
EBITDA	1,035	948	980	894	949	734	784	320
Depn & Amortn	180	140	172	194	216	229	175	282
Income Before Taxes	636	587	614	459	442	201	335	(314)
Income Taxes	(17)	194	165	7	112	(400)	(62)	(2)
Net Income	557	282	324	334	226	528	309	(362)
Average Shares	148	154	162	161	162	165	169	165
Balance Sheet								
Current Assets	2,750	2,603	2,649	2,242	2,457	2,234	2,062	1,845
Total Assets	7,490	6,868	6,899	6,532	6,774	6,979	6,358	6,545
Current Liabilities	2,518	2,285	2,377	1,925	2,072	2,083	1,956	1,943
Long-Term Obligations	3,289	3,337	2,649	2,739	3,247	3,354	3,420	3,192
Total Liabilities	7,652	7,341	6,995	6,538	7,091	6,964	6,903	6,781
Stockholders' Equity	(162)	(473)	(96)	(6)	(317)	15	(545)	(236)
Shares Outstanding	143	148	155	161	159	159	162	166
Statistical Record								
Return on Assets %	7.74	4.10	4.82	5.02	3.28	7.92	4.79	N.M.
EBITDA Margin %	12.22	10.97	12.34	11.26	11.43	9.50	11.23	4.63
Net Margin %	6.58	3.26	4.08	4.21	2.72	6.83	4.43	N.M.
Asset Turnover	1.18	1.26	1.18	1.19	1.20	1.16	1.08	0.94
Current Ratio	1.09	1.14	1.11	1.16	1.19	1.07	1.05	0.95
Debt to Equity	...	...	...	...	...	223.60	...	...
Price Range	38.79-32.69	41.19-29.30	33.85-22.66	29.21-17.87	29.33-14.05	27.18-21.10	21.51-14.77	20.26-12.42
P/E Ratio	10.34-8.72	22.51-16.01	16.93-11.33	14.18-8.67	21.10-10.11	8.52-6.61	11.82-8.12	...

Address: One Crown Way,	Web Site: www.crowncork.com	Auditors: PricewaterhouseCoopers LLP
Philadelphia, PA 19154-4599	Officers: John W. Conway - Chairman, President,	Investor Contact: 215-698-5341
Telephone: 215-698-5100	Chief Executive Officer Timothy J. Donahue -	Transfer Agents: Wells Fargo
	President, Executive Vice President, Chief Financial	Shareowner Services, Mendota Heights,
	Officer, Chief Operating Officer	MN

216

CSX CORP.

Exchange	Symbol	Price	52Wk Range	Yield	P/E
NYS	CSX	$24.63 (3/28/2013)	24.63-19.01	2.27	13.76

*7 Year Price Score 111.09 *NYSE Composite Index=100   *12 Month Price Score 97.64

Interim Earnings (Per Share)

Qtr.	Mar	Jun	Sep	Dec
2008	0.28	0.31	0.31	0.21
2009	0.21	0.26	0.25	0.26
2010	0.26	0.36	0.36	0.38
2011	0.35	0.46	0.43	0.43
2012	0.43	0.49	0.44	0.43

Interim Dividends (Per Share)

Amt	Decl	Ex	Rec	Pay
0.14Q	05/09/2012	05/29/2012	05/31/2012	06/15/2012
0.14Q	07/11/2012	08/29/2012	08/31/2012	09/14/2012
0.14Q	10/03/2012	11/28/2012	11/30/2012	12/14/2012
0.14Q	02/13/2013	02/26/2013	02/28/2013	03/15/2013

Indicated Div: $0.56

Valuation Analysis

		Institutional Holding	
Forecast EPS	$1.78 (04/06/2013)	No of Institutions	940
Market Cap	$25.1 Billion	Shares	701,543,744
Book Value	$9.0 Billion	% Held	64.80
Price/Book	2.80		
Price/Sales	2.14		

Business Summary: Rail (MIC: 7.4.3 SIC: 4011 NAIC: 482111)

CSX provides rail-based transportation services including rail service and transport of intermodal containers and trailers. Co.'s CSX Transportation, Inc. subsidiary provides a link to the transportation supply chain via its rail network, which serves population centers in 23 states east of the Mississippi River, the District of Columbia and Ontario and Quebec, Canada. Co.'s CSX Intermodal Terminals, Inc. subsidiary operates a system of intermodal terminals, mainly in the eastern U.S. and performs drayage services (the pickup and delivery of intermodal shipments). The Total Distribution Services, Inc. subsidiary serves the automotive industry with distribution centers and storage locations.

Recent Developments: For the year ended Dec 28 2012, net income increased 2.0% to US$1.86 billion from US$1.82 billion in the prior year. Revenues were US$11.76 billion, up 0.1% from US$11.74 billion the year before. Operating income was US$3.46 billion versus US$3.42 billion in the prior year, an increase of 1.1%. Direct operating expenses declined 1.5% to US$7.24 billion from US$7.35 billion in the comparable period the year before. Indirect operating expenses increased 8.5% to US$1.06 billion from US$976.0 million in the equivalent prior-year period.

Prospects: Our evaluation of CSX Corp. as of Apr. 7, 2013 is the result of our systematic analysis on three basic characteristics: earnings strength, relative valuation, and recent stock price movement. The company has managed to produce a neutral trend in earnings per share over the past 5 quarters. However, while recent estimates for the company have been lowered by analysts, CSX has posted better than expected results. Based on operating earnings yield, the company is undervalued when compared to all of the companies in our coverage universe. Share price changes over the past year indicates that CSX will perform poorly over the near term.

Financial Data
(US$ in Millions)

	12/28/2012	12/30/2011	12/31/2010	12/25/2009	12/26/2008	12/28/2007	12/29/2006	12/30/2005
Earnings Per Share	1.79	1.67	1.35	0.97	1.11	1.00	0.94	0.84
Cash Flow Per Share	2.85	3.23	2.79	1.76	2.43	1.70	1.56	0.86
Tang Book Value Per Share	8.81	8.00	7.75	7.44	6.81	7.10	6.81	6.08
Dividends Per Share	0.540	0.447	0.327	0.293	0.257	0.180	0.110	0.072
Dividend Payout %	30.17	26.75	24.14	30.24	23.05	18.06	11.70	8.53
Income Statement								
Total Revenue	11,756	11,743	10,636	9,041	11,255	10,030	9,566	8,618
EBITDA	4,584	4,411	4,044	3,216	3,532	3,177	3,080	2,273
Depn & Amortn	1,059	976	947	908	904	883	867	833
Income Before Taxes	2,964	2,888	2,546	1,761	2,146	1,932	1,862	1,055
Income Taxes	1,105	1,066	983	624	781	706	531	316
Net Income	1,859	1,822	1,563	1,152	1,365	1,336	1,310	1,145
Average Shares	1,040	1,089	1,153	1,187	1,225	1,344	1,397	1,368
Balance Sheet								
Current Assets	2,801	2,935	2,855	2,570	2,391	2,491	2,672	2,372
Total Assets	30,571	29,473	28,141	27,036	26,288	25,534	25,129	24,232
Current Liabilities	2,627	2,687	2,537	1,865	2,404	2,671	2,522	2,979
Long-Term Obligations	9,052	8,734	8,051	7,895	7,512	6,470	5,362	5,093
Total Liabilities	21,583	21,018	19,455	18,190	18,240	16,849	16,187	16,278
Stockholders' Equity	8,988	8,455	8,686	8,846	8,048	8,685	8,942	7,954
Shares Outstanding	1,020	1,049	1,111	1,180	1,171	1,223	1,313	1,309
Statistical Record								
Return on Assets %	6.21	6.34	5.57	4.33	5.28	5.29	5.32	4.70
Return on Equity %	21.37	21.32	17.54	13.68	16.36	15.20	15.55	15.55
EBITDA Margin %	38.99	37.56	38.02	35.57	31.38	31.67	32.20	26.38
Net Margin %	15.81	15.52	14.70	12.74	12.13	13.32	13.69	13.29
Asset Turnover	0.39	0.41	0.38	0.34	0.44	0.40	0.39	0.35
Current Ratio	1.07	1.09	1.13	1.38	0.99	0.93	1.06	0.80
Debt to Equity	1.01	1.03	0.93	0.89	0.93	0.74	0.60	0.64
Price Range	23.68-19.01	27.01-18.39	21.54-14.11	16.80-6.97	23.02-10.41	17.09-11.30	12.64-8.20	8.52-6.17
P/E Ratio	13.23-10.62	16.17-11.01	15.95-10.45	17.32-7.18	20.74-9.38	17.09-11.30	13.44-8.73	10.14-7.34
Average Yield %	2.50	1.92	1.82	2.39	1.45	1.27	1.04	0.99

Address: 500 Water Street, 15th floor, Jacksonville, FL 32202	**Web Site:** www.csx.com	**Auditors:** Ernst & Young LLP
Telephone: 904-359-3200	**Officers:** Michael J. Ward - Chairman, President, Chief Executive Officer Oscar Munoz - Executive Vice President, Chief Financial Officer, Chief Operating Officer	**Investor Contact:** 180-052-15571
		Transfer Agents: Computershare Shareowner Services, Pittsburgh, PA

CULLEN/FROST BANKERS, INC.

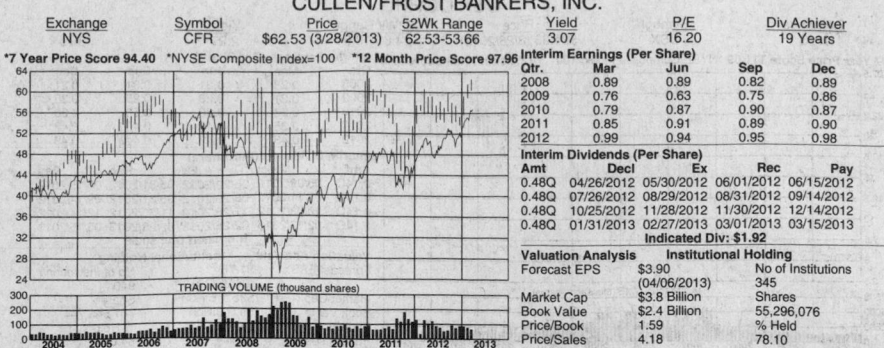

Exchange	Symbol	Price	52Wk Range	Yield	P/E	Div Achiever
NYS	CFR	$62.53 (3/28/2013)	62.53-53.66	3.07	16.20	19 Years

*7 Year Price Score 94.40   *NYSE Composite Index=100   *12 Month Price Score 97.96

Interim Earnings (Per Share)

Qtr.	Mar	Jun	Sep	Dec
2008	0.89	0.89	0.82	0.89
2009	0.76	0.63	0.75	0.86
2010	0.79	0.87	0.90	0.87
2011	0.85	0.91	0.89	0.90
2012	0.99	0.94	0.95	0.98

Interim Dividends (Per Share)

Amt	Decl	Ex	Rec	Pay
0.48Q	04/26/2012	05/30/2012	06/01/2012	06/15/2012
0.48Q	07/26/2012	08/29/2012	08/31/2012	09/14/2012
0.48Q	10/25/2012	11/28/2012	11/30/2012	12/14/2012
0.48Q	01/31/2013	02/27/2013	03/01/2013	03/15/2013

Indicated Div: $1.92

Valuation Analysis / **Institutional Holding**

Forecast EPS	$3.90 (04/06/2013)	No of Institutions 345
Market Cap	$3.8 Billion	Shares 55,296,076
Book Value	$2.4 Billion	% Held 78.10
Price/Book	1.59	
Price/Sales	4.18	

Business Summary: Banking (MIC: 5.1.1 SIC: 6021 NAIC: 522110)

Cullen/Frost Bankers is a financial holding company and a bank holding company. Through its subsidiaries, Co. provides a range of products and services throughout numerous Texas markets. Co. provides commercial and consumer banking services, as well as trust and investment management, mutual funds, investment banking, insurance, brokerage, leasing, asset-based lending, treasury management and item processing services. Co.'s operations are managed along two reportable operating segments consisting of Banking and Frost Wealth Advisors. As of Dec 31 2012, Co. had total assets of $23.12 billion and total deposits of $19.50 billion.

Recent Developments: For the year ended Dec 31 2012, net income increased 9.4% to US$238.0 million from US$217.5 million in the prior year. Net interest income increased 4.0% to US$604.9 million from US$581.8 million in the prior year. Provision for loan losses was US$10.1 million versus US$27.4 million in the prior year, a decrease of 63.3%. Non-interest income fell 0.4% to US$288.8 million from US$290.0 million, while non-interest expense advanced 3.0% to US$575.1 million.

Prospects: Our evaluation of Cullen/Frost Bankers Inc. as of Apr. 7, 2013 is the result of our systematic analysis on three basic characteristics: earnings strength, relative valuation, and recent stock price movement. The company has managed to produce a neutral trend in earnings per share over the past 5 quarters and while recent estimates for the company have remained steady, CFR has posted better than expected results. Based on operating earnings yield, the company is undervalued when compared to all of the companies in our coverage universe. Share price changes over the past year indicates that CFR will perform poorly over the near term.

Financial Data
(US$ in Thousands)

	12/31/2012	12/31/2011	12/31/2010	12/31/2009	12/31/2008	12/31/2007	12/31/2006	12/31/2005
Earnings Per Share	3.86	3.54	3.44	3.00	3.50	3.55	3.42	3.07
Cash Flow Per Share	4.88	4.49	7.03	4.61	3.97	3.41	(0.96)	2.52
Tang Book Value Per Share	30.48	28.48	24.95	22.44	20.41	15.66	13.61	14.65
Dividends Per Share	1.900	1.830	1.780	1.710	1.660	1.540	1.320	1.165
Dividend Payout %	49.22	51.69	51.74	57.00	47.43	43.38	38.60	37.95
Income Statement								
Interest Income	631,612	623,017	617,339	623,036	675,651	768,847	683,959	509,827
Interest Expense	26,751	41,241	53,880	86,357	141,626	250,110	214,796	118,561
Net Interest Income	604,861	581,776	563,459	536,679	534,025	518,737	469,163	391,266
Provision for Losses	10,080	27,445	43,611	65,392	37,823	14,660	14,150	10,250
Non-Interest Income	288,782	290,002	282,033	293,706	287,322	268,231	240,747	230,379
Non-Interest Expense	575,093	558,098	535,541	532,238	486,645	462,446	410,353	367,007
Income Before Taxes	308,475	286,235	266,340	232,755	296,879	309,862	285,407	244,388
Income Taxes	70,523	68,700	57,576	53,721	89,624	97,791	91,816	78,965
Net Income	237,952	217,535	208,764	179,034	207,255	212,071	193,591	165,423
Average Shares	61,643	61,277	60,585	59,513	59,285	59,713	56,642	53,803
Balance Sheet								
Net Loans & Leases	9,119,395	7,884,982	7,990,704	8,242,471	8,733,838	7,677,023	7,277,299	6,004,730
Total Assets	23,124,069	20,317,245	17,617,092	16,288,038	15,034,142	13,485,014	13,224,189	11,741,437
Total Deposits	19,497,366	16,756,748	14,479,342	13,313,310	11,508,937	10,529,673	10,387,909	9,146,394
Total Liabilities	20,706,587	18,033,708	15,555,412	14,393,614	13,270,615	12,007,926	11,847,306	10,759,201
Stockholders' Equity	2,417,482	2,283,537	2,061,680	1,894,424	1,763,527	1,477,088	1,376,883	982,236
Shares Outstanding	61,479	61,263	60,909	60,038	59,416	58,662	59,839	54,482
Statistical Record								
Return on Assets %	1.09	1.15	1.23	1.14	1.45	1.59	1.55	1.53
Return on Equity %	10.10	10.01	10.55	9.79	12.76	14.86	16.41	18.33
Net Interest Margin %	95.76	93.38	91.27	86.14	79.04	67.47	68.60	76.74
Efficiency Ratio %	62.48	61.13	59.55	58.06	50.54	44.59	44.38	49.58
Loans to Deposits	0.47	0.47	0.55	0.62	0.76	0.73	0.70	0.66
Price Range	60.67-53.66	62.57-44.29	62.01-50.00	53.19-36.61	62.75-45.38	56.84-48.10	59.44-52.26	56.05-42.45
P/E Ratio	15.72-13.90	17.68-12.51	18.03-14.53	17.73-12.20	17.93-12.97	16.01-13.55	17.38-15.28	18.26-13.83
Average Yield %	3.36	3.36	3.27	3.61	3.13	2.94	2.36	2.40

Address: 100 W. Houston Street, San Antonio, TX 78205	Web Site: www.frostbank.com	Auditors: Ernst & Young LLP
Telephone: 210-220-4011	Officers: Richard W. Evans - Chairman, President, Chief Executive Officer Phillip D. Green - Group	Investor Contact: 210-220-5632
Fax: 210-220-5578	Executive Vice President, Chief Financial Officer	Transfer Agents: Bank of New York Mellon Corporation, Pittsburgh, PA

CUMMINS, INC.

Exchange	Symbol	Price	52Wk Range	Yield	P/E
NYS	CMI	$115.81 (3/28/2013)	121.71-83.53	1.73	13.36

*7 Year Price Score 137.32 *NYSE Composite Index=100 *12 Month Price Score 103.36

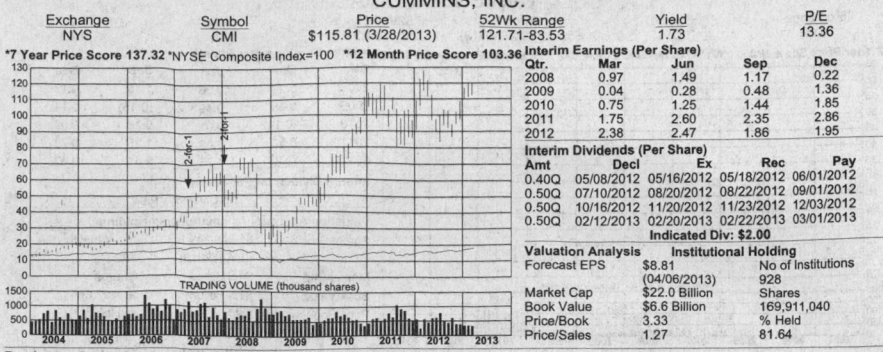

Interim Earnings (Per Share)

Qtr.	Mar	Jun	Sep	Dec
2008	0.97	1.49	1.17	0.22
2009	0.04	0.28	0.48	1.36
2010	0.75	1.25	1.44	1.85
2011	1.75	2.60	2.35	2.86
2012	2.38	2.47	1.86	1.95

Interim Dividends (Per Share)

Amt	Decl	Ex	Rec	Pay
0.40Q	05/08/2012	05/16/2012	05/18/2012	06/01/2012
0.50Q	07/10/2012	08/20/2012	08/22/2012	09/01/2012
0.50Q	10/16/2012	11/20/2012	11/23/2012	12/03/2012
0.50Q	02/12/2013	02/20/2013	02/22/2013	03/01/2013

Indicated Div: $2.00

Valuation Analysis

		Institutional Holding	
Forecast EPS	$8.81 (04/06/2013)	No of Institutions	928
Market Cap	$22.0 Billion	Shares	169,911,040
Book Value	$6.6 Billion	% Held	81.64
Price/Book	3.33		
Price/Sales	1.27		

Business Summary: Auto Parts (MIC: 1.8.2 SIC: 3519 NAIC: 333618)

Cummins is a diesel engine manufacturer. Co.'s operating segments consist of: engine, which produces engines and parts for sale to customers in on-highway and various industrial markets; components, which sells filtration products, exhaust aftertreatment systems, turbochargers and fuel systems; power generation, which provides power systems which sells engines, generator sets and alternators; and distribution, which includes wholly-owned and partially-owned distributorships engaged in wholesaling engines, generator sets and service parts, as well as performing service and repair activities on Co.'s products and maintaining relationships with various original equipment manufacturers.

Recent Developments: For the year ended Dec 31 2012, net income decreased 10.7% to US$1.74 billion from US$1.95 billion in the prior year. Revenues were US$17.33 billion, down 4.0% from US$18.05 billion the year before. Operating income was US$2.25 billion versus US$2.68 billion in the prior year, a decrease of 15.9%. Direct operating expenses declined 4.7% to US$12.83 billion from US$13.46 billion in the comparable period the year before. Indirect operating expenses increased 18.1% to US$2.25 billion from US$1.91 billion in the equivalent prior-year period.

Prospects: Our evaluation of Cummins Inc. as of Apr. 7, 2013 is the result of our systematic analysis on three basic characteristics: earnings strength, relative valuation, and recent stock price movement. The company has generated a negative trend in earnings per share over the past 5 quarters and while recent estimates for the company have been raised by analysts, CMI has posted better than expected results. Based on operating earnings yield, the company is undervalued when compared to all of the companies in our coverage universe. Share price changes over the past year indicates that CMI will perform in line with the market over the near term.

Financial Data

(US$ in Thousands)	12/31/2012	12/31/2011	12/31/2010	12/31/2009	12/31/2008	12/31/2007	12/31/2006	12/31/2005
Earnings Per Share	8.67	9.55	5.28	2.16	3.84	3.70	3.55	2.75
Cash Flow Per Share	8.07	10.74	5.11	5.76	5.05	4.08	4.41	4.30
Tang Book Value Per Share	30.50	25.66	20.63	15.80	13.14	14.20	11.12	7.56
Dividends Per Share	1.800	1.325	0.875	0.700	0.600	0.430	0.330	0.300
Dividend Payout %	20.76	13.87	16.57	32.41	15.63	11.62	9.29	10.90
Income Statement								
Total Revenue	17,334,000	18,048,000	13,226,000	10,800,000	14,342,000	13,048,000	11,362,000	9,918,000
EBITDA	2,565,000	2,945,000	1,884,000	936,000	1,464,000	1,447,000	1,398,000	1,143,000
Depn & Amortn	287,000	264,000	248,000	269,000	262,000	256,000	266,000	260,000
Income Before Taxes	2,271,000	2,671,000	1,617,000	640,000	1,178,000	1,169,000	1,083,000	798,000
Income Taxes	533,000	725,000	477,000	156,000	360,000	381,000	324,000	216,000
Net Income	1,645,000	1,848,000	1,040,000	428,000	755,000	739,000	715,000	550,000
Average Shares	189,668	193,597	197,148	197,695	196,530	199,900	203,106	204,400
Balance Sheet								
Current Assets	7,167,000	7,091,000	6,289,000	5,003,000	4,713,000	4,815,000	4,488,000	3,916,000
Total Assets	12,548,000	11,668,000	10,402,000	8,816,000	8,519,000	8,195,000	7,465,000	6,885,000
Current Liabilities	3,136,000	3,657,000	3,260,000	2,432,000	2,639,000	2,711,000	2,399,000	2,218,000
Long-Term Obligations	698,000	658,000	709,000	637,000	629,000	555,000	647,000	1,213,000
Total Liabilities	5,945,000	6,176,000	5,732,000	5,043,000	5,289,000	4,786,000	4,663,000	5,021,000
Stockholders' Equity	6,603,000	5,492,000	4,670,000	3,773,000	3,230,000	3,409,000	2,802,000	1,864,000
Shares Outstanding	189,800	192,000	197,800	201,300	201,300	202,200	208,400	186,000
Statistical Record								
Return on Assets %	13.55	16.75	10.82	4.94	9.01	9.44	9.97	8.20
Return on Equity %	27.13	36.37	24.64	12.22	22.68	23.80	30.65	33.69
EBITDA Margin %	14.80	16.32	14.24	8.67	10.21	11.09	12.30	11.52
Net Margin %	9.49	10.24	7.86	3.96	5.26	5.66	6.29	5.55
Asset Turnover	1.43	1.64	1.38	1.25	1.71	1.67	1.58	1.48
Current Ratio	2.29	1.94	1.93	2.06	1.79	1.78	1.87	1.77
Debt to Equity	0.11	0.12	0.15	0.17	0.19	0.16	0.23	0.65
Price Range	128.00-83.53	120.18-79.91	111.25-45.16	50.55-18.45	73.87-17.78	70.08-28.57	34.48-22.72	23.31-15.96
P/E Ratio	14.76-9.63	12.58-8.37	21.07-8.55	23.40-8.54	19.24-4.63	18.94-7.72	9.71-6.40	8.48-5.80
Average Yield %	1.76	1.32	1.16	1.91	1.17	0.86	1.17	1.52

Address: 500 Jackson Street, Box 3005, Columbus, IN 47202-3005 **Telephone:** 812-377-5000 **Fax:** 812-377-4937	**Web Site:** www.cummins.com **Officers:** Norman Thomas Linebarger - Chairman, President, Chief Executive Officer, Executive Vice President, Vice President, Chief Financial Officer, Chief Operating Officer, Division Officer Jean S. Blackwell - Executive Vice President, Division Officer	**Auditors:** PricewaterhouseCoopers LLP **Investor Contact:** 812-377-3121 **Transfer Agents:** Wells Fargo Shareownwner Services, St. Paul, MN

CVR ENERGY INC

Exchange	Symbol	Price	52Wk Range	Yield	P/E
NYS	CVI	$51.62 (3/28/2013)	61.40-23.95	N/A	11.92

*7 Year Price Score N/A *NYSE Composite Index=100 *12 Month Price Score 132.56

Interim Earnings (Per Share)

Qtr.	Mar	Jun	Sep	Dec
2008	0.26	0.36	1.16	0.13
2009	0.36	0.49	(0.16)	0.11
2010	(0.14)	0.01	0.27	0.02
2011	0.52	1.42	1.25	0.75
2012	(0.29)	1.75	2.41	0.47

Interim Dividends (Per Share)

No Dividends Paid

Valuation Analysis

		Institutional Holding	
Forecast EPS	$5.94	No of Institutions	
	(04/05/2013)	182	
Market Cap	$4.5 Billion	Shares	
Book Value	$1.5 Billion	91,437,864	
Price/Book	2.94	% Held	
Price/Sales	0.52	N/A	

Business Summary: Refining & Marketing (MIC: 9.1.2 SIC: 5989 NAIC: 454319)

CVR Energy is an independent petroleum refiner and marketer of transportation fuels. Co. has two business segments: petroleum and nitrogen fertilizer. Co.'s petroleum business operates a coking medium-sour crude oil refinery in Coffeyville, KS, and a crude oil unit refinery in Wynnewood, OK. In addition, Co. owns and operates a crude oil gathering system, a rack marketing division supplying product through tanker trucks, as well as a pipeline system. Co.'s nitrogen fertilizer business is operated by CVR Partners, LP, which produces nitrogen fertilizers in the form of ammonia and an aqueous solution of urea and ammonium nitrate used as a fertilizer.

Recent Developments: For the year ended Dec 31 2012, net income increased 9.0% to US$412.6 million from US$378.6 million in the prior year. Revenues were US$8.57 billion, up 70.4% from US$5.03 billion the year before. Operating income was US$1.03 billion versus US$566.6 million in the prior year, an increase of 82.7%. Direct operating expenses rose 68.8% to US$7.22 billion from US$4.28 billion in the comparable period the year before. Indirect operating expenses increased 69.5% to US$313.4 million from US$185.0 million in the equivalent prior-year period.

Prospects: Our evaluation of CVR Energy Inc. as of Apr. 7, 2013 is the result of our systematic analysis on three basic characteristics: earnings strength, relative valuation, and recent stock price movement. The company has suffered a very negative trend in earnings per share over the past 5 quarters. However, while recent estimates for the company have been lowered by analysts, CVI has posted better than expected results. Based on operating earnings yield, the company is undervalued when compared to all of the companies in our coverage universe. Share price changes over the past year indicates that CVI will perform very well over the near term.

Financial Data

(US$ in Thousands)	12/31/2012	12/31/2011	12/31/2010	12/31/2009	12/31/2008	12/31/2007	12/31/2006	12/31/2005
Earnings Per Share	4.33	3.94	0.16	0.80	1.90	...	...	...
Cash Flow Per Share	8.76	3.22	2.61	0.99	0.96	...	...	...
Tang Book Value Per Share	17.09	12.79	7.50	7.09	6.24	4.17	...	...
Income Statement								
Total Revenue	8,567,327	5,029,113	4,079,768	3,136,329	5,016,103	2,966,864	3,037,567	1,454,260
EBITDA	847,773	738,693	166,603	227,923	349,632	(7,462)	406,182	(132,385)
Depn & Amortn	135,030	95,251	90,473	86,814	84,168	71,184	54,341	25,705
Income Before Taxes	638,175	588,122	28,073	98,589	227,846	(138,672)	311,411	(182,125)
Income Taxes	225,584	209,563	13,783	29,235	63,911	(81,639)	119,840	(62,968)
Net Income	378,605	345,776	14,290	69,354	163,935	(56,824)	191,571	(119,157)
Average Shares	87,392	87,766	86,789	86,342	86,224	...	...	...
Balance Sheet								
Current Assets	1,761,079	1,356,783	599,357	425,976	373,411	557,881	342,453	...
Total Assets	3,610,895	3,119,291	1,740,184	1,614,494	1,610,483	1,856,068	1,449,480	...
Current Liabilities	625,631	587,559	265,715	190,624	244,909	536,443	230,200	...
Long-Term Obligations	897,078	853,903	468,954	474,726	479,503	484,328	769,202	...
Total Liabilities	2,085,740	1,967,679	1,050,611	960,679	1,031,016	1,412,553	1,366,053	...
Stockholders' Equity	1,525,155	1,151,612	689,573	653,815	579,467	443,515	83,427	...
Shares Outstanding	86,831	86,808	86,413	86,329	86,243	86,141	...	...
Statistical Record								
Return on Assets %	11.22	14.23	0.85	4.30	9.43	N.M.	...	...
Return on Equity %	28.21	37.56	2.13	11.25	31.96	N.M.	...	...
EBITDA Margin %	9.90	14.69	4.08	7.27	6.97	N.M.	13.37	N.M.
Net Margin %	4.42	6.88	0.35	2.21	3.27	N.M.	6.31	N.M.
Asset Turnover	2.54	2.07	2.43	1.95	2.89	1.80	...	...
Current Ratio	2.81	2.31	2.26	2.23	1.52	1.04	1.49	...
Debt to Equity	0.59	0.74	0.68	0.73	0.83	1.09	9.22	...
Price Range	49.49-19.72	28.88-14.65	15.25-6.74	13.63-3.42	29.55-2.25	25.70-20.25	...	...
P/E Ratio	11.43-4.55	7.33-3.72	95.31-42.13	17.04-4.28	15.55-1.18	...	...	...

Address: 2277 Plaza Drive, Suite 500, Sugar Land, TX 77479 **Telephone:** 281-207-3200	**Web Site:** www.cvrenergy.com **Officers:** Carl C. Icahn - Chairman John J. Lipinski - Chairman, President, Chief Executive Officer	**Auditors:** KPMG LLP

CVS CAREMARK CORPORATION

Exchange	Symbol	Price	52Wk Range	Yield	P/E
NYS	CVS	$54.99 (3/28/2013)	55.30-43.25	1.64	18.15

*7 Year Price Score 115.64 *NYSE Composite Index=100 *12 Month Price Score 101.83

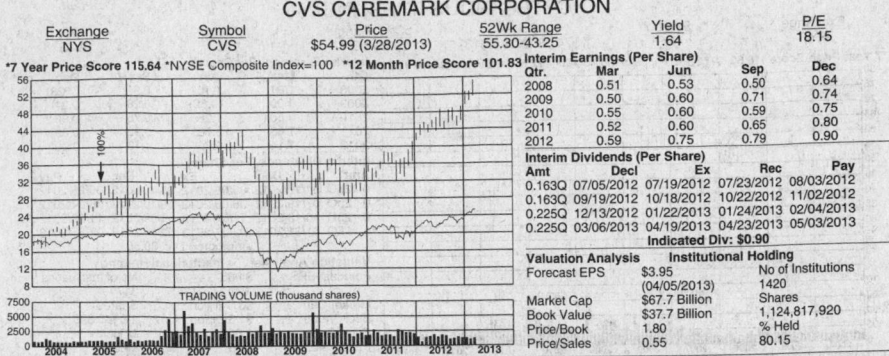

Interim Earnings (Per Share)

Qtr.	Mar	Jun	Sep	Dec
2008	0.51	0.53	0.50	0.64
2009	0.50	0.60	0.71	0.74
2010	0.55	0.60	0.59	0.75
2011	0.52	0.60	0.65	0.80
2012	0.59	0.75	0.79	0.90

Interim Dividends (Per Share)

Amt	Decl	Ex	Rec	Pay
0.163Q	07/05/2012	07/19/2012	07/23/2012	08/03/2012
0.163Q	09/19/2012	10/18/2012	10/22/2012	11/02/2012
0.225Q	12/13/2012	01/22/2013	01/24/2013	02/04/2013
0.225Q	03/06/2013	04/19/2013	04/23/2013	05/03/2013

Indicated Div: $0.90

Valuation Analysis — **Institutional Holding**

Forecast EPS	$3.95	No of Institutions
	(04/05/2013)	1420
Market Cap	$67.7 Billion	Shares
Book Value	$37.7 Billion	1,124,817,920
Price/Book	1.80	% Held
Price/Sales	0.55	80.15

Business Summary: Retail - Food & Beverage, Drug & Tobacco (MIC: 2.1.2 SIC: 5912 NAIC: 446110)

CVS Caremark is a pharmacy health care provider. Co. has three reportable segments: Pharmacy Services, which provides a range of pharmacy benefit management services, including mail order and pharmacy services, formulary management, discounted drug purchase arrangements, Medicare Part D services, retail pharmacy network management services, prescription management systems, clinical services and disease management services; Retail Pharmacy, which sells prescription drugs and an assortment of general merchandise through its CVS/pharmacy® and Longs Drugs® retail stores and online through CVS.com®; and Corporate, which provides management and administrative services to support Co.

Recent Developments: For the year ended Dec 31 2012, income from continuing operations increased 11.3% to US$3.88 billion from US$3.49 billion a year earlier. Net income increased 12.1% to US$3.88 billion from US$3.46 billion in the prior year. Revenues were US$123.13 billion, up 15.0% from US$107.10 billion the year before. Operating income was US$7.23 billion versus US$6.33 billion in the prior year, an increase of 14.2%. Direct operating expenses rose 16.3% to US$100.63 billion from US$86.54 billion in the comparable period the year before. Indirect expenses increased 7.4% to US$15.28 billion from US$14.23 billion in the equivalent prior-year period.

Prospects: Our evaluation of CVS Caremark Corp. as of Apr. 7, 2013 is the result of our systematic analysis on three basic characteristics: earnings strength, relative valuation, and recent stock price movement. The company has managed to produce a neutral trend in earnings per share over the past 5 quarters and while recent estimates for the company have remained steady, CVS has posted better than expected results. Based on operating earnings yield, the company is undervalued when compared to all of the companies in our coverage universe. Share price changes over the past year indicates that CVS will perform poorly over the near term.

Financial Data
(US$ in Thousands)

	12/31/2012	12/31/2011	12/31/2010	12/31/2009	12/31/2008	12/29/2007	12/30/2006	12/31/2005
Earnings Per Share	3.03	2.57	2.49	2.55	2.18	1.92	1.60	1.45
Cash Flow Per Share	5.23	4.38	3.50	2.81	2.73	2.44	2.13	1.99
Tang Book Value Per Share	1.26	1.33	1.65	N.M.	N.M.	N.M.	6.29	6.77
Dividends Per Share	0.650	0.500	0.500	0.350	0.305	0.258	0.229	0.155	0.145
Dividend Payout %	21.45	19.46	14.06	11.96	11.83	11.91	9.69	10.00
Income Statement								
Total Revenue	123,133,000	107,100,000	96,413,000	98,729,000	87,471,900	76,329,500	43,813,800	37,006,200
EBITDA	8,180,000	7,898,000	7,634,000	7,827,000	7,370,400	5,887,900	2,602,800	2,148,100
Depn & Amortn	1,300,000	1,568,000	1,469,000	1,389,000	1,274,200	1,094,600	161,200	128,600
Income Before Taxes	6,323,000	5,746,000	5,629,000	5,913,000	5,536,700	4,358,700	2,225,800	1,909,000
Income Taxes	2,441,000	2,258,000	2,190,000	2,205,000	2,192,600	1,721,700	856,900	684,300
Net Income	3,877,000	3,461,000	3,427,000	3,696,000	3,212,100	2,637,000	1,368,900	1,224,700
Average Shares	1,280,000	1,347,000	1,377,000	1,450,000	1,469,100	1,371,800	853,200	841,600
Balance Sheet								
Current Assets	19,852,000	18,594,000	17,706,000	17,537,000	16,526,200	14,149,400	10,391,500	8,392,700
Total Assets	65,912,000	64,543,000	62,169,000	61,641,000	60,959,900	54,721,900	20,569,800	15,283,400
Current Liabilities	13,790,000	11,956,000	11,070,000	12,300,000	13,489,900	10,766,300	7,000,700	4,583,900
Long-Term Obligations	9,133,000	9,208,000	8,652,000	8,756,000	8,057,200	8,349,700	2,870,400	1,594,100
Total Liabilities	28,208,000	26,492,000	24,469,000	25,873,000	26,385,500	23,400,000	10,652,200	6,952,200
Stockholders' Equity	37,704,000	38,051,000	37,700,000	35,768,000	34,574,400	31,321,900	9,917,600	8,331,200
Shares Outstanding	1,231,000	1,298,000	1,363,000	1,391,000	1,438,765	1,436,457	825,737	814,308
Statistical Record								
Return on Assets %	5.93	5.46	5.54	6.03	5.51	7.02	7.66	8.23
Return on Equity %	10.21	9.14	9.33	10.51	9.67	12.82	15.04	16.03
EBITDA Margin %	6.64	7.37	7.92	7.93	8.37	7.71	5.94	5.80
Net Margin %	3.15	3.23	3.55	3.74	3.67	3.45	3.12	3.31
Asset Turnover	1.88	1.69	1.56	1.61	1.50	2.03	2.45	2.49
Current Ratio	1.44	1.56	1.60	1.43	1.23	1.31	1.48	1.83
Debt to Equity	0.24	0.24	0.23	0.24	0.23	0.27	0.29	0.19
Price Range	49.24-41.46	41.16-32.06	37.37-26.98	38.01-23.98	44.12-24.42	42.25-30.79	35.95-26.35	31.25-22.25
P/E Ratio	16.25-13.68	16.02-12.47	15.01-10.84	14.91-9.40	20.24-11.20	22.01-16.04	22.47-16.47	21.55-15.34
Average Yield %	1.43	1.39	1.08	0.97	0.71	0.62	0.51	0.53

Address: One CVS Drive, Woonsocket, RI 02895	Web Site: www.cvscaremark.com	Auditors: Ernst & Young LLP
Telephone: 401-765-1500	Officers: Larry J. Merlo - President, Chief Executive Officer Troyen A. Brennan - Executive Vice President, Chief Medical Officer	Investor Contact: 800-201-0938
Fax: 401-762-2137		Transfer Agents: Computershare, Pittsburgh, PA

CYTEC INDUSTRIES, INC.

Exchange	Symbol	Price	52Wk Range	Yield	P/E
NYS	CYT	$74.08 (3/28/2013)	78.43-55.77	0.67	18.43

*7 Year Price Score 116.53 *NYSE Composite Index=100 ***12 Month Price Score 102.94**

Interim Earnings (Per Share)

Qtr.	Mar	Jun	Sep	Dec
2008	1.01	1.16	0.96	(7.28)
2009	0.00	(0.52)	0.26	0.21
2010	0.50	1.26	0.75	0.96
2011	1.66	0.70	0.98	0.89
2012	1.14	0.76	1.13	0.99

Interim Dividends (Per Share)

Amt	Decl	Ex	Rec	Pay
0.125Q	04/19/2012	05/08/2012	05/10/2012	05/25/2012
0.125Q	07/19/2012	08/08/2012	08/10/2012	08/24/2012
0.125Q	10/18/2012	11/07/2012	11/09/2012	11/26/2012
0.125Q	01/31/2013	02/07/2013	02/11/2013	02/25/2013

Indicated Div: $0.50

Valuation Analysis

		Institutional Holding	
Forecast EPS	$4.85	No. of Institutions	317
	(04/05/2013)		
Market Cap	$3.3 Billion	Shares	44,145,888
Book Value	$1.8 Billion	% Held	78.53
Price/Book	1.85		
Price/Sales	1.95		

Business Summary: Specialty Chemicals (MIC: 8.3.2 SIC: 2899 NAIC: 325998)

Cytec Industries is a materials and chemicals company. Co.'s products serve a range of end markets including aerospace and industrial materials, mining and plastics. At Dec 31 2012, Co. conducted its operations through four reportable business segments: Engineered Materials, which includes aerospace composites and structural adhesives, industrial composites and materials and carbon fibers for aerospace, and other markets; Umeco, which includes composites structural materials and composite process materials; In-Process Separation, which includes mining chemicals and phosphines products; and Additive Technologies, which includes polymer additives, specialty additives, and formulated resins.

Recent Developments: For the year ended Dec 31 2012, net income decreased 9.9% to US$190.1 million from US$210.9 million in the prior year. Revenues were US$1.71 billion, up 20.6% from US$1.42 billion the year before. Operating income was US$163.6 million versus US$155.5 million in the prior year, an increase of 5.2%. Direct operating expenses rose 19.1% to US$1.18 billion from US$992.2 million in the comparable period the year before. Indirect operating expenses increased 35.3% to US$363.0 million from US$268.2 million in the equivalent prior-year period.

Prospects: Our evaluation of Cytec Industries Inc. as of Apr. 7, 2013 is the result of our systematic analysis on three basic characteristics: earnings strength, relative valuation, and recent stock price movement. The company has generated a negative trend in earnings per share over the past 5 quarters. However, while recent estimates for the company have been mixed, CYT has posted better than expected results. Based on operating earnings yield, the company is about fairly valued when compared to all of the companies in our coverage universe. Share price changes over the past year indicates that CYT will perform well over the near term.

Financial Data

(US$ in Thousands)	12/31/2012	12/31/2011	12/31/2010	12/31/2009	12/31/2008	12/31/2007	12/31/2006	12/31/2005
Earnings Per Share	4.02	4.24	3.46	(0.05)	(4.16)	4.20	4.01	1.27
Cash Flow Per Share	6.80	4.37	5.65	11.70	4.77	5.60	4.24	5.14
Tang Book Value Per Share	24.25	15.55	14.11	9.39	7.44	7.17	0.87	N.M.
Dividends Per Share	0.500	0.500	0.050	0.163	0.500	0.400	0.400	0.400
Dividend Payout %	12.44	11.79	1.45	...	...	9.52	9.98	31.50
Income Statement								
Total Revenue	1,708,100	3,073,100	2,748,300	2,789,500	3,639,900	3,503,800	3,329,500	2,925,700
EBITDA	229,300	403,000	350,200	193,600	35,600	463,300	466,600	256,700
Depn & Amortn	67,600	135,300	122,700	174,100	153,300	139,600	149,000	141,100
Income Before Taxes	131,600	231,900	194,300	(4,700)	(152,900)	281,800	262,100	35,600
Income Taxes	37,300	64,800	50,500	(2,900)	47,400	76,700	69,200	(14,400)
Net Income	188,000	207,800	172,300	(2,500)	(198,800)	206,500	194,900	59,100
Average Shares	46,786	49,003	49,865	48,306	47,800	49,224	48,629	46,382
Balance Sheet								
Current Assets	1,216,700	1,287,800	1,311,400	1,140,900	1,187,900	1,276,100	1,153,400	1,122,600
Total Assets	3,922,100	3,536,700	3,673,900	3,559,400	3,625,600	4,061,700	3,831,500	3,810,500
Current Liabilities	807,400	521,900	579,600	575,400	507,200	686,900	611,900	625,900
Long-Term Obligations	567,400	635,900	641,500	658,400	806,400	705,300	900,400	1,225,500
Total Liabilities	2,123,100	1,850,100	1,943,300	2,000,500	2,150,900	2,131,800	2,261,400	2,572,400
Stockholders' Equity	1,799,000	1,686,600	1,730,600	1,558,900	1,474,700	1,929,900	1,570,100	1,238,100
Shares Outstanding	44,946	45,508	49,444	48,722	47,063	47,535	47,622	46,298
Statistical Record								
Return on Assets %	5.03	5.76	4.76	N.M.	N.M.	5.23	5.10	1.96
Return on Equity %	10.76	12.16	10.48	N.M.	N.M.	11.80	13.88	5.51
EBITDA Margin %	13.42	13.11	12.74	6.94	0.98	13.22	14.01	8.77
Net Margin %	11.01	6.76	6.27	N.M.	N.M.	5.89	5.85	2.02
Asset Turnover	0.46	0.85	0.76	0.78	0.94	0.89	0.87	0.97
Current Ratio	1.51	2.47	2.26	1.98	2.34	1.86	1.88	1.79
Debt to Equity	0.32	0.38	0.37	0.42	0.55	0.37	0.57	0.99
Price Range	70.69-45.95	59.19-32.49	60.85-36.42	39.20-16.58	63.77-16.28	71.78-53.83	62.40-45.89	54.25-39.52
P/E Ratio	17.58-11.43	13.96-7.66	17.59-10.53	...	...	17.09-12.82	15.56-11.44	42.72-31.12
Average Yield %	0.80	1.01	0.11	0.65	1.06	0.65	0.73	0.87

Address: Five Garret Mountain Plaza, Woodland Park, NJ 07424 **Telephone:** 973-357-3100	**Web Site:** www.cytec.com **Officers:** Shane D. Fleming - Chairman, President, Chief Executive Officer David M. Drillock - Vice President, Chief Financial Officer	**Auditors:** KPMG LLP **Investor Contact:** 973-357-3299 **Transfer Agents:** Computershare

DAVITA HEALTHCARE PARTNERS INC

Exchange	Symbol	Price	52Wk Range	Yield	P/E
NYS	DVA	$118.59 (3/28/2013)	123.35-80.23	N/A	21.68

*7 Year Price Score 136.64 *NYSE Composite Index=100 *12 Month Price Score 106.30

Interim Earnings (Per Share)

Qtr.	Mar	Jun	Sep	Dec
2008	0.80	0.90	0.89	0.94
2009	0.92	1.02	1.06	1.06
2010	1.04	1.04	1.15	0.72
2011	0.96	1.03	1.42	1.56
2012	1.46	0.99	1.50	1.51

Interim Dividends (Per Share)

No Dividends Paid

Valuation Analysis		Institutional Holding	
Forecast EPS	$7.48	No of Institutions	
	(04/05/2013)	535	
Market Cap	$12.5 Billion	Shares	
Book Value	$3.8 Billion	98,654,424	
Price/Book	3.32	% Held	
Price/Sales	1.53	96.88	

TRADING VOLUME (thousand shares)

Business Summary: Diagnostic & Health Related Services (MIC: 4.2.2 SIC: 8092 NAIC: 621492)

DaVita HealthCare Partners operates kidney dialysis centers and provides related lab services in outpatient dialysis centers and in contracted hospitals across the U.S. Co. also operates other ancillary services and strategic initiatives, which include its international operations that relate primarily to its core business of providing kidney dialysis services. On Dec 31 2011, Co. provided administrative services through a network of 1,809 outpatient dialysis centers located in the U.S. throughout 43 states and the District of Columbia. Also, Co. operated or provided administrative services to 11 outpatient dialysis centers located in three countries outside of the U.S.

Recent Developments: For the year ended Dec 31 2012, income from continuing operations increased 8.5% to US$641.5 million from US$591.3 million a year earlier. Net income increased 11.8% to US$641.2 million from US$573.4 million in the prior year. Revenues were US$8.19 billion, up 21.6% from US$6.73 billion the year before. Operating income was US$1.30 billion versus US$1.15 billion in the prior year, an increase of 12.3%. Direct operating expenses rose 20.4% to US$5.58 billion from US$4.63 billion in the comparable period the year before. Indirect operating expenses increased 38.9% to US$1.31 billion from US$943.5 million in the equivalent prior-year period.

Prospects: Our evaluation of Davita HealthCare Partners Inc. as of Apr. 7, 2013 is the result of our systematic analysis on three basic characteristics: earnings strength, relative valuation, and recent stock price movement. The company has managed to produce a neutral trend in earnings per share over the past 5 quarters. However, while recent estimates for the company have been mixed, DVA has posted better than expected results. Based on operating earnings yield, the company is about fairly valued when compared to all of the companies in our coverage universe. Share price changes over the past year indicates that DVA will perform well over the near term.

Financial Data
(US$ in Thousands)

	12/31/2012	12/31/2011	12/31/2010	12/31/2009	12/31/2008	12/31/2007	12/31/2006	12/31/2005
Earnings Per Share	5.47	4.96	3.94	4.06	3.53	3.55	2.74	2.20
Cash Flow Per Share	11.43	12.47	8.27	6.44	5.27	5.03	5.02	4.82
Income Statement								
Total Revenue	8,186,280	6,731,806	6,447,391	6,108,800	5,660,173	5,264,151	4,880,662	2,973,918
EBITDA	1,573,291	1,397,979	1,136,380	1,156,052	1,035,182	1,063,659	913,182	575,937
Depn & Amortn	299,810	249,060	219,314	214,515	201,006	178,990	160,717	105,254
Income Before Taxes	984,927	907,829	735,459	755,782	609,460	627,522	475,759	331,097
Income Taxes	359,845	325,292	260,239	278,465	235,300	245,744	186,430	123,675
Net Income	536,017	478,001	405,683	422,684	374,160	381,778	289,691	228,643
Average Shares	97,971	96,532	103,059	104,167	105,939	107,418	105,793	104,068
Balance Sheet								
Current Assets	2,878,794	2,281,608	2,622,854	2,302,521	2,128,304	1,976,250	1,709,496	1,654,408
Total Assets	16,018,596	8,892,172	8,114,424	7,558,236	7,286,091	6,943,960	6,491,816	6,279,762
Current Liabilities	2,018,174	1,153,116	924,345	1,046,941	1,163,063	1,086,496	1,112,172	989,733
Long-Term Obligations	8,326,534	4,417,624	4,233,850	3,532,217	3,622,421	3,683,887	3,730,380	4,085,435
Total Liabilities	12,255,459	6,751,097	6,136,002	5,423,170	5,333,633	5,211,710	5,245,892	5,429,153
Stockholders' Equity	3,763,137	2,141,075	1,978,422	2,135,066	1,952,458	1,732,250	1,245,924	850,609
Shares Outstanding	105,498	93,641	96,001	103,062	103,753	107,130	104,636	101,935
Statistical Record								
Return on Assets %	4.29	5.62	5.18	5.69	5.24	5.68	4.54	5.20
Return on Equity %	18.11	23.21	19.72	20.68	20.25	25.64	27.64	33.29
EBITDA Margin %	19.22	20.77	17.63	18.92	18.29	20.21	18.71	19.37
Net Margin %	6.55	7.10	6.29	6.92	6.61	7.25	5.94	7.69
Asset Turnover	0.66	0.79	0.82	0.82	0.79	0.78	0.76	0.68
Current Ratio	1.43	1.98	2.84	2.20	1.83	1.82	1.54	1.67
Debt to Equity	2.21	2.06	2.14	1.65	1.86	2.13	2.99	4.80
Price Range	114.98-71.13	89.36-60.64	74.11-56.83	61.55-42.34	60.01-42.48	66.53-51.54	60.27-47.59	53.59-39.26
P/E Ratio	21.02-14.10	18.02-12.23	18.81-14.42	15.16-10.43	17.00-12.03	18.74-14.52	22.00-17.37	24.36-17.85

Address: 2000 16th Street, Denver, CO 80202	**Web Site:** www.davita.com	**Auditors:** KPMG LLP
Telephone: 303-405-2100	**Officers:** Kent J. Thiry - Chairman, Co-Chairman, Chief Executive Officer Robert Margolis - Co-Chairman	**Investor Contact:** 310-536-2585
		Transfer Agents: Computershare

DANA HOLDING CORP

Exchange	Symbol	Price	52Wk Range	Yield	P/E
NYS	DAN	$17.83 (3/28/2013)	18.15-11.31	1.12	12.74

*7 Year Price Score N/A   *NYSE Composite Index=100   *12 Month Price Score 109.47

TRADING VOLUME (thousand shares)

Interim Earnings (Per Share)

Qtr.	Mar	Jun	Sep	Dec
2008	(0.29)	(1.47)	(2.79)	(2.64)
2009	(1.64)	(0.08)	(0.45)	(2.02)
2010	(0.28)	0.00	0.22	(0.15)
2011	(0.26)	0.32	0.51	0.33
2012	0.33	0.40	0.26	0.41

Interim Dividends (Per Share)

Amt	Decl	Ex	Rec	Pay
0.05Q	04/25/2012	05/09/2012	05/11/2012	06/01/2012
0.05Q	07/26/2012	08/08/2012	08/10/2012	08/31/2012
0.05Q	10/26/2012	11/07/2012	11/09/2012	11/30/2012
0.05Q	02/27/2013	03/13/2013	03/15/2013	04/05/2013

Indicated Div: $0.20

Valuation Analysis / **Institutional Holding**

Forecast EPS	$1.92 (04/06/2013)	No of Institutions	326
Market Cap	$2.6 Billion	Shares	156,489,184
Book Value	$1.8 Billion	% Held	0.01
Price/Book	1.43		
Price/Sales	0.37		

Business Summary: Auto Parts (MIC: 1.8.2 SIC: 3714 NAIC: 336399)

Dana Holding is a holding company. Through its subsidiaries, Co. is engaged as a supplier of driveline products, power technologies such as sealing and thermal management products, and service parts for vehicle manufacturers. Co. serves three primary markets: light vehicle, medium/heavy and off-highway. Co. has four business units: Light Vehicle Driveline, Commercial Vehicle, Off-Highway and Power Technologies. Co. owns or has licensed numerous trademarks that are registered in many countries, which includes its Spicer®, Victor Reinz® and Long® trademarks.

Recent Developments: For the year ended Dec 31 2012, income from continuing operations increased 31.3% to US$315.0 million from US$240.0 million a year earlier. Net income increased 35.8% to US$315.0 million from US$232.0 million in the prior year. Revenues were US$7.22 billion, down 4.2% from US$7.54 billion the year before. Operating income was US$448.0 million versus US$385.0 million in the prior year, an increase of 16.4%. Direct operating expenses declined 6.0% to US$6.25 billion from US$6.65 billion in the comparable period the year before. Indirect operating expenses increased 2.7% to US$526.0 million from US$512.0 million in the equivalent prior-year period.

Prospects: Our evaluation of Dana Holding Corp. as of Apr. 7, 2013 is the result of our systematic analysis on three basic characteristics: earnings strength, relative valuation, and recent stock price movement. The company has generated a negative trend in earnings per share over the past 5 quarters and while recent estimates for the company have been mixed, DAN has posted better than expected results. Based on operating earnings yield, the company is undervalued when compared to all of the companies in our coverage universe. Share price changes over the past year indicates that DAN will perform well over the near term.

Financial Data
(US$ in Thousands)

	12/31/2012	12/31/2011	12/31/2010	12/31/2009	12/31/2008	12/31/2007	12/31/2006
Earnings Per Share	1.40	1.02	(0.16)	(4.19)	(7.20)	(3.68)	(4.92)
Cash Flow Per Share	2.28	2.52	2.04	1.89	(8.94)	(0.35)	0.35
Tang Book Value Per Share	4.48	3.29	3.24	2.58	5.66	...	...
Dividends Per Share	0.200	...	...	...	...	...	...
Dividend Payout %	14.29	...	...	...	...	...	...
Income Statement							
Total Revenue	7,224,000	7,592,000	6,109,000	5,228,000	7,344,000	8,721,000	8,504,000
EBITDA	701,000	655,000	408,000	58,000	(119,000)	(45,000)	(215,000)
Depn & Amortn	277,000	307,000	314,000	397,000	350,000	279,000	278,000
Income Before Taxes	364,000	296,000	35,000	(454,000)	(563,000)	(387,000)	(571,000)
Income Taxes	51,000	85,000	31,000	(27,000)	107,000	62,000	66,000
Net Income	300,000	219,000	10,000	(431,000)	(691,000)	(551,000)	(739,000)
Average Shares	214,700	215,300	140,800	110,200	100,100	150,300	150,000
Balance Sheet							
Current Assets	2,953,000	3,049,000	2,933,000	2,582,000	2,733,000	3,792,000	3,324,000
Total Assets	5,144,000	5,305,000	5,099,000	5,064,000	5,593,000	6,425,000	6,734,000
Current Liabilities	1,310,000	1,493,000	1,407,000	1,156,000	1,446,000	2,952,000	2,086,000
Long-Term Obligations	803,000	831,000	780,000	969,000	1,181,000	19,000	722,000
Total Liabilities	3,301,000	3,568,000	3,414,000	3,385,000	3,579,000	7,207,000	7,568,000
Stockholders' Equity	1,843,000	1,737,000	1,685,000	1,679,000	2,014,000	(782,000)	(834,000)
Shares Outstanding	148,264	147,319	144,126	139,414	100,065	150,200	150,300
Statistical Record							
Return on Assets %	5.73	4.21	0.20	N.M.	N.M.	N.M.	N.M.
Return on Equity %	16.71	12.80	0.59	N.M.	N.M.	...	...
EBITDA Margin %	9.70	8.63	6.68	1.11	N.M.	N.M.	N.M.
Net Margin %	4.15	2.88	0.16	N.M.	N.M.	N.M.	N.M.
Asset Turnover	1.38	1.46	1.20	0.98	1.22	1.33	1.20
Current Ratio	2.25	2.04	2.08	2.23	1.89	1.28	1.59
Debt to Equity	0.44	0.48	0.46	0.58	0.59	...	...
Price Range	16.49-11.31	18.99-9.95	17.65-9.20	10.95-0.20	12.75-0.40	...	...
P/E Ratio	11.78-8.08	18.62-9.75	...	...	...	...	...
Average Yield %	1.44	...	...	...	...	...	...

Address: 3939 Technology Drive, Maumee, OH 43537	Web Site: www.dana.com	Auditors: PricewaterhouseCoopers LLP
Telephone: 419-887-3000	Officers: Roger J. Wood - President, Chief Executive Officer William G. Quigley - Executive Vice President, Chief Financial Officer	Transfer Agents: Wells Fargo Shareowner Services
Fax: 419-535-4643		

224

DANAHER CORP.

Exchange	Symbol	Price	52Wk Range	Yield	P/E
NYS	DHR	$62.15 (3/28/2013)	62.65-49.53	0.16	18.50

*7 Year Price Score 118.63 *NYSE Composite Index=100 *12 Month Price Score 102.55

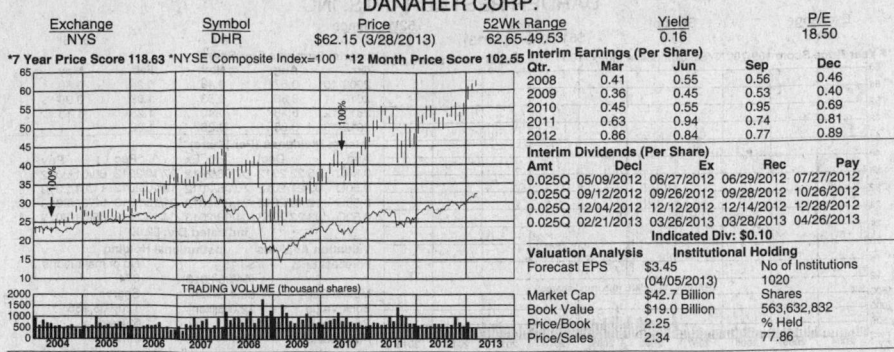

Interim Earnings (Per Share)

Qtr.	Mar	Jun	Sep	Dec
2008	0.41	0.55	0.56	0.46
2009	0.36	0.45	0.53	0.40
2010	0.45	0.55	0.95	0.69
2011	0.63	0.94	0.74	0.81
2012	0.86	0.84	0.77	0.89

Interim Dividends (Per Share)

Amt	Decl	Ex	Rec	Pay
0.025Q	05/09/2012	06/27/2012	06/29/2012	07/27/2012
0.025Q	09/12/2012	09/26/2012	09/28/2012	10/26/2012
0.025Q	12/04/2012	12/12/2012	12/14/2012	12/28/2012
0.025Q	02/21/2013	03/26/2013	03/28/2013	04/26/2013

Indicated Div: $0.10

Valuation Analysis / **Institutional Holding**

Forecast EPS	$3.45 (04/05/2013)	No of Institutions	1020
Market Cap	$42.7 Billion	Shares	563,632,832
Book Value	$19.0 Billion	% Held	77.86
Price/Book	2.25		
Price/Sales	2.34		

TRADING VOLUME (thousand shares)

Business Summary: Industrial Machinery & Equipment (MIC: 7.2.1 SIC: 3823 NAIC: 334513)

Danaher has five segments: Test and Measurement, which provides electronic measurement instruments and monitoring, management and optimization tools; Environmental, which provides products that help protect water supply and air quality; Life Sciences and Diagnostics, which provides a range of analytical instruments, reagents, consumables, software and services; Dental, which provides a range of consumables, equipment and services for the dental market; and Industrial Technologies, which designs and manufactures components and systems that are incorporated by original equipment manufacturers and systems integrators for sale into a set of applications and end-markets.

Recent Developments: For the year ended Dec 31 2012, income from continuing operations increased 18.8% to US$2.30 billion from US$1.94 billion a year earlier. Net income increased 10.1% to US$2.39 billion from US$2.17 billion in the prior year. Revenues were US$18.26 billion, up 13.5% from US$16.09 billion the year before. Operating income was US$3.17 billion versus US$2.62 billion in the prior year, an increase of 20.9%. Direct operating expenses rose 11.8% to US$8.85 billion from US$7.91 billion in the comparable period the year before. Indirect operating expenses increased 12.4% to US$6.25 billion from US$5.56 billion in the equivalent prior-year period.

Prospects: Our evaluation of Danaher Corp. as of Apr. 7, 2013 is the result of our systematic analysis on three basic characteristics: earnings strength, relative valuation, and recent stock price movement. The company has managed to produce a neutral trend in earnings per share over the past 5 quarters and while recent estimates for the company have remained steady, DHR has posted better than expected results. Based on operating earnings yield, the company is about fairly valued when compared to all of the companies in our coverage universe. Share price changes over the past year indicates that DHR will perform well over the near term.

Financial Data
(US$ in Thousands)

	12/31/2012	12/31/2011	12/31/2010	12/31/2009	12/31/2008	12/31/2007	12/31/2006	12/31/2005
Earnings Per Share	3.36	3.11	2.64	1.73	1.98	2.10	1.74	1.38
Cash Flow Per Share	4.91	3.88	3.19	2.81	2.90	2.64	2.51	1.95
Dividends Per Share	0.100	0.090	0.080	0.065	0.060	0.055	0.040	0.035
Dividend Payout %	2.98	2.89	3.03	3.76	3.04	2.63	2.30	2.54
Income Statement								
Total Revenue	18,260,400	16,090,540	13,202,602	11,184,938	12,697,456	11,025,917	9,596,404	7,984,704
EBITDA	3,593,000	2,868,219	2,632,641	1,727,000	2,063,474	1,914,651	1,735,210	1,300,668
Depn & Amortn	497,800	350,660	197,998	184,524	193,997	173,942	217,217	36,000
Income Before Taxes	2,940,900	2,381,069	2,319,937	1,424,854	1,749,307	1,637,099	1,446,172	1,234,442
Income Taxes	711,500	512,562	549,705	273,150	431,676	423,101	324,143	336,642
Net Income	2,392,200	2,172,264	1,793,000	1,151,704	1,317,631	1,369,904	1,122,029	897,800
Average Shares	713,100	701,191	683,275	671,484	671,726	658,918	650,502	655,966
Balance Sheet								
Current Assets	7,587,800	6,272,357	5,729,513	5,220,628	4,187,119	4,049,767	3,394,902	2,945,019
Total Assets	32,941,000	29,949,447	22,217,130	19,595,420	17,490,128	17,471,935	12,864,151	9,163,109
Current Liabilities	4,206,100	4,172,028	3,304,744	2,760,960	2,745,097	2,899,853	2,459,556	2,268,586
Long-Term Obligations	5,287,600	5,206,800	2,783,907	2,889,023	2,553,170	3,395,764	2,422,861	857,771
Total Liabilities	13,924,500	13,044,713	8,506,117	7,965,244	7,681,566	8,386,247	6,219,491	4,082,759
Stockholders' Equity	19,016,500	16,904,783	13,711,010	11,630,176	9,808,562	9,085,688	6,644,660	5,080,350
Shares Outstanding	687,500	687,730	656,360	645,470	636,760	635,968	616,484	611,142
Statistical Record								
Return on Assets %	7.59	8.33	8.58	6.21	7.52	9.03	10.19	10.17
Return on Equity %	13.28	14.19	14.15	10.74	13.91	17.42	19.14	18.51
EBITDA Margin %	19.68	17.83	19.94	15.44	16.25	17.37	18.08	16.29
Net Margin %	13.10	13.50	13.58	10.30	10.38	12.42	11.69	11.24
Asset Turnover	0.58	0.62	0.63	0.60	0.72	0.73	0.87	0.90
Current Ratio	1.80	1.50	1.73	1.89	1.53	1.40	1.38	1.30
Debt to Equity	0.28	0.31	0.20	0.25	0.26	0.37	0.36	0.17
Price Range	56.83-48.33	55.77-40.42	47.37-35.08	38.05-24.02	43.87-24.73	44.31-34.94	37.49-27.15	29.04-24.28
P/E Ratio	16.91-14.38	17.93-13.00	17.94-13.29	21.99-13.88	22.16-12.49	21.10-16.64	21.55-15.60	21.04-17.59
Average Yield %	0.19	0.18	0.20	0.21	0.17	0.14	0.12	0.13

Address: 2200 Pennsylvania Avenue, N.W., Suite 800W, Washington, DC 20037-1701 **Telephone:** 202-828-0850 **Fax:** 202-828-0860	**Web Site:** www.danaher.com **Officers:** Steven M. Rales - Chairman H. Lawrence Culp - President, Chief Executive Officer	**Auditors:** Ernst & Young LLP **Investor Contact:** 202-828-0850 **Transfer Agents:** Computershare, Providence, RI

DARDEN RESTAURANTS, INC.

Exchange	Symbol	Price	52Wk Range	Yield	P/E
NYS	DRI	$51.68 (3/28/2013)	57.21-44.44	3.87	15.76

*7 Year Price Score 109.70 *NYSE Composite Index=100 *12 Month Price Score 86.73

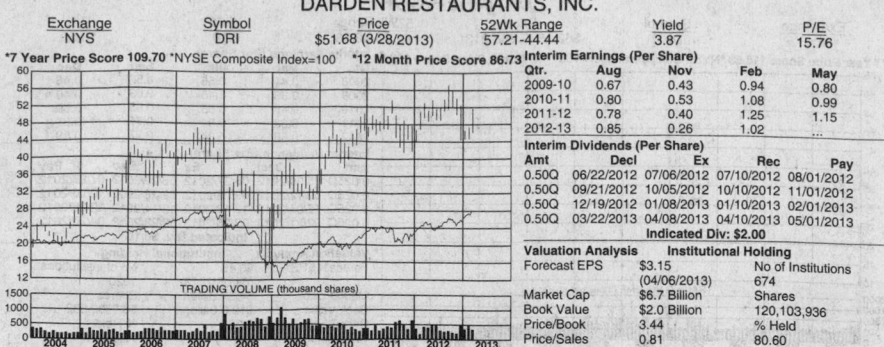

Interim Earnings (Per Share)

Qtr.	Aug	Nov	Feb	May
2009-10	0.67	0.43	0.94	0.80
2010-11	0.80	0.53	1.08	0.99
2011-12	0.78	0.40	1.25	1.15
2012-13	0.85	0.26	1.02	...

Interim Dividends (Per Share)

Amt	Decl	Ex	Rec	Pay
0.50Q	06/22/2012	07/06/2012	07/10/2012	08/01/2012
0.50Q	09/21/2012	10/05/2012	10/10/2012	11/01/2012
0.50Q	12/19/2012	01/08/2013	01/10/2013	02/01/2013
0.50Q	03/22/2013	04/08/2013	04/10/2013	05/01/2013

Indicated Div: $2.00

Valuation Analysis

		Institutional Holding	
Forecast EPS	$3.15 (04/06/2013)	No of Institutions	674
Market Cap	$6.7 Billion	Shares	120,103,936
Book Value	$2.0 Billion	% Held	80.60
Price/Book	3.44		
Price/Sales	0.81		

TRADING VOLUME (thousand shares)

Business Summary: Hotels, Restaurants & Travel (MIC: 2.2.1 SIC: 5812 NAIC: 722110)

Darden Restaurants and its subsidiaries owns and operates Red Lobster®, Olive Garden®, LongHorn Steakhouse®, The Capital Grille®, Bahama Breeze®, Seasons 52®, Eddie V's Prime Seafood® and Wildfish Seafood Grille® restaurant brands located in the U.S. and Canada. Except for three restaurants in Central Florida that are owned by joint ventures, Co., through its subsidiaries, owns and operates all of its restaurants in the U.S. and Canada. As of May 27 2012, Co. operated 1,994 restaurants in the U.S. and Canada and franchised five LongHorn Steakhouse restaurants in Puerto Rico, 22 Red Lobster restaurants in Japan, and one Red Lobster restaurant in Dubai, to unaffiliated franchisees.

Recent Developments: For the quarter ended Feb 24 2013, income from continuing operations decreased 18.0% to US$134.5 million from US$164.1 million in the year-earlier quarter. Net income decreased 18.1% to US$134.4 million from US$164.1 million in the year-earlier quarter. Revenues were US$2.26 billion, up 4.6% from US$2.16 billion the year before. Direct operating expenses rose 7.7% to US$1.75 billion from US$1.63 billion in the comparable period the year before. Indirect operating expenses increased 5.8% to US$332.7 million from US$314.6 million in the equivalent prior-year period.

Prospects: Our evaluation of Darden Restaurants Inc. as of Apr. 7, 2013 is the result of our systematic analysis on three basic characteristics: earnings strength, relative valuation, and recent stock price movement. The company has generated a negative trend in earnings per share over the past 5 quarters. However, while recent estimates for the company have been mixed, DRI has posted better than expected results. Based on operating earnings yield, the company is undervalued when compared to all of the companies in our coverage universe. Share price changes over the past year indicates that DRI will perform very poorly over the near term.

Financial Data

(US$ in Thousands)	9 Mos	6 Mos	3 Mos	05/27/2012	05/29/2011	05/30/2010	05/31/2009	05/25/2008
Earnings Per Share	3.28	3.51	3.65	3.57	3.39	2.84	2.65	2.60
Cash Flow Per Share	6.97	7.37	7.00	5.87	6.56	6.50	5.61	5.48
Tang Book Value Per Share	3.63	2.97	6.66	5.97	6.67	6.09	4.09	2.62
Dividends Per Share	1.930	1.860	1.790	1.720	1.280	1.000	0.800	0.720
Dividend Payout %	58.84	52.99	49.04	48.18	37.76	35.21	30.19	27.69
Income Statement								
Total Revenue	6,253,000	3,994,800	2,034,800	7,998,700	7,500,200	7,113,100	7,217,500	6,626,500
EBITDA	464,600	285,800	176,500	1,095,400	1,060,800	941,700	906,300	848,400
Depn & Amortn	9,300	5,500	2,300	355,800	319,600	304,200	286,400	248,000
Income Before Taxes	362,600	189,500	146,300	638,000	647,600	543,600	512,500	514,700
Income Taxes	83,300	44,700	35,300	161,500	168,900	136,600	140,700	145,200
Net Income	278,800	144,400	110,800	475,500	476,300	404,500	372,200	377,200
Average Shares	131,500	131,700	131,000	133,220	140,300	142,400	140,400	145,100
Balance Sheet								
Current Assets	853,400	800,600	726,800	757,600	663,800	678,500	554,800	467,900
Total Assets	6,957,800	6,832,700	6,020,400	5,944,200	5,466,600	5,247,400	5,025,200	4,730,600
Current Liabilities	1,535,400	1,543,600	1,860,900	1,774,100	1,286,800	1,254,600	1,096,100	1,136,200
Long-Term Obligations	2,555,400	2,557,000	1,507,800	1,508,100	1,463,300	1,466,300	1,691,200	1,694,200
Total Liabilities	5,007,500	4,969,300	4,160,400	4,102,200	3,530,400	3,353,400	3,419,200	3,321,500
Stockholders' Equity	1,950,300	1,863,400	1,860,000	1,842,000	1,936,200	1,894,000	1,606,000	1,409,100
Shares Outstanding	129,812	129,357	128,607	129,000	134,600	140,630	139,300	140,500
Statistical Record								
Return on Assets %	6.67	7.24	8.26	8.36	8.92	7.90	7.51	9.94
Return on Equity %	23.08	25.70	25.50	25.24	24.94	23.18	24.29	30.22
EBITDA Margin %	7.43	6.40	8.67	13.69	14.14	13.24	12.56	12.80
Net Margin %	4.46	3.61	5.45	5.94	6.35	5.69	5.16	5.69
Asset Turnover	1.29	1.29	1.39	1.41	1.40	1.39	1.46	1.75
Current Ratio	0.56	0.52	0.39	0.43	0.52	0.54	0.51	0.41
Debt to Equity	1.31	1.37	0.81	0.82	0.76	0.77	1.05	1.20
Price Range	57.21-44.44	57.21-41.82	53.87-41.53	53.63-41.53	52.03-37.61	48.68-30.31	40.26-13.54	47.08-20.99
P/E Ratio	17.44-13.55	16.30-11.91	14.76-11.38	15.02-11.63	15.35-11.09	17.14-10.67	15.19-5.11	18.11-8.07
Average Yield %	3.81	3.68	3.69	3.58	2.80	2.72	2.75	1.92

Address: 1000 Darden Center Drive, Orlando, FL 32837	**Web Site:** www.darden.com	**Auditors:** KPMG LLP
Telephone: 407-245-4000	**Officers:** Clarence Otis - Chairman, Chief Executive Officer, Executive Vice President, Senior Vice President, Vice President, Chief Financial Officer, Treasurer Andrew H. Madsen - President, Chief Operating Officer	**Transfer Agents:** Wells Fargo Shareowner Services, South St. Paul, MN

DDR CORP.

Exchange	Symbol	Price	52Wk Range	Yield	P/E
NYS	DDR	$17.42 (3/28/2013)	17.71-13.36	2.84	N/A

*7 Year Price Score 53.32   ***NYSE Composite Index=100**   ***12 Month Price Score 103.20**

Interim Earnings (Per Share)

Qtr.	Mar	Jun	Sep	Dec
2008	0.28	0.25	0.23	(1.58)
2009	0.59	(1.64)	(0.90)	(0.40)
2010	(0.15)	(0.39)	(0.10)	(0.38)
2011	0.01	(0.10)	(0.18)	(0.08)
2012	(0.08)	(0.16)	0.04	(0.02)

Interim Dividends (Per Share)

Amt	Decl	Ex	Rec	Pay
0.12Q	05/16/2012	06/15/2012	06/19/2012	07/06/2012
0.12Q	08/29/2012	09/12/2012	09/14/2012	10/02/2012
0.12Q	11/08/2012	12/13/2012	12/17/2012	01/04/2013
0.135Q	01/07/2013	03/12/2013	03/14/2013	04/02/2013

Indicated Div: $0.50

Valuation Analysis

		Institutional Holding	
Forecast EPS	$0.19	No of Institutions	
	(04/05/2013)	294	
Market Cap	$5.5 Billion	Shares	
Book Value	$3.3 Billion	284,518,720	
Price/Book	1.64	% Held	
Price/Sales	6.84	N/A	

Business Summary: REITs (MIC: 5.3.1 SIC: 6798 NAIC: 525930)

DDR is a real estate investment trust. Co. owns, manages and develops a portfolio of shopping centers and, to a lesser extent, office properties. As of Dec 31 2011, Co.'s portfolio consisted of 432 shopping centers (including 177 shopping centers owned through unconsolidated joint ventures and two shopping centers that are otherwise consolidated by Co.) in which Co. had an economic interest and five office properties. These properties consist of shopping centers, lifestyle centers and enclosed malls. At Dec 31 2011, Co. owned and/or managed more than 122.8 million total square feet of gross leasable area, which includes all of the aforementioned properties and 49 properties managed by Co.

Recent Developments: For the year ended Dec 31 2012, loss from continuing operations was US$14.8 million compared with a loss of US$7.9 million a year earlier. Net loss amounted to US$25.3 million versus a net loss of US$19.4 million in the prior year. Revenues were US$800.4 million, up 6.7% from US$749.8 million the year before. Revenues from property income rose 7.8% to US$749.8 million from US$695.8 million in the corresponding earlier year.

Prospects: Our evaluation of DDR Corp. as of Apr. 7, 2013 is the result of our systematic analysis on three basic characteristics: earnings strength, relative valuation, and recent stock price movement. The company has managed to produce a neutral trend in earnings per share over the past 5 quarters. Because the company lacks sufficient analyst estimate data, we place greater weight on the historical EPS trend as the measure of earnings strength. Based on operating earnings yield, the company is overvalued when compared to all of the companies in our coverage universe. Share price changes over the past year indicates that DDR will perform in line with the market over the near term.

Financial Data
(US$ in Thousands)

	12/31/2012	12/31/2011	12/31/2010	12/31/2009	12/31/2008	12/31/2007	12/31/2006	12/31/2005
Earnings Per Share	(0.21)	(0.28)	(1.03)	(2.51)	(0.83)	1.85	1.81	2.08
Cash Flow Per Share	1.04	1.01	1.14	1.44	3.53	3.43	3.10	3.28
Tang Book Value Per Share	8.93	9.49	9.85	11.34	16.30	20.01	16.30	16.96
Dividends Per Share	0.480	0.220	0.080	0.440	2.070	2.640	2.360	2.160
Dividend Payout %	...	...	...	...	...	142.70	130.39	103.85
Income Statement								
Total Revenue	800,375	771,018	803,069	819,307	931,472	944,851	818,098	727,176
EBITDA	448,625	568,559	631,859	833,139	494,704	633,301	556,949	499,721
Depn & Amortn	265,195	245,069	240,573	244,861	256,666	234,125	201,283	178,134
Income Before Taxes	(22,195)	103,604	172,168	362,444	(701)	146,666	143,254	149,386
Income Taxes	1,160	1,044	47,992	(691)	(17,434)	(14,642)	(2,481)	342
Net Income	(25,822)	(15,854)	(209,358)	(356,593)	(57,776)	276,047	253,264	282,643
Average Shares	291,726	271,472	244,712	158,816	119,987	121,497	109,613	109,142
Balance Sheet								
Current Assets	249,778	283,557	267,290	343,651	381,423	326,416	198,700	168,115
Total Assets	8,055,837	7,469,425	7,768,090	8,426,606	9,018,325	9,089,816	7,179,753	6,862,977
Current Liabilities	370,234	286,949	139,807	141,389	175,981	227,480	206,050	176,985
Long-Term Obligations	4,319,143	4,104,584	4,302,000	5,178,663	5,917,364	5,591,014	4,248,812	3,891,001
Total Liabilities	4,713,699	4,423,741	4,671,488	5,563,417	6,333,640	6,090,991	4,683,570	4,292,696
Stockholders' Equity	3,342,138	3,045,684	3,096,602	2,863,189	2,684,685	2,998,825	2,496,183	2,570,281
Shares Outstanding	314,261	276,280	255,555	201,085	128,418	119,448	108,986	108,947
Statistical Record								
Return on Assets %	N.M.	N.M.	N.M.	N.M.	N.M.	3.39	3.61	4.54
Return on Equity %	N.M.	N.M.	N.M.	N.M.	N.M.	10.05	10.00	11.03
EBITDA Margin %	56.05	73.74	78.68	101.69	53.11	67.03	68.08	68.72
Net Margin %	N.M.	N.M.	N.M.	N.M.	N.M.	29.22	30.96	38.87
Asset Turnover	0.10	0.10	0.10	0.09	0.10	0.12	0.12	0.12
Current Ratio	0.67	0.99	1.91	2.43	2.17	1.43	0.96	0.95
Debt to Equity	1.29	1.35	1.39	1.81	2.20	1.86	1.70	1.51
Price Range	15.86-12.28	15.14-10.17	14.09-8.25	10.45-1.43	45.47-2.75	71.38-37.69	66.11-47.80	49.08-38.91
P/E Ratio	...	...	...	...	...	38.58-20.37	36.52-26.41	23.60-18.71
Average Yield %	3.26	1.69	0.69	7.14	6.79	4.68	4.34	4.88

Address: 3300 Enterprise Parkway, Beachwood, OH 44122
Telephone: 216-755-5500

Web Site: www.ddrc.com
Officers: Daniel B. Hurwitz - President, Chief Executive Officer David J. Oakes - Senior Executive Vice President, Chief Financial Officer

Auditors: PricewaterhouseCoopers LLP
Transfer Agents: Computershare

DEAN FOODS CO.

Exchange	Symbol	Price	52Wk Range	Yield	P/E
NYS	DF	$18.13 (3/28/2013)	18.94-11.47	N/A	21.33

*7 Year Price Score 67.74 *NYSE Composite Index=100 *12 Month Price Score 101.88

Interim Earnings (Per Share)

Qtr.	Mar	Jun	Sep	Dec
2008	0.21	0.31	0.24	0.43
2009	0.48	0.38	0.27	0.27
2010	0.24	0.25	0.13	(0.11)
2011	0.14	(0.28)	(8.39)	(0.05)
2012	0.20	0.30	0.20	0.15

Interim Dividends (Per Share)

No Dividends Paid

Valuation Analysis

		Institutional Holding	
Forecast EPS	$1.09	No of Institutions	414
	(04/06/2013)		
Market Cap	$3.4 Billion	Shares	
Book Value	$357.2 Million		175,090,944
Price/Book	9.42	% Held	
Price/Sales	0.29		87.46

Business Summary: Food (MIC: 1.2.1 SIC: 5143 NAIC: 424430)

Dean Foods is a food and beverage company. Co. has two segments: Fresh Dairy Direct, a processor and distributor of milk and other dairy products, with products such as milk, ice cream, cultured dairy products, creamers, ice cream mix and other dairy products, sold under local and regional brands and private labels; and The WhiteWave Foods Company, which manufactures, markets and sells branded plant-based foods and beverages, such as Silk® soy, almond and coconut milks, Alpro® and Provamel® soy, almond and hazelnut drinks and food products, coffee creamers and beverages, including International Delight® and LAND O LAKES®, and dairy products, such as Horizon Organic® milk.

Recent Developments: For the year ended Dec 31 2012, net income amounted to US$161.0 million versus a net loss of US$1.59 billion in the prior year. Revenues were US$11.46 billion, down 1.5% from US$11.64 billion the year before. Operating income was US$427.8 million versus a loss of US$1.95 billion in the prior year. Direct operating expenses declined 3.4% to US$8.56 billion from US$8.86 billion in the comparable period the year before. Indirect operating expenses decreased 47.7% to US$2.47 billion from US$4.73 billion in the equivalent prior-year period.

Prospects: Our evaluation of Dean Foods Co. as of Apr. 7, 2013 is the result of our systematic analysis on three basic characteristics: earnings strength, relative valuation, and recent stock price movement. The company has generated a negative trend in earnings per share over the past 5 quarters. However, while recent estimates for the company have been lowered by analysts, DF has posted better than expected results. Based on operating earnings yield, the company is undervalued when compared to all of the companies in our coverage universe. Share price changes over the past year indicates that DF will perform very well over the near term.

Financial Data

(US$ in Thousands)	12/31/2012	12/31/2011	12/31/2010	12/31/2009	12/31/2008	12/31/2007	12/31/2006	12/31/2005
Earnings Per Share	0.85	(8.59)	0.50	1.38	1.20	0.96	1.61	2.13
Cash Flow Per Share	2.38	2.45	2.94	3.85	4.80	2.69	4.19	3.82
Dividends Per Share	...	...	...	...	...	15.000	...	...
Dividend Payout %	...	...	...	...	...	1,562.50	...	...
Income Statement								
Total Revenue	11,462,277	13,055,493	12,122,887	11,158,388	12,454,613	11,821,903	10,098,555	10,505,560
EBITDA	675,077	(1,789,108)	410,818	635,954	617,593	554,415	657,960	615,180
Depn & Amortn	246,583	10,539	11,295	9,637	9,836	6,744	7,700	7,300
Income Before Taxes	263,922	(2,052,598)	151,222	379,823	299,677	214,469	455,713	438,896
Income Taxes	146,509	(456,811)	73,482	152,065	114,837	84,007	175,450	166,423
Net Income	158,622	(1,575,621)	91,491	240,308	183,770	131,353	225,414	327,531
Average Shares	186,131	183,388	182,861	173,858	153,395	137,291	139,762	153,438
Balance Sheet								
Current Assets	2,202,778	1,716,322	1,816,216	1,628,969	1,481,193	1,531,984	1,379,290	1,476,968
Total Assets	5,687,091	5,754,363	7,956,667	7,843,941	7,040,192	7,033,356	6,770,173	7,050,884
Current Liabilities	1,340,993	1,495,542	1,440,965	1,478,525	1,427,267	932,516	1,336,556	1,137,330
Long-Term Obligations	3,077,258	3,563,389	3,893,275	3,980,627	4,173,725	5,247,105	2,872,193	3,328,592
Total Liabilities	5,329,904	5,857,761	6,457,142	6,491,995	6,481,958	6,982,089	4,960,774	5,178,805
Stockholders' Equity	357,187	(103,398)	1,499,525	1,351,946	558,234	51,267	1,809,399	1,872,079
Shares Outstanding	185,563	183,745	182,255	180,854	154,036	132,236	128,371	134,209
Statistical Record								
Return on Assets %	2.77	N.M.	1.16	3.23	2.60	1.90	3.26	4.42
Return on Equity %	124.66	N.M.	6.42	25.16	60.14	14.12	12.25	14.45
EBITDA Margin %	5.89	N.M.	3.39	5.70	4.96	4.69	6.52	5.86
Net Margin %	1.38	N.M.	0.75	2.15	1.48	1.11	2.23	3.12
Asset Turnover	2.00	1.90	1.53	1.50	1.77	1.71	1.46	1.42
Current Ratio	1.64	1.15	1.26	1.10	1.04	1.64	1.03	1.30
Debt to Equity	8.62	...	2.60	2.94	7.48	102.35	1.59	1.78
Price Range	18.79-10.56	13.88-7.97	18.53-7.26	21.92-15.90	28.90-11.51	48.31-24.30	43.51-34.70	39.45-26.93
P/E Ratio	22.11-12.42	...	37.06-14.52	15.88-11.52	24.08-9.59	50.32-25.31	27.02-21.55	18.52-12.65
Average Yield %	...	...	...	...	...	45.33	...	...

Address: 2711 North Haskell Avenue, Suite 3400, Dallas, TX 75204	Web Site: www.deanfoods.com	Auditors: Deloitte & Touche LLP
Telephone: 214-303-3400	Officers: Gregg L. Engles - Chairman, Chief Executive Officer Gregg A. Tanner - Chief Executive Officer, Executive Vice President, Chief Supply Chain Officer	Transfer Agents: The Bank of New York, New York, NY
Fax: 214-528-9929		

DEERE & CO.

Exchange	Symbol	Price	52Wk Range	Yield	P/E
NYS	DE	$85.98 (3/28/2013)	95.05-70.59	2.37	10.76

*7 Year Price Score 112.37 *NYSE Composite Index=100 *12 Month Price Score 99.90

Interim Earnings (Per Share)

Qtr.	Jan	Apr	Jul	Oct
2009-10	0.57	1.28	1.44	1.07
2010-11	1.20	2.12	1.69	1.62
2011-12	1.30	2.61	1.98	1.75
2012-13	1.65	...	...	...

Interim Dividends (Per Share)

Amt	Decl	Ex	Rec	Pay
0.46Q	05/30/2012	06/27/2012	06/29/2012	08/01/2012
0.46Q	08/29/2012	09/26/2012	09/28/2012	11/01/2012
0.46Q	12/05/2012	12/27/2012	12/31/2012	02/01/2013
0.51Q	02/27/2013	03/26/2013	03/28/2013	05/01/2013

Indicated Div: $2.04

Valuation Analysis

		Institutional Holding	
Forecast EPS	$8.55	No of Institutions	
	(04/05/2013)	1172	
Market Cap	$33.5 Billion	Shares	
Book Value	$7.5 Billion	278,051,744	
Price/Book	4.48	% Held	
Price/Sales	0.91	61.16	

TRADING VOLUME (thousand shares)

Business Summary: Construction Services (MIC: 7.5.4 SIC: 3523 NAIC: 332212)

Deere & Company operates in three business segments. The agriculture and turf segment primarily manufactures and distributes a line of agriculture and turf equipment and related service parts, including loaders; combines, and corn pickers among others. The construction and forestry segment primarily manufactures and distributes a range of machines and service parts used in construction, earthmoving, material handling and timber harvesting, including backhoe loaders; crawler dozers and loaders; and excavators among others. The financial services segment primarily finances sales and leases by Co.'s dealers of new and used agriculture and turf equipment and construction and forestry equipment.

Recent Developments: For the quarter ended Jan 31 2013, net income increased 21.6% to US$649.6 million from US$534.4 million in the year-earlier quarter. Revenues were US$7.42 billion, up 9.7% from US$6.77 billion the year before. Direct operating expenses rose 9.6% to US$5.01 billion from US$4.58 billion in the comparable period the year before. Indirect operating expenses increased 5.1% to US$1.46 billion from US$1.39 billion in the equivalent prior-year period.

Prospects: Our evaluation of Deere & Co. as of Apr. 7, 2013 is the result of our systematic analysis on three basic characteristics: earnings strength, relative valuation, and recent stock price movement. The company has managed to produce a neutral trend in earnings per share over the past 5 quarters. However, while recent estimates for the company have been mixed, DE has posted better than expected results. Based on operating earnings yield, the company is undervalued when compared to all of the companies in our coverage universe. Share price changes over the past year indicates that DE will perform well over the near term.

Financial Data

(US$ in Thousands)	3 Mos	10/31/2012	10/31/2011	10/31/2010	10/31/2009	10/31/2008	10/31/2007	10/31/2006
Earnings Per Share	7.99	7.63	6.63	4.35	2.06	4.70	4.00	3.59
Cash Flow Per Share	2.95	2.93	5.57	5.38	4.69	4.51	6.14	2.08
Tang Book Value Per Share	16.56	15.00	13.97	12.26	8.61	12.19	13.17	13.92
Dividends Per Share	1.840	1.790	1.520	1.160	1.120	1.060	0.910	0.780
Dividend Payout %	23.03	23.46	22.93	26.67	54.37	22.55	22.75	21.73
Income Statement								
Total Revenue	7,421,400	36,157,100	32,012,500	26,004,600	23,112,400	28,437,600	24,082,200	22,147,800
EBITDA	1,403,300	6,072,200	5,498,200	4,376,600	2,957,200	4,796,800	4,123,700	3,460,300
Depn & Amortn	277,100	555,000	516,000	540,000	575,000	536,000	297,000	269,000
Income Before Taxes	946,100	4,734,400	4,222,800	3,025,200	1,339,800	3,123,800	2,675,500	2,173,800
Income Taxes	289,000	1,659,400	1,423,600	1,161,600	460,000	1,111,200	883,000	741,600
Net Income	649,700	3,064,700	2,799,900	1,865,000	873,500	2,052,800	1,821,700	1,693,800
Average Shares	393,000	401,500	422,400	428,600	424,400	436,300	455,000	471,600
Balance Sheet								
Current Assets	16,541,600	16,942,400	13,478,600	11,510,500	10,760,300	10,174,900	9,919,800	8,969,400
Total Assets	55,169,600	56,265,800	48,207,400	43,266,800	41,132,600	38,734,600	38,575,700	34,720,400
Current Liabilities	17,646,400	19,092,000	17,552,100	14,220,500	12,585,000	15,084,200	15,737,800	12,787,500
Long-Term Obligations	22,170,200	22,453,400	16,960,000	16,815,000	17,392,000	13,899,000	11,798,000	11,584,000
Total Liabilities	47,685,900	49,423,700	41,407,100	36,976,500	36,313,900	32,201,900	31,419,900	27,229,200
Stockholders' Equity	7,483,700	6,842,100	6,800,300	6,290,300	4,818,700	6,532,700	7,155,800	7,491,200
Shares Outstanding	389,556	387,805	406,069	422,180	423,242	422,296	439,636	454,466
Statistical Record								
Return on Assets %	6.13	5.85	6.12	4.42	2.19	5.30	4.97	4.96
Return on Equity %	44.66	44.81	42.78	33.58	15.39	29.91	24.87	23.62
EBITDA Margin %	18.91	16.79	17.18	16.83	12.79	16.87	17.12	15.62
Net Margin %	8.75	8.48	8.75	7.17	3.78	7.22	7.56	7.65
Asset Turnover	0.71	0.69	0.70	0.62	0.58	0.73	0.66	0.65
Current Ratio	0.94	0.89	0.77	0.81	0.86	0.67	0.63	0.70
Debt to Equity	2.96	3.28	2.49	2.67	3.61	2.13	1.65	1.55
Price Range	95.05-70.59	88.40-70.59	99.24-61.72	77.25-46.30	48.38-24.83	94.69-29.89	77.45-42.41	45.67-30.34
P/E Ratio	11.90-8.83	11.59-9.25	14.97-9.31	17.76-10.64	23.49-12.05	20.15-6.36	19.36-10.60	12.72-8.45
Average Yield %	2.26	2.26	1.83	1.93	2.84	1.41	1.57	2.02

Address: One John Deere Place,	Web Site: www.johndeere.com	Auditors: Deloitte & Touche LLP
Moline, IL 61265	Officers: Samuel R. Allen - Chairman, President,	Investor Contact: 309-765-4491
Telephone: 309-765-8000	Chief Executive Officer, Chief Operating Officer,	Transfer Agents: BNY Mellon
Fax: 309-765-9929	Division Officer Rajesh Kalathur - Senior Vice	Shareowner Services, Pittsburgh, PA
	President, Chief Financial Officer	

DELTA AIR LINES, INC. (DE)

Exchange	Symbol	Price	52Wk Range	Yield	P/E
NYS	DAL	$16.51 (3/28/2013)	17.07-8.55	N/A	13.87

*7 Year Price Score N/A *NYSE Composite Index=100 *12 Month Price Score 123.93

TRADING VOLUME (thousand shares)

Interim Earnings (Per Share)

Qtr.	Mar	Jun	Sep	Dec
2008	(16.15)	(2.64)	(0.13)	(0.17)
2009	(0.96)	(0.31)	(0.19)	(0.03)
2010	(0.31)	0.55	0.43	0.02
2011	(0.38)	0.23	0.65	0.50
2012	0.15	(0.20)	1.23	0.01

Interim Dividends (Per Share)

No Dividends Paid

Valuation Analysis **Institutional Holding**

Forecast EPS	$2.61	No of Institutions
	(04/06/2013)	516
Market Cap	$14.1 Billion	Shares
Book Value	N/A	719,406,080
Price/Book	N/A	% Held
Price/Sales	0.38	N/A

Business Summary: Airlines/Air Freight (MIC: 7.4.4 SIC: 4512 NAIC: 481111)

Delta Air Lines provides scheduled air transportation for passengers and cargo throughout the U.S. and around the world. Co.'s route network is centered around a system of hub and international gateway airports that Co. operates in Amsterdam, Atlanta, Cincinnati, Detroit, Memphis, Minneapolis-St. Paul, New York - LaGuardia, New York-JFK, Paris-Charles de Gaulle, Salt Lake City, Seattle and Tokyo-Narita. Each of these hub operations includes flights that gather and distribute traffic from markets in the geographic region surrounding the hub or gateway to domestic and international cities and to other hubs or gateways.

Recent Developments: For the year ended Dec 31 2012, net income increased 18.1% to US$1.01 billion from US$854.0 million in the prior year. Revenues were US$36.67 billion, up 4.4% from US$35.12 billion the year before. Operating income was US$2.18 billion versus US$1.98 billion in the prior year, an increase of 10.1%. Direct operating expenses rose 3.6% to US$21.66 billion from US$20.91 billion in the comparable period the year before. Indirect operating expenses increased 4.9% to US$12.84 billion from US$12.23 billion in the equivalent prior-year period.

Prospects: Our evaluation of Delta Air Lines Inc. as of Apr. 7, 2013 is the result of our systematic analysis on three basic characteristics: earnings strength, relative valuation, and recent stock price movement. The company has suffered a very negative trend in earnings per share over the past 5 quarters. However, while recent estimates for the company have been mixed, DAL has posted better than expected results. Based on operating earnings yield, the company is undervalued when compared to all of the companies in our coverage universe. Share price changes over the past year indicates that DAL will perform very well over the near term.

Financial Data
(US$ in Thousands)

	12/31/2012	12/31/2011	12/31/2010	12/31/2009	12/31/2008	12/31/2007	04/30/2007	12/31/2006
Earnings Per Share	1.19	1.01	0.70	(1.50)	(19.08)	0.79	4.63	(31.58)
Cash Flow Per Share	2.92	3.38	3.40	1.67	(3.64)	0.85	15.80	5.05
Income Statement								
Total Revenue	36,670,000	35,115,000	31,755,000	28,063,000	22,697,000	13,358,000	5,796,000	17,171,000
EBITDA	3,430,000	3,263,000	3,520,000	1,576,000	(7,162,000)	1,579,000	1,928,000	(6,058,000)
Depn & Amortn	1,400,000	1,400,000	1,727,000	1,906,000	1,266,000	778,000	386,000	109,000
Income Before Taxes	1,025,000	769,000	608,000	(1,581,000)	(9,041,000)	525,000	1,294,000	(6,968,000)
Income Taxes	16,000	(85,000)	15,000	(344,000)	(119,000)	211,000	(4,000)	(765,000)
Net Income	1,009,000	854,000	593,000	(1,237,000)	(8,922,000)	314,000	1,298,000	(6,203,000)
Average Shares	850,000	844,000	843,000	827,000	468,000	395,200	233,700	196,500
Balance Sheet								
Current Assets	8,272,000	7,729,000	7,307,000	7,741,000	8,904,000	5,240,000	...	5,385,000
Total Assets	44,550,000	43,499,000	43,188,000	43,539,000	45,014,000	32,423,000	...	19,622,000
Current Liabilities	13,270,000	12,701,000	11,385,000	9,797,000	11,022,000	6,605,000	...	5,769,000
Long-Term Obligations	11,082,000	11,847,000	13,179,000	15,665,000	15,411,000	7,986,000	...	6,509,000
Total Liabilities	46,681,000	44,895,000	42,291,000	43,294,000	44,140,000	22,310,000	...	33,215,000
Stockholders' Equity	(2,131,000)	(1,396,000)	897,000	245,000	874,000	10,113,000	...	(13,593,000)
Shares Outstanding	851,402	845,245	834,723	783,954	695,136	294,718	...	197,335
Statistical Record								
Return on Assets %	2.29	1.97	1.37	N.M.	N.M.	1.21	...	N.M.
Return on Equity %	...	...	103.85	N.M.	N.M.	...	...	...
EBITDA Margin %	9.35	9.29	11.08	5.62	N.M.	11.82	33.26	N.M.
Net Margin %	2.75	2.43	1.87	N.M.	N.M.	2.35	22.39	N.M.
Asset Turnover	0.83	0.81	0.73	0.63	0.58	0.51	...	0.87
Current Ratio	0.62	0.61	0.64	0.79	0.81	0.79	...	0.93
Debt to Equity	...	...	14.69	63.94	17.63	0.79	...	...
Price Range	12.10-8.01	13.00-6.62	14.93-9.96	12.38-3.93	18.53-4.64	21.51-14.17	22.79-20.45	...
P/E Ratio	10.17-6.73	12.87-6.55	21.33-14.23	...	...	27.23-17.94	4.92-4.42	...

Address: Post Office Box 20706, Atlanta, GA 30320-6001 Telephone: 404-715-2600	Web Site: www.delta.com Officers: Edward H. Bastian - President Richard H. Anderson - Chief Executive Officer	Auditors: Ernst & Young LLP Transfer Agents: Wells Fargo Shareowner Services, St. Paul, MN

DELUXE CORP.

Exchange	Symbol	Price	52Wk Range	Yield	P/E
NYS	DLX	$41.40 (3/28/2013)	42.18-21.51	2.42	12.47

*7 Year Price Score 114.88 *NYSE Composite Index=100 *12 Month Price Score 121.32

Interim Earnings (Per Share)

Qtr.	Mar	Jun	Sep	Dec
2008	0.53	0.63	0.27	0.54
2009	0.24	0.54	0.56	0.60
2010	0.65	0.65	0.98	0.68
2011	0.63	0.68	0.71	0.78
2012	0.86	0.82	0.81	0.83

Interim Dividends (Per Share)

Amt	Decl	Ex	Rec	Pay
0.25Q	05/01/2012	05/17/2012	05/21/2012	06/04/2012
0.25Q	08/01/2012	08/16/2012	08/20/2012	09/04/2012
0.25Q	10/25/2012	11/15/2012	11/19/2012	12/03/2012
0.25Q	01/24/2013	02/13/2013	02/15/2013	03/04/2013

Indicated Div: $1.00

Valuation Analysis

		Institutional Holding	
Forecast EPS	$3.63 (04/05/2013)	No of Institutions	305
Market Cap	$2.1 Billion	Shares	47,424,936
Book Value	$432.9 Million	% Held	85.90
Price/Book	4.84		
Price/Sales	1.38		

Business Summary: Printing (MIC: 7.5.5 SIC: 2761 NAIC: 323116)

Deluxe is engaged in providing products and services to small businesses and financial institutions. Co. operates three business segments: Small Business Services, Financial Services and Direct Checks. Co. offers services such as web design, hosting and other web services, logo design, search engine optimization and marketing, social media marketing, and digital printing services designed to fulfill the sales and marketing needs of small businesses, as well as products such as business cards, greeting cards, postcards, brochures and apparel. Co. also offers various customer acquisition programs, marketing communications services and package insert programs.

Recent Developments: For the year ended Dec 31 2012, income from continuing operations increased 17.9% to US$170.5 million from US$144.6 million a year earlier. Net income increased 17.9% to US$170.5 million from US$144.6 million in the prior year. Revenues were US$1.51 billion, up 6.9% from US$1.42 billion the year before. Operating income was US$302.0 million versus US$271.1 million in the prior year, an increase of 11.4%. Direct operating expenses rose 6.3% to US$524.4 million from US$493.4 million in the comparable period the year before. Indirect operating expenses increased 5.4% to US$688.5 million from US$653.1 million in the equivalent prior-year period.

Prospects: Our evaluation of Deluxe Corp. as of Apr. 7, 2013 is the result of our systematic analysis on three basic characteristics: earnings strength, relative valuation, and recent stock price movement. The company has managed to produce a neutral trend in earnings per share over the past 5 quarters and while recent estimates for the company have remained steady, DLX has posted better than expected results. Based on operating earnings yield, the company is undervalued when compared to all of the companies in our coverage universe. Share price changes over the past year indicates that DLX will perform very well over the near term.

Financial Data

(US$ in Thousands)	12/31/2012	12/31/2011	12/31/2010	12/31/2009	12/31/2008	12/31/2007	12/31/2006	12/31/2005
Earnings Per Share	3.32	2.80	2.96	1.94	1.97	2.76	1.96	3.09
Cash Flow Per Share	4.79	4.61	4.16	4.06	3.89	4.76	4.69	3.53
Dividends Per Share	1.000	1.000	1.000	1.000	1.000	1.000	1.300	1.600
Dividend Payout %	30.12	35.71	33.78	51.55	50.76	36.23	66.33	51.78
Income Statement								
Total Revenue	1,514,917	1,417,596	1,402,237	1,344,195	1,468,662	1,606,367	1,639,654	1,716,294
EBITDA	408,982	389,020	354,029	269,066	316,636	386,749	343,459	493,746
Depn & Amortn	111,382	125,139	73,915	67,765	106,039	113,801	144,257	187,703
Income Before Taxes	250,753	216,084	235,949	155,021	160,176	217,654	142,541	250,734
Income Taxes	80,261	71,489	82,554	55,656	54,304	74,139	41,983	92,771
Net Income	170,492	144,595	152,624	99,365	101,634	143,515	100,954	157,521
Average Shares	51,076	51,415	51,325	50,925	51,350	51,932	51,230	50,936
Balance Sheet								
Current Assets	219,743	192,575	171,237	159,499	167,086	191,945	202,117	213,938
Total Assets	1,412,440	1,388,809	1,308,691	1,211,210	1,218,985	1,210,755	1,267,132	1,425,875
Current Liabilities	220,110	300,367	211,512	243,048	283,637	297,588	664,503	491,085
Long-Term Obligations	652,581	656,131	748,122	742,753	773,896	775,086	576,590	902,805
Total Liabilities	979,505	1,086,120	1,082,493	1,094,000	1,165,919	1,169,648	1,332,805	1,507,901
Stockholders' Equity	432,935	302,689	226,198	117,210	53,066	41,107	(65,673)	(82,026)
Shares Outstanding	50,614	50,826	51,338	51,189	51,131	51,887	51,519	50,735
Statistical Record								
Return on Assets %	12.14	10.72	12.11	8.18	8.34	11.58	7.50	10.77
Return on Equity %	46.23	54.68	88.89	116.71	215.26	...	...	...
EBITDA Margin %	27.00	27.44	25.25	20.02	21.56	24.08	20.95	28.77
Net Margin %	11.25	10.20	10.88	7.39	6.92	8.93	6.16	9.18
Asset Turnover	1.08	1.05	1.11	1.11	1.21	1.30	1.22	1.17
Current Ratio	1.00	0.64	0.81	0.66	0.59	0.65	0.30	0.44
Debt to Equity	1.51	2.17	3.31	6.34	14.58	18.86	...	...
Price Range	32.24-21.51	28.12-18.05	23.85-14.79	17.93-6.23	32.89-8.28	44.67-25.63	31.37-13.57	42.90-30.11
P/E Ratio	9.71-6.48	10.04-6.45	8.06-5.00	9.24-3.21	16.70-4.20	16.18-9.29	16.01-6.92	13.88-9.74
Average Yield %	3.76	4.21	5.06	7.23	5.59	2.79	5.84	4.19

Address: 3680 Victoria Street North, Shoreview, MN 55126-2966
Telephone: 651-483-7111
Fax: 651-483-7337

Web Site: www.deluxe.com
Officers: Lee J. Schram - Chief Executive Officer
Anthony C. Scarfone - Senior Vice President, Secretary, General Counsel

Auditors: PricewaterhouseCoopers LLP
Investor Contact: 651-787-1068
Transfer Agents: Wells Fargo
Shareowner Services, St. Paul, MN

DENBURY RESOURCES, INC. (DE)

Exchange	Symbol	Price	52Wk Range	Yield	P/E
NYS	DNR	$18.65 (3/28/2013)	19.50-13.46	N/A	13.81

*7 Year Price Score 80.18   *NYSE Composite Index=100   *12 Month Price Score 102.51

Interim Earnings (Per Share)

Qtr.	Mar	Jun	Sep	Dec
2008	0.29	0.45	0.63	0.18
2009	(0.07)	(0.35)	0.11	0.02
2010	0.33	0.34	0.07	0.01
2011	(0.04)	0.64	0.68	0.14
2012	0.29	0.54	0.22	0.30

Interim Dividends (Per Share)
No Dividends Paid

Valuation Analysis

	Institutional Holding	
Forecast EPS $1.25 (04/05/2013)	No of Institutions 508	
Market Cap $7.0 Billion	Shares	
Book Value $5.1 Billion	380,198,112	
Price/Book 1.37	% Held	
Price/Sales 2.85	92.23	

Business Summary: Production & Extraction (MIC: 9.1.1 SIC: 1311 NAIC: 213112)

Denbury Resources is an oil and natural gas company. Co. is primarily engaged as an oil and natural gas producer in Mississippi and Montana, owner of carbon dioxide reserves east of the Mississippi River used for tertiary oil recovery, as well as certain operating acreage in the Rocky Mountain and Gulf Coast regions. Co.'s oil and natural gas reserves in the Gulf Coast region are situated in Mississippi, Texas, Louisiana and Alabama, and in the Rocky Mountain region are situated in Montana, North Dakota, Utah, and Wyoming. As of Dec 31 2011, Co.'s total estimated proved reserves consisted of 357.7 million barrels of oil and 625.21 billion cubic feet of natural gas.

Recent Developments: For the year ended Dec 31 2012, net income decreased 8.4% to US$525.4 million from US$573.3 million in the prior year. Revenues were US$2.46 billion, up 6.4% from US$2.31 billion the year before. Direct operating expenses rose 4.9% to US$547.1 million from US$521.7 million in the comparable period the year before. Indirect operating expenses increased 21.9% to US$1.05 billion from US$863.6 million in the equivalent prior-year period.

Prospects: Our evaluation of Denbury Resources Inc. as of Apr. 7, 2013 is the result of our systematic analysis on three basic characteristics: earnings strength, relative valuation, and recent stock price movement. The company has generated a negative trend in earnings per share over the past 5 quarters. However, while recent estimates for the company have been mixed, DNR has posted better than expected results. Based on operating earnings yield, the company is undervalued when compared to all of the companies in our coverage universe. Share price changes over the past year indicates that DNR will perform poorly over the near term.

Financial Data
(US$ in Thousands)

	12/31/2012	12/31/2011	12/31/2010	12/31/2009	12/31/2008	12/31/2007	12/31/2006	12/31/2005
Earnings Per Share	1.35	1.43	0.72	(0.30)	1.54	1.00	0.82	0.69
Cash Flow Per Share	3.65	3.04	2.31	2.15	3.17	2.38	1.98	1.62
Tang Book Value Per Share	10.20	9.18	7.87	6.89	7.43	5.74	4.60	3.20
Income Statement								
Total Revenue	2,456,472	2,309,324	1,921,791	882,493	1,365,702	971,950	731,536	560,392
EBITDA	1,532,671	1,514,555	1,089,490	156,907	873,262	624,293	503,141	365,764
Depn & Amortn	522,233	426,150	434,307	238,323	221,792	200,049	150,768	100,059
Income Before Taxes	856,857	924,045	479,070	(128,846)	618,874	393,414	328,798	247,727
Income Taxes	331,497	350,712	193,543	(47,033)	235,832	140,267	127,117	81,570
Net Income	525,360	573,333	271,723	(75,156)	388,396	253,147	202,457	166,471
Average Shares	388,938	400,958	376,255	246,917	252,530	252,101	247,547	239,268
Balance Sheet								
Current Assets	1,542,754	684,113	864,318	255,762	415,199	240,359	183,269	299,183
Total Assets	11,139,342	10,184,424	9,065,063	4,269,978	3,589,674	2,771,077	2,139,837	1,505,069
Current Liabilities	616,421	661,267	579,345	393,790	386,067	264,633	200,398	154,064
Long-Term Obligations	3,104,462	2,669,729	2,416,208	1,301,068	852,767	680,330	514,173	379,461
Total Liabilities	6,024,453	5,377,926	4,684,356	2,297,741	1,749,606	1,366,699	1,033,778	771,407
Stockholders' Equity	5,114,889	4,806,498	4,380,707	1,972,237	1,840,068	1,404,378	1,106,059	733,662
Shares Outstanding	375,561	388,980	400,212	261,773	247,559	244,749	240,272	229,396
Statistical Record								
Return on Assets %	4.91	5.96	4.08	N.M.	12.18	10.31	11.11	13.33
Return on Equity %	10.56	12.48	8.55	N.M.	23.88	20.17	22.01	26.11
EBITDA Margin %	62.39	65.58	56.69	17.78	63.94	64.23	68.78	65.27
Net Margin %	21.39	24.83	14.14	N.M.	28.44	26.05	27.68	29.71
Asset Turnover	0.23	0.24	0.29	0.22	0.43	0.40	0.40	0.45
Current Ratio	2.50	1.03	1.49	0.65	1.08	0.91	0.91	1.94
Debt to Equity	0.61	0.56	0.55	0.66	0.46	0.48	0.46	0.52
Price Range	20.91-13.46	24.86-10.68	19.79-13.55	18.48-9.94	39.64-5.75	30.15-13.03	18.30-12.07	12.81-6.21
P/E Ratio	15.49-9.97	17.38-7.59	27.49-18.82	...	25.74-3.73	30.15-13.03	22.32-14.73	18.57-9.01

Address: 5320 Legacy Drive, Plano, TX 75024 Telephone: 972-673-2000 Fax: 972-673-2150	Web Site: www.denbury.com Officers: Wieland F. Wettstein - Chairman Phil Rykhoek - Chief Executive Officer	Auditors: PricewaterhouseCoopers LLP Investor Contact: 972-673-2028 Transfer Agents: American Stock Transfer and Trust Company, New York, NY

DEVON ENERGY CORP.

Exchange	Symbol	Price	52Wk Range	Yield	P/E
NYS	DVN	$56.42 (3/28/2013)	72.33-51.15	1.56	N/A

*7 Year Price Score 72.71 *NYSE Composite Index=100 *12 Month Price Score 89.04

Interim Earnings (Per Share)

Qtr.	Mar	Jun	Sep	Dec
2008	1.66	2.88	5.87	(15.25)
2009	(8.92)	0.70	1.12	1.51
2010	2.66	1.58	4.79	1.32
2011	0.97	6.50	2.50	1.32
2012	0.97	1.18	(1.80)	(0.89)

Interim Dividends (Per Share)

Amt	Decl	Ex	Rec	Pay
0.20Q	06/06/2012	09/12/2012	09/14/2012	09/28/2012
0.20Q	09/12/2012	12/12/2012	12/14/2012	12/31/2012
0.20Q	11/28/2012	03/13/2013	03/15/2013	03/29/2013
0.22Q	03/06/2013	06/12/2013	06/14/2013	06/28/2013

Indicated Div: $0.88

Valuation Analysis

		Institutional Holding	
Forecast EPS	$3.65	No of Institutions	
	(04/06/2013)	1137	
Market Cap	$22.9 Billion	Shares	
Book Value	$21.3 Billion	353,785,920	
Price/Book	1.08	% Held	
Price/Sales	2.41	77.88	

Business Summary: Production & Extraction (MIC: 9.1.1 SIC: 1311 NAIC: 211111)

Devon Energy is an independent energy company engaged primarily in the exploration, development and production of oil, natural gas and natural gas liquids. Co.'s operations are located in the U.S. and Canada. Co.'s U.S. properties are comprised of Barnett Shale, Cana-Woodford Shale, Permian Basin, Gulf Coast/East Texas, Rocky Mountains, Granite Wash, and Mississippian. Co.'s Canada properties are comprised of Canadian Oil Sands and Lloydminster. Co. also owns natural gas pipelines, plants and treatment facilities in its producing areas. As of Dec 31 2012, Co. had 3.01 billion barrels of oil equivalent of proved reserves.

Recent Developments: For the year ended Dec 31 2012, loss from continuing operations was US$185.0 million compared with income of US$2.13 billion a year earlier. Net loss amounted to US$206.0 million versus net income of US$4.70 billion in the prior year. Revenues were US$9.50 billion, down 17.0% from US$11.45 billion the year before. Direct operating expenses declined 6.9% to US$3.32 billion from US$3.57 billion in the comparable period the year before. Indirect operating expenses increased 22.6% to US$3.99 billion from US$3.26 billion in the equivalent prior-year period.

Prospects: Our evaluation of Devon Energy Corp. as of Apr. 7, 2013 is the result of our systematic analysis on three basic characteristics: earnings strength, relative valuation, and recent stock price movement. The company has enjoyed a very positive trend in earnings per share over the past 5 quarters. However, while recent estimates for the company have been mixed, DVN has posted better than expected results. Based on operating earnings yield, the company is about fairly valued when compared to all of the companies in our coverage universe. Share price changes over the past year indicates that DVN will perform very poorly over the near term.

Financial Data

(US$ in Thousands)	12/31/2012	12/31/2011	12/31/2010	12/31/2009	12/31/2008	12/31/2007	12/31/2006	12/31/2005
Earnings Per Share	(0.52)	11.25	10.31	(5.58)	(4.85)	8.00	6.34	6.26
Cash Flow Per Share	12.36	15.11	12.59	10.79	21.13	14.95	13.56	12.25
Tang Book Value Per Share	37.44	38.19	30.53	21.58	25.88	35.64	26.43	20.65
Dividends Per Share	0.800	0.670	0.640	0.640	0.640	0.560	0.450	0.300
Dividend Payout %	...	5.96	6.21	...	...	7.00	7.10	4.79
Income Statement								
Total Revenue	9,502,000	11,454,000	9,940,000	8,015,000	15,211,000	11,362,000	10,578,000	10,741,000
EBITDA	2,900,000	6,890,000	5,861,000	(2,069,000)	(195,000)	7,512,000	6,875,000	7,276,000
Depn & Amortn	2,811,000	2,248,000	1,930,000	2,108,000	3,509,000	2,858,000	2,442,000	2,191,000
Income Before Taxes	(317,000)	4,290,000	3,568,000	(4,526,000)	(4,033,000)	4,224,000	4,012,000	4,552,000
Income Taxes	(132,000)	2,156,000	1,235,000	(1,773,000)	(954,000)	1,078,000	1,189,000	1,622,000
Net Income	(206,000)	4,704,000	4,550,000	(2,479,000)	(2,148,000)	3,606,000	2,846,000	2,930,000
Average Shares	400,000	414,000	436,000	439,000	444,000	450,000	448,000	470,000
Balance Sheet								
Current Assets	8,971,000	9,305,000	5,555,000	2,992,000	2,684,000	3,914,000	3,212,000	4,206,000
Total Assets	43,326,000	41,117,000	32,927,000	29,686,000	31,908,000	41,456,000	35,063,000	30,273,000
Current Liabilities	6,003,000	6,738,000	4,583,000	3,802,000	3,135,000	3,657,000	4,645,000	2,934,000
Long-Term Obligations	8,455,000	5,969,000	3,819,000	5,847,000	5,661,000	6,924,000	5,568,000	5,957,000
Total Liabilities	22,048,000	19,687,000	13,674,000	14,116,000	14,848,000	19,450,000	17,621,000	15,411,000
Stockholders' Equity	21,278,000	21,430,000	19,253,000	15,570,000	17,060,000	22,006,000	17,442,000	14,862,000
Shares Outstanding	406,000	403,700	431,500	446,700	443,700	444,214	444,029	443,451
Statistical Record								
Return on Assets %	N.M.	12.71	14.53	N.M.	N.M.	9.43	8.71	9.77
Return on Equity %	N.M.	23.13	26.13	N.M.	N.M.	18.28	17.62	20.54
EBITDA Margin %	30.52	60.15	58.96	N.M.	N.M.	66.12	64.99	67.74
Net Margin %	N.M.	41.07	45.77	N.M.	N.M.	31.74	26.90	27.28
Asset Turnover	0.22	0.31	0.32	0.26	0.41	0.30	0.32	0.36
Current Ratio	1.49	1.38	1.21	0.79	0.86	1.07	0.69	1.43
Debt to Equity	0.40	0.28	0.20	0.38	0.33	0.31	0.32	0.40
Price Range	75.81-51.15	93.10-53.34	78.51-59.79	74.20-38.84	124.36-59.50	93.50-63.28	74.03-49.10	70.18-36.60
P/E Ratio	...	8.28-4.74	7.61-5.80	...	...	11.69-7.91	11.68-7.74	11.21-5.85
Average Yield %	1.31	0.88	0.95	1.06	0.67	0.72	0.71	0.57

Address: 333 West Sheridan, Oklahoma City, OK 73102-5015
Telephone: 405-235-3611

Web Site: www.devonenergy.com
Officers: J. Larry Nichols - Executive Chairman John Richels - President, Chief Executive Officer

Auditors: KPMG LLP
Investor Contact: 405-552-8172
Transfer Agents: Computershare Trust Company, N.A, Providence, RI

DEVRY INC.

Exchange	Symbol	Price	52Wk Range	Yield	P/E
NYS	DV	$31.75 (3/28/2013)	34.48-18.35	1.07	13.23

*7 Year Price Score 54.82   *NYSE Composite Index=100   *12 Month Price Score 104.93

Interim Earnings (Per Share)

Qtr.	Sep	Dec	Mar	Jun
2009-10	0.76	1.00	1.12	0.99
2010-11	1.03	1.25	1.32	1.08
2011-12	0.83	0.13	1.00	0.13
2012-13	0.49	0.78	...	...

Interim Dividends (Per Share)

Amt	Decl	Ex	Rec	Pay
0.12S	05/23/2011	06/16/2011	06/20/2011	07/12/2011
0.15S	11/03/2011	12/06/2011	12/08/2011	01/10/2012
0.15S	05/14/2012	06/19/2012	06/21/2012	07/12/2012
0.17S	11/08/2012	11/28/2012	11/30/2012	12/19/2012

Indicated Div: $0.34

Valuation Analysis

		Institutional Holding	
Forecast EPS	$2.65 (04/06/2013)	No of Institutions	292
Market Cap	$2.0 Billion	Shares	63,368,892
Book Value	$1.4 Billion	% Held	91.43
Price/Book	1.44		
Price/Sales	0.99		

TRADING VOLUME (thousand shares)

Business Summary: Educational Services (MIC: 2.2.2 SIC: 8299 NAIC: 611519)

DeVry is a provider of educational services. Co. provides its programs through several institutions including: DeVry University, which provides associate, bachelor's and master's degree programs in technology, healthcare technology, business and management; Ross University, which provides medical and veterinary medical education; Chamberlain College of Nursing, which provides associate, bachelor's and master's degree programs in nursing; and Becker Professional Education, which prepares candidates for professional certification examination, education programs and seminars in accounting and finance, as well as training for designations such as Association of Chartered Certified Accounts.

Recent Developments: For the quarter ended Dec 31 2012, net income increased 452.0% to US$51.2 million from US$9.3 million in the year-earlier quarter. Revenues were US$505.2 million, down 3.6% from US$524.0 million the year before. Operating income was US$65.9 million versus US$13.8 million in the prior-year quarter, an increase of 379.1%. Direct operating expenses rose 0.9% to US$243.4 million from US$241.2 million in the comparable period the year before. Indirect operating expenses decreased 27.2% to US$195.9 million from US$269.1 million in the equivalent prior-year period.

Prospects: Our evaluation of DeVRY Inc. as of Apr. 7, 2013 is the result of our systematic analysis on three basic characteristics: earnings strength, relative valuation, and recent stock price movement. The company has enjoyed a very positive trend in earnings per share over the past 5 quarters and while recent estimates for the company have been mixed, DV has posted better than expected results. Based on operating earnings yield, the company is undervalued when compared to all of the companies in our coverage universe. Share price changes over the past year indicates that DV will perform very poorly over the near term.

Financial Data

(US$ in Thousands)	6 Mos	3 Mos	06/30/2012	06/30/2011	06/30/2010	06/30/2009	06/30/2008	06/30/2007
Earnings Per Share	2.40	1.75	2.09	4.68	3.87	2.28	1.73	1.07
Cash Flow Per Share	3.71	3.93	4.12	5.84	5.49	3.49	2.78	1.77
Tang Book Value Per Share	8.47	7.93	8.05	9.77	6.62	2.96	5.40	4.13
Dividends Per Share	0.320	0.300	0.300	0.240	0.200	0.160	0.120	0.100
Dividend Payout %	13.33	17.14	14.35	5.13	5.17	7.02	6.94	9.35
Income Statement								
Total Revenue	987,980	482,736	2,089,781	2,182,371	1,915,181	1,461,453	1,091,833	933,473
EBITDA	158,933	68,722	285,081	552,208	463,352	274,701	197,143	138,266
Depn & Amortn	47,238	22,932	77,149	58,033	51,225	39,825	34,808	35,979
Income Before Taxes	110,236	44,860	206,138	494,432	412,622	237,352	172,276	104,940
Income Taxes	27,190	13,038	63,757	163,602	132,639	71,700	46,744	28,752
Net Income	82,275	31,989	141,565	330,403	279,909	165,613	125,532	76,188
Average Shares	64,536	65,109	67,705	70,620	72,267	72,516	72,406	71,400
Balance Sheet								
Current Assets	450,771	546,053	401,114	624,650	499,647	385,446	325,588	218,985
Total Assets	1,914,066	2,020,320	1,838,616	1,850,503	1,627,826	1,434,299	1,018,356	844,113
Current Liabilities	337,528	474,249	315,209	316,431	343,854	392,017	210,692	165,875
Long-Term Obligations	...	...	...	...	...	20,000	...	...
Total Liabilities	517,708	652,561	482,223	460,987	448,445	507,357	262,367	202,147
Stockholders' Equity	1,396,358	1,367,759	1,356,393	1,389,516	1,179,381	926,942	755,989	641,966
Shares Outstanding	63,287	63,782	64,722	68,635	71,030	71,233	71,377	71,131
Statistical Record								
Return on Assets %	8.21	5.76	7.65	19.00	18.28	13.50	13.44	8.88
Return on Equity %	11.45	8.39	10.28	25.72	26.58	19.68	17.91	12.63
EBITDA Margin %	16.09	14.24	13.64	25.30	24.19	18.80	18.06	14.81
Net Margin %	8.33	6.63	6.77	15.14	14.62	11.33	11.50	8.16
Asset Turnover	1.06	1.02	1.13	1.25	1.25	1.19	1.17	1.09
Current Ratio	1.34	1.15	1.27	1.97	1.45	0.98	1.55	1.32
Debt to Equity	...	...	...	...	...	0.02	...	...
Price Range	42.09-18.35	46.44-18.35	66.55-26.58	61.86-37.50	74.25-45.11	62.63-39.03	61.19-32.40	35.76-19.90
P/E Ratio	17.54-7.65	26.54-10.49	31.84-12.72	13.22-8.01	19.19-11.66	27.47-17.12	35.37-18.73	33.42-18.60
Average Yield %	1.13	0.95	0.77	0.48	0.35	0.31	0.25	0.37

Address: 3005 Highland Parkway, Downers Grove, IL 60515
Telephone: 630-515-7700
Fax: 630-571-0317

Web Site: www.devryinc.com
Officers: Daniel M. Hamburger - President, Chief Executive Officer David J. Pauldine - Executive Vice President

Auditors: PricewaterhouseCoopers LLP
Investor Contact: 630-353-3800
Transfer Agents: Computershares Investor Services, L.L.C., Chicago, IL

DIAMOND OFFSHORE DRILLING, INC.

Exchange	Symbol	Price	52Wk Range	Yield	P/E
NYS	DO	$69.56 (3/28/2013)	76.48-56.18	0.72	13.43

*7 Year Price Score 72.12 *NYSE Composite Index=100 ***12 Month Price Score 97.31**

Interim Earnings (Per Share)

Qtr.	Mar	Jun	Sep	Dec
2008	2.09	2.99	2.23	2.11
2009	2.51	2.79	2.62	1.98
2010	2.09	1.61	1.43	1.74
2011	1.80	1.92	1.85	1.35
2012	1.33	1.45	1.28	1.12

Interim Dividends (Per Share)

Amt	Decl	Ex	Rec	Pay
0.125Q	10/18/2012	10/31/2012	11/01/2012	12/03/2012
0.75Sp	10/18/2012	10/31/2012	11/01/2012	12/03/2012
0.75Sp	02/05/2013	02/14/2013	02/19/2013	03/01/2013
0.125Q	02/05/2013	02/14/2013	02/19/2013	03/01/2013

Indicated Div: $0.50

Valuation Analysis

		Institutional Holding	
Forecast EPS	$4.48 (04/06/2013)	No of Institutions	546
Market Cap	$9.7 Billion	Shares	143,148,176
Book Value	$4.6 Billion	% Held	98.01
Price/Book	2.11		
Price/Sales	3.24		

TRADING VOLUME (thousand shares)

Business Summary: Equipment & Services (MIC: 9.1.3 SIC: 1381 NAIC: 213111)

Diamond Offshore Drilling is engaged in providing contract drilling services. Through its fleet, Co. provides a range of services in both the floater market (ultra-deepwater, deepwater and mid-water) as well as the non-floater, or jack-up, market. Co. provides offshore drilling services to a customer base that includes independent oil and gas companies and government-owned oil companies. As of Dec 31 2012, Co. had a fleet of 44 offshore drilling rigs, consisting of 32 semisubmersibles, seven jack-ups and five drillships, four of which are under construction.

Recent Developments: For the year ended Dec 31 2012, net income decreased 25.1% to US$720.5 million from US$962.5 million in the prior year. Revenues were US$2.99 billion, down 10.1% from US$3.32 billion the year before. Operating income was US$962.4 million versus US$1.26 billion in the prior year, a decrease of 23.3%. Direct operating expenses declined 1.8% to US$1.59 billion from US$1.61 billion in the comparable period the year before. Indirect operating expenses decreased 3.2% to US$438.1 million from US$452.5 million in the equivalent prior-year period.

Prospects: Our evaluation of Diamond Offshore Drilling Inc. as of Apr. 7, 2013 is the result of our systematic analysis on three basic characteristics: earnings strength, relative valuation, and recent stock price movement. The company has enjoyed a very positive trend in earnings per share over the past 5 quarters. However, while recent estimates for the company have been mixed, DO has posted better than expected results. Based on operating earnings yield, the company is undervalued when compared to all of the companies in our coverage universe. Share price changes over the past year indicates that DO will perform in line with the market over the near term.

Financial Data
(US$ in Thousands)

	12/31/2012	12/31/2011	12/31/2010	12/31/2009	12/31/2008	12/31/2007	12/31/2006	12/31/2005
Earnings Per Share	5.18	6.92	6.87	9.89	9.43	6.12	5.12	1.91
Cash Flow Per Share	9.41	10.21	9.22	10.91	11.62	8.77	5.89	3.02
Tang Book Value Per Share	32.92	31.17	27.78	26.11	24.09	20.72	17.95	14.38
Dividends Per Share	3.500	3.500	5.250	8.000	6.125	5.750	2.000	0.375
Dividend Payout %	67.57	50.58	76.42	80.89	64.95	93.95	39.06	19.63
Income Statement								
Total Revenue	2,986,508	3,322,419	3,322,974	3,631,284	3,544,057	2,567,723	2,052,572	1,221,002
EBITDA	1,352,300	1,644,352	1,816,982	2,259,990	2,132,865	1,467,362	1,153,048	555,866
Depn & Amortn	392,913	398,612	393,177	346,446	286,900	235,200	200,500	183,700
Income Before Taxes	918,081	1,179,271	1,336,016	1,868,431	1,847,613	1,246,537	966,332	356,395
Income Taxes	197,604	216,729	380,559	492,212	536,593	399,996	259,485	96,058
Net Income	720,477	962,542	955,457	1,376,219	1,311,020	846,541	706,847	260,337
Average Shares	139,048	139,038	139,070	139,097	139,073	138,945	138,781	141,351
Balance Sheet								
Current Assets	2,132,943	1,992,683	1,863,498	1,723,370	1,466,733	1,265,190	1,481,547	1,281,878
Total Assets	7,235,286	6,964,157	6,726,984	6,264,261	4,938,762	4,341,465	4,132,839	3,606,922
Current Liabilities	485,546	427,291	626,288	413,475	509,087	453,011	333,509	268,986
Long-Term Obligations	1,496,066	1,495,823	1,495,593	1,495,375	503,280	503,071	964,310	977,654
Total Liabilities	2,658,892	2,631,094	2,865,272	2,633,619	1,590,125	1,464,398	1,813,331	1,753,595
Stockholders' Equity	4,576,394	4,333,063	3,861,712	3,630,642	3,348,637	2,877,067	2,319,508	1,853,327
Shares Outstanding	139,031	139,027	139,026	139,026	139,001	138,870	129,216	128,925
Statistical Record								
Return on Assets %	10.12	14.06	14.71	24.57	28.18	19.98	18.27	7.45
Return on Equity %	16.13	23.49	25.50	39.44	42.00	32.58	33.88	14.97
EBITDA Margin %	45.28	49.49	54.68	62.24	60.18	57.15	56.18	45.53
Net Margin %	24.12	28.97	28.75	37.90	36.99	32.97	34.44	21.32
Asset Turnover	0.42	0.49	0.51	0.65	0.76	0.61	0.53	0.35
Current Ratio	4.39	4.66	2.98	4.17	2.88	2.79	4.44	4.77
Debt to Equity	0.33	0.35	0.39	0.41	0.15	0.17	0.42	0.53
Price Range	72.43-55.61	80.14-52.90	106.34-56.94	107.01-54.29	145.68-55.45	148.51-73.65	96.15-63.90	71.31-38.25
P/E Ratio	13.98-10.74	11.58-7.64	15.48-8.29	10.82-5.49	15.45-5.88	24.27-12.03	18.78-12.48	37.34-20.03
Average Yield %	5.36	5.18	7.12	9.68	5.58	5.85	2.54	0.71

Address: 15415 Katy Freeway, Houston, TX 77094
Telephone: 281-492-5300
Fax: 281-492-5316

Web Site: www.diamondoffshore.com
Officers: James S. Tisch - Chairman Lawrence R. Dickerson - President, Chief Executive Officer

Auditors: Deloitte & Touche LLP
Investor Contact: 281-492-5393
Transfer Agents: BNY Mellon Shareholder Services, Pittsburgh, PA

235

DICK'S SPORTING GOODS, INC

Exchange	Symbol	Price	52Wk Range	Yield	P/E
NYS	DKS	$47.30 (3/28/2013)	53.93-44.58	1.06	20.48

*7 Year Price Score 144.33 ***NYSE Composite Index=100** ***12 Month Price Score 90.54**

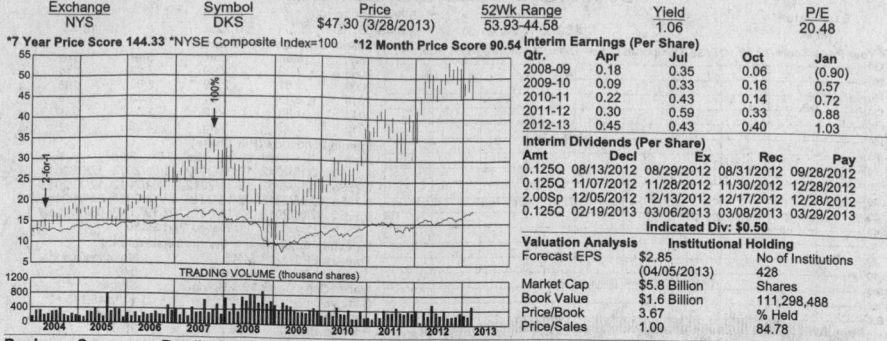

Interim Earnings (Per Share)

Qtr.	Apr	Jul	Oct	Jan
2008-09	0.18	0.35	0.06	(0.90)
2009-10	0.09	0.33	0.16	0.57
2010-11	0.22	0.43	0.14	0.72
2011-12	0.30	0.59	0.33	0.88
2012-13	0.45	0.43	0.40	1.03

Interim Dividends (Per Share)

Amt	Decl	Ex	Rec	Pay
0.125Q	08/13/2012	08/29/2012	08/31/2012	09/28/2012
0.125Q	11/07/2012	11/28/2012	11/30/2012	12/28/2012
2.00Sp	12/05/2012	12/13/2012	12/17/2012	12/28/2012
0.125Q	02/19/2013	03/06/2013	03/08/2013	03/29/2013

Indicated Div: $0.50

Valuation Analysis / **Institutional Holding**

Forecast EPS	$2.85 (04/05/2013)	No of Institutions	428
Market Cap	$5.8 Billion	Shares	111,298,488
Book Value	$1.6 Billion	% Held	84.78
Price/Book	3.67		
Price/Sales	1.00		

Business Summary: Retail - Specialty (MIC: 2.1.3 SIC: 5941 NAIC: 451110)

Dick's Sporting Goods is a sporting goods retailer providing a range of brand name sporting goods equipment, apparel and footwear. Co. also owns and operates Golf Galaxy, LLC (Golf Galaxy). As of Jan 28 2012, Co. operated 480 Dick's stores in 43 states and 81 Golf Galaxy stores in 30 states, the majority of which are located across the eastern half of U.S. Co.'s merchandise categories are comprised of Apparel, which includes athletic apparel, outerwear and sportswear; Footwear, which consists of athletic shoes for running, walking, tennis, fitness and cross training, basketball and hiking; and Hardlines, which includes equipment and accessories for team sports, golf and fitness and cycling.

Recent Developments: For the year ended Feb 2 2013, net income increased 10.2% to US$290.7 million from US$263.9 million in the prior year. Revenues were US$5.84 billion, up 12.0% from US$5.21 billion the year before. Operating income was US$523.7 million versus US$432.0 million in the prior year, an increase of 21.2%. Direct operating expenses rose 10.6% to US$4.00 billion from US$3.62 billion in the comparable period the year before. Indirect operating expenses increased 13.0% to US$1.31 billion from US$1.16 billion in the equivalent prior-year period.

Prospects: Our evaluation of Dick's Sporting Goods Inc. as of Apr. 7, 2013 is the result of our systematic analysis on three basic characteristics: earnings strength, relative valuation, and recent stock price movement. The company has managed to produce a neutral trend in earnings per share over the past 5 quarters. However, while recent estimates for the company have been lowered by analysts, DKS has posted results that fell short of analysts expectations. Based on operating earnings yield, the company is about fairly valued when compared to all of the companies in our coverage universe. Share price changes over the past year indicates that DKS will perform well over the near term.

Financial Data

(US$ in Thousands)	02/02/2013	01/28/2012	01/29/2011	01/30/2010	01/31/2009	02/02/2008	02/03/2007	01/28/2006
Earnings Per Share	2.31	2.10	1.50	1.15	(0.31)	1.33	1.01	0.68
Cash Flow Per Share	3.55	3.42	3.36	3.56	1.44	2.41	1.88	1.71
Tang Book Value Per Share	10.47	11.39	9.37	7.27	5.77	4.54	4.37	2.57
Dividends Per Share	2.500	0.500	...	...	...	...	...	...
Dividend Payout %	108.23	23.81	...	...	...	...	...	...
Income Statement								
Total Revenue	5,836,119	5,211,802	4,871,492	4,412,835	4,130,128	3,888,422	3,114,162	2,624,987
EBITDA	621,159	558,994	418,627	325,971	125,336	344,717	252,639	184,454
Depn & Amortn	125,300	113,100	107,100	100,400	92,600	75,900	54,929	49,861
Income Before Taxes	489,825	432,026	297,511	223,176	21,773	257,527	187,685	121,634
Income Taxes	199,116	168,120	115,434	87,817	56,867	102,491	75,074	48,654
Net Income	290,709	263,906	182,077	135,359	(35,094)	155,036	112,611	72,980
Average Shares	125,995	125,768	121,724	117,955	111,662	116,504	110,790	107,958
Balance Sheet								
Current Assets	1,595,889	1,868,393	1,564,330	1,222,361	1,049,864	1,069,694	869,779	614,017
Total Assets	2,887,807	2,996,452	2,597,536	2,245,333	1,966,524	2,035,635	1,524,265	1,187,789
Current Liabilities	1,000,768	940,146	848,543	795,675	615,475	761,948	564,983	471,269
Long-Term Obligations	7,762	151,596	139,846	141,265	181,258	181,185	180,865	181,020
Total Liabilities	1,300,483	1,363,707	1,233,955	1,162,106	1,070,942	1,147,115	903,715	772,996
Stockholders' Equity	1,587,324	1,632,745	1,363,581	1,083,227	895,582	888,520	620,550	414,793
Shares Outstanding	123,005	121,333	118,729	114,808	112,338	111,145	106,170	100,552
Statistical Record								
Return on Assets %	9.72	9.46	7.54	6.45	N.M.	8.73	8.17	6.44
Return on Equity %	17.76	17.66	14.92	13.72	N.M.	20.60	21.40	20.09
EBITDA Margin %	10.64	10.73	8.59	7.39	3.03	8.87	8.11	7.03
Net Margin %	4.98	5.06	3.74	3.07	N.M.	3.99	3.62	2.78
Asset Turnover	1.95	1.87	2.02	2.10	2.07	2.19	2.26	2.32
Current Ratio	1.59	1.99	1.84	1.54	1.71	1.40	1.54	1.30
Debt to Equity	N.M.	0.09	0.10	0.13	0.20	0.20	0.29	0.44
Price Range	53.93-40.80	42.58-29.86	37.81-22.46	26.05-10.77	33.40-9.56	35.84-24.66	27.90-17.62	20.07-13.50
P/E Ratio	23.35-17.66	20.28-14.22	25.21-14.97	22.65-9.37	...	26.95-18.55	27.62-17.45	29.51-19.85
Average Yield %	5.12	1.33	...	...	...	...	...	...

Address: 345 Court Street, Coraopolis, PA 15108
Telephone: 724-273-3400

Web Site: www.dickssportinggoods.com
Officers: Edward W. Stack - Chairman, Chief Executive Officer William J. Colombo - Vice-Chairman, Chief Marketing Officer

Auditors: Deloitte & Touche LLP
Transfer Agents: American Stock Transfer & Trust Company, New York, NY

236

DIEBOLD, INC.

Exchange	Symbol	Price	52Wk Range	Yield	P/E	Div Achiever
NYS	DBD	$30.32 (3/28/2013)	40.68-27.61	3.79	24.65	59 Years

*7 Year Price Score 85.11 *NYSE Composite Index=100 *12 Month Price Score 81.07

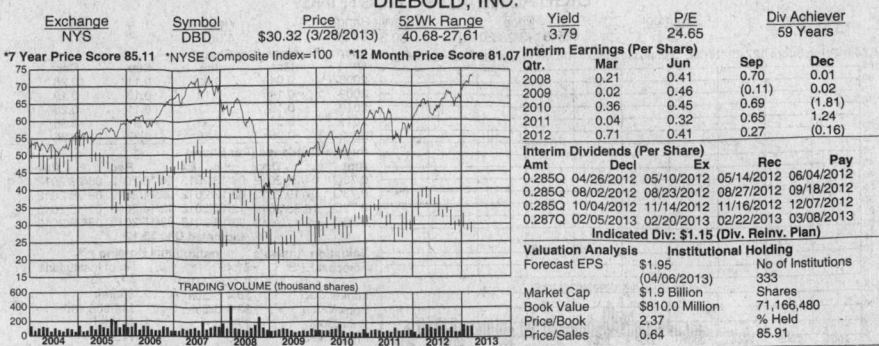

Interim Earnings (Per Share)

Qtr.	Mar	Jun	Sep	Dec
2008	0.21	0.41	0.70	0.01
2009	0.02	0.46	(0.11)	0.02
2010	0.36	0.45	0.69	(1.81)
2011	0.04	0.32	0.65	1.24
2012	0.71	0.41	0.27	(0.16)

Interim Dividends (Per Share)

Amt	Decl	Ex	Rec	Pay
0.285Q	04/26/2012	05/10/2012	05/14/2012	06/04/2012
0.285Q	08/02/2012	08/23/2012	08/27/2012	09/18/2012
0.285Q	10/04/2012	11/14/2012	11/16/2012	12/07/2012
0.287Q	02/05/2013	02/20/2013	02/22/2013	03/08/2013

Indicated Div: $1.15 (Div. Reinv. Plan)

Valuation Analysis / **Institutional Holding**

Forecast EPS	$1.95 (04/06/2013)	No of Institutions	333
Market Cap	$1.9 Billion	Shares	71,166,480
Book Value	$810.0 Million	% Held	85.91
Price/Book	2.37		
Price/Sales	0.64		

Business Summary: Computer Hardware & Equipment (MIC: 6.2.1 SIC: 3578 NAIC: 333313)

Diebold is engaged in providing integrated software-led services and self-service delivery and security systems to primarily the financial, commercial, government and retail markets. Co. has two lines of business: Self-Service Solutions and Security Solutions. The Self-Service Solutions supplies an integrated line of self-service technologies and services, including comprehensive automated teller machine (ATM) outsourcing, ATM security, deposit and payment terminals and software in many countries around the world. The Security Solutions include physical and advanced electronic security systems.

Recent Developments: For the year ended Dec 31 2012, income from continuing operations decreased 42.3% to US$87.5 million from US$151.6 million a year earlier. Net income decreased 44.5% to US$84.4 million from US$152.1 million in the prior year. Revenues were US$2.99 billion, up 5.5% from US$2.84 billion the year before. Operating income was US$124.7 million versus US$155.6 million in the prior year, a decrease of 19.8%. Direct operating expenses rose 7.4% to US$2.26 billion from US$2.10 billion in the comparable period the year before. Indirect operating expenses increased 5.4% to US$611.4 million from US$580.3 million in the equivalent prior-year period.

Prospects: Our evaluation of Diebold Inc. as of Apr. 7, 2013 is the result of our systematic analysis on three basic characteristics: earnings strength, relative valuation, and recent stock price movement. The company has generated a negative trend in earnings per share over the past 5 quarters. However, while recent estimates for the company have been lowered by analysts, DBD has posted results that fell short of analysts expectations. Based on operating earnings yield, the company is about fairly valued when compared to all of the companies in our coverage universe. Share price changes over the past year indicates that DBD will perform very poorly over the near term.

Financial Data

(US$ in Thousands)	12/31/2012	12/31/2011	12/31/2010	12/31/2009	12/31/2008	12/31/2007	12/31/2006	12/31/2005
Earnings Per Share	1.23	2.24	(0.31)	0.39	1.33	0.59	1.29	1.36
Cash Flow Per Share	2.14	3.35	4.15	4.52	4.30	2.28	3.76	1.66
Tang Book Value Per Share	8.49	9.18	10.53	8.98	8.14	9.84	9.62	11.11
Dividends Per Share	1.140	1.120	1.080	1.040	1.000	0.940	0.860	0.820
Dividend Payout %	92.68	50.00	...	266.67	75.19	159.32	66.67	60.29
Income Statement								
Total Revenue	2,991,693	2,835,848	2,823,793	2,718,292	3,170,080	2,964,837	2,906,232	2,587,049
EBITDA	199,203	249,397	86,915	209,344	247,917	171,489	207,455	211,468
Depn & Amortn	51,447	50,549	51,425	50,085	55,295	45,549	40,385	49,877
Income Before Taxes	117,426	164,392	(2,397)	123,807	147,375	83,703	131,046	145,080
Income Taxes	29,905	12,815	14,561	44,477	37,425	35,797	37,902	55,347
Net Income	78,454	144,815	(20,252)	26,026	88,583	39,541	86,547	96,746
Average Shares	63,914	64,792	65,907	66,867	66,492	66,673	66,885	70,966
Balance Sheet								
Current Assets	1,814,857	1,732,355	1,714,036	1,588,085	1,614,118	1,630,532	1,595,681	1,427,880
Total Assets	2,592,987	2,517,443	2,519,790	2,554,865	2,537,936	2,631,126	2,514,279	2,353,193
Current Liabilities	838,855	824,217	809,765	743,091	735,397	750,638	598,736	580,031
Long-Term Obligations	617,534	606,154	550,368	540,000	594,588	609,264	665,481	454,722
Total Liabilities	1,783,024	1,690,457	1,558,635	1,508,486	1,591,335	1,516,292	1,422,878	1,200,344
Stockholders' Equity	809,963	826,986	961,155	1,046,379	946,601	1,114,834	1,091,401	1,152,849
Shares Outstanding	63,240	62,513	65,717	66,327	66,114	65,965	65,595	68,721
Statistical Record								
Return on Assets %	3.06	5.75	N.M.	1.02	3.42	1.54	3.56	4.31
Return on Equity %	9.56	16.20	N.M.	2.61	8.57	3.58	7.71	8.02
EBITDA Margin %	6.66	8.79	3.08	7.70	7.82	5.78	7.14	8.17
Net Margin %	2.62	5.11	N.M.	0.96	2.79	1.33	2.98	3.74
Asset Turnover	1.17	1.13	1.11	1.07	1.22	1.15	1.19	1.15
Current Ratio	2.16	2.10	2.12	2.14	2.19	2.17	2.67	2.46
Debt to Equity	0.76	0.73	0.57	0.52	0.63	0.55	0.61	0.39
Price Range	40.68-28.26	36.94-24.76	34.87-25.94	32.93-19.05	40.30-23.37	54.25-28.89	46.93-37.01	57.58-33.37
P/E Ratio	33.07-22.98	16.49-11.05	...	84.44-48.85	30.30-17.57	91.95-48.97	36.38-28.69	42.34-24.54
Average Yield %	3.31	3.58	3.58	3.85	3.02	2.08	2.05	1.74

Address: 5995 Mayfair Road, P.O. Box 3077, North Canton, OH 44720-8077 **Telephone:** 330-490-4000	**Web Site:** www.diebold.com **Officers:** Henry D.G. Wallace - Executive Chairman, Acting Chief Executive Officer Bradley C. Richardson - Executive Vice President, Chief Financial Officer	**Auditors:** KPMG LLP **Transfer Agents:** Wells Fargo Shareowner Services

DIGITAL REALTY TRUST, INC.

Exchange	Symbol	Price	52Wk Range	Yield	P/E
NYS	DLR	$66.91 (3/28/2013)	80.31-59.28	4.66	45.21

*7 Year Price Score 127.29 *NYSE Composite Index=100   *12 Month Price Score 87.79

Interim Earnings (Per Share)

Qtr.	Mar	Jun	Sep	Dec
2008	0.04	0.05	0.11	0.20
2009	0.14	0.13	0.16	0.19
2010	0.18	0.11	0.11	0.28
2011	0.33	0.33	0.31	0.35
2012	0.36	0.38	0.37	0.36

Interim Dividends (Per Share)

Amt	Decl	Ex	Rec	Pay
0.73Q	04/23/2012	06/13/2012	06/15/2012	06/29/2012
0.73Q	07/19/2012	09/12/2012	09/14/2012	09/28/2012
0.73Q	10/30/2012	12/12/2012	12/14/2012	01/15/2013
0.78Q	02/12/2013	03/13/2013	03/15/2013	03/29/2013

Indicated Div: $3.12

Valuation Analysis

		Institutional Holding	
Forecast EPS	$1.46	No of Institutions	
	(04/06/2013)	497	
Market Cap	$8.4 Billion	Shares	
Book Value	$3.5 Billion	144,606,480	
Price/Book	2.41	% Held	
Price/Sales	6.55	110.16	

Business Summary: REITs (MIC: 5.3.1 SIC: 6798 NAIC: 525930)

Digital Realty Trust is a real estate investment trust. Through its ownership of about 95.6% of Digital Realty Trust, L.P., Co. owns, acquires, develops, and redevelops technology-related real estate. Co. provides Turn-Key Datacenter® and Powered Base Building® datacenter applications to its tenants across a variety of industry ranging from information technology and Internet enterprises, to manufacturing and financial services. As of Dec 31 2011, excluding three properties held as investments in unconsolidated joint ventures, Co. owned 101 properties, of which 85 are located throughout North America, 15 in Europe and one in Asia, totaling approximately 18.3 million rentable square feet.

Recent Developments: For the year ended Dec 31 2012, net income increased 33.3% to US$216.0 million from US$162.1 million in the prior year. Revenues were US$1.28 billion, up 20.4% from US$1.06 billion the year before. Revenues from property income rose 19.7% to US$1.27 billion from US$1.06 billion in the corresponding earlier year.

Prospects: Our evaluation of Digital Realty Trust Inc. as of Apr. 7, 2013 is the result of our systematic analysis on three basic characteristics: earnings strength, relative valuation, and recent stock price movement. The company has managed to produce a neutral trend in earnings per share over the past 5 quarters. However, while recent estimates for the company have been lowered by analysts, DLR has posted results that fell short of analysts expectations. Based on operating earnings yield, the company is overvalued when compared to all of the companies in our coverage universe. Share price changes over the past year indicates that DLR will perform poorly over the near term.

Financial Data

(US$ in Thousands)	12/31/2012	12/31/2011	12/31/2010	12/31/2009	12/31/2008	12/31/2007	12/31/2006	12/31/2005
Earnings Per Share	1.48	1.32	0.68	0.62	0.41	0.34	0.47	0.25
Cash Flow Per Share	4.68	4.07	4.26	3.74	3.16	1.75	2.85	3.45
Tang Book Value Per Share	23.14	18.42	16.02	11.67	11.33	10.93	10.14	8.28
Dividends Per Share	2.920	2.720	2.020	1.470	1.260	1.169	1.081	0.996
Dividend Payout %	197.30	206.06	297.06	237.10	307.32	343.75	230.05	398.50
Income Statement								
Total Revenue	1,279,067	1,062,710	865,401	637,142	527,445	395,247	281,903	208,809
EBITDA	907,154	772,848	655,275	474,622	361,838	282,349	217,152	127,967
Depn & Amortn	393,995	327,400	281,455	211,316	177,879	133,792	89,126	63,467
Income Before Taxes	357,943	299,358	237,052	175,617	124,975	86,440	77,377	25,378
Net Income	210,334	156,265	102,294	87,662	67,661	40,592	31,392	16,101
Average Shares	116,006	99,169	86,013	77,020	70,435	62,572	37,442	24,221
Balance Sheet								
Current Assets	268,617	186,376	142,118	156,216	157,912	116,094	81,698	40,640
Total Assets	8,819,214	6,098,566	5,329,483	3,745,059	3,279,669	2,809,464	2,186,219	1,529,170
Current Liabilities	739,861	390,588	288,841	188,233	197,268	198,488	108,084	52,508
Long-Term Obligations	4,278,565	2,940,210	2,806,954	1,784,444	1,395,673	1,367,738	1,122,638	749,067
Total Liabilities	5,350,909	3,575,649	3,366,965	2,186,064	1,786,842	1,765,548	1,476,447	1,142,673
Stockholders' Equity	3,468,305	2,522,917	1,962,518	1,558,995	1,492,827	1,043,916	709,772	386,497
Shares Outstanding	125,140	106,039	91,159	76,812	73,306	65,406	54,257	27,363
Statistical Record								
Return on Assets %	2.81	2.73	2.25	2.50	2.22	1.63	1.69	1.27
Return on Equity %	7.00	6.97	5.81	5.74	5.32	4.63	5.73	5.75
EBITDA Margin %	70.92	72.72	75.72	74.49	68.60	71.44	77.03	61.28
Net Margin %	16.44	14.70	11.82	13.76	12.83	10.27	11.14	7.71
Asset Turnover	0.17	0.19	0.19	0.18	0.17	0.16	0.15	0.16
Current Ratio	0.36	0.48	0.49	0.83	0.80	0.58	0.76	0.77
Debt to Equity	1.23	1.17	1.43	1.14	0.93	1.31	1.58	1.94
Price Range	80.31-59.28	67.14-50.63	63.94-46.69	50.28-26.33	49.28-21.29	43.99-33.15	37.22-22.75	23.71-13.20
P/E Ratio	54.26-40.05	50.86-38.36	94.03-68.66	81.10-42.47	120.20-51.93	129.38-97.50	79.19-48.40	94.84-52.80
Average Yield %	4.13	4.61	3.58	3.77	3.34	3.03	3.77	5.81

Address: Four Embarcadero Center, Suite 3200, San Francisco, CA 94111 Telephone: 415-738-6500 Fax: 415-738-6501	Web Site: www.digitalrealty.com Officers: Dennis E. Singleton - Interim Chairman Michael F. Foust - Chief Executive Officer	Auditors: KPMG LLP Investor Contact: 415-738-6500 Transfer Agents: American Stock Transfer & Trust Company, LLC, Brooklyn, NY

DILLARD'S INC.

Exchange	Symbol	Price	52Wk Range	Yield	P/E
NYS	DDS	$78.55 (3/28/2013)	89.05-61.02	0.25	11.43

*7 Year Price Score 197.46 *NYSE Composite Index=100 *12 Month Price Score 100.03

Interim Earnings (Per Share)

Qtr.	Apr	Jul	Oct	Jan
2008-09	0.04	(0.51)	(0.76)	(2.02)
2009-10	0.10	(0.36)	0.11	1.08
2010-11	0.68	0.10	0.22	1.65
2011-12	1.31	0.32	4.31	2.72
2012-13	1.89	0.63	1.01	3.32

Interim Dividends (Per Share)

Amt	Decl	Ex	Rec	Pay
0.05Q	08/15/2012	09/26/2012	09/28/2012	11/01/2012
0.05Q	11/26/2012	12/05/2012	12/07/2012	12/21/2012
5.00Sp	11/26/2012	12/05/2012	12/07/2012	12/21/2012
0.05Q	02/28/2013	03/26/2013	03/28/2013	05/06/2013

Indicated Div: $0.20

Valuation Analysis | **Institutional Holding**

Forecast EPS	$7.00
	(04/05/2013)
Market Cap	$3.8 Billion
Book Value	$2.0 Billion
Price/Book	1.90
Price/Sales	0.56

No of Institutions: 287
Shares: 44,326,004
% Held: 76.11

TRADING VOLUME (thousand shares)

Business Summary: Retail - General Merchandise/Department Stores (MIC: 2.1.1 SIC: 5311 NAIC: 452111)

Dillard's is a fashion apparel, cosmetics and home furnishing retailer. Co. operates in two reportable segments: the operation of retail department stores and a general contracting construction company. As of Jan 28 2012, Co. operated 304 Dillard's stores, including 16 clearance centers, and an Internet store providing a range of merchandise including fashion apparel for women, men and children, accessories, cosmetics, home furnishings and other consumer goods. Co. also operates a general contracting construction company, CDI Contractors, LLC and CDI Contractors, Inc., whose business includes constructing and remodeling stores for Co.

Recent Developments: For the year ended Feb 2 2013, net income decreased 27.6% to US$336.0 million from US$463.9 million in the prior year. Revenues were US$6.75 billion, up 5.4% from US$6.41 billion the year before. Direct operating expenses rose 4.9% to US$4.25 billion from US$4.05 billion in the comparable period the year before. Indirect operating expenses increased 3.2% to US$2.02 billion from US$1.96 billion in the equivalent prior-year period.

Prospects: Our evaluation of Dillard's Inc. as of Apr. 7, 2013 is the result of our systematic analysis on three basic characteristics: earnings strength, relative valuation, and recent stock price movement. The company has managed to produce a neutral trend in earnings per share over the past 5 quarters. However, while recent estimates for the company have been mixed, DDS has posted results that fell short of analysts expectations. Based on operating earnings yield, the company is undervalued when compared to all of the companies in our coverage universe. Share price changes over the past year indicates that DDS will perform very well over the near term.

Financial Data

(US$ in Thousands)	02/02/2013	01/28/2012	01/29/2011	01/30/2010	01/31/2009	02/02/2008	02/03/2007	01/28/2006
Earnings Per Share	6.87	8.52	2.67	0.93	(3.25)	0.68	3.05	1.49
Cash Flow Per Share	10.69	9.39	7.66	7.53	4.73	3.25	4.46	4.54
Tang Book Value Per Share	41.24	41.50	34.79	31.21	30.65	33.02	31.85	29.08
Dividends Per Share	5.200	0.190	0.160	0.160	0.160	0.160	0.160	0.160
Dividend Payout %	75.69	2.23	5.99	17.20	...	23.53	5.25	10.74
Income Statement								
Total Revenue	6,751,595	6,399,765	6,253,535	6,226,628	6,988,440	7,370,806	7,810,067	7,707,993
EBITDA	809,346	726,728	604,508	421,528	(7,184)	451,074	642,484	543,355
Depn & Amortn	260,000	258,000	262,000	263,000	284,000	299,000	301,000	302,000
Income Before Taxes	479,750	396,669	268,716	84,525	(380,005)	60,518	253,842	135,785
Income Taxes	145,060	(62,518)	84,450	12,690	(140,520)	13,010	20,580	14,300
Net Income	335,962	463,909	179,620	68,531	(241,065)	53,761	245,646	121,485
Average Shares	48,911	54,448	67,174	73,783	74,278	79,103	80,475	81,661
Balance Sheet								
Current Assets	1,491,980	1,591,729	1,701,926	1,749,529	1,686,755	1,945,188	2,047,846	2,150,479
Total Assets	4,048,744	4,306,137	4,374,166	4,606,327	4,745,844	5,338,129	5,408,015	5,516,919
Current Liabilities	767,116	870,364	831,212	769,022	913,665	1,184,170	977,115	1,147,392
Long-Term Obligations	822,309	823,938	908,629	970,009	981,805	985,904	1,184,939	1,290,752
Total Liabilities	2,078,569	2,254,118	2,287,446	2,302,224	2,494,729	2,824,018	2,821,062	3,176,378
Stockholders' Equity	1,970,175	2,052,019	2,086,720	2,304,103	2,251,115	2,514,111	2,586,953	2,340,541
Shares Outstanding	47,769	49,441	59,977	73,831	73,454	75,166	80,141	79,294
Statistical Record								
Return on Assets %	7.91	10.72	4.01	1.47	N.M.	1.00	4.42	2.17
Return on Equity %	16.44	22.48	8.20	3.02	N.M.	2.11	9.81	5.22
EBITDA Margin %	11.99	11.36	9.67	6.77	N.M.	6.12	8.23	7.05
Net Margin %	4.98	7.25	2.87	1.10	N.M.	0.73	3.15	1.58
Asset Turnover	1.59	1.48	1.40	1.34	1.39	1.38	1.41	1.38
Current Ratio	1.94	1.83	2.05	2.28	1.85	1.64	2.10	1.87
Debt to Equity	0.42	0.40	0.44	0.42	0.44	0.39	0.46	0.55
Price Range	89.05-43.89	60.28-38.56	41.96-15.61	20.02-3.00	22.96-2.78	39.90-14.93	36.09-24.23	28.14-19.40
P/E Ratio	12.96-6.39	7.08-4.53	15.72-5.85	21.53-3.23	...	58.68-21.96	11.83-7.94	18.89-13.02
Average Yield %	7.26	0.40	0.60	1.45	1.37	0.58	0.53	0.68

Address: 1600 Cantrell Road, Little Rock, AR 72201	**Web Site:** www.dillards.com	**Auditors:** KPMG LLP
Telephone: 501-376-5200	**Officers:** William T. Dillard - Chairman, Chief Executive Officer Alex Dillard - President	**Investor Contact:** 501-376-5965
Fax: 501-376-5917		**Transfer Agents:** Registrar and Transfer Company, Cranford, NJ

DISCOVER FINANCIAL SERVICES

Exchange	Symbol	Price	52Wk Range	Yield	P/E
NYS	DFS	$44.84 (3/28/2013)	45.02-30.72	1.25	10.05

*7 Year Price Score N/A *NYSE Composite Index=100 *12 Month Price Score 99.62

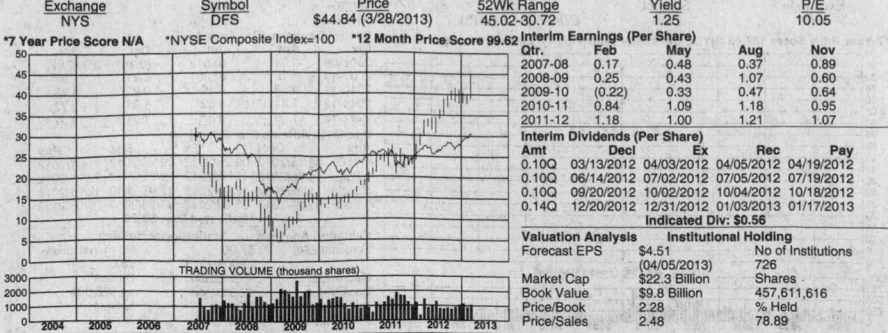

Interim Earnings (Per Share)

Qtr.	Feb	May	Aug	Nov
2007-08	0.17	0.48	0.37	0.89
2008-09	0.25	0.43	1.07	0.60
2009-10	(0.22)	0.33	0.47	0.64
2010-11	0.84	1.09	1.18	0.95
2011-12	1.18	1.00	1.21	1.07

Interim Dividends (Per Share)

Amt	Decl	Ex	Rec	Pay
0.10Q	03/13/2012	04/03/2012	04/05/2012	04/19/2012
0.10Q	06/14/2012	07/02/2012	07/05/2012	07/19/2012
0.10Q	09/20/2012	10/02/2012	10/04/2012	10/18/2012
0.14Q	12/20/2012	12/31/2012	01/03/2013	01/17/2013

Indicated Div: $0.56

Valuation Analysis

Forecast EPS	$4.51 (04/05/2013)
Market Cap	$22.3 Billion
Book Value	$9.8 Billion
Price/Book	2.28
Price/Sales	2.48

Institutional Holding

No of Institutions	726
Shares	457,611,616
% Held	78.89

Business Summary: Credit & Lending (MIC: 5.4.1 SIC: 6141 NAIC: 522210)

Discover Financial Services is a bank holding company. Co. manages its business activities in two segments: Direct Banking, which includes Discover card-branded credit cards issued to individuals and small businesses on the Discover network and other consumer banking products and services, including private student loans, personal loans, home loans, prepaid cards and other consumer lending and deposit products; and Payment Services, which includes PULSE, Diners Club and its network partners business, which includes credit, debit and prepaid cards issued on the Discover Networks by third parties. At Nov 30 2012, Co. had total assets of $75.28 billion and total deposits of $42.16 billion.

Recent Developments: For the year ended Nov 30 2012, net income increased 5.3% to US$2.35 billion from US$2.23 billion in the prior year. Net interest income increased 10.5% to US$5.37 billion from US$4.86 billion in the prior year. Provision for loan losses was US$848.0 million versus US$1.01 billion in the prior year, a decrease of 16.3%. Non-interest income rose 3.4% to US$2.28 billion from US$2.21 billion, while non-interest expense advanced 20.1% to US$3.05 billion.

Prospects: Our evaluation of Discover Financial Services as of Apr. 7, 2013 is the result of our systematic analysis on three basic characteristics: earnings strength, relative valuation, and recent stock price movement. The company has managed to produce a neutral trend in earnings per share over the past 5 quarters. Because the company lacks sufficient analyst estimate data, we place greater weight on the historical EPS trend as the measure of earnings strength. Based on operating earnings yield, the company is undervalued when compared to all of the companies in our coverage universe. Share price changes over the past year indicates that DFS will perform in line with the market over the near term.

Financial Data
(US$ in Thousands)

	11/30/2012	11/30/2011	11/30/2010	11/30/2009	11/30/2008	11/30/2007	11/30/2006	11/30/2005
Earnings Per Share	4.46	4.06	1.22	2.39	1.92	1.23	...	...
Cash Flow Per Share	5.84	6.66	7.12	7.13	9.37	4.27	...	...
Tang Book Value Per Share	17.56	14.75	11.04	12.57	11.37	10.98	5,039,867.00	4,278,405.00
Dividends Per Share	0.400	0.200	0.080	0.120	0.240	0.060	...	...
Dividend Payout %	8.97	4.93	6.56	5.02	12.50	4.88	...	...
Income Statement								
Total Revenue	8,984,000	8,550,313	8,241,217	7,913,039	6,929,416	6,434,288	5,997,465	5,111,848
Income Before Taxes	3,753,000	3,511,244	1,268,859	2,120,898	1,657,605	945,196	1,582,305	924,256
Income Taxes	1,408,000	1,284,536	504,071	844,713	594,692	356,566	505,689	346,341
Net Income	2,345,000	2,226,708	764,788	1,276,185	927,750	588,630	1,076,616	577,915
Average Shares	520,000	542,626	548,760	511,803	483,470	478,878	...	...
Balance Sheet								
Total Assets	75,283,000	68,783,937	60,784,968	46,020,987	39,892,382	37,376,105	29,067,242	26,943,923
Total Liabilities	65,505,000	60,541,726	54,328,122	37,585,440	33,976,559	31,776,683	23,292,470	22,343,474
Stockholders' Equity	9,778,000	8,242,211	6,456,846	8,435,547	5,915,823	5,599,422	5,774,772	4,600,449
Shares Outstanding	497,871	528,830	544,681	542,922	479,986	477,688	1,000.00	1,000.00
Statistical Record								
Return on Assets %	3.25	3.44	1.43	2.97	2.39	1.77	...	...
Return on Equity %	25.96	30.30	10.27	17.78	16.07	10.35	...	...
Net Margin %	26.10	26.04	9.28	16.13	13.39	9.15	17.95	11.31
Asset Turnover	0.12	0.13	0.15	0.18	0.18	0.19	...	...
Price Range	41.61-23.07	27.52-18.02	19.09-12.43	17.08-4.89	19.25-6.67	31.70-16.25	...	...
P/E Ratio	9.33-5.17	6.78-4.44	15.65-10.19	7.15-2.05	10.03-3.47	25.77-13.21	...	...
Average Yield %	1.19	0.87	0.53	1.14	1.61	0.27	...	...

Address: 2500 Lake Cook Road, Riverwoods, IL 60015
Telephone: 224-405-0900

Web Site: www.discover.com
Officers: David W. Nelms - Chairman, Chief Executive Officer Roger C. Hochschild - President, Chief Operating Officer

Auditors: Deloitte & Touche LLP
Investor Contact: 224-405-4555
Transfer Agents: Computershare, Jersey City, NJ

DISNEY (WALT) CO. (THE)

Exchange	Symbol	Price	52Wk Range	Yield	P/E
NYS	DIS	$56.80 (3/28/2013)	57.75-40.99	1.32	18.32

*7 Year Price Score 126.99 *NYSE Composite Index=100 *12 Month Price Score 103.12

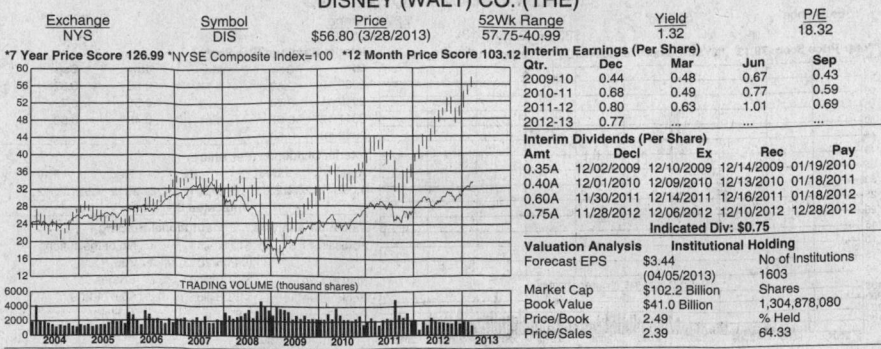

Interim Earnings (Per Share)

Qtr.	Dec	Mar	Jun	Sep
2009-10	0.44	0.48	0.67	0.43
2010-11	0.68	0.49	0.77	0.59
2011-12	0.80	0.63	1.01	0.69
2012-13	0.77	...	...	...

Interim Dividends (Per Share)

Amt	Decl	Ex	Rec	Pay
0.35A	12/02/2009	12/10/2009	12/14/2009	01/19/2010
0.40A	12/01/2010	12/09/2010	12/13/2010	01/18/2011
0.60A	11/30/2011	12/14/2011	12/16/2011	01/18/2012
0.75A	11/28/2012	12/06/2012	12/10/2012	12/28/2012

Indicated Div: $0.75

Valuation Analysis

Forecast EPS $3.44 (04/05/2013)
Market Cap $102.2 Billion
Book Value $41.0 Billion
Price/Book 2.49
Price/Sales 2.39

Institutional Holding

No of Institutions 1603
Shares 1,304,878,080
% Held 64.33

Business Summary: Entertainment (MIC: 2.3.2 SIC: 7812 NAIC: 512110)

Walt Disney is an entertainment company with operations in five segments: Media Networks, which operates the ESPN, Disney Channels Worldwide, ABC Family, SOAPnet and UTV/Bindass cable television and radio networks; Parks and Resorts, which operates the Walt Disney World and other Disneyland resorts; Studio Entertainment, which produces and acquires live-action and animated motion pictures for distribution to the theatrical, home entertainment, and television markets; Consumer Products, which licenses trade names, characters and visual and literary properties to retailers, show promoters, and publishers; and Interactive, which produces and distributes console, online and mobile games.

Recent Developments: For the quarter ended Dec 29 2012, net income decreased 5.5% to US$1.44 billion from US$1.52 billion in the year-earlier quarter. Revenues were US$11.34 billion, up 5.2% from US$10.78 billion the year before. Indirect operating expenses increased 7.6% to US$9.25 billion from US$8.59 billion in the equivalent prior-year period.

Prospects: Our evaluation of Disney (Walt) Co. as of Apr. 7, 2013 is the result of our systematic analysis on three basic characteristics: earnings strength, relative valuation, and recent stock price movement. The company has generated a negative trend in earnings per share over the past 5 quarters and while recent estimates for the company have been mixed, DIS has posted better than expected results. Based on operating earnings yield, the company is undervalued when compared to all of the companies in our coverage universe. Share price changes over the past year indicates that DIS will perform well over the near term.

Financial Data
(US$ in Thousands)

	3 Mos	09/29/2012	10/01/2011	10/02/2010	10/03/2009	09/27/2008	09/29/2007	09/30/2006
Earnings Per Share	3.10	3.13	2.52	2.03	1.76	2.28	2.25	1.64
Cash Flow Per Share	4.15	4.45	3.73	3.44	2.68	2.89	2.70	3.03
Tang Book Value Per Share	3.36	5.41	4.61	4.40	5.39	4.25	3.15	3.10
Dividends Per Share	...	0.600	0.400	0.350	0.350	0.350	0.310	0.270
Dividend Payout %	...	19.17	15.87	17.24	19.89	15.35	13.78	16.46
Income Statement								
Total Revenue	11,341,000	42,278,000	40,893,000	38,063,000	36,149,000	37,843,000	35,510,000	34,285,000
EBITDA	2,504,000	10,989,000	9,642,000	8,198,000	7,127,000	8,872,000	9,292,000	7,002,000
Depn & Amortn	514,000	1,987,000	1,841,000	1,602,000	1,580,000	1,527,000	1,459,000	1,436,000
Income Before Taxes	1,918,000	8,633,000	7,458,000	6,187,000	5,081,000	6,821,000	7,240,000	4,974,000
Income Taxes	590,000	3,087,000	2,785,000	2,314,000	2,049,000	2,673,000	2,874,000	1,890,000
Net Income	1,382,000	5,682,000	4,807,000	3,963,000	3,307,000	4,427,000	4,687,000	3,374,000
Average Shares	1,800,000	1,818,000	1,909,000	1,948,000	1,875,000	1,948,000	2,092,000	2,076,000
Balance Sheet								
Current Assets	14,322,000	13,709,000	13,757,000	12,225,000	11,889,000	11,666,000	11,314,000	9,562,000
Total Assets	80,642,000	74,898,000	72,124,000	69,206,000	63,117,000	62,497,000	60,928,000	59,998,000
Current Liabilities	14,498,000	12,813,000	12,088,000	11,000,000	8,934,000	11,591,000	11,391,000	10,210,000
Long-Term Obligations	12,633,000	10,981,000	11,210,000	10,354,000	11,721,000	11,351,000	12,166,000	11,135,000
Total Liabilities	39,626,000	35,139,000	34,739,000	31,687,000	29,383,000	30,174,000	30,175,000	28,178,000
Stockholders' Equity	41,016,000	39,759,000	37,385,000	37,519,000	33,734,000	32,323,000	30,753,000	31,820,000
Shares Outstanding	1,800,000	1,780,000	1,762,200	1,896,900	1,818,300	1,822,900	1,962,200	2,064,000
Statistical Record								
Return on Assets %	7.25	7.75	6.82	6.01	5.18	7.19	7.77	5.98
Return on Equity %	14.31	14.77	12.87	11.15	9.85	14.08	15.02	11.66
EBITDA Margin %	22.08	25.99	23.58	21.54	19.72	23.44	26.17	20.42
Net Margin %	12.19	13.44	11.76	10.41	9.15	11.70	13.20	9.84
Asset Turnover	0.55	0.58	0.58	0.58	0.57	0.61	0.59	0.61
Current Ratio	0.99	1.07	1.14	1.11	1.33	1.01	0.99	0.94
Debt to Equity	0.31	0.28	0.30	0.28	0.35	0.35	0.40	0.35
Price Range	52.97-37.50	52.92-29.00	44.07-29.55	37.56-27.24	30.69-15.59	35.47-28.12	35.86-29.95	30.48-22.53
P/E Ratio	17.09-12.10	16.91-9.27	17.49-11.73	18.50-13.42	17.44-8.86	15.56-12.33	15.94-13.31	18.59-13.74
Average Yield %	...	1.40	1.04	1.07	1.53	1.09	0.92	1.00

Address: 500 South Buena Vista Street, Burbank, CA 91521
Telephone: 818-560-1000

Web Site: www.disney.com
Officers: John Ennis Pepper - Chairman Robert A. Iger - President, Chief Executive Officer

Auditors: PricewaterhouseCoopers LLP
Investor Contact: 818-553-7200
Transfer Agents: The Walt Disney Company, Glendale, CA

DOLBY LABORATORIES INC

Exchange	Symbol	Price	52Wk Range	Yield	P/E
NYS	DLB	$33.56 (3/28/2013)	45.11-28.98	11.92	14.66

*7 Year Price Score 78.13 *NYSE Composite Index=100 *12 Month Price Score 84.85

Interim Earnings (Per Share)

Qtr.	Dec	Mar	Jun	Sep
2009-10	0.59	0.74	0.55	0.57
2010-11	0.76	0.72	0.55	0.72
2011-12	0.67	0.81	0.48	0.50
2012-13	0.50	...	...	...

Interim Dividends (Per Share)

Amt	Decl	Ex	Rec	Pay
4.00U	12/11/2012	12/19/2012	12/21/2012	12/27/2012

Indicated Div: $4.00

Valuation Analysis		Institutional Holding	
Forecast EPS	$1.89	No of Institutions	
	(04/05/2013)	306	
Market Cap	$3.4 Billion	Shares	
Book Value	$1.3 Billion	46,071,208	
Price/Book	2.57	% Held	
Price/Sales	3.68	39.83	

Business Summary: Manufacturing (MIC: 6.1.1 SIC: 3663 NAIC: 334220)

Dolby Laboratories provides video and audio products for the film production, cinema, and television broadcast industries. Co. sells digital cinema servers, which load, store, decrypt, and decode encrypted digital film files, as well as digital three-dimensional products and its reference monitor. Co. also sells cinema processors, and to a lesser extent, broadcast products used to encode and distribute content to viewers. Co. also provides related digital cinema processors and media adapters, as well as digital cinema accessories. Co. also licenses its technologies, such as Dolby Digital, Dolby Digital Plus, and Dolby TrueHD to original equipment manufacturers and software vendors.

Recent Developments: For the quarter ended Dec 28 2012, net income decreased 29.8% to US$51.5 million from US$73.4 million in the year-earlier quarter. Revenues were US$236.6 million, up 1.0% from US$234.2 million the year before. Operating income was US$67.0 million versus US$101.3 million in the prior-year quarter, a decrease of 33.8%. Direct operating expenses rose 25.5% to US$25.6 million from US$20.4 million in the comparable period the year before. Indirect operating expenses increased 28.0% to US$144.0 million from US$112.5 million in the equivalent prior-year period.

Prospects: Our evaluation of Dolby Laboratories Inc. as of Apr. 7, 2013 is the result of our systematic analysis on three basic characteristics: earnings strength, relative valuation, and recent stock price movement. The company has generated a negative trend in earnings per share over the past 5 quarters. However, while recent estimates for the company have been mixed, DLB has posted better than expected results. Based on operating earnings yield, the company is undervalued when compared to all of the companies in our coverage universe. Share price changes over the past year indicates that DLB will perform poorly over the near term.

Financial Data
(US$ in Thousands)

	3 Mos	09/28/2012	09/30/2011	09/24/2010	09/25/2009	09/26/2008	09/28/2007	09/29/2006
Earnings Per Share	2.29	2.46	2.75	2.46	2.11	1.74	1.26	0.80
Cash Flow Per Share	3.53	3.66	3.56	2.89	2.42	2.38	1.50	1.26
Tang Book Value Per Share	9.75	13.41	12.33	10.19	8.77	6.36	6.55	5.18
Dividends Per Share	4.000	...	...	...	...	...	...	...
Dividend Payout %	174.67	...	...	...	...	...	...	...
Income Statement								
Total Revenue	236,602	926,264	955,505	922,713	719,503	640,231	482,028	391,542
EBITDA	71,539	393,376	454,740	448,217	374,589	298,439	197,571	140,278
Depn & Amortn	3,794	30,600	24,100	17,800	13,500	12,400	11,200	10,600
Income Before Taxes	69,059	368,991	440,643	437,012	371,419	301,802	209,416	146,637
Income Taxes	17,582	103,857	130,061	154,185	127,073	100,770	65,131	55,833
Net Income	51,349	264,302	309,267	283,447	242,991	199,458	142,831	89,549
Average Shares	103,523	107,541	112,554	115,388	115,367	114,781	113,573	111,658
Balance Sheet								
Current Assets	618,558	970,286	1,158,598	1,060,413	900,838	691,869	733,418	572,632
Total Assets	1,551,950	1,960,798	1,884,387	1,711,772	1,581,315	1,336,146	991,697	739,288
Current Liabilities	144,465	156,840	159,385	165,756	156,584	200,673	143,204	92,854
Long-Term Obligations	...	...	...	...	5,825	7,782	9,691	10,893
Total Liabilities	224,173	240,529	220,874	238,035	240,207	286,893	194,541	145,000
Stockholders' Equity	1,327,777	1,720,269	1,663,513	1,473,737	1,341,108	1,049,253	797,156	594,288
Shares Outstanding	101,819	103,095	109,420	112,084	113,849	112,474	110,250	107,261
Statistical Record								
Return on Assets %	13.89	13.78	16.92	17.26	16.70	17.18	16.55	13.55
Return on Equity %	15.90	15.66	19.40	20.19	20.39	21.66	20.59	17.02
EBITDA Margin %	30.24	42.47	47.59	48.58	52.06	46.61	40.99	35.83
Net Margin %	21.70	28.53	32.37	30.72	33.77	31.15	29.63	22.87
Asset Turnover	0.53	0.48	0.52	0.56	0.49	0.55	0.56	0.59
Current Ratio	4.28	6.19	7.27	6.40	5.75	3.45	5.12	6.17
Debt to Equity	...	...	...	...	N.M.	0.01	0.01	0.02
Price Range	45.11-28.98	45.11-26.28	69.51-27.44	69.37-37.40	42.10-24.86	52.73-33.62	38.15-18.72	23.54-15.00
P/E Ratio	19.70-12.66	18.34-10.68	25.28-9.98	28.20-15.20	19.95-11.78	30.30-19.32	30.28-14.90	29.42-18.75
Average Yield %	11.00	...	...	...	...	...	...	...

Address: 100 Potrero Avenue, San Francisco, CA 94103-4813 Telephone: 415-558-0200	Web Site: www.dolby.com Officers: Peter Gotcher - Chairman Kevin J. Yeaman - President, Chief Executive Officer	Auditors: KPMG LLP Transfer Agents: Computershare Trust Company, Providence, RI

DOLE FOOD CO., INC.

Exchange	Symbol	Price	52Wk Range	Yield	P/E
NYS	DOLE	$10.90 (3/28/2013)	14.35-8.35	N/A	N/A

*7 Year Price Score N/A   *NYSE Composite Index=100   *12 Month Price Score 94.08

Interim Earnings (Per Share)

Qtr.	Mar	Jun	Oct	Dec
2009	1.99	0.39	(1.04)	0.18
2010	0.25	0.37	(0.58)	(0.44)
2011	0.01	0.93	(0.56)	0.05
2012	0.19	0.73	(0.17)	(2.38)

Interim Dividends (Per Share)

No Dividends Paid

Valuation Analysis

		Institutional Holding	
Forecast EPS	$0.58	No of Institutions	
	(04/05/2013)	164	
Market Cap	$972.2 Million	Shares	
Book Value	$686.1 Million	58,061,228	
Price/Book	1.42	% Held	
Price/Sales	0.23	N/A	

Business Summary: Food (MIC: 1.2.1 SIC: 0161 NAIC: 111219)

Dole Food Company is a producer, marketer and distributor of fruit and vegetables. Co. has three business segments: fresh fruit, fresh vegetables and packaged foods. The fresh fruit segment contains several operating divisions that produce and market fruit to wholesale, retail and institutional customers worldwide. The fresh vegetables segment produces and markets vegetables and salads to wholesale, retail and institutional customers, primarily in North America and Europe. The packaged foods segment contains several operating divisions that produce and market packaged foods including fruit, juices, frozen fruit and snack foods.

Recent Developments: For the year ended Dec 29 2012, income from continuing operations decreased 98.8% to US$1.2 million from US$101.8 million a year earlier. Net loss amounted to US$141.6 million versus net income of US$41.8 million in the prior year. Revenues were US$4.25 billion, down 11.1% from US$4.78 billion the year before. Operating income was US$16.6 million versus US$101.0 million in the prior year, a decrease of 83.6%. Direct operating expenses declined 11.4% to US$3.88 billion from US$4.38 billion in the comparable period the year before. Indirect operating expenses increased 16.4% to US$351.2 million from US$301.6 million in the equivalent prior-year period.

Prospects: Our evaluation of Dole Food Company Inc. as of Apr. 7, 2013 is the result of our systematic analysis on three basic characteristics: earnings strength, relative valuation, and recent stock price movement. The company has suffered a very negative trend in earnings per share over the past 5 quarters. However, while recent estimates for the company have been lowered by analysts, DOLE has posted results that fell short of analysts expectations. Based on operating earnings yield, the company is overvalued when compared to all of the companies in our coverage universe. Share price changes over the past year indicates that DOLE will perform well over the near term.

Financial Data

(US$ in Thousands)	12/29/2012	12/31/2011	01/01/2011	01/02/2010	01/03/2009	12/29/2007	12/30/2006
Earnings Per Share	(1.64)	0.44	(0.39)	1.43	2.34	(1.12)	(1.74)
Cash Flow Per Share	0.52	0.06	1.69	4.83	0.85	0.90	...
Tang Book Value Per Share	1.69	N.M.	N.M.	N.M.	N.M.	N.M.	...
Income Statement							
Total Revenue	4,246,708	7,223,836	6,892,614	6,778,521	7,619,952	6,820,812	5,990,863
EBITDA	109,462	279,911	240,433	412,268	403,465	310,843	304,912
Depn & Amortn	96,000	99,500	110,400	115,800	142,913	159,711	153,758
Income Before Taxes	5,897	42,646	(27,722)	97,670	92,522	(36,194)	(16,421)
Income Taxes	10,755	6,521	13,394	22,684	(48,015)	4,054	22,609
Net Income	(144,463)	38,359	(34,124)	84,085	121,005	(57,506)	(89,627)
Average Shares	87,840	88,081	87,451	58,775	51,710	51,710	51,710
Balance Sheet							
Current Assets	2,744,691	1,810,345	1,898,255	1,737,199	1,987,967	1,846,514	...
Total Assets	4,229,711	4,270,071	4,256,990	4,107,023	4,364,619	4,642,884	...
Current Liabilities	1,479,200	1,080,370	1,203,081	960,564	1,456,920	1,152,732	...
Long-Term Obligations	1,512,646	1,641,112	1,564,325	1,552,680	1,798,556	2,316,208	...
Total Liabilities	3,543,636	3,477,567	3,464,821	3,268,048	3,961,719	4,317,876	...
Stockholders' Equity	686,135	792,504	792,169	838,975	402,900	325,008	...
Shares Outstanding	89,189	88,952	88,611	88,233	51,710	51,710	...
Statistical Record							
Return on Assets %	N.M.	0.90	N.M.	1.99	2.64	...	...
Return on Equity %	N.M.	4.85	N.M.	13.58	32.71	...	...
EBITDA Margin %	2.58	3.87	3.49	6.08	5.29	4.56	5.09
Net Margin %	N.M.	0.53	N.M.	1.24	1.59	N.M.	N.M.
Asset Turnover	1.00	1.70	1.65	1.60	1.66	...	...
Current Ratio	1.86	1.68	1.58	1.81	1.36	1.60	...
Debt to Equity	2.20	2.07	1.97	1.85	4.46	7.13	...
Price Range	14.35-8.05	14.87-8.05	13.55-8.64	12.50-11.37	...	...	...
P/E Ratio	...	33.80-18.30	...	8.74-7.95	...	...	...

Address: One Dole Drive, Westlake Village, CA 91362 **Telephone:** 818-879-6600	**Web Site:** www.dole.com **Officers:** David H. Murdock - Chairman, Chief Executive Officer C. Michael Carter - Executive Vice President, Corporate Secretary, General Counsel, President, Chief Operating Officer	**Auditors:** Deloitte & Touche LLP **Investor Contact:** 818-879-6600 **Transfer Agents:** Wells Fargo Shareholder Services, St. Paul, MN

DOLLAR GENERAL CORP

Exchange	Symbol	Price	52Wk Range	Yield	P/E
NYS	DG	$50.58 (3/28/2013)	55.06-42.33	N/A	17.75

*7 Year Price Score N/A ***NYSE Composite Index=100** ***12 Month Price Score 90.15**

Interim Earnings (Per Share)

Qtr.	Apr	Jul	Oct	Jan
2010-11	0.39	0.41	0.37	0.64
2011-12	0.45	0.42	0.50	0.85
2012-13	0.63	0.64	0.62	0.96

Interim Dividends (Per Share)

No Dividends Paid

Valuation Analysis		Institutional Holding	
Forecast EPS	$3.28	No of Institutions	
	(04/06/2013)	546	
Market Cap	$16.5 Billion	Shares	
Book Value	$5.0 Billion	368,411,040	
Price/Book	3.32	% Held	
Price/Sales	1.03	N/A	

Business Summary: Retail - General Merchandise/Department Stores (MIC: 2.1.1 SIC: 5331 NAIC: 452990)

Dollar General is a discount retailer. As of Mar 2 2012, Co. operated 9,961 stores located in 39 states, primarily in the southern, southwestern, midwestern and eastern U.S. Co. provides a selection of merchandise, including consumables, seasonal, home products and apparel. Consumables includes paper and cleaning products; food; beverages and snacks; health and beauty; and pet. Seasonal products include decorations, hardware, automotive and home office supplies. Home products includes kitchen supplies, cookware, candles, craft supplies and kitchen, bed and bath soft goods. Apparel includes casual everyday apparel, as well as socks, underwear, disposable diapers, shoes and accessories.

Recent Developments: For the year ended Feb 1 2013, net income increased 24.3% to US$952.7 million from US$766.7 million in the prior year. Revenues were US$16.02 billion, up 8.2% from US$14.81 billion the year before. Operating income was US$1.66 billion versus US$1.49 billion in the prior year, an increase of 11.0%. Direct operating expenses rose 8.2% to US$10.94 billion from US$10.11 billion in the comparable period the year before. Indirect operating expenses increased 7.0% to US$3.43 billion from US$3.21 billion in the equivalent prior-year period.

Prospects: Our evaluation of Dollar General Inc. as of Apr. 7, 2013 is the result of our systematic analysis on three basic characteristics: earnings strength, relative valuation, and recent stock price movement. The company has managed to produce a neutral trend in earnings per share over the past 5 quarters. However, while recent estimates for the company have been mixed, DG has posted better than expected results. Based on operating earnings yield, the company is undervalued when compared to all of the companies in our coverage universe. Share price changes over the past year indicates that DG will perform poorly over the near term.

Financial Data

(US$ in Thousands)	02/01/2013	02/03/2012	01/28/2011	01/29/2010	01/30/2009	02/01/2008	07/06/2007	02/02/2007
Earnings Per Share	2.85	2.22	1.82	1.04	...	...	...	0.77
Cash Flow Per Share	3.41	3.03	2.42	2.08	...	...	...	2.28
Tang Book Value Per Share	N.M.	N.M.	N.M.	N.M.	N.M.	N.M.	...	9.78
Dividends Per Share	...	...	...	...	...	...	...	0.350
Dividend Payout %	...	...	...	...	...	...	...	45.45
Income Statement								
Total Revenue	16,022,128	14,807,188	13,035,000	11,796,380	10,457,668	5,571,493	3,923,753	9,169,822
EBITDA	1,902,520	1,673,889	1,474,664	1,098,816	773,774	359,405	92,748	447,876
Depn & Amortn	277,200	243,700	215,700	201,100	190,500	116,900	83,500	199,600
Income Before Taxes	1,497,394	1,225,289	984,972	552,116	194,403	(6,593)	3,995	220,363
Income Taxes	544,732	458,604	357,115	212,674	86,221	(1,775)	11,993	82,420
Net Income	952,662	766,685	627,857	339,442	108,182	(4,818)	(7,998)	137,943
Average Shares	334,469	345,117	344,800	324,836	...	...	...	179,148
Balance Sheet								
Current Assets	2,677,113	2,275,074	2,367,825	1,845,449	1,870,125	1,517,744	...	1,742,748
Total Assets	10,367,682	9,688,520	9,546,222	8,863,519	8,889,199	8,656,431	...	3,040,514
Current Liabilities	1,738,547	1,509,902	1,365,373	1,206,500	1,075,235	858,241	...	832,871
Long-Term Obligations	2,771,336	2,617,891	3,287,070	3,399,715	4,122,956	4,278,756	...	261,958
Total Liabilities	5,382,352	5,013,938	5,482,590	5,454,735	6,043,580	5,943,436	...	1,294,767
Stockholders' Equity	4,985,330	4,674,582	4,063,632	3,408,784	2,845,619	2,712,995	...	1,745,747
Shares Outstanding	327,069	338,089	341,507	340,586	317,844	317,418	...	178,534
Statistical Record								
Return on Assets %	9.53	7.84	6.84	3.83	1.24	...	...	4.59
Return on Equity %	19.78	17.26	16.85	10.88	3.90	...	...	7.98
EBITDA Margin %	11.87	11.30	11.31	9.31	7.40	6.45	2.36	4.88
Net Margin %	5.95	5.18	4.82	2.88	1.03	N.M.	N.M.	1.50
Asset Turnover	1.60	1.51	1.42	1.33	1.20	...	...	3.05
Current Ratio	1.54	1.51	1.73	1.53	1.74	1.77	...	2.09
Debt to Equity	0.56	0.56	0.81	1.00	1.45	1.58	...	0.15
Price Range	55.06-41.64	42.70-26.85	33.28-21.71	24.55-22.15	...	...	...	...
P/E Ratio	19.32-14.61	19.23-12.09	18.29-11.93	23.61-21.30	...	...	...	...

Address: 100 Mission Ridge, Goodlettsville, TN 37072 **Telephone:** 615-855-4000 **Fax:** 615-855-5527	**Web Site:** www.dollargeneral.com **Officers:** Richard W. Dreiling - Chairman, Chief Executive Officer David M. Tehle - Executive Vice President, Chief Financial Officer	**Auditors:** Ernst & Young LLP **Investor Contact:** 615-855-4000 **Transfer Agents:** Wells Fargo Bank, N.A., St. Paul, MN

DOMINION RESOURCES INC

Exchange	Symbol	Price	52Wk Range	Yield	P/E
NYS	D	$58.18 (3/28/2013)	58.18-49.19	3.87	109.77

*7 Year Price Score 108.43 *NYSE Composite Index=100 *12 Month Price Score 97.41

Interim Earnings (Per Share)

Qtr.	Mar	Jun	Sep	Dec
2008	1.18	0.51	0.87	0.60
2009	0.42	0.76	1.00	(0.02)
2010	0.29	2.98	0.98	0.53
2011	0.82	0.58	0.69	0.35
2012	0.86	0.45	0.36	(1.15)

Interim Dividends (Per Share)

Amt	Decl	Ex	Rec	Pay
0.527Q	05/08/2012	05/30/2012	06/01/2012	06/20/2012
0.527Q	08/10/2012	08/29/2012	08/31/2012	09/20/2012
0.527Q	10/18/2012	11/28/2012	11/30/2012	12/20/2012
0.563Q	01/25/2013	02/26/2013	02/28/2013	03/20/2013

Indicated Div: $2.25

Valuation Analysis   **Institutional Holding**

Forecast EPS	$3.35	No of Institutions
	(04/05/2013)	1001
Market Cap	$33.5 Billion	Shares
Book Value	$10.8 Billion	355,218,432
Price/Book	3.10	% Held
Price/Sales	2.56	57.04

Business Summary: Electric Utilities (MIC: 3.1.1 SIC: 4911 NAIC: 221121)

Dominion Resources is engaged in producing and transporting energy. Co.'s operations include Virginia Electric and Power Company, that generates, transmits and distributes electricity for sale in Virginia and North Carolina. Co. has three primary segments: Dominion Virginia Power, including regulated electric distribution and transmission, and nonregulated retail energy marketing (electric and gas); Dominion Generation, including regulated and merchant electric fleet; and Dominion Energy, including gas transmission, distribution and storage, liquefied natural gas import and storage, and producer services. As of Dec 31 2012, Co. served nearly 6.0 million customers in 15 states.

Recent Developments: For the year ended Dec 31 2012, income from continuing operations decreased 75.8% to US$351.0 million from US$1.45 billion a year earlier. Net income decreased 76.9% to US$329.0 million from US$1.43 billion in the prior year. Revenues were US$13.09 billion, down 7.4% from US$14.15 billion the year before. Operating income was US$1.16 billion versus US$2.89 billion in the prior year, a decrease of 60.1%. Direct operating expenses rose 5.6% to US$10.18 billion from US$9.64 billion in the comparable period the year before. Indirect operating expenses increased 8.9% to US$1.76 billion from US$1.61 billion in the equivalent prior-year period.

Prospects: Our evaluation of Dominion Resources Inc. as of Apr. 7, 2013 is the result of our systematic analysis on three basic characteristics: earnings strength, relative valuation, and recent stock price movement. The company has enjoyed a very positive trend in earnings per share over the past 5 quarters and while recent estimates for the company have been mixed, D has posted results that were in line with analysts expectations. Based on operating earnings yield, the company is about fairly valued when compared to all of the companies in our coverage universe. Share price changes over the past year indicates that D will perform poorly over the near term.

Financial Data

(US$ in Thousands)	12/31/2012	12/31/2011	12/31/2010	12/31/2009	12/31/2008	12/31/2007	12/31/2006	12/31/2005
Earnings Per Share	0.53	2.45	4.76	2.17	3.16	3.88	1.97	1.50
Cash Flow Per Share	7.20	5.21	3.10	6.38	4.59	(0.38)	5.73	3.83
Tang Book Value Per Share	12.43	13.90	14.58	12.35	10.50	9.65	11.81	9.16
Dividends Per Share	2.110	1.970	1.830	1.750	1.580	1.460	1.380	1.340
Dividend Payout %	398.11	80.41	38.45	80.65	50.00	37.63	70.23	89.33
Income Statement								
Total Revenue	13,093,000	14,379,000	15,197,000	15,131,000	16,290,000	15,674,000	16,482,000	18,041,000
EBITDA	2,822,000	4,328,000	7,127,000	4,129,000	4,742,000	7,186,000	3,609,000	2,721,000
Depn & Amortn	1,443,000	1,288,000	1,258,000	1,319,000	1,191,000	1,533,000	106,000	130,000
Income Before Taxes	497,000	2,171,000	5,037,000	1,916,000	2,715,000	4,494,000	2,489,000	1,616,000
Income Taxes	146,000	745,000	2,057,000	612,000	879,000	1,783,000	920,000	582,000
Net Income	302,000	1,408,000	2,808,000	1,287,000	1,834,000	2,539,000	1,380,000	1,033,000
Average Shares	573,900	574,600	590,100	593,700	580,800	655,200	703,200	688,800
Balance Sheet								
Current Assets	5,140,000	5,430,000	5,400,000	6,817,000	7,661,000	6,656,000	8,098,000	10,129,000
Total Assets	46,838,000	45,614,000	42,817,000	42,554,000	42,053,000	39,123,000	49,269,000	52,660,000
Current Liabilities	7,763,000	6,962,000	5,773,000	6,833,000	7,794,000	7,746,000	11,229,000	14,480,000
Long-Term Obligations	16,851,000	17,394,000	15,758,000	15,481,000	14,956,000	13,235,000	14,791,000	14,653,000
Total Liabilities	36,013,000	33,911,000	30,563,000	31,112,000	31,719,000	29,460,000	36,099,000	42,006,000
Stockholders' Equity	10,825,000	11,703,000	12,254,000	11,442,000	10,334,000	9,663,000	13,170,000	10,654,000
Shares Outstanding	576,000	570,000	581,000	599,000	583,000	577,000	698,000	694,000
Statistical Record								
Return on Assets %	0.65	3.18	6.58	3.04	4.51	5.74	2.71	2.11
Return on Equity %	2.67	11.75	23.70	11.82	18.29	22.24	11.58	9.25
EBITDA Margin %	21.55	30.10	46.90	27.29	29.11	45.85	21.90	15.08
Net Margin %	2.31	9.79	18.48	8.51	11.26	16.20	8.37	5.73
Asset Turnover	0.28	0.33	0.36	0.36	0.40	0.35	0.32	0.37
Current Ratio	0.66	0.78	0.94	1.00	0.98	0.86	0.72	0.70
Debt to Equity	1.56	1.49	1.29	1.35	1.45	1.37	1.12	1.38
Price Range	54.97-49.19	53.53-42.26	44.92-36.27	39.61-27.29	48.11-33.58	48.99-40.00	42.01-34.52	43.25-33.35
P/E Ratio	103.72-92.81	21.85-17.25	9.44-7.62	18.25-12.58	15.22-10.63	12.63-10.31	21.32-17.52	28.83-22.23
Average Yield %	4.05	4.13	4.42	5.21	3.78	3.33	3.60	3.58

Address: 120 Tredegar Street, Richmond, VA 23219	**Web Site:** www.dom.com	**Auditors:** Deloitte & Touche LLP
Telephone: 804-819-2000	**Officers:** Thomas F. Farrell - Chairman, President, Chief Executive Officer, Division Officer Mark F. McGettrick - Executive Vice President, Chief Financial Officer	**Investor Contact:** 804 819-2150
Fax: 804-775-5819		**Transfer Agents:** Dominion Resources Services, Inc.

DOMTAR CORP

Exchange	Symbol	Price	52Wk Range	Yield	P/E
NYS	UFS	$78.97 (3/28/2013)	98.35-70.25	2.28	16.59

*7 Year Price Score N/A *NYSE Composite Index=100 ***12 Month Price Score 90.41**

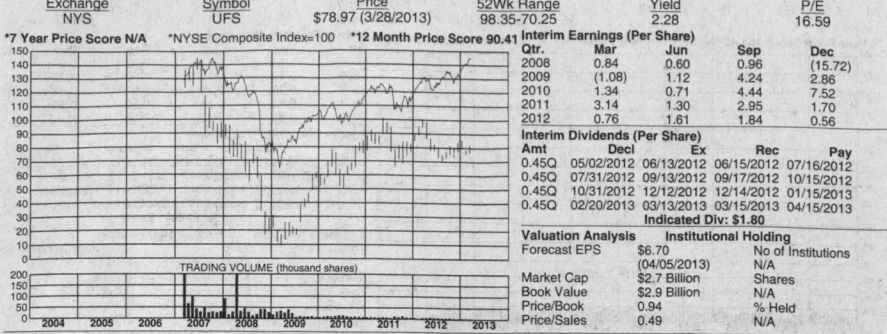

Interim Earnings (Per Share)

Qtr.	Mar	Jun	Sep	Dec
2008	0.84	0.60	0.96	(15.72)
2009	(1.08)	1.12	4.24	2.86
2010	1.34	0.71	4.44	7.52
2011	3.14	1.30	2.95	1.70
2012	0.76	1.61	1.84	0.56

Interim Dividends (Per Share)

Amt	Decl	Ex	Rec	Pay
0.45Q	05/02/2012	06/13/2012	06/15/2012	07/16/2012
0.45Q	07/31/2012	09/13/2012	09/17/2012	10/15/2012
0.45Q	10/31/2012	12/12/2012	12/14/2012	01/15/2013
0.45Q	02/20/2013	03/13/2013	03/15/2013	04/15/2013

Indicated Div: $1.80

Valuation Analysis

		Institutional Holding	
Forecast EPS	$6.70 (04/05/2013)	No of Institutions	N/A
Market Cap	$2.7 Billion	Shares	N/A
Book Value	$2.9 Billion	% Held	N/A
Price/Book	0.94		
Price/Sales	0.49		

Business Summary: Paper & Forest Products (MIC: 8.1.2 SIC: 2621 NAIC: 322110)

Domtar designs, manufactures, markets and distributes a range of fiber-based products. Co. is a manufacturer and marketer of uncoated freesheet paper in North America for a range of customers, including merchants and retail outlets. Co. operates in three reportable segments: Pulp and Paper, which comprises the manufacturing, sale and distribution of communication, specialty and packaging papers, as well as softwood, fluff and hardwood market pulp; Distribution, which involves the purchasing, warehousing, sale and distribution of its paper products and those of other manufacturers; and Personal Care, which consists of the manufacturing, sale and distribution of adult incontinence products.

Recent Developments: For the year ended Dec 31 2012, net income decreased 52.9% to US$172.0 million from US$365.0 million in the prior year. Revenues were US$5.48 billion, down 2.3% from US$5.61 billion the year before. Operating income was US$367.0 million versus US$592.0 million in the prior year, a decrease of 38.0%. Direct operating expenses rose 3.6% to US$4.32 billion from US$4.17 billion in the comparable period the year before. Indirect operating expenses decreased 6.5% to US$794.0 million from US$849.0 million in the equivalent prior-year period.

Prospects: Our evaluation of Domtar Corp. as of Apr. 7, 2013 is the result of our systematic analysis on three basic characteristics: earnings strength, relative valuation, and recent stock price movement. The company has produced a positive trend in earnings per share over the past 5 quarters and while recent estimates for the company have been raised by analysts, UFS has posted results that fell short of analysts expectations. Based on operating earnings yield, the company is undervalued when compared to all of the companies in our coverage universe. Share price changes over the past year indicates that UFS will perform poorly over the near term.

Financial Data

(US$ in Thousands)	12/31/2012	12/31/2011	12/31/2010	12/31/2009	12/31/2008	12/30/2007	12/31/2006	12/31/2006
Earnings Per Share	4.76	9.08	14.00	7.18	(13.32)	1.80	(25.68)	...
Cash Flow Per Share	15.26	22.13	27.24	18.42	4.56	15.38	15.08	
Tang Book Value Per Share	67.32	72.10	75.56	61.27	50.02	69.12	34,812,000.00	
Dividends Per Share	1.700	1.300	0.750	...	...	...	...	
Dividend Payout %	35.71	14.32	5.36	...	...	...	...	
Income Statement								
Total Revenue	5,482,000	5,612,000	5,850,000	5,465,000	6,394,000	5,947,000	3,306,000	...
EBITDA	752,000	968,000	998,000	1,020,000	26,000	741,000	(245,000)	...
Depn & Amortn	385,000	376,000	395,000	405,000	463,000	471,000	311,000	...
Income Before Taxes	236,000	505,000	448,000	490,000	(570,000)	99,000	(556,000)	...
Income Taxes	58,000	133,000	(157,000)	180,000	3,000	29,000	53,000	
Net Income	172,000	365,000	605,000	310,000	(573,000)	70,000	(609,000)	...
Average Shares	36,100	40,200	43,200	43,200	42,958	39,658	23,675	
Balance Sheet								
Current Assets	2,015,000	1,934,000	2,000,000	2,202,000	1,655,000	1,798,000	889,000	
Total Assets	6,123,000	5,869,000	6,026,000	6,519,000	6,104,000	7,748,000	3,998,000	...
Current Liabilities	758,000	716,000	725,000	771,000	743,000	895,000	268,000	
Long-Term Obligations	1,128,000	837,000	825,000	1,701,000	2,110,000	2,213,000	32,000	
Total Liabilities	3,246,000	2,897,000	2,824,000	3,857,000	3,961,000	4,551,000	1,083,000	...
Stockholders' Equity	2,877,000	2,972,000	3,202,000	2,662,000	2,143,000	3,197,000	2,915,000	...
Shares Outstanding	34,238	36,131	41,635	42,062	41,219	39,264	83.33	...
Statistical Record								
Return on Assets %	2.86	6.14	9.65	4.91	N.M.	1.20	...	...
Return on Equity %	5.87	11.82	20.63	12.90	N.M.	2.30	...	...
EBITDA Margin %	13.72	17.25	17.06	18.66	0.41	12.46	N.M.	...
Net Margin %	3.14	6.50	10.34	5.67	N.M.	1.18	N.M.	...
Asset Turnover	0.91	0.94	0.93	0.87	0.92	1.02	...	...
Current Ratio	2.66	2.70	2.76	2.86	2.23	2.01	3.32	...
Debt to Equity	0.39	0.28	0.26	0.64	0.98	0.69	0.01	...
Price Range	99.74-70.25	101.02-66.16	84.58-49.91	61.30-9.12	96.12-16.80	145.20-81.96	...	...
P/E Ratio	20.95-14.76	11.13-7.29	6.04-3.56	8.54-1.27	...	80.67-45.53	...	...
Average Yield %	2.07	1.55	1.14	...	...	...	...	...

Address: 395 de Maisonneuve Blvd. West, Montreal, H3A 1L6 **Telephone:** 514-848-5555	**Web Site:** www.domtar.com **Officers:** Harold H. MacKay - Chairman John D. Williams - President, Chief Executive Officer	**Auditors:** PricewaterhouseCoopers LLP **Investor Contact:** 514-848-5555 **Transfer Agents:** Computershare Investor Services, Inc, Toronto, ON, Canada

DR PEPPER SNAPPLE GROUP INC

Exchange	Symbol	Price	52Wk Range	Yield	P/E
NYS	DPS	$46.95 (3/28/2013)	46.95-39.14	3.24	15.86

*7 Year Price Score N/A *NYSE Composite Index=100 *12 Month Price Score 94.52

Interim Earnings (Per Share)

Qtr.	Mar	Jun	Sep	Dec
2008	0.00	0.42	0.41	(2.44)
2009	0.52	0.62	0.59	0.44
2010	0.35	0.74	0.60	0.49
2011	0.50	0.77	0.71	0.77
2012	0.48	0.83	0.84	0.81

Interim Dividends (Per Share)

Amt	Decl	Ex	Rec	Pay
0.34Q	05/16/2012	06/14/2012	06/18/2012	07/06/2012
0.34Q	08/09/2012	09/13/2012	09/17/2012	10/05/2012
0.34Q	11/16/2012	12/13/2012	12/17/2012	01/04/2013
0.38Q	02/13/2013	03/13/2013	03/15/2013	04/05/2013

Indicated Div: $1.52

Valuation Analysis / **Institutional Holding**

Forecast EPS	$3.08	No of Institutions
	(04/06/2013)	498
Market Cap	$9.6 Billion	Shares
Book Value	$2.3 Billion	212,684,448
Price/Book	4.23	% Held
Price/Sales	1.61	N/A

TRADING VOLUME (thousand shares)

Business Summary: Beverages (MIC: 1.2.2 SIC: 2086 NAIC: 312111)

Dr Pepper Snapple Group is a brand owner, manufacturer and distributor of non-alcoholic beverages in the U.S., Canada and Mexico with a range of flavored carbonated soft drinks (CSDs) and non-carbonated beverages (NCBs), including ready-to-drink teas, juices, juice drinks and mixers. In the CSD market, Co.'s key brands are Dr Pepper, Canada Dry, 7UP, Squirt, Crush, A&W, Sunkist soda, Schweppes and Sun Drop. In the NCB market segment in the U.S., Co. participates in the ready-to-drink tea, juice, juice drinks and mixer categories. Co.'s key NCB brands are Snapple, Hawaiian Punch, Mott's, and Clamato. Co.'s segments are: Beverage Concentrates, Packaged Beverages and Latin America Beverages.

Recent Developments: For the year ended Dec 31 2012, net income increased 3.8% to US$629.0 million from US$606.0 million in the prior year. Revenues were US$6.00 billion, up 1.6% from US$5.90 billion the year before. Operating income was US$1.09 billion versus US$1.02 billion in the prior year, an increase of 6.6%. Direct operating expenses rose 0.6% to US$2.50 billion from US$2.49 billion in the comparable period the year before. Indirect operating expenses increased 0.4% to US$2.40 billion from US$2.39 billion in the equivalent prior-year period.

Prospects: Our evaluation of Dr Pepper Snapple Group Inc. as of Apr. 7, 2013 is the result of our systematic analysis on three basic characteristics: earnings strength, relative valuation, and recent stock price movement. The company has managed to produce a neutral trend in earnings per share over the past 5 quarters and while recent estimates for the company have remained steady, DPS has posted results that fell short of analysts expectations. Based on operating earnings yield, the company is undervalued when compared to all of the companies in our coverage universe. Share price changes over the past year indicates that DPS will perform in line with the market over the near term.

Financial Data
(US$ in Thousands)

	12/31/2012	12/31/2011	12/31/2010	12/31/2009	12/31/2008	12/31/2007	12/31/2006	01/01/2006
Earnings Per Share	2.96	2.74	2.17	2.17	(1.23)	...	...	...
Cash Flow Per Share	2.17	3.48	10.54	3.40	2.78	...	...	...
Dividends Per Share	1.360	1.210	0.900	0.150	...	...	...	...
Dividend Payout %	45.95	44.16	41.47	6.91	...	...	...	...
Income Statement								
Total Revenue	5,995,000	5,903,000	5,636,000	5,531,000	5,710,000	5,748,000	4,735,000	3,205,000
EBITDA	1,341,000	1,234,000	1,131,000	1,274,000	(9,000)	1,126,000	1,110,000	1,005,000
Depn & Amortn	240,000	198,000	185,000	167,000	141,000	120,000	94,000	48,000
Income Before Taxes	978,000	925,000	821,000	868,000	(375,000)	817,000	805,000	787,000
Income Taxes	349,000	320,000	294,000	315,000	(61,000)	322,000	298,000	321,000
Net Income	629,000	606,000	528,000	555,000	(312,000)	497,000	510,000	477,000
Average Shares	212,300	221,200	242,600	255,200	254,000	...	...	...
Balance Sheet								
Current Assets	1,335,000	1,757,000	1,309,000	1,279,000	1,237,000	2,739,000	1,632,000	...
Total Assets	8,928,000	9,283,000	8,859,000	8,776,000	8,638,000	10,528,000	9,346,000	...
Current Liabilities	1,232,000	1,915,000	1,338,000	854,000	801,000	1,135,000	1,691,000	...
Long-Term Obligations	2,554,000	2,256,000	1,687,000	2,960,000	3,522,000	2,912,000	3,084,000	...
Total Liabilities	6,648,000	7,020,000	6,400,000	5,589,000	6,031,000	5,507,000	6,096,000	...
Stockholders' Equity	2,280,000	2,263,000	2,459,000	3,187,000	2,607,000	5,021,000	3,250,000	...
Shares Outstanding	205,292	212,130	223,936	254,109	253,685	...	...	...
Statistical Record								
Return on Assets %	6.89	6.68	5.99	6.37	N.M.	5.00	...	...
Return on Equity %	27.62	25.67	18.70	19.16	N.M.	12.02	...	...
EBITDA Margin %	22.37	20.90	20.07	23.03	N.M.	19.59	23.44	31.36
Net Margin %	10.49	10.27	9.37	10.03	N.M.	8.65	10.77	14.88
Asset Turnover	0.66	0.65	0.64	0.64	0.59	0.58	...	...
Current Ratio	1.08	0.92	0.98	1.50	1.54	2.41	0.97	...
Debt to Equity	1.12	1.00	0.69	0.93	1.35	0.58	0.95	...
Price Range	45.91-37.33	42.81-33.73	40.10-26.84	30.09-11.90	27.95-13.78	...	...	...
P/E Ratio	15.51-12.61	15.62-12.31	18.48-12.37	13.87-5.48	...	...	...	...
Average Yield %	3.22	3.18	2.57	0.67	...	...	...	...

Address: 5301 Legacy Drive, Plano, TX 75024 **Telephone:** 972-673-7000	**Web Site:** www.drpeppersnapplegroup.com **Officers:** Wayne R. Sanders Chairman Larry D. Young - President, Chief Executive Officer	**Auditors:** Deloitte & Touche LLP **Investor Contact:** 972-673-7935 **Transfer Agents:** Computershare Investor Services, Canton, MA

247

DONALDSON CO. INC.

Exchange	Symbol	Price	52Wk Range	Yield	P/E	Div Achiever
NYS	DCI	$36.19 (3/28/2013)	38.04-31.40	1.11	22.20	17 Years

*7 Year Price Score 129.39 *NYSE Composite Index=100   *12 Month Price Score 97.11

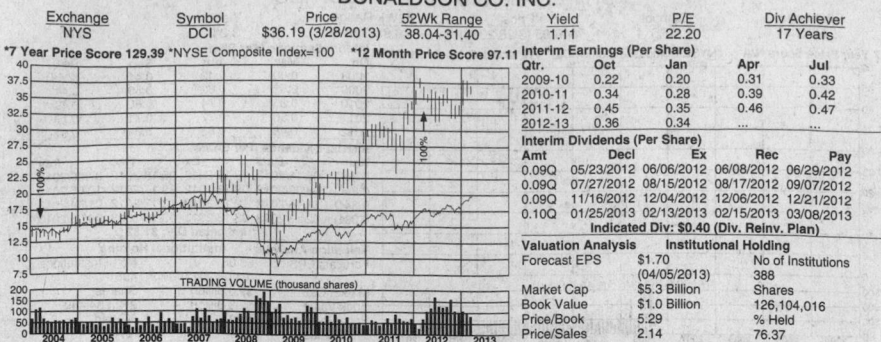

Interim Earnings (Per Share)

Qtr.	Oct	Jan	Apr	Jul
2009-10	0.22	0.20	0.31	0.33
2010-11	0.34	0.28	0.39	0.42
2011-12	0.45	0.35	0.46	0.47
2012-13	0.36	0.34	...	...

Interim Dividends (Per Share)

Amt	Decl	Ex	Rec	Pay
0.09Q	05/23/2012	06/06/2012	06/08/2012	06/29/2012
0.09Q	07/27/2012	08/15/2012	08/17/2012	09/07/2012
0.09Q	11/16/2012	12/04/2012	12/06/2012	12/21/2012
0.10Q	01/25/2013	02/13/2013	02/15/2013	03/08/2013

Indicated Div: $0.40 (Div. Reinv. Plan)

Valuation Analysis   **Institutional Holding**

Forecast EPS	$1.70 (04/05/2013)	No of Institutions 388
Market Cap	$5.3 Billion	Shares
Book Value	$1.0 Billion	126,104,016
Price/Book	5.29	% Held
Price/Sales	2.14	76.37

Business Summary: Industrial Machinery & Equipment (MIC: 7.2.1 SIC: 3564 NAIC: 333411)

Donaldson is a manufacturer of filtration systems and replacement parts. Co.'s product mix includes air and liquid filtration systems and exhaust and emission control products. Co. has two segments. Co.'s Engine Products segment consist of air filtration systems, exhaust and emissions systems, liquid filtration systems, and replacement filters. Co.'s Industrial Products segment consist of dust, fume, and mist collectors, compressed air purification systems, air filtration systems for gas turbines, PTFE membrane-based products, and specialized air filtration systems for applications including computer hard disk drives.

Recent Developments: For the quarter ended Jan 31 2013, net income decreased 5.6% to US$50.8 million from US$53.8 million in the year-earlier quarter. Revenues were US$596.0 million, up 2.6% from US$580.9 million the year before. Operating income was US$71.2 million versus US$74.8 million in the prior-year quarter, a decrease of 4.8%. Direct operating expenses rose 4.5% to US$397.1 million from US$380.1 million in the comparable period the year before. Indirect operating expenses increased 1.4% to US$127.8 million from US$126.0 million in the equivalent prior-year period.

Prospects: Our evaluation of Donaldson Co. Inc. as of Apr. 7, 2013 is the result of our systematic analysis on three basic characteristics: earnings strength, relative valuation, and recent stock price movement. The company has managed to produce a neutral trend in earnings per share over the past 5 quarters and while recent estimates for the company have remained steady, DCI has posted results that fell short of analysts expectations. Based on operating earnings yield, the company is about fairly valued when compared to all of the companies in our coverage universe. Share price changes over the past year indicates that DCI will perform in line with the market over the near term.

Financial Data
(US$ in Thousands)

	6 Mos	3 Mos	07/31/2012	07/31/2011	07/31/2010	07/31/2009	07/31/2008	07/31/2007
Earnings Per Share	1.63	1.64	1.73	1.44	1.05	0.83	1.06	0.92
Cash Flow Per Share	1.80	1.78	1.72	1.59	1.30	1.78	1.09	0.73
Tang Book Value Per Share	5.40	5.07	4.75	4.70	3.42	2.94	3.60	2.87
Dividends Per Share	0.350	0.335	0.320	0.268	0.235	0.228	0.210	0.180
Dividend Payout %	21.47	20.43	18.50	18.64	22.38	27.25	19.81	19.67
Income Statement								
Total Revenue	1,184,983	588,947	2,493,248	2,294,029	1,877,064	1,868,629	2,232,521	1,918,828
EBITDA	185,979	95,375	437,569	379,288	295,351	231,343	305,113	266,020
Depn & Amortn	32,896	16,026	55,300	54,500	53,200	52,900	52,400	46,600
Income Before Taxes	147,527	76,678	370,780	312,263	230,176	161,425	236,163	204,861
Income Taxes	42,601	22,565	106,479	86,972	64,013	29,518	64,210	54,144
Net Income	104,926	54,113	264,301	225,291	166,163	131,907	171,953	150,717
Average Shares	149,988	151,524	152,940	157,196	158,355	158,344	162,422	164,871
Balance Sheet								
Current Assets	1,032,840	1,048,413	1,085,662	1,066,582	860,215	676,767	853,757	673,644
Total Assets	1,718,668	1,712,498	1,730,082	1,726,093	1,499,506	1,333,996	1,548,622	1,319,017
Current Liabilities	485,011	444,929	498,523	496,244	389,256	300,084	516,707	458,944
Long-Term Obligations	120,375	202,473	203,483	205,748	256,192	253,674	176,475	129,004
Total Liabilities	714,488	757,316	820,068	791,382	752,873	645,378	808,587	694,319
Stockholders' Equity	1,004,180	955,182	910,014	934,711	746,633	688,618	740,035	624,698
Shares Outstanding	146,882	146,791	147,662	150,794	152,841	154,695	155,243	158,285
Statistical Record								
Return on Assets %	14.52	14.45	15.25	13.97	11.73	9.15	11.96	12.34
Return on Equity %	25.72	27.11	28.58	26.80	23.15	18.47	25.13	25.73
EBITDA Margin %	15.69	16.19	17.55	16.53	15.73	12.38	13.67	13.86
Net Margin %	8.85	9.19	10.60	9.82	8.85	7.06	7.70	7.85
Asset Turnover	1.46	1.43	1.44	1.42	1.32	1.30	1.55	1.57
Current Ratio	2.13	2.36	2.18	2.15	2.21	2.26	1.65	1.47
Debt to Equity	0.12	0.21	0.22	0.22	0.34	0.37	0.24	0.21
Price Range	38.20-31.40	38.20-30.97	38.20-23.31	31.29-20.95	23.84-16.44	23.97-11.00	25.77-17.96	19.27-16.00
P/E Ratio	23.44-19.26	23.29-18.88	22.08-13.47	21.73-14.55	22.70-15.66	28.88-13.25	24.32-16.94	20.95-17.39
Average Yield %	1.01	0.97	0.97	0.98	1.13	1.34	0.99	1.01

Address: 1400 West 94th Street, Minneapolis, MN 55431 Telephone: 952-887-3131	Web Site: www.donaldson.com Officers: William M. Cook - Chairman, President, Chief Executive Officer Charles J. McMurray - Senior Vice President, Chief Administrative Officer	Auditors: PricewaterhouseCoopers LLP Investor Contact: 952-887-3753 Transfer Agents: Wells Fargo Shareowner Services, St. Paul, MN

DOUGLAS EMMETT INC

	Exchange	Symbol	Price	52Wk Range	Yield	P/E
	NYS	DEI	$24.93 (3/28/2013)	25.32-21.10	2.89	155.81

*7 Year Price Score N/A   *NSYE Composite Index=100   *12 Month Price Score 96.23

Interim Earnings (Per Share)

Qtr.	Mar	Jun	Sep	Dec
2008	(0.02)	(0.08)	(0.08)	(0.05)
2009	(0.02)	(0.06)	(0.07)	(0.07)
2010	(0.07)	(0.07)	(0.03)	(0.05)
2011	0.00	(0.04)	0.03	0.03
2012	0.04	0.05	0.04	0.04

Interim Dividends (Per Share)

Amt	Decl	Ex	Rec	Pay
0.15Q	05/24/2012	06/27/2012	06/29/2012	07/13/2012
0.15Q	09/13/2012	09/26/2012	09/28/2012	10/15/2012
0.18Q	12/06/2012	12/27/2012	12/31/2012	01/15/2013
0.18Q	03/07/2013	03/26/2013	03/28/2013	04/15/2013

Indicated Div: $0.72

Valuation Analysis / **Institutional Holding**

Forecast EPS $0.31 (04/05/2013) — No of Institutions 243

Market Cap $3.5 Billion — Shares 150,358,624

Book Value $2.0 Billion — % Held 99.92

Price/Book 1.78

Price/Sales 6.08

Business Summary: REITs (MIC: 5.3.1 SIC: 6798 NAIC: 525930)

Douglas Emmett is a self-administered and self-managed real estate investment trust. Through Co.'s interest in Douglas Emmett Properties, LP and its subsidiaries, as well as its investment in Co.'s unconsolidated institutional real estate funds, Co. owns or partially owns, manages, leases, acquires and develops real estate, consisting primarily of office and multifamily properties. As of Dec 31 2011, Co. owned a consolidated portfolio of 50 office properties (including ancillary retail space) and nine multifamily properties, as well as the fee interests in two parcels of land. Co. has two reportable segments: Office Properties and Multifamily Properties.

Recent Developments: For the year ended Dec 31 2012, net income increased to US$28.3 million from US$2.3 million in the prior year. Revenues were US$579.0 million, up 0.6% from US$575.3 million the year before.

Prospects: Our evaluation of Douglas Emmett Inc. as of Apr. 7, 2013 is the result of our systematic analysis on three basic characteristics: earnings strength, relative valuation, and recent stock price movement. The company has suffered a very negative trend in earnings per share over the past 5 quarters and while recent estimates for the company have remained steady, DEI has posted results that fell short of analysts expectations. Based on operating earnings yield, the company is overvalued when compared to all of the companies in our coverage universe. Share price changes over the past year indicates that DEI will perform poorly over the near term.

Financial Data

(US$ in Thousands)	12/31/2012	12/31/2011	12/31/2010	12/31/2009	12/31/2008	12/31/2007	12/31/2006
Earnings Per Share	0.16	0.01	(0.22)	(0.22)	(0.23)	(0.12)	(0.18)
Cash Flow Per Share	1.50	1.65	1.54	1.48	1.51	1.37	...
Tang Book Value Per Share	13.97	14.17	14.63	14.64	14.40	16.42	18.05
Dividends Per Share	0.630	0.490	0.400	0.400	0.750	0.700	0.120
Dividend Payout %	393.75	...	...	...	...	...	...
Income Statement							
Total Revenue	578,999	575,337	570,844	571,060	608,094	518,220	86,995
EBITDA	325,923	306,663	320,876	334,140	399,586	350,832	29,272
Depn & Amortn	1,710	2,867	6,971	3,279	245,352	209,600	32,689
Income Before Taxes	177,520	155,341	146,998	151,637	(35,913)	(18,689)	(29,543)
Net Income	22,942	1,451	(26,423)	(27,064)	(27,993)	(13,008)	(20,591)
Average Shares	173,120	159,966	122,714	121,552	120,725	112,645	115,005
Balance Sheet							
Current Assets	378,596	412,803	281,280	88,882	24,995	21,066	19,955
Total Assets	6,103,807	6,231,602	6,279,289	6,059,932	6,760,804	6,189,968	6,200,118
Current Liabilities	171,914	193,074	212,300	256,894	322,997	331,605	357,856
Long-Term Obligations	3,441,140	3,624,156	3,668,133	3,273,459	3,692,785	3,105,677	2,789,702
Total Liabilities	4,124,151	4,366,496	4,452,228	4,266,569	4,985,615	4,360,129	4,088,345
Stockholders' Equity	1,979,656	1,865,106	1,827,061	1,793,363	1,775,189	1,829,839	2,111,773
Shares Outstanding	141,245	131,070	124,131	121,596	121,897	109,833	115,005
Statistical Record							
Return on Assets %	0.37	0.02	N.M.	N.M.	N.M.	N.M.	...
Return on Equity %	1.19	0.08	N.M.	N.M.	N.M.	N.M.	...
EBITDA Margin %	56.29	53.30	56.21	58.51	65.71	67.70	33.65
Net Margin %	3.96	0.25	N.M.	N.M.	N.M.	N.M.	N.M.
Asset Turnover	0.09	0.09	0.09	0.09	0.09	0.08	...
Current Ratio	2.20	2.14	1.32	0.35	0.08	0.06	0.06
Debt to Equity	1.74	1.94	2.01	1.83	2.08	1.70	1.32
Price Range	24.48-18.46	21.05-15.54	18.56-13.00	14.85-6.36	24.97-8.26	29.01-22.61	26.60-23.03
P/E Ratio	153.00-115.38	N.M.	...	...	...	...	...
Average Yield %	2.78	2.63	2.51	3.73	3.68	2.74	0.48

Address: 808 Wilshire Boulevard, 2nd Floor, Santa Monica, CA 90401
Telephone: 310-255-7700

Web Site: www.douglasemmett.com
Officers: Dan A. Emmett - Chairman Jordan L. Kaplan - President, Chief Executive Officer

Auditors: Ernst & Young LLP
Investor Contact: 310-255-7751
Transfer Agents: Computershare Investor Services

249

DOVER CORP

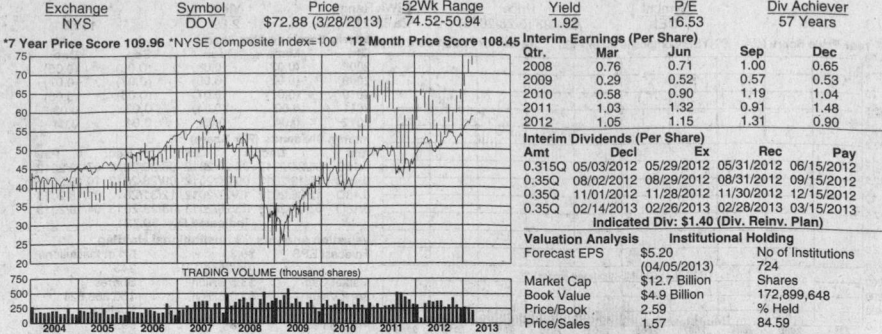

Exchange	Symbol	Price	52Wk Range	Yield	P/E	Div Achiever
NYS	DOV	$72.88 (3/28/2013)	74.52-50.94	1.92	16.53	57 Years

*7 Year Price Score 109.96 *NYSE Composite Index=100 *12 Month Price Score 108.45

Interim Earnings (Per Share)

Qtr.	Mar	Jun	Sep	Dec
2008	0.76	0.71	1.00	0.65
2009	0.29	0.52	0.57	0.53
2010	0.58	0.90	1.19	1.04
2011	1.03	1.32	0.91	1.48
2012	1.05	1.15	1.31	0.90

Interim Dividends (Per Share)

Amt	Decl	Ex	Rec	Pay
0.315Q	05/03/2012	05/29/2012	05/31/2012	06/15/2012
0.35Q	08/02/2012	08/29/2012	08/31/2012	09/15/2012
0.35Q	11/01/2012	11/28/2012	11/30/2012	12/15/2012
0.35Q	02/14/2013	02/26/2013	02/28/2013	03/15/2013

Indicated Div: $1.40 (Div. Reinv. Plan)

Valuation Analysis / Institutional Holding

Forecast EPS	$5.20 (04/05/2013)	No of Institutions 724
Market Cap	$12.7 Billion	Shares 172,899,648
Book Value	$4.9 Billion	% Held
Price/Book	2.59	84.59
Price/Sales	1.57	

Business Summary: Industrial Machinery & Equipment (MIC: 7.2.1 SIC: 3559 NAIC: 333220)

Dover is a manufacturer focusing on equipment and components, systems, and support services. Co.'s segments are: Communication Technologies, engages in the design and manufacture of products and components in the consumer electronics, medical technology, aerospace/defense, and telecom/other markets; Energy, provides applications for the extraction and handling of oil and gas in the drilling, production, and downstream markets; Engineered Systems, which is comprised of two platforms, Fluid Solutions and Refrigeration & Industrial; and Printing & Identification, provides printing, coding, and dispensing applications for the consumer goods, food, pharmaceutical, and industrial markets.

Recent Developments: For the year ended Dec 31 2012, income from continuing operations increased 7.8% to US$833.1 million from US$773.2 million a year earlier. Net income decreased 9.4% to US$811.1 million from US$895.2 million in the prior year. Revenues were US$8.10 billion, up 10.0% from US$7.37 billion the year before. Operating income was US$1.27 billion versus US$1.12 billion in the prior year, an increase of 12.6%. Direct operating expenses rose 10.5% to US$5.00 billion from US$4.52 billion in the comparable period the year before. Indirect operating expenses increased 7.0% to US$1.84 billion from US$1.72 billion in the equivalent prior-year period.

Prospects: Our evaluation of Dover Corp. as of Apr. 7, 2013 is the result of our systematic analysis on three basic characteristics: earnings strength, relative valuation, and recent stock price movement. The company has enjoyed a very positive trend in earnings per share over the past 5 quarters. However, while recent estimates for the company have been mixed, DOV has posted better than expected results. Based on operating earnings yield, the company is undervalued when compared to all of the companies in our coverage universe. Share price changes over the past year indicates that DOV will perform well over the near term.

Financial Data
(US$ in Thousands)

	12/31/2012	12/31/2011	12/31/2010	12/31/2009	12/31/2008	12/31/2007	12/31/2006	12/31/2005
Earnings Per Share	4.41	4.74	3.70	1.91	3.12	3.26	2.73	2.50
Cash Flow Per Share	6.93	5.69	5.09	4.31	5.35	4.48	4.31	3.25
Tang Book Value Per Share	N.M.	N.M.	1.35	N.M.	N.M.	N.M.	N.M.	N.M.
Dividends Per Share	1.330	1.180	1.070	1.020	0.900	0.770	0.710	0.660
Dividend Payout %	30.16	24.89	28.92	53.40	28.85	23.62	26.01	26.40
Income Statement								
Total Revenue	8,104,339	7,950,140	7,132,648	5,775,689	7,568,888	7,226,089	6,511,623	6,078,380
EBITDA	1,419,201	1,386,757	1,195,340	751,593	1,201,356	1,127,012	1,032,453	847,194
Depn & Amortn	160,489	175,997	163,915	159,600	159,300	150,400	132,600	131,400
Income Before Taxes	1,137,571	1,095,164	925,084	491,618	946,019	887,604	822,869	643,588
Income Taxes	304,452	248,799	217,176	119,724	251,261	234,331	219,541	169,135
Net Income	811,070	895,243	700,104	356,438	590,831	661,080	561,782	510,142
Average Shares	183,993	188,887	189,170	186,736	189,269	202,918	205,497	204,177
Balance Sheet								
Current Assets	3,027,844	3,397,130	3,261,871	2,522,707	2,614,185	2,544,238	2,271,506	1,975,925
Total Assets	10,443,940	9,501,450	8,562,894	7,882,403	7,867,304	8,069,770	7,626,658	6,573,032
Current Liabilities	1,986,628	1,202,981	1,194,386	969,176	1,237,580	1,681,192	1,433,980	1,207,454
Long-Term Obligations	2,189,350	2,186,230	1,790,886	1,825,260	1,860,729	1,452,003	1,480,491	1,344,173
Total Liabilities	5,524,711	4,570,895	4,036,332	3,798,795	4,074,438	4,123,597	3,815,636	3,243,509
Stockholders' Equity	4,919,230	4,930,555	4,526,562	4,083,608	3,792,866	3,946,173	3,811,022	3,329,523
Shares Outstanding	174,717	183,591	186,488	186,876	185,996	194,038	204,316	202,850
Statistical Record								
Return on Assets %	8.11	9.91	8.51	4.53	7.39	8.42	7.91	8.25
Return on Equity %	16.42	18.93	16.26	9.05	15.23	17.04	15.73	15.82
EBITDA Margin %	17.51	17.44	16.76	13.01	15.87	15.60	15.86	13.94
Net Margin %	10.01	11.26	9.82	6.17	7.81	9.15	8.63	8.39
Asset Turnover	0.81	0.88	0.87	0.73	0.95	0.92	0.92	0.98
Current Ratio	1.52	2.82	2.73	2.60	2.11	1.51	1.58	1.64
Debt to Equity	0.45	0.44	0.40	0.45	0.49	0.37	0.39	0.40
Price Range	65.71-50.94	69.84-44.64	58.96-41.05	42.87-22.06	54.18-23.97	54.44-44.34	51.58-41.49	41.94-34.70
P/E Ratio	14.90-11.55	14.73-9.42	15.94-11.09	22.45-11.55	17.37-7.68	16.70-13.60	18.89-15.20	16.78-13.88
Average Yield %	2.24	1.97	2.20	2.99	2.14	1.57	1.49	1.69

Address: 3005 Highland Parkway, Downers Grove, IL 60515 **Telephone:** 630-541-1540	**Web Site:** www.dovercorporation.com **Officers:** Robert W. Cremin - Chairman Robert A. Livingston - President, Chief Executive Officer	**Auditors:** PricewaterhouseCoopers LLP **Investor Contact:** 212-849-4539 **Transfer Agents:** Mellon Invester Services, South Hackensack, NJ

DOW CHEMICAL CO.

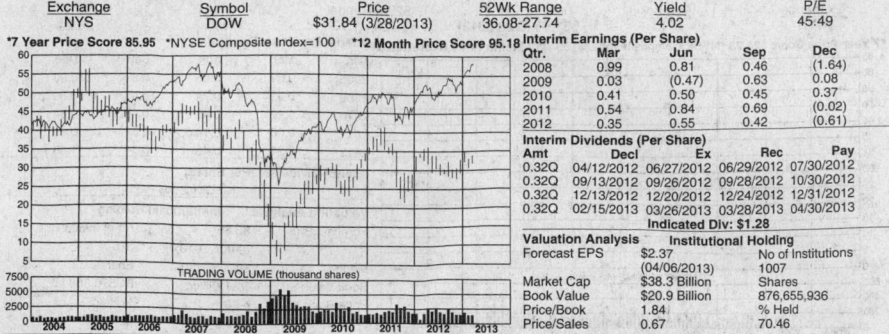

Exchange	Symbol	Price	52Wk Range	Yield	P/E
NYS	DOW	$31.84 (3/28/2013)	36.08-27.74	4.02	45.49

*7 Year Price Score 85.95 *NYSE Composite Index=100 *12 Month Price Score 95.18

Interim Earnings (Per Share)

Qtr.	Mar	Jun	Sep	Dec
2008	0.99	0.81	0.46	(1.64)
2009	0.03	(0.47)	0.63	0.08
2010	0.41	0.50	0.45	0.37
2011	0.54	0.84	0.69	(0.02)
2012	0.35	0.55	0.42	(0.61)

Interim Dividends (Per Share)

Amt	Decl	Ex	Rec	Pay
0.32Q	04/12/2012	06/27/2012	06/29/2012	07/30/2012
0.32Q	09/13/2012	09/26/2012	09/28/2012	10/30/2012
0.32Q	12/13/2012	12/20/2012	12/24/2012	12/31/2012
0.32Q	02/15/2013	03/26/2013	03/28/2013	04/30/2013

Indicated Div: $1.28

Valuation Analysis

		Institutional Holding	
Forecast EPS	$2.37	No of Institutions	
	(04/06/2013)	1007	
Market Cap	$38.3 Billion	Shares	
Book Value	$20.9 Billion	876,655,936	
Price/Book	1.84	% Held	
Price/Sales	0.67	70.46	

Business Summary: Plastics (MIC: 8.4.2 SIC: 2821 NAIC: 325211)

Dow Chemical is engaged in manufacturing and supplying products used primarily as raw materials in the manufacture of customer products and services. Co. serves the following industries: appliance; automotive; agricultural; building and construction; chemical processing; electronics; furniture; housewares; oil and gas; packaging; paints, coatings and adhesives; personal care; pharmaceutical; processed foods; pulp and paper; textile and carpet; utilities; and water treatment. Co. conducts its operations through six segments: Electronic and Functional Materials, Coatings and Infrastructure Solutions, Agricultural Sciences, Performance Materials, Performance Plastics and Feedstocks and Energy.

Recent Developments: For the year ended Dec 31 2012, net income decreased 60.5% to US$1.10 billion from US$2.78 billion in the prior year. Revenues were US$56.79 billion, down 5.3% from US$59.99 billion the year before. Direct operating expenses declined 6.3% to US$47.79 billion in the comparable period the year before. Indirect operating expenses increased 33.2% to US$6.61 billion from US$4.96 billion in the equivalent prior-year period.

Prospects: Our evaluation of Dow Chemical Co. as of Apr. 7, 2013 is the result of our systematic analysis on three basic characteristics: earnings strength, relative valuation, and recent stock price movement. The company has enjoyed a very positive trend in earnings per share over the past 5 quarters and while recent estimates for the company have remained steady, DOW has posted results that fell short of analysts expectations. Based on operating earnings yield, the company is undervalued when compared to all of the companies in our coverage universe. Share price changes over the past year indicates that DOW will perform in line with the market over the near term.

Financial Data
(US$ in Millions)

	12/31/2012	12/31/2011	12/31/2010	12/31/2009	12/31/2008	12/31/2007	12/31/2006	12/31/2005
Earnings Per Share	0.70	2.05	1.72	0.32	0.62	2.99	3.82	4.62
Cash Flow Per Share	3.47	3.38	3.64	1.99	5.05	4.70	4.32	4.64
Tang Book Value Per Share	N.M.	0.24	N.M.	N.M.	10.59	17.05	15.00	13.17
Dividends Per Share	1.210	0.900	0.600	0.600	1.680	1.635	1.500	1.340
Dividend Payout %	172.86	43.90	34.88	187.50	270.97	54.68	39.27	29.00
Income Statement								
Total Revenue	56,786	59,985	53,674	44,875	57,514	53,513	49,124	46,307
EBITDA	4,892	6,352	5,924	4,061	3,204	5,592	6,398	7,958
Depn & Amortn	2,535	2,673	2,798	2,690	2,108	2,031	1,954	1,959
Income Before Taxes	1,129	2,378	1,690	(161)	534	3,107	4,013	5,435
Income Taxes	565	817	481	(97)	667	1,244	1,155	1,782
Net Income	1,182	2,742	2,310	648	579	2,887	3,724	4,515
Average Shares	1,176	1,158	1,143	1,053	939	965	974	976
Balance Sheet								
Current Assets	23,684	23,422	23,781	19,560	16,060	18,654	17,209	17,404
Total Assets	69,605	69,224	69,588	65,937	45,474	48,801	45,581	45,934
Current Liabilities	11,493	13,634	13,896	13,106	13,108	12,445	10,601	10,663
Long-Term Obligations	19,919	18,310	20,605	19,152	8,042	7,581	8,036	9,186
Total Liabilities	48,728	46,943	47,749	45,382	31,463	28,412	27,516	29,610
Stockholders' Equity	20,877	22,281	21,839	20,555	14,011	20,389	18,065	16,324
Shares Outstanding	1,203	1,184	1,167	1,150	924	940	958	967
Statistical Record								
Return on Assets %	1.70	3.95	3.41	1.16	1.22	6.12	8.14	9.83
Return on Equity %	5.46	12.43	10.90	3.75	3.36	15.02	21.66	30.51
EBITDA Margin %	8.61	10.59	11.04	9.05	5.57	10.45	13.02	17.19
Net Margin %	2.08	4.57	4.30	1.44	1.01	5.39	7.58	9.75
Asset Turnover	0.82	0.86	0.79	0.81	1.22	1.13	1.07	1.01
Current Ratio	2.06	1.72	1.71	1.49	1.23	1.50	1.62	1.63
Debt to Equity	0.95	0.82	0.94	0.93	0.57	0.37	0.44	0.56
Price Range	36.08-27.74	41.34-21.51	34.41-22.97	29.42-6.33	42.88-15.09	47.67-39.27	44.93-33.54	56.42-40.63
P/E Ratio	51.54-39.63	20.17-10.49	20.01-13.35	91.94-19.78	69.16-24.34	15.94-13.13	11.76-8.78	12.21-8.79
Average Yield %	3.86	2.76	2.09	3.25	5.05	3.75	3.75	2.86

Address: 2030 Dow Center, Midland, MI 48674 **Telephone:** 989-636-1000 **Fax:** 989-636-3518	**Web Site:** www.dow.com **Officers:** Andrew N. Liveris - Chairman, President, Chief Executive Officer William F. Banholzer - Executive Vice President, Chief Technology Officer	**Auditors:** Deloitte & Touche LLP **Investor Contact:** 800-422-8193 **Transfer Agents:** Computershare, Inc. Pittsburgh, PA

DRESSER-RAND GROUP INC

Exchange	Symbol	Price	52Wk Range	Yield	P/E
NYS	DRC	$61.66 (3/28/2013)	63.24-41.13	N/A	26.24

*7 Year Price Score 124.73 *NYSE Composite Index=100 ***12 Month Price Score 106.54**

Interim Earnings (Per Share)

Qtr.	Mar	Jun	Sep	Dec
2008	0.32	0.55	0.57	0.93
2009	0.42	0.74	0.91	0.50
2010	0.27	0.43	0.46	0.64
2011	0.00	0.14	0.51	0.89
2012	0.31	0.45	0.54	1.05

Interim Dividends (Per Share)

No Dividends Paid

Valuation Analysis   **Institutional Holding**

Forecast EPS	$3.36	No of Institutions
	(04/06/2013)	316
Market Cap	$4.7 Billion	Shares
Book Value	$1.1 Billion	81,570,368
Price/Book	4.28	% Held
Price/Sales	1.71	92.45

Business Summary: Equipment & Services (MIC: 9.1.3 SIC: 3511 NAIC: 333611)

Dresser-Rand Group is a supplier of rotating equipment for the oil, gas, chemical, petrochemical, process, power, military and other industries. Co.'s rotating equipment is also supplied to the environmental market space within energy infrastructure. Co. has two segments: new units, which manufactures turbo and reciprocating compression equipment, steam turbines, gas turbines and gas and diesel engines; and aftermarket parts and services, which consists of support applications for installed equipment and the operation and maintenance of several types of energy plants. The aftermarket parts and services segment includes engineering, manufacturing, sales and administrative support.

Recent Developments: For the year ended Dec 31 2012, net income increased 51.2% to US$182.9 million from US$121.0 million in the prior year. Revenues were US$2.74 billion, up 18.4% from US$2.31 billion the year before. Operating income was US$335.9 million versus US$258.7 million in the prior year, an increase of 29.8%. Direct operating expenses rose 20.2% to US$2.00 billion from US$1.67 billion in the comparable period the year before. Indirect operating expenses increased 2.9% to US$396.2 million from US$385.0 million in the equivalent prior-year period.

Prospects: Our evaluation of Dresser-Rand Group Inc. as of Apr. 7, 2013 is the result of our systematic analysis on three basic characteristics: earnings strength, relative valuation, and recent stock price movement. The company has suffered a very negative trend in earnings per share over the past 5 quarters. However, while recent estimates for the company have been lowered by analysts, DRC has posted results that fell short of analysts expectations. Based on operating earnings yield, the company is about fairly valued when compared to all of the companies in our coverage universe. Share price changes over the past year indicates that DRC will perform well over the near term.

Financial Data
(US$ in Thousands)

	12/31/2012	12/31/2011	12/31/2010	12/31/2009	12/31/2008	12/31/2007	12/31/2006	12/31/2005
Earnings Per Share	2.35	1.53	1.80	2.57	2.36	1.25	0.92	0.56
Cash Flow Per Share	1.23	1.39	4.64	1.59	2.80	2.53	1.92	3.19
Tang Book Value Per Share	N.M.	N.M.	2.17	1.16	N.M.	N.M.	N.M.	N.M.
Income Statement								
Total Revenue	2,736,400	2,311,600	1,953,600	2,289,600	2,194,700	1,665,000	1,501,527	1,208,203
EBITDA	392,000	291,400	280,100	375,700	361,300	236,500	216,193	134,851
Depn & Amortn	56,100	47,400	31,400	32,000	30,600	32,100	31,000	24,700
Income Before Taxes	275,700	182,300	215,700	311,900	301,300	167,600	137,316	53,114
Income Taxes	92,800	62,400	69,000	101,100	103,600	60,900	58,557	15,459
Net Income	179,000	119,700	146,700	210,800	197,700	106,700	78,759	37,095
Average Shares	76,276	78,319	81,545	81,876	83,837	85,586	85,453	66,547
Balance Sheet								
Current Assets	1,356,000	1,151,000	1,084,200	936,300	907,800	825,700	669,032	549,415
Total Assets	3,333,000	3,042,400	2,304,700	2,150,200	2,052,200	1,950,900	1,771,329	1,657,871
Current Liabilities	963,000	926,800	669,100	585,400	736,300	620,500	471,500	393,180
Long-Term Obligations	1,014,900	987,900	370,000	370,000	370,100	370,300	505,565	598,137
Total Liabilities	2,241,800	2,170,700	1,217,400	1,137,600	1,292,000	1,145,700	1,139,458	1,143,211
Stockholders' Equity	1,091,200	871,700	1,087,300	1,012,600	760,200	805,200	631,871	514,660
Shares Outstanding	75,675	75,363	80,436	82,513	81,958	85,826	85,477	85,476
Statistical Record								
Return on Assets %	5.60	4.48	6.59	10.03	9.85	5.73	4.59	2.18
Return on Equity %	18.19	12.22	13.97	23.78	25.19	14.85	13.74	7.67
EBITDA Margin %	14.33	12.61	14.34	16.41	16.46	14.20	14.40	11.16
Net Margin %	6.54	5.18	7.51	9.21	9.01	6.41	5.25	3.07
Asset Turnover	0.86	0.86	0.88	1.09	1.09	0.89	0.88	0.71
Current Ratio	1.41	1.24	1.62	1.60	1.23	1.33	1.42	1.40
Debt to Equity	0.93	1.13	0.34	0.37	0.49	0.46	0.80	1.16
Price Range	56.14-41.13	55.85-35.69	43.29-29.58	32.66-17.19	41.76-12.74	43.48-22.97	27.94-18.60	25.99-19.80
P/E Ratio	23.89-17.50	36.50-23.33	24.05-16.43	12.71-6.69	17.69-5.40	34.78-18.38	30.37-20.22	46.41-35.36

Address: West8 Tower, Suite 1000, 10205 Westheimer Road, Houston, TX 77042 Telephone: 713-354-6100	Web Site: www.dresser-rand.com Officers: William E. Macaulay - Chairman Vincent R. Volpe - President, Chief Executive Officer	Auditors: PricewaterhouseCoopers LLP Investor Contact: 713-973-5497 Transfer Agents: Computershare, Pittsburgh, PA

252

DRIL-QUIP, INC.

Exchange	Symbol	Price	52Wk Range	Yield	P/E
NYS	DRQ	$87.17 (3/28/2013)	88.00-58.72	N/A	29.65

*7 Year Price Score 117.57 *NYSE Composite Index=100 *12 Month Price Score 106.76

TRADING VOLUME (thousand shares)

Interim Earnings (Per Share)

Qtr.	Mar	Jun	Sep	Dec
2008	0.62	0.68	0.69	0.64
2009	0.63	0.68	0.63	0.72
2010	0.64	0.70	0.69	0.52
2011	0.54	0.55	0.58	0.69
2012	0.71	0.74	0.73	0.76

Interim Dividends (Per Share)

No Dividends Paid

Valuation Analysis		Institutional Holding	
Forecast EPS	$3.63	No of Institutions	
	(04/06/2013)	276	
Market Cap	$3.5 Billion	Shares	
Book Value	$1.1 Billion	44,540,268	
Price/Book	3.31	% Held	
Price/Sales	4.81	97.33	

Business Summary: Equipment & Services (MIC: 9.1.3 SIC: 3533 NAIC: 333132)

Dril-Quip designs, manufactures, sells and services offshore drilling and production equipment. Co.'s principal products consist of subsea and surface wellheads, subsea and surface production trees, subsea control systems and manifolds, mudline hanger systems, specialy connectors and associated pipe, drilling and production riser systems, liner hangers, wellhead connectors and diverters. Co. also provides technical advisory assistance on an as-requested basis during installation of its products, as well as rework and reconditioning services for customer-owned its products. Co.'s customers may rent or purchase running tools from Co. for use in the installation and retrieval of its products.

Recent Developments: For the year ended Dec 31 2012, net income increased 25.1% to US$119.2 million from US$95.3 million in the prior year. Revenues were US$733.0 million, up 21.9% from US$601.3 million the year before. Operating income was US$161.7 million versus US$129.6 million in the prior year, an increase of 24.7%. Direct operating expenses rose 24.8% to US$451.7 million from US$361.8 million in the comparable period the year before. Indirect operating expenses increased 8.9% to US$119.7 million from US$109.9 million in the equivalent prior-year period.

Prospects: Our evaluation of Dril-Quip Inc. as of Apr. 7, 2013 is the result of our systematic analysis on three basic characteristics: earnings strength, relative valuation, and recent stock price movement. The company has managed to produce a neutral trend in earnings per share over the past 5 quarters and while recent estimates for the company have been raised by analysts, DRQ has posted better than expected results. Based on operating earnings yield, the company is about fairly valued when compared to all of the companies in our coverage universe. Share price changes over the past year indicates that DRQ will perform in line with the market over the near term.

Financial Data

(US$ in Thousands)	12/31/2012	12/31/2011	12/31/2010	12/31/2009	12/31/2008	12/31/2007	12/31/2006	12/31/2005
Earnings Per Share	2.94	2.36	2.55	2.66	2.62	2.63	2.15	0.90
Cash Flow Per Share	(0.20)	2.54	2.69	3.48	1.02	2.04	2.36	(0.48)
Tang Book Value Per Share	26.35	23.03	20.68	17.78	14.34	14.52	11.58	8.55
Income Statement								
Total Revenue	733,031	601,342	566,251	540,204	542,771	495,557	442,742	340,829
EBITDA	187,916	152,652	159,588	160,037	158,567	154,038	137,497	62,623
Depn & Amortn	26,224	23,013	20,875	17,997	16,854	15,653	15,087	15,426
Income Before Taxes	162,122	130,004	138,903	142,391	144,984	146,290	125,373	47,410
Income Taxes	42,913	34,737	36,677	37,250	39,399	38,349	38,482	14,843
Net Income	119,209	95,267	102,226	105,141	105,585	107,941	86,891	32,567
Average Shares	40,523	40,322	40,060	39,538	40,292	41,007	40,342	36,206
Balance Sheet								
Current Assets	924,388	799,302	688,249	617,356	514,274	552,598	465,055	311,216
Total Assets	1,231,447	1,085,858	948,551	817,246	680,609	699,822	594,935	428,262
Current Liabilities	155,089	151,000	111,329	104,625	113,739	98,406	117,805	90,324
Long-Term Obligations	...	...	58	316	896	2,054	2,876	3,113
Total Liabilities	165,015	160,614	120,537	112,161	121,159	107,327	127,438	98,800
Stockholders' Equity	1,066,432	925,244	828,014	705,085	559,450	592,495	467,497	329,462
Shares Outstanding	40,475	40,175	40,041	39,658	39,022	40,793	40,357	38,543
Statistical Record								
Return on Assets %	10.26	9.37	11.58	14.04	15.26	16.67	16.98	8.90
Return on Equity %	11.94	10.87	13.34	16.63	18.28	20.37	21.81	11.93
EBITDA Margin %	25.64	25.39	28.18	29.63	29.21	31.08	31.06	18.37
Net Margin %	16.26	15.84	18.05	19.46	19.45	21.78	19.63	9.56
Asset Turnover	0.63	0.59	0.64	0.72	0.78	0.77	0.87	0.93
Current Ratio	5.96	5.29	6.18	5.90	4.52	5.62	3.95	3.45
Debt to Equity	...	...	N.M.	N.M.	N.M.	N.M.	0.01	0.01
Price Range	76.61-58.72	81.36-49.38	82.28-40.95	58.79-18.38	64.21-14.30	62.56-33.55	44.15-25.24	27.00-11.59
P/E Ratio	26.06-19.97	34.47-20.92	32.27-16.06	22.10-6.91	24.51-5.46	23.79-12.76	20.53-11.74	29.99-12.87

Address: 6401 N. Eldridge Parkway, Houston, TX 77041 Telephone: 713-939-7711	Web Site: www.dril-quip.com Officers: John V. Lovoi - Chairman Larry E. Reimert - Co-Chairman	Auditors: BDO USA, LLP Investor Contact: 713-939-7711 Transfer Agents: Computershare, Jersey City, NJ

DST SYSTEMS INC. (DE)

Exchange	Symbol	Price	52Wk Range	Yield	P/E
NYS	DST	$71.27 (3/28/2013)	71.27-49.72	1.68	10.07

*7 Year Price Score 93.90   *NYSE Composite Index=100   *12 Month Price Score 109.10

Interim Earnings (Per Share)

Qtr.	Mar	Jun	Sep	Dec
2008	1.12	0.86	0.91	1.37
2009	1.47	0.97	1.21	1.19
2010	1.58	2.00	1.16	1.99
2011	1.14	1.17	0.76	0.88
2012	1.22	3.17	1.87	0.81

Interim Dividends (Per Share)

Amt	Decl	Ex	Rec	Pay
0.35Q	09/20/2011	10/12/2011	10/14/2011	11/04/2011
0.40Q	02/24/2012	03/14/2012	03/16/2012	04/10/2012
0.40Q	10/04/2012	10/17/2012	10/19/2012	11/08/2012
0.30Q	01/30/2013	02/14/2013	02/19/2013	03/15/2013

Indicated Div: $1.20

Valuation Analysis   **Institutional Holding**

Forecast EPS	$4.56	No of Institutions
	(04/06/2013)	330
Market Cap	$3.2 Billion	Shares
Book Value	$1.1 Billion	32,436,658
Price/Book	2.92	% Held
Price/Sales	1.23	60.19

Business Summary: IT Services (MIC: 6.3.1 SIC: 7374 NAIC: 518210)

DST Systems provides information processing and software services and products. Co. has two operating segments: Financial Services, providing shareowner recordkeeping and distribution support, participant recordkeeping, investment management, business process management and customer contact, medical and pharmacy claims administration processing, and electronic file systems; and Output Solutions, providing single source print and electronic statement and billing output applications. In addition, investments in Co.'s real estate subsidiaries and affiliates, equity securities, private equity investments and certain financial interests have been aggregated into its Investments and Other segment.

Recent Developments: For the year ended Dec 31 2012, net income increased 81.8% to US$324.0 million from US$178.2 million in the prior year. Revenues were US$2.58 billion, up 7.9% from US$2.39 billion the year before. Operating income was US$157.3 million versus US$260.1 million in the prior year, a decrease of 39.5%. Indirect operating expenses increased 13.7% to US$2.42 billion from US$2.13 billion in the equivalent prior-year period.

Prospects: Our evaluation of DST Systems Inc. as of Apr. 7, 2013 is the result of our systematic analysis on three basic characteristics: earnings strength, relative valuation, and recent stock price movement. The company has produced a positive trend in earnings per share over the past 5 quarters and while recent estimates for the company have been mixed, DST has posted better than expected results. Based on operating earnings yield, the company is undervalued when compared to all of the companies in our coverage universe. Share price changes over the past year indicates that DST will perform well over the near term.

Financial Data

(US$ in Thousands)	12/31/2012	12/31/2011	12/31/2010	12/31/2009	12/31/2008	12/31/2007	12/31/2006	12/31/2005
Earnings Per Share	7.08	3.95	6.73	4.84	4.28	12.35	3.78	5.39
Cash Flow Per Share	4.80	8.85	7.56	7.31	8.53	0.85	5.47	2.23
Tang Book Value Per Share	11.40	3.72	11.79	8.31	1.78	16.56	5.58	.5.60
Dividends Per Share	0.800	0.700	0.600	...	...	...	...	...
Dividend Payout %	11.30	17.72	8.92	...	...	...	...	...
Income Statement								
Total Revenue	2,576,600	2,388,700	2,328,500	2,217,900	2,285,400	2,302,500	2,235,800	2,515,100
EBITDA	669,900	419,900	613,800	483,100	450,700	1,514,000	533,500	872,800
Depn & Amortn	139,100	121,100	127,500	123,700	119,700	127,100	125,400	148,000
Income Before Taxes	487,300	252,300	440,200	317,200	275,600	1,326,600	330,800	658,200
Income Taxes	195,500	95,800	159,100	112,900	67,400	514,500	105,600	278,400
Net Income	324,000	183,100	318,500	241,600	242,900	874,700	272,900	424,600
Average Shares	45,800	46,300	47,300	50,000	56,700	70,700	72,100	78,700
Balance Sheet								
Current Assets	954,300	766,900	997,200	678,900	556,400	739,000	652,500	760,400
Total Assets	3,392,500	3,428,600	3,339,400	2,912,800	2,509,400	3,395,900	3,119,100	3,029,500
Current Liabilities	1,378,500	1,073,700	1,104,900	1,281,200	652,200	1,526,200	1,596,500	1,622,300
Long-Term Obligations	492,200	1,059,500	923,300	563,800	1,345,400	97,200	493,200	541,400
Total Liabilities	2,312,800	2,608,600	2,515,000	2,278,400	2,271,200	2,236,800	2,546,800	2,533,800
Stockholders' Equity	1,079,700	820,000	824,400	634,400	238,200	1,159,100	572,300	495,700
Shares Outstanding	44,300	44,100	46,200	49,100	49,700	60,800	65,700	71,700
Statistical Record								
Return on Assets %	9.47	5.41	10.19	8.91	8.20	26.85	8.88	13.24
Return on Equity %	34.02	22.27	43.67	55.37	34.67	101.04	51.10	68.40
EBITDA Margin %	26.00	17.58	26.36	21.78	19.72	65.75	23.86	34.70
Net Margin %	12.57	7.67	13.68	10.89	10.63	37.99	12.21	16.88
Asset Turnover	0.75	0.71	0.74	0.82	0.77	0.71	0.73	0.78
Current Ratio	0.69	0.71	0.90	0.53	0.85	0.48	0.41	0.47
Debt to Equity	0.46	1.29	1.12	0.89	5.65	0.08	0.86	1.09
Price Range	62.33-46.33	56.10-41.23	46.61-35.68	47.31-25.89	82.55-32.04	88.23-63.05	63.89-55.31	62.14-44.38
P/E Ratio	8.80-6.54	14.20-10.44	6.93-5.30	9.77-5.35	19.29-7.49	7.14-5.11	16.90-14.63	11.53-8.23
Average Yield %	1.48	1.44	1.44	...	...	...	...	...

Address: 333 West 11th Street, Kansas City, MO 64105 **Telephone:** 816-435-1000	**Web Site:** www.dstsystems.com **Officers:** Stephen C. Hooley - President, Chief Operating Officer, Chief Executive Officer Jonathan J. Boehm - Executive Vice President	**Auditors:** PricewaterhouseCoopers LLP **Investor Contact:** 816-435-8684 **Transfer Agents:** Computershare Trust Company, N.A., Providence, RI

DSW INC

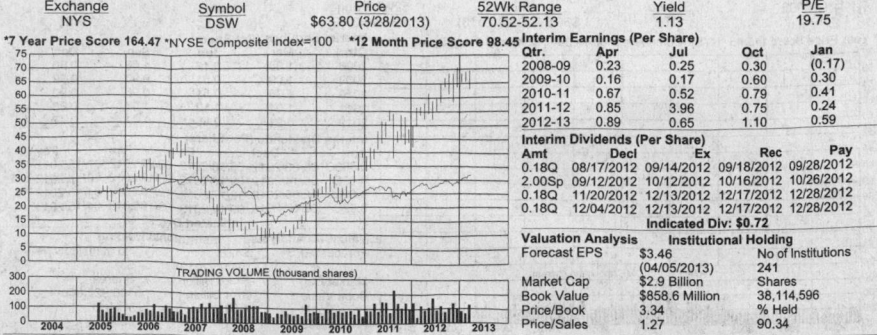

Exchange	Symbol	Price	52Wk Range	Yield	P/E
NYS	DSW	$63.80 (3/28/2013)	70.52-52.13	1.13	19.75

*7 Year Price Score 164.47   *NYSE Composite Index=100   *12 Month Price Score 98.45

Interim Earnings (Per Share)

Qtr.	Apr	Jul	Oct	Jan
2008-09	0.23	0.25	0.30	(0.17)
2009-10	0.16	0.17	0.60	0.30
2010-11	0.67	0.52	0.79	0.41
2011-12	0.85	3.96	0.75	0.24
2012-13	0.89	0.65	1.10	0.59

Interim Dividends (Per Share)

Amt	Decl	Ex	Rec	Pay
0.18Q	08/17/2012	09/14/2012	09/18/2012	09/28/2012
2.00Sp	09/12/2012	10/12/2012	10/16/2012	10/26/2012
0.18Q	11/20/2012	12/13/2012	12/17/2012	12/28/2012
0.18Q	12/04/2012	12/13/2012	12/17/2012	12/28/2012

Indicated Div: $0.72

Valuation Analysis		Institutional Holding	
Forecast EPS	$3.46 (04/05/2013)	No of Institutions	241
Market Cap	$2.9 Billion	Shares	38,114,596
Book Value	$858.6 Million	% Held	90.34
Price/Book	3.34		
Price/Sales	1.27		

Business Summary: Retail - Apparel and Accessories (MIC: 2.1.5 SIC: 5661 NAIC: 448210)

DSW is a footwear and accessories specialty retailer. Co. provides an assortment of brand name and designer dress, casual and athletic footwear for women and men, as well as accessories through its DSW stores and dsw.com. Co. also provides kids' shoes on dsw.com. Co. has two segments: the DSW segment, which includes DSW stores and dsw.com; and the leased business division segment. As of Jan 28 2012, Co. operated a total of 326 stores located in 40 states. Co. has registered a number of trademarks, service marks and domain names in the U.S. and internationally, including DSW®, DSW Shoe Warehouse® and DSW Designer Shoe Warehouse®.

Recent Developments: For the year ended Feb 2 2013, income from continuing operations decreased 27.5% to US$145.2 million from US$200.3 million a year earlier. Net income decreased 25.1% to US$146.4 million from US$195.5 million in the prior year. Revenues were US$2.26 billion, up 11.5% from US$2.02 billion the year before. Operating income was US$236.8 million versus US$151.5 million in the prior year, an increase of 56.4%. Direct operating expenses rose 11.9% to US$1.53 billion from US$1.37 billion in the comparable period the year before. Indirect operating expenses decreased 2.9% to US$487.9 million from US$502.5 million in the equivalent prior-year period.

Prospects: Our evaluation of DSW Inc. as of Apr. 7, 2013 is the result of our systematic analysis on three basic characteristics: earnings strength, relative valuation, and recent stock price movement. The company has managed to produce a neutral trend in earnings per share over the past 5 quarters. However, while recent estimates for the company have been lowered by analysts, DSW has posted results that fell short of analysts expectations. Based on expected earnings growth, the company is about fairly valued when compared to all of the companies in our coverage universe. Share price changes over the past year indicates that DSW will perform very well over the near term.

Financial Data

(US$ in Thousands)	02/02/2013	01/28/2012	01/29/2011	01/30/2010	01/31/2009	02/02/2008	02/03/2007	01/28/2006
Earnings Per Share	3.23	4.54	2.40	1.23	0.61	1.21	1.48	1.00
Cash Flow Per Share	5.73	6.10	3.21	3.74	2.21	1.62	1.98	2.94
Tang Book Value Per Share	18.50	17.57	13.91	11.37	9.99	9.17	7.81	6.21
Dividends Per Share	2.870	2.300	...	...	...	...	...	...
Dividend Payout %	88.85	50.66	...	...	...	...	...	...
Income Statement								
Total Revenue	2,257,778	2,024,329	1,822,376	1,602,605	1,462,944	1,405,615	1,279,060	1,144,061
EBITDA	301,638	207,773	223,067	137,466	78,133	106,494	121,518	90,445
Depn & Amortn	64,836	56,323	47,984	46,378	36,454	25,173	20,804	20,333
Income Before Taxes	240,613	142,269	177,279	91,891	44,285	87,291	107,627	62,607
Income Taxes	95,427	(58,069)	69,655	37,150	17,383	33,516	42,163	25,426
Net Income	146,439	174,788	107,624	54,741	26,902	53,775	65,464	37,181
Average Shares	45,303	37,138	44,918	44,517	44,218	44,273	44,222	37,347
Balance Sheet								
Current Assets	821,790	868,007	717,181	606,990	454,047	451,622	457,971	378,117
Total Assets	1,262,103	1,207,900	1,008,897	850,756	721,197	693,882	608,303	507,715
Current Liabilities	275,311	307,549	253,716	224,719	158,326	168,905	159,267	139,589
Total Liabilities	403,524	421,313	368,133	325,875	255,613	260,402	233,724	202,999
Stockholders' Equity	858,579	786,587	640,764	524,881	465,584	433,480	374,579	304,716
Shares Outstanding	45,012	43,291	44,187	43,891	44,018	43,966	43,941	43,892
Statistical Record								
Return on Assets %	11.67	15.81	11.61	6.98	3.81	8.28	11.54	8.26
Return on Equity %	17.51	24.56	18.52	11.08	6.00	13.35	18.96	15.42
EBITDA Margin %	13.36	10.26	12.24	8.58	5.34	7.58	9.50	7.91
Net Margin %	6.49	8.63	5.91	3.42	1.84	3.83	5.12	3.25
Asset Turnover	1.80	1.83	1.97	2.04	2.07	2.16	2.26	2.54
Current Ratio	2.98	2.82	2.83	2.70	2.87	2.67	2.88	2.71
Price Range	70.52-49.41	55.31-33.29	40.21-21.92	26.91-6.67	20.41-8.00	44.11-15.90	41.14-26.73	27.70-17.71
P/E Ratio	21.83-15.30	12.18-7.33	16.75-9.13	21.88-5.42	33.46-13.11	36.45-13.14	27.80-18.06	27.70-17.71
Average Yield %	4.76	5.00	...	...	...	...	...	...

Address: 810 DSW Drive, Columbus, OH 43219
Telephone: 614-237-7100

Web Site: www.dswinc.com
Officers: Jay L. Schottenstein - Chairman, Chief Executive Officer Deborah L. Ferree - Vice-Chairman, President, Executive Vice President, Chief Merchandising Officer

Auditors: Deloitte & Touche LLP
Investor Contact: 855-893-8691
Transfer Agents: Computershare Investor Services

DTE ENERGY CO.

Exchange	Symbol	Price	52Wk Range	Yield	P/E
NYS	DTE	$68.34 (3/28/2013)	68.34-53.83	3.63	19.25

*7 Year Price Score 115.45 *NYSE Composite Index=100 *12 Month Price Score 100.97

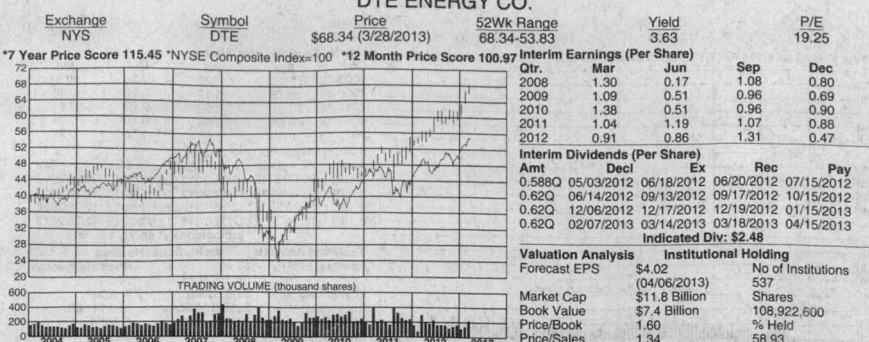

Interim Earnings (Per Share)

Qtr.	Mar	Jun	Sep	Dec
2008	1.30	0.17	1.08	0.80
2009	1.09	0.51	0.96	0.69
2010	1.38	0.51	0.96	0.90
2011	1.04	1.19	1.07	0.88
2012	0.91	0.86	1.31	0.47

Interim Dividends (Per Share)

Amt	Decl	Ex	Rec	Pay
0.588Q	05/03/2012	06/18/2012	06/20/2012	07/15/2012
0.62Q	06/14/2012	09/13/2012	09/17/2012	10/15/2012
0.62Q	12/06/2012	12/17/2012	12/19/2012	01/15/2013
0.62Q	02/07/2013	03/14/2013	03/18/2013	04/15/2013

Indicated Div: $2.48

Valuation Analysis | **Institutional Holding**

Forecast EPS	$4.02 (04/06/2013)	No of Institutions 537
Market Cap	$11.8 Billion	Shares 108,922,600
Book Value	$7.4 Billion	% Held
Price/Book	1.60	58.93
Price/Sales	1.34	

TRADING VOLUME (thousand shares)

Business Summary: Electric Utilities (MIC: 3.1.1 SIC: 4911 NAIC: 221111)

DTE Energy is a holding company. Through its subsidiary, Detroit Edison Company, Co. was engaged in the generation, purchase, distribution and sale of electricity to approximately 2.1 million customers in southeastern Michigan as of Dec 31 2012. Through its subsidiary, DTE Gas Company, Co. was engaged in the purchase, storage, transportation, distribution and sale of natural gas to approximately 1.2 million customers throughout Michigan as of Dec 31 2012 and the sale of storage and transportation capacity. Co.'s other businesses are involved in natural gas pipelines, gathering and storage; power and industrial projects; energy marketing and trading operations.

Recent Developments: For the year ended Dec 31 2012, income from continuing operations decreased 6.8% to US$674.0 million from US$723.0 million a year earlier. Net income decreased 14.2% to US$618.0 million from US$720.0 million in the prior year. Revenues were US$8.79 billion, down 0.8% from US$8.86 billion the year before. Operating income was US$1.28 billion versus US$1.42 billion in the prior year, a decrease of 10.0%. Direct operating expenses rose 0.6% to US$6.19 billion from US$6.15 billion in the comparable period the year before. Indirect operating expenses increased 2.8% to US$1.32 billion from US$1.29 billion in the equivalent prior-year period.

Prospects: Our evaluation of DTE Energy Co. as of Apr. 7, 2013 is the result of our systematic analysis on three basic characteristics: earnings strength, relative valuation, and recent stock price movement. The company has generated a negative trend in earnings per share over the past 5 quarters and while recent estimates for the company have remained steady, DTE has posted results that fell short of analysts expectations. Based on operating earnings yield, the company is undervalued when compared to all of the companies in our coverage universe. Share price changes over the past year indicates that DTE will perform in line with the market over the near term.

Financial Data
(US$ in Thousands)

	12/31/2012	12/31/2011	12/31/2010	12/31/2009	12/31/2008	12/31/2007	12/31/2006	12/31/2005
Earnings Per Share	3.55	4.18	3.74	3.24	3.36	5.70	2.43	3.05
Cash Flow Per Share	12.88	11.88	10.86	11.09	9.60	6.66	8.23	5.72
Tang Book Value Per Share	30.29	29.05	27.36	25.39	23.85	23.22	21.00	20.88
Dividends Per Share	2.415	2.322	2.180	2.120	2.120	2.120	2.075	2.060
Dividend Payout %	68.03	55.56	58.29	65.43	63.10	37.19	85.39	67.54
Income Statement								
Total Revenue	8,791,000	8,897,000	8,557,000	8,014,000	9,329,000	8,506,000	9,022,000	9,022,000
EBITDA	1,465,000	1,536,000	1,552,000	1,374,000	1,357,000	1,705,000	1,817,000	1,831,000
Depn & Amortn	75,000	65,000	65,000	66,000	54,000	42,000	1,014,000	872,000
Income Before Taxes	960,000	987,000	950,000	782,000	819,000	1,155,000	324,000	497,000
Income Taxes	286,000	267,000	311,000	247,000	288,000	364,000	137,000	202,000
Net Income	610,000	711,000	630,000	532,000	546,000	971,000	433,000	537,000
Average Shares	172,000	170,000	169,000	164,000	163,000	170,000	178,000	176,000
Balance Sheet								
Current Assets	2,915,000	3,196,000	3,167,000	2,877,000	3,328,000	3,995,000	3,961,000	4,682,000
Total Assets	26,339,000	26,009,000	24,896,000	24,195,000	24,590,000	23,754,000	23,785,000	23,335,000
Current Liabilities	2,768,000	2,628,000	2,749,000	2,645,000	3,013,000	4,231,000	4,164,000	4,920,000
Long-Term Obligations	7,014,000	7,187,000	7,089,000	7,370,000	7,741,000	6,971,000	7,474,000	7,080,000
Total Liabilities	18,966,000	19,000,000	18,174,000	17,917,000	18,595,000	17,901,000	17,936,000	17,566,000
Stockholders' Equity	7,373,000	7,009,000	6,722,000	6,278,000	5,995,000	5,853,000	5,849,000	5,769,000
Shares Outstanding	172,351	169,247	169,428	165,400	163,019	163,232	177,138	177,814
Statistical Record								
Return on Assets %	2.32	2.79	2.57	2.18	2.25	4.09	1.84	2.41
Return on Equity %	8.46	10.36	9.69	8.67	9.19	16.60	7.45	9.49
EBITDA Margin %	16.66	17.26	18.14	17.14	14.55	20.04	20.14	20.29
Net Margin %	6.94	7.99	7.36	6.64	5.85	11.42	4.80	5.95
Asset Turnover	0.33	0.35	0.35	0.33	0.38	0.36	0.38	0.40
Current Ratio	1.05	1.22	1.15	1.09	1.10	0.94	0.95	0.95
Debt to Equity	0.95	1.03	1.05	1.17	1.29	1.19	1.28	1.23
Price Range	62.10-52.96	55.05-44.03	48.97-41.50	44.64-23.61	45.23-30.42	54.20-43.96	49.19-39.00	48.11-41.81
P/E Ratio	17.49-14.92	13.17-10.53	13.09-11.10	13.78-7.29	13.46-9.05	9.51-7.71	20.24-16.05	15.77 13.71
Average Yield %	4.17	4.69	4.76	6.28	5.25	4.35	4.87	4.56

Address: One Energy Plaza, Detroit, MI 48226-1279	Web Site: www.dteenergy.cm	Auditors: PricewaterhouseCoopers LLP
Telephone: 313-235-4000	Officers: Gerard M. Anderson - Chairman, President, Chief Executive Officer David E. Meador - Executive Vice President, Chief Financial Officer	Investor Contact: 313-235-4200 Transfer Agents: Wells Fargo Shareowner Services, St. Paul, MN

DU PONT (E.I.) DE NEMOURS & CO

Exchange	Symbol	Price	52Wk Range	Yield	P/E
NYS	DD	$49.16 (3/28/2013)	53.80-41.95	3.50	16.66

*7 Year Price Score 98.84   *NYSE Composite Index=100   *12 Month Price Score 91.85

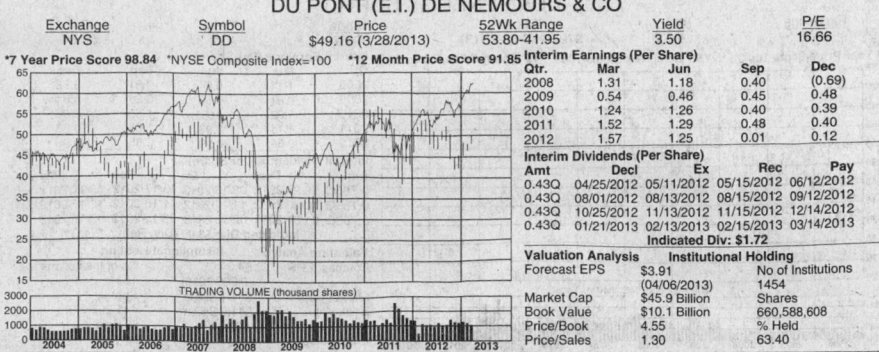

Interim Earnings (Per Share)

Qtr.	Mar	Jun	Sep	Dec
2008	1.31	1.18	0.40	(0.69)
2009	0.54	0.46	0.45	0.48
2010	1.24	1.26	0.40	0.39
2011	1.52	1.29	0.48	0.40
2012	1.57	1.25	0.01	0.12

Interim Dividends (Per Share)

Amt	Decl	Ex	Rec	Pay
0.43Q	04/25/2012	05/11/2012	05/15/2012	06/12/2012
0.43Q	08/01/2012	08/13/2012	08/15/2012	09/12/2012
0.43Q	10/25/2012	11/13/2012	11/15/2012	12/14/2012
0.43Q	01/21/2013	02/13/2013	02/15/2013	03/14/2013

Indicated Div: $1.72

Valuation Analysis   Institutional Holding

Forecast EPS	$3.91	No of Institutions
	(04/06/2013)	1454
Market Cap	$45.9 Billion	Shares
Book Value	$10.1 Billion	660,588,608
Price/Book	4.55	% Held
Price/Sales	1.30	63.40

Business Summary: Diversified Chemicals (MIC: 8.3.1 SIC: 2821 NAIC: 325211)

Du Pont (E.I.) de Nemours & Co is a science company. Subsidiaries and affiliates of Co. conducts manufacturing, seed production or selling activities and some are distributors of products manufactured by it. Co. consists of 13 businesses which are aggregated into eight reportable segments. Co.'s reportable segments are Agriculture, Electronics & Communications, Industrial Biosciences, Nutrition & Health, Performance Chemicals, Performance Materials, Safety & Protection and Pharmaceuticals. Co.'s primary products are corn hybrids, photopolymers and electronic materials, fluorochemicals, fluoropolymers, engineering polymers, packaging and industrial polymers, and elastomers, among others.

Recent Developments: For the year ended Dec 31 2012, income from continuing operations decreased 21.0% to US$2.49 billion from US$3.16 billion a year earlier. Net income decreased 19.9% to US$2.81 billion from US$3.51 billion in the prior year. Revenues were US$35.31 billion, up 2.6% from US$34.42 billion the year before. Direct operating expenses rose 2.9% to US$25.60 billion from US$24.87 billion in the comparable period the year before. Indirect operating expenses increased 14.3% to US$6.59 billion from US$5.77 billion in the equivalent prior-year period.

Prospects: Our evaluation of Du Pont (E.I.) de Nemours & Co as of Apr. 7, 2013 is the result of our systematic analysis on three basic characteristics: earnings strength, relative valuation, and recent stock price movement. The company has managed to produce a neutral trend in earnings per share over the past 5 quarters and while recent estimates for the company have been raised by analysts, DD has posted better than expected results. Based on operating earnings yield, the company is undervalued when compared to all of the companies in our coverage universe. Share price changes over the past year indicates that DD will perform poorly over the near term.

Financial Data

(US$ in Thousands)	12/31/2012	12/31/2011	12/31/2010	12/31/2009	12/31/2008	12/31/2007	12/31/2006	12/31/2005
Earnings Per Share	2.95	3.68	3.28	1.92	2.20	3.22	3.38	2.07
Cash Flow Per Share	5.18	5.55	5.02	5.24	3.46	4.68	4.05	2.59
Tang Book Value Per Share	0.12	N.M.	4.06	2.53	2.26	6.64	4.99	4.24
Dividends Per Share	1.700	1.640	1.640	1.640	1.640	1.520	1.480	1.460
Dividend Payout %	57.63	44.57	50.00	85.42	74.55	47.20	43.79	70.53
Income Statement								
Total Revenue	35,310,000	38,719,000	32,733,000	27,328,000	31,836,000	30,653,000	28,982,000	28,491,000
EBITDA	5,358,000	6,383,000	5,676,000	4,347,000	4,486,000	5,757,000	5,400,000	5,434,000
Depn & Amortn	1,779,000	1,654,000	1,375,000	1,755,000	1,719,000	1,584,000	1,611,000	1,358,000
Income Before Taxes	3,115,000	4,282,000	3,711,000	2,184,000	2,391,000	3,743,000	3,329,000	3,558,000
Income Taxes	622,000	772,000	659,000	415,000	381,000	748,000	196,000	1,468,000
Net Income	2,788,000	3,474,000	3,031,000	1,755,000	2,007,000	2,988,000	3,148,000	2,053,000
Average Shares	942,197	941,029	921,655	908,712	907,371	925,402	928,600	988,954
Balance Sheet								
Current Assets	21,191,000	18,058,000	19,059,000	17,288,000	15,311,000	13,160,000	12,870,000	12,422,000
Total Assets	49,736,000	48,492,000	40,410,000	38,185,000	36,209,000	34,131,000	31,777,000	33,250,000
Current Liabilities	13,549,000	11,185,000	9,389,000	9,390,000	9,710,000	8,541,000	7,940,000	7,463,000
Long-Term Obligations	10,465,000	11,736,000	10,137,000	9,528,000	7,638,000	5,955,000	6,013,000	6,783,000
Total Liabilities	39,648,000	39,899,000	31,132,000	30,970,000	29,084,000	22,995,000	22,355,000	24,343,000
Stockholders' Equity	10,088,000	8,593,000	9,278,000	7,215,000	7,125,000	11,136,000	9,422,000	8,907,000
Shares Outstanding	933,016	926,123	917,310	903,814	902,374	899,289	922,067	919,610
Statistical Record								
Return on Assets %	5.66	7.82	7.71	4.72	5.69	9.07	9.68	5.96
Return on Equity %	29.77	38.88	36.75	24.48	21.92	29.07	34.35	20.24
EBITDA Margin %	15.17	16.49	17.34	15.91	14.09	18.78	18.63	19.07
Net Margin %	7.90	8.97	9.26	6.42	6.30	9.75	10.86	7.21
Asset Turnover	0.72	0.87	0.83	0.73	0.90	0.93	0.89	0.83
Current Ratio	1.56	1.61	2.03	1.84	1.58	1.54	1.62	1.66
Debt to Equity	1.04	1.37	1.09	1.32	1.07	0.53	0.64	0.76
Price Range	53.80-41.95	56.79-38.49	50.02-32.19	35.38-16.14	52.25-21.95	53.35-42.58	49.47-38.88	54.55-37.83
P/E Ratio	18.24-14.22	15.43-10.46	15.25-9.81	18.43-8.41	23.75-9.98	16.57-13.22	14.64-11.50	26.35-18.28
Average Yield %	3.46	3.29	4.04	5.79	3.94	3.08	3.46	3.24

Address: 1007 Market Street, Wilmington, DE 19898 Telephone: 302-774-1000 Fax: 302-774-0748	Web Site: www.dupont.com Officers: Ellen J. Kullman - Chairwoman, Chief Executive Officer Nicholas C. Fanandakis - Executive Vice President, Senior Vice President, Chief Financial Officer	Auditors: PricewaterhouseCoopers LLP Investor Contact: 302-774-4994 Transfer Agents: Computershare Trust Company, N.A., Providence, RI

DUKE ENERGY CORP

Exchange	Symbol	Price	52Wk Range	Yield	P/E
NYS	DUK	$72.59 (3/28/2013)	72.59-59.87	4.22	23.64

*7 Year Price Score 106.32 ***NYSE Composite Index=100** ***12 Month Price Score 97.65**

Interim Earnings (Per Share)

Qtr.	Mar	Jun	Sep	Dec
2008	1.11	0.84	0.51	0.78
2009	0.81	0.63	0.24	0.81
2010	1.02	(0.51)	1.53	0.96
2011	1.14	0.99	1.05	0.66
2012	0.66	0.99	0.85	0.56

Interim Dividends (Per Share)

Amt	Decl	Ex	Rec	Pay
0.765Q	06/26/2012	08/15/2012	08/17/2012	09/17/2012
0.765Q	10/30/2012	11/14/2012	11/16/2012	12/17/2012
0.765Q	01/04/2013	02/13/2013	02/15/2013	03/18/2013

Indicated Div: $3.06 (Div. Reinv. Plan)

Valuation Analysis **Institutional Holding**

Forecast EPS	$4.34 (04/06/2013)	No of Institutions 1211
Market Cap	$51.1 Billion	Shares 441,258,272
Book Value	$41.0 Billion	% Held
Price/Book	1.25	N/A
Price/Sales	2.60	

TRADING VOLUME (thousand shares)

Business Summary: Electric Utilities (MIC: 3.1.1 SIC: 4931 NAIC: 221122)

Duke Energy is an energy company. Co.'s segments include U.S. Franchised Electric and Gas (USFE&G), Commercial Power and International Energy. USFE&G generates, transmits, distributes and sells electricity in central and western North Carolina, western South Carolina, central, north central and southern Indiana, northern Kentucky, and in southwestern Ohio. Commercial Power owns, operates and manages power plants and engages in the wholesale marketing and procurement of electric power. International Energy operates and manages power generation facilities and sells and markets electric power, natural gas, and natural gas liquids outside the U.S.

Recent Developments: For the year ended Dec 31 2012, income from continuing operations increased 1.9% to US$1.75 billion from US$1.71 billion a year earlier. Net income increased 4.0% to US$1.78 billion from US$1.71 billion in the prior year. Revenues were US$19.62 billion, up 35.1% from US$14.53 billion the year before. Operating income was US$3.13 billion versus US$2.78 billion in the prior year, an increase of 12.6%. Direct operating expenses rose 41.0% to US$12.57 billion from US$8.92 billion in the comparable period the year before. Indirect operating expenses increased 38.3% to US$3.92 billion from US$2.84 billion in the equivalent prior-year period.

Prospects: Our evaluation of Duke Energy Corp. Holding Co as of Apr. 7, 2013 is the result of our systematic analysis on three basic characteristics: earnings strength, relative valuation, and recent stock price movement. The company has generated a negative trend in earnings per share over the past 5 quarters and while recent estimates for the company have been mixed, DUK has posted better than expected results. Based on operating earnings yield, the company is undervalued when compared to all of the companies in our coverage universe. Share price changes over the past year indicates that DUK will perform poorly over the near term.

Financial Data
(US$ in Thousands)

	12/31/2012	12/31/2011	12/31/2010	12/31/2009	12/31/2008	12/31/2007	12/31/2006	12/31/2005
Earnings Per Share	3.07	3.84	3.00	2.49	3.21	3.54	4.71	5.64
Cash Flow Per Share	9.11	8.27	10.27	8.03	7.87	7.64	9.61	9.00
Tang Book Value Per Share	34.40	41.68	41.08	38.52	36.76	37.65	40.63	40.94
Dividends Per Share	1.530	2.970	2.910	2.820	2.700	2.580	3.780	3.510
Dividend Payout %	49.84	77.34	97.00	113.25	84.11	72.88	80.25	62.23
Income Statement								
Total Revenue	19,624,000	14,529,000	14,272,000	12,731,000	13,207,000	12,720,000	15,184,000	16,746,000
EBITDA	6,147,000	5,137,000	4,861,000	4,281,000	4,438,000	4,460,000	5,469,000	6,746,000
Depn & Amortn	2,652,000	2,026,000	1,994,000	1,846,000	1,834,000	1,888,000	2,215,000	1,884,000
Income Before Taxes	2,303,000	2,305,000	2,094,000	1,761,000	1,993,000	2,079,000	2,191,000	3,875,000
Income Taxes	705,000	752,000	890,000	758,000	616,000	712,000	843,000	1,283,000
Net Income	1,768,000	1,706,000	1,320,000	1,075,000	1,362,000	1,500,000	1,863,000	1,824,000
Average Shares	575,000	444,333	439,666	431,333	422,666	422,000	396,000	323,333
Balance Sheet								
Current Assets	10,122,000	6,880,000	6,223,000	5,766,000	5,273,000	4,925,000	6,940,000	7,957,000
Total Assets	113,856,000	62,526,000	59,090,000	57,040,000	53,077,000	49,704,000	68,700,000	54,723,000
Current Liabilities	10,029,000	5,528,000	3,897,000	4,088,000	4,345,000	5,708,000	6,613,000	8,418,000
Long-Term Obligations	36,351,000	18,679,000	17,935,000	16,113,000	13,250,000	9,498,000	18,118,000	14,547,000
Total Liabilities	72,900,000	39,754,000	36,568,000	35,290,000	32,089,000	28,505,000	42,598,000	38,284,000
Stockholders' Equity	40,956,000	22,772,000	22,522,000	21,750,000	20,988,000	21,199,000	26,102,000	16,439,000
Shares Outstanding	704,000	445,333	443,000	436,333	424,000	420,666	419,000	309,333
Statistical Record								
Return on Assets %	2.00	2.81	2.27	1.95	2.64	2.53	3.02	3.31
Return on Equity %	5.53	7.53	5.96	5.03	6.44	6.34	8.76	11.09
EBITDA Margin %	31.32	35.36	34.06	33.63	33.60	35.06	36.02	40.28
Net Margin %	9.01	11.74	9.25	8.44	10.31	11.79	12.27	10.89
Asset Turnover	0.22	0.24	0.25	0.23	0.26	0.21	0.25	0.30
Current Ratio	1.01	1.24	1.60	1.41	1.21	0.86	1.05	0.95
Debt to Equity	0.89	0.82	0.80	0.74	0.63	0.45	0.69	0.88
Price Range	69.84-59.87	66.18-51.75	55.59-46.83	53.43-35.43	61.41-43.29	63.00-51.09	58.89-47.48	52.66-42.81
P/E Ratio	22.75-19.50	17.23-13.48	18.53-15.61	21.46-14.23	19.13-13.49	17.80-14.43	12.50-10.08	9.34-7.59
Average Yield %	2.36	5.22	5.71	6.24	5.15	4.45	7.31	7.27

Address: 550 South Tryon Street, Charlotte, NC 28202-4200 Telephone: 704-382-3853 Fax: 704-382-0230	Web Site: www.duke-energy.com Officers: James E. Rogers - Chairman, Executive Chairman, President, Chief Executive Officer Marc E. Manly - Executive Vice President, Group Executive, Chief Legal Officer, Corporate Secretary, Division Officer	Auditors: Deloitte & Touche LLP Investor Contact: 704-382-4070 Transfer Agents: Duke Energy, Charlotte, NC

DUKE REALTY CORP.

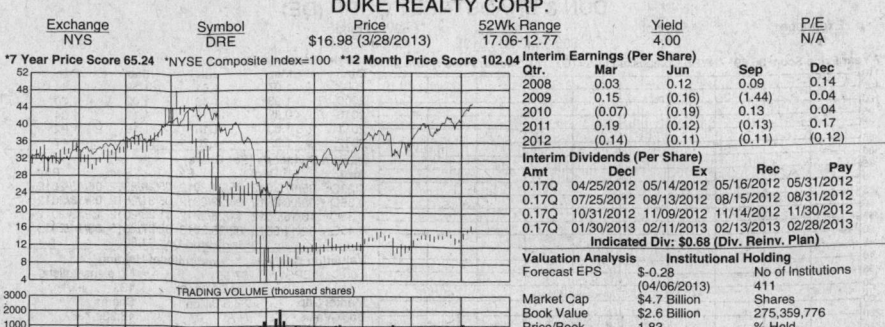

Exchange	Symbol	Price	52Wk Range	Yield	P/E
NYS	DRE	$16.98 (3/28/2013)	17.06-12.77	4.00	N/A

*7 Year Price Score 65.24   *NYSE Composite Index=100   *12 Month Price Score 102.04

Interim Earnings (Per Share)

Qtr.	Mar	Jun	Sep	Dec
2008	0.03	0.12	0.09	0.14
2009	0.15	(0.16)	(1.44)	0.04
2010	(0.07)	(0.19)	0.13	0.04
2011	0.19	(0.12)	(0.13)	0.17
2012	(0.14)	(0.11)	(0.11)	(0.12)

Interim Dividends (Per Share)

Amt	Decl	Ex	Rec	Pay
0.17Q	04/25/2012	05/14/2012	05/16/2012	05/31/2012
0.17Q	07/25/2012	08/13/2012	08/15/2012	08/31/2012
0.17Q	10/31/2012	11/09/2012	11/14/2012	11/30/2012
0.17Q	01/30/2013	02/11/2013	02/13/2013	02/28/2013

Indicated Div: $0.68 (Div. Reinv. Plan)

Valuation Analysis

		Institutional Holding	
Forecast EPS	$-0.28	No of Institutions	
	(04/06/2013)	411	
Market Cap	$4.7 Billion	Shares	
Book Value	$2.6 Billion	275,359,776	
Price/Book	1.83	% Held	
Price/Sales	4.28	N/A	

Business Summary: REITs (MIC: 5.3.1 SIC: 6798 NAIC: 525930)

Duke Realty is a self-administered and self-managed real estate investment trust and is the sole general partner of Duke Realty Limited Partnership. As of Dec 31 2012, Co. owned or jointly controlled 774 industrial, office, medical office and other properties. As of the same date, Co. owned, including through ownership interests in unconsolidated joint ventures, more than 4,600 acres of land and controlled an additional 1,600 acres through purchase options. Co. had four reportable operating segments at Dec 31 2012, the first three of which consist of the ownership and rental of industrial, office and medical office real estate investments and its Service Operations segment.

Recent Developments: For the year ended Dec 31 2012, loss from continuing operations was US$87.8 million compared with a loss of US$2.8 million a year earlier. Net loss amounted to US$75.9 million versus net income of US$96.3 million in the prior year. Revenues were US$1.11 billion, down 12.3% from US$1.26 billion the year before. Revenues from property income rose 12.3% to US$834.4 million from US$742.9 million in the corresponding earlier year.

Prospects: Our evaluation of Duke Realty Corp. as of Apr. 7, 2013 is the result of our systematic analysis on three basic characteristics: earnings strength, relative valuation, and recent stock price movement. The company has managed to produce a neutral trend in earnings per share over the past 5 quarters. Because the company lacks sufficient analyst estimate data, we place greater weight on the historical EPS trend as the measure of earnings strength. Based on operating earnings yield, the company is overvalued when compared to all of the companies in our coverage universe. Share price changes over the past year indicates that DRE will perform poorly over the near term.

Financial Data

(US$ in Thousands)	12/31/2012	12/31/2011	12/31/2010	12/31/2009	12/31/2008	12/31/2007	12/31/2006	12/31/2005
Earnings Per Share	(0.48)	0.11	(0.07)	(1.67)	0.38	1.55	1.07	2.17
Cash Flow Per Share	1.11	1.34	1.64	1.99	4.36	2.33	2.04	2.86
Tang Book Value Per Share	7.04	7.59	8.09	8.52	12.16	13.72	12.15	13.33
Dividends Per Share	0.680	0.680	0.680	0.760	1.930	1.910	0.182	2.113
Dividend Payout %	...	618.18	...	...	507.89	123.23	17.00	97.35
Income Statement								
Total Revenue	1,109,440	1,274,274	1,393,603	1,344,089	1,367,870	1,170,099	1,193,433	1,136,387
EBITDA	414,918	480,821	530,277	192,782	337,324	371,332	360,141	349,102
Depn & Amortn	262,825	267,222	271,058	266,803	246,441	214,477	206,999	204,377
Income Before Taxes	(92,563)	(8,796)	20,370	(293,031)	94,924	168,990	163,592	150,569
Income Taxes	(103)	(194)	(1,126)	(6,070)	...	...	...	...
Net Income	(75,868)	96,309	65,262	(271,490)	113,996	279,467	204,147	355,662
Average Shares	267,900	259,598	238,920	201,206	155,041	149,614	149,393	155,877
Balance Sheet								
Current Assets	216,229	382,211	173,565	318,615	248,815	254,683	262,688	204,057
Total Assets	7,560,101	7,004,437	7,644,276	7,304,279	7,690,883	7,661,981	7,238,595	5,647,560
Current Liabilities	319,071	282,480	302,702	283,481	326,114	354,838	342,228	277,625
Long-Term Obligations	4,446,170	3,809,589	4,207,079	3,854,032	4,298,478	4,316,460	3,961,845	2,600,651
Total Liabilities	4,968,687	4,289,751	4,698,666	4,378,934	4,869,125	4,911,948	4,735,012	3,194,762
Stockholders' Equity	2,591,414	2,714,686	2,945,610	2,925,345	2,821,758	2,750,033	2,503,583	2,452,798
Shares Outstanding	279,423	252,927	252,195	224,029	148,420	146,175	133,921	134,697
Statistical Record								
Return on Assets %	N.M.	1.31	0.87	N.M.	1.48	3.75	3.17	6.16
Return on Equity %	N.M.	3.40	2.22	N.M.	4.08	10.64	8.24	13.48
EBITDA Margin %	37.40	37.73	38.05	14.34	24.66	31.74	30.18	30.72
Net Margin %	N.M.	7.56	4.68	N.M.	8.33	23.88	17.11	31.30
Asset Turnover	0.15	0.17	0.19	0.18	0.18	0.16	0.19	0.20
Current Ratio	0.68	1.35	0.57	1.12	0.76	0.72	0.77	0.74
Debt to Equity	1.72	1.40	1.43	1.32	1.52	1.57	1.58	1.06
Price Range	15.77-12.02	15.51-9.70	14.32-10.37	13.16-4.39	26.94-4.17	48.21-24.76	43.95-33.33	34.72-29.40
P/E Ratio	...	141.00-88.18	...	...	70.89-10.97	31.10-15.97	41.07-31.15	16.00-13.55
Average Yield %	4.82	5.31	5.48	7.80	9.23	5.19	0.49	6.54

Address: 600 East 96th Street, Suite 100, Indianapolis, IN 46240	Web Site: www.dukerealty.com	Auditors: KPMG LLP
Telephone: 317-808-6000	**Officers:** Dennis D. Oklak - Chairman, President, Chief Executive Officer Howard L. Feinsand - Executive Vice President, Secretary, General Counsel	**Investor Contact:** 317-808-6060
Fax: 317-808-6770		**Transfer Agents:** American Stock Transfer & Trust Company, New York, NY

DUN & BRADSTREET CORP (DE)

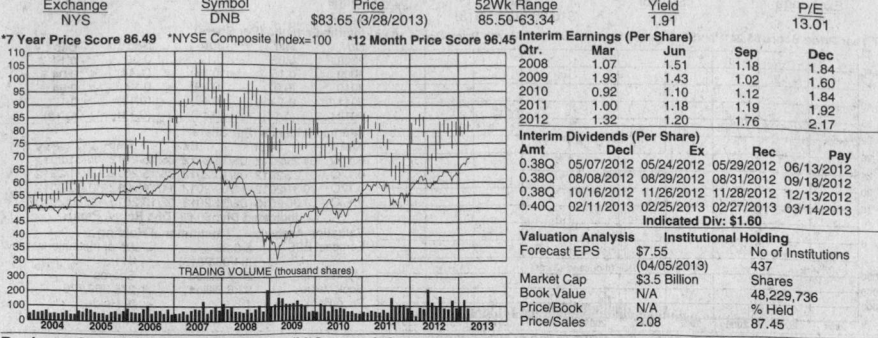

Exchange	Symbol	Price	52Wk Range	Yield	P/E
NYS	DNB	$83.65 (3/28/2013)	85.50-63.34	1.91	13.01

*7 Year Price Score 86.49 *NYSE Composite Index=100 *12 Month Price Score 96.45

Interim Earnings (Per Share)

Qtr.	Mar	Jun	Sep	Dec
2008	1.07	1.51	1.18	1.84
2009	1.93	1.43	1.02	1.60
2010	0.92	1.10	1.12	1.84
2011	1.00	1.18	1.19	1.92
2012	1.32	1.20	1.76	2.17

Interim Dividends (Per Share)

Amt	Decl	Ex	Rec	Pay
0.38Q	05/07/2012	05/24/2012	05/29/2012	06/13/2012
0.38Q	08/08/2012	08/29/2012	08/31/2012	09/18/2012
0.38Q	10/16/2012	11/26/2012	11/28/2012	12/13/2012
0.40Q	02/11/2013	02/25/2013	02/27/2013	03/14/2013

Indicated Div: $1.60

Valuation Analysis

		Institutional Holding	
Forecast EPS	$7.55 (04/05/2013)	No of Institutions	437
Market Cap	$3.5 Billion	Shares	48,229,736
Book Value	N/A	% Held	87.45
Price/Book	N/A		
Price/Sales	2.08		

Business Summary: Business Services (MIC: 7.5.2 SIC: 7323 NAIC: 561450)

Dun & Bradstreet is a provider of commercial information on businesses. Customers uses Co.'s products and services, including D&B Risk Management Solutions™, to mitigate credit and supplier risk; D&B Sales & Marketing Solutions™, to enhance marketing databases; and D&B Internet Solutions, that enable business personnel to research companies, executives and industries. Co. operates in three segments: North America, which consisted of its operations in the U.S. and Canada; Asia Pacific, which consisted of its operations in Australia, Japan, China and India; and Europe and other International Markets, which consisted of its operations in the U.K., the Netherlands, Belgium and Latin America.

Recent Developments: For the year ended Dec 31 2012, net income increased 14.0% to US$296.5 million from US$260.2 million in the prior year. Revenues were US$1.66 billion, down 5.4% from US$1.76 billion the year before. Operating income was US$432.1 million versus US$424.8 million in the prior year, an increase of 1.7%. Direct operating expenses declined 11.3% to US$521.0 million from US$587.1 million in the comparable period the year before. Indirect operating expenses decreased 4.9% to US$709.9 million from US$746.6 million in the equivalent prior-year period.

Prospects: Our evaluation of Dun & Bradstreet Corp. as of Apr. 7, 2013 is the result of our systematic analysis on three basic characteristics: earnings strength, relative valuation, and recent stock price movement. The company has managed to produce a neutral trend in earnings per share over the past 5 quarters. However, while recent estimates for the company have been lowered by analysts, DNB has posted results that fell short of analysts expectations. Based on operating earnings yield, the company is undervalued when compared to all of the companies in our coverage universe. Share price changes over the past year indicates that DNB will perform poorly over the near term.

Financial Data
(US$ in Thousands)

	12/31/2012	12/31/2011	12/31/2010	12/31/2009	12/31/2008	12/31/2007	12/31/2006	12/31/2005
Earnings Per Share	6.43	5.28	4.98	5.99	5.60	4.99	3.70	3.19
Cash Flow Per Share	7.83	6.40	6.40	7.07	8.00	6.76	4.82	3.91
Dividends Per Share	1.520	1.440	1.400	1.360	1.200	1.000	...	...
Dividend Payout %	23.64	27.27	28.11	22.70	21.43	20.04	...	...
Income Statement								
Total Revenue	1,663,000	1,758,500	1,676,600	1,687,000	1,726,300	1,599,200	1,531,300	1,443,600
EBITDA	428,200	415,900	444,200	485,900	485,100	457,900	412,300	375,500
Depn & Amortn	11,200	12,300	12,400	10,700	10,300	10,600	10,400	10,900
Income Before Taxes	378,300	368,100	387,900	432,500	438,900	426,300	388,900	354,200
Income Taxes	83,100	109,200	137,900	112,100	128,000	135,800	146,800	133,600
Net Income	295,500	260,300	252,100	319,400	310,600	298,100	240,700	221,200
Average Shares	46,000	49,300	50,400	52,900	55,500	59,800	65,100	69,415
Balance Sheet								
Current Assets	747,400	726,900	668,300	759,600	695,800	718,300	645,000	759,300
Total Assets	1,991,800	1,977,100	1,905,500	1,749,400	1,586,000	1,658,800	1,360,100	1,613,400
Current Liabilities	876,700	953,500	927,700	859,100	908,500	910,000	805,500	1,029,100
Long-Term Obligations	1,290,700	963,900	972,000	961,800	904,300	724,800	458,900	100
Total Liabilities	3,009,200	2,721,000	2,559,900	2,495,100	2,442,200	2,098,900	1,759,200	1,535,800
Stockholders' Equity	(1,017,400)	(743,900)	(654,400)	(745,700)	(856,200)	(440,100)	(399,100)	77,600
Shares Outstanding	41,300	47,700	49,600	51,200	53,300	56,800	60,100	67,057
Statistical Record								
Return on Assets %	14.85	13.41	13.80	19.15	19.09	19.75	16.19	13.62
Return on Equity %	...	...	...	...	...	...	...	335.66
EBITDA Margin %	25.75	23.65	26.49	28.80	28.10	28.63	26.92	26.01
Net Margin %	17.77	14.80	15.04	18.93	17.99	18.64	15.72	15.32
Asset Turnover	0.84	0.91	0.92	1.01	1.06	1.06	1.03	0.89
Current Ratio	0.85	0.76	0.72	0.88	0.77	0.79	0.80	0.74
Price Range	86.50-63.34	86.45-59.25	84.37-65.90	84.64-69.80	98.78-64.40	106.63-82.28	84.25-65.50	67.88-55.04
P/E Ratio	13.45-9.85	16.37-11.22	16.94-13.23	14.13-11.65	17.64-11.50	21.37-16.49	22.77-17.70	21.28-17.25
Average Yield %	1.95	1.94	1.90	1.75	1.40	1.07	...	...

Address: 103 JFK Parkway, Short Hills, NJ 07078 Telephone: 973-921-5500	Web Site: www.dnb.com Officers: Sara Mathew - Chairman, President, Chief Executive Officer, Chief Operating Officer, Region Officer, Chief Financial Officer Paul D. Ballew - Chief	Auditors: PricewaterhouseCoopers LLP Investor Contact: 973-921-5914 Transfer Agents: Computershare Trust Company, N.A., Providence, RI

EAGLE MATERIALS INC

Exchange	Symbol	Price	52Wk Range	Yield	P/E
NYS	EXP	$66.63 (3/28/2013)	71.57-29.84	0.60	52.05

*7 Year Price Score 125.85 *NYSE Composite Index=100 *12 Month Price Score 127.58

Interim Earnings (Per Share)

Qtr.	Jun	Sep	Dec	Mar
2009-10	0.27	0.28	0.11	0.01
2010-11	0.24	0.22	0.12	(0.24)
2011-12	0.07	0.14	0.07	0.20
2012-13	0.31	0.40	0.37	...

Interim Dividends (Per Share)

Amt	Decl	Ex	Rec	Pay
0.10Q	05/24/2012	06/20/2012	06/22/2012	07/20/2012
0.10Q	09/06/2012	09/28/2012	10/02/2012	11/02/2012
0.10Q	11/15/2012	12/19/2012	12/21/2012	01/23/2013
0.10Q	02/28/2013	04/04/2013	04/08/2013	05/03/2013

Indicated Div: $0.40

Valuation Analysis		Institutional Holding	
Forecast EPS	$1.64	No of Institutions	
	(04/05/2013)	291	
Market Cap	$3.3 Billion	Shares	
Book Value	$687.5 Million	45,890,968	
Price/Book	4.78	% Held	
Price/Sales	5.48	N/A	

Business Summary: Construction Materials (MIC: 8.5.1 SIC: 3241 NAIC: 327310)

Eagle Materials is a holding company. Through its subsidiaries and joint venture, Co. is a producer of building products used in residential, industrial, commercial and infrastructure construction. Co. has four segments: Cement, Gypsum Wallboard, Recycled Paperboard, and Concrete and Aggregates. These operations include the mining of limestone and the manufacture, production, distribution and sale of Portland cement, the mining of gypsum and the manufacture and sale of gypsum wallboard, the manufacture and sale of recycled paperboard to the gypsum wallboard industry and other paperboard converters, the sale of readymix concrete and the mining and sale of aggregates such as sand and gravel.

Recent Developments: For the quarter ended Dec 31 2012, net income increased 520.6% to US$18.0 million from US$2.9 million in the year-earlier quarter. Revenues were US$164.7 million, up 33.3% from US$123.6 million the year before. Direct operating expenses rose 20.1% to US$133.5 million from US$111.1 million in the comparable period the year before. Indirect operating expenses decreased 97.8% to US$124,000 from US$5.7 million in the equivalent prior-year period.

Prospects: Our evaluation of Eagle Materials Inc. as of Apr. 7, 2013 is the result of our systematic analysis on three basic characteristics: earnings strength, relative valuation, and recent stock price movement. The company has generated a negative trend in earnings per share over the past 5 quarters. However, while recent estimates for the company have been mixed, EXP has posted results that fell short of analysts expectations. Based on operating earnings yield, the company is overvalued when compared to all of the companies in our coverage universe. Share price changes over the past year indicates that EXP will perform very well over the near term.

Financial Data

(US$ in Thousands)	9 Mos	6 Mos	3 Mos	03/31/2012	03/31/2011	03/31/2010	03/31/2009	03/31/2008
Earnings Per Share	1.28	0.98	0.72	0.42	0.34	0.66	0.95	2.12
Cash Flow Per Share	2.57	2.24	1.76	1.37	1.00	1.48	1.83	2.29
Tang Book Value Per Share	10.61	7.74	7.35	7.10	6.93	6.69	6.31	5.81
Dividends Per Share	0.400	0.400	0.400	0.300	0.400	0.400	0.600	0.800
Dividend Payout %	31.25	40.82	55.56	71.43	117.65	60.61	63.16	37.74
Income Statement								
Total Revenue	483,444	318,701	154,042	495,023	462,180	467,905	602,182	749,553
EBITDA	99,735	63,342	29,754	58,905	107,103	86,300	108,677	175,076
Depn & Amortn	39,780	25,444	12,661	48,900	48,200	49,700	50,000	43,600
Income Before Taxes	49,270	30,821	13,416	(6,616)	42,383	15,140	29,757	110,402
Income Taxes	23,429	14,108	5,936	3,180	1,913	10,347	20,419	46,616
Net Income	49,911	31,931	13,978	18,732	14,849	28,950	41,764	97,768
Average Shares	49,249	45,353	45,078	44,515	44,251	44,038	43,897	46,145
Balance Sheet								
Current Assets	243,323	193,807	194,818	191,841	174,626	161,274	175,283	180,626
Total Assets	1,456,820	974,888	980,396	985,145	982,810	1,013,776	1,066,668	1,114,847
Current Liabilities	110,452	93,464	77,661	77,043	70,350	71,864	64,249	107,276
Long-Term Obligations	483,259	212,259	249,259	262,259	287,000	303,000	355,000	400,000
Total Liabilities	769,273	472,777	496,454	512,634	523,246	568,414	638,841	709,160
Stockholders' Equity	687,547	502,111	483,942	472,511	459,564	445,362	427,827	405,687
Shares Outstanding	49,351	45,438	45,362	45,269	44,447	43,830	43,589	43,430
Statistical Record								
Return on Assets %	4.83	4.46	3.25	1.90	1.49	2.78	3.83	9.35
Return on Equity %	10.25	9.10	6.77	4.01	3.28	6.63	10.02	20.49
EBITDA Margin %	20.63	19.88	19.32	11.90	23.17	18.44	18.05	23.36
Net Margin %	10.32	10.02	9.07	3.78	3.21	6.19	6.94	13.04
Asset Turnover	0.49	0.57	0.54	0.50	0.46	0.45	0.55	0.72
Current Ratio	2.20	2.07	2.51	2.49	2.48	2.24	2.73	1.68
Debt to Equity	0.70	0.42	0.52	0.56	0.62	0.68	0.83	0.99
Price Range	58.60-26.15	47.41-16.25	37.34-15.68	35.81-15.68	32.79-21.79	29.75-22.18	37.86-14.41	50.95-29.05
P/E Ratio	45.78-20.43	48.38-16.58	51.86-21.78	85.26-37.33	96.44-64.09	45.08-33.61	39.85-15.17	24.03-13.70
Average Yield %	1.00	1.26	1.51	1.20	1.47	1.54	2.44	1.99

Address: 3811 Turtle Creek Blvd., Suite 1100, Dallas, TX 75219	Web Site: www.eaglematerials.com	Auditors: Ernst & Young LLP
Telephone: 214-432-2000	Officers: Laurence E. Hirsch - Chairman Steven R. Rowley - President, Chief Executive Officer, Chief Operating Officer	Investor Contact: 214-432-2000
Fax: 214-432-2100		Transfer Agents: Computershare, Inc., Providence, RI

EASTMAN CHEMICAL CO.

Exchange	Symbol	Price	52Wk Range	Yield	P/E
NYS	EMN	$69.87 (3/28/2013)	74.78-43.26	1.72	23.85

*7 Year Price Score 143.50 *NYSE Composite Index=100 *12 Month Price Score 112.44

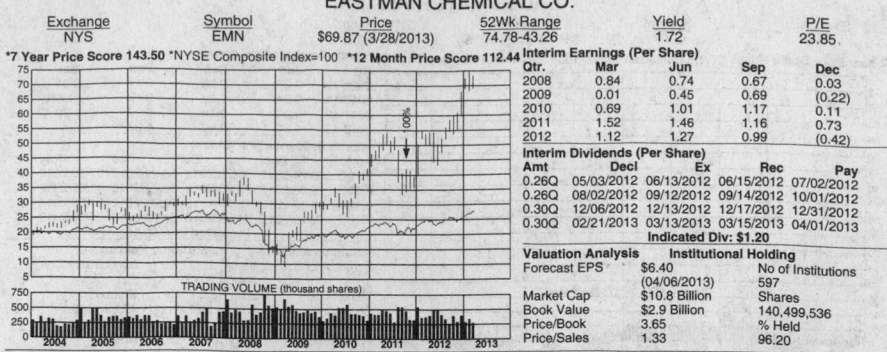

Interim Earnings (Per Share)

Qtr.	Mar	Jun	Sep	Dec
2008	0.84	0.74	0.67	0.03
2009	0.01	0.45	0.69	(0.22)
2010	0.69	1.01	1.17	0.11
2011	1.52	1.46	1.16	0.73
2012	1.12	1.27	0.99	(0.42)

Interim Dividends (Per Share)

Amt	Decl	Ex	Rec	Pay
0.26Q	05/03/2012	06/13/2012	06/15/2012	07/02/2012
0.26Q	08/02/2012	09/12/2012	09/14/2012	10/01/2012
0.30Q	12/06/2012	12/13/2012	12/17/2012	12/31/2012
0.30Q	02/21/2013	03/13/2013	03/15/2013	04/01/2013

Indicated Div: $1.20

Valuation Analysis

		Institutional Holding	
Forecast EPS	$6.40 (04/06/2013)	No of Institutions	597
Market Cap	$10.8 Billion	Shares	140,499,536
Book Value	$2.9 Billion	% Held	96.20
Price/Book	3.65		
Price/Sales	1.33		

Business Summary: Plastics (MIC: 8.4.2 SIC: 2821 NAIC: 325211)

Eastman Chemical is a chemicals company that produces materials, chemicals, and fibers in five segments: Additives and Functional Products manufacture chemicals for products in the coatings and tire industries; Adhesives and Plasticizers manufactures resins and plasticizers; Advanced Materials produces and markets copolyesters, cellulose esters, interlayers, and aftermarket window film products; Fibers manufactures and sells acetate tow and triacetin plasticizers, solution-dyed acetate yarns, cellulose acetate flake and acetyl raw materials; and Specialty Fluids and Intermediates provides products that include intermediates based on oxo and acetyl chemistries and performance chemicals.

Recent Developments: For the year ended Dec 31 2012, income from continuing operations decreased 27.0% to US$443.0 million from US$607.0 million a year earlier. Net income decreased 31.4% to US$444.0 million from US$647.0 million in the prior year. Revenues were US$8.10 billion, up 12.9% from US$7.18 billion the year before. Operating income was US$800.0 million versus US$937.0 million in the prior year, a decrease of 14.6%. Direct operating expenses rose 13.0% to US$6.34 billion from US$5.61 billion in the comparable period the year before. Indirect operating expenses increased 52.2% to US$962.0 million from US$632.0 million in the equivalent prior-year period.

Prospects: Our evaluation of Eastman Chemical Co. as of Apr. 7, 2013 is the result of our systematic analysis on three basic characteristics: earnings strength, relative valuation, and recent stock price movement. The company has produced a positive trend in earnings per share over the past 5 quarters. However, while recent estimates for the company have been mixed, EMN has posted better than expected results. Based on operating earnings yield, the company is undervalued when compared to all of the companies in our coverage universe. Share price changes over the past year indicates that EMN will perform very well over the near term.

Financial Data

(US$ in Millions)	12/31/2012	12/31/2011	12/31/2010	12/31/2009	12/31/2008	12/31/2007	12/31/2006	12/31/2005
Earnings Per Share	2.93	4.86	2.96	0.93	2.27	1.79	2.46	3.40
Cash Flow Per Share	7.73	4.47	3.99	5.23	4.33	4.42	3.71	4.76
Tang Book Value Per Share	N.M.	10.69	8.86	8.28	8.47	11.08	10.27	7.97
Dividends Per Share	1.080	0.990	0.895	0.880	0.880	0.880	0.885	0.880
Dividend Payout %	36.86	20.37	30.24	95.14	38.68	49.16	36.05	25.84
Income Statement								
Total Revenue	8,102	7,178	5,842	5,047	6,726	6,830	7,450	7,059
EBITDA	1,101	1,301	973	566	755	845	950	997
Depn & Amortn	309	261	238	262	256	313	294	287
Income Before Taxes	649	964	636	226	429	470	576	610
Income Taxes	206	307	211	90	101	149	167	226
Net Income	437	696	438	136	346	300	409	557
Average Shares	149	143	147	146	152	167	166	163
Balance Sheet								
Current Assets	2,594	2,302	2,047	1,735	1,423	2,293	2,422	1,924
Total Assets	11,619	6,184	5,986	5,515	5,281	6,009	6,173	5,773
Current Liabilities	1,364	1,114	1,070	800	832	1,122	1,059	1,051
Long-Term Obligations	4,779	1,445	1,598	1,604	1,442	1,535	1,589	1,621
Total Liabilities	8,676	4,314	4,359	4,002	3,728	3,927	4,144	4,161
Stockholders' Equity	2,943	1,870	1,627	1,513	1,553	2,082	2,029	1,612
Shares Outstanding	153	136	141	144	144	159	167	163
Statistical Record								
Return on Assets %	4.90	11.44	7.62	2.52	6.11	4.93	6.85	9.57
Return on Equity %	18.11	39.81	27.90	8.87	18.99	14.59	22.47	39.84
EBITDA Margin %	13.59	18.12	16.66	11.21	11.23	12.37	12.75	14.12
Net Margin %	5.39	9.70	7.50	2.69	5.14	4.39	5.49	7.89
Asset Turnover	0.91	1.18	1.02	0.93	1.19	1.12	1.25	1.21
Current Ratio	1.90	2.07	1.91	2.17	1.71	2.04	2.29	1.83
Debt to Equity	1.62	0.77	0.98	1.06	0.93	0.74	0.78	1.01
Price Range	68.05-40.09	54.08-33.31	42.04-25.82	30.70-9.00	38.76-13.41	35.62-28.95	30.61-23.85	30.68-22.35
P/E Ratio	23.23-13.68	11.13-6.85	14.20-8.72	33.01-9.68	17.07-5.91	19.90-16.17	12.45-9.70	9.02-6.57
Average Yield %	2.03	2.23	2.67	4.13	3.01	2.73	3.29	3.25

Address: 200 South Wilcox Drive, Kingsport, TN 37662 Telephone: 423-229-2000 Fax: 423-229-2145	Web Site: www.eastman.com Officers: James P. Rogers - Chairman, Chief Executive Officer Mark J. Costa - Executive Vice President, Chief Marketing Officer	Auditors: PricewaterhouseCoopers LLP Investor Contact: 212-835-1620 Transfer Agents: American Stock Transfer & Trust Company, New York, NY

EATON CORP PLC

Exchange	Symbol	Price	52Wk Range	Yield	P/E
NYS	ETN	$61.25 (3/28/2013)	63.42-37.04	2.74	17.70

*7 Year Price Score 108.51 *NYSE Composite Index=100 *12 Month Price Score 113.56

Interim Earnings (Per Share)

Qtr.	Mar	Jun	Sep	Dec
2008	0.82	1.01	0.94	0.47
2009	(0.15)	0.09	0.57	0.63
2010	0.46	0.67	0.79	0.83
2011	0.83	0.97	1.07	1.07
2012	0.91	1.12	1.02	0.41

Interim Dividends (Per Share)

Amt	Decl	Ex	Rec	Pay
0.42Q	02/27/2013	03/07/2013	03/11/2013	03/22/2013

Indicated Div: $1.68

Valuation Analysis

		Institutional Holding	
Forecast EPS	$4.35	No of Institutions	
	(04/05/2013)	N/A	
Market Cap	$28.8 Billion	Shares	
Book Value	$15.1 Billion	N/A	
Price/Book	1.91	% Held	
Price/Sales	1.77	N/A	

Business Summary: Electrical Equipment (MIC: 7.3.1 SIC: 3599 NAIC: 336399)

Eaton is a power management company. The Electrical Americas and Electrical Rest of World segments are engaged in electrical components and systems for power quality, distribution and control. The Hydraulics segment provides hydraulics components, systems and services for industrial and mobile equipment. The Aerospace segment is a supplier of aerospace fuel, hydraulics and pneumatic systems for commercial and military use. The Truck segment is engaged in the design, manufacture and marketing of drivetrain and powertrain systems and components for commercial vehicles. The Automotive segment supplies automotive drivetrain and powertrain systems for cars, light trucks and commercial vehicles.

Recent Developments: For the year ended Dec 31 2012, net income decreased 9.8% to US$1.22 billion from US$1.35 billion in the prior year. Revenues were US$16.31 billion, up 1.6% from US$16.05 billion the year before. Direct operating expenses rose 1.7% to US$11.45 billion from US$11.26 billion in the comparable period the year before. Indirect operating expenses increased 5.6% to US$3.33 billion from US$3.16 billion in the equivalent prior-year period.

Prospects: Our evaluation of Eaton Corp PLC as of Apr. 7, 2013 is the result of our systematic analysis on three basic characteristics: earnings strength, relative valuation, and recent stock price movement. The company has generated a negative trend in earnings per share over the past 5 quarters and while recent estimates for the company have remained steady, ETN has posted results that fell short of analysts expectations. Based on operating earnings yield, the company is undervalued when compared to all of the companies in our coverage universe. Share price changes over the past year indicates that ETN will perform very well over the near term.

Financial Data
(US$ in Millions)

	12/31/2012	12/31/2011	12/31/2010	12/31/2009	12/31/2008	12/31/2007	12/31/2006	12/31/2005
Earnings Per Share	3.46	3.93	2.73	1.14	3.26	3.31	3.11	2.62
Cash Flow Per Share	4.77	3.69	3.82	4.23	4.41	3.94	4.76	3.78
Tang Book Value Per Share	N.M.	N.M.	N.M.	N.M.	N.M.	N.M.	0.35	0.04
Dividends Per Share	1.520	1.360	0.540	1.000	1.000	0.510	0.740	0.620
Dividend Payout %	43.93	34.61	19.78	88.11	30.67	48.11	23.79	23.71
Income Statement								
Total Revenue	16,311	16,049	13,715	11,873	15,376	13,033	12,370	11,115
EBITDA	2,057	2,227	1,723	1,026	1,877	1,657	1,527	1,495
Depn & Amortn	598	556	551	573	592	469	434	409
Income Before Taxes	1,251	1,553	1,036	303	1,128	1,041	989	996
Income Taxes	31	201	99	(82)	73	82	77	191
Net Income	1,217	1,350	929	383	1,058	994	950	805
Average Shares	350	342	339	335	324	300	305	308
Balance Sheet								
Current Assets	7,844	5,826	5,506	4,524	4,795	4,767	4,408	3,578
Total Assets	35,848	17,873	17,252	16,282	16,655	13,430	11,417	10,218
Current Liabilities	5,431	3,637	3,233	2,689	3,745	3,659	3,407	2,968
Long-Term Obligations	9,762	3,366	3,382	3,349	3,190	2,432	1,774	1,830
Total Liabilities	20,762	10,404	9,890	9,505	10,338	8,258	7,311	6,440
Stockholders' Equity	15,086	7,469	7,362	6,777	6,317	5,172	4,106	3,778
Shares Outstanding	470	334	339	332	330	292	292	297
Statistical Record								
Return on Assets %	4.52	7.69	5.54	2.33	7.01	8.00	8.78	8.34
Return on Equity %	10.76	18.21	13.14	5.85	18.37	21.43	24.10	21.80
EBITDA Margin %	12.61	13.88	12.56	8.64	12.21	12.71	12.34	13.45
Net Margin %	7.46	8.41	6.77	3.23	6.88	7.63	7.68	7.24
Asset Turnover	0.61	0.91	0.82	0.72	1.02	1.05	1.14	1.15
Current Ratio	1.44	1.60	1.70	1.68	1.28	1.30	1.29	1.21
Debt to Equity	0.65	0.45	0.46	0.49	0.50	0.47	0.43	0.48
Price Range	54.66-37.04	56.22-34.16	51.09-30.62	33.10-15.14	48.48-19.39	51.27-36.90	39.45-31.50	36.18-28.34
P/E Ratio	15.80-10.71	14.31-8.69	18.71-11.22	29.04-13.28	14.87-5.95	15.49-11.15	12.68-10.13	13.81-10.82
Average Yield %	3.25	2.85	1.33	3.97	2.78	1.24	2.05	1.94

Address: 70 Sir John Rogerson?s Quay, Dublin 2, 44114-2584	Web Site: www.eaton.com	Auditors: Ernst & Young LLP
Telephone: 440-523-5000	Officers: Alexander M. Cutler - Chairman, President, Chief Executive Officer Richard H. Fearon - Vice-Chairman, Chief Financial Officer, Chief Planning Officer	Investor Contact: 216-523-4205 Transfer Agents: Computershare Shareowner Services, Jersey City, NJ

EATON VANCE CORP

Exchange	Symbol	Price	52Wk Range	Yield	P/E	Div Achiever
NYS	EV	$41.83 (3/28/2013)	41.83-23.21	1.91	24.61	31 Years

*7 Year Price Score 87.10   *NYSE Composite Index=100   *12 Month Price Score 119.85

TRADING VOLUME (thousand shares)

Interim Earnings (Per Share)

Qtr.	Jan	Apr	Jul	Oct
2009-10	0.37	0.29	0.34	0.41
2010-11	0.30	0.50	0.55	0.40
2011-12	0.40	0.44	0.43	0.45
2012-13	0.38	...	...	...

Interim Dividends (Per Share)

Amt	Decl	Ex	Rec	Pay
0.19Q	07/10/2012	07/27/2012	07/31/2012	08/10/2012
0.20Q	10/18/2012	10/29/2012	10/31/2012	11/14/2012
0.20Q	12/04/2012	12/13/2012	12/17/2012	12/20/2012
1.00Sp	12/04/2012	12/12/2012	12/14/2012	12/20/2012

Indicated Div: $0.80

Valuation Analysis / **Institutional Holding**

Forecast EPS	$2.18 (04/06/2013)	No of Institutions 378
Market Cap	$5.0 Billion	Shares
Book Value	$575.9 Million	97,957,752
Price/Book	8.72	% Held
Price/Sales	4.08	81.17

Business Summary: Wealth Management (MIC: 5.5.2 SIC: 6282 NAIC: 523930)

Eaton Vance manages and distributes a range of investment products and services, and is engaged in a number of investment areas, including tax-managed equity, value equity, equity income, structured emerging market equity, floating-rate bank loan, municipal bond, investment grade, and bond investing. Co. also serves institutional clients who access investment management services on a direct basis. Co. manages investments for a range of clients in the institutional marketplace, including corporations, endowments, foundations, family offices, and public and private employee retirement plans. As of Oct 31 2011, Co. had $188.20 billion in assets under management.

Recent Developments: For the quarter ended Jan 31 2013, net income decreased 4.2% to US$62.1 million from US$64.9 million in the year-earlier quarter. Revenues were US$318.5 million, up 7.8% from US$295.6 million the year before. Operating income was US$100.7 million versus US$92.8 million in the prior-year quarter, an increase of 8.5%. Indirect operating expenses increased 7.4% to US$217.8 million from US$202.8 million in the equivalent prior-year period.

Prospects: Our evaluation of Eaton Vance Corp. as of Apr. 7, 2013 is the result of our systematic analysis on three basic characteristics: earnings strength, relative valuation, and recent stock price movement. The company has enjoyed a very positive trend in earnings per share over the past 5 quarters and while recent estimates for the company have been mixed, EV has posted results that fell short of analysts expectations. Based on operating earnings yield, the company is about fairly valued when compared to all of the companies in our coverage universe. Share price changes over the past year indicates that EV will perform well over the near term.

Financial Data

(US$ in Thousands)

	3 Mos	10/31/2012	10/31/2011	10/31/2010	10/31/2009	10/31/2008	10/31/2007	10/31/2006
Earnings Per Share	1.70	1.72	1.75	1.40	1.08	1.57	1.06	1.17
Cash Flow Per Share	1.00	1.59	1.49	0.82	1.41	1.31	2.14	2.06
Tang Book Value Per Share	2.22	3.42	2.17	1.70	1.11	0.67	0.76	2.89
Dividends Per Share	1.780	0.770	0.730	0.660	0.625	0.605	0.630	0.400
Dividend Payout %	104.71	44.77	41.71	47.14	57.87	38.54	59.43	34.19
Income Statement								
Total Revenue	318,517	1,209,036	1,260,031	1,121,661	890,371	1,095,800	1,084,100	862,194
EBITDA	112,280	428,309	420,380	373,163	251,700	355,765	238,632	271,819
Depn & Amortn	4,600	16,900	15,800	15,400	14,100	10,400	7,900	4,000
Income Before Taxes	94,889	403,738	381,376	326,961	207,663	322,847	238,349	263,002
Income Taxes	35,939	142,385	156,844	126,263	71,044	125,154	93,200	102,245
Net Income	49,805	203,465	214,902	174,298	130,107	195,663	142,811	159,377
Average Shares	119,112	115,126	119,975	122,632	120,728	124,483	135,252	137,004
Balance Sheet								
Current Assets	415,227	632,423	657,959	499,274	488,162	484,801	610,152	329,367
Total Assets	1,803,533	1,979,491	1,831,300	1,280,607	1,075,067	968,355	966,831	668,195
Current Liabilities	125,450	227,985	210,723	258,001	188,323	191,431	217,699	139,645
Long-Term Obligations	911,583	946,605	977,699	500,000	500,000	500,000	500,000	...
Total Liabilities	1,227,664	1,367,419	1,370,885	870,322	727,959	728,228	737,663	171,710
Stockholders' Equity	575,869	612,072	460,415	410,285	347,108	240,127	229,168	496,485
Shares Outstanding	120,049	116,291	115,623	118,326	117,519	115,811	118,169	126,435
Statistical Record								
Return on Assets %	11.32	10.65	13.81	14.80	12.73	20.17	17.47	23.25
Return on Equity %	39.15	37.84	49.36	46.03	44.31	83.16	39.36	33.50
EBITDA Margin %	35.25	35.43	33.36	33.27	28.27	32.47	22.01	31.53
Net Margin %	15.64	16.83	17.06	15.54	14.61	17.86	13.17	18.49
Asset Turnover	0.68	0.63	0.81	0.95	0.87	1.13	1.33	1.26
Current Ratio	3.31	2.77	3.12	1.94	2.59	2.53	2.80	2.36
Debt to Equity	1.58	1.55	2.12	1.22	1.44	2.08	2.18	...
Price Range	36.36-23.21	29.70-21.78	33.92-20.84	35.72-25.90	30.67-12.36	50.03-16.70	50.03-29.87	31.10-24.14
P/E Ratio	21.39-13.65	17.27-12.66	19.38-11.91	25.51-18.50	28.40-11.44	31.87-10.64	47.20-28.18	26.58-20.63
Average Yield %	6.28	2.92	2.52	2.17	2.60	1.65	1.65	1.47

Address: Two International Place, Boston, MA 02110 **Telephone:** 617-482-8260 **Fax:** 617-482-2396	**Web Site:** www.eatonvance.com **Officers:** Thomas E. Faust - Chairman, President, Chief Executive Officer Duncan W. Richardson - Executive Vice President, Chief Equity Investment Officer	**Auditors:** Deloitte & Touche LLP **Investor Contact:** 617-482-8260 **Transfer Agents:** ComputerShare Investor Services, Providence, RI

ECOLAB, INC.

Exchange	Symbol	Price	52Wk Range	Yield	P/E	Div Achiever
NYS	ECL	$80.18 (3/28/2013)	80.18-59.92	1.15	34.12	20 Years

*7 Year Price Score 124.19 *NYSE Composite Index=100 *12 Month Price Score 103.08

Interim Earnings (Per Share)

Qtr.	Mar	Jun	Sep	Dec
2008	0.41	0.55	0.50	0.34
2009	0.24	0.41	0.60	0.48
2010	0.40	0.54	0.74	0.55
2011	0.40	0.53	0.65	0.33
2012	0.17	0.62	0.80	0.77

Interim Dividends (Per Share)

Amt	Decl	Ex	Rec	Pay
0.20Q	05/03/2012	06/15/2012	06/19/2012	07/16/2012
0.20Q	08/02/2012	09/14/2012	09/18/2012	10/15/2012
0.23Q	12/06/2012	12/14/2012	12/18/2012	12/28/2012
0.23Q	02/22/2013	03/01/2013	03/05/2013	04/15/2013

Indicated Div: $0.92 (Div. Reinv. Plan)

Valuation Analysis / **Institutional Holding**

Forecast EPS	$3.54	No of Institutions
	(04/06/2013)	789
Market Cap	$23.6 Billion	Shares
Book Value	$6.1 Billion	247,530,096
Price/Book	3.89	% Held
Price/Sales	2.00	95.77

Business Summary: Specialty Chemicals (MIC: 8.3.2 SIC: 2842 NAIC: 325612)

Ecolab has six segments: U.S. Cleaning & Sanitizing, which provides cleaning and sanitizing products; U.S. Other Services, which provides pest elimination and kitchen equipment repair and maintenance; International Cleaning, Sanitizing & Other Services, which provide cleaning and sanitizing products as well as pest elimination service; Global Water, which provides water treatment and process improvement offerings; Global Paper, which serves the process chemicals and water treatment needs of the pulp and paper industry; and Global Energy, which serves the process chemicals and water treatment needs of the petroleum and petrochemical industries in upstream and downstream applications.

Recent Developments: For the year ended Dec 31 2012, net income increased 51.4% to US$701.3 million from US$463.3 million in the prior year. Revenues were US$11.84 billion, up 74.1% from US$6.80 billion the year before. Operating income was US$1.29 billion versus US$753.8 million in the prior year, an increase of 71.0%. Direct operating expenses rose 86.5% to US$6.48 billion from US$3.48 billion in the comparable period the year before. Indirect operating expenses increased 58.3% to US$4.07 billion from US$2.57 billion in the equivalent prior-year period.

Prospects: Our evaluation of Ecolab Inc. as of Apr. 7, 2013 is the result of our systematic analysis on three basic characteristics: earnings strength, relative valuation, and recent stock price movement. The company has enjoyed a very positive trend in earnings per share over the past 5 quarters and while recent estimates for the company have been raised by analysts, ECL has posted better than expected results. Based on operating earnings yield, the company is about fairly valued when compared to all of the companies in our coverage universe. Share price changes over the past year indicates that ECL will perform well over the near term.

Financial Data

(US$ in Thousands)	12/31/2012	12/31/2011	12/31/2010	12/31/2009	12/31/2008	12/31/2007	12/31/2006	12/31/2005
Earnings Per Share	2.35	1.91	2.23	1.74	1.80	1.70	1.43	1.23
Cash Flow Per Share	4.10	2.89	4.07	2.94	3.06	3.23	2.49	2.31
Tang Book Value Per Share	N.M.	N.M.	2.23	1.16	N.M.	1.33	1.67	2.00
Dividends Per Share	0.830	0.725	0.640	0.575	0.530	0.475	0.415	0.362
Dividend Payout %	35.32	37.96	28.70	33.05	29.44	27.94	29.02	29.47
Income Statement								
Total Revenue	11,838,700	6,798,500	6,089,700	5,900,600	6,137,500	5,469,600	4,895,814	4,534,832
EBITDA	1,757,300	1,084,800	1,112,800	971,300	998,500	928,200	847,442	765,132
Depn & Amortn	468,000	331,000	306,000	290,000	286,000	260,900	235,800	222,712
Income Before Taxes	1,012,600	679,600	747,700	620,100	650,900	616,300	567,224	498,182
Income Taxes	311,300	216,300	216,600	201,400	202,800	189,100	198,609	178,701
Net Income	703,600	462,500	530,300	417,300	448,100	427,200	368,615	319,481
Average Shares	298,900	242,100	237,600	239,900	249,300	251,800	257,144	260,098
Balance Sheet								
Current Assets	4,892,000	5,396,000	1,869,900	1,814,200	1,691,100	1,717,300	1,853,557	1,421,666
Total Assets	17,572,300	18,240,800	4,872,200	5,020,900	4,756,900	4,722,800	4,419,365	3,796,628
Current Liabilities	3,052,700	3,166,300	1,324,800	1,250,200	1,441,900	1,518,300	1,502,730	1,119,357
Long-Term Obligations	5,736,100	6,613,200	656,400	868,800	799,300	599,900	557,058	519,374
Total Liabilities	11,495,300	12,574,100	2,743,000	3,020,000	3,185,300	2,787,100	2,739,135	2,147,418
Stockholders' Equity	6,077,000	5,666,700	2,129,200	2,000,900	1,571,600	1,935,700	1,680,230	1,649,210
Shares Outstanding	294,722	291,974	232,512	236,594	236,179	246,825	251,336	254,143
Statistical Record								
Return on Assets %	3.92	4.00	10.72	8.54	9.43	9.35	8.97	8.50
Return on Equity %	11.95	11.87	25.68	23.36	25.48	23.63	22.14	19.89
EBITDA Margin %	14.84	15.96	18.27	16.46	16.27	16.97	17.31	16.87
Net Margin %	5.94	6.80	8.71	7.07	7.30	7.81	7.53	7.05
Asset Turnover	0.66	0.59	1.23	1.21	1.29	1.20	1.19	1.21
Current Ratio	1.60	1.70	1.41	1.45	1.17	1.13	1.23	1.27
Debt to Equity	0.94	1.17	0.31	0.43	0.51	0.31	0.33	0.31
Price Range	72.72-58.02	57.81-44.53	52.30-41.33	47.48-29.85	51.24-30.62	52.30-40.16	46.19-33.85	36.76-31.06
P/E Ratio	30.94-24.69	30.27-23.31	23.45-18.53	27.29-17.16	28.47-17.01	30.76-23.62	32.30-23.67	29.89-25.25
Average Yield %	1.27	1.40	1.36	1.45	1.21	1.07	1.02	1.10

Address: 370 Wabasha Street North, St. Paul, MN 55102 **Telephone:** 651-293-2233	**Web Site:** www.ecolab.com **Officers:** Douglas M. Baker - Chairman, President, Chief Executive Officer Thomas W. Handley - President, Chief Operating Officer, Senior Executive Vice President, Division Officer	**Auditors:** PricewaterhouseCoopers LLP **Investor Contact:** 612-293-2809 **Transfer Agents:** Computershare Trust Company, N.A., Canton, MA

EDISON INTERNATIONAL

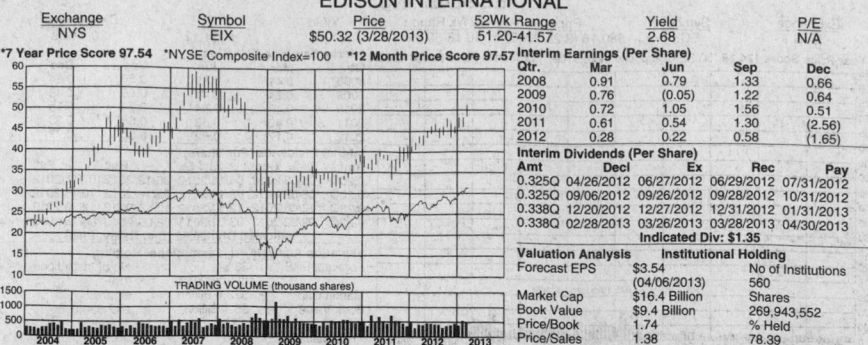

Exchange	Symbol	Price	52Wk Range	Yield	P/E
NYS	EIX	$50.32 (3/28/2013)	51.20-41.57	2.68	N/A

*7 Year Price Score 97.54   *NYSE Composite Index=100   *12 Month Price Score 97.57

Interim Earnings (Per Share)

Qtr.	Mar	Jun	Sep	Dec
2008	0.91	0.79	1.33	0.66
2009	0.76	(0.05)	1.22	0.64
2010	0.72	1.05	1.56	0.51
2011	0.61	0.54	1.30	(2.56)
2012	0.28	0.22	0.58	(1.65)

Interim Dividends (Per Share)

Amt	Decl	Ex	Rec	Pay
0.325Q	04/26/2012	06/27/2012	06/29/2012	07/31/2012
0.325Q	09/06/2012	09/26/2012	09/28/2012	10/31/2012
0.338Q	12/20/2012	12/27/2012	12/31/2012	01/31/2013
0.338Q	02/28/2013	03/26/2013	03/28/2013	04/30/2013

Indicated Div: $1.35

Valuation Analysis / **Institutional Holding**

Forecast EPS	$3.54
	(04/06/2013)
Market Cap	$16.4 Billion
Book Value	$9.4 Billion
Price/Book	1.74
Price/Sales	1.38

No of Institutions	560
Shares	269,943,552
% Held	78.39

Business Summary: Electric Utilities (MIC: 3.1.1 SIC: 4911 NAIC: 221111)

Edison International is a holding company. Through its subsidiary, Southern California Edison Company (SCE), Co. supplies electricity to commercial, residential, industrial, public authorities, and agricultural and other customers in southern California. SCE supplies electricity to its customers through transmission facilities, which include sub-transmission facilities located in California, Nevada and Arizona, and its distribution systems located in California. At Dec 31 2012, SCE served its service territory through approximately 5.0 million customer accounts. Co. is also the parent company of subsidiaries that are engaged in businesses related to the delivery or use of electricity.

Recent Developments: For the year ended Dec 31 2012, net loss amounted to US$92.0 million versus net income of US$22.0 million in the prior year. Revenues were US$11.86 billion, up 12.0% from US$10.59 billion the year before. Operating income was US$2.29 billion versus US$2.06 billion in the prior year, an increase of 10.9%. Direct operating expenses rose 13.7% to US$8.04 billion from US$7.07 billion in the comparable period the year before. Indirect operating expenses increased 5.6% to US$1.53 billion from US$1.45 billion in the equivalent prior-year period.

Prospects: Our evaluation of Edison International as of Apr. 7, 2013 is the result of our systematic analysis on three basic characteristics: earnings strength, relative valuation, and recent stock price movement. The company has produced a positive trend in earnings per share over the past 5 quarters and while recent estimates for the company have been raised by analysts, EIX has posted better than expected results. Based on operating earnings yield, the company is undervalued when compared to all of the companies in our coverage universe. Share price changes over the past year indicates that EIX will perform in line with the market over the near term.

Financial Data
(US$ in Thousands)

	12/31/2012	12/31/2011	12/31/2010	12/31/2009	12/31/2008	12/31/2007	12/31/2006	12/31/2005
Earnings Per Share	(0.56)	(0.11)	3.82	2.58	3.68	3.31	3.57	3.43
Cash Flow Per Share	10.20	11.98	10.67	9.34	6.76	9.79	11.02	6.79
Tang Book Value Per Share	28.95	30.86	32.48	30.20	31.99	28.73	26.47	22.51
Dividends Per Share	1.313	1.285	1.265	1.245	1.225	1.175	1.100	1.020
Dividend Payout %	...	...	33.12	48.26	33.29	35.50	30.81	29.74
Income Statement								
Total Revenue	11,862,000	12,760,000	12,409,000	12,361,000	14,112,000	13,113,000	12,622,000	11,852,000
EBITDA	4,005,000	2,310,000	3,863,000	3,050,000	3,970,000	3,693,000	3,694,000	3,470,000
Depn & Amortn	1,634,000	1,889,000	1,640,000	1,538,000	1,419,000	1,375,000	1,280,000	1,168,000
Income Before Taxes	1,860,000	(350,000)	1,551,000	812,000	1,913,000	1,720,000	1,776,000	1,620,000
Income Taxes	267,000	(288,000)	354,000	(98,000)	596,000	492,000	582,000	457,000
Net Income	(183,000)	(37,000)	1,256,000	849,000	1,215,000	1,098,000	1,181,000	1,137,000
Average Shares	330,000	326,000	329,000	327,000	329,000	331,000	330,000	332,000
Balance Sheet								
Current Assets	2,672,000	4,484,000	4,422,000	4,430,000	7,353,000	4,265,000	5,482,000	5,959,000
Total Assets	44,394,000	48,039,000	45,530,000	41,444,000	44,615,000	37,562,000	36,261,000	34,791,000
Current Liabilities	3,744,000	4,348,000	3,952,000	3,787,000	6,697,000	4,280,000	4,303,000	4,959,000
Long-Term Obligations	9,231,000	13,689,000	12,371,000	10,437,000	10,950,000	9,016,000	9,101,000	8,833,000
Total Liabilities	34,962,000	37,984,000	34,947,000	30,696,000	34,191,000	28,203,000	27,637,000	27,457,000
Stockholders' Equity	9,432,000	10,055,000	10,583,000	9,841,000	10,424,000	9,359,000	8,624,000	7,334,000
Shares Outstanding	325,811	325,811	325,811	325,811	325,811	325,811	325,811	325,811
Statistical Record								
Return on Assets %	N.M.	N.M.	2.89	1.97	2.95	2.97	3.32	3.34
Return on Equity %	N.M.	N.M.	12.30	8.38	12.25	12.21	14.80	16.83
EBITDA Margin %	33.76	18.10	31.13	24.67	28.13	28.16	29.27	29.28
Net Margin %	N.M.	N.M.	10.12	6.87	8.61	8.37	9.36	9.59
Asset Turnover	0.26	0.27	0.29	0.29	0.34	0.36	0.36	0.35
Current Ratio	0.71	1.03	1.12	1.17	1.10	1.00	1.27	1.20
Debt to Equity	0.98	1.36	1.17	1.06	1.05	0.96	1.06	1.20
Price Range	47.96-39.98	41.52-33.29	39.19-31.15	36.39-23.73	54.99-29.58	59.76-42.94	46.95-38.32	48.92-30.71
P/E Ratio	...	...	10.26-8.15	14.10-9.20	14.94-8.04	18.05-12.97	13.15-10.73	14.26-8.95
Average Yield %	2.97	3.37	3.37	4.30	3.95	2.69	2.21	2.93

Address: 2244 Walnut Grove Avenue,	Web Site: www.edisoninvestor.com	Auditors: PricewaterhouseCoopers LLP
P.O. Box 976, Rosemead, CA 91770	Officers: Theodore F. Craver - Chairman, President,	Transfer Agents: Wells Fargo Bank,
Telephone: 626-302-2222	Chief Executive Officer W. James Scilacci - Executive	N.A., South St. Paul, MN
	Vice President, Chief Financial Officer, Treasurer	

EDWARDS LIFESCIENCES CORP

Exchange	Symbol	Price	52Wk Range	Yield	P/E
NYS	EW	$82.16 (3/28/2013)	109.75-68.44	N/A	33.13

*7 Year Price Score 163.60 *NYSE Composite Index=100 *12 Month Price Score 87.32

Interim Earnings (Per Share)

Qtr.	Mar	Jun	Sep	Dec
2008	0.16	0.34	0.28	0.33
2009	0.52	0.41	0.63	0.40
2010	0.40	0.48	0.40	0.54
2011	0.53	0.48	0.43	0.53
2012	0.55	0.57	0.58	0.77

Interim Dividends (Per Share)

Amt	Decl	Ex	Rec	Pay
100%	04/12/2010	05/28/2010	05/14/2010	05/27/2010

Valuation Analysis | **Institutional Holding**

Forecast EPS	$3.26	No of Institutions
	(04/05/2013)	526
Market Cap	$9.4 Billion	Shares
Book Value	$1.5 Billion	110,453,616
Price/Book	6.35	% Held
Price/Sales	4.94	89.88

Business Summary: Medical Instruments & Equipment (MIC: 4.3.1 SIC: 3842 NAIC: 339113)

Edwards Lifesciences provides products and technologies to treat cardiovascular disease or critically ill patients. Co.'s products and technologies are categorized into four main areas: Heart Valve Therapy, including tissue heart valves and heart valve repair products; Critical Care, including hemodynamic monitoring systems used to measure a patient's cardiovascular function, and disposable pressure transducers; Cardiac Surgery Systems, including products for use during cardiac surgery, including cannulae, embolic protection devices and other products used during cardiopulmonary bypass procedures; and Vascular, including a line of balloon catheter-based products, surgical clips and inserts.

Recent Developments: For the year ended Dec 31 2012, net income increased 23.9% to US$293.2 million from US$236.7 million in the prior year. Revenues were US$1.90 billion, up 13.2% from US$1.68 billion the year before. Direct operating expenses rose 1.0% to US$494.6 million from US$489.8 million in the comparable period the year before. Indirect operating expenses increased 11.2% to US$1.01 billion from US$910.3 million in the equivalent prior-year period.

Prospects: Our evaluation of Edwards Lifesciences Corp. as of Apr. 7, 2013 is the result of our systematic analysis on three basic characteristics: earnings strength, relative valuation, and recent stock price movement. The company has produced a positive trend in earnings per share over the past 5 quarters. However, while recent estimates for the company have been mixed, EW has posted better than expected results. Based on operating earnings yield, the company is about fairly valued when compared to all of the companies in our coverage universe. Share price changes over the past year indicates that EW will perform very well over the near term.

Financial Data
(US$ in Thousands)

	12/31/2012	12/31/2011	12/31/2010	12/31/2009	12/31/2008	12/31/2007	12/31/2006	12/31/2005
Earnings Per Share	2.48	1.98	1.83	1.95	1.10	0.94	1.05	0.64
Cash Flow Per Share	3.24	2.74	2.21	1.47	1.37	1.83	1.97	1.15
Tang Book Value Per Share	8.99	8.07	8.05	6.65	4.17	3.20	2.56	1.80
Income Statement								
Total Revenue	1,899,600	1,678,600	1,447,000	1,321,400	1,237,700	1,091,100	1,037,000	997,900
EBITDA	434,700	327,300	309,700	343,500	202,300	189,200	214,200	182,600
Depn & Amortn	44,000	44,000	40,000	38,000	36,800	38,000	39,200	56,200
Income Before Taxes	391,100	283,600	268,200	304,400	164,400	149,800	172,300	116,700
Income Taxes	97,900	46,900	50,200	75,300	35,500	36,800	41,800	37,400
Net Income	293,200	236,700	218,000	229,100	128,900	113,000	130,500	79,300
Average Shares	118,300	119,400	119,200	117,400	119,200	125,400	127,800	124,600
Balance Sheet								
Current Assets	1,291,900	1,168,500	1,032,600	889,200	691,900	581,700	531,600	514,200
Total Assets	2,221,500	1,980,500	1,767,200	1,615,500	1,400,200	1,345,100	1,246,800	1,229,100
Current Liabilities	347,400	335,200	337,800	290,500	258,500	375,400	226,200	194,200
Long-Term Obligations	189,300	150,400	...	90,300	175,500	61,700	235,900	316,100
Total Liabilities	742,200	642,600	459,000	457,600	521,400	510,100	497,400	539,100
Stockholders' Equity	1,479,300	1,337,900	1,308,200	1,157,900	878,800	835,000	749,400	690,000
Shares Outstanding	114,300	114,100	115,000	113,600	111,800	113,200	115,400	119,049
Statistical Record								
Return on Assets %	13.92	12.63	12.89	15.19	9.36	8.72	10.54	6.77
Return on Equity %	20.76	17.89	17.68	22.50	15.00	14.26	18.13	12.03
EBITDA Margin %	22.88	19.50	21.40	26.00	16.34	17.34	20.66	18.30
Net Margin %	15.43	14.10	15.07	17.34	10.41	10.36	12.58	7.95
Asset Turnover	0.90	0.90	0.86	0.88	0.90	0.84	0.84	0.85
Current Ratio	3.72	3.49	3.06	3.06	2.68	1.55	2.35	2.65
Debt to Equity	0.13	0.11	...	0.08	0.20	0.07	0.31	0.46
Price Range	109.75-68.43	91.36-62.40	84.75-42.91	43.89-26.56	33.09-21.30	26.38-22.98	24.16-20.68	23.38-19.73
P/E Ratio	44.25-27.59	46.14-31.52	46.31-23.45	22.51-13.62	30.08-19.36	28.06-24.45	23.00-19.69	36.53-30.84

Address: One Edwards Way, Irvine, CA 92614	Web Site: www.edwards.com	Auditors: PricewaterhouseCoopers LLP
Telephone: 949-250-2500	Officers: Michael A. Mussallem - Chairman, Chief Executive Officer Donald E. Bobo - Corporate Vice-President	Investor Contact: 949-250-2806 Transfer Agents: ComputerShare Investor Services, Providence, RI

EMC CORP. (MA)

Exchange	Symbol	Price	52Wk Range	Yield	P/E
NYS	EMC	$23.89 (3/28/2013)	29.85-22.83	N/A	19.42

*7 Year Price Score 120.16 *NYSE Composite Index=100 *12 Month Price Score 87.37

Interim Earnings (Per Share)

Qtr.	Mar	Jun	Sep	Dec
2008	0.13	0.18	0.20	0.14
2009	0.10	0.10	0.14	0.19
2010	0.17	0.20	0.22	0.29
2011	0.21	0.24	0.27	0.38
2012	0.27	0.29	0.28	0.39

Interim Dividends (Per Share)

No Dividends Paid

Valuation Analysis

		Institutional Holding	
Forecast EPS	$1.86	No of Institutions	
	(04/05/2013)	1553	
Market Cap	$50.3 Billion	Shares	
Book Value	$22.4 Billion	1,886,504,704	
Price/Book	2.25	% Held	
Price/Sales	2.32	82.34	

TRADING VOLUME (thousand shares)

Business Summary: Computer Hardware & Equipment (MIC: 6.2.1 SIC: 3572 NAIC: 334112)

EMC develops, delivers and supports the Information Technology industry's range of information infrastructure and virtual infrastructure technologies, applications and services. Co. manages its business in two categories: Information Infrastructure and VMware Virtual Infrastructure. Co.'s Information Infrastructure business comprises three segments: Information Storage, which provides a portfolio of enterprise storage systems and software, RSA Information Security and Information Intelligence Group. Co.'s VMware Virtual Infrastructure business, which is represented by Co.'s majority equity stake in VMware, Inc., is engaged in virtualization infrastructure applications.

Recent Developments: For the year ended Dec 31 2012, net income increased 10.6% to US$2.89 billion from US$2.61 billion in the prior year. Revenues were US$21.71 billion, up 8.5% from US$20.01 billion the year before. Operating income was US$3.96 billion versus US$3.44 billion in the prior year, an increase of 15.1%. Direct operating expenses rose 3.0% to US$8.08 billion from US$7.84 billion in the comparable period the year before. Indirect operating expenses increased 10.9% to US$9.67 billion from US$8.73 billion in the equivalent prior-year period.

Prospects: Our evaluation of EMC Corp. as of Apr. 7, 2013 is the result of our systematic analysis on three basic characteristics: earnings strength, relative valuation, and recent stock price movement. The company has enjoyed a very positive trend in earnings per share over the past 5 quarters and while recent estimates for the company have remained steady, EMC has posted better than expected results. Based on operating earnings yield, the company is undervalued when compared to all of the companies in our coverage universe. Share price changes over the past year indicates that EMC will perform poorly over the near term.

Financial Data

(US$ in Thousands)	12/31/2012	12/31/2011	12/31/2010	12/31/2009	12/31/2008	12/31/2007	12/31/2006	12/31/2005
Earnings Per Share	1.23	1.10	0.88	0.53	0.64	0.77	0.54	0.47
Cash Flow Per Share	2.98	2.76	2.21	1.65	1.74	1.50	0.95	0.93
Tang Book Value Per Share	3.08	2.46	1.94	2.51	2.58	2.40	1.56	3.20
Income Statement								
Total Revenue	21,713,902	20,007,588	17,015,126	14,025,910	14,876,163	13,230,205	11,155,090	9,663,955
EBITDA	4,662,818	4,147,636	3,381,628	2,122,575	2,337,680	2,662,724	1,879,541	2,062,931
Depn & Amortn	780,300	727,900	595,300	565,500	561,100	530,300	455,400	402,700
Income Before Taxes	3,803,615	3,249,270	2,607,983	1,374,576	1,702,806	2,059,569	1,390,018	1,652,243
Income Taxes	917,598	640,385	638,297	252,775	312,514	378,446	162,664	519,078
Net Income	2,732,613	2,461,337	1,899,995	1,088,077	1,345,567	1,665,668	1,223,982	1,133,165
Average Shares	2,205,639	2,229,113	2,147,931	2,055,146	2,079,853	2,157,873	2,286,304	2,432,582
Balance Sheet								
Current Assets	12,208,609	11,582,683	9,783,322	10,538,302	10,665,029	10,053,102	6,520,587	6,573,976
Total Assets	38,068,685	34,268,179	30,833,284	26,812,003	23,874,575	22,284,654	18,566,247	16,790,383
Current Liabilities	10,303,996	10,376,210	9,378,014	5,148,167	5,218,436	4,408,208	3,881,104	3,673,858
Long-Term Obligations	...	...	...	3,100,290	3,450,000	3,450,000	3,450,000	126,963
Total Liabilities	15,711,542	15,309,146	13,429,244	11,262,121	10,832,612	9,763,337	8,240,540	4,724,953
Stockholders' Equity	22,357,143	18,959,033	17,404,040	15,549,882	13,041,963	12,521,317	10,325,707	12,065,430
Shares Outstanding	2,106,959	2,048,890	2,069,246	2,052,441	2,012,938	2,102,187	2,122,339	2,384,147
Statistical Record								
Return on Assets %	7.53	7.56	6.59	4.29	5.81	8.15	6.92	7.04
Return on Equity %	13.19	13.54	11.53	7.61	10.50	14.58	10.93	9.61
EBITDA Margin %	21.47	20.73	19.87	15.13	15.71	20.13	16.85	21.35
Net Margin %	12.58	12.30	11.17	7.76	9.05	12.59	10.97	11.73
Asset Turnover	0.60	0.61	0.59	0.55	0.64	0.65	0.63	0.60
Current Ratio	1.18	1.12	1 04	2.05	2.04	2.28	1.68	1.79
Debt to Equity	...	...	...	0.20	0.26	0.28	0.33	0.01
Price Range	29.88-21.72	28.47-20.28	23.09-16.63	18.44-9.85	18.53-8.85	25.39-12.93	14.58-9.65	14.87-11.47
P/E Ratio	24.29-17.66	25.88-18.44	26.24-18.90	34.79-18.58	28.95-13.83	32.97-16.79	27.00-17.87	31.64-24.40

Address: 176 South Street, Hopkinton, MA 01748 **Telephone:** 508-435-1000 **Fax:** 508-435-5222	**Web Site:** www.emc.com **Officers:** Joseph M. Tucci - Chairman, President, Chief Executive Officer William J. Teuber - Vice-Chairman	**Auditors:** PricewaterhouseCoopers LLP **Investor Contact:** 508-293-7137 **Transfer Agents:** BNY Mellon Shareowner Services, Pittsburgh, PA

EMCOR GROUP, INC.

Exchange	Symbol	Price	52Wk Range	Yield	P/E
NYS	EME	$42.39 (3/28/2013)	42.39-25.76	0.57	19.63

*7 Year Price Score 103.34 *NYSE Composite Index=100 *12 Month Price Score 114.53

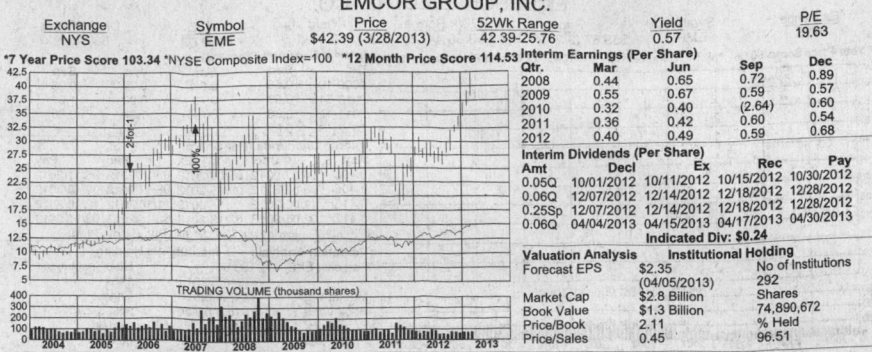

Interim Earnings (Per Share)

Qtr.	Mar	Jun	Sep	Dec
2008	0.44	0.65	0.72	0.89
2009	0.55	0.67	0.59	0.57
2010	0.32	0.40	(2.64)	0.60
2011	0.36	0.42	0.60	0.54
2012	0.40	0.49	0.59	0.68

Interim Dividends (Per Share)

Amt	Decl	Ex	Rec	Pay
0.05Q	10/01/2012	10/11/2012	10/15/2012	10/30/2012
0.06Q	12/07/2012	12/14/2012	12/18/2012	12/28/2012
0.25Sp	12/07/2012	12/14/2012	12/18/2012	12/28/2012
0.06Q	04/04/2013	04/15/2013	04/17/2013	04/30/2013

Indicated Div: $0.24

Valuation Analysis | **Institutional Holding**

Forecast EPS	$2.35 (04/05/2013)	No of Institutions	292
Market Cap	$2.8 Billion	Shares	74,890,672
Book Value	$1.3 Billion	% Held	96.51
Price/Book	2.11		
Price/Sales	0.45		

Business Summary: Construction Services (MIC: 7.5.4 SIC: 1731 NAIC: 238210)

EMCOR Group is an electrical and mechanical construction and facilities services firm. Co. is engaged in providing construction services relating to electrical and mechanical systems in various facilities and in providing services for the operation, maintenance and management of various aspects of such facilities. Co. has the following reportable segments: U.S. electrical construction and facilities services; U.S. mechanical construction and facilities services; U.S. facilities services; U. K. construction and facilities services; and other international construction and facilities services.

Recent Developments: For the year ended Dec 31 2012, income from continuing operations increased 19.5% to US$148.9 million from US$124.6 million a year earlier. Net income increased 11.4% to US$148.9 million from US$133.7 million in the prior year. Revenues were US$6.35 billion, up 13.1% from US$5.61 billion the year before. Operating income was US$250.0 million versus US$210.8 million in the prior year, an increase of 18.6%. Direct operating expenses rose 13.5% to US$5.54 billion from US$4.88 billion in the comparable period the year before. Indirect operating expenses increased 6.4% to US$556.4 million from US$523.2 million in the equivalent prior-year period.

Prospects: Our evaluation of EMCOR Group Inc. as of Apr. 7, 2013 is the result of our systematic analysis on three basic characteristics: earnings strength, relative valuation, and recent stock price movement. The company has managed to produce a neutral trend in earnings per share over the past 5 quarters and while recent estimates for the company have remained steady, EME has posted better than expected results. Based on operating earnings yield, the company is undervalued when compared to all of the companies in our coverage universe. Share price changes over the past year indicates that EME will perform well over the near term.

Financial Data

(US$ in Thousands)	12/31/2012	12/31/2011	12/31/2010	12/31/2009	12/31/2008	12/31/2007	12/31/2006	12/31/2005
Earnings Per Share	2.16	1.91	(1.31)	2.38	2.71	1.90	1.33	0.94
Cash Flow Per Share	2.76	2.24	1.03	5.45	5.11	4.02	3.31	2.30
Tang Book Value Per Share	6.51	4.48	7.52	5.44	2.57	1.06	6.03	5.06
Dividends Per Share	0.510	0.050	...	...	...	...	...	...
Dividend Payout %	23.61	2.62	...	...	...	...	...	...
Income Statement								
Total Revenue	6,346,679	5,613,459	5,121,285	5,547,942	6,785,242	5,927,152	5,021,036	4,714,547
EBITDA	310,929	264,543	(12,269)	281,402	325,934	216,837	122,295	84,323
Depn & Amortn	60,962	53,750	16,417	18,977	23,357	17,012	4,251	3,192
Income Before Taxes	244,248	201,352	(38,189)	259,270	300,723	203,800	121,939	75,545
Income Taxes	95,362	76,764	52,395	96,193	116,588	77,706	30,484	9,738
Net Income	146,584	130,826	(86,691)	160,756	182,204	126,808	86,634	60,042
Average Shares	67,738	68,375	66,393	67,445	67,117	66,731	65,480	63,669
Balance Sheet								
Current Assets	2,044,453	1,936,653	1,980,167	1,977,365	2,010,740	1,935,790	1,662,413	1,389,803
Total Assets	3,107,070	3,014,076	2,755,542	2,981,894	3,008,404	2,871,643	2,089,023	1,778,941
Current Liabilities	1,294,519	1,330,913	1,232,699	1,334,605	1,513,155	1,514,223	1,208,348	1,045,316
Long-Term Obligations	154,112	153,335	151,184	150,251	196,218	223,453	1,239	1,406
Total Liabilities	1,760,990	1,779,342	1,602,599	1,763,823	1,965,059	1,986,602	1,378,714	1,163,505
Stockholders' Equity	1,346,080	1,234,734	1,152,943	1,218,071	1,043,345	885,041	710,309	615,436
Shares Outstanding	66,964	66,444	66,660	66,187	65,520	65,196	63,655	62,207
Statistical Record								
Return on Assets %	4.78	4.53	N.M.	5.37	6.18	5.11	4.48	3.34
Return on Equity %	11.33	10.96	N.M.	14.22	18.85	15.90	13.07	10.20
EBITDA Margin %	4.90	4.71	N.M.	5.07	4.80	3.66	2.44	1.79
Net Margin %	2.31	2.33	N.M.	2.90	2.69	2.14	1.73	1.27
Asset Turnover	2.07	1.95	1.79	1.85	2.30	2.39	2.60	2.62
Current Ratio	1.58	1.46	1.61	1.48	1.33	1.28	1.38	1.33
Debt to Equity	0.11	0.12	0.13	0.12	0.19	0.25	N.M.	N.M.
Price Range	34.70-25.76	32.65-18.58	29.89-22.33	27.69-13.56	34.63-11.28	38.31-23.52	31.31-17.79	18.06-10.54
P/E Ratio	16.06-11.93	17.09-9.73	...	11.63-5.70	12.78-4.16	20.16-12.38	23.54-13.37	19.21-11.21
Average Yield %	1.76	0.18	...	...	...	...	...	...

Address: 301 Merritt Seven, Norwalk, CT 06851-1092 Telephone: 203-849-7800	Web Site: www.emcorgroup.com Officers: Frank T. MacInnis - Chairman, Chief Executive Officer Anthony J. Guzzi - President, Chief Operating Officer	Auditors: Ernst & Young LLP Investor Contact: 203-849-7938 Transfer Agents: BNY Mellon Shareowner Services, New York, NY

EMERSON ELECTRIC CO.

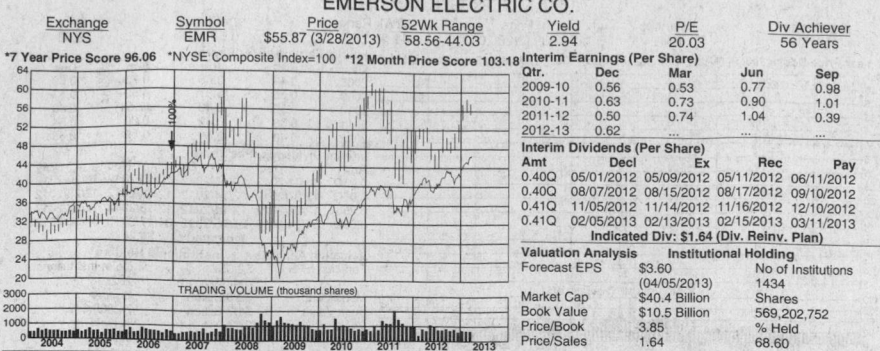

Exchange	Symbol	Price	52Wk Range	Yield	P/E	Div Achiever
NYS	EMR	$55.87 (3/28/2013)	58.56-44.03	2.94	20.03	56 Years

*7 Year Price Score 96.06   *NYSE Composite Index=100   *12 Month Price Score 103.18

Interim Earnings (Per Share)

Qtr.	Dec	Mar	Jun	Sep
2009-10	0.56	0.53	0.77	0.98
2010-11	0.63	0.73	0.90	1.01
2011-12	0.50	0.74	1.04	0.39
2012-13	0.62	...	...	...

Interim Dividends (Per Share)

Amt	Decl	Ex	Rec	Pay
0.40Q	05/01/2012	05/09/2012	05/11/2012	06/11/2012
0.40Q	08/07/2012	08/15/2012	08/17/2012	09/10/2012
0.41Q	11/05/2012	11/14/2012	11/16/2012	12/10/2012
0.41Q	02/05/2013	02/13/2013	02/15/2013	03/11/2013

Indicated Div: $1.64 (Div. Reinv. Plan)

Valuation Analysis   **Institutional Holding**

Forecast EPS	$3.60 (04/05/2013)	No of Institutions 1434
Market Cap	$40.4 Billion	Shares 569,202,752
Book Value	$10.5 Billion	% Held
Price/Book	3.85	68.60
Price/Sales	1.64	

Business Summary: Electrical Equipment (MIC: 7.3.1 SIC: 3679 NAIC: 334419)

Emerson Electric designs and supplies products and technology, and delivers engineering services and applications in a range of industrial, commercial and consumer markets globally. Co.'s segments include: Process Management, providing measurement, control and diagnostic capabilities for automated industrial processes; Industrial Automation, bringing integrated manufacturing applications to several industries; Network Power, providing power conditioning and environmental control; Climate Technologies, for household and commercial comfort; and Commercial & Residential Solutions, providing tools for personnel and homeowners, home and commercial storage systems, and appliance applications.

Recent Developments: For the quarter ended Dec 31 2012, net income increased 22.3% to US$466.0 million from US$381.0 million in the year-earlier quarter. Revenues were US$5.55 billion, up 4.6% from US$5.31 billion the year before. Direct operating expenses rose 2.8% to US$3.35 billion from US$3.25 billion in the comparable period the year before. Indirect operating expenses increased 3.0% to US$1.39 billion from US$1.35 billion in the equivalent prior-year period.

Prospects: Our evaluation of Emerson Electric Co. as of Apr. 7, 2013 is the result of our systematic analysis on three basic characteristics: earnings strength, relative valuation, and recent stock price movement. The company has managed to produce a neutral trend in earnings per share over the past 5 quarters and while recent estimates for the company have remained steady, EMR has posted better than expected results. Based on operating earnings yield, the company is undervalued when compared to all of the companies in our coverage universe. Share price changes over the past year indicates that EMR will perform in line with the market over the near term.

Financial Data
(US$ in Thousands)

	3 Mos	09/30/2012	09/30/2011	09/30/2010	09/30/2009	09/30/2008	09/30/2007	09/30/2006
Earnings Per Share	2.79	2.67	3.27	2.84	2.27	3.06	2.66	2.24
Cash Flow Per Share	4.53	4.17	4.32	4.39	4.09	4.21	3.80	3.08
Tang Book Value Per Share	0.85	0.60	N.M.	N.M.	0.73	2.49	2.30	2.08
Dividends Per Share	1.610	1.600	1.380	1.340	1.320	1.200	1.050	0.890
Dividend Payout %	57.71	59.93	42.20	47.18	58.15	39.22	39.47	39.73
Income Statement								
Total Revenue	5,553,000	24,412,000	24,222,000	21,039,000	20,915,000	24,807,000	22,572,000	20,133,000
EBITDA	668,000	4,085,000	4,637,000	3,878,000	3,288,000	4,417,000	3,923,000	3,438,000
Depn & Amortn	(59,000)	746,000	783,000	738,000	651,000	638,000	588,000	547,000
Income Before Taxes	673,000	3,115,000	3,631,000	2,879,000	2,417,000	3,591,000	3,107,000	2,684,000
Income Taxes	207,000	1,091,000	1,127,000	848,000	693,000	1,137,000	971,000	839,000
Net Income	454,000	1,968,000	2,480,000	2,164,000	1,724,000	2,412,000	2,136,000	1,845,000
Average Shares	726,900	734,600	753,500	757,000	758,700	789,400	803,900	824,400
Balance Sheet								
Current Assets	10,086,000	10,126,000	9,345,000	8,363,000	7,653,000	9,331,000	8,065,000	7,330,000
Total Assets	23,771,000	23,818,000	23,861,000	22,843,000	19,763,000	21,040,000	19,680,000	18,672,000
Current Liabilities	7,203,000	7,133,000	6,465,000	5,849,000	4,956,000	6,573,000	5,546,000	5,374,000
Long-Term Obligations	3,542,000	3,787,000	4,324,000	4,586,000	3,998,000	3,297,000	3,372,000	3,128,000
Total Liabilities	13,293,000	13,523,000	13,462,000	13,051,000	11,208,000	11,927,000	10,908,000	10,518,000
Stockholders' Equity	10,478,000	10,295,000	10,399,000	9,792,000	8,555,000	9,113,000	8,772,000	8,154,000
Shares Outstanding	722,641	724,113	738,877	752,690	751,872	771,216	788,434	804,693
Statistical Record								
Return on Assets %	8.69	8.23	10.62	10.16	8.45	11.81	11.14	10.28
Return on Equity %	19.85	18.97	24.57	23.59	19.52	26.90	25.24	23.72
EBITDA Margin %	12.03	16.73	19.14	18.43	15.72	17.81	17.38	17.08
Net Margin %	8.18	8.06	10.24	10.29	8.24	9.72	9.46	9.16
Asset Turnover	1.04	1.02	1.04	0.99	1.03	1.22	1.18	1.12
Current Ratio	1.40	1.42	1.45	1.43	1.54	1.42	1.45	1.36
Debt to Equity	0.34	0.37	0.42	0.47	0.47	0.36	0.38	0.38
Price Range	53.25-44.03	52.67-40.69	61.85-41.31	53.62-37.75	41.24-24.87	58.32-38.46	53.37-41.10	43.73-33.97
P/E Ratio	19.09-15.78	19.73-15.24	18.91-12.63	18.88-13.29	18.17-10.96	19.06-12.57	20.06-15.45	19.52-15.16
Average Yield %	3.27	3.28	2.54	2.91	3.93	2.32	2.31	2.24

Address: 8000 W. Florissant Avenue, P.O. Box 4100, St. Louis, MO 63136 Telephone: 314-553-2000	Web Site: www.emerson.com Officers: David N. Farr - Chairman, President, Chief Executive Officer Edward L. Monser - President, Chief Operating Officer	Auditors: KPMG LLP Investor Contact: 314-553-2197 Transfer Agents: BNY Mellon Shareowner Services LLC, Pittsburgh, PA

ENBRIDGE ENERGY PARTNERS, L.P.

Exchange	Symbol	Price	52Wk Range	Yield	P/E
NYS	EEP	$30.14 (3/28/2013)	31.40-27.15	7.18	23.73

*7 Year Price Score 100.38 *NYSE Composite Index=100 *12 Month Price Score 90.20

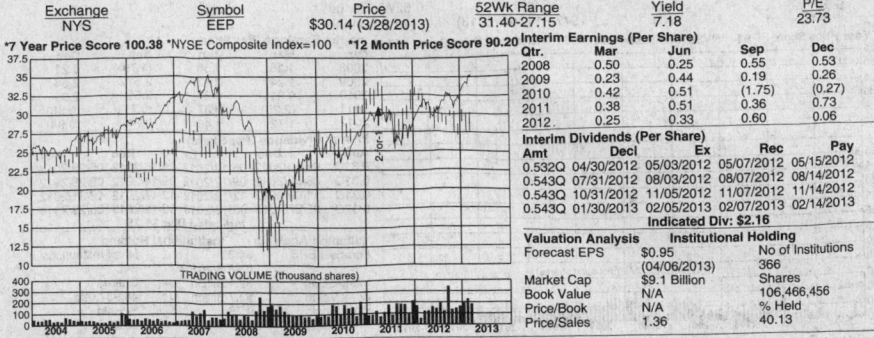

Interim Earnings (Per Share)

Qtr.	Mar	Jun	Sep	Dec
2008	0.50	0.25	0.55	0.53
2009	0.23	0.44	0.19	0.26
2010	0.42	0.51	(1.75)	(0.27)
2011	0.38	0.51	0.36	0.73
2012	0.25	0.33	0.60	0.06

Interim Dividends (Per Share)

Amt	Decl	Ex	Rec	Pay
0.532Q	04/30/2012	05/03/2012	05/07/2012	05/15/2012
0.543Q	07/31/2012	08/03/2012	08/07/2012	08/14/2012
0.543Q	10/31/2012	11/05/2012	11/07/2012	11/14/2012
0.543Q	01/30/2013	02/05/2013	02/07/2013	02/14/2013

Indicated Div: $2.16

Valuation Analysis / **Institutional Holding**

Forecast EPS	$0.95	No of Institutions
	(04/06/2013)	366
Market Cap	$9.1 Billion	Shares
Book Value	N/A	106,466,456
Price/Book	N/A	% Held
Price/Sales	1.36	40.13

Business Summary: Equipment & Services (MIC: 9.1.3 SIC: 4619 NAIC: 486990)

Enbridge Energy Partners owns and operates crude oil and liquid petroleum transportation and storage assets, along with natural gas gathering, treating, processing, transmission and marketing assets in the U.S. Co. conducts its business through three operating segments: liquids, natural gas and marketing. As of Dec 31 2012, Co.'s portfolio of assets included: 6,500 miles of crude oil gathering and transportation lines; 35,000,000 barrels of crude oil storage and terminaling capacity; natural gas gathering and transportation lines totaling 11,400 miles; and nine natural gas treating and 25 natural gas processing facilities with an aggregate capacity of 3,105,000,000 cubic feet per day.

Recent Developments: For the year ended Dec 31 2012, net income decreased 18.8% to US$550.1 million from US$677.2 million in the prior year. Revenues were US$6.71 billion, down 26.4% from US$9.11 billion the year before. Operating income was US$893.2 million versus US$996.8 million in the prior year, a decrease of 10.4%. Direct operating expenses declined 34.9% to US$4.72 billion from US$7.24 billion in the comparable period the year before. Indirect operating expenses increased 26.0% to US$1.09 billion from US$868.1 million in the equivalent prior-year period.

Prospects: Our evaluation of Enbridge Energy Partners, L.P. as of Apr. 7, 2013 is the result of our systematic analysis on three basic characteristics: earnings strength, relative valuation, and recent stock price movement. The company has generated a negative trend in earnings per share over the past 5 quarters. However, while recent estimates for the company have been lowered by analysts, EEP has posted results that fell short of analysts expectations. Based on operating earnings yield, the company is overvalued when compared to all of the companies in our coverage universe. Share price changes over the past year indicates that EEP will perform very poorly over the near term.

Financial Data

(US$ in Thousands)	12/31/2012	12/31/2011	12/31/2010	12/31/2009	12/31/2008	12/31/2007	12/31/2006	12/31/2005
Earnings Per Share	1.27	1.99	(1.09)	1.12	1.81	1.23	1.81	0.53
Cash Flow Per Share	2.92	3.99	1.58	3.13	2.79	2.68	2.29	2.15
Dividends Per Share	2.152	2.092	2.024	1.980	1.940	1.863	1.850	1.850
Dividend Payout %	169.45	105.15	...	176.79	106.89	152.04	102.21	349.06
Income Statement								
Total Revenue	6,706,100	9,109,800	7,736,100	5,731,800	10,060,000	7,282,600	6,509,000	6,476,900
EBITDA	1,248,000	1,343,100	456,000	899,300	814,200	487,400	530,500	437,800
Depn & Amortn	344,800	339,800	311,200	269,300	223,400	165,600	135,100	138,200
Income Before Taxes	558,200	682,700	(130,000)	401,400	410,200	222,000	284,900	191,900
Income Taxes	8,100	5,500	7,900	8,500	7,000	5,100	...	...
Net Income	493,100	624,000	(198,500)	316,600	403,200	249,500	284,900	89,200
Average Shares	290,600	262,300	239,200	232,800	194,200	172,600	140,400	124,200
Balance Sheet								
Current Assets	1,087,900	1,319,400	1,219,900	869,900	1,124,500	959,700	1,009,300	985,300
Total Assets	12,796,800	11,370,100	10,441,000	8,988,300	8,300,900	6,891,600	5,223,800	4,428,400
Current Liabilities	1,634,000	1,450,200	1,317,900	1,065,000	1,136,200	1,124,400	961,600	971,300
Long-Term Obligations	5,819,700	5,146,100	5,114,700	3,791,200	3,353,400	2,992,900	2,066,100	1,834,700
Total Liabilities	8,342,400	7,203,500	7,020,900	5,259,500	4,574,000	4,320,100	3,180,400	3,064,600
Shares Outstanding	303,232	284,435	252,195	235,489	228,907	181,578	155,191	131,113
Statistical Record								
Return on Assets %	4.07	5.72	N.M.	3.66	5.29	4.12	5.90	2.18
EBITDA Margin %	18.61	14.74	5.89	15.69	8.09	6.69	8.15	6.76
Net Margin %	7.35	6.85	N.M.	5.52	4.01	3.43	4.38	1.38
Asset Turnover	0.55	0.84	0.80	0.66	1.32	1.20	1.35	1.58
Current Ratio	0.67	0.91	0.93	0.82	0.99	0.85	1.05	1.01
Price Range	33.50-27.15	34.30-25.28	31.21-23.10	26.88-12.52	26.49-11.89	30.91-24.27	25.34-21.05	28.40-21.08
P/E Ratio	26.38-21.38	17.24-12.70	...	24.00-11.18	14.64-6.57	25.13-19.73	14.00-11.63	53.58-39.77
Average Yield %	7.17	6.88	7.41	9.97	8.81	6.97	8.02	7.15

Address: 1100 Louisiana Street, Suite 3300, Houston, TX 77002 **Telephone:** 713-821-2000 **Fax:** 713-821-2230	**Web Site:** www.enbridgepartners.com **Officers:** Jeffrey A. Connelly - Chairman Terrance L. McGill - President, Holding/Parent Company Officer	**Auditors:** PricewaterhouseCoopers LLP **Investor Contact:** 866-337-4636 **Transfer Agents:** Computershare, Providence, RI

ENDURANCE SPECIALTY HOLDINGS LTD

Exchange	Symbol	Price	52Wk Range	Yield	P/E
NYS	ENH	$47.81 (3/28/2013)	47.81-34.09	2.61	15.94

*7 Year Price Score 96.91 *NYSE Composite Index=100 *12 Month Price Score 102.86

Interim Earnings (Per Share)

Qtr.	Mar	Jun	Sep	Dec
2008	1.15	1.56	(1.79)	0.22
2009	1.24	2.42	2.51	2.54
2010	0.91	0.97	2.51	2.05
2011	(2.25)	0.87	(0.71)	(0.88)
2012	1.72	1.48	0.74	(0.94)

Interim Dividends (Per Share)

Amt	Decl	Ex	Rec	Pay
0.31Q	05/10/2012	06/13/2012	06/15/2012	06/29/2012
0.31Q	08/09/2012	09/12/2012	09/14/2012	09/28/2012
0.31Q	11/09/2012	12/13/2012	12/17/2012	12/31/2012
0.32Q	02/27/2013	03/13/2013	03/15/2013	03/29/2013

Indicated Div: $1.25

Valuation Analysis

Forecast EPS	$4.30 (04/06/2013)
Market Cap	$2.1 Billion
Book Value	$2.7 Billion
Price/Book	0.76
Price/Sales	0.91

Institutional Holding

No of Institutions	242
Shares	48,937,096
% Held	95.25

Business Summary: General Insurance (MIC: 5.2.1 SIC: 6331 NAIC: 524126)

Endurance Specialty Holdings is a holding company. Through its operating subsidiaries, Co. focuses on underwriting personal and commercial property and casualty insurance and reinsurance. Co.'s business is organized into two business segments: Insurance and Reinsurance. Co.'s Insurance segment is comprised of six lines of business: agriculture, professional lines, casualty, property, healthcare liability, as well as surety and other specialty lines. Co.'s Reinsurance segment is comprised of five lines of business: catastrophe, casualty, property, aerospace and marine, as well as surety and other specialty.

Recent Developments: For the year ended Dec 31 2012, net income amounted to US$162.5 million versus a net loss of US$93.7 million in the prior year. Revenues were US$2.26 billion, up 7.3% from US$2.10 billion the year before. Net premiums earned were US$2.01 billion versus US$1.93 billion in the prior year, an increase of 4.3%. Net investment income rose 17.9% to US$173.3 million from US$147.0 million a year ago.

Prospects: Our evaluation of Endurance Specialty Holdings Ltd. as of Apr. 7, 2013 is the result of our systematic analysis on three basic characteristics: earnings strength, relative valuation, and recent stock price movement. The company has suffered a very negative trend in earnings per share over the past 5 quarters. However, while recent estimates for the company have been mixed, ENH has posted better than expected results. Based on operating earnings yield, the company is overvalued when compared to all of the companies in our coverage universe. Share price changes over the past year indicates that ENH will perform poorly over the near term.

Financial Data
(US$ in Thousands)

	12/31/2012	12/31/2011	12/31/2010	12/31/2009	12/31/2008	12/31/2007	12/31/2006	12/31/2005
Earnings Per Share	3.00	(2.95)	6.38	8.69	1.32	7.17	6.73	(3.60)
Cash Flow Per Share	6.39	6.99	8.00	8.44	8.28	7.43	10.16	12.87
Tang Book Value Per Share	58.48	55.98	56.30	46.95	34.94	38.06	33.39	27.20
Dividends Per Share	1.240	4.080	2.940	2.940	...	2.940	...	...
Dividend Payout %	41.33	...	46.08	33.83	...	41.00	...	...
Income Statement								
Premium Income	2,013,900	1,931,393	1,741,113	1,633,192	1,766,485	1,594,800	1,638,574	1,723,694
Total Revenue	2,256,335	2,103,034	1,958,379	1,907,358	1,835,322	1,859,376	1,877,071	1,896,425
Benefits & Claims	1,520,995	1,632,666	1,038,100	866,640	1,135,431	749,081	827,630	1,650,943
Income Before Taxes	165,862	(116,740)	371,898	524,696	89,063	542,069	527,959	(271,632)
Income Taxes	3,346	(23,006)	7,160	(11,408)	(9,561)	20,962	29,833	(51,148)
Net Income	162,516	(93,734)	364,738	536,104	98,624	521,107	498,126	(220,484)
Average Shares	42,601	40,214	53,728	58,874	62,795	70,539	71,755	62,029
Balance Sheet								
Total Assets	8,794,972	8,292,615	7,979,405	7,666,694	7,272,470	7,270,727	6,925,554	6,352,537
Total Liabilities	6,084,375	5,681,450	5,131,252	4,879,411	5,065,187	4,758,468	4,627,680	4,479,994
Stockholders' Equity	2,710,597	2,611,165	2,848,153	2,787,283	2,207,283	2,512,259	2,297,874	1,872,543
Shares Outstanding	43,116	43,086	47,218	55,115	57,203	60,364	66,480	66,138
Statistical Record								
Return on Assets %	1.90	N.M.	4.66	7.18	1.35	7.34	7.50	N.M.
Return on Equity %	6.09	N.M.	12.94	21.47	4.17	21.67	23.89	N.M.
Loss Ratio %	75.52	84.53	59.62	53.06	64.28	46.97	50.51	95.78
Net Margin %	7.20	(4.46)	18.62	28.11	5.37	28.03	26.54	(11.63)
Price Range	42.36-34.09	50.43-32.19	46.64-34.86	38.44-19.71	42.29-20.00	43.20-33.35	37.89-29.80	39.64-30.16
P/E Ratio	14.12-11.36	...	7.31-5.46	4.42-2.27	32.04-15.15	6.03-4.65	5.63-4.43	...
Average Yield %	3.20	9.96	7.53	9.50	...	7.68	...	...

Address: Wellesley House, 90 Pitts Bay Road, Pembroke, HM 08 **Telephone:** 441-278-0400	**Web Site:** www.endurance.bm **Officers:** William H. Bolinder - Chairman David S. Cash - Chief Executive Officer	**Auditors:** Ernst & Young Ltd. **Investor Contact:** 441-278-0988 **Transfer Agents:** EquiServe Trust Company, N.A., Providence, Rhode Island

ENERGEN CORP.

Exchange	Symbol	Price	52Wk Range	Yield	P/E	Div Achiever
NYS	EGN	$52.01 (3/28/2013)	55.50-40.85	1.12	14.82	30 Years

*7 Year Price Score 87.53   *NYSE Composite Index=100   *12 Month Price Score 91.91

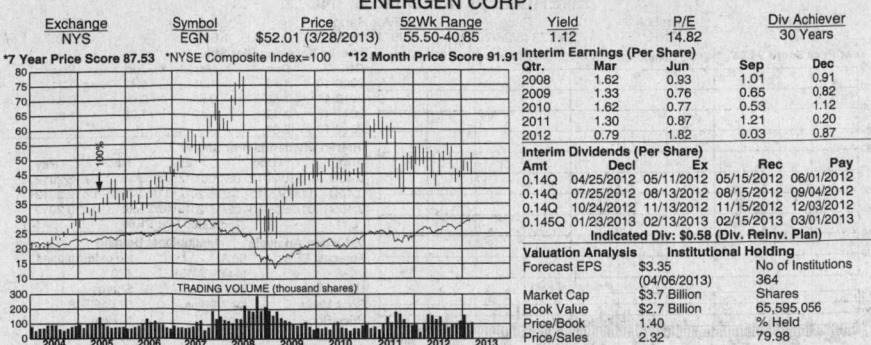

Interim Earnings (Per Share)

Qtr.	Mar	Jun	Sep	Dec
2008	1.62	0.93	1.01	0.91
2009	1.33	0.76	0.65	0.82
2010	1.62	0.77	0.53	1.12
2011	1.30	0.87	1.21	0.20
2012	0.79	1.82	0.03	0.87

Interim Dividends (Per Share)

Amt	Decl	Ex	Rec	Pay
0.14Q	04/25/2012	05/11/2012	05/15/2012	06/01/2012
0.14Q	07/25/2012	08/13/2012	08/15/2012	09/04/2012
0.14Q	10/24/2012	11/13/2012	11/15/2012	12/03/2012
0.145Q	01/23/2013	02/13/2013	02/15/2013	03/01/2013

Indicated Div: $0.58 (Div. Reinv. Plan)

Valuation Analysis | **Institutional Holding**

Forecast EPS	$3.35	No of Institutions
	(04/06/2013)	364
Market Cap	$3.7 Billion	Shares
Book Value	$2.7 Billion	65,595,056
Price/Book	1.40	% Held
Price/Sales	2.32	79.98

Business Summary: Production & Extraction (MIC: 9.1.1 SIC: 4924 NAIC: 221210)

Energen is an energy holding company. Through its principal subsidiaries, Energen Resources Corporation (Energen Resources) and Alabama Gas Corporation (Alagasco), Co. is engaged in the development, acquisition, exploration and production of oil, natural gas and natural gas liquids in the continental U.S. and in the purchase, distribution and sale of natural gas in central and north Alabama. As of Dec 31 2011, Energen Resources' proved oil and gas reserves totaled 343.1 million barrels of oil equivalent, most of which were located in the Permian Basin, the San Juan Basin and Colorado and the Black Warrior Basin, and Alagasco served customers in 181 cities and communities in 28 counties.

Recent Developments: For the year ended Dec 31 2012, net income decreased 2.3% to US$253.6 million from US$259.6 million in the prior year. Revenues were US$1.62 billion, up 9.0% from US$1.48 billion the year before. Operating income was US$459.4 million versus US$448.3 million in the prior year, an increase of 2.5%. Direct operating expenses declined 5.0% to US$620.1 million from US$652.6 million in the comparable period the year before. Indirect operating expenses increased 40.5% to US$537.7 million from US$382.6 million in the equivalent prior-year period.

Prospects: Our evaluation of Energen Corp. as of Apr. 7, 2013 is the result of our systematic analysis on three basic characteristics: earnings strength, relative valuation, and recent stock price movement. The company has managed to produce a neutral trend in earnings per share over the past 5 quarters. However, while recent estimates for the company have been mixed, EGN has posted results that fell short of analysts expectations. Based on operating earnings yield, the company is undervalued when compared to all of the companies in our coverage universe. Share price changes over the past year indicates that EGN will perform very poorly over the near term.

Financial Data

(US$ in Thousands)	12/31/2012	12/31/2011	12/31/2010	12/31/2009	12/31/2008	12/31/2007	12/31/2006	12/31/2005
Earnings Per Share	3.51	3.59	4.04	3.57	4.47	4.28	3.73	2.35
Cash Flow Per Share	10.17	10.57	9.34	9.48	7.93	6.76	6.66	4.59
Tang Book Value Per Share	37.14	33.79	30.02	27.77	26.74	19.47	17.06	12.15
Dividends Per Share	0.560	0.540	0.520	0.500	0.480	0.460	0.440	0.400
Dividend Payout %	15.95	15.04	12.87	14.01	10.74	10.75	11.80	17.02
Income Statement								
Total Revenue	1,617,169	1,483,479	1,578,534	1,440,420	1,568,910	1,435,060	1,393,986	1,128,394
EBITDA	882,535	734,144	744,884	674,759	745,352	685,118	619,291	448,896
Depn & Amortn	419,598	283,997	247,865	235,084	188,413	161,377	142,086	131,719
Income Before Taxes	397,381	405,325	457,797	400,296	514,958	476,641	428,553	270,377
Income Taxes	143,819	145,701	166,990	143,971	193,043	167,429	155,030	97,491
Net Income	253,562	259,624	290,807	256,325	321,915	309,233	273,570	173,012
Average Shares	72,316	72,332	72,050	71,885	72,030	72,180	73,278	73,714
Balance Sheet								
Current Assets	425,120	444,168	486,283	515,606	643,041	449,030	489,579	478,491
Total Assets	6,175,890	5,237,416	4,363,560	3,803,118	3,775,404	3,079,653	2,836,887	2,618,226
Current Liabilities	1,159,782	543,879	818,611	520,761	510,101	606,230	570,642	688,309
Long-Term Obligations	1,103,528	1,153,700	405,254	410,786	561,631	562,365	582,490	683,236
Total Liabilities	3,499,200	2,805,253	2,209,517	1,814,875	1,862,114	1,700,995	1,634,818	1,725,548
Stockholders' Equity	2,676,690	2,432,163	2,154,043	1,988,243	1,913,290	1,378,658	1,202,069	892,678
Shares Outstanding	72,069	71,970	71,761	71,602	71,544	70,816	70,445	73,493
Statistical Record								
Return on Assets %	4.43	5.41	7.12	6.76	9.37	10.45	10.03	7.21
Return on Equity %	9.90	11.32	14.04	13.14	19.50	23.96	26.12	20.40
EBITDA Margin %	54.57	49.49	47.19	46.84	47.51	47.74	44.43	39.78
Net Margin %	15.68	17.50	18.42	17.80	20.52	21.55	19.63	15.33
Asset Turnover	0.28	0.31	0.39	0.38	0.46	0.49	0.51	0.47
Current Ratio	0.37	0.82	0.59	0.99	1.26	0.74	0.86	0.70
Debt to Equity	0.41	0.47	0.19	0.21	0.29	0.41	0.48	0.77
Price Range	55.50-40.85	65.01-38.80	49.76-42.08	48.26-23.57	79.40-23.30	69.18-43.99	47.38-32.77	43.40-27.14
P/E Ratio	15.81-11.64	18.11-10.81	12.32-10.42	13.52-6.60	17.76-5.21	16.16-10.28	12.70-8.79	18.47-11.55
Average Yield %	1.15	1.00	1.13	1.32	0.86	0.83	1.13	1.15

Address: 605 Richard Arrington Jr. Boulevard North, Birmingham, AL 35203-2707
Telephone: 205-326-2700

Web Site: www.energen.com
Officers: James T. McManus - Chairman, President, Chief Executive Officer, Chief Operating Officer Charles W. Porter - Vice President, Chief Financial Officer, Treasurer

Auditors: PricewaterhouseCoopers LLP
Investor Contact: 205-326-8421
Transfer Agents: Computershare Shareowner Services LLC, Jersey City, NJ

ENERGIZER HOLDINGS, INC.

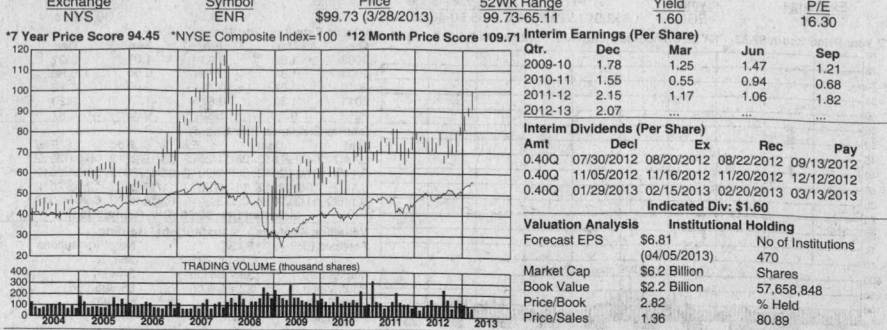

Exchange	Symbol	Price	52Wk Range	Yield	P/E
NYS	ENR	$99.73 (3/28/2013)	99.73-65.11	1.60	16.30

*7 Year Price Score 94.45 *NYSE Composite Index=100 *12 Month Price Score 109.71

Interim Earnings (Per Share)

Qtr.	Dec	Mar	Jun	Sep
2009-10	1.78	1.25	1.47	1.21
2010-11	1.55	0.55	0.94	0.68
2011-12	2.15	1.17	1.06	1.82
2012-13	2.07	...	...	...

Interim Dividends (Per Share)

Amt	Decl	Ex	Rec	Pay
0.40Q	07/30/2012	08/20/2012	08/22/2012	09/13/2012
0.40Q	11/05/2012	11/16/2012	11/20/2012	12/12/2012
0.40Q	01/29/2013	02/15/2013	02/20/2013	03/13/2013
		Indicated Div: $1.60		

Valuation Analysis

		Institutional Holding	
Forecast EPS	$6.81 (04/05/2013)	No of Institutions	470
Market Cap	$6.2 Billion	Shares	57,658,848
Book Value	$2.2 Billion	% Held	80.89
Price/Book	2.82		
Price/Sales	1.36		

Business Summary: Household & Personal Products (MIC: 1.7.1 SIC: 3699 NAIC: 335912)

Energizer Holdings is a manufacturer and marketer of primary batteries, portable lighting and personal care products in the wet shave, skin care, feminine care and infant care categories. Co.'s operations are managed via two segments: Personal Care, which includes Wet Shave products sold under the Schick, Wilkinson Sword, Edge, Skintimate and Personna brand names, Skin Care products sold under the Banana Boat, Hawaiian Tropic, Wet Ones and Playtex brand names, and Feminine Care and Infant Care products sold under the Playtex and Diaper Genie brand names; and Household Products, which manufactures and markets product portfolios in household batteries, other batteries and lighting products.

Recent Developments: For the quarter ended Dec 31 2012, net income decreased 9.7% to US$129.8 million from US$143.8 million in the year-earlier quarter. Revenues were US$1.19 billion, down 0.5% from US$1.20 billion the year before. Direct operating expenses declined 0.4% to US$630.9 million from US$633.6 million in the comparable period the year before. Indirect operating expenses increased 4.7% to US$372.9 million from US$356.1 million in the equivalent prior-year period.

Prospects: Our evaluation of Energizer Holdings Inc. as of Apr. 7, 2013 is the result of our systematic analysis on three basic characteristics: earnings strength, relative valuation, and recent stock price movement. The company has managed to produce a neutral trend in earnings per share over the past 5 quarters and while recent estimates for the company have remained steady, ENR has posted better than expected results. Based on operating earnings yield, the company is undervalued when compared to all of the companies in our coverage universe. Share price changes over the past year indicates that ENR will perform in line with the market over the near term.

Financial Data
(US$ in Thousands)

	3 Mos	09/30/2012	09/30/2011	09/30/2010	09/30/2009	09/30/2008	09/30/2007	09/30/2006
Earnings Per Share	6.12	6.22	3.72	5.72	4.72	5.59	5.51	4.14
Cash Flow Per Share	10.93	9.71	5.93	9.32	7.84	8.08	7.85	6.09
Dividends Per Share	0.800	0.400	...	...	...	...	...	...
Dividend Payout %	13.07	6.43	...	...	...	...	...	...
Income Statement								
Total Revenue	1,192,500	4,567,200	4,645,700	4,248,300	3,999,800	4,331,000	3,365,100	3,076,900
EBITDA	230,100	829,400	681,900	788,100	701,000	775,900	630,000	543,600
Depn & Amortn	...	136,700	154,500	119,300	111,000	121,400	104,600	109,100
Income Before Taxes	188,700	565,400	406,000	543,400	445,300	473,200	434,200	356,600
Income Taxes	58,900	156,500	144,800	140,400	147,500	143,900	112,800	95,700
Net Income	129,800	408,900	261,200	403,000	297,800	329,300	321,400	260,900
Average Shares	62,600	65,700	70,300	70,500	63,100	58,900	58,300	63,100
Balance Sheet								
Current Assets	2,575,300	2,522,600	2,392,600	2,429,500	2,125,800	2,026,800	2,011,400	1,635,100
Total Assets	6,745,300	6,731,200	6,663,400	6,387,900	6,149,000	5,816,700	3,553,000	3,132,600
Current Liabilities	1,233,300	1,307,500	1,159,300	1,253,500	1,159,500	1,361,700	1,122,900	926,900
Long-Term Obligations	2,138,700	2,138,600	2,206,500	2,022,500	2,288,500	2,589,500	1,372,000	1,625,000
Total Liabilities	4,548,900	4,661,700	4,562,100	4,288,300	4,386,700	4,820,400	2,899,100	2,920,200
Stockholders' Equity	2,196,400	2,069,500	2,101,300	2,099,600	1,762,300	996,300	653,900	212,400
Shares Outstanding	62,045	61,522	67,075	70,355	69,521	58,182	57,311	56,672
Statistical Record								
Return on Assets %	5.88	6.09	4.00	6.43	4.98	7.01	9.61	8.56
Return on Equity %	18.42	19.55	12.44	20.87	21.59	39.80	74.20	78.41
EBITDA Margin %	19.30	18.16	14.68	18.55	17.53	17.92	18.72	17.67
Net Margin %	10.88	8.95	5.62	9.49	7.45	7.60	9.55	8.48
Asset Turnover	0.68	0.68	0.71	0.68	0.67	0.92	1.01	1.01
Current Ratio	2.09	1.93	2.06	1.94	1.83	1.49	1.79	1.76
Debt to Equity	0.97	1.03	1.05	0.96	1.30	2.60	2.10	7.65
Price Range	82.74-65.11	79.74-64.35	81.65-64.98	71.26-49.76	82.21-30.96	118.94-67.93	113.65-65.64	71.99-46.27
P/E Ratio	13.52-10.64	12.82-10.35	21.95-17.47	12.46-8.70	17.42-6.56	21.28-12.15	20.63-11.91	17.39-11.18
Average Yield %	1.08	0.55	...	...	...	...	...	...

Address: 533 Maryville University Drive, St. Louis, MO 63141 **Telephone:** 314-985-2000	**Web Site:** www.energizer.com **Officers:** J. Patrick Mulcahy - Chairman Ward M. Klein - Chief Executive Officer	**Auditors:** PricewaterhouseCoopers LLP **Investor Contact:** 314-982-2013 **Transfer Agents:** Continental Stock Transfer & Trust Company, New York, NY

ENERGY TRANSFER EQUITY L P

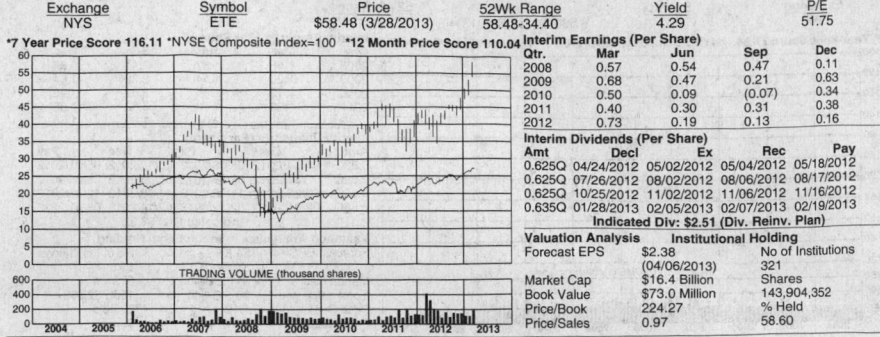

Exchange	Symbol	Price	52Wk Range	Yield	P/E
NYS	ETE	$58.48 (3/28/2013)	58.48-34.40	4.29	51.75

*7 Year Price Score 116.11 *NYSE Composite Index=100 *12 Month Price Score 110.04

Interim Earnings (Per Share)

Qtr.	Mar	Jun	Sep	Dec
2008	0.57	0.54	0.47	0.11
2009	0.68	0.47	0.21	0.63
2010	0.50	0.09	(0.07)	0.34
2011	0.40	0.30	0.31	0.38
2012	0.73	0.19	0.13	0.16

Interim Dividends (Per Share)

Amt	Decl	Ex	Rec	Pay
0.625Q	04/24/2012	05/02/2012	05/04/2012	05/18/2012
0.625Q	07/26/2012	08/02/2012	08/06/2012	08/17/2012
0.625Q	10/25/2012	11/02/2012	11/06/2012	11/16/2012
0.635Q	01/28/2013	02/05/2013	02/07/2013	02/19/2013

Indicated Div: $2.51 (Div. Reinv. Plan)

Valuation Analysis / **Institutional Holding**

Forecast EPS	$2.38 (04/06/2013)	No of Institutions	321
Market Cap	$16.4 Billion	Shares	143,904,352
Book Value	$73.0 Million	% Held	58.60
Price/Book	224.27		
Price/Sales	0.97		

Business Summary: Equipment & Services (MIC: 9.1.3 SIC: 4922 NAIC: 486210)

Energy Transfer Equity is engaged in energy-related services. Co.'s segments consist of its investments in Energy Transfer Partners, L.P. (ETP) and in Regency Energy Partners LP (Regency). ETP owns and operates a portfolio of energy assets. ETP has pipeline operations in Arizona, Arkansas, Colorado, Louisiana, New Mexico, Utah and West Virginia and Texas. Regency is engaged in the gathering and processing, contract compression, treating and transportation of natural gas and the transportation, fractionation and storage of natural gas liquids. Its assets are located in Texas, Louisiana, Arkansas, Pennsylvania, California, Mississippi, Alabama, West Virginia, Kansas, Colorado and Oklahoma.

Recent Developments: For the year ended Dec 31 2012, income from continuing operations increased 160.5% to US$1.38 billion from US$531.0 million a year earlier. Net income increased 141.3% to US$1.27 billion from US$528.0 million in the prior year. Revenues were US$16.96 billion, up 107.1% from US$8.19 billion the year before. Operating income was US$1.36 billion versus US$1.24 billion in the prior year, an increase of 9.9%. Direct operating expenses rose 133.0% to US$14.15 billion from US$6.08 billion in the comparable period the year before. Indirect operating expenses increased 65.3% to US$1.45 billion from US$878.0 million in the equivalent prior-year period.

Prospects: Our evaluation of Energy Transfer Equity L.P. as of Apr. 7, 2013 is the result of our systematic analysis on three basic characteristics: earnings strength, relative valuation, and recent stock price movement. The company has produced a positive trend in earnings per share over the past 5 quarters. However, while recent estimates for the company have been lowered by analysts, ETE has posted results that fell short of analysts expectations. Based on operating earnings yield, the company is overvalued when compared to all of the companies in our coverage universe. Share price changes over the past year indicates that ETE will perform well over the near term.

Financial Data
(US$ in Thousands)

	12/31/2012	12/31/2011	12/31/2010	12/31/2009	12/31/2008	12/31/2007	08/31/2007	08/31/2006
Earnings Per Share	1.13	1.38	0.86	1.98	1.68	0.41	1.55	0.79
Cash Flow Per Share	4.03	6.17	4.88	3.25	3.69	0.49	...	2.32
Dividends Per Share	2.500	2.350	2.160	2.105	1.950	1.458	1.381	0.295
Dividend Payout %	221.24	170.29	251.16	106.31	116.07	355.73	89.10	37.38
Income Statement								
Total Revenue	16,964,000	8,240,703	6,598,132	5,417,295	9,293,367	2,349,342	6,792,037	7,859,096
EBITDA	3,044,000	1,723,365	1,276,985	1,448,495	1,234,202	374,074	1,014,035	718,627
Depn & Amortn	801,000	556,569	394,698	304,129	256,910	77,847	175,851	133,595
Income Before Taxes	1,225,000	427,942	286,342	686,503	683,727	192,852	558,198	434,386
Income Taxes	54,000	16,883	13,738	9,229	3,808	9,949	11,391	23,015
Net Income	304,000	309,811	192,758	442,473	375,044	92,677	319,360	107,140
Average Shares	266,722	222,968	222,941	222,898	222,829	222,829	204,578	133,820
Balance Sheet								
Current Assets	5,597,000	1,455,444	1,291,010	1,267,959	1,180,995	1,403,796	1,050,578	1,302,735
Total Assets	48,904,000	20,896,793	17,378,730	12,160,509	11,069,902	9,462,094	8,183,089	5,924,141
Current Liabilities	5,845,000	1,841,313	1,081,075	889,745	1,208,921	1,241,433	932,815	1,020,787
Long-Term Obligations	21,440,000	10,946,864	9,346,067	7,750,998	7,190,357	5,870,106	5,198,676	3,205,646
Total Liabilities	46,718,000	20,772,165	17,187,119	12,160,351	11,153,334	9,477,757	8,230,221	5,878,390
Stockholders' Equity	73,000	71,144	70,943	...	...	...	...	...
Shares Outstanding	279,955	222,972	222,941	222,898	222,829	222,829	222,828	124,360
Statistical Record								
Return on Assets %	0.87	1.62	1.31	3.81	3.64	0.90	...	1.98
Return on Equity %	420.65	436.09	...	...	...	...	...	...
EBITDA Margin %	17.94	20.91	19.35	26.74	13.28	15.92	14.93	9.14
Net Margin %	1.79	3.76	2.92	8.17	4.04	3.94	4.70	1.36
Asset Turnover	0.48	0.43	0.45	0.47	0.90	0.23	...	1.45
Current Ratio	0.96	0.79	1.19	1.43	0.98	1.13	1.13	1.28
Debt to Equity	293.70	153.87	131.74	...	...	...	...	...
Price Range	47.79-34.40	46.23-32.07	40.46-28.15	30.88-16.18	35.25-13.29	37.00-31.70	42.92-26.20	27.37-21.60
P/E Ratio	42.29-30.44	33.50-23.24	47.05-32.73	15.60-8.17	20.98-7.91	90.24-77.32	27.69-16.90	34.65-27.34
Average Yield %	5.90	5.87	6.18	8.34	7.14	4.21	4.03	1.18

Address: 3738 Oak Lawn Avenue, Dallas, TX 75219 Telephone: 214-981-0700	Web Site: www.energytransfer.com Officers: Kelcy L. Warren - Chairman, Chief Executive Officer John W. McReynolds - President, Chief Financial Officer	Auditors: Grant Thornton LLP Investor Contact: 214-981-0795 Transfer Agents: American Stock Transfer & Trust Company

ENTERGY CORP.

Exchange	Symbol	Price	52Wk Range	Yield	P/E
NYS	ETR	$63.24 (3/28/2013)	73.06-61.45	5.25	13.29

*7 Year Price Score 71.94   *NYSE Composite Index=100   *12 Month Price Score 87.61

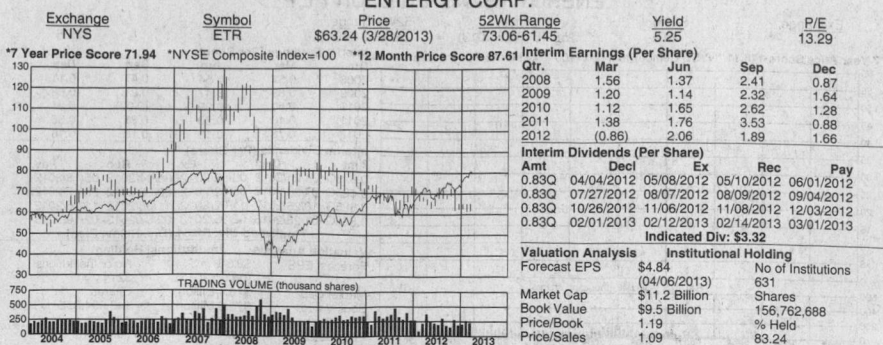

Interim Earnings (Per Share)

Qtr.	Mar	Jun	Sep	Dec
2008	1.56	1.37	2.41	0.87
2009	1.20	1.14	2.32	1.64
2010	1.12	1.65	2.62	1.28
2011	1.38	1.76	3.53	0.88
2012	(0.86)	2.06	1.89	1.66

Interim Dividends (Per Share)

Amt	Decl	Ex	Rec	Pay
0.83Q	04/04/2012	05/08/2012	05/10/2012	06/01/2012
0.83Q	07/27/2012	08/07/2012	08/09/2012	09/04/2012
0.83Q	10/26/2012	11/06/2012	11/08/2012	12/03/2012
0.83Q	02/01/2013	02/12/2013	02/14/2013	03/01/2013

Indicated Div: $3.32

Valuation Analysis

		Institutional Holding	
Forecast EPS	$4.84	No of Institutions	
	(04/06/2013)	631	
Market Cap	$11.2 Billion	Shares	
Book Value	$9.5 Billion	156,762,688	
Price/Book	1.19	% Held	
Price/Sales	1.09	83.24	

TRADING VOLUME (thousand shares)

Business Summary: Electric Utilities (MIC: 3.1.1 SIC: 4911 NAIC: 221122)

Entergy is an integrated energy company engaged in electric power production and retail electric distribution operations. Co. operates two segments: Utility, which generates, transmits, distributes, and sells electric power, and operates a natural gas distribution business; and Entergy Wholesale Commodities, which owns and operates nuclear power plants in the northern U.S., and sells electric power produced by those plants to wholesale customers. Co. also owns interests in non-nuclear power plants that sell electric power to wholesale customers. As of Dec 31 2012, Co.'s utility business delivered electricity to 2.8 million utility customers in Arkansas, Louisiana, Mississippi, and Texas.

Recent Developments: For the year ended Dec 31 2012, net income decreased 36.5% to US$868.4 million from US$1.37 billion in the prior year. Revenues were US$10.30 billion, down 8.3% from US$11.23 billion the year before. Operating income was US$1.30 billion versus US$2.01 billion in the prior year, a decrease of 35.4%. Direct operating expenses declined 3.4% to US$7.12 billion from US$7.37 billion in the comparable period the year before. Indirect operating expenses increased 1.8% to US$1.88 billion from US$1.84 billion in the equivalent prior-year period.

Prospects: Our evaluation of Entergy Corp. as of Apr. 7, 2013 is the result of our systematic analysis on three basic characteristics: earnings strength, relative valuation, and recent stock price movement. The company has managed to produce a neutral trend in earnings per share over the past 5 quarters and while recent estimates for the company have been mixed, ETR has posted better than expected results. Based on operating earnings yield, the company is undervalued when compared to all of the companies in our coverage universe. Share price changes over the past year indicates that ETR will perform poorly over the near term.

Financial Data

(US$ in Thousands)	12/31/2012	12/31/2011	12/31/2010	12/31/2009	12/31/2008	12/31/2007	12/31/2006	12/31/2005
Earnings Per Share	4.76	7.55	6.66	6.30	6.20	5.60	5.36	4.19
Cash Flow Per Share	16.54	17.63	21.11	15.22	17.36	13.02	16.48	6.98
Tang Book Value Per Share	50.65	49.73	46.64	44.70	41.72	40.37	40.29	37.64
Dividends Per Share	3.320	3.320	3.240	3.000	3.000	2.580	2.160	2.160
Dividend Payout %	69.75	43.97	48.65	47.62	48.39	46.07	40.30	51.55
Income Statement								
Total Revenue	10,302,079	11,229,073	11,487,577	10,745,650	13,093,756	11,484,398	10,932,158	10,106,247
EBITDA	3,112,375	3,783,583	3,982,587	3,507,237	3,516,222	3,180,755	2,868,738	2,853,828
Depn & Amortn	1,771,649	1,745,455	1,705,331	1,281,838	1,220,269	1,131,610	1,035,153	1,001,852
Income Before Taxes	899,218	1,653,635	1,887,544	1,891,583	1,835,248	1,646,090	1,482,398	1,526,851
Income Taxes	30,855	286,263	617,239	632,740	602,998	514,417	443,044	559,284
Net Income	868,363	1,367,372	1,270,305	1,251,050	1,220,566	1,134,849	1,132,602	923,758
Average Shares	177,737	178,370	187,814	195,838	201,011	202,780	211,452	214,441
Balance Sheet								
Current Assets	3,683,126	3,622,703	4,339,083	4,534,161	5,160,389	3,958,247	3,325,434	4,056,294
Total Assets	43,202,502	40,701,699	38,685,276	37,364,597	36,616,818	33,643,002	31,082,731	30,851,269
Current Liabilities	4,106,321	4,950,699	2,776,249	3,193,997	3,765,894	3,256,754	2,465,130	3,127,914
Long-Term Obligations	11,954,859	10,082,134	11,359,235	11,059,971	11,517,382	9,948,573	8,986,120	8,999,498
Total Liabilities	33,724,902	31,459,918	29,878,138	28,439,894	28,339,197	25,469,169	22,539,931	22,662,548
Stockholders' Equity	9,477,600	9,241,781	8,807,138	8,924,703	8,277,621	8,173,833	8,542,800	8,188,721
Shares Outstanding	177,807	176,355	178,745	189,118	189,358	193,120	202,667	207,529
Statistical Record								
Return on Assets %	2.06	3.44	3.34	3.38	3.46	3.51	3.66	3.12
Return on Equity %	9.25	15.15	14.33	14.55	14.80	13.58	13.54	10.96
EBITDA Margin %	30.21	33.69	34.67	32.64	26.85	27.70	26.24	28.24
Net Margin %	8.43	12.18	11.06	11.64	9.32	9.88	10.36	9.14
Asset Turnover	0.24	0.28	0.30	0.29	0.37	0.35	0.35	0.34
Current Ratio	0.90	0.73	1.56	1.42	1.37	1.22	1.35	1.30
Debt to Equity	1.26	1.09	1.29	1.24	1.39	1.22	1.05	1.10
Price Range	73.06-62.04	74.18-59.57	84.07-69.43	85.44-60.53	126.07-68.25	124.15-90.45	93.28-67.67	78.43-64.88
P/E Ratio	15.35-13.03	9.83-7.89	12.62-10.42	13.56-9.61	20.33-11.01	22.17-16.15	17.40-12.63	18.72-15.48
Average Yield %	4.91	4.86	4.21	3.97	2.92	2.39	2.83	3.01

Address: 639 Loyola Avenue, New Orleans, LA 70113
Telephone: 504-576-4000
Fax: 504-576-4428

Web Site: www.entergy.com
Officers: J. Wayne Leonard - Chairman, Chief Executive Officer Leo P. Denault - Chairman, Chief Executive Officer, Executive Vice President, Chief Financial Officer

Auditors: Deloitte & Touche LLP
Investor Contact: 504-576-4879
Transfer Agents: BNY Mellon Shareowner Services, Jersey City, NJ

ENTERPRISE PRODUCTS PARTNERS L.P.

Exchange	Symbol	Price	52Wk Range	Yield	P/E	Div Achiever
NYS	EPD	$60.29 (3/28/2013)	60.29-46.23	4.27	22.25	14 Years

*7 Year Price Score 131.58 *NYSE Composite Index=100   *12 Month Price Score 99.88

Interim Earnings (Per Share)

Qtr.	Mar	Jun	Sep	Dec
2008	0.51	0.52	0.38	0.43
2009	0.41	0.32	0.36	0.64
2010	0.50	0.46	0.47	(0.29)
2011	0.49	0.51	0.55	0.83
2012	0.73	0.64	0.66	0.68

Interim Dividends (Per Share)

Amt	Decl	Ex	Rec	Pay
0.627Q	04/13/2012	04/26/2012	04/30/2012	05/09/2012
0.635Q	07/11/2012	07/27/2012	07/31/2012	08/08/2012
0.65Q	09/20/2012	10/29/2012	10/31/2012	11/08/2012
0.66Q	01/14/2013	01/29/2013	01/31/2013	02/07/2013

Indicated Div: $2.57 (Div. Reinv. Plan)

Valuation Analysis   Institutional Holding

Forecast EPS	$2.73	No of Institutions
	(04/05/2013)	757
Market Cap	$54.5 Billion	Shares
Book Value	N/A	249,975,600
Price/Book	N/A	% Held
Price/Sales	1.28	27.58

Business Summary: Equipment & Services (MIC: 9.1.3 SIC: 4922 NAIC: 486210)

Enterprise Products Partners is a North American provider of midstream energy services to producers and consumers of natural gas, natural gas liquids (NGLs), crude oil, refined products and certain petrochemicals. Co.'s midstream energy operations include: natural gas gathering, treating, processing, transportation and storage; NGL transportation, fractionation, storage, and import and export terminaling; crude oil and refined products transportation, storage, and terminaling; offshore production platforms; petrochemical transportation and services; and a marine transportation business that operates primarily on the U.S. inland and Intracoastal Waterway systems and in the Gulf of Mexico.

Recent Developments: For the year ended Dec 31 2012, net income increased 16.3% to US$2.43 billion from US$2.09 billion in the prior year. Revenues were US$42.58 billion, down 3.9% from US$44.31 billion the year before. Operating income was US$3.11 billion versus US$2.86 billion in the prior year, an increase of 8.7%. Direct operating expenses declined 4.7% to US$39.37 billion from US$41.32 billion in the comparable period before. Indirect operating expenses decreased 21.7% to US$106.0 million from US$135.4 million in the equivalent prior-year period.

Prospects: Our evaluation of Enterprise Products Partners L.P. as of Apr. 7, 2013 is the result of our systematic analysis on three basic characteristics: earnings strength, relative valuation, and recent stock price movement. The company has generated a negative trend in earnings per share over the past 5 quarters and while recent estimates for the company have remained steady, EPD has posted better than expected results. Based on operating earnings yield, the company is about fairly valued when compared to all of the companies in our coverage universe. Share price changes over the past year indicates that EPD will perform poorly over the near term.

Financial Data
(US$ in Thousands)

	12/31/2012	12/31/2011	12/31/2010	12/31/2009	12/31/2008	12/31/2007	12/31/2006	12/31/2005
Earnings Per Share	2.71	2.38	1.15	1.73	1.85	0.96	1.22	0.91
Cash Flow Per Share	3.35	4.04	8.38	4.88	2.82	3.67	2.84	1.65
Dividends Per Share	2.533	2.405	2.285	2.165	2.045	1.915	1.795	1.660
Dividend Payout %	93.45	101.05	198.70	125.14	110.54	199.48	147.13	182.42
Income Statement								
Total Revenue	42,583,100	44,313,000	33,739,300	25,510,900	21,905,656	16,950,125	13,990,969	12,256,959
EBITDA	4,018,000	3,588,700	2,833,600	2,446,800	1,823,911	1,267,980	1,189,754	982,539
Depn & Amortn	900,500	776,600	745,700	678,100	466,054	414,901	350,800	328,700
Income Before Taxes	2,346,500	2,069,100	1,347,800	1,129,200	962,694	549,916	608,520	423,290
Income Taxes	(17,200)	27,200	26,100	25,300	26,401	15,257	21,323	8,362
Net Income	2,428,000	2,088,300	320,800	1,030,900	954,021	533,674	601,155	419,508
Average Shares	893,200	859,900	278,500	487,800	437,582	434,427	414,759	382,963
Balance Sheet								
Current Assets	5,843,100	6,068,700	5,507,100	4,246,900	2,163,720	2,537,885	1,922,158	1,971,447
Total Assets	35,934,400	34,125,100	31,360,800	26,151,600	17,957,535	16,608,007	13,989,718	12,591,016
Current Liabilities	7,755,700	7,432,400	5,880,200	4,536,000	2,223,149	3,044,683	1,984,921	1,890,271
Long-Term Obligations	14,655,200	14,029,400	13,281,200	11,346,400	9,108,410	6,906,145	5,295,590	4,833,781
Total Liabilities	22,746,700	22,011,700	19,986,600	16,639,500	11,872,547	10,476,358	7,509,485	6,911,707
Shares Outstanding	903,333	886,140	848,202	610,444	441,435	435,297	432,408	389,109
Statistical Record								
Return on Assets %	6.91	6.38	1.12	4.67	5.50	3.49	4.52	3.51
EBITDA Margin %	9.44	8.10	8.40	9.59	8.33	7.48	8.50	8.02
Net Margin %	5.70	4.71	0.95	4.04	4.36	3.15	4.30	3.42
Asset Turnover	1.21	1.35	1.17	1.16	1.26	1.11	1.05	1.03
Current Ratio	0.75	0.82	0.94	0.94	0.97	0.83	0.97	1.04
Price Range	54.88-46.23	46.41-37.50	44.30-30.34	32.15-17.95	32.48-17.26	33.33-28.00	29.80-23.90	27.70-23.47
P/E Ratio	20.25-17.06	19.50-15.76	38.52-26.38	18.58-10.38	17.56-9.33	34.72-29.17	24.43-19.59	30.44-25.79
Average Yield %	4.94	5.64	6.23	8.37	7.36	6.16	6.89	6.42

Address: 1100 Louisiana Street, 10th Floor, Houston, TX 77002 **Telephone:** 713-381-6500	**Web Site:** www.epplp.com **Officers:** Michael A. Creel - President, Chief Executive Officer W. Randall Fowler - Executive Vice President, Chief Financial Officer	**Auditors:** Deloitte & Touche LLP **Investor Contact:** 866-230-0745 **Transfer Agents:** Wells Fargo Shareowner Services, South St. Paul, MN

EOG RESOURCES, INC.

Exchange	Symbol	Price	52Wk Range	Yield	P/E	Div Achiever
NYS	EOG	$128.07 (3/28/2013)	134.10-83.96	0.59	60.70	13 Years

*7 Year Price Score 108.83 *NYSE Composite Index=100 *12 Month Price Score 104.68

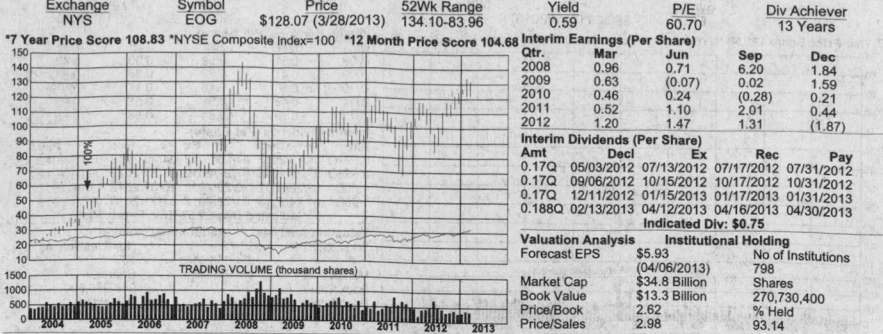

Interim Earnings (Per Share)

Qtr.	Mar	Jun	Sep	Dec
2008	0.96	0.71	6.20	1.84
2009	0.63	(0.07)	0.02	1.59
2010	0.46	0.24	(0.28)	0.21
2011	0.52	1.10	2.01	0.44
2012	1.20	1.47	1.31	(1.87)

Interim Dividends (Per Share)

Amt	Decl	Ex	Rec	Pay
0.17Q	05/03/2012	07/13/2012	07/17/2012	07/31/2012
0.17Q	09/06/2012	10/15/2012	10/17/2012	10/31/2012
0.17Q	12/11/2012	01/15/2013	01/17/2013	01/31/2013
0.188Q	02/13/2013	04/12/2013	04/16/2013	04/30/2013

Indicated Div: $0.75

Valuation Analysis

Forecast EPS	$5.93
	(04/06/2013)
Market Cap	$34.8 Billion
Book Value	$13.3 Billion
Price/Book	2.62
Price/Sales	2.98

Institutional Holding

No of Institutions	798
Shares	270,730,400
% Held	93.14

Business Summary: Production & Extraction (MIC: 9.1.1 SIC: 1311 NAIC: 211111)

EOG Resources, together with its subsidiaries, explores for, develops, produces and markets crude oil and natural gas primarily in producing basins in the U.S., Canada, The Republic of Trinidad and Tobago, the U.K., The People's Republic of China, the Argentine Republic and, from time to time, select other international areas. As of Dec 31 2012, Co.'s total estimated net proved reserves were 1.81 billion barrels of oil equivalent, of which 701.0 million barrels (MMBbl) were crude oil and condensate reserves, 320.0 MMBbl were natural gas liquids reserves and 4,740.00 billion cubic feet, or 790.0 million barrels of oil equivalent were natural gas reserves.

Recent Developments: For the year ended Dec 31 2012, net income decreased 47.7% to US$570.3 million from US$1.09 billion in the prior year. Revenues were US$11.68 billion, up 15.4% from US$10.13 billion the year before. Operating income was US$1.48 billion versus US$2.11 billion in the prior year, a decrease of 30.0%. Direct operating expenses rose 13.2% to US$1.90 billion from US$1.68 billion in the comparable period the year before. Indirect operating expenses increased 31.1% to US$8.30 billion from US$6.33 billion in the equivalent prior-year period.

Prospects: Our evaluation of EOG Resources Inc. as of Apr. 7, 2013 is the result of our systematic analysis on three basic characteristics: earnings strength, relative valuation, and recent stock price movement. The company has generated a negative trend in earnings per share over the past 5 quarters and while recent estimates for the company have been raised by analysts, EOG has posted better than expected results. Based on operating earnings yield, the company is about fairly valued when compared to all of the companies in our coverage universe. Share price changes over the past year indicates that EOG will perform well over the near term.

Financial Data
(US$ in Thousands)

	12/31/2012	12/31/2011	12/31/2010	12/31/2009	12/31/2008	12/31/2007	12/31/2006	12/31/2005
Earnings Per Share	2.11	4.10	0.63	2.17	9.72	4.37	5.24	5.13
Cash Flow Per Share	19.52	17.43	10.80	11.74	18.73	11.88	10.66	9.92
Tang Book Value Per Share	48.91	46.99	40.27	39.59	36.11	28.33	22.76	17.42
Dividends Per Share	0.670	0.635	0.610	0.570	0.465	0.330	0.220	0.150
Dividend Payout %	31.75	15.49	96.83	26.27	4.78	7.55	4.20	2.92
Income Statement								
Total Revenue	11,682,636	10,126,115	6,099,896	4,786,959	7,127,143	4,190,791	3,904,415	3,620,213
EBITDA	4,663,995	4,636,543	2,479,488	2,522,100	5,125,072	2,743,191	2,772,888	2,681,901
Depn & Amortn	3,169,703	2,516,381	1,941,926	1,549,188	1,326,875	1,065,545	817,089	654,258
Income Before Taxes	1,280,740	1,909,799	407,976	872,011	3,746,539	1,630,868	1,912,641	1,965,137
Income Taxes	710,461	818,676	247,322	325,384	1,309,620	540,950	612,756	705,561
Net Income	570,279	1,091,123	160,654	546,627	2,436,919	1,089,918	1,299,885	1,259,576
Average Shares	270,762	266,268	254,500	251,884	250,542	247,637	246,100	243,975
Balance Sheet								
Current Assets	3,589,884	3,253,938	2,527,446	1,839,541	2,108,451	1,292,039	1,350,080	1,563,238
Total Assets	27,336,578	24,838,797	21,624,233	18,118,667	15,951,226	12,088,907	9,402,160	7,753,320
Current Liabilities	2,924,058	2,522,319	2,220,099	1,345,560	1,764,916	1,474,170	1,255,012	1,172,041
Long-Term Obligations	5,905,602	5,009,166	5,003,341	2,760,000	1,860,000	1,185,000	733,442	858,992
Total Liabilities	14,051,814	12,197,893	11,392,601	8,120,625	6,936,729	5,098,813	3,802,489	3,437,028
Stockholders' Equity	13,284,764	12,640,904	10,231,632	9,998,042	9,014,497	6,990,094	5,599,671	4,316,292
Shares Outstanding	271,632	269,019	254,077	252,508	249,631	246,524	243,735	242,074
Statistical Record								
Return on Assets %	2.18	4.70	0.81	3.21	17.33	10.14	15.15	18.59
Return on Equity %	4.39	9.54	1.59	5.75	30.37	17.31	26.22	34.69
EBITDA Margin %	39.92	45.79	40.65	52.69	71.91	65.46	71.02	74.08
Net Margin %	4.88	10.78	2.63	11.42	34.19	26.01	33.29	34.79
Asset Turnover	0.45	0.44	0.31	0.28	0.51	0.39	0.46	0.53
Current Ratio	1.23	1.29	1.14	1.37	1.19	0.88	1.08	1.33
Debt to Equity	0.44	0.40	0.49	0.28	0.21	0.17	0.13	0.20
Price Range	124.37-83.96	119.67-68.41	113.72-86.62	100.58-45.59	143.41-59.59	91.02-59.96	84.81-57.36	80.84-32.48
P/E Ratio	58.94-39.79	29.19-16.69	180.51-137.49	46.35-21.01	14.75-6.13	20.83-13.72	16.19-10.95	15.76-6.33
Average Yield %	0.62	0.64	0.63	0.78	0.46	0.44	0.32	0.26

Address: 1111 Bagby, Sky Lobby 2, Houston, TX 77002 Telephone: 713-651-7000	Web Site: www.eogresources.com Officers: Mark G. Papa - Chairman, Chief Executive Officer William R. Thomas - President, Senior Executive Vice President	Auditors: Deloitte & Touche LLP Investor Contact: 713-651-7000 Transfer Agents: Computershare Trust Company, N.A., Providence, RI

EQT CORP.

Exchange	Symbol	Price	52Wk Range	Yield	P/E
NYS	EQT	$67.75 (3/28/2013)	68.18-44.00	0.18	55.53

*7 Year Price Score 105.99 *NYSE Composite Index=100 *12 Month Price Score 103.22

Interim Earnings (Per Share)

Qtr.	Mar	Jun	Sep	Dec
2008	0.57	0.44	0.73	0.26
2009	0.55	0.20	0.02	0.42
2010	0.65	0.20	0.24	0.50
2011	0.82	0.58	1.19	0.60
2012	0.48	0.21	0.21	0.32

Interim Dividends (Per Share)

Amt	Decl	Ex	Rec	Pay
0.22Q	04/18/2012	05/09/2012	05/11/2012	06/01/2012
0.22Q	07/12/2012	08/08/2012	08/10/2012	09/01/2012
0.22Q	10/17/2012	11/07/2012	11/09/2012	12/01/2012
0.03Q	01/16/2013	02/13/2013	02/15/2013	03/01/2013

Indicated Div: $0.12

Valuation Analysis | **Institutional Holding**

Forecast EPS	$1.95	No of Institutions
	(04/05/2013)	530
Market Cap	$10.2 Billion	Shares
Book Value	$3.6 Billion	131,369,392
Price/Book	2.82	% Held
Price/Sales	6.20	N/A

TRADING VOLUME (thousand shares)

Business Summary: Production & Extraction (MIC: 9.1.1 SIC: 4923 NAIC: 221210)

EQT conducts its business through three business segments. The EQT Production segment includes Co.'s exploration for, and development and production of, natural gas, natural gas liquids and crude oil in the Appalachian Basin. EQT Midstream's operations include the natural gas gathering, transportation, storage and marketing activities of Co., including ownership and operation of EQT Midstream Partners, LP. Distribution's operations primarily comprise the state-regulated natural gas distribution activities of Co. As of Dec 31 2012, Co. had 6.00 trillion cubic feet of natural gas equivalent of proved natural gas and crude oil reserves.

Recent Developments: For the year ended Dec 31 2012, net income decreased 59.1% to US$196.4 million from US$479.8 million in the prior year. Revenues were US$1.64 billion, unchanged from the year before. Operating income was US$470.5 million versus US$861.3 million in the prior year, a decrease of 45.4%. Direct operating expenses declined 10.9% to US$228.4 million from US$256.5 million in the comparable period the year before. Indirect operating expenses increased 80.5% to US$942.7 million from US$522.1 million in the equivalent prior-year period.

Prospects: Our evaluation of EQT Corp. as of Apr. 7, 2013 is the result of our systematic analysis on three basic characteristics: earnings strength, relative valuation, and recent stock price movement. The company has enjoyed a very positive trend in earnings per share over the past 5 quarters. However, while recent estimates for the company have been lowered by analysts, EQT has posted better than expected results. Based on operating earnings yield, the company is overvalued when compared to all of the companies in our coverage universe. Share price changes over the past year indicates that EQT will perform in line with the market over the near term.

Financial Data
(US$ in Thousands)

	12/31/2012	12/31/2011	12/31/2010	12/31/2009	12/31/2008	12/31/2007	12/31/2006	12/31/2005
Earnings Per Share	1.22	3.19	1.57	1.19	2.00	2.10	1.80	2.10
Cash Flow Per Share	5.47	6.13	5.47	5.55	3.99	3.52	5.16	(2.58)
Tang Book Value Per Share	24.01	24.04	20.64	16.43	15.67	8.98	7.78	2.96
Dividends Per Share	0.880	0.880	0.880	0.880	0.880	0.880	0.870	0.820
Dividend Payout %	72.13	27.59	56.05	73.95	44.00	41.90	48.33	39.05
Income Statement								
Total Revenue	1,641,608	1,639,934	1,322,708	1,269,827	1,576,488	1,361,406	1,267,910	1,253,724
EBITDA	985,611	1,234,754	743,990	554,945	600,020	556,250	472,645	548,814
Depn & Amortn	499,118	339,297	270,285	196,078	136,816	109,802	100,122	93,527
Income Before Taxes	301,707	759,129	345,548	247,088	404,810	398,779	325,471	410,850
Income Taxes	105,296	279,360	127,520	96,668	154,920	144,395	109,706	153,038
Net Income	183,395	479,769	227,700	156,929	255,604	257,483	220,286	260,055
Average Shares	150,506	150,209	145,232	131,482	128,106	122,839	122,113	123,715
Balance Sheet								
Current Assets	852,845	1,690,134	827,940	695,166	927,182	742,247	701,450	1,097,223
Total Assets	8,849,862	8,772,719	7,098,438	5,957,257	5,329,662	3,936,971	3,256,911	3,342,285
Current Liabilities	570,465	804,910	596,984	612,674	1,042,608	1,519,308	1,079,779	2,092,496
Long-Term Obligations	2,502,969	2,527,627	1,943,200	1,949,200	1,249,200	753,500	753,500	763,434
Total Liabilities	5,246,042	5,178,889	4,019,742	3,806,227	3,279,569	2,839,499	2,310,631	2,987,817
Stockholders' Equity	3,603,820	3,593,830	3,078,696	2,151,030	2,050,093	1,097,472	946,280	354,468
Shares Outstanding	150,109	149,477	149,153	130,931	130,866	122,155	121,603	119,906
Statistical Record								
Return on Assets %	2.08	6.05	3.49	2.78	5.50	7.16	6.68	7.95
Return on Equity %	5.08	14.38	8.71	7.47	16.20	25.20	33.87	42.31
EBITDA Margin %	60.04	75.29	56.25	43.70	38.06	40.86	37.28	43.77
Net Margin %	11.17	29.26	17.21	12.36	16.21	18.91	17.37	20.74
Asset Turnover	0.19	0.21	0.20	0.23	0.34	0.38	0.38	0.38
Current Ratio	1.50	2.10	1.39	1.13	0.89	0.49	0.65	0.52
Debt to Equity	0.69	0.70	0.63	0.91	0.61	0.69	0.80	2.15
Price Range	62.74-44.00	68.35-44.42	47.37-32.54	45.74-27.77	75.11-22.94	56.63-39.67	44.45-31.77	39.35-28.16
P/E Ratio	51.43-36.07	21.43-13.92	30.17-20.73	38.44-23.34	37.56-11.47	26.97-18.89	24.69-17.65	18.74-13.41
Average Yield %	1.64	1.64	2.19	2.34	1.71	1.77	2.37	2.45

Address: 625 Liberty Avenue, Pittsburgh, PA 15222
Telephone: 412-553-5700
Fax: 412-553-5732

Web Site: www.eqt.com
Officers: David L. Porges - Chairman, President, Chief Executive Officer Philip P. Conti - Senior Vice President, Chief Financial Officer

Auditors: Ernst & Young LLP
Investor Contact: 412-553-7833
Transfer Agents: Computershare

EQUIFAX, INC.

Exchange	Symbol	Price	52Wk Range	Yield	P/E
NYS	EFX	$57.59 (3/28/2013)	59.72-42.50	1.53	25.94

*7 Year Price Score 122.00 *NYSE Composite Index=100 ***12 Month Price Score 104.21**

Interim Earnings (Per Share)

Qtr.	Mar	Jun	Sep	Dec
2008	0.50	0.54	0.56	0.50
2009	0.43	0.47	0.47	0.47
2010	0.44	0.56	0.61	0.50
2011	0.46	0.28	0.54	0.60
2012	0.58	0.62	0.64	0.38

Interim Dividends (Per Share)

Amt	Decl	Ex	Rec	Pay
0.18Q	05/03/2012	05/23/2012	05/25/2012	06/15/2012
0.18Q	08/17/2012	08/28/2012	08/30/2012	09/14/2012
0.18Q	11/08/2012	11/20/2012	11/23/2012	12/14/2012
0.22Q	02/06/2013	02/20/2013	02/22/2013	03/15/2013

Indicated Div: $0.88

Valuation Analysis

		Institutional Holding	
Forecast EPS	$3.60 (04/05/2013)	No of Institutions	513
Market Cap	$6.9 Billion	Shares	136,682,352
Book Value	$1.9 Billion	% Held	86.02
Price/Book	3.59		
Price/Sales	3.21		

Business Summary: Business Services (MIC: 7.5.2 SIC: 7323 NAIC: 561450)

Equifax is a provider of information services. Co. has five segments: U.S. Consumer Information Solutions, which provides consumer information products to businesses; international, which includes its Canada Consumer, Europe and Latin America business units; TALX Workforce Solutions, which enables clients to verify income and employment, and outsource and automate certain payroll-related and human resources management processes; North America Personal Solutions, which provides products to monitor, manage and protect credit, credit score and identity information; and North America Commercial Solutions, which provides credit, financial, marketing and other information regarding businesses.

Recent Developments: For the year ended Dec 31 2012, income from continuing operations increased 16.9% to US$280.8 million from US$240.2 million a year earlier. Net income increased 16.2% to US$280.8 million from US$241.7 million in the prior year. Revenues were US$2.16 billion, up 10.2% from US$1.96 billion the year before. Operating income was US$489.0 million versus US$471.0 million in the prior year, an increase of 3.8%. Direct operating expenses rose 9.3% to US$829.1 million from US$758.8 million in the comparable period the year before. Indirect operating expenses increased 15.4% to US$842.4 million from US$730.0 million in the equivalent prior-year period.

Prospects: Our evaluation of Equifax Inc. as of Apr. 7, 2013 is the result of our systematic analysis on three basic characteristics: earnings strength, relative valuation, and recent stock price movement. The company has produced a positive trend in earnings per share over the past 5 quarters and while recent estimates for the company have remained steady, EFX has posted better than expected results. Based on operating earnings yield, the company is about fairly valued when compared to all of the companies in our coverage universe. Share price changes over the past year indicates that EFX will perform well over the near term.

Financial Data
(US$ in Thousands)	12/31/2012	12/31/2011	12/31/2010	12/31/2009	12/31/2008	12/31/2007	12/31/2006	12/31/2005
Earnings Per Share	2.22	1.88	2.11	1.83	2.09	2.02	2.12	1.86
Cash Flow Per Share	4.13	3.35	2.83	3.31	3.46	3.41	2.94	2.60
Dividends Per Share	0.720	0.640	0.280	0.160	0.160	0.160	0.160	0.150
Dividend Payout %	32.43	34.04	13.27	8.74	7.66	7.92	7.55	8.06
Income Statement								
Total Revenue	2,160,500	1,959,800	1,859,500	1,824,500	1,935,700	1,843,000	1,546,300	1,443,400
EBITDA	659,000	628,200	599,100	572,400	638,800	616,900	535,100	513,400
Depn & Amortn	163,400	164,900	167,800	158,800	155,400	127,700	82,800	82,200
Income Before Taxes	440,200	408,200	375,200	356,600	412,100	430,700	420,400	395,600
Income Taxes	159,400	168,000	131,900	116,100	133,100	151,900	141,400	144,200
Net Income	272,100	232,900	266,700	233,900	272,800	272,700	274,500	246,500
Average Shares	122,500	123,700	126,500	127,900	130,400	135,100	129,400	132,200
Balance Sheet								
Current Assets	529,700	452,300	429,200	416,800	353,800	425,000	345,200	280,400
Total Assets	4,511,100	3,508,600	3,433,600	3,550,500	3,260,300	3,523,900	1,790,600	1,831,500
Current Liabilities	646,500	362,800	319,500	492,200	318,000	546,900	582,100	294,500
Long-Term Obligations	1,447,400	966,000	978,900	990,900	1,187,400	1,165,200	173,900	463,800
Total Liabilities	2,577,900	1,806,200	1,742,200	1,949,300	1,947,900	2,124,700	952,500	1,011,200
Stockholders' Equity	1,933,200	1,702,400	1,691,400	1,601,200	1,312,400	1,399,200	838,100	820,300
Shares Outstanding	120,400	119,600	122,600	126,200	126,300	129,700	124,700	129,200
Statistical Record								
Return on Assets %	6.77	6.71	7.64	6.87	8.02	10.26	15.16	14.55
Return on Equity %	14.93	13.73	16.20	16.06	20.07	24.38	33.10	36.68
EBITDA Margin %	30.50	32.05	32.22	31.37	33.00	33.47	34.61	35.57
Net Margin %	12.59	11.88	14.34	12.82	14.09	14.80	17.75	17.08
Asset Turnover	0.54	0.56	0.53	0.54	0.57	0.69	0.85	0.85
Current Ratio	0.82	1.25	1.34	0.85	1.11	0.78	0.59	0.95
Debt to Equity	0.75	0.57	0.58	0.62	0.90	0.83	0.21	0.57
Price Range	54.93-38.42	39.81-28.79	36,40-27.78	31.50-19.79	39.68-19.99	46.26-35.33	41.38-31.29	38.76-27.23
P/E Ratio	24.74-17.31	21.18-15.31	17.25-13.17	17.21-10.81	18.99-9.56	22.90-17.49	19.52-14.76	20.84-14.64
Average Yield %	1.56	1.82	0.87	0.60	0.49	0.40	0.44	0.44

Address: 1550 Peachtree Street, N.W., Atlanta, GA 30309	Web Site: www.equifax.com	Auditors: Ernst & Young LLP
Telephone: 404-885-8000	Officers: Richard F. Smith - Chairman, Chief Executive Officer Nuala M. King - Senior Vice President, Controller	Investor Contact: 404-885-8804
Fax: 404-885-8682		Transfer Agents: SunTrust Bank Stock Transfer Department, Atlanta, GA

EQUITY LIFESTYLE PROPERTIES INC

Exchange	Symbol	Price	52Wk Range	Yield	P/E
NYS	ELS	$76.80 (3/28/2013)	76.80-63.82	2.60	58.18

*7 Year Price Score 115.17 *NYSE Composite Index=100 *12 Month Price Score 98.89

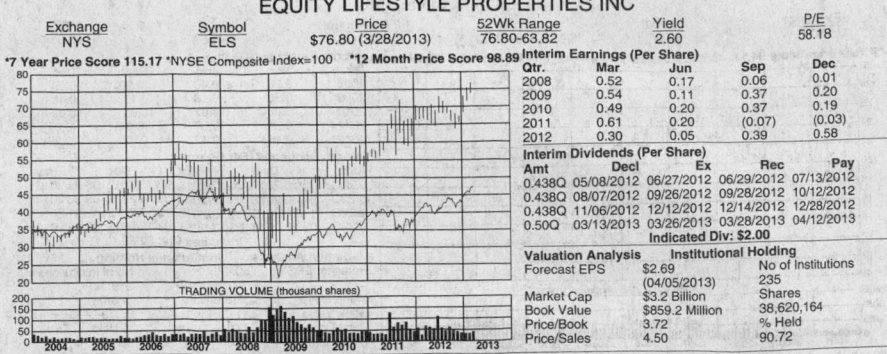

Interim Earnings (Per Share)

Qtr.	Mar	Jun	Sep	Dec
2008	0.52	0.17	0.06	0.01
2009	0.54	0.11	0.37	0.20
2010	0.49	0.20	0.37	0.19
2011	0.61	0.20	(0.07)	(0.03)
2012	0.30	0.05	0.39	0.58

Interim Dividends (Per Share)

Amt	Decl	Ex	Rec	Pay
0.438Q	05/08/2012	06/27/2012	06/29/2012	07/13/2012
0.438Q	08/07/2012	09/26/2012	09/28/2012	10/12/2012
0.438Q	11/06/2012	12/12/2012	12/14/2012	12/28/2012
0.50Q	03/13/2013	03/26/2013	03/28/2013	04/12/2013

Indicated Div: $2.00

Valuation Analysis		Institutional Holding	
Forecast EPS	$2.69	No of Institutions	
	(04/05/2013)	235	
Market Cap	$3.2 Billion	Shares	
Book Value	$859.2 Million	38,620,164	
Price/Book	3.72	% Held	
Price/Sales	4.50	90.72	

Business Summary: REITs (MIC: 5.3.1 SIC: 6798 NAIC: 525930)
Equity Lifestyle Properties is a fully integrated owner and operator of lifestyle-oriented properties (Properties). Co. leases individual developed areas with access to utilities for placement of factory built homes, cottages, cabins or recreational vehicles. The operations of Co. are conducted primarily through MHC Operating Limited Partnership. Co.'s Realty Systems, Inc. subsidiary is engaged in the business of purchasing and selling or leasing homes that are located in Properties owned and managed by Co. As of Dec 31 2011, Co. owned or had an ownership interest in a portfolio of 382 Properties located throughout the U.S. and Canada, consisting of 141,132 residential sites.

Recent Developments: For the year ended Dec 31 2012, income from continuing operations increased 75.2% to US$74.5 million from US$42.5 million a year earlier. Net income increased 75.2% to US$74.5 million from US$42.5 million in the prior year. Revenues were US$709.9 million, up 20.5% from US$589.2 million the year before. Revenues from property income rose 20.6% to US$690.0 million from US$572.3 million in the corresponding earlier year.

Prospects: Our evaluation of Equity Lifestyle Properties Inc. as of Apr. 7, 2013 is the result of our systematic analysis on three basic characteristics: earnings strength, relative valuation, and recent stock price movement. The company has enjoyed a very positive trend in earnings per share over the past 5 quarters. Because the company lacks sufficient analyst estimate data, we place greater weight on the historical EPS trend as the measure of earnings strength. Based on operating earnings yield, the company is overvalued when compared to all of the companies in our coverage universe. Share price changes over the past year indicates that ELS will perform poorly over the near term.

Financial Data
(US$ in Thousands)

	12/31/2012	12/31/2011	12/31/2010	12/31/2009	12/31/2008	12/31/2007	12/31/2006	12/31/2005
Earnings Per Share	1.32	0.64	1.25	1.22	0.75	1.31	0.69	(0.10)
Cash Flow Per Share	5.73	4.93	5.35	5.45	4.64	5.10	4.24	3.91
Tang Book Value Per Share	17.38	22.55	7.33	7.20	3.14	2.91	1.97	1.40
Dividends Per Share	1.750	1.500	1.200	1.100	0.800	0.600	0.300	0.100
Dividend Payout %	132.58	234.38	96.00	90.16	106.67	45.80	43.48	...
Income Statement								
Total Revenue	709,877	580,073	511,361	489,934	443,485	413,451	412,786	386,480
EBITDA	298,065	226,687	223,099	215,361	199,848	207,683	197,028	179,607
Depn & Amortn	105,578	86,463	73,347	73,670	68,700	65,419	62,581	58,782
Income Before Taxes	67,963	40,556	58,601	48,499	34,813	40,926	33,261	21,399
Net Income	74,458	42,504	60,397	56,261	18,303	32,102	16,632	(2,333)
Average Shares	45,431	40,330	35,518	32,944	30,498	30,414	30,241	29,927
Balance Sheet								
Current Assets	115,929	158,489	109,145	187,838	94,729	81,421	95,035	113,325
Total Assets	3,398,226	3,496,101	2,048,395	2,166,319	2,091,647	2,033,695	2,055,831	1,948,874
Current Liabilities	204,058	212,138	175,318	163,991	133,010	85,586	78,707	68,698
Long-Term Obligations	2,269,866	2,284,683	1,412,919	1,547,901	1,662,403	1,659,392	1,717,212	1,638,281
Total Liabilities	2,538,978	2,569,774	1,821,365	1,947,789	2,012,934	1,962,754	2,008,713	1,916,358
Stockholders' Equity	859,248	926,327	227,030	218,530	78,713	70,941	47,118	32,516
Shares Outstanding	41,596	41,078	30,972	30,350	25,051	24,348	23,928	23,295
Statistical Record								
Return on Assets %	2.15	1.53	2.87	2.64	0.88	1.57	0.83	N.M.
Return on Equity %	8.32	7.37	27.11	37.86	24.39	54.38	41.77	N.M.
EBITDA Margin %	41.99	39.08	43.63	43.96	45.06	50.23	47.73	46.47
Net Margin %	10.49	7.33	11.81	11.48	4.13	7.76	4.03	N.M.
Asset Turnover	0.21	0.21	0.24	0.23	0.21	0.20	0.21	0.20
Current Ratio	0.57	0.75	0.62	1.15	0.71	0.95	1.21	1.65
Debt to Equity	2.64	2.47	6.22	7.08	21.12	23.39	36.44	50.38
Price Range	72.99-63.82	72.10-54.57	59.42-46.80	50.87-29.84	54.25-23.91	59.67-44.33	54.92-41.40	47.85-33.03
P/E Ratio	55.30-48.35	112.66-85.27	47.54-37.44	41.70-24.46	72.33-31.88	45.55-33.84	79.59-60.00	...
Average Yield %	2.57	2.44	2.27	2.68	1.77	1.16	0.64	0.25

Address: Two North Riverside Plaza, Suite 800, Chicago, IL 60606 Telephone: 312-279-1400	Web Site: www.equitylifestyle.com Officers: Samuel Zell - Chairman Howard Walker - Vice-Chairman	Auditors: Ernst & Young LLP Investor Contact: 800-247-5279 Transfer Agents: American Stock Transfer & Trust Company, LLC, New York, NY

EQUITY ONE, INC.

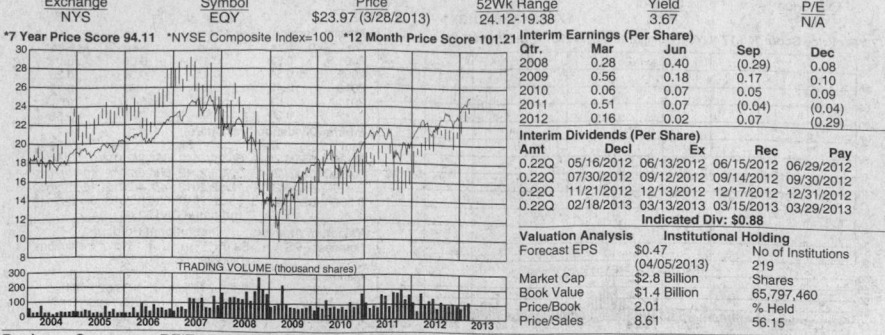

Exchange	Symbol	Price	52Wk Range	Yield	P/E
NYS	EQY	$23.97 (3/28/2013)	24.12-19.38	3.67	N/A

*7 Year Price Score 94.11   *NYSE Composite Index=100   *12 Month Price Score 101.21

Interim Earnings (Per Share)

Qtr.	Mar	Jun	Sep	Dec
2008	0.28	0.40	(0.29)	0.08
2009	0.56	0.18	0.17	0.10
2010	0.06	0.07	0.05	0.09
2011	0.51	0.07	(0.04)	(0.04)
2012	0.16	0.02	0.07	(0.29)

Interim Dividends (Per Share)

Amt	Decl	Ex	Rec	Pay
0.22Q	05/16/2012	06/13/2012	06/15/2012	06/29/2012
0.22Q	07/30/2012	09/12/2012	09/14/2012	09/30/2012
0.22Q	11/21/2012	12/13/2012	12/17/2012	12/31/2012
0.22Q	02/18/2013	03/13/2013	03/15/2013	03/29/2013

Indicated Div: $0.88

Valuation Analysis

		Institutional Holding	
Forecast EPS	$0.47 (04/05/2013)	No of Institutions	219
Market Cap	$2.8 Billion	Shares	65,797,460
Book Value	$1.4 Billion	% Held	56.15
Price/Book	2.01		
Price/Sales	8.61		

Business Summary: REITs (MIC: 5.3.1 SIC: 6798 NAIC: 525930)

Equity One is a real estate investment trust that owns, manages, acquires, develops and redevelops shopping centers primarily located in supply constrained suburban and urban communities. Co.'s segments by geographical area are: South Florida; North Florida and the Southeast; Northeast; West Coast; and Other/Non-Retail. Co.'s consolidated portfolio consists mainly of grocery-anchored shopping centers. At Dec 31 2011, Co.'s consolidated property portfolio comprised of 165 properties, including 144 shopping centers, nine development or redevelopment properties, six non-retail properties and six land parcels. Co. also had joint venture interests in 17 shopping centers and two office buildings.

Recent Developments: For the year ended Dec 31 2012, loss from continuing operations was US$6.8 million compared with income of US$26.9 million a year earlier. Net income decreased 83.3% to US$7.2 million from US$43.2 million in the prior year. Revenues were US$325.6 million, up 16.2% from US$280.2 million the year before. Revenues from property income rose 16.3% to US$323.1 million from US$277.9 million in the corresponding earlier year.

Prospects: Our evaluation of Equity One Inc. as of Apr. 7, 2013 is the result of our systematic analysis on three basic characteristics: earnings strength, relative valuation, and recent stock price movement. The company has enjoyed a very positive trend in earnings per share over the past 5 quarters. However, while recent estimates for the company have been mixed, EQY has posted results that fell short of analysts expectations. Based on operating earnings yield, the company is overvalued when compared to all of the companies in our coverage universe. Share price changes over the past year indicates that EQY will perform in line with the market over the near term.

Financial Data

(US$ in Thousands)	12/31/2012	12/31/2011	12/31/2010	12/31/2009	12/31/2008	12/31/2007	12/31/2006	12/31/2005
Earnings Per Share	(0.04)	0.29	0.27	0.99	0.47	0.95	2.38	1.24
Cash Flow Per Share	1.34	0.93	0.78	1.16	1.17	1.46	1.29	1.59
Tang Book Value Per Share	10.76	11.69	11.87	11.60	11.63	12.07	12.51	12.70
Dividends Per Share	0.880	0.880	0.880	1.120	1.200	1.200	2.200	1.170
Dividend Payout %	...	303.45	325.93	113.13	255.32	126.32	92.44	94.35
Income Statement								
Total Revenue	325,611	291,925	285,224	271,390	239,029	246,613	233,421	252,964
EBITDA	49,906	77,946	88,796	135,186	93,595	172,958	148,235	177,959
Depn & Amortn	(12,469)	(10,584)	(7,487)	(6,775)	(3,708)	(4,586)	(2,612)	(1,006)
Income Before Taxes	(9,800)	18,378	18,361	68,511	36,452	110,881	96,389	127,215
Income Taxes	(2,503)	(5,064)	(3,765)	(5,017)	1,015	...	...	...
Net Income	(3,477)	33,621	25,112	83,817	35,008	69,385	176,955	92,741
Average Shares	114,233	110,241	91,710	83,857	74,222	73,362	74,324	74,790
Balance Sheet								
Current Assets	42,178	121,314	53,514	57,776	17,564	69,921	20,514	17,702
Total Assets	3,502,668	3,219,342	2,681,864	2,452,320	2,036,263	2,174,384	2,051,849	2,052,033
Current Liabilities	55,248	50,514	32,885	33,251	27,778	30,499	36,565	40,161
Long-Term Obligations	1,599,350	1,309,071	1,202,873	1,216,891	1,069,715	1,188,839	1,069,656	1,021,324
Total Liabilities	2,105,942	1,802,026	1,395,957	1,387,785	1,126,765	1,258,452	1,126,171	1,079,304
Stockholders' Equity	1,396,726	1,417,316	1,285,907	1,064,535	909,498	915,932	925,678	972,729
Shares Outstanding	116,938	112,599	102,327	86,131	76,198	73,300	72,756	75,409
Statistical Record								
Return on Assets %	N.M.	1.14	0.98	3.73	1.66	3.28	8.62	4.59
Return on Equity %	N.M.	2.49	2.14	8.49	3.83	7.54	18.64	9.74
EBITDA Margin %	15.33	26.70	31.13	49.81	39.16	70.13	63.51	70.35
Net Margin %	N.M.	11.52	8.80	30.88	14.65	28.14	75.81	36.66
Asset Turnover	0.10	0.10	0.11	0.12	0.11	0.12	0.11	0.13
Current Ratio	0.76	2.40	1.63	1.74	0.63	2.29	0.56	0.44
Debt to Equity	1.15	0.92	0.94	1.14	1.18	1.30	1.16	1.05
Price Range	21.96-17.02	20.05-14.89	19.88-14.72	17.70-9.74	26.44-10.43	29.30-21.49	28.14-20.48	24.47-19.85
P/E Ratio	...	69.14-51.34	73.63-54.52	17.88-9.84	56.26-22.19	30.84-22.62	11.82-8.61	19.73-16.01
Average Yield %	4.30	4.91	5.03	7.73	5.78	4.56	9.23	5.23

Address: 1600 N.E. Miami Gardens Drive, North Miami Beach, FL 33179	Web Site: www.equityone.net	Auditors: Ernst & Young LLP
Telephone: 305-947-1664	Officers: Chaim Katzman - Chairman Michael Berfield - Executive Vice President	Investor Contact: 305-947-1664
		Transfer Agents: American Stock Transfer & Trust Company, New York, NY

282

EQUITY RESIDENTIAL

Exchange	Symbol	Price	52Wk Range	Yield	P/E
NYS	EQR	$55.06 (3/28/2013)	65.47-54.06	2.91	20.39

*7 Year Price Score 114.07 *NYSE Composite Index=100   *12 Month Price Score 87.31

Interim Earnings (Per Share)

Qtr.	Mar	Jun	Sep	Dec
2008	0.51	0.47	0.64	(0.13)
2009	0.28	0.35	0.48	0.15
2010	0.19	0.02	0.09	0.66
2011	0.42	1.85	0.35	0.33
2012	0.47	0.33	0.72	1.18

Interim Dividends (Per Share)

Amt	Decl	Ex	Rec	Pay
0.338Q	06/08/2012	06/20/2012	06/22/2012	07/13/2012
0.338Q	09/11/2012	09/19/2012	09/21/2012	10/12/2012
0.767Q	12/07/2012	12/19/2012	12/21/2012	01/11/2013
0.40Q	03/12/2013	03/20/2013	03/22/2013	04/12/2013

Indicated Div: $1.60

Valuation Analysis		Institutional Holding	
Forecast EPS	$0.81 (04/06/2013)	No of Institutions	599
Market Cap	$17.9 Billion	Shares	337,574,528
Book Value	$7.3 Billion	% Held	105.96
Price/Book	2.46		
Price/Sales	8.43		

Business Summary: REITs (MIC: 5.3.1 SIC: 6798 NAIC: 525930)

Equity Residential is a real estate investment trust focused on the acquisition, development and management of apartment properties. Co. is the general partner of, and at Dec 31 2012 owned an approximate 95.9% ownership interest in ERP Operating Limited Partnership (ERPOP), an Illinois limited partnership. All of Co.'s property ownership, development and related business operations are conducted through ERPOP and those entities/subsidiaries owned or controlled by ERPOP. As of Dec 31 2012, Co., directly or indirectly through investments in title holding entities, owned all or a portion of 403 properties located in 13 states and the District of Columbia consisting of 115,370 apartment units.

Recent Developments: For the year ended Dec 31 2012, income from continuing operations increased 439.1% to US$311.6 million from US$57.8 million a year earlier. Net income decreased 5.8% to US$881.2 million from US$935.2 million in the prior year. Revenues were US$2.12 billion, up 12.8% from US$1.88 billion the year before. Revenues from property income rose 12.8% to US$2.11 billion from US$1.87 billion in the corresponding earlier year.

Prospects: Our evaluation of Equity Residential Properties Trust as of Apr. 7, 2013 is the result of our systematic analysis on three basic characteristics: earnings strength, relative valuation, and recent stock price movement. The company has enjoyed a very positive trend in earnings per share over the past 5 quarters. However, while recent estimates for the company have been mixed, EQR has posted better than expected results. Based on operating earnings yield, the company is overvalued when compared to all of the companies in our coverage universe. Share price changes over the past year indicates that EQR will perform poorly over the near term.

Financial Data

(US$ in Thousands)	12/31/2012	12/31/2011	12/31/2010	12/31/2009	12/31/2008	12/31/2007	12/31/2006	12/31/2005
Earnings Per Share	2.70	2.95	0.95	1.27	1.49	3.39	3.50	2.79
Cash Flow Per Share	3.45	2.71	2.59	2.46	2.79	2.84	2.60	2.50
Tang Book Value Per Share	22.27	18.38	16.85	17.28	17.55	18.00	18.73	16.79
Dividends Per Share	1.780	1.580	1.470	1.640	1.930	1.870	1.790	1.740
Dividend Payout %	65.93	53.56	154.74	129.13	129.53	55.16	51.14	62.37
Income Statement								
Total Revenue	2,123,715	1,989,463	1,995,519	1,943,711	2,103,204	2,038,084	1,990,436	1,954,937
EBITDA	1,476,136	1,230,368	1,108,945	1,139,962	1,136,560	1,202,407	1,136,911	1,109,419
Depn & Amortn	684,992	663,616	673,403	600,375	602,908	616,414	592,637	528,958
Income Before Taxes	312,108	80,509	(45,481)	22,965	44,850	90,695	108,020	189,870
Income Taxes	539	728	334	2,808	5,286	...	...	...
Net Income	881,204	935,197	295,983	382,029	420,092	989,622	1,072,844	861,793
Average Shares	319,766	312,065	282,888	290,015	290,060	302,235	315,579	310,785
Balance Sheet								
Current Assets	872,161	546,850	624,988	562,588	1,062,895	324,281	678,020	201,935
Total Assets	17,201,000	16,659,303	16,184,194	15,417,515	16,535,110	15,689,777	15,062,219	14,098,945
Current Liabilities	441,759	367,692	339,800	319,916	428,507	437,505	401,231	387,931
Long-Term Obligations	8,529,244	9,721,061	9,948,076	9,392,570	10,501,246	9,508,733	8,057,656	7,591,073
Total Liabilities	9,911,187	10,990,288	11,094,008	10,370,176	11,537,816	10,627,259	9,177,997	8,703,605
Stockholders' Equity	7,289,813	5,669,015	5,090,186	5,047,339	4,997,294	5,062,518	5,884,222	5,395,340
Shares Outstanding	325,054	297,508	290,197	279,959	272,786	269,554	293,551	289,536
Statistical Record								
Return on Assets %	5.19	5.69	1.87	2.39	2.60	6.44	7.36	6.44
Return on Equity %	13.56	17.38	5.84	7.61	8.33	18.08	19.02	16.47
EBITDA Margin %	69.51	61.84	55.57	58.65	54.04	59.00	57.12	56.75
Net Margin %	41.49	47.01	14.83	19.65	19.97	48.56	53.90	44.08
Asset Turnover	0.13	0.12	0.13	0.12	0.13	0.13	0.14	0.15
Current Ratio	1.97	1.49	1.84	1.76	2.48	0.74	1.69	0.52
Debt to Equity	1.17	1.71	1.95	1.86	2.10	1.88	1.37	1.41
Price Range	65.47-54.06	63.68-49.66	52.29-31.86	36.00-16.71	49.00-22.13	56.35-34.24	54.73-39.99	41.99-31.20
P/E Ratio	24.25-20.02	21.59-16.83	55.04-33.54	28.35-13.16	32.89-14.85	16.62-10.10	15.64-11.43	15.05-11.18
Average Yield %	3.00	2.79	3.35	6.45	5.02	4.17	3.81	4.78

Address: Two North Riverside Plaza, Chicago, IL 60606 Telephone: 312-474-1300 Fax: 312-454-8703	Web Site: www.equityresidential.com Officers: Samuel Zell - Chairman David J. Neithercut - President, Chief Executive Officer	Auditors: Ernst & Young LLP Investor Contact: 888-879-6356 Transfer Agents: Computershare Services LLC, Providence, RI

ESSEX PROPERTY TRUST, INC.

Exchange	Symbol	Price	52Wk Range	Yield	P/E	Div Achiever
NYS	ESS	$150.58 (3/28/2013)	160.33-138.08	3.21	44.16	18 Years

*7 Year Price Score 116.33 *NYSE Composite Index=100   *12 Month Price Score 92.35

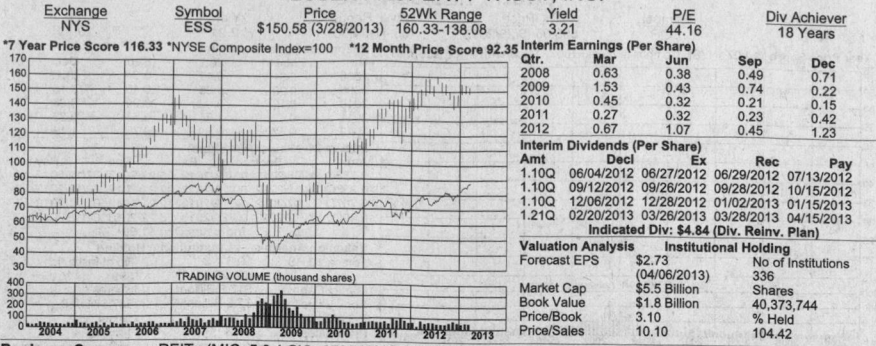

Interim Earnings (Per Share)

Qtr.	Mar	Jun	Sep	Dec
2008	0.63	0.38	0.49	0.71
2009	1.53	0.43	0.74	0.22
2010	0.45	0.32	0.21	0.15
2011	0.27	0.32	0.23	0.42
2012	0.67	1.07	0.45	1.23

Interim Dividends (Per Share)

Amt	Decl	Ex	Rec	Pay
1.10Q	06/04/2012	06/27/2012	06/29/2012	07/13/2012
1.10Q	09/12/2012	09/26/2012	09/28/2012	10/15/2012
1.10Q	12/06/2012	12/28/2012	01/02/2013	01/15/2013
1.21Q	02/20/2013	03/26/2013	03/28/2013	04/15/2013

Indicated Div: $4.84 (Div. Reinv. Plan)

Valuation Analysis		Institutional Holding	
Forecast EPS	$2.73 (04/06/2013)	No of Institutions	336
Market Cap	$5.5 Billion	Shares	40,373,744
Book Value	$1.8 Billion	% Held	104.42
Price/Book	3.10		
Price/Sales	10.10		

Business Summary: REITs (MIC: 5.3.1 SIC: 6798 NAIC: 525930)

Essex Property Trust is a self-administered and self-managed real estate investment trust. Co. owns all of its interest in its real estate investments directly or indirectly through Essex Portfolio, L.P. (the Operating Partnership). Co. is the sole general partner of the Operating Partnership. Co. is engaged primarily in the ownership, operation, management, acquisition, development and redevelopment of predominantly apartment communities. As of Dec 31 2012, Co. owned or held an interest in 163 communities, aggregating 33,468 units, located along the West Coast, as well as five commercial, and nine active development projects with 2,495 units in various stages of development.

Recent Developments: For the year ended Dec 31 2012, income from continuing operations increased 165.1% to US$129.6 million from US$48.9 million a year earlier. Net income increased 142.7% to US$139.6 million from US$57.5 million in the prior year. Revenues were US$543.4 million, up 15.0% from US$472.5 million the year before. Revenues from property income rose 14.2% to US$531.9 million from US$465.7 million in the corresponding earlier year.

Prospects: Our evaluation of Essex Property Trust Inc. as of Apr. 7, 2013 is the result of our systematic analysis on three basic characteristics: earnings strength, relative valuation, and recent stock price movement. The company has managed to produce a neutral trend in earnings per share over the past 5 quarters. Because the company lacks sufficient analyst estimate data, we place greater weight on the historical EPS trend as the measure of earnings strength. Based on operating earnings yield, the company is overvalued when compared to all of the companies in our coverage universe. Share price changes over the past year indicates that ESS will perform poorly over the near term.

Financial Data

(US$ in Thousands)	12/31/2012	12/31/2011	12/31/2010	12/31/2009	12/31/2008	12/31/2007	12/31/2006	12/31/2005
Earnings Per Share	3.41	1.24	1.14	2.91	2.21	4.24	2.45	3.32
Cash Flow Per Share	7.61	6.66	5.92	6.37	7.17	7.78	6.93	5.41
Tang Book Value Per Share	46.52	40.37	36.05	35.79	36.59	36.63	31.31	24.14
Dividends Per Share	4.400	4.160	4.130	4.120	4.080	3.720	3.360	3.240
Dividend Payout %	129.03	335.48	362.28	141.58	184.62	87.74	137.14	97.59
Income Statement								
Total Revenue	543,425	475,558	415,732	411,389	412,895	388,523	348,074	327,291
EBITDA	409,754	393,618	327,455	228,737	267,155	240,265	212,608	210,104
Depn & Amortn	170,686	152,542	125,904	116,902	110,860	100,389	83,036	80,075
Income Before Taxes	138,824	149,382	113,966	25,819	78,092	58,881	56,674	56,415
Income Taxes	...	...	...	...	...	400	525	2,538
Net Income	125,284	47,070	35,934	37,108	65,354	115,638	62,748	79,716
Average Shares	35,124	32,628	29,734	29,746	25,346	25,100	23,551	23,388
Balance Sheet								
Current Assets	201,002	176,107	177,448	209,083	147,666	75,036	43,014	36,651
Total Assets	4,847,223	4,036,964	3,732,887	3,254,637	3,164,823	2,980,323	2,485,840	2,239,290
Current Liabilities	115,302	94,440	90,178	82,591	88,952	86,669	63,524	55,478
Long-Term Obligations	2,818,683	2,360,858	2,258,745	1,847,442	1,760,647	1,657,691	1,411,554	1,354,918
Total Liabilities	3,078,070	2,595,088	2,578,592	2,197,192	2,173,993	2,044,093	1,727,719	1,658,323
Stockholders' Equity	1,769,153	1,441,876	1,154,295	1,057,445	990,830	936,230	758,121	580,967
Shares Outstanding	36,442	33,888	31,324	28,849	26,395	24,876	23,416	23,033
Statistical Record								
Return on Assets %	2.81	1.21	1.03	1.16	2.12	4.23	2.66	3.58
Return on Equity %	7.78	3.63	3.25	3.62	6.76	13.65	9.37	13.60
EBITDA Margin %	75.40	82.77	78.77	55.60	64.70	61.84	61.08	64.19
Net Margin %	23.05	9.90	8.64	9.02	15.83	29.76	18.03	24.36
Asset Turnover	0.12	0.12	0.12	0.13	0.13	0.14	0.15	0.15
Current Ratio	1.74	1.86	1.97	2.53	1.66	0.87	0.68	0.66
Debt to Equity	1.59	1.64	1.96	1.75	1.78	1.77	1.86	2.33
Price Range	160.33-136.94	146.48-110.77	116.94-77.66	87.34-50.76	129.00-63.95	146.40-95.34	133.47-94.42	93.15-69.10
P/E Ratio	47.02-40.16	118.13-89.33	102.58-68.12	30.01-17.44	58.37-28.94	34.53-22.49	54.48-38.54	28.06-20.81
Average Yield %	2.95	3.20	4.06	5.93	3.87	3.08	2.95	3.92

Address: 925 East Meadow Drive, Palo Alto, CA 94303 Telephone: 650-494-3700	Web Site: www.essexpropertytrust.com Officers: George M. Marcus - Chairman Michael J. Schall - President, Chief Executive Officer, Senior Executive Vice President, Chief Operating Officer	Auditors: KPMG LLP Investor Contact: 650-494-3700 Transfer Agents: Computershare Investor Services, LLC, Chicago, IL

ESTERLINE TECHNOLOGIES CORP

Exchange	Symbol	Price	52Wk Range	Yield	P/E
NYS	ESL	$75.70 (3/28/2013)	77.40-51.98	N/A	20.68

*7 Year Price Score 110.76 *NYSE Composite Index=100 *12 Month Price Score 103.44

Interim Earnings (Per Share)

Qtr.	Jan	Apr	Jul	Oct
2009-10	0.42	0.98	1.30	1.95
2010-11	0.97	1.47	1.21	0.62
2011-12	0.73	1.44	(0.55)	1.97
2012-13	0.80	...	...	...

Interim Dividends (Per Share)

No Dividends Paid

Valuation Analysis		Institutional Holding	
Forecast EPS	$5.63	No of Institutions	
	(04/05/2013)	259	
Market Cap	$2.3 Billion	Shares	
Book Value	$1.7 Billion	32,257,082	
Price/Book	1.42	% Held	
Price/Sales	1.18	95.68	

Business Summary: Electronic Instruments & Related Products (MIC: 6.2.3 SIC: 3823 NAIC: 333220)

Esterline Technologies designs, manufactures and markets engineered products. Co. has three segments: Avionics & Controls, which focuses on integrated cockpit systems, technology interface systems for commercial and military aircraft, and land- and sea-based military vehicles, communication systems, military audio and data products, medical equipment and other industrial applications; Sensors & Systems, which includes operations that produce high-precision temperature and pressure sensors, electrical power switching, and other systems; and Advanced Materials, which focuses on thermally engineered components, elastomer products, and combustible ordnance and warfare countermeasure devices.

Recent Developments: For the quarter ended Jan 25 2013, net income increased 10.2% to US$25.1 million from US$22.8 million in the year-earlier quarter. Revenues were US$458.0 million, down 2.7% from US$470.9 million the year before. Operating income was US$38.7 million versus US$37.0 million in the prior-year quarter, an increase of 4.5%. Direct operating expenses declined 4.9% to US$297.6 million from US$312.8 million in the comparable period the year before. Indirect operating expenses increased 0.5% to US$121.7 million from US$121.1 million in the equivalent prior-year period.

Prospects: Our evaluation of Esterline Technologies Corp. as of Apr. 7, 2013 is the result of our systematic analysis on three basic characteristics: earnings strength, relative valuation, and recent stock price movement. The company has generated a negative trend in earnings per share over the past 5 quarters. However, while recent estimates for the company have been mixed, ESL has posted better than expected results. Based on operating earnings yield, the company is undervalued when compared to all of the companies in our coverage universe. Share price changes over the past year indicates that ESL will perform poorly over the near term.

Financial Data
(US$ in Thousands)

	3 Mos	10/26/2012	10/28/2011	10/29/2010	10/30/2009	10/31/2008	10/26/2007	10/27/2006
Earnings Per Share	3.66	3.60	4.27	4.66	4.00	4.03	3.52	2.15
Cash Flow Per Share	7.57	6.33	6.32	6.02	5.29	3.96	4.73	1.45
Tang Book Value Per Share	N.M.	N.M.	N.M.	9.38	3.16	5.37	3.39	3.93
Income Statement								
Total Revenue	457,962	1,992,318	1,717,985	1,526,601	1,425,438	1,483,172	1,266,555	972,275
EBITDA	66,629	241,706	239,583	226,470	187,168	207,098	181,150	118,601
Depn & Amortn	27,971	52,400	42,500	39,500	39,189	41,095	34,273	26,757
Income Before Taxes	28,315	143,533	158,482	134,749	120,924	140,455	114,956	73,196
Income Taxes	2,394	29,958	24,938	24,504	13,511	26,563	22,519	16,716
Net Income	25,111	112,535	133,040	141,920	119,798	120,533	92,284	55,615
Average Shares	31,423	31,282	31,154	30,477	29,951	29,908	26,252	25,818
Balance Sheet								
Current Assets	1,047,990	1,035,693	1,039,313	1,076,585	796,597	777,330	729,998	468,338
Total Assets	3,235,404	3,227,117	3,378,586	2,587,738	2,314,247	1,922,102	2,050,306	1,290,451
Current Liabilities	383,310	396,346	418,361	324,377	294,239	321,119	309,900	200,599
Long-Term Obligations	803,329	838,060	1,020,028	598,972	520,158	388,248	455,002	282,307
Total Liabilities	1,580,283	1,616,636	1,815,751	1,174,942	1,061,226	895,761	928,480	582,462
Stockholders' Equity	1,655,121	1,610,481	1,562,835	1,412,796	1,253,021	1,026,341	1,121,826	707,989
Shares Outstanding	30,960	30,869	30,613	30,279	29,773	29,636	29,364	25,489
Statistical Record								
Return on Assets %	3.52	3.42	4.47	5.81	5.67	5.97	5.54	4.64
Return on Equity %	7.22	7.11	8.97	10.68	10.54	11.04	10.11	8.39
EBITDA Margin %	14.55	12.13	13.95	14.83	13.13	13.96	14.30	12.20
Net Margin %	5.48	5.65	7.74	9.30	8.40	8.13	7.29	5.72
Asset Turnover	0.61	0.60	0.58	0.62	0.67	0.73	0.76	0.81
Current Ratio	2.73	2.61	2.48	3.32	2.71	2.42	2.36	2.33
Debt to Equity	0.49	0.52	0.65	0.42	0.42	0.38	0.41	0.40
Price Range	75.20-51.98	75.20-48.71	81.96-48.54	60.44-37.71	43.50-19.22	62.44-26.87	58.06-36.94	46.28-31.40
P/E Ratio	20.55-14.20	20.89-13.53	19.19-11.37	12.97-8.09	10.88-4.80	15.49-6.67	16.49-10.49	21.53-14.60

Address: 500 108th Avenue N.E., Bellevue, WA 98004 **Telephone:** 425-453-9400	**Web Site:** www.esterline.com **Officers:** Robert W. Cremin - Chairman Richard Bradley Lawrence - President, Chief Executive Officer, Chief Operating Officer	**Auditors:** Ernst & Young LLP **Investor Contact:** 425-453-9400 **Transfer Agents:** Mellon Investor Services LLC, Ridgefield , NJ

EVEREST RE GROUP LTD

Exchange	Symbol	Price	52Wk Range	Yield	P/E
NYS	RE	$129.86 (3/28/2013)	130.64-92.45	1.48	8.22

*7 Year Price Score 106.57 *NYSE Composite Index=100 *12 Month Price Score 105.49

Interim Earnings (Per Share)

Qtr.	Mar	Jun	Sep	Dec
2008	1.24	2.47	(3.80)	(0.26)
2009	1.77	4.43	3.75	3.28
2010	(0.38)	2.70	3.11	5.37
2011	(5.81)	2.41	1.16	0.75
2012	5.68	4.08	4.82	1.18

Interim Dividends (Per Share)

Amt	Decl	Ex	Rec	Pay
0.48Q	05/09/2012	05/25/2012	05/30/2012	06/13/2012
0.48Q	08/15/2012	08/27/2012	08/29/2012	09/19/2012
0.48Q	11/14/2012	11/26/2012	11/28/2012	12/12/2012
0.48Q	02/20/2013	03/04/2013	03/06/2013	03/20/2013

Indicated Div: $1.92

Valuation Analysis | **Institutional Holding**

Valuation Analysis		Institutional Holding	
Forecast EPS	$14.12 (04/06/2013)	No of Institutions	394
Market Cap	$6.7 Billion	Shares	50,905,104
Book Value	$6.7 Billion	% Held	89.42
Price/Book	0.99		
Price/Sales	1.36		

Business Summary: General Insurance (MIC: 5.2.1 SIC: 6331 NAIC: 524126)

Everest Re Group is a holding company. Through its subsidiaries, Co. principally provides reinsurance and insurance in the U.S., Bermuda and international markets. Co.'s segments include: U.S. Reinsurance, which writes property and casualty reinsurance and specialty lines of business, including Marine, Aviation, Surety and accident and health business within the U.S.; Insurance, which writes property and casualty insurance, including medical stop loss insurance within the U.S. and Canada; International, which focuses on the international reinsurance markets; and Bermuda, which writes property and casualty reinsurance through its Bermuda and U.K. based subsidiaries.

Recent Developments: For the year ended Dec 31 2012, net income amounted to US$829.0 million versus a net loss of US$80.5 million in the prior year. Revenues were US$4.92 billion, up 4.9% from US$4.69 billion the year before. Net premiums earned were US$4.16 billion versus US$4.10 billion in the prior year, an increase of 1.5%. Net investment income fell 3.2% to US$600.2 million from US$620.0 million a year ago.

Prospects: Our evaluation of Everest Re Group Ltd. as of Apr. 7, 2013 is the result of our systematic analysis on three basic characteristics: earnings strength, relative valuation, and recent stock price movement. The company has generated a negative trend in earnings per share over the past 5 quarters and while recent estimates for the company have been raised by analysts, RE has posted better than expected results. Based on operating earnings yield, the company is undervalued when compared to all of the companies in our coverage universe. Share price changes over the past year indicates that RE will perform well over the near term.

Financial Data
(US$ in Thousands)

	12/31/2012	12/31/2011	12/31/2010	12/31/2009	12/31/2008	12/31/2007	12/31/2006	12/31/2005
Earnings Per Share	15.79	(1.49)	10.70	13.22	(0.30)	13.19	12.87	(3.79)
Cash Flow Per Share	12.76	12.26	16.22	12.94	10.72	13.54	9.83	18.49
Tang Book Value Per Share	130.96	112.99	115.45	102.90	80.77	90.43	78.53	64.08
Dividends Per Share	1.920	1.920	1.920	1.920	1.920	1.920	0.600	...
Dividend Payout %	12.16	...	17.94	14.52		14.56	4.66	...
Income Statement								
Premium Income	4,164,628	4,101,347	3,934,625	3,894,098	3,694,301	3,997,498	3,853,153	3,963,093
Total Revenue	4,922,810	4,693,961	4,705,807	4,498,578	3,527,579	4,782,047	4,517,300	4,555,099
Benefits & Claims	2,745,265	3,726,204	2,945,712	2,374,058	2,438,972	2,548,138	2,434,420	3,724,317
Income Before Taxes	939,526	(233,947)	591,238	939,321	(83,607)	1,027,956	991,750	(280,921)
Income Taxes	110,572	(153,461)	(19,516)	132,332	(64,849)	188,681	150,922	(62,254)
Net Income	828,954	(80,486)	610,754	806,989	(18,758)	839,275	840,828	(218,667)
Average Shares	52,067	53,916	56,786	60,847	61,674	63,629	65,324	57,649
Balance Sheet								
Total Assets	19,777,907	18,893,555	18,407,971	18,001,312	16,846,590	17,999,482	17,107,570	16,474,539
Total Liabilities	13,044,440	12,822,180	12,124,454	11,899,590	11,886,235	12,314,712	11,999,883	12,334,845
Stockholders' Equity	6,733,467	6,071,375	6,283,517	6,101,722	4,960,355	5,684,770	5,107,687	4,139,694
Shares Outstanding	51,417	53,736	54,428	59,300	61,414	62,863	65,043	64,600
Statistical Record								
Return on Assets %	4.28	N.M.	3.35	4.63	N.M.	4.78	5.01	N.M.
Return on Equity %	12.91	N.M.	9.86	14.59	N.M.	15.55	18.19	N.M.
Loss Ratio %	65.92	90.85	74.87	60.97	66.02	63.74	63.18	93.98
Net Margin %	16.84	(1.71)	12.98	17.94	(0.53)	17.55	18.61	(4.80)
Price Range	114.60-83.35	93.76-73.50	88.82-69.24	92.49-58.69	105.04-60.75	114.08-92.53	103.03-85.91	107.34-82.20
P/E Ratio	7.26-5.28	...	8.30-6.47	7.00-4.44	...	8.65-7.02	8.01-6.67	...
Average Yield %	1.90	2.28	2.37	2.49	2.26	1.89	0.63	...

Address: Wessex House, 2nd Floor, 45 Reid Street, Hamilton, HM DX Telephone: 441-295-0006	Web Site: www.everestre.com Officers: Joseph V. Taranto - Chairman, Chief Executive Officer Dominic James Addesso - President, Executive Vice President, Chief Financial Officer	Auditors: PricewaterhouseCoopers LLP Investor Contact: 908-604-3169 Transfer Agents: Computershare Trust Company, N.A., Providence, RI

EXCO RESOURCES INC.

Exchange	Symbol	Price	52Wk Range	Yield	P/E
NYS	XCO	$7.13 (3/28/2013)	8.93-5.77	2.81	N/A

*7 Year Price Score 43.89 *NYSE Composite Index=100 *12 Month Price Score 86.30

Interim Earnings (Per Share)

Qtr.	Mar	Jun	Sep	Dec
2008	(1.89)	(2.83)	(0.80)	(6.97)
2009	(5.21)	(0.34)	2.03	1.15
2010	0.54	2.62	0.30	(0.34)
2011	0.10	0.38	0.39	(0.77)
2012	(1.32)	(2.32)	(1.62)	(1.25)

Interim Dividends (Per Share)

Amt	Decl	Ex	Rec	Pay
0.04Q	05/31/2012	06/13/2012	06/15/2012	06/29/2012
0.04Q	09/04/2012	09/12/2012	09/14/2012	09/28/2012
0.04Q	11/28/2012	12/12/2012	12/14/2012	12/28/2012
0.05Q	03/01/2013	03/13/2013	03/15/2013	03/29/2013

Indicated Div: $0.20

Valuation Analysis

Forecast EPS	$0.36
	(04/06/2013)
Market Cap	$1.6 Billion
Book Value	$149.4 Million
Price/Book	10.38
Price/Sales	2.84

Institutional Holding

No of Institutions	271
Shares	202,295,056
% Held	84.54

TRADING VOLUME (thousand shares)

Business Summary: Production & Extraction (MIC: 9.1.1 SIC: 1311 NAIC: 211111)

EXCO Resources is an independent oil and natural gas company engaged in the exploration, exploitation, development and production of onshore U.S. oil and natural gas properties with a focus on shale resource plays. Co.'s principal operations are conducted in certain key U.S. oil and natural gas areas including East Texas, North Louisiana, Appalachia and the Permian Basin in West Texas. In addition to its oil and natural gas producing operations, Co. owns 50% interests in two midstream joint ventures located in East Texas, North Louisiana and Appalachia.

Recent Developments: For the year ended Dec 31 2012, net loss amounted to US$1.39 billion versus net income of US$22.6 million in the prior year. Revenues were US$546.6 million, down 27.5% from US$754.2 million the year before. Operating loss was US$1.42 billion versus a loss of US$169.6 million in the prior year. Direct operating expenses rose 6.1% to US$207.5 million from US$195.5 million in the comparable period the year before. Indirect operating expenses increased 140.9% to US$1.75 billion from US$728.3 million in the equivalent prior-year period.

Prospects: Our evaluation of Exco Resources Inc. as of Apr. 7, 2013 is the result of our systematic analysis on three basic characteristics: earnings strength, relative valuation, and recent stock price movement. The company has enjoyed a very positive trend in earnings per share over the past 5 quarters and while recent estimates for the company have been raised by analysts, XCO has posted better than expected results. Based on operating earnings yield, the company is undervalued when compared to all of the companies in our coverage universe. Share price changes over the past year indicates that XCO will perform poorly over the near term.

Financial Data
(US$ in Thousands)

	12/31/2012	12/31/2011	12/31/2010	12/31/2009	12/31/2008	12/31/2007	12/31/2006	12/31/2005
Earnings Per Share	(6.50)	0.10	3.11	(2.35)	(11.81)	(0.80)	1.41	...
Cash Flow Per Share	2.40	2.00	1.60	2.05	6.34	5.54	2.35	...
Tang Book Value Per Share	N.M.	6.18	6.20	2.78	4.09	25.22	6.81	N.M.
Dividends Per Share	0.160	0.160	0.140	0.050	...	...	...	...
Dividend Payout %	...	160.00	4.50	...	...	...	...	...
Income Statement								
Total Revenue	546,609	754,201	515,226	585,835	1,490,258	906,510	559,449	72,170
EBITDA	(1,035,469)	423,628	905,022	(89,478)	(1,351,357)	676,854	452,088	59,151
Depn & Amortn	312,944	372,715	201,977	269,597	475,509	385,752	140,455	16,452
Income Before Taxes	(1,421,905)	(10,110)	657,512	(506,236)	(1,988,504)	109,752	226,762	23,285
Income Taxes	...	...	1,608	(9,501)	(255,033)	60,096	89,401	7,321
Net Income	(1,393,285)	22,596	671,926	(496,804)	(1,733,471)	49,656	138,954	15,964
Average Shares	214,321	216,705	215,735	211,266	153,346	104,364	98,453	...
Balance Sheet								
Current Assets	361,866	678,008	520,460	402,038	513,040	311,300	236,710	340,506
Total Assets	2,323,732	3,791,587	3,477,420	2,358,894	4,822,352	5,955,771	3,707,057	1,507,637
Current Liabilities	237,931	287,399	285,698	212,914	322,873	278,167	190,924	471,380
Long-Term Obligations	1,848,912	1,887,828	1,588,269	1,196,277	3,019,738	2,099,171	2,081,653	461,802
Total Liabilities	2,174,339	2,233,255	1,936,868	1,499,306	3,489,851	2,847,751	2,527,207	1,164,956
Stockholders' Equity	149,393	1,558,332	1,540,552	859,588	1,332,501	3,108,020	1,179,850	342,681
Shares Outstanding	217,586	216,706	213,197	211,905	210,968	104,578	104,162	1,000.00
Statistical Record								
Return on Assets %	N.M.	0.62	23.03	N.M.	N.M.	1.03	5.33	1.31
Return on Equity %	N.M.	1.46	55.99	N.M.	N.M.	2.32	18.25	5.84
EBITDA Margin %	N.M.	56.17	175.66	N.M.	N.M.	74.67	80.81	81.96
Net Margin %	N.M.	3.00	130.41	N.M.	N.M.	5.48	24.84	22.12
Asset Turnover	0.18	0.21	0.18	0.16	0.28	0.19	0.21	0.06
Current Ratio	1.52	2.36	1.82	1.89	1.59	1.12	1.24	0.72
Debt to Equity	12.38	1.21	1.03	1.39	2.27	0.68	1.76	1.35
Price Range	10.32-5.77	20.95-9.48	22.22-13.44	22.13-7.72	38.01-4.29	19.48-13.72	17.90-9.79	...
P/E Ratio	...	209.50-94.80	7.14-4.32	...	...	...	12.70-6.94	...
Average Yield %	2.15	0.98	0.81	...	...	...	...	...

Address: 12377 Merit Drive, Suite 1700, LB 82, Dallas, TX 75251	**Web Site:** www.excoresources.com	**Auditors:** KPMG LLP
Telephone: 214-368-2084	**Officers:** Douglas H. Miller - Chairman, Chief Executive Officer Stephen F. Smith - Vice-Chairman, President, Chief Financial Officer	**Investor Contact:** 214-706-3310
Fax: 214-368-2087		**Transfer Agents:** Continental Stock Transfer & Trust Company, New York, NY

EXELON CORP.

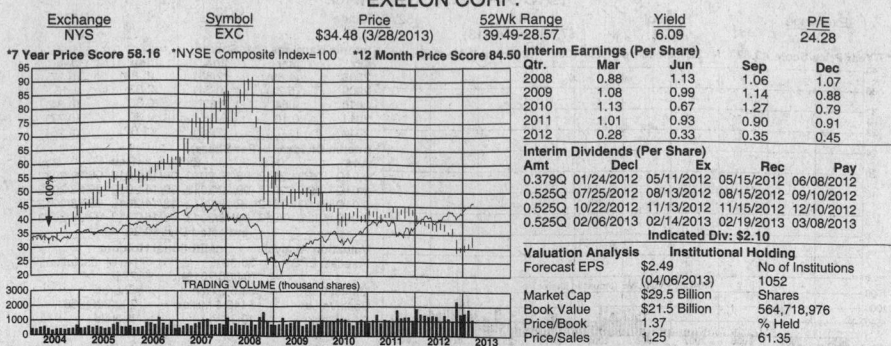

Exchange	Symbol	Price	52Wk Range	Yield	P/E
NYS	EXC	$34.48 (3/28/2013)	39.49-28.57	6.09	24.28

*7 Year Price Score 58.16 *NYSE Composite Index=100 *12 Month Price Score 84.50

Interim Earnings (Per Share)

Qtr.	Mar	Jun	Sep	Dec
2008	0.88	1.13	1.06	1.07
2009	1.08	0.99	1.14	0.88
2010	1.13	0.67	1.27	0.79
2011	1.01	0.93	0.90	0.91
2012	0.28	0.33	0.35	0.45

Interim Dividends (Per Share)

Amt	Decl	Ex	Rec	Pay
0.379Q	01/24/2012	05/11/2012	05/15/2012	06/08/2012
0.525Q	07/25/2012	08/13/2012	08/15/2012	09/10/2012
0.525Q	10/22/2012	11/13/2012	11/15/2012	12/10/2012
0.525Q	02/06/2013	02/14/2013	02/19/2013	03/08/2013

Indicated Div: $2.10

Valuation Analysis | **Institutional Holding**

Forecast EPS	$2.49 (04/06/2013)	No of Institutions 1052
Market Cap	$29.5 Billion	Shares
Book Value	$21.5 Billion	564,718,976
Price/Book	1.37	% Held
Price/Sales	1.25	61.35

TRADING VOLUME (thousand shares)

Business Summary: Electric Utilities (MIC: 3.1.1 SIC: 4931 NAIC: 221122)

Exelon is a utility services holding company. The business of Co.'s Exelon Generation Company, LLC (Generation) subsidiary consists of its owned and contracted electric generating facilities and investments in generation ventures that are marketed through its customer-facing activities. Co. also engages in the energy delivery businesses through its other subsidiaries, Commonwealth Edison Company (ComEd), PECO Energy Company (PECO) and Baltimore Gas and Electric Company (BGE). Co. has nine segments consisting of Generation's six power marketing segments (Mid-Atlantic, Midwest, New England, New York, Electric Reliability Council of Texas, and other regions in Generation), ComEd, PECO and BGE.

Recent Developments: For the year ended Dec 31 2012, net income decreased 53.1% to US$1.17 billion from US$2.50 billion in the prior year. Revenues were US$23.49 billion, up 23.2% from US$19.06 billion the year before. Operating income was US$2.38 billion versus US$4.48 billion in the prior year, a decrease of 46.9%. Direct operating expenses rose 45.5% to US$18.12 billion from US$12.45 billion in the comparable period the year before. Indirect operating expenses increased 36.0% to US$2.90 billion from US$2.13 billion in the equivalent prior-year period.

Prospects: Our evaluation of Exelon Corp. as of Apr. 7, 2013 is the result of our systematic analysis on three basic characteristics: earnings strength, relative valuation, and recent stock price movement. The company has enjoyed a very positive trend in earnings per share over the past 5 quarters and while recent estimates for the company have been mixed, EXC has posted results that fell short of analysts expectations. Based on operating earnings yield, the company is undervalued when compared to all of the companies in our coverage universe. Share price changes over the past year indicates that EXC will perform very poorly over the near term.

Financial Data

(US$ in Thousands)	12/31/2012	12/31/2011	12/31/2010	12/31/2009	12/31/2008	12/31/2007	12/31/2006	12/31/2005
Earnings Per Share	1.42	3.75	3.87	4.09	4.13	4.05	2.35	1.36
Cash Flow Per Share	7.49	7.32	7.93	9.25	9.93	6.71	7.22	3.21
Tang Book Value Per Share	22.10	17.86	16.65	15.31	12.93	11.50	10.99	8.34
Dividends Per Share	2.100	2.100	2.100	2.100	2.025	1.760	1.600	1.600
Dividend Payout %	147.89	56.00	54.26	51.34	49.03	43.46	68.09	117.65
Income Statement								
Total Revenue	23,489,000	18,924,000	18,644,000	17,318,000	18,859,000	18,916,000	15,655,000	15,357,000
EBITDA	7,556,000	8,408,000	8,986,000	8,506,000	4,952,000	6,565,000	5,253,000	4,192,000
Depn & Amortn	4,754,000	3,782,000	3,948,000	3,380,000	91,000	1,520,000	1,487,000	1,334,000
Income Before Taxes	1,889,000	3,953,000	4,221,000	4,445,000	4,060,000	4,278,000	2,907,000	2,029,000
Income Taxes	627,000	1,457,000	1,658,000	1,712,000	1,317,000	1,446,000	1,206,000	944,000
Net Income	1,171,000	2,495,000	2,563,000	2,707,000	2,737,000	2,736,000	1,592,000	923,000
Average Shares	819,000	665,000	663,000	662,000	662,000	676,000	676,000	676,000
Balance Sheet								
Current Assets	10,133,000	5,489,000	6,398,000	5,441,000	5,368,000	5,051,000	4,992,000	4,637,000
Total Assets	78,554,000	55,092,000	52,240,000	49,180,000	47,817,000	45,894,000	44,319,000	42,389,000
Current Liabilities	7,784,000	4,989,000	4,240,000	4,238,000	4,080,000	5,995,000	5,795,000	6,563,000
Long-Term Obligations	18,854,000	12,189,000	12,004,000	11,385,000	12,592,000	11,965,000	11,911,000	11,760,000
Total Liabilities	56,843,000	40,620,000	38,593,000	36,453,000	36,683,000	35,670,000	34,259,000	33,177,000
Stockholders' Equity	21,518,000	14,472,000	13,647,000	12,727,000	11,134,000	10,224,000	10,060,000	9,212,000
Shares Outstanding	854,781	663,368	661,845	659,798	658,154	660,879	670,000	666,409
Statistical Record								
Return on Assets %	1.75	4.65	5.05	5.58	5.83	6.07	3.67	2.17
Return on Equity %	6.49	17.75	19.44	22.69	25.56	26.98	16.52	9.86
EBITDA Margin %	32.17	44.43	48.20	49.12	26.26	34.71	33.55	27.30
Net Margin %	4.99	13.18	13.75	15.63	14.51	14.46	10.17	6.01
Asset Turnover	0.35	0.35	0.37	0.36	0.40	0.42	0.36	0.36
Current Ratio	1.30	1.10	1.51	1.28	1.32	0.84	0.86	0.71
Debt to Equity	0.88	0.84	0.88	0.89	1.13	1.17	1.18	1.28
Price Range	42.07-28.57	45.34-39.77	49.66-37.63	57.81-40.15	91.64-45.00	86.18-59.05	63.46-51.54	56.92-42.03
P/E Ratio	29.63-20.12	12.09-10.61	12.83-9.72	14.13-9.82	22.19-10.90	21.28-14.58	27.00-21.93	41.85-30.90
Average Yield %	5.72	4.95	4.95	4.25	2.75	2.40	2.77	3.24

Address: 10 South Dearborn Street, P.O. Box 805379, Chicago, IL 60680-5379 **Telephone:** 312-394-7398	**Web Site:** www.exeloncorp.com **Officers:** Mayo A. Shattuck - Executive Chairman Christopher M. Crane - President, Chief Executive Officer, Chief Operating Officer	**Auditors:** PricewaterhouseCoopers LLP **Investor Contact:** 312-394-2345 **Transfer Agents:** Wells Fargo

EXTRA SPACE STORAGE INC

Exchange	Symbol	Price	52Wk Range	Yield	P/E
NYS	EXR	$39.27 (3/28/2013)	40.41-27.48	2.55	34.45

*7 Year Price Score 163.85 *NYSE Composite Index=100 *12 Month Price Score 105.04

Interim Earnings (Per Share)

Qtr.	Mar	Jun	Sep	Dec
2008	0.10	0.12	0.15	0.23
2009	0.34	(0.09)	0.07	0.07
2010	0.04	0.07	0.09	0.10
2011	0.09	0.12	0.16	0.17
2012	0.21	0.22	0.37	0.34

Interim Dividends (Per Share)

Amt	Decl	Ex	Rec	Pay
0.20Q	06/04/2012	06/13/2012	06/15/2012	06/29/2012
0.20Q	09/06/2012	09/13/2012	09/17/2012	09/28/2012
0.25Q	11/08/2012	12/06/2012	12/10/2012	12/31/2012
0.25Q	02/21/2013	03/13/2013	03/15/2013	03/29/2013

Indicated Div: $1.00

Valuation Analysis

		Institutional Holding	
Forecast EPS	$1.02	No of Institutions	
	(04/06/2013)	280	
Market Cap	$4.3 Billion	Shares	
Book Value	$1.5 Billion	111,297,824	
Price/Book	2.92	% Held	
Price/Sales	10.62	100.23	

Business Summary: REITs (MIC: 5.3.1 SIC: 6798 NAIC: 525930)

Extra Space Storage is a real estate investment trust. Co. owns, operates, manages, acquires, develops and redevelops self-storage facilities. Co. has three segments: property management, acquisition and development, which includes managing, acquiring, developing and selling self-storage facilities; rental operations, which includes rental operations of self-storage facilities; and tenant reinsurance, which includes the reinsurance of risks relating to the loss of goods stored by tenants in Co.'s self storage facilities. As of Dec 31 2011, Co. had direct and indirect equity interests in 697 storage facilities. Co. also managed 185 properties for franchisees or third parties.

Recent Developments: For the year ended Dec 31 2012, net income increased 118.6% to US$127.7 million from US$58.4 million in the prior year. Revenues were US$409.4 million, up 24.1% from US$329.8 million the year before. Revenues from property income rose 29.1% to US$346.9 million from US$268.7 million in the corresponding earlier year.

Prospects: Our evaluation of Extra Space Storage Inc. as of Apr. 7, 2013 is the result of our systematic analysis on three basic characteristics: earnings strength, relative valuation, and recent stock price movement. The company has generated a negative trend in earnings per share over the past 5 quarters and while recent estimates for the company have been raised by analysts, EXR has posted better than expected results. Based on operating earnings yield, the company is overvalued when compared to all of the companies in our coverage universe. Share price changes over the past year indicates that EXR will perform well over the near term.

Financial Data

(US$ in Thousands)	12/31/2012	12/31/2011	12/31/2010	12/31/2009	12/31/2008	12/31/2007	12/31/2006	12/31/2005
Earnings Per Share	1.14	0.54	0.30	0.37	0.61	0.53	0.27	(0.14)
Cash Flow Per Share	2.10	1.57	1.20	0.94	1.26	1.57	1.35	0.42
Tang Book Value Per Share	13.44	10.71	10.02	10.16	10.13	9.42	10.03	9.28
Dividends Per Share	0.850	0.560	0.400	0.380	1.000	0.933	0.910	0.910
Dividend Payout %	74.56	103.70	133.33	102.70	163.93	175.94	337.04	...
Income Statement								
Total Revenue	409,396	329,830	281,497	280,476	273,251	238,866	197,264	134,728
EBITDA	261,722	234,971	198,797	184,589	192,584	174,433	139,795	99,587
Depn & Amortn	80,342	63,597	54,703	56,280	49,031	43,110	35,367	29,913
Income Before Taxes	115,752	108,189	84,062	64,923	87,191	80,725	55,944	28,750
Income Taxes	5,413	1,155	4,162	4,300	...	...	...	...
Net Income	127,689	58,423	33,374	39,093	46,888	36,094	14,876	(4,966)
Average Shares	106,523	96,683	92,050	91,082	81,913	70,503	59,291	35,481
Balance Sheet								
Current Assets	78,720	85,031	99,829	191,358	125,105	67,728	140,336	90,997
Total Assets	3,223,477	2,516,250	2,248,468	2,407,556	2,291,008	2,054,075	1,669,825	1,420,192
Current Liabilities	137,299	260,079	203,324	135,531	64,953	31,346	20,800	20,591
Long-Term Obligations	1,496,425	1,154,484	1,083,467	1,309,237	1,275,880	1,322,363	951,012	869,851
Total Liabilities	1,731,670	1,497,303	1,367,067	1,523,377	1,418,545	1,434,154	1,026,270	940,064
Stockholders' Equity	1,491,807	1,018,947	881,401	884,179	872,463	619,921	643,555	480,128
Shares Outstanding	110,737	94,783	87,587	86,721	85,790	65,784	64,167	51,765
Statistical Record								
Return on Assets %	4.44	2.45	1.43	1.66	2.15	1.94	0.96	N.M.
Return on Equity %	10.14	6.15	3.78	4.45	6.27	5.71	2.65	N.M.
EBITDA Margin %	63.93	71.24	70.62	65.81	70.48	73.03	70.87	73.92
Net Margin %	31.19	17.71	11.86	13.94	17.16	15.11	7.54	N.M.
Asset Turnover	0.14	0.14	0.12	0.12	0.13	0.13	0.13	0.12
Current Ratio	0.57	0.33	0.49	1.41	1.93	2.16	6.75	4.42
Debt to Equity	1.00	1.13	1.23	1.48	1.46	2.13	1.48	1.81
Price Range	36.39-24.00	24.48-17.40	17.57-11.08	12.09-5.10	17.70-6.47	20.44-13.15	18.90-14.49	16.56-12.62
P/E Ratio	31.92-21.05	45.33-32.22	58.57-36.93	32.68-13.78	29.02-10.61	38.57-24.81	70.00-53.67	...
Average Yield %	2.74	2.70	2.74	4.36	7.04	5.55	5.54	6.39

Address: 2795 East Cottonwood Parkway, Suite 400, Salt Lake City, UT 84121 **Telephone:** 801-365-4600	**Web Site:** www.extraspace.com **Officers:** Spencer F. Kirk - Chairman, President, Chief Executive Officer P. Scott Stubbs - Executive Vice President, Chief Financial Officer	**Auditors:** Ernst & Young LLP **Investor Contact:** 801-365-4597 **Transfer Agents:** American Stock Transfer & Trust Company

EXXON MOBIL CORP.

Exchange	Symbol	Price	52Wk Range	Yield	P/E	Div Achiever
NYS	XOM	$90.11 (3/28/2013)	93.48-77.60	2.53	9.29	30 Years

*7 Year Price Score 100.02 *NYSE Composite Index=100 *12 Month Price Score 94.05

Interim Earnings (Per Share)

Qtr.	Mar	Jun	Sep	Dec
2008	2.03	2.22	2.86	1.58
2009	0.92	0.81	0.98	1.27
2010	1.33	1.60	1.44	1.85
2011	2.14	2.18	2.13	1.97
2012	2.00	3.41	2.09	2.20

Interim Dividends (Per Share)

Amt	Decl	Ex	Rec	Pay
0.57Q	04/25/2012	05/10/2012	05/14/2012	06/11/2012
0.57Q	07/25/2012	08/09/2012	08/13/2012	09/10/2012
0.57Q	10/25/2012	11/07/2012	11/09/2012	12/10/2012
0.57Q	01/30/2013	02/07/2013	02/11/2013	03/11/2013

Indicated Div: $2.28 (Div. Reinv. Plan)

Valuation Analysis

		Institutional Holding	
Forecast EPS	$8.03 (04/06/2013)	No of Institutions	2313
Market Cap	$405.7 Billion	Shares	2,567,675,904
Book Value	$165.9 Billion	% Held	47.07
Price/Book	2.45		
Price/Sales	0.84		

Business Summary: Refining & Marketing (MIC: 9.1.2 SIC: 2911 NAIC: 324110)

Exxon Mobil is engaged in the energy business. Co.'s principal business consists of the exploration for, and production of, crude oil and natural gas, manufacture of petroleum products and transportation and sale of crude oil, natural gas and petroleum products. Co. is a manufacturer and marketer of commodity petrochemicals, including olefins, aromatics, polyethylene and polypropylene plastics and a range of products. Co. also has interests in electric power generation facilities. As of Dec 31 2012, Co. had 25.16 billion barrels of oil-equivalent proved reserves.

Recent Developments: For the year ended Dec 31 2012, net income increased 13.0% to US$47.68 billion from US$42.21 billion in the prior year. Revenues were US$482.30 billion, down 0.8% from US$486.43 billion the year before. Direct operating expenses declined 1.3% to US$337.92 billion from US$342.39 billion in the comparable period the year before. Indirect operating expenses decreased 7.4% to US$65.32 billion from US$70.54 billion in the equivalent prior-year period.

Prospects: Our evaluation of Exxon Mobil Corp. as of Apr. 7, 2013 is the result of our systematic analysis on three basic characteristics: earnings strength, relative valuation, and recent stock price movement. The company has generated a negative trend in earnings per share over the past 5 quarters and while recent estimates for the company have been raised by analysts, XOM has posted better than expected results. Based on operating earnings yield, the company is undervalued when compared to all of the companies in our coverage universe. Share price changes over the past year indicates that XOM will perform in line with the market over the near term.

Financial Data

(US$ in Thousands)	12/31/2012	12/31/2011	12/31/2010	12/31/2009	12/31/2008	12/31/2007	12/31/2006	12/31/2005
Earnings Per Share	9.70	8.42	6.22	3.98	8.69	7.28	6.62	5.71
Cash Flow Per Share	12.10	11.36	9.91	5.89	11.57	9.43	8.34	7.68
Tang Book Value Per Share	36.84	32.61	29.49	23.39	22.70	22.62	19.87	18.13
Dividends Per Share	2.180	1.850	1.740	1.660	1.550	1.370	1.280	1.140
Dividend Payout %	22.47	21.97	27.97	41.71	17.84	18.82	19.34	19.96
Income Statement								
Total Revenue	482,295,000	486,429,000	383,221,000	310,586,000	477,359,000	404,552,000	377,635,000	370,680,000
EBITDA	94,941,000	89,087,000	67,978,000	47,242,000	96,449,000	83,124,000	79,472,000	70,181,000
Depn & Amortn	15,888,000	15,583,000	14,760,000	11,917,000	12,379,000	12,250,000	11,416,000	10,253,000
Income Before Taxes	78,726,000	73,257,000	52,959,000	34,777,000	83,397,000	70,474,000	67,402,000	59,432,000
Income Taxes	31,045,000	31,051,000	21,561,000	15,119,000	36,530,000	29,864,000	27,902,000	23,302,000
Net Income	44,880,000	41,060,000	30,460,000	19,280,000	45,220,000	40,610,000	39,500,000	36,130,000
Average Shares	4,627,999	4,874,999	4,896,999	4,847,999	5,202,999	5,576,999	5,969,999	6,321,999
Balance Sheet								
Current Assets	64,460,000	72,963,000	58,984,000	55,235,000	72,266,000	85,963,000	75,777,000	73,342,000
Total Assets	333,795,000	331,052,000	302,510,000	233,323,000	228,052,000	242,082,000	219,015,000	208,335,000
Current Liabilities	64,139,000	77,505,000	62,633,000	52,061,000	49,100,000	58,312,000	48,817,000	46,307,000
Long-Term Obligations	7,928,000	9,322,000	12,227,000	7,129,000	7,025,000	7,183,000	6,645,000	6,220,000
Total Liabilities	167,932,000	176,656,000	155,671,000	122,754,000	115,087,000	120,320,000	105,171,000	97,149,000
Stockholders' Equity	165,863,000	154,396,000	146,839,000	110,569,000	112,965,000	121,762,000	113,844,000	111,186,000
Shares Outstanding	4,501,999	4,733,999	4,978,999	4,726,999	4,975,999	5,381,999	5,728,999	6,132,999
Statistical Record								
Return on Assets %	13.46	12.96	11.37	8.36	19.18	17.61	18.49	17.90
Return on Equity %	27.95	27.26	23.67	17.25	38.42	34.47	35.11	33.93
EBITDA Margin %	19.69	18.31	17.74	15.21	20.20	20.55	21.04	18.93
Net Margin %	9.31	8.44	7.95	6.21	9.47	10.04	10.46	9.75
Asset Turnover	1.45	1.54	1.43	1.35	2.03	1.75	1.77	1.84
Current Ratio	1.01	0.94	0.94	1.06	1.47	1.47	1.55	1.58
Debt to Equity	0.05	0.06	0.08	0.06	0.06	0.06	0.06	0.06
Price Range	93.48-77.60	87.98-68.03	73.42-56.57	81.64-62.22	94.56-62.35	95.05-69.86	78.73-56.65	64.98-49.49
P/E Ratio	9.64-8.00	10.45-8.08	11.80-9.09	20.51-15.63	10.88-7.17	13.06-9.60	11.89-8.56	11.38-8.67
Average Yield %	2.52	2.32	2.68	2.34	1.87	1.64	1.96	1.96

Address: 5959 Las Colinas Boulevard, Irving, TX 75039-2298 Telephone: 972-444-1000 Fax: 972-444-1505	Web Site: www.exxonmobil.com Officers: Rex W. Tillerson - Chairman, Chief Executive Officer Mark W. Albers - Senior Vice President	Auditors: PricewaterhouseCoopers LLP Investor Contact: 180-025-21800 Transfer Agents: Computershare Trust Company, N.A., Providence, RI

FACTSET RESEARCH SYSTEMS INC.

Exchange	Symbol	Price	52Wk Range	Yield	P/E	Div Achiever
NYS	FDS	$92.60 (3/28/2013)	108.52-87.45	1.34	21.89	13 Years

*7 Year Price Score 118.78 *NYSE Composite Index=100 *12 Month Price Score 92.08

Interim Earnings (Per Share)

Qtr.	Nov	Feb	May	Aug
2009-10	0.74	0.75	0.81	0.83
2010-11	0.88	0.95	0.92	0.86
2011-12	0.99	1.02	1.05	1.07
2012-13	1.11	1.00	...	...

Interim Dividends (Per Share)

Amt	Decl	Ex	Rec	Pay
0.31Q	05/08/2012	05/29/2012	05/31/2012	06/19/2012
0.31Q	08/08/2012	08/29/2012	08/31/2012	09/18/2012
0.31Q	11/15/2012	11/28/2012	11/30/2012	12/18/2012
0.31Q	02/21/2013	02/26/2013	02/28/2013	03/19/2013

Indicated Div: $1.24

Valuation Analysis

		Institutional Holding	
Forecast EPS	$4.59 (04/05/2013)	No of Institutions	364
Market Cap	$4.0 Billion	Shares	49,783,288
Book Value	$547.2 Million	% Held	93.29
Price/Book	7.37		
Price/Sales	4.84		

Business Summary: Internet & Software (MIC: 6.3.2 SIC: 7371 NAIC: 541511)

FactSet Research Systems is a provider of integrated financial information and analytical applications to the investment community. By consolidating content from databases with analytics on a single platform, Co. supports the investment process from initial research to published results for buy and sell-side professionals. Co.'s applications provide users access to company analysis, multicompany comparisons, industry analysis, company screening, portfolio analysis, predictive risk measurements, alphatesting, portfolio optimization and simulation, real-time news and quotes and tools to value and analyze fixed income securities and portfolios.

Recent Developments: For the quarter ended Feb 28 2013, net income decreased 4.7% to US$44.5 million from US$46.7 million in the year-earlier quarter. Revenues were US$213.1 million, up 6.9% from US$199.4 million the year before. Operating income was US$56.2 million versus US$67.1 million in the prior-year quarter, a decrease of 16.3%. Direct operating expenses rose 12.3% to US$75.8 million from US$67.5 million in the comparable period the year before. Indirect operating expenses increased 25.3% to US$81.1 million from US$64.7 million in the equivalent prior-year period.

Prospects: Our evaluation of FactSet Research Systems Inc. as of Apr. 7, 2013 is the result of our systematic analysis on three basic characteristics: earnings strength, relative valuation, and recent stock price movement. The company has generated a negative trend in earnings per share over the past 5 quarters. However, while recent estimates for the company have been mixed, FDS has posted better than expected results. Based on operating earnings yield, the company is about fairly valued when compared to all of the companies in our coverage group. Share price changes over the past year indicates that FDS will perform well over the near term.

Financial Data
(US$ in Thousands)

	6 Mos	3 Mos	08/31/2012	08/31/2011	08/31/2010	08/31/2009	08/31/2008	08/31/2007
Earnings Per Share	4.23	4.25	4.12	3.61	3.13	2.97	2.50	2.14
Cash Flow Per Share	5.26	5.14	5.17	4.51	4.52	4.41	2.97	3.19
Tang Book Value Per Share	6.07	6.72	5.94	5.34	4.96	5.84	4.57	4.68
Dividends Per Share	1.240	1.200	1.160	1.000	0.860	0.760	0.600	0.360
Dividend Payout %	29.31	28.24	28.16	27.70	27.48	25.59	24.00	16.82
Income Statement								
Total Revenue	424,167	211,085	805,793	726,510	641,059	622,023	575,519	475,801
EBITDA	146,043	80,430	300,805	266,858	250,981	238,222	211,947	183,576
Depn & Amort	18,010	8,917	26,100	27,900	28,800	26,100	22,900	20,700
Income Before Taxes	128,033	71,513	274,705	238,958	222,181	212,122	189,047	162,876
Income Taxes	33,726	21,744	85,896	67,912	71,970	67,172	64,030	53,309
Net Income	94,307	49,769	188,809	171,046	150,211	144,950	125,017	109,567
Average Shares	44,455	44,984	45,810	47,355	48,004	48,789	50,080	51,284
Balance Sheet								
Current Assets	284,561	320,046	299,125	273,170	265,145	299,410	234,523	252,332
Total Assets	669,978	711,856	694,143	657,440	644,608	633,137	587,274	523,750
Current Liabilities	94,813	95,333	113,176	109,423	109,276	99,363	92,626	90,650
Total Liabilities	122,798	125,343	141,879	142,252	142,202	132,308	121,803	114,439
Stockholders' Equity	547,180	586,513	552,264	515,188	502,406	500,829	465,471	409,311
Shares Outstanding	43,579	44,342	44,279	45,055	46,024	46,739	47,968	48,348
Statistical Record								
Return on Assets %	28.61	28.07	27.86	26.27	23.51	23.75	22.44	22.34
Return on Equity %	34.98	34.38	35.28	33.62	29.95	30.00	28.50	28.53
EBITDA Margin %	34.43	38.10	37.33	36.73	39.15	38.30	36.83	38.58
Net Margin %	22.23	23.58	23.43	23.54	23.43	23.30	21.72	23.03
Asset Turnover	1.25	1.19	1.19	1.12	1.00	1.02	1.03	0.97
Current Ratio	3.00	3.36	2.64	2.50	2.43	3.01	2.53	2.78
Price Range	108.52-86.17	108.52-86.16	108.52-82.24	111.76-73.55	78.69-54.95	63.59-33.18	73.53-44.53	69.36-43.32
P/E Ratio	25.65-20.37	25.53-20.27	26.34-19.96	30.96-20.37	25.14-17.56	21.41-11.17	29.41-17.81	32.41-20.24
Average Yield %	1.30	1.26	1.23	1.05	1.24	1.62	1.00	0.61

Address: 601 Merritt 7, Norwalk, CT 06851
Telephone: 203-810-1000
Fax: 203-810-1001

Web Site: www.factset.com
Officers: Philip A. Hadley - Chairman, Chief Executive Officer Charles J. Snyder - Vice-Chairman

Auditors: PricewaterhouseCoopers LLP
Transfer Agents: BNY Mellon Shareowner Services

FAIR ISAAC CORP

Exchange	Symbol	Price	52Wk Range	Yield	P/E
NYS	FICO	$45.69 (3/28/2013)	47.86-38.51	0.18	18.42

*7 Year Price Score 127.94 *NYSE Composite Index=100 *12 Month Price Score 95.17

Interim Earnings (Per Share)

Qtr.	Dec	Mar	Jun	Sep
2009-10	0.37	0.28	0.40	0.38
2010-11	0.40	0.19	0.58	0.63
2011-12	0.81	0.55	0.59	0.69
2012-13	0.65	...	...	...

Interim Dividends (Per Share)

Amt	Decl	Ex	Rec	Pay
0.02Q	04/30/2012	05/10/2012	05/14/2012	05/30/2012
0.02Q	08/22/2012	09/06/2012	09/10/2012	09/26/2012
0.02Q	11/06/2012	12/03/2012	12/05/2012	12/19/2012
0.02Q	02/12/2013	02/21/2013	02/25/2013	03/13/2013

Indicated Div: $0.08

Valuation Analysis / **Institutional Holding**

Forecast EPS	$2.80 (04/05/2013)
No of Institutions	273
Market Cap	$1.6 Billion
Book Value	$508.7 Million
Shares	38,235,260
Price/Book	3.19
% Held	90.75
Price/Sales	2.33

Business Summary: Internet & Software (MIC: 6.3.2 SIC: 7389 NAIC: 541512)

Fair Isaac provides analytical products, credit scoring and credit account management products and services. Co. is organized into the following three segments: Applications, which includes pre-configured Decision Management applications designed for a specific type of business problem or process, such as marketing, account origination, and customer management, as well as associated services; Scores, which includes Co.'s business-to-business scoring applications and services, Co.'s myFICO® applications for consumers, and associated services; and Tools, which is composed of software tools that clients use to create their own custom Decision Management applications, and associated services.

Recent Developments: For the quarter ended Dec 31 2012, net income decreased 21.9% to US$23.4 million from US$30.0 million in the year-earlier quarter. Revenues were US$190.0 million, up 11.5% from US$170.3 million the year before. Operating income was US$43.0 million versus US$52.1 million in the prior-year quarter, a decrease of 17.4%. Direct operating expenses rose 22.1% to US$56.1 million from US$46.0 million in the comparable period the year before. Indirect operating expenses increased 25.7% to US$90.9 million from US$72.3 million in the equivalent prior-year period.

Prospects: Our evaluation of Fair, Isaac & Co. Inc. as of Apr. 7, 2013 is the result of our systematic analysis on three basic characteristics: earnings strength, relative valuation, and recent stock price movement. The company has managed to produce a neutral trend in earnings per share over the past 5 quarters and while recent estimates for the company have remained steady, FICO has posted results that fell short of analysts expectations. Based on operating earnings yield, the company is undervalued when compared to all of the companies in our coverage universe. Share price changes over the past year indicates that FICO will perform well over the near term.

Financial Data

(US$ in Thousands)	3 Mos	09/30/2012	09/30/2011	09/30/2010	09/30/2009	09/30/2008	09/30/2007	09/30/2006
Earnings Per Share	2.48	2.64	1.79	1.42	1.33	1.70	1.82	1.59
Cash Flow Per Share	3.35	3.71	3.46	2.36	3.12	3.24	3.20	3.13
Dividends Per Share	0.080	0.080	0.080	0.080	0.080	0.080	0.080	0.080
Dividend Payout %	3.23	3.03	4.47	5.63	6.02	4.71	4.40	5.03
Income Statement								
Total Revenue	190,020	676,423	619,683	605,643	630,735	744,842	822,236	825,365
EBITDA	42,910	189,204	151,868	145,641	156,725	162,671	199,127	201,304
Depn & Amortn	8	21,544	24,241	30,901	38,391	38,143	50,226	48,791
Income Before Taxes	35,043	136,243	97,455	92,304	97,570	112,995	149,662	159,192
Income Taxes	11,622	44,239	25,893	27,847	32,105	31,809	45,012	55,706
Net Income	23,421	92,004	71,562	64,457	65,102	83,952	104,650	103,486
Average Shares	36,151	36,063	39,988	45,308	48,776	49,373	57,548	65,125
Balance Sheet								
Current Assets	251,374	259,325	364,481	347,175	442,558	351,702	422,751	413,310
Total Assets	1,176,114	1,158,611	1,129,468	1,123,716	1,303,888	1,275,253	1,275,771	1,321,205
Current Liabilities	189,003	209,605	146,498	122,147	114,588	122,631	525,924	537,029
Long-Term Obligations	455,000	455,000	504,000	512,000	570,000	570,000	170,000	...
Total Liabilities	667,386	684,205	663,974	648,802	703,619	713,312	709,457	551,177
Stockholders' Equity	508,728	474,406	465,494	474,914	600,269	561,941	566,314	770,028
Shares Outstanding	35,478	34,839	37,084	39,882	48,156	48,473	51,064	59,369
Statistical Record								
Return on Assets %	7.42	8.02	6.35	5.31	5.05	6.56	8.06	7.75
Return on Equity %	17.60	19.52	15.22	11.99	11.20	14.84	15.66	13.14
EBITDA Margin %	22.58	27.97	24.51	24.05	24.85	21.84	24.22	24.39
Net Margin %	12.33	13.60	11.55	10.64	10.32	11.27	12.73	12.54
Asset Turnover	0.60	0.59	0.55	0.50	0.49	0.58	0.63	0.62
Current Ratio	1.33	1.24	2.49	2.84	3.86	2.87	0.80	0.77
Debt to Equity	0.89	0.96	1.08	1.08	0.95	1.01	0.30	...
Price Range	47.86-35.49	45.95-20.26	31.61-21.19	26.57-18.07	24.22-9.90	39.98-19.08	42.59-35.03	48.21-33.25
P/E Ratio	19.30-14.31	17.41-7.67	17.66-11.84	18.71-12.73	18.21-7.44	23.52-11.22	23.40-19.25	30.32-20.91
Average Yield %	0.19	0.20	0.30	0.35	0.49	0.30	0.21	0.20

Address: 181 Metro Drive, Suite 700, San Jose, CA 95110-1346
Telephone: 408-535-1500

Web Site: www.fico.com
Officers: A. George Battle - Chairman William J. Lansing - Chief Executive Officer

Auditors: Deloitte & Touche LLP
Investor Contact: 800-213-5542
Transfer Agents: Computershare Shareowner Services, Pittsburgh, PA

FAIRCHILD SEMICONDUCTOR INTERNATIONAL, INC.

Exchange	Symbol	Price	52Wk Range	Yield	P/E
NYS	FCS	$14.14 (3/28/2013)	15.59-11.30	N/A .	74.42

*7 Year Price Score 92.73 *NYSE Composite Index=100 *12 Month Price Score 96.75

Interim Earnings (Per Share)

Qtr.	Mar	Jun	Sep	Dec
2008	0.14	0.05	0.21	(1.75)
2009	(0.41)	(0.20)	0.02	0.10
2010	0.18	0.34	0.28	0.40
2011	0.33	0.34	0.28	0.17
2012	0.01	0.09	0.19	(0.11)

Interim Dividends (Per Share)

No Dividends Paid

Valuation Analysis   **Institutional Holding**

Forecast EPS	$0.62	No of Institutions
	(04/06/2013)	271
Market Cap	$1.8 Billion	Shares
Book Value	$1.4 Billion	141,565,984
Price/Book	1.31	% Held
Price/Sales	1.28	98.39

TRADING VOLUME (thousand shares)

Business Summary: Semiconductors (MIC: 6.2.4 SIC: 3674 NAIC: 334413)

Fairchild Semiconductor International designs, develops, manufactures and markets power analog, power discrete and certain non-power semiconductor products. Co.'s products are used in a variety of electronic applications, including computers and internet hardware; communications; networking and storage equipment; industrial power supply and instrumentation equipment; consumer electronics such as digital cameras, displays, audio/video devices and household appliances; and automotive applications. Co.'s business is organized into three principal product groups: Mobile, Computing, Consumer and Communication; Power Conversion, Industrial and Automotive; and Standard Discrete and Standard Linear.

Recent Developments: For the year ended Dec 30 2012, net income decreased 83.1% to US$24.6 million from US$145.5 million in the prior year. Revenues were US$1.41 billion, down 11.5% from US$1.59 billion the year before. Operating income was US$44.7 million versus US$164.9 million in the prior year, a decrease of 72.9%. Direct operating expenses declined 6.4% to US$963.9 million from US$1.03 billion in the comparable period the year before. Indirect operating expenses increased 0.8% to US$397.3 million from US$394.3 million in the equivalent prior-year period.

Prospects: Our evaluation of Fairchild Semiconductor International Inc. as of Apr. 7, 2013 is the result of our systematic analysis on three basic characteristics: earnings strength, relative valuation, and recent stock price movement. The company has enjoyed a very positive trend in earnings per share over the past 5 quarters. However, while recent estimates for the company have been mixed, FCS has posted results that fell short of analysts expectations. Based on operating earnings yield, the company is overvalued when compared to all of the companies in our coverage universe. Share price changes over the past year indicates that FCS will perform well over the near term.

Financial Data

(US$ in Thousands)	12/30/2012	12/25/2011	12/26/2010	12/27/2009	12/28/2008	12/30/2007	12/31/2006	12/25/2005
Earnings Per Share	0.19	1.12	1.20	(0.49)	(1.35)	0.51	0.67	(2.01)
Cash Flow Per Share	1.42	2.13	2.68	1.53	1.50	1.54	1.49	1.26
Tang Book Value Per Share	9.09	8.66	7.58	6.34	6.46	6.00	6.53	5.41
Income Statement								
Total Revenue	1,405,900	1,588,800	1,599,700	1,187,500	1,574,200	1,670,200	1,651,100	1,425,100
EBITDA	164,600	312,800	338,200	115,100	(9,700)	228,700	235,100	141,800
Depn & Amortn	135,300	150,500	156,300	160,400	136,600	127,000	116,800	150,200
Income Before Taxes	23,700	157,700	174,700	(63,300)	(168,600)	82,100	98,800	(36,500)
Income Taxes	(900)	12,200	21,500	(3,100)	(1,200)	18,100	15,400	204,700
Net Income	24,600	145,500	153,200	(60,200)	(167,400)	64,000	83,400	(241,200)
Average Shares	129,000	130,300	128,000	123,800	124,300	126,300	124,400	120,200
Balance Sheet								
Current Assets	832,000	853,000	843,100	781,200	778,900	885,500	1,028,500	874,500
Total Assets	1,883,900	1,936,900	1,849,100	1,762,400	1,849,800	2,132,600	2,045,600	1,928,300
Current Liabilities	204,900	258,200	282,000	195,500	194,100	444,800	262,500	229,700
Long-Term Obligations	250,100	300,100	316,900	466,900	529,900	385,900	589,700	641,000
Total Liabilities	513,900	612,400	670,400	733,500	789,900	910,900	911,200	919,800
Stockholders' Equity	1,370,000	1,324,500	1,178,700	1,028,900	1,059,900	1,221,700	1,134,400	1,008,500
Shares Outstanding	126,924	125,826	124,525	124,044	123,298	124,134	122,729	120,529
Statistical Record								
Return on Assets %	1.27	7.71	8.51	N.M.	N.M.	3.07	4.13	N.M.
Return on Equity %	1.80	11.66	13.92	N.M.	N.M.	5.45	7.66	N.M.
EBITDA Margin %	11.71	19.69	21.14	9.69	N.M.	13.69	14.24	9.95
Net Margin %	1.75	9.16	9.58	N.M.	N.M.	3.83	5.05	N.M.
Asset Turnover	0.72	0.84	0.89	0.66	0.79	0.80	0.82	0.66
Current Ratio	4.06	3.30	2.99	4.00	4.01	1.99	3.92	3.81
Debt to Equity	0.18	0.23	0.27	0.45	0.50	0.32	0.52	0.64
Price Range	15.54-11.30	20.97-10.40	15.65-7.73	11.33-2.87	15.02-3.19	20.43-14.38	21.76-15.01	18.24-12.98
P/E Ratio	81.79-59.47	18.72-9.29	13.04-6.44	...	...	40.06-28.20	32.48-22.40	...

Address: 3030 Orchard Parkway, San Jose, CA 95134 **Telephone:** 408-822-2000	**Web Site:** www.fairchildsemi.com **Officers:** Mark S. Thompson - Chairman, President, Chief Executive Officer Vijay Ullal - President, Chief Operating Officer	**Auditors:** KPMG LLP **Investor Contact:** 207-775-8660 **Transfer Agents:** Computershare Trust Co., N.A., Canton, MA

FAMILY DOLLAR STORES, INC.

Exchange	Symbol	Price	52Wk Range	Yield	P/E	Div Achiever
NYS	FDO	$59.05 (3/28/2013)	73.26-54.87	1.76	16.18	36 Years

*7 Year Price Score 147.09 *NYSE Composite Index=100 *12 Month Price Score 82.62

Interim Earnings (Per Share)

Qtr.	Nov	Feb	May	Aug
2009-10	0.49	0.81	0.77	0.56
2010-11	0.58	0.98	0.91	0.67
2011-12	0.68	1.15	1.06	0.69
2012-13	0.69	1.21	...	...

Interim Dividends (Per Share)

Amt	Decl	Ex	Rec	Pay
0.21Q	05/10/2012	06/13/2012	06/15/2012	07/13/2012
0.21Q	09/04/2012	09/12/2012	09/14/2012	10/15/2012
0.21Q	12/04/2012	12/12/2012	12/14/2012	12/27/2012
0.26Q	03/04/2013	03/13/2013	03/15/2013	04/15/2013

Indicated Div: $1.04

Valuation Analysis / **Institutional Holding**

Forecast EPS	$3.95	No of Institutions
	(04/11/2013)	553
Market Cap	$6.8 Billion	Shares
Book Value	$1.4 Billion	127,294,944
Price/Book	4.76	% Held
Price/Sales	0.68	87.73

TRADING VOLUME (thousand shares)

Business Summary: Retail - General Merchandise/Department Stores (MIC: 2.1.1 SIC: 5331 NAIC: 452990)

Family Dollar Stores operates a chain of general merchandise retail discount stores. Co.'s primary product categories are: consumables, such as household chemicals, paper products, food, health and beauty aids, hardware and automotive supplies, and pet food and supplies; home products, such as blankets, sheets and towels, housewares, giftware, and home decor; apparel and accessories, such as men's, women's, boys' and girls' and infants' clothing, shoes, and fashion accessories; and seasonal and electronics, such as toys, stationery and school supplies, and pre-paid cellular phones and services. As of Sept. 29, 2012, Co. operated 7,475 stores in 45 states and the District of Columbia.

Recent Developments: For the quarter ended Mar 2 2013, net income increased 2.7% to US$140.1 million from US$136.4 million in the year-earlier quarter. Revenues were US$2.89 billion, up 17.7% from US$2.46 billion the year before. Operating income was US$217.0 million versus US$215.3 million in the prior-year quarter, an increase of 0.8%. Direct operating expenses rose 20.3% to US$1.93 billion from US$1.60 billion in the comparable period the year before. Indirect operating expenses increased 16.8% to US$750.1 million from US$642.1 million in the equivalent prior-year period.

Prospects: Our evaluation of Family Dollar Stores Inc. as of Apr. 7, 2013 is the result of our systematic analysis on three basic characteristics: earnings strength, relative valuation, and recent stock price movement. The company has managed to produce a neutral trend in earnings per share over the past 5 quarters. However, while recent estimates for the company have been mixed, FDO has posted results that fell short of analysts expectations. Based on operating earnings yield, the company is undervalued when compared to all of the companies in our coverage universe. Share price changes over the past year indicates that FDO will perform poorly over the near term.

Financial Data

(US$ in Thousands)	6 Mos	3 Mos	08/25/2012	08/27/2011	08/28/2010	08/29/2009	08/30/2008	09/01/2007
Earnings Per Share	3.65	3.59	3.58	3.12	2.62	2.07	1.66	1.62
Cash Flow Per Share	2.50	3.36	3.16	4.29	4.37	3.80	3.69	2.74
Tang Book Value Per Share	12.39	11.68	11.25	9.26	10.90	10.38	8.98	8.19
Dividends Per Share	0.840	0.810	0.780	0.670	0.520	0.520	0.480	0.440
Dividend Payout %	23.01	22.56	21.79	21.47	22.14	25.12	28.92	27.16
Income Statement								
Total Revenue	5,315,685	2,421,688	9,331,005	8,547,835	7,866,971	7,400,606	6,983,628	6,834,305
EBITDA	350,947	130,549	893,528	819,104	747,635	617,077	514,904	532,693
Depn & Amortn	(6,971)	(2,857)	204,500	179,500	172,037	159,808	149,598	144,060
Income Before Taxes	344,021	126,284	663,938	617,158	563,858	450,925	361,762	381,896
Income Taxes	123,597	46,005	241,698	228,713	205,723	159,659	128,689	139,042
Net Income	220,424	80,279	422,240	388,445	358,135	291,266	233,073	242,854
Average Shares	115,920	116,197	118,058	124,486	136,596	140,522	140,494	149,599
Balance Sheet								
Current Assets	1,950,679	1,941,418	1,768,170	1,533,844	1,660,208	1,599,438	1,344,091	1,537,280
Total Assets	3,771,982	3,687,446	3,373,065	2,996,205	2,982,057	2,842,722	2,661,782	2,624,156
Current Liabilities	1,281,927	1,326,396	1,065,657	1,017,055	1,054,487	1,059,707	1,068,985	1,130,303
Long-Term Obligations	500,199	500,158	516,320	532,370	250,000	250,000	250,000	250,000
Total Liabilities	2,347,310	2,334,853	2,075,438	1,909,131	1,560,503	1,402,662	1,407,699	1,449,515
Stockholders' Equity	1,424,672	1,352,593	1,297,627	1,087,074	1,421,554	1,440,060	1,254,083	1,174,641
Shares Outstanding	114,952	115,790	115,362	117,353	130,452	138,795	139,704	143,344
Statistical Record								
Return on Assets %	12.39	12.40	13.30	13.03	12.33	10.61	8.84	9.28
Return on Equity %	32.20	33.77	35.51	31.05	25.10	21.68	19.25	20.05
EBITDA Margin %	6.60	5.39	9.58	9.58	9.50	8.34	7.37	7.79
Net Margin %	4.15	3.32	4.53	4.54	4.55	3.94	3.34	3.55
Asset Turnover	2.92	2.82	2.94	2.87	2.71	2.70	2.65	2.61
Current Ratio	1.52	1.46	1.66	1.51	1.57	1.51	1.26	1.36
Debt to Equity	0.35	0.37	0.40	0.49	0.18	0.17	0.20	0.21
Price Range	73.26-54.49	73.26-53.63	73.26-49.00	55.74-41.38	43.56-25.95	34.63-21.96	29.31-15.85	35.23-24.56
P/E Ratio	20.07-14.93	20.41-14.94	20.46-13.69	17.87-13.26	16.63-9.90	16.73-10.61	17.66-9.55	21.75-15.16
Average Yield %	1.31	1.28	1.29	1.36	1.70	1.82	2.18	1.44

Address: P.O. Box 1017, 10401 Monroe Road, Charlotte, NC 28201-1017 Telephone: 704-847-6961	Web Site: Officers: Howard R. Levine - Chairman, President, Chief Executive Officer, Chief Operating Officer Michael K. Bloom - President, Chief Operating Officer	Auditors: PricewaterhouseCoopers LLP Transfer Agents: American Stock Transfer & Trust Company, LLC, Brooklyn, NY

FEDERAL REALTY INVESTMENT TRUST (MD)

Exchange	Symbol	Price	52Wk Range	Yield	P/E	Div Achiever
NYS	FRT	$108.04 (3/28/2013)	110.03-94.95	2.70	45.97	45 Years

*7 Year Price Score 116.10 *NYSE Composite Index=100 ***12 Month Price Score 94.59**

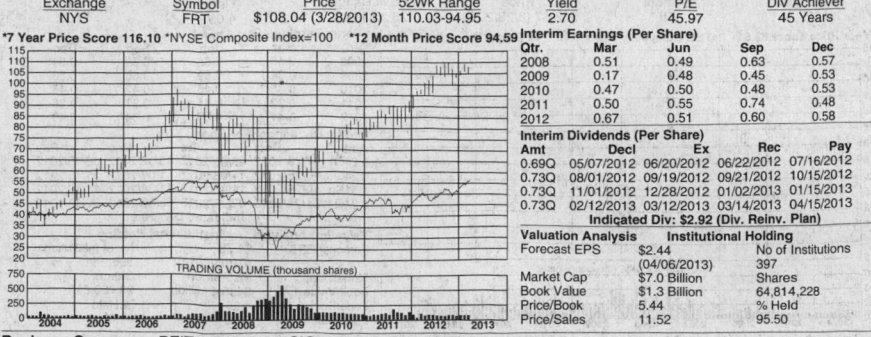

Interim Earnings (Per Share)

Qtr.	Mar	Jun	Sep	Dec
2008	0.51	0.49	0.63	0.57
2009	0.17	0.48	0.45	0.53
2010	0.47	0.50	0.48	0.53
2011	0.50	0.55	0.74	0.48
2012	0.67	0.51	0.60	0.58

Interim Dividends (Per Share)

Amt	Decl	Ex	Rec	Pay
0.69Q	05/07/2012	06/20/2012	06/22/2012	07/16/2012
0.73Q	08/01/2012	09/19/2012	09/21/2012	10/15/2012
0.73Q	11/01/2012	12/28/2012	01/02/2013	01/15/2013
0.73Q	02/12/2013	03/12/2013	03/14/2013	04/15/2013

Indicated Div: $2.92 (Div. Reinv. Plan)

Valuation Analysis		Institutional Holding	
Forecast EPS	$2.44	No of Institutions	
	(04/06/2013)	397	
Market Cap	$7.0 Billion	Shares	
Book Value	$1.3 Billion	64,814,228	
Price/Book	5.44	% Held	
Price/Sales	11.52	95.50	

Business Summary: REITs (MIC: 5.3.1 SIC: 6798 NAIC: 525930)

Federal Realty Investment Trust is an equity real estate investment trust. Co. is engaged in the ownership, management, and redevelopment of retail and mixed-use properties located primarily in certain metropolitan markets in the Northeast and Mid-Atlantic regions of the U.S., as well as in California. As of Dec 31 2012, Co. owned or had a majority interest in community and neighborhood shopping centers and mixed-use properties, which are operated as 88 retail real estate projects comprising approximately 19.6 million square feet. A joint venture in which Co. owns a 30% interest owned seven retail real estate projects totaling approximately 1.0 million square feet as of Dec 31 2012.

Recent Developments: For the year ended Dec 31 2012, income from continuing operations increased 9.7% to US$144.4 million from US$131.6 million a year earlier. Net income increased 4.4% to US$156.2 million from US$149.6 million in the prior year. Revenues were US$608.0 million, up 9.9% from US$553.1 million the year before. Revenues from property income rose 10.0% to US$602.6 million from US$548.0 million in the corresponding earlier year.

Prospects: Our evaluation of Federal Realty Investment Trust as of Apr. 7, 2013 is the result of our systematic analysis on three basic characteristics: earnings strength, relative valuation, and recent stock price movement. The company has enjoyed a very positive trend in earnings per share over the past 5 quarters. Because the company lacks sufficient analyst estimate data, we place greater weight on the historical EPS trend as the measure of earnings strength. Based on operating earnings yield, the company is overvalued when compared to all of the companies in our coverage universe. Share price changes over the past year indicates that FRT will perform in line with the market over the near term.

Financial Data
(US$ in Thousands)

	12/31/2012	12/31/2011	12/31/2010	12/31/2009	12/31/2008	12/31/2007	12/31/2006	12/31/2005
Earnings Per Share	2.35	2.28	1.98	1.63	2.19	3.45	1.92	1.94
Cash Flow Per Share	4.63	3.92	4.20	4.30	3.88	3.82	3.45	3.32
Tang Book Value Per Share	19.70	18.98	18.53	19.06	18.73	18.84	14.17	12.10
Dividends Per Share	2.840	2.720	2.660	2.620	2.520	2.370	2.460	2.370
Dividend Payout %	120.85	119.30	134.34	160.74	115.07	68.70	128.13	122.16
Income Statement								
Total Revenue	608,018	553,059	544,674	531,019	520,525	485,892	451,022	410,330
EBITDA	399,058	356,369	348,550	324,336	330,020	318,380	297,571	268,310
Depn & Amortn	142,039	126,568	119,817	115,093	111,069	105,966	97,879	91,503
Income Before Taxes	144,372	131,554	127,107	102,356	120,704	101,970	99,429	90,456
Net Income	151,925	143,917	122,790	98,304	129,787	195,537	118,712	114,612
Average Shares	64,056	62,603	61,324	59,830	58,914	56,543	53,962	53,050
Balance Sheet								
Current Assets	166,497	199,925	129,607	255,916	134,691	152,437	99,744	87,331
Total Assets	3,898,565	3,659,908	3,159,553	3,222,309	3,092,776	2,989,297	2,688,606	2,350,852
Current Liabilities	181,571	160,948	155,926	161,571	136,978	146,205	139,662	128,164
Long-Term Obligations	2,208,602	2,110,410	1,767,149	1,793,848	1,745,785	1,638,460	1,696,930	1,390,143
Total Liabilities	2,611,753	2,443,816	2,009,720	2,044,972	1,978,174	1,874,665	1,904,528	1,576,005
Stockholders' Equity	1,286,812	1,216,092	1,149,833	1,177,337	1,114,602	1,114,632	784,078	774,847
Shares Outstanding	64,815	63,544	61,526	61,242	58,985	58,645	55,320	52,890
Statistical Record								
Return on Assets %	4.01	4.22	3.85	3.11	4.26	6.89	4.71	4.96
Return on Equity %	12.11	12.17	10.55	8.58	11.61	20.60	15.23	14.64
EBITDA Margin %	65.63	64.44	63.99	61.08	63.40	65.52	65.98	65.39
Net Margin %	24.99	26.02	22.54	18.51	24.93	40.24	26.32	27.93
Asset Turnover	0.16	0.16	0.17	0.17	0.17	0.17	0.18	0.18
Current Ratio	0.92	1.24	0.83	1.58	0.98	1.04	0.71	0.68
Debt to Equity	1.72	1.74	1.54	1.52	1.57	1.47	2.16	1.79
Price Range	110.03-89.23	92.45-75.31	84.32-63.07	70.49-38.82	88.37-44.87	97.12-73.82	87.15-61.63	65.73-46.50
P/E Ratio	46.82-37.97	40.55-33.03	42.59-31.85	43.25-23.82	40.35-20.49	28.15-21.40	45.39-32.10	33.88-23.97
Average Yield %	2.79	3.22	3.53	4.70	3.52	2.76	3.40	4.17

Address: 1626 East Jefferson Street, Rockville, MD 20852 **Telephone:** 301-998-8100	**Web Site:** www.federalrealty.com **Officers:** Donald C. Wood - President, Chief Executive Officer Dawn M. Becker - Executive Vice President, Chief Operating Officer, Secretary, General Counsel	**Auditors:** Grant Thornton LLP **Investor Contact:** 301-998-8265 **Transfer Agents:** American Stock Transfer & Trust Company, New York, NY

FEDERATED INVESTORS INC (PA)

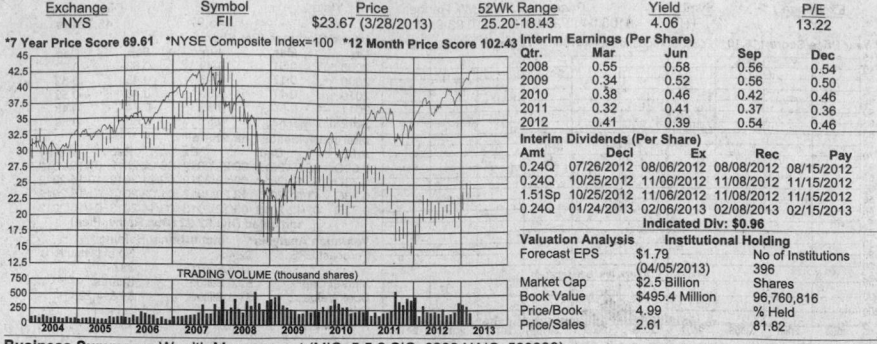

Exchange	Symbol	Price	52Wk Range	Yield	P/E
NYS	FII	$23.67 (3/28/2013)	25.20-18.43	4.06	13.22

*7 Year Price Score 69.61   *NYSE Composite Index=100   *12 Month Price Score 102.43

Interim Earnings (Per Share)

Qtr.	Mar	Jun	Sep	Dec
2008	0.55	0.58	0.56	0.54
2009	0.34	0.52	0.56	0.50
2010	0.38	0.46	0.42	0.46
2011	0.32	0.41	0.37	0.36
2012	0.41	0.39	0.54	0.46

Interim Dividends (Per Share)

Amt	Decl	Ex	Rec	Pay
0.24Q	07/26/2012	08/06/2012	08/08/2012	08/15/2012
0.24Q	10/25/2012	11/06/2012	11/08/2012	11/15/2012
1.51Sp	10/25/2012	11/06/2012	11/08/2012	11/15/2012
0.24Q	01/24/2013	02/06/2013	02/08/2013	02/15/2013

Indicated Div: $0.96

Valuation Analysis / **Institutional Holding**

Forecast EPS	$1.79
	(04/05/2013)
Market Cap	$2.5 Billion
Book Value	$495.4 Million
Price/Book	4.99
Price/Sales	2.61

No of Institutions
396
Shares
96,760,816
% Held
81.82

TRADING VOLUME (thousand shares)

Business Summary: Wealth Management (MIC: 5.5.2 SIC: 6282 NAIC: 523930)

Federated Investors is a provider of investment management products and related financial services. Co. sponsors, markets and provides investment-related services to various investment products, including mutual funds and Separate Accounts (which include separately managed accounts, institutional accounts, sub-advised funds and other managed products) in both domestic and international markets. Co. markets these funds to banks, broker/dealers and other financial intermediaries who use them to meet the needs of their customers, including retail investors, corporations and retirement plans. As of Dec 31 2012, Co. had $379.80 billion in assets under management.

Recent Developments: For the year ended Dec 31 2012, net income increased 27.4% to US$197.6 million from US$155.1 million in the prior year. Revenues were US$945.7 million, up 5.7% from US$895.1 million the year before. Operating income was US$312.6 million versus US$257.5 million in the prior year, an increase of 21.4%. Indirect operating expenses decreased 0.7% to US$633.1 million from US$637.7 million in the equivalent prior-year period.

Prospects: Our evaluation of Federated Investors Inc. as of Apr. 7, 2013 is the result of our systematic analysis on three basic characteristics: earnings strength, relative valuation, and recent stock price movement. The company has managed to produce a neutral trend in earnings per share over the past 5 quarters. However, while recent estimates for the company have been lowered by analysts, FII has posted better than expected results. Based on operating earnings yield, the company is undervalued when compared to all of the companies in our coverage universe. Share price changes over the past year indicates that FII will perform in line with the market over the near term.

Financial Data

(US$ in Thousands)	12/31/2012	12/31/2011	12/31/2010	12/31/2009	12/31/2008	12/31/2007	12/31/2006	12/31/2005
Earnings Per Share	1.79	1.45	1.73	1.92	2.22	2.12	1.86	1.48
Cash Flow Per Share	3.14	1.13	2.16	2.75	3.09	3.24	2.82	1.75
Tang Book Value Per Share	N.M.	N.M.	N.M.	N.M.	N.M.	0.39	0.39	1.59
Dividends Per Share	2.470	0.960	2.220	0.960	3.690	0.810	0.690	0.575
Dividend Payout %	137.99	66.21	128.32	50.00	166.22	38.21	37.10	38.85
Income Statement								
Total Revenue	945,706	895,114	951,943	1,175,950	1,223,680	1,127,644	978,858	909,216
EBITDA	316,611	254,671	308,620	334,318	381,000	372,473	332,870	301,949
Depn & Amortn	8,100	8,300	7,500	7,500	24,588	25,602	25,011	20,465
Income Before Taxes	308,511	246,371	301,120	326,818	356,793	352,443	310,366	290,216
Income Taxes	110,883	91,288	111,957	118,278	128,168	129,207	113,719	116,719
Net Income	188,088	150,906	179,114	197,292	224,317	217,471	197,729	160,283
Average Shares	100,313	100,632	99,993	100,056	100,855	102,606	106,288	108,252
Balance Sheet								
Current Assets	300,062	366,511	373,170	184,787	116,832	206,291	182,051	346,423
Total Assets	1,090,061	1,150,856	1,153,504	912,433	846,610	840,971	810,294	896,621
Current Liabilities	181,134	187,356	214,352	196,998	217,838	164,571	131,907	166,300
Long-Term Obligations	276,250	318,750	365,686	118,556	156,497	62,701	112,987	159,784
Total Liabilities	594,629	608,897	661,705	384,226	423,236	266,956	280,919	356,292
Stockholders' Equity	495,432	541,959	491,799	528,207	423,374	574,015	529,375	540,329
Shares Outstanding	104,450	103,752	103,673	102,943	102,271	101,758	103,863	107,042
Statistical Record								
Return on Assets %	16.74	13.10	17.34	22.43	26.51	26.34	23.17	17.32
Return on Equity %	36.16	29.20	35.12	41.47	44.86	39.42	36.97	32.12
EBITDA Margin %	33.48	28.45	32.42	28.43	31.14	33.03	34.01	33.21
Net Margin %	19.89	16.86	18.82	16.78	18.33	19.29	20.20	17.63
Asset Turnover	0.84	0.78	0.92	1.34	1.45	1.37	1.15	0.98
Current Ratio	1.66	1.96	1.74	0.94	0.54	1.25	1.38	2.08
Debt to Equity	0.56	0.59	0.74	0.22	0.37	0.11	0.21	0.30
Price Range	23.45-15.83	28.00-14.38	28.01-20.17	28.02-16.80	44.39-16.14	43.00-31.44	39.93-30.12	37.85-27.03
P/E Ratio	13.10-8.84	19.31-9.92	16.19-11.66	14.59-8.75	20.00-7.27	20.28-14.83	21.47-16.19	25.57-18.26
Average Yield %	12.01	4.35	9.26	4.00	11.34	2.14	1.99	1.84

Address: Federated Investors Tower,	Web Site: www.federatedinvestors.com	Auditors: Ernst & Young LLP
Pittsburgh, PA 15222-3779	Officers: John F. Donahue - Chairman Gordon J.	Transfer Agents: ComputerShare
Telephone: 412-288-1900	Ceresino - Vice-Chairman	Investor Services, Providence, RI

FEDEX CORP

Exchange	Symbol	Price	52Wk Range	Yield	P/E
NYS	FDX	$98.20 (3/28/2013)	109.07-84.34	0.57	17.20

*7 Year Price Score 91.93 *NSE Composite Index=100 *12 Month Price Score 103.73

Interim Earnings (Per Share)

Qtr.	Aug	Nov	Feb	May
2009-10	0.58	1.10	0.76	1.33
2010-11	1.20	0.89	0.73	1.75
2011-12	1.46	1.57	1.65	1.74
2012-13	1.45	1.39	1.13	...

Interim Dividends (Per Share)

Amt	Decl	Ex	Rec	Pay
0.14Q	06/04/2012	06/14/2012	06/18/2012	07/02/2012
0.14Q	08/17/2012	09/06/2012	09/10/2012	10/01/2012
0.14Q	11/02/2012	11/19/2012	11/21/2012	12/17/2012
0.14Q	02/15/2013	03/07/2013	03/11/2013	04/01/2013

Indicated Div: $0.56

Valuation Analysis

Forecast EPS	$6.07 (04/06/2013)
Market Cap	$31.1 Billion
Book Value	$16.1 Billion
Price/Book	1.93
Price/Sales	0.71

Institutional Holding

No of Institutions	1002
Shares	259,909,456
% Held	76.70

TRADING VOLUME (thousand shares)

Business Summary: Airlines/Air Freight (MIC: 7.4.4 SIC: 4513 NAIC: 492110)

FedEx provides a portfolio of transportation, e-commerce and business services through several companies under the FedEx brand. These companies are included in four business segments. The Federal Express Corporation segment provides delivery within one to three business days. The FedEx Ground Package System, Inc. segment provides small-package ground delivery services. The FedEx Freight, Inc. segment provides less-than-truckload freight services, as well as Co.'s FedEx Freight Priority and FedEx Freight Economy services. The FedEx Corporate Services, Inc. segment provides Co.'s other companies with sales, marketing, information technology, communications and back-office support.

Recent Developments: For the quarter ended Feb 28 2013, net income decreased 30.7% to US$361.0 million from US$521.0 million in the year-earlier quarter. Revenues were US$10.95 billion, up 3.7% from US$10.56 billion the year before. Operating income was US$589.0 million versus US$813.0 million in the prior-year quarter, a decrease of 27.6%. Direct operating expenses rose 6.0% to US$4.75 billion from US$4.48 billion in the comparable period the year before. Indirect operating expenses increased 6.5% to US$5.62 billion from US$5.27 billion in the equivalent prior-year period.

Prospects: Our evaluation of FedEx Corp. as of Apr. 7, 2013 is the result of our systematic analysis on three basic characteristics: earnings strength, relative valuation, and recent stock price movement. The company has managed to produce a neutral trend in earnings per share over the past 5 quarters. However, while recent estimates for the company have been lowered by analysts, FDX has posted results that fell short of analysts expectations. Based on operating earnings yield, the company is undervalued when compared to all of the companies in our coverage universe. Share price changes over the past year indicates that FDX will perform very well over the near term.

Financial Data
(US$ in Thousands)

	9 Mos	6 Mos	3 Mos	05/31/2012	05/31/2011	05/31/2010	05/31/2009	05/31/2008
Earnings Per Share	5.71	6.23	6.41	6.41	4.57	3.76	0.31	3.60
Cash Flow Per Share	15.22	13.96	15.49	15.31	12.83	10.06	8.85	11.24
Tang Book Value Per Share	42.10	40.33	38.77	38.93	40.68	36.98	36.53	36.53
Dividends Per Share	0.550	0.680	0.530	0.520	0.480	0.440	0.440	0.400
Dividend Payout %	9.63	10.91	8.27	8.11	10.50	11.70	141.94	11.11
Income Statement								
Total Revenue	32,852,000	21,899,000	10,792,000	42,680,000	39,304,000	34,734,000	35,497,000	37,953,000
EBITDA	3,784,000	2,612,000	1,310,000	5,280,000	4,242,000	3,865,000	2,536,000	3,870,000
Depn & Amortn	1,764,000	1,165,000	573,000	2,100,000	1,900,000	1,900,000	1,800,000	1,800,000
Income Before Taxes	1,983,000	1,419,000	727,000	3,141,000	2,265,000	1,894,000	677,000	2,016,000
Income Taxes	725,000	522,000	268,000	1,109,000	813,000	710,000	579,000	891,000
Net Income	1,258,000	897,000	459,000	2,032,000	1,452,000	1,184,000	98,000	1,125,000
Average Shares	317,000	315,000	316,000	317,000	317,000	314,000	312,000	312,000
Balance Sheet								
Current Assets	9,745,000	9,159,000	8,877,000	9,056,000	8,285,000	7,284,000	7,116,000	7,244,000
Total Assets	31,830,000	31,312,000	30,691,000	29,903,000	27,385,000	24,902,000	24,244,000	25,633,000
Current Liabilities	5,099,000	4,828,000	4,809,000	5,374,000	4,882,000	4,645,000	4,524,000	5,368,000
Long-Term Obligations	1,991,000	2,241,000	2,242,000	1,250,000	1,667,000	1,668,000	1,930,000	1,506,000
Total Liabilities	15,718,000	15,769,000	15,667,000	15,176,000	12,165,000	11,091,000	10,618,000	11,107,000
Stockholders' Equity	16,112,000	15,543,000	15,024,000	14,727,000	15,220,000	13,811,000	13,626,000	14,526,000
Shares Outstanding	317,000	317,000	317,000	317,000	317,000	314,000	312,000	311,000
Statistical Record								
Return on Assets %	5.97	6.59	6.93	7.07	5.55	4.82	0.39	4.52
Return on Equity %	11.06	12.51	13.19	13.53	10.00	8.63	0.70	8.25
EBITDA Margin %	11.52	11.93	12.14	12.37	10.79	11.13	7.14	10.20
Net Margin %	3.83	4.10	4.25	4.76	3.69	3.41	0.28	2.96
Asset Turnover	1.45	1.45	1.47	1.49	1.50	1.41	1.42	1.53
Current Ratio	1.91	1.90	1.85	1.69	1.70	1.57	1.57	1.35
Debt to Equity	0.12	0.14	0.15	0.08	0.11	0.12	0.14	0.10
Price Range	107.33-84.34	95.82-77.29	95.82-65.15	98.50-65.15	98.32-70.11	95.62-50.05	93.69-34.28	117.25-82.55
P/E Ratio	18.80-14.77	15.38-12.41	14.95-10.16	15.37-10.16	21.51-15.34	25.43-13.31	302.23-110.58	32.57-22.93
Average Yield %	0.60	0.77	0.62	0.61	0.55	0.57	0.67	0.40

Address: 942 South Shady Grove Road, Memphis, TN 38120 **Telephone:** 901-818-7500	**Web Site:** **Officers:** Frederick W. Smith - Chairman, President, Chief Executive Officer Robert B. Carter - Executive Vice President, Chief Information Officer	**Auditors:** Ernst & Young LLP **Investor Contact:** 901-818-7200 **Transfer Agents:** Computershare, Providence, R.I.

FIDELITY NATIONAL FINANCIAL INC

Exchange	Symbol	Price	52Wk Range	Yield	P/E
NYS	FNF	$25.23 (3/28/2013)	26.14-17.70	2.54	9.41

*7 Year Price Score 108.35 *NYSE Composite Index=100 *12 Month Price Score 106.86

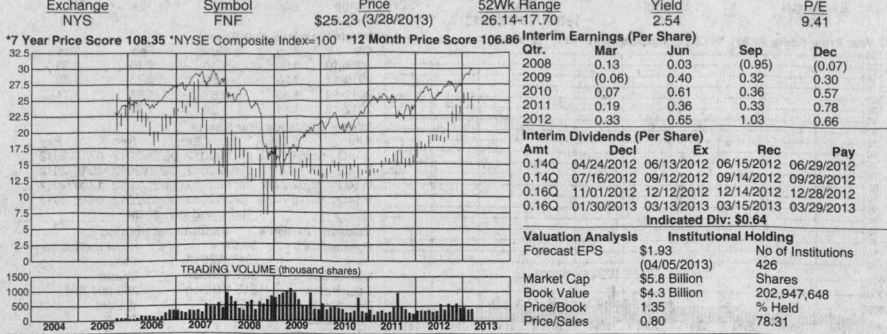

Interim Earnings (Per Share)

Qtr.	Mar	Jun	Sep	Dec
2008	0.13	0.03	(0.95)	(0.07)
2009	(0.06)	0.40	0.32	0.30
2010	0.07	0.61	0.36	0.57
2011	0.19	0.36	0.33	0.78
2012	0.33	0.65	1.03	0.66

Interim Dividends (Per Share)

Amt	Decl	Ex	Rec	Pay
0.14Q	04/24/2012	06/13/2012	06/15/2012	06/29/2012
0.14Q	07/16/2012	09/12/2012	09/14/2012	09/28/2012
0.16Q	11/01/2012	12/12/2012	12/14/2012	12/28/2012
0.16Q	01/30/2013	03/13/2013	03/15/2013	03/29/2013

Indicated Div: $0.64

Valuation Analysis / Institutional Holding

Valuation Analysis		Institutional Holding	
Forecast EPS	$1.93	No of Institutions	
	(04/05/2013)	426	
Market Cap	$5.8 Billion	Shares	
Book Value	$4.3 Billion	202,947,648	
Price/Book	1.35	% Held	
Price/Sales	0.80	78.31	

Business Summary: General Insurance (MIC: 5.2.1 SIC: 6361 NAIC: 524127)

Fidelity National Financial is provider of title insurance, mortgage services and other services. As of Dec 31 2012, Co. had four reporting segments: Fidelity National Title Group , which provides core title insurance and escrow and other title related services; Remy International, Inc., which is a designer, manufacturer, remanufacturer, marketer and distributor of aftermarket and original equipment electrical components; Restaurant Group; which consists of the operations of Co.'s American Blue Ribbon Holdings, LLC and J. Alexander's LLC subsidiaries; and Corporate and Other segment includes the operations of the parent holding company and other smaller operations.

Recent Developments: For the year ended Dec 31 2012, income from continuing operations increased 109.1% to US$606.6 million from US$290.1 million a year earlier. Net income increased 61.4% to US$611.7 million from US$379.1 million in the prior year. Revenues were US$7.20 billion, up 48.8% from US$4.84 billion the year before. Net premiums earned were US$3.84 billion versus US$3.26 billion in the prior year, an increase of 17.6%.

Prospects: Our evaluation of Fidelity National Financial Inc. as of Apr. 7, 2013 is the result of our systematic analysis on three basic characteristics: earnings strength, relative valuation, and recent stock price movement. The company has generated a negative trend in earnings per share over the past 5 quarters. However, while recent estimates for the company have been mixed, FNF has posted better than expected results. Based on operating earnings yield, the company is undervalued when compared to all of the companies in our coverage universe. Share price changes over the past year indicates that FNF will perform well over the near term.

Financial Data
(US$ in Thousands)

	12/31/2012	12/31/2011	12/31/2010	12/31/2009	12/31/2008	12/31/2007	12/31/2006	12/31/2005
Earnings Per Share	2.68	1.66	1.61	0.97	(0.85)	0.59	2.39	3.11
Cash Flow Per Share	2.80	0.57	0.81	1.69	0.02	1.58	3.96	4.02
Tang Book Value Per Share	7.48	9.16	7.85	7.16	4.87	7.93	9.67	8.19
Dividends Per Share	0.580	0.480	0.690	0.600	1.050	1.200	1.170	0.250
Dividend Payout %	21.64	28.92	42.86	61.86	...	203.39	48.95	8.04
Income Statement								
Premium Income	3,836,500	3,261,100	3,641,200	3,927,600	2,695,009	3,800,458	4,606,200	4,948,966
Total Revenue	7,201,700	4,839,600	5,740,300	5,828,400	4,329,095	5,524,010	9,436,101	6,315,861
Benefits & Claims	279,300	222,300	402,900	392,600	630,404	653,876	486,334	354,710
Income Before Taxes	843,400	414,800	562,400	344,900	(295,393)	176,513	943,202	868,304
Income Taxes	246,700	134,400	185,600	106,800	(125,542)	46,776	350,871	327,351
Net Income	606,500	369,500	370,100	222,300	(179,016)	129,769	437,761	538,981
Average Shares	226,000	222,700	229,300	228,500	209,974	219,989	182,861	173,575
Balance Sheet								
Total Assets	9,902,600	7,862,100	7,887,500	7,934,400	8,368,240	7,556,414	7,259,559	5,900,533
Total Liabilities	5,634,600	4,229,400	4,460,400	4,608,500	5,562,667	4,312,326	3,785,191	3,420,496
Stockholders' Equity	4,268,000	3,632,700	3,427,100	3,325,900	2,805,573	3,244,088	3,474,368	2,480,037
Shares Outstanding	228,545	220,677	223,748	230,217	214,902	213,036	221,413	174,319
Statistical Record								
Return on Assets %	6.81	4.69	4.68	2.73	N.M.	1.75	6.65	9.82
Return on Equity %	15.31	10.47	10.96	7.25	N.M.	3.86	14.70	20.90
Loss Ratio %	7.28	6.82	11.07	10.00	23.39	17.21	10.56	7.17
Net Margin %	8.42	7.63	6.45	3.81	(4.14)	2.35	4.64	8.53
Price Range	24.21-15.93	17.12-13.12	15.77-12.78	22.83-12.44	20.38-7.04	28.43-13.49	25.60-18.03	26.00-20.30
P/E Ratio	9.03-5.94	10.31-7.90	9.80-7.94	23.54-12.82	...	48.19-22.86	10.71-7.54	8.36-6.53
Average Yield %	2.95	3.17	4.84	4.87	3.87	7.16	5.65	1.10

Address: 601 Riverside Avenue, Jacksonville, FL 32204	Web Site: www.fnf.com	Auditors: KPMG LLP
Telephone: 904-854-8100	Officers: William P. Foley - Chairman Frank P. Willey - Vice-Chairman	Investor Contact: 904-854-8120
		Transfer Agents: Continental Stock Transfer & Trust Company, New York, NY

FIDELITY NATIONAL INFORMATION SERVICES INC

Exchange	Symbol	Price	52Wk Range	Yield	P/E
NYS	FIS	$39.62 (3/28/2013)	39.62-30.71	2.22	25.56

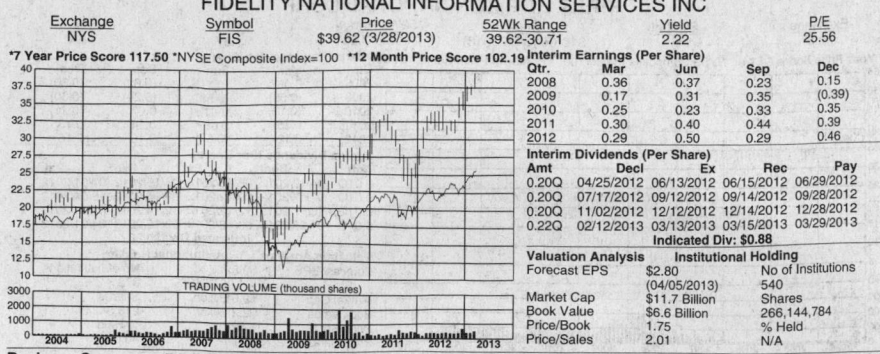

*7 Year Price Score 117.50 *NYSE Composite Index=100 *12 Month Price Score 102.19

Interim Earnings (Per Share)

Qtr.	Mar	Jun	Sep	Dec
2008	0.36	0.37	0.23	0.15
2009	0.17	0.31	0.35	(0.39)
2010	0.25	0.23	0.33	0.35
2011	0.30	0.40	0.44	0.39
2012	0.29	0.50	0.29	0.46

Interim Dividends (Per Share)

Amt	Decl	Ex	Rec	Pay
0.20Q	04/25/2012	06/13/2012	06/15/2012	06/29/2012
0.20Q	07/17/2012	09/12/2012	09/14/2012	09/28/2012
0.20Q	11/02/2012	12/12/2012	12/14/2012	12/28/2012
0.22Q	02/12/2013	03/13/2013	03/15/2013	03/29/2013

Indicated Div: $0.88

Valuation Analysis **Institutional Holding**

Forecast EPS	$2.80	No of Institutions	
	(04/05/2013)	540	
Market Cap	$11.7 Billion	Shares	
Book Value	$6.6 Billion	266,144,784	
Price/Book	1.75	% Held	
Price/Sales	2.01	N/A	

Business Summary: Business Services (MIC: 7.5.2 SIC: 6159 NAIC: 522320)

Fidelity National Information Services has three segments: Financial Solutions, which provides software and services for the processing, customer channel, treasury, cash management, wealth management and capital market operations of financial institution customers; Payment Solutions, which provides software and services for the Electronic Fund Transfer, card processing, item processing, bill payment, and government and healthcare payments processing needs of its customers; and International Solutions, which provides banking applications, channel applications, card and merchant services, item processing and check risk management services to financial institutions, card issuers and retailers.

Recent Developments: For the year ended Dec 31 2012, income from continuing operations increased 13.3% to US$560.3 million from US$494.6 million a year earlier. Net income was unchanged at US$481.1 million versus US$481.1 million the prior year. Non-interest income rose 3.2% to US$5.81 billion from US$5.63 billion, while non-interest expense advanced 3.3% to US$4.73 billion.

Prospects: Our evaluation of Fidelity National Information Services Inc. as of Apr. 7, 2013 is the result of our systematic analysis on three basic characteristics: earnings strength, relative valuation, and recent stock price movement. The company has managed to produce a neutral trend in earnings per share over the past 5 quarters and while recent estimates for the company have remained steady, FIS has posted results that fell short of analysts expectations. Based on operating earnings yield, the company is undervalued when compared to all of the companies in our coverage universe. Share price changes over the past year indicates that FIS will perform in line with the market over the near term.

Financial Data
(US$ in Thousands)

	12/31/2012	12/31/2011	12/31/2010	12/31/2009	12/31/2008	12/31/2007	12/31/2006	12/31/2005
Earnings Per Share	1.55	1.53	1.15	0.44	1.11	2.86	1.37	2.06
Cash Flow Per Share	3.58	3.90	3.10	3.02	3.10	2.40	2.66	2.08
Tang Book Value Per Share	N.M.	N.M.	N.M.	N.M.	N.M.	N.M.	N.M.	3.10
Dividends Per Share	0.800	0.200	0.200	0.200	0.200	0.200	3.950	0.200
Dividend Payout %	51.61	13.07	17.39	45.45	18.02	6.99	288.32	9.71
Income Statement								
Total Revenue	5,807,600	5,745,700	5,269,500	3,769,500	3,446,000	4,758,016	4,132,602	1,117,141
EBITDA	1,171,700	1,113,800	912,600	367,900	424,800	1,151,642	689,403	207,790
Depn & Amortn	117,800	110,700	123,000	81,300	88,400	115,600	97,700	20,400
Income Before Taxes	831,200	744,300	616,300	156,000	179,200	812,245	403,630	174,558
Income Taxes	270,900	239,000	215,300	52,100	57,600	300,530	150,150	68,927
Net Income	461,200	469,600	404,500	105,900	214,800	561,222	259,087	130,319
Average Shares	297,500	307,000	352,000	239,400	193,500	196,546	189,196	63,391
Balance Sheet								
Current Assets	1,844,200	1,682,700	1,673,000	1,666,100	1,179,800	1,829,495	1,300,539	444,902
Total Assets	13,549,700	13,848,300	14,161,800	13,997,600	7,514,000	9,794,583	7,630,560	972,435
Current Liabilities	1,256,800	1,354,900	1,285,900	1,234,700	852,200	1,254,214	880,515	233,562
Long-Term Obligations	4,231,600	4,550,600	4,935,200	3,016,600	2,409,000	4,003,383	2,947,840	227,881
Total Liabilities	6,908,800	7,345,300	7,758,600	5,688,700	3,981,200	6,013,404	4,487,816	513,165
Stockholders' Equity	6,640,900	6,503,000	6,403,200	8,308,900	3,532,800	3,781,179	3,142,744	459,270
Shares Outstanding	294,100	292,900	301,900	374,500	190,900	194,700	190,991	62,815
Statistical Record								
Return on Assets %	3.36	3.35	2.87	0.98	2.48	6.44	6.02	13.76
Return on Equity %	7.00	7.28	5.50	1.79	5.86	16.21	14.39	34.32
EBITDA Margin %	20.18	19.38	17.32	9.76	12.33	24.20	16.68	18.60
Net Margin %	7.94	8.17	7.68	2.81	6.23	11.80	6.27	11.67
Asset Turnover	0.42	0.41	0.37	0.35	0.40	0.55	0.96	1.18
Current Ratio	1.47	1.24	1.30	1.35	1.38	1.46	1.48	1.90
Debt to Equity	0.64	0.70	0.77	0.36	0.68	1.06	0.94	0.50
Price Range	36.97-26.43	33.54-22.55	29.90-22.28	25.70-15.52	24.23-12.47	32.12-22.47	24.60-18.79	23.00-18.26
P/E Ratio	23.85-17.05	21.92-14.74	26.00-19.37	58.41-35.27	21.83-11.23	11.23-7.86	17.96-13.72	11.17-8.86
Average Yield %	2.47	0.69	0.76	0.96	1.00	0.76	18.40	0.98

Address: 601 Riverside Avenue, Jacksonville, FL 32204 Telephone: 904-435-6000	Web Site: www.fisglobal.com Officers: Frank R. Martire - Chairman, President, Chief Executive Officer Gary A. Norcross - Corporate Executive Vice President, Chief Operating Officer	Auditors: KPMG LLP Investor Contact: 904-854-3282 Transfer Agents: Computershare Investor Services, LLC, Chicago, IL

FIRST HORIZON NATIONAL CORP

Exchange	Symbol	Price	52Wk Range	Yield	P/E
NYS	FHN	$10.68 (3/28/2013)	11.26-7.55	1.87	N/A

*7 Year Price Score 54.74   *NYSE Composite Index=100   *12 Month Price Score 104.58

Interim Earnings (Per Share)

Qtr.	Mar	Jun	Sep	Dec
2008	0.06	(0.11)	(0.62)	(0.30)
2009	(0.39)	(0.58)	(0.24)	(0.30)
2010	(0.12)	0.01	0.07	(0.21)
2011	0.15	0.08	0.14	0.13
2012	0.12	(0.50)	0.10	0.16

Interim Dividends (Per Share)

Amt	Decl	Ex	Rec	Pay
0.01Q	04/19/2012	06/13/2012	06/15/2012	07/01/2012
0.01Q	07/17/2012	09/12/2012	09/14/2012	10/01/2012
0.01Q	10/17/2012	12/12/2012	12/14/2012	01/01/2013
0.05Q	01/23/2013	03/13/2013	03/15/2013	04/01/2013

Indicated Div: $0.20

Valuation Analysis

		Institutional Holding	
Forecast EPS	$0.82	No of Institutions	
	(04/06/2013)	373	
Market Cap	$2.6 Billion	Shares	
Book Value	$2.2 Billion	215,342,240	
Price/Book	1.18	% Held	
Price/Sales	1.77	80.69	

Business Summary: Banking (MIC: 5.1.1 SIC: 6021 NAIC: 522110)

First Horizon National is a financial holding company. Through its subsidiary, Co. provides, among others, general banking services; discount brokerage and full-service brokerage; correspondent banking; retail and commercial insurance sales as agent; mortgage banking services; and services related to health savings accounts. Also, through FTN Financial, Co. provides: fixed income sales and trading; and underwriting of bank-eligible securities and other fixed-income securities. At Dec 31 2011, Co. had four business segments: Regional Banking, Capital Markets, Corporate, and Non-Strategic. Also, as of such date, Co. had total assets of $24.80 billion and total deposits of $16.20 billion.

Recent Developments: For the year ended Dec 31 2012, loss from continuing operations was US$16.4 million compared with income of US$142.0 million a year earlier. Net loss amounted to US$16.3 million versus net income of US$142.6 million in the prior year. Net interest income decreased 1.7% to US$688.7 million from US$700.8 million in the prior year. Provision for loan losses was US$78.0 million versus US$44.0 million in the prior year, an increase of 77.3%. Non-interest income fell 14.6% to US$671.3 million from US$786.0 million, while non-interest expense advanced 7.0% to US$1.38 billion.

Prospects: Our evaluation of First Horizon National Corp. as of Apr. 7, 2013 is the result of our systematic analysis on three basic characteristics: earnings strength, relative valuation, and recent stock price movement. The company has produced a positive trend in earnings per share over the past 5 quarters and while recent estimates for the company have remained steady, FHN has posted results that were in line with analysts expectations. Based on operating earnings yield, the company is overvalued when compared to all of the companies in our coverage universe. Share price changes over the past year indicates that FHN will perform well over the near term.

Financial Data
(US$ in Thousands)

	12/31/2012	12/31/2011	12/31/2010	12/31/2009	12/31/2008	12/31/2007	12/31/2006	12/31/2005
Earnings Per Share	(0.11)	0.50	(0.25)	(1.49)	(1.10)	(1.35)	3.62	3.40
Cash Flow Per Share	1.49	0.17	3.26	3.56	23.51	0.90	13.07	3.97
Tang Book Value Per Share	7.98	8.10	7.52	7.67	10.61	8.09	7.08	7.12
Dividends Per Share	0.040	0.040	...	...	0.400	1.800	1.800	1.740
Dividend Payout %	...	8.00	...	...	...	...	49.72	51.18
Income Statement								
Interest Income	798,953	832,437	880,286	992,939	1,606,725	2,305,959	2,329,111	1,840,174
Interest Expense	110,286	131,605	149,448	216,471	711,643	1,365,317	1,332,174	856,147
Net Interest Income	688,667	700,832	730,838	776,468	895,082	940,642	996,937	984,027
Provision for Losses	78,000	44,000	270,000	880,000	1,080,000	272,765	83,129	67,678
Non-Interest Income	671,329	786,011	955,692	1,233,531	1,491,313	859,949	1,166,893	1,399,756
Non-Interest Expense	1,383,701	1,292,995	1,367,133	1,550,533	1,656,052	1,843,433	1,742,621	1,670,932
Income Before Taxes	(101,705)	149,848	49,397	(420,534)	(349,657)	(315,607)	338,080	645,173
Income Taxes	(85,262)	15,836	(19,083)	(174,945)	(156,814)	(140,731)	87,278	204,075
Net Income	(27,759)	131,196	50,201	(269,837)	(191,960)	(170,111)	462,914	438,000
Average Shares	248,349	262,861	235,699	220,412	180,711	125,843	127,917	128,950
Balance Sheet								
Net Loans & Leases	16,833,556	16,426,673	16,493,062	17,679,471	20,995,634	25,512,765	24,762,197	24,846,573
Total Assets	25,520,140	24,789,384	24,698,952	26,068,678	31,021,980	37,015,461	37,918,259	36,579,061
Total Deposits	16,629,709	16,213,009	15,208,231	14,867,215	14,241,814	17,032,285	20,213,232	23,437,770
Total Liabilities	23,306,099	22,399,912	22,316,112	23,061,375	27,447,348	34,584,588	35,160,599	33,971,476
Stockholders' Equity	2,214,041	2,389,472	2,382,840	3,007,303	3,574,632	2,430,873	2,757,660	2,607,585
Shares Outstanding	243,597	257,468	263,366	221,980	205,282	126,366	124,865	126,222
Statistical Record								
Return on Assets %	N.M.	0.53	0.20	N.M.	N.M.	N.M.	1.24	1.32
Return on Equity %	N.M.	5.50	1.86	N.M.	N.M.	N.M.	17.26	18.84
Net Interest Margin %	86.20	84.19	83.02	78.20	55.71	40.79	42.80	53.47
Efficiency Ratio %	94.11	79.89	74.46	69.64	53.45	58.23	49.85	51.57
Loans to Deposits	1.01	1.01	1.08	1.19	1.47	1.50	1.23	1.06
Price Range	10.89-7.55	12.53-5.63	14.83-9.24	13.68-6.52	18.42-4.20	37.60-15.00	35.62-30.99	37.11-29.27
P/E Ratio	...	25.06-11.26	...	...	...	...	9.84-8.56	10.92-8.61
Average Yield %	0.44	0.43	...	...	3.95	6.33	5.41	5.15

Address: 165 Madison Avenue, Memphis, TN 38103 Telephone: 901-523-4444	Web Site: www.fhnc.com Officers: D. Bryan Jordan - Chairman, President, Chief Executive Officer Thomas C. Adams - Executive Vice President, Chief Investment Officer, Treasurer, Funds Management Manager	Auditors: KPMG LLP Investor Contact: 800-410-4577 Transfer Agents: Wells Fargo Shareowner Services

FIRSTENERGY CORP.

Exchange	Symbol	Price	52Wk Range	Yield	P/E
NYS	FE	$42.20 (3/28/2013)	50.87-38.90	5.21	N/A

*7 Year Price Score 77.55 *NYSE Composite Index=100 *12 Month Price Score 83.92

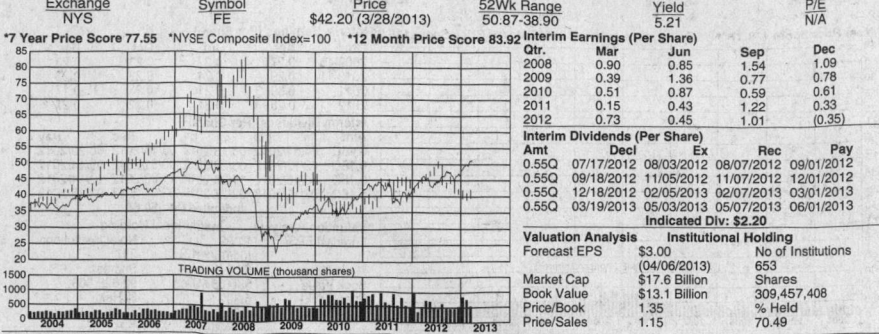

Interim Earnings (Per Share)

Qtr.	Mar	Jun	Sep	Dec
2008	0.90	0.85	1.54	1.09
2009	0.39	1.36	0.77	0.78
2010	0.51	0.87	0.59	0.61
2011	0.15	0.43	1.22	0.33
2012	0.73	0.45	1.01	(0.35)

Interim Dividends (Per Share)

Amt	Decl	Ex	Rec	Pay
0.55Q	07/17/2012	08/03/2012	08/07/2012	09/01/2012
0.55Q	09/18/2012	11/05/2012	11/07/2012	12/01/2012
0.55Q	12/18/2012	02/05/2013	02/07/2013	03/01/2013
0.55Q	03/19/2013	05/03/2013	05/07/2013	06/01/2013

Indicated Div: $2.20

Valuation Analysis   **Institutional Holding**

Forecast EPS	$3.00	No of Institutions
	(04/06/2013)	653
Market Cap	$17.6 Billion	Shares
Book Value	$13.1 Billion	309,457,408
Price/Book	1.35	% Held
Price/Sales	1.15	70.49

Business Summary: Electric Utilities (MIC: 3.1.1 SIC: 4911 NAIC: 221121)

FirstEnergy is a public utility holding company. Through its utility operating subsidiaries, Ohio Edison Company, The Cleveland Electric Illuminating Company, The Toledo Edison Company, Pennsylvania Power Company, Jersey Central Power & Light Company, Metropolitan Edison Company, Pennsylvania Electric Company, Monongahela Power Company, The Potomac Edison Company and West Penn Power Company (the Utilities), Co. is engaged in providing electric service. The Utilities' combined service areas encompass approximately 65,000 square miles in Ohio, Pennsylvania, West Virginia, Maryland, New Jersey and New York.

Recent Developments: For the year ended Dec 31 2012, net income decreased 11.3% to US$771.0 million from US$869.0 million in the prior year. Revenues were US$15.30 billion, down 5.2% from US$16.15 billion the year before. Operating income was US$2.18 billion versus US$1.70 billion in the prior year, an increase of 28.2%. Direct operating expenses declined 6.1% to US$10.48 billion from US$11.16 billion in the comparable period the year before. Indirect operating expenses decreased 19.5% to US$2.65 billion from US$3.29 billion in the equivalent prior-year period.

Prospects: Our evaluation of FirstEnergy Corp. as of Apr. 7, 2013 is the result of our systematic analysis on three basic characteristics: earnings strength, relative valuation, and recent stock price movement. The company has produced a positive trend in earnings per share over the past 5 quarters and while recent estimates for the company have been raised by analysts, FE has posted results that fell short of analysts expectations. Based on operating earnings yield, the company is undervalued when compared to all of the companies in our coverage universe. Share price changes over the past year indicates that FE will perform very poorly over the near term.

Financial Data
(US$ in Thousands)

	12/31/2012	12/31/2011	12/31/2010	12/31/2009	12/31/2008	12/31/2007	12/31/2006	12/31/2005
Earnings Per Share	1.84	2.21	2.57	3.29	4.38	4.22	3.81	2.61
Cash Flow Per Share	5.54	7.68	10.12	8.11	7.28	5.54	5.98	6.77
Tang Book Value Per Share	15.87	16.35	9.74	9.79	8.88	11.06	9.83	9.64
Dividends Per Share	2.200	2.200	2.200	2.200	2.200	2.000	1.800	1.668
Dividend Payout %	119.57	99.55	85.60	66.87	50.23	47.39	47.24	63.89
Income Statement								
Total Revenue	15,303,000	16,258,000	13,339,000	12,967,000	13,627,000	12,802,000	11,501,000	11,989,000
EBITDA	3,377,000	...	2,668,000	2,819,000	3,498,000	...	3,344,000	2,858,000
Depn & Amortn	...	...	746,000	736,000	677,000	638,000	596,000	589,000
Income Before Taxes	1,324,000	1,443,000	1,242,000	1,235,000	2,119,000	2,192,000	2,053,000	1,627,000
Income Taxes	553,000	574,000	482,000	245,000	777,000	883,000	795,000	754,000
Net Income	770,000	885,000	784,000	1,006,000	1,342,000	1,309,000	1,254,000	861,000
Average Shares	419,000	401,000	305,000	306,000	307,000	310,000	327,000	330,000
Balance Sheet								
Current Assets	...	3,355,000	3,698,000	3,320,000	3,053,000	2,230,000	2,083,000	2,317,000
Total Assets	...	47,326,000	34,805,000	34,304,000	33,521,000	32,068,000	31,196,000	31,841,000
Current Liabilities	7,605,000	4,855,000	4,698,000	5,288,000	7,098,000	5,148,000	5,255,000	5,453,000
Long-Term Obligations	15,179,000	15,716,000	12,579,000	11,908,000	9,100,000	8,869,000	8,535,000	8,155,000
Total Liabilities	37,322,000	34,046,000	26,260,000	25,745,000	25,238,000	23,091,000	22,161,000	22,653,000
Stockholders' Equity	13,084,000	13,280,000	8,545,000	8,559,000	8,283,000	8,977,000	9,035,000	9,188,000
Shares Outstanding	...	418,216	304,835	304,835	304,835	304,835	319,205	329,836
Statistical Record								
Return on Assets %	...	2.16	2.27	2.97	4.08	4.14	3.98	2.74
Return on Equity %	5.83	8.11	9.17	11.95	15.51	14.53	13.76	9.69
EBITDA Margin %	22.07	21.54	20.00	21.74	25.67	27.91	29.08	23.84
Net Margin %	5.03	5.44	5.88	7.76	9.85	10.22	10.90	7.18
Asset Turnover	0.31	0.40	0.39	0.38	0.41	0.40	0.36	0.38
Current Ratio	0.50	0.69	0.79	0.63	0.43	0.43	0.40	0.42
Debt to Equity	1.16	1.18	1.47	1.39	1.10	0.99	0.94	0.89
Price Range	50.87-40.72	46.02-36.25	47.03-34.03	52.96-35.79	83.21-45.45	74.76-57.90	61.31-48.20	52.73-38.26
P/E Ratio	27.65-22.13	20.82-16.40	18.30-13.24	16.10-10.88	19.00-10.38	17.72-13.72	16.09-12.65	20.20-14.66
Average Yield %	4.88	5.24	5.77	5.08	3.22	3.04	3.32	3.65

Address: 76 South Main Street, Akron, OH 44308 **Telephone:** 800-736-3402	**Web Site:** www.firstenergycorp.com **Officers:** Anthony J. Alexander - President, Chief Executive Officer Mark T. Clark - Executive Vice President, Chief Financial Officer	**Auditors:** PricewaterhouseCoopers LLP **Investor Contact:** 800-736-3402 **Transfer Agents:** American Stock Transfer & Trust Company, LLC, New York, NY

FLOWERS FOODS, INC.

Exchange	Symbol	Price	52Wk Range	Yield	P/E
NYS	FLO	$32.94 (3/28/2013)	32.94-18.87	1.94	33.61

*7 Year Price Score 118.37 *NYSE Composite Index=100 *12 Month Price Score 116.98

Interim Earnings (Per Share)

Qtr.	Apr	Jul	Oct	Dec
2009-10	0.27	0.22	0.23	0.23
2010-11	0.29	0.24	0.23	0.23
2011	0.30	0.21	0.23	0.17
2012	0.28	0.21	0.22	0.27

Interim Dividends (Per Share)

Amt	Decl	Ex	Rec	Pay
0.16Q	06/01/2012	06/13/2012	06/15/2012	06/29/2012
0.16Q	08/17/2012	08/29/2012	08/31/2012	09/14/2012
0.16Q	11/16/2012	11/28/2012	11/30/2012	12/14/2012
0.16Q	02/15/2013	02/27/2013	03/01/2013	03/15/2013

Indicated Div: $0.64

Valuation Analysis / **Institutional Holding**

Forecast EPS	$1.39	No of Institutions
	(04/05/2013)	297
Market Cap	$4.6 Billion	Shares
Book Value	$858.6 Million	92,628,808
Price/Book	5.30	% Held
Price/Sales	1.50	63.38

Business Summary: Food (MIC: 1.2.1 SIC: 2053 NAIC: 311813)

Flowers Foods is a producer and marketer of bakery products. Co. operates through two business segments: direct-store-delivery (DSD) and warehouse delivery (warehouse). The DSD segment focuses on the production and marketing of bakery products to U.S. customers in the Southeast, Mid-Atlantic, and Southwest as well as select markets in the Northeast, California and Nevada primarily through its DSD system. The warehouse segment produces snack cakes and breads and rolls that are shipped both fresh and frozen to national retail, foodservice, vending, and co-pack customers through their warehouse channels.

Recent Developments: For the year ended Dec 29 2012, net income increased 10.3% to US$136.1 million from US$123.4 million in the prior year. Revenues were US$3.05 billion, up 9.8% from US$2.77 billion the year before. Operating income was US$218.5 million versus US$189.0 million in the prior year, an increase of 15.6%. Direct operating expenses rose 9.8% to US$1.62 billion from US$1.47 billion in the comparable period the year before. Indirect operating expenses increased 8.9% to US$1.21 billion from US$1.11 billion in the equivalent prior-year period.

Prospects: Our evaluation of Flowers Foods Inc. as of Apr. 7, 2013 is the result of our systematic analysis on three basic characteristics: earnings strength, relative valuation, and recent stock price movement. The company has enjoyed a very positive trend in earnings per share over the past 5 quarters and while recent estimates for the company have been raised by analysts, FLO has posted better than expected results. Based on operating earnings yield, the company is about fairly valued when compared to all of the companies in our coverage universe. Share price changes over the past year indicates that FLO will perform poorly over the near term.

Financial Data
(US$ in Thousands)

	12/29/2012	12/31/2011	01/01/2011	01/02/2010	01/03/2009	12/29/2007	12/30/2006	12/31/2005
Earnings Per Share	0.98	0.90	0.99	0.94	0.85	0.68	0.58	0.43
Cash Flow Per Share	1.59	0.99	2.24	1.71	0.68	1.58	1.11	0.82
Tang Book Value Per Share	1.45	2.93	3.67	3.00	2.36	4.05	3.41	3.24
Dividends Per Share	0.630	0.583	0.517	0.450	0.383	0.306	0.211	0.170
Dividend Payout %	64.29	64.81	52.02	47.87	44.92	44.93	36.26	39.93
Income Statement								
Total Revenue	3,046,491	2,773,356	2,573,769	2,600,849	2,414,892	2,036,674	1,888,654	1,715,869
EBITDA	311,911	276,526	284,962	281,433	253,002	209,281	181,193	158,186
Depn & Amortn	93,400	87,500	79,100	75,100	70,300	64,600	62,700	58,900
Income Before Taxes	208,772	191,966	210,380	207,759	190,051	153,085	123,439	105,623
Income Taxes	72,651	68,538	73,333	74,047	67,744	54,970	45,304	39,861
Net Income	136,101	123,428	137,047	130,297	119,233	94,615	81,043	61,231
Average Shares	138,449	136,881	138,162	139,099	139,554	138,552	138,899	143,052
Balance Sheet								
Current Assets	464,451	378,570	313,714	338,955	352,243	269,234	242,116	237,570
Total Assets	1,995,849	1,553,998	1,325,489	1,351,442	1,353,244	987,535	906,590	851,069
Current Liabilities	354,958	268,419	242,772	221,772	265,069	213,645	185,242	174,275
Long-Term Obligations	535,016	283,406	98,870	225,905	263,879	22,508	79,126	74,403
Total Liabilities	1,137,229	795,030	529,699	635,497	718,525	331,320	343,727	338,698
Stockholders' Equity	858,620	758,968	795,790	715,945	634,719	656,215	562,863	512,371
Shares Outstanding	138,273	135,981	135,972	137,189	139,120	137,856	136,013	135,715
Statistical Record								
Return on Assets %	7.69	8.60	10.27	9.66	10.02	10.02	9.25	7.11
Return on Equity %	16.88	15.92	18.18	19.35	18.17	15.57	15.12	11.35
EBITDA Margin %	10.24	9.97	11.07	10.82	10.48	10.28	9.59	9.22
Net Margin %	4.47	4.45	5.32	5.01	4.94	4.65	4.29	3.57
Asset Turnover	1.72	1.93	1.93	1.93	2.03	2.16	2.15	1.99
Current Ratio	1.31	1.41	1.29	1.53	1.33	1.26	1.31	1.36
Debt to Equity	0.62	0.37	0.12	0.32	0.42	0.03	0.14	0.15
Price Range	24.13-18.45	22.97-16.22	18.01-15.61	17.53-13.65	21.41-14.51	16.61-11.82	13.52-11.45	13.50-8.18
P/E Ratio	24.62-18.83	25.52-18.02	18.20-15.77	18.65-14.52	25.18-17.07	24.43-17.39	23.30-19.74	31.40-19.02
Average Yield %	3.01	3.07	3.07	2.91	2.19	2.17	1.72	1.63

Address: 1919 Flowers Circle, Thomasville, GA 31757 Telephone: 229-226-9110	Web Site: www.flowersfoods.com Officers: George E. Deese - Executive Chairman, Chairman, Chief Executive Officer Allen L. Shiver - President, Chief Executive Officer	Auditors: PricewaterhouseCoopers LLP Investor Contact: 229-227-2348 Transfer Agents: Computershare, Providence, RI

FLOWSERVE CORP.

Exchange	Symbol	Price	52Wk Range	Yield	P/E
NYS	FLS	$167.71 (3/28/2013)	169.06-100.16	1.00	19.71

*7 Year Price Score 125.12 *NYSE Composite Index=100 *12 Month Price Score 112.44

TRADING VOLUME (thousand shares)

Interim Earnings (Per Share)

Qtr.	Mar	Jun	Sep	Dec
2008	1.53	2.13	2.04	2.03
2009	1.64	1.92	2.07	1.96
2010	1.42	1.62	1.84	1.99
2011	1.72	1.76	1.92	2.24
2012	1.69	1.98	2.07	2.78

Interim Dividends (Per Share)

Amt	Decl	Ex	Rec	Pay
0.36Q	05/17/2012	06/27/2012	06/29/2012	07/13/2012
0.36Q	08/15/2012	09/26/2012	09/28/2012	10/12/2012
0.36Q	11/15/2012	12/27/2012	12/31/2012	01/14/2013
0.42Q	02/21/2013	03/26/2013	03/28/2013	04/12/2013

Indicated Div: $1.68

Valuation Analysis

		Institutional Holding	
Forecast EPS	$10.20	No of Institutions	
	(04/06/2013)	587	
Market Cap	$8.1 Billion	Shares	
Book Value	$1.9 Billion	48,280,908	
Price/Book	4.27	% Held	
Price/Sales	1.70	74.73	

Business Summary: Industrial Machinery & Equipment (MIC: 7.2.1 SIC: 3561 NAIC: 333911)

Flowserve develops and manufactures flow control equipment for the movement, control and protection of the flow of materials in its customers' critical processes. Co.'s product portfolio of pumps, valves, seals, automation and aftermarket services supports global infrastructure industries, including oil and gas, chemical, power generation and water management, and certain industrial markets. Through Co.'s manufacturing platform and global network of Quick Response Centers, it provides a range of aftermarket equipment services, such as installation, diagnostics, repair and retrofitting. Co.'s segments are: Engineered Product Division; Industrial Product Division; and Flow Control Division.

Recent Developments: For the year ended Dec 31 2012, net income increased 5.0% to US$450.8 million from US$429.2 million in the prior year. Revenues were US$4.75 billion, up 5.3% from US$4.51 billion the year before. Operating income was US$675.8 million versus US$618.7 million in the prior year, an increase of 9.2%. Direct operating expenses rose 5.8% to US$3.17 billion from US$3.00 billion in the comparable period the year before. Indirect operating expenses increased 1.1% to US$905.2 million from US$895.0 million in the equivalent prior-year period.

Prospects: Our evaluation of Flowserve Corp. as of Apr. 7, 2013 is the result of our systematic analysis on three basic characteristics: earnings strength, relative valuation, and recent stock price movement. The company has produced a positive trend in earnings per share over the past 5 quarters and while recent estimates for the company have remained steady, FLS has posted results that fell short of analysts expectations. Based on operating earnings yield, the company is about fairly valued when compared to all of the companies in our coverage universe. Share price changes over the past year indicates that FLS will perform very well over the near term.

Financial Data

(US$ in Thousands)	12/31/2012	12/31/2011	12/31/2010	12/31/2009	12/31/2008	12/31/2007	12/31/2006	12/31/2005
Earnings Per Share	8.51	7.64	6.88	7.59	7.74	4.46	2.02	0.21
Cash Flow Per Share	9.86	3.93	6.38	7.72	7.15	7.39	2.92	2.30
Tang Book Value Per Share	14.26	19.69	17.13	14.68	7.56	5.42	0.47	N.M.
Dividends Per Share	1.440	1.280	1.160	1.080	1.000	0.600	...	...
Dividend Payout %	16.92	16.75	16.86	14.23	12.92	13.45	...	...
Income Statement								
Total Revenue	4,751,339	4,510,201	4,032,036	4,365,262	4,473,473	3,762,694	3,061,063	2,695,277
EBITDA	725,751	693,897	606,654	662,913	668,672	446,668	277,237	200,898
Depn & Amortn	88,572	90,653	60,300	57,200	52,600	49,500	46,700	46,900
Income Before Taxes	594,613	568,644	513,628	568,955	573,171	341,373	172,456	83,272
Income Taxes	160,766	158,524	141,596	156,460	147,721	104,294	73,238	37,092
Net Income	448,339	428,582	388,290	427,887	442,413	255,774	115,032	11,835
Average Shares	52,656	56,102	56,415	56,362	57,180	57,289	56,905	56,690
Balance Sheet								
Current Assets	2,740,216	2,628,354	2,523,744	2,499,322	2,332,425	1,896,771	1,302,881	1,071,199
Total Assets	4,810,958	4,622,614	4,459,910	4,248,894	4,023,694	3,520,421	2,869,235	2,575,538
Current Liabilities	1,590,625	1,470,321	1,456,375	1,458,083	1,607,996	1,250,180	884,036	694,922
Long-Term Obligations	869,116	451,523	476,230	539,373	545,617	550,795	556,519	652,769
Total Liabilities	2,920,739	2,352,801	2,356,888	2,452,781	2,655,927	2,227,444	1,848,649	1,743,704
Stockholders' Equity	1,890,219	2,269,813	2,103,022	1,796,113	1,367,767	1,292,977	1,020,586	831,834
Shares Outstanding	48,135	53,906	55,059	54,956	55,215	56,309	56,022	55,974
Statistical Record								
Return on Assets %	9.48	9.44	8.92	10.34	11.70	8.01	4.23	0.45
Return on Equity %	21.50	19.60	19.92	27.05	33.16	22.11	12.42	1.39
EBITDA Margin %	15.27	15.39	15.05	15.19	14.95	11.87	9.06	7.45
Net Margin %	9.44	9.50	9.63	9.80	9.89	6.80	3.76	0.44
Asset Turnover	1.00	0.99	0.93	1.06	1.18	1.18	1.12	1.03
Current Ratio	1.72	1.79	1.73	1.71	1.45	1.52	1.47	1.54
Debt to Equity	0.46	0.20	0.23	0.30	0.40	0.43	0.55	0.78
Price Range	146.80-100.16	134.99-70.00	119.32-83.01	107.03-44.51	141.35-37.92	101.00-48.98	60.75-40.91	39.56-23.70
P/E Ratio	17.25-11.77	17.67-9.16	17.34-12.07	14.10-5.86	18.26-4.90	22.65-10.98	30.07-20.25	188.38-112.86
Average Yield %	1.19	1.19	1.12	1.40	1.02	0.86	...	...

Address: 5215 N. O'Connor Boulevard, Suite 2300, Irving, TX 75039	Web Site: www.flowserve.com	Auditors: PricewaterhouseCoopers LLP
Telephone: 972-443-6500	Officers: Mark A. Blinn - President, Chief Executive Officer Mark D. Dailey - Senior Vice President, Chief Administrative Officer	Transfer Agents: Wells Fargo Bank, N.A., South St. Paul, MN
Fax: 972-443-6800		

FLUOR CORP.

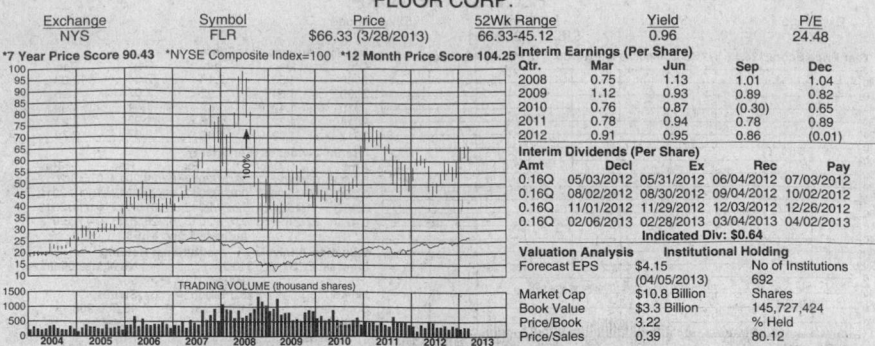

Exchange	Symbol	Price	52Wk Range	Yield	P/E
NYS	FLR	$66.33 (3/28/2013)	66.33-45.12	0.96	24.48

*7 Year Price Score 90.43 *NYSE Composite Index=100 *12 Month Price Score 104.25

Interim Earnings (Per Share)

Qtr.	Mar	Jun	Sep	Dec
2008	0.75	1.13	1.01	1.04
2009	1.12	0.93	0.89	0.82
2010	0.76	0.87	(0.30)	0.65
2011	0.78	0.94	0.78	0.89
2012	0.91	0.95	0.86	(0.01)

Interim Dividends (Per Share)

Amt	Decl	Ex	Rec	Pay
0.16Q	05/03/2012	05/31/2012	06/04/2012	07/03/2012
0.16Q	08/02/2012	08/30/2012	09/04/2012	10/02/2012
0.16Q	11/01/2012	11/29/2012	12/03/2012	12/26/2012
0.16Q	02/06/2013	02/28/2013	03/04/2013	04/02/2013

Indicated Div: $0.64

Valuation Analysis

		Institutional Holding	
Forecast EPS	$4.15 (04/05/2013)	No of Institutions	692
Market Cap	$10.8 Billion	Shares	145,727,424
Book Value	$3.3 Billion	% Held	80.12
Price/Book	3.22		
Price/Sales	0.39		

Business Summary: Construction Services (MIC: 7.5.4 SIC: 1629 NAIC: 541330)

Fluor is a holding company. Through its subsidiaries, Co. is a services firm engaged in providing engineering, procurement, construction and maintenance as well as project management services. Co.'s business is organized into five principal segments: Oil & Gas, Industrial & Infrastructure, Government, Global Services and Power. In addition, Co.'s subsidiary, Fluor Constructors International, Inc., which is organized and operates separately from the rest of Co.'s business, provides unionized management and construction services in the U.S. and Canada, both independently and as a subcontractor on projects in each of Co.'s segments.

Recent Developments: For the year ended Dec 31 2012, net income decreased 18.2% to US$571.1 million from US$698.1 million in the prior year. Revenues were US$27.58 billion, up 17.9% from US$23.38 billion the year before. Direct operating expenses rose 20.1% to US$26.69 billion from US$22.23 billion in the comparable period the year before. Indirect operating expenses increased 3.0% to US$151.5 million from US$147.1 million in the equivalent prior-year period.

Prospects: Our evaluation of Fluor Corp. as of Apr. 7, 2013 is the result of our systematic analysis on three basic characteristics: earnings strength, relative valuation, and recent stock price movement. The company has produced a positive trend in earnings per share over the past 5 quarters and while recent estimates for the company have been raised by analysts, FLR has posted better than expected results. Based on operating earnings yield, the company is undervalued when compared to all of the companies in our coverage universe. Share price changes over the past year indicates that FLR will perform in line with the market over the near term.

Financial Data
(US$ in Thousands)

	12/31/2012	12/31/2011	12/31/2010	12/31/2009	12/31/2008	12/31/2007	12/31/2006	12/31/2005
Earnings Per Share	2.71	3.40	1.98	3.75	3.93	2.92	1.48	1.31
Cash Flow Per Share	3.75	5.16	3.09	5.02	5.34	5.19	1.72	2.41
Tang Book Value Per Share	19.96	19.53	19.32	17.99	14.23	12.38	9.39	8.92
Dividends Per Share	0.640	0.500	0.500	0.500	0.500	0.400	0.400	0.320
Dividend Payout %	23.62	14.71	25.25	13.33	12.72	13.68	27.12	24.43
Income Statement								
Total Revenue	27,577,135	23,381,399	20,849,349	21,990,297	22,325,894	16,691,033	14,078,506	13,161,051
EBITDA	946,368	1,187,395	739,566	1,304,621	1,223,042	755,393	503,814	396,329
Depn & Amortn	212,381	201,939	190,584	182,011	163,305	146,809	126,158	104,124
Income Before Taxes	733,505	1,001,816	559,596	1,136,788	1,114,402	649,093	381,990	299,582
Income Taxes	162,438	303,729	118,514	403,913	393,944	115,774	118,538	72,309
Net Income	456,330	593,728	357,496	684,889	720,458	533,319	263,452	227,273
Average Shares	168,491	174,564	180,988	180,862	183,460	182,178	178,392	173,312
Balance Sheet								
Current Assets	6,094,137	5,880,623	5,562,825	5,122,088	4,668,662	4,059,500	3,323,586	3,108,222
Total Assets	8,276,043	8,270,276	7,614,923	7,178,483	6,423,721	5,796,179	4,874,870	4,574,445
Current Liabilities	3,887,114	3,840,111	3,523,383	3,301,398	3,162,610	2,860,094	2,406,267	2,339,335
Long-Term Obligations	520,205	513,500	17,759	17,740	17,722	17,704	187,129	92,023
Total Liabilities	4,934,748	4,874,751	4,117,924	3,872,950	3,752,639	3,521,720	3,144,398	2,943,887
Stockholders' Equity	3,341,295	3,395,525	3,496,999	3,305,533	2,671,082	2,274,459	1,730,472	1,630,558
Shares Outstanding	162,359	168,979	176,425	178,824	181,555	177,364	176,082	174,176
Statistical Record								
Return on Assets %	5.50	7.48	4.83	10.07	11.76	10.00	5.58	5.32
Return on Equity %	13.51	17.23	10.51	22.92	29.06	26.63	15.68	15.32
EBITDA Margin %	3.43	5.08	3.55	5.93	5.48	4.53	3.58	3.01
Net Margin %	1.65	2.54	1.71	3.11	3.23	3.20	1.87	1.73
Asset Turnover	3.32	2.94	2.82	3.23	3.64	3.13	2.98	3.08
Current Ratio	1.57	1.53	1.58	1.55	1.48	1.42	1.38	1.33
Debt to Equity	0.16	0.15	0.01	0.01	0.01	0.01	0.11	0.06
Price Range	63.99-45.12	75.63-45.49	66.63-41.76	58.21-30.46	98.64-29.56	84.05-37.96	50.98-37.20	39.08-25.18
P/E Ratio	23.61-16.65	22.24-13.38	33.65-21.09	15.52-8.12	25.10-7.52	28.78-13.00	34.44-25.14	29.83-19.23
Average Yield %	1.17	0.80	1.01	1.10	0.75	0.70	0.94	1.05

Address: 6700 Las Colinas Boulevard, Irving, TX 75039
Telephone: 469-398-7000

Web Site: www.fluor.com
Officers: David T. Seaton - Chairman, Chief Executive Officer, Chief Operating Officer Glenn Gilkey - Senior Vice President

Auditors: Ernst & Young LLP
Investor Contact: 469-398-7189
Transfer Agents: Computershare, Pittsburgh, PA

FMC CORP.

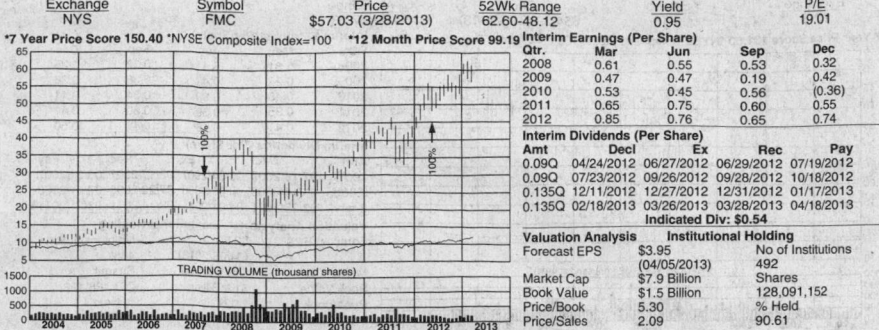

Exchange	Symbol	Price	52Wk Range	Yield	P/E
NYS	FMC	$57.03 (3/28/2013)	62.60-48.12	0.95	19.01

*7 Year Price Score 150.40 *NYSE Composite Index=100 *12 Month Price Score 99.19

Interim Earnings (Per Share)

Qtr.	Mar	Jun	Sep	Dec
2008	0.61	0.55	0.53	0.32
2009	0.47	0.47	0.19	0.42
2010	0.53	0.45	0.56	(0.36)
2011	0.65	0.75	0.60	0.55
2012	0.85	0.76	0.65	0.74

Interim Dividends (Per Share)

Amt	Decl	Ex	Rec	Pay
0.09Q	04/24/2012	06/27/2012	06/29/2012	07/19/2012
0.09Q	07/23/2012	09/26/2012	09/28/2012	10/18/2012
0.135Q	12/11/2012	12/27/2012	12/31/2012	01/17/2013
0.135Q	02/18/2013	03/26/2013	03/28/2013	04/18/2013

Indicated Div: $0.54

Valuation Analysis / **Institutional Holding**

Forecast EPS	$3.95	No of Institutions
	(04/05/2013)	492
Market Cap	$7.9 Billion	Shares
Book Value	$1.5 Billion	128,091,152
Price/Book	5.30	% Held
Price/Sales	2.09	90.61

Business Summary: Diversified Chemicals (MIC: 8.3.1 SIC: 2812 NAIC: 325181)

FMC is a chemical company serving agricultural, consumer and industrial markets. Co. operates in three business segments: Agricultural Products, which develops, markets and sells crop protection chemicals; Specialty Chemicals, which consists of Co.'s BioPolymer and lithium businesses and focuses on food ingredients, pharmaceutical additives for binding, encapsulation and disintegrant applications, ultrapure biopolymers for medical devices and lithium for energy storage, specialty polymers and pharmaceutical synthesis in industrial uses; and Industrial Chemicals, which manufactures a range of inorganic materials, including soda ash, hydrogen peroxide, specialty peroxygens and silicates.

Recent Developments: For the year ended Dec 31 2012, income from continuing operations increased 12.5% to US$465.9 million from US$414.0 million a year earlier. Net income increased 14.0% to US$435.7 million from US$382.2 million in the prior year. Revenues were US$3.75 billion, up 11.0% from US$3.38 billion the year before. Direct operating expenses rose 8.9% to US$2.41 billion from US$2.21 billion in the comparable period the year before. Indirect operating expenses increased 17.7% to US$683.0 million from US$580.1 million in the equivalent prior-year period.

Prospects: Our evaluation of FMC Corp. as of Apr. 7, 2013 is the result of our systematic analysis on three basic characteristics: earnings strength, relative valuation, and recent stock price movement. The company has managed to produce a neutral trend in earnings per share over the past 5 quarters and while recent estimates for the company have been mixed, FMC has posted results that were in line with analysts expectations. Based on operating earnings yield, the company is undervalued when compared to all of the companies in our coverage universe. Share price changes over the past year indicates that FMC will perform very well over the near term.

Financial Data
(US$ in Thousands)

	12/31/2012	12/31/2011	12/31/2010	12/31/2009	12/31/2008	12/31/2007	12/31/2006	12/31/2005
Earnings Per Share	3.00	2.55	1.18	1.56	2.01	0.85	0.83	0.74
Cash Flow Per Share	2.61	2.68	2.45	2.09	2.08	1.79	1.72	1.44
Tang Book Value Per Share	7.05	5.92	6.55	5.98	4.87	5.88	5.58	5.26
Dividends Per Share	0.405	0.300	0.250	0.250	0.240	0.203	0.180	...
Dividend Payout %	13.50	11.76	21.19	16.03	11.94	23.68	21.56	...
Income Statement								
Total Revenue	3,748,300	3,377,900	3,116,300	2,826,200	3,115,300	2,632,900	2,347,000	2,150,200
EBITDA	757,300	688,400	496,500	443,100	606,800	341,500	368,300	307,800
Depn & Amortn	99,100	101,100	109,400	108,400	106,100	113,800	116,400	119,500
Income Before Taxes	612,900	547,900	347,800	307,700	468,800	192,800	219,000	130,200
Income Taxes	146,700	136,500	132,000	53,000	125,400	29,000	68,700	82,300
Net Income	416,200	365,900	172,500	228,500	304,600	132,400	132,000	116,600
Average Shares	138,813	143,308	146,160	146,602	151,592	155,198	158,152	156,744
Balance Sheet								
Current Assets	2,181,800	1,869,400	1,646,200	1,487,700	1,432,800	1,194,100	1,067,800	1,067,300
Total Assets	4,373,600	3,743,500	3,319,900	3,136,200	2,993,900	2,733,400	2,735,000	2,740,000
Current Liabilities	1,135,400	919,900	963,400	709,200	759,100	751,400	702,500	659,300
Long-Term Obligations	908,800	779,100	503,000	588,000	592,900	419,600	523,500	639,800
Total Liabilities	2,893,600	2,502,900	2,188,400	2,059,800	2,091,000	1,669,100	1,715,500	1,780,700
Stockholders' Equity	1,480,300	1,240,600	1,131,500	1,076,400	902,900	1,064,300	1,019,500	959,300
Shares Outstanding	137,670	139,674	142,971	145,037	145,019	150,258	153,270	154,062
Statistical Record								
Return on Assets %	10.23	10.36	5.34	7.46	10.61	4.84	4.82	4.08
Return on Equity %	30.51	30.85	15.63	23.09	30.88	12.71	13.34	12.70
EBITDA Margin %	20.20	20.38	15.93	15.68	19.48	12.97	15.69	14.31
Net Margin %	11.10	10.83	5.54	8.09	9.78	5.03	5.62	5.42
Asset Turnover	0.92	0.96	0.97	0.92	1.08	0.96	0.86	0.75
Current Ratio	1.92	2.03	1.71	2.10	1.89	1.59	1.52	1.62
Debt to Equity	0.61	0.63	0.44	0.55	0.66	0.39	0.51	0.67
Price Range	58.59-43.48	46.43-32.91	40.70-25.40	29.00-17.64	39.83-15.00	29.43-17.82	19.29-13.05	15.65-10.86
P/E Ratio	19.53-14.49	18.21-12.91	34.49-21.53	18.59-11.30	19.82-7.46	34.62-20.96	23.24-15.72	21.15-14.67
Average Yield %	0.77	0.75	0.78	1.01	0.83	0.91	1.13	...

Address: 1735 Market Street, Philadelphia, PA 19103	Web Site: www.fmc.com	Auditors: KPMG LLP
Telephone: 215-299-6000	Officers: Pierre R. Brondeau - Chairman, President, Chief Executive Officer Paul Graves - Executive Vice President, Chief Financial Officer	Investor Contact: 215-299-6119
Fax: 215-299-6618		Transfer Agents: Wells Fargo Bank, N.A., South St. Paul, MN

FMC TECHNOLOGIES, INC.

Exchange	Symbol	Price	52Wk Range	Yield	P/E
NYS	FTI	$54.39 (3/28/2013)	54.39-37.68	N/A	30.56

*7 Year Price Score 131.50 *NYSE Composite Index=100 *12 Month Price Score 104.45

Interim Earnings (Per Share)

Qtr.	Mar	Jun	Sep	Dec
2008	0.31	0.41	0.32	0.35
2009	0.28	0.42	0.36	0.38
2010	0.40	0.39	0.34	0.41
2011	0.35	0.39	0.50	0.41
2012	0.41	0.46	0.41	0.50

Interim Dividends (Per Share)

Amt	Decl	Ex	Rec	Pay
100%	07/18/2007	09/04/2007	08/17/2007	08/31/2007
0.00U	07/14/2008	08/01/2008	07/22/2008	07/31/2008
2-for-1	02/25/2011	04/01/2011	03/14/2011	03/31/2011

Valuation Analysis

		Institutional Holding	
Forecast EPS	$2.20	No of Institutions	
	(04/06/2013)	488	
Market Cap	$12.9 Billion	Shares	
Book Value	$1.8 Billion	237,488,192	
Price/Book	7.02	% Held	
Price/Sales	2.10	96.39	

Business Summary: Equipment & Services (MIC: 9.1.3 SIC: 3533 NAIC: 333132)

FMC Technologies designs, manufactures and services systems and products, including subsea production and processing systems, surface wellhead production systems, high pressure fluid control equipment, measurement solutions and marine loading systems for the energy industry. Co. operates in three business segments: Subsea Technologies, which provides subsea systems, schilling robotics, and multiphase and wetgas meters; Surface Technologies, which provides surface wellhead, fluid control and completions services; and Energy Infrastructure, which provides measurement, loading and transfer, material handling, blending and transfer, separation, direct drive, and automation and control systems.

Recent Developments: For the year ended Dec 31 2012, net income increased 7.8% to US$434.8 million from US$403.5 million in the prior year. Revenues were US$6.15 billion, up 20.6% from US$5.10 billion the year before. Direct operating expenses rose 21.9% to US$4.83 billion from US$3.97 billion in the comparable period the year before. Indirect operating expenses increased 25.1% to US$713.7 million from US$570.4 million in the equivalent prior-year period.

Prospects: Our evaluation of FMC Technologies Inc. as of Apr. 7, 2013 is the result of our systematic analysis on three basic characteristics: earnings strength, relative valuation, and recent stock price movement. The company has managed to produce a neutral trend in earnings per share over the past 5 quarters. However, while recent estimates for the company have been lowered by analysts, FTI has posted better than expected results. Based on operating earnings yield, the company is overvalued when compared to all of the companies in our coverage universe. Share price changes over the past year indicates that FTI will perform poorly over the near term.

Financial Data
(US$ in Thousands)

	12/31/2012	12/31/2011	12/31/2010	12/31/2009	12/31/2008	12/31/2007	12/31/2006	12/31/2005
Earnings Per Share	1.78	1.64	1.53	1.44	1.39	1.13	0.98	0.38
Cash Flow Per Share	0.58	0.68	0.80	2.39	0.98	2.19	0.56	(0.11)
Tang Book Value Per Share	3.76	4.33	3.74	2.77	1.99	2.89	2.60	1.91
Income Statement								
Total Revenue	6,151,400	5,099,000	4,125,600	4,405,400	4,550,900	4,615,400	3,790,700	3,226,700
EBITDA	740,900	647,100	627,400	605,700	565,500	538,900	361,700	223,600
Depn & Amortn	113,100	86,100	80,700	78,300	57,700	64,500	56,500	53,300
Income Before Taxes	601,200	552,800	537,900	517,900	506,300	465,100	298,500	164,800
Income Taxes	166,400	149,300	159,600	155,100	152,000	156,500	84,500	56,200
Net Income	430,000	399,800	375,500	361,800	361,300	302,800	276,300	106,100
Average Shares	240,900	243,200	245,400	251,400	259,400	267,600	280,800	283,200
Balance Sheet								
Current Assets	3,488,300	2,787,900	2,345,300	2,225,600	2,443,700	2,104,000	1,690,200	1,428,100
Total Assets	5,902,900	4,271,000	3,644,200	3,509,500	3,586,300	3,211,100	2,487,800	2,095,600
Current Liabilities	1,970,400	2,232,900	1,495,400	1,678,500	1,962,500	1,785,200	1,208,200	1,058,200
Long-Term Obligations	1,580,400	36,000	351,100	391,600	472,000	112,200	212,600	252,600
Total Liabilities	4,066,000	2,846,400	2,332,500	2,406,700	2,889,800	2,189,400	1,601,800	1,396,100
Stockholders' Equity	1,836,900	1,424,600	1,311,700	1,102,800	696,500	1,021,700	886,000	699,500
Shares Outstanding	237,100	237,800	239,600	243,600	249,800	258,600	269,200	272,400
Statistical Record								
Return on Assets %	8.43	10.10	10.50	10.20	10.60	10.63	12.06	5.32
Return on Equity %	26.30	29.22	31.10	40.22	41.94	31.75	34.85	15.58
EBITDA Margin %	12.04	12.69	15.21	13.75	12.43	11.68	9.54	6.93
Net Margin %	6.99	7.84	9.10	8.21	7.94	6.56	7.29	3.29
Asset Turnover	1.21	1.29	1.15	1.24	1.34	1.62	1.65	1.62
Current Ratio	1.77	1.25	1.57	1.33	1.25	1.18	1.40	1.35
Debt to Equity	0.86	0.03	0.27	0.36	0.68	0.11	0.24	0.36
Price Range	54.36-37.68	53.77-35.96	44.56-23.80	29.42-11.90	38.38-10.17	31.74-13.17	16.93-10.68	10.39-6.89
P/E Ratio	30.54-21.17	32.79-21.93	29.12-15.56	20.43-8.26	27.61-7.32	28.08-11.66	17.27-10.90	27.34-18.14

Address: 5875 N. Sam Houston Parkway W., Houston, TX 77086 Telephone: 281-591-4000	Web Site: www.fmctechnologies.com Officers: John T. Gremp - Chairman, President, Chief Executive Officer Robert L. Potter - President, Executive Vice President	Auditors: KPMG LLP Investor Contact: 281-591-4080 Transfer Agents: National City Bank, Cleveland, OH

FOOT LOCKER, INC.

Exchange	Symbol	Price	52Wk Range	Yield	P/E
NYS	FL	$34.24 (3/28/2013)	37.27-28.01	2.34	13.27

*7 Year Price Score 150.57 *NYSE Composite Index=100 *12 Month Price Score 94.21

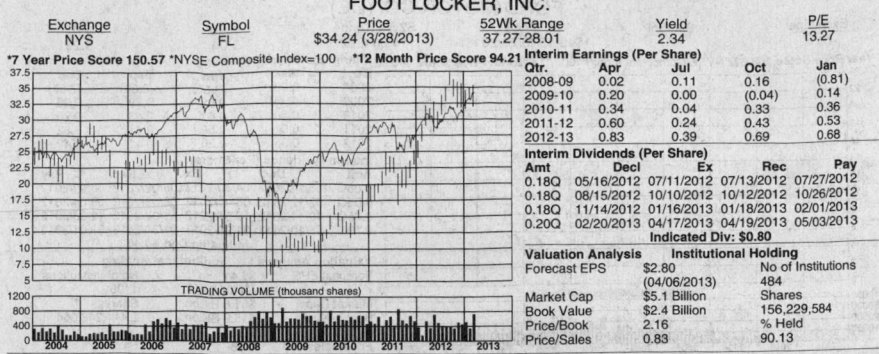

Interim Earnings (Per Share)

Qtr.	Apr	Jul	Oct	Jan
2008-09	0.02	0.11	0.16	(0.81)
2009-10	0.20	0.00	(0.04)	0.14
2010-11	0.34	0.04	0.33	0.36
2011-12	0.60	0.24	0.43	0.53
2012-13	0.83	0.39	0.69	0.68

Interim Dividends (Per Share)

Amt	Decl	Ex	Rec	Pay
0.18Q	05/16/2012	07/11/2012	07/13/2012	07/27/2012
0.18Q	08/15/2012	10/10/2012	10/12/2012	10/26/2012
0.18Q	11/14/2012	01/16/2013	01/18/2013	02/01/2013
0.20Q	02/20/2013	04/17/2013	04/19/2013	05/03/2013

Indicated Div: $0.80

Valuation Analysis		Institutional Holding	
Forecast EPS	$2.80	No of Institutions	
	(04/06/2013)	484	
Market Cap	$5.1 Billion	Shares	
Book Value	$2.4 Billion	156,229,584	
Price/Book	2.16	% Held	
Price/Sales	0.83	90.13	

Business Summary: Retail - Apparel and Accessories (MIC: 2.1.5 SIC: 5661 NAIC: 448210)

Foot Locker is a retailer of athletic footwear and apparel. Through its subsidiaries, Co. operates in two segments: Athletic Stores, which serves as an athletic footwear and apparel retailer whose formats include Foot Locker, Lady Foot Locker, Kids Foot Locker, Champs Sports, Footaction, and CCS; and Direct-to-Customers, which reflects CCS and Footlocker.com, Inc., which sells, through its affiliates, including Eastbay, Inc., to customers through catalogs, mobile devices, and Internet websites. As of Jan 28 2012, Co. operated 3,369 primarily mall-based stores in the U.S., Canada, Europe, Australia, and New Zealand.

Recent Developments: For the year ended Feb 2 2013, net income increased 42.8% to US$397.0 million from US$278.0 million in the prior year. Revenues were US$6.18 billion, up 9.9% from US$5.62 billion the year before. Direct operating expenses rose 8.4% to US$4.15 billion from US$3.83 billion in the comparable period the year before. Indirect operating expenses increased 4.8% to US$1.43 billion from US$1.36 billion in the equivalent prior-year period.

Prospects: Our evaluation of Foot Locker Inc. as of Apr. 7, 2013 is the result of our systematic analysis on three basic characteristics: earnings strength, relative valuation, and recent stock price movement. The company has generated a negative trend in earnings per share over the past 5 quarters. However, while recent estimates for the company have been lowered by analysts, FL has posted better than expected results. Based on operating earnings yield, the company is undervalued when compared to all of the companies in our coverage universe. Share price changes over the past year indicates that FL will perform well over the near term.

Financial Data
(US$ in Thousands)

	02/02/2013	01/28/2012	01/29/2011	01/30/2010	01/31/2009	02/02/2008	02/03/2007	01/28/2006
Earnings Per Share	2.58	1.80	1.07	0.30	(0.52)	0.33	1.60	1.68
Cash Flow Per Share	2.71	3.26	2.10	2.22	2.49	1.84	1.20	2.29
Tang Book Value Per Share	14.61	12.61	11.69	10.89	10.76	12.36	12.37	10.59
Dividends Per Share	0.720	0.660	0.600	0.600	0.600	0.500	0.395	0.315
Dividend Payout %	27.91	36.67	56.07	200.00	...	151.52	24.69	18.75
Income Statement								
Total Revenue	6,182,000	5,623,000	5,049,000	4,854,000	5,237,000	5,437,000	5,750,000	5,653,000
EBITDA	730,000	551,000	372,000	195,000	35,000	117,000	570,000	586,000
Depn & Amortn	118,000	110,000	106,000	112,000	130,000	166,000	175,000	171,000
Income Before Taxes	607,000	435,000	257,000	73,000	(100,000)	(50,000)	392,000	405,000
Income Taxes	210,000	157,000	88,000	26,000	(21,000)	(99,000)	145,000	142,000
Net Income	397,000	278,000	169,000	48,000	(80,000)	51,000	251,000	264,000
Average Shares	154,000	154,400	156,700	156,300	154,000	155,600	156,800	157,600
Balance Sheet								
Current Assets	2,363,000	2,079,000	1,934,000	1,772,000	1,764,000	2,064,000	2,034,000	2,014,000
Total Assets	3,367,000	3,050,000	2,896,000	2,816,000	2,877,000	3,248,000	3,249,000	3,312,000
Current Liabilities	636,000	548,000	489,000	433,000	418,000	501,000	516,000	717,000
Long-Term Obligations	133,000	135,000	137,000	138,000	142,000	221,000	220,000	275,000
Total Liabilities	990,000	940,000	871,000	868,000	953,000	977,000	954,000	1,285,000
Stockholders' Equity	2,377,000	2,110,000	2,025,000	1,948,000	1,924,000	2,271,000	2,295,000	2,027,000
Shares Outstanding	150,070	151,619	154,620	156,541	154,918	154,474	155,703	155,504
Statistical Record								
Return on Assets %	12.17	9.38	5.93	1.69	N.M.	1.57	7.53	8.08
Return on Equity %	17.41	13.48	8.53	2.49	N.M.	2.24	11.43	13.73
EBITDA Margin %	11.81	9.80	7.37	4.02	0.67	2.15	9.91	10.37
Net Margin %	6.42	4.94	3.35	0.99	N.M.	0.94	4.37	4.67
Asset Turnover	1.90	1.90	1.77	1.71	1.71	1.68	1.72	1.73
Current Ratio	3.72	3.79	3.96	4.09	4.22	4.12	3.94	2.81
Debt to Equity	0.06	0.06	0.07	0.07	0.07	0.10	0.10	0.14
Price Range	37.27-26.24	26.67-16.77	19.81-11.61	12.57-7.28	17.89-5.49	24.21-9.84	27.32-21.27	29.58-19.00
P/E Ratio	14.45-10.17	14.82-9.32	18.51-10.85	41.90-24.27	...	73.36-29.82	17.07-13.29	17.61-11.31
Average Yield %	2.21	3.04	3.97	5.65	4.88	2.72	1.67	1.29

Address: 112 West 34th Street, New York, NY 10120 Telephone: 212-720-3700	Web Site: www.footlocker-inc.com Officers: Ken C. Hicks - Chairman, President, Chief Executive Officer Richard A. Johnson - Executive Vice President, Chief Operating Officer, Division Officer	Auditors: KPMG LLP Transfer Agents: BNY Mellon Shareowner Services, Pittsburgh, PA

FORD MOTOR CO. (DE)

Exchange	Symbol	Price	52Wk Range	Yield	P/E
NYS	F	$13.15 (3/28/2013)	14.30-8.92	3.04	9.26

*7 Year Price Score 106.57 ***NYSE Composite Index=100** ***12 Month Price Score 105.92**

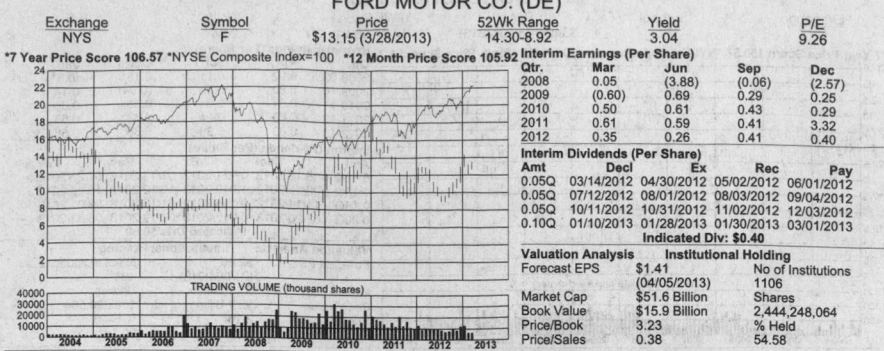

Interim Earnings (Per Share)

Qtr.	Mar	Jun	Sep	Dec
2008	0.05	(3.88)	(0.06)	(2.57)
2009	(0.60)	0.69	0.29	0.25
2010	0.50	0.61	0.43	0.29
2011	0.61	0.59	0.41	3.32
2012	0.35	0.26	0.41	0.40

Interim Dividends (Per Share)

Amt	Decl	Ex	Rec	Pay
0.05Q	03/14/2012	04/30/2012	05/02/2012	06/01/2012
0.05Q	07/12/2012	08/01/2012	08/03/2012	09/04/2012
0.05Q	10/11/2012	10/31/2012	11/02/2012	12/03/2012
0.10Q	01/10/2013	01/28/2013	01/30/2013	03/01/2013

Indicated Div: $0.40

Valuation Analysis		Institutional Holding	
Forecast EPS	$1.41	No of Institutions	
	(04/05/2013)	1106	
Market Cap	$51.6 Billion	Shares	
Book Value	$15.9 Billion	2,444,248,064	
Price/Book	3.23	% Held	
Price/Sales	0.38	54.58	

Business Summary: Autos- Manufacturing (MIC: 1.8.1 SIC: 3711 NAIC: 336111)

Ford Motor is engaged in producing automobiles. Co.'s vehicle brands are Ford and Lincoln. Co. also sells parts and accessories, primarily to its dealerships and to authorized parts distributors. Also, through its wholly-owned subsidiary, Ford Motor Credit Company LLC, Co. provides automotive financing products to and through automotive dealers. Co.'s business is divided in two sectors: Automotive and Financial Services. Reportable segments in the Automotive sector include: Ford North America; Ford South America; Ford Europe; and Ford Asia Pacific Africa. Reportable segments in the Financial Services sector include: Ford Motor Credit Company and Other Financial Services.

Recent Developments: For the year ended Dec 31 2012, net income decreased 72.0% to US$5.66 billion from US$20.22 billion in the prior year. Revenues were US$134.25 billion, down 1.5% from US$136.26 billion the year before. Direct operating expenses declined 0.7% to US$112.58 billion from US$113.35 billion in the comparable period the year before. Indirect operating expenses increased 1.5% to US$15.38 billion from US$15.16 billion in the equivalent prior-year period.

Prospects: Our evaluation of Ford Motor Co. as of Apr. 7, 2013 is the result of our systematic analysis on three basic characteristics: earnings strength, relative valuation, and recent stock price movement. The company has enjoyed a very positive trend in earnings per share over the past 5 quarters. However, while recent estimates for the company have been lowered by analysts, F has posted better than expected results. Based on operating earnings yield, the company is undervalued when compared to all of the companies in our coverage universe. Share price changes over the past year indicates that F will perform well over the near term.

Financial Data
(US$ in Millions)

	12/31/2012	12/31/2011	12/31/2010	12/31/2009	12/31/2008	12/31/2007	12/31/2006	12/31/2005
Earnings Per Share	1.42	4.94	1.90	0.86	(6.46)	(1.38)	(6.72)	1.05
Cash Flow Per Share	2.36	2.58	3.33	5.36	(0.08)	8.63	5.12	11.74
Tang Book Value Per Share	4.04	3.93	...	...	...	1.61	...	3.76
Dividends Per Share	0.200	0.050	...	...	...	...	0.250	0.400
Dividend Payout %	14.08	1.01	...	...	...	...	...	38.10
Income Statement								
Total Revenue	134,252	136,264	128,954	118,308	146,277	172,455	160,123	177,089
EBITDA	14,343	15,758	17,001	8,650	2,454	9,105	(1,679)	12,272
Depn & Amortn	3,655	3,533	3,876	4,094	6,584	3,474	6,488	4,167
Income Before Taxes	7,132	8,181	6,611	3,016	(14,567)	(4,135)	(15,472)	1,711
Income Taxes	2,056	(11,541)	592	69	63	(1,294)	(2,646)	(512)
Net Income	5,665	20,213	6,561	2,717	(14,672)	(2,723)	(12,613)	2,024
Average Shares	4,016	4,112	3,450	3,313	2,274	1,978	1,877	2,135
Balance Sheet								
Current Assets	43,305	41,667	41,487	48,278	48,078	60,919	67,200	52,814
Total Assets	190,554	178,348	164,687	194,850	218,328	279,264	278,554	269,476
Current Liabilities	73,428	73,038	75,091	77,073	111,139	109,556	115,000	111,450
Long-Term Obligations	66,296	59,177	62,324	88,427	90,224	107,478	109,593	94,428
Total Liabilities	174,607	163,320	165,360	202,670	235,639	273,636	282,019	256,519
Stockholders' Equity	15,947	15,028	(673)	(7,820)	(17,311)	5,628	(3,465)	12,957
Shares Outstanding	3,923	3,801	3,779	3,369	2,397	2,208	1,880	1,864
Statistical Record								
Return on Assets %	3.06	11.78	3.65	1.32	N.M.	N.M.	N.M.	0.72
Return on Equity %	36.48	281.62	...	...	N.M.	N.M.	N.M.	13.96
EBITDA Margin %	10.68	11.56	13.18	7.31	1.68	5.28	N.M.	6.93
Net Margin %	4.22	14.83	5.09	2.30	N.M.	N.M.	N.M.	1.14
Asset Turnover	0.73	0.79	0.72	0.57	0.59	0.62	0.58	0.63
Current Ratio	0.59	0.57	0.55	0.63	0.43	0.56	0.58	0.47
Debt to Equity	4.16	3.94	...	...	...	19.10	...	7.29
Price Range	12.96-8.92	18.79-9.37	17.00-9.88	10.20-1.58	8.48-1.26	9.64-6.70	9.19-6.19	14.71-7.65
P/E Ratio	9.13-6.28	3.80-1.90	8.95-5.20	11.86-1.84	...	...	...	14.01-7.29
Average Yield %	1.83	0.38	...	...	...	...	3.25	3.85

Address: One American Road, Dearborn, MI 48126	Web Site: www.corporate.ford.com	Auditors: PricewaterhouseCoopers LLP
Telephone: 313-322-3000	Officers: William Clay Ford - Chairman Alan R. Mulally - President, Chief Executive Officer	Investor Contact: 180-055-55259
Fax: 313-222-4177		Transfer Agents: Computershare Trust Company, N.A., Providence, RI

FOREST CITY ENTERPRISES, INC.

Exchange	Symbol	Price	52Wk Range	Yield	P/E
NYS	FCE A	$17.77 (3/28/2013)	17.77-12.98	N/A	888.50

*7 Year Price Score 52.35 *NYSE Composite Index=100 *12 Month Price Score 99.08

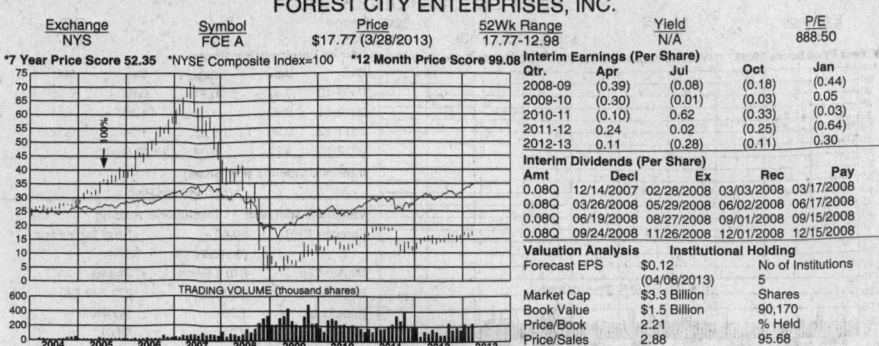

Interim Earnings (Per Share)

Qtr.	Apr	Jul	Oct	Jan
2008-09	(0.39)	(0.08)	(0.18)	(0.44)
2009-10	(0.30)	(0.01)	(0.03)	0.05
2010-11	(0.10)	0.62	(0.33)	(0.03)
2011-12	0.24	0.02	(0.25)	(0.64)
2012-13	0.11	(0.28)	(0.11)	0.30

Interim Dividends (Per Share)

Amt	Decl	Ex	Rec	Pay
0.08Q	12/14/2007	02/28/2008	03/03/2008	03/17/2008
0.08Q	03/26/2008	05/29/2008	06/02/2008	06/17/2008
0.08Q	06/19/2008	08/27/2008	09/01/2008	09/15/2008
0.08Q	09/24/2008	11/26/2008	12/01/2008	12/15/2008

Valuation Analysis

	Institutional Holding
Forecast EPS $0.12	No of Institutions
(04/06/2013)	5
Market Cap $3.3 Billion	Shares
Book Value $1.5 Billion	90,170
Price/Book 2.21	% Held
Price/Sales 2.88	95.68

Business Summary: Property, Real Estate & Development (MIC: 5.3.2 SIC: 6512 NAIC: 531120)

Forest City Enterprises principally engages in the ownership, development, management and acquisition of commercial and residential real estate and land in 28 states and the District of Columbia. Co. operates through three business units, all of which are reportable segments: Commercial Group; Residential Group; and Land Development Group. As of Jan 31 2012, the Commercial Group owned interests in 96 completed properties including: 49 office properties; 17 regional malls; 28 specialty retail centers; and two hotels. At Jan 31 2012, the Residential Group's operating portfolio consisted of 33,819 apartment units in 120 properties and 14,104 military housing units.

Recent Developments: For the year ended Jan 31 2013, loss from continuing operations was US$17.2 million compared with a loss of US$106.5 million a year earlier. Net income amounted to US$36.3 million versus a net loss of US$568,000 in the prior year. Revenues were US$1.13 billion, up 7.9% from US$1.05 billion the year before.

Prospects: Our evaluation of Forest City Enterprises Inc. as of Apr. 7, 2013 is the result of our systematic analysis on three basic characteristics: earnings strength, relative valuation, and recent stock price movement. The company has enjoyed a very positive trend in earnings per share over the past 5 quarters. Because the company lacks sufficient analyst estimate data, we place greater weight on the historical EPS trend as the measure of earnings strength. Based on operating earnings yield, the company is overvalued when compared to all of the companies in our coverage universe. Share price changes over the past year indicates that FCE.A will perform in line with the market over the near term.

Financial Data

(US$ in Thousands)	01/31/2013	01/31/2012	01/31/2011	01/31/2010	01/31/2009	01/31/2008	01/31/2007	01/31/2006
Earnings Per Share	0.02	(0.61)	0.30	(0.22)	(1.09)	0.51	1.70	0.81
Cash Flow Per Share	2.44	1.78	1.54	3.01	2.89	2.66	3.05	3.40
Tang Book Value Per Share	7.51	6.74	7.09	6.47	6.40	7.89	10.07	8.78
Dividends Per Share	...	...	...	...	0.320	0.300	0.260	0.220
Dividend Payout %	...	...	...	...	...	58.82	15.29	27.16
Income Statement								
Total Revenue	1,134,687	1,089,977	1,177,661	1,257,222	1,290,390	1,295,620	1,168,835	1,200,775
EBITDA	383,992	336,329	729,930	556,197	544,148	505,625	469,415	500,770
Depn & Amortn	240,437	237,793	265,234	286,885	320,511	253,521	206,053	196,413
Income Before Taxes	(79,759)	(110,387)	202,182	(26,953)	(101,764)	(3,415)	31,296	59,337
Income Taxes	(11,204)	(64,344)	69,720	(19,550)	(29,154)	3,064	34,412	23,238
Net Income	36,425	(86,486)	58,660	(30,651)	(112,200)	52,425	177,251	83,519
Average Shares	172,621	168,170	173,437	139,825	102,755	102,261	104,454	102,603
Balance Sheet								
Current Assets	1,169,834	1,166,296	1,316,653	1,067,862	985,939	921,786	834,289	950,262
Total Assets	10,612,432	10,504,283	11,769,209	11,916,711	11,422,917	10,251,597	8,981,604	7,990,341
Current Liabilities	1,093,963	1,112,462	1,074,042	1,181,493	1,277,199	1,015,844	772,964	674,949
Long-Term Obligations	6,773,629	6,698,052	8,118,053	8,793,008	8,496,219	7,408,384	6,321,399	5,930,506
Total Liabilities	9,135,540	9,037,217	10,239,810	10,768,085	10,608,775	9,279,481	7,955,793	7,095,959
Stockholders' Equity	1,476,892	1,467,066	1,529,399	1,148,626	814,142	972,116	1,025,811	894,382
Shares Outstanding	183,957	169,162	165,449	155,324	102,878	102,589	101,882	101,844
Statistical Record								
Return on Assets %	0.34	N.M.	0.50	N.M.	N.M.	0.55	2.09	1.09
Return on Equity %	2.47	N.M.	4.38	N.M.	N.M.	5.25	18.46	9.83
EBITDA Margin %	33.84	30.86	61.98	44.24	42.17	39.03	40.16	41.70
Net Margin %	3.21	N.M.	4.98	N.M.	N.M.	4.05	15.16	6.96
Asset Turnover	0.11	0.10	0.10	0.11	0.12	0.13	0.14	0.16
Current Ratio	1.07	1.05	1.23	0.90	0.77	0.91	1.08	1.41
Debt to Equity	4.59	4.57	5.31	7.66	10.44	7.62	6.16	6.63
Price Range	17.33-12.98	19.26-9.76	16.98-10.70	13.76-3.41	41.60-3.42	72.23-35.38	61.58-37.79	40.71-28.98
P/E Ratio	866.50-649.00	...	56.60-35.67	...	...	141.63-69.37	36.22-22.23	50.26-35.78
Average Yield %	...	...	...	...	1.22	0.52	0.52	0.63

Address: Terminal Tower, Suite 1100, 50 Public Square, Cleveland, OH 44113	Web Site: www.forestcity.net	Auditors: PricewaterhouseCoopers LLP
Telephone: 216-621-6060	Officers: Charles A. Ratner - Chairman, President, Chief Executive Officer, Chief Operating Officer Samuel H. Miller - Co-Chairman Emeritus, Co-Chairman, Treasurer	Investor Contact: 216-416-3558 Transfer Agents: Wells Fargo Shareowner Services, St. Paul, MN

FOREST LABORATORIES, INC.

Exchange	Symbol	Price	52Wk Range	Yield	P/E
NYS	FRX	$38.04 (3/28/2013)	38.15-32.07	N/A	88.47

*7 Year Price Score 89.08   *NYSE Composite Index=100   *12 Month Price Score 96.43

Interim Earnings (Per Share)

Qtr.	Jun	Sep	Dec	Mar
2009-10	0.87	0.61	0.69	0.08
2010-11	0.39	1.00	1.11	1.11
2011-12	0.90	0.91	1.04	0.72
2012-13	0.21	0.08	(0.58)	...

Interim Dividends (Per Share)

No Dividends Paid

Valuation Analysis   **Institutional Holding**

Forecast EPS	$0.40	No of Institutions
	(04/05/2013)	577
Market Cap	$10.1 Billion	Shares
Book Value	$5.7 Billion	271,242,720
Price/Book	1.79	% Held
Price/Sales	3.01	93.01

Business Summary: Pharmaceuticals (MIC: 4.1.1 SIC: 2834 NAIC: 325412)

Forest Laboratories develops, manufactures and sells branded forms of drug products, most of which require a physician's prescription. Co.'s principal products include: Namenda®, its N-methyl-D-aspartate antagonist for the treatment of moderate and severe Alzheimer's disease; Bystolic®, its beta-blocker for the treatment of hypertension; Savella®, its serotonin and norepinephrine inhibitor for the management of fibromyalgia; Teflaro®, a hospital-based injectable cephalosporin antibiotic for the treatment of adults with skin and skin structure infections and community-acquired bacterial pneumonia; and Daliresp®, as a treatment for patients with severe chronic obstructive pulmonary disease.

Recent Developments: For the quarter ended Dec 31 2012, net loss amounted to US$153.6 million versus net income of US$278.4 million in the year-earlier quarter. Revenues were US$722.7 million, down 40.2% from US$1.21 billion the year before. Direct operating expenses declined 41.6% to US$153.3 million from US$262.7 million in the comparable period the year before. Indirect operating expenses increased 28.3% to US$753.7 million from US$587.3 million in the equivalent prior-year period.

Prospects: Our evaluation of Forest Laboratories Inc. as of Apr. 7, 2013 is the result of our systematic analysis on three basic characteristics: earnings strength, relative valuation, and recent stock price movement. The company has suffered a very negative trend in earnings per share over the past 5 years. However, while recent estimates for the company have been mixed, FRX has posted results that fell short of analysts expectations. Based on operating earnings yield, the company is overvalued when compared to all of the companies in our coverage universe. Share price changes over the past year indicates that FRX will perform in line with the market over the near term.

Financial Data
(US$ in Thousands)

	9 Mos	6 Mos	3 Mos	03/31/2012	03/31/2011	03/31/2010	03/31/2009	03/31/2008
Earnings Per Share	0.43	2.05	2.88	3.57	3.59	2.25	2.52	3.06
Cash Flow Per Share	2.00	3.26	4.30	5.26	3.94	3.36	3.52	3.78
Tang Book Value Per Share	10.52	10.88	10.99	10.77	16.63	14.58	11.94	10.19
Income Statement								
Total Revenue	2,304,454	1,581,764	821,127	4,586,044	4,419,700	4,192,862	3,922,782	3,836,329
EBITDA	32,515	179,464	110,696	1,278,640	1,379,993	995,711	1,013,800	1,257,498
Depn & Amortn	108,191	70,849	35,267	40,952	42,257	45,025	43,266	47,101
Income Before Taxes	(75,676)	108,615	75,429	1,237,688	1,337,736	950,686	970,534	1,210,397
Income Taxes	1,870	32,553	20,144	258,630	290,966	268,303	202,791	242,464
Net Income	(77,546)	76,062	55,285	979,058	1,046,770	682,383	767,743	967,933
Average Shares	266,018	267,169	268,972	274,016	291,175	303,781	304,400	316,133
Balance Sheet								
Current Assets	2,876,855	3,271,819	3,555,380	3,586,195	5,259,673	4,579,191	3,785,954	2,907,504
Total Assets	7,485,310	7,537,462	7,446,011	7,491,755	6,922,454	6,223,531	5,196,808	4,525,367
Current Liabilities	945,990	860,073	845,895	929,309	937,858	979,646	817,828	610,825
Total Liabilities	1,817,394	1,750,393	1,701,933	1,814,938	1,423,574	1,333,624	1,082,217	810,050
Stockholders' Equity	5,667,916	5,787,069	5,744,078	5,676,817	5,498,880	4,889,907	4,114,591	3,715,317
Shares Outstanding	266,101	265,967	268,595	265,621	286,119	302,390	301,615	311,407
Statistical Record								
Return on Assets %	1.55	7.50	10.58	13.55	15.93	11.95	15.79	23.60
Return on Equity %	2.07	9.98	14.08	17.47	20.15	15.16	19.61	28.64
EBITDA Margin %	1.41	11.35	13.48	27.88	31.22	23.75	25.84	32.78
Net Margin %	N.M.	4.81	6.73	21.35	23.68	16.27	19.57	25.23
Asset Turnover	0.45	0.53	0.58	0.63	0.67	0.73	0.81	0.94
Current Ratio	3.04	3.80	4.20	3.86	5.61	4.67	4.63	4.76
Price Range	37.42-30.43	36.49-28.55	40.17-28.55	40.17-28.55	34.33-24.36	32.47-21.19	41.13-18.79	55.25-35.44
P/E Ratio	87.02-70.77	17.80-13.93	13.95-9.91	11.25-8.00	9.56-6.79	14.43-9.42	16.32-7.46	18.06-11.58

Address: 909 Third Avenue, New York, NY 10022-4731 Telephone: 212-421-7850 Fax: 212-750-9152	Web Site: www.frx.com Officers: Howard Solomon - Chairman, President, Chief Executive Officer Francis I. Perier - Executive Vice President, Chief Financial Officer	Auditors: BDO USA, LLP Transfer Agents: Mellon Investor Services, LLC, Ridgefield Park, NJ

FOREST OIL CORP.

Exchange	Symbol	Price	52Wk Range	Yield	P/E
NYS	FST	$5.26 (3/28/2013)	13.32-5.26	N/A	N/A

*7 Year Price Score 32.82 *NYSE Composite Index=100 *12 Month Price Score 73.10

TRADING VOLUME (thousand shares)

Interim Earnings (Per Share)

Qtr.	Mar	Jun	Sep	Dec
2008	(0.05)	(0.78)	4.77	(15.43)
2009	(12.32)	0.36	1.53	0.61
2010	0.97	0.29	0.60	0.14
2011	(0.03)	0.34	0.72	0.16
2012	(0.29)	(4.44)	(3.97)	(2.48)

Interim Dividends (Per Share)

No Dividends Paid

Valuation Analysis		Institutional Holding	
Forecast EPS	$0.28	No of Institutions	
	(04/06/2013)	285	
Market Cap	$622.0 Million	Shares	
Book Value	N/A	139,691,568	
Price/Book	N/A	% Held	
Price/Sales	1.03	108.29	

Business Summary: Production & Extraction (MIC: 9.1.1 SIC: 1311 NAIC: 211111)

Forest Oil is an oil and gas company engaged in the acquisition, exploration, development, and production of oil, natural gas, and natural gas liquids primarily in North America. Co.'s primary areas consist of a portfolio of tight-gas sands and shale plays that have exposure to oil, natural gas and natural gas liquids. Co.'s primary operational areas are in the Texas Panhandle Area, the Eagle Ford Shale in South Texas, and the East Texas / North Louisiana Area. As of Dec 31 2012, Co. had estimated proved reserves of 1,363 Bcfe and estimated proved undeveloped reserves of 425 Bcfe.

Recent Developments: For the year ended Dec 31 2012, loss from continuing operations was US$1.29 billion compared with income of US$98.3 million a year earlier. Net loss amounted to US$1.29 billion versus net income of US$142.8 million in the prior year. Revenues were US$605.7 million; down 14.0% from US$704.6 million the year before. Direct operating expenses rose 2.2% to US$156.9 million from US$153.5 million in the comparable period the year before. Indirect operating expenses increased 395.7% to US$1.41 billion from US$284.8 million in the equivalent prior-year period.

Prospects: Our evaluation of Forest Oil Corp. as of Apr. 7, 2013 is the result of our systematic analysis on three basic characteristics: earnings strength, relative valuation, and recent stock price movement. The company has suffered a very negative trend in earnings per share over the past 5 quarters. However, while recent estimates for the company have been lowered by analysts, FST has posted better than expected results. Based on operating earnings yield, the company is undervalued when compared to all of the companies in our coverage universe. Share price changes over the past year indicates that FST will perform in line with the market over the near term.

Financial Data

(US$ in Thousands)	12/31/2012	12/31/2011	12/31/2010	12/31/2009	12/31/2008	12/31/2007	12/31/2006	12/31/2005
Earnings Per Share	(11.21)	1.19	2.00	(8.85)	(11.46)	2.18	2.66	2.41
Cash Flow Per Share	3.22	3.56	4.81	5.72	11.91	9.31	6.79	10.24
Tang Book Value Per Share	...	8.33	9.65	7.33	14.63	24.28	21.39	25.48
Income Statement								
Total Revenue	605,659	704,557	854,751	768,455	1,647,163	1,083,892	819,992	1,072,045
EBITDA	(693,205)	556,834	749,289	(966,499)	(943,141)	734,926	593,317	675,570
Depn & Amortn	280,458	219,684	251,618	303,622	532,181	390,338	266,881	368,679
Income Before Taxes	(1,115,494)	187,395	348,148	(1,433,608)	(1,601,001)	231,426	254,649	245,488
Income Taxes	173,437	89,135	120,627	(510,475)	(574,678)	62,395	90,903	93,358
Net Income	(1,288,931)	137,842	227,521	(923,133)	(1,026,323)	169,306	168,502	151,568
Average Shares	114,958	112,868	111,498	104,336	89,591	77,751	63,431	62,878
Balance Sheet								
Current Assets	125,080	210,672	481,683	729,992	473,049	361,374	261,000	315,925
Total Assets	2,201,862	3,381,151	3,785,388	3,684,690	5,282,798	5,695,548	3,189,072	3,645,546
Current Liabilities	226,325	340,837	629,374	535,020	521,411	738,382	263,941	522,916
Long-Term Obligations	1,862,088	1,693,044	1,582,280	1,865,836	2,735,661	1,503,035	1,204,709	1,769,614
Total Liabilities	2,244,686	2,188,038	2,432,601	2,605,536	3,609,886	3,283,737	1,755,066	1,961,024
Stockholders' Equity	(42,824)	1,193,113	1,352,787	1,079,154	1,672,912	2,411,811	1,434,006	1,684,522
Shares Outstanding	118,245	114,525	113,594	112,337	97,039	88,379	62,998	62,687
Statistical Record								
Return on Assets %	N.M.	3.85	6.09	N.M.	N.M.	3.81	4.93	4.48
Return on Equity %	N.M.	10.83	18.71	N.M.	N.M.	8.80	10.81	9.60
EBITDA Margin %	N.M.	79.03	87.66	N.M.	N.M.	67.80	72.36	63.02
Net Margin %	N.M.	19.56	26.62	N.M.	N.M.	15.62	20.55	14.14
Asset Turnover	0.22	0.20	0.23	0.17	0.30	0.24	0.24	0.32
Current Ratio	0.55	0.62	0.77	1.36	0.91	0.49	0.99	0.60
Debt to Equity	...	1.42	1.17	1.73	1.64	0.62	0.84	1.05
Price Range	14.80-5.72	28.57-8.89	27.82-16.01	17.63-7.61	56.10-8.79	37.17-20.84	28.52-20.25	26.10-14.20
P/E Ratio	...	24.01-7.47	13.91-8.00	...	...	17.05-9.56	10.72-7.61	10.83-5.89

Address: 707 17th Street, Suite 3600, Denver, CO 80202 Telephone: 303-812-1400	Web Site: www.forestoil.com Officers: Patrick R. McDonald - President, Interim Chief Executive Officer, Chief Executive Officer Michael N. Kennedy - Executive Vice President, Chief Financial Officer	Auditors: Ernst & Young LLP Transfer Agents: Computershare Shareowner Services LLC, Jersey City, NJ

FORTUNE BRANDS HOME & SECURITY, INC.

Exchange	Symbol	Price	52Wk Range	Yield	P/E
NYS	FBHS	$37.43 (3/28/2013)	37.67-20.15	N/A	52.72

*7 Year Price Score N/A *NYSE Composite Index=100 *12 Month Price Score 117.90

TRADING VOLUME (thousand shares)

Interim Earnings (Per Share)

Qtr.	Mar	Jun	Sep	Dec
2011	(0.07)	0.28	0.13	(0.55)
2012	0.08	0.29	0.24	0.10

Interim Dividends (Per Share)

No Dividends Paid

Valuation Analysis — **Institutional Holding**

Forecast EPS	$1.22	No of Institutions
	(04/05/2013)	341
Market Cap	$6.1 Billion	Shares
Book Value	$2.4 Billion	142,117,536
Price/Book	2.58	% Held
Price/Sales	1.71	N/A

Business Summary: Household Appliances, Electronics & Goods (MIC: 1.5.1 SIC: 3442 NAIC: 332321)

Fortune Brands Home & Security is a holding company. Through its subsidiaries, Co. provides home and security products. Co. has four business segments: Kitchen and Bath Cabinetry, which includes custom, semi-custom and stock cabinetry for the kitchen, bath and home; Plumbing and Accessories, which includes faucets, bath furnishings, accessories and kitchen sinks; Advanced Material Windows and Door Systems, which includes residential fiberglass and steel entry door systems, vinyl-framed windows and patio doors, and urethane millwork; and Security and Storage, which includes locks, safety and security devices, tool storage and garage organization products.

Recent Developments: For the year ended Dec 31 2012, net income amounted to US$119.7 million versus a net loss of US$34.6 million in the prior year. Revenues were US$3.59 billion, up 7.9% from US$3.33 billion the year before. Operating income was US$161.7 million versus a loss of US$15.6 million in the prior year. Direct operating expenses rose 3.8% to US$2.42 billion from US$2.33 billion in the comparable period the year before. Indirect operating expenses were unchanged at US$1.01 billion versus the equivalent prior-year period.

Prospects: Our evaluation of Fortune Brands Home & Security Inc. as of Apr. 7, 2013 is the result of our systematic analysis on three basic characteristics: earnings strength, relative valuation, and recent stock price movement. The company has managed to produce a neutral trend in earnings per share over the past 5 quarters and while recent estimates for the company have been mixed, FBHS has posted better than expected results. Based on operating earnings yield, the company is overvalued when compared to all of the companies in our coverage universe. Share price changes over the past year indicates that FBHS will perform very well over the near term.

Financial Data

(US$ in Thousands)	12/31/2012	12/31/2011	12/31/2010	12/31/2009	12/31/2008
Earnings Per Share	0.71	(0.23)	57,223.00	(41,877.00)	(641,931.00)
Cash Flow Per Share	1.76	1.13	138,900.00	269,300.00	
Tang Book Value Per Share	1.93	0.36	...	...	...
Dividends Per Share	...	3.540			
Income Statement					
Total Revenue	3,591,100	3,328,600	3,233,500	3,006,800	3,759,100
EBITDA	264,000	94,300	300,400	181,500	(447,100)
Depn & Amortn	101,300	111,500	111,600	131,100	143,000
Income Before Taxes	154,000	(43,600)	72,500	(34,800)	(717,700)
Income Taxes	34,300	(9,000)	14,100	6,300	(76,500)
Net Income	118,700	(35,600)	57,200	(41,900)	(641,900)
Average Shares	166,100	155,200	1,000.00	1,000.00	1,000.00
Balance Sheet					
Current Assets	1,228,000	953,500	1,467,800	1,369,400	
Total Assets	3,873,700	3,637,900	4,259,400	4,191,200	...
Current Liabilities	632,600	597,800	576,500	553,000	...
Long-Term Obligations	297,500	389,300	3,230,800	3,248,800	
Total Liabilities	1,492,600	1,517,100	4,317,800	4,353,400	...
Stockholders' Equity	2,381,100	2,120,800	(58,400)	(162,200)	...
Shares Outstanding	163,855	156,008	1,000.00	1,000.00	1,000.00
Statistical Record					
Return on Assets %	3.15	N.M.	1.35	...	...
Return on Equity %	5.26	N.M.	...	...	...
EBITDA Margin %	7.35	2.83	9.29	6.04	N.M.
Net Margin %	3.31	N.M.	1.77	N.M.	N.M.
Asset Turnover	0.95	0.84	0.77	...	...
Current Ratio	1.94	1.60	2.55	2.48	...
Debt to Equity	0.12	0.18	...	...	...
Price Range	30.33-16.82	17.03-12.20	...	...	...
P/E Ratio	42.72-23.69	...	...	...	...
Average Yield %	...	23.37	...	...	...

Address: 520 Lake Cook Road, Deerfield, IL 60015-5611 Telephone: 847-484-4400	Web Site: www.FBHS.com Officers: Christopher J. Klein - President, Chief Executive Officer Lauren S. Tashma - Senior Vice President, Secretary, General Counsel	Auditors: PricewaterhouseCoopers LLP Transfer Agents: Wells Fargo Shareowner Services, St. Paul, MN

FRANKLIN RESOURCES, INC.

Exchange	Symbol	Price	52Wk Range	Yield	P/E	Div Achiever
NYS	BEN	$150.81 (3/28/2013)	150.81-102.05	0.77	16.46	23 Years

*7 Year Price Score 104.51 *NYSE Composite Index=100 *12 Month Price Score 105.82

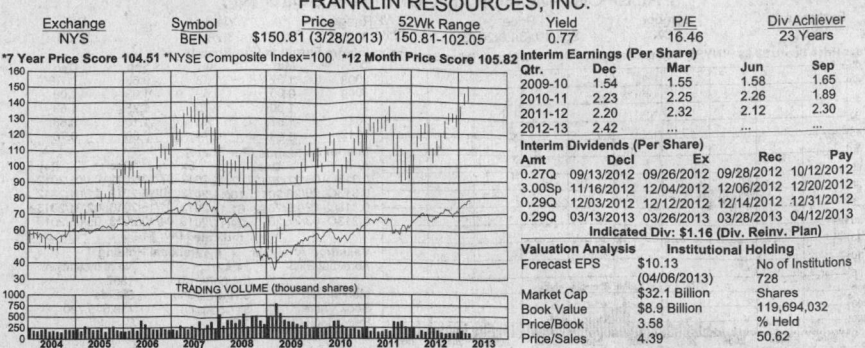

Interim Earnings (Per Share)
Qtr.	Dec	Mar	Jun	Sep
2009-10	1.54	1.55	1.58	1.65
2010-11	2.23	2.25	2.26	1.89
2011-12	2.20	2.32	2.12	2.30
2012-13	2.42	...	...	...

Interim Dividends (Per Share)
Amt	Decl	Ex	Rec	Pay
0.27Q	09/13/2012	09/26/2012	09/28/2012	10/12/2012
3.00Sp	11/16/2012	12/04/2012	12/06/2012	12/20/2012
0.29Q	12/03/2012	12/12/2012	12/14/2012	12/31/2012
0.29Q	03/13/2013	03/26/2013	03/28/2013	04/12/2013

Indicated Div: $1.16 (Div. Reinv. Plan)

Valuation Analysis
		Institutional Holding	
Forecast EPS	$10.13	No of Institutions	
	(04/06/2013)	728	
Market Cap	$32.1 Billion	Shares	
Book Value	$8.9 Billion	119,694,032	
Price/Book	3.58	% Held	
Price/Sales	4.39	50.62	

Business Summary: Wealth Management (MIC: 5.5.2 SIC: 6282 NAIC: 523930)

Franklin Resources is a holding company that, together with its subsidiaries, operates as Franklin Templeton Investments®. Co. is a global investment management organization. Co. provides investment choices under its Franklin®, Templeton®, Mutual Series®, Bissett®, Fiduciary Trust®, Darby® and Balanced Equity Management® brand names. In addition to investment management, Co.'s services include fund administration, sales, distribution, shareholder services, transfer agency, trustee, custodial and other fiduciary services, as well as select private banking services. At Sep 30 2012, Co.'s total assets under management were $749.90 billion.

Recent Developments: For the quarter ended Dec 31 2012, net income increased 2.2% to US$504.7 million from US$493.7 million in the year-earlier quarter. Revenues were US$1.90 billion, up 11.7% from US$1.70 billion the year before. Operating income was US$685.1 million versus US$632.4 million in the prior-year quarter, an increase of 8.3%. Direct operating expenses rose 15.9% to US$730.9 million from US$630.6 million in the comparable period the year before. Indirect operating expenses increased 10.7% to US$485.8 million from US$438.9 million in the equivalent prior-year period.

Prospects: Our evaluation of Franklin Resources Inc. as of Apr. 7, 2013 is the result of our systematic analysis on three basic characteristics: earnings strength, relative valuation, and recent stock price movement. The company has managed to produce a neutral trend in earnings per share over the past 5 quarters and while recent estimates for the company have been raised by analysts, BEN has posted better than expected results. Based on operating earnings yield, the company is undervalued when compared to all of the companies in our coverage universe. Share price changes over the past year indicates that BEN will perform in line with the market over the near term.

Financial Data
(US$ in Thousands)	3 Mos	09/30/2012	09/30/2011	09/30/2010	09/30/2009	09/30/2008	09/30/2007	09/30/2006
Earnings Per Share	9.16	8.95	8.62	6.33	3.87	6.67	7.03	4.86
Cash Flow Per Share	5.60	4.97	7.34	7.30	2.78	5.95	6.72	5.01
Tang Book Value Per Share	30.85	33.27	29.29	25.54	24.54	21.72	21.49	18.57
Dividends Per Share	4.100	3.080	1.000	4.090	0.830	0.750	0.609	0.360
Dividend Payout %	44.76	34.41	11.60	64.61	21.45	11.24	8.53	7.41
Income Statement								
Total Revenue	1,901,800	7,101,000	7,140,039	5,852,999	4,194,087	6,032,386	6,205,769	5,050,726
EBITDA	759,600	2,701,700	2,723,200	2,121,149	1,296,718	2,181,766	2,687,140	1,878,809
Depn & Amortn	53,900	67,900	71,500	67,700	61,500	58,200	198,619	14,022
Income Before Taxes	694,300	2,609,600	2,625,277	2,049,860	1,263,365	2,208,236	2,465,301	1,835,566
Income Taxes	211,400	762,700	803,424	618,312	384,314	648,376	692,363	567,998
Net Income	516,100	1,931,400	1,923,580	1,445,689	896,778	1,588,213	1,772,938	1,267,568
Average Shares	211,800	214,400	222,084	227,353	231,454	238,281	252,118	261,745
Balance Sheet								
Current Assets	6,245,400	6,996,500	8,372,635	6,932,798	5,948,987	5,494,883	5,896,637	5,443,823
Total Assets	14,354,200	14,751,500	13,775,843	10,708,088	9,468,463	9,176,520	9,943,250	9,499,859
Current Liabilities	1,747,000	1,709,100	2,202,253	1,662,390	1,390,120	1,534,720	2,129,405	1,825,762
Long-Term Obligations	2,462,500	2,839,100	2,083,926	949,903	57,000	227,433	162,125	627,919
Total Liabilities	5,406,400	5,550,200	5,251,112	2,981,094	1,836,290	2,102,156	2,610,975	2,815,131
Stockholders' Equity	8,947,800	9,201,300	8,524,731	7,726,994	7,632,173	7,074,364	7,332,275	6,684,728
Shares Outstanding	212,524	212,208	217,693	224,007	229,324	232,777	245,469	253,249
Statistical Record								
Return on Assets %	14.17	13.50	15.71	14.33	9.62	16.57	18.24	13.78
Return on Equity %	22.84	21.73	23.67	18.83	12.20	21.99	25.30	20.50
EBITDA Margin %	39.94	38.05	38.14	36.24	30.92	36.17	43.30	37.20
Net Margin %	27.14	27.20	26.94	24.70	21.38	26.33	28.57	25.10
Asset Turnover	0.53	0.50	0.58	0.58	0.45	0.63	0.64	0.55
Current Ratio	3.57	4.09	3.80	4.17	4.28	3.58	2.77	2.98
Debt to Equity	0.28	0.31	0.24	0.12	0.01	0.03	0.02	0.09
Price Range	133.34-96.26	128.00-90.38	137.26-95.64	121.31-84.97	103.46-38.66	142.21-83.01	143.95-103.87	105.79-78.24
P/E Ratio	14.56-10.51	14.30-10.10	15.92-11.10	19.16-13.42	26.73-9.99	21.32-12.45	20.48-14.78	21.77-16.10
Average Yield %	3.46	2.78	0.83	3.92	1.23	0.72	0.48	0.39

Address: One Franklin Parkway, San Mateo, CA 94403
Telephone: 650-312-2000
Fax: 650-312-3655

Web Site: www.franklinresources.com
Officers: Charles B. Johnson - Chairman Rupert H. Johnson - Vice-Chairman

Auditors: PricewaterhouseCoopers LLP
Investor Contact: 650-312-4091
Transfer Agents: BNY Mellon, Pittsburgh, PA

FREEPORT-MCMORAN COPPER & GOLD INC.

Exchange	Symbol	Price	52Wk Range	Yield	P/E
NYS	FCX	$33.10 (3/28/2013)	42.64-30.81	3.78	10.38

*7 Year Price Score 83.69   *NYSE Composite Index=100   ***12 Month Price Score 85.70**

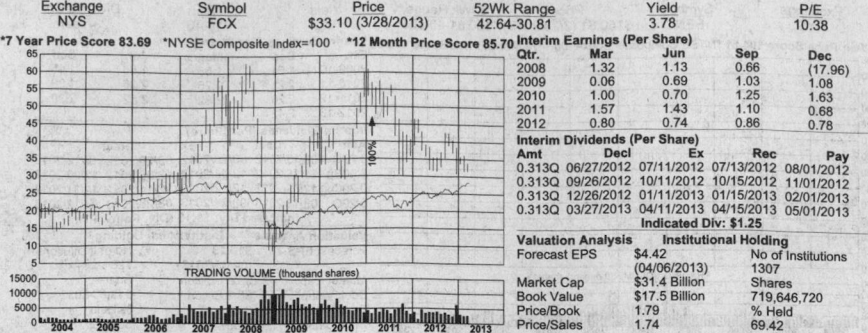

Interim Earnings (Per Share)

Qtr.	Mar	Jun	Sep	Dec
2008	1.32	1.13	0.66	(17.96)
2009	0.06	0.69	1.03	1.08
2010	1.00	0.70	1.25	1.63
2011	1.57	1.43	1.10	0.68
2012	0.80	0.74	0.86	0.78

Interim Dividends (Per Share)

Amt	Decl	Ex	Rec	Pay
0.313Q	06/27/2012	07/11/2012	07/13/2012	08/01/2012
0.313Q	09/26/2012	10/11/2012	10/15/2012	11/01/2012
0.313Q	12/26/2012	01/11/2013	01/15/2013	02/01/2013
0.313Q	03/27/2013	04/11/2013	04/15/2013	05/01/2013

Indicated Div: $1.25

Valuation Analysis   **Institutional Holding**

Forecast EPS	$4.42 (04/06/2013)	No of Institutions 1307
Market Cap	$31.4 Billion	Shares
Book Value	$17.5 Billion	719,646,720
Price/Book	1.79	% Held
Price/Sales	1.74	69.42

Business Summary: Non-Precious Metals (MIC: 8.2.2 SIC: 1021 NAIC: 212234)

Freeport-McMoRan Copper & Gold is a mining company. Co.'s portfolio of assets includes the Grasberg minerals district in Indonesia, mining operations in North and South America, and the Tenke Fungurume minerals district in the Democratic Republic of Congo. Co.'s products include copper concentrate, cathode and continuous cast copper rod; gold products; molybdenum and molybdenum-based chemicals; as well as cobalt hydroxide, silver and other metals such as rhenium and magnetite. At Dec 31 2012, Co. had consolidated recoverable proven and probable reserves of 116.50 billion pounds of copper, 32.5 million ounces of gold, 3.42 billion pounds of molybdenum, and 321.4 million ounces of silver.

Recent Developments: For the year ended Dec 31 2012, net income decreased 30.7% to US$3.98 billion from US$5.75 billion in the prior year. Revenues were US$18.01 billion, down 13.7% from US$20.88 billion the year before. Operating income was US$5.81 billion versus US$9.14 billion in the prior year, a decrease of 36.4%. Direct operating expenses rose 5.9% to US$11.56 billion from US$10.92 billion in the comparable period the year before. Indirect operating expenses decreased 22.6% to US$635.0 million from US$820.0 million in the equivalent prior-year period.

Prospects: Our evaluation of Freeport-McMoRan Copper & Gold Inc. as of Apr. 7, 2013 is the result of our systematic analysis on three basic characteristics: earnings strength, relative valuation, and recent stock price movement. The company has enjoyed a very positive trend in earnings per share over the past 5 quarters. However, while recent estimates for the company have been lowered by analysts, FCX has posted better than expected results. Based on operating earnings yield, the company is undervalued when compared to all of the companies in our coverage universe. Share price changes over the past year indicates that FCX will perform poorly over the near term.

Financial Data

(US$ in Thousands)	12/31/2012	12/31/2011	12/31/2010	12/31/2009	12/31/2008	12/31/2007	12/31/2006	12/31/2005
Earnings Per Share	3.19	4.78	4.57	2.93	(14.86)	3.75	3.31	2.34
Cash Flow Per Share	3.97	6.99	6.86	5.31	4.40	9.13	4.89	4.31
Tang Book Value Per Share	18.13	16.16	12.88	6.86	2.22	10.03	3.41	1.99
Dividends Per Share	1.188	1.500	0.950	0.075	0.906	0.625	2.375	1.250
Dividend Payout %	37.23	31.38	20.79	2.56	...	16.67	71.64	53.53
Income Statement								
Total Revenue	18,010,000	20,880,000	18,982,000	15,040,000	17,796,000	16,939,000	5,790,500	4,179,118
EBITDA	6,852,000	10,056,000	10,102,000	7,539,000	(10,826,000)	7,888,000	3,127,507	2,418,383
Depn & Amortn	1,179,000	926,000	1,128,000	1,137,000	1,899,000	1,264,000	232,539	259,108
Income Before Taxes	5,487,000	8,818,000	8,512,000	5,816,000	(13,309,000)	6,111,000	2,819,381	2,027,636
Income Taxes	1,510,000	3,087,000	2,983,000	2,307,000	(2,844,000)	2,400,000	1,201,175	915,068
Net Income	3,980,000	5,747,000	5,544,000	3,534,000	(11,067,000)	2,977,000	1,456,509	995,127
Average Shares	954,000	955,000	949,000	938,000	764,000	794,000	442,996	440,940
Balance Sheet								
Current Assets	10,297,000	10,047,000	9,851,000	7,433,000	5,233,000	5,903,000	2,151,037	2,022,382
Total Assets	35,440,000	32,070,000	29,386,000	25,996,000	23,353,000	40,661,000	5,389,802	5,550,206
Current Liabilities	3,343,000	2,940,000	3,763,000	3,002,000	3,158,000	3,869,000	972,449	1,368,978
Long-Term Obligations	3,525,000	3,533,000	4,660,000	6,330,000	7,284,000	7,180,000	660,999	1,002,598
Total Liabilities	17,897,000	16,428,000	16,882,000	16,877,000	17,580,000	22,427,000	2,944,701	3,707,212
Stockholders' Equity	17,543,000	15,642,000	12,504,000	9,119,000	5,773,000	18,234,000	2,445,101	1,842,994
Shares Outstanding	949,000	948,000	945,000	860,000	768,000	766,000	393,930	373,612
Statistical Record								
Return on Assets %	11.76	18.70	20.02	14.32	N.M.	12.93	26.63	18.71
Return on Equity %	23.92	40.84	51.28	47.46	N.M.	28.79	67.93	66.20
EBITDA Margin %	38.05	48.16	53.22	50.13	N.M.	46.57	54.01	57.87
Net Margin %	22.10	27.52	29.21	23.50	N.M.	17.57	25.15	23.81
Asset Turnover	0.53	0.68	0.69	0.61	0.55	0.74	1.06	0.79
Current Ratio	3.08	3.42	2.62	2.48	1.66	1.53	2.21	1.48
Debt to Equity	0.20	0.23	0.37	0.69	1.26	0.39	0.27	0.54
Price Range	46.50-30.81	60.92-29.87	60.05-29.09	43.66-11.07	62.93-8.40	58.93-25.25	36.05-21.88	27.68-16.03
P/E Ratio	14.58-9.66	12.74-6.25	13.14-6.37	14.90-3.78	...	15.71-6.73	10.89-6.61	11.83-6.85
Average Yield %	3.19	3.17	2.33	0.27	2.24	1.52	8.36	5.98

Address: 333 North Central Avenue, Phoenix, AZ 85004-2189 Telephone: 602-366-8100	Web Site: www.fcx.com Officers: James R. Moffett - Chairman B. M. Rankin - Vice-Chairman	Auditors: Ernst & Young LLP Investor Contact: 602-366-8400 Transfer Agents: Computershare Shareowner Services LLC, Jersey City, NJ

FREESCALE SEMICONDUCTOR LTD

Exchange	Symbol	Price	52Wk Range	Yield	P/E
NYS	FSL	$14.89 (3/28/2013)	16.02-7.64	N/A	N/A

*7 Year Price Score N/A   *NYSE Composite Index=100   ***12 Month Price Score 122.84**

Interim Earnings (Per Share)

Qtr.	Mar	Jun	Sep	Dec
2010	(1.31)	(2.73)	(0.79)	(0.52)
2011	(0.75)	(0.79)	(0.36)	0.03
2012	(0.04)	(0.14)	(0.10)	(0.14)

Interim Dividends (Per Share)

No Dividends Paid

Valuation Analysis   **Institutional Holding**

Forecast EPS	$0.45	No of Institutions
	(04/05/2013)	119
Market Cap	$3.7 Billion	Shares
Book Value	N/A	657,609,984
Price/Book	N/A	% Held
Price/Sales	0.94	N/A

Business Summary: Semiconductors (MIC: 6.2.4 SIC: 3674 NAIC: 334413)

Freescale Semiconductor is engaged in embedded processing applications. An embedded processing solution is the combination of embedded processors, complementary semiconductor devices and software. Co.'s embedded processor products include microcontrollers, single-and multi-core microprocessors, digital signal controllers, applications processors and digital signal processors. Co. also provides complementary semiconductor products, including radio frequency, power management, analog, mixed-signal devices and sensors. Co. sells its products directly to original equipment manufacturers, distributors, original design manufacturers and contract manufacturers.

Recent Developments: For the year ended Dec 31 2012, net loss amounted to US$102.0 million versus a net loss of US$410.0 million in the prior year. Revenues were US$3.95 billion, down 13.7% from US$4.57 billion the year before. Operating income was US$463.0 million versus US$274.0 million in the prior year, an increase of 69.0%. Direct operating expenses declined 13.9% to US$2.30 billion from US$2.68 billion in the comparable period the year before. Indirect operating expenses decreased 27.3% to US$1.18 billion from US$1.62 billion in the equivalent prior-year period.

Prospects: Our evaluation of Freescale Semiconductor Ltd as of Apr. 7, 2013 is the result of our systematic analysis on three basic characteristics: earnings strength, relative valuation, and recent stock price movement. The company has suffered a very negative trend in earnings per share over the past 5 quarters and while recent estimates for the company have been mixed, FSL has posted better than expected results. Based on operating earnings yield, the company is overvalued when compared to all of the companies in our coverage universe. Share price changes over the past year indicates that FSL will perform in line with the market over the near term.

Financial Data

(US$ in Millions)	12/31/2012	12/31/2011	12/31/2010	12/31/2009	12/31/2008
Earnings Per Share	(0.41)	(1.82)	(5.35)	3.81	(40.47)
Cash Flow Per Share	1.41	0.44	2.00	0.39	...
Income Statement					
Total Revenue	3,945	4,572	4,458	3,508	5,226
EBITDA	602	806	460	2,192	(6,029)
Depn & Amortn	192	625	955	1,134	1,751
Income Before Taxes	(100)	(382)	(1,078)	502	(8,482)
Income Taxes	2	28	(25)	(246)	(543)
Net Income	(102)	(410)	(1,053)	748	(7,939)
Average Shares	251	227	197	196	197
Balance Sheet					
Current Assets	2,058	2,232	2,492	2,683	...
Total Assets	3,171	3,415	4,269	5,093	...
Current Liabilities	872	800	1,019	895	...
Long-Term Obligations	6,375	6,590	7,584	7,438	...
Total Liabilities	7,702	7,895	9,203	8,987	...
Stockholders' Equity	(4,531)	(4,480)	(4,934)	(3,894)	...
Shares Outstanding	249	246	196	196	196
Statistical Record					
EBITDA Margin %	15.26	17.63	10.32	62.49	N.M.
Net Margin %	N.M.	N.M.	N.M.	21.32	N.M.
Asset Turnover	1.19	1.19	0.95	...	...
Current Ratio	2.36	2.79	2.45	3.00	...
Price Range	17.68-7.64	20.02-10.50	...	...	...

Address: 6501 William Cannon Drive West, Austin, TX 78735 **Telephone:** 512-895-2000	**Web Site:** www.freescale.com **Officers:** J. Daniel McCranie - Non-Executive Chairman Gregg A. Lowe - President, Chief Executive Officer	**Auditors:** KPMG LLP **Investor Contact:** 512-895-2454 **Transfer Agents:** Computershare

FTI CONSULTING INC.

Exchange	Symbol	Price	52Wk Range	Yield	P/E
NYS	FCN	$37.66 (3/28/2013)	38.09-23.11	N/A	N/A

7 Year Price Score 65.91 **NYSE Composite Index=100** **12 Month Price Score 103.91**

TRADING VOLUME (thousand shares)

Interim Earnings (Per Share)

Qtr.	Mar	Jun	Sep	Dec
2008	0.59	0.66	0.51	0.58
2009	0.60	0.69	0.70	0.71
2010	0.29	0.52	0.47	0.23
2011	0.48	0.40	0.70	0.92
2012	0.43	0.18	0.55	(2.09)

Interim Dividends (Per Share)

No Dividends Paid

Valuation Analysis		Institutional Holding	
Forecast EPS	$2.48	No of Institutions	
	(04/11/2013)	229	
Market Cap	$1.5 Billion	Shares	
Book Value	$1.1 Billion	44,440,744	
Price/Book	1.44	% Held	
Price/Sales	0.97	86.65	

Business Summary: Business Services (MIC: 7.5.2 SIC: 8742 NAIC: 541618)

FTI Consulting is a business advisory firm. Co. operates five segments: Corporate Finance/Restructuring, which provides advise on a range of areas, including restructuring; Forensic and Litigation Consulting, which provides dispute advisory, investigations, forensic accounting, business intelligence assessments, data analytics and risk mitigation services; Economic Consulting, which provides analysis of economic issues; Technology, which provides electronic discovery and information management consulting, software and services; and Strategic Communications, which provides advice and consulting services relating to financial and corporate communications and investor relations, among others.

Recent Developments: For the year ended Dec 31 2012, net loss amounted to US$37.0 million versus net income of US$103.9 million in the prior year. Revenues were US$1.58 billion, up 0.6% from US$1.57 billion the year before. Operating income was US$59.0 million versus US$205.4 million in the prior year, a decrease of 71.3%. Direct operating expenses rose 2.5% to US$980.5 million from US$956.9 million in the comparable period the year before. Indirect operating expenses increased 32.9% to US$537.3 million from US$404.4 million in the equivalent prior-year period.

Prospects: Our evaluation of FTI Consulting Inc. as of Apr. 7, 2013 is the result of our systematic analysis on three basic characteristics: earnings strength, relative valuation, and recent stock price movement. The company has enjoyed a very positive trend in earnings per share over the past 5 quarters. However, while recent estimates for the company have been lowered by analysts, FCN has posted better than expected results. Based on operating earnings yield, the company is undervalued when compared to all of the companies in our coverage universe. Share price changes over the past year indicates that FCN will perform very poorly over the near term.

Financial Data

(US$ in Thousands)	12/31/2012	12/31/2011	12/31/2010	12/31/2009	12/31/2008	12/31/2007	12/31/2006	12/31/2005
Earnings Per Share	(0.92)	2.39	1.51	2.70	2.34	2.00	1.04	1.35
Cash Flow Per Share	2.97	4.23	4.28	5.02	4.05	1.81	1.61	2.43
Income Statement								
Total Revenue	1,576,871	1,566,768	1,401,461	1,399,946	1,293,145	1,001,270	707,933	539,545
EBITDA	107,222	253,258	240,004	319,156	283,688	216,023	117,170	116,910
Depn & Amortn	52,768	48,371	77,266	52,502	44,824	30,015	11,175	6,534
Income Before Taxes	3,114	153,127	117,440	227,025	205,631	149,790	79,165	97,187
Income Taxes	40,100	49,224	45,550	83,999	80,196	57,669	37,141	40,819
Net Income	(36,986)	103,903	71,890	143,026	125,435	92,121	42,024	56,368
Average Shares	40,316	43,473	47,471	53,044	53,603	45,974	40,526	41,787
Balance Sheet								
Current Assets	674,375	770,954	788,715	499,915	552,454	661,527	294,949	298,135
Total Assets	2,275,452	2,411,084	2,414,359	2,077,338	2,088,169	1,858,624	1,391,156	959,464
Current Liabilities	304,197	497,837	289,282	406,202	423,909	381,062	178,459	104,927
Long-Term Obligations	717,024	643,579	785,563	417,397	418,592	731,197	577,275	348,431
Total Liabilities	1,207,220	1,304,882	1,247,040	973,124	964,342	1,201,918	839,890	505,195
Stockholders' Equity	1,068,232	1,106,202	1,167,319	1,104,214	1,123,827	972,250	565,100	454,269
Shares Outstanding	40,755	41,484	46,144	46,985	50,934	48,979	41,890	39,000
Statistical Record								
Return on Assets %	N.M.	4.31	3.20	6.87	6.34	5.67	3.58	6.76
Return on Equity %	N.M.	9.14	6.33	12.84	11.94	11.98	8.25	11.86
EBITDA Margin %	6.80	16.16	17.13	22.80	21.94	21.57	16.55	21.67
Net Margin %	N.M.	6.63	5.13	10.22	9.70	9.20	5.94	10.45
Asset Turnover	0.67	0.65	0.62	0.67	0.65	0.62	0.60	0.65
Current Ratio	2.22	1.55	2.73	1.23	1.30	1.74	1.65	2.84
Debt to Equity	0.67	0.58	0.67	0.38	0.37	0.75	1.02	0.77
Price Range	44.22-23.11	43.77-32.99	48.06-31.61	56.13-36.54	74.19-41.16	62.78-26.09	29.17-20.00	30.31-18.23
P/E Ratio	...	18.31-13.80	31.83-21.15	20.79-13.53	31.71-17.59	31.39-13.05	28.05-19.23	22.45-13.50

Address: 777 South Flagler Drive, Suite 1500 West Tower, West Palm Beach, FL 33401 Telephone: 561-515-1900	Web Site: www.fticonsulting.com Officers: Dennis J. Shaughnessy - Chairman Dominic DiNapoli - Vice-Chairman	Auditors: KPMG LLP Investor Contact: 617-747-1791 Transfer Agents: American Stock Transfer & Trust Company, New York, NY

FULLER (H.B.) COMPANY

Exchange	Symbol	Price	52Wk Range	Yield	P/E	Div Achiever
NYS	FUL	$39.08 (3/28/2013)	42.31-28.34	0.87	15.15	45 Years

*7 Year Price Score 123.33 *NYSE Composite Index=100 *12 Month Price Score 112.43

Interim Earnings (Per Share)

Qtr.	Feb	May	Aug	Nov
2009-10	0.38	0.22	0.38	0.44
2010-11	0.29	0.50	0.47	0.53
2011-12	0.31	0.04	1.64	0.49
2012-13	0.41	...	...	...

Interim Dividends (Per Share)

Amt	Decl	Ex	Rec	Pay
0.085Q	04/12/2012	04/24/2012	04/26/2012	05/10/2012
0.085Q	06/28/2012	07/10/2012	07/12/2012	07/26/2012
0.085Q	09/26/2012	10/09/2012	10/11/2012	10/25/2012
0.085Q	01/24/2013	02/05/2013	02/07/2013	02/21/2013

Indicated Div: $0.34 (Div. Reinv. Plan)

Valuation Analysis

		Institutional Holding	
Forecast EPS	$2.62 (04/06/2013)	No of Institutions	219
Market Cap	$2.0 Billion	Shares	54,025,592
Book Value	$804.2 Million	% Held	87.83
Price/Book	2.44		
Price/Sales	0.97		

TRADING VOLUME (thousand shares)

Business Summary: Specialty Chemicals (MIC: 8.3.2 SIC: 2891 NAIC: 325520)

H.B. Fuller is a formulator, manufacturer and marketer of adhesives, sealants, and chemical products. Co.'s North America Adhesives, Europe, India, Middle East and Africa, Latin America Adhesives and Asia Pacific segments produce and supply industrial and performance adhesives products for applications in various markets, including assembly (appliances, filters, construction), packaging (food and beverage containers), converting, nonwoven and hygiene, performance wood (windows, doors), textile, flexible packaging, graphic arts and envelope. The Construction Products segment includes products used for tile setting and heating, ventilation, and air conditioning and insulation applications.

Recent Developments: For the quarter ended Mar 2 2013, income from continuing operations increased 52.7% to US$20.8 million from US$13.6 million in the year-earlier quarter. Net income increased 35.5% to US$20.8 million from US$15.3 million in the year-earlier quarter. Revenues were US$479.8 million, up 38.9% from US$345.5 million the year before. Direct operating expenses rose 42.7% to US$346.5 million from US$242.8 million in the comparable period the year before. Indirect operating expenses increased 26.3% to US$103.0 million from US$81.5 million in the equivalent prior-year period.

Prospects: Our evaluation of Fuller (H.B.) Company as of Apr. 7, 2013 is the result of our systematic analysis on three basic characteristics: earnings strength, relative valuation, and recent stock price movement. The company has produced a positive trend in earnings per share over the past 5 quarters. However, while recent estimates for the company have been lowered by analysts, FUL has posted results that fell short of analysts expectations. Based on operating earnings yield, the company is undervalued when compared to all of the companies in our coverage universe. Share price changes over the past year indicates that FUL will perform very well over the near term.

Financial Data

(US$ in Thousands)	3 Mos	12/01/2012	12/03/2011	11/27/2010	11/28/2009	11/29/2008	12/01/2007	12/02/2006
Earnings Per Share	2.58	2.48	1.79	1.43	1.70	0.36	1.68	2.23
Cash Flow Per Share	1.89	2.20	2.06	1.53	1.48	0.85	2.35	3.20
Tang Book Value Per Share	6.48	5.82	9.38	7.96	7.12	6.17	7.92	6.84
Dividends Per Share	0.340	0.330	0.295	0.278	0.270	0.263	0.256	0.249
Dividend Payout %	13.18	13.31	16.48	19.44	15.88	72.92	15.24	11.15
Income Statement								
Total Revenue	479,842	1,886,239	1,557,552	1,356,161	1,234,659	1,391,554	1,400,258	1,472,391
EBITDA	46,424	162,100	154,763	127,847	155,964	53,151	179,346	152,927
Depn & Amortn	15,643	54,490	31,054	30,361	34,709	34,369	36,349	39,460
Income Before Taxes	25,454	89,548	114,992	87,718	114,620	10,208	136,887	100,031
Income Taxes	7,120	30,479	34,951	25,307	36,728	(5,693)	37,712	23,682
Net Income	20,677	125,622	89,105	70,877	83,654	18,889	102,173	134,213
Average Shares	51,027	50,618	49,866	49,608	49,117	51,835	60,991	60,065
Balance Sheet								
Current Assets	780,638	799,344	596,590	533,617	473,656	479,057	635,950	669,094
Total Assets	1,765,410	1,786,320	1,227,709	1,153,457	1,100,445	1,081,328	1,364,602	1,478,471
Current Liabilities	321,803	350,119	254,985	231,333	236,008	229,954	297,835	342,442
Long-Term Obligations	474,299	475,112	179,611	200,978	162,713	204,000	137,000	224,000
Total Liabilities	961,174	1,008,047	522,505	521,523	509,091	545,717	565,609	700,679
Stockholders' Equity	804,236	778,273	705,204	631,934	591,354	535,611	798,993	777,792
Shares Outstanding	50,314	49,903	49,449	49,194	48,657	48,447	57,436	59,931
Statistical Record								
Return on Assets %	8.67	8.36	7.36	6.31	7.69	1.55	7.21	10.41
Return on Equity %	17.06	16.98	13.11	11.62	14.89	2.84	13.00	19.76
EBITDA Margin %	9.67	8.59	9.94	9.43	12.63	3.82	12.81	10.39
Net Margin %	4.31	6.66	5.72	5.23	6.78	1.36	7.30	9.12
Asset Turnover	1.34	1.26	1.29	1.21	1.13	1.14	0.99	1.14
Current Ratio	2.43	2.28	2.34	2.31	2.01	2.08	2.14	1.95
Debt to Equity	0.59	0.61	0.25	0.32	0.28	0.38	0.17	0.29
Price Range	41.92-28.34	34.00-21.34	25.19-17.06	24.56-18.69	22.88-9.76	27.41-12.94	31.35-24.11	27.54-15.65
P/E Ratio	16.25-10.98	13.71-8.60	14.07-9.53	17.17-13.07	13.46-5.74	76.14-35.94	18.66-14.35	12.35-7.02
Average Yield %	1.05	1.21	1.37	1.30	1.55	1.20	0.94	1.14

Address: 1200 Willow Lake Boulevard, St. Paul, MN 55110-5101	Web Site: www.hbfuller.com	Auditors: KPMG LLP
Telephone: 651-236-5900	Officers: Lee R. Mitau - Chairman James J. Owens - President, Chief Executive Officer	Investor Contact: 651-236-5062
Fax: 651-236-5161		Transfer Agents: Wells Fargo Shareowner Services, Minnesota, MN

GALLAGHER (ARTHUR J.) & CO.

Exchange	Symbol	Price	52Wk Range	Yield	P/E
NYS	AJG	$41.31 (3/28/2013)	41.31-33.84	3.39	25.98

*7 Year Price Score 115.19 *NYSE Composite Index=100 *12 Month Price Score 98.85

Interim Earnings (Per Share)

Qtr.	Mar	Jun	Sep	Dec
2008	(0.07)	0.44	0.40	0.04
2009	0.27	0.44	0.41	0.16
2010	0.28	0.42	0.44	0.52
2011	0.14	0.37	0.41	0.35
2012	0.24	0.59	0.50	0.26

Interim Dividends (Per Share)

Amt	Decl	Ex	Rec	Pay
0.34Q	04/25/2012	06/27/2012	06/29/2012	07/13/2012
0.34Q	07/26/2012	09/26/2012	09/28/2012	10/15/2012
0.34Q	10/24/2012	11/29/2012	12/03/2012	12/20/2012
0.35Q	01/24/2013	02/28/2013	03/04/2013	03/20/2013

Indicated Div: $1.40

Valuation Analysis

Forecast EPS	$2.15 (04/06/2013)
Market Cap	$5.2 Billion
Book Value	$1.7 Billion
Price/Book	3.13
Price/Sales	2.06

Institutional Holding

No of Institutions	390
Shares	111,278,560
% Held	87.81

Business Summary: Brokers & Intermediaries (MIC: 5.2.3 SIC: 6411 NAIC: 524210)

Arthur J. Gallagher & Co. is engaged in providing insurance brokerage and third-party claims settlement and administration services to entities in the U.S. and abroad. Co. operates three segments: Brokerage, which is comprised of retail and wholesale brokerage operations; Risk Management, which provides contract claim settlement and administration services for enterprises that choose to self-insure some or all of their property/casualty coverages and for insurance companies that choose to outsource some or all of their property/casualty claims departments; and Corporate, which includes financial information related to Co.'s debt and clean energy investments and others.

Recent Developments: For the year ended Dec 31 2012, income from continuing operations increased 35.3% to US$195.0 million from US$144.1 million a year earlier. Net income increased 35.3% to US$195.0 million from US$144.1 million in the prior year. Revenues were US$2.52 billion, up 18.1% from US$2.13 billion the year before.

Prospects: Our evaluation of Gallagher (Arthur J.) & Co. as of Apr. 7, 2013 is the result of our systematic analysis on three basic characteristics: earnings strength, relative valuation, and recent stock price movement. The company has generated a negative trend in earnings per share over the past 5 quarters. However, while recent estimates for the company have been mixed, AJG has posted results that fell short of analysts expectations. Based on operating earnings yield, the company is about fairly valued when compared to all of the companies in our coverage universe. Share price changes over the past year indicates that AJG will perform poorly over the near term.

Financial Data
(US$ in Thousands)

	12/31/2012	12/31/2011	12/31/2010	12/31/2009	12/31/2008	12/31/2007	12/31/2006	12/31/2005
Earnings Per Share	1.59	1.28	1.66	1.28	0.82	1.43	1.31	0.32
Cash Flow Per Share	2.83	2.53	2.21	2.10	1.71	2.63	1.08	2.01
Tang Book Value Per Share	N.M.	N.M.	N.M.	N.M.	N.M.	N.M.	3.40	3.67
Dividends Per Share	1.360	1.320	1.280	1.280	1.280	1.240	1.200	1.120
Dividend Payout %	85.53	103.13	77.11	100.00	156.10	86.71	91.60	350.00
Income Statement								
Total Revenue	2,520,300	2,134,700	1,864,200	1,729,300	1,645,000	1,623,300	1,534,000	1,483,900
EBITDA	286,700	243,700	235,300	241,700	193,600	229,400	184,900	29,900
Depn & Amortn	41,400	35,900	32,300	30,600	30,000	29,300	31,800	32,700
Income Before Taxes	245,300	207,800	203,000	211,100	163,600	200,100	153,100	(2,800)
Income Taxes	50,300	63,700	39,700	78,000	52,200	45,500	24,600	(31,400)
Net Income	195,000	144,100	174,100	128,600	77,300	138,800	128,500	30,800
Average Shares	122,500	112,500	105,100	100,600	94,200	97,100	98,400	96,100
Balance Sheet								
Current Assets	2,429,500	2,199,400	1,726,000	1,540,000	1,702,000	2,275,800	2,376,200	2,401,800
Total Assets	5,352,300	4,483,500	3,596,000	3,250,300	3,271,300	3,556,800	3,420,100	3,389,500
Current Liabilities	2,362,900	2,073,600	1,577,300	1,474,400	1,858,600	2,232,200	2,401,300	2,386,300
Long-Term Obligations	725,000	675,000	550,000	550,000	400,000	400,000	25,900	107,600
Total Liabilities	3,693,700	3,239,900	2,489,300	2,357,400	2,532,800	2,841,300	2,556,000	2,620,400
Stockholders' Equity	1,658,600	1,243,600	1,106,700	892,900	738,500	715,500	864,100	769,100
Shares Outstanding	125,600	114,700	108,400	102,500	96,400	92,000	98,400	95,700
Statistical Record								
Return on Assets %	3.95	3.57	5.09	3.94	2.26	3.98	3.77	0.93
Return on Equity %	13.40	12.26	17.41	15.77	10.60	17.57	15.74	4.03
EBITDA Margin %	11.38	11.42	12.62	13.98	11.77	14.13	12.05	2.01
Net Margin %	7.74	6.75	9.34	7.44	4.70	8.55	8.38	2.08
Asset Turnover	0.51	0.53	0.54	0.53	0.48	0.47	0.45	0.45
Current Ratio	1.03	1.06	1.09	1.04	0.92	1.02	0.99	1.01
Debt to Equity	0.44	0.54	0.50	0.62	0.54	0.56	0.03	0.14
Price Range	37.73-32.76	33.82-24.51	29.65-22.00	25.91-15.04	28.54-22.10	31.08-24.19	31.76-24.56	32.68-26.50
P/E Ratio	23.73-20.60	26.42-19.15	17.86-13.25	20.24-11.75	34.80-26.95	21.73-16.92	24.24-18.75	102.13-82.81
Average Yield %	3.84	4.51	5.00	5.93	5.14	4.39	4.31	3.87

Address: Two Pierce Place, Itasca, IL 60143-3141
Telephone: 630-773-3800
Fax: 630-285-4000

Web Site: www.ajg.com
Officers: J. Patrick Gallagher - Chairman, President, Chief Executive Officer Douglas K. Howell - Corporate Vice-President, Chief Financial Officer

Auditors: Ernst & Young LLP
Investor Contact: 630-285-3501
Transfer Agents: Computershare Investor Services, Canton, MA

GAMESTOP CORP

Exchange	Symbol	Price	52Wk Range	Yield	P/E
NYS	GME	$27.97 (3/28/2013)	27.97-15.73	3.93	N/A

*7 Year Price Score 69.17   *NYSE Composite Index=100   *12 Month Price Score 106.74

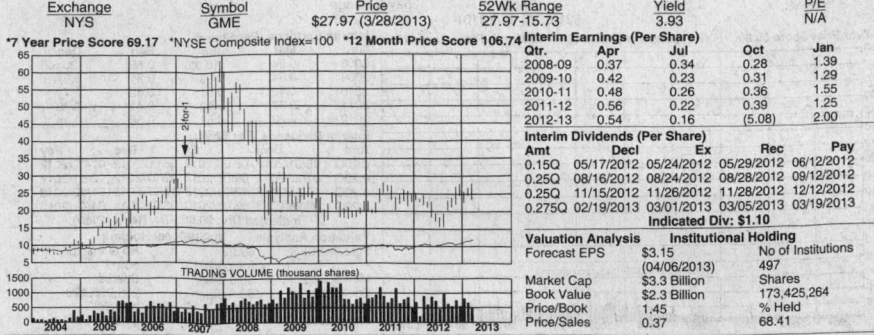

Interim Earnings (Per Share)

Qtr.	Apr	Jul	Oct	Jan
2008-09	0.37	0.34	0.28	1.39
2009-10	0.42	0.23	0.31	1.29
2010-11	0.48	0.26	0.36	1.55
2011-12	0.56	0.22	0.39	1.25
2012-13	0.54	0.16	(5.08)	2.00

Interim Dividends (Per Share)

Amt	Decl	Ex	Rec	Pay
0.15Q	05/17/2012	05/24/2012	05/29/2012	06/12/2012
0.25Q	08/16/2012	08/24/2012	08/28/2012	09/12/2012
0.25Q	11/15/2012	11/26/2012	11/28/2012	12/12/2012
0.275Q	02/19/2013	03/01/2013	03/05/2013	03/19/2013

Indicated Div: $1.10

Valuation Analysis / **Institutional Holding**

Forecast EPS	$3.15 (04/06/2013)	No of Institutions	497
Market Cap	$3.3 Billion	Shares	173,425,264
Book Value	$2.3 Billion	% Held	68.41
Price/Book	1.45		
Price/Sales	0.37		

Business Summary: Retail - Appliances and Electronics (MIC: 2.1.7 SIC: 5734 NAIC: 443120)

GameStop is a video game retailer. Co. provides video game products, personal computer (PC) entertainment software, and related products, such as video game accessories and strategy guides, as well as mobile devices such as tablets, phones and music players. Co. also operates electronic commerce Web sites, including www.gamestop.com. The network also includes: www.kongregate.com, a browser-based game site; Game Informer magazine, a multi-platform video game publication; Spawn Labs, a streaming technology company; and a digital PC distribution platform available at www.gamestop.com/pcgames. As of Jan 28 2012, Co. operated 6,683 stores in the U.S., Australia, Canada and Europe.

Recent Developments: For the year ended Feb 2 2013, net loss amounted to US$269.8 million versus net income of US$338.5 million in the prior year. Revenues were US$8.89 billion, down 7.0% from US$9.55 billion the year before. Operating loss was US$41.6 million versus an income of US$569.9 million in the prior year. Direct operating expenses declined 9.3% to US$6.24 billion from US$6.87 billion in the comparable period the year before. Indirect operating expenses increased 27.7% to US$2.69 billion from US$2.11 billion in the equivalent prior-year period.

Prospects: Our evaluation of GameStop Corp. as of Apr. 7, 2013 is the result of our systematic analysis on three basic characteristics: earnings strength, relative valuation, and recent stock price movement. The company has managed to produce a neutral trend in earnings per share over the past 5 quarters. However, while recent estimates for the company have been lowered by analysts, GME has posted better than expected results. Based on operating earnings yield, the company is undervalued when compared to all of the companies in our coverage universe. Share price changes over the past year indicates that GME will perform very poorly over the near term.

Financial Data
(US$ in Thousands)

	02/02/2013	01/28/2012	01/29/2011	01/30/2010	01/31/2009	02/02/2008	02/03/2007	01/28/2006
Earnings Per Share	(2.13)	2.41	2.65	2.25	2.38	1.75	1.00	0.81
Cash Flow Per Share	4.92	4.48	3.91	3.93	3.37	3.19	2.78	2.52
Tang Book Value Per Share	6.34	5.95	4.43	3.26	1.16	2.86	N.M.	N.M.
Dividends Per Share	0.800	...	...	...	...	...	...	...
Income Statement								
Total Revenue	8,886,700	9,550,500	9,473,700	9,077,997	8,805,897	7,093,962	5,318,900	3,091,783
EBITDA	138,500	760,600	838,400	800,839	822,886	626,938	443,914	260,936
Depn & Amortn	180,100	191,700	181,800	169,129	150,098	138,108	116,294	68,204
Income Before Taxes	(44,900)	549,100	621,400	588,533	633,951	441,056	254,296	159,922
Income Taxes	224,900	210,600	214,600	212,804	235,669	152,765	96,046	59,138
Net Income	(269,700)	339,900	408,000	377,265	398,282	288,291	158,250	100,784
Average Shares	126,400	141,000	154,000	167,875	167,671	164,844	158,284	124,972
Balance Sheet								
Current Assets	2,010,900	1,997,300	2,154,800	2,127,304	1,818,041	1,794,717	1,440,341	1,121,265
Total Assets	4,133,600	4,847,400	5,063,800	4,955,527	4,512,590	3,775,891	3,349,584	3,015,119
Current Liabilities	1,715,300	1,633,900	1,747,800	1,655,676	1,562,711	1,260,557	1,087,057	887,674
Long-Term Obligations	...	...	249,000	447,343	545,712	574,473	843,723	963,463
Total Liabilities	1,847,300	1,805,300	2,166,500	2,232,170	2,212,909	1,913,445	1,973,706	1,900,406
Stockholders' Equity	2,286,300	3,042,100	2,897,300	2,723,157	2,299,681	1,862,446	1,375,878	1,114,713
Shares Outstanding	118,200	136,800	146,000	158,662	163,843	161,007	152,305	145,594
Statistical Record								
Return on Assets %	N.M.	6.88	8.17	7.99	9.64	8.11	4.89	5.14
Return on Equity %	N.M.	11.48	14.56	15.06	19.19	17.85	12.50	12.19
EBITDA Margin %	1.56	7.96	8.85	8.82	9.34	8.84	8.35	8.44
Net Margin %	N.M.	3.56	4.31	4.16	4.52	4.06	2.98	3.26
Asset Turnover	1.95	1.93	1.90	1.92	2.13	2.00	1.64	1.58
Current Ratio	1.17	1.22	1.23	1.28	1.16	1.42	1.32	1.26
Debt to Equity	...	...	0.09	0.16	0.24	0.31	0.61	0.86
Price Range	27.83-15.73	28.21-19.50	25.46-17.20	32.42-19.64	57.04-17.50	63.30-25.57	29.01-18.34	19.59-9.30
P/E Ratio	...	11.71-8.09	9.61-6.49	14.41-8.73	23.97-7.35	36.17-14.61	29.01-18.34	24.19-11.48
Average Yield %	3.69	...	...	...	...	...	...	...

Address: 625 Westport Parkway, Grapevine, TX 76051
Telephone: 817-424-2000

Web Site: www.gamestop.com
Officers: Daniel A. DeMatteo - Executive Chairman
Tony D. Bartel - President

Auditors: BDO USA, LLP
Investor Contact: 817-424-2000
Transfer Agents: Computershare Shareowner Services, Pittsburg, PA

GANNETT CO INC

Exchange	Symbol	Price	52Wk Range	Yield	P/E
NYS	GCI	$21.87 (3/28/2013)	22.07-12.33	3.66	12.22

*7 Year Price Score 60.50 *NYSE Composite Index=100 *12 Month Price Score 111.65

Interim Earnings (Per Share)

Qtr.	Mar	Jun	Sep	Dec
2008	0.84	(10.03)	0.69	(20.62)
2009	0.34	0.30	0.31	0.57
2010	0.49	0.81	0.42	0.71
2011	0.37	0.62	0.41	0.49
2012	0.28	0.51	0.56	0.44

Interim Dividends (Per Share)

Amt	Decl	Ex	Rec	Pay
0.20Q	05/01/2012	06/06/2012	06/08/2012	07/02/2012
0.20Q	07/23/2012	09/05/2012	09/07/2012	10/01/2012
0.20Q	10/23/2012	12/05/2012	12/07/2012	01/02/2013
0.20Q	02/26/2013	03/06/2013	03/08/2013	04/01/2013

Indicated Div: $0.80 (Div. Reinv. Plan)

Valuation Analysis

		Institutional Holding	
Forecast EPS	$2.22 (04/05/2013)	No of Institutions	558
Market Cap	$5.0 Billion	Shares	233,258,128
Book Value	$2.4 Billion	% Held	91.30
Price/Book	2.14		
Price/Sales	0.94		

TRADING VOLUME (thousand shares)

Business Summary: Publishing (MIC: 2.3.3 SIC: 2711 NAIC: 511110)

Gannett is an international media and marketing company operating primarily in the U.S. and the U.K. Co. has three segments: Publishing, Digital and Broadcasting (television). The Publishing Segment includes the operations of 99 daily publications in the U.S., U.K. and Guam, about 500 non-daily local publications in the U.S. and Guam and more than 200 such titles in the U.K. The Digital Segment includes Co.'s CareerBuilder, LLC, Point Roll, Inc., ShopLocal, Inc. and Reviewed.com subsidiaries. Through its Broadcasting Segment, Co. owns and operates 23 television stations with affiliated digital platforms sites.

Recent Developments: For the year ended Dec 30 2012, income from continuing operations decreased 5.0% to US$475.0 million from US$500.1 million a year earlier. Net income decreased 5.0% to US$475.0 million from US$500.1 million in the prior year. Revenues were US$5.35 billion, up 2.2% from US$5.24 billion the year before. Operating income was US$789.8 million versus US$830.8 million in the prior year, a decrease of 4.9%. Direct operating expenses declined 0.6% to US$2.94 billion from US$2.96 billion in the comparable period the year before. Indirect operating expenses increased 11.8% to US$1.62 billion from US$1.45 billion in the equivalent prior-year period.

Prospects: Our evaluation of Gannett Co Inc. as of Apr. 7, 2013 is the result of our systematic analysis on three basic characteristics: earnings strength, relative valuation, and recent stock price movement. The company has managed to produce a neutral trend in earnings per share over the past 5 quarters. However, while recent estimates for the company have been mixed, GCI has posted better than expected results. Based on operating earnings yield, the company is undervalued when compared to all of the companies in our coverage universe. Share price changes over the past year indicates that GCI will perform very well over the near term.

Financial Data

(US$ in Thousands)	12/30/2012	12/25/2011	12/26/2010	12/27/2009	12/28/2008	12/30/2007	12/31/2006	12/25/2005
Earnings Per Share	1.79	1.89	2.43	1.51	(29.11)	4.52	4.90	5.05
Cash Flow Per Share	3.20	3.41	3.25	3.72	4.47	5.79	6.16	5.86
Dividends Per Share	0.800	0.240	0.160	0.160	1.600	1.420	1.200	1.120
Dividend Payout %	44.69	12.70	6.58	10.60	...	31.42	24.49	22.18
Income Statement								
Total Revenue	5,353,197	5,239,989	5,438,678	5,612,993	6,767,650	7,439,460	8,033,354	7,598,939
EBITDA	992,528	1,015,243	1,214,490	990,791	(6,477,997)	1,942,713	2,279,475	2,298,734
Depn & Amortn	194,039	197,373	214,684	242,809	262,198	285,125	276,770	276,186
Income Before Taxes	648,020	644,730	826,820	572,234	(6,931,040)	1,408,184	1,719,482	1,817,855
Income Taxes	195,400	152,800	244,013	193,800	(658,400)	473,300	558,700	606,600
Net Income	424,280	458,748	588,201	355,270	(6,647,565)	1,055,612	1,160,782	1,244,654
Average Shares	236,690	242,768	241,605	236,027	228,345	233,740	236,756	246,256
Balance Sheet								
Current Assets	1,072,720	1,075,545	1,139,134	1,049,042	1,245,944	1,343,255	1,532,019	1,462,071
Total Assets	6,379,886	6,616,450	6,816,844	7,148,432	7,796,814	15,887,727	16,223,804	15,743,396
Current Liabilities	934,516	901,937	893,186	900,103	1,153,141	962,163	1,116,948	1,096,341
Long-Term Obligations	1,432,100	1,760,363	2,352,242	3,061,951	3,816,942	4,098,338	5,210,021	5,438,273
Total Liabilities	4,029,272	4,288,559	4,653,090	5,544,507	6,740,932	6,870,568	7,841,541	8,172,834
Stockholders' Equity	2,350,614	2,327,891	2,163,754	1,603,925	1,055,882	9,017,159	8,382,263	7,570,562
Shares Outstanding	230,042	237,036	239,509	237,156	228,123	230,202	234,743	238,045
Statistical Record								
Return on Assets %	6.42	6.85	8.45	4.77	N.M.	6.59	7.14	8.02
Return on Equity %	17.84	20.48	31.31	26.79	N.M.	12.17	14.32	15.86
EBITDA Margin %	18.54	19.37	22.33	17.65	N.M.	26.11	28.38	30.25
Net Margin %	7.93	8.75	10.82	6.33	N.M.	14.19	14.45	16.38
Asset Turnover	0.81	0.78	0.78	0.75	0.57	0.46	0.49	0.49
Current Ratio	1.15	1.19	1.28	1.17	1.08	1.40	1.37	1.33
Debt to Equity	0.61	0.76	1.09	1.91	3.61	0.45	0.62	0.72
Price Range	18.97-12.33	17.19-8.55	18.67-11.76	15.63-1.95	39.00-6.09	63.11-35.30	64.80-51.67	82.41-59.19
P/E Ratio	10.60-6.89	9.10-4.52	7.68-4.84	10.35-1.29	...	13.96-7.81	13.22-10.54	16.32-11.72
Average Yield %	5.19	1.09	1.09	2.29	7.20	2.77	2.08	1.53

Address: 7950 Jones Branch Drive, McLean, VA 22107-0910 Telephone: 703-854-6000	Web Site: www.gannett.com Officers: Marjorie Magner - Chairwoman Gracia C. Martore - President, Acting Chief Executive Officer, Chief Executive Officer, Chief Operating Officer, Chief Financial Officer	Auditors: Ernst & Young LLP Investor Contact: 703-854-6917 Transfer Agents: Wells Fargo Shareowner Services, St. Paul, MN

GARDNER DENVER, INC.

Exchange	Symbol	Price	52Wk Range	Yield	P/E
NYS	GDI	$75.11 (3/28/2013)	76.00-48.15	0.27	14.23

*7 Year Price Score 115.35 *NYSE Composite Index=100 *12 Month Price Score 102.87

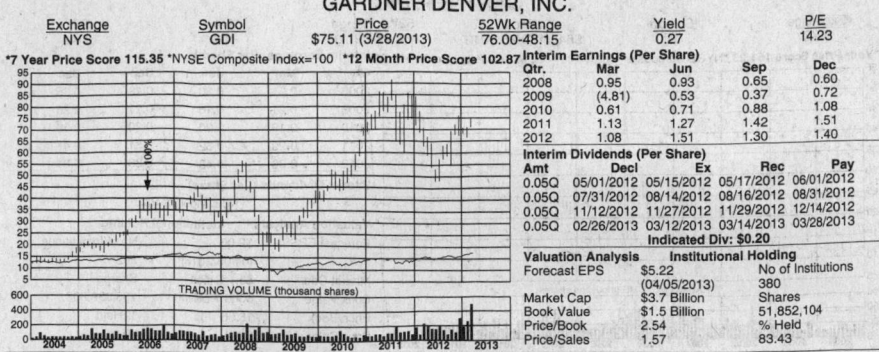

Interim Earnings (Per Share)

Qtr.	Mar	Jun	Sep	Dec
2008	0.95	0.93	0.65	0.60
2009	(4.81)	0.53	0.37	0.72
2010	0.61	0.71	0.88	1.08
2011	1.13	1.27	1.42	1.51
2012	1.08	1.51	1.30	1.40

Interim Dividends (Per Share)

Amt	Decl	Ex	Rec	Pay
0.05Q	05/01/2012	05/15/2012	05/17/2012	06/01/2012
0.05Q	07/31/2012	08/14/2012	08/16/2012	08/31/2012
0.05Q	11/12/2012	11/27/2012	11/29/2012	12/14/2012
0.05Q	02/26/2013	03/12/2013	03/14/2013	03/28/2013

Indicated Div: $0.20

Valuation Analysis | **Institutional Holding**

Forecast EPS	$5.22	No of Institutions
	(04/05/2013)	380
Market Cap	$3.7 Billion	Shares
Book Value	$1.5 Billion	51,852,104
Price/Book	2.54	% Held
Price/Sales	1.57	83.43

Business Summary: Industrial Machinery & Equipment (MIC: 7.2.1 SIC: 3561 NAIC: 333911)

Gardner Denver designs, manufactures and markets engineered industrial machinery and related parts and services. Co. is a manufacturer of compressors and vacuum products for industrial applications. Co. also designs, manufactures, markets, and services a group of pumps, water jetting systems and related aftermarket parts used in oil and natural gas well drilling, servicing and production and in industrial cleaning and maintenance. In addition, Co. manufactures loading arms, swivel joints, couplers and valves used to load and unload ships, tank trucks and rail cars. Co.'s divisional operations are combined into two product groups: Industrial Products Group and Engineered Products Group.

Recent Developments: For the year ended Dec 31 2012, net income decreased 5.4% to US$264.5 million from US$279.5 million in the prior year. Revenues were US$2.36 billion, down 0.6% from US$2.37 billion the year before. Operating income was US$372.7 million versus US$400.7 million in the prior year, a decrease of 7.0%. Direct operating expenses declined 0.8% to US$1.55 billion from US$1.56 billion in the comparable period the year before. Indirect operating expenses increased 6.0% to US$431.6 million from US$407.1 million in the equivalent prior-year period.

Prospects: Our evaluation of Gardner Denver Inc. as of Apr. 7, 2013 is the result of our systematic analysis on three basic characteristics: earnings strength, relative valuation, and recent stock price movement. The company has generated a negative trend in earnings per share over the past 5 quarters and while recent estimates for the company have been raised by analysts, GDI has posted better than expected results. Based on operating earnings yield, the company is undervalued when compared to all of the companies in our coverage universe. Share price changes over the past year indicates that GDI will perform in line with the market over the near term.

Financial Data
(US$ in Thousands)

	12/31/2012	12/31/2011	12/31/2010	12/31/2009	12/31/2008	12/31/2007	12/31/2006	12/31/2005
Earnings Per Share	5.28	5.33	3.28	(3.18)	3.12	3.80	2.49	1.37
Cash Flow Per Share	5.81	5.80	3.87	4.07	5.27	3.41	3.19	2.41
Tang Book Value Per Share	8.77	4.97	6.05	3.06	0.92	5.00	N.M.	N.M.
Dividends Per Share	0.200	0.200	0.200	0.050	...	...	...	...
Dividend Payout %	3.79	3.75	6.10	...	...	...	...	...
Income Statement								
Total Revenue	2,355,525	2,370,903	1,895,104	1,778,145	2,018,332	1,868,844	1,669,176	1,214,552
EBITDA	440,046	462,662	315,523	(41,178)	320,433	353,155	290,203	164,399
Depn & Amortn	63,778	60,284	60,248	68,731	61,484	58,584	52,209	38,322
Income Before Taxes	361,562	386,981	231,851	(138,394)	233,466	268,360	200,615	95,644
Income Taxes	97,069	107,439	56,897	24,905	67,485	63,256	67,707	28,693
Net Income	263,266	277,563	172,962	(165,185)	165,981	205,104	132,908	66,951
Average Shares	49,816	52,053	52,727	51,890	53,141	54,043	53,460	48,890
Balance Sheet								
Current Assets	1,105,377	1,015,734	828,537	718,511	857,564	701,528	579,718	586,267
Total Assets	2,490,192	2,365,568	2,027,098	1,939,048	2,340,125	1,905,607	1,750,231	1,715,060
Current Liabilities	762,481	505,754	359,600	323,530	397,382	312,202	326,344	313,844
Long-Term Obligations	9,727	326,133	250,682	330,935	506,700	263,987	383,459	542,641
Total Liabilities	1,038,577	1,088,277	849,935	886,878	1,141,377	745,894	897,701	1,056,771
Stockholders' Equity	1,451,615	1,277,291	1,177,163	1,052,170	1,198,748	1,159,713	852,530	658,289
Shares Outstanding	49,144	50,650	52,181	52,191	51,785	53,546	52,625	51,998
Statistical Record								
Return on Assets %	10.81	12.64	8.72	N.M.	7.80	11.22	7.67	4.88
Return on Equity %	19.24	22.62	15.52	N.M.	14.04	20.39	17.59	12.59
EBITDA Margin %	18.68	19.51	16.65	N.M.	15.88	18.90	17.39	13.54
Net Margin %	11.18	11.71	9.13	N.M.	8.22	10.97	7.96	5.51
Asset Turnover	0.97	1.08	0.96	0.83	0.95	1.02	0.96	0.89
Current Ratio	1.45	2.01	2.30	2.22	2.16	2.25	1.78	1.87
Debt to Equity	0.01	0.26	0.21	0.31	0.42	0.23	0.45	0.82
Price Range	84.24-48.15	91.50-59.76	70.87-38.93	43.56-17.66	56.80-18.04	45.80-30.55	40.25-24.30	25.72-16.52
P/E Ratio	15.95-9.12	17.17-11.21	21.61-11.87	...	18.21-5.78	12.05-8.04	16.16-9.76	18.77-12.06
Average Yield %	0.32	0.26	0.39	0.17	...	...	...	...

Address: 1500 Liberty Ridge Drive, Suite 3000, Wayne, PA 19087 **Telephone:** 610-249-2000	**Web Site:** www.gardnerdenver.com **Officers:** Frank J. Hansen - Chairman Michael M. Larsen - President, Interim Chief Executive Officer, Chief Executive Officer, Vice President, Chief Financial Officer	**Auditors:** KPMG **Investor Contact:** 610-249-2009 **Transfer Agents:** Wells Fargo Bank, N.A., South St. Paul, MN

GARTNER, INC.

Exchange	Symbol	Price	52Wk Range	Yield	P/E
NYS	IT	$54.41 (3/28/2013)	54.41-39.78	N/A	31.45

*7 Year Price Score 151.23 *NYSE Composite Index=100 *12 Month Price Score 101.29

Interim Earnings (Per Share)

Qtr.	Mar	Jun	Sep	Dec
2008	0.21	0.30	0.19	0.35
2009	0.21	0.18	0.21	0.26
2010	0.19	0.20	0.20	0.36
2011	0.29	0.32	0.31	0.47
2012	0.36	0.43	0.33	0.61

Interim Dividends (Per Share)

No Dividends Paid

Valuation Analysis

		Institutional Holding	
Forecast EPS	$2.06	No of Institutions	
	(04/05/2013)	302	
Market Cap	$5.1 Billion	Shares	
Book Value	$306.7 Million	135,999,808	
Price/Book	16.56	% Held	
Price/Sales	3.14	90.81	

Business Summary: IT Services (MIC: 6.3.1 SIC: 8741 NAIC: 561110)

Gartner is an information technology research and advisory company. Co. provides independent and objective research and analysis on the information technology, computer hardware, software, communications and related technology industries. Co. manages its business through three reportable segments: Research, Consulting and Events. The Research segment consists primarily of subscription-based research products, access to research inquiry, peer networking services, and membership programs. The Consulting segment consists primarily of consulting, measurement engagements, and advisory services. The Events segment consists of various symposia, conferences and exhibitions.

Recent Developments: For the year ended Dec 31 2012, net income increased 21.2% to US$165.9 million from US$136.9 million in the prior year. Revenues were US$1.62 billion, up 10.0% from US$1.47 billion the year before. Operating income was US$245.7 million versus US$214.1 million in the prior year, an increase of 14.8%. Direct operating expenses rose 8.3% to US$659.1 million from US$608.8 million in the comparable period the year before. Indirect operating expenses increased 10.1% to US$711.0 million from US$645.8 million in the equivalent prior-year period.

Prospects: Our evaluation of Gartner Inc. as of Apr. 7, 2013 is the result of our systematic analysis on three basic characteristics: earnings strength, relative valuation, and recent stock price movement. The company has managed to produce a neutral trend in earnings per share over the past 5 quarters and while recent estimates for the company have remained steady, IT has posted better than expected results. Based on operating earnings yield, the company is overvalued when compared to all of the companies in our coverage universe. Share price changes over the past year indicates that IT will perform in line with the market over the near term.

Financial Data
(US$ in Thousands)

	12/31/2012	12/31/2011	12/31/2010	12/31/2009	12/31/2008	12/31/2007	12/31/2006	12/31/2005
Earnings Per Share	1.73	1.39	0.96	0.85	1.05	0.68	0.50	(0.02)
Cash Flow Per Share	2.99	2.66	2.15	1.71	1.93	1.43	0.94	0.24
Income Statement								
Total Revenue	1,615,808	1,468,588	1,288,454	1,139,800	1,279,065	1,189,198	1,060,321	989,004
EBITDA	274,257	244,176	185,526	158,594	191,525	162,706	136,606	52,236
Depn & Amortn	29,802	32,025	35,825	27,036	27,515	26,391	34,153	35,726
Income Before Taxes	235,596	202,184	134,085	115,526	144,741	114,161	85,872	5,438
Income Taxes	69,693	65,282	37,800	32,562	47,598	40,608	27,680	7,875
Net Income	165,903	136,902	96,285	82,964	103,871	73,553	58,192	(2,437)
Average Shares	95,842	98,846	99,834	97,549	99,028	108,328	116,203	112,253
Balance Sheet								
Current Assets	927,466	705,785	621,102	557,825	554,524	557,790	484,033	462,119
Total Assets	1,621,277	1,379,872	1,285,658	1,215,279	1,093,065	1,133,210	1,039,793	1,026,617
Current Liabilities	1,070,000	921,137	811,152	898,173	792,409	876,012	803,883	642,768
Long-Term Obligations	115,000	150,000	180,000	124,000	238,500	157,500	150,000	180,000
Total Liabilities	1,314,604	1,198,088	1,098,602	1,102,744	1,114,381	1,115,712	1,013,475	880,029
Stockholders' Equity	306,673	181,784	187,056	112,535	(21,316)	17,498	26,318	146,588
Shares Outstanding	93,361	93,343	95,988	95,877	93,880	99,031	104,064	114,334
Statistical Record								
Return on Assets %	11.03	10.27	7.70	7.19	9.31	6.77	5.63	N.M.
Return on Equity %	67.74	74.23	64.28	181.90	...	335.74	67.31	N.M.
EBITDA Margin %	16.97	16.63	14.40	13.91	14.97	13.68	12.88	5.28
Net Margin %	10.27	9.32	7.47	7.28	8.12	6.19	5.49	N.M.
Asset Turnover	1.07	1.10	1.03	0.99	1.15	1.09	1.03	1.05
Current Ratio	0.87	0.77	0.77	0.62	0.70	0.64	0.60	0.72
Debt to Equity	0.37	0.83	0.96	1.10	...	9.00	5.70	1.23
Price Range	51.01-34.67	43.01-32.19	33.75-18.04	20.16-8.38	27.81-13.53	28.22-16.38	20.75-13.01	14.09-8.16
P/E Ratio	29.49-20.04	30.94-23.16	35.16-18.79	23.72-9.86	26.49-12.89	41.50-24.09	41.50-26.02	...

Address: P.O. Box 10212, 56 Top Gallant Road, Stamford, CT 06902-7700	Web Site: www.gartner.com	Auditors: KPMG LLP
Telephone: 203-316-1111	Officers: James C. Smith - Chairman Eugene A. Hall - Chief Executive Officer	Transfer Agents: Mellon Investor Services L.L.C., Ridgefield Park, NJ

GATX CORP.

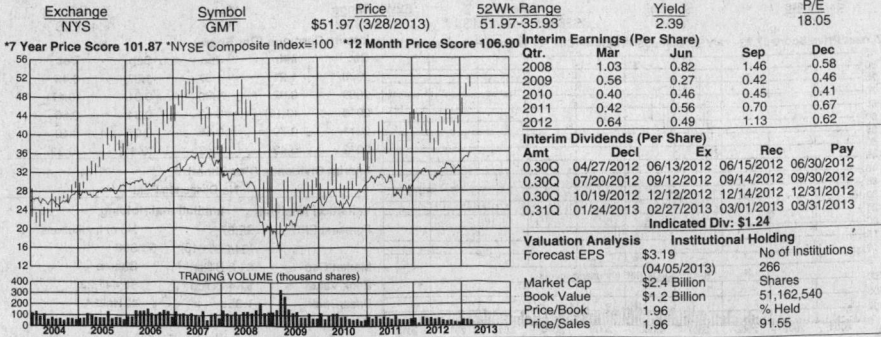

Exchange	Symbol	Price	52Wk Range	Yield	P/E
NYS	GMT	$51.97 (3/28/2013)	51.97-35.93	2.39	18.05

*7 Year Price Score 101.87 *NYSE Composite Index=100 *12 Month Price Score 106.90

Interim Earnings (Per Share)

Qtr.	Mar	Jun	Sep	Dec
2008	1.03	0.82	1.46	0.58
2009	0.56	0.27	0.42	0.46
2010	0.40	0.46	0.45	0.41
2011	0.42	0.56	0.70	0.67
2012	0.64	0.49	1.13	0.62

Interim Dividends (Per Share)

Amt	Decl	Ex	Rec	Pay
0.30Q	04/27/2012	06/13/2012	06/15/2012	06/30/2012
0.30Q	07/20/2012	09/12/2012	09/14/2012	09/30/2012
0.30Q	10/19/2012	12/12/2012	12/14/2012	12/31/2012
0.31Q	01/24/2013	02/27/2013	03/01/2013	03/31/2013

Indicated Div: $1.24

Valuation Analysis / **Institutional Holding**

Forecast EPS	$3.19	No of Institutions
	(04/05/2013)	266
Market Cap	$2.4 Billion	Shares
Book Value	$1.2 Billion	51,162,540
Price/Book	1.96	% Held
Price/Sales	1.96	91.55

TRADING VOLUME (thousand shares)

Business Summary: Rail (MIC: 7.4.3 SIC: 4741 NAIC: 488210)

GATX is engaged in leasing, operating and managing assets primarily in the rail and marine markets. As of Dec 31 2011, Co. had three financial reporting segments: Rail, which is principally engaged in leasing tank and freight railcars and locomotives in North America and Europe; American Steamship Company, which owns and operates a fleet of U.S. flagged vessels on the Great Lakes, providing waterborne transportation of dry bulk commodities for a range of industrial customers; and Portfolio Management, which provides leasing, asset remarketing and asset management services to the marine and industrial equipment markets.

Recent Developments: For the year ended Dec 31 2012, net income increased 23.9% to US$137.3 million from US$110.8 million in the prior year. Revenues were US$1.24 billion, up 4.3% from US$1.19 billion the year before. Indirect operating expenses increased 2.0% to US$1.00 billion from US$984.8 million in the equivalent prior-year period.

Prospects: Our evaluation of GATX Corp. as of Apr. 7, 2013 is the result of our systematic analysis on three basic characteristics: earnings strength, relative valuation, and recent stock price movement. The company has generated a negative trend in earnings per share over the past 5 quarters and while recent estimates for the company have remained steady, GMT has posted better than expected results. Based on operating earnings yield, the company is about fairly valued when compared to all of the companies in our coverage universe. Share price changes over the past year indicates that GMT will perform in line with the market over the near term.

Financial Data
(US$ in Thousands)

	12/31/2012	12/31/2011	12/31/2010	12/31/2009	12/31/2008	12/31/2007	12/31/2006	12/31/2005
Earnings Per Share	2.88	2.35	1.72	1.70	3.89	3.76	2.00	(0.29)
Cash Flow Per Share	7.89	6.61	5.25	5.70	7.63	6.81	5.75	5.68
Tang Book Value Per Share	24.57	22.22	22.02	21.80	21.12	21.82	20.58	18.50
Dividends Per Share	1.200	1.160	1.120	1.120	1.080	0.960	0.840	0.800
Dividend Payout %	41.67	49.36	65.12	65.88	27.76	25.53	42.00	...
Income Statement								
Total Revenue	1,243,200	1,308,500	1,204,900	1,153,900	1,443,100	1,346,000	1,229,100	1,134,600
EBITDA	559,800	386,700	325,500	335,200	488,800	450,000	399,800	184,900
Depn & Amortn	249,400	238,500	228,100	227,300	219,200	191,400	173,700	212,700
Income Before Taxes	143,800	148,200	97,400	107,900	269,600	258,600	226,100	(27,800)
Income Taxes	26,100	37,400	16,600	26,500	73,600	72,800	75,600	(12,700)
Net Income	137,300	110,800	80,800	81,400	196,000	203,700	111,700	(14,300)
Average Shares	47,600	47,200	47,000	48,800	51,000	55,400	62,101	50,106
Balance Sheet								
Current Assets	620,600	713,800	542,300	439,900	540,900	572,600	775,700	608,400
Total Assets	6,055,400	5,857,500	5,442,400	5,206,400	5,191,500	4,725,600	4,644,000	5,244,400
Current Liabilities	451,000	164,200	230,200	193,800	271,700	366,900	182,000	234,400
Long-Term Obligations	3,294,300	3,518,500	3,060,900	2,842,000	2,684,200	2,112,400	2,192,300	2,815,600
Total Liabilities	4,811,200	4,730,200	4,328,700	4,103,800	4,066,900	3,576,100	3,481,000	4,222,100
Stockholders' Equity	1,244,200	1,127,300	1,113,700	1,102,600	1,124,600	1,149,500	1,163,000	1,022,300
Shares Outstanding	46,898	46,653	46,360	46,101	48,725	47,899	51,997	50,618
Statistical Record								
Return on Assets %	2.30	1.96	1.52	1.57	3.94	4.35	2.26	N.M.
Return on Equity %	11.55	9.89	7.29	7.31	17.19	17.62	10.22	N.M.
EBITDA Margin %	45.03	29.55	27.01	29.05	33.87	33.43	32.53	16.30
Net Margin %	11.04	8.47	6.71	7.05	13.58	15.13	9.09	N.M.
Asset Turnover	0.21	0.23	0.23	0.22	0.29	0.29	0.25	0.21
Current Ratio	1.38	4.35	2.36	2.27	1.99	1.56	4.26	2.60
Debt to Equity	2.65	3.12	2.75	2.58	2.39	1.84	1.89	2.75
Price Range	44.90-35.93	44.33-29.70	36.77-25.94	32.90-13.87	51.50-21.89	52.25-34.80	48.15-35.99	41.52-26.34
P/E Ratio	15.59-12.48	18.86-12.64	21.38-15.08	19.35-8.16	13.24-5.63	13.90-9.26	24.07-18.00	...
Average Yield %	2.88	3.14	3.76	4.32	2.83	2.13	2.03	2.30

Address: 222 West Adams Street, Chicago, IL 60606-5314 **Telephone:** 312-621-6200	**Web Site:** www.gatx.com **Officers:** Brian A. Kenney - Chairman, President, Chief Executive Officer James F. Earl - Executive Vice President, Chief Operating Officer	**Auditors:** Ernst & Young LLP **Investor Contact:** 312-621-6262 **Transfer Agents:** Computershare Shareowner Services LLC, Jersey City, NJ

GENERAL CABLE CORP. (DE)

Exchange	Symbol	Price	52Wk Range	Yield	P/E
NYS	BGC	$36.63 (3/28/2013)	36.63-23.92	N/A	457.88

*7 Year Price Score 67.73 *NYSE Composite Index=100 *12 Month Price Score 105.96

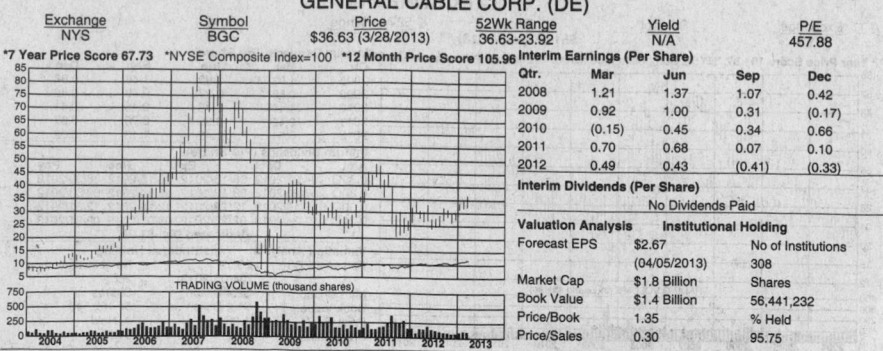

Interim Earnings (Per Share)

Qtr.	Mar	Jun	Sep	Dec
2008	1.21	1.37	1.07	0.42
2009	0.92	1.00	0.31	(0.17)
2010	(0.15)	0.45	0.34	0.66
2011	0.70	0.68	0.07	0.10
2012	0.49	0.43	(0.41)	(0.33)

Interim Dividends (Per Share)

No Dividends Paid

Valuation Analysis		Institutional Holding	
Forecast EPS	$2.67	No of Institutions	
	(04/05/2013)	308	
Market Cap	$1.8 Billion	Shares	
Book Value	$1.4 Billion	56,441,232	
Price/Book	1.35	% Held	
Price/Sales	0.30	95.75	

Business Summary: Electrical Equipment (MIC: 7.3.1 SIC: 3357 NAIC: 335929)

General Cable is engaged in the development, design, manufacture, marketing and distribution of copper, aluminum and fiber optic wire and cable products for use in the energy, industrial, construction, specialty and communications markets. Co. additionally engages in the design, integration, and installation on a turn-key basis for products such as high and extra-high voltage terrestrial and submarine systems. Co.'s three segments include North America, Europe and Mediterranean, and Rest of World. Co.'s product categories consist of electric utility, electrical infrastructure, communications, construction, and red mill.

Recent Developments: For the year ended Dec 31 2012, net income decreased 85.4% to US$9.8 million from US$67.1 million in the prior year. Revenues were US$6.01 billion, up 2.5% from US$5.87 billion the year before. Operating income was US$194.8 million versus US$230.1 million in the prior year, a decrease of 15.3%. Direct operating expenses rose 2.7% to US$5.40 billion from US$5.26 billion in the comparable period the year before. Indirect operating expenses increased 11.1% to US$419.4 million from US$377.6 million in the equivalent prior-year period.

Prospects: Our evaluation of General Cable Corp. as of Apr. 7, 2013 is the result of our systematic analysis on three basic characteristics: earnings strength, relative valuation, and recent stock price movement. The company has generated a negative trend in earnings per share over the past 5 quarters. However, while recent estimates for the company have been mixed, BGC has posted better than expected results. Based on operating earnings yield, the company is about fairly valued when compared to all of the companies in our coverage universe. Share price changes over the past year indicates that BGC will perform in line with the market over the near term.

Financial Data
(US$ in Thousands)

	12/31/2012	12/31/2011	12/31/2010	12/31/2009	12/31/2008	12/31/2007	12/31/2006	12/31/2005
Earnings Per Share	0.08	1.57	1.31	2.06	4.07	3.82	2.60	0.41
Cash Flow Per Share	5.79	1.87	1.90	10.51	4.38	4.53	1.88	2.94
Tang Book Value Per Share	19.36	21.09	21.18	17.52	6.39	5.60	8.26	5.79
Income Statement								
Total Revenue	6,014,300	5,866,700	4,864,900	4,385,200	6,230,100	4,614,800	3,665,100	2,380,800
EBITDA	284,800	313,700	279,100	341,900	469,700	393,200	281,300	145,500
Depn & Amortn	102,200	97,400	84,800	84,800	75,500	55,800	45,500	47,500
Income Before Taxes	82,300	124,800	122,700	174,100	338,400	307,800	200,200	61,000
Income Taxes	74,200	42,500	47,200	58,400	112,700	99,400	64,900	21,800
Net Income	9,800	85,200	76,900	116,600	217,200	208,600	135,300	39,200
Average Shares	51,100	53,700	53,100	52,800	53,400	54,600	52,000	41,900
Balance Sheet								
Current Assets	3,234,600	2,887,100	2,805,700	2,462,700	2,477,700	2,577,600	1,734,300	1,069,500
Total Assets	4,919,900	4,370,400	4,327,700	3,924,100	3,840,400	3,798,000	2,218,700	1,523,200
Current Liabilities	1,977,600	1,522,800	1,420,200	1,182,100	1,411,000	1,865,500	995,200	690,900
Long-Term Obligations	938,900	892,600	864,500	869,300	1,216,100	897,900	685,100	445,200
Total Liabilities	3,566,600	2,971,800	2,845,700	2,653,900	3,132,000	3,146,700	1,784,300	1,229,900
Stockholders' Equity	1,353,300	1,398,600	1,482,000	1,270,200	708,400	651,300	434,400	293,300
Shares Outstanding	49,693	49,697	52,116	52,008	51,775	52,430	52,002	49,520
Statistical Record								
Return on Assets %	0.21	1.96	1.86	3.00	5.67	6.93	7.23	2.86
Return on Equity %	0.71	5.92	5.59	11.79	31.86	38.43	37.19	13.18
EBITDA Margin %	4.74	5.35	5.74	7.80	7.54	8.52	7.68	6.11
Net Margin %	0.16	1.45	1.58	2.66	3.49	4.52	3.69	1.65
Asset Turnover	1.29	1.35	1.18	1.13	1.63	1.53	1.96	1.74
Current Ratio	1.64	1.90	1.98	2.08	1.76	1.38	1.74	1.55
Debt to Equity	0.69	0.64	0.58	0.68	1.72	1.38	1.58	1.52
Price Range	34.54-23.92	48.54-20.89	35.64-21.80	42.50-13.65	73.28-7.62	83.90-42.36	45.10-19.90	20.66-11.14
P/E Ratio	431.75-299.00	30.92-13.31	27.21-16.64	20.63-6.63	18.00-1.87	21.96-11.09	17.35-7.65	50.39-27.17

Address: 4 Tessneer Drive, Highland Heights, KY 41076-9753
Telephone: 859-572-8000
Fax: 859-572-8458

Web Site: www.generalcable.com
Officers: Gregory B. Kenny - President, Chief Executive Officer Emmanuel Sabonnadiere - Executive Vice President, Region Officer

Auditors: Deloitte & Touche LLP
Investor Contact: 859-572-8373
Transfer Agents: Computershare Investor Services, Canton, MA

GENERAL DYNAMICS CORP.

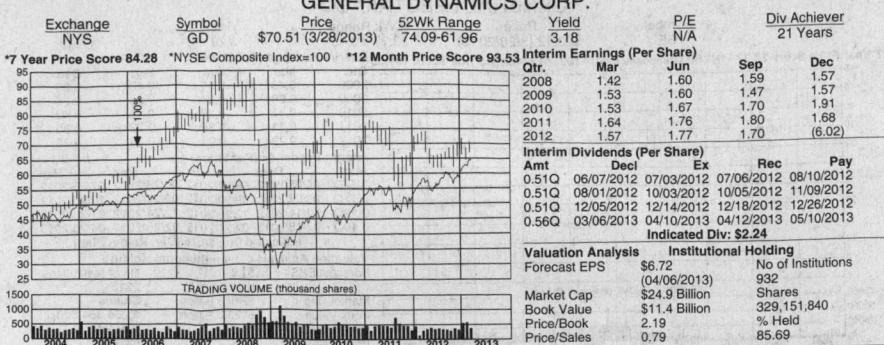

Exchange	Symbol	Price	52Wk Range	Yield	P/E	Div Achiever
NYS	GD	$70.51 (3/28/2013)	74.09-61.96	3.18	N/A	21 Years

*7 Year Price Score 84.28   *NYSE Composite Index=100   *12 Month Price Score 93.53

Interim Earnings (Per Share)

Qtr.	Mar	Jun	Sep	Dec
2008	1.42	1.60	1.59	1.57
2009	1.53	1.60	1.47	1.57
2010	1.53	1.67	1.70	1.91
2011	1.64	1.76	1.80	1.68
2012	1.57	1.77	1.70	(6.02)

Interim Dividends (Per Share)

Amt	Decl	Ex	Rec	Pay
0.51Q	06/07/2012	07/03/2012	07/06/2012	08/10/2012
0.51Q	08/01/2012	10/03/2012	10/05/2012	11/09/2012
0.51Q	12/05/2012	12/14/2012	12/18/2012	12/26/2012
0.56Q	03/06/2013	04/10/2013	04/12/2013	05/10/2013

Indicated Div: $2.24

Valuation Analysis / **Institutional Holding**

Forecast EPS	$6.72	No of Institutions
	(04/06/2013)	932
Market Cap	$24.9 Billion	Shares
Book Value	$11.4 Billion	329,151,840
Price/Book	2.19	% Held
Price/Sales	0.79	85.69

Business Summary: Aerospace (MIC: 7.1.1 SIC: 3721 NAIC: 336411)

General Dynamics is an aerospace and defense company. Co. has four business groups: Aerospace, which produces Gulfstream aircraft, provides aircraft services and performs aircraft completions for other original equipment manufacturers; Combat Systems, which designs and manufactures combat vehicles, weapons systems and munitions; Marine Systems, which designs, constructs and repairs surface ships and submarines; and Information Systems and Technology, which provides communications and information technology products and services. Co.'s key customer is the U.S. government. Co. also has business with international governments and a base of corporate and individual buyers of business aircraft.

Recent Developments: For the year ended Dec 31 2012, loss from continuing operations was US$332.0 million compared with income of US$2.55 billion a year earlier. Net loss amounted to US$332.0 million versus net income of US$2.53 billion in the prior year. Revenues were US$31.51 billion, down 3.6% from US$32.68 billion the year before. Operating income was US$833.0 million versus US$3.83 billion in the prior year, a decrease of 78.2%. Direct operating expenses declined 1.5% to US$26.41 billion from US$26.82 billion in the comparable period the year before. Indirect operating expenses increased 110.3% to US$4.27 billion from US$2.03 billion in the equivalent prior-year period.

Prospects: Our evaluation of General Dynamics Corp. as of Apr. 7, 2013 is the result of our systematic analysis on three basic characteristics: earnings strength, relative valuation, and recent stock price movement. The company has produced a positive trend in earnings per share over the past 5 quarters. However, while recent estimates for the company have been lowered by analysts, GD has posted results that fell short of analysts expectations. Based on operating earnings yield, the company is undervalued when compared to all of the companies in our coverage universe. Share price changes over the past year indicates that GD will perform poorly over the near term.

Financial Data

(US$ in Millions)	12/31/2012	12/31/2011	12/31/2010	12/31/2009	12/31/2008	12/31/2007	12/31/2006	12/31/2005
Earnings Per Share	(0.94)	6.87	6.81	6.17	6.17	5.08	4.56	3.61
Cash Flow Per Share	7.58	8.89	7.83	7.41	7.83	7.23	5.27	5.12
Tang Book Value Per Share	N.M.	N.M.	N.M.	N.M.	N.M.	4.59	0.25	1.40
Dividends Per Share	2.510	1.830	1.640	1.490	1.340	1.100	0.890	0.780
Dividend Payout %	...	26.64	24.08	24.15	21.72	21.65	19.52	21.61
Income Statement								
Total Revenue	31,513	32,677	32,466	31,981	29,300	27,240	24,063	21,244
EBITDA	1,317	4,451	4,516	4,235	4,263	3,685	3,145	2,319
Depn & Amortn	620	592	569	562	593	568	517	101
Income Before Taxes	541	3,718	3,790	3,513	3,604	3,047	2,527	2,100
Income Taxes	873	1,166	1,162	1,106	1,126	967	817	632
Net Income	(332)	2,526	2,624	2,394	2,459	2,072	1,856	1,461
Average Shares	353	367	385	387	398	408	406	404
Balance Sheet								
Current Assets	15,744	15,368	14,186	13,249	11,950	12,298	9,880	9,173
Total Assets	34,309	34,883	32,545	31,077	28,373	25,733	22,376	19,591
Current Liabilities	11,620	11,145	11,177	10,371	10,360	9,164	7,824	6,907
Long-Term Obligations	3,908	3,907	2,430	3,159	3,113	2,118	2,774	2,781
Total Liabilities	22,919	21,651	19,229	18,654	18,320	13,965	12,549	11,446
Stockholders' Equity	11,390	13,232	13,316	12,423	10,053	11,768	9,827	8,145
Shares Outstanding	353	356	372	385	386	403	405	400
Statistical Record								
Return on Assets %	N.M.	7.49	8.25	8.05	9.06	8.61	8.85	7.87
Return on Equity %	N.M.	19.03	20.39	21.30	22.48	19.19	20.65	19.06
EBITDA Margin %	4.18	13.62	13.91	13.24	14.55	13.53	13.07	10.92
Net Margin %	N.M.	7.73	8.08	7.49	8.39	7.61	7.71	6.88
Asset Turnover	0.91	0.97	1.02	1.08	1.08	1.13	1.15	1.14
Current Ratio	1.35	1.38	1.27	1.28	1.15	1.34	1.26	1.33
Debt to Equity	0.34	0.30	0.18	0.25	0.31	0.18	0.28	0.34
Price Range	74.09-61.96	78.11-55.67	78.67-55.87	70.66-36.31	94.60-48.54	94.00-73.95	77.69-56.80	60.53-49.38
P/E Ratio	...	11.37-8.10	11.55-8.20	11.45-5.88	15.33-7.87	18.50-14.56	17.04-12.46	16.77-13.68
Average Yield %	3.74	2.66	2.43	2.62	1.70	1.35	1.33	1.41

Address: 2941 Fairview Park Drive, Suite 100, Falls Church, VA 22042-4513 Telephone: 703-876-3000	Web Site: www.generaldynamics.com Officers: Phebe N. Novakovic - President, Chief Executive Officer, Chief Operating Officer, Executive Vice President, Senior Vice President John P. Casey - Executive Vice President, Vice President	Auditors: KPMG LLP Investor Contact: 703-876-3748 Transfer Agents: Computershare Trust Company N.A., Providence, RI

GENERAL ELECTRIC CO

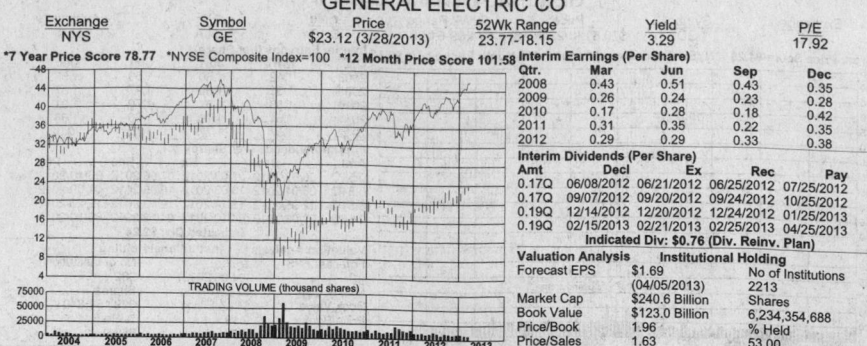

Exchange	Symbol	Price	52Wk Range	Yield	P/E
NYS	GE	$23.12 (3/28/2013)	23.77-18.15	3.29	17.92

*7 Year Price Score 78.77 ***NYSE Composite Index=100** ***12 Month Price Score 101.58**

Interim Earnings (Per Share)

Qtr.	Mar	Jun	Sep	Dec
2008	0.43	0.51	0.43	0.35
2009	0.26	0.24	0.23	0.28
2010	0.17	0.28	0.18	0.42
2011	0.31	0.35	0.22	0.35
2012	0.29	0.29	0.33	0.38

Interim Dividends (Per Share)

Amt	Decl	Ex	Rec	Pay
0.17Q	06/08/2012	06/21/2012	06/25/2012	07/25/2012
0.17Q	09/07/2012	09/20/2012	09/24/2012	10/25/2012
0.19Q	12/14/2012	12/20/2012	12/24/2012	01/25/2013
0.19Q	02/15/2013	02/21/2013	02/25/2013	04/25/2013

Indicated Div: $0.76 (Div. Reinv. Plan)

Valuation Analysis

		Institutional Holding	
Forecast EPS	$1.69	No of Institutions	
	(04/05/2013)	2213	
Market Cap	$240.6 Billion	Shares	
Book Value	$123.0 Billion	6,234,354,688	
Price/Book	1.96	% Held	
Price/Sales	1.63	53.00	

Business Summary: Electrical Equipment (MIC: 7.3.1 SIC: 3699 NAIC: 335999)

General Electric is an infrastructure and financial services corporation. Co.'s segments include: Power & Water, which is engaged in the field of development, implementation and improvement of products and technologies that harness resources; Oil & Gas, which helps oil and gas companies make use of energy resources; Energy Management, which provides integrated electrical products and systems used to distribute, protect and control energy and equipment; Aviation, which is a provider of jet engines and related services; Home & Business Solutions, which sells and services home appliances; and GE Capital, which provides a range of financial services and products, among others.

Recent Developments: For the year ended Dec 31 2012, income from continuing operations increased 2.6% to US$14.90 billion from US$14.52 billion a year earlier. Net income decreased 4.0% to US$13.86 billion from US$14.44 billion in the prior year. Revenues were US$147.36 billion, up 0.0% from US$147.29 billion the year before. Direct operating expenses rose 7.9% to US$81.06 billion from US$75.14 billion in the comparable period the year before. Indirect operating expenses decreased 2.6% to US$36.39 billion from US$37.36 billion in the equivalent prior-year period.

Prospects: Our evaluation of General Electric Co as of Apr. 7, 2013 is the result of our systematic analysis on three basic characteristics: earnings strength, relative valuation, and recent stock price movement. The company has enjoyed a very positive trend in earnings per share over the past 5 quarters. However, while recent estimates for the company have been mixed, GE has posted better than expected results. Based on operating earnings yield, the company is undervalued when compared to all of the companies in our coverage universe. Share price changes over the past year indicates that GE will perform well over the near term.

Financial Data
(US$ in Millions)

	12/31/2012	12/31/2011	12/31/2010	12/31/2009	12/31/2008	12/31/2007	12/31/2006	12/31/2005
Earnings Per Share	1.29	1.23	1.06	1.01	1.72	2.17	2.00	1.54
Cash Flow Per Share	2.97	3.15	3.39	2.32	4.81	4.51	2.96	3.56
Tang Book Value Per Share	3.61	3.00	4.19	3.73	0.75	1.83	2.52	2.64
Dividends Per Share	0.700	0.610	0.460	0.610	1.240	1.150	1.030	0.910
Dividend Payout %	54.26	49.59	43.40	60.40	72.09	53.00	51.50	59.09
Income Statement								
Total Revenue	147,359	147,300	150,211	156,783	182,515	172,738	163,391	149,702
EBITDA	31,529	36,375	31,940	31,213	48,082	53,190	46,603	39,715
Depn & Amortn	1,615	1,732	1,749	2,100	2,091	1,889	1,789	1,413
Income Before Taxes	17,406	20,098	14,208	10,344	19,782	27,514	25,528	23,115
Income Taxes	2,504	5,732	1,050	(1,090)	1,052	4,130	3,954	3,854
Net Income	13,641	14,151	11,644	11,025	17,410	22,208	20,829	16,353
Average Shares	10,564	10,620	10,678	10,615	10,098	10,218	10,394	10,611
Balance Sheet								
Current Assets	162,740	165,198	153,043	152,646	124,718	96,331	87,456	87,480
Total Assets	685,328	717,242	751,216	781,818	797,769	795,337	697,239	673,342
Current Liabilities	221,403	253,379	224,075	218,399	248,610	246,113	220,514	204,927
Long-Term Obligations	236,084	243,459	293,323	338,215	330,067	319,015	260,804	212,281
Total Liabilities	562,302	600,804	632,280	664,527	693,104	679,778	584,925	563,988
Stockholders' Equity	123,026	116,438	118,936	117,291	104,665	115,559	112,314	109,354
Shares Outstanding	10,405	10,573	10,615	10,663	10,536	9,987	10,277	10,484
Statistical Record								
Return on Assets %	1.94	1.93	1.52	1.40	2.18	2.98	3.04	2.30
Return on Equity %	11.36	12.02	9.86	9.93	15.77	19.49	18.79	14.89
EBITDA Margin %	21.40	24.69	21.26	19.91	26.34	30.79	28.52	26.53
Net Margin %	9.26	9.61	7.75	7.03	9.54	12.86	12.75	10.92
Asset Turnover	0.21	0.20	0.20	0.20	0.23	0.23	0.24	0.21
Current Ratio	0.74	0.65	0.68	0.70	0.50	0.39	0.40	0.43
Debt to Equity	1.92	2.09	2.47	2.88	3.15	2.76	2.32	1.94
Price Range	23.12-18.15	21.52-14.69	19.50-13.88	17.07-6.66	38.43-12.84	42.12-34.09	38.15-32.11	37.18-32.68
P/E Ratio	17.92-14.07	17.50-11.94	18.40-13.09	16.90-6.59	22.34-7.47	19.41-15.71	19.07-16.06	24.14-21.22
Average Yield %	3.46	3.36	2.78	4.56	4.43	3.04	3.00	2.58

Address: 3135 Easton Turnpike, Fairfield, CT 06828-0001 **Telephone:** 203-373-2211 **Fax:** 203-373-3131	**Web Site:** www.ge.com **Officers:** Jeffrey R. Immelt - Chairman, President, Chief Executive Officer Michael A. Neal - Vice-Chairman, Division Officer	**Auditors:** KPMG LLP **Investor Contact:** 203-373-2460 **Transfer Agents:** The Bank of New York Mellon Corporation

GENERAL GROWTH PROPERTIES INC

Exchange	Symbol	Price	52Wk Range	Yield	P/E
NYS	GGP	$19.88 (3/28/2013)	20.99-15.96	2.41	N/A

*7 Year Price Score 69.49   *NYSE Composite Index=100   *12 Month Price Score 96.83

TRADING VOLUME (thousand shares)

Interim Earnings (Per Share)

Qtr.	Mar	Jun	Sep	Dec
2011	0.00	(0.22)	(0.08)	(0.10)
2012	(0.21)	(0.12)	(0.23)	0.03

Interim Dividends (Per Share)

Amt	Decl	Ex	Rec	Pay
0.10Q	05/01/2012	07/12/2012	07/16/2012	07/30/2012
0.11Q	08/01/2012	10/11/2012	10/15/2012	10/29/2012
0.11Q	11/26/2012	12/12/2012	12/14/2012	01/04/2013
0.12Q	02/04/2013	04/12/2013	04/16/2013	04/30/2013

Indicated Div: $0.48 (Div. Reinv. Plan)

Valuation Analysis

Forecast EPS	$0.31
	(04/06/2013)
Market Cap	$18.7 Billion
Book Value	$7.6 Billion
Price/Book	2.45
Price/Sales	7.43

Institutional Holding

No of Institutions	N/A
Shares	N/A
% Held	N/A

Business Summary: REITs (MIC: 5.3.1 SIC: 6798 NAIC: 525930)

General Growth Properties is a self-administered and self-managed real estate investment trust. Co. is a real estate owner and operator of regional malls with an ownership interest in 136 regional malls in 41 states as of Dec 31 2011. Co., through its subsidiaries and affiliates, operates, manages, develops and acquires retail and other rental properties, primarily regional malls, which are primarily located throughout the U.S. Substantially all of Co.'s business is conducted through GGP Limited Partnership (Operating Partnership), in which Co. holds approximately a 99% common equity ownership of the Operating Partnership.

Recent Developments: For the year ended Dec 31 2012, loss from continuing operations was US$494.6 million compared with a loss of US$206.2 million a year earlier. Net loss amounted to US$471.5 million versus a net loss of US$306.8 million in the prior year. Revenues were US$2.51 billion, up 2.7% from US$2.44 billion the year before. Revenues from property income rose 2.4% to US$2.36 billion from US$2.31 billion in the corresponding earlier year.

Prospects: Our evaluation of General Growth Properties Inc. as of Apr. 7, 2013 is the result of our systematic analysis on three basic characteristics: earnings strength, relative valuation, and recent stock price movement. The company has produced a positive trend in earnings per share over the past 5 quarters. Because the company lacks sufficient analyst estimate data, we place greater weight on the historical EPS trend as the measure of earnings strength. Based on operating earnings yield, the company is overvalued when compared to all of the companies in our coverage universe. Share price changes over the past year indicates that GGP will perform in line with the market over the near term.

Financial Data

(US$ in Thousands)	12/31/2012	12/31/2011	12/31/2010	11/09/2010	12/31/2009	12/31/2008	12/31/2007	12/31/2006
Earnings Per Share	(0.52)	(0.37)	(0.27)	(3.74)	(4.11)	0.10	1.18	0.24
Cash Flow Per Share	0.86	0.53	(0.38)	0.15	2.79	2.12	2.90	3.38
Tang Book Value Per Share	6.99	7.50	8.70	...	0.88	3.87	2.63	5.34
Dividends Per Share	0.420	0.400	0.380	...	0.190	1.500	1.850	1.680
Dividend Payout %	...	...	...	...	...	1,500.00	156.78	700.00
Income Statement								
Total Revenue	2,511,850	2,742,942	416,542	2,406,944	3,135,814	3,361,525	3,261,801	3,256,283
EBITDA	350,236	1,734,610	34,644	1,478,671	546,682	1,935,402	1,692,789	1,858,543
Depn & Amortn	105,871	1,086,639	153,797	569,307	708,016	706,831	614,928	670,091
Income Before Taxes	(563,805)	(308,177)	(257,560)	(338,556)	(1,469,296)	(67,728)	(87,595)	82,600
Income Taxes	9,091	9,256	(8,929)	(60,573)	(14,610)	23,461	(294,160)	98,984
Net Income	(481,233)	(313,172)	(254,216)	(1,185,758)	(1,284,689)	26,260	287,954	59,273
Average Shares	938,049	981,136	945,248	316,918	311,993	262,195	244,538	242,054
Balance Sheet								
Current Assets	885,675	791,327	1,135,410	...	1,058,437	554,327	487,812	440,981
Total Assets	27,282,405	29,518,151	32,367,379	...	28,149,774	29,557,330	28,814,319	25,241,445
Current Liabilities	1,170,509	1,882,067	1,846,169	...	1,513,271	1,065,430	1,145,827	961,692
Long-Term Obligations	16,186,356	17,335,706	18,047,957	...	7,300,772	24,853,313	24,282,139	20,521,967
Total Liabilities	19,660,707	21,034,822	22,288,277	...	27,326,811	27,802,582	27,357,623	23,577,366
Stockholders' Equity	7,621,698	8,483,329	10,079,102	...	822,963	1,754,748	1,456,696	1,664,079
Shares Outstanding	939,049	935,307	941,880	...	312,381	268,903	243,898	242,066
Statistical Record								
Return on Assets %	N.M.	N.M.	N.M.	...	N.M.	0.09	1.07	0.23
Return on Equity %	N.M.	N.M.	N.M.	...	N.M.	1.63	18.45	3.30
EBITDA Margin %	13.94	63.24	8.32	61.43	17.43	57.58	51.90	57.08
Net Margin %	N.M.	N.M.	N.M.	N.M.	N.M.	0.78	8.83	1.82
Asset Turnover	0.09	0.09	0.01	...	0.11	0.11	0.12	0.13
Current Ratio	0.76	0.42	0.62	...	0.70	0.52	0.43	0.46
Debt to Equity	2.12	2.04	1.79	...	8.87	14.16	16.67	12.33
Price Range	20.99-14.36	16.90-11.01	16.91-13.91	17.30-8.69	12.64-0.32	42.61-0.34	65.13-39.42	54.15-41.18
P/E Ratio	...	...	...	...	...	426.08-3.40	55.20-33.41	225.61-171.58
Average Yield %	2.34	2.78	2.52	...	6.67	5.90	3.45	3.60

Address: 110 N. Wacker Dr., Chicago, IL 60606 **Telephone:** 312-960-5000	**Web Site:** www.ggp.com **Officers:** John Bucksbaum - Chairman Thomas H. Nolan - President, Chief Operating Officer	**Auditors:** Deloitte & Touche LLP **Investor Contact:** 312-960-5529 **Transfer Agents:** American Stock Transfer & Trust Company, LLC, Brooklyn, NY

327

GENERAL MILLS, INC.

Exchange	Symbol	Price	52Wk Range	Yield	P/E
NYS	GIS	$49.31 (3/28/2013)	49.31-37.55	3.08	18.06

*7 Year Price Score 107.75 *NYSE Composite Index=100 *12 Month Price Score 103.89

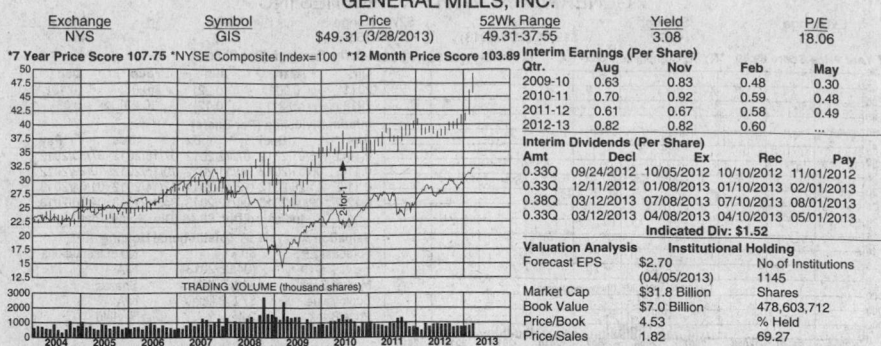

Interim Earnings (Per Share)

Qtr.	Aug	Nov	Feb	May
2009-10	0.63	0.83	0.48	0.30
2010-11	0.70	0.92	0.59	0.48
2011-12	0.61	0.67	0.58	0.49
2012-13	0.82	0.82	0.60	...

Interim Dividends (Per Share)

Amt	Decl	Ex	Rec	Pay
0.33Q	09/24/2012	10/05/2012	10/10/2012	11/01/2012
0.33Q	12/11/2012	01/08/2013	01/10/2013	02/01/2013
0.38Q	03/12/2013	07/08/2013	07/10/2013	08/01/2013
0.33Q	03/12/2013	04/08/2013	04/10/2013	05/01/2013

Indicated Div: $1.52

Valuation Analysis

		Institutional Holding	
Forecast EPS	$2.70 (04/05/2013)	No of Institutions	1145
Market Cap	$31.8 Billion	Shares	478,603,712
Book Value	$7.0 Billion	% Held	69.27
Price/Book	4.53		
Price/Sales	1.82		

Business Summary: Food (MIC: 1.2.1 SIC: 2043 NAIC: 311230)

General Mills is a manufacturer and marketer of branded consumer foods sold through retail stores. Co. is also a supplier of branded and unbranded food products to the foodservice and commercial baking industries. Co.'s major product categories in the U.S. are ready-to-eat cereals, refrigerated yogurt, ready-to-serve soup, dry dinners, shelf stable and frozen vegetables, refrigerated and frozen dough products, dessert and baking mixes, frozen pizza and pizza snacks, grain, fruit and savory snacks, and a variety of organic products including granola bars, cereal, and soup. Co. has three operating segments: U.S. Retail; International; and Bakeries and Foodservice.

Recent Developments: For the quarter ended Feb 24 2013, net income increased 2.9% to US$412.6 million in the year-earlier quarter. Revenues were US$4.43 billion, up 7.5% from US$4.12 billion the year before. Operating income was US$642.1 million versus US$668.6 million in the prior-year quarter, a decrease of 4.0%. Direct operating expenses rose 11.3% to US$2.91 billion from US$2.61 billion in the comparable period the year before. Indirect operating expenses increased 5.0% to US$880.6 million from US$838.8 million in the equivalent prior-year period.

Prospects: Our evaluation of General Mills Inc. as of Apr. 7, 2013 is the result of our systematic analysis on three basic characteristics: earnings strength, relative valuation, and recent stock price movement. The company has generated a negative trend in earnings per share over the past 5 quarters and while recent estimates for the company have been raised by analysts, GIS has posted better than expected results. Based on operating earnings yield, the company is undervalued when compared to all of the companies in our coverage universe. Share price changes over the past year indicates that GIS will perform poorly over the near term.

Financial Data
(US$ in Thousands)

	9 Mos	6 Mos	3 Mos	05/27/2012	05/29/2011	05/30/2010	05/31/2009	05/25/2008
Earnings Per Share	2.73	2.71	2.56	2.35	2.70	2.24	1.90	1.86
Cash Flow Per Share	4.46	3.96	3.77	3.72	2.38	3.32	2.71	2.60
Dividends Per Share	1.295	1.270	1.245	1.220	1.120	0.960	0.860	0.785
Dividend Payout %	47.44	46.86	48.63	51.91	41.48	42.86	45.26	42.32
Income Statement								
Total Revenue	13,363,400	8,932,800	4,051,000	16,657,900	14,880,200	14,796,500	14,691,300	13,652,100
EBITDA	2,683,500	1,895,200	919,300	3,103,900	3,247,100	3,063,200	2,776,500	2,687,000
Depn & Amortn	432,300	286,100	139,200	541,500	472,600	457,100	453,600	459,200
Income Before Taxes	2,016,100	1,450,600	697,100	2,210,500	2,428,200	2,204,500	1,932,900	1,806,100
Income Taxes	577,700	403,500	158,100	709,600	721,100	771,200	720,400	622,200
Net Income	1,488,900	1,090,500	548,900	1,567,300	1,798,300	1,530,500	1,304,400	1,294,700
Average Shares	665,100	664,500	667,400	666,700	664,800	683,300	687,000	693,800
Balance Sheet								
Current Assets	4,365,800	4,565,500	5,217,400	3,691,400	3,902,000	3,480,000	3,534,900	3,620,000
Total Assets	22,793,400	22,952,900	22,635,300	21,096,800	18,674,500	17,678,900	17,874,800	19,041,600
Current Liabilities	4,282,600	5,736,400	5,975,500	3,843,200	3,659,200	3,769,100	3,606,000	4,856,300
Long-Term Obligations	6,631,900	5,571,900	5,462,000	6,161,900	5,542,500	5,268,500	5,754,800	4,348,700
Total Liabilities	15,776,700	15,969,200	15,990,100	14,675,100	12,309,000	12,276,000	12,700,100	12,825,800
Stockholders' Equity	7,016,700	6,983,700	6,645,200	6,421,700	6,365,500	5,402,900	5,174,700	6,215,800
Shares Outstanding	644,300	645,900	644,800	648,500	644,800	656,500	656,000	675,000
Statistical Record								
Return on Assets %	8.20	8.14	7.68	7.90	9.92	8.63	6.95	6.98
Return on Equity %	26.03	26.66	26.03	24.58	30.65	29.02	22.53	22.51
EBITDA Margin %	20.08	21.22	22.69	18.63	21.82	20.70	18.90	19.68
Net Margin %	11.14	12.21	13.55	9.41	12.09	10.34	8.88	9.48
Asset Turnover	0.79	0.77	0.76	0.84	0.82	0.83	0.78	0.74
Current Ratio	1.02	0.80	0.87	0.96	1.07	0.92	0.98	0.75
Debt to Equity	0.95	0.80	0.82	0.96	0.87	0.98	1.11	0.70
Price Range	45.67-37.55	41.05-37.55	41.05-36.68	41.05-34.95	39.95-33.57	36.95-25.59	35.08-23.61	31.25-26.43
P/E Ratio	16.73-13.75	15.15-13.86	16.04-14.33	17.47-14.87	14.80-12.43	16.50-11.42	18.46-12.43	16.80-14.21
Average Yield %	3.26	3.24	3.20	3.16	3.07	2.92	2.86	2.71

Address: Number One General Mills Boulevard, Minneapolis, MN 55426
Telephone: 763-764-7600
Fax: 763-764-7384

Web Site: www.generalmills.com
Officers: Kendall J. Powell - Chairman, Chief Executive Officer Y. Marc Belton - Executive Vice President

Auditors: KPMG LLP
Investor Contact: 180-024-55703
Transfer Agents: Wells Fargo Bank Minnesota, NA, Mendota Heights, MN

GENERAL MOTORS CO.

Exchange	Symbol	Price	52Wk Range	Yield	P/E
NYS	GM	$27.82 (3/28/2013)	30.60-18.80	N/A	9.53

*7 Year Price Score N/A   *NYSE Composite Index=100   *12 Month Price Score 105.22

Interim Earnings (Per Share)

Qtr.	Mar	Jun	Sep	Dec
2010	0.55	0.85	1.20	0.27
2011	1.77	1.54	1.03	0.28
2012	0.60	0.90	0.89	0.54

Interim Dividends (Per Share)

No Dividends Paid

Valuation Analysis		Institutional Holding	
Forecast EPS	$3.36	No of Institutions	
	(04/06/2013)	639	
Market Cap	$38.0 Billion	Shares	
Book Value	$36.2 Billion	592,096,384	
Price/Book	1.05	% Held	
Price/Sales	0.25	N/A	

Business Summary: Autos- Manufacturing (MIC: 1.8.1 SIC: 3711 NAIC: 336111)

General Motors designs, builds and sells cars, trucks and automobile parts. Co. also provides financing services through General Motors Financial Company, Inc. Co.'s automotive operations are conducted through four segments: GM North America (GMNA), GM Europe, GM International Operations and GM South America. GMNA serves customers in North America with vehicles developed, manufactured and/or marketed under the Buick, Cadillac, Chevrolet and GMC brands. Outside North America Co.'s vehicles are developed, manufactured and/or marketed under the Buick, Cadillac, Chevrolet, GMC, Holden, Opel, and Vauxhall brands. Co. sells its products to dealers for retail sales, and to fleet customers.

Recent Developments: For the year ended Dec 31 2012, net income decreased 33.9% to US$6.14 billion from US$9.29 billion in the prior year. Revenues were US$152.26 billion, up 1.3% from US$150.28 billion the year before. Operating loss was US$30.36 billion versus an income of US$5.66 billion in the prior year. Direct operating expenses rose 7.8% to US$141.44 billion from US$131.17 billion in the comparable period the year before. Indirect operating expenses increased 206.2% to US$41.18 billion from US$13.45 billion in the equivalent prior-year period.

Prospects: Our evaluation of General Motors Co. as of Apr. 7, 2013 is the result of our systematic analysis on three basic characteristics: earnings strength, relative valuation, and recent stock price movement. The company has generated a negative trend in earnings per share over the past 5 quarters. However, while recent estimates for the company have been mixed, GM has posted results that fell short of analysts' expectations. Based on operating earnings yield, the company is undervalued when compared to all of the companies in our coverage universe. Share price changes over the past year indicates that GM will perform well over the near term.

Financial Data

(US$ in Millions)	12/31/2012	12/31/2011	12/31/2010	12/31/2009	07/09/2009	12/31/2008	12/31/2007
Earnings Per Share	2.92	4.58	2.89	(3.58)	178.55	(53.47)	(68.12)
Cash Flow Per Share	6.75	5.32	4.52	0.78	(57.55)	(20.78)	...
Tang Book Value Per Share	12.49	N.M.	N.M.	N.M.	...	...	...
Dividends Per Share	...	...	...	...	...	0.500	1.000
Income Statement							
Total Revenue	152,256	150,276	135,592	57,474	47,115	148,979	179,984
EBITDA	(22,705)	9,782	9,643	(2,359)	117,817	(11,122)	5,535
Depn & Amortn	7,908	4,108	4,363	2,657	6,829	9,931	9,439
Income Before Taxes	(30,257)	5,985	5,737	(5,283)	106,396	(23,288)	(5,101)
Income Taxes	(34,831)	(110)	672	(1,000)	(1,166)	1,766	36,863
Net Income	6,188	9,190	6,172	(4,297)	109,118	(30,943)	(38,542)
Average Shares	1,675	1,668	1,624	1,239	611	579	566
Balance Sheet							
Current Assets	69,996	60,247	53,053	59,247	...	44,267	...
Total Assets	149,422	144,603	138,898	136,295	...	91,039	...
Current Liabilities	53,992	48,932	47,157	52,435	...	75,608	...
Long-Term Obligations	10,532	11,650	9,974	5,562	...	29,018	...
Total Liabilities	113,178	106,483	102,718	108,048	...	176,599	...
Stockholders' Equity	36,244	38,120	36,180	28,247	...	(85,560)	...
Shares Outstanding	1,366	1,564	1,500	1,500	...	610	...
Statistical Record							
Return on Assets %	4.20	6.48	4.49	N.M.	...	...	...
Return on Equity %	16.60	24.74	19.16	...	...	...	...
EBITDA Margin %	N.M.	6.51	7.11	N.M.	250.06	N.M.	3.08
Net Margin %	4.06	6.12	4.55	N.M.	231.60	N.M.	N.M.
Asset Turnover	1.03	1.06	0.99	0.51	...	...	...
Current Ratio	1.30	1.23	1.13	1.13	...	0.59	...
Debt to Equity	0.29	0.31	0.28	0.20	...	...	...
Price Range	28.83-18.80	38.98-19.05	36.86-33.25	...	...	...	...
P/E Ratio	9.87-6.44	8.51-4.16	12.75-11.51	...	...	...	...

Address: 300 Renaissance Center,	Web Site: www.gm.com	Auditors: Deloitte & Touche LLP
Detroit, MI 48265-3000	Officers: Daniel F. Akerson - Chairman, Chief	Investor Contact: 313-667-1669
Telephone: 313-556-5000	Executive Officer Stephen J. Girsky - Vice-Chairman	Transfer Agents: Computershare Trust Company N.A.

GENPACT LTD

*7 Year Price Score N/A   *NYSE Composite Index=100   *12 Month Price Score 96.27

Interim Earnings (Per Share)

Qtr.	Mar	Jun	Sep	Dec
2008	0.09	0.11	0.15	0.21
2009	0.14	0.11	0.15	0.16
2010	0.13	0.12	0.18	0.20
2011	0.16	0.17	0.21	0.27
2012	0.17	0.27	0.11	0.23

Interim Dividends (Per Share)

Amt	Decl	Ex	Rec	Pay
2.24U	08/30/2012	09/06/2012	09/10/2012	09/24/2012

Valuation Analysis

		Institutional Holding	
Forecast EPS	$1.02	No of Institutions	
	(04/05/2013)	177	
Market Cap	$4.1 Billion	Shares	
Book Value	$1.2 Billion	130,207,032	
Price/Book	3.51	% Held	
Price/Sales	2.16	N/A	

Business Summary: Business Services (MIC: 7.5.2 SIC: 7389 NAIC: 541618)

Genpact is engaged in managing business process and technology management services. Co.'s services include Finance and Accounting, Smart Decision Services, Supply Chain and Procurement, Enterprise Application Services, IT Management Services, and Collections and Customer Services. Co.'s Smart Decision Services is comprised of analytics, re-engineering, and risk management services. Co. provides its services across a range of industries which includes banking and insurance, capital markets, consumer packaged goods and retail, pharmaceuticals, manufacturing, and healthcare.

Recent Developments: For the year ended Dec 31 2012, net income decreased 3.4% to US$184.6 million from US$191.1 million in the prior year. Revenues were US$1.90 billion, up 18.8% from US$1.60 billion the year before. Operating income was US$264.3 million versus US$216.2 million in the prior year, an increase of 22.2%. Direct operating expenses rose 15.2% to US$1.16 billion from US$1.00 billion in the comparable period the year before. Indirect operating expenses increased 26.5% to US$479.9 million from US$379.3 million in the equivalent prior-year period.

Prospects: Our evaluation of Genpact Ltd. as of Apr. 7, 2013 is the result of our systematic analysis on three basic characteristics: earnings strength, relative valuation, and recent stock price movement. The company has generated a negative trend in earnings per share over the past 5 quarters and while recent estimates for the company have remained steady, G has posted better than expected results. Based on operating earnings yield, the company is about fairly valued when compared to all of the companies in our coverage universe. Share price changes over the past year indicates that G will perform well over the near term.

Financial Data

(US$ in Thousands)	12/31/2012	12/31/2011	12/31/2010	12/31/2009	12/31/2008	12/31/2007	12/31/2006	12/31/2005
Earnings Per Share	0.78	0.81	0.63	0.58	0.57	0.12	(0.15)	(0.02)
Cash Flow Per Share	1.38	1.20	0.74	0.73	0.99	1.11	0.52	...
Tang Book Value Per Share	0.44	1.77	3.96	2.82	1.15	2.55	N.M.	...
Dividends Per Share	2.240	...	...	...	...	...	...	...
Dividend Payout %	287.18	...	...	...	...	...	...	...
Income Statement								
Total Revenue	1,901,971	1,600,436	1,258,963	1,120,071	1,040,847	822,684	613,047	491,894
EBITDA	348,457	323,415	247,060	229,151	212,722	166,567	118,477	92,899
Depn & Amortn	69,351	67,279	65,672	71,141	74,520	77,380	74,250	75,315
Income Before Taxes	262,992	262,059	184,247	161,124	144,349	81,608	33,922	10,707
Income Taxes	78,419	70,656	34,203	25,466	8,823	16,543	(5,850)	(6,397)
Net Income	178,216	184,294	142,181	127,301	125,141	56,423	39,772	17,104
Average Shares	229,532	226,354	224,838	220,066	218,444	142,739	70,987	71,274
Balance Sheet								
Current Assets	1,128,767	985,119	935,780	847,140	744,334	671,861	242,900	...
Total Assets	2,605,927	2,403,387	1,893,461	1,747,565	1,696,326	1,743,466	1,081,292	...
Current Liabilities	517,818	661,828	322,548	395,583	426,611	271,440	263,846	...
Long-Term Obligations	659,412	75,631	2,489	28,329	74,006	105,887	125,589	...
Total Liabilities	1,437,516	970,329	414,789	550,169	854,533	492,737	456,597	...
Stockholders' Equity	1,168,411	1,433,058	1,478,672	1,197,396	841,793	1,250,729	624,695	...
Shares Outstanding	225,480	222,347	220,916	217,433	214,560	212,101	67,762	...
Statistical Record								
Return on Assets %	7.10	8.58	7.81	7.39	7.26	3.99	...	...
Return on Equity %	13.66	12.66	10.63	12.49	11.93	6.02	...	...
EBITDA Margin %	18.32	20.21	19.62	20.46	20.44	20.25	19.33	18.89
Net Margin %	9.37	11.52	11.29	11.37	12.02	6.86	6.49	3.48
Asset Turnover	0.76	0.74	0.69	0.65	0.60	0.58	...	...
Current Ratio	2.18	1.49	2.90	2.14	1.74	2.48	0.92	...
Debt to Equity	0.56	0.05	N.M.	0.02	0.09	0.08	0.20	...
Price Range	18.66-14.45	17.83-13.09	18.50-13.50	15.21-7.25	16.04-6.34	17.68-13.37	...	...
P/E Ratio	23.92-18.53	22.01-16.16	29.37-21.43	26.22-12.50	28.14-11.12	147.33-111.42	...	...
Average Yield %	13.70	...	...	...	...	...	...	...

Address: Canon's Court, 22 Victoria Street, Hamilton, HM12 **Telephone:** 441-295-2244	**Web Site:** www.genpact.com **Officers:** Robert G. Scott - Interim Non-Executive Chairman N. V. Tyagarajan - President, Chief Executive Officer	**Auditors:** KPMG LLP **Transfer Agents:** Computershare, Providence, RI

GENUINE PARTS CO.

Exchange	Symbol	Price	52Wk Range	Yield	P/E	Div Achiever
NYS	GPC	$78.00 (3/28/2013)	78.00-58.53	2.76	18.84	56 Years

*7 Year Price Score 119.59 *NYSE Composite Index=100 *12 Month Price Score 103.23

Interim Earnings (Per Share)

Qtr.	Mar	Jun	Sep	Dec
2008	0.75	0.81	0.81	0.56
2009	0.56	0.65	0.67	0.62
2010	0.63	0.78	0.83	0.75
2011	0.80	0.96	0.97	0.86
2012	0.93	1.08	1.11	1.03

Interim Dividends (Per Share)

Amt	Decl	Ex	Rec	Pay
0.495Q	04/23/2012	06/06/2012	06/08/2012	07/02/2012
0.495Q	08/20/2012	09/05/2012	09/07/2012	10/01/2012
0.495Q	11/19/2012	12/05/2012	12/07/2012	01/02/2013
0.537Q	02/19/2013	03/06/2013	03/08/2013	04/01/2013

Indicated Div: $2.15 (Div. Reinv. Plan)

Valuation Analysis

	Institutional Holding
Forecast EPS $4.50 (04/05/2013)	No of Institutions 713
Market Cap $12.1 Billion	Shares 127,932,264
Book Value $3.0 Billion	% Held 73.88
Price/Book 4.03	
Price/Sales 0.93	

Business Summary: Retail - General Merchandise/Department Stores (MIC: 2.1.1 SIC: 5013 NAIC: 423120)

Genuine Parts is engaged in the distribution of automotive replacement parts, industrial replacement parts, office products and electrical/electronic materials. Co. has four segments: automotive, which distributes replacement parts for automobiles, trucks, and other vehicles; industrial, which distributes industrial bearings, mechanical and fluid power transmission equipment, including hydraulic and pneumatic products; office products, which distributes a office products, computer supplies, office furniture, and business electronics; and electrical/electronic materials, which distributes materials including insulating and conductive materials for use in electronic and electrical apparatus.

Recent Developments: For the year ended Dec 31 2012, net income increased 14.7% to US$648.0 million from US$565.1 million in the prior year. Revenues were US$13.01 billion, up 4.5% from US$12.46 billion the year before. Direct operating expenses rose 4.3% to US$9.24 billion from US$8.85 billion in the comparable period the year before. Indirect operating expenses increased 2.2% to US$2.75 billion from US$2.70 billion in the equivalent prior-year period.

Prospects: Our evaluation of Genuine Parts Co. as of Apr. 7, 2013 is the result of our systematic analysis on three basic characteristics: earnings strength, relative valuation, and recent stock price movement. The company has managed to produce a neutral trend in earnings per share over the past 5 quarters and while recent estimates for the company have been raised by analysts, GPC has posted better than expected results. Based on operating earnings yield, the company is about fairly valued when compared to all of the companies in our coverage universe. Share price changes over the past year indicates that GPC will perform poorly over the near term.

Financial Data
(US$ in Thousands)

	12/31/2012	12/31/2011	12/31/2010	12/31/2009	12/31/2008	12/31/2007	12/31/2006	12/31/2005
Earnings Per Share	4.14	3.58	3.00	2.50	2.92	2.98	2.76	2.50
Cash Flow Per Share	5.82	3.99	4.29	5.30	3.26	3.79	2.53	2.53
Tang Book Value Per Share	16.15	16.08	16.39	15.42	13.58	15.86	14.59	15.21
Dividends Per Share	1.980	1.800	1.640	1.600	1.560	1.460	1.350	1.250
Dividend Payout %	47.83	50.28	54.67	64.00	53.42	48.99	48.91	50.00
Income Statement								
Total Revenue	13,013,868	12,458,877	11,207,589	10,057,512	11,015,263	10,843,195	10,457,942	9,783,050
EBITDA	1,052,405	924,616	794,581	675,694	803,050	935,774	875,915	774,593
Depn & Amortn	12,991	6,774	4,737	3,644	2,861	87,702	73,423	65,529
Income Before Taxes	1,018,932	890,806	761,783	644,165	768,468	816,745	770,916	709,064
Income Taxes	370,891	325,690	286,272	244,590	293,051	310,406	295,511	271,630
Net Income	648,041	565,116	475,511	399,575	475,417	506,339	475,405	437,434
Average Shares	156,420	157,660	158,461	159,707	162,986	170,135	172,486	175,007
Balance Sheet								
Current Assets	4,820,131	4,576,596	4,414,887	4,032,828	3,871,420	4,053,012	3,835,127	3,806,882
Total Assets	6,807,061	5,879,591	5,465,044	5,004,689	4,786,350	4,774,069	4,496,984	4,771,538
Current Liabilities	2,487,638	1,812,073	1,971,814	1,408,284	1,287,103	1,547,976	1,198,768	1,249,104
Long-Term Obligations	283,748	534,186	262,622	513,504	512,708	263,707	512,248	500,000
Total Liabilities	3,809,174	3,096,356	2,671,225	2,383,359	2,462,018	2,057,353	1,946,993	2,077,581
Stockholders' Equity	2,997,887	2,783,235	2,793,819	2,621,330	2,324,332	2,716,716	2,549,991	2,693,957
Shares Outstanding	154,841	155,651	157,636	158,917	159,442	166,065	170,530	173,032
Statistical Record								
Return on Assets %	10.19	9.96	9.08	8.16	9.92	10.92	10.26	9.48
Return on Equity %	22.36	20.27	17.56	16.16	18.81	19.23	18.13	16.70
EBITDA Margin %	8.09	7.42	7.09	6.72	7.29	8.63	8.38	7.92
Net Margin %	4.98	4.54	4.24	3.97	4.32	4.67	4.55	4.47
Asset Turnover	2.05	2.20	2.14	2.05	2.30	2.34	2.26	2.12
Current Ratio	1.94	2.53	2.24	2.86	3.01	2.62	3.20	3.05
Debt to Equity	0.09	0.19	0.09	0.20	0.22	0.10	0.20	0.19
Price Range	66.38-58.53	61.96-46.73	51.50-36.96	39.38-25.06	46.30-31.21	51.43-46.30	48.02-40.26	46.50-40.98
P/E Ratio	16.03-14.14	17.31-13.05	17.17-12.32	15.75-10.02	15.86-10.69	17.26-15.54	17.40-14.59	18.60-16.39
Average Yield %	3.16	3.34	3.80	4.63	3.84	2.98	3.09	2.87

Address: 2999 Circle 75 Parkway, Atlanta, GA 30339	Web Site: www.genpt.com	Auditors: Ernst & Young LLP
Telephone: 770-953-1700	Officers: Thomas C. Gallagher - Chairman, President, Chief Executive Officer, Chief Operating Officer Jerry W. Nix - Vice-Chairman, Executive Vice President, Senior Vice President, Chief Financial Officer	Investor Contact: 770-953-1700
Fax: 770-956-2211		Transfer Agents: Computershare, Providence, RI

GENWORTH FINANCIAL, INC. (HOLDING CO)

Exchange	Symbol	Price	52Wk Range	Yield	P/E
NYS	GNW	$10.00 (3/28/2013)	10.51-4.12	N/A	15.38

*7 Year Price Score 36.29 *NYSE Composite Index=100 *12 Month Price Score 128.67

Interim Earnings (Per Share)

Qtr.	Mar	Jun	Sep	Dec
2008	0.27	(0.25)	(0.60)	(0.74)
2009	(1.08)	(0.11)	0.04	0.12
2010	0.36	0.08	0.17	(0.32)
2011	0.17	(0.20)	0.06	0.22
2012	0.09	0.16	0.07	0.33

Interim Dividends (Per Share)

Dividend Payment Suspended

Valuation Analysis

	Institutional Holding
Forecast EPS $1.21	No of Institutions
(04/06/2013)	489
Market Cap $4.9 Billion	Shares
Book Value $16.5 Billion	419,133,888
Price/Book 0.30	% Held
Price/Sales 0.49	78.90

Business Summary: General Insurance (MIC: 5.2.1 SIC: 6311 NAIC: 524113)

Genworth Financial is a holding company. Through its subsidiaries, Co. provides insurance, wealth management, investment and financial services. Co. operates through three divisions: Insurance and Wealth Management, Mortgage Insurance and Corporate and Runoff. Under these divisions, there are six business segments: U.S. Life Insurance, which provides insurance and fixed annuity products; International Protection, which provides payment protection coverages; Wealth Management, which provides wealth management products; International Mortgage Insurance and U.S. Mortgage Insurance, which provide mortgage insurance products; as well as Runoff, which includes products which are no longer sold.

Recent Developments: For the year ended Dec 31 2012, net income increased 178.2% to US$523.0 million from US$188.0 million in the prior year. Revenues were US$10.02 billion, down 3.3% from US$10.37 billion the year before. Net premiums earned were US$5.04 billion versus US$5.71 billion in the prior year, a decrease of 11.7%. Net investment income fell 1.1% to US$3.34 billion from US$3.38 billion a year ago.

Prospects: Our evaluation of Genworth Financial Inc. as of Apr. 7, 2013 is the result of our systematic analysis on three basic characteristics: earnings strength, relative valuation, and recent stock price movement. The company has suffered a very negative trend in earnings per share over the past 5 quarters. However, while recent estimates for the company have been lowered by analysts, GNW has posted better than expected results. Based on operating earnings yield, the company is undervalued when compared to all of the companies in our coverage universe. Share price changes over the past year indicates that GNW will perform in line with the market over the near term.

Financial Data
(US$ in Millions)

	12/31/2012	12/31/2011	12/31/2010	12/31/2009	12/31/2008	12/31/2007	12/31/2006	12/31/2005
Earnings Per Share	0.65	0.25	0.29	(1.02)	(1.32)	2.73	2.83	2.52
Cash Flow Per Share	1.95	6.37	2.73	4.28	12.53	10.90	9.57	7.32
Tang Book Value Per Share	30.34	29.96	24.06	20.49	14.93	25.15	24.27	23.52
Dividends Per Share	...	...	...	...	0.400	0.370	0.315	0.270
Dividend Payout %	...	...	...	...	...	13.55	11.13	10.71
Income Statement								
Premium Income	5,038	5,705	5,854	6,019	6,777	6,330	6,487	6,297
Total Revenue	10,023	10,344	10,089	9,069	9,948	11,125	11,029	10,504
Income Before Taxes	712	314	76	(792)	(942)	1,606	1,918	1,798
Income Taxes	189	53	(209)	(393)	(370)	452	594	577
Net Income	323	122	142	(460)	(572)	1,220	1,328	1,221
Average Shares	494	493	493	451	433	447	469	484
Balance Sheet								
Total Assets	113,312	114,302	112,395	108,187	107,389	114,315	110,871	105,292
Total Liabilities	96,775	97,761	98,534	95,911	98,463	100,837	97,541	91,982
Stockholders' Equity	16,537	16,541	13,861	12,276	8,926	13,478	13,330	13,310
Shares Outstanding	492	491	490	489	433	436	443	471
Statistical Record								
Return on Assets %	0.28	0.11	0.13	N.M.	N.M.	1.08	1.23	1.17
Return on Equity %	1.95	0.80	1.09	N.M.	N.M.	9.10	9.97	9.33
Net Margin %	3.22	1.18	1.41	(5.07)	(5.75)	10.97	12.04	11.62
Price Range	9.34-4.12	14.31-4.92	18.96-10.59	13.34-0.84	25.45-0.90	37.00-23.33	36.24-31.78	34.98-25.72
P/E Ratio	14.37-6.34	57.24-19.68	65.38-36.52	...	...	13.55-8.55	12.81-11.23	13.88-10.21
Average Yield %	...	...	...	...	2.52	1.16	0.93	0.90

Address: 6620 West Broad Street, Richmond, VA 23230 Telephone: 804-281-6000	Web Site: www.genworth.com Officers: Thomas J. McInerney - President, Chief Executive Officer Martin P. Klein - Acting President, Acting Chief Executive Officer, Senior Vice President, Chief Financial Officer	Auditors: KPMG LLP Transfer Agents: Computershare Shareowner Services LLC, Pittsburgh, PA

GLOBAL PARTNERS LP

Exchange	Symbol	Price	52Wk Range	Yield	P/E
NYS	GLP	$35.85 (3/28/2013)	37.81-20.19	5.93	20.96

*7 Year Price Score 99.56 *NYSE Composite Index=100 ***12 Month Price Score 120.26**

Interim Earnings (Per Share)

Qtr.	Mar	Jun	Sep	Dec
2008	0.63	(0.09)	0.08	0.78
2009	1.40	0.07	0.15	0.91
2010	1.06	(0.07)	0.03	0.31
2011	0.39	(0.04)	0.08	0.46
2012	(0.06)	0.66	0.24	0.82

Interim Dividends (Per Share)

Amt	Decl	Ex	Rec	Pay
0.50Q	04/20/2012	05/02/2012	05/04/2012	05/15/2012
0.525Q	07/19/2012	08/01/2012	08/03/2012	08/14/2012
0.532Q	10/25/2012	11/01/2012	11/05/2012	11/14/2012
0.57Q	01/22/2013	02/01/2013	02/05/2013	02/14/2013

Indicated Div: $2.13

Valuation Analysis   **Institutional Holding**

Forecast EPS	$3.25	No of Institutions
	(04/05/2013)	45
Market Cap	$987.3 Million	Shares
Book Value	N/A	11,083,321
Price/Book	N/A	% Held
Price/Sales	0.06	50.43

TRADING VOLUME (thousand shares)

Business Summary: Equipment & Services (MIC: 9.1.3 SIC: 5171 NAIC: 424710)

Global Partners engages in the wholesale and commercial distribution of refined petroleum products, renewable fuels and small amounts of natural gas and crude oil and provides ancillary services. Co.'s Wholesale segment sells gasoline, home heating oil, diesel, kerosene and residual oil to unbranded and Mobil-branded retail gasoline stations and other resellers of transportation fuels, home heating oil retailers and wholesale distributors. Co.'s Commercial segment sells and delivers unbranded gasoline, home heating oil, diesel, kerosene, residual oil and small amounts of natural gas and renewable fuel to end user customers in the public sector and to commercial and industrial end users.

Recent Developments: For the year ended Dec 31 2012, net income increased 141.5% to US$46.7 million from US$19.4 million in the prior year. Revenues were US$17.63 billion, up 18.8% from US$14.84 billion the year before. Operating income was US$84.6 million versus US$50.6 million in the prior year, an increase of 67.1%. Direct operating expenses rose 18.2% to US$17.29 billion from US$14.63 billion in the comparable period the year before. Indirect operating expenses increased 56.6% to US$248.9 million from US$159.0 million in the equivalent prior-year period.

Prospects: Looking ahead, Co. should benefit from a number of growth opportunities that logistics and marketing focused. For example, in Columbus, ND, Co. has completed its new 100,000 barrel storage tank and loading facility as part of the development of that location as a hub for the gathering, storage, transportation and marketing of crude oil and associated petroleum products. Co. has also have completed a rail expansion at its Albany, NY terminal, increasing the terminal's capacity to receive products via rail from 55,000 barrels per day to 160,000 barrels per day. According to Co., this increased rail capacity now allows the terminal to offload two 120-car unit trains per day.

Financial Data
(US$ in Thousands)

	12/31/2012	12/31/2011	12/31/2010	12/31/2009	12/31/2008	12/31/2007	12/31/2006	12/31/2005
Earnings Per Share	1.71	0.87	1.59	2.51	1.40	1.38	2.46	0.70
Cash Flow Per Share	8.78	(0.82)	(5.33)	(4.70)	7.57	(9.25)	(4.83)	...
Dividends Per Share	2.058	2.000	1.958	1.950	1.950	1.873	1.719	...
Dividend Payout %	120.32	229.89	123.11	77.69	139.29	135.69	69.86	...
Income Statement								
Total Revenue	17,625,997	14,835,729	7,801,559	5,818,411	9,019,123	6,757,834	4,472,418	1,248,899
EBITDA	123,088	75,029	64,948	61,551	53,206	71,612	51,541	14,425
Depn & Amortn	38,500	24,400	15,600	10,800	10,200	6,000	4,513	1,345
Income Before Taxes	48,320	19,420	27,038	35,563	22,207	48,204	35,127	10,394
Income Taxes	1,577	68	...	1,429	1,152	1,191	1,666	986
Net Income	46,743	19,352	27,038	34,134	21,055	47,013	33,461	9,408
Average Shares	26,567	21,474	16,597	13,279	13,071	12,444	11,285	11,284
Balance Sheet								
Current Assets	1,506,933	1,412,864	1,197,645	862,858	693,307	960,865	596,073	519,340
Total Assets	2,329,752	1,868,851	1,672,316	1,052,703	889,262	1,159,227	638,887	554,756
Current Liabilities	1,045,195	771,054	751,681	567,635	494,712	789,910	447,790	290,613
Long-Term Obligations	762,754	731,095	593,502	312,089	225,290	190,240	83,239	183,158
Total Liabilities	1,893,291	1,553,562	1,395,500	895,283	745,794	998,876	535,648	478,447
Shares Outstanding	27,540	21,792	19,105	13,253	13,300	13,300	11,515	11,515
Statistical Record								
Return on Assets %	2.22	1.09	1.98	3.52	2.05	5.23	5.61	...
EBITDA Margin %	0.70	0.51	0.83	1.06	0.59	1.06	1.15	1.16
Net Margin %	0.27	0.13	0.35	0.59	0.23	0.70	0.75	0.75
Asset Turnover	8.37	8.38	5.73	5.99	8.78	7.52	7.49	...
Current Ratio	1.44	1.83	1.59	1.52	1.40	1.22	1.33	1.79
Price Range	27.81-20.19	29.83-14.86	27.60-19.58	26.99-9.21	28.19-6.75	39.80-23.94	25.98-19.35	24.20-18.27
P/E Ratio	16.26-11.81	34.29-17.08	17.36-12.31	10.75-3.67	20.14-4.82	28.84-17.35	10.56-7.87	34.57-26.10
Average Yield %	8.67	8.53	8.13	10.64	11.63	5.94	7.95	...

Address: P.O. Box 9161, 800 South Street, Waltham, MA 02454-9161 Telephone: 781-894-8800	Web Site: www.globalp.com Officers: Alfred A. Slifka - Chairman Richard Slifka - Vice-Chairman	Auditors: Ernst & Young LLP Investor Contact: 617-542-5300 Transfer Agents: American Stock Transfer and Trust Company, New Yor, NY

GLOBAL PAYMENTS, INC.

Exchange	Symbol	Price	52Wk Range	Yield	P/E
NYS	GPN	$49.66 (3/28/2013)	51.00-39.88	0.16	21.59

*7 Year Price Score 91.32 *NYSE Composite Index=100 *12 Month Price Score 101.20

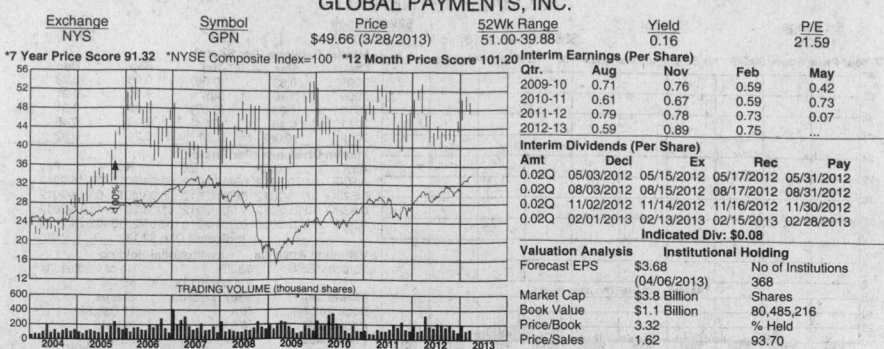

Interim Earnings (Per Share)

Qtr.	Aug	Nov	Feb	May
2009-10	0.71	0.76	0.59	0.42
2010-11	0.61	0.67	0.59	0.73
2011-12	0.79	0.78	0.73	0.07
2012-13	0.59	0.89	0.75	...

Interim Dividends (Per Share)

Amt	Decl	Ex	Rec	Pay
0.02Q	05/03/2012	05/15/2012	05/17/2012	05/31/2012
0.02Q	08/03/2012	08/15/2012	08/17/2012	08/31/2012
0.02Q	11/02/2012	11/14/2012	11/16/2012	11/30/2012
0.02Q	02/01/2013	02/13/2013	02/15/2013	02/28/2013

Indicated Div: $0.08

Valuation Analysis		Institutional Holding	
Forecast EPS	$3.68	No of Institutions	
	(04/06/2013)	368	
Market Cap	$3.8 Billion	Shares	
Book Value	$1.1 Billion	80,485,216	
Price/Book	3.32	% Held	
Price/Sales	1.62	93.70	

Business Summary: Business Services (MIC: 7.5.2 SIC: 7389 NAIC: 522320)

Global Payments is a provider of electronic payments transaction processing services for consumers, merchants, Independent Sales Organizations, financial institutions, government agencies and multi-national corporations located throughout the U.S., Canada, the U.K., Spain, the Asia-Pacific region, the Czech Republic, and the Russian Federation. Co. serves as an intermediary to facilitate electronic payment transactions. Co. operates two segments, North America Merchant Services and International Merchant Services, which target customers in industries such as financial institutions, gaming, government, health care, restaurants, retail, universities, nonprofit organizations and utilities.

Recent Developments: For the quarter ended Feb 28 2013, net income decreased 4.4% to US$62.8 million from US$65.7 million in the year-earlier quarter. Revenues were US$578.7 million, up 8.5% from US$533.5 million the year before. Operating income was US$90.8 million versus US$92.3 million in the prior-year quarter, a decrease of 1.7%. Direct operating expenses rose 12.0% to US$217.5 million from US$194.2 million in the comparable period the year before. Indirect operating expenses increased 9.5% to US$270.5 million from US$247.0 million in the equivalent prior-year period.

Prospects: Our evaluation of Global Payments Inc. as of Apr. 7, 2013 is the result of our systematic analysis on three basic characteristics: earnings strength, relative valuation, and recent stock price movement. The company has enjoyed a very positive trend in earnings per share over the past 5 quarters. However, while recent estimates for the company have been lowered by analysts, GPN has posted results that fell short of analysts expectations. Based on operating earnings yield, the company is undervalued when compared to all of the companies in our coverage universe. Share price changes over the past year indicates that GPN will perform well over the near term.

Financial Data
(US$ in Thousands)

	9 Mos	6 Mos	3 Mos	05/31/2012	05/31/2011	05/31/2010	05/31/2009	05/31/2008
Earnings Per Share	2.30	2.28	2.17	2.37	2.60	2.48	0.46	2.01
Cash Flow Per Share	3.32	3.37	6.37	(2.19)	8.89	5.74	4.80	3.42
Tang Book Value Per Share	N.M.	N.M.	1.57	2.00	0.79	1.09	2.04	5.70
Dividends Per Share	0.080	0.080	0.080	0.080	0.080	0.080	0.080	0.080
Dividend Payout %	3.48	3.51	3.69	3.38	3.08	3.23	17.39	3.98
Income Statement								
Total Revenue	1,757,571	1,178,825	590,287	2,203,847	1,859,802	1,642,468	1,601,524	1,274,229
EBITDA	329,935	222,631	91,713	406,445	413,786	391,982	227,683	295,399
Depn & Amortn	42,091	25,561	11,225	99,096	82,192	68,703	66,254	44,040
Income Before Taxes	269,333	183,086	78,926	300,447	324,207	310,389	161,427	261,403
Income Taxes	76,986	53,553	24,764	82,881	95,076	87,379	87,249	90,588
Net Income	175,320	116,858	46,675	188,161	209,238	203,317	37,217	162,754
Average Shares	78,324	79,144	79,043	79,431	80,478	82,120	80,992	80,979
Balance Sheet								
Current Assets	1,146,862	1,489,920	1,336,881	1,248,739	1,847,975	968,264	595,188	617,410
Total Assets	3,076,224	3,428,721	2,805,492	2,688,143	3,350,531	2,039,326	1,676,821	1,445,907
Current Liabilities	673,828	1,037,470	1,045,946	837,285	1,444,364	672,471	336,177	217,752
Long-Term Obligations	883,462	777,988	285,464	236,565	268,217	272,965	167,610	...
Total Liabilities	1,929,137	2,194,757	1,656,540	1,515,959	2,165,996	1,178,062	629,806	319,089
Stockholders' Equity	1,147,087	1,233,964	1,148,952	1,172,184	1,184,535	861,264	1,047,015	1,126,818
Shares Outstanding	76,749	78,724	78,819	78,551	80,334	79,646	80,445	79,636
Statistical Record								
Return on Assets %	6.34	5.95	6.19	6.21	7.76	10.94	2.38	12.27
Return on Equity %	15.18	15.11	14.81	15.92	20.46	21.31	3.42	15.57
EBITDA Margin %	18.77	18.89	15.54	18.44	22.25	23.87	14.22	23.18
Net Margin %	9.98	9.91	7.91	8.54	11.25	12.38	2.32	12.77
Asset Turnover	0.83	0.76	0.82	0.73	0.69	0.88	1.03	0.96
Current Ratio	1.70	1.44	1.28	1.49	1.28	1.44	1.77	2.84
Debt to Equity	0.77	0.63	0.25	0.20	0.23	0.32	0.16	...
Price Range	53.48-39.88	53.48-39.88	53.48-39.33	53.48-39.33	53.39-36.10	54.15-35.94	49.77-27.59	47.56-35.75
P/E Ratio	23.25-17.34	23.46-17.49	24.65-18.12	22.57-16.59	20.53-13.88	21.83-14.49	108.20-59.98	23.66-17.79
Average Yield %	0.18	0.18	0.18	0.17	0.18	0.18	0.21	0.19

Address: 10 Glenlake Parkway, North Tower, Atlanta, GA 30328	**Web Site:** www.globalpaymentsinc.com	**Auditors:** Deloitte & Touche LLP
Telephone: 770-829-8000	**Officers:** Paul R. Garcia - Chairman, Chief Executive Officer Jeffrey Steven Sloan - President	**Investor Contact:** 770-829-8234
		Transfer Agents: Computershare Trust Company, N.A, Canton, MA

GRACE (W.R.) CO. (DE)

Exchange	Symbol	Price	52Wk Range	Yield	P/E
NYS	GRA	$77.51 (3/28/2013)	78.51-48.01	N/A	63.02

*7 Year Price Score 179.97 *NYSE Composite Index=100 *12 Month Price Score 108.93

TRADING VOLUME (thousand shares)

Interim Earnings (Per Share)

Qtr.	Mar	Jun	Sep	Dec
2008	0.19	0.34	0.39	0.61
2009	(0.54)	0.26	0.61	0.64
2010	0.76	0.69	0.74	0.61
2011	0.72	1.00	1.07	0.77
2012	0.80	0.90	0.99	(1.47)

Interim Dividends (Per Share)

No Dividends Paid

Valuation Analysis		Institutional Holding	
Forecast EPS	$4.50	No of Institutions	
	(04/05/2013)	285	
Market Cap	$5.9 Billion	Shares	
Book Value	$308.4 Million	63,750,216	
Price/Book	18.99	% Held	
Price/Sales	1.86	82.12	

Business Summary: Specialty Chemicals (MIC: 8.3.2 SIC: 2819 NAIC: 331311)

Grace (W.R.) is engaged in the production and sale of chemicals and specialty materials through its two segments: Grace Davison and Grace Construction Products. Grace Davison markets its products, including refining technologies, materials technologies and specialty technologies products, to a range of industrial customers, including those in the energy and refining industry, consumer, industrial and packaging industries, petrochemical and biochemical industries and the pharmaceutical and life sciences industries. Grace Construction Products produces and sells construction chemicals and building materials including concrete admixtures and fibers, additives, and fire protection materials.

Recent Developments: For the year ended Dec 31 2012, net income decreased 64.6% to US$95.1 million from US$268.8 million in the prior year. Revenues were US$3.16 billion, down 1.8% from US$3.21 billion the year before. Direct operating expenses declined 3.0% to US$1.99 billion from US$2.05 billion in the comparable period the year before. Indirect operating expenses increased 42.5% to US$1.11 billion from US$777.8 million in the equivalent prior-year period.

Prospects: Co. anticipates 2012 sales of $3.10 billion to $3.20 billion, reflecting improved sales volumes and base pricing, offset by lower rare earth surcharges and unfavorable currency translation. Consolidated gross margin is forecast in the high end of Co.'s 35.0% to 37.0% target range with raw material inflation moderating. Separately, on Aug. 28, 2012, Co. announced the groundbreaking for its new production facility for waterproofing products in the central Chinese city of Ezhou. Slated for completion in the second half of 2013, the new facility is expected to double Co.'s regional production capacity for specialty waterproofing products sold to Chinese customers and exported to other markets.

Financial Data
(US$ in Thousands)

	12/31/2012	12/31/2011	12/31/2010	12/31/2009	12/31/2008	12/31/2007	12/31/2006	12/31/2005
Earnings Per Share	1.23	3.57	2.78	0.98	1.68	1.12	0.27	1.00
Cash Flow Per Share	6.04	2.95	4.51	6.00	0.02	1.26	2.25	0.81
Tang Book Value Per Share	0.38	N.M.	...	...	...	...	...	...
Income Statement								
Total Revenue	3,155,500	3,211,900	2,675,000	2,825,000	3,317,000	3,115,200	2,826,517	2,569,500
EBITDA	204,800	530,400	378,000	240,900	310,300	270,400	240,500	306,300
Depn & Amortn	119,000	120,000	115,600	113,000	118,700	113,400	113,500	114,000
Income Before Taxes	39,300	368,300	222,100	91,000	141,200	92,600	60,800	140,600
Income Taxes	(37,300)	114,700	32,500	11,500	4,300	(5,800)	8,100	21,300
Net Income	94,100	269,400	207,100	71,200	121,500	80,300	18,300	67,300
Average Shares	76,300	75,500	74,400	72,600	72,500	71,600	68,300	67,300
Balance Sheet								
Current Assets	2,440,200	2,149,100	1,904,200	1,628,700	1,498,200	1,578,500	1,368,800	1,253,600
Total Assets	5,090,200	4,496,700	4,271,700	3,968,200	3,875,500	3,869,000	3,637,400	3,517,200
Current Liabilities	646,300	635,600	532,900	494,700	533,100	521,100	448,600	377,100
Long-Term Obligations	35,800	21,600	15,500	10,900	600	300	200	400
Total Liabilities	4,781,800	4,337,300	4,347,400	4,267,400	4,302,400	4,255,600	4,187,200	4,112,500
Stockholders' Equity	308,400	159,400	(75,700)	(299,200)	(426,900)	(386,600)	(549,800)	(595,300)
Shares Outstanding	75,565	73,886	73,120	72,283	72,157	71,627	68,915	66,922
Statistical Record								
Return on Assets %	1.96	6.14	5.03	1.82	3.13	2.14	0.51	1.91
Return on Equity %	40.12	643.73	...	...	...	...	...	...
EBITDA Margin %	6.49	16.51	14.13	8.53	9.35	8.68	8.51	11.92
Net Margin %	2.98	8.39	7.74	2.52	3.66	2.58	0.65	2.62
Asset Turnover	0.66	0.73	0.65	0.72	0.85	0.83	0.79	0.73
Current Ratio	3.78	3.38	3.57	3.29	2.81	3.03	3.05	3.32
Debt to Equity	0.12	0.14	...	...	...	...	...	...
Price Range	68.51-46.16	52.06-31.39	36.22-19.73	26.17-4.07	27.79-3.01	30.65-18.86	20.35-8.12	13.79-6.75
P/E Ratio	55.70-37.53	14.58-8.79	13.03-7.10	26.70-4.15	16.54-1.79	27.37-16.84	75.37-30.07	13.79-6.75

Address: 7500 Grace Drive, Columbia, MD 21044 **Telephone:** 410-531-4000	**Web Site:** www.grace.com **Officers:** Alfred E. Festa - Chairman, President, Chief Executive Officer Gregory E. Poling - President, Chief Operating Officer, Vice President	**Auditors:** PricewaterhouseCoopers LLP **Investor Contact:** 410-.53-1.4167 **Transfer Agents:** Computershare, Pittsburgh, PA

GRACO INC.

Exchange	Symbol	Price	52Wk Range	Yield	P/E	Div Achiever
NYS	GGG	$58.03 (3/28/2013)	59.54-42.22	1.72	23.98	13 Years

*7 Year Price Score 118.42 *NYSE Composite Index=100 *12 Month Price Score 104.51

Interim Earnings (Per Share)

Qtr.	Mar	Jun	Sep	Dec
2008	0.57	0.69	0.54	0.18
2009	0.05	0.19	0.29	0.28
2010	0.34	0.41	0.50	0.44
2011	0.61	0.61	0.60	0.47
2012	0.58	0.56	0.60	0.69

Interim Dividends (Per Share)

Amt	Decl	Ex	Rec	Pay
0.225Q	06/08/2012	07/12/2012	07/16/2012	08/01/2012
0.225Q	09/14/2012	10/18/2012	10/22/2012	11/07/2012
0.25Q	12/07/2012	01/17/2013	01/22/2013	02/06/2013
0.25Q	02/15/2013	04/11/2013	04/15/2013	05/01/2013

Indicated Div: $1.00

Valuation Analysis

		Institutional Holding	
Forecast EPS	$2.91 (04/05/2013)	No of Institutions	325
Market Cap	$3.5 Billion	Shares	
Book Value	$454.1 Million		57,930,144
Price/Book	7.77	% Held	
Price/Sales	3.48		82.66

Business Summary: Industrial Machinery & Equipment (MIC: 7.2.1 SIC: 3561 NAIC: 333911)

Graco and its subsidiaries design, manufacture and sell equipment that equipment that pumps, meters, mixes, dispenses and sprays a variety of fluids and semi-solids. Co. has three reportable segments: Industrial, which markets equipment and pre-engineered packages for moving and applying paints, coatings, sealants, adhesives and other fluids; Contractor, which markets sprayers for architectural coatings for painting, corrosion control, texture, and line striping; and Lubrication, which markets products to move and dispense lubricants for oil change facilities, service garages, fleet service centers, automobile dealerships, the mining industry and industrial lubrication applications.

Recent Developments: For the year ended Dec 28 2012, net income increased 4.8% to US$149.1 million from US$142.3 million in the prior year. Revenues were US$1.01 billion, up 13.1% from US$895.3 million the year before. Operating income was US$224.7 million versus US$219.5 million in the prior year, an increase of 2.4%. Direct operating expenses rose 16.9% to US$461.9 million from US$395.1 million in the comparable period the year before. Indirect operating expenses increased 16.1% to US$325.9 million from US$280.7 million in the equivalent prior-year period.

Prospects: Our evaluation of Graco Inc. as of Apr. 7, 2013 is the result of our systematic analysis on three basic characteristics: earnings strength, relative valuation, and recent stock price movement. The company has enjoyed a very positive trend in earnings per share over the past 5 quarters and while recent estimates for the company have been raised by analysts, GGG has posted better than expected results. Based on operating earnings yield, the company is about fairly valued when compared to all of the companies in our coverage universe. Share price changes over the past year indicates that GGG will perform in line with the market over the near term.

Financial Data

(US$ in Thousands)	12/28/2012	12/30/2011	12/31/2010	12/25/2009	12/26/2008	12/28/2007	12/29/2006	12/30/2005
Earnings Per Share	2.42	2.32	1.69	0.81	1.99	2.32	2.17	1.80
Cash Flow Per Share	3.15	2.70	1.65	2.45	2.70	2.73	2.30	2.23
Tang Book Value Per Share	1.94	3.50	2.38	1.28	0.37	2.19	3.20	2.87
Dividends Per Share	0.900	0.840	0.800	0.760	0.740	0.660	0.580	0.520
Dividend Payout %	37.19	36.21	47.34	93.83	37.19	28.45	26.73	28.89
Income Statement								
Total Revenue	1,012,456	895,283	744,065	579,212	817,270	841,339	816,468	731,702
EBITDA	258,799	239,459	173,924	95,221	207,112	251,769	243,512	209,028
Depn & Amortn	22,200	20,600	21,200	21,700	20,900	19,500	18,200	18,300
Income Before Taxes	217,326	209,728	148,540	68,667	178,579	228,836	224,366	189,354
Income Taxes	68,200	67,400	45,700	19,700	57,700	76,000	74,600	63,500
Net Income	149,126	142,328	102,840	48,967	120,879	152,836	149,766	125,854
Average Shares	61,711	61,370	60,803	60,229	60,835	65,984	68,977	69,862
Balance Sheet								
Current Assets	776,996	582,970	252,408	188,993	260,595	248,832	238,983	213,898
Total Assets	1,321,734	874,309	530,474	476,434	579,850	536,724	511,603	445,630
Current Liabilities	151,671	131,282	119,754	103,815	121,160	125,877	128,929	111,581
Long-Term Obligations	556,480	300,000	70,255	86,260	180,000	107,060	...	...
Total Liabilities	867,620	551,569	266,360	266,780	412,216	292,050	180,599	157,946
Stockholders' Equity	454,114	322,740	264,114	209,654	167,634	244,674	331,004	287,684
Shares Outstanding	60,766	59,747	60,047	59,999	59,516	61,963	66,804	68,387
Statistical Record								
Return on Assets %	13.62	20.32	20.10	9.30	21.71	29.24	31.38	30.88
Return on Equity %	38.50	48.64	42.71	26.03	58.80	53.24	48.55	48.68
EBITDA Margin %	25.56	26.75	23.37	16.44	25.34	29.92	29.83	28.57
Net Margin %	14.73	15.90	13.82	8.45	14.79	18.17	18.34	17.20
Asset Turnover	0.92	1.28	1.45	1.10	1.47	1.61	1.71	1.80
Current Ratio	5.12	4.44	2.11	1.82	2.15	1.98	1.85	1.92
Debt to Equity	1.23	0.93	0.27	0.41	1.07	0.44	...	...
Price Range	56.01-39.96	53.84-32.47	40.29-26.38	30.70-14.48	41.84-17.67	46.07-36.25	48.95-36.48	40.68-31.83
P/E Ratio	23.14-16.51	23.21-14.00	23.84-15.61	37.90-17.88	21.03-8.88	19.86-15.63	22.56-16.81	22.60-17.68
Average Yield %	1.84	1.96	2.51	3.18	2.17	1.66	1.39	1.44

Address: 88-11th Avenue Northeast, Minneapolis, MN 55413 Telephone: 612-623-6000 Fax: 612-623-6777	Web Site: www.graco.com Officers: Lee R. Mitau - Chairman Patrick J. McHale - President, Chief Executive Officer	Auditors: Deloitte & Touche LLP Transfer Agents: Wells Fargo Bank, N.A., St. Paul, MN

GRAINGER (W.W.) INC.

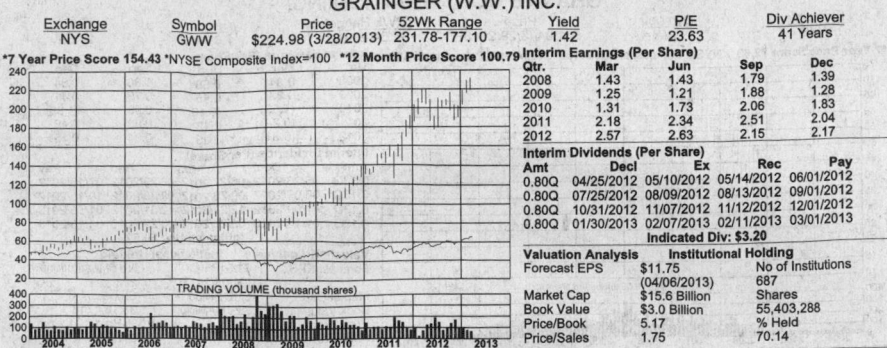

Exchange	Symbol	Price	52Wk Range	Yield	P/E	Div Achiever
NYS	GWW	$224.98 (3/28/2013)	231.78-177.10	1.42	23.63	41 Years

*7 Year Price Score 154.43 *NYSE Composite Index=100 *12 Month Price Score 100.79

Interim Earnings (Per Share)

Qtr.	Mar	Jun	Sep	Dec
2008	1.43	1.43	1.79	1.39
2009	1.25	1.21	1.88	1.28
2010	1.31	1.73	2.06	1.83
2011	2.18	2.34	2.51	2.04
2012	2.57	2.63	2.15	2.17

Interim Dividends (Per Share)

Amt	Decl	Ex	Rec	Pay
0.80Q	04/25/2012	05/10/2012	05/14/2012	06/01/2012
0.80Q	07/25/2012	08/09/2012	08/13/2012	09/01/2012
0.80Q	10/31/2012	11/07/2012	11/12/2012	12/01/2012
0.80Q	01/30/2013	02/07/2013	02/11/2013	03/01/2013
		Indicated Div: $3.20		

Valuation Analysis / **Institutional Holding**

Forecast EPS	$11.75	No of Institutions
	(04/06/2013)	687
Market Cap	$15.6 Billion	Shares
Book Value	$3.0 Billion	55,403,288
Price/Book	5.17	% Held
Price/Sales	1.75	70.14

Business Summary: Electrical Equipment (MIC: 7.3.1 SIC: 5099 NAIC: 423990)

W.W. Grainger is a distributor of maintenance, repair and operating supplies and other related products and services used by businesses and institutions primarily in the U.S. and Canada. Co. has two segments: The U.S. and Canada. The U.S. segment provides material handling equipment, safety and security supplies, lighting and electrical products, power and hand tools, pumps and plumbing supplies, cleaning and maintenance supplies, forestry and agriculture equipment, building and home inspection supplies, vehicle and fleet components and many other items. The Canada segment reflects the operations of Acklands - Grainger Inc., which is a distributor of industrial and safety supplies.

Recent Developments: For the year ended Dec 31 2012, net income increased 4.9% to US$698.8 million from US$666.4 million in the prior year. Revenues were US$8.95 billion, up 10.8% from US$8.08 billion the year before. Operating income was US$1.13 billion versus US$1.05 billion in the prior year, an increase of 7.5%. Direct operating expenses rose 10.2% to US$5.03 billion from US$4.57 billion in the comparable period the year before. Indirect operating expenses increased 13.3% to US$2.79 billion from US$2.46 billion in the equivalent prior-year period.

Prospects: Our evaluation of Grainger (W.W.) Inc. as of Apr. 7, 2013 is the result of our systematic analysis on three basic characteristics: earnings strength, relative valuation, and recent stock price movement. The company has managed to produce a neutral trend in earnings per share over the past 5 quarters and while recent estimates for the company have been mixed, GWW has posted results that fell short of analysts expectations. Based on operating earnings yield, the company is about fairly valued when compared to all of the companies in our coverage universe. Share price changes over the past year indicates that GWW will perform in line with the market over the near term.

Financial Data
(US$ in Thousands)

	12/31/2012	12/31/2011	12/31/2010	12/31/2009	12/31/2008	12/31/2007	12/31/2006	12/31/2005
Earnings Per Share	9.52	9.07	6.93	5.62	6.04	4.94	4.24	3.78
Cash Flow Per Share	11.66	10.71	8.42	9.93	6.90	5.69	4.97	4.83
Tang Book Value Per Share	35.70	30.30	26.20	25.08	24.35	23.47	23.40	23.48
Dividends Per Share	3.060	2.520	2.080	1.780	1.550	1.340	1.110	0.920
Dividend Payout %	32.14	27.78	30.01	31.67	25.66	27.13	26.18	24.34
Income Statement								
Total Revenue	8,950,045	8,078,185	7,182,158	6,221,991	6,850,032	6,418,014	5,883,654	5,526,636
EBITDA	1,290,256	1,207,436	1,010,610	860,779	918,562	802,693	699,061	627,628
Depn & Amortn	159,049	149,200	149,678	147,531	139,570	131,999	118,568	108,782
Income Before Taxes	1,117,789	1,051,213	853,960	705,840	769,576	679,845	600,063	529,865
Income Taxes	418,940	385,115	340,196	276,565	297,863	261,741	219,624	186,350
Net Income	689,881	658,423	510,865	430,466	475,355	420,120	383,399	346,324
Average Shares	71,181	71,176	72,138	74,891	78,750	85,044	90,523	91,588
Balance Sheet								
Current Assets	2,900,640	2,694,900	2,238,071	2,131,515	2,144,109	1,800,817	1,862,086	1,997,868
Total Assets	5,014,598	4,716,062	3,904,377	3,726,332	3,515,417	3,094,028	3,046,088	3,107,921
Current Liabilities	1,080,041	1,387,925	869,303	776,799	761,734	826,403	706,323	726,964
Long-Term Obligations	467,048	175,055	420,446	437,500	488,228	4,895	4,895	4,895
Total Liabilities	1,990,686	2,087,277	1,699,161	1,562,612	1,481,612	995,920	868,473	818,945
Stockholders' Equity	3,023,912	2,628,785	2,205,216	2,163,720	2,033,805	2,098,108	2,177,615	2,288,976
Shares Outstanding	69,478	69,962	69,377	72,276	74,781	79,459	84,067	89,715
Statistical Record								
Return on Assets %	14.14	15.28	13.39	11.89	14.34	13.68	12.46	11.71
Return on Equity %	24.34	27.24	23.39	20.51	22.95	19.65	17.17	15.90
EBITDA Margin %	14.42	14.95	14.07	13.83	13.41	12.51	11.88	11.36
Net Margin %	7.71	8.15	7.11	6.92	6.94	6.55	6.52	6.27
Asset Turnover	1.83	1.87	1.88	1.72	2.07	2.09	1.91	1.87
Current Ratio	2.69	1.94	2.57	2.74	2.81	2.18	2.64	2.75
Debt to Equity	0.15	0.07	0.19	0.20	0.24	N.M.	N.M.	N.M.
Price Range	219.90-177.10	192.31-126.11	138.65-96.83	101.43-61.37	93.10-59.92	98.45-69.34	79.73-60.62	71.97-52.29
P/E Ratio	23.10-18.60	21.20-13.90	20.01-13.97	18.05-10.92	15.41-9.92	19.93-14.04	18.80-14.30	19.04-13.83
Average Yield %	1.52	1.67	1.86	2.13	1.91	1.57	1.56	1.48

Address: 100 Grainger Parkway, Lake Forest, IL 60045-5201	**Web Site:** www.grainger.com	**Auditors:** Ernst & Young LLP
Telephone: 847-535-1000	**Officers:** James T. Ryan - Chairman, President, Chief Executive Officer, Chief Operating Officer Laura D. Brown - Senior Vice President	**Investor Contact:** 847-535-0409
Fax: 847-535-0878		**Transfer Agents:** Computershare Trust Company, N.A., Providence, RI

GRANITE CONSTRUCTION INC.

Exchange	Symbol	Price	52Wk Range	Yield	P/E
NYS	GVA	$31.84 (3/28/2013)	37.54-21.66	1.63	27.69

*7 Year Price Score 72.63 ***NYSE Composite Index=100** ***12 Month Price Score 103.00**

Interim Earnings (Per Share)

Qtr.	Mar	Jun	Sep	Dec
2008	0.34	0.68	1.36	0.84
2009	0.23	0.46	0.79	0.41
2010	(1.09)	(0.18)	0.99	(1.32)
2011	(0.24)	0.13	0.93	0.48
2012	(0.31)	0.05	0.94	0.45

Interim Dividends (Per Share)

Amt	Decl	Ex	Rec	Pay
0.13Q	05/23/2012	06/27/2012	06/29/2012	07/13/2012
0.13Q	08/09/2012	09/26/2012	09/28/2012	10/15/2012
0.13Q	11/09/2012	12/27/2012	12/31/2012	01/15/2013
0.13Q	01/17/2013	03/26/2013	03/29/2013	04/15/2013

Indicated Div: $0.52

Valuation Analysis

Forecast EPS	$1.51
	(04/05/2013)
Market Cap	$1.2 Billion
Book Value	$830.0 Million
Price/Book	1.49
Price/Sales	0.59

Institutional Holding

No of Institutions	228
Shares	36,167,716
% Held	81.16

Business Summary: Construction Services (MIC: 7.5.4 SIC: 1629 NAIC: 237990)

Granite Construction is a holding company. Co.'s reportable segments are: Construction, which performs heavy civil construction projects focused on construction and improvement of streets, roads, highways, bridges, site work and other infrastructure projects; Large Project Construction, which include highways, mass transit facilities, bridges, tunnels, waterway locks and dams, pipelines, canals and airport infrastructure; Construction Materials, which mines and processes aggregates and operates plants that produce construction materials for internal use and for sale to third parties; and Real Estate, which purchases, develops, operates, sells and invests in real estate related projects.

Recent Developments: For the year ended Dec 31 2012, net income decreased 9.3% to US$59.9 million from US$66.1 million in the prior year. Revenues were US$2.08 billion, up 3.7% from US$2.01 billion the year before. Operating income was US$80.8 million versus US$99.3 million in the prior year, a decrease of 18.6%. Direct operating expenses rose 4.9% to US$1.85 billion from US$1.76 billion in the comparable period the year before. Indirect operating expenses increased 3.5% to US$153.9 million from US$148.7 million in the equivalent prior-year period.

Prospects: Our evaluation of Granite Construction Inc. as of Apr. 7, 2013 is the result of our systematic analysis on three basic characteristics: earnings strength, relative valuation, and recent stock price movement. The company has managed to produce a neutral trend in earnings per share over the past 5 quarters. However, while recent estimates for the company have been lowered by analysts, GVA has posted results that fell short of analysts expectations. Based on operating earnings yield, the company is overvalued when compared to all of the companies in our coverage universe. Share price changes over the past year indicates that GVA will perform very well over the near term.

Financial Data
(US$ in Thousands)

	12/31/2012	12/31/2011	12/31/2010	12/31/2009	12/31/2008	12/31/2007	12/31/2006	12/31/2005
Earnings Per Share	1.15	1.31	(1.56)	1.90	3.21	2.71	1.94	2.02
Cash Flow Per Share	2.38	2.42	0.78	1.71	6.82	5.75	6.35	3.61
Tang Book Value Per Share	20.00	20.66	19.64	21.50	20.06	17.75	16.60	14.91
Dividends Per Share	0.520	0.520	0.520	0.520	0.520	0.430	0.400	0.400
Dividend Payout %	45.22	39.69	...	27.37	16.20	15.87	20.62	19.80
Income Statement								
Total Revenue	2,083,037	2,009,531	1,762,965	1,963,479	2,674,244	2,737,914	2,969,604	2,641,352
EBITDA	138,818	150,724	(37,472)	216,562	316,144	253,931	161,940	136,873
Depn & Amortn	51,800	56,000	64,900	74,700	84,100	81,300	70,700	700
Income Before Taxes	79,041	87,240	(107,132)	131,155	234,488	193,189	110,860	140,814
Income Taxes	21,109	23,348	(43,928)	38,650	67,692	65,470	38,678	41,413
Net Income	45,283	51,161	(58,983)	73,500	122,404	112,065	80,509	83,150
Average Shares	39,076	38,473	37,820	37,683	38,106	41,389	41,471	41,249
Balance Sheet								
Current Assets	1,022,057	909,722	913,856	1,006,718	1,102,563	1,127,513	1,083,205	976,948
Total Assets	1,729,487	1,547,799	1,535,533	1,709,575	1,743,455	1,786,418	1,632,838	1,472,230
Current Liabilities	531,272	448,468	438,777	506,113	626,621	729,945	763,443	609,147
Long-Term Obligations	270,148	208,501	242,351	244,688	250,687	268,417	78,576	124,415
Total Liabilities	899,534	748,602	774,502	878,924	975,946	1,086,219	938,294	850,670
Stockholders' Equity	829,953	799,197	761,031	830,651	767,509	700,199	694,544	621,560
Shares Outstanding	38,730	38,682	38,745	38,635	38,266	39,450	41,833	41,682
Statistical Record								
Return on Assets %	2.76	3.32	N.M.	4.26	6.92	6.55	5.19	6.05
Return on Equity %	5.54	6.56	N.M.	9.20	16.63	16.07	12.23	14.19
EBITDA Margin %	6.66	7.50	N.M.	11.03	11.82	9.27	5.45	5.18
Net Margin %	2.17	2.55	N.M.	3.74	4.58	4.09	2.71	3.15
Asset Turnover	1.27	1.30	1.09	1.14	1.51	1.60	1.91	1.92
Current Ratio	1.92	2.03	2.08	1.99	1.76	1.54	1.42	1.60
Debt to Equity	0.33	0.26	0.32	0.29	0.33	0.38	0.11	0.20
Price Range	34.43-21.66	29.26-17.15	35.82-21.44	44.78-27.36	49.09-22.67	73.38-32.68	63.29-37.06	39.61-22.50
P/E Ratio	29.94-18.83	22.34-13.09	...	23.57-14.40	15.29-7.06	27.08-12.06	32.62-19.10	19.61-11.14
Average Yield %	1.89	2.13	1.89	1.51	1.51	0.78	0.84	1.33

Address: 585 West Beach Street, Watsonville, CA 95076 **Telephone:** 831-724-1011	**Web Site:** www.graniteconstruction.com **Officers:** David H. Watts - Chairman Mark E. Boitano - Executive Vice President	**Auditors:** PricewaterhouseCoopers LLP **Investor Contact:** 831-761-4741 **Transfer Agents:** Computershare, Canton, MA

GREAT PLAINS ENERGY, INC.

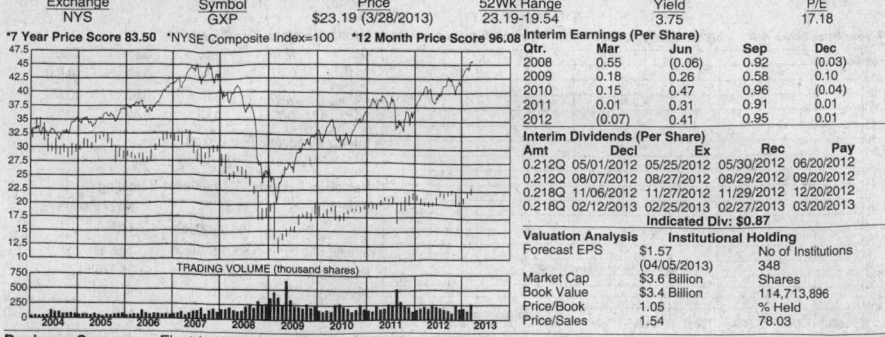

Exchange	Symbol	Price	52Wk Range	Yield	P/E
NYS	GXP	$23.19 (3/28/2013)	23.19-19.54	3.75	17.18

*7 Year Price Score 83.50   *NYSE Composite Index=100   *12 Month Price Score 96.08

Interim Earnings (Per Share)

Qtr.	Mar	Jun	Sep	Dec
2008	0.55	(0.06)	0.92	(0.03)
2009	0.18	0.26	0.58	0.10
2010	0.15	0.47	0.96	(0.04)
2011	0.01	0.31	0.91	0.01
2012	(0.07)	0.41	0.95	0.01

Interim Dividends (Per Share)

Amt	Decl	Ex	Rec	Pay
0.212Q	05/01/2012	05/25/2012	05/30/2012	06/20/2012
0.212Q	08/07/2012	08/27/2012	08/29/2012	09/20/2012
0.218Q	11/06/2012	11/27/2012	11/29/2012	12/20/2012
0.218Q	02/12/2013	02/25/2013	02/27/2013	03/20/2013

Indicated Div: $0.87

Valuation Analysis / **Institutional Holding**

Forecast EPS	$1.57	No of Institutions
	(04/05/2013)	348
Market Cap	$3.6 Billion	Shares
Book Value	$3.4 Billion	114,713,896
Price/Book	1.05	% Held
Price/Sales	1.54	78.03

Business Summary: Electric Utilities (MIC: 3.1.1 SIC: 4911 NAIC: 221122)

Great Plains Energy is a public utility holding company. Co.'s wholly owned direct subsidiaries with operations or active subsidiaries are as follows: Kansas City Power & Light Company (KCP&L), an integrated, regulated electric utility that provides electricity to customers primarily in the states of Missouri and Kansas. KCP&L has one active wholly owned subsidiary, Kansas City Power & Light Receivables Company; and KCP&L Greater Missouri Operations Company (GMO), an integrated, regulated electric utility that primarily provides electricity to customers in the state of Missouri. GMO also provides regulated steam service to certain customers in the St. Joseph, MO area.

Recent Developments: For the year ended Dec 31 2012, net income increased 14.8% to US$199.9 million from US$174.2 million in the prior year. Revenues were US$2.31 billion, down 0.3% from US$2.32 billion the year before. Operating income was US$538.9 million versus US$479.8 million in the prior year, an increase of 12.3%. Direct operating expenses declined 4.2% to US$1.32 billion from US$1.38 billion in the comparable period the year before. Indirect operating expenses decreased 2.1% to US$447.3 million from US$456.7 million in the equivalent prior-year period.

Prospects: Our evaluation of Great Plains Energy Inc. as of Apr. 7, 2013 is the result of our systematic analysis on three basic characteristics: earnings strength, relative valuation, and recent stock price movement. The company has produced a positive trend in earnings per share over the past 5 quarters. However, while recent estimates for the company have been lowered by analysts, GXP has posted better than expected results. Based on operating earnings yield, the company is undervalued when compared to all of the companies in our coverage universe. Share price changes over the past year indicates that GXP will perform poorly over the near term.

Financial Data
(US$ in Thousands)

	12/31/2012	12/31/2011	12/31/2010	12/31/2009	12/31/2008	12/31/2007	12/31/2006	12/31/2005
Earnings Per Share	1.35	1.25	1.53	1.14	1.51	1.85	1.61	2.15
Cash Flow Per Share	4.55	3.27	4.09	2.59	4.32	3.91	3.96	5.59
Tang Book Value Per Share	20.65	20.50	20.02	19.37	21.39	18.18	16.70	16.37
Dividends Per Share	0.855	0.835	0.830	0.830	1.660	1.660	1.660	1.660
Dividend Payout %	63.33	66.80	54.25	72.81	109.93	89.73	103.11	77.21
Income Statement								
Total Revenue	2,309,900	2,318,000	2,255,500	1,965,000	1,670,100	3,267,100	2,675,349	2,604,882
EBITDA	856,300	782,500	845,800	668,700	545,200	329,800	431,577	459,071
Depn & Amortn	330,600	305,000	349,100	306,000	249,100	3,300	182,972	173,145
Income Before Taxes	304,900	259,100	311,900	181,800	184,800	232,700	177,384	212,139
Income Taxes	104,600	84,800	99,000	29,500	63,800	71,500	47,822	39,691
Net Income	199,900	174,400	211,700	150,100	154,500	159,200	127,630	162,310
Average Shares	147,200	138,700	136,900	129,800	101,200	85,200	78,170	74,700
Balance Sheet								
Current Assets	723,700	619,100	611,600	612,500	603,800	654,900	570,782	490,918
Total Assets	9,647,300	9,118,000	8,818,200	8,482,800	7,869,300	4,826,700	4,335,660	3,833,726
Current Liabilities	1,449,500	1,634,900	1,339,300	958,300	1,337,400	990,200	1,202,993	402,922
Long-Term Obligations	2,756,800	2,742,300	2,942,700	3,213,000	2,556,600	1,102,900	607,510	1,140,880
Total Liabilities	6,268,300	6,119,100	5,893,300	5,651,300	5,279,700	3,219,800	2,954,744	2,571,299
Stockholders' Equity	3,379,000	2,998,900	2,924,900	2,831,500	2,589,600	1,606,900	1,380,916	1,262,427
Shares Outstanding	153,529	136,141	135,713	135,423	119,255	86,234	80,351	74,740
Statistical Record								
Return on Assets %	2.12	1.94	2.45	1.84	2.43	3.48	3.12	4.25
Return on Equity %	6.25	5.89	7.36	5.54	7.34	10.66	9.66	13.29
EBITDA Margin %	37.07	33.76	37.50	34.03	32.64	10.09	16.13	17.62
Net Margin %	8.65	7.52	9.39	7.64	9.25	4.87	4.77	6.23
Asset Turnover	0.25	0.26	0.26	0.24	0.26	0.71	0.65	0.68
Current Ratio	0.50	0.38	0.46	0.64	0.45	0.66	0.47	1.22
Debt to Equity	0.82	0.91	1.01	1.13	0.99	0.69	0.44	0.90
Price Range	22.81-19.54	21.97-16.53	19.63-16.85	20.34-11.17	29.32-17.09	33.18-26.99	32.80-27.33	32.63-27.27
P/E Ratio	16.90-14.47	17.58-13.22	12.83-11.01	17.84-9.80	19.42-11.32	17.94-14.59	20.37-16.98	15.18-12.68
Average Yield %	4.08	4.15	4.49	5.02	6.96	5.48	5.60	5.45

Address: 1200 Main Street, Kansas City, MO 64105
Telephone: 816-556-2200

Web Site: www.greatplainsenergy.com
Officers: William H. Downey - Executive Vice-Chairman, President, Chief Operating Officer Terry Bassham - Chief Executive Officer, Executive Vice President

Auditors: Deloitte & Touche LLP
Investor Contact: 816-654-1763
Transfer Agents: Computershare Trust Company, N.A, Providence, RI

GREEN DOT CORP

Exchange	Symbol	Price	52Wk Range	Yield	P/E
NYS	GDOT	$16.71 (3/28/2013)	26.91-9.06	N/A	15.62

*7 Year Price Score N/A   *NYSE Composite Index=100   *12 Month Price Score 86.83

Interim Earnings (Per Share)

Qtr.	Mar	Jun	Sep	Dec
2010	0.27	0.58	0.40	(0.64)
2011	0.58	0.54	0.60	(0.53)
2012	0.78	0.54	0.48	(0.73)

Interim Dividends (Per Share)

No Dividends Paid

Valuation Analysis

		Institutional Holding	
Forecast EPS	$1.18	No of Institutions	
	(04/05/2013)	142	
Market Cap	$601.5 Million	Shares	
Book Value	$327.8 Million	25,776,512	
Price/Book	1.84	% Held	
Price/Sales	1.10	N/A	

TRADING VOLUME (thousand shares)

Business Summary: Credit & Lending (MIC: 5.4.1 SIC: 7389 NAIC: 522210)

Green Dot is a financial services company providing money management applications to a base of U.S. consumers. Co.'s principal products and services consist of Green Dot-branded general purpose reloadable prepaid debit (GPR) cards, co-branded GPR cards, and MoneyPak and point-of-sale, swipe reload transactions facilitated by the Green Dot Network. Co. also services general purpose gift cards. GPR cards are designed for general spending purposes and can be used where their applicable payment network, such as Visa or MasterCard, is accepted. Co. sells its cards and provides its reload services nationwide at approximately 59,000 retail store locations.

Recent Developments: For the year ended Dec 31 2012, net income decreased 9.3% to US$47.2 million from US$52.1 million in the prior year. Revenues were US$546.3 million, up 16.9% from US$467.4 million the year before. Operating income was US$72.1 million versus US$83.4 million in the prior year, a decrease of 13.6%. Indirect operating expenses increased 23.5% to US$474.1 million from US$383.9 million in the equivalent prior-year period.

Prospects: Our evaluation of Green Dot Corp as of Apr. 7, 2013 is the result of our systematic analysis on three basic characteristics: earnings strength, relative valuation, and recent stock price movement. The company has generated a negative trend in earnings per share over the past 5 quarters and while recent estimates for the company have been raised by analysts, GDOT has posted better than expected results. Based on operating earnings yield, the company is undervalued when compared to all of the companies in our coverage universe. Share price changes over the past year indicates that GDOT will perform very poorly over the near term.

Financial Data

(US$ in Thousands)	12/31/2012	12/31/2011	12/31/2010	12/31/2009	07/31/2009	07/31/2008	07/31/2007
Earnings Per Share	1.07	1.19	0.98	0.29	0.52	0.26	(0.05)
Cash Flow Per Share	2.95	2.35	3.40	1.51	2.93	3.25	...
Tang Book Value Per Share	8.25	6.84	3.95	3.11	0.91	1.10	...
Income Statement							
Total Revenue	546,285	467,398	363,888	112,757	234,816	168,126	83,624
EBITDA	90,240	95,749	76,919	25,614	68,270	33,578	4,655
Depn & Amortn	18,100	12,300	7,600	2,300	4,600	4,400	3,500
Income Before Taxes	76,138	84,013	69,632	23,427	64,065	29,596	1,301
Income Taxes	28,919	31,930	27,400	9,764	26,902	12,261	(3,346)
Net Income	47,219	52,083	42,232	13,663	37,163	17,335	4,647
Average Shares	42,083	61,887	52,578	15,425	15,712	14,154	11,100
Balance Sheet							
Current Assets	530,219	337,025	249,893	145,377	94,099	82,044	...
Total Assets	725,728	425,859	285,758	183,108	123,269	97,246	...
Current Liabilities	379,407	161,654	111,508	104,732	76,804	63,198	...
Total Liabilities	397,964	172,663	120,627	111,744	81,031	65,962	...
Stockholders' Equity	327,764	253,196	165,131	71,364	42,238	31,284	...
Shares Outstanding	35,995	35,442	41,853	12,860	12,040	11,753	10,194
Statistical Record							
Return on Assets %	8.18	14.64	18.01	6.87	33.71	...	...
Return on Equity %	16.21	24.90	35.71	18.76	101.09	...	...
EBITDA Margin %	16.52	20.49	21.14	22.72	29.07	19.97	5.57
Net Margin %	8.64	11.14	11.61	12.12	15.83	10.31	5.56
Asset Turnover	0.95	1.31	1.55	0.57	2.13	...	...
Current Ratio	1.40	2.08	2.24	1.39	1.23	1.30	...
Price Range	32.36-9.06	64.29-26.42	64.68-42.95	...	...	...	...
P/E Ratio	30.24-8.47	54.03-22.20	66.00-43.83	...	...	...	...

Address: 3645 E. Foothill Blvd., Pasadena, CA 91107
Telephone: 626-765-2000

Web Site: www.greendot.com
Officers: Steven W. Streit - Chairman, President, Chief Executive Officer Samuel Altman - Executive Vice President

Auditors: Ernst & Young LLP
Investor Contact: 626-765-2427
Transfer Agents: Computershare Trust Company, N.A.

GREENHILL & CO INC

Exchange	Symbol	Price	52Wk Range	Yield	P/E
NYS	GHL	$53.38 (3/28/2013)	61.79-31.93	3.37	38.68

*7 Year Price Score 65.72   *NYSE Composite Index=100   *12 Month Price Score 115.63

Interim Earnings (Per Share)

Qtr.	Mar	Jun	Sep	Dec
2008	0.68	1.04	(0.42)	0.44
2009	0.47	0.35	1.01	0.56
2010	0.02	0.57	0.47	0.06
2011	(0.05)	0.69	0.28	0.52
2012	0.53	0.07	0.28	0.50

Interim Dividends (Per Share)

Amt	Decl	Ex	Rec	Pay
0.45Q	04/18/2012	06/04/2012	06/06/2012	06/20/2012
0.45Q	07/18/2012	08/31/2012	09/05/2012	09/19/2012
0.45Q	10/17/2012	12/03/2012	12/05/2012	12/19/2012
0.45Q	01/23/2013	03/04/2013	03/06/2013	03/20/2013

Indicated Div: $1.80

Valuation Analysis / **Institutional Holding**

Forecast EPS	$2.35	No of Institutions
	(04/05/2013)	205
Market Cap	$1.5 Billion	Shares
Book Value	$302.2 Million	% Held
Price/Book	4.97	96.94
Price/Sales	5.27	

Business Summary: Finance Intermediaries & Services (MIC: 5.5.1 SIC: 6211 NAIC: 523110)

Greenhill & Co is an investment bank. Co. provides advice on domestic and cross-border mergers, acquisitions, and similar corporate finance matters. In its financing advisory and restructuring practice, Co. provides advice on valuation, restructuring alternatives, capital structures, and sales or recapitalizations to debtors, creditors, governments and companies experiencing financial distress as well as potential acquirers of distressed companies and assets. In its private capital and real estate capital advisory business, Co. assists fund managers and sponsors in raising capital for new funds and provides advisory services to private equity and real estate funds and other organizations.

Recent Developments: For the year ended Dec 31 2012, net income decreased 5.6% to US$42.1 million from US$44.6 million in the prior year. Revenues were US$285.1 million, down 3.0% from US$294.0 million the year before. Indirect operating expenses decreased 4.8% to US$214.6 million from US$225.3 million in the equivalent prior-year period.

Prospects: Our evaluation of Greenhill & Co Inc. as of Apr. 7, 2013 is the result of our systematic analysis on three basic characteristics: earnings strength, relative valuation, and recent stock price movement. The company has enjoyed a very positive trend in earnings per share over the past 5 quarters. However, while recent estimates for the company have been lowered by analysts, GHL has posted results that fell short of analysts expectations. Based on operating earnings yield, the company is overvalued when compared to all of the companies in our coverage universe. Share price changes over the past year indicates that GHL will perform very well over the near term.

Financial Data

(US$ in Thousands)	12/31/2012	12/31/2011	12/31/2010	12/31/2009	12/31/2008	12/31/2007	12/31/2006	12/31/2005
Earnings Per Share	1.38	1.44	1.12	2.39	1.74	4.01	2.55	1.81
Cash Flow Per Share	3.09	3.15	2.22	2.07	(0.49)	5.08	1.31	2.00
Tang Book Value Per Share	3.21	4.80	5.49	7.63	6.51	4.62	4.83	3.92
Dividends Per Share	1.800	1.800	1.800	1.800	1.800	1.260	0.700	0.440
Dividend Payout %	130.43	125.00	160.71	75.31	103.45	31.42	27.45	24.31
Income Statement								
Total Revenue	285,079	293,993	278,329	298,646	221,873	400,422	290,646	221,152
EBITDA	78,731	78,718	67,014	119,306	86,031	184,454	122,166	92,496
Depn & Amortn	7,240	8,009	5,986	4,117	4,592	4,229	3,009	2,495
Income Before Taxes	70,475	68,669	58,951	113,893	77,858	177,201	119,157	90,000
Income Taxes	28,383	24,086	19,530	42,736	29,392	61,833	41,633	32,636
Net Income	42,092	44,577	34,526	71,240	48,978	115,276	75,666	55,532
Average Shares	30,561	31,034	30,776	29,753	28,214	28,728	29,627	30,671
Balance Sheet								
Current Assets	106,322	116,454	111,314	105,475	93,539	220,910	124,615	111,511
Total Assets	386,970	460,743	508,678	328,389	265,779	374,213	297,731	234,941
Current Liabilities	83,458	113,189	135,815	94,836	65,712	228,814	139,939	116,996
Total Liabilities	84,811	114,542	138,196	96,337	67,530	231,067	142,170	120,226
Stockholders' Equity	302,159	346,201	370,481	232,052	198,249	143,146	155,561	114,715
Shares Outstanding	28,148	28,647	29,341	27,977	27,981	26,729	28,522	29,229
Statistical Record								
Return on Assets %	9.90	9.20	8.25	23.98	15.26	34.31	28.41	26.96
Return on Equity %	12.95	12.44	11.46	33.11	28.61	77.18	55.99	45.90
EBITDA Margin %	27.62	26.78	24.08	39.95	38.77	46.06	42.03	41.82
Net Margin %	14.77	15.16	12.40	23.85	22.07	28.79	26.03	25.11
Asset Turnover	0.67	0.61	0.67	1.01	0.69	1.19	1.09	1.07
Current Ratio	1.27	1.03	0.82	1.11	1.42	0.97	0.89	0.95
Price Range	53.33-31.93	83.84-27.31	88.86-61.13	95.63-56.11	85.00-45.52	75.80-51.05	75.70-51.20	57.70-27.00
P/E Ratio	38.64-23.14	58.22-18.97	79.34-54.58	40.01-23.48	48.85-26.16	18.90-12.73	29.69-20.08	31.88-14.92
Average Yield %	4.19	3.52	2.38	2.37	2.83	1.90	1.14	1.10

Address: 300 Park Avenue, New York, NY 10022	**Web Site:** www.greenhill.com	**Auditors:** Ernst & Young LLP
Telephone: 212-389-1500	**Officers:** Robert F. Greenhill - Chairman Scott L. Bok - Chief Executive Officer	**Investor Contact:** 212-389-1800
		Transfer Agents: American Stock Transfer & Trust Company, New York, NY

341

GREIF INC

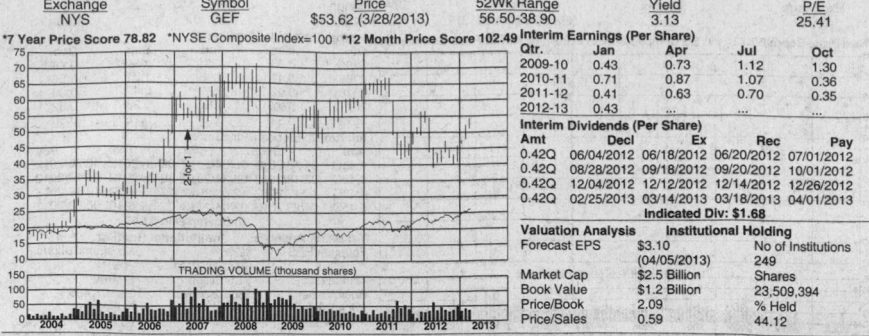

Exchange	Symbol	Price	52Wk Range	Yield	P/E
NYS	GEF	$53.62 (3/28/2013)	56.50-38.90	3.13	25.41

*7 Year Price Score 78.82   *NYSE Composite Index=100   *12 Month Price Score 102.49

Interim Earnings (Per Share)

Qtr.	Jan	Apr	Jul	Oct
2009-10	0.43	0.73	1.12	1.30
2010-11	0.71	0.87	1.07	0.36
2011-12	0.41	0.63	0.70	0.35
2012-13	0.43	...	...	...

Interim Dividends (Per Share)

Amt	Decl	Ex	Rec	Pay
0.42Q	06/04/2012	06/18/2012	06/20/2012	07/01/2012
0.42Q	08/28/2012	09/18/2012	09/20/2012	10/01/2012
0.42Q	12/04/2012	12/12/2012	12/14/2012	12/26/2012
0.42Q	02/25/2013	03/14/2013	03/18/2013	04/01/2013

Indicated Div: $1.68

Valuation Analysis   **Institutional Holding**

Forecast EPS	$3.10 (04/05/2013)	No of Institutions 249
Market Cap	$2.5 Billion	Shares
Book Value	$1.2 Billion	23,509,394
Price/Book	2.09	% Held
Price/Sales	0.59	44.12

Business Summary: Containers & Packaging (MIC: 8.1.3 SIC: 2655 NAIC: 322214)

Greif is a producer of industrial packaging products and services. Co. has four business segments: Rigid Industrial Packaging and Services, which provides steel, fibre and plastic drums, rigid intermediate bulk containers, closure systems, as well as services such as container life cycle services, blending, filling and other packaging services, logistics and warehousing; Flexible Products and Services, which produces flexible intermediate bulk containers, industrial and consumer shipping sacks and multiwall bag products; Paper Packaging, which produces containerboard and corrugated products; and Land Management, which focuses on the harvesting and regeneration of its U.S. timber properties.

Recent Developments: For the quarter ended Jan 31 2013, net income increased 14.9% to US$26.2 million from US$22.8 million in the year-earlier quarter. Revenues were US$1.01 billion, up 1.6% from US$992.8 million the year before. Operating income was US$64.6 million versus US$56.5 million in the prior-year quarter, an increase of 14.3%. Direct operating expenses rose 0.7% to US$821.3 million from US$815.4 million in the comparable period the year before. Indirect operating expenses increased 1.5% to US$122.7 million from US$120.9 million in the equivalent prior-year period.

Prospects: Our evaluation of Greif Bros. Corp. as of Apr. 7, 2013 is the result of our systematic analysis on three basic characteristics: earnings strength, relative valuation, and recent stock price movement. The company has enjoyed a very positive trend in earnings per share over the past 5 quarters and while recent estimates for the company have been raised by analysts, GEF has posted results that fell short of analysts expectations. Based on operating earnings yield, the company is about fairly valued when compared to all of the companies in our coverage universe. Share price changes over the past year indicates that GEF will perform poorly over the near term.

Financial Data
(US$ in Thousands)

	3 Mos	10/31/2012	10/31/2011	10/31/2010	10/31/2009	10/31/2008	10/31/2007	10/31/2006
Earnings Per Share	2.11	2.17	3.01	3.58	2.28	3.99	2.65	2.42
Cash Flow Per Share	8.38	9.98	3.65	3.78	5.69	2.98	8.33	4.96
Tang Book Value Per Share	0.50	0.55	0.01	8.39	7.86	9.40	8.79	10.67
Dividends Per Share	1.680	1.680	1.680	1.600	1.520	1.320	0.920	0.600
Dividend Payout %	79.62	77.42	55.81	44.69	66.67	33.08	34.72	24.84
Income Statement								
Total Revenue	1,008,600	4,269,500	4,247,954	3,461,537	2,792,217	3,776,756	3,322,294	2,628,475
EBITDA	99,700	408,400	445,665	416,776	315,954	454,435	346,747	326,664
Depn & Amortn	39,500	131,400	122,700	98,500	88,600	92,900	89,600	82,800
Income Before Taxes	38,600	187,100	243,413	252,489	173,761	311,907	211,635	207,871
Income Taxes	12,500	56,800	71,077	40,571	37,706	73,610	53,544	63,816
Net Income	24,900	126,100	176,040	209,985	132,433	234,354	156,368	142,119
Average Shares	25,400	25,200	25,044	24,959	24,639	24,378	24,172	23,726
Balance Sheet								
Current Assets	1,126,500	1,064,000	1,305,337	1,165,889	833,761	922,650	841,785	793,037
Total Assets	3,942,940	3,856,900	4,207,282	3,498,445	2,812,510	2,745,898	2,652,711	2,188,001
Current Liabilities	795,900	862,000	929,768	761,811	562,097	671,801	648,910	491,299
Long-Term Obligations	1,305,200	1,175,300	1,345,138	953,066	721,108	673,171	622,685	481,408
Total Liabilities	2,727,700	2,656,100	2,971,931	2,219,724	1,719,937	1,690,087	1,652,799	1,343,990
Stockholders' Equity	1,215,200	1,200,800	1,235,351	1,278,721	1,092,573	1,055,811	999,912	844,011
Shares Outstanding	47,466	47,403	47,092	47,169	46,937	46,644	46,698	46,299
Statistical Record								
Return on Assets %	3.06	3.12	4.57	6.65	4.77	8.66	6.46	6.98
Return on Equity %	9.92	10.32	14.00	17.71	12.33	22.74	16.96	18.05
EBITDA Margin %	9.88	9.57	10.49	12.04	11.32	12.03	10.44	12.43
Net Margin %	2.47	2.95	4.14	6.07	4.74	6.21	4.71	5.41
Asset Turnover	1.07	1.06	1.10	1.10	1.00	1.40	1.37	1.29
Current Ratio	1.42	1.23	1.40	1.53	1.48	1.37	1.30	1.61
Debt to Equity	1.07	0.98	1.09	0.75	0.66	0.64	0.62	0.57
Price Range	56.50-38.90	56.50-38.90	67.04-41.65	60.83-46.52	57.32-26.22	71.05-33.85	63.84-45.40	47.51-28.77
P/E Ratio	26.78-18.44	26.04-17.93	22.27-13.84	16.99-12.99	25.14-11.50	17.81-8.48	24.09-17.13	19.63-11.89
Average Yield %	3.67	3.63	2.82	2.86	3.65	2.13	1.63	1.76

Address: 425 Winter Road, Delaware, OH 43015
Telephone: 740-549-6000

Web Site: www.greif.com
Officers: Michael J. Gasser - Chairman David B. Fischer - President, Chief Executive Officer

Auditors: Ernst & Young, LLP
Investor Contact: 740-549-6000
Transfer Agents: National City Bank, Cleveland, OH

GROUP 1 AUTOMOTIVE, INC.

Exchange	Symbol	Price	52Wk Range	Yield	P/E
NYS	GPI	$60.07 (3/28/2013)	69.30-44.29	1.00	14.34

*7 Year Price Score 135.01 *NYSE Composite Index=100   ***12 Month Price Score 98.29**

Interim Earnings (Per Share)

Qtr.	Mar	Jun	Sep	Dec
2008	0.73	0.76	(0.91)	(1.96)
2009	0.37	0.43	0.78	(0.09)
2010	0.34	0.54	0.83	0.46
2011	0.66	1.06	0.94	0.80
2012	0.97	1.20	1.32	0.69

Interim Dividends (Per Share)

Amt	Decl	Ex	Rec	Pay
0.15Q	05/08/2012	05/30/2012	06/01/2012	06/15/2012
0.15Q	08/16/2012	08/30/2012	09/04/2012	09/18/2012
0.15Q	11/16/2012	11/29/2012	12/03/2012	12/17/2012
0.15Q	02/14/2013	02/27/2013	03/01/2013	03/15/2013

Indicated Div: $0.60

Valuation Analysis

		Institutional Holding	
Forecast EPS	$5.14	No of Institutions	
	(04/06/2013)	218	
Market Cap	$1.4 Billion	Shares	
Book Value	$892.8 Million	31,197,964	
Price/Book	1.53	% Held	
Price/Sales	0.18	106.72	

Business Summary: Retail - Automotive (MIC: 2.1.4 SIC: 5511 NAIC: 441110)

Group 1 Automotive is an operator in the automotive retail industry. Through its dealerships, Co. sells new and used cars and light trucks; arranges related vehicle financing; service and insurance contracts; provides automotive maintenance and repair services; and sells vehicle parts. Co. performs both warranty and non-warranty service work at its dealerships, primarily for the vehicle brand(s) sold at a particular location. As of Dec 31 2012, Co. owned and operated 142 franchises, representing 31 brands of automobiles, at 111 dealership locations and 28 collision service centers in the U.S. and 15 franchises at ten dealerships and three collision centers in the U.K.

Recent Developments: For the year ended Dec 31 2012, net income increased 21.6% to US$100.2 million from US$82.4 million in the prior year. Revenues were US$7.48 billion, up 23.0% from US$6.08 billion the year before. Operating income was US$230.0 million versus US$193.5 million in the prior year, an increase of 18.9%. Direct operating expenses rose 24.2% to US$6.36 billion from US$5.12 billion in the comparable period the year before. Indirect operating expenses increased 15.7% to US$887.3 million from US$767.1 million in the equivalent prior-year period.

Prospects: Our evaluation of Group 1 Automotive Inc. as of Apr. 7, 2013 is the result of our systematic analysis on three basic characteristics: earnings strength, relative valuation, and recent stock price movement. The company has generated a negative trend in earnings per share over the past 5 quarters and while recent estimates for the company have been raised by analysts, GPI has posted results that fell short of analysts expectations. Based on operating earnings yield, the company is undervalued when compared to all of the companies in our coverage universe. Share price changes over the past year indicates that GPI will perform in line with the market over the near term.

Financial Data

(US$ in Thousands)	12/31/2012	12/31/2011	12/31/2010	12/31/2009	12/31/2008	12/31/2007	12/31/2006	12/31/2005
Earnings Per Share	4.19	3.47	2.16	1.49	(1.39)	2.90	3.62	2.24
Cash Flow Per Share	(3.47)	9.00	(3.01)	15.50	7.55	0.16	2.21	15.31
Tang Book Value Per Share	5.03	4.62	4.95	2.53	N.M.	N.M.	0.68	3.74
Dividends Per Share	0.590	0.480	0.100	...	0.470	0.560	0.550	...
Dividend Payout %	14.08	13.83	4.63	...	...	19.31	15.19	...
Income Statement								
Total Revenue	7,476,100	6,079,765	5,509,169	4,525,707	5,654,087	6,392,997	6,083,484	5,969,590
EBITDA	261,496	220,603	168,731	142,071	50,187	200,511	222,913	183,426
Depn & Amortn	31,500	27,100	26,500	25,800	25,700	20,900	18,100	18,900
Income Before Taxes	160,735	132,094	80,904	54,851	(50,806)	106,023	139,348	108,407
Income Taxes	60,526	49,700	30,600	20,006	(21,316)	38,071	50,958	38,138
Net Income	100,209	82,394	50,304	34,845	(31,493)	67,952	88,390	54,231
Average Shares	22,688	22,409	23,317	23,325	22,671	23,406	24,446	24,229
Balance Sheet								
Current Assets	1,566,181	1,175,584	1,019,234	822,038	1,096,624	1,260,084	1,178,012	1,105,828
Total Assets	3,023,015	2,476,343	2,201,964	1,969,414	2,310,085	2,505,297	2,113,955	1,833,618
Current Liabilities	1,395,518	1,044,947	894,934	718,813	1,004,496	1,069,531	940,958	968,632
Long-Term Obligations	555,016	482,601	412,950	444,141	601,999	674,838	428,639	158,074
Total Liabilities	2,130,226	1,669,243	1,417,596	1,249,258	1,688,732	1,820,816	1,421,115	1,206,825
Stockholders' Equity	892,789	807,100	784,368	720,156	621,353	684,481	692,840	626,793
Shares Outstanding	22,726	22,707	23,793	24,479	23,946	23,105	24,261	24,016
Statistical Record								
Return on Assets %	3.63	3.52	2.41	1.63	N.M.	2.94	4.48	2.87
Return on Equity %	11.76	10.35	6.69	5.19	N.M.	9.87	13.40	9.08
EBITDA Margin %	3.50	3.63	3.06	3.14	0.89	3.14	3.66	3.07
Net Margin %	1.34	1.36	0.91	0.77	N.M.	1.06	1.45	0.91
Asset Turnover	2.71	2.60	2.64	2.12	2.34	2.77	3.08	3.16
Current Ratio	1.12	1.13	1.14	1.14	1.09	1.18	1.25	1.14
Debt to Equity	0.62	0.60	0.53	0.62	0.97	0.99	0.62	0.25
Price Range	65.51-44.29	51.80-33.93	42.29-22.49	34.47-7.42	29.08-5.65	54.51-23.71	63.18-32.02	32.72-24.04
P/E Ratio	15.63-10.57	14.93-9.78	19.58-10.41	23.13-4.98	...	18.80-8.18	17.45-8.85	14.61-10.73
Average Yield %	1.06	1.15	0.32	...	2.37	1.44	1.12	...

Address: 800 Gessner, Suite 500,	Web Site: www.group1auto.com	Auditors: Ernst & Young LLP
Houston, TX 77024	Officers: John L. Adams - Non-Executive Chairman	Transfer Agents: American Stock
Telephone: 713-647-5700	Earl J. Hesterberg - President, Chief Executive Officer	Transfer & Trust Company LLC
Fax: 713-647-5858		

GUESS ?, INC.

Exchange	Symbol	Price	52Wk Range	Yield	P/E
NYS	GES	$24.83 (3/28/2013)	33.54-22.66	3.22	12.11

*7 Year Price Score 70.55   *NYSE Composite Index=100   ***12 Month Price Score 91.88**

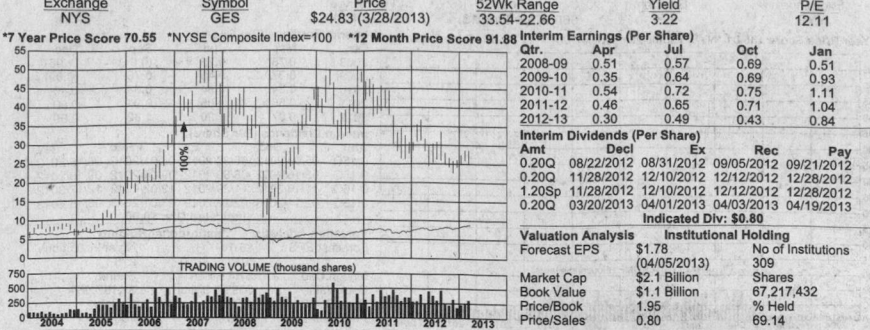

Interim Earnings (Per Share)

Qtr.	Apr	Jul	Oct	Jan
2008-09	0.51	0.57	0.69	0.51
2009-10	0.35	0.64	0.69	0.93
2010-11	0.54	0.72	0.75	1.11
2011-12	0.46	0.65	0.71	1.04
2012-13	0.30	0.49	0.43	0.84

Interim Dividends (Per Share)

Amt	Decl	Ex	Rec	Pay
0.20Q	08/22/2012	08/31/2012	09/05/2012	09/21/2012
0.20Q	11/28/2012	12/10/2012	12/12/2012	12/28/2012
1.20Sp	11/28/2012	12/10/2012	12/12/2012	12/28/2012
0.20Q	03/20/2013	04/01/2013	04/03/2013	04/19/2013

Indicated Div: $0.80

Valuation Analysis   **Institutional Holding**

Forecast EPS	$1.78 (04/05/2013)	No of Institutions 309
Market Cap	$2.1 Billion	Shares
Book Value	$1.1 Billion	67,217,432
Price/Book	1.95	% Held
Price/Sales	0.80	69.14

Business Summary: Retail - Apparel and Accessories (MIC: 2.1.5 SIC: 2331 NAIC: 315212)

GUESS® designs, markets, distributes and licenses collections of apparel and accessories for men, women and children. Co.'s apparel is marketed under various trademarks including GUESS, GUESS®, GUESS U.S.A., GUESS Jeans, GUESS® and Triangle Design, MARCIANO, GUESS Kids, and Baby GUESS. The lines include clothing, including jeans, pants, skirts, dresses, shorts, blouses, shirts, jackets, knitwear and intimate apparel. Co. also grants licenses to manufacture and distribute a range of products that complement its apparel lines, including eyewear, watches, handbags, footwear, kids' and infants' apparel, leather apparel, swimwear, fragrance, jewelry and other fashion accessories..

Recent Developments: For the year ended Feb 2 2013, net income decreased 32.9% to US$181.5 million from US$270.7 million in the prior year. Revenues were US$2.66 billion, down 1.1% from US$2.69 billion the year before. Operating income was US$274.5 million versus US$397.2 million in the prior year, a decrease of 30.9%. Direct operating expenses rose 3.9% to US$1.59 billion from US$1.53 billion in the comparable period the year before. Indirect operating expenses increased 4.4% to US$792.6 million from US$759.0 million in the equivalent prior-year period.

Prospects: Our evaluation of GUESS ® Inc. as of Apr. 7, 2013 is the result of our systematic analysis on three basic characteristics: earnings strength, relative valuation, and recent stock price movement. The company has produced a positive trend in earnings per share over the past 5 quarters. However, while recent estimates for the company have been lowered by analysts, GES has posted better than expected results. Based on operating earnings yield, the company is undervalued when compared to all of the companies in our coverage universe. Share price changes over the past year indicates that GES will perform in line with the market over the near term.

Financial Data

(US$ in Thousands)	02/02/2013	01/28/2012	01/29/2011	01/30/2010	01/31/2009	02/02/2008	02/03/2007	12/31/2006
Earnings Per Share	2.05	2.86	3.11	2.61	2.28	1.99	0.09	1.34
Cash Flow Per Share	3.07	3.99	3.80	3.95	2.48	1.91	0.83	1.53
Tang Book Value Per Share	12.09	12.67	11.01	10.51	7.94	6.40	4.26	4.18
Dividends Per Share	2.000	0.800	2.680	0.450	0.360	0.280	...	...
Dividend Payout %	97.56	27.97	86.17	17.24	15.79	14.07	...	...
Income Statement								
Total Revenue	2,658,605	2,688,048	2,487,294	2,128,466	2,093,390	1,749,916	135,952	1,185,184
EBITDA	282,739	400,438	424,780	370,261	325,344	313,400	13,013	200,245
Depn & Amortn	2,501	2,242	3,739	7,853	7,906	6,041	320	2,745
Income Before Taxes	280,614	399,341	421,377	361,929	318,809	311,463	12,720	195,997
Income Taxes	99,128	128,691	126,874	115,599	103,784	124,099	4,885	72,715
Net Income	178,744	265,500	289,508	242,761	213,562	186,472	7,980	123,168
Average Shares	86,540	91,948	92,115	91,592	93,570	93,695	93,120	92,074
Balance Sheet								
Current Assets	1,107,225	1,261,482	1,163,580	1,123,089	894,189	814,739	563,467	558,892
Total Assets	1,713,506	1,844,475	1,685,804	1,530,175	1,246,566	1,186,228	843,322	836,925
Current Liabilities	384,966	420,036	431,016	341,679	335,884	388,291	279,529	283,896
Long-Term Obligations	8,314	10,206	12,218	14,137	14,586	18,724	17,336	18,018
Total Liabilities	626,514	668,845	630,928	509,964	470,528	529,254	404,598	405,865
Stockholders' Equity	1,086,992	1,175,630	1,054,876	1,020,211	776,038	656,974	438,724	431,060
Shares Outstanding	85,367	89,631	92,290	92,736	92,329	94,337	93,105	92,088
Statistical Record								
Return on Assets %	9.89	15.08	18.05	17.53	17.61	18.43	10.20	16.75
Return on Equity %	15.54	23.87	27.98	27.10	29.89	34.13	19.70	34.24
EBITDA Margin %	10.63	14.90	17.08	17.40	15.54	17.91	9.57	16.90
Net Margin %	6.72	9.88	11.64	11.41	10.20	10.66	5.87	10.39
Asset Turnover	1.47	1.53	1.55	1.54	1.73	1.73	1.74	1.61
Current Ratio	2.88	3.00	2.70	3.29	2.66	2.10	2.02	1.97
Debt to Equity	0.01	0.01	0.01	0.01	0.02	0.03	0.04	0.04
Price Range	36.72-22.66	47.52-26.30	50.95-31.24	45.28-13.16	45.01-10.62	54.98-32.59	37.42-32.35	32.55-17.18
P/E Ratio	17.91-11.05	16.62-9.20	16.38-10.05	17.35-5.04	19.74-4.66	27.63-16.38	415.83-359.44	24.29-12.82
Average Yield %	7.10	2.20	6.55	1.50	1.15	0.63	...	...

Address: 1444 South Alameda Street, Los Angeles, CA 90021 Telephone: 213-765-3100	Web Site: www.guess.com Officers: Maurice Marciano - Chairman Paul Marciano - Vice-Chairman, Chief Executive Officer	Auditors: Ernst & Young LLP Investor Contact: 213-765-5578 Transfer Agents: ComputerShare Investor Services, Providence, RI

HALLIBURTON COMPANY

Exchange	Symbol	Price	52Wk Range	Yield	P/E
NYS	HAL	$40.41 (3/28/2013)	43.32-26.70	1.24	14.23

*7 Year Price Score 90.10   *NYSE Composite Index=100   *12 Month Price Score 110.01

Interim Earnings (Per Share)

Qtr.	Mar	Jun	Sep	Dec
2008	0.64	0.55	(0.02)	0.52
2009	0.42	0.29	0.29	0.27
2010	0.23	0.53	0.60	0.66
2011	0.56	0.80	0.74	0.98
2012	0.68	0.79	0.65	0.72

Interim Dividends (Per Share)

Amt	Decl	Ex	Rec	Pay
0.09Q	05/16/2012	06/04/2012	06/06/2012	06/27/2012
0.09Q	07/18/2012	08/31/2012	09/05/2012	09/26/2012
0.09Q	11/14/2012	12/04/2012	12/06/2012	12/27/2012
0.125Q	02/20/2013	03/04/2013	03/06/2013	03/27/2013

Indicated Div: $0.50

Valuation Analysis		Institutional Holding	
Forecast EPS	$3.00	No of Institutions	
	(04/06/2013)	1121	
Market Cap	$37.5 Billion	Shares	
Book Value	$15.8 Billion	795,322,752	
Price/Book	2.38	% Held	
Price/Sales	1.32	78.50	

Business Summary: Equipment & Services (MIC: 9.1.3 SIC: 1389 NAIC: 213112)

Halliburton is a provider of services and products to the energy industry related to the exploration, development, and production of oil and natural gas. Co. serves major, national, and independent oil and natural gas companies throughout the world and operates under two segments: Completion and Production, which delivers cementing, stimulation, intervention, pressure control, chemicals, artificial lift, and completion services; and Drilling and Evaluation, which provides field and reservoir modeling, drilling, evaluation, and wellbore placement services. Co. has manufacturing operations in various locations, including the U.S., Canada, Malaysia, Mexico, Singapore, and the U.K.

Recent Developments: For the year ended Dec 31 2012, income from continuing operations decreased 14.1% to US$2.59 billion from US$3.01 billion a year earlier. Net income decreased 7.0% to US$2.65 billion from US$2.84 billion in the prior year. Revenues were US$28.50 billion, up 14.8% from US$24.83 billion the year before. Operating income was US$4.16 billion versus US$4.74 billion in the prior year, a decrease of 12.2%. Direct operating expenses rose 21.5% to US$24.07 billion from US$19.81 billion in the comparable period the year before. Indirect operating expenses decreased 2.1% to US$275.0 million from US$281.0 million in the equivalent prior-year period.

Prospects: Our evaluation of Halliburton Co. as of Apr. 7, 2013 is the result of our systematic analysis on three basic characteristics: earnings strength, relative valuation, and recent stock price movement. The company has generated a negative trend in earnings per share over the past 5 quarters. However, while recent estimates for the company have been lowered by analysts, HAL has posted better than expected results. Based on operating earnings yield, the company is undervalued when compared to all of the companies in our coverage universe. Share price changes over the past year indicates that HAL will perform well over the near term.

Financial Data

(US$ in Thousands)	12/31/2012	12/31/2011	12/31/2010	12/31/2009	12/31/2008	12/31/2007	12/31/2006	12/31/2005
Earnings Per Share	2.84	3.08	2.01	1.27	1.70	3.68	2.23	2.27
Cash Flow Per Share	3.94	4.01	2.44	2.67	3.04	2.99	3.61	0.69
Tang Book Value Per Share	14.67	12.40	9.95	8.46	7.43	6.90	6.61	5.45
Dividends Per Share	0.360	0.360	0.360	0.360	0.360	0.345	0.300	0.250
Dividend Payout %	12.68	11.69	17.91	28.35	21.18	9.38	13.45	11.01
Income Statement								
Total Revenue	28,503,000	24,829,000	17,973,000	14,675,000	18,279,000	15,264,000	22,576,000	20,994,000
EBITDA	5,748,000	6,071,000	4,071,000	2,898,000	4,022,000	4,073,000	3,989,000	3,139,000
Depn & Amortn	1,628,000	1,359,000	1,119,000	931,000	738,000	583,000	527,000	504,000
Income Before Taxes	3,822,000	4,449,000	2,655,000	1,682,000	3,163,000	3,460,000	3,449,000	2,492,000
Income Taxes	1,235,000	1,439,000	853,000	518,000	1,211,000	907,000	1,144,000	79,000
Net Income	2,635,000	2,839,000	1,835,000	1,145,000	1,538,000	3,499,000	2,348,000	2,358,000
Average Shares	928,000	922,000	911,000	902,000	904,000	950,000	1,054,000	1,038,000
Balance Sheet								
Current Assets	13,086,000	11,577,000	8,886,000	8,638,000	7,411,000	7,573,000	11,183,000	9,327,000
Total Assets	27,410,000	23,677,000	18,297,000	16,538,000	14,385,000	13,135,000	16,820,000	15,010,000
Current Liabilities	4,752,000	4,121,000	2,757,000	2,889,000	2,781,000	2,411,000	4,727,000	4,437,000
Long-Term Obligations	4,820,000	4,820,000	3,824,000	3,824,000	2,586,000	2,627,000	2,786,000	2,813,000
Total Liabilities	11,645,000	10,479,000	7,924,000	7,810,000	6,660,000	6,269,000	9,444,000	8,638,000
Stockholders' Equity	15,765,000	13,198,000	10,373,000	8,728,000	7,725,000	6,866,000	7,376,000	6,372,000
Shares Outstanding	929,000	921,000	910,000	902,000	895,000	880,000	998,000	1,028,000
Statistical Record								
Return on Assets %	10.29	13.53	10.54	7.41	11.15	23.36	14.75	15.31
Return on Equity %	18.15	24.09	19.21	13.92	21.02	49.14	34.16	45.77
EBITDA Margin %	20.17	24.45	22.65	19.75	22.00	26.68	17.67	14.95
Net Margin %	9.24	11.43	10.21	7.80	8.41	22.92	10.40	11.23
Asset Turnover	1.11	1.18	1.03	0.95	1.32	1.02	1.42	1.36
Current Ratio	2.75	2.81	3.22	2.99	2.66	3.14	2.37	2.10
Debt to Equity	0.31	0.37	0.37	0.44	0.33	0.38	0.38	0.44
Price Range	38.51-26.70	57.27-28.68	41.15-21.15	31.75-14.78	53.91-13.46	41.48-28.27	41.66-26.57	34.70-18.79
P/E Ratio	13.56-9.40	18.59-9.31	20.47-10.52	25.00-11.64	31.71-7.92	11.27-7.68	18.68-11.91	15.29-8.28
Average Yield %	1.09	0.84	1.15	1.57	1.00	1.00	0.87	0.97

Address: 3000 North Sam Houston Parkway East, Houston, TX 77032 Telephone: 281-871-2699	Web Site: www.halliburton.com Officers: David J. Lesar - Chairman, President, Chief Executive Officer Albert O. Cornelison - Executive Vice President, General Counsel	Auditors: KPMG LLP Investor Contact: 888-669-3920 Transfer Agents: Computershare

HANESBRANDS INC

Exchange	Symbol	Price	52Wk Range	Yield	P/E
NYS	HBI	$45.56 (3/28/2013)	45.56-24.78	N/A	27.78

*7 Year Price Score N/A   *NYSE Composite Index=100   *12 Month Price Score 112.90

Interim Earnings (Per Share)

Qtr.	Mar	Jun	Sep	Dec
2008	0.38	0.60	0.17	0.20
2009	(0.20)	0.32	0.43	(0.01)
2010	0.37	0.87	0.63	0.29
2011	0.49	0.87	0.91	0.41
2012	(0.27)	0.01	1.10	0.80

Interim Dividends (Per Share)

No Dividends Paid

Valuation Analysis **Institutional Holding**

Forecast EPS	$3.40	No of Institutions
	(04/06/2013)	375
Market Cap	$4.5 Billion	Shares
Book Value	$886.9 Million	101,128,264
Price/Book	5.05	% Held
Price/Sales	0.99	97.91

TRADING VOLUME (thousand shares)

Business Summary: Apparel, Footwear & Accessories (MIC: 1.4.2 SIC: 2389 NAIC: 313312)

Hanesbrands is a consumer goods company. Co. is engaged in designing, manufacturing, sourcing and selling a range of basic apparel such as T-shirts, bras, panties, men's underwear, kids' underwear, casualwear, activewear, socks and hosiery. Co.'s apparel brands include Hanes, Champion, C9 by Champion, Bali, Playtex, Just My Size, L'eggs, barely there, Wonderbra, Gear for Sports, Zorba, Sol y Oro and Rinbros. Co. operates four segments: Innerwear, Outerwear, Direct to Consumer and International.

Recent Developments: For the year ended Dec 29 2012, income from continuing operations decreased 4.2% to US$232.4 million from US$242.6 million a year earlier. Net income decreased 38.2% to US$164.7 million from US$266.7 million in the prior year. Revenues were US$4.53 billion, up 2.1% from US$4.43 billion the year before. Operating income was US$440.1 million versus US$447.1 million in the prior year, a decrease of 1.6%. Direct operating expenses rose 5.6% to US$3.11 billion from US$2.94 billion in the comparable period the year before. Indirect operating expenses decreased 6.3% to US$979.9 million from US$1.05 billion in the equivalent prior-year period.

Prospects: Our evaluation of Hanesbrands Inc. as of Apr. 7, 2013 is the result of our systematic analysis on three basic characteristics: earnings strength, relative valuation, and recent stock price movement. The company has enjoyed a very positive trend in earnings per share over the past 5 quarters and while recent estimates for the company have been raised by analysts, HBI has posted better than expected results. Based on operating earnings yield, the company is undervalued when compared to all of the companies in our coverage universe. Share price changes over the past year indicates that HBI will perform poorly over the near term.

Financial Data

(US$ in Thousands)	12/29/2012	12/31/2011	01/01/2011	01/02/2010	01/03/2009	12/29/2007	12/30/2006	07/01/2006
Earnings Per Share	1.64	2.69	2.16	0.54	1.34	1.30	0.77	...
Cash Flow Per Share	5.58	1.72	1.38	4.37	1.85	3.75	0.94	...
Tang Book Value Per Share	3.39	0.80	N.M.	N.M.	N.M.	N.M.	N.M.	...
Income Statement								
Total Revenue	4,525,721	4,637,143	4,326,713	3,891,275	4,248,770	4,474,537	2,250,473	4,472,832
EBITDA	492,836	562,629	470,579	318,310	433,259	515,010	256,085	547,804
Depn & Amortn	93,036	90,725	86,612	96,755	115,145	131,676	73,412	114,204
Income Before Taxes	262,945	315,607	233,731	58,276	163,037	184,126	111,920	416,320
Income Taxes	30,502	48,919	22,438	6,993	35,868	57,999	37,781	93,827
Net Income	164,681	266,688	211,293	51,283	127,169	126,127	74,139	322,493
Average Shares	100,269	99,251	97,774	95,668	95,164	96,741	96,620	...
Balance Sheet								
Current Assets	2,027,525	2,330,791	2,147,671	1,822,557	2,110,325	2,094,334	2,071,180	3,755,812
Total Assets	3,631,700	4,034,669	3,790,002	3,326,564	3,534,049	3,439,483	3,435,620	4,891,075
Current Liabilities	875,668	933,719	829,350	878,975	748,284	688,982	611,181	1,611,954
Long-Term Obligations	1,317,500	1,807,777	1,990,735	1,727,547	2,130,907	2,315,250	2,484,000	2,786
Total Liabilities	2,744,834	3,353,608	3,227,328	2,991,845	3,348,894	3,150,579	3,366,349	1,661,941
Stockholders' Equity	886,866	681,061	562,674	334,719	185,155	288,904	69,271	3,229,134
Shares Outstanding	98,269	97,517	96,207	95,396	93,520	95,232	96,312	...
Statistical Record								
Return on Assets %	4.31	6.84	5.95	1.50	3.59	3.68	1.29	7.09
Return on Equity %	21.06	43.00	47.22	19.78	52.78	70.62	3.71	11.09
EBITDA Margin %	10.89	12.13	10.88	8.18	10.20	11.51	11.38	12.25
Net Margin %	3.64	5.75	4.88	1.32	2.99	2.82	3.29	7.21
Asset Turnover	1.18	1.19	1.22	1.14	1.20	1.31	0.39	0.98
Current Ratio	2.32	2.50	2.59	2.07	2.82	3.04	3.39	2.33
Debt to Equity	1.49	2.65	3.54	5.16	11.51	8.01	35.86	N.M.
Price Range	36.50-22.19	33.26-21.84	30.81-21.67	25.97-5.78	37.50-9.39	32.75-24.04	24.71-18.00	...
P/E Ratio	22.26-13.53	12.36-8.12	14.26-10.03	48.09-10.70	27.99-7.01	25.19-18.49	32.09-23.38	...

Address: 1000 East Hanes Mill Road, Winston-Salem, NC 27105 Telephone: 336-519-8080	Web Site: www.hanesbrands.com Officers: Richard A. Noll - Chairman, Chief Executive Officer William J. Nictakis - President, Chief Commercial Officer, Co-Chief Operating Officer	Auditors: PricewaterhouseCoopers LLP Transfer Agents: ComputerShare Investor Services, Providence, RI

HANOVER INSURANCE GROUP INC

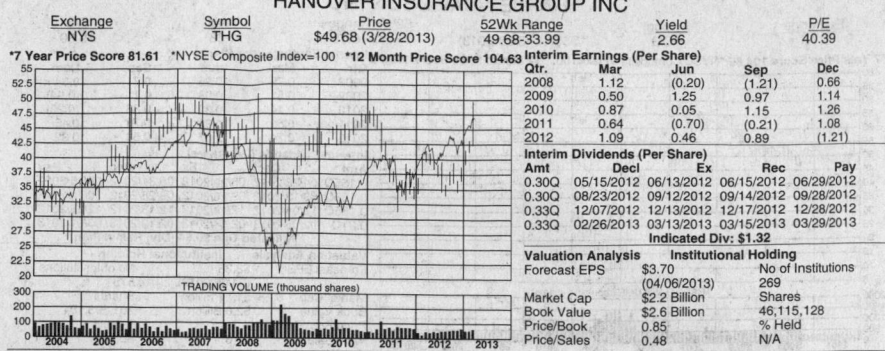

<table>
Exchange	Symbol	Price	52Wk Range	Yield	P/E
NYS	THG	$49.68 (3/28/2013)	49.68-33.99	2.66	40.39
</table>

*7 Year Price Score 81.61   *NYSE Composite Index=100   *12 Month Price Score 104.63

Interim Earnings (Per Share)

Qtr.	Mar	Jun	Sep	Dec
2008	1.12	(0.20)	(1.21)	0.66
2009	0.50	1.25	0.97	1.14
2010	0.87	0.05	1.15	1.26
2011	0.64	(0.70)	(0.21)	1.08
2012	1.09	0.46	0.89	(1.21)

Interim Dividends (Per Share)

Amt	Decl	Ex	Rec	Pay
0.30Q	05/15/2012	06/13/2012	06/15/2012	06/29/2012
0.30Q	08/23/2012	09/12/2012	09/14/2012	09/28/2012
0.33Q	12/07/2012	12/13/2012	12/17/2012	12/28/2012
0.33Q	02/26/2013	03/13/2013	03/15/2013	03/29/2013

Indicated Div: $1.32

Valuation Analysis

		Institutional Holding	
Forecast EPS	$3.70 (04/06/2013)	No of Institutions	269
Market Cap	$2.2 Billion	Shares	46,115,128
Book Value	$2.6 Billion	% Held	N/A
Price/Book	0.85		
Price/Sales	0.48		

Business Summary: General Insurance (MIC: 5.2.1 SIC: 6331 NAIC: 524126)

The Hanover Insurance Group is a holding company. Co.'s primary business operations include insurance products and services provided through four operating segments. These operating segments are: Commercial Lines, which includes commercial multiple peril, commercial automobile, workers' compensation and other commercial coverages; Personal Lines, which includes personal automobile, homeowners and other personal coverages; Chaucer, which includes marine and aviation, energy, property, U.K. motor, and casualty; and Other Property and Casualty, which markets investment management services to institutions, pension funds and other organizations.

Recent Developments: For the year ended Dec 31 2012, income from continuing operations increased 46.3% to US$46.1 million from US$31.5 million a year earlier. Net income increased 52.3% to US$55.9 million from US$36.7 million in the prior year. Revenues were US$4.59 billion, up 16.8% from US$3.93 billion the year before. Net premiums earned were US$4.24 billion versus US$3.60 billion in the prior year, an increase of 17.8%. Net investment income rose 7.1% to US$276.6 million from US$258.2 million a year ago.

Prospects: Our evaluation of Hanover Insurance Group Inc. as of Apr. 7, 2013 is the result of our systematic analysis on three basic characteristics: earnings strength, relative valuation, and recent stock price movement. The company has suffered a very negative trend in earnings per share over the past 5 quarters and while recent estimates for the company have been raised by analysts, THG has posted better than expected results. Based on operating earnings yield, the company is overvalued when compared to all of the companies in our coverage universe. Share price changes over the past year indicates that THG will perform very poorly over the near term.

Financial Data
(US$ in Thousands)

	12/31/2012	12/31/2011	12/31/2010	12/31/2009	12/31/2008	12/31/2007	12/31/2006	12/31/2005
Earnings Per Share	1.23	0.81	3.34	3.86	0.40	4.83	3.27	(6.02)
Cash Flow Per Share	9.11	4.90	1.83	1.81	4.07	1.42	0.81	2.86
Tang Book Value Per Share	54.41	52.11	50.81	46.05	33.74	41.95	36.75	33.95
Dividends Per Share	1.230	1.125	1.000	0.750	0.450	0.400	0.300	0.250
Dividend Payout %	100.00	138.89	29.94	19.43	112.50	8.28	9.17	...
Income Statement								
Premium Income	4,239,100	3,598,600	2,841,000	2,546,400	2,484,900	2,404,800	2,254,600	2,198,200
Total Revenue	4,590,700	3,931,600	3,152,200	2,834,100	2,680,400	2,786,800	2,644,100	2,624,300
Benefits & Claims	2,974,400	2,550,800	1,856,300	1,639,200	...	...	...	...
Income Before Taxes	28,700	22,300	211,100	270,900	164,400	348,400	279,400	71,300
Income Taxes	(17,400)	(9,600)	57,900	83,100	79,900	109,200	87,700	(5,200)
Net Income	55,900	37,100	154,800	197,200	20,600	253,100	170,300	(325,200)
Average Shares	45,300	45,800	46,300	51,100	51,700	52,400	52,200	54,000
Balance Sheet								
Total Assets	13,484,900	12,624,400	8,569,900	8,042,700	9,230,200	9,815,600	9,856,600	10,634,000
Total Liabilities	10,889,500	10,114,600	6,109,400	5,684,100	7,343,000	7,516,600	7,857,400	8,682,700
Stockholders' Equity	2,595,400	2,509,800	2,460,500	2,358,600	1,887,200	2,299,000	1,999,200	1,951,300
Shares Outstanding	44,300	44,600	44,900	47,500	50,900	51,800	51,100	53,700
Statistical Record								
Return on Assets %	0.43	0.35	1.86	2.28	0.22	2.57	1.66	N.M.
Return on Equity %	2.18	1.49	6.42	9.29	0.98	11.78	8.62	N.M.
Loss Ratio %	70.17	70.88	65.34	64.37	...	...	...	...
Net Margin %	1.22	0.94	4.91	6.96	0.77	9.08	6.44	(12.39)
Price Range	41.39-33.99	48.82-31.22	47.73-40.51	45.23-28.49	51.00-31.92	49.76-41.14	54.11-41.17	42.11-30.27
P/E Ratio	33.65-27.63	60.27-38.54	14.29-12.13	11.72-7.38	127.50-79.80	10.30-8.52	16.55-12.59	...
Average Yield %	3.25	2.83	2.25	1.96	1.05	0.87	0.64	0.67
</table>

<table>
Address: 440 Lincoln Street, Worcester, MA 01653 Telephone: 508-855-1000 Fax: 508-855-6332	Web Site: www.hanover.com Officers: Micheal P. Angelini - Chairman Frederick H. Eppinger - President, Chief Executive Officer	Auditors: PricewaterhouseCoopers LLP Investor Contact: 508-855-2063 Transfer Agents: Computershare, Jersey City, NJ
</table>

HARLEY-DAVIDSON INC

Exchange	Symbol	Price	52Wk Range	Yield	P/E
NYS	HOG	$53.30 (3/28/2013)	55.41-40.79	1.58	19.60

*7 Year Price Score 104.65 *NYSE Composite Index=100 *12 Month Price Score 102.03

Interim Earnings (Per Share)

Qtr.	Mar	Jun	Sep	Dec
2008	0.79	0.95	0.71	0.34
2009	0.51	0.08	0.11	(0.94)
2010	0.14	0.30	0.38	(0.20)
2011	0.51	0.81	0.78	0.46
2012	0.74	1.07	0.59	0.32

Interim Dividends (Per Share)

Amt	Decl	Ex	Rec	Pay
0.155Q	04/28/2012	05/29/2012	05/31/2012	06/15/2012
0.155Q	09/13/2012	09/26/2012	09/28/2012	10/12/2012
0.155Q	12/04/2012	12/14/2012	12/18/2012	12/28/2012
0.21Q	02/05/2013	02/14/2013	02/19/2013	03/01/2013

Indicated Div: $0.84 (Div. Reinv. Plan)

Valuation Analysis

		Institutional Holding	
Forecast EPS	$3.38	No of Institutions	
	(04/06/2013)	578	
Market Cap	$12.1 Billion	Shares	
Book Value	$2.6 Billion	201,803,184	
Price/Book	4.71	% Held	
Price/Sales	2.16	80.05	

Business Summary: Autos- Manufacturing (MIC: 1.8.1 SIC: 3751 NAIC: 336991)

Harley-Davidson is the parent company for the groups of companies doing business as Harley-Davidson Motor Company and Harley-Davidson Financial Services (HDFS). Co. operates in two segments: Motorcycles & Related Products (Motorcycles), which designs, manufactures and sells at wholesale heavyweight (street legal with engine displacement of 651+cc) Harley-Davidson motorcycles as well as a line of motorcycle parts, accessories, general merchandise and related services; as well as Financial Services, which provides wholesale and retail financing and provides insurance and insurance-related programs primarily to Harley-Davidson dealers and their retail customers through HDFS.

Recent Developments: For the year ended Dec 31 2012, income from continuing operations increased 13.8% to US$623.9 million from US$548.1 million a year earlier. Net income increased 4.1% to US$623.9 million from US$599.1 million in the prior year. Revenues were US$5.58 billion, up 5.1% from US$5.31 billion the year before. Operating income was US$1.00 billion versus US$830.0 million in the prior year, an increase of 20.5%. Direct operating expenses rose 2.6% to US$3.44 billion from US$3.35 billion in the comparable period the year before. Indirect operating expenses increased 1.0% to US$1.14 billion from US$1.13 billion in the equivalent prior-year period.

Prospects: Our evaluation of Harley-Davidson Inc. as of Apr. 7, 2013 is the result of our systematic analysis on three basic characteristics: earnings strength, relative valuation, and recent stock price movement. The company has managed to produce a neutral trend in earnings per share over the past 5 quarters and while recent estimates for the company have been mixed, HOG has posted results that fell short of analysts expectations. Based on operating earnings yield, the company is undervalued when compared to all of the companies in our coverage universe. Share price changes over the past year indicates that HOG will perform well over the near term.

Financial Data
(US$ in Thousands)

	12/31/2012	12/31/2011	12/31/2010	12/31/2009	12/31/2008	12/31/2007	12/31/2006	12/31/2005
Earnings Per Share	2.72	2.55	0.62	(0.24)	2.79	3.74	3.93	3.41
Cash Flow Per Share	3.52	3.80	4.99	2.62	(2.92)	3.20	2.88	3.43
Tang Book Value Per Share	11.18	10.37	9.24	8.86	8.49	9.70	10.45	11.05
Dividends Per Share	0.620	0.475	0.400	0.400	1.290	1.060	0.810	0.625
Dividend Payout %	22.79	18.63	64.52	...	46.24	28.34	20.61	18.33
Income Statement								
Total Revenue	5,580,506	5,311,713	4,859,336	4,781,909	5,971,277	6,143,044	6,185,577	5,673,832
EBITDA	1,176,523	1,018,338	735,997	446,684	1,280,800	1,651,991	1,838,009	1,693,464
Depn & Amortn	168,978	180,408	255,171	246,344	242,281	204,172	213,769	205,705
Income Before Taxes	961,512	792,664	390,469	178,660	1,033,977	1,447,819	1,624,240	1,487,759
Income Taxes	337,587	244,586	130,800	108,019	379,259	513,976	581,087	528,155
Net Income	623,925	599,114	146,545	(55,116)	654,718	933,843	1,043,153	959,604
Average Shares	229,229	234,918	234,787	233,573	234,477	249,882	265,273	281,035
Balance Sheet								
Current Assets	4,050,936	4,542,206	4,066,626	4,341,949	5,377,881	3,467,314	3,550,633	3,145,237
Total Assets	9,170,773	9,674,164	9,430,740	9,155,518	7,828,625	5,656,606	5,532,150	5,255,209
Current Liabilities	1,503,082	2,698,618	2,013,782	2,268,224	2,603,757	1,905,079	1,595,677	873,112
Long-Term Obligations	4,370,544	3,843,886	4,520,591	4,114,039	2,176,238	980,000	870,000	1,000,000
Total Liabilities	6,613,149	7,253,908	7,223,874	7,047,400	5,713,022	3,281,115	2,775,413	2,171,604
Stockholders' Equity	2,557,624	2,420,256	2,206,866	2,108,118	2,115,603	2,375,491	2,756,737	3,083,605
Shares Outstanding	226,100	230,540	235,520	234,313	232,764	238,485	258,052	274,001
Statistical Record								
Return on Assets %	6.60	6.27	1.58	N.M.	9.68	16.69	19.34	17.87
Return on Equity %	25.00	25.90	6.79	N.M.	29.08	36.39	35.72	30.45
EBITDA Margin %	21.08	19.17	15.15	9.34	21.45	26.89	29.71	29.85
Net Margin %	11.18	11.28	3.02	N.M.	10.96	15.20	16.86	16.91
Asset Turnover	0.59	0.56	0.52	0.56	0.88	1.10	1.15	1.06
Current Ratio	2.70	1.68	2.02	1.91	2.07	1.82	2.23	3.60
Debt to Equity	1.71	1.59	2.05	1.95	1.03	0.41	0.32	0.32
Price Range	53.49-39.33	45.91-32.10	35.49-21.51	29.58-8.20	46.71-11.90	73.85-44.96	75.50-47.96	62.18-44.40
P/E Ratio	19.67-14.46	18.00-12.59	57.24-34.69	...	16.74-4.27	19.75-12.02	19.21-12.20	18.23-13.02
Average Yield %	1.35	1.24	1.40	2.03	3.78	1.83	1.41	1.18

Address: 3700 West Juneau Avenue, Milwaukee, WI 53208 **Telephone:** 414-342-4680 **Fax:** 414-343-4621	**Web Site:** www.harley-davidson.com **Officers:** Barry K. Allen - Chairman Keith E. Wandell - President, Chief Executive Officer	**Auditors:** Ernst & Young LLP **Investor Contact:** 187-743-78625 **Transfer Agents:** Computershare, Inc., Providence, RI

HARMAN INTERNATIONAL INDUSTRIES, INC.

Exchange	Symbol	Price	52Wk Range	Yield	P/E
NYS	HAR	$44.63 (3/28/2013)	50.25-35.70	1.34	9.83

*7 Year Price Score 73.95   *NYSE Composite Index=100   *12 Month Price Score 93.16

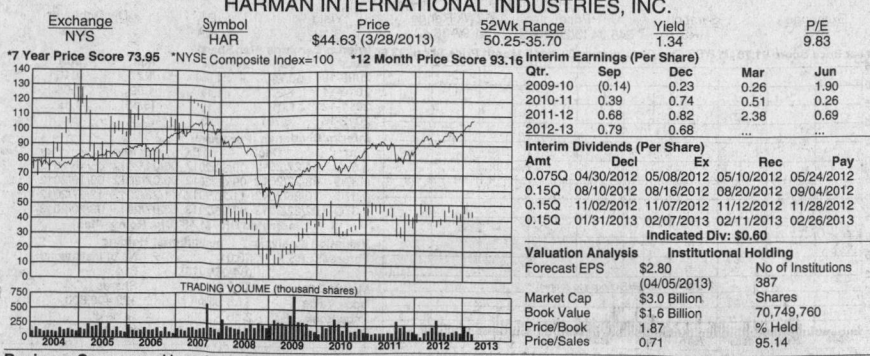

Interim Earnings (Per Share)

Qtr.	Sep	Dec	Mar	Jun
2009-10	(0.14)	0.23	0.26	1.90
2010-11	0.39	0.74	0.51	0.26
2011-12	0.68	0.82	2.38	0.69
2012-13	0.79	0.68	...	...

Interim Dividends (Per Share)

Amt	Decl	Ex	Rec	Pay
0.075Q	04/30/2012	05/08/2012	05/10/2012	05/24/2012
0.15Q	08/10/2012	08/16/2012	08/20/2012	09/04/2012
0.15Q	11/02/2012	11/07/2012	11/12/2012	11/28/2012
0.15Q	01/31/2013	02/07/2013	02/11/2013	02/26/2013

Indicated Div: $0.60

Valuation Analysis / **Institutional Holding**

Forecast EPS	$2.80	No of Institutions
	(04/05/2013)	387
Market Cap	$3.0 Billion	Shares
Book Value	$1.6 Billion	70,749,760
Price/Book	1.87	% Held
Price/Sales	0.71	95.14

Business Summary: Household Appliances, Electronics & Goods (MIC: 1.5.1 SIC: 3651 NAIC: 334310)

Harman International Industries is engaged in the development, manufacturing and marketing of audio products and electronic systems, and audio and infotainment systems. Co. has three segments: Infotainment, which designs, manufactures and markets infotainment systems for vehicle applications to be installed as original equipment by automotive manufacturers; Lifestyle, which designs, manufactures and markets automotive audio systems for vehicle applications to be installed as original equipment by automotive manufacturers, and loudspeaker and electronics for home and mobile applications; and Professional, which designs, manufactures and markets loudspeakers, headphones, and mixing consoles.

Recent Developments: For the quarter ended Dec 31 2012, net income decreased 19.9% to US$47.5 million from US$59.3 million in the year-earlier quarter. Revenues were US$1.06 billion, down 6.3% from US$1.13 billion the year before. Operating income was US$68.4 million versus US$95.4 million in the prior-year quarter, a decrease of 28.3%. Direct operating expenses declined 4.6% to US$783.8 million from US$821.5 million in the comparable period the year before. Indirect operating expenses decreased 3.2% to US$203.4 million from US$210.2 million in the equivalent prior-year period.

Prospects: Our evaluation of Harman International Industries Inc. as of Apr. 7, 2013 is the result of our systematic analysis on three basic characteristics: earnings strength, relative valuation, and recent stock price movement. The company has generated a negative trend in earnings per share over the past 5 quarters and while recent estimates for the company have remained steady, HAR has posted results that fell short of analysts expectations. Based on operating earnings yield, the company is undervalued when compared to all of the companies in our coverage universe. Share price changes over the past year indicates that HAR will perform in line with the market over the near term.

Financial Data
(US$ in Thousands)

	6 Mos	3 Mos	06/30/2012	06/30/2011	06/30/2010	06/30/2009	06/30/2008	06/30/2007
Earnings Per Share	4.54	4.68	4.57	1.90	2.25	(7.19)	1.73	4.72
Cash Flow Per Share	2.82	3.91	3.76	4.67	3.42	1.34	5.14	3.30
Tang Book Value Per Share	21.20	20.56	20.05	18.65	14.80	12.87	15.44	16.71
Dividends Per Share	0.450	0.375	0.300	0.050	...	0.037	0.050	0.050
Dividend Payout %	9.91	8.01	6.56	2.63	...	...	2.89	1.06
Income Statement								
Total Revenue	2,053,835	998,193	4,364,078	3,772,345	3,364,428	2,891,022	4,112,503	3,551,144
EBITDA	197,925	104,261	391,379	298,296	206,946	(365,300)	285,474	510,867
Depn & Amortn	54,200	26,500	110,100	115,500	127,654	147,457	152,342	127,162
Income Before Taxes	134,043	71,766	261,153	160,220	49,077	(519,696)	124,484	382,205
Income Taxes	31,999	17,211	(68,388)	24,304	8,610	(97,897)	17,119	70,186
Net Income	102,044	54,555	329,541	135,916	158,769	(422,551)	107,786	313,963
Average Shares	69,734	69,471	72,083	71,635	70,595	58,766	62,182	66,449
Balance Sheet								
Current Assets	2,061,025	2,146,368	2,116,245	2,108,155	1,673,979	1,510,531	1,439,081	1,233,153
Total Assets	3,104,815	3,187,551	3,169,464	3,058,495	2,556,215	2,492,353	2,826,925	2,508,868
Current Liabilities	967,247	1,352,587	1,381,900	1,047,581	863,451	743,530	906,952	815,981
Long-Term Obligations	270,047	...	...	378,401	363,902	628,854	427,313	57,661
Total Liabilities	1,485,518	1,613,101	1,639,853	1,634,837	1,421,323	1,518,528	1,487,079	1,014,827
Stockholders' Equity	1,619,297	1,574,450	1,529,611	1,423,658	1,134,892	973,825	1,339,846	1,494,041
Shares Outstanding	67,856	67,813	67,286	69,920	69,530	69,329	58,518	65,238
Statistical Record								
Return on Assets %	10.46	10.79	10.55	4.84	6.29	N.M.	4.03	12.91
Return on Equity %	20.98	22.44	22.26	10.62	15.06	N.M.	7.59	23.07
EBITDA Margin %	9.64	10.44	8.97	7.91	6.15	N.M.	6.94	14.39
Net Margin %	4.97	5.47	7.55	3.60	4.72	N.M.	2.62	8.84
Asset Turnover	1.37	1.39	1.40	1.34	1.33	1.09	1.54	1.46
Current Ratio	2.13	1.59	1.53	2.01	1.94	2.03	1.59	1.51
Debt to Equity	0.17	...	...	0.27	0.32	0.65	0.32	0.04
Price Range	50.70-35.70	50.70-26.20	50.70-26.20	51.58-29.12	52.51-17.89	44.34-9.41	117.74-37.08	122.59-76.32
P/E Ratio	11.17-7.86	10.83-5.60	11.09-5.73	27.15-15.33	23.34-7.95	...	68.06-21.43	25.97-16.17
Average Yield %	1.04	0.89	0.74	0.12	...	0.17	0.07	0.05

Address: 400 Atlantic Street, Suite 1500, Stamford, CT 06901 Telephone: 203-328-3500	Web Site: www.harman.com Officers: Dinesh C. Paliwal - Chairman, President, Chief Executive Officer Herbert K. Parker - Executive Vice President, Chief Financial Officer	Auditors: KPMG LLP Transfer Agents: Computershare Shareowner Services, Jersey City, NJ

HARRIS CORP.

Exchange	Symbol	Price	52Wk Range	Yield	P/E	Div Achiever
NYS	HRS	$46.34 (3/28/2013)	51.97-38.43	3.19	N/A	11 Years

*7 Year Price Score 91.70 ***NYSE Composite Index=100** ***12 Month Price Score 93.60**

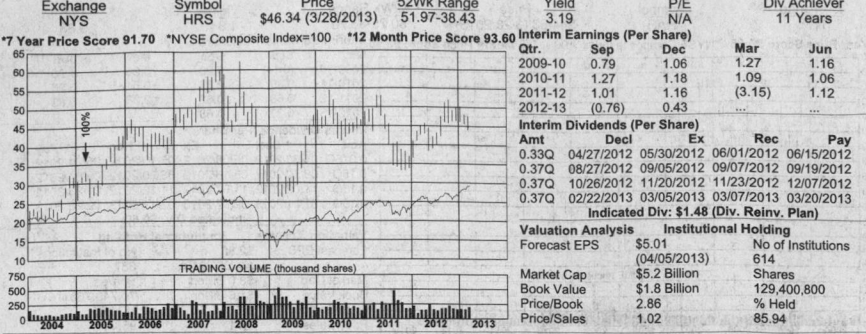

Interim Earnings (Per Share)
Qtr.	Sep	Dec	Mar	Jun
2009-10	0.79	1.06	1.27	1.16
2010-11	1.27	1.18	1.09	1.06
2011-12	1.01	1.16	(3.15)	1.12
2012-13	(0.76)	0.43	...	...

Interim Dividends (Per Share)
Amt	Decl	Ex	Rec	Pay
0.33Q	04/27/2012	05/30/2012	06/01/2012	06/15/2012
0.37Q	08/27/2012	09/05/2012	09/07/2012	09/19/2012
0.37Q	10/26/2012	11/20/2012	11/23/2012	12/07/2012
0.37Q	02/22/2013	03/05/2013	03/07/2013	03/20/2013

Indicated Div: $1.48 (Div. Reinv. Plan)

Valuation Analysis / Institutional Holding
Forecast EPS	$5.01 (04/05/2013)	No of Institutions	614
Market Cap	$5.2 Billion	Shares	129,400,800
Book Value	$1.8 Billion	% Held	85.94
Price/Book	2.86		
Price/Sales	1.02		

Business Summary: Defense (MIC: 7.1.2 SIC: 3812 NAIC: 339111)

Harris is an international communications and information technology (IT) company. Co. has three segments: RF communications, which supplies tactical radio communications and embedded encryption applications for military, government and commercial organizations and also of communications systems and equipment for public safety, utility and transportation markets; integrated network solutions, which provides networking capabilities to support government, energy, maritime and healthcare customers; and government communications systems, which conducts research, develops, produces, integrates and supports communications and IT for civilian, intelligence and defense government customers.

Recent Developments: For the quarter ended Dec 31 2012, income from continuing operations increased 2.7% to US$138.5 million from US$134.8 million in the year-earlier quarter. Net income decreased 66.1% to US$44.8 million from US$132.3 million in the year-earlier quarter. Revenues were US$1.29 billion, down 1.8% from US$1.31 billion the year before. Direct operating expenses declined 1.2% to US$845.4 million from US$856.0 million in the comparable period the year before. Indirect operating expenses decreased 2.4% to US$214.2 million from US$219.4 million in the equivalent prior-year period.

Prospects: Our evaluation of Harris Corp. as of Apr. 7, 2013 is the result of our systematic analysis on three basic characteristics: earnings strength, relative valuation, and recent stock price movement. The company has managed to produce a neutral trend in earnings per share over the past 5 quarters. However, while recent estimates for the company have been lowered by analysts, HRS has posted better than expected results. Based on operating earnings yield, the company is undervalued when compared to all of the companies in our coverage universe. Share price changes over the past year indicates that HRS will perform well over the near term.

Financial Data
(US$ in Thousands)	6 Mos	3 Mos	06/29/2012	07/01/2011	07/02/2010	07/03/2009	06/27/2008	06/29/2007
Earnings Per Share	(2.36)	(1.63)	0.26	4.60	4.28	0.28	3.26	3.43
Cash Flow Per Share	7.61	8.00	7.49	6.67	6.24	4.96	4.12	3.32
Tang Book Value Per Share	N.M.	N.M.	N.M.	N.M.	2.48	0.20	2.69	N.M.
Dividends Per Share	1.400	1.310	1.220	1.000	0.880	0.800	0.600	0.440
Dividend Payout %	...	...	469.23	21.74	20.56	285.71	18.40	12.83
Income Statement								
Total Revenue	2,548,400	1,261,500	5,451,300	5,924,600	5,206,100	5,005,000	5,311,000	4,243,000
EBITDA	512,000	249,500	1,095,200	1,103,700	1,020,900	628,400	792,800	774,900
Depn & Amortn	69,700	34,500	143,000	135,400	110,000	93,500	105,900	86,600
Income Before Taxes	387,800	187,600	841,500	880,700	840,300	485,300	638,500	660,700
Income Taxes	121,000	59,300	286,000	293,600	278,700	172,900	201,500	190,900
Net Income	(37,300)	(85,800)	30,600	588,000	561,600	37,900	444,200	480,400
Average Shares	112,900	112,600	114,800	126,300	130,000	133,200	136,500	141,100
Balance Sheet								
Current Assets	2,259,200	2,358,400	2,600,400	2,216,800	1,995,700	1,859,400	2,046,700	1,828,800
Total Assets	5,241,300	5,354,300	5,592,800	6,172,800	4,734,700	4,465,100	4,558,600	4,406,000
Current Liabilities	1,163,200	1,255,300	1,414,400	1,430,500	1,042,900	1,109,700	995,000	1,638,100
Long-Term Obligations	1,879,200	1,882,900	1,883,000	1,887,200	1,176,600	1,177,300	831,800	408,900
Total Liabilities	3,418,500	3,507,900	3,653,900	3,670,800	2,545,100	2,596,000	2,284,600	2,502,200
Stockholders' Equity	1,822,800	1,846,400	1,938,900	2,502,000	2,189,600	1,869,100	2,274,000	1,903,800
Shares Outstanding	112,396	112,951	112,147	123,118	127,460	131,370	133,594	129,577
Statistical Record								
Return on Assets %	N.M.	N.M.	0.52	10.81	12.24	0.83	9.94	12.76
Return on Equity %	N.M.	N.M.	1.38	25.13	27.75	1.80	21.32	27.02
EBITDA Margin %	20.09	19.78	20.09	18.63	19.61	12.56	14.93	18.26
Net Margin %	N.M.	N.M.	0.56	9.92	10.79	0.76	8.36	11.32
Asset Turnover	0.89	0.92	0.93	1.09	1.13	1.09	1.19	1.13
Current Ratio	1.94	1.88	1.84	1.55	1.91	1.68	2.06	1.12
Debt to Equity	1.03	1.02	0.97	0.75	0.54	0.63	0.37	0.21
Price Range	51.97-36.04	51.34-33.23	45.70-33.23	53.13-41.18	54.41-27.51	51.03-26.32	62.31-43.42	52.61-36.13
P/E Ratio			175.77-127.81	11.55-8.95	12.71-6.43	182.26-93.99	19.11-13.32	15.34-10.53
Average Yield %	3.16	3.18	3.08	2.16	2.06	2.20	1.13	1.00

Address: 1025 West NASA Boulevard, Melbourne, FL 32919
Telephone: 321-727-9100

Web Site: www.harris.com
Officers: Thomas A. Dattilo - Chairman William M. Brown - President, Chief Executive Officer

Auditors: Ernst & Young LLP
Investor Contact: 321-727-9383
Transfer Agents: Mellon Investor Services LLC, Jersey City, NJ

HARRIS TEETER SUPERMARKETS, INC.

Exchange	Symbol	Price	52Wk Range	Yield	P/E
NYS	HTSI	$42.71 (3/28/2013)	44.03-35.72	1.40	22.96

*7 Year Price Score 105.75 *NYSE Composite Index=100 ***12 Month Price Score 96.79**

Interim Earnings (Per Share)

Qtr.	Dec	Mar	Jun	Sep
2009-10	0.49	0.57	0.59	0.66
2010-11	0.78	0.61	0.66	(0.18)
2011-12	0.28	0.62	0.32	0.46
2012-13	0.46	...	...	...

Interim Dividends (Per Share)

Amt	Decl	Ex	Rec	Pay
0.14Q	08/16/2012	09/05/2012	09/07/2012	10/01/2012
0.50Sp	11/15/2012	12/12/2012	12/14/2012	12/31/2012
0.15Q	11/15/2012	12/12/2012	12/14/2012	01/01/2013
0.15Q	02/21/2013	03/06/2013	03/08/2013	04/01/2013

Indicated Div: $0.60

Valuation Analysis | **Institutional Holding**

Forecast EPS	$2.31	No of Institutions
	(04/05/2013)	215
Market Cap	$2.1 Billion	Shares
Book Value	$1.0 Billion	50,503,464
Price/Book	2.05	% Held
Price/Sales	0.46	N/A

Business Summary: Retail - Food & Beverage, Drug & Tobacco (MIC: 2.1.2 SIC: 5411 NAIC: 445110)

Harris Teeter Supermarkets, through its primary subsidiary Harris Teeter, Inc., is engaged in operating a regional chain of supermarkets. These supermarkets provide an assortment of groceries, produce, meat and seafood, bakery items, wines, as well as non-food items such as health and beauty care, general merchandise and floral. In addition, Co. operates pharmacies in its supermarkets. Retail supermarket operations are supported by two Co.-owned distribution centers and one Co.-owned dairy production facility. As of Oct 2 2012, Co. operated 208 supermarkets located in North Carolina, Virginia, South Carolina, Maryland, Tennessee, Delaware, District of Columbia, Florida and Georgia.

Recent Developments: For the quarter ended Jan 1 2013, income from continuing operations decreased 11.7% to US$22.8 million from US$25.8 million in the year-earlier quarter. Net income increased 67.0% to US$22.8 million from US$13.7 million in the year-earlier quarter. Revenues were US$1.16 billion, up 3.7% from US$1.12 billion the year before. Operating income was US$40.5 million versus US$46.3 million in the prior-year quarter, a decrease of 12.6%. Direct operating expenses rose 4.2% to US$826.4 million from US$792.7 million in the comparable period the year before. Indirect operating expenses increased 4.9% to US$294.3 million from US$280.6 million in the equivalent prior-year period.

Prospects: Our evaluation of Harris Teeter Supermarkets, Innc. as of Apr. 7, 2013 is the result of our systematic analysis on three basic characteristics: earnings strength, relative valuation, and recent stock price movement. The company has produced a positive trend in earnings per share over the past quarters and while recent estimates for the company have remained steady, HTSI has posted results that fell short of analysts expectations. Based on operating earnings yield, the company is about fairly valued when compared to all of the companies in our coverage universe. Share price changes over the past year indicates that HTSI will perform in line with the market over the near term.

Financial Data
(US$ in Thousands)

	3 Mos	10/02/2012	10/02/2011	10/03/2010	09/27/2009	09/28/2008	09/30/2007	10/01/2006
Earnings Per Share	1.86	1.68	1.87	2.31	1.78	2.00	1.68	1.52
Cash Flow Per Share	4.27	4.24	5.63	4.97	4.89	4.76	4.48	3.39
Tang Book Value Per Share	20.11	20.35	19.44	17.80	16.23	16.35	14.56	13.24
Dividends Per Share	1.070	0.550	0.520	0.480	0.480	0.480	0.440	0.440
Dividend Payout %	57.53	32.74	27.81	20.78	26.97	24.00	26.19	28.95
Income Statement								
Total Revenue	1,161,099	4,535,414	4,285,565	4,400,450	4,077,822	3,992,397	3,639,208	3,265,856
EBITDA	76,952	305,433	340,815	333,619	281,084	288,149	249,200	216,416
Depn & Amortn	36,496	134,455	140,717	135,338	125,487	114,405	100,798	88,900
Income Before Taxes	36,203	154,567	181,115	178,405	138,783	154,595	131,055	114,021
Income Taxes	13,395	54,640	69,657	65,297	52,225	57,359	49,803	41,061
Net Income	22,808	82,512	91,247	112,041	85,964	96,752	80,688	72,336
Average Shares	49,156	49,053	48,852	48,600	48,337	48,295	48,139	47,687
Balance Sheet								
Current Assets	579,131	634,393	759,673	544,971	474,286	477,156	456,264	425,445
Total Assets	1,891,966	1,952,488	1,984,424	1,889,886	1,844,321	1,696,407	1,529,689	1,362,936
Current Liabilities	387,124	451,638	479,373	402,047	402,865	410,803	382,770	327,326
Long-Term Obligations	207,417	208,271	283,428	296,131	355,561	310,953	255,857	228,269
Total Liabilities	863,039	914,869	1,015,149	997,437	1,032,142	872,572	793,079	692,419
Stockholders' Equity	1,028,927	1,037,619	969,275	892,449	812,179	823,835	736,610	670,517
Shares Outstanding	49,469	49,292	49,147	48,901	48,545	48,278	48,127	47,557
Statistical Record								
Return on Assets %	4.85	4.18	4.72	5.90	4.87	6.01	5.59	5.65
Return on Equity %	9.05	8.20	9.83	12.93	10.54	12.43	11.50	11.34
EBITDA Margin %	6.63	6.73	7.95	7.58	6.89	7.22	6.85	6.63
Net Margin %	1.96	1.82	2.13	2.55	2.11	2.42	2.22	2.21
Asset Turnover	2.42	2.30	2.22	2.32	2.31	2.48	2.52	2.55
Current Ratio	1.50	1.40	1.58	1.36	1.18	1.16	1.19	1.30
Debt to Equity	0.20	0.20	0.29	0.33	0.44	0.38	0.35	0.34
Price Range	44.40-35.72	44.96-37.23	45.57-33.58	36.99-24.93	32.52-19.17	39.55-30.00	35.67-25.65	26.43-19.60
P/E Ratio	23.87-19.20	26.76-22.16	24.37-17.96	16.01-10.79	18.27-10.77	19.77-15.00	21.23-15.27	17.39-12.89
Average Yield %	2.71	1.36	1.34	1.56	1.89	1.39	1.48	1.90

Address: 701 Crestdale Road, Matthews, NC 28105 **Telephone:** 704-844-3100	**Web Site:** www.harristeeter.com **Officers:** Thomas W. Dickson - Chairman, President, Chief Executive Officer Frederick J. Morganthall - President, Chief Operating Officer	**Auditors:** KPMG LLP **Investor Contact:** 704-844-7536 **Transfer Agents:** McGuireWoods LL P

HARSCO CORP.

Exchange	Symbol	Price	52Wk Range	Yield	P/E
NYS	HSC	$24.77 (3/28/2013)	25.82-18.75	3.31	N/A

*7 Year Price Score 56.05   *NYSE Composite Index=100   *12 Month Price Score 102.91

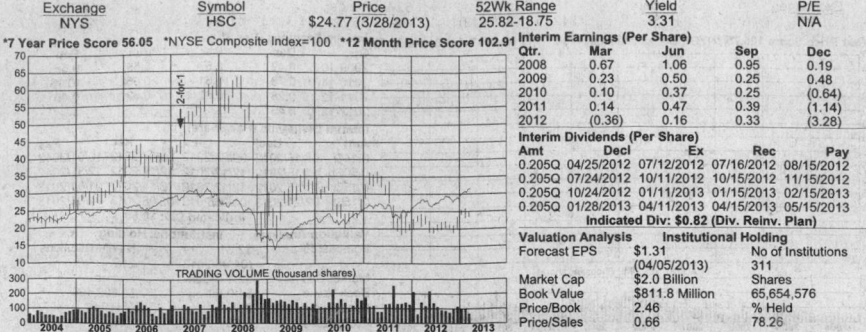

Interim Earnings (Per Share)

Qtr.	Mar	Jun	Sep	Dec
2008	0.67	1.06	0.95	0.19
2009	0.23	0.50	0.25	0.48
2010	0.10	0.37	0.25	(0.64)
2011	0.14	0.47	0.39	(1.14)
2012	(0.36)	0.16	0.33	(3.28)

Interim Dividends (Per Share)

Amt	Decl	Ex	Rec	Pay
0.205Q	04/25/2012	07/12/2012	07/16/2012	08/15/2012
0.205Q	07/24/2012	10/11/2012	10/15/2012	11/15/2012
0.205Q	10/24/2012	01/11/2013	01/15/2013	02/15/2013
0.205Q	01/28/2013	04/11/2013	04/15/2013	05/15/2013

Indicated Div: $0.82 (Div. Reinv. Plan)

Valuation Analysis

	Institutional Holding	
Forecast EPS	$1.31 (04/05/2013)	No of Institutions 311
Market Cap	$2.0 Billion	Shares
Book Value	$811.8 Million	65,654,576
Price/Book	2.46	% Held
Price/Sales	0.66	78.26

Business Summary: Industrial Machinery & Equipment (MIC: 7.2.1 SIC: 3291 NAIC: 327910)

Harsco provides industrial services and other products. Co. has four segments: Harsco Metals & Minerals, which provides on-site, outsourced services to the metals industries; Harsco Infrastructure, which provides rental and sales of scaffolding, shoring, concrete forming and other access-related applications; Harsco Rail, which provides equipment and services for the maintenance, repair and construction of railway track; and Harsco Industrial, which consists of: Harsco Industrial IKG, which manufactures industrial grating products; Harsco Industrial Air-X-Changers, which supplies air-cooled heat exchangers; and Harsco Industrial Patterson-Kelley, which manufactures heat transfer products.

Recent Developments: For the year ended Dec 31 2012, loss from continuing operations was US$253.2 million compared with a loss of US$7.5 million a year earlier. Net loss amounted to US$254.1 million versus a net loss of US$9.6 million in the prior year. Revenues were US$3.05 billion, down 7.8% from US$3.30 billion the year before. Operating loss was US$174.8 million versus an income of US$87.6 million in the prior year. Direct operating expenses declined 8.6% to US$2.35 billion from US$2.57 billion in the comparable period the year before. Indirect operating expenses increased 35.2% to US$871.3 million from US$644.5 million in the equivalent prior-year period.

Prospects: Our evaluation of Harsco Corp. as of Apr. 7, 2013 is the result of our systematic analysis on three basic characteristics: earnings strength, relative valuation, and recent stock price movement. The company has managed to produce a neutral trend in earnings per share over the past 5 quarters and while recent estimates for the company have remained steady, HSC has posted results that fell short of analysts expectations. Based on operating earnings yield, the company is about fairly valued when compared to all of the companies in our coverage universe. Share price changes over the past year indicates that HSC will perform well over the near term.

Financial Data

(US$ in Thousands)	12/31/2012	12/31/2011	12/31/2010	12/31/2009	12/31/2008	12/31/2007	12/31/2006	12/31/2005
Earnings Per Share	(3.16)	(0.14)	0.08	1.47	2.87	3.53	2.33	1.86
Cash Flow Per Share	2.46	3.70	4.98	5.41	6.85	5.60	4.88	3.79
Tang Book Value Per Share	3.78	4.99	7.70	7.76	7.99	7.78	5.30	4.25
Dividends Per Share	0.820	0.820	0.820	0.795	0.780	0.710	0.650	0.600
Dividend Payout %	...	...	1,025.00	54.08	27.18	20.11	27.96	32.26
Income Statement								
Total Revenue	3,046,018	3,302,740	3,038,678	2,990,577	3,967,822	3,688,160	3,423,293	2,766,210
EBITDA	77,115	363,670	357,665	501,632	719,835	735,202	603,866	464,087
Depn & Amortn	251,905	276,021	279,234	282,976	307,847	277,397	245,397	195,139
Income Before Taxes	(218,495)	41,665	20,476	158,838	342,436	381,390	301,700	230,195
Income Taxes	35,251	49,848	4,276	18,509	91,820	117,598	97,523	64,771
Net Income	(254,612)	(11,510)	6,754	118,777	240,945	299,492	196,398	156,657
Average Shares	80,632	80,736	80,761	80,586	84,029	84,724	84,430	84,160
Balance Sheet								
Current Assets	1,066,443	1,159,431	1,154,946	1,169,338	1,205,488	1,345,337	1,231,622	1,101,023
Total Assets	2,975,969	3,338,877	3,469,220	3,639,240	3,562,970	3,905,430	3,326,423	2,975,804
Current Liabilities	637,575	782,268	767,864	751,102	888,426	873,970	910,775	748,403
Long-Term Obligations	957,428	853,800	849,724	901,734	891,817	1,012,087	864,817	905,859
Total Liabilities	2,164,127	2,162,498	2,037,526	2,165,663	2,149,294	2,339,311	2,180,059	1,981,910
Stockholders' Equity	811,842	1,176,379	1,431,694	1,473,577	1,413,676	1,566,119	1,146,364	993,894
Shares Outstanding	80,584	80,477	80,514	80,353	80,174	84,459	84,037	83,566
Statistical Record								
Return on Assets %	N.M.	N.M.	0.19	3.30	6.43	8.28	6.23	5.84
Return on Equity %	N.M.	N.M.	0.46	8.23	16.13	22.08	18.35	16.42
EBITDA Margin %	2.53	11.01	11.77	16.77	18.14	19.93	17.64	16.78
Net Margin %	N.M.	N.M.	0.22	3.97	6.07	8.12	5.74	5.66
Asset Turnover	0.96	0.97	0.85	0.83	1.06	1.02	1.09	1.03
Current Ratio	1.67	1.48	1.50	1.56	1.36	1.54	1.35	1.47
Debt to Equity	1.18	0.73	0.59	0.61	0.63	0.65	0.75	0.91
Price Range	24.27-18.75	36.49-18.24	35.23-19.94	37.37-17.34	64.07-18.04	65.75-37.21	44.01-34.28	34.70-24.97
P/E Ratio	...	...	440.37-249.25	25.42-11.80	22.32-6.29	18.63-10.54	18.89-14.71	18.66-13.42
Average Yield %	3.91	2.92	3.02	2.73	1.65	1.37	1.65	2.02

Address: 350 Poplar Church Road, Camp Hill, PA 17011	Web Site: www.harsco.com	Auditors: PricewaterhouseCoopers LLP
Telephone: 717-763-7064	**Officers:** Richard C. Neuffer - Vice-Chairman Patrick K. Decker - President, Chief Executive Officer	**Investor Contact:** 717-975-5677
Fax: 717-763-6424		**Transfer Agents:** Computershare, Jersey City, NJ

HARTFORD FINANCIAL SERVICES GROUP INC.

Exchange	Symbol	Price	52Wk Range	Yield	P/E
NYS	HIG	$25.80 (3/28/2013)	26.46-15.93	1.55	N/A

*7 Year Price Score 41.73   *NYSE Composite Index=100   *12 Month Price Score 110.03

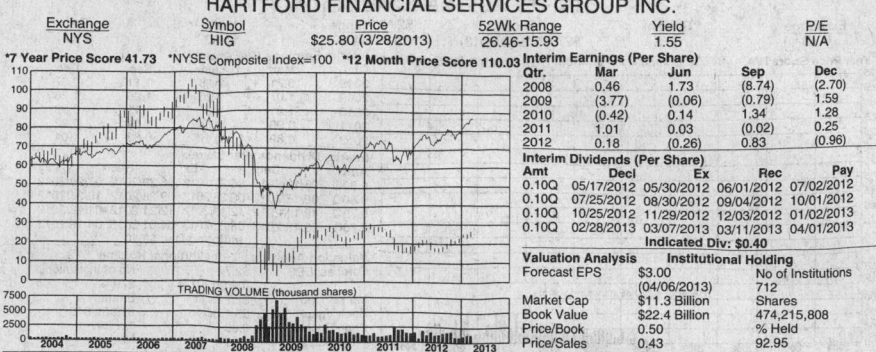

Interim Earnings (Per Share)

Qtr.	Mar	Jun	Sep	Dec
2008	0.46	1.73	(8.74)	(2.70)
2009	(3.77)	(0.06)	(0.79)	1.59
2010	(0.42)	0.14	1.34	1.28
2011	1.01	0.03	(0.02)	0.25
2012	0.18	(0.26)	0.83	(0.96)

Interim Dividends (Per Share)

Amt	Decl	Ex	Rec	Pay
0.10Q	05/17/2012	05/30/2012	06/01/2012	07/02/2012
0.10Q	07/25/2012	08/30/2012	09/04/2012	10/01/2012
0.10Q	10/25/2012	11/29/2012	12/03/2012	01/02/2013
0.10Q	02/28/2013	03/07/2013	03/11/2013	04/01/2013

Indicated Div: $0.40

Valuation Analysis / **Institutional Holding**

Forecast EPS	$3.00
	(04/06/2013)
Market Cap	$11.3 Billion
Book Value	$22.4 Billion
Price/Book	0.50
Price/Sales	0.43

No of Institutions 712
Shares 474,215,808
% Held 92.95

Business Summary: General Insurance (MIC: 5.2.1 SIC: 6331 NAIC: 524210)

Hartford Financial Services Group is a financial and insurance holding company. Through its subsidiaries, Co. provides investment products and life, property, and casualty insurance to both individual and business customers in the U.S. Co. has four divisions: Commercial Markets, which consist of the Property & Casualty Commercial and Group Benefits segments; Consumer Markets, which provides automobile, homeowners and home-based business coverages; Wealth Management, which consists of the reporting segments of Individual Annuity, Individual Life, Retirement Plans and Mutual Funds; and Runoff Operations, which includes Life Other Operations and Property & Casualty Other Operations.

Recent Developments: For the year ended Dec 31 2012, loss from continuing operations was US$33.0 million compared with income of US$626.0 million a year earlier. Net loss amounted to US$38.0 million versus net income of US$712.0 million in the prior year. Revenues were US$26.41 billion, up 20.8% from US$21.86 billion the year before. Net premiums earned were US$13.63 billion versus US$14.09 billion in the prior year, a decrease of 3.2%. Net investment income rose 202.2% to US$8.80 billion from US$2.91 billion a year ago.

Prospects: Our evaluation of Hartford Financial Services Group Inc. as of Apr. 7, 2013 is the result of our systematic analysis on three basic characteristics: earnings strength, relative valuation, and recent stock price movement. The company has generated a negative trend in earnings per share over the past 5 quarters and while recent estimates for the company have been raised by analysts, HIG has posted better than expected results. Based on operating earnings yield, the company is undervalued when compared to all of the companies in our coverage universe. Share price changes over the past year indicates that HIG will perform in line with the market over the near term.

Financial Data
(US$ in Thousands)

	12/31/2012	12/31/2011	12/31/2010	12/31/2009	12/31/2008	12/31/2007	12/31/2006	12/31/2005
Earnings Per Share	(0.18)	1.30	2.49	(2.93)	(8.99)	9.24	8.69	7.44
Cash Flow Per Share	6.11	5.11	7.67	8.59	13.63	18.94	18.26	12.52
Tang Book Value Per Share	48.67	48.24	42.07	35.77	27.31	55.69	53.07	45.03
Dividends Per Share	0.400	0.400	0.200	0.200	1.910	2.030	1.700	1.170
Dividend Payout %	...	30.77	8.03	...	...	21.97	19.56	15.73
Income Statement								
Premium Income	13,631,000	14,088,000	14,055,000	14,424,000	15,503,000	15,619,000	15,025,000	14,359,000
Total Revenue	26,412,000	21,859,000	22,383,000	24,701,000	9,219,000	25,916,000	26,500,000	27,083,000
Income Before Taxes	(527,000)	230,000	2,264,000	(1,728,000)	(4,591,000)	4,005,000	3,602,000	2,985,000
Income Taxes	(494,000)	(346,000)	584,000	(841,000)	(1,842,000)	1,056,000	857,000	711,000
Net Income	(38,000)	662,000	1,680,000	(887,000)	(2,749,000)	2,949,000	2,745,000	2,274,000
Average Shares	437,700	478,000	481,500	346,300	306,700	319,100	315,900	305,600
Balance Sheet								
Total Assets	298,513,000	304,064,000	318,346,000	307,717,000	287,583,000	360,361,000	326,710,000	285,557,000
Total Liabilities	276,066,000	281,154,000	298,035,000	289,852,000	278,315,000	341,157,000	307,834,000	270,232,000
Stockholders' Equity	22,447,000	22,910,000	20,311,000	17,865,000	9,268,000	19,204,000	18,876,000	15,325,000
Shares Outstanding	436,305	442,539	444,549	383,007	300,578	313,842	323,315	302,152
Statistical Record								
Return on Assets %	N.M.	0.21	0.54	N.M.	N.M.	0.86	0.90	0.83
Return on Equity %	N.M.	3.06	8.80	N.M.	N.M.	15.49	16.05	15.38
Net Margin %	(0.14)	3.03	7.51	(3.59)	(29.82)	11.38	10.36	8.40
Price Range	22.88-15.93	30.80-14.92	29.64-19.09	29.20-3.62	87.19-4.95	106.02-85.44	93.61-79.24	89.00-65.51
P/E Ratio	...	23.69-11.48	11.90-7.67	...	...	11.47-9.25	10.77-9.12	11.96-8.81
Average Yield %	2.07	1.73	0.81	1.17	3.38	2.14	1.99	1.55

Address: One Hartford Plaza, Hartford, CT 06155
Telephone: 860-547-5000

Web Site: www.thehartford.com
Officers: Liam E. McGee - Chairman, President, Chief Executive Officer Andrew J. Pinkes - Executive Vice President

Auditors: Deloitte & Touche LLP
Investor Contact: 860-547-8691
Transfer Agents: Computershare, Inc., Jersey City, NJ

HATTERAS FINANCIAL CORP

Exchange	Symbol	Price	52Wk Range	Yield	P/E
NYS	HTS	$27.43 (3/28/2013)	29.67-24.40	11.30	7.47

*7 Year Price Score N/A *NYSE Composite Index=100 *12 Month Price Score 90.37

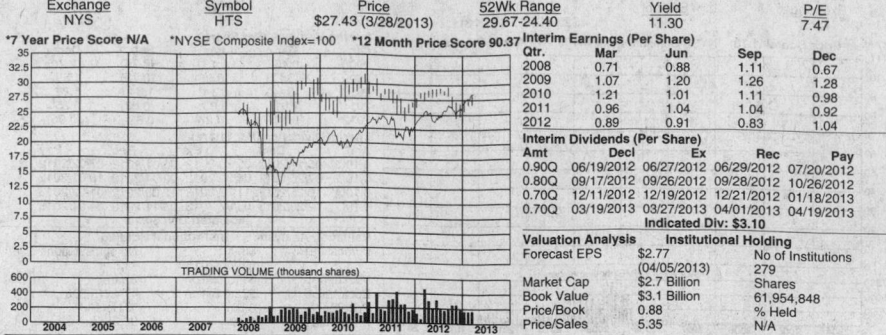

Interim Earnings (Per Share)

Qtr.	Mar	Jun	Sep	Dec
2008	0.71	0.88	1.11	0.67
2009	1.07	1.20	1.26	1.28
2010	1.21	1.01	1.11	0.98
2011	0.96	1.04	1.04	0.92
2012	0.89	0.91	0.83	1.04

Interim Dividends (Per Share)

Amt	Decl	Ex	Rec	Pay
0.90Q	06/19/2012	06/27/2012	06/29/2012	07/20/2012
0.80Q	09/17/2012	09/26/2012	09/28/2012	10/26/2012
0.70Q	12/11/2012	12/19/2012	12/21/2012	01/18/2013
0.70Q	03/19/2013	03/27/2013	04/01/2013	04/19/2013

Indicated Div: $3.10

Valuation Analysis

		Institutional Holding	
Forecast EPS	$2.77 (04/05/2013)	No of Institutions	279
Market Cap	$2.7 Billion	Shares	61,954,848
Book Value	$3.1 Billion	% Held	N/A
Price/Book	0.88		
Price/Sales	5.35		

TRADING VOLUME (thousand shares)

Business Summary: REITs (MIC: 5.3.1 SIC: 6798 NAIC: 525930)

Hatteras Financial is an externally-managed mortgage real estate investment trust that invests primarily in single-family residential mortgage pass-through securities guaranteed or issued by a U.S. Government agency (such as the Government National Mortgage Association), or by a U.S. Government-sponsored entity (such as the Federal National Mortgage Association), and the Federal Home Loan Mortgage Corporation. Co. refers to these securities as agency securities. Co. is externally-managed and advised by its manager, Atlantic Capital Advisors LLC.

Recent Developments: For the year ended Dec 31 2012, net income increased 22.8% to US$349.2 million from US$284.4 million in the prior year. Revenues were US$506.3 million, up 18.8% from US$426.1 million the year before.

Prospects: Our evaluation of Hatteras Financial Corp. as of Apr. 7, 2013 is the result of our systematic analysis on three basic characteristics: earnings strength, relative valuation, and recent stock price movement. The company has managed to produce a neutral trend in earnings per share over the past 5 quarters. However, while recent estimates for the company have been mixed, HTS has posted better than expected results. Based on operating earnings yield, the company is undervalued when compared to all of the companies in our coverage universe. Share price changes over the past year indicates that HTS will perform poorly over the near term.

Financial Data
(US$ in Thousands)

	12/31/2012	12/31/2011	12/31/2010	12/31/2009	12/31/2008	12/31/2007
Earnings Per Share	3.67	3.97	4.30	4.82	3.48	0.15
Cash Flow Per Share	4.70	4.67	4.47	5.02	3.39	...
Tang Book Value Per Share	28.28	27.08	24.84	25.74	20.35	19.76
Dividends Per Share	3.300	3.900	4.400	4.500	2.800	...
Dividend Payout %	89.92	98.24	102.33	93.36	80.46	...
Income Statement						
Total Revenue	506,308	426,120	265,016	283,115	198,372	7,296
EBITDA	512,450	378,054	211,504	193,933	85,636	1,324
Depn & Amortn	163,205	93,681	42,004	19,533	6,507	76
Income Before Taxes	349,245	284,373	169,500	174,400	79,129	1,248
Net Income	349,245	284,373	169,500	174,400	79,129	1,248
Average Shares	93,185	71,708	39,454	36,216	22,766	8,368
Balance Sheet						
Current Assets	717,390	752,417	310,172	358,666	247,687	26,998
Total Assets	26,404,118	18,586,719	10,006,979	7,416,402	5,460,326	1,646,388
Current Liabilities	23,087,309	16,287,364	8,789,814	6,441,243	4,661,217	1,481,032
Total Liabilities	23,331,254	16,506,531	8,861,495	6,484,689	4,724,039	1,481,032
Stockholders' Equity	3,072,864	2,080,188	1,145,484	931,713	736,287	165,356
Shares Outstanding	98,822	76,823	46,115	36,200	36,186	8,368
Statistical Record						
Return on Assets %	1.55	1.99	1.95	2.71	2.22	...
Return on Equity %	13.52	17.63	16.32	20.91	17.50	...
EBITDA Margin %	101.21	88.72	79.81	68.50	43.17	18.15
Net Margin %	68.98	66.74	63.96	61.60	39.89	17.11
Asset Turnover	0.02	0.03	0.03	0.04	0.06	...
Current Ratio	0.03	0.05	0.04	0.06	0.05	0.02
Price Range	29.67-24.40	30.86-23.81	31.63-24.20	33.25-21.99	26.99-17.70	...
P/E Ratio	8.08-6.65	7.77-6.00	7.36-5.63	6.90-4.56	7.76-5.09	...
Average Yield %	11.79	14.08	15.57	16.61	11.93	...

Address: 110 Oakwood Drive, Suite 340, Winston Salem, NC 27103
Telephone: 336-760-9347

Web Site: www.hatfin.com
Officers: Michael R. Hough - Chairman, Chief Executive Officer Benjamin M. Hough - President, Chief Operating Officer

Auditors: Ernst & Young LLP
Investor Contact: 310-954-1343
Transfer Agents: Wells Fargo Shareowner Services, South Saint Paul, MN

HAWAIIAN ELECTRIC INDUSTRIES, INC.

Exchange	Symbol	Price	52Wk Range	Yield	P/E
NYS	HE	$27.71 (3/28/2013)	29.24-24.00	4.47	19.51

*7 Year Price Score 98.90   *NYSE Composite Index=100   *12 Month Price Score 93.80

Interim Earnings (Per Share)

Qtr.	Mar	Jun	Sep	Dec
2008	0.41	0.06	0.44	0.16
2009	0.22	0.17	0.37	0.15
2010	0.29	0.31	0.35	0.26
2011	0.30	0.28	0.50	0.35
2012	0.40	0.40	0.49	0.13

Interim Dividends (Per Share)

Amt	Decl	Ex	Rec	Pay
0.31Q	05/08/2012	05/17/2012	05/21/2012	06/13/2012
0.31Q	08/02/2012	08/13/2012	08/15/2012	09/12/2012
0.31Q	11/07/2012	11/15/2012	11/19/2012	12/12/2012
0.31Q	02/06/2013	02/19/2013	02/21/2013	03/13/2013

Indicated Div: $1.24

Valuation Analysis / **Institutional Holding**

Forecast EPS	$1.65 (04/05/2013)	No of Institutions	281
Market Cap	$2.7 Billion	Shares	34,843,920
Book Value	$1.6 Billion	% Held	34.46
Price/Book	1.67		
Price/Sales	0.80		

Business Summary: Electric Utilities (MIC: 3.1.1 SIC: 4911 NAIC: 221122)

Hawaiian Electric Industries is a holding company with its principal subsidiaries engaged in electric utility and banking businesses operating primarily in the State of Hawaii. Co.'s subsidiary, Hawaiian Electric Company, Inc. and its operating utility subsidiaries, Hawaii Electric Light Company, Inc. and Maui Electric Company, Limited, are regulated electric public utilities. Co. also owns directly or indirectly the following subsidiaries: American Savings Holdings, Inc. and its subsidiary, American Savings Bank, F.S.B.; HEI Properties, Inc., a company holding passive, venture capital investments; Hawaiian Electric Industries Capital Trusts II and III; and The Old Oahu Tug Service, Inc.

Recent Developments: For the year ended Dec 31 2012, net income increased 0.3% to US$140.5 million from US$140.1 million in the prior year. Revenues were US$3.37 billion, up 4.1% from US$3.24 billion the year before. Operating income was US$284.2 million versus US$289.7 million in the prior year, a decrease of 1.9%. Direct operating expenses rose 4.7% to US$3.07 billion from US$2.94 billion in the comparable period the year before. Indirect operating expenses increased 6.1% to US$17.3 million from US$16.3 million in the equivalent prior-year period.

Prospects: Our evaluation of Hawaiian Electric Industries Inc. as of Apr. 7, 2013 is the result of our systematic analysis on three basic characteristics: earnings strength, relative valuation, and recent stock price movement. The company has generated a negative trend in earnings per share over the past 5 quarters and while recent estimates for the company have been mixed, HE has posted better than expected results. Based on operating earnings yield, the company is undervalued when compared to all of the companies in our coverage universe. Share price changes over the past year indicates that HE will perform in line with the market over the near term.

Financial Data

(US$ in Thousands)	12/31/2012	12/31/2011	12/31/2010	12/31/2009	12/31/2008	12/31/2007	12/31/2006	12/31/2005
Earnings Per Share	1.42	1.44	1.21	0.91	1.07	1.03	1.33	1.56
Cash Flow Per Share	2.41	2.62	3.65	3.11	3.04	2.64	3.53	2.70
Tang Book Value Per Share	15.79	15.45	15.16	14.69	14.82	14.70	12.80	14.34
Dividends Per Share	1.240	1.240	1.240	1.240	1.240	1.240	1.240	1.240
Dividend Payout %	87.32	86.11	102.48	136.26	115.89	120.39	93.23	79.49
Income Statement								
Total Revenue	3,374,995	3,242,335	2,664,982	2,309,590	3,218,920	2,536,418	2,460,904	2,215,564
EBITDA	441,592	443,812	416,750	351,168	362,634	354,942	385,038	408,525
Depn & Amortn	150,389	148,152	154,523	151,282	150,977	147,881	141,184	133,892
Income Before Taxes	217,407	216,052	183,247	128,824	139,256	131,057	171,055	201,344
Income Taxes	76,859	75,932	67,822	43,923	48,978	46,278	63,054	73,900
Net Income	140,548	140,120	115,425	83,011	90,278	84,779	108,001	126,689
Average Shares	97,338	95,820	93,693	91,516	84,720	82,419	81,373	81,200
Balance Sheet								
Current Assets	678,507	712,351	695,411	842,802	581,865	602,066	603,704	556,184
Total Assets	10,149,132	9,592,731	9,085,344	8,925,002	9,295,082	10,293,916	9,891,209	9,951,577
Current Liabilities	4,552,246	4,380,070	4,230,555	4,287,743	4,363,759	4,641,339	4,917,325	5,569,307
Long-Term Obligations	1,618,782	1,573,299	1,602,261	1,662,443	1,892,474	3,052,768	2,701,770	2,078,493
Total Liabilities	8,520,974	8,026,489	7,567,414	7,483,354	7,871,335	8,984,196	8,761,676	8,700,654
Stockholders' Equity	1,628,158	1,566,242	1,517,930	1,441,648	1,423,747	1,309,720	1,129,533	1,250,923
Shares Outstanding	97,928	96,038	94,690	92,520	90,515	83,431	81,461	80,983
Statistical Record								
Return on Assets %	1.42	1.50	1.28	0.91	0.92	0.84	1.09	1.30
Return on Equity %	8.78	9.09	7.80	5.79	6.59	6.95	9.07	10.15
EBITDA Margin %	13.08	13.69	15.64	15.20	11.27	13.99	15.65	18.44
Net Margin %	4.16	4.32	4.33	3.59	2.80	3.34	4.39	5.72
Asset Turnover	0.34	0.35	0.30	0.25	0.33	0.25	0.25	0.23
Current Ratio	0.15	0.16	0.16	0.20	0.13	0.13	0.12	0.10
Debt to Equity	0.99	1.00	1.06	1.15	1.33	2.33	2.39	1.66
Price Range	29.24-24.00	26.75-21.06	24.75-18.78	22.46-12.24	29.29-21.40	27.43-20.51	*28.93-25.78	29.76-24.71
P/E Ratio	20.59-16.90	18.58-14.62	20.45-15.52	24.68-13.45	27.37-20.00	26.63-19.91	21.75-19.38	19.08-15.84
Average Yield %	4.69	5.04	5.52	6.88	5.03	5.17	4.58	4.64

Address: 1001 Bishop Street, Suite 2900, Honolulu, HI 96813 Telephone: 808-543-5662 Fax: 808-543-7966	Web Site: www.hei.com Officers: Jeffrey N. Watanabe - Chairman Constance H. Lau - President, Chief Executive Officer	Auditors: PricewaterhouseCoopers LLP Investor Contact: 808-543-7384 Transfer Agents: Continental Stock Transfer & Trust Company, New York, NY

HCA HOLDINGS INC

Exchange	Symbol	Price	52Wk Range	Yield	P/E
NYS	HCA	$40.63 (3/28/2013)	40.63-24.40	N/A	11.64

*7 Year Price Score N/A   *NYSE Composite Index=100   *12 Month Price Score 112.04

TRADING VOLUME (thousand shares)

Interim Earnings (Per Share)

Qtr.	Mar	Jun	Sep	Dec
2010	0.89	0.67	0.55	0.65
2011	0.52	0.43	0.11	3.93
2012	1.18	0.85	0.78	0.68

Interim Dividends (Per Share)

Amt	Decl	Ex	Rec	Pay
2.00U	02/06/2012	02/14/2012	02/16/2012	02/29/2012
2.50U	10/23/2012	10/31/2012	11/02/2012	11/16/2012
2.00U	12/06/2012	12/13/2012	12/17/2012	12/21/2012

Valuation Analysis   Institutional Holding

Forecast EPS	$3.19	No of Institutions	
	(04/06/2013)	418	
Market Cap	$18.0 Billion	Shares	
Book Value	N/A	354,938,432	
Price/Book	N/A	% Held	
Price/Sales	0.55	N/A	

Business Summary: Hospitals & Health Care Facilities (MIC: 4.2.1 SIC: 8062 NAIC: 622110)

HCA Holdings is a holding company. Through its subsidiaries, partnerships and joint ventures (affiliates), Co. owns and operates hospitals and related health care entities. At Dec 31 2011, these affiliates owned and operated 163 hospitals, comprised of 157 general, acute care hospitals, five psychiatric hospitals, and one rehabilitation hospital, and operated 108 freestanding surgery centers. Co.'s facilities are located in 20 states and England. Co.'s general, acute care hospitals provide a range of services to accommodate such medical specialties as internal medicine, surgery, cardiology, oncology, neurosurgery, orthopedics and obstetrics, as well as diagnostic and emergency services.

Recent Developments: For the year ended Dec 31 2012, net income decreased 29.4% to US$2.01 billion from US$2.84 billion in the prior year. Revenues were US$33.01 billion, up 11.2% from US$29.68 billion the year before. Direct operating expenses rose 10.4% to US$5.72 billion from US$5.18 billion in the comparable period the year before. Indirect operating expenses increased 16.5% to US$24.40 billion from US$20.94 billion in the equivalent prior-year period.

Prospects: Our evaluation of HCA Holdings, Inc. as of Apr. 7, 2013 is the result of our systematic analysis on three basic characteristics: earnings strength, relative valuation, and recent stock price movement. The company has generated a negative trend in earnings per share over the past 5 quarters. However, while recent estimates for the company have been mixed, HCA has posted better than expected results. Based on operating earnings yield, the company is undervalued when compared to all of the companies in our coverage universe. Share price changes over the past year indicates that HCA will perform very well over the near term.

Financial Data

(US$ in Millions)	12/31/2012	12/31/2011	12/31/2010	12/31/2009	12/31/2008
Earnings Per Share	3.49	4.97	2.76	2.44	1.56
Cash Flow Per Share	9.46	8.25	7.23	6.45	...
Dividends Per Share	6.500	...	9.430	...	...
Dividend Payout %	186.25	...	341.67	...	...
Income Statement					
Total Revenue	33,013	29,682	30,683	30,052	28,374
EBITDA	21,129	6,801	5,462	5,162	4,380
Depn & Amortn	16,473	1,461	1,416	1,419	1,412
Income Before Taxes	2,858	3,303	1,949	1,756	947
Income Taxes	888	719	658	627	268
Net Income	1,605	2,465	1,207	1,054	673
Average Shares	459	495	437	432	430
Balance Sheet					
Current Assets	7,763	7,233	6,919	6,577	...
Total Assets	28,075	26,898	23,852	24,131	...
Current Liabilities	6,172	5,554	4,269	4,313	...
Long-Term Obligations	27,495	25,645	27,633	24,824	...
Total Liabilities	37,735	35,156	35,778	33,117	...
Stockholders' Equity	(9,660)	(8,258)	(11,926)	(8,986)	...
Shares Outstanding	443	437	427	426	425
Statistical Record					
Return on Assets %	5.82	9.71	5.03	...	...
EBITDA Margin %	64.00	22.91	17.80	17.18	15.44
Net Margin %	4.86	8.30	3.93	3.51	2.37
Asset Turnover	1.20	1.17	1.28	...	...
Current Ratio	1.26	1.30	1.62	1.52	...
Price Range	33.87-20.80	35.24-17.66	...	...	...
P/E Ratio	9.70-5.96	7.09-3.55	...	...	...
Average Yield %	23.25	...	...	...	...

Address: One Park Plaza, Nashville, TN 37203	Web Site: www.hcahealthcare.com	Auditors: Ernst & Young LLP
Telephone: 615-344-9551	Officers: Richard M. Bracken - Chairman, Chief Executive Officer R. Milton Johnson - President, Chief Financial Officer	Investor Contact: 615-344-2688 Transfer Agents: Wells Fargo Shareowner Services, St. Paul, MN

HCC INSURANCE HOLDINGS, INC.

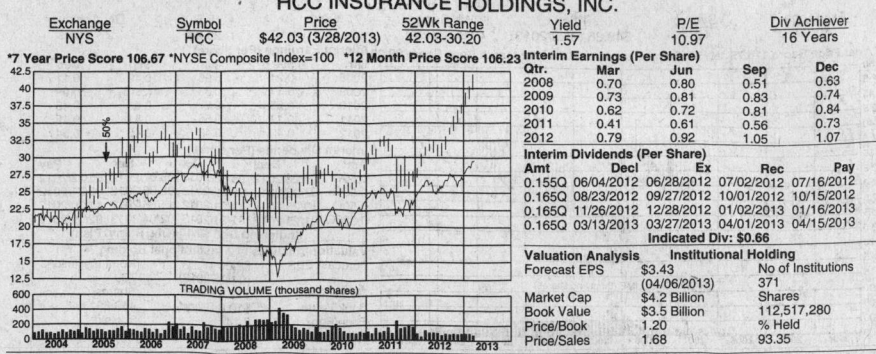

Exchange	Symbol	Price	52Wk Range	Yield	P/E	Div Achiever
NYS	HCC	$42.03 (3/28/2013)	42.03-30.20	1.57	10.97	16 Years

*7 Year Price Score 106.67 *NYSE Composite Index=100 *12 Month Price Score 106.23

Interim Earnings (Per Share)

Qtr.	Mar	Jun	Sep	Dec
2008	0.70	0.80	0.51	0.63
2009	0.73	0.81	0.83	0.74
2010	0.62	0.72	0.81	0.84
2011	0.41	0.61	0.56	0.73
2012	0.79	0.92	1.05	1.07

Interim Dividends (Per Share)

Amt	Decl	Ex	Rec	Pay
0.155Q	06/04/2012	06/28/2012	07/02/2012	07/16/2012
0.165Q	08/23/2012	09/27/2012	10/01/2012	10/15/2012
0.165Q	11/26/2012	12/28/2012	01/02/2013	01/16/2013
0.165Q	03/13/2013	03/27/2013	04/01/2013	04/15/2013

Indicated Div: $0.66

Valuation Analysis / **Institutional Holding**

Forecast EPS	$3.43
	(04/06/2013)
Market Cap	$4.2 Billion
Book Value	$3.5 Billion
Price/Book	1.20
Price/Sales	1.68

No of Institutions	371
Shares	112,517,280
% Held	93.35

Business Summary: General Insurance (MIC: 5.2.1 SIC: 6331 NAIC: 524126)

HCC Insurance Holdings is an insurance holding company. Co. underwrites a range of non-correlated specialty insurance products, including property and casualty, accident and health, surety, and credit product lines. Co. markets its products through a network of independent agents and brokers, managing general agents and directly to consumers. As of Dec 31 2012, Co.'s businesses were managed through five underwriting segments: U.S. Property and Casualty, Professional Liability, Accident and Health, U.S. Surety and Credit and International; and its Investing segment. Co.'s agencies underwrite insurance products and provide claims management services, primarily for its insurance companies.

Recent Developments: For the year ended Dec 31 2012, net income increased 53.3% to US$391.2 million from US$255.2 million in the prior year. Revenues were US$2.53 billion, up 6.4% from US$2.37 billion the year before. Net premiums earned were US$2.24 billion versus US$2.13 billion in the prior year, an increase of 5.4%. Net investment income rose 4.9% to US$222.6 million from US$212.3 million a year ago.

Prospects: Our evaluation of HCC Insurance Holdings Inc. as of Apr. 7, 2013 is the result of our systematic analysis on three basic characteristics: earnings strength, relative valuation, and recent stock price movement. The company has generated a negative trend in earnings per share over the past 5 quarters and while recent estimates for the company have been mixed, HCC has posted better than expected results. Based on operating earnings yield, the company is undervalued when compared to all of the companies in our coverage universe. Share price changes over the past year indicates that HCC will perform in line with the market over the near term.

Financial Data
(US$ in Thousands)

	12/31/2012	12/31/2011	12/31/2010	12/31/2009	12/31/2008	12/31/2007	12/31/2006	12/31/2005
Earnings Per Share	3.83	2.30	2.99	3.11	2.64	3.38	2.93	1.79
Cash Flow Per Share	6.58	3.86	3.65	5.19	4.39	6.44	5.87	5.92
Tang Book Value Per Share	26.32	23.24	21.53	19.37	15.69	14.46	11.64	10.48
Dividends Per Share	0.640	0.600	0.560	0.520	0.470	0.420	0.375	0.282
Dividend Payout %	16.71	26.09	18.73	16.72	17.80	12.43	12.80	15.74
Income Statement								
Premium Income	2,242,625	2,127,170	2,041,924	2,037,235	2,007,774	1,985,086	1,709,189	1,369,988
Total Revenue	2,525,827	2,374,005	2,302,254	2,313,928	2,279,423	2,388,373	2,075,295	1,644,342
Benefits & Claims	1,305,511	1,399,247	1,213,029	1,215,759	1,211,873	1,183,947	1,011,856	921,197
Income Before Taxes	554,427	355,006	489,827	518,551	436,312	585,870	509,834	278,747
Income Taxes	163,187	99,763	144,731	164,683	131,544	190,441	167,549	85,647
Net Income	391,240	255,243	345,096	353,868	304,768	395,429	342,285	195,860
Average Shares	100,456	109,240	114,077	113,058	115,474	116,997	116,736	109,437
Balance Sheet								
Total Assets	10,267,807	9,625,253	9,064,082	8,834,391	8,332,383	8,074,645	7,630,132	7,026,066
Total Liabilities	6,725,195	6,333,239	5,767,650	5,803,208	5,693,042	5,634,280	5,587,329	5,332,370
Stockholders' Equity	3,542,612	3,292,014	3,296,432	3,031,183	2,639,341	2,440,365	2,042,803	1,693,696
Shares Outstanding	100,928	104,101	114,968	114,051	113,444	115,069	111,731	110,803
Statistical Record								
Return on Assets %	3.92	2.73	3.86	4.12	3.70	5.04	4.67	3.02
Return on Equity %	11.42	7.75	10.91	12.48	11.97	17.64	18.32	12.98
Loss Ratio %	58.21	65.78	59.41	59.68	60.36	59.64	59.20	67.24
Net Margin %	15.49	10.75	14.99	14.91	13.37	16.56	16.49	11.91
Price Range	37.64-27.16	33.09-24.89	29.09-24.18	28.95-20.39	28.75-16.75	34.24-26.57	35.09-28.58	32.86-21.34
P/E Ratio	9.83-7.09	14.39-10.82	9.73-8.09	9.31-6.56	10.89-6.34	10.13-7.86	11.98-9.75	18.36-11.92
Average Yield %	1.97	2.03	2.09	2.05	1.97	1.37	1.18	1.07

Address: 13403 Northwest Freeway, Houston, TX 77040-6094 **Telephone:** 713-690-7300	**Web Site:** www.hcc.com **Officers:** Robert A. Rosholt - Chairman Christopher J.B. Williams - President, Chief Executive Officer	**Auditors:** PricewaterhouseCoopers LLP **Investor Contact:** 704-462-1000 **Transfer Agents:** American Stock Transfer & Trust Company, New York, NY

HCP, INC.

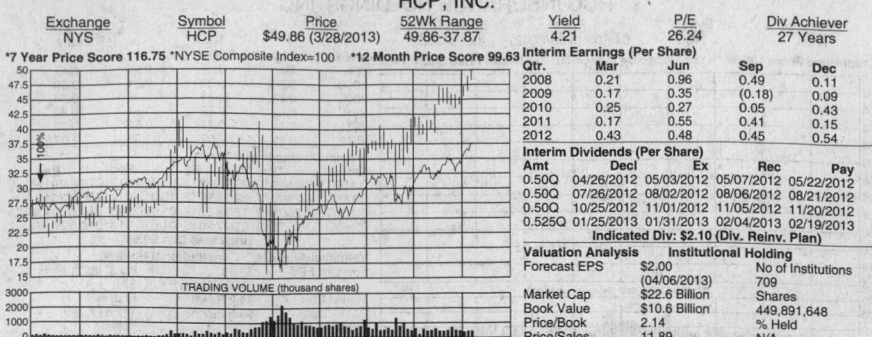

Exchange	Symbol	Price	52Wk Range	Yield	P/E	Div Achiever
NYS	HCP	$49.86 (3/28/2013)	49.86-37.87	4.21	26.24	27 Years

*7 Year Price Score 116.75 *NYSE Composite Index=100 *12 Month Price Score 99.63

Interim Earnings (Per Share)

Qtr.	Mar	Jun	Sep	Dec
2008	0.21	0.96	0.49	0.11
2009	0.17	0.35	(0.18)	0.09
2010	0.25	0.27	0.05	0.43
2011	0.17	0.55	0.41	0.15
2012	0.43	0.48	0.45	0.54

Interim Dividends (Per Share)

Amt	Decl	Ex	Rec	Pay
0.50Q	04/26/2012	05/03/2012	05/07/2012	05/22/2012
0.50Q	07/26/2012	08/02/2012	08/06/2012	08/21/2012
0.50Q	10/25/2012	11/01/2012	11/05/2012	11/20/2012
0.525Q	01/25/2013	01/31/2013	02/04/2013	02/19/2013

Indicated Div: $2.10 (Div. Reinv. Plan)

Valuation Analysis

		Institutional Holding	
Forecast EPS	$2.00 (04/06/2013)	No of Institutions	709
Market Cap	$22.6 Billion	Shares	449,891,648
Book Value	$10.6 Billion	% Held	N/A
Price/Book	2.14		
Price/Sales	11.89		

TRADING VOLUME (thousand shares)

Business Summary: REITs (MIC: 5.3.1 SIC: 6798 NAIC: 525930)

HCP is a real estate investment trust engaged in investing primarily in real estate serving the healthcare industry. Co. acquires, develops, leases, manages and disposes of healthcare real estate, and provides financing to healthcare providers. Co.'s portfolio is comprised of investments in the following five healthcare segments: senior housing, post-acute/skilled nursing, life science, medical office and hospital. Co. makes investments within its healthcare segments using the following five investment products: properties under lease, debt investments, developments and redevelopments, investment management and investments in senior housing operations.

Recent Developments: For the year ended Dec 31 2012, income from continuing operations increased 48.5% to US$812.9 million from US$547.3 million a year earlier. Net income increased 52.7% to US$846.8 million from US$554.5 million in the prior year. Revenues were US$1.90 billion, up 11.0% from US$1.71 billion the year before. Revenues from property income rose 9.3% to US$1.25 billion from US$1.15 billion in the corresponding earlier year.

Prospects: Our evaluation of HCP Inc. as of Apr. 7, 2013 is the result of our systematic analysis on three basic characteristics: earnings strength, relative valuation, and recent stock price movement. The company has enjoyed a very positive trend in earnings per share over the past 5 quarters. Because the company lacks sufficient analyst estimate data, we place greater weight on the historical EPS trend as the measure of earnings strength. Based on operating earnings yield, the company is about fairly valued when compared to all of the companies in our coverage universe. Share price changes over the past year indicates that HCP will perform in line with the market over the near term.

Financial Data
(US$ in Thousands)

	12/31/2012	12/31/2011	12/31/2010	12/31/2009	12/31/2008	12/31/2007	12/31/2006	12/31/2005
Earnings Per Share	1.90	1.29	1.00	0.40	1.79	2.71	2.66	1.12
Cash Flow Per Share	2.42	1.82	1.90	1.88	2.39	2.18	2.25	2.09
Tang Book Value Per Share	21.95	20.37	19.70	17.22	17.18	14.50	12.74	7.90
Dividends Per Share	2.000	1.920	1.860	1.840	1.820	1.780	1.700	1.680
Dividend Payout %	105.26	148.84	186.00	460.00	101.68	65.68	63.91	150.00
Income Statement								
Total Revenue	1,900,722	1,725,386	1,255,134	1,157,030	1,025,818	982,509	619,087	477,276
EBITDA	1,171,691	919,658	671,199	388,871	409,768	363,304	333,942	277,380
Depn & Amortn	(2,232)	(4,510)	(6,378)	(14,780)	(8,440)	(6,056)	(797)	(1,912)
Income Before Taxes	756,793	504,831	388,927	104,754	226,558	88,012	121,435	172,091
Income Taxes	(1,636)	1,249	412	1,924	4,292	...	...	...
Net Income	832,540	538,891	330,709	146,151	448,495	589,015	417,547	173,057
Average Shares	428,316	400,218	306,900	274,631	239,296	209,254	149,226	135,560
Balance Sheet								
Current Assets	319,671	101,740	1,107,524	188,985	126,851	177,588	91,713	36,925
Total Assets	19,915,555	17,408,475	13,331,923	12,209,735	11,849,826	12,521,772	10,012,749	3,597,265
Current Liabilities	399,902	399,620	461,878	509,856	444,345	511,895	334,138	68,718
Long-Term Obligations	8,693,820	7,722,619	4,646,345	5,656,143	5,937,456	7,510,907	6,202,015	1,956,946
Total Liabilities	9,364,318	8,374,993	5,374,556	6,429,198	6,648,555	8,418,063	6,718,713	2,197,499
Stockholders' Equity	10,551,237	9,033,482	7,957,367	5,780,537	5,201,271	4,103,709	3,294,036	1,399,766
Shares Outstanding	453,191	408,629	370,924	293,548	253,601	216,818	198,599	136,193
Statistical Record								
Return on Assets %	4.45	3.51	2.59	1.21	3.67	5.23	6.14	5.17
Return on Equity %	8.48	6.34	4.81	2.66	9.61	15.92	17.79	12.28
EBITDA Margin %	61.64	53.30	53.48	33.61	39.95	36.98	53.94	58.12
Net Margin %	43.80	31.23	26.35	12.63	43.72	59.95	67.45	36.26
Asset Turnover	0.10	0.11	0.10	0.10	0.08	0.09	0.09	0.14
Current Ratio	0.80	0.25	2.40	0.37	0.29	0.35	0.27	0.54
Debt to Equity	0.82	0.85	0.58	0.98	1.14	1.83	1.88	1.40
Price Range	47.21-37.87	41.76-28.77	37.97-27.06	32.84-16.08	41.25-15.80	41.88-25.76	36.88-25.55	28.68-23.45
P/E Ratio	24.85-19.93	32.37-22.30	37.97-27.06	82.10-40.20	23.04-8.83	15.45-9.51	13.86-9.61	25.61-20.94
Average Yield %	4.65	5.19	5.60	7.43	5.75	5.34	5.84	6.43

Address: 3760 Kilroy Airport Way, Suite 300, Long Beach, CA 90806 **Telephone:** 562-733-5100	**Web Site:** www.hcpi.com **Officers:** James F. Flaherty - Chairman, President, Chief Executive Officer Paul F. Gallagher - Executive Vice President, Chief Investment Officer	**Auditors:** Deloitte & Touche LLP **Investor Contact:** 562-733-5309 **Transfer Agents:** Wells Fargo Bank, N.A., South St. Paul, MN

HEALTH CARE REIT INC.

Exchange	Symbol	Price	52Wk Range	Yield	P/E
NYS	HCN	$67.91 (3/28/2013)	67.91-52.40	4.51	69.30

*7 Year Price Score 113.92 *NYSE Composite Index=100 *12 Month Price Score 100.23

Interim Earnings (Per Share)

Qtr.	Mar	Jun	Sep	Dec
2008	0.35	1.74	0.57	0.16
2009	0.56	0.53	0.17	0.24
2010	0.21	0.37	0.01	0.25
2011	0.15	0.39	0.21	0.14
2012	0.19	0.25	0.16	0.37

Interim Dividends (Per Share)

Amt	Decl	Ex	Rec	Pay
0.74Q	04/26/2012	05/04/2012	05/08/2012	05/21/2012
0.74Q	07/26/2012	08/03/2012	08/07/2012	08/20/2012
0.74Q	10/25/2012	11/02/2012	11/06/2012	11/20/2012
0.765Q	01/24/2013	02/01/2013	02/05/2013	02/20/2013

Indicated Div: $3.06

Valuation Analysis

Forecast EPS	$1.17 (04/06/2013)
Market Cap	$17.7 Billion
Book Value	$10.3 Billion
Price/Book	1.72
Price/Sales	9.70

Institutional Holding

No of Institutions	641
Shares	232,293,408
% Held	103.22

Business Summary: REITs (MIC: 5.3.1 SIC: 6798 NAIC: 525930)

Health Care REIT is a real estate investment trust that invests in seniors housing and health care real estate. As of Dec 31 2010, Co.'s portfolio consisted of 937 properties in 46 states. Co. has three segments: seniors housing triple-net, which includes independent living/continuing care retirement communities, assisted living facilities, Alzheimer's/dementia facilities, skilled nursing/post-acute facilities and combinations thereof; seniors housing operating, which includes independent living facilities, assisted living facilities, Alzheimer's facilities and combinations thereof; and medical facilities, which includes medical office buildings, hospitals and life science buildings.

Recent Developments: For the year ended Dec 31 2012, income from continuing operations increased 54.3% to US$180.5 million from US$117.0 million a year earlier. Net income increased 38.6% to US$294.8 million from US$212.7 million in the prior year. Revenues were US$1.82 billion, up 37.0% from US$1.33 billion the year before. Revenues from property income rose 31.5% to US$1.08 billion from US$821.6 million in the corresponding earlier year.

Prospects: Our evaluation of Health Care Reit Inc. as of Apr. 7, 2013 is the result of our systematic analysis on three basic characteristics: earnings strength, relative valuation, and recent stock price movement. The company has enjoyed a very positive trend in earnings per share over the past 5 quarters. Because the company lacks sufficient analyst estimate data, we place greater weight on the historical EPS trend as the measure of earnings strength. Based on operating earnings yield, the company is overvalued when compared to all of the companies in our coverage universe. Share price changes over the past year indicates that HCN will perform poorly over the near term.

Financial Data

(US$ in Thousands)	12/31/2012	12/31/2011	12/31/2010	12/31/2009	12/31/2008	12/31/2007	12/31/2006	12/31/2005
Earnings Per Share	0.98	0.90	0.83	1.49	2.81	1.46	1.31	1.15
Cash Flow Per Share	3.64	3.39	2.86	3.34	3.57	3.35	3.51	3.21
Tang Book Value Per Share	35.35	31.44	28.96	28.43	27.90	24.26	22.40	19.85
Dividends Per Share	2.960	2.835	2.740	2.720	2.700	2.279	2.881	2.460
Dividend Payout %	302.04	315.00	330.12	182.55	96.09	156.10	219.92	213.91
Income Statement								
Total Revenue	1,822,099	1,421,162	680,530	568,973	551,214	486,022	322,824	281,847
EBITDA	734,588	594,378	294,899	340,360	323,702	280,277	204,171	163,982
Depn & Amortn	548,935	437,949	216,856	178,622	172,031	154,852	100,654	84,828
Income Before Taxes	185,653	156,429	78,043	161,738	151,671	125,425	103,517	79,154
Income Taxes	7,612	1,388	364	168	1,306	...	...	...
Net Income	294,840	212,716	128,884	192,927	288,111	141,402	102,750	84,286
Average Shares	225,953	174,401	128,208	114,612	94,309	79,409	62,045	54,499
Balance Sheet								
Current Assets	1,141,421	233,102	210,639	58,713	177,440	30,269	36,216	36,237
Total Assets	19,549,109	14,924,606	9,451,734	6,367,186	6,193,118	5,213,856	4,280,610	2,972,164
Long-Term Obligations	8,531,899	7,240,752	4,469,736	2,414,022	2,863,772	2,704,668	2,145,786	1,500,818
Total Liabilities	9,254,308	7,799,842	4,848,883	2,570,147	2,981,532	2,809,500	2,301,817	1,541,408
Stockholders' Equity	10,294,801	7,124,764	4,602,851	3,797,039	3,211,586	2,404,356	1,978,793	1,430,756
Shares Outstanding	260,373	192,275	147,097	123,385	104,703	85,496	73,192	58,124
Statistical Record								
Return on Assets %	1.71	1.75	1.63	3.07	5.04	2.98	2.83	3.05
Return on Equity %	3.38	3.63	3.07	5.51	10.23	6.45	6.03	6.09
EBITDA Margin %	40.32	41.82	43.33	59.82	58.73	57.67	63.25	58.18
Net Margin %	16.18	14.97	18.94	33.91	52.27	29.09	31.83	29.90
Asset Turnover	0.11	0.12	0.09	0.09	0.10	0.10	0.09	0.10
Debt to Equity	0.83	1.02	0.97	0.64	0.89	1.12	1.08	1.05
Price Range	62.24-52.40	54.98-41.11	51.71-40.00	46.19-27.27	53.81-31.32	48.13-35.87	43.02-32.88	39.18-31.70
P/E Ratio	63.51-53.47	61.09-45.68	62.30-48.19	31.00-18.30	19.15-11.15	32.97-24.57	32.84-25.10	34.07-27.57
Average Yield %	5.16	5.62	6.08	7.12	6.00	5.30	7.28	6.97

Address: 4500 Dorr Street, Toledo, OH 43615	Web Site: www.hcreit.com	Auditors: Ernst & Young LLP
Telephone: 419-247-2800	**Officers:** George L. Chapman - Chairman, President, President (frmr), Chief Executive Officer, Executive Vice President, General Counsel Scott M. Brinker - Executive Vice President, Senior Vice President, Vice President	**Investor Contact:** 419-247-2800
Fax: 419-247-2826		**Transfer Agents:** BNY Mellon Shareowner Services, Jersey City, NJ

HEALTH MANAGEMENT ASSOCIATES, INC.

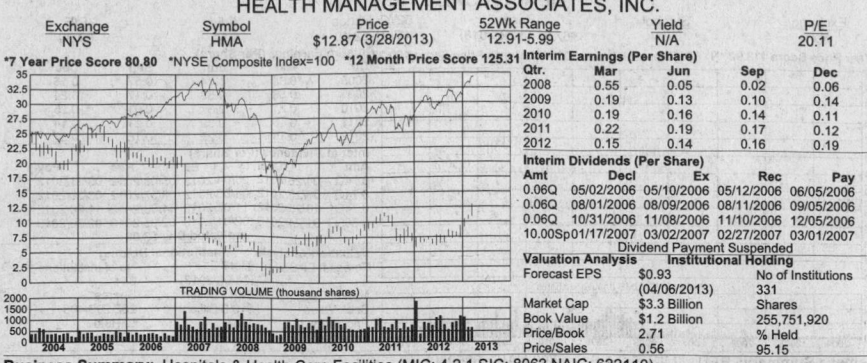

Exchange	Symbol	Price	52Wk Range	Yield	P/E
NYS	HMA	$12.87 (3/28/2013)	12.91-5.99	N/A	20.11

*7 Year Price Score 80.80 ***NYSE Composite Index=100** ***12 Month Price Score 125.31**

Interim Earnings (Per Share)

Qtr.	Mar	Jun	Sep	Dec
2008	0.55	0.05	0.02	0.06
2009	0.19	0.13	0.10	0.14
2010	0.19	0.16	0.14	0.11
2011	0.22	0.19	0.17	0.12
2012	0.15	0.14	0.16	0.19

Interim Dividends (Per Share)

Amt	Decl	Ex	Rec	Pay
0.06Q	05/02/2006	05/10/2006	05/12/2006	06/05/2006
0.06Q	08/01/2006	08/09/2006	08/11/2006	09/05/2006
0.06Q	10/31/2006	11/08/2006	11/10/2006	12/05/2006
10.00Sp	01/17/2007	03/02/2007	02/27/2007	03/01/2007

Dividend Payment Suspended

Valuation Analysis | **Institutional Holding**

Forecast EPS	$0.93	No of Institutions
	(04/06/2013)	331
Market Cap	$3.3 Billion	Shares
Book Value	$1.2 Billion	255,751,920
Price/Book	2.71	% Held
Price/Sales	0.56	95.15

TRADING VOLUME (thousand shares)

Business Summary: Hospitals & Health Care Facilities (MIC: 4.2.1 SIC: 8062 NAIC: 622110)

Health Management Associates operates general acute care hospitals and other health care facilities in non-urban communities. At Dec 31 2011, Co. operated 66 hospitals with a total of 10,330 licensed beds. Co.'s services include general surgery, internal medicine, obstetrics, emergency room care, radiology, oncology, diagnostic care, coronary care, and pediatric services. Co. also provides outpatient services such as one-day surgery, laboratory, x-ray, respiratory therapy, cardiology, and physical therapy. Some of Co.'s hospitals provide services in, among other areas, cardiology, neuro-surgery, oncology, radiation therapy, computer-assisted tomography scanning, lithotripsy, and obstetrics.

Recent Developments: For the year ended Dec 31 2012, income from continuing operations decreased 3.6% to US$198.9 million from US$206.3 million a year earlier. Net income decreased 6.2% to US$191.2 million from US$203.9 million in the prior year. Revenues were US$5.88 billion, up 15.5% from US$5.09 billion the year before. Indirect operating expenses increased 16.8% to US$5.58 billion from US$4.78 billion in the equivalent prior-year period.

Prospects: Our evaluation of Health Management Associates Inc. as of Apr. 7, 2013 is the result of our systematic analysis on three basic characteristics: earnings strength, relative valuation, and recent stock price movement. The company has enjoyed a very positive trend in earnings per share over the past 5 quarters and while recent estimates for the company have been mixed, HMA has posted results that fell short of analysts expectations. Based on operating earnings yield, the company is undervalued when compared to all of the companies in our coverage universe. Share price changes over the past year indicates that HMA will perform in line with the market over the near term.

Financial Data

(US$ in Thousands)	12/31/2012	12/31/2011	12/31/2010	12/31/2009	12/31/2008	12/31/2007	12/31/2006	12/31/2005
Earnings Per Share	0.64	0.70	0.60	0.56	0.68	0.49	0.75	0.31
Cash Flow Per Share	2.34	2.16	1.76	1.80	1.74	1.33	1.86	0.37
Tang Book Value Per Share	0.75	N.M.	N.M.	N.M.	N.M.	N.M.	6.19	5.87
Dividends Per Share	...	...	...	...	...	10.000	0.240	0.180
Dividend Payout %	...	...	...	...	...	2,040.82	32.00	58.06
Income Statement								
Total Revenue	5,878,238	5,804,451	5,114,997	4,617,143	4,451,611	4,392,086	4,056,599	917,186
EBITDA	1,052,917	820,062	708,744	667,743	830,764	616,182	538,007	169,511
Depn & Amortn	438,889	284,910	209,800	208,700	217,200	206,400	182,500	39,700
Income Before Taxes	301,481	312,405	287,271	241,102	374,815	187,822	304,210	125,586
Income Taxes	102,622	106,071	101,223	81,747	135,505	69,587	117,107	48,679
Net Income	164,220	178,710	150,069	138,182	167,225	119,879	182,749	75,541
Average Shares	256,710	255,037	251,106	246,965	244,671	245,119	243,340	244,697
Balance Sheet								
Current Assets	1,471,248	1,410,138	1,193,072	1,072,922	1,051,081	1,066,107	1,012,004	1,010,282
Total Assets	6,400,789	6,004,189	4,910,085	4,604,099	4,555,529	4,643,919	4,490,952	4,091,224
Current Liabilities	972,423	803,824	555,630	525,897	490,271	597,646	472,021	931,795
Long-Term Obligations	3,433,260	3,489,489	2,983,719	3,004,672	3,186,893	3,566,355	1,297,047	619,179
Total Liabilities	5,184,414	5,034,405	4,187,703	4,066,451	4,401,232	4,562,891	2,084,830	1,827,049
Stockholders' Equity	1,216,375	969,784	722,382	537,648	154,297	81,028	2,406,122	2,264,175
Shares Outstanding	256,394	254,156	250,880	248,517	244,221	242,866	240,707	240,648
Statistical Record								
Return on Assets %	2.64	3.27	3.15	3.02	3.63	2.62	4.26	1.59
Return on Equity %	14.99	21.12	23.82	39.94	141.73	9.64	7.83	2.84
EBITDA Margin %	17.91	14.13	13.86	14.46	18.66	14.03	13.26	18.48
Net Margin %	2.79	3.08	2.93	2.99	3.76	2.73	4.50	8.24
Asset Turnover	0.95	1.06	1.08	1.01	0.97	0.96	0.95	0.19
Current Ratio	1.51	1.75	2.15	2.04	2.14	1.78	2.14	1.08
Debt to Equity	2.82	3.60	4.13	5.59	20.65	44.01	0.54	0.27
Price Range	9.32-5.78	11.62-6.32	9.78-6.23	8.43-1.53	7.96-0.95	21.35-5.80	22.75-19.27	26.61-20.99
P/E Ratio	14.56-9.03	16.60-9.03	16.30-10.38	15.05-2.73	11.71-1.40	43.57-11.84	30.33-25.69	85.84-67.71
Average Yield %	...	...	...	...	...	94.08	1.16	0.76

Address: 5811 Pelican Bay Boulevard, Suite 500, Naples, FL 34108-2710 **Telephone:** 239-598-3131	**Web Site:** www.hma.com **Officers:** William J. Schoen - Chairman Gary D. Newsome - President, Chief Executive Officer	**Auditors:** Ernst & Young LLP **Investor Contact:** 239-598-3131 **Transfer Agents:** American Stock Transfer & Trust Company, New York, NY

HEALTH NET, INC.

Exchange NYS	Symbol HNT	Price $28.62 (3/28/2013)	52Wk Range 40.51-17.97	Yield N/A	P/E 19.47

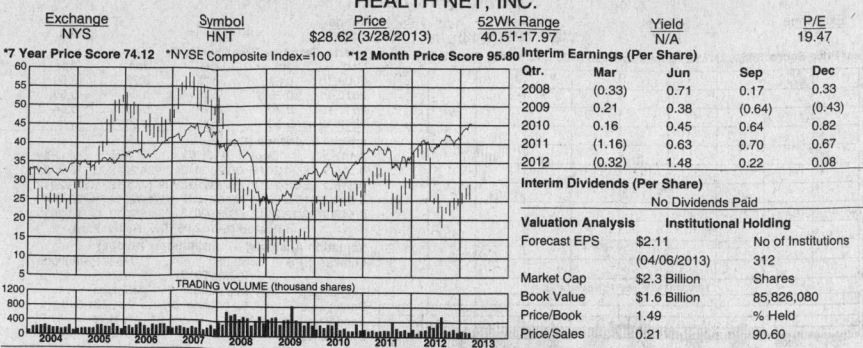

*7 Year Price Score 74.12   *NYSE Composite Index=100   *12 Month Price Score 95.80

Interim Earnings (Per Share)

Qtr.	Mar	Jun	Sep	Dec
2008	(0.33)	0.71	0.17	0.33
2009	0.21	0.38	(0.64)	(0.43)
2010	0.16	0.45	0.64	0.82
2011	(1.16)	0.63	0.70	0.67
2012	(0.32)	1.48	0.22	0.08

Interim Dividends (Per Share)

No Dividends Paid

Valuation Analysis		Institutional Holding	
Forecast EPS	$2.11	No of Institutions	
	(04/06/2013)	312	
Market Cap	$2.3 Billion	Shares	
Book Value	$1.6 Billion	85,826,080	
Price/Book	1.49	% Held	
Price/Sales	0.21	90.60	

Business Summary: Hospitals & Health Care Facilities (MIC: 4.2.1 SIC: 6324 NAIC: 524114)

Health Net is a holding company. Through its subsidiaries, Co. operates within three reportable segments: West Region Operations, which includes the operations of its commercial, Medicare and Medicaid health plans, its health and life insurance companies and its behavioral health and pharmaceutical services subsidiaries; Government Contracts, which includes the TRICARE program, the Military and Family Life Consultant Program and other health care-related government contracts; and Northeast Operations, which includes the operations of its businesses that are adjudicating run out claims and providing limited other administrative services to UnitedHealth Group Incorporated and its affiliates.

Recent Developments: For the year ended Dec 31 2012, income from continuing operations decreased 57.9% to US$25.7 million from US$61.1 million a year earlier. Net income increased 69.2% to US$122.1 million from US$72.1 million in the prior year. Revenues were US$11.29 billion, down 1.1% from US$11.42 billion the year before. Net premiums earned were US$10.46 billion versus US$9.88 billion in the prior year, an increase of 5.9%. Net investment income rose 11.2% to US$82.4 million from US$74.2 million a year ago.

Prospects: Our evaluation of Health Net Inc. as of Apr. 7, 2013 is the result of our systematic analysis on three basic characteristics: earnings strength, relative valuation, and recent stock price movement. The company has enjoyed a very positive trend in earnings per share over the past 5 quarters and while recent estimates for the company have remained steady, HNT has posted results that fell short of analysts expectations. Based on operating earnings yield, the company is about fairly valued when compared to all of the companies in our coverage universe. Share price changes over the past year indicates that HNT will perform very poorly over the near term.

Financial Data
(US$ in Thousands)

	12/31/2012	12/31/2011	12/31/2010	12/31/2009	12/31/2008	12/31/2007	12/31/2006	12/31/2005
Earnings Per Share	1.47	0.80	2.06	(0.47)	0.88	1.70	2.78	1.99
Cash Flow Per Share	0.39	1.17	2.76	2.38	(1.49)	5.44	2.41	1.69
Tang Book Value Per Share	11.98	9.96	11.25	10.23	8.76	9.20	8.38	7.38
Income Statement								
Total Revenue	11,289,092	11,901,036	13,619,852	15,713,241	15,366,589	14,108,271	12,908,350	11,940,533
EBITDA	92,770	239,946	397,045	58,548	230,841	421,701	551,476	451,195
Depn & Amortn	27,900	28,800	31,300	42,900	40,800	30,300	21,500	30,300
Income Before Taxes	31,650	178,998	330,865	(25,239)	147,132	358,904	478,797	376,264
Income Taxes	5,969	106,878	126,622	23,765	52,129	165,207	149,484	146,479
Net Income	122,063	72,120	204,243	(49,004)	95,003	193,697	329,313	229,785
Average Shares	83,112	89,970	99,232	103,849	107,610	113,829	118,310	115,641
Balance Sheet								
Current Assets	3,049,964	2,664,440	3,227,295	3,244,835	3,545,066	3,701,104	3,217,846	2,911,618
Total Assets	3,934,390	3,607,669	4,131,693	4,282,651	4,816,350	4,933,055	4,297,022	3,940,722
Current Liabilities	1,638,096	1,417,580	1,900,653	1,929,514	2,212,770	2,312,017	2,109,503	1,839,076
Long-Term Obligations	499,095	511,390	398,685	498,480	652,268	510,434	300,000	387,954
Total Liabilities	2,377,360	2,164,523	2,437,277	2,586,868	3,064,224	3,057,473	2,518,057	2,351,647
Stockholders' Equity	1,557,030	1,443,146	1,694,416	1,695,783	1,752,126	1,875,582	1,778,965	1,589,075
Shares Outstanding	81,301	81,957	94,647	103,155	103,708	110,299	117,508	114,716
Statistical Record								
Return on Assets %	3.23	1.86	4.85	N.M.	1.94	4.20	8.00	6.05
Return on Equity %	8.11	4.60	12.05	N.M.	5.22	10.60	19.56	16.06
EBITDA Margin %	0.82	2.02	2.92	0.37	1.50	2.99	4.27	3.78
Net Margin %	1.08	0.61	1.50	N.M.	0.62	1.37	2.55	1.92
Asset Turnover	2.99	3.08	3.24	3.45	3.14	3.06	3.13	3.14
Current Ratio	1.86	1.88	1.70	1.68	1.60	1.60	1.53	1.58
Debt to Equity	0.32	0.35	0.24	0.24	0.37	0.27	0.17	0.24
Price Range	40.51-17.97	33.75-21.07	29.35-21.83	24.36-10.89	52.39-7.78	58.75-46.12	53.24-37.21	52.58-28.02
P/E Ratio	27.56-12.22	42.19-26.34	14.25-10.60	...	59.53-8.84	34.56-27.13	19.15-13.38	26.42-14.08

Address: 21650 Oxnard Street, Woodland Hills, CA 91367 Telephone: 818-676-6000 Fax: 818-676-6000	Web Site: www.healthnet.com Officers: Roger F. Greaves - Chairman Jay M. Gellert - President, Chief Executive Officer	Auditors: Deloitte & Touche LLP Transfer Agents: Wells Fargo Bank, N.A., Mendota Heights, MN

HEINZ (H.J.) CO.

Exchange	Symbol	Price	52Wk Range	Yield	P/E
NYS	HNZ	$72.27 (3/28/2013)	72.66-51.95	2.85	23.54

*7 Year Price Score 109.29 *NYSE Composite Index=100 *12 Month Price Score 109.63

TRADING VOLUME (thousand shares)

Interim Earnings (Per Share)

Qtr.	Jul	Oct	Jan	Apr
2009-10	0.67	0.73	0.72	0.60
2010-11	0.75	0.78	0.84	0.69
2011-12	0.70	0.73	0.88	0.54
2012-13	0.80	0.90	0.83	...

Interim Dividends (Per Share)

Amt	Decl	Ex	Rec	Pay
0.515Q	05/24/2012	06/20/2012	06/24/2012	07/10/2012
0.515Q	08/28/2012	09/13/2012	09/17/2012	10/10/2012
0.515Q	11/30/2012	12/07/2012	12/11/2012	12/26/2012
0.515Q	03/13/2013	03/21/2013	03/25/2013	04/10/2013

Indicated Div: $2.06 (Div. Reinv. Plan)

Valuation Analysis

		Institutional Holding	
Forecast EPS	$3.55 (04/05/2013)	No of Institutions	1074
Market Cap	$23.2 Billion	Shares	231,731,248
Book Value	$3.0 Billion	% Held	64.53
Price/Book	7.65		
Price/Sales	2.00		

Business Summary: Food (MIC: 1.2.1 SIC: 2033 NAIC: 311421)

Heinz (H. J.) manufactures and markets a line of food products, primarily ketchup, condiments and sauces, frozen food, soups, beans and pasta meals, infant nutrition and other food products. Co.'s products are sold through its own sales organizations and through independent brokers, agents and distributors to chain, wholesale, cooperative and independent grocery accounts, convenience stores, bakeries, pharmacies, mass merchants, club stores, foodservice distributors and institutions, including hotels, restaurants, hospitals, health-care facilities, and certain government agencies. Co.'s segments include North American consumer products, Europe, Asia/Pacific, and U.S. Foodservice.

Recent Developments: For the quarter ended Jan 27 2013, income from continuing operations increased 7.1% to US$311.5 million from US$290.8 million in the year-earlier quarter. Net income decreased 5.0% to US$272.8 million from US$287.2 million in the year-earlier quarter. Revenues were US$2.93 billion, up 2.0% from US$2.87 billion the year before. Operating income was US$467.9 million versus US$426.5 million in the prior-year quarter, an increase of 9.7%. Direct operating expenses declined 0.8% to US$1.83 billion from US$1.84 billion in the comparable period the year before. Indirect operating expenses increased 5.2% to US$638.7 million from US$607.1 million in the equivalent prior-year period.

Prospects: Our evaluation of Heinz (H.J.) Co. as of Apr. 7, 2013 is the result of our systematic analysis on three basic characteristics: earnings strength, relative valuation, and recent stock price movement. The company has generated a negative trend in earnings per share over the past 5 quarters and while recent estimates for the company have remained steady, HNZ has posted better than expected results. Based on operating earnings yield, the company is about fairly valued when compared to all of the companies in our coverage universe. Share price changes over the past year indicates that HNZ will perform well over the near term.

Financial Data
(US$ in Thousands)

	9 Mos	6 Mos	3 Mos	04/29/2012	04/27/2011	04/28/2010	04/29/2009	04/30/2008
Earnings Per Share	3.07	3.12	2.95	2.85	3.06	2.71	2.90	2.63
Cash Flow Per Share	4.45	4.33	4.30	4.62	4.96	4.01	3.73	3.76
Dividends Per Share	2.025	1.990	1.955	1.920	1.800	1.680	1.660	1.520
Dividend Payout %	65.96	63.78	66.27	67.37	58.82	61.99	57.24	57.79
Income Statement								
Total Revenue	8,538,315	5,618,434	2,791,224	11,649,079	10,706,588	10,494,983	10,148,082	10,070,778
EBITDA	1,518,299	968,779	497,134	1,785,725	1,925,662	1,840,078	1,853,060	1,830,028
Depn & Amortn	256,409	170,742	84,530	342,793	298,660	299,050	281,375	288,897
Income Before Taxes	1,071,116	670,894	347,591	1,183,443	1,374,169	1,290,454	1,296,200	1,217,794
Income Taxes	169,957	92,624	61,587	243,535	368,221	358,514	373,128	372,869
Net Income	817,017	547,471	258,027	923,159	989,510	864,892	923,072	844,925
Average Shares	323,218	323,058	322,843	323,321	323,042	318,113	318,063	321,717
Balance Sheet								
Current Assets	3,908,872	3,897,500	3,658,600	3,882,236	3,753,542	3,051,125	2,945,021	3,325,566
Total Assets	11,929,104	11,911,976	11,519,874	11,983,293	12,230,645	10,075,711	9,664,184	10,565,043
Current Liabilities	3,376,349	3,296,384	3,143,805	2,647,961	4,161,460	2,175,359	2,062,846	2,670,060
Long-Term Obligations	3,930,592	4,120,661	4,111,048	4,779,981	3,078,128	4,559,152	5,076,186	4,730,946
Total Liabilities	8,898,523	9,046,607	8,939,486	9,224,704	9,121,683	8,184,366	8,444,246	8,677,223
Stockholders' Equity	3,030,581	2,865,369	2,580,388	2,758,589	3,108,962	1,891,345	1,219,938	1,887,820
Shares Outstanding	320,651	320,658	320,233	320,226	321,278	317,692	314,859	311,467
Statistical Record								
Return on Assets %	8.31	8.39	8.09	7.56	8.90	8.79	9.15	8.23
Return on Equity %	33.75	35.35	33.39	31.21	39.69	55.75	59.57	45.43
EBITDA Margin %	17.78	17.24	17.81	15.33	17.99	17.53	18.26	18.17
Net Margin %	9.57	9.74	9.24	7.92	9.24	8.24	9.10	8.39
Asset Turnover	0.97	0.96	0.98	0.95	0.96	1.07	1.01	0.98
Current Ratio	1.16	1.18	1.16	1.47	0.90	1.40	1.43	1.25
Debt to Equity	1.30	1.44	1.59	1.73	0.99	2.41	4.16	2.51
Price Range	60.72-51.73	58.42-49.91	55.27-48.82	54.92-48.82	51.23-43.16	47.57-33.99	52.61-30.73	48.62-41.90
P/E Ratio	19.78-16.85	18.72-16.00	18.74-16.55	19.27-17.13	16.74-14.10	17.55-12.54	18.14-10.60	18.49-15.93
Average Yield %	3.65	3.68	3.70	3.66	3.78	4.11	3.89	3.32

Address: One PPG Place, Pittsburgh, PA 15222 Telephone: 412-456-5700 Fax: 412-456-6128	Web Site: www.heinz.com Officers: William R. Johnson - Chairman, President, Chief Executive Officer Theodore N. Bobby - Executive Vice President, Corporate Secretary, General Counsel	Auditors: PricewaterhouseCoopers LLP Investor Contact: 412-456-1048 Transfer Agents: Wells Fargo Shareowner Services, South St. Paul, MN

HELIX ENERGY SOLUTIONS GROUP INC

Exchange	Symbol	Price	52Wk Range	Yield	P/E
NYS	HLX	$22.88 (3/28/2013)	25.37-15.07	N/A	N/A

*7 Year Price Score 77.04 *NYSE Composite Index=100 ***12 Month Price Score 112.53**

Interim Earnings (Per Share)

Qtr.	Mar	Jun	Sep	Dec
2008	0.79	0.96	0.65	(9.39)
2009	0.50	0.94	0.04	(0.52)
2010	(0.17)	(0.82)	0.25	(0.48)
2011	0.24	0.39	0.43	0.16
2012	0.62	0.42	0.14	(1.62)

Interim Dividends (Per Share)

No Dividends Paid

Valuation Analysis   Institutional Holding

Forecast EPS	$1.12	No of Institutions
	(04/06/2013)	335
Market Cap	$2.4 Billion	Shares
Book Value	$1.4 Billion	96,550,488
Price/Book	1.74	% Held
Price/Sales	2.86	N/A

TRADING VOLUME (thousand shares)

Business Summary: Equipment & Services (MIC: 9.1.3 SIC: 1389 NAIC: 213112)

Helix Energy Solutions Group is an offshore energy company that provides field development and other contracting services to the energy market and to its own oil and gas properties. Co.'s operations are conducted through two lines of business: contracting services, which provides offshore services comprising of well operations, robotics, subsea construction, and production facilities; and oil and gas, which engages in prospect generation, exploration, development and production activities located in the Gulf of Mexico. At Dec 31 2012, Co.'s estimated proved reserves for its 37 fields in the Gulf of Mexico on the Outer Continental Shelf totaled approximately 15.8 MMBOE.

Recent Developments: For the year ended Dec 31 2012, loss from continuing operations was US$66.8 million compared with income of US$37.9 million a year earlier. Net loss amounted to US$43.1 million versus net income of US$133.1 million in the prior year. Revenues were US$846.1 million, up 20.5% from US$702.0 million the year before. Operating loss was US$68.5 million versus an income of US$63.0 million in the prior year. Direct operating expenses rose 44.2% to US$796.2 million from US$552.3 million in the comparable period the year before. Indirect operating expenses increased 36.7% to US$118.4 million from US$86.6 million in the equivalent prior-year period.

Prospects: Our evaluation of Helix Energy Solutions Group Inc. as of Apr. 7, 2013 is the result of our systematic analysis on three basic characteristics: earnings strength, relative valuation, and recent stock price movement. The company has suffered a very negative trend in earnings per share over the past 5 quarters. However, while recent estimates for the company have been lowered by analysts, HLX has posted results that fell short of analysts expectations. Based on operating earnings yield, the company is overvalued when compared to all of the companies in our coverage universe. Share price changes over the past year indicates that HLX will perform very well over the near term.

Financial Data

(US$ in Thousands)	12/31/2012	12/31/2011	12/31/2010	12/31/2009	12/31/2008	12/31/2007	12/31/2006	12/31/2005
Earnings Per Share	(0.44)	1.22	(1.22)	0.96	(6.99)	3.34	3.87	1.86
Cash Flow Per Share	4.32	5.43	3.19	4.19	4.82	4.62	6.08	3.13
Tang Book Value Per Share	12.57	12.88	11.35	12.77	9.18	8.56	8.06	7.50
Income Statement								
Total Revenue	846,109	1,398,607	1,199,838	1,461,687	2,148,349	1,767,445	1,366,924	799,472
EBITDA	29,781	561,110	235,355	558,348	(104,440)	902,864	817,703	334,902
Depn & Amortn	116,016	328,986	333,228	277,190	341,117	338,424	195,924	113,215
Income Before Taxes	(134,395)	136,328	(183,176)	229,663	(526,969)	504,996	587,145	214,128
Income Taxes	(59,158)	14,903	(39,598)	95,822	89,977	174,928	257,156	75,019
Net Income	(46,297)	129,979	(126,988)	156,054	(630,848)	320,478	347,394	152,568
Average Shares	104,449	104,953	103,857	105,720	90,650	95,938	89,874	82,205
Balance Sheet								
Current Assets	804,107	944,242	740,854	565,560	950,307	727,269	923,900	372,053
Total Assets	3,386,580	3,582,347	3,592,020	3,779,533	5,070,338	5,452,353	4,290,187	1,660,864
Current Liabilities	453,046	396,176	367,797	368,488	672,798	678,979	613,376	251,665
Long-Term Obligations	1,002,621	1,147,444	1,347,753	1,348,315	1,968,502	1,725,541	1,454,469	440,703
Total Liabilities	1,993,195	2,159,944	2,330,416	2,368,276	3,844,693	3,550,787	2,709,239	976,564
Stockholders' Equity	1,393,385	1,422,403	1,261,604	1,411,257	1,225,645	1,901,566	1,580,948	684,300
Shares Outstanding	105,763	105,530	105,592	104,281	91,972	91,385	90,628	77,694
Statistical Record								
Return on Assets %	N.M.	3.62	N.M.	3.53	N.M.	6.58	11.68	11.30
Return on Equity %	N.M.	9.69	N.M.	11.84	N.M.	18.40	30.67	24.92
EBITDA Margin %	3.52	40.12	19.62	38.20	N.M.	51.08	59.82	41.89
Net Margin %	N.M.	9.29	N.M.	10.68	N.M.	18.13	25.41	19.08
Asset Turnover	0.24	0.39	0.33	0.33	0.41	0.36	0.46	0.59
Current Ratio	1.77	2.38	2.01	1.53	1.41	1.07	1.51	1.48
Debt to Equity	0.72	0.81	1.07	0.96	1.61	0.91	0.92	0.64
Price Range	20.75-15.07	20.76-11.30	16.87-8.70	16.59-2.70	42.57-4.00	46.84-28.00	44.59-28.53	39.51-19.20
P/E Ratio	...	17.02-9.26	...	17.28-2.81	...	14.02-8.38	11.52-7.37	21.24-10.32

Address: 400 North Sam Houston Parkway East, Suite 400, Houston, TX 77060 **Telephone:** 281-618-0400	**Web Site:** www.HelixESG.com **Officers:** Owen E. Kratz - Chairman, President, Chief Executive Officer Anthony Tripodo - Executive Vice President, Chief Financial Officer	**Auditors:** Ernst & Young LLP **Transfer Agents:** Wells Fargo Bank Shareowner Services, St. Paul, MN

HELMERICH & PAYNE, INC.

Exchange	Symbol	Price	52Wk Range	Yield	P/E	Div Achiever
NYS	HP	$60.70 (3/28/2013)	67.94-39.18	0.99	11.04	36 Years

*7 Year Price Score 108.30 *NYSE Composite Index=100 *12 Month Price Score 113.86

Interim Earnings (Per Share)

Qtr.	Dec	Mar	Jun	Sep
2009-10	0.59	0.43	(0.34)	0.77
2010-11	0.96	0.91	1.01	1.12
2011-12	1.32	1.18	1.38	1.46
2012-13	1.48	...	...	...

Interim Dividends (Per Share)

Amt	Decl	Ex	Rec	Pay
0.07Q	06/07/2012	08/13/2012	08/15/2012	08/31/2012
0.07Q	09/05/2012	11/13/2012	11/15/2012	11/30/2012
0.15Q	12/04/2012	02/13/2013	02/15/2013	03/01/2013
0.15Q	03/06/2013	05/13/2013	05/15/2013	05/31/2013

Indicated Div: $0.60

Valuation Analysis / **Institutional Holding**

Forecast EPS	$5.35 (04/05/2013)	No of Institutions	599
Market Cap	$6.4 Billion	Shares	111,326,696
Book Value	$4.0 Billion	% Held	89.94
Price/Book	1.62		
Price/Sales	1.98		

TRADING VOLUME (thousand shares)

Business Summary: Production & Extraction (MIC: 9.1.1 SIC: 1381 NAIC: 213111)

Helmerich & Payne is the holding company for Helmerich & Payne International Drilling Co., a drilling contractor with land and offshore operations in the U.S., South America, Africa and the Middle East. Co.'s contract drilling business is composed of three business segments: U.S. Land, Offshore and International Land. Co. is also engaged in the ownership, development and operation of commercial real estate, and through its subsidiary, TerraVici Drilling Solutions, Inc., in the research and development of rotary steerable technology. Co.'s real estate investments located within Tulsa, OK, include a shopping center, multi-tenant industrial warehouse properties and undeveloped real estate.

Recent Developments: For the quarter ended Dec 31 2012, income from continuing operations increased 10.6% to US$159.6 million from US$144.3 million in the year-earlier quarter. Net income increased 10.6% to US$159.6 million from US$144.3 million in the year-earlier quarter. Revenues were US$844.6 million, up 15.3% from US$732.6 million the year before. Operating income was US$240.5 million versus US$230.5 million in the prior-year quarter, an increase of 4.3%. Direct operating expenses rose 19.4% to US$466.9 million from US$391.0 million in the comparable period the year before. Indirect operating expenses increased 23.5% to US$137.2 million from US$111.0 million in the equivalent prior-year period.

Prospects: Our evaluation of Helmerich & Payne Inc. as of Apr. 7, 2013 is the result of our systematic analysis on three basic characteristics: earnings strength, relative valuation, and recent stock price movement. The company has managed to produce a neutral trend in earnings per share over the past 5 quarters. However, while recent estimates for the company have been mixed, HP has posted better than expected results. Based on operating earnings yield, the company is undervalued when compared to all of the companies in our coverage universe. Share price changes over the past year indicates that HP will perform well over the near term.

Financial Data

(US$ in Thousands)	3 Mos	09/30/2012	09/30/2011	09/30/2010	09/30/2009	09/30/2008	09/30/2007	09/30/2006
Earnings Per Share	5.50	5.34	3.99	1.45	3.32	4.34	4.27	2.77
Cash Flow Per Share	10.44	9.34	9.17	4.37	8.52	5.84	5.43	2.83
Tang Book Value Per Share	37.56	36.28	30.54	26.53	25.43	21.53	17.54	13.30
Dividends Per Share	0.280	0.280	0.250	0.210	0.200	0.185	0.180	0.169
Dividend Payout %	5.09	5.24	6.27	14.48	6.02	4.26	4.22	6.09
Income Statement								
Total Revenue	844,572	3,151,802	2,543,894	1,875,162	1,894,038	2,036,543	1,629,658	1,224,813
EBITDA	353,814	1,297,402	1,017,939	716,241	820,777	924,346	842,287	539,374
Depn & Amortn	106,599	387,549	315,468	262,658	236,437	210,766	146,042	101,583
Income Before Taxes	246,333	902,580	687,067	438,236	575,815	699,929	690,353	440,981
Income Taxes	86,722	328,971	252,399	152,155	232,381	255,557	250,984	154,391
Net Income	159,603	581,045	434,186	156,312	353,545	461,738	449,261	293,858
Average Shares	107,412	108,377	108,632	107,404	106,650	106,424	105,128	106,091
Balance Sheet								
Current Assets	979,432	895,228	956,313	652,804	522,932	690,647	498,964	428,691
Total Assets	5,934,288	5,721,085	5,003,891	4,265,370	4,161,024	3,588,045	2,885,369	2,134,712
Current Liabilities	427,233	381,164	416,729	232,638	301,906	308,957	226,612	264,548
Long-Term Obligations	195,000	195,000	235,000	360,000	420,000	475,000	445,000	175,000
Total Liabilities	1,943,893	1,886,087	1,733,844	1,457,905	1,478,015	1,322,571	1,069,853	752,820
Stockholders' Equity	3,990,395	3,834,998	3,270,047	2,807,465	2,683,009	2,265,474	1,815,516	1,381,892
Shares Outstanding	106,240	105,697	107,086	105,819	105,486	105,222	103,484	103,869
Statistical Record								
Return on Assets %	10.66	10.81	9.37	3.71	9.12	14.23	17.90	15.47
Return on Equity %	16.04	16.31	14.29	5.69	14.29	22.57	28.10	23.88
EBITDA Margin %	41.89	41.16	40.01	38.20	43.33	45.39	51.68	44.04
Net Margin %	18.90	18.44	17.07	8.34	18.67	22.67	27.57	23.99
Asset Turnover	0.58	0.59	0.55	0.45	0.49	0.63	0.65	0.64
Current Ratio	2.29	2.35	2.29	2.81	1.73	2.24	2.20	1.62
Debt to Equity	0.05	0.05	0.07	0.13	0.16	0.21	0.25	0.13
Price Range	65.13-39.18	65.13-37.39	72.60-40.26	48.58-33.42	43.19-18.10	76.99-30.40	36.43-21.75	39.95-22.02
P/E Ratio	11.84-7.12	12.20-7.00	18.20-10.09	33.50-23.05	13.01-5.45	17.74-7.00	8.53-5.09	14.42-7.95
Average Yield %	0.55	0.55	0.44	0.52	0.69	0.39	0.61	0.56

Address: 1437 South Boulder Avenue, Suite 1400, Tulsa, OK 74119-3623 Telephone: 918-742-5531 Fax: 918-742-0237	Web Site: www.hpinc.com Officers: Hans Helmerich - Chairman, President, Chief Executive Officer John W. Lindsay - President, Executive Vice President, Chief Operating Officer	Auditors: Ernst & Young LLP Investor Contact: 918-588-5207 Transfer Agents: Computershare Trust Company, N.A., Providence, RI

HERBALIFE LTD.

Exchange	Symbol	Price	52Wk Range	Yield	P/E
NYS	HLF	$37.45 (3/28/2013)	72.69-26.06	3.20	9.25

*7 Year Price Score 143.46 *NYSE Composite Index=100 *12 Month Price Score 74.69

TRADING VOLUME (thousand shares)

Interim Earnings (Per Share)

Qtr.	Mar	Jun	Sep	Dec
2008	0.47	0.51	0.45	0.27
2009	0.34	0.39	0.46	0.44
2010	0.41	0.66	0.61	0.65
2011	0.70	0.88	0.87	0.86
2012	0.88	1.10	1.04	1.04

Interim Dividends (Per Share)

Amt	Decl	Ex	Rec	Pay
0.30Q	04/30/2012	05/11/2012	05/15/2012	05/30/2012
0.30Q	07/30/2012	08/10/2012	08/14/2012	08/30/2012
0.30Q	10/29/2012	11/09/2012	11/14/2012	11/28/2012
0.30Q	02/19/2013	03/01/2013	03/05/2013	03/19/2013

Indicated Div: $1.20

Valuation Analysis		Institutional Holding	
Forecast EPS	$4.65	No of Institutions	
	(04/05/2013)	421	
Market Cap	$4.0 Billion	Shares	
Book Value	$420.8 Million	122,549,976	
Price/Book	9.51	% Held	
Price/Sales	0.98	100.04	

Business Summary: Household & Personal Products (MIC: 1.7,1 SIC: 5122 NAIC: 424210)

Herbalife is a global nutrition company that sells weight management, meals and snacks, sports and fitness, energy and targeted nutritional products as well as personal care products. Co. distributes and sells its products via a network of independent distributors, using the direct selling channel. As of Dec 31 2012, Co. sold its products in 88 countries to and via a network of approximately 3.2 million independent distributors. In China, Co. sells its products through, sales representatives, sales officers, independent service providers and in retail stores. Co. categorizes its products into four groups: weight management, targeted nutrition, energy, sports & fitness and Outer Nutrition.

Recent Developments: For the year ended Dec 31 2012, net income increased 15.7% to US$477.2 million from US$412.6 million in the prior year. Revenues were US$4.07 billion, up 17.9% from US$3.45 billion the year before. Operating income was US$661.4 million versus US$562.3 million in the prior year, an increase of 17.6%. Direct operating expenses rose 19.5% to US$812.6 million from US$680.1 million in the comparable period the year before. Indirect operating expenses increased 17.5% to US$2.60 billion from US$2.21 billion in the equivalent prior-year period.

Prospects: Our evaluation of Herbalife Ltd. as of Apr. 7, 2013 is the result of our systematic analysis on three basic characteristics: earnings strength, relative valuation, and recent stock price movement. The company has managed to produce a neutral trend in earnings per share over the past 5 quarters and while recent estimates for the company have been raised by analysts, HLF has posted better than expected results. Based on operating earnings yield, the company is undervalued when compared to all of the companies in our coverage universe. Share price changes over the past year indicates that HLF will perform very poorly over the near term.

Financial Data

(US$ in Thousands)	12/31/2012	12/31/2011	12/31/2010	12/31/2009	12/31/2008	12/31/2007	12/31/2006
Earnings Per Share	4.05	3.30	2.34	1.61	1.68	1.31	0.96
Cash Flow Per Share	5.04	4.33	3.20	2.33	2.13	1.95	1.30
Tang Book Value Per Share	0.04	1.23	0.62	N.M.	N.M.	N.M.	N.M.
Dividends Per Share	1.200	0.730	0.450	0.400	0.800	0.600	...
Dividend Payout %	29.63	22.12	19.27	24.84	23.81	22.81	...
Income Statement							
Total Revenue	4,072,330	3,454,537	2,734,226	2,324,577	2,359,213	2,145,839	1,885,534
EBITDA	732,347	631,170	455,212	358,231	380,952	346,457	284,246
Depn & Amortn	70,900	68,900	67,700	62,200	48,700	33,300	27,300
Income Before Taxes	650,906	559,779	380,095	290,928	319,030	302,584	217,405
Income Taxes	173,716	147,201	89,562	87,582	97,840	111,133	74,266
Net Income	477,190	412,578	290,533	203,346	221,190	191,451	143,139
Average Shares	117,856	124,846	124,512	126,194	131,538	145,428	149,018
Balance Sheet							
Current Assets	963,848	768,819	595,586	513,502	484,768	487,096	455,707
Total Assets	1,703,944	1,446,209	1,232,220	1,146,050	1,121,318	1,067,243	1,016,933
Current Liabilities	716,891	548,689	470,816	429,966	401,899	375,618	323,492
Long-Term Obligations	431,305	202,079	175,046	237,931	336,514	360,491	179,839
Total Liabilities	1,283,189	886,021	745,008	786,739	879,587	884,999	663,043
Stockholders' Equity	420,755	560,188	487,212	359,311	241,731	182,244	353,890
Shares Outstanding	106,900	115,800	117,800	120,400	122,800	128,800	143,200
Statistical Record							
Return on Assets %	30.21	30.81	24.43	17.94	20.16	18.37	...
Return on Equity %	97.03	78.78	68.64	67.66	104.06	71.42	...
EBITDA Margin %	17.98	18.27	16.65	15.41	16.15	16.15	15.08
Net Margin %	11.72	11.94	10.63	8.75	9.38	8.92	7.59
Asset Turnover	2.58	2.58	2.30	2.05	2.15	2.06	...
Current Ratio	1.34	1.40	1.27	1.19	1.21	1.30	1.41
Debt to Equity	1.03	0.36	0.36	0.66	1.39	1.98	0.51
Price Range	72.69-26.06	62.36-31.88	35.45-18.61	21.99-6.14	25.00-7.52	22.87-14.87	20.66-14.42
P/E Ratio	17.95-6.43	18.90-9.66	15.15-7.96	13.66-3.81	14.88-4.48	17.46-11.35	21.52-15.02
Average Yield %	2.27	1.48	1.72	2.79	2.46	1.60	

Address: P.O. Box 309GT, Ugland House, South Church Street, George Town, KY1-1104 **Telephone:** 213-745-0500	**Web Site:** www.herbalife.com **Officers:** Michael O. Johnson - Chairman, Chief Executive Officer Desmond Walsh - President	**Auditors:** KPMG LLP **Transfer Agents:** Mellon Investor Services LLC, Richfield, NJ, U.S.

HERSHEY COMPANY (THE)

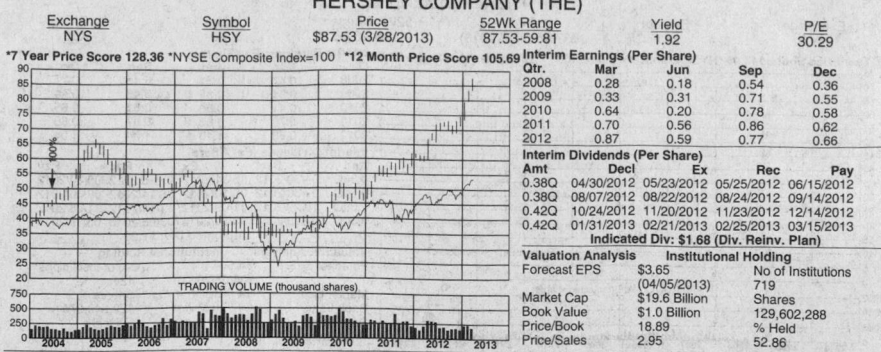

Exchange	Symbol	Price	52Wk Range	Yield	P/E
NYS	HSY	$87.53 (3/28/2013)	87.53-59.81	1.92	30.29

***7 Year Price Score 128.36** *NYSE Composite Index=100 ***12 Month Price Score 105.69**

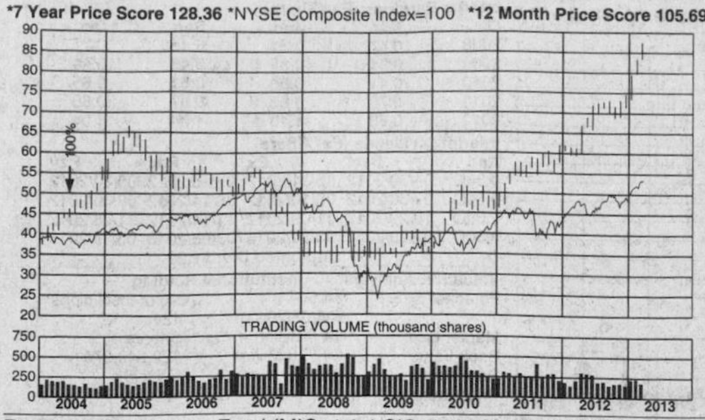

Interim Earnings (Per Share)

Qtr.	Mar	Jun	Sep	Dec
2008	0.28	0.18	0.54	0.36
2009	0.33	0.31	0.71	0.55
2010	0.64	0.20	0.78	0.58
2011	0.70	0.56	0.86	0.62
2012	0.87	0.59	0.77	0.66

Interim Dividends (Per Share)

Amt	Decl	Ex	Rec	Pay
0.38Q	04/30/2012	05/23/2012	05/25/2012	06/15/2012
0.38Q	08/07/2012	08/22/2012	08/24/2012	09/14/2012
0.42Q	10/24/2012	11/20/2012	11/23/2012	12/14/2012
0.42Q	01/31/2013	02/21/2013	02/25/2013	03/15/2013

Indicated Div: $1.68 (Div. Reinv. Plan)

Valuation Analysis		Institutional Holding
Forecast EPS	$3.65 (04/05/2013)	No of Institutions 719
Market Cap	$19.6 Billion	Shares 129,602,288
Book Value	$1.0 Billion	
Price/Book	18.89	% Held
Price/Sales	2.95	52.86

Business Summary: Food (MIC: 1.2.1 SIC: 2064 NAIC: 311320)

Hershey is engaged in the business of manufacturing, marketing, selling and distributing chocolate and sugar confectionery products; pantry items, such as baking ingredients, toppings and beverages; and gum and mint refreshment products. At Dec 31 2012, Co. sold its products under more than 80 brand names in about 70 countries. Co.'s three operating segments comprise geographic regions including the U.S.; the Americas, which include Canada, Mexico, Brazil, Central and South America, Puerto Rico and its export business in this region; and Asia, Europe, the Middle East and Africa, including exports to these areas. Co.'s two business units are: chocolate; and sweets and refreshment units.

Recent Developments: For the year ended Dec 31 2012, net income increased 5.1% to US$660.9 million from US$629.0 million in the prior year. Revenues were US$6.64 billion, up 9.3% from US$6.08 billion the year before. Operating income was US$1.11 billion versus US$1.06 billion in the prior year, an increase of 5.3%. Direct operating expenses rose 6.6% to US$3.78 billion from US$3.55 billion in the comparable period the year before. Indirect operating expenses increased 18.4% to US$1.75 billion from US$1.48 billion in the equivalent prior-year period.

Prospects: Our evaluation of Hershey Foods Corp. as of Apr. 7, 2013 is the result of our systematic analysis on three basic characteristics: earnings strength, relative valuation, and recent stock price movement. The company has enjoyed a very positive trend in earnings per share over the past 5 quarters and while recent estimates for the company have been raised by analysts, HSY has posted results that fell short of analysts expectations. Based on operating earnings yield, the company is about fairly valued when compared to all of the companies in our coverage universe. Share price changes over the past year indicates that HSY will perform well over the near term.

Financial Data

(US$ in Thousands)	12/31/2012	12/31/2011	12/31/2010	12/31/2009	12/31/2008	12/31/2007	12/31/2006	12/31/2005
Earnings Per Share	2.89	2.74	2.21	1.90	1.36	0.93	2.34	1.99
Cash Flow Per Share	4.85	2.56	3.96	4.68	2.28	3.40	3.07	1.89
Tang Book Value Per Share	1.05	0.98	1.12	0.10	N.M.	N.M.	0.18	1.63
Dividends Per Share	1.560	1.380	1.280	1.190	1.190	1.135	1.030	0.930
Dividend Payout %	53.98	50.36	57.92	62.63	87.50	122.04	44.02	46.73
Income Statement								
Total Revenue	6,644,252	6,080,788	5,671,009	5,298,668	5,132,768	4,946,716	4,944,230	4,835,974
EBITDA	1,321,185	1,270,791	1,102,414	944,001	839,389	769,752	1,192,469	1,078,943
Depn & Amortn	210,037	215,763	197,116	182,411	249,491	310,925	199,911	218,032
Income Before Taxes	1,015,579	962,845	808,864	671,131	492,022	340,242	876,502	772,926
Income Taxes	354,648	333,883	299,065	235,137	180,617	126,088	317,441	279,682
Net Income	660,931	628,962	509,799	435,994	311,405	214,154	559,061	493,244
Average Shares	228,337	229,919	230,313	228,995	228,697	231,449	239,071	248,292
Balance Sheet								
Current Assets	2,113,485	2,046,558	2,005,217	1,385,434	1,344,945	1,426,574	1,417,812	1,408,940
Total Assets	4,754,839	4,412,199	4,272,732	3,675,031	3,634,719	4,247,113	4,157,565	4,295,236
Current Liabilities	1,471,110	1,173,775	1,298,845	910,628	1,270,212	1,618,770	1,453,538	1,518,223
Long-Term Obligations	1,530,967	1,748,500	1,541,825	1,502,730	1,505,954	1,279,965	1,248,128	942,755
Total Liabilities	3,718,090	3,563,177	3,370,416	2,954,572	3,316,520	3,654,191	3,474,142	3,274,160
Stockholders' Equity	1,036,749	849,022	902,316	720,459	318,199	592,922	683,423	1,021,076
Shares Outstanding	223,786	225,205	227,030	227,998	227,035	227,049	230,263	240,524
Statistical Record								
Return on Assets %	14.38	14.48	12.83	11.93	7.88	5.10	13.23	12.19
Return on Equity %	69.91	71.83	62.83	83.95	68.17	33.56	65.60	46.74
EBITDA Margin %	19.88	20.90	19.44	17.82	16.35	15.56	24.12	22.31
Net Margin %	9.95	10.34	8.99	8.23	6.07	4.33	11.31	10.20
Asset Turnover	1.45	1.40	1.43	1.45	1.30	1.18	1.17	1.20
Current Ratio	1.44	1.74	1.54	1.52	1.06	0.88	0.98	0.93
Debt to Equity	1.48	2.06	1.71	2.09	4.73	2.16	1.83	0.92
Price Range	74.64-59.49	62.00-46.37	51.76-35.79	41.80-30.75	42.73-32.48	56.22-38.25	57.00-49.34	66.65-53.14
P/E Ratio	25.83-20.58	22.63-16.92	23.42-16.19	22.00-16.18	31.42-23.88	60.45-41.13	24.36-21.09	33.49-26.70
Average Yield %	2.29	2.48	2.81	3.24	3.24	2.34	1.94	1.55

Address: 100 Crystal A Drive, Hershey, PA 17033
Telephone: 717-534-4200
Fax: 717-531-6161

Web Site: www.hersheys.com
Officers: John P. Bilbrey - President, Chief Executive Officer Humberto P. Alfonso - Executive Vice President, Senior Vice President, Chief Financial Officer, Chief Administrative Officer

Auditors: KPMG LLP
Investor Contact: 800-539-0261
Transfer Agents: Computershare, Jersey City, NJ

HERTZ GLOBAL HOLDINGS INC

Exchange	Symbol	Price	52Wk Range	Yield	P/E
NYS	HTZ	$22.26 (3/28/2013)	22.26-10.62	N/A	41.22

*7 Year Price Score N/A   *NYSE Composite Index=100   *12 Month Price Score 120.61

Interim Earnings (Per Share)

Qtr.	Mar	Jun	Sep	Dec
2008	(0.18)	0.16	0.05	(3.77)
2009	(0.51)	0.01	0.15	(0.07)
2010	(0.37)	(0.06)	0.36	(0.07)
2011	(0.32)	0.12	0.47	0.11
2012	(0.13)	0.21	0.55	(0.09)

Interim Dividends (Per Share)

No Dividends Paid

Valuation Analysis		Institutional Holding	
Forecast EPS	$1.90	No of Institutions	
	(04/05/2013)	389	
Market Cap	$9.4 Billion	Shares	
Book Value	$2.5 Billion	563,943,744	
Price/Book	3.74	% Held	
Price/Sales	1.04	102.84	

Business Summary: Hotels, Restaurants & Travel (MIC: 2.2.1 SIC: 7514 NAIC: 532111)

Hertz Global Holdings is a holding company. Through its subsidiaries, Co. is engaged principally in the business of renting cars, crossovers and light trucks, as well as renting industrial, construction and material handling equipment. Co.'s range of equipment for rental includes earthmoving equipment, material handling equipment, aerial and electrical equipment, air compressors, generators, pumps, small tools, compaction equipment and construction-related trucks. In addition, Co.'s Hertz Claim Management Corporation subsidiary provides claim administration services to Co. and, to a lesser extent, to third parties. Co. operated from about 8,500 locations in 150 countries as of Dec 31 2011.

Recent Developments: For the year ended Dec 31 2012, net income increased 24.2% to US$243.1 million from US$195.7 million in the prior year. Revenues were US$9.02 billion, up 8.7% from US$8.30 billion the year before. Direct operating expenses rose 5.0% to US$4.80 billion from US$4.57 billion in the comparable period the year before. Indirect operating expenses increased 15.3% to US$3.13 billion from US$2.71 billion in the equivalent prior-year period.

Prospects: Our evaluation of Hertz Global Holdings Inc. as of Apr. 7, 2013 is the result of our systematic analysis on three basic characteristics: earnings strength, relative valuation, and recent stock price movement. The company has produced a positive trend in earnings per share over the past 5 quarters and while recent estimates for the company have been raised by analysts, HTZ has posted better than expected results. Based on operating earnings yield, the company is undervalued when compared to all of the companies in our coverage universe. Share price changes over the past year indicates that HTZ will perform poorly over the near term.

Financial Data

(US$ in Thousands)	12/31/2012	12/31/2011	12/31/2010	12/31/2009	12/31/2008	12/31/2007	12/31/2006	12/31/2005
Earnings Per Share	0.54	0.40	(0.12)	(0.34)	(3.74)	0.81	0.48	(0.09)
Cash Flow Per Share	6.45	5.37	5.36	4.78	6.48	9.62	10.78	...
Dividends Per Share	...	...	...	...	...	...	1.120	...
Dividend Payout %	...	...	...	...	...	...	233.33	...
Income Statement								
Total Revenue	9,020,807	8,298,380	7,562,534	7,101,507	8,525,055	8,685,631	8,058,405	154,469
EBITDA	3,420,591	3,056,094	2,756,171	2,601,993	1,895,635	3,505,309	3,117,354	43,930
Depn & Amortn	2,325,056	2,037,657	2,008,647	2,157,110	2,433,294	2,243,067	2,016,046	51,413
Income Before Taxes	450,545	324,270	(13,593)	(171,009)	(1,382,807)	386,820	200,651	(33,218)
Income Taxes	207,466	128,540	17,068	(59,660)	(196,847)	102,571	67,994	(12,243)
Net Income	243,079	176,170	(48,044)	(126,022)	(1,206,746)	264,559	115,943	(21,346)
Average Shares	448,209	444,778	411,941	371,456	322,701	325,487	243,354	229,500
Balance Sheet								
Current Assets	3,097,213	2,940,178	4,025,728	2,769,548	3,332,910	3,201,181	2,995,726	3,061,829
Total Assets	23,286,038	17,673,527	17,332,221	16,002,419	16,451,367	19,255,662	18,677,401	18,580,879
Current Liabilities	2,298,209	2,151,750	2,123,995	1,791,849	2,197,570	2,220,992	1,723,745	1,617,266
Long-Term Obligations	15,448,624	11,317,090	11,306,429	10,364,163	10,972,297	11,960,126	12,276,184	12,515,005
Total Liabilities	20,778,752	15,438,871	15,217,400	13,922,271	14,980,749	16,342,273	16,142,839	16,314,697
Stockholders' Equity	2,507,286	2,234,656	2,114,821	2,080,148	1,470,618	2,913,389	2,534,562	2,266,182
Shares Outstanding	421,485	417,022	413,462	410,245	322,987	321,862	320,618	229,500
Statistical Record								
Return on Assets %	1.18	1.01	N.M.	N.M.	N.M.	1.39	0.62	...
Return on Equity %	10.22	8.10	N.M.	N.M.	N.M.	9.71	4.83	...
EBITDA Margin %	37.92	36.83	36.45	36.64	22.24	40.36	38.68	28.44
Net Margin %	2.69	2.12	N.M.	N.M.	N.M.	3.05	1.44	N.M.
Asset Turnover	0.44	0.47	0.45	0.44	0.48	0.46	0.43	...
Current Ratio	1.35	1.37	1.90	1.55	1.52	1.44	1.74	1.89
Debt to Equity	6.16	5.06	5.35	4.98	7.46	4.11	4.84	5.52
Price Range	16.65-10.62	17.25-8.11	14.75-8.51	12.38-2.00	15.89-1.55	26.78-14.95	17.39-14.75	
P/E Ratio	30.83-19.67	43.13-20.27	...	...	...	33.06-18.46	36.23-30.73	
Average Yield %	...	...	...	...	...	...	6.96	...

Address: 225 Brae Boulevard, Park Ridge, NJ 07656-0713 **Telephone:** 201-307-2000	**Web Site:** www.hertz.com **Officers:** Mark P. Frissora - Chairman, Chief Executive Officer Elyse Douglas - Executive Vice President, Chief Financial Officer	**Auditors:** PricewaterhouseCoopers LLP **Investor Contact:** 201-307-2100 **Transfer Agents:** Computershare Trust Company, N.A., Providence, RI

HESS CORP

Exchange	Symbol	Price	52Wk Range	Yield	P/E
NYS	HES	$71.61 (3/28/2013)	72.51-39.95	0.56	12.04

*7 Year Price Score 75.28   *NYSE Composite Index=100   *12 Month Price Score 115.72

Interim Earnings (Per Share)

Qtr.	Mar	Jun	Sep	Dec
2008	2.34	2.76	2.37	(0.23)
2009	(0.18)	0.31	1.05	1.10
2010	1.65	1.15	3.52	0.16
2011	2.74	1.78	0.88	(0.39)
2012	1.60	1.61	1.64	1.10

Interim Dividends (Per Share)

Amt	Decl	Ex	Rec	Pay
0.10Q	06/06/2012	06/14/2012	06/18/2012	06/29/2012
0.10Q	09/05/2012	09/13/2012	09/17/2012	09/28/2012
0.10Q	12/05/2012	12/13/2012	12/17/2012	12/31/2012
0.10Q	03/04/2013	03/13/2013	03/15/2013	03/29/2013

Indicated Div: $0.40

Valuation Analysis

		Institutional Holding	
Forecast EPS	$6.20 (04/06/2013)	No of Institutions	739
Market Cap	$24.5 Billion	Shares	274,827,072
Book Value	$21.1 Billion	% Held	
Price/Book	1.16	N/A	
Price/Sales	0.64		

Business Summary: Production & Extraction (MIC: 9.1.1 SIC: 1382 NAIC: 211111)

Hess operates in two segments, Exploration and Production (E&P) and Marketing and Refining (M&R). The E&P segment explores for, develops, produces, purchases, transports and sells crude oil and natural gas. The M&R segment purchases, markets and trades refined petroleum products, natural gas and electricity. Co. also operates terminals and retail gasoline stations, most of which include convenience stores, that are located on the East Coast of the U.S. As of Dec 31 2012, Co. had total proved developed and undeveloped reserves of 1.55 billion barrels of oil equivalent.

Recent Developments: For the year ended Dec 31 2012, net income increased 23.1% to US$2.06 billion from US$1.68 billion in the prior year. Revenues were US$38.37 billion, up 1.3% from US$37.87 billion the year before. Direct operating expenses declined 5.0% to US$27.84 billion from US$29.30 billion in the comparable period the year before. Indirect operating expenses increased 11.2% to US$6.80 billion from US$6.11 billion in the equivalent prior-year period.

Prospects: Our evaluation of Hess Corp. as of Apr. 7, 2013 is the result of our systematic analysis on three basic characteristics: earnings strength, relative valuation, and recent stock price movement. The company has generated a negative trend in earnings per share over the past 5 quarters. However, while recent estimates for the company have been lowered by analysts, HES has posted results that were in line with analysts expectations. Based on operating earnings yield, the company is undervalued when compared to all of the companies in our coverage universe. Share price changes over the past year indicates that HES will perform poorly over the near term.

Financial Data
(US$ in Thousands)

	12/31/2012	12/31/2011	12/31/2010	12/31/2009	12/31/2008	12/31/2007	12/31/2006	12/31/2005
Earnings Per Share	5.95	5.01	6.47	2.27	7.24	5.74	6.07	3.98
Cash Flow Per Share	16.68	14.79	13.90	9.40	14.20	11.21	12.55	6.75
Tang Book Value Per Share	55.29	47.68	42.29	37.16	33.98	26.67	21.77	18.97
Dividends Per Share	0.400	0.400	0.400	0.400	0.400	0.400	0.400	0.400
Dividend Payout %	6.72	7.98	6.18	17.62	5.52	6.97	6.59	10.05
Income Statement								
Total Revenue	38,373,000	37,871,000	34,613,000	29,569,000	41,094,000	31,924,000	28,720,000	23,255,000
EBITDA	7,106,000	5,250,000	5,989,000	4,136,000	6,996,000	5,536,000	5,465,000	3,475,000
Depn & Amortn	2,949,000	2,406,000	2,317,000	2,254,000	2,029,000	1,576,000	1,224,000	1,025,000
Income Before Taxes	3,738,000	2,461,000	3,311,000	1,522,000	4,700,000	3,704,000	4,040,000	2,226,000
Income Taxes	1,675,000	785,000	1,173,000	715,000	2,340,000	1,872,000	2,124,000	984,000
Net Income	2,025,000	1,703,000	2,125,000	740,000	2,360,000	1,832,000	1,916,000	1,242,000
Average Shares	340,300	339,898	328,277	325,965	325,847	319,312	315,667	312,105
Balance Sheet								
Current Assets	8,387,000	8,339,000	8,780,000	7,987,000	7,332,000	6,926,000	5,848,000	5,290,000
Total Assets	43,441,000	39,136,000	35,396,000	29,465,000	28,589,000	26,131,000	22,404,000	19,115,000
Current Liabilities	8,382,000	8,100,000	7,613,000	6,850,000	7,730,000	8,024,000	6,739,000	6,447,000
Long-Term Obligations	7,324,000	6,005,000	5,537,000	4,319,000	3,812,000	3,918,000	3,745,000	3,759,000
Total Liabilities	22,351,000	20,620,000	18,707,000	16,081,000	16,282,000	16,357,000	14,293,000	12,829,000
Stockholders' Equity	21,090,000	18,516,000	16,689,000	13,384,000	12,307,000	9,774,000	8,111,000	6,286,000
Shares Outstanding	341,527	339,976	337,681	327,229	326,133	320,600	315,018	279,198
Statistical Record								
Return on Assets %	4.89	4.57	6.55	2.55	8.60	7.55	9.23	7.01
Return on Equity %	10.20	9.67	14.13	5.76	21.32	20.49	26.62	20.90
EBITDA Margin %	18.52	13.86	17.30	13.99	17.02	17.34	19.03	14.94
Net Margin %	5.28	4.50	6.14	2.50	5.74	5.74	6.67	5.34
Asset Turnover	0.93	1.02	1.07	1.02	1.50	1.32	1.38	1.31
Current Ratio	1.00	1.03	1.15	1.17	0.95	0.86	0.87	0.82
Debt to Equity	0.35	0.32	0.33	0.32	0.31	0.40	0.46	0.60
Price Range	67.00-39.95	87.03-49.46	76.54-49.69	68.04-47.50	133.80-38.45	104.40-47.31	56.02-38.50	46.46-26.33
P/E Ratio	11.26-6.71	17.37-9.87	11.83-7.68	29.97-20.93	18.48-5.31	18.19-8.24	9.23-6.34	11.67-6.62
Average Yield %	0.77	0.57	0.66	0.71	0.45	0.65	0.84	1.09

Address: 1185 Avenue of the Americas, New York, NY 10036 **Telephone:** 212-997-8500	**Web Site:** www.hess.com **Officers:** John B. Hess - Chairman, Chief Executive Officer Gregory P. Hill - Executive Vice President, Division Officer	**Auditors:** Ernst & Young LLP **Investor Contact:** 212-536-8940 **Transfer Agents:** BNY Mellon Shareowner Services, Jersey City, NJ

HEWLETT-PACKARD CO

Exchange	Symbol	Price	52Wk Range	Yield	P/E
NYS	HPQ	$23.84 (3/28/2013)	25.25-11.71	2.21	N/A

*7 Year Price Score 43.68 *NYSE Composite Index=100 ***12 Month Price Score 99.88**

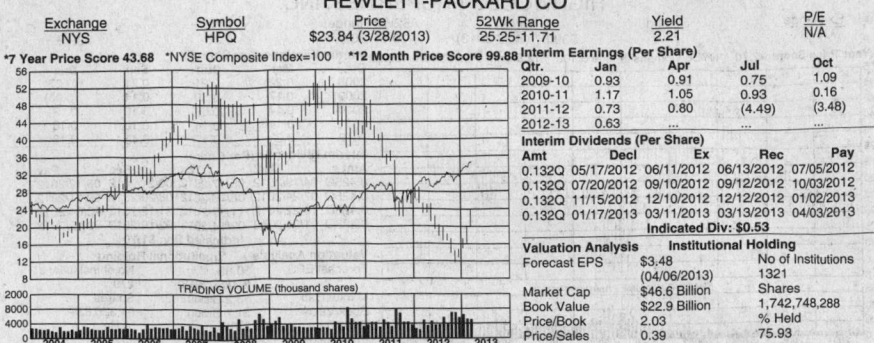

Interim Earnings (Per Share)

Qtr.	Jan	Apr	Jul	Oct
2009-10	0.93	0.91	0.75	1.09
2010-11	1.17	1.05	0.93	0.16
2011-12	0.73	0.80	(4.49)	(3.48)
2012-13	0.63	...	...	...

Interim Dividends (Per Share)

Amt	Decl	Ex	Rec	Pay
0.132Q	05/17/2012	06/11/2012	06/13/2012	07/05/2012
0.132Q	07/20/2012	09/10/2012	09/12/2012	10/03/2012
0.132Q	11/15/2012	12/10/2012	12/12/2012	01/02/2013
0.132Q	01/17/2013	03/11/2013	03/13/2013	04/03/2013

Indicated Div: $0.53

Valuation Analysis

		Institutional Holding	
Forecast EPS	$3.48 (04/06/2013)	No of Institutions	1321
Market Cap	$46.6 Billion	Shares	1,742,748,288
Book Value	$22.9 Billion	% Held	75.93
Price/Book	2.03		
Price/Sales	0.39		

TRADING VOLUME (thousand shares)

Business Summary: Computer Hardware & Equipment (MIC: 6.2.1 SIC: 3571 NAIC: 334111)

Hewlett-Packard is a provider of products, technologies, software, applications and services to individual consumers, businesses enterprises, including customers in the government, health and education sectors. Co.'s portolio include: personal computing and other access devices; multi-vendor customer services; imaging and printing-related products and services; and enterprise information technology infrastructure. As of Oct 31 2012, Co.'s operations were organized into seven business segments: the Personal Systems; Services; Printing; Services; Enterprise Servers, Storage and Networking; Software; HP Financial Services; and Corporate Investments.

Recent Developments: For the quarter ended Jan 31 2013, net income decreased 16.1% to US$1.23 billion from US$1.47 billion in the year-earlier quarter. Revenues were US$28.36 billion, down 5.6% from US$30.04 billion the year before. Operating income was US$1.75 billion versus US$2.04 billion in the prior-year quarter, a decrease of 14.2%. Direct operating expenses declined 5.5% to US$22.03 billion from US$23.31 billion in the comparable period the year before. Indirect operating expenses decreased 2.2% to US$4.58 billion from US$4.68 billion in the equivalent prior-year period.

Prospects: Our evaluation of Hewlett-Packard Co as of Apr. 7, 2013 is the result of our systematic analysis on three basic characteristics: earnings strength, relative valuation, and recent stock price movement. The company has managed to produce a neutral trend in earnings per share over the past 5 quarters and while recent estimates for the company have been raised by analysts, HPQ has posted better than expected results. Based on operating earnings yield, the company is undervalued when compared to all of the companies in our coverage universe. Share price changes over the past year indicates that HPQ will perform very poorly over the near term.

Financial Data

(US$ in Millions)	3 Mos	10/31/2012	10/31/2011	10/31/2010	10/31/2009	10/31/2008	10/31/2007	10/31/2006
Earnings Per Share	(6.54)	(6.41)	3.32	3.69	3.14	3.25	2.68	2.18
Cash Flow Per Share	6.11	5.34	6.04	5.14	5.60	5.86	3.66	4.08
Tang Book Value Per Share	N.M.	N.M.	N.M.	N.M.	0.34	N.M.	4.91	6.57
Dividends Per Share	0.516	0.504	0.400	0.320	0.320	0.320	0.320	0.320
Dividend Payout %	...	...	12.05	8.67	10.19	9.85	11.94	14.68
Income Statement								
Total Revenue	28,359	120,357	127,245	126,033	114,552	118,364	104,286	91,658
EBITDA	2,102	(5,973)	14,684	15,758	14,186	13,840	11,416	8,889
Depn & Amortn	350	5,084	5,007	4,784	4,771	3,367	2,683	2,304
Income Before Taxes	1,573	(11,933)	8,982	10,974	9,415	10,473	9,177	7,191
Income Taxes	341	717	1,908	2,213	1,755	2,144	1,913	993
Net Income	1,232	(12,650)	7,074	8,761	7,660	8,329	7,264	6,198
Average Shares	1,956	1,974	2,128	2,373	2,438	2,568	2,717	2,853
Balance Sheet								
Current Assets	49,552	50,637	51,021	54,184	52,539	51,728	47,402	48,264
Total Assets	106,701	108,768	129,517	124,503	114,799	113,331	88,699	81,981
Current Liabilities	44,386	46,666	50,442	49,403	43,003	52,939	39,260	35,850
Long-Term Obligations	21,752	21,789	22,551	15,258	13,980	7,676	4,997	2,490
Total Liabilities	83,806	86,332	90,892	84,054	74,282	74,389	50,173	43,837
Stockholders' Equity	22,895	22,436	38,625	40,449	40,517	38,942	38,526	38,144
Shares Outstanding	1,953	1,962	1,990	2,204	2,365	2,416	2,581	2,733
Statistical Record								
Return on Assets %	N.M.	N.M.	5.57	7.32	6.72	8.22	8.51	7.78
Return on Equity %	N.M.	N.M.	17.89	21.64	19.28	21.44	18.95	16.46
EBITDA Margin %	7.41	N.M.	11.54	12.50	12.38	11.69	10.95	9.70
Net Margin %	4.34	N.M.	5.56	6.95	6.69	7.04	6.97	6.76
Asset Turnover	1.02	1.01	1.00	1.05	1.00	1.17	1.22	1.15
Current Ratio	1.12	1.09	1.01	1.10	1.22	0.98	1.21	1.35
Debt to Equity	0.95	0.97	0.58	0.38	0.35	0.20	0.13	0.07
Price Range	29.07-11.71	29.07-13.85	48.99-22.20	54.52-38.00	48.74-25.53	53.41-31.18	52.87-38.22	39.87-28.04
P/E Ratio	...	...	14.76-6.69	14.78-10.30	15.52-8.13	16.43-9.59	19.73-14.26	18.29-12.86
Average Yield %	2.70	2.26	1.07	0.67	0.85	0.70	0.72	0.98

Address: 3000 Hanover Street, Palo Alto, CA 94304 Telephone: 650-857-1501	Web Site: www.hp.com Officers: Ralph V. Whitworth - Non-Executive Chairman Margaret C. Whitman - President, Chief Executive Officer	Auditors: Ernst & Young LLP Transfer Agents: ComputerShare Investor Services, Chicago, IL

HIGHWOODS PROPERTIES, INC.

Exchange	Symbol	Price	52Wk Range	Yield	P/E
NYS	HIW	$39.57 (3/28/2013)	39.57-30.97	4.30	38.79

*7 Year Price Score 92.70 *NYSE Composite Index=100 ***12 Month Price Score 100.82**

Interim Earnings (Per Share)

Qtr.	Mar	Jun	Sep	Dec
2008	0.22	0.21	0.21	(0.27)
2009	0.17	0.50	0.14	(0.05)
2010	0.14	0.50	0.10	0.12
2011	0.14	0.14	0.10	0.16
2012	0.23	0.17	0.43	0.18

Interim Dividends (Per Share)

Amt	Decl	Ex	Rec	Pay
0.425Q	04/19/2012	05/17/2012	05/21/2012	06/12/2012
0.425Q	07/24/2012	08/16/2012	08/20/2012	09/11/2012
0.425Q	10/22/2012	11/07/2012	11/12/2012	12/04/2012
0.425Q	01/30/2012	02/14/2013	02/19/2013	03/12/2013

Indicated Div: $1.70

Valuation Analysis   **Institutional Holding**

Forecast EPS	$0.69	No of Institutions
	(04/05/2013)	279
Market Cap	$3.2 Billion	Shares
Book Value	$1.2 Billion	91,326,824
Price/Book	2.74	% Held
Price/Sales	6.16	112.31

TRADING VOLUME (thousand shares)

Business Summary: REITs (MIC: 5.3.1 SIC: 6798 NAIC: 525930)

Highwoods Properties is a real estate investment trust that provides leasing, management, development, construction and other customer-related services for its properties and for third parties. Co. primarily conducts its activities through Highwoods Realty Limited Partnership (the "Operating Partnership").

Recent Developments: For the year ended Dec 31 2012, income from continuing operations increased 30.0% to US$50.7 million from US$39.0 million a year earlier. Net income increased 75.6% to US$84.2 million from US$48.0 million in the prior year. Revenues were US$516.1 million, up 11.4% from US$463.4 million the year before. Revenues from property income rose 10.6% to US$506.5 million from US$458.0 million in the corresponding earlier year.

Prospects: Our evaluation of Highwoods Properties Inc. as of Apr. 7, 2013 is the result of our systematic analysis on three basic characteristics: earnings strength, relative valuation, and recent stock price movement. The company has managed to produce a neutral trend in earnings per share over the past 5 quarters. Because the company lacks sufficient analyst estimate data, we place greater weight on the historical EPS trend as the measure of earnings strength. Based on operating earnings yield, the company is overvalued when compared to all of the companies in our coverage universe. Share price changes over the past year indicates that HIW will perform poorly over the near term.

Financial Data

(US$ in Thousands)	12/31/2012	12/31/2011	12/31/2010	12/31/2009	12/31/2008	12/31/2007	12/31/2006	12/31/2005
Earnings Per Share	1.02	0.54	0.86	0.76	0.37	1.31	0.62	0.58
Cash Flow Per Share	2.54	2.70	2.66	2.78	2.68	2.86	2.67	2.87
Tang Book Value Per Share	14.08	13.12	13.98	14.68	16.02	15.51	16.19	17.29
Dividends Per Share	1.700	1.700	1.700	1.700	1.700	1.700	1.700	1.700
Dividend Payout %	166.67	314.81	197.67	223.68	459.46	129.77	274.19	293.10
Income Statement								
Total Revenue	516,102	482,852	463,321	454,026	461,003	437,059	416,798	410,701
EBITDA	299,864	276,021	296,186	227,817	216,311	249,500	229,381	233,203
Depn & Amortn	165,420	147,786	141,019	116,819	112,299	109,546	103,775	110,851
Income Before Taxes	45,683	39,623	68,157	32,389	9,352	46,030	31,850	21,756
Net Income	84,235	47,971	72,303	61,694	31,992	90,745	53,744	62,458
Average Shares	79,678	76,189	75,578	72,079	63,238	61,547	61,362	53,732
Balance Sheet								
Current Assets	173,550	173,957	132,756	134,209	119,681	116,984	110,428	102,574
Total Assets	3,350,428	3,180,992	2,871,835	2,887,101	2,946,170	2,926,955	2,844,853	2,908,978
Current Liabilities	172,146	148,821	106,716	117,328	135,609	157,766	156,737	127,455
Long-Term Obligations	1,888,520	1,934,657	1,556,059	1,506,861	1,638,859	1,677,058	1,500,659	1,505,770
Total Liabilities	2,190,288	2,198,779	1,788,073	1,759,141	1,846,279	1,904,922	1,737,122	1,727,359
Stockholders' Equity	1,160,140	982,213	1,083,762	1,127,960	1,099,891	1,022,033	1,107,731	1,181,619
Shares Outstanding	80,311	72,647	71,690	71,285	63,571	57,167	56,211	54,028
Statistical Record								
Return on Assets %	2.57	1.59	2.51	2.12	1.09	3.14	1.87	2.03
Return on Equity %	7.84	4.64	6.54	5.54	3.01	8.52	4.70	4.90
EBITDA Margin %	58.10	57.16	63.93	50.18	46.92	57.09	55.03	56.78
Net Margin %	16.32	9.93	15.61	13.59	6.94	20.76	12.89	15.21
Asset Turnover	0.16	0.16	0.16	0.16	0.16	0.15	0.14	0.13
Current Ratio	1.01	1.17	1.24	1.14	0.88	0.74	0.70	0.80
Debt to Equity	1.63	1.97	1.44	1.34	1.49	1.64	1.35	1.27
Price Range	35.48-29.71	36.92-26.51	35.16-26.54	34.84-16.57	37.94-15.59	46.95-28.89	41.31-29.20	31.75-24.40
P/E Ratio	34.78-29.13	68.37-49.09	40.88-30.86	45.84-21.80	102.54-42.14	35.84-22.05	66.63-47.10	54.74-42.07
Average Yield %	5.17	5.30	5.46	6.64	5.58	4.47	4.88	6.02

Address: 3100 Smoketree Court, Suite 600, Raleigh, NC 27604
Telephone: 919-872-4924
Fax: 919-431-1439

Web Site: www.highwoods.com
Officers: O. Temple Sloan - Chairman Edward J. Fritsch - President, Chief Executive Officer

Auditors: Deloitte & Touche LLP
Investor Contact: 919-431-1529
Transfer Agents: Wells Fargo Shareholder Services, Mendota Heights, MN

HILL-ROM HOLDINGS, INC.

Exchange	Symbol	Price	52Wk Range	Yield	P/E
NYS	HRC	$35.22 (3/28/2013)	35.22-25.30	1.42	19.68

*7 Year Price Score 91.23 *NYSE Composite Index=100 *12 Month Price Score 102.55

TRADING VOLUME (thousand shares)

Interim Earnings (Per Share)

Qtr.	Dec	Mar	Jun	Sep
2009-10	0.31	0.38	0.48	0.80
2010-11	0.55	0.52	0.02	1.00
2011-12	0.53	0.40	0.37	0.63
2012-13	0.39	...	...	...

Interim Dividends (Per Share)

Amt	Decl	Ex	Rec	Pay
0.125Q	05/02/2012	06/13/2012	06/15/2012	06/29/2012
0.125Q	09/04/2012	09/12/2012	09/14/2012	09/28/2012
0.125Q	12/03/2012	12/12/2012	12/14/2012	12/28/2012
0.125Q	03/04/2013	03/13/2013	03/15/2013	03/29/2013

Indicated Div: $0.50

Valuation Analysis

		Institutional Holding	
Forecast EPS	$2.09	No of Institutions	
	(04/05/2013)	26	
Market Cap	$2.1 Billion	Shares	
Book Value	$820.9 Million	4,647,947	
Price/Book	2.59	% Held	
Price/Sales	1.26	N/A	

Business Summary: Medical Instruments & Equipment (MIC: 4.3.1 SIC: 3841 NAIC: 339112)

Hill-Rom Holdings is a manufacturer and provider of medical technologies and related services for the health care industry, including patient support systems and non-invasive therapeutic products. Co. operates and manages its business within three reportable segments: North America, which sells and rents its patient support and near-patient technologies and services, as well as its health information technology applications, in the U.S. and Canada; Surgical and Respiratory Care, which sells and rents its surgical and respiratory care products in various settings; and International, which sells and rents similar products as its North America segment in regions outside of the U.S. and Canada.

Recent Developments: For the quarter ended Dec 31 2012, net income decreased 27.1% to US$24.0 million from US$32.9 million in the year-earlier quarter. Revenues were US$428.4 million, up 12.4% from US$381.1 million the year before. Operating income was US$37.1 million versus US$49.6 million in the prior-year quarter, a decrease of 25.2%. Direct operating expenses rose 20.9% to US$237.0 million from US$196.0 million in the comparable period the year before. Indirect operating expenses increased 13.9% to US$154.3 million from US$135.5 million in the equivalent prior-year period.

Prospects: Our evaluation of Hil-Rom Holdings, Inc. as of Apr. 7, 2013 is the result of our systematic analysis on three basic characteristics: earnings strength, relative valuation, and recent stock price movement. The company has managed to produce a neutral trend in earnings per share over the past 5 quarters and while recent estimates for the company have remained steady, HRC has posted better than expected results. Based on operating earnings yield, the company is undervalued when compared to all of the companies in our coverage universe. Share price changes over the past year indicates that HRC will perform poorly over the near term.

Financial Data
(US$ in Thousands)

	3 Mos	09/30/2012	09/30/2011	09/30/2010	09/30/2009	09/30/2008	09/30/2007	09/30/2006
Earnings Per Share	1.79	1.94	2.09	1.97	(6.47)	1.85	3.07	3.59
Cash Flow Per Share	4.34	4.20	3.52	2.22	3.61	4.32	4.62	0.47
Tang Book Value Per Share	3.28	3.07	8.57	7.80	6.29	8.49	11.19	9.12
Dividends Per Share	0.500	0.487	0.430	0.410	0.410	0.775	1.138	1.130
Dividend Payout %	27.93	25.13	20.57	20.81	...	41.89	37.05	31.48
Income Statement								
Total Revenue	428,400	1,634,300	1,591,700	1,469,600	1,386,900	1,507,700	2,023,700	1,962,900
EBITDA	610,900	243,900	242,500	264,400	(294,100)	140,300	353,300	400,400
Depn & Amortn	573,300	73,900	74,300	72,800	74,300	33,700	39,600	40,100
Income Before Taxes	35,300	163,500	159,700	182,900	(378,800)	92,300	291,500	339,000
Income Taxes	11,300	42,700	26,200	56,900	26,200	25,200	100,900	117,500
Net Income	24,000	120,800	133,300	125,300	(405,000)	115,800	190,600	221,200
Average Shares	61,106	62,120	63,899	63,739	62,581	62,622	62,115	61,576
Balance Sheet								
Current Assets	682,400	681,800	791,700	739,200	695,100	772,300	894,400	763,900
Total Assets	1,615,000	1,627,600	1,299,100	1,245,600	1,232,600	1,689,900	2,117,000	1,952,200
Current Liabilities	371,700	378,100	334,000	288,700	344,300	394,700	339,600	325,200
Long-Term Obligations	234,600	237,500	50,800	98,500	99,700	100,200	348,600	347,000
Total Liabilities	794,100	815,000	557,400	538,100	623,300	607,300	839,200	820,500
Stockholders' Equity	820,900	812,600	741,700	707,500	609,300	1,082,600	1,277,800	1,131,700
Shares Outstanding	60,319	60,796	61,686	62,786	62,667	62,508	61,991	61,415
Statistical Record								
Return on Assets %	7.89	8.23	10.48	10.11	N.M.	6.07	9.37	10.58
Return on Equity %	14.08	15.50	18.40	19.03	N.M.	9.79	15.82	21.11
EBITDA Margin %	142.60	14.92	15.24	17.99	N.M.	9.31	17.46	20.40
Net Margin %	5.60	7.39	8.37	8.53	N.M.	7.68	9.42	11.27
Asset Turnover	1.19	1.11	1.25	1.19	0.95	0.79	0.99	0.94
Current Ratio	1.84	1.80	2.37	2.56	2.02	1.96	2.63	2.35
Debt to Equity	0.29	0.29	0.07	0.14	0.16	0.09	0.27	0.31
Price Range	35.96-25.30	35.96-25.30	47.48-27.37	35.89-19.59	30.31-8.89	33.46-24.38	36.29-29.34	31.18-24.19
P/E Ratio	20.09-14.13	18.54-13.04	22.72-13.10	18.22-9.94	...	18.09-13.18	11.82-9.56	8.68-6.74
Average Yield %	1.65	1.56	1.10	1.48	2.43	2.70	3.51	4.15

Address: 1069 State Route 46 East, Batesville, IN 47006-8835 **Telephone:** 812-934-7777 **Fax:** 812-934-7364	**Web Site:** www.Hill-Rom.com **Officers:** Rolf A. Classon - Chairman John J. Greisch - President, Chief Executive Officer	**Auditors:** PricewaterhouseCoopers LLP **Investor Contact:** 812-931-2199 **Transfer Agents:** Computershare Trust Company, Providence, RI

HILLENBRAND INC

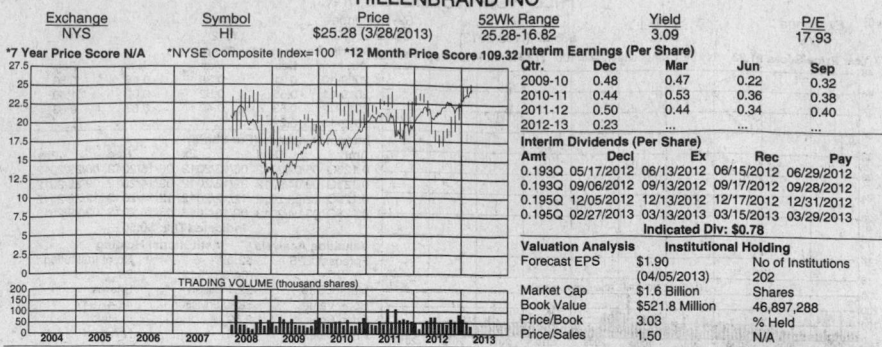

Exchange	Symbol	Price	52Wk Range	Yield	P/E
NYS	HI	$25.28 (3/28/2013)	25.28-16.82	3.09	17.93

*7 Year Price Score N/A   *NYSE Composite Index=100   *12 Month Price Score 109.32

Interim Earnings (Per Share)

Qtr.	Dec	Mar	Jun	Sep
2009-10	0.48	0.47	0.22	0.32
2010-11	0.44	0.53	0.36	0.38
2011-12	0.50	0.44	0.34	0.40
2012-13	0.23	...	...	...

Interim Dividends (Per Share)

Amt	Decl	Ex	Rec	Pay
0.193Q	05/17/2012	06/13/2012	06/15/2012	06/29/2012
0.193Q	09/06/2012	09/13/2012	09/17/2012	09/28/2012
0.195Q	12/05/2012	12/13/2012	12/17/2012	12/31/2012
0.195Q	02/27/2013	03/13/2013	03/15/2013	03/29/2013

Indicated Div: $0.78

Valuation Analysis

Forecast EPS	$1.90 (04/05/2013)
Market Cap	$1.6 Billion
Book Value	$521.8 Million
Price/Book	3.03
Price/Sales	1.50

Institutional Holding

No of Institutions	202
Shares	46,897,288
% Held	N/A

Business Summary: Miscellaneous Consumer Services (MIC: 2.2.3 SIC: 3995 NAIC: 339995)

Hillenbrand manufactures and sells business-to-business products and services. Co. has two segments: the Process Equipment Group, which designs, produces, markets, sells, and services bulk solids material handling equipment and systems for a variety of industries, including plastics, food, chemicals, pharmaceuticals, power generation, coal mining, pulp and paper, frac sand, industrial minerals, agribusiness, recycling, wood and forest products, and biomass energy generation; and Batesville®, which designs, manufactures and sells funeral service products, such as burial caskets, cremation caskets, containers, cremation vaults and urns to licensed funeral directors operating funeral homes.

Recent Developments: For the quarter ended Dec 31 2012, net income decreased 53.4% to US$14.6 million from US$31.3 million in the year-earlier quarter. Revenues were US$305.2 million, up 31.8% from US$231.6 million the year before. Operating income was US$24.1 million versus US$33.4 million in the prior-year quarter, a decrease of 27.8%. Direct operating expenses rose 41.1% to US$194.6 million from US$137.9 million in the comparable period the year before. Indirect operating expenses increased 43.4% to US$86.5 million from US$60.3 million in the equivalent prior-year period.

Prospects: Our evaluation of Hillenbrand Inc. as of Apr. 7, 2013 is the result of our systematic analysis on three basic characteristics: earnings strength, relative valuation, and recent stock price movement. The company has managed to produce a neutral trend in earnings per share over the past 5 quarters and while recent estimates for the company have remained steady, HI has posted better than expected results. Based on operating earnings yield, the company is undervalued when compared to all of the companies in our coverage universe. Share price changes over the past year indicates that HI will perform in line with the market over the near term.

Financial Data
(US$ in Thousands)

	3 Mos	09/30/2012	09/30/2011	09/30/2010	09/30/2009	09/30/2008	09/30/2007	09/30/2006
Earnings Per Share	1.41	1.68	1.71	1.49	1.66	1.49	...	...
Cash Flow Per Share	2.10	2.22	3.06	1.91	2.00	1.62	...	...
Tang Book Value Per Share	N.M.	N.M.	N.M.	N.M.	4.65	4.33	...	...
Dividends Per Share	0.772	0.770	0.760	0.750	0.740	0.365	...	...
Dividend Payout %	54.79	45.83	44.44	50.34	44.58	24.50	...	...
Income Statement								
Total Revenue	305,200	983,200	883,400	749,200	649,100	678,100	667,200	674,600
EBITDA	40,200	164,400	176,100	152,500	169,700	162,800	171,400	192,600
Depn & Amortn	15,000	18,700	19,100	17,200	14,900	15,400	14,400	13,800
Income Before Taxes	20,700	133,300	152,400	143,300	166,200	153,300	157,000	178,800
Income Taxes	5,900	30,100	51,700	54,100	58,500	60,100	57,500	65,600
Net Income	14,300	104,800	106,100	92,300	102,300	93,200	99,500	113,200
Average Shares	62,600	62,400	62,000	61,900	61,700	62,500	...	...
Balance Sheet								
Current Assets	665,700	305,300	380,100	322,800	232,900	181,600	170,200	171,500
Total Assets	2,033,000	1,087,500	1,180,700	1,052,100	561,100	545,300	316,600	329,400
Current Liabilities	439,600	151,800	136,200	118,000	134,900	186,000	75,800	77,000
Long-Term Obligations	757,700	271,600	431,500	403,400	...	...	...	...
Total Liabilities	1,511,200	581,200	737,600	680,200	257,100	256,900	135,700	136,900
Stockholders' Equity	521,800	506,300	443,100	371,900	304,000	288,400	180,900	192,500
Shares Outstanding	62,600	62,600	62,500	62,300	61,900	62,100	...	...
Statistical Record								
Return on Assets %	5.49	9.22	9.50	11.44	18.49	21.57	30.80	...
Return on Equity %	17.91	22.02	26.04	27.31	34.54	39.61	53.29	...
EBITDA Margin %	13.17	16.72	19.93	20.36	26.14	24.01	25.69	28.55
Net Margin %	4.69	10.66	12.01	12.32	15.76	13.74	14.91	16.78
Asset Turnover	0.66	0.86	0.79	0.93	1.17	1.57	2.07	...
Current Ratio	1.51	2.01	2.79	2.74	1.73	0.98	2.25	2.23
Debt to Equity	1.45	0.54	0.97	1.08	...	...	...	...
Price Range	23.90-16.82	23.90-16.82	24.08-17.86	25.77-17.85	20.97-13.96	24.29-18.00	...	...
P/E Ratio	16.95-11.93	14.23-10.01	14.08-10.44	17.30-11.98	12.63-8.41	16.30-12.08	...	...
Average Yield %	3.82	3.79	3.55	3.57	4.18	1.66	...	...

Address: One Batesville Boulevard, Batesville, IN 47006
Telephone: 812-934-7500

Web Site: www.hillenbrandinc.com
Officers: Ray J. Hillenbrand - Chairman James A. Henderson - Vice-Chairman

Auditors: PricewaterhouseCoopers LLP
Investor Contact: 812-931-6000
Transfer Agents: Computershare Trust Company, N. A., Providence, RI

HILLSHIRE BRANDS CO

Exchange	Symbol	Price	52Wk Range	Yield	P/E
NYS	HSH	$35.15 (3/28/2013)	111.60-24.46	1.42	5.87

*7 Year Price Score 57.01 ***NYSE Composite Index=100** ***12 Month Price Score 67.89**

Interim Earnings (Per Share)

Qtr.	Sep	Dec	Mar	Jun
2009-10	2.05	2.65	(2.45)	1.35
2010-11	1.45	6.85	1.25	1.00
2011-12	(1.85)	3.95	0.00	5.03
2012-13	0.43	0.53	...	...

Interim Dividends (Per Share)

Amt	Decl	Ex	Rec	Pay
0.125Q	08/08/2012	08/30/2012	09/04/2012	10/05/2012
0.125Q	10/25/2012	11/29/2012	12/03/2012	12/31/2012
0.125Q	01/23/2013	02/27/2013	03/01/2013	04/05/2013

Indicated Div: $0.50 (Div. Reinv. Plan)

Valuation Analysis		Institutional Holding	
Forecast EPS	$1.72	No of Institutions	
	(04/05/2013)	479	
Market Cap	$4.3 Billion	Shares	
Book Value	$367.0 Million	203,515,968	
Price/Book	11.77	% Held	
Price/Sales	2.02	N/A	

TRADING VOLUME (thousand shares)

Business Summary: Food (MIC: 1.2.1 SIC: 2013 NAIC: 311612)

Hillshire Brands is a manufacturer of meat-centric food products. Co. sells a range of packaged meat products that include hot dogs, corn dogs, breakfast sausages, dinner sausages and lunchmeats as well as frozen baked products and specialty items including cakes and cheesecakes. Co.'s operations are organized around three business segments: Retail, which sells packaged meat and frozen bakery products to retail customers in North America; Foodservice/Other, which sells meat and bakery products to foodservice customers in North America; and Australian Bakery, which sells bakery and other food products to retail and foodservice customers in Australia and other parts of the Pacific Rim region.

Recent Developments: For the quarter ended Dec 29 2012, income from continuing operations increased 480.0% to US$58.0 million from US$10.0 million in the year-earlier quarter. Net income decreased 86.2% to US$65.0 million from US$470.0 million in the year-earlier quarter. Revenues were US$1.06 billion, up 0.7% from US$1.05 billion the year before. Operating income was US$99.0 million versus US$23.0 million in the prior-year quarter, an increase of 330.4%. Direct operating expenses declined 3.6% to US$728.0 million from US$755.0 million in the comparable period the year before. Indirect operating expenses decreased 15.3% to US$233.0 million from US$275.0 million in the equivalent prior-year period.

Prospects: Our evaluation of Hillshire Brands Co. as of Apr. 7, 2013 is the result of our systematic analysis on three basic characteristics: earnings strength, relative valuation, and recent stock price movement. The company has produced a positive trend in earnings per share over the past 5 quarters and while recent estimates for the company have remained steady, HSH has posted better than expected results. Based on operating earnings yield, the company is about fairly valued when compared to all of the companies in our coverage universe. Share price changes over the past year indicates that HSH will perform poorly over the near term.

Financial Data

(US$ in Thousands)	6 Mos	3 Mos	06/30/2012	07/02/2011	07/03/2010	06/27/2009	06/28/2008	06/30/2007
Earnings Per Share	5.99	9.41	7.13	10.30	3.65	2.60	(0.55)	3.40
Cash Flow Per Share	2.80	3.89	2.10	3.61	6.81	6.44	4.25	3.33
Tang Book Value Per Share	N.M.	N.M.	N.M.	6.92	N.M.	N.M.	N.M.	N.M.
Dividends Per Share	0.250	0.125	1.150	2.300	2.200	2.200	2.100	2.000
Dividend Payout %	4.17	1.33	16.13	22.33	60.27	84.62	...	58.82
Income Statement								
Total Revenue	2,034,000	1,011,000	4,094,000	8,681,000	10,793,000	12,881,000	13,212,000	12,278,000
EBITDA	269,000	130,000	301,000	874,000	1,286,000	1,096,000	663,000	1,095,000
Depn & Amortn	86,000	43,000	266,000	302,000	368,000	383,000	403,000	539,000
Income Before Taxes	164,000	78,000	(37,000)	487,000	795,000	588,000	160,000	419,000
Income Taxes	57,000	27,000	(15,000)	149,000	153,000	224,000	201,000	(7,000)
Net Income	118,000	53,000	845,000	1,287,000	506,000	364,000	(79,000)	504,000
Average Shares	123,000	123,000	119,000	125,000	138,200	140,600	143,000	148,600
Balance Sheet								
Current Assets	1,030,000	1,012,000	1,002,000	4,584,000	3,810,000	3,830,000	4,467,000	5,643,000
Total Assets	2,467,000	2,452,000	2,450,000	9,533,000	8,836,000	9,417,000	10,830,000	12,190,000
Current Liabilities	706,000	756,000	833,000	4,122,000	2,723,000	2,846,000	3,841,000	4,301,000
Long-Term Obligations	936,000	942,000	939,000	1,936,000	2,718,000	2,745,000	2,340,000	2,803,000
Total Liabilities	2,100,000	2,141,000	2,215,000	7,588,000	7,349,000	7,381,000	8,019,000	9,575,000
Stockholders' Equity	367,000	311,000	235,000	1,945,000	1,487,000	2,036,000	2,811,000	2,615,000
Shares Outstanding	122,936	122,252	120,644	117,419	132,423	139,131	141,271	144,886
Statistical Record								
Return on Assets %	13.37	19.38	14.14	14.05	5.45	3.61	N.M.	3.78
Return on Equity %	60.06	116.27	77.74	75.21	28.26	15.06	N.M.	19.96
EBITDA Margin %	13.23	12.86	7.35	10.07	11.92	8.51	5.02	8.92
Net Margin %	5.80	5.24	20.64	14.83	4.69	2.83	N.M.	4.10
Asset Turnover	0.40	0.55	0.69	0.95	1.16	1.28	1.15	0.92
Current Ratio	1.46	1.34	1.20	1.11	1.40	1.35	1.16	1.31
Debt to Equity	2.55	3.03	4.00	1.00	1.83	1.35	0.83	1.07
Price Range	111.60-24.46	111.60-24.46	111.60-28.99	98.30-67.15	74.75-46.00	74.50-34.15	87.35-60.90	90.60-68.21
P/E Ratio	18.63-4.08	11.86-2.60	15.65-4.07	9.54-6.52	20.48-12.60	28.65-13.13	...	26.65-20.06
Average Yield %	0.39	0.16	1.20	2.78	3.57	4.25	2.78	2.45

Address: 400 South Jefferson Street, Chicago, IL 60607	Web Site: www.hillshirebrands.com	Auditors: PricewaterhouseCoopers LLP
Telephone: 312-614-6000	Officers: Sean M. Connolly - Chief Executive Officer Kent B. Magill - Executive Vice President, General Counsel, Corporate Secretary	Investor Contact: 163-059-88100
Fax: 312-558-4913		Transfer Agents: Computershare, Pittsburgh, PA

HNI CORP

*7 Year Price Score 83.79 *NYSE Composite Index=100 *12 Month Price Score 107.01

Interim Earnings (Per Share)

Qtr.	Mar	Jun	Sep	Dec
2008	0.09	0.30	0.44	0.19
2009	(0.27)	(0.03)	0.39	(0.24)
2010	(0.13)	0.10	0.34	0.28
2011	(0.04)	0.10	0.55	0.40
2012	0.00	0.15	0.53	0.39

Interim Dividends (Per Share)

Amt	Decl	Ex	Rec	Pay
0.24Q	05/08/2012	05/16/2012	05/18/2012	06/01/2012
0.24Q	08/07/2012	08/15/2012	08/17/2012	08/31/2012
0.24Q	11/08/2012	11/15/2012	11/19/2012	11/30/2012
0.24Q	02/13/2013	02/21/2013	02/25/2013	03/04/2013

Indicated Div: $0.96

Valuation Analysis / **Institutional Holding**

Forecast EPS	$1.35 (04/05/2013)	No of Institutions	168
Market Cap	$1.6 Billion	Shares	41,747,872
Book Value	$420.4 Million	% Held	67.05
Price/Book	3.80		
Price/Sales	0.80		

Business Summary: Office Equipment & Furniture (MIC: 7.5.1 SIC: 2522 NAIC: 337214)

HNI is a provider of office furniture and hearth products. Co.'s office furniture segment manufactures and markets a line of metal and wood commercial and home office furniture which includes storage products, desks, credenzas, chairs, tables, bookcases, freestanding office partitions and panel systems and other related products, under brands such as, HON®, Allsteel®, Maxon®, Gunlocke®, Paoli®, HBF®, Artco Bell™, basyx™ and Lamex®. Co.'s hearth products segment manufactures and markets a line of gas, electric, wood and biomass burning fireplaces, inserts, stoves, facings and accessories, under Heatilator®, Heat & Glo®, Quadra-Fire®, Harman Stove® and PelPro® brand names.

Recent Developments: For the year ended Dec 29 2012, income from continuing operations increased 5.6% to US$48.3 million from US$45.7 million a year earlier. Net income increased 5.6% to US$48.3 million from US$45.7 million in the prior year. Revenues were US$2.00 billion, up 9.3% from US$1.83 billion the year before. Operating income was US$87.6 million versus US$81.5 million in the prior year, an increase of 7.5%. Direct operating expenses rose 10.1% to US$1.31 billion from US$1.19 billion in the comparable period the year before. Indirect operating expenses increased 7.9% to US$601.6 million from US$557.6 million in the equivalent prior-year period.

Prospects: Our evaluation of HNI Corp. as of Apr. 7, 2013 is the result of our systematic analysis on three basic characteristics: earnings strength, relative valuation, and recent stock price movement. The company has generated a negative trend in earnings per share over the past 5 quarters and while recent estimates for the company have remained steady, HNI has posted results that fell short of analysts expectations. Based on operating earnings yield, the company is overvalued when compared to all of the companies in our coverage universe. Share price changes over the past year indicates that HNI will perform well over the near term.

Financial Data

(US$ in Thousands)	12/29/2012	12/31/2011	01/01/2011	01/02/2010	01/03/2009	12/29/2007	12/30/2006	12/31/2005
Earnings Per Share	1.07	1.01	0.59	(0.14)	1.02	2.57	2.45	2.50
Cash Flow Per Share	3.21	3.01	2.10	4.32	3.87	6.25	3.20	3.69
Tang Book Value Per Share	2.94	3.31	3.29	3.51	4.07	4.51	5.10	6.78
Dividends Per Share	0.950	0.920	0.860	0.860	0.860	0.780	0.720	0.620
Dividend Payout %	88.79	91.09	145.76	...	84.31	30.35	29.39	24.80
Income Statement								
Total Revenue	2,004,003	1,833,450	1,686,728	1,656,289	2,477,587	2,570,472	2,679,803	2,450,572
EBITDA	130,987	127,774	116,540	78,859	155,038	261,831	275,919	281,060
Depn & Amortn	43,360	46,287	58,630	74,867	70,155	68,173	69,503	65,514
Income Before Taxes	77,604	70,159	46,478	(7,673)	69,190	176,726	193,232	214,709
Income Taxes	29,278	24,411	16,797	(1,414)	23,634	57,141	63,670	77,295
Net Income	48,967	45,986	26,941	(6,442)	45,450	120,378	123,375	137,420
Average Shares	45,819	45,694	45,808	44,888	44,433	46,925	50,374	55,033
Balance Sheet								
Current Assets	404,940	434,040	408,161	360,271	417,841	489,072	504,174	486,598
Total Assets	1,079,631	1,054,258	997,880	994,326	1,165,629	1,206,976	1,226,359	1,140,271
Current Liabilities	395,885	388,910	361,351	300,142	373,625	384,461	358,542	358,174
Long-Term Obligations	150,372	150,540	150,111	200,000	267,343	281,091	285,974	103,869
Total Liabilities	659,272	635,201	589,895	575,042	716,796	748,068	730,440	546,327
Stockholders' Equity	420,359	419,057	407,985	419,284	448,833	458,908	495,919	593,944
Shares Outstanding	44,951	44,855	44,840	45,093	44,324	44,834	47,905	51,848
Statistical Record								
Return on Assets %	4.60	4.49	2.71	N.M.	3.77	9.92	10.45	12.75
Return on Equity %	11.70	11.15	6.53	N.M.	9.85	25.28	22.70	21.82
EBITDA Margin %	6.54	6.97	6.91	4.76	6.26	10.19	10.30	11.47
Net Margin %	2.44	2.51	1.60	N.M.	1.83	4.68	4.60	5.61
Asset Turnover	1.88	1.79	1.70	1.54	2.05	2.12	2.27	2.27
Current Ratio	1.02	1.12	1.13	1.20	1.12	1.27	1.41	1.36
Debt to Equity	0.36	0.36	0.37	0.48	0.60	0.61	0.58	0.17
Price Range	31.68-21.95	33.75-16.23	34.38-23.17	28.95-7.80	35.96-9.69	51.61-34.87	61.55-38.81	61.53-38.89
P/E Ratio	29.61-20.51	33.42-16.07	58.27-39.27	...	35.25-9.50	20.08-13.57	25.12-15.84	24.61-15.56
Average Yield %	3.59	3.63	3.14	4.53	3.77	1.85	1.47	1.22

Address: 408 East Second Street, Muscatine, IA 52761-0071	Web Site: www.hnicorp.com	Auditors: PricewaterhouseCoopers LLP
Telephone: 563-272-7400	Officers: Stanley A. Askren - Chairman, President, Chief Executive Officer Bradley D. Determan - Executive Vice President	Investor Contact: 563-272-7400
Fax: 563-264-7217		Transfer Agents: Wells Fargo Shareowner Services, Mendota Heights, MN

HOLLYFRONTIER CORP.

Exchange	Symbol	Price	52Wk Range	Yield	P/E
NYS	HFC	$51.45 (3/28/2013)	58.43-28.20	2.33	6.14

*7 Year Price Score 149.50 *NYSE Composite Index=100 *12 Month Price Score 122.90

Interim Earnings (Per Share)

Qtr.	Mar	Jun	Sep	Dec
2008	0.09	0.12	0.50	0.50
2009	0.22	0.14	0.23	(0.40)
2010	(0.27)	0.62	0.48	0.14
2011	0.79	1.79	2.48	0.79
2012	1.16	2.39	2.94	1.94

Interim Dividends (Per Share)

Amt	Decl	Ex	Rec	Pay
0.50Sp	11/01/2012	11/13/2012	11/15/2012	11/30/2012
0.20Q	11/01/2012	12/06/2012	12/10/2012	12/21/2012
0.30Q	02/20/2013	03/13/2013	03/15/2013	04/02/2013
0.50Q	02/20/2013	03/01/2013	03/05/2013	03/19/2013

Indicated Div: $1.20

Valuation Analysis

		Institutional Holding	
Forecast EPS	$6.88 (04/06/2013)	No of Institutions	508
Market Cap	$10.5 Billion	Shares	175,948,448
Book Value	$6.1 Billion	% Held	N/A
Price/Book	1.73		
Price/Sales	0.52		

TRADING VOLUME (thousand shares)

Business Summary: Refining & Marketing (MIC: 9.1.2 SIC: 2911 NAIC: 324110)

HollyFrontier is an independent petroleum refiner that produces light products such as gasoline, diesel fuel, jet fuel, lubricant products and asphalt. Co. has two reporting segments: Refining, which involves the purchase and refining of crude oil and wholesale and branded marketing of refined products; and Holly Energy Partners, L.P. (HEP), which is engaged in pipeline transportation, rental and terminalling operations as well as pipeline transportation services provided for Co.'s refining operations. As of Dec 31 2012, Co. owned a 44.0% interest in HEP, including the 2.0% general partner interest.

Recent Developments: For the year ended Dec 31 2012, net income increased 66.1% to US$1.76 billion from US$1.06 billion in the prior year. Revenues were US$20.09 billion, up 30.1% from US$15.44 billion the year before. Operating income was US$2.88 billion versus US$1.73 billion in the prior year, an increase of 66.6%. Direct operating expenses rose 24.9% to US$15.84 billion from US$12.68 billion in the comparable period the year before. Indirect operating expenses increased 32.9% to US$1.37 billion from US$1.03 billion in the equivalent prior-year period.

Prospects: Our evaluation of HollyFrontier Corp. as of Apr. 7, 2013 is the result of our systematic analysis on three basic characteristics: earnings strength, relative valuation, and recent stock price movement. The company has produced a positive trend in earnings per share over the past 5 quarters. However, while recent estimates for the company have been mixed, HFC has posted results that fell short of analysts' expectations. Based on operating earnings yield, the company is undervalued when compared to all of the companies in our coverage universe. Share price changes over the past year indicates that HFC will perform very well over the near term.

Financial Data
(US$ in Thousands)

	12/31/2012	12/31/2011	12/31/2010	12/31/2009	12/31/2008	12/31/2007	12/31/2006	12/31/2005
Earnings Per Share	8.38	6.42	0.97	0.20	1.19	2.99	2.29	1.33
Cash Flow Per Share	8.08	8.44	2.66	2.10	1.54	3.85	2.15	2.04
Tang Book Value Per Share	18.25	13.70	5.78	5.06	5.15	5.64	4.21	3.21
Dividends Per Share	3.100	1.337	0.300	0.300	0.300	0.230	0.145	0.095
Dividend Payout %	36.99	20.83	30.93	153.85	25.21	7.69	6.33	7.17
Income Statement								
Total Revenue	20,090,724	15,439,528	8,322,929	4,834,268	5,867,668	4,791,742	4,023,217	3,212,745
EBITDA	3,067,372	1,841,434	356,998	155,585	257,366	502,132	402,161	311,319
Depn & Amortn	182,900	125,000	94,000	78,400	54,800	35,800	40,270	43,817
Income Before Taxes	2,785,072	1,639,395	189,970	41,884	189,435	480,335	370,572	269,302
Income Taxes	1,027,962	581,991	59,312	7,460	64,826	165,316	136,603	101,424
Net Income	1,727,172	1,023,397	103,964	19,533	120,558	334,128	266,566	167,658
Average Shares	206,184	159,294	107,218	101,206	101,098	111,700	116,420	126,488
Balance Sheet								
Current Assets	4,470,265	4,659,124	1,703,435	1,283,011	530,623	1,034,621	806,852	775,929
Total Assets	10,328,997	10,314,621	3,701,475	3,145,939	1,874,225	1,663,945	1,237,869	1,142,900
Current Liabilities	1,654,444	2,629,061	1,389,855	1,025,112	462,158	818,080	559,393	577,367
Long-Term Obligations	1,336,238	1,214,742	810,561	707,458	341,914	...	...	...
Total Liabilities	4,276,043	5,110,611	3,004,056	2,526,900	1,332,685	1,070,151	771,775	765,549
Stockholders' Equity	6,052,954	5,204,010	697,419	619,039	541,540	593,794	466,094	377,351
Shares Outstanding	203,551	209,332	106,529	106,132	99,886	105,232	110,633	117,505
Statistical Record								
Return on Assets %	16.69	14.60	3.04	0.78	6.80	23.03	22.39	15.78
Return on Equity %	30.60	34.68	15.79	3.37	21.18	63.05	63.21	46.75
EBITDA Margin %	15.27	11.93	4.29	3.22	4.39	10.48	10.00	9.69
Net Margin %	8.60	6.63	1.25	0.40	2.05	6.97	6.63	5.22
Asset Turnover	1.94	2.20	2.43	1.93	3.31	3.30	3.38	3.02
Current Ratio	2.70	1.77	1.23	1.25	1.15	1.26	1.44	1.34
Debt to Equity	0.22	0.23	1.16	1.14	0.63	...	...	...
Price Range	47.38-25.24	38.20-20.39	20.49-11.93	16.43-8.54	27.98-5.50	39.94-22.82	27.84-14.19	16.18-6.34
P/E Ratio	5.65-3.01	5.95-3.18	21.12-12.29	82.15-42.67	23.52-4.63	13.36-7.63	12.16-6.20	12.16-4.77
Average Yield %	8.63	4.56	2.08	2.57	1.74	0.75	0.68	0.83

Address: 2828 N. Harwood, Suite 1300, Dallas, TX 75201 Telephone: 214-871-3555	Web Site: www.hollycorp.com Officers: Michael C. Jennings - Chairman, President, Chief Executive Officer Matthew P. Clifton - Executive Chairman	Auditors: Ernst & Young LLP Investor Contact: 214-954-6510 Transfer Agents: Wells Fargo Shareowner Services, Saint Paul, MN

HOME DEPOT INC

Exchange	Symbol	Price	52Wk Range	Yield	P/E
NYS	HD	$69.78 (3/28/2013)	71.37-47.02	2.24	23.26

*7 Year Price Score 144.32 *NYSE Composite Index=100 *12 Month Price Score 106.95

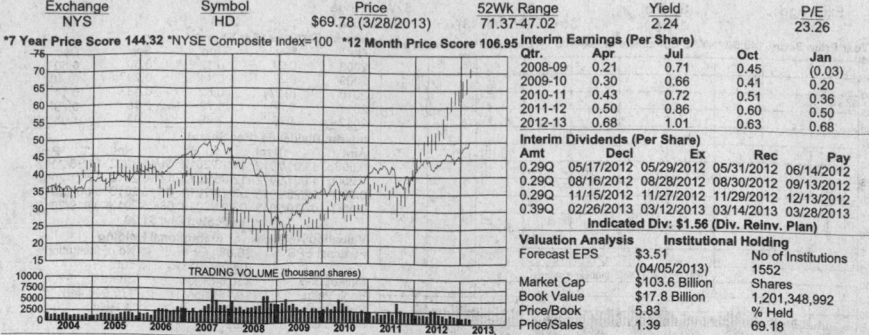

Interim Earnings (Per Share)

Qtr.	Apr	Jul	Oct	Jan
2008-09	0.21	0.71	0.45	(0.03)
2009-10	0.30	0.66	0.41	0.20
2010-11	0.43	0.72	0.51	0.36
2011-12	0.50	0.86	0.60	0.50
2012-13	0.68	1.01	0.63	0.68

Interim Dividends (Per Share)

Amt	Decl	Ex	Rec	Pay
0.29Q	05/17/2012	05/29/2012	05/31/2012	06/14/2012
0.29Q	08/16/2012	08/28/2012	08/30/2012	09/13/2012
0.29Q	11/15/2012	11/27/2012	11/29/2012	12/13/2012
0.39Q	02/26/2013	03/12/2013	03/14/2013	03/28/2013

Indicated Div: $1.56 (Div. Reinv. Plan)

Valuation Analysis		Institutional Holding	
Forecast EPS	$3.51	No of Institutions	
	(04/05/2013)	1552	
Market Cap	$103.6 Billion	Shares	
Book Value	$17.8 Billion	1,201,348,992	
Price/Book	5.83	% Held	
Price/Sales	1.39	69.18	

Business Summary: Retail - Hardware & Home Improvement (MIC: 2.1.8 SIC: 5211 NAIC: 444110)

Home Depot is a home improvement retailer. Co. operates the Home Depot stores, which stock about 30,000 to 40,000 different kinds of building materials, home improvement supplies and lawn and garden products. Co. also provides over 600,000 products through its Home Depot and Home Decorators Collection websites. As of Feb 3 2013, Co. had 2,256 The Home Depot stores, which included 1,976 stores in the U.S., including the Commonwealth of Puerto Rico and the territories of the U.S. Virgin Islands and Guam; 180 stores in Canada; as well as 100 stores in Mexico. The Home Depot stores serve three primary customer groups: Do-It-Yourself, Do-It-For-Me and Professional.

Recent Developments: For the year ended Feb 3 2013, net income increased 16.8% to US$4.54 billion from US$3.88 billion in the prior year. Revenues were US$74.75 billion, up 6.2% from US$70.40 billion the year before. Operating income was US$7.77 billion versus US$6.66 billion in the prior year, an increase of 16.6%. Direct operating expenses rose 6.0% to US$48.91 billion from US$46.13 billion in the comparable period the year before. Indirect operating expenses increased 2.7% to US$18.08 billion from US$17.60 billion in the equivalent prior-year period.

Prospects: Our evaluation of Home Depot Inc. as of Apr. 7, 2013 is the result of our systematic analysis on three basic characteristics: earnings strength, relative valuation, and recent stock price movement. The company has managed to produce a neutral trend in earnings per share over the past 5 quarters and while recent estimates for the company have been raised by analysts, HD has posted better than expected results. Based on operating earnings yield, the company is about fairly valued when compared to all of the companies in our coverage universe. Share price changes over the past year indicates that HD will perform well over the near term.

Financial Data

(US$ in Thousands)	02/03/2013	01/29/2012	01/30/2011	01/31/2010	02/01/2009	02/03/2008	01/28/2007	01/29/2006
Earnings Per Share	3.00	2.47	2.01	1.57	1.34	2.37	2.79	2.72
Cash Flow Per Share	4.58	4.27	2.79	3.05	3.30	3.05	3.74	3.04
Tang Book Value Per Share	11.19	10.92	10.91	10.73	9.81	9.77	9.50	11.12
Dividends Per Share	1.160	1.040	0.945	0.900	0.900	0.900	0.675	0.400
Dividend Payout %	38.67	42.11	47.01	57.32	67.16	37.97	24.19	14.71
Income Statement								
Total Revenue	74,754,000	70,395,000	67,997,000	66,176,000	71,288,000	77,349,000	90,837,000	81,511,000
EBITDA	9,450,000	8,343,000	7,557,000	6,609,000	6,261,000	9,148,000	11,559,000	10,942,000
Depn & Amortn	1,684,000	1,682,000	1,718,000	1,806,000	1,902,000	1,906,000	1,886,000	1,579,000
Income Before Taxes	7,221,000	6,068,000	5,273,000	3,982,000	3,590,000	6,620,000	9,308,000	9,282,000
Income Taxes	2,686,000	2,185,000	1,935,000	1,362,000	1,278,000	2,410,000	3,547,000	3,444,000
Net Income	4,535,000	3,883,000	3,338,000	2,661,000	2,260,000	4,395,000	5,761,000	5,838,000
Average Shares	1,511,000	1,570,000	1,658,000	1,692,000	1,686,000	1,856,000	2,062,000	2,147,000
Balance Sheet								
Current Assets	15,372,000	14,520,000	13,479,000	13,900,000	13,362,000	14,674,000	18,000,000	15,346,000
Total Assets	41,084,000	40,518,000	40,125,000	40,877,000	41,164,000	44,324,000	52,263,000	44,482,000
Current Liabilities	11,462,000	9,376,000	10,122,000	10,363,000	11,153,000	12,706,000	12,931,000	12,901,000
Long-Term Obligations	9,475,000	10,758,000	8,707,000	8,662,000	9,667,000	11,383,000	11,643,000	2,672,000
Total Liabilities	23,307,000	22,620,000	21,236,000	21,484,000	23,387,000	26,610,000	27,233,000	17,573,000
Stockholders' Equity	17,777,000	17,898,000	18,889,000	19,393,000	17,777,000	17,714,000	25,030,000	26,909,000
Shares Outstanding	1,484,000	1,537,000	1,623,000	1,698,000	1,696,000	1,690,000	1,970,000	2,124,000
Statistical Record								
Return on Assets %	10.94	9.66	8.26	6.50	5.30	8.95	11.94	14.04
Return on Equity %	25.01	21.17	17.49	14.36	12.77	20.23	22.24	22.93
EBITDA Margin %	12.64	11.85	11.11	9.99	8.78	11.83	12.72	13.42
Net Margin %	6.07	5.52	4.91	4.02	3.17	5.68	6.34	7.16
Asset Turnover	1.80	1.75	1.68	1.62	1.67	1.58	1.88	1.96
Current Ratio	1.34	1.55	1.33	1.34	1.20	1.15	1.39	1.19
Debt to Equity	0.53	0.60	0.46	0.45	0.54	0.64	0.47	0.10
Price Range	67.82-44.33	45.41-28.51	37.98-27.07	29.29-18.00	30.16-18.51	41.76-24.71	43.81-33.13	43.95-35.09
P/E Ratio	22.61-14.80	18.38-11.54	18.90-13.47	18.66-11.46	22.51-13.81	17.62-10.43	15.70-11.87	16.16-12.90
Average Yield %	2.10	2.83	2.97	3.54	3.56	2.57	1.77	1.00

Address: 2455 Paces Ferry Road, N.W., Atlanta, GA 30339 Telephone: 770-433-8211 Fax: 770-431-2707	Web Site: www.homedepot.com Officers: Francis S. Blake - Chairman, Chief Executive Officer Carol B. Tome - Executive Vice President, Chief Financial Officer	Auditors: KPMG LLP Investor Contact: 770-384-2871 Transfer Agents: Computershare Trust Company, N.A., Providence, RI

HOME PROPERTIES INC

Exchange	Symbol	Price	52Wk Range	Yield	P/E
NYS	HME	$63.42 (3/28/2013)	66.22-57.14	4.42	23.58

*7 Year Price Score 105.01 *NYSE Composite Index=100   *12 Month Price Score 93.14

Interim Earnings (Per Share)

Qtr.	Mar	Jun	Sep	Dec
2008	0.80	0.28	0.23	0.84
2009	0.33	0.18	0.16	0.37
2010	·0.07	0.14	0.15	0.18
2011	0.19	0.20	0.20	0.30
2012	0.31	0.28	0.71	1.38

Interim Dividends (Per Share)

Amt	Decl	Ex	Rec	Pay
0.66Q	05/03/2012	05/11/2012	05/15/2012	05/25/2012
0.66Q	08/02/2012	08/10/2012	08/14/2012	08/24/2012
0.66Q	11/01/2012	11/13/2012	11/15/2012	11/27/2012
0.70Q	02/04/2013	02/12/2013	02/14/2013	02/26/2013

Indicated Div: $2.80

Valuation Analysis

		Institutional Holding	
Forecast EPS	$1.26	No of Institutions	
	(04/06/2013)	318	
Market Cap	$3.3 Billion	Shares	
Book Value	$1.3 Billion	49,027,624	
Price/Book	2.47	% Held	
Price/Sales	5.07	99.40	

Business Summary: REITs (MIC: 5.3.1 SIC: 6798 NAIC: 525930)

Home Properties is a self-administered and self-managed real estate investment trust that owns, operates, acquires, develops and rehabilitates apartment communities. Co.'s properties are regionally focused, primarily in selected Northeast and Mid-Atlantic regions of the U.S. Co. conducts its business through Home Properties, L.P. (the Operating Partnership) and a management company, Home Properties Resident Services, Inc. At Dec 31 2012, Co. held 83.2% of the limited partnership units in the Operating Partnership. Co., through its affiliates described above, as of Dec 31 2012, owned and operated 121 communities with 42,635 apartment units.

Recent Developments: For the year ended Dec 31 2012, income from continuing operations increased 84.9% to US$80.9 million from US$43.8 million a year earlier. Net income increased 243.3% to US$163.6 million from US$47.7 million in the prior year. Revenues were US$644.3 million, up 14.7% from US$561.6 million the year before. Revenues from property income rose 14.7% to US$644.0 million from US$561.4 million in the corresponding earlier year.

Prospects: Our evaluation of Home Properties of New York Inc. as of Apr. 7, 2013 is the result of our systematic analysis on three basic characteristics: earnings strength, relative valuation, and recent stock price movement. The company has generated a negative trend in earnings per share over the past 5 quarters. Because the company lacks sufficient analyst estimate data, we place greater weight on the historical EPS trend as the measure of earnings strength. Based on operating earnings yield, the company is overvalued when compared to all of the companies in our coverage universe. Share price changes over the past year indicates that HME will perform poorly over the near term.

Financial Data
(US$ in Thousands)

	12/31/2012	12/31/2011	12/31/2010	12/31/2009	12/31/2008	12/31/2007	12/31/2006	12/31/2005
Earnings Per Share	2.69	0.89	0.54	1.04	2.15	1.73	3.15	2.33
Cash Flow Per Share	5.36	4.72	4.36	4.53	4.99	4.91	4.98	4.16
Tang Book Value Per Share	25.65	23.87	19.00	19.08	19.94	20.49	21.01	19.14
Dividends Per Share	2.640	2.480	2.320	2.680	2.650	2.610	2.570	2.530
Dividend Payout %	98.14	278.65	429.63	257.69	123.26	150.87	81.59	108.58
Income Statement								
Total Revenue	644,348	579,973	516,579	503,609	509,950	505,188	453,992	443,801
EBITDA	373,130	321,519	277,330	268,220	280,649	272,904	246,074	234,658
Depn & Amortn	166,379	143,272	126,466	120,041	115,811	112,584	101,695	100,115
Income Before Taxes	80,942	47,664	26,738	25,365	45,879	40,937	37,606	36,645
Net Income	163,622	47,664	26,318	47,078	69,666	61,544	110,485	81,512
Average Shares	50,382	42,545	37,169	33,172	32,332	33,794	33,337	32,328
Balance Sheet								
Current Assets	80,973	69,037	75,054	67,007	64,826	63,783	216,627	65,678
Total Assets	4,451,492	4,153,206	3,634,703	3,268,034	3,317,207	3,216,423	3,240,418	2,977,870
Current Liabilities	51,811	50,752	51,907	49,690	56,019	52,426	53,249	49,474
Long-Term Obligations	2,777,527	2,663,336	2,618,932	2,302,281	2,323,331	2,189,289	2,124,313	1,850,483
Total Liabilities	3,130,524	2,999,538	2,913,810	2,606,922	2,670,529	2,548,362	2,484,801	2,321,058
Stockholders' Equity	1,320,968	1,153,668	720,893	661,112	646,678	668,061	755,617	656,812
Shares Outstanding	51,508	48,321	37,949	34,655	32,431	32,600	33,103	31,184
Statistical Record								
Return on Assets %	3.79	1.22	0.76	1.43	2.13	1.91	3.55	2.81
Return on Equity %	13.19	5.09	3.81	7.20	10.57	8.65	15.64	11.84
EBITDA Margin %	57.91	55.44	53.69	53.26	55.03	54.02	54.20	52.87
Net Margin %	25.39	8.22	5.09	9.35	13.66	12.18	24.34	18.37
Asset Turnover	0.15	0.15	0.15	0.15	0.16	0.16	0.15	0.15
Current Ratio	1.56	1.36	1.45	1.35	1.16	1.22	4.07	1.33
Debt to Equity	2.10	2.31	3.63	3.48	3.59	3.28	2.81	2.82
Price Range	66.22-54.89	66.92-52.62	56.34-43.12	48.90-24.78	60.39-26.00	64.65-41.53	63.52-41.70	46.27-36.05
P/E Ratio	24.62-20.41	75.19-59.12	104.33-79.85	47.02-23.83	28.09-12.09	37.37-24.01	20.17-13.24	19.86-15.47
Average Yield %	4.34	4.22	4.68	7.31	5.57	4.91	4.76	6.17

Address: 850 Clinton Square, Rochester, NY 14604 **Telephone:** 585-546-4900	**Web Site:** www.homeproperties.com **Officers:** Edward J. Pettinella - President, Chief Executive Officer David P. Gardner - Executive Vice President, Chief Financial Officer	**Auditors:** PricewaterhouseCoopers LLP **Investor Contact:** 716-546-4900 **Transfer Agents:** Computershare Shareowner Services LLC, Ridgefield Park, NJ

HONEYWELL INTERNATIONAL, INC.

Exchange	Symbol	Price	52Wk Range	Yield	P/E
NYS	HON	$75.35 (3/28/2013)	75.48-52.92	2.18	20.42

*7 Year Price Score 111.74 *NYSE Composite Index=100 *12 Month Price Score 106.26

Interim Earnings (Per Share)

Qtr.	Mar	Jun	Sep	Dec
2008	0.85	0.96	0.97	0.97
2009	0.54	0.60	0.80	0.91
2010	0.50	0.60	0.64	0.85
2011	0.88	1.02	1.10	(0.38)
2012	1.04	1.14	1.20	0.31

Interim Dividends (Per Share)

Amt	Decl	Ex	Rec	Pay
0.373Q	04/23/2012	05/16/2012	05/18/2012	06/08/2012
0.373Q	07/25/2012	08/16/2012	08/20/2012	09/10/2012
0.41Q	10/26/2012	11/16/2012	11/20/2012	12/10/2012
0.41Q	02/14/2013	02/21/2013	02/25/2013	03/11/2013

Indicated Div: $1.64

Valuation Analysis

		Institutional Holding	
Forecast EPS	$4.95	No of Institutions	
	(04/05/2013)	1203	
Market Cap	$59.0 Billion	Shares	
Book Value	$13.1 Billion	695,870,208	
Price/Book	4.49	% Held	
Price/Sales	1.57	81.62	

Business Summary: Auto Parts (MIC: 1.8.2 SIC: 3714 NAIC: 336312)

Honeywell International is engaged in providing aerospace products and services, control, sensing and security technologies for buildings, homes and industry, turbochargers, automotive products, specialty chemicals, electronic materials, process technology for refining and petrochemicals, and energy products for homes, business and transportation. Co. manages its business operations through four businesses that are reported as operating segments: Aerospace; Automation and Control Solutions; Performance Materials and Technologies; and Transportation Systems.

Recent Developments: For the year ended Dec 31 2012, income from continuing operations increased 57.2% to US$2.93 billion from US$1.87 billion a year earlier. Net income increased 41.3% to US$2.93 billion from US$2.07 billion in the prior year. Revenues were US$37.67 billion, up 3.1% from US$36.53 billion the year before. Direct operating expenses declined 0.9% to US$28.29 billion from US$28.56 billion in the comparable period the year before. Indirect operating expenses decreased 3.4% to US$5.22 billion from US$5.40 billion in the equivalent prior-year period.

Prospects: Our evaluation of Honeywell International Inc. as of Apr. 7, 2013 is the result of our systematic analysis on three basic characteristics: earnings strength, relative valuation, and recent stock price movement. The company has generated a negative trend in earnings per share over the past 5 quarters and while recent estimates for the company have been raised by analysts, HON has posted better than expected results. Based on operating earnings yield, the company is undervalued when compared to all of the companies in our coverage universe. Share price changes over the past year indicates that HON will perform in line with the market over the near term.

Financial Data

(US$ in Thousands)	12/31/2012	12/31/2011	12/31/2010	12/31/2009	12/31/2008	12/31/2007	12/31/2006	12/31/2005
Earnings Per Share	3.69	2.61	2.59	2.85	3.76	3.16	2.52	1.94
Cash Flow Per Share	4.48	3.63	5.43	5.24	5.13	5.12	3.91	2.88
Tang Book Value Per Share	N.M.	N.M.	N.M.	N.M.	N.M.	N.M.	0.09	1.95
Dividends Per Share	1.528	1.370	1.210	1.210	1.100	1.000	0.907	0.825
Dividend Payout %	41.40	52.49	46.72	42.46	29.26	31.65	36.01	42.53
Income Statement								
Total Revenue	37,665,000	36,529,000	33,370,000	30,908,000	36,556,000	34,589,000	31,367,000	27,653,000
EBITDA	4,783,000	3,248,000	3,884,000	4,085,000	4,794,000	4,361,000	3,715,000	3,041,000
Depn & Amortn	660,000	699,000	724,000	707,000	702,000	675,000	650,000	578,000
Income Before Taxes	3,830,000	2,231,000	2,814,000	2,952,000	3,738,000	3,311,000	2,785,000	2,199,000
Income Taxes	944,000	417,000	808,000	789,000	1,009,000	877,000	720,000	742,000
Net Income	2,926,000	2,067,000	2,022,000	2,153,000	2,792,000	2,444,000	2,083,000	1,655,000
Average Shares	791,900	791,600	780,900	755,720	743,530	774,227	826,278	852,334
Balance Sheet								
Current Assets	17,598,000	16,134,000	15,011,000	13,936,000	13,263,000	13,685,000	12,304,000	11,962,000
Total Assets	41,853,000	39,808,000	37,834,000	36,004,000	35,490,000	33,805,000	30,941,000	32,294,000
Current Liabilities	13,045,000	12,275,000	11,717,000	11,147,000	12,289,000	11,941,000	10,135,000	10,430,000
Long-Term Obligations	6,395,000	6,881,000	5,755,000	6,246,000	5,865,000	5,419,000	3,909,000	3,082,000
Total Liabilities	28,728,000	29,002,000	27,168,000	27,160,000	28,303,000	24,583,000	21,221,000	21,040,000
Stockholders' Equity	13,125,000	10,806,000	10,666,000	8,844,000	7,187,000	9,222,000	9,720,000	11,254,000
Shares Outstanding	782,800	774,700	783,000	764,209	734,586	746,553	800,591	829,483
Statistical Record								
Return on Assets %	7.15	5.32	5.48	6.02	8.04	7.55	6.59	5.22
Return on Equity %	24.39	19.25	20.73	26.86	33.94	25.81	19.86	14.71
EBITDA Margin %	12.70	8.89	11.64	13.22	13.11	12.61	11.84	11.00
Net Margin %	7.77	5.66	6.06	6.97	7.64	7.07	6.64	5.98
Asset Turnover	0.92	0.94	0.90	0.86	1.05	1.07	0.99	0.87
Current Ratio	1.35	1.31	1.28	1.25	1.08	1.15	1.21	1.15
Debt to Equity	0.49	0.64	0.54	0.71	0.82	0.59	0.40	0.27
Price Range	64.29-52.92	62.00-41.94	53.72-36.87	41.31-23.23	62.43-23.67	61.77-44.13	45.46-35.84	39.30-33.21
P/E Ratio	17.42-14.34	23.75-16.07	20.74-14.24	14.49-8.15	16.60-6.30	19.55-13.97	18.04-14.22	20.26-17.12
Average Yield %	2.59	2.54	2.74	3.54	2.27	1.84	2.23	2.23

Address: 101 Columbia Road, Morris Township, NJ 07962 **Telephone:** 973-455-2000 **Fax:** 973-455-4807	**Web Site:** www.honeywell.com **Officers:** David M. Cote - Chairman, Chief Executive Officer David J. Anderson - Senior Vice President, Chief Financial Officer	**Auditors:** PricewaterhouseCoopers LLP **Investor Contact:** 973-455-2222 **Transfer Agents:** American Stock Transfer & Trust Company, LLC, New York, NY

HORACE MANN EDUCATORS CORP.

Exchange	Symbol	Price	52Wk Range	Yield	P/E
NYS	HMN	$20.85 (3/28/2013)	22.00-16.46	3.74	8.31

*7 Year Price Score 103.51 *NYSE Composite Index=100 *12 Month Price Score 102.68

Interim Earnings (Per Share)

Qtr.	Mar	Jun	Sep	Dec
2008	0.34	0.11	(0.79)	0.57
2009	0.33	0.46	0.48	0.54
2010	0.55	0.56	0.49	0.36
2011	0.62	(0.30)	0.56	0.80
2012	0.64	0.32	0.78	0.77

Interim Dividends (Per Share)

Amt	Decl	Ex	Rec	Pay
0.13Q	05/23/2012	06/07/2012	06/11/2012	06/29/2012
0.13Q	09/06/2012	09/13/2012	09/17/2012	09/28/2012
0.16Q	12/05/2012	12/13/2012	12/17/2012	12/31/2012
0.195Q	03/06/2013	03/14/2013	03/18/2013	03/29/2013

Indicated Div: $0.78

Valuation Analysis / **Institutional Holding**

Forecast EPS	$1.95 (04/06/2013)	No of Institutions	200
Market Cap	$820.8 Million	Shares	42,643,512
Book Value	$1.2 Billion	% Held	98.07
Price/Book	0.66		
Price/Sales	0.81		

Business Summary: General Insurance (MIC: 5.2.1 SIC: 6331 NAIC: 524126)

Horace Mann Educators is an insurance holding company. Through its subsidiaries, Co. markets and underwrites personal lines of property and casualty (primarily private passenger automobile and homeowners) insurance, retirement annuities (primarily tax-qualified products) and life insurance in the U.S. Co.'s principal insurance subsidiaries are Horace Mann Life Insurance Company, Horace Mann Insurance Company, Horace Mann Property & Casualty Insurance Company, Teachers Insurance Company, and Horace Mann Lloyds. Co. markets its products primarily to K-12 teachers, administrators and other employees of public schools and their families.

Recent Developments: For the year ended Dec 31 2012, net income increased 47.3% to US$103.9 million from US$70.5 million in the prior year. Revenues were US$1.01 billion, up 1.3% from US$998.3 million the year before. Net premiums earned were US$670.5 million versus US$667.1 million in the prior year, an increase of 0.5%. Net investment income rose 6.1% to US$306.0 million from US$288.3 million a year ago.

Prospects: Our evaluation of Horace Mann Educators Corp. as of Apr. 7, 2013 is the result of our systematic analysis on three basic characteristics: earnings strength, relative valuation, and recent stock price movement. The company has suffered a very negative trend in earnings per share over the past 5 quarters and while recent estimates for the company have remained steady, HMN has posted better than expected results. Based on operating earnings yield, the company is undervalued when compared to all of the companies in our coverage universe. Share price changes over the past year indicates that HMN will perform in line with the market over the near term.

Financial Data
(US$ in Thousands)

	12/31/2012	12/31/2011	12/31/2010	12/31/2009	12/31/2008	12/31/2007	12/31/2006	12/31/2005
Earnings Per Share	2.51	1.70	1.97	1.81	0.27	1.86	2.19	1.67
Cash Flow Per Share	5.12	2.91	4.01	4.57	4.08	4.67	4.32	3.85
Tang Book Value Per Share	30.44	26.13	21.00	17.15	10.27	15.16	13.90	12.03
Dividends Per Share	0.550	0.460	0.350	0.237	0.367	0.420	0.420	0.420
Dividend Payout %	21.91	27.06	17.77	13.12	136.11	22.58	19.18	25.15
Income Statement								
Premium Income	670,527	667,118	672,675	659,590	658,532	654,257	653,922	664,939
Total Revenue	1,010,814	998,300	974,711	937,427	834,818	887,005	873,807	869,412
Income Before Taxes	149,173	94,878	111,291	103,507	178	117,071	140,293	94,044
Income Taxes	45,307	24,398	30,429	30,021	(10,739)	34,283	41,585	16,771
Net Income	103,866	70,480	80,862	73,486	10,917	82,788	98,708	77,273
Average Shares	41,388	41,436	41,013	40,532	40,588	44,610	45,773	47,884
Balance Sheet								
Total Assets	8,167,726	7,483,737	7,005,541	6,343,113	5,507,718	6,259,313	6,329,687	5,840,607
Total Liabilities	6,921,923	6,396,811	6,125,534	5,623,568	5,058,873	5,566,035	5,672,606	5,260,016
Stockholders' Equity	1,245,803	1,086,926	880,007	719,545	448,845	693,278	657,081	580,591
Shares Outstanding	39,367	39,775	39,655	39,184	39,061	42,240	43,091	42,972
Statistical Record								
Return on Assets %	1.32	0.97	1.21	1.24	0.19	1.32	1.62	1.38
Return on Equity %	8.88	7.17	10.11	12.58	1.91	12.26	15.95	13.36
Net Margin %	10.28	7.06	8.30	7.84	1.31	9.33	11.30	8.89
Price Range	19.96-14.11	18.37-10.74	19.29-11.50	14.55-6.19	18.94-5.26	22.59-16.35	20.79-16.22	20.60-16.01
P/E Ratio	7.95-5.62	10.81-6.32	9.79-5.84	8.04-3.42	70.15-19.48	12.15-8.79	9.49-7.41	12.34-9.59
Average Yield %	3.10	3.08	2.20	2.21	2.60	2.06	2.27	2.25

Address: 1 Horace Mann Plaza, Springfield, IL 62715-0001
Telephone: 217-789-2500

Web Site: www.horacemann.com
Officers: Joseph J. Melone - Chairman Matthew P. Sharpe - Executive Vice President

Auditors: KPMG LLP
Investor Contact: 217-788-5738
Transfer Agents: American Stock Transfer & Trust Company, New York, NY

HORMEL FOODS CORP.

Exchange	Symbol	Price	52Wk Range	Yield	P/E	Div Achiever
NYS	HRL	$41.32 (3/28/2013)	41.32-27.48	1.65	22.22	46 Years

*7 Year Price Score 124.40 ***NYSE Composite Index=100** ***12 Month Price Score 111.64**

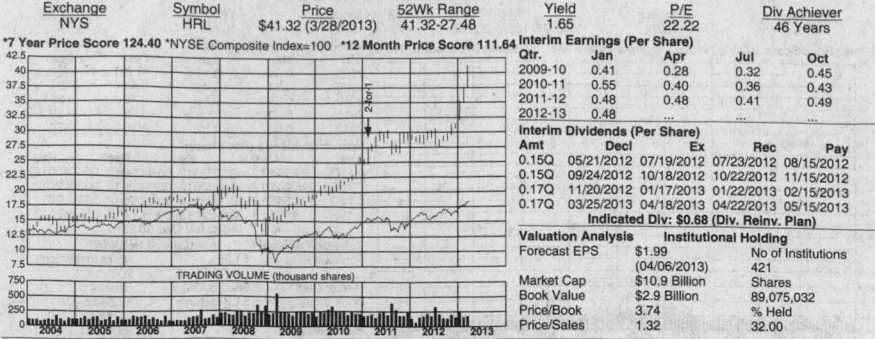

Interim Earnings (Per Share)

Qtr.	Jan	Apr	Jul	Oct
2009-10	0.41	0.28	0.32	0.45
2010-11	0.55	0.40	0.36	0.43
2011-12	0.48	0.48	0.41	0.49
2012-13	0.48	...	...	...

Interim Dividends (Per Share)

Amt	Decl	Ex	Rec	Pay
0.15Q	05/21/2012	07/19/2012	07/23/2012	08/15/2012
0.15Q	09/24/2012	10/18/2012	10/22/2012	11/15/2012
0.17Q	11/20/2012	01/17/2013	01/22/2013	02/15/2013
0.17Q	03/25/2013	04/18/2013	04/22/2013	05/15/2013

Indicated Div: $0.68 (Div. Reinv. Plan)

Valuation Analysis — **Institutional Holding**

Forecast EPS	$1.99	No of Institutions
	(04/06/2013)	421
Market Cap	$10.9 Billion	Shares
Book Value	$2.9 Billion	89,075,032
Price/Book	3.74	% Held
Price/Sales	1.32	32.00

Business Summary: Food (MIC: 1.2.1 SIC: 2011 NAIC: 311611)

Hormel Foods is a processor of meat and food products. Co.'s business is reported in five segments: Grocery Products, which process, market, and sell shelf-stable food products primarily in the retail market; Refrigerated Foods, which processes markets, and sells pork and beef products; Jennie-O Turkey Store, which processes, markets, and sells turkey products; Specialty Foods, which package and sell sugar and sugar substitute products, salt and pepper products, liquid portion products, dessert mixes, ready-to-drink products, sports nutrition products, gelatin products, and private label canned meats; and All Other, which manufactures, markets, and sells Co.'s products internationally.

Recent Developments: For the quarter ended Jan 27 2013, net income increased 1.3% to US$131.0 million from US$129.3 million in the year-earlier quarter. Revenues were US$2.12 billion, up 3.8% from US$2.04 billion the year before. Operating income was US$198.2 million versus US$195.9 million in the prior-year quarter, an increase of 1.2%. Direct operating expenses rose 4.1% to US$1.77 billion from US$1.70 billion in the comparable period the year before. Indirect operating expenses increased 3.2% to US$146.0 million from US$141.5 million in the equivalent prior-year period.

Prospects: Our evaluation of Hormel Foods Corp. as of Apr. 7, 2013 is the result of our systematic analysis on three basic characteristics: earnings strength, relative valuation, and recent stock price movement. The company has managed to produce a neutral trend in earnings per share over the past 5 quarters and while recent estimates for the company have remained steady, HRL has posted results that fell short of analysts expectations. Based on operating earnings yield, the company is about fairly valued when compared to all of the companies in our coverage universe. Share price changes over the past year indicates that HRL will perform in line with the market over the near term.

Financial Data
(US$ in Thousands)

	3 Mos	10/28/2012	10/30/2011	10/31/2010	10/25/2009	10/26/2008	10/28/2007	10/29/2006
Earnings Per Share	1.86	1.86	1.74	1.46	1.26	1.04	1.09	1.02
Cash Flow Per Share	1.92	1.97	1.85	1.79	2.06	1.01	1.23	1.19
Tang Book Value Per Share	8.22	7.85	7.17	6.13	5.10	4.60	4.15	4.02
Dividends Per Share	0.620	0.600	0.510	0.420	0.380	0.370	0.300	0.280
Dividend Payout %	33.33	32.26	29.31	28.77	30.04	35.58	27.65	27.32
Income Statement								
Total Revenue	2,116,241	8,230,670	7,895,089	7,220,719	6,533,671	6,754,903	6,193,032	5,745,481
EBITDA	218,206	854,452	849,168	769,572	669,288	647,168	619,308	578,998
Depn & Amortn	29,844	128,469	133,641	136,123	137,502	137,742	138,858	132,842
Income Before Taxes	187,078	719,644	692,079	611,425	523,354	453,301	466,367	425,990
Income Taxes	65,876	253,374	239,640	224,775	182,169	172,036	167,945	144,404
Net Income	129,716	500,050	474,195	395,587	342,813	285,500	301,892	286,139
Average Shares	269,140	268,891	271,915	270,698	270,978	274,256	278,302	279,122
Balance Sheet								
Current Assets	2,399,845	2,320,684	1,998,231	1,858,166	1,574,733	1,438,178	1,231,725	1,141,671
Total Assets	4,622,830	4,563,966	4,244,391	4,053,918	3,692,055	3,616,471	3,393,650	3,060,306
Current Liabilities	737,386	786,300	778,186	1,101,213	685,029	781,233	664,777	585,014
Long-Term Obligations	250,000	250,000	250,000	...	350,000	350,000	350,005	350,054
Total Liabilities	1,695,692	1,744,511	1,587,809	1,653,261	1,568,603	1,608,899	1,508,867	1,257,394
Stockholders' Equity	2,927,138	2,819,455	2,656,582	2,400,657	2,123,452	2,007,572	1,884,783	1,802,912
Shares Outstanding	264,680	263,044	263,963	265,963	267,187	269,041	271,354	274,679
Statistical Record								
Return on Assets %	11.28	11.39	11.46	10.05	9.41	8.17	9.38	9.75
Return on Equity %	17.71	18.31	18.80	17.21	16.64	14.71	16.42	16.99
EBITDA Margin %	10.31	10.38	10.76	10.66	10.24	9.58	10.00	10.08
Net Margin %	6.13	6.08	6.01	5.48	5.25	4.23	4.87	4.98
Asset Turnover	1.87	1.87	1.91	1.83	1.79	1.93	1.92	1.96
Current Ratio	3.25	2.95	2.57	1.69	2.30	1.84	1.85	1.95
Debt to Equity	0.09	0.09	0.09	...	0.16	0.17	0.19	0.19
Price Range	35.34-27.48	30.68-27.48	30.37-22.80	22.96-18.15	19.11-12.51	21.23-14.24	19.75-15.88	19.01-15.85
P/E Ratio	19.00-14.77	16.49-14.77	17.45-13.10	15.73-12.43	15.16-9.92	20.42-13.69	18.11-14.57	18.64-15.54
Average Yield %	2.09	2.07	1.87	2.04	2.32	1.95	1.62	1.61

Address: 1 Hormel Place, Austin, MN 55912-3680
Telephone: 507-437-5611
Fax: 507-437-5489

Web Site: www.hormel.com
Officers: Jeffrey M. Ettinger - Chairman, President, Chief Executive Officer Jody H. Feragen - Executive Vice President, Chief Financial Officer

Auditors: Ernst & Young LLP
Investor Contact: 507-437-5944
Transfer Agents: Wells Fargo Bank N.A., South St. Paul, MN

HORTON (D.R.) INC.

Exchange	Symbol	Price	52Wk Range	Yield	P/E
NYS	DHI	$24.30 (3/28/2013)	25.43-14.05	0.62	8.53

*7 Year Price Score 113.25 *NYSE Composite Index=100 *12 Month Price Score 109.81

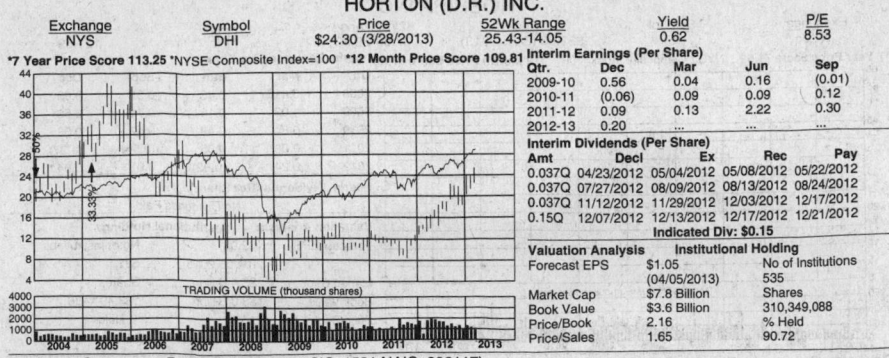

Interim Earnings (Per Share)

Qtr.	Dec	Mar	Jun	Sep
2009-10	0.56	0.04	0.16	(0.01)
2010-11	(0.06)	0.09	0.09	0.12
2011-12	0.09	0.13	2.22	0.30
2012-13	0.20	...	...	...

Interim Dividends (Per Share)

Amt	Decl	Ex	Rec	Pay
0.037Q	04/23/2012	05/04/2012	05/08/2012	05/22/2012
0.037Q	07/27/2012	08/09/2012	08/13/2012	08/24/2012
0.037Q	11/12/2012	11/29/2012	12/03/2012	12/17/2012
0.15Q	12/07/2012	12/13/2012	12/17/2012	12/21/2012

Indicated Div: $0.15

Valuation Analysis		Institutional Holding	
Forecast EPS	$1.05	No of Institutions	
	(04/05/2013)	535	
Market Cap	$7.8 Billion	Shares	
Book Value	$3.6 Billion	310,349,088	
Price/Book	2.16	% Held	
Price/Sales	1.65	90.72	

Business Summary: Builders (MIC: 2.2.5 SIC: 1531 NAIC: 236117)

D.R. Horton is a homebuilding company. Co. constructs and sells homes primarily under the name of D.R. Horton, America's Builder. Co.'s homebuilding operations involve the sale of completed homes, with a lesser amount, the sale of land and lots. In addition to building single-family detached homes, Co. builds attached homes, such as town homes, duplexes, triplexes and condominiums. Through its financial services operations, Co. provides mortgage financing and title agency services to homebuyers in several of its homebuilding markets. Co.'s subsidiary title companies provide title insurance policies, examination and closing services, primarily to its homebuilding customers.

Recent Developments: For the quarter ended Dec 31 2012, net income increased 139.4% to US$66.3 million from US$27.7 million in the year-earlier quarter. Revenues were US$1.28 billion, up 40.6% from US$906.6 million the year before. Direct operating expenses rose 36.0% to US$1.00 billion from US$737.0 million in the comparable period the year before. Indirect operating expenses increased 17.5% to US$164.9 million from US$140.4 million in the equivalent prior-year period.

Prospects: Our evaluation of Horton (D.R.) Inc. as of Apr. 7, 2013 is the result of our systematic analysis on three basic characteristics: earnings strength, relative valuation, and recent stock price movement. The company has generated a negative trend in earnings per share over the past 5 quarters and while recent estimates for the company have remained steady, DHI has posted better than expected results. Based on operating earnings yield, the company is about fairly valued when compared to all of the companies in our coverage universe. Share price changes over the past year indicates that DHI will perform very well over the near term.

Financial Data

(US$ in Thousands)	3 Mos	09/30/2012	09/30/2011	09/30/2010	09/30/2009	09/30/2008	09/30/2007	09/30/2006
Earnings Per Share	2.85	2.77	0.23	0.77	(1.72)	(8.34)	(2.27)	3.90
Cash Flow Per Share	(2.96)	(0.93)	0.05	2.23	3.60	5.94	4.32	(3.81)
Tang Book Value Per Share	11.12	11.07	8.24	8.15	7.07	8.90	17.44	18.75
Dividends Per Share	0.300	0.150	0.150	0.150	0.150	0.450	0.600	0.440
Dividend Payout %	10.53	5.42	65.22	19.48	...	...	...	11.28
Income Statement								
Total Revenue	1,275,100	4,354,000	3,636,800	4,400,200	3,657,600	6,646,100	11,296,500	15,051,300
EBITDA	120,000	278,400	74,300	194,900	(439,800)	(2,547,300)	(901,800)	2,041,700
Depn & Amortn	10,400	18,800	19,900	17,200	25,700	53,200	64,300	56,500
Income Before Taxes	107,900	242,900	12,100	99,500	(552,300)	(2,631,800)	(951,200)	1,987,100
Income Taxes	41,600	(713,400)	(59,700)	(145,600)	(7,000)	1,800	(238,700)	753,800
Net Income	66,300	956,300	71,800	245,100	(545,300)	(2,633,600)	(712,500)	1,233,300
Average Shares	364,100	359,000	318,500	318,600	316,900	315,700	314,100	316,200
Balance Sheet								
Current Assets	5,955,000	5,821,500	4,778,800	5,125,700	5,968,600	6,746,700	9,613,100	12,179,000
Total Assets	7,347,300	7,248,200	5,358,400	5,938,600	6,756,600	7,709,600	11,556,300	14,820,700
Current Liabilities	394,900	377,600	294,500	186,700	347,600	485,000	978,700	2,232,800
Long-Term Obligations	2,593,700	2,493,100	1,704,800	2,171,800	3,208,600	3,544,900	3,989,000	4,886,900
Total Liabilities	3,736,900	3,656,100	2,737,800	3,325,400	4,497,000	4,875,300	5,969,400	8,367,800
Stockholders' Equity	3,610,400	3,592,100	2,620,600	2,613,200	2,259,600	2,834,300	5,586,900	6,452,900
Shares Outstanding	321,264	320,891	316,043	318,823	317,480	316,660	314,914	313,246
Statistical Record								
Return on Assets %	15.65	15.13	1.27	3.86	N.M.	N.M.	N.M.	9.02
Return on Equity %	31.78	30.70	2.74	10.06	N.M.	N.M.	N.M.	20.88
EBITDA Margin %	9.41	6.39	2.04	4.43	N.M.	N.M.	N.M.	13.56
Net Margin %	5.20	21.96	1.97	5.57	N.M.	N.M.	N.M.	8.19
Asset Turnover	0.74	0.69	0.64	0.69	0.51	0.69	0.86	1.10
Current Ratio	15.08	15.42	16.23	27.45	17.17	13.91	9.82	5.45
Debt to Equity	0.72	0.69	0.65	0.83	1.42	1.25	0.71	0.76
Price Range	22.37-12.96	22.37-8.45	13.50-8.94	14.97-9.71	13.79-4.34	17.31-9.57	30.86-12.81	41.39-20.00
P/E Ratio	7.85-4.55	8.08-3.05	58.70-38.87	19.44-12.61	...	...	10.61-5.13	
Average Yield %	1.71	0.98	1.33	1.29	1.61	3.39	2.68	1.47

Address: 301 Commerce Street, Suite 500, Fort Worth, TX 76102 **Telephone:** 817-390-8200	**Web Site:** www.drhorton.com **Officers:** Donald R. Horton - Chairman Donald J. Tomnitz - Vice-Chairman, President, Chief Executive Officer	**Auditors:** PricewaterhouseCoopers LLP **Investor Contact:** 817-390-8200 **Transfer Agents:** American Stock Transfer & Trust Co., New York, NY

HOSPIRA INC

Exchange	Symbol	Price	52Wk Range	Yield	P/E
NYS	HSP	$32.83 (3/28/2013)	37.60-28.89	N/A	121.59

*7 Year Price Score 71.59   *NYSE Composite Index=100   *12 Month Price Score 87.89

Interim Earnings (Per Share)

Qtr.	Mar	Jun	Sep	Dec
2008	0.41	0.43	0.51	0.65
2009	1.03	0.16	0.71	0.58
2010	0.84	0.49	0.42	0.36
2011	0.88	0.85	(0.54)	(1.27)
2012	0.24	(0.02)	0.01	0.04

Interim Dividends (Per Share)

No Dividends Paid

Valuation Analysis

		Institutional Holding	
Forecast EPS	$2.03	No of Institutions	
	(04/05/2013)	531	
Market Cap	$5.4 Billion	Shares	
Book Value	$3.0 Billion	167,401,488	
Price/Book	1.78	% Held	
Price/Sales	1.33	85.08	

TRADING VOLUME (thousand shares)

Business Summary: Pharmaceuticals (MIC: 4.1.1 SIC: 2834 NAIC: 325412)

Hospira is a global provider of injectable drugs and infusion technologies. Co. product line includes specialty injectable pharmaceuticals such as generic injectables and proprietary specialty injectables; other pharmaceuticals, which include intravenous solutions, nutritionals and contract manufacturing services; as well as medication management products, which include infusion pumps and dedicated administration sets, Hospira MedNet™ safety software system and related services, gravity administration sets and other device products. Co.'s portfolio of products is used by hospitals and alternate site providers, such as clinics, home healthcare providers and long-term care facilities.

Recent Developments: For the year ended Dec 31 2012, net income amounted to US$44.2 million versus a net loss of US$9.4 million in the prior year. Revenues were US$4.09 billion, up 0.9% from US$4.06 billion the year before. Operating income was US$58.8 million versus US$56.8 million in the prior year, an increase of 3.5%. Direct operating expenses rose 12.0% to US$2.98 billion from US$2.66 billion in the comparable period the year before. Indirect operating expenses decreased 21.3% to US$1.05 billion from US$1.34 billion in the equivalent prior-year period.

Prospects: Our evaluation of Hospira Inc. as of Apr. 7, 2013 is the result of our systematic analysis on three basic characteristics: earnings strength, relative valuation, and recent stock price movement. The company has enjoyed a very positive trend in earnings per share over the past 5 quarters. However, while recent estimates for the company have been lowered by analysts, HSP has posted better than expected results. Based on operating earnings yield, the company is undervalued when compared to all of the companies in our coverage universe. Share price changes over the past year indicates that HSP will perform very poorly over the near term.

Financial Data
(US$ in Thousands)

	12/31/2012	12/31/2011	12/31/2010	12/31/2009	12/31/2008	12/31/2007	12/31/2006	12/31/2005
Earnings Per Share	0.27	(0.06)	2.11	2.47	1.99	0.85	1.48	1.46
Cash Flow Per Share	2.89	2.62	1.90	5.87	3.66	3.51	2.70	3.59
Tang Book Value Per Share	10.26	9.10	7.11	5.96	1.28	N.M.	8.03	7.57
Income Statement								
Total Revenue	4,092,100	4,057,100	3,917,200	3,879,300	3,629,500	3,436,238	2,688,505	2,626,696
EBITDA	286,100	311,700	728,600	775,100	835,000	594,468	495,364	491,590
Depn & Amortn	247,600	256,100	245,900	291,600	320,600	287,247	156,717	156,291
Income Before Taxes	(41,900)	(27,100)	391,500	384,800	407,500	187,786	324,697	322,075
Income Taxes	(51,000)	27,900	34,300	(19,100)	86,600	51,028	87,018	86,437
Net Income	44,200	(9,400)	357,200	403,900	320,900	136,758	237,679	235,638
Average Shares	166,000	165,500	169,500	163,200	161,300	160,164	160,424	161,634
Balance Sheet								
Current Assets	2,760,400	2,570,700	2,477,500	2,526,200	2,149,300	1,841,020	1,522,890	1,561,165
Total Assets	6,088,600	5,779,100	6,046,300	5,502,900	5,074,100	5,084,666	2,847,587	2,789,182
Current Liabilities	1,029,200	847,800	931,600	881,900	1,047,500	794,289	606,226	596,236
Long-Term Obligations	1,706,800	1,711,900	1,714,400	1,707,300	1,834,000	2,184,385	702,044	695,285
Total Liabilities	3,046,900	2,841,100	2,862,800	2,879,200	3,297,700	3,339,442	1,486,498	1,461,315
Stockholders' Equity	3,041,700	2,938,000	3,183,500	2,623,700	1,776,400	1,745,224	1,361,089	1,327,867
Shares Outstanding	165,300	164,700	166,700	163,500	159,600	158,611	155,884	161,668
Statistical Record								
Return on Assets %	0.74	N.M.	6.19	7.64	6.30	3.45	8.43	9.18
Return on Equity %	1.47	N.M.	12.30	18.36	18.17	8.81	17.68	20.39
EBITDA Margin %	6.99	7.68	18.60	19.98	23.01	17.30	18.43	18.72
Net Margin %	1.08	N.M.	9.12	10.41	8.84	3.98	8.84	8.97
Asset Turnover	0.69	0.69	0.68	0.73	0.71	0.87	0.95	1.02
Current Ratio	2.68	3.03	2.66	2.86	2.05	2.32	2.51	2.62
Debt to Equity	0.56	0.58	0.54	0.65	1.03	1.25	0.52	0.52
Price Range	38.14-28.89	58.13-27.29	59.75-48.56	51.11-21.38	43.80-25.36	44.51-33.85	47.63-31.17	44.88-28.45
P/E Ratio	141.26-107.00	...	28.32-23.01	20.69-8.66	22.01-12.74	52.36-39.82	32.18-21.06	30.74-19.49

Address: 275 North Field Drive, Lake Forest, IL 60045
Telephone: 224-212-2000

Web Site: www.hospira.com
Officers: F. Michael Ball - Chief Executive Officer
Thomas E. Werner - Senior Vice President, Chief Financial Officer

Auditors: Deloitte & Touche LLP
Investor Contact: 224-212-2711
Transfer Agents: ComputerShare Investor Services, Providence, RI

HOSPITALITY PROPERTIES TRUST

Exchange	Symbol	Price	52Wk Range	Yield	P/E
NYS	HPT	$27.44 (3/28/2013)	27.63-21.47	6.85	32.67

*7 Year Price Score 79.94 *NYSE Composite Index=100 ***12 Month Price Score 99.18**

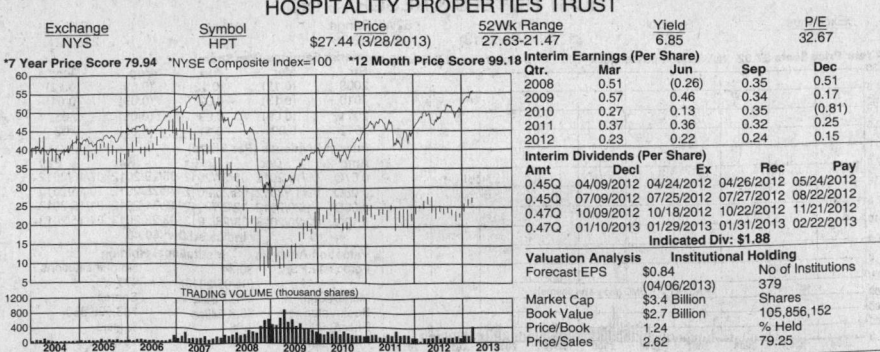

Interim Earnings (Per Share)

Qtr.	Mar	Jun	Sep	Dec
2008	0.51	(0.26)	0.35	0.51
2009	0.57	0.46	0.34	0.17
2010	0.27	0.13	0.35	(0.81)
2011	0.37	0.36	0.32	0.25
2012	0.23	0.22	0.24	0.15

Interim Dividends (Per Share)

Amt	Decl	Ex	Rec	Pay
0.45Q	04/09/2012	04/24/2012	04/26/2012	05/24/2012
0.45Q	07/09/2012	07/25/2012	07/27/2012	08/22/2012
0.47Q	10/09/2012	10/18/2012	10/22/2012	11/21/2012
0.47Q	01/10/2013	01/29/2013	01/31/2013	02/22/2013

Indicated Div: $1.88

Valuation Analysis

		Institutional Holding	
Forecast EPS	$0.84	No of Institutions	
	(04/06/2013)	379	
Market Cap	$3.4 Billion	Shares	105,856,152
Book Value	$2.7 Billion	% Held	
Price/Book	1.24		79.25
Price/Sales	2.62		

Business Summary: REITs (MIC: 5.3.1 SIC: 6798 NAIC: 525930)

Hospitality Properties Trust is a real estate investment trust which invests in real estate used in hospitality industries. At Dec 31 2011, Co. owned 288 hotels with 42,632 rooms or suites, and 185 travel centers located in 44 states in the U.S., Canada and Puerto Rico. At Dec 31 2011, Co.'s hotels were operated as, among others, Courtyard by Marriott®, Candlewood Suites®, Staybridge Suites®, Residence Inn by Marriott®, Crowne Plaza Hotels & Resorts®, Hyatt Place®, InterContinental Hotels & Resorts®, and Marriott Hotels and Resorts®. 145 of Co.'s travel centers were operated under the TravelCenters of America® brand names and 40 were operated under the Petro Stopping Centers® brand name.

Recent Developments: For the year ended Dec 31 2012, net income decreased 20.2% to US$151.9 million from US$190.4 million in the prior year. Revenues were US$1.30 billion, up 7.2% from US$1.21 billion the year before. Revenues from property income fell 1.4% to US$300.4 million from US$304.6 million in the corresponding earlier year.

Prospects: Our evaluation of Hospitality Properties Trust as of Apr. 7, 2013 is the result of our systematic analysis on three basic characteristics: earnings strength, relative valuation, and recent stock price movement. The company has enjoyed a very positive trend in earnings per share over the past 5 quarters. Because the company lacks sufficient analyst estimate data, we place greater weight on the historical EPS trend as the measure of earnings strength. Based on operating earnings yield, the company is overvalued when compared to all of the companies in our coverage universe. Share price changes over the past year indicates that HPT will perform poorly over the near term.

Financial Data
(US$ in Thousands)

	12/31/2012	12/31/2011	12/31/2010	12/31/2009	12/31/2008	12/31/2007	12/31/2006	12/31/2005
Earnings Per Share	0.84	1.30	(0.07)	1.51	1.11	3.27	2.20	1.75
Cash Flow Per Share	2.94	2.88	2.77	2.96	3.99	4.17	3.71	3.47
Tang Book Value Per Share	18.54	19.50	20.01	21.90	23.54	25.52	27.40	24.64
Dividends Per Share	1.820	1.800	1.800	0.770	3.080	3.030	2.940	2.170
Dividend Payout %	216.67	138.46	...	50.99	277.48	92.66	133.64	124.00
Income Statement								
Total Revenue	1,296,982	1,210,333	1,085,488	1,037,247	1,252,674	1,285,419	1,039,415	834,412
EBITDA	556,072	560,490	405,654	598,861	526,257	592,503	397,478	329,852
Depn & Amortn	267,010	234,647	245,212	256,914	243,232	221,978	146,988	134,686
Income Before Taxes	153,219	191,803	21,990	198,537	135,841	230,008	169,039	129,903
Income Taxes	1,612	1,502	638	5,196	1,846	2,191	...	...
Net Income	151,923	190,440	21,351	193,341	133,995	330,968	169,039	129,903
Average Shares	123,574	123,470	123,403	107,984	93,944	93,109	73,279	69,866
Balance Sheet								
Current Assets	60,793	181,524	85,503	155,482	54,476	51,535	580,619	47,631
Total Assets	5,635,125	5,133,573	5,192,286	5,548,370	5,576,405	5,679,307	3,957,463	3,114,607
Current Liabilities	178,969	218,557	220,822	262,878	305,250	313,482	310,093	298,780
Long-Term Obligations	2,722,358	2,115,714	2,111,223	2,193,561	2,668,288	2,579,391	1,199,830	960,372
Total Liabilities	2,901,327	2,334,271	2,332,045	2,456,439	2,973,538	2,892,873	1,509,923	1,259,152
Stockholders' Equity	2,733,798	2,799,302	2,860,241	3,091,931	2,602,867	2,786,434	2,447,540	1,855,455
Shares Outstanding	123,637	123,521	123,444	123,380	93,991	93,892	86,284	71,920
Statistical Record								
Return on Assets %	2.81	3.69	0.40	3.48	2.37	6.87	4.78	4.48
Return on Equity %	5.48	6.73	0.72	6.79	4.96	12.65	7.86	7.34
EBITDA Margin %	42.87	46.31	37.37	57.74	42.01	46.09	38.24	39.53
Net Margin %	11.71	15.73	1.97	18.64	10.70	25.75	16.26	15.57
Asset Turnover	0.24	0.23	0.20	0.19	0.22	0.27	0.29	0.29
Current Ratio	0.34	0.83	0.39	0.59	0.18	0.16	1.87	0.16
Debt to Equity	1.00	0.76	0.74	0.71	1.03	0.93	0.49	0.52
Price Range	27.63-21.47	25.71-19.05	27.98-19.15	24.02-9.09	36.98-7.20	48.84-32.22	48.19-38.12	43.12-36.19
P/E Ratio	32.89-25.56	19.78-14.65	...	15.91-6.02	33.32-6.49	14.94-9.85	21.90-17.33	24.64-20.68
Average Yield %	7.49	7.74	7.96	4.90	12.52	7.24	6.97	5.48

Address: Two Newton Place, 255	Web Site: www.hptreit.com	Auditors: Ernst & Young LLP
Washington Street, Suite 300, Newton,	Officers: John G. Murray - President, Chief Operating	Investor Contact: 617-796-8232
MA 02458-1634	Officer, Assistant Secretary Ethan S. Bornstein -	Transfer Agents: Wells Fargo
Telephone: 617-964-8389	Senior Vice President	Shareowner Services, Mendota Heights, MN

HOST HOTELS & RESORTS INC

Exchange	Symbol	Price	52Wk Range	Yield	P/E
NYS	HST	$17.49 (3/28/2013)	17.73-13.78	2.29	218.62

*7 Year Price Score 87.02 *NYSE Composite Index=100 *12 Month Price Score 99.58

Interim Earnings (Per Share)

Qtr.	Mar	Jun	Sep	Dec
2009	(0.12)	(0.12)	(0.09)	(0.12)
2010	(0.13)	0.02	(0.09)	(0.01)
2011	(0.09)	0.09	(0.05)	0.03
2012	0.00	0.11	(0.05)	0.02

Interim Dividends (Per Share)

Amt	Decl	Ex	Rec	Pay
0.07Q	06/18/2012	06/27/2012	06/29/2012	07/16/2012
0.08Q	09/17/2012	09/26/2012	09/28/2012	10/15/2012
0.09Q	11/29/2012	12/27/2012	12/31/2012	01/15/2013
0.10Q	02/20/2013	03/26/2013	03/28/2013	04/15/2013

Indicated Div: $0.40

Valuation Analysis

		Institutional Holding	
Forecast EPS	$0.34 (04/05/2013)	No of Institutions	477
Market Cap	$12.7 Billion	Shares	
Book Value	$6.8 Billion	% Held	798,506,880
Price/Book	1.86		104.30
Price/Sales	2.40		

Business Summary: REITs (MIC: 5.3.1 SIC: 6798 NAIC: 525930)

Host Hotels & Resorts is a real estate investment trust. Co. owns properties and conducts operations through Host Hotels & Resorts, L.P., of which it is the sole general partner and in which, as of Dec 31 2012, it held approximately 98.6% of the partnership interests. As of Feb 25 2013, Co.'s consolidated lodging portfolio consisted of 118 hotels containing approximately 62,600 rooms, with the majority located in the U.S., and 15 properties located in Canada, New Zealand, Chile, Australia, Mexico and Brazil. Co. is also developing two hotels in Rio de Janeiro, Brazil. In addition, Co. owns non-controlling interests in a joint venture in Europe and a joint venture in Asia/Pacific.

Recent Developments: For the year ended Dec 31 2012, income from continuing operations was US$13.0 million compared with a loss of US$10.0 million a year earlier. Net income amounted to US$63.0 million versus a net loss of US$16.0 million in the prior year. Revenues were US$5.29 billion, up 7.4% from US$4.92 billion the year before.

Prospects: Our evaluation of Host Marriott Corp. as of Apr. 7, 2013 is the result of our systematic analysis on three basic characteristics: earnings strength, relative valuation, and recent stock price movement. The company has enjoyed a very positive trend in earnings per share over the past 5 quarters. However, while recent estimates for the company have been mixed, HST has posted results that fell short of analysts expectations. Based on operating earnings yield, the company is overvalued when compared to all of the companies in our coverage universe. Share price changes over the past year indicates that HST will perform poorly over the near term.

Financial Data

(US$ in Millions)	12/31/2012	12/31/2011	12/31/2010	12/31/2009	12/31/2008	12/31/2007	12/31/2006	12/31/2005
Earnings Per Share	0.08	(0.02)	(0.21)	(0.45)	0.76	1.33	1.48	0.38
Cash Flow Per Share	1.09	0.95	0.79	0.94	1.95	1.92	1.83	1.45
Tang Book Value Per Share	9.42	9.47	9.33	9.43	10.32	10.23	9.83	6.03
Dividends Per Share	0.300	0.140	0.040	0.250	0.650	1.000	0.760	0.410
Dividend Payout %	375.00	...	...	...	85.53	75.19	51.35	107.89
Income Statement								
Total Revenue	5,286	4,998	4,437	4,158	5,288	5,426	4,888	3,881
EBITDA	395	337	219	158	1,342	962	782	606
Depn & Amortn	3	3	1	41	591	3	4	5
Income Before Taxes	42	(17)	(158)	(255)	430	574	361	179
Income Taxes	31	(1)	(31)	(39)	(3)	3	5	24
Net Income	61	(15)	(130)	(252)	427	727	738	166
Average Shares	719	693	656	587	552	554	483	355
Balance Sheet								
Current Assets	453	862	1,154	1,695	552	553	558	293
Total Assets	12,994	13,068	12,411	12,555	11,951	11,812	11,808	8,245
Current Liabilities	194	175	208	174	119	315	243	165
Long-Term Obligations	5,411	5,753	5,477	5,837	5,952	5,625	5,878	5,370
Total Liabilities	6,169	6,391	6,108	6,366	6,434	6,371	6,586	5,828
Stockholders' Equity	6,825	6,677	6,303	6,189	5,517	5,441	5,222	2,417
Shares Outstanding	724	705	675	646	525	522	521	361
Statistical Record								
Return on Assets %	0.47	N.M.	N.M.	N.M.	3.58	6.16	7.36	1.99
Return on Equity %	0.90	N.M.	N.M.	N.M.	7.77	13.64	19.32	6.90
EBITDA Margin %	7.47	6.74	4.94	3.80	25.38	17.73	16.00	15.61
Net Margin %	1.15	N.M.	N.M.	N.M.	8.07	13.40	15.10	4.28
Asset Turnover	0.40	0.39	0.36	0.34	0.44	0.46	0.49	0.47
Current Ratio	2.34	4.93	5.55	9.74	4.64	1.76	2.30	1.78
Debt to Equity	0.79	0.86	0.87	0.94	1.08	1.03	1.13	2.22
Price Range	17.25-13.78	19.77-10.17	17.87-10.60	12.13-3.40	18.76-5.06	28.71-16.71	25.60-18.95	19.05-15.49
P/E Ratio	215.63-172.25	...	...	...	24.68-6.66	21.59-12.56	17.30-12.80	50.13-40.76
Average Yield %	1.93	0.90	0.28	2.99	4.72	4.28	3.50	2.39

Address: 6903 Rockledge Drive, Suite 1500, Bethesda, MD 20817
Telephone: 240-744-1000
Fax: 240-380-6338

Web Site: www.hosthotels.com
Officers: Richard E. Marriott - Chairman W. Edward Walter - President, Chief Executive Officer

Auditors: KPMG LLP
Investor Contact: 240-744-5800
Transfer Agents: Computershare Trust Company, N.A, Providence, RI

HOWARD HUGHES CORP

Exchange	Symbol	Price	52Wk Range	Yield	P/E
NYS	HHC	$83.81 (3/28/2013)	83.97-56.76	N/A	N/A

*7 Year Price Score N/A   *NYSE Composite Index=100   *12 Month Price Score 104.05

TRADING VOLUME (thousand shares)

Interim Earnings (Per Share)

Qtr.	Mar	Jun	Sep	Dec
2011	(3.02)	0.22	(0.14)	0.79
2012	(2.96)	0.27	(1.30)	0.00

Interim Dividends (Per Share)

No Dividends Paid

Valuation Analysis / Institutional Holding

Valuation Analysis		Institutional Holding	
Forecast EPS	$0.39	No of Institutions	
	(04/05/2013)	190	
Market Cap	$3.3 Billion	Shares	
Book Value	$2.3 Billion	32,028,020	
Price/Book	1.44	% Held	
Price/Sales	8.78	N/A	

Business Summary: Property, Real Estate & Development (MIC: 5.3.2 SIC: 6552 NAIC: 531312)

Howard Hughes is a developer and operator of master planned communities and mixed-use properties. Co. operates its business in three segments: Master Planned Communities, Operating Assets and Strategic Developments. Co.'s Master Planned Communities segment primarily consists of the development and sale of residential and commercial land, primarily in large-scale projects. Co.'s Operating Assets segment contains 26 properties and investments, consisting primarily of commercial mixed-use, retail and office properties that are generating revenue. Co.'s Strategic Developments segment is made up of near, medium and long-term development projects for 19 of its real estate properties.

Recent Developments: For the year ended Dec 31 2012, net loss amounted to US$127.5 million versus net income of US$148.5 million in the prior year. Revenues were US$376.9 million, up 36.7% from US$275.7 million the year before. Revenues from property income rose 35.4% to US$346.7 million from US$256.1 million in the corresponding earlier year.

Prospects: Our evaluation of Howard Hughes Corp as of Feb. 19, 2012 is the result of our systematic analysis on three basic characteristics: earnings strength, relative valuation, and recent stock price movement. The company has suffered a very negative trend in earnings per share over the past 5 quarters. Because the company lacks sufficient analyst estimate data, we place greater weight on the historical EPS trend as the measure of earnings strength. Based on operating earnings yield, the company is overvalued when compared to all of the companies in our coverage universe. Share price changes over the past year indicates that HHC will perform poorly over the near term.

Financial Data
(US$ in Thousands)

	12/31/2012	12/31/2011	12/31/2010	12/31/2009	12/31/2008	12/31/2007
Earnings Per Share	(3.36)	1.17	(1.84)	...	...	...
Cash Flow Per Share	4.00	2.28	...	...	...	...
Tang Book Value Per Share	58.36	61.26	57.47	...	...	...
Income Statement						
Total Revenue	376,886	275,691	142,719	136,348	172,507	260,498
EBITDA	(113,357)	125,703	(638,185)	(675,530)	(24,180)	(63,614)
Depn & Amortn	19,455	14,012	14,582	17,145	15,637	20,883
Income Before Taxes	(124,339)	121,567	(654,820)	(691,963)	(38,712)	(82,993)
Income Taxes	6,887	(18,325)	(633,459)	(23,969)	2,703	(10,643)
Net Income	(127,543)	148,470	(69,230)	(703,816)	(17,909)	(3,899)
Average Shares	38,127	38,982	37,726	...	...	...
Balance Sheet						
Current Assets	680,397	696,934	655,315	20,563	22,325	...
Total Assets	3,503,042	3,395,149	3,022,707	2,905,227	3,443,956	...
Current Liabilities	503,733	459,073	524,940	917,008	1,099,674	...
Long-Term Obligations	688,312	606,477	318,660	208,860	358,467	...
Total Liabilities	1,197,804	1,070,564	844,424	1,402,607	1,459,944	...
Stockholders' Equity	2,305,238	2,324,585	2,178,283	1,502,620	1,984,012	...
Shares Outstanding	39,498	37,945	37,904	...	...	...
Statistical Record						
Return on Assets %	N.M.	4.63	...	N.M.	...	...
Return on Equity %	N.M.	6.59	...	N.M.	...	...
EBITDA Margin %	N.M.	45.60	N.M.	N.M.	N.M.	N.M.
Net Margin %	N.M.	53.85	N.M.	N.M.	N.M.	N.M.
Asset Turnover	0.11	0.09	...	0.04	...	...
Current Ratio	1.35	1.52	1.25	0.02	0.02	...
Debt to Equity	0.30	0.26	0.15	0.14	0.18	...
Price Range	75.12-44.27	76.48-37.31	56.00-36.90	...	...	...
P/E Ratio	...	65.37-31.89	...	...	...	...

Address: 13355 Noel Road, 22nd Floor, Dallas, TX 75240 Telephone: 214-741-7744	Web Site: www.howardhughes.com Officers: William A. Ackman - Chairman Grant Herlitz - President	Auditors: Ernst & Young LLP Transfer Agents: BNY Mellon, New York, NY

385

HUBBELL INC.

Exchange	Symbol	Price	52Wk Range	Yield	P/E
NYS	HUB A	$97.11 (3/28/2013)	97.73-72.82	1.85	19.42

*7 Year Price Score 136.10 *NYSE Composite Index=100 *12 Month Price Score 103.95

Interim Earnings (Per Share)

Qtr.	Mar	Jun	Sep	Dec
2008	0.85	1.09	1.18	0.82
2009	0.60	0.70	1.01	0.84
2010	0.64	0.95	1.18	0.82
2011	0.82	1.07	1.37	1.17
2012	1.05	1.29	1.45	1.20

Interim Dividends (Per Share)

Amt	Decl	Ex	Rec	Pay
0.41Q	06/06/2012	06/14/2012	06/18/2012	07/11/2012
0.41Q	09/12/2012	09/20/2012	09/24/2012	10/11/2012
0.45Q	12/04/2012	12/12/2012	12/14/2012	12/26/2012
0.45Q	02/07/2013	02/27/2013	03/01/2013	03/15/2013

Indicated Div: $1.80

Valuation Analysis

Forecast EPS	$5.46 (04/05/2013)
Market Cap	$5.8 Billion
Book Value	$1.7 Billion
Price/Book	3.46
Price/Sales	1.89

Institutional Holding

No of Institutions	56
Shares	5,513,436
% Held	3.31

Business Summary: Electrical Equipment (MIC: 7.3.1 SIC: 3613 NAIC: 334417)

Hubbell is engaged in the design, manufacture and sale of electrical and electronic products for a range of non-residential and residential construction, industrial and utility applications. Co. operates two segments:Electrical and Power. The Electrical segment comprises of electrical systems products and lighting products. The Power segment comprises of a variety of electrical distribution, transmission, substation and telecommunications products.

Recent Developments: For the year ended Dec 31 2012, net income increased 11.8% to US$302.1 million from US$270.2 million in the prior year. Revenues were US$3.04 billion, up 6.0% from US$2.87 billion the year before. Operating income was US$471.8 million versus US$423.8 million in the prior year, an increase of 11.3%. Direct operating expenses rose 4.3% to US$2.03 billion from US$1.95 billion in the comparable period the year before. Indirect operating expenses increased 8.1% to US$540.4 million from US$499.9 million in the equivalent prior-year period.

Prospects: Our evaluation of Hubbell Inc. as of Apr. 7, 2013 is the result of our systematic analysis on three basic characteristics: earnings strength, relative valuation, and recent stock price movement. The company has managed to produce a neutral trend in earnings per share over the past 5 quarters and while recent estimates for the company have been mixed, HUB.B has posted better than expected results. Based on operating earnings yield, the company is about fairly valued when compared to all of the companies in our coverage universe. Share price changes over the past year indicates that HUB.B will perform in line with the market over the near term.

Financial Data

(US$ in Thousands)	12/31/2012	12/31/2011	12/31/2010	12/31/2009	12/31/2008	12/31/2007	12/31/2006	12/31/2005
Earnings Per Share	5.00	4.42	3.59	3.15	3.94	3.50	2.59	2.67
Cash Flow Per Share	5.89	5.61	4.44	7.00	5.68	5.70	2.32	3.02
Tang Book Value Per Share	10.43	7.96	12.11	9.29	7.53	10.63	9.62	10.58
Dividends Per Share	1.680	1.520	1.440	1.400	1.380	1.320	1.320	1.320
Dividend Payout %	33.60	34.39	40.11	44.44	35.03	37.71	50.97	49.44
Income Statement								
Total Revenue	3,044,400	2,871,600	2,541,200	2,355,600	2,704,400	2,533,900	2,414,300	2,104,900
EBITDA	516,700	466,500	398,600	292,546	389,200	344,900	279,200	277,700
Depn & Amortn	44,100	45,800	47,100	46	43,900	43,100	42,300	42,700
Income Before Taxes	441,800	389,800	320,400	261,600	317,900	284,200	221,500	215,700
Income Taxes	139,700	119,600	101,600	80,300	95,200	75,900	63,400	50,600
Net Income	299,700	267,900	217,200	180,100	222,700	208,300	158,100	165,100
Average Shares	59,800	60,400	60,300	57,000	56,500	59,500	61,100	61,800
Balance Sheet								
Current Assets	1,456,200	1,353,500	1,226,100	917,900	919,100	788,000	814,400	820,100
Total Assets	2,947,000	2,846,500	2,705,800	2,464,500	2,115,500	1,863,400	1,751,500	1,667,000
Current Liabilities	447,240	492,100	445,000	418,500	425,000	419,500	382,300	360,500
Long-Term Obligations	596,700	596,300	595,700	497,200	497,400	199,400	199,300	199,200
Total Liabilities	1,285,800	1,378,700	1,246,600	1,166,300	1,107,400	780,600	736,000	668,900
Stockholders' Equity	1,661,200	1,467,800	1,459,200	1,298,200	1,008,100	1,082,600	1,015,500	998,100
Shares Outstanding	59,236	59,179	60,696	59,660	56,267	57,927	60,178	61,090
Statistical Record								
Return on Assets %	10.32	9.65	8.40	7.86	11.16	11.52	9.25	9.98
Return on Equity %	19.10	18.31	15.75	15.62	21.25	19.86	15.70	17.00
EBITDA Margin %	16.97	16.25	15.69	12.42	14.39	13.61	11.56	13.19
Net Margin %	9.84	9.33	8.55	7.65	8.23	8.22	6.55	7.84
Asset Turnover	1.05	1.03	0.98	1.03	1.36	1.40	1.41	1.27
Current Ratio	3.25	2.75	2.76	2.19	2.16	1.88	2.13	2.27
Debt to Equity	0.36	0.41	0.41	0.38	0.49	0.18	0.20	0.20
Price Range	86.48-67.80	72.70-47.97	61.10-38.46	48.05-22.15	51.60-25.88	58.15-43.39	53.28-43.78	54.00-42.67
P/E Ratio	17.30-13.56	16.45-10.85	17.02-10.71	15.25-7.03	13.10-6.57	16.61-12.40	20.57-16.90	20.22-15.98
Average Yield %	2.12	2.44	2.94	3.86	3.39	2.52	2.74	2.78

Address: 40 Waterview Drive, Shelton, CT 06484	Web Site: www.hubbell.com	Auditors: PicewaterhouseCoopers LLP
Telephone: 475-882-4000	Officers: Timothy H. Powers - Chairman, President, Chief Executive Officer David G. Nord - President, Chief Executive Officer, Senior Vice President, Chief Operating Officer, Chief Financial Officer	Transfer Agents: Mellon Investor Services, L.L.C., Jersey City, NJ

HUMANA INC.

Exchange	Symbol	Price	52Wk Range	Yield	P/E
NYS	HUM	$69.11 (3/28/2013)	91.85-61.60	1.50	9.25

*7 Year Price Score 110.64 *NYSE Composite Index=100   *12 Month Price Score 90.60

Interim Earnings (Per Share)

Qtr.	Mar	Jun	Sep	Dec
2008	0.47	1.24	1.09	1.04
2009	1.22	1.67	1.78	1.48
2010	1.52	2.00	2.32	0.63
2011	1.86	2.71	2.67	1.22
2012	1.49	2.16	2.62	1.20

Interim Dividends (Per Share)

Amt	Decl	Ex	Rec	Pay
0.26Q	04/30/2012	06/27/2012	06/29/2012	07/27/2012
0.26Q	08/24/2012	09/26/2012	09/28/2012	10/26/2012
0.26Q	10/18/2012	12/27/2012	12/31/2012	01/25/2013
0.26Q	02/27/2013	03/26/2013	03/28/2013	04/26/2013

Indicated Div: $1.04

Valuation Analysis

Forecast EPS	$7.90 (04/06/2013)
Market Cap	$10.9 Billion
Book Value	$8.8 Billion
Price/Book	1.24
Price/Sales	0.28

Institutional Holding

No of Institutions	626
Shares	160,658,512
% Held	88.98

Business Summary: Life & Health (MIC: 5.2.2 SIC: 6324 NAIC: 524114)

Humana is a holding company. Through its subsidiaries, Co. is engaged in providing insurance products and health and wellness services. Co. has three reportable segments: Retail, consisting of Medicare and commercial fully-insured medical and specialty health insurance benefits, including dental, vision, and other supplemental health and financial protection products, marketed to individuals; Employer Group, consisting of similar health insurance benefits as in its Retail segment, but marketed to employer groups; and Health and Well-Being Services, including services related to health and wellness, including provider services, pharmacy, integrated wellness, and home care services.

Recent Developments: For the year ended Dec 31 2012, net income decreased 13.9% to US$1.22 billion from US$1.42 billion in the prior year. Revenues were US$39.13 billion, up 6.2% from US$36.83 billion the year before. Net premiums earned were US$37.01 billion versus US$35.11 billion in the prior year, an increase of 5.4%.

Prospects: Our evaluation of Humana Inc. as of Apr. 7, 2013 is the result of our systematic analysis on three basic characteristics: earnings strength, relative valuation, and recent stock price movement. The company has enjoyed a very positive trend in earnings per share over the past 5 quarters. However, while recent estimates for the company have been mixed, HUM has posted better than expected results. Based on operating earnings yield, the company is undervalued when compared to all of the companies in our coverage universe. Share price changes over the past year indicates that HUM will perform very poorly over the near term.

Financial Data

(US$ in Thousands)	12/31/2012	12/31/2011	12/31/2010	12/31/2009	12/31/2008	12/31/2007	12/31/2006	12/31/2005
Earnings Per Share	7.47	8.46	6.47	6.15	3.83	4.91	2.90	1.87
Cash Flow Per Share	11.88	12.57	13.36	8.49	5.86	7.34	10.28	3.87
Tang Book Value Per Share	32.89	32.46	25.86	22.23	14.77	13.91	10.46	7.41
Dividends Per Share	1.030	0.750	...	...	...	...	...	...
Dividend Payout %	13.79	8.87	...	...	...	...	...	...
Income Statement								
Premium Income	37,009,000	35,106,000	32,712,323	29,926,751	28,064,844	24,434,347	20,729,182	14,001,591
Total Revenue	39,126,000	36,832,000	33,868,208	30,960,414	28,946,372	25,289,989	21,416,537	14,418,127
Benefits & Claims	30,985,000	28,823,000	27,087,874	24,775,002	23,708,233	20,270,531	...	...
Income Before Taxes	1,911,000	2,235,000	1,749,562	1,601,760	992,848	1,289,300	762,085	421,714
Income Taxes	689,000	816,000	650,172	562,085	345,694	455,616	274,662	113,231
Net Income	1,222,000	1,419,000	1,099,390	1,039,675	647,154	833,684	487,423	308,483
Average Shares	163,457	167,827	169,798	169,071	169,187	169,820	167,996	165,374
Balance Sheet								
Total Assets	19,979,000	17,708,000	16,103,253	14,153,494	13,041,760	12,879,074	10,127,496	6,869,614
Total Liabilities	11,132,000	9,645,000	9,179,197	8,377,491	8,584,570	8,850,137	7,073,610	4,395,509
Stockholders' Equity	8,847,000	8,063,000	6,924,056	5,776,003	4,457,190	4,028,937	3,053,886	2,474,105
Shares Outstanding	158,331	164,004	168,449	170,180	168,825	170,018	166,606	163,216
Statistical Record								
Return on Assets %	6.47	8.39	7.27	7.65	4.98	7.25	5.74	4.92
Return on Equity %	14.41	18.94	17.31	20.32	15.21	23.54	17.63	13.52
Loss Ratio %	83.72	82.10	82.81	82.79	84.48	82.96	...	...
Net Margin %	3.12	3.85	3.25	3.36	2.24	3.30	2.28	2.14
Price Range	95.50-61.60	89.83-54.74	60.64-43.56	45.80-18.77	86.98-24.56	78.46-52.25	67.97-41.60	55.29-29.10
P/E Ratio	12.78-8.25	10.62-6.47	9.37-6.73	7.45-3.05	22.71-6.41	15.98-10.64	23.44-14.34	29.57-15.56
Average Yield %	1.33	1.01	...	...	...	...	...	...

Address: 500 West Main Street, Louisville, KY 40202
Telephone: 502-580-1000

Web Site: www.humana.com
Officers: Michael B. McCallister - Chairman, President, Chief Executive Officer Bruce D. Broussard - President, Chief Executive Officer

Auditors: PricewaterhouseCoopers LLP
Investor Contact: 866-355-1252
Transfer Agents: American Stock Transfer & Trust Company, LLC, Brooklyn, NY

HUNTSMAN CORP

Exchange	Symbol	Price	52Wk Range	Yield	P/E
NYS	HUN	$18.59 (3/28/2013)	19.43-11.39	2.69	12.31

*7 Year Price Score 90.47   *NYSE Composite Index=100   *12 Month Price Score 108.81

Interim Earnings (Per Share)

Qtr.	Mar	Jun	Sep	Dec
2008	0.03	0.10	(0.09)	2.55
2009	(1.24)	1.51	(0.29)	0.28
2010	(0.73)	0.47	0.23	0.12
2011	0.26	0.47	(0.14)	0.43
2012	0.68	0.52	0.48	(0.17)

Interim Dividends (Per Share)

Amt	Decl	Ex	Rec	Pay
0.10Q	05/07/2012	06/13/2012	06/15/2012	06/29/2012
0.10Q	08/06/2012	09/12/2012	09/14/2012	09/28/2012
0.10Q	11/12/2012	12/12/2012	12/14/2012	12/31/2012
0.125Q	02/12/2013	03/13/2013	03/15/2013	03/29/2013

Indicated Div: $0.50

Valuation Analysis | **Institutional Holding**

Forecast EPS	$1.62 (04/05/2013)	No of Institutions 378
Market Cap	$4.4 Billion	Shares
Book Value	$1.8 Billion	172,333,456
Price/Book	2.50	% Held
Price/Sales	0.40	67.78

Business Summary: Specialty Chemicals (MIC: 8.3.2 SIC: 2899 NAIC: 424690)

Huntsman manufactures differentiated organic chemical products and of inorganic chemical products. Co. operates through its subsidiary, Huntsman International. Co.'s products comprise a range of chemicals and formulations which it markets to a group of consumer and industrial customers. Co.'s products are used in a range of applications, including those in the adhesives, aerospace, automotive, construction products, consumer products, electronics, medical, packaging, paints and coatings, power generation, refining, synthetic fiber, textile chemicals and dye industries. Co. operates in five segments: Polyurethanes, Performance Products, Advanced Materials, Textile Effects and Pigments.

Recent Developments: For the year ended Dec 31 2012, income from continuing operations increased 50.6% to US$378.0 million from US$251.0 million a year earlier. Net income increased 46.9% to US$373.0 million from US$254.0 million in the prior year. Revenues were US$11.19 billion, down 0.3% from US$11.22 billion the year before. Operating income was US$845.0 million versus US$606.0 million in the prior year, an increase of 39.4%. Direct operating expenses declined 2.4% to US$9.15 billion from US$9.38 billion in the comparable period the year before. Indirect operating expenses decreased 3.6% to US$1.19 billion from US$1.23 billion in the equivalent prior-year period.

Prospects: Our evaluation of Hunisman Corp. as of Apr. 7, 2013 is the result of our systematic analysis on three basic characteristics: earnings strength, relative valuation, and recent stock price movement. The company has suffered a very negative trend in earnings per share over the past 5 quarters. However, while recent estimates for the company have been mixed, HUN has posted better than expected results. Based on operating earnings yield, the company is undervalued when compared to all of the companies in our coverage universe. Share price changes over the past year indicates that HUN will perform well over the near term.

Financial Data

(US$ in Thousands)	12/31/2012	12/31/2011	12/31/2010	12/31/2009	12/31/2008	12/31/2007	12/31/2006	12/31/2005
Earnings Per Share	1.51	1.02	0.11	0.48	2.60	(0.74)	0.99	(0.35)
Cash Flow Per Share	3.25	1.54	(0.25)	4.72	3.30	(0.23)	4.05	4.42
Tang Book Value Per Share	6.66	6.18	6.72	6.94	5.84	5.76	5.31	4.20
Dividends Per Share	0.400	0.400	0.400	0.400	0.400	0.400	...	...
Dividend Payout %	26.49	39.22	363.64	83.33	15.38	...	...	...
Income Statement								
Total Revenue	11,187,000	11,221,000	9,250,000	7,763,000	10,215,000	9,650,800	10,623,600	12,961,600
EBITDA	1,165,000	999,000	588,000	1,114,000	1,277,000	679,500	1,124,900	945,100
Depn & Amortn	399,000	398,000	363,000	394,000	359,000	376,800	430,300	464,500
Income Before Taxes	540,000	352,000	(4,000)	482,000	655,000	17,100	343,900	54,000
Income Taxes	169,000	109,000	29,000	370,000	190,000	(12,100)	(49,000)	23,500
Net Income	363,000	247,000	27,000	114,000	609,000	(172,100)	229,800	(34,600)
Average Shares	240,600	241,700	236,000	238,300	234,263	232,792	233,100	220,500
Balance Sheet								
Current Assets	4,119,000	3,946,000	4,008,000	4,140,000	3,240,000	3,095,200	3,336,600	3,096,000
Total Assets	8,884,000	8,657,000	8,714,000	8,626,000	8,058,000	8,165,600	8,444,900	8,870,500
Current Liabilities	2,181,000	1,826,000	2,053,000	1,811,000	1,605,000	1,975,300	2,073,100	1,887,700
Long-Term Obligations	3,418,000	3,734,000	3,631,000	3,786,000	3,683,000	3,505,000	3,457,400	4,413,300
Total Liabilities	7,111,000	6,995,000	6,924,000	6,782,000	6,448,000	6,339,000	6,708,300	7,349,900
Stockholders' Equity	1,773,000	1,662,000	1,790,000	1,844,000	1,610,000	1,826,600	1,736,600	1,520,600
Shares Outstanding	238,273	235,746	236,799	234,081	233,553	221,036	220,652	220,451
Statistical Record								
Return on Assets %	4.13	2.84	0.31	1.37	7.49	N.M.	2.65	N.M.
Return on Equity %	21.08	14.31	1.49	6.60	35.35	N.M.	14.11	N.M.
EBITDA Margin %	10.41	8.90	6.36	14.35	12.50	7.04	10.59	7.29
Net Margin %	3.24	2.20	0.29	1.47	5.96	N.M.	2.16	N.M.
Asset Turnover	1.27	1.29	1.07	0.93	1.26	1.16	1.23	1.42
Current Ratio	1.89	2.16	1.95	2.29	2.02	1.57	1.61	1.64
Debt to Equity	1.93	2.25	2.03	2.05	2.29	1.92	1.99	2.90
Price Range	17.07-9.82	20.95-8.78	16.66-8.30	11.51-2.11	25.70-2.96	28.07-18.49	23.22-15.82	28.56-16.74
P/E Ratio	11.30-6.50	20.54-8.61	151.45-75.45	23.98-4.40	9.88-1.14	...	23.45-15.98	...
Average Yield %	2.84	2.61	3.40	6.34	2.45	1.75	...	...

Address: 500 Huntsman Way, Salt Lake City, UT 84108 **Telephone:** 801-584-5700	**Web Site:** www.huntsman.com **Officers:** Jon M. Huntsman - Chairman Peter R Huntsman - President, Chief Executive Officer	**Auditors:** Deloitte & Touche LLP **Investor Contact:** 801-584-5959 **Transfer Agents:** Computershare Shareowner Services, Providence, RI

HYATT HOTELS CORP

Exchange	Symbol	Price	52Wk Range	Yield	P/E
NYS	H	$43.23 (3/28/2013)	43.81-33.74	N/A	81.57

*7 Year Price Score N/A   *NYSE Composite Index=100   *12 Month Price Score 99.13

TRADING VOLUME (thousand shares)

Interim Earnings (Per Share)

Qtr.	Mar	Jun	Sep	Dec
2009	0.09	(0.34)	0.04	(0.08)
2010	0.03	0.14	0.17	(0.02)
2011	0.06	0.21	0.08	0.31
2012	0.06	0.24	0.14	0.09

Interim Dividends (Per Share)

No Dividends Paid

Valuation Analysis		Institutional Holding	
Forecast EPS	$0.79	No of Institutions	197
	(04/05/2013)		
Market Cap	$7.0 Billion	Shares	
Book Value	$4.8 Billion		48,842,348
Price/Book	1.45	% Held	
Price/Sales	1.77		N/A

Business Summary: Hotels, Restaurants & Travel (MIC: 2.2.1 SIC: 7011 NAIC: 721110)

Hyatt Hotels is a hospitality company. Co. manages, franchises, owns and develops hotels, resorts and residential and vacation ownership properties. Co.'s hotels and resorts operate under Park Hyatt, Andaz, Hyatt, Grand Hyatt and Hyatt Regency brands. Co.'s two select service brands are Hyatt Place and Hyatt House, an extended stay brand. Co. develops, sells or manages vacation ownership properties in select locations as part of the Hyatt Residence Club. Co. also manages, provides services to or licenses its trademarks with respect to residential ownership units that are adjacent to a Hyatt-branded hotel. As of Dec 31 2012, Co.'s global portfolio consisted of 500 Hyatt-branded properties.

Recent Developments: For the year ended Dec 31 2012, income from continuing operations decreased 21.6% to US$87.0 million from US$111.0 million a year earlier. Net income decreased 21.6% to US$87.0 million from US$111.0 million in the prior year. Revenues were US$3.95 billion, up 6.8% from US$3.70 billion the year before. Direct operating expenses rose 5.5% to US$3.12 billion from US$2.96 billion in the comparable period the year before. Indirect operating expenses increased 13.8% to US$669.0 million from US$588.0 million in the equivalent prior-year period.

Prospects: Our evaluation of Hyatt Hotels Corp. as of Apr. 7, 2013 is the result of our systematic analysis on three basic characteristics: earnings strength, relative valuation, and recent stock price movement. The company has generated a negative trend in earnings per share over the past 5 quarters. However, while recent estimates for the company have been lowered by analysts, H has posted better than expected results. Based on operating earnings yield, the company is overvalued when compared to all of the companies in our coverage universe. Share price changes over the past year indicates that H will perform poorly over the near term.

Financial Data
(US$ in Thousands)

	12/31/2012	12/31/2011	12/31/2010	12/31/2009	12/31/2008	12/31/2007	12/31/2006
Earnings Per Share	0.53	0.67	0.32	(0.30)	1.31	2.01	2.29
Cash Flow Per Share	3.02	2.33	2.58	1.82	2.24	2.69	...
Tang Book Value Per Share	26.53	26.38	27.23	26.57	26.60	23.97	...
Income Statement							
Total Revenue	3,949,000	3,698,000	3,527,000	3,332,000	3,837,000	3,738,000	3,471,000
EBITDA	470,000	399,000	405,000	219,000	511,100	649,400	667,600
Depn & Amortn	327,000	288,000	265,000	255,000	233,200	201,300	181,800
Income Before Taxes	117,000	79,000	128,000	(47,000)	190,000	463,000	511,000
Income Taxes	8,000	(28,000)	37,000	(10,000)	90,000	208,000	193,000
Net Income	88,000	113,000	66,000	(43,000)	168,000	270,000	315,000
Average Shares	165,377	169,240	174,354	151,486	128,061	134,634	137,558
Balance Sheet							
Current Assets	1,758,000	1,591,000	2,165,000	1,989,000	1,057,000	1,065,000	...
Total Assets	7,640,000	7,507,000	7,243,000	7,155,000	6,119,000	6,248,000	...
Current Liabilities	618,000	568,000	596,000	495,000	653,000	697,000	...
Long-Term Obligations	1,229,000	1,221,000	714,000	840,000	1,209,000	1,288,000	...
Total Liabilities	2,819,000	2,689,000	2,125,000	2,139,000	2,555,000	2,814,000	...
Stockholders' Equity	4,821,000	4,818,000	5,118,000	5,016,000	3,564,000	3,434,000	...
Shares Outstanding	162,066	165,162	173,953	173,875	119,830	119,823	...
Statistical Record							
Return on Assets %	1.16	1.53	0.92	N.M.	2.71	...	...
Return on Equity %	1.82	2.27	1.30	N.M.	4.79	...	...
EBITDA Margin %	11.90	10.79	11.48	6.57	13.32	17.37	19.23
Net Margin %	2.23	3.06	1.87	N.M.	4.38	7.22	9.08
Asset Turnover	0.52	0.50	0.49	0.50	0.62	...	...
Current Ratio	2.84	2.80	3.63	4.02	1.62	1.53	...
Debt to Equity	0.25	0.25	0.14	0.17	0.34	0.38	...
Price Range	44.10-33.74	49.57-29.79	46.19-28.63	30.31-27.90	...	...	...
P/E Ratio	83.21-63.66	73.99-44.46	144.34-89.47	...	...	...	...

Address: 71 South Wacker Drive, 12th Floor, Chicago, IL 60606
Telephone: 312-750-1234

Web Site: www.hyatt.com
Officers: Thomas J. Pritzker - Executive Chairman
Mark S. Hoplamazian - President, Chief Executive Officer

Auditors: Deloitte & Touche LLP
Investor Contact: 312-750-1234
Transfer Agents: Wells Fargo Shareowner Services, South St. Paul, MN

IDACORP, INC.

Exchange	Symbol	Price	52Wk Range	Yield	P/E
NYS	IDA	$48.27 (3/28/2013)	48.27-38.28	3.15	14.32

*7 Year Price Score 108.67 *NYSE Composite Index=100 *12 Month Price Score 100.88

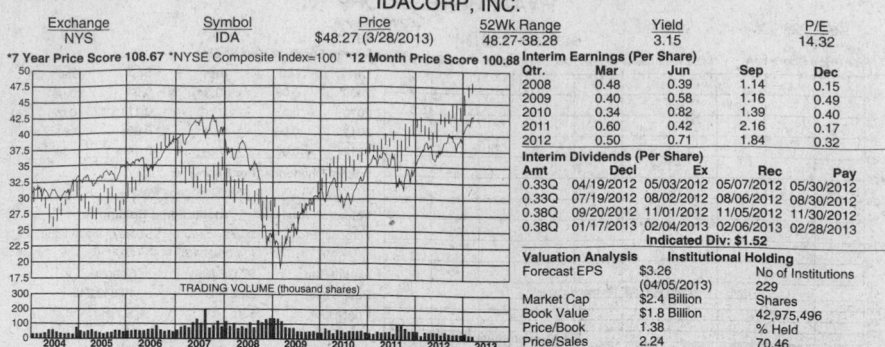

Interim Earnings (Per Share)

Qtr.	Mar	Jun	Sep	Dec
2008	0.48	0.39	1.14	0.15
2009	0.40	0.58	1.16	0.49
2010	0.34	0.82	1.39	0.40
2011	0.60	0.42	2.16	0.17
2012	0.50	0.71	1.84	0.32

Interim Dividends (Per Share)

Amt	Decl	Ex	Rec	Pay
0.33Q	04/19/2012	05/03/2012	05/07/2012	05/30/2012
0.33Q	07/19/2012	08/02/2012	08/06/2012	08/30/2012
0.38Q	09/20/2012	11/01/2012	11/05/2012	11/30/2012
0.38Q	01/17/2013	02/04/2013	02/06/2013	02/28/2013

Indicated Div: $1.52

Valuation Analysis **Institutional Holding**

Forecast EPS	$3.26	No of Institutions
	(04/05/2013)	229
Market Cap	$2.4 Billion	Shares
Book Value	$1.8 Billion	42,975,496
Price/Book	1.38	% Held
Price/Sales	2.24	70.46

Business Summary: Electric Utilities (MIC: 3.1.1 SIC: 4911 NAIC: 221122)

IDACORP is a holding company. Co.'s principal operating subsidiary is Idaho Power Company ("Idaho Power"). Idaho Power is an electric utility engaged in the generation, transmission, distribution, sale, and purchase of electric energy. Idaho Power's service territory covers southern Idaho and eastern Oregon. Idaho Power holds franchises, in the form of right-of-way arrangements, in 71 cities in Idaho and nine cities in Oregon and holds certificates from the respective public utility regulatory authorities to serve all or a portion of 25 counties in Idaho and three counties in Oregon. As of Dec 31 2012, Idaho Power supplied electric energy to approximately 501,000 business customers.

Recent Developments: For the year ended Dec 31 2012, net income increased 1.2% to US$168.9 million from US$166.9 million in the prior year. Revenues were US$1.08 billion, up 5.3% from US$1.03 billion the year before. Operating income was US$242.6 million versus US$155.4 million in the prior year, an increase of 56.2%. Direct operating expenses declined 4.1% to US$795.5 million from US$829.5 million in the comparable period the year before. Indirect operating expenses increased 1.4% to US$42.5 million from US$41.9 million in the equivalent prior-year period.

Prospects: Our evaluation of Idacorp Inc. as of Apr. 7, 2013 is the result of our systematic analysis on three basic characteristics: earnings strength, relative valuation, and recent stock price movement. The company has suffered a very negative trend in earnings per share over the past 5 quarters. Because the company lacks sufficient analyst estimate data, we place greater weight on the historical EPS trend as the measure of earnings strength. Based on operating earnings yield, the company is undervalued when compared to all of the companies in our coverage universe. Share price changes over the past year indicates that IDA will perform in line with the market over the near term.

Financial Data
(US$ in Thousands)

	12/31/2012	12/31/2011	12/31/2010	12/31/2009	12/31/2008	12/31/2007	12/31/2006	12/31/2005
Earnings Per Share	3.37	3.36	2.95	2.64	2.17	1.86	2.51	1.50
Cash Flow Per Share	4.98	6.27	6.34	6.04	3.02	1.83	3.97	3.82
Tang Book Value Per Share	34.71	32.78	30.56	28.67	27.20	26.14	24.95	23.35
Dividends Per Share	1.370	1.200	1.200	1.200	1.200	1.200	1.200	1.200
Dividend Payout %	40.65	35.71	40.68	45.45	55.30	64.52	47.81	80.00
Income Statement								
Total Revenue	1,080,662	1,026,756	1,036,029	1,049,800	960,414	879,394	926,291	859,488
EBITDA	393,185	305,246	329,756	331,206	296,753	267,240	279,164	238,950
Depn & Amortn	123,941	119,789	115,921	110,626	102,086	103,072	99,824	101,485
Income Before Taxes	195,375	113,931	138,721	147,770	121,611	100,827	118,365	77,294
Income Taxes	26,113	(52,133)	(731)	22,362	19,200	13,731	15,377	12,920
Net Income	168,761	166,694	142,798	124,350	98,414	82,339	107,403	63,661
Average Shares	50,010	49,558	48,340	47,182	45,332	44,291	42,874	42,279
Balance Sheet								
Current Assets	367,253	310,972	460,635	310,406	266,284	266,707	266,531	297,520
Total Assets	5,319,516	4,960,609	4,676,055	4,238,727	4,022,845	3,653,308	3,445,130	3,364,126
Current Liabilities	351,303	368,247	449,059	218,229	395,668	375,315	410,334	293,585
Long-Term Obligations	1,466,632	1,387,550	1,488,287	1,409,730	1,183,451	1,156,880	928,648	1,023,580
Total Liabilities	3,560,763	3,302,955	3,143,942	2,841,392	2,720,408	2,445,993	2,320,947	2,338,875
Stockholders' Equity	1,758,753	1,657,654	1,532,113	1,397,335	1,302,437	1,207,315	1,124,183	1,025,251
Shares Outstanding	50,156	49,951	49,405	47,896	46,920	45,062	43,833	42,417
Statistical Record								
Return on Assets %	3.27	3.46	3.20	3.01	2.56	2.32	3.15	1.93
Return on Equity %	9.85	10.45	9.75	9.21	7.82	7.06	9.99	6.26
EBITDA Margin %	36.38	29.73	31.83	31.55	30.90	30.39	30.14	27.80
Net Margin %	15.62	16.23	13.78	11.85	10.25	9.36	11.59	7.41
Asset Turnover	0.21	0.21	0.23	0.25	0.25	0.25	0.27	0.26
Current Ratio	1.05	0.84	1.03	1.42	0.67	0.71	0.65	1.01
Debt to Equity	0.83	0.84	0.97	1.01	1.01	0.91	0.83	1.00
Price Range	44.80-38.28	42.55-34.31	37.62-30.44	32.63-21.02	35.22-23.82	39.09-30.49	40.12-29.88	32.00-26.53
P/E Ratio	13.29-11.36	12.66-10.21	12.75-10.32	12.36-7.96	16.23-10.98	21.02-16.39	15.98-11.90	21.33-17.69
Average Yield %	3.28	3.21	3.10	3.44	4.46	3.96	3.54	4.10

Address: 1221 W. Idaho Street, Boise, ID 83702-5627 **Telephone:** 208-388-2200	**Web Site:** www.idacorpinc.com **Officers:** Jon H. Miller - Chairman J. Lamont Keen - President, Chief Executive Officer	**Auditors:** Deloitte & Touche LLP **Investor Contact:** 208-388-2664 **Transfer Agents:** Wells Fargo Shareowner Services, South St. Paul, MN

IDEX CORPORATION

Exchange	Symbol	Price	52Wk Range	Yield	P/E
NYS	IEX	$53.42 (3/28/2013)	53.62-36.00	1.50	118.71

*7 Year Price Score 110.77 *NYSE Composite Index=100 ***12 Month Price Score 108.04**

Interim Earnings (Per Share)

Qtr.	Mar	Jun	Sep	Dec
2008	0.50	0.56	0.23	0.31
2009	0.28	0.34	0.37	0.41
2010	0.45	0.49	0.47	0.50
2011	0.57	0.60	0.58	0.57
2012	0.62	0.65	0.60	(1.42)

Interim Dividends (Per Share)

Amt	Decl	Ex	Rec	Pay
0.20Q	04/10/2012	04/18/2012	04/20/2012	04/30/2012
0.20Q	06/25/2012	07/12/2012	07/16/2012	07/31/2012
0.20Q	09/25/2012	10/11/2012	10/15/2012	10/31/2012
0.20Q	12/06/2012	01/09/2013	01/11/2013	01/31/2013

Indicated Div: $0.80

Valuation Analysis

		Institutional Holding	
Forecast EPS	$2.94	No of Institutions	
	(04/05/2013)	341	
Market Cap	$4.4 Billion	Shares	
Book Value	$1.5 Billion	86,218,768	
Price/Book	3.02	% Held	
Price/Sales	2.26	98.99	

Business Summary: Industrial Machinery & Equipment (MIC: 7.2.1 SIC: 3561 NAIC: 333911)

IDEX sells pumps, flow meters and other fluidics systems and components and engineered products. Co. has four segments: Fluid & Metering Technologies, which designs, produces and distributes positive displacement pumps, flow meters, injectors, and other fluid-handling pump modules and systems; Health & Science Technologies, which designs, produces and distributes fluidics, roll compaction and drying systems; and Fire & Safety/Diversified Products, which produces firefighting pumps and controls, rescue tools, lifting bags and stainless steel banding and clamping devices.

Recent Developments: For the year ended Dec 31 2012, net income decreased 80.6% to US$37.6 million from US$193.9 million in the prior year. Revenues were US$1.95 billion, up 6.3% from US$1.84 billion the year before. Operating income was US$128.2 million versus US$304.7 million in the prior year, a decrease of 57.9%. Direct operating expenses rose 4.6% to US$1.15 billion from US$1.10 billion in the comparable period the year before. Indirect operating expenses increased 55.6% to US$675.5 million from US$434.0 million in the equivalent prior-year period.

Prospects: Our evaluation of IDEX Corp. as of Apr. 7, 2013 is the result of our systematic analysis on three basic characteristics: earnings strength, relative valuation, and recent stock price movement. The company has managed to produce a neutral trend in earnings per share over the past 5 quarters and while recent estimates for the company have been mixed, IEX has posted better than expected results. Based on operating earnings yield, the company is about fairly valued when compared to all of the companies in our coverage universe. Share price changes over the past year indicates that IEX will perform well over the near term.

Financial Data
(US$ in Thousands)

	12/31/2012	12/31/2011	12/31/2010	12/31/2009	12/31/2008	12/31/2007	12/31/2006	12/31/2005
Earnings Per Share	0.45	2.32	1.90	1.40	1.60	1.89	1.81	1.39
Cash Flow Per Share	3.93	2.64	2.29	2.67	2.76	2.46	2.01	1.88
Tang Book Value Per Share	N.M.	N.M.	N.M.	N.M.	N.M.	N.M.	N.M.	1.29
Dividends Per Share	0.770	0.660	0.570	0.480	0.480	0.460	0.380	0.320
Dividend Payout %	171.11	28.45	30.00	34.29	30.00	24.34	20.96	23.08
Income Statement								
Total Revenue	1,954,258	1,838,451	1,513,073	1,329,661	1,489,471	1,358,631	1,154,940	1,043,275
EBITDA	169,939	338,717	273,765	210,501	235,165	268,239	222,377	184,059
Depn & Amortn	41,485	35,504	25,741	24,496	17,610	9,722	4,131	708
Income Before Taxes	86,204	273,881	231,874	168,827	198,703	235,164	201,893	168,928
Income Taxes	48,574	80,024	74,774	55,436	67,343	79,300	68,171	59,125
Net Income	37,630	193,857	157,100	113,391	131,360	155,145	146,671	109,803
Average Shares	83,641	83,543	81,983	80,727	82,320	82,086	80,976	79,080
Balance Sheet								
Current Assets	881,865	789,161	692,758	451,712	505,205	637,138	417,908	347,501
Total Assets	2,785,390	2,836,107	2,381,695	2,098,157	2,176,317	1,989,594	1,670,821	1,244,180
Current Liabilities	291,427	258,278	353,668	189,682	219,255	198,953	187,252	153,296
Long-Term Obligations	779,241	806,366	408,450	391,754	548,144	448,901	353,770	156,899
Total Liabilities	1,320,392	1,322,972	1,006,035	830,053	1,008,755	826,871	691,549	421,170
Stockholders' Equity	1,464,998	1,513,135	1,375,660	1,268,104	1,167,562	1,162,723	979,272	823,010
Shares Outstanding	82,726	83,233	82,069	80,970	80,302	81,579	80,545	79,190
Statistical Record								
Return on Assets %	1.34	7.43	7.01	5.31	6.29	8.48	10.06	9.04
Return on Equity %	2.52	13.42	11.88	9.31	11.24	14.49	16.28	14.29
EBITDA Margin %	8.70	18.42	18.09	15.83	15.79	19.74	19.25	17.64
Net Margin %	1.93	10.54	10.38	8.53	8.82	11.42	12.70	10.52
Asset Turnover	0.69	0.70	0.68	0.62	0.71	0.74	0.79	0.86
Current Ratio	3.03	3.06	1.96	2.38	2.30	3.20	2.23	2.27
Debt to Equity	0.53	0.53	0.30	0.31	0.47	0.39	0.36	0.19
Price Range	46.53-36.00	47.08-29.80	40.04-27.85	32.42-16.74	40.71-18.30	41.50-30.74	35.43-27.16	30.13-24.65
P/E Ratio	103.40-80.00	20.29-12.84	21.07-14.66	23.16-11.96	25.44-11.44	21.96-16.26	19.57-15.01	21.68-17.73
Average Yield %	1.88	1.67	1.71	1.87	1.53	1.28	1.23	1.18

Address: 1925 West Field Court, Lake Forest, IL 60045	Web Site: www.idexcorp.com	Auditors: Deloitte & Touche LLP
Telephone: 847-498-7070	Officers: Andrew K. Silvernail - Chief Executive Officer Harold Morgan - Vice President	Investor Contact: 847-498-7070
		Transfer Agents: BNY Mellon Shareowner Services, Chicago, IL

IHS INC

Exchange	Symbol	Price	52Wk Range	Yield	P/E
NYS	IHS	$104.72 (3/28/2013)	118.63-84.39	N/A	44.00

*7 Year Price Score 141.07 *NYSE Composite Index=100 ***12 Month Price Score 96.64**

TRADING VOLUME (thousand shares)

Interim Earnings (Per Share)

Qtr.	Feb	May	Aug	Nov
2009-10	0.42	0.60	0.53	0.63
2010-11	0.47	0.59	0.60	0.40
2011-12	0.35	0.66	0.66	0.69
2012-13	0.37	...	...	...

Interim Dividends (Per Share)

No Dividends Paid

Valuation Analysis | Institutional Holding

Forecast EPS	$4.34	No of Institutions	
	(04/05/2013)	320	
Market Cap	$6.9 Billion	Shares	
Book Value	$1.5 Billion	65,273,192	
Price/Book	4.46	% Held	
Price/Sales	4.38	89.44	

Business Summary: Business Services (MIC: 7.5.2 SIC: 7375 NAIC: 519190)

IHS is a source of information in areas that shape business landscape. Businesses and governments in more than 165 countries rely on the content, analysis and delivery methods of Co. to make decisions and develop strategies. Co. is organized by geographies into three business segments: Americas, which includes the U.S., Canada, and Latin America; EMEA, which includes Europe, the Middle East, and Africa; and APAC, or Asia Pacific. Co. provides services within five customer workflows, which are Strategy, Planning, and Analysis; Energy Technical; Product Design; Supply Chain; and Environment, Health, Safety and Sustainability. Co. also sells its products to government agencies and entities.

Recent Developments: For the quarter ended Feb 28 2013, net income increased 5.1% to US$24.7 million from US$23.5 million in the year-earlier quarter. Revenues were US$382.5 million, up 11.6% from US$342.7 million the year before. Operating income was US$36.4 million versus US$35.1 million in the prior-year quarter, an increase of 3.8%. Direct operating expenses rose 9.2% to US$160.1 million from US$146.6 million in the comparable period the year before. Indirect operating expenses increased 15.5% to US$186.1 million from US$161.1 million in the equivalent prior-year period.

Prospects: Our evaluation of IHS Inc. as of Apr. 7, 2013 is the result of our systematic analysis on three basic characteristics: earnings strength, relative valuation, and recent stock price movement. The company has produced a positive trend in earnings per share over the past 5 quarters. However, while recent estimates for the company have been lowered by analysts, IHS has posted better than expected results. Based on operating earnings yield, the company is overvalued when compared to all of the companies in our coverage universe. Share price changes over the past year indicates that IHS will perform very well over the near term.

Financial Data

(US$ in Thousands)	3 Mos	11/30/2012	11/30/2011	11/30/2010	11/30/2009	11/30/2008	11/30/2007	11/30/2006
Earnings Per Share	2.38	2.37	2.06	2.18	2.11	1.57	1.39	0.99
Cash Flow Per Share	6.28	4.76	5.27	4.16	3.72	3.04	2.38	2.05
Tang Book Value Per Share	N.M.	N.M.	N.M.	N.M.	N.M.	N.M.	1.12	2.52
Income Statement								
Total Revenue	382,525	1,529,869	1,325,638	1,075,460	967,300	844,030	688,392	550,770
EBITDA	68,879	243,387	196,268	205,443	194,916	147,111	127,667	95,613
Depn & Amortn	32,479	36,100	23,800	18,700	15,100	13,600	11,400	15,714
Income Before Taxes	30,624	187,713	161,984	185,362	178,687	134,191	122,331	85,026
Income Taxes	5,953	29,564	26,695	43,994	41,580	38,512	38,827	26,879
Net Income	24,671	158,168	135,415	141,315	134,963	98,993	83,775	56,345
Average Shares	66,701	66,735	65,716	64,719	63,940	62,957	74,176	70,406
Balance Sheet								
Current Assets	876,072	863,883	698,078	552,734	413,234	317,817	402,247	380,922
Total Assets	3,567,949	3,549,211	3,073,037	2,155,702	1,675,588	1,436,180	1,323,807	944,301
Current Liabilities	978,457	876,937	816,857	578,268	549,177	545,926	392,395	338,471
Long-Term Obligations	882,723	890,922	658,911	275,095	141	...	37	74
Total Liabilities	2,029,042	1,964,853	1,688,308	979,621	661,910	635,125	482,899	379,110
Stockholders' Equity	1,538,907	1,584,358	1,384,729	1,176,081	1,013,678	801,055	840,908	565,191
Shares Outstanding	65,577	65,577	65,121	64,248	63,283	62,802	62,508	58,792
Statistical Record								
Return on Assets %	4.71	4.76	5.18	7.38	8.67	7.15	7.39	6.43
Return on Equity %	10.74	10.63	10.58	12.91	14.87	12.02	11.92	10.81
EBITDA Margin %	18.01	15.91	14.81	19.10	20.15	17.43	18.55	17.36
Net Margin %	6.45	10.34	10.22	13.14	13.95	11.73	12.17	10.23
Asset Turnover	0.46	0.46	0.51	0.56	0.62	0.61	0.61	0.63
Current Ratio	0.90	0.99	0.85	0.96	0.75	0.58	1.03	1.13
Debt to Equity	0.57	0.56	0.48	0.23	N.M.	...	N.M.	N.M.
Price Range	118.63-84.39	118.63-82.39	89.53-68.62	75.28-49.32	54.45-34.06	71.50-29.98	70.14-36.74	37.37-18.05
P/E Ratio	49.84-35.46	50.05-34.76	43.46-33.31	34.53-22.62	25.81-16.14	45.54-19.10	50.46-26.43	37.75-18.23

Address: 15 Inverness Way East, Englewood, CO 80112 Telephone: 303-790-0600	Web Site: www.ihs.com Officers: Jerre L. Stead - Chairman, Chief Executive Officer Scott Key - President, Senior Vice President, Chief Operating Officer	Auditors: Ernst & Young LLP Investor Contact: 303-397-2969 Transfer Agents: American Stock Transfer & Trust Company, New York, NY

ILLINOIS TOOL WORKS, INC.

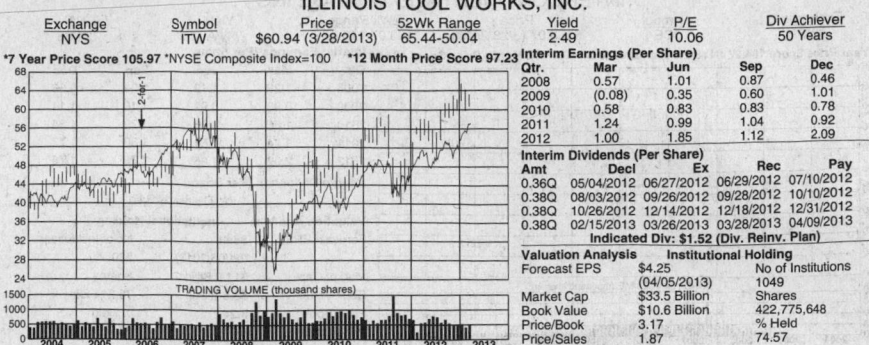

Exchange	Symbol	Price	52Wk Range	Yield	P/E	Div Achiever
NYS	ITW	$60.94 (3/28/2013)	65.44-50.04	2.49	10.06	50 Years

*7 Year Price Score 105.97 *NYSE Composite Index=100 *12 Month Price Score 97.23

Interim Earnings (Per Share)

Qtr.	Mar	Jun	Sep	Dec
2008	0.57	1.01	0.87	0.46
2009	(0.08)	0.35	0.60	1.01
2010	0.58	0.83	0.83	0.78
2011	1.24	0.99	1.04	0.92
2012	1.00	1.85	1.12	2.09

Interim Dividends (Per Share)

Amt	Decl	Ex	Rec	Pay
0.36Q	05/04/2012	06/27/2012	06/29/2012	07/10/2012
0.38Q	08/03/2012	09/26/2012	09/28/2012	10/10/2012
0.38Q	10/26/2012	12/14/2012	12/18/2012	12/31/2012
0.38Q	02/15/2013	03/26/2013	03/28/2013	04/09/2013

Indicated Div: $1.52 (Div. Reinv. Plan)

Valuation Analysis

		Institutional Holding	
Forecast EPS	$4.25	No of Institutions	
	(04/05/2013)	1049	
Market Cap	$33.5 Billion	Shares	
Book Value	$10.6 Billion	422,775,648	
Price/Book	3.17	% Held	
Price/Sales	1.87	74.57	

TRADING VOLUME (thousand shares)

Business Summary: Industrial Machinery & Equipment (MIC: 7.2.1 SIC: 3569 NAIC: 333999)

Illinois Tool Works manufactures industrial products and equipment. Co. operates in the following segments: Transportation, which produces components, fasteners, fluids and polymers; Power Systems & Electronics, which produces equipment and consumables associated with power conversion, metallurgy and electronics; Industrial Packaging, which produces steel, plastic and paper products and equipment; Food Equipment, which produces commercial food equipment and provides service; Construction Products, which produce construction fastening systems and truss products; Polymers & Fluids, which produces adhesives, sealants, and hygiene products; and All Other, which contains all other segments.

Recent Developments: For the year ended Dec 31 2012, income from continuing operations increased 23.7% to US$2.50 billion from US$2.02 billion a year earlier. Net income increased 38.6% to US$2.87 billion from US$2.07 billion in the prior year. Revenues were US$17.92 billion, up 0.8% from US$17.79 billion the year before. Operating income was US$2.85 billion versus US$2.73 billion in the prior year, an increase of 4.2%. Direct operating expenses declined 0.5% to US$11.46 billion from US$11.52 billion in the comparable period the year before. Indirect operating expenses increased 2.4% to US$3.62 billion from US$3.54 billion in the equivalent prior-year period.

Prospects: Our evaluation of Illinois Tool Works Inc. as of Apr. 7, 2013 is the result of our systematic analysis on three basic characteristics: earnings strength, relative valuation, and recent stock price movement. The company has generated a negative trend in earnings per share over the past 5 quarters. However, while recent estimates for the company have been lowered by analysts, ITW has posted results that were in line with analysts expectations. Based on operating earnings yield, the company is undervalued when compared to all of the companies in our coverage universe. Share price changes over the past year indicates that ITW will perform well over the near term.

Financial Data
(US$ in Thousands)

	12/31/2012	12/31/2011	12/31/2010	12/31/2009	12/31/2008	12/31/2007	12/31/2006	12/31/2005
Earnings Per Share	6.06	4.19	3.03	1.89	2.91	3.36	3.01	2.60
Cash Flow Per Share	4.40	3.98	3.12	4.29	4.27	4.50	3.65	3.23
Tang Book Value Per Share	5.05	5.35	5.62	4.43	2.78	6.92	6.94	6.89
Dividends Per Share	1.480	1.400	1.300	1.240	1.180	0.980	0.750	0.610
Dividend Payout %	24.42	33.41	42.90	65.61	40.55	29.17	24.92	23.46
Income Statement								
Total Revenue	17,924,000	17,786,583	15,870,376	13,877,048	15,869,354	16,170,611	14,055,049	12,921,792
EBITDA	3,487,000	3,336,416	2,913,307	2,035,248	2,990,379	3,184,402	2,943,859	2,623,780
Depn & Amortn	613,000	591,845	548,278	674,170	675,630	521,493	443,906	383,074
Income Before Taxes	3,633,000	2,592,714	2,211,993	1,213,790	2,191,366	2,580,979	2,445,246	2,181,569
Income Taxes	1,108,000	575,700	684,800	244,300	608,100	754,900	727,500	686,700
Net Income	2,870,000	2,071,384	1,527,193	947,009	1,519,003	1,869,862	1,717,746	1,494,869
Average Shares	473,200	494,646	503,350	501,921	521,213	556,030	569,892	575,434
Balance Sheet								
Current Assets	7,960,000	6,849,346	5,968,401	5,923,718	5,923,718	6,165,655	5,206,405	4,111,605
Total Assets	19,309,000	17,983,514	16,250,273	16,081,984	15,213,083	15,525,862	13,880,439	11,445,643
Current Liabilities	2,651,000	2,976,727	3,093,592	2,835,638	4,875,581	2,960,285	2,636,584	2,000,731
Long-Term Obligations	4,589,000	3,488,198	2,511,959	2,914,874	1,243,693	1,888,839	955,610	958,321
Total Liabilities	8,748,000	7,965,723	6,879,997	7,273,777	7,549,608	6,174,537	4,862,931	3,898,748
Stockholders' Equity	10,561,000	10,017,791	9,370,276	8,808,207	7,663,475	9,351,325	9,017,508	7,546,895
Shares Outstanding	549,551	483,608	497,744	502,336	499,114	530,096	558,749	561,627
Statistical Record								
Return on Assets %	15.35	12.10	9.45	6.05	9.86	12.72	13.57	13.11
Return on Equity %	27.82	21.37	16.80	11.50	17.81	20.36	20.74	19.70
EBITDA Margin %	19.45	18.76	18.36	14.67	18.84	19.69	20.95	20.31
Net Margin %	16.01	11.65	9.62	6.82	9.57	11.56	12.22	11.57
Asset Turnover	0.96	1.04	0.98	0.89	1.03	1.10	1.11	1.13
Current Ratio	3.00	2.30	1.93	2.00	1.21	2.08	1.97	2.06
Debt to Equity	0.43	0.35	0.27	0.33	0.16	0.20	0.11	0.13
Price Range	62.95-47.79	59.02-40.15	53.73-40.77	51.02-26.19	55.23-28.75	60.00-45.89	53.29-42.00	47.15-39.43
P/E Ratio	10.39-7.89	14.09-9.58	17.73-13.46	26.99-13.86	18.98-9.88	17.86-13.66	17.70-13.95	18.13-15.17
Average Yield %	2.61	2.74	2.79	3.20	2.61	1.82	1.61	1.42

Address: 3600 West Lake Avenue, Glenview, IL 60026-1215	Web Site: www.itw.com	Auditors: Deloitte & Touche LLP
Telephone: 847-724-7500	Officers: E. Scott Santi - Vice-Chairman, President, Chief Executive Officer, Acting Chief Executive Officer, Chief Operating Officer David C. Parry - Executive Vice President, Vice-Chairman	Investor Contact: 847-657-4104
		Transfer Agents: Computershare Investor Services LLC, Canton, MA

INTERCONTINENTALEXCHANGE INC

Exchange	Symbol	Price	52Wk Range	Yield	P/E
NYS	ICE	$163.07 (3/28/2013)	163.07-118.47	N/A	21.68

*7 Year Price Score 104.27 *NYSE Composite Index=100 *12 Month Price Score 104.90

Interim Earnings (Per Share)

Qtr.	Mar	Jun	Sep	Dec
2008	1.29	1.19	1.04	0.66
2009	0.98	0.97	1.18	1.14
2010	1.36	1.36	1.29	1.34
2011	1.74	1.64	1.80	1.73
2012	2.02	1.95	1.79	1.76

Interim Dividends (Per Share)

No Dividends Paid

Valuation Analysis		Institutional Holding	
Forecast EPS	$8.48	No of Institutions	
	(04/06/2013)	530	
Market Cap	$11.8 Billion	Shares	
Book Value	$3.6 Billion	75,214,224	
Price/Book	3.24	% Held	
Price/Sales	8.67	95.26	

Business Summary: Finance Intermediaries & Services (MIC: 5.5.1 SIC: 6231 NAIC: 523210)

IntercontinentalExchange is an operator of regulated markets and clearing houses, including futures exchanges, over-the-counter (OTC), markets, derivatives clearing houses and post-trade services. Co. operates these marketplaces for trading and clearing a range of energy, environmental and agricultural commodities, credit default swaps, equity indexes and currency contracts. Co. provides electronic platforms for the trading of products in both the futures and OTC markets together with clearing services, post-trade processing and market data. Through its distributed electronic markets, Co. brings together buyers and sellers of derivative and physical commodities and financial contracts.

Recent Developments: For the year ended Dec 31 2012, net income increased 7.7% to US$561.7 million from US$521.7 million in the prior year. Revenues were US$1.36 billion, up 2.7% from US$1.33 billion the year before. Operating income was US$827.0 million versus US$793.1 million in the prior year, an increase of 4.3%. Indirect operating expenses increased 0.3% to US$536.0 million from US$534.4 million in the equivalent prior-year period.

Prospects: Our evaluation of IntercontinentalExchange Inc. as of Apr. 7, 2013 is the result of our systematic analysis on three basic characteristics: earnings strength, relative valuation, and recent stock price movement. The company has managed to produce a neutral trend in earnings per share over the past 5 quarters and while recent estimates for the company have been raised by analysts, ICE has posted better than expected results. Based on operating earnings yield, the company is about fairly valued when compared to all of the companies in our coverage universe. Share price changes over the past year indicates that ICE will perform poorly over the near term.

Financial Data

(US$ in Thousands)	12/31/2012	12/31/2011	12/31/2010	12/31/2009	12/31/2008	12/31/2007	12/31/2006	12/31/2005
Earnings Per Share	7.52	6.90	5.35	4.27	4.17	3.39	2.40	(0.39)
Cash Flow Per Share	10.05	9.74	7.25	6.67	5.26	4.17	2.58	0.94
Tang Book Value Per Share	12.51	5.03	N.M.	3.15	N.M.	N.M.	6.42	2.82
Income Statement								
Total Revenue	1,362,965	1,327,491	1,149,944	994,788	813,078	574,293	313,799	155,865
EBITDA	888,368	848,824	687,694	560,366	513,933	388,410	215,009	69,318
Depn & Amortn	61,400	56,500	50,100	-45,700	32,400	23,200	10,800	11,800
Income Before Taxes	789,692	759,239	610,142	493,705	473,496	358,434	212,543	59,995
Income Taxes	227,955	237,498	202,375	179,551	172,524	117,822	69,275	19,585
Net Income	551,576	509,673	398,298	315,988	300,972	240,612	143,268	40,410
Average Shares	73,366	73,895	74,476	74,090	72,164	70,980	59,599	53,218
Balance Sheet								
Current Assets	33,750,087	32,605,391	23,575,778	19,459,851	12,552,588	1,142,094	340,917	164,015
Total Assets	37,214,842	36,147,864	26,642,259	21,884,875	14,959,581	2,796,345	493,211	265,770
Current Liabilities	32,245,697	31,800,314	23,127,384	18,967,832	12,311,642	910,961	37,899	26,394
Long-Term Obligations	969,500	837,500	325,750	208,500	332,500	184,375	...	...
Total Liabilities	33,571,465	33,026,339	23,864,709	19,485,143	12,952,282	1,319,489	38,743	33,147
Stockholders' Equity	3,643,377	3,121,525	2,777,550	2,399,732	2,007,299	1,476,856	454,468	232,623
Shares Outstanding	72,474	72,425	73,303	73,489	72,364	69,711	58,125	55,511
Statistical Record								
Return on Assets %	1.50	1.62	1.64	1.72	3.38	14.63	37.75	17.08
Return on Equity %	16.26	17.28	15.39	14.34	17.23	24.92	41.70	21.14
EBITDA Margin %	65.18	63.94	59.80	56.33	63.21	67.63	68.52	44.47
Net Margin %	40.47	38.39	34.64	31.76	37.02	41.90	45.66	25.93
Asset Turnover	0.04	0.04	0.05	0.05	0.09	0.35	0.83	0.66
Current Ratio	1.05	1.03	1.02	1.03	1.02	1.25	9.00	6.21
Debt to Equity	0.27	0.27	0.12	0.09	0.17	0.12	...	...
Price Range	142.37-112.15	134.72-103.91	126.94-93.92	119.74-50.92	192.50-50.69	194.50-115.72	113.21-36.90	39.25-31.97
P/E Ratio	18.93-14.91	19.52-15.06	23.73-17.56	28.04-11.93	46.16-12.16	57.37-34.14	47.17-15.38	...

Address: 2100 RiverEdge Parkway, Suite 500, Atlanta, GA 30328 Telephone: 770-857-4700 Fax: 770-857-4755	Web Site: www.theice.com Officers: Jeffrey C. Sprecher - Chairman, Chief Executive Officer Charles A. Vice - President, Chief Operating Officer	Auditors: Ernst & Young LLP Investor Contact: 770-857-4726 Transfer Agents: Computershare Investor Services, Canton, MA

INERGY L.P.

Exchange	Symbol	Price	52Wk Range	Yield	P/E
NYS	NRGY	$20.43 (3/28/2013)	21.94-15.69	6.51	4.80

*7 Year Price Score 59.15 ***NYSE Composite Index=100** ***12 Month Price Score 95.81**

Interim Earnings (Per Share)

Qtr.	Dec	Mar	Jun	Sep
2009-10	0.49	1.09	(0.79)	(1.12)
2010-11	0.72	0.30	(0.32)	(0.45)
2011-12	(0.03)	0.31	(0.17)	4.11
2012-13	0.01	...	...	...

Interim Dividends (Per Share)

Amt	Decl	Ex	Rec	Pay
0.375Q	07/26/2012	08/03/2012	08/07/2012	08/14/2012
0.00Q	08/21/2012	09/17/2012	08/29/2012	09/14/2012
0.29Q	10/26/2012	11/05/2012	11/07/2012	11/14/2012
0.29Q	01/25/2013	02/05/2013	02/07/2013	02/14/2013

Indicated Div: $1.33

Valuation Analysis / Institutional Holding

Forecast EPS	$0.20	No of Institutions
	(04/05/2013)	179
Market Cap	$2.7 Billion	Shares
Book Value	N/A	60,324,256
Price/Book	N/A	% Held
Price/Sales	1.51	44.56

TRADING VOLUME (thousand shares)

Business Summary: Equipment & Services (MIC: 9.1.3 SIC: 4612 NAIC: 221210)

Inergy is a partnership holding company that owns and operates energy midstream infrastructure and a natural gas liquids (NGL) marketing, supply and logistics business. Co.'s midstream infrastructure business consists of storage and transportation operations, which are conducted primarily through its subsidiary, Inergy Midstream, L.P. (Inergy Midstream). Co.'s NGL marketing, supply and logistics business utilizes its West Coast processing, fractionation and storage operations and other NGL facilities that it owns or controls. In addition, through Inergy Midstream, Co. owns US Salt, LLC, a mining and salt production company, which produces evaporated salt products.

Recent Developments: For the quarter ended Dec 31 2012, net income amounted to US$2.8 million versus a net loss of US$3.6 million in the year-earlier quarter. Revenues were US$438.6 million, down 34.4% from US$668.6 million the year before. Operating income was US$10.4 million versus US$48.1 million in the prior-year quarter, a decrease of 78.4%. Direct operating expenses declined 26.5% to US$358.6 million from US$487.8 million in the comparable period the year before. Indirect operating expenses decreased 47.6% to US$69.6 million from US$132.7 million in the equivalent prior-year period.

Prospects: Our evaluation of Inergy L.P. as of Apr. 7, 2013 is the result of our systematic analysis on three basic characteristics: earnings strength, relative valuation, and recent stock price movement. The company has suffered a very negative trend in earnings per share over the past 5 quarters. However, while recent estimates for the company have been lowered by analysts, NRGY has posted results that fell short of analysts expectations. Based on operating earnings yield, the company is overvalued when compared to all of the companies in our coverage universe. Share price changes over the past year indicates that NRGY will perform very well over the near term.

Financial Data
(US$ in Thousands)

	3 Mos	09/30/2012	09/30/2011	09/30/2010	09/30/2009	09/30/2008	09/30/2007	09/30/2006
Earnings Per Share	4.26	4.22	0.15	(0.37)	1.00	0.57	0.61	(0.20)
Cash Flow Per Share	1.89	1.91	1.08	2.72	4.46	3.68	3.52	2.52
Dividends Per Share	1.745	2.160	2.820	2.760	2.600	2.440	2.280	2.135
Dividend Payout %	40.96	51.18	1,880.00	...	260.00	428.07	373.77	...
Income Statement								
Total Revenue	438,600	2,006,800	2,153,800	1,786,000	1,570,600	1,878,900	1,483,100	1,387,561
EBITDA	50,600	799,100	258,200	266,100	262,000	201,800	179,400	118,920
Depn & Amortn	39,600	147,800	154,600	126,300	88,800	73,700	59,700	54,600
Income Before Taxes	2,900	567,700	(9,900)	48,800	103,500	67,200	67,700	10,478
Income Taxes	100	1,800	700	100	700	700	700	667
Net Income	1,300	554,900	17,600	48,000	101,400	65,100	67,000	9,811
Average Shares	131,582	131,589	117,684	64,533	53,736	49,851	47,875	41,407
Balance Sheet								
Current Assets	316,900	278,500	427,400	1,015,000	246,800	372,100	298,600	295,586
Total Assets	2,678,900	2,207,600	3,340,900	3,097,100	2,133,100	2,137,600	1,744,400	1,639,035
Current Liabilities	237,800	239,000	309,800	232,400	257,200	449,100	310,800	308,249
Long-Term Obligations	1,024,200	739,800	1,845,600	1,661,100	1,071,300	1,046,100	684,700	642,804
Total Liabilities	1,565,300	1,161,400	2,194,900	1,907,800	1,333,700	1,499,800	1,003,200	962,883
Shares Outstanding	131,740	131,677	131,313	77,731	59,807	50,715	49,764	45,005
Statistical Record								
Return on Assets %	18.49	19.95	0.55	1.84	4.75	3.34	3.96	0.62
EBITDA Margin %	11.54	39.82	11.99	14.90	16.68	10.74	12.10	8.57
Net Margin %	0.30	27.65	0.82	2.69	6.46	3.46	4.52	0.71
Asset Turnover	0.59	0.72	0.67	0.68	0.74	0.97	0.88	0.88
Current Ratio	1.33	1.17	1.38	4.37	0.96	0.83	0.96	0.96
Price Range	24.42-15.69	28.74-15.69	42.03-25.02	43.78-28.98	30.44-13.23	34.90-20.82	37.85-26.91	28.83-24.90
P/E Ratio	5.73-3.68	6.81-3.72	280.20-166.80	...	30.44-13.23	61.23-36.53	62.05-44.11	...
Average Yield %	9.27	10.61	7.67	7.57	11.34	8.55	7.08	7.95

Address: Two Brush Creek Boulevard, Suite 200, Kansas City, MO 64112
Telephone: 816-842-8181

Web Site: www.inergylp.com
Officers: John J. Sherman - President, Chief Executive Officer R. Brooks Sherman - President, Executive Vice President, Senior Vice President, Chief Financial Officer

Auditors: Ernst & Young LLP
Investor Contact: 816-842-8181
Transfer Agents: American Stock Transfer & Trust Company, New York, NY

INGERSOLL-RAND PLC

Exchange	Symbol	Price	52Wk Range	Yield	P/E
NYS	IR	$55.01 (3/28/2013)	56.47-38.64	1.53	16.77

*7 Year Price Score 105.43 ***NYSE Composite Index=100** ***12 Month Price Score 106.56**

Interim Earnings (Per Share)

Qtr.	Mar	Jun	Sep	Dec
2008	0.66	0.88	0.70	(10.97)
2009	(0.08)	0.38	0.65	0.41
2010	0.00	0.58	0.68	0.62
2011	(0.22)	0.26	0.25	0.72
2012	0.31	1.16	1.03	0.78

Interim Dividends (Per Share)

Amt	Decl	Ex	Rec	Pay
0.16Q	08/03/2012	09/11/2012	09/13/2012	09/28/2012
0.16Q	10/03/2012	12/12/2012	12/14/2012	12/28/2012
0.21Q	12/07/2012	03/08/2013	03/12/2013	03/28/2013
0.21Q	04/03/2013	06/12/2013	06/14/2013	06/28/2013

Indicated Div: $0.84

Valuation Analysis		Institutional Holding	
Forecast EPS	$3.60 (04/06/2013)	No of Institutions	N/A
Market Cap	$16.3 Billion	Shares	
Book Value	$7.1 Billion	N/A	
Price/Book	2.27	% Held	
Price/Sales	1.16	N/A	

Business Summary: Industrial Machinery & Equipment (MIC: 7.2.1 SIC: 3585 NAIC: 333415)

Ingersoll-Rand is engaged in the design, manufacture, sale and service of industrial and commercial products that include brand names such as Club Car®, Ingersoll-Rand®, Schlage®, Thermo King®, and Trane®. Co. has four business segments: Climate Solutions, which provides refrigeration and heating, ventilation and air conditioning (HVAC) products; Residential Solutions, which provides mechanical and electronic locks, HVAC systems, and portable security systems; Industrial Technologies, which provides compressed air systems, tools, pumps, and material handling equipment; and Security Technologies, which provides electronic and biometric access control systems and software, and exit devices.

Recent Developments: For the year ended Dec 31 2012, income from continuing operations increased 146.4% to US$1.05 billion from US$426.1 million a year earlier. Net income increased 182.7% to US$1.04 billion from US$369.3 million in the prior year. Revenues were US$14.03 billion, down 5.1% from US$14.78 billion the year before. Operating income was US$1.51 billion versus US$860.3 million in the prior year, an increase of 75.0%. Direct operating expenses declined 7.0% to US$9.76 billion from US$10.49 billion in the comparable period the year before. Indirect operating expenses decreased 19.2% to US$2.77 billion from US$3.43 billion in the equivalent prior-year period.

Prospects: Our evaluation of Ingersoll-Rand Plc. as of Apr. 7, 2013 is the result of our systematic analysis on three basic characteristics: earnings strength, relative valuation, and recent stock price movement. The company has generated a negative trend in earnings per share over the past 5 quarters and while recent estimates for the company have been mixed, IR has posted better than expected results. Based on operating earnings yield, the company is undervalued when compared to all of the companies in our coverage universe. Share price changes over the past year indicates that IR will perform well over the near term.

Financial Data
(US$ in Thousands)

	12/31/2012	12/31/2011	12/31/2010	12/31/2009	12/31/2008	12/31/2007	12/31/2006	12/31/2005
Earnings Per Share	3.28	1.01	1.89	1.37	(8.73)	13.43	3.20	3.09
Cash Flow Per Share	3.88	3.65	2.14	5.40	1.10	3.08	3.04	2.40
Tang Book Value Per Share	N.M.	N.M.	N.M.	N.M.	N.M.	11.70	0.21	1.47
Dividends Per Share	0.640	0.430	0.280	0.500	0.720	0.720	0.680	...
Dividend Payout %	19.51	42.51	14.81	36.50	...	5.36	21.25	...
Income Statement								
Total Revenue	14,034,900	14,782,000	14,079,100	13,195,300	13,227,400	8,763,100	11,409,300	10,546,900
EBITDA	1,758,600	1,107,100	1,524,900	1,102,000	(2,408,400)	1,163,100	1,610,200	1,610,500
Depn & Amortn	238,800	236,200	261,800	262,100	201,200	112,300	163,500	195,700
Income Before Taxes	1,282,600	616,800	995,100	551,000	(2,759,400)	950,800	1,314,900	1,270,500
Income Taxes	227,000	187,200	224,800	71,300	(208,600)	204,400	231,700	204,700
Net Income	1,018,600	343,200	642,200	451,300	(2,624,800)	3,966,700	1,032,500	1,054,200
Average Shares	310,600	339,300	339,800	329,100	303,700	295,300	323,100	341,300
Balance Sheet								
Current Assets	4,942,700	5,182,600	5,370,700	4,827,300	5,399,700	7,700,700	4,095,900	4,248,200
Total Assets	18,492,900	18,754,200	19,990,900	19,991,000	20,924,500	14,376,200	12,145,900	11,756,400
Current Liabilities	4,161,300	4,124,500	4,224,900	3,978,200	5,511,400	3,235,700	3,613,600	3,199,700
Long-Term Obligations	2,269,300	2,879,300	2,922,300	3,219,900	2,773,700	712,700	905,200	1,184,300
Total Liabilities	11,345,100	11,826,600	12,009,900	12,889,200	14,263,100	6,468,300	6,741,100	5,994,400
Stockholders' Equity	7,147,800	6,927,600	7,981,000	7,101,800	6,661,400	7,907,900	5,404,800	5,762,000
Shares Outstanding	295,583	297,116	328,164	320,589	318,792	272,613	306,762	360,740
Statistical Record								
Return on Assets %	5.45	1.77	3.21	2.21	N.M.	29.91	8.64	9.10
Return on Equity %	14.43	4.60	8.52	6.56	N.M.	59.59	18.49	18.34
EBITDA Margin %	12.53	7.49	10.83	8.35	N.M.	13.27	14.11	15.27
Net Margin %	7.26	2.32	4.56	3.42	N.M.	45.27	9.05	10.00
Asset Turnover	0.75	0.76	0.70	0.65	0.75	0.66	0.95	0.91
Current Ratio	1.19	1.26	1.27	1.21	0.98	2.38	1.13	1.33
Debt to Equity	0.32	0.42	0.37	0.45	0.42	0.09	0.17	0.21
Price Range	48.87-31.86	52.08-26.48	47.36-31.26	37.23-11.84	46.58-12.08	55.99-38.75	47.63-35.29	43.66-35.40
P/E Ratio	14.90-9.71	51.56-26.22	25.06-16.54	27.18-8.64	...	4.17-2.89	14.88-11.03	14.13-11.46
Average Yield %	1.59	1.09	0.75	2.02	2.10	1.48	1.69	...

Address: 170/175 Lakeview Dr., Airside Business Park, Dublin Telephone: 018-707-400	Web Site: www.irco.com Officers: Michael W. Lamach - Chairman, President, Chief Executive Officer, Chief Operating Officer James R. Bolch - President, Senior Vice President	Auditors: PricewaterhouseCoopers LLP Investor Contact: 704-655-4469 Transfer Agents: The Bank of New York Mellon, New York, NY

INGRAM MICRO INC.

Exchange	Symbol	Price	52Wk Range	Yield	P/E
NYS	IM	$19.68 (3/28/2013)	20.14-14.46	N/A	9.89

*7 Year Price Score 86.13   *NYSE Composite Index=100   *12 Month Price Score 103.07

Interim Earnings (Per Share)

Qtr.	Mar	Jun	Sep	Dec
2008	0.37	0.35	0.27	(3.36)
2009	0.17	0.15	0.25	0.64
2010	0.42	0.41	0.41	0.71
2011	0.34	0.37	0.15	0.67
2012	0.58	0.40	0.35	0.66

Interim Dividends (Per Share)

No Dividends Paid

Valuation Analysis   Institutional Holding

Forecast EPS	$2.15	No of Institutions
	(04/06/2013)	292
Market Cap	$3.0 Billion	Shares
Book Value	$3.6 Billion	171,883,728
Price/Book	0.82	% Held
Price/Sales	0.08	92.08

Business Summary: Computer Hardware & Equipment (MIC: 6.2.1 SIC: 5045 NAIC: 423430)

Ingram Micro is engaged in the distribution of information technology (IT) products and supply chain, mobile device lifecycle services and logistics solutions. Co. operates in North America, Europe, Asia-Pacific, Middle East and Africa, and Latin America. Co.'s product categories include IT Peripherals; Systems; Software; and Networking. Co.'s services include: supply chain services; integration services; technical support; training services; financial and credit services; marketing services; analytics services; e-commerce services; reseller community hosting services; managed services; cloud services; managed print services; personnel services; and mobility logistics services.

Recent Developments: For the year ended Dec 29 2012, net income increased 25.2% to US$305.9 million from US$244.2 million in the prior year. Revenues were US$37.83 billion, up 4.1% from US$36.33 billion the year before. Operating income was US$462.4 million versus US$458.6 million in the prior year, an increase of 0.8%. Direct operating expenses rose 4.0% to US$35.79 billion from US$34.42 billion in the comparable period the year before. Indirect operating expenses increased 8.5% to US$1.57 billion from US$1.45 billion in the equivalent prior-year period.

Prospects: Our evaluation of Ingram Micro Inc. as of Apr. 7, 2013 is the result of our systematic analysis on three basic characteristics: earnings strength, relative valuation, and recent stock price movement. The company has generated a negative trend in earnings per share over the past 5 quarters. However, while recent estimates for the company have been mixed, IM has posted better than expected results. Based on operating earnings yield, the company is undervalued when compared to all of the companies in our coverage universe. Share price changes over the past year indicates that IM will perform poorly over the near term.

Financial Data
(US$ in Thousands)

	12/29/2012	12/31/2011	01/01/2011	01/02/2010	01/03/2009	12/29/2007	12/30/2006	12/31/2005
Earnings Per Share	1.99	1.53	1.94	1.22	(2.37)	1.56	1.56	1.32
Cash Flow Per Share	0.30	1.90	1.12	1.48	3.27	1.67	0.31	0.05
Tang Book Value Per Share	18.70	21.40	19.90	18.32	16.46	15.57	13.44	11.09
Income Statement								
Total Revenue	37,827,299	36,328,701	34,588,984	29,515,446	34,362,152	35,047,089	31,357,477	28,808,312
EBITDA	462,369	491,989	534,011	356,927	(267,523)	504,705	474,145	410,983
Depn & Amortn	20,711	57,282	61,549	68,590	68,404	64,078	61,187	64,338
Income Before Taxes	396,184	387,871	438,061	269,248	(382,138)	385,238	367,333	301,937
Income Taxes	90,275	143,631	120,001	67,110	12,783	109,330	101,567	85,031
Net Income	305,909	244,240	318,060	202,138	(394,921)	275,908	265,766	216,906
Average Shares	153,717	159,588	163,861	165,565	166,542	176,951	170,875	164,331
Balance Sheet								
Current Assets	10,166,379	8,618,402	8,590,088	7,746,905	6,674,837	7,920,667	6,746,073	6,071,298
Total Assets	11,480,448	9,146,516	9,084,032	8,179,350	7,083,473	8,975,001	7,704,307	7,034,990
Current Liabilities	6,761,831	5,509,875	5,235,186	4,796,660	4,034,659	5,087,611	4,467,781	4,105,484
Long-Term Obligations	943,275	300,000	531,127	302,424	356,664	387,500	270,714	455,650
Total Liabilities	7,869,195	5,873,739	5,842,850	5,167,537	4,427,628	5,548,059	4,783,832	4,596,392
Stockholders' Equity	3,611,253	3,272,777	3,241,182	3,011,813	2,655,845	3,426,942	2,920,475	2,438,598
Shares Outstanding	150,320	149,484	158,745	164,383	161,330	172,942	169,408	162,366
Statistical Record								
Return on Assets %	2.97	2.69	3.69	2.66	N.M.	3.32	3.62	3.12
Return on Equity %	8.91	7.52	10.20	7.15	N.M.	8.72	9.95	9.30
EBITDA Margin %	1.22	1.35	1.54	1.21	N.M.	1.44	1.51	1.43
Net Margin %	0.81	0.67	0.92	0.68	N.M.	0.79	0.85	0.75
Asset Turnover	3.68	4.00	4.02	3.88	4.21	4.21	4.27	4.14
Current Ratio	1.50	1.56	1.64	1.62	1.65	1.56	1.51	1.48
Debt to Equity	0.26	0.09	0.16	0.10	0.13	0.11	0.09	0.19
Price Range	19.72-14.46	21.50-15.75	19.25-14.87	18.80-9.82	19.95-9.29	22.02-18.10	21.00-16.64	20.80-14.66
P/E Ratio	9.91-7.27	14.05-10.29	9.92-7.66	15.41-8.05	...	14.12-11.60	13.46-10.67	15.76-11.11

Address: 1600 E. St. Andrew Place, Santa Ana, CA 92705-4926
Telephone: 714-566-1000
Fax: 714-566-7604

Web Site: www.ingrammicro.com
Officers: Dale R. Laurance - Chairman Alain Monie - President, Chief Operating Officer

Auditors: PricewaterhouseCoopers LLP
Investor Contact: 714-382-5013
Transfer Agents: Computershare Trust Company, N.A., Providence, RI

INGREDION INC

Exchange	Symbol	Price	52Wk Range	Yield	P/E
NYS	INGR	$72.32 (3/28/2013)	72.32-45.59	2.10	13.22

*7 Year Price Score 127.48 *NYSE Composite Index=100 *12 Month Price Score 105.32

Interim Earnings (Per Share)

Qtr.	Mar	Jun	Sep	Dec
2008	0.85	0.90	1.15	0.62
2009	0.22	(1.13)	0.70	0.74
2010	0.57	0.48	0.48	0.67
2011	1.97	1.01	1.12	1.22
2012	1.21	1.40	1.45	1.41

Interim Dividends (Per Share)

Amt	Decl	Ex	Rec	Pay
0.20Q	05/15/2012	06/28/2012	07/02/2012	07/25/2012
0.26Q	09/20/2012	10/01/2012	10/03/2012	10/25/2012
0.26Q	12/14/2012	12/27/2012	12/31/2012	01/25/2013
0.38Q	03/20/2013	03/27/2013	04/01/2013	04/25/2013

Indicated Div: $1.52

Valuation Analysis | **Institutional Holding**

Forecast EPS	$5.87	No of Institutions
	(04/05/2013)	444
Market Cap	$5.6 Billion	Shares
Book Value	$2.4 Billion	76,408,920
Price/Book	2.29	% Held
Price/Sales	0.85	N/A

Business Summary: Food (MIC: 1.2.1 SIC: 2046 NAIC: 311221)

Ingredion is a manufacturer and supplier of starch and sweetener ingredients to a range of industries such as packaged food, beverage, paper and corrugated products, textile and personal care, and corn oil markets. Co.'s product line includes starches and sweeteners, animal feed products and edible corn oils. Co.'s starch-based products include both foot-grade and industrial starches. Co.'s sweetener products include glucose corn syrups, high maltose corn syrups, high fructose corn syrup, caramel color, dextrose, polyols, maltodextrins and glucose and corn syrup solids. Co. has four reportable business segments: North America, South America, Asia Pacific and Europe, Middle East and Africa.

Recent Developments: For the year ended Dec 31 2012, net income increased 2.6% to US$434.0 million from US$423.0 million in the prior year. Revenues were US$6.53 billion, up 5.0% from US$6.22 billion the year before. Operating income was US$668.0 million versus US$671.0 million in the prior year, a decrease of 0.4%. Direct operating expenses rose 3.9% to US$5.29 billion from US$5.09 billion in the comparable period the year before. Indirect operating expenses increased 25.3% to US$570.0 million from US$455.0 million in the equivalent prior-year period.

Prospects: Our evaluation of Ingredion Inc as of Apr. 7, 2013 is the result of our systematic analysis on three basic characteristics: earnings strength, relative valuation, and recent stock price movement. The company has generated a negative trend in earnings per share over the past 5 quarters and while recent estimates for the company have been raised by analysts, INGR has posted better than expected results. Based on operating earnings yield, the company is undervalued when compared to all of the companies in our coverage universe. Share price changes over the past year indicates that INGR will perform poorly over the near term.

Financial Data

(US$ in Thousands)	12/31/2012	12/31/2011	12/31/2010	12/31/2009	12/31/2008	12/31/2007	12/31/2006	12/31/2005
Earnings Per Share	5.47	5.32	2.20	0.54	3.52	2.59	1.63	1.19
Cash Flow Per Share	9.54	3.93	5.21	7.82	(1.06)	3.45	3.10	3.28
Tang Book Value Per Share	20.13	15.75	12.85	19.49	14.03	16.35	13.36	11.93
Dividends Per Share	0.920	0.660	0.560	0.560	0.510	0.380	0.240	0.280
Dividend Payout %	16.82	12.41	25.45	103.70	14.49	14.67	14.72	23.53
Income Statement								
Total Revenue	6,532,000	6,219,000	4,367,000	3,672,000	3,944,000	3,391,000	2,621,000	2,360,000
EBITDA	874,000	880,000	492,000	277,000	571,000	468,000	338,000	285,000
Depn & Amortn	211,000	211,000	155,000	130,000	128,000	125,000	114,000	106,000
Income Before Taxes	596,000	593,000	275,000	115,000	405,000	305,000	196,000	147,000
Income Taxes	167,000	170,000	99,000	68,000	130,000	102,000	69,000	55,000
Net Income	428,000	416,000	169,000	41,000	267,000	198,000	124,000	90,000
Average Shares	78,200	78,200	76,800	75,500	75,900	76,500	75,800	75,564
Balance Sheet								
Current Assets	2,360,000	2,102,000	1,753,000	1,045,000	1,297,000	1,089,000	837,000	685,000
Total Assets	5,592,000	5,317,000	5,071,000	2,952,000	3,207,000	3,103,000	2,662,000	2,389,000
Current Liabilities	933,000	926,000	891,000	565,000	859,000	674,000	517,000	424,000
Long-Term Obligations	1,724,000	1,801,000	1,681,000	408,000	660,000	519,000	480,000	471,000
Total Liabilities	3,155,000	3,213,000	3,095,000	1,257,000	1,809,000	1,479,000	1,288,000	1,150,000
Stockholders' Equity	2,437,000	2,104,000	1,976,000	1,695,000	1,398,000	1,624,000	1,374,000	1,239,000
Shares Outstanding	77,031	75,882	76,023	74,386	74,043	73,250	74,302	73,791
Statistical Record								
Return on Assets %	7.83	8.01	4.21	1.33	8.44	6.87	4.91	3.78
Return on Equity %	18.80	20.39	9.21	2.65	17.62	13.21	9.49	7.65
EBITDA Margin %	13.38	14.15	11.27	7.54	14.48	13.80	12.90	12.08
Net Margin %	6.55	6.69	3.87	1.12	6.77	5.84	4.73	3.81
Asset Turnover	1.19	1.20	1.09	1.19	1.25	1.18	1.04	0.99
Current Ratio	2.53	2.27	1.97	1.85	1.51	1.62	1.62	1.62
Debt to Equity	0.71	0.86	0.85	0.24	0.47	0.32	0.35	0.38
Price Range	66.59-45.59	59.36-37.74	47.27-26.61	32.26-17.95	50.75-19.58	49.12-30.79	37.21-23.68	30.14-18.05
P/E Ratio	12.17-8.33	11.16-7.09	21.49-12.10	59.74-33.24	14.42-5.56	18.97-11.89	22.83-14.53	25.33-15.17
Average Yield %	1.65	1.33	1.56	2.23	1.37	0.95	0.78	1.17

Address: 5 Westbrook Corporate Center, Westchester, IL 60154	Web Site: www.cornproducts.com	Auditors: KPMG LLP
Telephone: 708-551-2600	Officers: Ilene S. Gordon - Chairman, President, Chief Executive Officer Cheryl K. Beebe - Executive Vice President, Chief Financial Officer	Investor Contact: 708-551-2592 Transfer Agents: The Bank of New York Mellon, New York, NY

INTEGRYS ENERGY GROUP INC

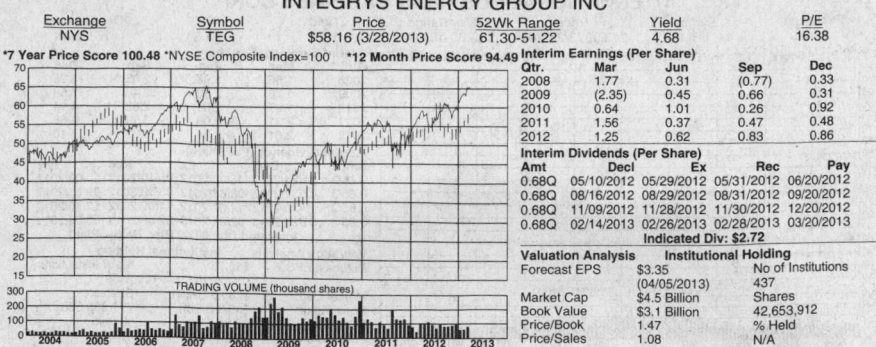

Exchange	Symbol	Price	52Wk Range	Yield	P/E
NYS	TEG	$58.16 (3/28/2013)	61.30-51.22	4.68	16.38

*7 Year Price Score 100.48 *NYSE Composite Index=100 *12 Month Price Score 94.49

Interim Earnings (Per Share)

Qtr.	Mar	Jun	Sep	Dec
2008	1.77	0.31	(0.77)	0.33
2009	(2.35)	0.45	0.66	0.31
2010	0.64	1.01	0.26	0.92
2011	1.56	0.37	0.47	0.48
2012	1.25	0.62	0.83	0.86

Interim Dividends (Per Share)

Amt	Decl	Ex	Rec	Pay
0.68Q	05/10/2012	05/29/2012	05/31/2012	06/20/2012
0.68Q	08/16/2012	08/29/2012	08/31/2012	09/20/2012
0.68Q	11/09/2012	11/28/2012	11/30/2012	12/20/2012
0.68Q	02/14/2013	02/26/2013	02/28/2013	03/20/2013

Indicated Div: $2.72

Valuation Analysis / **Institutional Holding**

Forecast EPS	$3.35	No of Institutions
	(04/05/2013)	437
Market Cap	$4.5 Billion	Shares
Book Value	$3.1 Billion	42,653,912
Price/Book	1.47	% Held
Price/Sales	1.08	N/A

Business Summary: Electric Utilities (MIC: 3.1.1 SIC: 4931 NAIC: 221111)

Integrys Energy Group is a holding company. Through its subsidiaries, Co. provides regulated electric and natural gas to residential, commercial and industrial, wholesale, and other customers, as well as non regulated retail energy supply and services to commercial, industrial, and residential customers. In addition, Co. has an approximate 34.0% interest in American Transmission Company LLC, which owns, maintains, monitors, and operates electric transmission assets in portions of Wisconsin, Michigan, Minnesota, and Illinois. Co. operates in five segments: natural gas utility, electric utility, Integrys Energy Services, electric transmission investment, and the holding company and other.

Recent Developments: For the year ended Dec 31 2012, income from continuing operations increased 27.8% to US$294.0 million from US$230.0 million a year earlier. Net income increased 23.3% to US$284.3 million from US$230.5 million in the prior year. Revenues were US$4.21 billion, down 10.1% from US$4.69 billion the year before. Operating income was US$467.5 million versus US$406.8 million in the prior year, an increase of 14.9%. Direct operating expenses declined 13.6% to US$3.40 billion from US$3.93 billion in the comparable period the year before. Indirect operating expenses increased 0.8% to US$347.1 million from US$344.5 million in the equivalent prior-year period.

Prospects: Our evaluation of Integrys Energy Group Inc. as of Apr. 7, 2013 is the result of our systematic analysis on three basic characteristics: earnings strength, relative valuation, and recent stock price movement. The company has generated a negative trend in earnings per share over the past 5 quarters. However, while recent estimates for the company have been lowered by analysts, TEG has posted results that fell short of analysts expectations. Based on operating earnings yield, the company is undervalued when compared to all of the companies in our coverage universe. Share price changes over the past year indicates that TEG will perform poorly over the near term.

Financial Data

(US$ in Thousands)	12/31/2012	12/31/2011	12/31/2010	12/31/2009	12/31/2008	12/31/2007	12/31/2006	12/31/2005
Earnings Per Share	3.55	2.87	2.83	(0.92)	1.64	3.50	3.67	4.07
Cash Flow Per Share	7.22	9.18	9.36	20.92	(3.25)	3.33	1.72	1.63
Tang Book Value Per Share	30.39	29.42	29.26	29.17	28.50	29.97	28.35	32.76
Dividends Per Share	2.720	2.720	2.720	2.720	2.680	2.563	2.280	2.240
Dividend Payout %	76.62	94.77	96.11	...	163.41	73.23	62.13	55.04
Income Statement								
Total Revenue	4,212,400	4,708,700	5,203,200	7,499,800	14,047,800	10,292,400	6,890,700	6,962,700
EBITDA	727,500	743,700	785,400	407,300	568,700	647,600	398,100	419,500
Depn & Amortn	250,700	250,100	265,800	230,900	234,700	216,100	106,100	142,800
Income Before Taxes	356,600	364,800	371,700	11,600	175,900	267,000	192,800	204,300
Income Taxes	149,800	133,900	148,200	83,200	51,200	86,000	45,000	46,700
Net Income	284,300	230,500	223,700	(68,800)	129,500	254,400	158,900	160,500
Average Shares	79,300	79,100	78,000	76,800	77,000	71,800	42,400	38,700
Balance Sheet								
Current Assets	1,659,100	1,803,300	2,050,400	3,512,200	5,890,800	3,726,300	2,927,400	2,507,800
Total Assets	10,327,400	9,983,200	9,816,800	11,847,900	14,272,500	11,234,400	6,861,700	5,455,200
Current Liabilities	1,813,300	1,646,700	1,657,800	3,147,600	5,714,000	3,248,200	2,906,400	2,331,800
Long-Term Obligations	1,931,700	1,872,000	2,161,600	2,394,700	2,288,000	2,265,100	1,287,200	867,100
Total Liabilities	7,250,500	6,970,700	6,859,900	8,938,200	11,121,800	7,947,500	5,277,000	4,099,900
Stockholders' Equity	3,076,900	3,012,500	2,956,900	2,909,700	3,150,700	3,286,900	1,584,700	1,355,300
Shares Outstanding	77,902	78,287	77,350	75,980	75,992	76,330	43,375	39,807
Statistical Record								
Return on Assets %	2.79	2.33	2.07	N.M.	1.01	2.81	2.58	3.24
Return on Equity %	9.31	7.72	7.63	N.M.	4.01	10.44	10.81	12.85
EBITDA Margin %	17.27	15.79	15.09	5.43	4.05	6.29	5.78	6.02
Net Margin %	6.75	4.90	4.30	N.M.	0.92	2.47	2.31	2.31
Asset Turnover	0.41	0.48	0.48	0.57	1.10	1.14	1.12	1.41
Current Ratio	0.91	1.10	1.24	1.12	1.03	1.15	1.01	1.08
Debt to Equity	0.63	0.62	0.73	0.82	0.73	0.69	0.81	0.64
Price Range	61.30-51.09	54.38-43.86	53.70-40.83	44.44-19.99	53.44-40.64	60.21-49.06	57.43-47.63	59.40-47.84
P/E Ratio	17.27-14.39	18.95-15.28	18.98-14.43	...	32.59-24.78	17.20-14.02	15.65-12.98	14.59-11.75
Average Yield %	5.00	5.41	5.71	8.07	5.54	4.82	4.43	4.10

Address: 130 East Randolph Street, Chicago, IL 60601-6207 **Telephone:** 312-228-5400	**Web Site:** www.integrysgroup.com **Officers:** Charles A. Schrock - Chairman, President, Chief Executive Officer Thomas P. Meinz - Executive Vice President, Chief External Affairs Officer	**Auditors:** Deloitte & Touche LLP **Investor Contact:** 920-433-1857 **Transfer Agents:** American Stock Transfer & Trust Company, LLC, Brooklyn, NY

INTERNATIONAL BUSINESS MACHINES CORP.

Exchange	Symbol	Price	52Wk Range	Yield	P/E	Div Achiever
NYS	IBM	$213.30 (3/28/2013)	215.80-183.09	1.59	14.84	17 Years

*7 Year Price Score 131.14 *NYSE Composite Index=100   *12 Month Price Score 95.37

Interim Earnings (Per Share)

Qtr.	Mar	Jun	Sep	Dec
2008	1.65	1.98	2.05	3.25
2009	1.70	2.32	2.40	3.59
2010	1.97	2.61	2.82	4.14
2011	2.31	3.00	3.19	4.58
2012	2.61	3.34	3.33	5.10

Interim Dividends (Per Share)

Amt	Decl	Ex	Rec	Pay
0.85Q	04/24/2012	05/08/2012	05/10/2012	06/09/2012
0.85Q	07/31/2012	08/08/2012	08/10/2012	09/10/2012
0.85Q	10/30/2012	11/07/2012	11/09/2012	12/10/2012
0.85Q	01/29/2013	02/06/2013	02/08/2013	03/09/2013

Indicated Div: $3.40 (Div. Reinv. Plan)

Valuation Analysis | **Institutional Holding**

Forecast EPS	$16.75 (04/06/2013)	No of Institutions	2139
Market Cap	$238.3 Billion	Shares	771,339,328
Book Value	$18.9 Billion	% Held	57.05
Price/Book	12.64		
Price/Sales	2.28		

TRADING VOLUME (thousand shares)

Business Summary: IT Services (MIC: 6.3.1 SIC: 7379 NAIC: 541519)

International Business Machines operates in five business segments: global technology services, which provides information technology infrastructure and business process services; global business services, which provides business outcomes across two business areas: Consulting and Application Management Services; software, which consists of middleware software that enables clients to integrate systems, processes and applications, and operating systems software; systems and technology, which provides clients with business applications requiring computing power and storage capabilities; and global financing, which facilitates clients' acquisition of Co.'s systems, software and services.

Recent Developments: For the year ended Dec 31 2012, net income increased 4.7% to US$16.60 billion from US$15.86 billion in the prior year. Revenues were US$104.51 billion, down 2.3% from US$106.92 billion the year before. Direct operating expenses declined 4.5% to US$54.21 billion from US$56.78 billion in the comparable period the year before. Indirect operating expenses were unchanged at US$29.85 billion versus the equivalent prior-year period.

Prospects: Our evaluation of International Business Machines Corp. as of Apr. 7, 2013 is the result of our systematic analysis on three basic characteristics: earnings strength, relative valuation, and recent stock price movement. The company has managed to produce a neutral trend in earnings per share over the past 5 quarters and while recent estimates for the company have remained steady, IBM has posted better than expected results. Based on operating earnings yield, the company is undervalued when compared to all of the companies in our coverage universe. Share price changes over the past year indicates that IBM will perform poorly over the near term.

Financial Data

(US$ in Thousands)	12/31/2012	12/31/2011	12/31/2010	12/31/2009	12/31/2008	12/31/2007	12/31/2006	12/31/2005
Earnings Per Share	14.37	13.06	11.52	10.01	8.93	7.18	6.11	4.87
Cash Flow Per Share	17.10	16.58	15.41	15.65	13.80	11.31	9.81	9.32
Tang Book Value Per Share	N.M.	N.M.	N.M.	N.M.	N.M.	8.72	8.93	13.97
Dividends Per Share	3.300	2.900	2.500	2.150	1.900	1.500	1.100	0.780
Dividend Payout %	22.96	22.21	21.70	21.48	21.28	20.89	18.00	16.02
Income Statement								
Total Revenue	104,507,000	106,916,000	99,870,000	95,758,000	103,630,000	98,786,000	91,424,000	91,134,000
EBITDA	26,928,000	26,093,000	24,830,000	23,440,000	22,495,000	19,736,000	18,042,000	17,327,000
Depn & Amortn	4,676,000	4,815,000	4,831,000	4,994,000	5,450,000	5,201,000	4,983,000	5,188,000
Income Before Taxes	21,902,000	21,003,000	19,723,000	18,138,000	16,715,000	14,489,000	13,317,000	12,226,000
Income Taxes	5,298,000	5,148,000	4,890,000	4,713,000	4,381,000	4,071,000	3,901,000	4,232,000
Net Income	16,604,000	15,855,000	14,833,000	13,425,000	12,334,000	10,418,000	9,492,000	7,934,000
Average Shares	1,155,449	1,213,767	1,287,355	1,341,352	1,381,773	1,450,570	1,553,535	1,627,632
Balance Sheet								
Current Assets	49,433,000	50,928,000	48,116,000	48,935,000	49,004,000	53,177,000	44,660,000	45,661,000
Total Assets	119,213,000	116,433,000	113,452,000	109,022,000	109,524,000	120,431,000	103,234,000	105,748,000
Current Liabilities	43,625,000	42,123,000	40,562,000	36,002,000	42,435,000	44,310,000	40,091,000	35,152,000
Long-Term Obligations	24,088,000	22,857,000	21,846,000	21,932,000	22,689,000	23,039,000	13,780,000	15,425,000
Total Liabilities	100,353,000	96,294,000	90,405,000	86,385,000	96,058,000	91,962,000	74,728,000	72,650,000
Stockholders' Equity	18,860,000	20,138,000	23,046,000	22,637,000	13,465,000	28,470,000	28,506,000	33,098,000
Shares Outstanding	1,117,367	1,163,182	1,227,993	1,305,337	1,339,095	1,385,234	1,506,482	1,573,979
Statistical Record								
Return on Assets %	14.05	13.79	13.33	12.29	10.70	9.32	9.08	7.38
Return on Equity %	84.92	73.43	64.94	74.37	58.66	36.57	30.82	25.25
EBITDA Margin %	25.77	24.41	24.86	24.48	21.71	19.98	19.73	19.01
Net Margin %	15.89	14.83	14.85	14.02	11.90	10.55	10.38	8.71
Asset Turnover	0.88	0.93	0.90	0.88	0.90	0.88	0.87	0.85
Current Ratio	1.13	1.21	1.19	1.36	1.15	1.20	1.11	1.30
Debt to Equity	1.28	1.14	0.95	0.97	1.69	0.81	0.48	0.47
Price Range	211.00-179.16	194.56-146.76	146.92-121.86	132.57-81.98	130.00-71.74	119.60-90.90	97.20-73.57	98.58-72.01
P/E Ratio	14.68-12.47	14.90-11.24	12.75-10.58	13.24-8.19	14.56-8.03	16.66-12.66	15.91-12.04	20.24-14.79
Average Yield %	1.67	1.70	1.90	1.97	1.73	1.42	1.32	0.93

Address: One New Orchard Road, Armonk, NY 10504 Telephone: 914-499-1900 Fax: 914-765-4190	Web Site: www.ibm.com Officers: Virginia M. Rometty - Chairman, President, Chief Executive Officer, Senior Vice President Bridget A. van Kralingen - Senior Vice President	Auditors: PricewaterhouseCoopers LLP Transfer Agents: Computershare Trust Company, N.A., Providence, RI

INTERNATIONAL FLAVORS & FRAGRANCES INC.

Exchange	Symbol	Price	52Wk Range	Yield	P/E	Div Achiever
NYS	IFF	$76.67 (3/28/2013)	76.86-53.33	1.77	24.81	10 Years

*7 Year Price Score 116.13 *NYSE Composite Index=100 ***12 Month Price Score 107.97**

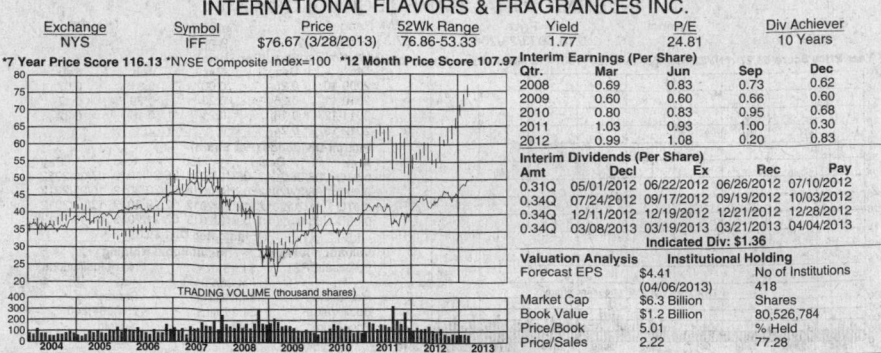

Interim Earnings (Per Share)

Qtr.	Mar	Jun	Sep	Dec
2008	0.69	0.83	0.73	0.62
2009	0.60	0.60	0.66	0.60
2010	0.80	0.83	0.95	0.68
2011	1.03	0.93	1.00	0.30
2012	0.99	1.08	0.20	0.83

Interim Dividends (Per Share)

Amt	Decl	Ex	Rec	Pay
0.31Q	05/01/2012	06/22/2012	06/26/2012	07/10/2012
0.34Q	07/24/2012	09/17/2012	09/19/2012	10/03/2012
0.34Q	12/11/2012	12/19/2012	12/21/2012	12/28/2012
0.34Q	03/08/2013	03/19/2013	03/21/2013	04/04/2013

Indicated Div: $1.36

Valuation Analysis | **Institutional Holding**

Forecast EPS	$4.41	No of Institutions
	(04/06/2013)	418
Market Cap	$6.3 Billion	Shares
Book Value	$1.2 Billion	80,526,784
Price/Book	5.01	% Held
Price/Sales	2.22	77.28

Business Summary: Specialty Chemicals (MIC: 8.3.2 SIC: 2869 NAIC: 325199)

International Flavors & Fragrances creates, manufacture and supplies flavors and fragrances for the food, beverage, personal care and household products industries. Co. operates in two business segments: Flavors and Fragrances. Flavors are the building blocks that impart taste in processed food and beverage products. Co.'s Flavors business includes four categories of products: savory; beverages; sweet, pharmaceutical and oral care; and dairy. Co.'s fragrances are a component in perfumes and consumer brands. Co.'s Fragrances business consists of three categories of products: fine fragrance and beauty care; functional fragrances; and fragrance ingredients.

Recent Developments: For the year ended Dec 31 2012, net income decreased 4.8% to US$254.1 million from US$266.9 million in the prior year. Revenues were US$2.82 billion, up 1.2% from US$2.79 billion the year before. Direct operating expenses declined 2.2% to US$1.65 billion from US$1.68 billion in the comparable period the year before. Indirect operating expenses increased 1.8% to US$688.9 million from US$676.9 million in the equivalent prior-year period.

Prospects: Our evaluation of International Flavors & Fragrances Inc. as of Apr. 7, 2013 is the result of our systematic analysis on three basic characteristics: earnings strength, relative valuation, and recent stock price movement. The company has produced a positive trend in earnings per share over the past 5 quarters. However, while recent estimates for the company have been mixed, IFF has posted results that fell short of analysts expectations. Based on operating earnings yield, the company is about fairly valued when compared to all of the companies in our coverage universe. Share price changes over the past year indicates that IFF will perform well over the near term.

Financial Data
(US$ in Thousands)

	12/31/2012	12/31/2011	12/31/2010	12/31/2009	12/31/2008	12/31/2007	12/31/2006	12/31/2005
Earnings Per Share	3.09	3.26	3.26	2.46	2.87	2.82	2.48	2.04
Cash Flow Per Share	3.98	2.35	3.96	3.72	2.78	3.63	2.91	1.89
Tang Book Value Per Share	6.70	4.89	3.55	0.61	N.M.	N.M.	1.78	1.54
Dividends Per Share	1.300	1.160	1.040	1.000	0.960	0.880	0.765	0.730
Dividend Payout %	42.07	35.58	31.90	40.65	33.45	31.21	30.85	35.78
Income Statement								
Total Revenue	2,821,446	2,788,018	2,622,862	2,326,158	2,389,372	2,276,638	2,095,390	1,993,393
EBITDA	561,835	493,512	487,544	344,520	360,683	383,097	353,674	285,215
Depn & Amortn	76,667	75,327	79,242	6,153	6,153	12,878	14,843	15,071
Income Before Taxes	443,415	373,546	359,593	276,549	280,522	328,684	313,282	246,188
Income Taxes	189,281	106,680	96,036	81,023	50,894	81,556	86,782	53,122
Net Income	254,134	266,866	263,557	195,526	229,628	247,128	226,500	193,066
Average Shares	81,833	81,467	80,440	79,094	79,964	87,633	91,369	94,826
Balance Sheet								
Current Assets	1,572,559	1,317,220	1,325,195	1,128,066	1,161,068	1,190,478	1,079,803	1,191,274
Total Assets	3,249,600	2,965,581	2,872,455	2,644,774	2,749,913	2,726,788	2,478,904	2,638,196
Current Liabilities	622,732	564,566	660,951	484,454	451,041	538,896	446,771	1,202,696
Long-Term Obligations	881,104	778,248	787,668	934,749	1,153,672	1,060,168	791,443	131,281
Total Liabilities	2,000,792	1,861,169	1,873,033	1,875,771	2,176,802	2,109,591	1,573,736	1,722,849
Stockholders' Equity	1,248,808	1,104,412	999,422	769,003	573,111	617,197	905,168	915,347
Shares Outstanding	81,626	80,921	80,210	79,157	78,661	80,995	89,417	92,714
Statistical Record								
Return on Assets %	8.16	9.14	9.55	7.25	8.36	9.49	8.85	7.72
Return on Equity %	21.54	25.37	29.81	29.14	38.48	32.47	24.88	21.15
EBITDA Margin %	19.91	17.70	18.59	14.81	15.10	16.83	16.88	14.31
Net Margin %	9.01	9.57	10.05	8.41	9.61	10.85	10.81	9.69
Asset Turnover	0.91	0.96	0.95	0.86	0.87	0.87	0.82	0.80
Current Ratio	2.53	2.33	2.00	2.33	2.57	2.21	2.42	0.99
Debt to Equity	0.71	0.70	0.79	1.22	2.01	1.72	0.87	0.14
Price Range	67.41-52.88	65.24-51.31	55.77-39.77	41.85-25.30	48.13-24.90	54.20-46.00	49.80-32.84	42.84-31.95
P/E Ratio	21.82-17.11	20.01-15.74	17.11-12.20	17.01-10.28	16.77-8.68	19.22-16.31	20.08-13.24	21.00-15.66
Average Yield %	2.21	1.97	2.21	2.94	2.43	1.76	2.01	1.96

Address: 521 West 57th Street, New York, NY 10019-2960 Telephone: 212-765-5500 Fax: 212-708-7132	Web Site: www.iff.com Officers: Douglas D. Tough - Chairman, Chief Executive Officer Kevin C. Berryman - Executive Vice President, Chief Financial Officer	Auditors: PricewaterhouseCoopers LLP Investor Contact: 212-708-7271 Transfer Agents: American Stock Transfer & Trust Company, New York, NY

INTERNATIONAL GAME TECHNOLOGY

Exchange	Symbol	Price	52Wk Range	Yield	P/E
NYS	IGT	$16.50 (3/28/2013)	17.31-11.10	1.94	17.74

*7 Year Price Score 53.27 ***NYSE Composite Index=100** ***12 Month Price Score 105.48**

Interim Earnings (Per Share)

Qtr.	Dec	Mar	Jun	Sep
2009-10	0.25	0.00	0.31	0.07
2010-11	0.25	0.23	0.29	0.17
2011-12	0.16	0.21	0.16	0.32
2012-13	0.24	...	...	...

Interim Dividends (Per Share)

Amt	Decl	Ex	Rec	Pay
0.06Q	06/06/2012	06/19/2012	06/21/2012	07/06/2012
0.06Q	08/22/2012	09/18/2012	09/20/2012	10/05/2012
0.07Q	11/20/2012	12/17/2012	12/19/2012	12/31/2012
0.08Q	03/04/2013	03/19/2013	03/21/2013	04/05/2013

Indicated Div: $0.32

Valuation Analysis

Forecast EPS	$1.28 (04/06/2013)
Market Cap	$4.4 Billion
Book Value	$1.3 Billion
Price/Book	3.48
Price/Sales	1.95

Institutional Holding

No of Institutions	468
Shares	251,094,240
% Held	73.35

TRADING VOLUME (thousand shares)

Business Summary: Hotels, Restaurants & Travel (MIC: 2.2.1 SIC: 7993 NAIC: 713290)

International Game Technology is a gaming company focusing in the design, development, manufacture, and marketing of casino games, gaming equipment and systems technology for land-based and online social gaming and wagering markets. Co. provides a range of casino-style games for land-based, online social gaming, online money wagering and mobile gaming markets with multi-line, multi-coin and multi-currency configurations. Land-based customers can combine Co.'s library of games with several gaming machine cabinets. In addition, Co.'s systems products include infrastructure and applications for casino management, customer relationship management, player management, and server-based gaming.

Recent Developments: For the quarter ended Dec 31 2012, income from continuing operations increased 29.8% to US$65.3 million from US$50.3 million in the year-earlier quarter. Net income increased 32.5% to US$65.3 million from US$49.3 million in the year-earlier quarter. Revenues were US$530.3 million, up 19.0% from US$445.5 million the year before. Operating income was US$118.4 million versus US$99.9 million in the prior-year quarter, an increase of 18.5%. Direct operating expenses rose 14.0% to US$220.8 million from US$193.6 million in the comparable period the year before. Indirect operating expenses increased 25.7% to US$191.1 million from US$152.0 million in the equivalent prior-year period.

Prospects: Our evaluation of International Game Technology as of Apr. 7, 2013 is the result of our systematic analysis on three basic characteristics: earnings strength, relative valuation, and recent stock price movement. The company has produced a positive trend in earnings per share over the past 5 quarters. However, while recent estimates for the company have been mixed, IGT has posted better than expected results. Based on operating earnings yield, the company is undervalued when compared to all of the companies in our coverage universe. Share price changes over the past year indicates that IGT will perform in line with the market over the near term.

Financial Data

(US$ in Thousands)	3 Mos	09/30/2012	09/30/2011	09/30/2010	09/30/2009	09/30/2008	09/30/2007	09/30/2006
Earnings Per Share	0.93	0.85	0.94	0.62	0.51	1.10	1.51	1.20
Cash Flow Per Share	1.79	1.54	2.05	1.99	1.86	1.58	2.49	1.85
Tang Book Value Per Share	N.M.	N.M.	0.14	N.M.	N.M.	N.M.	0.29	2.06
Dividends Per Share	0.250	0.240	0.240	0.240	0.325	0.506	0.520	0.500
Dividend Payout %	26.88	28.24	25.53	38.71	63.73	50.91	34.44	41.67
Income Statement								
Total Revenue	530,300	2,150,700	1,957,000	1,987,200	2,114,000	2,528,600	2,621,400	2,511,700
EBITDA	175,800	660,000	733,700	650,300	582,200	909,500	1,065,900	967,700
Depn & Amortn	57,700	240,300	226,200	236,800	276,800	286,000	265,500	235,400
Income Before Taxes	97,700	342,800	427,900	313,000	238,000	590,800	804,800	746,900
Income Taxes	32,400	93,100	135,600	88,700	89,000	248,300	296,600	273,300
Net Income	65,300	245,900	283,600	186,000	149,000	342,500	508,200	473,600
Average Shares	267,900	290,400	299,800	297,800	294,500	310,400	336,100	355,800
Balance Sheet								
Current Assets	1,166,500	1,263,300	1,409,900	1,202,400	1,233,700	1,470,100	1,287,000	1,375,700
Total Assets	4,176,500	4,285,100	4,154,400	4,007,000	4,388,200	4,557,400	4,167,500	3,902,700
Current Liabilities	562,900	630,300	534,700	582,300	624,500	736,700	691,500	1,246,600
Long-Term Obligations	1,775,500	1,846,400	1,646,300	1,674,300	2,169,500	2,247,100	1,503,000	200,000
Total Liabilities	2,923,100	3,087,300	2,712,000	2,772,700	3,420,900	3,648,400	2,714,800	1,860,700
Stockholders' Equity	1,253,400	1,197,800	1,442,400	1,234,300	967,300	909,000	1,452,700	2,042,000
Shares Outstanding	264,500	266,100	297,400	298,100	296,600	294,700	316,900	334,200
Statistical Record								
Return on Assets %	6.29	5.81	6.95	4.43	3.33	7.83	12.59	12.20
Return on Equity %	19.12	18.58	21.19	16.90	15.88	28.93	29.08	23.99
EBITDA Margin %	33.15	30.69	37.49	32.72	27.54	35.97	40.66	38.53
Net Margin %	12.31	11.43	14.49	9.36	7.05	13.55	19.39	18.86
Asset Turnover	0.54	0.51	0.48	0.47	0.47	0.58	0.65	0.65
Current Ratio	2.07	2.00	2.64	2.06	1.98	2.00	1.86	1.10
Debt to Equity	1.42	1.54	1.14	1.36	2.24	2.47	1.03	0.10
Price Range	17.78-11.10	17.79-11.10	18.95-13.54	22.22-13.82	23.05-7.12	49.06-16.07	48.26-34.21	41.66-25.93
P/E Ratio	19.12-11.94	20.93-13.06	20.16-14.40	35.84-22.29	45.20-13.96	44.60-14.61	31.96-22.66	34.72-21.61
Average Yield %	1.74	1.58	1.46	1.32	2.33	1.72	1.27	1.45

Address: 6355 South Buffalo Drive, Las Vegas, NV 89113 **Telephone:** 702-669-7777	**Web Site:** www.IGT.com **Officers:** Philip G. Satre - Chairman Patti S. Hart - President, Chief Executive Officer	**Auditors:** PricewaterhouseCoopers LLP **Investor Contact:** 866-296-4232 **Transfer Agents:** Wells Fargo Shareowner Services, South St. Paul, MN

INTERNATIONAL PAPER CO.

Exchange	Symbol	Price	52Wk Range	Yield	P/E
NYS	IP	$46.58 (3/28/2013)	47.00-27.81	2.58	25.88

*7 Year Price Score 111.65 *NYSE Composite Index=100 *12 Month Price Score 112.05

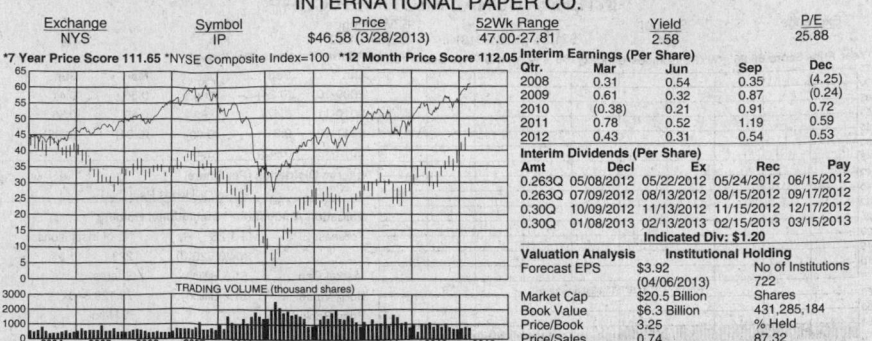

TRADING VOLUME (thousand shares)

Interim Earnings (Per Share)

Qtr.	Mar	Jun	Sep	Dec
2008	0.31	0.54	0.35	(4.25)
2009	0.61	0.32	0.87	(0.24)
2010	(0.38)	0.21	0.91	0.72
2011	0.78	0.52	1.19	0.59
2012	0.43	0.31	0.54	0.53

Interim Dividends (Per Share)

Amt	Decl	Ex	Rec	Pay
0.263Q	05/08/2012	05/22/2012	05/24/2012	06/15/2012
0.263Q	07/09/2012	08/13/2012	08/15/2012	09/17/2012
0.30Q	10/09/2012	11/13/2012	11/15/2012	12/17/2012
0.30Q	01/08/2013	02/13/2013	02/15/2013	03/15/2013

Indicated Div: $1.20

Valuation Analysis		Institutional Holding	
Forecast EPS	$3.92	No of Institutions	
	(04/06/2013)	722	
Market Cap	$20.5 Billion	Shares	
Book Value	$6.3 Billion	431,285,184	
Price/Book	3.25	% Held	
Price/Sales	0.74	87.32	

Business Summary: Paper & Forest Products (MIC: 8.1.2 SIC: 2621 NAIC: 322121)

International Paper is a paper and packaging company with markets and manufacturing operations in North America, Europe, Latin America, Russia, Asia and North Africa. Co.'s businesses are separated into four segments: Industrial Packaging; Printing Papers; Consumer Packaging; and Distribution. Co.'s Industrial Packaging segment is a manufacturer of containerboard. Co.'s Printing Papers segment is a producer of printing and writing papers. Co.'s Consumer Packaging segment is a producer of solid bleached sulfate board. Co.'s Distribution segment includes the operations of xpedx, which is a wholesale distribution marketer in several customer and product segments in North America.

Recent Developments: For the year ended Dec 31 2012, income from continuing operations decreased 41.4% to US$754.0 million from US$1.29 billion a year earlier. Net income decreased 40.2% to US$799.0 million from US$1.34 billion in the prior year. Revenues were US$27.83 billion, up 6.9% from US$26.03 billion the year before. Direct operating expenses rose 8.6% to US$20.59 billion from US$18.96 billion in the comparable period the year before. Indirect operating expenses increased 9.4% to US$5.55 billion from US$5.08 billion in the equivalent prior-year period.

Prospects: Our evaluation of International Paper Co, as of Apr. 7, 2013 is the result of our systematic analysis on three basic characteristics: earnings strength, relative valuation, and recent stock price movement. The company has enjoyed a very positive trend in earnings per share over the past 5 quarters and while recent estimates for the company have been raised by analysts, IP has posted better than expected results. Based on operating earnings yield, the company is about fairly valued when compared to all of the companies in our coverage universe. Share price changes over the past year indicates that IP will perform well over the near term.

Financial Data

(US$ in Millions)	12/31/2012	12/31/2011	12/31/2010	12/31/2009	12/31/2008	12/31/2007	12/31/2006	12/31/2005
Earnings Per Share	1.80	3.07	1.48	1.55	(3.05)	2.70	2.18	2.21
Cash Flow Per Share	6.80	6.19	3.79	10.95	6.32	4.40	2.57	3.11
Tang Book Value Per Share	4.52	9.78	10.34	8.62	5.01	11.81	11.10	6.75
Dividends Per Share	1.087	0.975	0.400	0.325	1.000	1.000	1.000	1.000
Dividend Payout %	60.42	31.76	27.03	20.97	...	37.04	45.87	45.25
Income Statement								
Total Revenue	27,833	26,034	25,179	23,366	24,829	21,890	21,995	24,097
EBITDA	3,095	3,262	2,830	3,340	686	3,037	4,867	2,555
Depn & Amortn	1,399	1,263	1,400	1,472	1,347	1,086	1,158	1,376
Income Before Taxes	1,024	1,458	822	1,199	(1,153)	1,654	3,188	586
Income Taxes	331	311	221	469	162	415	1,889	(285)
Net Income	794	1,341	644	663	(1,282)	1,168	1,050	1,100
Average Shares	440	437	434	428	421	433	488	509
Balance Sheet								
Current Assets	8,905	10,456	8,028	7,551	7,360	6,735	8,637	7,409
Total Assets	32,153	26,993	25,368	25,548	26,913	24,159	24,034	28,771
Current Liabilities	4,998	4,738	4,503	4,012	4,755	3,842	4,641	4,844
Long-Term Obligations	9,696	9,189	8,358	8,729	11,246	6,353	6,531	11,023
Total Liabilities	25,849	20,373	18,534	19,525	22,744	15,487	16,071	20,420
Stockholders' Equity	6,304	6,620	6,834	6,023	4,169	8,672	7,963	8,351
Shares Outstanding	439	436	437	433	427	425	453	490
Statistical Record								
Return on Assets %	2.68	5.12	2.53	2.53	N.M.	4.85	3.98	3.49
Return on Equity %	12.25	19.93	10.02	13.01	N.M.	14.04	12.87	13.25
EBITDA Margin %	11.12	12.53	11.24	14.29	2.76	13.87	22.13	10.60
Net Margin %	2.85	5.15	2.56	2.84	N.M.	5.34	4.77	4.56
Asset Turnover	0.94	0.99	0.99	0.89	0.97	0.91	0.83	0.77
Current Ratio	1.78	2.21	1.78	1.88	1.55	1.75	1.86	1.53
Debt to Equity	1.54	1.39	1.22	1.45	2.70	0.73	0.82	1.32
Price Range	39.84-27.81	32.86-22.65	28.63-19.88	27.66-4.09	33.50-10.36	41.46-31.66	37.61-30.80	42.01-27.15
P/E Ratio	22.13-15.45	10.70-7.38	19.34-13.43	17.85-2.64	...	15.36-11.73	17.25-14.13	19.01-12.29
Average Yield %	3.24	3.46	1.64	1.98	4.03	2.78	2.95	2.98

Address: 6400 Poplar Avenue, Memphis, TN 38197 Telephone: 901-419-7000	Web Site: www.internationalpaper.com Officers: John V. Faraci - Chairman, Chief Executive Officer John N. Balboni - Senior Vice President, Chief Information Officer	Auditors: Deloitte & Touche LLP Investor Contact: 901-419-1731 Transfer Agents: Computershare, Jersey City, NJ

INTERNATIONAL RECTIFIER CORP.

Exchange	Symbol	Price	52Wk Range	Yield	P/E
NYS	IRF	$21.15 (3/28/2013)	22.64-14.69	N/A	N/A

*7 Year Price Score 66.06 *NYSE Composite Index=100 *12 Month Price Score 102.46

Interim Earnings (Per Share)

Qtr.	Sep	Dec	Mar	Jun
2009-10	(0.24)	0.39	0.56	0.41
2010-11	0.47	0.62	0.69	0.56
2011-12	0.31	(0.09)	(0.04)	(0.98)
2012-13	(0.42)	(0.47)	...	...

Interim Dividends (Per Share)

No Dividends Paid

Valuation Analysis   **Institutional Holding**

Forecast EPS	$-1.26	No of Institutions
	(04/05/2013)	223
Market Cap	$1.5 Billion	Shares
Book Value	$1.2 Billion	79,129,840
Price/Book	1.19	% Held
Price/Sales	1.47	99.08

TRADING VOLUME (thousand shares)

Business Summary: Semiconductors (MIC: 6.2.4 SIC: 3674 NAIC: 334413)

International Rectifier designs, manufactures and markets power management semiconductors. Co.'s products include power metal oxide semiconductor field effect transistors (MOSFETs), analog and mixed signal integrated circuits, digital integrated circuits, radiation-resistant power MOSFETs, insulated gate bipolar transistors, direct current (DC)-DC converters, digital controllers, power modules, and automotive product packages. Co.'s semiconductors are used in a variety of applications including automotive, networking, industrial motors, displays, consumer electronics, servers, personal computers, game stations, household appliances, satellites, telecommunications, and renewable energy.

Recent Developments: For the quarter ended Dec 23 2012, net loss amounted to US$32.7 million versus a net loss of US$6.3 million in the year-earlier quarter. Revenues were US$223.8 million, down 2.7% from US$230.1 million the year before. Operating loss was US$34.7 million versus a loss of US$3.3 million in the prior-year quarter. Direct operating expenses rose 17.5% to US$174.7 million from US$148.7 million in the comparable period the year before. Indirect operating expenses decreased 1.1% to US$83.8 million from US$84.7 million in the equivalent prior-year period.

Prospects: Our evaluation of International Rectifier Corp. as of Apr. 7, 2013 is the result of our systematic analysis on three basic characteristics: earnings strength, relative valuation, and recent stock price movement. The company has enjoyed a very positive trend in earnings per share over the past 5 quarters. Because the company lacks sufficient analyst estimate data, we place greater weight on the historical EPS trend as the measure of earnings strength. Based on operating earnings yield, the company is overvalued when compared to all of the companies in our coverage universe. Share price changes over the past year indicates that IRF will perform well over the near term.

Financial Data

(US$ in Thousands)	6 Mos	3 Mos	06/24/2012	06/26/2011	06/27/2010	06/28/2009	06/29/2008	06/30/2007
Earnings Per Share	(1.91)	(1.53)	(0.79)	2.33	1.13	(3.42)	(0.86)	1.07
Cash Flow Per Share	1.34	0.45	0.59	2.32	0.74	(0.57)	0.50	2.56
Tang Book Value Per Share	16.65	17.02	17.27	17.16	15.77	14.73	18.34	18.97
Income Statement								
Total Revenue	476,314	252,492	1,050,588	1,176,577	895,297	740,419	984,830	1,202,469
EBITDA	(53,648)	(20,177)	(63,771)	154,446	21,789	(159,364)	(131,284)	122,655
Depn & Amortn	3,360	1,680	8,369	6,768	4,375	4,408	4,656	2,209
Income Before Taxes	(56,968)	(21,825)	(71,807)	157,792	28,635	(152,078)	(106,847)	136,482
Income Taxes	4,529	6,950	(16,757)	(8,754)	(52,192)	95,339	(44,205)	62,995
Net Income	(61,497)	(28,775)	(55,050)	166,546	80,827	(247,417)	(62,642)	77,742
Average Shares	69,144	69,283	69,270	70,523	71,248	72,295	72,819	72,933
Balance Sheet								
Current Assets	813,406	830,878	868,046	966,931	910,335	761,405	764,849	1,414,022
Total Assets	1,450,313	1,486,923	1,531,823	1,670,984	1,440,917	1,401,307	1,874,912	2,647,405
Current Liabilities	185,707	186,095	213,043	273,728	209,634	208,561	247,239	952,025
Total Liabilities	220,821	231,130	255,496	313,072	249,472	266,055	423,961	1,114,145
Stockholders' Equity	1,229,492	1,255,793	1,276,327	1,357,912	1,191,445	1,135,252	1,450,951	1,533,260
Shares Outstanding	69,180	69,135	69,231	69,899	70,324	71,192	72,826	72,811
Statistical Record								
Return on Assets %	N.M.	N.M.	N.M.	10.73	5.70	N.M.	N.M.	3.02
Return on Equity %	N.M.	N.M.	N.M.	13.10	6.97	N.M.	N.M.	4.96
EBITDA Margin %	N.M.	N.M.	N.M.	13.13	2.43	N.M.	N.M.	10.20
Net Margin %	N.M.	N.M.	N.M.	14.16	9.03	N.M.	N.M.	6.47
Asset Turnover	0.65	0.64	0.66	0.76	0.63	0.45	0.44	0.47
Current Ratio	4.38	4.46	4.07	3.53	4.34	3.65	3.09	1.49
Price Range	23.65-14.69	24.88-16.25	28.60-17.62	34.56-18.22	25.10-14.23	22.57-9.62	39.50-19.76	43.95-32.38
P/E Ratio	...	...	...	14.83-7.82	22.21-12.59	...	...	41.07-30.26

Address: 101 N. Sepulveda Blvd., El Segundo, CA 90245	Web Site: www.irf.com	Auditors: Ernst & Young LLP
Telephone: 310-726-8000	Officers: Richard J. Dahl - Chairman Oleg Kahykin - President, Chief Executive Officer	Investor Contact: 310-252-7731
Fax: 310-322-3332		Transfer Agents: Mellon Investor Services LLC, Jersey City, NJ

INTERPUBLIC GROUP OF COMPANIES INC.

Exchange	Symbol	Price	52Wk Range	Yield	P/E
NYS	IPG	$13.03 (3/28/2013)	13.38-9.45	2.30	13.86

*7 Year Price Score 106.81 ***NYSE Composite Index=100** ***12 Month Price Score 104.67**

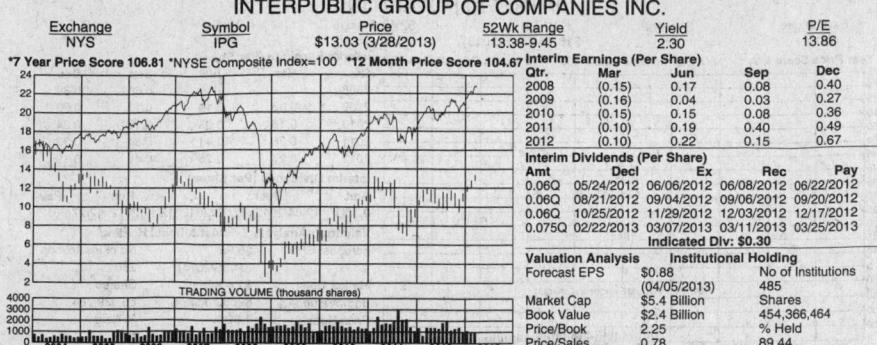

Interim Earnings (Per Share)

Qtr.	Mar	Jun	Sep	Dec
2008	(0.15)	0.17	0.08	0.40
2009	(0.16)	0.04	0.03	0.27
2010	(0.15)	0.15	0.08	0.36
2011	(0.10)	0.19	0.40	0.49
2012	(0.10)	0.22	0.15	0.67

Interim Dividends (Per Share)

Amt	Decl	Ex	Rec	Pay
0.06Q	05/24/2012	06/06/2012	06/08/2012	06/22/2012
0.06Q	08/21/2012	09/04/2012	09/06/2012	09/20/2012
0.06Q	10/25/2012	11/29/2012	12/03/2012	12/17/2012
0.075Q	02/22/2013	03/07/2013	03/11/2013	03/25/2013

Indicated Div: $0.30

Valuation Analysis / **Institutional Holding**

Forecast EPS	$0.88	No of Institutions	
	(04/05/2013)	485	
Market Cap	$5.4 Billion	Shares	
Book Value	$2.4 Billion	454,366,464	
Price/Book	2.25	% Held	
Price/Sales	0.78	89.44	

TRADING VOLUME (thousand shares)

Business Summary: Advertising (MIC: 2.3.4 SIC: 7311 NAIC: 541810)

Interpublic Group of Companies is engaged in providing advertising and marketing services. Co. has two reportable segments. Within its Integrated Agency Networks segment, Co.'s agencies provide an array of global communications and marketing services. In addition, Co.'s domestic integrated agencies provide a range of advertising, marketing communications services and/or marketing services. Co.'s Constituency Management Group segment provides clients with various services, including public relations, meeting and event production, sports and entertainment marketing, corporate and brand identity and marketing consulting.

Recent Developments: For the year ended Dec 31 2012, net income decreased 15.8% to US$464.6 million from US$551.5 million in the prior year. Revenues were US$6.96 billion, down 0.8% from US$7.01 billion the year before. Operating income was US$678.3 million versus US$687.2 million in the prior year, a decrease of 1.3%. Indirect operating expenses decreased 0.8% to US$6.28 billion from US$6.33 billion in the equivalent prior-year period.

Prospects: Our evaluation of Interpublic Group of Cos. Inc. as of Apr. 7, 2013 is the result of our systematic analysis on three basic characteristics: earnings strength, relative valuation, and recent stock price movement. The company has managed to produce a neutral trend in earnings per share over the past 5 quarters. However, while recent estimates for the company have been mixed, IPG has posted better than expected results. Based on operating earnings yield, the company is undervalued when compared to all of the companies in our coverage universe. Share price changes over the past year indicates that IPG will perform in line with the market over the near term.

Financial Data
(US$ in Thousands)

	12/31/2012	12/31/2011	12/31/2010	12/31/2009	12/31/2008	12/31/2007	12/31/2006	12/31/2005
Earnings Per Share	0.94	0.99	0.47	0.19	0.52	0.26	(0.19)	(0.68)
Cash Flow Per Share	0.82	0.59	1.73	1.16	1.87	0.65	0.02	(0.05)
Dividends Per Share	0.240	0.240	...	...	...	...	...	...
Dividend Payout %	25.53	24.24	...	...	...	...	...	...
Income Statement								
Total Revenue	6,956,200	7,014,600	6,531,900	6,027,600	6,962,700	6,554,200	6,190,800	6,274,300
EBITDA	903,100	968,100	690,600	503,600	751,700	521,500	267,800	82,600
Depn & Amortn	124,300	130,700	129,000	150,600	158,900	168,700	167,400	167,300
Income Before Taxes	674,800	738,400	450,600	232,400	471,500	235,700	(5,000)	(186,600)
Income Taxes	213,300	190,200	171,300	90,100	156,600	58,900	18,700	81,900
Net Income	446,700	532,300	261,100	121,300	295,000	167,600	(31,700)	(262,900)
Average Shares	481,400	540,600	542,100	508,100	518,300	503,100	428,100	424,800
Balance Sheet								
Current Assets	8,738,300	8,286,800	8,453,500	7,637,700	7,487,600	7,685,800	7,208,800	7,497,400
Total Assets	13,493,900	12,876,600	13,070,800	12,263,100	12,125,200	12,458,100	11,864,100	11,945,200
Current Liabilities	7,701,700	8,032,600	7,740,900	6,905,600	6,877,000	7,120,600	6,663,000	6,856,500
Long-Term Obligations	2,060,800	1,210,900	1,583,300	1,638,000	1,786,900	2,044,100	2,248,600	2,183,000
Total Liabilities	11,073,300	10,414,900	10,541,800	9,765,400	9,649,600	10,125,900	9,923,500	9,999,900
Stockholders' Equity	2,420,600	2,461,700	2,529,000	2,497,700	2,475,600	2,332,200	1,940,600	1,945,300
Shares Outstanding	417,500	449,500	489,100	486,100	476,600	471,200	468,600	429,900
Statistical Record								
Return on Assets %	3.38	4.10	2.06	0.99	2.39	1.38	N.M.	N.M.
Return on Equity %	18.25	21.33	10.39	4.88	12.24	7.84	N.M.	N.M.
EBITDA Margin %	12.98	13.80	10.57	8.35	10.80	7.96	4.33	1.32
Net Margin %	6.42	7.59	4.00	2.01	4.24	2.56	N.M.	N.M.
Asset Turnover	0.53	0.54	0.52	0.49	0.56	0.54	0.52	0.52
Current Ratio	1.13	1.03	1.09	1.11	1.09	1.08	1.08	1.09
Debt to Equity	0.85	0.49	0.63	0.66	0.72	0.88	1.16	1.12
Price Range	11.97-9.45	13.20-6.95	11.11-6.35	7.59-3.20	10.39-2.61	13.81-8.10	12.35-7.86	13.68-9.14
P/E Ratio	12.73-10.05	13.33-7.02	23.64-13.51	39.95-16.84	19.98-5.02	53.12-31.15	...	...
Average Yield %	2.20	2.30	...	...	...	...	...	...

Address: 1114 Avenue of the Americas, New York, NY 10036	Web Site: www.interpublic.com	Auditors: PricewaterhouseCoopers LLP
Telephone: 212-704-1200	Officers: Michael I. Roth - Chairman, Chief Executive Officer Philippe Krakowsky - Executive Vice President, Chief Strategy Officer, Chief Talent Officer	Transfer Agents: Computershare Shareowner Services LLC, Jersey City, NJ

INTREPID POTASH INC

Exchange	Symbol	Price	52Wk Range	Yield	P/E
NYS	IPI	$18.76 (3/28/2013)	25.13-18.76	N/A	16.17

*7 Year Price Score N/A *NYSE Composite Index=100 *12 Month Price Score 85.43

Interim Earnings (Per Share)

Qtr.	Mar	Jun	Sep	Dec
2008	...	...	0.66	0.30
2009	0.33	0.19	0.13	0.09
2010	0.16	0.05	0.16	0.24
2011	0.38	0.41	0.34	0.33
2012	0.27	0.25	0.44	0.19

Interim Dividends (Per Share)

Amt	Decl	Ex	Rec	Pay
0.75U	12/04/2012	12/13/2012	12/17/2012	12/27/2012

Valuation Analysis   **Institutional Holding**

Forecast EPS	$0.95	No of Institutions
	(04/05/2013)	230
Market Cap	$1.4 Billion	Shares
Book Value	$905.7 Million	55,039,784
Price/Book	1.56	% Held
Price/Sales	3.13	N/A

Business Summary: Agricultural Chemicals (MIC: 8.3.3 SIC: 1474 NAIC: 212391)

Intrepid Potash is a producer of muriate of potash and is engaged in the production and marketing of potash and langbeinite, another mineral containing potassium that is produced from langbeinite ore. Co.'s potash and langbeinite are marketed under the name of Trio®. Co. also produces salt, magnesium chloride, and metal recovery salts from its potash mining processes. As of Dec 31 2011, Co. owned five active potash production facilities: three in or near Carlsbad, NM (West, East, and North) and two in Utah (Moab and Wendover) and had estimated productive capacity to produce approximately 870,000 tons of potash and approximately 270,000 tons of langbeinite annually.

Recent Developments: For the year ended Dec 31 2012, net income decreased 20.1% to US$87.4 million from US$109.4 million in the prior year. Revenues were US$451.3 million, up 1.9% from US$443.0 million the year before. Operating income was US$135.4 million versus US$173.9 million in the prior year, a decrease of 22.1%. Direct operating expenses rose 9.5% to US$281.2 million from US$256.7 million in the comparable period the year before. Indirect operating expenses increased 181.4% to US$34.7 million from US$12.3 million in the equivalent prior-year period.

Prospects: Our evaluation of Intrepid Potash Inc. as of Apr. 7, 2013 is the result of our systematic analysis on three basic characteristics: earnings strength, relative valuation, and recent stock price movement. The company has generated a negative trend in earnings per share over the past 5 quarters. However, while recent estimates for the company have been lowered by analysts, IPI has posted better than expected results. Based on operating earnings yield, the company is undervalued when compared to all of the companies in our coverage universe. Share price changes over the past year indicates that IPI will perform in line with the market over the near term.

Financial Data
(US$ in Thousands)

	12/31/2012	12/31/2011	12/31/2010	12/31/2009	12/31/2008
Earnings Per Share	1.16	1.45	0.60	0.74	1.31
Cash Flow Per Share	2.49	2.31	1.64	1.08	...
Tang Book Value Per Share	12.03	11.58	10.09	9.45	8.71
Dividends Per Share	0.750	...	...	...	...
Dividend Payout %	64.66	...	...	...	...
Income Statement					
Total Revenue	451,316	442,954	359,304	301,803	305,914
EBITDA	183,588	210,187	103,452	110,219	167,112
Depn & Amortn	47,599	35,787	27,715	17,327	7,192
Income Before Taxes	136,927	175,261	75,043	92,247	157,765
Income Taxes	49,484	65,850	29,758	36,905	59,592
Net Income	87,443	109,411	45,285	55,342	98,173
Average Shares	75,336	75,281	75,154	75,042	74,988
Balance Sheet					
Current Assets	162,356	276,645	208,822	204,339	198,376
Total Assets	994,623	932,870	828,884	768,990	705,077
Current Liabilities	67,388	49,675	45,405	35,932	38,939
Total Liabilities	88,887	61,737	71,043	59,768	53,478
Stockholders' Equity	905,736	871,133	757,841	709,222	651,599
Shares Outstanding	75,312	75,207	75,110	75,032	74,846
Statistical Record					
Return on Assets %	9.05	12.42	5.67	7.51	...
Return on Equity %	9.82	13.43	6.17	8.13	...
EBITDA Margin %	40.68	47.45	28.79	36.52	54.63
Net Margin %	19.38	24.70	12.60	18.34	32.09
Asset Turnover	0.47	0.50	0.45	0.41	...
Current Ratio	2.41	5.57	4.60	5.69	5.09
Price Range	26.11-18.95	40.00-20.94	37.29-19.57	33.65-14.49	73.23-14.34
P/E Ratio	22.51-16.34	27.59-14.44	62.15-32.62	45.47-19.58	55.90-10.95
Average Yield %	3.34	...	...	...	...

Address: 707 17th Street, Suite 4200, Denver, CO 80202 Telephone: 303-296-3006	Web Site: www.intrepidpotash.com Officers: Robert P. Jornayvaz - Executive Chairman, Chief Executive Officer Hugh E. Harvey - Executive Deputy Chairman	Auditors: KPMG LLP Investor Contact: 303-296-3006 Transfer Agents: Computershare Trust Company, New York, NY

INVESCO LTD

Exchange	Symbol	Price	52Wk Range	Yield	P/E
NYS	IVZ	$28.96 (3/28/2013)	29.13-20.49	2.38	19.44

*7 Year Price Score 99.06   *NYSE Composite Index=100   *12 Month Price Score 102.02

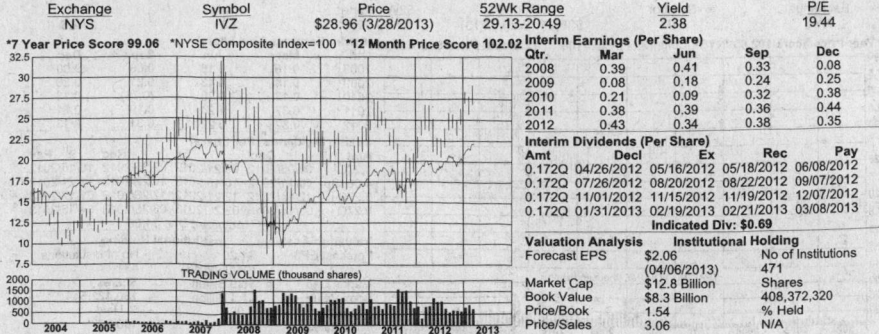

Interim Earnings (Per Share)

Qtr.	Mar	Jun	Sep	Dec
2008	0.39	0.41	0.33	0.08
2009	0.08	0.18	0.24	0.25
2010	0.21	0.09	0.32	0.38
2011	0.38	0.39	0.36	0.44
2012	0.43	0.34	0.38	0.35

Interim Dividends (Per Share)

Amt	Decl	Ex	Rec	Pay
0.172Q	04/26/2012	05/16/2012	05/18/2012	06/08/2012
0.172Q	07/26/2012	08/20/2012	08/22/2012	09/07/2012
0.172Q	11/01/2012	11/15/2012	11/19/2012	12/07/2012
0.172Q	01/31/2013	02/19/2013	02/21/2013	03/08/2013

Indicated Div: $0.69

Valuation Analysis	Institutional Holding	
Forecast EPS $2.06 (04/06/2013)	No of Institutions 471	
Market Cap $12.8 Billion	Shares 408,372,320	
Book Value $8.3 Billion	% Held	
Price/Book 1.54	N/A	
Price/Sales 3.06		

TRADING VOLUME (thousand shares)

Business Summary: Wealth Management (MIC: 5.5.2 SIC: 6282 NAIC: 523930)

Invesco is an independent global investment management company that is engaged in providing a range of investment products and services to retail and institutional clients. Co.'s sole business is investment management. Co. has three principal distribution channels: Retail, Institutional, and Private Wealth Management, and its asset classes include money market, fixed income, balanced, equity and alternatives. Co. operated in the institutional and retail segments of the investment management industry in North America, Europe and Asia-Pacific, serving clients in more than 100 countries at Dec 31 2012. Also, at such date, Co. had $687.70 billion in assets under management.

Recent Developments: For the year ended Dec 31 2012, net income decreased 5.6% to US$587.3 million from US$622.0 million in the prior year. Revenues were US$4.18 billion, up 2.1% from US$4.09 billion the year before. Operating income was US$871.5 million versus US$898.1 million in the prior year, a decrease of 3.0%. Indirect operating expenses increased 3.5% to US$3.31 billion from US$3.19 billion in the equivalent prior-year period.

Prospects: Our evaluation of Invesco Ltd as of Apr. 7, 2013 is the result of our systematic analysis on three basic characteristics: earnings strength, relative valuation, and recent stock price movement. The company has enjoyed a very positive trend in earnings per share over the past 5 quarters and while recent estimates for the company have been raised by analysts, IVZ has posted results that fell short of analysts expectations. Based on operating earnings yield, the company is undervalued when compared to all of the companies in our coverage universe. Share price changes over the past year indicates that IVZ will perform poorly over the near term.

Financial Data

(US$ in Thousands)	12/31/2012	12/31/2011	12/31/2010	12/31/2009	12/31/2008	12/31/2007	12/31/2006
Earnings Per Share	1.49	1.57	1.01	0.76	1.21	1.64	1.19
Cash Flow Per Share	1.81	2.08	0.82	0.87	1.28	2.30	1.15
Tang Book Value Per Share	N.M.	N.M.	N.M.	0.71	N.M.	N.M.	...
Dividends Per Share	0.640	0.477	0.433	0.407	0.520	0.372	0.357
Dividend Payout %	42.95	30.41	42.82	53.62	42.98	22.68	30.00
Income Statement							
Total Revenue	4,177,000	4,092,200	3,487,700	2,627,300	3,307,600	3,878,900	3,246,700
EBITDA	847,500	925,600	816,200	462,800	697,500	1,282,600	1,147,800
Depn & Amortn	65,400	117,400	96,700	77,600	47,600	64,100	67,500
Income Before Taxes	829,800	877,600	793,600	330,500	610,200	1,195,700	1,030,000
Income Taxes	272,200	286,100	197,000	148,200	236,000	357,300	254,600
Net Income	677,100	729,700	465,700	322,500	481,700	673,600	482,700
Average Shares	453,800	464,700	463,200	423,600	397,500	410,300	406,100
Balance Sheet							
Current Assets	3,907,600	3,834,100	4,274,500	3,121,000	2,378,900	4,194,400	3,709,000
Total Assets	17,492,400	19,347,000	20,444,100	10,909,600	9,756,900	12,925,200	12,228,500
Current Liabilities	2,713,000	2,974,400	3,264,500	2,298,400	2,103,400	3,640,900	3,365,400
Long-Term Obligations	1,186,000	1,069,600	1,315,700	745,700	862,000	1,276,400	979,000
Total Liabilities	9,175,600	11,227,900	12,179,500	3,996,700	4,067,400	6,334,600	6,064,500
Stockholders' Equity	8,316,800	8,119,100	8,264,600	6,912,900	5,689,500	6,590,600	6,164,000
Shares Outstanding	441,400	446,000	460,100	431,677	378,417	424,767	...
Statistical Record							
Return on Assets %	3.67	3.67	2.97	3.12	4.24	5.36	...
Return on Equity %	8.22	8.91	6.14	5.12	7.82	10.56	...
EBITDA Margin %	20.29	22.62	23.40	17.62	21.09	33.07	35.35
Net Margin %	16.21	17.83	13.35	12.27	14.56	17.37	14.87
Asset Turnover	0.23	0.21	0.22	0.25	0.29	0.31	...
Current Ratio	1.44	1.29	1.31	1.36	1.13	1.15	1.10
Debt to Equity	0.14	0.13	0.16	0.11	0.15	0.19	0.16
Price Range	26.84-20.35	27.42-14.85	24.24-16.63	23.97-9.51	31.38-8.84	32.00-22.09	24.65-15.87
P/E Ratio	18.01-13.66	17.46-9.46	24.00-16.47	31.54-12.51	25.93-7.31	19.51-13.47	20.71-13.34
Average Yield %	2.69	2.18	2.08	2.28	2.33	1.46	1.78

Address: 1555 Peachtree Street N.E., Suite 1800, Atlanta, GA 30309	Web Site: www.invesco.com	Auditors: PricewaterhouseCoopers LLP
Telephone: 404-892-0896	Officers: Rex D. Adams - Chairman Martin L. Flanagan - President, Chief Executive Officer	Investor Contact: 404-439-4605
Fax: 207-065-3962		Transfer Agents: BNY Mellon Shareowner Services, Pittsburg, PA

IRON MOUNTAIN INC

Exchange	Symbol	Price	52Wk Range	Yield	P/E
NYS	IRM	$36.31 (3/28/2013)	37.69-27.41	2.97	37.05

*7 Year Price Score 102.65 *NYSE Composite Index=100 ***12 Month Price Score 98.90**

Interim Earnings (Per Share)

Qtr.	Mar	Jun	Sep	Dec
2008	0.16	0.18	0.06	0.00
2009	0.14	0.43	0.21	0.30
2010	0.12	0.20	(0.76)	0.16
2011	0.37	1.24	0.19	0.21
2012	0.32	0.22	0.31	0.13

Interim Dividends (Per Share)

Amt	Decl	Ex	Rec	Pay
0.27Q	09/06/2012	09/21/2012	09/25/2012	10/15/2012
4.061Sp	10/11/2012	10/18/2012	10/22/2012	11/21/2012
0.27Q	12/14/2012	12/21/2012	12/26/2012	01/17/2013
0.27Q	03/14/2013	03/21/2013	03/25/2013	04/15/2013

Indicated Div: $1.08

Valuation Analysis | **Institutional Holding**

Forecast EPS	$1.20 (04/05/2013)	No of Institutions 431
Market Cap	$6.9 Billion	Shares
Book Value	$1.1 Billion	180,422,544
Price/Book	6.00	% Held
Price/Sales	2.30	100.96

TRADING VOLUME (thousand shares)

Business Summary: Business Services (MIC: 7.5.2 SIC: 4225 NAIC: 493110)

Iron Mountain is an information management services company. Co.'s information management services can be divided into three main service categories: records management services, consisting primarily of the archival storage of records, both physical and digital, for long periods of time; data protection & recovery services, relating to the off-site vaulting of data for disaster recovery and business continuity purposes for both physical and electronic records; and information destruction services, consisting primarily of its physical shredding operations. Co. provides its services to commercial, legal, banking, health care, accounting, insurance, entertainment and government organizations.

Recent Developments: For the year ended Dec 31 2012, income from continuing operations decreased 25.5% to US$183.5 million from US$246.4 million a year earlier. Net income decreased 56.2% to US$174.8 million from US$399.6 million in the prior year. Revenues were US$3.01 billion, unchanged from the year before. Operating income was US$557.0 million versus US$571.2 million in the prior year, a decrease of 2.5%. Direct operating expenses rose 2.6% to US$1.28 billion from US$1.25 billion in the comparable period the year before. Indirect operating expenses decreased 2.3% to US$1.17 billion from US$1.20 billion in the equivalent prior-year period.

Prospects: Our evaluation of Iron Mountain Inc. as of Apr. 7, 2013 is the result of our systematic analysis on three basic characteristics: earnings strength, relative valuation, and recent stock price movement. The company has enjoyed a very positive trend in earnings per share over the past 5 quarters. However, while recent estimates for the company have been lowered by analysts, IRM has posted results that fell short of analysts expectations. Based on operating earnings yield, the company is overvalued when compared to all of the companies in our coverage universe. Share price changes over the past year indicates that IRM will perform well over the near term.

Financial Data
(US$ in Thousands)

	12/31/2012	12/31/2011	12/31/2010	12/31/2009	12/31/2008	12/31/2007	12/31/2006	12/31/2005
Earnings Per Share	0.98	2.02	(0.27)	1.08	0.40	0.76	0.64	0.56
Cash Flow Per Share	2.49	3.16	3.09	3.04	2.66	2.42	1.89	1.92
Dividends Per Share	5.121	0.938	0.375	...	...	...	...	...
Dividend Payout %	522.60	46.41	...	...	...	...	...	...
Income Statement								
Total Revenue	3,005,255	3,014,703	3,127,549	3,013,595	3,055,134	2,730,035	2,350,342	2,078,155
EBITDA	821,563	848,794	628,451	844,194	716,121	674,272	606,921	551,300
Depn & Amortn	280,598	290,638	306,670	283,571	254,619	222,655	187,745	170,698
Income Before Taxes	298,366	352,900	100,795	332,833	224,867	223,024	224,218	197,018
Income Taxes	114,873	106,488	149,787	110,527	142,924	69,010	93,795	81,484
Net Income	171,708	395,538	(53,900)	220,877	82,037	153,094	128,863	111,099
Average Shares	174,867	195,938	201,991	204,271	203,290	202,062	200,463	198,105
Balance Sheet								
Current Assets	1,024,092	914,450	1,055,178	1,211,425	976,392	822,396	679,721	554,168
Total Assets	6,358,339	6,041,258	6,395,799	6,846,834	6,356,854	6,307,921	5,209,521	4,766,140
Current Liabilities	904,953	849,030	854,934	814,714	729,597	765,677	638,647	591,996
Long-Term Obligations	3,732,116	3,280,268	2,912,465	3,211,223	3,207,464	3,232,848	2,605,711	2,503,526
Total Liabilities	5,208,368	4,795,570	4,439,954	4,705,692	4,554,074	4,512,466	3,656,248	3,396,011
Stockholders' Equity	1,149,971	1,245,688	1,955,845	2,141,142	1,802,780	1,795,455	1,553,273	1,370,129
Shares Outstanding	190,005	172,140	200,064	203,546	201,931	200,693	199,109	197,494
Statistical Record								
Return on Assets %	2.76	6.36	N.M.	3.35	1.29	2.66	2.58	2.41
Return on Equity %	14.30	24.71	N.M.	11.20	4.55	9.14	8.82	8.58
EBITDA Margin %	27.34	28.16	20.09	28.01	23.44	24.70	25.82	26.53
Net Margin %	5.71	13.12	N.M.	7.33	2.69	5.61	5.48	5.35
Asset Turnover	0.48	0.48	0.47	0.46	0.48	0.47	0.47	0.45
Current Ratio	1.13	1.08	1.23	1.49	1.34	1.07	1.06	0.94
Debt to Equity	3.25	2.63	1.49	1.50	1.78	1.80	1.68	1.83
Price Range	37.69-27.41	35.40-24.39	28.39-20.25	31.95-17.07	37.02-17.64	38.54-25.54	29.85-22.94	29.81-18.01
P/E Ratio	38.46-27.97	17.52-12.07	...	29.58-15.81	92.55-44.10	50.71-33.61	46.65-35.84	53.24-32.17
Average Yield %	16.15	3.07	1.58	...	...	...	...	...

Address: 745 Atlantic Avenue, Boston, MA 02111
Telephone: 617-535-4766

Web Site: www.ironmountain.com
Officers: William L. Meaney - President, Chief Executive Officer Brian P. McKeon - Executive Vice President, Chief Financial Officer

Auditors: Deloitte & Touche LLP
Investor Contact: 617-535-4766
Transfer Agents: The Bank of New York, New York, NY

ITC HOLDINGS CORP

Exchange	Symbol	Price	52Wk Range	Yield	P/E
NYS	ITC	$89.26 (3/28/2013)	89.26-66.99	1.69	24.79

*7 Year Price Score 122.11 *NYSE Composite Index=100 *12 Month Price Score 102.07

TRADING VOLUME (thousand shares)

Interim Earnings (Per Share)

Qtr.	Mar	Jun	Sep	Dec
2008	0.53	0.57	0.56	0.53
2009	0.57	0.61	0.74	0.66
2010	0.67	0.71	0.75	0.71
2011	0.81	0.83	0.85	0.82
2012	0.88	0.81	0.98	0.92

Interim Dividends (Per Share)

Amt	Decl	Ex	Rec	Pay
0.352Q	05/23/2012	05/31/2012	06/04/2012	06/15/2012
0.378Q	08/16/2012	08/30/2012	09/04/2012	09/17/2012
0.378Q	11/08/2012	11/29/2012	12/03/2012	12/17/2012
0.378Q	02/13/2013	02/27/2013	03/01/2013	03/15/2013

Indicated Div: $1.51

Valuation Analysis | Institutional Holding

Forecast EPS	$4.90 (04/05/2013)	No of Institutions 320
Market Cap	$4.7 Billion	Shares
Book Value	$1.4 Billion	56,457,100
Price/Book	3.30	% Held
Price/Sales	5.62	100.51

Business Summary: Electric Utilities (MIC: 3.1.1 SIC: 4911 NAIC: 221121)

ITC Holdings is a holding company. Through its regulated operating subsidiaries, International Transmission Company; Michigan Electric Transmission Company, LLC; ITC Midwest LLC; and ITC Great Plains, LLC, Co. is engaged in the transmission of electricity in the U.S. Co. operates high-voltage systems in Michigan's Lower Peninsula and portions of Iowa, Minnesota, Illinois, Missouri and Kansas that transmit electricity from generating stations to local distribution facilities connected to its systems. In addition, Co. has other subsidiaries focused primarily on business development activities.

Recent Developments: For the year ended Dec 31 2012, net income increased 9.4% to US$187.9 million from US$171.7 million in the prior year. Revenues were US$830.5 million, up 9.7% from US$757.4 million the year before. Operating income was US$431.1 million versus US$397.8 million in the prior year, an increase of 8.4%. Indirect operating expenses increased 11.1% to US$399.5 million from US$359.6 million in the equivalent prior-year period.

Prospects: Our evaluation of ITC Holdings Corp. as of Apr. 7, 2013 is the result of our systematic analysis on three basic characteristics: earnings strength, relative valuation, and recent stock price movement. The company has enjoyed a very positive trend in earnings per share over the past 5 quarters and while recent estimates for the company have been mixed, ITC has posted better than expected results. Based on operating earnings yield, the company is about fairly valued when compared to all of the companies in our coverage universe. Share price changes over the past year indicates that ITC will perform poorly over the near term.

Financial Data
(US$ in Thousands)

	12/31/2012	12/31/2011	12/31/2010	12/31/2009	12/31/2008	12/31/2007	12/31/2006	12/31/2005
Earnings Per Share	3.60	3.31	2.84	2.58	2.19	1.68	0.92	1.06
Cash Flow Per Share	6.43	7.57	8.55	5.45	4.01	3.21	1.77	1.96
Tang Book Value Per Share	7.97	5.10	2.31	0.19	N.M.	N.M.	N.M.	2.68
Dividends Per Share	1.460	1.375	1.310	1.250	1.190	1.130	1.075	0.525
Dividend Payout %	40.56	41.54	46.13	48.45	54.34	67.26	116.85	49.53
Income Statement								
Total Revenue	830,535	757,397	696,843	621,015	617,877	426,249	223,622	205,274
EBITDA	526,542	482,471	434,873	402,278	372,694	242,364	125,024	109,147
Depn & Amortn	97,300	85,800	77,800	76,800	85,600	58,700	40,100	30,200
Income Before Taxes	296,508	266,434	227,932	208,472	176,470	109,946	46,852	53,609
Income Taxes	108,632	94,749	82,254	77,572	67,262	36,650	13,658	18,938
Net Income	187,876	171,685	145,678	130,900	109,208	73,296	33,223	34,671
Average Shares	51,563	51,078	50,398	50,077	49,770	43,541	36,236	32,729
Balance Sheet								
Current Assets	198,226	201,528	251,742	294,013	167,273	76,057	109,673	72,603
Total Assets	5,564,809	4,823,366	4,307,873	4,029,716	3,714,565	3,213,297	2,128,797	916,639
Current Liabilities	1,003,311	315,467	182,404	146,678	166,178	106,427	99,566	52,658
Long-Term Obligations	2,495,298	2,645,022	2,496,896	2,434,398	2,248,253	2,243,424	1,262,278	517,315
Total Liabilities	4,149,954	3,564,474	3,190,440	3,018,193	2,785,502	2,650,222	1,596,553	653,338
Stockholders' Equity	1,414,855	1,258,892	1,117,433	1,011,523	929,063	563,075	532,244	263,301
Shares Outstanding	52,248	51,323	50,715	50,084	49,654	42,916	42,395	33,228
Statistical Record								
Return on Assets %	3.61	3.76	3.49	3.38	3.14	2.74	2.18	4.02
Return on Equity %	14.01	14.45	13.69	13.49	14.60	13.38	8.35	15.08
EBITDA Margin %	63.40	63.70	62.41	64.78	60.32	56.86	55.91	53.17
Net Margin %	22.62	22.67	20.91	21.08	17.67	17.20	14.86	16.89
Asset Turnover	0.16	0.17	0.17	0.16	0.18	0.16	0.15	0.24
Current Ratio	0.20	0.64	1.38	2.00	1.01	0.71	1.10	1.38
Debt to Equity	1.76	2.10	2.23	2.41	2.42	3.98	2.37	1.96
Price Range	79.62-66.99	77.66-61.98	62.90-49.05	52.39-32.60	58.59-35.00	57.49-38.00	40.13-25.03	29.99-26.40
P/E Ratio	22.12-18.61	23.46-18.73	22.15-17.27	20.31-12.64	26.75-15.98	34.22-22.62	43.62-27.21	28.29-24.91
Average Yield %	1.96	1.94	2.31	2.84	2.34	2.45	3.56	1.88

Address: 27175 Energy Way, Novi, MI 48377 Telephone: 248-946-3000	Web Site: www.itc-holdings.com Officers: Joseph L. Welch - President, Chief Executive Officer, Treasurer Jon E. Jipping - Executive Vice President, Chief Operating Officer	Auditors: Deloitte & Touche LLP Investor Contact: 248-374-7045 Transfer Agents: Computershare Trust Company N.A, Providence, RI

ITT CORPORATION

Exchange	Symbol	Price	52Wk Range	Yield	P/E
NYS	ITT	$28.43 (3/28/2013)	29.16-17.14	N/A	21.38

*7 Year Price Score 62.87   *NYSE Composite Index=100   *12 Month Price Score 111.58

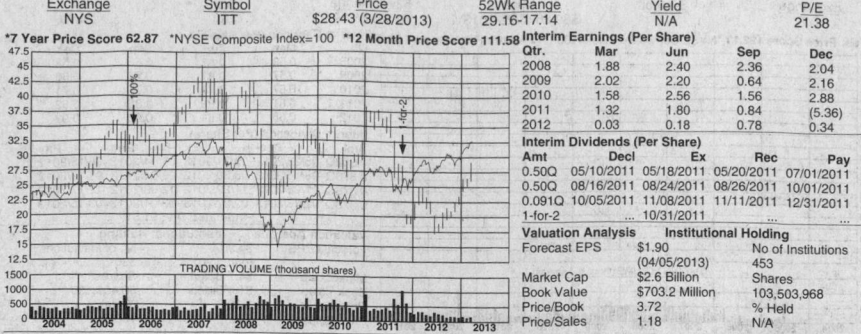

Interim Earnings (Per Share)

Qtr.	Mar	Jun	Sep	Dec
2008	1.88	2.40	2.36	2.04
2009	2.02	2.20	0.64	2.16
2010	1.58	2.56	1.56	2.88
2011	1.32	1.80	0.84	(5.36)
2012	0.03	0.18	0.78	0.34

Interim Dividends (Per Share)

Amt	Decl	Ex	Rec	Pay
0.50Q	05/10/2011	05/18/2011	05/20/2011	07/01/2011
0.50Q	08/16/2011	08/24/2011	08/26/2011	10/01/2011
0.091Q	10/05/2011	11/08/2011	11/11/2011	12/31/2011
1-for-2	...	10/31/2011	...	...

Valuation Analysis   **Institutional Holding**

Forecast EPS	$1.90	No of Institutions	
	(04/05/2013)	453	
Market Cap	$2.6 Billion	Shares	
Book Value	$703.2 Million	103,503,968	
Price/Book	3.72	% Held	
Price/Sales	1.18	N/A	

TRADING VOLUME (thousand shares)

Business Summary: Industrial Machinery & Equipment (MIC: 7.2.1 SIC: 3561 NAIC: 333911)

ITT is a global industrial company engaged in the engineering and manufacture of components for the operation of systems and manufacturing processes in the electronics, energy & mining, transportation, aerospace, and industrial markets. Co. operates through four segments: Industrial Process, which consists of industrial pumping and complementary equipment; Motion Technologies, which consists of friction and shock and vibration equipment; Interconnect Solutions, which consists of electronic connectors; and Control Technologies, which consists of fluid handling, motion control and vibration and shock isolation products.

Recent Developments: For the year ended Dec 31 2012, income from continuing operations was US$109.5 million compared with a loss of US$576.5 million a year earlier. Net income amounted to US$125.4 million versus a net loss of US$129.5 million in the prior year. Revenues were US$2.23 billion, up 6.8% from US$2.09 billion the year before. Operating income was US$151.5 million versus a loss of US$244.9 million in the prior year. Direct operating expenses rose 7.4% to US$1.55 billion from US$1.44 billion in the comparable period the year before. Indirect operating expenses decreased 40.6% to US$528.7 million from US$889.9 million in the equivalent prior-year period.

Prospects: Our evaluation of ITT Corporation as of Apr. 7, 2013 is the result of our systematic analysis on three basic characteristics: earnings strength, relative valuation, and recent stock price movement. The company has produced a positive trend in earnings per share over the past 5 quarters and while recent estimates for the company have been raised by analysts, ITT has posted results that fell short of analysts expectations. Based on operating earnings yield, the company is undervalued when compared to all of the companies in our coverage universe. Share price changes over the past year indicates that ITT will perform in line with the market over the near term.

Financial Data

(US$ in Thousands)	12/31/2012	12/31/2011	12/31/2010	12/31/2009	12/31/2008	12/31/2007	12/31/2006	12/31/2005
Earnings Per Share	1.33	(1.40)	8.60	7.00	8.66	8.06	6.20	3.82
Cash Flow Per Share	2.65	(3.48)	13.42	13.91	12.36	8.84	8.47	8.08
Tang Book Value Per Share	N.M.	0.89	N.M.	N.M.	N.M.	N.M.	3.27	2.76
Dividends Per Share	0.364	0.091	2.000	1.700	1.400	1.120	0.880	0.720
Dividend Payout %	27.37	...	23.26	24.29	16.17	13.90	14.19	18.85
Income Statement								
Total Revenue	2,227,800	2,119,000	10,995,000	10,904,500	11,694,800	9,003,300	7,807,900	7,427,300
EBITDA	201,000	(189,000)	1,092,000	1,193,000	1,475,300	1,149,200	982,600	677,000
Depn & Amortn	54,600	57,000	190,000	292,600	278,300	185,400	194,500	196,600
Income Before Taxes	149,100	(318,000)	818,000	825,200	1,087,500	898,500	727,300	448,100
Income Taxes	39,600	260,000	164,000	174,500	312,300	265,500	227,600	133,700
Net Income	125,400	(130,000)	798,000	643,700	794,700	742,100	581,100	359,500
Average Shares	94,100	92,800	92,650	91,950	91,700	92,000	93,700	94,250
Balance Sheet								
Current Assets	1,540,400	1,762,000	4,394,000	4,255,800	4,064,200	4,929,800	3,347,700	2,772,000
Total Assets	3,386,100	3,671,000	12,438,000	11,129,100	10,480,200	11,552,700	7,430,000	7,063,400
Current Liabilities	805,300	834,000	2,745,000	2,615,600	4,030,500	5,456,300	2,759,400	2,560,400
Long-Term Obligations	...	4,000	1,354,000	1,430,800	467,900	483,000	500,400	516,300
Total Liabilities	2,682,900	2,977,000	7,933,000	7,250,800	7,420,300	7,607,900	4,565,200	4,340,000
Stockholders' Equity	703,200	694,000	4,505,000	3,878,300	3,059,900	3,944,800	2,864,800	2,723,400
Shares Outstanding	92,100	93,500	92,000	91,450	90,850	90,745	91,508	92,318
Statistical Record								
Return on Assets %	3.54	N.M.	6.77	5.96	7.19	7.82	8.02	5.01
Return on Equity %	17.90	N.M.	19.04	18.56	22.63	21.80	20.80	14.19
EBITDA Margin %	9.02	N.M.	9.93	10.94	12.62	12.76	12.58	9.12
Net Margin %	5.63	N.M.	7.26	5.90	6.80	8.24	7.44	4.84
Asset Turnover	0.63	0.26	0.93	1.01	1.06	0.95	1.08	1.04
Current Ratio	1.91	2.11	1.60	1.63	1.01	0.90	1.21	1.08
Debt to Equity	...	0.01	0.30	0.37	0.15	0.12	0.17	0.19
Price Range	24.95-17.14	38.27-18.80	36.07-26.44	35.24-20.07	42.62-22.60	45.30-35.25	36.06-28.31	35.76-25.04
P/E Ratio	18.76-12.89	...	4.19-3.07	5.03-2.87	4.92-2.61	5.62-4.37	5.82-4.57	9.36-6.55
Average Yield %	1.72	0.29	6.55	5.91	4.00	2.81	2.70	2.36

Address: 1133 Westchester Avenue, White Plains, NY 10604 Telephone: 914-641-2000	Web Site: www.itt.com Officers: Denise L. Ramos - President, Chief Executive Officer, Senior Vice President, Chief Financial Officer Aris C. Chicles - Executive Vice President, Senior Vice President, Director	Auditors: Deloitte & Touche LLP Transfer Agents: The Bank of New York, New York, NY

ITT EDUCATIONAL SERVICES, INC.

Exchange	Symbol	Price	52Wk Range	Yield	P/E
NYS	ESI	$13.78 (3/28/2013)	68.83-12.36	N/A	2.36

*7 Year Price Score 39.72 ***NYSE Composite Index=100** ***12 Month Price Score 39.58**

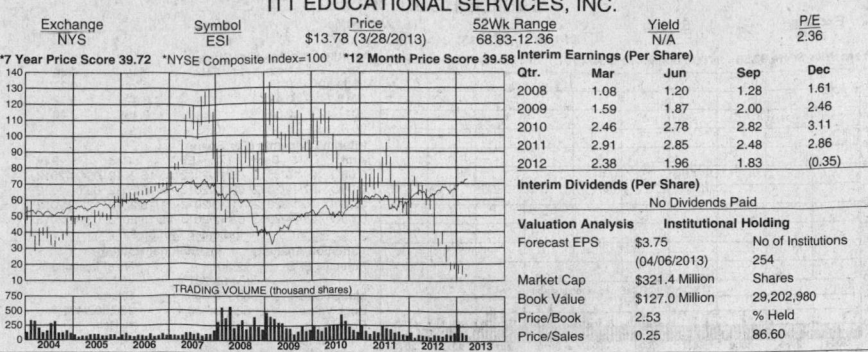

Interim Earnings (Per Share)

Qtr.	Mar	Jun	Sep	Dec
2008	1.08	1.20	1.28	1.61
2009	1.59	1.87	2.00	2.46
2010	2.46	2.78	2.82	3.11
2011	2.91	2.85	2.48	2.86
2012	2.38	1.96	1.83	(0.35)

Interim Dividends (Per Share)

No Dividends Paid

Valuation Analysis **Institutional Holding**

Forecast EPS	$3.75	No of Institutions
	(04/06/2013)	254
Market Cap	$321.4 Million	Shares
Book Value	$127.0 Million	29,202,980
Price/Book	2.53	% Held
Price/Sales	0.25	86.60

Business Summary: Educational Services (MIC: 2.2.2 SIC: 8299 NAIC: 611710)

ITT Educational Services is a provider of postsecondary degree programs. As of Dec. 31, 2012, Co. was providing master, bachelor and associate degree programs to approximately 61,000 students. As of Dec. 31, 2012, Co. had 149 locations (including 147 campuses and two learning sites) in 39 states. Co. provides one or more of its online programs to students who are located in 48 states. As of Dec. 31, 2012, the ITT Technical Institutes were providing 52 degree programs in various fields of study across the following schools of study: Information Technology, Electronics Technology, Drafting and Design, Business, Criminal Justice, and Breckinridge School of Nursing and Health Sciences.

Recent Developments: For the year ended Dec 31 2012, net income decreased 54.4% to US$140.5 million from US$307.8 million in the prior year. Revenues were US$1.29 billion, down 14.2% from US$1.50 billion the year before. Operating income was US$232.8 million versus US$507.1 million in the prior year, a decrease of 54.1%. Direct operating expenses declined 2.5% to US$539.2 million from US$553.1 million in the comparable period the year before. Indirect operating expenses increased 17.1% to US$515.2 million from US$439.8 million in the equivalent prior-year period.

Prospects: Our evaluation of ITT Educational Services Inc. as of Apr. 7, 2013 is the result of our systematic analysis on three basic characteristics: earnings strength, relative valuation, and recent stock price movement. The company has generated a negative trend in earnings per share over the past 5 quarters and while recent estimates for the company have been mixed, ESI has posted better than expected results. Based on operating earnings yield, the company is undervalued when compared to all of the companies in our coverage universe. Share price changes over the past year indicates that ESI will perform very poorly over the near term.

Financial Data
(US$ in Thousands)

	12/31/2012	12/31/2011	12/31/2010	12/31/2009	12/31/2008	12/31/2007	12/31/2006	12/31/2005
Earnings Per Share	5.85	11.13	11.17	7.91	5.17	3.71	2.72	2.33
Cash Flow Per Share	4.40	14.14	16.84	8.04	4.44	4.43	3.84	3.34
Tang Book Value Per Share	5.44	6.47	4.27	4.42	4.85	1.78	2.53	6.75
Income Statement								
Total Revenue	1,287,209	1,499,949	1,596,529	1,319,194	1,015,333	869,508	757,764	688,003
EBITDA	262,109	534,932	640,313	513,687	350,101	265,280	203,164	181,219
Depn & Amortn	29,320	27,856	26,764	24,895	22,230	23,249	21,641	15,672
Income Before Taxes	230,414	508,153	614,135	491,357	329,765	244,486	189,627	174,291
Income Taxes	89,949	200,401	239,969	191,094	126,793	92,894	71,111	64,579
Net Income	140,465	307,752	374,166	300,263	202,972	151,592	118,516	109,712
Average Shares	23,999	27,655	33,501	37,942	39,243	40,883	43,629	47,112
Balance Sheet								
Current Assets	384,965	456,288	414,097	390,962	431,045	349,823	380,952	437,008
Total Assets	672,230	728,818	674,780	616,705	623,859	540,953	560,320	592,491
Current Liabilities	306,949	345,047	356,151	284,792	264,553	291,924	284,505	251,139
Long-Term Obligations	140,000	150,000	150,000	150,000	150,000	150,000	150,000	...
Total Liabilities	545,276	560,019	546,710	460,120	436,008	470,395	456,375	283,897
Stockholders' Equity	126,954	168,799	128,070	156,585	187,851	70,558	103,945	308,594
Shares Outstanding	23,324	26,099	29,993	35,446	38,716	39,693	41,039	45,691
Statistical Record								
Return on Assets %	20.00	43.85	57.94	48.41	34.76	27.53	20.56	20.21
Return on Equity %	94.73	207.33	262.89	174.35	156.66	173.74	57.46	40.36
EBITDA Margin %	20.36	35.66	40.11	38.94	34.48	30.51	26.81	26.34
Net Margin %	10.91	20.52	23.44	22.76	19.99	17.43	15.64	15.95
Asset Turnover	1.83	2.14	2.47	2.13	1.74	1.58	1.31	1.27
Current Ratio	1.25	1.32	1.16	1.37	1.63	1.20	1.34	1.74
Debt to Equity	1.10	0.89	1.17	0.96	0.80	2.13	1.44	...
Price Range	74.21-16.52	95.44-50.37	119.20-51.46	133.21-85.38	97.61-45.93	130.47-68.24	70.79-56.00	62.46-42.88
P/E Ratio	12.69-2.82	8.58-4.53	10.67-4.61	16.84-10.79	18.88-8.88	35.17-18.39	26.03-20.59	26.81-18.40

Address: 13000 North Meridian Street, Carmel, IN 46032-1404	**Web Site:** www.ittesi.com	**Auditors:** PricewaterhouseCoopers LLP
Telephone: 317-706-9200	**Officers:** Kevin M. Modany - Chairman, Chief Executive Officer Daniel M. Fitzpatrick - Executive Vice President, Chief Financial Officer	**Transfer Agents:** The Bank of New York, New York, NY

JABIL CIRCUIT, INC.

Exchange	Symbol	Price	52Wk Range	Yield	P/E
NYS	JBL	$18.48 (3/28/2013)	25.41-16.97	1.73	10.15

*7 Year Price Score 97.55   *NYSE Composite Index=100   *12 Month Price Score 87.72

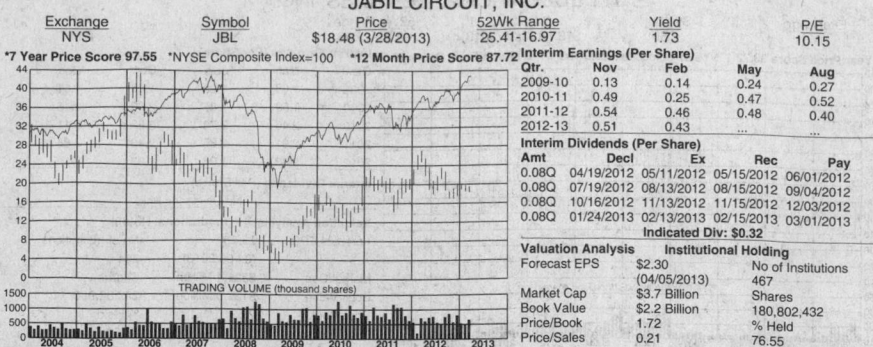

Interim Earnings (Per Share)

Qtr.	Nov	Feb	May	Aug
2009-10	0.13	0.14	0.24	0.27
2010-11	0.49	0.25	0.47	0.52
2011-12	0.54	0.46	0.48	0.40
2012-13	0.51	0.43	...	...

Interim Dividends (Per Share)

Amt	Decl	Ex	Rec	Pay
0.08Q	04/19/2012	05/11/2012	05/15/2012	06/01/2012
0.08Q	07/19/2012	08/13/2012	08/15/2012	09/04/2012
0.08Q	10/16/2012	11/13/2012	11/15/2012	12/03/2012
0.08Q	01/24/2013	02/13/2013	02/15/2013	03/01/2013

Indicated Div: $0.32

Valuation Analysis

		Institutional Holding	
Forecast EPS	$2.30 (04/05/2013)	No of Institutions	467
Market Cap	$3.7 Billion	Shares	180,802,432
Book Value	$2.2 Billion	% Held	76.55
Price/Book	1.72		
Price/Sales	0.21		

Business Summary: Electrical Equipment (MIC: 7.3.1 SIC: 3672 NAIC: 334412)

Jabil Circuit is a provider of electronic manufacturing services. Co. provides electronics design, production and product management services to companies in the aerospace, automotive, computing, consumer, defense, industrial, networking, peripherals, solar, storage and telecommunications industries. Co.'s business units provide its customers with varying combinations of the following services: integrated design and engineering; design and implementation of product testing; parallel global production; enclosure services; systems assembly, direct order fulfillment and configure to order; injection molding, metal, plastics, precision machining and automation; and aftermarket services.

Recent Developments: For the quarter ended Feb 28 2013, net income decreased 10.3% to US$88.1 million from US$98.2 million in the year-earlier quarter. Revenues were US$4.42 billion, up 4.3% from US$4.24 billion the year before. Operating income was US$149.0 million versus US$150.2 million in the prior-year quarter, a decrease of 0.8%. Direct operating expenses rose 4.6% to US$4.09 billion from US$3.91 billion in the comparable period the year before. Indirect operating expenses increased 2.1% to US$175.5 million from US$171.9 million in the equivalent prior-year period.

Prospects: Our evaluation of Jabil Circuit Inc. as of Apr. 7, 2013 is the result of our systematic analysis on three basic characteristics: earnings strength, relative valuation, and recent stock price movement. The company has enjoyed a very positive trend in earnings per share over the past 5 quarters. However, while recent estimates for the company have been lowered by analysts, JBL has posted results that fell short of analysts expectations. Based on operating earnings yield, the company is undervalued when compared to all of the companies in our coverage universe. Share price changes over the past year indicates that JBL will perform poorly over the near term.

Financial Data

(US$ in Thousands)	6 Mos	3 Mos	08/31/2012	08/31/2011	08/31/2010	08/31/2009	08/31/2008	08/31/2007
Earnings Per Share	1.82	1.85	1.87	1.73	0.78	(5.63)	0.65	0.35
Cash Flow Per Share	4.62	3.29	3.07	3.86	1.99	2.69	2.00	0.90
Tang Book Value Per Share	9.69	9.21	9.18	8.56	6.87	6.15	6.90	5.73
Dividends Per Share	0.320	0.320	0.320	0.280	0.280	0.280	0.280	0.280
Dividend Payout %	17.58	17.30	17.11	16.18	35.90	...	43.08	80.00
Income Statement								
Total Revenue	9,054,269	4,637,018	17,151,941	16,518,827	13,409,411	11,684,538	12,779,703	12,290,592
EBITDA	323,121	172,163	966,513	894,899	606,813	(638,251)	515,783	405,798
Depn & Amortn	6,922	3,451	353,525	319,151	283,334	292,039	276,288	239,747
Income Before Taxes	258,345	139,618	508,900	481,187	247,267	(1,005,133)	157,193	94,513
Income Taxes	64,672	34,034	112,811	98,229	76,501	160,898	25,119	21,401
Net Income	194,380	105,847	394,687	381,063	168,840	(1,165,212)	133,892	73,236
Average Shares	206,804	207,816	211,181	220,719	217,597	207,002	206,158	206,972
Balance Sheet								
Current Assets	5,897,273	5,946,076	5,639,328	5,135,360	4,654,018	3,676,826	4,139,137	3,666,293
Total Assets	8,247,641	8,185,500	7,803,141	7,057,940	6,367,747	5,317,858	7,032,137	6,295,232
Current Liabilities	4,228,588	4,269,490	3,858,996	3,889,888	3,605,174	2,685,926	3,047,640	2,990,847
Long-Term Obligations	1,653,708	1,656,058	1,658,326	1,112,594	1,018,930	1,036,873	1,099,473	760,477
Total Liabilities	6,071,538	6,111,787	5,698,084	5,190,820	4,789,701	3,882,696	4,316,412	3,852,221
Stockholders' Equity	2,176,103	2,073,713	2,105,057	1,867,120	1,578,046	1,435,162	2,715,725	2,443,011
Shares Outstanding	202,643	202,140	206,028	203,416	210,496	208,022	206,380	204,574
Statistical Record								
Return on Assets %	4.91	5.04	5.30	5.68	2.89	N.M.	2.00	1.25
Return on Equity %	18.12	19.52	19.82	22.12	11.21	N.M.	5.18	3.09
EBITDA Margin %	3.57	3.71	5.64	5.42	4.53	N.M.	4.04	3.30
Net Margin %	2.15	2.28	2.30	2.31	1.26	N.M.	1.05	0.60
Asset Turnover	2.29	2.27	2.30	2.46	2.30	1.89	1.91	2.10
Current Ratio	1.39	1.39	1.46	1.32	1.29	1.37	1.36	1.23
Debt to Equity	0.76	0.80	0.79	0.60	0.65	0.72	0.40	0.31
Price Range	27.13-16.97	27.13-16.97	27.13-15.76	22.98-10.25	18.36-10.25	16.15-3.16	25.32-9.03	31.05-20.07
P/E Ratio	14.91-9.32	14.66-9.17	14.51-8.43	13.28-5.92	23.54-13.14	...	38.95-13.89	88.71-57.34
Average Yield %	1.55	1.52	1.52	1.54	1.93	3.73	1.77	1.12

Address: 10560 Dr. Martin Luther King, Jr. Street North, St. Petersburg, FL 33716 Telephone: 727-577-9749 Fax: 727-579-8529	Web Site: www.jabil.com Officers: Timothy L. Main - Chairman, President, Chief Executive Officer Thomas A. Sansone - Vice-Chairman	Auditors: Ernst & Young LLP Investor Contact: 727-803-3349 Transfer Agents: Computershare, Providence, RI

JACOBS ENGINEERING GROUP, INC.

Exchange	Symbol	Price	52Wk Range	Yield	P/E
NYS	JEC	$56.24 (3/28/2013)	56.24-34.40	N/A	18.75

*7 Year Price Score 76.71   *NYSE Composite Index=100   *12 Month Price Score 110.31

TRADING VOLUME (thousand shares)

Interim Earnings (Per Share)

Qtr.	Dec	Mar	Jun	Sep
2009-10	0.58	0.62	0.15	0.61
2010-11	0.52	0.63	0.71	0.74
2011-12	0.70	0.65	0.76	0.83
2012-13	0.76	...	...	...

Interim Dividends (Per Share)

No Dividends Paid

Valuation Analysis

		Institutional Holding
Forecast EPS	$3.35	No of Institutions
	(04/05/2013)	582
Market Cap	$7.3 Billion	Shares
Book Value	$3.8 Billion	127,237,336
Price/Book	1.91	% Held
Price/Sales	0.66	86.74

Business Summary: Construction Services (MIC: 7.5.4 SIC: 1629 NAIC: 236210)

Jacobs Engineering Group is a technical services firm. Co. provides technical and construction services to a range of industrial, commercial, and governmental clients. Co.'s categories of services are: Project Services, including engineering, design, architecture, interiors, planning, and environmental services; Process, Scientific, and Systems Consulting services, including services related to scientific testing, analysis, and consulting activities; Construction services, encompassing field construction services and modular construction activities; and Operations and Maintenance services, including services performed in connection with operating facilities on behalf of clients.

Recent Developments: For the quarter ended Dec 28 2012, net income increased 14.3% to US$104.5 million from US$91.4 million in the year-earlier quarter. Revenues were US$2.76 billion, up 4.9% from US$2.63 billion the year before. Operating income was US$160.3 million versus US$142.0 million in the prior-year quarter, an increase of 12.9%. Direct operating expenses rose 5.1% to US$2.32 billion from US$2.21 billion in the comparable period the year before. Indirect operating expenses decreased 1.3% to US$275.5 million from US$279.1 million in the equivalent prior-year period.

Prospects: Our evaluation of Jacobs Engineering Group Inc. as of Apr. 7, 2013 is the result of our systematic analysis on three basic characteristics: earnings strength, relative valuation, and recent stock price movement. The company has enjoyed a very positive trend in earnings per share over the past 5 quarters and while recent estimates for the company have been raised by analysts, JEC has posted better than expected results. Based on operating earnings yield, the company is undervalued when compared to all of the companies in our coverage universe. Share price changes over the past year indicates that JEC will perform poorly over the near term.

Financial Data
(US$ in Thousands)

	3 Mos	09/28/2012	09/30/2011	10/01/2010	10/02/2009	09/30/2008	09/30/2007	09/30/2006
Earnings Per Share	3.00	2.94	2.60	1.96	3.21	3.38	2.35	1.64
Cash Flow Per Share	3.11	2.36	1.89	1.59	4.32	2.58	3.04	1.92
Tang Book Value Per Share	14.02	11.30	10.24	13.03	13.19	10.28	9.92	7.18
Income Statement								
Total Revenue	2,759,641	10,893,778	10,381,664	9,915,517	11,467,376	11,252,159	8,473,970	7,421,270
EBITDA	183,390	699,797	615,913	485,512	700,886	719,504	486,597	338,174
Depn & Amortn	24,475	100,824	95,370	88,495	86,342	73,126	49,700	40,600
Income Before Taxes	156,311	593,336	516,661	391,934	624,773	657,411	448,642	305,287
Income Taxes	51,788	202,382	181,440	145,647	224,919	236,669	161,512	108,404
Net Income	99,010	378,954	331,029	245,974	399,854	420,742	287,130	196,883
Average Shares	129,669	128,692	127,235	125,790	124,534	124,357	122,226	120,374
Balance Sheet								
Current Assets	3,695,372	3,612,077	3,157,353	2,767,042	2,818,449	2,750,234	2,278,078	1,817,961
Total Assets	6,936,678	6,839,433	6,049,428	4,683,917	4,428,614	4,278,238	3,389,421	2,853,884
Current Liabilities	1,750,800	1,747,052	2,058,045	1,239,453	1,295,901	1,576,997	1,276,434	1,041,195
Long-Term Obligations	513,113	528,260	2,042	509	737	55,675	40,450	77,673
Total Liabilities	3,098,991	3,116,960	2,736,440	1,824,869	1,802,701	2,033,091	1,545,759	1,430,670
Stockholders' Equity	3,837,687	3,722,473	3,312,988	2,859,048	2,625,913	2,245,147	1,843,662	1,423,214
Shares Outstanding	130,240	129,935	127,784	125,909	124,229	122,701	120,221	117,991
Statistical Record								
Return on Assets %	5.94	5.90	6.19	5.41	9.13	10.94	9.20	7.56
Return on Equity %	10.67	10.80	10.76	8.99	16.33	20.52	17.58	15.36
EBITDA Margin %	6.65	6.42	5.93	4.90	6.11	6.39	5.74	4.56
Net Margin %	3.59	3.48	3.19	2.48	3.49	3.74	3.39	2.65
Asset Turnover	1.69	1.70	1.94	2.18	2.62	2.93	2.71	2.85
Current Ratio	2.11	2.07	1.53	2.23	2.17	1.74	1.78	1.75
Debt to Equity	0.13	0.14	N.M.	N.M.	N.M.	0.02	0.02	0.05
Price Range	47.61-34.40	47.61-31.55	53.01-31.88	49.97-34.02	54.31-26.27	101.58-47.60	77.16-36.24	46.46-29.65
P/E Ratio	15.87-11.47	16.19-10.73	20.39-12.26	25.49-17.36	16.92-8.18	30.05-14.08	32.83-15.42	28.33-18.08

Address: 155 North Lake Avenue, Pasadena, CA 91101	**Web Site:** www.jacobs.com	**Auditors:** Ernst & Young LLP
Telephone: 626-578-3500	**Officers:** Craig L. Martin - President, Chief Executive Officer Thomas R. Hammond - Executive Vice President	**Transfer Agents:** Wells Fargo Shareowner Services, South St. Paul, MN
Fax: 626-568-7144		

JANUS CAPITAL GROUP INC

Exchange NYS	Symbol JNS	Price $9.40 (3/28/2013)	52Wk Range 9.83-6.80	Yield 2.55	P/E 17.09

*7 Year Price Score 48.78 *NYSE Composite Index=100 *12 Month Price Score 103.77

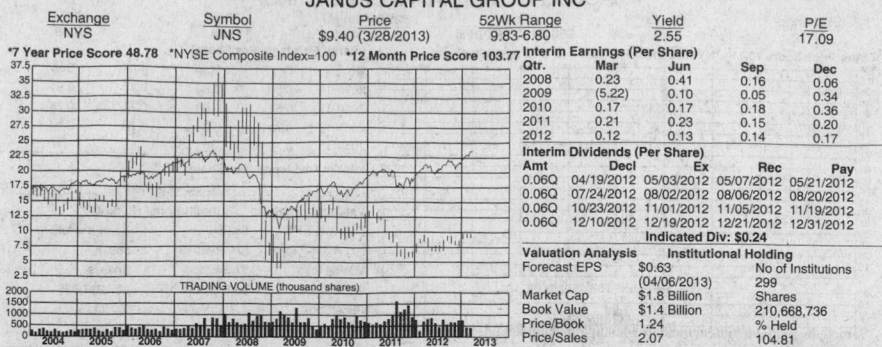

Interim Earnings (Per Share)

Qtr.	Mar	Jun	Sep	Dec
2008	0.23	0.41	0.16	0.06
2009	(5.22)	0.10	0.05	0.34
2010	0.17	0.17	0.18	0.36
2011	0.21	0.23	0.15	0.20
2012	0.12	0.13	0.14	0.17

Interim Dividends (Per Share)

Amt	Decl	Ex	Rec	Pay
0.06Q	04/19/2012	05/03/2012	05/07/2012	05/21/2012
0.06Q	07/24/2012	08/02/2012	08/06/2012	08/20/2012
0.06Q	10/23/2012	11/01/2012	11/05/2012	11/19/2012
0.06Q	12/10/2012	12/19/2012	12/21/2012	12/31/2012

Indicated Div: $0.24

Valuation Analysis

		Institutional Holding	
Forecast EPS	$0.63 (04/06/2013)	No of Institutions	299
Market Cap	$1.8 Billion	Shares	210,668,736
Book Value	$1.4 Billion	% Held	104.81
Price/Book	1.24		
Price/Sales	2.07		

Business Summary: Wealth Management (MIC: 5.5.2 SIC: 6282 NAIC: 523930)

Janus Capital Group is engaged in providing investment management, administration, distribution and related services to financial advisors, individuals and institutional clients through mutual funds, other pooled investment vehicles, separate accounts and subadvised relationships (investment products) in both domestic and international markets. Through its subsidiaries, Co. provides investment management competencies across a range of disciplines including fundamental U.S. and global equities (growth and value), mathematical equities, fixed income and alternatives. Co.'s investment products are distributed through three primary channels: Retail Intermediary, Institutional and International.

Recent Developments: For the year ended Dec 31 2012, net income decreased 27.1% to US$111.9 million from US$153.4 million in the prior year. Revenues were US$850.0 million, down 13.4% from US$981.9 million the year before. Operating income was US$214.5 million versus US$311.8 million in the prior year, a decrease of 31.2%. Indirect operating expenses decreased 5.2% to US$635.5 million from US$670.1 million in the equivalent prior-year period.

Prospects: Our evaluation of Janus Capital Group Inc. as of Apr. 7, 2013 is the result of our systematic analysis on three basic characteristics: earnings strength, relative valuation, and recent stock price movement. The company has produced a positive trend in earnings per share over the past 5 quarters and while recent estimates for the company have been raised by analysts, JNS has posted better than expected results. Based on operating earnings yield, the company is undervalued when compared to all of the companies in our coverage universe. Share price changes over the past year indicates that JNS will perform well over the near term.

Financial Data
(US$ in Thousands)

	12/31/2012	12/31/2011	12/31/2010	12/31/2009	12/31/2008	12/31/2007	12/31/2006	12/31/2005
Earnings Per Share	0.55	0.78	0.88	(4.55)	0.85	0.65	0.66	0.40
Cash Flow Per Share	1.13	1.23	1.37	1.06	1.49	1.65	1.49	1.25
Tang Book Value Per Share	N.M.	N.M.	N.M.	N.M.	N.M.	N.M.	N.M.	0.88
Dividends Per Share	0.290	0.150	0.040	0.040	0.040	0.040	0.040	0.040
Dividend Payout %	52.73	19.23	4.55	...	4.71	6.15	6.06	10.00
Income Statement								
Total Revenue	850,000	981,900	1,015,700	848,700	1,037,900	1,117,000	1,026,700	953,100
EBITDA	234,400	297,100	322,500	(661,200)	292,800	383,500	283,800	217,300
Depn & Amortn	13,400	14,000	15,000	15,600	15,900	14,200	21,400	20,100
Income Before Taxes	176,600	232,800	245,000	(750,400)	206,800	322,900	230,100	168,600
Income Taxes	64,700	79,400	76,400	(6,300)	68,800	116,400	81,900	67,900
Net Income	102,300	142,900	159,900	(757,100)	136,900	116,300	133,600	87,800
Average Shares	185,100	184,200	182,000	166,500	160,700	178,600	203,500	219,100
Balance Sheet								
Current Assets	888,400	835,900	893,300	630,600	583,900	953,900	925,100	1,003,700
Total Assets	2,660,400	2,644,000	2,726,800	2,530,300	3,336,700	3,564,100	3,537,900	3,628,500
Current Liabilities	159,500	148,800	420,800	187,100	156,600	226,700	185,600	267,800
Long-Term Obligations	545,100	595,200	586,700	792,000	1,106,000	1,127,700	537,200	262,200
Total Liabilities	1,242,500	1,330,800	1,555,300	1,529,200	1,728,600	1,840,600	1,231,500	1,047,300
Stockholders' Equity	1,417,900	1,313,200	1,171,500	1,001,100	1,608,100	1,723,500	2,306,400	2,581,200
Shares Outstanding	187,522	187,035	184,100	182,024	157,890	166,287	193,479	216,035
Statistical Record								
Return on Assets %	3.85	5.32	6.08	N.M.	3.96	3.28	3.73	2.37
Return on Equity %	7.47	11.50	14.72	N.M.	8.20	5.77	5.47	3.30
EBITDA Margin %	27.58	30.26	31.75	N.M.	28.21	34.33	27.64	22.80
Net Margin %	12.04	14.55	15.74	N.M.	13.19	10.41	13.01	9.21
Asset Turnover	0.32	0.37	0.39	0.29	0.30	0.31	0.29	0.26
Current Ratio	5.57	5.62	2.12	3.37	3.73	4.21	4.98	3.75
Debt to Equity	0.38	0.45	0.50	0.79	0.69	0.65	0.23	0.10
Price Range	9.55-6.60	14.54-5.63	15.72-8.81	15.82-3.95	32.85-5.28	36.80-19.43	24.15-15.80	19.93-12.99
P/E Ratio	17.36-12.00	18.64-7.22	17.86-10.01	...	38.65-6.21	56.62-29.89	36.59-23.94	49.83-32.48
Average Yield %	3.57	1.60	0.34	0.37	0.18	0.15	0.20	0.26

Address: 151 Detroit Street, Denver, CO 80206 Telephone: 303-333-3863	Web Site: www.janus.com Officers: Glenn S. Schafer - Chairman Richard M. Weil - Chief Executive Officer	Auditors: Deloitte & Touche LLP Transfer Agents: Wells Fargo Shareowner Services, Saint Paul, MN

JARDEN CORP.

Exchange	Symbol	Price	52Wk Range	Yield	P/E
NYS	JAH	$42.85 (3/28/2013)	43.70-25.29	N/A	20.70

*7 Year Price Score 138.92 *NYSE Composite Index=100 *12 Month Price Score 114.12

TRADING VOLUME (thousand shares)

Interim Earnings (Per Share)

Qtr.	Mar	Jun	Sep	Dec
2008	0.04	0.37	0.55	(1.49)
2009	0.08	0.35	0.55	(0.01)
2010	(0.44)	0.29	0.60	0.35
2011	0.14	0.55	0.69	0.17
2012	0.27	0.72	0.67	0.43

Interim Dividends (Per Share)

Amt	Decl	Ex	Rec	Pay
0.058Q	07/01/2011	07/07/2011	07/11/2011	07/29/2011
0.058Q	09/23/2011	09/29/2011	10/03/2011	10/31/2011
0.058Q	12/15/2011	12/29/2011	01/03/2012	01/31/2012
3-for-2	02/14/2013	03/19/2013	02/25/2013	03/18/2013

Div. Payment Suspended by Co.

Valuation Analysis

		Institutional Holding	
Forecast EPS	$3.23	No of Institutions	
	(04/06/2013)	374	
Market Cap	$5.0 Billion	Shares	
Book Value	$1.8 Billion	77,476,104	
Price/Book	2.86	% Held	
Price/Sales	0.75	87.70	

Business Summary: Leisure Equipment (MIC: 1.6.1 SIC: 3949 NAIC: 339920)

Jarden is a consumer products company. Co. operates three primary business segments: Outdoor Solutions, which manufactures or sources, markets and distributes consumer products for outdoor and outdoor-related activities; Consumer Solutions, which manufactures or sources, markets, and distributes a line of household products, including kitchen appliances and home environment products; and Branded Consumables, which manufactures or sources, markets and distributes a line of consumer products, consumable and fundamental household staples. In addition to the three primary business segments, Co.'s Process Solutions segment manufactures, markets and distributes a variety of plastic products.

Recent Developments: For the year ended Dec 31 2012, net income increased 19.1% to US$243.9 million from US$204.7 million in the prior year. Revenues were US$6.70 billion, up 0.2% from US$6.68 billion the year before. Operating income was US$576.8 million versus US$522.9 million in the prior year, an increase of 10.3%. Direct operating expenses declined 1.0% to US$4.77 billion from US$4.82 billion in the comparable period the year before. Indirect operating expenses increased 0.9% to US$1.35 billion from US$1.34 billion in the equivalent prior-year period.

Prospects: Our evaluation of Jarden Corp. as of Apr. 7, 2013 is the result of our systematic analysis on three basic characteristics: earnings strength, relative valuation, and recent stock price movement. The company has generated a negative trend in earnings per share over the past 5 quarters and while recent estimates for the company have been raised by analysts, JAH has posted better than expected results. Based on operating earnings yield, the company is undervalued when compared to all of the companies in our coverage universe. Share price changes over the past year indicates that JAH will perform well over the near term.

Financial Data

(US$ in Thousands)	12/31/2012	12/31/2011	12/31/2010	12/31/2009	12/31/2008	12/31/2007	12/31/2006	12/31/2005
Earnings Per Share	2.07	1.54	0.79	1.01	(0.52)	0.25	1.06	0.15
Cash Flow Per Share	4.08	3.23	2.16	5.08	2.21	2.83	2.41	3.04
Dividends Per Share		0.058	0.230	0.220	0.100	...	...	...
Dividend Payout %	2.78	14.94	27.73	9.87	...	...	...	...
Income Statement								
Total Revenue	6,696,100	6,679,900	6,022,700	5,152,600	5,383,300	4,660,100	3,846,300	3,189,066
EBITDA	711,800	655,100	534,300	500,500	250,400	301,300	363,500	236,086
Depn & Amortn	135,000	145,000	127,000	113,600	104,300	85,000	67,900	56,100
Income Before Taxes	391,500	330,400	229,500	239,400	(32,600)	66,600	188,000	95,668
Income Taxes	147,600	125,700	122,800	110,700	26,300	38,500	82,000	34,952
Net Income	243,900	204,700	106,700	128,700	(58,900)	28,100	106,000	60,716
Average Shares	118,200	132,900	134,700	127,200	112,800	109,950	99,750	82,050
Balance Sheet								
Current Assets	3,810,400	3,493,500	3,370,800	2,988,000	2,729,100	2,550,200	1,563,700	1,464,447
Total Assets	7,710,600	7,116,700	7,093,000	6,023,600	5,727,000	5,868,100	3,882,600	3,524,608
Current Liabilities	1,728,700	1,463,700	1,677,200	1,484,500	1,354,400	1,280,400	724,100	714,527
Long-Term Obligations	3,293,400	2,890,100	2,806,000	2,145,900	2,436,900	2,449,500	1,421,800	1,455,050
Total Liabilities	5,951,000	5,204,700	5,272,500	4,256,800	4,342,800	4,329,500	2,625,200	2,520,762
Stockholders' Equity	1,759,600	1,912,000	1,820,500	1,766,800	1,384,200	1,538,600	1,257,400	1,003,846
Shares Outstanding	117,300	136,350	137,700	135,300	113,400	115,200	107,400	102,099
Statistical Record								
Return on Assets %	3.28	2.88	1.63	2.19	N.M.	0.58	2.86	2.66
Return on Equity %	13.25	10.97	5.95	8.17	N.M.	2.01	9.38	9.08
EBITDA Margin %	10.63	9.81	8.87	9.71	4.65	6.47	9.45	7.40
Net Margin %	3.64	3.06	1.77	2.50	N.M.	0.60	2.76	1.90
Asset Turnover	0.90	0.94	0.92	0.88	0.93	0.96	1.04	1.40
Current Ratio	2.20	2.39	2.01	2.01	2.01	1.99	2.16	2.05
Debt to Equity	1.87	1.51	1.54	1.21	1.76	1.59	1.13	1.45
Price Range	37.05-19.86	24.49-17.25	23.39-17.22	21.05-5.89	18.00-5.28	29.93-15.39	25.58-15.89	27.61-18.88
P/E Ratio	17.90-9.59	15.90-11.20	29.61-21.80	20.84-5.83	...	119.71-61.57	24.13-14.99	184.04-125.90
Average Yield %	0.20	1.07	1.07	0.73	...	...	...	...

Address: 555 Theodore Fremd Avenue, Rye, NY 10580 Telephone: 914-967-9400	Web Site: www.jarden.com Officers: Martin E. Franklin - Executive Chairman Ian G.H. Ashken - Vice-Chairman, Chief Financial Officer	Auditors: PricewaterhouseCoopers LLP Investor Contact: 203-682-8200 Transfer Agents: Computershare Trust Company, N.A, Providence, RI

JOHNSON CONTROLS INC

Exchange	Symbol	Price	52Wk Range	Yield	P/E
NYS	JCI	$35.07 (3/28/2013)	35.09-23.51	2.17	20.51

*7 Year Price Score 85.64   *NYSE Composite Index=100   *12 Month Price Score 102.74

Interim Earnings (Per Share)

Qtr.	Dec	Mar	Jun	Sep
2009-10	0.52	0.40	0.61	0.66
2010-11	0.55	0.51	0.52	0.78
2011-12	0.60	0.53	0.61	0.05
2012-13	0.52	...	...	...

Interim Dividends (Per Share)

Amt	Decl	Ex	Rec	Pay
0.18Q	05/23/2012	06/06/2012	06/08/2012	07/03/2012
0.18Q	07/25/2012	09/05/2012	09/07/2012	10/02/2012
0.19Q	11/14/2012	12/05/2012	12/07/2012	12/28/2012
0.19Q	01/23/2013	03/06/2013	03/08/2013	04/02/2013

Indicated Div: $0.76 (Div. Reinv. Plan)

Valuation Analysis

		Institutional Holding	
Forecast EPS	$2.60	No of Institutions	
	(04/05/2013)	881	
Market Cap	$24.0 Billion	Shares	
Book Value	$11.9 Billion	559,264,320	
Price/Book	2.02	% Held	
Price/Sales	0.57	78.86	

Business Summary: Auto Parts (MIC: 1.8.2 SIC: 2531 NAIC: 561790)

Johnson Controls operates in three primary businesses: Building Efficiency, which provides heating, ventilating and air conditioning systems, building management systems, controls, security and mechanical equipment, as well as residential air conditioning and heating systems and industrial refrigeration products; Automotive Experience, which designs and manufactures interior products and systems for passenger cars and light trucks, including seating and overhead systems, door systems, floor consoles, instrument panels, cockpits and integrated electronics; and Power Solutions, which designs and manufactures lead-acid automotive batteries for the replacement and original equipment markets.

Recent Developments: For the quarter ended Dec 31 2012, net income decreased 16.3% to US$384.0 million from US$459.0 million in the year-earlier quarter. Revenues were US$10.42 billion, unchanged from the year before. Direct operating expenses rose 0.4% to US$8.91 billion from US$8.88 billion in the comparable period the year before. Indirect operating expenses increased 1.6% to US$1.05 billion from US$1.04 billion in the equivalent prior-year period.

Prospects: Our evaluation of Johnson Controls Inc. as of Apr. 7, 2013 is the result of our systematic analysis on three basic characteristics: earnings strength, relative valuation, and recent stock price movement. The company has suffered a very negative trend in earnings per share over the past 5 quarters and while recent estimates for the company have been mixed, JCI has posted better than expected results. Based on operating earnings yield, the company is undervalued when compared to all of the companies in our coverage universe. Share price changes over the past year indicates that JCI will perform poorly over the near term.

Financial Data
(US$ in Thousands)

	3 Mos	09/30/2012	09/30/2011	09/30/2010	09/30/2009	09/30/2008	09/30/2007	09/30/2006
Earnings Per Share	1.71	1.78	2.36	2.19	(0.57)	1.63	2.09	1.74
Cash Flow Per Share	2.86	2.28	1.59	2.25	1.54	3.24	3.24	2.43
Tang Book Value Per Share	5.57	5.31	4.53	4.20	2.77	3.63	3.37	1.10
Dividends Per Share	0.730	0.720	0.640	0.520	0.520	0.520	0.440	0.373
Dividend Payout %	42.69	40.45	27.12	23.74	...	31.90	21.05	21.41
Income Statement								
Total Revenue	10,422,000	41,955,000	40,833,000	34,305,000	28,497,000	38,062,000	34,624,000	32,235,000
EBITDA	679,000	2,074,000	2,544,000	2,200,000	504,000	1,991,000	2,250,000	1,979,000
Depn & Amortn	223,000	824,000	731,000	691,000	745,000	783,000	732,000	705,000
Income Before Taxes	395,000	1,250,000	1,813,000	1,509,000	(241,000)	1,208,000	1,518,000	1,026,000
Income Taxes	96,000	237,000	370,000	197,000	32,000	321,000	300,000	63,000
Net Income	354,000	1,226,000	1,624,000	1,491,000	(338,000)	979,000	1,252,000	1,028,000
Average Shares	686,700	688,600	689,900	682,500	595,300	601,400	599,200	589,800
Balance Sheet								
Current Assets	12,828,000	12,673,000	12,015,000	10,652,000	9,826,000	10,676,000	10,872,000	9,264,000
Total Assets	31,232,000	30,884,000	29,676,000	25,743,000	24,088,000	24,987,000	24,105,000	21,921,000
Current Liabilities	10,768,000	10,855,000	10,782,000	9,910,000	8,716,000	9,810,000	9,920,000	8,146,000
Long-Term Obligations	5,413,000	5,321,000	4,533,000	2,652,000	3,168,000	3,201,000	3,255,000	4,166,000
Total Liabilities	19,374,000	19,329,000	18,634,000	15,672,000	14,950,000	15,563,000	15,198,000	14,566,000
Stockholders' Equity	11,858,000	11,555,000	11,042,000	10,071,000	9,138,000	9,424,000	8,907,000	7,355,000
Shares Outstanding	684,321	682,307	680,164	673,726	668,531	590,796	593,766	587,321
Statistical Record								
Return on Assets %	3.84	4.04	5.86	5.98	N.M.	3.98	5.44	5.40
Return on Equity %	10.18	10.82	15.38	15.52	N.M.	10.65	15.40	15.33
EBITDA Margin %	6.52	4.94	6.23	6.41	1.77	5.23	6.50	6.14
Net Margin %	3.40	2.92	3.98	4.35	N.M.	2.57	3.62	3.19
Asset Turnover	1.38	1.38	1.47	1.38	1.16	1.55	1.50	1.69
Current Ratio	1.19	1.17	1.11	1.07	1.13	1.09	1.10	1.14
Debt to Equity	0.46	0.46	0.41	0.26	0.35	0.34	0.37	0.57
Price Range	35.58-23.51	35.58-23.51	42.71-26.37	35.01-23.77	30.33-8.68	44.42-28.33	42.12-23.98	30.00-20.09
P/E Ratio	20.81-13.75	19.99-13.21	18.10-11.17	15.99-10.85	...	27.25-17.38	20.15-11.47	17.24-11.55
Average Yield %	2.49	2.39	1.72	1.79	2.75	1.51	1.33	1.51

Address: 5757 North Green Bay Avenue, Milwaukee, WI 53209
Telephone: 414-524-1200

Web Site: www.johnsoncontrols.com
Officers: Stephen A. Roell - Chairman, Vice-Chairman, President, Chief Executive Officer, Executive Vice President, Senior Vice President, Vice President, Chief Financial Officer Alex A. Molinaroli - Vice-Chairman, Vice President, Division Officer

Auditors: PricewaterhouseCoopers LLP
Investor Contact: 414-524-2375
Transfer Agents: Wells Fargo Bank, N.A., St. Paul, MN

JOHNSON & JOHNSON

Exchange	Symbol	Price	52Wk Range	Yield	P/E	Div Achiever
NYS	JNJ	$81.53 (3/28/2013)	81.53-61.78	2.99	21.12	50 Years

*7 Year Price Score 97.00   *NYSE Composite Index=100   *12 Month Price Score 102.28

Interim Earnings (Per Share)

Qtr.	Mar	Jun	Sep	Dec
2008	1.26	1.17	1.17	0.97
2009	1.26	1.15	1.20	0.79
2010	1.62	1.23	1.23	0.70
2011	1.25	1.00	1.15	0.09
2012	1.41	0.50	1.05	0.90

Interim Dividends (Per Share)

Amt	Decl	Ex	Rec	Pay
0.61Q	04/26/2012	05/24/2012	05/29/2012	06/12/2012
0.61Q	07/16/2012	08/24/2012	08/28/2012	09/11/2012
0.61Q	10/17/2012	11/23/2012	11/27/2012	12/11/2012
0.61Q	01/02/2013	02/22/2013	02/26/2013	03/12/2013

Indicated Div: $2.44 (Div. Reinv. Plan)

Valuation Analysis		Institutional Holding	
Forecast EPS	$5.40	No of Institutions	
	(04/06/2013)	2319	
Market Cap	$226.5 Billion	Shares	
Book Value	$64.8 Billion	2,080,929,408	
Price/Book	3.49	% Held	
Price/Sales	3.37	66.41	

Business Summary: Pharmaceuticals (MIC: 4.1.1 SIC: 2834 NAIC: 325412)

Johnson & Johnson is a holding company. Through its subsidiaries, Co. engages in three business segments. The Consumer segment includes products used in the baby care, skin care, oral care, wound care and women's health care fields, as well as nutritional and over-the-counter pharmaceutical products, and wellness and prevention platforms. The Pharmaceutical segment includes products in the areas of anti-infective, antipsychotic, contraceptive, gastrointestinal, hematology, immunology, infectious diseases, neurology, oncology, pain management, thrombosis and vaccines. The Medical Devices and Diagnostics segment includes products used principally by physicians, nurses, hospitals, and clinics.

Recent Developments: For the year ended Dec 30 2012, net income increased 8.7% to US$10.51 billion from US$9.67 billion in the prior year. Revenues were US$67.22 billion, up 3.4% from US$65.03 billion the year before. Direct operating expenses rose 6.4% to US$21.66 billion from US$20.36 billion in the comparable period the year before. Indirect operating expenses increased 2.1% to US$29.70 billion from US$29.09 billion in the equivalent prior-year period.

Prospects: Our evaluation of Johnson & Johnson as of Apr. 7, 2013 is the result of our systematic analysis on three basic characteristics: earnings strength, relative valuation, and recent stock price movement. The company has produced a positive trend in earnings per share over the past 5 quarters and while recent estimates for the company have remained steady, JNJ has posted better than expected results. Based on operating earnings yield, the company is undervalued when compared to all of the companies in our coverage universe. Share price changes over the past year indicates that JNJ will perform poorly over the near term.

Financial Data
(US$ in Millions)

	12/30/2012	01/01/2012	01/02/2011	01/03/2010	12/28/2008	12/30/2007	12/31/2006	01/01/2006
Earnings Per Share	3.86	3.49	4.78	4.40	4.57	3.63	3.73	3.46
Cash Flow Per Share	5.61	5.24	5.97	5.91	5.36	5.30	4.87	4.00
Tang Book Value Per Share	4.91	8.37	8.97	7.04	5.35	5.12	3.67	8.64
Dividends Per Share	2.400	2.250	2.110	1.930	1.795	1.620	1.455	1.275
Dividend Payout %	62.18	64.47	44.14	43.86	39.28	44.63	39.01	36.85
Income Statement								
Total Revenue	67,224	65,030	61,587	61,897	63,747	61,095	53,324	50,514
EBITDA	17,889	15,993	20,243	18,891	19,791	15,871	16,015	15,244
Depn & Amortn	3,646	3,152	2,948	2,775	2,788	2,744	2,194	2,021
Income Before Taxes	13,775	12,361	16,947	15,755	16,929	13,283	14,587	13,656
Income Taxes	3,261	2,689	3,613	3,489	3,980	2,707	3,534	3,245
Net Income	10,853	9,672	13,334	12,266	12,949	10,576	11,053	10,411
Average Shares	2,813	2,776	2,789	2,790	2,836	2,911	2,962	3,013
Balance Sheet								
Current Assets	46,116	54,316	47,307	39,541	34,377	29,945	22,975	31,394
Total Assets	121,347	113,644	102,908	94,682	84,912	80,954	70,556	58,025
Current Liabilities	24,262	22,811	23,072	21,731	20,852	19,837	19,161	12,635
Long-Term Obligations	11,489	12,969	9,156	8,223	8,120	7,074	2,014	2,017
Total Liabilities	56,521	56,564	46,329	44,094	42,401	37,635	31,238	20,154
Stockholders' Equity	64,826	57,080	56,579	50,588	42,511	43,319	39,318	37,871
Shares Outstanding	2,779	2,725	2,739	2,755	2,770	2,841	2,894	2,975
Statistical Record								
Return on Assets %	9.26	8.96	13.53	13.44	15.66	14.00	17.24	18.75
Return on Equity %	17.85	17.07	24.95	25.92	30.26	25.67	28.72	29.96
EBITDA Margin %	26.61	24.59	32.87	30.52	31.05	25.98	30.03	30.18
Net Margin %	16.14	14.87	21.65	19.82	20.31	17.31	20.73	20.61
Asset Turnover	0.57	0.60	0.63	0.68	0.77	0.81	0.83	0.91
Current Ratio	1.90	2.38	2.05	1.82	1.65	1.51	1.20	2.48
Debt to Equity	0.18	0.23	0.16	0.16	0.19	0.16	0.05	0.05
Price Range	72.52-61.78	67.92-57.66	66.03-57.02	64.96-46.60	72.22-55.33	68.40-59.77	69.10-56.80	69.40-60.04
P/E Ratio	18.79-16.01	19.46-16.52	13.81-11.93	14.76-10.59	15.80-12.11	18.84-16.47	18.53-15.23	20.06-17.35
Average Yield %	3.58	3.54	3.39	3.34	2.76	2.53	2.34	1.97

Address: One Johnson & Johnson Plaza, New Brunswick, NJ 08933	**Web Site:** www.jnj.com	**Auditors:** PricewaterhouseCoopers LLP
Telephone: 732-524-0400	**Officers:** Alex Gorsky - Chairman, Chief Executive	**Investor Contact:** 800-950-5089
Fax: 732-214-0332	Officer, Division Officer Dominic J. Caruso - Vice President, Chief Financial Officer	**Transfer Agents:** Computershare Trust Company, Canton, MA

JONES LANG LASALLE INC

Exchange	Symbol	Price	52Wk Range	Yield	P/E
NYS	JLL	$99.41 (3/28/2013)	100.69-64.67	0.40	21.47

*7 Year Price Score 96.64 ***NYSE Composite Index=100** ***12 Month Price Score 112.07**

Interim Earnings (Per Share)

Qtr.	Mar	Jun	Sep	Dec
2008	0.09	0.73	0.43	1.19
2009	(1.78)	(0.40)	0.46	1.39
2010	0.01	0.72	0.84	1.91
2011	0.03	0.99	0.76	1.91
2012	0.31	0.83	1.10	2.38

Interim Dividends (Per Share)

Amt	Decl	Ex	Rec	Pay
0.15S	04/26/2011	05/12/2011	05/16/2011	06/15/2011
0.15S	11/02/2011	11/10/2011	11/15/2011	12/15/2011
0.20S	05/01/2012	05/11/2012	05/15/2012	06/15/2012
0.20S	10/29/2012	11/13/2012	11/15/2012	12/14/2012

Indicated Div: $0.40

Valuation Analysis / **Institutional Holding**

Forecast EPS	$6.21 (04/06/2013)	No of Institutions	321
Market Cap	$4.4 Billion	Shares	41,735,280
Book Value	$2.0 Billion	% Held	91.25
Price/Book	2.24		
Price/Sales	1.11		

TRADING VOLUME (thousand shares)

Business Summary: Property, Real Estate & Development (MIC: 5.3.2 SIC: 6531 NAIC: 531210)

Jones Lang LaSalle is a financial and services firm focusing in real estate. As of Dec 31 2012, Co. had over 200 corporate offices worldwide and operations in more than 1,000 locations in 70 countries. Co. provides real estate and investment management services on a local, regional and global basis to owner, occupier, investor and developer clients. Co. manages its operations as four business segments: The three geographic regions of Real Estate Services (RES): Americas, Europe, Middle East and Africa, Asia Pacific; and Investment Management, which provides investment management services to institutional investors and individuals.

Recent Developments: For the year ended Dec 31 2012, net income increased 26.1% to US$208.8 million from US$165.6 million in the prior year. Revenues were US$3.93 billion, up 9.7% from US$3.58 billion the year before.

Prospects: Our evaluation of Jones Lang LaSalle Inc. as of Apr. 7, 2013 is the result of our systematic analysis on three basic characteristics: earnings strength, relative valuation, and recent stock price movement. The company has generated a negative trend in earnings per share over the past 5 quarters. However, while recent estimates for the company have been lowered by analysts, JLL has posted results that fell short of analysts expectations. Based on operating earnings yield, the company is about fairly valued when compared to all of the companies in our coverage universe. Share price changes over the past year indicates that JLL will perform well over the near term.

Financial Data
(US$ in Thousands)

	12/31/2012	12/31/2011	12/31/2010	12/31/2009	12/31/2008	12/31/2007	12/31/2006	12/31/2005
Earnings Per Share	4.63	3.70	3.48	(0.11)	2.44	7.64	5.24	3.12
Cash Flow Per Share	7.45	4.90	9.09	6.50	1.01	12.79	11.85	3.84
Tang Book Value Per Share	1.17	N.M.	2.23	N.M.	N.M.	8.66	5.26	5.56
Dividends Per Share	0.400	0.300	0.200	0.200	0.750	0.850	0.600	0.250
Dividend Payout %	8.64	8.11	5.75	...	30.74	11.13	11.45	8.01
Income Statement								
Total Revenue	3,932,830	3,584,544	2,925,613	2,480,736	2,697,586	2,652,075	2,013,578	1,390,610
EBITDA	355,603	313,805	379,208	250,716	307,730	462,540	338,267	198,027
Depn & Amortn	66,200	62,600	118,550	134,312	156,267	114,091	94,188	66,276
Income Before Taxes	254,230	215,614	214,856	61,386	120,895	335,385	229,825	127,752
Income Taxes	69,244	56,387	49,038	5,677	28,743	87,595	63,825	36,236
Net Income	208,316	164,384	153,902	(3,595)	84,883	257,832	176,401	103,672
Average Shares	44,799	44,367	44,084	38,543	34,205	33,577	33,447	33,109
Balance Sheet								
Current Assets	1,515,529	1,300,884	1,194,841	939,918	999,768	1,070,976	807,445	531,098
Total Assets	4,351,499	3,932,636	3,349,861	3,096,933	3,077,025	2,291,874	1,729,948	1,144,769
Current Liabilities	1,661,971	1,348,617	1,296,312	1,095,095	987,885	1,063,932	830,446	522,635
Long-Term Obligations	444,000	463,000	197,500	175,000	483,942	29,205	32,398	26,697
Total Liabilities	2,400,316	2,241,507	1,780,930	1,718,004	2,009,343	1,281,341	979,568	608,766
Stockholders' Equity	1,951,183	1,691,129	1,568,931	1,378,929	1,067,682	1,010,533	750,380	536,003
Shares Outstanding	44,054	43,470	42,659	41,843	34,561	31,722	36,592	35,199
Statistical Record								
Return on Assets %	5.01	4.51	4.77	N.M.	3.15	12.82	12.27	9.61
Return on Equity %	11.39	10.08	10.44	N.M.	8.15	29.28	27.43	19.86
EBITDA Margin %	9.04	8.75	12.96	10.11	11.41	17.44	16.80	14.24
Net Margin %	5.29	4.59	5.26	N.M.	3.15	9.72	8.76	7.46
Asset Turnover	0.95	0.98	0.91	0.80	1.00	1.32	1.40	1.29
Current Ratio	0.91	0.96	0.92	0.86	1.01	1.01	0.97	1.02
Debt to Equity	0.23	0.27	0.13	0.13	0.45	0.03	0.04	0.05
Price Range	87.08-63.21	107.72-47.04	88.51-57.01	61.57-16.94	90.19-19.18	123.17-70.48	93.21-52.75	52.48-34.54
P/E Ratio	18.81-13.65	29.11-12.71	25.43-16.38	...	36.96-7.86	16.12-9.23	17.79-10.07	16.82-11.07
Average Yield %	0.53	0.37	0.27	0.53	1.34	0.83	0.75	0.55

Address: 200 East Randolph Drive, Chicago, IL 60601
Telephone: 312-782-5800
Fax: 312-782-4339

Web Site: www.joneslanglasalle.com
Officers: Sheila A. Penrose - Chairman Colin Dyer - President, Chief Executive Officer

Auditors: KPMG LLP
Investor Contact: 312-782-5800
Transfer Agents: Computershare, Jersey City, NJ

JOY GLOBAL INC

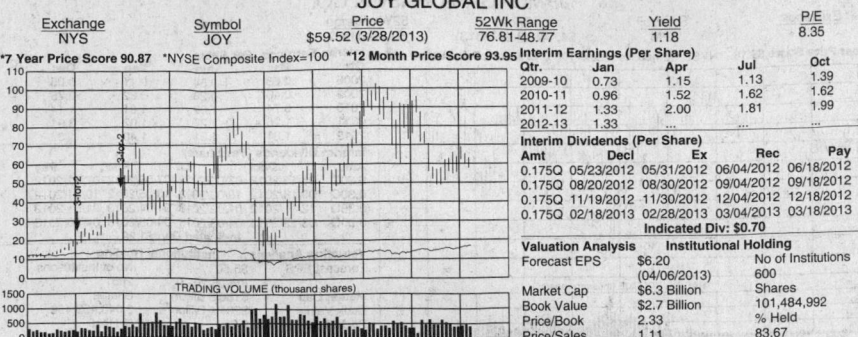

Exchange	Symbol	Price	52Wk Range	Yield	P/E
NYS	JOY	$59.52 (3/28/2013)	76.81-48.77	1.18	8.35

*7 Year Price Score 90.87 *NYSE Composite Index=100 ***12 Month Price Score 93.95**

Interim Earnings (Per Share)

Qtr.	Jan	Apr	Jul	Oct
2009-10	0.73	1.15	1.13	1.39
2010-11	0.96	1.52	1.62	1.62
2011-12	1.33	2.00	1.81	1.99
2012-13	1.33	...	...	...

Interim Dividends (Per Share)

Amt	Decl	Ex	Rec	Pay
0.175Q	05/23/2012	05/31/2012	06/04/2012	06/18/2012
0.175Q	08/20/2012	08/30/2012	09/04/2012	09/18/2012
0.175Q	11/19/2012	11/30/2012	12/04/2012	12/18/2012
0.175Q	02/18/2013	02/28/2013	03/04/2013	03/18/2013

Indicated Div: $0.70

Valuation Analysis

Forecast EPS $6.20 (04/06/2013)
Market Cap $6.3 Billion
Book Value $2.7 Billion
Price/Book 2.33
Price/Sales 1.11

Institutional Holding

No of Institutions 600
Shares 101,484,992
% Held 83.67

TRADING VOLUME (thousand shares)

Business Summary: Industrial Machinery & Equipment (MIC: 7.2.1 SIC: 3532 NAIC: 333131)

Joy Global is a manufacturer and servicer of mining equipment for the extraction of coal and other minerals and ores. Co.'s equipment is used in mining regions to mine coal, copper, iron ore, oil sands, and other minerals. Co. operates in two reportable segments: Underground Mining Machinery, which is a manufacturer of underground mining equipment for the extraction of coal and other bedded minerals and provides service locations near mining regions; and Surface Mining Equipment, which is a producer of surface mining equipment for the extraction of ores and minerals and provides operational support for several types of equipment used in surface mining.

Recent Developments: For the quarter ended Jan 25 2013, net income decreased 0.2% to US$142.1 million from US$142.5 million in the year-earlier quarter. Revenues were US$1.15 billion, up 1.2% from US$1.14 billion the year before. Operating income was US$221.2 million versus US$213.7 million in the prior-year quarter, an increase of 3.5%. Direct operating expenses rose 0.0% to US$773.1 million from US$772.8 million in the comparable period the year before. Indirect operating expenses increased 3.9% to US$155.6 million from US$149.7 million in the equivalent prior-year period.

Prospects: Our evaluation of Joy Global Inc. as of Apr. 7, 2013 is the result of our systematic analysis on three basic characteristics: earnings strength, relative valuation, and recent stock price movement. The company has generated a negative trend in earnings per share over the past 5 quarters. However, while recent estimates for the company have been mixed, JOY has posted better than expected results. Based on operating earnings yield, the company is undervalued when compared to all of the companies in our coverage universe. Share price changes over the past year indicates that JOY will perform well over the near term.

Financial Data
(US$ in Thousands)

	3 Mos	10/26/2012	10/28/2011	10/29/2010	10/30/2009	10/31/2008	10/26/2007	10/28/2006
Earnings Per Share	7.13	7.13	5.72	4.40	4.41	3.45	2.51	3.38
Cash Flow Per Share	5.19	4.19	4.82	5.67	4.42	5.28	3.48	2.72
Tang Book Value Per Share	6.84	5.72	10.83	10.15	4.84	2.07	5.98	7.18
Dividends Per Share	0.700	0.700	0.700	0.700	0.700	0.625	0.600	0.450
Dividend Payout %	9.82	9.82	12.24	15.91	15.87	18.12	23.90	13.31
Income Statement								
Total Revenue	1,149,877	5,660,889	4,403,906	3,524,334	3,598,314	3,418,934	2,547,322	2,401,710
EBITDA	241,247	1,256,359	979,644	747,293	756,672	597,585	513,903	487,119
Depn & Amortn	20,095	83,800	59,500	51,500	49,300	48,800	39,900	37,900
Income Before Taxes	205,999	1,105,131	895,833	679,024	682,640	527,087	449,059	450,357
Income Taxes	63,860	337,870	264,831	217,525	227,990	153,950	169,275	35,501
Net Income	142,137	762,021	609,656	461,499	454,650	374,278	279,784	416,421
Average Shares	107,237	106,889	106,537	104,905	103,104	108,425	111,630	123,276
Balance Sheet								
Current Assets	3,136,781	3,156,077	3,564,007	2,361,927	1,950,027	1,738,129	1,537,795	1,227,875
Total Assets	6,176,798	6,142,503	5,426,354	3,284,041	3,008,279	2,644,313	2,134,903	1,954,005
Current Liabilities	1,716,460	1,780,817	1,724,571	1,023,324	926,784	1,140,351	753,539	599,981
Long-Term Obligations	1,294,200	1,306,625	1,356,412	396,326	523,890	540,967	396,257	98,145
Total Liabilities	3,464,249	3,565,314	3,474,559	1,928,647	2,194,540	2,111,839	1,410,909	1,034,376
Stockholders' Equity	2,712,549	2,577,189	1,951,795	1,355,394	813,739	532,474	723,994	919,629
Shares Outstanding	106,205	105,926	105,113	103,529	103,021	102,707	107,682	117,542
Statistical Record								
Return on Assets %	12.34	13.21	14.04	14.71	16.13	15.41	13.76	23.18
Return on Equity %	31.59	33.74	36.97	42.67	67.73	58.61	34.23	52.61
EBITDA Margin %	20.98	22.19	22.24	21.20	21.03	17.48	20.17	20.28
Net Margin %	12.36	13.46	13.84	13.09	12.64	10.95	10.98	17.34
Asset Turnover	0.92	0.98	1.01	1.12	1.28	1.41	1.25	1.34
Current Ratio	1.83	1.77	2.07	2.31	2.10	1.52	2.04	2.05
Debt to Equity	0.48	0.51	0.69	0.29	0.64	1.02	0.55	0.11
Price Range	95.71-48.77	95.71-48.77	102.36-60.49	73.12-44.47	56.55-15.21	88.18-20.90	64.38-37.35	71.68-30.04
P/E Ratio	13.42-6.84	13.42-6.84	17.90-10.58	16.62-10.11	12.82-3.45	25.56-6.06	25.65-14.88	21.21-8.89
Average Yield %	1.10	1.02	0.81	1.23	2.24	0.99	1.22	0.96

Address: 100 East Wisconsin Avenue, Suite 2780, Milwaukee, WI 53202
Telephone: 414-319-8500

Web Site: www.joyglobal.com
Officers: John Nils Hanson - Chairman, President, Chief Executive Officer Michael W. Sutherlin - President, Chief Executive Officer

Auditors: Ernst & Young LLP
Investor Contact: 414-319-8507
Transfer Agents: The American Stock Transfer & Trust Company, New York, NY

JPMORGAN CHASE & CO.

Exchange	Symbol	Price	52Wk Range	Yield	P/E
NYS	JPM	$47.46 (3/28/2013)	51.00-31.00	2.53	9.13

*7 Year Price Score 89.18   *NYSE Composite Index=100   *12 Month Price Score 108.69

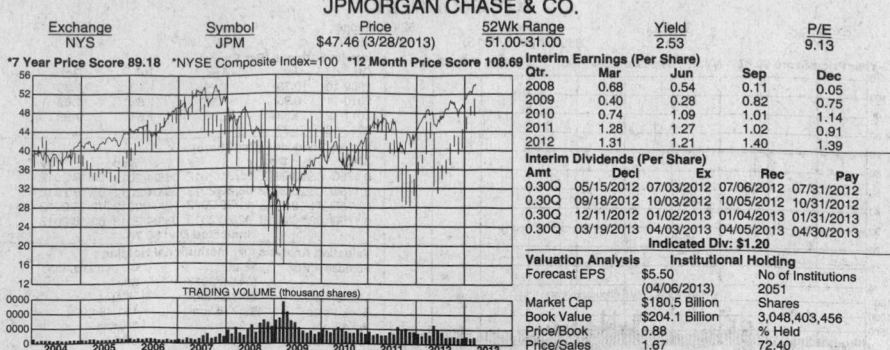

Interim Earnings (Per Share)

Qtr.	Mar	Jun	Sep	Dec
2008	0.68	0.54	0.11	0.05
2009	0.40	0.28	0.82	0.75
2010	0.74	1.09	1.01	1.14
2011	1.28	1.27	1.02	0.91
2012	1.31	1.21	1.40	1.39

Interim Dividends (Per Share)

Amt	Decl	Ex	Rec	Pay
0.30Q	05/15/2012	07/03/2012	07/06/2012	07/31/2012
0.30Q	09/18/2012	10/03/2012	10/05/2012	10/31/2012
0.30Q	12/11/2012	01/02/2013	01/04/2013	01/31/2013
0.30Q	03/19/2013	04/03/2013	04/05/2013	04/30/2013

Indicated Div: $1.20

Valuation Analysis / Institutional Holding

Forecast EPS	$5.50 (04/06/2013)	No of Institutions	2051
Market Cap	$180.5 Billion	Shares	3,048,403,456
Book Value	$204.1 Billion	% Held	72.40
Price/Book	0.88		
Price/Sales	1.67		

Business Summary: Banking (MIC: 5.1.1 SIC: 6021 NAIC: 522110)

JPMorgan Chase is a financial holding company. Through its subsidiaries, Co. provides investment banking, financial services for consumers and small businesses, commercial banking, financial transaction processing, asset management and private equity. Co.'s activities are organized into four segments. Co.'s consumer business is the consumer and community banking segment. Co.'s wholesale businesses comprise the corporate and investment bank, commercial banking, and asset management segments. Under the J.P. Morgan and Chase brands, Co. serves a number of corporate, institutional and government clients. As of Dec 31 2012, Co. had total assets of $2.36 trillion and deposits of $1.19 trillion.

Recent Developments: For the year ended Dec 31 2012, net income increased 12.2% to US$21.28 billion from US$18.98 billion in the prior year. Net interest income decreased 5.8% to US$44.91 billion from US$47.69 billion in the prior year. Provision for loan losses was US$3.39 billion versus US$7.57 billion in the prior year, a decrease of 55.3%. Non-interest income rose 5.2% to US$52.12 billion from US$49.55 billion, while non-interest expense advanced 2.9% to US$64.73 billion.

Prospects: Our evaluation of J.P. Morgan Chase & Co. as of Apr. 7, 2013 is the result of our systematic analysis on three basic characteristics: earnings strength, relative valuation, and recent stock price movement. The company has managed to produce a neutral trend in earnings per share over the past 5 quarters. However, while recent estimates for the company have been mixed, JPM has posted better than expected results. Based on operating earnings yield, the company is undervalued when compared to all of the companies in our coverage universe. Share price changes over the past year indicates that JPM will perform in line with the market over the near term.

Financial Data
(US$ in Millions)

	12/31/2012	12/31/2011	12/31/2010	12/31/2009	12/31/2008	12/31/2007	12/31/2006	12/31/2005
Earnings Per Share	5.20	4.48	3.98	2.26	1.37	4.38	4.04	2.38
Cash Flow Per Share	6.57	24.60	(0.95)	31.56	6.58	(32.48)	(14.29)	(6.94)
Tang Book Value Per Share	36.01	31.05	26.02	22.50	19.27	18.77	16.11	14.02
Dividends Per Share	1.150	0.800	0.200	0.530	1.520	1.440	1.360	1.360
Dividend Payout %	22.12	17.86	5.03	23.45	110.95	32.88	33.66	57.14
Income Statement								
Interest Income	56,063	61,293	63,782	66,350	73,018	71,387	59,107	45,200
Interest Expense	11,153	13,604	12,781	15,198	34,239	44,981	37,865	25,369
Net Interest Income	44,910	47,689	51,001	51,152	38,779	26,406	21,242	19,831
Provision for Losses	3,385	7,574	16,639	32,015	20,979	6,864	3,270	3,483
Non-Interest Income	52,121	49,545	51,693	49,282	28,473	44,966	40,195	34,702
Non-Interest Expense	64,729	62,911	61,196	52,352	43,500	41,703	38,281	38,835
Income Before Taxes	28,917	26,749	24,859	16,067	2,773	22,805	19,886	12,215
Income Taxes	7,633	7,773	7,489	4,415	(926)	7,440	6,237	3,732
Net Income	21,284	18,976	17,370	11,728	5,605	15,365	14,444	8,483
Average Shares	3,823	3,921	3,977	3,880	3,606	3,509	3,574	3,558
Balance Sheet								
Net Loans & Leases	711,860	696,111	660,661	601,856	721,734	510,140	475,848	412,058
Total Assets	2,359,141	2,265,792	2,117,605	2,031,989	2,175,052	1,562,147	1,351,520	1,198,942
Total Deposits	1,193,593	1,127,806	930,369	938,367	1,009,277	740,728	638,788	554,991
Total Liabilities	2,155,072	2,082,219	1,941,499	1,866,624	2,008,168	1,438,926	1,235,730	1,091,731
Stockholders' Equity	204,069	183,573	176,106	165,365	166,884	123,221	115,790	107,211
Shares Outstanding	3,804	3,773	3,911	3,942	3,733	3,368	3,462	3,487
Statistical Record								
Return on Assets %	0.92	0.87	0.84	0.56	0.30	1.05	1.13	0.72
Return on Equity %	10.95	10.55	10.17	7.06	3.85	12.86	12.95	7.97
Net Interest Margin %	80.11	77.80	79.96	77.09	53.11	36.99	35.94	43.87
Efficiency Ratio %	59.83	56.76	53.00	45.27	42.86	35.84	38.55	48.60
Loans to Deposits	0.60	0.62	0.71	0.64	0.72	0.69	0.74	0.74
Price Range	46.27-31.00	48.00-28.38	47.81-35.63	47.16-15.90	49.85-22.72	53.20-40.46	48.95-38.05	40.20-33.27
P/E Ratio	8.90-5.96	10.71-6.33	12.01-8.95	20.87-7.04	36.39-16.58	12.15-9.24	12.12-9.42	16.89-13.98
Average Yield %	2.93	2.03	0.50	1.49	3.82	3.02	3.10	3.77

Address: 270 Park Avenue, New York, NY 10017	Web Site: www.jpmorganchase.com	Auditors: PricewaterhouseCoopers LLP
Telephone: 212-270-6000	Officers: James Dimon - Chairman, President, Chief Executive Officer Douglas L. Braunstein - Vice-Chairman, Chief Financial Officer	Investor Contact: 212-270-7325
Fax: 212-270-1648		Transfer Agents: Computershare Shareowner Services, LLC, Pittsburgh, PA

JUNIPER NETWORKS INC

Exchange	Symbol	Price	52Wk Range	Yield	P/E
NYS	JNPR	$18.54 (3/28/2013)	22.73-14.27	N/A	52.97

*7 Year Price Score 68.91 ***NYSE Composite Index=100** ***12 Month Price Score 101.10**

Interim Earnings (Per Share)

Qtr.	Mar	Jun	Sep	Dec
2008	0.20	0.22	0.27	0.26
2009	(0.01)	0.03	0.16	0.04
2010	0.30	0.24	0.25	0.35
2011	0.24	0.21	0.16	0.19
2012	0.03	0.11	0.03	0.18

Interim Dividends (Per Share)

No Dividends Paid

Valuation Analysis — **Institutional Holding**

Forecast EPS	$1.16 (04/06/2013)	No of Institutions	503
Market Cap	$9.4 Billion	Shares	509,454,336
Book Value	$7.0 Billion	% Held	86.48
Price/Book	1.35		
Price/Sales	2.16		

Business Summary: Peripherals (MIC: 6.2.2 SIC: 3661 NAIC: 334210)

Juniper Networks designs, develops, and sells products and services that serves the networking requirements of service providers, enterprises, governments, and research and public sector organizations. Co. has two segments: Platform Systems Division, which provides scalable routing and switching products used in service provider, enterprise, and public sector networks to control and direct network traffic between data centers, core, edge, aggregation, campus, Wide Area Networks, branch, and consumer and business devices; and Software Solutions Division, which provides software focused on network security and network services applications for service providers and enterprise customers.

Recent Developments: For the year ended Dec 31 2012, net income decreased 56.1% to US$186.5 million from US$425.0 million in the prior year. Revenues were US$4.37 billion, down 1.9% from US$4.45 billion the year before. Operating income was US$308.1 million versus US$618.5 million in the prior year, a decrease of 50.2%. Direct operating expenses rose 4.8% to US$1.66 billion from US$1.58 billion in the comparable period the year before. Indirect operating expenses increased 6.7% to US$2.40 billion from US$2.25 billion in the equivalent prior-year period.

Prospects: Our evaluation of Juniper Networks Inc. as of Apr. 7, 2013 is the result of our systematic analysis on three basic characteristics: earnings strength, relative valuation, and recent stock price movement. The company has enjoyed a very positive trend in earnings per share over the past 5 quarters. However, while recent estimates for the company have been lowered by analysts, JNPR has posted better than expected results. Based on operating earnings yield, the company is about fairly valued when compared to all of the companies in our coverage universe. Share price changes over the past year indicates that JNPR will perform very well over the near term.

Financial Data
(US$ in Thousands)

	12/31/2012	12/31/2011	12/31/2010	12/31/2009	12/31/2008	12/31/2007	12/31/2006	12/31/2005
Earnings Per Share	0.35	0.79	1.15	0.22	0.93	0.62	(1.76)	0.59
Cash Flow Per Share	1.23	1.86	1.55	1.52	1.65	1.46	1.33	1.16
Tang Book Value Per Share	5.53	5.77	4.87	4.14	4.20	3.09	4.08	3.04
Income Statement								
Total Revenue	4,365,400	4,448,709	4,093,266	3,315,912	3,572,376	2,836,088	2,303,580	2,063,957
EBITDA	492,800	759,082	927,384	449,677	841,320	599,079	(829,759)	585,780
Depn & Amortn	159,400	147,566	151,030	143,416	162,029	187,696	168,023	138,800
Income Before Taxes	291,500	571,716	778,154	312,061	728,891	510,583	(897,049)	502,199
Income Taxes	105,000	146,704	158,781	196,833	217,142	149,753	104,388	148,170
Net Income	186,500	425,136	618,402	116,999	511,749	360,830	(1,001,437)	354,029
Average Shares	526,200	541,417	538,790	534,015	551,433	579,145	567,454	598,907
Balance Sheet								
Current Assets	3,600,700	4,439,661	3,214,370	2,878,959	2,816,206	2,555,115	2,521,806	1,818,456
Total Assets	9,832,100	9,983,820	8,467,851	7,590,263	7,187,341	6,885,406	7,368,395	8,026,599
Current Liabilities	1,422,000	1,466,703	1,471,976	1,375,785	1,056,610	1,379,843	762,617	627,400
Long-Term Obligations	999,200	999,034	...	...	...	...	399,944	399,959
Total Liabilities	2,833,100	2,894,638	1,859,651	1,768,127	1,285,936	1,531,546	1,253,311	1,126,889
Stockholders' Equity	6,999,000	7,089,182	6,608,200	5,822,136	5,901,405	5,353,860	6,115,084	6,899,710
Shares Outstanding	508,400	526,409	525,378	519,341	526,752	522,815	569,234	568,243
Statistical Record								
Return on Assets %	1.88	4.61	7.70	1.58	7.25	5.06	N.M.	4.71
Return on Equity %	2.64	6.21	9.95	2.00	9.07	6.29	N.M.	5.49
EBITDA Margin %	11.29	17.06	22.66	13.56	23.55	21.12	N.M.	28.38
Net Margin %	4.27	9.56	15.11	3.53	14.33	12.72	N.M.	17.15
Asset Turnover	0.44	0.48	0.51	0.45	0.51	0.40	0.30	0.27
Current Ratio	2.53	3.03	2.18	2.09	2.67	1.85	3.31	2.90
Debt to Equity	0.14	0.14	...	...	...	...	0.07	0.06
Price Range	23.88-14.27	44.46-17.08	37.90-22.82	28.22-12.67	33.20-13.84	37.65-17.74	22.38-12.20	27.19-19.75
P/E Ratio	68.23-40.77	56.28-21.62	32.96-19.84	128.27-57.59	35.70-14.88	60.72-28.61	...	46.08-33.47

Address: 1194 North Mathilda Avenue, Sunnyvale, CA 94089 **Telephone:** 408-745-2000 **Fax:** 408-745-2100	**Web Site:** www.juniper.net **Officers:** Scott G. Kriens - Chairman Pradeep S. Sindhu - Vice-Chairman, Chief Technical Officer	**Auditors:** Ernst & Young LLP **Investor Contact:** 408-936-5396 **Transfer Agents:** Wells Fargo Shareowner Services, South St. Paul, MN

KANSAS CITY SOUTHERN

Exchange	Symbol	Price	52Wk Range	Yield	P/E
NYS	KSU	$110.90 (3/28/2013)	110.90-62.54	0.78	32.33

*7 Year Price Score 162.55 *NYSE Composite Index=100 *12 Month Price Score 117.11

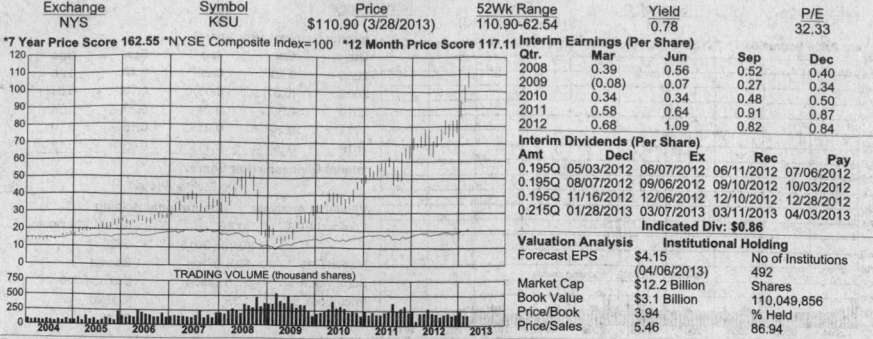

Interim Earnings (Per Share)

Qtr.	Mar	Jun	Sep	Dec
2008	0.39	0.56	0.52	0.40
2009	(0.08)	0.07	0.27	0.34
2010	0.34	0.34	0.48	0.50
2011	0.58	0.64	0.91	0.87
2012	0.68	1.09	0.82	0.84

Interim Dividends (Per Share)

Amt	Decl	Ex	Rec	Pay
0.195Q	05/03/2012	06/07/2012	06/11/2012	07/06/2012
0.195Q	08/07/2012	09/06/2012	09/10/2012	10/03/2012
0.195Q	11/16/2012	12/06/2012	12/10/2012	12/28/2012
0.215Q	01/28/2013	03/07/2013	03/11/2013	04/03/2013

Indicated Div: $0.86

TRADING VOLUME (thousand shares)

Valuation Analysis

		Institutional Holding	
Forecast EPS	$4.15 (04/06/2013)	No of Institutions	492
Market Cap	$12.2 Billion	Shares	110,049,856
Book Value	$3.1 Billion	% Held	86.94
Price/Book	3.94		
Price/Sales	5.46		

Business Summary: Rail (MIC: 7.4.3 SIC: 4011 NAIC: 482111)

Kansas City Southern is a holding company. Co. has domestic and international rail operations in North America that are focused on the north/south freight corridor connecting commercial and industrial markets in the central U.S. with industrial cities in Mexico. As of Dec 31 2012, Co.'s coordinated rail network comprised approximately 6,300 route miles extending from the midwest and southeast portions of the U.S. south into Mexico and connects with all other Class I railroads, providing shippers with an alternative to other railroad routes and giving direct access to Mexico and the southeast and southwest U.S. through alternate interchange hubs.

Recent Developments: For the year ended Dec 31 2012, net income increased 14.3% to US$379.4 million from US$331.9 million in the prior year. Revenues were US$2.24 billion, up 6.7% from US$2.10 billion the year before. Operating income was US$715.9 million versus US$611.6 million in the prior year, an increase of 17.1%. Direct operating expenses rose 3.2% to US$746.5 million from US$723.3 million in the comparable period the year before. Indirect operating expenses increased 1.7% to US$776.2 million from US$763.4 million in the equivalent prior-year period.

Prospects: Our evaluation of Kansas City Southern Industries Inc. as of Apr. 7, 2013 is the result of our systematic analysis on three basic characteristics: earnings strength, relative valuation, and recent stock price movement. The company has managed to produce a neutral trend in earnings per share over the past 5 quarters. However, while recent estimates for the company have been mixed, KSU has posted better than expected results. Based on operating earnings yield, the company is overvalued when compared to all of the companies in our coverage universe. Share price changes over the past year indicates that KSU will perform well over the near term.

Financial Data

(US$ in Thousands)	12/31/2012	12/31/2011	12/31/2010	12/31/2009	12/31/2008	12/31/2007	12/31/2006	12/31/2005
Earnings Per Share	3.43	3.00	1.67	0.61	1.86	1.57	1.08	1.10
Cash Flow Per Share	6.12	5.90	4.96	3.14	5.43	5.03	3.59	2.37
Tang Book Value Per Share	28.06	25.10	23.62	21.33	7.91	6.55	3.59	0.66
Dividends Per Share	0.780	...	...	...	11.620	38.530	...	...
Dividend Payout %	22.74	...	...	...	624.73	2,454.14	...	...
Income Statement								
Total Revenue	2,238,600	2,098,300	1,814,800	1,480,200	1,852,100	1,742,800	1,659,700	1,352,000
EBITDA	896,300	752,100	612,500	452,100	466,800	462,500	408,300	334,300
Depn & Amortn	198,800	186,200	184,900	182,500	97,200	95,900	93,800	127,700
Income Before Taxes	597,100	436,800	269,500	95,900	230,700	209,900	147,300	73,100
Income Taxes	237,000	123,100	109,200	34,600	64,500	67,100	45,400	(7,100)
Net Income	377,300	330,300	180,200	68,000	183,900	153,800	108,900	100,900
Average Shares	110,080	109,830	107,534	93,649	98,602	97,616	92,386	92,747
Balance Sheet								
Current Assets	522,300	642,500	598,200	613,800	690,700	645,700	606,000	466,800
Total Assets	6,395,900	6,173,000	5,640,900	5,479,100	5,442,700	4,928,200	4,637,300	4,423,600
Current Liabilities	424,800	437,400	431,200	410,800	1,096,300	1,098,700	637,400	573,700
Long-Term Obligations	1,547,600	1,602,800	1,621,600	1,911,900	1,448,700	1,105,000	1,631,800	1,663,900
Total Liabilities	3,299,300	3,408,500	3,209,800	3,420,300	3,531,200	3,201,900	3,054,900	2,997,400
Stockholders' Equity	3,096,600	2,764,500	2,431,100	2,058,800	1,911,500	1,726,300	1,582,400	1,426,200
Shares Outstanding	110,131	109,910	102,648	96,213	91,463	76,975	75,920	73,412
Statistical Record								
Return on Assets %	5.99	5.59	3.24	1.25	3.54	3.22	2.40	2.94
Return on Equity %	12.84	12.71	8.03	3.43	10.08	9.30	7.24	8.23
EBITDA Margin %	40.04	35.84	33.75	30.54	25.20	26.54	24.60	24.73
Net Margin %	16.85	15.74	9.93	4.59	9.93	8.82	6.56	7.46
Asset Turnover	0.36	0.36	0.33	0.27	0.36	0.36	0.37	0.39
Current Ratio	1.23	1.47	1.39	1.49	0.63	0.59	0.95	0.81
Debt to Equity	0.50	0.58	0.67	0.93	0.76	0.64	1.03	1.17
Price Range	83.82-62.54	69.17-46.00	49.98-29.70	34.13-12.62	55.00-16.59	42.50-28.37	30.00-22.32	25.56-16.09
P/E Ratio	24.44-18.23	23.06-15.33	29.93-17.78	55.95-20.69	29.57-8.92	27.07-18.07	27.78-20.67	23.24-14.63

Address: 427 West 12th Street, Kansas City, MO 64105
Telephone: 816-983-1303
Fax: 816-556-0297

Web Site: www.kcsouthern.com
Officers: Michael R. Haverty - Executive Chairman, Chief Executive Officer David L. Starling - President, Chief Executive Officer

Auditors: KPMG LLP
Investor Contact: 816-983-1551
Transfer Agents: Computershare Trust Company, N.A, Providence, RI

KAR AUCTION SERVICES INC.

Exchange	Symbol	Price	52Wk Range	Yield	P/E
NYS	KAR	$20.03 (3/28/2013)	22.19-14.60	3.79	30.35

*7 Year Price Score N/A   *NYSE Composite Index=100   *12 Month Price Score 104.30

Interim Earnings (Per Share)

Qtr.	Mar	Jun	Sep	Dec
2010	0.06	0.21	0.19	0.05
2011	0.29	(0.11)	0.23	0.10
2012	0.19	0.17	0.14	0.16

Interim Dividends (Per Share)

Amt	Decl	Ex	Rec	Pay
0.19Q	11/30/2012	12/17/2012	12/19/2012	12/28/2012
0.19Q	02/20/2013	03/21/2013	03/25/2013	04/04/2013

Indicated Div: $0.76

Valuation Analysis   Institutional Holding

Forecast EPS	$1.17	No of Institutions	
	(04/05/2013)	N/A	
Market Cap	$2.7 Billion	Shares	
Book Value	$1.4 Billion	N/A	
Price/Book	1.90	% Held	
Price/Sales	1.39	N/A	

Business Summary: Retail - Automotive (MIC: 2.1.4 SIC: 5521 NAIC: 441120)

KAR Auction Services is a holding company. Through its subsidiaries, Co. provides vehicle and salvage auction services in North America. Co.'s segments are ADESA Inc. Auctions, which provides online and physical auctions of vehicle as well as ancillary services such as inspections, storage, transportation, reconditioning and titling, and other services; Insurance Auto Auctions, Inc., which provides salvage processing services such as selling total loss and recovered theft vehicles; and Automotive Finance Corporation, which provides short-term, inventory-secured financing, known as floorplan financing. At Dec 31 2011, Co. had 69 whole car auction locations and 159 salvage auction locations.

Recent Developments: For the year ended Dec 31 2012, net income increased 27.4% to US$92.0 million from US$72.2 million in the prior year. Revenues were US$1.96 billion, up 4.1% from US$1.89 billion the year before. Operating income was US$267.0 million versus US$281.9 million in the prior year, a decrease of 5.3%. Direct operating expenses rose 5.0% to US$1.09 billion from US$1.04 billion in the comparable period the year before. Indirect operating expenses increased 7.0% to US$609.3 million from US$569.2 million in the equivalent prior-year period.

Prospects: Our evaluation of KAR Aucton Services Inc. as of Apr. 7, 2013 is the result of our systematic analysis on three basic characteristics: earnings strength, relative valuation, and recent stock price movement. The company has produced a positive trend in earnings per share over the past 5 quarters and while recent estimates for the company have been raised by analysts, KAR has posted better than expected results. Based on operating earnings yield, the company is about fairly valued when compared to all of the companies in our coverage universe. Share price changes over the past year indicates that KAR will perform very well over the near term.

Financial Data

(US$ in Thousands)	12/31/2012	12/31/2011	12/31/2010	12/31/2009	12/31/2008	12/31/2007
Earnings Per Share	0.66	0.52	0.51	...	...	...
Cash Flow Per Share	2.12	2.25	3.47	2.32	...	...
Dividends Per Share	0.190	...	...	...	...	...
Dividend Payout %	28.79	...	...	...	...	...
Income Statement						
Total Revenue	1,963,400	1,886,300	1,815,000	1,729,600	1,771,400	1,102,800
EBITDA	343,400	304,800	309,200	289,200	60,400	179,900
Depn & Amortn	72,400	71,700	71,000	82,300	92,800	65,900
Income Before Taxes	151,600	90,000	96,800	34,300	(247,600)	(48,300)
Income Taxes	59,600	17,800	27,200	11,100	(31,400)	(10,000)
Net Income	92,000	72,200	69,600	23,200	(216,200)	(38,300)
Average Shares	139,000	137,800	135,900	108,100	...	...
Balance Sheet						
Current Assets	1,581,400	1,373,200	1,254,700	941,900	752,700	901,800
Total Assets	4,922,300	4,779,100	4,525,000	4,251,300	4,157,600	4,530,800
Current Liabilities	1,286,900	1,196,200	966,800	642,400	448,400	459,700
Long-Term Obligations	1,774,600	1,816,900	1,875,700	2,047,300	2,522,900	2,601,100
Total Liabilities	3,478,600	3,435,900	3,280,400	3,109,800	3,406,900	3,517,200
Stockholders' Equity	1,443,700	1,343,200	1,244,600	1,141,500	750,700	1,013,600
Shares Outstanding	136,657	136,271	135,493	134,509	106,853	106,863
Statistical Record						
Return on Assets %	1.89	1.55	1.59	0.55	N.M.	...
Return on Equity %	6.58	5.58	5.83	2.45	N.M.	...
EBITDA Margin %	17.49	16.16	17.04	16.72	3.41	16.31
Net Margin %	4.69	3.83	3.83	1.34	N.M.	N.M.
Asset Turnover	0.40	0.41	0.41	0.41	0.41	...
Current Ratio	1.23	1.15	1.30	1.47	1.68	1.96
Debt to Equity	1.23	1.35	1.51	1.79	3.36	2.57
Price Range	20.63-13.49	20.91-11.52	15.73-11.19	13.79-11.80	...	...
P/E Ratio	31.26-20.44	40.21-22.15	30.84-21.94	...	...	...
Average Yield %	1.11	...	...	...	...	...

Address: 13085 Hamilton Crossing Boulevard, Carmel, IN 46032
Telephone: 800-923-3725

Web Site: www.karauctionservices.com
Officers: Brian T. Clingen - Chairman, Chief Executive Officer James P. Hallett - Chief Executive Officer

Auditors: KPMG LLP
Investor Contact: 317-249-4390

KB HOME

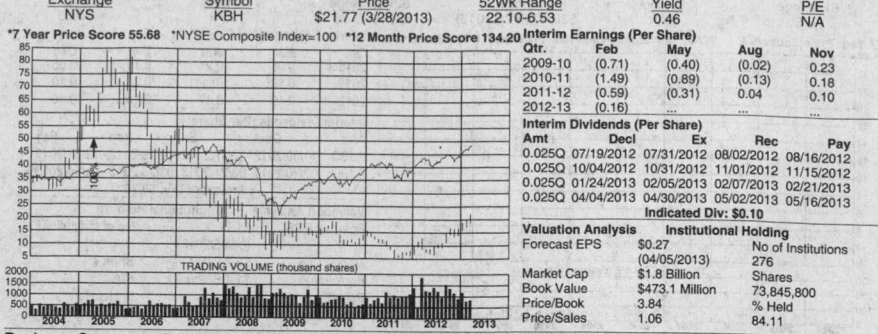

Exchange	Symbol	Price	52Wk Range	Yield	P/E
NYS	KBH	$21.77 (3/28/2013)	22.10-6.53	0.46	N/A

*7 Year Price Score 55.68   *NYSE Composite Index=100   *12 Month Price Score 134.20

Interim Earnings (Per Share)

Qtr.	Feb	May	Aug	Nov
2009-10	(0.71)	(0.40)	(0.02)	0.23
2010-11	(1.49)	(0.89)	(0.13)	0.18
2011-12	(0.59)	(0.31)	0.04	0.10
2012-13	(0.16)	...	...	...

Interim Dividends (Per Share)

Amt	Decl	Ex	Rec	Pay
0.025Q	07/19/2012	07/31/2012	08/02/2012	08/16/2012
0.025Q	10/04/2012	10/31/2012	11/01/2012	11/15/2012
0.025Q	01/24/2013	02/05/2013	02/07/2013	02/21/2013
0.025Q	04/04/2013	04/30/2013	05/02/2013	05/16/2013

Indicated Div: $0.10

Valuation Analysis

		Institutional Holding	
Forecast EPS	$0.27 (04/05/2013)	No of Institutions	276
Market Cap	$1.8 Billion	Shares	73,845,800
Book Value	$473.1 Million	% Held	84.11
Price/Book	3.84		
Price/Sales	1.06		

Business Summary: Builders (MIC: 2.2.5 SIC: 1531 NAIC: 236115)

KB Home constructs and sells homes under the name KB Home. Co.'s homebuilding operations, which is comprised of four segments, provides a range of homes designed primarily for first-time, move-up and adult homebuyers, including attached and detached single-family residential homes, townhomes and condominiums. Co. provides homes in development communities, at urban in-fill locations and as part of mixed-use projects. Co.'s homebuilding reporting segments conducts operations in the following states: California, Arizona, Nevada, New Mexico, Colorado, Texas, Florida, Maryland, North Carolina and Virginia. Co.'s financial services segment provide insurance and title services to its homebuyers.

Recent Developments: For the quarter ended Feb 28 2013, net loss amounted to US$12.5 million versus a net loss of US$45.8 million in the year-earlier quarter. Revenues were US$405.2 million, up 59.2% from US$254.6 million the year before. Direct operating expenses rose 47.9% to US$344.1 million from US$232.7 million in the comparable period the year before. Indirect operating expenses increased 15.4% to US$59.1 million from US$51.2 million in the equivalent prior-year period.

Prospects: Our evaluation of KB HOME as of Apr. 7, 2013 is the result of our systematic analysis on three basic characteristics: earnings strength, relative valuation, and recent stock price movement. The company has produced a positive trend in earnings per share over the past 5 quarters and while recent estimates for the company have been raised by analysts, KBH has posted better than expected results. Based on operating earnings yield, the company is overvalued when compared to all of the companies in our coverage universe. Share price changes over the past year indicates that KBH will perform very well over the near term.

Financial Data

(US$ in Thousands)	3 Mos	11/30/2012	11/30/2011	11/30/2010	11/30/2009	11/30/2008	11/30/2007	11/30/2006
Earnings Per Share	(0.33)	(0.76)	(2.32)	(0.90)	(1.33)	(12.59)	(12.04)	5.82
Cash Flow Per Share	(0.84)	0.45	(4.51)	(1.74)	4.56	4.39	15.48	9.08
Tang Book Value Per Share	5.66	4.29	5.03	7.18	8.03	9.27	19.91	30.09
Dividends Per Share	0.100	0.138	0.250	0.250	0.250	0.813	1.000	1.000
Dividend Payout %	...	...	...	...	...	...	...	17.18
Income Statement								
Total Revenue	405,219	1,560,115	1,315,866	1,589,996	1,824,850	3,033,936	6,416,526	11,003,792
EBITDA	2,993	(9,964)	(94,282)	(7,631)	(226,136)	(844,965)	(1,329,896)	790,234
Depn & Amortn	971	1,600	2,000	3,300	5,200	9,400	17,300	20,200
Income Before Taxes	(13,014)	(80,850)	(144,615)	(77,140)	(275,584)	(832,721)	(1,331,550)	757,457
Income Taxes	100	(20,100)	(2,400)	(7,000)	(209,400)	8,200	(46,000)	215,700
Net Income	(12,458)	(58,953)	(178,768)	(69,368)	(101,784)	(976,131)	(929,414)	482,351
Average Shares	79,401	77,106	77,043	76,889	76,660	77,509	77,172	82,856
Balance Sheet								
Current Assets	2,678,323	2,338,519	2,277,339	2,824,647	3,128,331	3,715,238	4,933,414	7,753,486
Total Assets	2,900,637	2,561,698	2,512,542	3,109,749	3,435,989	4,044,300	5,705,956	9,014,464
Current Liabilities	310,709	165,936	147,543	276,180	387,279	541,294	699,851	1,071,265
Long-Term Obligations	1,963,753	1,722,815	1,583,571	1,775,529	1,820,370	1,941,537	2,161,794	3,125,803
Total Liabilities	2,427,502	2,184,892	2,069,885	2,477,871	2,728,765	3,213,695	3,855,269	6,091,716
Stockholders' Equity	473,135	376,806	442,657	631,878	707,224	830,605	1,850,687	2,922,748
Shares Outstanding	83,549	87,837	87,956	88,053	88,072	89,607	89,525	89,374
Statistical Record								
Return on Assets %	N.M.	N.M.	N.M.	N.M.	N.M.	N.M.	N.M.	5.76
Return on Equity %	N.M.	N.M.	N.M.	N.M.	N.M.	N.M.	N.M.	16.71
EBITDA Margin %	0.74	N.M.	N.M.	N.M.	N.M.	N.M.	N.M.	7.18
Net Margin %	N.M.	N.M.	N.M.	N.M.	N.M.	N.M.	N.M.	4.38
Asset Turnover	0.64	0.61	0.47	0.49	0.49	0.62	0.87	1.31
Current Ratio	8.62	14.09	15.44	10.23	8.08	6.86	7.05	7.24
Debt to Equity	4.15	4.57	3.58	2.81	2.57	2.34	1.17	1.07
Price Range	19.82-6.53	16.90-6.34	15.71-5.27	19.33-9.80	20.51-8.11	28.75-8.02	55.64-18.92	81.66-39.03
P/E Ratio	...	...	...	...	...	...	...	14.03-6.71
Average Yield %	0.81	1.32	2.40	1.83	1.71	4.01	2.52	1.79

Address: 10990 Wilshire Boulevard, Los Angeles, CA 90024
Telephone: 310-231-4000
Fax: 310-231-4222

Web Site: www.kbhome.com
Officers: Jeffrey T. Mezger - President, Chief Executive Officer Jeff J. Kaminski - Executive Vice President, Chief Financial Officer

Auditors: Ernst & Young LLP
Investor Contact: 310-231-4000
Transfer Agents: Computershare Shareowner Services LLC, Jersey City, NJ

KBR INC

Exchange	Symbol	Price	52Wk Range	Yield	P/E
NYS	KBR	$32.08 (3/28/2013)	35.51-22.91	1.00	33.07

*7 Year Price Score N/A   *NYSE Composite Index=100   *12 Month Price Score 97.45

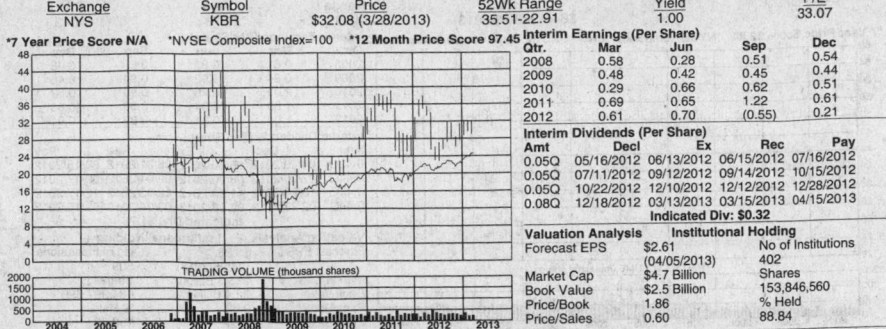

Interim Earnings (Per Share)

Qtr.	Mar	Jun	Sep	Dec
2008	0.58	0.28	0.51	0.54
2009	0.48	0.42	0.45	0.44
2010	0.29	0.66	0.62	0.51
2011	0.69	0.65	1.22	0.61
2012	0.61	0.70	(0.55)	0.21

Interim Dividends (Per Share)

Amt	Decl	Ex	Rec	Pay
0.05Q	05/16/2012	06/13/2012	06/15/2012	07/16/2012
0.05Q	07/11/2012	09/12/2012	09/14/2012	10/15/2012
0.05Q	10/22/2012	12/10/2012	12/12/2012	12/28/2012
0.08Q	12/18/2012	03/13/2013	03/15/2013	04/15/2013

Indicated Div: $0.32

Valuation Analysis   Institutional Holding

Forecast EPS	$2.61	No of Institutions
	(04/05/2013)	402
Market Cap	$4.7 Billion	Shares
Book Value	$2.5 Billion	153,846,560
Price/Book	1.86	% Held
Price/Sales	0.60	88.84

TRADING VOLUME (thousand shares)

Business Summary: Construction Services (MIC: 7.5.4 SIC: 1629 NAIC: 237120)

KBR is an engineering, construction and services company. Co.'s Hydrocarbons business group provides services ranging from prefeasibility studies to front-end engineering design, and construction to commissioning of process facilities. Co.'s Infrastructure, Government and Power (IGP) business group serves the IGP industries, providing products and services to industrial commercial, defense and governmental agencies. Co.'s Services business group provides construction, construction management, fabrication, operations/ maintenance, commissioning/startup and turnaround to a variety of markets. Co.'s Other business group comprises of the Ventures business unit and its other operations.

Recent Developments: For the year ended Dec 31 2012, net income decreased 62.6% to US$202.0 million from US$540.0 million in the prior year. Revenues were US$7.92 billion, down 14.5% from US$9.26 billion the year before. Operating income was US$299.0 million versus US$587.0 million in the prior year, a decrease of 49.1%. Direct operating expenses declined 14.3% to US$7.25 billion from US$8.46 billion in the comparable period the year before. Indirect operating expenses increased 75.4% to US$370.0 million from US$211.0 million in the equivalent prior-year period.

Prospects: Our evaluation of KBR Inc. as of Apr. 7, 2013 is the result of our systematic analysis on three basic characteristics: earnings strength, relative valuation, and recent stock price movement. The company has generated a negative trend in earnings per share over the past 5 quarters. However, while recent estimates for the company have been lowered by analysts, KBR has posted better than expected results. Based on operating earnings yield, the company is undervalued when compared to all of the companies in our coverage universe. Share price changes over the past year indicates that KBR will perform in line with the market over the near term.

Financial Data
(US$ in Thousands)

	12/31/2012	12/31/2011	12/31/2010	12/31/2009	12/31/2008	12/31/2007	12/31/2006	12/31/2005
Earnings Per Share	0.97	3.16	2.07	1.79	1.91	1.79	1.20	1.76
Cash Flow Per Share	0.96	4.33	3.52	(0.23)	0.74	1.48	6.65	3.88
Tang Book Value Per Share	11.27	9.66	7.75	9.60	7.95	11.88	8.94	...
Dividends Per Share	0.200	0.200	0.200	0.200	0.200	...	...	...
Dividend Payout %	20.62	6.33	9.66	11.17	10.47	...	...	...
Income Statement								
Total Revenue	7,921,000	9,261,000	10,099,000	12,105,000	11,581,000	8,745,000	9,633,000	10,146,000
EBITDA	360,000	661,000	665,000	588,000	582,000	321,000	277,000	517,000
Depn & Amortn	65,000	71,000	62,000	55,000	49,000	41,000	47,000	56,000
Income Before Taxes	288,000	572,000	586,000	532,000	568,000	342,000	220,000	433,000
Income Taxes	86,000	32,000	191,000	168,000	212,000	138,000	129,000	182,000
Net Income	144,000	480,000	327,000	290,000	319,000	302,000	168,000	240,000
Average Shares	149,000	151,000	157,000	161,000	167,000	169,000	140,000	136,000
Balance Sheet								
Current Assets	3,668,000	3,442,000	3,262,000	3,641,000	4,142,000	4,056,000	3,898,000	3,510,000
Total Assets	5,767,000	5,673,000	5,417,000	5,327,000	5,884,000	5,203,000	5,407,000	5,182,000
Current Liabilities	2,277,000	2,284,000	2,347,000	2,291,000	3,043,000	2,623,000	2,983,000	2,566,000
Long-Term Obligations	84,000	88,000	92,000	...	...	...	2,000	792,000
Total Liabilities	3,225,000	3,178,000	3,171,000	3,039,000	3,832,000	2,936,000	3,620,000	3,926,000
Stockholders' Equity	2,542,000	2,495,000	2,246,000	2,288,000	2,052,000	2,267,000	1,787,000	1,256,000
Shares Outstanding	147,584	148,143	151,132	160,363	161,725	169,709	167,643	...
Statistical Record								
Return on Assets %	2.51	8.66	6.09	5.17	5.74	5.69	3.17	...
Return on Equity %	5.70	20.25	14.42	13.36	14.73	14.90	11.04	...
EBITDA Margin %	4.54	7.14	6.58	4.86	5.03	3.67	2.88	5.10
Net Margin %	1.82	5.18	3.24	2.40	2.75	3.45	1.74	2.37
Asset Turnover	1.38	1.67	1.88	2.16	2.08	1.65	1.82	...
Current Ratio	1.61	1.51	1.39	1.59	1.36	1.55	1.31	1.37
Debt to Equity	0.03	0.04	0.04	...	...	...	N.M.	0.63
Price Range	37.93-22.91	39.12-22.20	30.90-17.60	24.49-11.71	40.38-9.86	44.01-20.00	27.01-20.75	...
P/E Ratio	39.10-23.62	12.38-7.03	14.93-8.50	13.68-6.54	21.14-5.16	24.59-11.17	22.51-17.29	...
Average Yield %	0.68	0.62	0.86	1.09	0.77	...	...	...

Address: 601 Jefferson Street, Suite 3400, Houston, TX 77002
Telephone: 713-753-3011

Web Site: www.kbr.com
Officers: William P. Utt - Chairman, President, Chief Executive Officer Farhan Mujib - Executive Vice President

Auditors: KPMG LLP
Investor Contact: 713-753-5082
Transfer Agents: American Stock Transfer & Trust Company, Brooklyn, NY

KELLOGG CO

Exchange	Symbol	Price	52Wk Range	Yield	P/E
NYS	K	$64.43 (3/28/2013)	64.60-46.51	2.73	24.13

*7 Year Price Score 92.84   *NYSE Composite Index=100   *12 Month Price Score 104.92

Interim Earnings (Per Share)

Qtr.	Mar	Jun	Sep	Dec
2008	0.81	0.82	0.89	0.48
2009	0.84	0.92	0.94	0.46
2010	1.09	0.79	0.90	0.52
2011	1.00	0.94	0.80	0.65
2012	1.00	0.84	0.82	0.01

Interim Dividends (Per Share)

Amt	Decl	Ex	Rec	Pay
0.43Q	04/20/2012	05/30/2012	06/01/2012	06/15/2012
0.44Q	07/20/2012	08/30/2012	09/04/2012	09/17/2012
0.44Q	10/26/2012	11/29/2012	12/03/2012	12/17/2012
0.44Q	02/22/2013	02/28/2013	03/04/2013	03/15/2013

Indicated Div: $1.76

Valuation Analysis

		Institutional Holding	
Forecast EPS	$3.88 (04/05/2013)	No of Institutions	809
Market Cap	$23.3 Billion	Shares	484,997,696
Book Value	$2.4 Billion	% Held	100.92
Price/Book	9.62		
Price/Sales	1.64		

Business Summary: Food (MIC: 1.2.1 SIC: 2043 NAIC: 311230)

Kellogg is engaged in the manufacture and marketing of cereal and convenience foods, such as cookies, crackers, toaster pastries, cereal bars, fruit-flavored snacks, frozen waffles and veggie foods. These products were, as of Feb 26 2013, manufactured by Co. in 18 countries and marketed in more than 180 countries. Co.'s cereal products are generally marketed under the Kellogg's name. Co. also markets cookies, crackers, crisps, and other convenience foods, under brands such as Kellogg's, Keebler, Cheez-It, Murray, Austin and Famous Amos. Co. has seven reportable segments: U.S. Morning Foods & Kashi; U.S. Snacks; U.S. Specialty; North America Other; Europe; Latin America; and Asia Pacific.

Recent Developments: For the year ended Dec 29 2012, net income increased 11.2% to US$961.0 million from US$864.0 million in the prior year. Revenues were US$14.20 billion, up 7.6% from US$13.20 billion the year before. Operating income was US$1.56 billion versus US$1.43 billion in the prior year, an increase of 9.5%. Direct operating expenses rose 8.9% to US$8.76 billion from US$8.05 billion in the comparable period the year before. Indirect operating expenses increased 3.9% to US$3.87 billion from US$3.73 billion in the equivalent prior-year period.

Prospects: Our evaluation of Kellogg Co as of Apr. 7, 2013 is the result of our systematic analysis on three basic characteristics: earnings strength, relative valuation, and recent stock price movement. The company has produced a positive trend in earnings per share over the past 5 quarters and while recent estimates for the company have been raised by analysts, K has posted better than expected results. Based on operating earnings yield, the company is about fairly valued when compared to all of the companies in our coverage universe. Share price changes over the past year indicates that K will perform poorly over the near term.

Financial Data

(US$ in Thousands)	12/29/2012	12/31/2011	01/01/2011	01/02/2010	01/03/2009	12/29/2007	12/30/2006	12/31/2005
Earnings Per Share	2.67	3.38	3.30	3.16	2.99	2.76	2.51	2.36
Cash Flow Per Share	4.92	4.42	2.69	4.31	3.26	3.81	3.56	2.78
Dividends Per Share	1.740	1.670	1.560	1.430	1.300	1.202	1.137	1.060
Dividend Payout %	65.17	49.41	47.27	45.25	43.48	43.55	45.30	44.92
Income Statement								
Total Revenue	14,197,000	13,198,000	12,397,000	12,575,000	12,822,000	11,776,000	10,906,700	10,177,200
EBITDA	2,034,000	2,334,000	2,382,000	2,363,000	2,316,000	2,238,000	2,131,700	2,117,200
Depn & Amortn	448,000	369,000	392,000	384,000	375,000	372,000	352,700	391,800
Income Before Taxes	1,325,000	1,732,000	1,742,000	1,684,000	1,633,000	1,547,000	1,471,600	1,425,100
Income Taxes	363,000	503,000	502,000	476,000	485,000	444,000	466,500	444,700
Net Income	961,000	1,231,000	1,247,000	1,212,000	1,148,000	1,103,000	1,004,100	980,400
Average Shares	360,000	364,000	378,000	384,000	385,000	400,000	400,400	415,600
Balance Sheet								
Current Assets	3,380,000	3,027,000	2,915,000	2,558,000	2,521,000	2,717,000	2,427,000	2,196,500
Total Assets	15,184,000	11,901,000	11,847,000	11,200,000	10,946,000	11,397,000	10,714,000	10,574,500
Current Liabilities	4,523,000	3,313,000	3,184,000	2,288,000	3,552,000	4,044,000	4,020,200	3,162,800
Long-Term Obligations	6,082,000	5,037,000	4,908,000	4,835,000	4,068,000	3,270,000	3,053,000	3,702,600
Total Liabilities	12,765,000	10,141,000	9,689,000	8,928,000	9,498,000	8,871,000	8,645,000	8,290,800
Stockholders' Equity	2,419,000	1,760,000	2,158,000	2,272,000	1,448,000	2,526,000	2,069,000	2,283,700
Shares Outstanding	361,266	357,301	365,604	381,379	381,861	390,051	397,697	405,329
Statistical Record								
Return on Assets %	7.12	10.40	10.85	10.98	10.11	10.00	9.46	9.20
Return on Equity %	46.12	63.01	56.45	65.34	56.84	48.14	46.26	43.30
EBITDA Margin %	14.33	17.68	19.21	18.79	18.06	19.00	19.54	20.80
Net Margin %	6.77	9.33	10.06	9.64	8.95	9.37	9.21	9.63
Asset Turnover	1.05	1.11	1.08	1.14	1.13	1.07	1.03	0.96
Current Ratio	0.75	0.91	0.92	1.12	0.71	0.67	0.60	0.69
Debt to Equity	2.51	2.86	2.27	2.13	2.81	1.29	1.48	1.62
Price Range	56.86-46.51	57.56-48.25	55.58-47.98	54.00-35.84	57.39-40.69	56.41-48.89	50.79-42.64	46.46-42.41
P/E Ratio	21.30-17.42	17.03-14.28	16.84-14.54	17.09-11.34	19.19-13.61	20.44-17.71	20.24-16.99	19.69-17.97
Average Yield %	3.38	3.13	3.01	3.12	2.57	2.29	2.40	2.37

Address: One Kellogg Square, P.O. Box 3599, Battle Creek, MI 49016-3599
Telephone: 269-961-2000
Fax: 616-961-2871

Web Site: www.kelloggcompany.com
Officers: James M. Jenness - Chairman John A. Bryant - President, Chief Executive Officer

Auditors: PricewaterhouseCoopers LLP
Investor Contact: 269-961-2800
Transfer Agents: Wells Fargo Bank, N.A., St. Paul, MN

KEMPER CORP. (DE)

Exchange	Symbol	Price	52Wk Range	Yield	P/E
NYS	KMPR	$32.61 (3/28/2013)	33.81-28.28	2.94	18.74

*7 Year Price Score 87.14   *NYSE Composite Index=100   *12 Month Price Score 95.32

Interim Earnings (Per Share)

Qtr.	Mar	Jun	Sep	Dec
2008	0.35	(0.05)	(0.63)	(0.16)
2009	(0.09)	0.67	1.00	1.06
2010	0.77	0.61	0.58	1.03
2011	0.89	(0.01)	0.08	0.42
2012	0.72	0.04	0.95	0.04

Interim Dividends (Per Share)

Amt	Decl	Ex	Rec	Pay
0.24Q	05/02/2012	05/10/2012	05/14/2012	05/29/2012
0.24Q	08/01/2012	08/09/2012	08/13/2012	08/27/2012
0.24Q	11/07/2012	11/15/2012	11/19/2012	12/04/2012
0.24Q	02/06/2013	02/14/2013	02/19/2013	03/05/2013

Indicated Div: $0.96

Valuation Analysis / **Institutional Holding**

Forecast EPS	$1.75	No of Institutions
	(04/05/2013)	185
Market Cap	$1.9 Billion	Shares
Book Value	$2.2 Billion	27,598,304
Price/Book	0.88	% Held
Price/Sales	0.77	N/A

Business Summary: General Insurance (MIC: 5.2.1 SIC: 6311 NAIC: 522298)

Kemper is an insurance holding company. Through its subsidiaries, Co. is engaged in providing life, health, automobile, homeowners and other insurance products to individuals and businesses. Co. operates four segments: Kemper Preferred, Kemper Specialty, Kemper Direct and Life and Health Insurance. These segments provide preferred and standard risk personal automobile insurance, homeowners insurance and other personal insurance, automobile insurance to individuals and businesses in the non-standard and specialty market, renters' insurance products and other affinity relationships, individual life, accident, health and property insurance.

Recent Developments: For the year ended Dec 31 2012, income from continuing operations increased 48.8% to US$91.8 million from US$61.7 million a year earlier. Net income increased 38.8% to US$103.4 million from US$74.5 million in the prior year. Revenues were US$2.46 billion, down 1.3% from US$2.50 billion the year before. Net premiums earned were US$2.11 billion versus US$2.17 billion in the prior year, a decrease of 3.1%. Net investment income fell 0.7% to US$295.9 million from US$298.0 million a year ago.

Prospects: Our evaluation of Kemper Corp. as of Apr. 7, 2013 is the result of our systematic analysis on three basic characteristics: earnings strength, relative valuation, and recent stock price movement. The company has suffered a very negative trend in earnings per share over the past 5 quarters and while recent estimates for the company have been mixed, KMPR has posted results that fell short of analysts expectations. Based on operating earnings yield, the company is about fairly valued when compared to all of the companies in our coverage universe. Share price changes over the past year indicates that KMPR will perform in line with the market over the near term.

Financial Data
(US$ in Thousands)

	12/31/2012	12/31/2011	12/31/2010	12/31/2009	12/31/2008	12/31/2007	12/31/2006	12/31/2005
Earnings Per Share	1.74	1.38	2.98	2.64	(0.47)	3.30	4.15	3.67
Cash Flow Per Share	1.11	(0.41)	0.95	2.63	1.10	3.84	4.51	5.46
Tang Book Value Per Share	31.65	31.61	29.50	25.43	21.09	30.86	28.95	26.46
Dividends Per Share	0.960	0.960	0.880	1.070	1.880	1.820	1.760	1.700
Dividend Payout %	55.17	69.57	29.53	40.53	...	55.15	42.41	46.32
Income Statement								
Premium Income	2,107,100	2,173,600	2,289,400	2,455,500	2,376,600	2,286,900	2,478,700	2,478,300
Total Revenue	2,462,300	2,495,000	2,743,400	2,933,400	2,742,200	2,919,800	3,075,500	3,048,100
Income Before Taxes	122,400	82,600	261,300	229,600	(90,000)	243,600	391,300	332,900
Income Taxes	30,600	11,700	77,400	66,400	(46,200)	55,800	117,400	82,700
Net Income	103,400	83,700	184,600	164,700	(29,600)	217,800	283,100	255,500
Average Shares	58,999	60,366	61,766	62,156	62,700	65,900	68,200	69,500
Balance Sheet								
Total Assets	8,009,100	8,085,900	8,358,500	8,573,500	8,818,800	9,405,000	9,321,400	9,198,300
Total Liabilities	5,847,400	5,869,800	6,245,100	6,655,900	7,170,200	7,107,200	7,037,400	7,040,600
Stockholders' Equity	2,161,700	2,216,100	2,113,400	1,917,600	1,648,600	2,297,800	2,284,000	2,157,700
Shares Outstanding	58,454	60,248	61,066	62,357	62,314	64,254	66,991	68,516
Statistical Record								
Return on Assets %	1.28	1.02	2.18	1.89	N.M.	2.33	3.06	2.84
Return on Equity %	4.71	3.87	9.16	9.24	N.M.	9.51	12.75	12.18
Net Margin %	4.20	3.35	6.73	5.61	(1.08)	7.46	9.21	8.38
Price Range	32.93-28.28	31.42-22.29	30.92-21.70	23.77-8.10	47.99-13.72	52.60-40.47	50.96-40.00	53.69-41.09
P/E Ratio	18.93-16.25	22.77-16.15	10.38-7.28	9.00-3.07	...	15.94-12.26	12.28-9.64	14.63-11.20
Average Yield %	3.17	3.46	3.45	6.48	6.37	3.84	3.83	3.61

Address: One East Wacker Drive, Chicago, IL 60601
Telephone: 312-661-4600

Web Site: www.kemper.com
Officers: Donald G. Southwell - Chairman, President, Chief Executive Officer Scott Renwick - Senior Vice President, Secretary, General Counsel

Auditors: Deloitte & Touche LLP
Transfer Agents: Computershare Trust Company, N.A, Providence, RI

427

KENNAMETAL INC.

Exchange	Symbol	Price	52Wk Range	Yield	P/E
NYS	KMT	$39.04 (3/28/2013)	46.18-30.89	1.64	12.72

*7 Year Price Score 105.08 *NYSE Composite Index=100 *12 Month Price Score 97.48

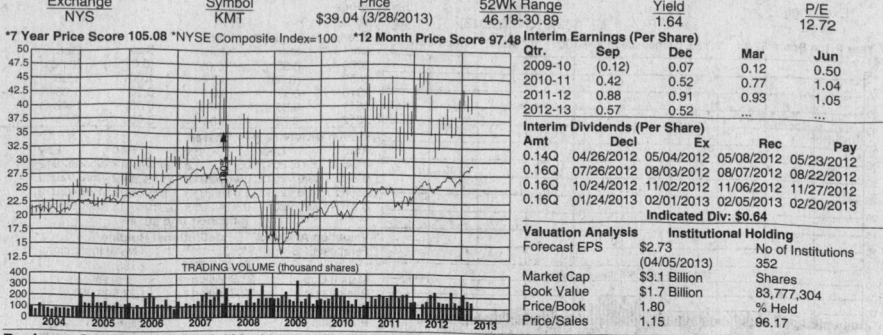

Interim Earnings (Per Share)
Qtr.	Sep	Dec	Mar	Jun
2009-10	(0.12)	0.07	0.12	0.50
2010-11	0.42	0.52	0.77	1.04
2011-12	0.88	0.91	0.93	1.05
2012-13	0.57	0.52	...	...

Interim Dividends (Per Share)
Amt	Decl	Ex	Rec	Pay
0.14Q	04/26/2012	05/04/2012	05/08/2012	05/23/2012
0.16Q	07/26/2012	08/03/2012	08/07/2012	08/22/2012
0.16Q	10/24/2012	11/02/2012	11/06/2012	11/27/2012
0.16Q	01/24/2013	02/01/2013	02/05/2013	02/20/2013

Indicated Div: $0.64

Valuation Analysis
		Institutional Holding	
Forecast EPS	$2.73	No of Institutions	
	(04/05/2013)	352	
Market Cap	$3.1 Billion	Shares	
Book Value	$1.7 Billion	83,777,304	
Price/Book	1.80	% Held	
Price/Sales	1.15	96.17	

Business Summary: Industrial Machinery & Equipment (MIC: 7.2.1 SIC: 3541 NAIC: 333512)

Kennametal is a supplier of tooling, engineered components and materials consumed in production processes. Co. engages in developing and manufacturing metalworking tools and wear-resistant engineered components and coatings using powder metallurgy. Co. also manufactures and markets tool holders, tool-holding systems and rotary-cutting tools, compacts and metallurgical powders, as well as products made from tungsten carbide or other materials used for custom-engineered and certain applications. Co. has two segments: Industrial, which serves customers that operate in industrial end markets; and Infrastructure, which serves customers that operate in the earthworks and energy sectors.

Recent Developments: For the quarter ended Dec 31 2012, net income decreased 41.8% to US$43.3 million from US$74.5 million in the year-earlier quarter. Revenues were US$633.1 million, down 1.3% from US$641.7 million the year before. Operating income was US$66.5 million versus US$94.0 million in the prior-year quarter, a decrease of 29.3%. Direct operating expenses rose 5.8% to US$433.7 million from US$409.9 million in the comparable period the year before. Indirect operating expenses decreased 3.5% to US$133.0 million from US$137.8 million in the equivalent prior-year period.

Prospects: Our evaluation of Kennametal Inc. as of Apr. 7, 2013 is the result of our systematic analysis on three basic characteristics: earnings strength, relative valuation, and recent stock price movement. The company has generated a negative trend in earnings per share over the past 5 quarters. However, while recent estimates for the company have been lowered by analysts, KMT has posted results that fell short of analysts expectations. Based on operating earnings yield, the company is undervalued when compared to all of the companies in our coverage universe. Share price changes over the past year indicates that KMT will perform well over the near term.

Financial Data
(US$ in Thousands)	6 Mos	3 Mos	06/30/2012	06/30/2011	06/30/2010	06/30/2009	06/30/2008	06/30/2007
Earnings Per Share	3.07	3.46	3.77	2.76	0.57	(1.64)	2.15	2.22
Cash Flow Per Share	3.42	3.74	3.60	2.81	2.04	2.63	3.63	2.59
Tang Book Value Per Share	9.58	9.14	8.50	12.01	8.19	7.78	11.00	8.34
Dividends Per Share	0.600	0.580	0.540	0.480	0.480	0.480	0.465	0.410
Dividend Payout %	19.54	16.76	14.32	17.39	84.21	...	21.63	18.47
Income Statement								
Total Revenue	1,262,603	629,459	2,736,246	2,403,493	1,884,067	1,999,859	2,705,129	2,385,493
EBITDA	186,863	94,274	521,257	412,364	198,234	11,129	361,273	357,300
Depn & Amortn	55,767	28,991	104,073	93,471	96,429	96,381	94,733	78,663
Income Before Taxes	118,170	59,327	389,969	296,133	76,602	(112,496)	234,812	249,496
Income Taxes	27,815	12,280	79,136	63,856	26,977	(11,205)	64,057	70,469
Net Income	88,532	46,390	307,230	229,727	46,419	(119,742)	167,775	174,243
Average Shares	80,986	81,405	81,439	83,173	81,690	73,122	78,201	78,546
Balance Sheet								
Current Assets	1,356,363	1,272,079	1,282,962	1,287,585	915,931	875,904	1,151,986	1,016,502
Total Assets	3,100,539	3,016,200	3,034,188	2,754,469	2,267,823	2,346,974	2,784,349	2,606,227
Current Liabilities	362,525	480,288	578,622	841,521	393,005	378,969	521,311	487,237
Long-Term Obligations	704,212	530,321	490,608	1,919	314,675	436,592	313,052	361,399
Total Liabilities	1,380,548	1,328,847	1,390,338	1,116,397	952,323	1,099,531	1,136,442	1,121,760
Stockholders' Equity	1,719,991	1,687,353	1,643,850	1,638,072	1,315,500	1,247,443	1,647,907	1,484,467
Shares Outstanding	79,151	79,616	80,085	81,129	81,903	73,232	76,858	77,972
Statistical Record								
Return on Assets %	8.71	10.01	10.59	9.15	2.01	N.M.	6.21	6.91
Return on Equity %	15.02	17.30	18.67	15.56	3.62	N.M.	10.68	12.54
EBITDA Margin %	14.80	14.98	19.05	17.16	10.52	0.56	13.36	14.98
Net Margin %	7.01	7.37	11.23	9.56	2.46	N.M.	6.20	7.30
Asset Turnover	0.94	0.96	0.94	0.96	0.82	0.78	1.00	0.95
Current Ratio	3.74	2.65	2.22	1.53	2.33	2.31	2.21	2.09
Debt to Equity	0.41	0.31	0.30	N.M.	0.24	0.35	0.19	0.24
Price Range	47.51-30.89	47.51-29.93	47.51-29.93	44.01-24.34	33.81-15.75	35.82-13.31	45.60-27.43	41.18-25.06
P/E Ratio	15.48-10.06	13.73-8.65	12.60-7.94	15.95-8.82	59.32-27.63	...	21.21-12.76	18.55-11.29
Average Yield %	1.55	1.51	1.40	1.35	1.87	2.16	1.27	1.31

Address: World Headquarters, 1600 Technology Way, P.O. Box 231, Latrobe, PA 15650-0231 **Telephone:** 724-539-5000 **Fax:** 724-539-4710	**Web Site:** www.kennametal.com **Officers:** Carlos M. Cardoso - Chairman, President, Chief Executive Officer, Vice President, Chief Operating Officer Paul J. DeMand - Vice President, Division Officer	**Auditors:** PricewaterhouseCoopers LLP **Investor Contact:** 724-539-6559 **Transfer Agents:** Computershare, Jersey City, NJ

428

KEYCORP

Exchange	Symbol	Price	52Wk Range	Yield	P/E
NYS	KEY	$9.96 (3/28/2013)	10.15-6.89	2.01	11.19

*7 Year Price Score 47.47 *NYSE Composite Index=100 *12 Month Price Score 104.44

Interim Earnings (Per Share)

Qtr.	Mar	Jun	Sep	Dec
2008	0.54	(2.70)	(0.10)	(1.17)
2009	(1.09)	(0.68)	(0.52)	(0.20)
2010	(0.11)	0.03	0.20	0.31
2011	0.19	0.25	0.22	0.20
2012	0.20	0.24	0.23	0.22

Interim Dividends (Per Share)

Amt	Decl	Ex	Rec	Pay
0.05Q	05/16/2012	05/24/2012	05/29/2012	06/15/2012
0.05Q	07/13/2012	08/24/2012	08/28/2012	09/14/2012
0.05Q	11/15/2012	11/23/2012	11/27/2012	12/14/2012
0.05Q	01/17/2013	03/01/2013	03/05/2013	03/15/2013

Indicated Div: $0.20 (Div. Reinv. Plan)

Valuation Analysis

		Institutional Holding	
Forecast EPS	$0.85	No of Institutions	
	(04/06/2013)	689	
Market Cap	$9.2 Billion	Shares	
Book Value	$10.3 Billion	791,297,408	
Price/Book	0.90	% Held	
Price/Sales	1.97	80.12	

Business Summary: Banking (MIC: 5.1.1 SIC: 6021 NAIC: 522110)

KeyCorp is a bank holding company. Through its subsidiaries, Co. provides a range of retail and commercial banking, commercial leasing, investment management, consumer finance and investment banking products and services to individual, corporate and institutional clients through two business segments: Key Community Bank and Key Corporate Bank. Co.'s bank and trust company subsidiaries also provide personal and corporate trust services, personal financial services, access to mutual funds, cash management services, investment banking and capital markets products, and international banking services. At Dec 31 2012, Co. had total assets of $89.24 billion and total deposits of $65.99 billion.

Recent Developments: For the year ended Dec 31 2012, income from continuing operations decreased 12.3% to US$856.0 million from US$976.0 million a year earlier. Net income decreased 7.2% to US$865.0 million from US$932.0 million in the prior year. Net interest income decreased 0.1% to US$2.26 billion from US$2.27 billion in the prior year. Provision for loan losses was US$229.0 million versus a credit for loan losses of US$60.0 million in the prior year. Non-interest income rose 8.8% to US$1.97 billion from US$1.81 billion, while non-interest expense advanced 4.2% to US$2.91 billion.

Prospects: Our evaluation of KeyCorp as of Apr. 7, 2013 is the result of our systematic analysis on three basic characteristics: earnings strength, relative valuation, and recent stock price movement. The company has produced a positive trend in earnings per share over the past 5 quarters and while recent estimates for the company have been raised by analysts, KEY has posted better than expected results. Based on operating earnings yield, the company is undervalued when compared to all of the companies in our coverage universe. Share price changes over the past year indicates that KEY will perform in line with the market over the near term.

Financial Data

(US$ in Thousands)	12/31/2012	12/31/2011	12/31/2010	12/31/2009	12/31/2008	12/31/2007	12/31/2006	12/31/2005
Earnings Per Share	0.89	0.87	0.44	(2.34)	(3.36)	2.32	2.57	2.73
Cash Flow Per Share	1.44	2.03	3.11	3.33	(0.49)	(0.50)	2.48	5.30
Tang Book Value Per Share	9.54	9.11	8.45	7.94	12.41	16.39	15.99	15.05
Dividends Per Share	0.180	0.100	0.040	0.092	1.000	1.460	1.380	1.300
Dividend Payout %	20.22	11.49	9.09	...	...	62.93	53.70	47.62
Income Statement								
Interest Income	2,705,000	2,889,000	3,408,000	3,795,000	4,629,000	5,644,000	5,380,000	4,617,000
Interest Expense	441,000	622,000	897,000	1,415,000	2,220,000	2,875,000	2,565,000	1,827,000
Net Interest Income	2,264,000	2,267,000	2,511,000	2,380,000	2,409,000	2,769,000	2,815,000	2,790,000
Provision for Losses	229,000	(60,000)	638,000	3,159,000	1,835,000	529,000	150,000	143,000
Non-Interest Income	1,967,000	1,808,000	1,954,000	2,035,000	1,870,000	2,229,000	2,127,000	2,078,000
Non-Interest Expense	2,907,000	2,790,000	3,034,000	3,554,000	3,578,000	3,248,000	3,149,000	3,137,000
Income Before Taxes	1,095,000	1,345,000	793,000	(2,298,000)	(1,134,000)	1,221,000	1,643,000	1,588,000
Income Taxes	239,000	369,000	186,000	(1,035,000)	334,000	280,000	450,000	459,000
Net Income	858,000	920,000	554,000	(1,335,000)	(1,468,000)	919,000	1,055,000	1,129,000
Average Shares	943,259	935,801	878,153	697,155	450,039	395,823	410,222	414,014
Balance Sheet								
Net Loans & Leases	52,533,000	49,299,000	48,970,000	56,679,000	75,728,000	74,359,000	68,519,000	68,893,000
Total Assets	89,236,000	88,785,000	91,843,000	93,287,000	104,531,000	99,983,000	92,337,000	93,126,000
Total Deposits	65,993,000	61,956,000	60,610,000	65,571,000	65,260,000	63,099,000	59,116,000	58,765,000
Total Liabilities	78,965,000	78,880,000	80,726,000	82,624,000	94,051,000	92,237,000	84,634,000	85,528,000
Stockholders' Equity	10,271,000	9,905,000	11,117,000	10,663,000	10,480,000	7,746,000	7,703,000	7,598,000
Shares Outstanding	925,768	953,007	880,607	878,534	495,002	388,792	399,153	406,623
Statistical Record								
Return on Assets %	0.96	1.02	0.60	N.M.	N.M.	0.96	1.14	1.23
Return on Equity %	8.48	8.75	5.09	N.M.	N.M.	11.90	13.79	15.34
Net Interest Margin %	83.70	78.47	73.68	62.71	52.04	49.06	52.32	60.43
Efficiency Ratio %	62.22	59.40	56.58	60.96	55.05	41.25	41.95	46.86
Loans to Deposits	0.80	0.80	0.81	0.86	1.16	1.18	1.16	1.17
Price Range	9.04-6.89	9.71-5.71	9.19-5.55	9.23-4.60	26.42-6.27	39.79-21.91	38.60-33.13	34.83-30.81
P/E Ratio	10.16-7.74	11.16-6.56	20.89-12.61	...	...	17.15-9.44	15.02-12.89	12.76-11.29
Average Yield %	2.22	1.27	0.51	1.45	6.19	4.32	3.78	3.94

Address: 127 Public Square, Cleveland, OH 44114-1306	Web Site: www.key.com	Auditors: Ernst & Young LLP
Telephone: 216-689-3000	Officers: Beth E. Mooney - Chairman, Vice-Chairman, President, Chief Executive Officer, Chief Operating Officer Thomas C. Stevens - Vice-Chairman, Chief Administrative Officer	Investor Contact: 216-689-4221 Transfer Agents: ComputerShare Investor Services, Providence, RI

KILROY REALTY CORP

Exchange	Symbol	Price $52.40 (3/28/2013)	52Wk Range 53.99-42.47	Yield 2.67	P/E 20.47

*7 Year Price Score 91.70   *NYSE Composite Index=100   *12 Month Price Score 100.92

Interim Earnings (Per Share)

Qtr.	Mar	Jun	Sep	Dec
2008	0.30	0.17	0.40	0.18
2009	0.23	0.25	0.17	(0.11)
2010	0.11	(0.04)	(0.01)	0.03
2011	0.01	(0.01)	0.17	0.69
2012	1.06	(0.02)	(0.04)	1.64

Interim Dividends (Per Share)

Amt	Decl	Ex	Rec	Pay
0.35Q	05/17/2012	06/27/2012	06/29/2012	07/17/2012
0.35Q	09/14/2012	09/26/2012	09/28/2012	10/17/2012
0.35Q	12/06/2012	12/27/2012	12/31/2012	01/15/2013
0.35Q	02/28/2013	03/26/2013	03/28/2013	04/17/2013

Indicated Div: $1.40

Valuation Analysis

Forecast EPS	$0.16
	(04/05/2013)
Market Cap	$3.9 Billion
Book Value	$2.2 Billion
Price/Book	1.79
Price/Sales	9.70

Institutional Holding

No of Institutions	274
Shares	88,014,976
% Held	109.34

Business Summary: REITs (MIC: 5.3.1 SIC: 6798 NAIC: 525930)

Kilroy Realty is a real estate investment trust, which owns, develops, acquires, and manages real estate assets, consisting primarily of Class A real estate properties in the coastal regions of Los Angeles, Orange County, San Diego County, the San Francisco Bay Area and greater Seattle. As of Dec 31 2012, Co. had a stabilized portfolio of 114 office properties encompassing an aggregate of 13,249,780 rentable sq. ft.; 4 development properties under construction, 1 redevelopment properties under construction and one lease-up property. Co. owns its interests in all of its office properties through Kilroy Services, LLC.

Recent Developments: For the year ended Dec 31 2012, income from continuing operations was US$5.4 million compared with a loss of US$3.7 million a year earlier. Net income increased 310.6% to US$277.1 million from US$67.5 million in the prior year. Revenues were US$404.9 million, up 19.9% from US$337.6 million the year before.

Prospects: Our evaluation of Kilroy Realty Corp. as of Apr. 7, 2013 is the result of our systematic analysis on three basic characteristics: earnings strength, relative valuation, and recent stock price movement. The company has generated a negative trend in earnings per share over the past 5 quarters. Because the company lacks sufficient analyst estimate data, we place greater weight on the historical EPS trend as the measure of earnings strength. Based on operating earnings yield, the company is overvalued when compared to all of the companies in our coverage universe. Share price changes over the past year indicates that KRC will perform in line with the market over the near term.

Financial Data

(US$ in Thousands)	12/31/2012	12/31/2011	12/31/2010	12/31/2009	12/31/2008	12/31/2007	12/31/2006	12/31/2005
Earnings Per Share	2.56	0.87	0.07	0.53	1.06	3.20	2.30	0.84
Cash Flow Per Share	2.59	2.44	2.42	3.23	4.44	4.56	1.97	4.04
Tang Book Value Per Share	26.66	21.18	19.84	18.70	18.38	19.70	19.33	16.27
Dividends Per Share	1.400	1.400	1.400	1.630	2.320	2.220	2.120	2.040
Dividend Payout %	54.69	160.92	2,000.00	307.55	218.87	69.38	92.17	242.86
Income Statement								
Total Revenue	404,912	367,131	301,980	279,434	289,968	258,472	251,244	241,715
EBITDA	209,613	199,897	164,214	148,364	160,582	145,277	152,550	106,277
Depn & Amortn	125,900	106,000	86,300	74,000	68,800	61,100	59,000	56,100
Income Before Taxes	5,447	5,059	18,937	29,545	51,323	48,281	51,662	11,628
Net Income	270,914	66,015	19,708	36,990	-44,121	113,822	81,864	33,819
Average Shares	69,639	56,717	49,513	38,732	32,669	32,526	31,389	28,710
Balance Sheet								
Current Assets	396,317	120,363	116,513	103,701	95,834	96,129	135,151	76,604
Total Assets	4,616,084	3,446,795	2,816,565	2,084,281	2,099,583	2,068,720	1,799,352	1,674,474
Current Liabilities	183,658	104,405	88,910	69,669	76,487	78,859	87,339	152,414
Long-Term Obligations	2,040,935	1,821,286	1,427,776	972,016	1,169,466	1,107,002	879,198	842,282
Total Liabilities	2,426,454	2,079,440	1,656,576	1,155,695	1,369,880	1,301,790	1,051,418	1,081,568
Stockholders' Equity	2,189,630	1,367,355	1,159,989	928,586	729,703	766,930	747,934	592,906
Shares Outstanding	74,926	58,819	52,349	43,148	33,086	32,765	32,398	28,970
Statistical Record								
Return on Assets %	6.70	2.11	0.80	1.77	2.11	5.89	4.71	2.07
Return on Equity %	15.19	5.22	1.89	4.46	5.88	15.03	12.21	5.55
EBITDA Margin %	51.77	54.45	54.38	53.09	55.38	56.21	60.72	43.97
Net Margin %	66.91	17.98	6.53	13.24	15.22	44.04	32.58	13.99
Asset Turnover	0.10	0.12	0.12	0.13	0.14	0.13	0.14	0.15
Current Ratio	2.16	1.15	1.31	1.49	1.25	1.22	1.55	0.50
Debt to Equity	0.93	1.33	1.23	1.05	1.60	1.44	1.18	1.42
Price Range	49.88-37.92	41.94-29.25	36.72-26.75	33.46-15.40	55.54-22.10	89.80-52.66	83.42-63.45	63.71-38.95
P/E Ratio	19.48-14.81	48.21-33.62	524.57-382.14	63.13-29.06	52.40-20.85	28.06-16.46	36.27-27.59	75.85-46.37
Average Yield %	3.05	3.75	4.34	6.72	5.15	3.20	2.90	4.15

Address: 12200 W. Olympic Boulevard, Suite 200, Los Angeles, CA 90064 Telephone: 310-481-8400	Web Site: www.kilroyrealty.com Officers: John B. Kilroy - Chairman, President, Chief Executive Officer Jeffrey C. Hawken - Executive Vice President, Chief Operating Officer	Auditors: Deloitte & Touche LLP Investor Contact: 310-481-8400 Transfer Agents: Computershare Shareowner Services LLC, Jersey City, NJ

KIMBERLY-CLARK CORP.

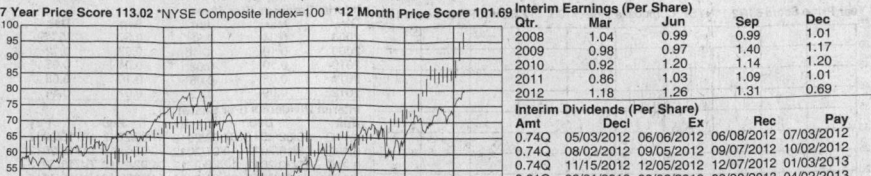

Exchange	Symbol	Price	52Wk Range	Yield	P/E	Div Achiever
NYS	KMB	$97.98 (3/28/2013)	97.98-73.53	3.31	22.17	38 Years

*7 Year Price Score 113.02 *NYSE Composite Index=100 *12 Month Price Score 101.69

Interim Earnings (Per Share)

Qtr.	Mar	Jun	Sep	Dec
2008	1.04	0.99	0.99	1.01
2009	0.98	0.97	1.40	1.17
2010	0.92	1.20	1.14	1.20
2011	0.86	1.03	1.09	1.01
2012	1.18	1.26	1.31	0.69

Interim Dividends (Per Share)

Amt	Decl	Ex	Rec	Pay
0.74Q	05/03/2012	06/06/2012	06/08/2012	07/03/2012
0.74Q	08/02/2012	09/05/2012	09/07/2012	10/02/2012
0.74Q	11/15/2012	12/05/2012	12/07/2012	01/03/2013
0.81Q	02/21/2013	03/06/2013	03/08/2013	04/02/2013

Indicated Div: $3.24 (Div. Reinv. Plan)

Valuation Analysis | **Institutional Holding**

Forecast EPS	$5.60	No of Institutions
	(04/06/2013)	1299
Market Cap	$38.1 Billion	Shares
Book Value	$5.5 Billion	302,704,352
Price/Book	6.89	% Held
Price/Sales	1.81	67.45

TRADING VOLUME (thousand shares)

Business Summary: Household & Personal Products (MIC: 1.7.1 SIC: 2679 NAIC: 322299)

Kimberly-Clark manufactures and markets products mostly made from natural or synthetic fibers. Co. has four segments: Personal Care, which produces disposable diapers, training and youth pants, swimpants, baby wipes, feminine and incontinence care products, and other products; Consumer Tissue, which produces facial and bathroom tissue, paper towels, napkins and related products; K-C Professional and Other, which produces products such as apparel, wipers, soaps, sanitizers, tissues and towels; and Health Care, which provides surgical and infection prevention products for the operating room, and a portfolio of medical devices focused on pain management, respiratory and digestive health.

Recent Developments: For the year ended Dec 31 2012, net income increased 8.6% to US$1.83 billion from US$1.68 billion in the prior year. Revenues were US$21.06 billion, up 1.0% from US$20.85 billion the year before. Operating income was US$2.69 billion versus US$2.44 billion in the prior year, an increase of 10.0%. Direct operating expenses declined 2.6% to US$14.31 billion from US$14.69 billion in the comparable period the year before. Indirect operating expenses increased 9.5% to US$4.06 billion from US$3.71 billion in the equivalent prior-year period.

Prospects: Our evaluation of Kimberly-Clark Corp. as of Apr. 7, 2013 is the result of our systematic analysis on three basic characteristics: earnings strength, relative valuation, and recent stock price movement. The company has managed to produce a neutral trend in earnings per share over the past 5 quarters and while recent estimates for the company have remained steady, KMB has posted better than expected results. Based on operating earnings yield, the company is about fairly valued when compared to all of the companies in our coverage universe. Share price changes over the past year indicates that KMB will perform in line with the market over the near term.

Financial Data
(US$ in Thousands)

	12/31/2012	12/31/2011	12/31/2010	12/31/2009	12/31/2008	12/31/2007	12/31/2006	12/31/2005
Earnings Per Share	4.42	3.99	4.45	4.52	4.04	4.09	3.25	3.28
Cash Flow Per Share	8.34	5.78	6.65	8.37	6.02	5.50	5.63	4.88
Tang Book Value Per Share	5.01	5.54	6.80	7.63	5.19	7.81	8.85	7.87
Dividends Per Share	2.960	2.800	2.640	2.400	2.320	2.120	1.960	1.800
Dividend Payout %	66.97	70.18	59.33	53.10	57.43	51.83	60.31	54.88
Income Statement								
Total Revenue	21,063,000	20,846,000	19,746,000	19,115,000	19,415,000	18,266,000	16,746,900	15,902,600
EBITDA	2,715,000	2,466,000	2,798,000	2,843,000	2,559,000	2,563,500	2,075,000	2,157,600
Depn & Amortn	29,000	24,000	25,000	18,000	12,000	14,000	39,000	26,000
Income Before Taxes	2,420,000	2,183,000	2,550,000	2,576,000	2,289,000	2,317,500	1,844,900	1,968,900
Income Taxes	768,000	660,000	788,000	746,000	618,000	536,500	469,200	438,400
Net Income	1,750,000	1,591,000	1,843,000	1,884,000	1,690,000	1,822,900	1,499,500	1,568,300
Average Shares	396,100	398,600	414,400	416,800	418,600	445,600	461,600	477,400
Balance Sheet								
Current Assets	6,589,000	6,283,000	6,328,000	5,864,000	5,813,000	6,096,600	5,269,700	4,783,100
Total Assets	19,873,000	19,373,000	19,864,000	19,209,000	18,089,000	18,439,700	17,067,000	16,303,200
Current Liabilities	6,091,000	5,397,000	5,338,000	4,923,000	4,752,000	4,928,600	5,015,800	4,642,900
Long-Term Obligations	5,070,000	5,426,000	5,120,000	4,792,000	4,882,000	4,393,900	2,276,000	2,594,700
Total Liabilities	14,339,000	13,577,000	13,406,000	12,751,000	13,200,000	12,211,400	10,176,200	9,987,600
Stockholders' Equity	5,534,000	5,796,000	6,458,000	6,458,000	4,889,000	6,228,300	6,890,800	6,315,600
Shares Outstanding	389,300	395,700	406,856	417,000	413,600	420,921	455,619	461,489
Statistical Record								
Return on Assets %	8.89	8.11	9.43	10.10	9.23	10.27	8.99	9.41
Return on Equity %	30.81	25.97	28.54	33.21	30.32	27.79	22.71	22.95
EBITDA Margin %	12.89	11.83	14.17	14.87	13.18	14.03	12.39	13.57
Net Margin %	8.31	7.63	9.33	9.86	8.70	9.98	8.95	9.86
Asset Turnover	1.07	1.06	1.01	1.02	1.06	1.03	1.00	0.95
Current Ratio	1.08	1.16	1.19	1.19	1.22	1.24	1.05	1.03
Debt to Equity	0.92	0.94	0.79	0.74	1.00	0.71	0.33	0.41
Price Range	87.93-71.13	74.00-62.57	66.91-58.86	66.82-43.41	69.50-50.74	71.98-65.76	68.13-56.66	68.15-55.97
P/E Ratio	19.89-16.09	18.55-15.68	15.04-13.23	14.78-9.60	17.20-12.56	17.60-16.08	20.96-17.43	20.78-17.06
Average Yield %	3.67	4.16	4.21	4.36	3.77	3.06	3.17	2.88

Address: P.O. Box 619100, Dallas, TX 75261-9100	**Web Site:** www.kimberly-clark.com	**Auditors:** Deloitte & Touche LLP
Telephone: 972-281-1200	**Officers:** Thomas J. Falk - Chairman, President, Chief Executive Officer Mark A. Buthman - Senior Vice President, Chief Financial Officer	**Investor Contact:** 972-281-1440
		Transfer Agents: ComputerShare Investor Services, Providence, RI

KIMCO REALTY CORP.

Exchange	Symbol	Price	52Wk Range	Yield	P/E
NYS	KIM	$22.40 (3/28/2013)	22.40-17.37	3.75	53.33

*7 Year Price Score 69.72   *NYSE Composite Index=100   *12 Month Price Score 101.40

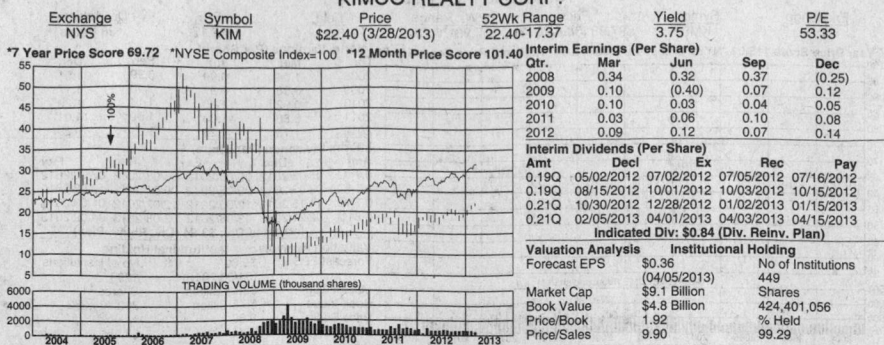

Interim Earnings (Per Share)

Qtr.	Mar	Jun	Sep	Dec
2008	0.34	0.32	0.37	(0.25)
2009	0.10	(0.40)	0.07	0.12
2010	0.10	0.03	0.04	0.05
2011	0.03	0.06	0.10	0.08
2012	0.09	0.12	0.07	0.14

Interim Dividends (Per Share)

Amt	Decl	Ex	Rec	Pay
0.19Q	05/02/2012	07/02/2012	07/05/2012	07/16/2012
0.19Q	08/15/2012	10/01/2012	10/03/2012	10/15/2012
0.21Q	10/30/2012	12/28/2012	01/02/2013	01/15/2013
0.21Q	02/05/2013	04/01/2013	04/03/2013	04/15/2013

Indicated Div: $0.84 (Div. Reinv. Plan)

Valuation Analysis | **Institutional Holding**

Forecast EPS	$0.36	No of Institutions	
	(04/05/2013)	449	
Market Cap	$9.1 Billion	Shares	
Book Value	$4.8 Billion	424,401,056	
Price/Book	1.92	% Held	
Price/Sales	9.90	99.29	

Business Summary: REITs (MIC: 5.3.1 SIC: 6798 NAIC: 525930)

Kimco Realty is a self-administered real estate investment trust engaged principally in the operation of neighborhood and community shopping centers which are anchored generally by discount department stores, supermarkets or drugstores. Co. also provides property management services for shopping centers owned by affiliated entities, various real estate joint ventures and unaffiliated third parties. As of Dec 31 2011, Co. had interests in 946 shopping center properties and 845 other property interests, primarily through its preferred equity investments, other real estate investments and non-retail properties located in 44 states, Puerto Rico, Canada, Mexico, Chile, Brazil and Peru.

Recent Developments: For the year ended Dec 31 2012, income from continuing operations increased 33.3% to US$212.0 million from US$159.0 million a year earlier. Net income increased 53.9% to US$280.3 million from US$182.1 million in the prior year. Revenues were US$922.3 million, up 7.1% from US$861.1 million the year before. Revenues from property income rose 7.2% to US$884.8 million from US$825.7 million in the corresponding earlier year.

Prospects: Our evaluation of Kimco Realty Corp. as of Apr. 7, 2013 is the result of our systematic analysis on three basic characteristics: earnings strength, relative valuation, and recent stock price movement. The company has produced a positive trend in earnings per share over the past 5 quarters. Because the company lacks sufficient analyst estimate data, we place greater weight on the historical EPS trend as the measure of earnings strength. Based on operating earnings yield, the company is overvalued when compared to all of the companies in our coverage universe. Share price changes over the past year indicates that KIM will perform in line with the market over the near term.

Financial Data

(US$ in Thousands)	12/31/2012	12/31/2011	12/31/2010	12/31/2009	12/31/2008	12/31/2007	12/31/2006	12/31/2005
Earnings Per Share	0.42	0.27	0.22	(0.15)	0.78	1.65	1.70	1.52
Cash Flow Per Share	1.18	1.10	1.18	1.15	2.20	2.64	1.90	1.81
Tang Book Value Per Share	11.69	11.51	12.14	11.96	14.66	15.40	13.42	10.46
Dividends Per Share	0.780	0.730	0.660	0.720	1.680	1.520	1.380	1.270
Dividend Payout %	185.71	270.37	300.00	...	215.38	92.12	81.18	83.55
Income Statement								
Total Revenue	922,304	873,694	849,549	786,887	758,704	681,553	593,880	522,545
EBITDA	522,236	540,049	542,367	363,712	490,754	452,027	427,437	393,320
Depn & Amortn	262,742	251,139	247,637	227,776	206,518	191,270	144,767	108,042
Income Before Taxes	34,069	80,441	89,598	(40,845)	127,764	78,034	164,199	185,917
Income Taxes	3,939	19,537	3,415	(36,622)	3,542	(44,490)	4,387	430
Net Income	266,073	169,051	142,868	(3,942)	249,902	442,830	428,259	363,628
Average Shares	406,689	407,669	406,201	350,077	258,843	257,058	244,615	230,868
Balance Sheet								
Current Assets	339,529	296,229	479,681	445,261	492,053	388,504	631,142	347,054
Total Assets	9,740,807	9,614,516	9,833,875	10,162,205	9,397,147	9,097,816	7,869,280	5,534,636
Current Liabilities	3,400,526	3,221,217	3,225,940	3,219,126	3,723,156	3,405,343	3,098,457	2,345,178
Long-Term Obligations	1,003,190	1,130,499	1,076,566	1,434,080	1,115,828	1,084,650	838,898	543,791
Total Liabilities	4,975,647	4,928,130	4,898,033	5,309,232	5,421,801	5,203,242	4,502,321	3,147,422
Stockholders' Equity	4,765,160	4,686,386	4,935,842	4,852,973	3,975,346	3,894,574	3,366,959	2,387,214
Shares Outstanding	407,782	406,937	406,423	405,532	271,080	252,803	250,870	228,059
Statistical Record								
Return on Assets %	2.74	1.74	1.43	N.M.	2.69	5.22	6.39	7.07
Return on Equity %	5.61	3.51	2.92	N.M.	6.33	12.20	14.89	15.73
EBITDA Margin %	56.62	61.81	63.84	46.22	64.68	66.32	71.97	75.27
Net Margin %	28.85	19.35	16.82	N.M.	32.94	64.97	72.11	69.59
Asset Turnover	0.10	0.09	0.08	0.08	0.08	0.08	0.09	0.10
Current Ratio	0.10	0.09	0.15	0.14	0.13	0.11	0.20	0.15
Debt to Equity	0.21	0.24	0.22	0.30	0.28	0.28	0.25	0.23
Price Range	21.03-16.27	20.30-14.11	18.14-12.59	20.45-6.97	42.95-11.26	53.41-35.30	46.88-32.73	33.25-26.20
P/E Ratio	50.07-38.74	75.19-52.26	82.45-57.23	...	55.06-14.44	32.37-21.39	27.58-19.25	21.88-17.23
Average Yield %	4.08	4.17	4.32	6.15	5.18	3.47	3.51	4.33

Address: 3333 New Hyde Park Road, New Hyde Park, NY 11042-0020	Web Site: www.kimcorealty.com	Auditors: PricewaterhouseCoopers LLP
Telephone: 516-869-9000	Officers: Milton Cooper - Chairman David B. Henry - Vice-Chairman, President, Chief Executive Officer, Chief Investment Officer	Investor Contact: 866-831-4297
Fax: 516-869-9001		Transfer Agents: Wells Fargo Shareowner Services, Saint Paul, MN

KINDRED HEALTHCARE INC

Exchange	Symbol	Price	52Wk Range	Yield	P/E
NYS	KND	$10.53 (3/28/2013)	12.53-7.79	N/A	N/A

*7 Year Price Score 51.89 *NYSE Composite Index=100 ***12 Month Price Score 98.31**

Interim Earnings (Per Share)

Qtr.	Mar	Jun	Sep	Dec
2008	0.38	0.56	(0.54)	0.54
2009	0.58	(0.19)	0.14	0.49
2010	0.38	0.41	0.12	0.52
2011	0.55	(0.13)	0.03	(1.56)
2012	0.35	0.29	0.14	(1.56)

Interim Dividends (Per Share)

No Dividends Paid

Valuation Analysis		Institutional Holding	
Forecast EPS	$1.20	No of Institutions	
	(04/05/2013)	198	
Market Cap	$561.0 Million	Shares	
Book Value	$1.3 Billion	55,678,588	
Price/Book	0.45	% Held	
Price/Sales	0.09	99.12	

Business Summary: Hospitals & Health Care Facilities (MIC: 4.2.1 SIC: 8059 NAIC: 623110)

Kindred Healthcare is a healthcare services company that through its subsidiaries operates long-term acute care (LTAC) hospitals, inpatient rehabilitation hospitals (IRFs), nursing and rehabilitation centers, assisted living facilities, a contract rehabilitation services business and a home health and hospice business. At Dec 31 2011, Co.'s hospital division operated 121 LTAC hospitals (8,597 licensed beds) and five IRFs (183 licensed beds) in 26 states. Co.'s nursing center division operated 224 nursing and rehabilitation centers (27,148 licensed beds) and six assisted living facilities (413 licensed beds) in 27 states. Co.'s rehabilitation division provided rehabilitation services.

Recent Developments: For the year ended Dec 31 2012, loss from continuing operations was US$32.4 million compared with a loss of US$48.1 million a year earlier. Net loss amounted to US$39.3 million versus a net loss of US$53.7 million in the prior year. Revenues were US$6.18 billion, up 12.3% from US$5.50 billion the year before. Indirect operating expenses increased 10.8% to US$6.07 billion from US$5.47 billion in the equivalent prior-year period.

Prospects: Our evaluation of Kindred Healthcare Inc. as of Apr. 7, 2013 is the result of our systematic analysis on three basic characteristics: earnings strength, relative valuation, and recent stock price movement. The company has enjoyed a very positive trend in earnings per share over the past 5 quarters. However, while recent estimates for the company have been mixed, KND has posted better than expected results. Based on operating earnings yield, the company is undervalued when compared to all of the companies in our coverage universe. Share price changes over the past year indicates that KND will perform very well over the near term.

Financial Data
(US$ in Thousands)

	12/31/2012	12/31/2011	12/31/2010	12/31/2009	12/31/2008	12/31/2007	12/31/2006	12/31/2005
Earnings Per Share	(0.78)	(1.16)	1.43	1.02	0.93	(1.17)	1.92	3.20
Cash Flow Per Share	5.07	3.32	5.42	6.10	4.83	4.21	3.32	7.05
Tang Book Value Per Share	N.M.	N.M.	17.63	20.99	20.00	18.60	19.27	21.45
Income Statement								
Total Revenue	6,181,291	5,521,763	4,359,697	4,270,007	4,151,396	4,220,266	4,266,661	3,923,999
EBITDA	293,737	169,744	217,244	234,407	231,930	200,365	248,729	323,875
Depn & Amortn	179,100	152,200	120,304	124,880	120,500	117,300	117,000	101,000
Income Before Taxes	6,741	(63,375)	89,854	101,727	96,057	66,021	117,808	214,777
Income Taxes	39,112	(7,104)	33,708	39,115	37,164	31,301	46,569	86,147
Net Income	(40,367)	(53,481)	56,491	40,111	36,285	(46,870)	78,711	144,909
Average Shares	51,659	46,230	38,954	38,502	38,906	39,983	40,923	45,239
Balance Sheet								
Current Assets	1,273,766	1,233,282	836,038	843,651	1,102,635	1,013,647	1,002,561	944,964
Total Assets	4,237,946	4,138,493	2,337,415	2,022,224	2,181,761	2,079,552	2,016,127	1,760,561
Current Liabilities	835,331	848,923	621,384	602,619	625,270	629,942	606,998	620,627
Long-Term Obligations	1,648,706	1,531,882	365,556	147,647	349,433	275,814	130,000	26,323
Total Liabilities	2,981,787	2,849,572	1,305,656	1,055,630	1,266,786	1,201,668	1,020,549	890,025
Stockholders' Equity	1,256,159	1,288,921	1,031,759	966,594	914,975	862,124	995,578	870,536
Shares Outstanding	53,280	52,116	39,495	39,104	38,909	38,339	39,978	37,331
Statistical Record								
Return on Assets %	N.M.	N.M.	2.59	1.91	1.70	N.M.	4.17	8.64
Return on Equity %	N.M.	N.M.	5.65	4.26	4.07	N.M.	8.44	18.22
EBITDA Margin %	4.75	3.07	4.98	5.49	5.59	4.75	5.83	8.25
Net Margin %	N.M.	N.M.	1.30	0.94	0.87	N.M.	1.84	3.69
Asset Turnover	1.47	1.71	2.00	2.03	1.94	2.06	2.26	2.34
Current Ratio	1.52	1.45	1.35	1.40	1.76	1.61	1.65	1.52
Debt to Equity	1.31	1.19	0.35	0.15	0.38	0.32	0.13	0.03
Price Range	13.41-7.79	28.55-7.68	19.59-11.61	19.84-10.91	32.49-8.51	28.19-17.42	24.53-15.55	32.34-19.09
P/E Ratio	...	...	13.70-8.12	19.45-10.70	34.94-9.15	...	12.78-8.10	10.11-5.97

Address: 680 South Fourth Street,	Web Site: www.kindredhealthcare.com	Auditors: PricewaterhouseCoopers LLP
Louisville, KY 40202-2412	Officers: Edward L. Kuntz - Chairman Benjamin A.	Investor Contact: 502-596-7734
Telephone: 502-596-7300	Breier - President, Executive Vice President, Chief	Transfer Agents: Computershare
	Operating Officer, Division Officer	

KINDER MORGAN ENERGY PARTNERS, L.P.

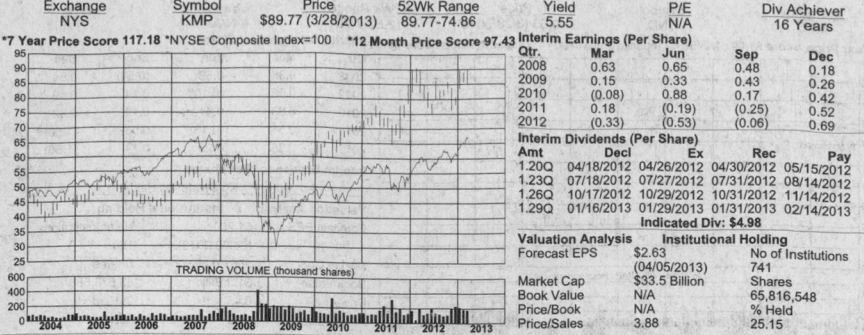

Exchange	Symbol	Price	52Wk Range	Yield	P/E	Div Achiever
NYS	KMP	$89.77 (3/28/2013)	89.77-74.86	5.55	N/A	16 Years

*7 Year Price Score 117.18 *NYSE Composite Index=100 *12 Month Price Score 97.43

Interim Earnings (Per Share)

Qtr.	Mar	Jun	Sep	Dec
2008	0.63	0.65	0.48	0.18
2009	0.15	0.33	0.43	0.26
2010	(0.08)	0.88	0.17	0.42
2011	0.18	(0.19)	(0.25)	0.52
2012	(0.33)	(0.53)	(0.06)	0.69

Interim Dividends (Per Share)

Amt	Decl	Ex	Rec	Pay
1.20Q	04/18/2012	04/26/2012	04/30/2012	05/15/2012
1.23Q	07/18/2012	07/27/2012	07/31/2012	08/14/2012
1.26Q	10/17/2012	10/29/2012	10/31/2012	11/14/2012
1.29Q	01/16/2013	01/29/2013	01/31/2013	02/14/2013

Indicated Div: $4.98

Valuation Analysis | **Institutional Holding**

Forecast EPS	$2.63 (04/05/2013)	No of Institutions	741
Market Cap	$33.5 Billion	Shares	65,816,548
Book Value	N/A	% Held	25.15
Price/Book	N/A		
Price/Sales	3.88		

Business Summary: Equipment & Services (MIC: 9.1.3 SIC: 4922 NAIC: 486210)

Kinder Morgan Energy Partners is a pipeline transportation and energy storage company. As of Dec 31 2012, Co. owned an interest in or operates approximately 46,000 miles of pipelines and 180 terminals. Co.'s pipelines transport natural gas, refined petroleum products, crude oil, carbon dioxide and other products, and its terminals store petroleum products and chemicals, and handle such products as ethanol, coal, petroleum coke and steel. Co. is also a producer and transporter of carbon dioxide (CO2), for oil recovery projects in North America. Co. has five business segments: Products Pipelines, Natural Gas Pipelines, CO2, Terminals and Kinder Morgan Canada.

Recent Developments: For the year ended Dec 31 2012, income from continuing operations increased 89.8% to US$2.03 billion from US$1.07 billion a year earlier. Net income increased 6.9% to US$1.36 billion from US$1.27 billion in the prior year. Revenues were US$8.64 billion, up 9.5% from US$7.89 billion the year before. Operating income was US$2.34 billion versus US$1.56 billion in the prior year, an increase of 50.3%. Direct operating expenses declined 5.2% to US$4.52 billion from US$4.77 billion in the comparable period the year before. Indirect operating expenses increased 13.9% to US$1.78 billion from US$1.56 billion in the equivalent prior-year period.

Prospects: Our evaluation of Kinder Morgan Energy Partners, L.P. as of Apr. 7, 2013 is the result of our systematic analysis on three basic characteristics: earnings strength, relative valuation, and recent stock price movement. The company has generated a negative trend in earnings per share over the past 5 quarters and while recent estimates for the company have been raised by analysts, KMP has posted better than expected results. Based on operating earnings yield, the company is overvalued when compared to all of the companies in our coverage universe. Share price changes over the past year indicates that KMP will perform poorly over the near term.

Financial Data

(US$ in Thousands)	12/31/2012	12/31/2011	12/31/2010	12/31/2009	12/31/2008	12/31/2007	12/31/2006	12/31/2005
Earnings Per Share	(0.22)	0.25	1.40	1.18	1.94	(0.09)	2.04	1.58
Cash Flow Per Share	9.03	8.81	7.88	7.52	8.67	7.35	5.60	6.08
Dividends Per Share	4.850	4.580	4.320	4.200	3.890	3.390	3.230	3.070
Dividend Payout %	...	1,832.00	308.57	355.93	200.52	...	158.33	194.30
Income Statement								
Total Revenue	8,642,000	8,211,200	8,077,700	7,003,400	11,740,300	9,217,700	8,954,583	9,787,128
EBITDA	3,359,000	2,400,200	2,476,300	2,388,400	2,249,200	1,345,400	1,659,060	1,350,731
Depn & Amortn	1,008,000	886,100	852,800	829,600	684,200	529,300	397,525	339,580
Income Before Taxes	1,716,000	1,003,100	1,138,600	1,149,800	1,176,800	424,700	930,036	752,290
Income Taxes	30,000	45,800	34,600	55,700	20,400	71,000	19,048	24,461
Net Income	1,339,000	1,257,800	1,316,300	1,267,500	1,304,800	590,300	972,143	812,227
Average Shares	351,000	326,100	307,100	281,500	257,200	236,900	224,914	212,429
Balance Sheet								
Current Assets	2,244,000	1,575,400	1,286,700	1,244,700	1,244,400	1,209,700	1,036,745	1,215,224
Total Assets	32,094,000	24,102,700	21,861,100	20,262,200	17,885,800	15,177,800	12,246,394	11,923,462
Current Liabilities	3,165,000	3,119,100	2,764,200	2,017,600	1,782,100	2,558,300	2,885,699	1,808,885
Long-Term Obligations	16,175,000	12,238,400	10,882,300	10,330,200	9,226,200	6,608,100	4,426,962	5,319,356
Total Liabilities	20,770,000	16,595,100	14,650,400	13,617,700	11,840,200	10,742,100	8,224,741	8,309,722
Shares Outstanding	373,188	336,500	316,101	296,872	266,280	247,966	230,431	220,237
Statistical Record								
Return on Assets %	4.75	5.47	6.25	6.65	7.87	4.30	8.04	7.23
EBITDA Margin %	38.87	29.23	30.66	34.10	19.16	14.60	18.53	13.80
Net Margin %	15.49	15.32	16.30	18.10	11.11	6.40	10.86	8.30
Asset Turnover	0.31	0.36	0.38	0.37	0.71	0.67	0.74	0.87
Current Ratio	0.71	0.51	0.47	0.62	0.70	0.47	0.36	0.67
Price Range	90.60-74.86	84.95-64.58	71.39-59.69	60.99-41.15	60.54-42.90	56.96-47.46	50.88-43.15	54.18-42.95
P/E Ratio	...	339.80-258.32	50.99-42.64	51.69-34.87	31.21-22.11	...	24.94-21.15	34.29-27.18
Average Yield %	5.90	6.27	6.48	8.15	7.08	6.48	6.96	6.25

Address: 1001 Louisiana Street, Suite 1000, Houston, TX 77002 **Telephone:** 713-369-9000	**Web Site:** www.kindermorgan.com **Officers:** Richard D. Kinder - Chairman, Chief Executive Officer, Holding/Parent Company Officer, Associate/Affiliate Company Officer C. Park Sharper - President, Holding/Parent Company Officer, Associate/Affiliate Company Officer	**Auditors:** PricewaterhouseCoopers LLP **Investor Contact:** 713-369-9449 **Transfer Agents:** Computershare Trust Company, N.A., Providence, RI

KINDER MORGAN INC.

Exchange	Symbol	Price	52Wk Range	Yield	P/E
NYS	KMI	$38.68 (3/28/2013)	39.85-30.76	3.83	110.51

*7 Year Price Score N/A *NYSE Composite Index=100 *12 Month Price Score 97.09

TRADING VOLUME (thousand shares)

Interim Earnings (Per Share)

Qtr.	Mar	Jun	Sep	Dec
2011	0.12	0.19	0.21	0.22
2012	0.03	(0.15)	0.19	0.24

Interim Dividends (Per Share)

Amt	Decl	Ex	Rec	Pay
0.32Q	04/18/2012	04/26/2012	04/30/2012	05/16/2012
0.35Q	07/18/2012	07/27/2012	07/31/2012	08/15/2012
0.36Q	10/17/2012	10/29/2012	10/31/2012	11/15/2012
0.37Q	01/16/2013	01/29/2013	01/31/2013	02/15/2013

Indicated Div: $1.48

Valuation Analysis   Institutional Holding

Forecast EPS	$1.19	No of Institutions
	(04/06/2013)	N/A
Market Cap	$40.1 Billion	Shares
Book Value	$13.9 Billion	N/A
Price/Book	2.89	% Held
Price/Sales	4.02	N/A

Business Summary: Equipment & Services (MIC: 9.1.3 SIC: 4923 NAIC: 221210)

Kinder Morgan owns and manages energy transportation and storage assets. Co. operates or owns an interest in pipelines that transport natural gas, gasoline, crude oil, carbon dioxide and other products; and terminals that store petroleum products, chemicals and handle bulk materials like coal and petroleum coke. Co.'s operations are conducted in the following business segments: natural gas pipelines, products pipelines, carbon dioxide, terminals, Kinder Morgan Canada, and other; all through its limited partner interests of Kinder Morgan Energy Partners, L.P. At Dec 31 2012, Co. had total proved reserves of 82.0 million barrels of crude oil and 6.1 million barrels of natural gas liquids.

Recent Developments: For the year ended Dec 31 2012, income from continuing operations increased 168.2% to US$1.20 billion from US$449.0 million a year earlier. Net income decreased 35.3% to US$427.0 million from US$660.0 million in the prior year. Revenues were US$9.97 billion, up 25.6% from US$7.94 billion the year before. Operating income was US$2.59 billion versus US$1.42 billion in the prior year, an increase of 82.2%. Direct operating expenses declined 0.2% to US$4.76 billion from US$4.77 billion in the comparable period the year before. Indirect operating expenses increased 49.7% to US$2.62 billion from US$1.75 billion in the equivalent prior-year period.

Prospects: Our evaluation of Kinder Morgan, Inc. as of Apr. 7, 2013 is the result of our systematic analysis on three basic characteristics: earnings strength, relative valuation, and recent stock price movement. The company has enjoyed a very positive trend in earnings per share over the past 5 quarters. However, while recent estimates for the company have been mixed, KMI has posted results that fell short of analysts expectations. Based on operating earnings yield, the company is overvalued when compared to all of the companies in our coverage universe. Share price changes over the past year indicates that KMI will perform poorly over the near term.

Financial Data

(US$ in Thousands)	12/31/2012	12/31/2011	12/31/2010	12/31/2009	12/31/2008
Earnings Per Share	0.35	0.74	...	...	...
Cash Flow Per Share	3.07	3.35	...	...	...
Dividends Per Share	1.340	0.740	...	...	...
Dividend Payout %	382.86	100.00	...	...	...
Income Statement					
Total Revenue	9,973,000	8,264,900	8,190,600	7,185,200	12,094,800
EBITDA	3,913,000	2,571,600	2,324,500	2,498,400	(1,573,600)
Depn & Amortn	1,324,000	1,022,200	1,025,500	1,047,500	897,200
Income Before Taxes	1,190,000	869,100	654,100	877,500	(3,099,100)
Income Taxes	139,000	362,800	167,600	326,600	304,300
Net Income	315,000	594,400	(41,300)	495,000	(3,599,300)
Average Shares	908,000	707,600	...	...	...
Balance Sheet					
Current Assets	3,674,000	1,663,300	1,786,900	1,380,300	1,317,200
Total Assets	68,185,000	30,717,000	28,908,100	27,581,000	25,444,900
Current Liabilities	5,209,000	4,529,000	3,644,100	2,319,200	2,014,700
Long-Term Obligations	32,000,000	14,356,400	13,812,900	13,240,700	12,126,800
Total Liabilities	54,320,000	27,396,500	25,469,000	23,410,500	21,040,600
Stockholders' Equity	13,865,000	3,320,500	3,439,100	4,170,500	4,404,300
Shares Outstanding	1,035,668	803,344	...	...	...
Statistical Record					
Return on Assets %	0.64	1.99	N.M.	1.87	...
Return on Equity %	3.66	17.59	N.M.	11.55	...
EBITDA Margin %	39.24	31.11	28.38	34.77	N.M.
Net Margin %	3.16	7.19	N.M.	6.89	N.M.
Asset Turnover	0.20	0.28	0.29	0.27	...
Current Ratio	0.71	0.37	0.49	0.60	0.65
Debt to Equity	2.31	4.32	4.02	3.17	2.75
Price Range	39.85-30.76	32.17-23.66	...	...	...
P/E Ratio	113.86-87.89	43.47-31.97	...	...	...
Average Yield %	3.88	2.60	...	...	...

Address: 1001 Louisiana Street, Suite 1000, Houston, TX 77002 Telephone: 713-369-9000	Web Site: www.kindermorgan.com Officers: Richard D. Kinder - Chairman, Chief Executive Officer C. Park Shaper - President	Auditors: PricewaterhouseCoopers LLP Investor Contact: 713-369-9449 Transfer Agents: Computershare Investor Services, Jersey City, NJ

KIRBY CORP.

Exchange	Symbol	Price	52Wk Range	Yield	P/E
NYS	KEX	$76.80 (3/28/2013)	77.03-45.39	N/A	20.59

*7 Year Price Score 119.20 *NYSE Composite Index=100 *12 Month Price Score 114.37

Interim Earnings (Per Share)

Qtr.	Mar	Jun	Sep	Dec
2008	0.68	0.74	0.77	0.72
2009	0.52	0.63	0.65	0.55
2010	0.46	0.54	0.57	0.59
2011	0.60	0.77	0.94	1.00
2012	0.91	0.85	0.95	1.03

Interim Dividends (Per Share)
No Dividends Paid

Valuation Analysis / Institutional Holding

Valuation Analysis		Institutional Holding	
Forecast EPS	$4.17	No of Institutions	
	(04/05/2013)	304	
Market Cap	$4.3 Billion	Shares	
Book Value	$1.7 Billion	57,936,640	
Price/Book	2.56	% Held	
Price/Sales	2.06	92.72	

Business Summary: Shipping (MIC: 7.4.2 SIC: 4449 NAIC: 483211)

Kirby is a domestic tank barge operator, transporting bulk liquid products throughout the Mississippi River System, on the Gulf Intracoastal Waterway, along the U.S. coasts and in Alaska and Hawaii. Co. transports petrochemicals, black oil products, refined petroleum products and agricultural chemicals by tank barge. In addition, Co. provides after-market service for diesel engines and reduction gears used in marine and power generation applications. Co. also distributes and services diesel engines and transmissions, pumps and compression products, and manufactures oilfield service equipment such as hydraulic fracturing equipment for land-based pressure pumping and oilfield service markets.

Recent Developments: For the year ended Dec 31 2012, net income increased 14.6% to US$212.6 million from US$185.5 million in the prior year. Revenues were US$2.11 billion, up 14.2% from US$1.85 billion the year before. Operating income was US$364.8 million versus US$312.3 million in the prior year, an increase of 16.8%. Direct operating expenses rose 14.8% to US$1.41 billion from US$1.23 billion in the comparable period the year before. Indirect operating expenses increased 9.2% to US$338.2 million from US$309.6 million in the equivalent prior-year period.

Prospects: Our evaluation of Kirby Corp. as of Apr. 7, 2013 is the result of our systematic analysis on three basic characteristics: earnings strength, relative valuation, and recent stock price movement. The company has managed to produce a neutral trend in earnings per share over the past 5 quarters and while recent estimates for the company have been raised by analysts, KEX has posted better than expected results. Based on operating earnings yield, the company is about fairly valued when compared to all of the companies in our coverage universe. Share price changes over the past year indicates that KEX will perform in line with the market over the near term.

Financial Data
(US$ in Thousands)

	12/31/2012	12/31/2011	12/31/2010	12/31/2009	12/31/2008	12/31/2007	12/31/2006	12/31/2005
Earnings Per Share	3.73	3.33	2.15	2.34	2.91	2.29	1.79	1.34
Cash Flow Per Share	5.86	5.76	4.60	6.01	4.59	4.45	2.87	2.83
Tang Book Value Per Share	19.42	17.20	17.31	15.30	12.33	10.10	7.71	7.26
Income Statement								
Total Revenue	2,112,658	1,850,417	1,109,557	1,082,158	1,360,154	1,172,625	984,218	795,722
EBITDA	519,578	447,559	306,480	319,587	370,304	307,826	240,466	182,138
Depn & Amortn	154,943	135,257	106,163	103,823	100,457	87,259	71,212	59,097
Income Before Taxes	340,250	294,400	189,357	204,684	255,783	200,283	154,053	110,258
Income Taxes	127,907	109,255	72,258	78,020	97,444	76,491	58,751	42,341
Net Income	209,438	183,026	116,249	125,941	157,168	123,341	95,451	68,781
Average Shares	55,674	54,413	53,466	53,313	54,020	53,764	53,304	51,562
Balance Sheet								
Current Assets	596,256	529,329	425,915	300,097	279,511	267,343	249,592	186,276
Total Assets	3,653,128	2,960,411	1,794,937	1,635,963	1,526,098	1,430,475	1,271,119	1,025,548
Current Liabilities	355,020	358,800	160,259	137,104	173,066	191,420	166,867	139,821
Long-Term Obligations	1,070,110	763,000	200,006	200,204	246,064	296,015	309,518	200,032
Total Liabilities	1,958,160	1,517,886	638,838	583,500	636,045	660,645	639,124	488,006
Stockholders' Equity	1,694,968	1,442,525	1,156,099	1,052,463	890,053	769,830	631,995	537,542
Shares Outstanding	56,585	55,744	53,557	53,837	53,489	53,531	52,983	51,942
Statistical Record								
Return on Assets %	6.32	7.70	6.78	7.97	10.60	9.13	8.31	7.13
Return on Equity %	13.31	14.09	10.53	12.97	18.89	17.60	16.32	14.14
EBITDA Margin %	24.59	24.19	27.62	29.53	27.23	26.25	24.43	22.89
Net Margin %	9.91	9.89	10.48	11.64	11.56	10.52	9.70	8.64
Asset Turnover	0.64	0.78	0.65	0.68	0.92	0.87	0.86	0.82
Current Ratio	1.68	1.48	2.66	2.19	1.62	1.40	1.50	1.33
Debt to Equity	0.63	0.53	0.17	0.19	0.28	0.38	0.49	0.37
Price Range	70.00-45.39	65.99-43.75	45.46-31.35	38.81-19.94	60.00-20.98	49.93-33.65	40.56-25.73	27.61-19.00
P/E Ratio	18.77-12.17	19.82-13.14	21.14-14.58	16.59-8.52	20.62-7.21	21.80-14.69	22.66-14.37	20.60-14.18

Address: 55 Waugh Drive, Suite 1000, Houston, TX 77007 **Telephone:** 713-435-1000 **Fax:** 713-435-1010	**Web Site:** www.kirbycorp.com **Officers:** C. Berdon Lawrence - Chairman Joseph H. Pyne - Chairman, Chief Executive Officer	**Auditors:** KPMG LLP **Transfer Agents:** Computershare Trust Company, N.A., Providence, RI

436

KOHL'S CORP.

Exchange	Symbol	Price	52Wk Range	Yield	P/E
NYS	KSS	$46.13 (3/28/2013)	55.11-41.81	3.03	11.06

*7 Year Price Score 81.81 *NYSE Composite Index=100 *12 Month Price Score 89.85

TRADING VOLUME (thousand shares)

Interim Earnings (Per Share)

Qtr.	Apr	Jul	Oct	Jan
2008-09	0.49	0.77	0.52	1.10
2009-10	0.45	0.75	0.63	1.40
2010-11	0.64	0.84	0.53	1.63
2011-12	0.73	1.08	0.80	1.74
2012-13	0.63	1.00	0.91	1.63

Interim Dividends (Per Share)

Amt	Decl	Ex	Rec	Pay
0.32Q	05/09/2012	06/04/2012	06/06/2012	06/27/2012
0.32Q	08/07/2012	08/31/2012	09/05/2012	09/26/2012
0.32Q	11/07/2012	12/03/2012	12/05/2012	12/26/2012
0.35Q	02/27/2013	03/11/2013	03/13/2013	03/27/2013

Indicated Div: $1.40

Valuation Analysis

Valuation Analysis		Institutional Holding	
Forecast EPS	$4.33 (04/06/2013)	No of Institutions	779
Market Cap	$10.2 Billion	Shares	226,603,216
Book Value	$6.0 Billion	% Held	82.55
Price/Book	1.69		
Price/Sales	0.53		

Business Summary: Retail - General Merchandise/Department Stores (MIC: 2.1.1 SIC: 5311 NAIC: 452111)

Kohl's is engaged in the operation of family-oriented department stores that sell apparel, footwear and accessories for women, men and children; soft home products such as sheets and pillows; and housewares. In addition, Co. provides on-line shopping on its website at www.Kohls.com. Co.'s stores feature private brands which are found Only at Kohl's as well as national brands. Co.'s new brands include Jennifer Lopez and Marc Anthony, Rock & Republic, Van Heusen, ELLE and Simply Vera Vera Wang, and Princess Vera Wang. As of Jan. 28, 2012, Co. operated 1,127 stores in 49 states.

Recent Developments: For the year ended Feb 2 2013, net income decreased 15.5% to US$986.0 million from US$1.17 billion in the prior year. Revenues were US$19.28 billion, up 2.5% from US$18.80 billion the year before. Operating income was US$1.89 billion versus US$2.16 billion in the prior year, a decrease of 12.4%. Direct operating expenses rose 5.7% to US$12.29 billion from US$11.63 billion in the comparable period the year before. Indirect operating expenses increased 1.6% to US$5.10 billion from US$5.02 billion in the equivalent prior-year period.

Prospects: Our evaluation of Kohl's Corp. as of Apr. 7, 2013 is the result of our systematic analysis on three basic characteristics: earnings strength, relative valuation, and recent stock price movement. The company has managed to produce a neutral trend in earnings per share over the past 5 quarters. However, while recent estimates for the company have been lowered by analysts, KSS has posted better than expected results. Based on operating earnings yield, the company is undervalued when compared to all of the companies in our coverage universe. Share price changes over the past year indicates that KSS will perform very poorly over the near term.

Financial Data

(US$ in Thousands)	02/02/2013	01/28/2012	01/29/2011	01/30/2010	01/31/2009	02/02/2008	02/03/2007	01/28/2006
Earnings Per Share	4.17	4.30	3.65	3.23	2.89	3.39	3.31	2.43
Cash Flow Per Share	5.30	7.96	5.53	7.34	5.57	3.89	9.18	2.57
Tang Book Value Per Share	27.24	26.35	27.18	24.92	21.41	18.95	16.74	16.62
Dividends Per Share	1.280	1.000	...	...	...	...	...	...
Dividend Payout %	30.70	23.26	...	...	...	...	...	...
Income Statement								
Total Revenue	19,279,000	18,804,000	18,391,000	17,178,000	16,389,000	16,473,734	15,544,184	13,402,217
EBITDA	2,723,000	2,936,000	2,570,000	2,303,000	2,079,000	2,245,077	2,189,868	1,711,368
Depn & Amortn	833,000	778,000	656,000	591,000	543,000	440,600	375,067	295,187
Income Before Taxes	1,561,000	1,859,000	1,782,000	1,588,000	1,425,000	1,742,061	1,774,445	1,345,790
Income Taxes	575,000	692,000	668,000	597,000	540,000	658,210	665,764	503,830
Net Income	986,000	1,167,000	1,114,000	991,000	885,000	1,083,851	1,108,681	841,960
Average Shares	237,000	271,000	306,000	306,000	307,000	320,087	334,771	346,772
Balance Sheet								
Current Assets	4,719,000	4,775,000	5,645,000	5,485,000	3,700,000	3,723,889	3,401,040	4,266,052
Total Assets	13,905,000	14,094,000	13,564,000	13,160,000	11,334,000	10,560,082	9,041,177	9,153,038
Current Liabilities	2,535,000	2,590,000	2,710,000	2,390,000	1,815,000	1,771,448	1,918,658	1,746,455
Long-Term Obligations	4,448,000	4,150,000	1,678,000	2,052,000	2,053,000	2,051,875	1,040,057	1,046,104
Total Liabilities	7,857,000	7,586,000	5,462,000	5,307,000	4,595,000	4,458,479	3,437,782	3,195,700
Stockholders' Equity	6,048,000	6,508,000	8,102,000	7,853,000	6,739,000	6,101,603	5,603,395	5,957,338
Shares Outstanding	222,000	247,000	291,000	307,000	305,000	310,468	320,986	345,088
Statistical Record								
Return on Assets %	6.93	8.46	8.36	8.11	8.11	11.09	11.99	9.86
Return on Equity %	15.45	16.02	14.00	13.62	13.82	18.57	18.87	15.46
EBITDA Margin %	14.12	15.61	13.97	13.41	12.69	13.63	14.09	12.77
Net Margin %	5.11	6.21	6.06	5.77	5.40	6.58	7.13	6.28
Asset Turnover	1.35	1.36	1.38	1.41	1.50	1.69	1.68	1.57
Current Ratio	1.86	1.84	2.08	2.29	2.04	2.10	1.77	2.44
Debt to Equity	0.74	0.64	0.21	0.26	0.30	0.34	0.19	0.18
Price Range	55.11-41.81	57.00-42.60	58.57-44.27	60.73-33.58	53.86-24.98	78.89-38.33	73.97-44.13	58.64-43.03
P/E Ratio	13.22-10.03	13.26-9.91	16.05-12.13	18.80-10.40	18.64-8.64	23.27-11.31	22.35-13.33	24.13-17.71
Average Yield %	2.63	1.95	...	...	...	...	...	...

Address: N56 W17000 Ridgewood Drive, Menomonee Falls, WI 53051	Web Site: www.kohls.com	Auditors: Ernst & Young LLP
Telephone: 262-703-7000	Officers: Kevin Mansell - Chairman, President, Chief Executive Officer Peggy Eskenasi - Senior Executive Vice President	Transfer Agents: Wells Fargo Shareowner Services, St. Paul, M
Fax: 262-703-6373		

KORN/FERRY INTERNATIONAL (DE)

Exchange	Symbol	Price	52Wk Range	Yield	P/E
NYS	KFY	$17.86 (3/28/2013)	19.25-12.71	N/A	25.51

*7 Year Price Score 78.06   *NYSE Composite Index=100   *12 Month Price Score 108.64

TRADING VOLUME (thousand shares)

Interim Earnings (Per Share)

Qtr.	Jul	Oct	Jan	Apr
2009-10	(0.33)	0.06	0.17	0.20
2010-11	0.24	0.30	0.30	0.43
2011-12	0.33	0.32	0.25	0.25
2012-13	0.22	0.03	0.20	...

Interim Dividends (Per Share)

No Dividends Paid

Valuation Analysis   **Institutional Holding**

Forecast EPS	$1.08	No of Institutions
	(04/05/2013)	179
Market Cap	$868.5 Million	Shares
Book Value	$658.2 Million	47,672,644
Price/Book	1.32	% Held
Price/Sales	1.06	94.10

Business Summary: Business Services (MIC: 7.5.2 SIC: 7361 NAIC: 541612)

Korn/Ferry International and its subsidiaries are engaged in the business of providing executive recruitment on a retained basis, outsourced recruiting and leadership and talent consulting services. Co. operates in two business segments: Executive Recruitment, which focuses on recruiting board-level, chief executive and other senior executive positions for clients and provides other related talent management consulting services; and High Impact Recruitment Solutions-Futurestep, which creates recruitment applications to meet certain workforce needs of organizations. Their services include recruitment process outsourcing, talent acquisition and management consulting services.

Recent Developments: For the quarter ended Jan 31 2013, net income decreased 19.1% to US$9.5 million from US$11.7 million in the year-earlier quarter. Revenues were US$210.3 million, up 8.0% from US$194.6 million the year before. Operating income was US$8.7 million versus US$16.2 million in the prior-year quarter, a decrease of 46.1%. Indirect operating expenses increased 12.9% to US$201.6 million from US$178.5 million in the equivalent prior-year period.

Prospects: Our evaluation of Korn/Ferry International as of Apr. 7, 2013 is the result of our systematic analysis on three basic characteristics: earnings strength, relative valuation, and recent stock price movement. The company has enjoyed a very positive trend in earnings per share over the past 5 quarters and while recent estimates for the company have been raised by analysts, KFY has posted better than expected results. Based on operating earnings yield, the company is undervalued when compared to all of the companies in our coverage universe. Share price changes over the past year indicates that KFY will perform well over the near term.

Financial Data
(US$ in Thousands)

	9 Mos	6 Mos	3 Mos	04/30/2012	04/30/2011	04/30/2010	04/30/2009	04/30/2008
Earnings Per Share	0.70	0.75	1.04	1.15	1.27	0.12	(0.23)	1.46
Cash Flow Per Share	1.37	1.33	1.70	1.53	2.12	(0.69)	0.07	2.48
Tang Book Value Per Share	6.94	8.57	9.08	9.03	7.92	6.39	6.90	7.58
Income Statement								
Total Revenue	611,094	400,822	196,023	826,759	776,251	599,649	676,128	835,642
EBITDA	45,419	28,329	19,734	96,612	104,910	18,837	15,311	102,294
Depn & Amortn	13,127	8,039	3,742	14,017	12,671	11,493	11,583	10,441
Income Before Taxes	30,571	18,929	15,393	80,804	89,704	4,722	(12,073)	98,990
Income Taxes	11,042	8,289	5,605	28,351	32,692	(485)	384	36,081
Net Income	21,096	11,614	10,418	54,303	58,874	5,298	(10,092)	66,211
Average Shares	48,015	47,834	47,655	47,261	46,280	45,457	43,522	45,528
Balance Sheet								
Current Assets	415,830	428,836	413,446	500,067	441,597	386,451	371,597	526,268
Total Assets	1,063,390	983,875	930,974	1,014,689	971,680	827,098	740,879	880,214
Current Liabilities	234,347	176,369	137,688	215,312	233,866	198,083	173,347	272,458
Total Liabilities	405,167	341,298	300,017	385,213	393,343	335,756	281,780	384,080
Stockholders' Equity	658,223	642,577	630,957	629,476	578,337	491,342	459,099	496,134
Shares Outstanding	48,630	48,590	48,430	47,913	47,003	45,979	44,729	44,593
Statistical Record								
Return on Assets %	3.29	3.68	5.35	5.45	6.55	0.68	N.M.	8.04
Return on Equity %	5.20	5.65	8.03	8.97	11.01	1.11	N.M.	14.21
EBITDA Margin %	7.43	7.07	10.07	11.69	13.51	3.14	2.26	12.24
Net Margin %	3.45	2.90	5.31	6.57	7.58	0.88	N.M.	7.92
Asset Turnover	0.81	0.84	0.88	0.83	0.86	0.76	0.83	1.02
Current Ratio	1.77	2.43	3.00	2.32	1.89	1.95	2.14	1.93
Price Range	17.18-12.71	18.60-12.71	21.27-11.52	23.90-11.52	24.75-12.95	18.61-9.75	19.44-7.61	26.89-14.00
P/E Ratio	24.54-18.16	24.80-16.95	20.45-11.08	20.78-10.02	19.49-10.20	155.08-81.25	...	18.42-9.59

Address: 1900 Avenue of the Stars, Suite 2600, Los Angeles, CA 90067 **Telephone:** 310-552-1834 **Fax:** 310-553-8640	**Web Site:** www.kornferry.com **Officers:** Gary D. Burnison - Chief Executive Officer, President Ana Dutra - Executive Vice President, Division Officer	**Auditors:** Ernst & Young LLP **Investor Contact:** 310-556-8550 **Transfer Agents:** Mellon Investor Services, South Hackensack, NJ

KROGER CO.

Exchange	Symbol	Price	52Wk Range	Yield	P/E
NYS	KR	$33.14 (3/28/2013)	33.14-21.11	1.81	11.96

*7 Year Price Score 91.38 *NYSE Composite Index=100 *12 Month Price Score 110.64

TRADING VOLUME (thousand shares)

Interim Earnings (Per Share)

Qtr.	May	Aug	Oct	Jan
2008-09	0.58	0.42	0.36	0.54
2009-10	0.66	0.39	(1.35)	0.40
2010-11	0.58	0.41	0.32	0.44
2011-12	0.70	0.46	0.33	(0.49)
2012-13	0.78	0.51	0.60	0.88

Interim Dividends (Per Share)

Amt	Decl	Ex	Rec	Pay
0.115Q	06/21/2012	08/13/2012	08/15/2012	09/01/2012
0.15Q	09/13/2012	11/13/2012	11/15/2012	12/01/2012
0.15Q	01/18/2013	02/13/2013	02/15/2013	03/01/2013
0.15Q	03/14/2013	05/13/2013	05/15/2013	06/01/2013

Indicated Div: $0.60

Valuation Analysis

		Institutional Holding	
Forecast EPS	$2.75	No of Institutions	
	(04/06/2013)	696	
Market Cap	$17.0 Billion	Shares	
Book Value	$4.2 Billion	504,413,024	
Price/Book	4.05	% Held	
Price/Sales	0.18	75.81	

Business Summary: Retail - Food & Beverage, Drug & Tobacco (MIC: 2.1.2 SIC: 5411 NAIC: 445110)

Kroger operates retail food and drug stores, multi-department stores, jewelry stores, and convenience stores. As of Jan 28 2012, Co. operated, either directly or through its subsidiaries, 2,435 supermarkets and multi-department stores, 1,090 of which had fuel centers. In addition to the supermarkets, as of Jan 28 2012, Co. operated through subsidiaries, 791 convenience stores and 348 fine jewelry stores. In addition, 83 convenience stores were operated through franchise agreements. The convenience stores provide a range of staple food items and general merchandise and, in most cases, sell gasoline. Co. also manufactures and processes some of the food for sale in its supermarkets.

Recent Developments: For the year ended Feb 2 2013, net income increased 153.0% to US$1.51 billion from US$596.0 million in the prior year. Revenues were US$96.75 billion, up 7.1% from US$90.37 billion the year before. Operating income was US$2.76 billion versus US$1.28 billion in the prior year, an increase of 116.3%. Direct operating expenses rose 7.5% to US$76.86 billion from US$71.49 billion in the comparable period the year before. Indirect operating expenses decreased 2.7% to US$17.13 billion from US$17.60 billion in the equivalent prior-year period.

Prospects: Our evaluation of Kroger Co. as of Apr. 7, 2013 is the result of our systematic analysis on three basic characteristics: earnings strength, relative valuation, and recent stock price movement. The company has produced a positive trend in earnings per share over the past 5 quarters and while recent estimates for the company have been raised by analysts, KR has posted better than expected results. Based on operating earnings yield, the company is undervalued when compared to all of the companies in our coverage universe. Share price changes over the past year indicates that KR will perform poorly over the near term.

Financial Data

(US$ in Thousands)	02/02/2013	01/28/2012	01/29/2011	01/30/2010	01/31/2009	02/02/2008	02/03/2007	01/28/2006
Earnings Per Share	2.77	1.01	1.74	0.11	1.90	1.69	1.54	1.31
Cash Flow Per Share	5.23	4.52	5.32	4.53	4.45	3.75	3.23	3.04
Tang Book Value Per Share	5.78	5.07	6.70	5.72	4.48	4.18	3.87	3.04
Dividends Per Share	0.495	0.430	0.390	0.365	0.345	0.290	0.195	...
Dividend Payout %	17.87	42.57	22.41	331.82	18.16	17.16	12.66	...
Income Statement								
Total Revenue	96,751,000	90,374,000	82,189,000	76,733,000	76,000,000	70,235,000	66,111,000	60,553,000
EBITDA	4,416,000	2,916,000	3,782,000	2,616,000	3,893,000	3,657,000	3,508,000	3,300,000
Depn & Amortn	1,652,000	1,638,000	1,600,000	1,525,000	1,447,000	1,356,000	1,272,000	1,265,000
Income Before Taxes	2,302,000	843,000	1,734,000	589,000	1,966,000	1,827,000	1,748,000	1,525,000
Income Taxes	794,000	247,000	601,000	532,000	717,000	646,000	633,000	567,000
Net Income	1,497,000	602,000	1,116,000	70,000	1,249,000	1,181,000	1,115,000	958,000
Average Shares	537,000	593,000	638,000	650,000	659,000	698,000	723,000	731,000
Balance Sheet								
Current Assets	7,959,000	7,325,000	7,621,000	7,450,000	7,206,000	7,114,000	6,755,000	6,466,000
Total Assets	24,652,000	23,476,000	23,505,000	23,093,000	23,211,000	22,299,000	21,215,000	20,482,000
Current Liabilities	11,057,000	9,105,000	8,070,000	7,714,000	7,629,000	8,689,000	7,581,000	6,715,000
Long-Term Obligations	6,145,000	6,850,000	7,304,000	7,477,000	7,505,000	6,529,000	6,154,000	6,678,000
Total Liabilities	20,445,000	19,495,000	18,209,000	18,261,000	18,035,000	17,385,000	16,292,000	16,092,000
Stockholders' Equity	4,207,000	3,981,000	5,296,000	4,832,000	5,176,000	4,914,000	4,923,000	4,390,000
Shares Outstanding	514,000	561,000	620,000	642,000	649,000	663,000	705,000	723,000
Statistical Record								
Return on Assets %	6.12	2.57	4.80	0.30	5.50	5.44	5.26	4.69
Return on Equity %	35.97	13.01	22.10	1.40	24.83	24.08	23.56	24.23
EBITDA Margin %	4.56	3.23	4.60	3.41	5.12	5.21	5.31	5.45
Net Margin %	1.55	0.67	1.36	0.09	1.64	1.68	1.69	1.58
Asset Turnover	3.96	3.86	3.54	3.32	3.35	3.24	3.12	2.96
Current Ratio	0.72	0.80	0.94	0.97	0.94	0.82	0.89	0.96
Debt to Equity	1.46	1.72	1.38	1.55	1.45	1.33	1.25	1.52
Price Range	27.89-21.11	25.83-21.40	23.86-19.16	24.67-19.46	30.35-22.50	31.41-24.80	25.85-18.27	20.62-15.27
P/E Ratio	10.07-7.62	25.57-21.19	13.71-11.01	224.27-176.91	15.97-11.84	18.59-14.67	16.79-11.86	15.74-11.66
Average Yield %	2.07	1.82	1.81	1.69	1.29	1.05	0.90	...

Address: 1014 Vine Street, Cincinnati, OH 45202	Web Site: www.kroger.com	Auditors: PricewaterhouseCoopers LLP
Telephone: 513-762-4000	Officers: David B. Dillon - Chairman, President, Chief Executive Officer, Executive Vice President, Chief Operating Officer W. Rodney McMullen - Vice-Chairman, President, Chief Operating Officer	Investor Contact: 513-762-4808
Fax: 513-762-1400		Transfer Agents: Wells Fargo Shareowner Services, St. Paul, MN

L-3 COMMUNICATIONS HOLDINGS, INC.

Exchange	Symbol	Price	52Wk Range	Yield	P/E
NYS	LLL	$80.92 (3/28/2013)	81.21-64.36	2.72	9.75

*7 Year Price Score 81.77 *NYSE Composite Index=100 *12 Month Price Score 98.43

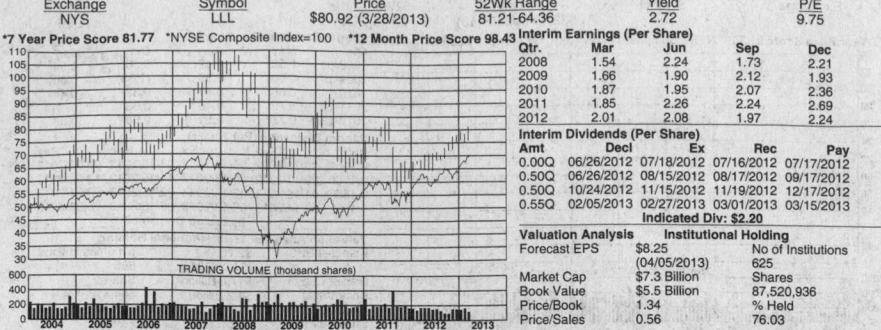

Interim Earnings (Per Share)

Qtr.	Mar	Jun	Sep	Dec
2008	1.54	2.24	1.73	2.21
2009	1.66	1.90	2.12	1.93
2010	1.87	1.95	2.07	2.36
2011	1.85	2.26	2.24	2.69
2012	2.01	2.08	1.97	2.24

Interim Dividends (Per Share)

Amt	Decl	Ex	Rec	Pay
0.00Q	06/26/2012	07/18/2012	07/16/2012	07/17/2012
0.50Q	06/26/2012	08/15/2012	08/17/2012	09/17/2012
0.50Q	10/24/2012	11/15/2012	11/19/2012	12/17/2012
0.55Q	02/05/2013	02/27/2013	03/01/2013	03/15/2013

Indicated Div: $2.20

Valuation Analysis

Institutional Holding	
Forecast EPS	$8.25
	(04/05/2013)
Market Cap	$7.3 Billion
Book Value	$5.5 Billion
Price/Book	1.34
Price/Sales	0.56

No of Institutions 625
Shares 87,520,936
% Held 76.03

TRADING VOLUME (thousand shares)

Business Summary: Aerospace (MIC: 7.1.1 SIC: 3812 NAIC: 334511)

L-3 Communications Holdings, through its wholly-owned subsidiary, L-3 Communications Corporation, is a contractor in Intelligence, Surveillance and Reconnaissance (ISR) systems, Command, Control, Communications (C3) systems, aircraft modernization and sustainment of aircraft, maritime vessels and ground vehicles, and national security systems. Co. also provides electronic systems used on military and commercial platforms. Co. has four reportable segments: Electronic Systems, C3ISR, Aircraft Modernization and Maintenance, and National Security Solutions. Co.'s customers include the U.S. Department of Defense and its contractors, and U.S. Government intelligence agencies, among others.

Recent Developments: For the year ended Dec 31 2012, income from continuing operations decreased 8.8% to US$788.0 million from US$864.0 million a year earlier. Net income decreased 15.3% to US$820.0 million from US$968.0 million in the prior year. Revenues were US$13.15 billion, down 0.1% from US$13.16 billion the year before. Operating income was US$1.35 billion versus US$1.40 billion in the prior year, a decrease of 3.4%. Direct operating expenses rose 0.7% to US$11.80 billion from US$11.72 billion in the comparable period the year before. Indirect operating expenses decreased 100.0% to nil from US$43.0 million in the equivalent prior-year period.

Prospects: Our evaluation of L-3 Communications Holdings Inc. as of Apr. 7, 2013 is the result of our systematic analysis on three basic characteristics: earnings strength, relative valuation, and recent stock price movement. The company has managed to produce a neutral trend in earnings per share over the past 5 quarters. However, while recent estimates for the company have been mixed, LLL has posted better than expected results. Based on operating earnings yield, the company is undervalued when compared to all of the companies in our coverage universe. Share price changes over the past year indicates that LLL will perform poorly over the near term.

Financial Data

(US$ in Thousands)	12/31/2012	12/31/2011	12/31/2010	12/31/2009	12/31/2008	12/31/2007	12/31/2006	12/31/2005
Earnings Per Share	8.30	9.03	8.25	7.61	7.72	5.98	4.22	4.20
Cash Flow Per Share	12.75	14.21	12.78	12.05	11.41	10.17	8.73	7.13
Dividends Per Share	2.000	1.800	1.600	1.400	1.200	1.000	0.750	0.500
Dividend Payout %	24.10	19.93	19.39	18.40	15.54	16.72	17.77	11.90
Income Statement								
Total Revenue	13,146,000	15,169,000	15,680,000	15,615,000	14,901,000	13,960,500	12,476,900	9,444,700
EBITDA	1,508,000	1,736,000	1,896,000	1,804,000	1,837,000	1,597,700	1,246,600	1,115,500
Depn & Amortn	170,000	173,000	164,000	158,000	152,000	149,600	135,700	113,300
Income Before Taxes	1,162,000	1,328,000	1,484,000	1,386,000	1,442,000	1,183,100	835,000	798,000
Income Taxes	374,000	360,000	518,000	475,000	502,000	418,000	298,500	279,800
Net Income	810,000	956,000	955,000	901,000	949,000	756,100	526,100	508,500
Average Shares	97,600	105,600	115,100	117,400	122,900	126,500	124,800	121,200
Balance Sheet								
Current Assets	4,571,000	5,244,000	5,078,000	5,151,000	4,961,000	4,763,100	3,929,800	3,643,500
Total Assets	13,826,000	15,497,000	15,451,000	14,813,000	14,485,000	14,390,700	13,286,700	11,909,100
Current Liabilities	2,597,000	2,690,000	2,733,000	2,482,000	2,707,000	2,581,700	2,376,400	1,854,300
Long-Term Obligations	3,653,000	4,135,000	4,136,000	4,128,000	4,556,000	4,559,100	4,566,300	4,644,000
Total Liabilities	8,363,000	8,862,000	8,687,000	8,246,000	8,654,000	8,401,800	7,980,800	7,418,400
Stockholders' Equity	5,463,000	6,635,000	6,764,000	6,567,000	5,831,000	5,988,900	5,305,900	4,490,700
Shares Outstanding	90,433	98,979	108,623	115,353	118,633	124,174	125,237	120,372
Statistical Record								
Return on Assets %	5.51	6.18	6.31	6.15	6.56	5.46	4.18	5.17
Return on Equity %	13.35	14.27	14.33	14.53	16.01	13.39	10.74	12.27
EBITDA Margin %	11.47	11.44	12.09	11.55	12.33	11.44	9.99	11.81
Net Margin %	6.16	6.30	6.09	5.77	6.37	5.42	4.22	5.38
Asset Turnover	0.89	0.98	1.04	1.07	1.03	1.01	0.99	0.96
Current Ratio	1.76	1.95	1.86	2.08	1.83	1.84	1.65	1.96
Debt to Equity	0.67	0.62	0.61	0.63	0.78	0.76	0.86	1.03
Price Range	77.91-64.17	84.70-56.53	93.55-63.88	84.88-55.27	109.78-56.89	110.00-76.75	83.39-63.86	81.06-62.56
P/E Ratio	9.39-7.73	9.38-6.26	11.34-7.74	11.15-7.26	14.22-7.37	18.39-12.83	19.76-15.13	19.30-14.90
Average Yield %	2.86	2.52	2.09	1.95	1.30	1.08	0.99	0.70

Address: 600 Third Avenue, New York, NY 10016 Telephone: 212-697-1111 Fax: 212-867-5249	Web Site: www.L-3Com.com Officers: Michael T. Strianese - Chairman, President, Chief Executive Officer Curtis Brunson - Executive Vice President	Auditors: PricewaterhouseCoopers LLP Investor Contact: 212-697-1111 Transfer Agents: Computershare Trust Company, Canton, MA

LABORATORY CORP. OF AMERICA HOLDINGS

Exchange	Symbol	Price	52Wk Range	Yield	P/E
NYS	LH	$90.20 (3/28/2013)	95.25-82.37	N/A	15.06

*7 Year Price Score 101.91 *NYSE Composite Index=100   *12 Month Price Score 93.42

TRADING VOLUME (thousand shares)

Interim Earnings (Per Share)

Qtr.	Mar	Jun	Sep	Dec
2008	1.14	0.92	1.02	1.10
2009	1.22	1.24	1.21	1.31
2010	1.25	1.46	1.34	1.24
2011	1.23	1.20	1.31	1.35
2012	1.63	1.56	1.53	1.27

Interim Dividends (Per Share)

No Dividends Paid

Valuation Analysis

		Institutional Holding	
Forecast EPS	$7.12	No of Institutions	
	(04/05/2013)	677	
Market Cap	$8.4 Billion	Shares	
Book Value	$2.7 Billion	105,068,712	
Price/Book	3.10	% Held	
Price/Sales	1.49	94.73	

Business Summary: Diagnostic & Health Related Services (MIC: 4.2.2 SIC: 8071 NAIC: 621511)

Laboratory Corporation of America Holdings is an independent clinical laboratory company. As of Dec 31 2012, Co. had a national network of 50 primary laboratories and about 1,800 patient service centers, along with a network of branches and STAT laboratories (laboratories that perform certain routine tests quickly). Through its network of laboratories, Co. provides a range of clinical laboratory tests that are used by the medical profession in routine testing, patient diagnosis, and in the monitoring and treatment of disease. Co. has also developed testing operations, such as oncology testing, human immunodeficiency virus genotyping and phenotyping, diagnostic genetics, and clinical trials.

Recent Developments: For the year ended Dec 31 2012, net income increased 9.7% to US$584.8 million from US$533.1 million in the prior year. Revenues were US$5.67 billion, up 2.3% from US$5.54 billion the year before. Operating income was US$1.02 billion versus US$948.4 million in the prior year, an increase of 7.9%. Direct operating expenses rose 4.7% to US$3.42 billion from US$3.27 billion in the comparable period the year before. Indirect operating expenses decreased 7.5% to US$1.23 billion from US$1.33 billion in the equivalent prior-year period.

Prospects: Our evaluation of Laboratory Corp. of America Holdings as of Apr. 7, 2013 is the result of our systematic analysis on three basic characteristics: earnings strength, relative valuation, and recent stock price movement. The company has produced a positive trend in earnings per share over the past 5 quarters and while recent estimates for the company have been raised by analysts, LH has posted better than expected results. Based on operating earnings yield, the company is undervalued when compared to all of the companies in our coverage universe. Share price changes over the past year indicates that LH will perform poorly over the near term.

Financial Data
(US$ in Thousands)

	12/31/2012	12/31/2011	12/31/2010	12/31/2009	12/31/2008	12/31/2007	12/31/2006	12/31/2005
Earnings Per Share	5.99	5.11	5.29	4.98	4.16	3.93	3.24	2.71
Cash Flow Per Share	8.77	8.56	8.58	8.03	7.10	6.08	5.10	4.30
Income Statement								
Total Revenue	5,671,400	5,542,300	5,003,900	4,694,700	4,505,200	4,068,200	3,590,800	3,327,600
EBITDA	2,102,600	1,951,700	2,019,700	1,064,400	997,100	922,300	838,000	714,000
Depn & Amortn	141,100	141,500	129,100	130,700	153,800	141,300	136,000	97,200
Income Before Taxes	1,867,000	1,722,700	1,820,600	870,800	771,300	724,400	654,200	582,400
Income Taxes	359,400	333,000	344,000	329,000	307,900	325,500	289,300	254,500
Net Income	583,100	519,700	558,700	543,300	464,500	476,800	431,600	386,200
Average Shares	97,400	101,800	105,400	109,100	111,800	121,300	134,700	144,900
Balance Sheet								
Current Assets	1,391,800	1,084,800	1,143,800	935,600	1,032,800	937,500	887,000	702,300
Total Assets	6,795,000	6,136,600	6,187,800	4,837,800	4,669,500	4,368,200	4,000,800	3,875,800
Current Liabilities	1,028,500	797,400	1,120,500	1,018,400	546,900	967,900	930,900	888,100
Long-Term Obligations	2,175,000	2,085,500	1,826,700	977,200	1,600,500	1,077,500	603,000	604,500
Total Liabilities	4,077,600	3,633,100	3,721,500	2,731,700	2,981,200	2,642,900	2,023,700	1,990,100
Stockholders' Equity	2,717,400	2,503,500	2,466,300	2,106,100	1,688,300	1,725,300	1,977,100	1,885,700
Shares Outstanding	93,500	97,800	102,400	105,300	108,200	111,000	122,200	126,500
Statistical Record								
Return on Assets %	8.99	8.43	10.13	11.43	10.25	11.39	10.96	10.33
Return on Equity %	22.28	20.91	24.42	28.64	27.14	25.76	22.35	19.88
EBITDA Margin %	37.07	35.21	40.36	22.67	22.13	22.67	23.34	21.46
Net Margin %	10.28	9.38	11.16	11.57	10.31	11.72	12.02	11.61
Asset Turnover	0.87	0.90	0.91	0.99	0.99	0.97	0.91	0.89
Current Ratio	1.35	1.36	1.02	0.92	1.89	0.97	0.95	0.79
Debt to Equity	0.80	0.83	0.74	0.46	0.95	0.62	0.30	0.32
Price Range	95.25-82.37	100.83-75.99	88.92-70.14	76.45-53.51	80.50-54.34	81.40-66.95	73.94-53.68	54.58-44.93
P/E Ratio	15.90-13.75	19.73-14.87	16.81-13.26	15.35-10.74	19.35-13.06	20.71-17.04	22.82-16.57	20.14-16.58

Address: 358 South Main Street, Burlington, NC 27215 Telephone: 336-229-1127	Web Site: www.labcorp.com Officers: Thomas P. Mac Mahon - Chairman David P. King - President, Chief Executive Officer	Auditors: PricewaterhouseCoopers LLP Investor Contact: 336-436-5076 Transfer Agents: American Stock Transfer & Trust Company, Brooklyn, NY

L BRANDS, INC

Exchange	Symbol	Price	52Wk Range	Yield	P/E
NYS	LTD	$44.66 (3/28/2013)	52.15-40.83	2.69	17.58

*7 Year Price Score 149.77 *NYSE Composite Index=100 *12 Month Price Score 87.48

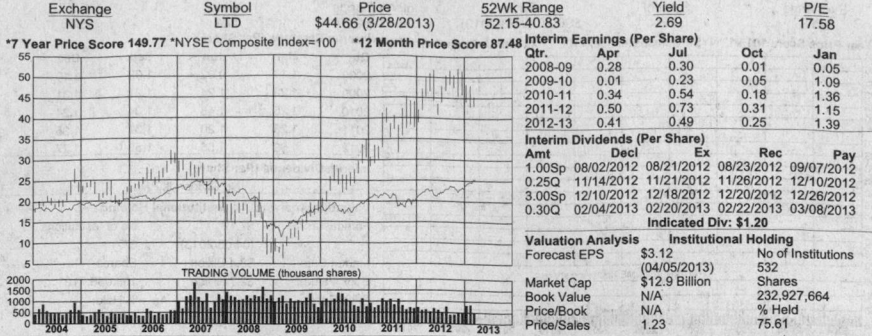

Interim Earnings (Per Share)

Qtr.	Apr	Jul	Oct	Jan
2008-09	0.28	0.30	0.01	0.05
2009-10	0.01	0.23	0.05	1.09
2010-11	0.34	0.54	0.18	1.36
2011-12	0.50	0.73	0.31	1.15
2012-13	0.41	0.49	0.25	1.39

Interim Dividends (Per Share)

Amt	Decl	Ex	Rec	Pay
1.00Sp	08/02/2012	08/21/2012	08/23/2012	09/07/2012
0.25Q	11/14/2012	11/21/2012	11/26/2012	12/10/2012
3.00Sp	12/10/2012	12/18/2012	12/20/2012	12/26/2012
0.30Q	02/04/2013	02/20/2013	02/22/2013	03/08/2013

Indicated Div: $1.20

Valuation Analysis

Valuation Analysis		Institutional Holding	
Forecast EPS	$3.12	No of Institutions	
	(04/05/2013)	532	
Market Cap	$12.9 Billion	Shares	
Book Value	N/A	232,927,664	
Price/Book	N/A	% Held	
Price/Sales	1.23	75.61	

Business Summary: Retail - Apparel and Accessories (MIC: 2.1.5 SIC: 5621 NAIC: 448120)

L Brands is a retailer of women's intimate and other apparel, beauty and personal care products and accessories. Co. sells its merchandise through specialty retail stores in the U.S. and Canada, which are primarily mall-based, and through websites, catalogue and international franchise, license and wholesale partners. Co. operates the following retail brands: Victoria's Secret, Victoria's Secret Pink, Bath & Body Works, La Senza and Henri Bendel. Co. has two reportable segments: Victoria's Secret, a retailer of women's intimate and other apparel; and Bath & Body Works, a retailer of home fragrance and personal care products. At Jan 28 2012, Co. operated a total of 2,941 stores.

Recent Developments: For the year ended Feb 2 2013, net income decreased 11.4% to US$753.0 million from US$850.0 million in the prior year. Revenues were US$10.46 billion, up 0.9% from US$10.36 billion the year before. Operating income was US$1.57 billion versus US$1.24 billion in the prior year, an increase of 27.1%. Direct operating expenses declined 3.7% to US$6.07 billion from US$6.31 billion in the comparable period the year before. Indirect operating expenses decreased 0.2% to US$2.81 billion from US$2.82 billion in the equivalent prior-year period.

Prospects: Our evaluation of L Brands, Inc. as of Apr. 7, 2013 is the result of our systematic analysis on three basic characteristics: earnings strength, relative valuation, and recent stock price movement. The company has produced a positive trend in earnings per share over the past 5 quarters. However, while recent estimates for the company have been lowered by analysts, LTD has posted better than expected results. Based on operating earnings yield, the company is undervalued when compared to all of the companies in our coverage universe. Share price changes over the past year indicates that LTD will perform poorly over the near term.

Financial Data
(US$ in Thousands)

	02/02/2013	01/28/2012	01/29/2011	01/30/2010	01/31/2009	02/02/2008	02/03/2007	01/28/2006
Earnings Per Share	2.54	2.70	2.42	1.37	0.65	1.89	1.68	1.66
Cash Flow Per Share	4.58	4.18	3.99	3.66	2.86	2.05	1.49	2.69
Tang Book Value Per Share	...	N.M.	N.M.	0.46	N.M.	N.M.	1.60	1.69
Dividends Per Share	5.000	3.800	4.600	0.600	0.600	0.600	0.600	0.600
Dividend Payout %	196.85	140.74	190.08	43.80	92.31	31.75	35.71	36.14
Income Statement								
Total Revenue	10,459,000	10,364,000	9,613,000	8,632,000	9,043,000	10,134,000	10,671,000	9,699,000
EBITDA	1,983,000	1,860,000	1,846,000	1,263,000	874,000	1,590,000	1,490,000	1,288,000
Depn & Amortn	386,000	387,000	387,000	387,000	371,000	352,000	316,000	299,000
Income Before Taxes	1,281,000	1,227,000	1,251,000	641,000	340,000	1,107,000	1,097,000	957,000
Income Taxes	528,000	377,000	446,000	202,000	233,000	411,000	422,000	291,000
Net Income	753,000	850,000	805,000	448,000	220,000	718,000	676,000	683,000
Average Shares	297,000	314,000	333,000	327,000	337,000	380,000	403,000	411,000
Balance Sheet								
Current Assets	2,205,000	2,368,000	2,592,000	3,250,000	2,867,000	2,919,000	2,771,000	2,784,000
Total Assets	6,019,000	6,108,000	6,451,000	7,173,000	6,972,000	7,437,000	7,093,000	6,346,000
Current Liabilities	1,538,000	1,526,000	1,504,000	1,322,000	1,255,000	1,374,000	1,709,000	1,575,000
Long-Term Obligations	4,477,000	3,481,000	2,507,000	2,723,000	2,897,000	2,905,000	1,665,000	1,669,000
Total Liabilities	7,034,000	5,971,000	4,975,000	4,990,000	5,098,000	5,218,000	4,138,000	3,875,000
Stockholders' Equity	(1,015,000)	137,000	1,476,000	2,183,000	1,874,000	2,219,000	2,955,000	2,471,000
Shares Outstanding	289,000	295,000	321,000	323,000	321,000	346,000	398,000	395,000
Statistical Record								
Return on Assets %	12.22	13.57	11.85	6.35	3.06	9.91	9.90	11.02
Return on Equity %	...	105.68	44.12	22.15	10.78	27.83	24.51	28.50
EBITDA Margin %	18.96	17.95	19.20	14.63	9.66	15.69	13.96	13.28
Net Margin %	7.20	8.20	8.37	5.19	2.43	7.09	6.33	7.04
Asset Turnover	1.70	1.65	1.42	1.22	1.26	1.40	1.56	1.56
Current Ratio	1.43	1.55	1.72	2.46	2.28	2.12	1.62	1.77
Debt to Equity	...	25.41	1.70	1.25	1.55	1.31	0.56	0.68
Price Range	52.15-40.83	45.22-29.13	34.90-19.65	20.46-6.26	22.06-7.13	29.67-15.05	32.10-22.93	25.12-18.81
P/E Ratio	20.53-16.07	16.75-10.79	14.42-8.12	14.93-4.57	33.94-10.97	15.70-7.96	19.11-13.65	15.13-11.33
Average Yield %	10.58	9.99	17.28	4.30	3.90	2.53	2.25	2.70

Address: Three Limited Parkway, P.O. Box 16000, Columbus, OH 43216
Telephone: 614-415-7000
Fax: 614-479-7440

Web Site: www.LimitedBrands.com
Officers: Leslie H. Wexner - Chairman, Chief Executive Officer Martyn R. Redgrave - Executive Vice President, Chief Administrative Officer, Senior Advisor

Auditors: Ernst & Young LLP
Investor Contact: 614-415-6400
Transfer Agents: American Stock Transfer & Trust Company, LLC

LAS VEGAS SANDS CORP

Exchange	Symbol	Price	52Wk Range	Yield	P/E
NYS	LVS	$56.35 (3/28/2013)	61.05-36.41	2.48	30.46

*7 Year Price Score 84.59   ***NYSE Composite Index=100**   ***12 Month Price Score 102.89**

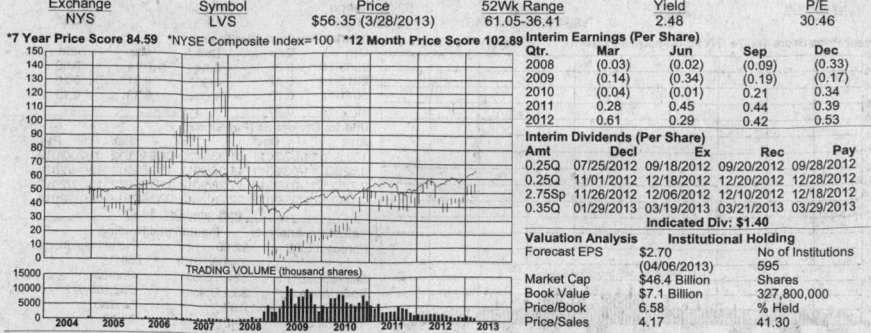

Interim Earnings (Per Share)

Qtr.	Mar	Jun	Sep	Dec
2008	(0.03)	(0.02)	(0.09)	(0.33)
2009	(0.14)	(0.34)	(0.19)	(0.17)
2010	(0.04)	(0.01)	0.21	0.34
2011	0.28	0.45	0.44	0.39
2012	0.61	0.29	0.42	0.53

Interim Dividends (Per Share)

Amt	Decl	Ex	Rec	Pay
0.25Q	07/25/2012	09/18/2012	09/20/2012	09/28/2012
0.25Q	11/01/2012	12/18/2012	12/20/2012	12/28/2012
2.75Sp	11/26/2012	12/06/2012	12/10/2012	12/18/2012
0.35Q	01/29/2013	03/19/2013	03/21/2013	03/29/2013

Indicated Div: $1.40

Valuation Analysis   Institutional Holding

Forecast EPS	$2.70	No of Institutions
	(04/06/2013)	595
Market Cap	$46.4 Billion	Shares
Book Value	$7.1 Billion	327,800,000
Price/Book	6.58	% Held
Price/Sales	4.17	41.30

Business Summary: Hotels, Restaurants & Travel (MIC: 2.2.1 SIC: 7011 NAIC: 721120)

Las Vegas Sands is a developer of properties that feature accommodations, gaming, entertainment and retail, convention and exhibition facilities, restaurants and other amenities. Through its 70.3% ownership of Sands China Ltd, Co. owns and operates resort properties in Macau, including The Venetian Macao Resort Hotel, the Four Seasons Hotel Macao, Cotai Strip, the Plaza Casino, and the Sands Macao. In Singapore, Co. owns and operates the Marina Bay Sands. In the U.S., Co.'s properties include The Venetian Resort Hotel Casino and The Palazzo Resort Hotel Casino, as well as the Sands Expo and Convention Center in Las Vegas, NV; and the Sands Casino Resort Bethlehem in Bethlehem, PA.

Recent Developments: For the year ended Dec 31 2012, net income was unchanged at US$1.88 billion versus US$1.88 billion the prior year. Revenues were US$11.13 billion, up 18.3% from US$9.41 billion the year before. Operating income was US$2.31 billion versus US$2.39 billion in the prior year, a decrease of 3.3%. Direct operating expenses rose 26.2% to US$6.21 billion from US$4.92 billion in the comparable period the year before. Indirect operating expenses increased 24.2% to US$2.61 billion from US$2.10 billion in the equivalent prior-year period.

Prospects: Our evaluation of Las Vegas Sands Corp. as of Apr. 7, 2013 is the result of our systematic analysis on three basic characteristics: earnings strength, relative valuation, and recent stock price movement. The company has produced a positive trend in earnings per share over the past 5 quarters. However, while recent estimates for the company have been mixed, LVS has posted results that fell short of analysts expectations. Based on operating earnings yield, the company is about fairly valued when compared to all of the companies in our coverage universe. Share price changes over the past year indicates that LVS will perform poorly over the near term.

Financial Data

(US$ in Thousands)	12/31/2012	12/31/2011	12/31/2010	12/31/2009	12/31/2008	12/31/2007	12/31/2006	12/31/2005
Earnings Per Share	1.85	1.56	0.51	(0.82)	(0.48)	0.33	1.24	0.80
Cash Flow Per Share	3.78	3.66	2.80	0.97	0.32	1.03	(0.56)	1.67
Tang Book Value Per Share	8.48	10.60	9.71	10.12	6.92	6.36	5.85	4.54
Dividends Per Share	3.750	...	...	...	...	...	...	...
Dividend Payout %	202.70	...	...	...	...	...	...	...
Income Statement								
Total Revenue	11,131,132	9,410,745	6,853,182	4,563,105	4,389,946	2,950,567	2,236,859	1,740,912
EBITDA	3,275,631	3,239,918	1,926,478	576,027	734,927	558,713	693,883	450,913
Depn & Amortn	977,743	876,540	772,707	637,906	560,913	248,090	119,975	99,796
Income Before Taxes	2,062,576	2,094,823	855,905	(372,627)	(228,025)	138,279	504,246	287,936
Income Taxes	180,763	211,704	74,302	(3,884)	(59,700)	21,591	62,243	4,250
Net Income	1,524,093	1,560,123	599,394	(354,479)	(163,558)	116,688	442,003	283,686
Average Shares	824,556	811,816	791,760	656,836	392,131	355,789	355,264	354,526
Balance Sheet								
Current Assets	4,477,514	5,397,152	4,058,907	5,623,674	3,741,276	1,379,086	1,093,557	644,706
Total Assets	22,163,652	22,244,123	21,044,308	20,572,106	17,144,113	11,466,517	7,126,458	3,879,739
Current Liabilities	2,622,823	2,498,706	2,600,413	1,839,305	1,530,416	1,493,273	734,648	460,368
Long-Term Obligations	10,132,265	9,577,131	9,373,755	10,852,147	10,356,115	7,517,997	4,136,152	1,625,901
Total Liabilities	15,101,810	14,393,434	13,877,938	13,654,838	12,403,716	9,206,243	5,051,304	2,270,201
Stockholders' Equity	7,061,842	7,850,689	7,166,370	6,917,268	4,740,397	2,260,274	2,075,154	1,609,538
Shares Outstanding	824,297	733,249	707,507	660,322	641,839	355,271	354,492	354,179
Statistical Record								
Return on Assets %	6.85	7.21	2.88	N.M.	N.M.	1.26	8.03	7.58
Return on Equity %	20.38	20.78	8.51	N.M.	N.M.	5.38	23.99	19.39
EBITDA Margin %	29.43	34.43	28.11	12.62	16.74	18.94	31.02	25.90
Net Margin %	13.69	16.58	8.75	N.M.	N.M.	3.95	19.76	16.30
Asset Turnover	0.50	0.43	0.33	0.24	0.31	0.32	0.41	0.47
Current Ratio	1.71	2.16	1.56	3.06	2.44	0.92	1.49	1.40
Debt to Equity	1.43	1.22	1.31	1.57	2.18	3.33	1.99	1.01
Price Range	61.05-36.41	50.60-36.34	52.80-14.94	19.56-1.42	103.05-3.23	144.56-72.83	97.00-38.68	50.79-29.69
P/E Ratio	33.00-19.68	32.44-23.29	103.53-29.29	...	...	438.06-220.70	78.23-31.19	63.49-37.11
Average Yield %	7.91	...	...	...	...	...	...	...

Address: 3355 Las Vegas Boulevard South, Las Vegas, NV 89109 **Telephone:** 702-414-1000	**Web Site:** www.lasvegassands.com **Officers:** Sheldon Gary Adelson - Chairman, Chief Executive Officer, Treasurer Michael Alan Leven - President, Chief Operating Officer	**Auditors:** PricewaterhouseCoopers LLP **Investor Contact:** 702-414-1221 **Transfer Agents:** American Stock Transfer & Trust Company, New York, NY

LAUDER (ESTEE) COS., INC. (THE)

Exchange	Symbol	Price	52Wk Range	Yield	P/E
NYS	EL	$64.03 (3/28/2013)	65.92-50.56	1.12	27.25

*7 Year Price Score 160.74 *NYSE Composite Index=100 *12 Month Price Score 97.80

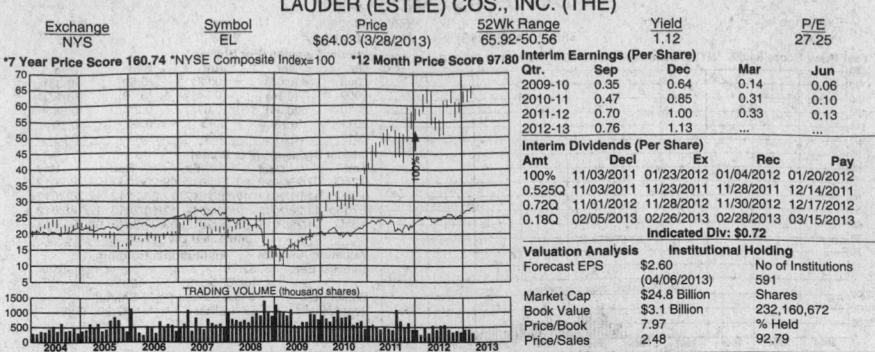

Interim Earnings (Per Share)

Qtr.	Sep	Dec	Mar	Jun
2009-10	0.35	0.64	0.14	0.06
2010-11	0.47	0.85	0.31	0.10
2011-12	0.70	1.00	0.33	0.13
2012-13	0.76	1.13	...	...

Interim Dividends (Per Share)

Amt	Decl	Ex	Rec	Pay
100%	11/03/2011	01/23/2012	01/04/2012	01/20/2012
0.525Q	11/03/2011	11/23/2011	11/28/2011	12/14/2011
0.72Q	11/01/2012	11/28/2012	11/30/2012	12/17/2012
0.18Q	02/05/2013	02/26/2013	02/28/2013	03/15/2013

Indicated Div: $0.72

Valuation Analysis

Forecast EPS	$2.60 (04/06/2013)
Market Cap	$24.8 Billion
Book Value	$3.1 Billion
Price/Book	7.97
Price/Sales	2.48

Institutional Holding

No of Institutions	591
Shares	232,160,672
% Held	92.79

TRADING VOLUME (thousand shares)

Business Summary: Household & Personal Products (MIC: 1.7.1 SIC: 2844 NAIC: 325620)

Estee Lauder Companies is a manufacturer and marketer of skin care, makeup, fragrance and hair care products. Co.'s products are sold under brand names including: Estee Lauder, Aramis, Clinique, Origins, MAC, Bobbi Brown, La Mer and Aveda. Co. is also the licensee for fragrances and/or cosmetics sold under brand names such as Tommy Hilfiger, Donna Karan, Michael Kors, Tom Ford and Coach. Co. sells its products via distribution channels such as department stores, specialty retailers, perfumeries, pharmacies, salons and spas. Co.'s products are also sold in Co.-operated stores, its own and authorized retailer websites, in-flight and duty-free shops, among others.

Recent Developments: For the quarter ended Dec 31 2012, net income increased 12.8% to US$449.4 million from US$398.4 million in the year-earlier quarter. Revenues were US$2.93 billion, up 7.1% from US$2.74 billion the year before. Operating income was US$653.1 million versus US$597.0 million in the prior-year quarter, an increase of 9.4%. Direct operating expenses rose 3.1% to US$568.0 million from US$551.0 million in the comparable period the year before. Indirect operating expenses increased 7.7% to US$1.71 billion from US$1.59 billion in the equivalent prior-year period.

Prospects: Our evaluation of Lauder (Estee) Cos. Inc. as of Apr. 7, 2013 is the result of our systematic analysis on three basic characteristics: earnings strength, relative valuation, and recent stock price movement. The company has generated a negative trend in earnings per share over the past 5 quarters and while recent estimates for the company have remained steady, EL has posted better than expected results. Based on operating earnings yield, the company is about fairly valued when compared to all of the companies in our coverage universe. Share price changes over the past year indicates that EL will perform in line with the market over the near term.

Financial Data

(US$ in Thousands)	6 Mos	3 Mos	06/30/2012	06/30/2011	06/30/2010	06/30/2009	06/30/2008	06/30/2007
Earnings Per Share	2.35	2.22	2.16	1.74	1.19	0.55	1.20	1.08
Cash Flow Per Share	3.02	2.68	2.89	2.61	2.42	1.77	1.77	1.62
Tang Book Value Per Share	5.26	5.04	4.27	3.86	2.75	1.86	1.93	1.12
Dividends Per Share	0.720	0.525	0.525	0.375	0.275	0.275	0.275	0.250
Dividend Payout %	30.64	23.65	24.31	21.55	23.11	50.00	22.92	23.15
Income Statement								
Total Revenue	5,482,500	2,549,500	9,713,600	8,810,000	7,795,800	7,323,800	7,910,800	7,037,500
EBITDA	1,311,400	559,100	1,609,100	1,372,900	1,041,700	658,600	1,044,600	948,000
Depn & Amortn	153,200	75,300	286,900	283,500	251,800	240,200	233,900	198,100
Income Before Taxes	1,109,900	448,900	1,261,100	1,025,500	688,300	342,700	743,900	711,000
Income Taxes	360,900	149,300	400,600	321,700	205,900	115,900	259,900	255,200
Net Income	747,000	299,500	856,900	700,800	478,300	218,400	473,800	449,200
Average Shares	394,700	395,500	397,000	402,400	401,400	395,400	394,200	415,600
Balance Sheet								
Current Assets	4,341,000	4,213,100	3,855,100	3,686,500	3,121,000	2,912,500	2,787,200	2,239,400
Total Assets	7,170,100	7,007,600	6,593,000	6,273,900	5,335,600	5,176,600	5,011,200	4,125,700
Current Liabilities	2,052,200	1,972,400	2,125,800	1,943,300	1,572,200	1,459,200	1,699,200	1,500,700
Long-Term Obligations	1,330,100	1,330,700	1,069,100	1,080,100	1,205,000	1,387,600	1,078,200	1,028,100
Total Liabilities	4,059,900	3,982,400	3,859,800	3,644,500	3,387,200	3,536,600	3,358,000	2,926,700
Stockholders' Equity	3,110,200	3,025,200	2,733,200	2,629,400	1,948,400	1,640,000	1,653,200	1,199,000
Shares Outstanding	386,915	387,209	388,897	394,562	395,447	393,388	389,814	388,656
Statistical Record								
Return on Assets %	13.74	13.36	13.28	12.07	9.10	4.29	10.34	11.36
Return on Equity %	32.38	31.92	31.87	30.62	26.66	13.26	33.13	31.84
EBITDA Margin %	23.92	21.93	16.57	15.58	13.36	8.99	13.20	13.47
Net Margin %	13.63	11.75	8.82	7.95	6.14	2.98	5.99	6.38
Asset Turnover	1.48	1.49	1.51	1.52	1.48	1.44	1.73	1.78
Current Ratio	2.12	2.14	1.81	1.90	1.99	2.00	1.64	1.49
Debt to Equity	0.43	0.44	0.39	0.41	0.62	0.85	0.65	0.86
Price Range	65.35-50.56	65.35-42.10	65.35-42.10	52.59-27.86	34.99-15.14	26.87-9.97	24.42-19.02	25.74-17.47
P/E Ratio	27.81-21.51	29.44-18.96	30.25-19.49	30.23-16.01	29.40-12.72	48.85-18.14	20.35-15.85	23.83-16.18
Average Yield %	1.23	0.93	0.96	0.94	1.11	1.59	1.25	1.17

Address: 767 Fifth Avenue, New York, NY 10153 Telephone: 212-572-4200	Web Site: www.elcompanies.com Officers: William P. Lauder - Executive Chairman Leonard A. Lauder - Chairman Emeritus	Auditors: KPMG LLP Investor Contact: 800-308-2334 Transfer Agents: Computershare Shareowner Services, Pittsburgh, PA

LAZARD LTD

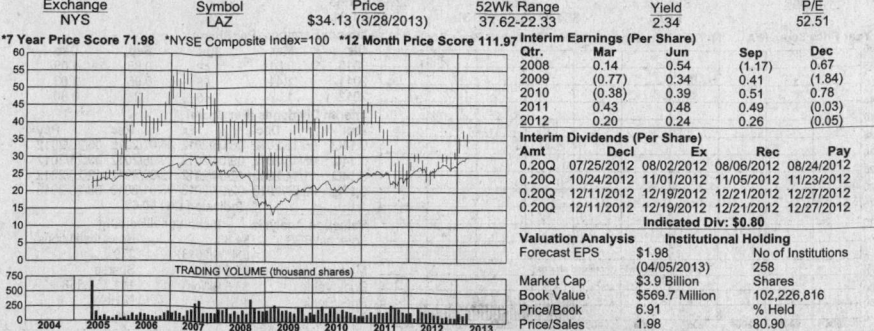

Exchange	Symbol	Price	52Wk Range	Yield	P/E
NYS	LAZ	$34.13 (3/28/2013)	37.62-22.33	2.34	52.51

*7 Year Price Score 71.98   *NYSE Composite Index=100   *12 Month Price Score 111.97

Interim Earnings (Per Share)

Qtr.	Mar	Jun	Sep	Dec
2008	0.14	0.54	(1.17)	0.67
2009	(0.77)	0.34	0.41	(1.84)
2010	(0.38)	0.39	0.51	0.78
2011	0.43	0.48	0.49	(0.03)
2012	0.20	0.24	0.26	(0.05)

Interim Dividends (Per Share)

Amt	Decl	Ex	Rec	Pay
0.20Q	07/25/2012	08/02/2012	08/06/2012	08/24/2012
0.20Q	10/24/2012	11/01/2012	11/05/2012	11/23/2012
0.20Q	12/11/2012	12/19/2012	12/21/2012	12/27/2012
0.20Q	12/11/2012	12/19/2012	12/21/2012	12/27/2012
		Indicated Div: $0.80		

Valuation Analysis

Forecast EPS	$1.98	Institutional Holding	
	(04/05/2013)	No of Institutions	258
Market Cap	$3.9 Billion	Shares	
Book Value	$569.7 Million		102,226,816
Price/Book	6.91	% Held	
Price/Sales	1.98		80.90

TRADING VOLUME (thousand shares)

Business Summary: Finance Intermediaries & Services (MIC: 5.5.1 SIC: 6282 NAIC: 523930)

Lazard is a holding company. Through its subsidiaries, Co. operates in two business segments: Co.'s Financial Advisory segment provides clients with a range of financial advisory services regarding mergers and acquisitions and other strategic matters, restructurings, capital structure, capital raising and various other financial matters, to corporations, governments, sovereigns, institutions and individual clients; and Co.'s Asset Management business provides investment management and advisory services, including equity, fixed income, cash management and alternative investment strategies, to its clients. As of Dec 31 2011, Co. had $141.04 billion in assets under management.

Recent Developments: For the year ended Dec 31 2012, net income decreased 51.3% to US$92.8 million from US$190.6 million in the prior year. Revenues were US$1.99 billion, up 3.9% from US$1.92 billion the year before. Operating income was US$123.9 million versus US$235.5 million in the prior year, a decrease of 47.4%. Direct operating expenses declined 9.5% to US$81.6 million from US$90.1 million in the comparable period the year before. Indirect operating expenses increased 12.2% to US$1.79 billion from US$1.59 billion in the equivalent prior-year period.

Prospects: Our evaluation of Lazard Ltd. as of Apr. 7, 2013 is the result of our systematic analysis on three basic characteristics: earnings strength, relative valuation, and recent stock price movement. The company has produced a positive trend in earnings per share over the past 5 quarters. However, while recent estimates for the company have been lowered by analysts, LAZ has posted better than expected results. Based on operating earnings yield, the company is about fairly valued when compared to all of the companies in our coverage universe. Share price changes over the past year indicates that LAZ will perform very well over the near term.

Financial Data
(US$ in Thousands)

	12/31/2012	12/31/2011	12/31/2010	12/31/2009	12/31/2008	12/31/2007	12/31/2006	12/31/2005
Earnings Per Share	0.65	1.36	1.36	(1.68)	0.06	2.79	2.31	1.45
Cash Flow Per Share	4.11	3.37	1.62	3.13	8.29	1.40	6.19	23.83
Tang Book Value Per Share	1.53	2.79	2.58	0.44	1.13	N.M.	...	...
Dividends Per Share	1.160	0.605	0.500	0.450	0.400	0.360	0.360	...
Dividend Payout %	178.46	44.49	36.76	...	666.67	12.90	15.58	...
Income Statement								
Total Revenue	1,994,013	1,919,638	2,003,077	1,638,408	1,697,106	2,054,799	1,597,809	1,379,807
EBITDA	163,099	271,994	274,229	(154,703)	29,736	439,818	367,809	359,646
Depn & Amortn	39,214	36,495	30,579	27,531	4,596	21,523	40,600	17,284
Income Before Taxes	123,885	235,499	243,650	(182,234)	25,140	418,295	327,209	342,362
Income Taxes	31,100	44,940	49,227	6,011	25,379	80,616	68,812	58,985
Net Income	84,309	174,917	174,979	(130,242)	3,138	155,042	92,985	143,486
Average Shares	129,325	137,629	138,469	78,311	60,874	62,212	44,166	37,561
Balance Sheet								
Current Assets	1,685,959	1,869,789	2,227,849	1,607,021	1,636,816	2,177,607	2,220,402	1,284,283
Total Assets	2,986,893	3,081,936	3,422,532	3,147,762	2,862,931	3,840,413	3,208,665	1,910,897
Current Liabilities	740,989	678,015	863,252	854,584	782,745	1,383,498	1,642,546	903,295
Long-Term Obligations	1,094,713	1,096,934	1,249,753	1,261,478	1,264,575	1,764,622	1,312,502	1,245,926
Total Liabilities	2,417,237	2,355,793	2,770,134	2,792,371	2,612,351	3,770,074	3,449,018	2,781,568
Stockholders' Equity	569,656	726,143	652,398	355,391	250,580	70,339	(240,353)	(870,671)
Shares Outstanding	115,413	119,517	112,850	86,315	66,918	50,032	51,439	37,500
Statistical Record								
Return on Assets %	2.77	5.38	5.33	N.M.	0.09	4.40	3.63	5.30
Return on Equity %	12.98	25.38	34.73	N.M.	1.95	...	...	...
EBITDA Margin %	8.18	14.17	13.69	N.M.	1.75	21.40	23.02	26.06
Net Margin %	4.23	9.11	8.74	N.M.	0.18	7.55	5.82	10.40
Asset Turnover	0.66	0.59	0.61	0.55	0.50	0.58	0.62	0.51
Current Ratio	2.28	2.76	2.58	1.88	2.09	1.57	1.35	1.42
Debt to Equity	1.92	1.51	1.92	3.55	5.05	25.09	...	...
Price Range	31.49-22.33	45.95-19.65	41.02-26.43	43.55-21.18	43.96-20.61	55.75-36.15	48.78-31.85	32.33-20.70
P/E Ratio	48.45-34.35	33.79-14.45	30.16-19.43	...	732.67-343.50	19.98-12.96	21.12-13.79	22.30-14.28
Average Yield %	4.18	1.78	1.42	1.33	1.13	0.77	0.91	...

Address: Clarendon House, 2 Church Street, Hamilton, HM 11 Telephone: 441-295-1422	Web Site: www.lazard.com Officers: Kenneth M. Jacobs - Chairman, Chief Executive Officer Steven J. Golub - Vice-Chairman, Division Officer	Auditors: Deloitte & Touche LLP Investor Contact: 877-266-8601 Transfer Agents: Computershare, Pittsburgh, PA

LEAR CORP.

Exchange	Symbol	Price	52Wk Range	Yield	P/E
NYS	LEA	$54.87 (3/28/2013)	56.46-34.81	1.24	4.27

*7 Year Price Score N/A   *NYSE Composite Index=100   *12 Month Price Score 113.88

Interim Earnings (Per Share)

Qtr.	Mar	Jun	Sep	Dec
2010	0.61	1.48	0.88	1.09
2011	1.44	1.65	0.95	1.03
2012	1.32	1.45	1.23	8.86

Interim Dividends (Per Share)

Amt	Decl	Ex	Rec	Pay
0.14Q	05/16/2012	06/05/2012	06/07/2012	06/26/2012
0.14Q	08/15/2012	09/04/2012	09/06/2012	09/25/2012
0.14Q	11/14/2012	12/04/2012	12/06/2012	12/26/2012
0.17Q	02/07/2013	02/27/2013	03/01/2013	03/20/2013

Indicated Div: $0.68

Valuation Analysis

		Institutional Holding	
Forecast EPS	$4.83 (04/06/2013)	No of Institutions	379
Market Cap	$5.3 Billion	Shares	
Book Value	$3.5 Billion		111,754,856
Price/Book	1.51	% Held	
Price/Sales	0.36	N/A	

Business Summary: Auto Parts (MIC: 1.8.2 SIC: 3714 NAIC: 336360)

Lear is engaged in supplying automotive manufacturers with automotive seat systems and related components, as well as electrical distribution systems and related components. Co. conducts its business in two operating segments: seating, which designs, manufactures, assemblies and supplies vehicle seating requirements and includes seat systems and related components, such as seat frames, recliner mechanisms, seat tracks, seat trim covers, headrests and seat foam; and electrical power management systems, which designs, manufactures, assemblies and supplies electrical distribution systems and components for powertrain vehicles, as well as for hybrid and electric vehicles.

Recent Developments: For the year ended Dec 31 2012, net income increased 130.9% to US$1.32 billion from US$570.4 million in the prior year. Revenues were US$14.57 billion, up 2.9% from US$14.16 billion the year before. Direct operating expenses rose 3.0% to US$13.35 billion from US$12.96 billion in the comparable period the year before. Indirect operating expenses decreased 0.3% to US$512.3 million from US$513.6 million in the equivalent prior-year period.

Prospects: Our evaluation of Lear Corp. as of Apr. 7, 2013 is the result of our systematic analysis on three basic characteristics: earnings strength, relative valuation, and recent stock price movement. The company has managed to produce a neutral trend in earnings per share over the past 5 quarters and while recent estimates for the company have been raised by analysts, LEA has posted better than expected results. Based on operating earnings yield, the company is undervalued when compared to all of the companies in our coverage universe. Share price changes over the past year indicates that LEA will perform in line with the market over the near term.

Financial Data
(US$ in Thousands)

	12/31/2012	12/31/2011	12/31/2010	12/31/2009	11/07/2009	12/31/2008	12/31/2007	12/31/2006
Earnings Per Share	12.85	5.08	4.05	(0.06)	5.28	(4.46)	1.54	(5.16)
Cash Flow Per Share	7.40	7.62	6.56	4.69	(3.78)	0.93	3.04	2.08
Tang Book Value Per Share	28.57	17.95	17.55	14.34	...	N.M.	N.M.	N.M.
Dividends Per Share	0.560	0.500	...	...	...	...	...	0.125
Dividend Payout %	4.36	9.84	...	...	...	...	...	...
Income Statement								
Total Revenue	14,567,000	14,156,500	11,954,600	1,580,900	8,158,700	13,570,500	15,995,000	17,838,900
EBITDA	938,400	901,700	740,100	17,000	1,303,000	(57,100)	814,000	(56,600)
Depn & Amortn	239,600	246,300	235,900	39,700	224,000	294,000	291,600	387,000
Income Before Taxes	648,900	615,700	448,800	(33,800)	927,600	(541,400)	323,200	(653,400)
Income Taxes	(638,000)	68,800	24,600	(24,200)	29,200	85,800	89,900	54,900
Net Income	1,282,800	540,700	438,300	(3,800)	818,200	(689,900)	241,500	(707,500)
Average Shares	99,825	106,344	108,122	69,050	155,119	154,484	156,428	137,214
Balance Sheet								
Current Assets	4,873,500	4,761,500	4,385,500	3,787,000	...	3,674,200	3,718,000	3,890,300
Total Assets	8,194,100	7,010,900	6,621,100	6,073,300	...	6,872,900	7,800,400	7,850,500
Current Liabilities	3,216,900	3,063,500	2,818,500	2,400,800	...	4,609,800	3,603,900	3,887,300
Long-Term Obligations	626,300	695,400	694,900	927,100	...	1,303,000	2,344,600	2,434,500
Total Liabilities	4,707,000	4,574,500	4,160,900	3,984,200	...	6,674,000	6,709,700	7,248,500
Stockholders' Equity	3,487,100	2,436,400	2,460,200	2,089,100	...	198,900	1,090,700	602,000
Shares Outstanding	95,942	100,686	105,176	73,909	154,807	154,807	154,379	152,503
Statistical Record								
Return on Assets %	16.83	7.93	6.91	N.M.	...	N.M.	3.09	N.M.
Return on Equity %	43.19	22.08	19.27	N.M.	...	N.M.	28.53	N.M.
EBITDA Margin %	6.44	6.37	6.19	1.08	15.97	N.M.	5.09	N.M.
Net Margin %	8.81	3.82	3.67	N.M.	10.03	N.M.	1.51	N.M.
Asset Turnover	1.91	2.08	1.88	0.24	...	1.84	2.04	2.21
Current Ratio	1.51	1.55	1.56	1.58	...	0.80	1.03	1.00
Debt to Equity	0.18	0.29	0.28	0.44	...	6.55	2.15	4.04
Price Range	47.01-34.81	55.96-36.03	49.88-31.81	34.29-28.13	...	...	...	...
P/E Ratio	3.66-2.71	11.02-7.09	12.31-7.85	...	...	...	...	...
Average Yield %	1.35	1.05	...	...	...	...	...	...

Address: 21557 Telegraph Road, Southfield, MI 48033 Telephone: 248-447-1500	Web Site: www.lear.com Officers: Robert E. Rossiter - Advisor, Chairman, President, Chief Executive Officer Matthew J. Simoncini - President, Chief Executive Officer, Senior Vice President, Chief Financial Officer, Chief Accounting Officer	Auditors: Ernst & Young LLP Investor Contact: 800-413-5327 Transfer Agents: BNY Mellon, New York, NY

LEGG MASON, INC.

Exchange	Symbol	Price	52Wk Range	Yield	P/E
NYS	LM	$32.15 (3/28/2013)	32.15-22.38	1.37	N/A

*7 Year Price Score 49.32   *NYSE Composite Index=100   *12 Month Price Score 101.70

Interim Earnings (Per Share)

Qtr.	Jun	Sep	Dec	Mar
2009-10	0.35	0.30	0.28	0.40
2010-11	0.30	0.50	0.41	0.43
2011-12	0.40	0.39	0.20	0.54
2012-13	(0.07)	0.60	(3.45)	...

Interim Dividends (Per Share)

Amt	Decl	Ex	Rec	Pay
0.11Q	05/01/2012	06/08/2012	06/12/2012	07/09/2012
0.11Q	07/27/2012	10/02/2012	10/04/2012	10/22/2012
0.11Q	10/26/2012	12/10/2012	12/12/2012	12/28/2012
0.11Q	02/01/2013	03/12/2013	03/14/2013	04/15/2013

Indicated Div: $0.44

Valuation Analysis

		Institutional Holding	
Forecast EPS	$-2.66	No of Institutions	
	(04/06/2013)	-450	
Market Cap	$4.1 Billion	Shares	
Book Value	$4.9 Billion	137,906,480	
Price/Book	0.84	% Held	
Price/Sales	1.60	' 77.46	

Business Summary: Wealth Management (MIC: 5.5.2 SIC: 6282 NAIC: 523920)

Legg Mason is an asset management holding company. Through its subsidiaries, Co. is engaged in providing investment management and related services. Co.'s investment advisory services include discretionary and non-discretionary management of separate investment accounts for institutional and individual investors. Co.'s investment products include proprietary mutual funds ranging from money market and other liquidity products to fixed income and equity funds, other domestic and offshore funds provided to both retail and institutional investors and funds-of-hedge funds. As of Mar 31 2012, Co. had total assets under management of US$643.32 billion.

Recent Developments: For the quarter ended Dec 31 2012, net loss amounted to US$458.6 million versus net income of US$35.1 million in the year-earlier quarter. Revenues were US$673.9 million, up 7.5% from US$627.0 million the year before. Operating loss was US$633.3 million versus an income of US$59.3 million in the prior-year quarter. Indirect operating expenses increased 130.3% to US$1.31 billion from US$567.7 million in the equivalent prior-year period.

Prospects: Our evaluation of Legg Mason Inc. as of Apr. 7, 2013 is the result of our systematic analysis on three basic characteristics: earnings strength, relative valuation, and recent stock price movement. The company has suffered a very negative trend in earnings per share over the past 5 quarters. Because the company lacks sufficient analyst estimate data, we place greater weight on the historical EPS trend as the measure of earnings strength. Based on operating earnings yield, the company is about fairly valued when compared to all of the companies in our coverage universe. Share price changes over the past year indicates that LM will perform poorly over the near term.

Financial Data

(US$ in Thousands)	9 Mos	6 Mos	3 Mos	03/31/2012	03/31/2011	03/31/2010	03/31/2009	03/31/2008
Earnings Per Share	(2.38)	1.27	1.06	1.54	1.63	1.32	(13.85)	1.86
Cash Flow Per Share	1.92	2.18	2.11	3.46	2.65	9.29	3.11	6.77
Tang Book Value Per Share	4.32	2.66	2.55	3.90	3.87	3.87	N.M.	N.M.
Dividends Per Share	0.410	0.350	0.350	0.320	0.200	0.120	0.960	0.960
Dividend Payout %	...	27.56	33.02	20.78	12.27	9.09	...	51.61
Income Statement								
Total Revenue	1,944,887	1,270,987	630,692	2,662,574	2,784,317	2,634,879	3,357,367	4,634,086
EBITDA	(475,820)	137,463	13,986	472,981	550,856	562,684	(2,923,219)	590,712
Depn & Amortn	41,824	28,261	14,676	93,795	102,748	114,078	138,445	141,083
Income Before Taxes	(559,253)	79,511	(17,981)	303,083	365,197	329,656	(3,153,857)	443,871
Income Taxes	(168,814)	11,400	(4,997)	72,052	119,434	118,676	(1,210,853)	175,995
Net Income	(382,531)	71,339	(9,458)	220,817	253,923	204,357	(1,947,928)	267,610
Average Shares	131,534	134,128	138,720	143,349	155,484	155,362	140,669	143,976
Balance Sheet								
Current Assets	1,829,585	1,831,260	1,679,006	2,457,794	2,446,556	2,559,146	2,859,387	4,685,752
Total Assets	7,115,060	7,874,899	7,799,007	8,555,747	8,707,756	8,613,711	9,321,354	11,830,352
Current Liabilities	518,297	599,314	507,214	975,782	968,972	1,045,355	1,281,193	2,739,447
Long-Term Obligations	1,344,435	1,371,776	1,375,295	1,407,321	1,479,396	1,165,180	2,965,204	1,825,654
Total Liabilities	2,196,751	2,418,399	2,342,617	2,878,456	2,937,372	2,771,987	4,866,877	5,209,849
Stockholders' Equity	4,918,309	5,456,500	5,456,390	5,677,291	5,770,384	5,841,724	4,454,477	6,620,503
Shares Outstanding	128,943	131,707	135,030	139,874	150,218	161,438	141,853	138,556
Statistical Record								
Return on Assets %	N.M.	2.18	1.85	2.55	2.93	2.28	N.M.	2.49
Return on Equity %	N.M.	3.19	2.70	3.85	4.37	3.97	N.M.	4.06
EBITDA Margin %	N.M.	10.82	2.22	17.76	19.78	21.36	N.M.	12.75
Net Margin %	N.M.	5.61	N.M.	8.29	9.12	7.76	N.M.	5.77
Asset Turnover	0.33	0.32	0.31	0.31	0.32	0.29	0.32	0.43
Current Ratio	3.53	3.06	3.31	2.52	2.52	2.45	2.23	1.71
Debt to Equity	0.27	0.25	0.25	0.25	0.26	0.20	0.67	0.28
Price Range	29.31-22.38	29.31-22.38	34.22-22.38	37.53-22.95	37.58-25.17	33.70-15.90	64.87-10.79	105.87-52.72
P/E Ratio	...	23.08-17.62	32.28-21.11	24.37-14.90	23.06-15.44	25.53-12.05	...	56.92-28.34
Average Yield %	1.59	1.36	1.32	1.11	0.62	0.45	2.90	1.15

Address: 100 International Drive, Baltimore, MD 21202 **Telephone:** 410-539-0000 **Fax:** 410-539-8010	**Web Site:** www.leggmason.com **Officers:** Joseph A. Sullivan - President, Acting Chief Executive Officer, Chief Diversity Officer, Senior Executive Vice President, Chief Administrative Officer Peter H. Nachtwey - Senior Executive Vice President, Chief Financial Officer	**Auditors:** PricewaterhouseCoopers LLP **Investor Contact:** 410-454-5246 **Transfer Agents:** American Stock Transfer & Trust Company, New York, NY

LEGGETT & PLATT, INC.

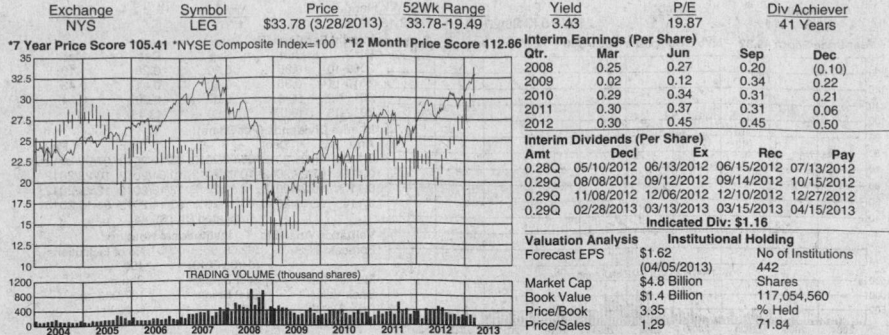

Exchange	Symbol	Price	52Wk Range	Yield	P/E	Div Achiever
NYS	LEG	$33.78 (3/28/2013)	33.78-19.49	3.43	19.87	41 Years

*7 Year Price Score 105.41 *NYSE Composite Index=100 *12 Month Price Score 112.86

Interim Earnings (Per Share)

Qtr.	Mar	Jun	Sep	Dec
2008	0.25	0.27	0.20	(0.10)
2009	0.02	0.12	0.34	0.22
2010	0.29	0.34	0.31	0.21
2011	0.30	0.37	0.31	0.06
2012	0.30	0.45	0.45	0.50

Interim Dividends (Per Share)

Amt	Decl	Ex	Rec	Pay
0.28Q	05/10/2012	06/13/2012	06/15/2012	07/13/2012
0.29Q	08/08/2012	09/12/2012	09/14/2012	10/15/2012
0.29Q	11/08/2012	12/06/2012	12/10/2012	12/27/2012
0.29Q	02/28/2013	03/13/2013	03/15/2013	04/15/2013

Indicated Div: $1.16

Valuation Analysis

		Institutional Holding	
Forecast EPS	$1.62 (04/05/2013)	No of Institutions	442
Market Cap	$4.8 Billion	Shares	
Book Value	$1.4 Billion		117,054,560
Price/Book	3.35	% Held	
Price/Sales	1.29		71.84

Business Summary: Furniture (MIC: 1.6.2 SIC: 2519 NAIC: 337121)

Leggett & Platt designs and produces a range of components and products. Co.'s operations are organized into four segments: Residential Furnishings, which supplies a variety of components used by bedding and upholstered furniture manufacturers in the assembly of their finished products; Commercial Fixturing and Components, which provides store fixtures and office furniture components; Industrial Materials, which supplies drawn steel wire and produces welded steel tubing; and Specialized Products, which designs, produces and sells components for automotive seating, specialized machinery and equipment, and service van interiors.

Recent Developments: For the year ended Dec 31 2012, income from continuing operations increased 58.6% to US$248.1 million from US$156.4 million a year earlier. Net income increased 60.2% to US$250.5 million from US$156.4 million in the prior year. Revenues were US$3.72 billion, up 2.3% from US$3.64 billion the year before. Operating income was US$341.3 million versus US$237.8 million in the prior year, an increase of 43.5%. Direct operating expenses was unchanged at US$2.97 billion versus the comparable period the year before. Indirect operating expenses decreased 4.9% to US$406.7 million from US$427.5 million in the equivalent prior-year period.

Prospects: Our evaluation of Leggett & Platt Inc. as of Apr. 7, 2013 is the result of our systematic analysis on three basic characteristics: earnings strength, relative valuation, and recent stock price movement. The company has produced a positive trend in earnings per share over the past 5 quarters. However, while recent estimates for the company have been mixed, LEG has posted better than expected results. Based on operating earnings yield, the company is about fairly valued when compared to all of the companies in our coverage universe. Share price changes over the past year indicates that LEG will perform in line with the market over the near term.

Financial Data

(US$ in Thousands)	12/31/2012	12/31/2011	12/31/2010	12/31/2009	12/31/2008	12/31/2007	12/31/2006	12/31/2005
Earnings Per Share	1.70	1.04	1.15	0.70	0.62	(0.06)	1.61	1.30
Cash Flow Per Share	3.11	2.26	2.40	3.55	2.59	3.42	2.57	2.33
Tang Book Value Per Share	1.67	1.82	2.90	3.06	3.72	5.74	5.72	5.55
Dividends Per Share	1.140	1.100	1.060	1.020	1.000	0.780	0.670	0.630
Dividend Payout %	67.06	105.77	92.17	145.71	161.29	...	41.61	48.46
Income Statement								
Total Revenue	3,720,800	3,636,000	3,359,100	3,055,100	4,076,100	4,306,400	5,505,400	5,299,300
EBITDA	457,400	354,700	410,800	360,600	368,100	357,700	657,400	567,300
Depn & Amortn	116,100	116,900	122,800	130,300	140,400	180,200	175,400	171,100
Income Before Taxes	304,400	206,200	255,500	198,400	188,000	128,400	434,800	356,200
Income Taxes	56,300	49,800	71,900	77,300	65,100	77,400	134,500	104,900
Net Income	248,200	153,300	176,600	111,800	104,400	(11,200)	300,300	251,300
Average Shares	145,963	146,999	153,268	159,964	168,186	179,827	186,832	193,574
Balance Sheet								
Current Assets	1,339,100	1,224,000	1,219,100	1,213,600	1,306,800	1,834,400	1,894,100	1,763,300
Total Assets	3,254,900	2,915,100	3,001,000	3,061,200	3,161,900	4,072,500	4,265,300	4,052,600
Current Liabilities	731,000	586,000	523,000	535,100	524,200	799,600	691,200	738,000
Long-Term Obligations	853,900	833,300	762,200	789,300	851,200	1,000,600	1,060,000	921,600
Total Liabilities	1,820,400	1,617,900	1,493,700	1,507,200	1,508,900	1,939,800	1,914,200	1,803,600
Stockholders' Equity	1,434,500	1,297,200	1,507,300	1,554,000	1,653,000	2,132,700	2,351,100	2,249,000
Shares Outstanding	142,100	139,400	146,200	148,793	155,813	168,725	178,000	182,576
Statistical Record								
Return on Assets %	8.02	5.18	5.83	3.59	2.88	N.M.	7.22	6.09
Return on Equity %	18.12	10.93	11.54	6.97	5.50	N.M.	13.06	11.02
EBITDA Margin %	12.29	9.76	12.23	11.80	9.03	8.31	11.94	10.71
Net Margin %	6.67	4.22	5.26	3.66	2.56	N.M.	5.45	4.74
Asset Turnover	1.20	1.23	1.11	0.98	1.12	1.03	1.32	1.28
Current Ratio	1.83	2.09	2.33	2.27	2.49	2.29	2.74	2.39
Debt to Equity	0.60	0.64	0.51	0.51	0.51	0.47	0.45	0.41
Price Range	27.85-19.49	26.37-17.87	25.02-18.26	20.82-10.21	23.98-12.24	24.62-17.27	26.96-22.39	29.44-18.55
P/E Ratio	16.38-11.46	25.36-17.18	21.76-15.88	29.74-14.59	38.68-19.74	...	16.75-13.91	22.65-14.27
Average Yield %	4.87	4.83	4.95	6.28	5.71	3.59	2.76	2.47

Address: No. 1 Leggett Road, Carthage, MO 64836	**Web Site:** www.leggett.com	**Auditors:** PricewaterhouseCoopers LLP
Telephone: 417-358-8131	**Officers:** David S. Haffner - Chairman, President, Chief Executive Officer, Executive Vice President, Chief Operating Officer Karl G. Glassman - President, Executive Vice President, Chief Operating Officer	**Investor Contact:** 417-358-8131
		Transfer Agents: Wells Fargo Shareowner Services, St. Paul, MN

LENDER PROCESSING SERVICES INC

Exchange	Symbol	Price	52Wk Range	Yield	P/E
NYS	LPS	$25.46 (3/28/2013)	30.63-21.44	1.57	30.67

*7 Year Price Score N/A *NYSE Composite Index=100 *12 Month Price Score 90.47

TRADING VOLUME (thousand shares)

Interim Earnings (Per Share)

Qtr.	Mar	Jun	Sep	Dec
2008	0.63	0.67	0.54	0.00
2009	0.53	0.78	0.78	0.78
2010	0.75	0.85	0.85	0.78
2011	0.63	0.25	0.48	(0.24)
2012	0.56	(0.45)	0.69	0.03

Interim Dividends (Per Share)

Amt	Decl	Ex	Rec	Pay
0.10Q	04/26/2012	06/05/2012	06/07/2012	06/21/2012
0.10Q	07/24/2012	09/04/2012	09/06/2012	09/20/2012
0.10Q	10/25/2012	12/04/2012	12/06/2012	12/20/2012
0.10Q	02/07/2013	03/05/2013	03/07/2013	03/21/2013

Indicated Div: $0.40

Valuation Analysis

		Institutional Holding	
Forecast EPS	$2.60 (04/05/2013)	No of Institutions	320
Market Cap	$2.2 Billion	Shares	78,732,032
Book Value	$542.9 Million	% Held	N/A
Price/Book	3.98		
Price/Sales	1.08		

Business Summary: Business Services (MIC: 7.5.2 SIC: 7389 NAIC: 523999)

Lender Processing Services is a provider of technology, data and services to the mortgage lending industry. Co. operates through two segments: Technology, Data and Analytics segment, which includes its mortgage servicing platform, a web-based workflow information system called Desktop, its other software and related service offerings, and its data and analytics businesses; and Transaction Services segment, which includes its origination services such as settlement and title agency services, appraisal services and other origination services, and includes its default services such as foreclosure administrative services, property inspection and preservation services as well as other services.

Recent Developments: For the year ended Dec 31 2012, income from continuing operations decreased 41.3% to US$79.4 million from US$135.2 million a year earlier. Net income decreased 27.1% to US$70.4 million from US$96.5 million in the prior year. Revenues were US$2.00 billion, up 0.7% from US$1.98 billion the year before. Operating income was US$232.9 million versus US$278.7 million in the prior year, a decrease of 16.4%. Direct operating expenses declined 1.0% to US$1.47 billion from US$1.48 billion in the comparable period the year before. Indirect operating expenses increased 33.6% to US$299.6 million from US$224.3 million in the equivalent prior-year period.

Prospects: Our evaluation of Lender Processing Services Inc. as of Apr. 7, 2013 is the result of our systematic analysis on three basic characteristics: earnings strength, relative valuation, and recent stock price movement. The company has generated a negative trend in earnings per share over the past 5 quarters and while recent estimates for the company have been mixed, LPS has posted better than expected results. Based on operating earnings yield, the company is undervalued when compared to all of the companies in our coverage universe. Share price changes over the past year indicates that LPS will perform poorly over the near term.

Financial Data
(US$ in Thousands)

	12/31/2012	12/31/2011	12/31/2010	12/31/2009	12/31/2008	12/31/2007	12/31/2006	12/31/2005
Earnings Per Share	0.83	1.13	3.23	2.87	...	...	...	...
Cash Flow Per Share	5.12	5.59	4.82	4.64	3.81	2.91	...	...
Dividends Per Share	0.400	0.400	0.400	0.400	0.200	...	...	...
Dividend Payout %	48.19	35.40	12.38	13.94	...	...	...	...
Income Statement								
Total Revenue	1,997,651	2,090,112	2,456,335	2,370,548	1,861,909	1,690,568	1,484,977	1,382,479
EBITDA	265,129	321,500	587,483	558,058	452,267	451,262	356,614	343,487
Depn & Amortn	32,000	31,500	30,300	26,100	20,500	27,200	29,200	26,800
Income Before Taxes	146,983	223,868	487,649	448,982	383,443	425,606	329,722	320,541
Income Taxes	67,546	81,062	185,305	171,735	146,667	164,734	127,984	124,160
Net Income	70,359	96,543	302,344	275,729	230,888	256,805	201,055	195,705
Average Shares	84,857	85,685	93,559	96,152	95,754	97,697	...	...
Balance Sheet								
Current Assets	684,107	530,836	559,274	550,144	553,707	407,536	355,105	...
Total Assets	2,445,834	2,245,415	2,251,843	2,197,304	2,103,633	1,962,043	1,879,800	...
Current Liabilities	598,360	457,986	465,727	369,374	382,765	168,193	199,141	...
Long-Term Obligations	1,068,125	1,109,850	1,104,247	1,249,250	1,402,350	...	...	...
Total Liabilities	1,902,938	1,757,427	1,725,629	1,741,446	1,912,484	291,004	302,269	...
Stockholders' Equity	542,896	487,988	526,214	455,858	191,149	1,671,039	1,577,531	...
Shares Outstanding	84,913	84,406	88,846	95,839	95,264	...	...	...
Statistical Record								
Return on Assets %	2.99	4.29	13.59	12.82	11.33	13.37	...	...
Return on Equity %	13.61	19.04	61.57	85.23	24.73	15.81	...	...
EBITDA Margin %	13.27	15.38	23.92	23.54	24.29	26.69	24.01	24.85
Net Margin %	3.52	4.62	12.31	11.63	12.40	15.19	13.54	14.16
Asset Turnover	0.85	0.93	1.10	1.10	0.91	0.88	...	...
Current Ratio	1.14	1.16	1.20	1.49	1.45	2.42	1.78	...
Debt to Equity	1.97	2.27	2.10	2.74	7.34	...	...	...
Price Range	30.63-14.40	34.16-13.11	42.44-26.39	43.99-24.90	35.93-18.11	...	...	...
P/E Ratio	36.90-17.35	30.23-11.60	13.14-8.17	15.33-8.68	...	...	...	...
Average Yield %	1.64	1.72	1.17	1.22	0.70	...	...	...

Address: 601 Riverside Avenue, Jacksonville, FL 32204 Telephone: 904-854-5100	Web Site: www.lpsvcs.com Officers: Lee A. Kennedy - Executive Chairman, President, Chief Executive Officer Hugh R. Harris - President, Chief Executive Officer	Auditors: KPMG LLP Investor Contact: 904-854-8640 Transfer Agents: Computershare Investor Services, Canton, MA

LENNAR CORP.

Exchange	Symbol	Price	52Wk Range	Yield	P/E
NYS	LEN	$41.48 (3/28/2013)	43.40-23.68	0.39	13.34

*7 Year Price Score 124.24 *NYSE Composite Index=100 ***12 Month Price Score 107.55**

TRADING VOLUME (thousand shares)

Interim Earnings (Per Share)

Qtr.	Feb	May	Aug	Nov
2007-08	(0.56)	(0.76)	(0.56)	(5.12)
2008-09	(0.98)	(0.76)	(0.97)	0.27
2009-10	(0.04)	0.21	0.16	0.17
2010-11	0.14	0.07	0.11	0.15
2011-12	0.08	2.06	0.40	0.55

Interim Dividends (Per Share)

Amt	Decl	Ex	Rec	Pay
0.04Q	04/11/2012	04/23/2012	04/25/2012	05/09/2012
0.04Q	06/26/2012	07/09/2012	07/11/2012	07/25/2012
0.04Q	10/01/2012	10/11/2012	10/15/2012	10/29/2012
0.04Q	01/17/2013	01/30/2013	02/01/2013	02/15/2013

Indicated Div: $0.16

Valuation Analysis / **Institutional Holding**

Forecast EPS	$1.65 (04/05/2013)	No of Institutions 538
Market Cap	$7.9 Billion	Shares
Book Value	$3.4 Billion	194,061,936
Price/Book	2.33	% Held
Price/Sales	1.94	94.42

Business Summary: Builders (MIC: 2.2.5 SIC: 1521 NAIC: 236115)

Lennar is a homebuilder, a provider of financial services and through its Rialto Investments (Rialto) segment, an investor, and manager of funds that invest in real estate assets. Co.'s homebuilding operations include the construction and sale of single-family attached and detached homes, as well as the purchase, development and sale of residential land directly and through unconsolidated entities in which it has investments. Co.'s Financial Services reportable segment provides mortgage financing, title insurance and closing services for both buyers of its homes and others. Co.'s Rialto reportable segment focuses on real estate investments and asset management.

Recent Developments: For the year ended Nov 30 2012, net income increased 484.1% to US$657.3 million from US$112.5 million in the prior year. Revenues were US$4.10 billion, up 32.6% from US$3.10 billion the year before. Direct operating expenses rose 26.2% to US$3.66 billion from US$2.90 billion in the comparable period the year before. Indirect operating expenses increased 33.7% to US$127.3 million from US$95.3 million in the equivalent prior-year period.

Prospects: Our evaluation of Lennar Corp. as of Apr. 7, 2013 is the result of our systematic analysis on three basic characteristics: earnings strength, relative valuation, and recent stock price movement. The company has suffered a very negative trend in earnings per share over the past 5 quarters and while recent estimates for the company have been raised by analysts, LEN has posted better than expected results. Based on operating earnings yield, the company is about fairly valued when compared to all of the companies in our coverage universe. Share price changes over the past year indicates that LEN will perform very well over the near term.

Financial Data
(US$ in Thousands)

	11/30/2012	11/30/2011	11/30/2010	11/30/2009	11/30/2008	11/30/2007	11/30/2006	11/30/2005
Earnings Per Share	3.11	0.48	0.51	(2.45)	(7.00)	(12.31)	3.69	8.23
Cash Flow Per Share	(2.27)	(1.40)	1.50	2.47	6.93	2.82	3.51	2.08
Tang Book Value Per Share	17.83	14.31	13.98	13.03	16.12	23.52	34.81	32.09
Dividends Per Share	0.160	0.160	0.160	0.160	0.520	0.640	0.640	0.573
Dividend Payout %	5.14	33.33	31.37	...	...	...	17.34	6.96
Income Statement								
Total Revenue	4,104,706	3,095,385	3,074,022	3,119,387	4,575,417	10,186,781	16,266,662	13,866,971
EBITDA	351,191	301,395	180,833	(536,996)	(471,408)	(2,659,491)	1,018,611	2,150,468
Depn & Amortn	49,531	42,141	20,080	21,641	35,061	56,764	50,011	79,558
Income Before Taxes	207,307	168,604	90,328	(629,487)	(506,469)	(2,716,255)	968,600	2,070,910
Income Taxes	(435,218)	(14,570)	(25,734)	(314,345)	547,557	(1,140,000)	348,780	815,284
Net Income	679,124	92,199	95,261	(417,141)	(1,109,085)	(1,941,081)	593,869	1,355,155
Average Shares	218,695	195,185	188,857	170,537	158,395	157,718	161,371	165,522
Balance Sheet								
Current Assets	6,609,544	5,750,638	5,644,973	6,036,779	6,084,297	5,538,717	8,676,984	9,095,001
Total Assets	10,362,206	9,154,671	8,787,851	7,314,791	7,424,898	9,102,747	12,408,266	12,541,225
Current Liabilities	220,690	201,101	168,006	169,596	246,727	668,909	1,093,793	1,737,032
Long-Term Obligations	4,005,051	3,362,759	3,128,154	2,978,909	2,770,718	2,836,873	2,613,503	2,592,772
Total Liabilities	6,947,442	6,458,203	6,178,902	4,871,312	4,801,891	5,280,628	6,706,894	7,289,814
Stockholders' Equity	3,414,764	2,696,468	2,608,949	2,443,479	2,623,007	3,822,119	5,701,372	5,251,411
Shares Outstanding	191,547	188,402	186,636	184,896	160,558	159,887	158,156	157,560
Statistical Record								
Return on Assets %	6.94	1.03	1.18	N.M.	N.M.	N.M.	4.76	12.49
Return on Equity %	22.16	3.48	3.77	N.M.	N.M.	N.M.	10.84	29.13
EBITDA Margin %	8.56	9.74	5.88	N.M.	N.M.	N.M.	6.26	15.51
Net Margin %	16.55	2.98	3.10	N.M.	N.M.	N.M.	3.65	9.77
Asset Turnover	0.42	0.35	0.38	0.42	0.55	0.95	1.30	1.28
Current Ratio	29.95	28.60	33.60	35.60	24.66	8.28	7.93	5.24
Debt to Equity	1.17	1.25	1.20	1.22	1.06	0.74	0.46	0.49
Price Range	39.05-18.23	21.38-12.71	20.71-11.63	17.38-5.87	21.81-3.64	56.11-14.49	65.95-40.07	68.27-44.27
P/E Ratio	12.56-5.86	44.54-26.48	40.61-22.80	...	...	...	17.87-10.86	8.30-5.38
Average Yield %	0.56	0.91	1.03	1.52	3.56	1.67	1.23	0.99

Address: 700 Northwest 107th Avenue, Miami, FL 33172 **Telephone:** 305-559-4000	**Web Site:** www.lennar.com **Officers:** Richard Beckwitt - President Stuart A. Miller - President, Chief Executive Officer	**Auditors:** Deloitte & Touche LLP **Transfer Agents:** ComputerShare Investor Services, Providence, RI

LENNOX INTERNATIONAL INC

Exchange	Symbol	Price	52Wk Range	Yield	P/E
NYS	LII	$63.49 (3/28/2013)	65.34-36.95	1.26	36.28

*7 Year Price Score 115.88 *NYSE Composite Index=100 *12 Month Price Score 112.46

TRADING VOLUME (thousand shares)

Interim Earnings (Per Share)

Qtr.	Mar	Jun	Sep	Dec
2008	0.10	0.88	0.96	0.21
2009	(0.33)	0.56	0.54	0.11
2010	(0.03)	0.86	0.76	0.51
2011	(0.13)	0.83	0.64	0.32
2012	(0.12)	0.87	0.57	0.43

Interim Dividends (Per Share)

Amt	Decl	Ex	Rec	Pay
0.18Q	05/09/2012	06/13/2012	06/15/2012	07/16/2012
0.20Q	09/20/2012	10/02/2012	10/04/2012	10/15/2012
0.20Q	12/07/2012	12/13/2012	12/17/2012	12/28/2012
0.20Q	03/15/2013	03/26/2013	03/28/2013	04/15/2013

Indicated Div: $0.80

Valuation Analysis / **Institutional Holding**

Forecast EPS	$3.40 (04/05/2013)	No of Institutions	257
Market Cap	$3.2 Billion	Shares	37,358,840
Book Value	$496.8 Million	% Held	63.07
Price/Book	6.42		
Price/Sales	1.08		

Business Summary: Metal Products (MIC: 8.2.3 SIC: 3585 NAIC: 333415)

Lennox International, through its subsidiaries, provides climate control products for the heating, ventilation, air conditioning and refrigeration markets. Co. has three segments: the Residential Heating and Cooling, which provides heating, air conditioning, and hearth products to the residential replacement residential and construction markets; the Commercial Heating and Cooling, which provides rooftop products, chillers and air handlers to light commercial, market; and the Refrigeration, which provides unit coolers, condensing units and commercial refrigeration products to the light commercial market.

Recent Developments: For the year ended Dec 31 2012, net income increased 1.9% to US$90.0 million from US$88.3 million in the prior year. Revenues were US$2.95 billion, up 3.8% from US$2.84 billion the year before. Operating income was US$219.1 million versus US$184.4 million in the prior year, an increase of 18.8%. Direct operating expenses rose 2.6% to US$2.23 billion from US$2.17 billion in the comparable period the year before. Indirect operating expenses increased 3.6% to US$503.2 million from US$485.5 million in the equivalent prior-year period.

Prospects: Our evaluation of Lennox International Inc. as of Apr. 7, 2013 is the result of our systematic analysis on three basic characteristics: earnings strength, relative valuation, and recent stock price movement. The company has generated a negative trend in earnings per share over the past 5 quarters and while recent estimates for the company have been mixed, LII has posted better than expected results. Based on operating earnings yield, the company is about fairly valued when compared to all of the companies in our coverage universe. Share price changes over the past year indicates that LII will perform very well over the near term.

Financial Data
(US$ in Thousands)

	12/31/2012	12/31/2011	12/31/2010	12/31/2009	12/31/2008	12/31/2007	12/31/2006	12/31/2005
Earnings Per Share	1.75	1.65	2.08	0.90	2.11	2.43	2.26	2.11
Cash Flow Per Share	4.35	1.45	3.40	4.06	3.22	3.59	2.86	3.56
Tang Book Value Per Share	5.43	3.19	5.92	6.17	4.11	8.79	8.41	8.03
Dividends Per Share	0.760	0.720	0.600	0.560	0.560	0.530	0.460	0.410
Dividend Payout %	43.43	43.64	28.85	62.22	26.54	21.81	20.35	19.43
Income Statement								
Total Revenue	2,949,400	3,303,600	3,096,400	2,847,500	3,481,400	3,749,700	3,671,100	3,366,200
EBITDA	263,700	198,200	232,800	154,700	262,000	303,200	259,100	252,300
Depn & Amortn	55,400	60,400	53,500	52,900	50,600	48,800	44,300	1,900
Income Before Taxes	191,200	121,000	166,500	93,600	197,700	247,600	210,400	235,000
Income Taxes	66,700	42,300	59,500	39,100	81,200	89,200	52,400	83,000
Net Income	90,000	88,300	116,200	51,100	122,800	169,000	166,000	150,700
Average Shares	51,400	53,400	55,800	56,600	58,300	69,400	73,500	73,700
Balance Sheet								
Current Assets	987,100	903,200	946,900	833,900	935,000	1,070,700	1,018,400	1,047,200
Total Assets	1,691,900	1,705,700	1,692,000	1,543,900	1,659,500	1,814,600	1,719,800	1,737,600
Current Liabilities	639,600	572,900	615,600	593,800	576,000	684,200	651,100	656,500
Long-Term Obligations	351,000	459,600	317,000	193,800	413,700	166,700	96,800	108,000
Total Liabilities	1,195,100	1,237,900	1,102,300	939,500	1,200,900	1,006,100	915,400	943,200
Stockholders' Equity	496,800	467,800	589,700	604,400	458,600	808,500	804,400	794,400
Shares Outstanding	50,232	50,844	53,696	56,274	55,106	62,052	67,155	71,035
Statistical Record								
Return on Assets %	5.28	5.20	7.18	3.19	7.05	9.56	9.60	9.26
Return on Equity %	18.61	16.70	19.46	9.61	19.33	20.96	20.77	23.78
EBITDA Margin %	8.94	6.00	7.52	5.43	7.53	8.09	7.06	7.50
Net Margin %	3.05	2.67	3.75	1.79	3.53	4.51	4.52	4.48
Asset Turnover	1.73	1.94	1.91	1.78	2.00	2.12	2.12	2.07
Current Ratio	1.54	1.58	1.54	1.40	1.62	1.56	1.56	1.60
Debt to Equity	0.71	0.98	0.54	0.32	0.90	0.21	0.12	0.14
Price Range	53.84-34.74	53.63-25.29	49.93-38.22	40.76-23.87	41.42-19.89	41.50-29.41	34.54-21.44	30.32-18.70
P/E Ratio	30.77-19.85	32.50-15.33	24.00-18.37	45.29-26.52	19.63-9.43	17.08-12.10	15.28-9.49	14.37-8.86
Average Yield %	1.70	1.77	1.38	1.70	1.68	1.55	1.66	1.75

Address: 2140 Lake Park Blvd., Richardson, TX 75080 Telephone: 972-497-5000	Web Site: www.lennoxinternational.com Officers: Todd M. Bluedorn - Chairman, Chief Executive Officer Michael J. Blatz - Executive Vice President, Division Officer	Auditors: KPMG LLP Investor Contact: 972-497-6670 Transfer Agents: Mellon Investor Services, South Hackensack, NJ

LEUCADIA NATIONAL CORP.

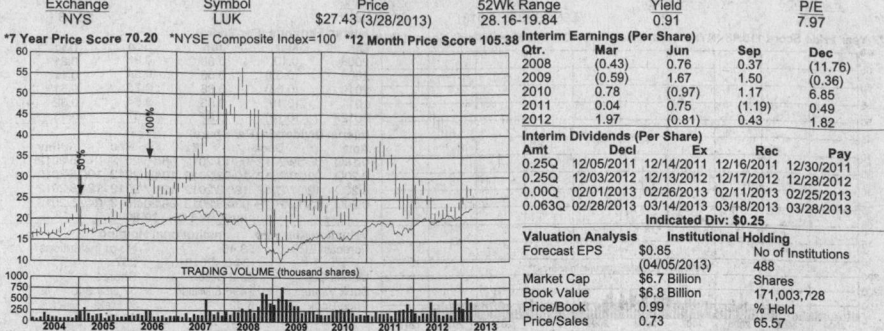

Exchange	Symbol	Price	52Wk Range	Yield	P/E
NYS	LUK	$27.43 (3/28/2013)	28.16-19.84	0.91	7.97

*7 Year Price Score 70.20   *NYSE Composite Index=100   *12 Month Price Score 105.38

Interim Earnings (Per Share)

Qtr.	Mar	Jun	Sep	Dec
2008	(0.43)	0.76	0.37	(11.76)
2009	(0.59)	1.67	1.50	(0.36)
2010	0.78	(0.97)	1.17	6.85
2011	0.04	0.75	(1.19)	0.49
2012	1.97	(0.81)	0.43	1.82

Interim Dividends (Per Share)

Amt	Decl	Ex	Rec	Pay
0.25Q	12/05/2011	12/14/2011	12/16/2011	12/30/2011
0.25Q	12/03/2012	12/13/2012	12/17/2012	12/28/2012
0.00Q	02/01/2013	02/26/2013	02/11/2013	02/25/2013
0.063Q	02/28/2013	03/14/2013	03/18/2013	03/28/2013

Indicated Div: $0.25

Valuation Analysis   Institutional Holding

Forecast EPS	$0.85 (04/05/2013)	No of Institutions 488
Market Cap	$6.7 Billion	Shares
Book Value	$6.8 Billion	171,003,728
Price/Book	0.99	% Held
Price/Sales	0.73	65.57

Business Summary: Paper & Forest Products (MIC: 8.1.2 SIC: 2499 NAIC: 321999)

Leucadia National is a holding company. Through its subsidiaries, Co. is engaged in a variety of businesses, including beef processing, manufacturing, land based contract oil and gas drilling, gaming entertainment, real estate activities, medical product development and winery operations. Co. also has an investment in the common stock of Jefferies Group, Inc., an investment bank, and Mueller Industries, Inc., a manufacturer of copper, brass, plastic, and aluminum products. In addition, Co. owns equity interests in operating businesses, including a broker-dealer engaged in making markets and trading of securities and a commercial mortgage origination and servicing business.

Recent Developments: For the year ended Dec 31 2012, income from continuing operations increased to US$866.3 million from US$13.1 million a year earlier. Net income increased to US$864.6 million from US$25.0 million in the prior year. Revenues were US$9.19 billion, up 540.8% from US$1.43 billion the year before. Direct operating expenses rose to US$7.57 billion from US$300.8 million in the comparable period the year before. Indirect operating expenses increased 44.5% to US$659.3 million from US$456.4 million in the equivalent prior-year period.

Prospects: Our evaluation of Leucadia National Corp. as of Apr. 7, 2013 is the result of our systematic analysis on three basic characteristics: earnings strength, relative valuation, and recent stock price movement. The company has enjoyed a very positive trend in earnings per share over the past 5 quarters. Because the company lacks sufficient analyst estimate data, we place greater weight on the historical EPS trend as the measure of earnings strength. Based on operating earnings yield, the company is undervalued when compared to all of the companies in our coverage universe. Share price changes over the past year indicates that LUK will perform poorly over the near term.

Financial Data

(US$ in Thousands)	12/31/2012	12/31/2011	12/31/2010	12/31/2009	12/31/2008	12/31/2007	12/31/2006	12/31/2005
Earnings Per Share	3.44	0.10	7.85	2.25	(11.00)	2.10	0.85	7.13
Cash Flow Per Share	0.90	0.04	1.77	(0.55)	0.04	(0.08)	0.42	1.49
Tang Book Value Per Share	24.18	21.66	28.36	17.62	10.87	24.67	17.72	16.55
Dividends Per Share	0.250	0.250	0.250	...	...	0.250	0.250	0.125
Dividend Payout %	7.27	250.00	3.18	...	...	11.90	29.41	1.75
Income Statement								
Total Revenue	9,193,689	1,570,768	1,320,004	1,119,002	1,080,653	1,154,895	862,672	1,041,147
EBITDA	1,229,214	888,098	598,542	(35,793)	(148,814)	96,892	237,212	396,035
Depn & Amortn	170,113	95,233	104,730	86,377	72,283	42,443	24,000	189,496
Income Before Taxes	966,520	680,988	369,003	(250,973)	(366,568)	(57,088)	133,820	138,163
Income Taxes	376,494	270,253	(1,133,318)	7,143	1,673,675	(559,771)	41,771	(1,131,082)
Net Income	854,466	25,231	1,939,312	550,280	(2,535,425)	484,294	189,399	1,636,041
Average Shares	248,914	244,573	247,672	247,849	230,494	234,653	231,884	231,274
Balance Sheet								
Current Assets	2,521,266	1,253,479	985,590	551,474	866,638	1,720,133	1,366,209	2,228,615
Total Assets	9,349,118	9,263,189	9,350,298	6,762,364	5,198,493	8,126,622	5,303,824	5,260,884
Current Liabilities	1,280,479	877,132	747,840	624,981	562,916	459,950	326,653	474,396
Long-Term Obligations	918,126	1,875,571	1,548,469	1,657,779	1,832,743	2,004,145	974,646	986,718
Total Liabilities	2,581,850	3,088,793	2,393,540	2,400,717	2,521,696	2,556,130	1,410,549	1,598,970
Stockholders' Equity	6,767,268	6,174,396	6,956,758	4,361,647	2,676,797	5,570,492	3,893,275	3,661,914
Shares Outstanding	244,582	244,582	243,808	243,288	238,498	222,574	216,351	216,058
Statistical Record								
Return on Assets %	9.16	0.27	24.07	9.20	N.M.	7.21	3.59	32.52
Return on Equity %	13.17	0.38	34.27	15.64	N.M.	10.23	5.01	55.27
EBITDA Margin %	13.37	56.54	45.34	N.M.	N.M.	8.39	27.50	38.04
Net Margin %	9.29	1.61	146.92	49.18	N.M.	41.93	21.95	157.14
Asset Turnover	0.99	0.17	0.16	0.19	0.16	0.17	0.16	0.21
Current Ratio	1.97	1.43	1.32	0.88	1.54	3.74	4.18	4.70
Debt to Equity	0.14	0.30	0.22	0.38	0.68	0.36	0.25	0.27
Price Range	29.72-19.84	39.02-20.42	29.52-18.89	26.33-10.85	56.33-13.51	51.62-26.61	32.16-23.77	24.41-16.41
P/E Ratio	8.64-5.77	390.20-204.20	3.76-2.41	11.70-4.82	...	24.58-12.67	37.84-27.97	3.42-2.30
Average Yield %	1.06	0.82	1.04	...	...	0.66	0.90	0.63

Address: 315 Park Avenue South, New York, NY 10010 Telephone: 212-460-1900 Fax: 212-598-4869	Web Site: www.leucadia.com Officers: Joseph S. Steinberg - President, Chairman Brian P. Friedman - President	Auditors: PricewaterhouseCoopers LLP Investor Contact: 212-460-1900 Transfer Agents: American Stock Transfer & Trust Company, New York, NY

LEVEL 3 COMMUNICATIONS, INC.

Exchange	Symbol	Price	52Wk Range	Yield	P/E
NYS	LVLT	$20.29 (3/28/2013)	26.72-18.12	N/A	N/A

*7 Year Price Score 52.29 *NYSE Composite Index=100 ***12 Month Price Score 90.74**

Interim Earnings (Per Share)

Qtr.	Mar	Jun	Sep	Dec
2008	(1.80)	(0.30)	(1.20)	0.45
2009	(1.20)	(1.20)	(1.50)	(1.65)
2010	(2.10)	(1.50)	(1.47)	(0.39)
2011	(1.80)	(1.65)	(1.75)	(0.33)
2012	(0.66)	(0.29)	(0.76)	(0.25)

Interim Dividends (Per Share)

No Dividends Paid

Valuation Analysis **Institutional Holding**

Forecast EPS	$-0.07	No of Institutions
	(04/05/2013)	333
Market Cap	$4.4 Billion	Shares
Book Value	$1.2 Billion	360,100,160
Price/Book	3.78	% Held
Price/Sales	0.69	N/A

Business Summary: Services (MIC: 6.1.2 SIC: 4813 NAIC: 517110)

Level 3 Communications is a facility based provider of a range of integrated communications services. Co. provides a range of communications services, which are: Core Network Services, which includes transport services, infrastructure services, data services, and local and enterprise voice services; Wholesale Voice Services, which includes voice over Internet Protocol local service, SIP Trunking, Primary Rate Interface service, long distance service and toll free service; and Other Communications Services, which includes managed modem and SBC Contract Services. Co. provides communications services to a range of wholesale and enterprise customers.

Recent Developments: For the year ended Dec 31 2012, loss from continuing operations was US$422.0 million compared with a loss of US$827.0 million a year earlier. Net loss amounted to US$422.0 million versus a net loss of US$756.0 million in the prior year. Revenues were US$6.38 billion, up 47.1% from US$4.33 billion the year before. Operating income was US$575.0 million versus US$52.0 million in the prior year, an increase of. Direct operating expenses rose 52.5% to US$2.60 billion from US$1.71 billion in the comparable period the year before. Indirect operating expenses increased 24.2% to US$3.20 billion from US$2.58 billion in the equivalent prior-year period.

Prospects: Our evaluation of Level 3 Communications Inc. as of Apr. 7, 2013 is the result of our systematic analysis on three basic characteristics: earnings strength, relative valuation, and recent stock price movement. The company has suffered a very negative trend in earnings per share over the past 5 quarters. Because the company lacks sufficient analyst estimate data, we place greater weight on the historical EPS trend as the measure of earnings strength. Based on operating earnings yield, the company is overvalued when compared to all of the companies in our coverage universe. Share price changes over the past year indicates that LVLT will perform poorly over the near term.

Financial Data
(US$ in Thousands)

	12/31/2012	12/31/2011	12/31/2010	12/31/2009	12/31/2008	12/31/2007	12/31/2006	12/31/2005
Earnings Per Share	(1.96)	(5.51)	(5.55)	(5.70)	(2.85)	(10.95)	(11.10)	(13.65)
Cash Flow Per Share	2.68	2.83	3.06	3.28	3.95	2.28	3.30	(2.57)
Income Statement								
Total Revenue	6,376,000	4,333,000	3,651,000	3,762,000	4,301,000	4,269,000	3,378,000	3,613,000
EBITDA	1,016,000	635,000	653,000	799,000	1,067,000	225,000	448,000	473,000
Depn & Amortn	659,000	706,000	781,000	823,000	832,000	838,000	652,000	657,000
Income Before Taxes	(374,000)	(786,000)	(713,000)	(617,000)	(284,000)	(1,136,000)	(788,000)	(679,000)
Income Taxes	48,000	41,000	(91,000)	1,000	6,000	(22,000)	2,000	8,000
Net Income	(422,000)	(756,000)	(622,000)	(618,000)	(290,000)	(1,114,000)	(744,000)	(638,000)
Average Shares	215,356	137,176	110,679	108,869	104,333	101,174	66,883	46,639
Balance Sheet								
Current Assets	1,842,000	1,707,000	972,000	1,259,000	1,244,000	1,229,000	2,389,000	1,677,000
Total Assets	13,307,000	13,188,000	8,355,000	9,062,000	9,638,000	10,245,000	9,994,000	8,277,000
Current Liabilities	1,802,000	1,658,000	956,000	1,519,000	1,052,000	958,000	929,000	1,435,000
Long-Term Obligations	8,516,000	8,385,000	6,268,000	5,755,000	6,394,000	6,832,000	7,357,000	6,023,000
Total Liabilities	12,136,000	11,995,000	8,512,000	8,571,000	8,762,000	9,175,000	9,620,000	8,753,000
Stockholders' Equity	1,171,000	1,193,000	(157,000)	491,000	876,000	1,070,000	374,000	(476,000)
Shares Outstanding	218,380	207,913	111,365	109,607	107,841	102,524	78,561	54,517
Statistical Record								
EBITDA Margin %	15.93	14.65	17.89	21.24	24.81	5.27	13.26	13.09
Asset Turnover	0.48	0.40	0.42	0.40	0.43	0.42	0.37	0.46
Current Ratio	1.02	1.03	1.02	0.83	1.18	1.28	2.57	1.17
Debt to Equity	7.27	7.03	...	11.72	7.30	6.39	19.67	...
Price Range	27.53-16.87	39.30-14.70	26.25-12.87	25.65-9.02	66.30-9.45	101.40-42.30	90.30-40.95	58.50-24.30

Address: 1025 Eldorado Blvd., Broomfield, CO 80021-8869 **Telephone:** 720-888-1000	**Web Site:** www.level3.com **Officers:** Walter Scott - Chairman Charles C. Miller - Vice-Chairman, Executive Vice President	**Auditors:** KPMG LLP **Investor Contact:** 877-585-8266 **Transfer Agents:** Wells Fargo Shareowner Services, Saint Paul, MN

LEXMARK INTERNATIONAL, INC.

Exchange	Symbol	Price	52Wk Range	Yield	P/E
NYS	LXK	$26.40 (3/28/2013)	33.19-16.77	4.55	17.25

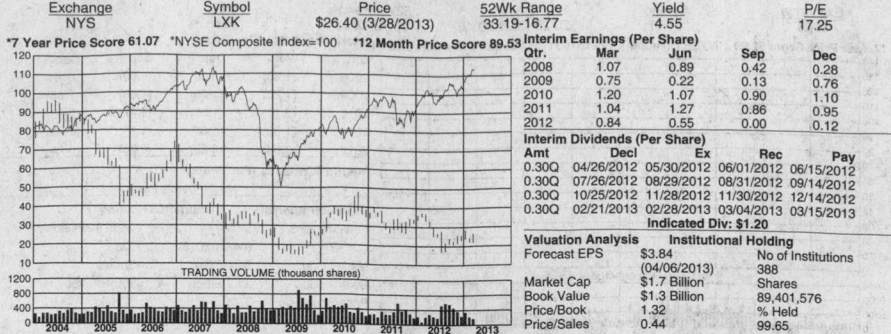

*7 Year Price Score 61.07 *NYSE Composite Index=100 ***12 Month Price Score 89.53**

Interim Earnings (Per Share)

Qtr.	Mar	Jun	Sep	Dec
2008	1.07	0.89	0.42	0.28
2009	0.75	0.22	0.13	0.76
2010	1.20	1.07	0.90	1.10
2011	1.04	1.27	0.86	0.95
2012	0.84	0.55	0.00	0.12

Interim Dividends (Per Share)

Amt	Decl	Ex	Rec	Pay
0.30Q	04/26/2012	05/30/2012	06/01/2012	06/15/2012
0.30Q	07/26/2012	08/29/2012	08/31/2012	09/14/2012
0.30Q	10/25/2012	11/28/2012	11/30/2012	12/14/2012
0.30Q	02/21/2013	02/28/2013	03/04/2013	03/15/2013

Indicated Div: $1.20

Valuation Analysis | **Institutional Holding**

Forecast EPS	$3.84	No of Institutions
	(04/06/2013)	388
Market Cap	$1.7 Billion	Shares
Book Value	$1.3 Billion	89,401,576
Price/Book	1.32	% Held
Price/Sales	0.44	99.65

TRADING VOLUME (thousand shares)

Business Summary: Peripherals (MIC: 6.2.2 SIC: 3577 NAIC: 334119)

Lexmark International is a developer, manufacturer and supplier of printing, imaging, device management, managed print services, document workflow, and business process and content management solutions. Co. operates two segments. The Imaging Solutions and Services segment offers a portfolio of monochrome and color laser printers and laser multifunction products as well as a range of supplies and services covering its printing products and technology solutions. The Perceptive Software segment offers a suite of enterprise content management, business process management, document output management, intelligent data capture and search software as well as associated industry specific solutions.

Recent Developments: For the year ended Dec 31 2012, net income decreased 66.9% to US$106.3 million from US$320.9 million in the prior year. Revenues were US$3.80 billion, down 9.0% from US$4.17 billion the year before. Operating income was US$187.1 million versus US$442.9 million in the prior year, a decrease of 57.8%. Direct operating expenses declined 7.5% to US$2.40 billion from US$2.59 billion in the comparable period the year before. Indirect operating expenses increased 6.6% to US$1.21 billion from US$1.14 billion in the equivalent prior-year period.

Prospects: Our evaluation of Lexmark International Inc. as of Apr. 7, 2013 is the result of our systematic analysis on three basic characteristics: earnings strength, relative valuation, and recent stock price movement. The company has managed to produce a neutral trend in earnings per share over the past 5 quarters and while recent estimates for the company have been mixed, LXK has posted results that fell short of analysts expectations. Based on operating earnings yield, the company is undervalued when compared to all of the companies in our coverage universe. Share price changes over the past year indicates that LXK will perform very poorly over the near term.

Financial Data

(US$ in Thousands)	12/31/2012	12/31/2011	12/31/2010	12/31/2009	12/31/2008	12/31/2007	12/31/2006	12/31/2005
Earnings Per Share	1.53	4.12	4.28	1.86	2.69	3.14	3.27	2.91
Cash Flow Per Share	6.01	5.07	6.62	5.14	5.41	5.92	6.53	4.76
Tang Book Value Per Share	10.53	14.34	13.41	12.98	10.45	13.50	10.67	12.77
Dividends Per Share	1.150	0.250	...	...	...	...	...	...
Dividend Payout %	75.16	6.07	...	...	...	...	...	...
Income Statement								
Total Revenue	3,797,600	4,173,000	4,199,700	3,879,900	4,528,400	4,973,900	5,108,100	5,221,500
EBITDA	417,200	639,500	628,800	417,500	473,000	519,300	636,700	684,300
Depn & Amortn	229,600	196,000	181,000	209,100	203,200	191,000	199,500	157,100
Income Before Taxes	158,000	413,600	421,500	187,000	275,900	349,500	459,300	553,700
Income Taxes	51,700	92,700	81,500	41,100	35,700	48,700	120,900	197,400
Net Income	106,300	320,900	340,000	145,900	240,200	300,800	338,400	356,300
Average Shares	69,500	77,900	79,500	78,600	89,200	95,800	103,500	122,300
Balance Sheet								
Current Assets	1,921,600	2,208,800	2,269,600	2,140,700	2,062,700	2,066,800	1,830,000	2,169,600
Total Assets	3,523,400	3,637,000	3,705,200	3,354,200	3,265,400	3,121,100	2,849,000	3,330,100
Current Liabilities	1,443,100	1,123,300	1,246,300	1,191,800	1,257,500	1,497,300	1,324,000	1,233,700
Long-Term Obligations	299,600	649,300	649,100	648,900	648,700	...	149,800	149,600
Total Liabilities	2,242,200	2,245,300	2,310,900	2,340,600	2,453,300	1,842,800	1,813,800	1,901,400
Stockholders' Equity	1,281,200	1,391,700	1,394,300	1,013,600	812,100	1,278,300	1,035,200	1,428,700
Shares Outstanding	63,900	71,400	78,600	78,100	77,700	94,700	97,000	111,900
Statistical Record								
Return on Assets %	2.96	8.74	9.63	4.41	7.50	10.08	10.95	9.56
Return on Equity %	7.93	23.04	28.24	15.98	22.92	26.00	27.47	20.29
EBITDA Margin %	10.99	15.32	14.97	10.76	10.45	10.44	12.46	13.11
Net Margin %	2.80	7.69	8.10	3.76	5.30	6.05	6.62	6.82
Asset Turnover	1.06	1.14	1.19	1.17	1.41	1.67	1.65	1.40
Current Ratio	1.33	1.97	1.82	1.80	1.64	1.38	1.38	1.76
Debt to Equity	0.23	0.47	0.47	0.64	0.80	...	0.14	0.10
Price Range	37.48-16.77	40.35-26.48	47.72-25.50	28.94-14.48	37.68-23.25	72.40-32.85	74.13-45.01	86.10-39.69
P/E Ratio	24.50-10.96	9.79-6.43	11.15-5.96	15.56-7.78	14.01-8.64	23.06-10.46	22.67-13.76	29.59-13.64
Average Yield %	4.34	0.77	...	...	...	...	...	...

Address: One Lexmark Centre Drive, 740 West New Circle Road, Lexington, KY 40550	**Web Site:** www.lexmark.com	**Auditors:** PricewaterhouseCoopers LLP
Telephone: 859-232-2000	**Officers:** Paul A. Rooke - Chairman, President, Chief Executive Officer, Executive Vice President, Division Officer John W. Gamble - Executive Vice President, Chief Financial Officer, Principal Accounting Officer	**Transfer Agents:** Computershare, Providence, RI

LIBERTY PROPERTY TRUST

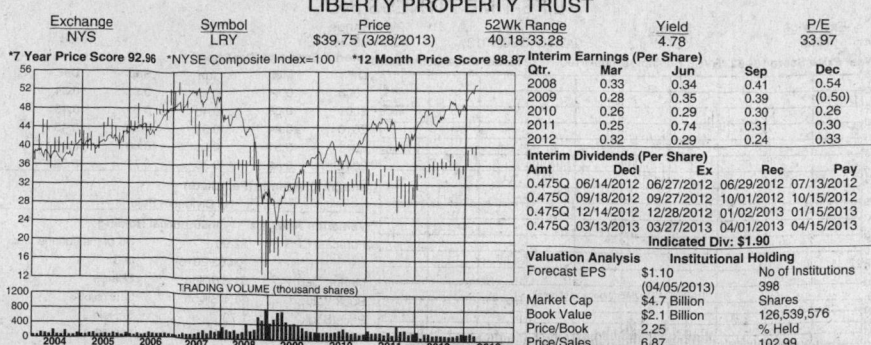

Exchange	Symbol	Price	52Wk Range	Yield	P/E
NYS	LRY	$39.75 (3/28/2013)	40.18-33.28	4.78	33.97

*7 Year Price Score 92.96 *NYSE Composite Index=100 *12 Month Price Score 98.87

Interim Earnings (Per Share)

Qtr.	Mar	Jun	Sep	Dec
2008	0.33	0.34	0.41	0.54
2009	0.28	0.35	0.39	(0.50)
2010	0.26	0.29	0.30	0.26
2011	0.25	0.74	0.31	0.30
2012	0.32	0.29	0.24	0.33

Interim Dividends (Per Share)

Amt	Decl	Ex	Rec	Pay
0.475Q	06/14/2012	06/27/2012	06/29/2012	07/13/2012
0.475Q	09/18/2012	09/27/2012	10/01/2012	10/15/2012
0.475Q	12/14/2012	12/28/2012	01/02/2013	01/15/2013
0.475Q	03/13/2013	03/27/2663	04/01/2013	04/15/2013

Indicated Div: $1.90

Valuation Analysis

		Institutional Holding	
Forecast EPS	$1.10	No of Institutions	
	(04/05/2013)	398	
Market Cap	$4.7 Billion	Shares	
Book Value	$2.1 Billion	126,539,576	
Price/Book	2.25	% Held	
Price/Sales	6.87	102.99	

TRADING VOLUME (thousand shares)

Business Summary: REITs (MIC: 5.3.1 SIC: 6798 NAIC: 525930)

Liberty Property Trust is a real estate investment trust. Substantially all of Co.'s operations are conducted by its subsidiary, Liberty Property Limited Partnership. Co. provides leasing, property management, development, and other tenant-related services for a portfolio of industrial and office properties which are located principally within the Mid-Atlantic, Southeastern, Midwestern and Southwestern U.S. and the U.K. As of Dec 31 2011, Co. owned and operated 332 industrial and 265 office properties; and 1,456 acres of developable land; as well as had an ownership interest, through unconsolidated joint ventures, in 47 industrial and 49 office properties and 615 acres of developable land.

Recent Developments: For the year ended Dec 31 2012, income from continuing operations decreased 4.4% to US$133.8 million from US$140.1 million a year earlier. Net income decreased 29.9% to US$147.8 million from US$210.7 million in the prior year. Revenues were US$685.6 million, up 3.4% from US$663.2 million the year before.

Prospects: Our evaluation of Liberty Property Trust as of Apr. 7, 2013 is the result of our systematic analysis on three basic characteristics: earnings strength, relative valuation, and recent stock price movement. The company has enjoyed a very positive trend in earnings per share over the past 5 quarters. Because the company lacks sufficient analyst estimate data, we place greater weight on the historical EPS trend as the measure of earnings strength. Based on operating earnings yield, the company is overvalued when compared to all of the companies in our coverage universe. Share price changes over the past year indicates that LRY will perform poorly over the near term.

Financial Data
(US$ in Thousands)

	12/31/2012	12/31/2011	12/31/2010	12/31/2009	12/31/2008	12/31/2007	12/31/2006	12/31/2005
Earnings Per Share	1.17	1.59	1.12	0.52	1.62	1.80	2.95	2.82
Cash Flow Per Share	2.71	2.77	2.65	2.78	2.86	4.22	3.86	4.14
Tang Book Value Per Share	17.65	18.96	19.05	19.68	20.44	20.52	20.59	19.34
Dividends Per Share	1.900	1.900	1.900	1.900	2.350	2.490	2.470	2.450
Dividend Payout %	162.39	119.50	169.64	365.38	145.06	138.33	83.73	86.88
Income Statement								
Total Revenue	685,552	667,594	746,830	744,257	748,520	698,747	666,719	680,730
EBITDA	382,305	390,291	427,445	431,646	431,660	400,566	390,229	407,663
Depn & Amortn	140,600	144,300	147,300	144,500	147,200	135,400	124,900	123,300
Income Before Taxes	131,364	132,370	140,864	149,080	142,293	147,613	155,336	163,368
Income Taxes	976	1,020	1,736	494	1,645	(709)	288	14,827
Net Income	137,436	183,999	127,762	56,376	151,942	164,831	266,574	249,351
Average Shares	117,694	115,303	113,606	108,002	93,804	91,803	90,492	88,376
Balance Sheet								
Current Assets	189,119	193,063	273,766	379,796	153,857	171,059	205,111	183,061
Total Assets	5,177,971	4,989,673	5,062,833	5,227,421	5,217,035	5,638,749	4,910,911	4,497,529
Current Liabilities	109,260	104,523	109,622	117,848	117,813	144,240	135,891	124,301
Long-Term Obligations	2,657,398	2,222,862	2,359,822	2,456,875	2,590,167	3,021,129	2,387,938	2,249,178
Total Liabilities	3,086,959	2,886,079	2,980,647	3,105,126	3,260,300	3,801,728	3,039,307	2,788,347
Stockholders' Equity	2,091,012	2,103,594	2,082,186	2,122,295	1,956,735	1,837,021	1,871,604	1,709,182
Shares Outstanding	118,470	116,102	114,280	112,625	98,784	91,567	90,913	88,356
Statistical Record								
Return on Assets %	2.70	3.66	2.48	1.08	2.79	3.12	5.67	5.76
Return on Equity %	6.54	8.79	6.08	2.76	7.99	8.89	14.89	15.09
EBITDA Margin %	55.77	58.46	57.23	58.00	57.67	57.33	58.53	59.89
Net Margin %	20.05	27.56	17.11	7.57	20.30	23.59	39.98	36.63
Asset Turnover	0.13	0.13	0.15	0.14	0.14	0.13	0.14	0.16
Current Ratio	1.73	1.85	2.50	3.22	1.31	1.19	1.51	1.47
Debt to Equity	1.27	1.06	1.13	1.16	1.32	1.64	1.28	1.32
Price Range	38.57-30.91	36.06-26.16	35.05-27.41	35.11-16.90	40.89-12.93	53.91-28.16	52.35-41.32	45.80-38.19
P/E Ratio	32.97-26.42	22.68-16.45	31.29-24.47	67.52-32.50	25.24-7.98	29.95-15.64	17.75-14.01	16.24-13.54
Average Yield %	5.36	5.87	5.99	7.35	7.65	5.81	5.35	5.87

Address: 500 Chesterfield Parkway, Malvern, PA 19355 **Telephone:** 610-648-1700 **Fax:** 610-644-4129	**Web Site:** www.libertyproperty.com **Officers:** William P. Hankowsky - Chairman, President, Chief Executive Officer George J. Alburger - Executive Vice President, Chief Financial Officer, Treasurer	**Auditors:** Ernst & Young LLP **Investor Contact:** 610-648-1704 **Transfer Agents:** Wells Fargo Shareholder Services, St. Paul, MN

LIFE-TIME FITNESS INC

Exchange	Symbol	Price	52Wk Range	Yield	P/E
NYS	LTM	$42.78 (3/28/2013)	52.31-39.36	N/A	16.08

*7 Year Price Score 104.52 *NYSE Composite Index=100 *12 Month Price Score 84.90

Interim Earnings (Per Share)

Qtr.	Mar	Jun	Sep	Dec
2008	0.44	0.50	0.55	0.34
2009	0.38	0.46	0.51	0.46
2010	0.44	0.53	0.57	0.45
2011	0.51	0.61	0.66	0.48
2012	0.62	0.73	0.77	0.56

Interim Dividends (Per Share)

No Dividends Paid

Valuation Analysis **Institutional Holding**

Forecast EPS	$2.90	No of Institutions
	(04/05/2013)	248
Market Cap	$1.8 Billion	Shares
Book Value	$1.1 Billion	52,975,588
Price/Book	1.72	% Held
Price/Sales	1.64	108.26

Business Summary: Sporting & Recreational (MIC: 2.2.4 SIC: 7997 NAIC: 713940)

Life Time Fitness is engaged in designing, building and operating sports and athletic, fitness, family recreation and spa centers in a resort-like environment in residential locations. Co.'s programs include a range of interest areas, such as group fitness, yoga, swimming, running, racquetball, squash, tennis, pilates, mixed combat arts, kids activities and camps, adult activities and leagues, rock climbing, cycling, basketball, personal training, weight loss and nutrition initiatives, spa, medi-spa and chiropractic services. As of Feb 28 2012, Co. operated 102 centers under the LIFE TIME FITNESS® and LIFE TIME ATHLETICsm brands primarily in suburban locations in 26 markets in the U.S.

Recent Developments: For the year ended Dec 31 2012, net income increased 20.4% to US$111.5 million from US$92.6 million in the prior year. Revenues were US$1.13 billion, up 11.2% from US$1.01 billion the year before. Operating income was US$208.2 million versus US$173.3 million in the prior year, an increase of 20.2%. Direct operating expenses rose 6.7% to US$655.9 million from US$614.9 million in the comparable period the year before. Indirect operating expenses increased 16.6% to US$262.8 million from US$225.5 million in the equivalent prior-year period.

Prospects: Our evaluation of Life-Time Fitness Inc. as of Apr. 7, 2013 is the result of our systematic analysis on three basic characteristics: earnings strength, relative valuation, and recent stock price movement. The company has managed to produce a neutral trend in earnings per share over the past 5 quarters and while recent estimates for the company have remained steady, LTM has posted better than expected results. Based on operating earnings yield, the company is undervalued when compared to all of the companies in our coverage universe. Share price changes over the past year indicates that LTM will perform in line with the market over the near term.

Financial Data

(US$ in Thousands)	12/31/2012	12/31/2011	12/31/2010	12/31/2009	12/31/2008	12/31/2007	12/31/2006	12/31/2005
Earnings Per Share	2.66	2.26	2.00	1.82	1.83	1.78	1.37	1.13
Cash Flow Per Share	6.17	5.65	4.83	4.74	4.68	3.79	3.48	3.12
Tang Book Value Per Share	23.40	21.74	19.54	17.60	16.27	14.49	10.55	8.57
Income Statement								
Total Revenue	1,126,947	1,013,674	912,844	837,001	769,621	655,786	511,897	390,116
EBITDA	325,247	274,378	255,778	242,175	221,964	197,277	148,771	120,313
Depn & Amortn	117,019	101,112	95,019	93,314	74,610	59,867	48,256	39,371
Income Before Taxes	182,753	153,128	132,964	118,523	117,802	111,967	83,159	66,866
Income Taxes	72,697	61,820	53,448	47,441	47,224	45,220	33,513	26,758
Net Income	111,538	92,617	80,692	72,384	71,821	68,019	50,565	41,213
Average Shares	41,972	40,930	40,385	39,870	39,342	38,127	36,779	36,339
Balance Sheet								
Current Assets	100,314	85,545	76,904	58,805	63,811	63,323	39,846	35,395
Total Assets	2,072,174	1,915,828	1,718,480	1,631,525	1,647,703	1,386,533	987,676	723,460
Current Liabilities	168,037	140,958	133,417	126,201	170,923	163,604	140,355	101,518
Long-Term Obligations	691,867	679,449	605,279	643,630	702,569	555,037	374,327	258,835
Total Liabilities	999,257	958,355	877,902	894,094	994,802	813,976	595,163	415,616
Stockholders' Equity	1,072,917	957,473	840,578	737,431	652,901	572,557	392,513	307,844
Shares Outstanding	43,149	42,428	41,924	41,410	39,612	39,137	36,817	35,570
Statistical Record								
Return on Assets %	5.58	5.10	4.82	4.41	4.72	5.73	5.91	6.36
Return on Equity %	10.96	10.30	10.23	10.41	11.69	14.10	14.44	14.76
EBITDA Margin %	28.86	27.07	28.02	28.93	28.84	30.08	29.06	30.84
Net Margin %	9.90	9.14	8.84	8.65	9.33	10.37	9.88	10.56
Asset Turnover	0.56	0.56	0.54	0.51	0.51	0.55	0.60	0.60
Current Ratio	0.60	0.61	0.58	0.47	0.37	0.39	0.28	0.35
Debt to Equity	0.64	0.71	0.72	0.87	1.08	0.97	0.95	0.84
Price Range	52.35-40.80	47.81-33.31	42.57-22.63	31.47-7.50	49.68-8.87	64.82-47.60	52.58-37.84	40.43-24.00
P/E Ratio	19.68-15.34	21.15-14.74	21.29-11.32	17.29-4.12	27.15-4.85	36.42-26.74	38.38-27.62	35.78-21.24

Address: 2902 Corporate Place, Chanhassen, MN 55317 Telephone: 952-947-0000	Web Site: www.lifetimefitness.com Officers: Bahram Akradi - Chairman, President, Chief Executive Officer Tami A. Kozikowski - Executive Vice President	Auditors: Deloitte & Touche LLP Investor Contact: 952-229-7427 Transfer Agents: Wells Fargo Shareowner Services, South St. Paul, MN

LILLY (ELI) & CO.

Exchange	Symbol	Price	52Wk Range	Yield	P/E
NYS	LLY	$56.79 (3/28/2013)	56.79-39.18	3.45	15.52

*7 Year Price Score 95.62 *NYSE Composite Index=100 *12 Month Price Score 107.40

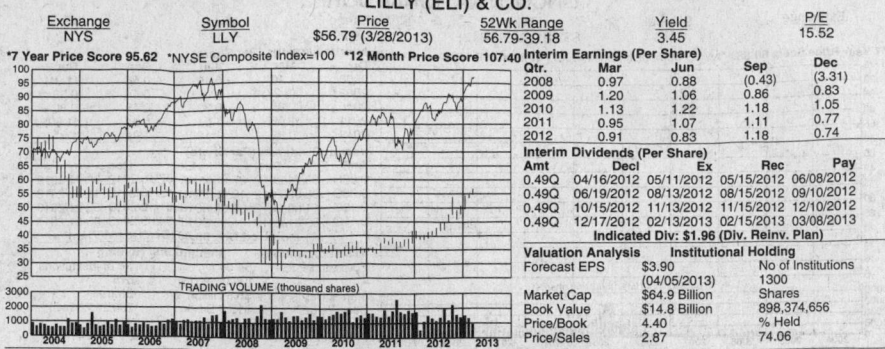

Interim Earnings (Per Share)

Qtr.	Mar	Jun	Sep	Dec
2008	0.97	0.88	(0.43)	(3.31)
2009	1.20	1.06	0.86	0.83
2010	1.13	1.22	1.18	1.05
2011	0.95	1.07	1.11	0.77
2012	0.91	0.83	1.18	0.74

Interim Dividends (Per Share)

Amt	Decl	Ex	Rec	Pay
0.49Q	04/16/2012	05/11/2012	05/15/2012	06/08/2012
0.49Q	06/19/2012	08/13/2012	08/15/2012	09/10/2012
0.49Q	10/15/2012	11/13/2012	11/15/2012	12/10/2012
0.49Q	12/17/2012	02/13/2013	02/15/2013	03/08/2013

Indicated Div: $1.96 (Div. Reinv. Plan)

Valuation Analysis **Institutional Holding**

Forecast EPS	$3.90	No of Institutions
	(04/05/2013)	1300
Market Cap	$64.9 Billion	Shares
Book Value	$14.8 Billion	898,374,656
Price/Book	4.40	% Held
Price/Sales	2.87	74.06

Business Summary: Pharmaceuticals (MIC: 4.1.1 SIC: 2834 NAIC: 325412)

Eli Lilly discovers, develops, manufactures, and markets products in two business segments: human pharmaceutical products and animal health products. Co.'s human pharmaceutical products include: neurosciences products, endocrinology products, oncology products, and cardiovascular products. Co.'s animal health products is comprised of products for food animals, which include Rumensin®, a cattle feed additive, and Tylan®, an antibiotic used to control certain diseases in cattle, swine, and poultry; as well as products for companion animals, which include Trifexis® and Comfortis®, a chewable tablet for dogs; and Reconcile®, for treatment of canine separation anxiety.

Recent Developments: For the year ended Dec 31 2012, net income decreased 6.0% to US$4.09 billion from US$4.35 billion in the prior year. Revenues were US$22.60 billion, down 6.9% from US$24.29 billion the year before. Direct operating expenses declined 5.4% to US$4.80 billion from US$5.07 billion in the comparable period the year before. Indirect operating expenses decreased 10.6% to US$12.40 billion from US$13.87 billion in the equivalent prior-year period.

Prospects: Our evaluation of Lilly (Eli) & Co. as of Apr. 7, 2013 is the result of our systematic analysis on three basic characteristics: earnings strength, relative valuation, and recent stock price movement. The company has enjoyed a very positive trend in earnings per share over the past 5 quarters and while recent estimates for the company have remained steady, LLY has posted better than expected results. Based on operating earnings yield, the company is undervalued when compared to all of the companies in our coverage universe. Share price changes over the past year indicates that LLY will perform well over the near term.

Financial Data
(US$ in Thousands)

	12/31/2012	12/31/2011	12/31/2010	12/31/2009	12/31/2008	12/31/2007	12/31/2006	12/31/2005
Earnings Per Share	3.66	3.90	4.58	3.94	(1.89)	2.71	2.45	1.81
Cash Flow Per Share	4.75	6.49	6.20	3.95	6.65	4.73	3.66	1.76
Tang Book Value Per Share	8.75	7.27	6.60	5.07	2.36	9.88	9.70	9.55
Dividends Per Share	1.960	1.960	1.960	1.960	1.880	1.700	1.600	1.520
Dividend Payout %	53.55	50.26	42.79	49.75	...	62.73	65.31	83.98
Income Statement								
Total Revenue	22,603,400	24,286,500	23,076,000	21,836,000	20,378,000	18,633,500	15,691,000	14,645,300
EBITDA	6,235,000	6,188,000	7,407,900	6,357,400	(558,300)	4,561,100	4,045,400	3,399,900
Depn & Amortn	754,000	732,400	749,100	813,500	731,700	682,300	627,400	577,200
Income Before Taxes	5,408,200	5,349,500	6,525,200	5,357,800	(1,307,600)	3,865,800	3,418,000	2,717,500
Income Taxes	1,319,600	1,001,800	1,455,700	1,029,000	764,300	923,800	755,300	715,900
Net Income	4,088,600	4,347,700	5,069,500	4,328,800	(2,071,900)	2,953,000	2,662,700	1,979,600
Average Shares	1,117,294	1,113,967	1,105,813	1,098,367	1,094,499	1,090,750	1,087,490	1,092,150
Balance Sheet								
Current Assets	13,038,700	14,248,200	14,840,000	12,486,500	12,453,300	12,256,900	9,694,400	10,795,800
Total Assets	34,398,900	33,659,800	31,001,400	27,460,900	29,212,600	26,787,800	21,955,400	24,580,800
Current Liabilities	8,389,500	8,930,900	7,101,400	6,568,100	13,109,700	5,268,300	5,085,500	5,716,300
Long-Term Obligations	5,519,400	5,464,700	6,770,500	6,634,700	4,615,500	4,593,500	3,494,400	5,763,500
Total Liabilities	19,633,700	20,118,100	18,581,100	17,937,200	22,477,300	13,123,400	10,974,700	13,788,900
Stockholders' Equity	14,765,200	13,541,700	12,420,300	9,523,700	6,735,300	13,664,400	10,980,700	10,791,900
Shares Outstanding	1,143,643	1,157,791	1,152,290	1,149,033	1,136,059	1,134,313	1,131,668	1,130,137
Statistical Record								
Return on Assets %	11.98	13.45	17.34	15.28	N.M.	12.12	11.44	8.01
Return on Equity %	28.81	33.49	46.20	53.25	N.M.	23.96	24.46	18.24
EBITDA Margin %	27.58	25.48	32.10	29.11	N.M.	24.48	25.78	23.21
Net Margin %	18.09	17.90	21.97	19.82	N.M.	15.85	16.97	13.52
Asset Turnover	0.66	0.75	0.79	0.77	0.73	0.76	0.67	0.59
Current Ratio	1.55	1.60	2.09	1.90	0.95	2.33	1.91	1.89
Debt to Equity	0.37	0.40	0.55	0.70	0.69	0.34	0.32	0.53
Price Range	53.81-38.64	41.75-33.63	38.06-32.25	40.57-27.47	57.18-29.91	60.56-49.09	58.86-50.41	60.44-49.76
P/E Ratio	14.70-10.56	10.71-8.62	8.31-7.04	10.30-6.97	...	22.35-18.11	24.02-20.58	33.39-27.49
Average Yield %	4.48	5.32	5.58	5.71	4.12	3.06	2.90	2.76

Address: Lilly Corporate Center, Indianapolis, IN 46285 Telephone: 317-276-2000	Web Site: www.lilly.com Officers: John C. Lechleiter - Chairman, President, Chief Executive Officer, Chief Operating Officer Derica W. Rice - Executive Vice President, Chief Financial Officer	Auditors: Ernst & Young LLP Investor Contact: 800-833-8699 Transfer Agents: Wells Fargo Shareowner Services, St. Paul, MN

LINCOLN NATIONAL CORP.

Exchange	Symbol	Price	52Wk Range	Yield	P/E
NYS	LNC	$32.61 (3/28/2013)	33.47-19.29	1.47	7.15

*7 Year Price Score 60.88   *NYSE Composite Index=100   *12 Month Price Score 112.79

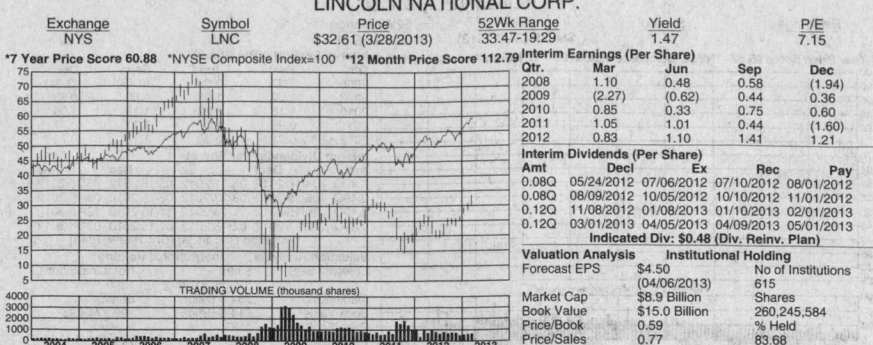

Interim Earnings (Per Share)

Qtr.	Mar	Jun	Sep	Dec
2008	1.10	0.48	0.58	(1.94)
2009	(2.27)	(0.62)	0.44	0.36
2010	0.85	0.33	0.75	0.60
2011	1.05	1.01	0.44	(1.60)
2012	0.83	1.10	1.41	1.21

Interim Dividends (Per Share)

Amt	Decl	Ex	Rec	Pay
0.08Q	05/24/2012	07/06/2012	07/10/2012	08/01/2012
0.08Q	08/09/2012	10/05/2012	10/10/2012	11/01/2012
0.12Q	11/08/2012	01/08/2013	01/10/2013	02/01/2013
0.12Q	03/01/2013	04/05/2013	04/09/2013	05/01/2013

Indicated Div: $0.48 (Div. Reinv. Plan)

Valuation Analysis | **Institutional Holding**

Forecast EPS	$4.50	No of Institutions	
	(04/06/2013)	615	
Market Cap	$8.9 Billion	Shares	
Book Value	$15.0 Billion	260,245,584	
Price/Book	0.59	% Held	
Price/Sales	0.77	83.68	

TRADING VOLUME (thousand shares)

Business Summary: Life & Health (MIC: 5.2.2 SIC: 6311 NAIC: 524113)

Lincoln National is a holding company, which operates multiple insurance and retirement businesses through subsidiary companies. Through its business segments, Co. sells a range of wealth protection, accumulation and retirement income products and services. These products include fixed and indexed annuities, variable annuities, universal life insurance (UL), variable universal life insurance, linked-benefit UL, term life insurance, employer-sponsored retirement plans and services, and group life, disability and dental. As of Dec 31 2011, Co. conducted its operations through four reportable segments: Annuities, Retirement Plan Services, Life Insurance and Group Protection.

Recent Developments: For the year ended Dec 31 2012, income from continuing operations increased 461.6% to US$1.29 billion from US$229.0 million a year earlier. Net income increased 494.1% to US$1.31 billion from US$221.0 million in the prior year. Revenues were US$11.53 billion, up 8.4% from US$10.64 billion the year before. Net premiums earned were US$2.46 billion versus US$2.29 billion in the prior year, an increase of 7.3%. Net investment income rose 1.0% to US$4.70 billion from US$4.65 billion a year ago.

Prospects: Our evaluation of Lincoln National Corp. (ID) as of Apr. 7, 2013 is the result of our systematic analysis on three basic characteristics: earnings strength, relative valuation, and recent stock price movement. The company has managed to produce a neutral trend in earnings per share over the past 5 quarters and while recent estimates for the company have been raised by analysts, LNC has posted better than expected results. Based on operating earnings yield, the company is undervalued when compared to all of the companies in our coverage universe. Share price changes over the past year indicates that LNC will perform in line with the market over the near term.

Financial Data
(US$ in Thousands)

	12/31/2012	12/31/2011	12/31/2010	12/31/2009	12/31/2008	12/31/2007	12/31/2006	12/31/2005
Earnings Per Share	4.56	0.92	2.54	(1.85)	0.22	4.43	5.13	4.72
Cash Flow Per Share	4.51	4.16	5.55	3.35	4.88	7.23	12.08	5.62
Tang Book Value Per Share	46.79	40.82	31.00	26.08	15.76	28.66	27.92	23.89
Dividends Per Share	0.320	0.200	0.040	0.240	1.660	1.580	1.520	1.460
Dividend Payout %	7.02	21.74	1.57	...	754.55	35.67	29.63	30.93
Income Statement								
Premium Income	2,462,000	2,294,000	2,176,000	2,064,000	2,096,000	1,945,000	1,406,000	308,398
Total Revenue	11,532,000	10,636,000	10,407,000	8,499,000	9,883,000	10,594,000	9,063,000	5,487,938
Benefits & Claims	3,538,000	3,345,000	3,330,000	2,836,000	3,157,000	2,698,000	4,170,000	2,365,620
Income Before Taxes	1,568,000	599,000	1,234,000	(521,000)	(25,000)	1,874,000	1,811,000	1,074,644
Income Taxes	282,000	297,000	283,000	(106,000)	(87,000)	553,000	495,000	243,589
Net Income	1,313,000	294,000	980,000	(485,000)	57,000	1,215,000	1,316,000	831,055
Average Shares	287,590	314,950	319,213	285,635	259,390	273,905	256,169	176,144
Balance Sheet								
Total Assets	218,869,000	202,906,000	193,824,000	177,433,000	163,136,000	191,435,000	178,494,000	124,787,566
Total Liabilities	203,896,000	188,742,000	181,018,000	165,733,000	155,159,000	179,717,000	166,293,000	118,403,177
Stockholders' Equity	14,973,000	14,164,000	12,806,000	11,700,000	7,977,000	11,718,000	12,201,000	6,384,389
Shares Outstanding	271,402	291,319	315,718	302,223	255,869	264,233	275,752	174,820
Statistical Record								
Return on Assets %	0.62	0.15	0.53	N.M.	0.03	0.66	0.87	0.69
Return on Equity %	8.99	2.18	8.00	N.M.	0.58	10.16	14.16	13.23
Loss Ratio %	143.70	145.82	153.03	137.40	150.62	138.71	296.59	767.07
Net Margin %	11.39	2.76	9.42	(5.71)	0.58	11.47	14.52	15.14
Price Range	27.29-19.29	32.49-14.32	32.90-20.97	27.84-5.01	58.22-5.07	74.46-56.16	66.46-52.20	53.89-41.95
P/E Ratio	5.98-4.23	35.32-15.57	12.95-8.26	...	264.64-23.05	16.81-12.68	12.96-10.18	11.42-8.89
Average Yield %	1.37	0.80	0.15	1.30	3.87	2.39	2.59	3.04

Address: 150 N. Radnor Chester Road, Suite A305, Radnor, PA 19087
Telephone: 484-583-1400

Web Site: www.lincolnfinancial.com
Officers: Dennis R. Glass - President, Chief Executive Officer Lisa M. Buckingham - Executive Vice President, Senior Vice President, Chief Human Resources Officer

Auditors: Ernst & Young LLP
Investor Contact: 800-237-2920
Transfer Agents: Computershare, South Hackensack, NJ

LINDSAY CORP

Exchange	Symbol	Price	52Wk Range	Yield	P/E	Div Achiever
NYS	LNN	$88.18 (3/28/2013)	94.57-54.66	0.52	18.37	10 Years

*7 Year Price Score 123.47 *NYSE Composite Index=100 *12 Month Price Score 109.99

TRADING VOLUME (thousand shares)

Interim Earnings (Per Share)

Qtr.	Nov	Feb	May	Aug
2009-10	0.53	0.48	0.50	0.48
2010-11	0.34	0.89	1.20	0.46
2011-12	0.23	1.00	1.47	0.68
2012-13	1.15	1.50	...	...

Interim Dividends (Per Share)

Amt	Decl	Ex	Rec	Pay
0.09Q	05/04/2012	05/15/2012	05/17/2012	05/31/2012
0.115Q	07/23/2012	08/15/2012	08/17/2012	08/31/2012
0.115Q	10/03/2012	11/14/2012	11/16/2012	11/30/2012
0.115Q	12/06/2012	02/12/2013	02/14/2013	02/28/2013

Indicated Div: $0.46

Valuation Analysis		Institutional Holding	
Forecast EPS	$5.29 (04/06/2013)	No of Institutions	245
Market Cap	$1.1 Billion	Shares	16,216,706
Book Value	$347.2 Million	% Held	93.72
Price/Book	3.27		
Price/Sales	1.82		

Business Summary: Construction Services (MIC: 7.5.4 SIC: 3523 NAIC: 333111)

Lindsay is engaged in providing a range of proprietary water management and road infrastructure products and services. Co.'s irrigation segment includes the manufacture and marketing of center pivot, lateral move, hose reel irrigation systems, repair and replacement parts, and the design, manufacture and servicing of water pumping stations and controls for the agriculture, golf, landscape and municipal markets. Co.'s infrastructure segment includes the manufacture and marketing of moveable barriers, specialty barriers, crash cushions and end terminals, road marking and road safety equipment, large diameter steel tubing, railroad signals and structures, and outsourced manufacturing services.

Recent Developments: For the quarter ended Feb 28 2013, net income increased 51.5% to US$19.4 million from US$12.8 million in the year-earlier quarter. Revenues were US$175.5 million, up 32.8% from US$132.1 million the year before. Operating income was US$29.4 million versus US$18.9 million in the prior-year quarter, an increase of 55.4%. Direct operating expenses rose 30.9% to US$125.2 million from US$95.6 million in the comparable period the year before. Indirect operating expenses increased 19.2% to US$20.9 million from US$17.5 million in the equivalent prior-year period.

Prospects: Our evaluation of Lindsay Corp. as of Apr. 7, 2013 is the result of our systematic analysis on three basic characteristics: earnings strength, relative valuation, and recent stock price movement. The company has generated a negative trend in earnings per share over the past 5 quarters and while recent estimates for the company have been raised by analysts, LNN has posted better than expected results. Based on operating earnings yield, the company is undervalued when compared to all of the companies in our coverage universe. Share price changes over the past year indicates that LNN will perform very well over the near term.

Financial Data

(US$ in Thousands)	6 Mos	3 Mos	08/31/2012	08/31/2011	08/31/2010	08/31/2009	08/31/2008	08/31/2007
Earnings Per Share	4.80	4.30	3.38	2.90	1.98	1.11	3.20	1.31
Cash Flow Per Share	5.74	4.68	4.12	3.43	1.91	4.68	2.55	0.87
Tang Book Value Per Share	22.81	21.16	20.11	17.05	13.97	12.49	11.52	8.37
Dividends Per Share	0.435	0.410	0.385	0.345	0.325	0.305	0.285	0.265
Dividend Payout %	9.06	9.53	11.39	11.90	16.41	27.48	8.91	20.23
Income Statement								
Total Revenue	322,909	147,370	551,255	478,890	358,440	336,228	475,087	281,857
EBITDA	58,070	25,518	74,696	65,961	46,087	29,235	68,811	29,170
Depn & Amortn	6,240	3,130	9,600	9,000	8,100	7,600	6,400	4,800
Income Before Taxes	51,871	22,383	65,108	56,514	36,782	20,539	61,111	24,133
Income Taxes	17,792	7,655	21,831	19,712	11,920	6,716	21,706	8,513
Net Income	34,079	14,728	43,277	36,802	24,862	13,823	39,405	15,620
Average Shares	12,882	12,853	12,810	12,692	12,585	12,461	12,324	11,964
Balance Sheet								
Current Assets	367,183	327,206	298,865	257,693	208,011	189,529	208,621	149,778
Total Assets	482,482	442,878	415,531	381,144	325,481	307,897	326,877	242,205
Current Liabilities	111,518	93,017	80,438	79,319	67,082	59,187	82,447	51,502
Long-Term Obligations	...	...	...	4,285	8,571	19,454	25,625	31,796
Total Liabilities	135,325	116,805	104,693	105,479	95,874	100,239	130,976	101,177
Stockholders' Equity	347,157	326,073	310,838	275,665	229,607	207,658	195,901	141,028
Shares Outstanding	12,855	12,833	12,723	12,676	12,486	12,365	12,211	11,746
Statistical Record								
Return on Assets %	14.08	13.32	10.83	10.42	7.85	4.36	13.81	7.19
Return on Equity %	19.41	18.36	14.72	14.57	11.37	6.85	23.33	11.93
EBITDA Margin %	17.98	17.32	13.55	13.77	12.86	8.69	14.48	10.35
Net Margin %	10.55	9.99	7.85	7.68	6.94	4.11	8.29	5.54
Asset Turnover	1.42	1.40	1.38	1.36	1.13	1.06	1.67	1.30
Current Ratio	3.29	3.52	3.72	3.25	3.10	3.20	2.53	2.91
Debt to Equity	...	...	...	0.02	0.04	0.09	0.13	0.23
Price Range	94.57-54.66	79.57-49.82	73.84-49.53	79.19-36.87	45.94-31.44	85.60-22.12	129.15-39.68	47.88-28.16
P/E Ratio	19.70-11.39	18.50-11.59	21.85-14.65	27.31-12.71	23.20-15.88	77.12-19.93	40.36-12.40	36.55-21.50
Average Yield %	0.61	0.63	0.63	0.55	0.86	0.78	0.37	0.77

Address: 2222 North 111th Street, Omaha, NE 68164	Web Site: www.lindsay.com	Auditors: KPMG LLP
Telephone: 402-829-6800	Officers: Michael N. Christodolou - Chairman Richard W. Parod - President, Chief Executive Officer	Investor Contact: 402-827-6579 Transfer Agents: Wells Fargo Shareowner Services, St. Paul, MN

LINKEDIN CORP

Exchange	Symbol	Price	52Wk Range	Yield	P/E
NYS	LNKD	$176.06 (3/28/2013)	181.48-91.09	N/A	926.63

*7 Year Price Score N/A   *NYSE Composite Index=100   *12 Month Price Score 127.19

TRADING VOLUME (thousand shares)

Interim Earnings (Per Share)

Qtr.	Mar	Jun	Sep	Dec
2010	0.00	0.02	0.02	0.03
2011	0.00	0.04	(0.02)	0.06
2012	0.04	0.03	0.02	0.10

Interim Dividends (Per Share)

No Dividends Paid

Valuation Analysis		Institutional Holding	
Forecast EPS	$1.33	No of Institutions	
	(04/06/2013)	386	
Market Cap	$19.1 Billion	Shares	
Book Value	$908.4 Million	81,888,416	
Price/Book	21.06	% Held	
Price/Sales	19.67	N/A	

Business Summary: Internet & Software (MIC: 6.3.2 SIC: 7371 NAIC: 541511)

LinkedIn is engaged in operating an online professional network on the Internet. Through Co.'s proprietary platform, members are able to create, manage and share their professional identity online, build and engage with their professional network, access shared information, and find business opportunities. Co.'s platform provides members with applications and tools to search, connect and communicate with business contacts, learn about career opportunities, join industry groups, research organizations and share information. Co.'s members create profiles that serve as their professional profiles and are accessible by any other member, as well as anyone with an Internet connection.

Recent Developments: For the year ended Dec 31 2012, net income increased 81.4% to US$21.6 million from US$11.9 million in the prior year. Revenues were US$972.3 million, up 86.2% from US$522.2 million the year before. Operating income was US$56.9 million versus US$25.8 million in the prior year, an increase of 120.0%. Direct operating expenses rose 54.1% to US$125.5 million from US$81.4 million in the comparable period the year before. Indirect operating expenses increased 90.4% to US$789.9 million from US$414.9 million in the equivalent prior-year period.

Prospects: Our evaluation of LinkedIn Corp as of Apr. 7, 2013 is the result of our systematic analysis on three basic characteristics: earnings strength, relative valuation, and recent stock price movement. The company has enjoyed a very positive trend in earnings per share over the past 5 quarters and while recent estimates for the company have been raised by analysts, LNKD has posted better than expected results. Based on operating earnings yield, the company is overvalued when compared to all of the companies in our coverage universe. Share price changes over the past year indicates that LNKD will perform well over the near term.

Financial Data

(US$ in Thousands)	12/31/2012	12/31/2011	12/31/2010	12/31/2009	12/31/2008
Earnings Per Share	0.19	0.11	0.07	(0.10)	(0.11)
Cash Flow Per Share	2.53	1.73	1.28	0.52	...
Tang Book Value Per Share	7.00	5.96	2.38	1.95	...
Income Statement					
Total Revenue	972,309	522,189	243,099	120,127	78,773
EBITDA	126,089	62,273	37,499	8,170	792
Depn & Amortn	70,000	39,500	18,597	11,645	6,243
Income Before Taxes	57,114	22,942	18,966	(3,125)	(4,232)
Income Taxes	35,504	11,030	3,581	848	290
Net Income	21,610	11,912	15,385	(3,973)	(4,522)
Average Shares	112,844	104,118	46,459	41,184	42,389
Balance Sheet					
Current Assets	1,018,797	725,927	172,206	121,158	...
Total Assets	1,382,330	873,697	238,188	148,559	...
Current Liabilities	415,379	226,659	105,472	49,273	...
Total Liabilities	473,906	248,718	113,958	51,496	...
Stockholders' Equity	908,424	624,979	124,230	97,063	...
Shares Outstanding	108,647	101,480	43,308	41,745	41,913
Statistical Record					
Return on Assets %	1.91	2.14	7.96	...	...
Return on Equity %	2.81	3.18	13.90	...	...
EBITDA Margin %	12.97	11.93	15.43	6.80	1.01
Net Margin %	2.22	2.28	6.33	N.M.	N.M.
Asset Turnover	0.86	0.94	1.26	...	...
Current Ratio	2.45	3.20	1.63	2.46	...
Price Range	123.23-61.79	109.97-59.07	...	...	...
P/E Ratio	648.58-325.21	999.73-537.00	...	...	...

Address: 2029 Stierlin Court, Mountain View, CA 94043 Telephone: 650-687-3600	Web Site: www.linkedin.com Officers: Reid G. Hoffman - Chairman Jeffrey Weiner - Chief Executive Officer	Auditors: Deloitte & Touche LLP Transfer Agents: Computershare Trust Company, N.A., Canton, MA

LIVE NATION ENTERTAINMENT, INC.

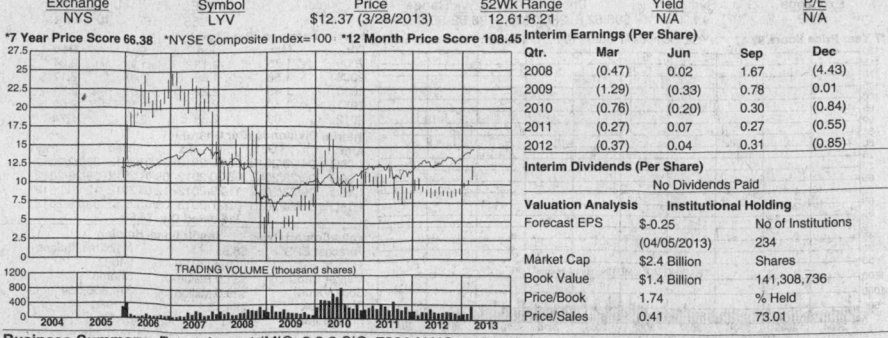

Exchange	Symbol	Price	52Wk Range	Yield		P/E
NYS	LYV	$12.37 (3/28/2013)	12.61-8.21	N/A		N/A

*7 Year Price Score 66.38 *NYSE Composite Index=100 *12 Month Price Score 108.45

Interim Earnings (Per Share)

Qtr.	Mar	Jun	Sep	Dec
2008	(0.47)	0.02	1.67	(4.43)
2009	(1.29)	(0.33)	0.78	0.01
2010	(0.76)	(0.20)	0.30	(0.84)
2011	(0.27)	0.07	0.27	(0.55)
2012	(0.37)	0.04	0.31	(0.85)

Interim Dividends (Per Share)

No Dividends Paid

Valuation Analysis | **Institutional Holding**

Forecast EPS	$-0.25	No of Institutions	
	(04/05/2013)	234	
Market Cap	$2.4 Billion	Shares	
Book Value	$1.4 Billion	141,308,736	
Price/Book	1.74	% Held	
Price/Sales	0.41	73.01	

Business Summary: Entertainment (MIC: 2.3.2 SIC: 7996 NAIC: 713110)

Live Nation Entertainment is engaged as a live entertainment and ticketing sales and marketing company. In addition, Co. operates artist management companies through its Front Line Management Group, Inc. subsidiary, and produces live music concerts. Co. owns, operates, has booking rights for and/or has an equity interest in 133 venues, including House of Blues® music venues and locations such as The Fillmore in San Francisco, the Hollywood Palladium, the Heineken Music Hall in Amsterdam and the O2 Dublin. As of Dec 31 2011, Co. conducted its businesses through five reportable segments: Concerts, Ticketing, Artist Nation, eCommerce and Sponsorship.

Recent Developments: For the year ended Dec 31 2012, loss from continuing operations was US$161.9 million compared with a loss of US$70.4 million a year earlier. Net loss amounted to US$161.9 million versus a net loss of US$70.4 million in the prior year. Revenues were US$5.82 billion, up 8.1% from US$5.38 billion the year before. Operating loss was US$21.6 million versus an income of US$18.3 million in the prior year. Direct operating expenses rose 9.5% to US$4.15 billion from US$3.79 billion in the comparable period the year before. Indirect operating expenses increased 7.2% to US$1.69 billion from US$1.58 billion in the equivalent prior-year period.

Prospects: Our evaluation of Live Nation Entertainment, Inc. as of Apr. 7, 2013 is the result of our systematic analysis on three basic characteristics: earnings strength, relative valuation, and recent stock price movement. The company has suffered a very negative trend in earnings per share over the past 5 quarters. Because the company lacks sufficient analyst estimate data, we place greater weight on the historical EPS trend as the measure of earnings strength. Based on operating earnings yield, the company is overvalued when compared to all of the companies in our coverage universe. Share price changes over the past year indicates that LYV will perform poorly over the near term.

Financial Data

(US$ in Thousands)	12/31/2012	12/31/2011	12/31/2010	12/31/2009	12/31/2008	12/31/2007	12/31/2006	12/31/2005
Earnings Per Share	(0.87)	(0.46)	(1.39)	(0.73)	(3.04)	(0.17)	(0.48)	(1.96)
Cash Flow Per Share	1.96	0.74	0.96	0.69	(0.69)	0.73	0.26	0.21
Tang Book Value Per Share	N.M.	N.M.	N.M.	0.20	N.M.	0.70	2.78	8.03
Income Statement								
Total Revenue	5,819,047	5,383,998	5,063,748	4,181,021	4,166,838	4,184,981	3,691,559	2,936,845
EBITDA	102,081	141,007	54,747	110,337	(135,910)	202,983	159,651	50,993
Depn & Amortn	124,593	129,177	135,573	162,694	148,222	120,828	128,167	64,622
Income Before Taxes	(142,082)	(104,369)	(193,582)	(116,329)	(336,963)	34,719	6,712	(63,619)
Income Taxes	29,736	(26,224)	15,154	11,333	(15,925)	43,592	37,210	61,488
Net Income	(163,227)	(83,016)	(228,390)	(60,179)	(231,765)	(11,936)	(31,442)	(130,619)
Average Shares	186,955	182,388	164,410	82,652	76,228	68,440	64,853	66,809
Balance Sheet								
Current Assets	1,812,812	1,576,790	1,603,497	717,866	639,818	834,408	738,109	755,692
Total Assets	5,290,806	5,087,771	5,195,560	2,341,759	2,478,657	2,752,103	2,225,002	1,776,584
Current Liabilities	1,768,172	1,492,553	1,474,221	752,234	771,237	905,470	773,960	701,620
Long-Term Obligations	1,677,955	1,663,056	1,677,714	699,037	837,076	786,261	607,425	341,136
Total Liabilities	3,935,388	3,626,668	3,831,144	1,649,442	1,816,395	1,845,037	1,546,340	1,099,884
Stockholders' Equity	1,355,418	1,461,103	1,364,416	692,317	662,262	907,066	678,662	676,700
Shares Outstanding	190,853	188,957	174,147	84,448	78,022	74,893	65,477	65,668
Statistical Record								
EBITDA Margin %	1.75	2.62	1.08	2.64	N.M.	4.85	4.32	1.74
Asset Turnover	1.12	1.05	1.34	1.73	1.59	1.68	1.85	1.80
Current Ratio	1.03	1.06	1.09	0.95	0.83	0.92	0.95	1.08
Debt to Equity	1.24	1.14	1.23	1.01	1.26	0.87	0.90	0.50
Price Range	10.88-8.21	12.26-7.33	16.70-8.43	8.90-2.52	17.48-3.06	25.05-12.56	24.58-12.93	13.30-10.55

Address: 9348 Civic Center Drive, Beverly Hills, CA 90210 **Telephone:** 310-867-7000	**Web Site:** www.livenation.com **Officers:** Irving L. Azoff - Executive Chairman Michael Rapino - President, Chief Executive Officer	**Auditors:** Ernst & Young LLP **Investor Contact:** 310-867-7000 **Transfer Agents:** Computershare

LOCKHEED MARTIN CORP.

Exchange	Symbol	Price	52Wk Range	Yield	P/E	Div Achiever
NYS	LMT	$96.52 (3/28/2013)	96.52-80.82	4.77	11.55	10 Years

*7 Year Price Score 92.47   *NYSE Composite Index=100   *12 Month Price Score 91.97

TRADING VOLUME (thousand shares)

Interim Earnings (Per Share)

Qtr.	Mar	Jun	Sep	Dec
2008	1.75	2.15	1.92	2.04
2009	1.68	1.88	2.07	2.17
2010	1.45	2.22	1.57	2.71
2011	1.50	2.14	2.10	2.08
2012	2.03	2.38	2.21	1.74

Interim Dividends (Per Share)

Amt	Decl	Ex	Rec	Pay
1.00Q	04/26/2012	05/30/2012	06/01/2012	06/22/2012
1.00Q	06/28/2012	08/30/2012	09/04/2012	09/28/2012
1.15Q	09/27/2012	11/29/2012	12/03/2012	12/28/2012
1.15Q	01/24/2013	02/27/2013	03/01/2013	03/29/2013

Indicated Div: $4.60

Valuation Analysis

Forecast EPS	$8.95 (04/05/2013)
Market Cap	$31.0 Billion
Book Value	$39.0 Million
Price/Book	794.43
Price/Sales	0.66

Institutional Holding

No of Institutions	946
Shares	314,856,064
% Held	87.59

Business Summary: Defense (MIC: 7.1.2 SIC: 3761 NAIC: 336414)

Lockheed Martin is a security and aerospace company. Co. has five segments: Aeronautics, which researches, designs, develops, manufactures, integrates, sustains, supports, and upgrades military aircraft; Information Systems & Global Solutions, which provides management services, information technology applications, and technology systems; Missiles and Fire Control, which provides air and missile defense systems, tactical missiles and air-to-ground precision strike weapon systems; Mission Systems and Training, which provides surface ship and submarine combat systems; and Space Systems, which provides satellites, defensive missile systems, and space transportation systems.

Recent Developments: For the year ended Dec 31 2012, income from continuing operations increased 2.9% to US$2.75 billion from US$2.67 billion a year earlier. Net income increased 3.4% to US$2.75 billion from US$2.66 billion in the prior year. Revenues were US$47.18 billion, up 1.5% from US$46.50 billion the year before. Operating income was US$4.43 billion versus US$4.02 billion in the prior year, an increase of 10.3%. Direct operating expenses rose 0.5% to US$42.99 billion from US$42.76 billion in the comparable period the year before. Indirect operating income amounted to US$238.0 million compared with an income of US$276.0 million in the equivalent prior-year period.

Prospects: Our evaluation of Lockheed Martin Corp. as of Apr. 7, 2013 is the result of our systematic analysis on three basic characteristics: earnings strength, relative valuation, and recent stock price movement. The company has generated a negative trend in earnings per share over the past 5 quarters. However, while recent estimates for the company have been lowered by analysts, LMT has posted better than expected results. Based on operating earnings yield, the company is undervalued when compared to all of the companies in our coverage universe. Share price changes over the past year indicates that LMT will perform poorly over the near term.

Financial Data
(US$ in Millions)

	12/31/2012	12/31/2011	12/31/2010	12/31/2009	12/31/2008	12/31/2007	12/31/2006	12/31/2005
Earnings Per Share	8.36	7.81	7.94	7.78	7.86	7.10	5.80	4.10
Cash Flow Per Share	4.81	12.66	9.74	8.25	11.03	10.19	8.84	7.25
Dividends Per Share	4.150	3.250	2.640	2.340	1.830	1.470	1.250	1.050
Dividend Payout %	49.64	41.61	33.25	30.08	23.28	20.70	21.55	25.61
Income Statement								
Total Revenue	47,182	46,499	45,803	45,189	42,731	41,862	39,620	37,213
EBITDA	5,443	4,993	4,189	4,288	4,960	4,477	3,788	2,885
Depn & Amortn	988	1,008	92	104	118	153	164	150
Income Before Taxes	4,072	3,631	3,826	4,002	4,413	4,165	3,462	2,508
Income Taxes	1,327	964	1,181	1,260	1,485	1,335	1,063	791
Net Income	2,745	2,655	2,926	3,024	3,217	3,033	2,529	1,825
Average Shares	328	339	368	388	409	427	436	445
Balance Sheet								
Current Assets	13,855	14,094	12,851	12,477	10,683	10,940	10,164	10,529
Total Assets	38,657	37,908	35,067	35,111	33,439	28,926	28,231	27,744
Current Liabilities	12,155	12,130	11,157	10,703	10,542	9,871	9,553	9,428
Long-Term Obligations	6,158	6,460	5,019	5,052	3,563	4,303	4,405	4,784
Total Liabilities	38,618	36,907	31,359	30,982	30,574	19,121	21,347	19,877
Stockholders' Equity	39	1,001	3,708	4,129	2,865	9,805	6,884	7,867
Shares Outstanding	321	321	346	373	393	409	421	432
Statistical Record								
Return on Assets %	7.15	7.28	8.34	8.82	10.29	10.61	9.04	6.85
Return on Equity %	526.44	112.76	74.67	86.47	50.64	36.35	34.29	24.52
EBITDA Margin %	11.54	10.74	9.15	9.49	11.61	10.69	9.56	7.75
Net Margin %	5.82	5.71	6.39	6.69	7.53	7.25	6.38	4.90
Asset Turnover	1.23	1.27	1.31	1.32	1.37	1.46	1.42	1.40
Current Ratio	1.14	1.16	1.15	1.17	1.01	1.11	1.06	1.12
Debt to Equity	157.90	6.45	1.35	1.22	1.24	0.44	0.64	0.61
Price Range	94.87-79.98	82.27-66.87	86.92-68.04	86.17-58.18	119.59-67.97	112.25-91.36	92.95-63.55	65.40-53.29
P/E Ratio	11.35-9.57	10.53-8.56	10.95-8.57	11.08-7.48	15.22-8.65	15.81-12.87	16.03-10.96	15.95-13.00
Average Yield %	4.67	4.21	3.49	3.07	1.83	1.46	1.59	1.71

Address: 6801 Rockledge Drive, Bethesda, MD 20817 **Telephone:** 301-897-6000	**Web Site:** www.lockheedmartin.com **Officers:** Robert J. Stevens - Executive Chairman, Chairman, Chief Executive Officer Marillyn A. Hewson - President, Chief Executive Officer, Chief Operating Officer, Executive Vice President	**Auditors:** Ernst & Young LLP **Investor Contact:** 301-897-6584 **Transfer Agents:** Computershare Trust Company, N.A, Providence, RI

LOEWS CORP.

Exchange	Symbol	Price	52Wk Range	Yield	P/E
NYS	L	$44.07 (3/28/2013)	44.64-38.30	0.57	30.82

*7 Year Price Score 94.22 *NYSE Composite Index=100 *12 Month Price Score 96.98

Interim Earnings (Per Share)

Qtr.	Mar	Jun	Sep	Dec
2008	1.05	9.54	(0.31)	(1.67)
2009	(1.49)	0.78	1.08	0.93
2010	0.99	0.87	0.09	-1.11
2011	0.92	0.62	0.40	0.68
2012	0.92	0.14	0.45	(0.08)

Interim Dividends (Per Share)

Amt	Decl	Ex	Rec	Pay
0.063Q	05/08/2012	05/30/2012	06/01/2012	06/14/2012
0.063Q	08/14/2012	08/29/2012	08/31/2012	09/14/2012
0.063Q	11/13/2012	11/28/2012	11/30/2012	12/14/2012
0.063Q	02/12/2013	03/06/2013	03/08/2013	03/15/2013

Indicated Div: $0.25

Valuation Analysis | **Institutional Holding**

Forecast EPS	$3.34 (04/06/2013)	No of Institutions: 547
Market Cap	$17.3 Billion	Shares
Book Value	$19.5 Billion	275,542,400
Price/Book	0.89	% Held
Price/Sales	1.19	56.67

Business Summary: General Insurance (MIC: 5.2.1 SIC: 6331 NAIC: 524126)

Loews is a holding company. Co. is engaged in commercial property and casualty insurance through its 90.0%-owned subsidiary, CNA Financial Corporation; the operation of offshore oil and gas drilling rigs through its 50.4% owned subsidiary, Diamond Offshore Drilling, Inc.; the transportation and storage of natural gas and natural gas liquids and gathering and processing of natural gas through its 55.0% owned subsidiary, Boardwalk Pipeline Partners, LP; the exploration, production and marketing of natural gas and oil through its wholly owned subsidiary, HighMount Exploration & Production LLC; and the operation of hotels through its wholly owned subsidiary, Loews Hotels Holding Corporation.

Recent Developments: For the year ended Dec 31 2012, income from continuing operations decreased 34.5% to US$1.11 billion from US$1.69 billion a year earlier. Net income decreased 34.5% to US$1.11 billion from US$1.69 billion in the prior year. Revenues were US$14.55 billion, up 3.0% from US$14.13 billion the year before. Net premiums earned were US$6.88 billion versus US$6.60 billion in the prior year, an increase of 4.2%. Net investment income rose 13.9% to US$2.35 billion from US$2.06 billion a year ago.

Prospects: Our evaluation of Loews Corp. as of Apr. 7, 2013 is the result of our systematic analysis on three basic characteristics: earnings strength, relative valuation, and recent stock price movement. The company has generated a negative trend in earnings per share over the past 5 quarters and while recent estimates for the company have remained steady, L has posted better than expected results. Based on operating earnings yield, the company is about fairly valued when compared to all of the companies in our coverage universe. Share price changes over the past year indicates that L will perform in line with the market over the near term.

Financial Data

(US$ in Thousands)	12/31/2012	12/31/2011	12/31/2010	12/31/2009	12/31/2008	12/31/2007	12/31/2006	12/31/2005
Earnings Per Share	1.43	2.63	3.07	1.30	9.05	3.65	3.75	1.72
Cash Flow Per Share	7.20	9.80	(0.11)	10.61	7.04	10.60	3.10	6.04
Tang Book Value Per Share	47.12	45.25	42.44	37.74	28.16	30.66	29.77	22.95
Dividends Per Share	0.250	0.250	0.250	0.250	0.250	0.250	0.237	0.200
Dividend Payout %	17.48	9.51	8.14	19.23	2.76	6.85	6.33	11.63
Income Statement								
Premium Income	6,882,000	6,603,000	6,515,000	6,721,000	7,150,000	7,482,000	7,603,100	7,568,600
Total Revenue	14,552,000	14,127,000	14,615,000	14,117,000	13,247,000	18,380,000	17,911,000	16,017,800
Benefits & Claims	5,896,000	5,489,000	4,985,000	5,290,000	5,723,000	6,009,000	6,046,200	6,998,700
Income Before Taxes	1,399,000	2,232,000	2,902,000	1,730,000	587,000	4,575,000	4,472,100	1,846,500
Income Taxes	289,000	536,000	895,000	345,000	7,000	1,481,000	1,450,700	490,400
Net Income	568,000	1,064,000	1,288,000	564,000	4,530,000	2,489,000	2,491,300	1,211,600
Average Shares	395,870	405,320	419,520	432,810	477,230	536,000	553,540	557,970
Balance Sheet								
Total Assets	80,021,000	75,375,000	76,277,000	74,070,000	69,857,000	76,079,000	76,880,900	70,675,600
Total Liabilities	60,562,000	56,540,000	57,827,000	57,171,000	56,731,000	58,488,000	60,379,100	57,583,500
Stockholders' Equity	19,459,000	18,835,000	18,450,000	16,899,000	13,126,000	17,591,000	16,501,800	13,092,100
Shares Outstanding	391,805	396,200	414,546	425,070	435,091	529,683	544,203	557,540
Statistical Record								
Return on Assets %	0.73	1.40	1.71	0.78	6.19	3.25	3.38	1.68
Return on Equity %	2.96	5.71	7.29	3.76	29.41	14.60	16.84	9.59
Loss Ratio %	85.67	83.13	76.52	78.71	80.04	80.31	79.52	92.47
Net Margin %	3.90	7.53	8.81	4.00	34.20	13.54	13.91	7.56
Price Range	43.17-37.31	44.26-33.50	40.08-31.12	36.65-18.02	50.72-20.07	53.01-40.37	41.92-30.75	32.60-22.46
P/E Ratio	30.19-26.09	16.83-12.74	13.06-10.14	28.19-13.86	5.60-2.22	14.52-11.06	11.18-8.20	18.95-13.06
Average Yield %	0.62	0.63	0.68	0.86	0.62	0.53	0.66	0.74

Address: 667 Madison Avenue, New York, NY 10065-8087 **Telephone:** 212-521-2000	**Web Site:** www.loews.com **Officers:** Jonathan M. Tisch - Co-Chairman Andrew H. Tisch - Co-Chairman	**Auditors:** Deloitte & Touche LLP **Investor Contact:** 212-521-2788 **Transfer Agents:** Computershare Shareowner Services, Jersey City, NJ

LORILLARD, INC.

Exchange	Symbol	Price	52Wk Range	Yield	P/E
NYS	LO	$40.35 (3/28/2013)	46.55-37.23	5.45	14.36

*7 Year Price Score 129.00 *NYSE Composite Index=100 *12 Month Price Score 89.70

Interim Earnings (Per Share)

Qtr.	Mar	Jun	Sep	Dec
2008	0.33	0.42	0.46	0.51
2009	0.36	0.57	0.48	0.51
2010	0.50	0.58	0.60	0.58
2011	0.57	0.68	0.65	0.77
2012	0.57	0.72	0.72	0.80

Interim Dividends (Per Share)

Amt	Decl	Ex	Rec	Pay
0.517Q	08/15/2012	08/29/2012	08/31/2012	09/10/2012
0.517Q	10/31/2012	11/28/2012	11/30/2012	12/10/2012
3-for-1	11/13/2012	01/16/2013	12/14/2012	01/15/2013
0.55Q	02/13/2013	02/27/2013	03/01/2013	03/11/2013

Indicated Div: $2.20

Valuation Analysis | **Institutional Holding**

Forecast EPS	$3.09	No of Institutions
	(04/05/2013)	580
Market Cap	$15.4 Billion	Shares
Book Value	N/A	139,148,848
Price/Book	N/A	% Held
Price/Sales	2.33	N/A

TRADING VOLUME (thousand shares)

Business Summary: Tobacco Products (MIC: 1.3.1 SIC: 2111 NAIC: 312221)

Lorillard is a manufacturer of cigarettes. Newport, Co.'s main cigarette brand, includes both menthol and non-menthol product offerings. In addition to the Newport brand, Co.'s product line has four additional brand families marketed under the Kent, True, Maverick, and Old Gold brand names. As of Dec 31 2012, these five brands included 39 different product offerings. Co., through its LOEC, Inc. subsidiary, is also an electronic cigarette company, which markets its products under the blu eCigs brand. Co. sells its products primarily to wholesale distributors, who in turn service retail outlets, chain store organizations, and government agencies, including the U.S. Armed Forces.

Recent Developments: For the year ended Dec 31 2012, net income decreased 1.5% to US$1.10 billion from US$1.12 billion in the prior year. Revenues were US$6.62 billion, up 2.4% from US$6.47 billion the year before. Operating income was US$1.88 billion versus US$1.89 billion in the prior year, a decrease of 0.7%. Direct operating expenses rose 2.9% to US$4.24 billion from US$4.12 billion in the comparable period the year before. Indirect operating expenses increased 11.8% to US$504.0 million from US$451.0 million in the equivalent prior-year period.

Prospects: Our evaluation of Lorillard Inc. as of Apr. 7, 2013 is the result of our systematic analysis on three basic characteristics: earnings strength, relative valuation, and recent stock price movement. The company has produced a positive trend in earnings per share over the past 5 quarters and while recent estimates for the company have been mixed, LO has posted better than expected results. Based on operating earnings yield, the company is undervalued when compared to all of the companies in our coverage universe. Share price changes over the past year indicates that LO will perform very poorly over the near term.

Financial Data
(US$ in Millions)

	12/31/2012	12/31/2011	12/31/2010	12/31/2009	12/31/2008	12/31/2007	12/31/2006	12/31/2005
Earnings Per Share	2.81	2.66	2.26	1.92	1.72	1.72	1.58	1.35
Cash Flow Per Share	3.00	2.83	2.40	2.10	1.89	1.69	1.49	...
Tang Book Value Per Share	...	...	...	0.19	1.25	1.94	2.48	...
Dividends Per Share	2.067	1.733	1.417	1.280	0.613	...	...	...
Dividend Payout %	73.55	65.08	62.68	66.67	35.73	...	...	...
Income Statement								
Total Revenue	6,623	6,466	5,932	5,233	4,204	3,969	3,755	3,568
EBITDA	1,921	1,932	1,764	1,578	1,446	1,317	1,287	1,129
Depn & Amortn	39	37	35	32	32	40	47	48
Income Before Taxes	1,728	1,770	1,635	1,519	1,435	1,349	1,318	1,135
Income Taxes	629	654	606	571	547	485	518	445
Net Income	1,099	1,116	1,029	948	887	898	826	706
Average Shares	390	418	455	493	516	521	521	521
Balance Sheet								
Current Assets	2,777	2,564	2,935	2,181	1,962	2,103	2,115	...
Total Assets	3,396	3,008	3,296	2,575	2,321	2,600	2,759	...
Current Liabilities	1,601	1,485	1,426	1,337	1,273	1,188	1,151	...
Long-Term Obligations	3,111	2,595	1,769	722	...	...	...	...
Total Liabilities	5,173	4,521	3,521	2,488	1,690	1,587	1,464	...
Stockholders' Equity	(1,777)	(1,513)	(225)	87	631	1,013	1,295	...
Shares Outstanding	382	396	441	468	504	522	522	521
Statistical Record								
Return on Assets %	34.23	35.41	35.05	38.73	35.95	33.51	...	...
Return on Equity %	...	...	...	264.07	107.61	77.82	...	...
EBITDA Margin %	29.00	29.88	29.74	30.15	34.40	33.18	34.27	31.64
Net Margin %	16.59	17.26	17.35	18.12	21.10	22.63	22.00	19.79
Asset Turnover	2.06	2.05	2.02	2.14	1.70	1.48	...	...
Current Ratio	1.73	1.73	2.06	1.63	1.54	1.77	1.84	...
Debt to Equity	...	...	...	8.30	...	...	...	...
Price Range	46.55-35.80	39.49-24.73	29.74-23.71	27.14-17.93	29.47-18.40	29.76-21.40	21.57-14.65	14.66-9.58
P/E Ratio	16.56-12.74	14.85-9.30	13.16-10.49	14.13-9.34	17.14-10.70	17.30-12.44	13.65-9.27	10.86-7.10
Average Yield %	5.00	5.12	5.43	5.53	2.63	...	...	...

Address: 714 Green Valley Road, Greensboro, NC 27408-7018
Telephone: 336-335-7000

Web Site: www.lorillard.com
Officers: Murray S. Kessler - Chairman, President, Chief Executive Officer David H. Taylor - Executive Vice President, Chief Financial Officer

Auditors: Deloitte & Touche LLP
Investor Contact: 336-335-7000
Transfer Agents: Mellon Investor Services LLC, South Hackensack, NJ

464

LOUISIANA-PACIFIC CORP.

Exchange	Symbol	Price	52Wk Range	Yield	P/E
NYS	LPX	$21.60 (3/28/2013)	22.18-8.04	N/A	108.00

*7 Year Price Score 110.58 *NYSE Composite Index=100 *12 Month Price Score 133.83

Interim Earnings (Per Share)

Qtr.	Mar	Jun	Sep	Dec
2008	(0.45)	(0.79)	(1.08)	(3.30)
2009	(0.30)	(0.28)	(0.12)	(0.42)
2010	(0.18)	0.16	(0.24)	(0.05)
2011	(0.18)	(0.27)	(0.49)	(0.42)
2012	(0.08)	(0.27)	0.22	0.33

Interim Dividends (Per Share)

Dividend Payment Suspended

Valuation Analysis | **Institutional Holding**

Forecast EPS	$1.30	No of Institutions
	(04/05/2013)	313
Market Cap	$3.0 Billion	Shares
Book Value	$1.0 Billion	142,496,816
Price/Book	2.89	% Held
Price/Sales	1.74	96.13

Business Summary: Paper & Forest Products (MIC: 8.1.2 SIC: 2493 NAIC: 321219)

Louisiana-Pacific is a manufacturer of building products. Co. provides building products to retail, wholesale, home building and industrial customers for home construction, repair and remodeling, and manufactured housing. Co. has four segments: North America oriented strand board (OSB), which manufactures and distributes OSB structural panel products; siding, which includes Smart Side® siding products, Canexel siding products, and other related products; engineered wood products, which includes laminated veneer lumber and laminated strand lumber, I-joists, plywood, and other related products; and South America, which includes products produced and or sold in South America.

Recent Developments: For the year ended Dec 31 2012, income from continuing operations was US$32.1 million compared with a loss of US$171.9 million a year earlier. Net income amounted to US$28.8 million versus a net loss of US$181.1 million in the prior year. Revenues were US$1.72 billion, up 26.4% from US$1.36 billion the year before. Operating income was US$107.4 million versus a loss of US$140.1 million in the prior year. Direct operating expenses rose 12.8% to US$1.40 billion from US$1.24 billion in the comparable period the year before. Indirect operating expenses decreased 18.8% to US$205.3 million from US$252.8 million in the equivalent prior-year period.

Prospects: Our evaluation of Louisiana-Pacific Corp. as of Apr. 7, 2013 is the result of our systematic analysis on three basic characteristics: earnings strength, relative valuation, and recent stock price movement. The company has produced a positive trend in earnings per share over the past 5 quarters and while recent estimates for the company have been raised by analysts, LPX has posted results that fell short of analysts expectations. Based on operating earnings yield, the company is about fairly valued when compared to all of the companies in our coverage universe. Share price changes over the past year indicates that LPX will perform very well over the near term.

Financial Data

(US$ in Thousands)	12/31/2012	12/31/2011	12/31/2010	12/31/2009	12/31/2008	12/31/2007	12/31/2006	12/31/2005
Earnings Per Share	0.20	(1.36)	(0.30)	(1.12)	(5.62)	(1.73)	1.17	4.15
Cash Flow Per Share	0.81	(0.30)	0.37	0.56	(1.38)	(0.09)	1.75	4.72
Tang Book Value Per Share	7.46	7.29	9.21	9.85	11.41	15.00	17.18	16.66
Dividends Per Share	...	...	...	...	0.300	0.600	0.600	0.475
Dividend Payout %	...	...	...	...	...	...	51.28	11.45
Income Statement								
Total Revenue	1,715,800	1,356,900	1,383,600	1,054,700	1,376,200	1,704,900	2,235,100	2,598,900
EBITDA	161,200	(48,300)	98,000	(17,800)	(603,800)	(125,500)	331,400	654,800
Depn & Amortn	73,900	78,900	82,000	80,000	100,400	109,800	128,000	135,100
Income Before Taxes	38,000	(184,100)	(47,900)	(169,400)	(753,300)	(270,600)	154,000	536,400
Income Taxes	7,600	(39,100)	(22,100)	(63,400)	(202,000)	(133,400)	24,200	61,300
Net Income	28,800	(181,300)	(39,000)	(121,400)	(578,800)	(179,900)	123,700	455,500
Average Shares	142,600	133,200	129,100	108,500	102,900	103,700	105,500	109,700
Balance Sheet								
Current Assets	995,600	656,800	713,600	838,800	502,700	1,075,900	1,504,000	1,797,200
Total Assets	2,331,000	2,139,900	2,410,600	2,247,400	2,188,700	3,229,300	3,436,400	3,598,000
Current Liabilities	239,300	139,500	135,000	306,900	165,900	488,600	264,900	346,100
Long-Term Obligations	782,700	715,900	714,500	337,600	472,600	485,800	644,600	734,800
Total Liabilities	1,297,200	1,139,000	1,192,800	997,900	1,006,400	1,409,800	1,369,000	1,555,100
Stockholders' Equity	1,033,800	1,000,900	1,217,800	1,249,500	1,182,300	1,819,500	2,067,400	2,042,900
Shares Outstanding	138,534	137,139	131,946	126,571	103,291	103,081	104,229	105,780
Statistical Record								
Return on Assets %	1.28	N.M.	N.M.	N.M.	N.M.	N.M.	3.52	12.92
Return on Equity %	2.82	N.M.	N.M.	N.M.	N.M.	N.M.	6.02	23.91
EBITDA Margin %	9.40	N.M.	7.08	N.M.	N.M.	N.M.	14.83	25.20
Net Margin %	1.68	N.M.	N.M.	N.M.	N.M.	N.M.	5.53	17.53
Asset Turnover	0.77	0.60	0.59	0.48	0.51	0.51	0.64	0.74
Current Ratio	4.16	4.71	5.29	2.73	3.03	2.20	5.68	5.19
Debt to Equity	0.76	0.72	0.59	0.27	0.40	0.27	0.31	0.36
Price Range	19.32-7.68	11.57-4.63	12.86-6.55	7.77-1.19	15.53-1.41	23.33-13.51	29.45-18.26	28.55-22.86
P/E Ratio	96.60-38.40	...	...	...	...	...	25.17-15.61	6.88-5.51
Average Yield %	...	...	...	...	3.41	3.18	2.59	1.86

Address: 414 Union Street, Nashville, TN 37219	**Web Site:** www.lpcorp.com	**Auditors:** Deloitte & Touche LLP
Telephone: 615-986-5600	**Officers:** E. Gary Cook - Chairman W. Bradley Southern - Senior Vice President, General Manager	**Investor Contact:** 800-756-8200
		Transfer Agents: EquiServe Trust Company, Providence, RI

LOWE'S COMPANIES INC

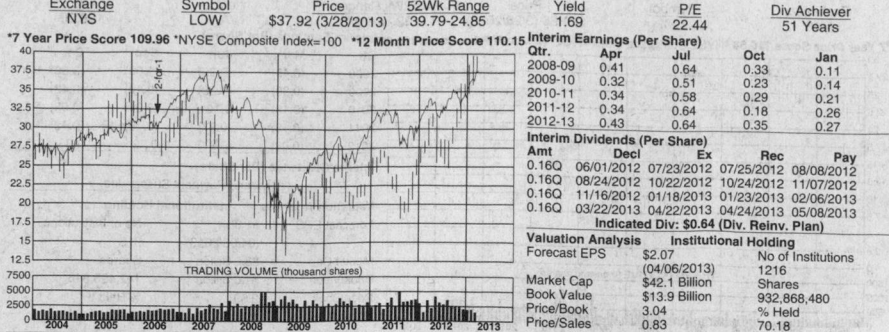

Exchange	Symbol	Price	52Wk Range	Yield	P/E	Div Achiever
NYS	LOW	$37.92 (3/28/2013)	39.79-24.85	1.69	22.44	51 Years

*7 Year Price Score 109.96 *NYSE Composite Index=100 ***12 Month Price Score 110.15**

Interim Earnings (Per Share)

Qtr.	Apr	Jul	Oct	Jan
2008-09	0.41	0.64	0.33	0.11
2009-10	0.32	0.51	0.23	0.14
2010-11	0.34	0.58	0.29	0.21
2011-12	0.34	0.64	0.18	0.26
2012-13	0.43	0.64	0.35	0.27

Interim Dividends (Per Share)

Amt	Decl	Ex	Rec	Pay
0.16Q	06/01/2012	07/23/2012	07/25/2012	08/08/2012
0.16Q	08/24/2012	10/22/2012	10/24/2012	11/07/2012
0.16Q	11/16/2012	01/18/2013	01/23/2013	02/06/2013
0.16Q	03/22/2013	04/22/2013	04/24/2013	05/08/2013

Indicated Div: $0.64 (Div. Reinv. Plan)

Valuation Analysis · **Institutional Holding**

Forecast EPS	$2.07
	(04/06/2013)
Market Cap	$42.1 Billion
Book Value	$13.9 Billion
Price/Book	3.04
Price/Sales	0.83

No of Institutions	1216
Shares	932,868,480
% Held	70.18

Business Summary: Retail - Hardware & Home Improvement (MIC: 2.1.8 SIC: 5211 NAIC: 444110)

Lowe's Companies is a home improvement retailer providing products in the following categories: plumbing, appliances, tools and outdoor power equipment, lawn and garden, electrical, lumber, seasonal living, paint, home fashions, storage and cleaning, flooring, millwork, building materials, hardware and cabinets and countertops. As of Feb 1 2013, Co. operated 1,754 stores, comprised of 1,715 stores across 50 U.S. states, 34 stores in Canada and five stores in Mexico. Co. provides national brand name merchandise such as Whirlpool® appliances and water heaters and Stainmaster® carpets, as well as private brands such as Portfolio® lighting products and Top Choice® lumber products, among others.

Recent Developments: For the year ended Feb 1 2013, net income increased 6.5% to US$1.96 billion from US$1.84 billion in the prior year. Revenues were US$50.52 billion, up 0.6% from US$50.21 billion the year before. Direct operating expenses rose 1.0% to US$33.19 billion from US$32.86 billion in the comparable period the year before. Indirect operating expenses decreased 1.8% to US$14.19 billion from US$14.44 billion in the equivalent prior-year period.

Prospects: Our evaluation of Lowe's Companies Inc. as of Apr. 7, 2013 is the result of our systematic analysis on three basic characteristics: earnings strength, relative valuation, and recent stock price movement. The company has produced a positive trend in earnings per share over the past 5 quarters and while recent estimates for the company have remained steady, LOW has posted better than expected results. Based on operating earnings yield, the company is about fairly valued when compared to all of the companies in our coverage universe. Share price changes over the past year indicates that LOW will perform well over the near term.

Financial Data

(US$ in Thousands)	02/01/2013	02/03/2012	01/28/2011	01/29/2010	01/30/2009	02/01/2008	02/02/2007	02/03/2006
Earnings Per Share	1.69	1.43	1.42	1.21	1.49	1.86	1.99	1.73
Cash Flow Per Share	3.28	3.37	2.76	2.78	2.84	2.94	2.94	2.43
Tang Book Value Per Share	12.48	13.32	13.38	13.07	12.28	11.04	10.31	9.14
Dividends Per Share	0.620	0.530	0.420	0.355	0.335	0.290	0.180	0.110
Dividend Payout %	36.69	37.06	29.58	29.34	22.48	15.59	9.05	6.36
Income Statement								
Total Revenue	50,521,000	50,208,000	48,815,000	47,220,000	48,230,000	48,283,000	46,927,000	43,243,000
EBITDA	5,083,000	4,757,000	5,146,000	4,726,000	5,325,000	6,071,000	6,314,000	5,644,000
Depn & Amortn	1,523,000	1,480,000	1,586,000	1,614,000	1,539,000	1,366,000	1,162,000	980,000
Income Before Taxes	3,137,000	2,906,000	3,228,000	2,825,000	3,506,000	4,511,000	4,998,000	4,506,000
Income Taxes	1,178,000	1,067,000	1,218,000	1,042,000	1,311,000	1,702,000	1,893,000	1,735,000
Net Income	1,959,000	1,839,000	2,010,000	1,783,000	2,195,000	2,809,000	3,105,000	2,771,000
Average Shares	1,152,000	1,273,000	1,403,000	1,464,000	1,472,000	1,510,000	1,566,000	1,606,000
Balance Sheet								
Current Assets	9,784,000	10,072,000	9,967,000	9,732,000	9,251,000	8,686,000	8,314,000	7,831,000
Total Assets	32,666,000	33,559,000	33,699,000	33,005,000	32,686,000	30,869,000	27,767,000	24,682,000
Current Liabilities	7,708,000	7,891,000	7,119,000	7,355,000	8,022,000	7,751,000	6,539,000	5,832,000
Long-Term Obligations	9,030,000	7,035,000	6,537,000	4,528,000	5,039,000	5,576,000	4,325,000	3,499,000
Total Liabilities	18,809,000	17,026,000	15,587,000	13,936,000	14,631,000	14,771,000	12,042,000	10,343,000
Stockholders' Equity	13,857,000	16,533,000	18,112,000	19,069,000	18,055,000	16,098,000	15,725,000	14,339,000
Shares Outstanding	1,110,000	1,241,000	1,354,000	1,459,000	1,470,000	1,458,000	1,524,500	1,568,200
Statistical Record								
Return on Assets %	5.93	5.38	6.04	5.44	6.93	9.61	11.87	11.88
Return on Equity %	12.93	10.44	10.84	9.63	12.89	17.70	20.71	21.07
EBITDA Margin %	10.06	9.47	10.54	10.01	11.04	12.57	13.45	13.05
Net Margin %	3.88	3.66	4.12	3.78	4.55	5.82	6.62	6.41
Asset Turnover	1.53	1.47	1.47	1.44	1.52	1.65	1.79	1.85
Current Ratio	1.27	1.28	1.40	1.32	1.15	1.12	1.27	1.34
Debt to Equity	0.65	0.43	0.36	0.24	0.28	0.35	0.28	0.24
Price Range	38.58-24.85	27.46-18.11	28.22-19.59	24.17-13.39	27.36-16.82	34.93-20.31	34.65-26.37	34.70-25.75
P/E Ratio	22.83-14.70	19.20-12.66	19.87-13.80	19.98-11.07	18.36-11.29	18.78-10.92	17.41-13.25	20.06-14.88
Average Yield %	2.03	2.24	1.81	1.74	1.50	1.01	0.59	0.36

Address: 1000 Lowe's Boulevard, Mooresville, NC 28117 **Telephone:** 704-758-1000	**Web Site:** www.lowes.com **Officers:** Robert A. Niblock - Chairman, President, Chief Executive Officer Maureen K. Ausura - Executive Vice President, Senior Vice President	**Auditors:** Deloitte & Touche LLP **Investor Contact:** 704-758-2033 **Transfer Agents:** Computershare Trust Company, N.A., Providence, RI

M & T BANK CORP

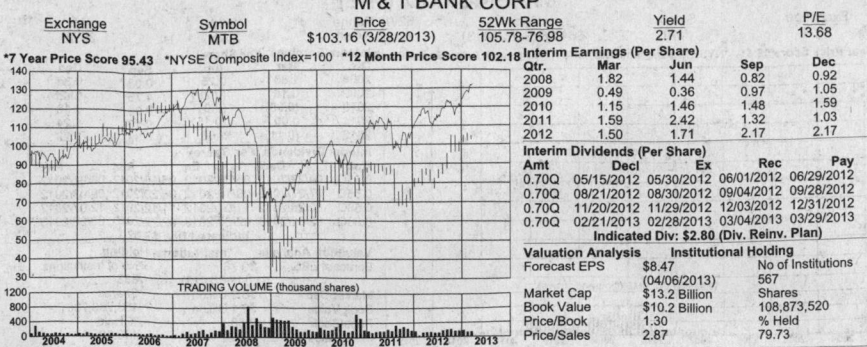

Exchange	Symbol	Price	52Wk Range	Yield	P/E
NYS	MTB	$103.16 (3/28/2013)	105.78-76.98	2.71	13.68

*7 Year Price Score 95.43 *NYSE Composite Index=100 ***12 Month Price Score 102.18**

Interim Earnings (Per Share)

Qtr.	Mar	Jun	Sep	Dec
2008	1.82	1.44	0.82	0.92
2009	0.49	0.36	0.97	1.05
2010	1.15	1.46	1.48	1.59
2011	1.59	2.42	1.32	1.03
2012	1.50	1.71	2.17	2.17

Interim Dividends (Per Share)

Amt	Decl	Ex	Rec	Pay
0.70Q	05/15/2012	05/30/2012	06/01/2012	06/29/2012
0.70Q	08/21/2012	08/30/2012	09/04/2012	09/28/2012
0.70Q	11/20/2012	11/29/2012	12/03/2012	12/31/2012
0.70Q	02/21/2013	02/28/2013	03/04/2013	03/29/2013

Indicated Div: $2.80 (Div. Reinv. Plan)

Valuation Analysis   **Institutional Holding**

Forecast EPS	$8.47	No of Institutions
	(04/06/2013)	567
Market Cap	$13.2 Billion	Shares
Book Value	$10.2 Billion	108,873,520
Price/Book	1.30	% Held
Price/Sales	2.87	79.73

Business Summary: Banking (MIC: 5.1.1 SIC: 6022 NAIC: 522110)

M&T Bank is a bank holding company. Through its subsidiaries, Co. provides individuals, corporations and other businesses, and institutions with commercial and retail banking services, including loans and deposits, trust, mortgage banking, asset management, insurance and other financial services. Banking activities are focused on consumers residing in New York State, Pennsylvania, Maryland, Delaware, Virginia and the District of Columbia. Co. has six reportable segments: Business Banking, Commercial Banking, Commercial Real Estate, Discretionary Portfolio, Residential Mortgage Banking and Retail Banking. At Dec 31 2011, Co. had total assets of $77.92 billion and deposits of $59.39 billion.

Recent Developments: For the year ended Dec 31 2012, net income increased 19.8% to US$1.03 billion from US$859.5 million in the prior year. Net interest income increased 8.7% to US$2.60 billion from US$2.39 billion in the prior year. Provision for loan losses was US$204.0 million versus US$270.0 million in the prior year, a decrease of 24.4%. Non-interest income rose 5.3% to US$1.67 billion from US$1.58 billion, while non-interest expense advanced 1.3% to US$2.51 billion.

Prospects: Our evaluation of M & T Bank Corp. as of Apr. 7, 2013 is the result of our systematic analysis on three basic characteristics: earnings strength, relative valuation, and recent stock price movement. The company has produced a positive trend in earnings per share over the past 5 quarters and while recent estimates for the company have been raised by analysts, MTB has posted results that fell short of analysts expectations. Based on operating earnings yield, the company is undervalued when compared to all of the companies in our coverage universe. Share price changes over the past year indicates that MTB will perform well over the near term.

Financial Data

(US$ in Thousands)	12/31/2012	12/31/2011	12/31/2010	12/31/2009	12/31/2008	12/31/2007	12/31/2006	12/31/2005
Earnings Per Share	7.54	6.35	5.69	2.89	5.01	5.95	7.37	6.73
Cash Flow Per Share	3.96	14.45	14.18	10.37	14.74	12.34	4.86	2.62
Tang Book Value Per Share	44.39	37.44	33.14	28.05	25.75	27.68	28.33	25.56
Dividends Per Share	2.800	2.800	2.800	2.800	2.800	2.600	2.250	1.750
Dividend Payout %	37.14	44.09	49.21	96.89	55.89	43.70	30.53	26.00
Income Statement								
Interest Income	2,941,685	2,792,087	2,729,795	2,725,197	3,277,591	3,544,813	3,314,093	2,788,694
Interest Expense	343,169	402,331	462,269	669,449	1,337,795	1,694,576	1,496,552	994,351
Net Interest Income	2,598,516	2,389,756	2,267,526	2,055,748	1,939,796	1,850,237	1,817,541	1,794,343
Provision for Losses	204,000	270,000	368,000	604,000	412,000	192,000	80,000	88,000
Non-Interest Income	1,667,270	1,582,912	1,108,100	1,048,106	938,979	932,989	1,045,852	949,718
Non-Interest Expense	2,509,260	2,478,068	1,914,837	1,980,563	1,726,996	1,627,689	1,551,751	1,485,142
Income Before Taxes	1,552,526	1,224,600	1,092,789	519,291	739,779	963,537	1,231,642	1,170,919
Income Taxes	523,028	365,121	356,628	139,400	183,892	309,278	392,453	388,736
Net Income	1,029,498	859,479	736,161	379,891	555,887	654,259	839,189	782,183
Average Shares	126,405	123,079	118,843	114,776	110,904	110,012	113,918	116,232
Balance Sheet								
Net Loans & Leases	65,645,097	59,187,715	51,087,441	51,058,664	48,212,559	47,262,123	42,297,349	39,692,982
Total Assets	83,008,803	77,924,287	68,021,263	68,880,399	65,815,757	64,875,639	57,064,905	55,146,406
Total Deposits	65,611,253	59,394,649	49,805,284	47,449,838	42,581,263	41,266,188	39,910,503	37,100,174
Total Liabilities	72,806,210	68,653,078	59,663,568	61,127,492	59,031,026	58,390,383	50,783,810	49,270,020
Stockholders' Equity	10,202,593	9,271,209	8,357,695	7,752,907	6,784,731	6,485,256	6,281,095	5,876,386
Shares Outstanding	128,176	125,683	119,702	118,222	110,365	109,852	110,216	112,059
Statistical Record								
Return on Assets %	1.28	1.18	1.08	0.56	0.85	1.07	1.50	1.45
Return on Equity %	10.54	9.75	9.14	5.23	8.36	10.25	13.81	13.48
Net Interest Margin %	88.33	85.59	83.07	75.43	59.18	52.20	54.84	64.34
Efficiency Ratio %	54.44	56.64	49.89	52.49	40.96	36.35	35.59	39.73
Loans to Deposits	1.00	1.00	1.03	1.08	1.13	1.15	1.06	1.07
Price Range	104.88-76.98	91.01-67.43	94.45-66.89	68.96-30.50	97.04-53.63	124.74-79.31	124.21-106.45	112.28-96.93
P/E Ratio	13.91-10.21	14.33-10.62	16.60-11.76	23.86-10.55	19.37-10.70	20.96-13.33	16.85-14.44	16.68-14.40
Average Yield %	3.17	3.44	3.41	5.22	3.60	2.43	1.92	1.67

Address: One M & T Plaza, Buffalo, NY 14203 Telephone: 716-842-5445	Web Site: www.mtb.com Officers: Robert G. Wilmers - Chairman, Chief Executive Officer Michael P. Pinto - Vice-Chairman	Auditors: PricewaterhouseCoopers LLP Investor Contact: 716-842-5138 Transfer Agents: Registrar and Transfer Company, Cranford, NJ

MACERICH CO. (THE)

Exchange	Symbol	Price	52Wk Range	Yield	P/E
NYS	MAC	$64.38 (3/28/2013)	64.38-54.68	3.60	25.65

*7 Year Price Score 95.51   *NYSE Composite Index=100   *12 Month Price Score 96.42

Interim Earnings (Per Share)

Qtr.	Mar	Jun	Sep	Dec
2008	1.30	0.25	0.08	0.84
2009	0.18	(0.29)	1.75	(0.26)
2010	(0.08)	(0.01)	0.06	0.18
2011	0.00	(0.15)	0.10	1.24
2012	(0.11)	1.00	0.33	1.29

Interim Dividends (Per Share)

Amt	Decl	Ex	Rec	Pay
0.55Q	04/27/2012	05/08/2012	05/10/2012	06/08/2012
0.55Q	07/27/2012	08/16/2012	08/20/2012	09/07/2012
0.58Q	10/25/2012	11/07/2012	11/12/2012	12/07/2012
0.58Q	02/01/2013	02/20/2013	02/22/2013	03/08/2013

Indicated Div: $2.32

Valuation Analysis   Institutional Holding

Forecast EPS	$0.78 (04/06/2013)	No of Institutions 383
Market Cap	$8.9 Billion	Shares
Book Value	$3.1 Billion	153,766,736
Price/Book	2.88	% Held
Price/Sales	10.04	106.02

Business Summary: REITs (MIC: 5.3.1 SIC: 6798 NAIC: 525930)

Macerich is a self-administered and self-managed real estate investment trust. Co. is involved in the acquisition, ownership, development, redevelopment, management and leasing of regional and community shopping centers located throughout the U.S. Co. is the sole general partner of, and owns a majority of the ownership interests in The Macerich Partnership, L.P. (the Operating Partnership). As of Dec 31 2012, the Operating Partnership owned or had an ownership interest in 61 regional shopping centers and nine community/power shopping centers. Co. conducts all of its operations through the Operating Partnership and its management companies.

Recent Developments: For the year ended Dec 31 2012, net income increased 116.7% to US$366.4 million from US$169.1 million in the prior year. Revenues were US$881.3 million, up 15.5% from US$763.4 million the year before. Revenues from property income rose 14.4% to US$835.8 million from US$730.4 million in the corresponding earlier year.

Prospects: Our evaluation of Macerich Co. as of Apr. 7, 2013 is the result of our systematic analysis on three basic characteristics: earnings strength, relative valuation, and recent stock price movement. The company has suffered a very negative trend in earnings per share over the past 5 quarters. Because the company lacks sufficient analyst estimate data, we place greater weight on the historical EPS trend as the measure of earnings strength. Based on operating earnings yield, the company is overvalued when compared to all of the companies in our coverage universe. Share price changes over the past year indicates that MAC will perform poorly over the near term.

Financial Data

(US$ in Thousands)	12/31/2012	12/31/2011	12/31/2010	12/31/2009	12/31/2008	12/31/2007	12/31/2006	12/31/2005
Earnings Per Share	2.51	1.18	0.19	1.45	2.47	1.00	3.19	0.88
Cash Flow Per Share	2.61	1.80	1.67	1.49	3.38	4.54	2.99	3.97
Tang Book Value Per Share	21.46	21.57	22.79	19.25	17.07	21.63	25.21	17.50
Dividends Per Share	2.230	2.050	2.100	2.600	3.200	2.930	2.750	2.630
Dividend Payout %	88.84	173.73	1,105.26	179.31	129.55	293.00	86.21	298.86
Income Statement								
Total Revenue	881,323	791,250	758,559	805,654	901,490	896,368	829,656	767,385
EBITDA	560,739	298,894	509,840	600,340	624,766	652,887	636,347	986,479
Depn & Amortn	271,025	235,884	221,799	221,276	192,511	181,810	171,015	148,116
Income Before Taxes	112,936	(132,275)	75,223	116,019	150,899	207,351	190,665	588,453
Income Taxes	(4,159)	(6,110)	(9,202)	(4,761)	1,126	(470)	33	(2,031)
Net Income	337,426	156,866	25,190	120,742	187,440	96,540	252,358	71,686
Average Shares	134,148	131,628	120,346	81,226	86,794	84,760	88,058	73,573
Balance Sheet								
Current Assets	271,862	269,801	638,097	263,064	274,553	320,198	483,685	298,937
Total Assets	9,311,209	7,938,549	7,645,010	7,252,471	8,090,435	8,121,134	7,562,163	7,178,944
Current Liabilities	388,425	371,968	328,263	336,679	403,891	393,102	304,575	308,076
Long-Term Obligations	5,261,370	4,206,074	3,892,070	4,531,634	5,975,269	5,762,958	4,993,879	5,424,730
Total Liabilities	6,233,680	5,125,212	4,754,731	5,394,900	6,726,136	6,494,760	5,685,637	6,017,615
Stockholders' Equity	3,077,529	2,813,337	2,890,279	-1,857,571	1,364,299	1,626,374	1,876,526	1,161,329
Shares Outstanding	137,507	132,153	130,452	96,667	76,883	72,311	71,567	59,941
Statistical Record								
Return on Assets %	3.90	2.01	0.34	1.57	2.31	1.23	3.42	1.21
Return on Equity %	11.42	5.50	1.06	7.50	12.50	5.51	16.61	6.60
EBITDA Margin %	63.62	37.77	67.21	74.52	69.30	72.84	76.70	128.55
Net Margin %	38.29	19.83	3.32	14.99	20.79	10.77	30.42	9.34
Asset Turnover	0.10	0.10	0.10	0.11	0.11	0.11	0.11	0.13
Current Ratio	0.70	0.73	1.94	0.78	0.68	0.81	1.59	0.97
Debt to Equity	1.71	1.50	1.35	2.44	4.38	3.54	2.66	4.67
Price Range	62.29-50.30	56.20-40.21	49.40-29.97	37.62-5.80	75.36-5.80	103.32-70.63	87.00-67.90	71.19-53.28
P/E Ratio	24.82-20.04	47.63-34.08	260.00-157.74	25.94-4.00	30.51-3.99	103.32-70.63	27.27-21.29	80.90-60.55
Average Yield %	3.89	4.18	5.15	12.33	5.82	3.40	3.71	4.21

Address: 401 Wilshire Boulevard, Suite 700, Santa Monica, CA 90401 **Telephone:** 310-394-6000	**Web Site:** www.macerich.com **Officers:** Arthur M. Coppola - Chairman, Chief Executive Officer Mace Siegel - Chairman Emeritus, Founder	**Auditors:** KPMG LLP **Transfer Agents:** Computershare Trust Company, N.A., Providence, RI

MACK CALI REALTY CORP

Exchange	Symbol	Price	52Wk Range	Yield	P/E
NYS	CLI	$28.61 (3/28/2013)	29.33-24.59	6.29	60.87

*7 Year Price Score 70.73   *NYSE Composite Index=100   *12 Month Price Score 94.85

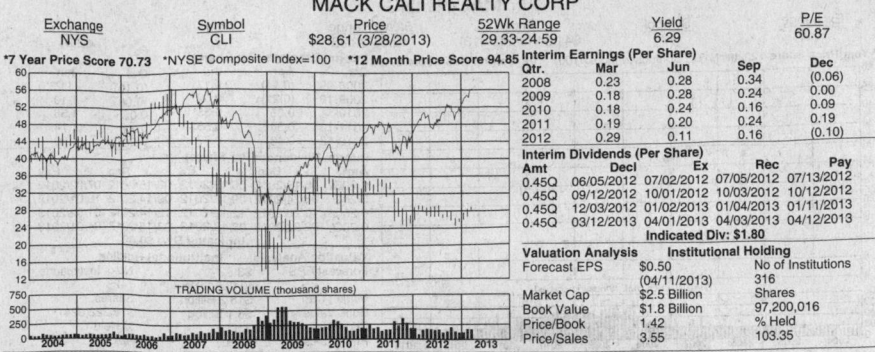

Interim Earnings (Per Share)

Qtr.	Mar	Jun	Sep	Dec
2008	0.23	0.28	0.34	(0.06)
2009	0.18	0.28	0.24	0.00
2010	0.18	0.24	0.16	0.09
2011	0.19	0.20	0.24	0.19
2012	0.29	0.11	0.16	(0.10)

Interim Dividends (Per Share)

Amt	Decl	Ex	Rec	Pay
0.45Q	06/05/2012	07/02/2012	07/05/2012	07/13/2012
0.45Q	09/12/2012	10/01/2012	10/03/2012	10/12/2012
0.45Q	12/03/2012	01/02/2013	01/04/2013	01/11/2013
0.45Q	03/12/2013	04/01/2013	04/03/2013	04/12/2013

Indicated Div: $1.80

Valuation Analysis / Institutional Holding

Forecast EPS	$0.50 (04/11/2013)	No of Institutions	316
Market Cap	$2.5 Billion	Shares	97,200,016
Book Value	$1.8 Billion	% Held	103.35
Price/Book	1.42		
Price/Sales	3.55		

TRADING VOLUME (thousand shares)

Business Summary: REITs (MIC: 5.3.1 SIC: 1542 NAIC: 525930)

Mack-Cali Realty is a self-administered and self-managed real estate investment trust that owns and operates a real estate portfolio comprised predominantly of Class A office and office/flex properties located primarily in the Northeast. Co. is engaged in providing commercial real estate leasing, management, acquisition, development and construction services on an in-house basis. As of Dec. 31, 2012, Co. owned or had interests in 278 properties plus developable land, aggregating approx. 31,700,000 sq. ft., which are leased to over 2,000 commercial tenants located in six states, primarily in the Northeast, and the District of Columbia.

Recent Developments: For the year ended Dec 31 2012, income from continuing operations decreased 40.5% to US$46.3 million from US$77.8 million a year earlier. Net income decreased 43.1% to US$46.3 million from US$81.4 million in the prior year. Revenues were US$704.7 million, down 0.6% from US$709.1 million the year before. Operating income was US$169.5 million versus US$199.9 million in the prior year, a decrease of 15.2%. Direct operating expenses declined 5.6% to US$186.8 million from US$197.8 million in the comparable period the year before. Indirect operating expenses increased 11.9% to US$348.5 million from US$311.4 million in the equivalent prior-year period.

Prospects: Our evaluation of Mack Cali Realty Corp. as of Apr. 7, 2013 is the result of our systematic analysis on three basic characteristics: earnings strength, relative valuation, and recent stock price movement. The company has managed to produce a neutral trend in earnings per share over the past 5 quarters. Because the company lacks sufficient analyst estimate data, we place greater weight on the historical EPS trend as the measure of earnings strength. Based on operating earnings yield, the company is overvalued when compared to all of the companies in our coverage universe. Share price changes over the past year indicates that CLI will perform poorly over the near term.

Financial Data
(US$ in Thousands)

	12/31/2012	12/31/2011	12/31/2010	12/31/2009	12/31/2008	12/31/2007	12/31/2006	12/31/2005
Earnings Per Share	0.47	0.81	0.67	0.71	0.79	1.61	2.28	1.51
Cash Flow Per Share	2.78	2.93	2.82	3.97	4.20	3.88	3.79	3.95
Tang Book Value Per Share	20.15	21.52	21.77	22.88	22.88	24.67	23.88	23.96
Dividends Per Share	1.800	1.800	1.800	1.990	2.560	2.560	2.530	2.520
Dividend Payout %	382.98	222.22	268.66	280.28	324.05	159.01	110.96	166.89
Income Statement								
Total Revenue	704,743	724,279	787,480	764,525	777,969	808,350	740,309	643,405
EBITDA	486,695	529,147	554,289	556,158	582,258	530,233	535,701	510,204
Depn & Amortn	198,966	199,932	197,853	201,599	194,553	186,424	177,001	164,031
Income Before Taxes	165,396	203,279	207,193	213,857	260,945	221,807	225,397	227,692
Net Income	46,269	81,387	63,439	63,728	53,726	110,466	144,666	95,488
Average Shares	99,996	98,962	92,477	88,389	80,648	82,500	77,901	74,189
Balance Sheet								
Current Assets	226,747	182,667	178,473	439,298	170,003	187,334	245,157	218,958
Total Assets	4,526,045	4,295,759	4,362,466	4,721,637	4,443,922	4,593,202	4,422,889	4,247,502
Current Liabilities	253,149	227,544	229,035	241,010	259,084	281,062	252,803	209,215
Long-Term Obligations	2,204,389	1,914,045	2,089,494	2,337,437	2,225,475	2,211,735	2,159,959	2,126,181
Total Liabilities	2,759,071	2,406,195	2,604,194	2,890,179	2,899,459	2,950,647	2,894,982	2,736,215
Stockholders' Equity	1,766,974	1,889,564	1,758,272	1,831,458	1,544,463	1,642,555	1,527,907	1,511,287
Shares Outstanding	87,536	87,799	79,605	78,969	66,419	65,558	62,925	62,019
Statistical Record								
Return on Assets %	1.05	1.88	1.40	1.39	1.19	2.45	3.34	2.36
Return on Equity %	2.52	4.46	3.53	3.78	3.36	6.97	9.52	6.25
EBITDA Margin %	69.06	73.06	70.39	72.75	74.84	65.59	72.36	79.30
Net Margin %	6.57	11.24	8.06	8.34	6.91	13.67	19.54	14.84
Asset Turnover	0.16	0.17	0.17	0.17	0.17	0.18	0.17	0.16
Current Ratio	0.90	0.80	0.78	1.82	0.66	0.67	0.97	1.05
Debt to Equity	1.25	1.01	1.19	1.28	1.44	1.35	1.41	1.41
Price Range	29.33-24.59	35.48-24.37	38.19-27.98	36.44-14.54	42.50-14.25	56.28-31.38	55.10-42.58	48.02-40.67
P/E Ratio	62.40-52.32	43.80-30.09	57.00-41.76	51.32-20.48	53.80-18.04	34.96-19.49	24.17-18.68	31.80-26.93
Average Yield %	6.58	5.78	5.47	7.52	7.77	5.78	5.26	5.72

Address: 343 Thornall Street, Edison, NJ 08837-2206
Telephone: 732-590-1000
Fax: 732-205-8237

Web Site: www.mack-cali.com
Officers: William L. Mack - Chairman Mitchell E. Hersh - President, Chief Executive Officer

Auditors: PricewaterhouseCoopers LLP
Transfer Agents: Computershare Trust Company, N.A., Providence, RI

MACYS INC

Exchange	Symbol	Price	52Wk Range	Yield	P/E
NYS	M	$41.84 (3/28/2013)	42.66-32.83	1.91	12.91

*7 Year Price Score 122.48 *NYSE Composite Index=100   *12 Month Price Score 97.33

Interim Earnings (Per Share)

Qtr.	Apr	Jul	Oct	Jan
2008-09	(0.14)	0.17	(0.10)	(11.33)
2009-10	(0.21)	0.02	(0.08)	1.10
2010-11	0.05	0.35	0.02	1.56
2011-12	0.30	0.55	0.32	1.74
2012-13	0.43	0.67	0.36	1.79

Interim Dividends (Per Share)

Amt	Decl	Ex	Rec	Pay
0.20Q	05/18/2012	06/13/2012	06/15/2012	07/02/2012
0.20Q	08/24/2012	09/12/2012	09/14/2012	10/01/2012
0.20Q	10/26/2012	12/12/2012	12/14/2012	01/02/2013
0.20Q	02/22/2013	03/13/2013	03/15/2013	04/01/2013

Indicated Div: $0.80

Valuation Analysis

		Institutional Holding	
Forecast EPS	$3.92	No of Institutions	
	(04/06/2013)	742	
Market Cap	$16.2 Billion	Shares	
Book Value	$6.1 Billion	370,222,624	
Price/Book	2.68	% Held	
Price/Sales	0.59	N/A	

Business Summary: Retail - General Merchandise/Department Stores (MIC: 2.1.1 SIC: 5311 NAIC: 452111)

Macy's is a retail organization operating stores and Internet websites that sell a range of merchandise, including apparel and accessories (men's, women's and children's), cosmetics, home furnishings and other consumer goods. As of Jan 28 2012, the operations of Co. included approximately 840 stores in 45 states, the District of Columbia, Guam and Puerto Rico under the names Macy's and Bloomingdale's as well as macys.com and bloomingdales.com. Co. also operates seven Bloomingdale's Outlet stores. Bloomingdale's Outlet stores sell a range of apparel and accessories, including women's ready-to-wear, men's, children's, women's shoes, fashion accessories, jewelry, handbags and intimate apparel.

Recent Developments: For the year ended Feb 2 2013, net income increased 6.3% to US$1.34 billion from US$1.26 billion in the prior year. Revenues were US$27.69 billion, up 4.9% from US$26.41 billion the year before. Operating income was US$2.66 billion versus US$2.41 billion in the prior year, an increase of 10.4%. Direct operating expenses rose 5.1% to US$16.54 billion from US$15.74 billion in the comparable period the year before. Indirect operating expenses increased 2.8% to US$8.49 billion from US$8.26 billion in the equivalent prior-year period.

Prospects: Our evaluation of Macy's Inc. as of Apr. 7, 2013 is the result of our systematic analysis on three basic characteristics: earnings strength, relative valuation, and recent stock price movement. The company has produced a positive trend in earnings per share over the past 5 quarters and while recent estimates for the company have remained steady, M has posted better than expected results. Based on operating earnings yield, the company is undervalued when compared to all of the companies in our coverage universe. Share price changes over the past year indicates that M will perform poorly over the near term.

Financial Data

(US$ in Thousands)	02/02/2013	01/28/2012	01/29/2011	01/30/2010	01/31/2009	02/02/2008	02/03/2007	01/28/2006
Earnings Per Share	3.24	2.92	1.98	0.83	(11.40)	1.97	1.81	3.24
Cash Flow Per Share	5.49	4.94	3.57	4.16	4.47	5.01	6.73	4.59
Tang Book Value Per Share	4.51	3.84	2.72	0.67	0.44	N.M.	4.36	5.34
Dividends Per Share	0.800	0.350	0.200	0.200	0.527	0.517	0.507	0.385
Dividend Payout %	24.69	11.99	10.10	24.10	...	26.27	28.04	11.88
Income Statement								
Total Revenue	27,686,000	26,405,000	25,003,000	23,489,000	24,892,000	26,313,000	26,970,000	22,390,000
EBITDA	2,561,000	2,450,000	1,935,000	1,104,000	(4,336,000)	1,906,000	1,905,000	2,457,000
Depn & Amortn	37,000	39,000	41,000	41,000	42,000	43,000	69,000	33,000
Income Before Taxes	2,102,000	1,968,000	1,320,000	507,000	(4,938,000)	1,320,000	1,446,000	2,044,000
Income Taxes	767,000	712,000	473,000	157,000	(135,000)	411,000	458,000	671,000
Net Income	1,335,000	1,256,000	847,000	350,000	(4,803,000)	893,000	995,000	1,406,000
Average Shares	412,200	430,400	427,300	423,200	421,200	451,800	547,700	434,600
Balance Sheet								
Current Assets	7,876,000	8,777,000	6,899,000	6,882,000	6,740,000	6,324,000	7,422,000	10,145,000
Total Assets	20,991,000	22,095,000	20,631,000	21,300,000	22,145,000	27,789,000	29,550,000	33,168,000
Current Liabilities	5,075,000	6,263,000	5,065,000	4,454,000	5,126,000	5,360,000	6,359,000	7,590,000
Long-Term Obligations	6,806,000	6,655,000	6,971,000	8,456,000	8,733,000	9,087,000	7,847,000	8,860,000
Total Liabilities	14,940,000	16,162,000	15,101,000	16,599,000	17,499,000	17,882,000	17,296,000	19,649,000
Stockholders' Equity	6,051,000	5,933,000	5,530,000	4,701,000	4,646,000	9,907,000	12,254,000	13,519,000
Shares Outstanding	387,701	414,181	423,300	420,843	420,083	419,745	496,900	546,800
Statistical Record								
Return on Assets %	6.10	5.90	4.05	1.62	N.M.	3.12	3.12	5.87
Return on Equity %	21.92	21.97	16.60	7.51	N.M.	8.08	7.60	14.32
EBITDA Margin %	9.25	9.28	7.74	4.70	N.M.	7.24	7.06	10.97
Net Margin %	4.82	4.76	3.39	1.49	N.M.	3.39	3.69	6.28
Asset Turnover	1.26	1.24	1.20	1.08	1.00	0.92	0.85	0.93
Current Ratio	1.55	1.40	1.36	1.55	1.31	1.18	1.17	1.34
Debt to Equity	1.12	1.12	1.26	1.80	1.88	0.92	0.64	0.66
Price Range	41.73-32.83	35.82-22.01	26.00-15.92	20.72-6.58	27.04-5.68	46.51-21.31	44.95-33.25	38.65-27.61
P/E Ratio	12.88-10.13	12.27-7.54	13.13-8.04	24.96-7.93	...	23.61-10.82	24.83-18.37	11.93-8.52
Average Yield %	2.09	1.26	0.91	1.44	2.95	1.44	1.33	1.16

Address: 151 West 34th Street, New York, NY 10001 Telephone: 212-494-1602 Fax: 212-494-1838	Web Site: www.macys.com Officers: Terry J. Lundgren - Chairman, President, Chief Executive Officer Thomas G. Cody - Vice-Chairman	Auditors: KPMG LLP Investor Contact: 513-579-7780 Transfer Agents: Computershare Shareowner Services, Pittsburgh, PA

MAGELLAN MIDSTREAM PARTNERS LP

Exchange	Symbol	Price	52Wk Range	Yield	P/E	Div Achiever
NYS	MMP	$53.43 (3/28/2013)	53.43-33.58	3.51	27.83	11 Years

*7 Year Price Score 147.51 *NYSE Composite Index=100 *12 Month Price Score 110.82

Interim Earnings (Per Share)

Qtr.	Mar	Jun	Sep	Dec
2008	0.28	0.25	0.24	0.26
2009	0.11	0.14	0.22	0.56
2010	0.30	0.48	0.26	0.40
2011	0.40	0.46	0.49	0.48
2012	0.41	0.61	0.22	0.67

Interim Dividends (Per Share)

Amt	Decl	Ex	Rec	Pay
0.471Q	07/26/2012	08/03/2012	08/07/2012	08/14/2012
2-for-1	08/30/2012	10/15/2012	09/28/2012	10/12/2012
0.485Q	10/24/2012	11/02/2012	11/06/2012	11/14/2012
0.50Q	01/22/2013	02/04/2013	02/06/2013	02/14/2013

Indicated Div: $1.88

Valuation Analysis — Institutional Holding

Forecast EPS	$2.21	No of Institutions
	(04/05/2013)	433
Market Cap	$12.1 Billion	Shares
Book Value	N/A	129,206,768
Price/Book	N/A	% Held
Price/Sales	6.82	108.94

Business Summary: Equipment & Services (MIC: 9.1.3 SIC: 4613 NAIC: 486910)

Magellan Midstream Partners is engaged in the transportation, storage and distribution of petroleum products. As of Dec 31 2011, Co.'s asset portfolio consisted of: petroleum pipeline system, which is comprised of 9,600 miles of pipeline and 50 terminals; petroleum terminals, which include storage terminal facilities and inland terminals; and ammonia pipeline system, which represents its 1,100-mile ammonia pipeline and six terminals. Petroleum products transported, stored and distributed through Co.'s petroleum pipeline system and petroleum terminals include refined petroleum products, liquefied petroleum gases, blendstocks, oils and feedstocks, crude oil and condensate, and biofuels.

Recent Developments: For the year ended Dec 31 2012, net income increased 5.3% to US$435.7 million from US$413.6 million in the prior year. Revenues were US$1.77 billion, up 1.3% from US$1.75 billion the year before. Operating income was US$552.1 million versus US$522.9 million in the prior year, an increase of 5.6%. Direct operating expenses declined 2.7% to US$985.6 million from US$1.01 billion in the comparable period the year before. Indirect operating expenses increased 10.0% to US$234.5 million from US$213.1 million in the equivalent prior-year period.

Prospects: Our evaluation of Magellan Midstream Partners L.P. as of Apr. 7, 2013 is the result of our systematic analysis on three basic characteristics: earnings strength, relative valuation, and recent stock price movement. The company has produced a positive trend in earnings per share over the past 5 quarters and while recent estimates for the company have been raised by analysts, MMP has posted better than expected results. Based on operating earnings yield, the company is about fairly valued when compared to all of the companies in our coverage universe. Share price changes over the past year indicates that MMP will perform well over the near term.

Financial Data
(US$ in Thousands)

	12/31/2012	12/31/2011	12/31/2010	12/31/2009	12/31/2008	12/31/2007	12/31/2006	12/31/2005
Earnings Per Share	1.92	1.83	1.43	1.11	1.03	0.82	0.71	0.64
Cash Flow Per Share	2.84	2.56	1.94	2.36	2.05	1.24	1.45	1.07
Dividends Per Share	1.784	1.556	1.454	1.420	1.360	1.246	1.143	0.983
Dividend Payout %	92.90	85.04	102.02	127.93	131.50	151.56	161.28	153.04
Income Statement								
Total Revenue	1,772,074	1,748,667	1,557,447	1,014,171	1,212,786	1,318,121	1,223,560	1,137,072
EBITDA	673,710	633,203	507,815	389,492	464,603	353,576	360,720	313,237
Depn & Amortn	126,700	118,900	107,300	95,600	69,600	62,200	59,300	54,900
Income Before Taxes	435,331	408,669	307,219	224,705	344,533	240,331	248,410	210,079
Income Taxes	2,622	1,866	1,371	1,661	1,987	1,568	...	...
Net Income	435,670	413,566	311,580	226,475	346,613	242,790	192,728	159,483
Average Shares	226,608	225,974	219,122	114,290	211,626	210,909	210,633	210,671
Balance Sheet								
Current Assets	700,278	612,190	384,583	323,968	165,583	205,082	177,018	185,689
Total Assets	4,420,067	4,045,001	3,717,900	3,163,148	2,296,115	2,101,194	1,952,649	1,876,518
Current Liabilities	392,620	311,055	275,047	229,397	195,258	220,645	518,389	185,895
Long-Term Obligations	2,393,408	2,151,775	1,906,148	1,680,004	1,083,930	916,414	526,742	792,730
Total Liabilities	2,904,365	2,581,598	2,262,592	1,966,794	1,340,673	1,230,030	1,146,167	1,068,528
Shares Outstanding	226,200	225,473	224,962	213,175	211,048	210,422	209,837	209,837
Statistical Record								
Return on Assets %	10.27	10.65	9.06	8.30	15.72	11.98	10.07	8.63
EBITDA Margin %	38.02	36.21	32.61	38.40	38.31	26.82	29.48	27.55
Net Margin %	24.59	23.65	20.01	22.33	28.58	18.42	15.75	14.03
Asset Turnover	0.42	0.45	0.45	0.37	0.55	0.65	0.64	0.62
Current Ratio	1.78	1.97	1.40	1.41	0.85	0.93	0.34	1.00
Price Range	45.34-32.51	34.48-26.59	28.59-20.52	21.66-12.90	22.24-11.07	25.50-18.95	19.62-15.41	17.65-14.64
P/E Ratio	23.61-16.93	18.84-14.53	20.00-14.35	19.52-11.62	21.59-10.75	31.10-23.11	27.63-21.70	27.58-22.88
Average Yield %	4.66	5.19	5.99	8.01	7.37	5.69	6.55	6.09

Address: Magellan GP, LLC, P.O. Box 22186, Tulsa, OK 74121-2186
Telephone: 918-574-7000

Web Site: www.magellanlp.com
Officers: Michael N. Mears - Chairman, President, Chief Executive Officer John D. Chandler - Senior Vice President, Chief Financial Officer

Auditors: Ernst & Young LLP
Investor Contact: 918-574-7650
Transfer Agents: Computershare Trust Company, N.A., Providence, RI

MANITOWOC CO., INC.

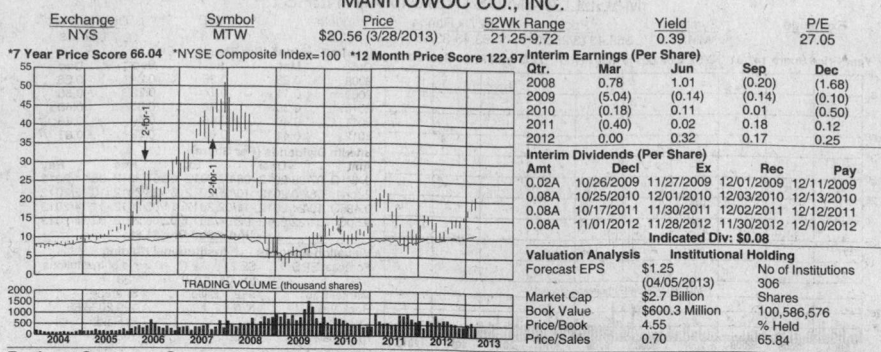

Exchange	Symbol	Price	52Wk Range	Yield	P/E
NYS	MTW	$20.56 (3/28/2013)	21.25-9.72	0.39	27.05

*7 Year Price Score 66.04   *NYSE Composite Index=100   *12 Month Price Score 122.97

Interim Earnings (Per Share)

Qtr.	Mar	Jun	Sep	Dec
2008	0.78	1.01	(0.20)	(1.68)
2009	(5.04)	(0.14)	(0.14)	(0.10)
2010	(0.18)	0.11	0.01	(0.50)
2011	(0.40)	0.02	0.18	0.12
2012	0.00	0.32	0.17	0.25

Interim Dividends (Per Share)

Amt	Decl	Ex	Rec	Pay
0.02A	10/26/2009	11/27/2009	12/01/2009	12/11/2009
0.08A	10/25/2010	12/01/2010	12/03/2010	12/13/2010
0.08A	10/17/2011	11/30/2011	12/02/2011	12/12/2011
0.08A	11/01/2012	11/28/2012	11/30/2012	12/10/2012

Indicated Div: $0.08

Valuation Analysis **Institutional Holding**

Forecast EPS	$1.25
	(04/05/2013)
Market Cap	$2.7 Billion
Book Value	$600.3 Million
Price/Book	4.55
Price/Sales	0.70

No of Institutions 306

Shares 100,586,576

% Held 65.84

Business Summary: Construction Services (MIC: 7.5.4 SIC: 3531 NAIC: 333120)

Manitowoc Company is a capital goods manufacturer operating in two principal markets: Cranes and Related Products (Crane) and Foodservice Equipment (Foodservice). Co.'s Crane segment provides lifting equipment for the construction industry including: lattice-boom cranes; tower cranes; mobile telescopic cranes; and boom trucks. Co.'s Foodservice segment manufactures commercial foodservice equipment including: primary cooking and warming equipment; ice-cube machines, ice flaker machines and storage bins; refrigerator and freezer equipment; warewashing equipment; beverage dispensers and related products; serving and storage equipment; and food preparation equipment.

Recent Developments: For the year ended Dec 31 2012, income from continuing operations increased 354.7% to US$92.3 million from US$20.3 million a year earlier. Net income amounted to US$92.6 million versus a net loss of US$17.7 million in the prior year. Revenues were US$3.93 billion, up 8.5% from US$3.62 billion the year before. Operating income was US$281.8 million versus US$218.4 million in the prior year, an increase of 29.0%. Direct operating expenses rose 7.2% to US$2.99 billion from US$2.79 billion in the comparable period the year before. Indirect operating expenses increased 7.3% to US$652.6 million from US$608.3 million in the equivalent prior-year period.

Prospects: Our evaluation of Manitowoc Co. Inc. as of Apr. 7, 2013 is the result of our systematic analysis on three basic characteristics: earnings strength, relative valuation, and recent stock price movement. The company has generated a negative trend in earnings per share over the past 5 quarters and while recent estimates for the company have remained steady, MTW has posted better than expected results. Based on operating earnings yield, the company is about fairly valued when compared to all of the companies in our coverage universe. Share price changes over the past year indicates that MTW will perform very well over the near term.

Financial Data
(US$ in Thousands)

	12/31/2012	12/31/2011	12/31/2010	12/31/2009	12/31/2008	12/31/2007	12/31/2006	12/31/2005
Earnings Per Share	0.76	(0.08)	(0.56)	(5.41)	(0.08)	2.64	1.33	0.54
Cash Flow Per Share	1.23	0.12	1.60	2.60	2.37	1.91	2.40	0.89
Tang Book Value Per Share	N.M.	N.M.	N.M.	N.M.	N.M.	4.85	1.23	N.M.
Dividends Per Share	0.080	0.080	0.080	0.080	0.080	0.075	0.070	0.070
Dividend Payout %	10.53	...	...	...	...	2.84	5.28	13.08
Income Statement								
Total Revenue	3,927,000	3,651,900	3,141,700	3,782,600	4,503,000	4,005,000	2,933,300	2,254,097
EBITDA	382,200	315,400	277,900	(371,500)	225,100	587,400	363,500	191,133
Depn & Amortn	106,600	120,900	125,500	131,100	91,800	88,100	72,300	63,509
Income Before Taxes	130,300	37,400	(44,600)	(705,400)	79,200	463,000	244,900	73,858
Income Taxes	38,000	15,900	23,900	(58,800)	1,500	129,400	78,400	14,772
Net Income	101,700	(10,500)	(73,400)	(704,200)	(10,700)	336,700	166,200	65,800
Average Shares	133,317	133,377	130,581	130,268	129,930	127,489	125,571	123,052
Balance Sheet								
Current Assets	1,328,000	1,239,800	1,160,600	1,259,900	2,134,300	1,575,600	1,142,700	953,383
Total Assets	4,057,300	3,965,200	4,009,300	4,278,700	6,065,400	2,868,700	2,219,500	1,961,777
Current Liabilities	1,145,900	1,104,600	1,025,500	1,142,200	1,618,100	1,074,600	935,400	690,254
Long-Term Obligations	1,732,000	1,810,900	1,935,600	2,027,500	2,473,000	217,500	264,300	474,000
Total Liabilities	3,457,000	3,481,800	3,527,400	3,670,800	4,765,600	1,518,800	1,445,000	1,418,449
Stockholders' Equity	600,300	483,400	481,900	607,900	1,299,800	1,349,900	774,500	543,328
Shares Outstanding	132,769	131,884	131,388	130,708	130,359	129,880	124,243	121,450
Statistical Record								
Return on Assets %	2.53	N.M.	N.M.	N.M.	N.M.	13.23	7.95	3.38
Return on Equity %	18.72	N.M.	N.M.	N.M.	N.M.	31.70	25.22	12.39
EBITDA Margin %	9.73	8.64	8.85	N.M.	5.00	14.67	12.39	8.48
Net Margin %	2.59	N.M.	N.M.	N.M.	N.M.	8.41	5.67	2.92
Asset Turnover	0.98	0.92	0.76	0.73	1.01	1.57	1.40	1.16
Current Ratio	1.16	1.12	1.13	1.10	1.32	1.47	1.22	1.38
Debt to Equity	2.89	3.75	4.02	3.34	1.90	0.16	0.34	0.87
Price Range	16.28-9.72	22.88-6.01	15.96-8.61	11.63-2.42	48.83-4.61	50.98-25.93	31.09-12.86	13.30-8.57
P/E Ratio	21.42-12.79	...	...	...	...	19.31-9.82	23.37-9.67	24.63-15.88
Average Yield %	0.61	0.55	0.69	1.14	0.28	0.20	0.31	0.64

Address: 2400 South 44th Street, Manitowoc, WI 54221-0066 **Telephone:** 920-684-4410	**Web Site:** www.manitowoc.com **Officers:** Glen E. Tellock - Chairman, President, Chief Executive Officer Carl J. Laurino - Senior Vice President, Chief Financial Officer	**Auditors:** PricewaterhouseCoopers LLP **Investor Contact:** 920-684-4410 **Transfer Agents:** Computershare Trust Company, N.A, Providence, RI

MANPOWERGROUP

Exchange	Symbol	Price	52Wk Range	Yield	P/E
NYS	MAN	$56.72 (3/28/2013)	57.31-32.41	1.52	22.96

*7 Year Price Score 69.49 *NYSE Composite Index=100 *12 Month Price Score 120.27

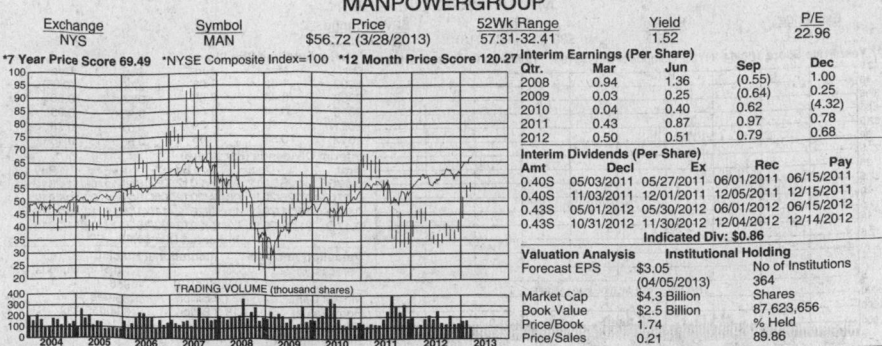

Interim Earnings (Per Share)

Qtr.	Mar	Jun	Sep	Dec
2008	0.94	1.36	(0.55)	1.00
2009	0.03	0.25	(0.64)	0.25
2010	0.04	0.40	0.62	(4.32)
2011	0.43	0.87	0.97	0.78
2012	0.50	0.51	0.79	0.68

Interim Dividends (Per Share)

Amt	Decl	Ex	Rec	Pay
0.40S	05/03/2011	05/27/2011	06/01/2011	06/15/2011
0.40S	11/03/2011	12/01/2011	12/05/2011	12/15/2011
0.43S	05/01/2012	05/30/2012	06/01/2012	06/15/2012
0.43S	10/31/2012	11/30/2012	12/04/2012	12/14/2012

Indicated Div: $0.86

Valuation Analysis   **Institutional Holding**

Forecast EPS	$3.05 (04/05/2013)	No of Institutions	364
Market Cap	$4.3 Billion	Shares	87,623,656
Book Value	$2.5 Billion	% Held	89.86
Price/Book	1.74		
Price/Sales	0.21		

Business Summary: Business Services (MIC: 7.5.2 SIC: 7363 NAIC: 561330)

Manpower is a provider of workforce services such as recruitment and assessment, training and development, outsourcing, and workforce consulting. Co.'s operating segments are: Americas, which include U.S. and Other Americas; Southern Europe, which include France, Italy and Other Southern Europe; Northern Europe; Asia Pacific Middle East (APME); and Right Management. The Americas, Southern Europe, Northern Europe and APME segments engages in the placement of contingent workers, and other workforce services, including recruitment and assessment, training and development, and ManpowerGroup Solutions. The Right Management segment consists of career management and workforce consulting services.

Recent Developments: For the year ended Dec 31 2012, net income decreased 21.5% to US$197.6 million from US$251.6 million in the prior year. Revenues were US$20.68 billion, down 6.0% from US$22.01 billion the year before. Operating income was US$411.7 million versus US$524.2 million in the prior year, a decrease of 21.5%. Direct operating expenses declined 5.8% to US$17.24 billion from US$18.30 billion in the comparable period the year before. Indirect operating expenses decreased 4.8% to US$3.03 billion from US$3.18 billion in the equivalent prior-year period.

Prospects: Our evaluation of ManpowerGroup as of Apr. 7, 2013 is the result of our systematic analysis on three basic characteristics: earnings strength, relative valuation, and recent stock price movement. The company has produced a positive trend in earnings per share over the past 5 quarters and while recent estimates for the company have remained steady, MAN has posted better than expected results. Based on operating earnings yield, the company is about fairly valued when compared to all of the companies in our coverage universe. Share price changes over the past year indicates that MAN will perform in line with the market over the near term.

Financial Data
(US$ in Thousands)

	12/31/2012	12/31/2011	12/31/2010	12/31/2009	12/31/2008	12/31/2007	12/31/2006	12/31/2005
Earnings Per Share	2.47	3.04	(3.26)	(0.12)	2.75	5.73	4.54	2.87
Cash Flow Per Share	4.16	0.85	2.25	5.29	10.04	5.20	4.17	3.03
Tang Book Value Per Share	14.73	14.31	13.05	15.00	14.05	15.76	13.88	10.19
Dividends Per Share	0.860	0.800	0.740	0.740	0.740	0.690	0.590	0.470
Dividend Payout %	34.82	26.32	...	...	26.91	12.04	13.00	16.38
Income Statement								
Total Revenue	20,678,000	22,006,000	18,866,500	16,038,700	21,552,800	20,500,300	17,562,500	16,080,400
EBITDA	504,100	619,800	(17,600)	124,300	607,200	919,200	606,500	526,400
Depn & Amortn	100,500	104,400	110,100	97,200	107,100	99,000	88,800	94,800
Income Before Taxes	368,400	479,900	(165,200)	(22,900)	458,300	791,200	481,900	394,700
Income Taxes	170,800	228,300	98,400	(13,700)	239,400	306,500	176,200	134,600
Net Income	197,600	251,600	(263,600)	(9,200)	218,900	484,700	398,000	260,100
Average Shares	80,100	82,800	81,000	78,300	79,700	84,600	87,700	91,100
Balance Sheet								
Current Assets	5,060,600	4,990,500	4,874,000	4,332,400	4,690,100	5,214,800	4,682,000	3,841,700
Total Assets	7,012,600	6,899,700	6,729,700	6,213,800	6,618,200	7,224,400	6,514,100	5,568,400
Current Liabilities	3,677,200	3,762,200	3,290,100	2,603,000	2,906,600	3,255,500	2,881,600	2,580,500
Long-Term Obligations	462,100	266,000	669,300	715,600	837,300	874,800	791,200	475,000
Total Liabilities	4,511,800	4,416,300	4,332,500	3,677,300	4,134,400	4,555,100	4,039,900	3,421,800
Stockholders' Equity	2,500,800	2,483,400	2,397,200	2,536,500	2,483,800	2,669,300	2,474,200	2,146,600
Shares Outstanding	76,647	79,903	81,759	78,576	77,964	79,872	85,070	87,372
Statistical Record								
Return on Assets %	2.83	3.69	N.M.	N.M.	3.15	7.06	6.59	4.56
Return on Equity %	7.91	10.31	N.M.	N.M.	8.47	18.85	17.23	12.04
EBITDA Margin %	2.44	2.82	N.M.	0.78	2.82	4.48	3.45	3.27
Net Margin %	0.96	1.14	N.M.	N.M.	1.02	2.36	2.27	1.62
Asset Turnover	2.96	3.23	2.92	2.50	3.11	2.98	2.91	2.82
Current Ratio	1.38	1.33	1.48	1.66	1.61	1.60	1.62	1.49
Debt to Equity	0.18	0.11	0.28	0.28	0.34	0.33	0.32	0.22
Price Range	47.90-32.41	68.67-32.32	65.14-40.58	61.48-23.75	70.35-23.60	95.05-56.20	76.77-46.14	48.65-38.55
P/E Ratio	19.39-13.12	22.59-10.63	...	...	25.58-8.58	16.59-9.81	16.91-10.16	16.95-13.43
Average Yield %	2.19	1.56	1.41	1.70	1.50	0.92	0.96	1.07

Address: 100 Manpower Place, Milwaukee, WI 53212	**Web Site:** www.manpower.com	**Auditors:** Deloitte & Touche LLP
Telephone: 414-961-1000	**Officers:** Jeffrey A. Joerres - Chairman, President,	**Investor Contact:** 414-906-6807
Fax: 414-332-0796	Chief Executive Officer Jonas Prising - Executive Vice President, Region Officer	**Transfer Agents:** Computershare, Providence, R.I.

MARATHON OIL CORP.

Exchange	Symbol	Price	52Wk Range	Yield	P/E
NYS	MRO	$33.72 (3/28/2013)	35.71-23.32	2.02	15.12

*7 Year Price Score 100.64 *NYSE Composite Index=100 ***12 Month Price Score 105.44**

Interim Earnings (Per Share)

Qtr.	Mar	Jun	Sep	Dec
2008	1.02	1.08	2.90	(0.05)
2009	0.40	0.58	0.58	0.50
2010	0.64	1.00	0.98	0.99
2011	1.39	1.39	0.57	0.78
2012	0.59	0.56	0.63	0.45

Interim Dividends (Per Share)

Amt	Decl	Ex	Rec	Pay
0.17Q	04/25/2012	05/14/2012	05/16/2012	06/11/2012
0.17Q	07/25/2012	08/14/2012	08/16/2012	09/10/2012
0.17Q	10/31/2012	11/19/2012	11/21/2012	12/10/2012
0.17Q	01/25/2013	02/15/2013	02/20/2013	03/11/2013

Indicated Div: $0.68

Valuation Analysis		Institutional Holding	
Forecast EPS	$3.10 (04/06/2013)	No of Institutions	956
Market Cap	$23.8 Billion	Shares	634,055,232
Book Value	$18.3 Billion	% Held	79.11
Price/Book	1.30		
Price/Sales	1.47		

TRADING VOLUME (thousand shares)

Business Summary: Production & Extraction (MIC: 9.1.1 SIC: 2911 NAIC: 324110)

Marathon Oil is an international energy company. Co.'s operations are organized into three reportable segments: Exploration and Production, which explores for, produces and markets liquid hydrocarbons and natural gas on a worldwide basis; Oil Sands Mining, which mines, extracts and transports bitumen from oil sands deposits in Alberta, Canada, and upgrades the bitumen to produce and market synthetic crude oil and vacuum gas oil; and Integrated Gas, which produces and markets products manufactured from natural gas, such as liquefied natural gas and methanol, in Equatorial Guinea. As of Dec 31 2012, Co. had total proved reserves of 2.02 billion barrels of oil equivalent.

Recent Developments: For the year ended Dec 31 2012, income from continuing operations decreased 7.3% to US$1.58 billion from US$1.71 billion a year earlier. Net income decreased 46.3% to US$1.58 billion from US$2.95 billion in the prior year. Revenues were US$16.22 billion, up 6.1% from US$15.28 billion the year before. Operating income was US$6.33 billion versus US$4.81 billion in the prior year, an increase of 31.6%. Direct operating expenses declined 15.6% to US$5.47 billion from US$6.48 billion in the comparable period the year before. Indirect operating expenses increased 10.7% to US$4.42 billion from US$3.99 billion in the equivalent prior-year period.

Prospects: Our evaluation of Marathon Oil Corp. as of Apr. 7, 2013 is the result of our systematic analysis on three basic characteristics: earnings strength, relative valuation, and recent stock price movement. The company has produced a positive trend in earnings per share over the past 5 quarters. However, while recent estimates for the company have been mixed, MRO has posted results that fell short of analysts expectations. Based on operating earnings yield, the company is undervalued when compared to all of the companies in our coverage universe. Share price changes over the past year indicates that MRO will perform in line with the market over the near term.

Financial Data

(US$ in Thousands)	12/31/2012	12/31/2011	12/31/2010	12/31/2009	12/31/2008	12/31/2007	12/31/2006	12/31/2005
Earnings Per Share	2.23	4.13	3.61	2.06	4.95	5.69	7.25	4.22
Cash Flow Per Share	5.67	9.19	8.27	7.43	9.54	9.45	7.67	6.65
Tang Book Value Per Share	25.12	23.60	31.54	28.94	28.27	22.59	18.73	13.90
Dividends Per Share	0.680	0.800	0.990	0.960	0.960	0.920	0.765	0.610
Dividend Payout %	30.49	19.37	27.42	46.60	19.39	16.17	10.55	14.45
Income Statement								
Total Revenue	16,221,000	15,282,000	73,621,000	54,139,000	78,569,000	65,207,000	65,449,000	63,673,000
EBITDA	8,821,000	6,827,000	8,174,000	6,124,000	9,215,000	8,420,000	10,466,000	5,301,000
Depn & Amortn	2,478,000	2,266,000	2,965,000	2,623,000	2,178,000	1,613,000	1,518,000	16,000
Income Before Taxes	6,113,000	4,427,000	5,122,000	3,441,000	6,973,000	6,846,000	8,969,000	5,157,000
Income Taxes	4,531,000	2,720,000	2,554,000	2,257,000	3,445,000	2,901,000	4,022,000	1,730,000
Net Income	1,582,000	2,946,000	2,568,000	1,463,000	3,528,000	3,956,000	5,234,000	3,032,000
Average Shares	710,000	714,000	712,000	711,000	713,000	695,000	722,054	718,162
Balance Sheet								
Current Assets	3,762,000	3,224,000	13,829,000	10,637,000	8,403,000	10,587,000	10,096,000	9,383,000
Total Assets	35,306,000	31,371,000	50,014,000	47,052,000	42,686,000	42,746,000	30,831,000	28,498,000
Current Liabilities	5,081,000	4,394,000	11,113,000	9,057,000	7,753,000	11,260,000	8,061,000	8,154,000
Long-Term Obligations	6,512,000	4,674,000	7,601,000	8,436,000	7,087,000	6,084,000	3,061,000	3,698,000
Total Liabilities	17,023,000	14,219,000	26,243,000	25,142,000	21,277,000	23,523,000	16,224,000	16,793,000
Stockholders' Equity	18,283,000	17,152,000	23,771,000	21,910,000	21,409,000	19,223,000	14,607,000	11,705,000
Shares Outstanding	707,000	704,000	710,000	708,000	706,000	710,000	695,541	733,491
Statistical Record								
Return on Assets %	4.73	7.24	5.29	3.26	8.24	10.75	17.64	11.68
Return on Equity %	8.90	14.40	11.24	6.75	17.32	23.39	39.78	30.60
EBITDA Margin %	54.38	44.67	11.10	11.31	11.73	12.91	15.99	8.33
Net Margin %	9.75	19.28	3.49	2.70	4.49	6.07	8.00	4.76
Asset Turnover	0.49	0.38	1.52	1.21	1.83	1.77	2.21	2.45
Current Ratio	0.74	0.73	1.24	1.17	1.08	0.94	1.25	1.15
Debt to Equity	0.36	0.27	0.32	0.39	0.33	0.32	0.21	0.32
Price Range	35.06-23.32	34.07-20.27	22.55-17.08	21.48-12.74	37.68-11.92	40.35-25.40	29.71-19.86	21.57-10.88
P/E Ratio	15.72-10.46	8.25-4.91	6.25-4.73	10.43-6.18	7.61-2.41	7.09-4.46	4.10-2.74	5.11-2.58
Average Yield %	2.34	2.81	5.00	5.24	3.66	2.78	3.12	3.74

Address: 5555 San Felipe Street, Houston, TX 77056-2723	Web Site: www.marathonoil.com	Auditors: PricewaterhouseCoopers LLP
Telephone: 713-629-6600	Officers: Clarence P. Cazalot - Chairman, President, Chief Executive Officer Janet F. Clark - Executive Vice President, Senior Vice President, Chief Financial Officer	Investor Contact: 713-296-4114 Transfer Agents: Computershare, Providence, R.I.

MARATHON PETROLEUM CORP.

Exchange	Symbol	Price	52Wk Range	Yield	P/E
NYS	MPC	$89.60 (3/28/2013)	91.13-34.28	1.56	9.06

*7 Year Price Score N/A *NYSE Composite Index=100 *12 Month Price Score 137.79

Interim Earnings (Per Share)

Qtr.	Mar	Jun	Sep	Dec
2010	0.00	1.13	0.77	0.00
2011	0.00	2.24	3.16	(0.21)
2012	1.70	2.38	3.59	2.24

Interim Dividends (Per Share)

Amt	Decl	Ex	Rec	Pay
0.25Q	04/25/2012	05/14/2012	05/16/2012	06/11/2012
0.35Q	07/25/2012	08/14/2012	08/16/2012	09/10/2012
0.35Q	10/31/2012	11/19/2012	11/21/2012	12/10/2012
0.35Q	01/30/2013	02/15/2013	02/20/2013	03/11/2013

Indicated Div: $1.40

Valuation Analysis

Forecast EPS	$10.64 (04/06/2013)
Market Cap	$29.8 Billion
Book Value	$11.7 Billion
Price/Book	2.55
Price/Sales	0.36

Institutional Holding

No of Institutions	728
Shares	278,851,584
% Held	N/A

TRADING VOLUME (thousand shares)

Business Summary: Refining & Marketing (MIC: 9.1.2 SIC: 1311 NAIC: 211111)

Marathon Petroleum is an independent petroleum refining, marketing and transportation company. Co. has three operating segments: Refining and Marketing, which refines crude oil and other feedstocks at Co.'s six refineries in the Gulf Coast and Midwest regions of the U.S., purchases ethanol and refined products for resale and distributes refined products; Speedway, which sells transportation fuels and convenience products in the retail market in the Midwest, primarily through Speedway® convenience stores; and Pipeline Transportation, which transports crude oil and other feedstocks to Co.'s refineries and other locations, and delivers refined products to wholesale and retail market areas.

Recent Developments: For the year ended Dec 31 2012, net income increased 42.0% to US$3.39 billion from US$2.39 billion in the prior year. Revenues were US$82.49 billion, up 4.7% from US$78.76 billion the year before. Operating income was US$5.35 billion versus US$3.75 billion in the prior year, an increase of 42.8%. Direct operating expenses rose 4.4% to US$68.67 billion from US$65.80 billion in the comparable period the year before. Indirect operating expenses decreased 8.0% to US$8.48 billion from US$9.22 billion in the equivalent prior-year period.

Prospects: Our evaluation of Marathon Petroleum Corp. as of Apr. 7, 2013 is the result of our systematic analysis on three basic characteristics: earnings strength, relative valuation, and recent stock price movement. The company has produced a positive trend in earnings per share over the past 5 quarters and while recent estimates for the company have been raised by analysts, MPC has posted better than expected results. Based on operating earnings yield, the company is undervalued when compared to all of the companies in our coverage universe. Share price changes over the past year indicates that MPC will perform very well over the near term.

Financial Data

(US$ in Millions)	12/31/2012	12/31/2011	12/31/2010	12/31/2009	12/31/2008
Earnings Per Share	9.89	6.67	...	...	...
Cash Flow Per Share	13.18	9.29	...	...	...
Tang Book Value Per Share	32.32	24.27	...	...	...
Dividends Per Share	1.200	0.450	...	...	...
Dividend Payout %	12.13	6.75	...	...	...
Income Statement					
Total Revenue	82,492	78,759	62,605	45,639	65,258
EBITDA	6,317	4,632	1,945	1,315	2,467
Depn & Amortn	995	891	941	670	606
Income Before Taxes	5,238	3,719	1,023	685	1,885
Income Taxes	1,845	1,330	400	236	670
Net Income	3,389	2,389	623	449	1,215
Average Shares	342	357	...	...	...
Balance Sheet					
Current Assets	13,029	12,001	10,056	7,900	...
Total Assets	27,223	25,745	23,232	21,254	...
Current Liabilities	8,203	9,591	8,620	6,637	...
Long-Term Obligations	3,342	3,292	3,231	2,601	...
Total Liabilities	15,529	16,240	14,988	12,082	...
Stockholders' Equity	11,694	9,505	8,244	9,172	...
Shares Outstanding	333	357	...	...	...
Statistical Record					
Return on Assets %	12.76	9.76	2.80	...	...
Return on Equity %	31.89	26.92	7.15	...	...
EBITDA Margin %	7.66	5.88	3.11	2.88	3.78
Net Margin %	4.11	3.03	1.00	0.98	1.86
Asset Turnover	3.11	3.22	2.81	...	...
Current Ratio	1.59	1.25	1.17	1.19	...
Debt to Equity	0.29	0.35	0.39	0.28	...
Price Range	63.00-30.96	44.97-27.06	...	...	...
P/E Ratio	6.37-3.13	6.74-4.06	...	...	...
Average Yield %	2.57	1.26	...	...	...

Address: 539 South Main Street, Findlay, OH 45840-3229 **Telephone:** 419-422-2121	**Web Site:** www.marathonpetroleum.com **Officers:** Gary R. Heminger - President, Chief Executive Officer Garry L. Peiffer - Executive Vice President	**Auditors:** PricewaterhouseCoopers LLP **Investor Contact:** 419-429-5640 **Transfer Agents:** Computershare Trust Company, N.A., Canton, MA

MARKEL CORP (HOLDING CO)

Exchange	Symbol	Price	52Wk Range	Yield	P/E
NYS	MKL	$503.50 (3/28/2013)	508.85-421.90	N/A	19.45

*7 Year Price Score 102.39 *NYSE Composite Index=100 ***12 Month Price Score 99.16**

Interim Earnings (Per Share)

Qtr.	Mar	Jun	Sep	Dec
2008	3.41	8.29	(14.46)	(3.32)
2009	1.67	3.34	6.02	9.50
2010	4.33	2.12	6.48	14.34
2011	0.85	3.11	5.48	5.18
2012	5.92	8.42	5.32	6.22

Interim Dividends (Per Share)

No Dividends Paid

Valuation Analysis

		Institutional Holding	
Forecast EPS	$19.75 (04/06/2013)	No of Institutions	309
Market Cap	$4.8 Billion	Shares	8,348,835
Book Value	$3.9 Billion		
Price/Book	1.25	% Held	75.49
Price/Sales	1.62		

Business Summary: General Insurance (MIC: 5.2.1 SIC: 6331 NAIC: 524126)

Markel is a financial holding company. Co.'s key business markets and underwrites insurance products via three segments: Excess and Surplus Lines, which writes property and casualty insurance outside of the standard market for hard-to-place risks; Specialty Admitted, which writes risks that, although hard-to-place in the standard market, must remain with an admitted insurance company for marketing and regulatory reasons; and London markets, which writes specialty property, casualty, professional liability, equine, marine, energy and trade credit insurance and reinsurance. Co. also owns interests in industrial and service businesses that operate outside of the specialty insurance market.

Recent Developments: For the year ended Dec 31 2012, net income increased 73.9% to US$258.2 million from US$148.5 million in the prior year. Revenues were US$3.00 billion, up 14.1% from US$2.63 billion the year before. Net premiums earned were US$2.15 billion versus US$1.98 billion in the prior year, an increase of 8.5%. Net investment income rose 7.0% to US$282.1 million from US$263.7 million a year ago.

Prospects: Our evaluation of Markel Corp. as of Apr. 7, 2013 is the result of our systematic analysis on three basic characteristics: earnings strength, relative valuation, and recent stock price movement. The company has suffered a very negative trend in earnings per share over the past 5 quarters and while recent estimates for the company have remained steady, MKL has posted better than expected results. Based on operating earnings yield, the company is about fairly valued when compared to all of the companies in our coverage universe. Share price changes over the past year indicates that MKL will perform poorly over the near term.

Financial Data
(US$ in Thousands)

	12/31/2012	12/31/2011	12/31/2010	12/31/2009	12/31/2008	12/31/2007	12/31/2006	12/31/2005
Earnings Per Share	25.89	14.60	27.27	20.52	(5.95)	40.64	39.40	14.80
Cash Flow Per Share	40.61	32.14	22.86	28.78	39.40	51.03	52.69	56.10
Tang Book Value Per Share	294.88	261.92	259.89	231.34	187.15	230.62	195.78	139.38
Income Statement								
Premium Income	2,147,128	1,979,340	1,730,921	1,815,835	2,022,184	2,117,294	2,184,381	1,938,461
Total Revenue	3,000,112	2,629,950	2,225,393	2,069,326	1,898,328	2,483,256	2,519,005	2,200,148
Benefits & Claims	1,154,068	1,209,986	946,229	992,863	1,269,025	1,096,203	1,132,579	1,299,983
Income Before Taxes	312,050	190,196	295,511	198,637	(161,016)	571,958	553,401	186,000
Income Taxes	53,802	41,710	27,782	(3,782)	(102,249)	166,289	160,899	38,085
Net Income	253,385	142,026	266,793	201,638	(58,767)	405,669	392,502	147,915
Average Shares	9,666	9,726	9,785	9,826	9,876	9,981	10,024	10,171
Balance Sheet								
Total Assets	12,556,588	11,532,103	10,825,589	10,241,896	9,477,690	10,134,419	10,088,131	9,814,098
Total Liabilities	8,667,931	8,144,590	7,654,066	7,467,536	7,297,016	7,493,257	7,791,738	8,108,665
Stockholders' Equity	3,888,657	3,387,513	3,171,523	2,774,360	2,180,674	2,641,162	2,296,393	1,705,433
Shares Outstanding	9,629	9,620	9,717	9,819	9,813	9,956	9,994	9,798
Statistical Record								
Return on Assets %	2.10	1.27	2.53	2.05	N.M.	4.01	3.94	1.54
Return on Equity %	6.95	4.33	8.97	8.14	N.M.	16.43	19.62	8.80
Loss Ratio %	53.75	61.13	54.67	54.68	62.76	51.77	51.85	67.06
Net Margin %	8.45	5.40	11.99	9.74	(3.10)	16.34	15.58	6.72
Price Range	500.68-399.12	425.68-347.36	387.72-321.32	363.00-211.00	491.10-245.25	545.50-458.91	481.50-319.50	367.91-307.69
P/E Ratio	19.34-15.42	29.16-23.79	14.22-11.78	17.69-10.28	...	13.42-11.29	12.22-8.11	24.86-20.79

Address: 4521 Highwoods Parkway, Glen Allen, VA 23060-6148 **Telephone:** 804-747-0136	**Web Site:** www.markelcorp.com **Officers:** Alan I. Kirshner - Chairman, Chief Executive Officer Steven A. Markel - Vice-Chairman	**Auditors:** KPMG LLP **Investor Contact:** 800-446-6671 **Transfer Agents:** American Stock Transfer & Trust Company, LLC, Brooklyn, NY

MARRIOTT INTERNATIONAL, INC.

Exchange	Symbol	Price	52Wk Range	Yield	P/E
NYS	MAR	$42.23 (3/28/2013)	42.23-34.11	1.23	24.55

*7 Year Price Score 103.79 *NYSE Composite Index=100 *12 Month Price Score 97.24

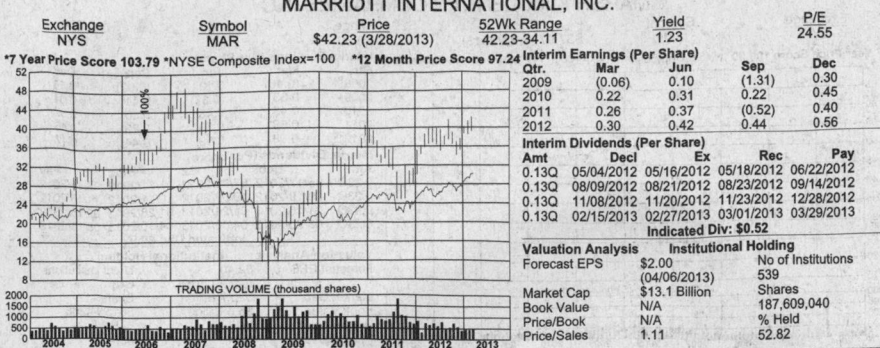

Interim Earnings (Per Share)

Qtr.	Mar	Jun	Sep	Dec
2009	(0.06)	0.10	(1.31)	0.30
2010	0.22	0.31	0.22	0.45
2011	0.26	0.37	(0.52)	0.40
2012	0.30	0.42	0.44	0.56

Interim Dividends (Per Share)

Amt	Decl	Ex	Rec	Pay
0.13Q	05/04/2012	05/16/2012	05/18/2012	06/22/2012
0.13Q	08/09/2012	08/21/2012	08/23/2012	09/14/2012
0.13Q	11/08/2012	11/20/2012	11/23/2012	12/28/2012
0.13Q	02/15/2013	02/27/2013	03/01/2013	03/29/2013

Indicated Div: $0.52

Valuation Analysis

		Institutional Holding	
Forecast EPS	$2.00	No of Institutions	
	(04/06/2013)	539	
Market Cap	$13.1 Billion	Shares	
Book Value	N/A	187,609,040	
Price/Book	N/A	% Held	
Price/Sales	1.11	52.82	

Business Summary: Hotels, Restaurants & Travel (MIC: 2.2.1 SIC: 7011 NAIC: 721110)

Marriott International is an operator, franchisor, and licensor of hotels and timeshare properties under various brand names. Co. also operates, markets, and develops residential properties and provides services to home/condominium owner associations. Co.'s operations are grouped into four business segments: North American Full-Service Lodging, North American Limited-Service Lodging, International Lodging, and Luxury Lodging. As of Dec 28 2012, Co. operated, franchised or licensed 3,801 lodging properties worldwide, with 660,394 rooms inclusive of 35 home and condominium products (3,927 units) for which Co. managed the related owners' associations.

Recent Developments: For the year ended Dec 28 2012, net income increased 188.4% to US$571.0 million from US$198.0 million in the prior year. Revenues were US$11.81 billion, down 4.1% from US$12.32 billion the year before. Operating income was US$940.0 million versus US$526.0 million in the prior year, an increase of 78.7%. Direct operating expenses declined 7.3% to US$10.23 billion from US$11.04 billion in the comparable period the year before. Indirect operating expenses decreased 14.2% to US$645.0 million from US$752.0 million in the equivalent prior-year period.

Prospects: Our evaluation of Marriott International Inc. as of Apr. 7, 2013 is the result of our systematic analysis on three basic characteristics: earnings strength, relative valuation, and recent stock price movement. The company has managed to produce a neutral trend in earnings per share over the past 5 quarters. However, while recent estimates for the company have been mixed, MAR has posted better than expected results. Based on operating earnings yield, the company is about fairly valued when compared to all of the companies in our coverage universe. Share price changes over the past year indicates that MAR will perform poorly over the near term.

Financial Data
(US$ in Millions)

	12/28/2012	12/30/2011	12/31/2010	01/01/2010	01/02/2009	12/28/2007	12/29/2006	12/30/2005
Earnings Per Share	1.72	0.55	1.21	(0.97)	0.99	1.75	1.41	1.45
Cash Flow Per Share	3.07	3.12	3.18	2.44	1.79	2.07	2.41	1.94
Tang Book Value Per Share	...	...	N.M.	N.M.	N.M.	N.M.	2.88	4.52
Dividends Per Share	0.490	0.388	0.207	0.087	0.338	0.287	0.240	0.200
Dividend Payout %	28.49	70.45	17.15		34.09	16.43	17.02	13.84
Income Statement								
Total Revenue	11,814	12,317	11,691	10,908	12,879	12,990	12,160	11,550
EBITDA	1,075	646	868	(108)	958	1,430	1,228	864
Depn & Amortn	93	127	138	151	155	162	155	156
Income Before Taxes	862	369	569	(352)	679	1,122	994	681
Income Taxes	278	158	93	(65)	350	441	286	94
Net Income	571	198	458	(346)	362	696	608	669
Average Shares	332	362	378	356	366	397	430	462
Balance Sheet								
Current Assets	1,475	1,324	3,382	2,851	3,368	3,572	3,314	2,010
Total Assets	6,342	5,910	8,983	7,933	8,903	8,942	8,588	8,530
Current Liabilities	2,773	2,558	2,501	2,287	2,533	2,876	2,522	1,992
Long-Term Obligations	2,528	1,816	2,691	2,234	2,975	2,790	1,818	1,681
Total Liabilities	7,627	6,691	7,398	6,791	7,523	7,513	5,970	5,278
Stockholders' Equity	(1,285)	(781)	1,585	1,142	1,380	1,429	2,618	3,252
Shares Outstanding	310	333	366	358	349	357	389	411
Statistical Record								
Return on Assets %	9.35	2.67	5.43	N.M.	3.99	7.96	7.12	7.80
Return on Equity %	...	49.39	33.68	N.M.	25.36	34.49	20.77	18.30
EBITDA Margin %	9.10	5.24	7.42	N.M.	7.44	11.01	10.10	7.48
Net Margin %	4.83	1.61	3.92	N.M.	2.81	5.36	5.00	5.79
Asset Turnover	1.93	1.66	1.39	1.30	1.42	1.49	1.42	1.35
Current Ratio	0.53	0.52	1.35	1.25	1.33	1.24	1.31	1.01
Debt to Equity	...	...	1.70	1.96	2.16	1.95	0.69	0.52
Price Range	41.60-29.17	40.11-24.88	40.64-24.59	26.81-11.94	35.27-11.80	49.02-29.76	45.45-31.21	33.32-27.45
P/E Ratio	24.19-16.96	72.93-45.23	33.59-20.32		35.62-11.92	28.01-17.00	32.24-22.13	22.98-18.93
Average Yield %	1.32	1.20	0.64	0.42	1.28	0.69	0.67	0.65

Address: 10400 Fernwood Road, Bethesda, MD 20817 Telephone: 301-380-3000	Web Site: www.marriott.com Officers: J. W. Marriott - Executive Chairman, Chief Executive Officer John W. Marriott - Vice-Chairman	Auditors: Ernst & Young LLP Transfer Agents: BNY Mellon Shareowner Services, Jersey City, NJ

MARSH & MCLENNAN COMPANIES INC.

Exchange	Symbol	Price	52Wk Range	Yield	P/E
NYS	MMC	$37.97 (3/28/2013)	37.97-30.80	2.42	17.83

*7 Year Price Score 109.20 *NYSE Composite Index=100 *12 Month Price Score 99.41

Interim Earnings (Per Share)

Qtr.	Mar	Jun	Sep	Dec
2008	(0.40)	0.13	(0.02)	0.16
2009	0.33	(0.37)	0.41	0.04
2010	0.45	0.43	0.30	0.37
2011	0.58	0.50	0.23	0.46
2012	0.63	0.59	0.44	0.47

Interim Dividends (Per Share)

Amt	Decl	Ex	Rec	Pay
0.23Q	05/17/2012	07/09/2012	07/11/2012	08/15/2012
0.23Q	09/19/2012	10/09/2012	10/11/2012	11/15/2012
0.23Q	01/16/2013	01/24/2013	01/28/2013	02/15/2013
0.23Q	03/20/2013	04/08/2013	04/10/2013	05/15/2013

Indicated Div: $0.92

Valuation Analysis / **Institutional Holding**

Forecast EPS	$2.40 (04/06/2013)	No of Institutions 648
Market Cap	$20.7 Billion	Shares
Book Value	$6.5 Billion	501,994,208
Price/Book	3.17	% Held
Price/Sales	1.74	83.47

Business Summary: Brokers & Intermediaries (MIC: 5.2.3 SIC: 6411 NAIC: 524210)

Marsh & McLennan Companies provides advice and services in the areas of risk, strategy and human capital. Co.'s Risk and Insurance Services segment, which is managed through Marsh and Guy Carpenter, provides risk management and insurance broking, reinsurance broking and insurance program management services for businesses, public entities, insurance companies, associations, professional services organizations, and private clients. Co. conducts business in its Consulting segment via: Mercer, which provides consulting, advice, and services in the areas of talent, health, retirement and investments; and Oliver Wyman Group, which provides management and economic and brand consulting services.

Recent Developments: For the year ended Dec 31 2012, income from continuing operations increased 22.6% to US$1.20 billion from US$982.0 million a year earlier. Net income increased 18.3% to US$1.20 billion from US$1.02 billion in the prior year. Revenues were US$11.92 billion, up 3.5% from US$11.53 billion the year before.

Prospects: Our evaluation of Marsh & McLennan Cos. Inc. as of Apr. 7, 2013 is the result of our systematic analysis on three basic characteristics: earnings strength, relative valuation, and recent stock price movement. The company has managed to produce a neutral trend in earnings per share over the past 5 quarters and while recent estimates for the company have remained steady, MMC has posted results that fell short of analysts expectations. Based on operating earnings yield, the company is undervalued when compared to all of the companies in our coverage universe. Share price changes over the past year indicates that MMC will perform in line with the market over the near term.

Financial Data
(US$ in Thousands)

	12/31/2012	12/31/2011	12/31/2010	12/31/2009	12/31/2008	12/31/2007	12/31/2006	12/31/2005
Earnings Per Share	2.13	1.79	1.55	0.42	(0.14)	4.53	1.76	0.74
Cash Flow Per Share	2.42	3.15	1.34	1.23	1.62	(0.43)	1.60	0.74
Tang Book Value Per Share	N.M.	N.M.	N.M.	N.M.	N.M.	0.12	N.M.	N.M.
Dividends Per Share	0.900	0.860	0.810	0.800	0.800	0.760	0.680	0.680
Dividend Payout %	42.25	48.04	52.26	190.48	...	16.78	38.64	91.89
Income Statement								
Total Revenue	11,924,000	11,526,000	10,550,000	10,493,000	11,587,000	11,350,000	11,921,000	11,652,000
EBITDA	1,925,000	1,640,000	1,048,000	565,000	323,000	1,461,000	2,042,000	1,436,000
Depn & Amortn	72,000	65,000	66,000	58,000	72,000	442,000	584,000	580,000
Income Before Taxes	1,696,000	1,404,000	769,000	283,000	79,000	847,000	1,219,000	571,000
Income Taxes	492,000	422,000	204,000	41,000	137,000	295,000	388,000	192,000
Net Income	1,176,000	993,000	855,000	227,000	(73,000)	2,475,000	990,000	404,000
Average Shares	552,000	551,000	544,000	524,000	514,000	546,000	557,000	543,000
Balance Sheet								
Current Assets	5,963,000	5,648,000	5,276,000	4,931,000	4,784,000	5,454,000	5,834,000	5,262,000
Total Assets	16,288,000	15,454,000	15,310,000	15,337,000	15,206,000	17,359,000	18,137,000	17,892,000
Current Liabilities	3,564,000	3,739,000	3,105,000	3,703,000	3,386,000	3,493,000	5,549,000	4,351,000
Long-Term Obligations	2,658,000	2,668,000	3,026,000	3,034,000	3,194,000	3,604,000	3,860,000	5,044,000
Total Liabilities	9,746,000	9,571,000	8,942,000	9,509,000	9,484,000	9,537,000	12,318,000	12,532,000
Stockholders' Equity	6,542,000	5,883,000	6,368,000	5,828,000	5,722,000	7,822,000	5,819,000	5,360,000
Shares Outstanding	545,507	539,178	540,509	529,674	514,266	520,392	551,913	545,583
Statistical Record								
Return on Assets %	7.39	6.46	5.58	1.49	N.M.	13.95	5.50	2.23
Return on Equity %	18.88	16.21	14.02	3.93	N.M.	36.29	17.71	7.76
EBITDA Margin %	16.14	14.23	9.93	5.38	2.79	12.87	17.13	12.32
Net Margin %	9.86	8.62	8.10	2.16	N.M.	21.81	8.30	3.47
Asset Turnover	0.75	0.75	0.69	0.69	0.71	0.64	0.66	0.64
Current Ratio	1.67	1.51	1.70	1.33	1.41	1.56	1.05	1.21
Debt to Equity	0.41	0.45	0.48	0.52	0.56	0.46	0.66	0.94
Price Range	35.78-30.72	32.00-25.71	27.48-20.57	25.39-17.74	33.58-21.29	33.19-24.20	32.73-24.77	33.09-26.93
P/E Ratio	16.80-14.42	17.88-14.36	17.73-13.27	60.45-42.24	...	7.33-5.34	18.60-14.07	44.72-36.39
Average Yield %	2.72	2.93	3.40	3.73	2.94	2.66	2.34	2.28

Address: 1166 Avenue Of The Americas, New York, NY 10036-2774 **Telephone:** 212-345-5000 **Fax:** 212-345-4809	**Web Site:** www.mmc.com **Officers:** David A. Nadler - Vice-Chairman Daniel S. Glaser - President, Chief Executive Officer, Chief Operating Officer, Division Officer	**Auditors:** Deloitte & Touche LLP **Transfer Agents:** Wells Fargo Shareowner Services, St. Paul, MN

MARTIN MARIETTA MATERIALS, INC.

Exchange	Symbol	Price	52Wk Range	Yield	P/E
NYS	MLM	$102.02 (3/28/2013)	104.88-64.56	1.57	55.75

*7 Year Price Score 80.27   *NYSE Composite Index=100   *12 Month Price Score 107.23

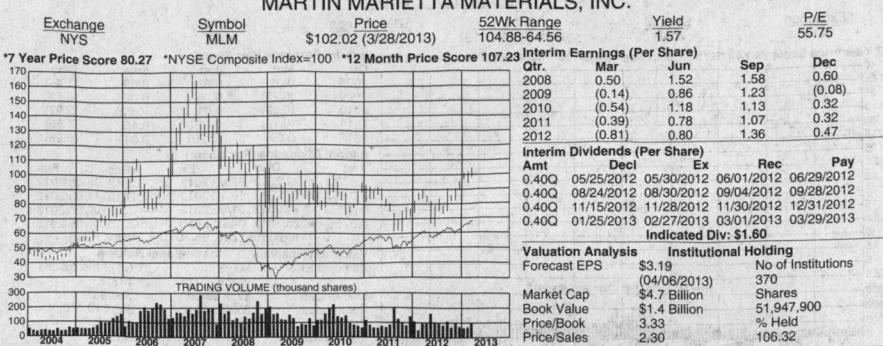

Interim Earnings (Per Share)

Qtr.	Mar	Jun	Sep	Dec
2008	0.50	1.52	1.58	0.60
2009	(0.14)	0.86	1.23	(0.08)
2010	(0.54)	1.18	1.13	0.32
2011	(0.39)	0.78	1.07	0.32
2012	(0.81)	0.80	1.36	0.47

Interim Dividends (Per Share)

Amt	Decl	Ex	Rec	Pay
0.40Q	05/25/2012	05/30/2012	06/01/2012	06/29/2012
0.40Q	08/24/2012	08/30/2012	09/04/2012	09/28/2012
0.40Q	11/15/2012	11/28/2012	11/30/2012	12/31/2012
0.40Q	01/25/2013	02/27/2013	03/01/2013	03/29/2013

Indicated Div: $1.60

Valuation Analysis / Institutional Holding

Forecast EPS	$3.19	No of Institutions
	(04/06/2013)	370
Market Cap	$4.7 Billion	Shares
Book Value	$1.4 Billion	51,947,900
Price/Book	3.33	% Held
Price/Sales	2.30	106.32

Business Summary: Construction Materials (MIC: 8.5.1 SIC: 1411 NAIC: 212311)

Martin Marietta Materials is engaged in the construction aggregates business. Co. operates four segments: the Mideast Group, Southeast Group, and West Group, collectively the Aggregates business, and the Specialty Products segment. The Aggregates business mines, processes and sells granite, limestone, sand, gravel, and other aggregate products for use in the public infrastructure, nonresidential and residential construction industries, agriculture, railroad ballast, chemical, and other uses. The Aggregates business also includes the operation of other construction materials businesses. The Specialty Products segment includes the magnesia-based chemical and dolomitic lime businesses.

Recent Developments: For the year ended Dec 31 2012, income from continuing operations increased 8.0% to US$86.0 million from US$79.6 million a year earlier. Net income increased 2.3% to US$85.5 million from US$83.6 million in the prior year. Revenues were US$2.04 billion, up 18.9% from US$1.71 billion the year before. Operating income was US$155.0 million versus US$161.0 million in the prior year, a decrease of 3.7%. Direct operating expenses rose 21.2% to US$1.71 billion from US$1.41 billion in the comparable period the year before. Indirect operating expenses increased 21.3% to US$171.0 million from US$141.0 million in the equivalent prior-year period.

Prospects: Our evaluation of Martin Marietta Materials Inc. as of Apr. 7, 2013 is the result of our systematic analysis on three basic characteristics: earnings strength, relative valuation, and recent stock price movement. The company has managed to produce a neutral trend in earnings per share over the past 5 quarters and while recent estimates for the company have been mixed, MLM has posted results that fell short of analysts expectations. Based on operating earnings yield, the company is overvalued when compared to all of the companies in our coverage universe. Share price changes over the past year indicates that MLM will perform well over the near term.

Financial Data

(US$ in Thousands)	12/31/2012	12/31/2011	12/31/2010	12/31/2009	12/31/2008	12/31/2007	12/31/2006	12/31/2005
Earnings Per Share	1.83	1.78	2.10	1.91	4.20	6.06	5.29	4.08
Cash Flow Per Share	4.85	5.68	5.93	7.24	8.24	9.27	7.44	6.83
Tang Book Value Per Share	16.17	16.15	17.14	16.05	9.30	8.76	14.99	12.81
Dividends Per Share	1.600	1.600	1.600	1.600	1.490	1.240	1.010	0.860
Dividend Payout %	87.43	89.89	76.19	83.77	35.48	20.46	19.09	21.08
Income Statement								
Total Revenue	2,037,667	1,713,823	1,782,857	1,702,603	2,120,081	2,207,141	2,206,401	2,004,243
EBITDA	328,192	329,162	374,578	364,772	485,575	586,900	527,669	444,237
Depn & Amortn	171,940	169,974	178,426	176,050	167,977	147,427	136,866	133,593
Income Before Taxes	102,913	100,602	127,696	115,262	243,299	378,580	350,444	268,047
Income Taxes	16,950	20,986	29,217	27,375	71,822	116,073	106,640	72,534
Net Income	84,474	82,379	97,012	85,159	176,256	262,749	245,422	192,666
Average Shares	45,970	45,793	45,659	44,190	41,965	43,347	46,367	47,279
Balance Sheet								
Current Assets	700,401	657,850	696,211	856,860	665,031	626,010	592,354	602,041
Total Assets	3,160,926	3,147,822	3,074,743	3,239,283	3,032,502	2,683,805	2,506,421	2,433,316
Current Liabilities	173,335	173,712	385,493	373,553	348,639	506,616	315,072	200,122
Long-Term Obligations	1,042,183	1,052,902	782,045	1,023,492	1,152,414	848,186	579,308	709,159
Total Liabilities	1,750,381	1,738,501	1,649,303	1,874,043	2,010,798	1,737,814	1,252,449	1,259,631
Stockholders' Equity	1,410,545	1,409,321	1,425,440	1,365,240	1,021,704	945,991	1,253,972	1,173,685
Shares Outstanding	46,002	45,726	45,579	45,399	41,462	41,318	44,851	45,727
Statistical Record								
Return on Assets %	2.67	2.65	3.07	2.73	6.15	10.12	9.94	8.05
Return on Equity %	5.97	5.81	6.95	7.16	17.87	23.89	20.22	16.56
EBITDA Margin %	16.11	19.21	21.01	21.42	22.90	26.59	23.92	22.16
Net Margin %	4.15	4.81	5.44	5.02	8.31	11.90	11.12	9.61
Asset Turnover	0.64	0.55	0.56	0.54	0.74	0.85	0.89	0.84
Current Ratio	4.04	3.79	1.81	2.29	1.91	1.24	1.88	3.01
Debt to Equity	0.74	0.75	0.55	0.75	1.13	0.90	0.46	0.76
Price Range	95.59-64.56	93.00-61.62	99.81-72.61	104.24-68.37	132.60-60.29	168.77-99.93	112.37-76.39	79.93-50.01
P/E Ratio	52.23-35.28	52.25-34.62	47.53-34.58	54.58-35.80	31.57-14.35	27.85-16.49	21.24-14.44	19.59-12.26
Average Yield %	1.96	2.03	1.88	1.88	1.45	0.92	1.11	1.32

Address: 2710 Wycliff Road, Raleigh, NC 27607-3033	Web Site: www.martinmarietta.com	Auditors: Ernst & Young LLP
Telephone: 919-781-4550	Officers: C. Howard Nye - President, Chief Executive Officer Philip J. Sipling - Executive Vice President, Division Officer	Investor Contact: 919-788-4367
Fax: 919-783-4552		Transfer Agents: American Stock Transfer & Trust Company, Brooklyn, NY

MASCO CORP.

Exchange	Symbol	Price	52Wk Range	Yield	P/E
NYS	MAS	$20.25 (3/28/2013)	20.94-11.73	1.48	N/A

*7 Year Price Score 79.74   *NYSE Composite Index=100   *12 Month Price Score 117.73

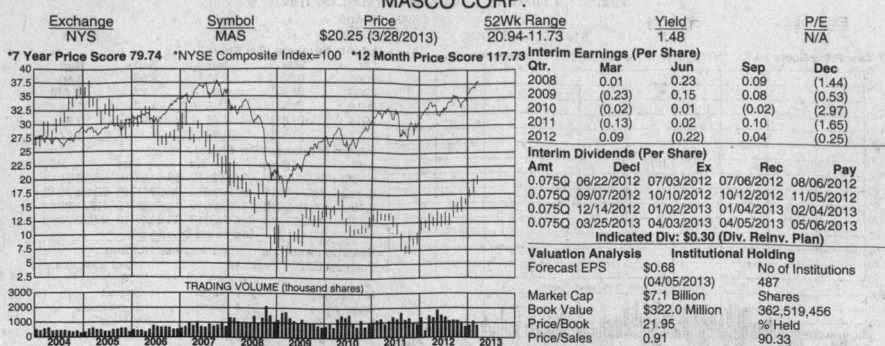

Interim Earnings (Per Share)

Qtr.	Mar	Jun	Sep	Dec
2008	0.01	0.23	0.09	(1.44)
2009	(0.23)	0.15	0.08	(0.53)
2010	(0.02)	0.01	(0.02)	(2.97)
2011	(0.13)	0.02	0.10	(1.65)
2012	0.09	(0.22)	0.04	(0.25)

Interim Dividends (Per Share)

Amt	Decl	Ex	Rec	Pay
0.075Q	06/22/2012	07/03/2012	07/06/2012	08/06/2012
0.075Q	09/07/2012	10/10/2012	10/12/2012	11/05/2012
0.075Q	12/14/2012	01/02/2013	01/04/2013	02/04/2013
0.075Q	03/25/2013	04/03/2013	04/05/2013	05/06/2013

Indicated Div: $0.30 (Div. Reinv. Plan)

Valuation Analysis | **Institutional Holding**

Forecast EPS	$0.68	No of Institutions
	(04/05/2013)	487
Market Cap	$7.1 Billion	Shares
Book Value	$322.0 Million	362,519,456
Price/Book	21.95	% Held
Price/Sales	0.91	90.33

Business Summary: Metal Products (MIC: 8.2.3 SIC: 2434 NAIC: 337110)

Masco manufactures, distributes and installs home improvement and building products. These products are sold for home improvement and new home construction through mass merchandisers, hardware stores, home centers, homebuilders, distributors and other outlets for consumers and contractors and direct to the consumer. Co. has five business segments aggregated by similarity in products and services which includes: cabinets and related products; plumbing products; installation and other services; decorative architectural products; and other specialty products.

Recent Developments: For the year ended Dec 31 2012, loss from continuing operations was US$41.0 million compared with a loss of US$423.0 million a year earlier. Net loss amounted to US$79.0 million versus a net loss of US$533.0 million in the prior year. Revenues were US$7.75 billion, up 3.7% from US$7.47 billion the year before. Operating income was US$271.0 million versus a loss of US$295.0 million in the prior year. Direct operating expenses rose 2.0% to US$5.79 billion from US$5.68 billion in the comparable period the year before. Indirect operating expenses decreased 19.2% to US$1.68 billion from US$2.08 billion in the equivalent prior-year period.

Prospects: Our evaluation of Masco Corp. as of Apr. 7, 2013 is the result of our systematic analysis on three basic characteristics: earnings strength, relative valuation, and recent stock price movement. The company has managed to produce a neutral trend in earnings per share over the past 5 quarters and while recent estimates for the company have been raised by analysts, MAS has posted better than expected results. Based on operating earnings yield, the company is overvalued when compared to all of the companies in our coverage universe. Share price changes over the past year indicates that MAS will perform very well over the near term.

Financial Data

(US$ in Thousands)	12/31/2012	12/31/2011	12/31/2010	12/31/2009	12/31/2008	12/31/2007	12/31/2006	12/31/2005
Earnings Per Share	(0.33)	(1.66)	(3.00)	(0.53)	(1.11)	1.03	1.22	2.19
Cash Flow Per Share	0.80	0.69	1.33	2.01	2.25	3.44	3.07	3.26
Tang Book Value Per Share	N.M.	N.M.	N.M.	N.M.	N.M.	N.M.	0.54	0.88
Dividends Per Share	0.300	0.300	0.300	0.460	0.925	0.910	0.860	0.780
Dividend Payout %	...	...	...	...	...	88.35	70.49	35.62
Income Statement								
Total Revenue	7,745,000	7,467,000	7,592,000	7,792,000	9,600,000	11,770,000	12,778,000	12,642,000
EBITDA	497,000	27,000	(266,000)	309,000	235,000	1,251,000	1,368,000	1,860,000
Depn & Amortn	202,000	246,000	261,000	237,000	220,000	226,000	230,000	208,000
Income Before Taxes	42,000	(472,000)	(777,000)	(151,000)	(211,000)	770,000	900,000	1,412,000
Income Taxes	83,000	(49,000)	225,000	(49,000)	132,000	336,000	412,000	518,000
Net Income	(114,000)	(575,000)	(1,043,000)	(183,000)	(391,000)	386,000	488,000	940,000
Average Shares	349,000	348,000	349,000	351,000	353,000	373,000	400,000	430,000
Balance Sheet								
Current Assets	3,217,000	3,429,000	3,464,000	3,451,000	3,300,000	3,808,000	5,115,000	5,123,000
Total Assets	6,875,000	7,297,000	8,140,000	9,175,000	9,483,000	10,907,000	12,325,000	12,559,000
Current Liabilities	1,862,000	2,363,000	1,487,000	1,781,000	1,547,000	1,908,000	3,389,000	2,894,000
Long-Term Obligations	3,422,000	3,222,000	4,032,000	3,604,000	3,915,000	3,966,000	3,533,000	3,915,000
Total Liabilities	6,553,000	6,770,000	6,756,000	6,546,000	6,637,000	6,882,000	7,854,000	7,711,000
Stockholders' Equity	322,000	527,000	1,384,000	2,629,000	2,846,000	4,025,000	4,471,000	4,848,000
Shares Outstanding	349,000	347,900	348,600	350,400	351,400	358,900	383,890	419,040
Statistical Record								
Return on Assets %	N.M.	N.M.	N.M.	N.M.	N.M.	3.32	3.92	7.49
Return on Equity %	N.M.	N.M.	N.M.	N.M.	N.M.	9.09	10.47	18.30
EBITDA Margin %	6.42	0.36	N.M.	3.97	2.45	10.63	10.71	14.71
Net Margin %	N.M.	N.M.	N.M.	N.M.	N.M.	3.28	3.82	7.44
Asset Turnover	1.09	0.97	0.88	0.84	0.94	1.01	1.03	1.01
Current Ratio	1.73	1.45	2.33	1.94	2.13	2.00	1.51	1.77
Debt to Equity	10.63	6.11	2.91	1.37	1.38	0.99	0.79	0.81
Price Range	17.08-10.98	14.77-6.91	18.35-10.05	15.13-3.67	23.33-7.44	33.93-20.94	33.20-26.00	38.03-27.37
P/E Ratio	...	...	...	...	...	32.94-20.33	27.21-21.31	17.37-12.50
Average Yield %	2.17	2.66	2.33	4.27	5.58	3.38	2.93	2.43

Address: 21001 Van Born Road, Taylor, MI 48180	Web Site: www.masco.com	Auditors: PricewaterhouseCoopers LLP
Telephone: 313-274-7400	Officers: Richard A. Manoogian - Chairman, President, Chief Executive Officer, Vice President	Investor Contact: 313-792-5500
Fax: 313-792-4177	Timothy Wadhams - President, Chief Executive Officer, Senior Vice President, Vice President, Chief Financial Officer	Transfer Agents: Computershare, Pittsburgh, PA

MASTERCARD INC

Exchange	Symbol	Price	52Wk Range	Yield	P/E
NYS	MA	$541.13 (3/28/2013)	541.13-391.78	0.44	24.66

*7 Year Price Score N/A   *NYSE Composite Index=100   *12 Month Price Score 103.71

TRADING VOLUME (thousand shares)

Interim Earnings (Per Share)

Qtr.	Mar	Jun	Sep	Dec
2008	3.38	(5.74)	(1.49)	1.84
2009	2.80	2.67	3.45	2.24
2010	3.46	3.49	3.94	3.16
2011	4.29	4.76	5.63	0.19
2012	5.36	5.55	6.17	4.87

Interim Dividends (Per Share)

Amt	Decl	Ex	Rec	Pay
0.30Q	06/05/2012	07/05/2012	07/09/2012	08/09/2012
0.30Q	09/11/2012	10/05/2012	10/10/2012	11/09/2012
0.30Q	12/04/2012	01/07/2013	01/09/2013	02/08/2013
0.60Q	02/05/2013	04/05/2013	04/09/2013	05/09/2013

Indicated Div: $2.40

Valuation Analysis

		Institutional Holding	
Forecast EPS	$25.50	No of Institutions	
	(04/06/2013)	1007	
Market Cap	$66.7 Billion	Shares	
Book Value	$6.9 Billion	101,615,456	
Price/Book	9.64	% Held	
Price/Sales	9.02	75.45	

Business Summary: Business Services (MIC: 7.5.2 SIC: 7389 NAIC: 525990)

MasterCard is a technology company in the payments industry that connects consumers, financial institutions, merchants, governments and businesses worldwide, enabling them to use electronic forms of payment instead of cash and checks. Co. provides a range of payment applications that enable the development and implementation of credit, debit, prepaid, commercial and related payment programs and applications for consumers and merchants. Co. manages a family of payment brands, including MasterCard®, Maestro® and Cirrus®. Co. processes payment transactions over the MasterCard Worldwide Network and provides support services to its customers and others.

Recent Developments: For the year ended Dec 31 2012, net income increased 44.9% to US$2.76 billion from US$1.90 billion in the prior year. Revenues were US$7.39 billion, up 10.1% from US$6.71 billion the year before. Operating income was US$3.94 billion versus US$2.71 billion in the prior year, an increase of 45.1%. Indirect operating expenses decreased 13.7% to US$3.45 billion from US$4.00 billion in the equivalent prior-year period.

Prospects: Our evaluation of MasterCard Inc. as of Apr. 7, 2013 is the result of our systematic analysis on three basic characteristics: earnings strength, relative valuation, and recent stock price movement. The company has managed to produce a neutral trend in earnings per share over the past 5 quarters. However, while recent estimates for the company have been mixed, MA has posted better than expected results. Based on operating earnings yield, the company is about fairly valued when compared to all of the companies in our coverage universe. Share price changes over the past year indicates that MA will perform well over the near term.

Financial Data
(US$ in Thousands)

	12/31/2012	12/31/2011	12/31/2010	12/31/2009	12/31/2008	12/31/2007	12/31/2006	12/31/2005
Earnings Per Share	21.94	14.85	14.05	11.16	(1.95)	8.00	0.37	2.67
Cash Flow Per Share	23.52	20.97	12.95	10.61	3.17	5.71	4.80	2.73
Tang Book Value Per Share	41.81	33.02	30.54	21.42	9.56	18.79	13.90	6.99
Dividends Per Share	1.050	0.600	0.600	0.600	0.600	0.540	0.090	...
Dividend Payout %	4.79	4.04	4.27	5.38	...	6.75	24.32	...
Income Statement								
Total Revenue	7,391,000	6,714,000	5,539,000	5,098,684	4,991,600	4,067,599	3,326,074	2,937,628
EBITDA	4,000,000	2,804,000	2,831,000	2,353,370	(329,273)	1,637,169	298,662	473,391
Depn & Amortn	84,000	77,000	70,000	76,121	59,097	49,311	43,445	46,304
Income Before Taxes	3,932,000	2,746,000	2,757,000	2,218,051	(383,213)	1,671,432	294,172	407,338
Income Taxes	1,174,000	842,000	910,000	755,427	(129,298)	585,546	243,982	140,619
Net Income	2,759,000	1,906,000	1,846,000	1,462,532	(253,915)	1,085,886	50,190	266,719
Average Shares	126,000	128,000	131,000	130,232	130,148	135,695	135,779	100,000
Balance Sheet								
Current Assets	9,357,000	7,741,000	6,454,000	5,003,147	4,311,507	4,591,741	3,577,229	2,227,898
Total Assets	12,462,000	10,693,000	8,837,000	7,470,279	6,475,849	6,260,041	5,082,470	3,700,544
Current Liabilities	4,906,000	4,217,000	3,143,000	3,167,131	2,990,451	2,363,342	1,811,590	1,556,703
Long-Term Obligations	...	...	...	21,598	19,387	149,824	229,668	229,489
Total Liabilities	5,545,000	4,825,000	3,632,000	3,966,519	4,548,494	3,232,734	2,718,111	2,531,396
Stockholders' Equity	6,917,000	5,868,000	5,205,000	3,503,760	1,927,355	3,027,307	2,364,359	1,169,148
Shares Outstanding	123,243	126,863	130,898	129,772	129,236	131,271	134,969	100,000
Statistical Record								
Return on Assets %	23.77	19.52	22.64	20.97	N.M.	19.15	1.14	7.66
Return on Equity %	43.04	34.43	42.39	53.86	N.M.	40.28	2.84	24.88
EBITDA Margin %	54.12	41.76	51.11	46.16	N.M.	40.25	8.98	16.11
Net Margin %	37.33	28.39	33.33	28.68	N.M.	26.70	1.51	9.08
Asset Turnover	0.64	0.69	0.68	0.73	0.78	0.72	0.76	0.84
Current Ratio	1.91	1.84	2.05	1.58	1.44	1.94	1.97	1.43
Debt to Equity	...	...	...	0.01	0.01	0.05	0.10	0.20
Price Range	498.53-339.06	380.96-220.85	267.22-191.98	258.36-119.18	320.00-121.09	223.20-96.41	105.48-43.90	...
P/E Ratio	22.72-15.45	25.65-14.87	19.02-13.66	23.15-10.68	...	27.90-12.05	285.08-118.65	...
Average Yield %	0.24	0.20	0.26	0.32	0.28	0.38	0.13	...

Address: 2000 Purchase Street, Purchase, NY 10577	Web Site: www.mastercard.com	Auditors: PricewaterhouseCoopers LLP
Telephone: 914-249-2000	Officers: Richard Haythornthwaite - Chairman Walter M. Macnee - Vice-Chairman	Transfer Agents: Computershare, Jersey City, NJ

MBIA INC.

Exchange	Symbol	Price	52Wk Range	Yield	P/E
NYS	MBI	$10.27 (3/28/2013)	13.02-6.81	N/A	1.62

*7 Year Price Score 40.19   *NYSE Composite Index=100   *12 Month Price Score 101.44

Interim Earnings (Per Share)

Qtr.	Mar	Jun	Sep	Dec
2008	(13.03)	7.14	(3.48)	(5.32)
2009	3.34	4.30	(3.50)	(1.16)
2010	(7.22)	6.32	(1.06)	2.22
2011	(5.68)	0.68	2.26	(3.19)
2012	0.05	2.98	0.04	3.26

Interim Dividends (Per Share)

Dividend Payment Suspended

Valuation Analysis

		Institutional Holding	
Forecast EPS	$0.49	No of Institutions	
	(04/06/2013)	336	
Market Cap	$2.0 Billion	Shares	
Book Value	$3.2 Billion	186,793,952	
Price/Book	0.63	% Held	
Price/Sales	0.83	91.29	

Business Summary: General Insurance (MIC: 5.2.1 SIC: 6351 NAIC: 524130)

MBIA provides financial guarantee insurance, as well as related reinsurance, advisory and portfolio services, for the public and structured finance markets, and asset management advisory services. Co.'s U.S. public finance insurance business is conducted through its National Public Finance Guarantee Corp. subsidiary and its structured finance and international insurance operations are conducted through MBIA Insurance Corp. and its subsidiaries. In its asset management advisory services business, Co.'s registered investment advisors provide fixed-income asset management services for third parties and the investment portfolios of Co. and its affiliates including the wind-down businesses.

Recent Developments: For the year ended Dec 31 2012, net income amounted to US$1.23 billion versus a net loss of US$1.32 billion in the prior year. Revenues were US$2.44 billion, compared with negative revenues of US$1.56 billion the year before. Net premiums earned were unchanged at US$605.0 million versus the prior year. Net investment income fell 38.0% to US$281.0 million from US$453.0 million a year ago.

Prospects: Our evaluation of MBIA Inc. as of Apr. 7, 2013 is the result of our systematic analysis on three basic characteristics: earnings strength, relative valuation, and recent stock price movement. The company has produced a positive trend in earnings per share over the past 5 quarters. Because the company lacks sufficient analyst estimate data, we place greater weight on the historical EPS trend as the measure of earnings strength. Based on operating earnings yield, the company is undervalued when compared to all of the companies in our coverage universe. Share price changes over the past year indicates that MBI will perform very well over the near term.

Financial Data

(US$ in Thousands)	12/31/2012	12/31/2011	12/31/2010	12/31/2009	12/31/2008	12/31/2007	12/31/2006	12/31/2005
Earnings Per Share	6.33	(6.69)	0.26	2.99	(12.29)	(15.17)	5.99	5.18
Cash Flow Per Share	(5.28)	(15.11)	(6.21)	(10.53)	(0.72)	8.07	5.00	5.83
Tang Book Value Per Share	16.22	8.80	14.02	12.50	4.41	28.53	52.84	48.95
Dividends Per Share	...	...	...	...	...	1.360	1.240	1.120
Dividend Payout %	...	...	...	...	...	...	20.70	21.62
Income Statement								
Premium Income	605,000	605,000	594,217	746,336	850,444	824,017	835,593	842,742
Total Revenue	2,435,000	(1,557,000)	893,798	2,954,021	(856,603)	(282,554)	2,712,256	2,300,507
Benefits & Claims	50,000	(80,000)	231,944	864,137	1,318,001	900,345	80,889	84,274
Income Before Taxes	1,598,000	(2,239,000)	(95,228)	1,216,881	(3,727,389)	(3,065,692)	1,133,263	1,015,948
Income Taxes	364,000	(920,000)	(147,757)	582,821	(1,054,696)	(1,143,744)	320,080	303,869
Net Income	1,234,000	(1,319,000)	52,529	634,060	(2,672,693)	(1,921,948)	819,288	710,986
Average Shares	194,904	197,019	203,021	208,156	217,521	126,670	136,694	137,220
Balance Sheet								
Total Assets	21,724,000	26,873,000	32,279,011	25,684,699	29,657,074	47,415,074	39,763,030	34,561,394
Total Liabilities	18,551,000	25,173,000	29,446,872	23,094,601	28,662,654	43,759,269	32,558,776	27,969,750
Stockholders' Equity	3,173,000	1,700,000	2,832,139	2,590,098	994,420	3,655,805	7,204,254	6,591,644
Shares Outstanding	195,671	193,143	199,745	204,667	207,920	125,372	134,835	133,047
Statistical Record								
Return on Assets %	5.06	N.M.	0.18	2.29	N.M.	N.M.	2.20	2.10
Return on Equity %	50.51	N.M.	1.94	35.38	N.M.	N.M.	11.88	10.80
Loss Ratio %	8.26	(13.22)	39.03	115.78	154.98	109.26	9.68	10.00
Net Margin %	50.68	...	5.88	21.46	...	...	30.21	30.91
Price Range	13.32-6.81	13.61-6.03	13.00-3.98	8.24-2.29	18.98-3.79	73.02-18.63	73.31-56.50	63.83-50.50
P/E Ratio	2.10-1.08	...	50.00-15.31	2.76-0.77	...	...	12.24-9.43	12.32-9.75
Average Yield %	...	...	...	...	...	2.31	2.03	1.92

Address: 113 King Street, Armonk, NY 10504
Telephone: 914-273-4545

Web Site: www.mbia.com
Officers: Joseph W. Brown - Chairman, Chief Executive Officer C. Edward Chaplin - Co-President, Chief Financial Officer, Chief Administrative Officer

Auditors: PricewaterhouseCoopers LLP
Investor Contact: 914-765-3190
Transfer Agents: Wells Fargo Shareowner Services, St. Paul, MN

MCCORMICK & CO., INC.

Exchange	Symbol	Price	52Wk Range	Yield	P/E	Div Achiever
NYS	MKC V	$73.55 (3/28/2013)	73.55-53.39	1.85	24.04	26 Years

*7 Year Price Score 129.75 *NYSE Composite Index=100 ***12 Month Price Score 101.13**

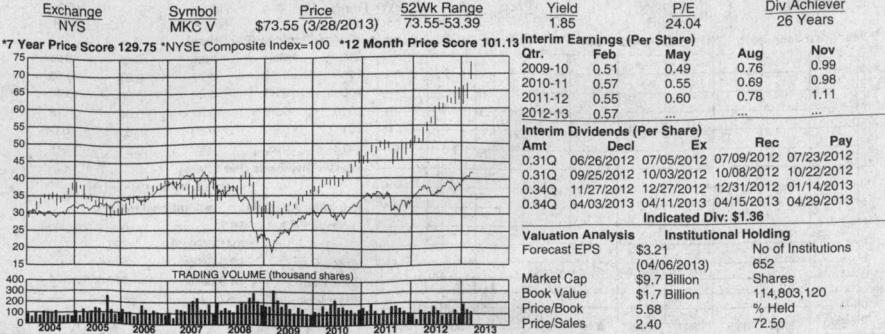

Interim Earnings (Per Share)

Qtr.	Feb	May	Aug	Nov
2009-10	0.51	0.49	0.76	0.99
2010-11	0.57	0.55	0.69	0.98
2011-12	0.55	0.60	0.78	1.11
2012-13	0.57	...	...	...

Interim Dividends (Per Share)

Amt	Decl	Ex	Rec	Pay
0.31Q	06/26/2012	07/05/2012	07/09/2012	07/23/2012
0.31Q	09/25/2012	10/03/2012	10/08/2012	10/22/2012
0.34Q	11/27/2012	12/27/2012	12/31/2012	01/14/2013
0.34Q	04/03/2013	04/11/2013	04/15/2013	04/29/2013

Indicated Div: $1.36

Valuation Analysis		Institutional Holding	
Forecast EPS	$3.21	No of Institutions	
	(04/06/2013)	652	
Market Cap	$9.7 Billion	Shares	
Book Value	$1.7 Billion	114,803,120	
Price/Book	5.68	% Held	
Price/Sales	2.40	72.50	

Business Summary: Food (MIC: 1.2.1 SIC: 2099 NAIC: 311942)

McCormick & Co. manufactures, markets and distributes spices, seasoning mixes, condiments and other flavorful products to the food industry-retail outlets, food manufacturers and foodservice businesses. Co. operates in two business segments: consumer and industrial. The consumer segment sells to retail outlets, including grocery, mass merchandise, warehouse clubs, discount and drug stores under the McCormick®, Lawry's®, Club House®, Zatarain's®, Thai Kitchen®, Simply Asia®, Ducros®, Schwartz®, Kamis®, Vahine®, and Kohinoor® brands. In the industrial segment, Co. provides a range of products to multinational food manufacturers and foodservice customers.

Recent Developments: For the quarter ended Feb 28 2013, net income increased 2.0% to US$76.0 million from US$74.5 million in the year-earlier quarter. Revenues were US$934.4 million, up 3.1% from US$906.7 million the year before. Operating income was US$112.0 million versus US$112.5 million in the prior-year quarter, a decrease of 0.4%. Direct operating expenses rose 3.9% to US$572.7 million from US$551.4 million in the comparable period the year before. Indirect operating expenses increased 2.8% to US$249.7 million from US$242.8 million in the equivalent prior-year period.

Prospects: Our evaluation of McCormick & Co. Inc. as of Apr. 7, 2013 is the result of our systematic analysis on three basic characteristics: earnings strength, relative valuation, and recent stock price movement. The company has managed to produce a neutral trend in earnings per share over the past 5 quarters. However, while recent estimates for the company have been mixed, MKC has posted better than expected results. Based on operating earnings yield, the company is about fairly valued when compared to all of the companies in our coverage universe. Share price changes over the past year indicates that MKC will perform well over the near term.

Financial Data

(US$ in Thousands)	3 Mos	11/30/2012	11/30/2011	11/30/2010	11/30/2009	11/30/2008	11/30/2007	11/30/2006
Earnings Per Share	3.06	3.04	2.79	2.75	2.27	1.94	1.73	1.50
Cash Flow Per Share	3.50	3.42	2.56	2.92	3.18	2.43	1.74	2.36
Dividends Per Share	1.270	1.240	1.120	1.040	0.960	0.880	0.800	0.720
Dividend Payout %	41.50	40.79	40.14	37.82	42.29	45.36	46.24	48.00
Income Statement								
Total Revenue	934,400	4,014,200	3,697,600	3,336,800	3,192,100	3,176,600	2,916,200	2,716,400
EBITDA	138,800	683,500	640,900	591,000	550,100	462,100	432,700	350,400
Depn & Amortn	26,200	102,800	98,300	79,000	80,800	67,600	69,700	73,700
Income Before Taxes	98,700	526,100	491,400	462,700	416,500	337,800	302,400	223,000
Income Taxes	28,100	139,800	142,600	118,000	133,000	100,600	92,200	64,700
Net Income	76,000	407,800	374,200	370,200	299,800	255,800	230,100	202,200
Average Shares	134,000	134,300	134,300	134,700	132,300	131,800	132,700	135,000
Balance Sheet								
Current Assets	1,211,500	1,285,400	1,222,900	1,015,900	970,500	968,300	983,100	899,400
Total Assets	4,086,100	4,165,400	4,087,800	3,419,700	3,387,800	3,220,300	2,787,500	2,568,000
Current Liabilities	1,115,500	1,187,600	993,300	834,800	818,200	1,034,100	861,300	780,500
Long-Term Obligations	776,000	779,200	1,029,700	779,900	875,000	885,200	573,500	569,600
Total Liabilities	2,378,900	2,482,500	2,486,100	1,966,000	2,053,200	2,165,000	1,702,400	1,634,700
Stockholders' Equity	1,707,200	1,682,900	1,601,700	1,453,700	1,334,600	1,055,300	1,085,100	933,300
Shares Outstanding	131,904	132,500	132,900	133,100	131,800	130,100	127,800	116,900
Statistical Record								
Return on Assets %	10.02	9.86	9.97	10.88	9.07	8.49	8.59	8.35
Return on Equity %	24.21	24.76	24.49	26.55	25.09	23.84	22.80	23.33
EBITDA Margin %	14.85	17.03	17.33	17.71	17.23	14.55	14.84	12.90
Net Margin %	8.13	10.16	10.12	11.09	9.39	8.05	7.89	7.44
Asset Turnover	0.99	0.97	0.99	0.98	0.97	1.05	1.09	1.12
Current Ratio	1.09	1.08	1.23	1.22	1.19	0.94	1.14	1.15
Debt to Equity	0.45	0.46	0.64	0.54	0.66	0.84	0.53	0.61
Price Range	67.32-50.34	66.37-48.54	51.00-43.98	44.81-35.56	36.45-28.53	41.97-28.79	39.58-34.16	38.92-29.82
P/E Ratio	22.00-16.45	21.83-15.97	18.28-15.76	16.29-12.93	16.06-12.57	21.63-14.84	22.88-19.75	25.95-19.88
Average Yield %	2.11	2.17	2.32	2.65	3.00	2.39	2.15	2.10

Address: 18 Loveton Circle, P.O. Box 6000, Sparks, MD 21152-6000	Web Site: www.mccormickcorporation.com	Auditors: Ernst & Young LLP
Telephone: 410-771-7301	Officers: Alan D. Wilson - Chairman, President, Chief Executive Officer Gordon M. Stetz - Executive Vice President, Chief Financial Officer	Investor Contact: 410-771-7244
Fax: 410-771-7462		Transfer Agents: Wells Fargo Bank, N.A., South St. Paul, MN

MCDERMOTT INTERNATIONAL, INC. (PANAMA)

Exchange	Symbol	Price	52Wk Range	Yield	P/E
NYS	MDR	$10.99 (3/28/2013)	13.47-9.24	N/A	12.63

*7 Year Price Score N/A *NYSE Composite Index=100 *12 Month Price Score 95.78

Interim Earnings (Per Share)

Qtr.	Mar	Jun	Sep	Dec
2008	0.54	0.77	0.37	0.18
2009	0.33	0.40	0.50	0.42
2010	0.26	0.32	0.09	0.18
2011	0.30	0.28	0.05	(0.04)
2012	0.26	0.22	0.21	0.18

Interim Dividends (Per Share)

No Dividends Paid

Valuation Analysis

		Institutional Holding	
Forecast EPS	$0.71	No of Institutions	
	(04/06/2013)	398	
Market Cap	$2.6 Billion	Shares	
Book Value	$1.9 Billion	226,665,664	
Price/Book	1.37	% Held	
Price/Sales	0.71	92.64	

TRADING VOLUME (thousand shares)

Business Summary: Industrial Machinery & Equipment (MIC: 7.2.1 SIC: 8711 NAIC: 541330)

McDermott International is an engineering, procurement, construction and installation (EPCI) company focused on designing and executing offshore oil and gas projects. Co. is a U.S.-based engineering and construction company focused on the upstream offshore oil and gas sector. Co. provides EPCI services by providing fixed and floating production facilities, pipeline installations and subsea systems from concept to commissioning. Co. supports its activities with project management and procurement services. Co.'s business segments consist of Asia Pacific, Atlantic, Caspian and the Middle East. The Caspian and Middle East operating segments are aggregated into the Middle East reporting segment.

Recent Developments: For the year ended Dec 31 2012, net income increased 43.7% to US$217.4 million from US$151.4 million in the prior year. Revenues were US$3.64 billion, up 5.7% from US$3.45 billion the year before. Operating income was US$319.3 million versus US$250.7 million in the prior year, an increase of 27.4%. Direct operating expenses rose 4.0% to US$3.10 billion from US$2.98 billion in the comparable period the year before. Indirect operating expenses increased 3.9% to US$222.3 million from US$214.0 million in the equivalent prior-year period.

Prospects: Our evaluation of McDermott International Inc. as of Apr. 7, 2013 is the result of our systematic analysis on three basic characteristics: earnings strength, relative valuation, and recent stock price movement. The company has generated a negative trend in earnings per share over the past 5 quarters. However, while recent estimates for the company have been lowered by analysts, MDR has posted results that fell short of analysts expectations. Based on operating earnings yield, the company is undervalued when compared to all of the companies in our coverage universe. Share price changes over the past year indicates that MDR will perform in line with the market over the near term.

Financial Data

(US$ in Thousands)	12/31/2012	12/31/2011	12/31/2010	12/31/2009	12/31/2008	12/31/2007	12/31/2006	12/31/2005
Earnings Per Share	0.87	0.59	0.85	1.66	1.86	2.66	1.50	0.91
Cash Flow Per Share	0.89	0.42	1.66	1.82	(0.22)	5.89	1.05	1.24
Tang Book Value Per Share	7.83	6.89	6.02	6.50	4.46	4.46	1.35	...
Income Statement								
Total Revenue	3,641,624	3,445,110	2,403,743	6,193,077	6,572,423	5,631,610	4,120,141	1,856,311
EBITDA	441,593	337,157	388,277	610,174	631,710	755,481	343,196	221,881
Depn & Amortn	86,400	82,200	75,800	146,500	119,700	91,200	61,000	44,266
Income Before Taxes	359,849	256,276	311,388	470,917	538,983	703,741	311,129	166,863
Income Taxes	129,204	87,124	41,182	131,846	157,812	137,637	19,152	9,409
Net Income	206,653	138,730	201,666	387,056	429,302	607,828	342,299	197,977
Average Shares	237,619	237,040	235,622	233,626	230,393	228,742	227,718	218,337
Balance Sheet								
Current Assets	1,789,789	1,537,185	1,285,638	2,357,921	2,216,985	2,757,500	2,140,478	993,099
Total Assets	3,333,627	2,992,814	2,598,688	4,849,110	4,601,693	4,411,486	3,594,187	1,668,286
Current Liabilities	1,113,011	1,021,776	865,007	2,009,032	2,208,345	2,696,532	2,479,581	763,293
Long-Term Obligations	88,562	84,794	46,748	56,714	6,109	10,609	15,242	207,861
Total Liabilities	1,446,296	1,333,176	1,149,660	3,041,913	3,285,521	3,244,481	3,205,807	1,751,584
Stockholders' Equity	1,887,331	1,659,638	1,449,028	1,807,197	1,316,172	1,167,005	388,380	(83,298)
Shares Outstanding	235,867	235,056	233,885	230,750	228,333	225,870	221,769	215,408
Statistical Record								
Return on Assets %	6.52	4.96	5.42	8.19	9.50	15.18	13.01	12.96
Return on Equity %	11.62	8.93	12.39	24.78	34.48	78.16	224.40	...
EBITDA Margin %	12.13	9.79	16.15	9.85	9.61	13.42	8.33	11.95
Net Margin %	5.67	4.03	8.39	6.25	6.53	10.79	8.31	10.67
Asset Turnover	1.15	1.23	0.65	1.31	1.45	1.41	1.57	1.22
Current Ratio	1.61	1.50	1.49	1.17	1.00	1.02	0.86	1.30
Debt to Equity	0.05	0.05	0.03	0.03	N.M.	0.01	0.04	...
Price Range	14.86-9.24	25.73-9.84	20.69-12.46	...	...	...	...	...
P/E Ratio	17.08-10.62	43.61-16.68	24.34-14.66	...	...	...	...	...

Address: 757 N. Eldridge Pkwy., Houston, TX 77079 Telephone: 281-870-5000	Web Site: www.mcdermott.com Officers: Stephen M. Johnson - Chairman, President, Chief Executive Officer, Chief Operating Officer John T. McCormack - Executive Vice President, Chief Operating Officer, Senior Vice President	Auditors: Deloitte & Touche LLP Investor Contact: 281-870-5165 Transfer Agents: EquiServe Trust Company NA, Providence, RI

MCDONALD'S CORP

Exchange	Symbol	Price	52Wk Range	Yield	P/E	Div Achiever
NYS	MCD	$99.69 (3/28/2013)	99.69-84.05	3.09	18.60	36 Years

*7 Year Price Score 121.93 *NYSE Composite Index=100 *12 Month Price Score 96.70

Interim Earnings (Per Share)

Qtr.	Mar	Jun	Sep	Dec
2008	0.81	1.04	1.05	0.87
2009	0.87	0.98	1.15	1.11
2010	1.00	1.13	1.29	1.16
2011	1.15	1.35	1.45	1.33
2012	1.23	1.32	1.43	1.38

Interim Dividends (Per Share)

Amt	Decl	Ex	Rec	Pay
0.70Q	05/23/2012	05/31/2012	06/04/2012	06/15/2012
0.70Q	07/19/2012	08/30/2012	09/04/2012	09/18/2012
0.77Q	09/20/2012	11/29/2012	12/03/2012	12/17/2012
0.77Q	01/30/2013	02/27/2013	03/01/2013	03/15/2013

Indicated Div: $3.08 (Div. Reinv. Plan)

Valuation Analysis / **Institutional Holding**

Forecast EPS	$5.79	No of Institutions
	(04/06/2013)	1810
Market Cap	$100.0 Billion	Shares
Book Value	$15.3 Billion	714,888,640
Price/Book	6.54	% Held
Price/Sales	3.63	61.89

Business Summary: Hotels, Restaurants & Travel (MIC: 2.2.1 SIC: 5812 NAIC: 722211)

McDonald's franchises and operates McDonald's restaurants. Co.'s reportable segments include the U.S., Europe, and Asia/Pacific, Middle East and Africa. Co.'s menu includes hamburgers and cheeseburgers, Big Mac, Quarter Pounder with Cheese, Filet-O-Fish, several chicken sandwiches, Chicken McNuggets, Snack Wraps, french fries, salads, oatmeal, shakes, McFlurry desserts, sundaes, soft serve cones, pies, soft drinks, coffee, McCafe beverages and other beverages. At Dec 31 2012, Co. had a total of 34,480 restaurants in 119 countries, including 27,882 that were franchised or licensed, and 6,598 were operated by Co.

Recent Developments: For the year ended Dec 31 2012, net income decreased 0.7% to US$5.46 billion from US$5.50 billion in the prior year. Revenues were US$27.57 billion, up 2.1% from US$27.01 billion the year before. Operating income was US$8.60 billion versus US$8.53 billion in the prior year, an increase of 0.9%. Direct operating expenses rose 2.6% to US$15.22 billion from US$14.84 billion in the comparable period the year before. Indirect operating expenses increased 2.8% to US$3.74 billion from US$3.64 billion in the equivalent prior-year period.

Prospects: Our evaluation of McDonald's Corp. as of Apr. 7, 2013 is the result of our systematic analysis on three basic characteristics: earnings strength, relative valuation, and recent stock price movement. The company has enjoyed a very positive trend in earnings per share over the past 5 quarters. However, while recent estimates for the company have been lowered by analysts, MCD has posted better than expected results. Based on operating earnings yield, the company is about fairly valued when compared to all of the companies in our coverage universe. Share price changes over the past year indicates that MCD will perform very poorly over the near term.

Financial Data
(US$ in Thousands)

	12/31/2012	12/31/2011	12/31/2010	12/31/2009	12/31/2008	12/31/2007	12/31/2006	12/31/2005
Earnings Per Share	5.36	5.27	4.58	4.11	3.76	1.98	2.83	2.04
Cash Flow Per Share	6.88	6.93	5.95	5.27	5.24	4.10	3.52	3.44
Tang Book Value Per Share	12.46	11.49	11.44	10.78	9.99	11.14	11.01	10.45
Dividends Per Share	2.870	2.530	2.260	2.050	1.625	1.500	1.000	0.670
Dividend Payout %	53.54	48.01	49.34	49.88	43.22	75.76	35.34	32.84
Income Statement								
Total Revenue	27,567,000	27,006,000	24,074,600	22,744,700	23,522,400	22,786,600	21,586,400	20,460,200
EBITDA	9,854,300	9,656,600	8,487,300	7,953,200	7,731,500	5,011,600	5,671,800	5,191,600
Depn & Amortn	1,402,200	1,329,600	1,200,400	1,160,800	1,161,600	1,145,000	1,180,200	1,186,700
Income Before Taxes	7,935,500	7,834,200	6,836,000	6,319,200	6,047,300	3,456,500	4,089,600	3,648,800
Income Taxes	2,614,200	2,509,100	2,054,000	1,936,000	1,844,800	1,237,100	1,293,400	1,099,400
Net Income	5,464,800	5,503,100	4,946,300	4,551,000	4,313,200	2,395,100	3,544,200	2,602,200
Average Shares	1,020,200	1,044,900	1,080,300	1,107,400	1,146,000	1,211,800	1,251,700	1,274,200
Balance Sheet								
Current Assets	4,922,100	4,403,000	4,368,500	3,416,300	3,517,600	3,581,900	3,625,300	5,849,700
Total Assets	35,386,500	32,989,900	31,975,200	30,224,900	28,461,500	29,391,700	29,023,800	29,988,800
Current Liabilities	3,403,100	3,509,200	2,924,700	2,988,700	2,537,900	4,498,500	3,008,100	4,036,300
Long-Term Obligations	13,632,500	12,133,800	11,497,000	10,560,300	10,186,000	7,310,000	8,416,500	8,937,400
Total Liabilities	20,092,900	18,599,700	17,341,000	16,191,000	15,078,900	14,111,900	13,565,500	14,842,700
Stockholders' Equity	15,293,600	14,390,200	14,634,200	14,033,900	13,382,600	15,279,800	15,458,300	15,146,100
Shares Outstanding	1,002,700	1,021,400	1,053,600	1,076,700	1,115,300	1,165,300	1,203,700	1,263,200
Statistical Record								
Return on Assets %	15.94	16.94	15.90	15.51	14.87	8.20	12.01	9.00
Return on Equity %	36.72	37.92	34.51	33.20	30.01	15.58	23.16	17.73
EBITDA Margin %	35.75	35.76	35.25	34.97	32.87	21.99	26.27	25.37
Net Margin %	19.82	20.38	20.55	20.01	18.34	10.51	16.42	12.72
Asset Turnover	0.80	0.83	0.77	0.78	0.81	0.78	0.73	0.71
Current Ratio	1.45	1.25	1.49	1.14	1.39	0.80	1.21	1.45
Debt to Equity	0.89	0.84	0.79	0.75	0.76	0.48	0.54	0.59
Price Range	101.74-84.05	100.81-72.67	80.34-61.45	64.53-50.86	65.95-50.75	63.13-42.91	44.36-31.94	35.50-27.70
P/E Ratio	18.98-15.68	19.13-13.79	17.54-13.42	15.70-12.37	17.54-13.50	31.88-21.67	15.67-11.29	17.40-13.58
Average Yield %	3.11	3.01	3.21	3.57	2.80	2.94	2.72	2.10

Address: One McDonald's Plaza, Oak Brook, IL 60523 Telephone: 630-623-3000	Web Site: www.mcdonalds.com Officers: Donald Thompson - President, Chief Executive Officer, Chief Operating Officer Richard Floersch - Executive Vice President, Chief Human Resources Officer	Auditors: Ernst & Young LLP Investor Contact: 630-623-7428 Transfer Agents: Computershare Trust Company, Providence, RI

MCGRAW-HILL COS., INC. (THE)

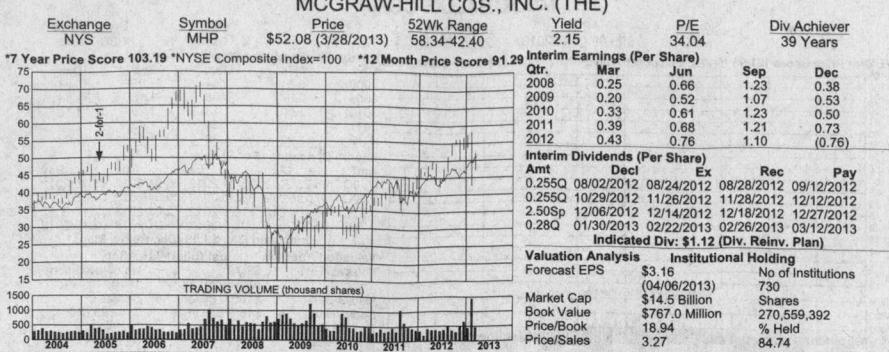

Exchange	Symbol	Price	52Wk Range	Yield	P/E	Div Achiever
NYS	MHP	$52.08 (3/28/2013)	58.34-42.40	2.15	34.04	39 Years

*7 Year Price Score 103.19 *NYSE Composite Index=100 *12 Month Price Score 91.29

Interim Earnings (Per Share)

Qtr.	Mar	Jun	Sep	Dec
2008	0.25	0.66	1.23	0.38
2009	0.20	0.52	1.07	0.53
2010	0.33	0.61	1.23	0.50
2011	0.39	0.68	1.21	0.73
2012	0.43	0.76	1.10	(0.76)

Interim Dividends (Per Share)

Amt	Decl	Ex	Rec	Pay
0.255Q	08/02/2012	08/24/2012	08/28/2012	09/12/2012
0.255Q	10/29/2012	11/26/2012	11/28/2012	12/12/2012
2.50Sp	12/06/2012	12/14/2012	12/18/2012	12/27/2012
0.28Q	01/30/2013	02/22/2013	02/26/2013	03/12/2013

Indicated Div: $1.12 (Div. Reinv. Plan)

Valuation Analysis — **Institutional Holding**

Forecast EPS	$3.16	No of Institutions
	(04/06/2013)	730
Market Cap	$14.5 Billion	Shares
Book Value	$767.0 Million	270,559,392
Price/Book	18.94	% Held
Price/Sales	3.27	84.74

TRADING VOLUME (thousand shares)

Business Summary: Publishing (MIC: 2.3.3 SIC: 2731 NAIC: 511130)

McGraw-Hill Companies is a content and analytics provider serving the capital, commodities and commercial markets. Co. has four segments: Standard & Poor's Ratings, which is a provider of credit ratings, providing investors and market participants with information and ratings benchmarks; S&P Capital IQ, which is a provider of financial research and analytical tools, combining cross-asset analytics and desktop services; S&P Dow Jones Indices, which is an index provider that maintains a range of valuation and index benchmarks; and Commodities & Commercial, which focuses in commercial and commodities markets that deliver access to information, data, analytic services and pricing benchmarks.

Recent Developments: For the year ended Dec 31 2012, income from continuing operations increased 16.0% to US$726.0 million from US$626.0 million a year earlier. Net income decreased 47.3% to US$492.0 million from US$934.0 million in the prior year. Revenues were US$4.45 billion, up 12.5% from US$3.95 billion the year before. Operating income was US$1.21 billion versus US$1.08 billion in the prior year, an increase of 12.4%. Direct operating expenses rose 4.9% to US$1.46 billion from US$1.39 billion in the comparable period the year before. Indirect operating expenses increased 19.8% to US$1.78 billion from US$1.49 billion in the equivalent prior-year period.

Prospects: Our evaluation of McGraw-Hill Cos. Inc. as of Apr. 7, 2013 is the result of our systematic analysis on three basic characteristics: earnings strength, relative valuation, and recent stock price movement. The company has managed to produce a neutral trend in earnings per share over the past 5 quarters. However, while recent estimates for the company have been mixed, MHP has posted better than expected results. Based on operating earnings yield, the company is undervalued when compared to all of the companies in our coverage universe. Share price changes over the past year indicates that MHP will perform poorly over the near term.

Financial Data

(US$ in Thousands)	12/31/2012	12/31/2011	12/31/2010	12/31/2009	12/31/2008	12/31/2007	12/31/2006	12/31/2005
Earnings Per Share	1.53	3.00	2.65	2.33	2.51	2.94	2.40	2.21
Cash Flow Per Share	2.67	4.51	4.71	4.23	3.69	5.11	4.23	4.16
Tang Book Value Per Share	N.M.	N.M.	N.M.	N.M.	N.M.	N.M.	1.00	2.04
Dividends Per Share	3.520	1.000	0.940	0.900	0.880	0.820	0.726	0.660
Dividend Payout %	230.07	33.33	35.47	38.63	35.06	27.89	30.25	29.86
Income Statement								
Total Revenue	4,450,000	6,246,000	6,168,331	5,951,782	6,355,055	6,772,281	6,255,138	6,003,642
EBITDA	1,352,000	1,609,000	1,592,146	1,421,220	1,533,156	1,824,102	1,580,041	1,516,149
Depn & Amortn	141,000	187,000	171,087	165,484	178,346	160,989	161,587	150,985
Income Before Taxes	1,130,000	1,347,000	1,339,416	1,178,869	1,279,186	1,622,532	1,404,823	1,359,962
Income Taxes	404,000	489,000	487,547	429,108	479,695	608,973	522,592	515,656
Net Income	437,000	911,000	828,063	730,502	799,491	1,013,559	882,231	844,306
Average Shares	284,600	304,000	312,220	313,296	318,687	344,785	366,878	382,570
Balance Sheet								
Current Assets	3,899,000	2,679,000	3,294,611	2,936,396	2,302,723	2,333,035	2,257,938	2,590,939
Total Assets	7,052,000	6,427,000	7,046,561	6,475,250	6,080,142	6,357,336	6,042,890	6,395,808
Current Liabilities	3,667,000	3,130,000	2,680,874	2,451,965	2,530,700	2,656,860	2,468,016	2,224,826
Long-Term Obligations	799,000	798,000	1,197,965	1,197,791	1,197,611	1,197,425	314	339
Total Liabilities	6,285,000	4,919,000	4,836,265	4,627,963	4,797,806	4,750,686	3,363,272	3,282,660
Stockholders' Equity	767,000	1,508,000	2,210,296	1,847,287	1,282,336	1,606,650	2,679,618	3,113,148
Shares Outstanding	279,000	276,000	307,621	315,340	314,405	322,367	353,958	372,698
Statistical Record								
Return on Assets %	6.47	13.52	12.25	11.64	12.82	16.35	14.19	13.77
Return on Equity %	38.31	49.00	40.82	46.68	55.20	47.29	30.46	27.69
EBITDA Margin %	30.38	25.76	25.81	23.88	24.12	26.93	25.26	25.25
Net Margin %	9.82	14.59	13.42	12.27	12.58	14.97	14.10	14.06
Asset Turnover	0.66	0.93	0.91	0.95	1.02	1.09	1.01	0.98
Current Ratio	1.06	0.86	1.23	1.20	0.91	0.88	0.91	1.16
Debt to Equity	1.04	0.53	0.54	0.65	0.93	0.75	N.M.	N.M.
Price Range	56.65-42.40	45.57-35.35	39.31-27.02	34.82-17.39	45.86-18.59	71.96-43.81	69.10-47.06	53.52-40.56
P/E Ratio	37.03-27.71	15.19-11.78	14.83-10.20	14.94-7.46	18.27-7.41	24.48-14.90	28.79-19.61	24.22-18.35
Average Yield %	7.17	2.45	2.86	3.22	2.41	1.38	1.28	1.42

Address: 1221 Avenue Of The Americas, New York, NY 10020
Telephone: 212-512-2000

Web Site: www.mcgraw-hill.com
Officers: Harold W. McGraw - Chairman, President, Chief Executive Officer Jack F. Callahan - Executive Vice President, Chief Financial Officer

Auditors: Ernst & Young LLP
Investor Contact: 866-436-8502
Transfer Agents: Computershare, Canton, MA

MCKESSON CORP.

Exchange	Symbol	Price	52Wk Range	Yield	P/E
NYS	MCK	$107.96 (3/28/2013)	111.23-85.48	0.74	16.43

*7 Year Price Score 128.03 *NYSE Composite Index=100 *12 Month Price Score 104.07

Interim Earnings (Per Share)

Qtr.	Jun	Sep	Dec	Mar
2009-10	1.06	1.11	1.19	1.26
2010-11	1.10	1.25	0.60	1.61
2011-12	1.13	1.18	1.20	2.08
2012-13	1.58	1.67	1.24	...

Interim Dividends (Per Share)

Amt	Decl	Ex	Rec	Pay
0.20Q	05/23/2012	06/06/2012	06/08/2012	07/02/2012
0.20Q	07/25/2012	08/30/2012	09/04/2012	10/01/2012
0.20Q	10/26/2012	11/29/2012	12/03/2012	01/02/2013
0.20Q	01/30/2013	02/27/2013	03/01/2013	04/01/2013

Indicated Div: $0.80

Valuation Analysis / Institutional Holding

Forecast EPS	$7.20 (04/06/2013)	No of Institutions	894
Market Cap	$25.1 Billion	Shares	221,851,808
Book Value	$7.6 Billion	% Held	80.22
Price/Book	3.29		
Price/Sales	0.20		

Business Summary: Pharmaceuticals (MIC: 4.1.1 SIC: 5122 NAIC: 541519)

McKesson delivers pharmaceuticals, medical supplies and health care information technologies. Co.'s McKesson Distribution Solutions segment distributes drugs, medical-surgical supplies and equipment and health and beauty care products, and provides specialty pharmaceutical systems and services for biotech and pharmaceutical manufacturers, and practice management, technology, clinical support and business services to oncology and other practices operating in the community setting. Co.'s McKesson Technology Solutions segment delivers clinical, patient care, financial, supply chain, management software, pharmacy automation for hospitals, as well as connectivity, outsourcing and other services.

Recent Developments: For the quarter ended Dec 31 2012, net income decreased 0.7% to US$298.0 million from US$300.0 million in the year-earlier quarter. Revenues were US$31.19 billion, up 1.1% from US$30.84 billion the year before. Operating income was US$485.0 million versus US$492.0 million in the prior-year quarter, a decrease of 1.4%. Direct operating expenses rose 0.8% over US$29.52 billion from US$29.27 billion in the comparable period the year before. Indirect operating expenses increased 10.1% to US$1.18 billion from US$1.07 billion in the equivalent prior-year period.

Prospects: Our evaluation of McKesson Corp. as of Apr. 7, 2013 is the result of our systematic analysis on three basic characteristics: earnings strength, relative valuation, and recent stock price movement. The company has managed to produce a neutral trend in earnings per share over the past 5 quarters and while recent estimates for the company have been mixed, MCK has posted results that fell short of analysts' expectations. Based on operating earnings yield, the company is undervalued when compared to all of the companies in our coverage universe. Share price changes over the past year indicates that MCK will perform well over the near term.

Financial Data

(US$ in Thousands)	9 Mos	6 Mos	3 Mos	03/31/2012	03/31/2011	03/31/2010	03/31/2009	03/31/2008
Earnings Per Share	6.57	6.53	6.04	5.59	4.57	4.62	2.95	3.32
Cash Flow Per Share	6.43	8.53	8.78	11.96	9.06	8.61	4.91	2.98
Tang Book Value Per Share	2.32	3.76	2.12	0.21	5.56	12.59	7.39	7.64
Dividends Per Share	0.800	0.800	0.800	0.800	0.720	0.480	0.480	0.240
Dividend Payout %	12.18	12.25	13.25	14.31	15.75	10.39	16.27	7.23
Income Statement								
Total Revenue	91,835,000	60,648,000	30,798,000	122,734,000	112,084,000	108,702,000	106,632,000	101,703,000
EBITDA	2,131,000	1,490,000	727,000	2,282,000	1,968,000	2,177,000	1,303,000	1,613,000
Depn & Amortn	428,000	282,000	140,000	140,000	139,000	148,000	133,000	124,000
Income Before Taxes	1,533,000	1,097,000	531,000	1,910,000	1,641,000	1,858,000	1,057,000	1,436,000
Income Taxes	454,000	316,000	151,000	516,000	505,000	601,000	241,000	468,000
Net Income	1,079,000	781,000	380,000	1,403,000	1,202,000	1,263,000	823,000	990,000
Average Shares	240,000	240,000	240,000	251,000	263,000	273,000	279,000	298,000
Balance Sheet								
Current Assets	23,439,000	23,091,000	22,054,000	23,603,000	22,357,000	21,504,000	18,671,000	17,786,000
Total Assets	33,433,000	32,968,000	31,748,000	33,093,000	30,886,000	28,189,000	25,267,000	24,603,000
Current Liabilities	20,208,000	20,750,000	20,097,000	21,686,000	18,726,000	17,012,000	15,606,000	15,348,000
Long-Term Obligations	3,973,000	3,073,000	3,072,000	3,072,000	3,587,000	2,293,000	2,290,000	1,795,000
Total Liabilities	25,784,000	25,253,000	24,545,000	26,262,000	23,666,000	20,657,000	19,074,000	18,482,000
Stockholders' Equity	7,649,000	7,715,000	7,203,000	6,831,000	7,220,000	7,532,000	6,193,000	6,121,000
Shares Outstanding	232,889	236,000	236,000	235,000	252,000	271,000	271,000	277,000
Statistical Record								
Return on Assets %	4.81	4.94	4.77	4.37	4.07	4.73	3.30	4.07
Return on Equity %	21.19	21.60	21.20	19.92	16.30	18.40	13.37	15.93
EBITDA Margin %	2.32	2.46	2.36	1.86	1.76	2.00	1.22	1.59
Net Margin %	1.17	1.29	1.23	1.14	1.07	1.16	0.77	0.97
Asset Turnover	3.71	3.80	3.94	3.83	3.79	4.07	4.28	4.18
Current Ratio	1.16	1.11	1.10	1.09	1.19	1.26	1.20	1.16
Debt to Equity	0.52	0.40	0.43	0.45	0.50	0.30	0.37	0.29
Price Range	99.62-75.89	96.67-69.35	93.75-69.35	88.59-69.35	80.64-58.05	66.72-33.87	58.85-28.60	67.92-51.66
P/E Ratio	15.16-11.55	14.80-10.62	15.52-11.48	15.85-12.41	17.65-12.70	14.44-7.33	19.95-9.69	20.46-15.56
Average Yield %	0.90	0.94	0.98	1.00	1.06	0.89	1.01	0.40

Address: One Post Street, San Francisco, CA 94104
Telephone: 415-983-8300
Fax: 415-983-8453

Web Site: www.mckesson.com
Officers: John H. Hammergren - Chairman, President, Chief Executive Officer Jeffrey C. Campbell - Executive Vice President, Chief Financial Officer

Auditors: Deloitte & Touche LLP
Investor Contact: 415-983-8391
Transfer Agents: Wells Fargo Shareowner Services, South St. Paul, MN

487

M.D.C. HOLDINGS, INC.

Exchange	Symbol	Price	52Wk Range	Yield	P/E
NYS	MDC	$36.65 (3/28/2013)	41.76-23.76	2.73	28.63

*7 Year Price Score 84.77   *NYSE Composite Index=100   *12 Month Price Score 102.44

Interim Earnings (Per Share)

Qtr.	Mar	Jun	Sep	Dec
2008	(1.58)	(2.18)	(2.55)	(1.92)
2009	(0.88)	(0.64)	(0.69)	2.72
2010	(0.45)	(0.08)	(0.22)	(0.65)
2011	(0.43)	(0.60)	(0.68)	(0.40)
2012	0.04	0.22	0.41	0.60

Interim Dividends (Per Share)

Amt	Decl	Ex	Rec	Pay
0.25Q	04/23/2012	05/07/2012	05/09/2012	05/23/2012
0.25Q	07/24/2012	08/06/2012	08/08/2012	08/22/2012
0.25Q	10/22/2012	11/05/2012	11/07/2012	11/21/2012
1.00A	12/13/2012	12/20/2012	12/24/2012	12/28/2012

Indicated Div: $1.00

Valuation Analysis   **Institutional Holding**

Forecast EPS	$1.70	No of Institutions
	(04/05/2013)	262
Market Cap	$1.8 Billion	Shares
Book Value	$880.9 Million	48,480,392
Price/Book	2.03	% Held
Price/Sales	1.48	92.77

Business Summary: Builders (MIC: 2.2.5 SIC: 1531 NAIC: 522292)

M.D.C. Holdings is engaged in two primary operations, homebuilding and financial services. Co.'s homebuilding operations consist of subsidiaries that purchase finished lots or develop lots to the extent necessary for the construction and sale of primarily single-family detached homes under the name Richmond American Homes. Co.'s financial services operation consists of its mortgage lending operations, which is the principal originator of mortgage loans for its homebuyers; insurance operations, which provide insurance coverage of homebuilding risks for its homebuilding subsidiaries and certain of its homebuilding subcontractors; and title operations.

Recent Developments: For the year ended Dec 31 2012, net income amounted to US$62.7 million versus a net loss of US$98.4 million in the prior year. Revenues were US$1.20 billion, up 42.7% from US$843.1 million the year before. Direct operating expenses rose 35.8% to US$1.00 billion from US$736.7 million in the comparable period the year before. Indirect operating expenses decreased 6.6% to US$167.3 million from US$179.1 million in the equivalent prior-year period.

Prospects: Our evaluation of M.D.C. Holdings Inc. as of Apr. 7, 2013 is the result of our systematic analysis on three basic characteristics: earnings strength, relative valuation, and recent stock price movement. The company has suffered a very negative trend in earnings per share over the past 5 quarters. However, while recent estimates for the company have been mixed, MDC has posted better than expected results. Based on operating earnings yield, the company is about fairly valued when compared to all of the companies in our coverage universe. Share price changes over the past year indicates that MDC will perform very well over the near term.

Financial Data

(US$ in Thousands)	12/31/2012	12/31/2011	12/31/2010	12/31/2009	12/31/2008	12/31/2007	12/31/2006	12/31/2005
Earnings Per Share	1.28	(2.12)	(1.40)	0.52	(8.24)	(13.94)	4.66	10.99
Cash Flow Per Share	(2.28)	(1.72)	(4.48)	4.35	10.36	12.97	8.08	(9.65)
Tang Book Value Per Share	17.97	17.98	20.87	22.82	23.16	32.05	47.77	43.54
Dividends Per Share	2.000	1.000	1.000	1.000	1.000	1.000	1.000	0.760
Dividend Payout %	156.25	...	...	192.31	...	...	21.46	6.92
Income Statement								
Total Revenue	1,203,023	844,168	958,655	898,303	1,458,108	2,933,249	4,801,742	4,884,160
EBITDA	40,625	(100,706)	(41,608)	(66,453)	(366,895)	(709,122)	392,552	863,555
Depn & Amortn	5,362	16,540	16,943	14,457	32,710	47,342	59,415	54,792
Income Before Taxes	61,115	(107,472)	(70,601)	(107,335)	(382,135)	(756,464)	333,137	808,763
Income Taxes	(1,584)	(9,082)	(5,831)	(132,014)	(1,590)	(119,524)	118,884	303,040
Net Income	62,699	(98,390)	(64,770)	24,679	(380,545)	(636,940)	214,253	505,723
Average Shares	48,064	46,796	46,628	46,919	46,159	45,687	45,971	46,036
Balance Sheet								
Current Assets	1,747,586	1,692,692	2,349,043	2,248,545	2,259,825	2,550,649	3,408,353	3,359,601
Total Assets	1,945,441	1,858,725	2,547,769	2,429,308	2,474,938	2,956,237	3,909,875	3,784,895
Current Liabilities	1,062,294	197,279	295,837	329,056	396,491	483,133	751,311	1,040,081
Long-Term Obligations	...	792,810	1,268,249	1,027,106	997,527	997,091	996,682	996,291
Total Liabilities	1,064,544	990,089	1,564,086	1,356,162	1,394,018	1,480,224	1,747,993	1,832,786
Stockholders' Equity	880,897	868,636	983,683	1,073,146	1,080,920	1,476,013	2,161,882	1,952,109
Shares Outstanding	48,698	47,957	47,142	47,017	46,666	46,053	45,165	44,630
Statistical Record								
Return on Assets %	3.29	N.M.	N.M.	1.01	N.M.	N.M.	5.57	15.38
Return on Equity %	7.15	N.M.	N.M.	2.29	N.M.	N.M.	10.42	30.00
EBITDA Margin %	3.38	N.M.	N.M.	N.M.	N.M.	N.M.	8.18	17.68
Net Margin %	5.21	N.M.	N.M.	2.75	N.M.	N.M.	4.46	10.35
Asset Turnover	0.63	0.38	0.39	0.37	0.54	0.85	1.25	1.49
Current Ratio	1.65	8.58	7.94	6.83	5.70	5.28	4.54	3.23
Debt to Equity	...	0.91	1.29	0.96	0.92	0.68	0.46	0.51
Price Range	40.62-17.77	31.80-15.39	38.94-24.63	38.65-23.38	48.15-22.74	60.00-32.34	68.10-40.43	88.17-61.98
P/E Ratio	31.73-13.88	...	...	74.33-44.96	...	...	14.61-8.68	8.02-5.64
Average Yield %	6.53	4.30	3.29	3.11	2.61	2.12	1.84	1.04

Address: 4350 South Monaco Street, Suite 500, Denver, CO 80237 Telephone: 303-773-1100	Web Site: www.richmondamerican.com Officers: Larry A. Mizel - Chairman, Chief Executive Officer David D. Mandarich - President, Chief Operating Officer	Auditors: Ernst & Young LLP Investor Contact: 303-977-3451 Transfer Agents: Continental Stock Transfer & Trust Company, New York, NY

MDU RESOURCES GROUP INC.

Exchange	Symbol	Price	52Wk Range	Yield	P/E	Div Achiever
NYS	MDU	$24.99 (3/28/2013)	24.99-19.76	2.76	N/A	22 Years

*7 Year Price Score 85.29 *NYSE Composite Index=100 *12 Month Price Score 99.67

Interim Earnings (Per Share)

Qtr.	Mar	Jun	Sep	Dec
2008	0.39	0.63	0.64	(0.07)
2009	(1.87)	0.30	0.50	0.40
2010	0.22	0.26	0.32	0.47
2011	0.23	0.24	0.34	0.32
2012	0.19	0.29	(0.16)	(0.33)

Interim Dividends (Per Share)

Amt	Decl	Ex	Rec	Pay
0.168Q	05/17/2012	06/12/2012	06/14/2012	07/01/2012
0.168Q	08/16/2012	09/11/2012	09/13/2012	10/01/2012
0.172Q	11/15/2012	12/11/2012	12/13/2012	12/31/2012
0.172Q	02/14/2013	03/12/2013	03/14/2013	04/01/2013

Indicated Div: $0.69 (Div. Reinv. Plan)

Valuation Analysis / **Institutional Holding**

Forecast EPS	$1.30	No of Institutions
	(04/05/2013)	395
Market Cap	$4.7 Billion	Shares
Book Value	$2.6 Billion	111,317,208
Price/Book	1.78	% Held
Price/Sales	1.16	54.04

Business Summary: Mining (MIC: 8.2.4 SIC: 1429 NAIC: 212319)

MDU Resources Group is a natural resource company. Through its subsidiaries, Co. operates the following segments: electric; natural gas distribution; pipeline and energy services; exploration and production; construction materials and contracting; construction services; and other. At Dec 31 2011, Co.'s electric segment served more than 127,000 residential, commercial, industrial and municipal customers in 177 communities and adjacent rural areas. Co. serves markets in portions of western North Dakota, eastern Montana, and northern South Dakota. At Dec 31 2011, Co. had total proved reserves of 585.91 billion cubic feet of natural gas equivalent.

Recent Developments: For the year ended Dec 31 2012, loss from continuing operations was US$14.3 million compared with income of US$226.0 million a year earlier. Net loss amounted to US$754,000 versus net income of US$213.0 million in the prior year. Revenues were US$4.08 billion, up 0.6% from US$4.05 billion the year before. Operating income was US$19.2 million versus US$406.4 million in the prior year, a decrease of 95.3%. Direct operating expenses was unchanged at US$3.13 billion versus the comparable period the year before. Indirect operating expenses increased 79.6% to US$927.1 million from US$516.3 million in the equivalent prior-year period.

Prospects: Our evaluation of MDU Resources Group Inc. as of Apr. 7, 2013 is the result of our systematic analysis on three basic characteristics: earnings strength, relative valuation, and recent stock price movement. The company has produced a positive trend in earnings per share over the past 5 quarters and while recent estimates for the company have remained steady, MDU has posted better than expected results. Based on operating earnings yield, the company is about fairly valued when compared to all of the companies in our coverage universe. Share price changes over the past year indicates that MDU will perform in line with the market over the near term.

Financial Data
(US$ in Thousands)

	12/31/2012	12/31/2011	12/31/2010	12/31/2009	12/31/2008	12/31/2007	12/31/2006	12/31/2005
Earnings Per Share	(0.01)	1.12	1.27	(0.67)	1.59	2.36	1.74	1.53
Cash Flow Per Share	3.09	3.32	2.93	4.57	4.28	3.10	3.66	2.71
Tang Book Value Per Share	10.49	11.15	10.71	10.10	11.44	11.31	10.49	9.04
Dividends Per Share	0.675	0.655	0.635	0.623	0.600	0.560	0.523	0.493
Dividend Payout %	...	58.48	50.00	...	37.74	23.73	30.08	32.31
Income Statement								
Total Revenue	4,075,431	4,050,492	3,909,695	4,176,501	5,003,278	4,247,896	4,070,684	3,455,414
EBITDA	385,054	756,282	747,588	186,776	882,069	867,370	816,005	684,077
Depn & Amortn	359,205	343,395	328,843	330,542	366,020	301,932	271,583	228,657
Income Before Taxes	(50,850)	331,533	335,734	(227,865)	434,522	493,201	472,327	400,670
Income Taxes	(31,146)	110,274	122,530	(96,092)	147,476	190,024	165,248	145,779
Net Income	(754)	213,026	240,659	(123,274)	293,673	432,120	315,757	275,083
Average Shares	188,826	188,905	188,229	185,175	183,807	182,902	181,392	179,490
Balance Sheet								
Current Assets	1,128,081	1,194,638	1,167,168	1,061,658	1,272,292	1,214,332	993,735	933,196
Total Assets	6,682,491	6,556,125	6,303,549	5,990,952	6,587,845	5,592,434	4,903,474	4,423,562
Current Liabilities	850,115	898,753	768,076	667,185	967,475	849,888	653,962	628,928
Long-Term Obligations	1,610,867	1,285,411	1,433,955	1,486,677	1,568,636	1,146,781	1,170,548	1,104,752
Total Liabilities	4,034,243	3,780,558	3,610,747	3,419,305	3,826,769	3,061,115	2,738,561	2,531,940
Stockholders' Equity	2,648,248	2,775,567	2,692,802	2,571,647	2,761,076	2,531,319	2,164,913	1,891,622
Shares Outstanding	188,830	188,793	188,362	187,850	183,669	182,407	181,018	179,856
Statistical Record								
Return on Assets %	N.M.	3.31	3.91	N.M.	4.81	8.23	6.77	6.74
Return on Equity %	N.M.	7.79	9.14	N.M.	11.07	18.40	15.57	15.40
EBITDA Margin %	9.45	18.67	19.12	4.47	17.63	20.42	20.05	19.80
Net Margin %	N.M.	5.26	6.16	N.M.	5.87	10.17	7.76	7.96
Asset Turnover	0.61	0.63	0.64	0.66	0.82	0.81	0.87	0.85
Current Ratio	1.33	1.33	1.52	1.59	1.32	1.43	1.52	1.48
Debt to Equity	0.61	0.46	0.53	0.58	0.57	0.45	0.54	0.58
Price Range	23.06-19.76	23.95-18.42	23.91-17.56	24.13-13.04	34.90-15.59	31.27-24.80	26.90-21.99	24.47-17.07
P/E Ratio	...	21.38-16.45	18.83-13.83	...	21.95-9.81	13.25-10.51	15.46-12.64	15.99-11.15
Average Yield %	3.09	3.06	3.06	3.22	2.22	2.02	2.18	2.48

Address: 1200 West Century Avenue, P.O. Box 5650, Bismarck, ND 58506-5650	Web Site: www.mdu.com	Auditors: Deloitte & Touche LLP
	Officers: Harry Jonathan Pearce - Chairman James Kent Wells - Vice-Chairman, Division Officer	Investor Contact: 866-866-8919
Telephone: 701-530-1000		Transfer Agents: Wells Fargo Bank, N.A., St. Paul, MN
Fax: 701-530-1731		

MEAD JOHNSON NUTRITION CO

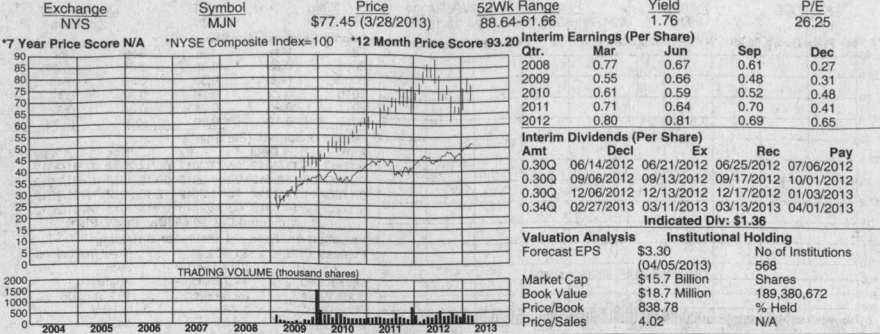

Exchange	Symbol	Price	52Wk Range	Yield	P/E
NYS	MJN	$77.45 (3/28/2013)	88.64-61.66	1.76	26.25

*7 Year Price Score N/A   *NYSE Composite Index=100   *12 Month Price Score 93.20

Interim Earnings (Per Share)

Qtr.	Mar	Jun	Sep	Dec
2008	0.77	0.67	0.61	0.27
2009	0.55	0.66	0.48	0.31
2010	0.61	0.59	0.52	0.48
2011	0.71	0.64	0.70	0.41
2012	0.80	0.81	0.69	0.65

Interim Dividends (Per Share)

Amt	Decl	Ex	Rec	Pay
0.30Q	06/14/2012	06/21/2012	06/25/2012	07/06/2012
0.30Q	09/06/2012	09/13/2012	09/17/2012	10/01/2012
0.30Q	12/06/2012	12/13/2012	12/17/2012	01/03/2013
0.34Q	02/27/2013	03/11/2013	03/13/2013	04/01/2013

Indicated Div: $1.36

Valuation Analysis

		Institutional Holding	
Forecast EPS	$3.30 (04/05/2013)	No of Institutions	568
Market Cap	$15.7 Billion	Shares	189,380,672
Book Value	$18.7 Million	% Held	N/A
Price/Book	838.78		
Price/Sales	4.02		

TRADING VOLUME (thousand shares)

Business Summary: Food (MIC: 1.2.1 SIC: 2026 NAIC: 311511)

Mead Johnson Nutrition manufactures, distributes and sells infant formulas, children's nutrition and other nutritional products. Co.'s pediatric nutrition products are grouped by category of feeding: infant formula products, which include formulas for routine feeding, formulas for mild feeding problems and specialty formula products, including formulas for severe intolerance, formulas for premature and low birth weight infants and medical nutrition products; children's nutrition products, which provide children with improved nutrition; and other products, which include pre-natal and post-natal nutritional supplements for expectant and nursing mothers, including Expecta and EnfaMama A+.

Recent Developments: For the year ended Dec 31 2012, net income increased 18.0% to US$612.4 million from US$519.0 million in the prior year. Revenues were US$3.90 billion, up 6.1% from US$3.68 billion the year before. Direct operating expenses rose 9.0% to US$1.49 billion from US$1.36 billion in the comparable period the year before. Indirect operating expenses increased 0.4% to US$1.55 billion from US$1.54 billion in the equivalent prior-year period.

Prospects: Our evaluation of Mead Johnson Nutrition Company as of Apr. 7, 2013 is the result of our systematic analysis on three basic characteristics: earnings strength, relative valuation, and recent stock price movement. The company has managed to produce a neutral trend in earnings per share over the past 5 quarters. However, while recent estimates for the company have been lowered by analysts, MJN has posted better than expected results. Based on operating earnings yield, the company is about fairly valued when compared to all of the companies in our coverage universe. Share price changes over the past year indicates that MJN will perform poorly over the near term.

Financial Data

(US$ in Thousands)	12/31/2012	12/31/2011	12/31/2010	12/31/2009	12/31/2008	12/31/2007	12/31/2006	12/31/2005
Earnings Per Share	2.95	2.47	2.20	1.99	2.32	...	...	...
Cash Flow Per Share	3.39	3.10	2.51	2.87	2.80	...	...	...
Tang Book Value Per Share	N.M.	...	...	...	...	2.40	...	...
Dividends Per Share	1.200	1.040	0.900	0.700	...	...	...	...
Dividend Payout %	40.68	42.11	40.91	35.18	...	...	...	...
Income Statement								
Total Revenue	3,901,300	3,677,000	3,141,600	2,826,500	2,882,400	2,576,400	2,345,100	2,201,800
EBITDA	925,800	831,300	737,500	729,900	739,800	704,100	672,700	660,100
Depn & Amortn	55,800	57,200	54,600	50,300	44,100	40,900	37,900	41,700
Income Before Taxes	805,000	721,900	634,300	587,000	652,400	663,200	634,800	618,400
Income Taxes	192,600	202,900	176,100	176,400	251,400	233,600	230,100	222,500
Net Income	604,500	508,500	452,700	399,600	393,900	422,500	398,200	389,800
Average Shares	204,300	205,000	205,100	200,600	170,000	...	...	...
Balance Sheet								
Current Assets	2,015,000	1,889,700	1,449,000	1,336,100	717,100	687,500	624,100	...
Total Assets	3,258,200	2,766,800	2,293,100	2,070,300	1,361,400	1,301,900	1,204,300	...
Current Liabilities	1,369,900	1,200,100	976,100	1,100,200	652,800	562,700	529,900	...
Long-Term Obligations	1,523,200	1,531,900	1,532,500	1,484,900	2,000,000	...	...	...
Total Liabilities	3,239,500	2,945,900	2,660,500	2,745,200	2,762,300	671,100	618,500	...
Stockholders' Equity	18,700	(179,100)	(367,400)	(674,900)	(1,400,900)	630,800	585,800	...
Shares Outstanding	202,520	203,700	204,700	204,500	204,500	200,000	...	...
Statistical Record								
Return on Assets %	20.01	20.10	20.75	23.29	29.50	33.72	...	...
Return on Equity %	...	...	...	...	...	69.46	...	...
EBITDA Margin %	23.73	22.61	23.48	25.82	25.67	27.33	28.69	29.98
Net Margin %	15.49	13.83	14.41	14.14	13.67	16.40	16.98	17.70
Asset Turnover	1.29	1.45	1.44	1.65	2.16	2.06	...	...
Current Ratio	1.47	1.57	1.48	1.21	1.10	1.22	1.18	...
Debt to Equity	81.45	...	...	...	...	...	...	...
Price Range	88.64-61.66	76.48-55.36	62.55-43.62	47.24-26.22	...	...	...	...
P/E Ratio	30.05-20.90	30.96-22.41	28.43-19.83	23.74-13.18	...	...	...	...
Average Yield %	1.59	1.56	1.69	1.97	...	...	...	...

Address: 2701 Patriot Blvd., Glenview, IL 60026
Telephone: 847-832-2420

Web Site: www.meadjohnson.com
Officers: James Milton Cornelius - Chairman Stephen W. Golsby - President, Chief Executive Officer

Auditors: Deloitte & Touche LLP
Investor Contact: 847-832-2182
Transfer Agents: Computershare Shareowner Services, Jersey City, NJ

MEADWESTVACO CORP.

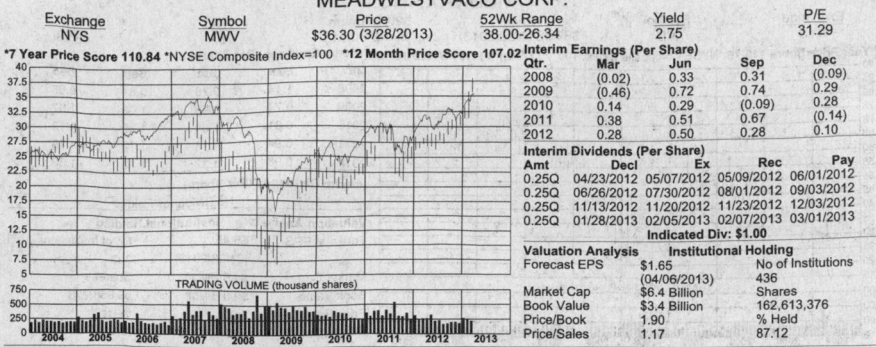

Exchange	Symbol	Price	52Wk Range	Yield	P/E
NYS	MWV	$36.30 (3/28/2013)	38.00-26.34	2.75	31.29

*7 Year Price Score 110.84 *NYSE Composite Index=100 *12 Month Price Score 107.02

Interim Earnings (Per Share)

Qtr.	Mar	Jun	Sep	Dec
2008	(0.02)	0.33	0.31	(0.09)
2009	(0.46)	0.72	0.74	0.29
2010	0.14	0.29	(0.09)	0.28
2011	0.38	0.51	0.67	(0.14)
2012	0.28	0.50	0.28	0.10

Interim Dividends (Per Share)

Amt	Decl	Ex	Rec	Pay
0.25Q	04/23/2012	05/07/2012	05/09/2012	06/01/2012
0.25Q	06/26/2012	07/30/2012	08/01/2012	09/03/2012
0.25Q	11/13/2012	11/20/2012	11/23/2012	12/03/2012
0.25Q	01/28/2013	02/05/2013	02/07/2013	03/01/2013

Indicated Div: $1.00

Valuation Analysis — **Institutional Holding**

Forecast EPS	$1.65
	(04/06/2013)
Market Cap	$6.4 Billion
Book Value	$3.4 Billion
Price/Book	1.90
Price/Sales	1.17

No of Institutions
436
Shares
162,613,376
% Held
87.12

Business Summary: Containers & Packaging (MIC: 8.1.3 SIC: 2653 NAIC: 322211)

MeadWestvaco provides packaging products and services to the healthcare, beauty and personal care, food, beverage, home and garden, tobacco, and agricultural industries. Co. produces packaging materials, and designs and produces packaging products, as well as paperboard for commercial printing. Co. also designs and produces corrugated packaging products. Also, Co. manufactures, markets and distributes chemicals derived from sawdust and other byproducts of the papermaking process in North America, Europe, South America and Asia. In addition, Co. has landholdings in the Southeastern region of the U.S., with operations in real estate development, forestry operations and leasing activities.

Recent Developments: For the year ended Dec 31 2012, income from continuing operations decreased 2.7% to US$215.0 million from US$221.0 million a year earlier. Net income decreased 16.8% to US$208.0 million from US$250.0 million in the prior year. Revenues were US$5.46 billion, up 2.7% from US$5.32 billion the year before. Direct operating expenses rose 3.2% to US$4.33 billion from US$4.19 billion in the comparable period the year before. Indirect operating expenses increased 0.2% to US$838.0 million from US$836.0 million in the equivalent prior-year period.

Prospects: Our evaluation of MeadWestvaco Corp. as of Apr. 7, 2013 is the result of our systematic analysis on three basic characteristics: earnings strength, relative valuation, and recent stock price movement. The company has suffered a very negative trend in earnings per share over the past 5 quarters and while recent estimates for the company have been mixed, MWV has posted results that fell short of analysts expectations. Based on operating earnings yield, the company is overvalued when compared to all of the companies in our coverage universe. Share price changes over the past year indicates that MWV will perform well over the near term.

Financial Data

(US$ in Thousands)	12/31/2012	12/31/2011	12/31/2010	12/31/2009	12/31/2008	12/31/2007	12/31/2006	12/31/2005
Earnings Per Share	1.16	1.42	0.62	1.30	0.52	1.56	0.52	0.14
Cash Flow Per Share	2.51	3.29	3.21	5.11	2.18	3.51	3.14	1.18
Tang Book Value Per Share	13.03	11.13	11.93	12.02	9.37	13.16	11.51	14.25
Dividends Per Share	1.000	1.000	0.940	0.920	0.920	0.920	0.920	0.920
Dividend Payout %	86.21	70.42	151.61	70.77	176.92	58.97	176.92	657.14
Income Statement								
Total Revenue	5,459,000	6,060,000	5,693,000	6,049,000	6,637,000	6,906,000	6,530,000	6,170,000
EBITDA	756,000	878,000	791,000	910,000	631,000	1,029,000	722,000	718,000
Depn & Amortn	306,000	315,000	307,000	350,000	381,000	430,000	433,000	404,000
Income Before Taxes	306,000	412,000	320,000	375,000	79,000	400,000	98,000	139,000
Income Taxes	91,000	160,000	54,000	150,000	(1,000)	115,000	5,000	16,000
Net Income	205,000	246,000	106,000	225,000	90,000	285,000	93,000	28,000
Average Shares	177,200	174,100	172,700	173,200	172,700	183,600	181,200	192,700
Balance Sheet								
Current Assets	2,066,000	2,242,000	2,446,000	2,530,000	2,161,000	2,167,000	2,015,000	2,030,000
Total Assets	8,908,000	8,763,000	8,814,000	9,021,000	8,455,000	9,837,000	9,285,000	8,908,000
Current Liabilities	1,106,000	1,480,000	1,226,000	1,245,000	1,274,000	1,455,000	1,465,000	1,042,000
Long-Term Obligations	2,100,000	1,880,000	2,042,000	2,153,000	2,309,000	2,375,000	2,372,000	2,417,000
Total Liabilities	5,548,000	5,581,000	5,528,000	5,615,000	5,488,000	6,129,000	5,752,000	5,425,000
Stockholders' Equity	3,360,000	3,182,000	3,286,000	3,406,000	2,967,000	3,708,000	3,533,000	3,483,000
Shares Outstanding	175,437	170,870	168,331	171,254	170,813	173,839	182,107	181,418
Statistical Record								
Return on Assets %	2.31	2.80	1.19	2.57	0.98	2.98	1.02	0.27
Return on Equity %	6.25	7.61	3.17	7.06	2.69	7.87	2.65	0.72
EBITDA Margin %	13.85	14.49	13.89	15.04	9.51	14.90	11.06	11.64
Net Margin %	3.76	4.06	1.86	3.72	1.36	4.13	1.42	0.45
Asset Turnover	0.62	0.69	0.64	0.69	0.72	0.72	0.72	0.60
Current Ratio	1.87	1.51	2.00	2.03	1.70	1.49	1.38	1.95
Debt to Equity	0.63	0.59	0.62	0.63	0.78	0.64	0.67	0.69
Price Range	31.87-26.23	30.60-21.08	26.33-18.87	26.07-6.98	27.89-8.52	32.52-25.57	27.45-22.11	30.20-22.53
P/E Ratio	27.47-22.61	21.55-14.85	42.47-30.43	20.05-5.37	53.64-16.38	20.84-16.39	52.78-42.52	215.72-160.92
Average Yield %	3.50	3.80	4.25	5.68	4.48	3.23	3.75	3.55

Address: 501 South 5th Street, Richmond, VA 23219-0501 Telephone: 804-444-1000	Web Site: www.mwv.com Officers: John A. Luke - Chairman, Chief Executive Officer, President James A. Buzzard - President, Executive Vice President	Auditors: PricewaterhouseCoopers LLP Transfer Agents: Computershare Shareowner Services

MEDNAX, INC.

Exchange	Symbol	Price	52Wk Range	Yield	P/E
NYS	MD	$89.63 (3/28/2013)	89.63-60.01	N/A	18.48

*7 Year Price Score 113.75 *NYSE Composite Index=100 ***12 Month Price Score 107.27**

TRADING VOLUME (thousand shares)

Interim Earnings (Per Share)

Qtr.	Mar	Jun	Sep	Dec
2008	1.14	0.78	0.81	0.85
2009	0.74	0.93	1.03	1.07
2010	0.81	1.04	1.29	1.12
2011	0.94	1.15	1.19	1.19
2012	0.98	1.22	1.32	1.32

Interim Dividends (Per Share)
No Dividends Paid

Valuation Analysis / Institutional Holding

Forecast EPS	$5.45	No of Institutions
	(04/06/2013)	333
Market Cap	$4.5 Billion	Shares
Book Value	$2.0 Billion	59,858,776
Price/Book	2.20	% Held
Price/Sales	2.47	N/A

Business Summary: Diagnostic & Health Related Services (MIC: 4.2.2 SIC: 8069 NAIC: 622310)

MEDNAX is a provider of physician services including newborn, maternal-fetal, pediatric subspecialties, and anesthesia care. At Dec 31 2012, Co.'s national network comprised over 2,100 affiliated physicians, including approx. 1,000 physicians who provide neonatal clinical care, in 34 states and Puerto Rico, primarily within hospital-based neonatal intensive care units (NICUs), to babies born prematurely or with medical complications. Co. also has over 200 affiliated physicians who provide maternal-fetal care to expectant mothers experiencing complicated pregnancies and obstetrical hospitalist services, as well as over 625 physicians who provide anesthesia care.

Recent Developments: For the year ended Dec 31 2012, net income increased 10.5% to US$240.9 million from US$218.0 million in the prior year. Revenues were US$1.82 billion, up 14.4% from US$1.59 billion the year before. Operating income was US$389.5 million versus US$355.4 million in the prior year, an increase of 9.6%. Indirect operating expenses increased 15.8% to US$1.43 billion from US$1.23 billion in the equivalent prior-year period.

Prospects: Our evaluation of Mednax, Inc. as of Apr. 7, 2013 is the result of our systematic analysis on three basic characteristics: earnings strength, relative valuation, and recent stock price movement. The company has produced a positive trend in earnings per share over the past 5 quarters. However, while recent estimates for the company have been mixed, MD has posted better than expected results. Based on operating earnings yield, the company is undervalued when compared to all of the companies in our coverage universe. Share price changes over the past year indicates that MD will perform well over the near term.

Financial Data
(US$ in Thousands)

	12/31/2012	12/31/2011	12/31/2010	12/31/2009	12/31/2008	12/31/2007	12/31/2006	12/31/2005
Earnings Per Share	4.85	4.47	4.26	3.78	3.59	2.86	2.52	1.86
Cash Flow Per Share	6.67	5.68	5.16	5.30	3.92	3.89	3.70	3.49
Tang Book Value Per Share	N.M.	N.M.	N.M.	N.M.	N.M.	1.83	1.81	0.25
Income Statement								
Total Revenue	1,816,612	1,588,248	1,401,559	1,288,264	1,068,277	917,644	818,554	693,700
EBITDA	407,216	371,884	327,845	301,811	254,411	235,155	209,510	158,743
Depn & Amortn	15,800	15,000	13,500	11,200	9,400	7,400	7,200	9,900
Income Before Taxes	388,171	353,245	311,152	287,700	241,418	227,006	201,278	146,581
Income Taxes	147,264	135,248	108,461	111,896	94,736	86,987	76,813	57,544
Net Income	240,907	217,997	202,691	175,804	169,201	142,722	124,465	89,037
Average Shares	49,691	48,796	47,570	46,471	47,161	49,904	49,387	47,860
Balance Sheet								
Current Assets	359,044	337,273	296,009	292,665	284,901	364,126	301,599	164,624
Total Assets	2,750,337	2,272,648	2,037,646	1,689,350	1,496,874	1,302,802	1,135,170	900,403
Current Liabilities	268,338	254,301	320,847	346,704	317,125	264,887	221,315	166,788
Long-Term Obligations	144,233	29,327	146,556	50,209	139,856	455	377	622
Total Liabilities	714,969	541,632	590,192	499,252	531,736	343,750	269,369	208,612
Stockholders' Equity	2,035,368	1,731,016	1,447,454	1,190,098	965,138	959,052	865,801	691,791
Shares Outstanding	50,019	48,933	47,937	46,963	45,642	48,421	48,861	47,458
Statistical Record								
Return on Assets %	9.57	10.12	10.88	11.04	12.05	11.71	12.23	10.54
Return on Equity %	12.76	13.72	15.37	16.31	17.54	15.64	15.98	14.10
EBITDA Margin %	22.42	23.41	23.39	23.43	23.82	25.63	25.60	22.88
Net Margin %	13.26	13.73	14.46	13.65	15.84	15.55	15.21	12.84
Asset Turnover	0.72	0.74	0.75	0.81	0.76	0.75	0.80	0.82
Current Ratio	1.34	1.33	0.92	0.84	0.90	1.37	1.36	0.99
Debt to Equity	0.07	0.02	0.10	0.04	0.14	N.M.	N.M.	N.M.
Price Range	81.35-60.01	75.18-58.62	68.35-46.34	61.21-25.02	71.69-24.33	68.62-48.53	52.34-41.86	45.31-30.80
P/E Ratio	16.77-12.37	16.82-13.11	16.04-10.88	16.19-6.62	19.97-6.78	23.99-16.97	20.77-16.61	24.36-16.56

Address: 1301 Concord Terrace, Sunrise, FL 33323 Telephone: 954-384-0175	Web Site: www.mednax.com Officers: Cesar L. Alvarez - Chairman Joseph M. Calabro - President, Chief Operating Officer	Auditors: PricewaterhouseCoopers LLP Transfer Agents: ComputerShare Investor Services, Providence, RI

MEDTRONIC, INC.

Exchange	Symbol	Price	52Wk Range	Yield	P/E	Div Achiever
NYS	MDT	$46.96 (3/28/2013)	47.22-35.89	2.21	13.89	35 Years

*7 Year Price Score 86.13   *NYSE Composite Index=100   *12 Month Price Score 101.89

Interim Earnings (Per Share)

Qtr.	Jul	Oct	Jan	Apr
2009-10	0.40	0.78	0.75	0.86
2010-11	0.76	0.52	0.86	0.72
2011-12	0.77	0.82	0.88	0.94
2012-13	0.84	0.63	0.97	...

Interim Dividends (Per Share)

Amt	Decl	Ex	Rec	Pay
0.26Q	06/21/2012	07/03/2012	07/06/2012	07/27/2012
0.26Q	08/23/2012	10/03/2012	10/05/2012	10/26/2012
0.26Q	12/06/2012	12/13/2012	12/17/2012	12/28/2012
0.26Q	02/14/2013	04/03/2013	04/05/2013	04/26/2013

Indicated Div: $1.04 (Div. Reinv. Plan)

Valuation Analysis   **Institutional Holding**

Forecast EPS	$3.69	No of Institutions
	(04/06/2013)	1308
Market Cap	$47.6 Billion	Shares
Book Value	$17.8 Billion	885,287,808
Price/Book	2.67	% Held
Price/Sales	2.90	73.54

Business Summary: Medical Instruments & Equipment (MIC: 4.3.1 SIC: 3845 NAIC: 334510)

Medtronic is a medical technology company. Co. develops, manufactures, and markets medical devices. Co.'s primary products include those for cardiac rhythm disorders, cardiovascular disease, neurological disorders, spinal conditions and musculoskeletal trauma, urological and digestive disorders, diabetes, and ear, nose, and throat conditions. Co. operates under two operating segments that manufacture and sell device-based medical therapies: cardiac and vascular group, which is composed of its Cardiac Rhythm Disease Management and CardioVascular businesses; and restorative therapies group, which is composed of its Spinal, Neuromodulation, Diabetes, and Surgical Technologies businesses.

Recent Developments: For the quarter ended Jan 25 2013, income from continuing operations increased 16.9% to US$988.0 million from US$845.0 million in the year-earlier quarter. Net income increased 5.7% to US$988.0 million from US$935.0 million in the year-earlier quarter. Revenues were US$4.03 billion, up 2.8% from US$3.92 billion the year before. Direct operating expenses rose 7.3% to US$999.0 million from US$931.0 million in the comparable period the year before. Indirect operating expenses decreased 3.2% to US$1.87 billion from US$1.93 billion in the equivalent prior-year period.

Prospects: Our evaluation of Medtronic Inc. as of Apr. 7, 2013 is the result of our systematic analysis on three basic characteristics: earnings strength, relative valuation, and recent stock price movement. The company has produced a positive trend in earnings per share over the past 5 quarters and while recent estimates for the company have remained steady, MDT has posted better than expected results. Based on operating earnings yield, the company is undervalued when compared to all of the companies in our coverage universe. Share price changes over the past year indicates that MDT will perform in line with the market over the near term.

Financial Data

(US$ in Thousands)	9 Mos	6 Mos	3 Mos	04/27/2012	04/29/2011	04/30/2010	04/24/2009	04/25/2008
Earnings Per Share	3.38	3.29	3.48	3.41	2.86	2.79	1.93	1.95
Cash Flow Per Share	4.71	4.32	4.50	4.25	3.48	3.67	3.48	3.09
Tang Book Value Per Share	4.67	4.68	4.67	4.37	3.41	3.35	1.95	1.62
Dividends Per Share	1.023	1.005	0.988	0.970	0.900	0.820	0.750	0.500
Dividend Payout %	30.25	30.55	28.38	28.45	31.47	29.39	38.86	25.64
Income Statement								
Total Revenue	12,130,000	8,103,000	4,008,000	16,184,000	15,933,000	15,817,000	14,599,000	13,515,000
EBITDA	3,269,000	2,045,000	1,144,000	5,127,000	4,465,000	4,669,000	3,041,000	3,193,000
Depn & Amortn	69,000	46,000	23,000	833,000	464,000	454,000	418,000	417,000
Income Before Taxes	3,097,000	1,942,000	1,088,000	4,145,000	3,723,000	3,969,000	2,594,000	2,885,000
Income Taxes	599,000	432,000	224,000	730,000	627,000	870,000	425,000	654,000
Net Income	2,498,000	1,510,000	864,000	3,617,000	3,096,000	3,099,000	2,169,000	2,231,000
Average Shares	1,021,000	1,027,800	1,037,100	1,059,900	1,081,700	1,109,400	1,124,000	1,142,100
Balance Sheet								
Current Assets	9,161,000	9,435,000	9,183,000	9,515,000	9,117,000	9,839,000	7,460,000	7,322,000
Total Assets	34,949,000	33,960,000	33,252,000	33,083,000	30,424,000	28,090,000	23,661,000	22,198,000
Current Liabilities	6,958,000	6,621,000	5,811,000	5,857,000	4,714,000	5,121,000	3,147,000	3,535,000
Long-Term Obligations	7,314,000	7,355,000	7,386,000	7,359,000	8,112,000	6,944,000	6,772,000	5,802,000
Total Liabilities	17,113,000	16,785,000	15,997,000	15,970,000	14,456,000	13,461,000	10,810,000	10,662,000
Stockholders' Equity	17,836,000	17,175,000	17,255,000	17,113,000	15,968,000	14,629,000	12,851,000	11,536,000
Shares Outstanding	1,013,805	1,011,357	1,020,138	1,037,194	1,070,162	1,097,342	1,119,140	1,124,926
Statistical Record								
Return on Assets %	10.44	10.46	11.38	11.42	10.61	11.78	9.49	10.73
Return on Equity %	19.93	20.26	21.79	21.93	20.29	22.19	17.84	19.87
EBITDA Margin %	26.95	25.24	28.54	31.68	28.02	29.52	20.83	23.63
Net Margin %	20.59	18.64	21.56	22.35	19.43	19.59	14.86	16.51
Asset Turnover	0.49	0.50	0.51	0.51	0.55	0.60	0.64	0.65
Current Ratio	1.32	1.43	1.58	1.62	1.93	1.92	2.37	2.07
Debt to Equity	0.41	0.43	0.43	0.43	0.51	0.47	0.53	0.50
Price Range	46.45-35.89	44.67-33.17	40.65-30.41	43.20-30.41	44.13-31.21	46.03-29.58	56.55-24.38	57.86-45.25
P/E Ratio	13.74-10.62	13.58-10.08	11.68-8.74	12.67-8.92	15.43-10.91	16.50-10.60	29.30-12.63	29.67-23.21
Average Yield %	2.55	2.60	2.70	2.62	2.42	2.09	1.81	0.98

Address: 710 Medtronic Parkway, Minneapolis, MN 55432 **Telephone:** 763-514-4000 **Fax:** 763-514-4879	Web Site: www.medtronic.com **Officers:** Omar Ishrak - Chairman, Chief Executive Officer Michael J. Coyle - Executive Vice President, Region Officer	Auditors: PricewaterhouseCoopers LLP **Transfer Agents:** Wells Fargo Bank, N.A., South St. Paul, MN

MEMC ELECTRONIC MATERIALS, INC.

Exchange	Symbol	Price	52Wk Range	Yield	P/E
NYS	WFR	$4.40 (3/28/2013)	5.66-1.54	N/A	N/A

*7 Year Price Score 10.59 *NYSE Composite Index=100 *12 Month Price Score 144.60

Interim Earnings (Per Share)

Qtr.	Mar	Jun	Sep	Dec
2008	(0.18)	0.76	0.80	0.31
2009	0.01	0.01	(0.29)	(0.04)
2010	(0.04)	0.06	0.08	0.05
2011	(0.02)	0.21	(0.41)	(6.46)
2012	(0.40)	(0.27)	0.16	(0.05)

Interim Dividends (Per Share)

No Dividends Paid

Valuation Analysis

		Institutional Holding	
Forecast EPS	$0.20	No of Institutions	
	(04/05/2013)	337	
Market Cap	$1.0 Billion	Shares	
Book Value	$575.3 Million	204,305,792	
Price/Book	1.77	% Held	
Price/Sales	0.40	80.91	

TRADING VOLUME (thousand shares)

Business Summary: Semiconductors (MIC: 6.2.4 SIC: 3674 NAIC: 334413)

MEMC Electronic Materials is engaged in the development, manufacture, and sale of silicon wafers. Through its subsidiary, SunEdison LLC, Co. develops solar energy projects. Co. has two reportable industry segments: Semiconductor Materials and Solar Energy. The Semiconductor Materials segment provides a range of wafers. Co.'s monocrystalline wafers for use in semiconductor applications range in size from 100 millimeter to 300 millimeter and are round in shape for semiconductor customers. The Solar Energy segment provides solar energy services that integrate the design, installation, financing, monitoring, operations and maintenance portions of the downstream solar market.

Recent Developments: For the year ended Dec 31 2012, net loss amounted to US$148.7 million versus a net loss of US$1.52 billion in the prior year. Revenues were US$2.53 billion, down 6.8% from US$2.72 billion the year before. Operating income was US$57.2 million versus a loss of US$1.30 billion in the prior year. Direct operating expenses declined 9.3% to US$2.19 billion from US$2.42 billion in the comparable period the year before. Indirect operating expenses decreased 82.5% to US$278.4 million from US$1.60 billion in the equivalent prior-year period.

Prospects: Our evaluation of MEMC Electronic Materials Inc. as of Apr. 7, 2013 is the result of our systematic analysis on three basic characteristics: earnings strength, relative valuation, and recent stock price movement. The company has produced a positive trend in earnings per share over the past 5 quarters. However, while recent estimates for the company have been mixed, WFR has posted better than expected results. Based on operating earnings yield, the company is overvalued when compared to all of the companies in our coverage universe. Share price changes over the past year indicates that WFR will perform very well over the near term.

Financial Data

(US$ in Thousands)	12/31/2012	12/31/2011	12/31/2010	12/31/2009	12/31/2008	12/31/2007	12/31/2006	12/31/2005
Earnings Per Share	(0.66)	(6.68)	0.15	(0.31)	1.69	3.56	1.61	1.10
Cash Flow Per Share	(1.14)	(0.07)	1.53	0.15	2.82	4.07	2.38	1.50
Tang Book Value Per Share	1.99	2.55	8.15	8.08	9.27	8.87	5.23	3.21
Income Statement								
Total Revenue	2,529,900	2,715,500	2,239,200	1,163,600	2,004,500	1,921,800	1,540,584	1,107,379
EBITDA	250,800	(1,093,700)	169,900	100	643,400	1,147,500	646,466	310,780
Depn & Amortn	200,600	217,700	158,900	122,800	103,000	79,300	68,224	55,305
Income Before Taxes	(81,500)	(1,384,100)	(12,500)	(100,200)	585,000	1,111,800	590,486	252,375
Income Taxes	64,900	73,100	(53,300)	(42,200)	195,400	282,200	214,833	(2,808)
Net Income	(150,600)	(1,536,000)	34,400	(68,300)	387,400	826,200	369,288	249,353
Average Shares	230,900	229,900	230,200	223,900	228,600	232,300	229,743	226,449
Balance Sheet								
Current Assets	1,459,200	1,885,900	1,737,300	1,249,600	1,454,200	1,589,500	899,514	436,278
Total Assets	4,701,600	4,881,600	4,611,900	3,566,500	2,936,700	2,887,200	1,765,524	1,148,103
Current Liabilities	1,135,800	1,436,900	1,284,100	509,100	472,600	444,200	257,818	224,909
Long-Term Obligations	2,267,100	1,778,900	610,600	384,400	26,100	25,600	29,373	34,821
Total Liabilities	4,126,300	4,143,700	2,360,200	1,397,900	854,700	852,200	598,631	436,766
Stockholders' Equity	575,300	737,900	2,251,700	2,168,600	2,082,000	2,035,000	1,166,893	711,337
Shares Outstanding	231,300	230,800	227,900	227,400	224,500	229,300	223,257	221,517
Statistical Record								
Return on Assets %	N.M.	N.M.	0.84	N.M.	13.27	35.51	25.35	23.11
Return on Equity %	N.M.	N.M.	1.56	N.M.	18.77	51.61	39.32	43.21
EBITDA Margin %	9.91	N.M.	7.59	0.01	32.10	59.71	41.96	28.06
Net Margin %	N.M.	N.M.	1.54	N.M.	19.33	42.99	23.97	22.52
Asset Turnover	0.53	0.57	0.55	0.36	0.69	0.83	1.06	1.03
Current Ratio	1.28	1.31	1.35	2.45	3.08	3.58	3.49	1.94
Debt to Equity	3.94	2.41	0.27	0.18	0.01	0.01	0.03	0.05
Price Range	5.19-1.54	14.84-3.67	16.82-9.41	20.94-11.98	88.49-10.45	94.02-40.29	48.75-23.40	23.68-10.74
P/E Ratio	...	...	112.13-62.73	...	52.36-6.18	26.41-11.32	30.28-14.53	21.53-9.76

Address: 501 Pearl Drive (City of O'Fallon), St. Peters, MO 63376 **Telephone:** 636-474-5000 **Fax:** 636-474-5158	**Web Site:** www.memc.com **Officers:** Emmanuel T. Hernandez - Chairman Ahmad R. Chatila - President, Chief Executive Officer	**Auditors:** KPMG LLP **Investor Contact:** 636-474-5226 **Transfer Agents:** Computershare Investor Services, L.L.C., Chicago, IL

MERCK & CO., INC

Exchange	Symbol	Price	52Wk Range	Yield	P/E
NYS	MRK	$44.20 (3/28/2013)	47.96-37.18	3.89	22.10

*7 Year Price Score 97.71   *NYSE Composite Index=100   *12 Month Price Score 93.01

Interim Earnings (Per Share)

Qtr.	Mar	Jun	Sep	Dec
2008	1.52	0.82	0.51	0.78
2009	0.67	0.74	1.62	2.62
2010	0.09	0.24	0.11	(0.16)
2011	0.34	0.65	0.55	0.49
2012	0.56	0.58	0.56	0.29

Interim Dividends (Per Share)

Amt	Decl	Ex	Rec	Pay
0.42Q	05/22/2012	06/13/2012	06/15/2012	07/09/2012
0.42Q	07/24/2012	09/13/2012	09/17/2012	10/05/2012
0.43Q	11/27/2012	12/13/2012	12/17/2012	01/08/2013
0.43Q	02/26/2013	03/13/2013	03/15/2013	04/05/2013

Indicated Div: $1.72 (Div. Reinv. Plan)

Valuation Analysis   Institutional Holding

Forecast EPS	$3.62	No of Institutions
	(04/05/2013)	1822
Market Cap	$133.8 Billion	Shares
Book Value	$53.0 Billion	2,322,806,016
Price/Book	2.52	% Held
Price/Sales	2.83	N/A

Business Summary: Pharmaceuticals (MIC: 4.1.1 SIC: 2834 NAIC: 325412)

Merck & Co. is a health care company that provides prescription medicines, vaccines, biologic therapies, animal health, and consumer care products, which it markets directly and through its joint ventures. Co.'s operations are comprised of four operating segments: pharmaceutical, which include therapeutic and preventive agents, generally sold by prescription, for the treatment of human disorders; animal health, which develops, manufactures and markets animal health products, including vaccines; consumer care, which develops, manufactures and markets over-the-counter, foot care and sun care products; and alliances, which includes Co.'s relationship with AstraZeneca LP.

Recent Developments: For the year ended Dec 31 2012, net income decreased 1.5% to US$6.30 billion from US$6.39 billion in the prior year. Revenues were US$47.27 billion, down 1.6% from US$48.05 billion the year before. Direct operating expenses declined 2.5% to US$16.45 billion from US$16.87 billion in the comparable period the year before. Indirect operating expenses decreased 8.4% to US$20.97 billion from US$22.90 billion in the equivalent prior-year period.

Prospects: Our evaluation of Merck & Co. Inc. as of Apr. 7, 2013 is the result of our systematic analysis on three basic characteristics: earnings strength, relative valuation, and recent stock price movement. The company has managed to produce a neutral trend in earnings per share over the past 5 quarters and while recent estimates for the company have been mixed, MRK has posted better than expected results. Based on operating earnings yield, the company is undervalued when compared to all of the companies in our coverage universe. Share price changes over the past year indicates that MRK will perform poorly over the near term.

Financial Data

(US$ in Thousands)	12/31/2012	12/31/2011	12/31/2010	12/31/2009	12/31/2008	12/31/2007	12/31/2006	12/31/2005
Earnings Per Share	2.00	2.02	0.28	5.65	3.64	1.49	2.03	2.10
Cash Flow Per Share	3.29	4.03	3.50	1.50	3.07	3.22	3.11	3.46
Tang Book Value Per Share	3.90	2.65	0.82	N.M.	7.97	7.37	7.00	7.48
Dividends Per Share	1.690	1.560	1.520	0.380	1.520	1.520	1.520	1.520
Dividend Payout %	84.50	77.23	542.86	6.73	41.76	102.01	74.88	72.38
Income Statement								
Total Revenue	47,267,000	48,047,000	45,987,000	27,428,300	23,850,300	24,197,700	22,636,000	22,011,900
EBITDA	15,557,000	14,701,000	9,079,000	15,880,600	8,622,200	2,147,000	5,926,700	5,837,100
Depn & Amortn	6,978,000	7,427,000	7,381,000	2,576,000	1,631,200	1,988,200	2,268,400	163,900
Income Before Taxes	8,097,000	6,724,000	1,066,000	13,056,800	7,371,100	515,600	4,047,500	5,768,600
Income Taxes	2,440,000	942,000	671,000	2,267,600	1,999,400	95,300	1,787,600	2,732,600
Net Income	6,168,000	6,272,000	861,000	12,901,300	7,808,400	3,275,400	4,433,800	4,631,300
Average Shares	3,076,000	3,094,000	3,120,000	2,273,200	2,145,300	2,192,900	2,187,700	2,200,400
Balance Sheet								
Current Assets	34,857,000	33,181,000	29,064,000	28,428,600	19,304,900	15,045,400	15,230,200	21,049,300
Total Assets	106,132,000	105,128,000	105,781,000	112,089,700	47,195,700	48,350,700	44,569,800	44,845,800
Current Liabilities	18,348,000	16,245,000	15,641,000	15,750,700	14,318,700	12,258,200	12,722,700	13,303,500
Long-Term Obligations	16,254,000	15,525,000	15,482,000	16,074,900	3,943,300	3,915,800	5,551,000	5,125,600
Total Liabilities	53,112,000	50,611,000	51,405,000	53,031,700	28,437,400	30,166,000	27,010,100	26,929,200
Stockholders' Equity	53,020,000	54,517,000	54,376,000	59,058,000	18,758,300	18,184,700	17,559,700	17,916,600
Shares Outstanding	3,026,636	3,040,839	3,082,107	3,108,223	2,107,690	2,172,503	2,167,786	2,181,924
Statistical Record								
Return on Assets %	5.82	5.95	0.79	16.20	16.30	7.05	9.92	10.60
Return on Equity %	11.44	11.52	1.52	33.16	42.16	18.33	25.00	26.31
EBITDA Margin %	32.91	30.60	19.74	57.90	36.15	8.87	26.18	26.52
Net Margin %	13.05	13.05	1.87	47.04	32.74	13.54	19.59	21.04
Asset Turnover	0.45	0.46	0.42	0.34	0.50	0.52	0.51	0.50
Current Ratio	1.90	2.04	1.86	1.80	1.35	1.23	1.20	1.58
Debt to Equity	0.31	0.28	0.28	0.27	0.21	0.22	0.32	0.29
Price Range	47.96-37.18	37.90-29.81	41.03-31.82	38.00-20.99	60.55-23.56	60.77-42.94	46.21-32.75	34.93-25.85
P/E Ratio	23.98-18.59	18.76-14.76	146.54-113.64	6.73-3.72	16.63-6.47	40.79-28.82	22.76-16.13	16.63-12.31
Average Yield %	4.08	4.57	4.22	1.28	4.09	3.00	3.97	4.96

Address: One Merck Drive, Whitehouse Station, NJ 08889-0100	Web Site: www.merck.com	Auditors: PricewaterhouseCoopers LLP
Telephone: 908-423-1000	Officers: Kenneth C. Frazier - Chairman, President, Chief Executive Officer Willie A. Deese - Executive Vice President, Division Officer	Investor Contact: 908-423-5881
Fax: 908-735-1500		Transfer Agents: Wells Fargo Bank, N.A., South St. Paul, MN

MERCURY GENERAL CORP.

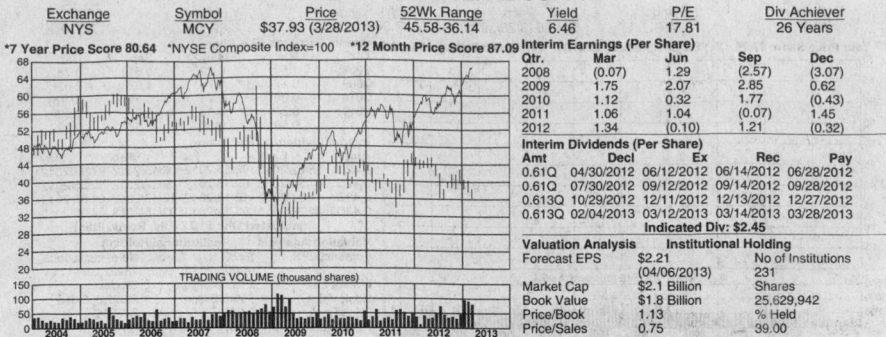

Exchange	Symbol	Price	52Wk Range	Yield	P/E	Div Achiever
NYS	MCY	$37.93 (3/28/2013)	45.58-36.14	6.46	17.81	26 Years

*7 Year Price Score 80.64   *NYSE Composite Index=100   *12 Month Price Score 87.09

Interim Earnings (Per Share)

Qtr.	Mar	Jun	Sep	Dec
2008	(0.07)	1.29	(2.57)	(3.07)
2009	1.75	2.07	2.85	0.62
2010	1.12	0.32	1.77	(0.43)
2011	1.06	1.04	(0.07)	1.45
2012	1.34	(0.10)	1.21	(0.32)

Interim Dividends (Per Share)

Amt	Decl	Ex	Rec	Pay
0.61Q	04/30/2012	06/12/2012	06/14/2012	06/28/2012
0.61Q	07/30/2012	09/12/2012	09/14/2012	09/28/2012
0.613Q	10/29/2012	12/11/2012	12/13/2012	12/27/2012
0.613Q	02/04/2013	03/12/2013	03/14/2013	03/28/2013

Indicated Div: $2.45

Valuation Analysis / **Institutional Holding**

Forecast EPS	$2.21	No of Institutions
	(04/06/2013)	231
Market Cap	$2.1 Billion	Shares
Book Value	$1.8 Billion	25,629,942
Price/Book	1.13	% Held
Price/Sales	0.75	39.00

TRADING VOLUME (thousand shares)

Business Summary: General Insurance (MIC: 5.2.1 SIC: 6331 NAIC: 524126)

Mercury General is an insurance holding company. Co. and its subsidiaries are primarily engaged in writing personal automobile insurance in a number of states, primarily in California. Co. also writes homeowners, commercial automobile and property, mechanical breakdown, fire, and umbrella insurance. Co. provides automobile policyholders the following types of coverage: collision, property damage liability, bodily injury liability, comprehensive, personal injury protection, underinsured and uninsured motorist, and other hazards. As of Dec 31 2012, Co. sold its policies through approximately 7,700 independent agents, of which over 1,300 are located in each of California and Florida.

Recent Developments: For the year ended Dec 31 2012, net income decreased 38.8% to US$116.9 million from US$191.2 million in the prior year. Revenues were US$2.78 billion, unchanged from the year before. Net premiums earned were unchanged at US$2.57 billion versus the prior year. Net investment income fell 6.4% to US$131.9 million from US$140.9 million a year ago.

Prospects: Our evaluation of Mercury General Corp. as of Apr. 7, 2013 is the result of our systematic analysis on three basic characteristics: earnings strength, relative valuation, and recent stock price movement. The company has managed to produce a neutral trend in earnings per share over the past 5 quarters. However, while recent estimates for the company have been lowered by analysts, MCY has posted results that fell short of analysts expectations. Based on operating earnings yield, the company is overvalued when compared to all of the companies in our coverage universe. Share price changes over the past year indicates that MCY will perform poorly over the near term.

Financial Data
(US$ in Thousands)

	12/31/2012	12/31/2011	12/31/2010	12/31/2009	12/31/2008	12/31/2007	12/31/2006	12/31/2005
Earnings Per Share	2.13	3.49	2.78	7.32	(4.42)	4.34	3.92	4.63
Cash Flow Per Share	2.69	2.89	1.68	3.45	1.18	3.95	6.62	8.98
Tang Book Value Per Share	31.90	32.10	30.87	30.33	27.28	34.02	31.54	29.44
Dividends Per Share	2.442	2.410	2.370	2.330	2.320	2.080	1.920	1.720
Dividend Payout %	114.67	69.05	85.25	31.83	...	47.93	48.98	37.15
Income Statement								
Premium Income	2,574,920	2,566,057	2,566,685	2,625,133	2,808,839	2,993,877	2,997,023	2,847,733
Total Revenue	2,783,370	2,777,285	2,775,885	3,121,493	2,414,196	3,178,750	3,168,743	2,991,913
Benefits & Claims	1,961,448	1,829,205	1,825,766	1,782,233	2,060,409	2,036,644	2,021,646	1,862,936
Income Before Taxes	135,310	245,099	182,390	571,541	(450,861)	315,036	312,409	352,639
Income Taxes	18,399	53,935	30,192	168,469	(208,742)	77,204	97,592	99,380
Net Income	116,911	191,164	152,198	403,072	(242,119)	237,832	214,817	253,259
Average Shares	54,922	54,845	54,826	55,092	54,917	54,829	54,786	54,717
Balance Sheet								
Total Assets	4,189,686	4,070,006	4,203,364	4,232,633	3,950,195	4,414,496	4,301,062	4,041,551
Total Liabilities	2,347,189	2,212,523	2,408,549	2,461,687	2,456,144	2,552,498	2,576,932	2,433,714
Stockholders' Equity	1,842,497	1,857,483	1,794,815	1,770,946	1,494,051	1,861,998	1,724,130	1,607,837
Shares Outstanding	54,922	54,856	54,803	54,776	54,763	54,729	54,669	54,605
Statistical Record								
Return on Assets %	2.82	4.62	3.61	9.85	N.M.	5.46	5.15	6.62
Return on Equity %	6.30	10.47	8.54	24.69	N.M.	13.26	12.89	16.51
Loss Ratio %	76.18	71.28	71.13	67.89	73.35	68.03	67.46	65.42
Net Margin %	4.20	6.88	5.48	12.91	(10.03)	7.48	6.78	8.46
Price Range	45.63-36.14	46.44-33.86	46.26-37.49	45.99-22.68	61.90-36.93	57.57-49.17	59.52-49.02	60.45-51.62
P/E Ratio	21.42-16.97	13.31-9.70	16.64-13.49	6.28-3.10	...	13.26-11.33	15.18-12.51	13.06-11.15
Average Yield %	5.85	5.97	5.64	6.66	4.85	3.90	3.54	3.04

Address: 4484 Wilshire Boulevard, Los Angeles, CA 90010 **Telephone:** 323-937-1060 **Fax:** 323-857-7116	**Web Site:** www.mercuryinsurance.com **Officers:** George Joseph - Chairman Gabriel Tirador - President, Chief Executive Officer	**Auditors:** KPMG LLP **Investor Contact:** 323-857-7123 **Transfer Agents:** Computershare, Jersey City, NJ

MEREDITH CORP.

Exchange	Symbol	Price	52Wk Range	Yield	P/E	Div Achiever
NYS	MDP	$38.26 (3/28/2013)	44.21-27.20	4.26	15.49	19 Years

*7 Year Price Score 81.30   *NYSE Composite Index=100   *12 Month Price Score 107.57

Interim Earnings (Per Share)

Qtr.	Sep	Dec	Mar	Jun
2009-10	0.40	0.42	0.73	0.73
2010-11	0.56	0.88	0.67	0.66
2011-12	0.48	0.70	0.47	0.66
2012-13	0.55	0.79	...	...

Interim Dividends (Per Share)

Amt	Decl	Ex	Rec	Pay
0.383Q	05/09/2012	05/29/2012	05/31/2012	06/15/2012
0.383Q	08/08/2012	08/29/2012	08/31/2012	09/14/2012
0.383Q	11/07/2012	11/28/2012	11/30/2012	12/14/2012
0.407Q	02/03/2013	02/26/2013	02/28/2013	03/15/2013

Indicated Div: $1.63

Valuation Analysis

Forecast EPS	$2.84 (04/05/2013)
Market Cap	$1.7 Billion
Book Value	$817.4 Million
Price/Book	2.08
Price/Sales	1.18

Institutional Holding

No of Institutions	255
Shares	48,401,424
% Held	91.05

Business Summary: Publishing (MIC: 2.3.3 SIC: 2721 NAIC: 511120)

Meredith is a media and marketing company serving American women. Co. has two business segments: the national media segment consists of magazine publishing, digital and mobile media, digital and customer relationship marketing, brand licensing, database-related activities, and other related operations; and the local media segment consists of network-affiliated television stations, related digital and mobile media, and video creation operations. As of June 30, 2012, Co. had 12 network-affiliated television stations across the U.S., and published more than 20 subscription magazines and more than 120 publications of other interest.

Recent Developments: For the quarter ended Dec 31 2012, net income increased 12.6% to US$35.6 million from US$31.6 million in the year-earlier quarter. Revenues were US$360.6 million, up 9.7% from US$328.7 million the year before. Operating income was US$57.5 million versus US$54.9 million in the prior-year quarter, an increase of 4.7%. Direct operating expenses rose 4.4% to US$134.1 million from US$128.4 million in the comparable period the year before. Indirect operating expenses increased 16.2% to US$169.0 million from US$145.4 million in the equivalent prior-year period.

Prospects: Our evaluation of Meredith Corp. as of Apr. 7, 2013 is the result of our systematic analysis on three basic characteristics: earnings strength, relative valuation, and recent stock price movement. The company has managed to produce a neutral trend in earnings per share over the past 5 quarters and while recent estimates for the company have remained steady, MDP has posted better than expected results. Based on operating earnings yield, the company is undervalued when compared to all of the companies in our coverage universe. Share price changes over the past year indicates that MDP will perform well over the near term.

Financial Data

(US$ in Thousands)	6 Mos	3 Mos	06/30/2012	06/30/2011	06/30/2010	06/30/2009	06/30/2008	06/30/2007
Earnings Per Share	2.47	2.38	2.31	2.78	2.28	(2.38)	2.83	3.31
Cash Flow Per Share	4.36	4.24	4.05	4.72	4.23	4.02	5.44	4.38
Dividends Per Share	1.530	1.530	1.403	0.970	0.910	0.880	0.800	0.690
Dividend Payout %	61.94	64.29	60.71	34.89	39.91	...	28.27	20.85
Income Statement								
Total Revenue	714,752	354,157	1,376,687	1,400,480	1,387,730	1,408,797	1,586,531	1,615,985
EBITDA	130,666	59,858	229,629	272,073	236,472	(77,066)	303,386	348,079
Depn & Amortn	27,908	14,553	43,858	46,782	54,088	58,062	61,881	59,830
Income Before Taxes	95,756	41,619	172,875	212,353	163,851	(155,249)	220,205	262,653
Income Taxes	35,330	16,764	68,503	80,743	59,888	(52,742)	86,100	93,823
Net Income	60,426	24,855	104,372	127,432	103,963	(107,084)	134,672	162,346
Average Shares	44,936	45,043	45,100	45,832	45,544	45,042	47,585	49,108
Balance Sheet								
Current Assets	389,696	383,783	359,436	333,738	381,427	340,140	403,090	452,640
Total Assets	2,055,931	2,045,706	2,016,299	1,712,829	1,727,316	1,669,303	2,059,620	2,089,951
Current Liabilities	430,528	411,412	482,586	408,992	438,306	349,216	443,137	487,029
Long-Term Obligations	315,000	355,000	275,000	145,000	250,000	380,000	410,000	375,000
Total Liabilities	1,238,579	1,244,986	1,218,854	937,844	1,038,971	1,059,920	1,271,765	1,256,750
Stockholders' Equity	817,352	800,720	797,445	774,985	688,345	609,383	787,855	833,201
Shares Outstanding	44,366	44,510	44,507	45,058	45,415	45,067	45,476	48,232
Statistical Record								
Return on Assets %	5.78	5.68	5.58	7.41	6.12	N.M.	6.47	7.86
Return on Equity %	13.86	13.61	13.24	17.42	16.02	N.M.	16.57	21.20
EBITDA Margin %	18.28	16.90	16.68	19.43	17.04	N.M.	19.12	21.54
Net Margin %	8.45	7.02	7.58	9.10	7.49	N.M.	8.49	10.05
Asset Turnover	0.74	0.74	0.74	0.81	0.82	0.76	0.76	0.78
Current Ratio	0.91	0.93	0.74	0.82	0.87	0.97	0.91	0.93
Debt to Equity	0.39	0.44	0.34	0.19	0.36	0.62	0.52	0.45
Price Range	37.26-27.20	37.26-21.48	34.76-21.48	36.81-29.26	37.81-23.93	30.08-10.88	62.42-28.29	63.25-46.18
P/E Ratio	15.09-11.01	15.66-9.03	15.05-9.30	13.24-10.53	16.58-10.50	...	22.06-10.00	19.11-13.95
Average Yield %	4.73	4.95	4.84	2.92	2.94	4.08	1.65	1.26

Address: 1716 Locust Street, Des Moines, IA 50309-3023	Web Site: www.meredith.com	Auditors: KPMG LLP
Telephone: 515-284-3000 **Fax:** 515-284-2700	**Officers:** Stephen M. Lacy - Chairman, President, Chief Executive Officer, Principal Accounting Officer, Principal Financial Officer, Acting Vice President Meredith D. Mell Frazier - Vice-Chairman	**Investor Contact:** 515-284-3357 **Transfer Agents:** Wells Fargo Bank, N.A., South St. Paul, MN

MERITOR INC

Exchange	Symbol	Price	52Wk Range	Yield	P/E
NYS	MTOR	$4.73 (3/28/2013)	8.23-3.94	N/A	8.60

*7 Year Price Score 38.33 *NYSE Composite Index=100 *12 Month Price Score 85.30

Interim Earnings (Per Share)

Qtr.	Dec	Mar	Jun	Sep
2009-10	0.00	0.16	(0.03)	0.02
2010-11	(0.03)	0.18	0.18	0.32
2011-12	(0.23)	0.21	0.50	0.06
2012-13	(0.22)	...	...	...

Interim Dividends (Per Share)

Dividend Payment Suspended

Valuation Analysis

	Institutional Holding	
Forecast EPS	$0.30	No of Institutions
	(04/05/2013)	208
Market Cap	$460.2 Million	Shares
Book Value	N/A	80,909,336
Price/Book	N/A	% Held
Price/Sales	0.11	N/A

Business Summary: Construction Services (MIC: 7.5.4 SIC: 3714 NAIC: 336350)

Meritor supplies a range of integrated systems and components to original equipment manufacturers (OEMs) and the aftermarket for the commercial vehicle, transportation and industrial sectors. Co. serves commercial truck, trailer, off-highway, military, bus and coach and other industrial OEMs and certain aftermarkets. Co.'s principal products are axles, undercarriages, drivelines, brakes and braking systems. Co. also sells other complimentary products, including third party and private label items, through its aftermarket distribution channels. These products include brake shoes and friction materials; automatic slack adjusters; yokes and shafts; and wheel-end hubs and drums, among others.

Recent Developments: For the quarter ended Dec 31 2012, loss from continuing operations was US$16.0 million compared with a loss of US$9.0 million in the year-earlier quarter. Net loss amounted to US$21.0 million versus a net loss of US$18.0 million in the year-earlier quarter. Revenues were US$891.0 million, down 23.1% from US$1.16 billion the year before. Operating income was US$14.0 million versus US$16.0 million in the prior-year quarter, a decrease of 12.5%. Direct operating expenses declined 23.3% to US$808.0 million from US$1.05 billion in the comparable period the year before. Indirect operating expenses decreased 23.3% to US$69.0 million from US$90.0 million in the equivalent prior-year period.

Prospects: Our evaluation of Meritor Inc. as of Apr. 7, 2013 is the result of our systematic analysis on three basic characteristics: earnings strength, relative valuation, and recent stock price movement. The company has suffered a very negative trend in earnings per share over the past 5 quarters. However, while recent estimates for the company have been lowered by analysts, MTOR has posted results that fell short of analysts expectations. Based on operating earnings yield, the company is undervalued when compared to all of the companies in our coverage universe. Share price changes over the past year indicates that MTOR will perform very poorly over the near term.

Financial Data
(US$ in Thousands)

	3 Mos	09/30/2012	10/02/2011	10/03/2010	09/30/2009	09/30/2008	09/30/2007	10/01/2006
Earnings Per Share	0.55	0.54	0.65	0.14	(16.72)	(1.40)	(3.11)	(2.52)
Cash Flow Per Share	(0.20)	0.81	0.44	2.47	(4.07)	2.25	0.51	6.37
Tang Book Value Per Share	...	...	...	...	...	N.M.	N.M.	5.58
Dividends Per Share	...	...	...	...	0.100	0.400	0.400	0.400
Income Statement								
Total Revenue	891,000	4,418,000	4,622,000	3,590,000	4,108,000	7,167,000	6,449,000	9,195,000
EBITDA	30,000	239,000	245,000	184,000	(214,000)	326,000	178,000	46,000
Depn & Amortn	16,000	59,000	61,000	66,000	76,000	140,000	125,000	165,000
Income Before Taxes	(15,000)	85,000	89,000	12,000	(376,000)	103,000	(57,000)	(252,000)
Income Taxes	10,000	56,000	77,000	48,000	707,000	217,000	(8,000)	(56,000)
Net Income	(21,000)	52,000	63,000	12,000	(1,212,000)	(101,000)	(219,000)	(175,000)
Average Shares	96,700	97,200	96,900	84,700	72,500	72,100	70,500	69,300
Balance Sheet								
Current Assets	1,141,000	1,298,000	1,459,000	1,721,000	1,316,000	2,452,000	2,389,000	3,093,000
Total Assets	2,341,000	2,501,000	2,663,000	2,879,000	2,508,000	4,674,000	4,789,000	5,513,000
Current Liabilities	917,000	1,028,000	1,253,000	1,390,000	1,289,000	2,137,000	2,079,000	2,549,000
Long-Term Obligations	1,032,000	1,042,000	950,000	1,029,000	1,080,000	1,063,000	1,130,000	1,184,000
Total Liabilities	3,382,000	3,524,000	3,658,000	3,933,000	3,785,000	4,212,000	4,246,000	4,506,000
Stockholders' Equity	(1,041,000)	(1,023,000)	(995,000)	(1,054,000)	(1,277,000)	462,000	543,000	944,000
Shares Outstanding	97,300	96,500	94,600	94,100	74,000	73,800	72,600	70,600
Statistical Record								
Return on Assets %	2.17	2.02	2.28	0.44	N.M.	N.M.	N.M.	N.M.
EBITDA Margin %	3.37	5.41	5.30	5.13	N.M.	4.55	2.76	0.50
Net Margin %	N.M.	1.18	1.36	0.33	N.M.	N.M.	N.M.	N.M.
Asset Turnover	1.70	1.72	1.67	1.32	1.14	1.51	1.26	1.62
Current Ratio	1.24	1.26	1.16	1.24	1.02	1.15	1.15	1.21
Debt to Equity	...	...	...	...	...	2.30	2.08	1.25
Price Range	8.67-3.94	10.24-3.99	22.62-6.63	16.80-6.85	13.04-0.35	17.00-9.37	23.52-13.91	17.63-12.90
P/E Ratio	15.76-7.16	18.96-7.39	34.80-10.20	120.00-48.93	...	...	...	...
Average Yield %	...	...	...	...	2.48	3.00	2.16	2.59

Address: 2135 West Maple Road, Troy, MI 48084-7186 **Telephone:** 248-435-1000 **Fax:** 248-435-1393	**Web Site:** www.Meritor.com **Officers:** Charles G. McClure - Chairman, President, Chief Executive Officer James D. Donlon - Executive Vice President	**Auditors:** Deloitte & Touche LLP **Transfer Agents:** Computershare Investor Services, Jersey City, NJ

METLIFE INC

Exchange	Symbol	Price	52Wk Range	Yield	P/E
NYS	MET	$38.02 (3/28/2013)	40.20-27.82	1.95	33.95

*7 Year Price Score 68.22 *NYSE Composite Index=100 *12 Month Price Score 100.34

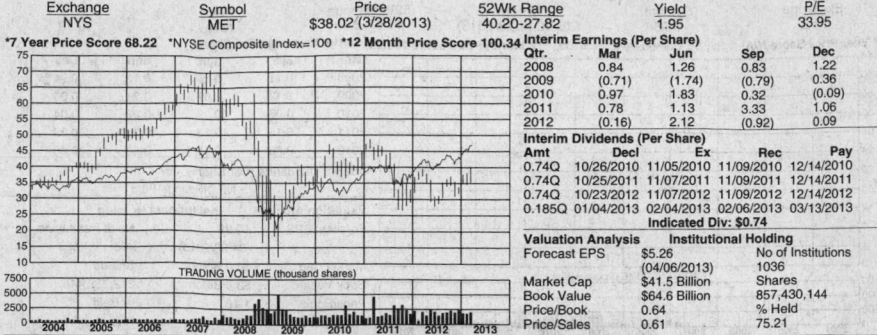

Interim Earnings (Per Share)

Qtr.	Mar	Jun	Sep	Dec
2008	0.84	1.26	0.83	1.22
2009	(0.71)	(1.74)	(0.79)	0.36
2010	0.97	1.83	0.32	(0.09)
2011	0.78	1.13	3.33	1.06
2012	(0.16)	2.12	(0.92)	0.09

Interim Dividends (Per Share)

Amt	Decl	Ex	Rec	Pay
0.74Q	10/26/2010	11/05/2010	11/09/2010	12/14/2010
0.74Q	10/25/2011	11/07/2011	11/09/2011	12/14/2011
0.74Q	10/23/2012	11/07/2012	11/09/2012	12/14/2012
0.185Q	01/04/2013	02/04/2013	02/06/2013	03/13/2013

Indicated Div: $0.74

Valuation Analysis

		Institutional Holding	
Forecast EPS	$5.26 (04/06/2013)	No of Institutions	1036
Market Cap	$41.5 Billion	Shares	857,430,144
Book Value	$64.6 Billion	% Held	75.21
Price/Book	0.64		
Price/Sales	0.61		

Business Summary: Life & Health (MIC: 5.2.2 SIC: 6311 NAIC: 524113)

MetLife is a provider of insurance, annuities and employee benefit programs throughout the U.S., Japan, Latin America, Asia, Europe and the Middle East. Through its subsidiaries and affiliates, Co. provides life insurance, annuities, property and casualty insurance, and other financial services to individuals, as well as group insurance and retirement and savings products and services to corporations and other institutions. Co. is organized into six segments, reflecting three geographic regions: Retail; Group, Voluntary and Worksite Benefits; Corporate Benefit Funding; and Latin America (collectively, the Americas); Asia; and Europe, the Middle East and Africa.

Recent Developments: For the year ended Dec 31 2012, income from continuing operations decreased 79.4% to US$1.31 billion from US$6.39 billion a year earlier. Net income decreased 78.8% to US$1.36 billion from US$6.42 billion in the prior year. Revenues were US$68.15 billion, down 3.0% from US$70.24 billion the year before. Net premiums earned were US$46.53 billion versus US$44.17 billion in the prior year, an increase of 5.4%. Net investment income rose 12.2% to US$21.98 billion from US$19.59 billion a year ago.

Prospects: Our evaluation of MetLife Inc. as of Apr. 7, 2013 is the result of our systematic analysis on three basic characteristics: earnings strength, relative valuation, and recent stock price movement. The company has generated a negative trend in earnings per share over the past 5 quarters and while recent estimates for the company have been mixed, MET has posted better than expected results. Based on operating earnings yield, the company is undervalued when compared to all of the companies in our coverage universe. Share price changes over the past year indicates that MET will perform poorly over the near term.

Financial Data
(US$ in Millions)

	12/31/2012	12/31/2011	12/31/2010	12/31/2009	12/31/2008	12/31/2007	12/31/2006	12/31/2005
Earnings Per Share	1.12	6.29	3.00	(2.89)	4.14	5.48	7.99	6.16
Cash Flow Per Share	15.98	9.71	9.06	4.65	14.52	13.39	8.67	10.69
Tang Book Value Per Share	50.03	45.34	37.49	34.28	23.59	41.51	38.43	32.08
Dividends Per Share	0.740	0.740	0.740	0.740	0.740	0.740	0.590	0.520
Dividend Payout %	66.07	11.76	24.67	...	17.87	13.50	7.38	8.44
Income Statement								
Premium Income	46,531	44,167	33,431	31,663	31,295	33,206	31,192	28,688
Total Revenue	68,150	70,262	52,717	41,058	50,989	53,007	48,396	44,776
Benefits & Claims	37,987	35,457	29,545	28,336	27,437	27,828	26,431	25,506
Income Before Taxes	1,442	10,026	3,958	(4,333)	5,067	6,279	4,455	4,553
Income Taxes	128	3,075	1,181	(2,015)	1,580	1,759	1,116	1,260
Net Income	1,324	6,981	2,790	(2,246)	3,209	4,317	6,293	4,714
Average Shares	1,076	1,068	889	818	744	762	770	755
Balance Sheet								
Total Assets	836,781	799,625	730,906	539,314	501,678	558,562	527,715	481,645
Total Liabilities	772,207	739,723	682,164	506,193	477,944	523,383	493,917	452,544
Stockholders' Equity	64,574	59,902	48,742	33,121	23,734	35,179	33,798	29,101
Shares Outstanding	1,091	1,057	985	818	793	729	751	757
Statistical Record								
Return on Assets %	0.16	0.91	0.44	N.M.	0.60	0.79	1.25	1.12
Return on Equity %	2.12	12.85	6.82	N.M.	10.86	12.52	20.01	18.16
Loss Ratio %	81.64	80.28	88.38	89.49	87.67	83.80	84.74	88.91
Net Margin %	1.94	9.94	5.29	(5.47)	6.29	8.14	13.00	10.53
Price Range	39.46-27.82	48.63-26.60	47.10-33.64	40.83-12.10	63.00-16.48	70.87-59.10	59.83-48.14	52.15-37.85
P/E Ratio	35.23-24.84	7.73-4.23	15.70-11.21	...	15.22-3.98	12.93-10.78	7.49-6.03	8.47-6.14
Average Yield %	2.18	1.90	1.84	2.36	1.46	1.14	1.11	1.15

Address: 200 Park Avenue, New York, NY 10166-0188 Telephone: 212-578-2211	Web Site: www.metlife.com Officers: C. Robert Henrikson - Chairman Steven A. Kandarian - President, Chief Executive Officer	Auditors: Deloitte & Touche LLP Transfer Agents: Mellon Investor Services L.L.C., Pittsburgh, PA

METROPCS COMMUNICATIONS INC

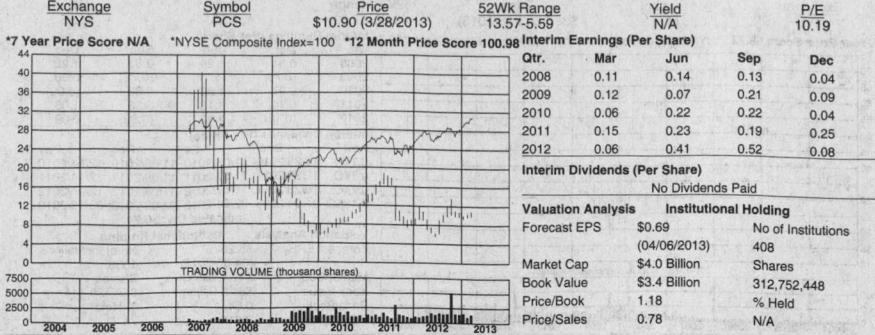

Exchange	Symbol	Price	52Wk Range	Yield	P/E
NYS	PCS	$10.90 (3/28/2013)	13.57-5.59	N/A	10.19

*7 Year Price Score N/A *NYSE Composite Index=100 *12 Month Price Score 100.98

Interim Earnings (Per Share)

Qtr.	Mar	Jun	Sep	Dec
2008	0.11	0.14	0.13	0.04
2009	0.12	0.07	0.21	0.09
2010	0.06	0.22	0.22	0.04
2011	0.15	0.23	0.19	0.25
2012	0.06	0.41	0.52	0.08

Interim Dividends (Per Share)

No Dividends Paid

Valuation Analysis / **Institutional Holding**

Forecast EPS	$0.69 (04/06/2013)	No of Institutions	408
Market Cap	$4.0 Billion	Shares	
Book Value	$3.4 Billion		312,752,448
Price/Book	1.18	% Held	
Price/Sales	0.78		N/A

TRADING VOLUME (thousand shares)

Business Summary: Services (MIC: 6.1.2 SIC: 4812 NAIC: 334220)

MetroPCS Communications is a facilities-based wireless broadband mobile communications provider. Co. provides wireless broadband mobile services under the MetroPCS® brand in selected areas in the U.S., including the Atlanta, Boston, Dallas/Fort Worth, Detroit, Las Vegas, Los Angeles, Miami, New York, Orlando/Jacksonville, Philadelphia, Sacramento, San Francisco, and Tampa/Sarasota areas. Co. provides a range of wireless broadband mobile communications services to its subscribers on a no long-term contract, paid-in-advance basis. Co.'s products and services include voice services, data services, custom calling features, and handsets. As of Dec 31 2011, Co. had over 9.3 million customers.

Recent Developments: For the year ended Dec 31 2012, net income increased 30.8% to US$394.2 million from US$301.3 million in the prior year. Revenues were US$5.10 billion, up 5.2% from US$4.85 billion the year before. Operating income was US$824.0 million versus US$747.5 million in the prior year, an increase of 10.2%. Direct operating expenses rose 0.6% to US$2.93 billion from US$2.91 billion in the comparable period the year before. Indirect operating expenses increased 13.6% to US$1.35 billion from US$1.19 billion in the equivalent prior-year period.

Prospects: Our evaluation of MetroPCS Communications Inc. as of Apr. 7, 2013 is the result of our systematic analysis on three basic characteristics: earnings strength, relative valuation, and recent stock price movement. The company has suffered a very negative trend in earnings per share over the past 5 quarters. However, while recent estimates for the company have been lowered by analysts, PCS has posted results that fell short of analysts expectations. Based on operating earnings yield, the company is undervalued when compared to all of the companies in our coverage universe. Share price changes over the past year indicates that PCS will perform poorly over the near term.

Financial Data
(US$ in Thousands)

	12/31/2012	12/31/2011	12/31/2010	12/31/2009	12/31/2008	12/31/2007	12/31/2006	12/31/2005
Earnings Per Share	1.07	0.82	0.54	0.49	0.42	0.28	0.10	0.62
Cash Flow Per Share	3.24	2.95	2.81	2.56	1.28	2.05	2.34	2.09
Tang Book Value Per Share	2.19	1.07	0.05	N.M.	N.M.	N.M.	N.M.	1.01
Income Statement								
Total Revenue	5,101,278	4,847,382	4,069,353	3,480,515	2,751,516	2,235,734	1,546,863	1,038,428
EBITDA	1,522,774	1,277,536	1,023,197	909,191	690,971	539,513	319,993	463,372
Depn & Amortn	641,425	538,835	449,732	377,856	255,319	178,202	135,028	87,895
Income Before Taxes	607,458	479,656	312,294	263,679	279,424	223,501	90,523	326,102
Income Taxes	213,286	178,346	118,879	86,835	129,986	123,098	36,717	127,425
Net Income	394,172	301,310	193,415	176,844	149,438	100,403	53,806	198,677
Average Shares	364,880	363,837	356,135	355,942	355,380	296,337	159,696	153,610
Balance Sheet								
Current Assets	3,187,303	2,743,593	1,593,885	1,491,391	1,043,884	1,732,884	758,527	612,102
Total Assets	10,189,415	9,482,931	7,918,580	7,386,017	6,422,148	5,806,130	4,153,122	2,158,981
Current Liabilities	847,803	816,723	802,420	797,469	742,356	580,490	435,629	235,617
Long-Term Obligations	4,724,112	4,711,021	3,757,287	3,625,949	3,057,983	2,986,177	2,580,000	902,864
Total Liabilities	6,830,508	6,555,331	5,377,004	5,097,875	4,387,825	3,957,384	3,245,374	1,321,390
Stockholders' Equity	3,358,907	2,927,600	2,541,576	2,288,142	2,034,323	1,848,746	907,748	837,591
Shares Outstanding	364,492	362,460	355,318	352,711	350,918	348,108	157,052	155,327
Statistical Record								
Return on Assets %	4.00	3.46	2.53	2.56	2.44	2.02	1.70	...
Return on Equity %	12.51	11.02	8.01	8.18	7.68	7.28	6.17	...
EBITDA Margin %	29.85	26.36	25.14	26.12	25.11	24.13	20.69	44.62
Net Margin %	7.73	6.22	4.75	5.08	5.43	4.49	3.48	19.13
Asset Turnover	0.52	0.56	0.53	0.50	0.45	0.45	0.49	...
Current Ratio	3.76	3.36	1.99	1.87	1.41	2.99	1.74	2.60
Debt to Equity	1.41	1.61	1.48	1.58	1.50	1.62	2.84	1.08
Price Range	13.57-5.59	18.69-7.51	12.74-5.53	18.75-5.85	21.83-10.71	40.33-15.10	...	...
P/E Ratio	12.68-5.22	22.79-9.16	23.59-10.24	38.27-11.94	51.98-25.50	144.04-53.93	...	...

Address: 2250 Lakeside Boulevard, Richardson, TX 75082-4304 Telephone: 214-570-5800	Web Site: www.metropcs.com Officers: Roger D. Linquist - Chairman, Chief Executive Officer J. Braxton Carter - Vice-Chairman, Chief Financial Officer	Auditors: Deloitte & Touche LLP Investor Contact: 214-570-4641 Transfer Agents: American Stock & Transfer & Trust Company, Brooklyn, NY

METTLER-TOLEDO INTERNATIONAL, INC.

Exchange	Symbol	Price	52Wk Range	Yield	P/E
NYS	MTD	$213.22 (3/28/2013)	221.56-148.68	N/A	23.33

*7 Year Price Score 136.00 *NYSE Composite Index=100 *12 Month Price Score 109.92

Interim Earnings (Per Share)

Qtr.	Mar	Jun	Sep	Dec
2008	1.06	1.38	1.52	1.83
2009	1.00	0.81	1.21	2.01
2010	1.10	1.49	1.82	2.39
2011	1.41	1.82	2.09	2.90
2012	1.62	1.93	2.28	3.32

Interim Dividends (Per Share)

No Dividends Paid

Valuation Analysis

Forecast EPS	$10.54
	(04/05/2013)
Market Cap	$6.5 Billion
Book Value	$827.2 Million
Price/Book	7.84
Price/Sales	2.77

Institutional Holding

No of Institutions	347
Shares	34,145,248
% Held	94.83

Business Summary: Biotechnology (MIC: 4.1.2 SIC: 3826 NAIC: 334516)

Mettler-Toledo International is a supplier of precision instruments and services. Co. provides weighing instruments for use in laboratory, industrial and food retailing applications. Co. also provides analytical instruments for use in life science, reaction engineering and real-time analytic systems used in drug and chemical compound development and process analytics instruments used for in-line measurement in production processes. In addition, Co. is a supplier of end-of-line inspection systems used in production and packaging for food, pharmaceutical and other industries. Co. has five segments: U.S. Operations, Swiss Operations, Western European Operations, Chinese Operations and Other.

Recent Developments: For the year ended Dec 31 2012, net income increased 7.9% to US$290.8 million from US$269.5 million in the prior year. Revenues were US$2.34 billion, up 1.4% from US$2.31 billion the year before. Direct operating expenses rose 0.9% to US$1.10 billion from US$1.09 billion in the comparable period the year before. Indirect operating expenses decreased 1.1% to US$834.6 million from US$843.5 million in the equivalent prior-year period.

Prospects: Our evaluation of Mettler-Toledo International Inc. as of Apr. 7, 2013 is the result of our systematic analysis on three basic characteristics: earnings strength, relative valuation, and recent stock price movement. The company has managed to produce a neutral trend in earnings per share over the past 5 quarters. However, while recent estimates for the company have been lowered by analysts, MTD has posted better than expected results. Based on operating earnings yield, the company is about fairly valued when compared to all of the companies in our coverage universe. Share price changes over the past year indicates that MTD will perform well over the near term.

Financial Data

(US$ in Thousands)	12/31/2012	12/31/2011	12/31/2010	12/31/2009	12/31/2008	12/31/2007	12/31/2006	12/31/2005
Earnings Per Share	9.14	8.21	6.80	5.03	5.79	4.70	3.86	2.52
Cash Flow Per Share	10.53	8.81	8.06	6.90	6.52	6.16	4.78	4.19
Tang Book Value Per Share	8.46	6.71	7.17	4.87	N.M.	1.14	2.48	3.16
Income Statement								
Total Revenue	2,341,528	2,309,328	1,968,178	1,728,853	1,973,344	1,793,748	1,594,912	1,482,472
EBITDA	438,786	404,092	357,256	279,513	320,446	290,534	248,408	201,041
Depn & Amortn	33,421	31,689	29,686	29,634	28,987	26,664	26,069	25,977
Income Before Taxes	382,601	349,177	307,513	224,762	266,069	242,867	204,847	160,184
Income Taxes	91,754	79,684	75,365	52,169	63,291	64,360	47,315	51,282
Net Income	290,847	269,493	232,148	172,593	202,778	178,507	157,532	108,902
Average Shares	31,824	32,839	34,140	34,290	35,048	37,952	40,785	43,285
Balance Sheet								
Current Assets	864,920	1,018,863	1,144,895	646,107	670,865	683,209	669,770	800,659
Total Assets	2,117,400	2,203,474	2,283,063	1,718,787	1,662,529	1,678,214	1,587,085	1,669,773
Current Liabilities	562,677	609,844	542,186	494,675	427,598	447,773	384,379	353,456
Long-Term Obligations	347,131	476,715	670,301	203,590	441,588	385,072	345,705	443,795
Total Liabilities	1,290,181	1,422,337	1,511,479	1,007,649	1,159,282	1,096,928	956,223	1,010,771
Stockholders' Equity	827,219	781,137	771,584	711,138	503,247	581,286	630,862	659,002
Shares Outstanding	30,410	31,590	32,425	33,851	33,595	35,638	38,430	41,404
Statistical Record								
Return on Assets %	13.43	12.01	11.60	10.21	12.11	10.93	9.67	6.91
Return on Equity %	36.07	34.71	31.31	28.42	37.29	29.45	24.43	15.78
EBITDA Margin %	18.74	17.50	18.15	16.17	16.24	16.20	15.58	13.56
Net Margin %	12.42	11.67	11.80	9.98	10.28	9.95	9.88	7.35
Asset Turnover	1.08	1.03	0.98	1.02	1.18	1.10	0.98	0.94
Current Ratio	1.54	1.67	2.11	1.31	1.57	1.53	1.74	2.27
Debt to Equity	0.42	0.61	0.87	0.29	0.88	0.66	0.55	0.67
Price Range	195.00-148.68	191.95-130.12	157.55-94.10	106.24-45.72	113.80-60.64	118.54-77.78	80.80-55.62	58.20-45.24
P/E Ratio	21.33-16.27	23.38-15.85	23.17-13.84	21.12-9.09	19.65-10.47	25.22-16.55	20.93-14.41	23.10-17.95

Address: Im Langacher, P.O. Box MT-100, Greifensee, CH 8606	Web Site: www.mt.com	Auditors: PricewaterhouseCoopers LLP
Telephone: 449-442-211	Officers: Robert F. Spoerry - Chairman Olivier A. Filliol - President, Chief Executive Officer	Investor Contact: 614-438-4748
Fax: 614-438-4646		Transfer Agents: Computershare Shareowner Services LLC, Jersey City, NJ

MGM RESORTS INTERNATIONAL

Exchange	Symbol	Price	52Wk Range	Yield	P/E
NYS	MGM	$13.15 (3/28/2013)	13.93-9.00	N/A	N/A

*7 Year Price Score 35.49   *NYSE Composite Index=100   *12 Month Price Score 103.20

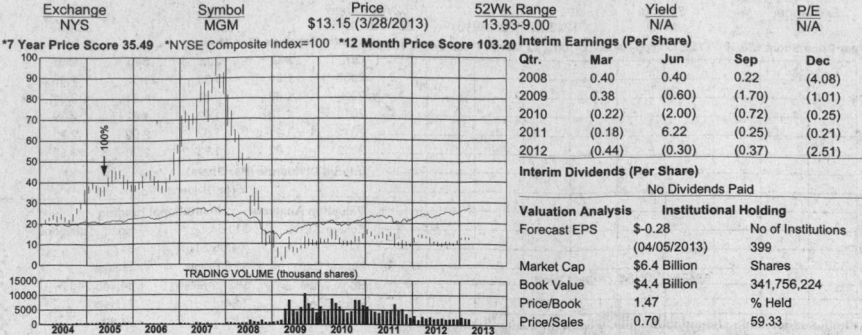

Interim Earnings (Per Share)

Qtr.	Mar	Jun	Sep	Dec
2008	0.40	0.40	0.22	(4.08)
2009	0.38	(0.60)	(1.70)	(1.01)
2010	(0.22)	(2.00)	(0.72)	(0.25)
2011	(0.18)	6.22	(0.25)	(0.21)
2012	(0.44)	(0.30)	(0.37)	(2.51)

Interim Dividends (Per Share)

No Dividends Paid

Valuation Analysis   **Institutional Holding**

Forecast EPS	$-0.28	No of Institutions
	(04/05/2013)	399
Market Cap	$6.4 Billion	Shares
Book Value	$4.4 Billion	341,756,224
Price/Book	1.47	% Held
Price/Sales	0.70	59.33

Business Summary: Hotels, Restaurants & Travel (MIC: 2.2.1 SIC: 7011 NAIC: 721120)

MGM Resorts International is a holding company. Through its subsidiaries, Co. owns and operates casino resorts, which provides gaming, hotel, convention, dining, entertainment, retail and other resort amenities. As of Dec 31 2011, Co. owned and operated casino resorts in Nevada including Bellagio, The Mirage, and Mandalay Bay; two resorts in Mississippi; a golf course located north of its Las Vegas Strip resorts, Primm Valley Golf Club at the California/Nevada state line and Fallen Oak golf course in Saucier, MS; and owned 51.0% in MGM China Holdings Ltd, which through MGM Grand Paradise, S.A, owned the MGM Macau resort and casino and the related gaming subconcession and land concession.

Recent Developments: For the year ended Dec 31 2012, net loss amounted to US$1.62 billion versus net income of US$3.23 billion in the prior year. Revenues were US$9.16 billion, up 16.7% from US$7.85 billion the year before. Direct operating expenses rose 17.8% to US$5.92 billion from US$5.03 billion in the comparable period the year before. Indirect operating expenses amounted to US$3.16 billion compared with an income of US$1.23 billion in the equivalent prior-year period.

Prospects: Our evaluation of MGM Resorts International as of Apr. 7, 2013 is the result of our systematic analysis on three basic characteristics: earnings strength, relative valuation, and recent stock price movement. The company has produced a positive trend in earnings per share over the past 5 quarters. Because the company lacks sufficient analyst estimate data, we place greater weight on the historical EPS trend as the measure of earnings strength. Based on operating earnings yield, the company is overvalued when compared to all of the companies in our coverage universe. Share price changes over the past year indicates that MGM will perform poorly over the near term.

Financial Data

(US$ in Thousands)	12/31/2012	12/31/2011	12/31/2010	12/31/2009	12/31/2008	12/31/2007	12/31/2006	12/31/2005
Earnings Per Share	(3.62)	5.62	(3.19)	(3.41)	(3.06)	5.31	2.22	1.50
Cash Flow Per Share	1.85	1.38	1.12	1.55	2.68	3.47	4.39	4.15
Tang Book Value Per Share	N.M.	N.M.	5.26	7.80	12.81	15.11	7.68	5.41
Income Statement								
Total Revenue	9,160,844	7,849,312	6,019,233	5,978,589	7,208,767	7,691,637	7,175,956	6,481,967
EBITDA	519,633	4,857,328	(193,874)	(373,987)	650,922	3,350,836	2,139,810	1,780,796
Depn & Amortn	1,001,086	910,946	721,406	740,125	788,856	704,632	650,823	593,893
Income Before Taxes	(1,597,811)	2,859,550	(2,028,860)	(1,877,239)	(730,700)	1,955,071	739,818	542,854
Income Taxes	(117,301)	(403,313)	(778,628)	(720,911)	186,298	757,883	341,930	235,644
Net Income	(1,767,691)	3,114,637	(1,437,397)	(1,291,682)	(855,286)	1,584,419	648,264	443,256
Average Shares	488,988	560,895	450,449	378,513	279,815	298,284	291,747	296,334
Balance Sheet								
Current Assets	2,507,092	2,812,720	1,455,645	3,053,501	1,533,030	1,175,386	1,514,751	1,018,583
Total Assets	26,284,738	27,766,276	18,961,045	22,518,210	23,274,716	22,727,686	22,146,238	20,699,420
Current Liabilities	1,925,671	1,744,764	1,246,221	2,383,601	3,002,576	1,724,687	1,648,100	1,534,568
Long-Term Obligations	13,589,283	13,470,167	12,047,698	12,976,037	12,416,552	11,175,229	12,994,869	12,355,433
Total Liabilities	21,919,190	21,679,698	15,962,500	18,647,778	19,300,355	16,666,983	18,296,689	17,464,348
Stockholders' Equity	4,365,548	6,086,578	2,998,545	3,870,432	3,974,361	6,060,703	3,849,549	3,235,072
Shares Outstanding	489,234	488,834	488,513	441,222	276,506	293,768	283,909	285,069
Statistical Record								
Return on Assets %	N.M.	13.33	N.M.	N.M.	N.M.	7.06	3.03	2.79
Return on Equity %	N.M.	68.57	N.M.	N.M.	N.M.	31.98	18.30	14.76
EBITDA Margin %	5.67	61.88	N.M.	N.M.	9.03	43.56	29.82	27.47
Net Margin %	N.M.	39.68	N.M.	N.M.	N.M.	20.60	9.03	6.84
Asset Turnover	0.34	0.34	0.29	0.26	0.31	0.34	0.33	0.41
Current Ratio	1.30	1.61	1.17	1.28	0.51	0.68	0.92	0.66
Debt to Equity	3.11	2.21	4.02	3.35	3.12	1.84	3.38	3.82
Price Range	14.71-9.00	16.76-8.23	16.64-9.01	16.10-1.89	84.02-8.79	99.75-56.90	57.80-34.65	46.00-33.35
P/E Ratio	...	2.98-1.46	...	...	...	18.79-10.72	26.04-15.61	30.67-22.23

Address: 3600 Las Vegas Boulevard South, Las Vegas, NV 89109 Telephone: 702-693-7120	Web Site: www.mgmresorts.com Officers: James J. Murren - Chairman, President, Chief Executive Officer William J. Hornbuckle - President, Chief Marketing Officer, Division Officer	Auditors: Deloitte & Touche LLP Transfer Agents: Computershare

MICHAEL KORS HOLDINGS LTD.

Exchange	Symbol	Price	52Wk Range	Yield	P/E
NYS	KORS	$56.79 (3/28/2013)	64.84-36.04	N/A	45.43

*7 Year Price Score N/A   *NYSE Composite Index=100   ***12 Month Price Score 108.20**

TRADING VOLUME (thousand shares)

Interim Earnings (Per Share)

Qtr.	Jun	Sep	Dec	Mar
2011-12	0.13	0.22	0.20	0.22
2012-13	0.34	0.49	...	...

Interim Dividends (Per Share)

No Dividends Paid

Valuation Analysis		Institutional Holding	
Forecast EPS	$1.84	No of Institutions	
	(04/05/2013)	332	
Market Cap	$11.3 Billion	Shares	
Book Value	$778.0 Million	148,753,632	
Price/Book	14.58	% Held	
Price/Sales	N/A	N/A	

Business Summary: Retail - Apparel and Accessories (MIC: 2.1.5 SIC: 5621 NAIC: 448120)

Michael Kors Holdings is a designer, marketer, distributor and retailer of branded women's apparel, footwear and accessories and men's apparel bearing the Michael Kors tradename and related trademarks with a presence in 85 countries. Co. offers two primary collections: the Michael Kors luxury collection and the MICHAEL Michael Kors collection. The Michael Kors collection offers accessories, footwear and apparel, including ready-to-wear womenswear and menswear. The MICHAEL Michael Kors collection offers accessories, primarily handbags, and small leather goods; footwear, exclusively in women's styles; and womenswear. Co. operates in three segments: retail, wholesale and licensing.

Recent Developments: For the quarter ended Sep 29 2012, net income increased 140.9% to US$97.8 million from US$40.6 million in the year-earlier quarter. Revenues were US$532.9 million, up 74.4% from US$305.5 million the year before. Operating income was US$157.9 million versus US$59.3 million in the prior-year quarter, an increase of 166.4%. Direct operating expenses rose 66.4% to US$217.0 million from US$130.4 million in the comparable period the year before. Indirect operating expenses increased 36.4% to US$158.0 million from US$115.8 million in the equivalent prior-year period.

Prospects: Co. attributes its recent strong North America wholesale segment top line gains to the continued successful conversion to shop-in-shops in department stores as well as higher comparable store sales. Co. is also experiencing strong sales gains in Europe, as well as increased revenue from its licensing segment. In view of that, for its fiscal year ended April 2013, Co. now expects total revenue to be in the range of $1.86 billion to $1.96 billion. Co. noted that its outlook assumes a comparable store sales increase of approximately 30%. Co. expects diluted earnings per share to be in the range of $1.48 to $1.50 for fiscal 2013.

Financial Data

(US$ in Thousands)	6 Mos	3 Mos	03/31/2012	04/02/2011	04/03/2010	03/28/2009
Earnings Per Share	1.25	0.98	0.78	0.40	0.22	0.08
Cash Flow Per Share	...	...	0.73	0.79	0.20	...
Tang Book Value Per Share	3.76	2.63	2.22	0.73	0.16	...
Income Statement						
Total Revenue	947,800	414,865	1,302,254	803,339	508,099	397,074
EBITDA	272,828	112,318	286,311	158,680	74,104	36,547
Depn & Amortn	2,307	...	36,000	23,600	17,100	12,700
Income Before Taxes	269,531	111,883	248,816	133,219	54,947	22,247
Income Taxes	103,058	43,238	101,452	60,713	15,699	9,208
Net Income	166,473	68,645	147,364	72,506	39,248	13,039
Average Shares	200,192	199,391	189,299	179,177	179,177	179,177
Balance Sheet						
Current Assets	887,308	569,192	464,063	245,398	154,023	...
Total Assets	1,119,484	787,920	674,425	399,495	281,852	...
Current Liabilities	277,089	196,248	165,006	127,725	102,760	...
Long-Term Obligations	...	...	...	101,650	103,500	...
Total Liabilities	341,506	252,270	218,188	267,469	226,135	...
Stockholders' Equity	777,978	535,650	456,237	132,026	55,717	...
Shares Outstanding	199,746	193,226	192,731	140,554	140,554	140,554
Statistical Record						
Return on Assets %	...	...	27.52	21.34	...	...
Return on Equity %	...	...	50.24	77.45	...	...
EBITDA Margin %	28.79	27.07	21.99	19.75	14.58	9.20
Net Margin %	17.56	16.55	11.32	9.03	7.72	3.28
Asset Turnover	...	...	2.43	2.36	...	...
Current Ratio	3.20	2.90	2.81	1.92	1.50	...
Debt to Equity	...	...	...	0.77	1.86	...
Price Range	57.35-24.10	49.59-24.10	49.59-24.10	...	...	...
P/E Ratio	45.88-19.28	50.60-24.59	63.58-30.90	...	...	...

Address: c/o Michael Kors Limited, Unit 1001, 10/F, Miramar Tower, 132 Nathan Road, Tsim Sha Tsui **Telephone:** 852-3928-5563	**Web Site:** www.michaelkors.com **Officers:** Michael Kors - Honorary Chairman, Chief Creative Officer John D. Idol - Chairman, Chief Executive Officer	**Auditors:** PricewaterhouseCoopers LLP **Investor Contact:** 203-682-8200 **Transfer Agents:** American Stock Transfer & Trust Company, LLC, Brooklyn, NY

MID-AMERICA APARTMENT COMMUNITIES INC

Exchange	Symbol	Price	52Wk Range	Yield	P/E
NYS	MAA	$69.06 (3/28/2013)	70.68-60.82	4.03	26.98

*7 Year Price Score 107.82 *NYSE Composite Index=100 *12 Month Price Score 94.62

Interim Earnings (Per Share)

Qtr.	Mar	Jun	Sep	Dec
2008	0.17	0.20	0.11	0.16
2009	0.28	0.25	0.12	0.21
2010	0.21	0.04	0.11	0.20
2011	0.24	0.20	0.37	0.50
2012	0.60	0.69	0.74	0.53

Interim Dividends (Per Share)

Amt	Decl	Ex	Rec	Pay
0.66Q	05/24/2012	07/11/2012	07/13/2012	07/31/2012
0.66Q	09/18/2012	10/11/2012	10/15/2012	10/31/2012
0.695Q	12/04/2012	01/11/2013	01/15/2013	01/31/2013
0.695Q	03/12/2013	04/11/2013	04/15/2013	04/30/2013

Indicated Div: $2.78

Valuation Analysis / **Institutional Holding**

Forecast EPS	$1.69 (04/06/2013)	No of Institutions 304
Market Cap	$2.9 Billion	Shares 41,880,732
Book Value	$918.8 Million	% Held 103.81
Price/Book	3.18	
Price/Sales	5.88	

Business Summary: REITs (MIC: 5.3.1 SIC: 6798 NAIC: 525930)

Mid-America Apartment Communities is a self-administered and self-managed real estate investment trust that focuses on acquiring, owning and operating apartment communities in the Sunbelt region of the U.S. As of Dec 31 2012, Co. owned 100% of 160 properties representing 47,809 apartment units. Four properties include retail components. As of the same date, Co. also had 33.33% ownership interests in Mid-America Multifamily Fund I, LLC and Mid-America Multifamily Fund II, LLC, which owned two properties containing 626 apartment units and four properties containing 1,156 apartment units, respectively. These apartment communities were located across 13 states.

Recent Developments: For the year ended Dec 31 2012, net income increased 114.4% to US$109.8 million from US$51.2 million in the prior year. Revenues were US$497.2 million, up 15.4% from US$430.8 million the year before. Revenues from property income rose 15.5% to US$496.3 million from US$429.8 million in the corresponding earlier year.

Prospects: Our evaluation of Mid-America Apartment Communities Inc. as of Apr. 7, 2013 is the result of our systematic analysis on three basic characteristics: earnings strength, relative valuation, and recent stock price movement. The company has generated a negative trend in earnings per share over the past 5 quarters. Because the company lacks sufficient analyst estimate data, we place greater weight on the historical EPS trend as the measure of earnings strength. Based on operating earnings yield, the company is overvalued when compared to all of the companies in our coverage universe. Share price changes over the past year indicates that MAA will perform poorly over the near term.

Financial Data

(US$ in Thousands)	12/31/2012	12/31/2011	12/31/2010	12/31/2009	12/31/2008	12/31/2007	12/31/2006	12/31/2005
Earnings Per Share	2.56	1.31	0.56	0.85	0.64	1.01	0.29	0.25
Cash Flow Per Share	5.13	4.66	4.20	4.83	5.11	4.66	4.32	4.66
Tang Book Value Per Share	21.61	18.44	14.86	14.75	14.52	15.53	17.69	16.21
Dividends Per Share	2.640	2.510	2.460	2.460	2.460	2.420	2.380	2.350
Dividend Payout %	103.13	191.60	439.29	289.41	384.38	239.60	820.69	940.00
Income Statement								
Total Revenue	497,165	448,992	402,229	378,544	369,851	352,957	325,999	297,455
EBITDA	324,007	280,212	253,331	248,817	250,382	243,245	233,972	210,943
Depn & Amortn	131,428	118,969	104,064	96,019	90,168	86,173	79,388	76,968
Income Before Taxes	133,828	102,631	93,271	95,704	98,204	92,620	91,072	75,224
Net Income	105,223	48,821	29,761	37,211	30,249	39,946	20,945	19,744
Average Shares	42,937	39,086	31,977	28,348	27,046	25,462	23,698	21,607
Balance Sheet								
Current Assets	9,883	58,679	47,456	14,380	9,840	20,916	9,690	19,598
Total Assets	2,751,068	2,530,468	2,176,048	1,986,826	1,921,955	1,783,822	1,746,646	1,570,457
Current Liabilities	11,255	8,401	8,508	10,491	9,939	9,552	10,443	9,707
Long-Term Obligations	1,673,848	1,649,755	1,500,193	1,399,596	1,323,056	1,264,620	1,196,349	1,140,046
Total Liabilities	1,832,303	1,808,100	1,653,781	1,553,458	1,508,004	1,380,292	1,297,580	1,207,931
Stockholders' Equity	918,765	722,368	522,267	433,368	413,951	403,530	449,066	362,526
Shares Outstanding	42,316	38,959	34,871	29,095	28,224	25,718	25,093	22,048
Statistical Record								
Return on Assets %	3.97	2.07	1.43	1.90	1.63	2.26	1.26	1.28
Return on Equity %	12.79	7.85	6.23	8.78	7.38	9.37	5.16	5.49
EBITDA Margin %	65.17	62.41	62.98	65.73	67.70	68.92	71.77	70.92
Net Margin %	21.16	10.87	7.40	9.83	8.18	11.32	6.42	6.64
Asset Turnover	0.19	0.19	0.19	0.19	0.20	0.20	0.20	0.19
Current Ratio	0.88	6.98	5.58	1.37	0.99	2.19	0.93	2.02
Debt to Equity	1.82	2.28	2.87	3.23	3.20	3.13	2.66	3.14
Price Range	70.20-58.49	73.25-55.35	64.23-45.58	49.61-22.99	59.60-24.04	60.48-42.75	65.81-49.35	49.96-36.17
P/E Ratio	27.42-22.85	55.92-42.25	114.70-81.39	58.36-27.05	93.13-37.56	59.88-42.33	226.93-170.17	199.84-144.68
Average Yield %	4.02	3.93	4.46	6.46	5.18	4.42	4.21	5.45

Address: 6584 Poplar Avenue, Memphis, TN 38138	**Web Site:** www.maac.com	**Auditors:** Ernst & Young LLP
Telephone: 901-682-6600	**Officers:** H. Eric Bolton - Chairman, President, Chief Executive Officer Albert M. Campbell - Executive Vice President, Chief Financial Officer, Treasurer, Director	**Investor Contact:** 901-682-6600
Fax: 901-682-6667		**Transfer Agents:** American Stock Transfer & Trust Company

MINE SAFETY APPLIANCES CO

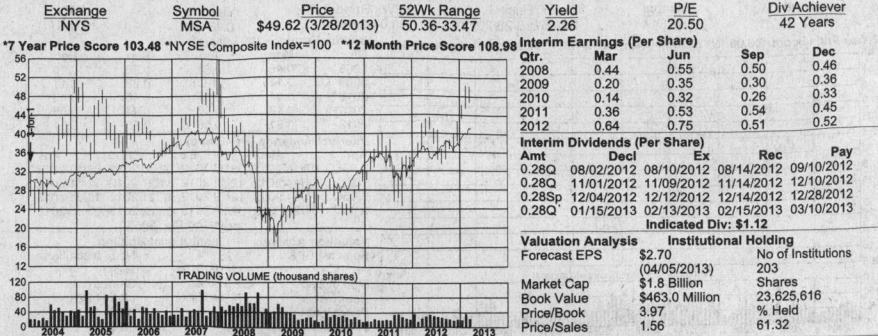

Exchange	Symbol	Price	52Wk Range	Yield	P/E	Div Achiever
NYS	MSA	$49.62 (3/28/2013)	50.36-33.47	2.26	20.50	42 Years

*7 Year Price Score 103.48 *NYSE Composite Index=100 *12 Month Price Score 108.98

Interim Earnings (Per Share)

Qtr.	Mar	Jun	Sep	Dec
2008	0.44	0.55	0.50	0.46
2009	0.20	0.35	0.30	0.36
2010	0.14	0.32	0.26	0.33
2011	0.36	0.53	0.54	0.45
2012	0.64	0.75	0.51	0.52

Interim Dividends (Per Share)

Amt	Deci	Ex	Rec	Pay
0.28Q	08/02/2012	08/10/2012	08/14/2012	09/10/2012
0.28Q	11/01/2012	11/09/2012	11/14/2012	12/10/2012
0.28Sp	12/04/2012	12/12/2012	12/14/2012	12/28/2012
0.28Q¹	01/15/2013	02/13/2013	02/15/2013	03/10/2013

Indicated Div: $1.12

Valuation Analysis   **Institutional Holding**

Forecast EPS	$2.70
	(04/05/2013)
Market Cap	$1.8 Billion
Book Value	$463.0 Million
Price/Book	3.97
Price/Sales	1.56

No of Institutions 203

Shares 23,625,616

% Held 61.32

Business Summary: Office Equipment & Furniture (MIC: 7.5.1 SIC: 3842 NAIC: 922160)

Mine Safety Appliances is engaged in the development, manufacture and supply of products for people's health and safety. Co.'s line of safety products is used by workers in the oil and gas, fire service, mining, construction and other industries, as well as the military. Co.'s product offering includes self-contained breathing apparatus, gas masks, gas detection instruments, head protection, respirators, thermal imaging cameras and fall protection equipments. Co. also provides an offering of consumer and contractor safety products through retail channels.

Recent Developments: For the year ended Dec 31 2012, net income increased 31.0% to US$91.8 million from US$70.0 million in the prior year. Revenues were US$1.18 billion, unchanged from the year before. Direct operating expenses declined 5.2% to US$666.2 million from US$703.0 million in the comparable period the year before. Indirect operating expenses increased 2.3% to US$379.4 million from US$370.8 million in the equivalent prior-year period.

Prospects: Our evaluation of Mine Safety Appliances Co as of Apr. 7, 2013 is the result of our systematic analysis on three basic characteristics: earnings strength, relative valuation, and recent stock price movement. The company has generated a negative trend in earnings per share over the past 5 quarters and while recent estimates for the company have remained steady, MSA has posted better than expected results. Based on operating earnings yield, the company is about fairly valued when compared to all of the companies in our coverage universe. Share price changes over the past year indicates that MSA will perform in line with the market over the near term.

Financial Data

(US$ in Thousands)	12/31/2012	12/31/2011	12/31/2010	12/31/2009	12/31/2008	12/31/2007	12/31/2006	12/31/2005
Earnings Per Share	2.42	1.87	1.05	1.21	1.96	1.86	1.73	2.19
Cash Flow Per Share	4.10	2.35	0.88	3.39	1.68	1.16	1.73	2.35
Tang Book Value Per Share	5.43	4.66	5.06	9.68	8.58	10.40	9.85	8.84
Dividends Per Share	1.380	1.030	0.990	0.960	0.940	0.840	0.680	0.520
Dividend Payout %	57.02	55.08	94.29	79.34	47.96	45.16	39.31	23.74
Income Statement								
Total Revenue	1,179,895	1,178,608	982,668	915,851	1,139,543	1,007,648	919,098	911,970
EBITDA	177,332	151,763	95,248	99,782	149,028	140,464	121,015	153,625
Depn & Amortn	31,681	32,828	29,192	27,362	27,647	24,363	22,147	24,345
Income Before Taxes	134,290	104,818	57,349	65,340	112,458	106,188	92,640	123,796
Income Taxes	42,529	34,773	18,290	22,003	42,036	38,600	28,722	42,013
Net Income	90,637	69,852	38,104	43,295	70,422	67,588	63,918	81,783
Average Shares	37,042	36,831	36,422	35,879	35,949	36,240	36,928	37,301
Balance Sheet								
Current Assets	463,548	458,849	477,389	434,025	477,775	497,050	416,859	377,226
Total Assets	1,111,746	1,115,052	1,197,188	875,228	875,810	1,016,306	898,620	725,357
Current Liabilities	188,800	171,770	181,741	168,450	219,687	209,189	127,435	130,859
Long-Term Obligations	272,333	334,046	367,094	82,114	94,082	103,726	112,541	45,834
Total Liabilities	648,791	681,386	745,820	438,612	482,044	554,775	460,767	342,960
Stockholders' Equity	462,955	433,666	451,368	436,616	393,766	461,531	437,853	382,397
Shares Outstanding	37,007	36,692	36,519	35,972	35,786	35,661	36,015	36,545
Statistical Record								
Return on Assets %	8.12	6.04	3.68	4.95	7.42	7.06	7.87	11.21
Return on Equity %	20.16	15.79	8.58	10.43	16.42	15.03	15.59	21.52
EBITDA Margin %	15.03	12.88	9.69	10.90	13.08	13.94	13.17	16.85
Net Margin %	7.68	5.93	3.88	4.73	6.18	6.71	6.95	8.97
Asset Turnover	1.06	1.02	0.95	1.05	1.20	1.05	1.13	1.25
Current Ratio	2.46	2.67	2.63	2.58	2.17	2.38	3.27	2.88
Debt to Equity	0.59	0.77	0.81	0.19	0.24	0.22	0.26	0.12
Price Range	43.40-32.88	40.22-24.84	32.37-22.73	29.54-15.97	51.87-20.04	56.00-37.39	43.50-34.45	51.00-34.45
P/E Ratio	17.93-13.59	21.51-13.28	30.83-21.65	24.41-13.20	26.46-10.22	30.11-20.10	25.14-19.91	23.29-15.73
Average Yield %	3.61	3.11	3.71	4.01	2.57	1.88	1.76	1.24

Address: 1000 Cranberry Woods Drive, Cranberry Township, PA 16066-5207
Telephone: 724-776-8600

Web Site: www.msasafety.com
Officers: John T. Ryan - Chairman William M. Lambert - President, Chief Executive Officer

Auditors: PricewaterhouseCoopers LLP
Investor Contact: 724-741-8221
Transfer Agents: Wells Fargo Bank, N.A., South St. Paul, MN

MINERALS TECHNOLOGIES, INC.

Exchange	Symbol	Price	52Wk Range	Yield	P/E
NYS	MTX	$41.51 (3/28/2013)	43.04-30.50	0.48	19.86

*7 Year Price Score 108.00 *NYSE Composite Index=100 *12 Month Price Score 106.32

Interim Earnings (Per Share)

Qtr.	Mar	Jun	Sep	Dec
2008	0.45	0.61	0.50	0.16
2009	0.11	(1.09)	0.23	0.11
2010	0.41	0.51	0.45	0.43
2011	0.43	0.45	0.44	0.56
2012	0.51	0.56	0.53	0.51

Interim Dividends (Per Share)

Amt	Decl	Ex	Rec	Pay
0.025Q	07/18/2012	08/28/2012	08/30/2012	09/13/2012
100%	11/14/2012	12/12/2012	11/27/2012	12/11/2012
0.05Q	11/14/2012	12/19/2012	12/21/2012	12/31/2012
0.05Q	01/23/2013	02/20/2013	02/22/2013	03/13/2013

Indicated Div: $0.20

Valuation Analysis

		Institutional Holding	
Forecast EPS	$2.25 (04/05/2013)	No of Institutions	225
Market Cap	$1.5 Billion	Shares	38,254,228
Book Value	$790.4 Million	% Held	98.35
Price/Book	1.84		
Price/Sales	1.44		

Business Summary: Specialty Chemicals (MIC: 8.3.2 SIC: 2819 NAIC: 325188)

Minerals Technologies is a resource- and technology-based company that develops, produces and markets a range of mineral, mineral-based and synthetic mineral products and supporting systems and services. Co. has two segments: specialty minerals, which produces and sells the synthetic mineral product precipitated calcium carbonate and processed mineral product quicklime, and mines mineral ores then processes and sells natural mineral products, primarily limestone and talc; and refractories, which produces and markets monolithic and shaped refractory materials and specialty products, services and application and measurement equipment, and calcium metal and metallurgical wire products.

Recent Developments: For the year ended Dec 31 2012, net income increased 8.6% to US$76.3 million from US$70.3 million in the prior year. Revenues were US$1.01 billion, down 3.8% from US$1.04 billion the year before. Operating income was US$110.0 million versus US$100.3 million in the prior year, an increase of 9.7%. Direct operating expenses declined 5.6% to US$786.2 million from US$832.7 million in the comparable period the year before. Indirect operating expenses decreased 2.3% to US$109.3 million from US$111.9 million in the equivalent prior-year period.

Prospects: Our evaluation of Minerals Technologies Inc. as of Apr. 7, 2013 is the result of our systematic analysis on three basic characteristics: earnings strength, relative valuation, and recent stock price movement. The company has generated a negative trend in earnings per share over the past 5 quarters. However, while recent estimates for the company have been mixed, MTX has posted better than expected results. Based on operating earnings yield, the company is about fairly valued when compared to all of the companies in our coverage universe. Share price changes over the past year indicates that MTX will perform well over the near term.

Financial Data
(US$ in Thousands)

	12/31/2012	12/31/2011	12/31/2010	12/31/2009	12/31/2008	12/31/2007	12/31/2006	12/31/2005
Earnings Per Share	2.09	1.87	1.79	(0.64)	1.72	(1.66)	1.26	1.29
Cash Flow Per Share	3.95	3.71	3.83	4.29	3.54	4.68	3.46	1.93
Tang Book Value Per Share	20.73	19.17	18.81	17.50	17.26	17.79	17.91	17.95
Dividends Per Share	0.125	0.100	0.100	0.100	0.100	0.100	0.100	0.100
Dividend Payout %	5.98	5.36	5.59	...	5.81	...	7.91	7.72
Income Statement								
Total Revenue	1,005,619	1,044,853	1,002,354	907,321	1,112,212	1,077,721	1,059,307	995,838
EBITDA	155,799	152,987	160,620	46,476	158,743	74,519	165,370	155,312
Depn & Amortn	48,700	55,900	61,200	69,000	76,200	80,400	79,800	72,600
Income Before Taxes	107,046	97,740	98,889	(23,140)	82,267	(11,499)	79,579	78,285
Income Taxes	30,777	27,486	28,963	(5,387)	24,079	11,266	24,588	23,289
Net Income	74,147	67,521	66,869	(23,796)	65,287	(63,514)	49,951	53,264
Average Shares	35,529	36,236	37,386	37,448	37,966	38,380	39,476	41,134
Balance Sheet								
Current Assets	764,485	720,289	675,572	600,713	531,547	473,310	411,762	377,200
Total Assets	1,211,189	1,164,955	1,116,105	1,072,138	1,067,620	1,128,893	1,193,124	1,156,303
Current Liabilities	250,098	180,902	155,237	152,914	150,853	167,149	212,063	231,252
Long-Term Obligations	8,478	85,449	92,621	92,621	97,221	111,006	113,351	40,306
Total Liabilities	420,778	423,343	360,582	347,977	356,036	377,720	440,567	385,141
Stockholders' Equity	790,411	741,612	755,523	724,161	711,584	751,173	752,557	771,162
Shares Outstanding	34,949	35,309	36,597	37,481	37,383	38,180	38,171	39,973
Statistical Record								
Return on Assets %	6.22	5.92	6.11	N.M.	5.93	N.M.	4.25	4.61
Return on Equity %	9.65	9.02	9.04	N.M.	8.90	N.M.	6.56	6.78
EBITDA Margin %	15.49	14.64	16.02	5.12	14.27	6.91	15.61	15.60
Net Margin %	7.37	6.46	6.67	N.M.	5.87	N.M.	4.72	5.35
Asset Turnover	0.84	0.92	0.92	0.85	1.01	0.93	0.90	0.86
Current Ratio	3.06	3.98	4.35	3.93	3.52	2.83	1.94	1.63
Debt to Equity	0.01	0.12	0.12	0.13	0.14	0.15	0.15	0.05
Price Range	39.92-28.79	35.05-23.38	33.41-22.86	28.20-13.38	36.21-18.95	35.45-28.40	30.64-24.00	34.41-25.80
P/E Ratio	19.10-13.77	18.74-12.50	18.66-12.77	...	21.05-11.01	...	24.31-19.05	26.68-20.00
Average Yield %	0.37	0.33	0.36	0.47	0.33	0.31	0.36	0.33

Address: 622 Third Avenue, New York, NY 10017-6707 Telephone: 212-878-1800	Web Site: www.mineralstech.com Officers: Joseph C. Muscari - Chairman, Chief Executive Officer Robert S. Wetherbee - President, Chief Executive Officer	Auditors: KPMG LLP Investor Contact: 212-878-1831 Transfer Agents: Computershare Trust Company, N. A., Providence, RI

MODINE MANUFACTURING CO

Exchange	Symbol	Price	52Wk Range	Yield	P/E
NYS	MOD	$9.10 (3/28/2013)	9.46-5.73	N/A	N/A

*7 Year Price Score 47.82   ***NYSE Composite Index=100**   ***12 Month Price Score 107.93**

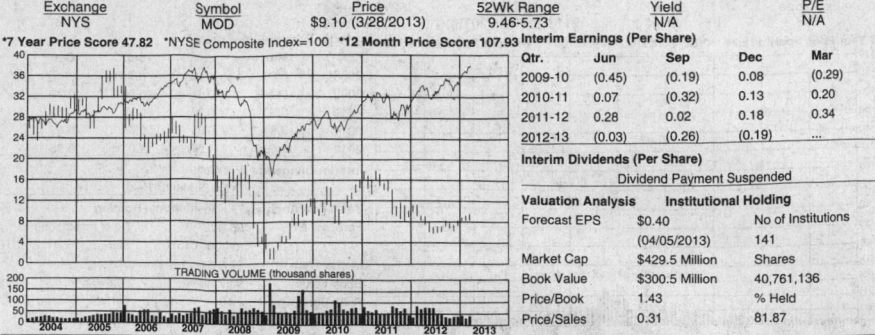

Interim Earnings (Per Share)

Qtr.	Jun	Sep	Dec	Mar
2009-10	(0.45)	(0.19)	0.08	(0.29)
2010-11	0.07	(0.32)	0.13	0.20
2011-12	0.28	0.02	0.18	0.34
2012-13	(0.03)	(0.26)	(0.19)	...

Interim Dividends (Per Share)

Dividend Payment Suspended

Valuation Analysis   Institutional Holding

Forecast EPS	$0.40	No of Institutions
	(04/05/2013)	141
Market Cap	$429.5 Million	Shares
Book Value	$300.5 Million	40,761,136
Price/Book	1.43	% Held
Price/Sales	0.31	81.87

Business Summary: Auto Parts (MIC: 1.8.2 SIC: 3714 NAIC: 336399)

Modine Manufacturing is a developer, manufacturer and marketer of heat exchangers and systems for use in on-highway and off-highway original equipment manufacturer vehicular applications, and to a range of building, industrial and refrigeration markets. Co.'s product lines include radiators and radiator cores, vehicular air conditioning, oil coolers, charge air coolers, heat-transfer packages and modules, building heating, ventilating and air conditioning equipment and exhaust gas recirculation coolers. Co. operates in North America, Europe (Austria, Germany, Hungary, Italy, the Netherlands, the U.K., and Russia), Brazil, South Africa, and Asia Pacific (China, India, Japan and South Korea).

Recent Developments: For the quarter ended Dec 31 2012, loss from continuing operations was US$8.4 million compared with income of US$8.8 million in the year-earlier quarter. Net loss amounted to US$8.4 million versus net income of US$9.1 million in the year-earlier quarter. Revenues were US$326.1 million, down 12.6% from US$373.3 million the year before. Operating loss was US$3.8 million versus an income of US$17.2 million in the prior-year quarter. Direct operating expenses declined 11.3% to US$277.9 million from US$313.2 million in the comparable period the year before. Indirect operating expenses increased 21.2% to US$52.0 million from US$42.9 million in the equivalent prior-year period.

Prospects: Our evaluation of Modine Manufacturing Co as of Apr. 7, 2013 is the result of our systematic analysis on three basic characteristics: earnings strength, relative valuation, and recent stock price movement. The company has suffered a very negative trend in earnings per share over the past 5 quarters and while recent estimates for the company have remained steady, MOD has posted results that fell short of analysts expectations. Based on operating earnings yield, the company is about fairly valued when compared to all of the companies in our coverage universe. Share price changes over the past year indicates that MOD will perform poorly over the near term.

Financial Data
(US$ in Thousands)

	9 Mos	6 Mos	3 Mos	03/31/2012	03/31/2011	03/31/2010	03/31/2009	03/31/2008
Earnings Per Share	(0.14)	0.23	0.51	0.82	0.13	(0.75)	(3.38)	(2.05)
Cash Flow Per Share	1.47	1.49	1.39	0.98	0.45	1.58	2.92	2.10
Tang Book Value Per Share	5.56	5.61	5.80	6.18	6.98	6.22	6.55	12.77
Dividends Per Share	...	...	...	...	...	...	0.300	0.700
Income Statement								
Total Revenue	1,016,400	690,298	350,376	1,577,152	1,448,235	1,163,234	1,408,714	1,849,373
EBITDA	34,500	25,120	17,708	116,857	101,067	76,956	(24,307)	67,163
Depn & Amortn	41,800	28,189	14,049	57,081	55,827	65,096	68,240	79,749
Income Before Taxes	(16,000)	(9,153)	825	48,041	12,226	(10,365)	(104,678)	(23,924)
Income Taxes	5,300	3,883	2,053	9,931	3,468	9,832	644	44,386
Net Income	(22,100)	(13,399)	(1,179)	38,461	6,180	(29,279)	(108,612)	(65,596)
Average Shares	46,700	46,584	46,546	46,881	46,729	39,298	32,077	32,030
Balance Sheet								
Current Assets	375,400	400,491	422,290	427,531	427,625	355,442	325,851	522,152
Total Assets	799,600	832,488	868,496	893,461	916,939	840,252	852,132	1,149,858
Current Liabilities	241,500	265,251	275,372	297,551	316,541	271,400	251,033	335,400
Long-Term Obligations	137,600	142,566	161,553	141,892	138,582	135,952	243,982	226,198
Total Liabilities	499,100	529,851	561,228	568,554	553,987	516,166	608,295	681,950
Stockholders' Equity	300,500	302,637	307,268	324,907	362,952	324,086	243,837	467,908
Shares Outstanding	47,200	47,103	47,103	46,767	46,546	46,261	32,241	32,293
Statistical Record								
Return on Assets %	N.M.	1.27	2.64	4.24	0.70	N.M.	N.M.	N.M.
Return on Equity %	N.M.	3.35	6.99	11.15	1.80	N.M.	N.M.	N.M.
EBITDA Margin %	3.39	3.64	5.05	7.41	6.98	6.62	N.M.	3.63
Net Margin %	N.M.	N.M.	N.M.	2.44	0.43	N.M.	N.M.	N.M.
Asset Turnover	1.71	1.68	1.65	1.74	1.65	1.37	1.41	1.64
Current Ratio	1.55	1.51	1.53	1.44	1.35	1.31	1.30	1.56
Debt to Equity	0.46	0.47	0.53	0.44	0.38	0.42	1.00	0.48
Price Range	11.25-5.73	11.62-5.73	16.00-5.73	17.85-8.12	17.73-7.43	12.50-2.50	18.91-0.83	28.94-11.62
P/E Ratio	...	50.52-24.91	31.37-11.24	21.77-9.90	136.38-57.15	...	...	...
Average Yield %	...	...	...	...	...	...	2.89	3.26

Address: 1500 DeKoven Avenue, Racine, WI 53403	**Web Site:** www.modine.com	**Auditors:** PricewaterhouseCoopers LLP
Telephone: 262-636-1200	**Officers:** Thomas A. Burke - President, Chief Executive Officer Thomas F. Marry - Executive Vice President, Chief Operating Officer, Region Officer	**Investor Contact:** 262-636-1687
Fax: 262-636-1424		**Transfer Agents:** Wells Fargo Bank, N.A., St. Paul, MN

MOHAWK INDUSTRIES, INC.

Exchange	Symbol	Price	52Wk Range	Yield	P/E
NYS	MHK	$113.12 (3/28/2013)	114.59-60.50	N/A	31.34

*7 Year Price Score 112.24 *NYSE Composite Index=100 *12 Month Price Score 120.97

Interim Earnings (Per Share)

Qtr.	Mar	Jun	Sep	Dec
2008	0.95	1.29	(21.70)	(1.87)
2009	(1.55)	0.67	0.50	0.29
2010	0.30	0.99	0.74	0.62
2011	0.34	0.88	0.68	0.62
2012	0.58	1.06	1.01	0.95

Interim Dividends (Per Share)

No Dividends Paid

Valuation Analysis   **Institutional Holding**

Forecast EPS	$5.30	No of Institutions
	(04/06/2013)	368
Market Cap	$7.8 Billion	Shares
Book Value	$3.7 Billion	64,410,544
Price/Book	2.10	% Held
Price/Sales	1.35	79.49

Business Summary: Furniture (MIC: 1.6.2 SIC: 2273 NAIC: 314110)

Mohawk Industries produces floor covering products for residential and commercial applications in the U.S. and residential applications in Europe. Co. has three segments: Mohawk, which designs, manufactures, sources, distributes and markets floor covering product lines, which include carpets, ceramic tile, laminate, rugs, carpet pad, hardwood and resilient for applications in remodeling and new construction; Dal-Tile, which designs, manufactures, sources, distributes and markets ceramic tile, porcelain tile and natural stone products; and Unilin, which designs, manufactures, sources, licenses, distributes and markets laminate and hardwood flooring used mainly in the residential market.

Recent Developments: For the year ended Dec 31 2012, net income increased 40.8% to US$250.9 million from US$178.2 million in the prior year. Revenues were US$5.79 billion, up 2.6% from US$5.64 billion the year before. Operating income was US$379.5 million versus US$315.5 million in the prior year, an increase of 20.3%. Direct operating expenses rose 1.7% to US$4.30 billion from US$4.23 billion in the comparable period the year before. Indirect operating expenses increased 0.8% to US$1.11 billion from US$1.10 billion in the equivalent prior-year period.

Prospects: Our evaluation of Mohawk Industries Inc. as of Apr. 7, 2013 is the result of our systematic analysis on three basic characteristics: earnings strength, relative valuation, and recent stock price movement. The company has produced a positive trend in earnings per share over the past 5 quarters and while recent estimates for the company have been raised by analysts, MHK has posted better than expected results. Based on operating earnings yield, the company is about fairly valued when compared to all of the companies in our coverage universe. Share price changes over the past year indicates that MHK will perform very well over the near term.

Financial Data
(US$ in Thousands)

	12/31/2012	12/31/2011	12/31/2010	12/31/2009	12/31/2008	12/31/2007	12/31/2006	12/31/2005
Earnings Per Share	3.61	2.52	2.65	(0.08)	(21.32)	10.32	6.70	5.30
Cash Flow Per Share	8.49	4.38	4.66	9.82	8.31	12.84	11.56	8.39
Tang Book Value Per Share	25.74	20.87	17.85	14.67	13.25	10.80	N.M.	N.M.
Income Statement								
Total Revenue	5,787,980	5,642,258	5,319,072	5,344,024	6,826,348	7,586,018	7,905,842	6,620,099
EBITDA	596,598	522,071	544,448	272,771	(938,835)	966,199	1,039,396	757,145
Depn & Amortn	217,393	220,580	218,649	223,453	212,281	207,613	189,388	133,333
Income Before Taxes	304,492	199,874	192,648	(77,713)	(1,278,166)	604,117	676,311	557,021
Income Taxes	53,599	21,649	2,713	(76,694)	180,062	(102,697)	220,478	198,826
Net Income	250,258	173,922	185,471	(5,499)	(1,458,228)	706,814	455,833	358,195
Average Shares	69,306	68,964	68,784	68,452	68,401	68,492	68,056	67,644
Balance Sheet								
Current Assets	2,550,046	2,398,164	2,248,613	2,359,000	2,246,249	2,449,720	2,378,911	2,340,487
Total Assets	6,303,684	6,206,228	6,098,926	6,391,446	6,446,175	8,680,050	8,178,394	7,991,523
Current Liabilities	828,649	1,101,346	1,048,914	884,022	876,916	1,211,500	1,595,763	1,111,914
Long-Term Obligations	1,327,729	1,200,184	1,302,994	1,801,572	1,860,001	2,021,395	2,207,547	3,194,561
Total Liabilities	2,584,067	2,790,443	2,827,370	3,190,623	3,292,372	3,972,693	4,463,131	4,964,403
Stockholders' Equity	3,719,617	3,415,785	3,271,556	3,200,823	3,153,803	4,707,357	3,715,263	3,027,120
Shares Outstanding	69,153	68,781	68,629	68,484	68,421	68,358	67,765	67,497
Statistical Record								
Return on Assets %	3.99	2.83	2.97	N.M.	N.M.	8.39	5.64	5.78
Return on Equity %	7.00	5.20	5.73	N.M.	N.M.	16.78	13.52	12.58
EBITDA Margin %	10.31	9.25	10.24	5.10	N.M.	12.74	13.15	11.44
Net Margin %	4.32	3.08	3.49	N.M.	N.M.	9.32	5.77	5.41
Asset Turnover	0.92	0.92	0.85	0.83	0.90	0.90	0.98	1.07
Current Ratio	3.08	2.18	2.14	2.67	2.56	2.02	1.49	2.10
Debt to Equity	0.36	0.35	0.40	0.56	0.59	0.43	0.59	1.06
Price Range	91.29-59.39	68.50-40.75	64.46-41.41	52.97-17.11	83.05-25.80	103.32-74.40	90.14-65.00	93.66-75.22
P/E Ratio	25.29-16.45	27.18-16.17	24.32-15.63	...	...	10.01-7.21	13.45-9.70	17.67-14.19

Address: 160 S. Industrial Blvd., Calhoun, GA 30701 Telephone: 706-629-7721	Web Site: www.mohawkind.com Officers: Jeffrey S. Lorberbaum - Chairman, Chief Executive Officer James T. Lucke - Vice President, General Counsel, Secretary	Auditors: KPMG LLP Investor Contact: 706-624-2695 Transfer Agents: American Stock Transfer & Trust Company, Addison, TX

508

MOLSON COORS BREWING CO.

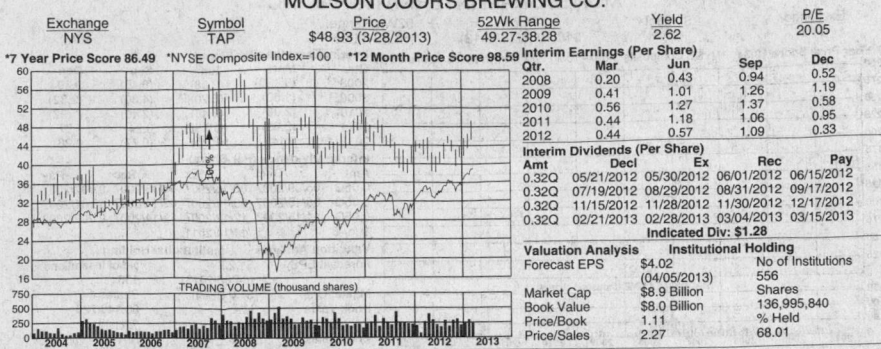

Exchange	Symbol	Price	52Wk Range	Yield	P/E
NYS	TAP	$48.93 (3/28/2013)	49.27-38.28	2.62	20.05

*7 Year Price Score 86.49   *NYSE Composite Index=100   *12 Month Price Score 98.59

Interim Earnings (Per Share)

Qtr.	Mar	Jun	Sep	Dec
2008	0.20	0.43	0.94	0.52
2009	0.41	1.01	1.26	1.19
2010	0.56	1.27	1.37	0.58
2011	0.44	1.18	1.06	0.95
2012	0.44	0.57	1.09	0.33

Interim Dividends (Per Share)

Amt	Decl	Ex	Rec	Pay
0.32Q	05/21/2012	05/30/2012	06/01/2012	06/15/2012
0.32Q	07/19/2012	08/29/2012	08/31/2012	09/17/2012
0.32Q	11/15/2012	11/28/2012	11/30/2012	12/17/2012
0.32Q	02/21/2013	02/28/2013	03/04/2013	03/15/2013

Indicated Div: $1.28

Valuation Analysis

		Institutional Holding	
Forecast EPS	$4.02	No of Institutions	
	(04/05/2013)	556	
Market Cap	$8.9 Billion	Shares	
Book Value	$8.0 Billion	136,995,840	
Price/Book	1.11	% Held	
Price/Sales	2.27	68.01	

Business Summary: Beverages (MIC: 1.2.2 SIC: 2082 NAIC: 312120)

Molson Coors Brewing is a holding company. Through its subsidiaries, Co. is engaged in the production of beers. Co. operates the following segments: Canada, which includes the production, marketing and sales of brands such as Coors Light and other brands in Canada; the U.S., which is comprised of Co.'s equity investment in MillerCoors LLC; and the U.K., which includes the production, marketing and sale of brands such as Carling in the U.K. and the Republic of Ireland; and Molson Coors International, which has operations in markets outside of the U.S., U.K., Canada and Central Europe, including Asia, continental Europe (outside of Central Europe), Mexico, Latin America and the Caribbean.

Recent Developments: For the year ended Dec 29 2012, income from continuing operations decreased 35.2% to US$437.6 million from US$674.8 million a year earlier. Net income decreased 35.1% to US$439.1 million from US$677.1 million in the prior year. Revenues were US$3.92 billion, up 11.4% from US$3.52 billion the year before. Operating income was US$867.4 million versus US$893.2 million in the prior year, a decrease of 2.9%. Direct operating expenses rose 14.8% to US$2.35 billion from US$2.05 billion in the comparable period the year before. Indirect operating expenses increased 21.5% to US$696.6 million from US$573.4 million in the equivalent prior-year period.

Prospects: Our evaluation of Molson Coors Brewing Co. as of Apr. 7, 2013 is the result of our systematic analysis on three basic characteristics: earnings strength, relative valuation, and recent stock price movement. The company has generated a negative trend in earnings per share over the past 5 quarters and while recent estimates for the company have been mixed, TAP has posted better than expected results. Based on operating earnings yield, the company is undervalued when compared to all of the companies in our coverage universe. Share price changes over the past year indicates that TAP will perform poorly over the near term.

Financial Data

(US$ in Thousands)	12/29/2012	12/31/2011	12/25/2010	12/26/2009	12/28/2008	12/30/2007	12/31/2006	12/25/2005
Earnings Per Share	2.44	3.63	3.78	3.87	2.09	2.74	2.09	0.84
Cash Flow Per Share	5.46	4.62	4.04	4.49	2.26	3.46	4.76	2.67
Tang Book Value Per Share	N.M.	8.94	8.86	5.77	4.13	N.M.	N.M.	N.M.
Dividends Per Share	1.280	1.240	1.080	0.920	0.760	0.640	0.640	0.640
Dividend Payout %	52.46	34.16	28.57	23.77	36.36	23.36	30.70	75.74
Income Statement								
Total Revenue	3,916,500	3,515,700	3,254,400	3,032,400	4,774,300	6,190,592	5,844,985	5,506,906
EBITDA	496,500	601,300	611,900	569,500	672,600	913,335	957,920	744,633
Depn & Amortn	230,300	177,000	159,600	146,900	230,100	283,400	363,000	326,400
Income Before Taxes	81,200	316,300	352,900	336,700	356,500	530,060	468,139	304,630
Income Taxes	154,500	99,400	138,700	(14,700)	102,900	4,186	82,405	50,264
Net Income	443,000	676,300	707,700	720,400	388,000	497,192	361,031	134,944
Average Shares	181,800	186,400	187,300	185,900	185,500	181,437	173,312	160,072
Balance Sheet								
Current Assets	1,748,000	2,118,000	2,220,900	1,762,800	1,107,100	1,776,814	1,458,356	1,468,242
Total Assets	16,212,200	12,423,800	12,697,600	12,021,100	10,416,600	13,451,566	11,603,413	11,799,265
Current Liabilities	2,598,500	1,277,200	1,333,900	1,580,900	986,100	1,735,577	1,800,116	2,236,616
Long-Term Obligations	3,422,500	1,914,900	1,959,600	1,412,700	1,831,700	2,260,596	2,129,845	2,136,668
Total Liabilities	8,245,300	4,775,900	4,898,800	4,941,500	4,436,300	6,302,175	5,786,057	6,474,548
Stockholders' Equity	7,966,900	7,647,900	7,798,800	7,079,600	5,980,300	7,149,391	5,817,356	5,324,717
Shares Outstanding	181,500	180,000	186,800	185,400	183,900	180,752	174,049	171,306
Statistical Record								
Return on Assets %	3.10	5.30	5.74	6.46	3.26	3.98	3.04	1.64
Return on Equity %	5.69	8.61	9.54	11.09	5.93	7.69	6.38	3.91
EBITDA Margin %	12.68	17.10	18.80	18.78	14.09	14.75	16.39	13.52
Net Margin %	11.31	19.24	21.75	23.76	8.13	8.03	6.18	2.45
Asset Turnover	0.27	0.28	0.26	0.27	0.40	0.50	0.49	0.67
Current Ratio	0.67	1.66	1.66	1.12	1.12	1.02	0.81	0.66
Debt to Equity	0.43	0.25	0.25	0.20	0.31	0.32	0.37	0.40
Price Range	46.00-38.28	50.51-38.00	50.93-38.90	50.49-31.44	59.26-35.41	57.23-37.72	38.38-31.18	39.75-29.05
P/E Ratio	18.85-15.69	13.91-10.47	13.47-10.29	13.05-8.12	28.35-16.94	20.89-13.77	18.36-14.92	47.32-34.58
Average Yield %	3.01	2.80	2.41	2.13	1.52	1.37	1.87	1.91

Address: 1555 Notre Dame Street East, Montreal, H2L 2R5	Web Site: www.molsoncoors.com	Auditors: PricewaterhouseCoopers LLP
Telephone: 514-521-1786	Officers: Andrew T. Molson - Vice-Chairman, Chairman Peter S. Swinburn - President, Chief Executive Officer	Investor Contact: 303-927-2312 Transfer Agents: Computershare Trust Company, N.A, Providence, RI

MONEYGRAM INTERNATIONAL INC

Exchange	Symbol	Price	52Wk Range	Yield	P/E
NYS	MGI	$18.10 (3/28/2013)	18.10-11.66	N/A	N/A

*7 Year Price Score 19.31 *NYSE Composite Index=100 *12 Month Price Score 98.50

Interim Earnings (Per Share)

Qtr.	Mar	Jun	Sep	Dec
2008	(35.20)	(0.88)	(6.40)	9.20
2009	(1.60)	(3.20)	(4.80)	(2.32)
2010	(2.08)	(2.48)	(2.40)	(1.92)
2011	(2.08)	(10.96)	0.24	1.77
2012	0.14	(0.35)	(0.77)	0.28

Interim Dividends (Per Share)

Amt	Decl	Ex	Rec	Pay
0.05Q	05/09/2007	06/13/2007	06/15/2007	07/02/2007
0.05Q	08/16/2007	09/12/2007	09/14/2007	10/01/2007
0.05Q	11/15/2007	12/12/2007	12/14/2007	01/02/2008
1-for-8		11/14/2011	...	...

Valuation Analysis — **Institutional Holding**

Forecast EPS	$1.23 (04/06/2013)	No of Institutions 136
Market Cap	$1.0 Billion	Shares
Book Value	N/A	60,140,720
Price/Book	N/A	% Held
Price/Sales	0.78	N/A

Business Summary: Business Services (MIC: 7.5.2 SIC: 7389 NAIC: 522320)

MoneyGram International is a payment services company. Co.'s products include global money transfers, bill payment applications and financial paper products. Co. conducts its business through its subsidiary MoneyGram Payment Systems, Inc., under the MoneyGram brand. Co. manages its business primarily through two segments: Global Funds Transfer, which provides money transfer and bill payment services to consumers, who may be unbanked or underbanked; and Financial Paper Products, which provides money orders to consumers through its retail and financial institution agent locations in the U.S. and Puerto Rico, and provides official check services for financial institutions in the U.S.

Recent Developments: For the year ended Dec 31 2012, net loss amounted to US$49.3 million versus net income of US$59.4 million in the prior year. Revenues were US$1.34 billion, up 7.5% from US$1.25 billion the year before. Operating income was US$52.4 million versus US$142.5 million in the prior year, a decrease of 63.2%. Direct operating expenses rose 9.4% to US$599.5 million from US$548.0 million in the comparable period the year before. Indirect operating expenses increased 23.7% to US$689.3 million from US$557.2 million in the equivalent prior-year period.

Prospects: Our evaluation of MoneyGram International Inc. as of Apr. 7, 2013 is the result of our systematic analysis on three basic characteristics: earnings strength, relative valuation, and recent stock price movement. The company has enjoyed a very positive trend in earnings per share over the past 5 quarters and while recent estimates for the company have been mixed, MGI has posted better than expected results. Based on operating earnings yield, the company is undervalued when compared to all of the companies in our coverage universe. Share price changes over the past year indicates that MGI will perform poorly over the near term.

Financial Data

(US$ in Thousands)	12/31/2012	12/31/2011	12/31/2010	12/31/2009	12/31/2008	12/31/2007	12/31/2006	12/31/2005
Earnings Per Share	(0.69)	(9.03)	(8.80)	(11.84)	(33.52)	(103.52)	11.60	10.48
Cash Flow Per Share	(0.78)	3.87	5.84	8.00	(448.93)	(34.37)	(35.12)	9.63
Tang Book Value Per Share	...	...	N.M.	...	...	...	22.05	19.25
Dividends Per Share	...	...	...	...	...	1.600	1.360	0.560
Dividend Payout %	...	...	...	...	...	...	11.72	5.34
Income Statement								
Total Revenue	1,341,200	1,247,769	1,166,653	1,171,902	927,118	157,537	1,159,559	971,236
EBITDA	105,400	170,790	206,161	139,406	(189,880)	(934,539)	220,547	184,327
Depn & Amortn	43,400	44,855	45,648	53,817	52,291	47,673	35,846	30,343
Income Before Taxes	(8,900)	39,770	58,380	(22,322)	(337,191)	(993,267)	176,773	146,376
Income Taxes	40,400	(19,636)	14,579	(20,416)	(75,806)	78,481	52,719	34,170
Net Income	(49,300)	59,406	43,801	(1,906)	(261,385)	(1,071,997)	124,054	112,946
Average Shares	71,500	48,576	10,398	10,312	10,307	10,352	10,727	10,746
Balance Sheet								
Current Assets	4,339,800	4,314,263	4,254,029	4,858,156	5,363,751	3,023,274	2,878,113	2,192,013
Total Assets	5,150,600	5,175,578	5,115,736	5,929,663	6,642,296	7,935,011	9,276,137	9,075,164
Current Liabilities	4,375,300	4,354,636	4,298,383	5,032,387	5,559,585	7,951,248	8,349,637	8,190,495
Long-Term Obligations	809,900	810,888	639,946	796,791	978,881	345,000	150,000	150,000
Total Liabilities	5,312,000	5,285,776	5,058,865	5,948,348	6,681,820	8,423,528	8,607,074	8,451,035
Stockholders' Equity	(161,400)	(110,198)	56,871	(18,685)	(39,524)	(488,517)	669,063	624,129
Shares Outstanding	57,856	57,834	10,452	10,314	10,319	10,330	10,533	10,731
Statistical Record								
Return on Assets %	N.M.	1.15	0.79	N.M.	N.M.	N.M.	1.35	1.28
Return on Equity %	...	...	229.41	...	...	N.M.	19.19	18.99
EBITDA Margin %	7.86	13.69	17.67	11.90	N.M.	N.M.	19.02	18.98
Net Margin %	N.M.	4.76	3.75	N.M.	N.M.	N.M.	10.70	11.63
Asset Turnover	0.26	0.24	0.21	0.19	0.13	0.02	0.13	0.11
Current Ratio	0.99	0.99	0.99	0.97	0.96	0.38	0.34	0.27
Debt to Equity	...	...	11.25	...	...	...	0.22	0.24
Price Range	19.26-11.66	31.68-16.25	30.48-16.08	26.32-8.00	122.96-6.80	250.64-109.68	289.60-199.76	217.92-143.52
P/E Ratio	...	...	...	...	...	...	24.97-17.22	20.79-13.69
Average Yield %	...	...	...	...	...	0.81	0.55	0.33

Address: 2828 N. Harwood St., 15th Floor, Dallas, TX 75201 **Telephone:** 214-999-7552	**Web Site:** www.moneygram.com **Officers:** Pamela H. Patsley - Executive Chairman, Chief Executive Officer Francis Aaron Henry - Executive Vice President, Secretary, General Counsel	**Auditors:** Deloitte & Touche LLP **Investor Contact:** 952-591-3840 **Transfer Agents:** Wells Fargo Shareowner Services, St. Paul, MN

MONSANTO CO.

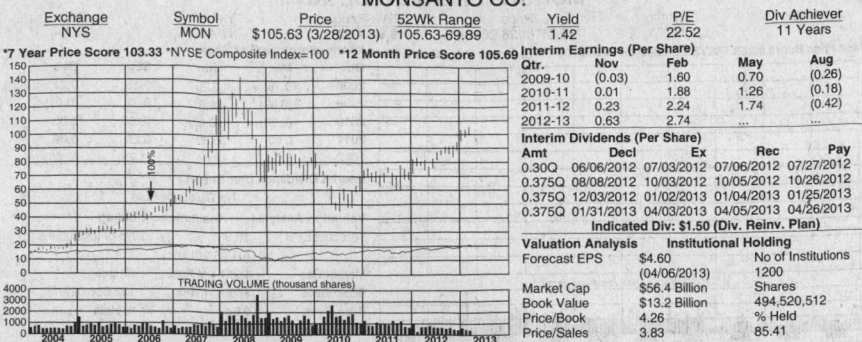

Exchange	Symbol	Price	52Wk Range	Yield	P/E	Div Achiever
NYS	MON	$105.63 (3/28/2013)	105.63-69.89	1.42	22.52	11 Years

*7 Year Price Score 103.33 *NYSE Composite Index=100 *12 Month Price Score 105.69

Interim Earnings (Per Share)

Qtr.	Nov	Feb	May	Aug
2009-10	(0.03)	1.60	0.70	(0.26)
2010-11	0.01	1.88	1.26	(0.18)
2011-12	0.23	2.24	1.74	(0.42)
2012-13	0.63	2.74	...	...

Interim Dividends (Per Share)

Amt	Decl	Ex	Rec	Pay
0.30Q	06/06/2012	07/03/2012	07/06/2012	07/27/2012
0.375Q	08/08/2012	10/03/2012	10/05/2012	10/26/2012
0.375Q	12/03/2012	01/02/2013	01/04/2013	01/25/2013
0.375Q	01/31/2013	04/03/2013	04/05/2013	04/26/2013

Indicated Div: $1.50 (Div. Reinv. Plan)

Valuation Analysis / **Institutional Holding**

Forecast EPS	$4.60 (04/06/2013)
Market Cap	$56.4 Billion
Book Value	$13.2 Billion
Price/Book	4.26
Price/Sales	3.83

No of Institutions	1200
Shares	494,520,512
% Held	85.41

Business Summary: Agricultural Chemicals (MIC: 8.3.3 SIC: 2879 NAIC: 325320)

Monsanto, along with its subsidiaries, is a provider of agricultural products for farmers. Co. has two business segments: Seeds and Genomics, and Agricultural Productivity. Through the Seeds and Genomics segment, Co. produces seed brands, including DEKALB, Asgrow, Deltapine, Seminis and De Ruiter, and develops biotechnology traits that assist farmers in controlling insects and weeds. Co. also provides other seed businesses with genetic material and biotechnology traits for their seed brands. Through the Agricultural Productivity segment, Co. manufactures Roundup and Harness brand herbicides and other herbicides and provides lawn-and-garden herbicide products for the residential market.

Recent Developments: For the quarter ended Feb 28 2013, income from continuing operations increased 22.7% to US$1.48 billion from US$1.21 billion in the year-earlier quarter. Net income increased 22.4% to US$1.48 billion from US$1.21 billion in the year-earlier quarter. Revenues were US$5.47 billion, up 15.2% from US$4.75 billion the year before. Operating income was US$2.11 billion versus US$1.81 billion in the prior-year quarter, an increase of 16.7%. Direct operating expenses rose 17.6% to US$2.40 billion from US$2.04 billion in the comparable period the year before. Indirect operating expenses increased 6.9% to US$958.0 million from US$896.0 million in the equivalent prior-year period.

Prospects: Our evaluation of Monsanto Co. as of Apr. 7, 2013 is the result of our systematic analysis on three basic characteristics: earnings strength, relative valuation, and recent stock price movement. The company has produced a positive trend in earnings per share over the past 5 quarters and while recent estimates for the company have been raised by analysts, MON has posted better than expected results. Based on operating earnings yield, the company is about fairly valued when compared to all of the companies in our coverage universe. Share price changes over the past year indicates that MON will perform well over the near term.

Financial Data
(US$ in Millions)

	6 Mos	3 Mos	08/31/2012	08/31/2011	08/31/2010	08/31/2009	08/31/2008	08/31/2007
Earnings Per Share	4.69	4.19	3.79	2.96	2.01	3.80	3.62	1.79
Cash Flow Per Share	6.05	6.56	5.70	5.25	2.57	4.09	5.09	3.41
Tang Book Value Per Share	15.91	14.21	13.40	12.84	10.42	10.02	8.59	6.35
Dividends Per Share	1.350	1.275	1.200	1.120	1.060	1.010	0.765	0.475
Dividend Payout %	28.78	30.43	31.66	37.84	52.74	26.58	21.13	26.54
Income Statement								
Total Revenue	8,411	2,939	13,504	11,822	10,502	11,724	11,365	8,563
EBITDA	2,887	644	3,724	3,075	2,202	3,573	3,477	1,880
Depn & Amortn	305	152	622	613	602	548	573	527
Income Before Taxes	2,546	464	2,988	2,374	1,494	2,967	2,926	1,336
Income Taxes	725	122	901	717	370	845	899	402
Net Income	1,822	339	2,045	1,607	1,109	2,109	2,024	993
Average Shares	540	540	540	542	550	555	559	555
Balance Sheet								
Current Assets	11,534	12,060	9,658	8,809	7,122	7,883	7,609	5,084
Total Assets	22,079	22,537	20,224	19,844	17,867	17,877	17,991	12,983
Current Liabilities	4,709	6,161	4,221	4,729	3,541	3,756	4,439	3,075
Long-Term Obligations	2,054	2,054	2,038	1,543	1,862	1,724	1,792	1,150
Total Liabilities	8,839	10,278	8,391	8,299	7,768	7,821	8,617	5,480
Stockholders' Equity	13,240	12,259	11,833	11,545	10,099	10,056	9,374	7,503
Shares Outstanding	534	535	534	535	540	545	548	545
Statistical Record								
Return on Assets %	11.82	10.51	10.18	8.52	6.21	11.76	13.03	8.04
Return on Equity %	20.05	19.38	17.45	14.85	11.00	21.71	23.92	14.16
EBITDA Margin %	34.32	21.91	27.58	26.01	20.97	30.48	30.59	21.95
Net Margin %	21.66	11.53	15.14	13.59	10.56	17.99	17.81	11.60
Asset Turnover	0.69	0.65	0.67	0.63	0.59	0.65	0.73	0.69
Current Ratio	2.45	1.96	2.29	1.86	2.01	2.10	1.71	1.65
Debt to Equity	0.16	0.17	0.17	0.13	0.18	0.17	0.19	0.15
Price Range	103.62-69.89	92.08-67.45	88.62-60.04	76.42-47.77	86.65-45.12	118.41-66.26	142.69-69.74	70.06-42.99
P/E Ratio	22.09-14.90	21.98-16.10	23.38-15.84	25.82-16.14	43.11-22.45	31.16-17.44	39.42-19.27	39.14-24.02
Average Yield %	1.56	1.57	1.57	1.69	1.54	1.23	0.70	0.85

Address: 800 North Lindbergh Blvd., St. Louis, MO 63167
Telephone: 314-694-1000
Fax: 314-694-1057

Web Site: www.monsanto.com
Officers: Hugh Grant - Chairman, President, Chief Executive Officer Brett D. Begemann - President, Executive Vice President, Executive Vice President, Chief Commercial Officer

Auditors: Deloitte & Touche LLP
Investor Contact: 888-725-9529
Transfer Agents: Computershare, Pittsburgh, PA

MONSTER WORLDWIDE INC

Exchange	Symbol	Price	52Wk Range	Yield	P/E
NYS	MWW	$5.07 (3/28/2013)	9.83-4.97	N/A	N/A

*7 Year Price Score 29.63   *NYSE Composite Index=100   *12 Month Price Score 70.13

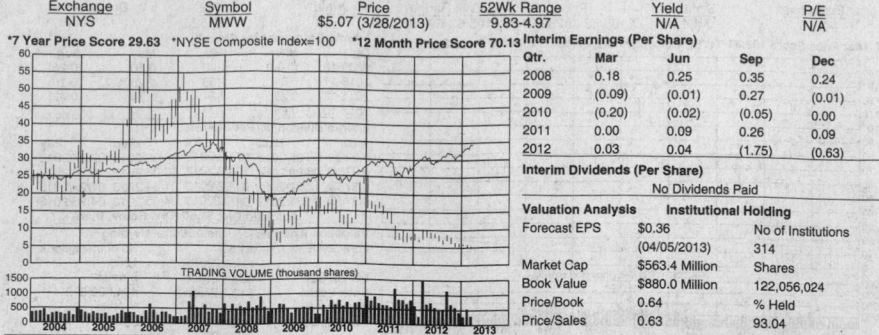

Interim Earnings (Per Share)

Qtr.	Mar	Jun	Sep	Dec
2008	0.18	0.25	0.35	0.24
2009	(0.09)	(0.01)	0.27	(0.01)
2010	(0.20)	(0.02)	(0.05)	0.00
2011	0.00	0.09	0.26	0.09
2012	0.03	0.04	(1.75)	(0.63)

Interim Dividends (Per Share)

No Dividends Paid

Valuation Analysis   **Institutional Holding**

Forecast EPS	$0.36	No of Institutions
	(04/05/2013)	314
Market Cap	$563.4 Million	Shares
Book Value	$880.0 Million	122,056,024
Price/Book	0.64	% Held
Price/Sales	0.63	93.04

TRADING VOLUME (thousand shares)

Business Summary: Business Services (MIC: 7.5.2 SIC: 2741 NAIC: 511199)

Monster Worldwide is the parent company of Monster®, a global online employment service provider. Co. operates three segments: Careers-North America, Careers-International and Internet Advertising & Fees. These segments provide the placement of job advertisements on the websites within the Monster network, access to the Monster network's of online resume databases, recruitment media services, other career-related services to customers, the display of advertisements on the Monster network of websites, and "click-throughs" on text based links and leads provided to advertisers throughout North America, Europe, and the Asia-Pacific region.

Recent Developments: For the year ended Dec 31 2012, income from continuing operations decreased 11.9% to US$58.2 million from US$66.1 million a year earlier. Net loss amounted to US$258.7 million versus net income of US$53.8 million in the prior year. Revenues were US$890.4 million, down 10.4% from US$993.6 million the year before. Operating income was US$32.2 million versus US$93.8 million in the prior year, a decrease of 65.7%. Indirect operating expenses decreased 4.6% to US$858.2 million from US$899.9 million in the equivalent prior-year period.

Prospects: Our evaluation of Monster Worldwide Inc. as of Apr. 7, 2013 is the result of our systematic analysis on three basic characteristics: earnings strength, relative valuation, and recent stock price movement. The company has managed to produce a neutral trend in earnings per share over the past 5 quarters and while recent estimates for the company have remained steady, MWW has posted better than expected results. Based on operating earnings yield, the company is about fairly valued when compared to all of the companies in our coverage universe. Share price changes over the past year indicates that MWW will perform in line with the market over the near term.

Financial Data
(US$ in Thousands)

	12/31/2012	12/31/2011	12/31/2010	12/31/2009	12/31/2008	12/31/2007	12/31/2006	12/31/2005
Earnings Per Share	(2.27)	0.43	(0.27)	0.16	1.03	1.12	0.28	0.86
Cash Flow Per Share	0.47	1.23	0.77	0.37	1.87	2.09	2.10	1.82
Tang Book Value Per Share	N.M.	N.M.	N.M.	1.37	0.85	3.67	3.65	1.47
Income Statement								
Total Revenue	890,392	1,040,105	914,133	905,142	1,343,627	1,351,309	1,116,676	986,917
EBITDA	78,195	138,200	17,133	45,909	224,153	254,655	262,721	206,712
Depn & Amortn	51,926	58,790	56,482	59,117	51,230	40,066	30,901	28,262
Income Before Taxes	26,269	73,410	(43,894)	(14,639)	187,238	240,057	248,344	182,646
Income Taxes	(32,978)	18,371	(14,405)	(37,883)	64,910	84,599	87,661	64,186
Net Income	(258,720)	53,797	(32,359)	18,927	124,793	146,399	37,137	107,432
Average Shares	113,995	123,923	120,608	121,170	121,167	130,755	131,247	125,038
Balance Sheet								
Current Assets	579,653	675,932	585,371	645,493	682,821	1,184,965	1,123,808	773,059
Total Assets	1,684,865	2,057,998	1,978,002	1,827,190	1,916,590	2,077,810	1,969,803	1,678,715
Current Liabilities	584,980	782,963	686,824	507,156	723,708	828,660	826,244	696,588
Long-Term Obligations	145,975	...	40,000	45,000	...	231	415	15,678
Total Liabilities	804,826	893,871	849,352	694,026	869,317	961,309	860,118	759,040
Stockholders' Equity	880,039	1,164,127	1,128,650	1,133,164	1,047,273	1,116,501	1,109,685	919,675
Shares Outstanding	111,129	117,628	121,113	119,659	118,614	123,775	128,564	125,465
Statistical Record								
Return on Assets %	N.M.	2.67	N.M.	1.01	6.23	7.23	2.04	6.67
Return on Equity %	N.M.	4.69	N.M.	1.74	11.50	13.15	3.66	12.83
EBITDA Margin %	8.78	13.29	1.87	5.07	16.68	18.85	23.53	20.95
Net Margin %	N.M.	5.17	N.M.	2.09	9.29	10.83	3.33	10.89
Asset Turnover	0.47	0.52	0.48	0.48	0.67	0.67	0.61	0.61
Current Ratio	0.99	0.86	0.85	1.27	0.94	1.43	1.36	1.11
Debt to Equity	0.17	...	0.04	0.04	...	N.M.	N.M.	0.02
Price Range	10.22-5.37	25.27-6.59	24.71-10.22	18.83-6.01	32.40-9.02	54.67-31.60	59.28-35.28	41.36-22.92
P/E Ratio	...	58.77-15.33	...	117.69-37.56	31.46-8.76	48.81-28.21	211.71-126.00	48.09-26.65

Address: 622 Third Avenue, New York, NY 10017 Telephone: 212-351-7000	Web Site: www.monster.com Officers: Salvatore Iannuzzi - Chairman, President, Chief Executive Officer James M. Langrock - Executive Vice President, Chief Financial Officer	Auditors: BDO USA, LLP Transfer Agents: Computershare Investor Services, Pittsburgh, PA

MOODY'S CORP.

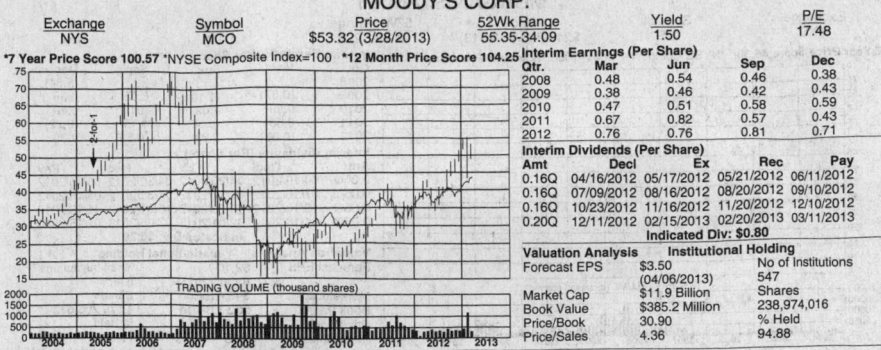

Exchange	Symbol	Price	52Wk Range	Yield	P/E
NYS	MCO	$53.32 (3/28/2013)	55.35-34.09	1.50	17.48

*7 Year Price Score 100.57 *NYSE Composite Index=100 *12 Month Price Score 104.25

Interim Earnings (Per Share)

Qtr.	Mar	Jun	Sep	Dec
2008	0.48	0.54	0.46	0.38
2009	0.38	0.46	0.42	0.43
2010	0.47	0.51	0.58	0.59
2011	0.67	0.82	0.57	0.43
2012	0.76	0.76	0.81	0.71

Interim Dividends (Per Share)

Amt	Decl	Ex	Rec	Pay
0.16Q	04/16/2012	05/17/2012	05/21/2012	06/11/2012
0.16Q	07/09/2012	08/16/2012	08/20/2012	09/10/2012
0.16Q	10/23/2012	11/16/2012	11/20/2012	12/10/2012
0.20Q	12/11/2012	02/15/2013	02/20/2013	03/11/2013

Indicated Div: $0.80

Valuation Analysis — **Institutional Holding**

Forecast EPS	$3.50 (04/06/2013)	No of Institutions 547
Market Cap	$11.9 Billion	Shares
Book Value	$385.2 Million	238,974,016
Price/Book	30.90	% Held
Price/Sales	4.36	94.88

Business Summary: Business Services (MIC: 7.5.2 SIC: 7323 NAIC: 561450)

Moody's provides credit ratings; credit and economic related research, data and analytical tools; risk management software; quantitative credit risk measures, credit portfolio management applications, training and financial credentialing and certification services; and outsourced research and analytical services. Co. operates two segments: Moody's Investors Service, which publishes credit ratings on debt obligations and the entities that issue such obligations, including corporate and governmental obligations, and commercial paper programs; and Moody's Analytics, which develops products and services for risk management activities of institutional participants in global financial markets.

Recent Developments: For the year ended Dec 31 2012, net income increased 21.1% to US$699.7 million from US$578.0 million in the prior year. Revenues were US$2.73 billion, up 19.7% from US$2.28 billion the year before. Operating income was US$1.08 billion versus US$888.4 million in the prior year, an increase of 21.3%. Indirect operating expenses increased 18.7% to US$1.65 billion from US$1.39 billion in the equivalent prior-year period.

Prospects: Our evaluation of Moody's Corp. as of Apr. 7, 2013 is the result of our systematic analysis on three basic characteristics: earnings strength, relative valuation, and recent stock price movement. The company has produced a positive trend in earnings per share over the past 5 quarters and while recent estimates for the company have remained steady, MCO has posted better than expected results. Based on operating earnings yield, the company is undervalued when compared to all of the companies in our coverage universe. Share price changes over the past year indicates that MCO will perform in line with the market over the near term.

Financial Data

(US$ in Thousands)	12/31/2012	12/31/2011	12/31/2010	12/31/2009	12/31/2008	12/31/2007	12/31/2006	12/31/2005
Earnings Per Share	3.05	2.49	2.15	1.69	1.87	2.58	2.58	1.84
Cash Flow Per Share	3.68	3.55	2.78	2.73	2.20	3.69	2.65	2.38
Tang Book Value Per Share	N.M.	...	...	...	...	...	N.M.	0.30
Dividends Per Share	0.640	0.535	0.420	0.400	0.400	0.320	0.280	0.203
Dividend Payout %	20.98	21.49	19.53	23.67	21.39	12.40	10.85	11.01
Income Statement								
Total Revenue	2,730,300	2,280,700	2,032,000	1,797,200	1,755,400	2,259,000	2,037,100	1,731,600
EBITDA	1,176,500	974,300	830,400	737,600	853,200	1,183,900	1,297,000	964,900
Depn & Amortn	93,500	79,200	66,300	64,100	75,100	42,900	39,500	35,200
Income Before Taxes	1,019,200	833,000	711,600	640,100	725,900	1,116,700	1,260,500	934,700
Income Taxes	324,300	261,800	201,000	239,100	268,200	415,200	506,600	373,900
Net Income	690,000	571,400	507,800	402,000	457,600	701,500	753,900	560,800
Average Shares	226,600	229,400	236,600	237,800	245,300	272,200	291,900	305,600
Balance Sheet								
Current Assets	2,525,700	1,424,400	1,343,000	1,012,900	809,100	989,100	1,001,900	1,051,800
Total Assets	3,960,900	2,876,100	2,540,300	2,003,300	1,773,400	1,714,600	1,497,700	1,457,200
Current Liabilities	1,164,900	1,134,000	933,800	1,236,000	1,393,100	1,349,200	700,000	578,900
Long-Term Obligations	1,607,400	1,172,500	1,228,300	746,200	750,000	600,000	300,000	300,000
Total Liabilities	3,575,700	3,045,100	2,849,900	2,609,500	2,767,800	2,498,200	1,330,300	1,147,800
Stockholders' Equity	385,200	(169,000)	(309,600)	(606,200)	(994,400)	(783,600)	167,400	309,400
Shares Outstanding	223,252	222,440	230,785	236,857	235,144	251,406	278,605	290,297
Statistical Record								
Return on Assets %	20.13	21.10	22.35	21.29	26.17	43.68	51.03	39.59
Return on Equity %	636.55	...	...	...	...	...	316.23	178.91
EBITDA Margin %	43.09	42.72	40.87	41.04	48.60	52.41	63.67	55.72
Net Margin %	25.27	25.05	24.99	22.37	26.07	31.05	37.01	32.39
Asset Turnover	0.80	0.84	0.89	0.95	1.00	1.41	1.38	1.22
Current Ratio	2.17	1.26	1.44	0.82	0.58	0.73	1.43	1.82
Debt to Equity	4.17	...	...	...	...	...	1.79	0.97
Price Range	51.54-34.09	41.75-26.54	30.54-18.75	31.23-16.04	45.77-15.63	74.84-35.39	72.45-50.30	62.30-40.01
P/E Ratio	16.90-11.18	16.77-10.66	14.20-8.72	18.48-9.49	24.48-8.36	29.01-13.72	28.08-19.50	33.86-21.74
Average Yield %	1.56	1.59	1.67	1.64	1.20	0.56	0.45	0.43

Address: 7 World Trade Center at 250 Greenwich Street, New York, NY 10007 Telephone: 212-553-0300 Fax: 212-553-4820	Web Site: www.moodys.com Officers: Raymond W. McDaniel - Chairman, Chief Executive Officer Linda S. Huber - Executive Vice President, Chief Financial Officer	Auditors: KPMG LLP Investor Contact: 212-553-4857 Transfer Agents: American Stock Transfer & Trust Company, LLC, Brooklyn, NY

MORGAN STANLEY

Exchange	Symbol	Price	52Wk Range	Yield	P/E
NYS	MS	$21.98 (3/28/2013)	24.32-12.36	0.91	N/A

*7 Year Price Score 45.38   *NYSE Composite Index=100   *12 Month Price Score 119.94

Interim Earnings (Per Share)

Qtr.	Mar	Jun	Sep	Dec
2008	...	...	...	(5.34)
2009	(0.57)	(1.10)	0.38	0.36
2010	0.99	1.09	(0.07)	0.48
2011	0.50	(0.38)	1.15	(0.22)
2012	(0.06)	0.29	(0.55)	0.30

Interim Dividends (Per Share)

Amt	Decl	Ex	Rec	Pay
0.05Q	04/19/2012	04/26/2012	04/30/2012	05/15/2012
0.05Q	07/19/2012	07/27/2012	07/31/2012	08/15/2012
0.05Q	10/18/2012	10/29/2012	10/31/2012	11/15/2012
0.05Q	01/18/2013	02/01/2013	02/05/2013	02/15/2013

Indicated Div: $0.20

Valuation Analysis

	Institutional Holding	
Forecast EPS	$2.10	No of Institutions
	(04/05/2013)	914
Market Cap	$43.4 Billion	Shares
Book Value	$62.1 Billion	1,679,205,632
Price/Book	0.70	% Held
Price/Sales	1.35	77.96

TRADING VOLUME (thousand shares)

Business Summary: Finance Intermediaries & Services (MIC: 5.5.1 SIC: 6211 NAIC: 523110)

Morgan Stanley is a financial holding company that provides its products and services to corporations, governments, financial institutions and individuals. Co.'s Institutional Securities segment includes capital raising, financial advisory services, corporate lending, and sales and trading activities in equity and fixed income securities. The Global Wealth Management Group includes Co.'s 65.0% interest in Morgan Stanley Smith Barney Holdings LLC. Co.'s Asset Management segment provides clients a range of equity, fixed income and alternative investments and merchant banking strategies. As of Dec 31 2012, Co. had total assets of $780.96 billion and total deposits of $83.27 billion.

Recent Developments: For the year ended Dec 31 2012, income from continuing operations decreased 83.9% to US$754.0 million from US$4.69 billion a year earlier. Net income decreased 84.6% to US$716.0 million from US$4.65 billion in the prior year. Revenues were US$32.04 billion, down 18.1% from US$39.14 billion the year before. Direct operating expenses declined 14.2% to US$5.92 billion from US$6.90 billion in the comparable period the year before. Indirect operating expenses decreased 2.1% to US$25.60 billion from US$26.14 billion in the equivalent prior-year period.

Prospects: Our evaluation of Morgan Stanley Dean Witter & Co. as of Apr. 7, 2013 is the result of our systematic analysis on three basic characteristics: earnings strength, relative valuation, and recent stock price movement. The company has managed to produce a neutral trend in earnings per share over the past 5 quarters and while recent estimates for the company have been mixed, MS has posted better than expected results. Based on operating earnings yield, the company is undervalued when compared to all of the companies in our coverage universe. Share price changes over the past year indicates that MS will perform well over the near term.

Financial Data

(US$ in Thousands)	12/31/2012	12/31/2011	12/31/2010	12/31/2009	12/31/2008	11/30/2008	11/30/2007	11/30/2006
Earnings Per Share	(0.02)	1.23	2.63	(0.77)	(1.62)	1.45	2.98	7.07
Cash Flow Per Share	12.98	4.04	29.58	(38.76)	(13.00)	71.21	(22.05)	(60.19)
Tang Book Value Per Share	25.41	25.72	23.95	18.28	24.59	27.24	24.71	29.54
Dividends Per Share	0.200	0.200	0.200	0.437	1.080	1.080	1.080	1.080
Dividend Payout %	...	16.26	7.60	...	...	74.48	36.24	15.28
Income Statement								
Interest Income	5,725,000	7,264,000	7,278,000	7,702,000	1,297,000	40,725,000	60,083,000	45,216,000
Interest Expense	5,924,000	6,907,000	6,414,000	6,712,000	1,124,000	37,523,000	57,302,000	41,937,000
Net Interest Income	(199,000)	357,000	864,000	990,000	173,000	3,202,000	2,781,000	3,279,000
Provision for Losses	...	...	...	...	...	...	...	756,000
Non-Interest Income	26,311,000	32,046,000	30,758,000	22,368,000	(1,141,000)	21,537,000	25,245,000	31,335,000
Non-Interest Expense	25,597,000	26,289,000	25,420,000	22,501,000	1,059,000	22,452,000	24,585,000	22,858,000
Income Before Taxes	515,000	6,114,000	6,202,000	857,000	(2,027,000)	2,287,000	3,441,000	11,000,000
Income Taxes	(239,000)	1,418,000	739,000	(336,000)	(732,000)	480,000	831,000	3,275,000
Net Income	68,000	4,110,000	4,703,000	1,346,000	(1,288,000)	1,707,000	3,209,000	7,472,000
Average Shares	1,918,811	1,675,271	1,411,268	1,185,414	1,002,058	1,095,704	1,054,240	1,054,796
Balance Sheet								
Net Loans & Leases	29,046,000	15,369,000	10,576,000	7,259,000	6,547,000	6,528,000	11,629,000	24,173,000
Total Assets	780,960,000	749,898,000	807,698,000	771,462,000	676,764,000	658,812,000	1,045,409,000	1,120,645,000
Total Deposits	83,266,000	65,662,000	63,812,000	62,215,000	51,355,000	42,755,000	31,179,000	28,343,000
Total Liabilities	718,851,000	687,849,000	750,487,000	724,774,000	628,011,000	607,981,000	1,014,140,000	1,085,215,000
Stockholders' Equity	62,109,000	62,049,000	57,211,000	46,688,000	48,753,000	50,831,000	31,269,000	35,430,000
Shares Outstanding	1,974,042	1,926,986	1,512,022	1,360,595	1,074,497	1,047,598	1,056,289	1,048,877
Statistical Record								
Return on Assets %	0.01	0.53	0.60	0.19	N.M.	0.20	0.30	0.74
Return on Equity %	0.11	6.89	9.05	2.82	N.M.	4.15	9.62	23.11
Net Interest Margin %	N.M.	4.91	11.87	12.85	13.34	7.86	4.63	7.25
Efficiency Ratio %	79.90	66.88	66.83	74.83	678.85	36.06	28.81	29.86
Loans to Deposits	0.35	0.23	0.17	0.12	0.13	0.15	0.37	0.85
Price Range	21.17-12.36	30.99-12.47	32.92-22.83	35.74-13.10	16.50-11.35	55.00-9.20	74.13-47.95	65.84-45.86
P/E Ratio	...	25.20-10.14	12.52-8.68	...	...	37.93-6.34	24.88-16.09	9.31-6.49
Average Yield %	1.21	0.92	0.74	1.62	7.34	2.81	1.64	2.01

Address: 1585 Broadway, New York, NY 10036
Telephone: 212-761-4000

Web Site: www.morganstanley.com
Officers: James P. Gorman - Chairman, President, Chief Executive Officer Gary G. Lynch - Vice-Chairman, Chief Legal Officer

Auditors: Deloitte & Touche LLP
Transfer Agents: Computershare, South Hackensack, NJ

MOSAIC CO (THE)

Exchange	Symbol	Price	52Wk Range	Yield	P/E
NYS	MOS	$59.61 (3/28/2013)	63.22-45.62	1.68	13.34

*7 Year Price Score 88.32 ***NYSE Composite Index=100** ***12 Month Price Score 99.09**

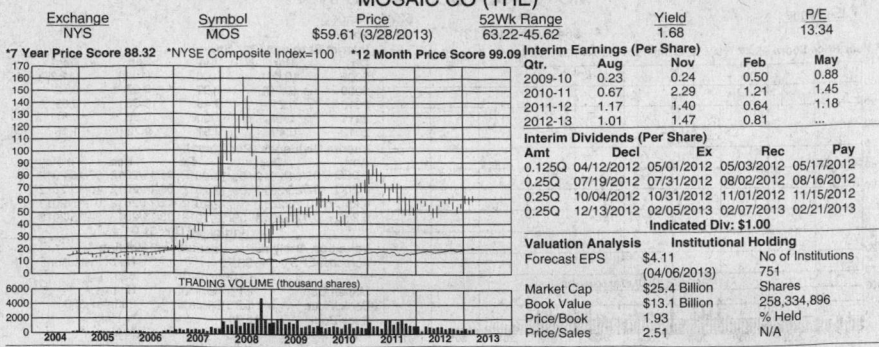

Interim Earnings (Per Share)

Qtr.	Aug	Nov	Feb	May
2009-10	0.23	0.24	0.50	0.88
2010-11	0.67	2.29	1.21	1.45
2011-12	1.17	1.40	0.64	1.18
2012-13	1.01	1.47	0.81	...

Interim Dividends (Per Share)

Amt	Decl	Ex	Rec	Pay
0.125Q	04/12/2012	05/01/2012	05/03/2012	05/17/2012
0.25Q	07/19/2012	07/31/2012	08/02/2012	08/16/2012
0.25Q	10/04/2012	10/31/2012	11/01/2012	11/15/2012
0.25Q	12/13/2012	02/05/2013	02/07/2013	02/21/2013

Indicated Div: $1.00

Valuation Analysis   **Institutional Holding**

Forecast EPS	$4.11 (04/06/2013)	No of Institutions 751
Market Cap	$25.4 Billion	Shares
Book Value	$13.1 Billion	258,334,896
Price/Book	1.93	% Held
Price/Sales	2.51	N/A

Business Summary: Agricultural Chemicals (MIC: 8.3.3 SIC: 2874 NAIC: 325312)

Mosaic is a producer and marketer of combined concentrated phosphate and potash crop nutrients for the agriculture industry. Co. mines phosphate rock and process rock into finished phosphate products in Florida and Louisiana; and mines potash in Saskatchewan, New Mexico, and Michigan. Co. also has other production, blending or distribution operations in Brazil, China, India, Argentina, and Chile; and an investment in a phosphate rock mine in Peru. Co. has two reportable segments: Phosphates, which sells phosphate-based crop nutrients and animal feed ingredients; and Potash, which sells potash, mainly as fertilizer, but also for use in industrial applications, and animal feed ingredients.

Recent Developments: For the quarter ended Feb 28 2013, net income increased 27.0% to US$345.4 million from US$271.9 million in the year-earlier quarter. Revenues were US$2.24 billion, up 2.3% from US$2.19 billion the year before. Operating income was US$419.1 million versus US$413.7 million in the prior-year quarter, an increase of 1.3%. Direct operating expenses were unchanged at US$1.67 billion versus the comparable period the year before. Indirect operating expenses increased 38.1% to US$149.3 million from US$108.1 million in the equivalent prior-year period.

Prospects: Our evaluation of Mosaic Co as of Apr. 7, 2013 is the result of our systematic analysis on three basic characteristics: earnings strength, relative valuation, and recent stock price movement. The company has produced a positive trend in earnings per share over the past 5 quarters. However, while recent estimates for the company have been mixed, MOS has posted better than expected results. Based on operating earnings yield, the company is undervalued when compared to all of the companies in our coverage universe. Share price changes over the past year indicates that MOS will perform in line with the market over the near term.

Financial Data
(US$ in Thousands)

	9 Mos	6 Mos	3 Mos	05/31/2012	05/31/2011	05/31/2010	05/31/2009	05/31/2008
Earnings Per Share	4.47	4.30	4.23	4.42	5.62	1.85	5.27	4.67
Cash Flow Per Share	5.31	5.39	5.85	6.20	5.44	3.05	2.80	5.74
Tang Book Value Per Share	26.48	26.29	25.07	23.83	21.97	15.62	15.21	10.94
Dividends Per Share	0.875	0.675	0.475	0.275	0.200	1.500	...	...
Dividend Payout %	19.57	15.70	11.23	6.22	3.56	81.08	...	...
Income Statement								
Total Revenue	7,281,900	5,041,300	2,505,100	11,107,800	9,937,800	6,759,100	10,298,000	9,812,600
EBITDA	2,012,000	1,408,800	718,300	3,118,300	3,723,800	1,684,300	3,309,500	3,131,000
Depn & Amortn	437,000	284,800	137,400	508,100	447,400	445,000	360,500	358,100
Income Before Taxes	1,388,600	1,134,300	586,800	2,628,900	3,271,300	1,189,700	2,905,700	2,682,400
Income Taxes	194,100	85,200	163,300	711,400	752,800	347,300	649,300	714,900
Net Income	1,402,800	1,058,200	429,400	1,930,200	2,514,600	827,100	2,350,200	2,082,800
Average Shares	427,100	427,000	426,700	436,500	447,500	446,600	446,200	445,700
Balance Sheet								
Current Assets	6,342,000	6,533,100	6,540,900	6,581,100	6,684,900	4,974,800	5,307,800	4,809,500
Total Assets	17,322,100	17,440,700	17,070,100	16,690,400	15,786,900	12,707,700	12,676,200	11,819,800
Current Liabilities	1,536,600	1,647,400	1,676,100	1,917,700	1,928,500	1,303,900	1,621,800	2,186,100
Long-Term Obligations	1,010,400	1,010,600	1,010,900	1,010,400	761,300	1,245,600	1,256,500	1,375,000
Total Liabilities	4,197,500	4,358,300	4,507,700	4,707,300	4,145,300	3,985,500	4,183,200	5,088,600
Stockholders' Equity	13,124,600	13,082,400	12,562,400	11,983,100	11,641,600	8,722,200	8,493,000	6,731,200
Shares Outstanding	425,747	425,676	425,641	425,470	446,572	445,439	444,513	443,925
Statistical Record								
Return on Assets %	11.49	11.06	11.03	11.85	17.65	6.52	19.19	19.80
Return on Equity %	15.32	15.08	14.80	16.30	24.70	9.61	30.87	38.06
EBITDA Margin %	27.63	27.95	28.67	28.07	37.47	24.92	32.14	31.91
Net Margin %	19.26	20.99	17.14	17.38	25.30	12.24	22.82	21.23
Asset Turnover	0.61	0.60	0.63	0.68	0.70	0.53	0.84	0.93
Current Ratio	4.13	3.97	3.90	3.43	3.47	3.82	3.27	2.20
Debt to Equity	0.08	0.08	0.08	0.08	0.07	0.14	0.15	0.20
Price Range	63.22-45.62	61.05-45.62	71.13-45.62	73.18-45.68	89.06-38.90	66.70-40.67	161.08-22.31	140.21-34.61
P/E Ratio	14.14-10.21	14.20-10.61	16.82-10.78	16.56-10.33	15.85-6.92	36.05-21.98	30.57-4.23	30.02-7.41
Average Yield %	1.59	1.25	0.86	0.47	0.30	2.80	...	...

Address: 3033 Campus Drive, Suite E490, Plymouth, MN 55441 **Telephone:** 800-918-8270 **Fax:** 763-577-2990	**Web Site:** www.mosaicco.com **Officers:** Robert L. Lumpkins - Chairman James T. Prokopanko - President, Chief Executive Officer	**Auditors:** KPMG LLP **Investor Contact:** 763-577-8213 **Transfer Agents:** American Stock Transfer & Trust Company, Brooklyn, NY

MOTOROLA SOLUTIONS INC.

Exchange	Symbol	Price	52Wk Range	Yield	P/E
NYS	MSI	$64.03 (3/28/2013)	64.03-45.17	1.62	21.63

*7 Year Price Score 95.47   *NYSE Composite Index=100   *12 Month Price Score 107.96

Interim Earnings (Per Share)

Qtr.	Mar	Jun	Sep	Dec
2008	(0.63)	0.00	(1.26)	(11.27)
2009	(0.70)	0.07	0.07	0.42
2010	0.21	0.49	0.35	0.89
2011	1.44	1.00	0.38	0.57
2012	0.49	0.61	0.72	1.15

Interim Dividends (Per Share)

Amt	Decl	Ex	Rec	Pay
0.22Q	05/01/2012	06/13/2012	06/15/2012	07/16/2012
0.26Q	07/25/2012	09/12/2012	09/14/2012	10/15/2012
0.26Q	10/26/2012	12/12/2012	12/14/2012	01/15/2013
0.26Q	01/17/2013	03/13/2013	03/15/2013	04/15/2013
		Indicated Div: $1.04		

Valuation Analysis

		Institutional Holding	
Forecast EPS	$3.72 (04/06/2013)	No of Institutions	699
Market Cap	$17.7 Billion	Shares	383,487,360
Book Value	$3.3 Billion	% Held	N/A
Price/Book	5.41		
Price/Sales	2.03		

Business Summary: Manufacturing (MIC: 6.1.1 SIC: 3663 NAIC: 334220)

Motorola Solutions is a provider of communication infrastructure, devices, software and services. Co. operates in two segments: Government, which designs, manufactures, sells, and provides services around voice and data communications systems, devices, security products and applications; and Enterprise, which includes sales of rugged and enterprise-grade mobile computers and tablets, laser/imaging/RFID based data capture products, wireless local area network and integrated digital enhanced network infrastructure and software. In addition, Co. provides design, installation, maintenance and optimization of equipment for public safety networks.

Recent Developments: For the year ended Dec 31 2012, income from continuing operations increased 18.5% to US$878.0 million from US$741.0 million a year earlier. Net income decreased 23.5% to US$881.0 million from US$1.15 billion in the prior year. Revenues were US$8.70 billion, up 6.0% from US$8.20 billion the year before. Operating income was US$1.26 billion versus US$858.0 million in the prior year, an increase of 46.4%. Direct operating expenses rose 7.2% to US$4.35 billion from US$4.06 billion in the comparable period the year before. Indirect operating expenses decreased 6.0% to US$3.09 billion from US$3.29 billion in the equivalent prior-year period.

Prospects: Our evaluation of Motorola Solutions Inc. as of Apr. 7, 2013 is the result of our systematic analysis on three basic characteristics: earnings strength, relative valuation, and recent stock price movement. The company has managed to produce a neutral trend in earnings per share over the past 5 quarters and while recent estimates for the company have remained steady, MSI has posted better than expected results. Based on operating earnings yield, the company is about fairly valued when compared to all of the companies in our coverage universe. Share price changes over the past year indicates that MSI will perform well over the near term.

Financial Data

(US$ in Millions)	12/31/2012	12/31/2011	12/31/2010	12/31/2009	12/31/2008	12/31/2007	12/31/2006	12/31/2005
Earnings Per Share	2.96	3.41	1.87	(0.14)	(13.09)	(0.14)	10.22	12.67
Cash Flow Per Share	3.65	2.54	4.60	1.92	0.75	2.38	10.01	13.04
Tang Book Value Per Share	5.96	11.73	21.95	18.48	16.95	28.84	42.76	40.92
Dividends Per Share	0.960	0.440	...	0.350	1.400	1.400	1.260	1.120
Dividend Payout %	32.43	12.90	...	...	...	...	12.33	8.84
Income Statement								
Total Revenue	8,698	8,203	19,282	22,044	30,146	36,622	42,879	36,843
EBITDA	1,489	1,177	1,378	716	(1,856)	425	4,847	6,981
Depn & Amortn	208	365	570	749	829	906	563	532
Income Before Taxes	1,215	738	677	(165)	(2,637)	(390)	4,610	6,520
Income Taxes	337	(3)	406	(77)	1,607	(285)	1,349	1,921
Net Income	881	1,158	633	(51)	(4,244)	(49)	3,661	4,578
Average Shares	297	339	338	327	323	330	357	361
Balance Sheet								
Current Assets	7,401	8,768	17,154	16,032	17,363	22,222	30,975	27,869
Total Assets	12,679	13,929	25,577	25,603	27,869	34,812	38,593	35,649
Current Liabilities	3,335	3,815	8,710	8,261	10,620	12,500	15,425	12,488
Long-Term Obligations	1,859	1,130	2,194	3,365	4,092	3,991	2,704	3,806
Total Liabilities	9,414	8,715	14,692	15,828	18,362	19,365	21,451	18,976
Stockholders' Equity	3,265	5,214	10,885	9,775	9,507	15,447	17,142	16,673
Shares Outstanding	276	318	336	330	325	323	342	357
Statistical Record								
Return on Assets %	6.60	5.86	2.47	N.M.	N.M.	N.M.	9.86	13.76
Return on Equity %	20.72	14.39	6.13	N.M.	N.M.	N.M.	21.65	30.52
EBITDA Margin %	17.12	14.35	7.15	3.25	N.M.	1.16	11.30	18.95
Net Margin %	10.13	14.12	3.28	N.M.	N.M.	N.M.	8.54	12.43
Asset Turnover	0.65	0.42	0.75	0.82	0.96	1.00	1.16	1.11
Current Ratio	2.22	2.30	1.97	1.94	1.63	1.78	2.01	2.23
Debt to Equity	0.57	0.22	0.20	0.34	0.43	0.26	0.16	0.23
Price Range	55.68-44.94	47.87-37.04	37.23-25.19	38.13-12.70	65.81-12.90	84.24-62.42	107.30-76.54	101.45-59.84
P/E Ratio	18.81-15.18	14.04-10.86	19.91-13.47	...	...	...	10.50-7.49	8.01-4.72
Average Yield %	1.94	1.02	...	1.33	4.06	1.92	1.38	1.43

Address: 1303 East Algonquin Road, Schaumburg, IL 60196 **Telephone:** 847-576-5000 **Fax:** 847-576-3477	**Web Site:** www.motorolasolutions.com **Officers:** Gregory Q. Brown - Chairman, President, Chief Executive Officer, Division Officer Eugene A. Delaney - Executive Vice President, Division Officer	**Auditors:** KPMG LLP **Investor Contact:** 847-576-6899 **Transfer Agents:** Computershare Shareowner Services, Jersey City, NJ

MSC INDUSTRIAL DIRECT CO., INC.

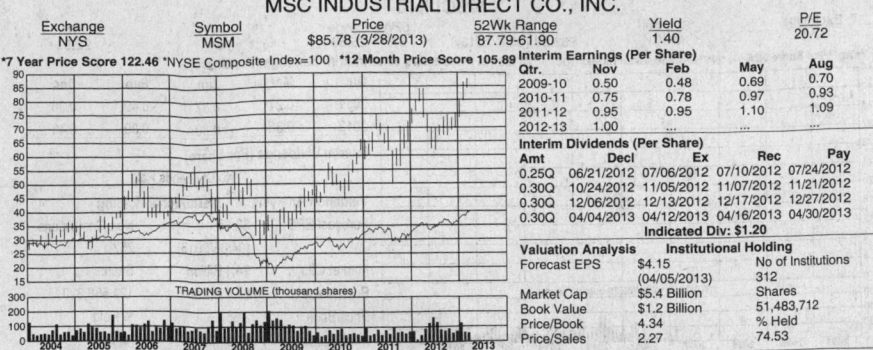

Exchange	Symbol	Price	52Wk Range	Yield	P/E
NYS	MSM	$85.78 (3/28/2013)	87.79-61.90	1.40	20.72

*7 Year Price Score 122.46 *NYSE Composite Index=100 *12 Month Price Score 105.89

Interim Earnings (Per Share)

Qtr.	Nov	Feb	May	Aug
2009-10	0.50	0.48	0.69	0.70
2010-11	0.75	0.78	0.97	0.93
2011-12	0.95	0.95	1.10	1.09
2012-13	1.00	...	...	...

Interim Dividends (Per Share)

Amt	Decl	Ex	Rec	Pay
0.25Q	06/21/2012	07/06/2012	07/10/2012	07/24/2012
0.30Q	10/24/2012	11/05/2012	11/07/2012	11/21/2012
0.30Q	12/06/2012	12/13/2012	12/17/2012	12/27/2012
0.30Q	04/04/2013	04/12/2013	04/16/2013	04/30/2013

Indicated Div: $1.20

Valuation Analysis **Institutional Holding**

Forecast EPS	$4.15 (04/05/2013)	No of Institutions 312
Market Cap	$5.4 Billion	Shares
Book Value	$1.2 Billion	51,483,712
Price/Book	4.34	% Held
Price/Sales	2.27	74.53

Business Summary: Industrial Machinery & Equipment (MIC: 7.2.1 SIC: 5084 NAIC: 423830)

MSC Industrial Direct Co. is a distributor of metalworking and maintenance, repair and operations supplies. Co. operates primarily in the U.S., through a network of customer fulfillment centers and branch offices. Co. provides approximately 600,000 stock-keeping units through its catalogs, specialty and promotional catalogs, brochures and the Internet, including its websites. Co.'s products include cutting tools, measuring instruments, tooling components, metalworking products, fasteners, flat stock, raw materials, abrasives, machinery hand and power tools, safety and janitorial supplies, plumbing supplies, materials handling products, power transmission components, and electrical supplies.

Recent Developments: For the quarter ended Dec 1 2012, net income increased 5.6% to US$63.2 million from US$59.8 million in the year-earlier quarter. Revenues were US$577.5 million, up 5.8% from US$545.7 million the year before. Operating income was US$102.4 million versus US$96.8 million in the prior-year quarter, an increase of 5.7%. Direct operating expenses rose 6.4% to US$312.4 million from US$293.6 million in the comparable period the year before. Indirect operating expenses increased 4.8% to US$162.7 million from US$155.3 million in the equivalent prior-year period.

Prospects: Our evaluation of MSC Industrial Direct Co. Inc. as of Apr. 7, 2013 is the result of our systematic analysis on three basic characteristics: earnings strength, relative valuation, and recent stock price movement. The company has managed to produce a neutral trend in earnings per share over the past 5 quarters and while recent estimates for the company have been mixed, MSM has posted better than expected results. Based on operating earnings yield, the company is about fairly valued when compared to all of the companies in our coverage universe. Share price changes over the past year indicates that MSM will perform in line with the market over the near term.

Financial Data
(US$ in Thousands)	3 Mos	09/01/2012	08/27/2011	08/28/2010	08/29/2009	08/30/2008	09/01/2007	08/26/2006
Earnings Per Share	4.14	4.09	3.43	2.37	2.00	3.04	2.59	2.00
Cash Flow Per Share	4.45	3.69	3.35	2.41	4.63	3.44	2.47	2.00
Tang Book Value Per Share	14.41	13.48	10.63	9.23	7.63	6.07	5.81	4.35
Dividends Per Share	1.050	1.000	1.880	0.820	0.800	0.740	0.640	0.540
Dividend Payout %	25.36	24.45	54.81	34.60	40.00	24.34	24.71	27.00
Income Statement								
Total Revenue	577,491	2,355,918	2,021,792	1,692,041	1,489,518	1,779,841	1,688,186	1,317,519
EBITDA	112,357	436,863	371,000	260,512	224,359	340,415	317,184	246,088
Depn & Amortn	10,021	24,676	21,470	18,709	19,610	19,329	26,031	24,951
Income Before Taxes	102,327	412,142	349,330	240,828	201,940	313,359	279,494	221,770
Income Taxes	39,140	153,111	130,544	90,455	76,818	117,116	105,564	85,381
Net Income	63,187	259,031	218,786	150,373	125,122	196,243	173,930	136,389
Average Shares	62,701	62,803	63,324	62,930	62,580	64,659	67,057	68,319
Balance Sheet								
Current Assets	974,607	920,111	758,434	676,536	682,714	622,676	589,802	527,473
Total Assets	1,507,953	1,444,876	1,244,423	1,153,323	1,157,547	1,102,726	1,075,327	1,014,298
Current Liabilities	173,035	170,515	172,202	190,285	255,838	250,601	173,287	152,727
Long-Term Obligations	2,243	2,189	...	...	39,365	98,473	142,200	192,986
Total Liabilities	260,339	257,765	251,311	253,443	352,011	391,114	347,450	375,025
Stockholders' Equity	1,247,614	1,187,111	993,112	899,880	805,536	711,612	727,877	639,273
Shares Outstanding	63,149	62,800	62,800	62,777	62,637	62,030	66,079	66,927
Statistical Record								
Return on Assets %	18.69	18.95	18.30	13.05	11.10	18.07	16.38	16.42
Return on Equity %	22.83	23.38	23.18	17.68	16.54	27.34	25.03	23.38
EBITDA Margin %	19.46	18.54	18.35	15.40	15.06	19.13	18.79	18.68
Net Margin %	10.94	10.99	10.82	8.89	8.40	11.03	10.30	10.35
Asset Turnover	1.70	1.72	1.69	1.47	1.32	1.64	1.59	1.59
Current Ratio	5.63	5.40	4.40	3.56	2.67	2.48	3.40	3.45
Debt to Equity	N.M.	N.M.	...	...	0.05	0.14	0.20	0.30
Price Range	84.27-61.90	84.27-56.13	75.04-44.57	57.47-38.92	51.82-27.43	54.50-35.13	57.33-37.44	54.72-31.97
P/E Ratio	20.36-14.95	20.60-13.72	21.88-12.99	24.25-16.42	25.91-13.72	17.93-11.56	22.14-14.46	27.36-15.98
Average Yield %	1.46	1.43	3.02	1.70	2.18	1.62	1.40	1.26

Address: 75 Maxess Road, Melville, NY 11747	**Web Site:** www.mscdirect.com	**Auditors:** Ernst & Young LLP
Telephone: 516-812-2000	**Officers:** Mitchell Jacobson - Chairman Erik Gershwind - President, Executive Vice President,	**Investor Contact:** 516-812-2000
Fax: 516-349-7096	Chief Operating Officer, Chief Executive Officer	**Transfer Agents:** Computershare Shareholder Services, Providence, RI

MSCI INC

Exchange	Symbol	Price	52Wk Range	Yield	P/E
NYS	MSCI	$33.93 (3/28/2013)	37.74-25.59	N/A	22.93

*7 Year Price Score N/A   *NYSE Composite Index=100   *12 Month Price Score 93.77

TRADING VOLUME (thousand shares)

Interim Earnings (Per Share)

Qtr.	Mar	Jun	Sep	Dec
2011	0.27	0.37	0.40	0.36
2012	0.35	0.30	0.39	0.43

Interim Dividends (Per Share)

No Dividends Paid

Valuation Analysis | Institutional Holding

Forecast EPS	$2.15	No of Institutions
	(04/05/2013)	257
Market Cap	$4.1 Billion	Shares
Book Value	$1.4 Billion	124,588,320
Price/Book	2.86	% Held
Price/Sales	4.29	N/A

Business Summary: Publishing (MIC: 2.3.3 SIC: 7389 NAIC: 523999)

MSCI is a provider of investment decision support tools as well as corporate governance and financial research and analysis services. Co.'s products include: its global equity indices and environmental, social and governance products marketed under the MSCI and MSCI Research brands, its market and credit risk analytics marketed under the RiskMetrics and Barra brands, its governance research and outsourced proxy voting and reporting services marketed under the ISS brand, its valuation models and risk management software marketed under the FEA brand and its forensic accounting risk research, legal and regulatory risk assessment and due diligence products marketed under the CFRA brand.

Recent Developments: For the year ended Dec 31 2012, net income increased 6.2% to US$184.2 million from US$173.5 million in the prior year. Revenues were US$950.1 million, up 5.5% from US$900.9 million the year before. Operating income was US$346.9 million versus US$322.0 million in the prior year, an increase of 7.7%. Direct operating expenses rose 3.9% to US$288.1 million from US$277.1 million in the comparable period the year before. Indirect operating expenses increased 4.4% to US$315.1 million from US$301.8 million in the equivalent prior-year period.

Prospects: Our evaluation of MSCI Inc. as of Apr. 7, 2013 is the result of our systematic analysis on three basic characteristics: earnings strength, relative valuation, and recent stock price movement. The company has enjoyed a very positive trend in earnings per share over the past 5 quarters. However, while recent estimates for the company have been lowered by analysts, MSCI has posted results that fell short of analysts expectations. Based on operating earnings yield, the company is undervalued when compared to all of the companies in our coverage universe. Share price changes over the past year indicates that MSCI will perform poorly over the near term.

Financial Data

(US$ in Thousands)	12/31/2012	12/31/2011	12/31/2010	11/30/2010	11/30/2009	11/30/2008	11/30/2007	11/30/2006
Earnings Per Share	1.48	1.41	0.11	0.81	0.80	0.67	0.96	0.86
Cash Flow Per Share	2.84	2.11	0.33	1.64	1.30	1.55	1.30	1.00
Tang Book Value Per Share	N.M.	N.M.	N.M.	N.M.	N.M.	N.M.	N.M.	6.25
Income Statement								
Total Revenue	950,141	900,941	72,524	662,901	442,948	430,961	369,886	310,698
EBITDA	426,881	403,589	33,906	262,834	187,905	161,933	157,588	113,994
Depn & Amortn	81,998	85,205	7,364	58,999	37,554	33,500	27,853	29,655
Income Before Taxes	289,409	263,413	20,556	153,491	131,721	109,643	133,292	99,469
Income Taxes	105,171	89,959	6,732	61,321	49,920	41,375	52,181	36,097
Net Income	184,238	173,454	13,824	92,170	81,801	68,268	81,111	71,445
Average Shares	123,204	122,276	121,803	113,357	102,475	101,194	84,624	83,900
Balance Sheet								
Current Assets	514,835	677,943	574,962	536,283	602,484	392,255	281,403	462,206
Total Assets	3,019,639	3,092,996	3,057,481	3,023,166	1,200,269	1,015,048	904,679	1,112,775
Current Liabilities	509,945	452,805	466,084	466,924	292,500	291,094	244,931	220,982
Long-Term Obligations	811,623	1,066,548	1,207,966	1,207,881	337,622	379,709	402,750	...
Total Liabilities	1,594,408	1,787,564	1,955,311	1,943,049	693,213	728,666	704,658	287,063
Stockholders' Equity	1,425,231	1,305,432	1,102,170	1,080,117	507,056	286,382	200,021	825,712
Shares Outstanding	120,114	121,212	119,594	119,522	104,781	100,063	100,011	29,323
Statistical Record								
Return on Assets %	6.01	5.64	0.60	4.36	7.39	7.09	8.04	6.61
Return on Equity %	13.46	14.41	1.58	11.61	20.62	27.99	15.82	9.03
EBITDA Margin %	44.93	44.80	46.75	39.65	42.42	37.57	42.60	36.69
Net Margin %	19.39	19.25	19.06	13.90	18.47	15.84	21.93	22.99
Asset Turnover	0.31	0.29	0.03	0.31	0.40	0.45	0.37	0.29
Current Ratio	1.01	1.50	1.23	1.15	2.06	1.35	1.15	2.09
Debt to Equity	0.57	0.82	1.10	1.12	0.67	1.33	2.01	...
Price Range	37.81-25.59	39.72-27.94	40.02-34.06	37.96-27.23	33.60-13.20	38.40-11.88	27.80-24.96	...
P/E Ratio	25.55-17.29	28.17-19.82	363.82-309.64	46.86-33.62	42.00-16.50	57.31-17.73	28.96-26.00	...

Address: 7 World Trade Center, 250 Greenwich Street, 49th Floor, New York, NY 10007
Telephone: 212-804-3900

Web Site: www.msci.com
Officers: Henry A. Fernandez - Chairman, President, Chief Executive Officer David C. Brierwood - Chief Operating Officer

Auditors: Deloitte & Touche LLP
Investor Contact: 212-804-5273
Transfer Agents: Mellon Investor Services LLC, Jersey City, NJ

MURPHY OIL CORP

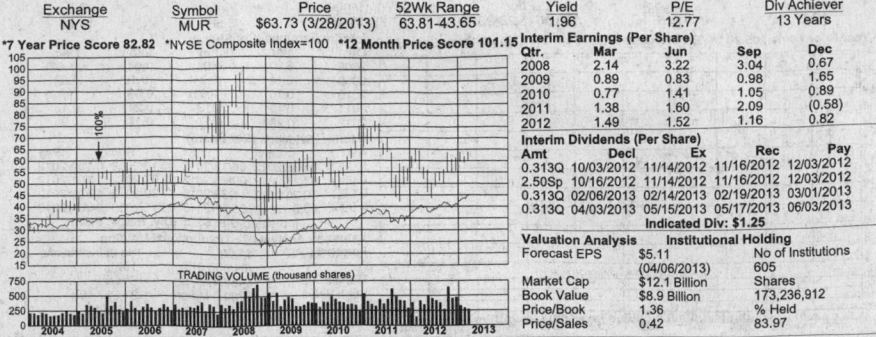

Exchange	Symbol	Price	52Wk Range	Yield	P/E	Div Achiever
NYS	MUR	$63.73 (3/28/2013)	63.81-43.65	1.96	12.77	13 Years

*7 Year Price Score 82.82 *NYSE Composite Index=100 *12 Month Price Score 101.15

Interim Earnings (Per Share)

Qtr.	Mar	Jun	Sep	Dec
2008	2.14	3.22	3.04	0.67
2009	0.89	0.83	0.98	1.65
2010	0.77	1.41	1.05	0.89
2011	1.38	1.60	2.09	(0.58)
2012	1.49	1.52	1.16	0.82

Interim Dividends (Per Share)

Amt	Decl	Ex	Rec	Pay
0.313Q	10/03/2012	11/14/2012	11/16/2012	12/03/2012
2.50Sp	10/16/2012	11/14/2012	11/16/2012	12/03/2012
0.313Q	02/06/2013	02/14/2013	02/19/2013	03/01/2013
0.313Q	04/03/2013	05/15/2013	05/17/2013	06/03/2013

Indicated Div: $1.25

Valuation Analysis | **Institutional Holding**

Forecast EPS	$5.11 (04/06/2013)	No of Institutions 605
Market Cap	$12.1 Billion	Shares 173,236,912
Book Value	$8.9 Billion	% Held 83.97
Price/Book	1.36	
Price/Sales	0.42	

Business Summary: Refining & Marketing (MIC: 9.1.2 SIC: 2911 NAIC: 324110)

Murphy Oil is a holding company. Co. operates two business activities: Exploration and Production, which explores for and produces crude oil, natural gas and natural gas liquids worldwide; and Refining and Marketing, which primarily consists of the sale of motor fuel and merchandise. The U.K. refining and marketing business consists of operations that refine crude oil and other feedstocks into petroleum products, buy and sell crude oil and refined products, and transport and market petroleum products. As of Dec 31 2012, Co. had 295.7 million barrels of proved reserves, 119.1 million barrels of proved synthetic oil reserves and 1.14 trillion cubic feet of natural gas reserves.

Recent Developments: For the year ended Dec 31 2012, income from continuing operations increased 32.2% to US$964.0 million from US$729.5 million a year earlier. Net income increased 11.2% to US$970.9 million from US$872.7 million in the prior year. Revenues were US$28.63 billion, up 3.6% from US$27.64 billion the year before. Direct operating expenses rose 2.6% to US$22.45 billion from US$21.88 billion in the comparable period the year before. Indirect operating expenses increased 6.6% to US$4.55 billion from US$4.27 billion in the equivalent prior-year period.

Prospects: Our evaluation of Murphy Oil Corp. as of Apr. 7, 2013 is the result of our systematic analysis on three basic characteristics: earnings strength, relative valuation, and recent stock price movement. The company has generated a negative trend in earnings per share over the past 5 quarters. However, while recent estimates for the company have been mixed, MUR has posted better than expected results. Based on operating earnings yield, the company is undervalued when compared to all of the companies in our coverage universe. Share price changes over the past year indicates that MUR will perform in line with the market over the near term.

Financial Data

(US$ in Thousands)	12/31/2012	12/31/2011	12/31/2010	12/31/2009	12/31/2008	12/31/2007	12/31/2006	12/31/2005
Earnings Per Share	4.99	4.49	4.13	4.35	9.06	4.01	3.37	4.51
Cash Flow Per Share	15.72	11.09	16.31	9.77	15.99	9.26	5.17	6.65
Tang Book Value Per Share	46.68	45.10	42.30	38.22	32.73	26.43	21.37	18.38
Dividends Per Share	3.675	1.100	1.050	1.000	0.875	0.675	0.525	0.450
Dividend Payout %	73.65	24.50	25.42	22.99	9.66	16.83	15.58	9.98
Income Statement								
Total Revenue	28,626,046	27,745,549	23,345,071	19,012,392	27,512,540	18,439,098	14,307,387	11,877,151
EBITDA	3,166,059	2,826,376	2,760,877	2,329,935	3,714,876	1,807,455	1,444,486	1,800,518
Depn & Amortn	1,528,145	1,234,693	1,311,918	1,028,371	852,348	545,159	406,529	419,694
Income Before Taxes	1,622,982	1,550,983	1,414,231	1,277,173	2,818,849	1,236,684	1,028,481	1,372,059
Income Taxes	658,936	810,051	616,150	536,656	1,078,565	470,703	390,146	534,156
Net Income	970,876	872,702	798,081	837,621	1,739,986	766,529	638,279	846,452
Average Shares	194,668	194,512	193,157	192,468	192,133	191,140	189,158	187,889
Balance Sheet								
Current Assets	4,108,583	3,447,671	3,550,693	3,375,695	2,846,964	2,886,792	2,107,091	1,838,946
Total Assets	17,522,643	14,138,138	14,233,243	12,756,359	11,149,098	10,535,849	7,445,727	6,368,511
Current Liabilities	3,409,081	2,824,928	2,930,910	2,181,608	1,888,146	2,109,262	1,311,105	1,287,008
Long-Term Obligations	2,245,201	249,553	939,350	1,353,183	1,026,222	1,516,156	840,275	609,574
Total Liabilities	8,580,608	5,359,741	6,033,693	5,410,333	4,870,153	5,469,675	3,393,051	2,907,521
Stockholders' Equity	8,942,035	8,778,397	8,199,550	7,346,026	6,278,945	5,066,174	4,052,676	3,460,990
Shares Outstanding	190,641	193,723	192,836	191,115	190,713	189,714	187,572	185,946
Statistical Record								
Return on Assets %	6.12	6.15	5.91	7.01	16.00	8.53	9.24	14.31
Return on Equity %	10.93	10.28	10.27	12.30	30.59	16.81	16.99	27.71
EBITDA Margin %	11.06	10.19	11.83	12.25	13.50	9.80	10.10	15.16
Net Margin %	3.39	3.15	3.42	4.41	6.32	4.16	4.46	7.13
Asset Turnover	1.80	1.96	1.73	1.59	2.53	2.05	2.07	2.01
Current Ratio	1.21	1.22	1.21	1.55	1.51	1.37	1.61	1.43
Debt to Equity	0.25	0.03	0.11	0.18	0.16	0.30	0.21	0.18
Price Range	64.76-43.65	77.48-42.10	75.37-48.44	64.66-38.18	100.93-37.00	85.38-45.93	59.15-45.12	55.98-38.05
P/E Ratio	12.98-8.75	17.26-9.38	18.25-11.73	14.86-8.78	11.14-4.08	21.29-11.45	17.55-13.39	12.41-8.44
Average Yield %	6.70	1.76	1.80	1.87	1.21	1.09	1.03	0.92

Address: 200 Peach Street, P.O. Box 7000, El Dorado, AR 71731-7000 **Telephone:** 870-862-6411 **Fax:** 870-864-3673	**Web Site:** www.murphyoilcorp.com **Officers:** Claiborne P. Deming - Chairman, President, Chief Executive Officer Steven A. Cosse - President, Chief Executive Officer, Executive Vice President, General Counsel	**Auditors:** KPMG LLP **Transfer Agents:** Computershare Trust Company, N.A., Chicago, IL

MYERS INDUSTRIES INC.

Exchange	Symbol	Price	52Wk Range	Yield	P/E
NYS	MYE	$13.96 (3/28/2013)	17.88-13.47	2.58	15.86

*7 Year Price Score 105.98 *NYSE Composite Index=100   *12 Month Price Score 86.00

Interim Earnings (Per Share)

Qtr.	Mar	Jun	Sep	Dec
2008	0.30	0.08	0.04	(1.67)
2009	0.14	(0.04)	(0.15)	0.03
2010	0.16	(0.03)	0.09	(1.43)
2011	0.19	0.13	0.21	0.18
2012	0.29	0.17	0.17	0.25

Interim Dividends (Per Share)

Amt	Decl	Ex	Rec	Pay
0.08Q	05/30/2012	06/13/2012	06/15/2012	07/02/2012
0.08Q	07/27/2012	09/05/2012	09/07/2012	10/01/2012
0.08Q	10/26/2012	11/28/2012	11/30/2012	12/28/2012
0.09Q	03/01/2013	03/07/2013	03/11/2013	04/01/2013

Indicated Div: $0.36 (Div. Reinv. Plan)

Valuation Analysis

	Institutional Holding	
Forecast EPS	$1.05	No of Institutions
	(04/05/2013)	157
Market Cap	$467.4 Million	Shares
Book Value	$230.0 Million	31,597,498
Price/Book	2.03	% Held
Price/Sales	0.59	84.71

Business Summary: Plastics (MIC: 8.4.2 SIC: 3089 NAIC: 326199)

Myers Industries manufactures a range of polymer products for industrial, agricultural, automotive, commercial and consumer markets. Co. is engaged in manufacturing plastic reusable material handling containers and pallets, as well as plastic horticultural pots, trays and flower planters. Other principal product lines include plastic storage and organization containers, plastic original equipment manufacturer parts, rubber tire repair products and custom plastic and rubber products. Co. is also a wholesale distributor of tools, equipment and supplies for the tire, wheel and undervehicle service industry.

Recent Developments: For the year ended Dec 31 2012, net income increased 22.3% to US$30.0 million from US$24.5 million in the prior year. Revenues were US$791.2 million, up 4.7% from US$755.7 million the year before. Operating income was US$51.9 million versus US$38.4 million in the prior year, an increase of 35.0%. Direct operating expenses rose 3.3% to US$575.9 million from US$557.4 million in the comparable period the year before. Indirect operating expenses increased 2.2% to US$163.4 million from US$159.9 million in the equivalent prior-year period.

Prospects: Our evaluation of Myers Industries Inc. as of Apr. 7, 2013 is the result of our systematic analysis on three basic characteristics: earnings strength, relative valuation, and recent stock price movement. The company has generated a negative trend in earnings per share over the past 5 quarters. However, while recent estimates for the company have been lowered by analysts, MYE has posted results that fell short of analysts expectations. Based on operating earnings yield, the company is undervalued when compared to all of the companies in our coverage universe. Share price changes over the past year indicates that MYE will perform well over the near term.

Financial Data

(US$ in Thousands)	12/31/2012	12/31/2011	12/31/2010	12/31/2009	12/31/2008	12/31/2007	12/31/2006	12/31/2005
Earnings Per Share	0.88	0.71	(1.21)	(0.02)	(1.26)	1.55	(1.97)	0.76
Cash Flow Per Share	1.80	1.86	1.29	2.05	1.75	2.76	2.33	1.94
Tang Book Value Per Share	4.27	4.31	4.31	3.57	3.43	3.34	3.21	1.83
Dividends Per Share	0.320	0.280	0.260	0.240	0.240	0.498	0.205	0.200
Dividend Payout %	36.36	39.44	...	...	...	32.10	...	26.32
Income Statement								
Total Revenue	791,188	755,654	737,618	701,834	867,830	918,793	779,984	903,679
EBITDA	84,863	72,623	(10,266)	53,405	4,862	110,278	89,135	91,988
Depn & Amortn	33,007	34,214	33,550	36,268	40,346	37,727	28,213	35,997
Income Before Taxes	47,341	33,687	(51,021)	8,833	(46,993)	57,051	45,074	40,407
Income Taxes	17,379	9,182	(8,187)	1,838	(768)	20,103	16,364	13,851
Net Income	29,962	24,505	(42,834)	(683)	(44,493)	54,736	(69,024)	26,556
Average Shares	34,109	34,743	35,304	35,266	35,211	35,249	35,044	34,724
Balance Sheet								
Current Assets	239,596	218,452	213,847	206,548	232,648	277,809	307,523	284,328
Total Assets	484,856	428,757	432,395	509,966	568,900	697,552	661,983	760,007
Current Liabilities	114,477	110,656	106,331	169,025	96,970	158,475	134,727	141,242
Long-Term Obligations	92,814	73,725	83,530	38,890	169,546	167,254	198,275	249,524
Total Liabilities	254,834	222,617	220,590	251,968	316,061	380,282	381,325	420,606
Stockholders' Equity	230,022	206,140	211,805	257,998	252,839	317,270	280,659	339,401
Shares Outstanding	33,480	33,420	35,315	35,286	35,235	35,180	35,067	34,806
Statistical Record								
Return on Assets %	6.54	5.69	N.M.	N.M.	N.M.	8.05	N.M.	3.44
Return on Equity %	13.70	11.73	N.M.	N.M.	N.M.	18.31	N.M.	7.75
EBITDA Margin %	10.73	9.61	N.M.	7.61	0.56	12.00	11.43	10.18
Net Margin %	3.79	3.24	N.M.	N.M.	N.M.	5.96	N.M.	2.94
Asset Turnover	1.73	1.75	1.57	1.30	1.37	1.35	1.10	1.17
Current Ratio	2.09	1.97	2.01	1.22	2.40	1.75	2.28	2.01
Debt to Equity	0.40	0.36	0.39	0.15	0.67	0.53	0.71	0.74
Price Range	17.88-12.36	13.56-8.77	11.44-6.34	11.00-2.91	14.63-5.01	22.55-13.57	18.62-14.24	14.70-9.36
P/E Ratio	20.32-14.05	19.10-12.35	...	...	...	14.55-8.75	...	19.34-12.32
Average Yield %	2.10	2.61	2.83	2.85	2.19	2.52	1.26	1.59

Address: 1293 South Main Street, Akron, OH 44301 **Telephone:** 330-253-5592	**Web Site:** www.myersindustries.com **Officers:** Richard P. Johnston - Chairman John C. Orr - President, Chief Executive Officer	**Auditors:** KPMG LLP **Investor Contact:** 330-253-5592 **Transfer Agents:** Computershare Investor Services, Canton, MA

NABORS INDUSTRIES LTD.

Exchange	Symbol	Price	52Wk Range	Yield	P/E
NYS	NBR	$16.22 (3/28/2013)	18.00-12.65	N/A	28.96

*7 Year Price Score 56.54 *NYSE Composite Index=100 *12 Month Price Score 101.25

Interim Earnings (Per Share)

Qtr.	Mar	Jun	Sep	Dec
2008	0.81	0.67	0.73	(0.28)
2009	0.44	(0.68)	0.10	(0.16)
2010	0.14	0.15	(0.14)	0.18
2011	0.28	0.65	0.25	(0.36)
2012	0.46	(0.25)	0.26	0.09

Interim Dividends (Per Share)

No Dividends Paid

Valuation Analysis		Institutional Holding	
Forecast EPS	$1.15	No of Institutions	
	(04/06/2013)	548	
Market Cap	$4.7 Billion	Shares	
Book Value	$6.0 Billion	256,757,120	
Price/Book	0.78	% Held	
Price/Sales	0.70	78.88	

Business Summary: Production & Extraction (MIC: 9.1.1 SIC: 1381 NAIC: 213111)

Nabors Industries is a holding company. Through its subsidiaries, Co. is a land drilling contractor and land well-servicing and workover contractor. As of Dec 31 2011, Co. marketed about 499 land drilling rigs for oil and gas land drilling operations in the U.S. Lower 48 states, Alaska, Canada, South America, Mexico, the Middle East, the Far East, the South Pacific, Russia and Africa; marketed approximately 581 and 174 rigs for land well-servicing and workover work in the U.S. and Canada, respectively; and a provider of offshore platform workover and drilling rigs, with 39 rigs, 12 jackup, and four barge rigs marketed in the U.S., including the Gulf of Mexico, and international markets.

Recent Developments: For the year ended Dec 31 2012, income from continuing operations decreased 30.1% to US$239.1 million from US$342.2 million a year earlier. Net income decreased 32.7% to US$164.7 million from US$244.7 million in the prior year. Revenues were US$6.75 billion, up 10.0% from US$6.14 billion the year before. Direct operating expenses rose 18.7% to US$4.48 billion from US$3.78 billion in the comparable period the year before. Indirect operating expenses increased 6.4% to US$1.99 billion from US$1.87 billion in the equivalent prior-year period.

Prospects: Our evaluation of Nabors Industries Ltd. as of Apr. 7, 2013 is the result of our systematic analysis on three basic characteristics: earnings strength, relative valuation, and recent stock price movement. The company has generated a negative trend in earnings per share over the past 5 quarters. However, while recent estimates for the company have been lowered by analysts, NBR has posted better than expected results. Based on operating earnings yield, the company is undervalued when compared to all of the companies in our coverage universe. Share price changes over the past year indicates that NBR will perform in line with the market over the near term.

Financial Data
(US$ in Thousands)	12/31/2012	12/31/2011	12/31/2010	12/31/2009	12/31/2008	12/31/2007	12/31/2006	12/31/2005
Earnings Per Share	0.56	0.83	0.33	(0.30)	1.93	3.25	3.40	2.00
Cash Flow Per Share	5.37	5.07	3.88	5.71	5.18	4.91	5.12	3.30
Tang Book Value Per Share	19.08	17.93	17.17	17.59	15.96	14.84	11.46	10.83
Income Statement								
Total Revenue	6,751,390	6,136,938	4,215,540	3,503,431	5,303,788	4,940,681	4,942,714	3,551,009
EBITDA	1,592,526	1,750,307	1,226,211	803,684	1,561,482	1,774,606	2,018,153	1,288,376
Depn & Amortn	1,066,291	1,005,905	871,121	773,852	668,238	585,573	500,673	369,579
Income Before Taxes	274,683	487,769	82,046	(235,116)	801,624	1,135,331	1,470,919	873,950
Income Taxes	32,628	142,605	(24,814)	(149,228)	250,451	239,664	450,183	225,255
Net Income	164,034	243,679	94,695	(85,546)	551,173	930,691	1,020,736	648,695
Average Shares	292,323	292,484	289,996	283,326	285,285	286,606	299,827	324,378
Balance Sheet								
Current Assets	3,132,857	3,088,314	2,612,930	2,176,664	2,166,593	2,205,112	2,504,856	2,617,308
Total Assets	12,656,022	12,912,140	11,646,569	10,644,690	10,467,982	10,103,382	9,142,303	7,230,407
Current Liabilities	1,132,382	1,802,562	2,154,380	608,622	1,128,859	1,494,132	854,360	1,352,456
Long-Term Obligations	4,379,336	4,348,490	3,064,126	3,940,605	3,887,711	3,306,433	4,004,074	1,251,751
Total Liabilities	6,641,905	7,255,137	6,249,219	5,477,034	5,775,863	5,589,261	5,605,650	3,472,267
Stockholders' Equity	6,014,117	5,657,003	5,397,350	5,167,656	4,692,119	4,514,121	3,536,653	3,758,140
Shares Outstanding	290,399	287,628	285,620	284,501	282,929	279,336	276,993	315,394
Statistical Record								
Return on Assets %	1.28	1.98	0.85	N.M.	5.34	9.67	12.47	9.91
Return on Equity %	2.80	4.41	1.79	N.M.	11.94	23.12	27.99	19.40
EBITDA Margin %	23.59	28.52	29.09	22.94	29.44	35.92	40.83	36.28
Net Margin %	2.43	3.97	2.25	N.M.	10.39	18.84	20.65	18.27
Asset Turnover	0.53	0.50	0.38	0.33	0.51	0.51	0.60	0.54
Current Ratio	2.77	1.71	1.21	3.58	1.92	1.48	2.93	1.94
Debt to Equity	0.73	0.77	0.57	0.76	0.83	0.73	1.13	0.33
Price Range	22.31-12.65	32.06-11.74	26.87-15.64	23.46-8.50	49.77-10.22	36.08-26.42	41.16-27.69	39.44-23.50
P/E Ratio	39.84-22.59	38.63-14.14	81.42-47.39	...	25.79-5.30	11.10-8.13	12.10-8.14	19.72-11.75

Address: Crown House, Second Floor, 4 Par-la-Ville Road, Hamilton, HM08 Telephone: 441-292-1510	Web Site: www.nabors.com Officers: Anthony G. Petrello - Deputy Chairman, President, Chief Executive Officer, Chief Operating Officer Robert Clark Wood - Principal Accounting Officer, Principal Financial Officer	Auditors: PricewaterhouseCoopers LLP Investor Contact: 713-874-0035 Transfer Agents: Computershare Trust Company, N.A., Providence, RI

NACCO INDUSTRIES INC.

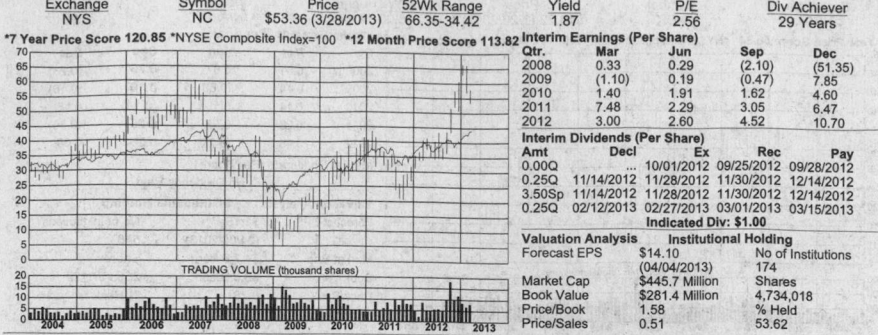

Exchange	Symbol	Price	52Wk Range	Yield	P/E	Div Achiever
NYS	NC	$53.36 (3/28/2013)	66.35-34.42	1.87	2.56	29 Years

*7 Year Price Score 120.85 *NYSE Composite Index=100 *12 Month Price Score 113.82

Interim Earnings (Per Share)

Qtr.	Mar	Jun	Sep	Dec
2008	0.33	0.29	(2.10)	(51.35)
2009	(1.10)	0.19	(0.47)	7.85
2010	1.40	1.91	1.62	4.60
2011	7.48	2.29	3.05	6.47
2012	3.00	2.60	4.52	10.70

Interim Dividends (Per Share)

Amt	Decl	Ex	Rec	Pay
0.00Q	...	10/01/2012	09/25/2012	09/28/2012
0.25Q	11/14/2012	11/28/2012	11/30/2012	12/14/2012
3.50Sp	11/14/2012	11/28/2012	11/30/2012	12/14/2012
0.25Q	02/12/2013	02/27/2013	03/01/2013	03/15/2013

Indicated Div: $1.00

Valuation Analysis

Forecast EPS	$14.10 (04/04/2013)
Market Cap	$445.7 Million
Book Value	$281.4 Million
Price/Book	1.58
Price/Sales	0.51

Institutional Holding

No of Institutions	174
Shares	4,734,018
% Held	53.62

Business Summary: Household Appliances, Electronics & Goods (MIC: 1.5.1 SIC: 3639 NAIC: 443111)

NACCO Industries is a holding company. Through its subsidiaries, Co. is engaged in the businesses of lift trucks, small appliances, specialty retail and mining. Co.'s NMHG Holding Co. subsidiary designs, engineers, manufactures, sells and services lift trucks and aftermarket parts. Co.'s Hamilton Beach Brands, Inc. subsidiary is a designer, marketer and distributor of small electric household appliances, and commercial products. Co.'s The Kitchen Collection, LLC subsidiary is a retailer of kitchenware and gourmet foods. Co.'s subsidiary, The North American Coal Corporation and its affiliated coal companies, mine and market coal as fuel for power generation and provide mining services.

Recent Developments: For the year ended Dec 31 2012, income from continuing operations decreased 46.9% to US$42.2 million from US$79.5 million a year earlier. Net income decreased 32.9% to US$108.7 million from US$162.1 million in the prior year. Revenues were US$873.4 million, up 10.5% from US$790.4 million the year before. Operating income was US$67.5 million versus US$64.1 million in the prior year, an increase of 5.3%. Direct operating expenses rose 11.5% to US$647.5 million from US$580.8 million in the comparable period the year before. Indirect operating expenses increased 8.9% to US$158.4 million from US$145.5 million in the equivalent prior-year period.

Prospects: Our evaluation of NACCO Industries Inc. as of Apr. 7, 2013 is the result of our systematic analysis on three basic characteristics: earnings strength, relative valuation, and recent stock price movement. The company has generated a negative trend in earnings per share over the past 5 quarters. Because the company lacks sufficient analyst estimate data, we place greater weight on the historical EPS trend as the measure of earnings strength. Based on operating earnings yield, the company is undervalued when compared to all of the companies in our coverage universe. Share price changes over the past year indicates that NC will perform very well over the near term.

Financial Data

(US$ in Thousands)	12/31/2012	12/31/2011	12/31/2010	12/31/2009	12/31/2008	12/31/2007	12/31/2006	12/31/2005
Earnings Per Share	20.82	19.28	9.53	6.47	(52.84)	10.80	12.89	7.60
Cash Flow Per Share	17.02	18.51	7.58	18.94	0.59	9.88	21.07	9.15
Tang Book Value Per Share	25.33	61.89	46.49	40.16	35.00	45.86	34.12	23.49
Dividends Per Share	5.378	2.120	2.085	2.067	2.045	1.980	1.905	1.847
Dividend Payout %	25.83	11.00	21.88	31.96	...	18.33	14.78	24.31
Income Statement								
Total Revenue	873,400	3,331,200	2,687,500	2,310,600	3,680,300	3,602,700	3,349,000	3,157,400
EBITDA	32,500	231,000	124,600	71,700	(372,200)	152,800	179,600	137,600
Depn & Amortn	15,200	45,600	48,700	50,700	57,600	57,600	59,500	60,400
Income Before Taxes	11,200	160,900	51,100	(8,000)	(462,800)	66,500	78,300	29,700
Income Taxes	15,800	51,700	17,400	20,500	18,600	23,100	27,800	13,100
Net Income	108,700	162,100	79,500	31,100	(437,600)	89,300	106,200	62,500
Average Shares	8,414	8,408	8,344	8,290	8,281	8,272	8,242	8,226
Balance Sheet								
Current Assets	486,800	1,375,100	1,214,200	967,600	1,141,200	1,434,800	1,153,800	1,073,700
Total Assets	776,300	1,801,400	1,658,300	1,488,700	1,687,900	2,428,200	2,156,300	2,094,000
Current Liabilities	227,200	891,200	663,500	479,300	675,300	856,500	751,000	704,700
Long-Term Obligations	135,400	129,100	355,300	377,600	400,500	439,500	359,900	406,200
Total Liabilities	494,900	1,225,200	1,210,900	1,092,100	1,331,200	1,536,100	1,363,200	1,390,700
Stockholders' Equity	281,400	576,200	447,400	396,600	356,700	892,100	793,100	703,300
Shares Outstanding	8,352	8,373	8,333	8,293	8,285	8,268	8,237	8,226
Statistical Record								
Return on Assets %	8.41	9.37	5.05	1.96	N.M.	3.90	5.00	3.02
Return on Equity %	25.28	31.67	18.84	8.26	N.M.	10.60	14.19	8.98
EBITDA Margin %	3.72	6.93	4.64	3.10	N.M.	4.24	5.36	4.36
Net Margin %	12.45	4.87	2.96	1.35	N.M.	2.48	3.17	1.98
Asset Turnover	0.68	1.93	1.71	1.45	1.78	1.57	1.58	1.53
Current Ratio	2.14	1.54	1.83	2.02	1.69	1.68	1.54	1.52
Debt to Equity	0.48	0.22	0.79	0.95	1.12	0.49	0.45	0.58
Price Range	60.69-31.20	43.53-20.73	41.34-15.66	24.58-4.80	41.86-9.68	60.32-31.39	59.17-41.54	42.44-32.91
P/E Ratio	2.91-1.50	2.26-1.08	4.34-1.64	3.80-0.74	...	5.59-2.91	4.59-3.22	5.58-4.33
Average Yield %	13.03	6.67	7.06	13.87	7.32	4.36	3.89	4.89

Address: 5875 Landerbrook Drive, Suite 220, Cleveland, OH 44124-4069
Telephone: 440-229-5151

Web Site: www.nacco.com
Officers: Alfred M. Rankin - Chairman, President, Chief Executive Officer Charles A. Bittenbender - Vice President, Secretary, General Counsel

Auditors: Ernst & Young LLP
Investor Contact: 440-449-9669
Transfer Agents: Computershare, Canton, MA

NATIONAL FUEL GAS CO. (NJ)

Exchange	Symbol	Price	52Wk Range	Yield	P/E	Div Achiever
NYS	NFG	$61.35 (3/28/2013)	61.35-42.17	2.38	22.56	41 Years

*7 Year Price Score 93.70   *NYSE Composite Index=100   *12 Month Price Score 105.29

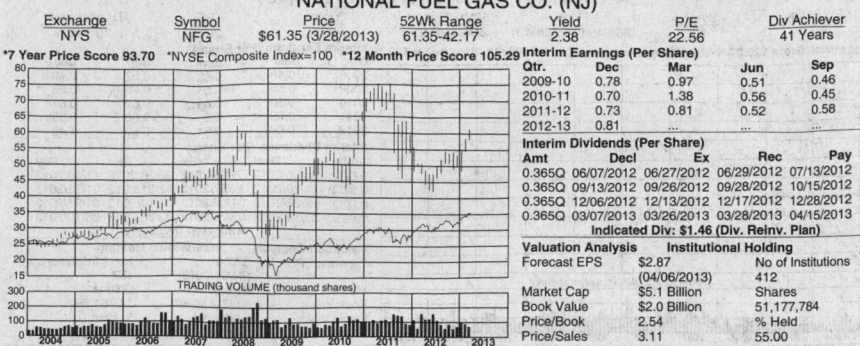

Interim Earnings (Per Share)

Qtr.	Dec	Mar	Jun	Sep
2009-10	0.78	0.97	0.51	0.46
2010-11	0.70	1.38	0.56	0.45
2011-12	0.73	0.81	0.52	0.58
2012-13	0.81	...	...	...

Interim Dividends (Per Share)

Amt	Decl	Ex	Rec	Pay
0.365Q	06/07/2012	06/27/2012	06/29/2012	07/13/2012
0.365Q	09/13/2012	09/26/2012	09/28/2012	10/15/2012
0.365Q	12/06/2012	12/13/2012	12/17/2012	12/28/2012
0.365Q	03/07/2013	03/26/2013	03/28/2013	04/15/2013

Indicated Div: $1.46 (Div. Reinv. Plan)

Valuation Analysis	Institutional Holding
Forecast EPS $2.87	No of Institutions
(04/06/2013)	412
Market Cap $5.1 Billion	Shares
Book Value $2.0 Billion	51,177,784
Price/Book 2.54	% Held
Price/Sales 3.11	55.00

Business Summary: Gas Utilities (MIC: 3.3.1 SIC: 4924 NAIC: 221210)

National Fuel Gas is a holding company. Through its subsidiaries, Co. operates in four segments: Utility, which sells natural gas to retail customers and provides natural gas transportation services; Pipeline and Storage, which provides interstate natural gas transportation and storage services; Exploration and Production, which engages in exploration for, and development and purchase of, natural gas and oil reserves; and Energy Marketing, which markets natural gas to industrial, wholesale, commercial, public authority and residential customers. At Sept. 30, 2012, Co. had proved developed and undeveloped reserves of 42.9 million barrels of oil and 988.43 billion cubic feet of natural gas.

Recent Developments: For the quarter ended Dec 31 2012, net income increased 11.9% to US$67.9 million from US$60.7 million in the year-earlier quarter. Revenues were US$452.9 million, up 4.7% from US$432.4 million the year before. Operating income was US$131.2 million versus US$118.4 million in the prior-year quarter, an increase of 10.8%. Direct operating expenses declined 1.1% to US$229.7 million from US$232.3 million in the comparable period the year before. Indirect operating expenses increased 12.5% to US$92.0 million from US$81.8 million in the equivalent prior-year period.

Prospects: Our evaluation of National Fuel Gas Co. as of Apr. 7, 2013 is the result of our systematic analysis on three basic characteristics: earnings strength, relative valuation, and recent stock price movement. The company has enjoyed a very positive trend in earnings per share over the past 5 quarters and while recent estimates for the company have been raised by analysts, NFG has posted better than expected results. Based on operating earnings yield, the company is about fairly valued when compared to all of the companies in our coverage universe. Share price changes over the past year indicates that NFG will perform in line with the market over the near term.

Financial Data

(US$ in Thousands)	3 Mos	09/30/2012	09/30/2011	09/30/2010	09/30/2009	09/30/2008	09/30/2007	09/30/2006
Earnings Per Share	2.72	2.63	3.09	2.73	1.25	3.18	3.96	1.61
Cash Flow Per Share	8.72	7.93	8.21	5.65	7.65	5.85	4.74	5.61
Tang Book Value Per Share	24.09	23.46	22.78	21.19	19.41	19.87	19.12	16.87
Dividends Per Share	1.450	1.440	1.400	1.360	1.320	1.270	1.220	1.180
Dividend Payout %	53.31	54.75	45.31	49.82	105.60	39.94	30.81	73.29
Income Statement								
Total Revenue	452,854	1,626,853	1,778,842	1,760,503	2,057,852	2,400,361	2,039,566	2,311,659
EBITDA	204,954	724,712	674,395	635,898	403,012	664,124	572,237	458,515
Depn & Amortn	72,331	271,530	226,527	191,809	173,410	170,623	170,803	179,615
Income Before Taxes	111,493	370,631	372,663	353,872	148,462	430,347	328,509	210,594
Income Taxes	43,549	150,554	164,381	137,227	51,120	167,922	131,813	76,086
Net Income	67,944	220,077	258,402	225,913	100,708	268,728	337,455	138,091
Average Shares	84,006	83,739	83,670	82,660	80,628	84,474	85,301	86,028
Balance Sheet								
Current Assets	394,369	355,576	385,312	775,377	776,970	499,478	554,138	519,453
Total Assets	6,108,197	5,935,142	5,284,742	5,105,625	4,769,129	4,130,187	3,888,412	3,734,331
Current Liabilities	772,899	734,479	528,618	524,324	318,507	374,571	439,346	290,345
Long-Term Obligations	1,149,000	1,149,000	899,000	1,049,000	1,249,000	999,000	799,000	1,095,675
Total Liabilities	4,091,987	3,975,047	3,392,857	3,359,654	3,179,893	2,526,588	2,258,293	2,290,769
Stockholders' Equity	2,016,210	1,960,095	1,891,885	1,745,971	1,589,236	1,603,599	1,630,119	1,443,562
Shares Outstanding	83,482	83,330	82,812	82,075	80,499	79,120	83,461	83,402
Statistical Record								
Return on Assets %	3.83	3.91	4.97	4.58	2.26	6.68	8.85	3.70
Return on Equity %	11.55	11.40	14.21	13.55	6.31	16.57	21.96	10.33
EBITDA Margin %	45.26	44.55	37.91	36.12	19.58	27.67	28.06	19.83
Net Margin %	15.00	13.53	14.53	12.83	4.89	11.20	16.55	5.97
Asset Turnover	0.28	0.29	0.34	0.36	0.46	0.60	0.54	0.62
Current Ratio	0.51	0.48	0.73	1.48	2.44	1.33	1.26	1.79
Debt to Equity	0.57	0.59	0.48	0.60	0.79	0.62	0.49	0.76
Price Range	55.75-42.17	63.58-42.17	75.40-48.68	54.32-42.98	47.83-27.06	61.93-39.55	47.76-35.59	38.78-29.53
P/E Ratio	20.50-15.50	24.17-16.03	24.40-15.75	19.90-15.74	38.26-21.65	19.47-12.44	12.06-8.99	24.09-18.34
Average Yield %	2.93	2.85	2.13	2.78	3.79	2.57	2.89	3.49

Address: 6363 Main Street, Williamsville, NY 14221 Telephone: 716-857-7000	Web Site: www.nationalfuelgas.com Officers: David F. Smith - Chairman, Chief Executive Officer Ronald J. Tanski - President, Chief Operating Officer, Chief Executive Officer	Auditors: PricewaterhouseCoopers LLP Investor Contact: 716-857-6987 Transfer Agents: Wells Fargo Shareowner Services, Saint Paul, MN

NATIONAL HEALTH INVESTORS, INC.

Exchange	Symbol	Price	52Wk Range	Yield	P/E	Div Achiever
NYS	NHI	$65.45 (3/28/2013)	66.91-47.29	4.25	20.08	10 Years

*7 Year Price Score 129.07 *NYSE Composite Index=100 *12 Month Price Score 109.40

Interim Earnings (Per Share)

Qtr.	Mar	Jun	Sep	Dec
2008	0.48	0.53	0.57	0.48
2009	0.55	0.55	0.63	0.58
2010	0.58	0.69	0.62	0.61
2011	0.69	0.90	0.68	0.65
2012	0.66	0.61	0.52	1.48

Interim Dividends (Per Share)

Amt	Decl	Ex	Rec	Pay
0.67Q	08/06/2012	09/26/2012	09/28/2012	11/09/2012
0.67Q	11/29/2012	12/27/2012	12/31/2012	01/31/2013
0.22Q	12/28/2012	01/08/2013	01/10/2013	01/31/2013
0.695Q	02/14/2013	03/26/2013	03/28/2013	05/10/2013

Indicated Div: $2.78

Valuation Analysis

		Institutional Holding	
Forecast EPS	$2.74 (04/05/2013)	No of Institutions	187
Market Cap	$1.8 Billion	Shares	14,781,352
Book Value	$457.2 Million	% Held	47.98
Price/Book	3.99		
Price/Sales	18.81		

Business Summary: REITs (MIC: 5.3.1 SIC: 6798 NAIC: 525930)

National Health Investors is a real estate investment trust which invests in income-producing health care properties primarily in the long-term care and senior housing industries. Co.'s investments include assisted living facilities, senior living campuses, independent living and hospitals. At Dec 31 2012, Co.'s continuing operations consisted of investments in real estate and mortgage notes receivable in 134 health care facilities located in 25 states consisting of 41 assisted living facilities, six senior living campuses, three independent living facilities, 78 skilled nursing facilities, two medical office buildings, four independent living and other notes receivable.

Recent Developments: For the year ended Dec 31 2012, income from continuing operations increased 2.0% to US$74.7 million from US$73.2 million a year earlier. Net income increased 12.0% to US$90.9 million from US$81.1 million in the prior year. Revenues were US$97.0 million, up 11.2% from US$87.2 million the year before. Revenues from property income rose 11.9% to US$85.1 million from US$76.1 million in the corresponding earlier year.

Prospects: Our evaluation of National Health Investors Inc. as of Apr. 7, 2013 is the result of our systematic analysis on three basic characteristics: earnings strength, relative valuation, and recent stock price movement. The company has enjoyed a very positive trend in earnings per share over the past 5 quarters. Because the company lacks sufficient analyst estimate data, we place greater weight on the historical EPS trend as the measure of earnings strength. Based on operating earnings yield, the company is about fairly valued when compared to all of the companies in our coverage universe. Share price changes over the past year indicates that NHI will perform well over the near term.

Financial Data

(US$ in Thousands)	12/31/2012	12/31/2011	12/31/2010	12/31/2009	12/31/2008	12/31/2007	12/31/2006	12/31/2005
Earnings Per Share	3.26	2.92	2.50	2.32	2.07	3.47	2.49	1.96
Cash Flow Per Share	3.09	2.77	2.80	2.51	2.42	2.40	2.08	2.13
Tang Book Value Per Share	16.41	15.98	15.98	15.73	15.58	16.08	15.55	15.27
Dividends Per Share	2.640	2.715	2.360	2.300	2.420	2.850	2.370	1.800
Dividend Payout %	80.98	92.98	94.40	99.14	116.91	82.13	95.18	91.84
Income Statement								
Total Revenue	96,953	82,702	78,396	64,221	63,005	62,313	150,724	157,382
EBITDA	86,677	88,445	74,808	65,516	60,344	83,726	68,058	62,514
Depn & Amortn	16,981	11,992	11,203	8,621	7,943	11,751	12,026	12,855
Income Before Taxes	69,696	72,760	62,137	58,136	55,451	79,041	62,921	53,708
Net Income	90,898	81,132	69,421	64,229	57,510	96,435	69,228	54,408
Average Shares	27,838	27,792	27,732	27,618	27,731	27,783	27,778	27,830
Balance Sheet								
Current Assets	21,542	25,776	8,063	47,907	101,976	77,255	183,898	138,050
Total Assets	705,981	579,563	509,341	459,360	457,106	500,732	595,464	587,932
Current Liabilities	33,350	37,105	27,615	23,863	23,389	44,945	50,138	42,369
Long-Term Obligations	203,250	97,300	37,765	...	3,987	9,512	113,492	117,453
Total Liabilities	248,799	136,078	66,841	24,748	27,491	54,594	163,793	162,964
Stockholders' Equity	457,182	443,485	442,500	434,612	429,615	446,138	431,671	424,968
Shares Outstanding	27,857	27,751	27,689	27,629	27,580	27,752	27,752	27,830
Statistical Record								
Return on Assets %	14.10	14.90	14.33	14.02	11.98	17.59	11.70	8.92
Return on Equity %	20.13	18.31	15.83	14.86	13.10	21.97	16.16	12.79
EBITDA Margin %	89.40	106.94	95.42	102.02	95.78	134.36	45.15	39.72
Net Margin %	93.75	98.10	88.55	100.01	91.28	154.76	45.93	34.57
Asset Turnover	0.15	0.15	0.16	0.14	0.13	0.11	0.25	0.26
Current Ratio	0.65	0.69	0.29	2.01	4.36	1.72	3.67	3.26
Debt to Equity	0.44	0.22	0.09	...	0.01	0.02	0.26	0.28
Price Range	57.14-43.70	49.19-38.03	48.31-32.03	37.64-21.77	34.60-18.62	35.50-27.20	33.50-23.48	30.90-25.28
P/E Ratio	17.53-13.40	16.85-13.02	19.32-12.81	16.22-9.38	16.71-9.00	10.23-7.84	13.45-9.43	15.77-12.90
Average Yield %	5.18	6.04	5.84	7.84	8.16	9.03	8.60	6.61

Address: 222 Robert Rose Drive, Murfreesboro, TN 37129
Telephone: 615-890-9100

Web Site: www.nhireit.com
Officers: W. Andrew Adams - Chairman, Chief Executive Officer, Acting Chief Financial Officer J. Justin Hutchens - President, Chief Executive Officer

Auditors: BDO USA, LLP
Investor Contact: 615-890-9100
Transfer Agents: Computershare Trust Company, N.A. Providence, RI

NATIONAL OILWELL VARCO INC

Exchange	Symbol	Price	52Wk Range	Yield	P/E
NYS	NOV	$70.75 (3/28/2013)	84.83-60.00	0.73	12.14

*7 Year Price Score 117.27 *NYSE Composite Index=100 *12 Month Price Score 87.94

Interim Earnings (Per Share)

Qtr.	Mar	Jun	Sep	Dec
2008	1.11	1.04	1.31	1.42
2009	1.13	0.53	0.92	0.94
2010	1.01	0.96	0.96	1.05
2011	0.96	1.13	1.25	1.35
2012	1.42	1.42	1.43	1.55

Interim Dividends (Per Share)

Amt	Decl	Ex	Rec	Pay
0.12Q	05/17/2012	06/13/2012	06/15/2012	06/29/2012
0.12Q	08/16/2012	09/12/2012	09/14/2012	09/28/2012
0.13Q	11/15/2012	12/05/2012	12/07/2012	12/21/2012
0.13Q	02/21/2013	03/13/2013	03/15/2013	03/29/2013

Indicated Div: $0.52

Valuation Analysis

		Institutional Holding	
Forecast EPS	$6.00	No of Institutions	
	(04/06/2013)	1114	
Market Cap	$30.2 Billion	Shares	394,929,760
Book Value	$20.2 Billion	% Held	85.53
Price/Book	1.49		
Price/Sales	1.51		

TRADING VOLUME (thousand shares)

Business Summary: Equipment & Services (MIC: 9.1.3 SIC: 3533 NAIC: 333132)

National Oilwell Varco is a provider of equipment and components used in oil and gas drilling and production operations, oilfield services, and supply chain integration services to the upstream oil and gas industry. Co.'s segments are: Rig Technology, which designs, manufactures, sells and services systems for the drilling, completion, and servicing of oil and gas wells; Petroleum Services & Supplies, which provides consumable goods and services used to drill, complete, remediate and workover oil and gas wells and service drill pipe, casing, and flowlines, among others; and Distribution & Transmission, which provides pipe, maintenance, repair and operating supplies and spare parts.

Recent Developments: For the year ended Dec 31 2012, net income increased 25.1% to US$2.48 billion from US$1.99 billion in the prior year. Revenues were US$20.04 billion, up 36.7% from US$14.66 billion the year before. Operating income was US$3.56 billion versus US$2.94 billion in the prior year, an increase of 21.1%. Direct operating expenses rose 44.7% to US$14.70 billion from US$10.16 billion in the comparable period the year before. Indirect operating expenses increased 14.2% to US$1.78 billion from US$1.56 billion in the equivalent prior-year period.

Prospects: Our evaluation of National-Oilwell Inc. as of Apr. 7, 2013 is the result of our systematic analysis on three basic characteristics: earnings strength, relative valuation, and recent stock price movement. The company has managed to produce a neutral trend in earnings per share over the past 5 quarters and while recent estimates for the company have remained steady, NOV has posted better than expected results. Based on operating earnings yield, the company is undervalued when compared to all of the companies in our coverage universe. Share price changes over the past year indicates that NOV will perform poorly over the near term.

Financial Data

(US$ in Thousands)	12/31/2012	12/31/2011	12/31/2010	12/31/2009	12/31/2008	12/31/2007	12/31/2006	12/31/2005
Earnings Per Share	5.83	4.70	3.98	3.52	4.90	3.76	1.94	0.91
Cash Flow Per Share	1.45	5.08	3.70	5.04	5.76	3.35	3.47	0.25
Tang Book Value Per Share	19.50	17.45	13.90	10.93	7.43	9.65	5.91	4.20
Dividends Per Share	0.490	0.450	0.410	1.100	...	...	...	...
Dividend Payout %	8.40	9.57	10.30	31.25				
Income Statement								
Total Revenue	20,041,000	14,658,000	12,156,000	12,712,000	13,431,400	9,789,000	7,025,800	4,644,500
EBITDA	3,809,000	3,177,000	2,660,000	2,454,000	3,163,500	2,179,700	1,099,000	561,000
Depn & Amortn	323,000	279,000	262,000	249,000	221,900	153,100	19,200	83,000
Income Before Taxes	3,447,000	2,876,000	2,361,000	2,161,000	2,918,900	2,028,900	1,049,200	430,000
Income Taxes	1,022,000	937,000	738,000	735,000	992,800	675,800	355,700	138,900
Net Income	2,491,000	1,994,000	1,667,000	1,469,000	1,952,000	1,337,100	684,000	286,900
Average Shares	427,000	424,000	419,000	417,000	398,700	355,400	353,600	316,600
Balance Sheet								
Current Assets	15,678,000	12,110,000	10,535,000	9,598,000	9,657,200	7,593,800	4,965,600	2,998,200
Total Assets	31,484,000	25,515,000	23,050,000	21,532,000	21,478,700	12,114,900	9,019,300	6,678,500
Current Liabilities	5,649,000	5,416,000	4,536,000	4,174,000	5,623,500	4,026,700	2,665,200	1,187,200
Long-Term Obligations	3,148,000	159,000	514,000	876,000	869,600	737,900	834,700	835,600
Total Liabilities	11,245,000	7,896,000	7,302,000	7,419,000	8,851,100	5,453,500	3,995,800	2,484,300
Stockholders' Equity	20,239,000	17,619,000	15,748,000	14,113,000	12,627,600	6,661,400	5,023,500	4,194,200
Shares Outstanding	426,928	423,900	421,141	418,451	417,350	356,867	351,143	348,724
Statistical Record								
Return on Assets %	8.72	8.21	7.48	6.83	11.59	12.65	8.71	6.19
Return on Equity %	13.12	11.95	11.17	10.99	20.18	22.89	14.84	10.45
EBITDA Margin %	19.01	21.67	21.88	19.30	23.55	22.27	15.64	12.08
Net Margin %	12.43	13.60	13.71	11.56	14.53	13.66	9.74	6.18
Asset Turnover	0.70	0.60	0.55	0.59	0.80	0.93	0.90	1.00
Current Ratio	2.78	2.24	2.32	2.30	1.72	1.89	1.86	2.53
Debt to Equity	0.16	0.01	0.03	0.06	0.07	0.11	0.17	0.20
Price Range	87.18-60.00	83.31-50.23	67.25-33.02	49.82-22.35	91.55-17.86	79.28-27.00	38.27-26.04	33.73-16.61
P/E Ratio	14.95-10.29	17.73-10.69	16.90-8.30	14.15-6.35	18.68-3.64	21.09-7.18	19.73-13.42	37.06-18.26
Average Yield %	0.66	0.63	0.91	3.06	...	...	...	...

Address: 7909 Parkwood Circle Drive, Houston, TX 77036-6565 **Telephone:** 713-346-7500	**Web Site:** www.nov.com **Officers:** Merrill A. Miller - Chairman, President, Chief Executive Officer Clay C. Williams - President, Executive Vice President, Senior Vice President, Chief Financial Officer, Chief Operating Officer	**Auditors:** Ernst & Young LLP **Investor Contact:** 713-346-7500 **Transfer Agents:** American Stock Transfer and Trust Company, New York, NY

NATIONAL RETAIL PROPERTIES INC

Exchange	Symbol	Price	52Wk Range	Yield	P/E	Div Achiever
NYS	NNN	$36.17 (3/28/2013)	36.17-26.10	4.34	32.59	23 Years

*7 Year Price Score 114.54 *NYSE Composite Index=100 *12 Month Price Score 103.65

Interim Earnings (Per Share)

Qtr.	Mar	Jun	Sep	Dec
2008	0.43	0.40	0.39	0.34
2009	0.32	0.32	0.26	(0.29)
2010	0.18	0.23	0.23	0.15
2011	0.23	0.23	0.24	0.27
2012	0.23	0.26	0.30	0.32

Interim Dividends (Per Share)

Amt	Decl	Ex	Rec	Pay
0.385Q	04/16/2012	04/26/2012	04/30/2012	05/15/2012
0.395Q	07/16/2012	07/27/2012	07/31/2012	08/15/2012
0.395Q	10/15/2012	10/29/2012	10/31/2012	11/15/2012
0.395Q	01/15/2013	01/29/2013	01/31/2013	02/15/2013

Indicated Div: $1.57 (Div. Reinv. Plan)

Valuation Analysis / **Institutional Holding**

Forecast EPS	$1.16 (04/06/2013)	No of Institutions 325
Market Cap	$4.0 Billion	Shares 106,132,704
Book Value	$2.3 Billion	% Held N/A
Price/Book	1.76	
Price/Sales	12.16	

Business Summary: REITs (MIC: 5.3.1 SIC: 6798 NAIC: 525930)

National Retail Properties is an integrated real estate investment trust. Co.'s assets include real estate assets, mortgages and notes receivable, and commercial mortgage residual interests. Co. acquires, owns, invests in and develops properties that are leased primarily to retail tenants under long-term net leases and are primarily held for investment. As of Dec 31 2012, Co. owned 1,622 properties with an aggregate gross leasable area of 19,168,000 sq. ft., located in 47 states.

Recent Developments: For the year ended Dec 31 2012, income from continuing operations increased 48.6% to US$128.5 million from US$86.5 million a year earlier. Net income increased 53.6% to US$141.9 million from US$92.4 million in the prior year. Revenues were US$331.8 million, up 27.6% from US$259.9 million the year before. Revenues from property income rose 28.3% to US$326.7 million from US$254.5 million in the corresponding earlier year.

Prospects: Our evaluation of National Retail Properties Inc. as of Apr. 7, 2013 is the result of our systematic analysis on three basic characteristics: earnings strength, relative valuation, and recent stock price movement. The company has managed to produce a neutral trend in earnings per share over the past 5 quarters. Because the company lacks sufficient analyst estimate data, we place greater weight on the historical EPS trend as the measure of earnings strength. Based on operating earnings yield, the company is overvalued versus all of the companies in our coverage universe. Share price changes over the past year indicates that NNN will perform in line with the market over the near term.

Financial Data
(US$ in Thousands)

	12/31/2012	12/31/2011	12/31/2010	12/31/2009	12/31/2008	12/31/2007	12/31/2006	12/31/2005
Earnings Per Share	1.11	0.96	0.80	0.60	1.56	2.26	3.05	1.56
Cash Flow Per Share	2.13	2.08	2.27	1.87	3.18	1.96	0.32	0.58
Tang Book Value Per Share	18.01	18.24	17.17	17.86	18.49	18.13	16.05	13.76
Dividends Per Share	1.560	1.530	1.510	1.500	1.480	1.400	1.320	1.300
Dividend Payout %	140.54	159.38	188.75	250.00	94.87	61.95	43.28	83.33
Income Statement								
Total Revenue	331,752	265,793	229,056	231,799	226,516	186,411	150,788	145,177
EBITDA	280,699	229,444	190,193	175,015	190,261	153,738	118,674	106,030
Depn & Amortn	83,096	65,017	55,278	54,332	45,429	32,831	24,316	22,129
Income Before Taxes	117,333	91,093	71,249	59,907	90,097	76,374	52,299	50,014
Income Taxes	(7,086)	779	475	(1,126)	(7,501)	(8,537)	(11,143)	(2,776)
Net Income	142,015	92,325	72,997	54,810	123,082	157,110	182,505	89,400
Average Shares	109,117	88,837	82,849	79,953	74,521	66,407	58,079	54,640
Balance Sheet								
Current Assets	58,416	62,846	61,317	84,892	90,682	121,933	103,535	126,057
Total Assets	3,988,026	3,434,429	2,713,575	2,590,962	2,649,362	2,539,605	1,916,785	1,733,416
Current Liabilities	191,727	80,708	168,342	7,471	34,108	142,714	40,329	181,587
Long-Term Obligations	1,412,592	1,273,509	972,685	987,346	1,026,304	930,270	748,737	698,745
Total Liabilities	1,691,741	1,431,931	1,186,092	1,026,722	1,107,153	1,132,320	820,280	905,329
Stockholders' Equity	2,296,285	2,002,498	1,527,483	1,564,240	1,542,209	1,407,285	1,096,505	828,087
Shares Outstanding	111,554	104,754	83,613	82,427	78,415	72,527	59,823	55,130
Statistical Record								
Return on Assets %	3.82	3.00	2.75	2.09	4.73	7.05	10.00	5.89
Return on Equity %	6.59	5.23	4.72	3.53	8.32	12.55	18.97	11.28
EBITDA Margin %	84.61	86.32	83.03	75.50	83.99	82.47	78.70	73.03
Net Margin %	42.81	34.74	31.87	23.65	54.34	84.28	121.03	61.58
Asset Turnover	0.09	0.09	0.09	0.09	0.09	0.08	0.08	0.10
Current Ratio	0.30	0.78	0.36	11.36	2.66	0.85	2.57	0.69
Debt to Equity	0.62	0.64	0.64	0.63	0.67	0.66	0.68	0.84
Price Range	32.25-26.10	27.30-22.92	27.73-19.45	22.29-12.96	24.57-10.53	26.11-20.77	23.97-18.90	21.53-18.16
P/E Ratio	29.05-23.51	28.44-23.88	34.66-24.31	37.15-21.60	15.75-6.75	11.55-9.19	7.86-6.20	13.80-11.64
Average Yield %	5.42	5.98	6.38	8.28	7.18	5.88	6.10	6.61

Address: 450 South Orange Avenue, Suite 900, Orlando, FL 32801 **Telephone:** 407-265-7348 **Fax:** 407-423-2894	**Web Site:** www.nnnreit.com **Officers:** Craig Macnab - Chairman, Chief Executive Officer Julian E. Whitehurst - President, Chief Operating Officer	**Auditors:** Ernst & Young LLP **Transfer Agents:** American Stock Transfer & Trust Company, Brooklyn, NY

NAVISTAR INTERNATIONAL CORP.

Exchange	Symbol	Price	52Wk Range	Yield	P/E
NYS	NAV	$34.57 (3/28/2013)	40.63-18.51	N/A	N/A

*7 Year Price Score 53.43   *NYSE Composite Index=100   *12 Month Price Score 100.03

Interim Earnings (Per Share)

Qtr.	Jan	Apr	Jul	Oct
2009-10	0.23	0.42	1.83	0.54
2010-11	(0.08)	0.93	18.24	3.60
2011-12	(2.19)	(2.50)	1.22	(40.07)
2012-13	(1.53)	...	...	...

Interim Dividends (Per Share)

No Dividends Paid

Valuation Analysis

Forecast EPS	$-2.80
	(04/05/2013)
Market Cap	$2.8 Billion
Book Value	N/A
Price/Book	N/A
Price/Sales	0.22

Institutional Holding

No of Institutions	241
Shares	95,494,384
% Held	111.21

Business Summary: Autos- Manufacturing (MIC: 1.8.1 SIC: 3711 NAIC: 336211)

Navistar International is a holding company. Through its subsidiaries, Co. is an international manufacturer of International® brand commercial and military trucks, IC Bus brand buses, MaxxForce® brand diesel engines, and recreational vehicles (RV) under the Monaco® RV family of brands, as well as a provider of service parts for all makes of trucks and trailers. Additionally, Co. is a private-label designer and manufacturer of diesel engines for the pickup truck, van, and sport-utility vehicle markets. Co. also provides retail, wholesale, and lease financing of its trucks and parts. Co. operates in four industry segments: Truck, Engine, Parts, and Financial Services.

Recent Developments: For the quarter ended Jan 31 2013, loss from continuing operations was US$99.0 million compared with a loss of US$131.0 million in the year-earlier quarter. Net loss amounted to US$108.0 million versus a net loss of US$140.0 million in the year-earlier quarter. Revenues were US$2.64 billion, down 12.4% from US$3.01 billion the year before. Direct operating expenses declined 13.7% to US$2.29 billion from US$2.65 billion in the comparable period the year before. Indirect operating expenses decreased 22.4% to US$434.0 million from US$559.0 million in the equivalent prior-year period.

Prospects: Our evaluation of Navistar International Corp. as of Apr. 7, 2013 is the result of our systematic analysis on three basic characteristics: earnings strength, relative valuation, and recent stock price movement. The company has produced a positive trend in earnings per share over the past 5 quarters. Because the company lacks sufficient analyst estimate data, we place greater weight on the historical EPS trend as the measure of earnings strength. Based on operating earnings yield, the company is overvalued when compared to all of the companies in our coverage universe. Share price changes over the past year indicates that NAV will perform very poorly over the near term.

Financial Data
(US$ in Millions)

	3 Mos	10/31/2012	10/31/2011	10/31/2010	10/31/2009	10/31/2008	10/31/2007	10/31/2006
Earnings Per Share	(42.88)	(43.56)	22.64	3.05	4.46	1.82	(1.70)	4.12
Cash Flow Per Share	6.95	8.80	12.09	15.44	17.15	15.80	2.52	(3.61)
Income Statement								
Total Revenue	2,637	12,948	13,958	12,145	11,569	14,724	12,295	14,200
EBITDA	18	(596)	937	882	875	957	687	1,052
Depn & Amortn	27	298	299	289	311	368	332	325
Income Before Taxes	(83)	(1,153)	391	340	313	120	(147)	296
Income Taxes	15	1,780	(1,458)	23	37	57	47	94
Net Income	(123)	(3,010)	1,723	223	320	134	(120)	301
Average Shares	80	69	76	73	71	73	70	74
Balance Sheet								
Current Assets	5,416	5,837	7,235	5,835	5,748	5,535	5,445	6,368
Total Assets	8,531	9,102	12,291	9,730	10,027	10,390	11,448	12,830
Current Liabilities	3,899	4,353	4,798	3,589	4,185	3,875	3,991	4,832
Long-Term Obligations	3,526	3,566	3,477	4,238	4,270	5,409	6,083	6,755
Total Liabilities	11,886	12,407	12,313	10,703	11,827	11,742	12,182	13,944
Stockholders' Equity	(3,355)	(3,305)	(22)	(973)	(1,800)	(1,352)	(734)	(1,114)
Shares Outstanding	80	79	70	71	70	71	70	70
Statistical Record								
Return on Assets %	N.M.	N.M.	15.65	2.26	3.13	1.22	N.M.	2.55
EBITDA Margin %	0.68	N.M.	6.71	7.26	7.56	6.50	5.59	7.41
Net Margin %	N.M.	N.M.	12.34	1.84	2.77	0.91	N.M.	2.12
Asset Turnover	1.25	1.21	1.27	1.23	1.13	1.34	1.01	1.20
Current Ratio	1.39	1.34	1.51	1.63	1.37	1.43	1.36	1.32
Price Range	47.20-18.51	47.20-18.51	70.17-30.68	56.89-32.18	47.27-15.87	78.99-21.99	73.65-27.10	30.28-20.95
P/E Ratio	...	...	3.10-1.36	18.65-10.55	10.60-3.56	43.40-12.08	...	7.35-5.08

Address: 2701 Navistar Drive, Lisle, IL 60532	Web Site: www.navistar.com	Auditors: KPMG LLP
Telephone: 331-332-5000	Officers: Troy A. Clarke - President, Chief Executive Officer, Chief Operating Officer, Division Officer	Investor Contact: 331-332-2143
Fax: 630-753-3982	Andrew J. Cederoth - Executive Vice President, Chief Financial Officer	Transfer Agents: Computershare Investor Services, Jersey City, NJ

NCR CORP.

Exchange	Symbol	Price	52Wk Range	Yield	P/E
NYS	NCR	$27.56 (3/28/2013)	29.18-20.25	N/A	30.97

*7 Year Price Score 113.01 *NYSE Composite Index=100 *12 Month Price Score 105.73

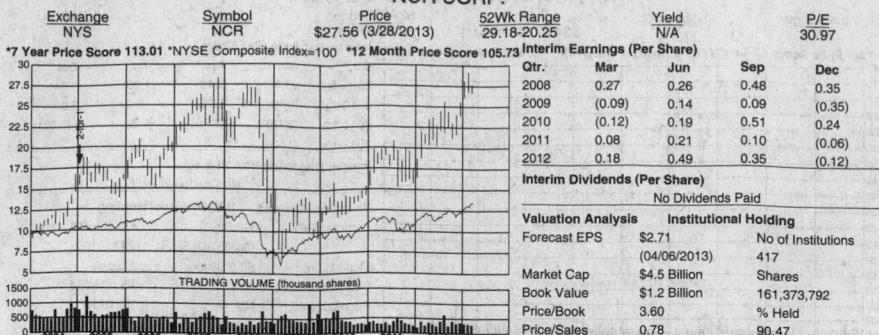

Interim Earnings (Per Share)

Qtr.	Mar	Jun	Sep	Dec
2008	0.27	0.26	0.48	0.35
2009	(0.09)	0.14	0.09	(0.35)
2010	(0.12)	0.19	0.51	0.24
2011	0.08	0.21	0.10	(0.06)
2012	0.18	0.49	0.35	(0.12)

Interim Dividends (Per Share)

No Dividends Paid

Valuation Analysis | **Institutional Holding**

Forecast EPS	$2.71	No of Institutions
	(04/06/2013)	417
Market Cap	$4.5 Billion	Shares
Book Value	$1.2 Billion	161,373,792
Price/Book	3.60	% Held
Price/Sales	0.78	90.47

Business Summary: Computer Hardware & Equipment (MIC: 6.2.1 SIC: 3578 NAIC: 334119)

NCR is a technology company that provides products and services that enable businesses to connect, interact and transact with their customers. Co.'s portfolio of self-service and assisted-service applications serve customers in the financial services, retail, hospitality, travel and gaming and entertainment industries and include automated teller machines, self-service kiosks and point of sale devices as well as software applications that can be used by consumers to enable them to interact with businesses from their computer or mobile device. Co. also resells third-party networking products and provides related service offerings in the telecommunications and technology sectors.

Recent Developments: For the year ended Dec 31 2012, income from continuing operations decreased 3.4% to US$140.0 million from US$145.0 million a year earlier. Net income increased 180.8% to US$146.0 million from US$52.0 million in the prior year. Revenues were US$5.73 billion, up 8.3% from US$5.29 billion the year before. Operating income was US$232.0 million versus US$212.0 million in the prior year, an increase of 9.4%. Direct operating expenses rose 6.7% to US$4.39 billion from US$4.11 billion in the comparable period the year before. Indirect operating expenses increased 14.7% to US$1.11 billion from US$970.0 million in the equivalent prior-year period.

Prospects: Our evaluation of NCR Corp. as of Apr. 7, 2013 is the result of our systematic analysis on three basic characteristics: earnings strength, relative valuation, and recent stock price movement. The company has generated a negative trend in earnings per share over the past 5 quarters and while recent estimates for the company have remained steady, NCR has posted better than expected results. Based on operating earnings yield, the company is undervalued when compared to all of the companies in our coverage universe. Share price changes over the past year indicates that NCR will perform very well over the near term.

Financial Data
(US$ in Thousands)

	12/31/2012	12/31/2011	12/31/2010	12/31/2009	12/31/2008	12/31/2007	12/31/2006	12/31/2005
Earnings Per Share	0.89	0.33	0.83	(0.21)	1.36	1.50	2.09	2.80
Cash Flow Per Share	(1.13)	2.37	1.51	1.40	2.50	0.84	2.68	3.29
Tang Book Value Per Share	N.M.	N.M.	4.81	2.91	2.25	9.50	9.68	10.49
Income Statement								
Total Revenue	5,730,000	5,443,000	4,819,000	4,612,000	5,315,000	4,970,000	6,142,000	6,028,000
EBITDA	282,000	153,000	160,000	(15,000)	397,000	311,000	626,000	645,000
Depn & Amortn	64,000	96,000	77,000	68,000	109,000	110,000	159,000	247,000
Income Before Taxes	182,000	49,000	86,000	(87,000)	289,000	232,000	478,000	396,000
Income Taxes	42,000	...	(28,000)	(57,000)	58,000	61,000	96,000	(133,000)
Net Income	146,000	53,000	134,000	(33,000)	228,000	274,000	382,000	529,000
Average Shares	163,800	161,000	161,200	158,900	167,900	182,700	182,900	189,100
Balance Sheet								
Current Assets	3,406,000	2,515,000	2,478,000	2,299,000	2,557,000	3,088,000	3,332,000	2,693,000
Total Assets	6,371,000	5,591,000	4,361,000	4,094,000	4,255,000	4,780,000	5,227,000	5,287,000
Current Liabilities	1,742,000	1,565,000	1,416,000	1,382,000	1,693,000	1,530,000	1,770,000	1,645,000
Long-Term Obligations	1,891,000	852,000	10,000	11,000	7,000	307,000	306,000	305,000
Total Liabilities	5,124,000	4,792,000	3,478,000	3,530,000	3,815,000	3,023,000	3,346,000	3,252,000
Stockholders' Equity	1,247,000	799,000	883,000	564,000	440,000	1,757,000	1,881,000	2,035,000
Shares Outstanding	162,800	157,600	159,700	159,600	158,100	178,200	178,900	181,700
Statistical Record								
Return on Assets %	2.43	1.07	3.17	N.M.	5.03	5.48	7.27	9.76
Return on Equity %	14.23	6.30	18.52	N.M.	20.70	15.06	19.51	25.67
EBITDA Margin %	4.92	2.81	3.32	N.M.	7.47	6.26	10.19	10.70
Net Margin %	2.55	0.97	2.78	N.M.	4.29	5.51	6.22	8.78
Asset Turnover	0.96	1.09	1.14	1.10	1.17	0.99	1.17	1.11
Current Ratio	1.96	1.61	1.75	1.66	1.51	2.02	1.88	1.64
Debt to Equity	1.52	1.07	0.01	0.02	0.02	0.17	0.16	0.15
Price Range	25.64-16.48	20.83-15.31	15.93-11.13	15.06-6.67	27.56-12.84	28.31-20.20	21.23-15.19	18.76-13.94
P/E Ratio	28.81-18.52	63.12-46.39	19.19-13.41	...	20.26-9.44	18.87-13.46	10.16-7.27	6.70-4.98

Address: 3097 Satellite Boulevard, Duluth, GA 30096 Telephone: 937-445-5000	Web Site: www.ncr.com Officers: William R. Nuti - Chairman, President, Chief Executive Officer John G. Bruno - Executive Vice President	Auditors: PricewaterhouseCoopers LLP Investor Contact: 800-225-5627 Transfer Agents: Computershare, Pittsburgh, PA

NEUSTAR, INC.

Exchange	Symbol	Price	52Wk Range	Yield	P/E
NYS	NSR	$46.53 (3/28/2013)	47.07-30.40	N/A	20.23

*7 Year Price Score 122.66 *NYSE Composite Index=100 *12 Month Price Score 107.35

Interim Earnings (Per Share)

Qtr.	Mar	Jun	Sep	Dec
2008	(0.06)	0.31	0.38	(0.55)
2009	0.32	0.32	0.32	0.37
2010	0.33	0.37	0.39	0.30
2011	0.96	0.43	0.51	0.27
2012	0.50	0.57	0.68	0.56

Interim Dividends (Per Share)

No Dividends Paid

Valuation Analysis | **Institutional Holding**

Forecast EPS	$3.34	No of Institutions
	(04/05/2013)	331
Market Cap	$3.1 Billion	Shares
Book Value	$646.6 Million	74,873,352
Price/Book	4.76	% Held
Price/Sales	3.70	90.87

Business Summary: Services (MIC: 6.1.2 SIC: 4899 NAIC: 517910)

NeuStar is a provider of information and analytics to the Internet, communications, entertainment, advertising and marketing industries. Co.'s services include registry services, managed domain name system services, Internet security services, caller identification services, and web performance monitoring services. Co. operates in three segments: carrier services, which include numbering services, order management services and Internet Protocol services; enterprise services, which include Internet infrastructure services and registry services; and information services, which include on-demand applications that help carriers and enterprises identify, verify, score and locate customers.

Recent Developments: For the year ended Dec 31 2012, income from continuing operations increased 26.3% to US$156.1 million from US$123.6 million a year earlier. Net income decreased 2.9% to US$156.1 million from US$160.8 million in the prior year. Revenues were US$831.4 million, up 34.0% from US$620.5 million the year before. Operating income was US$276.7 million versus US$209.0 million in the prior year, an increase of 32.4%. Direct operating expenses rose 34.8% to US$186.0 million from US$138.0 million in the comparable period the year before. Indirect operating expenses increased 34.9% to US$368.8 million from US$273.4 million in the equivalent prior-year period.

Prospects: Our evaluation of Neustar Inc. as of Apr. 7, 2013 is the result of our systematic analysis on three basic characteristics: earnings strength, relative valuation, and recent stock price movement. The company has enjoyed a very positive trend in earnings per share over the past 5 quarters and while recent estimates for the company have been raised by analysts, NSR has posted better than expected results. Based on operating earnings yield, the company is undervalued when compared to all of the companies in our coverage universe. Share price changes over the past year indicates that NSR will perform well over the near term.

Financial Data

(US$ in Thousands)	12/31/2012	12/31/2011	12/31/2010	12/31/2009	12/31/2008	12/31/2007	12/31/2006	12/31/2005
Earnings Per Share	2.30	2.16	1.40	1.34	0.06	1.17	0.94	0.72
Cash Flow Per Share	4.54	3.10	1.94	2.36	2.26	1.92	1.62	1.78
Tang Book Value Per Share	N.M.	N.M.	6.15	5.07	3.41	3.11	1.13	1.93
Income Statement								
Total Revenue	831,388	620,455	526,812	480,385	488,845	429,172	332,957	242,469
EBITDA	319,404	242,377	209,904	200,561	90,964	172,446	140,423	108,468
Depn & Amortn	42,700	34,100	34,900	30,200	26,700	22,800	17,800	16,000
Income Before Taxes	243,100	204,711	174,935	169,006	65,981	153,111	125,347	92,753
Income Taxes	87,013	81,137	68,726	67,865	61,687	60,776	51,353	37,251
Net Income	156,087	160,823	106,209	101,141	4,294	92,335	73,899	55,398
Average Shares	67,956	74,496	76,065	75,465	75,903	79,235	78,267	77,046
Balance Sheet								
Current Assets	525,756	339,395	460,725	434,768	268,689	310,136	135,675	181,983
Total Assets	1,526,724	1,382,638	733,874	647,804	519,166	616,661	448,259	281,771
Current Liabilities	157,430	145,398	115,504	118,505	104,053	99,266	81,705	68,313
Long-Term Obligations	577,505	586,727	4,076	10,766	11,933	10,923	3,925	4,459
Total Liabilities	880,116	880,004	137,762	143,367	132,513	136,126	107,113	95,608
Stockholders' Equity	646,608	502,634	596,112	504,437	386,653	480,535	341,146	186,163
Shares Outstanding	66,174	66,154	73,632	74,460	73,979	76,987	74,368	68,349
Statistical Record								
Return on Assets %	10.70	15.20	15.37	17.33	0.75	17.34	20.25	22.46
Return on Equity %	27.09	29.27	19.30	22.70	0.99	22.47	28.03	37.59
EBITDA Margin %	38.42	39.06	39.84	41.75	18.61	40.18	42.17	44.73
Net Margin %	18.77	25.92	20.16	21.05	0.88	21.51	22.19	22.85
Asset Turnover	0.57	0.59	0.76	0.82	0.86	0.81	0.91	0.98
Current Ratio	3.34	2.33	3.99	3.67	2.58	3.12	1.66	2.66
Debt to Equity	0.89	1.17	0.01	0.02	0.03	0.02	0.01	0.02
Price Range	43.20-30.40	34.38-22.55	27.00-20.40	24.19-13.62	30.33-14.46	36.12-26.69	37.25-26.67	32.51-25.60
P/E Ratio	18.78-13.22	15.92-10.44	19.29-14.57	18.05-10.16	505.50-241.00	30.87-22.81	39.63-28.37	45.15-35.56

Address: 21575 Ridgetop Circle, Sterling, VA 20166	Web Site: www.neustar.biz	Auditors: Ernst & Young LLP
Telephone: 571-434-5400	Officers: Scott Blake Harris - General Counsel, Senior Vice President Lisa A. Hook - President, Chief Executive Officer	Investor Contact: 571-434-3455 Transfer Agents: American Stock Transfer & Trust Company, Brooklyn, NY

NEW JERSEY RESOURCES CORP

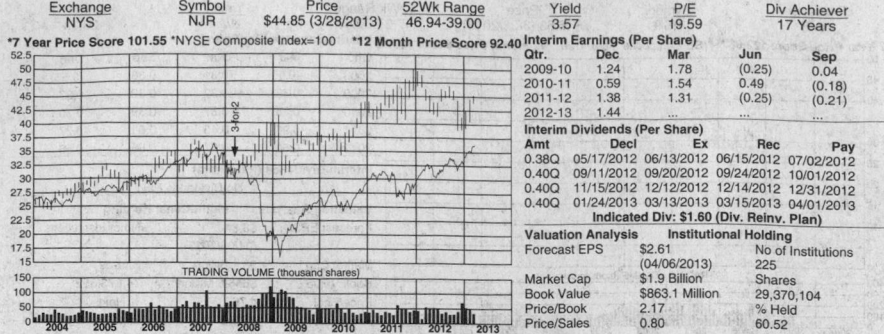

Exchange	Symbol	Price	52Wk Range	Yield	P/E	Div Achiever
NYS	NJR	$44.85 (3/28/2013)	46.94-39.00	3.57	19.59	17 Years

*7 Year Price Score 101.55 *NYSE Composite Index=100   *12 Month Price Score 92.40

Interim Earnings (Per Share)

Qtr.	Dec	Mar	Jun	Sep
2009-10	1.24	1.78	(0.25)	0.04
2010-11	0.59	1.54	0.49	(0.18)
2011-12	1.38	1.31	(0.25)	(0.21)
2012-13	1.44	...	...	...

Interim Dividends (Per Share)

Amt	Decl	Ex	Rec	Pay
0.38Q	05/17/2012	06/13/2012	06/15/2012	07/02/2012
0.40Q	09/11/2012	09/20/2012	09/24/2012	10/01/2012
0.40Q	11/15/2012	12/12/2012	12/14/2012	12/31/2012
0.40Q	01/24/2013	03/13/2013	03/15/2013	04/01/2013

Indicated Div: $1.60 (Div. Reinv. Plan)

Valuation Analysis / **Institutional Holding**

Forecast EPS	$2.61 (04/06/2013)	No of Institutions 225
Market Cap	$1.9 Billion	Shares
Book Value	$863.1 Million	29,370,104
Price/Book	2.17	% Held
Price/Sales	0.80	60.52

Business Summary: Gas Utilities (MIC: 3.3.1 SIC: 4924 NAIC: 221210)

New Jersey Resources is a holding company providing retail and wholesale energy services to customers in states from the Gulf Coast and Mid-Continent regions to the Appalachian and Northeast regions, the West Coast and Canada. Co. operates four business segments: Natural Gas Distribution, which consists of regulated energy and off-system, capacity and storage management operations; Clean Energy Ventures, which consists of capital investments in renewable energy projects; Energy Services, which consists of unregulated wholesale energy operations; and Energy Holdings, which consists of investments in the midstream natural gas market, such as natural gas transportation and storage facilities.

Recent Developments: For the quarter ended Dec 31 2012, net income increased 5.0% to US$60.2 million from US$57.4 million in the year-earlier quarter. Revenues were US$736.0 million, up 14.6% from US$642.4 million the year before. Operating income was US$87.2 million versus US$75.2 million in the prior-year quarter, an increase of 15.9%. Direct operating expenses rose 14.3% to US$606.8 million from US$531.0 million in the comparable period the year before. Indirect operating expenses increased 16.0% to US$42.0 million from US$36.2 million in the equivalent prior-year period.

Prospects: Our evaluation of New Jersey Resources Corp. as of Apr. 7, 2013 is the result of our systematic analysis on three basic characteristics: earnings strength, relative valuation, and recent stock price movement. The company has produced a positive trend in earnings per share over the past 5 quarters and while recent estimates for the company have been mixed, NJR has posted results that fell short of analysts expectations. Based on operating earnings yield, the company is undervalued when compared to all of the companies in our coverage universe. Share price changes over the past year indicates that NJR will perform poorly over the near term.

Financial Data
(US$ in Thousands)

	3 Mos	09/30/2012	09/30/2011	09/30/2010	09/30/2009	09/30/2008	09/30/2007	09/30/2006
Earnings Per Share	2.29	2.23	2.44	2.82	0.64	2.70	1.55	1.87
Cash Flow Per Share	2.00	1.23	6.05	3.37	6.34	3.15	2.92	(0.55)
Tang Book Value Per Share	20.64	19.55	18.74	17.62	16.59	17.28	15.50	14.24
Dividends Per Share	1.560	1.540	1.440	1.360	1.240	1.107	1.013	0.960
Dividend Payout %	68.12	69.06	59.02	48.23	193.75	40.99	65.24	51.43
Income Statement								
Total Revenue	736,019	2,248,923	3,009,209	2,639,304	2,592,460	3,816,210	3,021,765	3,299,608
EBITDA	98,759	152,461	181,948	226,575	83,621	245,185	168,080	188,963
Depn & Amortn	11,303	41,643	35,200	33,192	31,142	39,367	36,536	34,753
Income Before Taxes	81,631	89,974	127,125	172,132	31,465	180,007	103,931	128,541
Income Taxes	23,980	7,729	37,665	64,692	8,488	68,085	40,312	50,022
Net Income	60,206	92,879	101,299	117,457	27,242	113,910	65,281	78,519
Average Shares	41,758	41,632	41,568	41,630	42,465	42,176	42,112	42,121
Balance Sheet								
Current Assets	771,436	647,344	732,367	785,008	684,189	1,109,666	799,866	965,516
Total Assets	2,948,660	2,770,005	2,649,444	2,563,133	2,321,030	2,625,392	2,230,745	2,398,928
Current Liabilities	796,899	653,139	703,384	705,798	556,165	893,969	703,266	897,155
Long-Term Obligations	530,000	525,169	426,797	428,925	455,492	455,117	383,184	332,332
Total Liabilities	2,085,566	1,956,140	1,873,187	1,837,650	1,631,304	1,898,434	1,585,948	1,777,266
Stockholders' Equity	863,094	813,865	776,257	725,483	689,726	726,958	644,797	621,662
Shares Outstanding	41,810	41,619	41,421	41,173	41,585	42,057	41,611	43,647
Statistical Record								
Return on Assets %	3.30	3.42	3.89	4.81	1.10	4.68	2.82	3.41
Return on Equity %	11.37	11.65	13.49	16.60	3.85	16.56	10.31	14.82
EBITDA Margin %	13.42	6.78	6.05	8.58	3.23	6.42	5.56	5.73
Net Margin %	8.18	4.13	3.37	4.45	1.05	2.98	2.16	2.38
Asset Turnover	0.81	0.83	1.15	1.08	1.05	1.57	1.31	1.43
Current Ratio	0.97	0.99	1.04	1.11	1.23	1.24	1.14	1.08
Debt to Equity	0.61	0.65	0.55	0.59	0.66	0.63	0.59	0.53
Price Range	49.62-39.00	50.01-40.77	47.14-39.17	39.22-34.03	41.47-29.38	38.90-29.81	37.00-30.83	34.01-27.69
P/E Ratio	21.67-17.03	22.43-18.28	19.32-16.05	13.91-12.07	64.80-45.91	14.41-11.04	23.87-19.89	18.19-14.81
Average Yield %	3.52	3.39	3.34	3.70	3.46	3.34	3.31	3.19

Address: 1415 Wyckoff Road, Wall, NJ 07719 Telephone: 732-938-1480	Web Site: www.njresources.com Officers: Laurence M. Downes - Chairman, President, Chief Executive Officer Glenn C. Lockwood - Executive Vice President, Chief Financial Officer	Auditors: Deloitte & Touche LLP Investor Contact: 732-938-1229 Transfer Agents: Wells Fargo Shareowner Services, St. Paul, MN

NEW YORK COMMUNITY BANCORP INC.

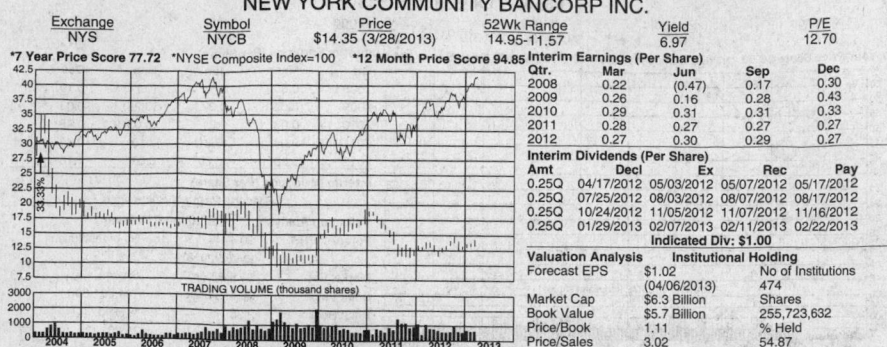

Exchange	Symbol	Price	52Wk Range	Yield	P/E
NYS	NYCB	$14.35 (3/28/2013)	14.95-11.57	6.97	12.70

*7 Year Price Score 77.72 *NYSE Composite Index=100 ***12 Month Price Score 94.85**

Interim Earnings (Per Share)

Qtr.	Mar	Jun	Sep	Dec
2008	0.22	(0.47)	0.17	0.30
2009	0.26	0.16	0.28	0.43
2010	0.29	0.31	0.31	0.33
2011	0.28	0.27	0.27	0.27
2012	0.27	0.30	0.29	0.27

Interim Dividends (Per Share)

Amt	Decl	Ex	Rec	Pay
0.25Q	04/17/2012	05/03/2012	05/07/2012	05/17/2012
0.25Q	07/25/2012	08/03/2012	08/07/2012	08/17/2012
0.25Q	10/24/2012	11/05/2012	11/07/2012	11/16/2012
0.25Q	01/29/2013	02/07/2013	02/11/2013	02/22/2013

Indicated Div: $1.00

Valuation Analysis

Forecast EPS	$1.02	**Institutional Holding**
	(04/06/2013)	No of Institutions 474
Market Cap	$6.3 Billion	Shares
Book Value	$5.7 Billion	255,723,632
Price/Book	1.11	% Held
Price/Sales	3.02	54.87

TRADING VOLUME (thousand shares)

Business Summary: Credit & Lending (MIC: 5.4.1 SIC: 6036 NAIC: 522120)

New York Community Bancorp is a bank holding company. Co. has two primary subsidiaries: New York Community Bank (Community Bank) and New York Commercial Bank (Commercial Bank). The Community Bank is a producer of multi-family loans, and it provides commercial real estate loans, acquisition, development, and construction loans, and commercial and industrial loans. Co. also originates one-to-four family loans mainly through its mortgage banking operation. The Commercial Bank provides installment loans, revolving lines of credit, and cash management services, as well as 24-hour banking online and by phone. At Dec 31 2011, Co. had total assets of $42.02 billion and deposits of $22.27 billion.

Recent Developments: For the year ended Dec 31 2012, net income increased 4.4% to US$501.1 million from US$480.0 million in the prior year. Net interest income decreased 3.4% to US$1.16 billion from US$1.20 billion in the prior year. Provision for loan losses was US$63.0 million versus US$100.4 million in the prior year, a decrease of 37.3%. Non-interest income rose 26.4% to US$297.4 million from US$235.3 million, while non-interest expense advanced 3.3% to US$593.8 million.

Prospects: Our evaluation of New York Community Bancorp Inc. as of Apr. 7, 2013 is the result of our systematic analysis on three basic characteristics: earnings strength, relative valuation, and recent stock price movement. The company has managed to produce a neutral trend in earnings per share over the past 5 quarters and while recent estimates for the company have been mixed, NYCB has posted results that fell short of analysts expectations. Based on operating earnings yield, the company is undervalued when compared to all of the companies in our coverage universe. Share price changes over the past year indicates that NYCB will perform poorly over the near term.

Financial Data

(US$ in Thousands)	12/31/2012	12/31/2011	12/31/2010	12/31/2009	12/31/2008	12/31/2007	12/31/2006	12/31/2005
Earnings Per Share	1.13	1.09	1.24	1.13	0.23	0.90	0.81	1.11
Cash Flow Per Share	1.31	1.90	(0.15)	0.60	0.73	0.96	1.02	1.74
Tang Book Value Per Share	6.93	6.77	6.91	6.52	4.91	5.05	4.86	4.66
Dividends Per Share	1.000	1.000	1.000	1.000	1.000	1.000	1.000	1.000
Dividend Payout %	88.50	91.74	80.65	88.50	434.78	111.11	123.46	90.09
Income Statement								
Interest Income	1,791,101	1,866,664	1,913,794	1,634,612	1,605,129	1,566,745	1,408,700	1,155,654
Interest Expense	631,080	666,243	733,831	729,287	929,634	950,215	847,134	583,651
Net Interest Income	1,160,021	1,200,421	1,179,963	905,325	675,495	616,530	561,566	572,003
Provision for Losses	62,988	100,420	102,903	63,000	7,700	...	...	...
Non-Interest Income	297,353	235,325	337,923	157,639	15,529	111,092	88,990	121,065
Non-Interest Expense	593,833	574,683	546,246	384,003	606,187	302,765	283,971	236,621
Income Before Taxes	780,909	734,577	837,471	593,149	53,794	402,099	348,714	444,714
Income Taxes	279,803	254,540	296,454	194,503	(24,090)	123,017	116,129	152,629
Net Income	501,106	480,037	541,017	398,646	77,884	279,082	232,585	292,085
Average Shares	437,712	436,143	434,186	351,939	335,371	311,102	286,261	262,497
Balance Sheet								
Net Loans & Leases	31,580,636	30,152,154	29,041,595	28,265,208	22,097,844	20,270,454	19,567,502	16,948,697
Total Assets	44,145,100	42,024,302	41,190,689	42,153,869	32,466,906	30,579,822	28,482,370	26,283,705
Total Deposits	24,877,521	22,274,130	21,809,051	22,316,411	14,292,454	13,157,333	12,619,004	12,104,899
Total Liabilities	38,488,836	36,458,598	35,664,469	36,786,967	28,247,660	26,397,509	24,792,533	22,958,828
Stockholders' Equity	5,656,264	5,565,704	5,526,220	5,366,902	4,219,246	4,182,313	3,689,837	3,324,877
Shares Outstanding	439,050	437,344	435,646	433,197	344,985	323,812	295,350	269,776
Statistical Record								
Return on Assets %	1.16	1.15	1.30	1.07	0.25	0.95	0.85	1.16
Return on Equity %	8.91	8.66	9.93	8.32	1.85	7.09	6.63	8.97
Net Interest Margin %	64.77	64.31	61.66	55.38	42.08	39.35	39.86	49.50
Efficiency Ratio %	28.43	27.34	24.26	21.43	37.40	18.04	18.96	18.53
Loans to Deposits	1.27	1.35	1.33	1.27	1.55	1.54	1.55	1.40
Price Range	14.95-11.57	18.97-11.32	19.30-14.42	14.65-7.90	20.59-11.02	19.42-15.90	18.01-15.85	20.57-15.76
P/E Ratio	13.23-10.24	17.40-10.39	15.56-11.63	12.96-6.99	89.52-47.91	21.58-17.67	22.23-19.57	18.53-14.20
Average Yield %	7.61	6.69	6.11	8.87	6.02	5.70	6.00	5.67

Address: 615 Merrick Avenue, Westbury, NY 11590 Telephone: 516-683-4100	Web Site: www.mynycb.com Officers: Joseph R. Ficalora - Chairman, President, Chief Executive Officer Thomas R. Cangemi - Senior Executive Vice President, Chief Financial Officer	Auditors: KPMG LLP Transfer Agents: Computershare, Jersey City, NJ

NEW YORK TIMES CO.

Exchange	Symbol	Price	52Wk Range	Yield	P/E
NYS	NYT	$9.80 (3/28/2013)	10.88-5.98	N/A	11.26

*7 Year Price Score 56.90   ***NYSE Composite Index=100**   ***12 Month Price Score 104.53**

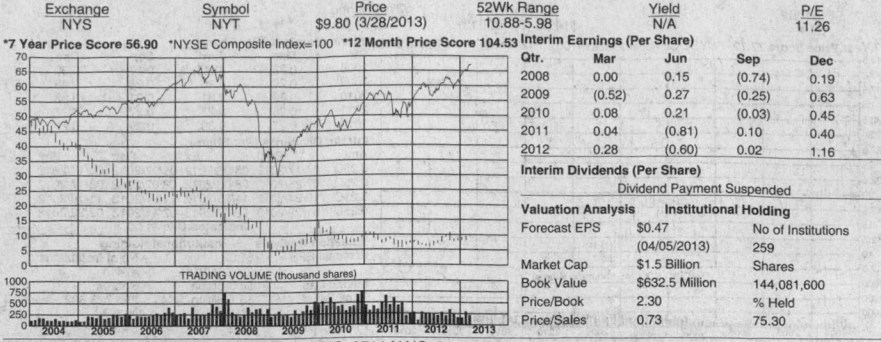

Interim Earnings (Per Share)

Qtr.	Mar	Jun	Sep	Dec
2008	0.00	0.15	(0.74)	0.19
2009	(0.52)	0.27	(0.25)	0.63
2010	0.08	0.21	(0.03)	0.45
2011	0.04	(0.81)	0.10	0.40
2012	0.28	(0.60)	0.02	1.16

Interim Dividends (Per Share)

Dividend Payment Suspended

Valuation Analysis	Institutional Holding	
Forecast EPS	$0.47	No of Institutions
	(04/05/2013)	259
Market Cap	$1.5 Billion	Shares
Book Value	$632.5 Million	144,081,600
Price/Book	2.30	% Held
Price/Sales	0.73	75.30

Business Summary: Publishing (MIC: 2.3.3 SIC: 2711 NAIC: 511110)

New York Times is a multimedia news and information company that includes newspapers, Internet businesses, investments in paper mills, and other investments. Co.'s businesses include two segments: News Media Group, which consists of The New York Times Media Group (includes The New York Times, the International Herald Tribune and NYTimes.com), and the New England Media Group (includes The Boston Globe, BostonGlobe.com, Boston.com, the Worcester Telegram & Gazette (the T&G), the T&G's Web site and Telegram.com and related businesses); and About Group, which consists of About.com, ConsumerSearch.com, Caloriecount.com websites, and related businesses.

Recent Developments: For the year ended Dec 30 2012, income from continuing operations increased 211.6% to US$159.8 million from US$51.3 million a year earlier. Net income amounted to US$133.3 million versus a net loss of US$40.2 million in the prior year. Revenues were US$1.99 billion, up 1.9% from US$1.95 billion the year before. Operating income was US$108.3 million versus US$143.7 million in the prior year, a decrease of 24.6%. Direct operating expenses rose 2.7% to US$832.2 million from US$810.6 million in the comparable period the year before. Indirect operating expenses increased 5.1% to US$1.05 billion from US$998.4 million in the equivalent prior-year period.

Prospects: Our evaluation of New York Times Co. as of Apr. 7, 2013 is the result of our systematic analysis on three basic characteristics: earnings strength, relative valuation, and recent stock price movement. The company has produced a positive trend in earnings per share over the past 5 quarters and while recent estimates for the company have remained steady, NYT has posted better than expected results. Based on operating earnings yield, the company is about fairly valued when compared to all of the companies in our coverage universe. Share price changes over the past year indicates that NYT will perform very well over the near term.

Financial Data
(US$ in Thousands)

	12/30/2012	12/25/2011	12/26/2010	12/27/2009	12/28/2008	12/30/2007	12/31/2006	12/25/2005
Earnings Per Share	0.87	(0.27)	0.71	0.14	(0.40)	1.45	(3.76)	1.78
Cash Flow Per Share	0.53	0.50	1.06	1.79	1.73	0.77	2.87	2.03
Tang Book Value Per Share	3.43	N.M.	N.M.	N.M.	N.M.	1.16	0.25	N.M.
Dividends Per Share	...	...	...	...	0.750	0.865	0.690	0.650
Dividend Payout %	...	...	...	...	...	59.66	...	36.52
Income Statement								
Total Revenue	1,990,080	2,323,401	2,393,463	2,440,439	2,948,856	3,195,077	3,289,903	3,372,775
EBITDA	426,890	197,951	364,198	198,584	87,020	397,490	(379,944)	593,934
Depn & Amortn	103,775	116,454	120,950	133,775	127,656	170,061	140,667	113,480
Income Before Taxes	260,300	(3,746)	158,186	(16,892)	(88,426)	187,587	(571,262)	436,053
Income Taxes	103,482	36,506	68,516	2,206	(5,726)	76,137	16,608	180,242
Net Income	133,173	(39,669)	107,704	19,891	(57,839)	208,704	(543,443)	259,753
Average Shares	152,693	147,190	152,600	146,367	143,777	144,158	144,579	145,877
Balance Sheet								
Current Assets	1,308,408	748,589	857,232	500,573	624,200	664,445	1,185,043	657,746
Total Assets	2,806,335	2,883,450	3,285,741	3,088,557	3,401,680	3,473,092	3,855,928	4,533,037
Current Liabilities	422,577	513,308	504,377	500,500	1,033,236	975,736	1,297,994	1,066,522
Long-Term Obligations	696,914	698,220	996,405	769,176	580,406	678,699	795,030	898,300
Total Liabilities	2,173,835	2,377,090	2,625,814	2,484,515	2,897,717	2,494,892	3,036,086	3,016,789
Stockholders' Equity	632,500	506,360	659,927	604,042	503,963	978,200	819,842	1,516,248
Shares Outstanding	148,605	147,846	146,151	144,513	143,804	143,727	143,859	145,215
Statistical Record								
Return on Assets %	4.61	N.M.	3.39	0.61	N.M.	5.71	N.M.	6.14
Return on Equity %	23.01	N.M.	17.09	3.60	N.M.	23.28	N.M.	17.86
EBITDA Margin %	21.45	8.52	15.22	8.14	2.95	12.44	N.M.	17.61
Net Margin %	6.69	N.M.	4.50	0.82	N.M.	6.53	N.M.	7.70
Asset Turnover	0.69	0.76	0.75	0.75	0.86	0.87	0.77	0.80
Current Ratio	3.10	1.46	1.70	1.00	0.60	0.68	0.91	0.62
Debt to Equity	1.10	1.38	1.51	1.27	1.15	0.69	0.97	0.59
Price Range	10.88-5.98	10.90-5.65	14.67-7.18	12.16-3.51	21.07-5.34	26.55-16.45	28.90-21.58	40.80-26.36
P/E Ratio	12.51-6.87	...	20.66-10.11	86.86-25.07	...	18.31-11.34	...	22.92-14.81
Average Yield %	...	...	...	...	5.08	3.86	2.81	1.98

Address: 620 Eighth Avenue, New York, NY 10018	Web Site: www.nytco.com	Auditors: Ernst & Young LLP
Telephone: 212-556-1234	Officers: Arthur Sulzberger - Chairman, Interim Chief Executive Officer Michael Golden - Vice-Chairman	Investor Contact: 212-556-5224 Transfer Agents: Computershare

NEWELL RUBBERMAID, INC.

Exchange	Symbol	Price	52Wk Range	Yield	P/E
NYS	NWL	$26.10 (3/28/2013)	26.10-16.67	2.30	19.05

*7 Year Price Score 91.58 *NYSE Composite Index=100 *12 Month Price Score 110.13

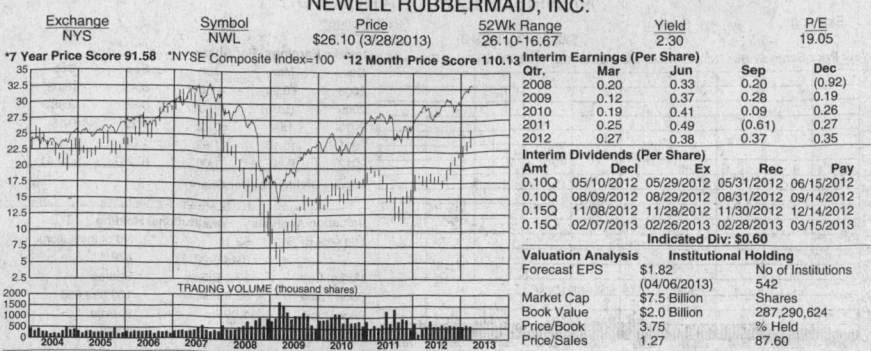

Interim Earnings (Per Share)

Qtr.	Mar	Jun	Sep	Dec
2008	0.20	0.33	0.20	(0.92)
2009	0.12	0.37	0.28	0.19
2010	0.19	0.41	0.09	0.26
2011	0.25	0.49	(0.61)	0.27
2012	0.27	0.38	0.37	0.35

Interim Dividends (Per Share)

Amt	Decl	Ex	Rec	Pay
0.10Q	05/10/2012	05/29/2012	05/31/2012	06/15/2012
0.10Q	08/09/2012	08/29/2012	08/31/2012	09/14/2012
0.15Q	11/08/2012	11/28/2012	11/30/2012	12/14/2012
0.15Q	02/07/2013	02/26/2013	02/28/2013	03/15/2013

Indicated Div: $0.60

Valuation Analysis

	Institutional Holding	
Forecast EPS	$1.82	No of Institutions
	(04/06/2013)	542
Market Cap	$7.5 Billion	Shares
Book Value	$2.0 Billion	287,290,624
Price/Book	3.75	% Held
Price/Sales	1.27	87.60

Business Summary: Plastics (MIC: 8.4.2 SIC: 3089 NAIC: 326299)

Newell Rubbermaid is a marketer of consumer and commercial products in six business segments: Home Solutions, such as food and home storage products, gourmet cookware, and cutlery; Writing, such as markers, highlighters, and variety of stationaries; Tools, such as industrial bandsaw blades and cutting tools for pipes; Commercial Products, such as hygiene systems; Baby and Parenting products, such as swings, highchairs, and car seats; and Specialty, such as convenience and window hardware, manual paint applicators, label makers and printers, and on-line postage. Co.'s products are marketed under a portfolio of brands, including Rubbermaid®, Graco®, Aprica®, and Levolor®, among other brands.

Recent Developments: For the year ended Dec 31 2012, income from continuing operations increased 196.9% to US$399.6 million from US$134.6 million a year earlier. Net income increased 220.5% to US$401.3 million from US$125.2 million in the prior year. Revenues were US$5.90 billion, up 0.6% from US$5.86 billion the year before. Operating income was US$651.9 million versus US$257.2 million in the prior year, an increase of 153.5%. Direct operating expenses rose 0.4% to US$3.67 billion from US$3.66 billion in the comparable period the year before. Indirect operating expenses decreased 19.0% to US$1.58 billion from US$1.95 billion in the equivalent prior-year period.

Prospects: Our evaluation of Newell Rubbermaid Inc. as of Apr. 7, 2013 is the result of our systematic analysis on three basic characteristics: earnings strength, relative valuation, and recent stock price movement. The company has managed to produce a neutral trend in earnings per share over the past 5 quarters and while recent estimates for the company have remained steady, NWL has posted better than expected results. Based on operating earnings yield, the company is undervalued when compared to all of the companies in our coverage universe. Share price changes over the past year indicates that NWL will perform well over the near term.

Financial Data
(US$ in Thousands)

	12/31/2012	12/31/2011	12/31/2010	12/31/2009	12/31/2008	12/31/2007	12/31/2006	12/31/2005
Earnings Per Share	1.37	0.42	0.96	0.97	(0.19)	1.68	1.40	0.91
Cash Flow Per Share	2.12	1.91	2.06	2.15	1.64	2.37	2.34	2.34
Dividends Per Share	0.430	0.290	0.200	0.255	0.840	0.840	0.840	0.840
Dividend Payout %	31.39	69.05	20.83	26.29	...	50.00	60.00	92.31
Income Statement								
Total Revenue	5,902,700	5,864,600	5,759,200	5,577,600	6,470,600	6,407,300	6,201,000	6,342,500
EBITDA	750,100	350,800	536,300	689,700	271,500	879,200	809,100	750,100
Depn & Amortn	106,700	110,600	118,000	122,100	131,100	143,200	159,500	202,500
Income Before Taxes	567,300	154,000	299,900	427,600	2,500	631,900	517,600	420,500
Income Taxes	166,300	17,900	7,500	142,700	53,600	149,700	44,200	61,700
Net Income	401,300	125,200	292,800	285,500	(52,300)	467,100	385,000	251,300
Average Shares	293,600	296,200	305,400	294,400	277,000	286,100	275,500	274,900
Balance Sheet								
Current Assets	2,271,100	2,148,000	2,132,000	2,182,100	2,393,800	2,651,700	2,476,900	2,472,800
Total Assets	6,222,000	6,160,900	6,405,300	6,423,900	6,792,500	6,682,900	6,310,500	6,445,800
Current Liabilities	1,570,800	1,660,900	1,665,900	1,759,500	2,205,900	2,563,800	1,896,600	1,797,500
Long-Term Obligations	1,706,500	1,809,300	2,063,900	2,015,300	2,118,300	1,197,400	1,972,300	2,429,700
Total Liabilities	4,225,300	4,311,800	4,503,300	4,645,200	5,178,300	4,435,600	4,420,300	4,802,600
Stockholders' Equity	1,996,700	1,849,100	1,902,000	1,778,700	1,614,200	2,247,300	1,890,200	1,643,200
Shares Outstanding	286,900	288,300	290,500	277,800	277,100	276,700	275,300	274,500
Statistical Record								
Return on Assets %	6.46	1.99	4.56	4.32	N.M.	7.19	6.04	3.83
Return on Equity %	20.81	6.68	15.91	16.83	N.M.	22.58	21.79	14.75
EBITDA Margin %	12.71	5.98	9.31	12.37	4.20	13.72	13.05	11.83
Net Margin %	6.80	2.13	5.08	5.12	N.M.	7.29	6.21	3.96
Asset Turnover	0.95	0.93	0.90	0.84	0.96	0.99	0.97	0.97
Current Ratio	1.45	1.29	1.28	1.24	1.09	1.03	1.31	1.38
Debt to Equity	0.85	0.98	1.09	1.13	1.31	0.53	1.04	1.48
Price Range	22.27-16.23	20.21-11.14	18.38-13.36	15.85-4.54	25.88-9.41	31.95-24.50	29.83-23.26	25.45-20.95
P/E Ratio	16.26-11.85	48.12-26.52	19.15-13.92	16.34-4.68	...	19.02-14.58	21.31-16.61	27.97-23.02
Average Yield %	2.30	1.79	1.23	2.24	4.53	2.90	3.16	3.66

Address: Three Glenlake Parkway, Atlanta, GA 30328
Telephone: 770-418-7000

Web Site: www.newellrubbermaid.com
Officers: Michael B. Polk - President, Chief Executive Officer William A. Burke - Executive Vice President, Chief Operating Officer, Division Officer

Auditors: Ernst & Young LLP
Investor Contact: 800-424-1941
Transfer Agents: ComputerShare Investor Services, Providence, RI

NEWFIELD EXPLORATION CO.

Exchange	Symbol	Price	52Wk Range	Yield	P/E
NYS	NFX	$22.42 (3/28/2013)	36.23-22.38	N/A	N/A

*7 Year Price Score 57.58   *NYSE Composite Index=100   *12 Month Price Score 78.84

Interim Earnings (Per Share)

Qtr.	Mar	Jun	Sep	Dec
2008	(0.50)	(1.89)	5.48	(6.03)
2009	(5.35)	(0.30)	0.58	0.88
2010	1.84	0.72	1.20	0.16
2011	(0.13)	1.62	1.99	0.50
2012	0.86	1.00	(0.24)	(10.41)

Interim Dividends (Per Share)

No Dividends Paid

Valuation Analysis   **Institutional Holding**

Forecast EPS	$2.13	No of Institutions
	(04/06/2013)	472
Market Cap	$3.0 Billion	Shares
Book Value	$2.8 Billion	136,699,696
Price/Book	1.09	% Held
Price/Sales	1.18	90.66

Business Summary: Production & Extraction (MIC: 9.1.1 SIC: 1311 NAIC: 211111)

Newfield Exploration is an independent energy company engaged in the exploration, development and production of crude oil, natural gas and natural liquids. Co.'s principal domestic areas of operation include the Mid-Continent, the Rocky Mountains and onshore Texas. Internationally, Co. focuses on offshore Malaysia and China. As of Dec 31 2011, Co. had total proved reserves of 3.91 trillion cubic feet equivalent, which consisted of 263.0 million barrels of crude oil or other liquid hydrocarbons and 2.33 trillion cubic feet of natural gas.

Recent Developments: For the year ended Dec 31 2012, net loss amounted to US$1.18 billion versus net income of US$539.0 million in the prior year. Revenues were US$2.57 billion, up 3.9% from US$2.47 billion the year before. Operating loss was US$967.0 million versus an income of US$736.0 million in the prior year. Direct operating expenses rose 9.6% to US$858.0 million from US$783.0 million in the comparable period the year before. Indirect operating expenses increased 181.1% to US$2.68 billion from US$952.0 million in the equivalent prior-year period.

Prospects: Our evaluation of Newfield Exploration Co. as of Apr. 7, 2013 is the result of our systematic analysis on three basic characteristics: earnings strength, relative valuation, and recent stock price movement. The company has managed to produce a neutral trend in earnings per share over the past 5 quarters. However, while recent estimates for the company have been lowered by analysts, NFX has posted results that fell short of analysts expectations. Based on operating earnings yield, the company is undervalued when compared to all of the companies in our coverage universe. Share price changes over the past year indicates that NFX will perform poorly over the near term.

Financial Data
(US$ in Thousands)

	12/31/2012	12/31/2011	12/31/2010	12/31/2009	12/31/2008	12/31/2007	12/31/2006	12/31/2005
Earnings Per Share	(8.80)	3.99	3.91	(4.18)	(2.88)	3.44	4.58	2.73
Cash Flow Per Share	8.47	11.86	12.35	12.14	6.60	9.02	10.90	8.87
Tang Book Value Per Share	20.54	29.11	24.90	20.81	24.66	26.79	23.22	18.16
Income Statement								
Total Revenue	2,567,000	2,471,000	1,883,000	1,338,000	2,225,000	1,783,000	1,673,000	1,762,000
EBITDA	104,000	1,700,000	1,571,000	(223,000)	214,000	1,031,000	1,616,000	1,090,000
Depn & Amortn	955,000	767,000	644,000	587,000	697,000	682,000	624,000	521,000
Income Before Taxes	(988,000)	840,000	829,000	(885,000)	(535,000)	294,000	949,000	543,000
Income Taxes	196,000	301,000	306,000	(343,000)	(162,000)	122,000	358,000	195,000
Net Income	(1,184,000)	539,000	523,000	(542,000)	(373,000)	450,000	591,000	348,000
Average Shares	135,000	135,000	134,000	130,000	129,000	131,000	129,000	128,000
Balance Sheet								
Current Assets	866,000	775,000	731,000	893,000	1,206,000	927,000	851,000	540,000
Total Assets	7,912,000	8,991,000	7,494,000	6,254,000	7,305,000	6,986,000	6,635,000	5,081,000
Current Liabilities	959,000	932,000	928,000	873,000	1,085,000	929,000	1,123,000	670,000
Long-Term Obligations	3,045,000	3,006,000	2,304,000	2,037,000	2,213,000	1,050,000	1,048,000	870,000
Total Liabilities	5,132,000	5,071,000	4,151,000	3,486,000	4,048,000	3,405,000	3,573,000	2,703,000
Stockholders' Equity	2,780,000	3,920,000	3,343,000	2,768,000	3,257,000	3,581,000	3,062,000	2,378,000
Shares Outstanding	135,314	134,684	134,246	133,004	132,077	131,335	129,183	127,540
Statistical Record								
Return on Assets %	N.M.	6.54	7.61	N.M.	N.M.	6.61	10.09	7.40
Return on Equity %	N.M.	14.84	17.12	N.M.	N.M.	13.55	21.73	15.84
EBITDA Margin %	4.05	68.80	83.43	N.M.	9.62	57.82	96.59	61.86
Net Margin %	N.M.	21.81	27.77	N.M.	N.M.	25.24	35.33	19.75
Asset Turnover	0.30	0.30	0.27	0.20	0.31	0.26	0.29	0.37
Current Ratio	0.90	0.83	0.79	1.02	1.11	1.00	0.76	0.81
Debt to Equity	1.10	0.77	0.69	0.74	0.68	0.29	0.34	0.37
Price Range	41.28-23.88	76.45-35.81	73.04-46.60	50.43-17.23	67.96-15.62	54.31-39.94	53.47-36.25	52.27-27.78
P/E Ratio	...	19.16-8.97	18.68-11.92	...	...	15.79-11.61	11.67-7.91	19.15-10.18

Address: 4 Waterway Square Place, Suite 100, The Woodlands, TX 77380 **Telephone:** 281-210-5100 **Fax:** 281-405-4242	**Web Site:** www.newfield.com **Officers:** Lee K. Boothby - Chairman, President, Chief Executive Officer Gary D. Packer - Executive Vice President, Chief Operating Officer	**Auditors:** PricewaterhouseCoopers LLP **Investor Contact:** 281-210-5201 **Transfer Agents:** American Stock Transfer & Trust Company, New York, NY

NEWMONT MINING CORP. (HOLDING CO.)

Exchange	Symbol	Price	52Wk Range	Yield	P/E
NYS	NEM	$41.89 (3/28/2013)	57.20-38.60	4.06	11.54

*7 Year Price Score 84.82   *NYSE Composite Index=100   *12 Month Price Score 80.65

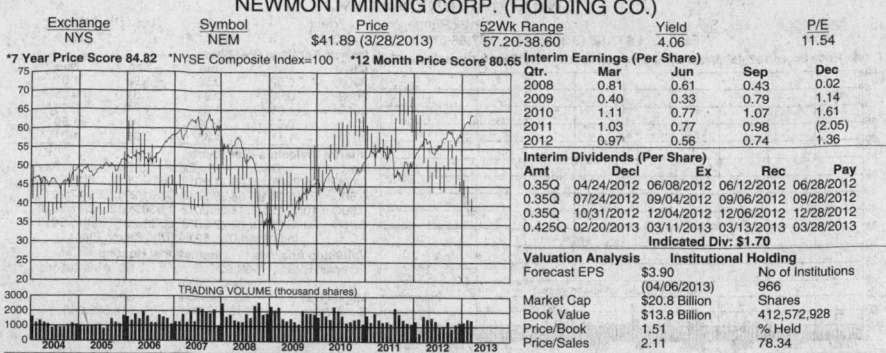

Interim Earnings (Per Share)

Qtr.	Mar	Jun	Sep	Dec
2008	0.81	0.61	0.43	0.02
2009	0.40	0.33	0.79	1.14
2010	1.11	0.77	1.07	1.61
2011	1.03	0.77	0.98	(2.05)
2012	0.97	0.56	0.74	1.36

Interim Dividends (Per Share)

Amt	Decl	Ex	Rec	Pay
0.35Q	04/24/2012	06/08/2012	06/12/2012	06/28/2012
0.35Q	07/24/2012	09/04/2012	09/06/2012	09/28/2012
0.35Q	10/31/2012	12/04/2012	12/06/2012	12/28/2012
0.425Q	02/20/2013	03/11/2013	03/13/2013	03/28/2013

Indicated Div: $1.70

Valuation Analysis | **Institutional Holding**

Forecast EPS	$3.90	No of Institutions
	(04/06/2013)	966
Market Cap	$20.8 Billion	Shares
Book Value	$13.8 Billion	412,572,928
Price/Book	1.51	% Held
Price/Sales	2.11	78.34

Business Summary: Precious Metals (MIC: 8.2.1 SIC: 1041 NAIC: 212221)

Newmont Mining is primarily a gold producer with operations and/or assets in the U.S., Australia, Peru, Indonesia, Ghana, New Zealand and Mexico. Co. is also engaged in the production of copper, principally through Batu Hijau in Indonesia and Boddington in Australia. Co.'s operating segments include: North America, which consists primarily of Nevada in the U.S. and La Herradura in Mexico; South America, which consists primarily of Yanacocha and Conga in Peru; Asia Pacific, which consists primarily of Boddington in Australia, Batu Hijau in Indonesia and other smaller operations in Australia and New Zealand; and Africa, which consists primarily of Ahafo and Akyem in Ghana.

Recent Developments: For the year ended Dec 31 2012, income from continuing operations increased 98.0% to US$2.19 billion from US$1.11 billion a year earlier. Net income increased 117.9% to US$2.12 billion from US$972.0 million in the prior year. Revenues were US$9.87 billion, down 4.7% from US$10.36 billion the year before. Direct operating expenses rose 8.9% to US$4.24 billion from US$3.89 billion in the comparable period the year before. Indirect operating expenses decreased 42.5% to US$2.55 billion from US$4.43 billion in the equivalent prior-year period.

Prospects: Our evaluation of Newmont Mining Corp. as of Apr. 7, 2013 is the result of our systematic analysis on three basic characteristics: earnings strength, relative valuation, and recent stock price movement. The company has produced a positive trend in earnings per share over the past 5 quarters. However, while recent estimates for the company have been lowered by analysts, NEM has posted better than expected results. Based on operating earnings yield, the company is undervalued when compared to all of the companies in our coverage universe. Share price changes over the past year indicates that NEM will perform poorly over the near term.

Financial Data
(US$ in Thousands)

	12/31/2012	12/31/2011	12/31/2010	12/31/2009	12/31/2008	12/31/2007	12/31/2006	12/31/2005
Earnings Per Share	3.63	0.73	4.55	2.66	1.87	(4.17)	1.75	0.72
Cash Flow Per Share	4.77	7.26	6.44	6.00	2.84	1.47	2.72	2.79
Tang Book Value Per Share	27.08	25.39	26.52	21.37	15.20	16.25	14.04	12.28
Dividends Per Share	1.400	1.000	0.500	0.400	0.400	0.400	0.400	0.400
Dividend Payout %	38.57	136.99	10.99	15.04	21.39	...	22.86	55.56
Income Statement								
Total Revenue	9,868,000	10,358,000	9,540,000	7,705,000	6,199,000	5,526,000	4,987,000	4,406,000
EBITDA	4,383,000	3,079,000	5,210,000	3,823,000	2,096,000	398,000	2,291,000	1,691,000
Depn & Amortn	1,032,000	1,036,000	945,000	806,000	747,000	695,000	636,000	588,000
Income Before Taxes	3,114,000	1,810,000	3,997,000	2,913,000	1,276,000	(352,000)	1,625,000	1,064,000
Income Taxes	869,000	713,000	856,000	788,000	113,000	200,000	424,000	314,000
Net Income	1,809,000	366,000	2,277,000	1,297,000	853,000	(1,886,000)	791,000	322,000
Average Shares	499,000	504,000	500,000	493,000	455,000	452,000	452,000	449,000
Balance Sheet								
Current Assets	5,945,000	5,388,000	7,253,000	5,822,000	2,361,000	2,672,000	2,642,000	3,036,000
Total Assets	29,650,000	27,474,000	25,663,000	22,299,000	15,839,000	15,598,000	15,601,000	13,992,000
Current Liabilities	3,141,000	3,940,000	2,747,000	2,320,000	1,596,000	1,500,000	1,739,000	1,350,000
Long-Term Obligations	6,288,000	3,624,000	4,182,000	4,652,000	3,373,000	2,683,000	1,752,000	1,733,000
Total Liabilities	15,877,000	14,578,000	12,318,000	11,596,000	8,737,000	8,050,000	6,264,000	5,616,000
Stockholders' Equity	13,773,000	12,896,000	13,345,000	10,703,000	7,102,000	7,548,000	9,337,000	8,376,000
Shares Outstanding	496,723	494,727	492,729	490,730	454,736	453,000	451,000	447,766
Statistical Record								
Return on Assets %	6.32	1.38	9.50	6.80	5.41	N.M.	5.35	2.41
Return on Equity %	13.53	2.79	18.94	14.57	11.61	N.M.	8.93	3.95
EBITDA Margin %	44.42	29.73	54.61	49.62	33.81	7.20	45.94	38.38
Net Margin %	18.33	3.53	23.87	16.83	13.76	N.M.	15.86	7.31
Asset Turnover	0.34	0.39	0.40	0.40	0.39	0.35	0.34	0.33
Current Ratio	1.89	1.37	2.64	2.51	1.48	1.78	1.52	2.25
Debt to Equity	0.46	0.28	0.31	0.43	0.47	0.36	0.19	0.21
Price Range	64.04-43.39	72.13-50.39	64.94-42.86	55.83-35.03	56.22-21.54	54.50-38.53	61.95-40.83	53.69-35.10
P/E Ratio	17.64-11.95	98.81-69.03	14.27-9.42	20.99-13.17	30.06-11.52	...	35.40-23.33	74.57-48.75
Average Yield %	2.75	1.70	0.89	0.92	0.92	0.91	0.79	0.95

Address: 6363 South Fiddler's Green Circle, Greenwood Village, CO 80111	**Web Site:** www.newmont.com	**Auditors:** PricewaterhouseCoopers LLP
Telephone: 303-863-7414	**Officers:** Gary J. Goldberg - President, Chief Executive Officer, Chief Operating Officer, Executive Vice President Alan R. Blank - Executive Vice President	**Investor Contact:** 303-837-5743
Fax: 303-837-5837		**Transfer Agents:** Computershare, Jersey City, NJ

NEXTERA ENERGY INC

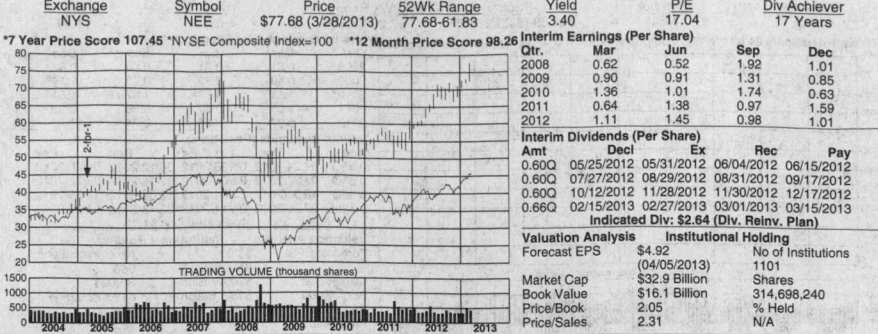

Exchange	Symbol	Price	52Wk Range	Yield	P/E	Div Achiever
NYS	NEE	$77.68 (3/28/2013)	77.68-61.83	3.40	17.04	17 Years

*7 Year Price Score 107.45 *NYSE Composite Index=100 *12 Month Price Score 98.26

Interim Earnings (Per Share)

Qtr.	Mar	Jun	Sep	Dec
2008	0.62	0.52	1.92	1.01
2009	0.90	0.91	1.31	0.85
2010	1.36	1.01	1.74	0.63
2011	0.64	1.38	0.97	1.59
2012	1.11	1.45	0.98	1.01

Interim Dividends (Per Share)

Amt	Decl	Ex	Rec	Pay
0.60Q	05/25/2012	05/31/2012	06/04/2012	06/15/2012
0.60Q	07/27/2012	08/29/2012	08/31/2012	09/17/2012
0.60Q	10/12/2012	11/28/2012	11/30/2012	12/17/2012
0.66Q	02/15/2013	02/27/2013	03/01/2013	03/15/2013

Indicated Div: $2.64 (Div. Reinv. Plan)

Valuation Analysis | **Institutional Holding**

Forecast EPS	$4.92 (04/05/2013)	No of Institutions 1101
Market Cap	$32.9 Billion	Shares 314,698,240
Book Value	$16.1 Billion	% Held
Price/Book	2.05	N/A
Price/Sales	2.31	

Business Summary: Electric Utilities (MIC: 3.1.1 SIC: 4911 NAIC: 221121)

NextEra Energy is a holding company. Through its subsidiaries, Florida Power & Light Company (FPL) and NextEra Energy Resources, LLC (NEER), Co. is engaged in providing retail and wholesale electric services. FPL is a rate-regulated electric utility engaged primarily in the generation, transmission, distribution and sale of electric energy in Florida. NEER produces the majority of its electricity from sources, including wind, solar and hydro. NEER also provides energy and capacity requirements services, owns a retail electricity provider serving customers in 13 states and the District of Columbia and engages in power and gas marketing and trading activities.

Recent Developments: For the year ended Dec 31 2012, net income decreased 0.6% to US$1.91 billion from US$1.92 billion in the prior year. Revenues were US$14.26 billion, down 7.1% from US$15.34 billion the year before. Operating income was US$3.28 billion versus US$3.26 billion in the prior year, an increase of 0.5%. Direct operating expenses declined 10.6% to US$8.28 billion from US$9.26 billion in the comparable period the year before. Indirect operating expenses decreased 4.2% to US$2.70 billion from US$2.82 billion in the equivalent prior-year period.

Prospects: Our evaluation of NextEra Energy Inc. as of Apr. 7, 2013 is the result of our systematic analysis on three basic characteristics: earnings strength, relative valuation, and recent stock price movement. The company has generated a negative trend in earnings per share over the past 5 quarters. However, while recent estimates for the company have been mixed, NEE has posted better than expected results. Based on operating earnings yield, the company is undervalued when compared to all of the companies in our coverage universe. Share price changes over the past year indicates that NEE will perform poorly over the near term.

Financial Data

(US$ in Thousands)	12/31/2012	12/31/2011	12/31/2010	12/31/2009	12/31/2008	12/31/2007	12/31/2006	12/31/2005
Earnings Per Share	4.56	4.59	4.74	3.97	4.07	3.27	3.23	2.29
Cash Flow Per Share	9.55	9.78	9.34	11.04	8.48	9.03	6.35	4.07
Tang Book Value Per Share	37.90	35.92	34.36	31.35	28.57	26.35	24.49	21.52
Dividends Per Share	2.400	2.200	2.000	1.890	1.780	1.640	1.500	1.420
Dividend Payout %	52.63	47.93	42.19	47.61	43.73	50.15	46.44	62.01
Income Statement								
Total Revenue	14,256,000	15,341,000	15,317,000	15,643,000	16,410,000	15,263,000	15,710,000	11,846,000
EBITDA	5,247,000	5,158,000	5,374,000	4,612,000	4,345,000	3,741,000	3,550,000	3,035,000
Depn & Amortn	1,772,000	1,844,000	2,092,000	2,004,000	1,643,000	1,479,000	1,421,000	1,496,000
Income Before Taxes	2,590,000	2,397,000	2,431,000	1,890,000	1,996,000	1,612,000	1,497,000	1,033,000
Income Taxes	692,000	529,000	532,000	327,000	450,000	368,000	397,000	272,000
Net Income	1,911,000	1,923,000	1,957,000	1,615,000	1,639,000	1,312,000	1,281,000	885,000
Average Shares	419,200	419,000	413,000	407,200	402,700	400,600	396,500	385,700
Balance Sheet								
Current Assets	5,237,000	4,872,000	5,258,000	4,337,000	5,392,000	3,779,000	4,999,000	4,987,000
Total Assets	64,439,000	57,188,000	52,994,000	48,458,000	44,821,000	40,123,000	35,991,000	33,004,000
Current Liabilities	8,879,000	6,719,000	6,904,000	6,449,000	7,689,000	5,758,000	6,493,000	7,267,000
Long-Term Obligations	23,177,000	20,810,000	18,013,000	16,300,000	13,833,000	11,280,000	9,591,000	8,039,000
Total Liabilities	48,371,000	42,245,000	38,533,000	35,491,000	33,140,000	29,388,000	26,061,000	24,505,000
Stockholders' Equity	16,068,000	14,943,000	14,461,000	12,967,000	11,681,000	10,735,000	9,930,000	8,499,000
Shares Outstanding	424,000	416,000	420,861	413,622	408,915	407,344	405,404	394,854
Statistical Record								
Return on Assets %	3.13	3.49	3.86	3.46	3.85	3.45	3.71	2.89
Return on Equity %	12.29	13.08	14.27	13.10	14.58	12.70	13.90	11.04
EBITDA Margin %	36.81	33.62	35.09	29.48	26.48	24.51	22.60	25.62
Net Margin %	13.40	12.54	12.78	10.32	9.99	8.60	8.15	7.47
Asset Turnover	0.23	0.28	0.30	0.34	0.39	0.40	0.46	0.39
Current Ratio	0.59	0.73	0.76	0.67	0.70	0.66	0.77	0.69
Debt to Equity	1.44	1.39	1.25	1.26	1.18	1.05	0.97	0.95
Price Range	72.05-58.79	61.08-50.17	56.03-45.57	60.05-41.78	72.03-37.08	72.56-53.85	55.10-38.03	47.84-36.03
P/E Ratio	15.80-12.89	13.31-10.93	11.82-9.61	15.13-10.52	17.70-9.11	22.19-16.47	17.06-11.77	20.89-15.73
Average Yield %	3.63	3.96	3.90	3.56	3.02	2.66	3.41	3.42

Address: 700 Universe Boulevard, Juno Beach, FL 33408	Web Site: www.nexteraenergy.com	Auditors: Deloitte & Touche LLP
Telephone: 561-694-4000	Officers: Lewis Hay - Executive Chairman, Chairman, Chief Executive Officer Moray P. Dewhurst - Vice-Chairman, Executive Vice President, Chief of Staff, Chief Financial Officer	Investor Contact: 561-694-4697
Fax: 561-694-4620		Transfer Agents: Computershare Investor Services, LLC, Canton, MA

NIELSEN HOLDINGS NV

Exchange	Symbol	Price	52Wk Range	Yield	P/E
NYS	NLSN	$35.82 (3/28/2013)	35.82-25.03	N/A	47.76

*7 Year Price Score N/A   *NYSE Composite Index=100   *12 Month Price Score 104.80

Interim Earnings (Per Share)

Qtr.	Mar	Jun	Sep	Dec
2010	0.15	0.27	0.04	0.01
2011	(0.55)	0.19	0.28	0.27
2012	0.07	0.28	0.29	0.11

Interim Dividends (Per Share)

No Dividends Paid

Valuation Analysis		Institutional Holding	
Forecast EPS	$2.16	No of Institutions	
	(04/05/2013)	198	
Market Cap	$13.0 Billion	Shares	
Book Value	$4.9 Billion	358,858,880	
Price/Book	2.63	% Held	
Price/Sales	2.31	N/A	

TRADING VOLUME (thousand shares)

Business Summary: Business Services (MIC: 7.5.2 SIC: 7389 NAIC: 561499)

Nielsen Holdings is an information and measurement company that provides clients with an understanding of consumers and consumer behavior. Co. aligns its business into three reporting segments: What Consumers Buy, which provides retail transactional measurement data, consumer behavior information and analytics primarily to businesses in the consumer packaged goods industry; What Consumers Watch, which provides viewership data and analytics primarily to the media and advertising industries across television, online and mobile devices; and Expositions, which operates a portfolio of business-to-business trade shows and conference events in the U.S.

Recent Developments: For the year ended Dec 31 2012, income from continuing operations increased 221.2% to US$273.0 million from US$85.0 million a year earlier. Net income increased 217.4% to US$273.0 million from US$86.0 million in the prior year. Revenues were US$5.61 billion, up 1.4% from US$5.53 billion the year before. Operating income was US$952.0 million versus US$794.0 million in the prior year, an increase of 19.9%. Direct operating expenses rose 1.8% to US$2.28 billion from US$2.24 billion in the comparable period the year before. Indirect operating expenses decreased 4.8% to US$2.38 billion from US$2.50 billion in the equivalent prior-year period.

Prospects: Our evaluation of Nielsen Holdings N.V. as of Apr. 7, 2013 is the result of our systematic analysis on three basic characteristics: earnings strength, relative valuation, and recent stock price movement. The company has produced a positive trend in earnings per share over the past 5 quarters and while recent estimates for the company have remained steady, NLSN has posted better than expected results. Based on operating earnings yield, the company is about fairly valued when compared to all of the companies in our coverage universe. Share price changes over the past year indicates that NLSN will perform in line with the market over the near term.

Financial Data
(US$ in Millions)

	12/31/2012	12/31/2011	12/31/2010	12/31/2009	12/31/2008	12/31/2007
Earnings Per Share	0.75	0.24	0.46	(1.79)	(2.61)	(1.57)
Cash Flow Per Share	2.16	1.82	1.96	1.89	1.39	...
Income Statement						
Total Revenue	5,612	5,532	5,126	4,808	4,806	4,458
EBITDA	1,000	746	926	195	552	431
Depn & Amortn	183	171	168	158	139	124
Income Before Taxes	408	104	103	(603)	(271)	(354)
Income Taxes	140	22	(46)	(197)	36	12
Net Income	273	84	130	(491)	(589)	(354)
Average Shares	366	357	279	273	226	225
Balance Sheet						
Current Assets	1,676	1,665	1,654	1,646	1,614	...
Total Assets	14,585	14,504	14,429	14,600	15,091	...
Current Liabilities	1,751	1,692	1,607	1,624	2,015	...
Long-Term Obligations	6,229	6,619	8,464	8,548	8,965	...
Total Liabilities	9,655	9,871	11,542	11,802	13,098	...
Stockholders' Equity	4,930	4,633	2,887	2,798	1,993	...
Shares Outstanding	362	359	276	276	226	...
Statistical Record						
Return on Assets %	1.87	0.58	0.90	N.M.	...	...
Return on Equity %	5.69	2.23	4.57	N.M.	...	...
EBITDA Margin %	17.82	13.49	18.06	4.06	11.49	9.67
Net Margin %	4.86	1.52	2.54	N.M.	N.M.	N.M.
Asset Turnover	0.38	0.38	0.35	0.32	...	...
Current Ratio	0.96	0.98	1.03	1.01	0.80	...
Debt to Equity	1.26	1.43	2.93	3.06	4.50	...
Price Range	31.80-25.03	32.06-25.00	...	...	...	...
P/E Ratio	42.40-33.37	133.58-104.17	...	...	...	...

Address: 770 Broadway, New York, NY 10003 Telephone: 646-654-5000	Web Site: www.nielsen.com Officers: James M. Kilts - Chairman Susan D. Whiting - Vice-Chairwoman	Auditors: Ernst & Young LLP Investor Contact: 646-654-4602 Transfer Agents: Computershare

NIKE, INC

Exchange	Symbol	Price	52Wk Range	Yield	P/E	Div Achiever
NYS	NKE	$59.01 (3/28/2013)	59.56-43.89	1.42	22.96	11 Years

*7 Year Price Score 127.95 *NYSE Composite Index=100 *12 Month Price Score 100.29

Interim Earnings (Per Share)

Qtr.	Aug	Nov	Feb	May
2009-10	0.52	0.38	0.51	0.53
2010-11	0.57	0.47	0.54	0.61
2011-12	0.68	0.50	0.60	0.58
2012-13	0.61	0.42	0.95	...

Interim Dividends (Per Share)

Amt	Decl	Ex	Rec	Pay
0.18Q	08/13/2012	08/30/2012	09/04/2012	10/01/2012
100%	11/15/2012	12/26/2012	12/10/2012	12/24/2012
0.21Q	11/15/2012	12/06/2012	12/10/2012	12/26/2012
0.21Q	02/14/2013	02/28/2013	03/04/2013	04/01/2013

Indicated Div: $0.84 (Div. Reinv. Plan)

Valuation Analysis | **Institutional Holding**
Forecast EPS	$2.66 (04/06/2013)	No of Institutions 1096
Market Cap	$52.7 Billion	Shares
Book Value	$10.7 Billion	607,359,936
Price/Book	4.94	% Held
Price/Sales	2.09	65.01

TRADING VOLUME (thousand shares)

Business Summary: Apparel, Footwear & Accessories (MIC: 1.4.2 SIC: 3021 NAIC: 316211)

NIKE is engaged in the design, marketing and distribution of athletic and sports-inspired footwear, apparel, equipment, accessories and services. Co.'s wholly-owned subsidiaries include Cole Haan, which designs, markets and distributes dress and casual shoes, handbags, accessories and coats; Converse Inc., which designs, markets and distributes athletic and casual footwear, apparel and accessories; Hurley International LLC, which designs, markets and distributes action sports and youth lifestyle footwear, apparel and accessories; and Umbro International Limited, which designs, distributes and licenses athletic and casual footwear, apparel and equipment, primarily for the sport of football.

Recent Developments: For the quarter ended Feb 28 2013, income from continuing operations increased 16.3% to US$662.0 million from US$569.0 million in the year-earlier quarter. Net income increased 54.6% to US$866.0 million from US$560.0 million in the year-earlier quarter. Revenues were US$6.19 billion, up 9.4% from US$5.66 billion the year before. Direct operating expenses rose 8.8% to US$3.45 billion from US$3.17 billion in the comparable period the year before. Indirect operating expenses increased 10.6% to US$1.88 billion from US$1.70 billion in the equivalent prior-year period.

Prospects: Our evaluation of NIKE Inc. as of Apr. 7, 2013 is the result of our systematic analysis on three basic characteristics: earnings strength, relative valuation, and recent stock price movement. The company has enjoyed a very positive trend in earnings per share over the past 5 quarters and while recent estimates for the company have been raised by analysts, NKE has posted better than expected results. Based on operating earnings yield, the company is about fairly valued when compared to all of the companies in our coverage universe. Share price changes over the past year indicates that NKE will perform very poorly over the near term.

Financial Data

(US$ in Thousands)	9 Mos	6 Mos	3 Mos	05/31/2012	05/31/2011	05/31/2010	05/31/2009	05/31/2008
Earnings Per Share	2.57	2.22	2.30	2.37	2.19	1.93	1.51	1.87
Cash Flow Per Share	2.96	2.84	2.59	2.06	1.91	3.26	1.79	1.95
Tang Book Value Per Share	11.37	10.61	10.33	10.53	9.78	9.40	8.27	6.75
Dividends Per Share	0.960	0.720	0.875	0.850	0.580	0.520	0.480	0.415
Dividend Payout %	37.35	32.43	38.04	35.94	26.42	26.94	31.68	22.19
Income Statement								
Total Revenue	18,616,000	12,429,000	6,669,000	24,128,000	20,862,000	19,014,000	19,176,100	18,627,000
EBITDA	2,723,000	1,774,000	916,000	3,359,000	3,183,000	2,846,900	2,282,000	2,729,400
Depn & Amortn	359,000	266,000	137,000	373,000	335,000	323,700	335,000	303,600
Income Before Taxes	2,370,000	1,512,000	782,000	2,983,000	2,844,000	2,516,900	1,956,500	2,502,900
Income Taxes	602,000	406,000	215,000	760,000	711,000	610,200	469,800	619,500
Net Income	1,817,000	951,000	567,000	2,223,000	2,133,000	1,906,700	1,486,700	1,883,400
Average Shares	911,700	913,100	922,800	939,600	971,400	987,800	981,400	1,008,200
Balance Sheet								
Current Assets	11,789,000	11,435,000	11,136,000	11,531,000	11,297,000	10,959,200	9,734,000	8,839,300
Total Assets	15,615,000	15,171,000	15,114,000	15,465,000	14,998,000	14,419,300	13,249,600	12,442,700
Current Liabilities	3,500,000	3,799,000	3,776,000	3,865,000	3,958,000	3,364,200	3,277,000	3,321,500
Long-Term Obligations	161,000	170,000	226,000	228,000	276,000	445,800	437,200	441,100
Total Liabilities	4,948,000	5,157,000	5,067,000	5,084,000	5,155,000	4,665,600	4,556,500	4,617,400
Stockholders' Equity	10,667,000	10,014,000	10,047,000	10,381,000	9,843,000	9,753,700	8,693,100	7,825,300
Shares Outstanding	893,614	896,000	901,104	916,000	936,000	968,000	971,000	982,200
Statistical Record								
Return on Assets %	15.56	13.86	14.34	14.55	14.50	13.78	11.57	16.24
Return on Equity %	22.70	20.75	21.51	21.92	21.77	20.67	18.00	25.30
EBITDA Margin %	14.63	14.27	13.74	13.92	15.26	14.97	11.90	14.65
Net Margin %	9.76	7.65	8.50	9.21	10.22	10.03	7.75	10.11
Asset Turnover	1.66	1.68	1.65	1.58	1.42	1.37	1.49	1.61
Current Ratio	3.37	3.01	2.95	2.98	2.85	3.26	2.97	2.66
Debt to Equity	0.02	0.02	0.02	0.02	0.03	0.05	0.05	0.06
Price Range	57.20-43.89	57.20-43.89	57.20-41.25	57.20-39.29	46.15-33.60	39.12-25.42	35.03-19.29	34.78-26.48
P/E Ratio	22.26-17.08	25.77-19.77	24.87-17.93	24.14-16.58	21.07-15.34	20.27-13.17	23.20-12.77	18.60-14.16
Average Yield %	1.89	1.43	1.76	1.76	1.45	1.64	1.78	1.36

Address: One Bowerman Drive, Beaverton, OR 97005-6453
Telephone: 503-671-6453

Web Site:
Officers: Philip H. Knight - Chairman Mark G. Parker - President, Chief Executive Officer

Auditors: PricewaterhouseCoopers LLP
Investor Contact: 180-064-08007
Transfer Agents: Computershare Trust Company, N.A., Providence, RI

NISOURCE INC. (HOLDING CO.)

Exchange	Symbol	Price	52Wk Range	Yield	P/E
NYS	NI	$29.34 (3/28/2013)	29.34-23.40	3.27	21.11

*7 Year Price Score 117.42 *NYSE Composite Index=100 *12 Month Price Score 101.20

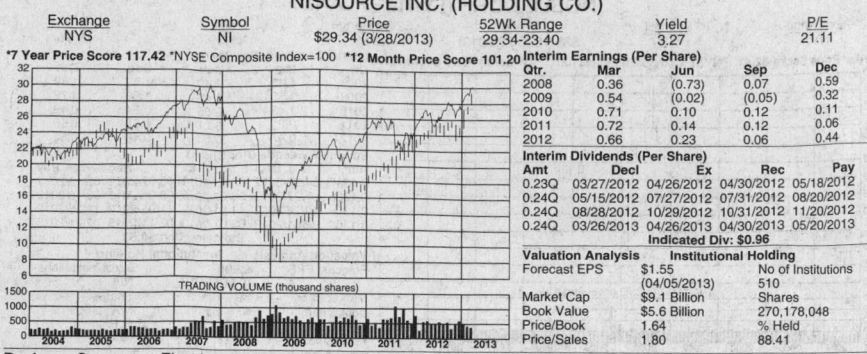

Interim Earnings (Per Share)

Qtr.	Mar	Jun	Sep	Dec
2008	0.36	(0.73)	0.07	0.59
2009	0.54	(0.02)	(0.05)	0.32
2010	0.71	0.10	0.12	0.11
2011	0.72	0.14	0.12	0.06
2012	0.66	0.23	0.06	0.44

Interim Dividends (Per Share)

Amt	Decl	Ex	Rec	Pay
0.23Q	03/27/2012	04/26/2012	04/30/2012	05/18/2012
0.24Q	05/15/2012	07/27/2012	07/31/2012	08/20/2012
0.24Q	08/28/2012	10/29/2012	10/31/2012	11/20/2012
0.24Q	03/26/2013	04/26/2013	04/30/2013	05/20/2013

Indicated Div: $0.96

Valuation Analysis

		Institutional Holding	
Forecast EPS	$1.55	No of Institutions	
	(04/05/2013)	510	
Market Cap	$9.1 Billion	Shares	
Book Value	$5.6 Billion	270,178,048	
Price/Book	1.64	% Held	
Price/Sales	1.80	88.41	

Business Summary: Electric Utilities (MIC: 3.1.1 SIC: 4931 NAIC: 221121)

NiSource is an energy holding company. Through its subsidiaries, Co. engages in three business segments: Gas Distribution Operations, which provides natural gas to customers in Ohio, Pennsylvania, Virginia, Kentucky, Maryland, northern Indiana and Massachusetts; Gas Transmission and Storage Operations, which owns and operates pipeline and operates underground natural gas storage systems; and Electric Operations, which generates, transmits and distributes electricity to customers in the northern part of Indiana and engages in electric wholesale and transmission transactions. At Dec 31 2012, Co. served more than 3.3 million natural gas customers and approximately 458,000 electric customers.

Recent Developments: For the year ended Dec 31 2012, income from continuing operations increased 39.3% to US$410.6 million from US$294.8 million a year earlier. Net income increased 39.1% to US$416.1 million from US$299.1 million in the prior year. Revenues were US$5.06 billion, down 15.3% from US$5.97 billion the year before. Operating income was US$1.04 billion versus US$890.1 million in the prior year, an increase of 17.1%. Direct operating expenses declined 39.4% to US$1.54 billion from US$2.55 billion in the comparable period the year before. Indirect operating expenses decreased 2.4% to US$2.48 billion from US$2.54 billion in the equivalent prior-year period.

Prospects: Our evaluation of NiSource Inc. as of Apr. 7, 2013 is the result of our systematic analysis on three basic characteristics: earnings strength, relative valuation, and recent stock price movement. The company has produced a positive trend in earnings per share over the past 5 quarters and while recent estimates for the company have been mixed, NI has posted better than expected results. Based on operating earnings yield, the company is about fairly valued when compared to all of the companies in our coverage universe. Share price changes over the past year indicates that NI will perform poorly over the near term.

Financial Data
(US$ in Thousands)

	12/31/2012	12/31/2011	12/31/2010	12/31/2009	12/31/2008	12/31/2007	12/31/2006	12/31/2005
Earnings Per Share	1.39	1.03	1.04	0.79	0.29	1.17	1.03	1.12
Cash Flow Per Share	4.36	3.10	2.61	6.06	2.13	2.77	4.24	2.63
Tang Book Value Per Share	5.13	3.63	3.36	3.10	2.63	3.56	3.29	3.08
Dividends Per Share	0.940	0.920	0.920	0.920	0.920	0.920	0.920	0.920
Dividend Payout %	67.63	89.32	88.46	116.46	317.24	78.63	89.32	82.14
Income Statement								
Total Revenue	5,061,200	6,019,100	6,422,000	6,649,400	8,874,200	7,939,800	7,490,000	7,899,100
EBITDA	1,578,600	1,372,000	1,413,700	1,375,200	1,482,500	1,429,600	1,432,100	1,393,100
Depr & Amortn	571,600	547,100	606,600	602,000	574,900	566,500	556,900	562,700
Income Before Taxes	593,900	452,500	421,100	381,000	542,900	474,700	496,600	433,000
Income Taxes	215,500	163,300	141,500	165,800	185,400	172,100	170,800	149,400
Net Income	416,100	299,100	292,000	217,700	79,000	321,400	282,200	306,500
Average Shares	300,400	288,500	280,100	275,800	275,449	274,700	273,400	273,000
Balance Sheet								
Current Assets	2,352,400	2,248,200	2,448,900	2,223,600	3,410,800	2,454,900	2,782,900	3,060,700
Total Assets	21,844,700	20,708,300	19,938,800	19,271,700	20,032,200	18,004,800	18,156,500	17,958,500
Current Liabilities	3,301,600	3,646,400	3,649,400	3,149,600	4,583,400	3,392,600	3,821,200	3,843,200
Long-Term Obligations	6,819,100	6,267,100	5,936,100	5,965,100	5,943,900	5,594,400	5,146,200	5,271,200
Total Liabilities	16,290,400	15,710,100	15,015,600	14,417,600	15,303,400	12,928,200	13,142,900	12,944,400
Stockholders' Equity	5,554,300	4,997,300	4,923,200	4,854,100	4,728,800	5,076,600	5,013,600	5,014,100
Shares Outstanding	310,280	281,853	278,855	276,638	274,261	274,176	273,654	272,622
Statistical Record								
Return on Assets %	1.95	1.47	1.49	1.11	0.41	1.78	1.56	1.75
Return on Equity %	7.87	6.03	5.97	4.54	1.61	6.37	5.63	6.20
EBITDA Margin %	31.19	22.79	22.01	20.68	16.71	18.01	19.12	17.64
Net Margin %	8.22	4.97	4.55	3.27	0.89	4.05	3.77	3.88
Asset Turnover	0.24	0.30	0.33	0.34	0.47	0.44	0.41	0.45
Current Ratio	0.71	0.62	0.67	0.71	0.74	0.72	0.73	0.80
Debt to Equity	1.23	1.25	1.21	1.23	1.26	1.10	1.03	1.05
Price Range	25.83-22.47	23.88-17.62	17.91-14.25	15.71-7.86	19.70-10.48	25.36-17.51	24.77-19.88	25.30-20.84
P/E Ratio	18.58-16.17	23.18-17.11	17.22-13.70	19.89-9.95	67.93-36.14	21.68-14.97	24.05-19.30	22.59-18.61
Average Yield %	3.83	4.53	5.67	7.65	5.69	4.28	4.22	3.98

Address: 801 East 86th Avenue, Merrillville, IN 46410 Telephone: 877-647-5990	Web Site: www.nisource.com Officers: Ian M. Rolland - Chairman Robert C. Skaggs - President, Chief Executive Officer	Auditors: Deloitte & Touche LLP Investor Contact: 219-647-5200 Transfer Agents: Computershare, Pittsburgh, PA

NOBLE CORP (SWITZERLAND)

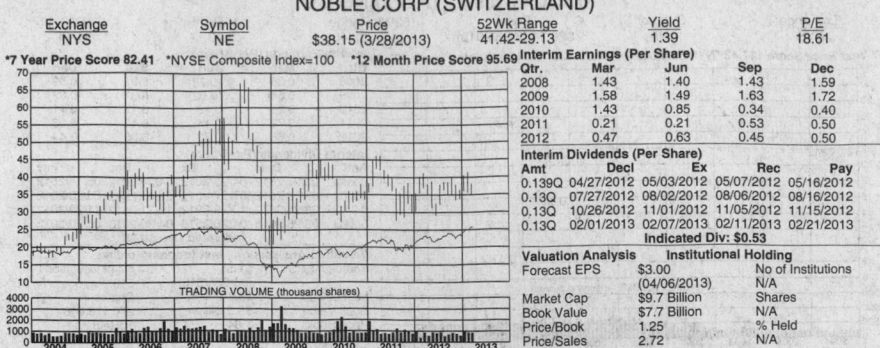

Exchange	Symbol	Price	52Wk Range	Yield	P/E
NYS	NE	$38.15 (3/28/2013)	41.42-29.13	1.39	18.61

*7 Year Price Score 82.41   *NYSE Composite Index=100   *12 Month Price Score 95.69

Interim Earnings (Per Share)

Qtr.	Mar	Jun	Sep	Dec
2008	1.43	1.40	1.43	1.59
2009	1.58	1.49	1.63	1.72
2010	1.43	0.85	0.34	0.40
2011	0.21	0.21	0.53	0.50
2012	0.47	0.63	0.45	0.50

Interim Dividends (Per Share)

Amt	Decl	Ex	Rec	Pay
0.139Q	04/27/2012	05/03/2012	05/07/2012	05/16/2012
0.13Q	07/27/2012	08/02/2012	08/06/2012	08/16/2012
0.13Q	10/26/2012	11/01/2012	11/05/2012	11/15/2012
0.13Q	02/01/2013	02/07/2013	02/11/2013	02/21/2013

Indicated Div: $0.53

Valuation Analysis / **Institutional Holding**

Forecast EPS	$3.00 (04/06/2013)
Market Cap	$9.7 Billion
Book Value	$7.7 Billion
Price/Book	1.25
Price/Sales	2.72

No of Institutions N/A
Shares N/A
% Held N/A

Business Summary: Equipment & Services (MIC: 9.1.3 SIC: 1381 NAIC: 213111)

Noble is an offshore drilling contractor for the oil and gas industry. Co. performs contract drilling services with its fleet of offshore drilling units located worldwide. Co. also has one floating production storage and offloading unit. Co.'s drilling fleet is composed of the following types of units: semisubmersibles, drillships, jackups, and submersibles. In addition, Co. performs services for drilling and workover activities covering two platforms off the east coast of Canada. Co. does not own or lease these platforms. Under its labor contracts, Co. provides the personnel required to manage and perform the drilling operations from a drilling platform owned by the operator.

Recent Developments: For the year ended Dec 31 2012, net income increased 52.9% to US$556.1 million from US$363.6 million in the prior year. Revenues were US$3.55 billion, up 31.6% from US$2.70 billion the year before. Operating income was US$783.8 million versus US$490.5 million in the prior year, an increase of 59.8%. Direct operating expenses rose 29.9% to US$1.92 billion from US$1.48 billion in the comparable period the year before. Indirect operating expenses increased 16.0% to US$845.7 million from US$728.8 million in the equivalent prior-year period.

Prospects: Our evaluation of Noble Corp. as of Apr. 7, 2013 is the result of our systematic analysis on three basic characteristics: earnings strength, relative valuation, and recent stock price movement. The company has generated a negative trend in earnings per share over the past 5 quarters. However, while recent estimates for the company have been lowered by analysts, NE has posted results that fell short of analysts expectations. Based on operating earnings yield, the company is about fairly valued when compared to all of the companies in our coverage universe. Share price changes over the past year indicates that NE will perform poorly over the near term.

Financial Data

(US$ in Thousands)	12/31/2012	12/31/2011	12/31/2010	12/31/2009	12/31/2008	12/31/2007	12/31/2006	12/31/2005
Earnings Per Share	2.05	1.46	3.02	6.42	5.85	4.48	2.67	1.08
Cash Flow Per Share	5.46	3.02	6.54	8.28	7.11	5.30	3.64	1.94
Tang Book Value Per Share	30.48	29.32	28.39	26.29	20.20	16.06	12.00	9.97
Dividends Per Share	...	...	0.880	0.180	0.910	0.120	0.080	...
Dividend Payout %	...	...	29.14	2.80	15.56	2.68	3.00	...
Income Statement								
Total Revenue	3,547,012	2,695,832	2,807,176	3,640,784	3,446,501	2,995,311	2,100,239	1,382,137
EBITDA	1,542,421	1,149,133	1,455,909	2,419,057	2,265,061	1,795,000	1,190,779	625,630
Depn & Amortn	758,621	658,640	539,829	408,313	356,658	292,987	253,325	241,752
Income Before Taxes	703,225	436,250	916,509	2,015,902	1,912,458	1,488,902	921,287	364,092
Income Taxes	147,088	72,625	143,077	337,260	351,463	282,891	189,421	67,396
Net Income	522,344	370,898	773,429	1,678,642	1,560,995	1,206,011	731,866	296,696
Average Shares	252,791	251,989	253,936	258,891	266,805	269,330	274,756	275,122
Balance Sheet								
Current Assets	1,305,325	1,059,612	830,728	1,483,190	1,240,341	860,191	569,980	522,455
Total Assets	14,607,774	13,495,159	11,221,321	8,396,896	7,102,331	5,876,006	4,585,914	4,346,367
Current Liabilities	911,449	827,180	720,381	433,947	678,993	492,772	426,260	259,335
Long-Term Obligations	4,634,375	4,071,964	2,686,484	750,946	750,789	774,182	684,469	1,129,325
Total Liabilities	6,884,608	6,088,638	4,058,318	1,608,464	1,811,616	1,567,684	1,356,921	1,614,633
Stockholders' Equity	7,723,166	7,406,521	7,163,003	6,788,432	5,290,715	4,308,322	3,228,993	2,731,734
Shares Outstanding	253,348	252,639	252,275	258,224	261,899	268,223	269,184	274,018
Statistical Record								
Return on Assets %	3.71	3.00	7.88	21.66	23.99	23.06	16.39	7.75
Return on Equity %	6.89	5.09	11.09	27.79	32.44	32.00	24.56	11.60
EBITDA Margin %	43.49	42.63	51.86	66.44	65.72	59.93	56.70	45.27
Net Margin %	14.73	13.76	27.55	46.11	45.29	40.26	34.85	21.47
Asset Turnover	0.25	0.22	0.29	0.47	0.53	0.57	0.47	0.36
Current Ratio	1.43	1.28	1.15	3.42	1.83	1.75	1.34	2.01
Debt to Equity	0.60	0.55	0.38	0.11	0.14	0.18	0.21	0.41
Price Range	41.25-29.13	46.12-27.68	44.87-27.04	44.78-20.81	67.98-20.62	56.85-33.87	42.63-29.97	37.77-23.66
P/E Ratio	20.12-14.21	31.59-18.96	14.86-8.95	6.98-3.24	11.62-3.52	12.69-7.56	15.96-11.22	34.97-21.90
Average Yield %	...	...	2.42	0.55	1.95	0.26	0.22	...

Address: Dorfstrasse 19A, Baar, 6340	**Web Site:** www.noblecorp.com	**Auditors:** PricewaterhouseCoopers LLP
Telephone: 417-616-555	**Officers:** David W. Williams - Chairman, President, Chief Executive Officer Julie J. Robertson - Executive Vice President, Secretary	**Investor Contact:** 281-276-6100
		Transfer Agents: Computershare Trust Company, N.A., Canton, MA

540

NOBLE ENERGY, INC.

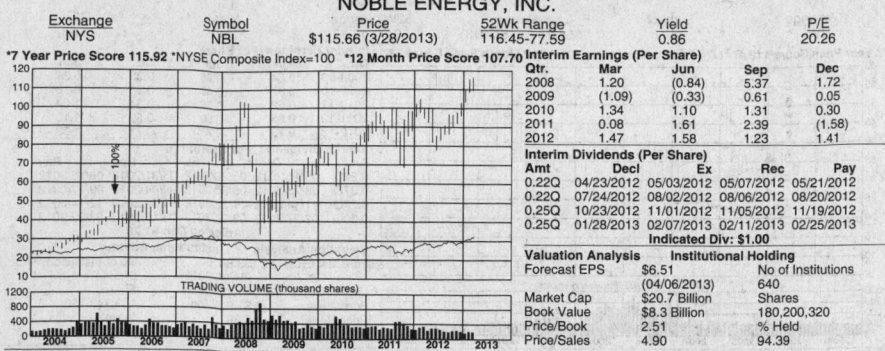

Exchange	Symbol	Price	52Wk Range	Yield	P/E
NYS	NBL	$115.66 (3/28/2013)	116.45-77.59	0.86	20.26

*7 Year Price Score 115.92 *NYSE Composite Index=100 *12 Month Price Score 107.70

Interim Earnings (Per Share)

Qtr.	Mar	Jun	Sep	Dec
2008	1.20	(0.84)	5.37	1.72
2009	(1.09)	(0.33)	0.61	0.05
2010	1.34	1.10	1.31	0.30
2011	0.08	1.61	2.39	(1.58)
2012	1.47	1.58	1.23	1.41

Interim Dividends (Per Share)

Amt	Decl	Ex	Rec	Pay
0.22Q	04/23/2012	05/03/2012	05/07/2012	05/21/2012
0.22Q	07/24/2012	08/02/2012	08/06/2012	08/20/2012
0.25Q	10/23/2012	11/01/2012	11/05/2012	11/19/2012
0.25Q	01/28/2013	02/07/2013	02/11/2013	02/25/2013

Indicated Div: $1.00

Valuation Analysis

		Institutional Holding	
Forecast EPS	$6.51	No of Institutions	
	(04/06/2013)	640	
Market Cap	$20.7 Billion	Shares	
Book Value	$8.3 Billion	180,200,320	
Price/Book	2.51	% Held	
Price/Sales	4.90	94.39	

Business Summary: Production & Extraction (MIC: 9.1.1 SIC: 1311 NAIC: 211111)

Noble Energy is an energy company engaged in oil and gas exploration and production. As of Dec 31 2012, Co. had operations in five main areas: the DJ Basin (onshore U.S.); the Marcellus Shale (onshore U.S.); the deepwater Gulf of Mexico (offshore U.S.); offshore West Africa; and offshore Eastern Mediterranean. Co.'s properties consist primarily of interests in developed and undeveloped crude oil and natural gas leases and concessions. As of the same date, Co. had total proved crude oil, condensate and natural gas liquids reserves of 357.0 million barrels; and total proved natural gas reserves of 4,964.00 billion cubic feet.

Recent Developments: For the year ended Dec 31 2012, income from continuing operations increased 134.2% to US$965.0 million from US$412.0 million a year earlier. Net income increased 126.7% to US$1.03 billion from US$453.0 million in the prior year. Revenues were US$4.22 billion, up 24.1% from US$3.40 billion the year before. Operating income was US$1.41 billion versus US$534.0 million in the prior year, an increase of 164.4%. Indirect operating expenses decreased 2.1% to US$2.81 billion from US$2.87 billion in the equivalent prior-year period.

Prospects: Our evaluation of Noble Energy Inc. as of Apr. 7, 2013 is the result of our systematic analysis on three basic characteristics: earnings strength, relative valuation, and recent stock price movement. The company has managed to produce a neutral trend in earnings per share over the past 5 quarters. However, while recent estimates for the company have been mixed, NBL has posted better than expected results. Based on operating earnings yield, the company is about fairly valued when compared to all of the companies in our coverage universe. Share price changes over the past year indicates that NBL will perform in line with the market over the near term.

Financial Data

(US$ in Thousands)	12/31/2012	12/31/2011	12/31/2010	12/31/2009	12/31/2008	12/31/2007	12/31/2006	12/31/2005
Earnings Per Share	5.71	2.54	4.10	(0.75)	7.58	5.45	3.79	4.12
Cash Flow Per Share	16.43	12.33	11.12	8.72	13.17	11.79	9.85	8.06
Tang Book Value Per Share	42.59	36.90	34.95	30.85	32.08	23.50	19.35	12.66
Dividends Per Share	0.910	0.800	0.720	0.720	0.660	0.435	0.275	0.150
Dividend Payout %	15.94	31.50	17.56	...	8.71	7.98	7.26	3.64
Income Statement								
Total Revenue	4,223,000	3,763,000	3,022,000	2,313,000	3,901,000	3,272,030	2,940,082	2,186,723
EBITDA	2,883,000	1,737,000	1,979,000	623,000	2,901,000	2,238,795	1,217,070	1,481,076
Depn & Amortn	1,403,000	965,000	883,000	816,000	791,000	758,271	3,808	424,875
Income Before Taxes	1,356,000	715,000	1,031,000	(264,000)	2,061,000	1,367,561	1,096,217	968,660
Income Taxes	391,000	262,000	306,000	(133,000)	711,000	423,697	417,789	322,940
Net Income	1,027,000	453,000	725,000	(131,000)	1,350,000	943,870	678,428	645,720
Average Shares	180,000	179,000	177,000	173,000	176,000	173,344	179,044	156,759
Balance Sheet								
Current Assets	2,771,000	2,418,000	1,838,000	1,678,000	2,158,000	1,569,267	1,068,546	1,175,511
Total Assets	17,554,000	16,444,000	13,282,000	11,807,000	12,384,000	10,830,896	9,588,625	8,878,033
Current Liabilities	2,532,000	2,268,000	1,422,000	990,000	1,174,000	1,635,743	1,184,262	1,240,145
Long-Term Obligations	3,736,000	4,100,000	2,272,000	2,037,000	2,241,000	1,851,087	1,800,810	2,030,533
Total Liabilities	9,296,000	9,179,000	6,434,000	5,650,000	6,075,000	6,022,089	5,474,808	5,787,889
Stockholders' Equity	8,258,000	7,265,000	6,848,000	6,157,000	6,309,000	4,808,807	4,113,817	3,090,144
Shares Outstanding	179,000	178,000	176,000	175,000	173,000	172,233	172,233	175,624
Statistical Record								
Return on Assets %	6.03	3.05	5.78	N.M.	11.60	9.24	7.35	10.48
Return on Equity %	13.20	6.42	11.15	N.M.	24.22	21.16	18.83	28.38
EBITDA Margin %	68.27	46.16	65.49	26.93	74.37	68.42	41.40	67.73
Net Margin %	24.32	12.04	23.99	N.M.	34.61	28.85	23.08	29.53
Asset Turnover	0.25	0.25	0.24	0.19	0.34	0.32	0.32	0.35
Current Ratio	1.09	1.07	1.29	1.69	1.84	0.96	0.90	0.95
Debt to Equity	0.45	0.56	0.33	0.33	0.36	0.38	0.44	0.66
Price Range	104.57-77.59	99.68-68.57	87.16-56.23	73.67-40.73	103.83-33.15	81.64-46.33	54.03-36.28	47.79-28.06
P/E Ratio	18.31-13.59	39.24-27.00	21.26-13.71	...	13.70-4.37	14.98-8.50	14.26-9.57	11.60-6.81
Average Yield %	0.98	0.90	0.98	1.20	0.94	0.68	0.60	0.40

Address: 100 Glenborough Drive, Suite 100, Houston, TX 77067 **Telephone:** 281-872-3100 **Fax:** 281-872-3111	**Web Site:** www.nobleenergyinc.com **Officers:** Charles D. Davidson - Chairman, President, Chief Executive Officer David L. Stover - President, Chief Operating Officer	**Auditors:** KPMG LLP **Investor Contact:** 281-.87-2.3125 **Transfer Agents:** Wells Fargo Bank, N. A., South St. Paul, MN

NORDSTROM, INC.

Exchange	Symbol	Price	52Wk Range	Yield	P/E
NYS	JWN	$55.23 (3/28/2013)	58.20-46.80	2.17	15.51

*7 Year Price Score 118.47 *NYSE Composite Index=100   *12 Month Price Score 92.32

Interim Earnings (Per Share)

Qtr.	Apr	Jul	Oct	Jan
2008-09	0.54	0.65	0.33	0.31
2009-10	0.37	0.48	0.38	0.78
2010-11	0.52	0.66	0.54	1.04
2011-12	0.65	0.80	0.59	1.10
2012-13	0.70	0.75	0.71	1.39

Interim Dividends (Per Share)

Amt	Decl	Ex	Rec	Pay
0.27Q	05/10/2012	05/29/2012	05/31/2012	06/15/2012
0.27Q	08/23/2012	08/30/2012	09/04/2012	09/17/2012
0.27Q	11/14/2012	11/28/2012	11/30/2012	12/14/2012
0.30Q	02/27/2013	03/07/2013	03/11/2013	03/22/2013

Indicated Div: $1.20

Valuation Analysis / **Institutional Holding**

Forecast EPS	$3.80 (04/06/2013)	No of Institutions 670
Market Cap	$10.9 Billion	Shares 133,743,720
Book Value	$1.9 Billion	% Held
Price/Book	5.69	56.66
Price/Sales	0.90	

Business Summary: Retail - General Merchandise/Department Stores (MIC: 2.1.1 SIC: 5651 NAIC: 448140)

Nordstrom is a fashion retailer. Co. has two segments: Retail and Credit. As of Mar 16 2012, the Retail segment included 116 Nordstrom branded full-line stores and online store, 105 off-price Nordstrom Rack stores and other retail channels, two Jeffrey boutiques, one treasure&bond store and one clearance store that operated under the name Last Chance. Through these retail channels, Co. provides a range of brand name and private label merchandise focused on apparel, shoes, cosmetics and accessories. Co.'s Credit segment includes its wholly owned federal savings bank, Nordstrom fsb, through which Co. provides a private label credit card, two Nordstrom VISA credit cards and a debit card.

Recent Developments: For the year ended Feb 2 2013, net income increased 7.6% to US$735.0 million from US$683.0 million in the prior year. Revenues were US$12.15 billion, up 11.7% from US$10.88 billion the year before. Operating income was US$1.25 billion versus US$1.25 billion in the prior year, an increase of 7.7%. Direct operating expenses rose 12.7% to US$7.43 billion from US$6.59 billion in the comparable period the year before. Indirect operating expenses increased 11.0% to US$3.37 billion from US$3.04 billion in the equivalent prior-year period.

Prospects: Our evaluation of Nordstrom Inc. as of Apr. 7, 2013 is the result of our systematic analysis on three basic characteristics: earnings strength, relative valuation, and recent stock price movement. The company has produced a positive trend in earnings per share over the past 5 quarters. However, while recent estimates for the company have been lowered by analysts, JWN has posted better than expected results. Based on operating earnings yield, the company is undervalued when compared to all of the companies in our coverage universe. Share price changes over the past year indicates that JWN will perform poorly over the near term.

Financial Data
(US$ in Thousands)

	02/02/2013	01/28/2012	01/29/2011	01/30/2010	01/31/2009	02/02/2008	02/03/2007	01/28/2006
Earnings Per Share	3.56	3.14	2.75	2.01	1.83	2.88	2.55	1.98
Cash Flow Per Share	5.38	5.53	5.39	5.79	3.93	0.66	4.31	2.86
Tang Book Value Per Share	8.82	8.58	9.03	6.98	5.37	4.81	7.90	7.26
Dividends Per Share	1.080	0.920	0.760	0.640	0.640	0.540	0.420	0.320
Dividend Payout %	30.34	29.30	27.64	31.84	34.97	18.75	16.47	16.16
Income Statement								
Total Revenue	12,148,000	10,877,000	9,700,000	8,627,000	8,573,000	8,828,000	8,560,698	7,722,860
EBITDA	1,711,000	1,574,000	1,391,000	1,105,000	1,060,000	1,480,000	1,396,638	1,173,503
Depn & Amortn	366,000	325,000	273,000	271,000	281,000	233,000	248,227	242,978
Income Before Taxes	1,185,000	1,119,000	991,000	696,000	648,000	1,173,000	1,105,653	885,225
Income Taxes	450,000	436,000	378,000	255,000	247,000	458,000	427,654	333,886
Net Income	735,000	683,000	613,000	441,000	401,000	715,000	677,999	551,339
Average Shares	206,700	217,700	222,600	219,700	219,200	249,000	265,712	277,776
Balance Sheet								
Current Assets	5,081,000	5,560,000	4,824,000	4,054,000	3,217,000	3,361,000	2,742,193	2,874,157
Total Assets	8,089,000	8,491,000	7,462,000	6,579,000	5,661,000	5,600,000	4,821,578	4,921,349
Current Liabilities	2,226,000	2,575,000	1,879,000	2,014,000	1,601,000	1,635,000	1,433,143	1,623,312
Long-Term Obligations	3,124,000	3,141,000	2,775,000	2,257,000	2,214,000	2,236,000	623,652	627,776
Total Liabilities	6,176,000	6,535,000	5,441,000	5,007,000	4,451,000	4,485,000	2,653,057	2,828,668
Stockholders' Equity	1,913,000	1,956,000	2,021,000	1,572,000	1,210,000	1,115,000	2,168,521	2,092,681
Shares Outstanding	197,000	207,600	218,000	217,700	215,400	221,000	257,313	269,549
Statistical Record								
Return on Assets %	8.72	8.59	8.76	7.23	7.14	13.76	13.69	11.61
Return on Equity %	37.38	34.44	34.22	31.79	34.59	43.67	31.31	28.49
EBITDA Margin %	14.08	14.47	14.34	12.81	12.36	16.76	16.31	15.20
Net Margin %	6.05	6.28	6.32	5.11	4.68	8.10	7.92	7.14
Asset Turnover	1.44	1.37	1.39	1.41	1.53	1.70	1.73	1.63
Current Ratio	2.28	2.16	2.57	2.01	2.01	2.06	1.91	1.77
Debt to Equity	1.63	1.61	1.37	1.44	1.83	2.01	0.29	0.30
Price Range	58.20-46.80	52.77-37.45	45.90-28.72	38.93-11.33	39.50-7.81	59.66-29.04	56.94-32.36	42.28-23.80
P/E Ratio	16.35-13.15	16.81-11.93	16.69-10.44	19.37-5.64	21.58-4.27	20.72-10.08	22.33-12.69	21.35-12.02
Average Yield %	2.00	1.97	1.98	2.47	2.37	1.16	1.01	0.98

Address: 1617 Sixth Avenue, Seattle, WA 98101	**Web Site:** www.nordstrom.com	**Auditors:** Deloitte & Touche LLP
Telephone: 206-628-2111	**Officers:** Blake W. Nordstrom - President, Co-President, Executive Vice President Peter E. Nordstrom - Executive Vice President, Division Officer	**Investor Contact:** 206-233-6564 **Transfer Agents:** Computershare, Pittsburgh, PA

NORFOLK SOUTHERN CORP.

Exchange	Symbol	Price	52Wk Range	Yield	P/E	Div Achiever
NYS	NSC	$77.08 (3/28/2013)	77.08-56.34	2.59	14.35	11 Years

*7 Year Price Score 105.58 *NYSE Composite Index=100 *12 Month Price Score 98.44

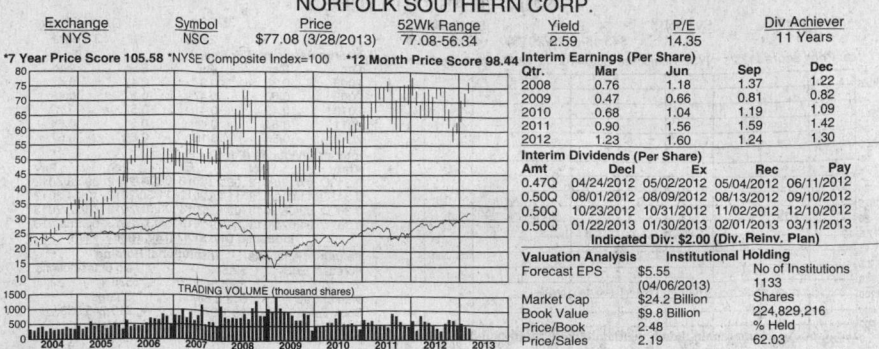

Interim Earnings (Per Share)

Qtr.	Mar	Jun	Sep	Dec
2008	0.76	1.18	1.37	1.22
2009	0.47	0.66	0.81	0.82
2010	0.68	1.04	1.19	1.09
2011	0.90	1.56	1.59	1.42
2012	1.23	1.60	1.24	1.30

Interim Dividends (Per Share)

Amt	Decl	Ex	Rec	Pay
0.47Q	04/24/2012	05/02/2012	05/04/2012	06/11/2012
0.50Q	08/01/2012	08/09/2012	08/13/2012	09/10/2012
0.50Q	10/23/2012	10/31/2012	11/02/2012	12/10/2012
0.50Q	01/22/2013	01/30/2013	02/01/2013	03/11/2013

Indicated Div: $2.00 (Div. Reinv. Plan)

Valuation Analysis		Institutional Holding	
Forecast EPS	$5.55 (04/06/2013)	No of Institutions	1133
Market Cap	$24.2 Billion	Shares	224,829,216
Book Value	$9.8 Billion	% Held	62.03
Price/Book	2.48		
Price/Sales	2.19		

Business Summary: Rail (MIC: 7.4.3 SIC: 4011 NAIC: 482111)

Norfolk Southern is primarily engaged in the rail transportation of raw materials, intermediate products, and finished goods in the Southeast, East, and Midwest and, via interchange with rail carriers, to and from the rest of the U.S. Co. also transports overseas freight through several Atlantic and Gulf Coast ports. Co. provides logistics services and intermodal network in the eastern half of the U.S. Co.'s system reaches several individual industries, electric generating facilities, mines, distribution centers, transload facilities, and other businesses located in its service area. At Dec 31 2012, Co.'s railroads operated in 22 states and the District of Columbia.

Recent Developments: For the year ended Dec 31 2012, net income decreased 8.7% to US$1.75 billion from US$1.92 billion in the prior year. Revenues were US$11.04 billion, down 1.2% from US$11.17 billion the year before. Operating income was US$3.12 billion versus US$3.21 billion in the prior year, a decrease of 2.8%. Direct operating expenses declined 2.0% to US$4.04 billion from US$4.12 billion in the comparable period the year before. Indirect operating expenses increased 1.0% to US$3.88 billion from US$3.84 billion in the equivalent prior-year period.

Prospects: Our evaluation of Norfolk Southern Corp. as of Apr. 7, 2013 is the result of our systematic analysis on three basic characteristics: earnings strength, relative valuation, and recent stock price movement. The company has generated a negative trend in earnings per share over the past 5 quarters and while recent estimates for the company have been mixed, NSC has posted better than expected results. Based on operating earnings yield, the company is undervalued when compared to all of the companies in our coverage universe. Share price changes over the past year indicates that NSC will perform poorly over the near term.

Financial Data

(US$ in Thousands)	12/31/2012	12/31/2011	12/31/2010	12/31/2009	12/31/2008	12/31/2007	12/31/2006	12/31/2005
Earnings Per Share	5.37	5.45	4.00	2.76	4.52	3.68	3.57	3.11
Cash Flow Per Share	9.53	9.34	7.41	5.07	7.27	5.99	5.43	5.21
Tang Book Value Per Share	31.08	30.00	29.85	28.06	26.23	25.64	24.19	22.66
Dividends Per Share	1.940	1.660	1.400	1.360	1.220	0.960	0.680	0.480
Dividend Payout %	36.13	30.46	35.00	49.28	26.99	26.09	19.05	15.43
Income Statement								
Total Revenue	11,040,000	11,172,000	9,516,000	7,969,000	10,661,000	9,432,000	9,407,000	8,527,000
EBITDA	4,152,000	4,214,000	3,643,000	2,904,000	3,968,000	3,411,000	3,449,000	3,023,000
Depn & Amortn	922,000	869,000	826,000	845,000	815,000	786,000	750,000	787,000
Income Before Taxes	2,734,000	2,896,000	2,351,000	1,600,000	2,731,000	2,202,000	2,282,000	1,777,000
Income Taxes	1,019,000	1,011,000	881,000	598,000	1,044,000	783,000	758,000	425,000
Net Income	1,749,000	1,916,000	1,496,000	1,034,000	1,716,000	1,464,000	1,481,000	1,281,000
Average Shares	325,500	351,300	371,800	372,100	380,000	397,800	414,700	412,300
Balance Sheet								
Current Assets	2,242,000	1,751,000	2,471,000	2,246,000	1,999,000	1,675,000	2,400,000	2,650,000
Total Assets	30,342,000	28,538,000	28,199,000	27,369,000	26,297,000	26,144,000	26,028,000	25,861,000
Current Liabilities	2,081,000	1,701,000	2,082,000	1,789,000	2,105,000	1,948,000	2,093,000	1,921,000
Long-Term Obligations	8,432,000	7,390,000	6,567,000	6,679,000	6,183,000	5,999,000	6,109,000	6,616,000
Total Liabilities	20,582,000	18,627,000	17,530,000	17,016,000	16,690,000	16,417,000	16,413,000	16,572,000
Stockholders' Equity	9,760,000	9,911,000	10,669,000	10,353,000	9,607,000	9,727,000	9,615,000	9,289,000
Shares Outstanding	314,034	330,386	357,362	369,019	366,233	379,297	397,419	409,885
Statistical Record								
Return on Assets %	5.92	6.75	5.38	3.85	6.53	5.61	5.71	5.06
Return on Equity %	17.73	18.62	14.23	10.36	17.70	15.14	15.67	14.83
EBITDA Margin %	37.61	37.72	38.28	36.44	37.22	36.16	36.66	35.45
Net Margin %	15.84	17.15	15.72	12.98	16.10	15.52	15.74	15.02
Asset Turnover	0.37	0.39	0.34	0.30	0.41	0.36	0.36	0.34
Current Ratio	1.08	1.03	1.19	1.26	0.95	0.86	1.15	1.38
Debt to Equity	0.86	0.75	0.62	0.65	0.64	0.62	0.64	0.71
Price Range	78.24-56.34	76.99-60.01	62.99-46.31	54.24-26.95	73.64-43.29	58.64-46.04	57.35-40.65	45.20-30.01
P/E Ratio	14.57-10.49	14.13-11.01	15.75-11.58	19.65-9.76	16.29-9.58	15.93-12.51	16.06-11.39	14.53-9.65
Average Yield %	2.83	2.41	2.47	3.23	2.10	1.85	1.38	1.31

Address: Three Commercial Place, Norfolk, VA 23510-2191 Telephone: 757-629-2680	Web Site: www.nscorp.com Officers: Charles W. Moorman - Chairman, President, Chief Executive Officer James A. Squires - Executive Vice President, Chief Financial Officer, Executive Vice President	Auditors: KPMG LLP Investor Contact: 757-629-2861 Transfer Agents: American Stock Transfer & Trust Company, LLC, Brooklyn, NY

NORTHEAST UTILITIES

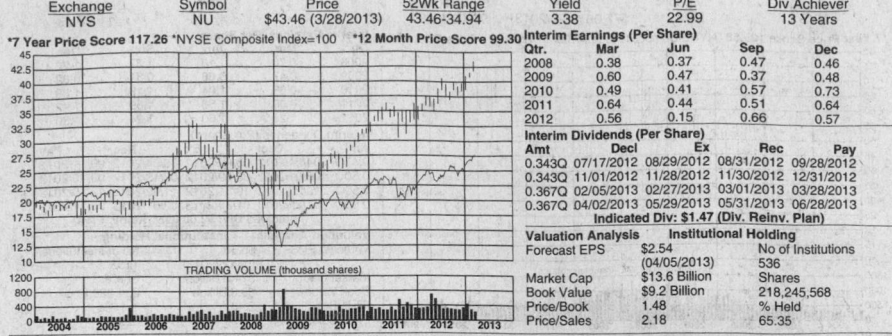

Exchange	Symbol	Price	52Wk Range	Yield	P/E	Div Achiever
NYS	NU	$43.46 (3/28/2013)	43.46-34.94	3.38	22.99	13 Years

*7 Year Price Score 117.26 *NYSE Composite Index=100 *12 Month Price Score 99.30

Interim Earnings (Per Share)

Qtr.	Mar	Jun	Sep	Dec
2008	0.38	0.37	0.47	0.46
2009	0.60	0.47	0.37	0.48
2010	0.49	0.41	0.57	0.73
2011	0.64	0.44	0.51	0.64
2012	0.56	0.15	0.66	0.57

Interim Dividends (Per Share)

Amt	Decl	Ex	Rec	Pay
0.343Q	07/17/2012	08/29/2012	08/31/2012	09/28/2012
0.343Q	11/01/2012	11/28/2012	11/30/2012	12/31/2012
0.367Q	02/05/2013	02/27/2013	03/01/2013	03/28/2013
0.367Q	04/02/2013	05/29/2013	05/31/2013	06/28/2013

Indicated Div: $1.47 (Div. Reinv. Plan)

Valuation Analysis / **Institutional Holding**

Forecast EPS	$2.54 (04/05/2013)	No of Institutions	536
Market Cap	$13.6 Billion	Shares	218,245,568
Book Value	$9.2 Billion	% Held	65.35
Price/Book	1.48		
Price/Sales	2.18		

Business Summary: Electric Utilities (MIC: 3.1.1 SIC: 4911 NAIC: 221122)

Northeast Utilities is a public utility holding company. Co.'s electric distribution segment consists of the distribution businesses of its utility subsidiaries: The Connecticut Light and Power Company (CL&P), Public Service Company of New Hampshire (PSNH) and Western Massachusetts Electric Company (WMECO). At Dec 31 2011, CL&P distributed electricity to about 1.2 million customers in Connecticut, PSNH distributed electricity to about 498,000 retail customers in New Hampshire and WEMCO distributed electricity to about.206,000 retail customers in the western region of Massachusetts. Co.'s regulated natural gas utility, Yankee Gas Services Company served about 208,000 customers in Connecticut.

Recent Developments: For the year ended Dec 31 2012, net income increased 33.1% to US$533.1 million from US$400.5 million in the prior year. Revenues were US$6.27 billion, up 40.5% from US$4.47 billion the year before. Operating income was US$1.12 billion versus US$794.2 million in the prior year, an increase of 40.8%. Direct operating expenses rose 33.2% to US$3.67 billion from US$2.75 billion in the comparable period the year before. Indirect operating expenses increased 62.1% to US$1.49 billion from US$918.2 million in the equivalent prior-year period.

Prospects: Our evaluation of Northeast Utilities as of Apr. 7, 2013 is the result of our systematic analysis on three basic characteristics: earnings strength, relative valuation, and recent stock price movement. The company has generated a negative trend in earnings per share over the past 5 quarters and while recent estimates for the company have remained steady, NU has posted results that fell short of analysts expectations. Based on operating earnings yield, the company is about fairly valued when compared to all of the companies in our coverage universe. Share price changes over the past year indicates that NU will perform in line with the market over the near term.

Financial Data
(US$ in Thousands)

	12/31/2012	12/31/2011	12/31/2010	12/31/2009	12/31/2008	12/31/2007	12/31/2006	12/31/2005
Earnings Per Share	1.89	2.22	2.19	1.91	1.67	1.59	3.05	(1.93)
Cash Flow Per Share	4.18	5.47	6.19	5.73	4.16	1.61	2.65	3.35
Tang Book Value Per Share	18.21	21.03	20.63	19.40	18.28	17.68	17.03	14.74
Dividends Per Share	1.323	1.100	1.025	0.950	0.825	0.775	0.725	0.675
Dividend Payout %	69.99	49.55	46.80	49.74	49.40	48.74	23.77	...
Income Statement								
Total Revenue	6,273,787	4,465,657	4,898,167	5,439,430	5,800,095	5,822,226	6,884,388	7,397,390
EBITDA	1,656,958	1,124,083	1,142,544	1,098,794	919,781	866,417	532,140	120,293
Depn & Amortn	519,010	302,192	300,737	309,618	278,588	265,297	243,822	236,921
Income Before Taxes	808,003	571,466	604,516	515,539	372,048	360,875	50,280	(386,429)
Income Taxes	274,926	170,953	210,409	179,947	105,661	109,420	(81,429)	(162,765)
Net Income	525,945	394,693	387,949	330,033	260,828	246,483	470,578	(253,488)
Average Shares	277,993	177,804	176,885	172,717	155,999	155,304	154,146	131,638
Balance Sheet								
Current Assets	2,227,295	1,357,472	1,317,742	1,267,854	1,505,564	1,286,256	1,731,051	2,376,843
Total Assets	28,302,824	15,647,066	14,522,042	14,057,679	13,988,480	11,581,822	11,303,236	12,569,075
Current Liabilities	3,643,690	1,947,682	1,238,075	979,412	1,703,462	1,206,150	1,363,835	1,975,230
Long-Term Obligations	7,200,156	4,614,913	4,632,866	4,492,935	4,103,162	3,483,599	2,960,435	3,027,288
Total Liabilities	19,065,774	11,634,396	10,594,666	10,363,577	10,851,968	8,551,787	8,388,857	10,023,631
Stockholders' Equity	9,237,050	4,012,670	3,927,376	3,694,102	3,136,512	3,030,035	2,914,379	2,545,444
Shares Outstanding	314,053	177,158	176,448	175,620	155,834	155,079	154,233	153,225
Statistical Record								
Return on Assets %	2.39	2.62	2.71	2.35	2.03	2.15	3.94	N.M.
Return on Equity %	7.92	9.94	10.18	9.66	8.44	8.29	17.24	N.M.
EBITDA Margin %	26.41	25.17	23.33	20.20	15.86	14.88	7.73	1.63
Net Margin %	8.38	8.84	7.92	6.07	4.50	4.23	6.84	N.M.
Asset Turnover	0.28	0.30	0.34	0.39	0.45	0.51	0.58	0.61
Current Ratio	0.61	0.70	1.06	1.29	0.88	1.07	1.27	1.20
Debt to Equity	0.78	1.15	1.18	1.22	1.31	1.15	1.02	1.19
Price Range	40.57-33.53	36.31-30.46	32.05-24.78	26.33-19.45	31.31-19.15	33.53-26.93	28.81-19.24	21.79-17.61
P/E Ratio	21.47-17.74	16.36-13.72	14.63-11.32	13.79-10.18	18.75-11.47	21.09-16.94	9.45-6.31	...
Average Yield %	3.53	3.23	3.64	4.16	3.24	2.60	3.28	3.48

Address: One Federal Street, Building 111-4, Springfield, MA 01105 **Telephone:** 413-785-5871	**Web Site:** www.nu.com **Officers:** Thomas J. May - President, Chief Executive Officer David R. McHale - Executive Vice President, Chief Financial Officer, Chief Administrative Officer	**Auditors:** Deloitte & Touche LLP **Investor Contact:** 860-728-4652 **Transfer Agents:** Computershare Investor Services, Canton, MA

NORTHROP GRUMMAN CORP

Exchange	Symbol	Price	52Wk Range	Yield	P/E
NYS	NOC	$70.15 (3/28/2013)	71.13-57.11	3.14	8.98

*7 Year Price Score 97.88   *NYSE Composite Index=100   *12 Month Price Score 93.41

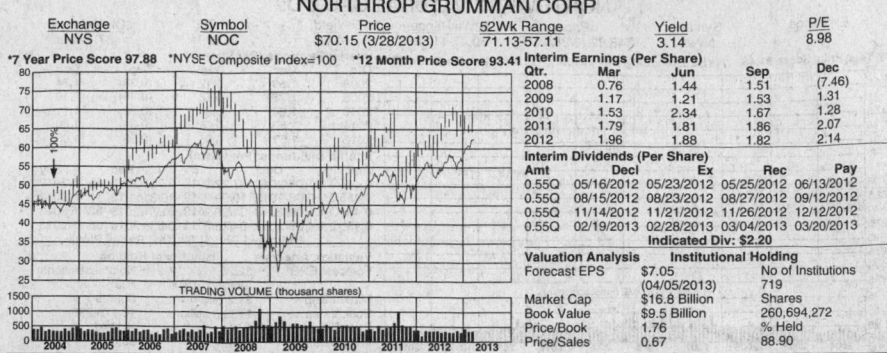

Interim Earnings (Per Share)

Qtr.	Mar	Jun	Sep	Dec
2008	0.76	1.44	1.51	(7.46)
2009	1.17	1.21	1.53	1.31
2010	1.53	2.34	1.67	1.28
2011	1.79	1.81	1.86	2.07
2012	1.96	1.88	1.82	2.14

Interim Dividends (Per Share)

Amt	Decl	Ex	Rec	Pay
0.55Q	05/16/2012	05/23/2012	05/25/2012	06/13/2012
0.55Q	08/15/2012	08/23/2012	08/27/2012	09/12/2012
0.55Q	11/14/2012	11/21/2012	11/26/2012	12/12/2012
0.55Q	02/19/2013	02/28/2013	03/04/2013	03/20/2013

Indicated Div: $2.20

Valuation Analysis

		Institutional Holding	
Forecast EPS	$7.05 (04/05/2013)	No of Institutions	719
Market Cap	$16.8 Billion	Shares	260,694,272
Book Value	$9.5 Billion	% Held	88.90
Price/Book	1.76		
Price/Sales	0.67		

Business Summary: Defense (MIC: 7.1.2 SIC: 3812 NAIC: 334511)

Northrop Grumman is a global security company providing systems, products and applications in unmanned systems, cybersecurity; command, control, communications and computers intelligence, surveillance, and reconnaissance; and logistics to government and commercial customers worldwide through its four sectors: Aerospace Systems, Electronic Systems, Information Systems and Technical Services. Co. provides a portfolio of capabilities and technologies that enable it to deliver systems for applications that range from undersea to outer space and into cyberspace.

Recent Developments: For the year ended Dec 31 2012, income from continuing operations decreased 5.2% to US$1.98 billion from US$2.09 billion a year earlier. Net income decreased 6.6% to US$1.98 billion from US$2.12 billion in the prior year. Revenues were US$25.22 billion, down 4.5% from US$26.41 billion the year before. Operating income was US$3.13 billion versus US$3.28 billion in the prior year, a decrease of 4.5%. Direct operating expenses declined 5.5% to US$19.64 billion from US$20.79 billion in the comparable period the year before. Indirect operating expenses increased 4.3% to US$2.45 billion from US$2.35 billion in the equivalent prior-year period.

Prospects: Our evaluation of Northrop Grumman Corp. as of Apr. 7, 2013 is the result of our systematic analysis on three basic characteristics: earnings strength, relative valuation, and recent stock price movement. The company has generated a negative trend in earnings per share over the past 5 quarters and while recent estimates for the company have been mixed, NOC has posted better than expected results. Based on operating earnings yield, the company is undervalued when compared to all of the companies in our coverage universe. Share price changes over the past year indicates that NOC will perform poorly over the near term.

Financial Data
(US$ in Thousands)

	12/31/2012	12/31/2011	12/31/2010	12/31/2009	12/31/2008	12/31/2007	12/31/2006	12/31/2005
Earnings Per Share	7.81	7.52	6.82	5.21	(3.77)	5.12	4.37	3.85
Cash Flow Per Share	10.59	7.64	8.26	6.68	9.57	8.46	5.08	7.37
Dividends Per Share	2.150	1.970	1.840	1.690	1.570	1.480	1.160	1.010
Dividend Payout %	27.53	26.20	26.98	32.44	...	28.91	26.54	26.23
Income Statement								
Total Revenue	25,218,000	26,412,000	34,757,000	33,755,000	33,887,000	32,018,000	30,148,000	30,721,000
EBITDA	3,625,000	3,766,000	3,482,000	3,132,000	499,000	3,572,000	3,148,000	3,151,000
Depn & Amortn	448,000	462,000	606,000	585,000	572,000	578,000	569,000	773,000
Income Before Taxes	2,965,000	3,083,000	2,595,000	2,266,000	(368,000)	2,686,000	2,276,000	2,044,000
Income Taxes	987,000	997,000	557,000	693,000	913,000	883,000	709,000	661,000
Net Income	1,978,000	2,118,000	2,053,000	1,686,000	(1,262,000)	1,790,000	1,542,000	1,400,000
Average Shares	253,400	281,600	301,100	323,300	334,500	354,300	358,600	363,200
Balance Sheet								
Current Assets	8,392,000	7,746,000	9,904,000	8,635,000	7,189,000	6,772,000	6,719,000	7,549,000
Total Assets	26,543,000	25,411,000	31,421,000	30,252,000	30,197,000	33,373,000	32,009,000	34,214,000
Current Liabilities	6,056,000	6,135,000	8,386,000	6,985,000	7,424,000	6,432,000	6,753,000	7,974,000
Long-Term Obligations	3,930,000	3,935,000	4,045,000	4,191,000	3,443,000	3,918,000	3,992,000	3,881,000
Total Liabilities	17,029,000	15,075,000	17,864,000	17,565,000	18,277,000	15,686,000	15,394,000	17,386,000
Stockholders' Equity	9,514,000	10,336,000	13,557,000	12,687,000	11,920,000	17,687,000	16,615,000	16,828,000
Shares Outstanding	239,209	253,889	290,956	306,865	327,012	337,834	345,921	347,357
Statistical Record								
Return on Assets %	7.59	7.45	6.66	5.58	N.M.	5.48	4.66	4.14
Return on Equity %	19.88	17.73	15.65	13.70	N.M.	10.44	9.22	8.35
EBITDA Margin %	14.37	14.26	10.02	9.28	1.47	11.16	10.44	10.26
Net Margin %	7.84	8.02	5.91	4.99	N.M.	5.59	5.11	4.56
Asset Turnover	0.97	0.93	1.13	1.12	1.06	0.98	0.91	0.91
Current Ratio	1.39	1.26	1.18	1.24	0.97	1.05	0.99	0.95
Debt to Equity	0.41	0.38	0.30	0.33	0.29	0.22	0.24	0.23
Price Range	71.13-57.11	70.33-49.26	62.94-49.08	51.56-31.16	74.91-31.03	76.64-60.74	64.62-54.10	54.53-46.49
P/E Ratio	9.11-7.31	9.35-6.55	9.23-7.20	9.90-5.98	...	14.97-11.86	14.79-12.38	14.16-12.08
Average Yield %	3.37	3.30	3.32	3.87	2.63	2.13	1.94	2.02

Address: 2980 Fairview Park Drive, Falls Church, VA 22042 **Telephone:** 703-280-2900	**Web Site:** www.northropgrumman.com **Officers:** Wesley G. Bush - Chairman, President, Chief Executive Officer, Vice President, Chief Financial Officer, Chief Operating Officer James F. Palmer - Corporate Vice-President, Chief Financial Officer	**Auditors:** Deloitte & Touche LLP **Investor Contact:** 703-280-4575 **Transfer Agents:** ComputerShare Investor Services, Providence, RI

NORTHWEST NATURAL GAS CO.

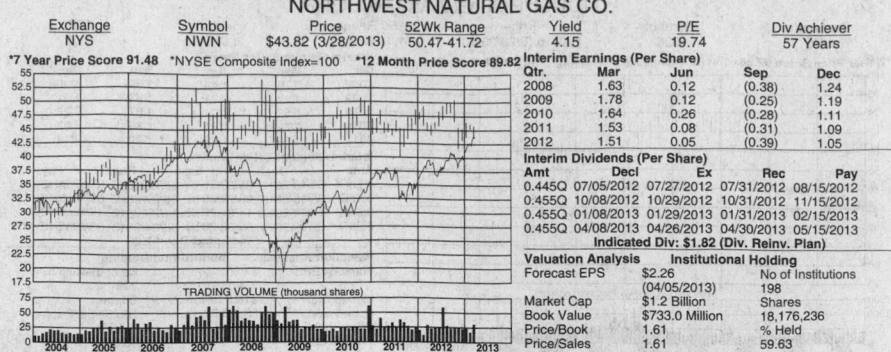

Exchange	Symbol	Price	52Wk Range	Yield	P/E	Div Achiever
NYS	NWN	$43.82 (3/28/2013)	50.47-41.72	4.15	19.74	57 Years

*7 Year Price Score 91.48 *NYSE Composite Index=100 *12 Month Price Score 89.82

Interim Earnings (Per Share)

Qtr.	Mar	Jun	Sep	Dec
2008	1.63	0.12	(0.38)	1.24
2009	1.78	0.12	(0.25)	1.19
2010	1.64	0.26	(0.28)	1.11
2011	1.53	0.08	(0.31)	1.09
2012	1.51	0.05	(0.39)	1.05

Interim Dividends (Per Share)

Amt	Decl	Ex	Rec	Pay
0.445Q	07/05/2012	07/27/2012	07/31/2012	08/15/2012
0.455Q	10/08/2012	10/29/2012	10/31/2012	11/15/2012
0.455Q	01/08/2013	01/29/2013	01/31/2013	02/15/2013
0.455Q	04/08/2013	04/26/2013	04/30/2013	05/15/2013

Indicated Div: $1.82 (Div. Reinv. Plan)

Valuation Analysis

		Institutional Holding	
Forecast EPS	$2.26 (04/05/2013)	No of Institutions	198
Market Cap	$1.2 Billion	Shares	18,176,236
Book Value	$733.0 Million	% Held	59.63
Price/Book	1.61		
Price/Sales	1.61		

TRADING VOLUME (thousand shares)

Business Summary: Gas Utilities (MIC: 3.3.1 SIC: 4924 NAIC: 221210)

Northwest Natural Gas is engaged in the distribution of natural gas. Co. operates in two segments: local gas distribution, which involves building and maintaining a pipeline distribution system, purchasing gas from producers and marketers, contracting for the transportation of gas over pipelines from regional supply basins to its service territory, and reselling the gas to customers; and gas storage, which includes natural gas storage services provided to customers primarily from two underground natural gas storage facilities, its Gill Ranch gas storage facility, and the non-utility portion of its Mist gas storage facility. Co. has operations in Oregon, Washington and California.

Recent Developments: For the year ended Dec 31 2012, net income decreased 6.3% to US$59.9 million from US$63.9 million in the prior year. Revenues were US$730.6 million, down 11.8% from US$828.1 million the year before. Operating income was US$142.2 million versus US$144.8 million in the prior year, a decrease of 1.8%. Direct operating expenses declined 22.5% to US$355.3 million from US$458.5 million in the comparable period the year before. Indirect operating expenses increased 3.7% to US$233.1 million from US$224.7 million in the equivalent prior-year period.

Prospects: Our evaluation of Northwest Natural Gas Co. as of Apr. 7, 2013 is the result of our systematic analysis on three basic characteristics: earnings strength, relative valuation, and recent stock price movement. The company has produced a positive trend in earnings per share over the past 5 quarters. However, while recent estimates for the company have been lowered by analysts, NWN has posted results that fell short of analysts expectations. Based on operating earnings yield, the company is about fairly valued when compared to all of the companies in our coverage universe. Share price changes over the past year indicates that NWN will perform poorly over the near term.

Financial Data

(US$ in Thousands)	12/31/2012	12/31/2011	12/31/2010	12/31/2009	12/31/2008	12/31/2007	12/31/2006	12/31/2005
Earnings Per Share	2.22	2.39	2.73	2.83	2.61	2.76	2.29	2.11
Cash Flow Per Share	6.28	8.75	4.76	9.07	1.31	6.85	5.39	2.87
Tang Book Value Per Share	27.23	26.70	25.99	24.88	23.71	22.52	21.97	21.28
Dividends Per Share	1.790	1.750	1.680	1.600	1.520	1.440	1.390	1.320
Dividend Payout %	80.63	73.22	61.54	56.54	58.24	52.17	60.70	62.56
Income Statement								
Total Revenue	730,607	848,796	812,106	1,012,711	1,037,855	1,033,193	1,013,172	910,486
EBITDA	220,133	219,322	227,807	225,033	219,691	224,174	203,331	189,797
Depn & Amortn	73,017	70,004	65,124	62,814	72,159	68,343	64,435	61,645
Income Before Taxes	103,959	107,280	122,129	121,793	110,203	118,557	99,649	90,869
Income Taxes	44,104	43,382	49,462	46,671	40,678	44,060	36,234	32,720
Net Income	59,855	63,898	72,667	75,122	69,525	74,497	63,415	58,149
Average Shares	26,907	26,744	26,657	26,576	26,594	26,995	27,657	27,621
Balance Sheet								
Current Assets	283,699	348,689	330,265	328,235	480,970	276,799	308,793	323,710
Total Assets	2,818,753	2,746,574	2,616,616	2,399,252	2,378,152	2,014,183	1,956,856	2,042,031
Current Liabilities	368,436	414,464	468,161	392,569	551,320	389,866	339,479	326,565
Long-Term Obligations	691,700	641,700	591,700	601,700	512,000	512,000	517,000	521,500
Total Liabilities	2,085,720	2,032,086	1,923,515	1,739,147	1,749,779	1,419,432	1,357,311	1,455,100
Stockholders' Equity	733,033	714,488	693,101	660,105	628,373	594,751	599,545	586,931
Shares Outstanding	26,917	26,756	26,668	26,533	26,501	26,407	27,283	27,579
Statistical Record								
Return on Assets %	2.15	2.38	2.90	3.14	3.16	3.75	3.17	3.08
Return on Equity %	8.25	9.08	10.74	11.66	11.34	12.48	10.69	10.07
EBITDA Margin %	30.13	25.84	28.05	22.22	21.17	21.70	20.07	20.85
Net Margin %	8.19	7.53	8.95	7.42	6.70	7.21	6.26	6.39
Asset Turnover	0.26	0.32	0.32	0.42	0.47	0.52	0.51	0.48
Current Ratio	0.77	0.84	0.71	0.84	0.87	0.71	0.91	0.99
Debt to Equity	0.94	0.90	0.85	0.91	0.81	0.86	0.86	0.89
Price Range	50.47-41.72	48.66-40.09	50.64-41.62	46.19-38.50	54.07-41.38	52.62-40.21	43.00-33.27	39.50-32.61
P/E Ratio	22.73-18.79	20.36-16.77	18.55-15.25	16.32-13.60	20.72-15.85	19.07-14.57	18.78-14.53	18.72-15.45
Average Yield %	3.83	3.86	3.63	3.73	3.28	3.12	3.74	3.68

Address: 220 N.W. Second Avenue, Portland, OR 97209 Telephone: 503-226-4211	Web Site: www.nwnatural.com Officers: Tod R. Hamachek - Chairman Gregg S. Kantor - President, Chief Executive Officer	Auditors: PricewaterhouseCoopers LLP Investor Contact: 503-226-4211ext.34 Transfer Agents: American Stock Transfer & Trust Company, Brooklyn, NY

NRG ENERGY INC

Exchange	Symbol	Price	52Wk Range	Yield	P/E
NYS	NRG	$26.49 (3/28/2013)	26.49-14.34	1.36	11.27

*7 Year Price Score 69.26   ***NYSE Composite Index=100**   ***12 Month Price Score 110.50**

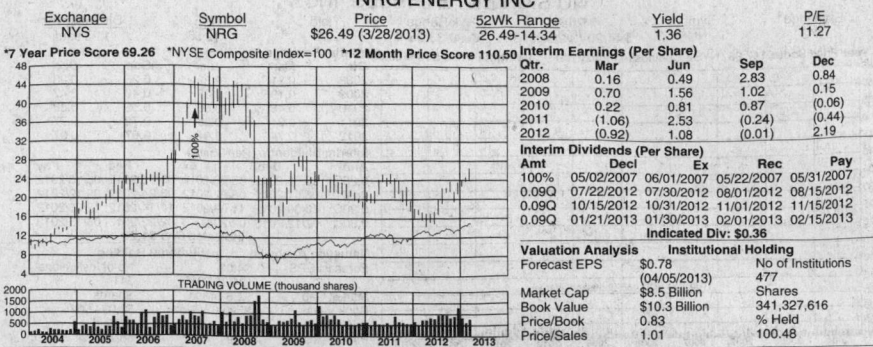

Interim Earnings (Per Share)

Qtr.	Mar	Jun	Sep	Dec
2008	0.16	0.49	2.83	0.84
2009	0.70	1.56	1.02	0.15
2010	0.22	0.81	0.87	(0.06)
2011	(1.06)	2.53	(0.24)	(0.44)
2012	(0.92)	1.08	(0.01)	2.19

Interim Dividends (Per Share)

Amt	Decl	Ex	Rec	Pay
100%	05/02/2007	06/01/2007	05/22/2007	05/31/2007
0.09Q	07/22/2012	07/30/2012	08/01/2012	08/15/2012
0.09Q	10/15/2012	10/31/2012	11/01/2012	11/15/2012
0.09Q	01/21/2013	01/30/2013	02/01/2013	02/15/2013

Indicated Div: $0.36

Valuation Analysis

		Institutional Holding	
Forecast EPS	$0.78 (04/05/2013)	No of Institutions	477
Market Cap	$8.5 Billion	Shares	341,327,616
Book Value	$10.3 Billion	% Held	100.48
Price/Book	0.83		
Price/Sales	1.01		

TRADING VOLUME (thousand shares)

Business Summary: Electric Utilities (MIC: 3.1.1 SIC: 4911 NAIC: 221121)

NRG Energy is wholesale power generation company. Co. is engaged in the ownership and operation of power generation facilities; the trading of energy, capacity and related products; and the transacting in and trading of fuel and transportation services. Co. is a retail electricity company engaged in the supply of electricity, energy services, and energy products to retail electricity customers in deregulated markets through its GenOn Energy, Inc., Green Mountain Energy Company, and Energy Plus Holdings LLC subsidiaries (collectively, the Retail Businesses). At Dec 31 2011, Co.'s Retail Businesses served approximately 2.1 million residential, business, commercial and industrial customers.

Recent Developments: For the year ended Dec 31 2012, net income increased 193.9% to US$579.0 million from US$197.0 million in the prior year. Revenues were US$8.42 billion, down 7.2% from US$9.08 billion the year before. Operating income was US$350.0 million versus US$635.0 million in the prior year, a decrease of 44.9%. Direct operating expenses declined 8.8% to US$6.09 billion from US$6.68 billion in the comparable period the year before. Indirect operating expenses increased 12.2% to US$1.99 billion from US$1.77 billion in the equivalent prior-year period.

Prospects: Our evaluation of NRG Energy Inc. as of Apr. 7, 2013 is the result of our systematic analysis on three basic characteristics: earnings strength, relative valuation, and recent stock price movement. The company has produced a positive trend in earnings per share over the past 5 quarters and while recent estimates for the company have been raised by analysts, NRG has posted results that were in line with analysts expectations. Based on operating earnings yield, the company is undervalued when compared to all of the companies in our coverage universe. Share price changes over the past year indicates that NRG will perform very well over the near term.

Financial Data

(US$ in Thousands)	12/31/2012	12/31/2011	12/31/2010	12/31/2009	12/31/2008	12/31/2007	12/31/2006	12/31/2005
Earnings Per Share	2.35	0.78	1.84	3.44	4.29	2.01	2.04	0.38
Cash Flow Per Share	4.94	4.86	6.44	8.58	6.09	6.32	1.58	0.40
Tang Book Value Per Share	22.03	19.47	18.85	16.88	16.94	9.29	9.17	11.24
Dividends Per Share	0.180	...	...	...	...	...	...	...
Dividend Payout %	7.66	...	...	...	...	...	...	...
Income Statement								
Total Revenue	8,422,000	9,079,000	8,849,000	8,952,000	6,885,000	5,989,000	5,623,000	2,708,000
EBITDA	1,022,000	151,000	1,345,000	2,415,000	2,020,000	1,425,000	929,000	230,000
Depn & Amortn	146,000	167,000	4,000	153,000	(270,000)	(156,000)	(490,000)	17,000
Income Before Taxes	215,000	(681,000)	709,000	1,628,000	1,670,000	892,000	820,000	16,000
Income Taxes	(327,000)	(843,000)	277,000	728,000	713,000	377,000	325,000	43,000
Net Income	559,000	197,000	477,000	942,000	1,188,000	586,000	621,000	84,000
Average Shares	234,000	241,000	254,000	271,200	275,000	288,000	300,000	170,000
Balance Sheet								
Current Assets	7,956,000	7,597,000	7,137,000	6,208,000	8,492,000	3,562,000	3,083,000	2,197,000
Total Assets	35,128,000	26,715,000	26,896,000	23,378,000	24,808,000	19,274,000	19,435,000	7,431,000
Current Liabilities	4,677,000	5,671,000	4,220,000	3,762,000	6,581,000	2,277,000	2,032,000	1,356,000
Long-Term Obligations	15,733,000	9,745,000	8,748,000	7,847,000	7,704,000	7,895,000	8,647,000	2,581,000
Total Liabilities	24,864,000	18,980,000	18,593,000	15,446,000	17,452,000	13,523,000	13,530,000	4,954,000
Stockholders' Equity	10,264,000	7,735,000	8,303,000	7,932,000	7,356,000	5,751,000	5,905,000	2,477,000
Shares Outstanding	322,606	227,519	247,197	253,995	234,356	236,734	244,647	161,403
Statistical Record								
Return on Assets %	1.80	0.73	1.90	3.91	5.38	3.03	4.62	1.10
Return on Equity %	6.19	2.46	5.88	12.32	18.08	10.05	14.82	3.25
EBITDA Margin %	12.13	1.66	15.20	26.98	29.34	23.79	16.52	8.49
Net Margin %	6.64	2.17	5.39	10.52	17.25	9.78	11.04	3.10
Asset Turnover	0.27	0.34	0.35	0.37	0.31	0.31	0.42	0.35
Current Ratio	1.70	1.34	1.69	1.65	1.29	1.56	1.52	1.62
Debt to Equity	1.53	1.26	1.05	0.99	1.05	1.37	1.46	1.04
Price Range	23.65-14.34	25.41-17.57	25.17-18.31	29.13-16.34	44.96-15.17	46.90-27.25	29.39-21.27	24.27-15.35
P/E Ratio	10.06-6.10	32.58-22.53	13.68-9.95	8.47-4.75	10.48-3.54	23.33-13.56	14.41-10.42	63.88-40.39
Average Yield %	0.96	...	...	...	...	...	...	...

Address: 211 Carnegie Center, Princeton, NJ 08540 **Telephone:** 609-524-4500	**Web Site:** www.nrgenergy.com **Officers:** Howard E. Cosgrove - Chairman David W. Crane - President, Chief Executive Officer	**Auditors:** KPMG LLP **Investor Contact:** 609-524-4526 **Transfer Agents:** BNY Mellon Shareowner Services, Jersey City, NJ

NU SKIN ENTERPRISES, INC.

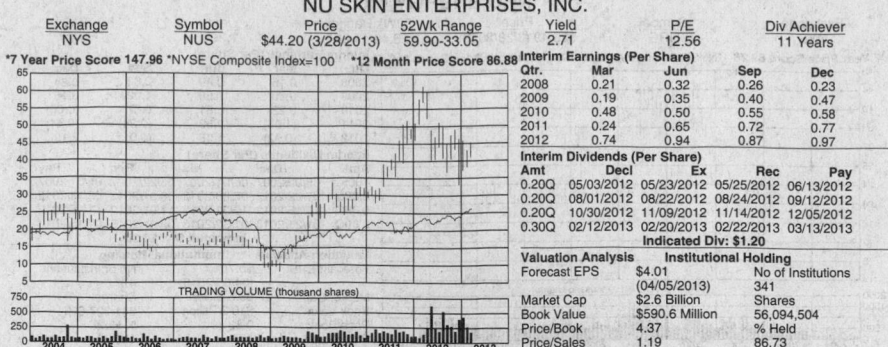

Exchange	Symbol	Price	52Wk Range	Yield	P/E	Div Achiever
NYS	NUS	$44.20 (3/28/2013)	59.90-33.05	2.71	12.56	11 Years

*7 Year Price Score 147.96 *NYSE Composite Index=100 *12 Month Price Score 86.88

Interim Earnings (Per Share)

Qtr.	Mar	Jun	Sep	Dec
2008	0.21	0.32	0.26	0.23
2009	0.19	0.35	0.40	0.47
2010	0.48	0.50	0.55	0.58
2011	0.24	0.65	0.72	0.77
2012	0.74	0.94	0.87	0.97

Interim Dividends (Per Share)

Amt	Decl	Ex	Rec	Pay
0.20Q	05/03/2012	05/23/2012	05/25/2012	06/13/2012
0.20Q	08/01/2012	08/22/2012	08/24/2012	09/12/2012
0.20Q	10/30/2012	11/09/2012	11/14/2012	12/05/2012
0.30Q	02/12/2013	02/20/2013	02/22/2013	03/13/2013

Indicated Div: $1.20

Valuation Analysis **Institutional Holding**

Forecast EPS	$4.01
	(04/05/2013)
Market Cap	$2.6 Billion
Book Value	$590.6 Million
Price/Book	4.37
Price/Sales	1.19

No of Institutions	341
Shares	56,094,504
% Held	86.73

Business Summary: Household & Personal Products (MIC: 1.7.1 SIC: 5122 NAIC: 424210)

NU Skin Enterprises is a direct selling company with operations in 52 markets worldwide. Co. develops and distributes personal care products and nutritional supplements under its Nu Skin and Pharmanex brands, respectively. Co.'s Nu Skin product line by category includes: core systems; targeted treatments; total care; cosmetic; and Epoch. Co.'s Pharmanex product line by category includes: nutritional; anti-aging, solutions; weight management; and Vitameal. In addition, Co. provides a limited number of other products and services, including household products and digital content storage. Co. sells its products to a network of independent distributors, except its operations in Mainland China.

Recent Developments: For the year ended Dec 31 2012, net income increased 44.6% to US$221.6 million from US$153.3 million in the prior year. Revenues were US$2.17 billion, up 24.4% from US$1.74 billion the year before. Operating income was US$340.8 million versus US$233.7 million in the prior year, an increase of 45.8%. Direct operating expenses rose 9.5% to US$353.2 million from US$322.6 million in the comparable period the year before. Indirect operating expenses increased 24.3% to US$1.48 billion from US$1.19 billion in the equivalent prior-year period.

Prospects: Our evaluation of NU Skin Enterprises Inc. as of Apr. 7, 2013 is the result of our systematic analysis on three basic characteristics: earnings strength, relative valuation, and recent stock price movement. The company has generated a negative trend in earnings per share over the past 5 quarters and while recent estimates for the company have been raised by analysts, NUS has posted better than expected results. Based on operating earnings yield, the company is undervalued when compared to all of the companies in our coverage universe. Share price changes over the past year indicates that NUS will perform very poorly over the near term.

Financial Data
(US$ in Thousands)

	12/31/2012	12/31/2011	12/31/2010	12/31/2009	12/31/2008	12/31/2007	12/31/2006	12/31/2005
Earnings Per Share	3.52	2.38	2.11	1.40	1.02	0.67	0.47	1.04
Cash Flow Per Share	5.12	3.61	3.01	2.11	1.62	0.75	1.09	1.63
Tang Book Value Per Share	6.60	6.07	4.52	2.89	1.83	1.21	1.65	2.15
Dividends Per Share	0.800	0.590	0.500	0.460	0.440	0.420	0.400	0.360
Dividend Payout %	22.73	24.79	23.70	32.86	43.14	62.69	85.11	34.62
Income Statement								
Total Revenue	2,169,664	1,743,991	1,537,259	1,331,058	1,247,646	1,157,667	1,115,409	1,180,930
EBITDA	370,742	252,469	230,313	162,924	125,053	95,578	76,376	143,651
Depn & Amortn	25,500	25,700	22,700	21,800	24,400	27,100	23,700	24,700
Income Before Taxes	345,242	226,769	207,613	141,124	100,653	68,478	52,676	118,951
Income Taxes	123,597	73,439	71,562	51,279	35,306	24,606	19,859	44,918
Net Income	221,645	153,330	136,051	89,845	65,347	43,872	32,817	74,033
Average Shares	63,025	64,546	64,547	64,296	64,132	65,584	70,506	71,356
Balance Sheet								
Current Assets	599,403	530,087	422,526	337,943	290,404	266,344	276,959	308,154
Total Assets	1,152,907	990,956	892,224	748,449	709,772	683,243	664,849	678,866
Current Liabilities	320,103	241,171	216,448	185,212	166,368	171,169	167,541	159,056
Long-Term Obligations	154,963	107,944	133,013	121,119	158,760	169,229	136,173	123,483
Total Liabilities	562,295	416,720	420,975	372,762	393,592	408,234	345,869	324,238
Stockholders' Equity	590,612	574,236	471,249	375,687	316,180	275,009	318,980	354,628
Shares Outstanding	58,400	62,300	62,100	62,800	63,400	63,400	69,700	70,100
Statistical Record								
Return on Assets %	20.62	16.28	16.58	12.32	9.36	6.51	4.88	11.49
Return on Equity %	37.95	29.33	32.13	25.97	22.05	14.77	9.74	22.75
EBITDA Margin %	17.09	14.48	14.98	12.24	10.02	8.26	6.85	12.16
Net Margin %	10.22	8.79	8.85	6.75	5.24	3.79	2.94	6.27
Asset Turnover	2.02	1.85	1.87	1.83	1.79	1.72	1.66	1.83
Current Ratio	1.87	2.20	1.95	1.82	1.75	1.56	1.65	1.94
Debt to Equity	0.26	0.19	0.28	0.32	0.50	0.62	0.43	0.35
Price Range	61.50-33.05	51.61-27.81	33.70-23.24	28.04-8.04	19.67-9.09	18.88-14.13	19.64-13.77	25.75-16.45
P/E Ratio	17.47-9.39	21.68-11.68	15.97-11.01	20.03-5.74	19.28-8.91	28.18-21.09	41.79-29.30	24.76-15.82
Average Yield %	1.70	1.55	1.75	2.78	2.84	2.49	2.31	1.69

Address: 75 West Center Street, Provo, UT 84601 **Telephone:** 801-345-1000 **Fax:** 801-345-5999	**Web Site:** www.nuskinenterprises.com **Officers:** Blake M. Roney - Chairman Steven J. Lund - Vice-Chairman	**Auditors:** PricewaterhouseCoopers LLP **Investor Contact:** 801-345-2657 **Transfer Agents:** American Stock Transfer & Trust, New York, NY

548

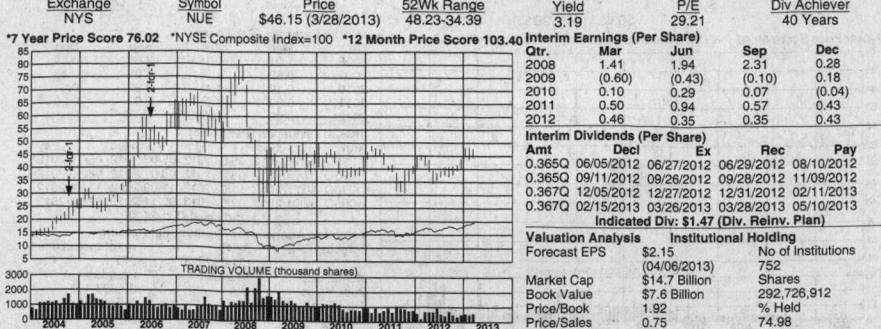

NUCOR CORP.

Exchange	Symbol	Price	52Wk Range	Yield	P/E	Div Achiever
NYS	NUE	$46.15 (3/28/2013)	48.23-34.39	3.19	29.21	40 Years

*7 Year Price Score 76.02   *NYSE Composite Index=100   *12 Month Price Score 103.40

Interim Earnings (Per Share)

Qtr.	Mar	Jun	Sep	Dec
2008	1.41	1.94	2.31	0.28
2009	(0.60)	(0.43)	(0.10)	0.18
2010	0.10	0.29	0.07	(0.04)
2011	0.50	0.94	0.57	0.43
2012	0.46	0.35	0.35	0.43

Interim Dividends (Per Share)

Amt	Decl	Ex	Rec	Pay
0.365Q	06/05/2012	06/27/2012	06/29/2012	08/10/2012
0.365Q	09/11/2012	09/26/2012	09/28/2012	11/09/2012
0.367Q	12/05/2012	12/27/2012	12/31/2012	02/11/2013
0.367Q	02/15/2013	03/26/2013	03/28/2013	05/10/2013

Indicated Div: $1.47 (Div. Reinv. Plan)

Valuation Analysis

Forecast EPS	$2.15
	(04/06/2013)
Market Cap	$14.7 Billion
Book Value	$7.6 Billion
Price/Book	1.92
Price/Sales	0.75

Institutional Holding

No of Institutions	752
Shares	292,726,912
% Held	74.98

Business Summary: Non-Precious Metals (MIC: 8.2.2 SIC: 3312 NAIC: 331111)

Nucor Corporation and its affiliates manufacture steel and steel products. Co. also produces direct reduced iron (DRI) for use in its steel mills. Co. operates in three segments: steel mills, which produce and distributes sheet steel, plate steel, structural steel and bar steel; steel products, which produce steel joists, joist girders, steel deck, fabricated concrete reinforcing steel, cold finished steel, steel fasteners, metal building systems, steel grating and metal, and wire and wire mesh; and raw materials, which produces direct reduced iron, broker ferrous and nonferrous metals, pig iron, hot briquetted iron, DRI, supply ferro-alloys, and process ferrous and nonferrous scrap metal.

Recent Developments: For the year ended Dec 31 2012, net income decreased 31.1% to US$593.1 million from US$861.0 million in the prior year. Revenues were US$19.43 billion, down 3.0% from US$20.02 billion the year before. Direct operating expenses declined 1.2% to US$17.92 billion from US$18.14 billion in the comparable period the year before. Indirect operating expenses increased 4.1% to US$468.2 million from US$449.6 million in the equivalent prior-year period.

Prospects: Our evaluation of Nucor Corp. as of Apr. 7, 2013 is the result of our systematic analysis on three basic characteristics: earnings strength, relative valuation, and recent stock price movement. The company has produced a positive trend in earnings per share over the past 5 quarters. However, while recent estimates for the company have been mixed, NUE has posted better than expected results. Based on operating earnings yield, the company is overvalued when compared to all of the companies in our coverage universe. Share price changes over the past year indicates that NUE will perform well over the near term.

Financial Data

(US$ in Thousands)	12/31/2012	12/31/2011	12/31/2010	12/31/2009	12/31/2008	12/31/2007	12/31/2006	12/31/2005
Earnings Per Share	1.58	2.45	0.42	(0.94)	5.98	4.94	5.68	4.13
Cash Flow Per Share	3.76	3.26	2.76	3.75	8.18	6.54	7.34	6.80
Tang Book Value Per Share	14.73	15.34	14.02	14.88	16.72	13.18	16.04	13.80
Dividends Per Share	1.462	1.452	1.442	1.410	1.910	2.440	2.150	0.925
Dividend Payout %	92.56	59.29	343.45	...	31.94	49.39	37.85	22.40
Income Statement								
Total Revenue	19,429,273	20,023,564	15,844,627	11,190,296	23,663,324	16,592,976	14,751,270	12,700,999
EBITDA	1,562,648	1,950,520	964,437	297,150	3,674,358	2,955,457	3,239,610	2,506,297
Depn & Amortn	534,010	522,571	512,147	494,035	479,484	403,172	363,936	375,054
Income Before Taxes	866,263	1,261,855	299,197	(331,637)	3,104,391	2,546,816	2,913,039	2,127,042
Income Taxes	259,814	390,828	60,792	(176,800)	959,480	781,368	936,137	706,084
Net Income	504,619	778,188	134,092	(293,613)	1,830,990	1,471,947	1,757,681	1,310,284
Average Shares	318,240	317,161	316,510	314,873	306,092	297,878	309,381	317,130
Balance Sheet								
Current Assets	5,661,364	6,708,081	5,861,175	5,182,248	6,397,486	5,073,249	4,675,036	4,071,553
Total Assets	14,152,059	14,570,350	13,921,910	12,571,904	13,874,443	9,826,122	7,884,989	7,138,787
Current Liabilities	2,029,568	2,396,059	1,504,438	1,227,057	1,854,192	1,582,036	1,450,028	1,255,699
Long-Term Obligations	3,380,200	3,630,200	4,280,200	3,080,200	3,086,200	2,250,300	922,300	922,300
Total Liabilities	6,510,488	7,095,465	6,801,840	5,181,378	5,945,239	4,713,205	3,059,000	2,858,999
Stockholders' Equity	7,641,571	7,474,885	7,120,070	7,390,526	7,929,204	5,112,917	4,825,989	4,279,788
Shares Outstanding	317,663	316,749	315,791	314,856	313,977	287,993	300,949	310,220
Statistical Record								
Return on Assets %	3.50	5.46	1.01	N.M.	15.41	16.62	23.40	19.75
Return on Equity %	6.66	10.66	1.85	N.M.	28.00	29.62	38.61	33.88
EBITDA Margin %	8.04	9.74	6.09	2.66	15.53	17.81	21.96	19.73
Net Margin %	2.60	3.89	0.85	N.M.	7.74	8.87	11.92	10.32
Asset Turnover	1.35	1.41	1.20	0.85	1.99	1.87	1.96	1.91
Current Ratio	2.79	2.80	3.90	4.22	3.45	3.21	3.22	3.24
Debt to Equity	0.44	0.49	0.60	0.42	0.39	0.44	0.19	0.22
Price Range	45.41-34.39	48.88-30.91	49.93-36.38	49.84-30.74	82.07-25.52	69.25-45.86	65.84-34.23	34.62-22.81
P/E Ratio	28.74-21.77	19.95-12.62	118.88-86.62	...	13.72-4.27	14.02-9.28	11.59-6.03	8.38-5.52
Average Yield %	3.66	3.57	3.45	3.28	3.37	4.07	4.21	3.26

Address: 1915 Rexford Road, Charlotte, NC 28211 **Telephone:** 704-366-7000 **Fax:** 704-362-4208	**Web Site:** www.nucor.com **Officers:** Daniel R. DiMicco - Chairman, Chief Executive Officer John J. Ferriola - President, Chief Executive Officer, Chief Operating Officer	**Auditors:** PricewaterhouseCoopers LLP **Transfer Agents:** American Stock Transfer & Trust Company, LLC, New York, NY

NUSTAR ENERGY L.P.

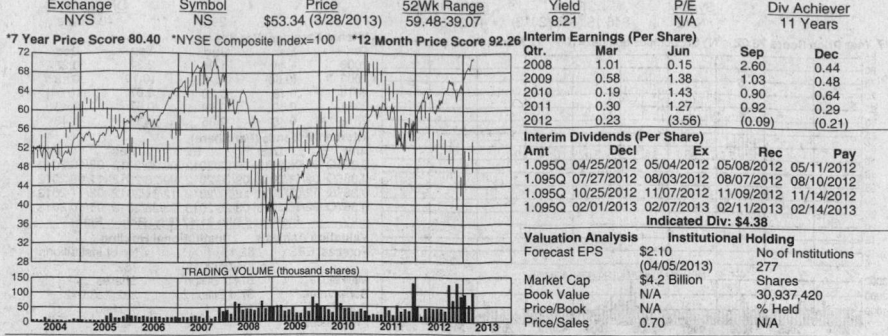

Exchange	Symbol	Price	52Wk Range	Yield	P/E	Div Achiever
NYS	NS	$53.34 (3/28/2013)	59.48-39.07	8.21	N/A	11 Years

*7 Year Price Score 80.40 *NYSE Composite Index=100 *12 Month Price Score 92.26

Interim Earnings (Per Share)

Qtr.	Mar	Jun	Sep	Dec
2008	1.01	0.15	2.60	0.44
2009	0.58	1.38	1.03	0.48
2010	0.19	1.43	0.90	0.64
2011	0.30	1.27	0.92	0.29
2012	0.23	(3.56)	(0.09)	(0.21)

Interim Dividends (Per Share)

Amt	Decl	Ex	Rec	Pay
1.095Q	04/25/2012	05/04/2012	05/08/2012	05/11/2012
1.095Q	07/27/2012	08/03/2012	08/07/2012	08/10/2012
1.095Q	10/25/2012	11/07/2012	11/09/2012	11/14/2012
1.095Q	02/01/2013	02/07/2013	02/11/2013	02/14/2013

Indicated Div: $4.38

Valuation Analysis		Institutional Holding	
Forecast EPS	$2.10 (04/05/2013)	No of Institutions	277
Market Cap	$4.2 Billion	Shares	30,937,420
Book Value	N/A	% Held	
Price/Book	N/A	N/A	
Price/Sales	0.70		

Business Summary: Refining & Marketing (MIC: 9.1.2 SIC: 4612 NAIC: 486110)

NuStar Energy engages in the terminalling and storage of petroleum products, the transportation of petroleum products and anhydrous ammonia, and petroleum refining marketing. Co. has three business segments: storage, which includes terminal and storage facilities that provide storage, handling and other services for petroleum products, specialty chemicals, crude oil and other liquids and storage tanks used to store and deliver crude oil; transportation, which consists of the transportation of refined petroleum products, crude oil and anhydrous ammonia; and asphalt and fuels marketing, which includes its asphalt operations, its fuels marketing operations and its San Antonio, TX refinery.

Recent Developments: For the year ended Dec 31 2012, loss from continuing operations was US$178.1 million compared with income of US$211.5 million a year earlier. Net loss amounted to US$227.2 million versus net income of US$221.6 million in the prior year. Revenues were US$5.96 billion, down 5.0% from US$6.27 billion the year before. Operating loss was US$30.1 million versus an income of US$301.8 million in the prior year. Direct operating expenses declined 4.0% to US$5.47 billion from US$5.70 billion in the comparable period the year before. Indirect operating expenses increased 90.2% to US$512.8 million from US$269.6 million in the equivalent prior-year period.

Prospects: Our evaluation of NuStar Energy L.P. as of Apr. 7, 2013 is the result of our systematic analysis on three basic characteristics: earnings strength, relative valuation, and recent stock price movement. The company has enjoyed a very positive trend in earnings per share over the past 5 quarters and while recent estimates for the company have been raised by analysts, NS has posted results that fell short of analysts expectations. Based on operating earnings yield, the company is overvalued when compared to all of the companies in our coverage universe. Share price changes over the past year indicates that NS will perform very poorly over the near term.

Financial Data

(US$ in Thousands)	12/31/2012	12/31/2011	12/31/2010	12/31/2009	12/31/2008	12/31/2007	12/31/2006	12/31/2005
Earnings Per Share	(3.61)	2.78	3.19	3.47	4.22	2.74	2.83	2.86
Cash Flow Per Share	4.09	1.45	5.76	3.27	9.10	4.72	5.36	5.32
Dividends Per Share	4.380	4.340	4.270	4.237	4.013	3.765	3.540	3.310
Dividend Payout %	...	156.12	133.86	122.12	95.08	137.41	125.09	115.73
Income Statement								
Total Revenue	5,955,676	6,575,255	4,403,061	3,855,871	4,828,770	1,475,014	1,135,674	659,557
EBITDA	101,210	467,903	462,691	441,275	473,112	334,229	311,578	220,361
Depn & Amortn	157,800	157,200	144,200	136,100	125,300	102,800	100,266	66,667
Income Before Taxes	(146,260)	227,022	240,211	225,791	256,994	154,913	149,885	110,069
Income Taxes	22,494	16,879	11,741	10,531	11,006	11,448	5,861	4,713
Net Income	(226,616)	221,461	238,970	224,875	254,018	150,298	149,530	111,073
Average Shares	72,957	65,018	62,946	55,232	53,182	47,158	46,809	35,023
Balance Sheet								
Current Assets	939,443	1,200,923	939,507	734,719	486,486	347,134	212,998	295,411
Total Assets	5,613,089	5,881,190	5,386,393	4,774,673	4,459,597	3,783,087	3,482,866	3,366,992
Current Liabilities	845,971	943,800	393,229	338,754	252,024	242,485	156,735	205,588
Long-Term Obligations	2,142,653	1,942,573	2,146,336	1,836,656	1,878,660	1,451,310	1,359,469	1,169,659
Total Liabilities	3,040,705	3,028,989	2,683,693	2,289,705	2,252,600	1,788,255	1,607,185	1,466,213
Shares Outstanding	77,886	70,756	64,610	60,210	54,460	49,409	46,809	46,809
Statistical Record								
Return on Assets %	N.M.	3.93	4.70	4.87	6.15	4.14	4.37	5.26
EBITDA Margin %	1.70	7.12	10.51	11.44	9.80	22.66	27.44	33.41
Net Margin %	N.M.	3.37	5.43	5.83	5.26	10.19	13.17	16.84
Asset Turnover	1.03	1.17	0.87	0.84	1.17	0.41	0.33	0.31
Current Ratio	1.11	1.27	2.39	2.17	1.93	1.43	1.36	1.44
Price Range	62.05-39.07	70.25-51.31	71.69-52.86	57.62-41.06	56.76-30.89	70.16-52.15	57.53-48.90	64.15-50.75
P/E Ratio	...	25.27-18.46	22.47-16.57	16.61-11.83	13.45-7.32	25.61-19.03	20.33-17.28	22.43-17.74
Average Yield %	8.34	7.01	7.08	8.29	8.48	6.02	6.86	5.63

Address: 19003 IH-10 West, San Antonio, TX 78257
Telephone: 210-918-2000

Web Site: www.nustarenergy.com
Officers: William E. Greehey - Chairman, Sister Company Officer Curtis V. Anastasio - President, Chief Executive Officer, Sister Company Officer

Auditors: KPMG LLP
Investor Contact: 210-918-3507
Transfer Agents: Computershare Investor Services, LLC, Canton, MA

NV ENERGY, INC.

Exchange	Symbol	Price	52Wk Range	Yield	P/E
NYS	NVE	$20.03 (3/28/2013)	20.24-15.51	3.79	14.84

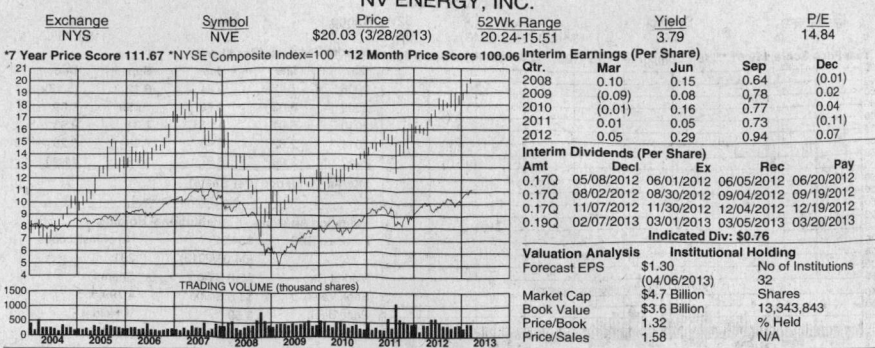

*7 Year Price Score 111.67 ***NYSE Composite Index=100** ***12 Month Price Score 100.06**

Interim Earnings (Per Share)

Qtr.	Mar	Jun	Sep	Dec
2008	0.10	0.15	0.64	(0.01)
2009	(0.09)	0.08	0,78	0.02
2010	(0.01)	0.16	0.77	0.04
2011	0.01	0.05	0.73	(0.11)
2012	0.05	0.29	0.94	0.07

Interim Dividends (Per Share)

Amt	Decl	Ex	Rec	Pay
0.17Q	05/08/2012	06/01/2012	06/05/2012	06/20/2012
0.17Q	08/02/2012	08/30/2012	09/04/2012	09/19/2012
0.17Q	11/07/2012	11/30/2012	12/04/2012	12/19/2012
0.19Q	02/07/2013	03/01/2013	03/05/2013	03/20/2013

Indicated Div: $0.76

Valuation Analysis | **Institutional Holding**

Forecast EPS	$1.30	No of Institutions
	(04/06/2013)	32
Market Cap	$4.7 Billion	Shares
Book Value	$3.6 Billion	13,343,843
Price/Book	1.32	% Held
Price/Sales	1.58	N/A

Business Summary: Electric Utilities (MIC: 3.1.1 SIC: 4931 NAIC: 221122)

NV Energy is a holding company. Co.'s subsidiaries, Nevada Power Company (NPC) and Sierra Pacific Power Company (SPPC), are public utilities that generate, transmit and distribute electric energy in Nevada and, in the case of SPPC, also deliver natural gas service. As of Dec 31 2012, Co. served approx. 1,200,000 electric customers, of which approx. 850,000 electric customers primarily in Las Vegas, North Las Vegas, Henderson and adjoining areas were served by NPC, and approx. 324,000 electric customers in an approx. 42,000 sq. mile area of western, central and northeastern Nevada, including the cities of Reno, Sparks, Carson City, and Elko were served by SPPC.

Recent Developments: For the year ended Dec 31 2012, net income increased 97.0% to US$321.9 million from US$163.4 million in the prior year. Revenues were US$2.98 billion, up 1.2% from US$2.94 billion the year before. Operating income was US$785.1 million versus US$610.7 million in the prior year, an increase of 28.6%. Direct operating expenses declined 8.3% to US$1.76 billion from US$1.91 billion in the comparable period the year before. Indirect operating expenses increased 4.8% to US$438.3 million from US$418.4 million in the equivalent prior-year period.

Prospects: Our evaluation of NV Energy, Inc. as of Apr. 7, 2013 is the result of our systematic analysis on three basic characteristics: earnings strength, relative valuation, and recent stock price movement. The company has generated a negative trend in earnings per share over the past 5 quarters and while recent estimates for the company have been raised by analysts, NVE has posted results that fell short of analysts expectations. Based on operating earnings yield, the company is undervalued when compared to all of the companies in our coverage universe. Share price changes over the past year indicates that NVE will perform in line with the market over the near term.

Financial Data
(US$ in Thousands)

	12/31/2012	12/31/2011	12/31/2010	12/31/2009	12/31/2008	12/31/2007	12/31/2006	12/31/2005
Earnings Per Share	1.35	0.69	0.96	0.78	0.89	0.89	1.33	0.44
Cash Flow Per Share	3.70	2.79	3.77	3.20	1.96	3.39	2.06	1.26
Tang Book Value Per Share	15.13	14.43	14.24	13.73	13.36	12.82	11.86	10.40
Dividends Per Share	0.640	0.490	0.450	0.410	0.340	0.160	...	...
Dividend Payout %	47.41	71.01	46.88	52.56	38.20	17.98	...	...
Income Statement								
Total Revenue	2,979,177	2,943,307	3,280,222	3,585,798	3,528,113	3,600,960	3,355,950	3,030,219
EBITDA	1,336,862	1,119,410	1,129,988	916,902	849,820	1,035,378	1,084,381	814,736
Depn & Amortn	541,119	524,032	443,713	321,921	263,325	483,140	401,930	404,329
Income Before Taxes	488,538	250,347	340,748	258,387	285,638	272,450	371,363	125,480
Income Taxes	166,592	86,915	113,764	75,451	95,354	87,555	145,605	43,173
Net Income	321,946	163,432	226,984	182,936	...	...	279,792	86,137
Average Shares	237,883	237,767	236,294	235,180	234,585	222,554	209,020	185,932
Balance Sheet								
Current Assets	911,049	772,520	731,938	747,075	770,276	868,420	933,207	1,122,889
Total Assets	11,984,136	11,635,128	11,669,668	11,413,463	11,345,980	9,464,750	8,832,076	7,870,546
Current Liabilities	1,019,307	891,855	1,255,895	946,379	969,383	718,979	576,074	744,667
Long-Term Obligations	4,669,798	5,008,931	4,924,109	5,303,357	5,266,982	4,137,864	4,001,542	3,817,122
Total Liabilities	8,426,765	8,229,049	8,318,850	8,189,541	8,214,794	6,468,175	6,209,779	5,760,392
Stockholders' Equity	3,557,371	3,406,079	3,350,818	3,223,922	3,131,186	2,996,575	2,622,297	2,110,154
Shares Outstanding	235,079	235,999	235,322	234,834	234,317	233,739	221,030	200,792
Statistical Record								
Return on Assets %	2.72	1.40	1.97	1.61	...	...	3.35	1.12
Return on Equity %	9.22	4.84	6.90	5.76	...	...	11.82	4.71
EBITDA Margin %	44.87	38.03	34.45	25.57	24.09	28.75	32.31	26.89
Net Margin %	10.81	5.55	6.92	5.10	...	...	8.34	2.84
Asset Turnover	0.25	0.25	0.28	0.32	0.34	0.39	0.40	0.39
Current Ratio	0.89	0.87	0.58	0.79	0.79	1.21	1.62	1.51
Debt to Equity	1.31	1.47	1.47	1.65	1.68	1.38	1.53	1.81
Price Range	19.01-15.51	16.42-12.48	14.29-11.08	12.67-8.00	16.98-7.25	19.29-14.63	17.48-12.78	15.22-9.30
P/E Ratio	14.08-11.49	23.80-18.09	14.89-11.54	16.24-10.26	19.08-8.15	21.67-16.44	13.14-9.61	34.59-21.14
Average Yield %	3.70	3.28	3.62	3.78	2.87	0.94	...	...

Address: 6226 West Sahara Avenue, Las Vegas, NV 89146 Telephone: 702-402-5000	Web Site: www.nvenergy.com Officers: Michael W. Yackira - Chief Executive Officer Dilek L. Samil - Executive Vice President, Senior Vice President, Chief Financial Officer, Chief Operating Officer, Treasurer	Auditors: Deloitte & Touche LLP Investor Contact: 702-402-5627 Transfer Agents: Wells Fargo Shareowner Services, South St. Paul, MN

NVR INC.

Exchange	Symbol	Price	52Wk Range	Yield	P/E
NYS	NVR	$1080 (3/28/2013)	1080.11-719.80	N/A	30.75

*7 Year Price Score 119.01 *NYSE Composite Index=100 *12 Month Price Score 107.72

Interim Earnings (Per Share)

Qtr.	Mar	Jun	Sep	Dec
2008	7.42	8.64	6.12	(5.17)
2009	3.02	6.79	11.59	9.69
2010	5.01	11.13	7.31	9.93
2011	2.52	6.48	7.98	6.26
2012	3.90	8.97	10.33	11.90

Interim Dividends (Per Share)

No Dividends Paid

Valuation Analysis / **Institutional Holding**

Forecast EPS	$54.32	No of Institutions
	(04/05/2013)	291
Market Cap	$5.3 Billion	Shares
Book Value	$1.5 Billion	4,799,555
Price/Book	3.59	% Held
Price/Sales	1.66	83.14

Business Summary: Builders (MIC: 2.2.5 SIC: 1531 NAIC: 236117)

NVR is engaged in the construction and sale of single-family detached homes, townhomes and condominium buildings. Co. also operates a mortgage banking and title services business. Co.'s mortgage banking operations are operated primarily through a wholly owned subsidiary, NVR Mortgage Finance, Inc. Co.'s homebuilding operations primarily construct and sell single-family detached homes, townhomes and condominium buildings under four trade names: Ryan Homes, NVHomes, Fox Ridge Homes and Heartland Homes.

Recent Developments: For the year ended Dec 31 2012, net income increased 39.5% to US$180.6 million from US$129.4 million in the prior year. Revenues were US$3.19 billion, up 19.6% from US$2.67 billion the year before. Direct operating expenses rose 18.9% to US$2.58 billion from US$2.17 billion in the comparable period the year before. Indirect operating expenses increased 15.5% to US$342.5 million from US$296.4 million in the equivalent prior-year period.

Prospects: Our evaluation of NVR Inc. as of Apr. 7, 2013 is the result of our systematic analysis on three basic characteristics: earnings strength, relative valuation, and recent stock price movement. The company has produced a positive trend in earnings per share over the past 5 quarters and while recent estimates for the company have remained steady, NVR has posted better than expected results. Based on operating earnings yield, the company is about fairly valued when compared to all of the companies in our coverage universe. Share price changes over the past year indicates that NVR will perform well over the near term.

Financial Data

(US$ in Thousands)	12/31/2012	12/31/2011	12/31/2010	12/31/2009	12/31/2008	12/31/2007	12/31/2006	12/31/2005
Earnings Per Share	35.12	23.01	33.42	31.26	17.04	54.14	88.05	89.61
Cash Flow Per Share	52.62	0.27	9.40	41.61	85.72	103.09	121.01	84.29
Tang Book Value Per Share	289.44	266.37	298.65	287.11	239.45	208.01	197.77	109.48
Income Statement								
Total Revenue	3,193,204	2,669,608	3,057,369	2,756,153	3,714,125	5,156,420	6,156,771	5,275,097
EBITDA	290,706	216,140	335,685	319,507	194,752	570,372	998,357	1,170,677
Depn & Amortn	8,100	6,672	7,263	9,713	13,641	17,036	14,158	10,690
Income Before Taxes	275,077	207,576	322,393	298,414	167,455	539,505	962,971	1,144,419
Income Taxes	94,489	78,156	116,388	106,234	66,563	205,550	375,559	446,860
Net Income	180,588	129,420	206,005	192,180	100,892	333,955	587,412	697,559
Average Shares	5,141	5,623	6,164	6,148	5,920	6,168	6,672	7,784
Balance Sheet								
Current Assets	1,830,732	1,013,482	1,624,721	1,668,868	1,548,213	1,353,063	1,289,735	971,501
Total Assets	2,604,842	1,779,485	2,260,061	2,395,770	2,103,236	2,194,416	2,473,808	2,269,588
Current Liabilities	283,819	213,267	182,454	203,361	214,750	362,914	455,074	544,825
Long-Term Obligations	603,562	6,596	99,681	147,880	210,389	286,283	356,632	463,141
Total Liabilities	1,124,365	404,686	519,687	638,508	729,447	1,065,041	1,321,734	1,592,426
Stockholders' Equity	1,480,477	1,374,799	1,740,374	1,757,262	1,373,789	1,129,375	1,152,074	677,162
Shares Outstanding	4,914	4,977	5,663	5,950	5,532	5,137	5,517	5,628
Statistical Record								
Return on Assets %	8.22	6.41	8.85	8.54	4.68	14.31	24.77	34.47
Return on Equity %	12.61	8.31	11.78	12.28	8.04	29.28	64.22	92.26
EBITDA Margin %	9.10	8.10	10.98	11.59	5.24	11.06	16.22	22.19
Net Margin %	5.66	4.85	6.74	6.97	2.72	6.48	9.54	13.22
Asset Turnover	1.45	1.32	1.31	1.23	1.72	2.21	2.60	2.61
Current Ratio	6.45	4.75	8.90	8.21	7.21	3.73	2.83	1.78
Debt to Equity	0.41	N.M.	0.06	0.08	0.15	0.25	0.31	0.68
Price Range	959.25-671.00	804.32-575.28	753.00-604.16	731.00-319.56	676.01-338.45	842.00-413.50	842.98-394.00	938.00-660.00
P/E Ratio	27.31-19.11	34.96-25.00	22.53-18.08	23.38-10.22	39.67-19.86	15.55-7.64	9.57-4.47	10.47-7.37

Address: 11700 Plaza America Drive, Suite 500, Reston, VA 20190 Telephone: 703-956-4000	Web Site: www.nvrinc.com Officers: Dwight C. Schar - Chairman Paul C. Saville - President, Chief Executive Officer	Auditors: KPMG LLP Transfer Agents: Computershare Trust Company, N.A, Providence, R

NYSE EURONEXT

Exchange	Symbol	Price	52Wk Range	Yield	P/E
NYS	NYX	$38.64 (3/28/2013)	38.64-22.28	3.11	27.80

*7 Year Price Score 56.00 *NYSE Composite Index=100 ***12 Month Price Score 121.31**

Interim Earnings (Per Share)

Qtr.	Mar	Jun	Sep	Dec
2008	0.87	0.73	0.66	(5.04)
2009	0.40	(0.70)	0.48	0.66
2010	0.50	0.70	0.49	0.52
2011	0.59	0.59	0.76	0.43
2012	0.34	0.49	0.44	0.13

Interim Dividends (Per Share)

Amt	Decl	Ex	Rec	Pay
0.30Q	04/30/2012	06/13/2012	06/15/2012	06/29/2012
0.30Q	08/03/2012	09/12/2012	09/14/2012	09/28/2012
0.30Q	11/06/2012	12/12/2012	12/14/2012	12/28/2012
0.30Q	02/05/2013	03/12/2013	03/14/2013	03/28/2013

Indicated Div: $1.20

Valuation Analysis | **Institutional Holding**

Forecast EPS	$2.31	No of Institutions	
	(04/06/2013)	545	
Market Cap	$9.4 Billion	Shares	
Book Value	$6.3 Billion	198,350,896	
Price/Book	1.47	% Held	
Price/Sales	2.49	73.20	

Business Summary: Finance Intermediaries & Services (MIC: 5.5.1 SIC: 6231 NAIC: 523210)

NYSE Euronext is a holding company. Through its subsidiaries, Co. is engaged in providing a range of products and services in cash equities, futures, options, swaps, exchange-traded products, bonds, clearing operations, market data, commercial technology services and carbon trading, to issuers, investors, financial institutions and market participants. Co. has three segments: Derivatives, which is comprised of its derivatives trading and clearing businesses; Cash Trading and Listings, which consists of its cash trading and listings businesses; and Information Services and Technology Solutions, which refers to its commercial technology transactions, data and infrastructure businesses.

Recent Developments: For the year ended Dec 31 2012, net income decreased 39.5% to US$365.0 million from US$603.0 million in the prior year. Revenues were US$3.75 billion, down 17.6% from US$4.55 billion the year before. Operating income was US$609.0 million versus US$850.0 million in the prior year, a decrease of 28.4%. Indirect operating expenses decreased 15.2% to US$3.14 billion from US$3.70 billion in the equivalent prior-year period.

Prospects: Our evaluation of NYSE Euronext Inc. as of Apr. 7, 2013 is the result of our systematic analysis on three basic characteristics: earnings strength, relative valuation, and recent stock price movement. The company has produced a positive trend in earnings per share over the past 5 quarters and while recent estimates for the company have been mixed, NYX has posted better than expected results. Based on operating earnings yield, the company is about fairly valued when compared to all of the companies in our coverage universe. Share price changes over the past year indicates that NYX will perform well over the near term.

Financial Data
(US$ in Thousands)

	12/31/2012	12/31/2011	12/31/2010	12/31/2009	12/31/2008	12/31/2007	12/31/2006	12/31/2005
Earnings Per Share	1.39	2.36	2.21	0.84	(2.78)	2.70	1.36	...
Cash Flow Per Share	2.53	3.83	2.25	1.80	2.71	2.97	1.46	...
Tang Book Value Per Share	N.M.	N.M.	N.M.	N.M.	N.M.	N.M.	3.51	...
Dividends Per Share	1.200	1.200	1.200	1.200	1.150	0.750	...	...
Dividend Payout %	86.33	50.85	54.30	142.86	...	27.78	...	...
Income Statement								
Total Revenue	3,749,000	4,552,000	4,425,000	4,687,000	4,703,000	4,158,000	2,375,950	1,633,173
EBITDA	779,000	1,042,000	1,019,000	534,000	(350,000)	1,162,000	464,169	194,309
Depn & Amortn	165,000	192,000	219,000	221,000	197,000	191,000	135,797	103,430
Income Before Taxes	478,000	734,000	692,000	203,000	(616,000)	911,000	328,372	90,879
Income Taxes	105,000	122,000	128,000	(7,000)	95,000	253,000	120,566	48,158
Net Income	348,000	619,000	577,000	219,000	(738,000)	643,000	204,977	40,749
Average Shares	250,000	263,000	262,000	261,000	265,000	238,000	150,175	...
Balance Sheet								
Current Assets	1,008,000	1,154,000	1,174,000	1,520,000	2,026,000	2,278,000	1,443,068	1,464,217
Total Assets	12,556,000	13,072,000	13,378,000	14,382,000	13,948,000	16,618,000	3,465,542	2,204,145
Current Liabilities	1,416,000	1,149,000	1,454,000	2,149,000	2,582,000	3,462,000	832,193	684,960
Long-Term Obligations	2,055,000	2,036,000	2,074,000	2,166,000	1,787,000	521,000	...	...
Total Liabilities	6,211,000	6,491,000	6,582,000	7,511,000	7,392,000	7,234,000	1,796,523	1,405,020
Stockholders' Equity	6,345,000	6,581,000	6,796,000	6,871,000	6,556,000	9,384,000	1,669,019	(8,656)
Shares Outstanding	242,000	258,000	261,000	260,000	259,000	265,000	156,327	...
Statistical Record								
Return on Assets %	2.71	4.68	4.16	1.55	N.M.	6.40	7.23	...
Return on Equity %	5.37	9.25	8.44	3.26	N.M.	11.63	24.69	...
EBITDA Margin %	20.78	22.89	23.03	11.39	N.M.	27.95	19.54	11.90
Net Margin %	9.28	13.60	13.04	4.67	N.M.	15.46	8.63	2.50
Asset Turnover	0.29	0.34	0.32	0.33	0.31	0.41	0.84	...
Current Ratio	0.71	1.00	0.81	0.71	0.78	0.66	1.73	2.14
Debt to Equity	0.32	0.31	0.31	0.32	0.27	0.06	...	...
Price Range	32.25-22.28	41.55-21.98	34.36-22.50	31.12-15.10	87.77-17.65	108.21-69.30	108.96-49.98	...
P/E Ratio	23.20-16.03	17.61-9.31	15.55-10.18	37.05-17.98	...	40.08-25.67	80.12-36.75	...
Average Yield %	4.61	3.78	4.18	4.80	2.27	0.89	...	...

Address: 11 Wall Street, New York, NY 10005 **Telephone:** 212-656-3000	**Web Site:** www.nyse.com **Officers:** Jan-Michiel Hessels - Chairman Marshall N. Carter - Deputy Chairman	**Auditors:** PricewaterhouseCoopers LLP **Investor Contact:** 212-656-5700 **Transfer Agents:** Computershare Shareholder Services, Providence, RI

OCCIDENTAL PETROLEUM CORP

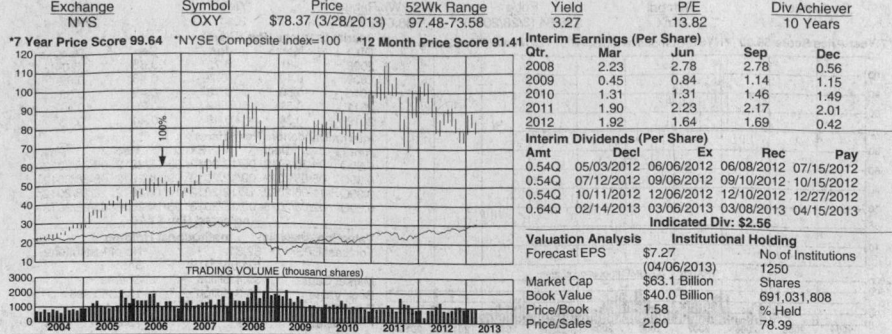

Exchange	Symbol	Price	52Wk Range	Yield	P/E	Div Achiever
NYS	OXY	$78.37 (3/28/2013)	97.48-73.58	3.27	13.82	10 Years

*7 Year Price Score 99.64   *NYSE Composite Index=100   *12 Month Price Score 91.41

Interim Earnings (Per Share)

Qtr.	Mar	Jun	Sep	Dec
2008	2.23	2.78	2.78	0.56
2009	0.45	0.84	1.14	1.15
2010	1.31	1.31	1.46	1.49
2011	1.90	2.23	2.17	2.01
2012	1.92	1.64	1.69	0.42

Interim Dividends (Per Share)

Amt	Decl	Ex	Rec	Pay
0.54Q	05/03/2012	06/06/2012	06/08/2012	07/15/2012
0.54Q	07/12/2012	09/06/2012	09/10/2012	10/15/2012
0.54Q	10/11/2012	12/06/2012	12/10/2012	12/27/2012
0.64Q	02/14/2013	03/06/2013	03/08/2013	04/15/2013

Indicated Div: $2.56

Valuation Analysis / **Institutional Holding**

Forecast EPS	$7.27 (04/06/2013)	No of Institutions	1250
Market Cap	$63.1 Billion	Shares	691,031,808
Book Value	$40.0 Billion	% Held	78.39
Price/Book	1.58		
Price/Sales	2.60		

Business Summary: Production & Extraction (MIC: 9.1.1 SIC: 1311 NAIC: 211111)

Occidental Petroleum's principal businesses consist of three segments: oil and gas, which explores for, develops and produces oil and condensate, natural gas liquids (NGLs) and natural gas; chemical, which mainly manufactures and markets basic chemicals and vinyls; and midstream, marketing and other, which gathers, processes, transports, stores, purchases and markets oil, condensate, NGLs, natural gas, carbon dioxide and power. As of Dec 31 2012, Co. had 3.30 billion barrels of oil equivalent of proved reserves, which consisted of 2.04 billion barrels of oil, 332.0 million barrels of NGLs and 5.57 trillion cubic feet of natural gas.

Recent Developments: For the year ended Dec 31 2012, income from continuing operations decreased 30.2% to US$4.64 billion from US$6.64 billion a year earlier. Net income decreased 32.1% to US$4.60 billion from US$6.77 billion in the prior year. Revenues were US$24.25 billion, up 0.6% from US$24.12 billion the year before. Direct operating expenses rose 6.2% to US$7.84 billion from US$7.39 billion in the comparable period the year before. Indirect operating expenses increased 43.7% to US$9.02 billion from US$6.28 billion in the equivalent prior-year period.

Prospects: Our evaluation of Occidental Petroleum Corp. as of Apr. 7, 2013 is the result of our systematic analysis on three basic characteristics: earnings strength, relative valuation, and recent stock price movement. The company has enjoyed a very positive trend in earnings per share over the past 5 quarters. However, while recent estimates for the company have been lowered by analysts, OXY has posted better than expected results. Based on operating earnings yield, the company is undervalued when compared to all of the companies in our coverage universe. Share price changes over the past year indicates that OXY will perform poorly over the near term.

Financial Data

(US$ in Thousands)	12/31/2012	12/31/2011	12/31/2010	12/31/2009	12/31/2008	12/31/2007	12/31/2006	12/31/2005
Earnings Per Share	5.67	8.32	5.56	3.58	8.35	6.44	4.86	6.46
Cash Flow Per Share	13.94	15.12	11.51	7.17	12.99	8.14	7.45	6.62
Tang Book Value Per Share	49.68	46.39	39.97	35.82	33.69	27.64	22.84	18.69
Dividends Per Share	2.160	1.840	1.470	1.310	1.210	0.940	0.800	0.645
Dividend Payout %	38.10	22.12	26.44	36.59	14.49	14.60	16.46	9.99
Income Statement								
Total Revenue	24,253,000	24,119,000	19,157,000	15,531,000	24,480,000	20,013,000	18,160,000	16,259,000
EBITDA	12,031,000	14,348,000	10,628,000	7,926,000	14,210,000	11,296,000	10,163,000	8,911,000
Depn & Amortn	4,511,000	3,591,000	3,153,000	3,117,000	2,710,000	2,379,000	2,042,000	1,485,000
Income Before Taxes	7,390,000	10,459,000	7,359,000	4,669,000	11,371,000	8,578,000	7,830,000	7,133,000
Income Taxes	3,118,000	4,201,000	2,995,000	1,918,000	4,629,000	3,507,000	3,466,000	2,020,000
Net Income	4,598,000	6,771,000	4,530,000	2,915,000	6,857,000	5,400,000	4,182,000	5,281,000
Average Shares	810,000	812,900	813,800	813,800	820,800	839,100	860,400	818,200
Balance Sheet								
Current Assets	9,492,000	11,542,000	13,059,000	8,086,000	7,172,000	8,595,000	6,006,000	6,574,000
Total Assets	64,210,000	60,044,000	52,432,000	44,229,000	41,537,000	36,519,000	32,355,000	26,108,000
Current Liabilities	7,290,000	7,947,000	7,825,000	6,092,000	6,134,000	6,266,000	4,724,000	4,280,000
Long-Term Obligations	7,023,000	5,871,000	5,111,000	2,557,000	2,049,000	1,741,000	2,619,000	2,873,000
Total Liabilities	24,194,000	22,424,000	19,948,000	15,148,000	14,237,000	13,696,000	13,171,000	11,076,000
Stockholders' Equity	40,016,000	37,620,000	32,484,000	29,081,000	27,300,000	22,823,000	19,184,000	15,032,000
Shares Outstanding	805,514	811,009	812,794	811,921	810,246	825,735	839,918	804,430
Statistical Record								
Return on Assets %	7.38	12.04	9.37	6.80	17.52	15.68	14.31	22.24
Return on Equity %	11.81	19.32	14.72	10.34	27.29	25.71	24.44	41.29
EBITDA Margin %	49.61	59.49	55.48	51.03	58.05	56.44	55.96	54.81
Net Margin %	18.96	28.07	23.65	18.77	28.01	26.98	23.03	32.48
Asset Turnover	0.39	0.43	0.40	0.36	0.63	0.58	0.62	0.68
Current Ratio	1.30	1.45	1.67	1.33	1.17	1.37	1.27	1.54
Debt to Equity	0.18	0.16	0.16	0.09	0.08	0.08	0.14	0.19
Price Range	105.46-73.58	115.74-68.58	99.03-72.23	84.48-47.56	97.85-40.72	78.10-43.08	53.89-42.00	44.40-27.81
P/E Ratio	18.60-12.98	13.91-8.24	17.81-12.99	23.60-13.28	11.72-4.88	12.13-6.69	11.09-8.64	6.87-4.30
Average Yield %	2.48	1.92	1.79	1.94	1.68	1.64	1.65	1.73

Address: 10889 Wilshire Boulevard, Los Angeles, CA 90024-4201	**Web Site:** www.oxy.com	**Auditors:** KPMG LLP
Telephone: 310-208-8800	**Officers:** Ray R. Irani - Executive Chairman, Chief Executive Officer Stephen I. Chazen - President, Chief Operating Officer, Chief Executive Officer	**Investor Contact:** 212-603-8111
Fax: 310-443-6690		**Transfer Agents:** Computershare Shareowner Services LLC, Jersey City, NY

OCEANEERING INTERNATIONAL, INC.

Exchange	Symbol	Price	52Wk Range	Yield	P/E
NYS	OII	$66.41 (3/28/2013)	66.48-43.76	1.08	24.97

*7 Year Price Score 146.68 *NYSE Composite Index=100 *12 Month Price Score 107.65

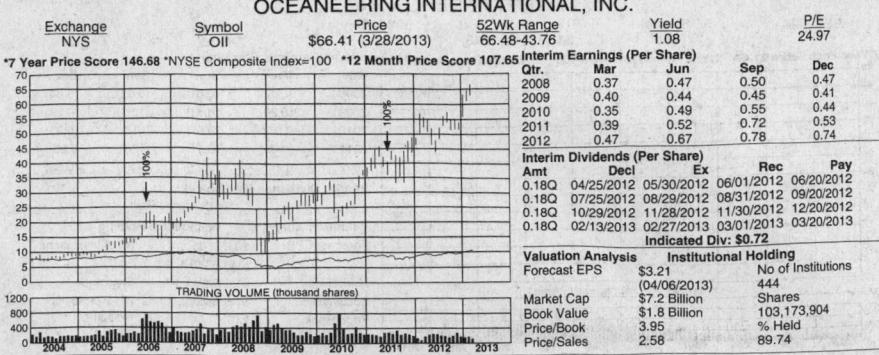

Interim Earnings (Per Share)

Qtr.	Mar	Jun	Sep	Dec
2008	0.37	0.47	0.50	0.47
2009	0.40	0.44	0.45	0.41
2010	0.35	0.49	0.55	0.44
2011	0.39	0.52	0.72	0.53
2012	0.47	0.67	0.78	0.74

Interim Dividends (Per Share)

Amt	Decl	Ex	Rec	Pay
0.18Q	04/25/2012	05/30/2012	06/01/2012	06/20/2012
0.18Q	07/25/2012	08/29/2012	08/31/2012	09/20/2012
0.18Q	10/29/2012	11/28/2012	11/30/2012	12/20/2012
0.18Q	02/13/2013	02/27/2013	03/01/2013	03/20/2013

Indicated Div: $0.72

Valuation Analysis / Institutional Holding

Forecast EPS	$3.21 (04/06/2013)	No of Institutions	444
Market Cap	$7.2 Billion	Shares	103,173,904
Book Value	$1.8 Billion	% Held	89.74
Price/Book	3.95		
Price/Sales	2.58		

Business Summary: Equipment & Services (MIC: 9.1.3 SIC: 1389 NAIC: 213112)

Oceaneering International is an oilfield provider of engineered services and products primarily to the offshore oil and gas industry, with a focus on deepwater applications. Co. also serves the defense and aerospace industries. As of Dec 31 2012, Co. has operations in the North Sea, West Africa, Brazil, Australia and Asia. Co. operates two business segments: services and products provided to the oil and gas industry, and all other services and products.

Recent Developments: For the year ended Dec 31 2012, net income increased 22.6% to US$289.0 million from US$235.7 million in the prior year. Revenues were US$2.78 billion, up 26.9% from US$2.19 billion the year before. Operating income was US$428.6 million versus US$334.8 million in the prior year, an increase of 28.0%. Direct operating expenses rose 28.0% to US$2.15 billion from US$1.68 billion in the comparable period the year before. Indirect operating expenses increased 14.6% to US$199.3 million from US$173.9 million in the equivalent prior-year period.

Prospects: Our evaluation of Oceaneering International Inc. as of Apr. 7, 2013 is the result of our systematic analysis on three basic characteristics: earnings strength, relative valuation, and recent stock price movement. The company has produced a positive trend in earnings per share over the past 5 quarters and while recent estimates for the company have remained steady, OII has posted better than expected results. Based on ongoing earnings yield, the company is about fairly valued when compared to all of the companies in our coverage universe. Share price changes over the past year indicates that OII will perform in line with the market over the near term.

Financial Data
(US$ in Thousands)

	12/31/2012	12/31/2011	12/31/2010	12/31/2009	12/31/2008	12/31/2007	12/31/2006	12/31/2005
Earnings Per Share	2.66	2.16	1.83	1.70	1.79	1.62	1.13	0.58
Cash Flow Per Share	4.05	2.66	4.05	3.82	2.25	1.91	1.40	0.90
Tang Book Value Per Share	13.46	11.33	11.52	9.96	7.79	7.29	5.60	4.22
Dividends Per Share	0.690	0.450	...	...	...	...	...	...
Dividend Payout %	25.94	20.83	...	...	...	...	...	...
Income Statement								
Total Revenue	2,782,604	2,192,663	1,917,045	1,822,081	1,977,421	1,743,080	1,280,198	998,543
EBITDA	599,015	485,519	462,225	416,565	432,908	381,379	271,628	173,306
Depn & Amortn	176,483	151,227	153,651	122,945	115,029	93,776	80,456	79,613
Income Before Taxes	420,249	334,084	303,144	286,533	305,301	273,468	178,982	84,096
Income Taxes	132,905	102,227	104,691	101,422	107,834	97,124	66,401	31,770
Net Income	289,017	235,658	200,531	188,353	199,386	180,374	124,494	62,680
Average Shares	108,617	109,001	109,534	110,052	111,444	111,510	109,982	107,296
Balance Sheet								
Current Assets	1,202,990	984,122	983,502	874,139	747,705	670,569	523,645	394,233
Total Assets	2,768,118	2,400,544	2,030,506	1,880,287	1,670,020	1,531,440	1,242,022	989,568
Current Liabilities	617,185	501,375	439,856	388,547	357,327	338,975	279,706	222,667
Long-Term Obligations	94,000	120,000	...	120,000	229,000	200,000	194,000	174,000
Total Liabilities	952,658	842,582	640,291	655,964	702,366	616,130	545,258	453,450
Stockholders' Equity	1,815,460	1,557,962	1,390,215	1,224,323	967,654	915,310	696,764	536,118
Shares Outstanding	107,907	108,034	108,230	109,835	108,950	110,150	108,880	107,117
Statistical Record								
Return on Assets %	11.15	10.64	10.26	10.61	12.42	13.01	11.16	6.93
Return on Equity %	17.09	15.99	15.34	17.19	21.12	22.38	20.20	12.66
EBITDA Margin %	21.53	22.14	24.11	22.86	21.89	21.88	21.22	17.36
Net Margin %	10.39	10.75	10.46	10.34	10.08	10.35	9.72	6.28
Asset Turnover	1.07	0.99	0.98	1.03	1.23	1.26	1.15	1.10
Current Ratio	1.95	1.96	2.24	2.25	2.09	1.98	1.87	1.77
Debt to Equity	0.05	0.08	...	0.10	0.24	0.22	0.28	0.32
Price Range	57.42-43.76	48.78-33.16	37.63-20.18	30.03-14.06	41.24-9.79	42.16-17.79	23.57-12.80	13.72-8.20
P/E Ratio	21.59-16.45	22.58-15.35	20.57-11.03	17.66-8.27	23.04-5.47	26.03-10.98	20.86-11.32	23.66-14.14
Average Yield %	1.34	1.10	...	...	...	...	...	...

Address: 11911 FM 529, Houston, TX 77041
Telephone: 713-329-4500
Fax: 713-329-4951

Web Site: www.oceaneering.com
Officers: John R. Huff - Chairman M. Kevin McEvoy - President, Chief Executive Officer

Auditors: Ernst & Young LLP
Investor Contact: 713-329-4500
Transfer Agents: Computershare Trust Company, N.A, Providence, R

OFFICE DEPOT, INC.

Exchange	Symbol	Price	52Wk Range	Yield	P/E
NYS	ODP	$3.93 (3/28/2013)	5.02-1.51	N/A	N/A

*7 Year Price Score 21.47 *NYSE Composite Index=100 ***12 Month Price Score 134.99**

Interim Earnings (Per Share)

Qtr.	Mar	Jun	Sep	Dec
2008	0.25	(0.01)	(0.02)	(5.64)
2009	(0.20)	(0.31)	(1.51)	(0.28)
2010	0.07	(0.07)	0.18	(0.21)
2011	(0.05)	(0.11)	0.28	0.05
2012	0.14	(0.23)	(0.25)	(0.06)

Interim Dividends (Per Share)

No Dividends Paid

Valuation Analysis

Forecast EPS	$0.06 (04/05/2013)
Market Cap	$1.1 Billion
Book Value	$1.0 Billion
Price/Book	1.07
Price/Sales	0.11

Institutional Holding

No of Institutions	288
Shares	224,871,984
% Held	74.83

Business Summary: Retail - Specialty (MIC: 2.1.3 SIC: 5112 NAIC: 453210)

Office Depot is a global supplier of office products and services under the Office Depot® brand and other proprietary brand names. Co. operates three segments: North American Retail Division, North American Business Solutions Division, and International Division. These segments sells an assortment of merchandise including general office supplies, computer supplies, business machines and related supplies, office furniture, printing, reproduction, mailing, shipping, and other services, personal computer support and network installation service, technology products, cleaning and breakroom supplies, certain services, and other solutions.

Recent Developments: For the year ended Dec 29 2012, net loss amounted to US$77.1 million versus net income of US$95.7 million in the prior year. Revenues were US$10.70 billion, down 6.9% from US$11.49 billion the year before. Operating loss was US$30.8 million versus an income of US$33.8 million in the prior year. Direct operating expenses declined 7.6% to US$7.45 billion from US$8.06 billion in the comparable period the year before. Indirect operating expenses decreased 3.4% to US$3.28 billion from US$3.39 billion in the equivalent prior-year period.

Prospects: Our evaluation of Office Depot Inc. as of Apr. 7, 2013 is the result of our systematic analysis on three basic characteristics: earnings strength, relative valuation, and recent stock price movement. The company has produced a positive trend in earnings per share over the past 5 quarters and while recent estimates for the company have remained steady, ODP has posted results that fell short of analysts expectations. Based on operating earnings yield, the company is overvalued when compared to all of the companies in our coverage universe. Share price changes over the past year indicates that ODP will perform very well over the near term.

Financial Data

(US$ in Thousands)	12/29/2012	12/31/2011	12/25/2010	12/26/2009	12/27/2008	12/29/2007	12/30/2006	12/31/2005
Earnings Per Share	(0.39)	0.22	(0.01)	(2.30)	(5.42)	1.43	1.79	0.87
Cash Flow Per Share	0.64	0.71	0.73	1.09	1.72	1.51	2.94	2.02
Tang Book Value Per Share	3.38	3.51	3.94	3.99	4.78	6.20	5.11	6.26
Income Statement								
Total Revenue	10,695,652	11,489,533	11,633,094	12,144,467	14,495,544	15,527,537	15,010,781	14,278,944
EBITDA	143,374	276,021	205,479	(26,920)	(1,274,210)	778,973	1,004,233	623,991
Depn & Amortn	152,100	211,410	208,319	221,000	245,100	266,700	245,900	252,300
Income Before Taxes	(75,423)	32,619	(56,675)	(311,152)	(1,577,583)	458,633	727,331	361,515
Income Taxes	1,697	(63,072)	(89,985)	287,572	(98,645)	63,018	211,196	87,723
Net Income	(77,111)	95,694	34,892	(596,465)	(1,478,938)	395,615	516,135	273,792
Average Shares	362,555	356,797	354,533	313,082	273,065	275,940	287,722	315,242
Balance Sheet								
Current Assets	2,696,190	2,744,132	3,090,655	3,206,329	3,122,387	3,715,714	3,455,125	3,530,062
Total Assets	4,010,779	4,250,984	4,652,366	4,890,346	5,268,226	7,256,540	6,570,102	6,098,525
Current Liabilities	2,045,968	2,047,437	2,343,445	2,428,205	2,625,744	2,973,416	2,969,927	2,468,751
Long-Term Obligations	485,331	659,820	659,820	662,740	688,788	607,462	570,752	569,098
Total Liabilities	2,962,937	3,148,277	3,517,962	3,748,623	3,905,276	4,172,696	3,959,991	3,359,304
Stockholders' Equity	1,047,842	1,102,707	1,134,404	1,141,723	1,362,950	3,083,844	2,610,111	2,739,221
Shares Outstanding	285,818	286,430	277,143	274,737	274,862	272,958	276,399	297,025
Statistical Record								
Return on Assets %	N.M.	2.11	0.73	N.M.	N.M.	5.74	8.17	4.19
Return on Equity %	N.M.	8.42	3.07	N.M.	N.M.	13.93	19.35	9.04
EBITDA Margin %	1.34	2.40	1.77	N.M.	N.M.	5.02	6.69	4.37
Net Margin %	N.M.	0.83	0.30	N.M.	N.M.	2.55	3.44	1.92
Asset Turnover	2.60	2.54	2.44	2.40	2.32	2.25	2.38	2.18
Current Ratio	1.32	1.34	1.32	1.32	1.19	1.25	1.16	1.43
Debt to Equity	0.46	0.59	0.58	0.58	0.51	0.20	0.22	0.21
Price Range	3.79-1.51	6.10-1.80	8.95-3.41	7.76-0.59	15.42-1.50	39.52-13.09	44.46-30.77	31.55-16.61
P/E Ratio	...	27.73-8.18	...	...	...	27.64-9.15	24.84-17.19	36.26-19.09

Address: 6600 North Military Trail, Boca Raton, FL 33496
Telephone: 561-438-4800
Fax: 561-265-4406

Web Site: www.officedepot.com
Officers: Neil R. Austrian - Chairman, Chief Executive Officer Steven M. Schmidt - President, Executive Vice President

Auditors: Deloitte & Touche LLP
Transfer Agents: BNY Mellon Shareowner Services, Pittsburgh, PA

OFFICEMAX INC (DE)

Exchange	Symbol	Price	52Wk Range	Yield	P/E
NYS	OMX	$11.61 (3/28/2013)	13.00-4.17	0.69	2.45

*7 Year Price Score 36.75   *NYSE Composite Index=100   *12 Month Price Score 143.56

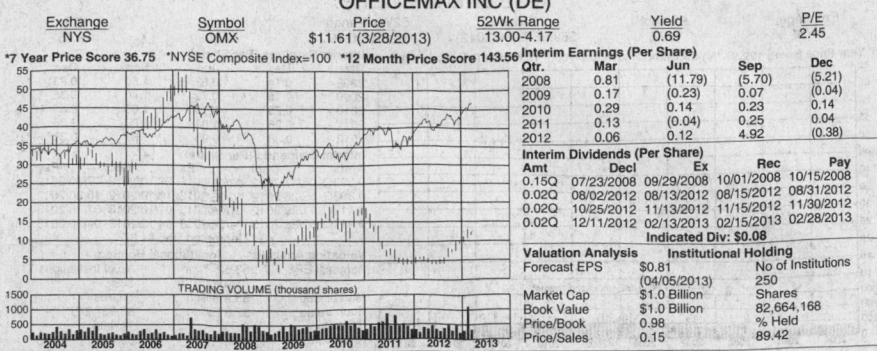

Interim Earnings (Per Share)

Qtr.	Mar	Jun	Sep	Dec
2008	0.81	(11.79)	(5.70)	(5.21)
2009	0.17	(0.23)	0.07	(0.04)
2010	0.29	0.14	0.23	0.14
2011	0.13	(0.04)	0.25	0.04
2012	0.06	0.12	4.92	(0.38)

Interim Dividends (Per Share)

Amt	Decl	Ex	Rec	Pay
0.15Q	07/23/2008	09/29/2008	10/01/2008	10/15/2008
0.02Q	08/02/2012	08/13/2012	08/15/2012	08/31/2012
0.02Q	10/25/2012	11/13/2012	11/15/2012	11/30/2012
0.02Q	12/11/2012	02/13/2013	02/15/2013	02/28/2013

Indicated Div: $0.08

Valuation Analysis

		Institutional Holding	
Forecast EPS	$0.81	No of Institutions	
	(04/05/2013)	250	
Market Cap	$1.0 Billion	Shares	
Book Value	$1.0 Billion	82,664,168	
Price/Book	0.98	% Held	
Price/Sales	0.15	89.42	

Business Summary: Retail - Specialty (MIC: 2.1.3 SIC: 5112 NAIC: 424120)

OfficeMax is engaged in both business-to-business and retail office products distribution. Co.'s OfficeMax, Contract segment markets and sells office supplies and paper, technology products and applications, office furniture and print and document services to corporate and government offices, as well as to small and medium-sized offices through field salespeople, outbound telesales, catalogs, the Internet and, in foreign markets, through office products stores. Co.'s OfficeMax, Retail segment markets and sells office supplies and paper, print and document services, technology products and applications and office furniture to small and medium-sized businesses and consumers via retail stores.

Recent Developments: For the year ended Dec 29 2012, net income increased to US$416.8 million from US$34.9 million in the prior year. Revenues were US$6.92 billion, down 2.8% from US$7.12 billion the year before. Operating income was US$24.3 million versus US$86.5 million in the prior year, a decrease of 71.9%. Direct operating expenses declined 3.3% to US$5.14 billion from US$5.31 billion in the comparable period the year before. Indirect operating expenses increased 2.2% to US$1.76 billion from US$1.72 billion in the equivalent prior-year period.

Prospects: Our evaluation of OfficeMax Inc. as of Apr. 7, 2013 is the result of our systematic analysis on three basic characteristics: earnings strength, relative valuation, and recent stock price movement. The company has managed to produce a neutral trend in earnings per share over the past 5 quarters. However, while recent estimates for the company have been lowered by analysts, OMX has posted better than expected results. Based on operating earnings yield, the company is undervalued when compared to all of the companies in our coverage universe. Share price changes over the past year indicates that OMX will perform very well over the near term.

Financial Data
(US$ in Thousands)

	12/29/2012	12/31/2011	12/25/2010	12/26/2009	12/27/2008	12/29/2007	12/30/2006	12/31/2005
Earnings Per Share	4.74	0.38	0.79	(0.03)	(21.90)	2.66	1.19	(0.99)
Cash Flow Per Share	2.14	0.61	1.04	4.65	2.96	0.94	5.15	(0.73)
Tang Book Value Per Share	10.66	5.32	5.72	4.52	2.18	10.77	6.86	3.64
Dividends Per Share	0.040	...	...	...	0.450	0.600	0.600	0.600
Dividend Payout %	0.84	...	...	...		22.56	50.42	...
Income Statement								
Total Revenue	6,920,384	7,121,167	7,150,007	7,212,050	8,267,008	9,081,962	8,965,707	9,157,660
EBITDA	769,657	170,991	247,370	115,177	(1,773,427)	496,366	327,176	139,301
Depn & Amortn	74,124	84,218	100,936	116,417	142,896	131,573	127,812	151,145
Income Before Taxes	669,540	57,637	115,736	(30,333)	(1,972,400)	331,462	166,005	(43,076)
Income Taxes	248,722	19,517	41,872	(28,758)	(306,481)	125,282	68,741	1,226
Net Income	416,790	34,894	71,155	667	(1,657,932)	207,373	91,721	(73,762)
Average Shares	87,939	86,997	86,512	77,483	75,862	76,374	73,713	78,745
Balance Sheet								
Current Assets	1,983,884	1,938,974	2,014,286	2,021,336	1,855,016	2,204,701	2,096,844	1,942,049
Total Assets	3,784,315	4,069,275	4,078,929	4,069,531	4,173,583	6,283,768	6,216,048	6,272,142
Current Liabilities	1,056,641	1,013,301	1,044,474	1,091,692	1,197,471	1,370,709	1,528,903	1,588,326
Long-Term Obligations	960,962	1,699,323	1,740,435	1,744,622	1,759,922	1,819,421	1,854,246	1,877,242
Total Liabilities	2,749,942	3,500,282	3,478,164	3,566,335	3,883,580	4,005,196	4,230,404	4,536,463
Stockholders' Equity	1,034,373	568,993	600,765	503,196	290,003	2,278,572	1,985,644	1,735,679
Shares Outstanding	86,883	86,158	85,057	84,624	75,977	75,397	74,903	70,804
Statistical Record								
Return on Assets %	10.64	0.84	1.75	0.02	N.M.	3.33	1.47	N.M.
Return on Equity %	52.13	5.87	12.93	0.17	N.M.	9.75	4.94	N.M.
EBITDA Margin %	11.12	2.40	3.46	1.60	N.M.	5.47	3.65	1.52
Net Margin %	6.02	0.49	1.00	0.01	N.M.	2.28	1.02	N.M.
Asset Turnover	1.77	1.72	1.76	1.75	1.59	1.46	1.44	1.33
Current Ratio	1.88	1.91	1.93	1.85	1.55	1.61	1.37	1.22
Debt to Equity	0.93	2.99	2.90	3.47	6.07	0.80	0.93	1.08
Price Range	10.16-4.17	18.54-4.00	19.59-9.74	14.08-1.95	24.82-3.27	54.54-20.54	51.17-24.84	34.50-24.35
P/E Ratio	2.14-0.88	48.79-10.53	24.80-12.33	...	...	20.50-7.72	43.00-20.87	...
Average Yield %	0.65	...	...	...	3.05	1.51	1.53	1.98

Address: 263 Shuman Boulevard, Naperville, IL 60563 **Telephone:** 630-438-7800	**Web Site:** www.officemax.com **Officers:** Ravichandra K. Saligram - President, Chief Executive Officer John Kenning - Executive Vice President	**Auditors:** KPMG LLP **Investor Contact:** 630-864-6800 **Transfer Agents:** Wells Fargo Bank Minnesota, N.A., South St. Paul, MN

OGE ENERGY CORP.

Exchange	Symbol	Price	52Wk Range	Yield	P/E
NYS	OGE	$69.98 (3/28/2013)	69.98-50.40	2.39	19.55

*7 Year Price Score 122.97 *NYSE Composite Index=100 *12 Month Price Score 101.34

Interim Earnings (Per Share)

Qtr.	Mar	Jun	Sep	Dec
2008	0.14	0.62	1.50	0.23
2009	0.18	0.72	1.40	0.35
2010	0.25	0.78	1.65	0.31
2011	0.25	1.04	1.80	0.36
2012	0.38	0.95	1.87	0.38

Interim Dividends (Per Share)

Amt	Decl	Ex	Rec	Pay
0.393Q	05/17/2012	07/06/2012	07/10/2012	07/30/2012
0.393Q	09/26/2012	10/05/2012	10/10/2012	10/30/2012
0.417Q	11/28/2012	01/08/2013	01/10/2013	01/30/2013
0.417Q	02/26/2013	04/08/2013	04/10/2013	04/30/2013

Indicated Div: $1.67

Valuation Analysis / **Institutional Holding**

Forecast EPS	$3.52 (04/06/2013)	No of Institutions	389
Market Cap	$6.9 Billion	Shares	63,937,248
Book Value	$2.8 Billion	% Held	55.03
Price/Book	2.50		
Price/Sales	1.88		

Business Summary: Electric Utilities (MIC: 3.1.1 SIC: 4911 NAIC: 221121)

OGE Energy is a holding company. Through its subsidiaries, Co. is an energy and energy services provider providing physical delivery and related services for both electricity and natural gas primarily in the south central U.S. Co. has three business segments: electric utility, which generates, transmits, distributes and sells electric energy ; natural gas transportation and storage, which delivers natural gas to most interstate and intrastate pipelines and end-users connected to its systems from the Arkoma and Anadarko basins; and natural gas gathering and processing, which provides well connect, gathering, measurement, treating, dehydration, compression and processing services.

Recent Developments: For the year ended Dec 31 2012, net income increased 5.9% to US$385.0 million from US$363.6 million in the prior year. Revenues were US$3.67 billion, down 6.2% from US$3.92 billion the year before. Operating income was US$676.9 million versus US$646.7 million in the prior year, an increase of 4.7%. Direct operating expenses declined 15.8% to US$1.92 billion from US$2.28 billion in the comparable period the year before. Indirect operating expenses increased 8.5% to US$1.08 billion from US$991.3 million in the equivalent prior-year period.

Prospects: Our evaluation of OGE Energy Corp. as of Apr. 7, 2013 is the result of our systematic analysis on three basic characteristics: earnings strength, relative valuation, and recent stock price movement. The company has produced a positive trend in earnings per share over the past 5 quarters. However, while recent estimates for the company have been lowered by analysts, OGE has posted better than expected results. Based on operating earnings yield, the company is about fairly valued when compared to all of the companies in our coverage universe. Share price changes over the past year indicates that OGE will perform very poorly over the near term.

Financial Data
(US$ in Thousands)

	12/31/2012	12/31/2011	12/31/2010	12/31/2009	12/31/2008	12/31/2007	12/31/2006	12/31/2005
Earnings Per Share	3.58	3.45	2.99	2.66	2.49	2.64	2.84	2.32
Cash Flow Per Share	10.58	8.52	8.04	6.80	6.75	3.58	6.26	4.94
Tang Book Value Per Share	26.32	24.33	23.46	21.04	20.29	18.31	17.59	14.82
Dividends Per Share	1.570	1.500	1.450	1.420	1.390	1.360	1.330	1.330
Dividend Payout %	43.85	43.48	48.49	53.38	55.82	51.52	46.83	57.33
Income Statement								
Total Revenue	3,671,200	3,915,900	3,716,900	2,869,700	4,070,700	3,797,600	4,005,600	5,948,200
EBITDA	1,058,400	971,800	893,500	780,800	663,400	644,300	617,800	510,800
Depn & Amortn	374,800	307,100	292,400	262,600	217,500	195,300	181,400	186,100
Income Before Taxes	520,100	524,300	461,400	382,200	332,600	360,900	346,600	237,900
Income Taxes	135,100	160,700	161,000	121,100	101,200	116,700	120,500	71,800
Net Income	355,000	342,900	295,300	258,300	231,400	244,200	262,100	211,000
Average Shares	99,100	99,200	98,900	97,200	92,800	92,500	92,100	90,800
Balance Sheet								
Current Assets	794,200	652,700	632,100	826,100	744,600	629,500	664,100	1,073,600
Total Assets	9,922,200	8,906,000	7,669,100	7,266,700	6,518,500	5,237,800	4,902,000	4,898,900
Current Liabilities	1,276,400	998,500	814,500	1,275,700	888,400	988,500	673,000	950,600
Long-Term Obligations	2,848,600	2,737,100	2,362,900	2,088,900	2,161,800	1,344,600	1,346,300	1,350,800
Total Liabilities	7,155,000	6,342,700	5,379,500	5,225,900	4,621,700	3,556,900	3,298,200	3,523,100
Stockholders' Equity	2,767,200	2,563,300	2,289,600	2,040,800	1,896,800	1,680,900	1,603,800	1,375,800
Shares Outstanding	98,800	98,100	97,600	97,000	93,500	91,800	91,200	90,600
Statistical Record								
Return on Assets %	3.76	4.14	3.95	3.75	3.93	4.82	5.35	4.32
Return on Equity %	13.28	14.13	13.64	13.12	12.90	14.87	17.59	15.86
EBITDA Margin %	28.83	24.82	24.04	27.21	16.30	16.97	15.42	8.59
Net Margin %	9.67	8.76	7.94	9.00	5.68	6.43	6.54	3.55
Asset Turnover	0.39	0.47	0.50	0.42	0.69	0.75	0.82	1.22
Current Ratio	0.62	0.65	0.78	0.65	0.84	0.64	0.99	1.13
Debt to Equity	1.03	1.07	1.03	1.02	1.14	0.80	0.84	0.98
Price Range	58.19-50.40	56.82-41.16	45.96-34.78	37.53-19.84	36.29-21.60	41.01-31.03	40.41-26.42	30.38-24.67
P/E Ratio	16.25-14.08	16.47-11.93	15.37-11.63	14.11-7.46	14.57-8.67	15.53-11.75	14.23-9.30	13.09-10.63
Average Yield %	2.89	3.03	3.64	4.93	4.50	3.74	3.98	4.85

Address: 321 North Harvey, P.O. Box 321, Oklahoma City, OK 73101-0321
Telephone: 405-553-3000

Web Site: www.oge.com
Officers: Peter B. Delaney - Chairman, President, Chief Executive Officer Sean Trauschke - Vice President, Chief Financial Officer

Auditors: Ernst & Young LLP
Transfer Agents: Computershare

OIL-DRI CORP. OF AMERICA

Exchange	Symbol	Price	52Wk Range	Yield	P/E	Div Achiever
NYS	ODC	$27.23 (3/28/2013)	28.82-18.45	2.64	22.69	10 Years

*7 Year Price Score 110.35 *NYSE Composite Index=100 *12 Month Price Score 107.87

Interim Earnings (Per Share)

Qtr.	Oct	Jan	Apr	Jul
2009-10	0.30	0.31	0.35	0.34
2010-11	0.35	0.25	0.26	0.40
2011-12	0.15	0.45	0.26	(0.01)
2012-13	0.64	0.31	...	...

Interim Dividends (Per Share)

Amt	Decl	Ex	Rec	Pay
0.17Q	03/15/2012	05/16/2012	05/18/2012	06/01/2012
0.18Q	06/14/2012	08/15/2012	08/17/2012	08/31/2012
0.18Q	10/16/2012	11/14/2012	11/16/2012	11/30/2012
0.36Q	12/04/2012	12/12/2012	12/14/2012	12/28/2012

Indicated Div: $0.72

Valuation Analysis

		Institutional Holding	
Forecast EPS	$1.26 (04/05/2013)	No of Institutions	62
Market Cap	$190.3 Million	Shares	3,904,098
Book Value	$89.8 Million	% Held	53.87
Price/Book	2.12		
Price/Sales	0.78		

Business Summary: Household & Personal Products (MIC: 1.7.1 SIC: 3999 NAIC: 339999)

Oil-Dri Corp of America develops, mines, manufactures and markets sorbent products principally produced from clay minerals, primarily consisting of montmorillonite and attapulgite and, to a lesser extent, other clay-like sorbent materials, such as Antelope shale. Co.'s principal products include cat litter, industrial and automotive floor absorbents, fluids purification and filtration bleaching clays, agricultural and horticultural chemical carriers, animal health and nutrition products and sports field products. Co. has two reportable operating segments, which are based on its primary customer groups: retail and wholesale products group and business to business products group.

Recent Developments: For the quarter ended Jan 31 2013, net income decreased 33.7% to US$2.1 million from US$3.2 million in the year-earlier quarter. Revenues were US$61.1 million, up 1.5% from US$60.2 million the year before. Operating income was US$3.4 million versus US$4.8 million in the prior-year quarter, a decrease of 29.9%. Direct operating expenses declined 1.7% to US$44.9 million from US$45.6 million in the comparable period the year before. Indirect operating expenses increased 32.5% to US$12.9 million from US$9.7 million in the equivalent prior-year period.

Prospects: Our evaluation of Oil-Dri Corp. of America as of Apr. 7, 2013 is the result of our systematic analysis on three basic characteristics: earnings strength, relative valuation, and recent stock price movement. The company has suffered a very negative trend in earnings per share over the past 5 quarters. Because the company lacks sufficient analyst estimate data, we place greater weight on the historical EPS trend as the measure of earnings strength. Based on operating earnings yield, the company is about fairly valued when compared to all of the companies in our coverage universe. Share price changes over the past year indicates that ODC will perform very well over the near term.

Financial Data

(US$ in Thousands)	6 Mos	3 Mos	07/31/2012	07/31/2011	07/31/2010	07/31/2009	07/31/2008	07/31/2007
Earnings Per Share	1.20	1.34	0.85	1.26	1.30	1.32	1.25	1.09
Cash Flow Per Share	3.47	4.01	3.33	1.87	3.70	2.25	1.63	2.50
Tang Book Value Per Share	11.96	11.92	11.40	12.39	11.95	11.59	11.35	10.67
Dividends Per Share	1.060	0.690	0.680	0.640	0.600	0.560	0.520	0.480
Dividend Payout %	88.33	51.49	80.00	50.79	46.15	42.42	41.60	44.04
Income Statement								
Total Revenue	122,539	61,417	240,681	226,755	219,050	236,245	232,359	212,117
EBITDA	9,995	6,527	19,677	22,636	21,395	22,141	20,057	18,038
Depn & Amortn	(3)	(2)	9,287	8,503	1,362	7,287	6,763	6,619
Income Before Taxes	9,088	6,057	8,361	12,141	12,814	13,309	12,175	10,445
Income Taxes	2,490	1,605	2,263	3,090	3,356	3,723	3,136	2,785
Net Income	6,598	4,452	6,098	9,051	9,458	9,586	9,039	7,660
Average Shares	6,922	6,879	7,062	7,103	7,275	7,242	7,215	7,028
Balance Sheet								
Current Assets	97,177	95,997	95,202	91,816	76,189	73,717	82,651	78,300
Total Assets	176,418	174,708	174,267	173,393	153,982	149,261	148,988	142,087
Current Liabilities	29,395	28,660	29,122	26,480	27,791	23,768	30,101	27,405
Long-Term Obligations	22,400	22,400	25,900	29,700	14,800	18,300	21,500	27,080
Total Liabilities	86,577	85,670	88,959	78,095	63,393	59,698	61,362	61,845
Stockholders' Equity	89,841	89,038	85,308	95,298	90,589	89,563	87,626	80,242
Shares Outstanding	6,988	6,936	6,924	7,156	7,000	7,108	7,045	6,893
Statistical Record								
Return on Assets %	4.78	5.46	3.50	5.53	6.24	6.43	6.19	5.44
Return on Equity %	8.94	10.28	6.73	9.74	10.50	10.82	10.74	9.98
EBITDA Margin %	8.16	10.63	8.18	9.98	9.77	9.37	8.63	8.50
Net Margin %	5.38	7.25	2.53	3.99	4.32	4.06	3.89	3.61
Asset Turnover	1.39	1.40	1.38	1.39	1.44	1.58	1.59	1.51
Current Ratio	3.31	3.35	3.27	3.47	2.74	3.10	2.75	2.86
Debt to Equity	0.25	0.25	0.30	0.31	0.16	0.20	0.25	0.34
Price Range	28.82-18.45	23.58-18.45	22.35-16.95	22.95-18.91	23.12-14.18	18.96-11.62	22.95-15.36	18.55-12.99
P/E Ratio	24.02-15.38	17.60-13.77	26.29-19.94	18.21-15.01	17.78-10.91	14.36-8.80	18.36-12.29	17.02-11.92
Average Yield %	4.73	3.26	3.39	3.06	3.40	3.47	2.80	2.91

Address: 410 North Michigan Avenue, Suite 400, Chicago, IL 60611-4213 Telephone: 312-321-1515 Fax: 312-321-9525	Web Site: www.oildri.com Officers: Richard M. Jaffee - Chairman Joseph C. Miller - Vice-Chairman	Auditors: PricewaterhouseCoopers LLP Investor Contact: 312-321-1515 Transfer Agents: ComputerShare Investor Services, Chicago, IL

OIL STATES INTERNATIONAL, INC.

Exchange	Symbol	Price	52Wk Range	Yield	P/E
NYS	OIS	$81.57 (3/28/2013)	86.65-61.28	N/A	10.07

*7 Year Price Score 134.97 *NYSE Composite Index=100 *12 Month Price Score 97.01

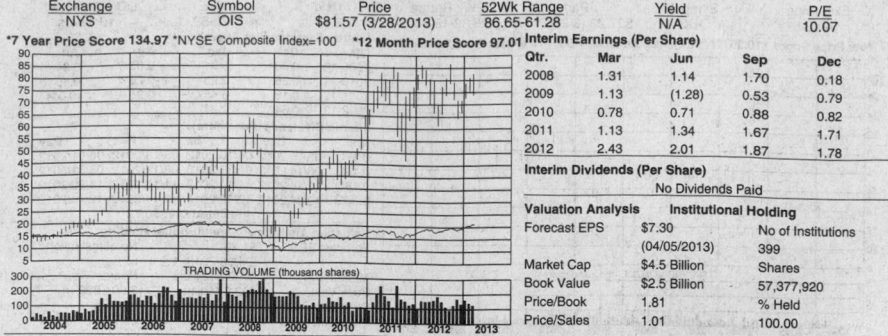

Interim Earnings (Per Share)

Qtr.	Mar	Jun	Sep	Dec
2008	1.31	1.14	1.70	0.18
2009	1.13	(1.28)	0.53	0.79
2010	0.78	0.71	0.88	0.82
2011	1.13	1.34	1.67	1.71
2012	2.43	2.01	1.87	1.78

Interim Dividends (Per Share)

No Dividends Paid

Valuation Analysis / **Institutional Holding**

Forecast EPS	$7.30	No of Institutions
	(04/05/2013)	399
Market Cap	$4.5 Billion	Shares
Book Value	$2.5 Billion	57,377,920
Price/Book	1.81	% Held
Price/Sales	1.01	100.00

Business Summary: Equipment & Services (MIC: 9.1.3 SIC: 3533 NAIC: 333132)

Oil States International provides products and services to natural resources companies. Co.'s segments are: Accomodations, which provides accommodation services for people working in remote locations; Offshore Products, including offshore development and drilling activities, bearing and connector products, subsea pipeline products, marine winches, mooring systems, cranes and rig equipment, blow-out preventer stack assembly, integration, and testing and repair services; Well Site Services, including completion-focused equipment and services and land drilling services; and Tubular Services, which distribute casing and tubing and provide threading, logistical and inventory management services.

Recent Developments: For the year ended Dec 31 2012, net income increased 39.1% to US$449.8 million from US$323.4 million in the prior year. Revenues were US$4.41 billion, up 26.8% from US$3.48 billion the year before. Operating income was US$683.8 million versus US$507.5 million in the prior year, an increase of 34.7%. Direct operating expenses rose 26.7% to US$3.29 billion from US$2.60 billion in the comparable period the year before. Indirect operating expenses increased 17.2% to US$436.3 million from US$372.4 million in the equivalent prior-year period.

Prospects: Our evaluation of Oil States International Inc. as of Apr. 7, 2013 is the result of our systematic analysis on three basic characteristics: earnings strength, relative valuation, and recent stock price movement. The company has generated a negative trend in earnings per share over the past 5 quarters. However, while recent estimates for the company have been lowered by analysts, OIS has posted results that fell short of analysts expectations. Based on operating earnings yield, the company is undervalued when compared to all of the companies in our coverage universe. Share price changes over the past year indicates that OIS will perform poorly over the near term.

Financial Data

(US$ in Thousands)	12/31/2012	12/31/2011	12/31/2010	12/31/2009	12/31/2008	12/31/2007	12/31/2006	12/31/2005
Earnings Per Share	8.10	5.86	3.19	1.18	4.33	3.99	3.89	2.41
Cash Flow Per Share	12.00	4.22	4.60	9.14	5.17	5.01	2.77	0.68
Tang Book Value Per Share	32.86	26.66	19.93	23.33	18.46	14.03	10.31	5.98
Income Statement								
Total Revenue	4,413,088	3,479,180	2,411,984	2,108,250	2,948,457	2,088,235	1,923,357	1,531,636
EBITDA	910,491	685,938	377,512	233,843	487,993	377,988	361,882	243,511
Depn & Amortn	216,500	174,900	121,600	114,700	99,000	66,500	50,500	47,576
Income Before Taxes	626,652	455,232	240,389	104,257	375,024	297,008	294,499	182,507
Income Taxes	177,047	131,647	72,023	46,097	156,349	96,986	104,013	60,694
Net Income	448,609	322,453	168,018	59,114	222,710	203,372	197,634	121,813
Average Shares	55,384	55,007	52,700	50,219	51,414	50,911	50,773	50,479
Balance Sheet								
Current Assets	1,826,092	1,489,659	1,100,004	925,568	1,237,484	865,667	783,989	663,744
Total Assets	4,439,962	3,703,641	3,015,999	1,932,386	2,299,247	1,929,626	1,571,094	1,342,872
Current Liabilities	518,532	474,949	554,175	315,223	536,505	304,911	280,416	262,697
Long-Term Obligations	1,279,805	1,142,505	731,732	164,074	474,948	487,102	391,729	402,109
Total Liabilities	1,975,557	1,741,485	1,388,093	551,538	1,080,254	844,799	731,258	708,888
Stockholders' Equity	2,464,405	1,962,156	1,627,906	1,380,848	1,218,993	1,084,827	839,836	633,984
Shares Outstanding	54,695	51,288	50,838	49,814	49,500	49,392	49,296	49,179
Statistical Record								
Return on Assets %	10.99	9.60	6.79	2.79	10.50	11.62	13.56	10.70
Return on Equity %	20.21	17.96	11.17	4.55	19.28	21.13	26.82	20.93
EBITDA Margin %	20.63	19.72	15.65	11.09	16.55	18.10	18.82	15.90
Net Margin %	10.17	9.27	6.97	2.80	7.55	9.74	10.28	7.95
Asset Turnover	1.08	1.04	0.97	1.00	1.39	1.19	1.32	1.35
Current Ratio	3.52	3.14	1.98	2.94	2.31	2.84	2.80	2.53
Debt to Equity	0.52	0.58	0.45	0.12	0.39	0.45	0.47	0.63
Price Range	86.65-61.28	85.50-46.95	65.31-34.20	39.82-11.47	63.57-14.93	50.89-27.08	42.95-25.40	36.57-17.95
P/E Ratio	10.70-7.57	14.59-8.01	20.47-10.72	33.75-9.72	14.68-3.45	12.75-6.79	11.04-6.53	15.17-7.45

Address: Three Allen Center, 333 Clay Street, Suite 4620, Houston, TX 77002 Telephone: 713-652-0582	Web Site: www.oilstatesintl.com Officers: Stephen A. Wells - Chairman Cindy B. Taylor - President, Chief Executive Officer	Auditors: Ernst & Young LLP Transfer Agents: Computershare, Pittsburgh, PA

OLD REPUBLIC INTERNATIONAL CORP.

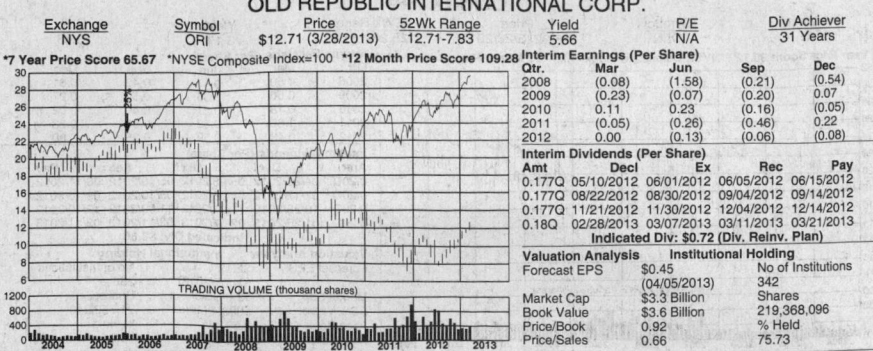

Exchange	Symbol	Price	52Wk Range	Yield	P/E	Div Achiever
NYS	ORI	$12.71 (3/28/2013)	12.71-7.83	5.66	N/A	31 Years

*7 Year Price Score 65.67   *NYSE Composite Index=100   *12 Month Price Score 109.28

Interim Earnings (Per Share)

Qtr.	Mar	Jun	Sep	Dec
2008	(0.08)	(1.58)	(0.21)	(0.54)
2009	(0.23)	(0.07)	(0.20)	0.07
2010	0.11	0.23	(0.16)	(0.05)
2011	(0.05)	(0.26)	(0.46)	0.22
2012	0.00	(0.13)	(0.06)	(0.08)

Interim Dividends (Per Share)

Amt	Decl	Ex	Rec	Pay
0.177Q	05/10/2012	06/01/2012	06/05/2012	06/15/2012
0.177Q	08/22/2012	08/30/2012	09/04/2012	09/14/2012
0.177Q	11/21/2012	11/30/2012	12/04/2012	12/14/2012
0.18Q	02/28/2013	03/07/2013	03/11/2013	03/21/2013

Indicated Div: $0.72 (Div. Reinv. Plan)

Valuation Analysis

		Institutional Holding	
Forecast EPS	$0.45 (04/05/2013)	No of Institutions	342
Market Cap	$3.3 Billion	Shares	219,368,096
Book Value	$3.6 Billion	% Held	75.73
Price/Book	0.92		
Price/Sales	0.66		

Business Summary: General Insurance (MIC: 5.2.1 SIC: 6351 NAIC: 524127)

Old Republic International is a holding company engaged in the business of insurance underwriting. Co. has three segments: General Insurance, which is characterized as a commercial lines insurance business with a focus on liability insurance coverages; Mortgage Guaranty, which protects mortgage lenders and investors from default related losses on residential mortgage loans made primarily to homebuyers who make down payments of less than 20.0% of the home's purchase price; and Title Insurance, which consists mainly of the issuance of policies to real estate purchasers and investors based upon searches of the public records, which contain information concerning interests in real property.

Recent Developments: For the year ended Dec 31 2012, net loss amounted to US$68.6 million versus a net loss of US$140.5 million in the prior year. Revenues were US$4.97 billion, up 7.0% from US$4.65 billion the year before. Net premiums earned were US$4.04 billion versus US$3.70 billion in the prior year, an increase of 9.4%. Net investment income fell 7.7% to US$336.3 million from US$364.5 million a year ago.

Prospects: Our evaluation of Old Republic International Corp. as of Apr. 7, 2013 is the result of our systematic analysis on three basic characteristics: earnings strength, relative valuation, and recent stock price movement. The company has suffered a very negative trend in earnings per share over the past 5 quarters and while recent estimates for the company have remained steady, ORI has posted results that fell short of analysts expectations. Based on operating earnings yield, the company is overvalued when compared to all of the companies in our coverage universe. Share price changes over the past year indicates that ORI will perform poorly over the near term.

Financial Data
(US$ in Thousands)

	12/31/2012	12/31/2011	12/31/2010	12/31/2009	12/31/2008	12/31/2007	12/31/2006	12/31/2005
Earnings Per Share	(0.27)	(0.55)	0.13	(0.42)	(2.41)	1.17	1.99	2.37
Cash Flow Per Share	2.07	(0.37)	(1.17)	2.26	2.44	3.73	4.35	3.83
Tang Book Value Per Share	13.86	14.55	15.90	16.17	15.55	19.71	18.91	17.53
Dividends Per Share	0.710	0.700	0.690	0.680	0.670	0.630	0.590	1.312
Dividend Payout %	...	...	530.77	...	...	53.85	29.65	55.36
Income Statement								
Premium Income	4,043,800	3,695,500	3,225,500	3,111,500	3,125,100	3,389,000	3,154,100	3,062,300
Total Revenue	4,970,100	4,645,500	4,102,700	3,803,600	3,237,700	4,091,000	3,794,200	3,805,900
Benefits & Claims	2,747,400	2,730,600	2,253,200	2,591,000	2,700,400	2,156,900	1,532,300	1,460,100
Income Before Taxes	...	...	27,600	...	...	...	...	...
Income Taxes	(59,800)	(96,100)	(2,500)	(174,400)	(260,800)	105,900	215,200	195,900
Net Income	(68,600)	(140,500)	30,100	(99,100)	(558,300)	272,400	464,800	551,400
Average Shares	255,812	255,045	241,327	235,657	231,484	232,912	233,034	232,108
Balance Sheet								
Total Assets	16,226,800	16,050,400	15,882,700	14,190,000	13,266,000	13,290,600	12,612,200	11,543,200
Total Liabilities	12,630,600	12,277,800	11,761,300	10,298,600	9,525,700	8,749,000	8,243,000	7,519,100
Stockholders' Equity	3,596,200	3,772,500	4,121,400	3,891,400	3,740,300	4,541,600	4,369,200	4,024,000
Shares Outstanding	259,490	259,328	259,222	240,685	240,520	230,472	231,047	229,575
Statistical Record								
Return on Assets %	N.M.	N.M.	0.20	N.M.	N.M.	2.10	3.85	4.99
Return on Equity %	N.M.	N.M.	0.75	N.M.	N.M.	6.11	11.08	13.98
Loss Ratio %	67.94	73.89	69.86	83.27	86.41	63.64	48.58	47.68
Net Margin %	(1.38)	(3.02)	0.73	(2.61)	(17.24)	6.66	12.25	14.49
Price Range	11.19-7.83	13.84-7.18	15.29-10.04	12.71-7.40	16.50-7.39	23.51-13.73	23.50-20.20	22.44-17.85
P/E Ratio	...	...	117.62-77.23	...	...	20.09-11.74	11.81-10.15	9.47-7.53
Average Yield %	7.29	6.36	5.42	6.36	5.49	3.19	2.71	6.55

Address: 307 North Michigan Avenue, Chicago, IL 60601
Telephone: 312-346-8100

Web Site: www.oldrepublic.com
Officers: Aldo C. Zucaro - Chairman, Chief Executive Officer James A. Kellogg - Executive Vice-Chairman

Auditors: KPMG LLP
Investor Contact: 800-468-9716
Transfer Agents: Wells Fargo Shareowner Services, St. Paul, MN

OLIN CORP.

Exchange	Symbol	Price	52Wk Range	Yield	P/E
NYS	OLN	$25.22 (3/28/2013)	25.23-18.51	3.17	13.63

*7 Year Price Score 98.72   *NYSE Composite Index=100   *12 Month Price Score 100.74

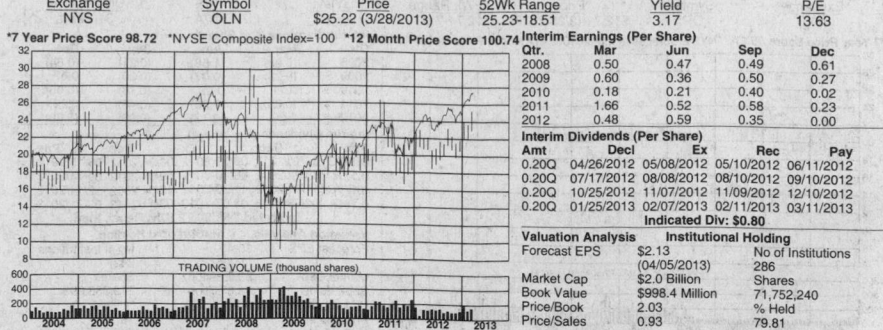

Interim Earnings (Per Share)

Qtr.	Mar	Jun	Sep	Dec
2008	0.50	0.47	0.49	0.61
2009	0.60	0.36	0.50	0.27
2010	0.18	0.21	0.40	0.02
2011	1.66	0.52	0.58	0.23
2012	0.48	0.59	0.35	0.00

Interim Dividends (Per Share)

Amt	Decl	Ex	Rec	Pay
0.20Q	04/26/2012	05/08/2012	05/10/2012	06/11/2012
0.20Q	07/17/2012	08/08/2012	08/10/2012	09/10/2012
0.20Q	10/25/2012	11/07/2012	11/09/2012	12/10/2012
0.20Q	01/25/2013	02/07/2013	02/11/2013	03/11/2013

Indicated Div: $0.80

Valuation Analysis   **Institutional Holding**

Forecast EPS	$2.13 (04/05/2013)
Market Cap	$2.0 Billion
Book Value	$998.4 Million
Price/Book	2.03
Price/Sales	0.93

No of Institutions 286
Shares 71,752,240
% Held 79.81

Business Summary: Diversified Chemicals (MIC: 8.3.1 SIC: 2812 NAIC: 325181)

Olin is a manufacturer concentrated in three segments: Chlor Alkali Products, which manufactures and sells chlorine/caustic soda, bleach, hydrochloric acid, potassium hydroxide and hydrogen; Chemical Distribution, which manufactures bleach products and distributes caustic soda, bleach products, potassium hydroxide and hydrochloric acid; and Winchester, which develops and manufactures small caliber ammunition for commercial customers, law enforcement agencies and militaries. Co.'s subsidiary, Olin Canada ULC, sells chlor alkali-related products within Canada and to the U.S.; and Winchester Australia Limited, loads and packs sporting and industrial ammunition in Australia, respectively.

Recent Developments: For the year ended Dec 31 2012, net income decreased 38.1% to US$149.6 million from US$241.7 million in the prior year. Revenues were US$2.18 billion, up 11.4% from US$1.96 billion the year before. Operating income was US$258.9 million versus US$223.9 million in the prior year, an increase of 15.6%. Direct operating expenses rose 11.1% to US$1.75 billion from US$1.57 billion in the comparable period the year before. , Indirect operating expenses increased 8.9% to US$177.8 million from US$163.3 million in the equivalent prior-year period.

Prospects: Our evaluation of Olin Corp. as of Apr. 7, 2013 is the result of our systematic analysis on three basic characteristics: earnings strength, relative valuation, and recent stock price movement. The company has managed to produce a neutral trend in earnings per share over the past 5 quarters and while recent estimates for the company have been raised by analysts, OLN has posted better than expected results. Based on operating earnings yield, the company is undervalued when compared to all of the companies in our coverage universe. Share price changes over the past year indicates that OLN will perform poorly over the near term.

Financial Data
(US$ in Thousands)

	12/31/2012	12/31/2011	12/31/2010	12/31/2009	12/31/2008	12/31/2007	12/31/2006	12/31/2005
Earnings Per Share	1.85	2.99	0.81	1.73	2.07	(0.12)	2.06	1.86
Cash Flow Per Share	3.48	2.70	1.46	2.56	1.52	2.76	0.89	3.91
Tang Book Value Per Share	1.23	4.23	6.47	6.42	4.98	4.86	6.37	4.89
Dividends Per Share	0.800	0.800	0.800	0.800	0.800	0.800	0.800	0.800
Dividend Payout %	43.24	26.76	98.77	46.24	38.65	...	38.83	43.01
Income Statement								
Total Revenue	2,184,700	1,961,100	1,585,900	1,531,500	1,764,500	1,276,800	3,151,800	2,357,700
EBITDA	358,500	498,300	158,300	254,400	294,800	115,700	164,400	189,500
Depn & Amortn	110,900	99,300	86,900	71,700	69,600	500	500	800
Income Before Taxes	222,200	369,800	47,000	172,200	218,100	104,700	155,400	187,100
Income Taxes	75,600	137,700	12,100	74,200	99,800	49,900	51,700	85,900
Net Income	149,600	241,700	64,800	135,700	157,700	(9,200)	149,700	133,300
Average Shares	81,000	80,800	79,900	78,300	76,100	74,300	72,800	71,600
Balance Sheet								
Current Assets	749,100	780,300	882,800	860,300	692,300	671,000	919,200	873,400
Total Assets	2,777,700	2,449,600	2,048,700	1,932,000	1,741,700	1,701,400	1,636,500	1,797,200
Current Liabilities	434,000	399,100	391,000	310,900	421,800	408,200	407,800	367,100
Long-Term Obligations	690,100	524,200	418,200	398,400	252,400	249,200	252,200	257,200
Total Liabilities	1,779,300	1,463,800	1,218,400	1,109,700	1,036,700	1,037,700	1,093,200	1,370,600
Stockholders' Equity	998,400	985,800	830,300	822,300	705,000	663,700	543,300	426,600
Shares Outstanding	80,200	80,100	79,579	78,721	77,304	74,504	73,322	71,875
Statistical Record								
Return on Assets %	5.71	10.75	3.26	7.39	9.14	N.M.	8.72	7.81
Return on Equity %	15.04	26.62	7.84	17.77	22.98	N.M.	30.87	34.07
EBITDA Margin %	16.41	25.41	9.98	16.61	16.71	9.06	5.22	8.04
Net Margin %	6.85	12.32	4.09	8.86	8.94	N.M.	4.75	5.65
Asset Turnover	0.83	0.87	0.80	0.83	1.02	0.77	1.84	1.38
Current Ratio	1.73	1.96	2.26	2.77	1.64	1.64	2.25	2.38
Debt to Equity	0.69	0.53	0.50	0.48	0.36	0.38	0.46	0.60
Price Range	23.19-18.51	26.40-16.71	22.33-15.40	19.30-9.05	30.14-12.60	23.52-16.14	22.51-14.46	25.00-17.15
P/E Ratio	12.54-10.01	8.83-5.59	27.57-19.01	11.16-5.23	14.56-6.09	...	10.93-7.02	13.44-9.22
Average Yield %	3.80	3.87	4.16	5.42	3.82	4.13	4.41	4.00

Address: 190 Carondelet Plaza, Suite 1530, Clayton, MO 63105-3443
Telephone: 314-480-1400

Web Site: www.olin.com
Officers: Joseph D. Rupp - Chairman, President, Chief Executive Officer George H. Pain - Senior Vice President, Secretary, General Counsel

Auditors: KPMG LLP
Investor Contact: 314-480-1452
Transfer Agents: Wells Fargo Shareowner Services, St. Paul, MN

OMEGA HEALTHCARE INVESTORS, INC.

Exchange	Symbol	Price	52Wk Range	Yield	P/E
NYS	OHI	$30.36 (3/28/2013)	30.36-20.19	5.93	27.11

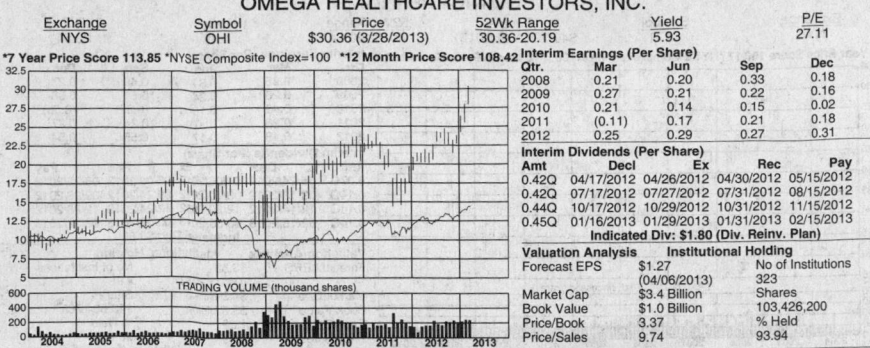

*7 Year Price Score 113.85 *NYSE Composite Index=100 *12 Month Price Score 108.42

Interim Earnings (Per Share)

Qtr.	Mar	Jun	Sep	Dec
2008	0.21	0.20	0.33	0.18
2009	0.27	0.21	0.22	0.16
2010	0.21	0.14	0.15	0.02
2011	(0.11)	0.17	0.21	0.18
2012	0.25	0.29	0.27	0.31

Interim Dividends (Per Share)

Amt	Decl	Ex	Rec	Pay
0.42Q	04/17/2012	04/26/2012	04/30/2012	05/15/2012
0.42Q	07/17/2012	07/27/2012	07/31/2012	08/15/2012
0.44Q	10/17/2012	10/29/2012	10/31/2012	11/15/2012
0.45Q	01/16/2013	01/29/2013	01/31/2013	02/15/2013

Indicated Div: $1.80 (Div. Reinv. Plan)

Valuation Analysis

		Institutional Holding	
Forecast EPS	$1.27	No of Institutions	
	(04/06/2013)	323	
Market Cap	$3.4 Billion	Shares	
Book Value	$1.0 Billion	103,426,200	
Price/Book	3.37	% Held	
Price/Sales	9.74	93.94	

Business Summary: REITs (MIC: 5.3.1 SIC: 6798 NAIC: 525930)

Omega Healthcare Investors is a self-administered real estate investment trust, investing in healthcare facilities, principally long-term care facilities located throughout the U.S. Co. has one reportable segment consisting of investments in healthcare related real estate properties. As of Dec 31 2011, Co.'s portfolio of investments consisted of 438 healthcare facilities located in 35 states and operated by 51 third-party operators. This portfolio was made up of: 385 skilled nursing facilities, 10 assisted living facilities and five specialty facilities; fixed rate mortgages on 32 long-term healthcare facilities; and six facilities and one parcel of land held-for-sale.

Recent Developments: For the year ended Dec 31 2012, net income increased 129.4% to US$120.7 million from US$52.6 million in the prior year. Revenues were US$350.5 million, up 19.9% from US$292.2 million the year before. Revenues from property income rose 15.0% to US$314.6 million from US$273.5 million in the corresponding earlier year.

Prospects: Our evaluation of Omega Healthcare Investors Inc. as of Apr. 7, 2013 is the result of our systematic analysis on three basic characteristics: earnings strength, relative valuation, and recent stock price movement. The company has managed to produce a neutral trend in earnings per share over the past 5 quarters. Because the company lacks sufficient analyst estimate data, we place greater weight on the historical EPS trend as the measure of earnings strength. Based on operating earnings yield, the company is overvalued when compared to all of the companies in our coverage universe. Share price changes over the past year indicates that OHI will perform poorly over the near term.

Financial Data
(US$ in Thousands)

	12/31/2012	12/31/2011	12/31/2010	12/31/2009	12/31/2008	12/31/2007	12/31/2006	12/31/2005
Earnings Per Share	1.12	0.46	0.52	0.87	0.94	0.90	0.78	0.45
Cash Flow Per Share	1.93	1.66	1.68	1.76	1.19	1.28	1.07	1.41
Tang Book Value Per Share	9.00	8.50	9.03	8.57	8.25	6.87	5.81	5.47
Dividends Per Share	1.690	1.550	1.370	1.200	1.190	1.080	0.960	0.850
Dividend Payout %	150.89	336.96	263.46	137.93	126.60	120.00	123.08	188.89
Income Statement								
Total Revenue	350,460	292,204	258,321	197,438	193,762	159,558	135,693	105,812
EBITDA	350,947	245,496	235,579	170,249	161,119	150,865	144,319	93,241
Depn & Amortn	124,182	106,031	86,646	49,084	43,994	39,439	38,732	28,539
Income Before Taxes	120,698	52,606	58,436	82,111	77,619	67,591	58,389	30,151
Income Taxes	...	...	...	...	(72)	(7)	2,347	...
Net Income	120,698	52,606	58,436	82,111	78,137	69,374	55,697	36,688
Average Shares	108,011	102,177	94,237	83,649	75,213	65,886	58,745	52,059
Balance Sheet								
Current Assets	163,551	135,127	122,139	93,214	81,540	69,075	56,040	9,833
Total Assets	2,982,005	2,557,312	2,304,007	1,655,033	1,364,467	1,182,287	1,175,370	1,015,729
Current Liabilities	...	...	...	...	...	73	5,646	...
Long-Term Obligations	1,824,932	1,551,400	1,176,965	738,149	548,197	573,709	676,141	566,229
Total Liabilities	1,970,676	1,678,828	1,299,941	789,806	576,479	596,160	709,916	586,048
Stockholders' Equity	1,011,329	878,484	1,004,066	865,227	787,988	586,127	465,454	429,681
Shares Outstanding	112,393	103,410	99,233	88,266	82,382	68,114	59,703	56,872
Statistical Record								
Return on Assets %	4.35	2.16	2.95	5.44	6.12	5.88	5.08	3.97
Return on Equity %	12.74	5.59	6.25	9.93	11.34	13.19	12.44	8.51
EBITDA Margin %	100.14	84.02	91.20	86.23	83.15	94.55	106.36	88.12
Net Margin %	34.44	18.00	22.62	41.59	40.33	43.48	41.05	34.67
Asset Turnover	0.13	0.12	0.13	0.13	0.15	0.14	0.12	0.11
Current Ratio	...	...	...	...	...	946.23	9.93	...
Debt to Equity	1.80	1.77	1.17	0.85	0.70	0.98	1.45	1.32
Price Range	24.75-19.19	24.27-14.42	23.67-17.67	19.85-11.83	19.66-10.72	19.08-12.69	17.94-11.50	14.16-10.56
P/E Ratio	22.10-17.13	52.76-31.35	45.52-33.98	22.82-13.60	20.91-11.40	21.20-14.10	23.00-14.74	31.47-23.47
Average Yield %	7.59	7.74	6.59	7.58	7.19	6.58	6.82	6.96

Address: 200 International Circle, Suite 3500, Hunt Valley, MD 21030 **Telephone:** 410-427-1700	**Web Site:** www.omegahealthcare.com **Officers:** Bernard J. Korman - Chairman C. Taylor Pickett - President, Chief Executive Officer	**Auditors:** Ernst & Young LLP **Investor Contact:** 410-427-1700 **Transfer Agents:** Registrar and Transfer Company, Cranford , NJ

OMNICARE INC.

Exchange	Symbol	Price	52Wk Range	Yield	P/E
NYS	OCR	$40.72 (3/28/2013)	40.72-29.64	1.38	23.54

*7 Year Price Score 100.17 *NYSE Composite Index=100 *12 Month Price Score 102.27

TRADING VOLUME (thousand shares)

Interim Earnings (Per Share)

Qtr.	Mar	Jun	Sep	Dec
2008	0.25	0.31	0.49	0.27
2009	0.26	0.24	0.61	0.68
2010	0.43	0.10	(0.89)	(0.56)
2011	0.26	(0.01)	0.24	0.27
2012	0.48	0.17	0.55	0.54

Interim Dividends (Per Share)

Amt	Decl	Ex	Rec	Pay
0.07Q	05/24/2012	06/06/2012	06/08/2012	06/22/2012
0.14Q	09/13/2012	09/20/2012	09/24/2012	09/28/2012
0.14Q	12/14/2012	12/20/2012	12/24/2012	12/28/2012
0.14Q	02/15/2013	03/05/2013	03/07/2013	03/22/2013

Indicated Div: $0.56

Valuation Analysis

		Institutional Holding	
Forecast EPS	$3.53 (04/06/2013)	No of Institutions	411
Market Cap	$4.3 Billion	Shares	143,634,768
Book Value	$3.5 Billion	% Held	98.63
Price/Book	1.22		
Price/Sales	0.69		

Business Summary: Diagnostic & Health Related Services (MIC: 4.2.2 SIC: 3841 NAIC: 339112)

Omnicare is a healthcare services company that specializes in the management of complex pharmaceutical care. Co. operates two segments: Long-Term Care Group and Specialty Care Group. The Long-Term Care Group provides pharmaceuticals and related pharmacy and ancillary services to long-term care facilities as well as chronic care facilities and other settings. The Specialty Care Group provides specialty pharmacy, commercialization services for the biopharmaceutical industry and to end-of-life pharmaceutical care management for hospice care agencies.

Recent Developments: For the year ended Dec 31 2012, income from continuing operations increased 20.6% to US$194.9 million from US$161.5 million a year earlier. Net income increased 124.2% to US$194.9 million from US$86.9 million in the prior year. Revenues were US$6.16 billion, down 0.4% from US$6.18 billion the year before. Operating income was US$447.2 million versus US$432.9 million in the prior year, an increase of 3.3%. Direct operating expenses declined 2.7% to US$4.68 billion from US$4.81 billion in the comparable period the year before. Indirect operating expenses increased 9.8% to US$1.04 billion from US$944.2 million in the equivalent prior-year period.

Prospects: Our evaluation of Omnicare Inc. as of Apr. 7, 2013 is the result of our systematic analysis on three basic characteristics: earnings strength, relative valuation, and recent stock price movement. The company has managed to produce a neutral trend in earnings per share over the past 5 quarters. However, while recent estimates for the company have been mixed, OCR has posted better than expected results. Based on operating earnings yield, the company is undervalued when compared to all of the companies in our coverage universe. Share price changes over the past year indicates that OCR will perform poorly over the near term.

Financial Data

(US$ in Thousands)	12/31/2012	12/31/2011	12/31/2010	12/31/2009	12/31/2008	12/31/2007	12/31/2006	12/31/2005
Earnings Per Share	1.73	0.76	(0.91)	1.80	1.32	0.94	1.50	2.10
Cash Flow Per Share	4.96	4.87	3.17	4.13	3.72	4.23	0.92	2.55
Dividends Per Share	0.420	0.153	0.110	0.090	0.090	0.090	0.090	0.090
Dividend Payout %	24.28	20.07	...	5.00	6.82	9.57	6.00	4.29
Income Statement								
Total Revenue	6,160,388	6,182,922	6,146,212	6,166,209	6,310,607	6,220,010	6,492,993	5,292,782
EBITDA	499,110	480,578	138,881	529,652	456,873	405,515	547,889	572,157
Depn & Amortn	51,932	47,053	47,614	49,440	52,636	54,857	57,110	44,741
Income Before Taxes	312,075	272,825	(73,991)	332,339	260,187	186,498	320,496	361,806
Income Taxes	117,201	111,293	11,799	97,523	104,079	72,442	136,924	135,315
Net Income	194,874	86,924	(106,109)	211,923	156,108	114,056	183,572	226,491
Average Shares	112,988	114,781	116,348	117,777	118,313	121,258	122,536	108,804
Balance Sheet								
Current Assets	2,088,859	2,297,371	2,457,796	2,219,607	2,371,693	2,456,150	2,424,828	2,360,895
Total Assets	6,989,264	7,193,110	7,363,413	7,324,104	7,459,718	7,593,779	7,398,471	7,157,405
Current Liabilities	482,014	540,067	594,651	620,049	640,789	652,160	552,401	1,000,504
Long-Term Obligations	2,030,030	1,968,274	2,106,758	1,980,239	2,731,163	2,820,751	2,955,120	2,719,392
Total Liabilities	3,483,552	3,397,674	3,547,469	3,448,111	4,038,334	4,302,076	4,235,020	4,215,359
Stockholders' Equity	3,505,712	3,795,436	3,815,944	3,875,993	3,421,384	3,291,703	3,163,451	2,942,046
Shares Outstanding	104,651	113,623	116,622	120,279	118,448	121,772	121,464	119,882
Statistical Record								
Return on Assets %	2.74	1.19	N.M.	2.87	2.07	1.52	2.52	4.10
Return on Equity %	5.32	2.28	N.M.	5.81	4.64	3.53	6.01	9.30
EBITDA Margin %	8.10	7.77	2.26	8.59	7.24	6.52	8.44	10.81
Net Margin %	3.16	1.41	N.M.	3.44	2.47	1.83	2.83	4.28
Asset Turnover	0.87	0.85	0.84	0.83	0.84	0.83	0.89	0.96
Current Ratio	4.33	4.25	4.13	3.58	3.70	3.77	4.39	2.36
Debt to Equity	0.58	0.52	0.55	0.51	0.80	0.86	0.93	0.92
Price Range	36.59-29.64	35.05-21.62	30.38-19.20	29.33-21.47	32.61-15.59	44.59-22.18	61.81-37.13	61.85-29.51
P/E Ratio	21.15-17.13	46.12-28.45	...	16.29-11.93	24.70-11.81	47.44-23.60	41.21-24.75	29.45-14.05
Average Yield %	1.25	0.52	0.42	0.36	0.37	0.24	0.18	0.23

Address: 900 Omnicare Center, 201 E. Fourth Street, Cincinnati, KY 45202	Web Site: www.omnicare.com	Auditors: PricewaterhouseCoopers LLP
Telephone: 513-719-2600	Officers: Nitin Sahney - President, Executive Vice President, Division Officer, Chief Operating Officer John L. Workman - President, Chief Executive Officer, Chief Financial Officer	Transfer Agents: BNY Mellon Shareowner Services, Jersey City, NJ

OMNICOM GROUP, INC.

Exchange	Symbol	Price	52Wk Range	Yield	P/E
NYS	OMC	$58.90 (3/28/2013)	60.05-45.62	2.72	16.32

*7 Year Price Score 103.50 ***NYSE Composite Index=100** ***12 Month Price Score 102.77**

Interim Earnings (Per Share)

Qtr.	Mar	Jun	Sep	Dec
2008	0.65	0.96	0.69	0.87
2009	0.53	0.75	0.53	0.73
2010	0.52	0.79	0.57	0.82
2011	0.69	0.96	0.72	0.96
2012	0.72	1.02	0.74	1.12

Interim Dividends (Per Share)

Amt	Decl	Ex	Rec	Pay
0.30Q	05/22/2012	06/12/2012	06/14/2012	07/11/2012
0.30Q	07/19/2012	09/20/2012	09/24/2012	10/09/2012
0.30Q	11/27/2012	12/12/2012	12/14/2012	12/31/2012
0.40Q	02/12/2013	03/01/2013	03/05/2013	04/02/2013

Indicated Div: $1.60

Valuation Analysis

		Institutional Holding	
Forecast EPS	$3.94 (04/05/2013)	No of Institutions	728
Market Cap	$15.4 Billion	Shares	284,657,792
Book Value	$3.5 Billion	% Held	88.86
Price/Book	4.46		
Price/Sales	1.09		

Business Summary: Advertising (MIC: 2.3.4 SIC: 7311 NAIC: 541810)

Omnicom Group is a holding company engaged in providing advertising, marketing, and corporate communications services. Co.'s services include, among others, advertising, marketing research, media planning and buying, crisis communications, mobile marketing, database management, custom publishing and organizational communications. Co. also provides package design, direct marketing, product placement, entertainment marketing, promotional marketing, public affairs, public relations, field marketing, recruitment communications, financial/corporate business-to-business advertising, reputation consulting, graphic arts, retail marketing, sports and event marketing, and investor relations services.

Recent Developments: For the year ended Dec 31 2012, net income increased 5.4% to US$1.12 billion from US$1.06 billion in the prior year. Revenues were US$14.22 billion, up 2.5% from US$13.87 billion the year before. Operating income was US$1.80 billion versus US$1.67 billion in the prior year, an increase of 8.0%. Direct operating expenses rose 1.3% to US$10.38 billion from US$10.25 billion in the comparable period the year before. Indirect operating expenses increased 4.3% to US$2.03 billion from US$1.95 billion in the equivalent prior-year period.

Prospects: Our evaluation of Omnicom Group Inc. as of Apr. 7, 2013 is the result of our systematic analysis on three basic characteristics: earnings strength, relative valuation, and recent stock price movement. The company has managed to produce a neutral trend in earnings per share over the past 5 quarters. However, while recent estimates for the company have been mixed, OMC has posted better than expected results. Based on operating earnings yield, the company is undervalued when compared to all of the companies in our coverage universe. Share price changes over the past year indicates that OMC will perform in line with the market over the near term.

Financial Data

(US$ in Thousands)	12/31/2012	12/31/2011	12/31/2010	12/31/2009	12/31/2008	12/31/2007	12/31/2006	12/31/2005
Earnings Per Share	3.61	3.33	2.70	2.53	3.17	2.95	2.50	2.18
Cash Flow Per Share	5.39	4.71	4.97	5.62	4.44	4.91	5.08	2.75
Dividends Per Share	1.200	1.000	0.800	0.600	0.600	0.575	0.500	0.463
Dividend Payout %	33.24	30.03	29.63	23.72	18.93	19.49	20.04	21.22
Income Statement								
Total Revenue	14,219,400	13,872,500	12,542,500	11,720,700	13,359,900	12,694,000	11,376,900	10,481,100
EBITDA	2,086,900	1,944,800	1,713,200	1,617,700	1,925,300	1,703,500	1,523,200	1,377,400
Depn & Amortn	282,700	273,700	253,000	242,800	235,900	44,400	39,700	37,600
Income Before Taxes	1,659,600	1,549,000	1,350,400	1,274,200	1,615,100	1,585,100	1,391,900	1,280,600
Income Taxes	527,100	505,800	460,200	433,600	542,700	536,900	466,900	435,300
Net Income	998,300	952,600	827,700	793,000	1,000,300	975,700	864,000	790,700
Average Shares	270,000	283,300	303,500	310,400	315,400	330,400	346,200	363,555
Balance Sheet								
Current Assets	11,661,400	10,421,500	10,194,100	8,788,500	8,564,900	10,504,200	9,646,800	7,967,400
Total Assets	22,151,900	20,505,400	19,566,100	17,920,700	17,318,400	19,271,700	18,164,400	15,919,900
Current Liabilities	11,875,800	11,671,000	11,023,100	10,082,500	9,754,200	11,227,200	10,296,100	8,700,300
Long-Term Obligations	4,448,500	3,182,900	2,342,600	2,220,600	3,054,300	3,054,700	3,054,700	2,357,500
Total Liabilities	18,691,100	17,001,100	15,985,600	13,725,900	13,795,600	15,180,000	14,293,100	11,971,900
Stockholders' Equity	3,460,800	3,504,300	3,580,500	4,194,800	3,522,800	4,091,700	3,871,300	3,948,000
Shares Outstanding	262,000	273,400	285,500	308,400	307,300	323,000	337,600	356,588
Statistical Record								
Return on Assets %	4.67	4.75	4.42	4.50	5.45	5.21	5.07	4.95
Return on Equity %	28.59	26.89	21.29	20.55	26.20	24.51	22.10	19.70
EBITDA Margin %	14.68	14.02	13.66	13.80	14.41	13.42	13.39	13.14
Net Margin %	7.02	6.87	6.60	6.77	7.49	7.69	7.59	7.54
Asset Turnover	0.66	0.69	0.67	0.67	0.73	0.68	0.67	0.66
Current Ratio	0.98	0.89	0.92	0.87	0.88	0.94	0.94	0.92
Debt to Equity	1.29	0.91	0.87	0.53	0.87	0.75	0.79	0.60
Price Range	54.23-44.04	50.90-35.95	47.51-33.77	39.84-22.06	49.90-22.23	54.84-46.05	52.96-39.48	45.53-38.20
P/E Ratio	15.02-12.20	15.29-10.80	17.60-12.51	15.75-8.72	15.74-7.01	18.59-15.61	21.18-15.79	20.89-17.52
Average Yield %	2.43	2.23	2.01	1.87	1.48	1.13	1.10	1.10

Address: 437 Madison Avenue, New York, NY 10022 **Telephone:** 212-415-3600 **Fax:** 212-415-3393	**Web Site:** www.omnicomgroup.com **Officers:** Bruce Crawford - Chairman Peter Mead - Vice-Chairman	**Auditors:** KPMG LLP **Investor Contact:** 212-415-3393 **Transfer Agents:** Wells Fargo Shareowner Services, Minneapolis, MN

ONEOK INC.

Exchange	Symbol	Price	52Wk Range	Yield	P/E	Div Achiever
NYS	OKE	$47.67 (3/28/2013)	49.39-39.49	3.02	27.88	10 Years

*7 Year Price Score 147.52   *NYSE Composite Index=100   *12 Month Price Score 95.45

Interim Earnings (Per Share)

Qtr.	Mar	Jun	Sep	Dec
2008	0.68	0.20	0.28	0.33
2009	0.58	0.20	0.23	0.44
2010	0.72	0.20	0.26	0.38
2011	0.58	0.26	0.28	0.54
2012	0.58	0.29	0.31	0.53

Interim Dividends (Per Share)

Amt	Decl	Ex	Rec	Pay
0.305Q	04/18/2012	04/26/2012	04/30/2012	05/15/2012
0.33Q	07/25/2012	08/02/2012	08/06/2012	08/15/2012
0.33Q	10/24/2012	11/01/2012	11/05/2012	11/14/2012
0.36Q	01/16/2013	01/29/2013	01/31/2013	02/14/2013

Indicated Div: $1.44

Valuation Analysis | **Institutional Holding**

Forecast EPS	$1.80 (04/05/2013)	No of Institutions	569
Market Cap	$9.8 Billion	Shares	146,832,544
Book Value	$2.1 Billion	% Held	67.00
Price/Book	4.59		
Price/Sales	0.77		

Business Summary: Gas Utilities (MIC: 3.3.1 SIC: 4923 NAIC: 221210)

Oneok is an energy company. As of Dec 31 2012, Co. owned 43.4% of ONEOK Partners, L.P. (ONEOK Partners), which is engaged in the gathering, processing, storage and transportation of natural gas in the U.S. In addition, as of this date, Co.'s Natural Gas Distribution segment provided natural gas distribution services to more than 2.0 million customers in Oklahoma, Kansas and Texas. Co. serves residential, commercial, industrial and transportation customers in all three states. In addition, Co.'s local distribution companies serve wholesale and public authority customers. Co.'s energy services business is engaged in providing natural gas marketing services to its customers across the U.S.

Recent Developments: For the year ended Dec 31 2012, income from continuing operations decreased 3.7% to US$729.3 million from US$757.5 million a year earlier. Net income decreased 2.1% to US$743.5 million from US$759.7 million in the prior year. Revenues were US$12.63 billion, down 14.7% from US$14.81 billion the year before. Operating income was US$1.10 billion versus US$1.16 billion in the prior year, a decrease of 4.9%. Direct operating expenses declined 17.3% to US$10.28 billion from US$12.43 billion in the comparable period the year before. Indirect operating expenses increased 2.2% to US$1.25 billion from US$1.22 billion in the equivalent prior-year period.

Prospects: Our evaluation of Oneok Inc. as of Apr. 7, 2013 is the result of our systematic analysis on three basic characteristics: earnings strength, relative valuation, and recent stock price movement. The company has managed to produce a neutral trend in earnings per share over the past 5 quarters. However, while recent estimates for the company have been mixed, OKE has posted better than expected results. Based on operating earnings yield, the company is about fairly valued when compared to all of the companies in our coverage universe. Share price changes over the past year indicates that OKE will perform poorly over the near term.

Financial Data
(US$ in Thousands)

	12/31/2012	12/31/2011	12/31/2010	12/31/2009	12/31/2008	12/31/2007	12/31/2006	12/31/2005
Earnings Per Share	1.71	1.68	1.55	1.44	1.48	1.40	1.34	2.53
Cash Flow Per Share	4.79	6.50	3.92	6.89	2.27	4.80	3.90	(0.89)
Tang Book Value Per Share	5.53	5.93	6.67	5.56	5.01	4.45	5.26	5.69
Dividends Per Share	1.270	1.080	0.910	0.820	0.780	0.700	0.610	0.545
Dividend Payout %	74.27	64.29	58.71	57.14	52.88	50.18	45.52	21.54
Income Statement								
Total Revenue	12,632,559	14,805,794	13,030,051	11,111,651	16,157,433	13,477,414	11,896,104	12,676,230
EBITDA	1,459,579	1,465,610	1,252,840	1,215,616	1,612,224	1,410,123	1,462,951	971,447
Depn & Amortn	335,852	312,288	307,317	288,991	243,927	227,964	235,543	183,394
Income Before Taxes	821,422	856,316	653,284	625,803	1,104,130	925,834	987,683	643,131
Income Taxes	215,195	226,048	213,834	207,321	194,071	184,597	193,764	242,521
Net Income	360,619	360,594	334,632	305,451	311,909	304,921	306,312	546,545
Average Shares	210,710	214,498	215,570	212,640	211,520	218,596	228,954	216,012
Balance Sheet								
Current Assets	2,764,660	2,318,812	2,379,045	2,588,464	3,377,602	2,951,475	3,238,600	4,405,793
Total Assets	15,855,275	13,696,635	12,499,175	12,827,683	13,126,062	11,062,034	10,504,721	10,013,466
Current Liabilities	2,812,994	3,246,175	3,151,112	3,338,912	4,193,764	2,881,667	2,064,177	4,795,341
Long-Term Obligations	6,515,372	4,529,551	3,686,542	4,334,204	4,112,581	4,215,046	4,030,855	2,024,070
Total Liabilities	13,725,666	11,458,062	10,050,552	10,620,489	11,037,892	9,092,726	8,288,763	8,218,709
Stockholders' Equity	2,129,609	2,238,573	2,448,623	2,207,194	2,088,170	1,969,308	2,215,958	1,794,757
Shares Outstanding	204,935	206,509	213,631	211,813	209,690	207,974	221,356	195,309
Statistical Record								
Return on Assets %	2.43	2.75	2.64	2.35	2.57	2.83	2.99	6.35
Return on Equity %	16.47	15.39	14.37	14.22	15.33	14.57	15.27	32.15
EBITDA Margin %	11.55	9.90	9.62	10.94	9.98	10.46	12.30	7.66
Net Margin %	2.85	2.44	2.57	2.75	1.93	2.26	2.57	4.31
Asset Turnover	0.85	1.13	1.03	0.86	1.33	1.25	1.16	1.47
Current Ratio	0.98	0.71	0.75	0.78	0.81	1.02	1.57	0.92
Debt to Equity	3.06	2.02	1.51	1.96	1.97	2.14	1.82	1.13
Price Range	49.39-39.49	43.35-27.69	27.84-20.31	22.29-9.10	25.32-11.59	27.43-20.06	22.13-13.28	17.86-13.32
P/E Ratio	28.88-23.09	25.80-16.48	17.96-13.10	15.48-6.32	17.10-7.83	19.59-14.33	16.51-9.91	7.06-5.26
Average Yield %	2.92	3.11	3.88	5.20	3.74	2.96	3.45	3.58

Address: 100 West Fifth Street, Tulsa, OK 74103	Web Site: www.oneok.com	Auditors: PricewaterhouseCoopers LLP
Telephone: 918-588-7000	Officers: John W. Gibson - Chairman, Vice-Chairman, President, Chief Executive Officer	Investor Contact: 918-588-7163
Fax: 918-588-7273	Terry K. Spencer - President	Transfer Agents: Wells Fargo Shareowner Services, St. Paul, MN

ORMAT TECHNOLOGIES INC

Exchange	Symbol	Price	52Wk Range	Yield	P/E
NYS	ORA	$20.65 (3/28/2013)	22.00-16.95	N/A	N/A

*7 Year Price Score 54.68   *NYSE Composite Index=100   *12 Month Price Score 97.31

Interim Earnings (Per Share)

Qtr.	Mar	Jun	Sep	Dec
2008	0.24	0.28	0.35	0.25
2009	0.32	0.35	0.52	0.32
2010	0.04	(0.03)	0.71	0.10
2011	(0.20)	0.18	0.02	(0.95)
2012	0.17	0.19	(0.01)	(4.89)

Interim Dividends (Per Share)

Amt	Decl	Ex	Rec	Pay
0.04Q	05/04/2011	05/16/2011	05/18/2011	05/25/2011
0.04Q	08/03/2011	08/12/2011	08/16/2011	08/25/2011
0.04Q	05/08/2012	05/17/2012	05/21/2012	05/30/2012
0.04Q	08/01/2012	08/10/2012	08/14/2012	08/23/2012

Valuation Analysis   **Institutional Holding**

Forecast EPS	$0.63	No of Institutions
	(04/06/2013)	130
Market Cap	$938.1 Million	Shares
Book Value	$695.1 Million	10,215,422
Price/Book	1.35	% Held
Price/Sales	1.82	19.68

TRADING VOLUME (thousand shares)

Business Summary: Electric Utilities (MIC: 3.1.1 SIC: 4911 NAIC: 221122)

Ormat Technologies is a holding company. Co. is engaged in the geothermal and recovered energy power business. Co. conducts its business in two segments: Electricity, which develops, builds, owns, and operates geothermal and recovered energy-based power plants in the U.S., and geothermal power plants in other countries, and sells the electricity they generate; and Product, which designs, manufactures and sells equipment for geothermal and recovered energy-based electricity generation, remote power units, and other power generating units and provide services relating to the engineering, procurement, construction, operation and maintenance of geothermal and recovered energy power plants.

Recent Developments: For the year ended Dec 31 2012, loss from continuing operations was US$206.0 million compared with a loss of US$42.7 million a year earlier. Net loss amounted to US$206.0 million versus a net loss of US$42.7 million in the prior year. Revenues were US$514.4 million, up 17.7% from US$437.0 million the year before. Operating loss was US$155.1 million versus an income of US$64.0 million in the prior year. Direct operating expenses rose 18.7% to US$380.0 million from US$320.1 million in the comparable period the year before. Indirect operating expenses increased 447.4% to US$289.5 million from US$52.9 million in the equivalent prior-year period.

Prospects: Our evaluation of Ormat Technologies Inc. as of Apr. 7, 2013 is the result of our systematic analysis on three basic characteristics: earnings strength, relative valuation, and recent stock price movement. The company has suffered a very negative trend in earnings per share over the past 5 quarters. However, while recent estimates for the company have been lowered by analysts, ORA has posted results that fell short of analysts expectations. Based on operating earnings yield, the company is overvalued when compared to all of the companies in our coverage universe. Share price changes over the past year indicates that ORA will perform poorly over the near term.

Financial Data

(US$ in Thousands)	12/31/2012	12/31/2011	12/31/2010	12/31/2009	12/31/2008	12/31/2007	12/31/2006	12/31/2005
Earnings Per Share	(4.54)	(0.95)	0.82	1.51	1.12	0.70	0.99	0.48
Cash Flow Per Share	1.96	2.92	2.23	2.44	2.64	1.52	2.11	4.28
Tang Book Value Per Share	14.52	18.93	19.79	19.04	17.67	13.73	10.25	4.26
Dividends Per Share	0.080	0.130	0.270	0.250	0.200	0.220	0.150	0.120
Dividend Payout %	...	...	32.93	16.56	17.86	31.43	15.15	25.00
Income Statement								
Total Revenue	514,408	437,009	373,230	415,244	344,833	295,919	268,937	237,992
EBITDA	(54,250)	164,402	151,581	159,754	101,335	86,601	100,577	95,192
Depn & Amortn	89,876	89,600	80,669	60,811	51,873	45,609	38,659	31,210
Income Before Taxes	(206,994)	6,770	30,782	83,341	44,903	20,574	37,517	12,973
Income Taxes	(3,500)	48,535	(1,098)	16,924	7,962	1,822	6,403	4,690
Net Income	(206,430)	(43,056)	37,318	68,851	49,832	27,376	34,447	15,177
Average Shares	45,431	45,431	45,452	45,533	44,298	38,880	34,707	31,563
Balance Sheet								
Current Assets	276,234	292,185	204,654	195,255	165,679	168,828	242,592	162,962
Total Assets	2,094,114	2,314,718	2,043,328	1,855,001	1,637,691	1,274,909	1,160,102	914,480
Current Liabilities	212,134	193,770	137,722	139,603	162,383	146,491	208,163	126,346
Long-Term Obligations	962,595	969,456	740,649	572,201	369,474	314,530	380,314	478,059
Total Liabilities	1,399,012	1,416,000	1,104,196	948,029	791,263	656,826	719,308	732,221
Stockholders' Equity	695,102	898,718	939,132	906,972	846,428	618,083	440,794	182,259
Shares Outstanding	45,430	45,430	45,430	45,430	45,353	41,530	38,101	31,562
Statistical Record								
Return on Assets %	N.M.	N.M.	1.91	3.94	3.41	2.25	3.32	1.72
Return on Equity %	N.M.	N.M.	4.04	7.85	6.79	5.17	11.06	8.67
EBITDA Margin %	N.M.	37.62	40.61	38.47	29.39	29.27	37.40	40.00
Net Margin %	N.M.	N.M.	10.00	16.58	14.45	9.25	12.81	6.38
Asset Turnover	0.23	0.20	0.19	0.24	0.24	0.24	0.26	0.27
Current Ratio	1.30	1.51	1.49	1.40	1.02	1.15	1.17	1.29
Debt to Equity	1.38	1.08	0.79	0.63	0.44	0.51	0.86	2.62
Price Range	22.00-16.25	31.18-14.43	38.00-26.13	43.33-22.89	56.12-22.85	57.00-33.72	43.42-27.75	28.77-13.91
P/E Ratio	...	...	46.34-31.87	28.70-15.16	50.11-20.40	81.43-48.17	43.86-28.03	59.94-28.98
Average Yield %	0.41	0.59	0.81	0.70	0.47	0.51	0.41	0.63

Address: 6225 Neil Road, Reno, NV 89511-1136	Web Site: www.ormat.com	Auditors: PricewaterhouseCoopers LLP
Telephone: 775-356-9029	Officers: Yoram Bronicki - President, Chief Operating Officer, Region Officer Yehudit Bronicki - Chief Executive Officer	Investor Contact: 775-356-9029
Fax: 775-356-9039		Transfer Agents: American Stock Transfer & Trust Company, New York, NY

OSHKOSH CORP

Exchange	Symbol	Price	52Wk Range	Yield	P/E
NYS	OSK	$42.49 (3/28/2013)	42.49-18.70	N/A	16.34

*7 Year Price Score 74.47   *NYSE Composite Index=100   *12 Month Price Score 129.48

Interim Earnings (Per Share)

Qtr.	Dec	Mar	Jun	Sep
2009-10	1.87	3.22	2.31	1.28
2010-11	1.09	0.74	0.75	0.42
2011-12	0.42	0.41	0.82	0.86
2012-13	0.51	...	...	...

Interim Dividends (Per Share)

Dividend Payment Suspended

Valuation Analysis   Institutional Holding

Forecast EPS	$3.02	No of Institutions
	(04/05/2013)	349
Market Cap	$3.5 Billion	Shares
Book Value	$1.8 Billion	79,078,832
Price/Book	1.98	% Held
Price/Sales	0.44	81.26

Business Summary: Construction Services (MIC: 7.5.4 SIC: 3711 NAIC: 336120)

Oshkosh is a designer, manufacturer and marketer of a range of vehicles and vehicle bodies. Co. operates four segments: access equipment, which provides aerial work platforms and telehandlers; defense, which provides tactical trucks and supply parts and services to the military; fire and emergency, which provides firefighting vehicles and equipment, aircraft rescue and firefighting vehicles, snow removal vehicles, simulators, ambulances and other emergency vehicles, and broadcast vehicles; and commercial, which provides concrete mixers, refuse collection vehicles, portable and stationary concrete batch plants and vehicle components, and field service vehicles and truck-mounted cranes.

Recent Developments: For the quarter ended Dec 31 2012, income from continuing operations increased 18.0% to US$46.5 million from US$39.4 million in the year-earlier quarter. Net income increased 18.3% to US$46.5 million from US$39.3 million in the year-earlier quarter. Revenues were US$1.76 billion, down 6.1% from US$1.88 billion the year before. Operating income was US$80.8 million versus US$75.4 million in the prior-year quarter, an increase of 7.2%. Direct operating expenses declined 8.4% to US$1.51 billion from US$1.65 billion in the comparable period the year before. Indirect operating expenses increased 13.3% to US$165.5 million from US$146.1 million in the equivalent prior-year period.

Prospects: Our evaluation of Oshkosh Corp. as of Apr. 7, 2013 is the result of our systematic analysis on three basic characteristics: earnings strength, relative valuation, and recent stock price movement. The company has enjoyed a very positive trend in earnings per share over the past 5 quarters and while recent estimates for the company have remained steady, OSK has posted better than expected results. Based on operating earnings yield, the company is undervalued when compared to all of the companies in our coverage universe. Share price changes over the past year indicates that OSK will perform very well over the near term.

Financial Data

(US$ in Thousands)	3 Mos	09/30/2012	09/30/2011	09/30/2010	09/30/2009	09/30/2008	09/30/2007	09/30/2006
Earnings Per Share	2.60	2.51	2.99	8.69	(14.37)	1.06	3.58	2.76
Cash Flow Per Share	2.79	2.93	4.27	6.89	11.75	5.26	5.52	2.42
Tang Book Value Per Share	N.M.	0.48	N.M.	N.M.	N.M.	N.M.	N.M.	3.85
Dividends Per Share	...	...	...	...	0.200	0.400	0.400	0.367
Dividend Payout %	...	...	...	...	...	37.74	11.17	13.32
Income Statement								
Total Revenue	1,761,000	8,180,900	7,584,700	9,842,400	5,295,200	7,138,300	6,307,300	3,427,388
EBITDA	111,300	484,100	641,800	1,539,400	(845,400)	541,100	652,400	354,787
Depn & Amortn	30,200	123,300	139,300	144,300	138,100	145,700	62,200	29,102
Income Before Taxes	66,900	286,700	416,500	1,211,500	(1,191,500)	190,400	395,700	324,938
Income Taxes	21,000	57,400	143,600	414,300	(19,700)	118,100	135,200	121,194
Net Income	46,500	230,800	273,400	790,000	(1,098,800)	79,300	268,100	205,529
Average Shares	91,181	91,893	91,573	90,954	76,473	74,836	74,830	74,399
Balance Sheet								
Current Assets	2,370,200	2,694,500	2,454,600	2,215,900	2,143,200	2,152,400	2,194,900	1,003,394
Total Assets	4,603,900	4,947,800	4,826,900	4,708,600	4,768,000	6,081,500	6,399,800	2,110,908
Current Liabilities	1,436,900	1,704,500	1,691,800	1,812,000	1,658,600	1,463,200	1,548,000	882,074
Long-Term Obligations	938,700	955,000	1,020,000	1,086,400	2,023,200	2,680,500	2,975,600	2,176
Total Liabilities	2,816,000	3,094,300	3,230,400	3,382,000	4,253,900	4,692,900	5,006,200	1,049,003
Stockholders' Equity	1,787,900	1,853,500	1,596,500	1,326,600	514,100	1,388,600	1,393,600	1,061,905
Shares Outstanding	83,347	91,557	91,323	90,662	89,431	74,428	74,207	73,751
Statistical Record								
Return on Assets %	5.18	4.71	5.73	16.67	N.M.	1.27	6.30	10.73
Return on Equity %	13.94	13.34	18.71	85.84	N.M.	5.68	21.84	21.86
EBITDA Margin %	6.32	5.92	8.46	15.64	N.M.	7.58	10.34	10.35
Net Margin %	2.64	2.82	3.60	8.03	N.M.	1.11	4.25	6.00
Asset Turnover	1.75	1.67	1.59	2.08	0.98	1.14	1.48	1.79
Current Ratio	1.65	1.58	1.45	1.22	1.29	1.47	1.42	1.14
Debt to Equity	0.53	0.52	0.64	0.82	3.94	1.93	2.14	N.M.
Price Range	31.42-18.70	29.76-14.51	39.27-15.74	43.84-24.88	34.20-3.92	62.55-9.09	65.76-44.00	65.51-41.50
P/E Ratio	12.08-7.19	11.86-5.78	13.13-5.26	5.04-2.86	...	59.01-8.58	18.37-12.29	23.74-15.04
Average Yield %	...	...	...	...	1.45	1.09	0.73	0.73

Address: P.O. Box 2566, Oshkosh, WI 54903-2566	**Web Site:** www.oshkoshcorporation.com	**Auditors:** Deloitte & Touche LLP
Telephone: 920-235-9151	**Officers:** Richard M. Donnelly - Chairman Charles L. Szews - President, Chief Executive Officer	**Investor Contact:** 920-966-5939
		Transfer Agents: Computershare Investor Services, LLC, Providence, RI

OWENS-ILLINOIS, INC.

Exchange	Symbol	Price	52Wk Range	Yield	P/E
NYS	OI	$26.65 (3/28/2013)	27.66-17.07	N/A	24.01

*7 Year Price Score 65.97   *NYSE Composite Index=100   *12 Month Price Score 113.14

TRADING VOLUME (thousand shares)

Interim Earnings (Per Share)

Qtr.	Mar	Jun	Sep	Dec
2008	1.04	1.35	0.46	(1.34)
2009	0.27	0.88	0.74	(0.94)
2010	0.50	0.85	0.84	(2.46)
2011	0.44	0.43	0.70	(4.68)
2012	0.72	0.80	0.54	(0.96)

Interim Dividends (Per Share)
No Dividends Paid

Valuation Analysis   Institutional Holding

Forecast EPS	$2.80	No of Institutions
	(04/06/2013)	417
Market Cap	$4.4 Billion	Shares
Book Value	$881.0 Million	159,033,536
Price/Book	4.96	% Held
Price/Sales	0.62	91.91

Business Summary: Containers & Packaging (MIC: 8.1.3 SIC: 3221 NAIC: 327213)

Owens-Illinois is a manufacturer of glass container products. Co. produces glass containers for alcoholic beverages, including beer, flavored malt beverages, spirits and wine. Co. also produces glass packaging for a range of food items, soft drinks, teas, juices and pharmaceuticals. Co. manufactures glass containers in a range of sizes, shapes and colors. Co.'s customers consist mainly of the food and beverage manufacturers.

Recent Developments: For the year ended Dec 31 2012, income from continuing operations was US$220.0 million compared with a loss of US$481.0 million a year earlier. Net income amounted to US$218.0 million versus a net loss of US$480.0 million in the prior year. Revenues were US$7.00 billion, down 4.9% from US$7.36 billion the year before. Direct operating expenses declined 5.7% to US$5.63 billion from US$5.97 billion in the comparable period the year before. Indirect operating expenses decreased 41.4% to US$1.05 billion from US$1.79 billion in the equivalent prior-year period.

Prospects: Our evaluation of Owens-Illinois Inc. as of Apr. 7, 2013 is the result of our systematic analysis on three basic characteristics: earnings strength, relative valuation, and recent stock price movement. The company has generated a negative trend in earnings per share over the past 5 quarters and while recent estimates for the company have remained steady, OI has posted better than expected results. Based on operating earnings yield, the company is undervalued when compared to all of the companies in our coverage universe. Share price changes over the past year indicates that OI will perform in line with the market over the near term.

Financial Data

(US$ in Thousands)	12/31/2012	12/31/2011	12/31/2010	12/31/2009	12/31/2008	12/31/2007	12/31/2006	12/31/2005
Earnings Per Share	1.11	(3.11)	(0.28)	0.95	1.52	7.99	(0.32)	(3.85)
Cash Flow Per Share	3.49	3.07	3.60	4.77	4.32	4.13	0.99	3.34
Income Statement								
Total Revenue	7,000,000	7,358,000	6,633,000	7,066,500	7,884,700	7,679,200	7,523,500	7,189,700
EBITDA	881,000	236,000	970,000	840,600	1,153,000	1,278,600	1,140,000	772,100
Depn & Amortn	378,000	405,000	369,000	374,800	431,000	423,400	509,200	524,000
Income Before Taxes	264,000	(472,000)	365,000	272,700	507,600	506,600	142,600	(218,600)
Income Taxes	108,000	85,000	129,000	127,500	236,700	147,800	126,500	367,100
Net Income	184,000	(510,000)	(47,000)	161,800	258,300	1,340,600	(27,500)	(558,600)
Average Shares	165,768	163,691	167,078	170,539	169,677	167,767	152,071	150,909
Balance Sheet								
Current Assets	2,648,000	2,694,000	2,738,000	2,796,700	2,444,700	2,694,600	2,432,700	2,282,300
Total Assets	8,598,000	8,926,000	9,754,000	8,727,400	7,976,500	9,324,600	9,320,700	9,521,800
Current Liabilities	2,162,000	2,245,000	2,079,000	2,034,300	2,003,300	2,529,500	2,365,700	1,821,900
Long-Term Obligations	3,454,000	3,627,000	3,924,000	3,257,500	2,940,300	3,013,500	4,719,400	5,018,700
Total Liabilities	7,717,000	8,087,000	7,939,000	7,189,200	6,935,900	7,137,200	8,964,000	8,797,900
Stockholders' Equity	881,000	839,000	1,815,000	1,538,200	1,040,600	2,187,400	356,700	723,900
Shares Outstanding	163,963	164,374	163,715	168,600	167,149	157,350	154,235	152,911
Statistical Record								
Return on Assets %	2.09	N.M.	N.M.	1.94	2.98	14.38	N.M.	N.M.
Return on Equity %	21.34	N.M.	N.M.	12.55	15.96	105.39	N.M.	N.M.
EBITDA Margin %	12.59	3.21	14.62	11.90	14.62	16.65	15.15	10.74
Net Margin %	2.63	N.M.	N.M.	2.29	3.28	17.46	N.M.	N.M.
Asset Turnover	0.80	0.79	0.72	0.85	0.91	0.82	0.80	0.71
Current Ratio	1.22	1.20	1.32	1.37	1.22	1.07	1.03	1.25
Debt to Equity	3.92	4.32	2.16	2.12	2.83	1.38	13.23	6.93
Price Range	24.67-17.07	33.01-14.04	37.63-25.06	38.86-9.73	59.90-16.31	50.08-18.55	22.21-13.22	27.25-18.01
P/E Ratio	22.23-15.38	...	...	40.91-10.24	39.41-10.73	6.27-2.32	...	...

Address: One Michael Owens Way, Perrysburg, OH 43551 **Telephone:** 567-336-5000	**Web Site:** www.o-i.com **Officers:** Albert P. L. Stroucken - Chairman, President, Chief Executive Officer Stephen P. Bramlage - Senior Vice President, Chief Financial Officer, Division Officer	**Auditors:** Ernst & Young LLP **Transfer Agents:** Computershare Trust Company, N.A., Providence, RI

OWENS CORNING

Exchange	Symbol	Price	52Wk Range	Yield	P/E
NYS	OC	$39.43 (3/28/2013)	43.39-26.13	N/A	N/A

*7 Year Price Score N/A   *NYSE Composite Index=100   *12 Month Price Score 109.42

Interim Earnings (Per Share)

Qtr.	Mar	Jun	Sep	Dec
2008	(0.12)	0.24	(6.36)	(0.39)
2009	(0.23)	0.26	0.63	(0.17)
2010	0.38	7.33	0.46	(0.82)
2011	0.19	0.62	1.01	0.41
2012	(0.38)	0.32	0.37	(0.47)

Interim Dividends (Per Share)

No Dividends Paid

Valuation Analysis

		Institutional Holding	
Forecast EPS	$2.00	No of Institutions	
	(04/06/2013)	287	
Market Cap	$4.7 Billion	Shares	
Book Value	$3.5 Billion	128,906,160	
Price/Book	1.32	% Held	
Price/Sales	0.90	96.72	

Business Summary: Construction Materials (MIC: 8.5.1 SIC: 3292 NAIC: 327910)

Owens Corning is a producer of glass fiber reinforcements and other materials for composites and of residential and commercial building materials. Co.'s products range from glass fiber used to reinforce composite materials for transportation, electronics, marine, infrastructure, wind-energy and other markets to insulation and roofing for residential, commercial and industrial applications. Co. operates within two reportable segments, Composites and Building Materials. Composites include Co.'s Reinforcements and Downstream businesses. Building Materials includes Co.'s Insulation and Roofing businesses. Through these lines of business, Co. manufactures and sells products worldwide.

Recent Developments: For the year ended Dec 31 2012, net loss amounted to US$16.0 million versus net income of US$281.0 million in the prior year. Revenues were US$5.17 billion, down 3.1% from US$5.34 billion the year before. Operating income was US$148.0 million versus US$461.0 million in the prior year, a decrease of 67.9%. Direct operating expenses rose 1.6% to US$4.38 billion from US$4.31 billion in the comparable period the year before. Indirect operating expenses increased 14.5% to US$649.0 million from US$567.0 million in the equivalent prior-year period.

Prospects: Our evaluation of Owens Corning as of Apr. 7, 2013 is the result of our systematic analysis on three basic characteristics: earnings strength, relative valuation, and recent stock price movement. The company has produced a positive trend in earnings per share over the past 5 quarters. However, while recent estimates for the company have been mixed, OC has posted results that fell short of analysts expectations. Based on operating earnings yield, the company is overvalued when compared to all of the companies in our coverage universe. Share price changes over the past year indicates that OC will perform well over the near term.

Financial Data
(US$ in Millions)

	12/31/2012	12/31/2011	12/31/2010	12/31/2009	12/31/2008	12/31/2007	12/31/2006	10/31/2006
Earnings Per Share	(0.16)	2.23	7.37	0.50	(6.56)	0.74	(0.51)	135.89
Cash Flow Per Share	2.76	2.36	3.89	4.33	1.51	1.42	0.12	(41.32)
Tang Book Value Per Share	11.41	12.27	11.85	4.12	3.30	12.26	8.22	...
Income Statement								
Total Revenue	5,172	5,335	4,997	4,803	5,847	4,978	909	5,552
EBITDA	402	757	505	496	505	455	(15)	9,612
Depn & Amortn	328	296	299	304	309	310	45	206
Income Before Taxes	(40)	353	96	81	80	23	(89)	9,165
Income Taxes	(28)	74	(840)	14	919	(8)	(28)	1,025
Net Income	(19)	276	933	64	(839)	96	(65)	8,140
Average Shares	119	123	126	127	127	129	128	59
Balance Sheet								
Current Assets	1,612	1,636	1,408	1,854	1,852	1,852	2,552	...
Total Assets	7,568	7,527	7,158	7,167	7,217	7,872	8,470	...
Current Liabilities	906	908	955	943	1,257	1,246	2,560	...
Long-Term Obligations	2,076	1,930	1,629	2,177	2,172	1,993	1,296	...
Total Liabilities	4,030	3,826	3,510	4,347	4,484	3,884	4,784	...
Stockholders' Equity	3,538	3,701	3,648	2,820	2,733	3,988	3,686	...
Shares Outstanding	118	120	124	127	127	130	130	...
Statistical Record								
Return on Assets %	N.M.	3.76	13.03	0.89	N.M.	1.17	N.M.	...
Return on Equity %	N.M.	7.51	28.85	2.31	N.M.	2.50	...	...
EBITDA Margin %	7.77	14.19	10.11	10.33	8.64	9.14	N.M.	173.13
Net Margin %	N.M.	5.17	18.67	1.33	N.M.	1.93	N.M.	146.61
Asset Turnover	0.68	0.73	0.70	0.67	0.77	0.61	0.11	...
Current Ratio	1.78	1.80	1.47	1.97	1.47	1.49	1.00	...
Debt to Equity	0.59	0.52	0.45	0.77	0.79	0.50	0.35	...
Price Range	37.05-26.13	38.51-20.55	36.18-22.98	26.59-5.33	28.13-10.51	36.06-19.90	31.65-25.98	28.75-27.60
P/E Ratio	...	17.27-9.22	4.91-3.12	53.18-10.66	...	48.73-26.89	...	0.21-0.20

Address: One Owens Corning Parkway, Toledo, OH 43659
Telephone: 419-248-8000

Web Site: www.owenscorning.com
Officers: Michael H. Thaman - Chairman, President, Chief Executive Officer David L. Johns - Senior Vice President, Chief Supply Chain & Information Technology Officer

Auditors: PricewaterhouseCoopers LLP
Investor Contact: 419-248-5748
Transfer Agents: Wells Fargo Shareowner Services, South Saint Paul, MN

OWENS & MINOR, INC.

Exchange	Symbol	Price	52Wk Range	Yield	P/E	Div Achiever
NYS	OMI	$32.56 (3/28/2013)	32.56-27.01	2.95	18.93	15 Years

*7 Year Price Score 94.70 *NYSE Composite Index=100 *12 Month Price Score 98.18

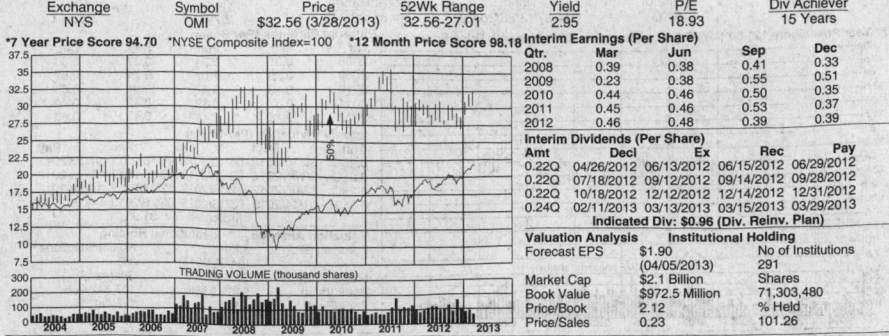

Interim Earnings (Per Share)

Qtr.	Mar	Jun	Sep	Dec
2008	0.39	0.38	0.41	0.33
2009	0.23	0.38	0.55	0.51
2010	0.44	0.46	0.50	0.35
2011	0.45	0.46	0.53	0.37
2012	0.46	0.48	0.39	0.39

Interim Dividends (Per Share)

Amt	Decl	Ex	Rec	Pay
0.22Q	04/26/2012	06/13/2012	06/15/2012	06/29/2012
0.22Q	07/18/2012	09/12/2012	09/14/2012	09/28/2012
0.22Q	10/18/2012	12/12/2012	12/14/2012	12/31/2012
0.24Q	02/11/2013	03/13/2013	03/15/2013	03/29/2013

Indicated Div: $0.96 (Div. Reinv. Plan)

Valuation Analysis / Institutional Holding

Forecast EPS	$1.90	No of Institutions
	(04/05/2013)	291
Market Cap	$2.1 Billion	Shares
Book Value	$972.5 Million	71,303,480
Price/Book	2.12	% Held
Price/Sales	0.23	101.26

Business Summary: Pharmaceuticals (MIC: 4.1.1 SIC: 5047 NAIC: 423450)

Owens & Minor is engaged in providing distribution, third-party logistics, and other supply-chain management services to healthcare providers and suppliers of medical and surgical products, and is a distributor of medical and surgical supplies to the acute-care market. Co. provides the distribution of finished medical and surgical products procured from suppliers to healthcare providers from distribution and service centers nationwide. Co. also provides distribution and supply-chain management services on an outsourced basis from facilities that are owned by customers, as well as third-party logistics services for the manufacturers and suppliers of healthcare and life-science products.

Recent Developments: For the year ended Dec 31 2012, net income decreased 5.4% to US$109.0 million from US$115.2 million in the prior year. Revenues were US$8.91 billion, up 3.2% from US$8.63 billion the year before. Operating income was US$196.8 million versus US$203.5 million in the prior year, a decrease of 3.3%. Direct operating expenses rose 2.7% to US$7.98 billion from US$7.77 billion in the comparable period the year before. Indirect operating expenses increased 11.3% to US$727.9 million from US$654.0 million in the equivalent prior-year period.

Prospects: Our evaluation of Owens & Minor Inc. as of Apr. 7, 2013 is the result of our systematic analysis on three basic characteristics: earnings strength, relative valuation, and recent stock price movement. The company has managed to produce a neutral trend in earnings per share over the past 5 quarters and while recent estimates for the company have remained steady, OMI has posted results that fell short of analysts expectations. Based on operating earnings yield, the company is about fairly valued when compared to all of the companies in our coverage universe. Share price changes over the past year indicates that OMI will perform poorly over the near term.

Financial Data

(US$ in Thousands)	12/31/2012	12/31/2011	12/31/2010	12/31/2009	12/31/2008	12/31/2007	12/31/2006	12/31/2005
Earnings Per Share	1.72	1.81	1.75	1.67	1.50	1.19	0.80	1.07
Cash Flow Per Share	3.47	1.09	3.92	2.68	1.02	3.64	(1.23)	2.28
Tang Book Value Per Share	10.36	10.20	9.23	7.86	6.58	5.06	3.89	4.19
Dividends Per Share	0.880	0.800	0.708	0.613	0.533	0.453	0.400	0.347
Dividend Payout %	51.16	44.20	40.44	36.80	35.56	37.99	50.00	32.30
Income Statement								
Total Revenue	8,908,145	8,627,912	8,123,608	8,037,624	7,243,237	6,800,466	5,533,736	4,822,414
EBITDA	222,853	224,715	213,936	216,875	194,625	157,413	101,753	124,332
Depn & Amortn	26,100	21,200	18,000	15,600	13,900	14,200	10,400	6,900
Income Before Taxes	183,356	189,833	181,613	188,247	164,726	120,230	78,080	105,574
Income Taxes	74,353	74,635	71,034	71,388	63,469	47,520	29,328	41,154
Net Income	109,003	115,198	110,579	104,658	93,327	72,710	48,752	64,420
Average Shares	62,844	62,924	62,563	62,083	62,244	60,984	60,700	60,084
Balance Sheet								
Current Assets	1,628,894	1,525,825	1,403,789	1,342,067	1,311,794	1,089,857	1,266,770	894,552
Total Assets	2,207,701	1,946,815	1,822,039	1,747,088	1,776,190	1,515,080	1,685,750	1,239,850
Current Liabilities	924,287	732,365	694,481	700,116	667,511	568,464	670,503	488,868
Long-Term Obligations	215,383	212,681	209,096	208,418	359,237	283,845	433,133	204,418
Total Liabilities	1,235,175	1,028,728	964,521	977,909	1,087,139	900,721	1,138,296	727,852
Stockholders' Equity	972,526	918,087	857,518	769,179	689,051	614,359	547,454	511,998
Shares Outstanding	63,271	63,449	63,433	62,869	62,161	61,311	60,385	59,835
Statistical Record								
Return on Assets %	5.23	6.11	6.20	5.94	5.66	4.54	3.33	5.43
Return on Equity %	11.50	12.98	13.60	14.35	14.28	12.52	9.20	13.25
EBITDA Margin %	2.50	2.60	2.63	2.70	2.69	2.31	1.84	2.58
Net Margin %	1.22	1.34	1.36	1.30	1.29	1.07	0.88	1.34
Asset Turnover	4.28	4.58	4.55	4.56	4.39	4.25	3.78	4.07
Current Ratio	1.76	2.08	2.02	1.92	1.97	1.92	1.89	1.83
Debt to Equity	0.22	0.23	0.24	0.27	0.52	0.46	0.79	0.40
Price Range	31.28-27.01	35.48-26.67	32.60-26.02	31.85-20.52	32.97-23.97	29.18-20.27	23.15-18.64	22.19-17.57
P/E Ratio	18.19-15.70	19.60-14.73	18.63-14.87	19.07-12.29	21.98-15.98	24.52-17.03	28.93-23.30	20.74-16.42
Average Yield %	3.02	2.58	2.45	2.31	1.84	1.84	1.93	1.79

Address: 9120 Lockwood Boulevard, Mechanicsville, VA 23116 **Telephone:** 804-723-7000 **Fax:** 804-270-7281	**Web Site:** www.owens-minor.com **Officers:** G. Gilmer Minor - Chairman Craig R. Smith - President, Chief Executive Officer	**Auditors:** KPMG LLP **Investor Contact:** 804-723-7555 **Transfer Agents:** Computershare Shareowner Services

PACKAGING CORP OF AMERICA

Exchange	Symbol	Price	52Wk Range	Yield	P/E
NYS	PKG	$44.87 (3/28/2013)	44.87-26.24	2.79	26.71

*7 Year Price Score 121.80 *NYSE Composite Index=100 *12 Month Price Score 112.83

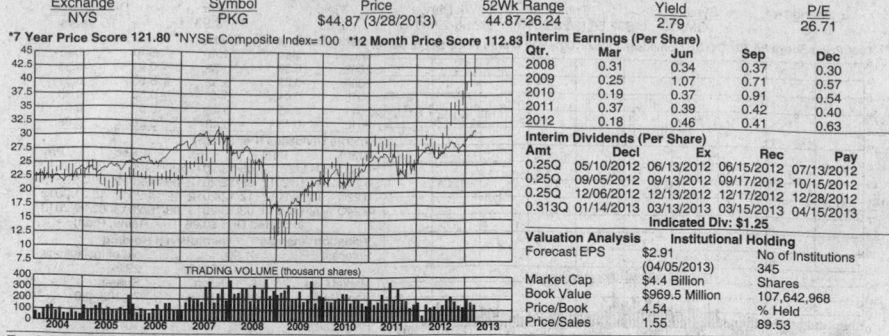

Interim Earnings (Per Share)

Qtr.	Mar	Jun	Sep	Dec
2008	0.31	0.34	0.37	0.30
2009	0.25	1.07	0.71	0.57
2010	0.19	0.37	0.91	0.54
2011	0.37	0.39	0.42	0.40
2012	0.18	0.46	0.41	0.63

Interim Dividends (Per Share)

Amt	Decl	Ex	Rec	Pay
0.25Q	05/10/2012	06/13/2012	06/15/2012	07/13/2012
0.25Q	09/05/2012	09/13/2012	09/17/2012	10/15/2012
0.25Q	12/06/2012	12/13/2012	12/17/2012	12/28/2012
0.313Q	01/14/2013	03/13/2013	03/15/2013	04/15/2013

Indicated Div: $1.25

Valuation Analysis

Valuation Analysis		Institutional Holding	
Forecast EPS	$2.91 (04/05/2013)	No of Institutions	345
Market Cap	$4.4 Billion	Shares	107,642,968
Book Value	$969.5 Million	% Held	89.53
Price/Book	4.54		
Price/Sales	1.55		

Business Summary: Containers & Packaging (MIC: 8.1.3 SIC: 2653 NAIC: 322211)

Packaging Corporation of America is producer of containerboard. Co.'s corrugated products manufacturing plants produce a variety of corrugated packaging products, including shipping containers used to protect and transport manufactured goods, multi-color boxes and displays. In addition, Co. is a producer of meat boxes and wax-coated boxes for the agricultural industry. Co.'s primary end-use markets for corrugated products are food, beverages and agricultural products; paper products; petroleum, plastic, synthetic and rubber products; general retail and wholesale trade; miscellaneous manufacturing; appliances, vehicles, and metal products; textile mill products and apparel; and other.

Recent Developments: For the year ended Dec 31 2012, net income increased 3.7% to US$163.8 million from US$158.0 million in the prior year. Revenues were US$2.84 billion, up 8.5% from US$2.62 billion the year before. Operating income was US$443.5 million versus US$272.7 million in the prior year, an increase of 62.6%. Direct operating expenses rose 6.1% to US$2.20 billion from US$2.08 billion in the comparable period the year before. Indirect operating expenses decreased 27.1% to US$196.2 million from US$269.2 million in the equivalent prior-year period.

Prospects: Our evaluation of Packaging Corp. of America as of Apr. 7, 2013 is the result of our systematic analysis on three basic characteristics: earnings strength, relative valuation, and recent stock price movement. The company has produced a positive trend in earnings per share over the past 5 quarters and while recent estimates for the company have been raised by analysts, PKG has posted results that fell short of analysts expectations. Based on operating earnings yield, the company is about fairly valued when compared to all of the companies in our coverage universe. Share price changes over the past year indicates that PKG will perform well over the near term.

Financial Data
(US$ in Thousands)

	12/31/2012	12/31/2011	12/31/2010	12/31/2009	12/31/2008	12/31/2007	12/31/2006	12/31/2005
Earnings Per Share	1.68	1.57	2.00	2.60	1.31	1.61	1.20	0.49
Cash Flow Per Share	4.18	3.48	3.44	3.01	2.61	2.87	2.38	2.26
Tang Book Value Per Share	8.80	8.60	9.38	8.23	6.19	6.76	6.12	5.96
Dividends Per Share	1.000	0.800	0.600	0.600	1.200	1.050	1.000	1.000
Dividend Payout %	59.52	50.96	30.00	23.08	91.60	65.22	83.33	204.08
Income Statement								
Total Revenue	2,843,877	2,620,111	2,435,606	2,147,589	2,360,493	2,316,006	2,187,046	1,993,658
EBITDA	609,459	434,249	339,382	500,654	385,112	438,052	377,027	254,794
Depn & Amortn	166,000	161,500	154,000	148,200	143,300	144,600	151,100	152,700
Income Before Taxes	380,559	243,504	153,104	316,971	210,143	267,868	194,724	74,002
Income Taxes	216,739	85,477	(52,331)	51,076	74,534	97,802	69,692	35,430
Net Income	163,820	158,027	205,435	265,895	135,609	170,066	125,032	52,604
Average Shares	97,497	100,376	102,608	102,358	103,593	105,459	104,485	108,098
Balance Sheet								
Current Assets	937,033	812,063	798,041	885,214	633,173	733,037	646,718	553,489
Total Assets	2,453,768	2,412,499	2,224,274	2,152,840	1,939,741	2,035,857	1,986,976	1,973,298
Current Liabilities	259,846	376,500	405,558	370,957	361,982	562,577	388,338	372,094
Long-Term Obligations	803,534	814,562	570,931	571,252	571,529	398,501	567,770	577,173
Total Liabilities	1,484,307	1,483,589	1,215,273	1,253,995	1,255,792	1,274,996	1,295,205	1,291,878
Stockholders' Equity	969,461	928,910	1,009,001	898,845	683,949	760,861	691,771	681,420
Shares Outstanding	98,142	98,322	102,308	103,018	102,397	105,018	104,611	103,686
Statistical Record								
Return on Assets %	6.71	6.82	9.39	12.99	6.80	8.46	6.31	2.59
Return on Equity %	17.21	16.31	21.54	33.60	18.72	23.41	18.21	7.02
EBITDA Margin %	21.43	16.57	13.93	23.31	16.31	18.91	17.24	12.78
Net Margin %	5.76	6.03	8.43	12.38	5.74	7.34	5.72	2.64
Asset Turnover	1.17	1.13	1.11	1.05	1.18	1.15	1.10	0.98
Current Ratio	3.61	2.16	1.97	2.39	1.75	1.30	1.67	1.49
Debt to Equity	0.83	0.88	0.57	0.64	0.84	0.52	0.82	0.85
Price Range	38.47-25.00	30.27-21.28	26.90-20.58	23.80-9.82	28.36-11.43	31.84-22.24	23.93-20.40	25.29-18.25
P/E Ratio	22.90-14.88	19.28-13.55	13.45-10.29	9.15-3.78	21.65-8.73	19.78-13.81	19.94-17.00	51.61-37.24
Average Yield %	3.21	2.98	2.52	3.50	5.52	4.00	4.43	4.54

Address: 1955 West Field Court, Lake Forest, IL 60045
Telephone: 847-482-3000

Web Site: www.packagingcorp.com
Officers: Paul T. Stecko - Executive Chairman
Thomas A. Hassfurther - Executive Vice President

Auditors: Ernst & Young LLP
Investor Contact: 877-454-2509
Transfer Agents: Computershare Trust Company N.A., Providence, RI

PALL CORP.

Exchange	Symbol	Price	52Wk Range	Yield	P/E
NYS	PLL	$68.37 (3/28/2013)	69.04-50.22	1.46	13.70

*7 Year Price Score 127.37 *NYSE Composite Index=100 *12 Month Price Score 103.47

Interim Earnings (Per Share)

Qtr.	Oct	Jan	Apr	Jul
2009-10	0.56	0.42	0.58	0.47
2010-11	0.61	0.64	0.60	0.83
2011-12	0.59	0.72	0.67	0.73
2012-13	2.92	0.67	...	...

Interim Dividends (Per Share)

Amt	Decl	Ex	Rec	Pay
0.21Q	04/19/2012	05/04/2012	05/08/2012	05/22/2012
0.21Q	07/11/2012	08/01/2012	08/03/2012	08/17/2012
0.25Q	09/26/2012	10/10/2012	10/12/2012	11/02/2012
0.25Q	01/17/2013	02/06/2013	02/08/2013	02/22/2013

Indicated Div: $1.00

Valuation Analysis

		Institutional Holding	
Forecast EPS	$3.08	No of Institutions	
	(04/05/2013)	528	
Market Cap	$7.6 Billion	Shares	
Book Value	$1.7 Billion	112,454,304	
Price/Book	4.47	% Held	
Price/Sales	2.85	91.85	

Business Summary: Industrial Machinery & Equipment (MIC: 7.2.1 SIC: 3569 NAIC: 333411)

Pall is a supplier of filtration, separation and purification technologies, principally made by Co., for the removal of solid, liquid and gaseous contaminants from a range of liquids and gases. Co. serves customers through two businesses globally: Life Sciences and Industrial. The Life Sciences business group is focused on developing, manufacturing and selling products to customers in the Medical, BioPharmaceuticals and Food & Beverage markets. The Industrial business group is focused on developing, manufacturing and selling products to customers in the Process Technologies, Aerospace and Microelectronics markets.

Recent Developments: For the quarter ended Jan 31 2013, income from continuing operations increased 7.6% to US$80.3 million from US$74.6 million in the year-earlier quarter. Net income decreased 9.4% to US$76.8 million from US$84.7 million in the year-earlier quarter. Revenues were US$662.5 million, up 3.5% from US$640.0 million the year before. Direct operating expenses rose 6.2% to US$320.5 million from US$301.9 million in the comparable period the year before. Indirect operating expenses decreased 0.1% to US$239.8 million from US$240.2 million in the equivalent prior-year period.

Prospects: Our evaluation of Pall Corp. as of Apr. 7, 2013 is the result of our systematic analysis on three basic characteristics: earnings strength, relative valuation, and recent stock price movement. The company has managed to produce a neutral trend in earnings per share over the past 5 quarters and while recent estimates for the company have been mixed, PLL has posted better than expected results. Based on operating earnings yield, the company is about fairly valued when compared to all of the companies in our coverage universe. Share price changes over the past year indicates that PLL will perform in line with the market over the near term.

Financial Data

(US$ in Thousands)	6 Mos	3 Mos	07/31/2012	07/31/2011	07/31/2010	07/31/2009	07/31/2008	07/31/2007
Earnings Per Share	4.99	5.04	2.71	2.67	2.03	1.64	1.76	1.02
Cash Flow Per Share	3.20	3.80	4.08	3.69	3.22	2.76	1.55	2.70
Tang Book Value Per Share	10.92	11.83	8.93	9.89	7.19	6.57	6.94	6.14
Dividends Per Share	0.880	0.880	0.770	0.670	0.610	0.420	0.620	0.350
Dividend Payout %	17.64	17.46	28.41	25.09	30.05	25.61	35.23	34.31
Income Statement								
Total Revenue	1,290,055	627,600	2,671,656	2,740,916	2,401,932	2,329,158	2,571,645	2,249,905
EBITDA	212,425	104,269	469,939	522,886	433,519	386,207	449,155	391,381
Depn & Amortn	...	...	82,852	84,461	91,474	87,285	91,024	91,796
Income Before Taxes	206,976	104,837	366,910	419,522	327,721	270,786	325,555	260,529
Income Taxes	37,492	15,672	85,963	104,026	86,473	75,167	108,276	133,032
Net Income	416,242	339,472	319,309	315,496	241,248	195,619	217,279	127,497
Average Shares	113,809	116,097	117,663	118,266	118,846	119,571	123,686	124,393
Balance Sheet								
Current Assets	2,040,156	2,096,832	1,852,457	1,809,208	1,702,759	1,570,450	1,659,639	1,606,377
Total Assets	3,453,093	3,520,428	3,347,892	3,232,416	2,999,212	2,840,812	2,956,746	2,708,846
Current Liabilities	803,478	710,110	852,128	790,007	637,205	717,390	573,963	832,190
Long-Term Obligations	474,492	488,683	490,706	491,954	741,353	577,666	747,051	591,591
Total Liabilities	1,749,520	1,717,619	1,837,857	1,742,595	1,816,862	1,726,214	1,817,511	1,648,245
Stockholders' Equity	1,703,573	1,802,809	1,510,035	1,489,821	1,182,350	1,114,598	1,139,235	1,060,601
Shares Outstanding	111,292	111,091	114,188	114,995	115,468	116,875	119,241	122,546
Statistical Record								
Return on Assets %	17.46	17.45	9.68	10.13	8.26	6.75	7.65	4.85
Return on Equity %	35.48	35.31	21.23	23.61	21.01	17.36	19.70	11.39
EBITDA Margin %	16.47	16.61	17.59	19.08	18.05	16.58	17.47	17.40
Net Margin %	32.27	54.09	11.95	11.51	10.04	8.40	8.45	5.67
Asset Turnover	0.80	0.80	0.81	0.88	0.82	0.80	0.91	0.86
Current Ratio	2.54	2.95	2.17	2.29	2.67	2.19	2.89	1.93
Debt to Equity	0.28	0.27	0.32	0.33	0.63	0.52	0.66	0.56
Price Range	69.04-50.22	65.02-49.64	64.24-41.00	59.09-34.19	41.32-28.98	42.19-18.82	42.77-34.66	48.87-25.36
P/E Ratio	13.84-10.06	12.90-9.85	23.70-15.13	22.13-12.81	20.35-14.28	25.73-11.48	24.30-19.69	47.91-24.86
Average Yield %	1.49	1.53	1.42	1.35	1.73	1.50	1.61	0.97

Address: 25 Harbor Park Drive, Port Washington, NY 11050	Web Site: www.pall.com	Auditors: KPMG LLP
Telephone: 516-484-5400	Officers: Ronald L. Hoffman - Chairman Lawrence D. Kingsley - President, Chief Executive Officer, Acting Chief Financial Officer	Investor Contact: 516-801-9871
Fax: 516-484-3649		Transfer Agents: Computershare Investor Services, Canton, MA

PANDORA MEDIA INC

Exchange	Symbol	Price	52Wk Range	Yield	P/E
NYS	P	$14.16 (3/28/2013)	14.27-7.18	N/A	N/A

*7 Year Price Score N/A   *NYSE Composite Index=100   *12 Month Price Score 112.61

TRADING VOLUME (thousand shares)

Interim Earnings (Per Share)

Qtr.	Apr	Jul	Oct	Jan
2010-11	(0.64)	(0.04)	(0.15)	(0.31)
2011-12	(0.61)	(0.04)	0.00	(0.06)
2012-13	(0.12)	(0.03)	0.01	(0.09)

Interim Dividends (Per Share)

No Dividends Paid

Valuation Analysis		Institutional Holding	
Forecast EPS	$0.01	No of Institutions	
	(04/05/2013)	188	
Market Cap	$2.4 Billion	Shares	
Book Value	$99.0 Million	170,419,088	
Price/Book	24.68	% Held	
Price/Sales	5.72	N/A	

Business Summary: Radio & Television (MIC: 2.3.1 SIC: 4832 NAIC: 515112)

Pandora Media provides internet radio in the U.S. Co. provides its service to listeners at no cost and generates revenue primarily from advertising. Co. also provides a subscription service to listeners. Co. provides service through two models: Free Service, which is advertising-based and allows listeners access to music and comedy catalogs and personalized playlist generating system for free across Co.'s delivery platforms; and Pandora One, which is a paid subscription service and allows unlimited listening time and provides access to 192 kbps audio on supported devices. As of Jan 2012, Co. had over 125.0 million registered users and as of Jan 31 2012, Co. had 47.0 million active users.

Recent Developments: For the year ended Jan 31 2013, net loss amounted to US$38.1 million versus a net loss of US$16.1 million in the prior year. Revenues were US$427.1 million, up 55.7% from US$274.3 million the year before. Operating loss was US$37.7 million versus a loss of US$11.0 million in the prior year. Direct operating expenses rose 69.6% to US$290.8 million from US$171.5 million in the comparable period the year before. Indirect operating expenses increased 52.9% to US$174.1 million from US$113.9 million in the equivalent prior-year period.

Prospects: Our evaluation of Pandora Media Inc as of Apr. 7, 2013 is the result of our systematic analysis on three basic characteristics: earnings strength, relative valuation, and recent stock price movement. The company has suffered a very negative trend in earnings per share over the past 5 quarters. Because the company lacks sufficient analyst estimate data, we place greater weight on the historical EPS trend as the measure of earnings strength. Based on operating earnings yield, the company is overvalued when compared to all of the companies in our coverage universe. Share price changes over the past year indicates that P will perform poorly over the near term.

Financial Data
(US$ in Thousands)

	01/31/2013	01/31/2012	01/31/2011	01/31/2010	01/31/2009
Earnings Per Share	(0.23)	(0.19)	(1.03)	(3.84)	(5.45)
Cash Flow Per Share	(0.00)	...	0.30	(4.24)	...
Tang Book Value Per Share	0.57	0.64	3.01	2.40	...
Income Statement					
Total Revenue	427,145	274,340	137,764	55,189	19,333
EBITDA	(30,603)	(10,975)	551	(14,817)	(26,149)
Depn & Amortn	7,100	4,500	1,600	1,100	1,200
Income Before Taxes	(38,143)	(16,032)	(1,630)	(16,753)	(28,228)
Income Taxes	5	75	134	...	...
Net Income	(38,148)	(16,107)	(1,764)	(16,753)	(28,228)
Average Shares	168,294	105,955	10,761	6,482	5,881
Balance Sheet					
Current Assets	198,614	160,125	88,776	37,677	...
Total Assets	218,832	178,015	99,209	40,277	...
Current Liabilities	115,970	70,907	52,061	18,748	...
Long-Term Obligations	...	...	837	4,095	...
Total Liabilities	119,843	73,475	55,557	23,242	...
Stockholders' Equity	98,989	104,540	43,652	17,035	...
Shares Outstanding	172,506	163,569	14,510	7,102	6,028
Statistical Record					
EBITDA Margin %	N.M.	N.M.	0.40	N.M.	N.M.
Asset Turnover	2.15	...	1.98	...	...
Current Ratio	1.71	2.26	1.71	2.01	...
Debt to Equity	...	...	0.02	0.24	...
Price Range	14.66-7.18	20.04-9.79	...	...	...

Address: 2101 Webster Street, Suite 1650, Oakland, CA 94612 **Telephone:** 510-451-4100	**Web Site:** www.pandora.com **Officers:** Joseph J. Kennedy - Chairman, President, Chief Executive Officer, Chief Financial Officer Thomas Conrad - Executive Vice President, Chief Technical Officer	**Auditors:** Ernst & Young LLP **Investor Contact:** 510-842-6960 **Transfer Agents:** Computershare Trust Company, N.A.

PARKER HANNIFIN CORP.

Exchange	Symbol	Price	52Wk Range	Yield	P/E	Div Achiever
NYS	PH	$91.58 (3/28/2013)	97.95-71.84	1.88	13.61	56 Years

*7 Year Price Score 111.56 *NYSE Composite Index=100 *12 Month Price Score 102.86

Interim Earnings (Per Share)

Qtr.	Sep	Dec	Mar	Jun
2009-10	0.45	0.64	0.94	1.36
2010-11	1.51	1.39	1.68	1.79
2011-12	1.91	1.56	2.01	1.96
2012-13	1.57	1.19	...	...

Interim Dividends (Per Share)

Amt	Decl	Ex	Rec	Pay
0.41Q	04/24/2012	05/08/2012	05/10/2012	06/01/2012
0.41Q	08/16/2012	08/24/2012	08/28/2012	09/07/2012
0.41Q	10/24/2012	11/07/2012	11/09/2012	12/07/2012
0.43Q	01/25/2013	02/06/2013	02/08/2013	03/01/2013

Indicated Div: $1.72 (Div. Reinv. Plan)

Valuation Analysis

		Institutional Holding	
Forecast EPS	$6.43	No of Institutions	
	(04/05/2013)	705	
Market Cap	$13.7 Billion	Shares	
Book Value	$5.3 Billion	127,762,880	
Price/Book	2.56	% Held	
Price/Sales	1.04	79.65	

Business Summary: Industrial Machinery & Equipment (MIC: 7.2.1 SIC: 3492 NAIC: 332912)

Parker Hannifin is a manufacturer of motion and control technologies and systems, including fluid power systems, electromechanical controls and related components. In addition to motion and control products, Co. is also a producer of fluid purification, fluid and fuel control, process instrumentation, air conditioning, refrigeration, electromagnetic shielding and thermal management products and systems. Co.'s technologies and systems are used in the products of its three principal business segments: Industrial; Aerospace; and Climate & Industrial Controls. Co.'s products are sold as original and replacement equipment through sales and distribution centers worldwide.

Recent Developments: For the quarter ended Dec 31 2012, net income decreased 25.3% to US$181.1 million from US$242.3 million in the year-earlier quarter. Revenues were US$3.07 billion, down 1.3% from US$3.11 billion the year before. Direct operating expenses rose 1.7% to US$2.42 billion from US$2.38 billion in the comparable period the year before. Indirect operating expenses increased 3.4% to US$381.1 million from US$368.7 million in the equivalent prior-year period.

Prospects: Our evaluation of Parker Hannifin Corp. as of Apr. 7, 2013 is the result of our systematic analysis on three basic characteristics: earnings strength, relative valuation, and recent stock price movement. The company has generated a negative trend in earnings per share over the past 5 quarters. However, while recent estimates for the company have been mixed, PH has posted better than expected results. Based on operating earnings yield, the company is undervalued when compared to all of the companies in our coverage universe. Share price changes over the past year indicates that PH will perform well over the near term.

Financial Data

(US$ in Thousands)	6 Mos	3 Mos	06/30/2012	06/30/2011	06/30/2010	06/30/2009	06/30/2008	06/30/2007
Earnings Per Share	6.73	7.10	7.45	6.37	3.40	3.13	5.53	4.67
Cash Flow Per Share	8.82	8.13	10.09	7.24	7.57	6.99	7.80	5.47
Tang Book Value Per Share	4.44	5.84	5.85	7.72	2.68	0.64	8.59	10.69
Dividends Per Share	1.620	1.580	1.540	1.250	1.010	1.000	0.840	0.693
Dividend Payout %	24.07	22.25	20.67	19.62	29.71	31.95	15.19	14.84
Income Statement								
Total Revenue	6,280,430	3,214,935	13,145,942	12,345,870	9,993,166	10,309,015	12,145,605	10,718,059
EBITDA	810,239	440,739	1,879,996	1,742,663	1,103,711	1,046,124	1,683,090	1,487,754
Depn & Amortn	163,827	81,172	210,508	229,238	245,295	252,599	257,570	245,058
Income Before Taxes	598,687	336,058	1,576,698	1,413,721	754,817	681,454	1,326,524	1,159,282
Income Taxes	177,625	96,110	421,206	356,571	198,452	172,939	377,058	329,236
Net Income	420,703	239,741	1,155,492	1,057,150	556,365	508,515	949,466	830,046
Average Shares	152,198	152,617	154,664	164,798	162,901	162,719	171,643	177,494
Balance Sheet								
Current Assets	4,095,747	4,200,082	4,498,114	4,305,256	3,588,796	3,123,781	4,095,625	3,386,175
Total Assets	11,461,361	11,134,578	11,170,282	10,886,805	9,910,382	9,855,902	10,386,854	8,441,413
Current Liabilities	2,488,260	2,366,465	2,486,013	2,391,043	2,204,891	2,005,754	2,183,256	1,925,245
Long-Term Obligations	1,509,238	1,511,799	1,503,946	1,691,086	1,413,634	1,839,705	1,952,452	1,089,916
Total Liabilities	6,135,644	5,993,454	6,273,767	5,502,951	5,542,417	5,576,277	5,127,883	3,729,748
Stockholders' Equity	5,325,717	5,141,124	4,896,515	5,383,854	4,367,965	4,279,625	5,258,971	4,711,665
Shares Outstanding	149,158	149,180	149,630	155,090	161,256	160,488	167,715	174,238
Statistical Record								
Return on Assets %	9.50	10.21	10.45	10.17	5.63	5.02	10.06	9.99
Return on Equity %	19.75	21.56	22.42	21.68	12.87	10.66	18.99	18.54
EBITDA Margin %	12.90	13.71	14.30	14.12	11.04	10.15	13.86	13.88
Net Margin %	6.70	7.46	8.79	8.56	5.57	4.93	7.82	7.74
Asset Turnover	1.20	1.22	1.19	1.19	1.01	1.02	1.29	1.29
Current Ratio	1.65	1.77	1.81	1.80	1.63	1.56	1.88	1.76
Debt to Equity	0.28	0.29	0.31	0.31	0.32	0.43	0.37	0.23
Price Range	90.75-71.84	90.75-60.81	91.58-60.81	98.49-54.80	71.23-39.98	72.33-27.86	86.15-60.32	68.39-46.50
P/E Ratio	13.48-10.67	12.78-8.56	12.29-8.16	15.46-8.60	20.95-11.76	23.11-8.90	15.58-10.91	14.65-9.96
Average Yield %	1.97	1.95	1.94	1.56	1.79	2.19	1.15	1.25

Address: 6035 Parkland Boulevard, Cleveland, OH 44124-4141 Telephone: 216-896-3000	Web Site: www.parker.com Officers: Donald E. Washkewicz - Chairman, President, Chief Executive Officer Jon P. Marten - Executive Vice President, Chief Financial Officer, Controller, Principal Accounting Officer, Principal Financial Officer	Auditors: Deloitte & Touche LLP Investor Contact: 216-896-2240 Transfer Agents: Wells Fargo Bank, N.A., St. Paul, MN

PEABODY ENERGY CORP

Exchange	Symbol	Price	52Wk Range	Yield	P/E
NYS	BTU	$21.15 (3/28/2013)	31.59-19.05	1.61	N/A

*7 Year Price Score 50.98   *NYSE Composite Index=100   ***12 Month Price Score 83.09**

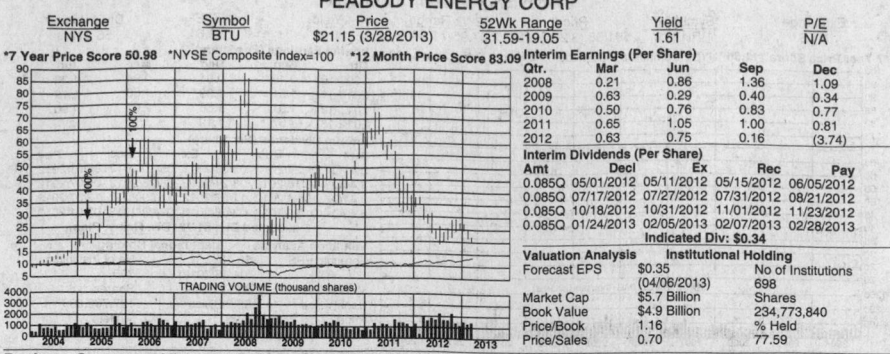

Interim Earnings (Per Share)

Qtr.	Mar	Jun	Sep	Dec
2008	0.21	0.86	1.36	1.09
2009	0.63	0.29	0.40	0.34
2010	0.50	0.76	0.83	0.77
2011	0.65	1.05	1.00	0.81
2012	0.63	0.75	0.16	(3.74)

Interim Dividends (Per Share)

Amt	Decl	Ex	Rec	Pay
0.085Q	05/01/2012	05/11/2012	05/15/2012	06/05/2012
0.085Q	07/17/2012	07/27/2012	07/31/2012	08/21/2012
0.085Q	10/18/2012	10/31/2012	11/01/2012	11/23/2012
0.085Q	01/24/2013	02/05/2013	02/07/2013	02/28/2013

Indicated Div: $0.34

Valuation Analysis

		Institutional Holding	
Forecast EPS	$0.35 (04/06/2013)	No of Institutions	698
Market Cap	$5.7 Billion	Shares	234,773,840
Book Value	$4.9 Billion	% Held	77.59
Price/Book	1.16		
Price/Sales	0.70		

Business Summary: Mining (MIC: 8.2.4 SIC: 1221 NAIC: 212111)

Peabody Energy engages in the mining of thermal coal and metallurgical coal. Co.'s mining operations are located in the U.S. and Australia, and include equity-affiliate mining operations in Australia and Venezuela. Co. also markets, brokers coal sales of other coal producers, and trades coal, freight and freight-related contracts. Co.'s other energy related commercial activities include participating in the development of a mine-mouth coal-fueled generating plant, the management of its coal reserve and real estate holdings, and the development of British thermal unit conversion and clean coal technologies. At Dec 31 2011, Co. had 9.01 billion tons of total proven and probable coal reserves.

Recent Developments: For the year ended Dec 31 2012, loss from continuing operations was US$470.9 million compared with income of US$1.01 billion a year earlier. Net loss amounted to US$575.1 million versus net income of US$946.3 million in the prior year. Revenues were US$8.08 billion, up 2.3% from US$7.90 billion the year before. Operating income was US$172.5 million versus US$1.60 billion in the prior year, a decrease of 89.2%. Direct operating expenses rose 8.3% to US$5.93 billion from US$5.48 billion in the comparable period the year before. Indirect operating expenses increased 139.8% to US$1.97 billion from US$822.6 million in the equivalent prior-year period.

Prospects: Our evaluation of Peabody Energy Corp. as of Apr. 7, 2013 is the result of our systematic analysis on three basic characteristics: earnings strength, relative valuation, and recent stock price movement. The company has suffered a very negative trend in earnings per share over the past 5 quarters. However, while recent estimates for the company have been lowered by analysts, BTU has posted better than expected results. Based on operating earnings yield, the company is overvalued when compared to all of the companies in our coverage universe. Share price changes over the past year indicates that BTU will perform in line with the market over the near term.

Financial Data
(US$ in Thousands)

	12/31/2012	12/31/2011	12/31/2010	12/31/2009	12/31/2008	12/31/2007	12/31/2006	12/31/2005
Earnings Per Share	(2.19)	3.52	2.85	1.66	3.51	0.98	2.23	1.58
Cash Flow Per Share	5.64	6.07	4.07	3.95	4.77	1.20	2.26	2.69
Tang Book Value Per Share	18.26	20.23	17.25	13.98	10.89	9.33	7.95	8.27
Dividends Per Share	0.340	0.340	0.295	0.250	0.240	0.240	0.240	0.170
Dividend Payout %	...	9.66	10.35	15.06	6.84	24.49	10.76	10.76
Income Statement								
Total Revenue	8,077,500	7,974,400	6,860,000	6,012,400	6,593,400	4,574,712	5,256,315	4,644,453
EBITDA	897,100	2,094,800	1,768,300	1,326,900	1,805,800	923,260	1,022,454	811,339
Depn & Amortn	663,400	482,200	440,900	413,000	412,900	368,744	384,620	323,052
Income Before Taxes	(147,400)	1,392,900	1,114,900	720,800	1,176,800	326,374	507,110	395,989
Income Taxes	262,300	363,200	308,100	193,800	185,800	(78,112)	(81,515)	960
Net Income	(585,700)	957,700	774,000	448,200	953,500	264,285	600,697	422,653
Average Shares	268,000	270,300	269,900	267,500	271,275	269,166	269,166	268,013
Balance Sheet								
Current Assets	2,575,500	3,005,900	2,958,200	2,189,000	1,971,300	1,927,293	1,274,340	1,324,644
Total Assets	15,809,000	16,733,000	11,363,100	9,955,300	9,822,400	9,668,307	9,514,056	6,852,006
Current Liabilities	1,674,100	1,823,700	1,513,700	1,312,400	1,856,200	2,186,986	1,367,531	1,022,923
Long-Term Obligations	6,205,100	6,556,400	2,706,800	2,738,200	3,139,200	3,138,727	3,168,069	1,382,921
Total Liabilities	10,904,100	11,247,900	6,702,400	6,205,600	6,918,600	7,148,636	7,175,530	4,673,539
Stockholders' Equity	4,904,900	5,485,100	4,660,700	3,749,700	2,903,800	2,519,671	2,338,526	2,178,467
Shares Outstanding	268,600	271,100	270,236	268,203	266,644	270,066	263,846	263,357
Statistical Record								
Return on Assets %	N.M.	6.82	7.26	4.53	9.76	2.76	7.34	6.49
Return on Equity %	N.M.	18.88	18.41	13.47	35.07	10.88	26.60	21.66
EBITDA Margin %	11.11	26.27	25.78	22.07	27.39	20.18	19.45	17.47
Net Margin %	N.M.	12.01	11.28	7.45	14.46	5.78	11.43	9.10
Asset Turnover	0.50	0.57	0.64	0.61	0.67	0.48	0.64	0.71
Current Ratio	1.54	1.65	1.95	1.67	1.06	0.88	0.93	1.29
Debt to Equity	1.27	1.20	0.58	0.73	1.08	1.25	1.35	0.63
Price Range	37.99-19.05	72.71-31.33	64.21-35.59	47.81-20.43	88.05-16.25	62.28-34.17	68.94-32.67	40.31-17.35
P/E Ratio	...	20.66-8.90	22.53-12.49	28.80-12.31	25.09-4.63	63.55-34.87	30.92-14.65	25.52-10.98
Average Yield %	1.26	0.64	0.62	0.75	0.45	0.53	0.53	0.61

Address: 701 Market Street, St. Louis, MO 63101-1826	Web Site: www.peabodyenergy.com	Auditors: Ernst & Young LLP
Telephone: 314-342-3400	Officers: Gregory H. Boyce - Chairman, Chief Executive Officer Michael C. Crews - Executive Vice President, Chief Financial Officer	Investor Contact: 314-342-7900 Transfer Agents: American Stock Transfer & Trust Company

PENNEY (J.C.) CO.,INC. (HOLDING CO.)

Exchange	Symbol	Price	52Wk Range	Yield	P/E
NYS	JCP	$15.11 (3/28/2013)	36.72-14.43	N/A	N/A

*7 Year Price Score 52.40   *NYSE Composite Index=100   *12 Month Price Score 70.99

Interim Earnings (Per Share)

Qtr.	Apr	Jul	Oct	Jan
2008-09	0.54	0.52	0.56	0.95
2009-10	0.11	0.00	0.11	0.86
2010-11	0.25	0.06	0.19	1.13
2011-12	0.28	0.07	(0.67)	(0.40)
2012-13	(0.75)	(0.67)	(0.56)	(2.51)

Interim Dividends (Per Share)

Dividend Payment Suspended

Valuation Analysis   Institutional Holding

Forecast EPS	$-2.21	No of Institutions	
	(04/06/2013)	531	
Market Cap	$3.3 Billion	Shares	
Book Value	$3.2 Billion		278,792,640
Price/Book	1.04	% Held	
Price/Sales	0.26		111.70

Business Summary: Retail - General Merchandise/Department Stores (MIC: 2.1.1 SIC: 5311 NAIC: 452111)

J.C. Penney Company is a holding company whose principal operating subsidiary is J. C. Penney Corporation, Inc. As of Jan 28 2012, Co. operated 1,102 JCPenney department stores in 49 states and Puerto Rico. Co.'s business consists of selling merchandise and services to consumers through its department stores and through the Internet website at jcp.com. Co. sells family apparel and footwear, accessories, fine and fashion jewelry, beauty products through Sephora inside jcpenney and home furnishings. In addition, Co.'s department stores provide its customers with services such as styling salon, optical, portrait photography and custom decorating.

Recent Developments: For the year ended Feb 2 2013, loss from continuing operations was US$985.0 million compared with a loss of US$152.0 million a year earlier. Net loss amounted to US$985.0 million versus a net loss of US$152.0 million in the prior year. Revenues were US$12.99 billion, down 24.8% from US$17.26 billion the year before. Operating loss was US$1.31 billion versus a loss of US$2.0 million in the prior year. Direct operating expenses declined 19.2% to US$8.92 billion from US$11.04 billion in the comparable period the year before. Indirect operating expenses decreased 13.6% to US$5.38 billion from US$6.22 billion in the equivalent prior-year period.

Prospects: Our evaluation of Penney (J.C.) Co.,Inc. as of Apr. 7, 2013 is the result of our systematic analysis on three basic characteristics: earnings strength, relative valuation, and recent stock price movement. The company has suffered a very negative trend in earnings per share over the past 5 quarters. Because the company lacks sufficient analyst estimate data, we place greater weight on the historical EPS trend as the measure of earnings strength. Based on operating earnings yield, the company is overvalued when compared to all of the companies in our coverage universe. Share price changes over the past year indicates that JCP will perform very poorly over the near term.

Financial Data

(US$ in Millions)	02/02/2013	01/28/2012	01/29/2011	01/30/2010	01/31/2009	02/02/2008	02/03/2007	01/28/2006
Earnings Per Share	(4.49)	(0.70)	1.63	1.08	2.57	4.93	4.96	4.26
Cash Flow Per Share	(0.04)	3.78	2.52	6.81	5.22	5.59	5.39	5.30
Tang Book Value Per Share	11.78	15.96	22.05	19.49	18.09	23.45	18.55	16.82
Dividends Per Share	0.200	0.800	0.800	0.800	0.800	0.800	0.720	0.500
Dividend Payout %	...	...	49.08	74.07	31.13	16.23	14.52	11.74
Income Statement								
Total Revenue	12,985	17,260	17,759	17,556	18,486	19,860	19,903	18,781
EBITDA	(767)	516	1,323	1,158	1,604	2,302	2,311	1,985
Depn & Amortn	543	518	511	495	469	426	389	372
Income Before Taxes	(1,536)	(229)	581	403	910	1,723	1,792	1,444
Income Taxes	(551)	(77)	203	154	343	618	658	467
Net Income	(985)	(152)	389	251	572	1,111	1,153	1,088
Average Shares	219	217	238	233	223	225	232	255
Balance Sheet								
Current Assets	3,683	5,081	6,370	6,652	6,220	6,751	6,648	6,702
Total Assets	9,781	11,424	13,042	12,581	12,011	14,309	12,673	12,461
Current Liabilities	2,583	2,756	2,647	3,249	2,794	3,338	3,492	2,762
Long-Term Obligations	2,956	2,871	3,099	2,999	3,505	3,505	3,010	3,444
Total Liabilities	6,610	7,414	7,582	7,803	7,856	8,997	8,385	8,454
Stockholders' Equity	3,171	4,010	5,460	4,778	4,155	5,312	4,288	4,007
Shares Outstanding	219	215	237	236	222	222	226	233
Statistical Record								
Return on Assets %	N.M.	N.M.	3.04	2.05	4.36	8.26	9.03	8.21
Return on Equity %	N.M.	N.M.	7.62	5.64	12.12	23.21	27.35	24.62
EBITDA Margin %	N.M.	2.99	7.45	6.60	8.68	11.59	11.61	10.57
Net Margin %	N.M.	N.M.	2.19	1.43	3.09	5.59	5.79	5.79
Asset Turnover	1.20	1.41	1.39	1.43	1.41	1.48	1.56	1.42
Current Ratio	1.43	1.84	2.41	2.05	2.23	2.02	1.90	2.43
Debt to Equity	0.93	0.72	0.57	0.63	0.84	0.66	0.70	0.86
Price Range	41.93-16.28	41.42-23.81	34.47-19.50	36.81-14.18	50.45-14.38	86.35-34.57	84.77-54.67	57.71-41.69
P/E Ratio	...	...	21.15-11.96	34.08-13.13	19.63-5.60	17.52-7.01	17.09-11.02	13.55-9.79
Average Yield %	0.76	2.43	2.84	2.94	2.41	1.21	1.06	0.99

Address: 6501 Legacy Drive, Plano, TX 75024 - 3698
Telephone: 972-431-1000
Fax: 972-591-9322

Web Site: www.jcpenney.net
Officers: Thomas J. Engibous - Chairman Myron E. Ullman - Chairman, Chief Executive Officer

Auditors: KPMG LLP
Investor Contact: 972-431-5500
Transfer Agents: BNY Mellon Shareowner Services, Pittsburgh, PA

PEPCO HOLDINGS INC.

Exchange	Symbol	Price	52Wk Range	Yield	P/E
NYS	POM	$21.40 (3/28/2013)	21.40-18.31	5.05	17.12

*7 Year Price Score 83.30   *NYSE Composite Index=100   *12 Month Price Score 96.19

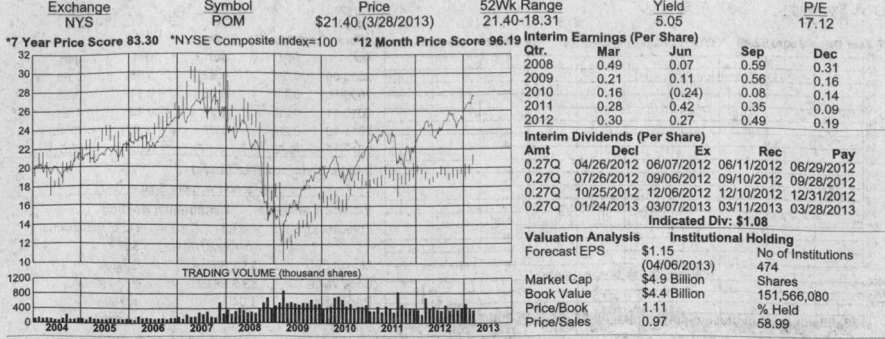

Interim Earnings (Per Share)

Qtr.	Mar	Jun	Sep	Dec
2008	0.49	0.07	0.59	0.31
2009	0.21	0.11	0.56	0.16
2010	0.16	(0.24)	0.08	0.14
2011	0.28	0.42	0.35	0.09
2012	0.30	0.27	0.49	0.19

Interim Dividends (Per Share)

Amt	Decl	Ex	Rec	Pay
0.27Q	04/26/2012	06/07/2012	06/11/2012	06/29/2012
0.27Q	07/26/2012	09/06/2012	09/10/2012	09/28/2012
0.27Q	10/25/2012	12/06/2012	12/10/2012	12/31/2012
0.27Q	01/24/2013	03/07/2013	03/11/2013	03/28/2013

Indicated Div: $1.08

Valuation Analysis		Institutional Holding	
Forecast EPS	$1.15 (04/06/2013)	No of Institutions	474
Market Cap	$4.9 Billion	Shares	151,566,080
Book Value	$4.4 Billion	% Held	58.99
Price/Book	1.11		
Price/Sales	0.97		

Business Summary: Electric Utilities (MIC: 3.1.1 SIC: 4931 NAIC: 221122)

Pepco Holdings is a holding company. Through its subsidiaries, Co. is engaged in the distribution, transmission and default supply of electricity and the delivery and supply of natural gas (Power Delivery). Co.'s regulated public utility subsidiaries are Potomac Electric Power Co., Delmarva Power & Light Co., and Atlantic City Electric Co., each of which owns and operates a network of wires, substations and other equipment that is classified either as transmission, distribution or common facilities. At Dec 31 2011, Co.'s Power Delivery business distributed electricity to over 1.8 million customers in the mid-Atlantic region and delivered natural gas to about 124,000 customers in Delaware.

Recent Developments: For the year ended Dec 31 2012, income from continuing operations increased 9.6% to US$285.0 million from US$260.0 million a year earlier. Net income increased 10.9% to US$285.0 million from US$257.0 million in the prior year. Revenues were US$5.08 billion, down 14.6% from US$5.95 billion the year before. Operating income was US$670.0 million versus US$637.0 million in the prior year, an increase of 5.2%. Direct operating expenses declined 19.2% to US$4.01 billion from US$4.97 billion in the comparable period the year before. Indirect operating expenses increased 14.6% to US$400.0 million from US$349.0 million in the equivalent prior-year period.

Prospects: Our evaluation of Pepco Holdings Inc. as of Apr. 7, 2013 is the result of our systematic analysis on three basic characteristics: earnings strength, relative valuation, and recent stock price movement. The company has generated a negative trend in earnings per share over the past 5 quarters. However, while recent estimates for the company have been lowered by analysts, POM has posted results that were in line with analysts expectations. Based on operating earnings yield, the company is about fairly valued when compared to all of the companies in our coverage universe. Share price changes over the past year indicates that POM will perform poorly over the near term.

Financial Data
(US$ in Thousands)

	12/31/2012	12/31/2011	12/31/2010	12/31/2009	12/31/2008	12/31/2007	12/31/2006	12/31/2005
Earnings Per Share	1.25	1.14	0.14	1.06	1.47	1.72	1.30	1.96
Cash Flow Per Share	2.58	3.04	3.63	2.74	2.02	4.10	1.06	5.22
Tang Book Value Per Share	13.21	12.87	12.54	12.82	12.69	13.01	11.48	11.58
Dividends Per Share	1.080	1.080	1.080	1.080	1.080	1.040	1.040	1.000
Dividend Payout %	86.40	94.74	771.43	101.89	73.47	60.47	80.00	51.02
Income Statement								
Total Revenue	5,081,000	5,920,000	7,039,000	9,259,000	10,700,000	9,366,400	8,362,900	8,065,500
EBITDA	1,158,000	1,091,000	850,000	1,101,000	1,161,000	1,198,100	1,140,000	1,363,800
Depn & Amortn	454,000	426,000	393,000	391,000	377,000	365,900	413,200	422,600
Income Before Taxes	440,000	412,000	151,000	343,000	473,000	512,000	404,600	619,600
Income Taxes	156,000	149,000	11,000	110,000	168,000	187,900	161,400	255,200
Net Income	285,000	257,000	32,000	235,000	300,000	334,200	248,300	371,200
Average Shares	230,000	226,000	224,000	221,000	204,000	194,100	190,700	189,300
Balance Sheet								
Current Assets	1,249,000	1,439,000	1,757,000	1,926,000	2,626,000	1,997,100	1,981,400	2,151,700
Total Assets	15,776,000	14,910,000	14,480,000	15,779,000	16,475,000	15,111,000	14,243,500	14,017,800
Current Liabilities	2,527,000	1,861,000	1,797,000	2,302,000	2,030,000	2,040,800	2,526,900	2,399,300
Long-Term Obligations	3,986,000	4,180,000	4,062,000	4,947,000	5,378,000	4,734,600	4,367,400	4,839,300
Total Liabilities	11,330,000	10,574,000	10,250,000	11,523,000	12,285,000	11,092,600	10,631,300	10,387,800
Stockholders' Equity	4,446,000	4,336,000	4,230,000	4,256,000	4,190,000	4,018,400	3,612,200	3,630,000
Shares Outstanding	230,015	227,500	225,082	222,269	218,906	200,512	191,932	189,817
Statistical Record								
Return on Assets %	1.85	1.75	0.21	1.46	1.89	2.28	1.76	2.71
Return on Equity %	6.47	6.00	0.75	5.56	7.29	8.76	6.86	10.53
EBITDA Margin %	22.79	18.43	12.08	11.89	10.85	12.79	13.63	16.91
Net Margin %	5.61	4.34	0.45	2.54	2.80	3.57	2.97	4.60
Asset Turnover	0.33	0.40	0.47	0.57	0.68	0.64	0.59	0.59
Current Ratio	0.49	0.77	0.98	0.84	1.29	0.98	0.78	0.90
Debt to Equity	0.90	0.96	0.96	1.16	1.28	1.18	1.21	1.33
Price Range	20.30-18.31	20.54-16.97	19.67-15.41	18.59-10.32	29.33-15.77	30.64-25.00	26.78-22.02	24.36-20.43
P/E Ratio	16.24-14.65	18.02-14.89	140.50-110.07	17.54-9.74	19.95-10.73	17.81-14.53	20.60-16.94	12.43-10.42
Average Yield %	5.59	5.67	5.61	7.43	4.57	3.75	4.33	4.50

Address: 701 Ninth Street, N.W., Washington, DC 20068	Web Site: www.pepcoholdings.com	Auditors: PricewaterhouseCoopers LLP
Telephone: 202-872-2000	Officers: Joseph M. Rigby - Chairman, President, Chief Executive Officer Anthony J. Kamerick - Executive Vice President, Senior Vice President, Chief Regulatory Officer, Chief Financial Officer	Investor Contact: 302-429-3004 Transfer Agents: American Stock Transfer & Trust Company, Brooklyn, NY

PEPSICO INC.

Exchange	Symbol	Price	52Wk Range	Yield	P/E	Div Achiever
NYS	PEP	$79.11 (3/28/2013)	79.11-64.85	2.72	20.18	41 Years

*7 Year Price Score 96.72 *NYSE Composite Index=100 *12 Month Price Score 98.55

Interim Earnings (Per Share)

Qtr.	Mar	Jun	Aug	Dec
2008	0.70	1.05	0.99	0.47
2009	0.72	1.06	1.09	0.90
2010	0.89	0.98	1.19	0.85
2011	0.71	1.17	1.25	0.89
2012	0.71	0.94	1.21	1.06

Interim Dividends (Per Share)

Amt	Decl	Ex	Rec	Pay
0.537Q	05/02/2012	05/30/2012	06/01/2012	06/29/2012
0.537Q	07/20/2012	09/05/2012	09/07/2012	09/28/2012
0.537Q	11/27/2012	12/05/2012	12/07/2012	01/02/2013
0.537Q	02/07/2013	02/27/2013	03/01/2013	03/29/2013

Indicated Div: $2.15 (Div. Reinv. Plan)

Valuation Analysis | **Institutional Holding**

Forecast EPS	$4.39	No of Institutions
	(04/06/2013)	1964
Market Cap	$122.1 Billion	Shares
Book Value	$22.3 Billion	1,187,206,528
Price/Book	5.48	% Held
Price/Sales	1.87	67.30

Business Summary: Beverages (MIC: 1.2.2 SIC: 2086 NAIC: 312111)

PepsiCo is a global food and beverage company. Co. makes, markets, sells and distributes a range of foods and beverages. Co. is organized into four business units: PepsiCo Americas Foods, which includes Frito-Lay North America, Quaker Foods North America and all of its Latin American food and snack businesses; PepsiCo Americas Beverages, which includes all of its North American and Latin American beverage businesses; PepsiCo Europe, which includes all beverage, food and snack businesses in Europe and South Africa; and PepsiCo Asia, Middle East and Africa (AMEA), which includes all beverage, food and snack businesses in AMEA, excluding South Africa. Co. is also comprised of six segments.

Recent Developments: For the year ended Dec 29 2012, net income decreased 3.8% to US$6.21 billion from US$6.46 billion in the prior year. Revenues were US$65.49 billion, down 1.5% from US$66.50 billion the year before. Operating income was US$9.11 billion versus US$9.63 billion in the prior year, a decrease of 5.4%. Direct operating expenses declined 1.0% to US$31.29 billion from US$31.59 billion in the comparable period the year before. Indirect operating expenses decreased 0.7% to US$25.09 billion from US$25.28 billion in the equivalent prior-year period.

Prospects: Our evaluation of PepsiCo Inc. as of Apr. 7, 2013 is the result of our systematic analysis on three basic characteristics: earnings strength, relative valuation, and recent stock price movement. The company has enjoyed a very positive trend in earnings per share over the past 5 quarters and while recent estimates for the company have remained steady, PEP has posted better than expected results. Based on operating earnings yield, the company is about fairly valued when compared to all of the companies in our coverage universe. Share price changes over the past year indicates that PEP will perform in line with the market over the near term.

Financial Data
(US$ in Thousands)

	12/29/2012	12/31/2011	12/25/2010	12/26/2009	12/27/2008	12/29/2007	12/30/2006	12/31/2005
Earnings Per Share	3.92	4.03	3.91	3.77	3.21	3.41	3.34	2.39
Cash Flow Per Share	5.46	5.58	5.33	4.37	4.46	4.29	3.70	3.45
Tang Book Value Per Share	N.M.	N.M.	N.M.	4.86	3.30	6.24	5.45	5.16
Dividends Per Share	2.127	2.025	1.890	1.775	1.650	1.425	1.160	1.010
Dividend Payout %	54.27	50.25	48.34	47.08	51.40	41.79	34.73	42.26
Income Statement								
Total Revenue	65,492,000	66,504,000	57,838,000	43,232,000	43,251,000	39,474,000	35,137,000	32,562,000
EBITDA	11,720,000	12,242,000	10,573,000	9,607,000	8,421,000	8,532,000	7,783,000	7,175,000
Depn & Amortn	2,608,000	2,609,000	2,241,000	1,563,000	1,486,000	1,362,000	1,344,000	1,253,000
Income Before Taxes	8,304,000	8,834,000	7,497,000	7,714,000	6,647,000	7,071,000	6,373,000	5,825,000
Income Taxes	2,090,000	2,372,000	1,894,000	2,100,000	1,879,000	1,973,000	1,347,000	2,304,000
Net Income	6,178,000	6,443,000	6,320,000	5,946,000	5,142,000	5,658,000	5,642,000	4,078,000
Average Shares	1,575,000	1,597,000	1,614,000	1,577,000	1,602,000	1,658,000	1,687,000	1,706,000
Balance Sheet								
Current Assets	18,720,000	17,441,000	17,569,000	12,571,000	10,806,000	10,151,000	9,130,000	10,454,000
Total Assets	74,638,000	72,882,000	68,153,000	39,848,000	35,994,000	34,628,000	29,930,000	31,727,000
Current Liabilities	17,089,000	18,154,000	15,892,000	8,756,000	8,787,000	7,753,000	6,860,000	9,406,000
Long-Term Obligations	23,544,000	20,568,000	19,999,000	7,400,000	7,858,000	4,203,000	2,550,000	2,313,000
Total Liabilities	52,344,000	52,294,000	46,989,000	23,044,000	23,888,000	17,394,000	14,562,000	17,476,000
Stockholders' Equity	22,294,000	20,588,000	21,164,000	16,804,000	12,106,000	17,234,000	15,368,000	14,251,000
Shares Outstanding	1,544,000	1,564,000	1,581,000	1,565,000	1,553,000	1,605,000	1,638,000	1,656,000
Statistical Record								
Return on Assets %	8.40	8.99	11.74	15.72	14.60	17.58	18.35	13.44
Return on Equity %	28.89	30.36	33.38	41.25	35.15	34.80	38.20	28.89
EBITDA Margin %	17.90	18.41	18.28	22.22	19.47	21.61	22.15	22.03
Net Margin %	9.43	9.69	10.93	13.75	11.89	14.33	16.06	12.52
Asset Turnover	0.89	0.93	1.07	1.14	1.23	1.23	1.14	1.07
Current Ratio	1.10	0.96	1.11	1.44	1.23	1.31	1.33	1.11
Debt to Equity	1.06	1.00	0.94	0.44	0.65	0.24	0.17	0.16
Price Range	73.58-62.28	71.78-59.99	68.11-58.96	64.23-45.81	79.57-50.29	78.69-62.16	65.91-56.77	59.90-51.57
P/E Ratio	18.77-15.89	17.81-14.89	17.42-15.08	17.04-12.15	24.79-15.67	23.08-18.23	19.73-17.00	25.06-21.58
Average Yield %	3.10	3.11	2.94	3.21	2.50	2.09	1.90	1.82

Address: 700 Anderson Hill Road, Purchase, NY 10577 **Telephone:** 914-253-2000 **Fax:** 914-253-2070	Web Site: www.pepsico.com **Officers:** Indra K. Nooyi - Chairman, President, Chief Executive Officer Zein Abdalla - Region Officer, President	Auditors: KPMG LLP **Transfer Agents:** Computershare Shareowner Services, LLC, Pittsburgh, PA

PERKINELMER, INC.

Exchange	Symbol	Price	52Wk Range	Yield	P/E
NYS	PKI	$33.64 (3/28/2013)	35.86-23.88	0.83	55.15

*7 Year Price Score 110.96 *NYSE Composite Index=100 *12 Month Price Score 106.67

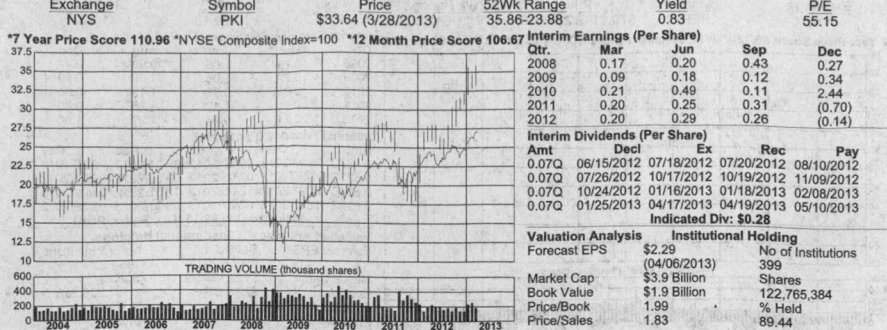

Interim Earnings (Per Share)

Qtr.	Mar	Jun	Sep	Dec
2008	0.17	0.20	0.43	0.27
2009	0.09	0.18	0.12	0.34
2010	0.21	0.49	0.11	2.44
2011	0.20	0.25	0.31	(0.70)
2012	0.20	0.29	0.26	(0.14)

Interim Dividends (Per Share)

Amt	Decl	Ex	Rec	Pay
0.07Q	06/15/2012	07/18/2012	07/20/2012	08/10/2012
0.07Q	07/26/2012	10/17/2012	10/19/2012	11/09/2012
0.07Q	10/24/2012	01/16/2013	01/18/2013	02/08/2013
0.07Q	01/25/2013	04/17/2013	04/19/2013	05/10/2013

Indicated Div: $0.28

Valuation Analysis | **Institutional Holding**

Forecast EPS	$2.29	No of Institutions
	(04/06/2013)	399
Market Cap	$3.9 Billion	Shares
Book Value	$1.9 Billion	122,765,384
Price/Book	1.99	% Held
Price/Sales	1.83	89.44

Business Summary: Biotechnology (MIC: 4.1.2 SIC: 3826 NAIC: 334516)

PerkinElmer is a provider of technology and services to the diagnostics, research, environmental, industrial and laboratory services markets. Co. operates its business in two segments: Human Health, which is engaged in developing diagnostics, tools, and applications to detect diseases earlier and to help in the discovery and development of new therapies, serving the diagnostics and research markets; and Environmental Health, which provides technologies and applications to facilitate the creation of food and consumer products, secure surroundings and enhanced energy resources, serving the environmental, industrial and laboratory services markets.

Recent Developments: For the year ended Dec 30 2012, income from continuing operations increased to US$68.4 million from US$1.2 million a year earlier. Net income increased 813.7% to US$69.9 million from US$7.7 million in the prior year. Revenues were US$2.12 billion, up 10.3% from US$1.92 billion the year before. Operating income was US$98.5 million versus US$91.1 million in the prior year, an increase of 8.1%. Direct operating expenses rose 7.6% to US$1.15 billion from US$1.07 billion in the comparable period the year before. Indirect operating expenses increased 14.3% to US$864.7 million from US$756.7 million in the equivalent prior-year period.

Prospects: Our evaluation of PerkinElmer Inc. as of Apr. 7, 2013 is the result of our systematic analysis on three basic characteristics: earnings strength, relative valuation, and recent stock price movement. The company has generated a negative trend in earnings per share over the past 5 quarters. However, while recent estimates for the company have been mixed, PKI has posted results that fell short of analysts expectations. Based on operating earnings yield, the company is undervalued when compared to all of the companies in our coverage universe. Share price changes over the past year indicates that PKI will perform very well over the near term.

Financial Data
(US$ In Thousands)

	12/30/2012	01/01/2012	01/02/2011	01/03/2010	12/28/2008	12/30/2007	12/31/2006	01/01/2006
Earnings Per Share	0.61	0.07	3.25	0.73	1.07	1.09	0.95	2.04
Cash Flow Per Share	1.34	2.00	1.41	1.26	1.86	1.73	1.02	1.61
Tang Book Value Per Share	N.M.	N.M.	N.M.	N.M.	N.M.	N.M.	0.45	1.91
Dividends Per Share	0.280	0.280	0.280	0.280	0.280	0.280	0.280	0.280
Dividend Payout %	45.90	400.00	8.62	38.36	26.17	25.69	29.47	13.73
Income Statement								
Total Revenue	2,115,205	1,921,287	1,704,346	1,812,202	1,937,465	1,787,331	1,546,358	1,473,831
EBITDA	131,227	118,153	205,443	181,398	201,260	195,826	185,903	129,030
Depn & Amortn	35,600	30,900	28,400	34,600	32,700	33,900	35,400	38,400
Income Before Taxes	50,587	64,354	161,984	130,677	147,361	151,289	150,736	66,660
Income Taxes	(17,854)	63,182	26,062	37,933	21,216	17,455	32,412	128
Net Income	69,940	7,655	383,919	85,599	126,409	131,686	119,583	268,108
Average Shares	114,860	113,864	117,982	116,590	118,687	120,605	126,512	131,140
Balance Sheet								
Current Assets	971,754	862,218	1,085,039	883,790	830,747	842,948	744,766	998,889
Total Assets	3,901,762	3,834,198	3,209,373	3,064,242	2,931,767	2,949,337	2,510,322	2,693,461
Current Liabilities	581,100	600,066	515,202	496,070	516,242	547,598	476,533	494,539
Long-Term Obligations	938,824	944,908	424,000	558,197	509,040	516,078	151,781	243,282
Total Liabilities	1,961,950	1,991,982	1,283,555	1,435,285	1,363,824	1,374,060	932,592	1,042,948
Stockholders' Equity	1,939,812	1,842,216	1,925,818	1,628,957	1,567,943	1,575,277	1,577,730	1,650,513
Shares Outstanding	115,036	113,157	115,715	117,023	117,112	117,585	123,255	130,109
Statistical Record								
Return on Assets %	1.81	0.22	12.27	2.81	4.31	4.84	4.61	10.20
Return on Equity %	3.71	0.41	21.66	5.27	8.07	8.38	7.43	17.29
EBITDA Margin %	6.20	6.15	12.05	10.01	10.39	10.96	12.02	8.75
Net Margin %	3.31	0.40	22.53	4.72	6.52	7.37	7.73	18.19
Asset Turnover	0.55	0.55	0.54	0.59	0.66	0.66	0.60	0.56
Current Ratio	1.67	1.44	2.11	1.78	1.61	1.54	1.56	2.02
Debt to Equity	0.48	0.51	0.22	0.34	0.32	0.33	0.10	0.15
Price Range	32.29-20.37	28.46-17.47	26.14-18.89	20.99-11.00	29.69-13.14	29.86-21.40	24.08-17.89	23.86-18.01
P/E Ratio	52.93-33.39	406.57-249.57	8.04-5.81	28.75-15.07	27.75-12.28	27.39-19.63	25.35-18.83	11.70-8.83
Average Yield %	1.02	1.18	1.24	1.68	1.24	1.14	1.32	1.33

Address: 940 Winter Street, Waltham, MA 02451	Web Site: www.perkinelmer.com	Auditors: Deloitte & Touche LLP
Telephone: 781-663-6900	Officers: Robert F. Friel - Chairman, President, Chief Executive Officer Frank Anders Wilson - Senior Vice President, Chief Financial Officer, Chief Accounting Officer	Investor Contact: 781-663-6900 Transfer Agents: Computershare Shareowner Services LLC, Jersey City, NJ

PENSKE AUTOMOTIVE GROUP INC

Exchange	Symbol	Price	52Wk Range	Yield	P/E
NYS	PAG	$33.36 (3/28/2013)	33.74-20.87	1.68	16.27

*7 Year Price Score 129.68 ***NYSE Composite Index=100** ***12 Month Price Score 104.25**

TRADING VOLUME (thousand shares)

Interim Earnings (Per Share)

Qtr.	Mar	Jun	Sep	Dec
2011	0.37	0.43	0.61	0.54
2012	0.52	0.54	0.45	0.53

Interim Dividends (Per Share)

Amt	Decl	Ex	Rec	Pay
0.11Q	04/19/2012	05/08/2012	05/10/2012	06/01/2012
0.12Q	07/19/2012	08/08/2012	08/10/2012	09/04/2012
0.13Q	10/18/2012	11/07/2012	11/12/2012	12/03/2012
0.14Q	01/29/2013	02/07/2013	02/11/2013	03/01/2013

Indicated Div: $0.56

Valuation Analysis

		Institutional Holding	
Forecast EPS	$2.54 (04/06/2013)	No of Institutions	198
Market Cap	$3.0 Billion	Shares	100,611,872
Book Value	$1.3 Billion	% Held	N/A
Price/Book	2.31		
Price/Sales	0.23		

Business Summary: Retail - Automotive (MIC: 2.1.4 SIC: 5511 NAIC: 441110)

Penske Automotive Group is a holding company. Through its subsidiaries, Co. is engaged in the sale of new and used motor vehicles and related products and services, including vehicle service, collision repair, and placement of finance and lease contracts, third-party insurance products and other aftermarket products. Co. has two segments: retail, consisting of its automotive retail operations; and PAG Investments, consisting of its investments in non-automotive retail operations. At Dec 31 2011, Co. operated 320 retail automotive franchises, of which 166 franchises are in the U.S. and 154 franchises are outside of the U.S. The franchises outside the U.S. are located primarily in the U.K.

Recent Developments: For the year ended Dec 31 2012, income from continuing operations increased 10.5% to US$194.7 million from US$176.2 million a year earlier. Net income increased 5.0% to US$187.2 million from US$178.3 million in the prior year. Revenues were US$13.16 billion, up 18.3% from US$11.13 billion the year before. Operating income was US$364.9 million versus US$295.6 million in the prior year, an increase of 23.4%. Direct operating expenses rose 19.1% to US$11.15 billion from US$9.37 billion in the comparable period the year before. Indirect operating expenses increased 12.4% to US$1.65 billion from US$1.47 billion in the equivalent prior-year period.

Prospects: Our evaluation of Penske Automotive Group Inc. as of Apr. 7, 2013 is the result of our systematic analysis on three basic characteristics: earnings strength, relative valuation, and recent stock price movement. The company has managed to produce a neutral trend in earnings per share over the past 5 quarters and while recent estimates for the company have been raised by analysts, PAG has posted better than expected results. Based on operating earnings yield, the company is undervalued when compared to all of the companies in our coverage universe. Share price changes over the past year indicates that PAG will perform well over the near term.

Financial Data
(US$ in Thousands)

	12/31/2012	12/31/2011	12/31/2010	12/31/2009	12/31/2008	12/31/2007	12/31/2006	12/31/2005
Earnings Per Share	2.05	1.94	1.18	0.83	(4.42)	1.35	1.32	1.26
Cash Flow Per Share	3.62	1.35	2.17	3.31	4.36	3.30	1.29	2.08
Tang Book Value Per Share	0.51	N.M.	0.25	N.M.	N.M.	N.M.	N.M.	N.M.
Dividends Per Share	0.460	0.240	...	...	0.360	0.300	0.270	0.225
Dividend Payout %	22.44	12.37	...	...	...	22.22	20.45	17.79
Income Statement								
Total Revenue	13,163,517	11,556,232	10,713,585	9,523,105	11,646,345	12,957,739	11,242,313	10,190,284
EBITDA	401,100	347,093	291,368	286,803	(345,838)	374,947	348,017	335,296
Depn & Amortn	53,995	48,903	48,884	67,277	53,822	50,957	44,863	42,599
Income Before Taxes	261,416	222,937	149,599	115,620	(519,025)	192,996	192,416	192,235
Income Taxes	94,330	71,933	57,912	45,386	(100,020)	67,310	67,845	69,760
Net Income	185,540	176,881	108,281	76,461	(411,901)	127,739	124,701	118,973
Average Shares	90,342	91,274	92,091	91,653	93,210	94,558	94,178	93,932
Balance Sheet								
Current Assets	2,773,083	2,192,600	2,008,443	1,743,464	2,006,510	2,301,609	2,286,689	1,879,645
Total Assets	5,378,990	4,502,299	4,069,832	3,796,007	3,963,161	4,668,553	4,469,802	3,594,173
Current Liabilities	2,693,556	2,149,672	1,958,792	1,629,817	1,880,112	2,096,039	1,752,957	1,664,750
Long-Term Obligations	918,024	846,777	769,285	933,966	1,087,932	830,106	1,168,666	576,690
Total Liabilities	4,074,775	3,366,314	3,028,282	2,853,546	3,179,435	3,247,094	3,174,149	2,448,441
Stockholders' Equity	1,304,215	1,135,985	1,041,550	942,461	783,726	1,421,459	1,295,653	1,145,732
Shares Outstanding	90,294	90,277	92,099	91,617	91,430	95,020	89,162	92,966
Statistical Record								
Return on Assets %	3.75	4.13	2.75	1.97	N.M.	2.80	3.09	3.34
Return on Equity %	15.17	16.25	10.92	8.86	N.M.	9.40	10.22	10.71
EBITDA Margin %	3.05	3.00	2.72	3.01	N.M.	2.89	3.10	3.29
Net Margin %	1.41	1.53	1.01	0.80	N.M.	0.99	1.11	1.17
Asset Turnover	2.66	2.70	2.72	2.45	2.69	2.84	2.79	2.86
Current Ratio	1.03	1.02	1.03	1.07	1.07	1.10	1.30	1.13
Debt to Equity	0.70	0.75	0.74	0.99	1.39	0.58	0.90	0.50
Price Range	32.11-18.58	23.96-15.06	17.42-10.94	21.20-4.84	21.94-5.12	24.42-17.46	24.21-18.95	19.73-12.87
P/E Ratio	15.66-9.06	12.35-7.76	14.76-9.27	25.54-5.83	...	18.09-12.93	18.34-14.36	15.66-10.21
Average Yield %	1.77	1.23	...	...	2.51	1.42	1.25	1.41

Address: 2555 Telegraph Road, Bloomfield Hills, MI 48302-0954 **Telephone:** 248-648-2500 **Fax:** 248-648-2525	**Web Site:** www.penskeautomotive.com **Officers:** Roger S. Penske - Chairman, Chief Executive Officer Robert H. Kurnick - President	**Auditors:** Deloitte & Touche LLP **Investor Contact:** 248-648-2540 **Transfer Agents:** ComputerShare Investor Services, Providence, RI

PFIZER INC

Exchange	Symbol	Price	52Wk Range	Yield	P/E
NYS	PFE	$28.86 (3/28/2013)	28.86-21.60	3.33	14.88

*7 Year Price Score 104.72 *NYSE Composite Index=100 *12 Month Price Score 103.49

Interim Earnings (Per Share)

Qtr.	Mar	Jun	Sep	Dec
2008	0.41	0.41	0.34	0.04
2009	0.40	0.34	0.43	0.07
2010	0.25	0.31	0.11	0.36
2011	0.28	0.33	0.48	0.19
2012	0.24	0.43	0.43	0.85

Interim Dividends (Per Share)

Amt	Decl	Ex	Rec	Pay
0.22Q	04/26/2012	05/09/2012	05/11/2012	06/05/2012
0.22Q	06/28/2012	08/01/2012	08/03/2012	09/05/2012
0.22Q	10/25/2012	11/07/2012	11/09/2012	12/04/2012
0.24Q	12/17/2012	01/30/2013	02/01/2013	03/05/2013

Indicated Div: $0.96 (Div. Reinv. Plan)

Valuation Analysis / **Institutional Holding**

Forecast EPS	$2.28 (04/05/2013)	No of Institutions 2083
Market Cap	$210.0 Billion	Shares
Book Value	$81.3 Billion	5,737,206,272
Price/Book	2.58	% Held
Price/Sales	3.56	68.78

Business Summary: Pharmaceuticals (MIC: 4.1.1 SIC: 2834 NAIC: 325412)

Pfizer is a research-based biopharmaceutical company. Co.'s Primary Care segment includes products prescribed by primary-care physicians. Co.'s Specialty Care and Oncology segment includes products prescribed by physicians who are specialists. Co.'s Established Products and Emerging Markets segment includes products that have lost patent protection or marketing rights and those sold in emerging markets. Co.'s Animal Health segment includes products and services to address disease in livestock and companion animals. Co.'s Consumer Healthcare segment includes non-prescription products in several therapeutic categories.

Recent Developments: For the year ended Dec 31 2012, income from continuing operations increased 13.4% to US$9.52 billion from US$8.40 billion a year earlier. Net income increased 45.3% to US$14.60 billion from US$10.05 billion in the prior year. Revenues were US$58.99 billion, down 9.6% from US$65.26 billion the year before. Direct operating expenses declined 19.5% to US$11.33 billion from US$14.08 billion in the comparable period the year before. Indirect operating expenses decreased 8.5% to US$35.57 billion from US$38.88 billion in the equivalent prior-year period.

Prospects: Our evaluation of Pfizer Inc. as of Apr. 7, 2013 is the result of our systematic analysis on three basic characteristics: earnings strength, relative valuation, and recent stock price movement. The company has enjoyed a very positive trend in earnings per share over the past 5 quarters and while recent estimates for the company have been mixed, PFE has posted better than expected results. Based on operating earnings yield, the company is undervalued when compared to all of the companies in our coverage universe. Share price changes over the past year indicates that PFE will perform in line with the market over the near term.

Financial Data

(US$ in Thousands)	12/31/2012	12/31/2011	12/31/2010	12/31/2009	12/31/2008	12/31/2007	12/31/2006	12/31/2005
Earnings Per Share	1.94	1.27	1.02	1.23	1.20	1.17	2.66	1.09
Cash Flow Per Share	2.29	2.59	1.43	2.37	2.70	1.93	2.43	2.00
Tang Book Value Per Share	N.M.	N.M.	N.M.	N.M.	2.71	3.41	3.65	1.89
Dividends Per Share	0.880	0.800	0.720	0.800	1.280	1.160	0.960	0.760
Dividend Payout %	45.36	62.99	70.59	65.04	106.67	99.15	36.09	69.72
Income Statement								
Total Revenue	58,986,000	67,425,000	67,809,000	50,009,000	48,296,000	48,418,000	48,371,000	51,298,000
EBITDA	18,396,000	19,570,000	16,223,000	13,709,000	11,590,000	11,307,000	15,852,000	14,674,000
Depn & Amortn	5,175,000	5,585,000	5,404,000	2,877,000	2,668,000	3,128,000	3,261,000	3,409,000
Income Before Taxes	12,080,000	12,762,000	9,422,000	10,345,000	9,694,000	9,278,000	13,028,000	11,534,000
Income Taxes	2,562,000	4,023,000	1,124,000	2,197,000	1,645,000	1,023,000	1,992,000	3,424,000
Net Income	14,570,000	10,009,000	8,257,000	8,635,000	8,104,000	8,144,000	19,337,000	8,085,000
Average Shares	7,508,001	7,870,001	8,074,001	7,045,001	6,750,001	6,939,001	7,274,001	7,411,001
Balance Sheet								
Current Assets	61,415,000	57,728,000	60,468,000	61,670,000	43,076,000	46,849,000	46,949,000	41,896,000
Total Assets	185,798,000	188,002,000	195,014,000	212,949,000	111,148,000	115,268,000	114,837,000	117,565,000
Current Liabilities	28,619,000	28,069,000	28,609,000	37,225,000	27,009,000	21,835,000	21,389,000	28,448,000
Long-Term Obligations	31,036,000	34,931,000	38,410,000	43,193,000	7,963,000	7,314,000	5,546,000	6,347,000
Total Liabilities	104,538,000	105,812,000	107,201,000	122,935,000	53,592,000	50,258,000	43,479,000	51,938,000
Stockholders' Equity	81,260,000	82,190,000	87,813,000	90,014,000	57,556,000	65,010,000	71,358,000	65,627,000
Shares Outstanding	7,276,001	7,575,001	8,012,001	8,070,001	6,746,001	6,761,001	7,124,001	7,361,001
Statistical Record								
Return on Assets %	7.77	5.23	4.05	5.33	7.14	7.08	16.64	6.70
Return on Equity %	17.78	11.78	9.29	11.70	13.19	11.94	28.23	12.08
EBITDA Margin %	31.19	29.02	23.92	27.41	24.00	23.35	32.77	28.61
Net Margin %	24.70	14.84	12.18	17.27	16.78	16.82	39.98	15.76
Asset Turnover	0.31	0.35	0.33	0.31	0.43	0.42	0.42	0.43
Current Ratio	2.15	2.06	2.11	1.66	1.59	2.15	2.20	1.47
Debt to Equity	0.38	0.43	0.44	0.48	0.14	0.11	0.08	0.10
Price Range	26.04-20.95	21.83-16.66	20.00-14.14	18.85-11.66	24.08-14.45	27.68-22.30	28.47-22.41	28.90-20.60
P/E Ratio	13.42-10.80	17.19-13.12	19.61-13.86	15.33-9.48	20.07-12.04	23.66-19.06	10.70-8.42	26.51-18.90
Average Yield %	3.79	4.10	4.29	5.08	6.62	4.59	3.74	2.97

Address: 235 East 42nd Street, New York, NY 10017 **Telephone:** 212-733-2323 **Fax:** 212-573-2641	**Web Site:** www.pfizer.com **Officers:** Ian C. Read - Chairman, President, Chief Executive Officer Frank A. D'Amelio - Executive Vice President, Chief Financial Officer, Senior Vice President	**Auditors:** KPMG LLP **Transfer Agents:** Computershare Trust Company, N.A., Canton, MA

PG&E CORP. (HOLDING CO.)

Exchange	Symbol	Price	52Wk Range	Yield	P/E
NYS	PCG	$44.53 (3/28/2013)	46.51-39.71	4.09	23.19

*7 Year Price Score 89.75 *NYSE Composite Index=100 *12 Month Price Score 91.94

Interim Earnings (Per Share)

Qtr.	Mar	Jun	Sep	Dec
2008	0.62	0.80	0.83	1.39
2009	0.65	1.02	0.83	0.71
2010	0.67	0.86	0.66	0.63
2011	0.50	0.91	0.50	0.20
2012	0.56	0.55	0.84	(0.04)

Interim Dividends (Per Share)

Amt	Decl	Ex	Rec	Pay
0.455Q	06/20/2012	06/28/2012	07/02/2012	07/15/2012
0.455Q	09/18/2012	09/27/2012	10/01/2012	10/15/2012
0.455Q	12/19/2012	12/27/2012	12/31/2012	01/15/2013
0.455Q	02/20/2013	03/26/2013	03/28/2013	04/15/2013

Indicated Div: $1.82

Valuation Analysis / **Institutional Holding**

Forecast EPS	$2.65	No of Institutions
	(04/06/2013)	594
Market Cap	$19.2 Billion	Shares
Book Value	$13.1 Billion	339,783,776
Price/Book	1.47	% Held
Price/Sales	1.28	78.20

Business Summary: Electric Utilities (MIC: 3.1.1 SIC: 4931 NAIC: 221122)

PG&E is a holding company. Through its subsidiary, Pacific Gas and Electric Company (Utility), Co. engages in electricity and natural gas distribution operations, electricity generation, and natural gas transportation and storage services. The Utility owns generation facilities located in California, and owns and operates natural gas transportation, storage, and distribution system in northern and central California. The Utility served approximately 5.2 million electricity distribution customers and about 4.4 million natural gas distribution customers at Dec 31 2012. The Utility is regulated by the California Public Utilities Commission and the Federal Energy Regulatory Commission.

Recent Developments: For the year ended Dec 31 2012, net income decreased 3.3% to US$830.0 million in the prior year. Revenues were US$15.04 billion, up 0.6% from US$14.96 billion the year before. Operating income was US$1.69 billion versus US$1.94 billion in the prior year, a decrease of 12.8%. Direct operating expenses rose 2.6% to US$11.08 billion from US$10.80 billion in the comparable period the year before. Indirect operating expenses increased 2.6% to US$2.27 billion from US$2.22 billion in the equivalent prior-year period.

Prospects: Our evaluation of PG&E Corp. as of Apr. 7, 2013 is the result of our systematic analysis on three basic characteristics: earnings strength, relative valuation, and recent stock price movement. The company has managed to produce a neutral trend in earnings per share over the past 5 quarters. However, while recent estimates for the company have been lowered by analysts, PCG has posted better than expected results. Based on operating earnings yield, the company is undervalued when compared to all of the companies in our coverage universe. Share price changes over the past year indicates that PCG will perform very poorly over the near term.

Financial Data

(US$ in Thousands)	12/31/2012	12/31/2011	12/31/2010	12/31/2009	12/31/2008	12/31/2007	12/31/2006	12/31/2005
Earnings Per Share	1.92	2.10	2.82	3.20	3.63	2.78	2.76	2.37
Cash Flow Per Share	11.48	9.32	8.39	8.26	7.68	7.25	7.84	6.48
Tang Book Value Per Share	30.35	29.35	28.55	27.83	26.57	23.19	21.55	20.28
Dividends Per Share	1.820	1.820	1.820	1.680	1.560	1.440	1.320	1.230
Dividend Payout %	94.79	86.67	64.54	52.50	42.98	51.80	47.83	51.90
Income Statement								
Total Revenue	15,040,000	14,956,000	13,841,000	13,399,000	14,628,000	13,237,000	12,539,000	11,703,000
EBITDA	4,035,000	4,206,000	4,486,000	4,313,000	4,106,000	4,038,000	3,851,000	3,649,000
Depn & Amortn	2,272,000	2,215,000	2,151,000	1,947,000	1,863,000	1,895,000	1,756,000	1,698,000
Income Before Taxes	1,067,000	1,298,000	1,660,000	1,694,000	1,609,000	1,545,000	1,545,000	1,448,000
Income Taxes	237,000	440,000	547,000	460,000	425,000	539,000	554,000	544,000
Net Income	830,000	858,000	1,113,000	1,234,000	1,338,000	1,006,000	991,000	917,000
Average Shares	425,000	402,000	392,000	386,000	358,000	353,000	349,000	378,000
Balance Sheet								
Current Assets	5,121,000	6,480,000	5,542,000	5,657,000	6,403,000	5,511,000	5,867,000	5,980,000
Total Assets	52,449,000	49,750,000	46,025,000	42,945,000	40,860,000	36,648,000	34,803,000	34,074,000
Current Liabilities	6,256,000	7,749,000	7,185,000	6,813,000	7,626,000	6,723,000	8,250,000	6,932,000
Long-Term Obligations	12,517,000	11,766,000	11,329,000	11,208,000	10,534,000	9,753,000	8,633,000	9,542,000
Total Liabilities	39,375,000	37,649,000	34,743,000	32,612,000	31,231,000	27,843,000	26,740,000	26,604,000
Stockholders' Equity	13,074,000	12,101,000	11,282,000	10,333,000	9,629,000	8,805,000	8,063,000	7,470,000
Shares Outstanding	430,718	412,257	395,227	371,272	362,346	379,646	374,181	368,268
Statistical Record								
Return on Assets %	1.62	1.79	2.50	2.94	3.44	2.82	2.88	2.67
Return on Equity %	6.58	7.34	10.30	12.36	14.48	11.93	12.76	11.19
EBITDA Margin %	26.83	28.12	32.41	32.19	28.07	30.51	30.71	31.18
Net Margin %	5.52	5.74	8.04	9.21	9.15	7.60	7.90	7.84
Asset Turnover	0.29	0.31	0.31	0.32	0.38	0.37	0.36	0.34
Current Ratio	0.82	0.84	0.77	0.83	0.84	0.82	0.71	0.86
Debt to Equity	0.96	0.97	1.00	1.08	1.08	1.11	1.07	1.28
Price Range	46.51-39.71	47.84-36.86	48.58-40.00	45.60-34.82	44.95-29.70	52.11-42.81	47.98-36.35	39.90-31.92
P/E Ratio	24.22-20.68	22.78-17.55	17.23-14.18	14.25-10.88	12.38-8.18	18.74-15.40	17.38-13.17	16.84-13.47
Average Yield %	4.23	4.23	4.09	4.26	4.02	3.07	3.23	3.40

Address: 77 Beale Street, P.O. Box 770000, San Francisco, CA 94177	Web Site: www.pgecorp.com	Auditors: Deloitte & Touche LLP
Telephone: 415-267-7000	Officers: Anthony F. Earley - Chairman, President, Chief Executive Officer, holding/Parent Company Officer Edward D. Halpin - Senior Vice President, Chief Nuclear Officer	Investor Contact: 415-972-7080
Fax: 415-267-7265		Transfer Agents: BNY Mellon Shareowner Services, Pittsburgh, PA

PHILIP MORRIS INTERNATIONAL INC

Exchange	Symbol	Price	52Wk Range	Yield	P/E
NYS	PM	$92.71 (3/28/2013)	93.74-81.91	3.67	17.93

*7 Year Price Score N/A   *NYSE Composite Index=100   *12 Month Price Score 94.56

Interim Earnings (Per Share)

Qtr.	Mar	Jun	Sep	Dec
2008	0.89	0.80	1.01	0.63
2009	0.74	0.79	0.93	0.80
2010	0.90	1.07	0.99	0.96
2011	1.06	1.35	1.35	1.09
2012	1.25	1.36	1.32	1.25

Interim Dividends (Per Share)

Amt	Decl	Ex	Rec	Pay
0.77Q	06/13/2012	06/25/2012	06/27/2012	07/12/2012
0.85Q	09/12/2012	09/25/2012	09/27/2012	10/11/2012
0.85Q	12/12/2012	12/24/2012	12/27/2012	01/11/2013
0.85Q	03/13/2013	03/26/2013	03/28/2013	04/12/2013

Indicated Div: $3.40

Valuation Analysis   **Institutional Holding**

Forecast EPS	$5.75 (04/06/2013)	No of Institutions 1558
Market Cap	$153.3 Billion	Shares
Book Value	N/A	1,199,731,456
Price/Book	N/A	% Held
Price/Sales	1.98	N/A

TRADING VOLUME (thousand shares)

Business Summary: Tobacco Products (MIC: 1.3.1 SIC: 2111 NAIC: 312221)

Philip Morris International is a holding company. Through its subsidiaries and affiliates, Co. is engaged in the manufacture and sale of cigarettes and other tobacco products in markets outside of the U.S. Co.'s portfolio of international and local brands include Marlboro, Merit, Parliament, Virginia Slims, L&M, Chesterfield, Bond Street, Lark, Muratti, Next, Philip Morris and Red & White. Co. also owns a number of local cigarette brands, such as Sampoerna, Dji Sam Soe and U Mild in Indonesia, Fortune, Champion and Hope in the Philippines, Diana in Italy, Optima and Apollo-Soyuz in Russia, Morven Gold in Pakistan, Boston in Colombia, Belmont, Canadian Classics and Number 7 in Canada.

Recent Developments: For the year ended Dec 31 2012, net income increased 3.1% to US$9.15 billion from US$8.88 billion in the prior year. Revenues were US$77.39 billion, up 1.4% from US$76.35 billion the year before. Operating income was US$13.85 billion versus US$13.33 billion in the prior year, an increase of 3.9%. Direct operating expenses rose 0.8% to US$56.39 billion from US$55.93 billion in the comparable period the year before. Indirect operating expenses increased 1.0% to US$7.16 billion from US$7.09 billion in the equivalent prior-year period.

Prospects: Our evaluation of Philip Morris International Inc. as of Apr. 7, 2013 is the result of our systematic analysis on three basic characteristics: earnings strength, relative valuation, and recent stock price movement. The company has produced a positive trend in earnings per share over the past 5 quarters. However, while recent estimates for the company have been lowered by analysts, PM has posted better than expected results. Based on operating earnings yield, the company is undervalued when compared to all of the companies in our coverage universe. Share price changes over the past year indicates that PM will perform poorly over the near term.

Financial Data
(US$ in Thousands)

	12/31/2012	12/31/2011	12/31/2010	12/31/2009	12/31/2008	12/31/2007	12/31/2006	12/31/2005
Earnings Per Share	5.17	4.85	3.92	3.24	3.32	40.17	40.97	37.47
Cash Flow Per Share	5.55	5.98	5.13	4.06	3.83	...	...	...
Tang Book Value Per Share	...	N.M.	N.M.	N.M.	N.M.	37.13	...	...
Dividends Per Share	3.240	2.820	2.440	2.240	1.540	43.830	18.530	51.210
Dividend Payout %	62.67	58.14	62.24	69.14	46.39	109.11	45.23	136.67
Income Statement								
Total Revenue	77,393,000	76,346,000	67,713,000	62,080,000	63,640,000	55,096,000	48,260,000	45,288,000
EBITDA	14,744,000	14,325,000	12,132,000	10,893,000	11,090,000	9,621,000	9,026,000	8,262,000
Depn & Amortn	898,000	993,000	932,000	853,000	842,000	748,000	658,000	527,000
Income Before Taxes	12,987,000	12,532,000	10,324,000	9,243,000	9,937,000	8,863,000	8,226,000	7,641,000
Income Taxes	3,833,000	3,653,000	2,826,000	2,691,000	2,787,000	2,564,000	1,829,000	1,835,000
Net Income	8,800,000	8,591,000	7,259,000	6,342,000	6,890,000	6,026,000	6,146,000	5,620,000
Average Shares	1,692,000	1,762,000	1,842,000	1,950,000	2,078,000	...	...	...
Balance Sheet								
Current Assets	16,590,000	14,859,000	13,756,000	14,682,000	14,939,000	15,052,000	11,925,000	...
Total Assets	37,670,000	35,488,000	35,050,000	34,552,000	32,972,000	32,043,000	26,120,000	...
Current Liabilities	17,016,000	14,794,000	12,804,000	11,178,000	10,144,000	8,551,000	6,989,000	...
Long-Term Obligations	17,639,000	14,828,000	13,370,000	13,672,000	11,377,000	5,578,000	2,222,000	...
Total Liabilities	41,146,000	35,259,000	31,544,000	28,836,000	25,472,000	16,642,000	11,853,000	...
Stockholders' Equity	(3,476,000)	229,000	3,506,000	5,716,000	7,500,000	15,401,000	14,267,000	...
Shares Outstanding	1,653,612	1,725,908	1,801,783	1,887,164	2,007,263	150,000	...	...
Statistical Record								
Return on Assets %	23.99	24.36	20.86	18.78	21.14	20.72	...	...
Return on Equity %	...	460.03	157.43	95.97	60.01	40.62	...	...
EBITDA Margin %	19.05	18.76	17.92	17.55	17.43	17.46	18.70	18.24
Net Margin %	11.37	11.25	10.72	10.22	10.83	10.94	12.74	12.41
Asset Turnover	2.11	2.16	1.95	1.84	1.95	1.89	...	...
Current Ratio	0.97	1.00	1.07	1.31	1.47	1.76	1.71	...
Debt to Equity	...	64.75	3.81	2.39	1.52	0.36	0.16	...
Price Range	93.74-73.26	79.10-56.02	60.82-43.17	51.55-32.34	55.95-36.63	...	...	...
P/E Ratio	18.13-14.17	16.31-11.55	15.52-11.01	15.91-9.98	16.85-11.03	...	...	...
Average Yield %	3.73	4.21	4.70	5.14	3.16	...	...	...

Address: 120 Park Avenue, New York, NY 10017	Web Site: www.pmi.com	Auditors: PricewaterhouseCoopers SA
Telephone: 917-663-2000	Officers: Louis C. Camilleri - Chairman, Chief Executive Officer Charles R. Wall - Vice-Chairman	Investor Contact: 191-766-32233
Fax: 917-663-5372		Transfer Agents: ComputerShare LLC, Providence, RI

PHILLIPS 66

Exchange	Symbol	Price	52Wk Range	Yield	P/E
NYS	PSX	$69.97 (3/28/2013)	69.97-29.35	1.45	10.80

*7 Year Price Score N/A   *NYSE Composite Index=100   *12 Month Price Score N/A

Interim Earnings (Per Share)

Qtr.	Mar	Jun	Sep	Dec
2012	...	1.86	2.51	1.11

Interim Dividends (Per Share)

Amt	Decl	Ex	Rec	Pay
0.20Q	07/11/2012	07/19/2012	07/23/2012	09/04/2012
0.25Q	10/03/2012	10/11/2012	10/15/2012	12/03/2012
0.313Q	02/11/2013	02/19/2013	02/21/2013	03/01/2013

Indicated Div: $1.02

Valuation Analysis | **Institutional Holding**

Forecast EPS	$7.68	No of Institutions
	(04/06/2013)	1007
Market Cap	$43.6 Billion	Shares
Book Value	$20.8 Billion	431,909,696
Price/Book	2.10	% Held
Price/Sales	0.24	N/A

TRADING VOLUME (thousand shares)

Business Summary: Refining & Marketing (MIC: 9.1.2 SIC: 2911 NAIC: 324110)

Phillips is a holding company. Through its subsidiaries, Co. is a petroleum refiner with a domestic net crude oil processing capacity of 1.8 million barrels per day, and a global net crude oil processing capacity of 2.2 million barrels per day. The Refining and Marketing segment purchases, refines, markets and transports crude oil and petroleum products, in the U.S., Europe and Asia, and also engages in power generation activities. The Midstream segment gathers, processes, transports and markets natural gas, and fractionates and markets natural gas liquids, predominantly in the U.S. The Chemicals segment manufactures and markets petrochemicals and plastics on a worldwide basis.

Recent Developments: For the year ended Dec 31 2012, net income decreased 13.6% to US$4.13 billion from US$4.78 billion in the prior year. Revenues were US$182.92 billion, down 8.8% from US$200.61 billion the year before. Direct operating expenses declined 10.4% to US$158.52 billion from US$176.91 billion in the comparable period the year before. Indirect operating expenses increased 4.1% to US$17.78 billion from US$17.08 billion in the equivalent prior-year period.

Prospects: Our evaluation of Phillips 66 Inc. as of Apr. 7, 2013 is the result of our systematic analysis on three basic characteristics: earnings strength, relative valuation, and recent stock price movement. The company has generated a negative trend in earnings per share over the past 5 quarters. However, while recent estimates for the company have been mixed, PSX has posted better than expected results. Based on operating earnings yield, the company is undervalued when compared to all of the companies in our coverage universe. Share price changes over the past year indicates that PSX will perform very poorly over the near term.

Financial Data

(US$ in Millions)	12/31/2012	12/31/2011	12/31/2010	12/31/2009
Earnings Per Share	6.48	...	...	...
Cash Flow Per Share	6.81	...	...	...
Tang Book Value Per Share	26.79	...	...	...
Dividends Per Share	0.450	...	...	...
Dividend Payout %	6.94	...	...	...
Income Statement				
Total Revenue	182,922	200,614	148,656	113,951
EBITDA	7,790	7,549	2,200	1,727
Depn & Amortn	913	908	880	879
Income Before Taxes	6,631	6,624	1,319	847
Income Taxes	2,500	1,844	579	368
Net Income	4,124	4,775	735	476
Average Shares	636	...	...	...
Balance Sheet				
Current Assets	17,962	13,948	14,704	...
Total Assets	48,073	43,211	44,955	...
Current Liabilities	12,482	12,384	12,503	...
Long-Term Obligations	6,961	361	388	...
Total Liabilities	27,298	19,947	18,954	...
Stockholders' Equity	20,775	23,264	26,001	...
Shares Outstanding	623	...	...	...
Statistical Record				
Return on Assets %	9.01	10.83	...	...
Return on Equity %	18.68	19.38	...	...
EBITDA Margin %	4.26	3.76	1.48	1.52
Net Margin %	2.25	2.38	0.49	0.42
Asset Turnover	4.00	4.55	...	...
Current Ratio	1.44	1.13	1.18	...
Debt to Equity	0.34	0.02	0.01	...
Price Range	53.58-29.35	...	...	...
P/E Ratio	8.27-4.53	...	...	...
Average Yield %	1.09	...	...	...

Address: 3010 Briarpark Drive, Houston, TX 77042
Telephone: 281-293-6600

Web Site: www.Phillips66.com
Officers: Greg C. Garland - Chairman, Chief Executive Officer Greg G. Maxwell - Executive Vice President, Chief Financial Officer

Auditors: Ernst & Young LLP
Investor Contact: 800-624-6440
Transfer Agents: Computershare Shareowner Services LLC

PIEDMONT NATURAL GAS CO., INC.

Exchange	Symbol	Price	52Wk Range	Yield	P/E	Div Achiever
NYS	PNY	$32.88 (3/28/2013)	33.57-28.77	3.77	18.37	33 Years

*7 Year Price Score 100.36 *NYSE Composite Index=100 *12 Month Price Score 95.47

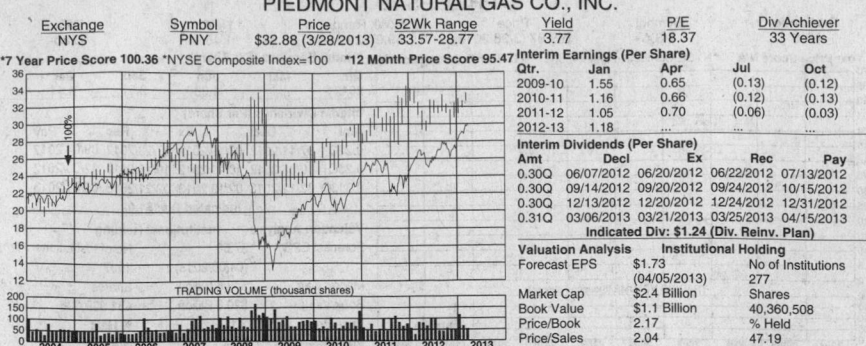

Interim Earnings (Per Share)

Qtr.	Jan	Apr	Jul	Oct
2009-10	1.55	0.65	(0.13)	(0.12)
2010-11	1.16	0.66	(0.12)	(0.13)
2011-12	1.05	0.70	(0.06)	(0.03)
2012-13	1.18	...	...	...

Interim Dividends (Per Share)

Amt	Decl	Ex	Rec	Pay
0.30Q	06/07/2012	06/20/2012	06/22/2012	07/13/2012
0.30Q	09/14/2012	09/20/2012	09/24/2012	10/15/2012
0.30Q	12/13/2012	12/20/2012	12/24/2012	12/31/2012
0.31Q	03/06/2013	03/21/2013	03/25/2013	04/15/2013

Indicated Div: $1.24 (Div. Reinv. Plan)

Valuation Analysis | **Institutional Holding**

Forecast EPS	$1.73 (04/05/2013)	No of Institutions	277
Market Cap	$2.4 Billion	Shares	40,360,508
Book Value	$1.1 Billion	% Held	47.19
Price/Book	2.17		
Price/Sales	2.04		

Business Summary: Gas Utilities (MIC: 3.3.1 SIC: 4924 NAIC: 221210)

Piedmont Natural Gas Company distributes natural gas to residential, commercial, industrial and power generation customers in portions of North Carolina, South Carolina and Tennessee. Co. has two reportable business segments: regulated utility, which is the gas distribution business that includes the operations of merchandising and related service work and home warranty programs, with activities conducted by Co.; and non-utility activities, consisting of Co.'s equity method investments in joint venture, energy-related businesses that are involved in unregulated retail natural gas marketing, and regulated interstate natural gas storage and intrastate natural gas transportation.

Recent Developments: For the quarter ended Jan 31 2013, net income increased 12.7% to US$85.9 million from US$76.2 million in the year-earlier quarter. Revenues were US$515.9 million, up 9.3% from US$471.8 million the year before. Operating income was US$86.2 million versus US$79.8 million in the prior-year quarter, an increase of 8.0%. Direct operating expenses rose 13.0% to US$284.3 million from US$251.6 million in the comparable period the year before. Indirect operating expenses increased 3.6% to US$145.4 million from US$140.4 million in the equivalent prior-year period.

Prospects: Our evaluation of Piedmont Natural Gas Co. Inc. as of Apr. 7, 2013 is the result of our systematic analysis on three basic characteristics: earnings strength, relative valuation, and recent stock price movement. The company has managed to produce a neutral trend in earnings per share over the past 5 quarters. However, while recent estimates for the company have been mixed, PNY has posted better than expected results. Based on operating earnings yield, the company is about fairly valued when compared to all of the companies in our coverage universe. Share price changes over the past year indicates that PNY will perform in line with the market over the near term.

Financial Data

(US$ in Thousands)	3 Mos	10/31/2012	10/31/2011	10/31/2010	10/31/2009	10/31/2008	10/31/2007	10/31/2006
Earnings Per Share	1.79	1.66	1.57	1.96	1.67	1.49	1.40	1.28
Cash Flow Per Share	4.04	4.22	4.32	4.99	4.71	0.94	3.14	1.37
Tang Book Value Per Share	14.48	13.54	13.11	12.67	12.00	11.45	11.18	11.07
Dividends Per Share	1.200	1.190	1.150	1.110	1.070	1.030	0.990	0.950
Dividend Payout %	67.04	71.69	73.25	56.63	64.07	69.13	70.71	74.22
Income Statement								
Total Revenue	515,875	1,122,780	1,433,905	1,552,295	1,638,116	2,089,108	1,711,292	1,924,628
EBITDA	163,448	294,209	329,873	313,711	332,090	340,601	297,432	293,381
Depn & Amortn	26,634	103,192	102,829	98,494	97,425	93,121	88,654	89,696
Income Before Taxes	132,357	170,920	183,052	171,506	187,990	188,207	151,506	151,375
Income Taxes	55,973	78,217	72,286	91,876	81,882	73,492	65,626	62,430
Net Income	85,923	119,847	113,568	141,954	122,824	110,007	104,387	97,189
Average Shares	72,725	72,278	72,266	72,525	73,461	73,612	74,472	76,156
Balance Sheet								
Current Assets	455,693	305,642	286,021	327,840	513,148	600,752	435,344	475,964
Total Assets	4,048,834	3,769,939	3,242,541	3,053,275	3,118,819	3,093,580	2,820,318	2,733,939
Current Liabilities	886,550	592,551	534,132	498,560	600,211	681,533	424,511	400,389
Long-Term Obligations	875,000	975,000	675,000	671,922	732,512	794,261	824,887	825,000
Total Liabilities	2,950,024	2,742,935	2,245,618	2,088,334	2,190,871	2,206,336	1,941,944	1,851,014
Stockholders' Equity	1,098,810	1,027,004	996,923	964,941	927,948	887,244	878,374	882,925
Shares Outstanding	72,512	72,250	72,318	72,282	73,266	73,246	74,208	75,464
Statistical Record								
Return on Assets %	3.45	3.41	3.61	4.60	3.95	3.71	3.76	3.64
Return on Equity %	12.17	11.81	11.58	15.00	13.53	12.43	11.85	11.00
EBITDA Margin %	31.68	26.20	23.01	20.21	20.27	16.30	17.38	15.24
Net Margin %	16.66	10.67	7.92	9.14	7.50	5.27	6.10	5.05
Asset Turnover	0.31	0.32	0.46	0.50	0.53	0.70	0.62	0.72
Current Ratio	0.51	0.52	0.54	0.66	0.85	0.88	1.03	1.19
Debt to Equity	0.80	0.95	0.68	0.70	0.79	0.90	0.94	0.93
Price Range	33.83-28.77	34.43-29.21	33.29-25.99	29.70-22.74	33.76-21.25	33.24-24.32	28.28-23.19	27.27-22.09
P/E Ratio	18.90-16.07	20.74-17.60	21.20-16.55	15.15-11.60	20.22-12.72	22.31-16.32	20.20-16.56	21.30-17.26
Average Yield %	3.82	3.74	3.88	4.18	4.15	3.81	3.78	3.86

Address: 4720 Piedmont Row Drive, Charlotte, NC 28210 Telephone: 704-364-3120	Web Site: www.piedmontng.com Officers: Thomas E. Skains - Chairman, President, Chief Executive Officer Victor M. Gaglio - Senior Vice President, Chief Utility Operations Officer	Auditors: Deloitte & Touche LLP Investor Contact: 704-731-4952 Transfer Agents: American Stock Transfer & Trust Company, Brooklyn, N

PIEDMONT OFFICE REALTY TRUST INC

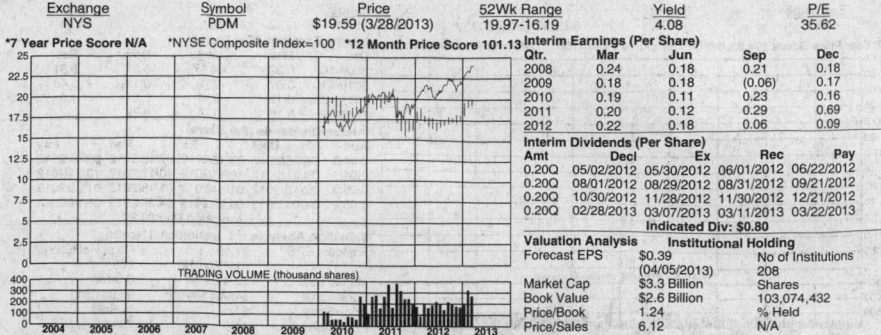

Exchange	Symbol	Price	52Wk Range	Yield	P/E
NYS	PDM	$19.59 (3/28/2013)	19.97-16.19	4.08	35.62

*7 Year Price Score N/A   *NYSE Composite Index=100   *12 Month Price Score 101.13

Interim Earnings (Per Share)

Qtr.	Mar	Jun	Sep	Dec
2008	0.24	0.18	0.21	0.18
2009	0.18	0.18	(0.06)	0.17
2010	0.19	0.11	0.23	0.16
2011	0.20	0.12	0.29	0.69
2012	0.22	0.18	0.06	0.09

Interim Dividends (Per Share)

Amt	Decl	Ex	Rec	Pay
0.20Q	05/02/2012	05/30/2012	06/01/2012	06/22/2012
0.20Q	08/01/2012	08/29/2012	08/31/2012	09/21/2012
0.20Q	10/30/2012	11/28/2012	11/30/2012	12/21/2012
0.20Q	02/28/2013	03/07/2013	03/11/2013	03/22/2013

Indicated Div: $0.80

Valuation Analysis / **Institutional Holding**

Forecast EPS	$0.39	No of Institutions
	(04/05/2013)	208
Market Cap	$3.3 Billion	Shares
Book Value	$2.6 Billion	103,074,432
Price/Book	1.24	% Held
Price/Sales	6.12	N/A

TRADING VOLUME (thousand shares)

Business Summary: REITs (MIC: 5.3.1 SIC: 6798 NAIC: 525930)

Piedmont Office Realty Trust is a real estate investment trust engaged in the acquisition and ownership of commercial real estate properties. Co. conducts business through Piedmont Operating Partnership, L.P. (Piedmont OP), a limited partnership, as well as performing the management of its buildings through two wholly-owned subsidiaries, Piedmont Government Services, LLC and Piedmont Office Management, LLC. As of Dec 31 2011, Co. owned interests in 79 office properties, plus five buildings owned through unconsolidated joint ventures and two industrial buildings.

Recent Developments: For the year ended Dec 31 2012, net income decreased 58.6% to US$93.2 million from US$225.1 million in the prior year. Revenues were US$536.4 million, up 0.5% from US$533.5 million the year before.

Prospects: Our evaluation of Piedmont Office Realty Trust Inc. as of Apr. 7, 2013 is the result of our systematic analysis on three basic characteristics: earnings strength, relative valuation, and recent stock price movement. The company has produced a positive trend in earnings per share over the past 5 quarters. Because the company lacks sufficient analyst estimate data, we place greater weight on the historical EPS trend as the measure of earnings strength. Based on operating earnings yield, the company is overvalued when compared to all of the companies in our coverage universe. Share price changes over the past year indicates that PDM will perform in line with the market over the near term.

Financial Data
(US$ in Thousands)

	12/31/2012	12/31/2011	12/31/2010	12/31/2009	12/31/2008	12/31/2007	12/31/2006
Earnings Per Share	0.55	1.30	0.70	0.47	0.81	0.84	0.87
Cash Flow Per Share	1.31	1.56	1.61	1.78	1.85	1.76	...
Tang Book Value Per Share	14.67	15.01	14.98	15.71	16.47	17.59	...
Dividends Per Share	0.800	1.260	1.260	1.260	1.760	1.760	1.760
Dividend Payout %	145.45	96.92	180.00	268.09	217.33	209.57	202.34
Income Statement							
Total Revenue	536,382	541,642	588,838	604,884	621,965	593,249	571,363
EBITDA	240,757	260,673	297,354	254,440	302,461	263,326	249,414
Depn & Amortn	113,649	109,730	104,490	106,073	99,745	95,081	95,296
Income Before Taxes	62,918	87,900	123,592	75,074	131,594	108,972	95,330
Net Income	93,204	225,041	120,379	74,700	131,314	133,610	133,324
Average Shares	170,441	172,980	170,967	158,580	159,722	160,755	153,897
Balance Sheet							
Current Assets	160,294	269,213	190,724	138,446	146,740	187,146	...
Total Assets	4,254,875	4,447,834	4,373,480	4,395,345	4,557,330	4,579,746	...
Current Liabilities	127,263	122,986	112,648	97,747	111,411	110,548	...
Long-Term Obligations	1,416,525	1,472,525	1,402,525	1,516,525	1,523,625	1,301,530	...
Total Liabilities	1,615,989	1,676,015	1,606,258	1,719,015	1,747,363	1,532,392	...
Stockholders' Equity	2,638,886	2,771,819	2,767,222	2,676,330	2,809,967	3,047,354	...
Shares Outstanding	167,556	172,629	172,658	158,916	159,633	162,991	155,293
Statistical Record							
Return on Assets %	2.14	5.10	2.75	1.67	2.87	...	...
Return on Equity %	3.44	8.13	4.42	2.72	4.47	...	...
EBITDA Margin %	44.89	48.13	50.50	42.06	48.63	44.39	43.65
Net Margin %	17.38	41.55	20.44	12.35	21.11	22.52	23.33
Asset Turnover	0.12	0.12	0.13	0.14	0.14	...	...
Current Ratio	1.26	2.19	1.69	1.42	1.32	1.69	...
Debt to Equity	0.54	0.53	0.51	0.57	0.54	0.43	...
Price Range	18.91-16.19	21.25-15.42	20.36-15.60	...	...	...	...
P/E Ratio	34.38-29.44	16.35-11.86	29.09-22.29	...	...	...	...
Average Yield %	4.60	6.70	6.73	...	...	...	...

Address: 11695 Johns Creek Parkway, Ste. 350, Johns Creek, GA 30097 Telephone: 770-418-8800	Web Site: www.piedmontreit.com Officers: W. Wayne Woody - Chairman Donald A. Miller - President, Chief Executive Officer	Auditors: Ernst & Young LLP Investor Contact: 866-354-3485 Transfer Agents: Computershare Inc.

PIER 1 IMPORTS INC.

Exchange	Symbol	Price	52Wk Range	Yield	P/E
NYS	PIR	$23.00 (3/28/2013)	23.39-15.21	0.87	14.11

*7 Year Price Score 194.03 *NYSE Composite Index=100 ***12 Month Price Score 108.84**

Interim Earnings (Per Share)

Qtr.	May	Aug	Nov	Feb
2009-10	0.32	(0.17)	0.37	0.31
2010-11	0.07	0.12	0.18	0.48
2011-12	0.12	0.14	0.21	1.01
2012-13	0.16	0.24	0.22	...

Interim Dividends (Per Share)

Amt	Decl	Ex	Rec	Pay
0.04Q	06/26/2012	07/16/2012	07/18/2012	08/01/2012
0.04Q	09/21/2012	10/15/2012	10/17/2012	10/31/2012
0.05Q	12/13/2012	01/14/2013	01/16/2013	01/30/2013
0.05Q	04/04/2013	04/22/2013	04/24/2013	05/08/2013
		Indicated Div: $0.20		

Valuation Analysis **Institutional Holding**

Forecast EPS	$1.19	No of Institutions
	(04/06/2013)	263
Market Cap	$2.4 Billion	Shares
Book Value	$484.4 Million	93,851,512
Price/Book	5.05	% Held
Price/Sales	1.50	79.96

Business Summary: Retail - Furniture & Home Furnishings (MIC: 2.1.6 SIC: 5719 NAIC: 442299)

Pier 1 Imports is an importer and retailer of decorative home furnishings and gifts. Co.'s decorative accessories merchandise group includes decorative accents, lamps, vases, dried and artificial flowers, baskets, ceramics, dinnerware, bath and fragrance products, and candles; while its furniture merchandise group includes furniture and furniture cushions, as well as decorations and mirrors. The retail operations of Co. consist of retail stores operating under the name Pier 1 Imports®. Also, Co. has merchandise primarily in store within a store locations in Mexico and El Salvador. As of Feb 25 2012, Co. operated 971 Pier 1 Imports stores in the U.S. and 81 Pier 1 Imports stores in Canada.

Recent Developments: For the quarter ended Nov 24 2012, net income increased 3.0% to US$23.7 million from US$23.0 million in the year-earlier quarter. Revenues were US$424.5 million, up 10.9% from US$382.7 million the year before. Operating income was US$38.8 million versus US$32.9 million in the prior-year quarter, an increase of 18.1%. Direct operating expenses rose 9.7% to US$238.3 million from US$217.2 million in the comparable period the year before. Indirect operating expenses increased 11.2% to US$147.4 million from US$132.6 million in the equivalent prior-year period.

Prospects: Our evaluation of Pier 1 Imports Inc. as of Apr. 7, 2013 is the result of our systematic analysis on three basic characteristics: earnings strength, relative valuation, and recent stock price movement. The company has managed to produce a neutral trend in earnings per share over the past 5 quarters. However, while recent estimates for the company have been lowered by analysts, PIR has posted better than expected results. Based on operating earnings yield, the company is about fairly valued when compared to all of the companies in our coverage universe. Share price changes over the past year indicates that PIR will perform well over the near term.

Financial Data

(US$ in Thousands)	9 Mos	6 Mos	3 Mos	02/25/2012	02/26/2011	02/27/2010	02/28/2009	03/01/2008
Earnings Per Share	1.63	1.62	1.52	1.48	0.85	0.86	(1.45)	(1.09)
Cash Flow Per Share	1.04	0.93	1.15	1.27	1.28	0.70	(0.36)	(0.95)
Tang Book Value Per Share	4.55	4.34	4.29	4.50	3.51	2.62	1.61	3.02
Dividends Per Share	0.120	0.080	0.040	...	...	...	...	...
Dividend Payout %	7.36	4.94	2.63					
Income Statement								
Total Revenue	1,153,260	728,734	361,119	1,533,611	1,396,470	1,290,852	1,320,677	1,511,832
EBITDA	92,351	54,266	22,761	176,000	127,145	76,584	(87,731)	(46,700)
Depn & Amortn	(6,198)	(5,461)	(4,652)	21,240	19,739	22,488	30,556	39,478
Income Before Taxes	101,347	62,891	28,027	164,107	103,544	32,051	(128,629)	(93,417)
Income Taxes	33,607	18,835	10,202	(4,831)	3,419	(54,796)	624	2,594
Net Income	67,740	44,056	17,825	168,938	100,125	86,847	(129,253)	(96,011)
Average Shares	107,308	107,447	110,564	114,390	117,484	100,715	88,912	88,083
Balance Sheet								
Current Assets	598,731	582,474	604,813	650,314	651,969	553,827	533,727	663,879
Total Assets	807,430	779,847	784,012	823,363	743,577	642,974	655,462	821,904
Current Liabilities	253,040	249,715	237,183	245,388	236,355	237,175	233,811	276,002
Long-Term Obligations	9,500	9,500	9,500	9,500	9,500	19,000	184,000	184,000
Total Liabilities	322,980	319,862	321,774	329,720	330,725	339,840	511,201	554,160
Stockholders' Equity	484,450	459,985	462,238	493,643	412,852	303,134	144,261	267,744
Shares Outstanding	106,371	105,988	107,741	109,720	117,484	115,587	89,874	88,607
Statistical Record								
Return on Assets %	24.07	24.63	22.37	21.62	14.48	13.41	N.M.	N.M.
Return on Equity %	42.39	44.20	38.67	37.38	28.05	38.93	N.M.	N.M.
EBITDA Margin %	8.01	7.45	6.30	11.48	9.10	5.93	N.M.	N.M.
Net Margin %	5.87	6.05	4.94	11.02	7.17	6.73	N.M.	N.M.
Asset Turnover	2.14	2.15	2.02	1.96	2.02	1.99	1.79	1.74
Current Ratio	2.37	2.33	2.55	2.65	2.76	2.34	2.28	2.41
Debt to Equity	0.02	0.02	0.02	0.02	0.02	0.06	1.28	0.69
Price Range	21.10-12.08	18.80-9.17	18.80-8.90	16.84-8.90	11.05-5.86	6.37-0.11	8.18-0.13	8.93-3.28
P/E Ratio	12.94-7.41	11.60-5.66	12.37-5.86	11.38-6.01	13.00-6.89	7.41-0.13	...	...
Average Yield %	0.70	0.54	0.30					

Address: 100 Pier 1 Place, Fort Worth, TX 76102	**Web Site:** www.pier1.com	**Auditors:** Ernst & Young LLP
Telephone: 817-252-8000	**Officers:** Alexander W. Smith - President, Chief Executive Officer Charles H. Turner - Executive Vice President, Chief Financial Officer	**Investor Contact:** 888-807-4371
Fax: 817-252-8174		**Transfer Agents:** Computershare, Jersey City, NJ

PINNACLE WEST CAPITAL CORP.

Exchange	Symbol	Price	52Wk Range	Yield	P/E
NYS	PNW	$57.89 (3/28/2013)	57.89-46.06	3.77	16.78

*7 Year Price Score 111.94 *NYSE Composite Index=100 ***12 Month Price Score 98.66**

Interim Earnings (Per Share)

Qtr.	Mar	Jun	Sep	Dec
2008	(0.04)	1.33	1.50	(0.38)
2009	(1.55)	0.68	1.84	(0.30)
2010	(0.06)	1.07	2.14	0.05
2011	(0.14)	0.79	2.32	0.11
2012	(0.08)	1.11	2.21	0.20

Interim Dividends (Per Share)

Amt	Decl	Ex	Rec	Pay
0.525Q	04/18/2012	04/27/2012	05/01/2012	06/01/2012
0.525Q	06/20/2012	07/30/2012	08/01/2012	09/04/2012
0.545Q	10/18/2012	10/31/2012	11/01/2012	12/03/2012
0.545Q	12/19/2012	01/30/2013	02/01/2013	03/01/2013

Indicated Div: $2.18 (Div. Reinv. Plan)

Valuation Analysis

		Institutional Holding	
Forecast EPS	$3.56	No of Institutions	
	(04/05/2013)	453	
Market Cap	$6.4 Billion	Shares	
Book Value	$4.0 Billion	86,892,808	
Price/Book	1.60	% Held	
Price/Sales	1.92	75.93	

TRADING VOLUME (thousand shares)

Business Summary: Electric Utilities (MIC: 3.1.1 SIC: 4911 NAIC: 221121)

Pinnacle West Capital is a holding company. Co.'s reportable business segment is its regulated electricity segment, which consists of regulated retail and wholesale electricity businesses and related activities, and includes electricity generation, transmission and distribution. Co.'s principal subsidiary, Arizona Public Service Company (APS) is an electric utility that provides either retail or wholesale electric service to most of the State of Arizona, with the major exceptions of about one-half of the Phoenix metropolitan area, the Tucson metropolitan area and Mohave County in northwestern Arizona. As of Dec 31 2011, APS provided electric service to approximately 1.1 million customers.

Recent Developments: For the year ended Dec 31 2012, income from continuing operations increased 17.8% to US$419.0 million from US$355.6 million a year earlier. Net income increased 12.6% to US$413.2 million from US$366.9 million in the prior year. Revenues were US$3.30 billion, up 1.9% from US$3.24 billion the year before. Operating income was US$851.8 million versus US$746.5 million in the prior year, an increase of 14.1%. Direct operating expenses declined 1.8% to US$1.88 billion from US$1.91 billion in the comparable period the year before. Indirect operating expenses decreased 1.8% to US$570.5 million from US$581.1 million in the equivalent prior-year period.

Prospects: Our evaluation of Pinnacle West Capital Corp. as of Apr. 7, 2013 is the result of our systematic analysis on three basic characteristics: earnings strength, relative valuation, and recent stock price movement. The company has generated a negative trend in earnings per share over the past 5 quarters. However, while recent estimates for the company have been mixed, PNW has posted better than expected results. Based on operating earnings yield, the company is undervalued when compared to all of the companies in our coverage universe. Share price changes over the past year indicates that PNW will perform in line with the market over the near term.

Financial Data
(US$ in Thousands)

	12/31/2012	12/31/2011	12/31/2010	12/31/2009	12/31/2008	12/31/2007	12/31/2006	12/31/2005
Earnings Per Share	3.45	3.09	3.27	0.67	2.40	3.05	3.27	1.82
Cash Flow Per Share	10.66	10.32	7.04	10.19	8.06	6.56	3.96	7.57
Tang Book Value Per Share	36.20	34.98	33.86	32.69	34.16	35.15	34.48	34.58
Dividends Per Share	2.120	2.100	2.100	2.100	2.100	2.100	2.025	1.925
Dividend Payout %	61.45	67.96	64.22	313.43	87.50	68.85	61.93	105.77
Income Statement								
Total Revenue	3,301,804	3,241,379	3,263,645	3,297,101	3,367,076	3,523,620	3,401,748	2,987,955
EBITDA	1,196,826	1,075,945	1,067,559	346,151	480,697	632,704	644,338	875,517
Depn & Amortn	364,546	338,627	350,326	35,000	33,000	37,000	39,000	381,000
Income Before Taxes	656,310	539,238	514,919	104,696	276,465	438,998	462,680	347,432
Income Taxes	237,317	183,604	164,321	37,827	65,407	150,920	156,418	126,892
Net Income	381,542	339,473	350,053	68,330	242,125	307,143	327,255	176,267
Average Shares	110,527	109,864	107,138	101,264	100,965	100,835	100,010	96,590
Balance Sheet								
Current Assets	1,005,726	956,470	931,930	928,737	882,482	947,447	1,474,662	1,891,392
Total Assets	13,379,615	13,111,018	12,362,703	11,808,155	11,620,093	11,243,712	11,455,943	11,322,645
Current Liabilities	1,083,542	1,342,705	1,310,736	1,083,160	1,505,928	1,384,967	1,458,560	2,272,073
Long-Term Obligations	3,199,088	3,019,054	3,045,794	3,370,524	3,031,603	3,127,125	3,232,633	2,608,455
Total Liabilities	9,406,809	9,289,168	8,679,376	8,492,046	8,174,114	7,712,101	8,009,827	7,897,681
Stockholders' Equity	3,972,806	3,821,850	3,683,327	3,316,109	3,445,979	3,531,611	3,446,116	3,424,964
Shares Outstanding	109,742	109,245	108,769	101,434	100,888	100,485	99,958	99,057
Statistical Record								
Return on Assets %	2.87	2.67	2.90	0.58	2.11	2.71	2.87	1.66
Return on Equity %	9.76	9.05	10.00	2.02	6.92	8.80	9.53	5.53
EBITDA Margin %	36.25	33.19	32.71	10.50	14.28	17.96	18.94	29.30
Net Margin %	11.56	10.47	10.73	2.07	7.19	8.72	9.62	5.90
Asset Turnover	0.25	0.25	0.27	0.28	0.29	0.31	0.30	0.28
Current Ratio	0.93	0.71	0.71	0.86	0.59	0.68	1.01	0.83
Debt to Equity	0.81	0.79	0.83	1.02	0.88	0.89	0.94	0.76
Price Range	54.32-46.06	48.71-37.98	42.37-34.50	37.73-23.00	42.50-26.95	51.60-37.10	50.92-38.70	46.39-39.85
P/E Ratio	15.74-13.35	15.76-12.29	12.96-10.55	56.31-34.33	17.71-11.23	16.92-12.16	15.57-11.83	25.49-21.90
Average Yield %	4.21	4.81	5.43	6.76	6.16	4.75	4.68	4.46

Address: 400 North Fifth Street, P.O. Box 53999, Phoenix, AZ 85072-3999
Telephone: 602-250-1000
Fax: 602-379-2625

Web Site: www.pinnaclewest.com
Officers: Donald E. Brandt - Chairman, President, Chief Executive Officer David P. Falck - Executive Vice President, Secretary, General Counsel

Auditors: Deloitte & Touche LLP
Investor Contact: 602-250-5511
Transfer Agents: Computershare Investor Services, Pittsburgh, PA

PIONEER NATURAL RESOURCES CO

Exchange	Symbol	Price	52Wk Range	Yield	P/E
NYS	PXD	$124.25 (3/28/2013)	132.45-78.78	0.06	82.83

*7 Year Price Score 150.12 *NYSE Composite Index=100 *12 Month Price Score 109.26

Interim Earnings (Per Share)

Qtr.	Mar	Jun	Sep	Dec
2008	1.09	1.32	(0.03)	(0.54)
2009	(0.13)	(0.80)	(0.06)	0.49
2010	2.08	1.41	0.94	0.65
2011	2.96	2.03	2.95	(0.97)
2012	1.68	(0.57)	0.15	0.22

Interim Dividends (Per Share)

Amt	Decl	Ex	Rec	Pay
0.04S	08/26/2011	09/28/2011	09/30/2011	10/14/2011
0.04S	02/23/2012	03/28/2012	03/30/2012	04/12/2012
0.04S	08/23/2012	09/26/2012	09/28/2012	10/12/2012
0.04S	02/21/2013	03/26/2013	03/28/2013	04/11/2013

Indicated Div: $0.08

Valuation Analysis / **Institutional Holding**

Forecast EPS	$4.64 (04/06/2013)	No of Institutions 590
Market Cap	$15.3 Billion	Shares
Book Value	$5.7 Billion	137,225,792
Price/Book	2.69	% Held
Price/Sales	4.75	106.81

Business Summary: Production & Extraction (MIC: 9.1.1 SIC: 1311 NAIC: 211111)

Pioneer Natural Resources is a holding company. Through its subsidiaries, Co. is an oil and gas exploration and production company. Co. explores for, develops and produces oil and gas reserves, and sells oil, natural gas liquid and gas units. Co. has field operations in the Permian Basin in West Texas, the Eagle Ford Shale play in South Texas, the Barnett Shale Combo play in North Texas, the Raton field in southeastern Colorado, the Hugoton field in southwest Kansas, the West Panhandle field in the Texas Panhandle and Alaska. As of Dec 31 2012, Co. had proved reserves of 1.09 billion barrels of oil equivalent.

Recent Developments: For the year ended Dec 31 2012, income from continuing operations decreased 59.1% to US$187.7 million from US$458.8 million a year earlier. Net income decreased 72.5% to US$242.8 million from US$881.9 million in the prior year. Revenues were US$3.23 billion, up 17.3% from US$2.75 billion the year before. Direct operating expenses rose 41.0% to US$1.45 billion from US$1.03 billion in the comparable period the year before. Indirect operating expenses increased 40.5% to US$1.50 billion from US$1.07 billion in the equivalent prior-year period.

Prospects: Our evaluation of Pioneer Natural Resources Co as of Apr. 7, 2013 is the result of our systematic analysis on three basic characteristics: earnings strength, relative valuation, and recent stock price movement. The company has generated a negative trend in earnings per share over the past 5 quarters. However, while recent estimates for the company have been mixed, PXD has posted results that fell short of analysts expectations. Based on operating earnings yield, the company is overvalued when compared to all of the companies in our coverage universe. Share price changes over the past year indicates that PXD will perform well over the near term.

Financial Data

(US$ in Thousands)	12/31/2012	12/31/2011	12/31/2010	12/31/2009	12/31/2008	12/31/2007	12/31/2006	12/31/2005
Earnings Per Share	1.50	6.88	5.08	(0.46)	1.85	3.06	5.81	3.80
Cash Flow Per Share	14.90	13.09	11.17	4.76	8.70	6.45	6.07	9.45
Tang Book Value Per Share	43.70	42.60	33.15	28.21	28.56	23.20	22.01	14.82
Dividends Per Share	0.080	0.080	0.080	0.080	0.300	0.270	0.250	0.220
Dividend Payout %	5.33	1.16	1.57	...	16.22	8.82	4.30	5.79
Income Statement								
Total Revenue	3,228,308	2,786,585	2,471,590	1,711,516	2,338,287	1,833,349	1,632,881	2,373,223
EBITDA	1,502,725	1,589,626	1,608,335	632,570	989,342	733,795	420,319	850,642
Depn & Amortn	830,689	603,896	523,808	541,293	387,677	241,475	1,670	3,914
Income Before Taxes	467,814	804,070	901,443	(82,084)	448,088	357,050	311,617	718,941
Income Taxes	280,141	345,308	384,458	50,263	205,639	112,645	136,666	291,728
Net Income	192,285	834,489	605,208	(52,106)	220,063	372,728	739,731	534,568
Average Shares	126,320	119,215	116,330	114,176	118,645	121,659	127,608	141,417
Balance Sheet								
Current Assets	1,050,355	1,479,297	1,197,183	616,118	486,911	765,055	536,558	623,804
Total Assets	13,069,030	11,524,161	9,679,102	8,867,265	9,163,178	8,616,981	7,355,399	7,329,234
Current Liabilities	1,034,790	1,011,798	769,220	571,191	694,997	994,169	886,979	1,033,355
Long-Term Obligations	3,721,193	2,528,905	2,601,670	2,761,011	2,964,047	2,755,491	1,497,162	2,058,412
Total Liabilities	7,379,676	6,035,367	5,558,519	5,331,077	5,581,029	5,574,259	4,370,728	5,112,132
Stockholders' Equity	5,689,354	5,488,794	4,120,583	3,536,188	3,582,149	3,042,722	2,984,671	2,217,102
Shares Outstanding	123,355	121,856	115,308	114,375	114,546	117,727	121,502	128,588
Statistical Record								
Return on Assets %	1.56	7.87	6.53	N.M.	2.47	4.67	10.07	7.65
Return on Equity %	3.43	17.37	15.81	N.M.	6.63	12.37	28.44	21.18
EBITDA Margin %	46.55	57.05	65.07	36.96	42.31	40.02	25.74	35.84
Net Margin %	5.96	29.95	24.49	N.M.	9.41	20.33	45.30	22.52
Asset Turnover	0.26	0.26	0.27	0.19	0.26	0.23	0.22	0.34
Current Ratio	1.02	1.46	1.56	1.08	0.70	0.77	0.60	0.60
Debt to Equity	0.65	0.46	0.63	0.78	0.83	0.91	0.50	0.93
Price Range	116.24-78.78	104.66-61.82	87.53-43.62	49.55-12.10	79.73-14.43	54.38-37.55	53.81-36.53	56.19-33.15
P/E Ratio	77.49-52.52	15.21-8.99	17.23-8.59	...	43.10-7.80	17.77-12.27	9.26-6.29	14.79-8.72
Average Yield %	0.08	0.09	0.13	0.28	0.61	0.59	0.58	0.49

Address: 5205 N. O'Connor Blvd., Suite 200, Irving, TX 75039
Telephone: 972-444-9001
Fax: 972-969-3587

Web Site: www.pxd.com
Officers: Scott D. Sheffield - Chairman, Chief Executive Officer Timothy L. Dove - President, Chief Operating Officer

Auditors: Ernst & Young LLP
Investor Contact: 972-969-4065
Transfer Agents: Continental Stock Transfer & Trust Company, New York, NY

PITNEY BOWES INC

Exchange	Symbol	Price	52Wk Range	Yield	P/E	Div Achiever
NYS	PBI	$14.86 (3/28/2013)	17.77-10.41	10.09	6.72	29 Years

*7 Year Price Score 43.59   *NYSE Composite Index=100   *12 Month Price Score 91.91

Interim Earnings (Per Share)

Qtr.	Mar	Jun	Sep	Dec
2008	0.56	0.61	0.47	0.36
2009	0.50	0.57	0.50	0.47
2010	0.38	0.30	0.43	0.30
2011	0.42	0.50	0.85	1.28
2012	0.79	0.50	0.38	0.55

Interim Dividends (Per Share)

Amt	Decl	Ex	Rec	Pay
0.375Q	04/09/2012	05/09/2012	05/11/2012	06/12/2012
0.375Q	07/09/2012	08/08/2012	08/10/2012	09/12/2012
0.375Q	11/02/2012	11/14/2012	11/16/2012	12/12/2012
0.375Q	01/31/2013	02/13/2013	02/15/2013	03/12/2013

Indicated Div: $1.50 (Div. Reinv. Plan)

Valuation Analysis

		Institutional Holding	
Forecast EPS	$1.92 (04/06/2013)	No of Institutions	582
Market Cap	$3.0 Billion	Shares	211,349,264
Book Value	$110.6 Million	% Held	86.78
Price/Book	26.98		
Price/Sales	0.61		

Business Summary: Office Equipment & Furniture (MIC: 7.5.1 SIC: 7372 NAIC: 511210)

Pitney Bowes is a provider of software, hardware and services that enables and integrates both physical and digital communications. Co. organizes its business activities within two groups based on the clients they primarily serve: Small and Medium Business Solutions as well as Enterprise Business Solutions. The Small and Medium Business Solutions group includes the North America Mailing and International Mailing reporting segments. The Enterprise Business Solutions group includes the Production Mail, Software, Management Services, Mail Services and Marketing Services reporting segments.

Recent Developments: For the year ended Dec 31 2012, income from continuing operations increased 8.4% to Dh454.3 million from US$418.9 million a year earlier. Net income decreased 27.1% to Dh463.5 million from US$635.9 million in the prior year. Revenues were Dh4.90 billion, down 4.3% from US$5.12 billion the year before. Direct operating expenses declined 2.0% to Dh2.35 billion from US$2.40 billion in the comparable period the year before. Indirect operating expenses decreased 12.9% to Dh1.95 billion from US$2.24 billion in the equivalent prior-year period.

Prospects: Our evaluation of Pitney Bowes Inc. as of Apr. 7, 2013 is the result of our systematic analysis on three basic characteristics: earnings strength, relative valuation, and recent stock price movement. The company has managed to produce a neutral trend in earnings per share over the past 5 quarters and while recent estimates for the company have been raised by analysts, PBI has posted better than expected results. Based on operating earnings yield, the company is undervalued when compared to all of the companies in our coverage universe. Share price changes over the past year indicates that PBI will perform very poorly over the near term.

Financial Data
(US$ in Thousands)

	12/31/2012	12/31/2011	12/31/2010	12/31/2009	12/31/2008	12/31/2007	12/31/2006	12/31/2005
Earnings Per Share	2.21	3.05	1.41	2.04	2.00	1.66	0.47	2.27
Cash Flow Per Share	3.29	4.56	4.62	3.99	4.74	4.85	(1.29)	2.36
Dividends Per Share	1.500	1.480	1.460	1.440	1.400	1.320	1.280	1.240
Dividend Payout %	67.87	48.52	103.55	70.59	70.00	79.52	272.34	54.63
Income Statement								
Total Revenue	4,904,015	5,277,974	5,425,254	5,569,171	6,262,305	6,129,795	5,730,018	5,492,183
EBITDA	1,003,999	825,547	978,801	1,166,882	1,236,427	1,220,682	1,438,286	1,367,582
Depn & Amortn	211,000	214,000	242,900	269,800	306,800	318,100	311,200	292,200
Income Before Taxes	604,613	414,281	534,577	693,176	713,177	660,711	914,490	867,124
Income Taxes	150,305	44,585	205,770	240,154	244,929	280,222	335,004	340,546
Net Income	445,163	617,480	292,379	423,445	419,793	366,781	105,347	526,578
Average Shares	201,366	202,766	206,753	207,322	209,699	221,219	225,443	231,771
Balance Sheet								
Current Assets	3,212,127	3,259,858	3,008,241	2,971,236	3,032,613	3,319,613	2,918,670	2,742,315
Total Assets	7,859,891	8,147,104	8,444,023	8,533,911	8,736,431	9,549,943	8,480,420	10,621,382
Current Liabilities	2,877,037	3,091,862	2,553,579	2,566,447	3,243,118	3,556,439	2,746,833	2,910,897
Long-Term Obligations	3,642,375	3,683,909	4,239,248	4,213,640	3,934,865	3,802,075	3,847,617	3,849,623
Total Liabilities	7,749,260	8,186,090	8,540,604	8,520,248	8,550,145	8,522,475	7,397,066	9,009,441
Stockholders' Equity	110,631	(38,986)	(96,581)	13,663	186,286	1,027,468	1,083,354	1,611,941
Shares Outstanding	200,884	199,751	203,431	207,197	206,181	214,514	220,613	226,707
Statistical Record								
Return on Assets %	5.55	7.44	3.44	4.90	4.58	4.07	1.10	5.15
Return on Equity %	1,239.30	...	...	423.55	68.98	34.75	7.82	32.79
EBITDA Margin %	20.47	15.64	18.04	20.95	19.74	19.91	25.10	24.90
Net Margin %	9.08	11.70	5.39	7.60	6.70	5.98	1.84	9.59
Asset Turnover	0.61	0.64	0.64	0.64	0.68	0.68	0.60	0.54
Current Ratio	1.12	1.05	1.18	1.16	0.94	0.93	1.06	0.94
Debt to Equity	32.92	...	...	308.40	21.12	3.70	3.55	2.39
Price Range	19.52-10.41	26.18-17.35	25.88-19.24	27.11-17.77	38.55-21.52	48.66-36.94	47.68-40.34	47.30-40.49
P/E Ratio	8.83-4.71	8.58-5.69	18.35-13.65	13.29-8.71	19.27-10.76	29.31-22.25	101.45-85.83	20.84-17.84
Average Yield %	10.13	6.71	6.44	6.25	4.29	2.92	2.94	2.84

Address: 1 Elmcroft Road, Stamford, CT 06926-0700 **Telephone:** 203-356-5000 **Fax:** 203-351-7336	**Web Site:** www.pb.com **Officers:** Michael I. Roth - Non-Executive Chairman Marc B. Lautenbach - President, Chief Executive Officer	**Auditors:** PricewaterhouseCoopers LLP **Investor Contact:** 203-351-6349 **Transfer Agents:** Computershare Trust Company, N.A, Providence, RI

PLAINS ALL AMERICAN PIPELINE, L.P.

Exchange	Symbol	Price	52Wk Range	Yield	P/E	Div Achiever
NYS	PAA	$56.48 (3/28/2013)	56.48-38.21	3.92	23.53	13 Years

*7 Year Price Score 136.26 *NYSE Composite Index=100 *12 Month Price Score 110.49

Interim Earnings (Per Share)

Qtr.	Mar	Jun	Sep	Dec
2008	0.28	0.07	0.57	0.28
2009	0.70	0.39	0.33	0.25
2010	0.40	0.33	0.14	0.34
2011	0.45	0.56	0.73	0.69
2012	0.51	0.93	0.27	0.70

Interim Dividends (Per Share)

Amt	Decl	Ex	Rec	Pay
2-for-1	08/17/2012	10/02/2012	09/17/2012	10/01/2012
0.542Q	10/04/2012	10/31/2012	11/02/2012	11/14/2012
0.563Q	01/07/2013	01/30/2013	02/01/2013	02/14/2013
0.575Q	04/08/2013	05/01/2013	05/03/2013	05/15/2013

Indicated Div: $2.21

Valuation Analysis / **Institutional Holding**

Forecast EPS	$2.87
	(04/06/2013)
Market Cap	$18.9 Billion
Book Value	N/A
Price/Book	N/A
Price/Sales	0.50

Institutional Holding	
No of Institutions	508
Shares	180,943,184
% Held	50.11

TRADING VOLUME (thousand shares)

Business Summary: Equipment & Services (MIC: 9.1.3 SIC: 4612 NAIC: 486110)

Plains All American Pipeline is a holding company. Co. is engaged in the transportation, storage, terminalling and marketing of crude oil, refined products and liquefied petroleum gas and other natural gas-related petroleum products (LPG). Co. is also engaged in the acquisition, development and operation of natural gas storage facilities. Co. has three segments: transportation, which transports crude oil and refined products on pipelines, gathering systems, trucks and barges; facilities, which provides storage, terminalling and throughput services; and supply and logistics, which consists of the sale of gathered and bulk-purchased crude oil, refined products and LPG volumes.

Recent Developments: For the year ended Dec 31 2012, net income increased 13.4% to US$1.13 billion from US$994.0 million in the prior year. Revenues were US$37.80 billion, up 10.3% from US$34.28 billion the year before. Operating income was US$1.43 billion versus US$1.30 billion in the prior year, an increase of 9.8%. Direct operating expenses rose 9.6% to US$35.55 billion from US$32.43 billion in the comparable period the year before. Indirect operating expenses increased 51.7% to US$824.0 million from US$543.0 million in the equivalent prior-year period.

Prospects: Our evaluation of Plains All American Pipeline, L.P. as of Apr. 7, 2013 is the result of our systematic analysis on three basic characteristics: earnings strength, relative valuation, and recent stock price movement. The company has generated a negative trend in earnings per share over the past 5 quarters. However, while recent estimates for the company have been mixed, PAA has posted better than expected results. Based on operating earnings yield, the company is undervalued when compared to all of the companies in our coverage universe. Share price changes over the past year indicates that PAA will perform well over the near term.

Financial Data
(US$ in Thousands)

	12/31/2012	12/31/2011	12/31/2010	12/31/2009	12/31/2008	12/31/2007	12/31/2006	12/31/2005
Earnings Per Share	2.40	2.44	1.20	1.66	1.34	1.26	1.44	1.36
Cash Flow Per Share	3.80	7.94	0.95	1.40	3.56	3.52	(1.70)	0.17
Dividends Per Share	2.110	1.952	1.877	1.811	1.748	1.641	1.435	1.288
Dividend Payout %	87.92	80.02	156.46	109.11	130.90	130.26	99.65	94.67
Income Statement								
Total Revenue	37,797,000	34,275,000	25,893,000	18,520,000	30,061,000	20,394,000	22,444,400	31,177,300
EBITDA	1,653,000	1,475,000	993,000	995,000	790,000	699,000	521,600	412,600
Depn & Amortn	222,000	196,000	235,000	216,000	196,000	181,000	91,300	79,200
Income Before Taxes	1,143,000	1,026,000	510,000	571,000	431,000	366,000	347,000	274,600
Income Taxes	54,000	45,000	(1,000)	6,000	8,000	16,000	300	...
Net Income	1,094,000	966,000	505,000	579,000	437,000	365,000	285,100	217,800
Average Shares	328,000	300,000	276,000	262,000	242,000	228,000	163,800	141,000
Balance Sheet								
Current Assets	5,147,000	4,351,000	4,381,000	3,658,000	2,596,000	3,673,000	3,157,600	1,805,200
Total Assets	19,235,000	15,381,000	13,703,000	12,358,000	10,032,000	9,906,000	8,714,900	4,120,300
Current Liabilities	5,183,000	4,511,000	4,215,000	3,782,000	2,960,000	3,729,000	3,024,700	1,793,300
Long-Term Obligations	6,320,000	4,520,000	4,631,000	4,142,000	3,259,000	2,624,000	2,626,300	951,700
Total Liabilities	12,598,000	9,931,000	9,361,000	8,262,000	6,480,000	6,482,000	5,738,100	2,789,600
Shares Outstanding	335,283	310,753	282,398	272,271	245,823	231,963	218,810	147,537
Statistical Record								
Return on Assets %	6.30	6.64	3.88	5.17	4.37	3.92	4.44	5.98
EBITDA Margin %	4.37	4.30	3.84	5.37	2.63	3.43	2.32	1.32
Net Margin %	2.89	2.82	1.95	3.13	1.45	1.79	1.27	0.70
Asset Turnover	2.18	2.36	1.99	1.65	3.01	2.19	3.50	8.56
Current Ratio	0.99	0.96	1.04	0.97	0.88	0.98	1.04	1.01
Price Range	46.76-36.40	36.73-28.52	32.41-25.84	26.52-17.34	26.00-13.01	32.52-24.58	26.23-20.21	23.76-18.35
P/E Ratio	19.48-15.17	15.05-11.69	27.00-21.53	15.97-10.45	19.40-9.71	25.81-19.51	18.21-14.03	17.47-13.49
Average Yield %	5.04	6.18	6.34	8.21	7.96	5.78	6.28	6.18

Address: 333 Clay Street, Suite 1600, Houston, TX 77002 **Telephone:** 713-646-4100	**Web Site:** www.paalp.com **Officers:** Greg L. Armstrong - Chairman, Chief Executive Officer Harry N. Pefanis - President, Chief Operating Officer	**Auditors:** PricewaterhouseCoopers LLP **Investor Contact:** 713-646-4222 **Transfer Agents:** American Stock Transfer & Trust Company, New York, NY

PLAINS EXPLORATION & PRODUCTION CO. L.P.

Exchange	Symbol	Price	52Wk Range	Yield	P/E
NYS	PXP	$47.47 (3/28/2013)	48.33-31.36	N/A	20.46

*7 Year Price Score 94.65 *NYSE Composite Index=100 *12 Month Price Score 105.94

Interim Earnings (Per Share)

Qtr.	Mar	Jun	Sep	Dec
2008	1.43	1.84	4.50	(14.24)
2009	0.05	0.37	0.30	0.36
2010	0.42	0.32	0.13	(0.14)
2011	0.49	0.87	(0.62)	0.69
2012	(0.64)	1.70	(0.41)	1.65

Interim Dividends (Per Share)

No Dividends Paid

Valuation Analysis		Institutional Holding	
Forecast EPS	$3.45	No of Institutions	
	(04/06/2013)	480	
Market Cap	$6.1 Billion	Shares	
Book Value	$3.5 Billion	121,760,200	
Price/Book	1.74	% Held	
Price/Sales	2.39	90.12	

Business Summary: Production & Extraction (MIC: 9.1.1 SIC: 1311 NAIC: 211111)

Plains Exploration & Production is an independent energy company engaged in the upstream oil and gas business. The upstream business acquires, develops, explores for and produces oil and gas. Co.'s upstream activities are located in the U.S. Co. owns oil and gas properties with principal operations in: Onshore California; Offshore California; the Gulf Coast Region; the Gulf of Mexico; and the Rocky Mountains. As of Dec 31 2012, Co. had estimated proved reserves of 440.4 million barrels of oil equivalent that consisted of 362.431 million barrels of oil and 468.025 million cubic feet of gas, of which 63.0% was proved developed.

Recent Developments: For the year ended Dec 31 2012, net income increased 65.9% to US$342.8 million from US$206.7 million in the prior year. Revenues were US$2.57 billion, up 30.6% from US$1.96 billion the year before. Operating income was US$615.7 million versus US$590.5 million in the prior year, an increase of 4.3%. Indirect operating expenses increased 41.9% to US$1.95 billion from US$1.37 billion in the equivalent prior-year period.

Prospects: Our evaluation of Plains Exploration & Production Co. L.P. as of Apr. 7, 2013 is the result of our systematic analysis on three basic characteristics: earnings strength, relative valuation, and recent stock price movement. The company has produced a positive trend in earnings per share over the past 5 quarters and while recent estimates for the company have been mixed, PXP has posted results that fell short of analysts expectations. Based on operating earnings yield, the company is about fairly valued when compared to all of the companies in our coverage universe. Share price changes over the past year indicates that PXP will perform in line with the market over the near term.

Financial Data (US$ in Thousands)	12/31/2012	12/31/2011	12/31/2010	12/31/2009	12/31/2008	12/31/2007	12/31/2006	12/31/2005
Earnings Per Share	2.32	1.44	0.73	1.09	(6.52)	1.99	7.64	(2.75)
Cash Flow Per Share	10.21	7.87	6.50	4.01	12.57	7.48	8.74	5.96
Tang Book Value Per Share	23.12	20.90	20.33	19.11	17.12	24.84	13.42	6.94
Income Statement								
Total Revenue	2,565,307	1,964,488	1,544,595	1,187,130	2,403,471	1,272,840	1,018,503	944,420
EBITDA	1,912,744	1,166,735	844,139	698,239	(415,154)	653,485	1,266,064	(101,534)
Depn & Amortn	1,101,108	664,478	533,416	407,248	621,484	316,078	216,782	187,915
Income Before Taxes	514,097	340,941	204,010	217,180	(1,153,629)	268,499	984,607	(344,870)
Income Taxes	171,310	134,262	100,745	80,875	(444,535)	109,748	384,897	(130,858)
Net Income	306,420	205,279	103,265	136,305	(709,094)	158,751	597,528	(214,012)
Average Shares	131,867	142,999	141,897	125,288	108,828	79,808	78,234	77,726
Balance Sheet								
Current Assets	1,839,730	1,441,377	402,887	306,635	1,476,441	674,920	184,796	293,332
Total Assets	17,298,283	9,791,472	8,894,937	7,734,731	7,111,915	9,693,351	2,463,228	2,741,942
Current Liabilities	980,001	626,186	533,689	682,551	993,645	818,046	460,192	363,998
Long-Term Obligations	9,979,369	3,760,952	3,344,717	2,649,689	2,805,000	3,305,000	235,500	797,375
Total Liabilities	13,781,805	6,526,836	5,511,972	4,535,750	4,734,635	6,355,104	1,332,545	2,023,605
Stockholders' Equity	3,516,478	3,264,636	3,382,965	3,198,981	2,377,280	3,338,247	1,130,683	718,337
Shares Outstanding	128,965	130,600	140,100	139,400	107,600	112,798	72,442	78,411
Statistical Record								
Return on Assets %	2.26	2.20	1.24	1.84	N.M.	2.61	22.96	N.M.
Return on Equity %	9.01	6.18	3.14	4.89	N.M.	7.10	64.63	N.M.
EBITDA Margin %	74.56	59.39	54.65	58.82	N.M.	51.34	124.31	N.M.
Net Margin %	11.94	10.45	6.69	11.48	N.M.	12.47	58.67	N.M.
Asset Turnover	0.19	0.21	0.19	0.16	0.29	0.21	0.39	0.35
Current Ratio	1.88	2.30	0.75	0.45	1.49	0.83	0.40	0.81
Debt to Equity	2.84	1.15	0.99	0.83	1.18	0.99	0.21	1.11
Price Range	46.94-31.36	41.41-21.31	35.10-19.34	32.37-15.75	78.30-16.31	55.98-35.51	49.18-31.70	45.68-24.25
P/E Ratio	20.23-13.52	28.76-14.80	48.08-26.49	29.70-14.45	...	28.13-17.84	6.44-4.15	...

Address: 700 Milam Street, Suite 3100, Houston, TX 77002 **Telephone:** 713-579-6000	**Web Site:** www.pxp.com **Officers:** James C. Flores - Chairman, President, Chief Executive Officer Winston M. Talbert - Executive Vice President, Chief Financial Officer	**Auditors:** PricewaterhouseCoopers LLP **Investor Contact:** 713-579-6000 **Transfer Agents:** American Stock Transfer & Trust, New York, NY

PLANTRONICS, INC.

Exchange	Symbol	Price	52Wk Range	Yield	P/E
NYS	PLT	$44.19 (3/28/2013)	45.61-28.95	0.91	18.65

*7 Year Price Score 116.39 *NYSE Composite Index=100 *12 Month Price Score 106.72

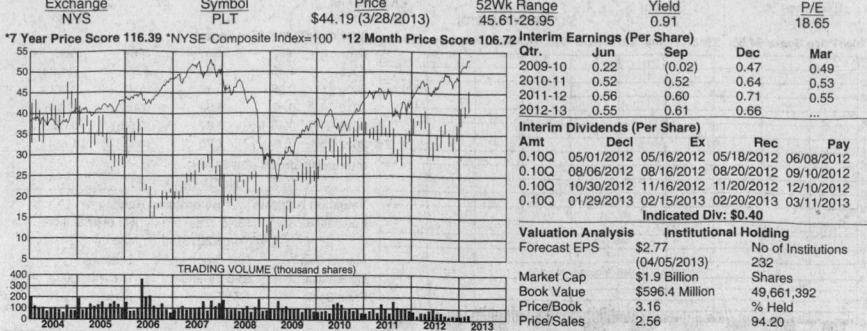

Interim Earnings (Per Share)

Qtr.	Jun	Sep	Dec	Mar
2009-10	0.22	(0.02)	0.47	0.49
2010-11	0.52	0.52	0.64	0.53
2011-12	0.56	0.60	0.71	0.55
2012-13	0.55	0.61	0.66	...

Interim Dividends (Per Share)

Amt	Decl	Ex	Rec	Pay
0.10Q	05/01/2012	05/16/2012	05/18/2012	06/08/2012
0.10Q	08/06/2012	08/16/2012	08/20/2012	09/10/2012
0.10Q	10/30/2012	11/16/2012	11/20/2012	12/10/2012
0.10Q	01/29/2013	02/15/2013	02/20/2013	03/11/2013

Indicated Div: $0.40

Valuation Analysis | **Institutional Holding**

Forecast EPS	$2.77 (04/05/2013)	No of Institutions 232
Market Cap	$1.9 Billion	Shares
Book Value	$596.4 Million	49,661,392
Price/Book	3.16	% Held
Price/Sales	2.56	94.20

Business Summary: Manufacturing (MIC: 6.1.1 SIC: 3661 NAIC: 334210)

Plantronics is a designer, manufacturer and marketer of lightweight communications headsets, telephone headset systems and accessories for the business and consumer markets under the Plantronics brand. Co.'s product categories include Office and Contact Center, which includes corded and cordless communication headsets, audio processors and telephone systems; Mobile, which includes Bluetooth® and corded products for mobile phone applications; Gaming and Computer Audio, which includes personal computer and gaming headsets; and Clarity, which includes products marketed for hearing impaired individuals.

Recent Developments: For the quarter ended Dec 31 2012, net income decreased 8.7% to US$28.2 million from US$30.9 million in the year-earlier quarter. Revenues were US$197.4 million, up 7.7% from US$183.2 million the year before. Operating income was US$34.6 million versus US$37.4 million in the prior-year quarter, a decrease of 7.5%. Direct operating expenses rose 9.4% to US$95.2 million from US$87.0 million in the comparable period the year before. Indirect operating expenses increased 14.9% to US$67.6 million from US$58.8 million in the equivalent prior-year period.

Prospects: Our evaluation of Plantronics Inc. as of Apr. 7, 2013 is the result of our systematic analysis on three basic characteristics: earnings strength, relative valuation, and recent stock price movement. The company has produced a positive trend in earnings per share over the past 5 quarters and while recent estimates for the company have been mixed, PLT has posted better than expected results. Based on operating earnings yield, the company is undervalued when compared to all of the companies in our coverage universe. Share price changes over the past year indicates that PLT will perform poorly over the near term.

Financial Data
(US$ in Thousands)

	9 Mos	6 Mos	3 Mos	03/31/2012	03/31/2011	03/31/2010	03/31/2009	03/31/2008
Earnings Per Share	2.37	2.42	2.41	2.41	2.21	1.16	(1.34)	1.39
Cash Flow Per Share	3.50	3.47	3.59	3.18	3.32	2.96	2.04	2.13
Tang Book Value Per Share	13.61	13.03	12.45	12.06	12.83	11.33	9.92	8.54
Dividends Per Share	0.350	0.300	0.250	0.200	0.200	0.200	0.200	0.200
Dividend Payout %	14.77	12.40	10.37	8.30	9.05	17.24	...	14.39
Income Statement								
Total Revenue	558,047	360,645	181,365	713,368	683,602	613,837	765,619	856,286
EBITDA	113,877	74,919	36,116	154,653	157,012	115,835	(55,372)	107,783
Depn & Amortn	12,658	8,306	4,020	13,300	16,300	18,200	25,800	28,400
Income Before Taxes	101,683	66,900	32,108	142,602	140,656	100,740	(84,716)	85,237
Income Taxes	23,990	17,413	8,545	33,566	31,413	24,287	(19,817)	16,842
Net Income	77,693	49,487	23,563	109,036	109,243	57,378	(64,899)	68,395
Average Shares	42,618	42,403	42,570	45,265	49,344	49,331	48,589	49,090
Balance Sheet								
Current Assets	532,992	554,487	549,128	524,174	617,720	569,592	463,555	450,203
Total Assets	725,457	702,414	683,997	672,470	744,647	655,351	633,120	741,393
Current Liabilities	94,282	83,884	85,197	86,193	93,602	69,616	85,970	115,214
Long-Term Obligations	20,000	29,000	42,000	37,000	...	...	...	...
Total Liabilities	129,084	129,634	143,184	145,226	109,795	84,017	107,753	162,773
Stockholders' Equity	596,373	572,780	540,813	527,244	634,852	571,334	525,367	578,620
Shares Outstanding	42,598	42,675	42,282	42,512	48,315	48,870	48,892	48,944
Statistical Record								
Return on Assets %	14.79	15.65	15.67	15.35	15.61	8.91	N.M.	9.80
Return on Equity %	18.26	19.15	19.08	18.71	18.11	10.46	N.M.	12.68
EBITDA Margin %	20.41	20.77	19.91	21.68	22.97	18.87	N.M.	12.59
Net Margin %	13.92	13.72	12.99	15.28	15.98	9.35	N.M.	7.99
Asset Turnover	1.07	1.08	1.06	1.00	0.98	0.95	1.11	1.23
Current Ratio	5.65	6.61	6.45	6.08	6.60	8.18	5.39	3.91
Debt to Equity	0.03	0.05	0.08	0.07	...	...	...	...
Price Range	40.80-28.95	40.80-27.45	40.80-27.45	40.26-27.45	38.20-26.79	32.13-11.91	26.06-7.84	32.71-17.82
P/E Ratio	17.22-12.22	16.86-11.34	16.93-11.39	16.71-11.39	17.29-12.12	27.70-10.27	...	23.53-12.82
Average Yield %	1.00	0.87	0.73	0.58	0.60	0.86	1.13	0.80

Address: 345 Encinal Street, Santa Cruz, CA 95060
Telephone: 831-426-5858

Web Site: www.plantronics.com
Officers: Marv Tseu - Chairman S. Kenneth Kannappan - President, Chief Executive Officer

Auditors: PricewaterhouseCoopers LLP
Investor Contact: 831-458-7533
Transfer Agents: Computershare Trust Company, N.A., Providence, RI

PLUM CREEK TIMBER CO., INC.

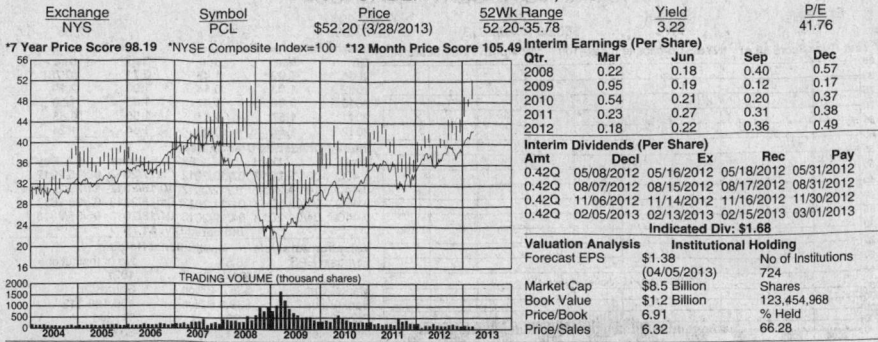

Exchange	Symbol	Price	52Wk Range	Yield	P/E
NYS	PCL	$52.20 (3/28/2013)	52.20-35.78	3.22	41.76

*7 Year Price Score 98.19 *NYSE Composite Index=100 *12 Month Price Score 105.49

Interim Earnings (Per Share)

Qtr.	Mar	Jun	Sep	Dec
2008	0.22	0.18	0.40	0.57
2009	0.95	0.19	0.12	0.17
2010	0.54	0.21	0.20	0.37
2011	0.23	0.27	0.31	0.38
2012	0.18	0.22	0.36	0.49

Interim Dividends (Per Share)

Amt	Decl	Ex	Rec	Pay
0.42Q	05/08/2012	05/16/2012	05/18/2012	05/31/2012
0.42Q	08/07/2012	08/15/2012	08/17/2012	08/31/2012
0.42Q	11/06/2012	11/14/2012	11/16/2012	11/30/2012
0.42Q	02/05/2013	02/13/2013	02/15/2013	03/01/2013

Indicated Div: $1.68

Valuation Analysis

		Institutional Holding	
Forecast EPS	$1.38	No of Institutions	
	(04/05/2013)	724	
Market Cap	$8.5 Billion	Shares	
Book Value	$1.2 Billion	123,454,968	
Price/Book	6.91	% Held	
Price/Sales	6.32	66.28	

TRADING VOLUME (thousand shares)

Business Summary: REITs (MIC: 5.3.1 SIC: 6798 NAIC: 525930)

Plum Creek Timber is a real estate investment trust. Co. manages its timberlands in two business segments, Northern Resources and Southern Resources. Co. also operates in the following business segments: Real Estate, which includes sales of timberlands and development of certain properties; Manufactured Products, which consists of lumber, plywood and medium density fiberboard products; and Other, which focuses on oil and natural gas production, mineral extraction and wind power development, along with communication and transportation rights of way. As of Dec 31 2011, Co. owned 6.6 million acres of timberlands located in 19 states within the Northwest, Southern and Northeast U.S.

Recent Developments: For the year ended Dec 31 2012, income from continuing operations increased 5.2% to US$203.0 million from US$193.0 million a year earlier. Net income increased 5.2% to US$203.0 million from US$193.0 million in the prior year. Revenues were US$1.34 billion, up 14.7% from US$1.17 billion the year before. Revenues from property income rose 16.9% to US$352.0 million from US$301.0 million in the corresponding earlier year.

Prospects: Our evaluation of Plum Creek Timber Co. Inc. as of Apr. 7, 2013 is the result of our systematic analysis on three basic characteristics: earnings strength, relative valuation, and recent stock price movement. The company has enjoyed a very positive trend in earnings per share over the past 5 quarters and while recent estimates for the company have been mixed, PCL has posted better than expected results. Based on operating earnings yield, the company is overvalued when compared to all of the companies in our coverage universe. Share price changes over the past year indicates that PCL will perform in line with the market over the near term.

Financial Data

(US$ in Thousands)	12/31/2012	12/31/2011	12/31/2010	12/31/2009	12/31/2008	12/31/2007	12/31/2006	12/31/2005
Earnings Per Share	1.25	1.19	1.31	1.44	1.37	1.61	1.75	1.92
Cash Flow Per Share	2.18	2.31	2.77	3.31	2.46	2.96	3.08	2.80
Tang Book Value Per Share	7.55	7.83	8.50	9.00	9.47	11.03	11.80	12.62
Dividends Per Share	1.680	1.680	1.680	1.680	1.680	1.680	1.600	1.520
Dividend Payout %	134.40	141.18	128.24	116.67	122.63	104.35	91.43	79.17
Income Statement								
Total Revenue	1,339,000	1,167,000	1,190,000	1,294,000	1,614,000	1,675,000	1,627,000	1,576,000
EBITDA	303,000	295,000	303,000	317,000	370,000	558,000	589,000	561,000
Depn & Amortn	22,000	20,000	19,000	20,000	31,000	134,000	128,000	113,000
Income Before Taxes	141,000	136,000	146,000	150,000	191,000	277,000	328,000	339,000
Income Taxes	(3,000)	(1,000)	1,000	(31,000)	(27,000)	(3,000)	13,000	8,000
Net Income	203,000	193,000	213,000	236,000	233,000	282,000	317,000	354,000
Average Shares	161,900	162,000	162,300	163,400	170,700	175,000	180,900	184,600
Balance Sheet								
Current Assets	508,000	454,000	410,000	519,000	699,000	456,000	513,000	574,000
Total Assets	4,384,000	4,259,000	4,251,000	4,448,000	4,780,000	4,664,000	4,661,000	4,812,000
Current Liabilities	472,000	815,000	375,000	183,000	307,000	303,000	281,000	375,000
Long-Term Obligations	2,598,000	2,073,000	2,426,000	2,728,000	2,807,000	2,376,000	2,198,000	2,019,000
Total Liabilities	3,161,000	2,996,000	2,877,000	2,982,000	3,208,000	2,763,000	2,572,000	2,487,000
Stockholders' Equity	1,223,000	1,263,000	1,374,000	1,466,000	1,572,000	1,901,000	2,089,000	2,325,000
Shares Outstanding	162,000	161,300	161,600	162,800	166,000	172,300	177,100	184,200
Statistical Record								
Return on Assets %	4.68	4.54	4.90	5.11	4.92	6.05	6.69	7.70
Return on Equity %	16.29	14.64	15.00	15.54	13.38	14.14	14.36	15.51
EBITDA Margin %	22.63	25.28	25.46	24.50	22.92	33.31	36.20	35.60
Net Margin %	15.16	16.54	17.90	18.24	14.44	16.84	19.48	22.46
Asset Turnover	0.31	0.27	0.27	0.28	0.34	0.36	0.34	0.34
Current Ratio	1.08	0.56	1.09	2.84	2.28	1.50	1.83	1.53
Debt to Equity	2.12	1.64	1.77	1.86	1.79	1.25	1.05	0.87
Price Range	44.82-35.78	44.00-33.75	43.52-33.51	38.40-23.79	56.00-28.31	48.22-37.59	39.85-33.51	39.34-34.19
P/E Ratio	35.86-28.62	36.97-28.36	33.22-25.58	26.67-16.52	40.88-20.66	29.95-23.35	22.77-19.15	20.49-17.81
Average Yield %	4.12	4.31	4.56	5.28	4.01	4.04	4.46	4.14

Address: 999 Third Avenue, Suite 4300, Seattle, WA 98104-4096
Telephone: 206-467-3600
Fax: 206-467-3795

Web Site: www.plumcreek.com
Officers: Rick R. Holley - President, Chief Executive Officer Thomas M. Lindquist - Executive Vice President, Chief Operating Officer

Auditors: Ernst & Young LLP
Investor Contact: 206-467-3600
Transfer Agents: Computershare Trust Company, N.A., Providence, RI

PNC FINANCIAL SERVICES GROUP (THE)

Exchange	Symbol	Price	52Wk Range	Yield	P/E
NYS	PNC	$66.50 (3/28/2013)	67.33-53.69	2.65	12.55

*7 Year Price Score 90.47   *NYSE Composite Index=100   *12 Month Price Score 95.87

Interim Earnings (Per Share)

Qtr.	Mar	Jun	Sep	Dec
2008	1.09	1.45	0.71	(0.78)
2009	1.03	0.14	1.00	2.19
2010	0.66	1.47	1.45	1.50
2011	1.57	1.67	1.55	0.85
2012	1.44	0.98	1.64	1.24

Interim Dividends (Per Share)

Amt	Decl	Ex	Rec	Pay
0.40Q	06/29/2012	07/13/2012	07/17/2012	08/05/2012
0.40Q	10/04/2012	10/12/2012	10/16/2012	11/05/2012
0.40Q	01/03/2013	01/11/2013	01/15/2013	02/05/2013
0.44Q	04/04/2013	04/12/2013	04/16/2013	05/05/2013

Indicated Div: $1.76

Valuation Analysis | **Institutional Holding**

Forecast EPS $6.51 (04/06/2013)	No of Institutions 1027
Market Cap $35.1 Billion	Shares 455,186,112
Book Value $39.0 Billion	% Held
Price/Book 0.90	80.06
Price/Sales 2.11	

Business Summary: Banking (MIC: 5.1.1 SIC: 6021 NAIC: 522110)

The PNC Financial Services Group is a bank holding company. Co. is engaged in retail banking, corporate and institutional banking, asset management, and residential mortgage banking. Co.'s primary geographic markets are located in Pennsylvania, Ohio, New Jersey, Michigan, Maryland, Illinois, Maryland, Indiana, Kentucky, Florida, Washington, D.C., Delaware, Virginia, Missouri, Wisconsin and Georgia. Co. operates through six segments: retail banking, corporate and institutional banking, asset management group, residential mortgage banking, BlackRock, and non-strategic assets portfolio. As of Dec 31 2011, Co. had total assets of $271.21 billion and deposits of $187.97 billion.

Recent Developments: For the year ended Dec 31 2012, income from continuing operations decreased 2.3% to US$3.00 billion from US$3.07 billion a year earlier. Net income decreased 2.3% to US$3.00 billion from US$3.07 billion in the prior year. Net interest income increased 10.8% to US$9.64 billion from US$8.70 billion in the prior year. Provision for loan losses was US$987.0 million versus US$1.15 billion in the prior year, a decrease of 14.3%. Non-interest income rose 4.4% to US$5.87 billion from US$5.63 billion, while non-interest expense advanced 16.2% to US$10.58 billion.

Prospects: Our evaluation of PNC Financial Services Group as of Apr. 7, 2013 is the result of our systematic analysis on three basic characteristics: earnings strength, relative valuation, and recent stock price movement. The company has produced a positive trend in earnings per share over the past 5 quarters and while recent estimates for the company have remained steady, PNC has posted better than expected results. Based on operating earnings yield, the company is undervalued when compared to all of the companies in our coverage universe. Share price changes over the past year indicates that PNC will perform poorly over the near term.

Financial Data

(US$ in Thousands)	12/31/2012	12/31/2011	12/31/2010	12/31/2009	12/31/2008	12/31/2007	12/31/2006	12/31/2005
Earnings Per Share	5.30	5.64	5.74	4.36	2.46	4.35	8.73	4.55
Cash Flow Per Share	12.94	11.52	9.31	12.67	21.49	(1.26)	9.08	(2.36)
Tang Book Value Per Share	46.48	42.26	35.82	19.61	13.13	15.55	23.02	13.98
Dividends Per Share	1.550	1.150	0.400	0.960	2.610	2.440	2.150	2.000
Dividend Payout %	29.25	20.39	6.97	22.02	106.10	56.09	24.63	43.96
Income Statement								
Interest Income	10,734,000	10,194,000	11,150,000	12,086,000	6,313,000	6,166,000	4,612,000	3,734,000
Interest Expense	1,094,000	1,494,000	1,920,000	3,003,000	2,490,000	3,251,000	2,367,000	1,580,000
Net Interest Income	9,640,000	8,700,000	9,230,000	9,083,000	3,823,000	2,915,000	2,245,000	2,154,000
Provision for Losses	987,000	1,152,000	2,502,000	3,930,000	1,517,000	315,000	124,000	21,000
Non-Interest Income	5,872,000	5,626,000	5,946,000	7,145,000	3,367,000	3,790,000	6,327,000	4,162,000
Non-Interest Expense	10,582,000	9,105,000	8,613,000	9,073,000	4,430,000	4,296,000	4,443,000	4,333,000
Income Before Taxes	3,943,000	4,069,000	4,061,000	3,225,000	1,243,000	2,094,000	4,005,000	1,962,000
Income Taxes	942,000	998,000	1,037,000	867,000	361,000	627,000	1,363,000	604,000
Net Income	3,001,000	3,071,000	3,397,000	2,403,000	882,000	1,467,000	2,595,000	1,325,000
Average Shares	529,000	526,000	520,000	455,000	347,066	335,157	296,522	289,840
Balance Sheet								
Net Loans & Leases	185,513,000	157,603,000	149,200,000	155,010,000	175,938,000	71,416,000	51,911,000	50,954,000
Total Assets	305,107,000	271,205,000	264,284,000	269,863,000	291,081,000	138,920,000	101,820,000	91,954,000
Total Deposits	213,142,000	187,966,000	183,390,000	186,922,000	192,865,000	82,696,000	66,301,000	60,275,000
Total Liabilities	266,104,000	237,152,000	234,042,000	239,921,000	265,659,000	124,066,000	91,032,000	83,391,000
Stockholders' Equity	39,003,000	34,053,000	30,242,000	29,942,000	25,422,000	14,854,000	10,788,000	8,563,000
Shares Outstanding	528,000	527,000	526,000	462,000	443,000	341,000	293,000	293,000
Statistical Record								
Return on Assets %	1.04	1.15	1.27	0.86	0.41	1.22	2.68	1.54
Return on Equity %	8.19	9.55	11.29	8.68	4.37	11.44	26.82	16.53
Net Interest Margin %	89.81	85.34	82.78	75.15	60.56	47.28	48.68	57.69
Efficiency Ratio %	63.72	57.55	50.38	47.18	45.76	43.15	40.62	54.88
Loans to Deposits	0.87	0.84	0.81	0.83	0.91	0.86	0.78	0.85
Price Range	67.33-53.69	64.94-42.98	69.64-50.36	57.01-18.51	81.21-42.68	76.23-64.09	74.98-62.41	65.00-49.38
P/E Ratio	12.70-10.13	11.51-7.62	12.13-8.77	13.08-4.25	33.01-17.35	17.52-14.73	8.59-7.15	14.29-10.85
Average Yield %	2.56	2.13	0.69	2.32	4.21	3.41	3.09	3.57

Address: One PNC Plaza, 249 Fifth Avenue, Pittsburgh, PA 15222-2707	Web Site: www.pnc.com	Auditors: PricewaterhouseCoopers LLP
Telephone: 412-762-2000	Officers: James E. Rohr - Executive Chairman, Chairman, Chief Executive Officer William S. Demchak - President	Investor Contact: 412-762-8257
Fax: 412-762-5798		Transfer Agents: Computershare Trust Company, N.A., Canton, MA

PNM RESOURCES INC

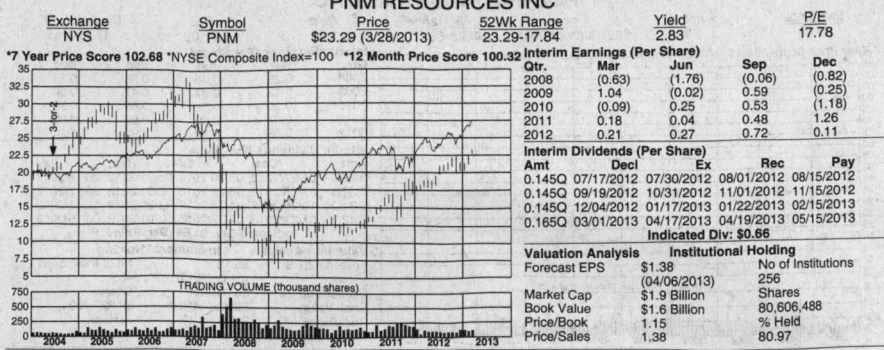

Exchange	Symbol	Price	52Wk Range	Yield	P/E
NYS	PNM	$23.29 (3/28/2013)	23.29-17.84	2.83	17.78

*7 Year Price Score 102.68 *NYSE Composite Index=100 *12 Month Price Score 100.32

Interim Earnings (Per Share)

Qtr.	Mar	Jun	Sep	Dec
2008	(0.63)	(1.76)	(0.06)	(0.82)
2009	1.04	(0.02)	0.59	(0.25)
2010	(0.09)	0.25	0.53	(1.18)
2011	0.18	0.04	0.48	1.26
2012	0.21	0.27	0.72	0.11

Interim Dividends (Per Share)

Amt	Decl	Ex	Rec	Pay
0.145Q	07/17/2012	07/30/2012	08/01/2012	08/15/2012
0.145Q	09/19/2012	10/31/2012	11/01/2012	11/15/2012
0.145Q	12/04/2012	01/17/2013	01/22/2013	02/15/2013
0.165Q	03/01/2013	04/17/2013	04/19/2013	05/15/2013

Indicated Div: $0.66

Valuation Analysis

Forecast EPS	$1.38 (04/06/2013)
Market Cap	$1.9 Billion
Book Value	$1.6 Billion
Price/Book	1.15
Price/Sales	1.38

Institutional Holding

No of Institutions	256
Shares	80,606,488
% Held	80.97

Business Summary: Electric Utilities (MIC: 3.1.1 SIC: 4911 NAIC: 221121)

PNM Resources is an investor-owned holding company of utilities providing electricity and energy products and services in New Mexico and Texas. Co.'s primary subsidiaries are Public Service Company of New Mexico (PNM) and Texas-New Mexico Power Company (TNMP). PNM Electric is an electric utility that provides electric generation, transmission, and distribution service to its rate-regulated customers. TNMP Electric is a regulated utility operating in Texas. TNMP Electric provides transmission and distribution services in Texas under the provisions of the Texas Electric Choice Act and the Texas Public Utility Regulatory Act.

Recent Developments: For the year ended Dec 31 2012, net income decreased 37.1% to US$120.1 million from US$190.9 million in the prior year. Revenues were US$1.34 billion, down 21.1% from US$1.70 billion the year before. Operating income was US$273.7 million versus US$257.3 million in the prior year, an increase of 6.4%. Direct operating expenses declined 32.0% to US$656.4 million from US$964.9 million in the comparable period the year before. Indirect operating expenses decreased 13.8% to US$412.3 million from US$478.5 million in the equivalent prior-year period.

Prospects: Our evaluation of PNM Resources Inc. as of Apr. 7, 2013 is the result of our systematic analysis on three basic characteristics: earnings strength, relative valuation, and recent stock price movement. The company has generated a negative trend in earnings per share over the past 5 quarters. However, while recent estimates for the company have been mixed, PNM has posted better than expected results. Based on operating earnings yield, the company is undervalued when compared to all of the companies in our coverage universe. Share price changes over the past year indicates that PNM will perform well over the near term.

Financial Data

(US$ in Thousands)	12/31/2012	12/31/2011	12/31/2010	12/31/2009	12/31/2008	12/31/2007	12/31/2006	12/31/2005
Earnings Per Share	1.31	1.96	(0.49)	1.36	(3.24)	0.96	1.73	1.00
Cash Flow Per Share	3.52	3.28	3.14	0.96	1.05	2.90	3.50	3.19
Tang Book Value Per Share	16.84	16.41	13.85	15.15	15.13	14.74	14.29	10.30
Dividends Per Share	0.560	0.500	0.500	0.500	0.710	0.910	0.860	0.770
Dividend Payout %	42.75	25.51	...	36.76	...	94.79	49.71	77.00
Income Statement								
Total Revenue	1,342,403	1,700,619	1,673,517	1,647,744	1,959,522	1,914,029	2,471,669	2,076,810
EBITDA	489,307	617,169	547,219	463,199	66,385	338,785	395,115	312,453
Depn & Amortn	206,499	195,366	186,067	147,296	150,474	144,323	103,191	160,591
Income Before Taxes	175,035	312,469	254,675	222,087	(192,948)	117,461	186,084	101,014
Income Taxes	54,910	121,535	(32,255)	28,818	(90,816)	3,226	63,970	32,861
Net Income	120,125	190,934	(31,124)	136,734	(270,644)	74,874	122,114	67,227
Average Shares	80,417	89,757	91,557	91,671	83,468	77,928	70,636	67,080
Balance Sheet								
Current Assets	442,191	462,819	543,880	578,205	752,633	605,877	690,875	596,297
Total Assets	5,372,583	5,204,613	5,225,083	5,359,921	6,147,982	5,872,136	6,165,624	5,124,709
Current Liabilities	434,103	373,268	520,124	563,273	1,428,388	1,584,069	1,310,851	723,496
Long-Term Obligations	1,669,760	1,671,626	1,563,595	1,565,206	1,379,011	1,231,859	1,765,907	1,746,395
Total Liabilities	3,752,867	3,619,099	3,576,812	3,598,675	4,390,047	4,168,196	4,460,799	3,826,721
Stockholders' Equity	1,619,716	1,585,514	1,648,271	1,761,246	1,757,935	1,703,940	1,704,825	1,297,988
Shares Outstanding	79,653	79,653	86,673	86,673	86,531	76,814	76,648	68,786
Statistical Record								
Return on Assets %	2.27	3.66	N.M.	2.38	N.M.	1.24	2.16	1.56
Return on Equity %	7.48	11.81	N.M.	7.77	N.M.	4.39	8.13	5.58
EBITDA Margin %	36.45	36.29	32.70	28.11	3.39	17.70	15.99	15.04
Net Margin %	8.95	11.23	N.M.	8.30	N.M.	3.91	4.94	3.24
Asset Turnover	0.25	0.33	0.32	0.29	0.33	0.32	0.44	0.48
Current Ratio	1.02	1.24	1.05	1.03	0.53	0.38	0.53	0.82
Debt to Equity	1.03	1.05	0.95	0.89	0.78	0.72	1.04	1.35
Price Range	22.32-17.52	19.11-12.98	13.93-10.94	12.88-6.20	21.45-7.86	34.00-21.45	31.80-22.99	30.26-24.06
P/E Ratio	17.04-13.37	9.75-6.62	...	9.47-4.56	...	35.42-22.34	18.38-13.29	30.26-24.06
Average Yield %	2.85	3.19	4.10	4.77	5.66	3.34	3.22	2.84

Address: 414 Silver Ave. S.W., Albuquerque, NM 87102-3289
Telephone: 505-241-2700

Web Site: www.pnmresources.com
Officers: Patricia K. Vincent-Collawn - Chairman, President, Chief Executive Officer Charles N. Eldred - Executive Vice President, Chief Financial Officer

Auditors: KPMG LLP
Investor Contact: 505-241-2211
Transfer Agents: Computershare

POLARIS INDUSTRIES INC.

Exchange	Symbol	Price	52Wk Range	Yield	P/E	Div Achiever
NYS	PII	$92.49 (3/28/2013)	93.23-68.63	1.82	21.02	17 Years

*7 Year Price Score 196.13 *NYSE Composite Index=100 *12 Month Price Score 99.70

Interim Earnings (Per Share)
Qtr.	Mar	Jun	Sep	Dec
2008	0.28	0.36	0.56	0.55
2009	0.13	0.27	0.47	0.66
2010	0.29	0.38	0.69	0.79
2011	0.67	0.69	0.95	0.90
2012	0.85	0.98	1.33	1.24

Interim Dividends (Per Share)
Amt	Decl	Ex	Rec	Pay
0.37Q	04/27/2012	05/30/2012	06/01/2012	06/15/2012
0.37Q	07/26/2012	08/29/2012	08/31/2012	09/17/2012
0.37Q	10/25/2012	11/28/2012	11/30/2012	12/17/2012
0.42Q	01/31/2013	02/27/2013	03/01/2013	03/15/2013

Indicated Div: $1.68 (Div. Reinv. Plan)

Valuation Analysis
		Institutional Holding	
Forecast EPS	$5.15	No of Institutions	453
	(04/06/2013)		
Market Cap	$6.3 Billion	Shares	53,327,280
Book Value	$690.5 Million	% Held	73.16
Price/Book	9.19		
Price/Sales	1.98		

Business Summary: Autos- Manufacturing (MIC: 1.8.1 SIC: 3799 NAIC: 336999)

Polaris Industries produces off-road vehicles (ORV), including all-terrain vehicles (ATVs) and side-by-side vehicles for recreational and utility use, snowmobiles, and on-road vehicles, including motorcycles and small electric vehicles, together with the related replacement parts, garments and accessories. Co.'s ORVs include ATVs and RANGER® and RZR® side-by-side vehicles; its snowmobiles include the Polaris snowmobile; and its On-Road Vehicles consist of Victory® and Indian® motorcycles and small vehicles. These products are sold through dealers and distributors principally located in the U.S., Canada and Europe.

Recent Developments: For the year ended Dec 31 2012, net income increased 37.2% to US$312.3 million from US$227.6 million in the prior year. Revenues were US$3.21 billion, up 20.8% from US$2.66 billion the year before. Operating income was US$478.4 million versus US$349.9 million in the prior year, an increase of 36.7%. Direct operating expenses rose 19.2% to US$2.28 billion from US$1.92 billion in the comparable period the year ago. Indirect operating expenses increased 14.4% to US$446.9 million from US$390.7 million in the equivalent prior-year period.

Prospects: Our evaluation of Polaris Industries Inc. as of Apr. 7, 2013 is the result of our systematic analysis on three basic characteristics: earnings strength, relative valuation, and recent stock price movement. The company has managed to produce a neutral trend in earnings per share over the past 5 quarters and while recent estimates for the company have remained steady, PII has posted better than expected results. Based on operating earnings yield, the company is about fairly valued when compared to all of the companies in our coverage universe. Share price changes over the past year indicates that PII will perform well over the near term.

Financial Data
(US$ in Thousands)	12/31/2012	12/31/2011	12/31/2010	12/31/2009	12/31/2008	12/31/2007	12/31/2006	12/31/2005
Earnings Per Share	4.40	3.20	2.14	1.52	1.75	1.53	1.29	1.64
Cash Flow Per Share	6.03	4.40	4.45	2.98	2.67	2.98	1.81	1.92
Tang Book Value Per Share	8.50	6.17	4.96	2.74	1.73	2.14	2.01	4.13
Dividends Per Share	1.480	0.900	0.800	0.780	0.760	0.680	0.620	0.560
Dividend Payout %	33.64	28.13	37.38	51.15	43.43	44.30	48.06	34.25
Income Statement								
Total Revenue	3,209,782	2,656,949	1,991,139	1,565,887	1,948,254	1,780,009	1,656,518	1,869,819
EBITDA	556,534	417,003	287,740	219,878	252,948	247,530	241,074	278,974
Depn & Amortn	70,580	66,390	66,519	64,593	66,112	62,093	71,164	67,936
Income Before Taxes	480,022	346,626	218,541	151,174	177,218	170,336	160,137	206,325
Income Taxes	167,533	119,051	71,403	50,157	59,667	57,738	50,988	64,348
Net Income	312,310	227,575	147,138	101,017	117,395	111,650	106,985	143,278
Average Shares	71,005	71,057	68,764	66,148	67,128	72,648	82,902	87,762
Balance Sheet								
Current Assets	1,017,841	878,676	808,145	491,500	443,612	447,556	392,961	373,988
Total Assets	1,486,492	1,228,024	1,061,647	763,653	751,148	769,881	778,791	768,956
Current Liabilities	631,029	615,531	584,210	343,074	404,833	388,246	361,420	375,614
Long-Term Obligations	104,292	104,600	100,000	200,000	200,000	200,000	250,000	18,000
Total Liabilities	795,962	727,968	690,656	559,112	614,121	596,899	611,420	399,299
Stockholders' Equity	690,530	500,056	370,991	204,541	137,027	172,982	167,371	369,657
Shares Outstanding	68,647	68,430	68,468	65,296	64,984	68,424	70,910	83,374
Statistical Record								
Return on Assets %	22.95	19.88	16.12	13.34	15.39	14.42	13.82	18.35
Return on Equity %	52.32	52.25	51.13	59.15	75.53	65.61	39.84	39.18
EBITDA Margin %	17.34	15.69	14.45	14.04	12.98	13.91	14.55	14.92
Net Margin %	9.73	8.57	7.39	6.45	6.03	6.27	6.46	7.66
Asset Turnover	2.36	2.32	2.18	2.07	2.55	2.30	2.14	2.39
Current Ratio	1.61	1.43	1.38	1.43	1.10	1.15	1.09	1.00
Debt to Equity	0.15	0.21	0.27	0.98	1.46	1.16	1.49	0.05
Price Range	88.35-54.67	65.53-35.75	40.35-21.29	24.37-7.29	26.25-10.10	28.87-21.35	27.28-18.10	36.92-22.22
P/E Ratio	20.08-12.43	20.48-11.17	18.86-9.95	16.03-4.80	15.00-5.77	18.87-13.95	21.15-14.03	22.52-13.55
Average Yield %	1.96	1.78	2.70	4.67	3.79	2.76	2.74	1.97

Address: 2100 Highway 55, Medina, MN 55340 **Telephone:** 763-542-0500	**Web Site:** www.polaris.com **Officers:** Scott W. Wine - Chairman, Chief Executive Officer Bennett J. Morgan - President, Chief Operating Officer	**Auditors:** Ernst & Young LLP **Investor Contact:** 763-513-3477 **Transfer Agents:** Wells Fargo Shareowner Services, Mendota Heights, MN

PPG INDUSTRIES, INC.

Exchange	Symbol	Price	52Wk Range	Yield	P/E	Div Achiever
NYS	PPG	$133.94 (3/28/2013)	144.21-92.09	1.76	22.10	41 Years

*7 Year Price Score 139.70 *NYSE Composite Index=100 *12 Month Price Score 106.96

Interim Earnings (Per Share)

Qtr.	Mar	Jun	Sep	Dec
2008	0.61	1.51	0.70	0.43
2009	(0.68)	0.89	0.96	0.86
2010	0.18	1.63	1.58	1.24
2011	1.40	2.12	1.96	1.39
2012	0.08	2.34	2.18	1.45

Interim Dividends (Per Share)

Amt	Decl	Ex	Rec	Pay
0.59Q	04/19/2012	05/08/2012	05/10/2012	06/12/2012
0.59Q	07/19/2012	08/08/2012	08/10/2012	09/12/2012
0.59Q	10/18/2012	11/07/2012	11/09/2012	12/12/2012
0.59Q	01/17/2013	02/20/2013	02/22/2013	03/12/2013

Indicated Div: $2.36 (Div. Reinv. Plan)

Valuation Analysis

		Institutional Holding	
Forecast EPS	$7.80	No of Institutions	
	(04/06/2013)	830	
Market Cap	$20.6 Billion	Shares	
Book Value	$4.1 Billion	131,376,200	
Price/Book	5.06	% Held	
Price/Sales	1.35	77.30	

Business Summary: Construction Materials (MIC: 8.5.1 SIC: 2851 NAIC: 325510)

PPG Industries operates in six segments. The Performance Coatings, Industrial Coatings and Architectural Coatings - Europe, Middle East and Africa segments supply protective and decorative finishes; factory-finished aluminum extrusions and steel and aluminum coils; marine and aircraft equipment; automotive original equipment, and other industrial and consumer products. The Optical and Specialty Materials segment is comprised of Co.'s optical products and silicas businesses. The Commodity Chemicals segment produces chlor-alkali and derivative products including caustic soda and chlorinated solvents. The Glass business segment is comprised of Co.'s flat glass and fiber glass businesses.

Recent Developments: For the year ended Dec 31 2012, net income decreased 12.2% to US$1.06 billion from US$1.21 billion in the prior year. Revenues were US$15.20 billion, up 2.1% from US$14.89 billion the year before. Direct operating expenses increased to US$9.07 billion from US$9.08 billion in the comparable period the year before. Indirect operating expenses increased 11.6% to US$4.71 billion from US$4.22 billion in the equivalent prior-year period.

Prospects: Our evaluation of PPG Industries Inc. as of Apr. 7, 2013 is the result of our systematic analysis on three basic characteristics: earnings strength, relative valuation, and recent stock price movement. The company has generated a negative trend in earnings per share over the past 5 quarters. However, while recent estimates for the company have been mixed, PPG has posted results that were in line with analysts expectations. Based on operating earnings yield, the company is undervalued when compared to all of the companies in our coverage universe. Share price changes over the past year indicates that PPG will perform very well over the near term.

Financial Data
(US$ in Thousands)

	12/31/2012	12/31/2011	12/31/2010	12/31/2009	12/31/2008	12/31/2007	12/31/2006	12/31/2005
Earnings Per Share	6.06	6.87	4.63	2.03	3.25	5.03	4.27	3.49
Cash Flow Per Share	11.62	9.13	7.96	8.16	8.23	6.05	6.82	6.28
Tang Book Value Per Share	1.41	N.M.	N.M.	N.M.	N.M.	12.59	7.63	8.46
Dividends Per Share	2.340	2.260	2.180	2.130	2.090	2.040	1.910	1.860
Dividend Payout %	38.61	32.90	47.08	104.93	64.31	40.56	44.73	53.30
Income Statement								
Total Revenue	15,200,000	14,885,000	13,423,000	12,239,000	15,849,000	11,206,000	11,037,000	10,201,000
EBITDA	1,917,000	2,074,000	1,751,000	1,141,000	1,561,000	1,608,000	1,432,000	1,341,000
Depn & Amortn	355,000	346,000	346,000	354,000	428,000	322,000	337,000	340,000
Income Before Taxes	1,391,000	1,560,000	1,250,000	622,000	905,000	1,213,000	1,026,000	933,000
Income Taxes	338,000	385,000	415,000	191,000	284,000	355,000	278,000	282,000
Net Income	941,000	1,095,000	769,000	336,000	538,000	834,000	711,000	596,000
Average Shares	155,100	159,300	165,900	165,500	165,400	165,900	166,500	170,900
Balance Sheet								
Current Assets	7,715,000	6,694,000	7,058,000	5,981,000	6,348,000	7,136,000	4,592,000	4,019,000
Total Assets	15,878,000	14,382,000	14,975,000	14,240,000	14,698,000	12,629,000	10,021,000	8,681,000
Current Liabilities	4,461,000	3,702,000	3,625,000	3,577,000	4,210,000	4,661,000	2,787,000	2,349,000
Long-Term Obligations	3,368,000	3,574,000	4,043,000	3,074,000	3,009,000	1,201,000	1,155,000	1,169,000
Total Liabilities	11,815,000	11,133,000	11,337,000	10,487,000	11,365,000	8,478,000	6,787,000	5,628,000
Stockholders' Equity	4,063,000	3,249,000	3,638,000	3,753,000	3,333,000	4,151,000	3,234,000	3,053,000
Shares Outstanding	153,566	151,888	160,381	165,667	164,198	163,800	164,081	165,277
Statistical Record								
Return on Assets %	6.20	7.46	5.26	2.32	3.93	7.36	7.60	6.77
Return on Equity %	25.67	31.80	20.81	9.48	14.34	22.59	22.62	17.99
EBITDA Margin %	12.61	13.93	13.04	9.32	9.85	14.35	12.97	13.15
Net Margin %	6.19	7.36	5.73	2.75	3.39	7.44	6.44	5.84
Asset Turnover	1.00	1.01	0.92	0.85	1.16	0.99	1.18	1.16
Current Ratio	1.73	1.81	1.95	1.67	1.51	1.53	1.65	1.71
Debt to Equity	0.83	1.10	1.11	0.82	0.90	0.29	0.36	0.38
Price Range	135.35-84.33	96.49-68.68	84.21-57.68	62.08-28.48	70.23-36.98	82.20-64.30	69.28-56.92	73.80-55.95
P/E Ratio	22.33-13.92	14.05-10.00	18.19-12.46	30.58-14.03	21.61-11.38	16.34-12.78	16.22-13.33	21.15-16.03
Average Yield %	2.19	2.68	3.17	4.39	3.59	2.82	2.98	2.88

Address: One PPG Place, Pittsburgh, PA 15272	Web Site: www.ppg.com	Auditors: PricewaterhouseCoopers LLP
Telephone: 412-434-3131	**Officers:** Charles E. Bunch - Chairman, President, Chief Executive Officer, Executive Vice President, Chief Operating Officer, Senior Vice President Viktoras R. Sekmakas - Executive Vice President	**Investor Contact:** 412-434-3740
Fax: 412-434-2571		**Transfer Agents:** Computershare, Pittsburgh, PA

PPL CORP

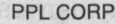

Exchange	Symbol	Price	52Wk Range	Yield	P/E	Div Achiever
NYS	PPL	$31.31 (3/28/2013)	31.31-26.77	4.69	12.04	13 Years

*7 Year Price Score 76.29   *NYSE Composite Index=100   ***12 Month Price Score 97.41**

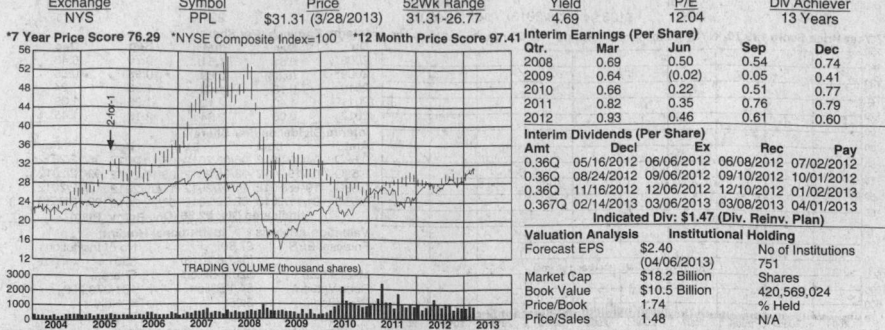

Interim Earnings (Per Share)

Qtr.	Mar	Jun	Sep	Dec
2008	0.69	0.50	0.54	0.74
2009	0.64	(0.02)	0.05	0.41
2010	0.86	0.22	0.51	0.77
2011	0.82	0.35	0.76	0.79
2012	0.93	0.46	0.61	0.60

Interim Dividends (Per Share)

Amt	Decl	Ex	Rec	Pay
0.36Q	05/16/2012	06/06/2012	06/08/2012	07/02/2012
0.36Q	08/24/2012	09/06/2012	09/10/2012	10/01/2012
0.36Q	11/16/2012	12/06/2012	12/10/2012	01/02/2013
0.367Q	02/14/2013	03/06/2013	03/08/2013	04/01/2013

Indicated Div: $1.47 (Div. Reinv. Plan)

Valuation Analysis

		Institutional Holding	
Forecast EPS	$2.40 (04/06/2013)	No of Institutions	751
Market Cap	$18.2 Billion	Shares	420,569,024
Book Value	$10.5 Billion	% Held	N/A
Price/Book	1.74		
Price/Sales	1.48		

Business Summary: Electric Utilities (MIC: 3.1.1 SIC: 4911 NAIC: 221122)

PPL is an energy and utility holding company. Through its subsidiaries, Co. generates electricity from power plants in the northeastern, northwestern and southeastern U.S.; markets energy mainly in the northeastern and northwestern portions of the U.S.; delivers electricity to customers in Pennsylvania, Kentucky, Virginia, Tennessee and the U.K. and natural gas to customers in Kentucky. As of Dec 31 2011, Co.'s subsidiary, Louisville Gas and Electric Company, provided electric service to about 394,000 customers in Louisville and adjacent areas in Kentucky. Also, at such date, Co. operated in four segments: Kentucky Regulated, International Regulated, Pennsylvania Regulated and Supply.

Recent Developments: For the year ended Dec 31 2012, net income increased 1.3% to US$1.53 billion from US$1.51 billion in the prior year. Revenues were US$12.29 billion, down 3.5% from US$12.74 billion the year before. Operating income was US$3.11 billion versus US$3.10 billion in the prior year, an increase of 0.3%. Direct operating expenses declined 5.7% to US$8.33 billion from US$8.83 billion in the comparable period the year before. Indirect operating expenses increased 4.9% to US$850.0 million from US$810.0 million in the equivalent prior-year period.

Prospects: Our evaluation of PPL Corp. as of Apr. 7, 2013 is the result of our systematic analysis on three basic characteristics: earnings strength, relative valuation, and recent stock price movement. The company has generated a negative trend in earnings per share over the past 5 quarters and while recent estimates for the company have been mixed, PPL has posted better than expected results. Based on operating earnings yield, the company is undervalued when compared to all of the companies in our coverage universe. Share price changes over the past year indicates that PPL will perform in line with the market over the near term.

Financial Data
(US$ in Thousands)

	12/31/2012	12/31/2011	12/31/2010	12/31/2009	12/31/2008	12/31/2007	12/31/2006	12/31/2005
Earnings Per Share	2.60	2.70	2.17	1.08	2.47	3.35	2.24	1.77
Cash Flow Per Share	4.75	4.55	4.71	4.92	4.24	4.13	4.62	3.66
Tang Book Value Per Share	9.27	9.77	11.34	10.80	9.91	11.33	9.35	7.72
Dividends Per Share	1.440	1.400	1.400	1.380	1.340	1.220	1.100	0.960
Dividend Payout %	55.38	51.85	64.52	127.78	54.25	36.42	49.11	54.24
Income Statement								
Total Revenue	12,286,000	12,737,000	8,521,000	7,556,000	8,044,000	6,498,000	6,899,000	6,219,000
EBITDA	4,146,000	4,053,000	2,391,000	1,449,000	2,265,000	2,171,000	2,068,000	1,772,000
Depn & Amortn	1,100,000	961,000	567,000	471,000	461,000	458,000	446,000	423,000
Income Before Taxes	2,090,000	2,201,000	1,239,000	596,000	1,378,000	1,300,000	1,181,000	864,000
Income Taxes	545,000	691,000	263,000	130,000	440,000	270,000	275,000	121,000
Net Income	1,526,000	1,495,000	938,000	407,000	930,000	1,288,000	865,000	678,000
Average Shares	581,626	550,952	431,569	376,406	376,526	385,111	386,769	383,737
Balance Sheet								
Current Assets	5,068,000	6,426,000	6,188,000	4,752,000	4,383,000	3,168,000	3,630,000	2,910,000
Total Assets	43,634,000	42,648,000	32,837,000	22,165,000	21,405,000	19,972,000	19,747,000	17,926,000
Current Liabilities	5,625,000	5,255,000	5,214,000	4,182,000	4,293,000	2,882,000	3,348,000	3,340,000
Long-Term Obligations	18,725,000	17,993,000	12,161,000	7,143,000	7,151,000	6,890,000	6,728,000	6,044,000
Total Liabilities	33,154,000	31,820,000	24,627,000	16,669,000	16,027,000	14,115,000	14,324,000	13,457,000
Stockholders' Equity	10,480,000	10,828,000	8,210,000	5,496,000	5,378,000	5,857,000	5,423,000	4,469,000
Shares Outstanding	581,944	578,405	483,391	377,183	375,000	373,271	385,039	380,145
Statistical Record								
Return on Assets %	3.53	3.96	3.41	1.87	4.48	6.49	4.59	3.80
Return on Equity %	14.28	15.71	13.69	7.49	16.51	22.84	17.49	15.48
EBITDA Margin %	33.75	31.82	28.06	19.18	28.16	33.41	29.98	28.49
Net Margin %	12.42	11.74	11.01	5.39	11.56	19.82	12.54	10.90
Asset Turnover	0.28	0.34	0.31	0.35	0.39	0.33	0.37	0.35
Current Ratio	0.90	1.22	1.19	1.14	1.02	1.10	1.08	0.87
Debt to Equity	1.79	1.66	1.48	1.30	1.33	1.18	1.24	1.35
Price Range	30.15-26.77	30.24-24.35	32.61-24.24	34.34-24.46	55.16-28.69	53.96-34.62	37.30-28.47	33.31-25.57
P/E Ratio	11.60-10.30	11.20-9.02	15.03-11.17	31.80-22.65	22.33-11.62	16.11-10.33	16.65-12.71	18.82-14.45
Average Yield %	5.07	5.11	5.14	4.50	3.10	2.69	3.41	3.30

Address: Two North Ninth Street, Allentown, PA 18101-1179 Telephone: 610-774-5151 Fax: 610-774-5106	Web Site: www.pplweb.com Officers: William H. Spence - President, Chief Executive Officer, Chief Operating Officer Paul A. Farr - Executive Vice President, Chief Financial Officer	Auditors: Ernst & Young LLP Investor Contact: 800-345-3085 Transfer Agents: Wells Fargo Bank, N.A., Shareowner Services, Mendota Heights, MN

PRAXAIR, INC.

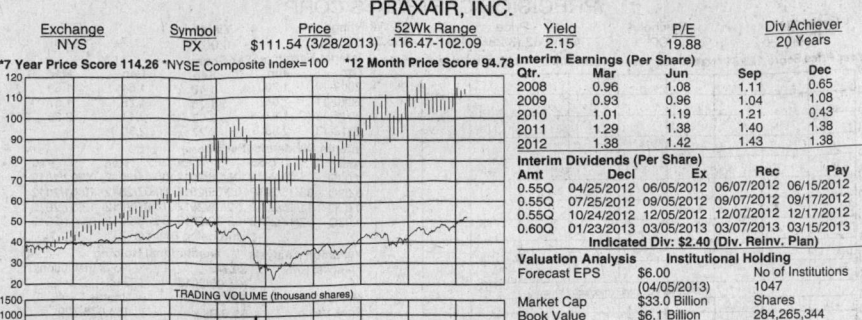

Exchange	Symbol	Price	52Wk Range	Yield	P/E	Div Achiever
NYS	PX	$111.54 (3/28/2013)	116.47-102.09	2.15	19.88	20 Years

*7 Year Price Score 114.26 *NYSE Composite Index=100 *12 Month Price Score 94.78

Interim Earnings (Per Share)

Qtr.	Mar	Jun	Sep	Dec
2008	0.96	1.08	1.11	0.65
2009	0.93	0.96	1.04	1.08
2010	1.01	1.19	1.21	0.43
2011	1.29	1.38	1.40	1.38
2012	1.38	1.42	1.43	1.38

Interim Dividends (Per Share)

Amt	Decl	Ex	Rec	Pay
0.55Q	04/25/2012	06/05/2012	06/07/2012	06/15/2012
0.55Q	07/25/2012	09/05/2012	09/07/2012	09/17/2012
0.55Q	10/24/2012	12/05/2012	12/07/2012	12/17/2012
0.60Q	01/23/2013	03/05/2013	03/07/2013	03/15/2013

Indicated Div: $2.40 (Div. Reinv. Plan)

Valuation Analysis

Forecast EPS	$6.00 (04/05/2013)
Market Cap	$33.0 Billion
Book Value	$6.1 Billion
Price/Book	5.45
Price/Sales	2.94

Institutional Holding

No of Institutions	1047
Shares	284,265,344
% Held	83.69

Business Summary: Specialty Chemicals (MIC: 8.3.2 SIC: 2819 NAIC: 325188)

Praxair is an industrial gases supplier. Co.'s primary products for its industrial gases business are atmospheric gases (oxygen, nitrogen, argon, rare gases) and process gases (carbon dioxide, helium, hydrogen, electronic gases, specialty gases, acetylene). Co. also designs, engineers, and builds equipment that produces industrial gases for internal use and external sale. Co. operates five segments: North America; Europe; South America; Asia; and surface technologies. The surface technologies segment is operated through Co.'s subsidiary, Praxair Surface Technologies, Inc., which supplies wear-resistant and high-temperature corrosion-resistant metallic and ceramic coatings and powders.

Recent Developments: For the year ended Dec 31 2012, net income increased 1.3% to US$1.74 billion from US$1.72 billion in the prior year. Revenues were US$11.22 billion, down 0.2% from US$11.25 billion the year before. Operating income was US$2.44 billion versus US$2.47 billion in the prior year, a decrease of 1.3%. Direct operating expenses declined 1.0% to US$6.40 billion from US$6.46 billion in the comparable period the year before. Indirect operating expenses increased 2.8% to US$2.39 billion from US$2.33 billion in the equivalent prior-year period.

Prospects: Our evaluation of Praxair Inc. as of Apr. 7, 2013 is the result of our systematic analysis on three basic characteristics: earnings strength, relative valuation, and recent stock price movement. The company has managed to produce a neutral trend in earnings per share over the past 5 quarters. However, while recent estimates for the company have been mixed, PX has posted better than expected results. Based on operating earnings yield, the company is about fairly valued when compared to all of the companies in our coverage universe. Share price changes over the past year indicates that PX will perform in line with the market over the near term.

Financial Data

(US$ in Thousands)	12/31/2012	12/31/2011	12/31/2010	12/31/2009	12/31/2008	12/31/2007	12/31/2006	12/31/2005
Earnings Per Share	5.61	5.45	3.84	4.01	3.80	3.62	3.00	2.20
Cash Flow Per Share	9.20	8.12	6.21	7.05	6.50	6.14	5.42	4.56
Tang Book Value Per Share	11.42	9.88	11.82	10.12	6.45	9.64	8.94	7.06
Dividends Per Share	2.200	2.000	1.800	1.600	1.500	1.200	1.000	0.720
Dividend Payout %	39.22	36.70	46.88	39.90	39.47	33.15	33.33	32.73
Income Statement								
Total Revenue	11,224,000	11,252,000	10,116,000	8,956,000	10,796,000	9,402,000	8,324,000	7,656,000
EBITDA	3,438,000	3,471,000	3,007,000	2,421,000	2,733,000	2,560,000	2,215,000	1,958,000
Depn & Amortn	1,001,000	1,003,000	925,000	846,000	850,000	774,000	696,000	665,000
Income Before Taxes	2,296,000	2,323,000	1,964,000	1,442,000	1,685,000	1,613,000	1,364,000	1,130,000
Income Taxes	586,000	641,000	768,000	169,000	465,000	419,000	355,000	376,000
Net Income	1,692,000	1,672,000	1,195,000	1,254,000	1,211,000	1,177,000	988,000	726,000
Average Shares	301,845	306,722	311,395	312,382	318,302	324,842	329,293	329,685
Balance Sheet								
Current Assets	2,792,000	2,607,000	2,378,000	2,223,000	2,301,000	2,408,000	2,059,000	2,133,000
Total Assets	18,090,000	16,356,000	15,274,000	14,317,000	13,054,000	13,382,000	11,102,000	10,491,000
Current Liabilities	2,479,000	2,535,000	2,110,000	1,813,000	2,979,000	2,650,000	1,758,000	2,001,000
Long-Term Obligations	6,685,000	5,838,000	5,155,000	4,757,000	3,709,000	3,364,000	2,981,000	2,926,000
Total Liabilities	12,026,000	10,868,000	9,482,000	9,002,000	9,045,000	8,240,000	6,548,000	6,589,000
Stockholders' Equity	6,064,000	5,488,000	5,792,000	5,315,000	4,009,000	5,142,000	4,554,000	3,902,000
Shares Outstanding	296,229	298,530	303,996	306,477	306,861	315,488	320,860	322,338
Statistical Record								
Return on Assets %	9.80	10.57	8.08	9.16	9.14	9.61	9.15	7.13
Return on Equity %	29.21	29.65	21.52	26.90	26.39	24.28	23.37	19.33
EBITDA Margin %	30.63	30.85	29.73	27.03	25.31	27.23	26.61	25.57
Net Margin %	15.07	14.86	11.81	14.00	11.22	12.52	11.87	9.48
Asset Turnover	0.65	0.71	0.68	0.65	0.81	0.77	0.77	0.75
Current Ratio	1.13	1.03	1.13	1.23	0.77	0.91	1.17	1.07
Debt to Equity	1.10	1.06	0.89	0.90	0.93	0.65	0.65	0.75
Price Range	116.47-102.09	111.30-88.93	95.97-74.01	84.89-53.93	99.50-47.80	91.75-58.85	63.54-50.59	54.08-41.07
P/E Ratio	20.76-18.20	20.42-16.32	24.99-19.27	21.17-13.45	26.18-12.58	25.35-16.26	21.18-16.98	24.58-18.67
Average Yield %	2.03	2.00	2.13	2.19	1.85	1.65	1.78	1.51

Address: 39 Old Ridgebury Road, Danbury, CT 06810-5113 **Telephone:** 203-837-2000 **Fax:** 203-837-2450	**Web Site:** www.praxair.com **Officers:** Stephen F. Angel - Chairman, Chief Executive Officer Scott E. Telesz - Executive Vice President, Senior Vice President	**Auditors:** PricewaterhouseCoopers LLP **Investor Contact:** 203-837-2210 **Transfer Agents:** Registrar and Transfer Company, Cranford, NJ

PRECISION CASTPARTS CORP.

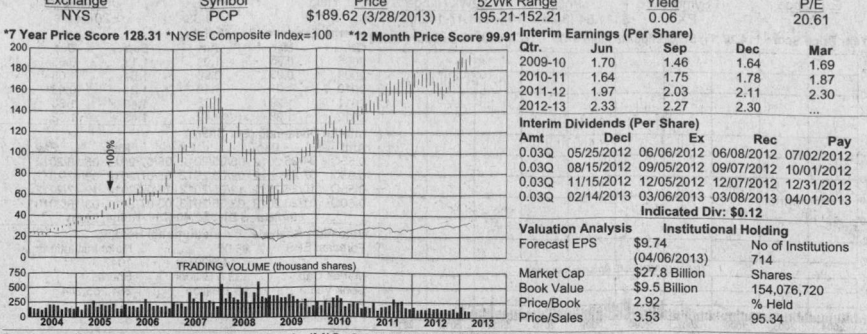

Exchange	Symbol	Price	52Wk Range	Yield	P/E
NYS	PCP	$189.62 (3/28/2013)	195.21-152.21	0.06	20.61

*7 Year Price Score 128.31 *NYSE Composite Index=100   *12 Month Price Score 99.91

Interim Earnings (Per Share)

Qtr.	Jun	Sep	Dec	Mar
2009-10	1.70	1.46	1.64	1.69
2010-11	1.64	1.75	1.78	1.87
2011-12	1.97	2.03	2.11	2.30
2012-13	2.33	2.27	2.30	...

Interim Dividends (Per Share)

Amt	Decl	Ex	Rec	Pay
0.03Q	05/25/2012	06/06/2012	06/08/2012	07/02/2012
0.03Q	08/15/2012	09/05/2012	09/07/2012	10/01/2012
0.03Q	11/15/2012	12/05/2012	12/07/2012	12/31/2012
0.03Q	02/14/2013	03/06/2013	03/08/2013	04/01/2013

Indicated Div: $0.12

Valuation Analysis

Forecast EPS	$9.74 (04/06/2013)
Market Cap	$27.8 Billion
Book Value	$9.5 Billion
Price/Book	2.92
Price/Sales	3.53

Institutional Holding

No of Institutions	714
Shares	154,076,720
% Held	95.34

Business Summary: Non-Precious Metals (MIC: 8.2.2 SIC: 3324 NAIC: 331512)

Precision Castparts is a manufacturer of metal components and products, and provides investment castings, forgings and fasteners/fastener systems for aerospace and industrial gas turbine applications. Co. provides investment castings and forgings for general industrial, armament, medical and other applications; nickel alloys in mill forms, as well as cobalt alloys, for the aerospace, chemical processing, oil and gas, pollution control and other industries; and seamless pipe for coal-fired, industrial gas turbine, and nuclear power plants. At Apr 1 2012, Co. manufactured metal components and products in three business segments: Investment Cast Products, Forged Products and Fastener Products.

Recent Developments: For the quarter ended Dec 30 2012, income from continuing operations increased 9.8% to US$340.4 million from US$310.1 million in the year-earlier quarter. Net income increased 10.0% to US$338.5 million from US$307.7 million in the year-earlier quarter. Revenues were US$2.04 billion, up 13.4% from US$1.80 billion the year before. Direct operating expenses rose 12.7% to US$1.39 billion from US$1.23 billion in the comparable period the year before. Indirect operating expenses increased 28.4% to US$145.9 million from US$113.6 million in the equivalent prior-year period.

Prospects: Our evaluation of Precision Castparts Corp. as of Apr. 7, 2013 is the result of our systematic analysis on three basic characteristics: earnings strength, relative valuation, and recent stock price movement. The company has managed to produce a neutral trend in earnings per share over the past 5 quarters. However, while recent estimates for the company have been mixed, PCP has posted results that fell short of analysts expectations. Based on operating earnings yield, the company is about fairly valued when compared to all of the companies in our coverage universe. Share price changes over the past year indicates that PCP will perform well over the near term.

Financial Data

(US$ in Thousands)	9 Mos	6 Mos	3 Mos	04/01/2012	04/03/2011	03/28/2010	03/29/2009	03/30/2008
Earnings Per Share	9.20	9.01	8.77	8.41	7.04	6.49	7.43	7.04
Cash Flow Per Share	9.27	8.69	8.60	7.21	7.16	6.48	7.93	6.63
Tang Book Value Per Share	6.97	21.65	22.05	24.91	26.56	18.13	16.42	12.28
Dividends Per Share	0.120	0.120	0.120	0.120	0.120	0.120	0.120	0.120
Dividend Payout %	1.30	1.33	1.37	1.43	1.70	1.85	1.62	1.70
Income Statement								
Total Revenue	5,939,700	3,896,500	1,969,700	7,214,600	6,220,100	5,486,600	6,827,900	6,852,100
EBITDA	1,680,200	1,107,000	561,100	1,971,800	1,651,100	1,565,000	1,716,900	1,629,900
Depn & Amortn	146,100	93,500	45,600	154,600	148,300	142,600	129,000	125,100
Income Before Taxes	1,520,700	1,010,400	514,300	1,812,000	1,493,800	1,409,300	1,577,500	1,462,500
Income Taxes	503,800	335,700	171,800	594,400	499,700	485,600	539,100	495,400
Net Income	1,012,400	674,400	341,700	1,224,100	1,013,500	921,800	1,044,500	987,300
Average Shares	146,800	146,400	146,400	145,600	143,900	142,100	140,600	140,200
Balance Sheet								
Current Assets	5,214,600	3,623,000	3,479,400	3,785,800	3,650,600	2,522,100	2,784,700	2,372,300
Total Assets	16,689,900	11,810,800	11,067,500	10,558,800	8,955,900	7,660,700	6,721,400	6,050,100
Current Liabilities	1,581,600	1,104,700	1,226,800	1,070,900	942,000	893,800	1,060,800	1,204,800
Long-Term Obligations	3,620,800	661,800	235,500	207,700	221,900	234,900	250,800	334,900
Total Liabilities	7,190,400	2,739,100	2,395,700	2,198,100	1,794,400	1,771,900	1,861,600	2,005,100
Stockholders' Equity	9,499,500	9,071,700	8,671,800	8,360,700	7,161,500	5,888,800	4,859,800	4,045,000
Shares Outstanding	146,452	145,537	145,348	145,257	143,711	141,883	139,873	139,027
Statistical Record								
Return on Assets %	10.03	12.16	12.52	12.58	12.00	12.85	16.40	17.51
Return on Equity %	15.31	15.66	15.83	15.82	15.28	17.20	23.52	28.77
EBITDA Margin %	28.29	28.41	28.49	27.33	26.54	28.52	25.15	23.79
Net Margin %	17.04	17.31	17.35	16.97	16.29	16.80	15.30	14.41
Asset Turnover	0.59	0.71	0.73	0.74	0.74	0.77	1.07	1.22
Current Ratio	3.30	3.28	2.84	3.54	3.88	2.82	2.63	1.97
Debt to Equity	0.38	0.07	0.03	0.02	0.03	0.04	0.05	0.08
Price Range	188.82-152.21	178.92-145.62	178.92-138.78	177.31-138.78	151.25-102.25	123.82-59.62	128.20-47.23	153.72-95.83
P/E Ratio	20.52-16.54	19.86-16.16	20.40-15.82	21.08-16.50	21.48-14.52	19.08-9.19	17.25-6.36	21.84-13.61
Average Yield %	0.07	0.07	0.07	0.07	0.09	0.13	0.15	0.10

Address: 4650 S.W. Macadam Avenue, Suite 400, Portland, OR 97239-4262 Telephone: 503-946-4800	Web Site: www.precast.com Officers: Mark Donegan - Chairman, Chief Executive Officer Kenneth D. Buck - Executive Vice President, Division Officer	Auditors: Deloitte & Touche LLP Investor Contact: 503-946-4850 Transfer Agents: The Bank of New York Mellon, Pittsburgh, PA

PRINCIPAL FINANCIAL GROUP, INC.

Exchange	Symbol	Price	52Wk Range	Yield	P/E
NYS	PFG	$34.03 (3/28/2013)	34.38-23.23	2.70	13.24

*7 Year Price Score 67.84 ***NYSE Composite Index=100** ***12 Month Price Score 105.65**

Interim Earnings (Per Share)

Qtr.	Mar	Jun	Sep	Dec
2008	0.67	0.64	0.35	(0.03)
2009	0.43	0.52	0.57	0.43
2010	0.59	0.42	0.44	0.61
2011	0.60	0.80	0.20	0.54
2012	0.66	0.58	0.60	0.73

Interim Dividends (Per Share)

Amt	Decl	Ex	Rec	Pay
0.18Q	05/22/2012	05/31/2012	06/04/2012	06/29/2012
0.21Q	08/21/2012	09/04/2012	09/06/2012	09/28/2012
0.21Q	10/25/2012	12/06/2012	12/10/2012	12/28/2012
0.23Q	01/31/2013	03/07/2013	03/11/2013	03/29/2013

Indicated Div: $0.92

Valuation Analysis

		Institutional Holding	
Forecast EPS	$3.23	No of Institutions	
	(04/06/2013)	425	
Market Cap	$10.0 Billion	Shares	
Book Value	$9.8 Billion	203,272,960	
Price/Book	1.02	% Held	
Price/Sales	1.08	64.85	

Business Summary: Life & Health (MIC: 5.2.2 SIC: 6321 NAIC: 524114)

Principal Financial Group is an insurance holding company. Through its subsidiaries, Co. is engaged in providing retirement services, insurance services and asset management. Co. provides businesses, individuals and institutional clients a range of financial products and services, including retirement, asset management and insurance through its family of financial services companies. Co. is also provider of corporate defined contribution plans in the U.S. Co. is also an employee stock ownership plan consultant. Co. organizes its businesses into the following segments: Retirement and Investor Services; Principal Global Investors; Principal International and U.S. Insurance Solutions.

Recent Developments: For the year ended Dec 31 2012, net income increased 19.7% to US$824.7 million from US$688.9 million in the prior year. Revenues were US$9.22 billion, up 6.3% from US$8.67 billion the year before. Net premiums earned were US$3.22 billion versus US$2.89 billion in the prior year, an increase of 11.4%. Net investment income fell 3.6% to US$3.25 billion from US$3.38 billion a year ago.

Prospects: Our evaluation of Principal Financial Group Inc. as of Apr. 7, 2013 is the result of our systematic analysis on three basic characteristics: earnings strength, relative valuation, and recent stock price movement. The company has managed to produce a neutral trend in earnings per share over the past 5 quarters and while recent estimates for the company have been raised by analysts, PFG has posted better than expected results. Based on operating earnings yield, the company is undervalued when compared to all of the companies in our coverage universe. Share price changes over the past year indicates that PFG will perform poorly over the near term.

Financial Data
(US$ in Thousands)

	12/31/2012	12/31/2011	12/31/2010	12/31/2009	12/31/2008	12/31/2007	12/31/2006	12/31/2005
Earnings Per Share	2.57	2.15	2.06	1.97	1.63	3.09	3.74	3.11
Cash Flow Per Share	10.33	8.63	8.72	7.54	8.56	11.15	8.35	8.28
Tang Book Value Per Share	28.40	27.45	26.68	20.86	4.52	23.31	24.28	26.09
Dividends Per Share	0.780	0.700	0.550	0.500	0.450	0.900	0.800	0.650
Dividend Payout %	30.35	32.56	26.70	25.38	27.61	29.13	21.39	20.90
Income Statement								
Premium Income	3,219,400	2,891,000	3,555,500	3,750,600	4,209,200	4,634,100	4,305,300	3,975,000
Total Revenue	9,215,100	8,709,600	9,158,600	8,849,100	9,935,900	10,906,500	9,870,500	9,007,700
Benefits & Claims	5,123,900	4,454,100	5,338,400	5,334,500	6,219,900	6,435,300	5,692,400	5,282,900
Income Before Taxes	959,400	987,600	841,300	745,800	453,600	1,048,200	1,328,700	1,124,300
Income Taxes	134,700	236,400	124,100	100,100	(4,500)	208,100	295,000	232,400
Net Income	805,900	715,000	699,300	622,700	458,100	860,300	1,064,300	919,000
Average Shares	300,400	317,600	323,000	298,900	261,100	268,100	275,500	289,900
Balance Sheet								
Total Assets	161,926,500	148,298,000	145,631,100	137,759,400	128,182,400	154,520,200	143,658,100	127,035,400
Total Liabilities	152,112,900	138,661,000	135,903,300	129,865,900	125,709,600	147,098,500	135,797,300	119,228,200
Stockholders' Equity	9,813,600	9,637,000	9,727,800	7,893,500	2,472,800	7,421,700	7,860,800	7,807,200
Shares Outstanding	293,800	301,100	320,400	319,000	259,300	259,100	268,400	280,600
Statistical Record								
Return on Assets %	0.52	0.49	0.49	0.47	0.32	0.58	0.79	0.76
Return on Equity %	8.26	7.38	7.94	12.01	9.23	11.26	13.59	11.97
Loss Ratio %	159.16	154.07	150.14	142.23	147.77	138.87	132.22	132.90
Net Margin %	8.75	8.21	7.64	7.04	4.61	7.89	10.78	10.20
Price Range	29.93-23.23	34.69-21.22	33.32-21.45	30.83-5.88	68.84-9.43	70.72-52.77	59.34-45.97	51.90-36.91
P/E Ratio	11.65-9.04	16.13-9.87	16.17-10.41	15.65-2.98	42.23-5.79	22.89-17.08	15.87-12.29	16.69-11.87
Average Yield %	2.90	2.47	2.07	2.45	1.04	1.47	1.51	1.50

Address: 711 High Street, Des Moines, IA 50392
Telephone: 515-247-5111

Web Site: www.principal.com
Officers: J. Barry Griswell - Chairman Larry D. Zimpleman - President, Chief Executive Officer, Chief Operating Officer, Division Officer

Auditors: Ernst & Young LLP
Investor Contact: 515-235-9500
Transfer Agents: ComputerShare Investor Services, Providence, RI

PROCTER & GAMBLE CO.

Exchange	Symbol	Price	52Wk Range	Yield	P/E	Div Achiever
NYS	PG	$77.06 (3/28/2013)	77.58-59.27	2.92	17.47	59 Years

*7 Year Price Score 95.75 *NYSE Composite Index=100 *12 Month Price Score 103.48

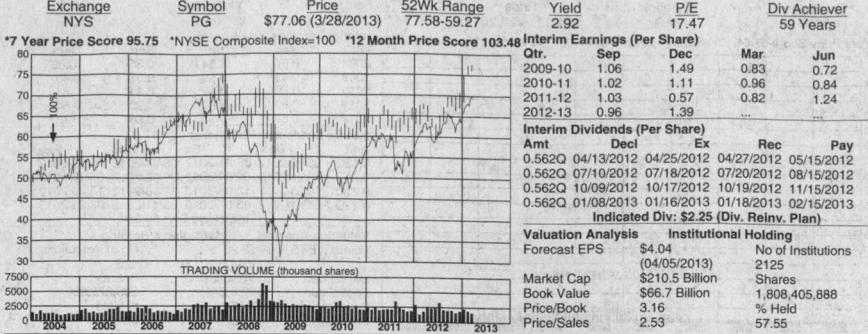

Interim Earnings (Per Share)

Qtr.	Sep	Dec	Mar	Jun
2009-10	1.06	1.49	0.83	0.72
2010-11	1.02	1.11	0.96	0.84
2011-12	1.03	0.57	0.82	1.24
2012-13	0.96	1.39	...	

Interim Dividends (Per Share)

Amt	Decl	Ex	Rec	Pay
0.562Q	04/13/2012	04/25/2012	04/27/2012	05/15/2012
0.562Q	07/10/2012	07/18/2012	07/20/2012	08/15/2012
0.562Q	10/09/2012	10/17/2012	10/19/2012	11/15/2012
0.562Q	01/08/2013	01/16/2013	01/18/2013	02/15/2013

Indicated Div: $2.25 (Div. Reinv. Plan)

Valuation Analysis | **Institutional Holding**

Forecast EPS	$4.04 (04/05/2013)	No of Institutions 2125
Market Cap	$210.5 Billion	Shares
Book Value	$66.7 Billion	1,808,405,888
Price/Book	3.16	% Held
Price/Sales	2.53	57.55

Business Summary: Household & Personal Products (MIC: 1.7.1 SIC: 2841 NAIC: 325611)

Procter & Gamble provides branded consumer packaged goods. Co. has five segments: Beauty, which provides antiperspirant and deodorant, cosmetics, hair care, and hair color; Grooming, which provides blades and razors, electronic hair removal devices, hair care appliances, pre and post shave products; Health Care, which provides feminine care, gastrointestinal, incontinence, rapid diagnostics, respiratory, toothbrush, toothpaste, and vitamins/minerals/supplements; Fabric Care and Home Care, which provides laundry detergents, dishwashing liquids, batteries, and pet care; and Baby Care and Family Care, which provides baby wipes, diapers and pants, paper towels, tissues, and toilet paper.

Recent Developments: For the quarter ended Dec 31 2012, income from continuing operations increased 143.8% to US$4.08 billion from US$1.67 billion in the year-earlier quarter. Net income increased 137.9% to US$4.08 billion from US$1.71 billion in the year-earlier quarter. Revenues were US$22.18 billion, up 2.0% from US$21.74 billion the year before. Operating income was US$4.49 billion versus US$2.68 billion in the prior-year quarter, an increase of 67.6%. Direct operating expenses rose 0.3% to US$10.88 billion from US$10.85 billion in the comparable period the year before. Indirect operating expenses decreased 17.2% to US$6.80 billion from US$8.21 billion in the equivalent prior-year period.

Prospects: Our evaluation of Procter & Gamble Co. as of Apr. 7, 2013 is the result of our systematic analysis on three basic characteristics: earnings strength, relative valuation, and recent stock price movement. The company has produced a positive trend in earnings per share over the past 5 quarters. However, while recent estimates for the company have been lowered by analysts, PG has posted better than expected results. Based on operating earnings yield, the company is about fairly valued when compared to all of the companies in our coverage universe. Share price changes over the past year indicates that PG will perform poorly over the near term.

Financial Data
(US$ in Millions)

	6 Mos	3 Mos	06/30/2012	06/30/2011	06/30/2010	06/30/2009	06/30/2008	06/30/2007
Earnings Per Share	4.41	3.59	3.66	3.93	4.11	4.26	3.64	3.04
Cash Flow Per Share	...	...	4.82	4.72	5.54	5.05	5.12	4.25
Dividends Per Share	2.211	2.174	2.137	1.970	1.802	1.640	1.450	1.280
Dividend Payout %	50.14	60.56	58.39	50.14	43.84	38.50	39.84	42.11
Income Statement								
Total Revenue	42,914	20,739	83,680	82,559	78,938	79,029	83,503	76,476
EBITDA	10,833	4,708	16,758	18,858	19,101	19,765	20,711	19,144
Depn & Amortn	1,448	710	3,204	2,838	3,108	3,082	3,166	3,130
Income Before Taxes	9,044	3,826	12,785	15,189	15,047	15,325	16,078	14,710
Income Taxes	2,115	973	3,468	3,392	4,101	4,032	4,003	4,370
Net Income	6,871	2,853	10,756	11,797	12,736	13,436	12,075	10,340
Average Shares	2,920	2,932	2,942	3,002	3,100	3,155	3,317	3,399
Balance Sheet								
Current Assets	25,601	24,124	21,910	21,970	18,782	21,905	24,515	24,031
Total Assets	139,903	135,888	132,244	138,354	128,172	134,833	143,992	138,014
Current Liabilities	26,230	24,898	24,907	27,293	24,282	30,901	30,958	30,717
Long-Term Obligations	23,607	23,563	21,080	22,033	21,360	20,652	23,581	23,375
Total Liabilities	73,222	71,589	68,805	70,714	67,057	71,734	74,498	71,254
Stockholders' Equity	66,681	64,299	63,439	67,640	61,115	63,099	69,494	66,760
Shares Outstanding	2,732	2,735	2,749	2,766	2,844	2,918	3,033	3,132
Statistical Record								
Return on Assets %	9.45	7.77	7.93	8.85	9.68	9.64	8.54	7.56
Return on Equity %	19.78	16.34	16.37	18.32	20.51	20.27	17.68	15.95
EBITDA Margin %	25.24	22.70	20.03	22.84	24.20	25.01	24.80	25.03
Net Margin %	16.01	13.76	12.85	14.29	16.13	17.00	14.46	13.52
Asset Turnover	0.61	0.61	0.62	0.62	0.60	0.57	0.59	0.56
Current Ratio	0.98	0.97	0.88	0.80	0.77	0.71	0.79	0.78
Debt to Equity	0.35	0.37	0.33	0.33	0.35	0.33	0.34	0.35
Price Range	70.76-59.27	69.76-59.27	67.90-58.51	67.46-59.34	64.53-51.10	73.15-44.18	74.67-60.49	66.09-55.60
P/E Ratio	16.05-13.44	19.43-16.51	18.55-15.99	17.17-15.10	15.70-12.43	17.17-10.37	20.51-16.62	21.74-18.29
Average Yield %	3.34	3.34	3.33	3.13	3.02	2.80	2.14	2.05

Address: One Procter & Gamble Plaza, Cincinnati, OH 45202 **Telephone:** 513-983-1100 **Fax:** 513-983-2062	**Web Site:** www.pg.com **Officers:** Robert A. McDonald - Chairman, President, Chief Executive Officer Werner Geissler - Vice-Chairman	**Auditors:** Deloitte & Touche LLP **Investor Contact:** 800-742-6253 **Transfer Agents:** The Procter & Gamble Company, Cincinnati, OH

PROGRESSIVE CORP. (OH)

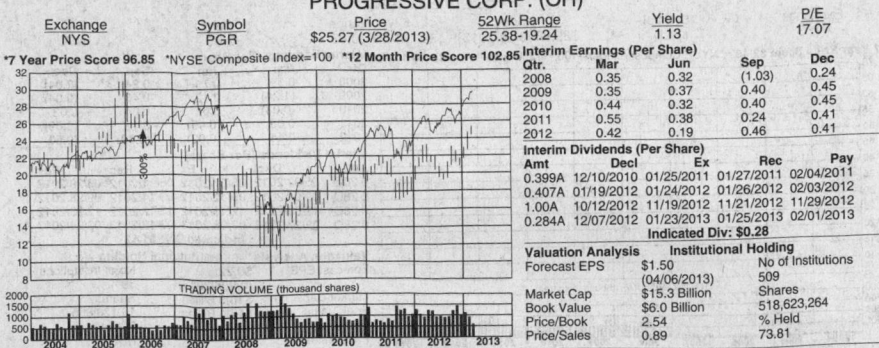

Exchange	Symbol	Price	52Wk Range	Yield	P/E
NYS	PGR	$25.27 (3/28/2013)	25.38-19.24	1.13	17.07

*7 Year Price Score 96.85   *NYSE Composite Index=100   *12 Month Price Score 102.85

Interim Earnings (Per Share)

Qtr.	Mar	Jun	Sep	Dec
2008	0.35	0.32	(1.03)	0.24
2009	0.35	0.37	0.40	0.45
2010	0.44	0.32	0.40	0.45
2011	0.55	0.38	0.24	0.41
2012	0.42	0.19	0.46	0.41

Interim Dividends (Per Share)

Amt	Decl	Ex	Rec	Pay
0.399A	12/10/2010	01/25/2011	01/27/2011	02/04/2011
0.407A	01/19/2012	01/24/2012	01/26/2012	02/03/2012
1.00A	10/12/2012	11/19/2012	11/21/2012	11/29/2012
0.284A	12/07/2012	01/23/2013	01/25/2013	02/01/2013

Indicated Div: $0.28

Valuation Analysis

		Institutional Holding	
Forecast EPS	$1.50 (04/06/2013)	No of Institutions	509
Market Cap	$15.3 Billion	Shares	518,623,264
Book Value	$6.0 Billion	% Held	73.81
Price/Book	2.54		
Price/Sales	0.89		

Business Summary: General Insurance (MIC: 5.2.1 SIC: 6331 NAIC: 524126)

Progressive is an insurance holding company. Through its insurance subsidiaries and affiliate, Co. provides personal and commercial automobile insurance and other property-casualty insurance and related services. Co.'s personal lines segment writes insurance for personal autos and recreational vehicles through both an independent insurance agency channel and a direct channel, while its commercial auto segment writes primary liability and physical damage insurance for automobiles and trucks owned by small businesses via the independent agency and direct channels. Co.'s service business provides policy issuance and claims adjusting services for the Commercial Auto Insurance Procedures/Plans.

Recent Developments: For the year ended Dec 31 2012, net income decreased 11.1% to US$902.3 million from US$1.02 billion in the prior year. Revenues were US$17.08 billion, up 8.3% from US$15.77 billion the year before. Net premiums earned were US$16.02 billion versus US$14.90 billion in the prior year, an increase of 7.5%. Net investment income fell 7.7% to US$443.0 million from US$480.0 million a year ago.

Prospects: Our evaluation of Progressive Corp. as of Apr. 7, 2013 is the result of our systematic analysis on three basic characteristics: earnings strength, relative valuation, and recent stock price movement. The company has enjoyed a very positive trend in earnings per share over the past 5 quarters and while recent estimates for the company have been mixed, PGR has posted better than expected results. Based on operating earnings yield, the company is about fairly valued when compared to all of the companies in our coverage universe. Share price changes over the past year indicates that PGR will perform poorly over the near term.

Financial Data

(US$ in Thousands)	12/31/2012	12/31/2011	12/31/2010	12/31/2009	12/31/2008	12/31/2007	12/31/2006	12/31/2005
Earnings Per Share	1.48	1.59	1.61	1.57	(0.10)	1.65	2.10	1.75
Cash Flow Per Share	2.80	2.37	2.55	2.23	2.31	2.52	2.61	2.53
Tang Book Value Per Share	9.94	9.47	9.13	8.55	6.23	7.26	9.15	7.74
Dividends Per Share	1.407	0.399	1.161	0.161	0.145	2.000	0.033	0.030
Dividend Payout %	95.08	25.08	72.13	10.27	...	121.21	1.55	1.72
Income Statement								
Premium Income	16,018,000	14,902,800	14,314,800	14,012,800	13,631,400	13,877,400	14,117,900	13,764,400
Total Revenue	17,083,900	15,508,100	14,963,300	14,563,600	12,840,100	14,686,800	14,786,400	14,303,400
Benefits & Claims	11,948,000	10,634,800	10,131,300	9,904,900	10,015,000	9,926,200	9,394,900	9,364,800
Income Before Taxes	1,317,700	1,487,000	1,565,200	1,556,900	(222,300)	1,693,000	2,433,200	2,058,900
Income Taxes	415,400	471,500	496,900	499,400	(152,300)	510,500	785,700	665,000
Net Income	902,300	1,015,500	1,068,300	1,057,500	(70,000)	1,182,500	1,647,500	1,393,900
Average Shares	607,800	636,900	663,300	672,200	673,900	718,500	783,800	799,300
Balance Sheet								
Total Assets	22,694,700	21,844,800	21,150,300	20,049,300	18,250,500	18,843,100	19,482,100	18,898,600
Total Liabilities	16,687,700	16,038,100	15,101,400	14,300,700	14,035,200	13,907,600	12,635,500	12,791,100
Stockholders' Equity	6,007,000	5,806,700	6,048,900	5,748,600	4,215,300	4,935,500	6,846,600	6,107,500
Shares Outstanding	604,600	613,000	662,400	672,600	676,500	680,200	748,000	789,200
Statistical Record								
Return on Assets %	4.04	4.72	5.19	5.52	N.M.	6.17	8.59	7.73
Return on Equity %	15.23	17.13	18.11	21.23	N.M.	20.07	25.44	24.75
Loss Ratio %	74.59	71.36	70.78	70.68	73.47	71.53	66.55	68.04
Net Margin %	5.28	6.55	7.14	7.26	(0.55)	8.05	11.14	9.75
Price Range	23.30-19.24	21.94-17.09	21.97-16.21	18.05-9.89	21.00-11.74	24.70-17.32	29.71-22.24	30.97-20.61
P/E Ratio	15.74-13.00	13.80-10.75	13.65-10.07	11.50-6.30	...	14.97-10.50	14.15-10.59	17.70-11.78
Average Yield %	6.64	2.02	5.95	1.05	0.84	9.29	0.13	0.12

Address: 6300 Wilson Mills Road, Mayfield Village, OH 44143	Web Site: www.progressive.com	Auditors: PricewaterhouseCoopers LLP
Telephone: 440-461-5000	Officers: Glenn M. Renwick - President, Chief Executive Officer M. Jeffrey Charney - Chief Marketing Officer	Investor Contact: 440-446-7165
Fax: 440-446-7168		Transfer Agents: American Stock Transfer & Trust Company, Brooklyn, NY

PROLOGIS INC

Exchange	Symbol	Price	52Wk Range	Yield	P/E
NYS	PLD	$39.98 (3/28/2013)	40.93-30.42	2.80	N/A

*7 Year Price Score 82.48   ***NYSE Composite Index=100**   ***12 Month Price Score 102.80**

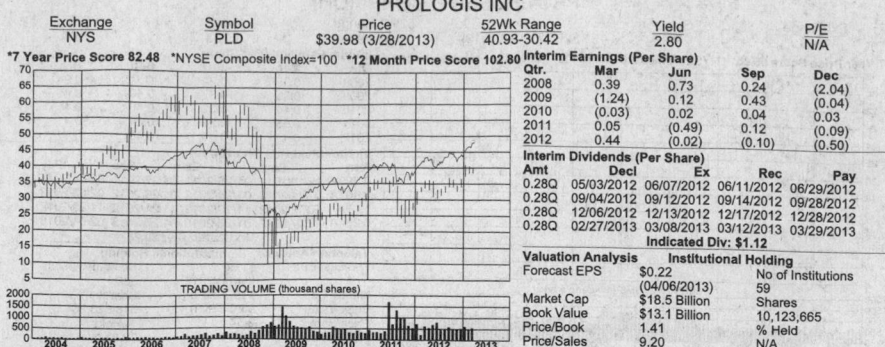

Interim Earnings (Per Share)

Qtr.	Mar	Jun	Sep	Dec
2008	0.39	0.73	0.24	(2.04)
2009	(1.24)	0.12	0.43	(0.04)
2010	(0.03)	0.02	0.04	0.03
2011	0.05	(0.49)	0.12	(0.09)
2012	0.44	(0.02)	(0.10)	(0.50)

Interim Dividends (Per Share)

Amt	Decl	Ex	Rec	Pay
0.28Q	05/03/2012	06/07/2012	06/11/2012	06/29/2012
0.28Q	09/04/2012	09/12/2012	09/14/2012	09/28/2012
0.28Q	12/06/2012	12/13/2012	12/17/2012	12/28/2012
0.28Q	02/27/2013	03/08/2013	03/12/2013	03/29/2013

Indicated Div: $1.12

Valuation Analysis

		Institutional Holding	
Forecast EPS	$0.22	No of Institutions	
	(04/06/2013)	59	
Market Cap	$18.5 Billion	Shares	
Book Value	$13.1 Billion	10,123,665	
Price/Book	1.41	% Held	
Price/Sales	9.20	N/A	

Business Summary: REITs (MIC: 5.3.1 SIC: 6798 NAIC: 525930)

Prologis is a real estate investment trust. Through its subsidiary, Prologis, L.P., Co. owns, acquires, develops and operates industrial properties in global, regional and other distribution markets throughout the Americas, Europe and Asia. Co.'s real estate operations segment represents the ownership of industrial properties, and its private capital segment represents the management of co-investment ventures and other unconsolidated investees. As of Dec 31 2011, Co. owned, or had investments in, on a consolidated basis or through unconsolidated investees, properties and development projects totaling approximately 600.0 million square feet (55.7 million square meters) in 22 countries.

Recent Developments: For the year ended Dec 31 2012, loss from continuing operations was US$93.2 million compared with a loss of US$267.2 million a year earlier. Net loss amounted to US$30.5 million versus a net loss of US$157.9 million in the prior year. Revenues were US$2.01 billion, up 38.2% from US$1.45 billion the year before. Revenues from property income rose 44.4% to US$1.87 billion from US$1.29 billion in the corresponding earlier year.

Prospects: Our evaluation of Prologis Inc. as of Apr. 7, 2013 is the result of our systematic analysis on three basic characteristics: earnings strength, relative valuation, and recent stock price movement. The company has generated a negative trend in earnings per share over the past 5 quarters. Because the company lacks sufficient analyst estimate data, we place greater weight on the historical EPS trend as the measure of earnings strength. Based on operating earnings yield, the company is overvalued when compared to all of the companies in our coverage universe. Share price changes over the past year indicates that PLD will perform in line with the market over the near term.

Financial Data

(US$ in Thousands)	12/31/2012	12/31/2011	12/31/2010	12/31/2009	12/31/2008	12/31/2007	12/31/2006	12/31/2005
Earnings Per Share	(0.18)	(0.51)	0.06	(0.37)	(0.67)	2.96	2.30	2.85
Cash Flow Per Share	1.01	0.56	1.56	1.80	3.08	2.47	3.83	3.52
Tang Book Value Per Share	27.04	28.52	18.36	18.20	23.27	25.61	21.67	20.28
Dividends Per Share	1.120	1.120	1.120	1.120	1.560	2.000	1.840	1.760
Dividend Payout %	...	...	1,866.67	...	...	67.57	80.00	61.75
Income Statement								
Total Revenue	2,005,961	1,533,291	633,500	633,842	715,045	669,671	729,896	676,149
EBITDA	1,151,775	801,552	349,717	201,721	296,507	585,567	564,544	504,905
Depn & Amortn	788,467	647,440	227,399	214,278	189,255	168,686	187,769	162,383
Income Before Taxes	(121,298)	(302,618)	(8,020)	(134,016)	(26,281)	289,936	211,545	199,529
Income Taxes	3,580	1,776	...	...	...	...	...	...
Net Income	(39,720)	(153,414)	27,119	(43,001)	(49,310)	314,260	224,072	257,807
Average Shares	459,895	370,534	161,988	134,321	97,403	99,808	91,106	87,873
Balance Sheet								
Current Assets	448,820	396,063	396,150	362,035	411,759	434,686	348,623	467,536
Total Assets	27,310,145	27,723,912	7,372,895	6,841,958	7,301,648	7,262,403	6,713,512	6,802,739
Current Liabilities	611,770	639,490	339,474	338,042	345,259	306,196	271,880	263,744
Long-Term Obligations	11,790,794	11,382,408	3,331,299	3,212,596	3,990,185	3,494,844	3,437,415	3,401,561
Total Liabilities	14,241,128	14,062,273	4,052,172	3,901,942	4,786,541	4,498,451	4,546,855	4,886,440
Stockholders' Equity	13,069,017	13,661,639	3,320,723	2,940,016	2,515,107	2,763,952	2,166,657	1,916,299
Shares Outstanding	461,770	458,597	168,736	149,258	98,469	99,210	89,662	85,814
Statistical Record								
Return on Assets %	N.M.	N.M.	0.38	N.M.	N.M.	4.50	3.32	3.91
Return on Equity %	N.M.	N.M.	0.87	N.M.	N.M.	12.75	10.98	14.37
EBITDA Margin %	57.42	52.28	55.20	31.83	41.47	87.44	77.35	74.67
Net Margin %	N.M.	N.M.	4.28	N.M.	N.M.	46.93	30.70	38.13
Asset Turnover	0.07	0.09	0.09	0.09	0.10	0.10	0.11	0.10
Current Ratio	0.73	0.62	1.17	1.07	1.19	1.42	1.28	1.77
Debt to Equity	0.90	0.83	1.00	1.09	1.59	1.26	1.59	1.78
Price Range	36.91-28.50	37.26-22.63	31.82-22.14	26.91-9.72	59.75-10.16	65.83-49.05	62.77-46.85	49.85-36.89
P/E Ratio	...	...	530.33-369.00	...	...	22.24-16.57	27.29-20.37	17.49-12.94
Average Yield %	3.33	3.55	4.23	5.67	3.51	3.42	3.42	4.17

Address: Pier 1, Bay 1, San Francisco, CA 94111	Web Site: www.prologis.com	Auditors: KPMG LLP
Telephone: 415-394-9000	Officers: Hamid R. Moghadam - Chairman, Chief Executive Officer, Co-Chief Executive Officer Tamra D. Browne - Senior Vice President, General Counsel, Secretary	Investor Contact: 415-733-9565
Fax: 415-394-9001		Transfer Agents: Computershare Trust Company, N.A., Providence, RI

PROSPERITY BANCSHARES INC.

Exchange	Symbol	Price	52Wk Range	Yield	P/E	Div Achiever
NYS	PB	$47.39 (3/28/2013)	47.50-39.10	1.81	14.67	13 Years

*7 Year Price Score 106.84 *NYSE Composite Index=100 *12 Month Price Score 98.60

TRADING VOLUME (thousand shares)

Interim Earnings (Per Share)

Qtr.	Mar	Jun	Sep	Dec
2008	0.52	0.52	0.33	0.49
2009	0.55	0.57	0.63	0.65
2010	0.66	0.68	0.69	0.70
2011	0.72	0.75	0.77	0.77
2012	0.77	0.78	0.82	0.86

Interim Dividends (Per Share)

Amt	Decl	Ex	Rec	Pay
0.195Q	06/04/2012	06/13/2012	06/15/2012	07/02/2012
0.195Q	09/04/2012	09/12/2012	09/14/2012	10/01/2012
0.215Q	10/24/2012	12/12/2012	12/14/2012	12/31/2012
0.215Q	03/05/2013	03/13/2013	03/15/2013	04/01/2013

Indicated Div: $0.86

Valuation Analysis

Forecast EPS	$3.48
	(04/05/2013)
Market Cap	$2.7 Billion
Book Value	$2.1 Billion
Price/Book	1.28
Price/Sales	5.40

Institutional Holding

No of Institutions	252
Shares	46,350,512
% Held	90.32

Business Summary: Banking (MIC: 5.1.1 SIC: 6022 NAIC: 522110)

Prosperity Bancshares is a financial holding company. Through its bank subsidiary, Prosperity Bank®, Co. provides its financial products and services to small and medium-sized businesses and consumers. Co. provides commercial mortgage and one-four family residential loans. Co. also provides commercial loans, loans for automobiles and other consumer durables, home equity loans, debit cards, internet banking and other cash management services and automated telephone banking. Co.'s deposit products include certificates of deposit, interest checking accounts, savings accounts and overdraft protection. As of Dec 31 2011, Co. had total assets of $9.82 billion and total deposits of $8.06 billion.

Recent Developments: For the year ended Dec 31 2012, net income increased 18.4% to US$167.9 million from US$141.7 million in the prior year. Net interest income increased 16.5% to US$380.7 million from US$326.7 million in the prior year. Provision for loan losses was US$6.1 million versus US$5.2 million in the prior year, an increase of 17.3%. Non-interest income rose 34.8% to US$75.5 million from US$56.0 million, while non-interest expense advanced 21.2% to US$198.5 million.

Prospects: Our evaluation of Prosperity Bancshares Inc. as of Apr. 7, 2013 is the result of our systematic analysis on three basic characteristics: earnings strength, relative valuation, and recent stock price movement. The company has enjoyed a very positive trend in earnings per share over the past 5 quarters and while recent estimates for the company have remained steady, PB has posted better than expected results. Based on operating earnings yield, the company is undervalued when compared to all of the companies in our coverage universe. Share price changes over the past year indicates that PB will perform in line with the market over the near term.

Financial Data

(US$ in Thousands)	12/31/2012	12/31/2011	12/31/2010	12/31/2009	12/31/2008	12/31/2007	12/31/2006	12/31/2005
Earnings Per Share	3.23	3.01	2.73	2.41	1.86	1.94	1.94	1.77
Cash Flow Per Share	4.04	4.65	3.81	1.59	2.72	5.50	2.39	2.46
Tang Book Value Per Share	14.99	13.25	10.70	9.43	7.43	7.41	6.62	6.48
Dividends Per Share	0.800	0.720	0.640	0.568	0.512	0.463	0.412	0.347
Dividend Payout %	24.77	23.92	23.44	23.55	27.55	23.84	21.26	19.63
Income Statement								
Interest Income	419,842	371,908	384,537	409,614	347,878	340,608	231,739	162,123
Interest Expense	39,136	45,240	66,389	102,513	120,149	140,173	93,594	51,226
Net Interest Income	380,706	326,668	318,148	307,101	227,729	200,435	138,145	110,897
Provision for Losses	6,100	5,200	13,585	28,775	9,867	760	504	480
Non-Interest Income	75,535	56,043	53,833	60,097	52,370	52,923	33,982	30,021
Non-Interest Expense	198,457	163,745	166,594	169,700	143,796	126,843	77,669	68,957
Income Before Taxes	251,684	213,766	191,802	168,723	126,436	125,755	93,954	71,481
Income Taxes	83,783	72,017	64,094	56,844	41,929	41,604	32,229	23,621
Net Income	167,901	141,749	127,708	111,879	84,507	84,151	61,725	47,860
Average Shares	51,941	47,017	46,832	46,354	45,479	43,310	31,893	27,024
Balance Sheet								
Net Loans & Leases	5,127,376	3,714,312	3,433,439	3,324,840	3,530,087	3,110,428	2,152,517	1,524,922
Total Assets	14,583,573	9,822,671	9,476,572	8,850,400	9,072,364	6,372,343	4,586,769	3,585,982
Total Deposits	11,641,844	8,060,254	7,454,920	7,258,550	7,303,297	4,966,407	3,725,678	2,920,318
Total Liabilities	12,494,184	8,255,406	8,024,233	7,499,155	7,817,258	5,244,912	3,922,358	3,121,265
Stockholders' Equity	2,089,389	1,567,265	1,452,339	1,351,245	1,255,106	1,127,431	664,411	464,717
Shares Outstanding	56,447	46,910	46,684	46,540	46,079	44,188	32,792	27,820
Statistical Record								
Return on Assets %	1.37	1.47	1.39	1.25	1.09	1.54	1.51	1.52
Return on Equity %	9.16	9.39	9.11	8.59	7.07	9.39	10.93	12.93
Net Interest Margin %	90.68	87.84	82.74	74.97	65.46	58.85	59.61	68.40
Efficiency Ratio %	40.06	38.26	38.00	36.13	35.93	32.23	29.23	35.89
Loans to Deposits	0.44	0.46	0.46	0.46	0.48	0.63	0.58	0.52
Price Range	47.31-39.10	46.50-31.67	43.53-28.49	40.98-20.33	39.00-23.04	37.09-28.18	36.07-28.81	31.70-25.19
P/E Ratio	14.65-12.11	15.45-10.52	15.95-10.44	17.00-8.44	20.97-12.39	19.12-14.53	18.59-14.85	17.91-14.23
Average Yield %	1.89	1.79	1.76	1.80	1.73	1.39	1.27	1.21

Address: Prosperity Bank Plaza, 4295 San Felipe, Houston, TX 77027 **Telephone:** 713-269-7199	**Web Site:** www.prosperitybanktx.com **Officers:** David Zalman - Chairman, President, Chief Executive Officer H. E. Timanus - Vice-Chairman	**Auditors:** Deloitte & Touche LLP **Investor Contact:** 713-693-9300 **Transfer Agents:** Computershare Investor Services, Golden, CO

607

PROTECTIVE LIFE CORP.

Exchange	Symbol	Price	52Wk Range	Yield	P/E
NYS	PL	$35.80 (3/28/2013)	35.86-24.93	2.01	9.78

*7 Year Price Score 87.02 *NYSE Composite Index=100 *12 Month Price Score 105.81

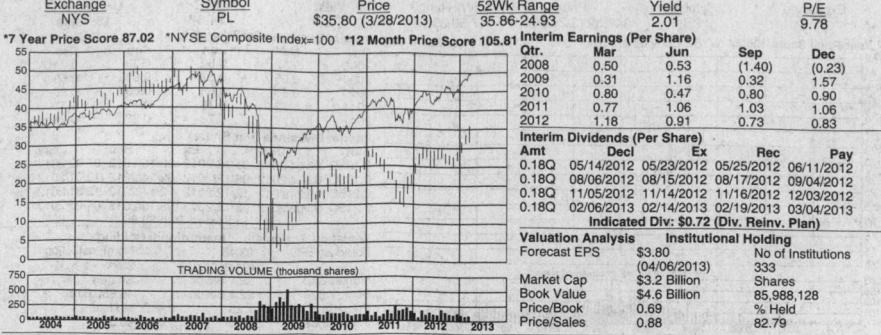

Interim Earnings (Per Share)

Qtr.	Mar	Jun	Sep	Dec
2008	0.50	0.53	(1.40)	(0.23)
2009	0.31	1.16	0.32	1.57
2010	0.80	0.47	0.80	0.90
2011	0.77	1.06	1.03	1.06
2012	1.18	0.91	0.73	0.83

Interim Dividends (Per Share)

Amt	Decl	Ex	Rec	Pay
0.18Q	05/14/2012	05/23/2012	05/25/2012	06/11/2012
0.18Q	08/06/2012	08/15/2012	08/17/2012	09/04/2012
0.18Q	11/05/2012	11/14/2012	11/16/2012	12/03/2012
0.18Q	02/06/2013	02/14/2013	02/19/2013	03/04/2013

Indicated Div: $0.72 (Div. Reinv. Plan)

Valuation Analysis

		Institutional Holding	
Forecast EPS	$3.80 (04/06/2013)	No of Institutions	333
Market Cap	$3.2 Billion	Shares	85,988,128
Book Value	$4.6 Billion	% Held	82.79
Price/Book	0.69		
Price/Sales	0.88		

Business Summary: Life & Health (MIC: 5.2.2 SIC: 6311 NAIC: 524113)

Protective Life is a holding company. Through its subsidiaries, Co. provides financial services through the production, distribution, and administration of insurance and investment products. Co.'s segments include: Life Marketing, which markets universal life, variable universal life, bank-owned life insurance products and level premium term insurance; Acquisitions, which acquires, converts, and services policies acquired from other companies; Annuities, which markets fixed and variable annuity products; Stable Value Products, which sells fixed and floating rate funding agreements; and Asset Protection, which markets extended service contracts and credit life and disability insurance.

Recent Developments: For the year ended Dec 31 2012, net income decreased 4.2% to US$302.5 million from US$315.6 million in the prior year. Revenues were US$3.62 billion, up 1.6% from US$3.57 billion the year before. Net premiums earned were US$1.47 billion versus US$1.41 billion in the prior year, an increase of 4.5%. Net investment income rose 2.3% to US$1.86 billion from US$1.82 billion a year ago.

Prospects: Our evaluation of Protective Life Corp. as of Apr. 7, 2013 is the result of our systematic analysis on three basic characteristics: earnings strength, relative valuation, and recent stock price movement. The company has generated a negative trend in earnings per share over the past 5 quarters and while recent estimates for the company have remained steady, PL has posted better than expected results. Based on operating earnings yield, the company is undervalued when compared to all of the companies in our coverage universe. Share price changes over the past year indicates that PL will perform poorly over the near term.

Financial Data
(US$ in Thousands)

	12/31/2012	12/31/2011	12/31/2010	12/31/2009	12/31/2008	12/31/2007	12/31/2006	12/31/2005
Earnings Per Share	3.66	3.92	2.97	3.34	(0.59)	4.05	3.94	3.46
Cash Flow Per Share	8.51	7.28	8.20	14.79	17.44	12.12	6.90	13.04
Tang Book Value Per Share	50.77	50.31	37.54	27.59	9.16	33.35	31.62	30.62
Dividends Per Share	0.700	0.620	0.540	0.480	0.815	0.890	0.840	0.760
Dividend Payout %	19.13	15.82	18.18	14.37	...	21.98	21.32	21.97
Income Statement								
Premium Income	1,468,442	1,405,465	1,217,054	1,162,646	1,109,743	1,126,339	946,122	728,923
Total Revenue	3,623,006	3,566,142	3,097,755	3,068,026	2,505,564	3,051,700	2,679,133	2,109,204
Benefits & Claims	2,326,040	2,233,473	2,089,429	1,977,979	1,976,541	1,893,707	1,637,215	1,253,367
Income Before Taxes	452,971	507,152	388,863	416,778	(75,131)	436,088	431,908	377,013
Income Taxes	150,519	167,837	129,067	145,290	(33,276)	146,522	150,347	130,446
Net Income	302,452	339,070	260,241	271,488	(41,855)	289,566	281,561	246,567
Average Shares	82,723	86,475	87,675	81,249	71,108	71,478	71,390	71,350
Balance Sheet								
Total Assets	57,384,672	52,932,085	47,562,786	42,311,587	39,572,449	41,786,041	39,795,294	28,966,993
Total Liabilities	52,769,489	48,711,620	44,231,699	39,832,766	38,811,354	39,329,280	37,482,219	26,783,333
Stockholders' Equity	4,615,183	4,220,465	3,331,087	2,478,821	761,095	2,456,761	2,313,075	2,183,660
Shares Outstanding	88,766	81,669	85,667	85,580	69,905	70,149	69,964	69,694
Statistical Record								
Return on Assets %	0.55	0.67	0.58	0.66	N.M.	0.71	0.82	0.88
Return on Equity %	6.83	8.98	8.96	16.76	N.M.	12.14	12.52	11.34
Loss Ratio %	158.40	158.91	171.68	170.13	178.11	168.13	173.04	171.95
Net Margin %	8.35	9.51	8.40	8.85	(1.67)	9.49	10.51	11.69
Price Range	30.25-23.19	29.49-14.25	27.37-16.55	23.97-2.92	43.69-5.73	50.83-39.80	50.40-43.04	44.83-37.39
P/E Ratio	8.27-6.34	7.52-3.64	9.22-5.57	7.18-0.87	...	12.55-9.83	12.79-10.92	12.96-10.81
Average Yield %	2.54	2.72	2.49	3.55	2.56	1.98	1.81	1.83

Address: 2801 Highway 280 South, Birmingham, AL 35223 **Telephone:** 205-268-1000	**Web Site:** www.protective.com **Officers:** John D. Johns - Chairman, President, Chief Executive Officer Richard J. Bielen - Vice-Chairman, Chief Financial Officer	**Auditors:** PricewaterhouseCoopers LLP **Investor Contact:** 205-268-3912 **Transfer Agents:** Computershare Shareowner Services LLC, Pittsburgh, PA

PRUDENTIAL FINANCIAL, INC.

Exchange	Symbol	Price	52Wk Range	Yield	P/E
NYS	PRU	$58.99 (3/28/2013)	64.50-44.74	2.71	62.76

*7 Year Price Score 77.39 *NYSE Composite Index=100 ***12 Month Price Score 97.06**

Interim Earnings (Per Share)

Qtr.	Mar	Jun	Sep	Dec
2008	0.20	1.35	(0.23)	(3.74)
2009	0.01	1.25	2.35	3.91
2010	1.15	1.70	2.46	0.44
2011	1.20	1.68	3.06	1.29
2012	(2.09)	4.64	(1.41)	(0.27)

Interim Dividends (Per Share)

Amt	Decl	Ex	Rec	Pay
1.15Q	11/09/2010	11/19/2010	11/23/2010	12/17/2010
1.45Q	11/08/2011	11/18/2011	11/22/2011	12/16/2011
1.60Q	11/07/2012	11/16/2012	11/20/2012	12/14/2012
0.40Q	02/12/2013	02/22/2013	02/26/2013	03/21/2013

Indicated Div: $1.60

Valuation Analysis

		Institutional Holding	
Forecast EPS	$7.80	No of Institutions	
	(04/06/2013)	792	
Market Cap	$27.4 Billion	Shares	
Book Value	$38.6 Billion	312,399,456	
Price/Book	0.71	% Held	
Price/Sales	0.32	60.80	

TRADING VOLUME (thousand shares)

Business Summary: Life & Health (MIC: 5.2.2 SIC: 6311 NAIC: 524113)

Prudential Financial is a holding company. Co. provides products and services such as life insurance, annuities, retirement-related services, mutual funds and investment management services through its subsidiaries or affiliates. Co.'s Financial Services Businesses include its U.S. Retirement Solutions and Investment Management, U.S. Individual Life and Group Insurance, and International Insurance divisions. The Closed Block Business includes in force participating insurance and annuity products and assets that are used for the payment of benefits and policyholders' dividends on these products. As of Dec 31 2011, Co. had about $900.70 billion of assets under management.

Recent Developments: For the year ended Dec 31 2012, income from continuing operations decreased 85.2% to US$532.0 million from US$3.60 billion a year earlier. Net income decreased 85.0% to US$547.0 million from US$3.64 billion in the prior year. Revenues were US$84.82 billion, up 73.0% from US$49.03 billion the year before. Net premiums earned were US$65.35 billion versus US$24.30 billion in the prior year, an increase of 168.9%. Net investment income rose 4.1% to US$13.66 billion from US$13.12 billion a year ago.

Prospects: Our evaluation of Prudential Financial Inc. as of Apr. 7, 2013 is the result of our systematic analysis on three basic characteristics: earnings strength, relative valuation, and recent stock price movement. The company has managed to produce a neutral trend in earnings per share over the past 5 quarters and while recent estimates for the company have been raised by analysts, PRU has posted results that fell short of analysts expectations. Based on operating earnings yield, the company is undervalued when compared to all of the companies in our coverage universe. Share price changes over the past year indicates that PRU will perform poorly over the near term.

Financial Data
(US$ in Millions)

	12/31/2012	12/31/2011	12/31/2010	12/31/2009	12/31/2008	12/31/2007	12/31/2006	12/31/2005
Earnings Per Share	0.94	7.22	5.75	7.63	(2.42)	7.61	6.50	6.34
Cash Flow Per Share	44.78	25.77	14.01	13.14	25.15	12.98	9.04	7.90
Tang Book Value Per Share	82.95	79.19	66.73	54.29	31.71	52.20	48.39	45.57
Dividends Per Share	1.600	1.450	1.150	0.700	0.580	1.150	0.950	0.780
Dividend Payout %	170.21	20.08	20.00	9.17	...	15.11	14.62	12.30
Income Statement								
Premium Income	65,354	24,338	18,260	16,545	15,468	14,351	13,908	13,685
Total Revenue	84,815	49,045	38,414	32,688	29,275	34,401	32,488	31,708
Benefits & Claims	65,131	23,614	18,285	16,346	16,531	14,749	14,283	13,840
Income Before Taxes	676	5,117	4,422	1,569	(1,118)	4,686	4,403	4,471
Income Taxes	204	1,599	1,310	21	(461)	1,245	1,248	869
Net Income	469	3,666	3,195	3,124	(1,073)	3,704	3,428	3,540
Average Shares	468	488	475	448	429	468	494	520
Balance Sheet								
Total Assets	709,298	624,521	539,854	480,203	445,011	485,814	454,266	417,776
Total Liabilities	670,723	587,298	507,439	455,008	431,589	462,357	431,374	395,013
Stockholders' Equity	38,575	37,223	32,415	25,195	13,422	23,457	22,892	22,763
Shares Outstanding	465	470	485	464	423	449	473	499
Statistical Record								
Return on Assets %	0.07	0.63	0.63	0.68	N.M.	0.79	0.79	0.86
Return on Equity %	1.23	10.53	11.09	16.18	N.M.	15.98	15.02	15.70
Loss Ratio %	99.66	97.03	100.14	98.80	106.87	102.77	102.70	101.13
Net Margin %	0.55	7.47	8.32	9.56	(3.67)	10.77	10.55	11.16
Price Range	64.65-44.74	67.32-43.91	65.82-47.02	54.63-11.29	93.04-13.73	103.17-84.28	86.84-71.47	77.96-52.62
P/E Ratio	68.78-47.60	9.32-6.08	11.45-8.18	7.16-1.48	...	13.56-11.07	13.36-11.00	12.30-8.30
Average Yield %	2.95	2.55	2.06	1.84	0.91	1.23	1.23	1.22

Address: 751 Broad Street, Newark, NJ 07102 **Telephone:** 973-802-6000	**Web Site:** www.investor.prudential.com **Officers:** John R. Strangfeld - Chairman, President, Chief Executive Officer, Division Officer Mark B. Grier - Vice-Chairman, Division Officer	**Auditors:** PricewaterhouseCoopers LLP **Transfer Agents:** Computershare Trust Company, N.A., Providence, RI

PUBLIC SERVICE ENTERPRISE GROUP INC.

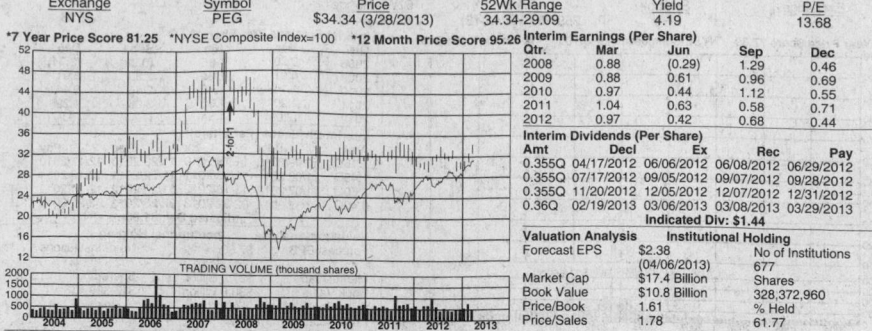

Exchange	Symbol	Price	52Wk Range	Yield	P/E
NYS	PEG	$34.34 (3/28/2013)	34.34-29.09	4.19	13.68

*7 Year Price Score 81.25 *NYSE Composite Index=100 *12 Month Price Score 95.26

Interim Earnings (Per Share)

Qtr.	Mar	Jun	Sep	Dec
2008	0.88	(0.29)	1.29	0.46
2009	0.88	0.61	0.96	0.69
2010	0.97	0.44	1.12	0.55
2011	1.04	0.63	0.58	0.71
2012	0.97	0.42	0.68	0.44

Interim Dividends (Per Share)

Amt	Decl	Ex	Rec	Pay
0.355Q	04/17/2012	06/06/2012	06/08/2012	06/29/2012
0.355Q	07/17/2012	09/05/2012	09/07/2012	09/28/2012
0.355Q	11/20/2012	12/05/2012	12/07/2012	12/31/2012
0.36Q	02/19/2013	03/06/2013	03/08/2013	03/29/2013
		Indicated Div: $1.44		

Valuation Analysis / **Institutional Holding**

Forecast EPS	$2.38	No of Institutions
	(04/06/2013)	677
Market Cap	$17.4 Billion	Shares
Book Value	$10.8 Billion	328,372,960
Price/Book	1.61	% Held
Price/Sales	1.78	61.77

Business Summary: Electric Utilities (MIC: 3.1.1 SIC: 4931 NAIC: 221119)

Public Service Enterprise Group is a holding company. Through its subsidiaries, Co. is engaged in the energy industry. Co.'s subsidiary, PSEG Power LLC, is a wholesale energy supply company. Co.'s Public Service Electric and Gas Company subsidiary is engaged in the transmission of electricity and distribution of electricity and natural gas in certain areas of New Jersey. Co.'s subsidiary, PSEG Energy Holdings L.L.C., owns and manages a portfolio of lease investments and solar generation projects. At Dec 31 2012, Co. provided distribution service to 2.2 million electric customers and 1.8 million gas customers in a service area that covers approximately 2,600 square miles across New Jersey.

Recent Developments: For the year ended Dec 31 2012, income from continuing operations decreased 9.4% to US$1.28 billion from US$1.41 billion a year earlier. Net income decreased 15.2% to US$1.28 billion from US$1.50 billion in the prior year. Revenues were US$9.78 billion, down 11.7% from US$11.08 billion the year before. Operating income was US$2.28 billion versus US$2.74 billion in the prior year, a decrease of 16.9%. Direct operating expenses declined 12.1% to US$6.35 billion from US$7.23 billion in the comparable period the year before. Indirect operating expenses increased 3.9% to US$1.15 billion from US$1.11 billion in the equivalent prior-year period.

Prospects: Our evaluation of Public Service Enterprise Group Inc. as of Apr. 7, 2013 is the result of our systematic analysis on three basic characteristics: earnings strength, relative valuation, and recent stock price movement. The company has managed to produce a neutral trend in earnings per share over the past 5 quarters and while recent estimates for the company have been mixed, PEG has posted better than expected results. Based on operating earnings yield, the company is undervalued when compared to all of the companies in our coverage universe. Share price changes over the past year indicates that PEG will perform poorly over the near term.

Financial Data
(US$ in Thousands)

	12/31/2012	12/31/2011	12/31/2010	12/31/2009	12/31/2008	12/31/2007	12/31/2006	12/31/2005
Earnings Per Share	2.51	2.96	3.08	3.14	2.34	2.62	1.47	1.36
Cash Flow Per Share	5.49	7.03	4.28	3.67	4.61	3.78	3.83	1.96
Tang Book Value Per Share	21.21	20.01	18.74	17.25	15.38	14.38	12.35	10.94
Dividends Per Share	1.420	1.370	1.370	1.330	1.290	1.170	1.140	1.120
Dividend Payout %	56.57	46.28	44.48	42.36	55.13	44.66	77.82	82.66
Income Statement								
Total Revenue	9,781,000	11,079,000	11,793,000	12,406,000	13,322,000	12,853,000	12,164,000	12,430,000
EBITDA	3,437,000	3,794,000	4,035,000	4,030,000	3,289,000	3,801,000	2,768,000	2,887,000
Depn & Amortn	1,227,000	1,135,000	1,110,000	959,000	894,000	897,000	947,000	859,000
Income Before Taxes	1,999,000	2,380,000	2,612,000	2,597,000	1,872,000	2,261,000	1,088,000	1,269,000
Income Taxes	736,000	977,000	1,059,000	1,044,000	926,000	1,060,000	454,000	541,000
Net Income	1,275,000	1,503,000	1,564,000	1,592,000	1,188,000	1,335,000	739,000	661,000
Average Shares	507,086	506,982	507,045	507,064	508,427	508,813	504,628	488,812
Balance Sheet								
Current Assets	3,869,000	3,911,000	5,051,000	3,646,000	3,999,000	4,928,000	3,662,000	4,830,000
Total Assets	31,725,000	29,821,000	29,909,000	28,730,000	29,049,000	28,392,000	28,570,000	29,815,000
Current Liabilities	3,777,000	2,957,000	3,485,000	3,214,000	3,410,000	4,290,000	3,406,000	4,757,000
Long-Term Obligations	6,687,000	7,461,000	7,819,000	7,645,000	8,005,000	8,662,000	10,370,000	11,279,000
Total Liabilities	20,945,000	19,551,000	20,276,000	19,862,000	21,198,000	21,013,000	21,743,000	23,713,000
Stockholders' Equity	10,780,000	10,270,000	9,633,000	8,868,000	7,851,000	7,379,000	6,827,000	6,102,000
Shares Outstanding	505,892	505,945	505,974	505,989	506,017	508,523	505,290	502,326
Statistical Record								
Return on Assets %	4.13	5.03	5.33	5.51	4.13	4.69	2.53	2.24
Return on Equity %	12.08	15.10	16.91	19.04	15.56	18.79	11.43	11.09
EBITDA Margin %	35.14	34.24	34.22	32.48	24.69	29.57	22.76	23.23
Net Margin %	13.04	13.57	13.26	12.83	8.92	10.39	6.08	5.32
Asset Turnover	0.32	0.37	0.40	0.43	0.46	0.45	0.42	0.42
Current Ratio	1.02	1.32	1.45	1.13	1.17	1.15	1.08	1.02
Debt to Equity	0.62	0.73	0.81	0.86	1.02	1.17	1.52	1.85
Price Range	34.00-29.09	34.81-28.84	34.78-29.11	33.86-24.02	51.62-24.99	49.61-32.48	36.09-29.77	33.85-24.84
P/E Ratio	13.55-11.59	11.76-9.74	11.29-9.45	10.78-7.65	22.06-10.68	18.94-12.40	24.55-20.26	24.89-18.26
Average Yield %	4.54	4.24	4.31	4.30	3.26	2.74	3.47	3.80

Address: 80 Park Plaza, P.O. Box 1171, Newark, NJ 07101-1171
Telephone: 973-430-7000

Web Site: www.pseg.com
Officers: Ralph Izzo - Chairman, President, Chief Executive Officer Caroline Dorsa - Executive Vice President, Chief Financial Officer

Auditors: Deloitte & Touche LLP
Investor Contact: 973-430-6566
Transfer Agents: Wells Fargo Shareowner Services, Mendota, MN

PULTEGROUP, INC.

Exchange	Symbol	Price	52Wk Range	Yield	P/E
NYS	PHM	$20.24 (3/28/2013)	21.67-7.69	N/A	37.48

*7 Year Price Score 89.17 *NYSE Composite Index=100 *12 Month Price Score 123.78

Interim Earnings (Per Share)

Qtr.	Mar	Jun	Sep	Dec
2008	(2.75)	(0.63)	(1.11)	(1.33)
2009	(2.02)	(0.74)	(1.15)	(0.06)
2010	(0.03)	0.20	(2.63)	(0.44)
2011	(0.10)	(0.15)	(0.34)	0.04
2012	(0.03)	0.11	0.30	0.16

Interim Dividends (Per Share)
Dividend Payment Suspended

Valuation Analysis	Institutional Holding
Forecast EPS $1.22 (04/05/2013)	No of Institutions 519
Market Cap $7.8 Billion	Shares
Book Value $2.2 Billion	325,195,520
Price/Book 3.57	% Held
Price/Sales 1.62	81.10

Business Summary: Builders (MIC: 2.2.5 SIC: 1531 NAIC: 236117)

PulteGroup is engaged in the homebuilding business, which includes the acquisition and development of land primarily for residential purposes within the U.S. and the construction of housing on such land. Through its brands, which include Pulte Homes, Del Webb, and Centex, Co. provides a variety of home designs, including single-family detached, townhouses, condominiums, and duplexes at different prices and with varying levels of options and amenities to its customer groups: entry-level, move-up, and active adult. Co.'s homebuilding operations are aggregated into six reportable segments: Northeast; Southeast; Florida; Texas; North; and Southwest.

Recent Developments: For the year ended Dec 31 2012, net income amounted to US$206.1 million versus a net loss of US$210.4 million in the prior year. Revenues were US$4.82 billion, up 16.5% from US$4.14 billion the year before. Direct operating expenses rose 11.6% to US$4.06 billion from US$3.64 billion in the comparable period the year before. Indirect operating expenses decreased 28.7% to US$576.7 million from US$808.9 million in the equivalent prior-year period.

Prospects: Our evaluation of Pultegroup Inc. as of Apr. 7, 2013 is the result of our systematic analysis on three basic characteristics: earnings strength, relative valuation, and recent stock price movement. The company has generated a negative trend in earnings per share over the past 5 quarters and while recent estimates for the company have been mixed, PHM has posted better than expected results. Based on operating earnings yield, the company is about fairly valued when compared to all of the companies in our coverage universe. Share price changes over the past year indicates that PHM will perform very well over the near term.

Financial Data

(US$ in Thousands)	12/31/2012	12/31/2011	12/31/2010	12/31/2009	12/31/2008	12/31/2007	12/31/2006	12/31/2005
Earnings Per Share	0.54	(0.55)	(2.90)	(3.94)	(5.81)	(8.94)	2.66	5.68
Cash Flow Per Share	1.99	0.05	1.53	2.46	4.80	4.83	(1.06)	0.07
Tang Book Value Per Share	5.28	4.64	4.50	5.54	10.59	16.35	23.82	21.49
Dividends Per Share	...	...	...	...	0.160	0.160	0.160	0.130
Dividend Payout %	...	...	...	...	...	...	6.02	2.29
Income Statement								
Total Revenue	4,819,998	4,136,690	4,569,290	4,084,389	6,289,458	9,263,094	14,274,408	14,694,535
EBITDA	192,301	(298,338)	(1,211,759)	(1,892,172)	(1,603,986)	(2,231,281)	1,252,675	2,254,964
Depn & Amortn	16,900	19,000	32,500	40,200	65,800	75,600	75,400	53,300
Income Before Taxes	179,495	(313,596)	(1,237,457)	(1,925,467)	(1,669,786)	(2,306,881)	1,177,275	2,201,664
Income Taxes	(27,591)	(99,912)	(137,817)	(792,552)	(209,486)	(222,486)	393,080	840,126
Net Income	206,145	(210,388)	(1,096,729)	(1,182,567)	(1,473,113)	(2,255,755)	687,471	1,491,913
Average Shares	384,564	379,877	378,585	300,179	253,512	252,192	258,621	262,801
Balance Sheet								
Current Assets	5,844,850	6,008,765	6,480,182	8,018,931	6,566,177	8,361,223	10,435,059	10,092,756
Total Assets	6,734,409	6,885,620	7,699,376	10,051,222	7,708,458	10,225,703	13,176,874	13,048,174
Current Liabilities	507,035	484,663	614,644	799,611	695,138	1,118,726	1,657,773	2,293,945
Long-Term Obligations	2,648,408	3,088,344	3,391,668	4,281,532	3,166,305	3,478,230	3,537,947	3,386,527
Total Liabilities	4,544,793	4,947,005	5,564,209	6,856,782	4,872,760	5,905,510	6,599,513	7,090,832
Stockholders' Equity	2,189,616	1,938,615	2,135,167	3,194,440	2,835,698	4,320,193	6,577,361	5,957,342
Shares Outstanding	386,608	382,607	382,027	380,690	258,169	257,098	255,315	257,030
Statistical Record								
Return on Assets %	3.02	N.M.	N.M.	N.M.	N.M.	N.M.	5.24	12.72
Return on Equity %	9.96	N.M.	N.M.	N.M.	N.M.	N.M.	10.97	28.47
EBITDA Margin %	3.99	N.M.	N.M.	N.M.	N.M.	N.M.	8.78	15.35
Net Margin %	4.28	N.M.	N.M.	N.M.	N.M.	N.M.	4.82	10.15
Asset Turnover	0.71	0.57	0.51	0.46	0.70	0.79	1.09	1.25
Current Ratio	11.53	12.40	10.54	10.03	9.45	7.47	6.29	4.40
Debt to Equity	1.21	1.59	1.59	1.34	1.12	0.81	0.54	0.57
Price Range	18.61-6.52	8.69-3.54	13.39-6.20	13.32-7.90	17.23-7.12	35.10-9.08	44.65-26.56	47.92-30.17
P/E Ratio	34.46-12.07	...	...	...	...	...	16.79-9.98	8.44-5.31
Average Yield %	...	...	...	...	1.30	0.73	0.48	0.33

Address: 100 Bloomfield Hills Parkway, Suite 300, Bloomfield Hills, MI 48304 Telephone: 248-647-2750	Web Site: www.pultegroupinc.com Officers: Richard J. Dugas - Chairman, President, Chief Executive Officer Roger A. Cregg - Executive Vice President, Chief Financial Officer	Auditors: Ernst & Young LLP Transfer Agents: Computershare Trust Company, N.A, Providence, RI

PVH CORP

Exchange	Symbol	Price	52Wk Range	Yield	P/E
NYS	PVH	$106.81 (3/28/2013)	125.07-72.70	0.14	18.20

*7 Year Price Score 157.69 *NYSE Composite Index=100 *12 Month Price Score 110.12

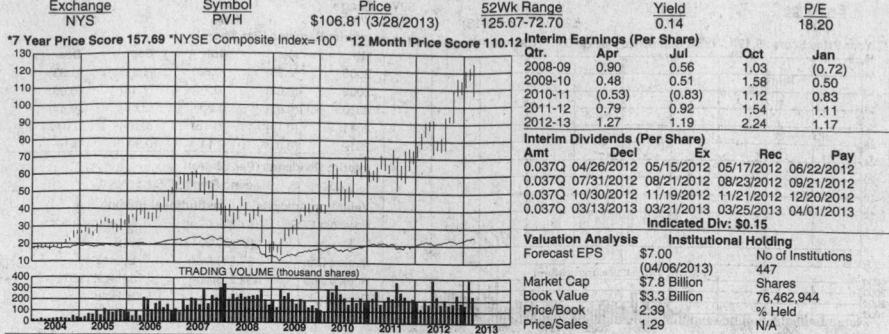

Interim Earnings (Per Share)

Qtr.	Apr	Jul	Oct	Jan
2008-09	0.90	0.56	1.03	(0.72)
2009-10	0.48	0.51	1.58	0.50
2010-11	(0.53)	(0.83)	1.12	0.83
2011-12	0.79	0.92	1.54	1.11
2012-13	1.27	1.19	2.24	1.17

Interim Dividends (Per Share)

Amt	Decl	Ex	Rec	Pay
0.037Q	04/26/2012	05/15/2012	05/17/2012	06/22/2012
0.037Q	07/31/2012	08/21/2012	08/23/2012	09/21/2012
0.037Q	10/30/2012	11/19/2012	11/21/2012	12/20/2012
0.037Q	03/13/2013	03/21/2013	03/25/2013	04/01/2013

Indicated Div: $0.15

Valuation Analysis / **Institutional Holding**

Forecast EPS	$7.00 (04/06/2013)	No of Institutions 447
Market Cap	$7.8 Billion	Shares
Book Value	$3.3 Billion	76,462,944
Price/Book	2.39	% Held
Price/Sales	1.29	N/A

Business Summary: Apparel, Footwear & Accessories (MIC: 1.4.2 SIC: 2321 NAIC: 315211)

PVH is an apparel company which is engaged in designing and marketing branded dress shirts, neckwear, sportswear, and, to a lesser extent, footwear and other related products. Additionally, Co. licenses its owned brands over a range of products. Co. manages its operation through its operating divisions, which are aggregated into seven reportable segments: Tommy Hilfiger North America; Tommy Hilfiger International; Calvin Klein Licensing; Other (Calvin Klein Apparel); Heritage Brand Wholesale Dress Furnishings; Heritage Brand Wholesale Sportswear; and Heritage Brand Retail. Co. owns the brands Calvin Klein and Tommy Hilfiger, as well as Van Heusen, IZOD, Bass, ARROW and Eagle.

Recent Developments: For the year ended Feb 3 2013, net income increased 57.4% to US$433.8 million from US$275.7 million in the prior year. Revenues were US$6.04 billion, up 2.6% from US$5.89 billion the year before. Direct operating expenses declined 1.4% to US$2.79 billion from US$2.83 billion in the comparable period the year before. Indirect operating expenses increased 0.9% to US$2.59 billion from US$2.56 billion in the equivalent prior-year period.

Prospects: Our evaluation of PVH Corp. as of Apr. 7, 2013 is the result of our systematic analysis on three basic characteristics: earnings strength, relative valuation, and recent stock price movement. The company has generated a negative trend in earnings per share over the past 5 quarters. However, while recent estimates for the company have been lowered by analysts, PVH has posted better than expected results. Based on operating earnings yield, the company is undervalued when compared to all of the companies in our coverage universe. Share price changes over the past year indicates that PVH will perform very well over the near term.

Financial Data
(US$ in Thousands)

	02/03/2013	01/29/2012	01/30/2011	01/31/2010	02/01/2009	02/03/2008	02/04/2007	01/29/2006
Earnings Per Share	5.87	4.36	0.80	3.08	1.76	3.21	2.64	1.85
Cash Flow Per Share	7.96	7.33	5.63	4.16	4.66	3.98	4.80	4.96
Tang Book Value Per Share	N.M.	N.M.	N.M.	0.20	N.M.	N.M.	N.M.	N.M.
Dividends Per Share	0.150	0.150	0.150	0.150	0.150	0.150	0.150	0.150
Dividend Payout %	2.56	3.44	18.75	4.87	8.52	4.67	5.68	8.11
Income Statement								
Total Revenue	6,042,999	5,890,624	4,636,848	2,398,731	2,491,935	2,425,175	2,090,648	1,908,848
EBITDA	777,339	670,781	302,012	284,772	221,536	351,274	298,620	238,365
Depn & Amortn	122,424	112,495	98,617	40,960	47,788	39,444	33,314	31,519
Income Before Taxes	537,665	430,198	76,573	211,583	146,304	294,821	248,433	178,269
Income Taxes	109,272	113,684	22,768	49,673	54,533	111,502	93,204	66,581
Net Income	433,840	317,881	53,805	161,910	91,771	183,319	155,229	111,688
Average Shares	73,876	72,923	67,378	52,506	52,200	57,082	53,483	51,695
Balance Sheet								
Current Assets	2,437,006	1,739,235	1,810,563	994,883	864,429	836,219	785,003	663,648
Total Assets	7,781,549	6,752,361	6,735,334	2,339,679	2,200,184	2,172,394	1,998,485	1,747,439
Current Liabilities	1,162,447	1,043,871	908,162	362,881	349,238	360,148	283,166	224,616
Long-Term Obligations	2,211,642	1,832,925	2,364,020	399,584	399,567	399,552	399,538	399,525
Total Liabilities	4,528,980	4,036,912	4,292,777	1,171,126	1,201,389	1,216,111	1,056,328	974,851
Stockholders' Equity	3,252,569	2,715,449	2,442,557	1,168,553	998,795	956,283	942,157	772,588
Shares Outstanding	72,910	68,048	67,065	51,902	51,486	51,283	55,849	43,196
Statistical Record								
Return on Assets %	5.87	4.73	1.19	7.15	4.21	8.81	8.15	6.79
Return on Equity %	14.30	12.36	2.99	14.98	9.41	19.37	17.81	15.98
EBITDA Margin %	12.86	11.39	6.51	11.87	8.89	14.48	14.28	12.49
Net Margin %	7.18	5.40	1.16	6.75	3.68	7.56	7.42	5.85
Asset Turnover	0.82	0.88	1.02	1.06	1.14	1.17	1.10	1.16
Current Ratio	2.10	1.67	1.99	2.74	2.48	2.32	2.77	2.95
Debt to Equity	0.68	0.67	0.97	0.34	0.40	0.42	0.42	0.52
Price Range	120.86-72.70	77.94-51.47	71.23-38.60	44.15-14.50	47.54-13.63	61.77-32.63	55.66-33.05	36.59-24.37
P/E Ratio	20.59-12.39	17.88-11.81	89.04-48.25	14.33-4.71	27.01-7.74	19.24-10.17	21.08-12.52	19.78-13.17
Average Yield %	0.16	0.23	0.27	0.45	0.46	0.29	0.36	0.49

Address: 200 Madison Avenue, New York, NY 10016
Telephone: 212-381-3500

Web Site: www.pvh.com
Officers: Emanuel Chirico - Chairman, Chief Executive Officer Allen E. Sirkin - President, Chief Operating Officer

Auditors: Ernst & Young LLP
Transfer Agents: Wells Fargo Bank, N.A., South St. Paul, MN

QEP RESOURCES INC

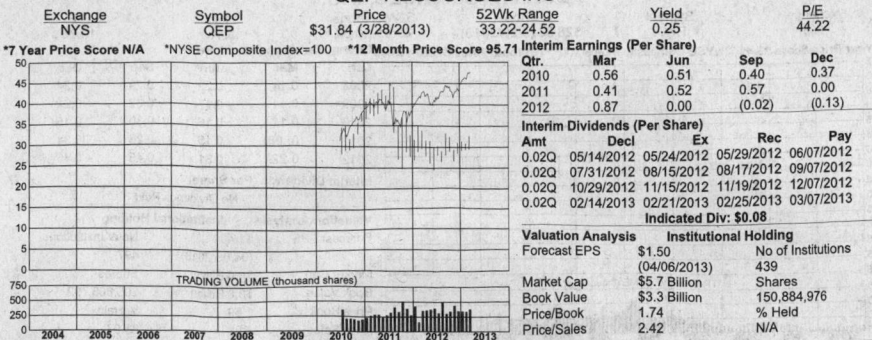

Exchange	Symbol	Price	52Wk Range	Yield	P/E
NYS	QEP	$31.84 (3/28/2013)	33.22-24.52	0.25	44.22

*7 Year Price Score N/A *NYSE Composite Index=100 *12 Month Price Score 95.71

Interim Earnings (Per Share)

Qtr.	Mar	Jun	Sep	Dec
2010	0.56	0.51	0.40	0.37
2011	0.41	0.52	0.57	0.00
2012	0.87	0.00	(0.02)	(0.13)

Interim Dividends (Per Share)

Amt	Decl	Ex	Rec	Pay
0.02Q	05/14/2012	05/24/2012	05/29/2012	06/07/2012
0.02Q	07/31/2012	08/15/2012	08/17/2012	09/07/2012
0.02Q	10/29/2012	11/15/2012	11/19/2012	12/07/2012
0.02Q	02/14/2013	02/21/2013	02/25/2013	03/07/2013

Indicated Div: $0.08

Valuation Analysis		Institutional Holding	
Forecast EPS	$1.50	No of Institutions	
	(04/06/2013)	439	
Market Cap	$5.7 Billion	Shares	
Book Value	$3.3 Billion	150,884,976	
Price/Book	1.74	% Held	
Price/Sales	2.42	N/A	

Business Summary: Production & Extraction (MIC: 9.1.1 SIC: 1311 NAIC: 211111)

QEP Resources is a holding company. Through its QEP Energy Company subsidiary (QEP Energy), Co. acquires, explores for, develops and produces natural gas, oil and natural gas liquids (NGLs). Co.'s other subsidiary, QEP Field Services Company, provides midstream field services, including natural gas gathering, processing, compression and treating services for affiliates and third parties. QEP Marketing Company, another subsidiary, markets affiliate and third-party natural gas and oil, and provides risk-management services. At Dec 31 2011, QEP Energy's total proved reserves for natural gas, oil, and NGL were 2.75 trillion cubic feet, 67.5 million barrels and 76.6 million barrels, respectively.

Recent Developments: For the year ended Dec 31 2012, income from continuing operations decreased 51.2% to US$132.0 million from US$270.4 million a year earlier. Net income decreased 51.2% to US$132.0 million from US$270.4 million in the prior year. Revenues were US$2.35 billion, down 25.6% from US$3.16 billion the year before. Operating loss was US$133.3 million versus an income of US$505.9 million in the prior year. Indirect operating expenses decreased 6.4% to US$2.48 billion from US$2.65 billion in the equivalent prior-year period.

Prospects: Our evaluation of QEP Resources Inc. as of Apr. 7, 2013 is the result of our systematic analysis on three basic characteristics: earnings strength, relative valuation, and recent stock price movement. The company has generated a negative trend in earnings per share over the past 5 quarters. However, while recent estimates for the company have been mixed, QEP has posted better than expected results. Based on operating earnings yield, the company is about fairly valued when compared to all of the companies in our coverage universe. Share price changes over the past year indicates that QEP will perform in line with the market over the near term.

Financial Data

(US$ in Thousands)	12/31/2012	12/31/2011	12/31/2010	12/31/2009	12/31/2008	12/31/2007
Earnings Per Share	0.72	1.50	1.84	...	...	...
Cash Flow Per Share	7.27	7.32	5.69	...	...	...
Tang Book Value Per Share	17.97	18.34	16.77	626.44	625.51	...
Dividends Per Share	0.080	0.080	0.040	...	...	...
Dividend Payout %	11.11	5.33	2.17	...	...	...
Income Statement						
Total Revenue	2,349,800	3,159,200	2,246,400	2,198,500	2,530,100	1,843,400
EBITDA	1,225,000	1,280,200	1,180,800	1,142,700	1,378,500	984,000
Depn & Amortn	910,200	769,500	645,800	619,500	411,500	296,000
Income Before Taxes	198,500	424,800	452,900	459,900	919,400	662,100
Income Taxes	66,500	154,400	167,000	163,800	324,900	241,300
Net Income	128,300	267,200	326,200	293,500	585,500	420,800
Average Shares	178,700	178,400	177,300	...	...	...
Balance Sheet						
Current Assets	649,700	818,600	654,200	543,200	894,400	...
Total Assets	9,108,500	7,442,700	6,785,300	6,419,400	6,234,400	...
Current Liabilities	761,900	637,800	624,300	613,600	719,500	...
Long-Term Obligations	3,206,900	1,679,400	1,472,300	1,348,700	1,299,100	...
Total Liabilities	5,842,500	4,141,200	3,775,000	3,665,600	3,484,500	...
Stockholders' Equity	3,266,000	3,301,500	3,010,300	2,753,800	2,749,900	...
Shares Outstanding	178,400	176,800	175,900	4,300	4,300	4,300
Statistical Record						
Return on Assets %	1.55	3.76	4.94	4.64	...	...
Return on Equity %	3.90	8.47	11.32	10.67	...	...
EBITDA Margin %	52.13	40.52	52.56	51.98	54.48	53.38
Net Margin %	5.46	8.46	14.52	13.35	23.14	22.83
Asset Turnover	0.28	0.44	0.34	0.35	...	...
Current Ratio	0.85	1.28	1.05	0.89	1.24	...
Debt to Equity	0.98	0.51	0.49	0.49	0.47	...
Price Range	34.90-24.52	45.15-24.82	38.12-28.18	...	...	...
P/E Ratio	48.47-34.06	30.10-16.55	20.72-15.32	...	...	...
Average Yield %	0.27	0.22	0.12	...	...	...

Address: 1050 17th Street, Suite 500, Denver, CO 80265	Web Site: www.qepres.com	Auditors: PricewaterhouseCoopers LLP
Telephone: 303-672-6900	Officers: Keith O. Rattie - Non-Executive Chairman	Investor Contact: 303-405-6665
	Charles B. Stanley - President, Chief Executive Officer	Transfer Agents: Wells Fargo Shareowner Services, Saint Paul, MN

QUANTA SERVICES, INC.

Exchange	Symbol	Price	52Wk Range	Yield	P/E
NYS	PWR	$28.58 (3/28/2013)	29.91-20.34	N/A	19.85

*7 Year Price Score 99.41   *NYSE Composite Index=100   *12 Month Price Score 105.45

Price chart and TRADING VOLUME (thousand shares) 2004–2013

Interim Earnings (Per Share)

Qtr.	Mar	Jun	Sep	Dec
2008	0.14	0.22	0.29	0.24
2009	0.11	0.17	0.32	0.22
2010	0.11	0.16	0.30	0.15
2011	(0.08)	0.15	0.25	0.31
2012	0.22	0.31	0.45	0.46

Interim Dividends (Per Share)

No Dividends Paid

Valuation Analysis — Institutional Holding

Valuation Analysis		Institutional Holding	
Forecast EPS	$1.40 (04/05/2013)	No of Institutions	497
Market Cap	$6.0 Billion	Shares	205,865,792
Book Value	$3.8 Billion	% Held	85.97
Price/Book	1.59		
Price/Sales	1.01		

Business Summary: Construction Services (MIC: 7.5.4 SIC: 1731 NAIC: 238210)

Quanta Services is a provider of infrastructure applications to the electric power, natural gas and oil pipeline and telecommunications industries, including the design, installation, upgrade, repair and maintenance of infrastructure within each of the industries it serves, such as electric power transmission and distribution networks, substation and renewable energy facilities, natural gas and oil transmission and distribution systems and facilities and wireline and wireless telecommunications networks. Co. has four segments: Electric Power Infrastructure Services, Natural Gas and Pipeline Infrastructure Services, Telecommunications Infrastructure Services and Fiber Optic Licensing.

Recent Developments: For the year ended Dec 31 2012, income from continuing operations increased 134.4% to US$305.7 million from US$130.4 million a year earlier. Net income increased 123.4% to US$322.7 million from US$144.4 million in the prior year. Revenues were US$5.92 billion, up 41.2% from US$4.19 billion the year before. Operating income was US$465.1 million versus US$194.8 million in the prior year, an increase of 138.7%. Direct operating expenses rose 37.2% to US$4.98 billion from US$3.63 billion in the comparable period the year before. Indirect operating expenses increased 28.8% to US$472.6 million from US$366.9 million in the equivalent prior-year period.

Prospects: Our evaluation of Quanta Services Inc. as of Apr. 7, 2013 is the result of our systematic analysis on three basic characteristics: earnings strength, relative valuation, and recent stock price movement. The company has generated a negative trend in earnings per share over the past 5 quarters and while recent estimates for the company have remained steady, PWR has posted better than expected results. Based on operating earnings yield, the company is about fairly valued when compared to all of the companies in our coverage universe. Share price changes over the past year indicates that PWR will perform very well over the near term.

Financial Data

(US$ in Thousands)	12/31/2012	12/31/2011	12/31/2010	12/31/2009	12/31/2008	12/31/2007	12/31/2006	12/31/2005
Earnings Per Share	1.44	0.62	0.72	0.81	0.88	0.89	0.15	0.25
Cash Flow Per Share	0.78	1.03	1.14	1.88	1.37	1.61	1.03	0.71
Tang Book Value Per Share	9.77	7.63	7.61	7.02	5.84	3.96	3.36	2.67
Income Statement								
Total Revenue	5,920,269	4,623,829	3,931,218	3,318,126	3,780,213	2,656,036	2,131,038	1,858,626
EBITDA	622,762	363,178	395,819	368,395	403,507	243,559	127,425	123,780
Depn & Amortn	157,991	146,053	146,068	125,852	114,000	74,659	49,400	55,000
Income Before Taxes	462,496	216,370	246,255	233,730	281,767	167,362	65,126	52,247
Income Taxes	158,859	71,954	90,698	70,195	115,026	34,222	47,643	22,690
Net Income	306,629	132,515	153,176	162,162	166,741	135,977	17,483	29,557
Average Shares	212,835	213,168	211,796	201,311	202,363	167,260	117,863	116,634
Balance Sheet								
Current Assets	2,201,727	1,765,154	1,596,364	1,582,792	1,381,491	1,304,762	990,629	831,010
Total Assets	5,140,757	4,699,114	4,341,212	4,116,954	3,554,787	3,387,832	1,639,157	1,554,785
Current Liabilities	881,179	781,076	500,395	495,688	451,798	757,429	334,456	258,071
Long-Term Obligations	...	...	...	126,608	143,750	143,750	413,750	450,091
Total Liabilities	1,374,209	1,317,162	975,657	1,007,771	896,821	1,202,689	910,074	851,047
Stockholders' Equity	3,766,548	3,381,952	3,365,555	3,109,183	2,657,966	2,185,143	729,083	703,738
Shares Outstanding	209,270	206,203	211,570	210,040	197,590	171,015	118,533	118,164
Statistical Record								
Return on Assets %	6.22	2.93	3.62	4.23	4.79	5.41	1.09	1.96
Return on Equity %	8.56	3.93	4.73	5.62	6.87	9.33	2.44	4.32
EBITDA Margin %	10.52	7.85	10.07	11.10	10.67	9.17	5.98	6.66
Net Margin %	5.18	2.87	3.90	4.89	4.41	5.12	0.82	1.59
Asset Turnover	1.20	1.02	0.93	0.87	1.09	1.06	1.33	1.23
Current Ratio	2.50	2.26	3.19	3.19	3.06	1.72	2.96	3.22
Debt to Equity	...	...	...	0.04	0.05	0.07	0.57	0.64
Price Range	27.60-20.34	24.03-15.46	23.03-17.05	25.41-15.91	35.22-10.72	33.00-18.80	19.83-12.31	14.54-7.25
P/E Ratio	19.17-14.13	38.76-24.94	31.99-23.68	31.37-19.64	40.02-12.18	37.08-21.12	132.20-82.07	58.16-29.00

Address: 2800 Post Oak Boulevard, Suite 2600, Houston, TX 77056 **Telephone:** 713-629-7600	**Web Site:** www.quantaservices.com **Officers:** James F. O'Neil - President, Chief Executive Officer, Chief Operating Officer James H. Haddox - Executive Vice President, Chief Financial Officer	**Auditors:** PricewaterhouseCoopers LLP **Investor Contact:** 713-341-,7260 **Transfer Agents:** American Stock Transfer & Trust Company, New York, NY

QUEST DIAGNOSTICS, INC.

Exchange	Symbol	Price	52Wk Range	Yield	P/E
NYS	DGX	$56.46 (3/28/2013)	64.68-54.62	2.13	16.32

*7 Year Price Score 96.45   *NYSE Composite Index=100   *12 Month Price Score 88.63

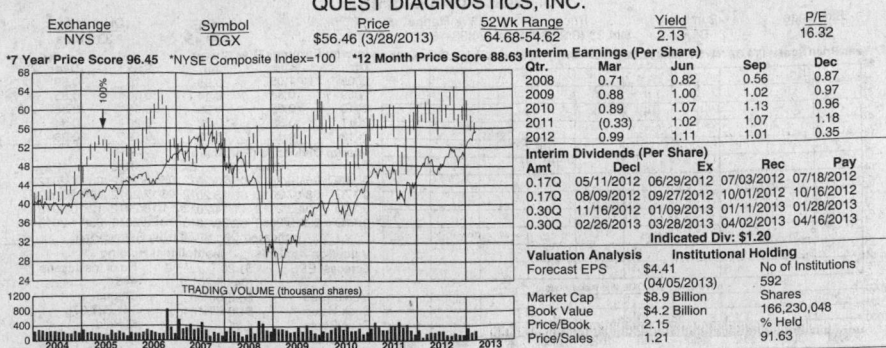

Interim Earnings (Per Share)

Qtr.	Mar	Jun	Sep	Dec
2008	0.71	0.82	0.56	0.87
2009	0.88	1.00	1.02	0.97
2010	0.89	1.07	1.13	0.96
2011	(0.33)	1.02	1.07	1.18
2012	0.99	1.11	1.01	0.35

Interim Dividends (Per Share)

Amt	Decl	Ex	Rec	Pay
0.17Q	05/11/2012	06/29/2012	07/03/2012	07/18/2012
0.17Q	08/09/2012	09/27/2012	10/01/2012	10/16/2012
0.30Q	11/16/2012	01/09/2013	01/11/2013	01/28/2013
0.30Q	02/26/2013	03/28/2013	04/02/2013	04/16/2013

Indicated Div: $1.20

Valuation Analysis | **Institutional Holding**

Forecast EPS	$4.41 (04/05/2013)	No of Institutions	592
Market Cap	$8.9 Billion	Shares	166,230,048
Book Value	$4.2 Billion	% Held	91.63
Price/Book	2.15		
Price/Sales	1.21		

Business Summary: Diagnostic & Health Related Services (MIC: 4.2.2 SIC: 8071 NAIC: 621511)

Quest Diagnostics is a provider of diagnostic testing, information and services. Co. is a provider of: clinical testing, which is generally is performed on whole blood, serum, plasma and other body fluids, such as urine, and specimens such as microbiology samples; and anatomic pathology services principally for the detection of cancer and are performed on tissues, such as biopsies, and other samples, such as human cells. Co.'s other operating segments include its non-clinical testing businesses and consist of its risk assessment services, clinical trials testing, healthcare information technology, and diagnostics products businesses.

Recent Developments: For the year ended Dec 31 2012, income from continuing operations increased 34.9% to US$666.5 million from US$494.1 million a year earlier. Net income increased 17.1% to US$592.1 million from US$505.7 million in the prior year. Revenues were US$7.38 billion, down 0.1% from US$7.39 billion the year before. Operating income was US$1.20 billion versus US$986.6 million in the prior year, an increase of 21.7%. Direct operating expenses was unchanged at US$4.36 billion versus the comparable period the year before. Indirect operating expenses decreased 11.0% to US$1.82 billion from US$2.04 billion in the equivalent prior-year period.

Prospects: Our evaluation of Quest Diagnostics Inc. as of Apr. 7, 2013 is the result of our systematic analysis on three basic characteristics: earnings strength, relative valuation, and recent stock price movement. The company has generated a negative trend in earnings per share over the past 5 quarters. However, while recent estimates for the company have been mixed, DGX has posted results that fell short of analysts expectations. Based on operating earnings yield, the company is undervalued when compared to all of the companies in our coverage universe. Share price changes over the past year indicates that DGX will perform poorly over the near term.

Financial Data
(US$ in Thousands)

	12/31/2012	12/31/2011	12/31/2010	12/31/2009	12/31/2008	12/31/2007	12/31/2006	12/31/2005
Earnings Per Share	3.46	2.92	4.05	3.87	2.97	1.74	2.94	2.66
Cash Flow Per Share	7.47	5.64	6.36	5.36	5.46	4.80	4.83	4.22
Dividends Per Share	0.680	0.400	0.400	0.400	0.400	0.400	0.390	0.345
Dividend Payout %	19.65	13.70	9.88	10.34	13.47	22.99	13.27	12.97
Income Statement								
Total Revenue	7,382,562	7,510,490	7,368,925	7,455,243	7,249,447	6,704,907	6,268,659	5,503,711
EBITDA	1,488,506	1,278,963	1,554,830	1,595,480	1,465,278	1,328,136	1,315,816	1,137,359
Depn & Amortn	281,047	281,102	253,964	256,687	264,593	237,879	195,687	176,124
Income Before Taxes	1,042,770	827,278	1,154,778	1,194,725	1,020,921	911,943	1,078,704	903,764
Income Taxes	401,897	349,000	425,531	460,474	386,768	358,574	407,581	364,177
Net Income	555,721	470,567	720,894	729,111	581,490	339,939	586,421	546,277
Average Shares	160,065	160,172	177,320	187,798	195,959	195,262	199,542	205,530
Balance Sheet								
Current Assets	1,560,997	1,401,260	1,605,417	1,679,425	1,496,819	1,374,357	1,191,018	1,069,497
Total Assets	9,283,863	9,313,379	8,527,630	8,563,643	8,403,830	8,565,693	5,661,482	5,306,115
Current Liabilities	1,047,603	1,561,159	1,214,268	1,059,212	1,224,761	1,288,297	1,150,870	1,101,292
Long-Term Obligations	3,354,173	3,370,522	2,641,160	2,936,792	3,078,089	3,377,212	1,239,105	1,255,386
Total Liabilities	5,120,816	5,620,507	4,494,150	4,574,004	4,798,934	5,241,451	2,642,311	2,543,131
Stockholders' Equity	4,163,047	3,692,872	4,033,480	3,989,639	3,604,896	3,324,242	3,019,171	2,762,984
Shares Outstanding	158,331	157,420	170,717	183,293	190,374	194,040	193,949	198,455
Statistical Record								
Return on Assets %	5.96	5.28	8.44	8.59	6.83	4.78	10.69	11.49
Return on Equity %	14.11	12.18	17.97	19.20	16.74	10.72	20.28	21.63
EBITDA Margin %	20.16	17.03	21.10	21.40	20.21	19.81	20.99	20.67
Net Margin %	7.53	6.27	9.78	9.78	8.02	5.07	9.35	9.93
Asset Turnover	0.79	0.84	0.86	0.88	0.85	0.94	1.14	1.16
Current Ratio	1.49	0.90	1.32	1.59	1.22	1.07	1.03	0.97
Debt to Equity	0.81	0.91	0.65	0.74	0.85	1.02	0.41	0.45
Price Range	64.68-54.62	60.83-46.02	61.61-43.50	62.07-43.46	56.54-40.27	58.33-48.17	64.28-48.70	54.50-44.51
P/E Ratio	18.69-15.79	20.83-15.76	15.21-10.74	16.04-11.23	19.04-13.56	33.52-27.68	21.86-16.56	20.49-16.73
Average Yield %	1.15	0.73	0.76	0.76	0.81	0.76	0.71	0.68

Address: Three Giralda Farms, Madison, NJ 07940	Web Site: www.questdiagnostics.com	Auditors: PricewaterhouseCoopers LLP
Telephone: 973-520-2700	Officers: Stephen H. Rusckowski - President, Chief Executive Officer Jon Roger Cohen - Senior Vice President, Chief Medical Officer	Investor Contact: 973-520-2900 Transfer Agents: ComputerShare Investor Services, Providence, RI

QUESTAR CORP.

Exchange	Symbol	Price	52Wk Range	Yield	P/E	Div Achiever
NYS	STR	$24.33 (3/28/2013)	24.33-18.50	2.79	20.45	33 Years

*7 Year Price Score 114.37 *NYSE Composite Index=100 *12 Month Price Score 105.00

Interim Earnings (Per Share)

Qtr.	Mar	Jun	Sep	Dec
2008	1.05	0.98	1.16	0.69
2009	0.38	0.44	0.56	0.85
2010	0.85	0.55	0.15	0.36
2011	0.39	0.22	0.20	0.34
2012	0.42	0.22	0.19	0.36

Interim Dividends (Per Share)

Amt	Decl	Ex	Rec	Pay
0.163Q	05/10/2012	05/23/2012	05/25/2012	06/11/2012
0.17Q	08/07/2012	08/15/2012	08/17/2012	09/10/2012
0.17Q	10/23/2012	11/14/2012	11/16/2012	12/10/2012
0.17Q	02/12/2013	02/20/2013	02/22/2013	03/11/2013

Indicated Div: $0.68 (Div. Reinv. Plan)

Valuation Analysis / **Institutional Holding**

Forecast EPS	$1.20 (04/05/2013)	No of Institutions 448
Market Cap	$4.3 Billion	Shares 141,327,376
Book Value	$1.0 Billion	% Held 73.57
Price/Book	4.11	
Price/Sales	3.87	

TRADING VOLUME (thousand shares)

Business Summary: Gas Utilities (MIC: 3.3.1 SIC: 1311 NAIC: 211111)

Questar is a natural gas holding company. Co. operates through wholly owned subsidiaries: Questar Gas Company ("Questar Gas"), which provides retail natural gas distribution in Utah, Wyoming and Idaho; Wexpro Company, which develops and produces natural gas on behalf of Questar Gas; and Questar Pipeline Company, which operates interstate natural gas pipelines and storage facilities in the western U.S. and provides other energy services. As of Dec 31 2012, Questar Gas was serving 930,760 sales and transportation customers.

Recent Developments: For the year ended Dec 31 2012, income from continuing operations increased 2.0% to US$212.0 million from US$207.9 million a year earlier. Net income increased 2.0% to US$212.0 million from US$207.9 million in the prior year. Revenues were US$1.10 billion, down 8.0% from US$1.19 billion the year before. Operating income was US$375.7 million versus US$366.9 million in the prior year, an increase of 2.4%. Direct operating expenses declined 25.0% to US$373.1 million from US$497.4 million in the comparable period the year before. Indirect operating expenses increased 6.1% to US$350.1 million from US$330.1 million in the equivalent prior-year period.

Prospects: Our evaluation of Questar Corp. as of Apr. 7, 2013 is the result of our systematic analysis on three basic characteristics: earnings strength, relative valuation, and recent stock price movement. The company has produced a positive trend in earnings per share over the past 5 quarters and while recent estimates for the company have been mixed, STR has posted better than expected results. Based on operating earnings yield, the company is about fairly valued when compared to all of the companies in our coverage universe. Share price changes over the past year indicates that STR will perform in line with the market over the near term.

Financial Data

(US$ in Thousands)	12/31/2012	12/31/2011	12/31/2010	12/31/2009	12/31/2008	12/31/2007	12/31/2006	12/31/2005
Earnings Per Share	1.19	1.16	1.91	2.23	3.88	2.88	2.54	1.87
Cash Flow Per Share	2.64	2.76	2.00	9.06	8.63	6.63	5.65	4.12
Tang Book Value Per Share	5.86	5.75	5.81	19.66	19.29	14.51	12.43	8.60
Dividends Per Share	0.665	0.620	0.540	0.505	0.492	0.485	0.465	0.445
Dividend Payout %	55.88	53.45	28.27	22.65	12.69	16.84	18.34	23.80
Income Statement								
Total Revenue	1,098,900	1,194,400	1,123,600	3,038,000	3,465,100	2,726,600	2,835,600	2,724,888
EBITDA	564,900	536,300	505,100	1,438,700	1,663,400	1,222,800	1,068,900	821,463
Depn & Amortn	189,200	169,400	161,800	714,600	502,100	375,800	316,100	259,734
Income Before Taxes	324,800	320,500	297,900	611,400	1,068,500	789,100	692,100	506,136
Income Taxes	116,500	116,400	109,400	222,000	378,000	290,600	255,500	187,923
Net Income	212,000	207,900	339,200	393,300	683,800	507,400	444,100	325,681
Average Shares	177,500	178,800	178,000	176,300	176,100	175,900	175,200	174,268
Balance Sheet								
Current Assets	345,700	335,400	399,600	831,100	1,185,000	658,900	753,400	755,840
Total Assets	3,757,100	3,532,800	3,373,600	8,897,700	8,630,700	5,944,200	5,064,700	4,357,073
Current Liabilities	546,700	568,800	655,100	948,100	1,131,600	998,700	678,900	873,574
Long-Term Obligations	1,138,200	993,000	898,500	2,179,900	2,078,900	1,021,000	1,022,400	983,200
Total Liabilities	2,721,500	2,499,300	2,337,500	5,395,500	5,212,700	3,366,300	2,859,200	2,807,270
Stockholders' Equity	1,035,600	1,033,500	1,036,100	3,502,200	3,418,000	2,577,900	2,205,500	1,549,803
Shares Outstanding	175,000	177,900	176,500	174,600	173,600	172,800	171,800	170,639
Statistical Record								
Return on Assets %	5.80	6.02	5.53	4.49	9.36	9.22	9.43	8.14
Return on Equity %	20.44	20.09	14.95	11.37	22.75	21.22	23.65	21.79
EBITDA Margin %	51.41	44.90	44.95	47.36	48.00	44.85	37.70	30.15
Net Margin %	19.29	17.41	30.19	12.95	19.73	18.61	15.66	11.95
Asset Turnover	0.30	0.35	0.18	0.35	0.47	0.50	0.60	0.68
Current Ratio	0.63	0.59	0.61	0.88	1.05	0.66	1.11	0.87
Debt to Equity	1.10	0.96	0.87	0.62	0.61	0.40	0.46	0.63
Price Range	21.24-18.50	20.02-16.41	18.08-12.83	13.87-8.14	23.65-7.13	18.66-12.40	14.51-10.97	14.38-7.55
P/E Ratio	17.85-15.55	17.26-14.15	9.47-6.72	6.22-3.65	6.09-1.84	6.48-4.30	5.71-4.32	7.69-4.04
Average Yield %	3.35	3.44	3.43	4.51	3.03	3.05	3.24	4.14

Address: 333 South State Street, P.O. Box 45433, Salt Lake City, UT 84145-0433 **Telephone:** 801-324-5900	**Web Site:** www.questar.com **Officers:** Keith O. Rattie - Chairman Ronald W. Jibson - President, Chief Executive Officer	**Auditors:** Ernst & Young LLP **Investor Contact:** 801-324-5218 **Transfer Agents:** Wells Fargo Shareowner Services, South St. Paul, MN

QUICKSILVER RESOURCES, INC.

Exchange	Symbol	Price	52Wk Range	Yield	P/E
NYS	KWK	$2.25 (3/28/2013)	5.75-1.67	N/A	N/A

*7 Year Price Score 22.10   *NYSE Composite Index=100   *12 Month Price Score 54.92

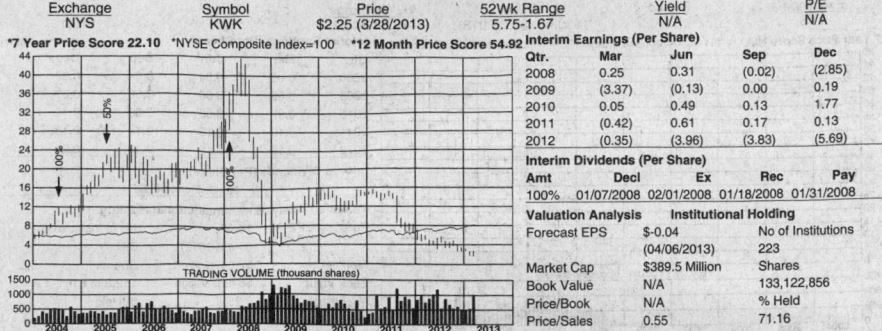

Interim Earnings (Per Share)

Qtr.	Mar	Jun	Sep	Dec
2008	0.25	0.31	(0.02)	(2.85)
2009	(3.37)	(0.13)	0.00	0.19
2010	0.05	0.49	0.13	1.77
2011	(0.42)	0.61	0.17	0.13
2012	(0.35)	(3.96)	(3.83)	(5.69)

Interim Dividends (Per Share)

Amt	Decl	Ex	Rec	Pay
100%	01/07/2008	02/01/2008	01/18/2008	01/31/2008

Valuation Analysis   **Institutional Holding**

Forecast EPS	$-0.04	No of Institutions
	(04/06/2013)	223
Market Cap	$389.5 Million	Shares
Book Value	N/A	133,122,856
Price/Book	N/A	% Held
Price/Sales	0.55	71.16

Business Summary: Production & Extraction (MIC: 9.1.1 SIC: 1311 NAIC: 211111)

Quicksilver Resources is an independent oil and gas company engaged in the acquisition, exploration, development and production of onshore oil and gas in North America. Co. focuses on unconventional reservoirs where hydrocarbons may be found in geological conditions, such as fractured shales, coalbeds and tight sands. Co.'s producing oil and gas properties in the U.S. are principally located in Texas, Colorado, Wyoming and Montana, and in Canada in Alberta and British Columbia. As of Dec 31 2011, Co.'s total proved reserves for natural gas, natural gas liquids and oil were 2.16 trillion cubic feet, 102.2 million barrels, and 3.0 million barrels, respectively.

Recent Developments: For the year ended Dec 31 2012, net loss amounted to US$2.35 billion versus net income of US$90.0 million in the prior year. Revenues were US$709.0 million, down 24.9% from US$943.6 million the year before. Operating loss was US$2.47 billion versus an income of US$122.6 million in the prior year. Direct operating expenses declined 14.5% to US$349.1 million from US$408.1 million in the comparable period the year before. Indirect operating expenses increased 584.3% to US$2.83 billion from US$413.0 million in the equivalent prior-year period.

Prospects: Our evaluation of Quicksilver Resources Inc. as of Apr. 7, 2013 is the result of our systematic analysis on three basic characteristics: earnings strength, relative valuation, and recent stock price movement. The company has managed to produce a neutral trend in earnings per share over the past 5 quarters. Because the company lacks sufficient analyst estimate data, we place greater weight on the historical EPS trend as the measure of earnings strength. Based on operating earnings yield, the company is overvalued when compared to all of the companies in our coverage universe. Share price changes over the past year indicates that KWK will perform very poorly over the near term.

Financial Data

(US$ in Thousands)	12/31/2012	12/31/2011	12/31/2010	12/31/2009	12/31/2008	12/31/2007	12/31/2006	12/31/2005
Earnings Per Share	(13.83)	0.52	2.45	(3.30)	(2.31)	2.86	0.57	0.54
Cash Flow Per Share	1.34	1.50	2.37	3.62	2.82	2.05	1.44	0.95
Tang Book Value Per Share	...	7.35	6.21	3.75	6.55	6.76	3.71	2.52
Income Statement								
Total Revenue	709,038	943,623	928,331	832,735	800,641	561,258	390,362	310,448
EBITDA	(2,320,501)	568,135	1,066,312	(515,812)	(374,454)	931,743	256,365	205,442
Depn & Amortn	163,624	225,763	202,603	201,387	194,823	124,936	80,870	56,642
Income Before Taxes	(2,648,176)	156,348	675,356	(912,300)	(671,787)	736,280	131,434	127,060
Income Taxes	(295,570)	57,863	252,886	(291,617)	(209,149)	256,508	38,150	40,702
Net Income	(2,352,606)	90,046	435,069	(557,473)	(373,994)	479,378	93,719	87,434
Average Shares	170,106	169,735	178,628	169,004	161,622	168,029	166,266	164,910
Balance Sheet								
Current Assets	207,513	300,427	238,172	219,938	393,336	190,401	170,964	113,584
Total Assets	1,381,788	3,995,462	3,512,334	3,612,882	4,500,571	2,775,846	1,882,912	1,243,094
Current Liabilities	167,791	334,173	463,100	366,660	418,499	358,575	199,389	212,190
Long-Term Obligations	2,063,206	1,903,431	1,746,716	2,427,523	2,605,025	813,817	919,117	506,039
Total Liabilities	2,514,585	2,733,543	2,452,926	2,976,884	3,405,862	1,707,491	1,307,246	859,479
Stockholders' Equity	(1,132,797)	1,261,919	1,059,408	635,998	1,094,709	1,068,355	575,666	383,615
Shares Outstanding	173,094	171,600	170,474	169,765	167,169	158,016	155,203	152,158
Statistical Record								
Return on Assets %	N.M.	2.40	12.21	N.M.	N.M.	20.58	6.00	8.20
Return on Equity %	N.M.	7.76	51.32	N.M.	N.M.	58.32	19.54	25.42
EBITDA Margin %	N.M.	60.21	114.86	N.M.	N.M.	166.01	65.67	66.18
Net Margin %	N.M.	9.54	46.87	N.M.	N.M.	85.41	24.01	28.16
Asset Turnover	0.26	0.25	0.26	0.21	0.22	0.24	0.25	0.29
Current Ratio	1.24	0.90	0.51	0.60	0.94	0.53	0.86	0.54
Debt to Equity	...	1.51	1.65	3.82	2.38	0.76	1.60	1.32
Price Range	7.08-2.68	15.67-6.35	16.24-10.94	16.30-4.00	43.73-4.06	30.36-16.72	25.14-14.84	24.55-11.25
P/E Ratio	...	30.13-12.21	6.63-4.47	...	...	10.61-5.85	44.10-26.03	45.45-20.84

Address: 801 Cherry Street, Suite 3700, Unit 19, Fort Worth, TX 76102	**Web Site:** www.qrinc.com	**Auditors:** Ernst & Young LLP
Telephone: 817-665-5000	**Officers:** Thomas F. Darden - Chairman Glenn M.	**Investor Contact:** 817-665-4023
Fax: 817-665-5004	Darden - President, Chief Executive Officer	**Transfer Agents:** Computershare

RACKSPACE HOSTING INC

Exchange	Symbol	Price	52Wk Range	Yield	P/E
NYS	RAX	$50.48 (3/28/2013)	79.24-41.22	N/A	67.31

*7 Year Price Score N/A   *NYSE Composite Index=100   *12 Month Price Score 92.51

TRADING VOLUME (thousand shares)

Interim Earnings (Per Share)

Qtr.	Mar	Jun	Sep	Dec
2008	0.05	0.04	0.04	0.06
2009	0.05	0.06	0.06	0.07
2010	0.07	0.08	0.09	0.10
2011	0.10	0.13	0.14	0.18
2012	0.17	0.18	0.19	0.21

Interim Dividends (Per Share)

No Dividends Paid

Valuation Analysis

Forecast EPS	$0.97 (04/06/2013)
Market Cap	$7.0 Billion
Book Value	$843.6 Million
Price/Book	8.25
Price/Sales	5.31

Institutional Holding

No of Institutions	334
Shares	112,334,616
% Held	82.93

Business Summary: Internet & Software (MIC: 6.3.2 SIC: 7371 NAIC: 541511)

Rackspace Hosting, through its operating subsidiaries, is a provider of cloud computing services. Co. provides a portfolio of cloud computing services, including Dedicated Cloud hosting and Public Cloud hosting. Dedicated Cloud refers to information technology services that Co. provides on a server or servers reserved for a customer. Public Cloud refers to pooled computing resources delivered on-demand over the Internet. Co. is also a provider for Hybrid Hosting, which combines the benefits of hosted computing on dedicated hardware and on pools of shared resources. In addition, Co. focuses on providing a service experience for its customers, which called Fanatical Support®.

Recent Developments: For the year ended Dec 31 2012, net income increased 38.0% to US$105.4 million from US$76.4 million in the prior year. Revenues were US$1.31 billion, up 27.7% from US$1.03 billion the year before. Operating income was US$172.7 million versus US$123.5 million in the prior year, an increase of 39.9%. Direct operating expenses rose 18.9% to US$367.5 million from US$309.1 million in the comparable period the year before. Indirect operating expenses increased 29.8% to US$769.0 million from US$592.5 million in the equivalent prior-year period.

Prospects: Our evaluation of Rackspace Hosting Inc. as of Apr. 7, 2013 is the result of our systematic analysis on three basic characteristics: earnings strength, relative valuation, and recent stock price movement. The company has generated a negative trend in earnings per share over the past 5 quarters. However, while recent estimates for the company have been lowered by analysts, RAX has posted results that fell short of analysts expectations. Based on operating earnings yield, the company is overvalued when compared to all of the companies in our coverage universe. Share price changes over the past year indicates that RAX will perform very well over the near term.

Financial Data
(US$ in Thousands)

	12/31/2012	12/31/2011	12/31/2010	12/31/2009	12/31/2008	12/31/2007	12/31/2006	12/31/2005
Earnings Per Share	0.75	0.55	0.35	0.24	0.19	0.17	0.19	0.11
Cash Flow Per Share	2.95	2.64	1.95	1.63	1.26	1.04	0.60	...
Tang Book Value Per Share	5.45	3.89	2.93	2.56	2.11	0.87	0.69	...
Income Statement								
Total Revenue	1,309,239	1,025,064	780,555	628,987	531,933	362,017	223,966	138,768
EBITDA	413,641	313,271	229,502	174,041	125,849	85,309	62,143	35,683
Depn & Amortn	240,900	189,800	149,900	118,800	85,700	54,700	30,900	18,900
Income Before Taxes	168,007	116,429	71,411	46,546	32,688	27,794	30,720	16,608
Income Taxes	62,589	40,018	25,053	16,328	10,985	9,965	10,900	5,836
Net Income	105,418	76,411	46,358	30,218	21,703	17,829	19,820	10,772
Average Shares	141,265	138,064	133,429	127,420	115,406	106,618	104,032	99,657
Balance Sheet								
Current Assets	425,245	263,365	185,445	191,669	292,495	58,143	27,928	...
Total Assets	1,295,551	1,026,482	761,577	668,645	685,261	301,813	132,983	...
Current Liabilities	255,439	237,749	189,142	158,194	132,524	108,727	46,102	...
Long-Term Obligations	62,326	72,216	70,052	116,078	255,560	83,351	9,490	...
Total Liabilities	451,904	427,059	322,714	319,218	415,577	204,940	62,493	...
Stockholders' Equity	843,647	599,423	438,863	349,427	269,684	96,873	70,490	...
Shares Outstanding	137,797	131,912	126,950	123,773	117,154	101,128	99,667	98,227
Statistical Record								
Return on Assets %	9.05	8.55	6.48	4.46	4.39	8.20	...	...
Return on Equity %	14.57	14.72	11.76	9.76	11.81	21.31	...	...
EBITDA Margin %	31.59	30.56	29.40	27.67	23.66	23.56	27.75	25.71
Net Margin %	8.05	7.45	5.94	4.80	4.08	4.92	8.85	7.76
Asset Turnover	1.12	1.15	1.09	0.93	1.07	1.67	...	...
Current Ratio	1.66	1.11	0.98	1.21	2.21	0.53	0.61	...
Debt to Equity	0.07	0.12	0.16	0.33	0.95	0.86	0.13	...
Price Range	74.27-41.22	46.19-29.78	31.74-15.51	23.06-4.38	11.71-4.79	...	...	...
P/E Ratio	99.03-54.96	83.98-54.15	90.69-44.31	96.08-18.25	61.63-25.21	...	...	...

Address: 5000 Walzem Road, San Antonio, TX 78218 Telephone: 210-312-4000	Web Site: www.rackspace.com Officers: Lewis J. Moorman - President, Chief Strategy Officer, Division Officer A. Lanham Napier - President, Chief Executive Officer	Auditors: KPMG LLP Investor Contact: 210-312-7291 Transfer Agents: American Stock & Transfer & Trust Company, Brooklyn, NY

RADIOSHACK CORP.

Exchange	Symbol	Price	52Wk Range	Yield	P/E
NYS	RSH	$3.36 (3/28/2013)	6.34-1.91	N/A	N/A

*7 Year Price Score 19.15   *NYSE Composite Index=100   *12 Month Price Score 92.54

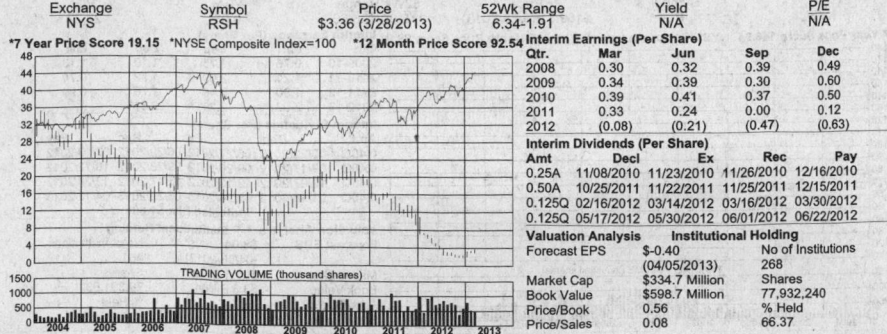

Interim Earnings (Per Share)

Qtr.	Mar	Jun	Sep	Dec
2008	0.30	0.32	0.39	0.49
2009	0.34	0.39	0.30	0.60
2010	0.39	0.41	0.37	0.50
2011	0.33	0.24	0.00	0.12
2012	(0.08)	(0.21)	(0.47)	(0.63)

Interim Dividends (Per Share)

Amt	Decl	Ex	Rec	Pay
0.25A	11/08/2010	11/23/2010	11/26/2010	12/16/2010
0.50A	10/25/2011	11/22/2011	11/25/2011	12/15/2011
0.125Q	02/16/2012	03/14/2012	03/16/2012	03/30/2012
0.125Q	05/17/2012	05/30/2012	06/01/2012	06/22/2012

Valuation Analysis

Institutional Holding	
Forecast EPS	$-0.40 (04/05/2013)
Market Cap	$334.7 Million
Book Value	$598.7 Million
Price/Book	0.56
Price/Sales	0.08

No of Institutions: 268
Shares: 77,932,240
% Held: 66.37

Business Summary: Retail - Appliances and Electronics (MIC: 2.1.7 SIC: 5731 NAIC: 443112)

RadioShack is engaged in the retail sale of consumer electronics goods and services. At Dec 31 2011, Co. operated 4,476 U.S. Co.-operated stores under the RadioShack brand throughout the U.S., Puerto Rico and the U.S. Virgin Islands. Co.'s product lines are categorized into three platforms: mobility platform, which includes postpaid and prepaid wireless handsets, commissions and residual income, prepaid wireless airtime and tablet devices; signature platform, which includes home entertainment, wireless, computer, and music accessories; and consumer electronics platform, which includes laptops, personal computing products, digital music players, telephones, cameras and digital televisions.

Recent Developments: For the year ended Dec 31 2012, loss from continuing operations was US$139.4 million compared with income of US$67.1 million a year earlier. Net loss amounted to US$139.4 million versus net income of US$72.2 million in the prior year. Revenues were US$4.26 billion, down 2.7% from US$4.38 billion the year before. Operating loss was US$60.9 million versus an income of US$155.1 million in the prior year. Direct operating expenses rose 5.0% to US$2.70 billion from US$2.57 billion in the comparable period the year before. Indirect operating expenses decreased 2.0% to US$1.62 billion from US$1.66 billion in the equivalent prior-year period.

Prospects: Our evaluation of RadioShack Corp. as of Apr. 7, 2013 is the result of our systematic analysis on three basic characteristics: earnings strength, relative valuation, and recent stock price movement. The company has enjoyed a very positive trend in earnings per share over the past 5 quarters. Because the company lacks sufficient analyst estimate data, we place greater weight on the historical EPS trend as the measure of earnings strength. Based on operating earnings yield, the company is overvalued when compared to all of the companies in our coverage universe. Share price changes over the past year indicates that RSH will perform very poorly over the near term.

Financial Data

(US$ in Thousands)	12/31/2012	12/31/2011	12/31/2010	12/31/2009	12/31/2008	12/31/2007	12/31/2006	12/31/2005
Earnings Per Share	(1.39)	0.70	1.68	1.63	1.49	1.74	0.54	1.79
Cash Flow Per Share	(0.43)	2.13	1.29	1.96	2.12	2.82	2.31	2.45
Tang Book Value Per Share	5.64	7.21	7.58	8.06	6.24	5.83	4.76	4.07
Dividends Per Share	0.250	0.500	0.250	0.250	0.250	0.250	0.250	0.250
Dividend Payout %	...	71.43	14.88	15.34	16.78	14.37	46.30	13.97
Income Statement								
Total Revenue	4,257,800	4,378,000	4,472,700	4,276,000	4,224,500	4,251,700	4,777,500	5,081,700
EBITDA	35,500	250,400	474,600	474,500	418,900	495,500	276,500	483,900
Depn & Amortn	97,000	99,400	99,200	106,700	99,300	112,700	128,200	123,800
Income Before Taxes	(114,100)	107,300	336,100	328,500	304,300	366,600	111,400	321,500
Income Taxes	25,300	40,200	130,000	123,500	111,900	129,800	38,000	51,600
Net Income	(139,400)	72,200	206,100	205,000	192,400	236,800	73,400	267,000
Average Shares	100,100	103,300	122,700	126,100	129,100	135,900	136,200	148,800
Balance Sheet								
Current Assets	1,981,900	1,812,800	1,778,700	2,015,700	1,792,000	1,566,800	1,599,600	1,627,300
Total Assets	2,299,100	2,175,100	2,175,400	2,429,300	2,283,500	1,989,600	2,070,000	2,205,100
Current Liabilities	978,200	663,600	908,100	654,500	637,200	748,000	984,200	986,300
Long-Term Obligations	499,000	670,600	331,800	627,800	732,500	348,200	345,800	494,900
Total Liabilities	1,700,400	1,421,800	1,332,900	1,381,000	1,466,200	1,219,900	1,416,200	1,616,300
Stockholders' Equity	598,700	753,300	842,500	1,048,300	817,300	769,700	653,800	588,800
Shares Outstanding	99,608	99,318	105,773	125,227	125,083	131,093	135,837	134,962
Statistical Record								
Return on Assets %	N.M.	3.32	8.95	8.70	8.98	11.67	3.43	11.31
Return on Equity %	N.M.	9.05	21.80	21.98	24.18	33.27	11.81	35.34
EBITDA Margin %	0.83	5.72	10.61	11.10	9.92	11.65	5.79	9.52
Net Margin %	N.M.	1.65	4.61	4.79	4.55	5.57	1.54	5.25
Asset Turnover	1.90	2.01	1.94	1.81	1.97	2.09	2.24	2.15
Current Ratio	2.03	2.73	1.96	3.08	2.81	2.09	1.63	1.65
Debt to Equity	0.83	0.89	0.39	0.60	0.90	0.45	0.53	0.84
Price Range	10.96-1.91	18.56-9.23	23.86-18.18	20.27-6.52	19.36-8.11	34.87-16.81	22.90-13.76	34.30-20.69
P/E Ratio	...	26.51-13.19	14.20-10.82	12.44-4.00	12.99-5.44	20.04-9.66	42.41-25.48	19.16-11.56
Average Yield %	5.69	3.64	1.21	1.77	1.69	1.01	1.38	0.97

Address: Mail Stop CF3-201, 300 RadioShack Circle, Fort Worth, TX 76102	Web Site: www.radioshack.com	Auditors: PricewaterhouseCoopers LLP
Telephone: 817-415-3011	Officers: James F. Gooch - President, Chief Executive Officer Joseph C. Magnacca - Chief Executive Officer	Investor Contact: 817-415-3021
Fax: 817-415-6808		Transfer Agents: Wells Fargo Bank, N.A., Mendota Heights, MN

RALPH LAUREN CORP

Exchange	Symbol	Price	52Wk Range	Yield	P/E
NYS	RL	$169.31 (3/28/2013)	178.06-136.60	0.95	22.22

*7 Year Price Score 146.94 *NYSE Composite Index=100 *12 Month Price Score 99.91

TRADING VOLUME (thousand shares)

Interim Earnings (Per Share)

Qtr.	Jun	Sep	Dec	Mar
2009-10	0.76	1.75	1.10	1.13
2010-11	1.21	2.09	1.72	0.74
2011-12	1.90	2.46	1.78	0.99
2012-13	2.03	2.29	2.31	...

Interim Dividends (Per Share)

Amt	Decl	Ex	Rec	Pay
0.40Q	05/22/2012	06/27/2012	06/29/2012	07/13/2012
0.40Q	09/17/2012	09/26/2012	09/28/2012	10/12/2012
0.40Q	12/07/2012	12/13/2012	12/17/2012	12/28/2012
0.40Q	03/18/2013	03/26/2013	03/28/2013	04/12/2013

Indicated Div: $1.60

Valuation Analysis

		Institutional Holding	
Forecast EPS	$8.04 (04/06/2013)	No of Institutions	481
Market Cap	$15.4 Billion	Shares	70,391,632
Book Value	$3.8 Billion	% Held	N/A
Price/Book	4.07		
Price/Sales	2.22		

Business Summary: Apparel, Footwear & Accessories (MIC: 1.4.2 SIC: 2329 NAIC: 315211)

Ralph Lauren designs, markets and distributes lifestyle products, including men's, women's and children's apparel, accessories (including footwear), fragrances and home furnishings. Co.'s brand names include Polo Ralph Lauren, Purple Label, Ralph Lauren Women's Collection, Black Label, Blue Label, Lauren by Ralph Lauren, Ralph Lauren Childrenswear, American Living, Chaps and Club Monaco, among others. As of Mar 31 2012, in addition to wholesale distribution, Co. sold directly to customers throughout the world via its 379 retail stores; its 474 concessions-based shop-within-shops; and its six e-commerce sites. Co. operates in three segments: Wholesale, Retail, and Licensing.

Recent Developments: For the quarter ended Dec 29 2012, net income increased 27.6% to US$215.7 million from US$169.0 million in the year-earlier quarter. Revenues were US$1.85 billion, up 2.2% from US$1.81 billion the year before. Operating income was US$304.4 million versus US$270.1 million in the prior-year quarter, an increase of 12.7%. Direct operating expenses declined 2.8% to US$752.0 million from US$774.0 million in the comparable period the year before. Indirect operating expenses increased 3.7% to US$789.7 million from US$761.5 million in the equivalent prior-year period.

Prospects: Our evaluation of Ralph Lauren Corp. as of Apr. 7, 2013 is the result of our systematic analysis on three basic characteristics: earnings strength, relative valuation, and recent stock price movement. The company has produced a positive trend in earnings per share over the past 5 quarters. However, while recent estimates for the company have been mixed, RL has posted better than expected results. Based on operating earnings yield, the company is about fairly valued when compared to all of the companies in our coverage universe. Share price changes over the past year indicates that RL will perform in line with the market over the near term.

Financial Data

(US$ in Thousands)	9 Mos	6 Mos	3 Mos	03/31/2012	04/02/2011	04/03/2010	03/28/2009	03/29/2008
Earnings Per Share	7.62	7.09	7.26	7.13	5.75	4.73	4.01	3.99
Cash Flow Per Share	10.96	9.95	10.21	9.58	7.19	9.02	7.83	6.82
Tang Book Value Per Share	26.87	25.93	23.21	24.70	20.11	17.99	14.31	10.71
Dividends Per Share	1.400	1.200	1.000	0.800	0.500	0.300	0.200	0.200
Dividend Payout %	18.37	16.93	13.77	11.22	8.70	6.34	4.99	5.01
Income Statement								
Total Revenue	5,301,500	3,455,400	1,593,400	6,859,500	5,660,300	4,978,900	5,018,900	4,880,100
EBITDA	958,000	650,700	296,100	1,066,800	869,100	726,400	617,300	694,200
Depn & Amortn	20,300	13,500	6,700	28,900	25,400	21,700	20,200	47,200
Income Before Taxes	925,300	628,900	285,100	1,024,400	833,100	694,900	592,500	646,000
Income Taxes	297,900	219,000	90,500	334,100	257,800	209,800	181,500	222,300
Net Income	622,800	407,100	193,400	681,000	567,600	479,500	406,000	419,800
Average Shares	93,300	93,400	95,100	95,500	98,700	101,300	101,300	105,200
Balance Sheet								
Current Assets	3,002,000	3,003,000	2,719,300	2,899,900	2,478,000	2,275,800	2,056,700	1,893,500
Total Assets	5,489,200	5,523,500	5,194,100	5,416,400	4,981,100	4,648,900	4,356,500	4,365,500
Current Liabilities	1,191,600	958,100	933,000	946,200	832,000	747,300	674,100	908,600
Long-Term Obligations	...	265,800	261,000	312,700	332,300	320,300	483,000	546,000
Total Liabilities	1,719,500	1,787,100	1,722,300	1,763,900	1,676,400	1,532,300	1,621,400	1,975,800
Stockholders' Equity	3,769,700	3,736,400	3,471,800	3,652,500	3,304,700	3,116,600	2,735,100	2,389,700
Shares Outstanding	90,700	91,500	91,100	92,700	94,500	98,200	99,200	99,500
Statistical Record								
Return on Assets %	13.26	12.36	13.60	13.14	11.82	10.48	9.34	10.36
Return on Equity %	19.65	18.83	20.69	19.63	17.73	16.12	15.89	17.82
EBITDA Margin %	18.07	18.83	18.58	15.55	15.35	14.59	12.30	14.23
Net Margin %	11.75	11.78	12.14	9.93	10.03	9.63	8.09	8.60
Asset Turnover	1.28	1.27	1.36	1.32	1.18	1.09	1.15	1.20
Current Ratio	2.52	3.13	2.91	3.06	2.98	3.05	3.05	2.08
Debt to Equity	...	0.07	0.08	0.09	0.10	0.10	0.18	0.23
Price Range	179.87-136.60	179.87-125.67	179.87-114.16	179.87-114.16	127.98-71.93	86.53-42.25	76.53-31.94	102.30-51.33
P/E Ratio	23.60-17.93	25.37-17.72	24.78-15.72	25.23-16.01	22.26-12.51	18.29-8.93	19.08-7.97	25.64-12.86
Average Yield %	0.90	0.83	0.67	0.56	0.52	0.43	0.37	0.26

Address: 650 Madison Avenue, New York, NY 10022 Telephone: 212-318-7000 Fax: 212-888-5780	Web Site: www.RalphLauren.com Officers: Ralph Lauren - Chairman, Chief Executive Officer Roger N. Farah - President, Chief Operating Officer	Auditors: Ernst & Young LLP Transfer Agents: The Bank of New York Mellon, Jersey City, NJ

RANGE RESOURCES CORP

Exchange	Symbol	Price	52Wk Range	Yield	P/E
NYS	RRC	$81.04 (3/28/2013)	82.46-54.57	0.20	1013.00

*7 Year Price Score 121.57 *NYSE Composite Index=100 *12 Month Price Score 105.75

TRADING VOLUME (thousand shares)

Interim Earnings (Per Share)

Qtr.	Mar	Jun	Sep	Dec
2008	0.01	(0.23)	1.81	0.60
2009	0.21	(0.26)	(0.19)	(0.11)
2010	0.48	0.06	(0.05)	(2.02)
2011	(0.16)	0.32	0.21	(0.02)
2012	(0.26)	0.34	(0.34)	0.33

Interim Dividends (Per Share)

Amt	Decl	Ex	Rec	Pay
0.04Q	06/01/2012	06/13/2012	06/15/2012	06/29/2012
0.04Q	08/31/2012	09/13/2012	09/17/2012	09/28/2012
0.04Q	11/30/2012	12/12/2012	12/14/2012	12/28/2012
0.04Q	03/01/2013	03/13/2013	03/15/2013	03/29/2013

Indicated Div: $0.16

Valuation Analysis		Institutional Holding	
Forecast EPS	$1.36	No of Institutions	
	(04/06/2013)	544	
Market Cap	$13.2 Billion	Shares	
Book Value	$2.4 Billion	178,748,992	
Price/Book	5.59	% Held	
Price/Sales	9.03	96.90	

Business Summary: Production & Extraction (MIC: 9.1.1 SIC: 1311 NAIC: 211111)

Range Resources is engaged in the exploration, development and acquisition of natural gas properties in the Appalachian and Southwestern regions of the U.S. The Appalachian region includes properties located in Pennsylvania, West Virginia and Virginia. The Southwestern region includes drilling, production and field operations in the Permian Basin of West Texas, the Delaware Basin of New Mexico, the East Texas Basin, as well as in the Texas Panhandle, Anadarko Basin of western Oklahoma, Ardmore Basin of southern Oklahoma, Nemaha Uplift of northern Oklahoma and Kansas and Mississippi. As of Dec 31 2011, Co. had total proved reserves 5.05 trillion cubic feet equivalent of gas.

Recent Developments: For the year ended Dec 31 2012, income from continuing operations decreased 69.6% to US$13.0 million from US$42.7 million a year earlier. Net income decreased 77.6% to US$13.0 million from US$58.0 million in the prior year. Revenues were US$1.46 billion, up 18.5% from US$1.23 billion the year before. Direct operating expenses rose 31.9% to US$308.4 million from US$233.7 million in the comparable period the year before. Indirect operating expenses increased 22.4% to US$1.12 billion from US$918.7 million in the equivalent prior-year period.

Prospects: Our evaluation of Range Resources Corp. as of Apr. 7, 2013 is the result of our systematic analysis on three basic characteristics: earnings strength, relative valuation, and recent stock price movement. The company has enjoyed a very positive trend in earnings per share over the past 5 quarters and while recent estimates for the company have been raised by analysts, RRC has posted better than expected results. Based on operating earnings yield, the company is overvalued when compared to all of the companies in our coverage universe. Share price changes over the past year indicates that RRC will perform well over the near term.

Financial Data
(US$ in Thousands)

	12/31/2012	12/31/2011	12/31/2010	12/31/2009	12/31/2008	12/31/2007	12/31/2006	12/31/2005
Earnings Per Share	0.08	0.36	(1.53)	(0.35)	2.22	1.54	1.14	0.86
Cash Flow Per Share	4.05	4.00	3.27	3.83	5.44	4.47	3.59	2.62
Tang Book Value Per Share	14.51	14.85	13.91	15.04	15.82	11.56	9.04	5.36
Dividends Per Share	0.160	0.160	0.160	0.160	0.160	0.130	0.090	0.060
Dividend Payout %	200.00	44.44	...	...	7.21	8.44	7.89	6.98
Income Statement								
Total Revenue	1,457,704	1,218,656	1,038,975	907,341	1,322,947	862,091	779,728	535,957
EBITDA	207,054	219,515	(218,551)	90,335	656,042	354,374	386,417	222,576
Depn & Amortn	13,200	16,200	16,200	31,700	13,700	10,900	7,500	6,400
Income Before Taxes	25,056	78,263	(365,943)	(58,732)	542,594	265,737	321,340	177,379
Income Taxes	12,054	35,557	(126,687)	(4,862)	196,436	98,761	123,726	66,368
Net Income	13,002	58,026	(239,256)	(53,870)	346,158	230,569	158,702	111,011
Average Shares	160,307	159,441	156,874	154,514	155,943	149,911	138,711	129,126
Balance Sheet								
Current Assets	327,614	315,263	261,714	175,280	404,311	261,814	320,337	207,977
Total Assets	6,728,735	5,845,470	5,498,586	5,395,881	5,562,543	4,016,508	3,187,674	2,018,985
Current Liabilities	455,143	511,932	430,562	314,104	353,514	305,433	232,356	321,760
Long-Term Obligations	2,878,185	1,974,967	1,960,536	1,707,833	1,790,668	1,150,658	1,048,782	616,148
Total Liabilities	4,371,343	3,453,050	3,274,825	3,017,292	3,104,710	2,288,486	1,931,513	1,322,062
Stockholders' Equity	2,357,392	2,392,420	2,223,761	2,378,589	2,457,833	1,728,022	1,256,161	696,923
Shares Outstanding	162,514	161,131	159,909	158,118	155,375	149,511	138,931	129,907
Statistical Record								
Return on Assets %	0.21	1.02	N.M.	N.M.	7.21	6.40	6.10	6.14
Return on Equity %	0.55	2.51	N.M.	N.M.	16.49	15.45	16.25	17.58
EBITDA Margin %	14.20	18.01	N.M.	9.96	49.59	41.11	49.56	41.53
Net Margin %	0.89	4.76	N.M.	N.M.	26.17	26.75	20.35	20.71
Asset Turnover	0.23	0.21	0.19	0.17	0.28	0.24	0.30	0.30
Current Ratio	0.72	0.62	0.61	0.56	1.14	0.86	1.38	0.65
Debt to Equity	1.22	0.83	0.88	0.72	0.73	0.67	0.83	0.88
Price Range	73.28-54.02	74.40-44.74	53.93-32.80	58.74-31.18	75.00-26.86	51.63-25.69	31.23-21.99	28.01-12.57
P/E Ratio	916.00-675.25	206.67-124.28	...	...	33.78-12.10	33.53-16.68	27.39-19.29	32.57-14.61
Average Yield %	0.25	0.28	0.37	0.36	0.31	0.35	0.34	0.31

Address: 100 Throckmorton Street, Suite 1200, Fort Worth, TX 76102 Telephone: 817-870-2601 Fax: 817-870-2316	Web Site: www.rangeresources.com Officers: John H. Pinkerton - Chairman, Chief Executive Officer Jeffrey L. Ventura - President, Chief Executive Officer, Chief Operating Officer	Auditors: Ernst & Young LLP Investor Contact: 817-869-4266 Transfer Agents: Computershare Investor Services, LLC, Cleveland, OH

RAYMOND JAMES FINANCIAL, INC.

Exchange	Symbol	Price	52Wk Range	Yield	P/E
NYS	RJF	$46.10 (3/28/2013)	48.12-31.77	1.21	20.22

*7 Year Price Score 113.80 *NYSE Composite Index=100 *12 Month Price Score 110.17

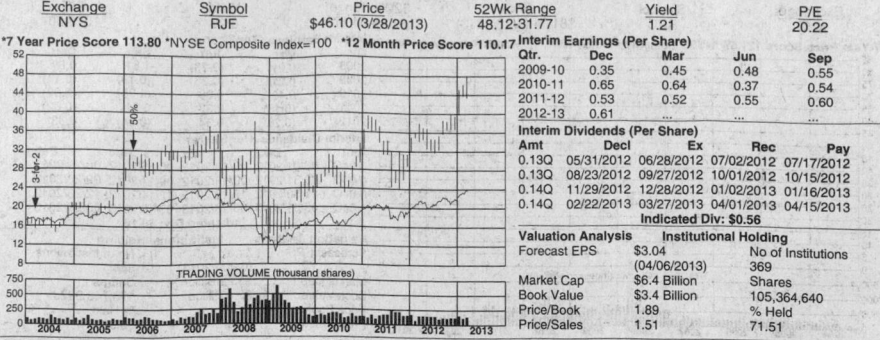

Interim Earnings (Per Share)

Qtr.	Dec	Mar	Jun	Sep
2009-10	0.35	0.45	0.48	0.55
2010-11	0.65	0.64	0.37	0.54
2011-12	0.53	0.52	0.55	0.60
2012-13	0.61	...	...	...

Interim Dividends (Per Share)

Amt	Decl	Ex	Rec	Pay
0.13Q	05/31/2012	06/28/2012	07/02/2012	07/17/2012
0.13Q	08/23/2012	09/27/2012	10/01/2012	10/15/2012
0.14Q	11/29/2012	12/28/2012	01/02/2013	01/16/2013
0.14Q	02/22/2013	03/27/2013	04/01/2013	04/15/2013

Indicated Div: $0.56

Valuation Analysis		Institutional Holding	
Forecast EPS	$3.04	No of Institutions	369
	(04/06/2013)		
Market Cap	$6.4 Billion	Shares	105,364,640
Book Value	$3.4 Billion	% Held	71.51
Price/Book	1.89		
Price/Sales	1.51		

Business Summary: Finance Intermediaries & Services (MIC: 5.5.1 SIC: 6211 NAIC: 523110)

Raymond James Financial is a financial holding company. Through its broker-dealer subsidiaries, Co. is engaged in various financial service businesses, including the underwriting, distribution, trading and brokerage of equity and debt securities and the sale of mutual funds and other investment products. In addition, other subsidiaries of Co. provide investment management services for retail and institutional clients, corporate and retail banking, and trust services. Co. operates in eight business segments: Private Client Group; Capital Markets; Asset Management; RJ Bank; Emerging Markets; Securities Lending ; Proprietary Capital; and Other.

Recent Developments: For the quarter ended Dec 31 2012, net income increased 53.6% to US$93.9 million from US$61.1 million in the year-earlier quarter. Revenues were US$1.14 billion, up 42.4% from US$798.8 million the year before. Direct operating expenses rose 74.7% to US$28.0 million from US$16.0 million in the comparable period the year before. Indirect operating expenses increased 41.9% to US$962.3 million from US$678.1 million in the equivalent prior-year period.

Prospects: Our evaluation of Raymond James Financial Inc. as of Apr. 7, 2013 is the result of our systematic analysis on three basic characteristics: earnings strength, relative valuation, and recent stock price movement. The company has enjoyed a very positive trend in earnings per share over the past 5 quarters. However, while recent estimates for the company have been mixed, RJF has posted better than expected results. Based on operating earnings yield, the company is undervalued when compared to all of the companies in our coverage universe. Share price changes over the past year indicates that RJF will perform well over the near term.

Financial Data

(US$ in Thousands)	3 Mos	09/30/2012	09/30/2011	09/30/2010	09/30/2009	09/30/2008	09/30/2007	09/30/2006
Earnings Per Share	2.28	2.20	2.19	1.83	1.29	1.97	2.11	1.85
Cash Flow Per Share	4.76	2.98	12.73	(8.56)	3.53	0.69	3.78	(0.35)
Tang Book Value Per Share	21.69	21.11	19.90	17.96	16.01	15.15	14.14	12.04
Dividends Per Share	0.530	0.520	0.520	0.440	0.440	0.440	0.400	0.320
Dividend Payout %	23.25	23.64	23.74	24.04	34.11	22.34	18.96	17.30
Income Statement								
Total Revenue	1,137,509	3,897,900	3,399,886	2,979,516	2,602,519	3,204,932	3,109,579	2,632,757
EBITDA	142,666	483,904	478,081	380,702	259,101	410,398	405,918	353,276
Depn & Amortn	(4,501)	15,983	27,336	24,558	22,700	27,850	23,421	19,369
Income Before Taxes	147,167	467,921	450,745	356,144	236,401	382,548	382,497	333,907
Income Taxes	53,273	175,656	182,894	133,625	96,024	151,776	141,794	127,724
Net Income	85,874	295,869	278,353	228,283	152,750	235,078	250,430	214,342
Average Shares	138,694	131,791	122,836	119,592	118,749	119,059	118,693	115,738
Balance Sheet								
Current Assets	11,916,542	8,694,956	8,961,474	9,243,879	9,381,277	11,538,116	9,608,271	7,681,900
Total Assets	22,275,971	21,160,265	18,006,995	17,883,081	18,226,728	20,731,859	16,254,168	11,516,650
Current Liabilities	17,194,912	16,069,177	14,383,200	14,853,785	15,500,311	18,501,299	14,037,981	9,578,371
Long-Term Obligations	1,271,477	1,410,806	711,950	432,428	493,278	109,333	228,703	319,499
Total Liabilities	18,896,170	17,891,325	15,419,376	15,580,265	16,194,265	18,847,954	14,496,354	10,052,781
Stockholders' Equity	3,379,801	3,268,940	2,587,619	2,302,816	2,032,463	1,883,905	1,757,814	1,463,869
Shares Outstanding	138,536	137,736	126,407	124,701	123,064	120,252	119,897	116,385
Statistical Record								
Return on Assets %	1.57	1.51	1.55	1.26	0.78	1.27	1.80	2.16
Return on Equity %	10.45	10.08	11.38	10.53	7.80	12.88	15.55	15.84
EBITDA Margin %	12.54	12.41	14.06	12.78	9.96	12.81	13.05	13.42
Net Margin %	7.55	7.59	8.19	7.66	5.87	7.33	8.05	8.14
Asset Turnover	0.21	0.20	0.19	0.17	0.13	0.17	0.22	0.26
Current Ratio	0.69	0.54	0.62	0.62	0.61	0.62	0.68	0.80
Debt to Equity	0.38	0.43	0.28	0.19	0.24	0.06	0.13	0.22
Price Range	39.82-31.77	38.59-24.11	39.46-24.42	31.12-22.11	32.98-11.48	38.25-20.65	35.12-27.75	31.40-20.40
P/E Ratio	17.46-13.93	17.54-10.96	18.02-11.15	17.01-12.08	25.57-8.90	19.42-10.48	16.64-13.15	16.97-11.03
Average Yield %	1.49	1.56	1.60	1.69	2.33	1.51	1.27	1.17

Address: 880 Carillon Parkway, St. Petersburg, FL 33716 **Telephone:** 727-567-1000	**Web Site:** www.raymondjames.com **Officers:** Thomas A. James - Chairman Francis S. Godbold - Vice-Chairman	**Auditors:** KPMG LLP **Investor Contact:** 727-567-5133 **Transfer Agents:** Computershare, Pittsburgh, PA

RAYONIER INC.

Exchange	Symbol	Price	52Wk Range	Yield	P/E
NYS	RYN	$59.67 (3/28/2013)	59.67-41.62	2.95	27.50

*7 Year Price Score 130.09 *NYSE Composite Index=100 *12 Month Price Score 105.50

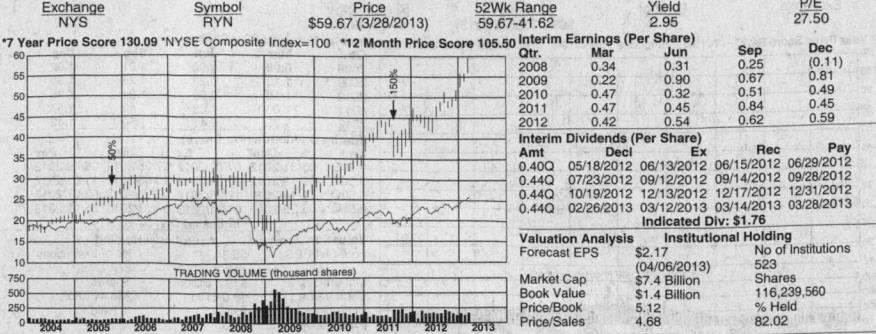

Interim Earnings (Per Share)

Qtr.	Mar	Jun	Sep	Dec
2008	0.34	0.31	0.25	(0.11)
2009	0.22	0.90	0.67	0.81
2010	0.47	0.32	0.51	0.49
2011	0.47	0.45	0.84	0.45
2012	0.42	0.54	0.62	0.59

Interim Dividends (Per Share)

Amt	Decl	Ex	Rec	Pay
0.40Q	05/18/2012	06/13/2012	06/15/2012	06/29/2012
0.44Q	07/23/2012	09/12/2012	09/14/2012	09/28/2012
0.44Q	10/19/2012	12/13/2012	12/17/2012	12/31/2012
0.44Q	02/26/2013	03/12/2013	03/14/2013	03/28/2013

Indicated Div: $1.76

Valuation Analysis

		Institutional Holding	
Forecast EPS	$2.17 (04/06/2013)	No of Institutions	523
Market Cap	$7.4 Billion	Shares	116,239,560
Book Value	$1.4 Billion	% Held	82.02
Price/Book	5.12		
Price/Sales	4.68		

Business Summary: REITs (MIC: 5.3.1 SIC: 6798 NAIC: 525930)

Rayonier is a real estate investment trust. Co. is a forest products company primarily engaged in activities associated with timberland management, the sale and entitlement of real estate, and the production and sale of cellulose fibers and fluff pulp. Co. operates in four reportable business segments: Forest Resources, which include all activities that relate to the harvesting of timber; Real Estate, which include all property sales, including those designated as higher and better use; Performance Fibers, which manufactures cellulose fibers and absorbent materials; and Wood Products, which manufactures and sells dimension lumber. The primary business of Co.'s Other segment is trading logs.

Recent Developments: For the year ended Dec 31 2012, net income increased 1.0% to US$278.7 million from US$276.0 million in the prior year. Revenues were US$1.57 billion, up 5.5% from US$1.49 billion the year before.

Prospects: Our evaluation of Rayonier Inc. as of Apr. 7, 2013 is the result of our systematic analysis on three basic characteristics: earnings strength, relative valuation, and recent stock price movement. The company has enjoyed a very positive trend in earnings per share over the past 5 quarters and while recent estimates for the company have remained steady, RYN has posted better than expected results. Based on operating earnings yield, the company is about fairly valued when compared to all of the companies in our coverage universe. Share price changes over the past year indicates that RYN will perform well over the near term.

Financial Data
(US$ in Thousands)

	12/31/2012	12/31/2011	12/31/2010	12/31/2009	12/31/2008	12/31/2007	12/31/2006	12/31/2005
Earnings Per Share	2.17	2.20	1.79	2.61	0.79	1.47	1.51	1.57
Cash Flow Per Share	3.62	3.55	4.12	2.59	2.88	2.78	2.68	2.39
Tang Book Value Per Share	11.66	10.84	10.34	9.61	7.81	8.36	7.95	7.75
Dividends Per Share	1.680	1.232	0.816	0.800	0.800	0.776	0.752	0.684
Dividend Payout %	77.42	56.00	45.67	30.69	100.84	52.67	49.91	43.48
Income Statement								
Total Revenue	1,571,000	1,488,642	1,315,233	1,168,567	1,232,100	1,224,654	1,229,807	1,180,708
EBITDA	585,435	508,963	432,484	577,222	391,327	400,767	366,701	368,959
Depn & Amortn	174,534	156,765	151,566	164,888	168,239	154,686	136,495	147,388
Income Before Taxes	366,526	302,274	231,770	361,703	179,946	197,514	190,748	192,258
Income Taxes	88,391	30,357	15,217	46,336	20,312	23,759	19,055	(16,948)
Net Income	278,685	276,005	217,586	312,541	152,036	174,269	176,418	182,839
Average Shares	128,702	125,394	121,868	120,030	119,143	118,380	117,238	116,466
Balance Sheet								
Current Assets	566,274	344,502	609,186	509,696	326,976	396,220	298,554	354,098
Total Assets	3,122,951	2,569,348	2,363,653	2,252,931	2,090,531	2,079,041	1,962,882	1,839,064
Current Liabilities	307,823	178,251	244,948	175,111	162,951	218,413	193,337	170,070
Long-Term Obligations	1,120,052	819,229	675,103	694,999	770,339	694,259	655,447	555,213
Total Liabilities	1,684,947	1,246,275	1,112,071	1,106,725	1,166,674	1,097,944	1,046,620	954,212
Stockholders' Equity	1,438,004	1,323,073	1,251,582	1,146,206	923,857	981,097	916,262	884,852
Shares Outstanding	123,332	122,035	121,023	119,312	118,221	117,325	115,319	114,138
Statistical Record								
Return on Assets %	9.76	11.19	9.43	14.39	7.27	8.62	9.28	9.69
Return on Equity %	20.13	21.44	18.15	30.20	15.92	18.37	19.59	21.75
EBITDA Margin %	37.27	34.19	32.88	49.40	31.76	32.72	29.82	31.25
Net Margin %	17.74	18.54	16.54	26.75	12.34	14.23	14.35	15.49
Asset Turnover	0.55	0.60	0.57	0.54	0.59	0.61	0.65	0.63
Current Ratio	1.84	1.93	2.49	2.91	2.01	1.81	1.54	2.08
Debt to Equity	0.78	0.62	0.54	0.61	0.83	0.71	0.72	0.63
Price Range	51.83-41.62	45.17-35.01	36.27-26.75	29.36-15.35	32.93-17.94	32.78-25.79	30.83-24.25	27.60-19.78
P/E Ratio	23.88-19.18	20.53-15.92	20.26-14.94	11.25-5.88	41.68-22.71	22.30-17.55	20.42-16.06	17.58-12.60
Average Yield %	3.60	3.00	2.59	3.27	2.91	2.62	2.78	2.90

Address: 1301 Riverplace Boulevard, Jacksonville, FL 32207 Telephone: 904-357-9100	Web Site: www.rayonier.com Officers: Lee M. Thomas - Chairman, President, Chief Executive Officer Paul G. Boynton - President, Chief Executive Officer, Chief Operating Officer	Auditors: Ernst & Young LLP Investor Contact: 904-357-9177 Transfer Agents: Computershare, Pittsburgh, PA

RAYTHEON CO.

Exchange	Symbol	Price	52Wk Range	Yield	P/E
NYS	RTN	$58.79 (3/28/2013)	59.28-49.30	3.74	10.41

*7 Year Price Score 94.27 *NYSE Composite Index=100 *12 Month Price Score 92.18

Interim Earnings (Per Share)

Qtr.	Mar	Jun	Sep	Dec
2008	0.92	1.00	1.01	1.02
2009	1.12	1.23	1.25	1.30
2010	1.16	0.55	1.94	1.25
2011	1.06	1.23	1.43	1.57
2012	1.32	1.41	1.50	1.42

Interim Dividends (Per Share)

Amt	Decl	Ex	Rec	Pay
0.50Q	05/31/2012	07/02/2012	07/05/2012	08/09/2012
0.50Q	09/19/2012	10/01/2012	10/03/2012	11/01/2012
0.50Q	11/14/2012	12/28/2012	01/02/2013	02/07/2013
0.55Q	03/20/2013	04/01/2013	04/03/2013	05/02/2013

Indicated Div: $2.20

Valuation Analysis

		Institutional Holding	
Forecast EPS	$5.34 (04/05/2013)	No of Institutions	877
Market Cap	$19.3 Billion	Shares	286,411,808
Book Value	$8.0 Billion	% Held	77.65
Price/Book	2.40		
Price/Sales	0.79		

Business Summary: Defense (MIC: 7.1.2 SIC: 3812 NAIC: 334511)

Raytheon is a technology company engaged in defense and other government markets throughout the world. Co. provides electronics, mission systems integration and other capabilities in the areas of sensing; effects; and command, control, communications and intelligence systems; and a range of mission support services. Co. serves both domestic and international customers, principally as a contractor on a portfolio of defense and related programs for government customers. Co. operates in six business segments: Integrated Defense Systems; Intelligence and Information Systems; Missile Systems; Network Centric Systems; Space and Airborne Systems; and Technical Services.

Recent Developments: For the year ended Dec 31 2012, income from continuing operations increased 1.2% to US$1.90 billion from US$1.88 billion a year earlier. Net income was unchanged at US$1.90 billion versus US$1.90 billion the prior year. Revenues were US$24.41 billion, down 1.5% from US$24.79 billion the year before. Operating income was US$2.99 billion versus US$2.83 billion in the prior year, an increase of 5.6%. Direct operating expenses declined 2.9% to US$19.09 billion from US$19.66 billion in the comparable period the year before. Indirect operating expenses increased 1.6% to US$2.33 billion from US$2.30 billion in the equivalent prior-year period.

Prospects: Our evaluation of Raytheon Co. as of Apr. 7, 2013 is the result of our systematic analysis on three basic characteristics: earnings strength, relative valuation, and recent stock price movement. The company has managed to produce a neutral trend in earnings per share over the past 5 quarters and while recent estimates for the company have been mixed, RTN has posted better than expected results. Based on operating earnings yield, the company is undervalued when compared to all of the companies in our coverage universe. Share price changes over the past year indicates that RTN will perform poorly over the near term.

Financial Data

(US$ in Thousands)	12/31/2012	12/31/2011	12/31/2010	12/31/2009	12/31/2008	12/31/2007	12/31/2006	12/31/2005
Earnings Per Share	5.65	5.28	4.88	4.89	3.95	5.79	2.85	1.92
Cash Flow Per Share	5.86	5.99	5.21	6.98	4.88	2.77	6.21	5.63
Tang Book Value Per Share	N.M.	N.M.	N.M.	N.M.	N.M.	1.15	N.M.	N.M.
Dividends Per Share	2.000	2.095	1.125	1.240	1.120	1.020	0.960	0.880
Dividend Payout %	35.40	39.68	23.05	25.36	28.35	17.62	33.68	45.83
Income Statement								
Total Revenue	24,414,000	24,857,000	25,183,000	24,881,000	23,174,000	21,301,000	20,291,000	21,894,000
EBITDA	3,289,000	3,159,000	2,846,000	3,338,000	2,855,000	2,546,000	2,176,000	2,054,000
Depn & Amortn	318,000	314,000	304,000	299,000	292,000	288,000	292,000	354,000
Income Before Taxes	2,779,000	2,690,000	2,432,000	2,930,000	2,498,000	2,225,000	1,688,000	1,440,000
Income Taxes	878,000	793,000	589,000	953,000	824,000	532,000	581,000	498,000
Net Income	1,888,000	1,866,000	1,840,000	1,935,000	1,672,000	2,578,000	1,283,000	871,000
Average Shares	334,200	353,600	377,000	395,700	423,700	445,659	450,875	453,302
Balance Sheet								
Current Assets	9,246,000	9,309,000	8,822,000	7,868,000	7,417,000	7,616,000	9,517,000	7,567,000
Total Assets	26,686,000	25,854,000	24,422,000	23,607,000	23,296,000	23,281,000	25,491,000	24,381,000
Current Liabilities	5,902,000	6,130,000	5,960,000	5,523,000	5,149,000	4,788,000	6,715,000	5,900,000
Long-Term Obligations	4,731,000	4,605,000	3,610,000	2,329,000	2,309,000	2,268,000	3,278,000	3,969,000
Total Liabilities	18,660,000	17,673,000	14,668,000	13,780,000	14,209,000	10,739,000	14,390,000	13,672,000
Stockholders' Equity	8,026,000	8,181,000	9,754,000	9,827,000	9,087,000	12,542,000	11,101,000	10,709,000
Shares Outstanding	328,000	339,000	359,000	378,000	400,000	426,196	445,870	446,373
Statistical Record								
Return on Assets %	7.17	7.42	7.66	8.25	7.16	10.57	5.15	3.59
Return on Equity %	23.23	20.81	18.79	20.46	15.42	21.81	11.77	8.19
EBITDA Margin %	13.47	12.71	11.30	13.42	12.32	11.95	10.72	9.38
Net Margin %	7.73	7.51	7.31	7.78	7.21	12.10	6.32	3.98
Asset Turnover	0.93	0.99	1.05	1.06	0.99	0.87	0.81	0.90
Current Ratio	1.57	1.52	1.48	1.42	1.44	1.59	1.42	1.28
Debt to Equity	0.59	0.56	0.37	0.24	0.25	0.18	0.30	0.37
Price Range	59.28-47.99	52.51-38.83	60.01-43.21	53.44-33.57	67.11-43.40	65.33-51.10	53.86-39.99	40.21-36.34
P/E Ratio	10.49-8.49	9.95-7.35	12.30-8.85	10.93-6.87	16.99-10.99	11.28-8.83	18.90-14.03	20.94-18.93
Average Yield %	3.70	4.48	2.22	2.69	1.92	1.78	2.08	2.29

Address: 870 Winter Street, Waltham, MA 02451	Web Site: www.raytheon.com	Auditors: PricewaterhouseCoopers LLP
Telephone: 781-522-3000	Officers: William H. Swanson - Chairman, Chief Executive Officer Thomas A. Kennedy - Executive Vice President, Chief Operating Officer, Vice President, Division Officer	Investor Contact: 877-786-7070 Transfer Agents: American Stock Transfer & Trust Co.

REALTY INCOME CORP.

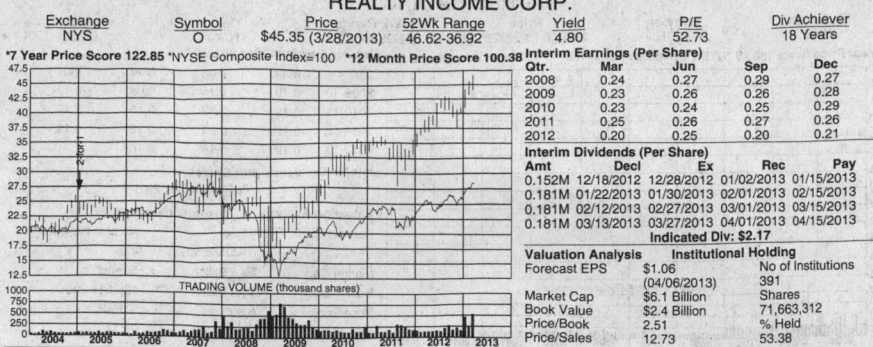

Exchange	Symbol	Price	52Wk Range	Yield	P/E	Div Achiever
NYS	O	$45.35 (3/28/2013)	46.62-36.92	4.80	52.73	18 Years

*7 Year Price Score 122.85 *NYSE Composite Index=100 *12 Month Price Score 100.38

Interim Earnings (Per Share)

Qtr.	Mar	Jun	Sep	Dec
2008	0.24	0.27	0.29	0.27
2009	0.23	0.26	0.26	0.28
2010	0.23	0.24	0.25	0.29
2011	0.25	0.26	0.27	0.26
2012	0.20	0.25	0.20	0.21

Interim Dividends (Per Share)

Amt	Decl	Ex	Rec	Pay
0.152M	12/18/2012	12/28/2012	01/02/2013	01/15/2013
0.181M	01/22/2013	01/30/2013	02/01/2013	02/15/2013
0.181M	02/12/2013	02/27/2013	03/01/2013	03/15/2013
0.181M	03/13/2013	03/27/2013	04/01/2013	04/15/2013

Indicated Div: $2.17

Valuation Analysis / **Institutional Holding**

Forecast EPS	$1.06 (04/06/2013)	No of Institutions	391
Market Cap	$6.1 Billion	Shares	71,663,312
Book Value	$2.4 Billion	% Held	53.38
Price/Book	2.51		
Price/Sales	12.73		

Business Summary: REITs (MIC: 5.3.1 SIC: 6798 NAIC: 525930)

Realty Income operates as an equity real estate investment trust (REIT). Co. invests in commercial real estate. Co. typically acquires properties under long-term leases with regional and national retailers and other commercial enterprises. Co.'s acquisition and investment activities generally focus on businesses providing goods and services that satisfy basic consumer and business needs. At Dec 31 2012, Co. owned 3,013 properties, located in 49 states, containing over 37.6 million leasable sq. ft., along with four properties owned by its wholly-owned taxable REIT subsidiary, Crest Net Lease, Inc.

Recent Developments: For the year ended Dec 31 2012, income from continuing operations increased 0.9% to US$146.0 million from US$144.6 million a year earlier. Net income increased 1.4% to US$159.2 million from US$157.0 million in the prior year. Revenues were US$475.5 million, up 15.9% from US$410.3 million the year before. Revenues from property income rose 15.9% to US$473.7 million from US$408.6 million in the corresponding earlier year.

Prospects: Our evaluation of Realty Income Corp. as of Apr. 7, 2013 is the result of our systematic analysis on three basic characteristics: earnings strength, relative valuation, and recent stock price movement. The company has produced a positive trend in earnings per share over the past 5 quarters. Because the company lacks sufficient analyst estimate data, we place greater weight on the historical EPS trend as the measure of earnings strength. Based on operating earnings yield, the company is overvalued when compared to all of the companies in our coverage universe. Share price changes over the past year indicates that O will perform well over the near term.

Financial Data
(US$ in Thousands)

	12/31/2012	12/31/2011	12/31/2010	12/31/2009	12/31/2008	12/31/2007	12/31/2006	12/31/2005
Earnings Per Share	0.86	1.05	1.01	1.03	1.06	1.16	1.11	1.12
Cash Flow Per Share	2.45	2.37	2.30	2.19	2.43	3.18	0.97	1.37
Tang Book Value Per Share	17.95	16.80	15.50	14.10	14.75	15.05	15.47	11.61
Dividends Per Share	1.778	1.738	1.723	1.708	1.667	1.571	1.448	1.353
Dividend Payout %	206.73	165.51	170.58	165.81	157.29	135.39	130.41	120.76
Income Statement								
Total Revenue	475,510	421,059	345,009	327,581	330,200	296,513	240,100	196,676
EBITDA	304,904	280,572	223,095	218,242	212,627	208,432	168,508	137,822
Depn & Amortn	158,933	129,435	101,679	96,109	95,781	81,049	62,443	48,605
Income Before Taxes	145,971	151,137	121,416	122,133	116,846	127,383	106,065	89,217
Net Income	159,152	157,032	130,784	131,127	131,841	140,409	110,781	99,119
Average Shares	132,884	126,189	105,942	103,581	101,209	100,333	89,917	80,208
Balance Sheet								
Current Assets	26,907	19,540	28,908	20,422	57,439	200,243	16,526	70,748
Total Assets	5,443,363	4,419,389	3,535,590	2,914,787	2,994,179	3,077,352	2,546,508	1,920,988
Current Liabilities	120,230	102,931	85,173	70,046	54,820	67,400	42,100	30,512
Long-Term Obligations	2,883,868	2,055,181	1,600,000	1,354,600	1,370,000	1,470,000	920,000	891,700
Total Liabilities	3,030,569	2,164,535	1,688,625	1,426,778	1,439,518	1,539,260	970,516	931,774
Stockholders' Equity	2,412,794	2,254,854	1,846,965	1,488,009	1,554,661	1,538,092	1,575,992	989,214
Shares Outstanding	133,452	133,223	118,058	104,286	104,211	101,082	100,746	83,696
Statistical Record								
Return on Assets %	3.22	3.95	4.06	4.44	4.33	4.99	4.96	5.89
Return on Equity %	6.80	7.66	7.84	8.62	8.50	9.02	8.64	10.42
EBITDA Margin %	64.12	66.63	64.66	66.62	64.39	70.29	70.18	70.08
Net Margin %	33.47	37.29	37.91	40.03	39.93	47.35	46.14	50.40
Asset Turnover	0.10	0.11	0.11	0.11	0.11	0.11	0.11	0.12
Current Ratio	0.22	0.19	0.34	0.29	1.05	2.97	0.39	2.32
Debt to Equity	1.20	0.91	0.87	0.91	0.88	0.96	0.58	0.90
Price Range	42.96-34.52	36.07-28.04	35.65-25.52	27.54-15.03	30.32-15.47	30.45-23.47	28.17-21.30	25.68-21.20
P/E Ratio	49.95-40.14	34.35-26.70	35.30-25.27	26.74-14.59	28.60-14.59	26.25-20.23	25.38-19.19	22.93-18.93
Average Yield %	4.51	5.12	5.44	7.63	6.98	5.70	6.03	5.72

Address: 600 La Terraza Boulevard, Escondido, CA 92025-3873
Telephone: 760-741-2111
Fax: 760-741-2235

Web Site: www.realtyincome.com
Officers: Thomas A. Lewis - Vice-Chairman, Chief Executive Officer Gary M. Malino - President, Co-President, Chief Operating Officer

Auditors: KPMG LLP
Investor Contact: 760-741-2111
Transfer Agents: Wells Fargo Shareowner Services, St. Paul, MN

RED HAT INC

Exchange	Symbol	Price	52Wk Range	Yield	P/E
NYS	RHT	$50.56 (3/28/2013)	61.95-47.41	N/A	68.32

*7 Year Price Score 150.46 *NYSE Composite Index=100   *12 Month Price Score 88.91

Interim Earnings (Per Share)

Qtr.	May	Aug	Nov	Feb
2009-10	0.10	0.15	0.08	0.12
2010-11	0.12	0.12	0.13	0.17
2011-12	0.17	0.20	0.19	0.19
2012-13	0.19	0.18	0.18	...

Interim Dividends (Per Share)

No Dividends Paid

Valuation Analysis		Institutional Holding	
Forecast EPS	$1.34	No of Institutions	475
	(04/05/2013)		
Market Cap	$9.8 Billion	Shares	
Book Value	$1.5 Billion		196,517,280
Price/Book	6.60	% Held	
Price/Sales	7.65		95.24

Business Summary: Internet & Software (MIC: 6.3.2 SIC: 7371 NAIC: 511210)

Red Hat, together with its subsidiaries, provides open source software technologies to the enterprise. These offerings include Co.'s core enterprise operating system platform, Red Hat Enterprise Linux, its enterprise middleware platform, Red Hat JBoss Middleware, as well as its virtualization, cloud, and storage offerings and other Red Hat enterprise technologies. Co. provides these software and services through content distribution and management services, Red Hat Network, Red Hat Network Satellite and Red Hat JBoss Operations Network. Co. also provides other infrastructure enterprise technologies, including storage, systems management, software development tools, and directory services.

Recent Developments: For the quarter ended Nov 30 2012, net income decreased 9.1% to US$34.8 million from US$38.2 million in the year-earlier quarter. Revenues were US$343.6 million, up 18.5% from US$290.0 million the year before. Operating income was US$49.9 million versus US$53.6 million in the prior-year quarter, a decrease of 6.8%. Direct operating expenses rose 17.5% to US$53.1 million from US$45.2 million in the comparable period the year before. Indirect operating expenses increased 25.8% to US$240.6 million from US$191.3 million in the equivalent prior-year period.

Prospects: Our evaluation of Red Hat Inc. as of Apr. 7, 2013 is the result of our systematic analysis on three basic characteristics: earnings strength, relative valuation, and recent stock price movement. The company has enjoyed a very positive trend in earnings per share over the past 5 quarters. However, while recent estimates for the company have been lowered by analysts, RHT has posted better than expected results. Based on operating earnings yield, the company is overvalued when compared to all of the companies in our coverage universe. Share price changes over the past year indicates that RHT will perform well over the near term.

Financial Data

(US$ in Thousands)	9 Mos	6 Mos	3 Mos	02/29/2012	02/28/2011	02/28/2010	02/28/2009	02/29/2008
Earnings Per Share	0.74	0.75	0.77	0.75	0.55	0.45	0.39	0.36
Cash Flow Per Share	2.36	2.35	2.21	2.02	1.53	1.36	1.24	1.05
Tang Book Value Per Share	3.84	3.96	3.77	3.67	3.71	3.01	2.87	2.71
Income Statement								
Total Revenue	980,932	637,327	314,731	1,133,103	909,277	748,236	652,572	523,016
EBITDA	196,082	130,767	66,874	231,214	175,987	137,485	149,230	150,792
Depn & Amortn	44,773	28,647	14,079	31,623	29,036	26,200	22,900	20,000
Income Before Taxes	157,693	106,568	55,089	208,009	153,694	121,502	121,532	124,540
Income Taxes	50,462	34,102	17,628	61,383	46,416	34,249	42,811	47,873
Net Income	107,231	72,466	37,461	146,626	107,278	87,253	78,721	76,667
Average Shares	195,666	195,795	195,937	196,451	196,353	193,546	211,344	221,313
Balance Sheet								
Current Assets	1,290,292	1,244,669	1,173,961	1,221,355	1,184,558	1,003,119	890,832	1,192,356
Total Assets	2,661,899	2,605,641	2,484,618	2,491,099	2,199,322	1,870,872	1,753,636	2,079,982
Current Liabilities	892,430	844,596	807,068	826,305	679,801	566,267	446,649	969,748
Total Liabilities	1,180,677	1,121,958	1,068,897	1,092,282	908,623	759,820	647,583	1,128,791
Stockholders' Equity	1,481,222	1,483,683	1,415,721	1,398,817	1,290,699	1,111,052	1,106,053	951,191
Shares Outstanding	193,479	193,211	192,888	192,654	193,046	187,351	189,998	190,859
Statistical Record								
Return on Assets %	5.68	5.97	6.41	6.24	5.27	4.81	4.11	3.96
Return on Equity %	9.91	10.31	11.04	10.87	8.93	7.87	7.65	8.63
EBITDA Margin %	19.99	20.52	21.25	20.41	19.35	18.37	22.87	28.83
Net Margin %	10.93	11.37	11.90	12.94	11.80	11.66	12.06	14.66
Asset Turnover	0.51	0.50	0.50	0.48	0.45	0.41	0.34	0.27
Current Ratio	1.45	1.47	1.45	1.48	1.74	1.77	1.99	1.23
Price Range	61.95-39.90	61.95-36.95	61.95-31.87	52.72-31.87	48.45-27.49	31.43-13.20	24.36-7.89	24.57-17.58
P/E Ratio	83.72-53.92	82.60-49.27	80.45-41.39	70.29-42.49	88.09-49.98	69.84-29.33	62.46-20.23	68.25-48.83

Address: 1801 Varsity Drive, Raleigh, NC 27606 Telephone: 919-754-3700	Web Site: www.redhat.com Officers: Henry Hugh Shelton - Chairman James M. Whitehurst - President, Chief Executive Officer	Auditors: PricewaterhouseCoopers LLP Investor Contact: 919-754-3700 Transfer Agents: Computershare

REGAL-BELOIT CORP.

Exchange	Symbol	Price	52Wk Range	Yield	P/E
NYS	RBC	$81.56 (3/28/2013)	84.67-57.04	0.93	17.58

*7 Year Price Score 115.61 *NYSE Composite Index=100 *12 Month Price Score 105.47

Interim Earnings (Per Share)

Qtr.	Mar	Jun	Sep	Dec
2008	0.97	1.14	1.09	0.67
2009	0.39	0.47	0.82	0.92
2010	0.98	1.07	1.14	0.65
2011	0.99	0.88	1.13	0.79
2012	1.16	1.49	1.29	0.70

Interim Dividends (Per Share)

Amt	Decl	Ex	Rec	Pay
0.19Q	04/30/2012	06/27/2012	06/29/2012	07/13/2012
0.19Q	07/27/2012	09/26/2012	09/28/2012	10/12/2012
0.19Q	10/26/2012	12/26/2012	12/28/2012	01/18/2013
0.19Q	01/25/2013	03/25/2013	03/27/2013	04/12/2013

Indicated Div: $0.76

Valuation Analysis — **Institutional Holding**

Forecast EPS	$5.18	No of Institutions
	(04/05/2013)	297
Market Cap	$3.7 Billion	Shares
Book Value	$2.0 Billion	45,395,516
Price/Book	1.87	% Held
Price/Sales	1.16	108.24

TRADING VOLUME (thousand shares)

Business Summary: Electrical Equipment (MIC: 7.3.1 SIC: 3621 NAIC: 335312)

Regal-Beloit is a manufacturer of electric motors and controls, electric generators and controls, and mechanical motion control products. Co. has two segments: Electrical and Mechanical. Co.'s electrical products primarily include motors used in commercial and residential heating, ventilation, air conditioning applications, a line of AC and DC commercial and industrial electric motors, electric generators and controls, drives and controls, and capacitors. Co.'s mechanical products primarily include gears and gearboxes, marine transmissions, manual valve actuators, and electrical connectivity devices. Co. sells its products to original equipment manufacturers, distributors and end-users.

Recent Developments: For the year ended Dec 29 2012, net income increased 26.8% to US$200.3 million from US$158.0 million in the prior year. Revenues were US$3.17 billion, up 12.8% from US$2.81 billion the year before. Operating income was US$312.8 million versus US$255.7 million in the prior year, an increase of 22.3%. Direct operating expenses rose 11.8% to US$2.40 billion from US$2.14 billion in the comparable period the year before. Indirect operating expenses increased 11.7% to US$458.2 million from US$410.3 million in the equivalent prior-year period.

Prospects: Our evaluation of Regal-Beloit Corp. as of Apr. 7, 2013 is the result of our systematic analysis on three basic characteristics: earnings strength, relative valuation, and recent stock price movement. The company has generated a negative trend in earnings per share over the past 5 quarters. However, while recent estimates for the company have been lowered by analysts, RBC has posted better than expected results. Based on operating earnings yield, the company is undervalued when compared to all of the companies in our coverage universe. Share price changes over the past year indicates that RBC will perform well over the near term.

Financial Data
(US$ in Thousands)

	12/29/2012	12/31/2011	01/01/2011	01/02/2010	12/27/2008	12/29/2007	12/30/2006	12/31/2005
Earnings Per Share	4.64	3.79	3.84	2.63	3.87	3.49	3.28	2.25
Cash Flow Per Share	8.44	6.70	4.60	8.98	4.93	6.44	3.04	3.78
Tang Book Value Per Share	11.34	2.45	10.65	10.36	1.02	2.37	5.17	1.83
Dividends Per Share	0.750	0.710	0.670	0.640	0.630	0.590	0.550	0.510
Dividend Payout %	16.16	18.73	17.45	24.33	16.28	16.91	16.77	22.67
Income Statement								
Total Revenue	3,166,900	2,808,332	2,237,978	1,826,277	2,246,249	1,802,497	1,619,545	1,428,707
EBITDA	394,800	320,740	290,653	209,250	276,394	242,975	224,840	165,747
Depn & Amortn	82,000	65,027	52,918	49,730	45,963	36,915	30,823	31,175
Income Before Taxes	269,900	226,337	220,729	137,955	204,201	184,937	174,842	112,924
Income Taxes	69,600	68,317	66,045	39,276	72,225	63,683	62,051	39,829
Net Income	195,600	152,290	149,379	95,048	128,587	118,347	109,806	69,557
Average Shares	42,100	40,144	38,921	36,131	33,250	33,920	33,504	30,878
Balance Sheet								
Current Assets	1,539,900	1,291,121	1,088,051	979,376	861,262	728,491	569,168	487,280
Total Assets	3,569,100	3,266,515	2,449,136	2,112,237	2,023,496	1,862,247	1,437,559	1,342,554
Current Liabilities	533,900	524,496	399,342	309,066	431,002	311,920	258,921	218,791
Long-Term Obligations	754,700	909,159	428,256	468,065	561,190	558,918	323,946	386,332
Total Liabilities	1,615,700	1,730,584	1,087,176	944,413	1,198,168	1,004,218	687,584	694,558
Stockholders' Equity	1,953,400	1,535,931	1,361,960	1,167,824	825,328	858,029	749,975	647,996
Shares Outstanding	44,900	41,579	38,615	37,399	31,398	31,331	31,037	30,655
Statistical Record								
Return on Assets %	5.74	5.34	6.57	4.52	6.64	7.19	7.92	5.16
Return on Equity %	11.24	10.54	11.84	9.38	15.32	14.76	15.75	11.73
EBITDA Margin %	12.47	11.42	12.99	11.46	12.30	13.48	13.88	11.60
Net Margin %	6.18	5.42	6.67	5.20	5.72	6.57	6.78	4.87
Asset Turnover	0.93	0.99	0.98	0.87	1.16	1.10	1.17	1.06
Current Ratio	2.88	2.46	2.72	3.17	2.00	2.34	2.20	2.23
Debt to Equity	0.39	0.59	0.31	0.40	0.68	0.65	0.43	0.60
Price Range	75.00-52.05	76.04-42.97	69.54-47.40	53.76-25.81	49.37-26.07	56.93-43.51	54.18-35.49	36.45-25.30
P/E Ratio	16.16-11.22	20.06-11.34	18.11-12.34	20.44-9.81	12.76-6.74	16.31-12.47	16.52-10.82	16.20-11.24
Average Yield %	1.15	1.14	1.13	1.54	1.60	1.23	1.24	1.67

Address: 200 State Street, Beloit, WI 53511 **Telephone:** 608-364-8800	**Web Site:** www.regalbeloit.com **Officers:** Henry W. Knueppel - Executive Chairman Peter C. Underwood - President, Secretary, General Counsel	**Auditors:** Deloitte & Touche LLP **Investor Contact:** 608-364-8800 **Transfer Agents:** ComputerShare Investor Services, Providence, RI

REGAL ENTERTAINMENT GROUP

Exchange	Symbol	Price	52Wk Range	Yield	P/E
NYS	RGC	$16.67 (3/28/2013)	16.67-12.86	5.04	17.92

*7 Year Price Score 81.01 ***NYSE Composite Index=100** ***12 Month Price Score 99.78**

Interim Earnings (Per Share)

Qtr.	Mar	Jun	Sep	Dec
2008	(0.02)	0.09	0.21	0.19
2009	0.14	0.26	(0.01)	0.23
2010	0.11	0.03	0.28	0.09
2011	(0.15)	0.23	0.16	0.03
2012	0.30	0.24	0.15	0.24

Interim Dividends (Per Share)

Amt	Decl	Ex	Rec	Pay
0.21Q	07/26/2012	09/06/2012	09/10/2012	09/18/2012
0.21Q	10/25/2012	12/03/2012	12/05/2012	12/14/2012
1.00Sp	11/29/2012	12/07/2012	12/11/2012	12/27/2012
0.21Q	02/07/2013	03/01/2013	03/05/2013	03/15/2013

Indicated Div: $0.84

Valuation Analysis / **Institutional Holding**

Forecast EPS	$0.99 (04/05/2013)	No of Institutions 294
Market Cap	$2.6 Billion	Shares 84,888,560
Book Value	N/A	% Held 52.39
Price/Book	N/A	
Price/Sales	0.92	

Business Summary: Entertainment (MIC: 2.3.2 SIC: 7832 NAIC: 512131)

Regal Entertainment is a holding company. Through its subsidiaries, Co. operates multi-screen theatres. Co. operates its theatre circuit using its Regal Cinemas, United Artists and Edwards brands. Most of Co.'s theatres provide amenities such as wall-to-wall and floor-to-ceiling screens, Sony Digital CinemaNULL 4K projection systems, digital stereo surround-sound, closed-captioning, multi-station concessions stands, computerized ticketing systems, stadium seating with cup holders and retractable armrests, and video game and party room areas adjacent to the theatre lobby. At Dec 29 2011, Co.'s theatre circuit consisted of 6,614 screens in 527 theatres in 37 states and the District of Columbia.

Recent Developments: For the year ended Dec 27 2012, net income increased 260.8% to US$144.7 million from US$40.1 million in the prior year. Revenues were US$2.82 billion, up 5.3% from US$2.68 billion the year before. Operating income was US$334.2 million versus US$221.3 million in the prior year, an increase of 51.0%. Direct operating expenses rose 4.9% to US$1.10 billion from US$1.05 billion in the comparable period the year before. Indirect operating expenses decreased 1.5% to US$1.39 billion from US$1.41 billion in the equivalent prior-year period.

Prospects: Our evaluation of Regal Entertainment Group as of Apr. 7, 2013 is the result of our systematic analysis on three basic characteristics: earnings strength, relative valuation, and recent stock price movement. The company has generated a negative trend in earnings per share over the past 5 quarters and while recent estimates for the company have been raised by analysts, RGC has posted better than expected results. Based on operating earnings yield, the company is about fairly valued when compared to all of the companies in our coverage universe. Share price changes over the past year indicates that RGC will perform poorly over the near term.

Financial Data

(US$ in Thousands)	12/27/2012	12/29/2011	12/30/2010	12/31/2009	01/01/2009	12/27/2007	12/28/2006	12/29/2005
Earnings Per Share	0.93	0.26	0.50	0.62	0.47	2.28	0.56	0.59
Cash Flow Per Share	2.25	2.31	1.70	2.69	1.74	5.29	2.05	2.65
Dividends Per Share	1.840	0.840	2.120	0.720	1.200	3.200	1.200	1.200
Dividend Payout %	197.85	323.08	424.00	116.13	255.32	140.35	214.29	203.39
Income Statement								
Total Revenue	2,824,200	2,681,700	2,807,900	2,893,900	2,771,900	2,661,200	2,598,100	2,516,700
EBITDA	522,300	371,300	459,500	485,000	420,100	888,800	473,800	480,500
Depn & Amortn	186,200	201,700	226,200	215,400	202,300	183,400	197,100	205,000
Income Before Taxes	201,100	19,900	85,200	118,600	93,500	592,500	151,500	158,200
Income Taxes	91,200	17,700	48,700	61,900	50,800	242,900	57,700	60,700
Net Income	144,800	40,300	77,600	95,500	72,500	363,000	86,300	91,800
Average Shares	154,990	154,556	154,517	154,092	153,742	159,474	155,124	154,330
Balance Sheet								
Current Assets	257,800	403,500	346,500	428,900	273,500	525,500	241,000	262,600
Total Assets	2,209,500	2,341,300	2,492,600	2,637,700	2,599,500	2,634,900	2,468,800	2,532,800
Current Liabilities	387,500	400,700	469,000	396,500	366,200	527,500	556,300	693,600
Long-Term Obligations	1,973,200	1,995,700	1,977,200	1,980,000	1,991,000	1,819,000	1,841,700	1,724,100
Total Liabilities	2,906,300	2,912,200	2,982,900	2,883,800	2,840,800	2,754,200	2,491,000	2,502,900
Stockholders' Equity	(696,800)	(570,900)	(490,300)	(246,100)	(241,300)	(119,300)	(22,200)	29,900
Shares Outstanding	155,452	154,573	154,303	154,001	153,509	153,227	150,357	147,363
Statistical Record								
Return on Assets %	6.38	1.67	3.03	3.66	2.73	14.26	3.46	3.63
Return on Equity %	...	...	...	...	...	...	2,247.72	186.15
EBITDA Margin %	18.49	13.85	16.36	16.76	15.16	33.40	18.24	19.09
Net Margin %	5.13	1.50	2.76	3.30	2.62	13.64	3.32	3.65
Asset Turnover	1.24	1.11	1.10	1.11	1.04	1.05	1.04	0.99
Current Ratio	0.67	1.01	0.74	1.08	0.75	1.00	0.43	0.38
Debt to Equity	...	...	...	...	...	...	...	57.66
Price Range	15.84-11.58	14.94-11.23	18.28-11.74	14.69-9.29	20.77-7.22	23.01-17.85	21.55-17.95	21.35-18.20
P/E Ratio	17.03-12.45	57.46-43.19	36.56-23.48	23.69-14.98	44.19-15.36	10.09-7.83	38.48-32.05	36.19-30.85
Average Yield %	13.27	6.42	14.62	5.80	7.51	14.95	6.11	6.10

Address: 7132 Regal Lane, Knoxville, TN 37918 Telephone: 865-922-1123	Web Site: www.regmovies.com Officers: Michael L. Campbell - Chairman, Executive Chairman Gregory W. Dunn - President, Chief Operating Officer	Auditors: KPMG LLP Investor Contact: 866-734-2534 Transfer Agents: Wells Fargo Bank Minnesota, National Association

REGENCY CENTERS CORP.

Exchange	Symbol	Price	52Wk Range	Yield	P/E
NYS	REG	$52.91 (3/28/2013)	53.44-42.13	3.50	N/A

*7 Year Price Score 83.65   *NYSE Composite Index=100   *12 Month Price Score 99.93

Interim Earnings (Per Share)

Qtr.	Mar	Jun	Sep	Dec
2008	0.38	0.45	0.78	0.05
2009	0.28	(0.23)	(1.05)	0.35
2010	0.15	0.08	0.12	(0.45)
2011	0.02	0.14	0.09	0.09
2012	0.14	0.06	0.13	(0.42)

Interim Dividends (Per Share)

Amt	Decl	Ex	Rec	Pay
0.463Q	05/01/2012	05/14/2012	05/16/2012	05/30/2012
0.463Q	07/27/2012	08/13/2012	08/15/2012	08/29/2012
0.463Q	11/02/2012	11/09/2012	11/14/2012	11/28/2012
0.463Q	01/28/2013	02/11/2013	02/13/2013	02/27/2013

Indicated Div: $1.85

Valuation Analysis / **Institutional Holding**

Forecast EPS	$0.72 (04/05/2013)	No of Institutions 318
Market Cap	$4.8 Billion	Shares
Book Value	$1.7 Billion	102,907,528
Price/Book	2.75	% Held
Price/Sales	9.59	103.77

Business Summary: REITs (MIC: 5.3.1 SIC: 6798 NAIC: 525930)

Regency Centers is a real estate investment trust. Co. is also the managing general partner in Regency Centers, L.P. (Operating Partnership). All of Co.'s operating, investing, and financing activities are performed through the Operating Partnership, its wholly-owned subsidiaries, and through its investments in real estate partnerships with third parties. At Dec 31 2011, Co. directly owned 217 shopping centers. Co. also owned partial ownership interests in 147 shopping centers. Co. leases space in its shopping centers to grocery stores, major retail anchors, side-shop retailers, and restaurants, including ground leasing or selling building pads (out-parcels) to these same types of tenants.

Recent Developments: For the year ended Dec 31 2012, income from continuing operations decreased 98.9% to US$505,000 from US$45.3 million a year earlier. Net income decreased 53.0% to US$26.2 million from US$55.8 million in the prior year. Revenues were US$496.9 million, up 0.8% from US$493.1 million the year before. Revenues from property income rose 2.7% to US$362.7 million from US$353.2 million in the corresponding earlier year.

Prospects: Our evaluation of Regency Centers Corp. as of Apr. 7, 2013 is the result of our systematic analysis on three basic characteristics: earnings strength, relative valuation, and recent stock price movement. The company has managed to produce a neutral trend in earnings per share over the past 5 quarters. Because the company lacks sufficient analyst estimate data, we place greater weight on the historical EPS trend as the measure of earnings strength. Based on operating earnings yield, the company is overvalued when compared to all of the companies in our coverage universe. Share price changes over the past year indicates that REG will perform in line with the market over the near term.

Financial Data
(US$ in Thousands)

	12/31/2012	12/31/2011	12/31/2010	12/31/2009	12/31/2008	12/31/2007	12/31/2006	12/31/2005
Earnings Per Share	(0.08)	0.35	(0.10)	(0.74)	1.66	2.65	2.89	2.23
Cash Flow Per Share	2.86	2.48	1.73	2.52	3.14	3.25	3.19	3.23
Tang Book Value Per Share	15.14	16.81	17.20	19.50	20.11	22.66	22.69	22.12
Dividends Per Share	1.850	1.850	1.850	2.112	2.900	2.640	2.380	2.200
Dividend Payout %	...	528.57	...	...	174.70	99.62	82.35	98.65
Income Statement								
Total Revenue	496,920	500,417	486,806	489,232	493,421	451,508	420,338	394,038
EBITDA	241,606	307,803	278,043	218,907	311,605	343,716	337,241	285,176
Depn & Amortn	139,555	145,152	131,305	121,934	109,757	96,757	91,824	86,235
Income Before Taxes	(10,078)	39,006	21,451	(12,266)	109,064	164,465	165,727	111,517
Income Taxes	13,224	...	...	...	...	...	...	...
Net Income	25,867	51,370	12,014	(36,704)	136,188	203,651	218,511	162,647
Average Shares	89,669	88,249	82,948	76,896	69,662	69,198	68,432	64,932
Balance Sheet								
Current Assets	152,592	160,814	140,232	217,393	156,767	138,652	121,196	145,809
Total Assets	3,853,458	3,987,071	3,973,648	3,973,806	4,142,375	4,143,012	3,671,785	3,616,215
Current Liabilities	145,331	122,278	111,837	109,773	152,966	175,915	151,457	121,076
Long-Term Obligations	1,941,891	1,982,440	2,094,469	1,886,380	2,135,571	2,007,975	1,575,386	1,613,942
Total Liabilities	2,122,693	2,178,716	2,272,213	2,098,639	2,446,290	2,272,626	1,818,468	1,827,390
Stockholders' Equity	1,730,765	1,808,355	1,701,435	1,875,167	1,696,085	1,870,386	1,853,317	1,788,825
Shares Outstanding	90,059	89,583	81,886	81,539	70,036	69,638	69,017	67,966
Statistical Record								
Return on Assets %	0.66	1.29	0.30	N.M.	3.28	5.21	6.00	4.74
Return on Equity %	1.46	2.93	0.67	N.M.	7.62	10.94	12.00	9.89
EBITDA Margin %	48.62	61.51	57.12	44.75	63.15	76.13	80.23	72.37
Net Margin %	5.21	10.27	2.47	N.M.	27.60	45.10	51.98	41.28
Asset Turnover	0.13	0.13	0.12	0.12	0.12	0.12	0.12	0.11
Current Ratio	1.05	1.32	1.25	1.98	1.02	0.79	0.80	1.20
Debt to Equity	1.12	1.10	1.23	1.01	1.26	1.07	0.85	0.90
Price Range	50.52-36.69	47.32-33.37	44.80-32.25	46.70-22.02	72.28-25.34	92.79-62.22	81.34-59.35	63.11-47.30
P/E Ratio	...	135.20-95.34	...	...	43.54-15.27	35.02-23.48	28.15-20.54	28.30-21.21
Average Yield %	4.04	4.49	4.84	6.27	5.11	3.50	3.58	4.00

Address: One Independent Drive, Suite 114, Jacksonville, FL 32202 **Telephone:** 904-598-7000	**Web Site:** www.regencycenters.com **Officers:** Martin E. Stein - Chairman, Chief Executive Officer Brian M. Smith - President, Chief Investment Officer	**Auditors:** KPMG LLP **Investor Contact:** 904-598-7000 **Transfer Agents:** Wells Fargo Bank, N.A., Mendota Heights, MN

REGIONS FINANCIAL CORP

Exchange	Symbol	Price	52Wk Range	Yield	P/E
NYS	RF	$8.19 (3/28/2013)	8.40-5.55	0.49	11.54

*7 Year Price Score 43.01 *NYSE Composite Index=100 ***12 Month Price Score 103.99**

Interim Earnings (Per Share)

Qtr.	Mar	Jun	Sep	Dec
2008	0.48	0.30	0.11	(8.98)
2009	0.04	(0.28)	(0.37)	(0.56)
2010	(0.21)	(0.28)	(0.17)	0.04
2011	0.01	0.04	0.08	(0.48)
2012	0.11	0.20	0.21	0.18

Interim Dividends (Per Share)

Amt	Decl	Ex	Rec	Pay
0.01Q	04/25/2012	06/13/2012	06/15/2012	07/02/2012
0.01Q	07/19/2012	09/12/2012	09/14/2012	10/01/2012
0.01Q	10/18/2012	12/12/2012	12/14/2012	01/02/2013
0.01Q	01/17/2013	03/13/2013	03/15/2013	04/01/2013

Indicated Div: $0.04

Valuation Analysis

		Institutional Holding	
Forecast EPS	$0.81 (04/06/2013)	No of Institutions	680
Market Cap	$11.6 Billion	Shares	1,069,650,816
Book Value	$15.5 Billion	% Held	70.31
Price/Book	0.75		
Price/Sales	1.93		

Business Summary: Banking (MIC: 5.1.1 SIC: 6021 NAIC: 522110)

Regions Financial is a financial holding company. Through its subsidiary, Regions Bank, Co. is engaged in providing commercial, retail and mortgage banking services, as well as other financial services in the fields of asset management, wealth management, securities brokerage, insurance and other specialty financing. Co. has three reportable segments: Business Services, Consumer Services and Wealth Management. Co. operates in the South, Midwest and Texas. As of Dec 31 2012, Co. had total assets of $121.35 billion, and deposits of $95.47 billion.

Recent Developments: For the year ended Dec 31 2012, income from continuing operations increased 523.8% to US$1.18 billion from US$189.0 million a year earlier. Net income amounted to US$1.12 billion versus a net loss of US$215.0 million in the prior year. Net interest income decreased 3.2% to US$3.30 billion from US$3.41 billion in the prior year. Provision for loan losses was US$213.0 million versus US$1.53 billion in the prior year, a decrease of 86.1%. Non-interest income fell 2.0% to US$2.10 billion from US$2.14 billion, while non-interest expense declined 8.7% to US$3.53 billion.

Prospects: Our evaluation of Regions Financial Corp. as of Apr. 7, 2013 is the result of our systematic analysis on three basic characteristics: earnings strength, relative valuation, and recent stock price movement. The company has generated a negative trend in earnings per share over the past 5 quarters and while recent estimates for the company have been mixed, RF has posted better than expected results. Based on operating earnings yield, the company is undervalued when compared to all of the companies in our coverage universe. Share price changes over the past year indicates that RF will perform well over the near term.

Financial Data
(US$ in Thousands)

	12/31/2012	12/31/2011	12/31/2010	12/31/2009	12/31/2008	12/31/2007	12/31/2006	12/31/2005
Earnings Per Share	0.71	(0.34)	(0.62)	(1.27)	(8.09)	1.76	2.67	2.15
Cash Flow Per Share	1.76	3.78	3.44	2.02	2.88	4.81	5.66	4.16
Tang Book Value Per Share	6.84	6.06	5.68	6.68	10.35	10.45	11.22	10.65
Dividends Per Share	0.040	0.040	0.040	0.130	0.960	1.460	1.760	1.360
Dividend Payout %	5.63	...	...	...	...	82.95	65.92	63.26
Income Statement								
Interest Income	3,903,000	4,252,000	4,689,000	5,332,000	6,563,390	8,074,663	5,694,258	4,310,375
Interest Expense	603,000	842,000	1,257,000	1,997,000	2,720,434	3,676,297	2,340,816	1,489,756
Net Interest Income	3,300,000	3,410,000	3,432,000	3,335,000	3,842,956	4,398,366	3,353,442	2,820,619
Provision for Losses	213,000	1,530,000	2,863,000	3,541,000	2,057,000	555,000	142,500	165,000
Non-Interest Income	2,100,000	2,143,000	3,531,000	3,755,000	3,073,231	2,855,835	2,062,104	1,813,432
Non-Interest Expense	3,526,000	3,862,000	4,985,000	4,751,000	10,791,614	4,660,351	3,314,031	3,046,956
Income Before Taxes	1,661,000	161,000	(885,000)	(1,202,000)	(5,932,427)	2,038,850	1,959,015	1,463,737
Income Taxes	482,000	(28,000)	(346,000)	(171,000)	(348,114)	645,687	605,870	421,551
Net Income	1,120,000	(215,000)	(539,000)	(1,031,000)	(5,595,774)	1,251,095	1,353,145	1,000,544
Average Shares	1,387,000	1,258,000	1,227,000	989,000	695,003	712,743	506,989	466,183
Balance Sheet								
Net Loans & Leases	73,459,000	76,042,000	81,164,000	89,071,000	96,874,973	94,778,527	98,414,950	59,153,041
Total Assets	121,347,000	127,050,000	132,351,000	142,318,000	146,247,810	141,041,717	143,369,021	84,785,600
Total Deposits	95,474,000	95,627,000	94,614,000	98,680,000	90,903,890	94,774,968	101,227,969	60,378,367
Total Liabilities	105,848,000	110,551,000	115,617,000	124,437,000	129,434,973	121,218,688	122,667,567	74,171,317
Stockholders' Equity	15,499,000	16,499,000	16,734,000	17,881,000	16,812,837	19,823,029	20,701,454	10,614,283
Shares Outstanding	1,413,339	1,258,816	1,256,236	1,192,609	691,365	693,635	730,075	456,347
Statistical Record								
Return on Assets %	0.90	N.M.	N.M.	N.M.	N.M.	0.88	1.19	1.18
Return on Equity %	6.98	N.M.	N.M.	N.M.	N.M.	6.17	8.64	9.37
Net Interest Margin %	84.55	80.20	73.19	62.55	58.55	54.47	58.89	65.44
Efficiency Ratio %	58.74	60.39	60.64	52.28	111.99	42.64	42.73	49.76
Loans to Deposits	0.77	0.80	0.86	0.90	1.07	1.00	0.97	0.98
Price Range	7.65-4.34	8.02-3.02	8.95-5.21	8.83-2.50	25.73-6.88	38.02-23.01	38.87-32.45	35.59-29.57
P/E Ratio	10.77-6.11	...	...	...	...	21.60-13.07	14.56-12.15	16.55-13.75
Average Yield %	0.62	0.70	0.57	2.64	6.39	4.53	4.93	4.10

Address: 1900 Fifth Avenue North, Birmingham, AL 35203	Web Site: www.regions.com	Auditors: Ernst & Young LLP
Telephone: 800-734-4667	Officers: O.B. Grayson Hall - Chairman, President, Chief Executive Officer, Chief Operating Officer, Head C. Matthew Lusco - Senior Executive Vice President, Chief Risk Officer	Investor Contact: 205-326-5807 Transfer Agents: Computershare Trust Company, N.A., Providence, RI

REGIS CORP.

Exchange	Symbol	Price	52Wk Range	Yield	P/E
NYS	RGS	$18.19 (3/28/2013)	19.46-15.92	1.32	N/A

*7 Year Price Score 69.02 *NYSE Composite Index=100 *12 Month Price Score 94.79

Interim Earnings (Per Share)

Qtr.	Sep	Dec	Mar	Jun
2009-10	0.14	0.30	(0.03)	0.31
2010-11	0.30	0.24	(0.45)	(0.29)
2011-12	0.15	(1.01)	(0.02)	(1.12)
2012-13	0.45	(0.22)	...	...

Interim Dividends (Per Share)

Amt	Decl	Ex	Rec	Pay
0.06Q	04/27/2012	05/07/2012	05/09/2012	05/23/2012
0.06Q	08/24/2012	08/31/2012	09/05/2012	09/19/2012
0.06Q	10/26/2012	11/06/2012	11/08/2012	11/22/2012
0.06Q	02/01/2013	02/08/2013	02/12/2013	02/26/2013

Indicated Div: $0.24

Valuation Analysis / Institutional Holding

Forecast EPS	$0.44	No of Institutions
	(04/05/2013)	199
Market Cap	$1.0 Billion	Shares
Book Value	$866.7 Million	69,512,792
Price/Book	1.19	% Held
Price/Sales	0.48	99.07

TRADING VOLUME (thousand shares)

Business Summary: Miscellaneous Consumer Services (MIC: 2.2.3 SIC: 7231 NAIC: 812112)

Regis primarily engages in the business of owning, operating and franchising hair and retail product salons. In addition to the primary hair and retail product salons, Co. owns Hair Club for Men and Women, a provider of hair restoration services. As of June 30 2012, Co. owned, franchised or held ownership interests in approximately 12,600 worldwide locations. Each of Co.'s salon concepts provide similar salon products and services and serve the mass market consumer marketplace. Co.'s hair restoration centers provide three hair restoration services; hair systems, hair transplants and hair therapy, which are targeted at the mass market consumer.

Recent Developments: For the quarter ended Dec 31 2012, loss from continuing operations was US$16.1 million compared with income of US$11.9 million in the year-earlier quarter. Net loss amounted to US$12.3 million versus a net loss of US$57.4 million in the year-earlier quarter. Revenues were US$506.2 million, down 3.8% from US$526.1 million the year before. Operating income was US$8.7 million versus US$11.9 million in the prior-year quarter, a decrease of 26.9%. Direct operating expenses declined 0.2% to US$339.2 million from US$339.9 million in the comparable period the year before. Indirect operating expenses decreased 9.2% to US$158.2 million from US$174.3 million in the equivalent prior-year period.

Prospects: Our evaluation of Regis Corp. as of Apr. 7, 2013 is the result of our systematic analysis on three basic characteristics: earnings strength, relative valuation, and recent stock price movement. The company has suffered a very negative trend in earnings per share over the past 5 quarters and while recent estimates for the company have remained steady, RGS has posted results that fell short of analysts expectations. Based on operating earnings yield, the company is about fairly valued when compared to all of the companies in our coverage universe. Share price changes over the past year indicates that RGS will perform in line with the market over the near term.

Financial Data
(US$ in Thousands)

	6 Mos	3 Mos	06/30/2012	06/30/2011	06/30/2010	06/30/2009	06/30/2008	06/30/2007
Earnings Per Share	(0.91)	(1.70)	(2.00)	(0.16)	0.75	(2.89)	1.95	1.82
Cash Flow Per Share	2.65	2.60	2.68	4.04	3.44	4.38	5.14	5.41
Tang Book Value Per Share	6.72	7.13	4.37	4.17	2.75	N.M.	N.M.	N.M.
Dividends Per Share	0.240	0.240	0.240	0.200	0.160	0.160	0.160	0.160
Dividend Payout %	...	...	...	...	21.33	...	8.21	8.79
Income Statement								
Total Revenue	1,011,525	505,360	2,273,779	2,325,869	2,358,434	2,429,787	2,738,865	2,626,588
EBITDA	64,612	32,183	34,387	92,548	189,718	214,173	282,970	274,641
Depn & Amortn	46,616	22,910	101,700	88,600	92,500	105,100	108,673	104,915
Income Before Taxes	39,731	27,170	(90,428)	(25,629)	53,214	78,766	138,099	127,956
Income Taxes	4,071	2,986	(5,279)	(9,496)	25,577	41,950	53,744	44,786
Net Income	26,158	28,538	(114,093)	(8,905)	42,740	(124,466)	85,204	83,170
Average Shares	56,794	68,589	57,137	56,704	66,753	43,026	43,587	45,623
Balance Sheet								
Current Assets	466,958	481,002	384,677	346,562	428,865	352,986	445,151	525,064
Total Assets	1,540,903	1,568,382	1,571,846	1,805,753	1,919,572	1,892,486	2,235,871	2,132,114
Current Liabilities	245,087	242,835	251,973	254,680	270,109	274,486	507,522	538,632
Long-Term Obligations	240,143	251,178	258,737	281,159	388,400	578,853	534,523	485,879
Total Liabilities	674,158	670,670	682,689	773,134	906,279	1,089,626	1,259,685	1,218,806
Stockholders' Equity	866,745	897,712	889,157	1,032,619	1,013,293	802,860	976,186	913,308
Shares Outstanding	56,615	57,527	57,415	57,710	57,561	43,881	43,070	44,164
Statistical Record								
Return on Assets %	N.M.	N.M.	N.M.	N.M.	2.24	N.M.	3.89	4.04
Return on Equity %	N.M.	N.M.	N.M.	N.M.	4.71	N.M.	8.99	9.32
EBITDA Margin %	6.39	6.37	1.51	3.98	8.04	8.81	10.33	10.46
Net Margin %	2.59	5.65	N.M.	N.M.	1.81	N.M.	3.11	3.17
Asset Turnover	1.33	1.32	1.34	1.25	1.24	1.18	1.25	1.28
Current Ratio	1.91	1.98	1.53	1.36	1.59	1.29	0.88	0.97
Debt to Equity	0.28	0.28	0.29	0.27	0.38	0.72	0.55	0.53
Price Range	19.46-15.21	19.22-13.93	18.61-12.92	21.51-13.14	20.36-12.23	31.46-8.56	39.07-22.67	43.29-32.78
P/E Ratio	...	...	...	...	...	27.15-16.31	20.04-11.63	23.79-18.01
Average Yield %	1.37	1.39	1.46	1.16	0.97	0.89	0.54	0.41

Address: 7201 Metro Boulevard, Edina, MN 55439 Telephone: 952-947-7777	Web Site: www.regiscorp.com Officers: Joseph L. Conner - Chairman Daniel J. Hanrahan - President, Chief Executive Officer	Auditors: PricewaterhouseCoopers LLP Investor Contact: 952-947-7777 Transfer Agents: Wells Fargo Bank Minnesota, N.A., South St. Paul, MN

REINSURANCE GROUP OF AMERICA, INC.

Exchange	Symbol	Price	52Wk Range	Yield	P/E
NYS	RGA	$59.67 (3/28/2013)	60.90-48.64	1.61	7.00

*7 Year Price Score N/A   *NYSE Composite Index=100   *12 Month Price Score 97.39

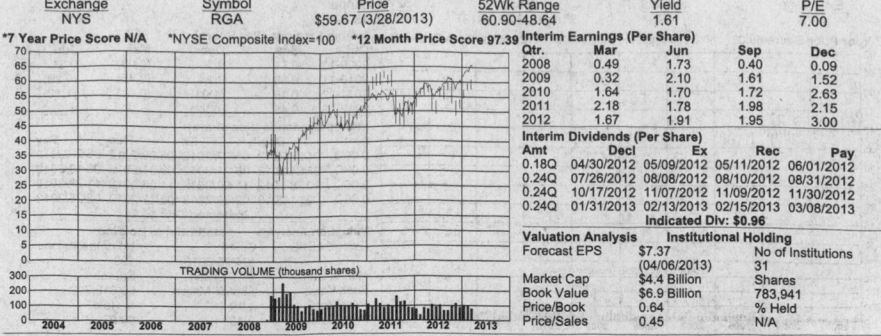

Interim Earnings (Per Share)

Qtr.	Mar	Jun	Sep	Dec
2008	0.49	1.73	0.40	0.09
2009	0.32	2.10	1.61	1.52
2010	1.64	1.70	1.72	2.63
2011	2.18	1.78	1.98	2.15
2012	1.67	1.91	1.95	3.00

Interim Dividends (Per Share)

Amt	Decl	Ex	Rec	Pay
0.18Q	04/30/2012	05/09/2012	05/11/2012	06/01/2012
0.24Q	07/26/2012	08/08/2012	08/10/2012	08/31/2012
0.24Q	10/17/2012	11/07/2012	11/09/2012	11/30/2012
0.24Q	01/31/2013	02/13/2013	02/15/2013	03/08/2013

Indicated Div: $0.96

Valuation Analysis

		Institutional Holding	
Forecast EPS	$7.37 (04/06/2013)	No of Institutions	31
Market Cap	$4.4 Billion	Shares	783,941
Book Value	$6.9 Billion	% Held	N/A
Price/Book	0.64		
Price/Sales	0.45		

Business Summary: Life & Health (MIC: 5.2.2 SIC: 6321 NAIC: 524130)

Reinsurance Group of America is an insurance holding company. Through its subsidiaries, Co. operates in five geographic-based operational segments: the U.S., which markets life and health reinsurance, reinsurance of asset-intensive products, and financial reinsurance; Canada, which is engaged in individual life reinsurance, as well as creditor, group life and health, critical illness, and longevity reinsurance; Europe and South Africa, which provides the reinsurance of life and health products; Asia Pacific, which provides the reinsurance of life, critical illness, health, disability income, and superannuation; and Corporate and Other, which includes investment income from invested assets.

Recent Developments: For the year ended Dec 31 2012, net income increased 15.7% to US$631.9 million from US$546.0 million in the prior year. Revenues were US$9.84 billion, up 11.5% from US$8.83 billion the year before. Net premiums earned were US$7.91 billion versus US$7.34 billion in the prior year, an increase of 7.8%. Net investment income rose 12.1% to US$1.44 billion from US$1.28 billion a year ago.

Prospects: Our evaluation of Reinsurance Group of America Inc. as of Apr. 7, 2013 is the result of our systematic analysis on three basic characteristics: earnings strength, relative valuation, and recent stock price movement. The company has produced a positive trend in earnings per share over the past 5 quarters and while recent estimates for the company have remained steady, RGA has posted better than expected results. Based on operating earnings yield, the company is undervalued when compared to all of the companies in our coverage universe. Share price changes over the past year indicates that RGA will perform poorly over the near term.

Financial Data

(US$ in Thousands)	12/31/2012	12/31/2011	12/31/2010	12/31/2009	12/31/2008	12/31/2007	12/31/2006	12/31/2005
Earnings Per Share	8.52	8.09	7.69	5.55	2.71	4.57	4.57	3.52
Cash Flow Per Share	26.70	17.80	25.19	18.74	11.34	15.48	13.82	9.58
Tang Book Value Per Share	93.47	83.65	68.71	52.99	36.03	51.42	45.85	41.38
Dividends Per Share	0.840	0.600	0.480	0.360	0.860	0.360	0.360	0.360
Dividend Payout %	9.86	7.42	6.24	6.49	13.28	7.88	7.88	10.23
Income Statement								
Premium Income	7,906,596	7,335,687	6,659,680	5,725,161	5,349,301	4,909,026	4,345,969	3,866,775
Total Revenue	9,840,911	8,829,538	8,261,730	7,066,822	5,681,203	5,718,361	5,193,691	4,584,765
Benefits & Claims	6,662,305	6,220,621	5,543,093	4,815,328	4,457,857	3,980,291	3,484,786	3,187,902
Income Before Taxes	919,223	834,380	863,817	592,345	280,392	474,918	451,388	356,346
Income Taxes	287,330	234,760	289,415	185,259	92,577	166,645	158,127	120,738
Net Income	631,893	599,620	574,402	407,086	176,796	293,834	288,210	224,180
Average Shares	74,153	74,108	74,694	73,327	65,271	64,231	63,062	63,724
Balance Sheet								
Total Assets	40,360,438	32,104,032	29,081,908	25,249,501	21,658,818	21,598,009	19,036,837	16,193,866
Total Liabilities	33,450,251	25,966,927	24,041,341	21,381,574	19,042,010	18,408,177	16,221,453	13,666,382
Stockholders' Equity	6,910,187	6,137,105	5,040,567	3,867,927	2,616,808	3,189,832	2,815,384	2,527,484
Shares Outstanding	73,927	73,367	73,363	72,989	72,623	62,031	61,410	61,075
Statistical Record								
Return on Assets %	1.74	1.96	2.11	1.74	0.82	1.45	1.64	1.48
Return on Equity %	9.66	10.73	12.90	12.56	6.07	9.79	10.79	9.33
Loss Ratio %	84.26	84.80	83.23	84.11	83.34	81.08	80.18	82.44
Net Margin %	6.42	6.79	6.95	5.76	3.11	5.14	5.55	4.89
Price Range	60.01-48.64	63.79-44.99	55.96-43.53	48.61-21.59	42.82-35.66	...	...	...
P/E Ratio	7.04-5.71	7.89-5.56	7.28-5.66	8.76-3.89	15.80-13.16	...	...	...
Average Yield %	1.53	1.06	0.98	0.93	0.92	...	...	...

Address: 1370 Timberlake Manor Parkway, Chesterfield, MO 63017 **Telephone:** 636-736-7000	**Web Site:** www.rgare.com **Officers:** A. Greig Woodring - President, Chief Executive Officer Jack B. Lay - Senior Executive Vice President, Chief Financial Officer	**Auditors:** Deloitte & Touche LLP **Investor Contact:** 636-300-8828 **Transfer Agents:** Mellon Investor Services, L.L.C.

RELIANCE STEEL & ALUMINUM CO.

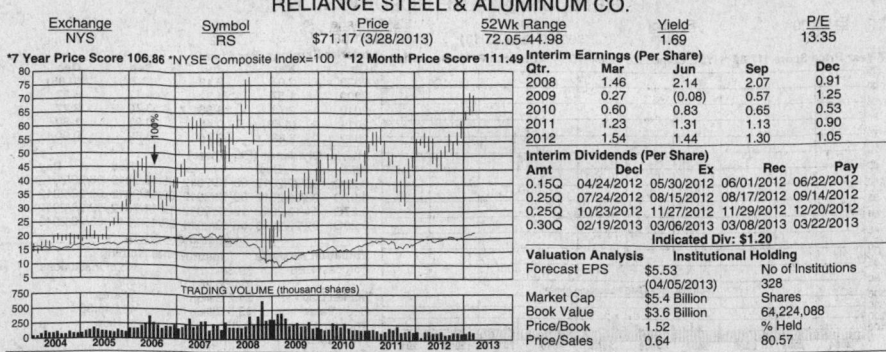

Exchange	Symbol	Price	52Wk Range	Yield	P/E
NYS	RS	$71.17 (3/28/2013)	72.05-44.98	1.69	13.35

*7 Year Price Score 106.86 *NYSE Composite Index=100 *12 Month Price Score 111.49

Interim Earnings (Per Share)

Qtr.	Mar	Jun	Sep	Dec
2008	1.46	2.14	2.07	0.91
2009	0.27	(0.08)	0.57	1.25
2010	0.60	0.83	0.65	0.53
2011	1.23	1.31	1.13	0.90
2012	1.54	1.44	1.30	1.05

Interim Dividends (Per Share)

Amt	Decl	Ex	Rec	Pay
0.15Q	04/24/2012	05/30/2012	06/01/2012	06/22/2012
0.25Q	07/24/2012	08/15/2012	08/17/2012	09/14/2012
0.25Q	10/23/2012	11/27/2012	11/29/2012	12/20/2012
0.30Q	02/19/2013	03/06/2013	03/08/2013	03/22/2013

Indicated Div: $1.20

Valuation Analysis

		Institutional Holding	
Forecast EPS	$5.53		No of Institutions
	(04/05/2013)		328
Market Cap	$5.4 Billion		Shares
Book Value	$3.6 Billion		64,224,088
Price/Book	1.52		% Held
Price/Sales	0.64		80.57

Business Summary: Non-Precious Metals (MIC: 8.2.2 SIC: 5051 NAIC: 423510)

Reliance Steel & Aluminum is a metals service center company. Co.'s network of metals service centers operates in more than 240 locations in 38 states in the U.S., and in ten other countries (Australia, Belgium, Canada, China, Malaysia, Mexico, Singapore, South Korea, the United Arab Emirates and the U.K.). Through this network, Co. provides metals processing services and distributes metal products, including alloy, aluminum, brass, copper, carbon steel, stainless steel, titanium and steel products, to manufacturers and end-users in the general manufacturing, non-residential construction, transportation, aerospace, energy, electronics and semiconductor fabrication and related industries.

Recent Developments: For the year ended Dec 31 2012, net income increased 16.9% to US$408.3 million from US$349.2 million in the prior year. Revenues were US$8.44 billion, up 3.8% from US$8.13 billion the year before. Operating income was US$659.2 million versus US$572.8 million in the prior year, an increase of 15.1%. Direct operating expenses rose 1.4% to US$6.24 billion from US$6.15 billion in the comparable period the year before. Indirect operating expenses increased 9.5% to US$1.55 billion from US$1.41 billion in the equivalent prior-year period.

Prospects: Our evaluation of Reliance Steel & Aluminum Co. as of Apr. 7, 2013 is the result of our systematic analysis on three basic characteristics: earnings strength, relative valuation, and recent stock price movement. The company has generated a negative trend in earnings per share over the past 5 quarters and while recent estimates for the company have been raised by analysts, RS has posted better than expected results. Based on operating earnings yield, the company is undervalued when compared to all of the companies in our coverage universe. Share price changes over the past year indicates that RS will perform well over the near term.

Financial Data

(US$ in Thousands)	12/31/2012	12/31/2011	12/31/2010	12/31/2009	12/31/2008	12/31/2007	12/31/2006	12/31/2005
Earnings Per Share	5.33	4.58	2.61	2.01	6.56	5.36	4.82	3.11
Cash Flow Per Share	7.98	3.14	2.88	12.84	9.07	8.45	2.61	4.13
Tang Book Value Per Share	17.19	13.38	12.84	10.83	8.51	10.09	8.02	9.74
Dividends Per Share	0.800	0.480	0.400	0.400	0.400	0.320	0.220	0.190
Dividend Payout %	15.01	10.48	15.33	19.90	6.10	5.97	4.56	6.12
Income Statement								
Total Revenue	8,442,300	8,134,700	6,312,795	5,318,132	8,718,844	7,265,610	5,748,376	3,370,722
EBITDA	859,900	741,700	508,660	376,107	946,853	813,310	693,455	413,817
Depn & Amortn	151,500	133,100	120,603	118,884	97,924	79,873	60,325	46,631
Income Before Taxes	607,200	509,400	295,704	194,098	766,556	654,727	571,438	341,964
Income Taxes	201,100	162,400	98,579	46,317	282,921	246,438	216,625	127,775
Net Income	403,500	343,800	194,353	148,158	482,777	407,955	354,507	205,437
Average Shares	75,694	75,041	74,472	73,701	73,597	76,064	73,599	66,194
Balance Sheet								
Current Assets	2,277,400	2,274,700	1,700,897	1,390,904	2,302,372	1,721,403	1,675,389	847,348
Total Assets	5,857,700	5,605,900	4,668,893	4,306,777	5,195,485	3,983,477	3,614,173	1,769,070
Current Liabilities	578,200	576,400	508,595	417,569	650,165	599,864	550,739	333,819
Long-Term Obligations	1,123,800	1,319,000	855,085	852,557	1,675,565	1,013,260	1,088,051	306,790
Total Liabilities	2,299,300	2,462,000	1,845,161	1,700,345	2,764,049	1,877,228	1,867,775	739,205
Stockholders' Equity	3,558,400	3,143,900	2,823,732	2,606,432	2,431,436	2,106,249	1,746,398	1,029,865
Shares Outstanding	76,042	75,007	74,639	73,750	73,312	74,906	75,702	66,217
Statistical Record								
Return on Assets %	7.02	6.69	4.33	3.12	10.49	10.74	13.17	12.33
Return on Equity %	12.01	11.52	7.16	5.88	21.22	21.18	25.54	22.18
EBITDA Margin %	10.19	9.12	8.06	7.07	10.86	11.19	12.06	12.28
Net Margin %	4.78	4.23	3.08	2.79	5.54	5.61	6.17	6.09
Asset Turnover	1.47	1.58	1.41	1.12	1.89	1.91	2.14	2.02
Current Ratio	3.94	3.95	3.34	3.33	3.54	2.87	3.04	2.54
Debt to Equity	0.32	0.42	0.30	0.33	0.69	0.48	0.62	0.30
Price Range	62.10-44.98	60.05-32.04	54.96-35.35	45.42-18.72	78.11-12.63	63.76-37.85	48.77-29.22	33.32-17.52
P/E Ratio	11.65-8.44	13.11-7.00	21.06-13.54	22.60-9.31	11.91-1.93	11.90-7.06	10.12-6.06	10.71-5.63
Average Yield %	1.50	1.00	0.90	1.15	0.81	0.74	0.58	0.82

Address: 350 South Grand Avenue, Suite 5100, Los Angeles, CA 90071 **Telephone:** 213-687-7700	**Web Site:** www.rsac.com **Officers:** David H. Hannah - Chairman, Chief Executive Officer Gregg J. Mollins - President, Chief Operating Officer	**Auditors:** KPMG LLP **Investor Contact:** 213-576-2428 **Transfer Agents:** American Stock Transfer & Trust Company, Brooklyn, NY

RENAISSANCERE HOLDINGS LTD.

Exchange	Symbol	Price	52Wk Range	Yield	P/E
NYS	RNR	$91.99 (3/28/2013)	91.99-71.86	1.22	8.19

*7 Year Price Score 117.69 *NYSE Composite Index=100 *12 Month Price Score 101.64

Interim Earnings (Per Share)

Qtr.	Mar	Jun	Sep	Dec
2008	2.05	2.13	(3.79)	(0.86)
2009	1.57	4.32	4.12	3.37
2010	2.73	3.66	3.70	2.27
2011	(4.69)	0.48	0.95	1.60
2012	3.88	2.75	3.62	0.99

Interim Dividends (Per Share)

Amt	Decl	Ex	Rec	Pay
0.27Q	05/22/2012	06/13/2012	06/15/2012	06/29/2012
0.27Q	08/08/2012	09/12/2012	09/14/2012	09/28/2012
0.27Q	11/13/2012	12/12/2012	12/14/2012	12/28/2012
0.28Q	02/20/2013	03/13/2013	03/15/2013	03/28/2013

Indicated Div: $1.12

Valuation Analysis | **Institutional Holding**

Forecast EPS	$9.38 (04/06/2013)	No of Institutions 308
Market Cap	$4.2 Billion	Shares
Book Value	$3.5 Billion	48,946,396
Price/Book	1.20	% Held
Price/Sales	2.98	77.82

Business Summary: General Insurance (MIC: 5.2.1 SIC: 6331 NAIC: 524130)

RenaissanceRe Holdings is a holding company. Co. is a global provider of reinsurance and insurance coverages and related services. Co.'s core products include property catastrophe reinsurance, which it primarily writes through its principal operating subsidiary Renaissance Reinsurance, its Lloyd's syndicate, RenaissanceRe Syndicate 1458 (Syndicate 1458), and joint ventures, principally DaVinci Reinsurance Ltd. (DaVinci) and Top Layer Reinsurance Ltd.; specialty reinsurance risks written through Renaissance Reinsurance, Syndicate 1458 and DaVinci; and other insurance products primarily written through Syndicate 1458. Co.'s reportable segments include: Reinsurance; Lloyd's; and Insurance.

Recent Developments: For the year ended Dec 31 2012, income from continuing operations was US$746.7 million compared with a loss of US$74.5 million a year earlier. Net income amounted to US$748.9 million versus a net loss of US$90.4 million in the prior year. Revenues were US$1.41 billion, up 28.4% from US$1.10 billion the year before. Net premiums earned were US$1.07 billion versus US$951.0 million in the prior year, an increase of 12.4%. Net investment income rose 41.8% to US$167.4 million from US$118.0 million a year ago.

Prospects: Our evaluation of RenaissanceRe Holdings Ltd. as of Apr. 7, 2013 is the result of our systematic analysis on three basic characteristics: earnings strength, relative valuation, and recent stock price movement. The company has suffered a very negative trend in earnings per share over the past 5 quarters and while recent estimates for the company have been raised by analysts, RNR has posted better than expected results. Based on operating earnings yield, the company is undervalued when compared to all of the companies in our coverage universe. Share price changes over the past year indicates that RNR will perform in line with the market over the near term.

Financial Data

(US$ in Thousands)	12/31/2012	12/31/2011	12/31/2010	12/31/2009	12/31/2008	12/31/2007	12/31/2006	12/31/2005
Earnings Per Share	11.23	(1.84)	12.31	13.40	(0.21)	7.93	10.57	(3.99)
Cash Flow Per Share	14.63	3.27	8.97	9.69	8.68	11.25	11.44	4.75
Tang Book Value Per Share	67.95	59.10	62.31	50.43	37.54	41.03	34.38	24.52
Dividends Per Share	1.080	1.040	1.000	0.960	0.920	0.880	0.840	0.800
Dividend Payout %	9.62	...	8.12	7.16	...	11.10	7.95	...
Income Statement								
Premium Income	1,069,355	951,049	864,921	1,273,816	1,386,824	1,424,369	1,529,777	1,402,709
Total Revenue	1,405,934	1,095,036	1,224,671	1,667,852	1,231,196	1,665,554	1,840,737	1,655,907
Income Before Taxes	748,091	(74,817)	792,358	1,061,753	84,721	758,400	942,204	(403,212)
Income Taxes	1,429	(315)	(6,124)	9,094	568	(18,432)	935	...
Net Income	600,909	(57,235)	744,731	881,158	29,020	612,436	797,110	(246,763)
Average Shares	49,603	50,747	55,641	61,210	63,411	71,825	72,073	71,900
Balance Sheet								
Total Assets	7,928,628	7,744,912	8,138,278	7,801,041	7,984,051	8,286,355	7,769,026	6,871,261
Total Liabilities	4,425,563	4,139,719	4,201,953	3,960,255	4,951,308	4,808,852	4,488,529	4,617,421
Stockholders' Equity	3,503,065	3,605,193	3,936,325	3,840,786	3,032,743	3,477,503	3,280,497	2,253,840
Shares Outstanding	45,542	51,542	54,109	61,744	61,503	68,920	72,140	71,522
Statistical Record								
Return on Assets %	7.65	N.M.	9.34	11.16	0.36	7.63	10.89	N.M.
Return on Equity %	16.86	N.M.	19.15	25.64	0.89	18.12	28.81	N.M.
Net Margin %	42.74	(5.23)	60.81	52.83	2.36	36.77	43.30	(14.90)
Price Range	82.76-71.69	75.05-60.13	64.23-51.41	56.80-41.99	60.24-35.16	65.82-49.70	60.50-41.28	52.08-36.55
P/E Ratio	7.37-6.38	...	5.22-4.18	4.24-3.13	...	8.30-6.27	5.72-3.91	...
Average Yield %	1.41	1.53	1.74	1.92	1.83	1.54	1.70	1.75

Address: Renaissance House, 12 Crow Lane, Pembroke, HM 19
Telephone: 441-295-4513

Web Site: www.renre.com
Officers: Kevin J. O'Donnell - President, Executive Vice President, Global Chief Underwriting Officer
Neill A. Currie - President, Chief Executive Officer

Auditors: Ernst & Young Ltd.
Investor Contact: 441-295-4513
Transfer Agents: Computershare Shareowner Services LLC, Jersey City, NJ

REPUBLIC SERVICES, INC.

Exchange	Symbol	Price	52Wk Range	Yield	P/E
NYS	RSG	$33.00 (3/28/2013)	33.00-25.39	2.85	21.29

*7 Year Price Score 89.14 *NYSE Composite Index=100 *12 Month Price Score 101.72

Interim Earnings (Per Share)

Qtr.	Mar	Jun	Sep	Dec
2008	0.41	0.22	0.48	(0.74)
2009	0.30	0.59	0.32	0.09
2010	0.17	0.42	0.35	0.39
2011	0.41	0.12	0.52	0.51
2012	0.38	0.40	0.42	0.35

Interim Dividends (Per Share)

Amt	Decl	Ex	Rec	Pay
0.22Q	04/26/2012	06/28/2012	07/02/2012	07/16/2012
0.235Q	07/26/2012	09/27/2012	10/01/2012	10/15/2012
0.235Q	11/01/2012	12/28/2012	01/02/2013	01/16/2013
0.235Q	02/07/2013	03/27/2013	04/01/2013	04/15/2013

Indicated Div: $0.94

Valuation Analysis / **Institutional Holding**

Forecast EPS	$1.91	No of Institutions
	(04/05/2013)	583
Market Cap	$11.9 Billion	Shares
Book Value	$7.7 Billion	322,893,312
Price/Book	1.55	% Held
Price/Sales	1.47	65.55

Business Summary: Sanitation Services (MIC: 7.5.3 SIC: 4953 NAIC: 562219)

Republic Services is engaged as a provider of non-hazardous solid waste collection, transfer station, recycling and disposal services. As of Dec 31 2012, Co. provided non-hazardous solid waste collection services for commercial, industrial, municipal and residential customers through 332 collection operations in 38 states and Puerto Rico. In addition, Co. owned or operated 195 transfer stations, 191 active solid waste landfills and 71 recycling centers. Co. also operated 69 landfill gas and renewable energy projects. Co. manages its operations through three geographic regions: East, Central, and West, which Co. has identified as its reportable segments.

Recent Developments: For the year ended Dec 31 2012, net income decreased 2.9% to US$572.1 million from US$588.9 million in the prior year. Revenues were US$8.12 billion, down 0.9% from US$8.19 billion the year before. Operating income was US$1.32 billion versus US$1.55 billion in the prior year, a decrease of 14.9%. Direct operating expenses rose 2.9% to US$5.01 billion from US$4.87 billion in the comparable period the year before. Indirect operating expenses increased 1.0% to US$1.79 billion from US$1.78 billion in the equivalent prior-year period.

Prospects: Our evaluation of Republic Services Inc. as of Apr. 7, 2013 is the result of our systematic analysis on three basic characteristics: earnings strength, relative valuation, and recent stock price movement. The company has generated a negative trend in earnings per share over the past 5 quarters and while recent estimates for the company have remained steady, RSG has posted results that fell short of analysts expectations. Based on operating earnings yield, the company is undervalued when compared to all of the companies in our coverage universe. Share price changes over the past year indicates that RSG will perform poorly over the near term.

Financial Data
(US$ in Thousands)

	12/31/2012	12/31/2011	12/31/2010	12/31/2009	12/31/2008	12/31/2007	12/31/2006	12/31/2005
Earnings Per Share	1.55	1.56	1.32	1.30	0.37	1.51	1.38	1.17
Cash Flow Per Share	4.11	4.70	3.74	3.68	2.60	3.48	2.61	3.59
Tang Book Value Per Share	N.M.	N.M.	N.M.	N.M.	N.M.	N.M.	N.M.	0.07
Dividends Per Share	0.910	0.840	0.780	0.760	0.720	0.553	0.400	0.347
Dividend Payout %	58.71	53.85	59.09	58.46	194.59	36.65	28.99	29.71
Income Statement								
Total Revenue	8,118,300	8,192,900	8,106,600	8,199,100	3,685,100	3,176,200	3,070,600	2,863,900
EBITDA	2,138,300	2,189,800	2,217,400	2,328,600	635,700	855,600	819,700	757,600
Depn & Amortn	926,900	843,600	833,700	869,900	354,100	305,500	296,000	278,800
Income Before Taxes	823,900	906,300	877,000	865,000	159,300	468,100	443,700	409,200
Income Taxes	251,800	317,400	369,500	368,500	85,400	177,900	164,100	155,500
Net Income	571,800	589,200	506,500	495,000	73,800	290,200	279,600	253,700
Average Shares	368,020	377,600	385,100	381,000	198,400	192,000	202,800	217,500
Balance Sheet								
Current Assets	1,231,300	1,265,700	1,246,100	1,264,900	1,325,700	413,800	393,400	482,300
Total Assets	19,616,900	19,551,500	19,461,900	19,540,300	19,921,400	4,467,800	4,429,400	4,550,500
Current Liabilities	1,695,000	1,897,500	2,676,500	2,548,700	2,565,800	628,700	602,200	667,000
Long-Term Obligations	7,051,100	6,887,000	5,865,100	6,419,600	7,198,500	1,565,500	1,544,600	1,472,100
Total Liabilities	11,913,600	11,870,200	11,615,400	11,975,800	12,640,000	3,164,000	3,007,300	2,944,700
Stockholders' Equity	7,703,300	7,681,300	7,846,500	7,564,500	7,281,400	1,303,800	1,422,100	1,605,800
Shares Outstanding	361,100	369,900	383,700	380,800	378,500	185,422	194,995	207,903
Statistical Record								
Return on Assets %	2.91	3.02	2.60	2.51	0.60	6.52	6.23	5.63
Return on Equity %	7.41	7.59	6.57	6.67	1.71	21.29	18.47	14.59
EBITDA Margin %	26.34	26.73	27.35	28.40	17.25	26.94	26.70	26.45
Net Margin %	7.04	7.19	6.25	6.04	2.00	9.14	9.11	8.86
Asset Turnover	0.41	0.42	0.42	0.42	0.30	0.71	0.68	0.64
Current Ratio	0.73	0.67	0.47	0.50	0.52	0.66	0.65	0.72
Debt to Equity	0.92	0.90	0.75	0.85	0.99	1.20	1.09	0.92
Price Range	31.14-25.39	32.94-24.76	32.65-25.62	29.57-15.85	35.05-18.43	34.85-26.61	29.34-24.65	25.39-20.23
P/E Ratio	20.09-16.38	21.12-15.87	24.73-19.41	22.75-12.19	94.73-49.81	23.08-17.62	21.26-17.86	21.70-17.29
Average Yield %	3.23	2.87	2.63	3.13	2.45	1.82	1.48	1.49

Address: 18500 North Allied Way, Phoenix, AZ 85054 Telephone: 480-627-2700	Web Site: www.republicservices.com Officers: James E. O'Connor - Chairman, Chief Executive Officer Harris W. Hudson - Vice-Chairman	Auditors: Ernst & Young LLP Transfer Agents: Wachovia Corp., Charlotte, NC

RESMED INC.

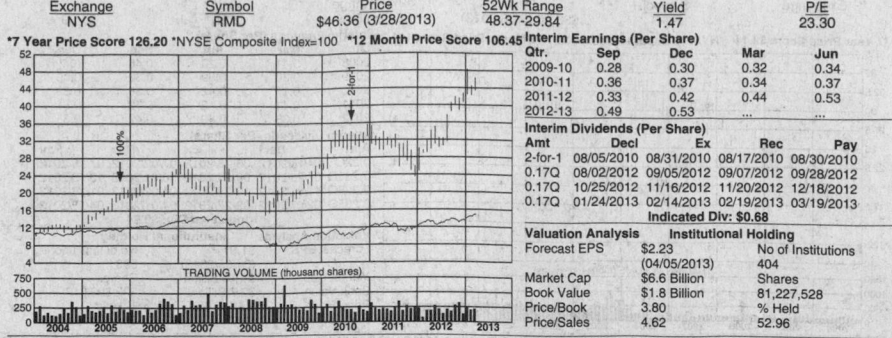

Exchange	Symbol	Price	52Wk Range	Yield	P/E
NYS	RMD	$46.36 (3/28/2013)	48.37-29.84	1.47	23.30

*7 Year Price Score 126.20 *NYSE Composite Index=100   *12 Month Price Score 106.45

Interim Earnings (Per Share)

Qtr.	Sep	Dec	Mar	Jun
2009-10	0.28	0.30	0.32	0.34
2010-11	0.36	0.37	0.34	0.37
2011-12	0.33	0.42	0.44	0.53
2012-13	0.49	0.53	...	...

Interim Dividends (Per Share)

Amt	Decl	Ex	Rec	Pay
2-for-1	08/05/2010	08/31/2010	08/17/2010	08/30/2010
0.17Q	08/02/2012	09/05/2012	09/07/2012	09/28/2012
0.17Q	10/25/2012	11/16/2012	11/20/2012	12/18/2012
0.17Q	01/24/2013	02/14/2013	02/19/2013	03/19/2013

Indicated Div: $0.68

Valuation Analysis

		Institutional Holding	
Forecast EPS	$2.23 (04/05/2013)	No of Institutions	404
Market Cap	$6.6 Billion	Shares	81,227,528
Book Value	$1.8 Billion	% Held	52.96
Price/Book	3.80		
Price/Sales	4.62		

TRADING VOLUME (thousand shares)

Business Summary: Medical Instruments & Equipment (MIC: 4.3.1 SIC: 3841 NAIC: 339112)

ResMed is a holding company. Through its operating subsidiaries, Co. is a developer, manufacturer and distributor of medical equipment for treating, diagnosing, and managing sleep-disordered breathing (SDB) and other respiratory disorders. SDB includes obstructive sleep apnea (OSA), and other respiratory disorders that occur during sleep. Co.'s treatment for OSA, nasal Continuous Positive Airway Pressure, deliver pressurized air, typically through a nasal mask, to prevent collapse of the upper airway during sleep. Co. has developed a number of products for SDB and other respiratory disorders including airflow generators, diagnostic products, mask systems, headgear and other accessories.

Recent Developments: For the quarter ended Dec 31 2012, net income increased 24.0% to US$77.9 million from US$62.9 million in the year-earlier quarter. Revenues were US$376.5 million, up 13.2% from US$332.7 million the year before. Operating income was US$92.1 million versus US$67.3 million in the prior-year quarter, an increase of 36.9%. Direct operating expenses rose 7.3% to US$143.8 million from US$134.0 million in the comparable period the year before. Indirect operating expenses increased 7.0% to US$140.6 million from US$131.5 million in the equivalent prior-year period.

Prospects: Our evaluation of ResMed Inc. as of Apr. 7, 2013 is the result of our systematic analysis on three basic characteristics: earnings strength, relative valuation, and recent stock price movement. The company has managed to produce a neutral trend in earnings per share over the past 5 quarters. However, while recent estimates for the company have been mixed, RMD has posted better than expected results. Based on operating earnings yield, the company is about fairly valued when compared to all of the companies in our coverage universe. Share price changes over the past year indicates that RMD will perform very well over the near term.

Financial Data

(US$ in Thousands)	6 Mos	3 Mos	06/30/2012	06/30/2011	06/30/2010	06/30/2009	06/30/2008	06/30/2007
Earnings Per Share	1.99	1.88	1.71	1.44	1.23	0.95	0.70	0.42
Cash Flow Per Share	2.48	2.61	2.62	1.86	1.25	1.58	0.89	0.59
Tang Book Value Per Share	9.86	9.55	9.13	9.54	6.99	5.76	5.27	4.37
Dividends Per Share	0.340	0.170	...	...	...	...	...	...
Dividend Payout %	17.09	9.04	...	...	...	...	...	...
Income Statement								
Total Revenue	716,269	339,731	1,368,515	1,243,148	1,092,357	920,735	835,397	716,332
EBITDA	177,469	85,066	316,839	287,810	254,601	198,539	155,588	98,393
Depn & Amortn	5,138	2,636	13,974	10,146	8,041	7,060	7,791	6,897
Income Before Taxes	189,301	90,901	331,945	303,707	260,589	201,684	157,855	97,973
Income Taxes	40,094	19,636	77,095	76,721	70,504	55,236	47,552	31,671
Net Income	149,207	71,265	254,850	226,986	190,085	146,448	110,303	66,302
Average Shares	146,689	146,055	149,316	157,195	155,098	154,226	157,424	156,506
Balance Sheet								
Current Assets	1,529,851	1,450,217	1,361,151	1,292,452	985,341	853,284	739,240	668,799
Total Assets	2,330,375	2,244,659	2,137,869	2,068,922	1,626,397	1,507,968	1,406,000	1,252,042
Current Liabilities	251,068	253,031	252,852	208,840	312,672	269,100	192,593	202,403
Long-Term Obligations	300,798	265,785	250,783	100,000	...	94,191	93,789	87,648
Total Liabilities	578,863	545,736	530,242	338,185	338,861	392,776	324,225	320,820
Stockholders' Equity	1,751,512	1,698,923	1,607,627	1,730,737	1,287,536	1,115,192	1,081,775	931,222
Shares Outstanding	143,384	143,057	142,021	151,668	151,345	150,502	151,950	155,234
Statistical Record								
Return on Assets %	13.30	13.19	12.08	12.29	12.13	10.05	8.28	5.87
Return on Equity %	17.55	16.97	15.23	15.04	15.82	13.33	10.93	7.94
EBITDA Margin %	24.78	25.04	23.15	23.15	23.31	21.56	18.62	13.74
Net Margin %	20.83	20.98	18.62	18.26	17.40	15.91	13.20	9.26
Asset Turnover	0.66	0.67	0.65	0.67	0.70	0.63	0.63	0.63
Current Ratio	6.09	5.73	5.38	6.19	3.15	3.17	3.84	3.30
Debt to Equity	0.17	0.16	0.16	0.06	...	0.08	0.09	0.09
Price Range	42.77-24.81	40.47-23.46	35.01-23.46	35.61-29.62	34.41-19.64	23.99-14.91	26.55-17.09	27.13-19.26
P/E Ratio	21.49-12.47	21.53-12.48	20.47-13.72	24.73-20.57	27.98-15.97	25.25-15.70	37.92-24.42	64.60-45.86
Average Yield %	0.17	0.55	...	...	...	...	...	...

Address: 9001 Spectrum Center Blvd., San Diego, CA 92123 **Telephone:** 858-836-5000	**Web Site:** www.resmed.com **Officers:** Peter C. Farrell - Chairman, President, Chief Executive Officer Robert D. Douglas - President, Chief Operating Officer, Region Officer, Office of the Chief Executive Officer	**Auditors:** KPMG LLP **Investor Contact:** 858-836-5971 **Transfer Agents:** Computershare Trust Company N.A., Canton, MA

REYNOLDS AMERICAN INC

Exchange	Symbol	Price	52Wk Range	Yield	P/E
NYS	RAI	$44.49 (3/28/2013)	46.68-39.65	5.30	19.86

*7 Year Price Score 121.08 *NYSE Composite Index=100 *12 Month Price Score 93.45

Interim Earnings (Per Share)

Qtr.	Mar	Jun	Sep	Dec
2008	0.85	0.62	0.36	0.45
2009	0.01	0.65	0.62	0.37
2010	0.14	0.58	0.65	0.54
2011	0.60	0.52	0.63	0.65
2012	0.47	0.78	0.74	0.26

Interim Dividends (Per Share)

Amt	Decl	Ex	Rec	Pay
0.59Q	05/03/2012	06/07/2012	06/11/2012	07/02/2012
0.59Q	07/12/2012	09/06/2012	09/10/2012	10/01/2012
0.59Q	11/29/2012	12/06/2012	12/10/2012	01/02/2013
0.59Q	02/07/2013	03/06/2013	03/08/2013	04/01/2013

Indicated Div: $2.36

Valuation Analysis / **Institutional Holding**

Forecast EPS	$3.21	No of Institutions
	(04/05/2013)	604
Market Cap	$24.6 Billion	Shares
Book Value	$5.3 Billion	283,167,296
Price/Book	4.68	% Held
Price/Sales	2.96	46.00

Business Summary: Tobacco Products (MIC: 1.3.1 SIC: 2111 NAIC: 312221)

Reynolds American is a holding company whose operating subsidiaries include a cigarette manufacturer, R. J. Reynolds Tobacco Company; a smokeless tobacco products manufacturer, American Snuff Company, LLC, referred to as American Snuff Co.; the manufacturer of the cigarette brand, Santa Fe Natural Tobacco Company, Inc.; and Niconovum AB, a marketer of nicotine replacement therapy products. Co.'s operating segments are: RJR Tobacco, which include several cigarettes brands such as CAMEL, PALL MALL, WINSTON, KOOL, DORAL and SALEM; American Snuff, which consists of the primary operations of American Snuff Co.; and Santa Fe, which manufactures and markets cigarettes and other tobacco products.

Recent Developments: For the year ended Dec 31 2012, income from continuing operations decreased 9.5% to US$1.27 billion from US$1.41 billion a year earlier. Net income decreased 9.5% to US$1.27 billion from US$1.41 billion in the prior year. Revenues were US$8.30 billion, down 2.8% from US$8.54 billion the year before. Operating income was US$2.21 billion versus US$2.40 billion in the prior year, a decrease of 7.7%. Direct operating expenses declined 3.2% to US$4.32 billion from US$4.46 billion in the comparable period the year before. Indirect operating expenses increased 5.4% to US$1.77 billion from US$1.68 billion in the equivalent prior-year period.

Prospects: Our evaluation of Reynolds American Inc. as of Apr. 7, 2013 is the result of our systematic analysis on three basic characteristics: earnings strength, relative valuation, and recent stock price movement. The company has managed to produce a neutral trend in earnings per share over the past 5 quarters and while recent estimates for the company have remained steady, RAI has posted better than expected results. Based on operating earnings yield, the company is undervalued when compared to all of the companies in our coverage universe. Share price changes over the past year indicates that RAI will perform in line with the market over the near term.

Financial Data
(US$ in Thousands)

	12/31/2012	12/31/2011	12/31/2010	12/31/2009	12/31/2008	12/31/2007	12/31/2006	12/31/2005
Earnings Per Share	2.24	2.40	1.91	1.65	2.29	2.21	2.05	1.76
Cash Flow Per Share	2.76	2.44	2.17	2.50	2.24	2.26	2.47	2.16
Dividends Per Share	2.330	2.150	1.840	1.725	1.700	1.600	1.375	1.050
Dividend Payout %	104.02	89.58	96.34	104.55	74.40	72.23	67.07	59.49
Income Statement								
Total Revenue	8,304,000	8,541,000	8,551,000	8,419,000	8,845,000	9,023,000	8,510,000	8,256,000
EBITDA	2,311,000	2,534,000	2,563,000	1,910,000	2,485,000	2,420,000	2,105,000	1,485,000
Depn & Amortn	131,000	138,000	151,000	144,000	142,000	143,000	162,000	41,000
Income Before Taxes	1,953,000	2,186,000	2,192,000	1,534,000	2,128,000	2,073,000	1,809,000	1,416,000
Income Taxes	681,000	780,000	863,000	572,000	790,000	766,000	673,000	431,000
Net Income	1,272,000	1,406,000	1,113,000	962,000	1,338,000	1,308,000	1,210,000	1,042,000
Average Shares	567,873	585,383	584,854	583,652	586,148	589,778	590,768	590,344
Balance Sheet								
Current Assets	4,812,000	4,307,000	4,802,000	5,495,000	5,019,000	4,992,000	4,935,000	5,065,000
Total Assets	16,557,000	16,254,000	17,078,000	18,009,000	18,154,000	18,629,000	18,178,000	14,519,000
Current Liabilities	3,769,000	4,276,000	4,372,000	4,340,000	3,923,000	3,903,000	4,092,000	4,149,000
Long-Term Obligations	5,035,000	3,206,000	3,701,000	4,136,000	4,486,000	4,515,000	4,389,000	1,558,000
Total Liabilities	11,300,000	10,003,000	10,568,000	11,511,000	11,917,000	11,163,000	11,135,000	7,966,000
Stockholders' Equity	5,257,000	6,251,000	6,510,000	6,498,000	6,237,000	7,466,000	7,043,000	6,553,000
Shares Outstanding	552,940	576,135	583,043	582,848	582,901	590,014	591,249	590,931
Statistical Record								
Return on Assets %	7.73	8.44	6.34	5.32	7.26	7.11	7.40	7.20
Return on Equity %	22.05	22.04	17.11	15.11	19.48	18.03	17.80	16.37
EBITDA Margin %	27.83	29.67	29.97	22.69	28.09	26.82	24.74	17.99
Net Margin %	15.32	16.46	13.02	11.43	15.13	14.50	14.22	12.62
Asset Turnover	0.50	0.51	0.49	0.47	0.48	0.49	0.52	0.57
Current Ratio	1.28	1.01	1.10	1.27	1.28	1.28	1.21	1.22
Debt to Equity	0.96	0.51	0.57	0.64	0.72	0.60	0.62	0.24
Price Range	46.68-39.23	41.86-31.80	33.40-25.30	26.97-16.08	35.18-19.23	35.52-29.32	33.09-24.13	24.35-19.28
P/E Ratio	20.84-17.51	17.44-13.25	17.49-13.25	16.35-9.75	15.36-8.40	16.07-13.26	16.14-11.77	13.84-10.96
Average Yield %	5.46	5.84	6.48	8.11	6.35	5.00	4.71	5.06

Address: 401 North Main Street, Winston-Salem, NC 27101 **Telephone:** 336-741-2000 **Fax:** 336-728-8888	**Web Site:** www.reynoldsamerican.com **Officers:** Daniel M. Delen - President, Chief Executive Officer Thomas R. Adams - Executive Vice President, Chief Financial Officer	**Auditors:** KPMG LLP **Investor Contact:** 336-741-5165 **Transfer Agents:** BNY Mellon Shareowner Services, Pittsburgh, PA

RITE AID CORP.

Exchange	Symbol	Price	52Wk Range	Yield	P/E
NYS	RAD	$1.90 (3/28/2013)	1.94-0.97	N/A	N/A

*7 Year Price Score 53.93   *NYSE Composite Index=100   *12 Month Price Score 116.67

TRADING VOLUME (thousand shares)

Interim Earnings (Per Share)

Qtr.	May	Aug	Nov	Feb
2009-10	(0.11)	(0.14)	(0.10)	(0.24)
2010-11	(0.09)	(0.23)	(0.09)	(0.24)
2011-12	(0.07)	(0.11)	(0.06)	(0.19)
2012-13	(0.03)	(0.05)	0.07	...

Interim Dividends (Per Share)

No Dividends Paid

Valuation Analysis   Institutional Holding

Forecast EPS	$-0.01	No of Institutions
	(04/06/2013)	266
Market Cap	$1.7 Billion	Shares
Book Value	N/A	405,586,368
Price/Book	N/A	% Held
Price/Sales	0.07	41.96

Business Summary: Retail - Food & Beverage, Drug & Tobacco (MIC: 2.1.2 SIC: 5912 NAIC: 446110)

Rite Aid, through its subsidiaries, operates retail drugstores. In its stores, Co. sells prescription drugs and an assortment of other merchandise including over-the-counter medications, health and beauty aids, personal care items, cosmetics, household items, beverages, convenience foods, greeting cards, merchandise and other everyday and convenience products, as well as photo processing. Co. has an alliance with GNC, a retailer of vitamin and mineral supplements, personal care, fitness and other health-related products, to open GNC stores-within-Rite Aid-stores. Co. also holds licenses to sell beer, wine and liquor, cigarettes and lottery tickets. At Mar 3 2012, Co. operated 4,667 stores.

Recent Developments: For the quarter ended Dec 1 2012, net income amounted to US$61.9 million versus a net loss of US$52.0 million in the year-earlier quarter. Revenues were US$6.24 billion, down 1.2% from US$6.31 billion the year before. Direct operating expenses declined 4.6% to US$4.43 billion from US$4.64 billion in the comparable period the year before. Indirect operating expenses increased 1.5% to US$1.75 billion from US$1.72 billion in the equivalent prior-year period.

Prospects: Our evaluation of Rite Aid Corp. as of Apr. 7, 2013 is the result of our systematic analysis on three basic characteristics: earnings strength, relative valuation, and recent stock price movement. The company has enjoyed a very positive trend in earnings per share over the past 5 quarters. Because the company lacks sufficient analyst estimate data, we place greater weight on the historical EPS trend as the measure of earnings strength. Based on operating earnings yield, the company is overvalued when compared to all of the companies in our coverage universe. Share price changes over the past year indicates that RAD will perform very poorly over the near term.

Financial Data
(US$ in Thousands)

	9 Mos	6 Mos	3 Mos	03/03/2012	02/26/2011	02/27/2010	02/28/2009	03/01/2008
Earnings Per Share	(0.20)	(0.33)	(0.39)	(0.43)	(0.64)	(0.59)	(3.49)	(1.54)
Cash Flow Per Share	0.68	0.39	0.28	0.30	0.45	(0.37)	0.43	0.11
Income Statement								
Total Revenue	18,937,018	12,699,171	6,468,287	26,121,222	25,214,907	25,669,117	26,289,268	24,326,846
EBITDA	630,373	336,564	147,142	433,790	333,926	385,127	(1,721,496)	485,367
Depn & Amortn	311,160	208,370	106,371	296,792	331,927	349,282	383,671	309,270
Income Before Taxes	(68,800)	(131,448)	(89,817)	(392,257)	(545,582)	(479,918)	(2,582,794)	(273,499)
Income Taxes	(63,818)	(64,595)	(61,729)	(23,686)	9,842	26,758	329,257	802,701
Net Income	(4,982)	(66,853)	(28,088)	(368,571)	(555,424)	(506,676)	(2,915,420)	(1,078,990)
Average Shares	917,808	889,645	887,516	885,819	882,947	880,843	840,812	723,923
Balance Sheet								
Current Assets	4,472,592	4,240,927	4,321,851	4,504,586	4,411,365	4,508,668	4,364,932	4,921,894
Total Assets	7,186,142	6,950,578	7,073,132	7,364,291	7,555,850	8,049,911	8,326,540	11,488,023
Current Liabilities	2,843,672	2,625,182	2,480,408	2,570,319	2,420,323	2,175,692	2,302,427	2,798,039
Long-Term Obligations	5,923,370	5,930,777	6,129,778	6,248,780	6,156,820	6,319,397	5,971,026	5,799,915
Total Liabilities	9,762,256	9,593,901	9,682,465	9,951,047	9,767,217	9,723,462	9,526,192	9,776,838
Stockholders' Equity	(2,576,114)	(2,643,323)	(2,609,333)	(2,586,756)	(2,211,367)	(1,673,551)	(1,199,652)	1,711,185
Shares Outstanding	903,827	903,786	899,074	898,687	890,297	887,636	886,113	830,209
Statistical Record								
EBITDA Margin %	3.33	2.65	2.27	1.66	1.32	1.50	N.M.	2.00
Asset Turnover	3.54	3.64	3.59	3.44	3.24	3.14	2.66	2.63
Current Ratio	1.57	1.62	1.74	1.75	1.82	2.07	1.90	1.76
Debt to Equity	...	...	...	...	...	...	...	3.39
Price Range	2.05-1.00	2.05-0.91	2.05-0.91	1.67-0.91	1.74-0.87	2.24-0.21	2.99-0.20	6.70-1.95

Address: 30 Hunter Lane, Camp Hill, PA 17011	Web Site: www.riteaid.com	Auditors: Deloitte & Touche LLP
Telephone: 717-761-2633	Officers: Mary F. Sammons - Chairman, President, Chief Executive Officer, Division Officer John T. Standley - President, Chief Executive Officer, Chief Operating Officer	Investor Contact: 717-975-3710
Fax: 717-975-5905		Transfer Agents: American Stock Transfer & Trust Company, New York, NY

RLI CORP.

Exchange	Symbol	Price	52Wk Range	Yield	P/E	Div Achiever
NYS	RLI	$71.85 (3/28/2013)	72.35-62.09	1.78	15.00	36 Years

*7 Year Price Score 103.93   *NYSE Composite Index=100   *12 Month Price Score 95.33

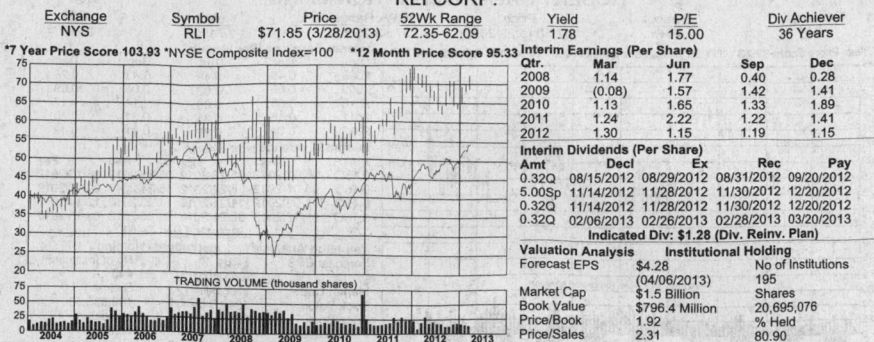

Interim Earnings (Per Share)

Qtr.	Mar	Jun	Sep	Dec
2008	1.14	1.77	0.40	0.28
2009	(0.08)	1.57	1.42	1.41
2010	1.13	1.65	1.33	1.89
2011	1.24	2.22	1.22	1.41
2012	1.30	1.15	1.19	1.15

Interim Dividends (Per Share)

Amt	Decl	Ex	Rec	Pay
0.32Q	08/15/2012	08/29/2012	08/31/2012	09/20/2012
5.00Sp	11/14/2012	11/28/2012	11/30/2012	12/20/2012
0.32Q	11/14/2012	11/28/2012	11/30/2012	12/20/2012
0.32Q	02/06/2013	02/26/2013	02/28/2013	03/20/2013

Indicated Div: $1.28 (Div. Reinv. Plan)

Valuation Analysis

		Institutional Holding	
Forecast EPS	$4.28	No of Institutions	
	(04/06/2013)	195	
Market Cap	$1.5 Billion	Shares	
Book Value	$796.4 Million	20,695,076	
Price/Book	1.92	% Held	
Price/Sales	2.31	80.90	

Business Summary: General Insurance (MIC: 5.2.1 SIC: 6331 NAIC: 524126)

RLI is an insurance holding company. Through its subsidiaries, Co. is engaged in underwriting selected property and casualty insurance. Co. has three segments: casualty, which includes general liability, commercial and personal umbrella, commercial transportation, Contractors Bonding and Insurance Company package business, executive products, and other products; property, which includes commercial fire, earthquake, wind, flood and collapse coverages as well as cargo, hull and protection and indemnity, marine liability, and inland marine; and surety, which engages in writing commercial and contract surety coverages, as well as those for the energy, petrochemical and refining industries.

Recent Developments: For the year ended Dec 31 2012, net income decreased 18.4% to US$103.3 million from US$126.6 million in the prior year. Revenues were US$660.8 million, up 6.7% from US$619.2 million the year before. Net premiums earned were US$576.6 million versus US$538.5 million in the prior year, an increase of 7.1%. Net investment income fell 7.6% to US$58.8 million from US$63.7 million a year ago.

Prospects: Our evaluation of RLI Corp. as of Apr. 7, 2013 is the result of our systematic analysis on three basic characteristics: earnings strength, relative valuation, and recent stock price movement. The company has produced a positive trend in earnings per share over the past 5 quarters and while recent estimates for the company have been raised by analysts, RLI has posted better than expected results. Based on operating earnings yield, the company is about fairly valued when compared to all of the companies in our coverage universe. Share price changes over the past year indicates that RLI will perform poorly over the near term.

Financial Data

(US$ in Thousands)	12/31/2012	12/31/2011	12/31/2010	12/31/2009	12/31/2008	12/31/2007	12/31/2006	12/31/2005
Earnings Per Share	4.79	6.09	6.00	4.32	3.60	7.30	5.27	4.07
Cash Flow Per Share	1.70	5.60	4.77	5.93	7.47	5.39	6.89	7.78
Tang Book Value Per Share	33.87	35.84	36.50	37.90	31.76	33.77	30.09	26.09
Dividends Per Share	6.260	6.190	8.150	1.080	0.990	0.870	0.750	0.630
Dividend Payout %	130.69	101.64	135.83	25.00	27.50	11.92	14.23	15.48
Income Statement								
Premium Income	576,571	538,452	493,382	491,961	528,764	544,478	530,338	491,307
Total Revenue	660,774	619,169	583,424	546,552	561,012	652,345	632,708	569,302
Benefits & Claims	271,645	200,084	201,332	203,388	247,174	190,868	256,889	251,170
Income Before Taxes	133,879	183,232	171,389	127,385	101,754	247,161	171,776	132,980
Income Taxes	39,386	59,138	51,058	38,592	27,922	78,609	52,254	36,742
Net Income	103,346	130,591	127,432	93,845	78,676	175,867	134,639	107,134
Average Shares	21,580	21,434	21,241	21,731	21,848	24,085	25,571	26,324
Balance Sheet								
Total Assets	2,644,632	2,695,170	2,514,592	2,538,653	2,419,401	2,626,523	2,771,296	2,735,870
Total Liabilities	1,848,269	1,876,318	1,723,216	1,706,403	1,711,247	1,852,101	2,014,776	2,042,929
Stockholders' Equity	796,363	818,852	791,376	832,250	708,154	774,422	756,520	692,941
Shares Outstanding	21,262	21,162	20,964	21,264	21,474	22,155	24,272	25,551
Statistical Record								
Return on Assets %	3.86	5.01	5.04	3.79	3.11	6.52	4.89	4.12
Return on Equity %	12.76	16.22	15.70	12.18	10.58	22.98	18.58	16.27
Loss Ratio %	47.11	37.16	40.81	41.34	46.75	35.06	48.44	51.12
Net Margin %	15.64	21.09	21.84	17.17	14.02	26.96	21.28	18.82
Price Range	74.44-62.09	74.16-50.98	61.09-49.91	61.17-43.13	66.61-44.64	60.82-51.00	57.41-45.16	55.68-40.28
P/E Ratio	15.54-12.96	12.18-8.37	10.18-8.32	14.16-9.98	18.50-12.40	8.33-6.99	10.89-8.57	13.68-9.90
Average Yield %	9.20	10.04	14.72	2.12	1.85	1.52	1.46	1.37

Address: 9025 North Lindbergh Drive, Peoria, IL 61615
Telephone: 309-692-1000
Fax: 309-692-1068

Web Site: www.rlicorp.com
Officers: Gerald D. Stephens - Chairman Jonathan E. Michael - President, Chief Executive Officer

Auditors: KPMG LLP
Investor Contact: 309-693-5880
Transfer Agents: Wells Fargo Shareholder Services, St. Paul, MN

ROBERT HALF INTERNATIONAL INC.

Exchange	Symbol	Price	52Wk Range	Yield	P/E
NYS	RHI	$37.53 (3/28/2013)	37.53-25.24	1.71	25.02

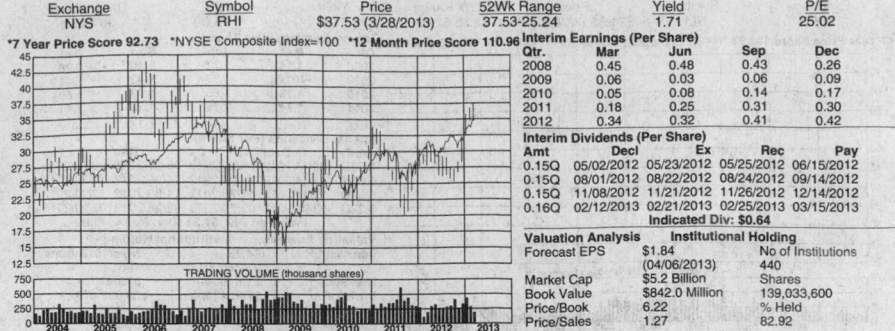

*7 Year Price Score 92.73   ***NYSE Composite Index=100**   ***12 Month Price Score 110.96**

Interim Earnings (Per Share)

Qtr.	Mar	Jun	Sep	Dec
2008	0.45	0.48	0.43	0.26
2009	0.06	0.03	0.06	0.09
2010	0.05	0.08	0.14	0.17
2011	0.18	0.25	0.31	0.30
2012	0.34	0.32	0.41	0.42

Interim Dividends (Per Share)

Amt	Decl	Ex	Rec	Pay
0.15Q	05/02/2012	05/23/2012	05/25/2012	06/15/2012
0.15Q	08/01/2012	08/22/2012	08/24/2012	09/14/2012
0.15Q	11/08/2012	11/21/2012	11/26/2012	12/14/2012
0.16Q	02/12/2013	02/21/2013	02/25/2013	03/15/2013

Indicated Div: $0.64

Valuation Analysis

		Institutional Holding	
Forecast EPS	$1.84 (04/06/2013)	No of Institutions	440
Market Cap	$5.2 Billion	Shares	139,033,600
Book Value	$842.0 Million	% Held	82.92
Price/Book	6.22		
Price/Sales	1.27		

TRADING VOLUME (thousand shares)

Business Summary: Business Services (MIC: 7.5.2 SIC: 7363 NAIC: 561320)

Robert Half International provides staffing and risk consulting services. Co.'s Accountemps, Robert Half Finance & Accounting, and Robert Half Management Resources divisions provide temporary, full-time, and project professionals in the fields of accounting and finance. Co.'s OfficeTeam division provides temporary administrative support personnel. Co.'s Robert Half Technology division provides information technology personnel. Co.'s Robert Half Legal division provides temporary, project, and full-time staffing of attorneys and support personnel within law firms and corporate legal departments. The Creative Group provides project staffing in the advertising, marketing, and web design fields.

Recent Developments: For the year ended Dec 31 2012, net income increased 40.0% to US$209.9 million from US$149.9 million in the prior year. Revenues were US$4.11 billion, up 8.8% from US$3.78 billion the year before. Direct operating expenses rose 7.6% to US$2.46 billion from US$2.29 billion in the comparable period the year before. Indirect operating expenses increased 5.3% to US$1.30 billion from US$1.24 billion in the equivalent prior-year period.

Prospects: Our evaluation of Robert Half International Inc. as of Apr. 7, 2013 is the result of our systematic analysis on three basic characteristics: earnings strength, relative valuation, and recent stock price movement. The company has managed to produce a neutral trend in earnings per share over the past 5 quarters and while recent estimates for the company have remained steady, RHI has posted better than expected results. Based on operating earnings yield, the company is about fairly valued when compared to all of the companies in our coverage universe. Share price changes over the past year indicates that RHI will perform well over the near term.

Financial Data
(US$ in Thousands)	12/31/2012	12/31/2011	12/31/2010	12/31/2009	12/31/2008	12/31/2007	12/31/2006	12/31/2005
Earnings Per Share	1.50	1.04	0.44	0.24	1.63	1.81	1.65	1.36
Cash Flow Per Share	2.09	1.82	1.23	1.65	2.94	2.57	2.27	1.95
Tang Book Value Per Share	4.58	4.30	4.41	4.78	5.26	4.99	5.15	4.72
Dividends Per Share	0.600	0.560	0.520	0.480	0.440	0.400	0.320	0.280
Dividend Payout %	40.00	53.85	118.18	200.00	26.99	22.10	19.39	20.59
Income Statement								
Total Revenue	4,111,213	3,776,976	3,175,093	3,036,547	4,600,554	4,645,666	4,013,546	3,338,439
EBITDA	391,772	300,680	170,547	130,586	487,325	548,718	510,535	432,555
Depn & Amortn	48,724	51,415	55,958	65,266	73,210	71,441	61,085	51,329
Income Before Taxes	344,245	250,216	115,168	66,763	419,276	490,404	466,202	392,174
Income Taxes	134,303	100,294	49,099	29,500	169,095	194,192	183,024	154,304
Net Income	209,942	149,922	66,069	37,263	250,181	296,212	283,178	237,870
Average Shares	139,409	141,790	144,028	146,611	153,289	163,479	171,712	174,382
Balance Sheet								
Current Assets	1,064,685	1,006,678	971,860	922,634	1,032,899	1,059,638	1,112,355	1,016,908
Total Assets	1,381,271	1,311,836	1,273,984	1,283,535	1,411,850	1,450,298	1,459,021	1,318,686
Current Liabilities	501,637	473,001	408,460	366,968	412,852	447,952	402,740	336,701
Long-Term Obligations	1,428	1,545	1,656	1,779	1,892	3,753	3,831	2,698
Total Liabilities	539,260	511,331	439,613	383,725	427,962	466,249	416,350	347,813
Stockholders' Equity	842,011	800,505	834,371	899,810	983,888	984,049	1,042,671	970,873
Shares Outstanding	139,438	142,085	146,182	148,645	150,943	158,057	167,847	170,681
Statistical Record								
Return on Assets %	15.55	11.60	5.17	2.76	17.43	20.36	20.39	18.90
Return on Equity %	25.49	18.34	7.62	3.96	25.36	29.23	28.13	25.27
EBITDA Margin %	9.53	7.96	5.37	4.30	10.59	11.81	12.72	12.96
Net Margin %	5.11	3.97	2.08	1.23	5.44	6.38	7.06	7.13
Asset Turnover	3.04	2.92	2.48	2.25	3.21	3.19	2.89	2.65
Current Ratio	2.12	2.13	2.38	2.51	2.50	2.37	2.76	3.02
Price Range	31.82-25.24	33.85-20.06	32.16-21.57	27.77-14.41	28.31-15.78	41.62-24.58	43.90-30.05	39.29-24.23
P/E Ratio	21.21-16.83	32.55-19.29	73.09-49.02	115.71-60.04	17.37-9.68	22.99-13.58	26.61-18.21	28.89-17.82
Average Yield %	2.12	2.04	1.92	2.14	1.87	1.18	0.86	0.91

Address: 2884 Sand Hill Road, Suite 200, Menlo Park, CA 94025 Telephone: 650-234-6000 Fax: 650-234-6999	Web Site: www.rhi.com Officers: Harold M. Messmer - Chairman, President, Chief Executive Officer M. Keith Waddell - Vice-Chairman, President, Chief Financial Officer, Treasurer	Auditors: PricewaterhouseCoopers LLP Transfer Agents: Mellon Investor Services LLC, New Jersey, NJ

ROCK-TENN CO.

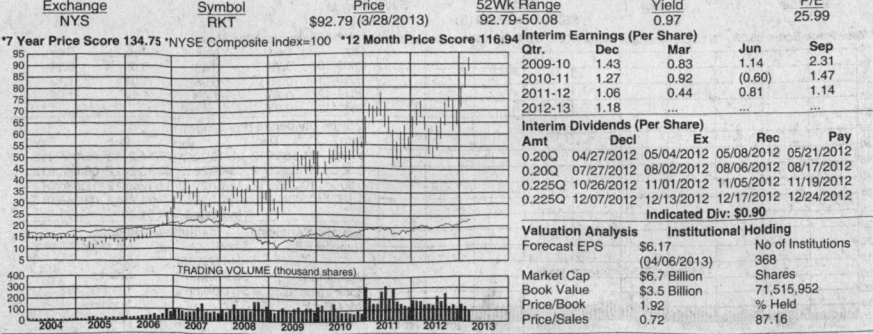

Exchange	Symbol	Price	52Wk Range	Yield	P/E
NYS	RKT	$92.79 (3/28/2013)	92.79-50.08	0.97	25.99

*7 Year Price Score 134.75 *NYSE Composite Index=100 ***12 Month Price Score 116.94**

Interim Earnings (Per Share)

Qtr.	Dec	Mar	Jun	Sep
2009-10	1.43	0.83	1.14	2.31
2010-11	1.27	0.92	(0.60)	1.47
2011-12	1.06	0.44	0.81	1.14
2012-13	1.18	...	...	...

Interim Dividends (Per Share)

Amt	Decl	Ex	Rec	Pay
0.20Q	04/27/2012	05/04/2012	05/08/2012	05/21/2012
0.20Q	07/27/2012	08/02/2012	08/06/2012	08/17/2012
0.225Q	10/26/2012	11/01/2012	11/05/2012	11/19/2012
0.225Q	12/07/2012	12/13/2012	12/17/2012	12/24/2012

Indicated Div: $0.90

Valuation Analysis

		Institutional Holding	
Forecast EPS	$6.17 (04/06/2013)	No of Institutions	368
Market Cap	$6.7 Billion	Shares	71,515,952
Book Value	$3.5 Billion	% Held	87.16
Price/Book	1.92		
Price/Sales	0.72		

Business Summary: Containers & Packaging (MIC: 8.1.3 SIC: 2631 NAIC: 322130)

Rock-Tenn is a manufacturer of corrugated and consumer packaging. Co. operates locations in the U.S., Canada, Mexico, Chile, Argentina, Puerto Rico and China. Co. operates in three segments: Corrugated Packaging, consisting of its containerboard mills and its corrugated converting operations; Consumer Packaging, consisting of its coated and uncoated paperboard mills, consumer packaging converting operations and merchandising display facilities; and Recycling, which consists of its recycled fiber brokerage and collection operations. Co.'s subsidiary, RTS, designs and manufactures solid fiber and corrugated partitions and die-cut paperboard components.

Recent Developments: For the quarter ended Dec 31 2012, net income increased 13.2% to US$86.9 million from US$76.8 million in the year-earlier quarter. Revenues were US$2.29 billion, up 0.9% from US$2.27 billion the year before. Operating income was US$170.4 million versus US$156.0 million in the prior-year quarter, an increase of 9.2%. Direct operating expenses was unchanged at US$1.88 billion versus the comparable period the year before. Indirect operating expenses increased 1.2% to US$239.1 million from US$236.2 million in the equivalent prior-year period.

Prospects: Our evaluation of Rock-Tenn Co. as of Apr. 7, 2013 is the result of our systematic analysis on three basic characteristics: earnings strength, relative valuation, and recent stock price movement. The company has enjoyed a very positive trend in earnings per share over the past 5 quarters and while recent estimates for the company have been raised by analysts, RKT has posted better than expected results. Based on operating earnings yield, the company is about fairly valued when compared to all of the companies in our coverage universe. Share price changes over the past year indicates that RKT will perform well over the near term.

Financial Data

(US$ in Thousands)	3 Mos	09/30/2012	09/30/2011	09/30/2010	09/30/2009	09/30/2008	09/30/2007	09/30/2006
Earnings Per Share	3.57	3.45	2.77	5.70	5.75	2.14	2.07	0.77
Cash Flow Per Share	11.01	9.20	9.29	9.83	10.28	6.42	6.19	4.25
Tang Book Value Per Share	11.58	10.51	10.40	2.85	N.M.	N.M.	4.13	2.57
Dividends Per Share	1.050	0.800	0.800	0.600	0.400	0.400	0.390	0.360
Dividend Payout %	29.41	23.19	28.88	10.53	6.96	18.69	18.84	46.75
Income Statement								
Total Revenue	2,287,100	9,207,600	5,399,600	3,001,400	2,812,300	2,838,900	2,315,800	2,138,100
EBITDA	308,300	938,700	546,100	499,400	544,700	334,900	278,400	193,700
Depn & Amortn	138,100	434,600	228,200	129,400	130,600	118,900	96,600	96,600
Income Before Taxes	141,100	385,700	214,000	294,600	317,400	129,000	130,700	43,100
Income Taxes	54,800	136,900	69,500	64,700	91,600	44,300	45,300	9,900
Net Income	86,000	249,100	141,500	225,600	222,300	81,800	81,700	28,700
Average Shares	72,700	72,100	50,500	39,100	38,700	38,200	39,500	37,000
Balance Sheet								
Current Assets	2,125,000	2,189,800	2,228,900	709,000	658,300	709,200	494,500	485,600
Total Assets	10,542,100	10,687,100	10,566,000	2,914,900	2,884,400	3,013,100	1,800,700	1,784,000
Current Liabilities	1,166,100	1,408,300	1,318,300	631,200	449,300	647,700	344,900	306,000
Long-Term Obligations	3,163,800	3,151,200	3,302,500	897,300	1,293,100	1,453,800	676,300	765,300
Total Liabilities	7,073,400	7,281,400	7,194,400	1,903,600	2,107,600	2,372,600	1,211,700	1,275,400
Stockholders' Equity	3,468,700	3,405,700	3,371,600	1,011,300	776,800	640,500	589,000	508,600
Shares Outstanding	71,797	70,884	70,467	38,903	38,707	38,228	37,988	37,688
Statistical Record								
Return on Assets %	2.45	2.34	2.09	7.78	7.54	3.39	4.56	1.60
Return on Equity %	7.47	7.33	6.44	25.23	31.37	13.27	14.89	5.95
EBITDA Margin %	13.48	10.19	10.11	16.64	19.37	11.80	12.02	9.06
Net Margin %	3.76	2.71	2.61	7.52	7.90	2.88	3.53	1.34
Asset Turnover	0.87	0.86	0.80	1.04	0.95	1.18	1.29	1.19
Current Ratio	1.82	1.55	1.69	1.12	1.47	1.09	1.43	1.59
Debt to Equity	0.91	0.93	0.98	0.89	1.66	2.27	1.15	1.50
Price Range	75.71-50.08	73.85-45.74	77.62-46.38	55.55-38.03	51.86-22.88	45.86-21.92	40.76-19.57	20.50-12.74
P/E Ratio	21.21-14.03	21.41-13.26	28.02-16.74	9.75-6.67	9.02-3.98	21.43-10.24	19.69-9.45	26.62-16.55
Average Yield %	1.64	1.31	1.31	1.23	1.13	1.28	1.30	2.35

Address: 504 Thrasher Street, Norcross, GA 30071 Telephone: 770-448-2193	Web Site: www.rocktenn.com Officers: James A. Rubright - Chairman, Chief Executive Officer Steven C. Voorhees - President, Executive Vice President, Chief Financial Officer, Chief Administrative Officer, Chief Operating Officer	Auditors: Ernst & Young LLP Investor Contact: 678-291-7900 Transfer Agents: ComputerShare Investor Services, Providence, RI

ROCKWELL COLLINS, INC.

Exchange	Symbol	Price	52Wk Range	Yield	P/E
NYS	COL	$63.12 (3/28/2013)	63.82-46.92	1.90	14.92

*7 Year Price Score 86.28   *NYSE Composite Index=100   *12 Month Price Score 101.93

Interim Earnings (Per Share)

Qtr.	Dec	Mar	Jun	Sep
2009-10	0.76	0.93	0.89	0.94
2010-11	0.96	0.96	1.01	1.13
2011-12	0.86	1.09	1.14	1.06
2012-13	0.94	...	...	...

Interim Dividends (Per Share)

Amt	Decl	Ex	Rec	Pay
0.30Q	04/18/2012	05/10/2012	05/14/2012	06/04/2012
0.30Q	07/25/2012	08/09/2012	08/13/2012	09/04/2012
0.30Q	10/23/2012	11/07/2012	11/12/2012	12/03/2012
0.30Q	01/29/2013	02/07/2013	02/11/2013	03/04/2013

Indicated Div: $1.20

Valuation Analysis

Forecast EPS	$4.60 (04/06/2013)
Market Cap	$8.6 Billion
Book Value	$1.1 Billion
Price/Book	8.21
Price/Sales	1.84

Institutional Holding

No of Institutions	533
Shares	121,505,592
% Held	72.59

Business Summary: Aerospace (MIC: 7.1.1 SIC: 3728 NAIC: 336413)

Rockwell Collins is engaged in the design, production and support of communications and aviation electronics for commercial and military customers. Co. serves a worldwide customer base through two business segments: Government Systems, which provides a range of electronic products, systems and services to customers including the U.S. Department of Defense, other ministries of defense, other government agencies and defense contractors around the world; and Commercial Systems, which supplies aviation electronics systems, products and services to customers located throughout the world. Co.'s Government Systems business also provides products and systems for ground and shipboard applications.

Recent Developments: For the quarter ended Dec 31 2012, net income increased 1.5% to US$132.0 million from US$130.0 million in the year-earlier quarter. Revenues were US$1.06 billion, down 2.9% from US$1.09 billion the year before. Direct operating expenses declined 3.1% to US$750.0 million from US$774.0 million in the comparable period the year before. Indirect operating expenses decreased 1.6% to US$124.0 million from US$126.0 million in the equivalent prior-year period.

Prospects: Our evaluation of Rockwell Collins Inc. as of Apr. 7, 2013 is the result of our systematic analysis on three basic characteristics: earnings strength, relative valuation, and recent stock price movement. The company has managed to produce a neutral trend in earnings per share over the past 5 quarters and while recent estimates for the company have remained steady, COL has posted better than expected results. Based on operating earnings yield, the company is undervalued when compared to all of the companies in our coverage universe. Share price changes over the past year indicates that COL will perform poorly over the near term.

Financial Data
(US$ in Millions)

	3 Mos	09/30/2012	09/30/2011	09/30/2010	09/30/2009	09/30/2008	09/30/2007	09/30/2006
Earnings Per Share	4.23	4.15	4.06	3.52	3.73	4.16	3.45	2.73
Cash Flow Per Share	4.74	3.67	4.26	4.53	4.01	3.85	3.63	3.46
Tang Book Value Per Share	N.M.	1.32	2.84	2.61	2.09	3.79	5.32	3.30
Dividends Per Share	1.140	1.080	0.960	0.960	0.960	0.800	0.640	0.560
Dividend Payout %	26.95	26.02	23.65	27.27	25.74	19.23	18.55	20.51
Income Statement								
Total Revenue	1,062	4,726	4,806	4,665	4,470	4,769	4,415	3,863
EBITDA	231	1,101	1,033	994	1,046	1,110	984	816
Depn & Amortn	43	231	177	186	174	152	140	127
Income Before Taxes	183	846	842	792	859	945	835	681
Income Taxes	56	248	240	241	273	275	258	212
Net Income	132	609	634	561	594	678	585	477
Average Shares	140	146	156	159	159	162	169	174
Balance Sheet								
Current Assets	2,793	2,787	2,889	2,689	2,362	2,338	2,169	1,927
Total Assets	5,313	5,314	5,389	5,064	4,645	4,144	3,750	3,278
Current Liabilities	1,915	1,440	1,495	1,452	1,359	1,740	1,459	1,324
Long-Term Obligations	573	779	528	525	532	228	223	245
Total Liabilities	4,261	4,055	3,866	3,582	3,353	2,736	2,177	2,072
Stockholders' Equity	1,052	1,259	1,523	1,482	1,292	1,408	1,573	1,206
Shares Outstanding	136	142	153	156	157	158	165	167
Statistical Record								
Return on Assets %	11.66	11.35	12.13	11.56	13.52	17.13	16.65	14.86
Return on Equity %	52.92	43.66	42.20	40.45	44.00	45.36	42.10	44.48
EBITDA Margin %	21.75	23.30	21.49	21.31	23.40	23.28	22.29	21.12
Net Margin %	12.43	12.89	13.19	12.03	13.29	14.22	13.25	12.35
Asset Turnover	0.90	0.88	0.92	0.96	1.02	1.20	1.26	1.20
Current Ratio	1.46	1.94	1.93	1.85	1.74	1.34	1.49	1.46
Debt to Equity	0.54	0.62	0.35	0.35	0.41	0.16	0.14	0.20
Price Range	59.96-46.92	59.96-46.92	67.20-44.89	67.84-48.15	51.14-27.85	75.86-45.47	74.50-55.15	60.32-43.80
P/E Ratio	14.17-11.09	14.45-11.31	16.55-11.06	19.27-13.68	13.71-7.47	18.24-10.93	21.59-15.99	22.10-16.04
Average Yield %	2.12	2.01	1.62	1.69	2.47	1.31	0.97	1.09

Address: 400 Collins Road NE, Cedar Rapids, IA 52498 **Telephone:** 319-295-1000	**Web Site:** www.rockwellcollins.com **Officers:** Clayton M. Jones - Chairman, President, Chief Executive Officer Bruce M. King - Senior Vice President	**Auditors:** Deloitte & Touche LLP **Investor Contact:** 319-295-7575 **Transfer Agents:** Wells Fargo Shareowner Services, St. Paul, MN

ROCKWELL AUTOMATION, INC.

Exchange	Symbol	Price	52Wk Range	Yield	P/E
NYS	ROK	$86.35 (3/28/2013)	91.45-61.52	2.41	17.27

*7 Year Price Score 111.38 *NYSE Composite Index=100 ***12 Month Price Score 106.77**

Interim Earnings (Per Share)

Qtr.	Dec	Mar	Jun	Sep
2009-10	0.53	0.95	0.83	0.91
2010-11	1.04	1.14	1.23	1.40
2011-12	1.27	1.16	1.33	1.37
2012-13	1.14	...	...	...

Interim Dividends (Per Share)

Amt	Decl	Ex	Rec	Pay
0.47Q	06/08/2012	08/09/2012	08/13/2012	09/10/2012
0.47Q	10/31/2012	11/08/2012	11/13/2012	12/10/2012
0.47Q	02/05/2013	02/14/2013	02/19/2013	03/11/2013
0.52Q	04/03/2013	05/09/2013	05/13/2013	06/10/2013

Indicated Div: $2.08

Valuation Analysis / **Institutional Holding**

Forecast EPS	$5.55	No of Institutions
	(04/05/2013)	645
Market Cap	$12.1 Billion	Shares
Book Value	$2.0 Billion	113,045,104
Price/Book	6.13	% Held
Price/Sales	1.92	69.56

Business Summary: Electrical Equipment (MIC: 7.3.1 SIC: 3829 NAIC: 334519)

Rockwell Automation is a provider of industrial automation power, control and information applications. Co. has two operating segments: Architecture and Software, which provides control platforms, software products, and other products including rotary and linear motion control products, sensors and machine safety components; and Control Products and Solutions, which include electro-mechanical and electronic motor starters, motor and circuit protection devices, signaling devices, packaged applications such as configured drives and motor control centers, as well as services including technical support and repair, asset management, training and predictive and preventative maintenance.

Recent Developments: For the quarter ended Dec 31 2012, net income decreased 11.9% to US$161.4 million from US$183.3 million in the year-earlier quarter. Revenues were US$1.49 billion, up 1.0% from US$1.47 billion the year before. Direct operating expenses rose 3.1% to US$881.9 million from US$855.2 million in the comparable period the year before. Indirect operating expenses increased 3.8% to US$390.1 million from US$375.8 million in the equivalent prior-year period.

Prospects: Our evaluation of Rockwell Automation Inc. as of Apr. 7, 2013 is the result of our systematic analysis on three basic characteristics: earnings strength, relative valuation, and recent stock price movement. The company has managed to produce a neutral trend in earnings per share over the past 5 quarters and while recent estimates for the company have been mixed, ROK has posted results that fell short of analysts expectations. Based on operating earnings yield, the company is undervalued when compared to all of the companies in our coverage universe. Share price changes over the past year indicates that ROK will perform well over the near term.

Financial Data
(US$ in Thousands)

	3 Mos	09/30/2012	09/30/2011	09/30/2010	09/30/2009	09/30/2008	09/30/2007	09/30/2006
Earnings Per Share	5.00	5.13	4.80	3.22	1.55	3.90	9.23	3.37
Cash Flow Per Share	7.72	5.07	4.51	3.48	3.72	4.06	2.80	2.41
Tang Book Value Per Share	5.19	4.96	4.07	2.33	1.21	3.65	4.29	4.40
Dividends Per Share	1.790	1.745	1.475	1.220	1.160	1.160	1.160	0.900
Dividend Payout %	35.80	34.02	30.73	37.89	74.84	29.74	12.57	26.71
Income Statement								
Total Revenue	1,489,200	6,259,400	6,000,400	4,857,000	4,332,500	5,697,800	5,003,900	5,561,400
EBITDA	267,800	1,156,800	1,052,400	727,000	459,300	985,500	940,300	1,092,400
Depn & Amortn	35,200	138,600	131,300	127,300	134,100	136,500	117,900	153,600
Income Before Taxes	217,200	965,900	867,600	544,200	273,900	808,900	788,600	888,300
Income Taxes	55,800	228,900	170,500	103,800	56,000	231,300	219,300	263,300
Net Income	161,400	737,000	697,800	464,300	220,700	577,600	1,487,800	607,000
Average Shares	141,200	143,400	145,200	144,000	142,500	148,200	161,200	179,900
Balance Sheet								
Current Assets	3,392,600	3,387,500	3,075,100	2,586,600	2,134,800	2,436,600	2,382,000	2,188,000
Total Assets	5,711,100	5,636,500	5,284,900	4,748,300	4,305,700	4,593,600	4,545,800	4,735,400
Current Liabilities	1,487,900	1,531,600	1,329,900	1,222,300	947,200	1,303,100	1,744,500	1,293,300
Long-Term Obligations	905,000	905,000	905,000	904,900	904,700	904,400	405,700	748,200
Total Liabilities	3,743,300	3,784,800	3,536,900	3,287,900	2,989,300	2,904,800	2,803,000	2,817,200
Stockholders' Equity	1,967,800	1,851,700	1,748,000	1,460,400	1,316,400	1,688,800	1,742,800	1,918,200
Shares Outstanding	139,800	139,800	141,900	141,700	142,100	143,200	149,400	170,800
Statistical Record								
Return on Assets %	13.01	13.46	13.91	10.26	4.96	12.61	32.06	13.11
Return on Equity %	37.41	40.84	43.50	33.44	14.69	33.57	81.28	34.03
EBITDA Margin %	17.98	18.48	17.54	14.97	10.60	17.30	18.79	19.64
Net Margin %	10.84	11.77	11.63	9.56	5.09	10.14	29.73	10.91
Asset Turnover	1.14	1.14	1.20	1.07	0.97	1.24	1.08	1.20
Current Ratio	2.28	2.21	2.31	2.12	2.25	1.87	1.37	1.69
Debt to Equity	0.46	0.49	0.52	0.62	0.69	0.54	0.23	0.39
Price Range	84.55-61.52	84.55-54.55	97.84-51.54	62.83-40.28	44.51-17.73	73.27-34.99	75.52-57.45	78.55-50.72
P/E Ratio	16.91-12.30	16.48-10.63	20.38-10.74	19.51-12.51	28.72-11.44	18.79-8.97	8.18-6.22	23.31-15.05
Average Yield %	2.40	2.40	1.95	2.36	3.75	2.06	1.80	1.41

Address: 1201 South Second Street, Milwaukee, WI 53204 Telephone: 414-382-2000	Web Site: www.rockwellautomation.com Officers: Keith D. Nosbusch - Chairman, President, Chief Executive Officer Sujeet Chand - Senior Vice President, Chief Technology Officer	Auditors: Deloitte & Touche LLP Investor Contact: 414-382-8511 Transfer Agents: Computershare Investor Services, South Hackensack, NJ

ROCKWOOD HOLDINGS INC

Exchange	Symbol	Price	52Wk Range	Yield	P/E
NYS	ROC	$65.44 (3/28/2013)	65.44-41.31	N/A	13.63

*7 Year Price Score 134.06 *NYSE Composite Index=100 *12 Month Price Score 112.82

Interim Earnings (Per Share)

Qtr.	Mar	Jun	Sep	Dec
2008	0.36	1.06	(0.04)	(9.28)
2009	(0.02)	0.02	0.13	0.14
2010	0.48	0.68	0.52	1.40
2011	2.24	1.18	0.95	0.79
2012	0.94	2.81	0.77	0.27

Interim Dividends (Per Share)

No Dividends Paid

Valuation Analysis

Forecast EPS	$3.77
	(04/05/2013)
Market Cap	$5.1 Billion
Book Value	$1.7 Billion
Price/Book	3.08
Price/Sales	1.46

Institutional Holding

No of Institutions	322
Shares	84,161,920
% Held	104.28

Business Summary: Specialty Chemicals (MIC: 8.3.2 SIC: 5169 NAIC: 424690)

Rockwood Holdings is a developer, manufacturer and marketer of chemicals and materials used for industrial and commercial purposes. Co. operates in four segments: Specialty Chemicals, which includes lithium compounds and chemicals, and surface treatment chemicals; Performance Additives, which includes color pigments and services, timber treatment chemicals and clay-based additives; Titanium Dioxide Pigments, which consists of titanium dioxide pigments, and zinc- and barium-based compounds; and Advanced Ceramics, which includes ceramic-on-ceramic ball head and liner components used in hip-joint prostheses systems, ceramic cutting tools and a range of other ceramic components.

Recent Developments: For the year ended Dec 31 2012, net income decreased 11.9% to US$398.2 million from US$451.9 million in the prior year. Revenues were US$3.51 billion, down 4.4% from US$3.67 billion the year before. Operating income was US$453.3 million versus US$567.3 million in the prior year, a decrease of 20.1%. Direct operating expenses declined 1.2% to US$2.35 billion from US$2.38 billion in the comparable period the year before. Indirect operating expenses decreased 2.8% to US$701.8 million from US$722.0 million in the equivalent prior-year period.

Prospects: Our evaluation of Rockwood Holdings Inc. as of Apr. 7, 2013 is the result of our systematic analysis on three basic characteristics: earnings strength, relative valuation, and recent stock price movement. The company has generated a negative trend in earnings per share over the past 5 quarters. However, while recent estimates for the company have been mixed, ROC has posted results that fell short of analysts expectations. Based on operating earnings yield, the company is about fairly valued when compared to all of the companies in our coverage universe. Share price changes over the past year indicates that ROC will perform well over the near term.

Financial Data

(US$ in Thousands)	12/31/2012	12/31/2011	12/31/2010	12/31/2009	12/31/2008	12/31/2007	12/31/2006	12/31/2005
Earnings Per Share	4.80	5.15	3.07	0.28	(7.95)	4.16	1.37	1.52
Cash Flow Per Share	56.78	5.87	6.43	4.99	4.00	4.99	4.10	4.41
Tang Book Value Per Share	4.57	0.19	N.M.	N.M.	N.M.	N.M.	N.M.	N.M.
Dividends Per Share	1.050	...	...	...	...	...	...	...
Dividend Payout %	21.88	...	...	...	...	...	...	...
Income Statement								
Total Revenue	3,506,900	3,669,300	3,191,600	2,962,900	3,380,100	3,136,400	2,975,200	3,121,200
EBITDA	622,600	742,100	534,700	411,300	(337,900)	515,800	487,900	536,600
Depn & Amortn	193,600	189,900	179,100	201,500	179,100	145,800	139,300	156,400
Income Before Taxes	342,300	456,100	204,500	31,700	(742,100)	161,900	152,900	164,600
Income Taxes	(55,900)	124,400	(24,600)	17,200	(23,900)	66,300	72,600	71,800
Net Income	383,500	411,300	239,400	21,100	(588,400)	317,100	103,000	95,800
Average Shares	79,943	79,865	78,093	74,851	73,983	76,279	75,044	60,002
Balance Sheet								
Current Assets	2,666,500	1,535,200	1,618,600	1,346,900	1,662,300	1,462,500	1,479,900	1,124,900
Total Assets	5,973,700	4,587,600	4,724,300	4,781,700	5,177,300	5,514,900	5,219,800	4,810,100
Current Liabilities	1,081,200	840,200	1,095,800	580,200	674,800	683,400	854,500	724,400
Long-Term Obligations	2,198,100	1,437,200	1,695,300	2,434,100	2,720,300	2,474,000	2,720,900	2,730,700
Total Liabilities	4,304,600	3,213,400	3,662,300	3,929,400	4,351,700	3,941,500	4,099,300	3,975,400
Stockholders' Equity	1,669,100	1,374,200	1,062,000	852,300	825,600	1,573,400	1,120,500	834,700
Shares Outstanding	78,466	76,936	75,897	74,165	74,061	73,895	73,785	73,779
Statistical Record								
Return on Assets %	7.24	8.83	5.04	0.42	N.M.	5.91	2.05	1.88
Return on Equity %	25.13	33.77	25.01	2.52	N.M.	23.54	10.54	12.83
EBITDA Margin %	17.75	20.22	16.75	13.88	N.M.	16.45	16.40	17.19
Net Margin %	10.94	11.21	7.50	0.71	N.M.	10.11	3.46	3.07
Asset Turnover	0.66	0.79	0.67	0.60	0.63	0.58	0.59	0.61
Current Ratio	2.47	1.83	1.48	2.32	2.46	2.14	1.73	1.55
Debt to Equity	1.32	1.05	1.60	2.86	3.29	1.57	2.43	3.27
Price Range	55.92-40.52	61.12-31.79	41.80-20.65	24.26-3.96	42.25-5.87	39.48-24.31	25.89-19.30	20.25-17.80
P/E Ratio	11.65-8.44	11.87-6.17	13.62-6.73	86.64-14.14	...	9.49-5.84	18.90-14.09	13.32-11.71
Average Yield %	2.21	...	...	...	...	...	...	...

Address: 100 Overlook Center, Princeton, NJ 08540	Web Site: www.rockwoodspecialties.com	Auditors: Deloitte & Touche LLP
Telephone: 609-514-0300	Officers: Seifi Ghasemi - Chairman, Chief Executive Officer Robert J. Zatta - Senior Vice President, Chief Financial Officer, Interim Principal Accounting Officer	Investor Contact: 609-734-6430 Transfer Agents: American Stock Transfer & Trust Company, New York, NY

ROLLINS, INC.

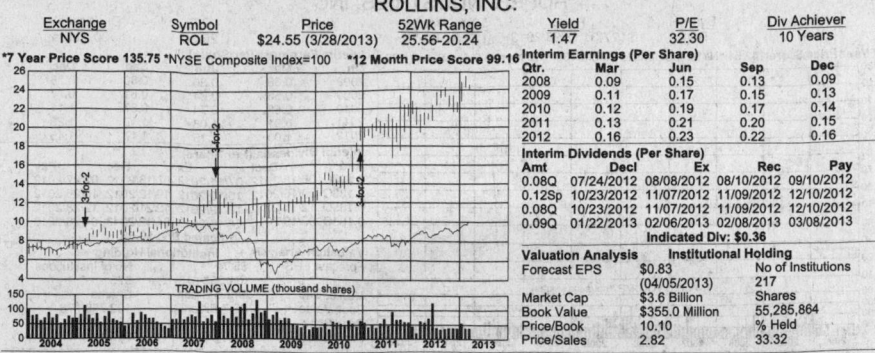

Exchange	Symbol	Price	52Wk Range	Yield	P/E	Div Achiever
NYS	ROL	$24.55 (3/28/2013)	25.56-20.24	1.47	32.30	10 Years

*7 Year Price Score 135.75 *NYSE Composite Index=100 *12 Month Price Score 99.16

Interim Earnings (Per Share)

Qtr.	Mar	Jun	Sep	Dec
2008	0.09	0.15	0.13	0.09
2009	0.11	0.17	0.15	0.13
2010	0.12	0.19	0.17	0.14
2011	0.13	0.21	0.20	0.15
2012	0.16	0.23	0.22	0.16

Interim Dividends (Per Share)

Amt	Decl	Ex	Rec	Pay
0.08Q	07/24/2012	08/08/2012	08/10/2012	09/10/2012
0.12Sp	10/23/2012	11/07/2012	11/09/2012	12/10/2012
0.08Q	10/23/2012	11/07/2012	11/09/2012	12/10/2012
0.09Q	01/22/2013	02/06/2013	02/08/2013	03/08/2013

Indicated Div: $0.36

Valuation Analysis

		Institutional Holding	
Forecast EPS	$0.83 (04/05/2013)	No of Institutions	217
Market Cap	$3.6 Billion	Shares	55,285,864
Book Value	$355.0 Million	% Held	33.32
Price/Book	10.10		
Price/Sales	2.82		

Business Summary: Business Services (MIC: 7.5.2 SIC: 7342 NAIC: 561710)

Rollins is an international service company providing pest and termite control services through its wholly-owned subsidiaries to both residential and commercial customers in North America with international franchises in Central America, the Caribbean, the Middle East, Asia, the Mediterranean, Europe and Africa. Orkin, LLC, a wholly-owned subsidiary of Co., provides pest control services and protection against termite damage, rodents and insects to homes and businesses, including hotels, food service establishments, food manufacturers, retailers and transportation companies.

Recent Developments: For the year ended Dec 31 2012, net income increased 10.5% to US$111.3 million from US$100.7 million in the prior year. Revenues were US$1.27 billion, up 5.5% from US$1.21 billion the year before. Direct operating expenses rose 5.0% to US$647.6 million from US$616.8 million in the comparable period the year before. Indirect operating expenses increased 4.3% to US$445.7 million from US$427.1 million in the equivalent prior-year period.

Prospects: Our evaluation of Rollins Inc. as of Apr. 7, 2013 is the result of our systematic analysis on three basic characteristics: earnings strength, relative valuation, and recent stock price movement. The company has managed to produce a neutral trend in earnings per share over the past 5 quarters. However, while recent estimates for the company have been mixed, ROL has posted results that fell short of analysts expectations. Based on operating earnings yield, the company is overvalued when compared to all of the companies in our coverage universe. Share price changes over the past year indicates that ROL will perform well over the near term.

Financial Data

(US$ in Thousands)	12/31/2012	12/31/2011	12/31/2010	12/31/2009	12/31/2008	12/31/2007	12/31/2006	12/31/2005
Earnings Per Share	0.76	0.69	0.61	0.56	0.46	0.43	0.37	0.34
Cash Flow Per Share	0.97	1.05	0.84	0.74	0.61	0.59	0.56	0.51
Tang Book Value Per Share	0.00	N.M.	N.M.	N.M.	N.M.	0.23	0.06	N.M.
Dividends Per Share	0.440	0.280	0.240	0.187	0.167	0.133	0.111	0.089
Dividend Payout %	57.89	40.58	39.34	33.33	36.23	31.25	29.76	26.31
Income Statement								
Total Revenue	1,270,909	1,205,064	1,136,890	1,073,958	1,020,564	894,920	858,878	802,417
EBITDA	191,868	176,716	159,957	143,129	127,920	116,024	106,652	110,652
Depn & Amortn	15,212	15,112	15,975	15,874	14,205	13,400	13,000	24,280
Income Before Taxes	176,642	161,096	143,545	126,291	112,954	104,913	95,159	87,955
Income Taxes	65,310	60,385	53,543	42,307	44,020	40,182	37,350	35,182
Net Income	111,332	100,711	90,002	83,984	68,934	64,731	57,809	52,773
Average Shares	146,306	146,946	148,231	149,623	150,121	152,113	154,971	156,987
Balance Sheet								
Current Assets	205,992	175,822	151,021	120,530	116,838	160,240	151,073	137,684
Total Assets	692,506	645,650	619,014	566,496	572,517	475,228	453,175	439,637
Current Liabilities	228,416	225,851	246,441	232,753	272,827	187,701	185,206	190,885
Long-Term Obligations	...	...	...	...	171	601	124	560
Total Liabilities	337,550	321,653	321,044	301,930	344,084	241,675	241,716	262,686
Stockholders' Equity	354,956	323,997	297,970	264,566	228,433	233,553	211,459	176,951
Shares Outstanding	146,015	146,250	147,181	148,356	150,061	150,953	152,754	153,024
Statistical Record								
Return on Assets %	16.59	15.93	15.18	14.75	13.12	13.94	12.95	12.30
Return on Equity %	32.71	32.38	32.00	34.07	29.76	29.09	29.77	30.64
EBITDA Margin %	15.10	14.66	14.07	13.33	12.53	12.96	12.42	13.79
Net Margin %	8.76	8.36	7.92	7.82	6.75	7.23	6.73	6.58
Asset Turnover	1.89	1.91	1.92	1.89	1.94	1.93	1.92	1.87
Current Ratio	0.90	0.78	0.61	0.52	0.43	0.85	0.82	0.72
Price Range	24.29-19.46	23.40-16.72	20.08-12.25	13.11-9.53	13.45-8.49	13.71-9.32	10.11-8.43	9.79-7.11
P/E Ratio	31.96-25.61	33.91-24.23	32.92-20.09	23.40-17.02	29.25-18.46	31.89-21.67	27.33-22.77	28.80-20.90
Average Yield %	1.98	1.40	1.59	1.59	1.48	1.20	1.20	1.04

Address: 2170 Piedmont Road N.E., Atlanta, GA 30324	Web Site: www.rollins.com	Auditors: Grant Thornton LLP
Telephone: 404-888-2000	Officers: R. Randall Rollins - Chairman Gary W. Rollins - Vice-Chairman, President, Chief Executive Officer, Chief Operating Officer	Investor Contact: 404-888-2000 Transfer Agents: American Stock Transfer and Trust Company, New Yor, NY

ROPER INDUSTRIES, INC

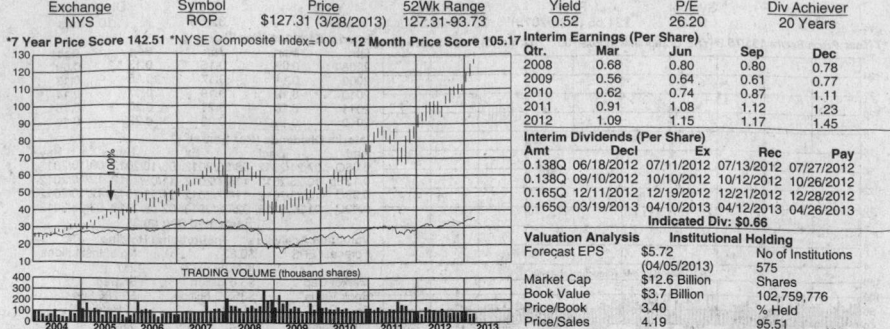

Exchange	Symbol	Price	52Wk Range	Yield	P/E	Div Achiever
NYS	ROP	$127.31 (3/28/2013)	127.31-93.73	0.52	26.20	20 Years

*7 Year Price Score 142.51 *NYSE Composite Index=100 *12 Month Price Score 105.17

Interim Earnings (Per Share)

Qtr.	Mar	Jun	Sep	Dec
2008	0.68	0.80	0.80	0.78
2009	0.56	0.64	0.61	0.77
2010	0.62	0.74	0.87	1.11
2011	0.91	1.08	1.12	1.23
2012	1.09	1.15	1.17	1.45

Interim Dividends (Per Share)

Amt	Decl	Ex	Rec	Pay
0.138Q	06/18/2012	07/11/2012	07/13/2012	07/27/2012
0.138Q	09/10/2012	10/10/2012	10/12/2012	10/26/2012
0.165Q	12/11/2012	12/19/2012	12/21/2012	12/28/2012
0.165Q	03/19/2013	04/10/2013	04/12/2013	04/26/2013

Indicated Div: $0.66

Valuation Analysis

		Institutional Holding	
Forecast EPS	$5.72 (04/05/2013)	No of Institutions	575
Market Cap	$12.6 Billion	Shares	102,759,776
Book Value	$3.7 Billion	% Held	95.51
Price/Book	3.40		
Price/Sales	4.19		

Business Summary: Electrical Equipment (MIC: 7.3.1 SIC: 3823 NAIC: 334513)

Roper Industries is engaged in designing, manufacturing and distributing radio frequency (RF) products and services, industrial technology products, energy systems and controls and medical and scientific imaging products and software. Co. markets these products and services to a range of markets including RF applications, medical, water, energy, research, education, software-as-a-service-based information networks, security and other markets. Co.'s segments include: Industrial Technology, Energy Systems and Controls, Medical & Scientific Imaging, and RF Technology.

Recent Developments: For the year ended Dec 31 2012, net income increased 13.1% to US$483.4 million from US$427.2 million in the prior year. Revenues were US$2.99 billion, up 7.0% from US$2.80 billion the year before. Operating income was US$757.6 million versus US$660.5 million in the prior year, an increase of 14.7%. Direct operating expenses rose 3.1% to US$1.32 billion from US$1.28 billion in the comparable period the year before. Indirect operating expenses increased 6.9% to US$914.1 million from US$855.0 million in the equivalent prior-year period.

Prospects: Our evaluation of Roper Industries Inc. as of Apr. 7, 2013 is the result of our systematic analysis on three basic characteristics: earnings strength, relative valuation, and recent stock price movement. The company has produced a positive trend in earnings per share over the past 5 quarters and while recent estimates for the company have been mixed, ROP has posted better than expected results. Based on operating earnings yield, the company is about fairly valued when compared to all of the companies in our coverage universe. Share price changes over the past year indicates that ROP will perform well over the near term.

Financial Data

(US$ in Thousands)	12/31/2012	12/31/2011	12/31/2010	12/31/2009	12/31/2008	12/31/2007	12/31/2006	12/31/2005
Earnings Per Share	4.86	4.34	3.34	2.58	3.06	2.68	2.13	1.74
Cash Flow Per Share	6.92	6.27	5.30	4.05	4.84	3.89	3.02	3.29
Dividends Per Share	0.715	0.440	0.380	0.330	0.290	0.260	0.235	0.212
Dividend Payout %	14.71	10.14	11.38	12.79	9.48	9.70	11.03	12.21
Income Statement								
Total Revenue	2,993,489	2,797,089	2,386,112	2,049,668	2,306,371	2,102,049	1,700,734	1,453,731
EBITDA	908,954	808,778	637,948	501,760	523,535	467,657	367,612	292,374
Depn & Amortn	154,748	140,143	123,021	103,448	33,900	31,805	29,939	28,413
Income Before Taxes	686,681	604,987	448,394	339,768	435,955	383,657	292,872	220,567
Income Taxes	203,321	177,740	125,814	100,287	149,440	133,624	99,548	67,392
Net Income	483,360	427,247	322,580	239,481	286,515	250,033	193,324	153,175
Average Shares	99,558	98,386	96,653	92,820	93,699	93,229	90,880	87,884
Balance Sheet								
Current Assets	1,245,542	1,115,473	998,091	870,745	858,307	951,137	627,495	498,207
Total Assets	7,071,104	5,319,411	5,069,524	4,327,736	3,971,538	3,453,184	2,995,359	2,522,306
Current Liabilities	1,086,210	554,196	539,645	478,011	619,208	667,530	587,649	505,625
Long-Term Obligations	1,503,107	1,015,110	1,247,703	1,040,962	1,033,689	727,489	726,881	620,958
Total Liabilities	3,383,378	2,124,321	2,318,617	1,906,246	1,967,800	1,663,378	1,508,520	1,272,518
Stockholders' Equity	3,687,726	3,195,096	2,750,907	2,421,490	2,003,738	1,789,806	1,486,839	1,249,788
Shares Outstanding	98,604	96,678	95,088	93,618	89,721	88,773	87,779	85,960
Statistical Record								
Return on Assets %	7.78	8.23	6.87	5.77	7.70	7.75	7.01	6.27
Return on Equity %	14.01	14.37	12.47	10.82	15.06	15.26	14.13	12.96
EBITDA Margin %	30.36	28.91	26.74	24.48	22.70	22.25	21.61	20.11
Net Margin %	16.15	15.27	13.52	11.68	12.42	11.89	11.37	10.54
Asset Turnover	0.48	0.54	0.51	0.49	0.62	0.65	0.62	0.59
Current Ratio	1.15	2.01	1.85	1.82	1.39	1.42	1.07	0.99
Debt to Equity	0.41	0.32	0.45	0.43	0.52	0.41	0.49	0.50
Price Range	113.14-88.02	88.45-65.91	78.43-50.08	55.04-36.96	67.70-35.19	70.81-48.61	51.31-38.46	40.71-28.39
P/E Ratio	23.28-18.11	20.38-15.19	23.48-14.99	21.33-14.33	22.12-11.50	26.42-18.14	24.09-18.06	23.40-16.31
Average Yield %	0.70	0.55	0.62	0.71	0.52	0.44	0.51	0.60

Address: 6901 Professional Parkway East, Suite 200, Sarasota, FL 34240	**Web Site:** www.roperind.com	**Auditors:** PricewaterhouseCoopers LLP
Telephone: 941-556-2601	**Officers:** Brian D. Jellison - Chairman, President, Chief Executive Officer John M. Humphrey - Vice President, Chief Financial Officer	**Investor Contact:** 941-556-2601
		Transfer Agents: American Stock Transfer & Trust Company, New York, NY

ROWAN COMPANIES PLC

Exchange	Symbol	Price	52Wk Range	Yield	P/E
NYS	RDC	$35.36 (3/28/2013)	37.32-28.99	N/A	24.22

*7 Year Price Score 92.80 *NYSE Composite Index=100 *12 Month Price Score 96.43

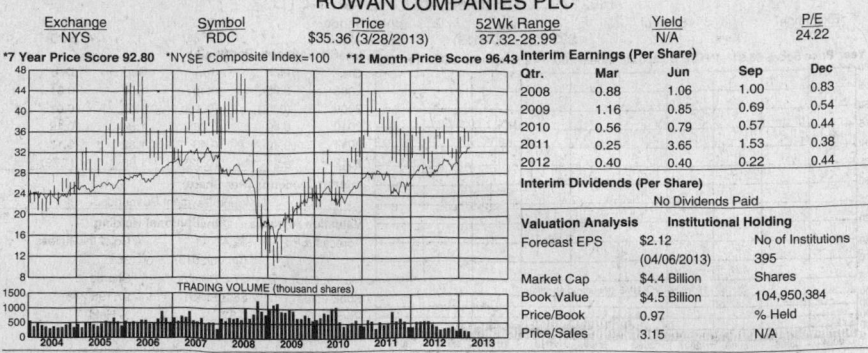

Interim Earnings (Per Share)

Qtr.	Mar	Jun	Sep	Dec
2008	0.88	1.06	1.00	0.83
2009	1.16	0.85	0.69	0.54
2010	0.56	0.79	0.57	0.44
2011	0.25	3.65	1.53	0.38
2012	0.40	0.40	0.22	0.44

Interim Dividends (Per Share)

No Dividends Paid

Valuation Analysis   **Institutional Holding**

Forecast EPS	$2.12	No of Institutions
	(04/06/2013)	395
Market Cap	$4.4 Billion	Shares
Book Value	$4.5 Billion	104,950,384
Price/Book	0.97	% Held
Price/Sales	3.15	N/A

Business Summary: Production & Extraction (MIC: 9.1.1 SIC: 1381 NAIC: 213111)

Rowan Companies is a provider of international and domestic offshore contract drilling services. Co. provides offshore contract drilling services utilizing a fleet of 31 self-elevating mobile offshore drilling platforms (jack-up rigs). Co. operates jack-up rigs capable of drilling depths up to 35,000 feet in maximum water depths ranging from 250 feet to 550 feet, depending on rig size and location. Co. conducts offshore drilling operations in various markets throughout the world. Co. has rigs in the Middle East, the U.S. Gulf of Mexico, the North Sea, Trinidad, Malaysia and Vietnam.

Recent Developments: For the year ended Dec 31 2012, net income decreased 75.5% to US$180.6 million from US$736.8 million in the prior year. Revenues were US$1.39 billion, up 48.3% from US$939.2 million the year before. Operating income was US$255.1 million versus US$149.6 million in the prior year, an increase of 70.5%. Direct operating expenses rose 48.0% to US$752.2 million from US$508.1 million in the comparable period the year before. Indirect operating expenses increased 36.9% to US$385.4 million from US$281.6 million in the equivalent prior-year period.

Prospects: Our evaluation of Rowan Cos. Plc as of Apr. 7, 2013 is the result of our systematic analysis on three basic characteristics: earnings strength, relative valuation, and recent stock price movement. The company has produced a positive trend in earnings per share over the past 5 quarters. However, while recent estimates for the company have been lowered by analysts, RDC has posted results that fell short of analysts expectations. Based on operating earnings yield, the company is undervalued when compared to all of the companies in our coverage universe. Share price changes over the past year indicates that RDC will perform well over the near term.

Financial Data
(US$ in Thousands)

	12/31/2012	12/31/2011	12/31/2010	12/31/2009	12/31/2008	12/31/2007	12/31/2006	12/31/2005
Earnings Per Share	1.46	5.83	2.36	3.24	3.77	4.31	2.85	2.08
Cash Flow Per Share	3.19	0.76	4.34	4.79	6.15	3.90	2.65	3.06
Tang Book Value Per Share	36.48	35.01	29.71	27.32	23.53	21.11	16.97	14.75
Dividends Per Share	...	...	...	...	0.100	0.100	0.250	0.250
Dividend Payout %	...	...	...	...	2.65	2.32	8.77	12.02
Income Statement								
Total Revenue	1,392,607	939,229	1,819,207	1,770,180	2,212,736	2,095,021	1,510,734	1,068,782
EBITDA	481,342	354,293	588,951	679,324	790,389	852,895	575,867	431,917
Depn & Amortn	247,900	204,872	186,563	171,445	141,395	118,796	89,971	81,291
Income Before Taxes	183,470	130,080	379,017	501,091	654,091	739,086	493,354	345,470
Income Taxes	(19,829)	(5,659)	99,022	133,587	226,463	255,286	176,377	127,633
Net Income	180,602	736,841	279,995	367,504	427,628	483,800	318,246	229,800
Average Shares	123,872	126,393	118,818	113,584	113,346	112,265	111,775	110,304
Balance Sheet								
Current Assets	1,552,550	821,715	1,324,769	1,549,797	1,369,187	1,302,967	1,102,849	1,208,132
Total Assets	7,699,487	6,597,845	6,217,457	5,210,694	4,548,892	3,875,305	3,435,398	2,975,183
Current Liabilities	294,094	348,371	529,230	568,272	744,642	495,589	516,706	340,613
Long-Term Obligations	2,009,598	1,089,335	1,133,745	787,490	355,560	420,482	485,404	550,326
Total Liabilities	3,167,763	2,271,858	2,465,147	2,100,324	1,889,076	1,526,867	1,561,352	1,355,444
Stockholders' Equity	4,531,724	4,325,987	3,752,310	3,110,370	2,659,816	2,348,438	1,874,046	1,619,739
Shares Outstanding	124,211	123,581	126,294	113,833	113,035	111,263	110,461	109,776
Statistical Record								
Return on Assets %	2.52	11.50	4.90	7.53	10.12	13.24	9.93	8.41
Return on Equity %	4.07	18.24	8.16	12.74	17.03	22.92	18.22	15.18
EBITDA Margin %	34.56	37.72	32.37	38.38	35.72	40.71	38.12	40.41
Net Margin %	12.97	78.45	15.39	20.76	19.33	23.09	21.07	21.50
Asset Turnover	0.19	0.15	0.32	0.36	0.52	0.57	0.47	0.39
Current Ratio	5.28	2.36	2.50	2.73	1.84	2.63	2.13	3.55
Debt to Equity	0.44	0.25	0.30	0.25	0.13	0.18	0.26	0.34
Price Range	38.78-28.99	44.19-29.12	34.91-21.48	27.31-10.33	47.34-12.10	45.70-29.72	47.95-29.64	38.88-24.83
P/E Ratio	26.56-19.86	7.58-4.99	14.79-9.10	8.43-3.19	12.56-3.21	10.60-6.90	16.82-10.40	18.69-11.94
Average Yield %					0.30	0.27	0.67	0.79

Address: 2800 Post Oak Boulevard, Suite 5450, Houston, TX 77056-6189 **Telephone:** 713-621-7800 **Fax:** 713-960-7660	**Web Site:** www.rowancompanies.com **Officers:** Henry E. Lentz - Chairman Thomas Peter Burke - President, Chief Operating Officer	**Auditors:** Deloitte & Touche LLP **Investor Contact:** 713-960-7517 **Transfer Agents:** Computershare Trust Company, N.A., Providence

ROYAL CARIBBEAN CRUISES LTD.

Exchange	Symbol	Price	52Wk Range	Yield	P/E
NYS	RCL	$33.22 (3/28/2013)	38.42-22.46	N/A	415.25

*7 Year Price Score 86.91 *NYSE Composite Index=100 ***12 Month Price Score 104.41**

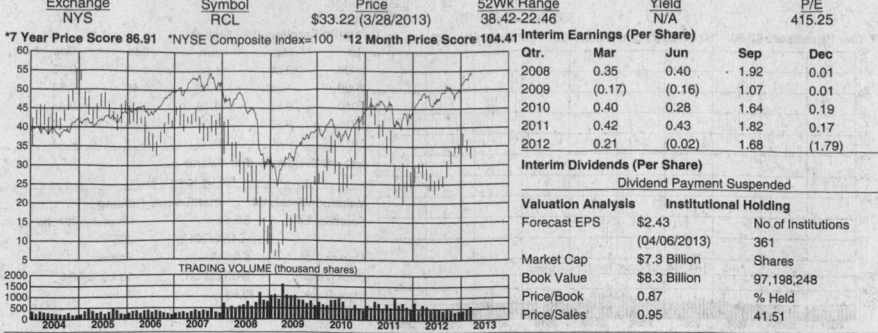

Interim Earnings (Per Share)

Qtr.	Mar	Jun	Sep	Dec
2008	0.35	0.40	1.92	0.01
2009	(0.17)	(0.16)	1.07	0.01
2010	0.40	0.28	1.64	0.19
2011	0.42	0.43	1.82	0.17
2012	0.21	(0.02)	1.68	(1.79)

Interim Dividends (Per Share)

Dividend Payment Suspended

Valuation Analysis   **Institutional Holding**

Forecast EPS	$2.43	No of Institutions
	(04/06/2013)	361
Market Cap	$7.3 Billion	Shares
Book Value	$8.3 Billion	97,198,248
Price/Book	0.87	% Held
Price/Sales	0.95	41.51

Business Summary: Hotels, Restaurants & Travel (MIC: 2.2.1 SIC: 4489 NAIC: 487210)

Royal Caribbean Cruises is a global cruise company. Co. owns five cruise brands which include, Royal Caribbean International, Celebrity Cruises, Pullmantur, Azamara Club Cruises, and CDF Croisieres de France. Co.'s ships operate on a range of worldwide itineraries that call on approximately 460 destinations. As of Dec 31 2011, Co. operated 39 ships with approx. 92,650 berths. Co.'s cruise brands provide an array of onboard services, amenities and activities including swimming pools, spa facilities, gaming facilities, lounges, bars, entertainment, retail shopping, libraries, recreational areas, cinemas, internet services and cafes, and shore excursions, among others.

Recent Developments: For the year ended Dec 31 2012, net income decreased 97.0% to US$18.3 million in the prior year. Revenues were US$7.69 billion, up 2.0% from US$7.54 billion the year before. Operating income was US$403.1 million versus US$931.6 million in the prior year, a decrease of 56.7%. Direct operating expenses rose 4.3% to US$5.16 billion from US$4.94 billion in the comparable period the year before. Indirect operating expenses increased 27.9% to US$2.13 billion from US$1.66 billion in the equivalent prior-year period.

Prospects: Our evaluation of Royal Caribbean Cruises Ltd. as of Apr. 7, 2013 is the result of our systematic analysis on three basic characteristics: earnings strength, relative valuation, and recent stock price movement. The company has enjoyed a very positive trend in earnings per share over the past 5 quarters. However, while recent estimates for the company have been lowered by analysts, RCL has posted better than expected results. Based on operating earnings yield, the company is undervalued when compared to all of the companies in our coverage universe. Share price changes over the past year indicates that RCL will perform very well over the near term.

Financial Data

(US$ in Thousands)	12/31/2012	12/31/2011	12/31/2010	12/31/2009	12/31/2008	12/31/2007	12/31/2006	12/31/2005
Earnings Per Share	0.08	2.77	2.51	0.75	2.68	2.82	2.94	3.26
Cash Flow Per Share	6.32	6.71	7.73	3.95	5.00	5.96	4.50	5.39
Tang Book Value Per Share	36.00	35.30	33.27	31.35	28.30	28.05	25.39	25.06
Dividends Per Share	...	...	...	...	0.450	0.150	...	...
Dividend Payout %	...	...	...	...	16.79	5.32	...	...
Income Statement								
Total Revenue	7,688,024	7,537,263	6,752,504	5,889,826	6,532,525	6,149,139	5,229,584	4,903,174
EBITDA	1,083,234	1,666,945	1,521,333	1,023,631	1,407,271	1,400,230	1,308,190	1,326,155
Depn & Amortn	730,493	702,426	643,716	568,214	520,353	483,066	421,645	402,069
Income Before Taxes	18,287	607,421	547,467	162,421	573,722	603,405	633,922	663,465
Net Income	18,287	607,421	547,467	162,421	573,722	603,405	633,922	715,956
Average Shares	219,457	219,229	217,711	215,295	214,195	214,255	221,485	234,714
Balance Sheet								
Current Assets	888,060	969,288	1,015,071	1,026,391	977,337	992,791	501,904	377,010
Total Assets	19,827,930	19,804,405	19,694,904	18,233,494	16,463,310	14,982,281	13,393,088	11,255,771
Current Liabilities	4,066,151	3,067,642	3,444,498	2,749,020	2,674,225	2,339,295	1,872,368	1,988,782
Long-Term Obligations	6,970,464	7,856,962	7,951,187	7,663,555	6,539,510	5,346,547	5,040,322	3,553,892
Total Liabilities	11,519,181	11,396,582	11,752,402	10,733,777	9,660,298	8,224,938	7,301,513	5,701,306
Stockholders' Equity	8,308,749	8,407,823	7,942,502	7,499,717	6,803,012	6,757,343	6,091,575	5,554,465
Shares Outstanding	218,771	217,057	215,903	213,949	212,822	212,482	211,503	210,361
Statistical Record								
Return on Assets %	0.09	3.08	2.89	0.94	3.64	4.25	5.14	6.17
Return on Equity %	0.22	7.43	7.09	2.27	8.44	9.39	10.89	13.82
EBITDA Margin %	14.09	22.12	22.53	17.38	21.54	22.77	25.02	27.05
Net Margin %	0.24	8.06	8.11	2.76	8.78	9.81	12.12	14.60
Asset Turnover	0.39	0.38	0.36	0.34	0.41	0.43	0.42	0.42
Current Ratio	0.22	0.32	0.29	0.37	0.37	0.42	0.27	0.19
Debt to Equity	0.84	0.93	1.00	1.02	0.96	0.79	0.83	0.64
Price Range	35.53-22.46	49.96-20.01	47.00-22.77	26.89-5.50	42.44-6.64	45.84-36.17	46.61-32.60	54.85-39.36
P/E Ratio	444.13-280.75	18.04-7.22	18.73-9.07	35.85-7.33	15.84-2.48	16.26-12.83	15.85-11.09	16.83-12.07
Average Yield %	...	...	...	...	1.73	0.36	...	...

Address: 1050 Caribbean Way, Miami, FL 33132 **Telephone:** 305-539-6000	**Web Site:** www.royalcaribbean.com **Officers:** Richard D. Fain - Chairman, Chief Executive Officer Brian J. Rice - Executive Vice President, Chief Financial Officer	**Auditors:** PricewaterhouseCoopers LLP **Investor Contact:** 305-982-2625 **Transfer Agents:** American Stock Transfer and Trust Company, Brooklyn, NY

RPC, INC.

Exchange	Symbol	Price	52Wk Range	Yield	P/E
NYS	RES	$15.17 (3/28/2013)	17.24-8.96	2.64	11.94

*7 Year Price Score 133.89 *NYSE Composite Index=100 ***12 Month Price Score 117.00**

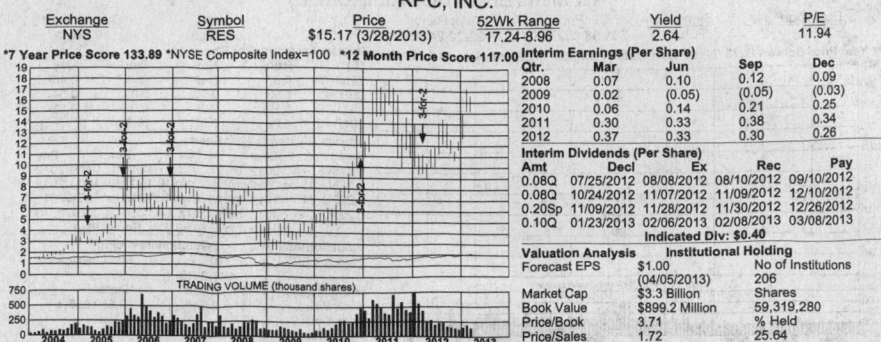

Interim Earnings (Per Share)

Qtr.	Mar	Jun	Sep	Dec
2008	0.07	0.10	0.12	0.09
2009	0.02	(0.05)	(0.05)	(0.03)
2010	0.06	0.14	0.21	0.25
2011	0.30	0.33	0.38	0.34
2012	0.37	0.33	0.30	0.26

Interim Dividends (Per Share)

Amt	Decl	Ex	Rec	Pay
0.08Q	07/25/2012	08/08/2012	08/10/2012	09/10/2012
0.08Q	10/24/2012	11/07/2012	11/09/2012	12/10/2012
0.20Sp	11/09/2012	11/28/2012	11/30/2012	12/26/2012
0.10Q	01/23/2013	02/06/2013	02/08/2013	03/08/2013

Indicated Div: $0.40

Valuation Analysis | **Institutional Holding**

Forecast EPS	$1.00 (04/05/2013)	No of Institutions	206
Market Cap	$3.3 Billion	Shares	59,319,280
Book Value	$899.2 Million	% Held	25.64
Price/Book	3.71		
Price/Sales	1.72		

Business Summary: Equipment & Services (MIC: 9.1.3 SIC: 1389 NAIC: 213112)

RPC is a holding company. Co. provides a range of oilfield services and equipment primarily to independent and major oil and gas companies engaged in the exploration, production and development of oil and gas properties throughout the U.S., including the southwest, mid-continent, Gulf of Mexico, Rocky Mountain and Appalachian regions, and in selected international markets. The services and equipment provided include pressure pumping services, downhole tool services, coiled tubing services, snubbing services, nitrogen services, the rental of drill pipe and other oilfield equipment, and well control. Co. has two reportable business segments, Technical Services and Support Services.

Recent Developments: For the year ended Dec 31 2012, net income decreased 7.4% to US$274.4 million from US$296.4 million in the prior year. Revenues were US$1.95 billion, up 7.5% from US$1.81 billion the year before. Operating income was US$442.4 million versus US$482.1 million in the prior year, a decrease of 8.2%. Direct operating expenses rose 11.4% to US$1.11 billion from US$992.7 million in the comparable period the year before. Indirect operating expenses increased 18.4% to US$396.7 million from US$335.0 million in the equivalent prior-year period.

Prospects: Our evaluation of RPC Inc. as of Apr. 7, 2013 is the result of our systematic analysis on three basic characteristics: earnings strength, relative valuation, and recent stock price movement. The company has generated a negative trend in earnings per share over the past 5 quarters. However, while recent estimates for the company have been lowered by analysts, RES has posted better than expected results. Based on operating earnings yield, the company is undervalued when compared to all of the companies in our coverage universe. Share price changes over the past year indicates that RES will perform very well over the near term.

Financial Data

(US$ in Thousands)	12/31/2012	12/31/2011	12/31/2010	12/31/2009	12/31/2008	12/31/2007	12/31/2006	12/31/2005
Earnings Per Share	1.27	1.35	0.67	(0.11)	0.38	0.40	0.50	0.30
Cash Flow Per Share	2.59	1.77	0.78	0.78	0.81	0.65	0.55	0.31
Tang Book Value Per Share	3.98	3.34	2.32	1.74	1.93	1.75	1.42	0.96
Dividends Per Share	0.520	0.213	0.093	0.098	0.107	0.089	0.059	0.032
Dividend Payout %	40.94	15.84	14.00	...	28.23	22.48	11.80	10.56
Income Statement								
Total Revenue	1,945,023	1,809,807	1,096,384	587,863	876,977	690,226	596,630	427,643
EBITDA	659,465	662,150	373,548	99,130	261,394	222,443	225,583	138,890
Depn & Amortn	214,900	179,900	133,400	130,600	118,400	78,500	46,698	39,100
Income Before Taxes	442,619	478,815	237,532	(33,499)	137,785	139,834	178,848	100,740
Income Taxes	168,183	182,434	90,790	(10,754)	54,382	52,785	68,054	34,256
Net Income	274,436	296,381	146,742	(22,745)	83,403	87,049	110,794	66,484
Average Shares	216,796	220,249	219,805	216,686	220,196	221,314	220,941	221,646
Balance Sheet								
Current Assets	567,827	626,555	398,678	219,454	292,823	235,060	182,254	142,843
Total Assets	1,367,163	1,338,211	887,871	649,043	793,461	701,015	474,307	311,785
Current Liabilities	164,511	179,466	117,504	67,773	92,329	90,722	70,952	49,955
Long-Term Obligations	107,000	203,300	121,250	90,300	174,450	156,400	35,600	...
Total Liabilities	467,931	575,619	348,976	239,320	344,377	291,743	139,020	79,284
Stockholders' Equity	899,232	762,592	538,895	409,723	449,084	409,272	335,287	232,501
Shares Outstanding	220,144	221,187	222,263	221,320	219,836	220,588	218,730	217,527
Statistical Record								
Return on Assets %	20.23	26.63	19.10	N.M.	11.13	14.81	28.19	23.14
Return on Equity %	32.94	45.54	30.94	N.M.	19.38	23.38	39.03	32.12
EBITDA Margin %	33.91	36.59	34.07	16.86	29.81	32.23	37.81	32.48
Net Margin %	14.11	16.38	13.38	N.M.	9.51	12.61	18.57	15.55
Asset Turnover	1.43	1.63	1.43	0.82	1.17	1.17	1.52	1.49
Current Ratio	3.45	3.49	3.39	3.24	3.17	2.59	2.57	2.86
Debt to Equity	0.12	0.27	0.22	0.22	0.39	0.38	0.11	...
Price Range	14.45-8.96	18.03-10.08	14.41-4.62	5.22-2.35	8.30-2.70	8.33-4.79	10.53-5.11	7.87-2.63
P/E Ratio	11.38-7.06	13.36-7.47	21.51-6.90	...	21.84-7.10	20.83-11.97	21.07-10.21	26.22-8.76
Average Yield %	4.56	1.51	1.23	2.46	1.81	1.35	0.86	0.77

Address: 2801 Buford Highway, Suite 520, Atlanta, GA 30329 Telephone: 404-321-2140 Fax: 404-321-2722	Web Site: www.rpc.net Officers: R. Randall Rollins - Chairman Richard A. Hubbell - President, Chief Executive Officer	Auditors: Grant Thornton LLP Investor Contact: 404-321-2172 Transfer Agents: American Stock Transfer & Trust Company, Brooklyn, NY

RPM INTERNATIONAL INC (DE)

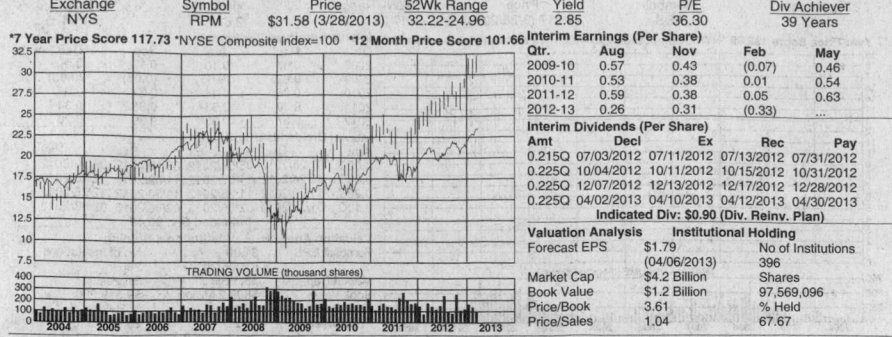

Exchange	Symbol	Price	52Wk Range	Yield	P/E	Div Achiever
NYS	RPM	$31.58 (3/28/2013)	32.22-24.96	2.85	36.30	39 Years

*7 Year Price Score 117.73 *NYSE Composite Index=100 *12 Month Price Score 101.66

Interim Earnings (Per Share)

Qtr.	Aug	Nov	Feb	May
2009-10	0.57	0.43	(0.07)	0.46
2010-11	0.53	0.38	0.01	0.54
2011-12	0.59	0.38	0.05	0.63
2012-13	0.26	0.31	(0.33)	...

Interim Dividends (Per Share)

Amt	Decl	Ex	Rec	Pay
0.215Q	07/03/2012	07/11/2012	07/13/2012	07/31/2012
0.225Q	10/04/2012	10/11/2012	10/15/2012	10/31/2012
0.225Q	12/07/2012	12/13/2012	12/17/2012	12/28/2012
0.225Q	04/02/2013	04/10/2013	04/12/2013	04/30/2013

Indicated Div: $0.90 (Div. Reinv. Plan)

Valuation Analysis

		Institutional Holding	
Forecast EPS	$1.79 (04/06/2013)	No of Institutions	396
Market Cap	$4.2 Billion	Shares	97,569,096
Book Value	$1.2 Billion	% Held	67.67
Price/Book	3.61		
Price/Sales	1.04		

Business Summary: Specialty Chemicals (MIC: 8.3.2 SIC: 2851 NAIC: 325510)

RPM International, through its subsidiaries, manufactures, markets and sells various specialty chemical product lines, including specialty paints, protective coatings, roofing systems, sealants and adhesives, for the industrial and consumer markets. Co. has two segments: the industrial segment (RPM Building Solutions Group, RPM Performance Coatings Group and RPM2 Group), which includes maintenance and protection products for roofing and waterproofing systems, flooring, corrosion control and other applications; and the consumer segment (Rust-Oleum Group and DAP Group), which includes rust-preventative, decorative paints, caulks, sealants, primers and other branded consumer products.

Recent Developments: For the quarter ended Feb 28 2013, net loss amounted to o42.2 million versus net income of US$7.9 million in the year-earlier quarter. Revenues were o843.7 million, up 9.1% from US$773.6 million the year before. Direct operating expenses rose 6.3% to o500.2 million from US$470.4 million in the comparable period the year before. Indirect operating expenses increased 39.7% to o387.5 million from US$277.5 million in the equivalent prior-year period.

Prospects: Our evaluation of RPM Inc. as of Apr. 7, 2013 is the result of our systematic analysis on three basic characteristics: earnings strength, relative valuation, and recent stock price movement. The company has managed to produce a neutral trend in earnings per share over the past 5 quarters. However, while recent estimates for the company have been mixed, RPM has posted better than expected results. Based on operating earnings yield, the company is undervalued when compared to all of the companies in our coverage universe. Share price changes over the past year indicates that RPM will perform well over the near term.

Financial Data

(US$ in Thousands)	9 Mos	6 Mos	3 Mos	05/31/2012	05/31/2011	05/31/2010	05/31/2009	05/31/2008
Earnings Per Share	0.87	1.25	1.32	1.65	1.45	1.39	0.93	0.39
Cash Flow Per Share	2.42	2.42	2.37	2.30	1.87	1.61	2.11	1.95
Tang Book Value Per Share	N.M.	N.M.	N.M.	N.M.	0.91	0.06	N.M.	N.M.
Dividends Per Share	0.880	0.870	0.860	0.855	0.835	0.815	0.790	0.745
Dividend Payout %	101.15	69.60	65.15	51.82	57.59	58.63	84.95	191.03
Income Statement								
Total Revenue	2,907,876	2,064,140	1,046,714	3,777,416	3,381,841	3,412,716	3,368,167	3,643,791
EBITDA	235,875	259,281	139,088	460,563	427,807	407,715	314,272	168,856
Depn & Amortn	62,542	40,926	19,358	73,339	72,385	84,023	84,879	82,838
Income Before Taxes	120,568	183,917	103,595	320,210	295,053	268,454	180,868	39,054
Income Taxes	38,519	59,150	34,195	94,526	91,885	87,327	61,252	(8,655)
Net Income	33,225	75,581	33,913	215,936	189,058	180,037	119,616	47,709
Average Shares	129,013	129,700	129,570	128,717	128,066	127,731	128,255	130,539
Balance Sheet								
Current Assets	1,751,459	1,798,540	1,794,861	1,811,337	1,867,970	1,448,736	1,552,916	1,783,975
Total Assets	3,922,921	3,965,570	3,671,807	3,560,020	3,515,029	3,004,024	3,409,921	3,763,567
Current Liabilities	730,956	698,609	706,322	759,792	735,289	631,494	849,162	846,361
Long-Term Obligations	1,392,381	1,413,101	1,199,513	1,112,952	1,106,304	924,308	762,295	1,066,687
Total Liabilities	2,763,939	2,722,618	2,445,567	2,376,364	2,251,865	1,924,551	2,266,250	2,627,011
Stockholders' Equity	1,158,982	1,242,952	1,226,240	1,183,656	1,263,164	1,079,473	1,143,671	1,136,556
Shares Outstanding	132,506	132,347	132,013	131,555	130,580	129,918	128,501	122,189
Statistical Record								
Return on Assets %	3.16	4.45	4.81	6.09	5.80	5.61	3.33	1.34
Return on Equity %	9.54	13.19	13.68	17.60	16.14	16.20	10.49	4.28
EBITDA Margin %	8.11	12.56	13.29	12.19	12.65	11.95	9.33	4.63
Net Margin %	1.14	3.66	3.24	5.72	5.59	5.28	3.55	1.31
Asset Turnover	1.09	1.07	1.07	1.06	1.04	1.06	0.94	1.02
Current Ratio	2.40	2.57	2.54	2.38	2.54	2.29	1.83	2.11
Debt to Equity	1.20	1.14	0.98	0.94	0.88	0.86	0.67	0.94
Price Range	31.96-23.79	29.18-22.85	28.01-17.53	26.93-17.40	25.22-16.37	22.69-13.28	25.07-9.24	24.63-17.92
P/E Ratio	36.74-27.34	23.34-18.28	21.22-13.28	16.32-10.55	17.39-11.29	16.32-9.55	26.96-9.94	63.15-45.95
Average Yield %	3.20	3.33	3.53	3.72	3.98	4.38	4.94	3.41

Address: 2628 Pearl Road, Medina, OH 44258	**Web Site:** www.rpminc.com	**Auditors:** Ernst & Young LLP
Telephone: 330-273-5090	**Officers:** Frank C. Sullivan - Chairman, Chief Executive Officer Ronald A. Rice - President, Chief Operating Officer	**Investor Contact:** 800-776-4488
Fax: 330-225-8743		**Transfer Agents:** Wells Fargo Shareowner Services, St. Paul, MN

RUBY TUESDAY, INC.

Exchange	Symbol	Price	52Wk Range	Yield	P/E
NYS	RT	$7.37 (3/28/2013)	9.06-5.68	N/A	N/A

*7 Year Price Score 53.13   *NYSE Composite Index=100   *12 Month Price Score 93.34

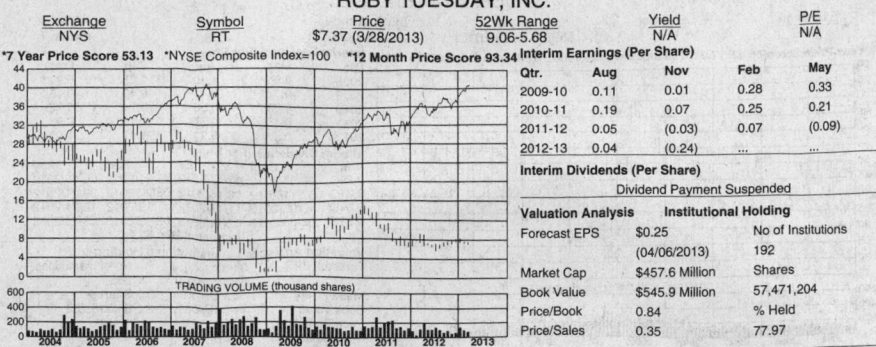

Interim Earnings (Per Share)

Qtr.	Aug	Nov	Feb	May
2009-10	0.11	0.01	0.28	0.33
2010-11	0.19	0.07	0.25	0.21
2011-12	0.05	(0.03)	0.07	(0.09)
2012-13	0.04	(0.24)	...	...

Interim Dividends (Per Share)

Dividend Payment Suspended

Valuation Analysis   **Institutional Holding**

Forecast EPS	$0.25	No of Institutions
	(04/06/2013)	192
Market Cap	$457.6 Million	Shares
Book Value	$545.9 Million	57,471,204
Price/Book	0.84	% Held
Price/Sales	0.35	77.97

Business Summary: Hotels, Restaurants & Travel (MIC: 2.2.1 SIC: 5812 NAIC: 722110)

Ruby Tuesday owns, operates and franchises the Ruby Tuesday concept in the bar and grill segment of casual dining. Ruby Tuesday restaurants serve American food with a variety of steaks, chicken, crab cakes, lobster, salmon, tilapia, fork-tender ribs, appetizers, handcrafted burgers, and others. Burger choices include such items as beef, turkey, and chicken. Co. also provides its RubyTueGo® curbside service and a delivered-meals catering program for businesses, organizations, and group events at both Co.-owned and franchised restaurants. As of June 5 2012, Co. owned and operated 714 restaurants located in 38 states and the District of Columbia.

Recent Developments: For the quarter ended Dec 4 2012, net loss amounted to US$15.1 million versus a net loss of US$2.0 million in the year-earlier quarter. Revenues were US$304.2 million, down 1.0% from US$307.4 million the year before. Direct operating expenses declined 3.1% to US$254.1 million from US$262.2 million in the comparable period the year before. Indirect operating expenses increased 68.0% to US$78.9 million from US$47.0 million in the equivalent prior-year period.

Prospects: Our evaluation of Ruby Tuesday Inc. as of Apr. 7, 2013 is the result of our systematic analysis on three basic characteristics: earnings strength, relative valuation, and recent stock price movement. The company has managed to produce a neutral trend in earnings per share over the past 5 quarters. However, while recent estimates for the company have been mixed, RT has posted results that fell short of analysts expectations. Based on operating earnings yield, the company is overvalued when compared to all of the companies in our coverage universe. Share price changes over the past year indicates that RT will perform poorly over the near term.

Financial Data

(US$ in Thousands)	6 Mos	3 Mos	06/05/2012	05/31/2011	06/01/2010	06/02/2009	06/03/2008	06/05/2007
Earnings Per Share	(0.22)	(0.01)	...	0.72	0.73	(0.35)	0.51	1.59
Cash Flow Per Share	1.22	1.63	1.76	1.82	2.29	2.00	1.98	3.24
Tang Book Value Per Share	8.65	8.91	8.87	8.85	8.34	7.88	7.82	7.93
Dividends Per Share	...	...	...	...	...	...	0.250	0.500
Dividend Payout %	...	...	...	...	...	...	49.02	31.45
Income Statement								
Total Revenue	637,154	332,921	1,325,836	1,265,162	1,194,796	1,248,556	1,360,304	1,410,227
EBITDA	17,327	23,149	72,293	128,756	75,093	(8,214)	59,302	154,128
Depn & Amortn	31,872	16,088	67,611	64,355	652	726	716	437
Income Before Taxes	(28,516)	271	(14,938)	52,048	58,086	(42,880)	27,234	133,726
Income Taxes	(16,047)	(2,328)	(14,750)	5,744	12,414	(24,948)	(2,678)	40,730
Net Income	(12,469)	2,599	(188)	46,878	45,344	(17,918)	26,377	91,668
Average Shares	62,005	62,956	62,916	64,948	61,870	51,395	51,688	57,633
Balance Sheet								
Current Assets	120,600	156,377	128,268	83,366	76,310	92,973	104,909	100,446
Total Assets	1,109,140	1,175,509	1,173,537	1,187,026	1,064,029	1,124,196	1,271,937	1,229,856
Current Liabilities	123,435	137,189	132,224	119,324	114,781	113,999	115,153	123,758
Long-Term Obligations	298,709	310,634	314,209	329,184	276,490	476,566	588,142	512,559
Total Liabilities	563,219	598,030	597,313	595,313	525,929	707,830	840,419	790,530
Stockholders' Equity	545,921	577,479	576,224	591,713	538,100	416,366	431,518	439,326
Shares Outstanding	62,095	63,828	64,038	65,098	64,492	52,806	52,772	53,240
Statistical Record								
Return on Assets %	N.M.	N.M.	N.M.	4.18	4.16	N.M.	2.11	7.66
Return on Equity %	N.M.	N.M.	N.M.	8.32	9.53	N.M.	6.07	19.02
EBITDA Margin %	2.72	6.95	5.45	10.18	6.29	N.M.	4.36	10.93
Net Margin %	N.M.	0.78	N.M.	3.71	3.80	N.M.	1.94	6.50
Asset Turnover	1.16	1.13	1.11	1.13	1.10	1.05	1.09	1.18
Current Ratio	0.98	1.14	0.97	0.70	0.66	0.82	0.91	0.81
Debt to Equity	0.55	0.54	0.55	0.56	0.51	1.14	1.36	1.17
Price Range	9.21-5.68	9.21-5.68	11.23-6.48	14.84-7.66	12.38-6.05	8.40-0.91	27.15-5.74	30.75-21.39
P/E Ratio	...	...	N.M.	20.61-10.64	16.96-8.29	...	53.24-11.25	19.34-13.45
Average Yield %	...	...	...	...	...	...	1.72	1.85

Address: 150 West Church Avenue, Maryville, TN 37801 **Telephone:** 865-379-5700 **Fax:** 865-379-6817	**Web Site:** www.rubytuesday.com **Officers:** Matthew A. Drapkin - Chairman James J. Buettgen - President, Chief Executive Officer	**Auditors:** KPMG LLP **Investor Contact:** 865-379-5757 **Transfer Agents:** Computershare Shareowner Services, Pittsburgh, PA

RYDER SYSTEM, INC.

Exchange	Symbol	Price	52Wk Range	Yield	P/E
NYS	R	$59.75 (3/28/2013)	61.42-33.40	2.08	14.61

*7 Year Price Score 86.43   *NYSE Composite Index=100   *12 Month Price Score 113.62

Interim Earnings (Per Share)

Qtr.	Mar	Jun	Sep	Dec
2008	0.96	1.10	1.25	0.21
2009	0.12	0.41	0.43	0.15
2010	0.23	0.56	0.74	0.72
2011	0.48	0.77	1.10	0.93
2012	0.67	0.91	1.47	1.05

Interim Dividends (Per Share)

Amt	Decl	Ex	Rec	Pay
0.29Q	05/04/2012	05/17/2012	05/21/2012	06/15/2012
0.31Q	07/11/2012	08/16/2012	08/20/2012	09/21/2012
0.31Q	10/05/2012	11/15/2012	11/19/2012	12/21/2012
0.31Q	02/08/2013	02/14/2013	02/19/2013	03/15/2013

Indicated Div: $1.24

Valuation Analysis

		Institutional Holding	
Forecast EPS	$4.81 (04/05/2013)	No of Institutions	365
Market Cap	$3.1 Billion	Shares	55,313,232
Book Value	$1.5 Billion	% Held	90.40
Price/Book	2.09		
Price/Sales	0.49		

Business Summary: Trucking (MIC: 7.4.1 SIC: 7513 NAIC: 532120)

Ryder System is engaged in providing transportation and supply chain management applications. Co. operates in two business segments: Fleet Management Solutions, which provides full service leasing, contract maintenance, contract-related maintenance and commercial rental of trucks, tractors and trailers to customers principally in the U.S., Canada and the U.K.; and Supply Chain Solutions (SCS), which provides supply chain consulting including distribution and transportation services in North America and Asia. The SCS segment also provides dedicated services, which includes vehicles and drivers as part of a dedicated transportation application in the U.S.

Recent Developments: For the year ended Dec 31 2012, income from continuing operations increased 17.2% to US$200.9 million from US$171.4 million a year earlier. Net income increased 23.7% to US$210.0 million from US$169.8 million in the prior year. Revenues were US$6.26 billion, up 3.4% from US$6.05 billion the year before. Direct operating expenses rose 4.1% to US$5.00 billion from US$4.81 billion in the comparable period the year before. Indirect operating expenses decreased 1.5% to US$950.4 million from US$965.3 million in the equivalent prior-year period.

Prospects: Our evaluation of Ryder System Inc. as of Apr. 7, 2013 is the result of our systematic analysis on three basic characteristics: earnings strength, relative valuation, and recent stock price movement. The company has enjoyed a very positive trend in earnings per share over the past 5 quarters and while recent estimates for the company have been mixed, R has posted better than expected results. Based on operating earnings yield, the company is undervalued when compared to all of the companies in our coverage universe. Share price changes over the past year indicates that R will perform poorly over the near term.

Financial Data

(US$ in Thousands)	12/31/2012	12/31/2011	12/31/2010	12/31/2009	12/31/2008	12/31/2007	12/31/2006	12/31/2005
Earnings Per Share	4.09	3.28	2.25	1.11	3.52	4.24	4.04	3.52
Cash Flow Per Share	22.42	20.63	19.88	17.90	22.28	18.59	14.02	12.22
Tang Book Value Per Share	19.52	16.74	19.08	21.93	19.95	29.32	25.48	21.81
Dividends Per Share	1.200	1.120	1.040	0.960	0.920	0.840	0.720	0.640
Dividend Payout %	29.34	34.15	46.22	86.49	26.14	19.81	17.82	18.18
Income Statement								
Total Revenue	6,256,967	6,050,534	5,136,435	4,887,254	6,203,743	6,565,995	6,306,643	5,740,847
EBITDA	1,383,351	1,284,813	1,150,140	1,169,327	1,350,638	1,381,500	1,276,822	1,217,977
Depn & Amortn	939,677	872,262	833,841	881,216	843,459	815,962	743,288	740,415
Income Before Taxes	303,121	279,387	186,305	143,769	349,922	405,464	392,973	357,088
Income Taxes	102,218	108,019	61,697	53,652	150,041	151,603	144,014	129,460
Net Income	209,769	169,777	118,170	61,945	199,881	253,861	248,959	226,929
Average Shares	50,740	50,878	51,884	55,094	56,790	59,845	61,578	64,560
Balance Sheet								
Current Assets	1,040,237	1,088,173	1,023,301	880,373	951,196	1,222,062	1,261,816	1,163,755
Total Assets	8,318,979	7,617,835	6,652,374	6,259,830	6,689,508	6,854,649	6,828,923	6,033,264
Current Liabilities	1,272,665	1,173,823	1,131,519	850,274	1,111,165	1,019,361	1,267,622	1,253,495
Long-Term Obligations	3,452,821	3,107,779	2,326,878	2,265,074	2,478,537	2,553,431	2,484,198	1,915,928
Total Liabilities	6,851,492	6,299,682	5,248,061	4,832,835	5,344,347	4,967,060	5,108,144	4,505,808
Stockholders' Equity	1,467,487	1,318,153	1,404,313	1,426,995	1,345,161	1,887,589	1,720,779	1,527,456
Shares Outstanding	51,371	51,143	51,174	53,419	55,658	58,041	60,721	61,869
Statistical Record								
Return on Assets %	2.63	2.38	1.83	0.96	2.94	3.71	3.87	3.89
Return on Equity %	15.03	12.47	8.35	4.47	12.33	14.07	15.33	14.94
EBITDA Margin %	22.11	21.23	22.39	23.93	21.77	21.04	20.25	21.22
Net Margin %	3.36	2.81	2.30	1.27	3.22	3.87	3.95	3.95
Asset Turnover	0.78	0.85	0.80	0.75	0.91	0.96	0.98	0.98
Current Ratio	0.82	0.93	0.90	1.04	0.86	1.20	1.00	0.93
Debt to Equity	2.35	2.36	1.66	1.59	1.84	1.35	1.44	1.25
Price Range	57.18-33.40	59.35-35.45	52.64-32.55	46.25-19.27	75.43-28.45	56.81-38.99	58.56-40.32	47.77-32.09
P/E Ratio	13.98-8.17	18.09-10.81	23.40-14.47	41.67-17.36	21.43-8.08	13.40-9.20	14.50-9.98	13.57-9.12
Average Yield %	2.63	2.25	2.47	2.83	1.60	1.65	1.44	1.63

Address: 11690 N.W. 105th Street, Miami, FL 33178 Telephone: 305-500-3726	Web Site: www.ryder.com Officers: Gregory T. Swienton - Executive Chairman, Chairman, Chief Executive Officer Robert E. Sanchez - President, Chief Executive Officer, Chief Operating Officer, Division Officer	Auditors: PricewaterhouseCoopers LLP Investor Contact: 305-500-4053 Transfer Agents: Wells Fargo Bank, N.A., St. Paul, MN

SAFEWAY INC.

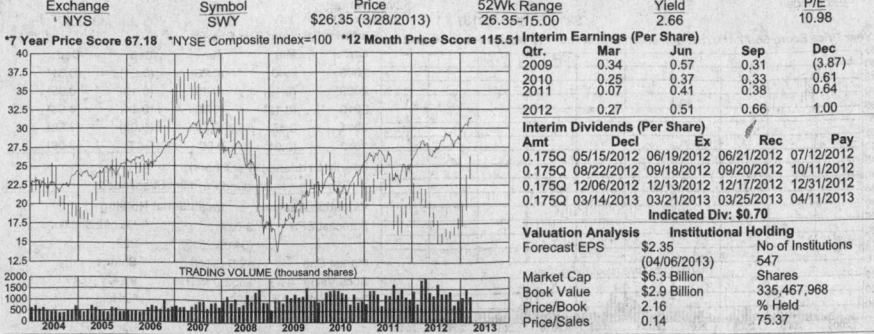

Exchange	Symbol	Price	52Wk Range	Yield	P/E
NYS	SWY	$26.35 (3/28/2013)	26.35-15.00	2.66	10.98

*7 Year Price Score 67.18 *NYSE Composite Index=100 *12 Month Price Score 115.51

Interim Earnings (Per Share)

Qtr.	Mar	Jun	Sep	Dec
2009	0.34	0.57	0.31	(3.87)
2010	0.25	0.37	0.33	0.61
2011	0.07	0.41	0.38	0.64
2012	0.27	0.51	0.66	1.00

Interim Dividends (Per Share)

Amt	Decl	Ex	Rec	Pay
0.175Q	05/15/2012	06/19/2012	06/21/2012	07/12/2012
0.175Q	08/22/2012	09/18/2012	09/20/2012	10/11/2012
0.175Q	12/06/2012	12/13/2012	12/17/2012	12/31/2012
0.175Q	03/14/2013	03/21/2013	03/25/2013	04/11/2013

Indicated Div: $0.70

Valuation Analysis

		Institutional Holding	
Forecast EPS	$2.35	No of Institutions	547
	(04/06/2013)		
Market Cap	$6.3 Billion	Shares	335,467,968
Book Value	$2.9 Billion	% Held	75.37
Price/Book	2.16		
Price/Sales	0.14		

TRADING VOLUME (thousand shares)

Business Summary: Retail - Food & Beverage, Drug & Tobacco (MIC: 2.1.2 SIC: 5411 NAIC: 445110)

Safeway is a food and drug retailer in North America, with 1,641 stores at Dec 29 2012. Co.'s U.S. retail operations are located principally in California, Hawaii, Oregon, Washington, Alaska, Colorado, Arizona, Texas, the Chicago metropolitan area and the Mid-Atlantic region. Co.'s Canadian retail operations are located principally in British Columbia, Alberta and Manitoba/Saskatchewan. Co. owns and operates GroceryWorks.com Operating Company, LLC, an online grocery channel doing business under the names Safeway.com and Vons.com. Co. also has a 49.0% ownership interest in Casa Ley, S.A. de C.V., which operates food and general merchandise stores in Western Mexico.

Recent Developments: For the year ended Dec 29 2012, income from continuing operations increased 9.3% to US$566.2 million from US$518.2 million a year earlier. Net income increased 15.4% to US$598.1 million from US$518.2 million in the prior year. Revenues were US$44.21 billion, up 1.3% from US$43.63 billion the year before. Operating income was US$1.10 billion versus US$1.13 billion in the prior year, a decrease of 2.7%. Direct operating expenses rose 2.0% to US$32.49 billion from US$31.84 billion in the comparable period the year before. Indirect operating expenses decreased 0.4% to US$10.62 billion from US$10.66 billion in the equivalent prior-year period.

Prospects: Our evaluation of Safeway Inc. as of Apr. 7, 2013 is the result of our systematic analysis on three basic characteristics: earnings strength, relative valuation, and recent stock price movement. The company has managed to produce a neutral trend in earnings per share over the past 5 quarters and while recent estimates for the company have been raised by analysts, SWY has posted better than expected results. Based on operating earnings yield, the company is undervalued when compared to all of the companies in our coverage universe. Share price changes over the past year indicates that SWY will perform poorly over the near term.

Financial Data

(US$ in Thousands)	12/29/2012	12/31/2011	01/01/2011	01/02/2010	01/03/2009	12/29/2007	12/30/2006	12/31/2005
Earnings Per Share	2.40	1.49	1.55	(2.66)	2.21	1.99	1.94	1.25
Cash Flow Per Share	6.41	5.91	4.90	6.19	5.10	4.99	4.90	4.21
Tang Book Value Per Share	10.26	10.83	12.40	11.64	10.25	9.76	7.44	5.60
Dividends Per Share	0.670	0.555	0.460	0.383	0.317	0.265	0.223	0.150
Dividend Payout %	27.92	37.25	29.68	...	14.36	13.29	11.47	12.00
Income Statement								
Total Revenue	44,206,500	43,630,200	41,050,000	40,850,700	44,104,000	42,286,000	40,185,000	38,416,000
EBITDA	2,296,700	2,331,600	2,371,900	584,200	1,902,100	2,869,000	2,633,300	2,191,800
Depn & Amortn	1,164,300	1,177,300	1,192,200	1,205,800	38,800	1,076,500	997,200	940,200
Income Before Taxes	828,400	882,100	881,200	(953,300)	1,504,600	1,403,600	1,240,000	849,000
Income Taxes	262,200	363,900	290,600	144,200	539,300	515,200	369,400	287,900
Net Income	596,500	516,700	589,800	(1,097,500)	965,300	888,400	870,600	561,100
Average Shares	245,900	343,800	379,600	412,900	436,300	445,700	447,800	449,800
Balance Sheet								
Current Assets	4,167,900	4,186,800	4,233,000	3,825,300	3,976,200	4,007,500	3,565,700	3,702,400
Total Assets	14,657,000	15,073,600	15,148,100	14,963,600	17,484,700	17,651,000	16,273,800	15,756,900
Current Liabilities	4,605,600	5,038,300	4,314,200	4,237,800	4,499,200	5,136,400	4,601,400	4,263,900
Long-Term Obligations	5,243,500	4,569,700	4,300,000	4,360,900	4,700,800	4,657,700	5,036,600	5,605,300
Total Liabilities	11,729,100	11,390,500	10,154,800	10,017,200	10,698,500	10,949,200	10,606,900	10,837,200
Stockholders' Equity	2,927,900	3,683,100	4,993,300	4,946,400	6,786,200	6,701,800	5,666,900	4,919,700
Shares Outstanding	239,500	296,600	368,000	388,300	428,900	440,100	440,100	449,400
Statistical Record								
Return on Assets %	4.02	3.43	3.93	N.M.	5.41	5.25	5.45	3.61
Return on Equity %	18.10	11.94	11.90	N.M.	14.08	14.40	16.49	12.20
EBITDA Margin %	5.20	5.34	5.78	1.43	4.31	6.78	6.55	5.71
Net Margin %	1.35	1.18	1.44	N.M.	2.19	2.10	2.17	1.46
Asset Turnover	2.98	2.90	2.73	2.52	2.47	2.50	2.52	2.47
Current Ratio	0.90	0.83	0.98	0.90	0.88	0.78	0.77	0.87
Debt to Equity	1.79	1.24	0.86	0.88	0.69	0.69	0.89	1.14
Price Range	22.88-15.00	25.42-16.06	26.94-18.79	24.06-17.24	34.21-17.92	38.00-30.56	35.31-22.37	26.05-17.92
P/E Ratio	9.53-6.25	17.06-10.78	17.38-12.12	...	15.48-8.11	19.10-15.36	18.20-11.53	20.84-14.34
Average Yield %	3.66	2.63	2.07	1.85	1.16	0.77	0.82	0.68

Address: 5918 Stoneridge Mall Road, Pleasanton, CA 94588-3229	**Web Site:** www.safeway.com		**Auditors:** Deloitte & Touche LLP
Telephone: 925-467-3000	**Officers:** Steven A. Burd - Chairman, President, Chief Executive Officer Robert L. Edwards - Executive Vice President, Chief Financial Officer, President		**Investor Contact:** 925-467-3717
Fax: 925-467-3323			**Transfer Agents:** Computershare Trust Company, N.A., Providence

ST. JOE CO. (THE)

Exchange	Symbol	Price	52Wk Range	Yield	P/E
NYS	JOE	$21.25 (3/28/2013)	24.38-14.40	N/A	303.57'

*7 Year Price Score 56.77   *NYSE Composite Index=100   *12 Month Price Score 102.66

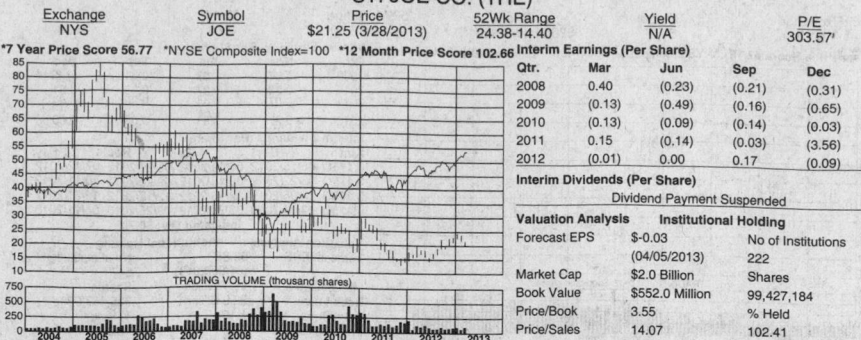

Interim Earnings (Per Share)

Qtr.	Mar	Jun	Sep	Dec
2008	0.40	(0.23)	(0.21)	(0.31)
2009	(0.13)	(0.49)	(0.16)	(0.65)
2010	(0.13)	(0.09)	(0.14)	(0.03)
2011	0.15	(0.14)	(0.03)	(3.56)
2012	(0.01)	0.00	0.17	(0.09)

Interim Dividends (Per Share)

Dividend Payment Suspended

Valuation Analysis		Institutional Holding	
Forecast EPS	$-0.03	No of Institutions	
	(04/05/2013)	222	
Market Cap	$2.0 Billion	Shares	
Book Value	$552.0 Million	99,427,184	
Price/Book	3.55	% Held	
Price/Sales	14.07	102.41	

Business Summary: Property, Real Estate & Development (MIC: 5.3.2 SIC: 6552 NAIC: 531190)

St. Joe is a real estate development company engaged in residential, commercial and industrial development and rural land sales in Northwest Florida. Co. has four segments: residential real estate, which plans and develops mixed-use resort, primary and seasonal residential communities on its existing land; commercial real estate, which plans, develops and entitles Co.'s land holdings for retail, multi-family, office, hotel, industrial uses and rental income; rural land sales, which markets and sells land for rural recreational, conservation, residential and timberland uses in Northwest Florida; and forestry, which focuses on the management and harvesting of Co.'s timber holdings.

Recent Developments: For the year ended Dec 31 2012, net income amounted to US$6.0 million versus a net loss of US$330.3 million in the prior year. Revenues were US$139.4 million, down 4.1% from US$145.3 million the year before. Revenues from property income rose 175.3% to US$56.0 million from US$20.3 million in the corresponding earlier year.

Prospects: Our evaluation of St. Joe Co. as of Apr. 7, 2013 is the result of our systematic analysis on three basic characteristics: earnings strength, relative valuation, and recent stock price movement. The company has suffered a very negative trend in earnings per share over the past 5 quarters. Because the company lacks sufficient analyst estimate data, we place greater weight on the historical EPS trend as the measure of earnings strength. Based on operating earnings yield, the company is overvalued when compared to all of the companies in our coverage universe. Share price changes over the past year indicates that JOE will perform very well over the near term.

Financial Data

(US$ in Thousands)	12/31/2012	12/31/2011	12/31/2010	12/31/2009	12/31/2008	12/31/2007	12/31/2006	12/31/2005
Earnings Per Share	0.07	(3.58)	(0.39)	(1.42)	(0.40)	0.53	0.69	1.66
Cash Flow Per Share	0.25	(0.11)	0.18	0.56	0.54	(2.84)	(1.95)	2.57
Tang Book Value Per Share	5.98	5.89	9.42	9.70	10.70	6.15	5.29	5.42
Dividends Per Share	...	...	...	...	...	0.480	0.640	0.600
Dividend Payout %	...	...	...	...	...	90.57	92.75	36.14
Income Statement								
Total Revenue	139,396	145,285	99,540	138,257	263,990	377,037	748,192	938,192
EBITDA	7,400	(379,993)	(35,234)	(203,563)	(14,700)	55,817	99,086	193,490
Depn & Amortn	2,400	2,800	3,400	4,500	6,200	7,400	9,600	10,500
Income Before Taxes	2,180	(386,714)	(47,246)	(209,220)	(25,383)	28,388	68,920	167,773
Income Taxes	387	(55,658)	(23,849)	(81,222)	(26,984)	869	25,157	64,332
Net Income	6,012	(330,279)	(35,864)	(130,019)	(35,883)	39,207	51,020	126,658
Average Shares	92,258	92,235	91,674	91,412	89,550	74,300	74,419	76,208
Balance Sheet								
Current Assets	170,191	167,023	189,558	237,702	197,848	89,370	88,803	261,510
Total Assets	645,521	661,291	1,051,695	1,098,140	1,218,278	1,263,966	1,560,395	1,591,946
Current Liabilities	41,995	44,519	64,984	91,250	92,636	152,305	250,611	214,396
Long-Term Obligations	36,062	53,458	54,651	39,508	49,560	541,181	627,056	554,446
Total Liabilities	93,496	117,730	179,571	203,228	229,649	783,625	1,099,315	1,102,948
Stockholders' Equity	552,025	543,561	872,124	894,912	988,629	480,341	461,080	488,998
Shares Outstanding	92,268	92,267	92,605	92,281	92,203	74,597	74,272	74,928
Statistical Record								
Return on Assets %	0.92	N.M.	N.M.	N.M.	N.M.	2.78	3.24	8.46
Return on Equity %	1.09	N.M.	N.M.	N.M.	N.M.	8.33	10.74	25.73
EBITDA Margin %	5.31	N.M.	N.M.	N.M.	N.M.	14.80	13.24	20.62
Net Margin %	4.31	N.M.	N.M.	N.M.	N.M.	10.40	6.82	13.50
Asset Turnover	0.21	0.17	0.09	0.12	0.21	0.27	0.47	0.63
Current Ratio	4.05	3.75	2.92	2.60	2.14	0.59	0.35	1.22
Debt to Equity	0.07	0.10	0.06	0.04	0.05	1.13	1.36	1.13
Price Range	23.08-14.40	29.50-12.94	37.13-17.25	33.90-14.59	46.01-19.77	61.06-27.23	67.99-41.92	84.73-59.89
P/E Ratio	329.71-205.71	...	...	...	...	115.21-51.38	98.54-60.75	51.04-36.08
Average Yield %	...	...	...	...	...	1.08	1.19	0.84

Address: 133 South WaterSound Parkway, WaterSound, FL 32413
Telephone: 904-301-4200

Web Site: www.joe.com
Officers: Bruce R. Berkowitz - Chairman Park Brady - Chief Executive Officer, Chief Operating Officer

Auditors: KPMG LLP
Investor Contact: 866-417-7132
Transfer Agents: American Stock Transfer & Trust Company, New York, NY

ST. JUDE MEDICAL, INC.

Exchange	Symbol	Price	52Wk Range	Yield	P/E
NYS	STJ	$40.44 (3/28/2013)	43.89-31.37	2.47	16.92

*7 Year Price Score 86.91 ***NYSE Composite Index=100** ***12 Month Price Score 98.75**

TRADING VOLUME (thousand shares)

Interim Earnings (Per Share)

Qtr.	Mar	Jun	Sep	Dec
2008	0.53	0.58	0.55	(0.55)
2009	0.58	0.63	0.48	0.57
2010	0.73	0.77	0.63	0.62
2011	0.71	0.72	0.69	0.39
2012	0.62	0.78	0.56	0.39

Interim Dividends (Per Share)

Amt	Decl	Ex	Rec	Pay
0.23Q	05/02/2012	06/27/2012	06/29/2012	07/31/2012
0.23Q	08/01/2012	09/26/2012	09/28/2012	10/31/2012
0.23Q	12/11/2012	12/27/2012	12/31/2012	01/31/2013
0.25Q	02/25/2013	03/26/2013	03/29/2013	04/30/2013

Indicated Div: $1.00

Valuation Analysis

		Institutional Holding	
Forecast EPS	$3.71	No of Institutions	
	(04/05/2013)	702	
Market Cap	$12.0 Billion	Shares	
Book Value	$4.1 Billion	284,202,400	
Price/Book	2.92	% Held	
Price/Sales	2.17	79.84	

Business Summary: Medical Instruments & Equipment (MIC: 4.3.1 SIC: 3845 NAIC: 334510)

St. Jude Medical develops, manufactures and distributes cardiovascular medical devices. Co.'s principal products are as follows: Cardiac Rhythm Management - tachycardia implantable cardioverter defibrillator systems and bradycardia pacemaker systems (pacemakers); Cardiovascular - vascular products, which include vascular closure products, pressure measurement guidewires, optical coherence tomography imaging products, vascular plugs and other vascular accessories, and structural heart products; Atrial Fibrillation - electrophysiology introducers and catheters, cardiac mapping, navigation and recording systems and ablation systems; and Neuromodulation - neurostimulation products.

Recent Developments: For the year ended Dec 29 2012, net income decreased 9.0% to US$752.0 million from US$826.0 million in the prior year. Revenues were US$5.50 billion, down 1.9% from US$5.61 billion the year before. Operating income was US$1.10 billion versus US$1.12 billion in the prior year, a decrease of 1.3%. Direct operating expenses rose 0.3% to US$1.54 billion from US$1.53 billion in the comparable period the year before. Indirect operating expenses decreased 3.3% to US$2.87 billion from US$2.96 billion in the equivalent prior-year period.

Prospects: Our evaluation of St. Jude Medical Inc. as of Apr. 7, 2013 is the result of our systematic analysis on three basic characteristics: earnings strength, relative valuation, and recent stock price movement. The company has managed to produce a neutral trend in earnings per share over the past 5 quarters. However, while recent estimates for the company have been mixed, STJ has posted better than expected results. Based on operating earnings yield, the company is undervalued when compared to all of the companies in our coverage universe. Share price changes over the past year indicates that STJ will perform poorly over the near term.

Financial Data

(US$ in Thousands)	12/29/2012	12/31/2011	01/01/2011	01/02/2010	01/03/2009	12/29/2007	12/30/2006	12/31/2005
Earnings Per Share	2.39	2.52	2.75	2.26	1.10	1.59	1.47	1.04
Cash Flow Per Share	4.27	3.98	3.89	2.56	2.71	2.54	1.81	1.97
Tang Book Value Per Share	1.11	2.08	1.30	2.65	2.19	2.25	2.14	1.84
Dividends Per Share	0.920	0.840	...	...	...	...	...	...
Dividend Payout %	38.49	33.33	...	...	...	...	...	...
Income Statement								
Total Revenue	5,503,000	5,611,696	5,164,771	4,681,273	4,363,251	3,779,277	3,302,447	2,915,280
EBITDA	1,269,000	1,287,082	1,528,173	1,314,774	769,315	899,848	839,260	688,273
Depn & Amortn	196,000	202,600	254,074	213,835	132,308	121,688	94,002	76,364
Income Before Taxes	1,005,000	1,019,071	1,208,803	1,057,393	630,741	744,305	720,641	621,404
Income Taxes	253,000	193,278	301,367	280,167	246,414	185,267	172,390	227,914
Net Income	752,000	825,793	907,436	777,226	384,327	559,038	548,251	393,490
Average Shares	314,800	327,094	330,488	344,359	349,722	352,444	372,830	379,106
Balance Sheet								
Current Assets	3,551,000	3,390,566	2,912,148	2,560,206	2,080,063	2,128,183	1,690,165	1,941,141
Total Assets	9,271,000	9,005,193	8,566,448	6,425,811	5,722,504	5,329,404	4,789,794	4,844,840
Current Liabilities	1,775,000	1,061,725	1,017,250	1,067,313	1,028,524	1,849,229	676,207	1,534,382
Long-Term Obligations	2,550,000	2,713,275	2,431,966	1,587,615	1,126,084	182,493	859,376	176,970
Total Liabilities	5,177,000	4,530,577	4,194,777	3,102,260	2,486,598	2,401,394	1,820,807	1,961,795
Stockholders' Equity	4,094,000	4,474,616	4,371,671	3,323,551	3,235,906	2,928,010	2,968,987	2,883,045
Shares Outstanding	295,648	319,615	329,018	324,537	345,332	342,846	353,932	367,904
Statistical Record								
Return on Assets %	8.25	9.42	12.14	12.83	6.84	11.08	11.41	9.75
Return on Equity %	17.60	18.72	23.65	23.76	12.27	19.01	18.79	15.08
EBITDA Margin %	23.06	22.94	29.59	28.09	17.63	23.81	25.41	23.61
Net Margin %	13.67	14.72	17.57	16.60	8.81	14.79	16.60	13.50
Asset Turnover	0.60	0.64	0.69	0.77	0.78	0.75	0.69	0.72
Current Ratio	2.00	3.19	2.86	2.40	2.02	1.15	2.50	1.27
Debt to Equity	0.62	0.61	0.56	0.48	0.35	0.06	0.29	0.06
Price Range	44.54-31.37	54.04-32.16	42.85-34.57	41.77-29.44	48.22-25.48	48.10-35.00	54.20-31.62	51.91-35.06
P/E Ratio	18.64-13.13	21.44-12.76	15.58-12.57	18.48-13.03	43.84-23.16	30.25-22.01	36.87-21.51	49.91-33.71
Average Yield %	2.37	1.89	...	...	...	...	...	...

Address: One St. Jude Medical Drive, St. Paul, MN 55117 **Telephone:** 651-756-2000 **Fax:** 651-490-4310	**Web Site:** www.sjm.com **Officers:** Daniel J. Starks - Chairman, President, Chief Executive Officer John C. Heinmiller - Executive Vice President, Chief Financial Officer	**Auditors:** Ernst & Young LLP **Investor Contact:** 651-.75-6.4347 **Transfer Agents:** Wells Fargo Shareowner Services, St. Paul, MN

SAIC INC

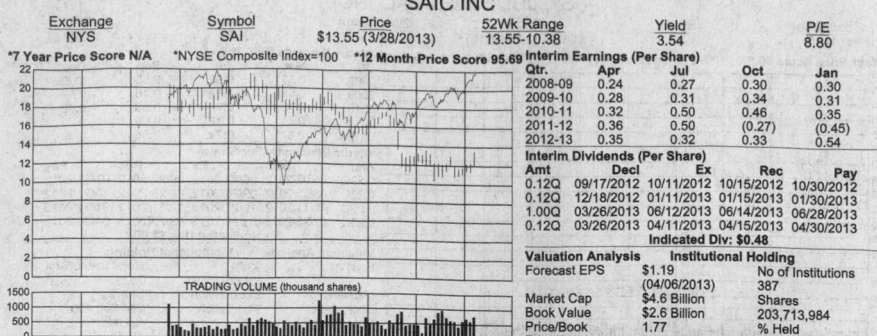

Exchange	Symbol	Price	52Wk Range	Yield	P/E
NYS	SAI	$13.55 (3/28/2013)	13.55-10.38	3.54	8.80

*7 Year Price Score N/A   *NYSE Composite Index=100   *12 Month Price Score 95.69

Interim Earnings (Per Share)

Qtr.	Apr	Jul	Oct	Jan
2008-09	0.24	0.27	0.30	0.30
2009-10	0.28	0.31	0.34	0.31
2010-11	0.32	0.50	0.46	0.35
2011-12	0.36	0.50	(0.27)	(0.45)
2012-13	0.35	0.32	0.33	0.54

Interim Dividends (Per Share)

Amt	Decl	Ex	Rec	Pay
0.12Q	09/17/2012	10/11/2012	10/15/2012	10/30/2012
0.12Q	12/18/2012	01/11/2013	01/15/2013	01/30/2013
1.00Q	03/26/2013	06/12/2013	06/14/2013	06/28/2013
0.12Q	03/26/2013	04/11/2013	04/15/2013	04/30/2013

Indicated Div: $0.48

Valuation Analysis

		Institutional Holding	
Forecast EPS	$1.19 (04/06/2013)	No of Institutions	387
Market Cap	$4.6 Billion	Shares	203,713,984
Book Value	$2.6 Billion	% Held	
Price/Book	1.77		53.09
Price/Sales	0.41		

TRADING VOLUME (thousand shares)

Business Summary: IT Services (MIC: 6.3.1 SIC: 7373 NAIC: 541330)

SAIC is a holding company. Through its subsidiary, Co. provides an array of scientific, engineering, systems integration and technical services. Co.'s segments include: Defense Solutions, which supports command and control, communications, modeling and simulation, logistics, readiness and sustainment and network operations; Health, Energy and Civil Solutions, which focuses on infrastructure, homeland security, safety and mission assurance, training, environmental assessments and restoration, engineering design, construction and information technology services; and Intelligence and Cybersecurity Solutions, which focuses on intelligence, surveillance, reconnaissance and cybersecurity.

Recent Developments: For the year ended Jan 31 2013, income from continuing operations was US$523.0 million compared with a loss of US$15.0 million a year earlier. Net income increased 789.8% to US$525.0 million from US$59.0 million in the prior year. Revenues were US$11.17 billion, up 6.4% from US$10.50 billion the year before. Operating income was US$734.0 million versus US$299.0 million in the prior year, an increase of 145.5%. Direct operating expenses rose 2.9% to US$9.81 billion from US$9.53 billion in the comparable period the year before. Indirect operating expenses decreased 5.7% to US$630.0 million from US$668.0 million in the equivalent prior-year period.

Prospects: Our evaluation of SAIC Inc. as of Apr. 7, 2013 is the result of our systematic analysis on three basic characteristics: earnings strength, relative valuation, and recent stock price movement. The company has managed to produce a neutral trend in earnings per share over the past 5 quarters. However, while recent estimates for the company have been lowered by analysts, SAI has posted better than expected results. Based on operating earnings yield, the company is undervalued when compared to all of the companies in our coverage universe. Share price changes over the past year indicates that SAI will perform very poorly over the near term.

Financial Data

(US$ in Millions)	01/31/2013	01/31/2012	01/31/2011	01/31/2010	01/31/2009	01/31/2008	01/31/2007	01/31/2006
Earnings Per Share	1.54	0.18	1.63	1.24	1.12	1.00	1.07	...
Cash Flow Per Share	1.03	2.30	2.02	1.61	1.47	0.85	2.00	...
Tang Book Value Per Share	0.68	0.52	1.66	1.94	3.56	4.03	5.17	0.10
Dividends Per Share	0.480	...	...	...	...	...	15.000	...
Dividend Payout %	31.17	...	...	...	...	...	1,401.87	...
Income Statement								
Total Revenue	11,173	10,587	11,117	10,846	10,070	8,935	8,294	...
EBITDA	855	430	1,071	965	859	737	660	...
Depn & Amortn	113	114	111	93	89	80	72	...
Income Before Taxes	658	207	883	798	712	623	613	...
Income Taxes	135	215	314	299	256	240	234	...
Net Income	525	59	618	497	452	415	391	...
Average Shares	333	336	366	390	405	417	364	...
Balance Sheet								
Current Assets	3,079	4,205	3,849	3,193	3,217	3,237	2,945	1,000.00
Total Assets	5,875	6,667	6,223	5,295	5,048	4,981	4,558	1,000.00
Current Liabilities	1,793	3,025	1,748	1,706	1,683	1,832	1,663	...
Long-Term Obligations	1,296	1,299	1,849	1,103	1,099	1,098	1,199	...
Total Liabilities	3,257	4,486	3,732	3,004	2,964	3,080	3,022	...
Stockholders' Equity	2,618	2,181	2,491	2,291	2,084	1,901	1,536	1,000.00
Shares Outstanding	342	341	362	388	210	179	92	0
Statistical Record								
Return on Assets %	8.35	0.92	10.73	9.61	8.99	8.70	17.16	...
Return on Equity %	21.82	2.53	25.85	22.72	22.62	24.15	50.91	...
EBITDA Margin %	7.65	4.06	9.63	8.90	8.53	8.25	7.96	...
Net Margin %	4.70	0.56	5.56	4.58	4.49	4.64	4.71	...
Asset Turnover	1.78	1.64	1.93	2.10	2.00	1.87	3.64	...
Current Ratio	1.72	1.39	2.20	1.87	1.91	1.77	1.77	...
Debt to Equity	0.50	0.60	0.74	0.48	0.53	0.58	0.78	...
Price Range	13.61-10.38	17.56-11.26	19.70-14.88	20.28-16.97	21.49-17.09	20.69-16.65	20.33-17.27	...
P/E Ratio	8.84-6.74	97.56-62.56	12.09-9.13	16.35-13.69	19.19-15.26	20.69-16.65	19.00-16.14	...
Average Yield %	4.07	...	...	...	...	...	80.41	...

Address: 1710 SAIC Drive, McLean, VA 22102
Telephone: 703-676-4300

Web Site: www.saic.com
Officers: A. Thomas Young - Chairman John P. Jumper - President, Chief Executive Officer

Auditors: Deloitte & Touche LLP
Investor Contact: 703-676-2283
Transfer Agents: BNY Mellon Shareowner Services

SAKS, INC.

Exchange	Symbol	Price	52Wk Range	Yield	P/E
NYS	SKS	$11.47 (3/28/2013)	11.97-9.72	N/A	27.98

*7 Year Price Score 82.17   *NYSE Composite Index=100   *12 Month Price Score 96.51

Interim Earnings (Per Share)

Qtr.	Apr	Jul	Oct	Jan
2008-09	0.13	(0.23)	(0.31)	(0.71)
2009-10	(0.04)	(0.39)	0.04	(0.03)
2010-11	0.11	(0.21)	0.20	0.16
2011-12	0.16	(0.05)	0.11	0.21
2012-13	0.18	(0.08)	0.14	0.13

Interim Dividends (Per Share)

No Dividends Paid

Valuation Analysis

Forecast EPS	$0.45
	(04/06/2013)
Market Cap	$1.7 Billion
Book Value	$1.1 Billion
Price/Book	1.49
Price/Sales	0.55

Institutional Holding

No of Institutions	255
Shares	96,182,896
% Held	59.92

TRADING VOLUME (thousand shares)

Business Summary: Retail - General Merchandise/Department Stores (MIC: 2.1.1 SIC: 5311 NAIC: 452111)

Saks is engaged as an omni-retailer providing a range of fashion apparel, shoes, accessories, jewelry, cosmetics, and gifts. The operations of Co. and its subsidiaries consist of Saks Fifth Avenue (SFA) stores, and SFA e-commerce operations as well as Saks Fifth Avenue OFF 5TH (OFF 5TH). SFA stores are principally free-standing stores in shopping places or anchor stores in regional malls. Customers may also purchase SFA products online at saks.com or by catalog. OFF 5TH stores are primarily located in mixed-use and off-price centers and provide a range of apparel, shoes, and accessories. As of Jan 28 2012, Co. operated 46 SFA stores and 60 OFF 5TH stores.

Recent Developments: For the year ended Feb 2 2013, income from continuing operations decreased 15.9% to US$62.9 million from US$74.8 million a year earlier. Net income decreased 15.9% to US$62.9 million from US$74.8 million in the prior year. Revenues were US$3.15 billion, up 4.4% from US$3.01 billion the year before. Operating income was US$138.5 million versus US$148.3 million in the prior year, a decrease of 6.6%. Direct operating expenses rose 4.7% to US$1.87 billion from US$1.79 billion in the comparable period the year before. Indirect operating expenses increased 5.5% to US$1.14 billion from US$1.08 billion in the equivalent prior-year period.

Prospects: Our evaluation of Saks Inc. as of Apr. 7, 2013 is the result of our systematic analysis on three basic characteristics: earnings strength, relative valuation, and recent stock price movement. The company has produced a positive trend in earnings per share over the past 5 quarters and while recent estimates for the company have remained steady, SKS has posted better than expected results. Based on operating earnings yield, the company is overvalued when compared to all of the companies in our coverage universe. Share price changes over the past year indicates that SKS will perform poorly over the near term.

Financial Data

(US$ in Thousands)	02/02/2013	01/28/2012	01/29/2011	01/30/2010	01/31/2009	02/02/2008	02/03/2007	01/28/2006
Earnings Per Share	0.41	0.45	0.30	(0.40)	(1.12)	0.31	0.40	0.16
Cash Flow Per Share	1.15	1.76	0.80	1.35	(0.01)	0.51	0.40	1.36
Tang Book Value Per Share	7.68	7.54	7.14	6.71	6.79	8.29	7.80	13.37
Dividends Per Share	...	...	...	...	...	...	8.000	...
Dividend Payout %	...	...	...	...	...	...	2,000.00	...
Income Statement								
Total Revenue	3,147,554	3,013,593	2,785,745	2,631,532	3,029,743	3,282,640	2,940,003	5,953,352
EBITDA	256,954	268,512	208,880	82,452	4,881	251,929	136,533	390,532
Depn & Amortn	120,377	118,513	118,669	135,135	134,669	134,635	128,522	210,116
Income Before Taxes	99,395	101,884	33,486	(102,163)	(169,094)	74,980	(42,125)	94,638
Income Taxes	36,513	27,094	(13,910)	(44,501)	(46,332)	27,507	(34,783)	72,290
Net Income	62,882	74,790	47,846	(57,919)	(154,941)	47,473	53,742	22,348
Average Shares	173,694	200,237	158,413	143,194	138,384	153,530	135,880	143,571
Balance Sheet								
Current Assets	1,082,122	1,085,674	1,060,769	925,950	874,380	1,126,135	1,250,841	1,644,651
Total Assets	2,090,247	2,128,465	2,143,100	2,135,701	2,165,008	2,371,024	2,544,303	3,850,725
Current Liabilities	545,337	396,712	481,907	379,781	370,428	781,038	862,780	845,050
Long-Term Obligations	260,603	367,962	359,250	493,320	635,400	253,346	450,010	722,736
Total Liabilities	940,398	921,681	979,535	1,064,091	1,199,388	1,195,418	1,448,164	1,851,342
Stockholders' Equity	1,149,849	1,206,784	1,163,565	1,071,610	965,620	1,175,606	1,096,139	1,999,383
Shares Outstanding	149,660	160,043	162,899	159,786	142,170	141,784	140,480	136,005
Statistical Record								
Return on Assets %	2.93	3.51	2.24	N.M.	N.M.	1.94	1.65	0.52
Return on Equity %	5.25	6.33	4.29	N.M.	N.M.	4.19	3.42	1.10
EBITDA Margin %	8.16	8.91	7.50	3.13	0.16	7.67	4.64	6.56
Net Margin %	2.00	2.48	1.72	N.M.	N.M.	1.45	1.83	0.38
Asset Turnover	1.47	1.41	1.31	1.23	1.34	1.34	0.90	1.40
Current Ratio	1.98	2.74	2.20	2.44	2.36	1.44	1.45	1.95
Debt to Equity	0.23	0.30	0.31	0.46	0.66	0.22	0.41	0.36
Price Range	11.97-9.72	12.97-7.81	12.12-6.32	7.44-1.55	17.91-2.40	22.69-15.09	20.63-14.26	24.43-13.80
P/E Ratio	29.20-23.71	28.82-17.36	40.40-21.07	...	...	73.19-48.68	51.57-35.65	152.69-86.25
Average Yield %	...	...	...	...	...	...	45.41	...

Address: 12 East 49th Street, New York, NY 10017	**Web Site:** www.saksincorporated.com	**Auditors:** PricewaterhouseCoopers LLP
Telephone: 212-940-5305	**Officers:** Stephen I. Sadove - Chairman, Chief Executive Officer Ronald L. Frasch - President, Chief Merchandising Officer	**Investor Contact:** 865-981-6243
		Transfer Agents: The Bank of New York, New York, NY

SALESFORCE.COM INC

Exchange	Symbol	Price	52Wk Range	Yield	P/E
NYS	CRM	$178.83 (3/28/2013)	186.37-121.37	N/A	N/A

*7 Year Price Score 162.42 *NYSE Composite Index=100 *12 Month Price Score 104.51

TRADING VOLUME (thousand shares)

Interim Earnings (Per Share)

Qtr.	Apr	Jul	Oct	Jan
2008-09	0.08	0.08	0.08	0.11
2009-10	0.15	0.17	0.16	0.15
2010-11	0.13	0.11	0.15	0.07
2011-12	0.00	(0.03)	(0.03)	(0.03)
2012-13	(0.14)	(0.07)	(1.55)	(0.14)

Interim Dividends (Per Share)

No Dividends Paid

Valuation Analysis

Forecast EPS	$1.97
	(04/05/2013)
Market Cap	$26.2 Billion
Book Value	$2.4 Billion
Price/Book	11.04
Price/Sales	8.58

Institutional Holding

No of Institutions	595
Shares	
	158,136,480
% Held	108.12

Business Summary: Internet & Software (MIC: 6.3.2 SIC: 7372 NAIC: 511210)

Salesforce.Com is a provider of enterprise cloud computing and social enterprise applications. Co. delivers customer relationship management applications via the Internet or cloud. Cloud computing refers to the use of Internet-based computing, storage and connectivity technology to deliver a variety of different services. Co.'s cloud applications for the social enterprise include: Sales Cloud; Service Cloud; Salesforce Chatter; Salesforce Radian6; and Salesforce Data.com. Co.'s cloud platforms for the social enterprise includes: The Force.com Platform; Heroku Platform; Database.com.; and The AppExchange. In addition, Co. provides consulting, deployment and training services to its customers.

Recent Developments: For the year ended Jan 31 2013, net loss amounted to US$270.4 million versus a net loss of US$11.6 million in the prior year. Revenues were US$3.05 billion, up 34.6% from US$2.27 billion the year before. Operating loss was US$110.7 million versus a loss of US$35.1 million in the prior year. Direct operating expenses rose 39.8% to US$683.6 million from US$488.9 million in the comparable period the year before. Indirect operating expenses increased 36.7% to US$2.48 billion from US$1.81 billion in the equivalent prior-year period.

Prospects: Our evaluation of Salesforce.com Inc. as of Apr. 7, 2013 is the result of our systematic analysis on three basic characteristics: earnings strength, relative valuation, and recent stock price movement. The company has produced a positive trend in earnings per share over the past 5 quarters and while recent estimates for the company have remained steady, CRM has posted better than expected results. Based on operating earnings yield, the company is overvalued when compared to all of the companies in our coverage universe. Share price changes over the past year indicates that CRM will perform very well over the near term.

Financial Data

(US$ in Thousands)	01/31/2013	01/31/2012	01/31/2011	01/31/2010	01/31/2009	01/31/2008	01/31/2007	01/31/2006
Earnings Per Share	(1.92)	(0.09)	0.47	0.63	0.35	0.15	0.00	0.24
Cash Flow Per Share	5.20	4.37	3.53	2.18	1.89	1.75	0.99	0.89
Tang Book Value Per Share	3.90	4.61	5.38	7.50	4.78	3.51	2.30	1.76
Income Statement								
Total Revenue	3,050,195	2,266,539	1,657,139	1,305,583	1,076,769	748,700	497,098	309,857
EBITDA	4,254	69,328	183,707	186,181	90,525	41,303	7,640	26,125
Depn & Amortn	101,100	85,600	54,500	41,800	27,600	19,583	9,928	5,584
Income Before Taxes	(127,794)	(33,317)	104,298	142,381	85,592	46,213	12,496	28,198
Income Taxes	142,651	(21,745)	34,601	57,689	37,557	23,385	9,795	(1,310)
Net Income	(270,445)	(11,572)	64,474	80,719	43,428	18,356	481	28,474
Average Shares	141,224	135,302	136,598	128,114	125,228	122,422	120,154	118,737
Balance Sheet								
Current Assets	2,015,880	1,672,222	1,074,924	1,706,159	1,068,557	740,811	419,096	303,217
Total Assets	5,528,956	4,164,154	3,091,165	2,460,201	1,479,822	1,089,593	664,832	434,749
Current Liabilities	2,917,624	2,323,471	1,276,466	908,130	766,966	605,917	376,999	234,625
Long-Term Obligations	...	...	472,538	450,198	...	...	6	184
Total Liabilities	3,157,711	2,498,053	1,814,674	1,416,399	808,038	637,534	383,041	238,378
Stockholders' Equity	2,371,245	1,666,101	1,276,491	1,043,802	671,784	452,059	281,791	196,371
Shares Outstanding	146,406	137,036	132,921	127,152	122,850	119,305	144,537	110,513
Statistical Record								
Return on Assets %	N.M.	N.M.	2.32	4.10	3.37	2.09	0.09	7.96
Return on Equity %	N.M.	N.M.	5.56	9.41	7.71	5.00	0.20	16.68
EBITDA Margin %	0.14	3.06	11.09	14.26	8.41	5.52	1.54	8.43
Net Margin %	N.M.	N.M.	3.89	6.18	4.03	2.45	0.10	9.19
Asset Turnover	0.63	0.62	0.60	0.66	0.84	0.85	0.90	0.87
Current Ratio	0.69	0.72	0.84	1.88	1.39	1.22	1.11	1.29
Debt to Equity	...	...	0.37	0.43	...	...	N.M.	N.M.
Price Range	178.07-116.80	159.32-97.48	150.58-62.08	74.82-25.77	74.43-21.96	64.99-38.86	44.00-21.85	42.65-13.07
P/E Ratio	...	...	320.38-132.09	118.76-40.90	212.66-62.74	433.27-259.07	N.M.	177.71-54.46

Address: The Landmark @ One Market, Suite 300, San Francisco, CA 94105	Web Site: www.salesforce.com	Auditors: Ernst & Young LLP
	Officers: Marc Benioff - Chairman, Chief Executive Officer Frank van Veenendaal - Vice-Chairman, Chief	Investor Contact: 415-536-6250
Telephone: 415-901-7000	Sales Officer, Division Officer	Transfer Agents: Computershare Investor Services, LLC

SALLY BEAUTY HOLDINGS INC

Exchange	Symbol	Price	52Wk Range	Yield	P/E
NYS	SBH	$29.38 (3/28/2013)	29.70-22.76	N/A	20.99

*7 Year Price Score N/A   *NYSE Composite Index=100   *12 Month Price Score 98.23

Interim Earnings (Per Share)

Qtr.	Dec	Mar	Jun	Sep
2009-10	0.14	0.19	0.22	0.23
2010-11	0.22	0.26	0.37	0.29
2011-12	0.16	0.35	0.37	0.36
2012-13	0.32	...	...	...

Interim Dividends (Per Share)

No Dividends Paid

Valuation Analysis / Institutional Holding

Forecast EPS	$1.60	No of Institutions
(04/05/2013)		342
Market Cap	$5.2 Billion	Shares
Book Value	N/A	177,414,464
Price/Book	N/A	% Held
Price/Sales	1.45	94.74

Business Summary: Retail - Specialty (MIC: 2.1.3 SIC: 5999 NAIC: 446120)

Sally Beauty Holdings is a holding company. Co. is a retailer and distributor of beauty supplies with operations primarily in North America, South America and Europe. Through its two business units, Sally Beauty Supply (SBS) and Beauty Systems Group (BSG), Co. sold and distributed beauty products through 4,315 company-owned stores, 184 franchised stores and 1,044 distributor sales consultants as of Sep 30 2012. SBS stores target retail consumers and salon personnel. BSG targets salons and salon personnel. Co. provides customers with beauty supplies, including hair color products, hair care products, hair dryers and hair styling appliances, skin and nail care products and other beauty items.

Recent Developments: For the quarter ended Dec 31 2012, net income increased 95.7% to US$59.0 million from US$30.1 million in the year-earlier quarter. Revenues were US$905.4 million, up 4.7% from US$864.8 million the year before. Operating income was US$121.9 million versus US$113.3 million in the prior-year quarter, an increase of 7.6%. Direct operating expenses rose 4.1% to US$461.1 million from US$443.0 million in the comparable period the year before. Indirect operating expenses increased 4.5% to US$322.5 million from US$308.6 million in the equivalent prior-year period.

Prospects: Our evaluation of Sally Beauty Holdings Inc. as of Apr. 7, 2013 is the result of our systematic analysis on three basic characteristics: earnings strength, relative valuation, and recent stock price movement. The company has produced a positive trend in earnings per share over the past 5 quarters and while recent estimates for the company have been raised by analysts, SBH has posted results that fell short of analysts expectations. Based on operating earnings yield, the company is about fairly valued when compared to all of the companies in our coverage universe. Share price changes over the past year indicates that SBH will perform poorly over the near term.

Financial Data
(US$ in Thousands)

	3 Mos	09/30/2012	09/30/2011	09/30/2010	09/30/2009	09/30/2008	09/30/2007	09/30/2006
Earnings Per Share	1.40	1.24	1.14	0.78	0.54	0.42	0.24	...
Cash Flow Per Share	1.66	1.62	1.59	1.19	1.23	0.61	1.07	...
Tang Book Value Per Share	...	...	...	...	...	...	...	595,564.00
Income Statement								
Total Revenue	905,441	3,523,644	3,269,131	2,916,090	2,636,600	2,648,191	2,513,772	2,373,100
EBITDA	122,771	550,355	495,769	383,330	337,736	325,115	267,485	218,201
Depn & Amortn	900	51,000	47,300	42,400	40,900	42,200	38,900	38,000
Income Before Taxes	95,146	360,943	335,939	227,948	164,814	123,799	82,613	180,109
Income Taxes	36,163	127,879	122,214	84,120	65,697	46,222	38,121	69,916
Net Income	58,983	233,064	213,725	143,828	99,117	77,577	44,492	110,193
Average Shares	183,386	188,610	188,093	184,088	183,306	182,704	182,375	...
Balance Sheet								
Current Assets	1,060,057	1,163,907	879,148	794,775	715,918	805,646	712,187	770,289
Total Assets	1,969,931	2,065,800	1,728,600	1,589,412	1,490,732	1,527,023	1,404,503	1,338,841
Current Liabilities	422,646	477,388	460,006	407,652	374,185	438,448	358,002	291,182
Long-Term Obligations	1,614,759	1,615,322	1,410,111	1,559,591	1,653,013	1,724,684	1,758,594	621
Total Liabilities	2,127,123	2,180,885	1,947,582	2,049,738	2,104,383	2,224,099	2,165,664	325,346
Stockholders' Equity	(157,192)	(115,085)	(218,982)	(460,326)	(613,651)	(697,076)	(761,161)	1,013,495
Shares Outstanding	176,058	180,241	184,057	182,230	181,858	181,516	180,909	1,000.00
Statistical Record								
Return on Assets %	13.92	12.25	12.88	9.34	6.57	5.28	3.24	8.59
Return on Equity %	...	...	...	...	...	...	35.26	11.52
EBITDA Margin %	13.56	15.62	15.17	13.15	12.81	12.28	10.64	9.19
Net Margin %	6.51	6.61	6.54	4.93	3.76	2.93	1.77	4.64
Asset Turnover	1.89	1.85	1.97	1.89	1.75	1.80	1.83	1.85
Current Ratio	2.51	2.44	1.91	1.95	1.91	1.91	1.84	2.65
Price Range	28.07-19.98	28.07-16.28	18.47-11.01	11.70-6.75	8.60-2.70	10.71-5.76	10.02-7.18	...
P/E Ratio	20.05-14.27	22.64-13.13	16.20-9.66	15.00-8.65	15.93-5.00	25.50-13.71	41.75-29.92	...

Address: 3001 Colorado Boulevard, Denton, TX 76210 Telephone: 940-898-7500	Web Site: www.sallybeauty.com Officers: Gary G. Winterhalter - Chairman, President, Chief Executive Officer Mark J. Flaherty - Senior Vice President, Chief Financial Officer	Auditors: KPMG LLP Investor Contact: 940-297-3877 Transfer Agents: Computershare Trust Company N.A., Providence, RI

659

SANDRIDGE ENERGY, INC.

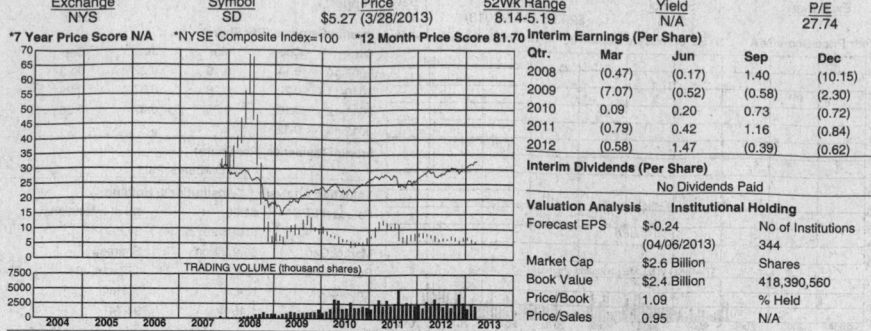

Exchange	Symbol	Price	52Wk Range	Yield	P/E
NYS	SD	$5.27 (3/28/2013)	8.14-5.19	N/A	27.74

*7 Year Price Score N/A   *NYSE Composite Index=100   *12 Month Price Score 81.70

Interim Earnings (Per Share)

Qtr.	Mar	Jun	Sep	Dec
2008	(0.47)	(0.17)	1.40	(10.15)
2009	(7.07)	(0.52)	(0.58)	(2.30)
2010	0.09	0.20	0.73	(0.72)
2011	(0.79)	0.42	1.16	(0.84)
2012	(0.58)	1.47	(0.39)	(0.62)

Interim Dividends (Per Share)

No Dividends Paid

Valuation Analysis

		Institutional Holding	
Forecast EPS	$-0.24 (04/06/2013)	No of Institutions	344
Market Cap	$2.6 Billion	Shares	
Book Value	$2.4 Billion	% Held	418,390,560
Price/Book	1.09	N/A	
Price/Sales	0.95		

Business Summary: Production & Extraction (MIC: 9.1.1 SIC: 1311 NAIC: 211111)

SandRidge Energy is an independent oil and natural gas company concentrating on development and production activities related to the exploitation of its holdings in the Mid-Continent area of Oklahoma and Kansas and in west Texas. Co.'s primary focus in the Mid-Continent area is the Mississippian formation, a shallow hydrocarbon system in northern Oklahoma and Kansas. Co.'s primary area of focus in west Texas is the Permian Basin. Co. also owns and operates other interests in the Mid-Continent, West Texas Overthrust, Gulf Coast and Gulf of Mexico. As of Dec 31 2011, Co.'s estimated proved reserves were 470.6 million barrels of oil equivalent, of which approximately 52.0% were oil.

Recent Developments: For the year ended Dec 31 2012, net income increased 51.8% to US$246.6 million from US$162.4 million in the prior year. Revenues were US$2.73 billion, up 93.0% from US$1.42 billion the year before. Operating income was US$325.2 million versus US$429.0 million in the prior year, a decrease of 24.2%. Direct operating expenses rose 185.4% to US$1.43 billion from US$500.6 million in the comparable period the year before. Indirect operating expenses increased 101.2% to US$977.2 million from US$485.6 million in the equivalent prior-year period.

Prospects: Our evaluation of Sandridge Energy as of Apr. 7, 2013 is the result of our systematic analysis on three basic characteristics: earnings strength, relative valuation, and recent stock price movement. The company has suffered a very negative trend in earnings per share over the past 5 quarters. Because the company lacks sufficient analyst estimate data, we place greater weight on the historical EPS trend as the measure of earnings strength. Based on operating earnings yield, the company is overvalued when compared to all of the companies in our coverage universe. Share price changes over the past year indicates that SD will perform well over the near term.

Financial Data

(US$ in Thousands)	12/31/2012	12/31/2011	12/31/2010	12/31/2009	12/31/2008	12/31/2007	12/31/2006	12/31/2005
Earnings Per Share	0.19	0.13	0.52	(10.15)	(9.26)	0.46	0.21	0.28
Cash Flow Per Share	1.72	1.19	1.34	1.78	3.71	3.28	0.91	1.05
Tang Book Value Per Share	4.83	3.38	3.20	...	4.78	15.80	11.89	3.79
Income Statement								
Total Revenue	2,730,965	1,415,213	931,736	591,044	1,181,814	677,452	388,242	284,857
EBITDA	1,095,372	787,902	335,042	(1,362,393)	(969,705)	429,966	92,906	54,264
Depn & Amortn	645,814	393,999	339,270	235,359	366,988	243,107	55,925	24,177
Income Before Taxes	146,209	156,571	(251,670)	(1,783,068)	(1,480,151)	75,097	21,186	25,016
Income Taxes	(100,362)	(5,817)	(446,680)	(8,716)	(38,328)	29,524	6,236	8,549
Net Income	141,571	108,065	190,565	(1,775,590)	(1,441,280)	50,221	15,621	15,575
Average Shares	456,015	406,645	315,349	175,005	155,619	110,041	74,664	56,737
Balance Sheet								
Current Assets	1,142,885	441,840	175,590	255,964	355,913	226,452	174,806	118,833
Total Assets	9,790,731	6,219,609	5,231,448	2,780,317	3,655,058	3,630,566	2,388,384	439,086
Current Liabilities	1,170,454	699,496	544,458	225,544	402,624	232,106	158,792	110,642
Long-Term Obligations	4,301,083	2,813,125	2,901,793	2,566,935	2,358,784	1,052,299	1,040,630	30,136
Total Liabilities	7,421,878	4,593,598	3,695,253	2,986,274	2,861,537	1,412,960	1,298,923	162,791
Stockholders' Equity	2,368,853	1,626,011	1,536,195	(205,957)	793,521	2,217,606	1,089,461	276,295
Shares Outstanding	490,359	411,953	406,360	208,715	166,046	140,391	91,604	72,917
Statistical Record								
Return on Assets %	1.76	1.89	4.76	N.M.	N.M.	1.67	1.10	5.02
Return on Equity %	7.07	6.83	28.65	N.M.	N.M.	3.04	2.29	9.57
EBITDA Margin %	40.11	55.67	35.96	N.M.	N.M.	63.47	23.93	19.05
Net Margin %	5.18	7.64	20.45	N.M.	N.M.	7.41	4.02	5.47
Asset Turnover	0.34	0.25	0.23	0.18	0.32	0.23	0.27	0.92
Current Ratio	0.98	0.63	0.32	1.13	0.88	0.98	1.10	1.07
Debt to Equity	1.82	1.73	1.89	...	2.97	0.47	0.96	0.11
Price Range	8.82-5.19	12.97-5.01	10.84-4.00	14.29-4.64	68.54-5.37	35.86-29.90	...	...
P/E Ratio	46.42-27.32	99.77-38.54	20.85-7.69	...	...	77.96-65.00	...	...

Address: 123 Robert S. Kerr Avenue, Oklahoma City, OK 73102 **Telephone:** 405-429-5500 **Fax:** 405-753-5975	**Web Site:** www.sandridgeenergy.com **Officers:** Tom L. Ward - Chairman, President, Chief Executive Officer James D. Bennett - Executive Vice President, Chief Financial Officer, Principal Financial Officer	**Auditors:** PricewaterhouseCoopers LLP **Investor Contact:** 405-429-5515 **Transfer Agents:** American Stock Transfer & Trust Company, LLC

SCANA CORP

Exchange	Symbol	Price	52Wk Range	Yield	P/E	Div Achiever
NYS	SCG	$51.16 (3/28/2013)	51.16-44.00	3.97	16.24	12 Years

*7 Year Price Score 105.20 *NYSE Composite Index=100 *12 Month Price Score 95.04

Interim Earnings (Per Share)

Qtr.	Mar	Jun	Sep	Dec
2008	0.94	0.48	0.80	0.73
2009	0.94	0.45	0.84	0.62
2010	1.02	0.43	0.79	0.74
2011	1.00	0.43	0.81	0.74
2012	0.91	0.54	0.91	0.78

Interim Dividends (Per Share)

Amt	Decl	Ex	Rec	Pay
0.495Q	05/03/2012	06/07/2012	06/11/2012	07/01/2012
0.495Q	08/02/2012	09/06/2012	09/10/2012	10/01/2012
0.495Q	10/24/2012	12/06/2012	12/10/2012	01/01/2013
0.507Q	02/20/2013	03/07/2013	03/11/2013	04/01/2013

Indicated Div: $2.03 (Div. Reinv. Plan)

Valuation Analysis

Forecast EPS	$3.34 (04/05/2013)
Market Cap	$6.8 Billion
Book Value	$4.2 Billion
Price/Book	1.63
Price/Sales	1.62

Institutional Holding

No of Institutions	487
Shares	72,592,464
% Held	48.95

TRADING VOLUME (thousand shares)

Business Summary: Electric Utilities (MIC: 3.1.1 SIC: 4931 NAIC: 221122)

SCANA is a holding company. Through its wholly-owned regulated subsidiaries, Co. is primarily engaged in the generation, transmission, distribution and sale of electricity in parts of South Carolina and in the purchase, transmission and sale of natural gas in portions of North Carolina and South Carolina. Through a wholly-owned nonregulated subsidiary, Co. markets natural gas to retail customers in Georgia and to wholesale customers primarily in the southeast. Other wholly- owned nonregulated subsidiaries provide fiber optic and other telecommunications services and provide service contracts to homeowners on certain home appliances and heating and air conditioning units.

Recent Developments: For the year ended Dec 31 2012, net income increased 8.5% to US$420.0 million from US$387.0 million in the prior year. Revenues were US$4.18 billion, down 5.3% from US$4.41 billion the year before. Operating income was US$859.0 million versus US$813.0 million in the prior year, an increase of 5.7%. Direct operating expenses declined 9.7% to US$2.75 billion from US$3.05 billion in the comparable period the year before. Indirect operating expenses increased 2.9% to US$563.0 million from US$547.0 million in the equivalent prior-year period.

Prospects: Our evaluation of SCANA Corp. as of Apr. 7, 2013 is the result of our systematic analysis on three basic characteristics: earnings strength, relative valuation, and recent stock price movement. The company has managed to produce a neutral trend in earnings per share over the past 5 quarters. However, while recent estimates for the company have been mixed, SCG has posted better than expected results. Based on operating earnings yield, the company is undervalued when compared to all of the companies in our coverage universe. Share price changes over the past year indicates that SCG will perform poorly over the near term.

Financial Data

(US$ in Thousands)	12/31/2012	12/31/2011	12/31/2010	12/31/2009	12/31/2008	12/31/2007	12/31/2006	12/31/2005
Earnings Per Share	3.15	2.97	2.98	2.85	2.95	2.74	2.68	2.81
Cash Flow Per Share	6.38	6.30	6.45	5.56	3.87	6.26	6.50	4.10
Tang Book Value Per Share	29.73	28.15	27.34	25.84	23.92	23.39	22.43	21.41
Dividends Per Share	1.980	1.940	1.900	1.880	1.840	1.760	1.680	1.560
Dividend Payout %	62.86	65.32	63.76	65.96	62.37	64.23	62.69	55.52
Income Statement								
Total Revenue	4,176,000	4,409,000	4,601,000	4,237,000	5,319,000	4,621,000	4,563,000	4,777,000
EBITDA	1,309,000	1,233,000	1,177,000	1,102,000	1,098,000	1,020,000	981,000	996,000
Depn & Amortn	412,000	394,000	377,000	347,000	344,000	341,000	333,000	510,000
Income Before Taxes	602,000	555,000	534,000	522,000	527,000	473,000	439,000	274,000
Income Taxes	182,000	168,000	159,000	167,000	189,000	140,000	119,000	(118,000)
Net Income	420,000	387,000	376,000	357,000	346,000	320,000	310,000	320,000
Average Shares	133,300	130,200	126,300	122,100	117,000	116,700	115,800	113,800
Balance Sheet								
Current Assets	1,527,000	1,491,000	1,631,000	1,521,000	1,836,000	1,301,000	1,376,000	1,464,000
Total Assets	14,616,000	13,534,000	12,968,000	12,094,000	11,502,000	10,165,000	9,817,000	9,519,000
Current Liabilities	1,811,000	1,642,000	1,867,000	1,256,000	1,155,000	1,721,000	1,405,000	1,500,000
Long-Term Obligations	4,949,000	4,622,000	4,152,000	4,483,000	4,361,000	2,879,000	3,067,000	2,948,000
Total Liabilities	10,462,000	9,645,000	9,266,000	8,686,000	8,344,000	7,092,000	6,857,000	6,728,000
Stockholders' Equity	4,154,000	3,889,000	3,702,000	3,408,000	3,158,000	3,073,000	2,960,000	2,791,000
Shares Outstanding	132,000	130,000	127,000	123,000	118,000	117,000	117,000	114,671
Statistical Record								
Return on Assets %	2.98	2.92	3.00	3.03	3.19	3.20	3.21	3.46
Return on Equity %	10.42	10.20	10.58	10.87	11.08	10.61	10.78	11.95
EBITDA Margin %	31.35	27.97	25.58	26.01	20.64	22.07	21.50	20.85
Net Margin %	10.06	8.78	8.17	8.43	6.50	6.92	6.79	6.70
Asset Turnover	0.30	0.33	0.37	0.36	0.49	0.46	0.47	0.52
Current Ratio	0.84	0.91	0.87	1.21	1.59	0.76	0.98	0.98
Debt to Equity	1.19	1.19	1.12	1.32	1.38	0.94	1.04	1.06
Price Range	49.65-43.71	45.34-35.12	41.69-34.55	38.44-26.37	42.51-30.03	45.26-36.70	41.99-37.16	43.40-37.10
P/E Ratio	15.76-13.88	15.27-11.82	13.99-11.59	13.49-9.25	14.41-10.18	16.52-13.39	15.67-13.87	15.44-13.20
Average Yield %	4.24	4.78	4.93	5.67	4.92	4.30	4.20	3.88

Address: 100 SCANA Parkway, Cayce, SC 29033 **Telephone:** 803-217-9000	**Web Site:** www.scana.com **Officers:** Kevin B. Marsh - Chairman, President, Chief Executive Officer, Chief Operating Officer Jimmy E. Addison - Senior Vice President, Chief Financial Officer	**Auditors:** Deloitte & Touche LLP **Investor Contact:** 803-217-9240 **Transfer Agents:** SCANA Corporation, Columbia, SC

SCHLUMBERGER LTD.

Exchange	Symbol	Price	52Wk Range	Yield	P/E
NYS	SLB	$74.89 (3/28/2013)	81.56-59.67	1.67	18.27

*7 Year Price Score 88.48   *NYSE Composite Index=100   *12 Month Price Score 99.38

Interim Earnings (Per Share)

Qtr.	Mar	Jun	Sep	Dec
2008	1.09	1.16	1.25	0.95
2009	0.78	0.51	0.65	0.66
2010	0.56	0.68	1.38	0.75
2011	0.69	0.98	0.96	1.05
2012	0.97	1.05	1.07	1.02

Interim Dividends (Per Share)

Amt	Decl	Ex	Rec	Pay
0.275Q	04/19/2012	05/30/2012	06/01/2012	07/13/2012
0.275Q	07/19/2012	08/29/2012	08/31/2012	10/12/2012
0.275Q	10/18/2012	11/29/2012	12/03/2012	01/11/2013
0.313Q	01/17/2013	02/15/2013	02/20/2013	04/12/2013

Indicated Div: $1.25

Valuation Analysis / **Institutional Holding**

Forecast EPS	$4.71 (04/06/2013)	No of Institutions 1714
Market Cap	$99.5 Billion	Shares 1,069,657,856
Book Value	$34.8 Billion	% Held 73.95
Price/Book	2.86	
Price/Sales	2.35	

Business Summary: Equipment & Services (MIC: 9.1.3 SIC: 3533 NAIC: 333132)

Schlumberger and its subsidiaries are engaged as a supplier of technology, project management and information services to customers in the international oil and gas exploration and production industry. Co. provides a range of products and services from exploration through production. Co. manages its business through three Groups: Reservoir Characterization, which consists of the technologies involved in finding and defining hydrocarbon resources; Drilling, which consists of the principal technologies involved in the drilling and positioning of oil and gas wells; and Production, which consists of the principal technologies involved in the lifetime production of oil and gas reservoirs.

Recent Developments: For the year ended Dec 31 2012, income from continuing operations increased 15.6% to US$5.47 billion from US$4.73 billion a year earlier. Net income increased 10.2% to US$5.52 billion from US$5.01 billion in the prior year. Revenues were US$42.32 billion, up 14.1% from US$37.09 billion the year before. Direct operating expenses rose 14.2% to US$33.06 billion from US$28.94 billion in the comparable period the year before. Indirect operating expenses increased 8.5% to US$2.07 billion from US$1.91 billion in the equivalent prior-year period.

Prospects: Our evaluation of Schlumberger Ltd. as of Apr. 7, 2013 is the result of our systematic analysis on three basic characteristics: earnings strength, relative valuation, and recent stock price movement. The company has managed to produce a neutral trend in earnings per share over the past 5 quarters. However, while recent estimates for the company have been lowered by analysts, SLB has posted better than expected results. Based on operating earnings yield, the company is undervalued when compared to all of the companies in our coverage universe. Share price changes over the past year indicates that SLB will perform well over the near term.

Financial Data

(US$ in Thousands)	12/31/2012	12/31/2011	12/31/2010	12/31/2009	12/31/2008	12/31/2007	12/31/2006	12/31/2005
Earnings Per Share	4.10	3.67	3.38	2.59	4.45	4.20	3.01	1.82
Cash Flow Per Share	5.11	4.57	4.40	4.43	5.75	5.27	4.05	2.55
Tang Book Value Per Share	11.57	9.17	8.90	10.90	9.09	7.39	3.84	3.69
Dividends Per Share	1.100	1.000	0.840	0.840	0.840	0.700	0.500	0.420
Dividend Payout %	26.83	27.25	24.85	32.43	18.88	16.67	16.61	23.08
Income Statement								
Total Revenue	42,321,000	39,669,000	28,931,000	22,975,000	27,564,767	23,708,037	19,517,194	14,716,951
EBITDA	10,431,000	9,336,000	7,763,000	6,631,000	9,368,215	8,852,994	6,744,484	4,519,789
Depn & Amortn	2,900,000	2,700,000	2,400,000	2,476,000	2,268,508	1,953,987	1,561,410	1,350,969
Income Before Taxes	7,191,000	6,338,000	5,156,000	3,934,000	6,852,455	6,624,449	4,948,158	2,971,730
Income Taxes	1,723,000	1,545,000	890,000	770,000	1,430,124	1,447,933	1,189,568	681,927
Net Income	5,490,000	4,997,000	4,267,000	3,134,000	5,434,801	5,176,516	3,709,851	2,206,967
Average Shares	1,339,000	1,361,000	1,263,000	1,214,000	1,223,894	1,238,675	1,242,196	1,229,716
Balance Sheet								
Current Assets	24,156,000	20,539,000	18,098,000	13,650,000	12,893,677	11,055,383	9,185,662	8,553,913
Total Assets	61,547,000	55,201,000	51,767,000	33,465,000	31,990,725	27,853,372	22,832,138	18,077,492
Current Liabilities	12,368,000	10,538,000	10,865,000	7,259,000	8,124,650	7,504,851	6,454,795	5,514,736
Long-Term Obligations	9,509,000	8,556,000	5,517,000	4,355,000	3,693,517	3,794,466	4,663,942	3,591,338
Total Liabilities	26,796,000	23,938,000	20,541,000	14,345,000	15,128,356	12,977,484	12,412,255	10,485,907
Stockholders' Equity	34,751,000	31,263,000	31,226,000	19,120,000	16,862,369	14,875,888	10,419,883	7,591,585
Shares Outstanding	1,328,255	1,333,775	1,361,171	1,194,812	1,194,100	1,195,616	1,178,543	1,177,604
Statistical Record								
Return on Assets %	9.38	9.34	10.01	9.58	18.11	20.43	18.14	12.95
Return on Equity %	16.59	15.99	16.95	17.42	34.15	40.93	41.19	32.20
EBITDA Margin %	24.65	23.53	26.83	28.86	33.99	37.34	34.56	30.71
Net Margin %	12.97	12.60	14.75	13.64	19.72	21.83	19.01	15.00
Asset Turnover	0.72	0.74	0.68	0.70	0.92	0.94	0.95	0.86
Current Ratio	1.95	1.95	1.67	1.88	1.59	1.47	1.42	1.55
Debt to Equity	0.27	0.27	0.18	0.23	0.22	0.26	0.45	0.47
Price Range	79.85-59.67	95.04-57.72	83.63-51.75	70.76-35.19	109.86-37.74	112.09-56.52	73.37-51.68	51.44-31.73
P/E Ratio	19.48-14.55	25.90-15.73	24.74-15.31	27.32-13.59	24.69-8.48	26.69-13.46	24.38-17.17	28.26-17.44
Average Yield %	1.55	1.24	1.29	1.57	1.02	0.83	0.80	1.07

Address: 42 Rue Saint-Dominique, Paris, 75007 **Telephone:** 713-375-3400	**Web Site:** www.slb.com **Officers:** Anthony Isaac - Chairman Paal Kibsgaard - Chief Executive Officer	**Auditors:** PricewaterhouseCoopers LLP **Investor Contact:** 713-375-3535 **Transfer Agents:** Computershare Trust Company, N.A., Providence, RI

SCHWAB (CHARLES) CORP.

Exchange	Symbol	Price	52Wk Range	Yield	P/E
NYS	SCHW	$17.69 (3/28/2013)	18.11-11.83	1.36	25.64

*7 Year Price Score 72.31 *NYSE Composite Index=100 *12 Month Price Score 111.13

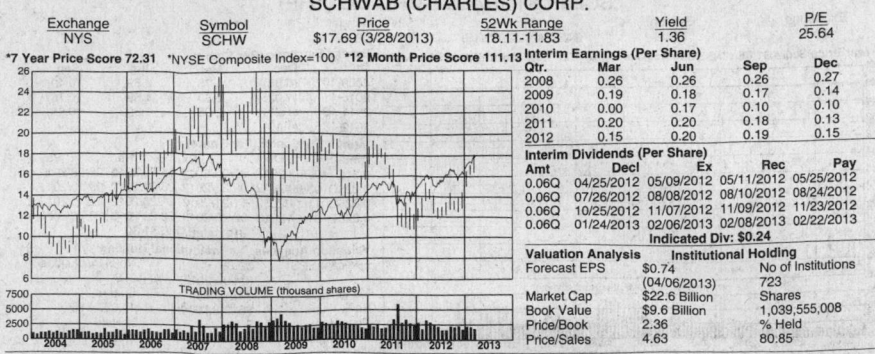

Interim Earnings (Per Share)

Qtr.	Mar	Jun	Sep	Dec
2008	0.26	0.26	0.26	0.27
2009	0.19	0.18	0.17	0.14
2010	0.00	0.17	0.10	0.10
2011	0.20	0.20	0.18	0.13
2012	0.15	0.20	0.19	0.15

Interim Dividends (Per Share)

Amt	Decl	Ex	Rec	Pay
0.06Q	04/25/2012	05/09/2012	05/11/2012	05/25/2012
0.06Q	07/26/2012	08/08/2012	08/10/2012	08/24/2012
0.06Q	10/25/2012	11/07/2012	11/09/2012	11/23/2012
0.06Q	01/24/2013	02/06/2013	02/08/2013	02/22/2013

Indicated Div: $0.24

Valuation Analysis

		Institutional Holding	
Forecast EPS	$0.74	No of Institutions	
	(04/06/2013)	723	
Market Cap	$22.6 Billion	Shares	
Book Value	$9.6 Billion	1,039,555,008	
Price/Book	2.36	% Held	
Price/Sales	4.63	80.85	

Business Summary: Finance Intermediaries & Services (MIC: 5.5.1 SIC: 6211 NAIC: 523120)

Charles Schwab is a savings and loan holding company. Co. is engaged, through its subsidiaries, in securities brokerage, banking, money management, and financial advisory services. Co. provides financial services to individuals and institutional clients through two segments: Investor Services and Institutional Services. The Investor Services segment provides retail brokerage and banking services to individual investors. The Institutional Services segment provides custodial, trading, and support services to independent investment advisors. The Institutional Services segment also provides retirement plan services, specialty brokerage services, and mutual fund clearing services.

Recent Developments: For the year ended Dec 31 2012, net income increased 7.4% to US$928.0 million from US$864.0 million in the prior year. Revenues were US$4.88 billion, up 4.1% from US$4.69 billion the year before. Indirect operating expenses increased 4.1% to US$3.43 billion from US$3.30 billion in the equivalent prior-year period.

Prospects: Our evaluation of Schwab (Charles) Corp. as of Apr. 7, 2013 is the result of our systematic analysis on three basic characteristics: earnings strength, relative valuation, and recent stock price movement. The company has produced a positive trend in earnings per share over the past 5 quarters. However, while recent estimates for the company have been mixed, SCHW has posted better than expected results. Based on operating earnings yield, the company is about fairly valued when compared to all of the companies in our coverage universe. Share price changes over the past year indicates that SCHW will perform well over the near term.

Financial Data
(US$ in Thousands)

	12/31/2012	12/31/2011	12/31/2010	12/31/2009	12/31/2008	12/31/2007	12/31/2006	12/31/2005
Earnings Per Share	0.69	0.70	0.38	0.68	1.05	1.97	0.95	0.55
Cash Flow Per Share	0.99	2.01	(0.01)	1.24	0.00	1.45	1.39	0.52
Tang Book Value Per Share	5.62	4.90	4.61	3.91	3.05	2.76	3.63	2.71
Dividends Per Share	0.240	0.240	0.240	0.240	0.220	1.200	0.135	0.089
Dividend Payout %	34.78	34.29	63.16	35.29	20.95	60.91	14.21	16.18
Income Statement								
Total Revenue	4,883,000	4,691,000	4,248,000	4,193,000	5,150,000	4,994,000	4,309,000	4,464,000
EBITDA	1,497,000	1,683,000	925,000	1,435,000	2,180,000	2,009,000	1,633,000	1,195,000
Depn & Amortn	47,000	291,000	146,000	159,000	152,000	156,000	157,000	10,000
Income Before Taxes	1,450,000	1,392,000	779,000	1,276,000	2,028,000	1,853,000	1,476,000	1,185,000
Income Taxes	522,000	528,000	325,000	489,000	798,000	733,000	585,000	455,000
Net Income	883,000	864,000	454,000	787,000	1,212,000	2,407,000	1,227,000	725,000
Average Shares	1,275,000	1,229,000	1,194,000	1,160,000	1,157,000	1,222,000	1,286,000	1,308,000
Balance Sheet								
Current Assets	55,559,000	46,608,000	39,667,000	36,717,000	28,641,000	36,807,000	33,332,000	36,046,000
Total Assets	133,637,000	108,553,000	92,568,000	75,431,000	51,675,000	42,286,000	48,992,000	47,351,000
Current Liabilities	120,775,000	97,441,000	82,840,000	67,439,000	45,197,000	36,034,000	33,463,000	40,999,000
Long-Term Obligations	1,632,000	2,001,000	2,006,000	1,512,000	883,000	899,000	388,000	514,000
Total Liabilities	124,048,000	100,839,000	86,342,000	70,358,000	47,614,000	38,554,000	43,984,000	42,901,000
Stockholders' Equity	9,589,000	7,714,000	6,226,000	5,073,000	4,061,000	3,732,000	5,008,000	4,450,000
Shares Outstanding	1,277,529	1,271,164	1,202,382	1,162,107	1,157,099	1,160,816	1,265,186	1,290,714
Statistical Record								
Return on Assets %	0.73	0.86	0.54	1.24	2.57	5.27	2.55	1.53
Return on Equity %	10.18	12.40	8.04	17.23	31.02	55.08	25.95	16.41
EBITDA Margin %	30.66	35.88	21.77	34.22	42.33	40.23	37.90	26.77
Net Margin %	18.08	18.42	10.69	18.77	23.53	48.20	28.48	16.24
Asset Turnover	0.04	0.05	0.05	0.07	0.11	0.11	0.09	0.09
Current Ratio	0.46	0.48	0.48	0.54	0.63	1.02	1.00	0.88
Debt to Equity	0.17	0.26	0.32	0.30	0.22	0.24	0.08	0.12
Price Range	15.38-11.61	19.45-10.75	19.88-12.76	19.49-11.34	26.00-14.59	25.55-17.76	19.36-14.26	16.00-9.87
P/E Ratio	22.29-16.83	27.79-15.36	52.32-33.58	28.66-16.68	24.76-13.90	12.97-9.02	20.38-15.01	29.09-17.95
Average Yield %	1.81	1.58	1.46	1.42	1.06	5.80	0.80	0.71

Address: 211 Main Street, San Francisco, CA 94105	Web Site: www.aboutschwab.com	Auditors: Deloitte & Touche LLP
Telephone: 415-667-7000	Officers: Charles R. Schwab - Chairman Walter W. Bettinger - President, Chief Executive Officer	Investor Contact: 415-667-1841
Fax: 415-627-8894		Transfer Agents: Wells Fargo Bank, N.A., Shareowner Services, St. Paul, MN

SCOTTS MIRACLE-GRO CO (THE)

Exchange	Symbol	Price	52Wk Range	Yield	P/E
NYS	SMG	$43.24 (3/28/2013)	55.00-38.17	3.01	24.02

*7 Year Price Score 91.65   ***NYSE Composite Index=100**   ***12 Month Price Score 93.27**

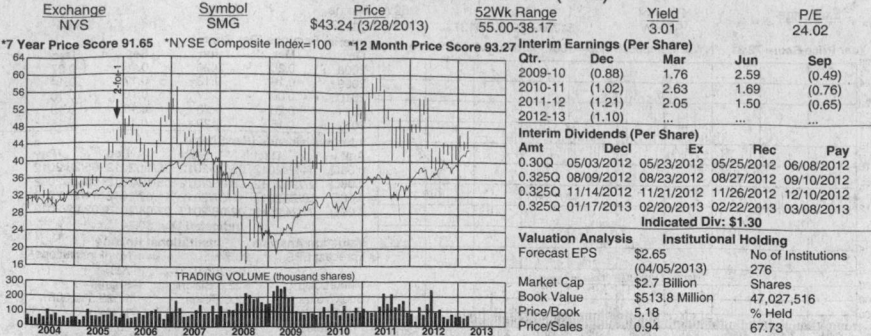

Interim Earnings (Per Share)

Qtr.	Dec	Mar	Jun	Sep
2009-10	(0.88)	1.76	2.59	(0.49)
2010-11	(1.02)	2.63	1.69	(0.76)
2011-12	(1.21)	2.05	1.50	(0.65)
2012-13	(1.10)	...	...	

Interim Dividends (Per Share)

Amt	Decl	Ex	Rec	Pay
0.30Q	05/03/2012	05/23/2012	05/25/2012	06/08/2012
0.325Q	08/09/2012	08/23/2012	08/27/2012	09/10/2012
0.325Q	11/14/2012	11/21/2012	11/26/2012	12/10/2012
0.325Q	01/17/2013	02/20/2013	02/22/2013	03/08/2013

Indicated Div: $1.30

Valuation Analysis

		Institutional Holding	
Forecast EPS	$2.65 (04/05/2013)	No of Institutions	276
Market Cap	$2.7 Billion	Shares	47,027,516
Book Value	$513.8 Million	% Held	67.73
Price/Book	5.18		
Price/Sales	0.94		

Business Summary: Agricultural Chemicals (MIC: 8.3.3 SIC: 2879 NAIC: 325320)

Scotts Miracle-Gro manufactures and markets branded consumer lawn and garden products. Co. has two segments: Global Consumer, which manufactures, markets and sells dry, granular slow-release lawn fertilizers, combination lawn fertilizer and control products, grass seed, spreaders, water-soluble, liquid and continuous release garden and indoor plant foods, plant care products, potting, garden and lawn soils, mulches and other growing media products, wild bird food, pesticide and rodenticide products; and Scotts LawnService®, which provides residential and commercial lawn fertilization, disease and insect control and other related services such as aeration, and tree and shrub fertilization.

Recent Developments: For the quarter ended Dec 29 2012, loss from continuing operations was US$68.3 million compared with a loss of US$73.1 million in the year-earlier quarter. Net loss amounted to US$67.7 million versus a net loss of US$73.9 million in the year-earlier quarter. Revenues were US$205.8 million, up 3.1% from US$199.6 million the year before. Operating loss was US$91.9 million versus a loss of US$99.0 million in the prior-year quarter. Direct operating expenses rose 0.4% to US$174.7 million from US$174.0 million in the comparable period the year before. Indirect operating expenses decreased 1.3% to US$123.0 million from US$124.6 million in the equivalent prior-year period.

Prospects: Our evaluation of Scotts Co. as of Apr. 7, 2013 is the result of our systematic analysis on three basic characteristics: earnings strength, relative valuation, and recent stock price movement. The company has produced a positive trend in earnings per share over the past 5 quarters. However, while recent estimates for the company have been mixed, SMG has posted better than expected results. Based on operating earnings yield, the company is about fairly valued when compared to all of the companies in our coverage universe. Share price changes over the past year indicates that SMG will perform in line with the market over the near term.

Financial Data
(US$ in Thousands)

	3 Mos	09/30/2012	09/30/2011	09/30/2010	09/30/2009	09/30/2008	09/30/2007	09/30/2006
Earnings Per Share	1.80	1.71	2.54	3.02	2.32	(0.17)	1.69	1.91
Cash Flow Per Share	3.03	2.51	1.89	4.46	4.07	3.11	3.78	2.70
Tang Book Value Per Share	N.M.	N.M.	N.M.	0.95	N.M.	N.M.	N.M.	2.99
Dividends Per Share	1.250	1.225	1.050	0.625	0.500	0.500	8.500	0.500
Dividend Payout %	69.44	71.64	41.34	20.70	21.55	...	502.96	26.18
Income Statement								
Total Revenue	205,800	2,826,100	2,835,700	3,139,900	3,141,500	2,981,800	2,871,800	2,697,100
EBITDA	(75,600)	314,200	316,100	453,800	315,000	151,900	310,200	303,500
Depn & Amortn	16,300	70,600	70,300	69,200	47,900	53,900	51,400	51,000
Income Before Taxes	(105,100)	181,800	194,800	337,800	210,700	15,800	188,100	212,900
Income Taxes	(36,800)	68,600	72,900	125,400	57,400	26,700	74,700	80,200
Net Income	(67,700)	106,500	167,900	204,100	153,300	(10,900)	113,400	132,700
Average Shares	61,400	62,100	66,200	67,600	66,100	64,500	67,000	69,400
Balance Sheet								
Current Assets	1,056,900	1,000,000	992,500	1,037,600	1,090,900	1,044,900	999,300	942,000
Total Assets	2,128,100	2,074,400	2,052,200	2,164,000	2,220,100	2,156,300	2,277,200	2,217,600
Current Liabilities	376,400	433,600	468,600	723,900	756,800	678,100	586,600	496,200
Long-Term Obligations	981,900	781,100	791,800	436,700	649,700	849,500	1,031,400	475,200
Total Liabilities	1,614,300	1,472,500	1,492,400	1,399,500	1,635,600	1,719,600	1,797,900	1,135,900
Stockholders' Equity	513,800	601,900	559,800	764,500	584,500	436,700	479,300	1,081,700
Shares Outstanding	61,500	61,300	60,800	65,000	63,800	61,800	64,100	66,600
Statistical Record								
Return on Assets %	5.25	5.15	7.96	9.31	7.01	N.M.	5.05	6.26
Return on Equity %	23.05	18.29	25.36	30.26	30.02	N.M.	14.53	12.59
EBITDA Margin %	N.M.	11.12	11.15	14.45	10.03	5.09	10.80	11.25
Net Margin %	N.M.	3.77	5.92	6.50	4.88	N.M.	3.95	4.92
Asset Turnover	1.31	1.37	1.35	1.43	1.44	1.34	1.28	1.27
Current Ratio	2.81	2.31	2.12	1.43	1.44	1.54	1.70	1.90
Debt to Equity	1.91	1.30	1.41	0.57	1.11	1.95	2.15	0.44
Price Range	55.00-38.17	55.00-38.17	60.27-40.41	51.87-37.84	44.17-20.58	45.89-16.92	57.04-40.86	50.24-37.57
P/E Ratio	30.56-21.21	32.16-22.32	23.73-15.91	17.18-12.53	19.04-8.87	...	33.75-24.18	26.30-19.67
Average Yield %	2.79	2.70	2.01	1.42	1.51	1.57	18.16	1.13

Address: 14111 Scottslawn Road, Marysville, OH 43041	Web Site: www.scotts.com	Auditors: Deloitte & Touche LLP
Telephone: 937-644-0011	Officers: James Hagedorn - Chairman, Chief Executive Officer Barry W. Sanders - President, Chief Operating Officer	Investor Contact: 937-644-0011
Fax: 937-644-7614		Transfer Agents: Wells Fargo Shareowner Services, St. Paul, MN

SCRIPPS NETWORKS INTERACTIVE INC

Exchange	Symbol	Price	52Wk Range	Yield	P/E
NYS	SNI	$64.34 (3/28/2013)	65.38-46.08	0.93	14.49

*7 Year Price Score N/A   *NYSE Composite Index=100   *12 Month Price Score 100.01

Interim Earnings (Per Share)

Qtr.	Mar	Jun	Sep	Dec
2008	0.00	0.33	0.35	(0.94)
2009	0.37	0.48	0.39	0.57
2010	0.43	0.63	0.61	0.78
2011	0.59	0.46	0.61	0.84
2012	0.73	0.93	0.78	2.00

Interim Dividends (Per Share)

Amt	Decl	Ex	Rec	Pay
0.12Q	05/16/2012	05/29/2012	05/31/2012	06/08/2012
0.12Q	07/31/2012	08/29/2012	08/31/2012	09/10/2012
0.12Q	11/14/2012	11/28/2012	11/30/2012	12/10/2012
0.15Q	02/14/2013	02/26/2013	02/28/2013	03/08/2013

Indicated Div: $0.60

Valuation Analysis

		Institutional Holding	
Forecast EPS	$3.59 (04/06/2013)	No of Institutions	433
Market Cap	$9.6 Billion	Shares	97,936,184
Book Value	$1.8 Billion	% Held	N/A
Price/Book	5.26		
Price/Sales	4.15		

Business Summary: Radio & Television (MIC: 2.3.1 SIC: 4841 NAIC: 515210)

Scripps Networks Interactive is a lifestyle content company with television and interactive brands. Co. operates in the media industry and has interests in national television networks and internet based media outlets. Co. manages its operations through its reportable operating segment: Lifestyle Media. The Lifestyle Media segment includes Co.'s national television networks, Home and Garden Television, Food Network, Travel Channel, DIY Network, Cooking Channel and Great American Country. This segment also includes websites that are associated with the aforementioned television brands and other Internet-based businesses serving food, home and travel related categories.

Recent Developments: For the year ended Dec 31 2012, income from continuing operations increased 33.5% to US$849.7 million from US$636.6 million a year earlier. Net income increased 47.7% to US$849.7 million from US$575.4 million in the prior year. Revenues were US$2.31 billion, up 11.3% from US$2.07 billion the year before. Operating income was US$914.4 million versus US$886.6 million in the prior year, an increase of 3.1%. Direct operating expenses rose 15.9% to US$610.8 million from US$526.9 million in the comparable period the year before. Indirect operating expenses increased 18.7% to US$782.0 million from US$658.6 million in the equivalent prior-year period.

Prospects: Our evaluation of Scripps Networks Interactive Inc. as of Apr. 7, 2013 is the result of our systematic analysis on three basic characteristics: earnings strength, relative valuation, and recent stock price movement. The company has managed to produce a neutral trend in earnings per share over the past 5 quarters. However, while recent estimates for the company have been mixed, SNI has posted results that fell short of analysts expectations. Based on operating earnings yield, the company is about fairly valued when compared to all of the companies in our coverage universe. Share price changes over the past year indicates that SNI will perform well over the near term.

Financial Data
(US$ in Thousands)

	12/31/2012	12/31/2011	12/31/2010	12/31/2009	12/31/2008	12/31/2007	12/31/2006	12/31/2005
Earnings Per Share	4.44	2.49	2.45	1.81	0.14	...	...	...
Cash Flow Per Share	4.03	4.43	2.92	3.17	3.36	...	...	...
Tang Book Value Per Share	3.97	3.90	2.84	0.19	3.70	...	...	...
Dividends Per Share	0.480	0.375	0.300	0.300	0.150	...	...	...
Dividend Payout %	10.81	15.06	12.24	16.57	107.14	...	...	...
Income Statement								
Total Revenue	2,307,182	2,072,048	2,067,162	1,541,248	1,590,637	1,441,265	1,323,469	1,002,461
EBITDA	1,035,304	959,490	869,920	585,911	381,965	184,414	538,825	405,711
Depn & Amortn	107,591	90,080	124,975	81,470	73,937	86,694	70,705	37,213
Income Before Taxes	876,899	833,289	709,778	501,631	293,821	60,950	414,075	331,537
Income Taxes	88,107	246,452	220,924	161,474	193,371	126,387	120,877	112,346
Net Income	681,478	411,558	410,972	299,326	23,557	(126,407)	191,924	58,848
Average Shares	153,327	165,572	168,009	165,381	164,131	...	...	...
Balance Sheet								
Current Assets	1,484,276	1,715,968	1,446,246	982,269	638,024	602,757	604,074	...
Total Assets	4,138,798	3,961,670	3,388,432	2,963,062	1,773,208	2,017,827	2,384,952	...
Current Liabilities	252,629	232,899	209,442	210,708	166,294	144,580	171,876	...
Long-Term Obligations	1,384,216	1,383,945	884,395	884,239	80,000	503,361	764,956	...
Total Liabilities	2,317,874	2,282,944	1,612,259	1,579,346	631,527	1,004,539	1,199,374	...
Stockholders' Equity	1,820,924	1,678,726	1,776,173	1,383,716	1,141,681	1,013,288	1,185,578	...
Shares Outstanding	148,887	157,145	167,647	165,781	163,752	...	...	...
Statistical Record								
Return on Assets %	16.78	11.20	12.94	12.64	1.24	N.M.	...	...
Return on Equity %	38.84	23.82	26.01	23.71	2.18	N.M.	...	...
EBITDA Margin %	44.87	46.31	42.08	38.02	24.01	12.80	40.71	40.47
Net Margin %	29.54	19.86	19.88	19.42	1.48	N.M.	14.50	5.87
Asset Turnover	0.57	0.56	0.65	0.65	0.84	0.65	...	...
Current Ratio	5.88	7.37	6.91	4.66	3.84	4.17	3.51	...
Debt to Equity	0.76	0.82	0.50	0.64	0.07	0.50	0.65	...
Price Range	63.72-42.53	53.36-36.15	53.33-38.62	42.21-18.51	43.00-20.55	...	...	...
P/E Ratio	14.35-9.58	21.43-14.52	21.77-15.76	23.32-10.23	307.14-146.79	...	...	...
Average Yield %	0.88	0.82	0.66	0.98	0.44	...	...	...

Address: 9721 Sherrill Boulevard, Knoxville, TN 37932 **Telephone:** 865-694-2700	**Web Site:** www.scrippsnetworksinteractive.com **Officers:** Kenneth W. Lowe - Chairman, President, Chief Executive Officer Anatolio B. Cruz - Executive Vice President, Chief Legal Officer, Secretary	**Auditors:** Deloitte & Touche LLP **Investor Contact:** 865-560-5007 **Transfer Agents:** BNY Mellon Shareowner Services, Pittsburgh, PA

SEACOR HOLDINGS INC

Exchange	Symbol	Price	52Wk Range	Yield	P/E
NYS	CKH	$73.68 (3/28/2013)	74.96-63.95	N/A	24.98

*7 Year Price Score 91.25   *NYSE Composite Index=100   *12 Month Price Score 94.64

Interim Earnings (Per Share)

Qtr.	Mar	Jun	Sep	Dec
2008	1.50	1.57	3.20	3.06
2009	2.36	1.91	1.23	1.04
2010	0.16	2.93	7.14	1.26
2011	0.52	0.42	0.18	0.79
2012	1.75	0.54	0.78	(0.11)

Interim Dividends (Per Share)

Amt	Decl	Ex	Rec	Pay
15.00Sp	11/18/2010	12/10/2010	12/14/2010	12/21/2010
5.00Sp	12/07/2012	12/13/2012	12/17/2012	12/26/2012

Valuation Analysis

		Institutional Holding	
Forecast EPS	$4.39	No of Institutions	
	(04/05/2013)	215	
Market Cap	$1.5 Billion	Shares	
Book Value	$1.7 Billion	20,068,132	
Price/Book	0.86	% Held	
Price/Sales	0.93	82.87	

Business Summary: Equipment & Services (MIC: 9.1.3 SIC: 4412 NAIC: 483111)

SEACOR Holdings is engaged in the business of owning, operating, investing in and marketing equipment, primarily to support offshore oil and gas activity, industrial aviation, and marine transportation industries. Co. operates a fleet of vessels and helicopters servicing oil and gas exploration, development and production facilities and U.S.-flag product tankers that transport petroleum, chemicals and crude products. Co. also operates inland river barges and towboats transporting grain, liquids and other bulk commodities and provides emergency preparedness and response services to oil, chemical, industrial and marine transportation clients, and government agencies in the U.S. and abroad.

Recent Developments: For the year ended Dec 31 2012, income from continuing operations decreased 0.4% to US$33.7 million from US$33.8 million a year earlier. Net income increased 43.4% to US$60.5 million from US$42.2 million in the prior year. Revenues were US$1.58 billion, up 22.5% from US$1.29 billion the year before. Operating income was US$88.5 million versus US$103.2 million in the prior year, a decrease of 14.3%. Direct operating expenses rose 26.0% to US$1.14 billion from US$908.2 million in the comparable period the year before. Indirect operating expenses increased 24.7% to US$348.1 million from US$279.1 million in the equivalent prior-year period.

Prospects: Our evaluation of SEACOR SMIT Inc. as of Apr. 7, 2013 is the result of our systematic analysis on three basic characteristics: earnings strength, relative valuation, and recent stock price movement. The company has produced a positive trend in earnings per share over the past 5 quarters and while recent estimates for the company have remained steady, CKH has posted results that fell short of analysts expectations. Based on operating earnings yield, the company is overvalued when compared to all of the companies in our coverage universe. Share price changes over the past year indicates that CKH will perform poorly over the near term.

Financial Data
(US$ in Thousands)

	12/31/2012	12/31/2011	12/31/2010	12/31/2009	12/31/2008	12/31/2007	12/31/2006	12/31/2005
Earnings Per Share	2.95	1.91	11.25	6.57	9.25	9.04	8.44	6.95
Cash Flow Per Share	9.29	9.78	18.66	14.92	13.92	16.39	14.86	11.00
Tang Book Value Per Share	84.47	81.34	79.64	83.10	76.69	67.82	60.22	51.60
Dividends Per Share	5.000	...	15.000	...	...	...	...	...
Dividend Payout %	169.49	...	133.33	...	...	...	...	...
Income Statement								
Total Revenue	1,581,200	2,141,942	2,649,368	1,711,338	1,655,956	1,359,230	1,323,445	972,004
EBITDA	275,914	231,783	566,847	424,691	508,854	503,138	523,693	349,049
Depn & Amortn	168,500	150,900	158,300	155,100	150,900	147,700	162,300	125,700
Income Before Taxes	77,145	53,394	373,479	215,014	325,841	351,251	345,707	194,398
Income Taxes	32,179	21,185	140,674	82,492	113,342	130,441	125,120	29,746
Net Income	61,215	41,056	244,724	143,810	223,688	241,648	234,394	170,709
Average Shares	20,775	21,466	21,757	23,388	24,699	27,266	28,350	25,272
Balance Sheet								
Current Assets	718,624	1,040,547	1,144,802	1,043,917	749,478	977,413	938,369	839,091
Total Assets	3,700,794	3,928,134	3,760,389	3,723,619	3,462,200	3,568,651	3,252,982	2,885,141
Current Liabilities	265,641	401,526	535,513	315,112	276,801	388,760	295,509	247,906
Long-Term Obligations	932,316	998,518	702,920	755,328	928,960	937,756	961,003	977,635
Total Liabilities	1,987,140	2,138,527	1,973,152	1,766,357	1,847,026	1,946,832	1,695,904	1,523,836
Stockholders' Equity	1,713,654	1,789,607	1,787,237	1,957,262	1,615,174	1,621,819	1,557,078	1,361,305
Shares Outstanding	19,887	20,933	21,399	22,612	20,017	22,575	24,518	24,818
Statistical Record								
Return on Assets %	1.60	1.07	6.54	4.00	6.35	7.08	7.64	7.34
Return on Equity %	3.49	2.30	13.07	8.05	13.78	15.20	16.06	15.84
EBITDA Margin %	17.45	10.82	21.40	24.82	30.73	37.02	39.57	35.91
Net Margin %	3.87	1.92	9.24	8.40	13.51	17.78	17.71	17.56
Asset Turnover	0.41	0.56	0.71	0.48	0.47	0.40	0.43	0.42
Current Ratio	2.71	2.59	2.14	3.31	2.71	2.51	3.18	3.38
Debt to Equity	0.54	0.56	0.39	0.39	0.58	0.58	0.62	0.72
Price Range	77.35-63.95	87.56-60.99	89.41-52.64	70.94-41.84	75.82-41.59	80.07-63.55	79.04-53.05	57.56-41.20
P/E Ratio	26.22-21.68	45.84-31.93	7.95-4.68	10.80-6.37	8.20-4.50	8.86-7.03	9.36-6.29	8.28-5.93
Average Yield %	7.16	...	23.25	...	...	...	...	...

Address: 2200 Eller Drive, P.O. Box 13038, Fort Lauderdale, FL 33316	Web Site: www.seacorholdings.com	Auditors: Ernst & Young LLP
Telephone: 954-523-2200	Officers: Charles L. Fabrikant - Chairman Oivind Lorentzen - Chief Executive Officer	Investor Contact: 954-523-2200
		Transfer Agents: American Stock Transfer & Trust Company, New York, NY

SEALED AIR CORP.

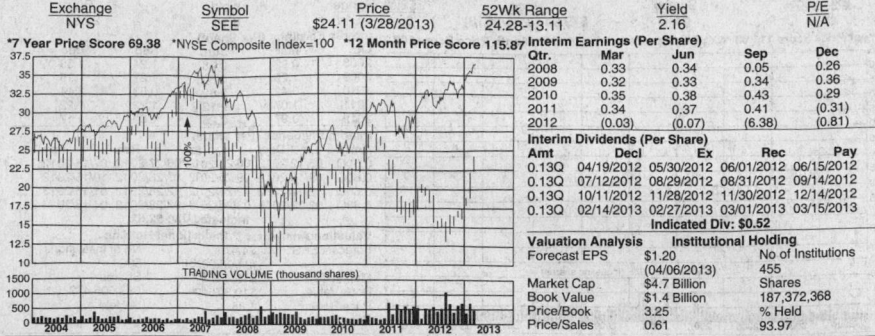

Exchange	Symbol	Price	52Wk Range	Yield	P/E
NYS	SEE	$24.11 (3/28/2013)	24.28-13.11	2.16	N/A

*7 Year Price Score 69.38   *NYSE Composite Index=100   *12 Month Price Score 115.87

Interim Earnings (Per Share)

Qtr.	Mar	Jun	Sep	Dec
2008	0.33	0.34	0.05	0.26
2009	0.32	0.33	0.34	0.36
2010	0.35	0.38	0.43	0.29
2011	0.34	0.37	0.41	(0.31)
2012	(0.03)	(0.07)	(6.38)	(0.81)

Interim Dividends (Per Share)

Amt	Decl	Ex	Rec	Pay
0.13Q	04/19/2012	05/30/2012	06/01/2012	06/15/2012
0.13Q	07/12/2012	08/29/2012	08/31/2012	09/14/2012
0.13Q	10/11/2012	11/28/2012	11/30/2012	12/14/2012
0.13Q	02/14/2013	02/27/2013	03/01/2013	03/15/2013

Indicated Div: $0.52

Valuation Analysis | **Institutional Holding**

Forecast EPS	$1.20	No of Institutions
	(04/06/2013)	455
Market Cap	$4.7 Billion	Shares
Book Value	$1.4 Billion	187,372,368
Price/Book	3.25	% Held
Price/Sales	0.61	93.97

Business Summary: Containers & Packaging (MIC: 8.1.3 SIC: 2671 NAIC: 322221)

Sealed Air is a holding company. Through its subsidiaries, Co. operates under three reportable segments: Food and Beverage, which provides solutions in the food and beverage production process; Institutional and Laundry, which provides solutions for facility hygiene, food safety and security in food service operations, and infection control to customers; and protective packaging, which provides a portfolio of protective packaging systems for use in a range of applications and industries globally. Co.'s Other category consists of medical applications, which products are sold to medical device manufacturers and pharmacy; and new ventures business, which include several development projects.

Recent Developments: For the year ended Dec 31 2012, loss from continuing operations was US$1.61 billion compared with income of US$138.5 million a year earlier. Net loss amounted to US$1.41 billion versus net income of US$149.1 million in the prior year. Revenues were US$7.65 billion, up 37.8% from US$5.55 billion the year before. Operating loss was US$1.42 billion versus an income of US$429.4 million in the prior year. Direct operating expenses rose 29.2% to US$5.10 billion from US$3.95 billion in the comparable period the year before. Indirect operating expenses increased 238.3% to US$3.96 billion from US$1.17 billion in the equivalent prior-year period.

Prospects: Our evaluation of Sealed Air Corp. as of Apr. 7, 2013 is the result of our systematic analysis on three basic characteristics: earnings strength, relative valuation, and recent stock price movement. The company has produced a positive trend in earnings per share over the past 5 quarters. However, while recent estimates for the company have been mixed, SEE has posted better than expected results. Based on operating earnings yield, the company is about fairly valued when compared to all of the companies in our coverage universe. Share price changes over the past year indicates that SEE will perform in line with the market over the near term.

Financial Data
(US$ in Thousands)

	12/31/2012	12/31/2011	12/31/2010	12/31/2009	12/31/2008	12/31/2007	12/31/2006	12/31/2005
Earnings Per Share	(7.31)	0.80	1.44	1.35	0.99	1.89	1.47	1.35
Cash Flow Per Share	2.09	2.35	3.05	3.51	2.56	2.36	2.67	2.16
Tang Book Value Per Share	N.M.	N.M.	2.88	1.58	N.M.	0.31	N.M.	N.M.
Dividends Per Share	0.520	0.520	0.500	0.480	0.480	0.400	0.300	...
Dividend Payout %	...	65.00	34.72	35.56	48.48	21.16	20.48	...
Income Statement								
Total Revenue	7,648,100	5,640,900	4,490,100	4,242,800	4,843,500	4,651,200	4,327,900	4,085,100
EBITDA	(1,197,900)	610,500	638,100	618,700	480,200	718,800	702,100	693,000
Depn & Amortn	304,000	189,500	143,500	142,800	143,900	142,100	170,800	177,800
Income Before Taxes	(1,874,600)	212,900	341,100	328,100	222,300	456,000	400,100	376,600
Income Taxes	(261,900)	67,000	87,500	85,600	42,400	103,000	126,000	120,800
Net Income	(1,410,300)	149,100	255,900	244,300	179,900	353,000	274,100	255,800
Average Shares	192,800	185,400	176,700	182,600	189,300	191,300	192,600	196,000
Balance Sheet								
Current Assets	3,222,400	3,262,600	2,040,000	2,073,400	1,672,700	1,936,100	1,756,700	1,695,400
Total Assets	9,437,200	11,496,700	5,399,400	5,420,100	4,986,000	5,438,300	5,020,900	4,864,200
Current Liabilities	2,333,600	2,383,500	1,447,700	1,433,800	1,622,200	1,741,600	1,406,100	1,533,500
Long-Term Obligations	4,540,800	5,010,900	1,399,200	1,626,300	1,289,900	1,531,600	1,826,600	1,813,000
Total Liabilities	7,993,400	8,539,200	2,994,800	3,220,500	3,061,400	3,418,700	3,366,100	3,472,100
Stockholders' Equity	1,443,800	2,957,500	2,404,600	2,199,600	1,924,600	2,019,600	1,654,800	1,392,100
Shares Outstanding	194,557	192,062	159,305	158,938	157,882	161,627	161,330	162,903
Statistical Record								
Return on Assets %	N.M.	1.76	4.73	4.70	3.44	6.75	5.55	5.26
Return on Equity %	N.M.	5.56	11.12	11.85	9.10	19.21	17.99	18.77
EBITDA Margin %	N.M.	10.82	14.21	14.58	9.91	15.45	16.22	16.96
Net Margin %	N.M.	2.64	5.70	5.76	3.71	7.59	6.33	6.26
Asset Turnover	0.73	0.67	0.83	0.82	0.93	0.89	0.88	0.84
Current Ratio	1.38	1.37	1.41	1.45	1.03	1.11	1.25	1.11
Debt to Equity	3.15	1.69	0.58	0.74	0.67	0.76	1.10	1.30
Price Range	20.71-13.11	28.52-15.61	25.59-18.84	22.65-10.43	28.18-12.61	33.72-22.41	32.77-22.91	28.22-23.01
P/E Ratio	...	35.65-19.51	17.77-13.08	16.78-7.73	28.46-12.74	17.84-11.86	22.30-15.58	20.90-17.04
Average Yield %	3.09	2.34	2.29	2.66	2.20	1.38	1.09	...

Address: 200 Riverfront Boulevard, Elmwood Park, NJ 07407-1033 **Telephone:** 201-791-7600	**Web Site:** www.sealedair.com **Officers:** William V. Hickey - Chairman, President, Chief Executive Officer Jerome A. Peribere - President, Chief Operating Officer	**Auditors:** KPMG LLP **Investor Contact:** 201-703-4210 **Transfer Agents:** BNY Mellon Shareowner Services, Jersey City, NJ

SEMPRA ENERGY

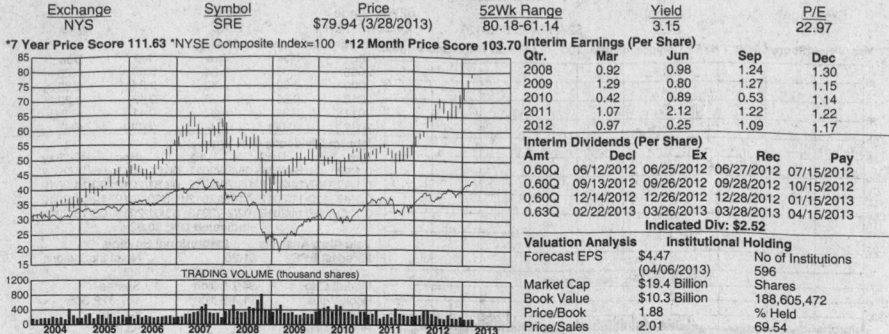

Exchange	Symbol	Price	52Wk Range	Yield	P/E
NYS	SRE	$79.94 (3/28/2013)	80.18-61.14	3.15	22.97

*7 Year Price Score 111.63 *NYSE Composite Index=100   *12 Month Price Score 103.70

Interim Earnings (Per Share)

Qtr.	Mar	Jun	Sep	Dec
2008	0.92	0.98	1.24	1.30
2009	1.29	0.80	1.27	1.15
2010	0.42	0.89	0.53	1.14
2011	1.07	2.12	1.22	1.22
2012	0.97	0.25	1.09	1.17

Interim Dividends (Per Share)

Amt	Decl	Ex	Rec	Pay
0.60Q	06/12/2012	06/25/2012	06/27/2012	07/15/2012
0.60Q	09/13/2012	09/26/2012	09/28/2012	10/15/2012
0.60Q	12/14/2012	12/26/2012	12/28/2012	01/15/2013
0.63Q	02/22/2013	03/26/2013	03/28/2013	04/15/2013

Indicated Div: $2.52

Valuation Analysis / **Institutional Holding**

Forecast EPS	$4.47 (04/06/2013)	No of Institutions 596
Market Cap	$19.4 Billion	Shares
Book Value	$10.3 Billion	188,605,472
Price/Book	1.88	% Held
Price/Sales	2.01	69.54

TRADING VOLUME (thousand shares)

Business Summary: Electric Utilities (MIC: 3.1.1 SIC: 4932 NAIC: 221210)

Sempra Energy is an energy services holding company whose business units develop energy infrastructure, operate utilities and provide related services to their customers. Co.'s operations are divided primarily between the Sempra Utilities and Sempra Global. The Sempra Utilities consist of two California regulated public utility companies: San Diego Gas & Electric Company and Southern California Gas Company. Sempra Global is a holding company for most of Co.'s subsidiaries that are not subject to California utility regulation. Sempra Global's principal business units, which provide energy-related services, are Sempra Generation, Sempra Pipelines & Storage, and Sempra Liquefied Natural Gas.

Recent Developments: For the year ended Dec 31 2012, net income decreased 33.4% to US$920.0 million from US$1.38 billion in the prior year. Revenues were US$9.65 billion, down 3.9% from US$10.04 billion the year before. Direct operating expenses declined 11.0% to US$3.69 billion from US$4.15 billion in the comparable period the year before. Indirect operating expenses increased 22.3% to US$4.72 billion from US$3.86 billion in the equivalent prior-year period.

Prospects: Our evaluation of Sempra Energy as of Apr. 7, 2013 is the result of our systematic analysis on three basic characteristics: earnings strength, relative valuation, and recent stock price movement. The company has managed to produce a neutral trend in earnings per share over the past 5 quarters and while recent estimates for the company have been mixed, SRE has posted better than expected results. Based on operating earnings yield, the company is about fairly valued when compared to all of the companies in our coverage universe. Share price changes over the past year indicates that SRE will perform in line with the market over the near term.

Financial Data
(US$ in Thousands)

	12/31/2012	12/31/2011	12/31/2010	12/31/2009	12/31/2008	12/31/2007	12/31/2006	12/31/2005
Earnings Per Share	3.48	5.62	2.98	4.52	4.43	4.16	5.38	3.65
Cash Flow Per Share	8.34	7.79	8.80	7.71	4.76	8.05	6.35	2.12
Tang Book Value Per Share	36.04	34.82	35.30	34.41	30.54	31.92	28.67	23.95
Dividends Per Share	2.400	1.920	1.560	1.560	1.370	1.240	1.200	1.160
Dividend Payout %	68.97	34.16	52.35	34.51	30.93	29.81	22.30	31.78
Income Statement								
Total Revenue	9,647,000	10,036,000	9,003,000	8,106,000	10,758,000	11,438,000	11,761,000	11,737,000
EBITDA	2,820,000	2,850,000	2,364,000	2,094,000	1,972,000	2,458,000	2,484,000	1,793,000
Depn & Amortn	1,090,000	978,000	867,000	775,000	687,000	686,000	657,000	646,000
Income Before Taxes	1,262,000	1,435,000	1,078,000	977,000	1,068,000	1,559,000	1,576,000	905,000
Income Taxes	59,000	366,000	102,000	422,000	438,000	524,000	641,000	42,000
Net Income	920,000	1,407,000	733,000	1,122,000	1,113,000	1,099,000	1,406,000	920,000
Average Shares	246,693	241,523	247,942	247,384	251,159	264,004	261,368	252,088
Balance Sheet								
Current Assets	3,695,000	2,332,000	3,353,000	2,295,000	2,476,000	11,338,000	12,016,000	13,318,000
Total Assets	36,499,000	33,356,000	30,283,000	28,512,000	26,400,000	30,091,000	28,949,000	29,213,000
Current Liabilities	4,258,000	4,163,000	3,786,000	3,888,000	3,612,000	10,394,000	10,349,000	12,157,000
Long-Term Obligations	11,621,000	10,078,000	8,980,000	7,460,000	6,544,000	4,553,000	4,525,000	4,823,000
Total Liabilities	26,197,000	23,498,000	21,156,000	19,405,000	18,431,000	21,752,000	21,438,000	23,053,000
Stockholders' Equity	10,282,000	9,838,000	9,027,000	9,007,000	7,969,000	8,339,000	7,511,000	6,160,000
Shares Outstanding	242,368	239,934	240,447	246,507	243,324	261,214	262,005	257,187
Statistical Record								
Return on Assets %	2.63	4.42	2.49	4.09	3.93	3.72	4.83	3.48
Return on Equity %	9.12	14.92	8.13	13.22	13.61	13.87	20.57	16.69
EBITDA Margin %	29.23	28.40	26.26	25.83	18.33	21.49	21.12	15.28
Net Margin %	9.54	14.02	8.14	13.84	10.35	9.61	11.95	7.84
Asset Turnover	0.28	0.32	0.31	0.30	0.38	0.39	0.40	0.44
Current Ratio	0.87	0.56	0.89	0.59	0.69	1.09	1.16	1.10
Debt to Equity	1.13	1.02	0.99	0.83	0.82	0.55	0.60	0.78
Price Range	72.74-54.83	55.50-45.59	55.98-44.51	56.88-36.72	62.57-36.99	66.29-52.21	56.78-43.36	47.49-35.75
P/E Ratio	20.90-15.76	9.88-8.11	18.79-14.94	12.58-8.12	14.12-8.35	15.94-12.55	10.55-8.06	13.01-9.79
Average Yield %	3.71	3.65	3.08	3.23	2.61	2.08	2.47	2.79

Address: 101 Ash Street, San Diego, CA 92101	Web Site: www.sempra.com	Auditors: Deloitte & Touche LLP
Telephone: 619-696-2000	Officers: Debra L. Reed - Chairman, Chief Executive Officer, Executive Vice President Mark A. Snell - President, Executive Vice President, Chief Financial Officer, Division Officer	Investor Contact: 877-736-7727 Transfer Agents: American Stock Transfer & Trust Company, Brooklyn, NY

SENIOR HOUSING PROPERTIES TRUST

Exchange	Symbol	Price	52Wk Range	Yield	P/E	Div Achiever
NYS	SNH	$26.83 (3/28/2013)	26.83-19.94	5.81	33.54	11 Years

*7 Year Price Score 95.26   *NYSE Composite Index=100   *12 Month Price Score 102.76

Interim Earnings (Per Share)

Qtr.	Mar	Jun	Sep	Dec
2008	0.26	0.22	0.25	0.28
2009	0.27	0.25	0.13	0.25
2010	0.24	0.19	0.22	0.26
2011	0.22	0.36	0.20	0.24
2012	0.20	0.20	0.15	0.25

Interim Dividends (Per Share)

Amt	Decl	Ex	Rec	Pay
0.38Q	07/09/2012	07/24/2012	07/26/2012	08/24/2012
0.39Q	10/09/2012	10/18/2012	10/22/2012	11/20/2012
0.39Q	01/10/2013	01/17/2013	01/22/2013	02/20/2013
0.39Q	04/02/2013	04/15/2013	04/17/2013	05/21/2013

Indicated Div: $1.56 (Div. Reinv. Plan)

Valuation Analysis | **Institutional Holding**

Forecast EPS	$1.00	No of Institutions
	(04/06/2013)	348
Market Cap	$4.7 Billion	Shares
Book Value	$2.6 Billion	154,746,416
Price/Book	1.79	% Held
Price/Sales	7.35	93.30

Business Summary: REITs (MIC: 5.3.1 SIC: 6798 NAIC: 525930)

Senior Housing Properties Trust is a real estate investment trust, investing in independent living communities, assisted living communities, nursing facilities and rehabilitation hospitals, properties leased to medical providers or medical related businesses, clinics and biotech laboratory tenants (MOBs), and wellness centers. As of Dec 31 2012, Co. owned 392 properties located in 40 states and Washington, D.C. Co.'s portfolio includes: 260 senior living communities; 120 properties leased to medical providers or medical related businesses, clinics and biotech laboratory tenants; and 10 wellness centers.

Recent Developments: For the year ended Dec 31 2012, net income decreased 10.3% to US$135.9 million from US$151.4 million in the prior year. Revenues were US$644.8 million, up 43.3% from US$450.0 million the year before. Revenues from property income rose 9.2% to US$460.8 million from US$422.2 million in the corresponding earlier year.

Prospects: Our evaluation of Senior Housing Properties Trust as of Apr. 7, 2013 is the result of our systematic analysis on three basic characteristics: earnings strength, relative valuation, and recent stock price movement. The company has produced a positive trend in earnings per share over the past 5 quarters and while recent estimates for the company have remained steady, SNH has posted results that fell short of analysts expectations. Based on operating earnings yield, the company is overvalued when compared to all of the companies in our coverage universe. Share price changes over the past year indicates that SNH will perform poorly over the near term.

Financial Data
(US$ in Thousands)

	12/31/2012	12/31/2011	12/31/2010	12/31/2009	12/31/2008	12/31/2007	12/31/2006	12/31/2005
Earnings Per Share	0.80	1.01	0.91	0.90	1.01	1.03	0.91	0.85
Cash Flow Per Share	1.67	1.71	1.68	1.72	1.75	1.63	1.55	1.52
Tang Book Value Per Share	14.99	15.20	15.00	14.92	15.12	14.09	13.14	12.78
Dividends Per Share	1.530	1.490	1.450	1.420	1.400	1.370	1.300	1.280
Dividend Payout %	191.25	147.52	159.34	157.78	138.61	133.01	142.86	150.59
Income Statement								
Total Revenue	644,842	450,017	339,009	297,780	235,537	188,022	179,806	163,187
EBITDA	393,522	361,668	286,050	244,305	207,230	170,442	157,215	143,101
Depn & Amortn	141,456	113,265	90,409	78,583	60,831	47,384	44,073	43,694
Income Before Taxes	135,943	151,592	116,786	109,318	106,245	85,303	66,122	52,774
Income Taxes	375	312	300	...	...	...	...	...
Net Income	135,884	151,419	116,485	109,715	106,511	85,303	66,101	58,705
Average Shares	169,176	149,577	128,092	121,863	105,153	83,168	72,529	68,757
Balance Sheet								
Current Assets	51,814	30,688	15,860	14,716	10,334	47,163	7,899	17,171
Total Assets	4,748,002	4,383,048	3,392,656	2,987,926	2,496,874	1,701,894	1,584,774	1,499,648
Current Liabilities	27,284	25,834	17,294	16,228	13,408	12,345	13,318	13,875
Long-Term Obligations	2,006,530	1,827,385	1,204,890	1,042,219	730,433	426,852	545,085	556,400
Total Liabilities	2,101,434	1,910,442	1,264,679	1,087,276	765,516	452,484	565,308	581,671
Stockholders' Equity	2,646,568	2,472,606	2,127,977	1,900,650	1,731,358	1,249,410	1,019,466	917,977
Shares Outstanding	176,553	162,646	141,854	127,377	114,542	88,691	77,613	71,812
Statistical Record								
Return on Assets %	2.97	3.89	3.65	4.00	5.06	5.19	4.29	3.98
Return on Equity %	5.29	6.58	5.78	6.04	7.13	7.52	6.82	6.49
EBITDA Margin %	61.03	80.37	84.38	82.04	87.98	90.65	87.44	87.69
Net Margin %	21.07	33.65	34.36	36.84	45.22	45.37	36.76	35.97
Asset Turnover	0.14	0.12	0.11	0.11	0.11	0.11	0.12	0.11
Current Ratio	1.90	1.19	0.92	0.91	0.77	3.82	0.59	1.24
Debt to Equity	0.76	0.74	0.57	0.55	0.42	0.34	0.53	0.61
Price Range	23.70-19.94	24.54-19.09	25.19-19.48	22.58-11.39	25.01-10.28	26.75-17.16	24.48-16.80	20.00-16.50
P/E Ratio	29.63-24.93	24.30-18.90	27.68-21.41	25.09-12.66	24.76-10.18	25.97-16.66	26.90-18.46	23.53-19.41
Average Yield %	6.94	6.57	6.54	8.12	6.85	6.12	6.73	7.09

Address: Two Newton Place, 255 Washington Street, Suite 300, Newton, MA 02458-1634 **Telephone:** 617-796-8350 **Fax:** 617-796-8349	**Web Site:** www.snhreit.com **Officers:** David J. Hegarty - President, Chief Operating Officer Richard A. Doyle - Chief Financial Officer, Treasurer	**Auditors:** Ernst & Young LLP **Transfer Agents:** Sullivan & Worcester LLP, Boston, MA

SENSIENT TECHNOLOGIES CORP.

Exchange	Symbol	Price	52Wk Range	Yield	P/E
NYS	SXT	$39.09 (3/28/2013)	39.37-33.81	2.25	15.70

*7 Year Price Score 109.93 *NYSE Composite Index=100 *12 Month Price Score 94.95

Interim Earnings (Per Share)

Qtr.	Mar	Jun	Sep	Dec
2008	0.43	0.53	0.50	0.43
2009	0.45	0.53	0.47	0.33
2010	0.48	0.58	0.59	0.52
2011	0.53	0.67	0.64	0.57
2012	0.58	0.70	0.66	0.55

Interim Dividends (Per Share)

Amt	Decl	Ex	Rec	Pay
0.22Q	04/26/2012	05/07/2012	05/09/2012	06/01/2012
0.22Q	07/19/2012	08/06/2012	08/08/2012	09/04/2012
0.22Q	10/18/2012	11/07/2012	11/09/2012	12/03/2012
0.22Q	01/18/2013	02/06/2013	02/08/2013	03/01/2013

Indicated Div: $0.88

Valuation Analysis		Institutional Holding	
Forecast EPS	$2.67 (04/06/2013)	No of Institutions	249
Market Cap	$1.9 Billion	Shares	53,086,320
Book Value	$1.2 Billion	% Held	88.49
Price/Book	1.68		
Price/Sales	1.33		

Business Summary: Specialty Chemicals (MIC: 8.3.2 SIC: 2816 NAIC: 325131)

Sensient Technologies is a manufacturer and marketer of colors, flavors and fragrances. Co. has two segments: Flavors & Fragrances Group, which develops, manufactures and supplies flavor and fragrance systems for the food, beverage, pharmaceutical, personal care and household-products industries; and Color Group, which develops, manufactures and supplies color systems for use in foods, beverages and pharmaceuticals, provides colors and other ingredients for cosmetics and pharmaceuticals, and provides technical colors for industrial applications and digital imaging. Through its Asia Pacific and China Groups, Co. markets its product line in the Pacific Rim under the Sensient name.

Recent Developments: For the year ended Dec 31 2012, net income increased 2.8% to US$123.9 million from US$120.5 million in the prior year. Revenues were US$1.46 billion, up 2.0% from US$1.43 billion the year before. Operating income was US$191.2 million versus US$190.8 million in the prior year, an increase of 0.2%. Direct operating expenses rose 1.5% to US$995.9 million from US$981.1 million in the comparable period the year before. Indirect operating expenses increased 5.1% to US$271.9 million from US$258.8 million in the equivalent prior-year period.

Prospects: Our evaluation of Sensient Technologies Corp. as of Apr. 7, 2013 is the result of our systematic analysis on three basic characteristics: earnings strength, relative valuation, and recent stock price movement. The company has managed to produce a neutral trend in earnings per share over the past 5 quarters and while recent estimates for the company have remained steady, SXT has posted results that fell short of analysts expectations. Based on operating earnings yield, the company is undervalued when compared to all of the companies in our coverage universe. Share price changes over the past year indicates that SXT will perform poorly over the near term.

Financial Data
(US$ in Thousands)

	12/31/2012	12/31/2011	12/31/2010	12/31/2009	12/31/2008	12/31/2007	12/31/2006	12/31/2005
Earnings Per Share	2.49	2.41	2.17	1.78	1.89	1.65	1.44	0.94
Cash Flow Per Share	2.80	2.87	3.17	2.86	1.82	2.25	2.16	2.36
Tang Book Value Per Share	13.91	11.86	10.59	9.00	7.57	6.82	5.16	4.04
Dividends Per Share	0.870	0.840	0.790	0.760	0.740	0.680	0.610	0.600
Dividend Payout %	34.94	34.85	36.41	42.70	39.15	41.21	42.36	63.83
Income Statement								
Total Revenue	1,459,050	1,430,789	1,328,180	1,201,412	1,252,620	1,184,778	1,098,774	1,023,930
EBITDA	238,200	235,594	216,686	189,146	206,044	191,682	172,321	140,983
Depn & Amortn	46,992	44,771	42,109	42,183	44,445	44,312	43,044	46,769
Income Before Taxes	174,307	171,384	154,193	123,175	129,293	111,243	93,529	58,477
Income Taxes	50,399	50,900	47,049	36,614	38,432	33,457	27,104	14,282
Net Income	123,908	120,484	107,144	86,561	90,861	77,786	66,425	44,195
Average Shares	49,822	49,937	49,424	48,641	48,131	47,257	46,204	47,067
Balance Sheet								
Current Assets	751,354	706,870	672,305	658,109	627,523	610,044	551,702	520,344
Total Assets	1,776,643	1,654,164	1,599,268	1,591,691	1,525,437	1,564,182	1,454,067	1,398,273
Current Liabilities	204,236	207,275	205,063	216,145	196,271	229,273	260,610	442,087
Long-Term Obligations	333,979	312,422	324,360	388,852	445,682	449,621	441,306	283,123
Total Liabilities	622,745	604,954	615,483	682,996	706,841	749,761	749,963	776,045
Stockholders' Equity	1,153,898	1,049,210	983,785	908,695	818,596	814,421	704,104	622,228
Shares Outstanding	49,690	49,916	49,609	48,772	48,156	47,351	46,569	46,334
Statistical Record								
Return on Assets %	7.20	7.41	6.72	5.55	5.87	5.15	4.66	3.06
Return on Equity %	11.22	11.85	11.32	10.02	11.10	10.24	10.02	6.90
EBITDA Margin %	16.33	16.47	16.31	15.74	16.45	16.18	15.68	13.77
Net Margin %	8.49	8.42	8.07	7.20	7.25	6.57	6.05	4.32
Asset Turnover	0.85	0.88	0.83	0.77	0.81	0.79	0.77	0.71
Current Ratio	3.68	3.41	3.28	3.04	3.20	2.66	2.12	1.18
Debt to Equity	0.29	0.30	0.33	0.43	0.54	0.55	0.63	0.46
Price Range	40.92-33.81	39.45-30.92	37.47-24.98	29.07-18.60	32.82-21.59	30.26-23.83	25.18-17.11	23.99-16.84
P/E Ratio	16.43-13.58	16.37-12.83	17.27-11.51	16.33-10.45	17.37-11.42	18.34-14.44	17.49-11.88	25.52-17.91
Average Yield %	2.37	2.36	2.66	3.10	2.64	2.55	2.99	3.00

Address: 777 East Wisconsin Avenue, Milwaukee, WI 53202-5304 Telephone: 414-271-6755 Fax: 414-347-4795	Web Site: www.sensient.com Officers: Kenneth P. Manning - Chairman, President, Chief Executive Officer, Chief Operating Officer Paul Manning - President, Chief Executive Officer, Division Officer	Auditors: Ernst & Young LLP Investor Contact: 800-558-9892 Transfer Agents: Wells Fargo Bank Minnesota, N.A., St. Paul, MN

SERVICE CORP. INTERNATIONAL

Exchange	Symbol	Price	52Wk Range	Yield	P/E
NYS	SCI	$16.73 (3/28/2013)	16.73-10.59	1.43	23.90

*7 Year Price Score 120.87 *NYSE Composite Index=100 *12 Month Price Score 107.90

Interim Earnings (Per Share)

Qtr.	Mar	Jun	Sep	Dec
2008	0.16	0.12	0.06	0.04
2009	0.14	0.09	0.12	0.14
2010	0.12	0.16	0.08	0.14
2011	0.16	0.11	0.15	0.19
2012	0.22	0.17	0.19	0.13

Interim Dividends (Per Share)

Amt	Decl	Ex	Rec	Pay
0.06Q	05/09/2012	07/11/2012	07/13/2012	07/31/2012
0.06Q	08/07/2012	10/11/2012	10/15/2012	10/31/2012
0.06Q	11/14/2012	12/12/2012	12/14/2012	12/31/2012
0.06Q	02/13/2013	03/13/2013	03/15/2013	03/28/2013

Indicated Div: $0.24

Valuation Analysis

		Institutional Holding	
Forecast EPS	$0.85	No of Institutions	
	(04/05/2013)	289	
Market Cap	$3.5 Billion	Shares	181,690,240
Book Value	$1.3 Billion	% Held	80.35
Price/Book	2.63		
Price/Sales	1.46		

Business Summary: Miscellaneous Consumer Services (MIC: 2.2.3 SIC: 7261 NAIC: 812210)

Service Corporation International provides deathcare products and services. Co.'s funeral service and cemetery operations consist of funeral service locations, cemeteries, funeral service/cemetery combination locations, crematoria, and related businesses. Co. provides funeral facilities and motor vehicles and preparation and embalming services. As of Dec 31 2012, Co. had 1,449 funeral service locations and 374 cemeteries (including 213 funeral service/cemetery combination locations) covering 43 states, eight Canadian provinces, the District of Columbia, and Germany.

Recent Developments: For the year ended Dec 31 2012, net income increased 5.4% to US$154.1 million from US$146.2 million in the prior year. Revenues were US$2.41 billion, up 4.1% from US$2.32 billion the year before. Operating income was US$399.8 million versus US$363.7 million in the prior year, an increase of 9.9%. Direct operating expenses rose 2.6% to US$1.89 billion from US$1.84 billion in the comparable period the year before. Indirect operating expenses increased 9.2% to US$125.4 million from US$114.8 million in the equivalent prior-year period.

Prospects: Our evaluation of Service Corp. International as of Apr. 7, 2013 is the result of our systematic analysis on three basic characteristics: earnings strength, relative valuation, and recent stock price movement. The company has managed to produce a neutral trend in earnings per share over the past 5 quarters and while recent estimates for the company have remained steady, SCI has posted better than expected results. Based on operating earnings yield, the company is about fairly valued when compared to all of the companies in our coverage universe. Share price changes over the past year indicates that SCI will perform well over the near term.

Financial Data
(US$ in Thousands)

	12/31/2012	12/31/2011	12/31/2010	12/31/2009	12/31/2008	12/31/2007	12/31/2006	12/31/2005
Earnings Per Share	0.70	0.61	0.50	0.49	0.37	0.85	0.19	(0.41)
Cash Flow Per Share	1.71	1.66	1.42	1.48	1.36	1.25	1.11	1.03
Tang Book Value Per Share	N.M.	N.M.	N.M.	0.46	N.M.	0.45	0.32	1.33
Dividends Per Share	0.280	0.190	0.160	0.160	0.160	0.120	0.100	0.075
Dividend Payout %	40.00	31.15	32.00	32.65	43.24	14.12	52.63	...
Income Statement								
Total Revenue	2,410,481	2,316,040	2,190,552	2,053,520	2,155,622	2,285,303	1,747,295	1,715,605
EBITDA	450,118	300,357	297,461	265,644	317,543	492,487	183,845	163,414
Depn & Amortn	137,660	25,591	25,197	21,698	137,836	115,700	84,000	60,327
Income Before Taxes	245,683	225,636	219,459	199,368	163,162	350,380	97,449	90,807
Income Taxes	91,548	79,404	92,458	76,275	65,717	143,670	44,845	34,122
Net Income	152,546	144,903	126,417	123,098	97,083	247,729	56,511	(126,730)
Average Shares	219,066	236,669	250,602	252,484	260,446	290,444	297,371	306,745
Balance Sheet								
Current Assets	286,199	328,093	381,918	377,461	355,510	421,327	238,337	650,383
Total Assets	9,683,568	9,327,812	9,190,540	8,890,981	8,110,883	8,932,244	9,729,389	7,536,692
Current Liabilities	412,104	385,608	366,627	365,515	326,782	426,440	407,947	271,956
Long-Term Obligations	1,916,621	1,861,116	1,832,380	1,840,532	1,821,404	1,820,106	1,912,696	1,175,463
Total Liabilities	8,340,541	7,935,718	7,711,084	7,408,205	6,817,704	7,440,161	8,134,614	5,948,206
Stockholders' Equity	1,343,027	1,392,094	1,479,456	1,482,776	1,293,179	1,492,083	1,594,775	1,588,486
Shares Outstanding	211,046	222,955	241,035	254,017	249,472	262,858	293,222	294,808
Statistical Record								
Return on Assets %	1.60	1.56	1.40	1.45	1.14	2.65	0.65	N.M.
Return on Equity %	11.12	10.09	8.54	8.87	6.95	16.05	3.55	N.M.
EBITDA Margin %	18.67	12.97	13.58	12.94	14.73	21.55	10.52	9.53
Net Margin %	6.33	6.26	5.77	5.99	4.50	10.84	3.23	N.M.
Asset Turnover	0.25	0.25	0.24	0.24	0.25	0.24	0.20	0.22
Current Ratio	0.69	0.85	1.04	1.03	1.09	0.99	0.58	2.39
Debt to Equity	1.43	1.34	1.24	1.24	1.41	1.22	1.20	0.74
Price Range	14.54-10.55	12.01-8.12	9.62-7.15	8.25-2.74	14.05-4.31	14.47-10.31	10.45-7.37	8.85-6.58
P/E Ratio	20.77-15.07	19.69-13.31	19.24-14.30	16.84-5.59	37.97-11.65	17.02-12.13	55.00-38.79	...
Average Yield %	2.25	1.84	1.92	2.77	1.70	0.96	1.17	0.96

Address: 1929 Allen Parkway, Houston, TX 77019 Telephone: 713-522-5141	Web Site: www.sci-corp.com Officers: Robert L. Waltrip - Chairman Thomas L. Ryan - President, Chief Executive Officer	Auditors: PricewaterhouseCoopers LLP Transfer Agents: BNY Mellon Shareholder Services, Pittsburgh, PA

SHERWIN-WILLIAMS CO.

Exchange	Symbol	Price	52Wk Range	Yield	P/E	Div Achiever
NYS	SHW	$168.89 (3/28/2013)	172.12-108.99	1.18	28.05	33 Years

*7 Year Price Score 164.99 *NYSE Composite Index=100 *12 Month Price Score 105.41

Interim Earnings (Per Share)

Qtr.	Mar	Jun	Sep	Dec
2008	0.64	1.45	1.50	0.43
2009	0.32	1.35	1.51	0.61
2010	0.30	1.64	1.60	0.68
2011	0.63	1.66	1.71	0.16
2012	0.95	2.17	2.24	0.65

Interim Dividends (Per Share)

Amt	Decl	Ex	Rec	Pay
0.39Q	04/18/2012	05/16/2012	05/18/2012	06/01/2012
0.39Q	07/18/2012	08/15/2012	08/17/2012	09/07/2012
0.39Q	10/18/2012	11/14/2012	11/16/2012	11/30/2012
0.50Q	02/13/2013	02/21/2013	02/25/2013	03/08/2013

Indicated Div: $2.00 (Div. Reinv. Plan)

Valuation Analysis / **Institutional Holding**

Forecast EPS	$7.85 (04/06/2013)
	No of Institutions 648
Market Cap	$17.4 Billion
	Shares 88,282,048
Book Value	$1.8 Billion
Price/Book	9.73
	% Held 72.06
Price/Sales	1.83

Business Summary: Specialty Chemicals (MIC: 8.3.2 SIC: 5231 NAIC: 444120)

Sherwin-Williams is engaged in the development, manufacture, distribution and sale of paint, coatings and related products to professional, industrial, commercial and retail customers primarily in North and South America with additional operations in the Caribbean region, Europe and Asia. Co. has four reportable operating segments: Paint Stores Group, Consumer Group, Global Finishes Group and Latin America Coatings Group. As of Dec 31 2012, there were 3,520 Co.-operated specialty paint stores in the Paint Stores Group; 302 Co.-operated branches in the Global Finishes Group; and 276 Co.-operated stores in the Latin America Coatings Group.

Recent Developments: For the year ended Dec 31 2012, net income increased 42.8% to US$631.0 million from US$441.9 million in the prior year. Revenues were US$9.53 billion, up 8.8% from US$8.77 billion the year before. Direct operating expenses rose 6.1% to US$5.33 billion from US$5.02 billion in the comparable period the year before. Indirect operating expenses increased 10.1% to US$3.27 billion from US$2.97 billion in the equivalent prior-year period.

Prospects: Our evaluation of Sherwin-Williams Co. as of Apr. 7, 2013 is the result of our systematic analysis on three basic characteristics: earnings strength, relative valuation, and recent stock price movement. The company has managed to produce a neutral trend in earnings per share over the past 5 quarters and while recent estimates for the company have been raised by analysts, SHW has posted results that fell short of analysts expectations. Based on operating earnings yield, the company is about fairly valued when compared to all of the companies in our coverage universe. Share price changes over the past year indicates that SHW will perform very well over the near term.

Financial Data

(US$ in Thousands)	12/31/2012	12/31/2011	12/31/2010	12/31/2009	12/31/2008	12/31/2007	12/31/2006	12/31/2005
Earnings Per Share	6.02	4.14	4.21	3.78	4.00	4.70	4.19	3.28
Cash Flow Per Share	8.71	7.11	6.60	7.57	7.48	6.87	6.11	5.24
Tang Book Value Per Share	1.81	N.M.	N.M.	N.M.	0.70	0.92	2.67	3.83
Dividends Per Share	1.560	1.460	1.440	1.420	1.400	1.260	1.000	0.820
Dividend Payout %	25.91	35.27	34.20	37.57	35.00	26.81	23.87	25.00
Income Statement								
Total Revenue	9,534,462	8,765,699	7,776,424	7,094,249	7,979,727	8,005,292	7,809,759	7,190,661
EBITDA	1,126,386	961,238	920,761	831,354	941,740	1,133,953	1,022,780	844,723
Depn & Amortn	179,202	180,904	175,311	170,904	165,511	163,479	145,917	143,517
Income Before Taxes	907,309	741,548	677,784	622,817	714,475	912,943	834,312	656,215
Income Taxes	276,225	299,688	215,299	186,969	237,599	297,365	258,254	191,601
Net Income	631,034	441,860	462,485	435,848	476,876	615,578	576,058	463,258
Average Shares	103,930	105,671	108,785	113,514	119,343	130,924	137,342	141,078
Balance Sheet								
Current Assets	3,149,238	2,261,593	2,213,722	1,770,019	1,909,205	2,069,580	2,450,281	1,894,385
Total Assets	6,234,737	5,229,252	5,169,235	4,323,855	4,415,759	4,855,340	4,995,087	4,369,195
Current Liabilities	1,876,436	2,162,661	2,063,940	1,393,668	1,936,736	2,141,385	2,074,815	1,554,371
Long-Term Obligations	1,632,165	639,231	648,326	782,670	303,727	293,454	291,876	486,996
Total Liabilities	4,442,933	3,712,333	3,559,795	2,832,905	2,810,111	3,069,613	3,002,727	2,638,583
Stockholders' Equity	1,791,804	1,516,919	1,609,440	1,490,950	1,605,648	1,785,727	1,992,360	1,730,612
Shares Outstanding	103,270	103,854	107,020	109,436	117,035	122,814	133,565	135,139
Statistical Record								
Return on Assets %	10.98	8.50	9.74	9.97	10.26	12.50	12.30	10.72
Return on Equity %	38.04	28.27	29.83	28.15	28.05	32.59	30.95	27.43
EBITDA Margin %	11.81	10.97	11.84	11.72	11.80	14.17	13.10	11.75
Net Margin %	6.62	5.04	5.95	6.14	5.98	7.69	7.38	6.44
Asset Turnover	1.66	1.69	1.64	1.62	1.72	1.63	1.67	1.66
Current Ratio	1.68	1.05	1.07	1.27	0.99	0.97	1.18	1.22
Debt to Equity	0.91	0.42	0.40	0.52	0.19	0.16	0.15	0.28
Price Range	158.59-91.00	90.08-69.57	84.50-58.00	63.75-42.98	63.36-45.06	72.99-57.65	64.61-41.29	48.63-40.75
P/E Ratio	26.34-15.12	21.76-16.80	20.07-13.78	16.87-11.37	15.84-11.27	15.53-12.27	15.42-9.85	14.83-12.42
Average Yield %	1.20	1.78	2.01	2.54	2.55	1.92	1.91	1.84

Address: 101 West Prospect Avenue, Cleveland, OH 44115-1075	**Web Site:** www.sherwin.com	**Auditors:** Ernst & Young LLP
Telephone: 216-566-2000	**Officers:** Christopher M. Connor - Chairman, Chief Executive Officer Robert J. Davisson - Division Officer	**Investor Contact:** 441-151-075
Fax: 216-566-3310		**Transfer Agents:** Wells Fargo Shareowner Services, St. Paul, M

SIGNET JEWELERS LTD

Exchange	Symbol	Price	52Wk Range	Yield	P/E
NYS	SIG	$67.00 (3/28/2013)	67.00-41.27	0.90	15.40

*7 Year Price Score 127.72 *NYSE Composite Index=100 *12 Month Price Score 112.21

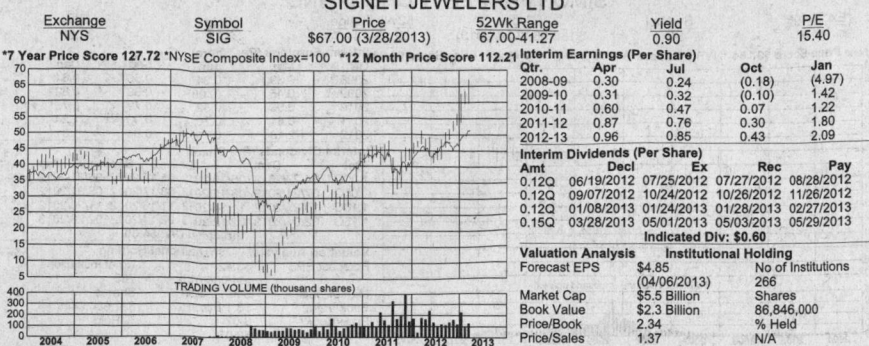

Interim Earnings (Per Share)

Qtr.	Apr	Jul	Oct	Jan
2008-09	0.30	0.24	(0.18)	(4.97)
2009-10	0.31	0.32	(0.10)	1.42
2010-11	0.60	0.47	0.07	1.22
2011-12	0.87	0.76	0.30	1.80
2012-13	0.96	0.85	0.43	2.09

Interim Dividends (Per Share)

Amt	Decl	Ex	Rec	Pay
0.12Q	06/19/2012	07/25/2012	07/27/2012	08/28/2012
0.12Q	09/07/2012	10/24/2012	10/26/2012	11/26/2012
0.12Q	01/08/2013	01/24/2013	01/28/2013	02/27/2013
0.15Q	03/28/2013	05/01/2013	05/03/2013	05/29/2013

Indicated Div: $0.60

Valuation Analysis | **Institutional Holding**

Forecast EPS	$4.85	No of Institutions
	(04/06/2013)	266
Market Cap	$5.5 Billion	Shares
Book Value	$2.3 Billion	86,846,000
Price/Book	2.34	% Held
Price/Sales	1.37	N/A

Business Summary: Retail - Specialty (MIC: 2.1.3 SIC: 5944 NAIC: 448310)

Signet Jewelers is a retailer of jewelry, watches and associated services. Co. has two geographical segments: the U.S., which operates retail stores in malls and off-mall locations as Kay Jewelers; destination superstores as Jared The Galleria Of Jewelry; and various regional brands such as JB Robinson Jewelers, Marks & Morgan Jewelers and Belden Jewelers; and the U.K. division, which operates retail stores situated in shopping malls under H.Samuel, Ernest Jones, and Leslie Davis trade names. As of Jan 28 2012, Co.'s U.S. division operated 1,318 stores in 50 states; and the U.K. division operated 535 stores, including 14 stores in the Republic of Ireland and three in the Channel Islands.

Recent Developments: For the year ended Feb 2 2013, net income increased 10.9% to US$359.9 million from US$324.4 million in the prior year. Revenues were US$3.98 billion, up 6.2% from US$3.75 billion the year before. Operating income was US$560.5 million versus US$507.4 million in the prior year, an increase of 10.5%. Direct operating expenses rose 5.8% to US$2.45 billion from US$2.31 billion in the comparable period the year before. Indirect operating expenses increased 5.0% to US$976.9 million from US$930.2 million in the equivalent prior-year period.

Prospects: Our evaluation of Signet Jewelers Limited as of Apr. 7, 2013 is the result of our systematic analysis on three basic characteristics: earnings strength, relative valuation, and recent stock price movement. The company has produced a positive trend in earnings per share over the past 5 quarters. However, while recent estimates for the company have been mixed, SIG has posted better than expected results. Based on operating earnings yield, the company is undervalued when compared to all of the companies in our coverage universe. Share price changes over the past year indicates that SIG will perform poorly over the near term.

Financial Data
(US$ in Thousands)

	02/02/2013	01/28/2012	01/29/2011	01/30/2010	01/31/2009	02/02/2008	02/02/2008	02/03/2007
Earnings Per Share	4.35	3.73	2.32	1.91	(4.62)	2.55	...	2.86
Cash Flow Per Share	3.74	3.78	3.79	6.06	1.93	1.66	...	2.27
Tang Book Value Per Share	28.32	26.32	22.18	20.74	18.59	1.02	...	...
Dividends Per Share	0.480	0.200	...	...	...	...	...	...
Dividend Payout %	11.03	5.36	...	...	...	...	...	...
Income Statement								
Total Revenue	3,983,400	3,749,200	3,437,400	3,290,700	3,344,300	3,665,300	...	3,559,200
EBITDA	659,900	599,800	470,300	384,700	(182,800)	472,600	...	503,200
Depn & Amortn	99,400	92,400	97,800	108,900	114,500	113,900	...	98,400
Income Before Taxes	556,900	502,100	300,400	241,800	(326,500)	336,200	...	387,300
Income Taxes	197,000	177,700	100,000	77,700	67,200	116,400	...	134,600
Net Income	359,900	324,400	200,400	164,100	(393,700)	219,800	...	252,700
Average Shares	82,800	87,000	86,400	85,700	85,200	86,100	...	88,300
Balance Sheet								
Current Assets	3,032,900	3,016,300	2,542,300	2,435,800	2,413,200	2,422,800	...	...
Total Assets	3,715,800	3,611,400	3,089,800	2,924,200	2,953,900	3,599,400	...	...
Current Liabilities	868,700	867,200	711,000	621,300	737,500	646,500	...	...
Long-Term Obligations	...	...	...	280,000	380,000	380,000	...	...
Total Liabilities	1,385,900	1,332,300	1,150,800	1,126,600	1,344,200	1,278,200	...	...
Stockholders' Equity	2,329,900	2,279,100	1,939,000	1,797,600	1,609,700	2,321,200	...	...
Shares Outstanding	81,400	86,600	86,200	85,500	85,300	1,705,500	...	...
Statistical Record								
Return on Assets %	9.66	9.71	6.68	5.60	N.M.	...	...	...
Return on Equity %	15.36	15.42	10.76	9.66	N.M.	...	...	...
EBITDA Margin %	16.57	16.00	13.68	11.69	N.M.	12.89	...	14.14
Net Margin %	9.03	8.65	5.83	4.99	N.M.	6.00	...	7.10
Asset Turnover	1.07	1.12	1.15	1.12	1.02	...	...	...
Current Ratio	3.49	3.48	3.58	3.92	3.27	3.75	...	...
Debt to Equity	...	...	...	0.16	0.24	0.16	...	...
Price Range	63.43-41.27	48.01-31.26	44.30-26.44	28.97-6.06	30.40-7.04	...	51.64-22.08	48.62-34.00
P/E Ratio	14.58-9.49	12.87-8.38	19.09-11.40	15.17-3.17	...	...	20.25-8.66	17.00-11.89
Average Yield %	0.98	0.47	...	...	...	...	...	...

| **Address:** Clarendon House, 2 Church Street, Hamilton, HM11
Telephone: 441-295-5872 | **Web Site:** www.signetjewelers.com
Officers: Michael W. Barnes - Chief Executive Officer Ronald W. Ristau - Chief Financial Officer | **Auditors:** KPMG LLP
Investor Contact: 440-207-3179700
Transfer Agents: Capita Registrars, Kent, United Kingdom |

SIMON PROPERTY GROUP, INC.

Exchange	Symbol	Price	52Wk Range	Yield	P/E
NYS	SPG	$158.56 (3/28/2013)	163.53-141.73	2.71	33.59

*7 Year Price Score 137.84 *NYSE Composite Index=100 *12 Month Price Score 94.94

Interim Earnings (Per Share)

Qtr.	Mar	Jun	Sep	Dec
2008	0.39	0.34	0.50	0.64
2009	0.45	(0.08)	0.38	0.32
2010	0.03	0.52	0.79	0.75
2011	0.61	0.70	0.93	1.24
2012	2.18	0.71	0.84	1.01

Interim Dividends (Per Share)

Amt	Decl	Ex	Rec	Pay
1.00Q	04/27/2012	05/15/2012	05/17/2012	05/31/2012
1.05Q	07/24/2012	08/15/2012	08/17/2012	08/31/2012
1.10Q	10/25/2012	11/14/2012	11/16/2012	11/30/2012
1.15Q	02/04/2013	02/12/2013	02/14/2013	02/28/2013

Indicated Div: $4.30

Valuation Analysis

Institutional Holding	
Forecast EPS	$3.42
	(04/06/2013)
Market Cap	$49.1 Billion
Book Value	$6.1 Billion
Price/Book	8.07
Price/Sales	10.07

No of Institutions 765
Shares 327,686,944
% Held 103.35

TRADING VOLUME (thousand shares)

Business Summary: REITs (MIC: 5.3.1 SIC: 6798 NAIC: 525930)

Simon Property Group is a self-administered and self-managed real estate investment trust. Co. owns, develops, and manages retail real estate properties, mainly regional malls, Premium Outlets®, The Mills®, and community/lifestyle centers. At Dec 31 2011, Co. owned or held an interest in 326 properties in the U.S., which consisted of 151 regional malls, 58 Premium Outlets, 66 community/lifestyle centers, 36 properties in the Mills Portfolio and 15 other shopping centers or outlet centers in 41 states and Puerto Rico. Co. also holds real estate interests in operating joint venture properties in Japan, South Korea, Mexico, and Malaysia.

Recent Developments: For the year ended Dec 31 2012, net income increased 38.0% to US$1.72 billion from US$1.25 billion in the prior year. Revenues were US$4.88 billion, up 13.3% from US$4.31 billion the year before. Revenues from property income rose 14.3% to US$4.55 billion from US$3.98 billion in the corresponding earlier year.

Prospects: Our evaluation of Simon Property Group Inc. as of Apr. 7, 2013 is the result of our systematic analysis on three basic characteristics: earnings strength, relative valuation, and recent stock price movement. The company has produced a positive trend in earnings per share over the past 5 quarters. Because the company lacks sufficient analyst estimate data, we place greater weight on the historical EPS trend as the measure of earnings strength. Based on operating earnings yield, the company is overvalued when compared to all of the companies in our coverage universe. Share price changes over the past year indicates that SPG will perform in line with the market over the near term.

Financial Data

(US$ in Thousands)	12/31/2012	12/31/2011	12/31/2010	12/31/2009	12/31/2008	12/31/2007	12/31/2006	12/31/2005
Earnings Per Share	4.72	3.48	2.10	1.05	1.87	1.95	2.19	1.82
Cash Flow Per Share	8.27	6.83	6.03	6.44	7.11	6.53	5.76	5.32
Tang Book Value Per Share	17.87	15.57	16.00	17.11	10.93	12.02	13.15	13.54
Dividends Per Share	4.100	3.500	2.600	2.700	3.600	3.360	3.040	2.800
Dividend Payout %	86.86	100.57	123.81	257.14	192.51	172.31	138.81	153.85
Income Statement								
Total Revenue	4,880,084	4,306,432	3,957,630	3,775,216	3,783,155	3,650,799	3,332,154	3,166,853
EBITDA	4,517,022	3,949,868	3,711,436	3,368,027	3,445,029	3,332,017	2,855,510	2,743,089
Depn & Amortn	1,301,304	1,112,438	1,016,027	1,009,490	956,827	875,284	812,718	806,638
Income Before Taxes	2,088,693	1,853,904	1,668,318	1,366,472	1,541,062	1,510,881	1,220,934	1,137,359
Net Income	1,719,632	1,245,900	753,514	387,262	463,636	491,239	563,840	475,749
Average Shares	303,138	293,573	291,350	268,472	225,883	223,776	221,927	221,130
Balance Sheet								
Current Assets	1,705,819	1,285,381	1,223,454	4,360,447	1,188,400	949,206	1,309,488	694,127
Total Assets	32,586,606	26,216,925	24,857,429	25,948,266	23,596,672	23,605,662	22,084,455	21,131,039
Current Liabilities	2,098,916	1,787,281	1,479,593	1,445,284	1,466,978	1,603,842	1,336,778	1,286,810
Long-Term Obligations	23,113,007	18,446,440	17,473,760	18,630,302	18,042,532	17,218,674	15,394,489	14,106,117
Total Liabilities	26,497,997	21,299,314	19,941,180	20,959,756	19,689,480	19,003,160	16,909,517	15,556,451
Stockholders' Equity	6,088,609	4,917,611	4,916,249	4,988,510	3,040,183	3,563,383	3,979,642	4,307,296
Shares Outstanding	309,895	293,856	292,961	285,748	231,319	223,034	221,431	220,361
Statistical Record								
Return on Assets %	5.83	4.88	2.97	1.56	1.96	2.15	2.61	2.20
Return on Equity %	31.16	25.34	15.22	9.65	14.00	13.02	13.61	10.63
EBITDA Margin %	92.56	91.72	93.78	89.21	91.06	91.27	85.70	86.62
Net Margin %	35.24	28.93	19.04	10.26	12.26	13.46	16.92	15.02
Asset Turnover	0.17	0.17	0.16	0.15	0.16	0.16	0.15	0.15
Current Ratio	0.81	0.72	0.83	3.02	0.81	0.59	0.98	0.54
Debt to Equity	3.80	3.75	3.55	3.73	5.93	4.83	3.87	3.27
Price Range	163.53-126.72	131.00-95.35	106.25-69.49	83.04-26.19	104.91-38.00	123.78-84.90	103.59-76.95	80.53-59.03
P/E Ratio	34.65-26.85	37.64-27.40	50.60-33.07	79.09-24.94	56.10-20.32	63.48-43.54	47.30-35.14	44.25-32.43
Average Yield %	2.74	3.08	2.95	4.87	4.28	3.29	3.51	4.01

Address: 225 West Washington Street, Indianapolis, IN 46204 Telephone: 317-636-1600 Fax: 317-685-7336	Web Site: www.simon.com Officers: David Simon - Chairman, Chief Executive Officer Herbert Simon - Chairman Emeritus, Chairman	Auditors: Ernst & Young LLP Investor Contact: 317-636-1600 Transfer Agents: Computershare Shareowner Services, Pittsburgh, PA

SJW CORP.

Exchange	Symbol	Price	52Wk Range	Yield	P/E	Div Achiever
NYS	SJW	$26.50 (3/28/2013)	28.09-22.69	2.75	22.46	45 Years

*7 Year Price Score 82.07   *NYSE Composite Index=100   *12 Month Price Score 101.30

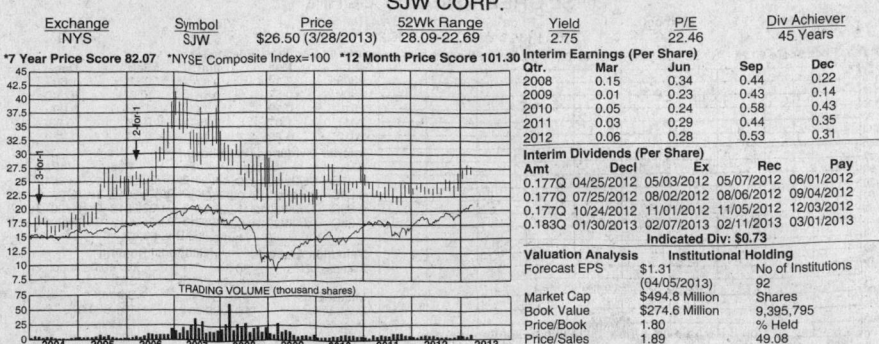

Interim Earnings (Per Share)

Qtr.	Mar	Jun	Sep	Dec
2008	0.15	0.34	0.44	0.22
2009	0.01	0.23	0.43	0.14
2010	0.05	0.24	0.58	0.43
2011	0.03	0.29	0.44	0.35
2012	0.06	0.28	0.53	0.31

Interim Dividends (Per Share)

Amt	Decl	Ex	Rec	Pay
0.177Q	04/25/2012	05/03/2012	05/07/2012	06/01/2012
0.177Q	07/25/2012	08/02/2012	08/06/2012	09/04/2012
0.177Q	10/24/2012	11/01/2012	11/05/2012	12/03/2012
0.183Q	01/30/2013	02/07/2013	02/11/2013	03/01/2013

Indicated Div: $0.73

Valuation Analysis · **Institutional Holding**

Forecast EPS	$1.31	No of Institutions
	(04/05/2013)	92
Market Cap	$494.8 Million	Shares
Book Value	$274.6 Million	9,395,795
Price/Book	1.80	% Held
Price/Sales	1.89	49.08

Business Summary: Water Utilities (MIC: 3.2.1 SIC: 4941 NAIC: 221310)

SJW is a holding company. Through its subsidiaries, Co. is engaged in the production, purchase, storage, purification, distribution, wholesale, and retail sale of water. Co.'s subsidiaries include: San Jose Water Company, a public utility providing water service in the metropolitan San Jose, CA area; SJW Land Company, which owns undeveloped land, owns and operates commercial buildings, and has a 70.0% limited partnership interest in 444 West Santa Clara Street, L.P.; SJWTX, Inc., a public utility providing water service in western Comal County and southern Blanco County; and Texas Water Alliance Limited, which is developing a water supply project in Texas.

Recent Developments: For the year ended Dec 31 2012, net income increased 6.9% to US$22.3 million from US$20.9 million in the prior year. Revenues were US$261.5 million, up 9.5% from US$239.0 million the year before. Operating income was US$55.3 million versus US$54.4 million in the prior year, an increase of 1.7%. Indirect operating expenses increased 11.7% to US$206.3 million from US$184.6 million in the equivalent prior-year period.

Prospects: Our evaluation of SJW Corp. as of Apr. 7, 2013 is the result of our systematic analysis on three basic characteristics: earnings strength, relative valuation, and recent stock price movement. The company has managed to produce a neutral trend in earnings per share over the past 5 quarters and while recent estimates for the company have remained steady, SJW has posted better than expected results. Based on operating earnings yield, the company is about fairly valued when compared to all of the companies in our coverage universe. Share price changes over the past year indicates that SJW will perform well over the near term.

Financial Data

(US$ in Thousands)	12/31/2012	12/31/2011	12/31/2010	12/31/2009	12/31/2008	12/31/2007	12/31/2006	12/31/2005
Earnings Per Share	1.18	1.11	1.30	0.81	1.15	1.04	2.08	1.18
Cash Flow Per Share	3.98	3.46	2.01	2.95	2.81	2.29	2.44	2.33
Tang Book Value Per Share	14.71	14.20	13.75	13.66	13.78	12.90	12.48	10.51
Dividends Per Share	0.710	0.690	0.680	0.660	0.645	0.605	0.565	0.535
Dividend Payout %	60.17	62.16	52.31	81.48	56.09	58.17	27.16	45.34
Income Statement								
Total Revenue	261,547	238,955	215,638	216,097	220,347	206,601	189,238	180,105
EBITDA	89,050	84,260	68,420	54,796	58,255	53,288	69,801	50,687
Depn & Amortn	31,005	29,141	26,331	23,655	22,067	20,956	20,095	18,654
Income Before Taxes	37,860	35,444	24,406	15,171	21,461	19,323	38,581	21,840
Income Taxes	15,542	14,566	...	10,280	...	12,549	...	...
Net Income	22,318	20,878	24,406	15,171	21,461	19,323	38,581	21,840
Average Shares	18,839	18,794	18,742	18,680	18,609	18,552	18,528	18,480
Balance Sheet								
Current Assets	42,911	68,915	38,027	28,010	31,961	31,591	59,475	31,692
Total Assets	1,087,499	1,038,810	935,362	878,474	850,877	767,326	705,864	587,709
Current Liabilities	49,107	28,288	29,155	31,958	43,323	32,954	37,246	20,944
Long-Term Obligations	335,598	343,848	295,704	246,879	216,613	216,312	163,648	145,281
Total Liabilities	812,895	774,806	680,330	625,718	596,551	530,392	477,682	391,801
Stockholders' Equity	274,604	264,004	255,032	252,756	254,326	236,934	228,182	195,908
Shares Outstanding	18,670	18,592	18,551	18,499	18,452	18,361	18,281	18,270
Statistical Record								
Return on Assets %	2.09	2.12	2.69	1.75	2.65	2.62	5.97	3.83
Return on Equity %	8.26	8.04	9.61	5.98	8.71	8.31	18.19	11.48
EBITDA Margin %	34.05	35.26	31.73	25.36	26.44	25.79	36.89	28.14
Net Margin %	8.53	8.74	11.32	7.02	9.74	9.35	20.39	12.13
Asset Turnover	0.25	0.24	0.24	0.25	0.27	0.28	0.29	0.32
Current Ratio	0.87	2.44	1.30	0.88	0.74	0.96	1.60	1.51
Debt to Equity	1.22	1.30	1.16	0.98	0.85	0.91	0.72	0.74
Price Range	26.62-22.69	26.47-21.10	28.23-21.76	29.94-18.72	34.67-21.17	43.00-28.19	39.50-21.56	27.69-16.15
P/E Ratio	22.56-19.23	23.85-19.01	21.72-16.74	36.96-23.11	30.15-18.88	41.35-27.11	18.99-10.37	23.47-13.68
Average Yield %	2.96	2.94	2.78	2.83	2.27	1.74	2.03	2.43

Address: 110 West Taylor Street, San Jose, CA 95110
Telephone: 408-279-7800

Web Site: www.sjwcorp.com
Officers: W. Richard Roth - President, Chief Executive Officer James P. Lynch - Chief Financial Officer, Treasurer

Auditors: KPMG LLP
Investor Contact: 800-.25-0.5147
Transfer Agents: American Stock Transfer & Trust Company, Brooklyn, NY

SL GREEN REALTY CORP.

Exchange	Symbol	Price	52Wk Range	Yield	P/E
NYS	SLG	$86.11 (3/28/2013)	86.29-70.91	1.53	49.49

*7 Year Price Score 90.29   *NYSE Composite Index=100   *12 Month Price Score 97.05

Interim Earnings (Per Share)

Qtr.	Mar	Jun	Sep	Dec
2008	2.14	2.37	0.58	1.60
2009	0.57	0.18	(0.03)	(0.10)
2010	0.19	1.75	1.42	0.09
2011	1.01	6.26	0.08	(0.03)
2012	0.29	1.14	0.09	0.22

Interim Dividends (Per Share)

Amt	Decl	Ex	Rec	Pay
0.25Q	06/22/2012	06/28/2012	07/02/2012	07/13/2012
0.25Q	09/17/2012	09/26/2012	09/28/2012	10/15/2012
0.33Q	11/27/2012	12/28/2012	01/02/2013	01/15/2013
0.33Q	03/20/2013	03/27/2013	04/01/2013	04/15/2013

Indicated Div: $1.32

Valuation Analysis   Institutional Holding

Forecast EPS	$0.34	No of Institutions
	(04/05/2013)	373
Market Cap	$7.9 Billion	Shares
Book Value	$6.5 Billion	101,800,072
Price/Book	1.21	% Held
Price/Sales	5.61	102.94

Business Summary: REITs (MIC: 5.3.1 SIC: 6798 NAIC: 525930)

SL Green Realty is a self-managed real estate investment trust. Co. is engaged in the business of owning, managing, leasing, acquiring and repositioning office properties in Manhattan, a borough of New York City. As of Dec 31 2012, Co.'s Manhattan office properties were comprised of 21 fee owned properties, including ownership in commercial condominium units, and six leasehold owned properties. As of the same date, Co.'s Suburban office properties were comprised of 24 fee owned properties and one leasehold property. Co. also held fee owned interests in nine unconsolidated Manhattan office properties and five unconsolidated Suburban office properties.

Recent Developments: For the year ended Dec 31 2012, net income decreased 69.0% to US$209.7 million from US$677.1 million in the prior year. Revenues were US$1.40 billion, up 10.8% from US$1.26 billion the year before. Revenues from property income rose 12.1% to US$1.08 billion from US$961.9 million in the corresponding earlier year.

Prospects: Our evaluation of SL Green Realty Corp. as of Apr. 7, 2013 is the result of our systematic analysis on three basic characteristics: earnings strength, relative valuation, and recent stock price movement. The company has suffered a very negative trend in earnings per share over the past 5 quarters. Because the company lacks sufficient analyst estimate data, we place greater weight on the historical EPS trend as the measure of earnings strength. Based on operating earnings yield, the company is overvalued when compared to all of the companies in our coverage universe. Share price changes over the past year indicates that SLG will perform poorly over the near term.

Financial Data
(US$ in Thousands)

	12/31/2012	12/31/2011	12/31/2010	12/31/2009	12/31/2008	12/31/2007	12/31/2006	12/31/2005
Earnings Per Share	1.74	7.33	3.45	0.54	6.69	10.78	4.38	3.20
Cash Flow Per Share	3.95	3.74	4.11	3.95	6.61	6.92	5.06	3.31
Tang Book Value Per Share	66.49	65.36	57.58	53.41	64.22	60.90	43.07	28.53
Dividends Per Share	1.080	0.550	0.400	0.675	2.737	2.888	2.500	2.220
Dividend Payout %	62.07	7.50	11.59	125.00	40.92	26.79	57.08	69.38
Income Statement								
Total Revenue	1,400,255	1,263,428	1,101,246	1,010,659	1,116,861	1,054,523	552,277	440,182
EBITDA	382,346	377,984	318,932	220,663	279,372	283,066	156,311	123,351
Depn & Amortn	306,800	254,500	209,700	210,400	204,900	170,900	66,900	54,200
Income Before Taxes	75,546	123,484	109,232	10,263	74,472	112,166	89,411	69,151
Net Income	196,405	647,410	300,575	57,544	409,759	660,410	220,719	157,419
Average Shares	92,873	86,244	79,761	72,044	60,598	61,885	48,495	45,504
Balance Sheet								
Current Assets	744,306	568,181	739,221	695,029	1,016,962	350,131	507,752	191,577
Total Assets	14,387,754	13,483,651	11,300,294	10,487,577	10,984,353	11,430,078	4,632,227	3,309,777
Current Liabilities	317,459	343,328	224,410	212,577	264,678	313,190	217,019	150,760
Long-Term Obligations	6,557,938	6,052,509	5,268,057	4,909,571	5,633,077	5,739,624	1,831,773	1,558,512
Total Liabilities	7,918,402	7,506,305	6,421,210	6,099,139	7,072,617	7,603,203	2,237,344	1,850,336
Stockholders' Equity	6,469,352	5,977,547	4,879,084	4,388,438	3,911,736	3,826,875	2,394,883	1,459,441
Shares Outstanding	91,250	85,783	78,306	77,515	57,044	58,759	49,840	42,456
Statistical Record								
Return on Assets %	1.41	5.22	2.76	0.54	3.65	8.22	5.56	5.19
Return on Equity %	3.15	11.93	6.49	1.39	10.56	21.23	11.45	11.21
EBITDA Margin %	27.31	29.92	28.96	21.83	25.01	26.84	28.30	28.02
Net Margin %	14.03	51.24	27.29	5.69	36.69	62.63	39.97	35.76
Asset Turnover	0.10	0.10	0.10	0.09	0.10	0.13	0.14	0.15
Current Ratio	2.34	1.65	3.29	3.27	3.84	1.12	2.34	1.27
Debt to Equity	1.01	1.01	1.08	1.12	1.44	1.50	0.76	1.07
Price Range	85.14-68.16	90.01-55.14	70.27-44.18	52.74-8.69	100.74-11.36	156.10-89.43	139.50-77.70	77.14-52.70
P/E Ratio	48.93-39.17	12.28-7.52	20.37-12.81	97.67-16.09	15.06-1.70	14.48-8.30	31.85-17.74	24.11-16.47
Average Yield %	1.40	0.75	0.67	2.42	3.75	2.30	2.35	3.48

Address: 420 Lexington Avenue, New York, NY 10170 **Telephone:** 212-594-2700	**Web Site:** www.slgreen.com **Officers:** Stephen L. Green - Chairman Andrew Mathias - President, Chief Investment Officer, Principal Operating Officer	**Auditors:** Ernst & Young LLP **Investor Contact:** 212-594-2700 **Transfer Agents:** Computershare

SM ENERGY CO.

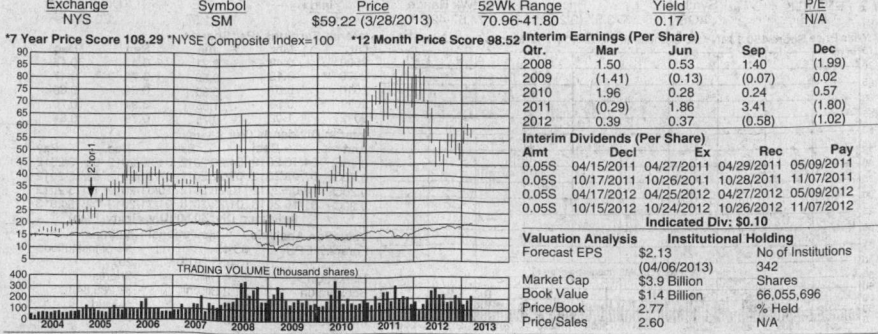

Exchange	Symbol	Price	52Wk Range	Yield	P/E
NYS	SM	$59.22 (3/28/2013)	70.96-41.80	0.17	N/A

*7 Year Price Score 108.29 *NYSE Composite Index=100 *12 Month Price Score 98.52

Interim Earnings (Per Share)

Qtr.	Mar	Jun	Sep	Dec
2008	1.50	0.53	1.40	(1.99)
2009	(1.41)	(0.13)	(0.07)	0.02
2010	1.96	0.28	0.24	0.57
2011	(0.29)	1.86	3.41	(1.80)
2012	0.39	0.37	(0.58)	(1.02)

Interim Dividends (Per Share)

Amt	Decl	Ex	Rec	Pay
0.05S	04/15/2011	04/27/2011	04/29/2011	05/09/2011
0.05S	10/17/2011	10/26/2011	10/28/2011	11/07/2011
0.05S	04/17/2012	04/25/2012	04/27/2012	05/09/2012
0.05S	10/15/2012	10/24/2012	10/26/2012	11/07/2012

Indicated Div: $0.10

Valuation Analysis

		Institutional Holding	
Forecast EPS	$2.13	No of Institutions	
	(04/06/2013)	342	
Market Cap	$3.9 Billion	Shares	
Book Value	$1.4 Billion	66,055,696	
Price/Book	2.77	% Held	
Price/Sales	2.60	N/A	

Business Summary: Production & Extraction (MIC: 9.1.1 SIC: 1311 NAIC: 211111)

SM Energy is an independent energy company engaged in the acquisition, exploration, development, and production of crude oil, natural gas, and natural gas liquids in onshore North America. Co.'s operations are concentrated in four core operating areas in the onshore U.S.: the South Texas & Gulf Coast Region; the Rocky Mountain Region; the Mid-Continent Region; and the Permian Region. As of Dec 31 2012, Co.'s estimated proved reserves for oil, gas and NGLs were 92.2 million barrels, 833.4 billion cubic feet, and 62.3 million barrels, respectively.

Recent Developments: For the year ended Dec 31 2012, net loss amounted to US$54.2 million versus net income of US$215.4 million in the prior year. Revenues were US$1.51 billion, down 6.1% from US$1.60 billion the year before. Operating loss was US$20.0 million versus an income of US$384.4 million in the prior year. Direct operating expenses rose 39.8% to US$1.12 billion from US$801.2 million in the comparable period the year before. Indirect operating expenses decreased 3.0% to US$405.4 million from US$417.7 million in the equivalent prior-year period.

Prospects: Our evaluation of SM Energy Co. as of Apr. 7, 2013 is the result of our systematic analysis on three basic characteristics: earnings strength, relative valuation, and recent stock price movement. The company has enjoyed a very positive trend in earnings per share over the past 5 quarters and while recent estimates for the company have been raised by analysts, SM has posted better than expected results. Based on operating earnings yield, the company is overvalued when compared to all of the companies in our coverage universe. Share price changes over the past year indicates that SM will perform poorly over the near term.

Financial Data
(US$ in Thousands)

	12/31/2012	12/31/2011	12/31/2010	12/31/2009	12/31/2008	12/31/2007	12/31/2006	12/31/2005
Earnings Per Share	(0.83)	3.19	3.04	(1.59)	1.45	2.94	2.94	2.33
Cash Flow Per Share	14.12	11.93	7.89	6.98	10.87	10.20	8.31	7.19
Tang Book Value Per Share	21.37	22.84	19.25	15.51	18.10	13.55	13.34	9.86
Dividends Per Share	0.100	0.100	0.100	0.100	0.100	0.100	0.100	0.100
Dividend Payout %	...	3.13	3.29	...	6.90	3.40	3.40	4.29
Income Statement								
Total Revenue	1,505,102	1,603,318	1,092,834	832,201	1,301,301	990,094	787,701	739,590
EBITDA	714,629	913,786	688,376	185,579	485,531	547,007	456,788	378,752
Depn & Amortn	734,646	529,402	349,605	316,414	314,330	227,596	154,522	132,758
Income Before Taxes	(83,517)	339,001	314,896	(159,464)	151,411	300,262	295,321	238,237
Income Taxes	(29,268)	123,585	118,059	(60,094)	59,858	110,550	105,306	86,301
Net Income	(54,249)	215,416	196,837	(99,370)	91,553	189,712	190,015	151,936
Average Shares	65,138	67,564	64,689	62,457	63,133	64,850	65,962	66,894
Balance Sheet								
Current Assets	340,564	463,204	274,645	209,046	311,794	269,941	226,940	203,931
Total Assets	4,199,529	3,798,980	2,744,321	2,360,936	2,695,016	2,571,680	1,899,097	1,268,747
Current Liabilities	541,546	505,805	502,053	296,671	296,601	362,545	204,070	198,994
Long-Term Obligations	1,440,000	985,069	323,673	454,902	587,500	572,500	433,980	99,885
Total Liabilities	2,785,063	2,336,040	1,525,795	1,387,366	1,567,531	1,708,335	1,155,723	699,427
Stockholders' Equity	1,414,466	1,462,940	1,218,526	973,570	1,127,485	863,345	743,374	569,320
Shares Outstanding	66,195	64,064	63,310	62,772	62,288	63,001	55,001	56,761
Statistical Record								
Return on Assets %	N.M.	6.58	7.71	N.M.	3.47	8.49	12.00	13.72
Return on Equity %	N.M.	16.07	17.96	N.M.	9.17	23.61	28.95	28.84
EBITDA Margin %	47.48	56.99	62.99	22.30	37.31	55.25	57.99	51.21
Net Margin %	N.M.	13.44	18.01	N.M.	7.04	19.16	24.12	20.54
Asset Turnover	0.38	0.49	0.43	0.33	0.49	0.44	0.50	0.67
Current Ratio	0.63	0.92	0.55	0.70	1.05	0.74	1.11	1.02
Debt to Equity	1.02	0.67	0.27	0.47	0.52	0.66	0.58	0.18
Price Range	83.35-41.80	86.80-56.04	58.93-31.64	37.22-11.58	64.64-15.31	44.07-31.80	45.28-34.34	40.28-19.57
P/E Ratio	...	27.21-17.57	19.38-10.41	...	44.58-10.56	14.99-10.82	15.40-11.68	17.29-8.40
Average Yield %	0.17	0.14	0.24	0.41	0.26	0.27	0.25	0.34

Address: 1775 Sherman Street, Suite 1200, Denver, CO 80203
Telephone: 303-861-8140
Fax: 303-861-0934

Web Site: www.sm-energy.com
Officers: William D. Sullivan - Chairman Javan D. Ottoson - President, Executive Vice President, Chief Operating Officer

Auditors: Ernst & Young LLP
Investor Contact: 303-837-2444
Transfer Agents: Computershare Trust Company NA, Golden, Co

SMITH (A.O.) CORP

Exchange	Symbol	Price	52Wk Range	Yield	P/E	Div Achiever
NYS	AOS	$73.57 (3/28/2013)	74.67-42.43	1.09	21.57	20 Years

*7 Year Price Score 150.13 *NYSE Composite Index=100 *12 Month Price Score 115.42

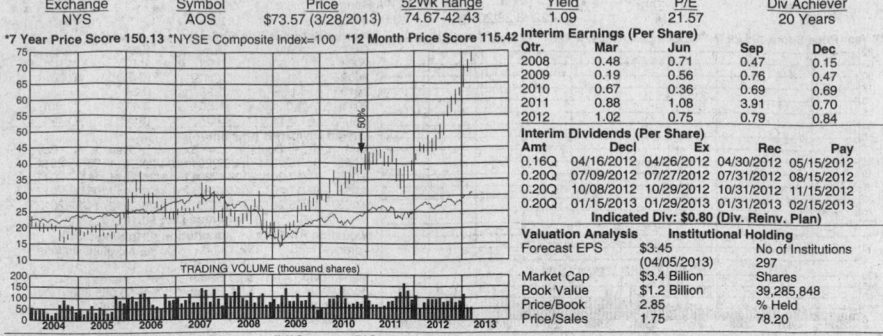

Interim Earnings (Per Share)

Qtr.	Mar	Jun	Sep	Dec
2008	0.48	0.71	0.47	0.15
2009	0.19	0.56	0.76	0.47
2010	0.67	0.36	0.69	0.69
2011	0.88	1.08	3.91	0.70
2012	1.02	0.75	0.79	0.84

Interim Dividends (Per Share)

Amt	Decl	Ex	Rec	Pay
0.16Q	04/16/2012	04/26/2012	04/30/2012	05/15/2012
0.20Q	07/09/2012	07/27/2012	07/31/2012	08/15/2012
0.20Q	10/08/2012	10/29/2012	10/31/2012	11/15/2012
0.20Q	01/15/2013	01/29/2013	01/31/2013	02/15/2013

Indicated Div: $0.80 (Div. Reinv. Plan)

Valuation Analysis		Institutional Holding	
Forecast EPS	$3.45 (04/05/2013)	No of Institutions	297
Market Cap	$3.4 Billion	Shares	39,285,848
Book Value	$1.2 Billion	% Held	78.20
Price/Book	2.85		
Price/Sales	1.75		

Business Summary: Metal Products (MIC: 8.2.3 SIC: 3621 NAIC: 335312)

A.O. Smith is a manufacturer of water heaters and boilers, serving a mix of residential and commercial end markets. Co. is comprised of two reporting segments: North America and Rest of World. Both segments manufacture and market lines of residential gas, gas tankless, oil and electric water heaters and commercial water heating equipment. Both segments primarily serve their respective regions of the world. The North America segment also manufactures and markets commercial water heating equipment, condensing and non-condensing boilers and water systems tanks. The Rest of World segment also manufactures and markets water treatment products, primarily for Asia.

Recent Developments: For the year ended Dec 31 2012, income from continuing operations increased 46.2% to US$162.6 million from US$111.2 million a year earlier. Net income decreased 48.1% to US$158.7 million from US$305.7 million in the prior year. Revenues were US$1.94 billion, up 13.4% from US$1.71 billion the year before. Direct operating expenses rose 7.5% to US$1.29 billion from US$1.20 billion in the comparable period the year before. Indirect operating expenses increased 22.6% to US$443.3 million from US$361.6 million in the equivalent prior-year period.

Prospects: Our evaluation of Smith (A.O.) Corp. as of Apr. 7, 2013 is the result of our systematic analysis on three basic characteristics: earnings strength, relative valuation, and recent stock price movement. The company has generated a negative trend in earnings per share over the past 5 quarters and while recent estimates for the company have been mixed, AOS has posted better than expected results. Based on operating earnings yield, the company is about fairly valued when compared to all of the companies in our coverage universe. Share price changes over the past year indicates that AOS will perform very well over the near term.

Financial Data
(US$ in Thousands)

	12/31/2012	12/31/2011	12/31/2010	12/31/2009	12/31/2008	12/31/2007	12/31/2006	12/31/2005
Earnings Per Share	3.41	6.57	2.42	2.26	1.80	1.90	1.65	1.03
Cash Flow Per Share	3.10	1.27	2.73	7.49	2.36	4.16	2.82	4.19
Tang Book Value Per Share	9.09	6.53	9.84	1.83	1.27	3.51	2.11	6.34
Dividends Per Share	0.720	0.600	0.540	0.513	0.493	0.467	0.440	0.427
Dividend Payout %	21.11	9.13	22.31	22.71	27.41	24.56	26.72	41.56
Income Statement								
Total Revenue	1,939,300	1,710,500	1,489,300	1,991,500	2,304,900	2,312,100	2,161,300	1,689,200
EBITDA	297,600	217,800	122,100	198,900	195,600	194,100	190,600	134,500
Depn & Amortn	54,600	47,000	40,800	67,500	66,300	67,500	60,900	52,800
Income Before Taxes	233,800	161,500	74,400	119,600	110,100	99,900	104,800	68,700
Income Taxes	71,200	50,300	17,300	29,600	27,900	11,700	28,600	22,200
Net Income	158,700	305,700	111,700	81,300	81,900	88,200	76,500	46,500
Average Shares	46,554	46,574	46,162	35,931	45,434	46,459	46,505	45,422
Balance Sheet								
Current Assets	1,107,200	1,208,700	896,000	740,000	781,300	767,600	760,000	576,000
Total Assets	2,265,200	2,349,000	2,112,000	1,901,300	1,883,900	1,854,400	1,839,900	1,292,700
Current Liabilities	499,000	519,900	536,800	491,300	505,000	472,600	437,300	307,600
Long-Term Obligations	225,100	443,000	242,400	232,100	317,300	379,600	432,100	162,400
Total Liabilities	1,071,100	1,263,200	1,230,600	1,130,600	1,242,800	1,096,600	1,155,300	679,800
Stockholders' Equity	1,194,100	1,085,800	881,400	770,700	641,100	757,800	684,600	612,900
Shares Outstanding	46,213	45,826	45,833	45,520	45,266	45,079	46,026	45,620
Statistical Record								
Return on Assets %	6.86	13.71	5.57	4.30	4.37	4.77	4.88	3.57
Return on Equity %	13.88	31.08	13.52	11.52	11.68	12.23	11.79	7.73
EBITDA Margin %	15.35	12.73	8.20	9.99	8.49	8.39	8.82	7.96
Net Margin %	8.18	17.87	7.50	4.08	3.55	3.81	3.54	2.75
Asset Turnover	0.84	0.77	0.74	1.05	1.23	1.25	1.38	1.30
Current Ratio	2.22	2.32	1.67	1.51	1.55	1.62	1.74	1.87
Debt to Equity	0.19	0.41	0.28	0.30	0.49	0.50	0.63	0.26
Price Range	63.58-41.04	44.65-30.43	43.07-27.64	29.96-14.19	31.33-16.29	34.10-21.86	37.77-22.70	24.75-16.75
P/E Ratio	18.65-12.04	6.80-4.63	17.80-11.42	13.26-6.28	17.41-9.05	17.95-11.51	22.89-13.76	24.03-16.27
Average Yield %	1.41	1.52	1.56	2.24	2.15	1.73	1.55	2.16

Address: 11270 West Park Place,	Web Site: www.aosmith.com	Auditors: Ernst & Young LLP
Milwaukee, WI 53224-9508	Officers: Paul W. Jones - Chairman, President, Chief	Investor Contact: 414-359-4130
Telephone: 414-359-4000	Executive Officer Ajita G. Rajendra - President, Chief	Transfer Agents: Wells Fargo Bank,
Fax: 414-359-4180	Operating Officer, Executive Vice President, Senior	N.A., South St. Paul, MN
	Vice President, Division Officer	

SMITHFIELD FOODS, INC.

Exchange	Symbol	Price	52Wk Range	Yield	P/E
NYS	SFD	$26.48 (3/28/2013)	26.85-17.82	N/A	17.19

*7 Year Price Score 87.47   *NYSE Composite Index=100   *12 Month Price Score 103.38

TRADING VOLUME (thousand shares)

Interim Earnings (Per Share)

Qtr.	Jul	Oct	Jan	Apr
2009-10	(0.75)	(0.17)	0.22	(0.02)
2010-11	0.46	0.86	1.21	0.59
2011-12	0.49	0.74	0.49	0.49
2012-13	0.40	0.07	0.58	...

Interim Dividends (Per Share)

No Dividends Paid

Valuation Analysis

		Institutional Holding	
Forecast EPS	$2.06	No of Institutions	
	(04/06/2013)	365	
Market Cap	$3.7 Billion	Shares	
Book Value	$3.2 Billion	130,306,112	
Price/Book	1.15	% Held	
Price/Sales	0.28	72.63	

Business Summary: Food (MIC: 1.2.1 SIC: 2011 NAIC: 311611)

Smithfield Foods is engaged in producing and marketing fresh meat and packaged meats products including smoked and boiled hams, bacon, and sausage. Co. has four segments: Pork, which produces pork and packaged meats products and markets them nationwide and to foreign markets; Hog Production, which consists of its hog production operations in the U.S. that develops breeding stock; International, which consists of its meat processing and distribution operations in Poland, Romania and the U.K., meat processing operations in Western Europe and Mexico, its hog production operations in Poland, Romania, and Mexico; and Corporate.

Recent Developments: For the quarter ended Jan 27 2013, net income increased 3.2% to US$81.5 million from US$79.0 million in the year-earlier quarter. Revenues were US$3.58 billion, up 3.0% from US$3.48 billion the year before. Operating income was US$136.3 million versus US$170.5 million in the prior-year quarter, a decrease of 20.1%. Direct operating expenses rose 5.0% to US$3.25 billion from US$3.10 billion in the comparable period the year before. Indirect operating expenses decreased 8.0% to US$192.5 million from US$209.3 million in the equivalent prior-year period.

Prospects: Our evaluation of Smithfield Foods Inc. as of Apr. 7, 2013 is the result of our systematic analysis on three basic characteristics: earnings strength, relative valuation, and recent stock price movement. The company has enjoyed a very positive trend in earnings per share over the past 5 quarters. However, while recent estimates for the company have been lowered by analysts, SFD has posted better than expected results. Based on operating earnings yield, the company is undervalued when compared to all of the companies in our coverage universe. Share price changes over the past year indicates that SFD will perform very poorly over the near term.

Financial Data

(US$ in Thousands)	9 Mos	6 Mos	3 Mos	04/29/2012	05/01/2011	05/02/2010	05/03/2009	04/27/2008
Earnings Per Share	1.54	1.45	2.12	2.21	3.12	(0.65)	(1.35)	0.96
Cash Flow Per Share	2.95	3.00	4.55	3.52	3.72	1.65	1.88	0.07
Tang Book Value Per Share	14.58	14.25	14.31	14.21	14.24	9.30	9.40	13.30
Income Statement								
Total Revenue	9,900,400	6,317,100	3,091,300	13,094,300	12,202,700	11,202,600	12,487,700	11,351,200
EBITDA	488,000	299,700	189,900	958,900	1,179,800	250,100	161,500	599,000
Depn & Amortn	176,100	117,700	58,800	238,600	227,400	236,900	264,000	258,000
Income Before Taxes	187,300	98,000	88,600	543,600	707,000	(253,200)	(311,600)	156,200
Income Taxes	47,000	32,800	27,600	172,400	236,100	(113,200)	(126,700)	72,800
Net Income	154,100	72,600	61,700	361,300	521,000	(101,400)	(190,300)	128,900
Average Shares	141,500	149,100	155,300	163,500	167,200	157,100	141,100	134,200
Balance Sheet								
Current Assets	3,438,700	3,657,200	3,329,300	3,299,000	3,337,900	3,320,300	2,784,500	3,850,000
Total Assets	7,621,000	7,788,900	7,372,300	7,422,200	7,611,800	7,708,900	7,202,500	8,867,900
Current Liabilities	1,515,600	1,611,900	1,665,100	1,136,300	1,227,900	1,191,900	1,286,800	1,676,000
Long-Term Obligations	1,852,400	1,851,700	1,372,900	1,900,900	1,978,600	2,918,400	2,649,900	3,474,400
Total Liabilities	4,419,800	4,521,200	4,081,500	4,034,900	4,066,300	4,953,300	4,641,100	5,819,700
Stockholders' Equity	3,201,200	3,267,700	3,290,800	3,387,300	3,545,500	2,755,600	2,561,400	3,048,200
Shares Outstanding	138,763	146,941	150,319	157,408	166,080	165,995	143,576	134,398
Statistical Record								
Return on Assets %	3.16	3.04	4.64	4.82	6.82	N.M.	N.M.	1.63
Return on Equity %	6.96	6.86	10.01	10.45	16.58	N.M.	N.M.	4.89
EBITDA Margin %	4.93	4.74	6.14	7.32	9.67	2.23	1.29	5.28
Net Margin %	1.56	1.15	2.00	2.76	4.27	N.M.	N.M.	1.14
Asset Turnover	1.78	1.71	1.78	1.75	1.60	1.51	1.53	1.44
Current Ratio	2.27	2.27	2.00	2.90	2.72	2.79	2.16	2.30
Debt to Equity	0.58	0.57	0.42	0.56	0.56	1.06	1.03	1.14
Price Range	24.05-17.82	24.97-17.82	24.97-17.82	24.97-18.11	24.76-13.79	21.35-9.87	31.78-5.60	34.95-24.45
P/E Ratio	15.62-11.57	17.22-12.29	11.78-8.42	11.30-8.19	7.94-4.42	...	...	36.41-25.47

Address: 200 Commerce Street, Smithfield, VA 23430 Telephone: 757-365-3000	Web Site: www.smithfieldfoods.com Officers: Joseph W. Luter - Chairman C. Larry Pope - President, Chief Executive Officer	Auditors: Ernst & Young LLP Investor Contact: 757-365-3050 Transfer Agents: ComputerShare Investor Services, Providence, RI

SOTHEBY'S

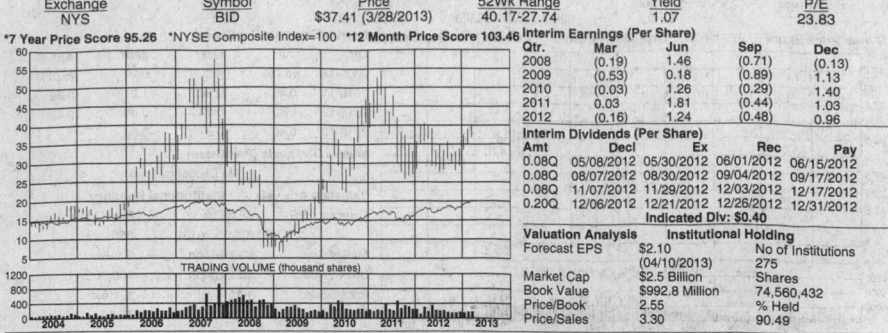

Exchange	Symbol	Price	52Wk Range	Yield	P/E
NYS	BID	$37.41 (3/28/2013)	40.17-27.74	1.07	23.83

*7 Year Price Score 95.26 ***NYSE Composite Index=100** ***12 Month Price Score 103.46**

Interim Earnings (Per Share)

Qtr.	Mar	Jun	Sep	Dec
2008	(0.19)	1.46	(0.71)	(0.13)
2009	(0.53)	0.18	(0.89)	1.13
2010	(0.03)	1.26	(0.29)	1.40
2011	0.03	1.81	(0.44)	1.03
2012	(0.16)	1.24	(0.48)	0.96

Interim Dividends (Per Share)

Amt	Decl	Ex	Rec	Pay
0.08Q	05/08/2012	05/30/2012	06/01/2012	06/15/2012
0.08Q	08/07/2012	08/30/2012	09/04/2012	09/17/2012
0.08Q	11/07/2012	11/29/2012	12/03/2012	12/17/2012
0.20Q	12/06/2012	12/21/2012	12/26/2012	12/31/2012

Indicated Div: $0.40

Valuation Analysis / **Institutional Holding**

Forecast EPS	$2.10	No of Institutions
	(04/10/2013)	275
Market Cap	$2.5 Billion	Shares
Book Value	$992.8 Million	74,560,432
Price/Book	2.55	% Held
Price/Sales	3.30	90.49

Business Summary: Miscellaneous Consumer Services (MIC: 2.2.3 SIC: 7389 NAIC: 453920)

Sotheby's is an auctioneer of authenticated fine and decorative art, jewelry and collectibles (collectively, art or works of art or artwork or property). Co.'s operations are organized under three segments: Auction, which functions principally as an agent by providing works of art for sale at auctions and by brokering private art sales, Finance, which provides certain collectors and art dealers with financing secured by works of art that Co. either has in its possession or permits borrowers to possess, and Dealer, which principally includes the activities of Noortman Master Paintings, an art dealer that sells works of art from inventory directly to private collectors and museums.

Recent Developments: For the year ended Dec 31 2012, net income decreased 36.8% to US$108.3 million from US$171.4 million in the prior year. Revenues were US$768.5 million, down 7.6% from US$831.8 million the year before. Operating income was US$214.4 million versus US$271.5 million in the prior year, a decrease of 21.0%. Direct operating expenses declined 6.9% to US$86.8 million from US$93.2 million in the comparable period the year before. Indirect operating expenses increased 0.0% to US$467.3 million from US$467.1 million in the equivalent prior-year period.

Prospects: Our evaluation of Sotheby's Holdings Inc. as of Apr. 7, 2013 is the result of our systematic analysis on three basic characteristics: earnings strength, relative valuation, and recent stock price movement. The company has enjoyed a very positive trend in earnings per share over the past 5 quarters. However, while recent estimates for the company have been mixed, BID has posted results that fell short of analysts expectations. Based on operating earnings yield, the company is about fairly valued when compared to all of the companies in our coverage universe. Share price changes over the past year indicates that BID will perform well over the near term.

Financial Data
(US$ in Thousands)

	12/31/2012	12/31/2011	12/31/2010	12/31/2009	12/31/2008	12/31/2007	12/31/2006	12/31/2005
Earnings Per Share	1.57	2.46	2.34	(0.10)	0.43	3.25	1.72	1.00
Cash Flow Per Share	(0.96)	5.99	5.15	2.43	(2.71)	(0.58)	4.48	0.97
Tang Book Value Per Share	14.43	13.19	11.24	8.35	7.97	8.56	3.92	1.95
Dividends Per Share	0.520	0.230	0.200	0.300	0.600	0.500	0.200	...
Dividend Payout %	33.12	9.35	8.55	...	139.53	15.38	11.63	...
Income Statement								
Total Revenue	768,492	831,836	774,309	484,958	691,559	917,722	664,809	513,508
EBITDA	220,215	286,085	286,259	75,546	99,426	317,785	218,393	144,718
Depn & Amortn	17,900	17,200	15,600	19,800	22,600	20,600	25,462	26,063
Income Before Taxes	159,436	231,389	225,579	15,395	48,477	283,019	165,783	90,913
Income Taxes	51,395	60,032	65,273	22,162	22,347	72,512	60,050	28,573
Net Income	108,292	171,416	160,950	(6,528)	28,269	213,139	107,049	61,602
Average Shares	68,527	68,850	67,322	65,208	65,500	65,600	62,100	61,900
Balance Sheet								
Current Assets	1,671,123	1,693,296	1,450,404	968,367	1,226,909	1,565,602	1,047,827	686,956
Total Assets	2,575,095	2,399,414	2,178,628	1,586,123	1,679,331	2,020,104	1,477,165	1,060,752
Current Liabilities	964,879	964,312	877,384	442,475	563,792	1,074,862	789,191	545,245
Long-Term Obligations	515,197	464,552	472,862	512,939	493,075	267,078	268,777	304,849
Total Liabilities	1,582,269	1,495,747	1,407,120	1,009,138	1,125,669	1,416,087	1,175,478	934,476
Stockholders' Equity	992,826	903,667	771,508	576,985	553,662	604,017	301,687	126,276
Shares Outstanding	67,779	67,407	67,320	67,157	67,279	66,563	64,795	57,847
Statistical Record								
Return on Assets %	4.34	7.49	8.55	N.M.	1.52	12.19	8.44	5.39
Return on Equity %	11.39	20.47	23.87	N.M.	4.87	47.07	50.03	34.02
EBITDA Margin %	28.66	34.39	36.97	15.58	14.38	34.63	32.85	28.18
Net Margin %	14.09	20.61	20.79	N.M.	4.09	23.22	16.10	12.00
Asset Turnover	0.31	0.36	0.41	0.30	0.37	0.52	0.52	0.45
Current Ratio	1.73	1.76	1.65	2.19	2.18	1.46	1.33	1.26
Debt to Equity	0.52	0.51	0.61	0.89	0.89	0.44	0.89	2.41
Price Range	40.51-27.74	54.41-25.84	46.80-22.11	24.40-6.35	38.58-7.64	57.64-30.71	38.00-18.55	19.43-13.52
P/E Ratio	25.80-17.67	22.12-10.50	20.00-9.45	...	89.72-17.77	17.74-9.45	22.09-10.78	19.43-13.52
Average Yield %	1.57	0.58	0.62	2.20	2.59	1.14	0.72	...

Address: 1334 York Avenue, New York, NY 10021	Web Site: www.sothebys.com	Auditors: Deloitte & Touche LLP
Telephone: 212-606-7000	Officers: Michael I. Sovern - Chairman The Duke of Devonshire - Deputy Chairman	Transfer Agents: Computershare Investor Services, Pittsburgh, PA

SMUCKER (J.M.) CO.

Exchange	Symbol	Price	52Wk Range	Yield	P/E	Div Achiever
NYS	SJM	$99.16 (3/28/2013)	99.16-73.65	2.10	21.01	15 Years

*7 Year Price Score 124.06 *NYSE Composite Index=100 *12 Month Price Score 103.49

TRADING VOLUME (thousand shares)

Interim Earnings (Per Share)

Qtr.	Jul	Oct	Jan	Apr
2009-10	0.83	1.18	1.14	1.01
2010-11	0.86	1.25	1.11	0.82
2011-12	0.98	1.12	1.03	0.94
2012-13	1.00	1.36	1.42	...

Interim Dividends (Per Share)

Amt	Decl	Ex	Rec	Pay
0.48Q	04/19/2012	05/09/2012	05/11/2012	06/01/2012
0.52Q	07/18/2012	08/08/2012	08/10/2012	09/04/2012
0.52Q	10/24/2012	11/14/2012	11/16/2012	12/03/2012
0.52Q	01/25/2013	02/13/2013	02/15/2013	03/01/2013

Indicated Div: $2.08 (Div. Reinv. Plan)

Valuation Analysis | **Institutional Holding**

Forecast EPS	$5.23	No of Institutions
	(04/06/2013)	689
Market Cap	$10.8 Billion	Shares
Book Value	$5.3 Billion	83,758,664
Price/Book	2.04	% Held
Price/Sales	1.82	70.32

Business Summary: Food (MIC: 1.2.1 SIC: 2033 NAIC: 311421)

Smucker (J.M.) markets and manufactures fruit spreads, retail packaged coffee, peanut butter, shortening and oils, ice cream toppings, sweetened condensed milk, and health and natural foods beverages in North America. Co.'s family of brands includes Smucker's, Folgers, Dunkin' Donuts, Jif, Crisco, Pillsbury, Eagle Brand, R.W. Knudsen Family, Hungry Jack, Cafe Bustelo, Cafe Pilon, White Lily, and Martha White in the U.S., along with Robin Hood, Five Roses, Carnation and Bick's in Canada. In addition to these brands, Co. markets products under numerous other brands, including Millstone, Dickinson's, Laura Scudder's, Adams, Double Fruit (Canada), and Santa Cruz Organic.

Recent Developments: For the quarter ended Jan 31 2013, net income increased 31.9% to US$154.2 million from US$116.8 million in the year-earlier quarter. Revenues were US$1.56 billion, up 6.3% from US$1.47 billion the year before. Operating income was US$258.3 million versus US$200.4 million in the prior-year quarter, an increase of 28.9%. Direct operating expenses rose 2.1% to US$1.02 billion from US$1.00 billion in the comparable period the year before. Indirect operating expenses increased 4.8% to US$277.9 million from US$265.3 million in the equivalent prior-year period.

Prospects: Our evaluation of Smucker (J.M.) Co. as of Apr. 7, 2013 is the result of our systematic analysis on three basic characteristics: earnings strength, relative valuation, and recent stock price movement. The company has managed to produce a neutral trend in earnings per share over the past 5 quarters and while recent estimates for the company have been mixed, SJM has posted better than expected results. Based on operating earnings yield, the company is about fairly valued when compared to all of the companies in our coverage universe. Share price changes over the past year indicates that SJM will perform in line with the market over the near term.

Financial Data

(US$ in Thousands)	9 Mos	6 Mos	3 Mos	04/30/2012	04/30/2011	04/30/2010	04/30/2009	04/30/2008
Earnings Per Share	4.72	4.33	4.09	4.06	4.05	4.15	3.12	3.00
Cash Flow Per Share	8.79	9.52	8.83	6.50	3.35	6.00	5.24	3.40
Tang Book Value Per Share	N.M.	N.M.	N.M.	N.M.	N.M.	N.M.	N.M.	0.98
Dividends Per Share	2.000	1.960	1.920	1.880	1.640	1.400	6.280	1.200
Dividend Payout %	42.37	45.27	46.94	46.31	40.49	33.73	201.28	40.00
Income Statement								
Total Revenue	4,558,007	2,998,449	1,369,703	5,525,782	4,825,743	4,605,289	3,757,933	2,524,774
EBITDA	884,365	565,187	254,704	939,886	950,041	901,372	531,000	342,171
Depn & Amortn	187,636	126,212	63,835	158,936	165,795	108,225	79,450	58,497
Income Before Taxes	625,477	391,483	167,265	701,158	717,164	730,753	396,065	254,788
Income Taxes	211,599	131,773	56,402	241,414	237,682	236,615	130,112	84,409
Net Income	413,878	259,710	110,863	459,744	479,482	494,138	265,953	170,379
Average Shares	107,548	108,296	109,448	112,262	117,119	119,081	85,285	56,720
Balance Sheet								
Current Assets	1,745,945	1,736,062	1,800,328	1,643,465	1,636,999	1,223,630	1,398,891	776,207
Total Assets	9,184,454	9,188,753	9,262,110	9,115,226	8,324,585	7,974,853	8,192,161	3,129,881
Current Liabilities	593,463	706,066	710,469	616,972	482,676	478,897	1,061,236	239,397
Long-Term Obligations	2,018,508	2,019,196	2,019,875	2,020,543	1,304,039	900,000	910,000	789,684
Total Liabilities	3,924,218	4,036,006	4,038,657	3,951,840	3,032,222	2,648,533	3,252,230	1,330,028
Stockholders' Equity	5,260,236	5,152,747	5,223,453	5,163,386	5,292,363	5,326,320	4,939,931	1,799,853
Shares Outstanding	108,482	108,458	110,438	110,284	114,172	119,119	118,422	54,622
Statistical Record								
Return on Assets %	5.62	5.22	5.09	5.26	5.88	6.11	4.70	5.84
Return on Equity %	9.73	9.14	8.69	8.77	9.03	9.63	7.89	9.45
EBITDA Margin %	19.40	18.85	18.60	17.01	19.69	19.57	14.13	13.55
Net Margin %	9.08	8.66	8.09	8.32	9.94	10.73	7.08	6.75
Asset Turnover	0.64	0.63	0.63	0.63	0.59	0.57	0.66	0.86
Current Ratio	2.94	2.46	2.53	2.66	3.39	2.56	1.32	3.24
Debt to Equity	0.38	0.39	0.39	0.39	0.25	0.17	0.18	0.44
Price Range	90.20-73.65	87.47-71.85	81.44-67.68	81.44-67.68	75.07-54.75	63.26-39.40	56.36-34.22	63.66-44.66
P/E Ratio	19.11-15.60	20.20-16.59	19.91-16.55	20.06-16.67	18.54-13.52	15.24-9.49	18.06-10.97	21.22-14.89
Average Yield %	2.45	2.48	2.52	2.46	2.59	2.58	13.91	2.25

Address: One Strawberry Lane, Orrville, OH 44667-0280 Telephone: 330-682-3000	Web Site: www.smucker.com Officers: Timothy P. Smucker - Chairman, Co-Chief Executive Officer Vincent C. Byrd - President, Chief Operating Officer	Auditors: Ernst & Young LLP Investor Contact: 330-684-3838 Transfer Agents: Computershare Investor Services, LLC, Canton, MA

681

SNAP-ON, INC.

Exchange	Symbol	Price	52Wk Range	Yield	P/E
NYS	SNA	$82.70 (3/28/2013)	82.70-57.63	1.84	15.90

*7 Year Price Score 125.79 *NYSE Composite Index=100 *12 Month Price Score 103.49

Interim Earnings (Per Share)

Qtr.	Mar	Jun	Sep	Dec
2008	0.97	1.15	0.94	1.01
2009	0.60	0.65	0.44	0.63
2010	0.63	0.78	0.80	0.99
2011	0.96	1.33	1.16	1.27
2012	1.21	1.30	1.26	1.43

Interim Dividends (Per Share)

Amt	Decl	Ex	Rec	Pay
0.34Q	04/26/2012	05/17/2012	05/21/2012	06/11/2012
0.34Q	08/02/2012	08/16/2012	08/20/2012	09/10/2012
0.38Q	11/01/2012	11/15/2012	11/19/2012	12/10/2012
0.38Q	02/13/2013	02/26/2013	02/28/2013	03/11/2013

Indicated Div: $1.52

Valuation Analysis **Institutional Holding**

Forecast EPS	$5.70 (04/05/2013)	No of Institutions	439
Market Cap	$4.8 Billion	Shares	52,757,536
Book Value	$1.8 Billion	% Held	82.37
Price/Book	2.67		
Price/Sales	1.55		

Business Summary: Industrial Machinery & Equipment (MIC: 7.2.1 SIC: 3429 NAIC: 332510)

Snap-on is a manufacturer and marketer of tools, equipment, diagnostics, repair information and systems applications. Co.'s products and services include hand and power tools, tool storage, diagnostic software, information and management systems, shop equipment and other applications for vehicle dealerships and repair centers, as well as for customers in industries, including aviation and aerospace, agriculture, construction, government and military, mining, natural resources, power generation and technical education. Co. provides training programs as well as after sales support for its customers. Co. also provides various financing programs to facilitate the sales of its products.

Recent Developments: For the year ended Dec 29 2012, net income increased 10.9% to US$314.6 million from US$283.8 million in the prior year. Revenues were US$3.10 billion, up 3.4% from US$3.00 billion the year before. Operating income was US$516.4 million versus US$475.1 million in the prior year, an increase of 8.7%. Direct operating expenses rose 2.2% to US$1.60 billion from US$1.57 billion in the comparable period the year before. Indirect operating expenses increased 2.8% to US$980.3 million from US$953.7 million in the equivalent prior-year period.

Prospects: Our evaluation of Snap-On Inc. as of Apr. 7, 2013 is the result of our systematic analysis on three basic characteristics: earnings strength, relative valuation, and recent stock price movement. The company has managed to produce a neutral trend in earnings per share over the past 5 quarters and while recent estimates for the company have remained steady, SNA has posted better than expected results. Based on operating earnings yield, the company is undervalued when compared to all of the companies in our coverage universe. Share price changes over the past year indicates that SNA will perform well over the near term.

Financial Data (US$ in Thousands)	12/29/2012	12/31/2011	01/01/2011	01/02/2010	01/03/2009	12/29/2007	12/30/2006	12/31/2005
Earnings Per Share	5.20	4.71	3.19	2.32	4.07	3.09	1.69	1.59
Cash Flow Per Share	5.67	2.21	2.43	6.03	3.68	4.00	3.50	3.84
Tang Book Value Per Share	13.86	9.39	6.83	4.67	2.90	3.94	0.72	8.17
Dividends Per Share	1.400	1.300	1.220	1.200	1.200	1.110	1.080	1.000
Dividend Payout %	26.92	27.60	38.24	51.72	29.48	35.92	63.91	62.89
Income Statement								
Total Revenue	3,099,200	2,996,500	2,681,500	2,420,800	2,934,700	2,904,200	2,522,400	2,362,200
EBITDA	592,100	547,300	403,600	325,900	457,000	406,000	218,400	221,900
Depn & Amortn	76,700	74,600	72,700	74,600	72,000	75,700	51,900	52,200
Income Before Taxes	460,200	412,900	277,400	205,300	357,800	284,200	145,900	148,000
Income Taxes	148,200	133,700	87,600	62,700	117,800	92,500	45,800	55,100
Net Income	306,100	276,300	186,500	134,200	236,700	181,200	100,100	92,900
Average Shares	58,900	58,700	58,400	57,900	58,100	58,600	59,200	58,400
Balance Sheet								
Current Assets	1,669,000	1,530,700	1,765,500	1,676,100	1,140,700	1,187,400	1,113,200	1,072,900
Total Assets	3,902,300	3,672,900	3,729,400	3,447,400	2,710,300	2,765,100	2,654,500	2,008,400
Current Liabilities	589,200	583,800	881,100	739,900	547,500	639,200	682,000	506,100
Long-Term Obligations	970,400	967,900	954,800	902,100	503,400	502,000	505,600	201,700
Total Liabilities	2,100,200	2,142,000	2,340,900	2,157,400	1,523,800	1,485,000	1,578,200	1,046,200
Stockholders' Equity	1,802,100	1,530,900	1,388,500	1,290,000	1,186,500	1,280,100	1,076,300	962,200
Shares Outstanding	58,254	58,224	58,181	57,745	57,441	57,429	58,578	61,162
Statistical Record								
Return on Assets %	8.10	7.49	5.21	4.37	8.51	6.71	4.31	4.33
Return on Equity %	18.42	18.98	13.96	10.87	18.88	15.42	9.85	8.99
EBITDA Margin %	19.10	18.26	15.05	13.46	15.57	13.98	8.66	9.39
Net Margin %	9.88	9.22	6.96	5.54	8.07	6.24	3.97	3.93
Asset Turnover	0.82	0.81	0.75	0.79	1.05	1.07	1.08	1.10
Current Ratio	2.83	2.62	2.00	2.27	2.08	1.86	1.63	2.12
Debt to Equity	0.54	0.63	0.69	0.70	0.42	0.39	0.47	0.21
Price Range	80.03-51.12	64.09-42.45	57.39-39.88	43.57-20.66	61.92-28.62	56.20-44.59	48.31-36.39	38.54-30.70
P/E Ratio	15.39-9.83	13.61-9.01	17.99-12.50	18.78-8.91	15.21-7.03	18.19-14.43	28.59-21.53	24.24-19.31
Average Yield %	2.11	2.35	2.65	3.62	2.43	2.23	2.59	2.88

Address: 2801 80th Street, Kenosha, WI 53143 **Telephone:** 262-656-5200 **Fax:** 262-656-5577	**Web Site:** www.snapon.com **Officers:** Jack D. Michaels - Chairman Nicholas T. Pinchuk - Chairman, President, Chief Executive Officer	**Auditors:** Deloitte & Touche LLP **Investor Contact:** 262-656-6121 **Transfer Agents:** Computershare Trust Company, N.A., Providence, RI

SOLERA HOLDINGS INC

Exchange	Symbol	Price	52Wk Range	Yield	P/E
NYS	SLH	$58.33 (3/28/2013)	58.33-37.00	0.86	40.51

*7 Year Price Score N/A   *NYSE Composite Index=100   *12 Month Price Score 108.64

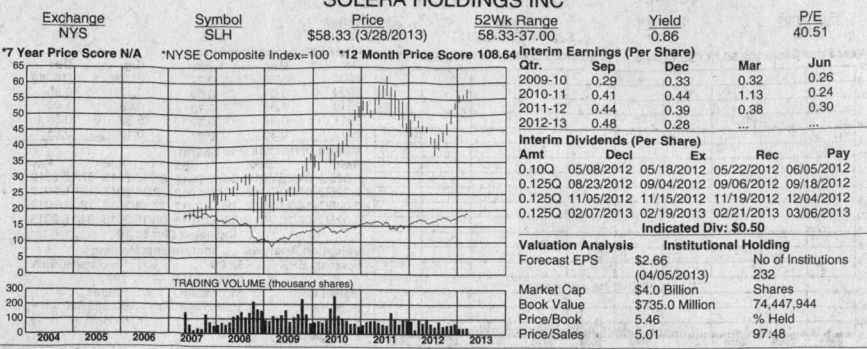

Interim Earnings (Per Share)

Qtr.	Sep	Dec	Mar	Jun
2009-10	0.29	0.33	0.32	0.26
2010-11	0.41	0.44	1.13	0.24
2011-12	0.44	0.39	0.38	0.30
2012-13	0.48	0.28	...	...

Interim Dividends (Per Share)

Amt	Decl	Ex	Rec	Pay
0.10Q	05/08/2012	05/18/2012	05/22/2012	06/05/2012
0.125Q	08/23/2012	09/04/2012	09/06/2012	09/18/2012
0.125Q	11/05/2012	11/15/2012	11/19/2012	12/04/2012
0.125Q	02/07/2013	02/19/2013	02/21/2013	03/06/2013

Indicated Div: $0.50

Valuation Analysis

		Institutional Holding	
Forecast EPS	$2.66 (04/05/2013)	No of Institutions	232
Market Cap	$4.0 Billion	Shares	74,447,944
Book Value	$735.0 Million	% Held	97.48
Price/Book	5.46		
Price/Sales	5.01		

Business Summary: Internet & Software (MIC: 6.3.2 SIC: 7371 NAIC: 541511)

Solera Holdings is a provider of software and services to the automobile insurance claims processing industry. Co. also provides products and services that complement its insurance claims processing software and services, including used vehicle validation, fraud detection software and services, salvage yard management software, disposition of salvage vehicles and data and analytics used by insurers in the re-underwriting of their insured drivers. Co.'s automobile insurance claims processing customers include insurance companies, collision repair facilities, independent assessors and automotive recyclers. Co. manages its business operations through two reportable segments: EMEA and Americas.

Recent Developments: For the quarter ended Dec 31 2012, net income decreased 27.9% to US$22.4 million from US$31.1 million in the year-earlier quarter. Revenues were US$209.2 million, up 7.2% from US$195.1 million the year before. Direct operating expenses rose 9.6% to US$65.6 million from US$59.9 million in the comparable period the year before. Indirect operating expenses increased 20.0% to US$112.0 million from US$93.3 million in the equivalent prior-year period.

Prospects: Our evaluation of Solera Holdings Inc. as of Apr. 7, 2013 is the result of our systematic analysis on three basic characteristics: earnings strength, relative valuation, and recent stock price movement. The company has produced a positive trend in earnings per share over the past 5 quarters and while recent estimates for the company have been mixed, SLH has posted better than expected results. Based on operating earnings yield, the company is about fairly valued when compared to all of the companies in our coverage universe. Share price changes over the past year indicates that SLH will perform very well over the near term.

Financial Data
(US$ in Thousands)

	6 Mos	3 Mos	06/30/2012	06/30/2011	06/30/2010	06/30/2009	06/30/2008	06/30/2007
Earnings Per Share	1.44	1.55	1.51	2.22	1.20	0.85	0.01	(2.82)
Cash Flow Per Share	3.27	3.50	3.17	3.01	2.73	1.92	1.84	1.36
Dividends Per Share	0.450	0.425	0.400	0.300	0.250	...	...	...
Dividend Payout %	31.25	27.42	26.49	13.51	20.83	...	...	...
Income Statement								
Total Revenue	404,952	195,719	790,207	684,697	631,348	557,691	539,853	471,960
EBITDA	154,278	79,603	241,797	205,226	179,044	145,058	179,516	93,838
Depn & Amortn	49,780	24,195	24,100	21,600	21,800	17,298	95,266	104,419
Income Before Taxes	69,712	38,108	164,104	154,630	126,342	92,801	42,176	(77,629)
Income Taxes	10,853	1,697	45,718	(14,427)	32,171	26,650	34,335	(773)
Net Income	53,409	33,641	106,988	157,377	84,432	57,825	598	(80,906)
Average Shares	69,062	69,094	70,527	70,683	69,763	67,732	64,737	33,865
Balance Sheet								
Current Assets	622,045	722,955	689,187	560,943	377,965	370,045	278,054	204,857
Total Assets	2,239,344	2,207,394	2,151,816	2,169,135	1,356,653	1,418,609	1,331,755	1,223,953
Current Liabilities	184,607	183,378	178,572	214,134	143,497	159,240	155,415	144,022
Long-Term Obligations	1,149,691	1,145,828	1,143,012	1,020,383	538,018	592,200	624,570	599,128
Total Liabilities	1,504,319	1,491,161	1,474,582	1,394,091	849,638	859,670	865,447	822,679
Stockholders' Equity	735,025	716,233	677,234	775,044	507,015	558,939	466,308	401,274
Shares Outstanding	68,835	68,753	68,895	70,795	70,017	69,531	64,816	64,813
Statistical Record								
Return on Assets %	4.74	5.07	4.94	8.93	6.08	4.20	0.05	N.M.
Return on Equity %	13.85	14.71	14.69	24.55	15.84	11.28	0.14	N.M.
EBITDA Margin %	38.10	40.67	30.60	29.97	28.36	26.01	33.25	19.88
Net Margin %	13.19	17.19	13.54	22.98	13.37	10.37	0.11	N.M.
Asset Turnover	0.38	0.36	0.36	0.39	0.45	0.41	0.42	0.38
Current Ratio	3.37	3.94	3.86	2.62	2.63	2.32	1.79	1.42
Debt to Equity	1.56	1.60	1.69	1.32	1.06	1.06	1.34	1.49
Price Range	53.86-37.00	54.64-37.00	62.26-40.68	59.16-36.20	40.03-24.11	31.12-15.71	28.28-17.19	19.38-17.25
P/E Ratio	37.40-25.69	35.25-23.87	41.23-26.94	26.65-16.31	33.36-20.09	36.61-18.48	N.M.	...
Average Yield %	0.99	0.94	0.81	0.62	0.75	...	...	...

Address: 7 Village Circle, Suite 100, Westlake, TX 76262 Telephone: 817-961-2100	Web Site: www.solerainc.com Officers: Tony Aquila - Chairman, President, Chief Executive Officer Abilio Jose Gonzalez - Senior Vice President	Auditors: Deloitte & Touche LLP Investor Contact: 858-946-1676 Transfer Agents: Computershare Trust Company N.A.

SONIC AUTOMOTIVE, INC.

Exchange	Symbol	Price	52Wk Range	Yield	P/E
NYS	SAH	$22.16 (3/28/2013)	25.15-12.16	0.45	14.48

*7 Year Price Score 102.55 *NYSE Composite Index=100 ***12 Month Price Score 114.06**

Interim Earnings (Per Share)

Qtr.	Mar	Jun	Sep	Dec
2008	0.35	0.27	(0.63)	(16.99)
2009	0.04	0.00	0.17	0.36
2010	0.08	0.16	0.23	1.00
2011	0.26	0.35	0.33	0.35
2012	0.35	0.47	0.18	0.53

Interim Dividends (Per Share)

Amt	Decl	Ex	Rec	Pay
0.025Q	04/23/2012	06/13/2012	06/15/2012	07/15/2012
0.025Q	07/23/2012	09/12/2012	09/14/2012	10/15/2012
0.025Q	10/23/2012	12/12/2012	12/14/2012	12/21/2012
0.025Q	02/20/2013	03/13/2013	03/15/2013	04/15/2013

Indicated Div: $0.10

Valuation Analysis

		Institutional Holding	
Forecast EPS	$2.00 (04/06/2013)	No of Institutions	197
Market Cap	$1.2 Billion	Shares	39,828,620
Book Value	$526.5 Million	% Held	67.62
Price/Book	2.24		
Price/Sales	0.14		

TRADING VOLUME (thousand shares)

Business Summary: Retail - Automotive (MIC: 2.1.4 SIC: 5511 NAIC: 441110)

Sonic Automotive is an automotive retailer. Co.'s dealerships provide services that include sales of both new and used cars and light trucks; sales of replacement parts, performance of vehicle maintenance, manufacturer warranty repairs, paint and collision repair services; as well as arrangement of extended service contracts, financing, insurance and other aftermarket products for its customers. As of Dec 31 2011, Co. operated 119 dealerships in 15 states (representing 30 different brands of cars and light trucks) and 23 collision repair centers.

Recent Developments: For the year ended Dec 31 2012, income from continuing operations increased 11.9% to US$91.3 million from US$81.5 million a year earlier. Net income increased 16.8% to US$89.1 million from US$76.3 million in the prior year. Revenues were US$8.37 billion, up 11.2% from US$7.52 billion the year before. Operating income was US$240.4 million versus US$219.5 million in the prior year, an increase of 9.5%. Direct operating expenses rose 12.1% to US$7.13 billion from US$6.36 billion in the comparable period the year before. Indirect operating expenses increased 5.9% to US$994.8 million from US$939.1 million in the equivalent prior-year period.

Prospects: Our evaluation of Sonic Automotive Inc. as of Apr. 7, 2013 is the result of our systematic analysis on three basic characteristics: earnings strength, relative valuation, and recent stock price movement. The company has managed to produce a neutral trend in earnings per share over the past 5 quarters and while recent estimates for the company have been raised by analysts, SAH has posted better than expected results. Based on operating earnings yield, the company is undervalued when compared to all of the companies in our coverage universe. Share price changes over the past year indicates that SAH will perform very well over the near term.

Financial Data
(US$ in Thousands)

	12/31/2012	12/31/2011	12/31/2010	12/31/2009	12/31/2008	12/31/2007	12/31/2006	12/31/2005
Earnings Per Share	1.53	1.29	1.49	0.62	(17.00)	2.13	1.85	2.12
Cash Flow Per Share	(1.25)	2.93	4.88	9.21	2.98	0.80	(1.46)	2.05
Tang Book Value Per Share	0.03	N.M.	N.M.	N.M.	N.M.	N.M.	N.M.	N.M.
Dividends Per Share	0.100	0.100	0.025	...	0.480	0.480	0.480	0.480
Dividend Payout %	6.54	7.75	1.68	...	...	22.54	25.95	22.64
Income Statement								
Total Revenue	8,365,468	7,871,274	6,880,844	6,131,709	6,034,776	8,336,933	7,972,074	7,884,842
EBITDA	279,121	269,462	223,226	198,262	(626,448)	330,507	294,114	275,092
Depn & Amortn	58,350	55,628	48,129	64,448	45,834	33,861	26,363	24,254
Income Before Taxes	141,233	126,029	78,421	22,359	(764,975)	189,213	165,357	164,181
Income Taxes	49,972	48,382	(17,504)	(33,251)	(130,848)	74,377	66,791	62,390
Net Income	89,101	76,254	89,929	31,548	(685,927)	95,502	81,117	91,861
Average Shares	60,406	65,464	65,794	55,832	40,356	46,941	46,265	45,533
Balance Sheet								
Current Assets	1,611,033	1,180,729	1,190,350	1,085,383	1,594,231	1,580,061	1,613,132	1,616,700
Total Assets	2,776,722	2,339,629	2,250,764	2,068,855	2,410,701	3,282,744	3,124,764	3,025,501
Current Liabilities	1,524,155	1,156,675	1,105,587	1,006,901	2,149,780	1,426,117	1,431,693	1,320,494
Long-Term Obligations	610,798	536,011	546,401	552,150	...	697,800	598,627	712,311
Total Liabilities	2,250,177	1,816,887	1,786,069	1,700,103	2,220,912	2,351,916	2,220,924	2,194,703
Stockholders' Equity	526,545	522,742	464,695	368,752	189,789	930,828	903,840	830,798
Shares Outstanding	53,239	52,629	52,787	52,128	40,092	41,327	42,720	41,975
Statistical Record								
Return on Assets %	3.47	3.32	4.16	1.41	N.M.	2.98	2.64	3.10
Return on Equity %	16.94	15.44	21.58	11.30	N.M.	10.41	9.35	11.48
EBITDA Margin %	3.34	3.42	3.24	3.23	N.M.	3.96	3.69	3.49
Net Margin %	1.07	0.97	1.31	0.51	N.M.	1.15	1.02	1.17
Asset Turnover	3.26	3.43	3.19	2.74	2.11	2.60	2.59	2.66
Current Ratio	1.06	1.02	1.08	1.08	0.74	1.11	1.13	1.22
Debt to Equity	1.16	1.03	1.18	1.50	...	0.75	0.66	0.86
Price Range	20.89-12.16	16.21-10.47	13.64-8.39	14.77-0.95	21.58-1.52	32.86-19.36	29.50-21.08	24.80-19.23
P/E Ratio	13.65-7.95	12.57-8.12	9.15-5.63	23.82-1.53	...	15.43-9.09	15.95-11.39	11.70-9.07
Average Yield %	0.58	0.73	0.24	...	3.70	1.75	1.93	2.15

Address: 4401 Colwick Road, Charlotte, NC 28211 **Telephone:** 704-566-2400 **Fax:** 704-536-5116	**Web Site:** www.sonicautomotive.com **Officers:** O. Bruton Smith - Chairman, Chief Executive Officer David B. Smith - Vice-Chairman, Executive Vice President	**Auditors:** Ernst & Young LLP **Investor Contact:** 888-766-4218 **Transfer Agents:** American Stock Transfer & Trust Company, New York, NY

SONOCO PRODUCTS CO.

Exchange	Symbol	Price	52Wk Range	Yield	P/E	Div Achiever
NYS	SON	$34.99 (3/28/2013)	34.99-29.20	3.43	18.32	29 Years

*7 Year Price Score 87.19 *NYSE Composite Index=100 *12 Month Price Score 96.43

Interim Earnings (Per Share)

Qtr.	Mar	Jun	Sep	Dec
2008	0.13	0.57	0.57	0.36
2009	0.23	0.33	0.47	0.47
2010	0.48	0.58	0.57	0.33
2011	0.56	0.52	0.76	0.29
2012	0.42	0.50	0.57	0.42

Interim Dividends (Per Share)

Amt	Decl	Ex	Rec	Pay
0.30Q	04/18/2012	05/16/2012	05/18/2012	06/08/2012
0.30Q	07/18/2012	08/15/2012	08/17/2012	09/10/2012
0.30Q	10/15/2012	11/14/2012	11/16/2012	12/10/2012
0.30Q	02/13/2013	02/25/2013	02/27/2013	03/08/2013

Indicated Div: $1.20 (Div. Reinv. Plan)

Valuation Analysis / **Institutional Holding**

Forecast EPS	$2.30 (04/06/2013)	No of Institutions	370
Market Cap	$3.5 Billion	Shares	74,403,656
Book Value	$1.5 Billion	% Held	64.58
Price/Book	2.37		
Price/Sales	0.74		

Business Summary: Containers & Packaging (MIC: 8.1.3 SIC: 2671 NAIC: 322221)

Sonoco Products is a manufacturer of industrial and consumer packaging products and a provider of packaging services. Co. has four segments: Consumer Packaging, which includes containers and trays, plastic bottles and jars, membrane ends and closures; Paper and Industrial Converted Products, which includes tubes and cores, construction tubes and forms, wire and cable reels and spools, and recycled paperboard, linerboard, and corrugating medium; Protective Packaging, which provides foam protective packaging, temperature-assurance packaging, and retail security packaging; and Packaging Services, which provides point-of-purchase displays, supply chain management services, and paper amenities.

Recent Developments: For the year ended Dec 31 2012, net income decreased 10.1% to US$196.1 million from US$218.0 million in the prior year. Revenues were US$4.79 billion, up 6.4% from US$4.50 billion the year before. Operating income was US$347.1 million versus US$322.5 million in the prior year, an increase of 7.6%. Direct operating expenses rose 5.4% to US$3.94 billion from US$3.74 billion in the comparable period the year before. Indirect operating expenses increased 14.3% to US$496.6 million from US$434.3 million in the equivalent prior-year period.

Prospects: Our evaluation of Sonoco Products Co. as of Apr. 7, 2013 is the result of our systematic analysis on three basic characteristics: earnings strength, relative valuation, and recent stock price movement. The company has produced a positive trend in earnings per share over the past 5 quarters and while recent estimates for the company have remained steady, SON has posted better than expected results. Based on operating earnings yield, the company is undervalued when compared to all of the companies in our coverage universe. Share price changes over the past year indicates that SON will perform very poorly over the near term.

Financial Data

(US$ in Thousands)	12/31/2012	12/31/2011	12/31/2010	12/31/2009	12/31/2008	12/31/2007	12/31/2006	12/31/2005
Earnings Per Share	1.91	2.13	1.96	1.50	1.63	2.10	1.92	1.61
Cash Flow Per Share	3.96	2.43	3.69	3.88	3.77	4.42	4.82	2.29
Tang Book Value Per Share	1.01	0.08	5.19	4.37	2.60	4.76	4.53	6.16
Dividends Per Share	1.190	1.150	1.110	1.080	1.070	1.020	0.950	0.910
Dividend Payout %	62.30	53.99	56.63	72.00	65.64	48.57	49.48	56.52
Income Statement								
Total Revenue	4,786,129	4,498,932	4,124,121	3,597,331	4,122,385	4,039,992	3,656,839	3,528,574
EBITDA	518,964	485,678	446,089	413,966	419,605	477,897	477,118	430,159
Depn & Amortn	171,905	163,198	156,529	161,180	170,032	170,013	157,000	155,412
Income Before Taxes	287,074	284,406	254,454	214,221	202,376	255,626	274,808	231,126
Income Taxes	103,759	78,423	64,485	66,818	54,797	55,186	93,329	84,174
Net Income	196,010	217,517	201,053	151,482	164,608	214,156	195,081	161,877
Average Shares	102,573	102,173	102,543	101,029	100,986	101,875	101,534	100,418
Balance Sheet								
Current Assets	1,499,896	1,312,791	1,157,516	996,573	929,990	1,027,679	942,798	885,500
Total Assets	4,176,065	3,986,170	3,281,014	3,062,580	3,086,466	3,340,243	2,916,678	2,981,740
Current Liabilities	1,044,235	836,483	780,649	805,639	698,196	758,081	659,824	620,486
Long-Term Obligations	1,099,454	1,232,966	603,941	462,743	656,847	804,339	712,089	657,075
Total Liabilities	2,687,079	2,574,375	1,789,223	1,696,199	1,923,491	1,898,706	1,697,610	1,718,426
Stockholders' Equity	1,488,986	1,411,795	1,491,791	1,366,381	1,162,975	1,441,537	1,219,068	1,263,314
Shares Outstanding	100,847	100,211	100,510	100,149	99,732	99,431	100,550	99,988
Statistical Record								
Return on Assets %	4.79	5.99	6.34	4.93	5.11	6.85	6.61	5.38
Return on Equity %	13.48	14.98	14.07	11.98	12.61	16.10	15.72	13.40
EBITDA Margin %	10.84	10.80	10.82	11.51	10.18	11.83	13.05	12.19
Net Margin %	4.10	4.83	4.88	4.21	3.99	5.30	5.33	4.59
Asset Turnover	1.17	1.24	1.30	1.17	1.28	1.29	1.24	1.17
Current Ratio	1.44	1.57	1.48	1.24	1.33	1.36	1.43	1.43
Debt to Equity	0.74	0.87	0.40	0.34	0.56	0.56	0.58	0.52
Price Range	34.49-29.20	36.80-27.34	34.83-26.95	30.31-16.95	35.61-21.22	44.89-28.51	38.64-29.25	30.48-25.68
P/E Ratio	18.06-15.29	17.28-12.84	17.77-13.75	20.21-11.30	21.85-13.02	21.38-13.58	20.13-15.23	18.93-15.95
Average Yield %	3.81	3.46	3.48	4.33	3.62	2.77	2.86	3.27

Address: 1 North Second Street, Hartsville, SC 29550 Telephone: 843-383-7000 Fax: 843-383-7008	Web Site: www.sonoco.com Officers: Harris E. DeLoach - Chairman, Chief Executive Officer Mancil Jack Sanders - President, Chief Operating Officer, Chief Executive Officer	Auditors: PricewaterhouseCoopers LLP Investor Contact: 843-339-6018 Transfer Agents: Continental Stock Transfer & Trust Company, New York, NY

SOUTH JERSEY INDUSTRIES, INC.

Exchange	Symbol	Price	52Wk Range	Yield	P/E	Div Achiever
NYS	SJI	$55.59 (3/28/2013)	55.81-46.35	3.18	18.72	13 Years

*7 Year Price Score 108.73 *NYSE Composite Index=100 *12 Month Price Score 98.31

Interim Earnings (Per Share)

Qtr.	Mar	Jun	Sep	Dec
2008	0.83	(0.45)	1.47	0.73
2009	1.06	0.17	(0.06)	0.78
2010	1.05	0.28	0.04	0.84
2011	1.72	0.20	(0.17)	1.23
2012	1.78	0.34	0.07	0.80

Interim Dividends (Per Share)

Amt	Decl	Ex	Rec	Pay
0.403Q	04/23/2012	06/07/2012	06/11/2012	07/03/2012
0.403Q	07/05/2012	09/06/2012	09/10/2012	10/02/2012
0.443Q	11/19/2012	12/06/2012	12/10/2012	12/28/2012
0.443Q	01/21/2013	03/07/2013	03/11/2013	04/02/2013

Indicated Div: $1.77 (Div. Reinv. Plan)

Valuation Analysis | **Institutional Holding**
Forecast EPS $3.30 — No of Institutions
(04/05/2013) — 200
Market Cap $1.8 Billion — Shares
Book Value $736.2 Million — 20,776,184
Price/Book 2.39 — % Held
Price/Sales 2.49 — 63.97

Business Summary: Gas Utilities (MIC: 3.3.1 SIC: 4924 NAIC: 221210)

South Jersey Industries is a holding company. Co. provides energy related products and services via its subsidiaries: South Jersey Gas Co., which distributes natural gas in the southernmost counties of New Jersey; South Jersey Resources Group, LLC, which markets wholesale natural gas storage, commodity and transportation in the mid-Atlantic, Appalachian and southern states; South Jersey Exploration, LLC, which owns oil, gas and mineral rights in the Marcellus Shale region in Pennsylvania; Marina Energy, LLC, which develops and operates on-site energy-related projects; South Jersey Energy Co., which acquires and markets natural gas and electricity; and South Jersey Energy Service Plus, LLC.

Recent Developments: For the year ended Dec 31 2012, income from continuing operations increased 3.2% to US$92.8 million from US$89.9 million a year earlier. Net income increased 2.6% to US$91.6 million from US$89.3 million in the prior year. Revenues were US$706.3 million, down 14.8% from US$828.6 million the year before. Operating income was US$109.9 million versus US$121.6 million in the prior year, a decrease of 9.6%. Direct operating expenses declined 17.3% to US$545.1 million from US$659.0 million in the comparable period the year before. Indirect operating expenses increased 7.1% to US$51.3 million from US$47.9 million in the equivalent prior-year period.

Prospects: Our evaluation of South Jersey Industries Inc. as of Apr. 7, 2013 is the result of our systematic analysis on three basic characteristics: earnings strength, relative valuation, and recent stock price movement. The company has generated a negative trend in earnings per share over the past 5 quarters. However, while recent estimates for the company have been lowered by analysts, SJI has posted results that fell short of analysts expectations. Based on operating earnings yield, the company is undervalued when compared to all of the companies in our coverage universe. Share price changes over the past year indicates that SJI will perform in line with the market over the near term.

Financial Data

(US$ in Thousands)	12/31/2012	12/31/2011	12/31/2010	12/31/2009	12/31/2008	12/31/2007	12/31/2006	12/31/2005
Earnings Per Share	2.97	2.97	2.22	1.94	2.58	2.10	2.44	1.69
Cash Flow Per Share	3.82	6.38	5.33	5.88	0.89	5.02	1.00	1.40
Tang Book Value Per Share	23.26	20.66	19.08	18.24	17.33	16.25	15.11	13.50
Dividends Per Share	1.650	1.498	1.355	1.222	1.107	1.005	0.920	0.863
Dividend Payout %	55.56	50.42	61.04	63.02	42.93	47.86	37.70	51.04
Income Statement								
Total Revenue	706,280	828,560	925,067	845,444	961,977	956,371	931,428	920,982
EBITDA	162,338	172,998	155,061	143,801	183,863	159,987	174,723	126,434
Depn & Amortn	41,336	35,749	34,018	31,280	29,237	27,942	26,249	24,031
Income Before Taxes	102,016	113,171	99,147	93,529	128,950	104,830	120,803	81,453
Income Taxes	11,479	22,502	28,811	34,302	51,948	43,056	49,683	33,767
Net Income	91,608	89,291	66,652	58,105	76,931	62,268	71,432	47,919
Average Shares	30,824	30,086	29,974	29,893	29,843	29,593	29,261	28,399
Balance Sheet								
Current Assets	394,837	340,609	423,837	368,355	435,084	328,330	371,724	357,463
Total Assets	2,631,440	2,247,510	2,076,615	1,782,008	1,793,427	1,529,441	1,573,032	1,436,146
Current Liabilities	651,844	587,971	640,524	478,784	499,907	328,311	422,794	403,106
Long-Term Obligations	601,400	424,213	340,000	312,793	332,784	357,896	358,022	319,066
Total Liabilities	1,895,226	1,623,396	1,506,518	1,238,407	1,278,173	1,048,361	1,129,996	1,044,961
Stockholders' Equity	736,214	624,114	570,097	543,601	515,254	481,080	443,036	391,185
Shares Outstanding	31,653	30,212	29,872	29,796	29,728	29,607	29,325	28,982
Statistical Record								
Return on Assets %	3.74	4.13	3.45	3.25	4.62	4.01	4.75	3.58
Return on Equity %	13.43	14.95	11.97	10.98	15.40	13.48	17.13	13.00
EBITDA Margin %	22.98	20.88	16.76	17.01	19.11	16.73	18.76	13.73
Net Margin %	12.97	10.78	7.21	6.87	8.00	6.51	7.67	5.20
Asset Turnover	0.29	0.38	0.48	0.47	0.58	0.62	0.62	0.69
Current Ratio	0.61	0.58	0.66	0.77	0.87	1.00	0.88	0.89
Debt to Equity	0.82	0.68	0.60	0.58	0.65	0.74	0.81	0.82
Price Range	56.93-46.35	57.49-43.44	54.01-37.53	39.94-32.66	39.85-28.01	40.43-31.96	33.90-26.00	32.00-25.18
P/E Ratio	19.17-15.61	19.36-14.63	24.33-16.91	20.59-16.84	15.45-10.86	19.25-15.22	13.89-10.66	18.93-14.90
Average Yield %	3.23	2.81	2.98	3.43	3.08	2.80	3.16	3.04

Address: 1 South Jersey Plaza, Folsom, NJ 08037
Telephone: 609-561-9000
Fax: 609-561-8225

Web Site: www.sjindustries.com
Officers: Edward J. Graham - Chairman, President, Chief Executive Officer David A. Kindlick - Senior Vice President, Chief Financial Officer

Auditors: Deloitte & Touche LLP
Investor Contact: 609-561-9000Ext.42
Transfer Agents: Computershare

SOUTHERN COMPANY (THE)

Exchange	Symbol	Price	52Wk Range	Yield	P/E	Div Achiever
NYS	SO	$46.92 (3/28/2013)	48.42-42.03	4.18	17.57	11 Years

*7 Year Price Score 107.46 *NYSE Composite Index=100   ***12 Month Price Score 91.65**

Interim Earnings (Per Share)

Qtr.	Mar	Jun	Sep	Dec
2008	0.47	0.54	1.00	0.24
2009	0.16	0.60	0.99	0.30
2010	0.60	0.61	0.97	0.17
2011	0.49	0.70	1.06	0.29
2012	0.42	0.71	1.11	0.44

Interim Dividends (Per Share)

Amt	Decl	Ex	Rec	Pay
0.49Q	04/16/2012	05/03/2012	05/07/2012	06/06/2012
0.49Q	07/16/2012	08/02/2012	08/06/2012	09/06/2012
0.49Q	10/15/2012	11/01/2012	11/05/2012	12/06/2012
0.49Q	01/18/2013	01/31/2013	02/04/2013	03/06/2013

Indicated Div: $1.96 (Div. Reinv. Plan)

Valuation Analysis

		Institutional Holding	
Forecast EPS	$2.76 (04/06/2013)	No of Institutions	1134
Market Cap	$40.7 Billion	Shares	421,662,304
Book Value	$19.4 Billion	% Held	45.84
Price/Book	2.10		
Price/Sales	2.46		

Business Summary: Electric Utilities (MIC: 3.1.1 SIC: 4911 NAIC: 221119)

Southern is a holding company. Through its subsidiaries, Alabama Power Company, Georgia Power Company, Gulf Power Company and Mississippi Power Company, each of which is an operating public utility company, Co. supplies electric service in the states of Alabama, Georgia, Florida, and Mississippi. In addition, Co. owns all of the common stock of Southern Power Company, which is also an operating public utility company that constructs, acquires, owns, and manages generation assets, including renewable energy projects, and sells electricity at market-based rates in the wholesale market.

Recent Developments: For the year ended Dec 31 2012, net income increased 6.5% to US$2.42 billion from US$2.27 billion in the prior year. Revenues were US$16.54 billion, down 6.3% from US$17.66 billion the year before. Operating income was US$4.46 billion versus US$4.23 billion in the prior year, an increase of 5.5%. Direct operating expenses declined 13.1% to US$9.39 billion from US$10.81 billion in the comparable period the year before. Indirect operating expenses increased 2.4% to US$2.68 billion from US$2.62 billion in the equivalent prior-year period.

Prospects: Our evaluation of Southern Company as of Apr. 7, 2013 is the result of our systematic analysis on three basic characteristics: earnings strength, relative valuation, and recent stock price movement. The company has produced a positive trend in earnings per share over the past 5 quarters. However, while recent estimates for the company have been mixed, SO has posted better than expected results. Based on operating earnings yield, the company is undervalued when compared to all of the companies in our coverage universe. Share price changes over the past year indicates that SO will perform poorly over the near term.

Financial Data

(US$ in Thousands)	12/31/2012	12/31/2011	12/31/2010	12/31/2009	12/31/2008	12/31/2007	12/31/2006	12/31/2005
Earnings Per Share	2.67	2.55	2.36	2.06	2.25	2.28	2.10	2.13
Cash Flow Per Share	5.61	6.89	4.80	4.10	4.39	4.49	3.80	3.40
Tang Book Value Per Share	21.52	20.75	19.65	18.61	18.46	17.63	16.23	15.22
Dividends Per Share	1.942	1.873	1.803	1.732	1.663	1.595	1.535	1.475
Dividend Payout %	72.75	73.43	76.38	84.10	73.89	69.96	73.10	69.25
Income Statement								
Total Revenue	16,537,000	17,657,000	17,456,000	15,743,000	17,127,000	15,353,000	14,356,000	13,554,000
EBITDA	6,713,000	6,392,000	5,768,000	5,275,000	5,183,000	4,920,000	4,658,000	4,414,000
Depn & Amortn	2,145,000	2,048,000	1,831,000	1,788,000	1,704,000	1,486,000	1,421,000	1,398,000
Income Before Taxes	3,749,000	3,487,000	3,066,000	2,605,000	2,646,000	2,593,000	2,412,000	2,305,000
Income Taxes	1,334,000	1,219,000	1,026,000	896,000	915,000	835,000	781,000	595,000
Net Income	2,415,000	2,268,000	2,040,000	1,708,000	1,742,000	1,734,000	1,573,000	1,591,000
Average Shares	879,000	864,000	837,000	796,000	774,848	761,000	748,000	749,000
Balance Sheet								
Current Assets	6,162,000	6,272,000	5,883,000	5,873,000	5,358,000	4,732,000	4,019,000	4,205,000
Total Assets	63,149,000	59,267,000	55,032,000	52,046,000	48,347,000	45,789,000	42,858,000	39,877,000
Current Liabilities	7,014,000	6,577,000	6,472,000	5,584,000	5,226,000	5,631,000	6,353,000	5,240,000
Long-Term Obligations	19,274,000	18,647,000	18,154,000	18,131,000	16,816,000	14,143,000	12,503,000	12,846,000
Total Liabilities	43,770,000	40,607,000	37,748,000	36,086,000	33,989,000	32,324,000	30,743,000	28,592,000
Stockholders' Equity	19,379,000	18,660,000	17,284,000	15,960,000	14,358,000	13,465,000	12,115,000	11,285,000
Shares Outstanding	867,768	865,125	843,500	819,500	777,600	763,600	746,400	741,448
Statistical Record								
Return on Assets %	3.93	3.97	3.81	3.40	3.69	3.91	3.80	4.14
Return on Equity %	12.66	12.62	12.27	11.27	12.49	13.56	13.44	14.38
EBITDA Margin %	40.59	36.20	33.04	33.51	30.26	32.05	32.45	32.57
Net Margin %	14.60	12.84	11.69	10.85	10.17	11.29	10.96	11.74
Asset Turnover	0.27	0.31	0.33	0.31	0.36	0.35	0.35	0.35
Current Ratio	0.88	0.95	0.91	1.05	1.03	0.84	0.63	0.80
Debt to Equity	0.99	1.00	1.05	1.14	1.17	1.05	1.03	1.14
Price Range	48.42-42.03	46.59-36.80	38.47-31.13	37.47-26.81	40.50-32.26	39.20-33.62	37.34-30.63	36.16-31.25
P/E Ratio	18.13-15.74	18.27-14.43	16.30-13.19	18.19-13.01	18.00-14.34	17.19-14.75	17.78-14.59	16.98-14.67
Average Yield %	4.28	4.64	5.13	5.52	4.59	4.39	4.42	4.34

Address: 30 Ivan Allen Jr. Boulevard, N.W., Atlanta, GA 30308	Web Site: www.southerncompany.com	Auditors: Deloitte & Touche LLP
Telephone: 404-506-5000	**Officers:** Thomas A. Fanning - Chairman, President, Chief Executive Officer, Executive Vice President, Chief Operating Officer W. Paul Bowers - Executive Vice President	**Investor Contact:** 404-506-5310
Fax: 404-506-0455		**Transfer Agents:** Computershare, Pittsburgh, PA

SOUTHERN COPPER CORP

Exchange	Symbol	Price	52Wk Range	Yield	P/E
NYS	SCCO	$37.57 (3/28/2013)	41.96-28.16	10.01	16.48

*7 Year Price Score 104.03 *NYSE Composite Index=100 *12 Month Price Score 100.14

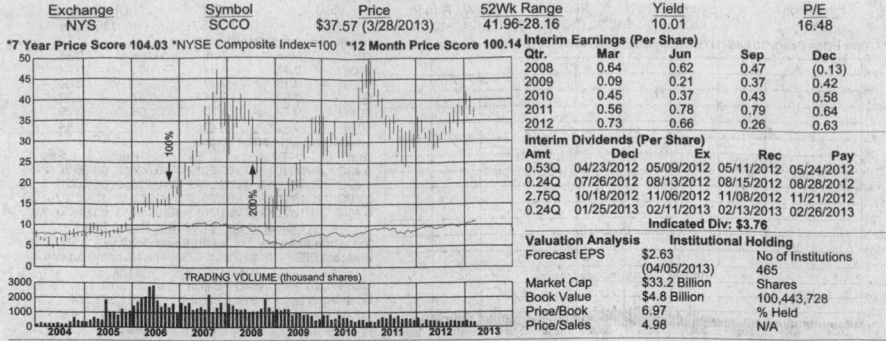

Interim Earnings (Per Share)

Qtr.	Mar	Jun	Sep	Dec
2008	0.64	0.62	0.47	(0.13)
2009	0.09	0.21	0.37	0.42
2010	0.45	0.37	0.43	0.58
2011	0.56	0.78	0.79	0.64
2012	0.73	0.66	0.26	0.63

Interim Dividends (Per Share)

Amt	Decl	Ex	Rec	Pay
0.53Q	04/23/2012	05/09/2012	05/11/2012	05/24/2012
0.24Q	07/26/2012	08/13/2012	08/15/2012	08/28/2012
2.75Q	10/18/2012	11/06/2012	11/08/2012	11/21/2012
0.24Q	01/25/2013	02/11/2013	02/13/2013	02/26/2013

Indicated Div: $3.76

Valuation Analysis / **Institutional Holding**

Forecast EPS	$2.63 (04/05/2013)	No of Institutions	465
Market Cap	$33.2 Billion	Shares	100,443,728
Book Value	$4.8 Billion	% Held	N/A
Price/Book	6.97		
Price/Sales	4.98		

Business Summary: Non-Precious Metals (MIC: 8.2.2 SIC: 1021 NAIC: 212234)

Southern Copper produces copper, molybdenum, zinc and silver. Co.'s mining, smelting and refining facilities are located in Peru and in Mexico, and it conducts exploration activities in those countries and in Argentina, Chile and Ecuador. Co.'s Peruvian copper operations involve mining, milling and flotation of copper ore to produce copper concentrates and molybdenum concentrates; the smelting of copper concentrates to produce anode copper; and the refining of anode copper to produce copper cathodes. Co. also produces molybdenum concentrate and refined silver. Co.'s Mexican operations are primarily engaged in the mining and processing of copper, molybdenum, zinc, silver, gold and lead.

Recent Developments: For the year ended Dec 31 2012, net income decreased 17.2% to US$1.94 billion from US$2.34 billion in the prior year. Revenues were US$6.67 billion, down 2.2% from US$6.82 billion the year before. Operating income was US$3.11 billion versus US$3.63 billion in the prior year, a decrease of 14.2%. Direct operating expenses rose 0.2% to US$2.77 billion from US$2.76 billion in the comparable period the year before. Indirect operating expenses increased 83.9% to US$791.2 million from US$430.1 million in the equivalent prior-year period.

Prospects: Our evaluation of Southern Copper Corp. as of Apr. 7, 2013 is the result of our systematic analysis on three basic characteristics: earnings strength, relative valuation, and recent stock price movement. The company has produced a positive trend in earnings per share over the past 5 quarters. However, while recent estimates for the company have been lowered by analysts, SCCO has posted better than expected results. Based on operating earnings yield, the company is undervalued when compared to all of the companies in our coverage universe. Share price changes over the past year indicates that SCCO will perform very well over the near term.

Financial Data

(US$ in Thousands)	12/31/2012	12/31/2011	12/31/2010	12/31/2009	12/31/2008	12/31/2007	12/31/2006	12/31/2005
Earnings Per Share	2.28	2.76	1.83	1.09	1.60	2.51	2.31	1.59
Cash Flow Per Share	2.36	2.45	2.26	1.13	1.95	3.06	2.33	1.86
Tang Book Value Per Share	5.26	4.59	4.44	4.43	3.82	4.22	4.01	3.63
Dividends Per Share	3.710	2.460	1.680	0.442	1.943	2.267	1.708	1.062
Dividend Payout %	162.72	89.13	91.80	40.55	121.46	90.31	74.06	66.99
Income Statement								
Total Revenue	6,669,266	6,818,721	5,149,500	3,734,280	4,850,820	6,085,672	5,460,221	4,112,629
EBITDA	3,164,216	3,907,380	2,863,067	1,766,661	2,402,434	3,701,628	3,263,183	2,258,867
Depn & Amortn	33,500	286,000	279,600	271,200	257,900	263,800	221,900	200,900
Income Before Taxes	2,973,542	3,448,688	2,430,780	1,404,434	2,093,782	3,411,860	3,006,029	2,002,367
Income Taxes	1,080,872	1,104,335	868,071	469,861	679,323	1,185,261	959,087	589,744
Net Income	1,934,632	2,336,424	1,554,051	929,381	1,406,593	2,216,370	2,037,640	1,400,148
Average Shares	848,346	845,901	850,000	850,697	878,713	883,398	883,383	883,368
Balance Sheet								
Current Assets	4,287,959	3,101,503	3,702,957	1,778,129	1,553,693	2,635,509	2,442,877	1,714,354
Total Assets	10,383,749	8,062,701	8,128,019	6,062,572	5,764,324	6,580,558	6,376,414	5,687,574
Current Liabilities	857,135	992,877	1,139,018	602,425	737,463	927,190	859,571	795,632
Long-Term Obligations	4,203,900	2,735,700	2,750,400	1,270,300	1,280,000	1,289,700	1,518,100	1,162,100
Total Liabilities	5,618,609	4,047,397	4,237,571	2,186,944	2,383,065	2,732,438	2,709,809	2,361,497
Stockholders' Equity	4,765,140	4,015,304	3,890,448	3,875,628	3,381,259	3,848,120	3,666,605	3,326,077
Shares Outstanding	884,596	850,000	850,000	850,000	854,900	883,396	884,596	883,368
Statistical Record								
Return on Assets %	20.92	28.86	21.90	15.72	22.73	34.21	33.78	33.80
Return on Equity %	43.95	59.11	40.02	25.61	38.81	58.99	58.28	55.48
EBITDA Margin %	47.44	57.30	55.60	47.31	49.53	60.83	59.76	54.93
Net Margin %	29.01	34.26	30.18	24.89	29.00	36.42	37.32	34.05
Asset Turnover	0.72	0.84	0.73	0.63	0.78	0.94	0.91	0.99
Current Ratio	5.00	3.12	3.25	2.95	2.11	2.84	2.84	2.15
Debt to Equity	0.88	0.68	0.71	0.33	0.38	0.34	0.41	0.35
Price Range	38.94-28.16	49.59-23.99	48.84-26.19	36.40-12.74	41.34-9.19	47.12-16.84	19.37-11.55	11.77-6.94
P/E Ratio	17.08-12.35	17.97-8.69	26.69-14.31	33.39-11.69	25.84-5.74	18.77-6.71	8.39-5.00	7.40-4.36
Average Yield %	11.20	7.04	4.93	1.84	7.03	7.23	11.25	12.08

Address: 1440 East Missouri Avenue, Suite 160, Phoenix, AZ 85014 Telephone: 602-264-1375	Web Site: www.southernperu.com Officers: German Larrea Mota Velasco - Chairman Oscar Gonzalez Rocha - President, Chief Executive Officer	Auditors: Galaz, Yamazaki, Ruiz Urquiza, S.C (member of Deloitte & Touche Tohmatsu) Investor Contact: 800-223-2064 Transfer Agents: Computershare, Jersey City, NJ

SOUTHWEST AIRLINES CO

Exchange	Symbol	Price	52Wk Range	Yield	P/E
NYS	LUV	$13.48 (3/28/2013)	13.48-7.88	0.30	24.07

*7 Year Price Score 72.69   *NYSE Composite Index=100   *12 Month Price Score 115.04

Interim Earnings (Per Share)

Qtr.	Mar	Jun	Sep	Dec
2008	0.05	0.44	(0.16)	(0.08)
2009	(0.12)	0.07	(0.02)	0.15
2010	0.01	0.15	0.27	0.17
2011	0.01	0.21	(0.18)	0.20
2012	0.13	0.30	0.02	0.11

Interim Dividends (Per Share)

Amt	Decl	Ex	Rec	Pay
0.01Q	05/16/2012	06/04/2012	06/06/2012	06/20/2012
0.01Q	07/26/2012	08/14/2012	08/16/2012	09/06/2012
0.01Q	11/15/2012	12/04/2012	12/06/2012	01/03/2013
0.01Q	01/31/2013	03/05/2013	03/07/2013	03/28/2013
			Indicated Div: $0.04	

Valuation Analysis / **Institutional Holding**

Forecast EPS	$1.02 (04/06/2013)	No of Institutions	607
Market Cap	$9.8 Billion	Shares	
Book Value	$7.0 Billion		617,101,824
Price/Book	1.41	% Held	
Price/Sales	0.58		73.29

Business Summary: Airlines/Air Freight (MIC: 7.4.4 SIC: 4512 NAIC: 481111)

Southwest Airlines operates Southwest Airlines (Southwest) and AirTran Airways (AirTran), passenger airlines that provide scheduled air transportation in the U.S. and near-international markets. Co. serves 97 destinations in 41 states, the District of Columbia, the Commonwealth of Puerto Rico, and six near-international countries including Mexico (Cancun, Mexico City, and Cabo San Lucas), Jamaica (Montego Bay), The Bahamas (Nassau), Aruba (Oranjestad), Dominican Republic (Punta Cana), and Bermuda. At Dec 31 2012, the total fleet operated by Southwest and AirTran combined consisted of 694 aircraft, including 606 Boeing 737s and 88 Boeing 717s.

Recent Developments: For the year ended Dec 31 2012, net income increased 136.5% to US$421.0 million from US$178.0 million in the prior year. Revenues were US$17.09 billion, up 9.1% from US$15.66 billion the year before. Operating income was US$623.0 million versus US$693.0 million in the prior year, a decrease of 10.1%. Direct operating expenses rose 10.0% to US$8.65 billion from US$7.87 billion in the comparable period the year before. Indirect operating expenses increased 10.1% to US$7.82 billion from US$7.10 billion in the equivalent prior-year period.

Prospects: Our evaluation of Southwest Airlines Co as of Apr. 7, 2013 is the result of our systematic analysis on three basic characteristics: earnings strength, relative valuation, and recent stock price movement. The company has suffered a very negative trend in earnings per share over the past 5 quarters and while recent estimates for the company have been raised by analysts, LUV has posted better than expected results. Based on operating earnings yield, the company is about fairly valued when compared to all of the companies in our coverage universe. Share price changes over the past year indicates that LUV will perform well over the near term.

Financial Data
(US$ in Thousands)

	12/31/2012	12/31/2011	12/31/2010	12/31/2009	12/31/2008	12/31/2007	12/31/2006	12/31/2005
Earnings Per Share	0.56	0.23	0.61	0.13	0.24	0.84	0.61	0.67
Cash Flow Per Share	2.74	1.79	2.09	1.33	(2.06)	3.76	1.77	2.83
Tang Book Value Per Share	8.06	7.45	8.34	7.36	6.69	9.45	8.23	8.33
Dividends Per Share	0.035	0.018	0.018	0.018	0.018	0.018	0.018	0.018
Dividend Payout %	6.16	7.83	2.95	13.85	7.50	2.14	2.95	2.69
Income Statement								
Total Revenue	17,088,000	15,658,000	12,104,000	10,350,000	11,023,000	9,861,000	9,086,000	7,584,000
EBITDA	1,636,000	1,197,000	1,496,000	920,000	944,000	1,624,000	1,282,000	1,412,000
Depn & Amortn	832,000	702,000	614,000	604,000	587,000	541,000	499,000	502,000
Income Before Taxes	685,000	323,000	745,000	164,000	278,000	1,058,000	790,000	874,000
Income Taxes	264,000	145,000	286,000	65,000	100,000	413,000	291,000	326,000
Net Income	421,000	178,000	459,000	99,000	178,000	645,000	499,000	548,000
Average Shares	757,000	775,000	747,000	741,000	739,000	768,000	824,000	814,000
Balance Sheet								
Current Assets	4,227,000	4,345,000	4,279,000	3,358,000	2,893,000	4,443,000	2,601,000	3,620,000
Total Assets	18,596,000	18,068,000	15,463,000	14,269,000	14,308,000	16,772,000	13,460,000	14,218,000
Current Liabilities	4,650,000	4,533,000	3,305,000	2,676,000	2,806,000	4,838,000	2,887,000	3,848,000
Long-Term Obligations	2,883,000	3,107,000	2,875,000	3,325,000	3,498,000	2,050,000	1,567,000	1,394,000
Total Liabilities	11,604,000	11,191,000	9,226,000	8,803,000	9,355,000	9,831,000	7,011,000	7,543,000
Stockholders' Equity	6,992,000	6,877,000	6,237,000	5,466,000	4,953,000	6,941,000	6,449,000	6,675,000
Shares Outstanding	730,319	772,560	747,434	742,790	739,992	734,797	783,309	801,641
Statistical Record								
Return on Assets %	2.29	1.06	3.09	0.69	1.14	4.27	3.61	4.29
Return on Equity %	6.05	2.71	7.84	1.90	2.98	9.63	7.60	8.98
EBITDA Margin %	9.57	7.64	12.36	8.89	8.56	16.47	14.11	18.62
Net Margin %	2.46	1.14	3.79	0.96	1.61	6.54	5.49	7.23
Asset Turnover	0.93	0.93	0.81	0.72	0.71	0.65	0.66	0.59
Current Ratio	0.91	0.96	1.29	1.25	1.03	0.92	0.90	0.94
Debt to Equity	0.41	0.45	0.46	0.61	0.71	0.30	0.24	0.21
Price Range	10.56-7.88	13.32-7.35	14.26-10.63	11.61-5.01	16.47-7.28	16.60-12.20	18.15-14.62	16.82-13.14
P/E Ratio	18.86-14.07	57.91-31.96	23.38-17.43	89.31-38.54	68.63-30.33	19.76-14.52	29.75-23.97	25.10-19.61
Average Yield %	0.39	0.17	0.14	0.23	0.14	0.12	0.11	0.12

Address: P.O. Box 36611, Dallas, TX 75235-1611	Web Site: www.southwest.com	Auditors: Ernst & Young LLP
Telephone: 214-792-4000	Officers: Gary C. Kelly - Chairman, President, Chief Executive Officer Robert E. Jordan - Executive Vice President, Executive Vice President, Chief Commercial Officer	Investor Contact: 214-792-4415
Fax: 214-792-5015		Transfer Agents: Wells Fargo Shareowner Services, Mendota Heights, MN

SOUTHWESTERN ENERGY COMPANY

Exchange	Symbol	Price	52Wk Range	Yield	P/E
NYS	SWN	$37.26 (3/28/2013)	38.86-25.82	N/A	N/A

*7 Year Price Score 89.79 *NYSE Composite Index=100 *12 Month Price Score 99.07

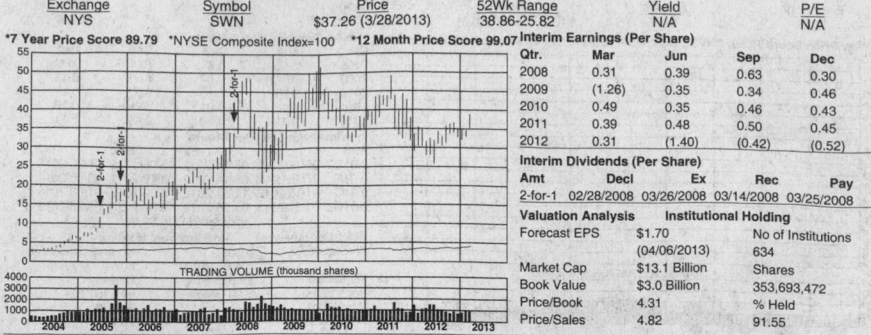

Interim Earnings (Per Share)

Qtr.	Mar	Jun	Sep	Dec
2008	0.31	0.39	0.63	0.30
2009	(1.26)	0.35	0.34	0.46
2010	0.49	0.35	0.46	0.43
2011	0.39	0.48	0.50	0.45
2012	0.31	(1.40)	(0.42)	(0.52)

Interim Dividends (Per Share)

Amt	Decl	Ex	Rec	Pay
2-for-1	02/28/2008	03/26/2008	03/14/2008	03/25/2008

Valuation Analysis   **Institutional Holding**

Forecast EPS	$1.70	No of Institutions
	(04/06/2013)	634
Market Cap	$13.1 Billion	Shares
Book Value	$3.0 Billion	353,693,472
Price/Book	4.31	% Held
Price/Sales	4.82	91.55

Business Summary: Production & Extraction (MIC: 9.1.1 SIC: 1311 NAIC: 211111)

Southwestern Energy is an independent energy company. Co. explores for and produces natural gas and oil, with operations focused on development of an unconventional natural gas reservoir located on the Arkansas side of the Arkoma Basin. Co. also has exploration and production activities in Pennsylvania, Texas, Arkansas and Oklahoma, and exploration operations in southern Arkansas and northern Louisiana, Colorado, Montana and Canada. Co.'s natural gas gathering and marketing activities support its exploration, development and production activities in Arkansas, Pennsylvania and Texas. At Dec 31 2012, Co.'s estimated proved natural gas and oil reserves were 4.02 trillion cubic feet equivalent.

Recent Developments: For the year ended Dec 31 2012, net loss amounted to US$707.1 million versus net income of US$637.8 million in the prior year. Revenues were US$2.72 billion, down 8.1% from US$2.95 billion the year before. Operating loss was US$1.12 billion versus an income of US$1.07 billion in the prior year. Direct operating expenses declined 11.9% to US$837.2 million from US$950.0 million in the comparable period the year before. Indirect operating expenses increased 222.5% to US$2.99 billion from US$928.1 million in the equivalent prior-year period.

Prospects: Our evaluation of Southwestern Energy Company as of Apr. 7, 2013 is the result of our systematic analysis on three basic characteristics: earnings strength, relative valuation, and recent stock price movement. The company has managed to produce a neutral trend in earnings per share over the past 5 quarters and while recent estimates for the company have been raised by analysts, SWN has posted better than expected results. Based on operating earnings yield, the company is about fairly valued when compared to all of the companies in our coverage universe. Share price changes over the past year indicates that SWN will perform in line with the market over the near term.

Financial Data
(US$ in Thousands)

	12/31/2012	12/31/2011	12/31/2010	12/31/2009	12/31/2008	12/31/2007	12/31/2006	12/31/2005
Earnings Per Share	(2.03)	1.82	1.73	(0.10)	1.64	0.64	0.47	0.47
Cash Flow Per Share	4.73	5.01	4.75	3.96	3.39	1.84	1.28	1.01
Tang Book Value Per Share	8.65	11.37	8.53	6.74	7.30	4.82	4.25	3.32
Income Statement								
Total Revenue	2,715,043	2,952,906	2,610,663	2,145,779	2,311,552	1,255,131	763,112	676,329
EBITDA	(299,836)	1,783,031	1,613,598	461,774	1,364,587	676,579	415,870	350,262
Depn & Amortn	814,710	707,966	591,943	495,291	416,151	295,332	152,519	99,558
Income Before Taxes	(1,150,203)	1,050,990	995,492	(52,155)	919,532	357,374	262,672	235,664
Income Taxes	(443,139)	413,221	391,659	(16,363)	350,999	135,855	99,399	86,431
Net Income	(707,064)	637,769	604,118	(35,650)	567,946	221,174	162,636	147,760
Average Shares	348,610	349,921	349,310	343,420	346,245	347,442	342,575	312,618
Balance Sheet								
Current Assets	808,912	978,278	580,893	564,501	889,265	363,341	323,836	461,064
Total Assets	6,737,527	7,902,897	6,017,463	4,770,250	4,760,158	3,622,716	2,379,069	1,868,524
Current Liabilities	767,771	884,913	693,983	536,416	792,861	430,895	378,860	302,386
Long-Term Obligations	1,668,273	1,342,100	1,093,000	997,500	674,200	977,600	136,600	100,000
Total Liabilities	3,701,655	3,933,593	3,052,587	2,439,025	2,252,328	1,976,216	944,426	758,220
Stockholders' Equity	3,035,872	3,969,304	2,964,876	2,331,225	2,507,830	1,646,500	1,434,643	1,110,304
Shares Outstanding	351,035	348,959	347,577	345,877	343,399	341,358	337,907	334,470
Statistical Record								
Return on Assets %	N.M.	9.16	11.20	N.M.	13.51	7.37	7.66	9.80
Return on Equity %	N.M.	18.39	22.81	N.M.	27.27	14.36	12.78	18.97
EBITDA Margin %	N.M.	60.38	61.81	21.52	59.03	53.91	54.50	51.79
Net Margin %	N.M.	21.60	23.14	N.M.	24.57	17.62	21.31	21.85
Asset Turnover	0.37	0.42	0.48	0.45	0.55	0.42	0.36	0.45
Current Ratio	1.05	1.11	0.84	1.05	1.12	0.84	0.85	1.52
Debt to Equity	0.55	0.34	0.37	0.43	0.27	0.59	0.10	0.09
Price Range	36.60-25.82	49.00-31.94	51.65-31.44	50.62-25.99	48.69-20.81	28.27-16.43	21.71-12.40	20.57-5.61
P/E Ratio	...	26.92-17.55	29.86-18.17	...	29.69-12.69	44.16-25.68	46.19-26.38	43.78-11.93

Address: 2350 North Sam Houston Parkway East, Suite 125, Houston, TX 77032 **Telephone:** 281-618-4700	**Web Site:** www.swn.com **Officers:** Steven L. Mueller - President, Chief Executive Officer William J. Way - Executive Vice President, Chief Operating Officer	**Auditors:** PricewaterhouseCoopers LLP **Investor Contact:** 281-.61-8.4847 **Transfer Agents:** Computershare Trust Company, N.A, Providence, RI

SPECTRA ENERGY CORP

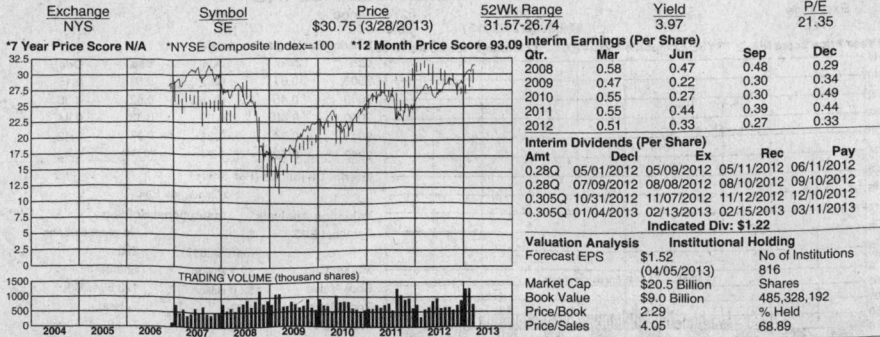

Exchange	Symbol	Price	52Wk Range	Yield	P/E
NYS	SE	$30.75 (3/28/2013)	31.57-26.74	3.97	21.35

*7 Year Price Score N/A   *NYSE Composite Index=100   *12 Month Price Score 93.09

Interim Earnings (Per Share)

Qtr.	Mar	Jun	Sep	Dec
2008	0.58	0.47	0.48	0.29
2009	0.47	0.22	0.30	0.34
2010	0.55	0.27	0.30	0.49
2011	0.55	0.44	0.39	0.44
2012	0.51	0.33	0.27	0.33

Interim Dividends (Per Share)

Amt	Decl	Ex	Rec	Pay
0.28Q	05/01/2012	05/09/2012	05/11/2012	06/11/2012
0.28Q	07/09/2012	08/08/2012	08/10/2012	09/10/2012
0.305Q	10/31/2012	11/07/2012	11/12/2012	12/10/2012
0.305Q	01/04/2013	02/13/2013	02/15/2013	03/11/2013

Indicated Div: $1.22

Valuation Analysis

		Institutional Holding	
Forecast EPS	$1.52	No of Institutions	
	(04/05/2013)	816	
Market Cap	$20.5 Billion	Shares	
Book Value	$9.0 Billion	485,328,192	
Price/Book	2.29	% Held	
Price/Sales	4.05	68.89	

TRADING VOLUME (thousand shares)

Business Summary: Equipment & Services (MIC: 9.1.3 SIC: 4923 NAIC: 486210)

Spectra Energy owns and operates natural gas-related energy assets. Co. operates in four segments: U.S. Transmission, which provides transportation and storage of natural gas in the northeastern and southeastern U.S. and the Maritime Provinces in Canada; Distribution, which provides natural gas distribution service in Ontario, Canada, and natural gas transportation and storage services; Western Canada Transmission & Processing, which provides natural gas liquids extraction, fractionation, transportation, storage and marketing to customers in western Canada and the northern tier of the U.S.; and Field Services, which gathers, processes, treats, compresses, transports and stores natural gas.

Recent Developments: For the year ended Dec 31 2012, income from continuing operations decreased 16.9% to US$1.05 billion from US$1.26 billion a year earlier. Net income decreased 18.3% to US$1.05 billion from US$1.28 billion in the prior year. Revenues were US$5.08 billion, down 5.2% from US$5.35 billion the year before. Operating income was US$1.58 billion versus US$1.76 billion in the prior year, a decrease of 10.7%. Direct operating expenses declined 9.2% to US$1.04 billion from US$1.14 billion in the comparable period the year before. Indirect operating expenses increased 0.7% to US$2.46 billion from US$2.45 billion in the equivalent prior-year period.

Prospects: Our evaluation of Spectra Energy Corp. as of Apr. 7, 2013 is the result of our systematic analysis on three basic characteristics: earnings strength, relative valuation, and recent stock price movement. The company has produced a positive trend in earnings per share over the past 5 quarters and while recent estimates for the company have been mixed, SE has posted better than expected results. Based on operating earnings yield, the company is about fairly valued when compared to all of the companies in our coverage universe. Share price changes over the past year indicates that SE will perform poorly over the near term.

Financial Data

(US$ in Millions)	12/31/2012	12/31/2011	12/31/2010	12/31/2009	12/31/2008	12/31/2007	12/31/2006	12/31/2005
Earnings Per Share	1.44	1.81	1.61	1.32	1.81	1.51	...	...
Cash Flow Per Share	2.96	3.36	2.17	2.74	2.89	2.32	...	...
Tang Book Value Per Share	6.68	5.60	5.40	4.91	3.53	4.60	2,132,000.00	...
Dividends Per Share	1.145	1.060	1.000	1.000	0.960	0.880	...	...
Dividend Payout %	79.51	58.56	62.11	75.76	53.04	58.28	...	...
Income Statement								
Total Revenue	5,075	5,351	4,945	4,552	5,074	4,742	4,532	9,454
EBITDA	2,485	2,529	2,356	2,096	2,093	1,994	1,829	3,736
Depn & Amortn	827	709	650	584	569	525	489	611
Income Before Taxes	1,033	1,195	1,076	902	910	862	767	2,491
Income Taxes	370	487	383	353	496	443	395	926
Net Income	940	1,184	1,049	848	1,129	957	1,244	674
Average Shares	656	653	650	643	624	635	...	...
Balance Sheet								
Current Assets	1,663	1,764	1,638	1,429	1,450	1,379	1,625	...
Total Assets	30,587	28,138	26,686	24,079	21,924	22,970	20,345	...
Current Liabilities	3,791	3,101	2,523	2,495	3,044	2,422	2,358	...
Long-Term Obligations	10,653	10,146	10,169	8,947	8,290	8,345	7,726	...
Total Liabilities	21,615	20,073	18,877	16,954	16,384	16,113	14,706	...
Stockholders' Equity	8,972	8,065	7,809	7,125	5,540	6,857	5,639	...
Shares Outstanding	668	651	649	647	611	632	1,000.00	...
Statistical Record								
Return on Assets %	3.19	4.32	4.13	3.69	5.02	4.42	...	...
Return on Equity %	11.00	14.92	14.05	13.39	18.16	15.32	...	...
EBITDA Margin %	48.97	47.26	47.64	46.05	41.25	42.05	40.36	39.52
Net Margin %	18.52	22.13	21.21	18.63	22.25	20.18	27.45	7.13
Asset Turnover	0.17	0.20	0.19	0.20	0.23	0.22	...	...
Current Ratio	0.44	0.57	0.65	0.57	0.48	0.57	0.69	...
Debt to Equity	1.19	1.26	1.30	1.26	1.50	1.22	1.37	...
Price Range	32.15-26.74	30.98-23.14	25.26-19.20	20.65-11.50	29.02-13.48	29.05-21.92	28.67-27.75	...
P/E Ratio	22.33-18.57	17.12-12.78	15.69-11.93	15.64-8.71	16.03-7.45	19.24-14.52	...	...
Average Yield %	3.88	3.93	4.50	5.88	4.13	3.45	...	...

Address: 5400 Westheimer Court, Houston, TX 77056 **Telephone:** 713-627-5400	**Web Site:** www.spectraenergy.com **Officers:** Gregory L. Ebel - President, Chief Executive Officer Sabra L. Harrington - Vice President, Controller	**Auditors:** Deloitte & Touche LLP **Transfer Agents:** Broadridge Corporate Issuer Solutions, Inc.

SPIRIT AEROSYSTEMS HOLDINGS INC

Exchange	Symbol	Price	52Wk Range	Yield	P/E
NYS	SPR	$18.99 (3/28/2013)	25.85-14.04	N/A	79.13

*7 Year Price Score N/A   *NYSE Composite Index=100   *12 Month Price Score 78.96

Interim Earnings (Per Share)

Qtr.	Mar	Jun	Sep	Dec
2008	0.61	0.62	0.53	0.15
2009	0.45	(0.06)	0.62	0.36
2010	0.40	0.39	0.33	0.44
2011	0.24	0.21	0.47	0.42
2012	0.52	0.24	(0.94)	0.42

Interim Dividends (Per Share)

No Dividends Paid

Valuation Analysis

		Institutional Holding	
Forecast EPS	$2.02	No of Institutions	
	(04/05/2013)	290	
Market Cap	$2.7 Billion	Shares	
Book Value	$2.0 Billion	123,594,760	
Price/Book	1.37	% Held	
Price/Sales	0.51	74.66	

Business Summary: Aerospace (MIC: 7.1.1 SIC: 3728 NAIC: 336413)

Spirit AeroSystems Holdings is an independent non-original equipment manufacturer aircraft parts designer and a manufacturer of commercial aerostructures. Co. also designs, engineers and manufactures structural components for military aircraft. As of Dec 31 2011, Co. and its subsidiaries were organized into three reporting segments: Fuselage Systems, which includes forward, mid and rear fuselage sections; Propulsion Systems, which includes struts/pylons, nacelles and related engine structural components; and Wing Systems, which includes wings and wing components and other miscellaneous structural parts.

Recent Developments: For the year ended Dec 31 2012, net income decreased 81.9% to US$34.8 million from US$192.4 million in the prior year. Revenues were US$5.40 billion, up 11.0% from US$4.86 billion the year before. Operating income was US$92.3 million versus US$356.1 million in the prior year, a decrease of 74.1%. Direct operating expenses rose 21.6% to US$5.25 billion from US$4.31 billion in the comparable period the year before. Indirect operating expenses decreased 69.3% to US$60.1 million from US$195.6 million in the equivalent prior-year period.

Prospects: Our evaluation of Spirit AeroSystems Holdings Inc. as of Apr. 7, 2013 is the result of our systematic analysis on three basic characteristics: earnings strength, relative valuation, and recent stock price movement. The company has generated a negative trend in earnings per share over the past 5 quarters and while recent estimates for the company have been mixed, SPR has posted better than expected results. Based on operating earnings yield, the company is undervalued when compared to all of the companies in our coverage universe. Share price changes over the past year indicates that SPR will perform very poorly over the near term.

Financial Data

(US$ in Thousands)	12/31/2012	12/31/2011	12/31/2010	12/31/2009	12/31/2008	12/31/2007	12/31/2006	12/29/2005
Earnings Per Share	0.24	1.35	1.55	1.37	1.91	2.13	0.14	(0.80)
Cash Flow Per Share	3.86	(0.34)	0.91	(0.10)	1.53	1.34	2.35	...
Tang Book Value Per Share	13.80	13.63	12.59	11.00	9.07	8.79	6.03	2.42
Income Statement								
Total Revenue	5,397,700	4,863,800	4,172,400	4,078,500	3,771,800	3,860,800	3,207,700	1,207,600
EBITDA	112,700	486,700	471,900	432,400	526,900	525,000	2,400	(37,900)
Depn & Amortn	18,600	129,200	115,300	123,000	122,400	97,400	52,800	28,600
Income Before Taxes	11,400	280,300	297,800	272,800	383,900	419,800	(71,500)	(76,600)
Income Taxes	(24,100)	86,900	78,200	80,900	118,500	122,900	(88,300)	13,700
Net Income	34,800	192,400	218,900	191,700	265,400	296,900	16,800	(90,300)
Average Shares	142,700	142,300	141,000	139,800	139,200	139,300	122,000	113,500
Balance Sheet								
Current Assets	3,355,400	3,155,800	3,294,700	2,852,900	2,433,300	1,842,800	1,420,500	862,100
Total Assets	5,415,300	5,042,400	5,102,000	4,473,800	3,760,300	3,339,900	2,722,200	1,656,600
Current Liabilities	1,067,000	913,500	1,164,800	982,200	743,300	675,000	569,700	311,500
Long-Term Obligations	1,165,900	1,152,000	1,187,300	591,100	580,900	579,000	594,300	710,000
Total Liabilities	3,418,900	3,078,200	3,291,600	2,900,500	2,463,300	2,073,300	1,863,200	1,330,800
Stockholders' Equity	1,996,400	1,964,200	1,810,400	1,573,300	1,297,000	1,266,600	859,000	325,800
Shares Outstanding	143,697	142,865	142,098	140,734	139,889	139,519	134,697	122,670
Statistical Record								
Return on Assets %	0.66	3.79	4.57	4.66	7.46	9.80	0.76	...
Return on Equity %	1.75	10.19	12.94	13.36	20.65	27.94	2.82	...
EBITDA Margin %	2.09	10.01	11.31	10.60	13.97	13.60	0.07	N.M.
Net Margin %	0.64	3.96	5.25	4.70	7.04	7.69	0.52	N.M.
Asset Turnover	1.03	0.96	0.87	0.99	1.06	1.27	1.46	...
Current Ratio	3.14	3.45	2.83	2.90	3.27	2.73	2.49	2.77
Debt to Equity	0.58	0.59	0.66	0.38	0.45	0.46	0.69	2.18
Price Range	25.85-14.04	26.16-14.40	23.88-16.50	20.42-8.22	34.50-7.80	40.50-27.98	33.47-28.31	...
P/E Ratio	107.71-58.50	19.38-10.67	15.41-10.65	14.91-6.00	18.06-4.08	19.01-13.14	239.07-202.21	...

Address: 3801 South Oliver, Wichita, KS 67210 **Telephone:** 316-526-9000	**Web Site:** www.spiritaero.com **Officers:** Robert D. Johnson - Chairman Larry A. Lawson - President, Chief Executive Officer	**Auditors:** PricewaterhouseCoopers LLP **Investor Contact:** 316-523-7040 **Transfer Agents:** Computershare, Pittsburgh, PA

SPRINT NEXTEL CORP

Exchange	Symbol	Price	52Wk Range	Yield	P/E
NYS	S	$6.21 (3/28/2013)	6.21-2.34	N/A	N/A

*7 Year Price Score 49.80 ***NYSE Composite Index=100** ***12 Month Price Score 116.40**

Interim Earnings (Per Share)

Qtr.	Mar	Jun	Sep	Dec
2008	(0.18)	(0.12)	(0.11)	(0.57)
2009	(0.21)	(0.13)	(0.17)	(0.33)
2010	(0.29)	(0.25)	(0.30)	(0.31)
2011	(0.15)	(0.28)	(0.10)	(0.43)
2012	(0.29)	(0.46)	(0.26)	(0.44)

Interim Dividends (Per Share)

Dividend Payment Suspended

Valuation Analysis

		Institutional Holding	
Forecast EPS	$-0.88 (04/06/2013)	No of Institutions	725
Market Cap	$18.7 Billion	Shares	
Book Value	$7.1 Billion		2,751,681,792
Price/Book	2.64	% Held	86.17
Price/Sales	0.53		

Business Summary: Services (MIC: 6.1.2 SIC: 4813 NAIC: 517110)

Sprint Nextel is a holding company. Through its subsidiaries, Co. is a communications company providing wireless and wireline communications products and services to individual consumers, businesses, government subscribers and resellers. Co. operates two segments: Wireless, which provides wireless services on a postpaid and prepaid payment basis to retail subscribers and also on a wholesale and affiliate basis, which includes the sale of wireless services that utilize the Sprint network but are sold under the wholesaler's brand; and Wireline, which provides wireline voice and data communications services to other communications companies and targeted business and consumer subscribers.

Recent Developments: For the year ended Dec 31 2012, net loss amounted to US$4.33 billion versus a net loss of US$2.89 billion in the prior year. Revenues were US$35.35 billion, up 4.9% from US$33.68 billion the year before. Operating loss was US$1.82 billion versus an income of US$108.0 million in the prior year. Direct operating expenses rose 9.6% to US$20.84 billion from US$19.02 billion in the comparable period the year before. Indirect operating expenses increased 12.1% to US$16.32 billion from US$14.56 billion in the equivalent prior-year period.

Prospects: Our evaluation of Sprint Nextel Corp. as of Apr. 7, 2013 is the result of our systematic analysis on three basic characteristics: earnings strength, relative valuation, and recent stock price movement. The company has enjoyed a very positive trend in earnings per share over the past 5 quarters. Because the company lacks sufficient analyst estimate data, we place greater weight on the historical EPS trend as the measure of earnings strength. Based on operating earnings yield, the company is overvalued when compared to all of the companies in our coverage universe. Share price changes over the past year indicates that S will perform very well over the near term.

Financial Data

(US$ in Thousands)	12/31/2012	12/31/2011	12/31/2010	12/31/2009	12/31/2008	12/31/2007	12/31/2006	12/31/2005
Earnings Per Share	(1.44)	(0.96)	(1.16)	(0.84)	(0.98)	(10.31)	0.45	0.87
Cash Flow Per Share	1.00	1.23	1.61	1.69	2.16	3.22	3.71	5.25
Tang Book Value Per Share	N.M.	N.M.	N.M.	N.M.	N.M.	N.M.	N.M.	0.96
Dividends Per Share	...	...	...	...	...	0.100	0.100	0.300
Dividend Payout %	...	...	...	...	...	...	22.22	34.48
Income Statement								
Total Revenue	35,345,000	33,679,000	32,563,000	32,260,000	35,635,000	40,146,000	41,028,000	34,680,000
EBITDA	4,913,000	4,560,000	4,525,000	4,586,000	3,287,000	(22,942,000)	8,459,000	8,842,000
Depn & Amortn	6,543,000	4,455,000	5,074,000	5,827,000	5,953,000	5,711,000	5,738,000	4,933,000
Income Before Taxes	(3,058,000)	(906,000)	(2,013,000)	(2,691,000)	(3,931,000)	(29,942,000)	1,489,000	2,796,000
Income Taxes	154,000	254,000	166,000	(1,058,000)	(1,264,000)	(365,000)	488,000	1,105,000
Net Income	(4,326,000)	(2,890,000)	(3,465,000)	(2,436,000)	(2,796,000)	(29,580,000)	1,329,000	1,785,000
Average Shares	3,002,000	2,995,000	2,988,000	2,886,000	2,854,000	2,868,000	2,972,000	2,054,000
Balance Sheet								
Current Assets	13,759,000	10,337,000	9,880,000	8,593,000	8,344,000	8,661,000	10,304,000	19,092,000
Total Assets	51,570,000	49,383,000	51,654,000	55,424,000	58,252,000	64,109,000	97,161,000	102,580,000
Current Liabilities	8,874,000	6,499,000	7,891,000	6,785,000	6,281,000	9,104,000	9,798,000	14,050,000
Long-Term Obligations	23,962,000	20,266,000	18,535,000	20,293,000	20,992,000	20,469,000	21,011,000	20,632,000
Total Liabilities	44,483,000	37,956,000	37,108,000	37,329,000	38,647,000	42,110,000	44,030,000	50,396,000
Stockholders' Equity	7,087,000	11,427,000	14,546,000	18,095,000	19,605,000	21,999,000	53,131,000	52,184,000
Shares Outstanding	3,010,000	2,996,000	2,988,000	2,973,000	2,857,000	2,845,000	2,897,000	2,961,000
Statistical Record								
Return on Assets %	N.M.	N.M.	N.M.	N.M.	N.M.	N.M.	1.33	2.48
Return on Equity %	N.M.	N.M.	N.M.	N.M.	N.M.	N.M.	2.52	5.41
EBITDA Margin %	13.90	13.54	13.90	14.22	9.22	N.M.	20.62	25.50
Net Margin %	N.M.	N.M.	N.M.	N.M.	N.M.	N.M.	3.24	5.15
Asset Turnover	0.70	0.67	0.61	0.57	0.58	0.50	0.41	0.48
Current Ratio	1.55	1.59	1.25	1.27	1.33	0.95	1.05	1.36
Debt to Equity	3.38	1.77	1.27	1.12	1.07	0.93	0.40	0.40
Price Range	5.78-2.12	5.93-2.16	5.29-3.15	5.58-1.83	13.13-1.37	23.34-13.13	24.23-16.08	24.41-19.68
P/E Ratio	...	...	...	...	...	...	53.85-35.73	28.06-22.63
Average Yield %	...	...	...	...	...	0.53	0.50	1.37

Address: 6200 Sprint Parkway, Overland Park, KS 66251
Telephone: 800-829-0965

Web Site: www.sprint.com
Officers: James H. Hance - Chairman Daniel R. Hesse - President, Chief Executive Officer

Auditors: KPMG LLP
Investor Contact: 800-259-3755
Transfer Agents: Computershare Trust Company, N. A., Canton, MA

SPX CORP.

Exchange	Symbol	Price	52Wk Range	Yield	P/E
NYS	SPW	$78.96 (3/28/2013)	82.00-58.83	1.27	15.24

*7 Year Price Score 87.97   *NYSE Composite Index=100   *12 Month Price Score 104.34

Interim Earnings (Per Share)

Qtr.	Mar	Jun	Sep	Dec
2008	1.13	1.74	2.13	(0.43)
2009	0.48	0.68	0.93	(1.45)
2010	0.44	1.57	0.78	1.29
2011	0.45	0.67	1.20	1.23
2012	0.26	0.93	1.16	2.84

Interim Dividends (Per Share)

Amt	Decl	Ex	Rec	Pay
0.25Q	05/25/2012	06/12/2012	06/14/2012	07/03/2012
0.25Q	08/23/2012	09/12/2012	09/14/2012	10/03/2012
0.25Q	11/27/2012	12/10/2012	12/12/2012	12/27/2012
0.25Q	02/21/2013	03/12/2013	03/14/2013	04/02/2013

Indicated Div: $1.00

Valuation Analysis

		Institutional Holding	
Forecast EPS	$4.97 (04/05/2013)	No of Institutions	376
Market Cap	$3.8 Billion	Shares	43,825,936
Book Value	$2.3 Billion	% Held	77.71
Price/Book	1.68		
Price/Sales	0.75		

Business Summary: Industrial Machinery & Equipment (MIC: 7.2.1 SIC: 3429 NAIC: 332510)

SPX is a global supplier of specialized, engineered solutions. Co. operates two segments: Flow Technology and Thermal Equipment and Services. The Flow Technology segment designs, manufactures and markets products and solutions used to process, blend, filter, dry, meter and transport fluids with a focus on original equipment installation and turnkey projects as well as comprehensive aftermarket support services. The Thermal Equipment and Services segment engineers, manufactures and services thermal heat transfer products.

Recent Developments: For the year ended Dec 31 2012, loss from continuing operations was US$78.4 million compared with income of US$155.6 million a year earlier. Net income increased 41.2% to US$262.0 million from US$185.6 million in the prior year. Revenues were US$5.10 billion, up 12.4% from US$4.54 billion the year before. Operating income was US$9.0 million versus US$286.5 million in the prior year, a decrease of 96.9%. Direct operating expenses rose 14.2% to US$3.73 billion from US$3.26 billion in the comparable period the year before. Indirect operating expenses increased 38.2% to US$1.37 billion from US$988.2 million in the equivalent prior-year period.

Prospects: Our evaluation of SPX Corp. as of Apr. 7, 2013 is the result of our systematic analysis on three basic characteristics: earnings strength, relative valuation, and recent stock price movement. The company has managed to produce a neutral trend in earnings per share over the past 5 quarters. However, while recent estimates for the company have been mixed, SPW has posted better than expected results. Based on operating earnings yield, the company is about fairly valued when compared to all of the companies in our coverage universe. Share price changes over the past year indicates that SPW will perform in line with the market over the near term.

Financial Data (US$ in Thousands)	12/31/2012	12/31/2011	12/31/2010	12/31/2009	12/31/2008	12/31/2007	12/31/2006	12/31/2005
Earnings Per Share	5.18	3.54	4.08	0.64	4.59	5.22	2.83	15.33
Cash Flow Per Share	1.39	6.39	5.10	9.54	7.61	8.02	1.03	(1.85)
Dividends Per Share	1.000	1.000	1.000	1.000	1.000	1.000	1.000	1.000
Dividend Payout %	19.31	28.25	24.51	156.25	21.79	19.16	35.34	6.52
Income Statement								
Total Revenue	5,100,200	5,461,900	4,886,800	4,850,800	5,855,700	4,822,300	4,313,300	4,292,200
EBITDA	134,100	390,000	395,400	241,800	558,600	494,800	359,500	165,200
Depn & Amortn	111,100	107,400	99,100	91,200	93,000	77,100	73,300	86,100
Income Before Taxes	(85,100)	191,300	214,500	66,000	360,500	349,900	236,000	27,300
Income Taxes	31,900	34,400	53,100	47,200	152,900	89,500	56,300	70,400
Net Income	259,200	180,600	205,600	31,700	247,900	294,200	170,700	1,090,000
Average Shares	50,031	50,946	50,347	49,797	54,062	56,307	60,724	71,084
Balance Sheet								
Current Assets	3,115,000	2,895,300	2,428,500	2,312,500	2,812,200	2,629,400	2,458,500	2,228,300
Total Assets	7,130,100	7,391,800	5,993,300	5,724,400	6,121,600	6,237,400	5,437,100	5,306,400
Current Liabilities	1,736,600	1,947,800	1,722,300	1,639,300	2,024,300	2,157,000	1,723,400	1,470,700
Long-Term Obligations	1,649,900	1,925,600	1,110,500	1,128,600	1,155,400	1,240,700	753,600	720,900
Total Liabilities	4,861,400	5,164,500	3,895,600	3,833,600	4,110,800	4,231,400	3,327,700	3,195,200
Stockholders' Equity	2,268,700	2,227,300	2,097,700	1,890,800	2,010,800	2,006,000	2,109,400	2,111,200
Shares Outstanding	48,303	51,073	50,294	49,367	51,128	52,792	58,766	62,563
Statistical Record								
Return on Assets %	3.56	2.70	3.51	0.54	4.00	5.04	3.18	16.91
Return on Equity %	11.50	8.35	10.31	1.62	12.31	14.30	8.09	51.43
EBITDA Margin %	2.63	7.14	8.09	4.98	9.54	10.26	8.33	3.85
Net Margin %	5.08	3.31	4.21	0.65	4.23	6.10	3.96	25.39
Asset Turnover	0.70	0.82	0.83	0.82	0.95	0.83	0.80	0.67
Current Ratio	1.79	1.49	1.41	1.41	1.39	1.22	1.43	1.52
Debt to Equity	0.73	0.86	0.53	0.60	0.57	0.62	0.36	0.34
Price Range	78.44-58.83	86.45-42.00	71.83-51.36	64.72-38.75	139.72-26.32	109.88-60.98	62.48-45.91	50.09-38.10
P/E Ratio	15.14-11.36	24.42-11.86	17.61-12.59	101.13-60.55	30.44-5.73	21.05-11.68	22.08-16.22	3.27-2.49
Average Yield %	1.46	1.44	1.61	1.96	1.06	1.19	1.85	2.26

Address: 13515 Ballantyne Corporate Place, Charlotte, NC 28277
Telephone: 704-752-4400
Fax: 704-752-4505

Web Site: www.spx.com
Officers: Christopher J. Kearney - Chairman, President, Chief Executive Officer Robert B. Foreman - Executive Vice President

Auditors: Deloitte & Touche LLP
Transfer Agents: Computershare, Providence, RI

694

STANCORP FINANCIAL GROUP INC

Exchange	Symbol	Price	52Wk Range	Yield	P/E	Div Achiever
NYS	SFG	$42.76 (3/28/2013)	42.76-29.08	2.17	13.71	13 Years

*7 Year Price Score 76.62   *NYSE Composite Index=100   *12 Month Price Score 103.22

Interim Earnings (Per Share)

Qtr.	Mar	Jun	Sep	Dec
2008	1.02	0.98	0.82	0.49
2009	0.67	1.15	1.21	1.23
2010	1.04	0.87	0.99	1.12
2011	0.73	0.42	1.07	0.88
2012	0.79	0.45	1.01	0.86

Interim Dividends (Per Share)

Amt	Decl	Ex	Rec	Pay
0.80A	11/09/2009	11/18/2009	11/20/2009	12/04/2009
0.86A	11/08/2010	11/17/2010	11/19/2010	12/03/2010
0.89A	11/15/2011	11/23/2011	11/28/2011	12/09/2011
0.93A	11/14/2012	11/20/2012	11/23/2012	12/07/2012

Indicated Div: $0.93

Valuation Analysis

		Institutional Holding	
Forecast EPS	$3.60 (04/06/2013)	No of Institutions	239
Market Cap	$1.9 Billion	Shares	39,097,240
Book Value	$2.2 Billion	% Held	79.74
Price/Book	0.88		
Price/Sales	0.66		

Business Summary: Life & Health (MIC: 5.2.2 SIC: 6321 NAIC: 524114)

StanCorp is a holding company and conducts business through wholly-owned operating subsidiaries throughout the U.S. Co. operates through two reportable segments: Insurance Services, which provides group life and accidental death and dismemberment insurance, group and individual disability insurance, group dental and group vision insurance, and absence management services to individuals and employer groups; and Asset Management, which provides 401(k) plans, 403(b) plans, 457 plans, defined benefit plans, money purchase pension plans, profit sharing plans and non-qualified deferred compensation products and services through an affiliated broker-dealer; as well as an Other category.

Recent Developments: For the year ended Dec 31 2012, net income increased 1.3% to US$138.5 million from US$136.7 million in the prior year. Revenues were US$2.90 billion, up 0.8% from US$2.87 billion the year before. Net premiums earned were US$2.16 billion versus US$2.15 billion in the prior year, an increase of 0.5%. Net investment income rose 2.6% to US$628.5 million from US$612.8 million a year ago.

Prospects: Our evaluation of Stancorp Financial Group Inc. as of Apr. 7, 2013 is the result of our systematic analysis on three basic characteristics: earnings strength, relative valuation, and recent stock price movement. The company has produced a positive trend in earnings per share over the past 5 quarters and while recent estimates for the company have remained steady, SFG has posted better than expected results. Based on operating earnings yield, the company is undervalued when compared to all of the companies in our coverage universe. Share price changes over the past year indicates that SFG will perform poorly over the near term.

Financial Data
(US$ in Thousands)

	12/31/2012	12/31/2011	12/31/2010	12/31/2009	12/31/2008	12/31/2007	12/31/2006	12/31/2005
Earnings Per Share	3.12	3.09	4.02	4.26	3.30	4.35	3.73	3.76
Cash Flow Per Share	8.46	5.66	7.59	9.02	7.38	9.37	7.21	7.34
Tang Book Value Per Share	48.02	44.60	40.64	35.59	27.44	29.07	27.33	25.84
Dividends Per Share	0.930	0.890	0.860	0.800	0.750	0.720	0.650	0.625
Dividend Payout %	29.81	28.80	21.39	18.78	22.73	16.55	17.43	16.62
Income Statement								
Premium Income	2,163,900	2,153,300	2,097,700	2,101,900	2,140,200	2,078,300	1,935,000	1,826,500
Total Revenue	2,898,400	2,874,700	2,765,100	2,770,000	2,667,000	2,709,200	2,492,900	2,337,200
Benefits & Claims	1,793,000	1,771,200	1,619,800	1,575,700	1,589,400	1,591,800	1,513,100	1,392,300
Income Before Taxes	183,400	195,100	282,800	315,700	241,100	341,700	309,700	325,600
Income Taxes	44,900	55,800	93,800	106,800	78,200	114,200	105,900	114,500
Net Income	138,500	139,300	189,000	208,900	162,900	227,500	203,800	211,100
Average Shares	44,359	45,016	47,006	49,044	49,292	52,344	54,688	56,076
Balance Sheet								
Total Assets	19,791,300	18,433,800	17,843,300	16,569,500	14,555,200	14,982,900	13,638,600	12,450,700
Total Liabilities	17,622,300	16,423,300	15,931,200	14,834,100	13,174,900	13,553,900	12,174,100	11,036,900
Stockholders' Equity	2,169,000	2,010,500	1,912,100	1,735,400	1,380,300	1,429,000	1,464,500	1,413,800
Shares Outstanding	44,419	44,268	46,159	47,744	48,989	49,155	53,592	54,712
Statistical Record								
Return on Assets %	0.72	0.77	1.10	1.34	1.10	1.59	1.56	1.78
Return on Equity %	6.61	7.10	10.36	13.41	11.57	15.72	14.16	15.00
Loss Ratio %	82.86	82.26	77.22	74.97	74.26	76.59	78.20	76.23
Net Margin %	4.78	4.85	6.84	7.54	6.11	8.40	8.18	9.03
Price Range	41.77-29.08	48.64-25.80	50.19-35.47	42.10-13.96	55.28-23.92	55.13-41.44	55.75-42.07	52.95-36.05
P/E Ratio	13.39-9.32	15.74-8.35	12.49-8.82	9.88-3.28	16.75-7.25	12.67-9.53	14.95-11.28	14.08-9.59
Average Yield %	2.63	2.31	2.03	2.50	1.63	1.46	1.34	1.48

Address: 1100 SW Sixth Avenue, Portland, OR 97204 **Telephone:** 971-321-7000	**Web Site:** www.stancorpfinancial.com **Officers:** J. Gregory Ness - Chairman, President, Chief Executive Officer Floyd F. Chadee - Senior Vice President, Chief Financial Officer	**Auditors:** Deloitte & Touche LLP **Investor Contact:** 971-321-6127 **Transfer Agents:** Computershare Shareowner Services

STANLEY BLACK & DECKER, INC.

Exchange	Symbol	Price	52Wk Range	Yield	P/E	Div Achiever
NYS	SWK	$80.97 (3/28/2013)	81.61-59.25	2.42	15.28	45 Years

*7 Year Price Score 113.42 *NYSE Composite Index=100 *12 Month Price Score 100.88

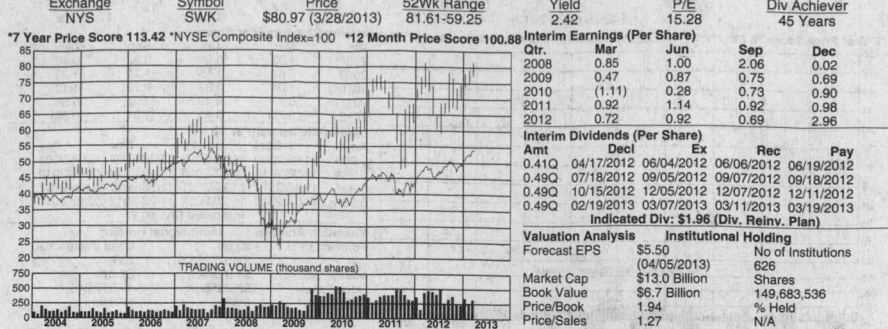

Interim Earnings (Per Share)

Qtr.	Mar	Jun	Sep	Dec
2008	0.85	1.00	2.06	0.02
2009	0.47	0.87	0.75	0.69
2010	(1.11)	0.28	0.73	0.90
2011	0.92	1.14	0.92	0.98
2012	0.72	0.92	0.69	2.96

Interim Dividends (Per Share)

Amt	Decl	Ex	Rec	Pay
0.41Q	04/17/2012	06/04/2012	06/06/2012	06/19/2012
0.49Q	07/18/2012	09/05/2012	09/07/2012	09/18/2012
0.49Q	10/15/2012	12/05/2012	12/07/2012	12/11/2012
0.49Q	02/19/2013	03/07/2013	03/11/2013	03/19/2013

Indicated Div: $1.96 (Div. Reinv. Plan)

Valuation Analysis

		Institutional Holding	
Forecast EPS	$5.50 (04/05/2013)	No of Institutions	626
Market Cap	$13.0 Billion	Shares	149,683,536
Book Value	$6.7 Billion	% Held	N/A
Price/Book	1.94		
Price/Sales	1.27		

Business Summary: Industrial Machinery & Equipment (MIC: 7.2.1 SIC: 3423 NAIC: 332212)

Stanley Black & Decker is a provider of power and hand tools, mechanical access applications, electronic security and monitoring systems, and products and services for various industrial applications. Co. operates in three business segments: construction and do-it-yourself, which is comprised of the Professional Power Tool and Accessories business, the Consumer Power Tool business, and the Hand Tools, Fasteners & Storage business; security, which is comprised of the Convergent Security Solutions and Mechanical Access Solutions businesses; as well as industrial, which is comprised of the Industrial and Automotive Repair, Engineered Fastening and Infrastructure businesses.

Recent Developments: For the year ended Dec 29 2012, income from continuing operations decreased 24.9% to US$449.5 million from US$598.4 million a year earlier. Net income increased 31.0% to US$883.8 million from US$674.6 million in the prior year. Revenues were US$10.19 billion, up 8.0% from US$9.44 billion the year before. Direct operating expenses rose 8.7% to US$6.49 billion from US$5.97 billion in the comparable period the year before. Indirect operating expenses increased 12.7% to US$3.18 billion from US$2.82 billion in the equivalent prior-year period.

Prospects: Our evaluation of Stanley Black & Decker, Inc. as of Apr. 7, 2013 is the result of our systematic analysis on three basic characteristics: earnings strength, relative valuation, and recent stock price movement. The company has produced a positive trend in earnings per share over the past 5 quarters and while recent estimates for the company have been mixed, SWK has posted better than expected results. Based on operating earnings yield, the company is undervalued when compared to all of the companies in our coverage universe. Share price changes over the past year indicates that SWK will perform in line with the market over the near term.

Financial Data
(US$ in Thousands)

	12/29/2012	12/31/2011	01/01/2011	01/02/2010	01/03/2009	12/29/2007	12/30/2006	12/31/2005
Earnings Per Share	5.30	3.97	1.32	2.79	3.92	4.00	3.46	3.16
Cash Flow Per Share	5.94	6.04	5.04	6.78	6.44	6.63	5.38	4.36
Tang Book Value Per Share	N.M.	N.M.	N.M.	N.M.	N.M.	N.M.	N.M.	4.59
Dividends Per Share	1.800	1.640	1.340	1.300	1.260	1.220	1.180	1.140
Dividend Payout %	33.96	41.31	101.52	46.59	32.14	30.50	34.10	36.08
Income Statement								
Total Revenue	10,190,500	10,376,400	8,409,600	3,737,100	4,426,200	4,483,800	4,018,600	3,285,300
EBITDA	1,107,000	1,303,200	744,500	534,900	559,100	697,900	501,400	445,500
Depn & Amortn	445,300	410,100	406,800	191,000	185,000	166,600	69,400	53,500
Income Before Taxes	527,600	779,800	237,100	283,300	301,300	451,100	367,100	358,200
Income Taxes	78,900	88,600	38,900	54,500	75,900	114,500	76,400	86,500
Net Income	883,800	674,600	198,200	224,300	313,300	336,600	289,500	269,600
Average Shares	166,701	170,105	150,167	80,396	79,874	84,045	83,704	85,405
Balance Sheet								
Current Assets	4,098,300	4,322,700	4,815,600	1,411,900	1,499,300	1,768,400	1,638,500	1,825,600
Total Assets	15,844,000	15,949,000	15,139,400	4,769,100	4,879,200	4,779,900	3,935,400	3,545,100
Current Liabilities	3,073,400	3,268,500	2,742,200	1,192,000	1,197,200	1,277,500	1,251,100	875,300
Long-Term Obligations	3,526,500	2,925,800	3,018,100	1,084,700	1,419,500	1,212,100	679,200	895,300
Total Liabilities	9,176,900	8,945,400	8,122,400	2,783,000	3,191,200	3,051,400	2,383,400	2,100,200
Stockholders' Equity	6,667,100	7,003,600	7,017,000	1,986,100	1,688,000	1,728,500	1,552,000	1,444,900
Shares Outstanding	159,952	169,045	166,347	80,478	78,876	80,378	81,841	83,791
Statistical Record								
Return on Assets %	5.57	4.35	2.00	4.66	6.38	7.75	7.76	8.45
Return on Equity %	12.97	9.65	4.42	12.24	18.04	20.58	19.37	20.28
EBITDA Margin %	10.86	12.56	8.85	14.31	12.63	15.56	12.48	13.56
Net Margin %	8.67	6.50	2.36	6.00	7.08	7.51	7.20	8.21
Asset Turnover	0.64	0.67	0.85	0.78	0.90	1.03	1.08	1.03
Current Ratio	1.33	1.32	1.76	1.18	1.25	1.38	1.31	2.09
Debt to Equity	0.53	0.42	0.43	0.55	0.84	0.70	0.44	0.62
Price Range	81.34-59.25	77.29-47.83	67.29-49.58	53.13-22.75	51.42-25.38	63.92-47.46	54.33-41.95	51.17-42.20
P/E Ratio	15.35-11.18	19.47-12.05	50.98-37.56	19.04-8.15	13.12-6.47	15.98-11.87	15.70-12.12	16.19-13.35
Average Yield %	2.55	2.43	2.30	3.38	2.88	2.17	2.40	2.46

Address: 1000 Stanley Drive, New Britain, CT 06053 **Telephone:** 860-225-5111 **Fax:** 860-827-3895	**Web Site:** www.stanleyworks.com **Officers:** John F. Lundgren - Chairman, President, Chief Executive Officer James M. Loree - President, Executive Vice President, Chief Operating Officer	**Auditors:** Ernst & Young LLP **Transfer Agents:** Computershare Investor Services, Canton, MA

STARWOOD HOTELS & RESORTS WORLDWIDE INC

Exchange	Symbol	Price	52Wk Range	Yield	P/E
NYS	HOT	$63.73 (3/28/2013)	63.73-48.46	1.96	22.28

*7 Year Price Score 102.42 *NYSE Composite Index=100 *12 Month Price Score 100.87

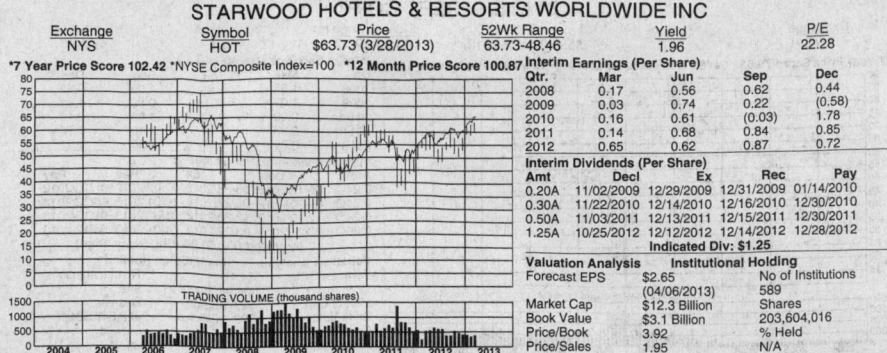

Interim Earnings (Per Share)

Qtr.	Mar	Jun	Sep	Dec
2008	0.17	0.56	0.62	0.44
2009	0.03	0.74	0.22	(0.58)
2010	0.16	0.61	(0.03)	1.78
2011	0.14	0.68	0.84	0.85
2012	0.65	0.62	0.87	0.72

Interim Dividends (Per Share)

Amt	Decl	Ex	Rec	Pay
0.20A	11/02/2009	12/29/2009	12/31/2009	01/14/2010
0.30A	11/22/2010	12/14/2010	12/16/2010	12/30/2010
0.50A	11/03/2011	12/13/2011	12/15/2011	12/30/2011
1.25A	10/25/2012	12/12/2012	12/14/2012	12/28/2012

Indicated Div: $1.25

Valuation Analysis

		Institutional Holding	
Forecast EPS	$2.65 (04/06/2013)	No of Institutions	589
Market Cap	$12.3 Billion	Shares	203,604,016
Book Value	$3.1 Billion	% Held	N/A
Price/Book	3.92		
Price/Sales	1.95		

Business Summary: Hotels, Restaurants & Travel (MIC: 2.2.1 SIC: 7011 NAIC: 721110)

Starwood Hotels & Resorts Worldwide is a hotel and leisure company. Co.'s hotel business provides hotels and resorts operated under brand names such as St. Regis®, The Luxury Collection®, W®, Westin®, Le Meridien®, Sheraton®, Four Points® by Sheraton, Aloft®, and Element®. Co.'s Starwood Vacation Ownership, Inc. subsidiary develops and operates vacation ownership resorts, and markets, sells and finances vacation ownership interests in the resorts. At Dec 31 2012, Co.'s hotel business included 1,121 owned, managed or franchised hotels with about 328,000 rooms, while its vacation ownership and residential business included 13 stand-alone vacation ownership resorts and residential properties.

Recent Developments: For the year ended Dec 31 2012, income from continuing operations decreased 6.0% to US$470.0 million from US$500.0 million a year earlier. Net income increased 15.4% to US$562.0 million from US$487.0 million in the prior year. Revenues were US$6.32 billion, up 12.4% from US$5.62 billion the year before. Operating income was US$912.0 million versus US$630.0 million in the prior year, an increase of 44.8%. Direct operating expenses rose 11.4% to US$4.80 billion from US$4.31 billion in the comparable period the year before. Indirect operating expenses decreased 11.1% to US$609.0 million from US$685.0 million in the equivalent prior-year period.

Prospects: Our evaluation of Starwood Hotels & Resorts Worldwide Inc. as of Apr. 7, 2013 is the result of our systematic analysis on three basic characteristics: earnings strength, relative valuation, and recent stock price movement. The company has generated a negative trend in earnings per share over the past 5 quarters. Because the company lacks sufficient analyst estimate data, we place greater weight on the historical EPS trend as the measure of earnings strength. Based on operating earnings yield, the company is fairly valued versus all of the companies in our coverage universe. Share price changes over the past year indicates that HOT will perform in line with the market over the near term.

Financial Data
(US$ in Thousands)

	12/31/2012	12/31/2011	12/31/2010	12/31/2009	12/31/2008	12/31/2007	12/31/2006	12/31/2005
Earnings Per Share	2.86	2.51	2.51	0.41	1.77	2.57	4.69	1.88
Cash Flow Per Share	6.12	3.39	4.17	3.17	3.56	4.41	2.35	3.52
Tang Book Value Per Share	5.76	4.58	2.09	N.M.	N.M.	N.M.	3.31	13.57
Dividends Per Share	1.250	0.500	0.300	0.200	0.900	0.900	0.420	...
Dividend Payout %	43.71	19.92	11.95	48.78	50.85	35.02	8.96	...
Income Statement								
Total Revenue	6,321,000	5,624,000	5,071,000	4,712,000	5,907,000	6,153,000	5,979,000	5,977,000
EBITDA	989,000	865,000	813,000	209,000	812,000	1,094,000	1,116,000	1,204,000
Depn & Amortn	226,000	235,000	252,000	274,000	291,000	280,000	280,000	387,000
Income Before Taxes	593,000	414,000	325,000	(292,000)	314,000	667,000	621,000	578,000
Income Taxes	148,000	(75,000)	27,000	(293,000)	76,000	189,000	(434,000)	219,000
Net Income	562,000	489,000	477,000	73,000	329,000	542,000	1,043,000	422,000
Average Shares	197,000	195,000	190,000	180,000	185,000	211,000	223,000	225,000
Balance Sheet								
Current Assets	1,919,000	2,534,000	2,306,000	1,491,000	2,166,000	1,824,000	1,810,000	2,283,000
Total Assets	8,861,000	9,560,000	9,776,000	8,761,000	9,703,000	9,622,000	9,280,000	12,454,000
Current Liabilities	2,029,000	1,992,000	2,161,000	2,027,000	2,688,000	2,101,000	2,461,000	2,879,000
Long-Term Obligations	1,656,000	2,596,000	3,215,000	2,955,000	3,502,000	3,590,000	1,827,000	2,926,000
Total Liabilities	5,724,000	6,606,000	7,305,000	6,937,000	8,082,000	7,546,000	6,272,000	7,243,000
Stockholders' Equity	3,137,000	2,954,000	2,471,000	1,824,000	1,621,000	2,076,000	3,008,000	5,211,000
Shares Outstanding	193,121	195,913	192,970	186,785	182,827	190,998	213,484	217,218
Statistical Record								
Return on Assets %	6.09	5.06	5.15	0.79	3.40	5.73	9.60	3.41
Return on Equity %	18.40	18.03	22.21	4.24	17.75	21.32	25.38	8.44
EBITDA Margin %	15.65	15.38	16.03	4.44	13.75	17.78	18.67	20.14
Net Margin %	8.89	8.69	9.41	1.55	5.57	8.81	17.44	7.06
Asset Turnover	0.68	0.58	0.55	0.51	0.61	0.65	0.55	0.48
Current Ratio	0.95	1.27	1.07	0.74	0.81	0.87	0.74	0.79
Debt to Equity	0.53	0.88	1.30	1.62	2.16	1.73	0.61	0.56
Price Range	60.70-48.46	65.09-36.90	62.41-33.32	37.31-9.52	55.60-11.44	75.09-43.30	65.61-50.19	...
P/E Ratio	21.22-16.94	25.93-14.70	24.86-13.27	91.00-23.22	31.41-6.46	29.22-16.85	13.99-10.70	...
Average Yield %	2.29	0.94	0.62	0.83	2.40	1.44	0.72	...

Address: One StarPoint, Stamford, CT 06902	**Web Site:** www.starwoodhotels.com	**Auditors:** Ernst & Young LLP
Telephone: 203-964-6000	**Officers:** Vasant M. Prabhu - Vice-Chairman, Executive Vice President, Chief Financial Officer Frits D. van Paasschen - President, Chief Executive Officer	**Investor Contact:** 203-351-3500 **Transfer Agents:** American Stock Transfer & Trust Company, Brooklyn, NY

STATE STREET CORP.

Exchange	Symbol	Price	52Wk Range	Yield	P/E
NYS	STT	$59.09 (3/28/2013)	60.53-39.17	1.76	14.07

*7 Year Price Score 79.63 *NYSE Composite Index=100 *12 Month Price Score 114.14

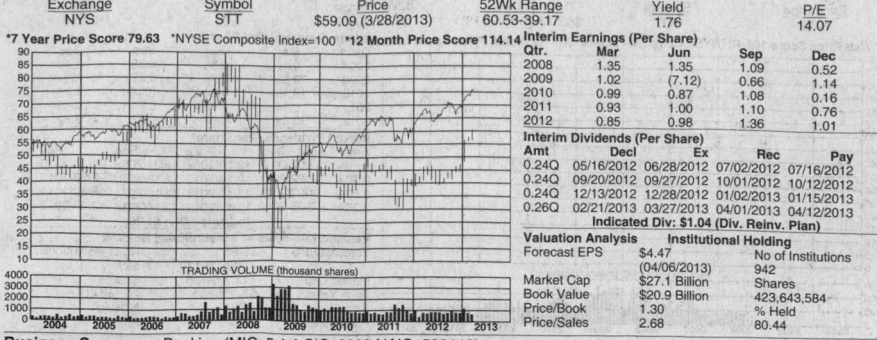

Interim Earnings (Per Share)

Qtr.	Mar	Jun	Sep	Dec
2008	1.35	1.35	1.09	0.52
2009	1.02	(7.12)	0.66	1.14
2010	0.99	0.87	1.08	0.16
2011	0.93	1.00	1.10	0.76
2012	0.85	0.98	1.36	1.01

Interim Dividends (Per Share)

Amt	Decl	Ex	Rec	Pay
0.24Q	05/16/2012	06/28/2012	07/02/2012	07/16/2012
0.24Q	09/20/2012	09/27/2012	10/01/2012	10/12/2012
0.24Q	12/13/2012	12/28/2012	01/02/2013	01/15/2013
0.26Q	02/21/2013	03/27/2013	04/01/2013	04/12/2013

Indicated Div: $1.04 (Div. Reinv. Plan)

Valuation Analysis

		Institutional Holding	
Forecast EPS	$4.47 (04/06/2013)	No of Institutions	942
Market Cap	$27.1 Billion	Shares	423,643,584
Book Value	$20.9 Billion	% Held	80.44
Price/Book	1.30		
Price/Sales	2.68		

Business Summary: Banking (MIC: 5.1.1 SIC: 6022 NAIC: 522110)

State Street is a financial holding company. Through its subsidiaries, Co. provides financial products and services to institutional investors. Co. has two lines of business: Investment Servicing, which provides, among others, custody, deposit-taking, product- and participant-level accounting, daily pricing and administration, master trust and master custody, record-keeping, cash management, foreign exchange, brokerage and other trading services; and Investment Management, which provides an array of investment management, investment research and other related services, such as securities finance. As of Dec 31 2012, Co. had total assets of $222.58 billion and deposits of $164.18 billion.

Recent Developments: For the year ended Dec 31 2012, net income increased 7.3% to US$2.06 billion from US$1.92 billion in the prior year. Net interest income increased 8.8% to US$2.54 billion from US$2.33 billion in the prior year. Credit for loan losses was US$3.0 million versus a provision for loan losses of nil in the prior year. Non-interest income fell 2.1% to US$7.11 billion from US$7.26 billion, while non-interest expense declined 2.4% to US$6.89 billion.

Prospects: Our evaluation of State Street Corp. as of Apr. 7, 2013 is the result of our systematic analysis on three basic characteristics: earnings strength, relative valuation, and recent stock price movement. The company has managed to produce a neutral trend in earnings per share over the past 5 quarters and while recent estimates for the company have been raised by analysts, STT has posted better than expected results. Based on operating earnings yield, the company is undervalued when compared to all of the companies in our coverage universe. Share price changes over the past year indicates that STT will perform in line with the market over the near term.

Financial Data

(US$ in Thousands)	12/31/2012	12/31/2011	12/31/2010	12/31/2009	12/31/2008	12/31/2007	12/31/2006	12/31/2005
Earnings Per Share	4.20	3.79	3.09	(4.31)	4.30	3.45	3.29	2.50
Cash Flow Per Share	3.84	6.85	1.66	(9.07)	(4.72)	8.15	2.96	7.52
Tang Book Value Per Share	25.87	22.14	19.13	16.43	10.46	12.28	16.35	13.70
Dividends Per Share	0.960	0.720	0.040	0.040	0.950	0.880	0.800	0.720
Dividend Payout %	22.86	19.00	1.29	...	22.09	25.51	24.32	28.80
Income Statement								
Interest Income	3,014,000	2,946,000	3,462,000	3,286,000	4,879,000	5,212,000	4,324,000	2,930,000
Interest Expense	476,000	613,000	763,000	722,000	2,229,000	3,482,000	3,214,000	2,023,000
Net Interest Income	2,538,000	2,333,000	2,699,000	2,564,000	2,650,000	1,730,000	1,110,000	907,000
Provision for Losses	(3,000)	...	25,000	149,000	...	...	...	...
Non-Interest Income	7,111,000	7,261,000	6,254,000	6,076,000	8,043,000	6,606,000	5,201,000	4,566,000
Non-Interest Expense	6,886,000	7,058,000	6,842,000	5,966,000	7,851,000	6,433,000	4,540,000	4,041,000
Income Before Taxes	2,766,000	2,536,000	2,086,000	2,525,000	2,842,000	1,903,000	1,771,000	1,432,000
Income Taxes	705,000	616,000	530,000	722,000	1,031,000	642,000	675,000	487,000
Net Income	2,061,000	1,920,000	1,556,000	(1,881,000)	1,811,000	1,261,000	1,106,000	838,000
Average Shares	481,129	496,072	497,924	474,003	416,100	365,488	335,732	334,636
Balance Sheet								
Net Loans & Leases	12,285,000	10,031,000	11,857,000	10,729,000	9,113,000	15,784,000	8,928,000	6,464,000
Total Assets	222,582,000	216,827,000	160,505,000	157,946,000	173,631,000	142,543,000	107,353,000	97,968,000
Total Deposits	164,181,000	157,287,000	98,345,000	90,062,000	112,225,000	95,789,000	65,646,000	59,646,000
Total Liabilities	201,713,000	197,429,000	142,718,000	143,455,000	160,857,000	131,244,000	100,101,000	91,601,000
Stockholders' Equity	20,869,000	19,398,000	17,787,000	14,491,000	12,774,000	11,299,000	7,252,000	6,367,000
Shares Outstanding	458,662	487,423	501,644	494,933	431,557	386,284	332,438	333,625
Statistical Record								
Return on Assets %	0.94	1.02	0.98	N.M.	1.14	1.01	1.08	0.87
Return on Equity %	10.21	10.33	9.64	N.M.	15.00	13.59	16.24	13.38
Net Interest Margin %	84.21	79.19	77.96	78.03	54.31	33.19	25.67	30.96
Efficiency Ratio %	68.01	69.15	70.42	63.73	60.76	54.43	47.66	53.91
Loans to Deposits	0.07	0.06	0.12	0.12	0.08	0.16	0.14	0.11
Price Range	47.01-38.78	50.06-30.38	48.07-32.81	55.17-14.89	85.37-28.69	82.24-59.48	68.36-54.49	59.29-40.68
P/E Ratio	11.19-9.23	13.21-8.02	15.56-10.62	...	19.85-6.67	23.84-17.24	20.78-16.56	23.72-16.27
Average Yield %	2.22	1.73	0.10	0.10	1.47	1.26	1.30	1.47

Address: One Lincoln Street, Boston, MA 02111 **Telephone:** 617-786-3000 **Fax:** 617-985-8055	**Web Site:** www.statestreet.com **Officers:** Joseph L. Hooley - Chairman, President, Chief Executive Officer, Chief Operating Officer Joseph C. Antonellis - Vice-Chairman	**Auditors:** Ernst & Young LLP **Transfer Agents:** American Stock Transfer & Trust Company, LLC, Brooklyn, NY

STEELCASE, INC.

Exchange	Symbol	Price	52Wk Range	Yield	P/E
NYS	SCS	$14.73 (3/28/2013)	15.41-7.87	2.72	23.38

*7 Year Price Score 86.04   ***NYSE Composite Index=100**   ***12 Month Price Score 122.39**

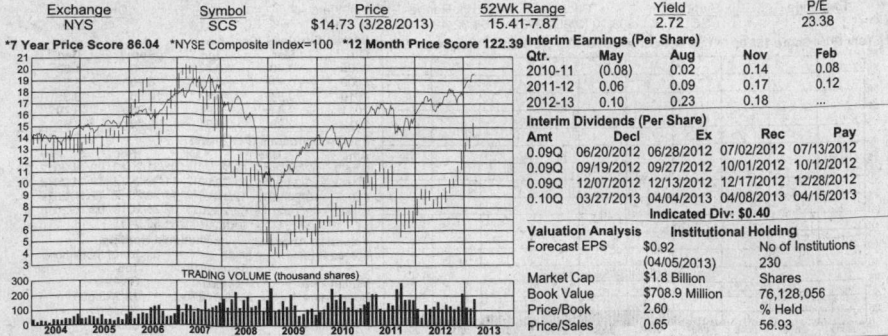

Interim Earnings (Per Share)

Qtr.	May	Aug	Nov	Feb
2010-11	(0.08)	0.02	0.14	0.08
2011-12	0.06	0.09	0.17	0.12
2012-13	0.10	0.23	0.18	...

Interim Dividends (Per Share)

Amt	Decl	Ex	Rec	Pay
0.09Q	06/20/2012	06/28/2012	07/02/2012	07/13/2012
0.09Q	09/19/2012	09/27/2012	10/01/2012	10/12/2012
0.09Q	12/07/2012	12/13/2012	12/17/2012	12/28/2012
0.10Q	03/27/2013	04/04/2013	04/08/2013	04/15/2013

Indicated Div: $0.40

Valuation Analysis

		Institutional Holding	
Forecast EPS	$0.92	No of Institutions	
	(04/05/2013)	230	
Market Cap	$1.8 Billion	Shares	
Book Value	$708.9 Million	76,128,056	
Price/Book	2.60	% Held	
Price/Sales	0.65	56.93	

Business Summary: Office Equipment & Furniture (MIC: 7.5.1 SIC: 2522 NAIC: 337211)

Steelcase provides products and services for the workplace. Co. operates under the Americas and EMEA segments plus an Other category. The Americas segment serves customers in the U.S, Canada and Latin America. Co.'s architecture, furniture and technology products is marketed to corporate, government, healthcare, education and retail customers via the Steelcase, Details, Coalesse, Nurture by Steelcase and Turnstone brands. The EMEA segment serves customers in Europe, the Middle East and Africa mainly under the Steelcase brand, with a focus on freestanding furniture systems, storage and seating applications. The Other category includes Co.'s Asia Pacific, PolyVision and Designtex businesses.

Recent Developments: For the quarter ended Nov 23 2012, net income increased 5.4% to US$23.6 million from US$22.4 million in the year-earlier quarter. Revenues were US$727.2 million, up 1.1% from US$719.4 million the year before. Operating income was US$38.4 million versus US$38.2 million in the prior-year quarter, an increase of 0.5%. Direct operating expenses rose 0.3% to US$501.3 million from US$499.6 million in the comparable period the year before. Indirect operating expenses increased 3.2% to US$187.5 million from US$181.6 million in the equivalent prior-year period.

Prospects: Our evaluation of Steelcase Inc. as of Apr. 7, 2013 is the result of our systematic analysis on three basic characteristics: earnings strength, relative valuation, and recent stock price movement. The company has generated a negative trend in earnings per share over the past 5 quarters. However, while recent estimates for the company have been lowered by analysts, SCS has posted better than expected results. Based on operating earnings yield, the company is about fairly valued when compared to all of the companies in our coverage universe. Share price changes over the past year indicates that SCS will perform very well over the near term.

Financial Data
(US$ in Thousands)

	9 Mos	6 Mos	3 Mos	02/24/2012	02/25/2011	02/26/2010	02/27/2009	02/29/2008
Earnings Per Share	0.63	0.62	0.48	0.43	0.15	(0.10)	(0.09)	0.93
Cash Flow Per Share	1.47	1.07	0.82	0.79	0.55	(0.08)	0.77	1.72
Tang Book Value Per Share	4.07	3.92	3.92	4.06	3.95	3.68	3.90	4.65
Dividends Per Share	0.330	0.300	0.270	0.240	0.160	0.200	0.530	2.350
Dividend Payout %	52.38	48.39	56.25	55.81	106.67	...	...	252.69
Income Statement								
Total Revenue	2,147,300	1,420,100	675,200	2,749,500	2,437,100	2,291,700	3,183,700	3,420,800
EBITDA	157,800	97,400	35,600	160,300	117,900	52,200	81,500	289,300
Depn & Amortn	42,500	27,400	13,600	52,700	61,200	69,400	79,100	84,000
Income Before Taxes	102,000	60,900	17,500	82,000	51,400	(32,300)	(8,800)	211,400
Income Taxes	35,700	22,200	6,500	25,300	31,000	(17,500)	2,900	78,200
Net Income	66,300	42,700	13,200	56,700	20,400	(13,600)	(11,700)	133,200
Average Shares	126,300	125,900	126,900	129,600	132,900	132,900	134,500	143,600
Balance Sheet								
Current Assets	779,100	735,600	680,400	702,100	1,012,300	643,600	751,400	934,700
Total Assets	1,766,700	1,699,100	1,663,400	1,701,000	1,996,500	1,677,200	1,750,000	2,124,400
Current Liabilities	522,400	483,800	449,700	461,900	736,800	433,700	519,600	683,000
Long-Term Obligations	287,200	287,800	288,400	288,900	291,300	293,400	250,800	250,500
Total Liabilities	1,057,800	1,010,800	976,700	992,400	1,278,100	979,600	1,017,200	1,213,500
Stockholders' Equity	708,900	688,300	686,700	708,600	718,400	697,600	732,800	910,900
Shares Outstanding	125,164	125,072	126,000	126,489	132,234	132,963	133,801	138,649
Statistical Record								
Return on Assets %	4.64	4.64	3.42	3.08	1.11	N.M.	N.M.	5.79
Return on Equity %	11.59	11.47	8.91	7.97	2.89	N.M.	N.M.	12.20
EBITDA Margin %	7.35	6.86	5.27	5.83	4.84	2.28	2.56	8.46
Net Margin %	3.09	3.01	1.95	2.06	0.84	N.M.	N.M.	3.89
Asset Turnover	1.62	1.64	1.53	1.49	1.33	1.34	1.65	1.49
Current Ratio	1.49	1.52	1.51	1.52	1.37	1.48	1.45	1.37
Debt to Equity	0.41	0.42	0.42	0.41	0.41	0.42	0.34	0.28
Price Range	11.06-6.26	9.73-5.45	11.78-5.45	11.93-5.45	11.09-6.21	7.51-3.82	14.20-4.03	20.41-13.17
P/E Ratio	17.56-9.94	15.69-8.79	24.54-11.35	27.74-12.67	73.93-41.40	...	...	21.95-14.16
Average Yield %	3.70	3.66	3.19	2.68	1.94	3.41	5.68	13.39

Address: 901 44th Street SE, Grand Rapids, MI 49508	Web Site: www.steelcase.com	Auditors: Deloitte & Touche LLP
Telephone: 616-247-2710	Officers: James P. Hackett - President, Chief Executive Officer Mark A. Baker - Senior Vice President, Global Operations Officer	Transfer Agents: Wells Fargo Bank, N.A., St. Paul, MN

STEPAN CO.

Exchange	Symbol	Price	52Wk Range	Yield	P/E	Div Achiever
NYS	SCL	$63.10 (3/28/2013)	64.32-42.13	1.01	18.08	45 Years

*7 Year Price Score 156.00 *NYSE Composite Index=100 *12 Month Price Score 113.42

Interim Earnings (Per Share)
Qtr.	Mar	Jun	Sep	Dec
2008	0.42	0.47	0.80	1.83
2009	0.71	0.92	0.90	3.31
2010	0.94	0.77	0.86	3.33
2011	0.84	0.94	0.85	3.79
2012	0.98	0.94	0.89	0.68

Interim Dividends (Per Share)
Amt	Decl	Ex	Rec	Pay
0.14Q	07/24/2012	08/29/2012	08/31/2012	09/14/2012
0.16Q	10/24/2012	11/28/2012	11/30/2012	12/14/2012
100%	10/24/2012	12/17/2012	11/30/2012	12/14/2012
0.16Q	02/19/2013	02/26/2013	02/28/2013	03/15/2013

Indicated Div: $0.64

Valuation Analysis
Forecast EPS	$4.36 (04/06/2013)
Market Cap	$1.4 Billion
Book Value	$479.0 Million
Price/Book	2.89
Price/Sales	0.77

Institutional Holding
No of Institutions	165
Shares	13,273,699
% Held	60.29

Business Summary: Specialty Chemicals (MIC: 8.3.2 SIC: 2843 NAIC: 325613)

Stepan is engaged in the production and sale of specialty and intermediate chemicals, which are sold to other manufacturers for use in a variety of end products. Co. has three reportable segments: surfactants, which are used in a variety of consumer and industrial cleaning compounds as well as in agricultural products, lubricating ingredients, biodiesel and other specialized applications; polymers, which is engaged in the sale of polyols and phthalic anhydride used in plastics, building materials and refrigeration systems; and specialty products, which are chemicals used in food, flavoring and pharmaceutical applications.

Recent Developments: For the year ended Dec 31 2012, net income increased 9.8% to US$79.7 million from US$72.6 million in the prior year. Revenues were US$1.80 billion, down 2.1% from US$1.84 billion the year before. Operating income was US$128.7 million versus US$118.5 million in the prior year, an increase of 8.7%. Direct operating expenses declined 4.7% to US$1.51 billion from US$1.59 billion in the comparable period the year before. Indirect operating expenses increased 18.8% to US$162.8 million from US$137.1 million in the equivalent prior-year period.

Prospects: Our evaluation of Stepan Co. as of Apr. 7, 2013 is the result of our systematic analysis on three basic characteristics: earnings strength, relative valuation, and recent stock price movement. The company has enjoyed a very positive trend in earnings per share over the past 5 quarters and while recent estimates for the company have remained steady, SCL has posted better than expected results. Based on operating earnings yield, the company is undervalued when compared to all of the companies in our coverage universe. Share price changes over the past year indicates that SCL will perform very well over the near term.

Financial Data
(US$ in Thousands)	12/31/2012	12/31/2011	12/31/2010	12/31/2009	12/31/2008	12/31/2007	12/31/2006	12/31/2005
Earnings Per Share	3.49	6.42	5.90	5.84	3.52	1.50	0.63	1.35
Cash Flow Per Share	5.11	7.47	6.51	16.86	3.04	5.05	4.25	4.67
Tang Book Value Per Share	21.01	36.12	32.11	26.76	19.07	19.40	16.43	15.07
Dividends Per Share	0.580	0.530	0.490	0.450	0.425	0.412	0.403	0.393
Dividend Payout %	16.62	8.26	8.31	7.71	12.07	27.50	63.89	29.07
Income Statement								
Total Revenue	1,803,737	1,843,092	1,431,122	1,276,382	1,600,130	1,329,901	1,172,583	1,078,377
EBITDA	181,339	164,704	149,834	144,282	104,017	71,037	55,470	62,935
Depn & Amortn	51,294	47,099	40,351	37,171	36,928	37,176	38,384	36,759
Income Before Taxes	120,446	108,510	103,142	100,840	57,575	24,131	8,201	18,375
Income Taxes	36,035	32,292	35,888	34,028	17,615	8,687	900	4,170
Net Income	79,396	71,976	65,427	63,049	37,172	15,118	6,670	13,159
Average Shares	22,730	11,220	11,090	10,796	10,549	10,113	9,284	9,725
Balance Sheet								
Current Assets	523,078	479,742	427,826	349,592	328,423	293,932	268,469	259,248
Total Assets	985,478	901,118	811,431	634,203	611,897	573,185	546,055	516,159
Current Liabilities	247,167	233,226	205,627	163,295	212,135	200,978	180,495	162,904
Long-Term Obligations	149,564	164,967	159,963	93,911	104,725	96,939	107,403	108,945
Total Liabilities	506,493	499,907	461,940	344,918	403,753	367,134	365,269	349,325
Stockholders' Equity	478,985	401,211	349,491	289,285	208,144	206,051	180,786	166,834
Shares Outstanding	21,965	10,246	10,105	9,948	9,632	9,309	9,207	9,040
Statistical Record								
Return on Assets %	8.39	8.41	9.05	10.12	6.26	2.70	1.26	2.61
Return on Equity %	17.99	19.18	20.49	25.35	17.90	7.82	3.84	7.85
EBITDA Margin %	10.05	8.94	10.47	11.30	6.50	5.34	4.73	5.84
Net Margin %	4.40	3.91	4.57	4.94	2.32	1.14	0.57	1.22
Asset Turnover	1.91	2.15	1.98	2.05	2.69	2.38	2.21	2.14
Current Ratio	2.12	2.06	2.08	2.14	1.55	1.46	1.49	1.59
Debt to Equity	0.31	0.41	0.46	0.32	0.50	0.47	0.59	0.65
Price Range	55.54-39.17	41.59-31.55	39.63-23.58	33.73-11.55	30.11-14.32	17.45-12.70	16.50-12.53	13.74-10.40
P/E Ratio	15.91-11.22	6.48-4.91	6.72-4.00	5.78-1.98	8.56-4.07	11.63-8.47	26.19-19.88	10.18-7.70
Average Yield %	1.26	1.46	1.52	1.93	2.02	2.73	2.74	3.26

Address: Edens & Winnetka Road, Northfield, IL 60093 **Telephone:** 847-446-7500	**Web Site:** www.stepan.com **Officers:** F. Quinn Stepan - Chairman F. Quinn Stepan - President, Chief Executive Officer	**Auditors:** Deloitte & Touche LLP **Investor Contact:** 847-446-7500 **Transfer Agents:** ComputerShare Investor Services, Chicago, IL

STERIS CORP.

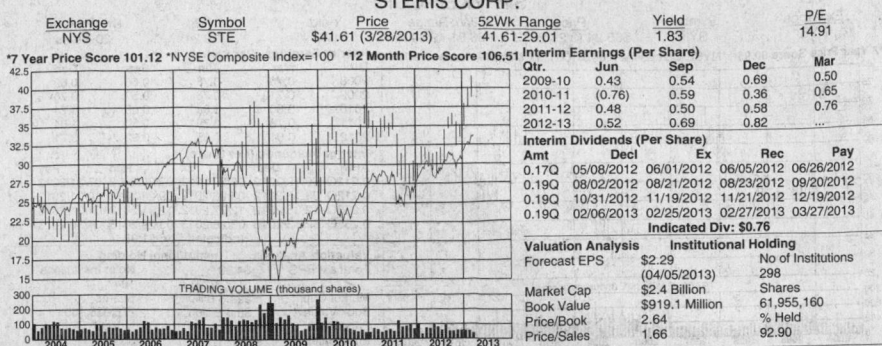

Exchange	Symbol	Price	52Wk Range	Yield	P/E
NYS	STE	$41.61 (3/28/2013)	41.61-29.01	1.83	14.91

*7 Year Price Score 101.12 *NYSE Composite Index=100 *12 Month Price Score 106.51

Interim Earnings (Per Share)

Qtr.	Jun	Sep	Dec	Mar
2009-10	0.43	0.54	0.69	0.50
2010-11	(0.76)	0.59	0.36	0.65
2011-12	0.48	0.50	0.58	0.76
2012-13	0.52	0.69	0.82	...

Interim Dividends (Per Share)

Amt	Decl	Ex	Rec	Pay
0.17Q	05/08/2012	06/01/2012	06/05/2012	06/26/2012
0.19Q	08/02/2012	08/21/2012	08/23/2012	09/20/2012
0.19Q	10/31/2012	11/19/2012	11/21/2012	12/19/2012
0.19Q	02/06/2013	02/25/2013	02/27/2013	03/27/2013

Indicated Div: $0.76

Valuation Analysis

Forecast EPS	$2.29
	(04/05/2013)
Market Cap	$2.4 Billion
Book Value	$919.1 Million
Price/Book	2.64
Price/Sales	1.66

Institutional Holding

No of Institutions	
298	
Shares	
61,955,160	
% Held	
92.90	

TRADING VOLUME (thousand shares)

Business Summary: Medical Instruments & Equipment (MIC: 4.3.1 SIC: 3842 NAIC: 339113)

STERIS is a provider of infection prevention and surgical products and services, focused primarily on the markets of healthcare, pharmaceutical and research. Co. operates in three business segments: Healthcare, which manufactures and sells infrastructure capital equipment, accessory, consumable, consumable, information support and service applications; Life Sciences, which manufactures and sells a range of capital equipment, formulated cleaning chemistries, and service applications; and STERIS Isomedix Services, which sells a range of contract materials processing services using gamma irradiation and ethylene oxide technologies through a network of facilities located in North America.

Recent Developments: For the quarter ended Dec 31 2012, net income increased 42.9% to US$48.1 million from US$33.6 million in the year-earlier quarter. Revenues were US$380.4 million, up 7.1% from US$355.2 million the year before. Operating income was US$67.1 million versus US$53.7 million in the prior-year quarter, an increase of 25.0%. Direct operating expenses rose 4.6% to US$227.3 million from US$217.2 million in the comparable period the year before. Indirect operating expenses increased 2.0% to US$86.0 million from US$84.3 million in the equivalent prior-year period.

Prospects: Our evaluation of Steris Corp, as of Apr. 7, 2013 is the result of our systematic analysis on three basic characteristics: earnings strength, relative valuation, and recent stock price movement. The company has managed to produce a neutral trend in earnings per share over the past 5 quarters and while recent estimates for the company have remained steady, STE has posted better than expected results. Based on operating earnings yield, the company is undervalued when compared to all of the companies in our coverage universe. Share price changes over the past year indicates that STE will perform well over the near term.

Financial Data

(US$ in Thousands)	9 Mos	6 Mos	3 Mos	03/31/2012	03/31/2011	03/31/2010	03/31/2009	03/31/2008
Earnings Per Share	2.79	2.55	2.36	2.31	0.85	2.16	1.86	1.20
Cash Flow Per Share	3.72	3.45	3.43	2.55	1.99	3.82	2.85	2.26
Tang Book Value Per Share	3.58	5.07	8.61	8.38	7.93	7.57	7.06	6.21
Dividends Per Share	0.720	0.700	0.680	0.660	0.560	2.440	0.300	0.230
Dividend Payout %	25.81	27.45	28.81	28.57	65.88	112.96	16.13	19.17
Income Statement								
Total Revenue	1,073,686	693,281	336,960	1,406,810	1,207,448	1,257,733	1,298,525	1,265,090
EBITDA	226,227	140,767	62,639	275,296	132,984	252,989	226,705	178,710
Depn & Amortn	48,508	30,188	14,337	52,980	47,772	19,277	51,260	55,165
Income Before Taxes	167,762	104,491	45,590	211,108	73,819	191,816	166,485	119,799
Income Taxes	49,166	33,992	15,236	74,993	22,554	63,349	55,800	42,693
Net Income	118,596	70,499	30,354	136,115	51,265	128,467	110,685	77,106
Average Shares	58,972	58,792	58,312	58,963	60,148	59,423	59,544	64,124
Balance Sheet								
Current Assets	622,133	605,686	655,505	651,883	705,806	576,457	553,130	513,376
Total Assets	1,765,072	1,632,732	1,403,346	1,405,696	1,426,685	1,238,402	1,216,939	1,239,292
Current Liabilities	227,808	231,708	270,214	278,395	344,746	197,129	202,026	230,359
Long-Term Obligations	520,890	434,340	210,000	210,000	210,000	210,000	210,000	179,280
Total Liabilities	845,952	752,371	571,202	584,295	639,116	484,688	499,203	533,140
Stockholders' Equity	919,120	880,361	832,144	821,401	787,569	753,714	717,736	706,152
Shares Outstanding	58,416	58,423	58,082	57,733	59,122	59,227	58,452	59,263
Statistical Record								
Return on Assets %	10.36	9.87	9.77	9.59	3.85	10.46	9.01	6.28
Return on Equity %	19.17	17.91	16.73	16.87	6.65	17.46	15.55	10.39
EBITDA Margin %	21.07	20.30	18.59	19.57	11.01	20.11	17.46	14.13
Net Margin %	11.05	10.17	9.01	9.68	4.25	10.21	8.52	6.09
Asset Turnover	0.93	0.96	1.01	0.99	0.91	1.02	1.06	1.03
Current Ratio	2.73	2.61	2.43	2.34	2.05	2.92	2.74	2.23
Debt to Equity	0.57	0.49	0.25	0.26	0.27	0.28	0.29	0.25
Price Range	36.63-28.10	36.12-27.38	36.72-27.38	36.72-27.38	37.83-28.35	35.25-22.58	38.38-19.25	31.21-23.20
P/E Ratio	13.13-10.07	14.16-10.74	15.56-11.60	15.90-11.85	44.51-33.35	16.32-10.45	20.63-10.35	26.01-19.33
Average Yield %	2.23	2.26	2.22	2.08	1.67	8.53	1.02	0.83

Address: 5960 Heisley Road, Mentor, OH 44060-1834	**Web Site:** www.steris-ir.com	**Auditors:** Ernst & Young LLP
Telephone: 440-354-2600	**Officers:** John P. Wareham - Chairman Walter M. Rosebrough - President, Chief Executive Officer	**Investor Contact:** 440-392-7245
		Transfer Agents: Computershare, Providence, RI

STRYKER CORP.

Exchange	Symbol	Price	52Wk Range	Yield	P/E	Div Achiever
NYS	SYK	$65.24 (3/28/2013)	66.81-49.84	1.62	19.24	20 Years

*7 Year Price Score 90.95   *NYSE Composite Index=100   *12 Month Price Score 106.09

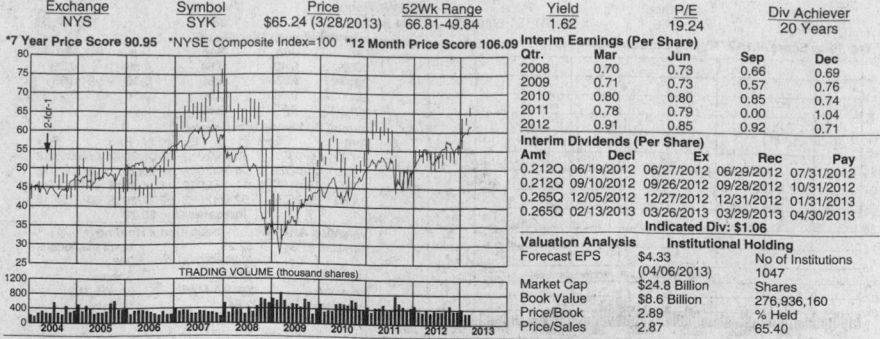

Interim Earnings (Per Share)
Qtr.	Mar	Jun	Sep	Dec
2008	0.70	0.73	0.66	0.69
2009	0.71	0.73	0.57	0.76
2010	0.80	0.80	0.85	0.74
2011	0.78	0.79	0.00	1.04
2012	0.91	0.85	0.92	0.71

Interim Dividends (Per Share)
Amt	Decl	Ex	Rec	Pay
0.212Q	06/19/2012	06/27/2012	06/29/2012	07/31/2012
0.212Q	09/10/2012	09/26/2012	09/28/2012	10/31/2012
0.265Q	12/05/2012	12/27/2012	12/31/2012	01/31/2013
0.265Q	02/13/2013	03/26/2013	03/29/2013	04/30/2013

Indicated Div: $1.06

Valuation Analysis
		Institutional Holding	
Forecast EPS	$4.33	No of Institutions	
	(04/06/2013)	1047	
Market Cap	$24.8 Billion	Shares	
Book Value	$8.6 Billion	276,936,160	
Price/Book	2.89	% Held	
Price/Sales	2.87	65.40	

Business Summary: Medical Instruments & Equipment (MIC: 4.3.1 SIC: 3841 NAIC: 339112)

Stryker is a medical technology company. Co. segregates its operations into three reportable business segments: Reconstructive, which provides products that consist primarily of implants used in hip and knee joint replacements and trauma and extremities surgeries; MedSurg, which provides products that include surgical equipment and surgical navigation systems, endoscopic and communications systems, patient handling and emergency medical equipment, and reprocessed and remanufactured medical devices, as well as other medical device products used in various medical specialties; and Neurotechnology and Spine, which provides products that include both neurosurgical and neurovascular devices.

Recent Developments: For the year ended Dec 31 2012, net income decreased 3.5% to US$1.30 billion from US$1.35 billion in the prior year. Revenues were US$8.66 billion, up 4.2% from US$8.31 billion the year before. Operating income was US$1.74 billion versus US$1.69 billion in the prior year, an increase of 3.3%. Direct operating expenses declined 1.1% to US$2.78 billion from US$2.81 billion in the comparable period the year before. Indirect operating expenses increased 8.5% to US$4.14 billion from US$3.81 billion in the equivalent prior-year period.

Prospects: Our evaluation of Stryker Corp. as of Apr. 7, 2013 is the result of our systematic analysis on three basic characteristics: earnings strength, relative valuation, and recent stock price movement. The company has managed to produce a neutral trend in earnings per share over the past 5 quarters and while recent estimates for the company have remained steady, SYK has posted better than expected results. Based on operating earnings yield, the company is undervalued when compared to all of the companies in our coverage universe. Share price changes over the past year indicates that SYK will perform in line with the market over the near term.

Financial Data
(US$ in Thousands)

	12/31/2012	12/31/2011	12/31/2010	12/31/2009	12/31/2008	12/31/2007	12/31/2006	12/31/2005
Earnings Per Share	3.39	3.45	3.19	2.77	2.78	2.44	1.89	1.64
Cash Flow Per Share	4.34	3.71	3.90	3.68	2.87	2.51	2.13	2.14
Tang Book Value Per Share	...	10.94	13.80	12.58	11.28	10.83	7.98	5.75
Dividends Per Share	0.902	0.752	0.630	0.250	0.400	0.330	0.220	0.110
Dividend Payout %	26.62	21.81	19.75	9.03	14.39	13.52	11.64	6.71
Income Statement								
Total Revenue	8,657,000	8,307,000	7,320,000	6,723,100	6,718,200	6,000,500	5,405,600	4,871,500
EBITDA	1,982,000	1,968,000	1,952,400	1,824,600	1,775,600	1,548,600	1,270,900	1,158,200
Depn & Amortn	277,000	282,000	222,800	200,700	195,400	178,500	167,100	154,900
Income Before Taxes	1,705,000	1,686,000	1,729,600	1,623,900	1,580,200	1,370,100	1,103,800	1,003,300
Income Taxes	407,000	341,000	456,200	516,500	432,400	383,400	326,100	328,100
Net Income	1,298,000	1,345,000	1,273,400	1,107,400	1,147,800	1,017,400	777,700	675,200
Average Shares	383,000	389,500	399,500	399,400	413,600	417,200	411,800	411,600
Balance Sheet								
Current Assets	8,148,000	7,211,000	7,631,400	5,851,200	4,979,300	4,904,900	3,534,300	2,870,100
Total Assets	13,206,000	12,405,000	10,895,100	9,071,300	7,603,300	7,354,000	5,873,800	4,944,100
Current Liabilities	1,876,000	1,828,000	1,605,000	1,441,000	1,462,100	1,333,000	1,351,500	1,248,800
Long-Term Obligations	1,746,000	1,751,000	996,500	...	...	...	...	184,200
Total Liabilities	4,609,000	4,722,000	3,721,500	2,476,200	2,196,600	1,975,500	1,682,800	1,692,300
Stockholders' Equity	8,597,000	7,683,000	7,173,600	6,595,100	5,406,700	5,378,500	4,191,000	3,251,800
Shares Outstanding	...	381,000	391,100	397,900	396,400	411,000	407,900	405,200
Statistical Record								
Return on Assets %	10.11	11.55	12.76	13.28	15.31	15.38	14.38	14.96
Return on Equity %	15.90	18.11	18.50	18.45	21.23	21.26	20.90	22.49
EBITDA Margin %	22.89	23.69	26.67	27.14	26.43	25.81	23.51	23.78
Net Margin %	14.99	16.19	17.40	16.47	17.08	16.96	14.39	13.86
Asset Turnover	0.67	0.71	0.73	0.81	0.90	0.91	1.00	1.08
Current Ratio	4.34	3.94	4.75	4.06	3.41	3.68	2.62	2.30
Debt to Equity	0.20	0.23	0.14	...	...	...	...	0.06
Price Range	56.57-49.84	65.07-43.80	58.89-42.88	52.20-31.19	74.72-36.48	76.48-55.12	55.45-40.88	56.10-39.80
P/E Ratio	16.69-14.70	18.86-12.70	18.46-13.44	18.84-11.26	26.88-13.12	31.34-22.59	29.34-21.63	34.21-24.27
Average Yield %	1.68	1.37	1.21	0.60	0.66	0.49	0.46	0.23

Address: 2825 Airview Boulevard, Kalamazoo, MI 49002
Telephone: 269-385-2600
Fax: 269-385-1062

Web Site: www.stryker.com
Officers: John W. Brown - Chairman Kevin Lobo - President, Chief Executive Officer, Division Officer

Auditors: Ernst & Young LLP
Investor Contact: 269-385-2600
Transfer Agents: American Stock Transfer & Trust Company, LLC, New York, NY

SUBURBAN PROPANE PARTNERS L.P.

Exchange	Symbol	Price	52Wk Range	Yield	P/E
NYS	SPH	$44.50 (3/28/2013)	45.35-34.80	7.71	101.14

*7 Year Price Score 84.64   *NYSE Composite Index=100   *12 Month Price Score 95.61

Interim Earnings (Per Share)

Qtr.	Dec	Mar	Jun	Sep
2009-10	1.36	2.78	(0.19)	(0.70)
2010-11	1.21	2.81	(0.19)	(0.61)
2011-12	0.65	1.38	(0.26)	(1.72)
2012-13	1.04	...	...	...

Interim Dividends (Per Share)

Amt	Decl	Ex	Rec	Pay
0.853Q	04/19/2012	04/27/2012	05/01/2012	05/08/2012
0.853Q	07/17/2012	07/27/2012	07/31/2012	08/07/2012
0.853Q	10/24/2012	11/02/2012	11/06/2012	11/13/2012
0.875Q	01/23/2013	02/01/2013	02/05/2013	02/12/2013

Indicated Div: $3.43

Valuation Analysis

		Institutional Holding	
Forecast EPS	$2.20 (04/05/2013)	No of Institutions	218
Market Cap	$2.5 Billion	Shares	17,350,544
Book Value	N/A	% Held	45.79
Price/Book	N/A		
Price/Sales	2.03		

TRADING VOLUME (thousand shares)

Business Summary: Gas Utilities (MIC: 3.3.1 SIC: 5999 NAIC: 453998)

Suburban Propane Partners is engaged in the distribution of propane, fuel oil and refined fuels, as well as the marketing of natural gas and electricity in deregulated markets. In support of its primary marketing and distribution operations, Co. installs and services a range of home comfort equipment, particularly in the areas of heating and ventilation. At Sep 29 2012, Co. served more than 1.2 million residential, commercial, industrial and agricultural customers through about 750 locations in 41 states. Co.'s operations are concentrated in the east and west coast regions of the U.S. Co. has three reportable segments: Propane, Fuel Oil and Refined Fuels, and Natural Gas and Electricity.

Recent Developments: For the quarter ended Dec 29 2012, net income increased 157.4% to US$59.8 million from US$23.2 million in the year-earlier quarter. Revenues were US$490.7 million, up 63.6% from US$299.9 million the year before. Operating income was US$84.5 million versus US$30.3 million in the prior-year quarter, an increase of 178.9%. Direct operating expenses rose 33.5% to US$245.1 million from US$183.6 million in the comparable period the year before. Indirect operating expenses increased 87.3% to US$161.1 million from US$86.0 million in the equivalent prior-year period.

Prospects: Our evaluation of Suburban Propane Partners L.P. as of Apr. 7, 2013 is the result of our systematic analysis on three basic characteristics: earnings strength, relative valuation, and recent stock price movement. The company has enjoyed a very positive trend in earnings per share over the past 5 quarters. However, while recent estimates for the company have been lowered by analysts, SPH has posted results that fell short of analysts expectations. Based on operating earnings yield, the company is about fairly valued when compared to all of the companies in our coverage universe. Share price changes over the past year indicates that SPH will perform very poorly over the near term.

Financial Data
(US$ in Thousands)

	3 Mos	09/29/2012	09/24/2011	09/25/2010	09/26/2009	09/27/2008	09/29/2007	09/30/2006
Earnings Per Share	0.44	0.05	3.22	3.24	4.96	4.70	3.89	2.83
Cash Flow Per Share	3.46	2.81	3.75	4.42	7.46	3.69	4.50	5.53
Dividends Per Share	3.410	3.410	3.408	3.350	3.255	3.087	2.763	2.475
Dividend Payout %	775.00	6,820.00	105.82	103.40	65.63	65.69	71.02	87.46
Income Statement								
Total Revenue	490,703	1,063,458	1,190,552	1,136,694	1,143,154	1,574,163	1,439,563	1,661,640
EBITDA	112,835	75,889	175,596	172,306	234,114	178,522	193,838	165,335
Depn & Amortn	28,359	35,237	32,368	28,411	28,123	28,394	29,242	33,151
Income Before Taxes	59,920	2,019	115,850	116,498	167,724	113,076	129,000	91,504
Income Taxes	132	137	884	1,182	2,486	1,903	5,653	764
Net Income	59,788	1,882	114,966	115,316	165,238	154,880	127,287	90,740
Average Shares	57,347	38,990	35,723	35,613	33,315	32,950	32,730	30,453
Balance Sheet								
Current Assets	406,523	338,280	297,822	296,427	307,556	359,551	282,211	235,351
Total Assets	2,928,931	2,884,448	956,459	970,260	977,514	1,035,713	975,218	953,886
Current Liabilities	279,739	253,715	151,514	164,514	180,059	223,615	196,410	192,616
Long-Term Obligations	1,420,096	1,422,078	348,169	347,953	349,415	531,772	548,538	548,304
Total Liabilities	1,822,859	1,792,705	598,241	605,423	617,797	815,637	808,941	853,185
Shares Outstanding	57,103	57,013	35,429	35,318	35,227	32,725	32,674	30,314
Statistical Record								
Return on Assets %	1.98	0.10	11.97	11.87	16.46	15.45	13.23	9.30
EBITDA Margin %	22.99	7.14	14.75	15.16	20.48	11.34	13.47	9.95
Net Margin %	12.18	0.18	9.66	10.14	14.45	9.84	8.84	5.46
Asset Turnover	0.65	0.54	1.24	1.17	1.14	1.57	1.50	1.70
Current Ratio	1.45	1.33	1.97	1.80	1.71	1.61	1.44	1.22
Price Range	47.95-34.80	48.65-34.80	58.75-41.04	54.10-41.24	45.88-22.64	48.15-33.99	49.16-33.61	35.43-24.04
P/E Ratio	108.98-79.09	973.00-696.00	18.25-12.75	16.70-12.73	9.25-4.56	10.24-7.23	12.64-8.64	12.52-8.49
Average Yield %	8.24	7.89	6.39	7.14	8.71	7.67	6.48	8.40

Address: 240 Route 10 West, Whippany, NJ 07981 Telephone: 973-887-5300	Web Site: www.suburbanpropane.com Officers: Harold R. Logan - Chairman Michael J. Dunn - President, Chief Executive Officer, Holding/Parent Company Officer	Auditors: PricewaterhouseCoopers LLP Investor Contact: 973-503-9252 Transfer Agents: Computershare Trust Company, N.A, Providence, RI

SUNOCO LOGISTICS PARTNERS L.P.

Exchange	Symbol	Price	52Wk Range	Yield	P/E	Div Achiever
NYS	SXL	$65.40 (3/28/2013)	67.75-32.63	3.00	59.45	10 Years

*7 Year Price Score 167.95 *NYSE Composite Index=100 *12 Month Price Score 121.71

Interim Earnings (Per Share)

Qtr.	Mar	Jun	Sep	Dec
2011	0.36	0.80	0.78	0.59
2012	0.77	1.28	1.09	(2.04)
2012	...	...	...	(2.04)

Interim Dividends (Per Share)

Amt	Decl	Ex	Rec	Pay
0.42Q	01/26/2012	02/06/2012	02/08/2012	02/14/2012
0.427Q	04/24/2012	05/07/2012	05/09/2012	05/15/2012
0.47Q	07/24/2012	08/06/2012	08/08/2012	08/14/2012
0.545Q	01/24/2013	02/06/2013	02/08/2013	02/14/2013

Indicated Div: $1.96

Valuation Analysis

Forecast EPS	$3.41 (04/05/2013)
Market Cap	$6.8 Billion
Book Value	N/A
Price/Book	N/A
Price/Sales	2.12

Institutional Holding

No of Institutions	226
Shares	48,506,364
% Held	43.55

Business Summary: Equipment & Services (MIC: 9.1.3 SIC: 4612 NAIC: 486110)

Sunoco Logistics Partners is principally engaged in the transport, terminalling and storage of crude oil and refined products. Co. also owns acquisition and marketing assets which are used to facilitate the purchase and sale of crude oil and refined products. Co.'s reporting segments are: Refined Products Pipelines, which serve Sunoco and other third parties; Terminal Facilities, which consist of 42 active refined product terminals; Crude Oil Pipelines, which transport crude oil principally in Oklahoma and Texas; and Crude Oil Acquisition and Marketing, which gathers, purchases, markets and sells crude oil using crude oil transport trucks and crude oil truck unloading facilities.

Recent Developments: For the year ended Dec 31 2012, net income decreased 55.9% to US$142.0 million from US$322.0 million in the prior year. Revenues were US$3.19 billion, down 70.7% from US$10.92 billion the year before. Operating income was US$164.0 million versus US$436.0 million in the prior year, a decrease of 62.4%. Direct operating expenses declined 71.4% to US$2.93 billion from US$10.26 billion in the comparable period the year before. Indirect operating expenses decreased 55.5% to US$97.0 million from US$218.0 million in the equivalent prior-year period.

Prospects: Notwithstanding lower lease acquisition margins and higher interest expense from financing acquisitions completed in 2006, Co.'s bottom line results are benefiting from an increase in revenues at its Nederland Terminal, operating results from the acquisitions completed in 2006 in the Western Pipeline System, higher revenues from its refined product terminals due to ethanol blending and product additives and increased other income related to the Aug 2006 acquisition of a 55.3% equity interest in the Mid-Valley Pipeline Company. Separately, on June 4 2007, Co. completely acquired a 50.0% interest in a refined products terminal located in Syracuse, NY from an affiliate of Exxon Mobil.

Financial Data
(US$ in Thousands)

	12/31/2012	10/04/2012	12/31/2011	12/31/2010	12/31/2009	12/31/2008	12/31/2007	12/31/2006
Earnings Per Share	1.10	3.14	2.54	3.11	2.16	1.66	1.12	0.95
Cash Flow Per Share	2.69	5.21	4.24	3.59	1.94	2.65	2.42	1.71
Dividends Per Share	1.835	1.731	1.610	1.505	1.370	1.222	1.108	1.008
Dividend Payout %	166.82	55.12	63.39	48.34	63.43	73.59	98.67	106.14
Income Statement								
Total Revenue	3,194,000	9,950,000	10,918,000	7,838,000	5,429,677	10,136,618	7,405,836	5,854,550
EBITDA	221,000	556,000	524,000	495,000	344,622	286,279	194,162	154,843
Depn & Amortn	57,000	78,000	88,000	66,000	49,578	40,687	38,007	36,649
Income Before Taxes	150,000	413,000	347,000	356,000	250,362	214,480	120,875	90,341
Income Taxes	8,000	24,000	25,000	8,000	...	...	...	...
Net Income	139,000	381,000	313,000	346,000	250,362	214,480	120,875	90,341
Average Shares	104,100	103,900	101,800	95,700	91,553	86,509	86,187	81,714
Balance Sheet								
Current Assets	2,390,000	...	2,506,000	1,799,000	1,425,518	825,237	1,303,678	962,584
Total Assets	10,361,000	...	5,477,000	4,188,000	3,098,606	2,308,249	2,504,642	2,082,077
Current Liabilities	2,131,000	...	2,535,000	1,711,000	1,333,336	859,060	1,368,838	980,207
Long-Term Obligations	1,732,000	...	1,448,000	1,229,000	868,424	747,631	515,104	491,910
Total Liabilities	4,289,000	...	4,381,000	3,223,000	2,236,992	1,638,349	1,913,597	1,499,166
Shares Outstanding	103,773	...	103,325	99,300	92,943	85,971	85,758	85,608
Statistical Record								
Return on Assets %	1.75	...	6.48	9.50	9.26	8.89	5.27	4.80
EBITDA Margin %	6.92	5.59	4.80	6.32	6.35	2.82	2.62	2.64
Net Margin %	4.35	3.83	2.87	4.41	4.61	2.12	1.63	1.54
Asset Turnover	0.40	...	2.26	2.15	2.01	4.20	3.23	3.11
Current Ratio	1.12	...	0.99	1.05	1.07	0.96	0.95	0.98
Price Range	51.90-45.06	50.04-32.63	39.76-25.24	27.86-20.67	22.96-15.05	17.98-9.70	20.99-16.23	16.96-13.20
P/E Ratio	47.18-40.96	15.94-10.39	15.65-9.94	8.96-6.65	10.63-6.97	10.83-5.85	18.74-14.49	17.85-13.89
Average Yield %	3.71	4.39	5.40	6.17	7.40	7.72	5.98	6.93

Address: 1818 Market Street, Suite 1500, Philadelphia, PA 19103	Web Site: www.sunocologistics.com	Auditors: Grant Thornton LLP
Telephone: 866-248-4344	Officers: Marshall S. McCrea - Chairman Michael J. Hennigan - President, Chief Executive Officer, Chief Operating Officer	Transfer Agents: American Stock Transfer & Trust Compan, New York, NY

SUNTRUST BANKS, INC.

Exchange	Symbol	Price	52Wk Range	Yield	P/E
NYS	STI	$28.81 (3/28/2013)	30.31-21.10	0.69	8.03

*7 Year Price Score 56.76   *NYSE Composite Index=100   *12 Month Price Score 100.20

Interim Earnings (Per Share)

Qtr.	Mar	Jun	Sep	Dec
2008	0.81	1.53	0.88	(1.09)
2009	(2.49)	(0.41)	(0.76)	(0.57)
2010	(0.46)	(0.11)	0.17	0.23
2011	0.08	0.33	0.39	0.13
2012	0.46	0.50	1.98	0.65

Interim Dividends (Per Share)

Amt	Decl	Ex	Rec	Pay
0.05Q	04/24/2012	05/30/2012	06/01/2012	06/15/2012
0.05Q	08/14/2012	08/29/2012	08/31/2012	09/14/2012
0.05Q	11/13/2012	11/28/2012	11/30/2012	12/14/2012
0.05Q	02/12/2013	02/27/2013	03/01/2013	03/15/2013

Indicated Div: $0.20 (Div. Reinv. Plan)

Valuation Analysis / **Institutional Holding**

Forecast EPS	$2.70	No of Institutions
	(04/06/2013)	717
Market Cap	$15.5 Billion	Shares
Book Value	$21.0 Billion	483,450,464
Price/Book	0.74	% Held
Price/Sales	1.38	79.30

Business Summary: Banking (MIC: 5.1.1 SIC: 6022 NAIC: 522110)

SunTrust Banks is a financial services holding company. Through its subsidiary, SunTrust Bank, Co. provides a line of financial services for consumers and businesses including deposit, credit, and trust and investment services. Additional subsidiaries provide mortgage banking, asset management, securities brokerage, and capital market services. Co. also provides a range of banking channels, including the internet, automated teller machines, and telebanking. Co. operates primarily in Florida, Georgia, Maryland, North Carolina, South Carolina, Tennessee, Virginia, and the District of Columbia. At Dec 31 2012, Co. had total assets of $173.44 billion and total deposits of $132.32 billion.

Recent Developments: For the year ended Dec 31 2012, net income increased 200.6% to US$1.98 billion from US$660.0 million in the prior year. Net interest income increased 0.7% to US$5.10 billion from US$5.07 billion in the prior year. Provision for loan losses was US$1.40 billion versus US$1.51 billion in the prior year, a decrease of 7.8%. Non-interest income rose 57.1% to US$5.37 billion from US$3.42 billion, while non-interest expense advanced 1.4% to US$6.32 billion.

Prospects: Our evaluation of SunTrust Banks Inc. as of Apr. 7, 2013 is the result of our systematic analysis on three basic characteristics: earnings strength, relative valuation, and recent stock price movement. The company has managed to produce a neutral trend in earnings per share over the past 5 quarters. However, while recent estimates for the company have been lowered by analysts, STI has posted better than expected results. Based on operating earnings yield, the company is undervalued when compared to all of the companies in our coverage universe. Share price changes over the past year indicates that STI will perform well over the near term.

Financial Data

(US$ in Thousands)	12/31/2012	12/31/2011	12/31/2010	12/31/2009	12/31/2008	12/31/2007	12/31/2006	12/31/2005
Earnings Per Share	3.59	0.94	(0.18)	(3.98)	2.13	4.55	2.82	5.47
Cash Flow Per Share	3.75	8.83	8.52	6.99	10.57	10.63	10.82	(13.14)
Tang Book Value Per Share	24.00	23.15	20.57	19.20	25.63	26.60	26.04	24.67
Dividends Per Share	0.200	0.120	0.040	0.220	2.850	2.920	2.440	2.200
Dividend Payout %	5.57	12.77	...	...	133.80	64.18	86.52	40.22
Income Statement								
Interest Income	5,867,000	6,181,000	6,343,000	6,709,747	8,327,382	10,035,920	9,792,020	7,731,309
Interest Expense	765,000	1,116,000	1,489,000	2,244,057	3,707,726	5,316,376	5,131,555	3,152,343
Net Interest Income	5,102,000	5,065,000	4,854,000	4,465,690	4,619,656	4,719,544	4,660,465	4,578,966
Provision for Losses	1,395,000	1,513,000	2,651,000	4,063,914	2,474,215	664,922	262,536	176,886
Non-Interest Income	5,373,000	3,421,000	3,729,000	3,710,278	4,473,463	3,428,684	3,468,372	3,155,044
Non-Interest Expense	6,307,000	6,237,000	5,841,000	6,523,052	5,878,678	5,223,977	4,868,195	4,690,729
Income Before Taxes	2,757,000	739,000	21,000	(2,450,354)	728,503	2,249,529	2,986,441	2,866,395
Income Taxes	773,000	79,000	(185,000)	(898,783)	(67,271)	615,514	868,970	879,156
Net Income	1,958,000	647,000	189,000	(1,563,683)	795,774	1,634,015	2,117,471	1,987,239
Average Shares	538,061	527,618	499,000	435,328	350,183	352,688	362,802	363,454
Balance Sheet								
Net Loans & Leases	122,695,000	122,391,000	116,502,000	115,224,667	128,679,575	129,888,185	132,199,934	127,222,380
Total Assets	173,442,000	176,859,000	172,874,000	174,164,735	189,137,961	179,573,933	182,161,609	179,712,841
Total Deposits	132,316,000	127,922,000	123,044,000	121,863,566	113,328,384	117,842,650	124,021,629	122,053,178
Total Liabilities	152,457,000	156,793,000	149,744,000	151,633,880	166,749,852	161,521,415	164,348,003	162,825,446
Stockholders' Equity	20,985,000	20,066,000	23,130,000	22,530,855	22,388,109	18,052,518	17,813,606	16,887,395
Shares Outstanding	538,959	536,967	500,436	499,156	354,515	348,411	354,902	361,984
Statistical Record								
Return on Assets %	1.11	0.37	0.11	N.M.	0.43	0.90	1.17	1.17
Return on Equity %	9.51	3.00	0.83	N.M.	3.92	9.11	12.20	12.09
Net Interest Margin %	86.96	81.94	76.53	66.56	55.48	47.03	47.59	59.23
Efficiency Ratio %	56.11	64.96	57.99	62.60	45.92	38.80	36.71	43.09
Loans to Deposits	0.93	0.96	0.95	0.95	1.14	1.10	1.07	1.04
Price Range	30.31-18.52	32.59-15.80	31.85-20.29	29.92-6.70	68.85-22.45	90.61-61.09	85.45-70.08	75.73-65.80
P/E Ratio	8.44-5.16	34.67-16.81	...	...	32.32-10.54	19.91-13.43	30.30-24.85	13.84-12.03
Average Yield %	0.81	0.50	0.16	1.24	6.07	3.65	3.18	3.05

Address: 303 Peachtree Street, N.E., Atlanta, GA 30308 Telephone: 404-588-7711	Web Site: www.suntrust.com Officers: William H. Rogers - Chairman, President, Chief Executive Officer Frances L. Breeden - Executive Vice President, Director	Auditors: Ernst & Young LLP Transfer Agents: Computershare, Providence, RI

705

SUPERIOR ENERGY SERVICES, INC.

Exchange	Symbol	Price	52Wk Range	Yield	P/E
NYS	SPN	$25.97 (3/28/2013)	27.29-17.89	N/A	10.73

*7 Year Price Score 68.35   *NYSE Composite Index=100   *12 Month Price Score 106.21

Interim Earnings (Per Share)

Qtr.	Mar	Jun	Sep	Dec
2008	1.24	0.89	1.22	1.09
2009	0.72	(0.88)	0.31	(1.47)
2010	0.27	0.30	0.42	0.04
2011	0.19	0.59	0.73	0.24
2012	0.42	0.89	0.59	0.47

Interim Dividends (Per Share)

No Dividends Paid

Valuation Analysis

		Institutional Holding	
Forecast EPS	$2.15 (04/05/2013)	No of Institutions	418
Market Cap	$4.1 Billion	Shares	
Book Value	$4.2 Billion		151,090,992
Price/Book	0.97	% Held	
Price/Sales	0.90		89.40

TRADING VOLUME (thousand shares)

Business Summary: Equipment & Services (MIC: 9.1.3 SIC: 1389 NAIC: 213112)

Superior Energy Services is a provider of oilfield services and equipment. Co. serves energy industry customers who focus on developing and producing oil and gas worldwide. Co. reports its operating results in four segments: Drilling Products and Services; Onshore Completion and Workover Services; Production Services; and Subsea and Technical Solutions. Co.'s products and services include: downhole drilling tools, surface rentals, pressure pumping, fluid handling, workover services, intervention services, pressure-control tools, pressure control services, completion tools and services, subsea construction, end-of-life services, and marine technical services.

Recent Developments: For the year ended Dec 31 2012, income from continuing operations increased 140.4% to US$383.1 million from US$159.4 million a year earlier. Net income increased 156.7% to US$365.9 million from US$142.6 million in the prior year. Revenues were US$4.57 billion, up 132.6% from US$1.96 billion the year before. Operating income was US$706.5 million versus US$296.4 million in the prior year, an increase of 138.4%. Direct operating expenses rose 157.0% to US$2.69 billion from US$1.05 billion in the comparable period the year before. Indirect operating expenses increased 88.6% to US$1.17 billion from US$621.5 million in the equivalent prior-year period.

Prospects: Our evaluation of Superior Energy Services Inc. as of Apr. 7, 2013 is the result of our systematic analysis on three basic characteristics: earnings strength, relative valuation, and recent stock price movement. The company has suffered a very negative trend in earnings per share over the past 5 quarters. However, while recent estimates for the company have been lowered by analysts, SPN has posted better than expected results. Based on earnings yield, the company is undervalued when compared to all of the companies in our coverage universe. Share price changes over the past year indicates that SPN will perform poorly over the near term.

Financial Data

(US$ in Thousands)	12/31/2012	12/31/2011	12/31/2010	12/31/2009	12/31/2008	12/31/2007	12/31/2006	12/31/2005
Earnings Per Share	2.42	1.76	1.03	(1.31)	4.45	3.41	2.32	0.85
Cash Flow Per Share	6.91	6.19	5.79	3.53	5.02	6.55	3.51	2.02
Tang Book Value Per Share	10.76	10.85	8.77	8.85	9.51	6.15	3.30	3.83
Income Statement								
Total Revenue	4,568,068	2,070,166	1,681,616	1,449,300	1,881,124	1,572,467	1,093,821	735,334
EBITDA	1,185,081	497,523	376,791	115,501	725,315	587,138	383,593	192,953
Depn & Amortn	480,000	224,600	207,700	202,800	163,600	121,300	79,300	68,600
Income Before Taxes	590,569	205,306	116,857	(137,279)	534,271	435,432	285,955	104,692
Income Taxes	225,020	79,146	43,285	(57,556)	196,922	151,372	103,605	38,172
Net Income	365,935	142,554	81,817	(102,323)	361,722	281,120	188,241	67,859
Average Shares	151,106	81,095	79,734	78,171	81,213	82,389	81,289	79,735
Balance Sheet								
Current Assets	1,460,357	883,222	764,052	863,563	646,849	471,005	419,787	304,302
Total Assets	7,802,886	4,048,145	2,907,533	2,516,665	2,491,633	2,257,249	1,874,478	1,097,250
Current Liabilities	772,065	393,533	505,887	228,379	298,244	292,431	243,095	149,184
Long-Term Obligations	1,814,500	1,685,087	681,635	848,665	710,830	711,151	711,505	216,596
Total Liabilities	3,571,807	2,594,546	1,626,982	1,338,620	1,272,100	1,276,570	1,163,790	572,876
Stockholders' Equity	4,231,079	1,453,599	1,280,551	1,178,045	1,219,533	980,679	710,688	524,374
Shares Outstanding	157,933	80,425	78,951	78,559	78,028	80,671	80,617	79,499
Statistical Record								
Return on Assets %	6.16	4.10	3.02	N.M.	15.19	13.61	12.67	6.46
Return on Equity %	12.84	10.43	6.66	N.M.	32.79	33.24	30.48	14.16
EBITDA Margin %	25.94	24.03	22.41	7.97	38.56	37.34	35.07	26.24
Net Margin %	8.01	6.89	4.87	N.M.	19.23	17.88	17.21	9.23
Asset Turnover	0.77	0.60	0.62	0.58	0.79	0.76	0.74	0.70
Current Ratio	1.89	2.24	1.51	3.78	2.17	1.61	1.73	2.04
Debt to Equity	0.43	1.16	0.53	0.72	0.58	0.73	1.00	0.41
Price Range	30.87-17.89	41.89-23.52	35.19-18.54	25.78-11.52	57.25-11.64	41.37-28.51	35.98-21.95	23.62-14.26
P/E Ratio	12.76-7.39	23.80-13.36	34.17-18.00	...	12.87-2.62	12.13-8.36	15.51-9.46	27.79-16.78

Address: 11000 Equity Drive, Suite 300, Houston, TX 77041
Telephone: 281-999-0047

Web Site: www.superiorenergy.com
Officers: Terence E. Hall - Executive Chairman David D. Dunlap - President, Chief Executive Officer

Auditors: KPMG LLP
Investor Contact: 281-999-0047
Transfer Agents: American Stock Transfer & Trust Company, New York, NY

SUPERVALU INC.

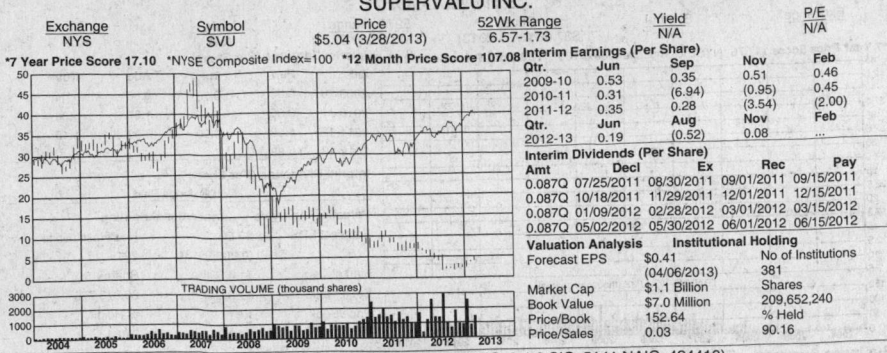

Exchange	Symbol	Price	52Wk Range	Yield	P/E
NYS	SVU	$5.04 (3/28/2013)	6.57-1.73	N/A	N/A

*7 Year Price Score 17.10   *NYSE Composite Index=100   *12 Month Price Score 107.08

Interim Earnings (Per Share)

Qtr.	Jun	Sep	Nov	Feb
2009-10	0.53	0.35	0.51	0.46
2010-11	0.31	(6.94)	(0.95)	0.45
2011-12	0.35	0.28	(3.54)	(2.00)
Qtr.	Jun	Aug	Nov	Feb
2012-13	0.19	(0.52)	0.08	...

Interim Dividends (Per Share)

Amt	Decl	Ex	Rec	Pay
0.087Q	07/25/2011	08/30/2011	09/01/2011	09/15/2011
0.087Q	10/18/2011	11/29/2011	12/01/2011	12/15/2011
0.087Q	01/09/2012	02/28/2012	03/01/2012	03/15/2012
0.087Q	05/02/2012	05/30/2012	06/01/2012	06/15/2012

Valuation Analysis   **Institutional Holding**

Forecast EPS	$0.41	No of Institutions
	(04/06/2013)	381
Market Cap	$1.1 Billion	Shares
Book Value	$7.0 Million	209,652,240
Price/Book	152.64	% Held
Price/Sales	0.03	90.16

Business Summary: Retail - Food & Beverage, Drug & Tobacco (MIC: 2.1.2 SIC: 5141 NAIC: 424410)

SUPERVALU operates in the grocery channel. Co. conducts its retail operations under the Acme, Albertsons, Cub Foods, Farm Fresh, Hornbacher's, Jewel-Osco, Lucky, Save-A-Lot, Shaw's, Shop 'n Save, Shoppers Food & Pharmacy and Star Market banners as well as in-store pharmacies under the Osco and Sav-on banners. In addition, Co. provides certain facilitative services between its independent retailers and vendors related to products that are delivered directly by suppliers to retail stores under programs developed by Co. These services include sourcing, invoicing and payment services. Co.'s business is classified into two reportable segments: Retail Food and Independent Business.

Recent Developments: For the quarter ended Dec 1 2012, net income amounted to US$16.0 million versus a net loss of US$750.0 million in the year-earlier quarter. Revenues were US$7.91 billion, down 5.0% from US$8.33 billion the year before. Operating income was US$157.0 million versus a loss of US$708.0 million in the prior-year period. Direct operating expenses declined 4.4% to US$6.23 billion from US$6.52 billion in the comparable period the year before. Indirect operating expenses decreased 39.5% to US$1.52 billion from US$2.52 billion in the equivalent prior-year period.

Prospects: Our evaluation of SUPERVALU Inc. as of Apr. 7, 2013 is the result of our systematic analysis on three basic characteristics: earnings strength, relative valuation, and recent stock price movement. The company has managed to produce a neutral trend in earnings per share over the past 5 quarters. However, while recent estimates for the company have been mixed, SVU has posted results that fell short of analysts expectations. Based on operating earnings yield, the company is undervalued when compared to all of the companies in our coverage universe. Share price changes over the past year indicates that SVU will perform very poorly over the near term.

Financial Data

(US$ in Thousands)	9 Mos	6 Mos	3 Mos	02/25/2012	02/26/2011	02/27/2010	02/28/2009	02/23/2008
Earnings Per Share	(2.25)	(5.87)	(5.07)	(4.91)	(7.13)	1.85	(13.51)	2.76
Cash Flow Per Share	4.22	4.20	4.90	4.99	5.50	6.97	7.15	8.23
Dividends Per Share	0.175	0.263	0.350	0.263	0.350	0.610	0.688	0.670
Dividend Payout %	...	...	...	...	...	32.97	...	24.28
Income Statement								
Total Revenue	26,542,000	18,629,000	10,590,000	36,100,000	37,534,000	40,597,000	44,564,000	44,048,000
EBITDA	1,004,000	646,000	485,000	271,000	(151,000)	2,053,000	(1,212,000)	2,595,000
Depn & Amortn	679,000	478,000	276,000	790,000	825,000	852,000	945,000	911,000
Income Before Taxes	(97,000)	(128,000)	54,000	(1,028,000)	(1,523,000)	632,000	(2,779,000)	977,000
Income Taxes	(43,000)	(58,000)	13,000	12,000	(13,000)	239,000	(2,855,000)	384,000
Net Income	(54,000)	(70,000)	41,000	(1,040,000)	(1,510,000)	393,000	(2,855,000)	593,000
Average Shares	214,000	212,000	214,000	212,000	212,000	213,000	211,000	215,000
Balance Sheet								
Current Assets	3,465,000	3,312,000	3,256,000	3,225,000	3,420,000	3,711,000	4,105,000	4,147,000
Total Assets	11,857,000	11,854,000	11,935,000	12,053,000	13,758,000	16,436,000	17,604,000	21,062,000
Current Liabilities	3,274,000	3,392,000	3,372,000	3,590,000	3,786,000	4,167,000	4,472,000	4,607,000
Long-Term Obligations	6,180,000	6,064,000	6,030,000	5,868,000	6,348,000	7,022,000	7,968,000	8,502,000
Total Liabilities	11,850,000	11,881,000	11,871,000	12,032,000	12,418,000	13,549,000	15,023,000	15,109,000
Stockholders' Equity	7,000	(27,000)	64,000	21,000	1,340,000	2,887,000	2,581,000	5,953,000
Shares Outstanding	212,000	214,000	214,000	212,000	212,000	212,000	212,000	212,000
Statistical Record								
Return on Assets %	N.M.	N.M.	N.M.	N.M.	N.M.	2.32	N.M.	2.78
Return on Equity %	N.M.	N.M.	N.M.	N.M.	N.M.	14.41	N.M.	10.56
EBITDA Margin %	3.78	3.47	4.58	0.75	N.M.	5.06	N.M.	5.89
Net Margin %	N.M.	N.M.	0.39	N.M.	N.M.	0.97	N.M.	1.35
Asset Turnover	2.82	2.77	2.78	2.80	2.49	2.39	2.27	2.07
Current Ratio	1.06	0.98	0.97	0.90	0.90	0.89	0.92	0.90
Debt to Equity	882.86	...	94.22	279.43	4.74	2.43	3.09	1.43
Price Range	8.46-1.73	8.72-1.73	9.67-4.06	11.38-6.40	17.47-7.23	17.67-12.35	35.62-9.02	49.67-26.65
P/E Ratio	...	...	...	...	...	9.55-6.68	...	18.00-9.66
Average Yield %	3.79	4.49	4.94	3.16	3.03	4.09	2.91	1.69

Address: 7075 Flying Cloud Drive, Eden Prairie, MN 55344 **Telephone:** 952-828-4000 **Fax:** 952-828-8998	**Web Site:** www.supervalu.com **Officers:** Sam K. Duncan - President, Chief Executive Officer Sherry M. Smith - Executive Vice President, Chief Financial Officer	**Auditors:** KPMG LLP **Investor Contact:** 952-828-4000 **Transfer Agents:** Wells Fargo Shareowner Services, St. Paul, MN

SYNNEX CORP

Exchange	Symbol	Price	52Wk Range	Yield	P/E
NYS	SNX	$37.00 (3/28/2013)	40.88-30.92	N/A	9.59

*7 Year Price Score 117.76 *NYSE Composite Index=100 *12 Month Price Score 100.49

TRADING VOLUME (thousand shares)

Interim Earnings (Per Share)

Qtr.	Feb	May	Aug	Nov
2009-10	0.98	0.70	0.86	1.04
2010-11	0.80	0.85	1.07	1.36
2011-12	1.02	0.90	0.93	1.15
2012-13	0.88	...	...	...

Interim Dividends (Per Share)

No Dividends Paid

Valuation Analysis

		Institutional Holding	
Forecast EPS	$3.80	No of Institutions	
	(04/06/2013)	221	
Market Cap	$1.4 Billion	Shares	
Book Value	$1.3 Billion	30,978,776	
Price/Book	1.01	% Held	
Price/Sales	0.13	81.84	

Business Summary: IT Services (MIC: 6.3.1 SIC: 7373 NAIC: 541512)

SYNNEX is a business process services company, servicing resellers, retailers and original equipment manufacturers. Co.'s primary business process services are wholesale distribution and business process outsourcing (BPO). Co. has two segments: distribution services and global business services (GBS). Co.'s distribution services segment distributes Information Technology systems, peripherals, system components, software, networking equipment, Consumer Electronics, and complementary products. Co.'s GBS segment provides a range of BPO services that include technical support, renewals management, direct sales, customer service, back office processing and information technology outsourcing.

Recent Developments: For the quarter ended Feb 28 2013, net income decreased 14.7% to US$33.4 million from US$39.2 million in the year-earlier quarter. Revenues were US$2.46 billion, unchanged from the year before. Operating income was US$55.9 million versus US$64.0 million in the prior-year quarter, a decrease of 12.6%. Direct operating expenses rose 0.6% to US$2.30 billion from US$2.29 billion in the comparable period the year before. Indirect operating expenses decreased 4.9% to US$100.1 million from US$105.3 million in the equivalent prior-year period.

Prospects: Our evaluation of Synnex Corp. as of Apr. 7, 2013 is the result of our systematic analysis on three basic characteristics: earnings strength, relative valuation, and recent stock price movement. The company has produced a positive trend in earnings per share over the past 5 quarters. However, while recent estimates for the company have been lowered by analysts, SNX has posted better than expected results. Based on operating earnings yield, the company is undervalued when compared to all of the companies in our coverage universe. Share price changes over the past year indicates that SNX will perform well over the near term.

Financial Data

(US$ in Thousands)	3 Mos	11/30/2012	11/30/2011	11/30/2010	11/30/2009	11/30/2008	11/30/2007	11/30/2006
Earnings Per Share	3.86	3.99	4.08	3.58	2.70	2.52	1.93	1.61
Cash Flow Per Share	5.71	6.62	6.12	(1.90)	8.01	1.66	(4.93)	(0.64)
Tang Book Value Per Share	30.92	30.06	25.87	23.19	20.62	16.90	15.53	15.19
Income Statement								
Total Revenue	2,460,839	10,285,507	10,409,840	8,614,141	7,719,197	7,768,230	7,004,120	6,343,514
EBITDA	63,429	284,113	279,896	216,985	172,311	162,781	129,305	106,593
Depn & Amortn	6,228	24,630	24,673	16,285	19,626	18,764	15,765	9,781
Income Before Taxes	51,708	236,553	229,718	183,586	138,702	129,586	98,666	80,153
Income Taxes	18,317	84,050	79,165	66,910	50,656	45,096	35,167	28,320
Net Income	33,369	151,376	150,331	127,948	92,088	83,797	63,127	51,385
Average Shares	38,030	37,908	36,833	35,757	34,013	33,263	32,674	32,014
Balance Sheet								
Current Assets	2,443,399	2,580,461	2,438,415	2,209,193	1,840,559	1,725,129	1,588,227	1,138,037
Total Assets	2,813,940	2,963,262	2,833,295	2,499,861	2,100,288	2,032,880	1,887,103	1,382,734
Current Liabilities	1,332,376	1,494,707	1,372,253	1,314,008	1,077,876	1,134,541	1,168,519	721,172
Long-Term Obligations	72,618	81,152	223,822	140,333	153,160	152,287	37,537	47,967
Total Liabilities	1,468,393	1,644,239	1,674,916	1,507,191	1,281,918	1,353,039	1,282,549	871,188
Stockholders' Equity	1,345,547	1,319,023	1,158,379	992,670	818,370	679,841	604,554	511,546
Shares Outstanding	36,711	36,628	36,164	35,570	33,602	31,954	31,328	30,477
Statistical Record								
Return on Assets %	5.32	5.21	5.64	5.56	4.46	4.26	3.86	4.17
Return on Equity %	11.45	12.19	13.98	14.13	12.29	13.01	11.31	10.83
EBITDA Margin %	2.58	2.76	2.69	2.52	2.23	2.10	1.85	1.68
Net Margin %	1.36	1.47	1.44	1.49	1.19	1.08	0.90	0.81
Asset Turnover	3.73	3.54	3.90	3.75	3.74	3.95	4.28	5.15
Current Ratio	1.83	1.73	1.78	1.68	1.71	1.52	1.36	1.58
Debt to Equity	0.05	0.06	0.19	0.14	0.19	0.22	0.06	0.09
Price Range	43.89-30.92	43.89-28.42	36.60-23.20	32.09-23.06	32.14-8.86	27.07-9.16	23.25-17.74	23.87-15.11
P/E Ratio	11.37-8.01	11.00-7.12	8.97-5.69	8.96-6.44	11.90-3.28	10.74-3.63	12.05-9.19	14.83-9.39

Address: 44201 Nobel Drive, Fremont, CA 94538
Telephone: 510-656-3333

Web Site: www.synnex.com
Officers: Dwight A. Steffensen - Chairman Kevin M. Murai - President, Chief Executive Officer, Co-Chief Executive Officer

Auditors: KPMG LLP
Investor Contact: Inv-est-orRelations
Transfer Agents: Computershare Trust Company, Providence, RI

SYNOVUS FINANCIAL CORP.

Exchange	Symbol	Price	52Wk Range	Yield	P/E
NYS	SNV	$2.77 (3/28/2013)	2.85-1.69	1.44	3.26

*7 Year Price Score 32.18   *NYSE Composite Index=100   *12 Month Price Score 107.82

Interim Earnings (Per Share)

Qtr.	Mar	Jun	Sep	Dec
2008	0.24	0.04	(0.12)	(1.93)
2009	(0.46)	(1.82)	(1.32)	(0.39)
2010	(0.47)	(0.36)	(0.25)	(0.21)
2011	(0.12)	(0.07)	0.02	0.02
2012	0.02	0.03	0.02	0.78

Interim Dividends (Per Share)

Amt	Decl	Ex	Rec	Pay
0.01Q	05/30/2012	06/12/2012	06/14/2012	07/02/2012
0.01Q	08/21/2012	09/18/2012	09/20/2012	10/01/2012
0.01Q	11/28/2012	12/11/2012	12/13/2012	01/02/2013
0.01Q	03/05/2013	03/19/2013	03/21/2013	04/01/2013

Indicated Div: $0.04 (Div. Reinv. Plan)

Valuation Analysis

Valuation Analysis		Institutional Holding	
Forecast EPS	$0.12	No of Institutions	
	(04/06/2013)	353	
Market Cap	$2.2 Billion	Shares	
Book Value	$3.6 Billion	631,355,520	
Price/Book	0.61	% Held	
Price/Sales	1.66	73.29	

TRADING VOLUME (thousand shares)

Business Summary: Banking (MIC: 5.1.1 SIC: 6021 NAIC: 522110)

Synovus Financial is a financial services company and a bank holding company. Through its subsidiary, Synovus Bank, Co. provides commercial banking services and retail banking services. Co.'s commercial banking services include cash management, asset management, capital markets services, institutional trust services and commercial, financial and real estate loans. Co.'s retail banking services include demand and savings deposits; mortgage, installment and other retail loans; investment and brokerage services; automated banking services; Internet based banking services; and credit card services. As of Dec 31 2011, Co. had total assets of $27.16 billion and total deposits of $22.41 billion.

Recent Developments: For the year ended Dec 31 2012, income from continuing operations was US$830.2 million compared with a loss of US$60.8 million a year earlier. Net income amounted to US$830.2 million versus a net loss of US$60.8 million in the prior year. Net interest income decreased 7.6% to US$854.1 million from US$924.2 million in the prior year. Provision for loan losses was US$320.4 million versus US$418.8 million in the prior year, a decrease of 23.5%. Non-interest income fell 7.4% to US$314.0 million from US$338.9 million, while non-interest expense declined 9.7% to US$816.2 million.

Prospects: Our evaluation of Synovus Financial Corp. as of Apr. 7, 2013 is the result of our systematic analysis on three basic characteristics: earnings strength, relative valuation, and recent stock price movement. The company has suffered a very negative trend in earnings per share over the past 5 quarters and while recent estimates for the company have remained steady, SNV has posted results that were in line with analysts expectations. Based on operating earnings yield, the company is overvalued when compared to all of the companies in our coverage universe. Share price changes over the past year indicates that SNV will perform well over the near term.

Financial Data

(US$ in Thousands)	12/31/2012	12/31/2011	12/31/2010	12/31/2009	12/31/2008	12/31/2007	12/31/2006	12/31/2005
Earnings Per Share	0.85	(0.15)	(1.24)	(3.99)	(1.77)	1.60	1.90	1.64
Cash Flow Per Share	0.60	0.82	1.35	1.16	2.53	2.04	2.43	1.99
Tang Book Value Per Share	3.28	2.35	2.58	3.84	8.50	8.77	7.96	6.44
Dividends Per Share	0.040	0.040	0.040	0.040	0.460	0.820	0.780	0.730
Dividend Payout %	4.71	...	...	...	...	51.25	41.05	44.51
Income Statement								
Interest Income	1,004,140	1,141,756	1,320,581	1,509,189	1,857,580	2,238,404	2,016,466	1,496,225
Interest Expense	150,023	217,602	334,248	498,879	779,687	1,089,456	882,592	527,378
Net Interest Income	854,117	924,154	986,333	1,010,310	1,077,893	1,148,948	1,133,874	968,847
Provision for Losses	320,369	418,795	1,131,274	1,805,599	699,883	170,208	75,148	82,532
Non-Interest Income	309,285	341,213	309,389	408,967	425,281	389,028	2,133,586	1,918,479
Non-Interest Expense	811,556	906,104	1,013,618	1,219,586	1,455,712	840,094	2,170,677	1,943,391
Income Before Taxes	31,477	(59,532)	(849,170)	(1,605,908)	(652,421)	527,674	1,021,635	861,403
Income Taxes	(798,732)	1,312	(15,151)	(171,977)	(77,695)	184,739	356,616	307,576
Net Income	830,209	(60,624)	(790,678)	(1,431,705)	(582,438)	526,305	616,917	516,446
Average Shares	910,102	785,272	685,186	372,943	329,319	329,863	324,232	314,815
Balance Sheet								
Net Loans & Leases	19,178,975	19,573,475	21,009,581	24,476,159	27,325,403	26,130,972	24,340,093	21,102,735
Total Assets	26,760,012	27,162,845	30,093,148	32,831,418	35,786,269	33,018,452	31,854,773	27,620,672
Total Deposits	21,057,044	22,411,752	24,500,304	27,433,533	28,617,179	24,959,816	24,294,447	20,784,365
Total Liabilities	23,190,581	24,335,393	27,095,230	29,980,377	31,999,111	29,576,862	28,146,123	24,671,343
Stockholders' Equity	3,569,431	2,827,452	2,997,918	2,851,041	3,787,158	3,441,590	3,708,650	2,949,329
Shares Outstanding	786,579	785,295	785,262	489,828	330,334	329,867	325,552	312,639
Statistical Record								
Return on Assets %	3.07	N.M.	N.M.	N.M.	N.M.	1.62	2.07	1.96
Return on Equity %	25.89	N.M.	N.M.	N.M.	N.M.	14.72	18.53	18.48
Net Interest Margin %	85.06	80.94	74.69	66.94	58.03	51.33	56.23	64.75
Efficiency Ratio %	61.79	61.10	62.19	63.58	63.77	31.97	52.30	56.91
Loans to Deposits	0.91	0.87	0.86	0.89	0.95	1.05	1.00	1.02
Price Range	2.55-1.53	2.90-0.98	3.82-1.96	8.30-1.49	13.49-6.68	14.60-9.86	13.55-11.27	13.10-11.58
P/E Ratio	3.00-1.80	...	...	...	...	9.13-6.16	7.13-5.93	7.99-7.06
Average Yield %	1.92	2.00	1.50	1.18	4.47	6.34	6.32	5.94

Address: 1111 Bay Avenue, Suite 500, Columbus, GA 31901
Telephone: 706-649-2311

Web Site: www.synovus.com
Officers: Kessel D. Stelling - Chairman, President, Chief Executive Officer Thomas J. Prescott - Executive Vice President, Chief Financial Officer

Auditors: KPMG LLP
Investor Contact: 706-649-5220
Transfer Agents: American Stock Transfer & Trust Company, LLC, Brooklyn, NY

SYSCO CORP.

Exchange	Symbol	Price	52Wk Range	Yield	P/E	Div Achiever
NYS	SYY	$35.17 (3/28/2013)	35.17-27.26	3.18	19.22	36 Years

*7 Year Price Score 91.69   *NYSE Composite Index=100   *12 Month Price Score 99.26

Interim Earnings (Per Share)

Qtr.	Sep	Dec	Mar	Jun
2009-10	0.55	0.45	0.42	0.57
2010-11	0.51	0.44	0.44	0.57
2011-12	0.51	0.43	0.44	0.52
2012-13	0.49	0.38	...	...

Interim Dividends (Per Share)

Amt	Decl	Ex	Rec	Pay
0.27Q	05/23/2012	07/03/2012	07/06/2012	07/27/2012
0.27Q	08/24/2012	10/03/2012	10/05/2012	10/26/2012
0.28Q	11/14/2012	01/02/2013	01/04/2013	01/25/2013
0.28Q	02/13/2013	04/03/2013	04/05/2013	04/26/2013

Indicated Div: $1.12 (Div. Reinv. Plan)

Valuation Analysis | **Institutional Holding**

Forecast EPS	$1.90	No of Institutions
	(04/05/2013)	1118
Market Cap	$20.6 Billion	Shares
Book Value	$4.9 Billion	551,086,976
Price/Book	4.20	% Held
Price/Sales	0.47	77.42

TRADING VOLUME (thousand shares)

Business Summary: Retail - Food & Beverage, Drug & Tobacco (MIC: 2.1.2 SIC: 5141 NAIC: 424410)

Sysco distributes food and related products to restaurants, healthcare and educational facilities, lodging establishments and other foodservice customers. Co. distributes a line of frozen foods, such as meats, fully prepared entrees, fruits, vegetables and desserts; canned and dry foods; meats; dairy products; beverage products; imported products; and fresh produce. Co. also supplies a range of non-food items, including paper products such as disposable napkins, plates and cups; tableware such as china and silverware; cookware such as pots, pans and utensils; restaurant and kitchen equipment and supplies; and cleaning supplies. Co.'s operations are located in the U.S., Canada and Ireland.

Recent Developments: For the quarter ended Dec 29 2012, net income decreased 11.5% to US$221.4 million from US$250.1 million in the year-earlier quarter. Revenues were US$10.80 billion, up 5.4% from US$10.24 billion the year before. Operating income was US$382.7 million versus US$427.0 million in the prior-year quarter, a decrease of 10.4%. Direct operating expenses rose 5.7% to US$8.88 billion from US$8.40 billion in the comparable period the year before. Indirect operating expenses increased 8.2% to US$1.53 billion from US$1.42 billion in the equivalent prior-year period.

Prospects: Our evaluation of Sysco Corp. as of Apr. 7, 2013 is the result of our systematic analysis on three basic characteristics: earnings strength, relative valuation, and recent stock price movement. The company has managed to produce a neutral trend in earnings per share over the past 5 quarters and while recent estimates for the company have remained steady, SYY has posted results that fell short of analysts expectations. Based on operating earnings yield, the company is about fairly valued when compared to all of the companies in our coverage universe. Share price changes over the past year indicates that SYY will perform poorly over the near term.

Financial Data

(US$ in Thousands)	6 Mos	3 Mos	06/30/2012	07/02/2011	07/03/2010	06/27/2009	06/28/2008	06/30/2007
Earnings Per Share	1.83	1.88	1.90	1.96	1.99	1.77	1.81	1.60
Cash Flow Per Share	2.13	2.32	2.40	1.87	1.47	2.67	2.64	2.28
Tang Book Value Per Share	5.03	5.18	4.96	5.01	3.69	3.08	3.17	2.99
Dividends Per Share	1.080	1.070	0.800	1.030	0.990	0.920	0.820	0.720
Dividend Payout %	59.02	56.91	42.11	52.55	49.75	51.98	45.30	45.00
Income Statement								
Total Revenue	21,883,806	11,086,916	42,380,939	39,323,489	37,243,495	36,853,330	37,522,111	35,042,075
EBITDA	1,115,256	601,923	2,282,298	2,319,721	2,336,766	2,248,218	2,255,448	2,067,931
Depn & Amortn	249,593	120,664	384,900	374,000	361,700	361,062	352,569	341,714
Income Before Taxes	802,553	450,391	1,784,002	1,827,454	1,849,589	1,770,834	1,791,338	1,621,215
Income Taxes	294,586	163,793	662,417	675,424	669,606	714,886	685,187	620,139
Net Income	507,967	286,598	1,121,585	1,152,030	1,179,983	1,055,948	1,106,151	1,001,076
Average Shares	589,751	589,838	588,991	588,691	593,590	596,069	610,970	626,366
Balance Sheet								
Current Assets	6,159,785	6,333,650	6,084,808	5,732,882	5,076,258	5,270,679	5,175,033	4,675,546
Total Assets	12,428,067	12,487,833	12,094,972	11,385,555	10,313,701	10,216,619	10,082,293	9,518,931
Current Liabilities	3,487,417	3,602,874	3,423,579	3,575,075	3,009,198	3,150,154	3,499,343	3,415,089
Long-Term Obligations	2,809,290	2,764,853	2,763,688	2,279,517	2,472,662	2,467,486	1,975,435	1,758,227
Total Liabilities	7,526,494	7,593,652	7,409,932	6,680,313	6,486,175	6,766,917	6,673,307	6,240,531
Stockholders' Equity	4,901,573	4,894,181	4,685,040	4,705,242	3,827,526	3,449,702	3,408,986	3,278,400
Shares Outstanding	585,355	587,243	585,946	591,577	588,406	590,026	601,232	611,840
Statistical Record								
Return on Assets %	9.02	9.24	9.58	10.65	11.31	10.43	11.32	10.85
Return on Equity %	22.46	23.16	23.95	27.08	31.90	30.88	33.17	31.71
EBITDA Margin %	5.10	5.43	5.39	5.90	6.27	6.10	6.01	5.90
Net Margin %	2.32	2.59	2.65	2.93	3.17	2.87	2.95	2.86
Asset Turnover	3.64	3.58	3.62	3.63	3.57	3.64	3.84	3.80
Current Ratio	1.77	1.76	1.78	1.60	1.69	1.67	1.48	1.37
Debt to Equity	0.57	0.56	0.59	0.48	0.65	0.72	0.58	0.54
Price Range	32.39-27.26	31.27-25.47	31.55-25.47	32.65-27.29	31.54-21.51	34.80-19.45	35.84-27.48	36.95-26.91
P/E Ratio	17.70-14.90	16.63-13.55	16.61-13.41	16.66-13.92	15.85-10.81	19.66-10.99	19.80-15.18	23.09-16.82
Average Yield %	3.62	3.70	2.79	3.50	3.60	3.63	2.63	2.17

Address: 1390 Enclave Parkway, Houston, TX 77077-2099
Telephone: 281-584-1390
Fax: 281-584-2880

Web Site: www.sysco.com
Officers: Manuel A. Fernandez - Executive Chairman
William J. DeLaney - President, Chief Executive Officer

Auditors: Ernst & Young LLP
Investor Contact: 281-584-2615
Transfer Agents: American Stock Transfer & Trust Company, New York, NY

TANGER FACTORY OUTLET CENTERS, INC.

Exchange	Symbol	Price	52Wk Range	Yield	P/E	Div Achiever
NYS	SKT	$36.18 (3/28/2013)	36.47-29.03	2.49	63.47	19 Years

*7 Year Price Score 129.38 *NYSE Composite Index=100 *12 Month Price Score 99.70

Interim Earnings (Per Share)

Qtr.	Mar	Jun	Sep	Dec
2008	0.09	0.00	0.14	0.13
2009	0.46	0.15	0.03	0.12
2010	0.01	0.04	0.14	0.12
2011	0.11	0.11	0.11	0.15
2012	0.09	0.12	0.16	0.20

Interim Dividends (Per Share)

Amt	Decl	Ex	Rec	Pay
0.21Q	07/05/2012	07/26/2012	07/30/2012	08/15/2012
0.21Q	10/04/2012	10/26/2012	10/30/2012	11/15/2012
0.21Q	01/03/2013	01/28/2013	01/30/2013	02/15/2013
0.225Q	04/04/2013	04/26/2013	04/30/2013	05/15/2013

Indicated Div: $0.90 (Div. Reinv. Plan)

Valuation Analysis

		Institutional Holding	
Forecast EPS	$0.71	No of Institutions	
	(04/05/2013)	293	
Market Cap	$3.4 Billion	Shares	
Book Value	$482.6 Million	89,120,312	
Price/Book	7.05	% Held	
Price/Sales	9.53	99.76	

Business Summary: REITs (MIC: 5.3.1 SIC: 6798 NAIC: 525930)

Tanger Factory Outlet Centers is a real estate investment trust, which develops, acquires, owns, operates and manages outlet shopping centers. Co.'s outlet centers and other assets are held by, and all of its operations are conducted by, Tanger Properties Limited Partnership and subsidiaries (Operating Partnership). Co. owns the majority of the units of partnership interest issued by the Operating Partnership, through its two wholly-owned subsidiaries, the Tanger GP Trust and the Tanger LP Trust. As of Dec 31 2011, Co. owned and operated 36 outlet centers, with a total gross leasable area of about 10.7 million square feet, and had partial ownership interests in three outlet centers.

Recent Developments: For the year ended Dec 31 2012, income from continuing operations increased 10.8% to US$56.5 million from US$51.0 million a year earlier. Net income increased 10.8% to US$56.5 million from US$51.0 million in the prior year. Revenues were US$357.0 million, up 13.3% from US$315.2 million the year before. Revenues from property income rose 13.7% to US$246.4 million from US$216.7 million in the corresponding earlier year.

Prospects: Our evaluation of Tanger Factory Outlet Centers Inc. as of Apr. 7, 2013 is the result of our systematic analysis on three basic characteristics: earnings strength, relative valuation, and recent stock price movement. The company has enjoyed a very positive trend in earnings per share over the past 5 quarters. Because the company lacks sufficient analyst estimate data, we place greater weight on the historical EPS trend as the measure of earnings strength. Based on operating earnings yield, the company is overvalued when compared to all of the companies in our coverage universe. Share price changes over the past year indicates that SKT will perform in line with the market over the near term.

Financial Data
(US$ in Thousands)

	12/31/2012	12/31/2011	12/31/2010	12/31/2009	12/31/2008	12/31/2007	12/31/2006	12/31/2005
Earnings Per Share	0.57	0.52	0.32	0.72	0.35	0.36	0.52	0.08
Cash Flow Per Share	1.80	1.64	1.48	1.77	1.56	1.60	1.44	1.48
Tang Book Value Per Share	3.85	5.31	3.61	3.81	1.32	1.60	1.97	1.92
Dividends Per Share	0.830	0.794	0.772	0.764	0.750	0.710	0.671	0.640
Dividend Payout %	145.61	152.64	241.41	106.08	211.27	197.22	130.34	800.00
Income Statement								
Total Revenue	356,997	315,223	276,303	271,685	245,391	228,765	211,711	202,799
EBITDA	183,285	164,136	137,426	171,590	119,794	121,965	109,435	114,352
Depn & Amortn	73,700	66,200	64,500	64,900	49,800	50,400	40,336	38,137
Income Before Taxes	59,771	52,554	38,806	69,007	31,551	31,499	28,324	33,288
Net Income	53,228	44,641	34,249	58,019	28,032	28,576	37,309	5,089
Average Shares	92,661	84,129	80,390	72,024	62,724	63,336	62,162	57,292
Balance Sheet								
Current Assets	10,335	7,894	6,481	3,267	4,977	2,412	8,453	5,567
Total Assets	1,672,425	1,621,815	1,216,934	1,178,861	1,121,855	1,060,280	1,040,877	1,000,605
Current Liabilities	48,233	51,413	63,425	46,110	69,159	70,998	48,598	37,418
Long-Term Obligations	1,093,537	1,025,542	714,616	584,611	795,319	706,345	678,579	663,607
Total Liabilities	1,189,816	1,161,253	850,005	716,190	893,799	811,076	766,201	750,391
Stockholders' Equity	482,609	460,562	366,929	462,671	228,056	249,204	274,676	250,214
Shares Outstanding	94,061	86,727	80,996	80,554	63,335	62,658	62,082	61,497
Statistical Record								
Return on Assets %	3.22	3.15	2.86	5.04	2.56	2.72	3.66	0.53
Return on Equity %	11.26	10.79	8.26	16.80	11.71	10.91	14.22	2.47
EBITDA Margin %	51.34	52.07	49.74	63.16	48.82	53.31	51.69	56.39
Net Margin %	14.91	14.16	12.40	21.36	11.42	12.49	17.62	2.51
Asset Turnover	0.22	0.22	0.23	0.24	0.22	0.22	0.21	0.21
Current Ratio	0.21	0.15	0.10	0.07	0.07	0.03	0.17	0.15
Debt to Equity	2.27	2.23	1.95	1.26	3.49	2.83	2.47	2.65
Price Range	34.43-28.10	29.82-22.39	25.85-18.68	20.68-12.96	22.39-13.10	22.02-16.61	20.05-14.74	14.93-10.82
P/E Ratio	60.40-49.30	57.35-43.06	80.78-58.36	28.72-18.00	63.96-37.43	61.17-46.13	38.55-28.35	186.63-135.25
Average Yield %	2.63	2.96	3.49	4.46	4.01	3.57	3.95	4.94

Address: 3200 Northline Avenue, Suite 360, Greensboro, NC 27408	Web Site: www.tangeroutlet.com	Auditors: PricewaterhouseCoopers LLP
Telephone: 336-292-3010	Officers: Steven B. Tanger - President, Chief Executive Officer Frank C. Marchisello - Executive Vice President, Chief Financial Officer, Secretary	Investor Contact: 336-834-6892 Transfer Agents: Computershare Trust Company, N.A, Providence, RI

TARGET CORP

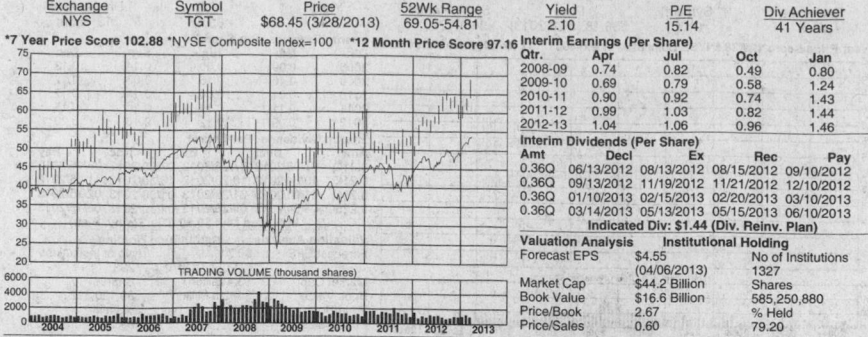

Exchange	Symbol	Price	52Wk Range	Yield	P/E	Div Achiever
NYS	TGT	$68.45 (3/28/2013)	69.05-54.81	2.10	15.14	41 Years

*7 Year Price Score 102.88 *NYSE Composite Index=100 *12 Month Price Score 97.16

Interim Earnings (Per Share)

Qtr.	Apr	Jul	Oct	Jan
2008-09	0.74	0.82	0.49	0.80
2009-10	0.69	0.79	0.58	1.24
2010-11	0.90	0.92	0.74	1.43
2011-12	0.99	1.03	0.82	1.44
2012-13	1.04	1.06	0.96	1.46

Interim Dividends (Per Share)

Amt	Decl	Ex	Rec	Pay
0.36Q	06/13/2012	08/13/2012	08/15/2012	09/10/2012
0.36Q	09/13/2012	11/19/2012	11/21/2012	12/10/2012
0.36Q	01/10/2013	02/15/2013	02/20/2013	03/10/2013
0.36Q	03/14/2013	05/13/2013	05/15/2013	06/10/2013

Indicated Div: $1.44 (Div. Reinv. Plan)

Valuation Analysis / **Institutional Holding**

Forecast EPS	$4.55 (04/06/2013)	No of Institutions 1327
Market Cap	$44.2 Billion	Shares 585,250,880
Book Value	$16.6 Billion	% Held 79.20
Price/Book	2.67	
Price/Sales	0.60	

TRADING VOLUME (thousand shares)

Business Summary: Retail - General Merchandise/Department Stores (MIC: 2.1.1 SIC: 5331 NAIC: 452990)
Target operates three segments. Co.'s U.S. Retail segment includes all of its merchandising operations. Co.'s U.S. Credit Card segment provides credit to its customers through its credit cards, the Target Credit Card and Target Visa, as well as the Target Debit Card. Co.'s Canadian segment includes costs incurred in the U.S. and Canada related to its Canadian retail market entry. Co. sells an assortment of general merchandise and food in its stores. Co.'s merchamdise product category includes household products, hardlines, apparel and accessories, food and pet supplies, and home furnishings and decor. As of Feb 2 2013, Co. had 1,778 stores in 49 states and the District of Columbia.

Recent Developments: For the year ended Feb 2 2013, net income increased 2.4% to US$3.00 billion from US$2.93 billion in the prior year. Revenues were US$73.30 billion, up 4.9% from US$69.87 billion the year before. Operating income was US$5.37 billion versus US$5.32 billion in the prior year, an increase of 0.9%. Direct operating expenses rose 5.6% to US$51.04 billion from US$48.31 billion in the comparable period the year before. Indirect operating expenses increased 4.1% to US$16.90 billion from US$16.24 billion in the equivalent prior-year period.

Prospects: Our evaluation of Target Corp. as of Apr. 7, 2013 is the result of our systematic analysis on three basic characteristics: earnings strength, relative valuation, and recent stock price movement. The company has managed to produce a neutral trend in earnings per share over the past 5 quarters. However, while recent estimates for the company have been mixed, TGT has posted results that fell short of analysts expectations. Based on operating earnings yield, the company is undervalued when compared to all of the companies in our coverage universe. Share price changes over the past year indicates that TGT will perform poorly over the near term.

Financial Data
(US$ in Millions)

	02/02/2013	01/28/2012	01/29/2011	01/30/2010	01/31/2009	02/02/2008	02/03/2007	01/28/2006
Earnings Per Share	4.52	4.28	4.00	3.30	2.86	3.33	3.21	2.71
Cash Flow Per Share	7.98	8.02	7.30	7.84	5.77	4.89	5.55	5.06
Tang Book Value Per Share	25.31	23.28	21.68	20.29	17.91	18.44	17.94	16.04
Dividends Per Share	1.320	1.100	0.840	0.660	0.600	0.520	0.440	0.360
Dividend Payout %	29.20	25.70	21.00	20.00	20.98	15.62	13.71	13.28
Income Statement								
Total Revenue	73,301	69,865	67,390	65,357	64,948	63,367	59,490	52,620
EBITDA	7,491	7,429	7,312	6,672	6,206	6,916	6,578	5,707
Depn & Amortn	2,120	2,107	2,060	1,999	1,804	1,644	1,509	1,384
Income Before Taxes	4,609	4,456	4,495	3,872	3,536	4,625	4,497	3,860
Income Taxes	1,610	1,527	1,575	1,384	1,322	1,776	1,710	1,452
Net Income	2,999	2,929	2,920	2,488	2,214	2,849	2,787	2,408
Average Shares	663	683	729	754	773	850	868	889
Balance Sheet								
Current Assets	16,388	16,449	17,213	18,424	17,488	18,906	14,706	14,405
Total Assets	48,163	46,630	43,705	44,533	44,106	44,560	37,349	34,995
Current Liabilities	14,031	14,287	10,070	11,327	10,512	11,782	11,117	9,588
Long-Term Obligations	14,654	13,697	15,607	15,118	17,490	15,126	8,675	9,119
Total Liabilities	31,605	30,809	28,218	29,186	30,394	29,253	21,716	20,790
Stockholders' Equity	16,558	15,821	15,487	15,347	13,712	15,307	15,633	14,205
Shares Outstanding	645	669	704	744	752	818	859	874
Statistical Record								
Return on Assets %	6.23	6.50	6.64	5.63	5.01	6.98	7.58	7.18
Return on Equity %	18.22	18.76	18.99	17.17	15.30	18.47	18.38	17.73
EBITDA Margin %	10.22	10.63	10.85	10.21	9.56	10.91	11.06	10.85
Net Margin %	4.09	4.19	4.33	3.81	3.41	4.50	4.68	4.58
Asset Turnover	1.52	1.55	1.53	1.48	1.47	1.55	1.62	1.57
Current Ratio	1.17	1.15	1.71	1.63	1.66	1.60	1.32	1.50
Debt to Equity	0.89	0.87	1.01	0.99	1.28	0.99	0.55	0.64
Price Range	65.44-50.33	55.55-46.33	60.77-48.64	52.02-25.37	57.89-26.96	70.14-48.08	62.35-45.28	59.98-46.28
P/E Ratio	14.48-11.13	12.98-10.82	15.19-12.16	15.76-7.69	20.24-9.43	21.06-14.44	19.42-14.11	22.13-17.08
Average Yield %	2.20	2.17	1.56	1.56	1.30	0.86	0.82	0.68

Address: 1000 Nicollet Mall, Minneapolis, MN 55403 Telephone: 612-304-6073 Fax: 612-370-5502	Web Site: www.target.com Officers: Gregg W. Steinhafel - Chairman, President, Chief Executive Officer Douglas A. Scovanner - Executive Vice President, Chief Financial Officer	Auditors: Ernst & Young LLP Investor Contact: 800-775-3110 Transfer Agents: Computershare Shareowner Services, Pittsburgh, PA

TARGA RESOURCES CORP

Exchange	Symbol	Price	52Wk Range	Yield	P/E
NYS	TRGP	$67.96 (3/28/2013)	67.96-40.54	2.69	74.68

*7 Year Price Score N/A   *NYSE Composite Index=100   *12 Month Price Score 115.17

Interim Earnings (Per Share)

Qtr.	Mar	Jun	Sep	Dec
2010	0.00	(48.10)	(3.77)	14.06
2011	0.16	0.25	0.12	0.20
2012	0.23	0.21	0.21	0.27

Interim Dividends (Per Share)

Amt	Decl	Ex	Rec	Pay
0.365Q	04/11/2012	04/19/2012	04/23/2012	05/16/2012
0.394Q	07/11/2012	07/19/2012	07/23/2012	08/15/2012
0.422Q	10/11/2012	10/18/2012	10/22/2012	11/15/2012
0.458Q	01/15/2013	01/24/2013	01/28/2013	02/15/2013

Indicated Div: $1.83

Valuation Analysis

		Institutional Holding	
Forecast EPS	$1.19	No of Institutions	
	(04/05/2013)	168	
Market Cap	$2.9 Billion	Shares	
Book Value	$144.1 Million	33,584,656	
Price/Book	19.95	% Held	
Price/Sales	0.49	N/A	

TRADING VOLUME (thousand shares)

Business Summary: Equipment & Services (MIC: 9.1.3 SIC: 4922 NAIC: 486210)

Targa Resources owns general and limited partner interests in Targa Resources Partners LP ("the Partnership"). The Partnership is engaged in the business of gathering, compressing, treating, processing and selling natural gas and storing, fractionating, treating, transporting and selling natural gas liquids ("NGL"s), NGL products, refined petroleum products and crude oil. The Partnership operates in two primary divisions: Natural Gas Gathering and Processing; and Logistics and Marketing.

Recent Developments: For the year ended Dec 31 2012, net income decreased 26.0% to US$159.3 million from US$215.4 million in the prior year. Revenues were US$5.89 billion, down 15.9% from US$6.99 billion the year before. Operating income was US$336.3 million versus US$351.1 million in the prior year, a decrease of 4.2%. Indirect operating expenses decreased 16.5% to US$5.55 billion from US$6.64 billion in the equivalent prior-year period.

Prospects: Our evaluation of Targa Resources Corp. as of Apr. 7, 2013 is the result of our systematic analysis on three basic characteristics: earnings strength, relative valuation, and recent stock price movement. The company has managed to produce a neutral trend in earnings per share over the past 5 quarters and while recent estimates for the company have been raised by analysts, TRGP has posted better than expected results. Based on operating earnings yield, the company is overvalued when compared to all of the companies in our coverage universe. Share price changes over the past year indicates that TRGP will perform poorly over the near term.

Financial Data
(US$ in Thousands)

	12/31/2012	12/31/2011	12/31/2010	12/31/2009	12/31/2008	12/31/2007
Earnings Per Share	0.91	0.74	(30.94)	...	...	...
Cash Flow Per Share	10.42	9.25	32.08	87.39	102.72	...
Tang Book Value Per Share	N.M.	3.73	3.41	100.43	111.50	...
Dividends Per Share	1.518	0.932	...	...	...	...
Dividend Payout %	166.76	125.89	...	...	...	...
Income Statement						
Total Revenue	5,885,700	6,994,500	5,469,200	4,536,000	7,998,900	7,297,200
EBITDA	534,900	542,500	378,700	409,500	454,800	444,800
Depn & Amortn	219,800	197,600	187,400	182,600	173,900	164,500
Income Before Taxes	194,300	233,200	80,400	94,800	139,700	118,000
Income Taxes	36,900	26,600	22,500	20,700	19,300	23,900
Net Income	38,100	30,700	(15,000)	29,300	37,300	56,100
Average Shares	41,800	41,400	6,500	3,842	3,793	3,448
Balance Sheet						
Current Assets	733,300	866,500	750,500	745,000	857,100	...
Total Assets	5,105,000	3,831,000	3,393,800	3,367,500	3,641,800	...
Current Liabilities	686,600	741,100	624,200	553,800	466,600	...
Long-Term Obligations	2,475,300	1,567,000	1,534,700	1,593,500	1,976,500	...
Total Liabilities	4,960,900	3,672,900	3,249,500	2,971,700	3,216,500	...
Stockholders' Equity	144,100	158,100	144,300	395,800	425,300	...
Shares Outstanding	42,294	42,398	42,292	3,940	3,814	3,660
Statistical Record						
Return on Assets %	0.85	0.85	N.M.	0.84	...	...
Return on Equity %	25.15	20.30	N.M.	7.14	...	...
EBITDA Margin %	9.09	7.76	6.92	9.03	5.69	6.10
Net Margin %	0.65	0.44	N.M.	0.65	0.47	0.77
Asset Turnover	1.31	1.94	1.62	1.29	...	...
Current Ratio	1.07	1.17	1.20	1.35	1.84	...
Debt to Equity	17.18	9.91	10.64	4.03	4.65	...
Price Range	52.84-39.62	41.05-26.68	27.53-24.70	...	...	...
P/E Ratio	58.07-43.54	55.47-36.05	...	...	...	...
Average Yield %	3.30	2.85	...	...	...	...

Address: 1000 Louisiana St., Suite 4300, Houston, TX 77002 Telephone: 713-584-1000	Web Site: www.targaresources.com Officers: Rene R. Joyce - Executive Chairman, Chief Executive Officer Michael A. Heim - President, Executive Vice President, Chief Operating Officer	Auditors: PricewaterhouseCoopers LLP Transfer Agents: Computershare Trust Company, N.A.

TAUBMAN CENTERS, INC.

Exchange	Symbol	Price	52Wk Range	Yield	P/E
NYS	TCO	$77.66 (3/28/2013)	82.29-70.71	2.58	56.69

*7 Year Price Score 136.29 *NYSE Composite Index=100 *12 Month Price Score 92.59

Interim Earnings (Per Share)

Qtr.	Mar	Jun	Sep	Dec
2008	0.09	0.01	0.17	(1.90)
2009	0.22	0.17	(1.77)	0.08
2010	0.11	0.14	0.01	0.60
2011	0.19	0.15	0.14	2.55
2012	0.30	0.27	0.35	0.45

Interim Dividends (Per Share)

Amt	Decl	Ex	Rec	Pay
0.463Q	06/07/2012	06/14/2012	06/18/2012	06/29/2012
0.463Q	09/05/2012	09/13/2012	09/17/2012	09/28/2012
0.463Q	11/30/2012	12/13/2012	12/17/2012	12/31/2012
0.50Q	03/08/2013	03/14/2013	03/18/2013	03/29/2013

Indicated Div: $2.00

Valuation Analysis

		Institutional Holding	
Forecast EPS	$1.54 (04/05/2013)	No of Institutions	330
Market Cap	$4.9 Billion	Shares	69,635,440
Book Value	N/A	% Held	101.56
Price/Book	N/A		
Price/Sales	6.57		

Business Summary: REITs (MIC: 5.3.1 SIC: 6798 NAIC: 525930)

Taubman Centers is a self-administered and self-managed real estate investment trust. The Taubman Realty Group Limited Partnership is a majority-owned partnership subsidiary of Co. that owns direct or indirect interests in all of Co.'s real estate properties. Co. owns, leases, acquires, disposes of, develops, expands, and manages shopping centers and interests therein. Co.'s owned portfolio as of Dec 31 2012 consisted of 24 urban and suburban shopping centers in 12 states which are located in metropolitan areas, including Charlotte, Dallas, Denver, Detroit, Los Angeles, Miami, Nashville, New York City, Orlando, Phoenix, Salt Lake City, San Francisco, Tampa, and Washington, D.C.

Recent Developments: For the year ended Dec 31 2012, income from continuing operations decreased 100.0% to nil from US$141.4 million a year earlier. Net income decreased 45.1% to US$157.8 million from US$287.4 million in the prior year. Revenues were US$748.0 million, up 16.0% from US$644.9 million the year before. Revenues from property income rose 17.5% to US$426.3 million from US$363.0 million in the corresponding earlier year.

Prospects: Our evaluation of Taubman Centers Inc. as of Apr. 7, 2013 is the result of our systematic analysis on three basic characteristics: earnings strength, relative valuation, and recent stock price movement. The company has suffered a very negative trend in earnings per share over the past 5 quarters. Because the company lacks sufficient analyst estimate data, we place greater weight on the historical EPS trend as the measure of earnings strength. Based on operating earnings yield, the company is overvalued when compared to all of the companies in our coverage universe. Share price changes over the past year indicates that TCO will perform in line with the market over the near term.

Financial Data
(US$ in Thousands)

	12/31/2012	12/31/2011	12/31/2010	12/31/2009	12/31/2008	12/31/2007	12/31/2006	12/31/2005
Earnings Per Share	1.37	3.03	0.86	(1.31)	(1.64)	0.90	0.40	0.87
Cash Flow Per Share	5.40	4.75	4.85	4.44	4.78	4.87	4.24	3.66
Tang Book Value Per Share	...	...	...	...	...	0.18	2.49	6.69
Dividends Per Share	1.850	1.763	1.866	1.660	1.660	1.540	1.290	1.160
Dividend Payout %	135.04	58.17	216.97	...	...	171.11	322.50	133.33
Income Statement								
Total Revenue	747,974	644,918	654,558	666,104	671,498	626,822	579,284	473,438
EBITDA	391,803	345,422	355,257	196,378	239,237	328,648	299,819	245,894
Depn & Amortn	134,900	127,200	144,900	139,700	138,700	128,400	128,500	109,300
Income Before Taxes	114,287	95,945	57,649	(88,992)	(46,860)	72,143	52,136	14,982
Income Taxes	4,964	610	734	1,657	1,117	...	...	...
Net Income	106,174	192,871	63,868	(53,512)	(72,025)	63,124	45,117	71,735
Average Shares	61,376	58,529	55,702	53,239	52,866	53,622	52,979	50,530
Balance Sheet								
Current Assets	109,237	380,759	70,611	65,701	110,708	101,610	65,376	207,694
Total Assets	3,268,495	3,336,792	2,546,873	2,606,853	3,071,792	3,151,307	2,826,622	2,797,580
Current Liabilities	661,391	447,403	418,224	390,581	438,369	418,458	369,225	352,257
Long-Term Obligations	2,952,030	3,145,602	2,656,560	2,691,019	2,796,821	2,700,980	2,319,538	2,089,948
Total Liabilities	3,524,113	3,552,916	2,910,634	2,935,410	3,241,749	3,137,932	2,688,763	2,442,205
Stockholders' Equity	(255,618)	(216,124)	(363,761)	(328,557)	(169,957)	13,375	137,859	355,375
Shares Outstanding	63,310	58,022	54,696	54,321	53,018	52,624	52,931	51,866
Statistical Record								
Return on Assets %	3.21	6.56	2.48	N.M.	N.M.	2.11	1.60	2.69
Return on Equity %	...	...	...	...	...	83.48	18.29	20.10
EBITDA Margin %	52.38	53.56	54.27	29.48	35.63	52.43	51.76	51.94
Net Margin %	14.19	29.91	9.76	N.M.	N.M.	10.07	7.79	15.15
Asset Turnover	0.23	0.22	0.25	0.23	0.22	0.21	0.21	0.18
Current Ratio	0.17	0.85	0.17	0.17	0.25	0.24	0.18	0.59
Debt to Equity	...	...	...	...	...	201.94	16.83	5.88
Price Range	81.34-62.03	62.71-48.27	50.76-31.66	37.66-13.56	58.05-18.69	63.22-47.07	50.86-35.61	36.04-26.60
P/E Ratio	59.37-45.28	20.70-15.93	59.02-36.81	...	...	70.24-52.30	127.15-89.03	41.43-30.57
Average Yield %	2.46	3.13	4.43	6.22	3.67	2.82	3.07	3.68

Address: 200 East Long Lake Road, Suite 300, Bloomfield Hills, MI 48304-2324 Telephone: 248-258-6800	Web Site: www.taubman.com Officers: Robert S. Taubman - Chairman, President, Chief Executive Officer Lisa A. Payne - Vice-Chairman, Chief Financial Officer	Auditors: KPMG LLP Investor Contact: 248-258-7367 Transfer Agents: Computershare Shareowner Services

TC PIPELINES, LP

Exchange	Symbol	Price	52Wk Range	Yield	P/E	Div Achiever
NYS	TCP	$48.49 (3/28/2013)	48.49-38.50	6.41	19.32	13 Years

*7 Year Price Score 99.57   *NYSE Composite Index=100   *12 Month Price Score 96.53

Interim Earnings (Per Share)

Qtr.	Mar	Jun	Sep	Dec
2008	0.87	0.47	0.72	0.67
2009	0.82	0.31	0.65	0.56
2010	0.71	0.59	0.82	0.79
2011	0.90	0.69	0.75	0.69
2012	0.71	0.60	0.64	0.55

Interim Dividends (Per Share)

Amt	Decl	Ex	Rec	Pay
0.77Q	04/24/2012	05/02/2012	05/04/2012	05/15/2012
0.78Q	07/25/2012	08/01/2012	08/03/2012	08/14/2012
0.78Q	10/25/2012	11/01/2012	11/05/2012	11/14/2012
0.78Q	01/18/2013	01/25/2013	01/29/2013	02/14/2013
			Indicated Div: $3.11	

Valuation Analysis

		Institutional Holding	
Forecast EPS	$2.32	No of Institutions	154
	(04/05/2013)	Shares	24,700,634
Market Cap	$2.6 Billion	% Held	44.03
Book Value	N/A		
Price/Book	N/A		
Price/Sales	13.37		

Business Summary: Equipment & Services (MIC: 9.1.3 SIC: 4922 NAIC: 486210)

TC PipeLines is managed by TC PipeLines GP, Inc. (its General Partner), which is an indirect, wholly-owned subsidiary of TransCanada Corporation (TransCanada). Through its subsidiaries, TransCanada owned about 33.3% equity interest in Co. at Dec 31 2011, including a 31.3% limited partner interest and an effective 2% general partner interest held by its General Partner. Co. has equity ownership interests in natural gas interstate pipeline systems, which transport natural gas from producing regions and import facilities to market hubs and consuming markets mainly in the Western and Midwestern U.S. and Central Canada. Co.'s pipeline systems are operated by subsidiaries of TransCanada.

Recent Developments: For the year ended Dec 31 2012, net income decreased 12.7% to US$137.0 million from US$157.0 million in the prior year. Revenues were US$194.0 million, down 13.4% from US$224.0 million the year before. Indirect operating expenses decreased 14.9% to US$57.0 million from US$67.0 million in the equivalent prior-year period.

Prospects: Our evaluation of TC PipeLines L.P. as of Apr. 7, 2013 is the result of our systematic analysis on three basic characteristics: earnings strength, relative valuation, and recent stock price movement. The company has managed to produce a neutral trend in earnings per share over the past 5 quarters. However, while recent estimates for the company have been mixed, TCP has posted results that fell short of analysts expectations. Based on operating earnings yield, the company is about fairly valued when compared to all of the companies in our coverage universe. Share price changes over the past year indicates that TCP will perform very poorly over the near term.

Financial Data
(US$ in Thousands)

	12/31/2012	12/31/2011	12/31/2010	12/31/2009	12/31/2008	12/31/2007	12/31/2006	12/31/2005
Earnings Per Share	2.51	3.02	2.91	2.34	2.75	2.51	2.39	2.70
Cash Flow Per Share	2.85	3.31	3.38	3.19	3.25	2.83	...	2.86
Dividends Per Share	3.100	3.040	2.940	2.870	2.775	2.565	2.325	2.300
Dividend Payout %	123.51	100.66	101.03	122.65	100.91	102.19	97.28	85.19
Income Statement								
Total Revenue	194,000	223,900	195,100	167,300	154,200	137,400	63,400	53,200
EBITDA	170,000	185,000	160,700	134,600	137,300	128,700	59,800	51,200
Depn & Amortn	11,000	15,200	15,000	14,700	6,900	6,300	200	...
Income Before Taxes	137,000	157,400	137,100	106,100	107,700	89,000	44,700	50,200
Net Income	137,000	157,400	137,100	106,100	107,700	89,000	44,700	50,200
Average Shares	53,500	51,100	46,200	38,700	34,900	34,900	17,500	17,500
Balance Sheet								
Current Assets	12,000	38,300	12,300	11,700	11,800	11,000	6,500	2,300
Total Assets	1,998,000	2,082,000	1,650,500	1,675,100	1,448,500	1,492,600	777,800	315,700
Current Liabilities	11,000	9,200	506,600	72,100	20,500	13,800	9,300	14,100
Long-Term Obligations	685,000	739,400	30,100	487,900	532,400	568,800	463,400	...
Total Liabilities	697,000	749,000	538,000	571,600	572,900	592,500	473,900	14,100
Shares Outstanding	53,472	53,472	46,227	46,227	34,856	34,856	17,500	17,500
Statistical Record								
Return on Assets %	6.70	8.43	8.25	6.79	7.30	7.84	...	15.50
EBITDA Margin %	87.63	82.63	82.37	80.45	89.04	93.67	94.32	96.24
Net Margin %	70.62	70.30	70.27	63.42	69.84	64.77	70.50	94.36
Asset Turnover	0.09	0.12	0.12	0.11	0.10	0.12	...	0.16
Current Ratio	1.09	4.16	0.02	0.16	0.58	0.80	0.70	0.16
Price Range	47.58-38.50	54.45-40.17	52.00-34.40	41.10-23.25	37.30-18.82	42.83-32.98	36.00-30.00	40.60-31.20
P/E Ratio	18.96-15.34	18.03-13.30	17.87-11.82	17.56-9.94	13.56-6.84	17.06-13.14	15.06-12.55	15.04-11.56
Average Yield %	7.05	6.36	7.05	8.61	8.71	6.80	7.08	6.61

Address: 717 Texas Street, Suite 2400, Houston, TX 77002-2761 **Telephone:** 877-290-2772	**Web Site:** www.tcpipelineslp.com **Officers:** Karl Johannson - Chairman, Associate/Affiliate Company Officer Steven D. Becker - President, Principal Executive Officer	**Auditors:** KPMG LLP (USA) **Investor Contact:** 877-.29-0.2772 **Transfer Agents:** Computershare, Pittsburgh, PA

TCF FINANCIAL CORP.

Exchange	Symbol	Price	52Wk Range	Yield	P/E
NYS	TCB	$14.96 (3/28/2013)	14.96-9.85	1.34	N/A

*7 Year Price Score 62.87   *NYSE Composite Index=100   *12 Month Price Score 108.50

Interim Earnings (Per Share)

Qtr.	Mar	Jun	Sep	Dec
2008	0.38	0.19	0.24	0.20
2009	0.17	0.08	0.14	0.15
2010	0.26	0.32	0.26	0.21
2011	0.20	0.19	0.20	0.12
2012	(1.78)	0.20	0.06	0.15

Interim Dividends (Per Share)

Amt	Decl	Ex	Rec	Pay
0.05Q	04/16/2012	04/25/2012	04/27/2012	05/31/2012
0.05Q	07/18/2012	08/13/2012	08/15/2012	08/31/2012
0.05Q	10/25/2012	11/13/2012	11/15/2012	11/30/2012
0.05Q	01/24/2013	02/13/2013	02/15/2013	02/28/2013

Indicated Div: $0.20 (Div. Reinv. Plan)

Valuation Analysis

		Institutional Holding	
Forecast EPS	$0.92	No of Institutions	279
	(04/06/2013)		
Market Cap	$2.4 Billion	Shares	159,612,688
Book Value	$1.9 Billion	% Held	91.71
Price/Book	1.31		
Price/Sales	1.78		

TRADING VOLUME (thousand shares)

Business Summary: Banking (MIC: 5.1.1 SIC: 6021 NAIC: 522110)

TCF Financial is a national bank holding company. Through its subsidiaries, Co. operates three segments: Lending, Funding and Support Services. The Lending segment includes retail lending, commercial banking, leasing and equipment finance, inventory finance and auto finance. The Funding segment includes branch banking and treasury services. The Support Services segment includes holding company and corporate functions that provide data processing, bank operations and other professional services. As of Dec 31 2012, Co. had total assets of $18.2 billion and total deposits of $14 billion.

Recent Developments: For the year ended Dec 31 2012, net loss amounted to US$212.9 million versus net income of US$109.4 million in the prior year. Net interest income increased 11.5% to US$780.0 million from US$699.7 million in the prior year. Provision for loan losses was US$247.4 million versus US$200.8 million in the prior year, an increase of 23.2%. Non-interest income rose 10.3% to US$490.4 million from US$444.4 million, while non-interest expense advanced 78.2% to US$1.36 billion.

Prospects: Our evaluation of TCF Financial Corp. as of Apr. 7, 2013 is the result of our systematic analysis on three basic characteristics: earnings strength, relative valuation, and recent stock price movement. The company has enjoyed a very positive trend in earnings per share over the past 5 quarters and while recent estimates for the company have remained steady, TCB has posted results that fell short of analysts expectations. Based on operating earnings yield, the company is about fairly valued when compared to all of the companies in our coverage universe. Share price changes over the past year indicates that TCB will perform in line with the market over the near term.

Financial Data

(US$ in Thousands)	12/31/2012	12/31/2011	12/31/2010	12/31/2009	12/31/2008	12/31/2007	12/31/2006	12/31/2005
Earnings Per Share	(1.37)	0.71	1.05	0.54	1.01	2.12	1.90	2.00
Cash Flow Per Share	3.12	3.22	3.72	2.87	4.37	2.85	2.80	1.16
Tang Book Value Per Share	8.41	10.24	9.23	7.92	7.79	7.48	6.75	6.04
Dividends Per Share	0.200	0.200	0.200	0.400	1.000	0.970	0.920	0.850
Dividend Payout %	...	28.17	19.05	74.07	99.01	45.75	48.42	42.50
Income Statement								
Interest Income	884,623	937,951	969,877	958,181	964,395	968,023	886,138	732,022
Interest Expense	104,604	238,263	270,675	325,175	370,722	417,846	348,608	214,332
Net Interest Income	780,019	699,688	699,202	633,006	593,673	550,177	537,530	517,690
Provision for Losses	247,443	200,843	236,437	258,536	192,045	56,992	20,689	5,022
Non-Interest Income	490,423	444,434	537,985	525,855	498,435	541,457	489,464	478,330
Non-Interest Expense	1,362,554	764,451	763,124	767,784	694,403	662,124	649,197	610,588
Income Before Taxes	(339,555)	178,828	237,626	132,541	205,660	372,518	357,108	380,410
Income Taxes	(132,858)	64,441	87,765	45,854	76,702	105,710	112,165	115,278
Net Income	(212,884)	109,394	146,564	87,097	128,958	266,808	244,943	265,132
Average Shares	159,268	154,509	138,812	126,593	125,308	125,830	129,225	132,741
Balance Sheet								
Net Loans & Leases	15,168,885	13,908,904	14,522,485	14,346,273	13,173,448	12,413,429	11,419,711	10,363,976
Total Assets	18,225,917	18,979,388	18,465,025	17,845,025	16,740,357	15,977,054	14,669,734	13,365,360
Total Deposits	14,050,786	12,202,004	11,585,115	11,568,319	10,243,352	9,576,549	9,769,250	9,110,694
Total Liabilities	16,362,544	17,111,255	16,993,362	16,709,813	15,246,581	14,878,042	13,636,360	12,366,888
Stockholders' Equity	1,863,373	1,868,133	1,471,663	1,175,362	1,493,776	1,099,012	1,033,374	998,472
Shares Outstanding	163,386	160,323	142,913	129,202	127,425	126,602	130,418	133,776
Statistical Record								
Return on Assets %	N.M.	0.58	0.81	0.50	0.79	1.74	1.75	2.06
Return on Equity %	N.M.	6.55	11.07	6.53	9.92	25.02	24.11	27.10
Net Interest Margin %	88.18	74.60	72.09	66.06	61.56	56.84	60.66	70.72
Efficiency Ratio %	99.09	55.30	50.61	51.74	47.47	43.86	47.19	50.45
Loans to Deposits	1.08	1.14	1.25	1.24	1.29	1.30	1.17	1.14
Price Range	12.44-9.85	16.99-8.79	18.87-13.07	16.51-9.00	23.58-9.95	28.98-17.32	28.11-24.48	32.14-24.84
P/E Ratio	...	23.93-12.38	17.97-12.45	30.57-16.67	23.35-9.85	13.67-8.17	14.79-12.88	16.07-12.42
Average Yield %	1.77	1.54	1.30	3.02	6.14	3.86	3.50	3.12

Address: 200 Lake Street East, Mail Code EX0-03-A, Wayzata, MN 55391-1693 Telephone: 952-745-2760	Web Site: www.tcfexpress.com Officers: William A. Cooper - Chairman, Chief Executive Officer Barry N. Winslow - Vice-Chairman, Chief Risk Officer	Auditors: KPMG LLP Transfer Agents: Computershare, Inc., Providence, RI

TD AMERITRADE HOLDING CORP

Exchange	Symbol	Price	52Wk Range	Yield	P/E
NYS	AMTD	$20.62 (3/28/2013)	21.41-15.21	1.75	19.45

*7 Year Price Score 88.03   *NYSE Composite Index=100   *12 Month Price Score 105.04

Interim Earnings (Per Share)

Qtr.	Dec	Mar	Jun	Sep
2009-10	0.23	0.27	0.30	0.20
2010-11	0.25	0.30	0.27	0.29
2011-12	0.27	0.25	0.28	0.26
2012-13	0.27	...	...	...

Interim Dividends (Per Share)

Amt	Decl	Ex	Rec	Pay
0.06Q	07/17/2012	07/27/2012	07/31/2012	08/14/2012
0.09Q	10/29/2012	11/07/2012	11/09/2012	11/23/2012
0.50Sp	12/10/2012	12/19/2012	12/21/2012	12/31/2012
0.09Q	01/22/2013	01/30/2013	02/01/2013	02/15/2013

Indicated Div: $0.36

Valuation Analysis

		Institutional Holding	
Forecast EPS	$1.12	No of Institutions	
	(04/06/2013)	370	
Market Cap	$11.3 Billion	Shares	
Book Value	$4.3 Billion	223,736,112	
Price/Book	2.64	% Held	
Price/Sales	4.26	N/A	

Business Summary: Finance Intermediaries & Services (MIC: 5.5.1 SIC: 6211 NAIC: 523120)

TD Ameritrade Holding is a holding company. Through its subsidiaries, Co. provides securities brokerage services and technology-based financial services to retail investors, traders and independent registered investment advisors (RIAs). Co. provides its services mainly through the Internet, a branch network and relationships with RIAs. Co.'s client offerings include TD Ameritrade® for self-directed retail investors, and TD Ameritrade Institutional, a provider of brokerage and custody services. Co.'s products and services include: common and preferred stock; exchange-traded funds; options; futures; foreign exchange; mutual funds; fixed income; margin lending; and cash management services.

Recent Developments: For the quarter ended Dec 31 2012, net income decreased 3.3% to US$147.0 million from US$152.0 million in the year-earlier quarter. Revenues were US$653.0 million, down 0.3% from US$654.8 million the year before. Operating income was US$241.0 million versus US$228.5 million in the prior-year quarter, an increase of 5.5%. Direct operating expenses rose 42.2% to US$2.0 million from US$1.4 million in the comparable period the year before. Indirect operating expenses decreased 3.5% to US$410.0 million from US$424.9 million in the equivalent prior-year period.

Prospects: Our evaluation of TD Ameritrade Holding Corp. as of Apr. 7, 2013 is the result of our systematic analysis on three basic characteristics: earnings strength, relative valuation, and recent stock price movement. The company has managed to produce a neutral trend in earnings per share over the past 5 quarters and while recent estimates for the company have been mixed, AMTD has posted better than expected results. Based on operating earnings yield, the company is about fairly valued when compared to all of the companies in our coverage universe. Share price changes over the past year indicates that AMTD will perform in line with the market over the near term.

Financial Data

(US$ in Thousands)	3 Mos	09/30/2012	09/30/2011	09/30/2010	09/30/2009	09/30/2008	09/30/2007	09/29/2006
Earnings Per Share	1.06	1.06	1.11	1.00	1.10	1.33	1.06	0.95
Cash Flow Per Share	3.03	1.08	1.39	1.00	1.04	1.67	0.96	0.89
Tang Book Value Per Share	1.65	1.88	1.13	0.31	N.M.	N.M.	N.M.	N.M.
Dividends Per Share	0.770	0.240	0.200	...	...	...	...	6.000
Dividend Payout %	72.64	22.64	18.02					631.58
Income Statement								
Total Revenue	653,000	2,647,000	2,767,485	2,566,756	2,423,091	2,786,972	2,632,413	2,139,351
EBITDA	266,000	1,026,000	1,145,614	1,057,406	1,173,345	1,401,224	1,207,345	993,579
Depn & Amortn	23,000	92,000	97,126	100,463	73,870	59,275	54,469	42,286
Income Before Taxes	237,000	906,000	1,016,471	912,085	1,059,405	1,263,502	1,034,703	857,305
Income Taxes	90,000	320,000	378,718	319,897	415,700	459,585	388,803	330,546
Net Income	147,000	586,000	637,753	592,188	643,705	803,917	645,900	526,759
Average Shares	551,000	554,000	576,462	591,922	587,252	603,133	608,263	555,465
Balance Sheet								
Current Assets	16,285,000	11,372,000	10,580,730	9,723,347	8,523,584	12,484,107	15,145,393	12,074,513
Total Assets	21,018,000	19,513,000	17,125,762	14,726,918	18,371,810	15,951,522	18,092,327	16,558,469
Current Liabilities	15,244,000	13,738,000	11,662,372	9,631,971	13,377,062	11,581,940	14,455,458	13,117,523
Long-Term Obligations	1,091,000	1,350,000	1,347,573	1,323,068	1,443,465	1,444,544	1,481,948	1,710,712
Total Liabilities	16,740,000	15,088,000	13,009,945	10,955,039	14,820,527	13,026,484	15,937,406	14,828,235
Stockholders' Equity	4,278,000	4,425,000	4,115,817	3,771,879	3,551,283	2,925,038	2,154,921	1,730,234
Shares Outstanding	547,000	545,000	554,285	576,134	587,109	593,130	594,688	607,626
Statistical Record								
Return on Assets %	2.83	3.19	4.00	3.58	3.75	4.71	3.72	3.20
Return on Equity %	13.81	13.68	16.17	16.17	19.88	31.56	33.16	32.51
EBITDA Margin %	40.74	38.76	41.40	41.20	48.42	50.28	45.86	46.44
Net Margin %	22.51	22.14	23.04	23.07	26.57	28.85	24.54	24.62
Asset Turnover	0.13	0.14	0.17	0.16	0.14	0.16	0.15	0.13
Current Ratio	1.07	0.83	0.91	1.01	0.64	1.08	1.05	0.92
Debt to Equity	0.26	0.31	0.33	0.35	0.41	0.49	0.69	0.99
Price Range	20.54-15.21	20.54-14.05	22.49-13.76	21.27-14.62	20.14-9.71	23.48-15.91	21.15-14.70	26.10-13.64
P/E Ratio	19.38-14.35	19.38-13.25	20.26-12.40	21.27-14.62	18.31-8.83	17.65-11.96	19.95-13.87	27.47-14.36
Average Yield %	4.52	1.41	1.07	...	...	...	...	30.44

Address: 4211 South 102nd Street, Omaha, NE 68127 **Telephone:** 402-331-7856 **Fax:** 402-597-7789	**Web Site:** www.amtd.com **Officers:** Joseph H. Moglia - Chairman Fredric J. Tomczyk - President, Chief Executive Officer	**Auditors:** Ernst & Young LLP **Investor Contact:** 800-237-8692 **Transfer Agents:** Computershare, Pittsburgh, PA

TE CONNECTIVITY LTD

Exchange	Symbol	Price	52Wk Range	Yield	P/E
NYS	TEL	$41.93 (3/28/2013)	42.54-30.51	2.00	15.94

*7 Year Price Score N/A *NYSE Composite Index=100 ***12 Month Price Score 105.89**

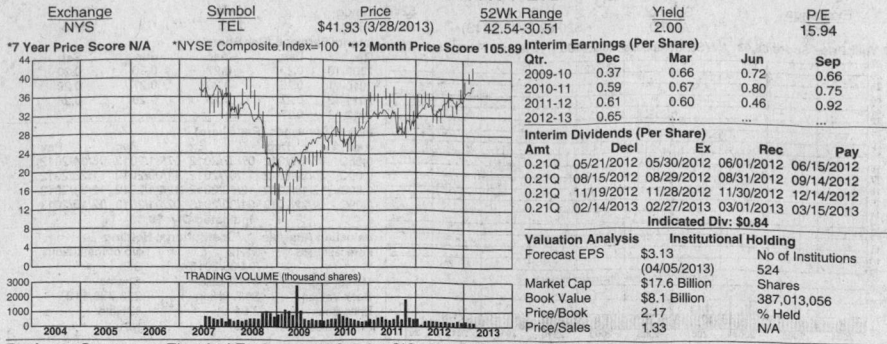

Interim Earnings (Per Share)

Qtr.	Dec	Mar	Jun	Sep
2009-10	0.37	0.66	0.72	0.66
2010-11	0.59	0.67	0.80	0.75
2011-12	0.61	0.60	0.46	0.92
2012-13	0.65	...	...	...

Interim Dividends (Per Share)

Amt	Decl	Ex	Rec	Pay
0.21Q	05/21/2012	05/30/2012	06/01/2012	06/15/2012
0.21Q	08/15/2012	08/29/2012	08/31/2012	09/14/2012
0.21Q	11/19/2012	11/28/2012	11/30/2012	12/14/2012
0.21Q	02/14/2013	02/27/2013	03/01/2013	03/15/2013

Indicated Div: $0.84

Valuation Analysis		Institutional Holding	
Forecast EPS	$3.13	No of Institutions	
	(04/05/2013)	524	
Market Cap	$17.6 Billion	Shares	
Book Value	$8.1 Billion	387,013,056	
Price/Book	2.17	% Held	
Price/Sales	1.33	N/A	

Business Summary: Electrical Equipment (MIC: 7.3.1 SIC: 5065 NAIC: 334111)

TE Connectivity designs and manufactures products that are designed to connect and protect the flow of power and data inside products used by consumers and industries. Co. operates through three reporting segments: Transportation Solutions, which provides electronic components, including connectors, relays, wire and cable, circuit protection devices, sensors, and heat shrink tubing and molded parts; Communications and Industrial Solutions, which supplies electronic components, including connectors, relays, circuit protection devices, antennas, and heat shrink tubing; and Network Solutions, which supplies infrastructure components and systems for the telecommunications and energy markets.

Recent Developments: For the quarter ended Dec 28 2012, income from continuing operations increased 16.3% to US$279.0 million from US$240.0 million in the year-earlier quarter. Net income increased 5.7% to US$277.0 million from US$262.0 million in the year-earlier quarter. Revenues were US$3.13 billion, down 1.1% from US$3.17 billion the year before. Operating income was US$293.0 million versus US$361.0 million in the prior-year quarter, a decrease of 18.8%. Direct operating expenses declined 3.7% to US$2.15 billion from US$2.23 billion in the comparable period the year before. Indirect operating expenses increased 19.6% to US$696.0 million from US$582.0 million in the equivalent prior-year period.

Prospects: Our evaluation of TE Connectivity Ltd. as of Apr. 7, 2013 is the result of our systematic analysis on three basic characteristics: earnings strength, relative valuation, and recent stock price movement. The company has enjoyed a very positive trend in earnings per share over the past 5 quarters. However, while recent estimates for the company have been lowered by analysts, TEL has posted better than expected results. Based on operating earnings yield, the company is undervalued when compared to all of the companies in our coverage universe. Share price changes over the past year indicates that TEL will perform in line with the market over the near term.

Financial Data

(US$ in Millions)	3 Mos	09/28/2012	09/30/2011	09/24/2010	09/25/2009	09/26/2008	09/28/2007	09/29/2006
Earnings Per Share	2.63	2.59	2.81	2.41	(7.09)	3.67	(1.11)	2.40
Cash Flow Per Share	5.05	4.58	4.00	3.72	2.90	2.05	3.10	3.36
Tang Book Value Per Share	5.90	5.47	7.63	7.77	7.52	7.59	7.34	...
Dividends Per Share	0.810	0.780	0.680	0.640	0.640	0.580	...	...
Dividend Payout %	30.80	30.12	24.20	26.56	...	15.80	...	...
Income Statement								
Total Revenue	3,134	13,282	14,312	12,070	10,256	14,834	13,460	12,300
EBITDA	219	2,070	2,274	2,182	(3,038)	2,836	1,032	1,896
Depn & Amortn	152	502	506	489	484	523	498	448
Income Before Taxes	34	1,415	1,629	1,558	(3,670)	2,157	356	1,240
Income Taxes	(245)	249	376	493	(576)	558	494	46
Net Income	277	1,112	1,245	1,103	(3,256)	1,782	(554)	1,193
Average Shares	426	430	443	457	459	486	497	497
Balance Sheet								
Current Assets	5,753	6,503	6,632	6,731	5,579	7,095	9,873	6,550
Total Assets	18,136	19,306	17,723	16,992	16,220	21,600	23,688	19,091
Current Liabilities	3,111	4,004	3,401	3,460	2,615	3,332	6,185	3,149
Long-Term Obligations	2,687	2,696	2,668	2,307	2,316	3,161	3,373	3,371
Total Liabilities	10,007	11,335	10,249	9,944	9,204	10,527	12,311	7,931
Stockholders' Equity	8,129	7,971	7,474	7,048	7,016	11,073	11,377	11,160
Shares Outstanding	420	422	423	443	458	463	497	...
Statistical Record								
Return on Assets %	6.33	6.02	7.06	6.66	N.M.	7.89	N.M.	...
Return on Equity %	14.37	14.44	16.87	15.73	N.M.	15.92	N.M.	...
EBITDA Margin %	6.99	15.59	15.89	18.08	N.M.	19.12	7.67	15.41
Net Margin %	8.84	8.37	8.70	9.14	N.M.	12.01	N.M.	9.70
Asset Turnover	0.74	0.72	0.81	0.73	0.54	0.66	0.63	...
Current Ratio	1.85	1.62	1.95	1.95	2.13	2.13	1.60	2.08
Debt to Equity	0.33	0.34	0.36	0.33	0.33	0.29	0.30	0.30
Price Range	37.95-30.49	37.30-27.25	38.51-27.86	32.85-21.12	27.66-7.44	40.12-26.90	40.30-32.45	...
P/E Ratio	14.43-11.59	14.40-10.52	13.70-9.91	13.63-8.76	...	10.93-7.33	...	...
Average Yield %	2.36	2.31	2.01	2.46	3.68	1.66	...	...

Address: Rheinstrasse 20, Schaffhausen, CH-8200	Web Site: www.tycoelectronics.com	Auditors: Deloitte & Touche LLP
Telephone: 526-336-661	Officers: Thomas J. Lynch - Chairman, Chief Executive Officer, Division Officer Robert W. Hau - Executive Vice President, Chief Financial Officer	Investor Contact: 610-893-9551
		Transfer Agents: Computershare Shareowner Services LLC, Jersey City, NJ

TECO ENERGY INC.

Exchange	Symbol	Price	52Wk Range	Yield	P/E
NYS	TE	$17.82 (3/28/2013)	18.45-16.21	4.94	18.00

*7 Year Price Score 94.56   *NYSE Composite Index=100   *12 Month Price Score 91.76

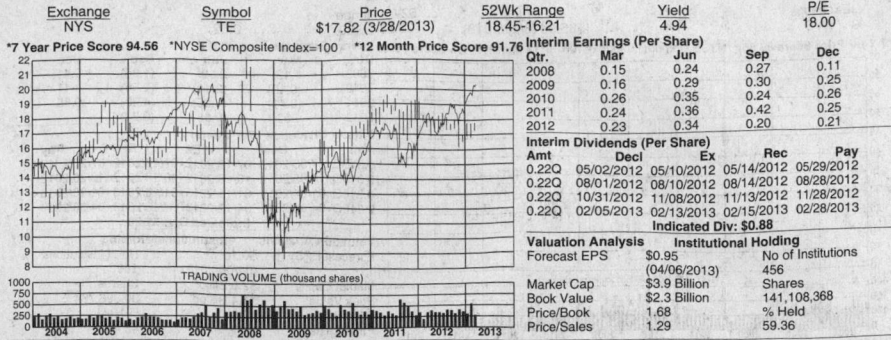

Interim Earnings (Per Share)

Qtr.	Mar	Jun	Sep	Dec
2008	0.15	0.24	0.27	0.11
2009	0.16	0.29	0.30	0.25
2010	0.26	0.35	0.24	0.26
2011	0.24	0.36	0.42	0.25
2012	0.23	0.34	0.20	0.21

Interim Dividends (Per Share)

Amt	Decl	Ex	Rec	Pay
0.22Q	05/02/2012	05/10/2012	05/14/2012	05/29/2012
0.22Q	08/01/2012	08/10/2012	08/14/2012	08/28/2012
0.22Q	10/31/2012	11/08/2012	11/13/2012	11/28/2012
0.22Q	02/05/2013	02/13/2013	02/15/2013	02/28/2013

Indicated Div: $0.88

Valuation Analysis — **Institutional Holding**

Forecast EPS	$0.95	No of Institutions
	(04/06/2013)	456
Market Cap	$3.9 Billion	Shares
Book Value	$2.3 Billion	141,108,368
Price/Book	1.68	% Held
Price/Sales	1.29	59.36

Business Summary: Electric Utilities (MIC: 3.1.1 SIC: 4911 NAIC: 221122)

TECO Energy is a holding company for regulated utilities and other businesses. Co. holds all of the common stock of Tampa Electric Company (Tampa Electric), as well as owns TECO Coal Corporation (Teco Coal) and TECO Guatemala, Inc. (TECO Guatemala). Tampa Electric provides retail electric service to more than 678,000 customers in West Central Florida while its Peoples Gas System division serves about 340,000 customers in Florida's metropolitan areas. TECO Coal operates surface and underground mines as well as coal processing facilities in eastern Kentucky, Tennessee and southwestern Virginia. TECO Guatemala has subsidiaries that have interests in independent power projects in Guatemala.

Recent Developments: For the year ended Dec 31 2012, income from continuing operations decreased 1.9% to US$246.0 million from US$250.8 million a year earlier. Net income decreased 21.9% to US$213.0 million from US$272.9 million in the prior year. Revenues were US$3.00 billion, down 6.6% from US$3.21 billion the year before. Operating income was US$556.5 million versus US$583.2 million in the prior year, a decrease of 4.6%. Direct operating expenses declined 9.5% to US$1.89 billion from US$2.09 billion in the comparable period the year before. Indirect operating expenses increased 2.2% to US$552.9 million from US$540.9 million in the equivalent prior-year period.

Prospects: Our evaluation of TECO Energy Inc. as of Apr. 7, 2013 is the result of our systematic analysis on three basic characteristics: earnings strength, relative valuation, and recent stock price movement. The company has managed to produce a neutral trend in earnings per share over the past 5 quarters. However, while recent estimates for the company have been mixed, TE has posted better than expected results. Based on operating earnings yield, the company is undervalued when compared to all of the companies in our coverage universe. Share price changes over the past year indicates that TE will perform poorly over the near term.

Financial Data
(US$ in Thousands)

	12/31/2012	12/31/2011	12/31/2010	12/31/2009	12/31/2008	12/31/2007	12/31/2006	12/31/2005
Earnings Per Share	0.99	1.27	1.11	1.00	0.77	1.97	1.18	1.31
Cash Flow Per Share	3.52	3.53	3.13	3.42	1.84	2.65	2.73	0.84
Tang Book Value Per Share	10.58	10.25	9.84	9.47	9.15	9.28	7.97	7.36
Dividends Per Share	0.880	0.850	0.815	0.800	0.795	0.775	0.760	0.760
Dividend Payout %	88.89	66.93	73.42	80.00	103.25	39.34	64.41	58.02
Income Statement								
Total Revenue	2,996,600	3,343,400	3,487,900	3,310,500	3,375,300	3,536,100	3,448,100	3,010,100
EBITDA	876,600	938,500	927,600	768,000	670,100	974,200	783,200	721,700
Depn & Amortn	309,300	306,600	297,100	275,200	257,300	254,000	270,300	267,600
Income Before Taxes	383,800	426,800	399,200	265,800	183,900	462,400	234,600	165,400
Income Taxes	137,800	153,900	170,000	98,600	94,400	214,200	118,700	101,900
Net Income	212,700	272,600	239,000	213,900	162,400	413,200	246,300	274,500
Average Shares	215,000	215,100	214,800	213,100	211,400	209,900	208,700	208,200
Balance Sheet								
Current Assets	856,800	797,900	757,600	651,600	765,400	789,800	1,285,700	1,272,200
Total Assets	7,356,500	7,322,200	7,194,600	7,219,500	7,147,400	6,765,200	7,361,800	7,170,100
Current Liabilities	602,200	1,019,700	752,300	771,300	784,300	617,600	1,350,400	925,900
Long-Term Obligations	2,972,700	2,687,300	3,148,100	3,201,600	3,206,600	3,158,400	3,212,600	3,709,200
Total Liabilities	5,064,700	5,055,600	5,024,900	5,134,100	5,139,700	4,748,200	5,632,800	5,578,400
Stockholders' Equity	2,291,800	2,266,600	2,169,700	2,085,400	2,007,700	2,017,000	1,729,000	1,591,700
Shares Outstanding	216,600	215,800	214,900	213,900	212,900	210,900	209,500	208,200
Statistical Record								
Return on Assets %	2.89	3.76	3.32	2.98	2.33	5.85	3.39	3.30
Return on Equity %	9.31	12.29	11.23	10.45	8.05	22.06	14.83	19.09
EBITDA Margin %	29.25	28.07	26.59	23.20	19.85	27.55	22.71	23.98
Net Margin %	7.10	8.15	6.85	6.46	4.81	11.69	7.14	9.12
Asset Turnover	0.41	0.46	0.48	0.46	0.48	0.50	0.47	0.36
Current Ratio	1.42	0.78	1.01	0.84	0.98	1.28	0.95	1.37
Debt to Equity	1.30	1.19	1.45	1.54	1.60	1.57	1.86	2.33
Price Range	19.17-16.21	19.60-16.12	17.90-14.69	16.61-8.60	21.96-10.72	18.50-15.13	17.67-14.50	19.21-14.94
P/E Ratio	19.36-16.37	15.43-12.69	16.13-13.23	16.61-8.60	28.52-13.92	9.39-7.68	14.97-12.29	14.66-11.40
Average Yield %	4.98	4.64	4.95	6.34	4.87	4.57	4.71	4.44

Address: 702 N. Franklin Street, Tampa, FL 33602 **Telephone:** 813-228-1111 **Fax:** 813-228-1670	**Web Site:** www.tecoenergy.com **Officers:** John B. Ramil - President, Chief Executive Officer Chalres A. Attal - Senior Vice President, Chief Legal Officer, General Counsel	**Auditors:** PricewaterhouseCoopers LLP **Investor Contact:** 800-810-2032 **Transfer Agents:** Computershare, Pittsburgh, PA

TEEKAY CORP

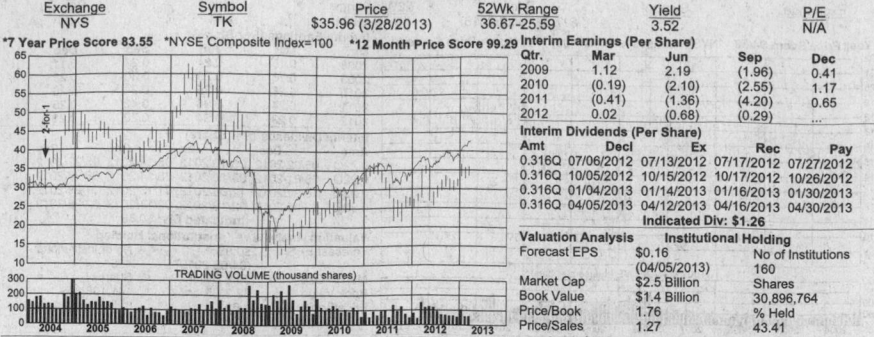

Exchange	Symbol	Price	52Wk Range	Yield	P/E
NYS	TK	$35.96 (3/28/2013)	36.67-25.59	3.52	N/A

*7 Year Price Score 83.55   *NYSE Composite Index=100   *12 Month Price Score 99.29

Interim Earnings (Per Share)

Qtr.	Mar	Jun	Sep	Dec
2009	1.12	2.19	(1.96)	0.41
2010	(0.19)	(2.10)	(2.55)	1.17
2011	(0.41)	(1.36)	(4.20)	0.65
2012	0.02	(0.68)	(0.29)	

Interim Dividends (Per Share)

Amt	Decl	Ex	Rec	Pay
0.316Q	07/06/2012	07/13/2012	07/17/2012	07/27/2012
0.316Q	10/05/2012	10/15/2012	10/17/2012	10/26/2012
0.316Q	01/04/2013	01/14/2013	01/16/2013	01/30/2013
0.316Q	04/05/2013	04/12/2013	04/16/2013	04/30/2013

Indicated Div: $1.26

Valuation Analysis

Forecast EPS	$0.16 (04/05/2013)
Market Cap	$2.5 Billion
Book Value	$1.4 Billion
Price/Book	1.76
Price/Sales	1.27

Institutional Holding

No of Institutions	160
Shares	30,896,764
% Held	43.41

TRADING VOLUME (thousand shares)

Business Summary: Equipment & Services (MIC: 9.1.3 SIC: 4412 NAIC: 483111)

Teekay is a provider of international crude oil and gas marine transportation services. Co. also provides offshore oil production, storage and offloading services. Co.'s shuttle tanker and FSO and FPSO segment includes its shuttle tanker operations, floating storage and off-take (or FSO) units, and its floating production, storage and offloading (or FPSO) units, which primarily operate under long-term fixed-rate contracts. Co.'s liquefied gas segment includes its liquefied natural gas and liquefied petroleum gas carriers that are subject to long-term, fixed-rate time-charter contracts. Co.'s conventional tanker segment includes its conventional crude oil tankers and product carriers.

Recent Developments: For the quarter ended Sep 30 2012, net loss amounted to US$10.5 million versus a net loss of US$342.3 million in the year-earlier quarter. Revenues were US$463.5 million, down 1.0% from US$468.1 million the year before. Operating income was US$48.4 million versus a loss of US$76.4 million in the prior-year quarter. Direct operating expenses declined 25.1% to US$29.7 million from US$39.6 million in the comparable period the year before. Indirect operating expenses decreased 23.7% to US$385.5 million from US$504.9 million in the equivalent prior-year period.

Prospects: Our evaluation of Teekay Corp. as of Apr. 7, 2013 is the result of our systematic analysis on three basic characteristics: earnings strength, relative valuation, and recent stock price movement. The company has enjoyed a very positive trend in earnings per share over the past 5 quarters. However, while recent estimates for the company have been lowered by analysts, TK has posted results that fell short of analysts expectations. Based on operating earnings yield, the company is overvalued when compared to all of the companies in our coverage universe. Share price changes over the past year indicates that TK will perform in line with the market over the near term.

Financial Data

(US$ in Thousands)	9 Mos	6 Mos	3 Mos	12/31/2011	12/31/2010	12/31/2009	12/31/2008	12/31/2007
Earnings Per Share	(0.30)	(4.21)	(4.89)	(5.25)	(3.67)	1.76	(6.48)	2.43
Cash Flow Per Share	4.58	3.46	3.73	1.53	5.65	5.08	(1.35)	3.48
Tang Book Value Per Share	...	15.07	15.89	16.39	22.49	25.08	22.07	27.39
Dividends Per Share	...	...	...	1.265	1.265	1.265	...	...
Dividend Payout %	...	...	...	...	...	71.88	...	...
Income Statement								
Total Revenue	1,441,012	977,475	495,564	1,953,782	2,068,878	2,172,049	3,193,655	2,406,622
EBITDA	606,222	24,959	51,514	162,576	353,841	663,072	585,711	861,438
Depn & Amortn	342,438	(35,907)	(17,777)	382,172	392,451	361,199	344,377	258,134
Income Before Taxes	141,490	(20,450)	29,037	(347,122)	(161,718)	180,424	(479,985)	397,904
Income Taxes	...	(5,417)	(3,568)	4,290	(6,340)	22,889	(56,176)	...
Net Income	(66,469)	(46,208)	1,066	(368,916)	(267,287)	128,412	(469,455)	181,251
Average Shares	69,372	69,231	70,146	70,234	72,862	73,058	72,493	74,735
Balance Sheet								
Current Assets	1,245,287	1,280,236	1,389,080	1,212,756	1,262,090	864,378	1,394,503	1,017,387
Total Assets	11,243,638	11,155,275	11,168,646	11,131,396	9,911,098	9,510,916	10,215,001	10,060,153
Current Liabilities	1,336,428	1,389,906	1,158,918	1,130,930	1,153,638	845,863	1,031,140	922,212
Long-Term Obligations	5,036,989	5,435,090	5,663,946	5,642,841	4,626,308	4,931,216	5,377,474	5,285,397
Total Liabilities	9,839,817	9,815,983	9,770,350	9,701,700	7,932,651	7,270,826	8,146,534	7,372,283
Stockholders' Equity	1,403,821	1,339,292	1,398,296	1,429,696	1,978,447	2,240,090	2,068,467	2,687,870
Shares Outstanding	...	69,266	69,178	68,732	72,012	72,694	72,512	72,772
Statistical Record								
Return on Assets %	N.M.	N.M.	N.M.	N.M.	N.M.	1.30	N.M.	2.04
Return on Equity %	N.M.	N.M.	N.M.	N.M.	N.M.	5.96	N.M.	6.95
EBITDA Margin %	42.07	2.55	10.40	8.32	17.10	30.53	18.34	35.79
Net Margin %	N.M.	N.M.	0.22	N.M.	N.M.	5.91	N.M.	7.53
Asset Turnover	0.18	0.19	0.19	0.19	0.21	0.22	0.31	0.27
Current Ratio	0.93	0.92	1.20	1.07	1.09	1.02	1.35	1.10
Debt to Equity	3.59	4.06	4.05	3.95	2.34	2.20	2.60	1.97
Price Range	36.12-21.43	36.12-21.43	37.18-21.43	37.18-21.43	33.81-21.40	25.24-11.84	53.30-11.51	62.66-42.52
P/E Ratio	...	...	...	...	...	14.34-6.73	...	25.79-17.50
Average Yield %	...	...	...	4.21	4.68	6.64	...	...

Address: 4th floor, Belvedere Building, 69 Pitts Bay Road, Hamilton, HM 08 **Telephone:** 441-298-2530	**Web Site:** www.teekay.com **Officers:** C. Sean Day - Chairman Peter Evensen - President, Chief Executive Officer	**Auditors:** KPMG LLP **Investor Contact:** 604-844-6654 **Transfer Agents:** ComputerShare Investor Services, Providence, RI

TELEFLEX INCORPORATED

Exchange	Symbol	Price	52Wk Range	Yield	P/E
NYS	TFX	$84.51 (3/28/2013)	84.51-57.73	1.61	N/A

*7 Year Price Score 100.81 *NYSE Composite Index=100 *12 Month Price Score 107.86

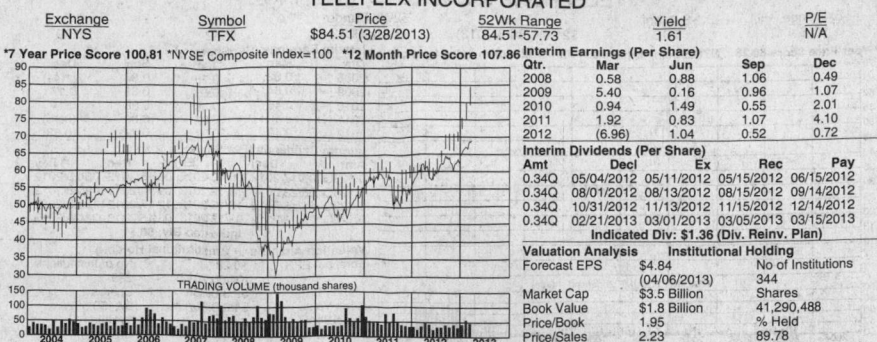

Interim Earnings (Per Share)

Qtr.	Mar	Jun	Sep	Dec
2008	0.58	0.88	1.06	0.49
2009	5.40	0.16	0.96	1.07
2010	0.94	1.49	0.55	2.01
2011	1.92	0.83	1.07	4.10
2012	(6.96)	1.04	0.52	0.72

Interim Dividends (Per Share)

Amt	Decl	Ex	Rec	Pay
0.34Q	05/04/2012	05/11/2012	05/15/2012	06/15/2012
0.34Q	08/01/2012	08/13/2012	08/15/2012	09/14/2012
0.34Q	10/31/2012	11/13/2012	11/15/2012	12/14/2012
0.34Q	02/21/2013	03/01/2013	03/05/2013	03/15/2013

Indicated Div: $1.36 (Div. Reinv. Plan)

Valuation Analysis | Institutional Holding

Forecast EPS	$4.84	No of Institutions	
	(04/06/2013)	344	
Market Cap	$3.5 Billion	Shares	
Book Value	$1.8 Billion	41,290,488	
Price/Book	1.95	% Held	
Price/Sales	2.23	89.78	

Business Summary: Medical Instruments & Equipment (MIC: 4.3.1 SIC: 3841 NAIC: 339112)

Teleflex is a provider of medical technology products. Co. primarily designs, develops, manufactures and supplies single-use medical devices used by hospitals and healthcare providers. Co. provides a platform of products, which it categorizes into four groups: Critical Care, which are used in a range of procedures for vascular access, anesthesia and airway management, respiratory care, treatment of urologic conditions and other procedures; Surgical Care, which includes ligation and closure products, access ports, and fluid management products; Cardiac Care, which includes diagnostic catheters and capital equipment; and Original Equipment Manufacturer and Development Services.

Recent Developments: For the year ended Dec 31 2012, loss from continuing operations was US$181.8 million compared with income of US$119.3 million a year earlier. Net loss amounted to US$189.1 million versus net income of US$325.0 million in the prior year. Revenues were US$1.55 billion, up 3.9% from US$1.49 billion the year before. Operating loss was US$97.4 million versus an income of US$229.6 million in the prior year. Direct operating expenses rose 2.4% to US$802.8 million from US$783.8 million in the comparable period the year before. Indirect operating expenses increased 76.5% to US$845.6 million from US$479.2 million in the equivalent prior-year period.

Prospects: Our evaluation of Teleflex Inc. as of Apr. 7, 2013 is the result of our systematic analysis on three basic characteristics: earnings strength, relative valuation, and recent stock price movement. The company has generated a negative trend in earnings per share over the past 5 quarters and while recent estimates for the company have been raised by analysts, TFX has posted better than expected results. Based on operating earnings yield, the company is about fairly valued when compared to all of the companies in our coverage universe. Share price changes over the past year indicates that TFX will perform in line with the market over the near term.

Financial Data
(US$ in Thousands)

	12/31/2012	12/31/2011	12/31/2010	12/31/2009	12/31/2008	12/31/2007	12/31/2006	12/25/2005
Earnings Per Share	(4.65)	7.92	4.99	7.59	3.01	3.73	3.49	3.39
Cash Flow Per Share	4.73	2.55	5.18	4.78	4.45	7.21	8.51	8.31
Tang Book Value Per Share	N.M.	N.M.	N.M.	3.04	N.M.	N.M.	17.31	15.79
Dividends Per Share	1.360	1.360	1.360	1.360	1.340	1.245	1.105	0.970
Dividend Payout %	...	17.17	27.25	17.92	44.52	33.38	31.66	28.61
Income Statement								
Total Revenue	1,551,009	1,528,911	1,801,705	1,890,062	2,420,949	1,934,332	2,646,757	2,514,552
EBITDA	(16,907)	303,377	319,152	370,825	451,207	245,556	352,284	347,850
Depn & Amortn	80,468	85,617	92,189	101,057	111,218	71,814	97,672	99,782
Income Before Taxes	(165,369)	148,703	147,793	182,846	220,977	109,348	219,027	207,915
Income Taxes	16,413	27,000	21,887	39,904	52,169	122,767	54,140	47,806
Net Income	(190,057)	323,329	201,094	302,994	119,774	146,484	139,430	138,817
Average Shares	40,859	40,801	40,280	39,936	39,832	39,259	39,988	40,958
Balance Sheet								
Current Assets	1,069,079	1,280,256	921,233	1,003,934	957,386	1,009,810	1,139,529	1,168,576
Total Assets	3,739,497	3,924,103	3,643,155	3,839,005	3,926,744	4,187,997	2,359,052	2,506,385
Current Liabilities	274,405	271,007	420,763	337,107	525,940	690,682	470,775	589,677
Long-Term Obligations	965,280	954,809	813,409	1,192,491	1,437,538	1,499,130	487,370	505,272
Total Liabilities	1,960,547	1,943,515	1,859,779	2,258,764	2,680,289	2,859,154	1,169,631	1,364,311
Stockholders' Equity	1,778,950	1,980,588	1,783,376	1,580,241	1,246,455	1,328,843	1,189,421	1,142,074
Shares Outstanding	40,972	40,740	39,995	39,755	39,684	39,451	39,018	40,357
Statistical Record								
Return on Assets %	N.M.	8.55	5.38	7.80	2.94	4.47	5.64	5.42
Return on Equity %	N.M.	17.18	11.96	21.44	9.28	11.63	11.77	12.36
EBITDA Margin %	N.M.	19.84	17.71	19.62	18.64	12.69	13.31	13.83
Net Margin %	N.M.	21.15	11.16	16.03	4.95	7.57	5.27	5.52
Asset Turnover	0.40	0.40	0.48	0.49	0.60	0.59	1.07	0.98
Current Ratio	3.90	4.72	2.19	2.98	1.82	1.46	2.42	1.98
Debt to Equity	0.54	0.48	0.46	0.75	1.15	1.13	0.41	0.44
Price Range	71.38-57.73	63.81-49.51	66.02-48.06	54.95-38.15	67.86-41.99	86.19-57.25	71.80-50.50	71.80-48.62
P/E Ratio	...	8.06-6.25	13.23-9.63	7.24-5.03	22.54-13.95	23.11-15.35	20.57-14.47	21.18-14.34
Average Yield %	2.13	2.33	2.39	2.88	2.41	1.74	1.79	1.63

Address: 155 South Limerick Road, Limerick, PA 19468	**Web Site:** www.teleflex.com	**Auditors:** PricewaterhouseCoopers LLP
Telephone: 610-948-5100	**Officers:** Benson F. Smith - Chairman, President, Chief Executive Officer Thomas E. Powell - Executive Vice President, Senior Vice President, Chief Financial Officer	**Investor Contact:** 610-948-2836
Fax: 610-948-5101		**Transfer Agents:** American Stock Transfer & Trust Company, New York, NY

TELEPHONE & DATA SYSTEMS, INC.

Exchange	Symbol	Price	52Wk Range	Yield	P/E
NYS	TDS	$21.07 (3/28/2013)	26.21-19.42	2.42	28.09

*7 Year Price Score 60.26   *NYSE Composite Index=100   *12 Month Price Score 91.17

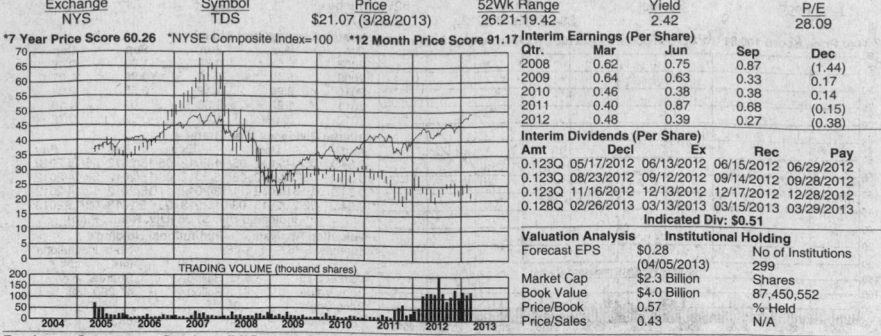

Interim Earnings (Per Share)

Qtr.	Mar	Jun	Sep	Dec
2008	0.62	0.75	0.87	(1.44)
2009	0.64	0.63	0.33	0.17
2010	0.46	0.38	0.38	0.14
2011	0.40	0.87	0.68	(0.15)
2012	0.48	0.39	0.27	(0.38)

Interim Dividends (Per Share)

Amt	Decl	Ex	Rec	Pay
0.123Q	05/17/2012	06/13/2012	06/15/2012	06/29/2012
0.123Q	08/23/2012	09/12/2012	09/14/2012	09/28/2012
0.123Q	11/16/2012	12/13/2012	12/17/2012	12/28/2012
0.128Q	02/26/2013	03/13/2013	03/15/2013	03/29/2013

Indicated Div: $0.51

Valuation Analysis

		Institutional Holding	
Forecast EPS	$0.28 (04/05/2013)	No of Institutions	299
Market Cap	$2.3 Billion	Shares	87,450,552
Book Value	$4.0 Billion	% Held	N/A
Price/Book	0.57		
Price/Sales	0.43		

Business Summary: Services (MIC: 6.1.2 SIC: 4813 NAIC: 517110)

Telephone and Data Systems is a telecommunications service company with wireless operations provided by its 84.0%-owned subsidiary, United States Cellular Corporation and wireline operations provided by its wholly owned subsidiary, TDS Telecommunications Corporation. At Dec 31 2011, Co. served 5.9 million U.S. Cellular customers and 1.1 million TDS Telecom equivalent access lines. Co. is also a 63.0% owner of Airadigm Communications, Inc., a Wisconsin-based wireless service provider. Co. also conducts printing and distribution services through its majority-owned subsidiary, Suttle-Straus, Inc.

Recent Developments: For the year ended Dec 31 2012, net income decreased 51.0% to US$122.7 million from US$250.2 million in the prior year. Revenues were US$5.35 billion, up 3.2% from US$5.18 billion the year before. Operating income was US$183.9 million versus US$362.5 million in the prior year, a decrease of 49.3%. Direct operating expenses rose 10.8% to US$2.27 billion from US$2.05 billion in the comparable period the year before. Indirect operating expenses increased 4.4% to US$2.89 billion from US$2.77 billion in the equivalent prior-year period.

Prospects: Our evaluation of Telephone and Data Systems Inc. as of Apr. 7, 2013 is the result of our systematic analysis on three basic characteristics: earnings strength, relative valuation, and recent stock price movement. The company has managed to produce a neutral trend in earnings per share over the past 5 quarters. However, while recent estimates for the company have been lowered by analysts, TDS has posted results that fell short of analysts expectations. Based on operating earnings yield, the company is overvalued when compared to all of the companies in our coverage universe. Share price changes over the past year indicates that TDS will perform well over the near term.

Financial Data
(US$ in Thousands)

	12/31/2012	12/31/2011	12/31/2010	12/31/2009	12/31/2008	12/31/2007	12/31/2006	12/31/2005
Earnings Per Share	0.75	1.83	1.36	1.77	0.80	3.22	1.37	1.91
Cash Flow Per Share	10.14	11.57	10.67	10.08	7.31	8.00	7.65	7.63
Tang Book Value Per Share	15.52	14.95	15.35	15.10	14.13	14.48	11.81	9.26
Dividends Per Share	0.490	0.470	0.450	0.430	0.410	0.390	0.370	0.350
Dividend Payout %	65.33	25.68	33.09	24.29	51.25	12.11	27.01	18.32
Income Statement								
Total Revenue	5,345,277	5,180,471	4,986,829	5,020,674	5,092,019	4,828,984	4,364,518	3,960,069
EBITDA	966,165	1,131,863	1,022,703	1,133,906	856,362	1,295,820	949,267	1,109,761
Depn & Amorth	785,300	741,600	734,800	724,100	694,400	692,900	681,200	655,800
Income Before Taxes	103,368	281,207	183,191	296,370	63,194	593,619	228,168	396,139
Income Taxes	73,582	113,503	92,283	133,376	30,093	269,054	116,459	140,572
Net Income	81,861	200,566	143,856	193,902	93,541	386,112	161,759	222,544
Average Shares	108,937	109,100	105,506	109,577	116,255	119,126	116,844	116,081
Balance Sheet								
Current Assets	1,763,437	1,705,680	1,596,076	1,644,142	1,628,936	3,875,588	2,973,084	1,778,969
Total Assets	8,623,900	8,201,005	7,762,519	7,608,784	7,652,416	9,894,143	10,599,514	10,404,565
Current Liabilities	924,608	874,133	810,633	780,296	773,287	2,799,519	2,084,731	1,056,104
Long-Term Obligations	1,721,571	1,529,857	1,499,862	1,492,908	1,621,422	1,632,226	1,633,308	1,633,519
Total Liabilities	4,611,539	4,238,014	3,947,767	3,830,647	3,884,077	5,966,945	7,028,231	7,050,089
Stockholders' Equity	4,012,361	3,962,991	3,814,752	3,778,137	3,768,339	3,927,198	3,571,283	3,354,476
Shares Outstanding	108,031	108,456	103,936	106,022	112,198	117,824	116,592	115,556
Statistical Record								
Return on Assets %	0.97	2.51	1.87	2.54	1.06	3.77	1.54	2.08
Return on Equity %	2.05	5.16	3.79	5.14	2.42	10.30	4.67	6.80
EBITDA Margin %	18.08	21.85	20.51	22.58	16.82	26.83	21.75	28.02
Net Margin %	1.53	3.87	2.88	3.86	1.84	8.00	3.71	5.62
Asset Turnover	0.63	0.65	0.65	0.66	0.58	0.47	0.42	0.37
Current Ratio	1.91	1.95	1.97	2.11	2.11	1.38	1.43	1.68
Debt to Equity	0.43	0.39	0.39	0.40	0.43	0.42	0.46	0.49
Price Range	28.61-19.42	31.86-18.42	32.04-25.28	30.86-22.19	58.30-22.50	68.00-48.60	50.60-33.95	40.91-34.52
P/E Ratio	38.15-25.89	17.41-10.07	23.56-18.59	17.44-12.54	72.88-28.13	21.12-15.09	36.93-24.78	21.42-18.07
Average Yield %	2.08	1.81	1.55	1.58	1.06	0.67	0.92	0.94

Address: 30 North LaSalle Street, Suite 4000, Chicago, IL 60602 **Telephone:** 312-630-1900 **Fax:** 312-630-1908	**Web Site:** www.teldta.com **Officers:** LeRoy T. Carlson - Chairman Emeritus LeRoy T. Carlson - President, Chief Executive Officer	**Auditors:** PricewaterhouseCoopers LLP **Investor Contact:** 312-592-5341 **Transfer Agents:** Computershare Trust Company, N.A., Canton, MA

TEMPUR-PEDIC INTERNATIONAL INC

Exchange	Symbol	Price	52Wk Range	Yield	P/E
NYS	TPX	$49.63 (3/28/2013)	87.26-21.02	N/A	29.19

*7 Year Price Score 111.44 *NYSE Composite Index=100   ***12 Month Price Score 102.29**

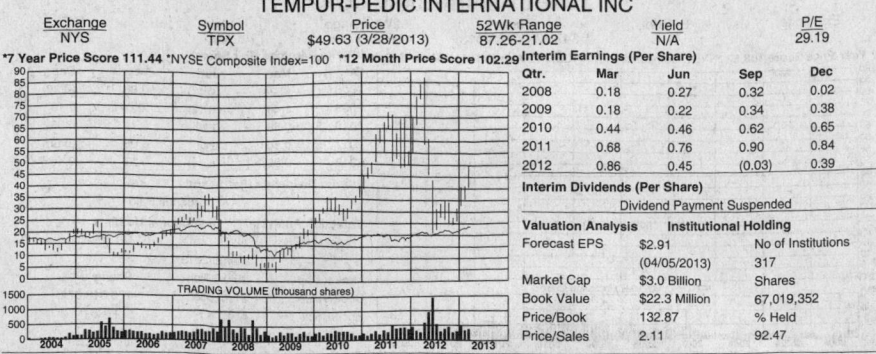

Interim Earnings (Per Share)

Qtr.	Mar	Jun	Sep	Dec
2008	0.18	0.27	0.32	0.02
2009	0.18	0.22	0.34	0.38
2010	0.44	0.46	0.62	0.65
2011	0.68	0.76	0.90	0.84
2012	0.86	0.45	(0.03)	0.39

Interim Dividends (Per Share)

Dividend Payment Suspended

Valuation Analysis | **Institutional Holding**

Forecast EPS	$2.91	No of Institutions
	(04/05/2013)	317
Market Cap	$3.0 Billion	Shares
Book Value	$22.3 Million	67,019,352
Price/Book	132.87	% Held
Price/Sales	2.11	92.47

Business Summary: Furniture (MIC: 1.6.2 SIC: 2515 NAIC: 337910)

Tempur-Pedic International is a manufacturer, marketer and distributor of mattresses and pillows, which it sells under the TEMPUR® and Tempur-Pedic® brands. Co.'s mattresses are composed of proprietary multi-layer, temperature sensitive, pressure-relieving TEMPUR® material that conforms to the body. Co.'s pillow offerings provide plush and pressure-relieving comfort as the temperature sensitive material conforms to the body. Co.'s other products include foundations used to support its mattress products, adjustable bed bases and other offerings such as cushions and other comfort products. Co. sells its mattresses and pillows through retail, direct, healthcare, and third party distributors.

Recent Developments: For the year ended Dec 31 2012, net income decreased 51.4% to US$106.8 million from US$219.6 million in the prior year. Revenues were US$1.40 billion, down 1.1% from US$1.42 billion the year before. Operating income was US$248.3 million versus US$340.5 million in the prior year, a decrease of 27.1%. Direct operating expenses rose 2.0% to US$688.3 million from US$674.8 million in the comparable period the year before. Indirect operating expenses increased 15.8% to US$466.3 million from US$402.6 million in the equivalent prior-year period.

Prospects: Our evaluation of Tempur-Pedic International Inc. as of Apr. 7, 2013 is the result of our systematic analysis on three basic characteristics: earnings strength, relative valuation, and recent stock price movement. The company has managed to produce a neutral trend in earnings per share over the past 5 quarters and while recent estimates for the company have been raised by analysts, TPX has posted better than expected results. Based on operating earnings yield, the company is about fairly valued when compared to all of the companies in our coverage universe. Share price changes over the past year indicates that TPX will perform very poorly over the near term.

Financial Data
(US$ in Thousands)

	12/31/2012	12/31/2011	12/31/2010	12/31/2009	12/31/2008	12/31/2007	12/31/2006	12/31/2005
Earnings Per Share	1.70	3.18	2.16	1.12	0.79	1.74	1.28	0.97
Cash Flow Per Share	3.08	3.71	2.62	1.80	2.65	1.58	1.95	1.04
Dividends Per Share	...	...	...	...	0.240	0.300	...	...
Dividend Payout %	...	...	...	...	30.38	17.24	...	...
Income Statement								
Total Revenue	1,402,900	1,417,938	1,105,421	831,156	927,818	1,106,722	945,045	836,732
EBITDA	278,900	369,258	273,365	174,396	162,888	272,896	219,526	207,758
Depn & Amortn	30,900	28,919	27,999	29,010	30,343	29,538	20,841	21,022
Income Before Taxes	229,200	328,391	230,865	128,037	107,422	212,874	174,765	166,472
Income Taxes	122,400	108,783	73,720	43,044	48,554	71,415	62,443	67,143
Net Income	106,800	219,608	157,145	84,993	58,868	141,459	112,322	99,329
Average Shares	62,900	69,149	72,792	76,048	74,909	81,256	87,530	102,144
Balance Sheet								
Current Assets	821,100	379,470	271,480	208,983	196,814	326,635	237,556	228,268
Total Assets	1,313,000	828,640	716,003	643,379	646,531	806,432	725,666	702,311
Current Liabilities	212,100	183,179	146,234	136,525	114,454	126,634	131,767	120,979
Long-Term Obligations	1,025,000	585,000	407,000	297,470	419,341	601,756	341,635	313,711
Total Liabilities	1,290,700	797,849	589,970	471,086	574,088	758,294	512,318	475,982
Stockholders' Equity	22,300	30,791	126,033	172,293	72,443	48,138	213,348	226,329
Shares Outstanding	59,700	63,770	68,484	75,112	74,833	74,534	83,222	92,448
Statistical Record								
Return on Assets %	9.95	28.43	23.12	13.18	8.08	18.47	15.73	14.80
Return on Equity %	401.23	280.07	105.35	69.46	97.37	108.20	51.09	45.15
EBITDA Margin %	19.88	26.04	24.73	20.98	17.56	24.66	23.23	24.83
Net Margin %	7.61	15.49	14.22	10.23	6.34	12.78	11.89	11.87
Asset Turnover	1.31	1.84	1.63	1.29	1.27	1.44	1.32	1.25
Current Ratio	3.87	2.07	1.86	1.53	1.72	2.58	1.80	1.89
Debt to Equity	45.96	19.00	3.23	1.73	5.79	12.50	1.60	1.39
Price Range	87.26-21.02	72.24-39.40	40.62-23.63	24.28-3.93	25.97-5.44	37.38-20.29	21.41-11.19	24.63-9.72
P/E Ratio	51.33-12.36	22.72-12.39	18.81-10.94	21.68-3.51	32.87-6.89	21.48-11.66	16.73-8.74	25.39-10.02
Average Yield %	...	...	...	...	2.07	1.06	...	...

Address: 1000 Tempur Way,	Web Site: www.tempurpedic.com	Auditors: Ernst & Young LLP
Lexington, KY 40511	Officers: P. Andrews McLane - Chairman Robert B.	Investor Contact: 800-805-3635
Telephone: 800-878-8889	Trussell - Vice-Chairman	Transfer Agents: American Stock Transfer & Trust Company, LLC

TENET HEALTHCARE CORP.

Exchange	Symbol	Price	52Wk Range	Yield	P/E
NYS	THC	$47.58 (3/28/2013)	47.58-17.56	N/A	36.60

*7 Year Price Score 108.62 *NYSE Composite Index=100 *12 Month Price Score 140.92

Interim Earnings (Per Share)

Qtr.	Mar	Jun	Sep	Dec
2008	(0.24)	(0.12)	0.88	(0.28)
2009	1.48	(0.12)	(0.04)	0.16
2010	0.68	0.20	6.72	0.56
2011	0.56	0.44	0.08	(0.60)
2012	0.52	(0.04)	0.37	0.44

Interim Dividends (Per Share)

No Dividends Paid

Valuation Analysis		Institutional Holding	
Forecast EPS	$2.79	No of Institutions	
	(04/06/2013)	383	
Market Cap	$5.0 Billion	Shares	
Book Value	$1.1 Billion	170,518,672	
Price/Book	4.36	% Held	
Price/Sales	0.55	N/A	

Business Summary: Hospitals & Health Care Facilities (MIC: 4.2.1 SIC: 8062 NAIC: 622110)

Tenet Healthcare is an investor-owned health care services company whose subsidiaries and affiliates as of Dec 31 2012 primarily operated 49 hospitals, 117 outpatient centers and Conifer Health Solutions (Conifer), which provides business process services to more than 600 hospital and other clients nationwide. With respect to business process services, Co. provides operational management for revenue cycle functions, including patient access, health information management, revenue integrity and patient financial services. Co. also provides patient communications services. Co.'s business lines are classified into two reportable business segments: hospital operations and other, and Conifer.

Recent Developments: For the year ended Dec 31 2012, income from continuing operations increased 102.9% to US$209.0 million from US$103.0 million a year earlier. Net income increased 41.5% to US$133.0 million from US$94.0 million in the prior year. Revenues were US$9.12 billion, up 5.4% from US$8.65 billion the year before. Operating income was US$749.0 million versus US$653.0 million in the prior year, an increase of 14.7%. Indirect operating expenses increased 4.6% to US$8.37 billion from US$8.00 billion in the equivalent prior-year period.

Prospects: Our evaluation of Tenet Healthcare Corp. as of Apr. 7, 2013 is the result of our systematic analysis on three basic characteristics: earnings strength, relative valuation, and recent stock price movement. The company has generated a negative trend in earnings per share over the past 5 quarters and while recent estimates for the company have been mixed, THC has posted results that fell short of analysts expectations. Based on operating earnings yield, the company is about fairly valued when compared to all of the companies in our coverage universe. Share price changes over the past year indicates that THC will perform very well over the near term.

Financial Data
(US$ in Millions)

	12/31/2012	12/31/2011	12/31/2010	12/31/2009	12/31/2008	12/31/2007	12/31/2006	12/31/2005
Earnings Per Share	1.30	0.48	8.16	1.48	0.20	(0.76)	(6.84)	(6.16)
Cash Flow Per Share	5.68	4.24	3.90	3.54	1.74	2.75	(3.92)	6.51
Tang Book Value Per Share	N.M.	N.M.	2.78	N.M.	N.M.	N.M.	N.M.	N.M.
Income Statement								
Total Revenue	9,119	8,854	9,205	9,014	8,663	8,852	8,701	9,614
EBITDA	1,198	979	1,007	1,036	834	646	(407)	56
Depn & Amortn	452	443	425	386	373	330	313	352
Income Before Taxes	334	161	158	205	43	(103)	(1,129)	(701)
Income Taxes	125	61	(977)	(23)	(25)	(58)	(262)	(87)
Net Income	133	94	1,152	197	25	(89)	(803)	(724)
Average Shares	108	121	140	126	119	118	117	117
Balance Sheet								
Current Assets	2,681	2,357	2,311	2,472	2,709	2,560	3,025	3,508
Total Assets	9,044	8,462	8,500	7,953	8,174	8,393	8,539	9,812
Current Liabilities	1,763	1,815	1,725	1,783	1,949	2,048	1,925	2,292
Long-Term Obligations	5,158	4,294	3,997	4,272	4,778	4,771	4,760	4,784
Total Liabilities	7,901	7,039	6,734	7,307	8,071	8,339	8,275	8,791
Stockholders' Equity	1,143	1,423	1,766	646	103	54	264	1,021
Shares Outstanding	104	103	121	120	119	118	117	117
Statistical Record								
Return on Assets %	1.52	1.11	14.00	2.44	0.30	N.M.	N.M.	N.M.
Return on Equity %	10.34	5.90	95.52	52.60	31.76	N.M.	N.M.	N.M.
EBITDA Margin %	13.14	11.06	10.94	11.49	9.63	7.30	N.M.	0.58
Net Margin %	1.46	1.06	12.51	2.19	0.29	N.M.	N.M.	N.M.
Asset Turnover	1.04	1.04	1.12	1.12	1.04	1.05	0.95	0.97
Current Ratio	1.52	1.30	1.34	1.39	1.39	1.25	1.57	1.53
Debt to Equity	4.51	3.02	2.26	6.61	46.39	88.35	18.03	4.69
Price Range	33.50-17.56	30.52-14.36	27.32-15.68	24.96-3.60	26.80-4.28	30.52-12.40	36.16-23.24	51.60-29.24
P/E Ratio	25.77-13.51	63.58-29.92	3.35-1.92	16.86-2.43	134.00-21.40	...	...	...

Address: 1445 Ross Avenue, Suite 1400, Dallas, TX 75202 Telephone: 469-893-2200 Fax: 888-896-9016	Web Site: www.tenethealth.com Officers: Edward A. Kangas - Chairman Trevor Fetter - President, Chief Executive Officer, Acting Chief Financial Officer	Auditors: Deloitte & Touche LLP Investor Contact: 469-893-6992 Transfer Agents: The Bank of New York Mellon, New York, NY

TENNANT CO.

Exchange	Symbol	Price	52Wk Range	Yield	P/E	Div Achiever
NYS	TNC	$48.56 (3/28/2013)	49.82-35.30	1.48	22.28	40 Years

*7 Year Price Score 113.42 *NYSE Composite Index=100 *12 Month Price Score 103.70

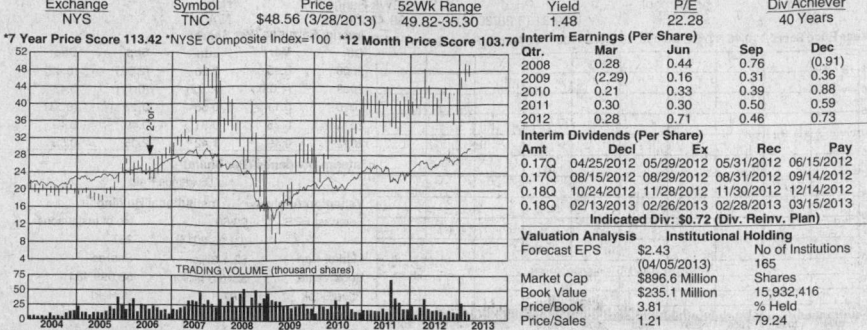

Interim Earnings (Per Share)

Qtr.	Mar	Jun	Sep	Dec
2008	0.28	0.44	0.76	(0.91)
2009	(2.29)	0.16	0.31	0.36
2010	0.21	0.33	0.39	0.88
2011	0.30	0.30	0.50	0.59
2012	0.28	0.71	0.46	0.73

Interim Dividends (Per Share)

Amt	Decl	Ex	Rec	Pay
0.17Q	04/25/2012	05/29/2012	05/31/2012	06/15/2012
0.17Q	08/15/2012	08/29/2012	08/31/2012	09/14/2012
0.18Q	10/24/2012	11/28/2012	11/30/2012	12/14/2012
0.18Q	02/13/2013	02/26/2013	02/28/2013	03/15/2013

Indicated Div: $0.72 (Div. Reinv. Plan)

Valuation Analysis **Institutional Holding**

Forecast EPS	$2.43 (04/05/2013)	No of Institutions 165
Market Cap	$896.6 Million	Shares
Book Value	$235.1 Million	15,932,416
Price/Book	3.81	% Held
Price/Sales	1.21	79.24

Business Summary: Industrial Machinery & Equipment (MIC: 7.2.1 SIC: 3589 NAIC: 333319)

Tennant is engaged in designing, manufacturing and marketing a range of products used to clean and coat surfaces in factories, office buildings, parking lots and streets, airports, hospitals, schools, warehouses, shopping centers and other retail environments. Co.'s products include equipment for maintaining surfaces in industrial, commercial and outdoor environments; chemical-free and other sustainable cleaning technologies; and coatings for protecting, repairing and upgrading floors and other surfaces. Co.'s customers include building service contract cleaners, as well as end-user businesses, healthcare facilities, schools and local, state and federal governments.

Recent Developments: For the year ended Dec 31 2012, net income increased 27.1% to US$41.6 million from US$32.7 million in the prior year. Revenues were US$739.0 million, down 2.0% from US$754.0 million the year before. Operating income was US$62.7 million versus US$49.6 million in the prior year, an increase of 26.3%. Direct operating expenses declined 4.9% to US$413.7 million from US$434.8 million in the comparable period the year before. Indirect operating expenses decreased 2.6% to US$262.6 million from US$269.5 million in the equivalent prior-year period.

Prospects: Our evaluation of Tennant Co. as of Apr. 7, 2013 is the result of our systematic analysis on three basic characteristics: earnings strength, relative valuation, and recent stock price movement. The company has generated a negative trend in earnings per share over the past 5 quarters. However, while recent estimates for the company have been mixed, TNC has posted better than expected results. Based on operating earnings yield, the company is about fairly valued when compared to all of the companies in our coverage universe. Share price changes over the past year indicates that TNC will perform poorly over the near term.

Financial Data

(US$ in Thousands)	12/31/2012	12/31/2011	12/31/2010	12/31/2009	12/31/2008	12/31/2007	12/31/2006	12/31/2005
Earnings Per Share	2.18	1.69	1.80	(1.42)	0.57	2.08	1.57	1.26
Cash Flow Per Share	2.56	3.02	2.26	4.06	2.05	2.13	2.17	2.45
Tang Book Value Per Share	10.50	9.39	8.95	7.19	6.51	11.78	10.60	9.21
Dividends Per Share	0.690	0.680	0.590	0.530	0.520	0.480	0.460	0.440
Dividend Payout %	31.65	40.24	32.78	...	91.23	23.08	29.30	34.92
Income Statement								
Total Revenue	738,980	753,998	667,667	595,875	701,405	664,218	598,981	552,908
EBITDA	79,410	68,304	54,239	(2,251)	40,837	73,657	55,052	46,906
Depn & Amortn	18,072	18,088	18,026	19,632	20,360	16,901	13,711	13,039
Income Before Taxes	59,890	48,730	34,727	(24,320)	17,575	57,712	43,302	34,994
Income Taxes	18,306	16,017	(76)	1,921	6,951	17,845	13,493	12,058
Net Income	41,584	32,713	34,803	(26,241)	10,624	39,867	29,809	22,936
Average Shares	19,102	19,360	19,332	18,507	18,581	19,146	18,989	18,210
Balance Sheet								
Current Assets	273,446	272,096	248,269	215,912	250,419	240,724	235,404	211,601
Total Assets	420,760	424,262	403,668	377,726	456,604	382,070	354,250	311,472
Current Liabilities	121,694	123,992	116,144	116,152	107,159	96,673	94,804	88,965
Long-Term Obligations	30,281	32,289	27,674	30,192	91,393	2,470	1,907	1,608
Total Liabilities	185,706	203,410	187,535	193,447	246,700	129,639	124,586	118,370
Stockholders' Equity	235,054	220,852	216,133	184,279	209,904	252,431	229,664	193,102
Shares Outstanding	18,464	18,834	19,038	18,750	18,284	18,499	18,753	18,382
Statistical Record								
Return on Assets %	9.82	7.90	8.91	N.M.	2.53	10.83	8.96	7.68
Return on Equity %	18.19	14.97	17.38	N.M.	4.58	16.54	14.10	12.49
EBITDA Margin %	10.75	9.06	8.12	N.M.	5.82	11.09	9.19	8.48
Net Margin %	5.63	4.34	5.21	N.M.	1.51	6.00	4.98	4.15
Asset Turnover	1.74	1.82	1.71	1.43	1.67	1.80	1.80	1.85
Current Ratio	2.25	2.19	2.14	1.86	2.34	2.49	2.48	2.38
Debt to Equity	0.13	0.15	0.13	0.16	0.44	0.01	0.01	0.01
Price Range	48.45-35.30	44.25-32.92	38.82-21.84	31.92-7.74	45.41-15.33	49.32-27.84	29.88-21.70	26.00-17.41
P/E Ratio	22.22-16.19	26.18-19.48	21.57-12.13	...	79.67-26.89	23.71-13.38	19.03-13.82	20.63-13.82
Average Yield %	1.67	1.73	1.86	2.61	1.65	1.27	1.78	2.20

Address: 701 North Lilac Drive, P.O. Box 1452, Minneapolis, MN 55440 **Telephone:** 763-540-1200 **Fax:** 612-513-2142	**Web Site:** www.tennantco.com **Officers:** H. Chris Killingstad - President, Chief Executive Officer Thomas Poulson - Vice President, Chief Financial Officer	**Auditors:** KPMG LLP **Investor Contact:** 763-540-1204 **Transfer Agents:** Wells Fargo Bank, N.A., St. Paul, MN

TENNECO INC

*7 Year Price Score 110.46 *NYSE Composite Index=100 ***12 Month Price Score 107.43**

TRADING VOLUME (thousand shares)

Interim Earnings (Per Share)

Qtr.	Mar	Jun	Sep	Dec
2008	0.13	0.26	(2.92)	(6.42)
2009	(1.05)	(0.72)	(0.17)	0.43
2010	0.11	0.66	0.17	(0.31)
2011	0.75	0.81	0.49	0.49
2012	0.49	1.42	2.05	0.55

Interim Dividends (Per Share)
No Dividends Paid

Valuation Analysis

		Institutional Holding	
Forecast EPS	$3.60 (04/05/2013)	No of Institutions	267
Market Cap	$2.4 Billion	Shares	58,099,484
Book Value	$246.0 Million	% Held	91.24
Price/Book	9.67		
Price/Sales	0.32		

Business Summary: Auto Parts (MIC: 1.8.2 SIC: 3714 NAIC: 336330)

Tenneco is a producer of emission control and ride control products and systems for light, commercial and specialty vehicle applications Co. serves both original equipment manufacturers and replacement markets through brands, including Monroe®, Rancho®, Clevite® Elastomers, Marzocchi®, Axios, Kinetic, and Fric-Rot ride control products and Walker®, Fonos, DynoMax®, Thrush, and Lukey emission control products. As a parts supplier, Co. produces individual component parts for vehicles as well as groups of components that are combined as modules or systems within vehicles. Co. operates in three geographic segments: North America; Europe, South America and India; and Asia Pacific.

Recent Developments:
For the year ended Dec 31 2012, net income increased 66.1% to US$304.0 million from US$183.0 million in the prior year. Revenues were US$7.36 billion, up 2.2% from US$7.21 billion the year before. Direct operating expenses rose 2.2% to US$6.17 billion from US$6.04 billion in the comparable period the year before. Indirect operating expenses decreased 2.7% to US$758.0 million from US$779.0 million in the equivalent prior-year period.

Prospects:
Our evaluation of Tenneco Automotive Inc. as of Apr. 7, 2013 is the result of our systematic analysis on three basic characteristics: earnings strength, relative valuation, and recent stock price movement. The company has suffered a very negative trend in earnings per share over the past 5 quarters. However, while recent estimates for the company have been mixed, TEN has posted results that fell short of analysts expectations. Based on operating earnings yield, the company is undervalued when compared to all of the companies in our coverage universe. Share price changes over the past year indicates that TEN will perform poorly over the near term.

Financial Data

(US$ in Thousands)	12/31/2012	12/31/2011	12/31/2010	12/31/2009	12/31/2008	12/31/2007	12/31/2006	12/31/2005
Earnings Per Share	4.50	2.55	0.63	(1.50)	(8.95)	(0.11)	1.10	1.29
Cash Flow Per Share	6.07	4.09	4.12	4.96	3.44	3.60	4.46	3.11
Tang Book Value Per Share	2.30	...	...	...	...	3.56	0.20	N.M.
Income Statement								
Total Revenue	7,363,000	7,205,000	5,937,000	4,649,000	5,916,000	6,184,000	4,685,000	4,441,000
EBITDA	633,000	586,000	497,000	313,000	219,000	457,000	515,000	392,000
Depn & Amortn	205,000	207,000	216,000	221,000	222,000	205,000	184,000	177,000
Income Before Taxes	323,000	271,000	132,000	(41,000)	(116,000)	88,000	195,000	85,000
Income Taxes	19,000	88,000	69,000	13,000	289,000	83,000	3,000	25,000
Net Income	275,000	157,000	39,000	(73,000)	(415,000)	(5,000)	51,000	58,000
Average Shares	61,083	61,520	60,998	48,572	46,406	45,809	46,755	45,321
Balance Sheet								
Current Assets	2,124,000	1,979,000	1,790,000	1,393,000	1,338,000	1,641,000	1,422,000	1,197,000
Total Assets	3,608,000	3,337,000	3,167,000	2,841,000	2,828,000	3,590,000	3,263,000	2,940,000
Current Liabilities	1,649,000	1,570,000	1,468,000	1,201,000	1,157,000	1,358,000	1,133,000	979,000
Long-Term Obligations	1,067,000	1,158,000	1,160,000	1,145,000	1,402,000	1,328,000	1,350,000	1,356,000
Total Liabilities	3,362,000	3,337,000	3,171,000	2,862,000	3,079,000	3,190,000	3,042,000	2,811,000
Stockholders' Equity	246,000	...	(4,000)	(21,000)	(251,000)	400,000	221,000	129,000
Shares Outstanding	60,494	60,452	60,247	59,495	47,019	46,597	45,790	44,249
Statistical Record								
Return on Assets %	7.90	4.83	1.30	N.M.	N.M.	N.M.	1.64	1.92
Return on Equity %	222.97	...	...	N.M.	N.M.	N.M.	29.14	41.58
EBITDA Margin %	8.60	8.13	8.37	6.73	3.70	7.39	10.99	8.83
Net Margin %	3.73	2.18	0.66	N.M.	N.M.	N.M.	1.09	1.31
Asset Turnover	2.11	2.22	1.98	1.64	1.84	1.80	1.51	1.47
Current Ratio	1.29	1.26	1.22	1.16	1.16	1.21	1.26	1.22
Debt to Equity	4.34	...	...	...	...	3.32	6.11	10.51
Price Range	39.76-24.72	46.58-23.90	43.03-17.68	19.30-0.70	29.81-1.73	37.16-23.25	27.45-19.92	20.03-12.00
P/E Ratio	8.84-5.49	18.27-9.37	68.30-28.06	...	...	...	24.95-18.11	15.53-9.30

Address: 500 North Field Drive, Lake Forest, IL 60045 **Telephone:** 847-482-5000	**Web Site:** www.tenneco.com **Officers:** Gregg M. Sherrill - Chairman, Chief Executive Officer Kenneth R. Trammell - Executive Vice President, Chief Financial Officer	**Auditors:** PricewaterhouseCoopers LLP **Investor Contact:** 847-482-5162 **Transfer Agents:** Wells Fargo Bank, N.A., South St. Paul, MN

TERADATA CORP (DE)

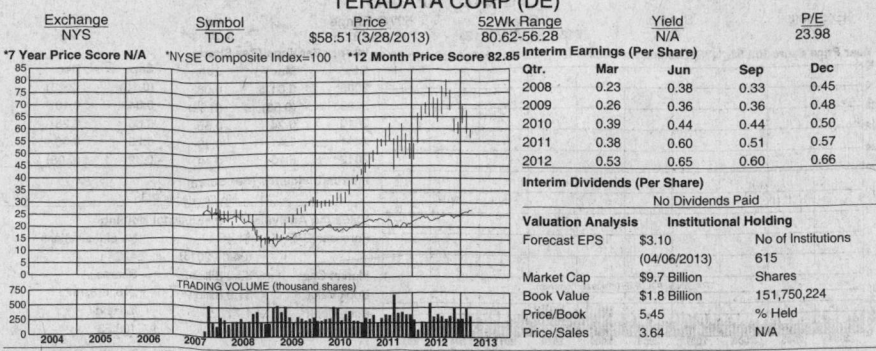

Exchange	Symbol	Price	52Wk Range	Yield	P/E
NYS	TDC	$58.51 (3/28/2013)	80.62-56.28	N/A	23.98

*7 Year Price Score N/A *NYSE Composite Index=100 *12 Month Price Score 82.85

Interim Earnings (Per Share)

Qtr.	Mar	Jun	Sep	Dec
2008	0.23	0.38	0.33	0.45
2009	0.26	0.36	0.36	0.48
2010	0.39	0.44	0.44	0.50
2011	0.38	0.60	0.51	0.57
2012	0.53	0.65	0.60	0.66

Interim Dividends (Per Share)

No Dividends Paid

Valuation Analysis

		Institutional Holding
Forecast EPS	$3.10	No of Institutions
	(04/06/2013)	615
Market Cap	$9.7 Billion	Shares
Book Value	$1.8 Billion	151,750,224
Price/Book	5.45	% Held
Price/Sales	3.64	N/A

Business Summary: IT Services (MIC: 6.3.1 SIC: 7372 NAIC: 511210)

Teradata is a provider of analytic data applications. Co.'s primary products include: Teradata analytic database software, which supports and manages mixed workloads and data warehousing functions; Teradata platform family, which supports massively parallel processing systems; Teradata logical data models, which used as blueprints for designing a data warehouse; Teradata Aster MapReduce platform, which analyzes multi-structured data sources and data types; Teradata analytic applications and tools, which include data mining and master data management; and Teradata integrated analytics, which enables businesses to convert businesses' data warehouse into an analytic services environment.

Recent Developments: For the year ended Dec 31 2012, net income increased 18.7% to US$419.0 million from US$353.0 million in the prior year. Revenues were US$2.67 billion, up 12.8% from US$2.36 billion the year before. Operating income was US$580.0 million versus US$456.0 million in the prior year, an increase of 27.2%. Direct operating expenses rose 9.8% to US$1.17 billion from US$1.07 billion in the comparable period the year before. Indirect operating expenses increased 8.8% to US$911.0 million from US$837.0 million in the equivalent prior-year period.

Prospects: Our evaluation of Teradata Corp. as of Apr. 7, 2013 is the result of our systematic analysis on three basic characteristics: earnings strength, relative valuation, and recent stock price movement. The company has managed to produce a neutral trend in earnings per share over the past 5 quarters. However, while recent estimates for the company have been lowered by analysts, TDC has posted better than expected results. Based on operating earnings yield, the company is about fairly valued when compared to all of the companies in our coverage universe. Share price changes over the past year indicates that TDC will perform well over the near term.

Financial Data
(US$ in Millions)

	12/31/2012	12/31/2011	12/31/2010	12/31/2009	12/31/2008	12/31/2007	12/31/2006	12/31/2005
Earnings Per Share	2.44	2.05	1.77	1.46	1.39	1.10	1.06	1.14
Cash Flow Per Share	3.41	3.05	2.47	2.65	2.46	2.14	1.21	...
Tang Book Value Per Share	2.95	2.68	5.57	4.14	3.38	2.65	...	...
Income Statement								
Total Revenue	2,665	2,362	1,936	1,709	1,762	1,702	1,547	1,467
EBITDA	667	514	474	393	343	388	357	339
Depn & Amortn	89	33	60	59	5	68	55	55
Income Before Taxes	578	481	414	334	338	322	302	284
Income Taxes	159	128	113	80	88	122	110	78
Net Income	419	353	301	254	250	200	192	206
Average Shares	171	171	170	173	179	181	180	180
Balance Sheet								
Current Assets	1,534	1,412	1,406	1,152	1,015	873	502	...
Total Assets	3,066	2,616	1,883	1,569	1,430	1,294	1,003	...
Current Liabilities	806	695	569	543	540	572	393	...
Long-Term Obligations	274	290	...	...	...	...	...	...
Total Liabilities	1,287	1,122	694	659	653	663	412	...
Stockholders' Equity	1,779	1,494	1,189	910	777	631	591	...
Shares Outstanding	165	167	168	168	173	181	...	...
Statistical Record								
Return on Assets %	14.71	15.69	17.44	16.94	18.31	17.41	...	...
Return on Equity %	25.53	26.31	28.68	30.11	35.41	32.73	...	...
EBITDA Margin %	25.03	21.76	24.48	23.00	19.47	22.80	23.08	23.11
Net Margin %	15.72	14.94	15.55	14.86	14.19	11.75	12.41	14.04
Asset Turnover	0.94	1.05	1.12	1.14	1.29	1.48	...	...
Current Ratio	1.90	2.03	2.47	2.12	1.88	1.53	1.28	...
Debt to Equity	0.15	0.19	...	...	...	...	...	...
Price Range	80.62-47.37	62.33-41.16	43.50-27.66	32.08-13.02	27.41-11.46	29.08-23.13	...	...
P/E Ratio	33.04-19.41	30.40-20.08	24.58-15.63	21.97-8.92	19.72-8.24	26.44-21.03	...	...

Address: 10000 Innovation Drive, Dayton, OH 45342 **Telephone:** 866-548-8348	**Web Site:** www.teradata.com **Officers:** James M. Ringler - Chairman Hermann Wimmer - Executive Vice President	**Auditors:** PricewaterhouseCoopers LLP **Investor Contact:** 937-242-4878 **Transfer Agents:** Computershare Shareowner Services

TERADYNE, INC.

Exchange	Symbol	Price	52Wk Range	Yield	P/E
NYS	TER	$16.22 (3/28/2013)	17.65-13.05	N/A	17.26

*7 Year Price Score 109.81 *NYSE Composite Index=100   *12 Month Price Score 98.96

Interim Earnings (Per Share)

Qtr.	Mar	Jun	Sep	Dec
2008	0.01	0.06	(0.13)	(2.28)
2009	(0.53)	(0.39)	0.04	0.10
2010	0.24	0.55	0.66	0.28
2011	0.41	0.39	0.25	0.60
2012	0.15	0.49	0.39	(0.08)

Interim Dividends (Per Share)

No Dividends Paid

Valuation Analysis

		Institutional Holding	
Forecast EPS	$1.46	No of Institutions	
	(04/06/2013)	426	
Market Cap	$3.0 Billion	Shares	
Book Value	$1.8 Billion	218,113,152	
Price/Book	1.71	% Held	
Price/Sales	1.84	108.53	

Business Summary: Semiconductors (MIC: 6.2.4 SIC: 3825 NAIC: 334515)

Teradyne is a global supplier of automatic test equipment. Co. designs, develops, manufactures and sells automatic test systems and applications used to test electronics in the consumer electronics, automotive, computing, telecommunications, wireless, and aerospace and defense industries. Co.'s automatic test equipment products and services include: semiconductor test systems; military/aerospace test instrumentation and systems, storage test systems, and circuit-board test and inspection systems; and wireless test systems. Co.'s customer base includes integrated device manufacturers, outsourced semiconductor assembly and test providers, and wafer foundries, among others.

Recent Developments: For the year ended Dec 31 2012, income from continuing operations decreased 36.9% to US$217.0 million from US$344.0 million a year earlier. Net income decreased 41.3% to US$217.0 million from US$369.9 million in the prior year. Revenues were US$1.66 billion, up 15.9% from US$1.43 billion the year before. Operating income was US$287.4 million versus US$231.5 million in the prior year, an increase of 24.1%. Direct operating expenses rose 7.5% to US$770.7 million from US$717.2 million in the comparable period the year before. Indirect operating expenses increased 24.6% to US$598.7 million from US$480.3 million in the equivalent prior-year period.

Prospects: Our evaluation of Teradyne Inc. as of Apr. 7, 2013 is the result of our systematic analysis on three basic characteristics: earnings strength, relative valuation, and recent stock price movement. The company has suffered a very negative trend in earnings per share over the past 5 quarters and while recent estimates for the company have remained steady, TER has posted better than expected results. Based on operating earnings yield, the company is undervalued when compared to all of the companies in our coverage universe. Share price changes over the past year indicates that TER will perform very well over the near term.

Financial Data

(US$ in Thousands)	12/31/2012	12/31/2011	12/31/2010	12/31/2009	12/31/2008	12/31/2007	12/31/2006	12/31/2005
Earnings Per Share	0.94	1.65	1.73	(0.77)	(2.33)	0.42	1.01	0.46
Cash Flow Per Share	2.16	1.48	3.15	0.70	0.95	0.70	2.31	0.07
Tang Book Value Per Share	5.91	4.14	5.49	2.93	3.06	6.70	6.84	5.96
Income Statement								
Total Revenue	1,656,750	1,429,061	1,608,650	819,407	1,107,042	1,102,280	1,376,818	1,075,232
EBITDA	415,868	327,254	496,265	(30,027)	(292,492)	111,534	270,371	(320)
Depn & Amortn	128,500	91,540	82,797	92,394	91,855	67,495	73,540	81,378
Income Before Taxes	265,976	218,637	394,512	(142,637)	(386,025)	79,243	230,395	(80,137)
Income Taxes	48,927	(129,256)	14,782	(8,800)	12,577	7,360	27,752	(19,680)
Net Income	217,049	373,809	379,730	(133,837)	(397,834)	77,711	198,757	90,648
Average Shares	230,246	226,820	226,807	173,604	170,593	185,374	204,414	196,283
Balance Sheet								
Current Assets	1,236,061	1,099,887	1,176,618	762,292	678,653	944,933	889,410	1,094,942
Total Assets	2,429,345	2,188,639	1,810,355	1,235,337	1,235,247	1,555,288	1,721,055	1,859,732
Current Liabilities	297,828	373,684	363,704	283,357	366,963	223,234	259,716	515,495
Long-Term Obligations	171,059	159,956	150,182	141,100	...	...	...	1,819
Total Liabilities	650,990	683,579	688,167	570,758	529,135	326,114	359,868	617,066
Stockholders' Equity	1,778,355	1,505,060	1,122,188	664,579	706,112	1,229,174	1,361,187	1,242,666
Shares Outstanding	187,908	183,587	182,035	174,908	169,651	173,088	188,952	197,011
Statistical Record								
Return on Assets %	9.37	18.70	24.94	N.M.	N.M.	4.74	11.10	4.79
Return on Equity %	13.18	28.46	42.50	N.M.	N.M.	6.00	15.27	7.63
EBITDA Margin %	25.10	22.90	30.85	N.M.	N.M.	10.12	19.64	N.M.
Net Margin %	13.10	26.16	23.61	N.M.	N.M.	7.05	14.44	8.43
Asset Turnover	0.72	0.71	1.06	0.66	0.79	0.67	0.77	0.57
Current Ratio	4.15	2.94	3.24	2.69	1.85	4.23	3.42	2.12
Debt to Equity	0.10	0.11	0.13	0.21	...	...	...	N.M.
Price Range	17.39-13.05	19.07-10.55	14.39-8.98	10.80-3.44	14.10-2.97	18.30-10.06	17.90-11.90	17.10-10.95
P/E Ratio	18.50-13.88	11.56-6.39	8.32-5.19	...	...	43.57-23.95	17.72-11.78	37.17-23.80

Address: 600 Riverpark Drive, North Reading, MA 01864 **Telephone:** 978-370-2700	**Web Site:** www.teradyne.com **Officers:** Mark E. Jagiela - President, Vice President, Division Officer Michael A. Bradley - President, Chief Executive Officer	**Auditors:** PricewaterhouseCoopers LLP **Investor Contact:** 978-370-2425 **Transfer Agents:** Computershare Trust Company, N.A, Providence, RI

TEREX CORP.

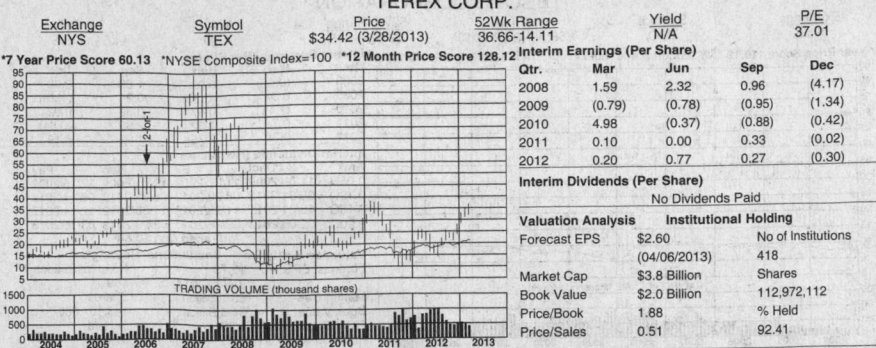

Exchange	Symbol	Price	52Wk Range	Yield	P/E
NYS	TEX	$34.42 (3/28/2013)	36.66-14.11	N/A	37.01

*7 Year Price Score 60.13   *NYSE Composite Index=100   *12 Month Price Score 128.12

Interim Earnings (Per Share)

Qtr.	Mar	Jun	Sep	Dec
2008	1.59	2.32	0.96	(4.17)
2009	(0.79)	(0.78)	(0.95)	(1.34)
2010	4.98	(0.37)	(0.88)	(0.42)
2011	0.10	0.00	0.33	(0.02)
2012	0.20	0.77	0.27	(0.30)

Interim Dividends (Per Share)

No Dividends Paid

Valuation Analysis   **Institutional Holding**

Forecast EPS	$2.60	No of Institutions
	(04/06/2013)	418
Market Cap	$3.8 Billion	Shares
Book Value	$2.0 Billion	112,972,112
Price/Book	1.88	% Held
Price/Sales	0.51	92.41

Business Summary: Industrial Machinery & Equipment (MIC: 7.2.1 SIC: 3537 NAIC: 333924)

Terex is an equipment manufacturer of a range of capital goods machinery products. Co. has five business segments: aerial work platforms, which provides aerial work platform equipment, telehandlers, light towers, bridge inspection equipment and utility equipment; construction, which provides construction equipment and their related components and replacement parts; cranes, which provides mobile telescopic cranes, tower cranes, lattice boom crawler cranes, lattice boom truck cranes, truck-mounted cranes (boom trucks), and port and rail equipment; material handling and port applications, which provides industrial cranes; and materials processing, which provides materials processing equipment.

Recent Developments: For the year ended Dec 31 2012, income from continuing operations increased 197.4% to US$101.4 million from US$34.1 million a year earlier. Net income increased 154.5% to US$103.6 million from US$40.7 million in the prior year. Revenues were US$7.35 billion, up 13.0% from US$6.50 billion the year before. Operating income was US$398.6 million versus US$81.2 million in the prior year, an increase of 390.9%. Direct operating expenses rose 6.5% to US$5.90 billion from US$5.54 billion in the comparable period the year before. Indirect operating expenses increased 19.1% to US$1.05 billion from US$879.1 million in the equivalent prior-year period.

Prospects: Our evaluation of Terex Corp. as of Apr. 7, 2013 is the result of our systematic analysis on three basic characteristics: earnings strength, relative valuation, and recent stock price movement. The company has suffered a very negative trend in earnings per share over the past 5 quarters. However, while recent estimates for the company have been mixed, TEX has posted results that fell short of analysts' expectations. Based on operating earnings yield, the company is undervalued when compared to all of the companies in our coverage universe. Share price changes over the past year indicates that TEX will perform very well over the near term.

Financial Data
(US$ in Thousands)

	12/31/2012	12/31/2011	12/31/2010	12/31/2009	12/31/2008	12/31/2007	12/31/2006	12/31/2005
Earnings Per Share	0.93	0.41	3.30	(3.88)	0.72	5.85	3.88	1.85
Cash Flow Per Share	2.64	0.17	(5.61)	(0.67)	1.87	3.53	4.81	2.75
Tang Book Value Per Share	2.62	1.18	14.71	10.62	13.45	16.39	11.06	6.14
Income Statement								
Total Revenue	7,348,400	6,504,600	4,418,200	4,043,100	9,889,600	9,137,700	7,647,600	6,380,400
EBITDA	421,400	302,700	(16,200)	(388,600)	473,000	1,031,500	754,300	445,900
Depn & Amortn	100,400	89,500	78,600	73,600	75,000	63,400	61,200	61,400
Income Before Taxes	155,600	84,500	(238,300)	(581,700)	314,100	919,300	614,700	289,800
Income Taxes	54,200	50,400	(26,800)	(132,100)	242,200	305,400	218,200	101,300
Net Income	105,800	45,200	358,500	(398,400)	71,900	613,900	399,900	188,500
Average Shares	113,900	110,700	108,700	102,600	99,700	104,900	103,000	102,200
Balance Sheet								
Current Assets	3,797,400	4,013,500	3,968,900	3,914,600	4,040,900	4,776,900	3,432,800	2,903,500
Total Assets	6,746,200	7,050,700	5,516,400	5,713,800	5,445,400	6,316,300	4,785,900	4,200,300
Current Liabilities	1,708,800	1,891,700	1,674,200	1,554,700	1,824,600	2,175,300	2,027,200	1,524,600
Long-Term Obligations	2,014,900	2,223,400	1,339,500	1,892,700	1,396,400	1,319,500	536,100	1,075,800
Total Liabilities	4,738,500	5,144,300	3,433,200	4,063,600	3,723,700	3,973,100	3,034,900	3,039,300
Stockholders' Equity	2,007,700	1,906,400	2,083,200	1,650,200	1,721,700	2,343,200	1,751,000	1,161,000
Shares Outstanding	109,900	108,800	108,100	107,300	94,000	100,300	101,100	98,600
Statistical Record								
Return on Assets %	1.53	0.72	6.38	N.M.	1.22	11.06	8.90	4.50
Return on Equity %	5.39	2.27	19.21	N.M.	3.53	29.99	27.47	16.42
EBITDA Margin %	5.73	4.65	N.M.	N.M.	4.78	11.29	9.86	6.99
Net Margin %	1.44	0.69	8.11	N.M.	0.73	6.72	5.23	2.95
Asset Turnover	1.06	1.04	0.79	0.72	1.68	1.65	1.70	1.52
Current Ratio	2.22	2.12	2.37	2.52	2.21	2.20	1.69	1.90
Debt to Equity	1.00	1.17	0.64	1.15	0.81	0.56	0.31	0.93
Price Range	28.11-14.11	38.30-9.61	31.04-17.30	24.11-7.57	74.80-9.33	94.13-56.57	66.29-30.42	31.16-18.16
P/E Ratio	30.23-15.17	93.41-23.44	9.41-5.24	...	103.89-12.96	16.09-9.67	17.09-7.84	16.85-9.81

Address: 200 Nyala Farm Road, Westport, CT 06880 **Telephone:** 203-222-7170 **Fax:** 203-222-7976	**Web Site:** www.terex.com **Officers:** Ronald M. DeFeo - Chairman, Chief Executive Officer Eric I. Cohen - Senior Vice President, Secretary, General Counsel	**Auditors:** PricewaterhouseCoopers LLP **Investor Contact:** 203-222-5943 **Transfer Agents:** American Stock Transfer & Trust Company, New York, NY

TESORO CORPORATION

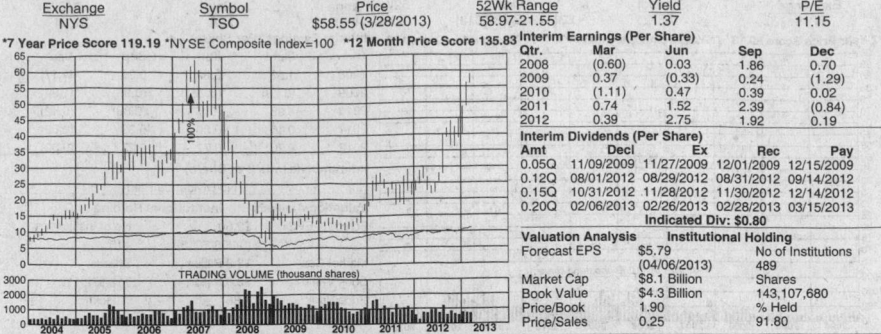

Exchange	Symbol	Price	52Wk Range	Yield	P/E
NYS	TSO	$58.55 (3/28/2013)	58.97-21.55	1.37	11.15

*7 Year Price Score 119.19 *NYSE Composite Index=100 ***12 Month Price Score 135.83**

Interim Earnings (Per Share)

Qtr.	Mar	Jun	Sep	Dec
2008	(0.60)	0.03	1.86	0.70
2009	0.37	(0.33)	0.24	(1.29)
2010	(1.11)	0.47	0.39	0.02
2011	0.74	1.52	2.39	(0.84)
2012	0.39	2.75	1.92	0.19

Interim Dividends (Per Share)

Amt	Decl	Ex	Rec	Pay
0.05Q	11/09/2009	11/27/2009	12/01/2009	12/15/2009
0.12Q	08/01/2012	08/29/2012	08/31/2012	09/14/2012
0.15Q	10/31/2012	11/28/2012	11/30/2012	12/14/2012
0.20Q	02/06/2013	02/26/2013	02/28/2013	03/15/2013

Indicated Div: $0.80

Valuation Analysis		Institutional Holding	
Forecast EPS	$5.79 (04/06/2013)	No of Institutions	489
Market Cap	$8.1 Billion	Shares	143,107,680
Book Value	$4.3 Billion	% Held	91.80
Price/Book	1.90		
Price/Sales	0.25		

Business Summary: Refining & Marketing (MIC: 9.1.2 SIC: 2911 NAIC: 324110)

Tesoro is an independent petroleum refiner and marketer. Through its subsidiaries, Co. manufactures and sells transportation fuels. Co. operates two segments: refining operating segment, which operates seven refineries in the western U.S., refines crude oil and other feedstocks into transportation fuels, such as gasoline and gasoline blendstocks, jet fuel and diesel fuel, as well as other products, including heavy fuel oils, liquefied petroleum gas, petroleum coke and asphalt; and retail operating segment, which sells transportation fuels and convenience products in 18 states through a network of 1,402 retail stations, primarily under the Tesoro®, Shell®, and USA Gasoline® brands.

Recent Developments: For the year ended Dec 31 2012, net income increased 36.8% to US$770.0 million from US$563.0 million in the prior year. Revenues were US$32.97 billion, up 8.8% from US$30.30 billion the year before. Operating income was US$1.40 billion versus US$1.08 billion in the prior year, an increase of 29.8%. Direct operating expenses rose 7.4% to US$29.00 billion from US$27.01 billion in the comparable period the year before. Indirect operating expenses increased 16.0% to US$2.57 billion from US$2.22 billion in the equivalent prior-year period.

Prospects: Our evaluation of Tesoro Petroleum Corp. as of Apr. 7, 2013 is the result of our systematic analysis on three basic characteristics: earnings strength, relative valuation, and recent stock price movement. The company has managed to produce a neutral trend in earnings per share over the past 5 quarters and while recent estimates for the company have been raised by analysts, TSO has posted results that fell short of analysts expectations. Based on operating earnings yield, the company is undervalued when compared to all of the companies in our coverage universe. Share price changes over the past year indicates that TSO will perform very well over the near term.

Financial Data
(US$ in Thousands)

	12/31/2012	12/31/2011	12/31/2010	12/31/2009	12/31/2008	12/31/2007	12/31/2006	12/31/2005
Earnings Per Share	5.25	3.81	(0.21)	(1.01)	2.00	4.06	5.73	3.60
Cash Flow Per Share	11.34	4.87	2.74	4.80	5.22	9.74	8.38	5.57
Tang Book Value Per Share	28.96	24.33	20.48	19.84	20.67	19.48	16.94	12.11
Dividends Per Share	0.270	...	...	0.350	0.400	0.350	0.200	0.100
Dividend Payout %	5.14	...	...	...	20.00	8.62	3.49	2.78
Income Statement								
Total Revenue	32,974,000	30,303,000	20,583,000	16,872,000	28,309,000	21,915,000	18,104,000	16,581,000
EBITDA	1,671,000	1,342,000	395,000	377,000	945,000	1,336,000	1,579,000	1,245,000
Depn & Amortn	295,000	262,000	266,000	439,000	412,000	369,000	262,000	203,000
Income Before Taxes	1,212,000	905,000	(25,000)	(188,000)	429,000	905,000	1,286,000	831,000
Income Taxes	442,000	342,000	4,000	(48,000)	151,000	339,000	485,000	324,000
Net Income	743,000	546,000	(29,000)	(140,000)	278,000	566,000	801,000	507,000
Average Shares	141,500	143,300	140,600	138,200	139,200	139,500	139,800	140,800
Balance Sheet								
Current Assets	4,636,000	4,151,000	2,928,000	2,223,000	1,646,000	2,600,000	2,811,000	2,215,000
Total Assets	10,702,000	9,892,000	8,732,000	8,070,000	7,433,000	8,128,000	5,904,000	5,097,000
Current Liabilities	2,881,000	3,249,000	2,496,000	1,889,000	1,441,000	2,494,000	1,672,000	1,502,000
Long-Term Obligations	1,587,000	1,283,000	1,843,000	1,837,000	1,609,000	1,657,000	1,029,000	1,044,000
Total Liabilities	6,451,000	6,224,000	5,517,000	4,983,000	4,215,000	5,076,000	3,402,000	3,210,000
Stockholders' Equity	4,251,000	3,668,000	3,215,000	3,087,000	3,218,000	3,052,000	2,502,000	1,887,000
Shares Outstanding	138,162	139,964	143,180	140,427	138,375	137,044	135,813	138,604
Statistical Record								
Return on Assets %	7.20	5.86	N.M.	N.M.	3.56	8.07	14.56	11.06
Return on Equity %	18.71	15.87	N.M.	N.M.	8.84	20.38	36.50	31.55
EBITDA Margin %	5.07	4.43	1.92	2.23	3.34	6.10	8.72	7.51
Net Margin %	2.25	1.80	N.M.	N.M.	0.98	2.58	4.42	3.06
Asset Turnover	3.19	3.25	2.45	2.18	3.63	3.12	3.29	3.62
Current Ratio	1.61	1.28	1.17	1.18	1.14	1.04	1.68	1.47
Debt to Equity	0.37	0.35	0.57	0.60	0.50	0.54	0.41	0.55
Price Range	44.73-21.55	29.18-17.98	18.68-10.54	19.11-10.89	47.75-6.80	64.48-31.73	37.52-27.11	34.93-14.52
P/E Ratio	8.52-4.10	7.66-4.72	...	...	23.88-3.40	15.88-7.81	6.55-4.73	9.70-4.03
Average Yield %	0.86	...	...	2.43	1.80	0.69	0.60	0.42

Address: 19100 Ridgewood Pkwy, San Antonio, TX 78259-1828 **Telephone:** 210-626-6000	**Web Site:** www.tsocorp.com **Officers:** Gregory J. Goff - President, Chief Executive Officer Charles S. Parrish - Executive Vice President, Secretary, General Counsel	**Auditors:** Ernst & Young LLP **Transfer Agents:** American Stock Transfer & Trust Company, New York, NY

TEVA PHARMACEUTICAL INDUSTRIES LTD

Exchange	Symbol	Price	52Wk Range	Yield	P/E
NYS	TEVA	$39.68 (3/28/2013)	45.87-36.95	2.20	17.64

*7 Year Price Score 79.73 *NYSE Composite Index=100 *12 Month Price Score 88.61

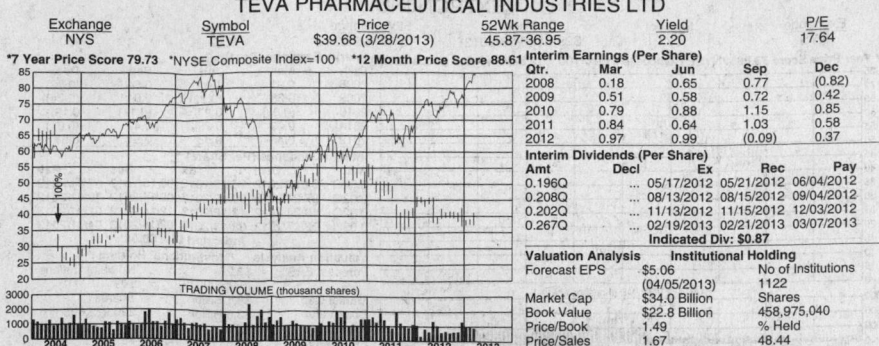

Interim Earnings (Per Share)

Qtr.	Mar	Jun	Sep	Dec
2008	0.18	0.65	0.77	(0.82)
2009	0.51	0.58	0.72	0.42
2010	0.79	0.88	1.15	0.85
2011	0.84	0.64	1.03	0.58
2012	0.97	0.99	(0.09)	0.37

Interim Dividends (Per Share)

Amt	Decl	Ex	Rec	Pay
0.196Q	...	05/17/2012	05/21/2012	06/04/2012
0.208Q	...	08/13/2012	08/15/2012	09/04/2012
0.202Q	...	11/13/2012	11/15/2012	12/03/2012
0.267Q	...	02/19/2013	02/21/2013	03/07/2013

Indicated Div: $0.87

Valuation Analysis

		Institutional Holding	
Forecast EPS	$5.06	No of Institutions	
	(04/05/2013)	1122	
Market Cap	$34.0 Billion	Shares	
Book Value	$22.8 Billion	458,975,040	
Price/Book	1.49	% Held	
Price/Sales	1.67	48.44	

Business Summary: Pharmaceuticals (MIC: 4.1.1 SIC: 2834 NAIC: 325412)

Teva Pharmaceutical Industries is a pharmaceutical company. Co.'s business includes three primary areas: Generic (Co. manufactures and sells generic pharmaceutical products in a variety of dosage forms, including tablets, capsules, ointments, creams, liquids, injectables and inhalants), Specialty (Co. produces medicines for Central Nervous System and respiratory therapeutic areas, oncology, women's health, and NTE activity) and OTC medicines (This product line includes the branded OTC medicines of Co. and P&G, in categories such as cough/cold and allergy, digestive wellness, vitamins, minerals and supplements, analgesics and skin medications).

Recent Developments: For the year ended Dec 31 2012, net income decreased 31.0% to US$1.91 billion from US$2.77 billion in the prior year. Revenues were US$20.32 billion, up 10.9% from US$18.31 billion the year before. Operating income was US$2.21 billion versus US$3.11 billion in the prior year, a decrease of 29.1%. Direct operating expenses rose 9.9% to US$9.67 billion from US$8.80 billion in the comparable period the year before. Indirect operating expenses increased 31.9% to US$8.45 billion from US$6.41 billion in the equivalent prior-year period.

Prospects: Our evaluation of Teva Pharmaceutical Industries Ltd. as of Apr. 7, 2013 is the result of our systematic analysis on three basic characteristics: earnings strength, relative valuation, and recent stock price movement. The company has generated a negative trend in earnings per share over the past 5 quarters. However, while recent estimates for the company have been lowered by analysts, TEVA has posted results that fell short of analysts expectations. Based on operating earnings yield, the company is undervalued when compared to all of the companies in our coverage universe. Share price changes over the past year indicates that TEVA will perform very poorly over the near term.

Financial Data
(US$ in Thousands)

	12/31/2012	12/31/2011	12/31/2010	12/31/2009	12/31/2008	12/31/2007	12/31/2006	12/31/2005
Earnings Per Share	2.25	3.09	3.67	2.23	0.78	2.38	0.69	1.59
Cash Flow Per Share	5.23	4.64	4.62	3.87	4.13	2.36	2.72	2.22
Tang Book Value Per Share	N.M.	N.M.	1.07	2.82	N.M.	4.42	1.47	5.54
Dividends Per Share	0.804	0.785	0.667	0.482	0.412	0.326	0.253	0.218
Dividend Payout %	35.73	25.40	18.18	21.64	52.77	13.70	36.71	13.71
Income Statement								
Total Revenue	20,317,000	18,312,000	16,121,000	13,899,000	11,085,000	9,408,000	8,408,000	5,250,400
EBITDA	2,633,000	3,467,000	4,319,000	3,313,000	1,323,000	2,916,000	1,232,000	1,555,600
Depn & Amortn	428,000	358,000	448,000	908,000	178,000	521,000	431,000	242,700
Income Before Taxes	1,819,000	2,956,000	3,646,000	2,203,000	827,000	2,353,000	706,000	1,308,600
Income Taxes	(137,000)	127,000	283,000	166,000	185,000	397,000	155,000	236,200
Net Income	1,963,000	2,759,000	3,331,000	2,000,000	635,000	1,952,000	546,000	1,072,300
Average Shares	873,000	893,000	921,000	896,000	820,000	830,000	805,000	680,800
Balance Sheet								
Current Assets	16,355,000	14,453,000	12,042,000	12,141,000	11,426,000	9,859,000	7,640,000	5,505,300
Total Assets	50,609,000	50,142,000	38,152,000	33,810,000	32,904,000	23,412,000	20,471,000	10,387,400
Current Liabilities	12,888,000	13,847,000	9,694,000	7,602,000	8,481,000	5,371,000	4,071,000	2,260,100
Long-Term Obligations	11,712,000	10,236,000	4,110,000	4,311,000	5,537,000	3,347,000	4,585,000	1,773,300
Total Liabilities	27,841,000	27,947,000	16,205,000	14,588,000	16,604,000	9,688,000	9,329,000	4,345,100
Stockholders' Equity	22,768,000	22,195,000	21,947,000	19,222,000	16,300,000	13,724,000	11,142,000	6,042,300
Shares Outstanding	857,000	883,000	897,000	885,000	851,000	768,000	758,000	646,700
Statistical Record								
Return on Assets %	3.89	6.25	9.26	6.00	2.25	8.90	3.54	10.71
Return on Equity %	8.71	12.50	16.18	11.26	4.22	15.70	6.35	18.76
EBITDA Margin %	12.96	18.93	26.79	23.84	11.94	30.99	14.65	29.63
Net Margin %	9.66	15.07	20.66	14.39	5.73	20.75	6.49	20.42
Asset Turnover	0.40	0.41	0.45	0.42	0.39	0.43	0.54	0.52
Current Ratio	1.27	1.04	1.24	1.60	1.35	1.84	1.88	2.44
Debt to Equity	0.51	0.46	0.19	0.22	0.34	0.24	0.41	0.29
Price Range	46.09-36.95	56.29-35.26	64.54-47.17	56.27-41.69	49.65-37.78	46.83-31.26	44.07-29.76	45.53-26.89
P/E Ratio	20.48-16.42	18.22-11.41	17.59-12.85	25.23-18.70	63.65-48.44	19.68-13.13	63.87-43.13	28.64-16.91
Average Yield %	1.94	1.72	1.21	1.00	0.91	0.80	0.69	0.65

Address: 5 Basel Street, P.O. Box 3190, Petach Tikva, 49131	Web Site: www.tevapharm.com	Auditors: Kesselman & Kesselman
Telephone: 392-672-67	Officers: Jeremy M. Levin - President, Chief Executive Officer Isaac Abravanel - Executive Vice President, Chief Integration Officer	

TEXTRON INC.

Exchange	Symbol	Price	52Wk Range	Yield	P/E
NYS	TXT	$29.81 (3/28/2013)	31.21-22.22	0.27	14.90

*7 Year Price Score 73.08 ***NYSE Composite Index=100** ***12 Month Price Score 103.23**

Interim Earnings (Per Share)

Qtr.	Mar	Jun	Sep	Dec
2008	0.91	1.02	0.84	(0.82)
2009	0.35	(0.22)	0.01	(0.24)
2010	(0.03)	0.27	(0.17)	0.19
2011	0.09	0.29	0.47	(0.04)
2012	0.40	0.58	0.51	0.51

Interim Dividends (Per Share)

Amt	Decl	Ex	Rec	Pay
0.02Q	04/25/2012	06/13/2012	06/15/2012	07/01/2012
0.02Q	07/24/2012	09/12/2012	09/14/2012	10/01/2012
0.02Q	10/24/2012	12/12/2012	12/14/2012	01/01/2013
0.02Q	02/27/2013	03/13/2013	03/15/2013	04/01/2013

Indicated Div: $0.08

Valuation Analysis

Forecast EPS	$2.25 (04/05/2013)
Market Cap	$8.1 Billion
Book Value	$3.0 Billion
Price/Book	2.70
Price/Sales	0.66

Institutional Holding

No of Institutions	509
Shares	229,972,608
% Held	78.16

Business Summary: Aerospace (MIC: 7.1.1 SIC: 3721 NAIC: 336411)

Textron has five segments: Cessna, which sells Citation jets, Caravan single-engine utility turboprops, single-engine piston aircraft and lift applications, and aftermarket services; Bell, which supplies military and commercial helicopters, tiltrotor aircraft, and related spare parts and services; Textron Systems, which includes unmanned aircraft systems, land and marine systems, weapons and sensors and various defense and aviation mission support products and services; Industrial, which provides fuel systems and functional components, golf, turf care and light transportation vehicles, and powered tools, testing and measurement equipment; and Finance, which is a commercial finance business.

Recent Developments: For the year ended Dec 29 2012, income from continuing operations increased 140.1% to US$581.0 million from US$242.0 million a year earlier. Net income increased 143.4% to US$589.0 million from US$242.0 million in the prior year. Revenues were US$12.24 billion, up 8.5% from US$11.28 billion the year before. Direct operating expenses rose 7.6% to US$10.02 billion from US$9.31 billion in the comparable period the year before. Indirect operating expenses decreased 15.5% to US$1.38 billion from US$1.63 billion in the equivalent prior-year period.

Prospects: Our evaluation of Textron Inc. as of Apr. 7, 2013 is the result of our systematic analysis on three basic characteristics: earnings strength, relative valuation, and recent stock price movement. The company has generated a negative trend in earnings per share over the past 5 quarters and while recent estimates for the company have remained steady, TXT has posted results that fell short of analysts expectations. Based on operating earnings yield, the company is undervalued when compared to all of the companies in our coverage universe. Share price changes over the past year indicates that TXT will perform in line with the market over the near term.

Financial Data
(US$ in Millions)

	12/29/2012	12/31/2011	01/01/2011	01/02/2010	01/03/2009	12/29/2007	12/30/2006	12/31/2005
Earnings Per Share	2.00	0.79	0.28	(0.12)	1.95	3.60	2.31	0.75
Cash Flow Per Share	3.32	3.84	3.60	3.87	3.00	4.21	3.81	3.89
Tang Book Value Per Share	4.95	3.98	4.86	4.42	2.06	4.81	4.83	8.01
Dividends Per Share	0.080	0.080	0.080	0.080	0.920	0.848	0.775	0.700
Dividend Payout %	4.00	10.13	28.57	...	47.18	23.54	33.55	93.96
Income Statement								
Total Revenue	12,237	11,275	10,525	10,500	14,246	13,225	11,490	10,043
EBITDA	1,368	900	664	471	1,395	2,054	1,703	1,313
Depn & Amortn	315	317	308	317	305	270	290	284
Income Before Taxes	841	337	86	(149)	658	1,300	975	739
Income Taxes	260	95	(6)	(76)	314	385	269	223
Net Income	589	242	86	(31)	486	917	601	203
Average Shares	294	307	302	262	249	254	260	272
Balance Sheet								
Current Assets	5,389	5,263	5,047	5,933	5,242	4,846	4,287	4,975
Total Assets	13,033	13,615	15,282	18,940	20,020	19,956	17,550	16,499
Current Liabilities	3,512	2,931	2,657	2,868	4,766	4,122	2,994	3,147
Long-Term Obligations	3,453	4,780	6,269	9,117	9,081	9,104	8,582	7,079
Total Liabilities	10,042	10,870	12,310	16,114	17,654	16,449	14,901	13,223
Stockholders' Equity	2,991	2,745	2,972	2,826	2,366	3,507	2,649	3,276
Shares Outstanding	271	278	275	272	242	250	251	260
Statistical Record								
Return on Assets %	4.43	1.68	0.50	N.M.	2.39	4.90	3.54	1.26
Return on Equity %	20.59	8.49	2.97	N.M.	16.28	29.87	20.34	5.88
EBITDA Margin %	11.18	7.98	6.31	4.49	9.79	15.53	14.82	13.07
Net Margin %	4.81	2.15	0.82	N.M.	3.41	6.93	5.23	2.02
Asset Turnover	0.92	0.78	0.62	0.54	0.70	0.71	0.68	0.62
Current Ratio	1.53	1.80	1.90	2.07	1.10	1.18	1.43	1.58
Debt to Equity	1.15	1.74	2.11	3.23	3.84	2.60	3.24	2.16
Price Range	28.89-18.64	28.50-14.88	24.55-16.07	20.73-3.75	71.30-11.69	73.38-44.08	49.19-37.88	40.02-32.92
P/E Ratio	14.45-9.32	36.08-18.84	87.68-57.39	...	36.56-5.99	20.38-12.24	21.29-16.40	53.37-43.90
Average Yield %	0.32	0.36	0.39	0.60	2.15	1.51	1.74	1.88

Address: 40 Westminster Street, Providence, RI 02903 Telephone: 401-421-2800 Fax: 401-421-2878	Web Site: www.textron.com Officers: Scott C. Donnelly - Chairman, President, Chief Executive Officer Frank T. Connor - Executive Vice President, Chief Financial Officer	Auditors: Ernst & Young LLP Investor Contact: 401-457-2288 Transfer Agents: American Stock & Transfer & Trust Company, Brooklyn, NY

THE GAP, INC.

Exchange	Symbol	Price	52Wk Range	Yield	P/E
NYS	GPS	$35.40 (3/28/2013)	37.27-25.23	1.69	15.19

*7 Year Price Score 136.57 *NYSE Composite Index=100   *12 Month Price Score 97.85

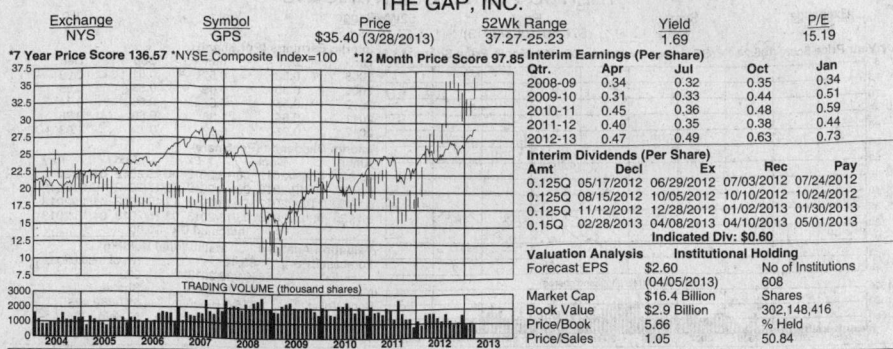

Interim Earnings (Per Share)

Qtr.	Apr	Jul	Oct	Jan
2008-09	0.34	0.32	0.35	0.34
2009-10	0.31	0.33	0.44	0.51
2010-11	0.45	0.36	0.48	0.59
2011-12	0.40	0.35	0.38	0.44
2012-13	0.47	0.49	0.63	0.73

Interim Dividends (Per Share)

Amt	Decl	Ex	Rec	Pay
0.125Q	05/17/2012	06/29/2012	07/03/2012	07/24/2012
0.125Q	08/15/2012	10/05/2012	10/10/2012	10/24/2012
0.125Q	11/12/2012	12/28/2012	01/02/2013	01/30/2013
0.15Q	02/28/2013	04/08/2013	04/10/2013	05/01/2013
			Indicated Div:	$0.60

Valuation Analysis   **Institutional Holding**

Forecast EPS	$2.60	No of Institutions
	(04/05/2013)	608
Market Cap	$16.4 Billion	Shares
Book Value	$2.9 Billion	302,148,416
Price/Book	5.66	% Held
Price/Sales	1.05	50.84

Business Summary: Retail - Apparel and Accessories (MIC: 2.1.5 SIC: 5651 NAIC: 448140)

The Gap is a retailer providing apparel, accessories and personal care products for men, women, children and babies under the Gap, Old Navy, Banana Republic, Piperlime and Athleta brands. Co. operates stores in the U.S., Canada, the U.K., France, Ireland, Japan, China and Italy. Co. also has franchise agreements with unaffiliated franchisees to operate Gap and Banana Republic throughout Asia, Australia, Eastern Europe, Latin America, the Middle East, and Africa. Under these agreements, third parties operate stores that sell apparel and related products under Co.'s brand names. Co.'s products are also available online. At Jan 28 2012, Co. had 3,263 Co.-operated and franchise store locations.

Recent Developments: For the year ended Feb 2 2013, net income increased 36.3% to US$1.14 billion from US$833.0 million in the prior year. Revenues were US$15.65 billion, up 7.6% from US$14.55 billion the year before. Operating income was US$1.94 billion versus US$1.44 billion in the prior year, an increase of 35.0%. Direct operating expenses rose 2.2% to US$9.48 billion from US$9.28 billion in the comparable period the year before. Indirect operating expenses increased 10.2% to US$4.23 billion from US$3.84 billion in the equivalent prior-year period.

Prospects: Our evaluation of The Gap Inc. as of Apr. 7, 2013 is the result of our systematic analysis on three basic characteristics: earnings strength, relative valuation, and recent stock price movement. The company has managed to produce a neutral trend in earnings per share over the past 5 quarters and while recent estimates for the company have been raised by analysts, GPS has posted better than expected results. Based on earnings yield, the company is undervalued when compared to all of the companies in our coverage universe. Share price changes over the past year indicates that GPS will perform in line with the market over the near term.

Financial Data

(US$ in Thousands)	02/02/2013	01/28/2012	01/29/2011	01/30/2010	01/31/2009	02/02/2008	02/03/2007	01/28/2006
Earnings Per Share	2.33	1.56	1.88	1.58	1.34	1.05	0.93	1.24
Cash Flow Per Share	3.95	2.58	2.75	2.79	1.98	2.64	1.48	1.77
Tang Book Value Per Share	5.57	5.32	6.64	6.96	6.04	5.82	6.36	6.33
Dividends Per Share	0.500	0.450	0.400	0.340	0.340	0.320	0.320	0.202
Dividend Payout %	21.46	28.85	21.28	21.52	25.37	30.48	34.41	16.31
Income Statement								
Total Revenue	15,651,000	14,549,000	14,664,000	14,197,000	14,526,000	15,763,000	15,943,000	16,023,000
EBITDA	2,497,000	2,026,000	2,611,000	2,464,000	2,199,000	1,940,000	1,777,000	2,370,000
Depn & Amortn	555,000	588,000	643,000	649,000	651,000	625,000	603,000	625,000
Income Before Taxes	1,861,000	1,369,000	1,982,000	1,816,000	1,584,000	1,406,000	1,264,000	1,793,000
Income Taxes	726,000	536,000	778,000	714,000	617,000	539,000	486,000	680,000
Net Income	1,135,000	833,000	1,204,000	1,102,000	967,000	833,000	778,000	1,113,000
Average Shares	488,000	533,000	641,000	699,000	719,000	794,000	835,973	902,305
Balance Sheet								
Current Assets	4,132,000	4,309,000	3,926,000	4,664,000	4,005,000	4,086,000	5,029,000	5,239,000
Total Assets	7,470,000	7,422,000	7,065,000	7,985,000	7,564,000	7,838,000	8,544,000	8,821,000
Current Liabilities	2,344,000	2,128,000	2,095,000	2,131,000	2,158,000	2,433,000	2,272,000	1,942,000
Long-Term Obligations	1,246,000	1,606,000	...	...	...	50,000	188,000	513,000
Total Liabilities	4,576,000	4,667,000	2,985,000	3,094,000	3,177,000	3,564,000	3,370,000	3,396,000
Stockholders' Equity	2,894,000	2,755,000	4,080,000	4,891,000	4,387,000	4,274,000	5,174,000	5,425,000
Shares Outstanding	463,000	485,000	588,000	676,000	694,000	734,000	813,870	856,986
Statistical Record								
Return on Assets %	15.00	11.53	16.04	14.21	12.59	10.20	8.82	11.83
Return on Equity %	39.53	24.44	26.92	23.82	22.39	17.68	14.44	21.54
EBITDA Margin %	15.95	13.93	17.81	17.36	15.14	12.31	11.15	14.79
Net Margin %	7.25	5.73	8.21	7.76	6.66	5.28	4.88	6.95
Asset Turnover	2.07	2.01	1.95	1.83	1.89	1.93	1.81	1.70
Current Ratio	1.76	2.02	1.87	2.19	1.86	1.68	2.21	2.70
Debt to Equity	0.43	0.58	...	...	...	0.01	0.04	0.09
Price Range	37.27-18.83	23.29-15.52	26.21-16.86	23.21-9.85	21.37-9.51	21.87-15.66	21.09-16.22	22.58-16.00
P/E Ratio	16.00-8.08	14.93-9.95	13.94-8.97	14.69-6.23	15.95-7.10	20.83-14.91	22.68-17.44	18.21-12.90
Average Yield %	1.64	2.33	1.94	1.92	2.04	1.71	1.74	1.03

Address: Two Folsom Street, San Francisco, CA 94105 Telephone: 415-427-0100	Web Site: www.gapinc.com Officers: Glenn K. Murphy - Chairman, Chief Executive Officer Michelle A. Banks - Executive Vice President, Chief Compliance Officer, Corporate Secretary, General Counsel	Auditors: Deloitte & Touche LLP Investor Contact: 415-427-0100 Transfer Agents: Wells Fargo Bank, N.A., South St. Paul, MN

THERMO FISHER SCIENTIFIC INC

Exchange	Symbol	Price	52Wk Range	Yield	P/E
NYS	TMO	$76.49 (3/28/2013)	77.70-48.63	0.78	23.83

*7 Year Price Score 106.24 *NYSE Composite Index=100 *12 Month Price Score 113.34

Interim Earnings (Per Share)

Qtr.	Mar	Jun	Sep	Dec
2008	0.53	0.57	0.51	0.68
2009	0.35	0.49	0.53	0.65
2010	0.56	0.57	0.66	0.74
2011	0.64	1.36	0.69	0.78
2012	0.75	0.63	0.79	1.03

Interim Dividends (Per Share)

Amt	Decl	Ex	Rec	Pay
0.13Q	05/24/2012	06/13/2012	06/15/2012	07/16/2012
0.13Q	07/12/2012	09/13/2012	09/17/2012	10/15/2012
0.15Q	11/08/2012	12/13/2012	12/17/2012	01/15/2013
0.15Q	02/27/2013	03/13/2013	03/15/2013	04/15/2013

Indicated Div: $0.60

Valuation Analysis

		Institutional Holding	
Forecast EPS	$5.42 (04/06/2013)	No of Institutions	993
Market Cap	$27.3 Billion	Shares	357,882,496
Book Value	$15.5 Billion	% Held	86.37
Price/Book	1.77		
Price/Sales	2.19		

Business Summary: Biotechnology (MIC: 4.1.2 SIC: 3829 NAIC: 334519)

Thermo Fisher Scientific provides analytical instruments, equipment, reagents and consumables, software and services for research, manufacturing, analysis, discovery and diagnostics. Co. has three segments: Analytical Technologies, which provides instruments, reagents, consumables, software and services that are used in the laboratory, on the production line and in the field; Specialty Diagnostics, which provides diagnostic test kits, reagents, culture media, instruments and associated products; and Laboratory Products and Services, which serves the pharmaceutical, biotechnology, academic, government and other research and industrial markets, as well as the clinical laboratory.

Recent Developments: For the year ended Dec 31 2012, income from continuing operations increased 23.0% to US$1.26 billion from US$1.02 billion a year earlier. Net income decreased 11.4% to US$1.18 billion from US$1.33 billion in the prior year. Revenues were US$12.51 billion, up 8.2% from US$11.56 billion the year before. Operating income was US$1.48 billion versus US$1.25 billion in the prior year, an increase of 18.5%. Direct operating expenses rose 6.6% to US$7.21 billion from US$6.76 billion in the comparable period the year before. Indirect operating expenses increased 7.6% to US$3.81 billion from US$3.54 billion in the equivalent prior-year period.

Prospects: Our evaluation of Thermo Fisher Scientific Inc. as of Apr. 7, 2013 is the result of our systematic analysis on three basic characteristics: earnings strength, relative valuation, and recent stock price movement. The company has produced a positive trend in earnings per share over the past 5 quarters. However, while recent estimates for the company have been mixed, TMO has posted better than expected results. Based on operating earnings yield, the company is undervalued when compared to all of the companies in our coverage universe. Share price changes over the past year indicates that TMO will perform well over the near term.

Financial Data

(US$ in Thousands)	12/31/2012	12/31/2011	12/31/2010	12/31/2009	12/31/2008	12/31/2007	12/31/2006	12/31/2005
Earnings Per Share	3.21	3.46	2.53	2.01	2.29	1.72	0.84	1.36
Cash Flow Per Share	5.59	4.44	3.71	4.02	3.39	3.52	2.07	1.68
Tang Book Value Per Share	N.M.	N.M.	0.13	0.27	N.M.	N.M.	N.M.	2.32
Dividends Per Share	0.540	...	...	...	...	...	...	...
Dividend Payout %	16.82	...	...	...	...	...	...	...
Income Statement								
Total Revenue	12,509,900	11,725,900	10,788,700	10,109,700	10,498,000	9,746,400	3,791,617	2,633,027
EBITDA	2,469,500	2,138,500	1,435,100	1,219,400	1,414,300	1,157,700	483,825	424,148
Depn & Amortn	983,700	863,500	198,300	190,300	189,900	185,700	240,773	123,272
Income Before Taxes	1,269,400	1,126,600	1,164,600	927,100	1,146,200	878,700	207,541	285,730
Income Taxes	11,000	107,000	131,500	75,800	160,900	101,700	43,054	87,597
Net Income	1,177,900	1,329,900	1,035,600	850,300	994,200	761,100	168,935	223,218
Average Shares	366,600	384,800	409,400	422,800	434,800	443,700	203,672	165,334
Balance Sheet								
Current Assets	4,834,800	4,821,900	4,135,000	4,530,900	4,345,900	3,665,300	3,659,536	1,353,900
Total Assets	27,444,600	26,833,700	21,349,400	21,625,000	21,090,000	21,207,400	21,262,238	4,251,569
Current Liabilities	2,093,300	3,113,100	1,709,800	1,639,300	1,540,200	1,901,600	2,152,321	791,662
Long-Term Obligations	7,031,200	5,755,200	2,031,300	2,064,000	2,043,500	2,045,900	2,180,705	468,630
Total Liabilities	11,979,900	11,795,600	5,988,400	6,194,100	6,163,400	6,719,100	7,350,411	1,458,257
Stockholders' Equity	15,464,700	15,038,100	15,361,000	15,430,900	14,926,600	14,488,300	13,911,827	2,793,312
Shares Outstanding	357,443	371,383	391,369	409,310	417,965	415,237	416,605	162,482
Statistical Record								
Return on Assets %	4.33	5.52	4.82	3.98	4.69	3.58	1.32	5.70
Return on Equity %	7.70	8.75	6.73	5.60	6.74	5.36	2.02	8.18
EBITDA Margin %	19.74	18.24	13.30	12.06	13.47	11.88	12.76	16.11
Net Margin %	9.42	11.34	9.60	8.41	9.47	7.81	4.46	8.48
Asset Turnover	0.46	0.49	0.50	0.47	0.50	0.46	0.30	0.67
Current Ratio	2.31	1.55	2.42	2.76	2.82	1.93	1.70	1.71
Debt to Equity	0.45	0.38	0.13	0.13	0.14	0.14	0.16	0.17
Price Range	65.28-45.95	65.57-43.54	55.94-42.12	49.03-32.39	62.70-28.90	59.51-44.16	46.16-30.28	31.78-24.24
P/E Ratio	20.34-14.31	18.95-12.58	22.11-16.65	24.39-16.11	27.38-12.62	34.60-25.67	54.95-36.05	23.37-17.82
Average Yield %	0.96	...	...	...	...	...	...	...

Address: 81 Wyman Street, Waltham, MA 02451	Web Site: www.thermofisher.com	Auditors: PricewaterhouseCoopers LLP
Telephone: 781-622-1000	Officers: Jim P. Manzi - Chairman Marc N. Casper - President, Chief Executive Officer	Investor Contact: 781-622-1111
Fax: 781-933-4476		Transfer Agents: American Stock Transfer & Trust Company, Brooklyn, NY

THOMSON REUTERS CORP

Exchange	Symbol	Price	52Wk Range	Yield	P/E
NYS	TRI	$32.96 (3/28/2013)	33.32-26.85	3.94	13.24

*7 Year Price Score 71.00   *NYSE Composite Index=100   *12 Month Price Score 99.82

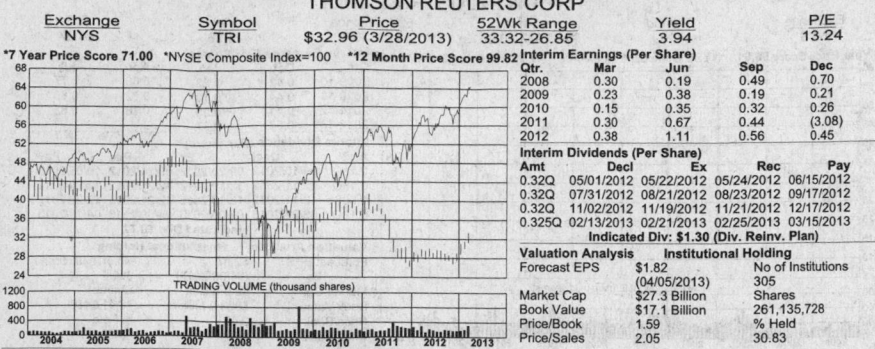

Interim Earnings (Per Share)

Qtr.	Mar	Jun	Sep	Dec
2008	0.30	0.19	0.49	0.70
2009	0.23	0.38	0.19	0.21
2010	0.15	0.35	0.32	0.26
2011	0.30	0.67	0.44	(3.08)
2012	0.38	1.11	0.56	0.45

Interim Dividends (Per Share)

Amt	Decl	Ex	Rec	Pay
0.32Q	05/01/2012	05/22/2012	05/24/2012	06/15/2012
0.32Q	07/31/2012	08/21/2012	08/23/2012	09/17/2012
0.32Q	11/02/2012	11/19/2012	11/21/2012	12/17/2012
0.325Q	02/13/2013	02/21/2013	02/25/2013	03/15/2013

Indicated Div: $1.30 (Div. Reinv. Plan)

Valuation Analysis   **Institutional Holding**

Forecast EPS	$1.82 (04/05/2013)	No of Institutions	305
Market Cap	$27.3 Billion	Shares	261,135,728
Book Value	$17.1 Billion	% Held	30.83
Price/Book	1.59		
Price/Sales	2.05		

TRADING VOLUME (thousand shares)

Business Summary: Publishing (MIC: 2.3.3 SIC: 2721 NAIC: 511120)

Thomson Reuters is engaged in the provision of information for the world's businesses and professionals. Co. delivers its insight to the financial, legal, tax and accounting, healthcare, science and media markets. Co.'s businesses are organized into the following two divisions: Professional, which consists of legal, tax and accounting, healthcare and science businesses; and Markets, which consists of financial and media businesses.

Recent Developments: For the year ended Dec 31 2012, net income amounted to US$2.12 billion versus a net loss of US$1.39 billion in the prior year. Revenues were US$13.28 billion, down 3.8% from US$13.81 billion the year before. Operating income was US$2.65 billion versus a loss of US$705.0 million in the prior year. Indirect operating expenses decreased 21.8% to US$11.51 billion from US$14.72 billion in the equivalent prior-year period.

Prospects: Our evaluation of Thomson Reuters Corp as of Apr. 7, 2013 is the result of our systematic analysis on three basic characteristics: earnings strength, relative valuation, and recent stock price movement. The company has generated a negative trend in earnings per share over the past 5 quarters and while recent estimates for the company have been mixed, TRI has posted better than expected results. Based on operating earnings yield, the company is about fairly valued when compared to all of the companies in our coverage universe. Share price changes over the past year indicates that TRI will perform poorly over the near term.

Financial Data

(US$ in Thousands)	12/31/2012	12/31/2011	12/31/2010	12/31/2009	12/31/2008	12/31/2007	12/31/2006
Earnings Per Share	2.49	(1.67)	1.08	1.01	1.68	6.20	1.73
Cash Flow Per Share	3.26	3.12	3.19	3.21	3.57	2.83	3.30
Tang Book Value Per Share	N.M.	N.M.	N.M.	N.M.	N.M.	4.83	0.56
Dividends Per Share	1.280	1.240	1.160	1.960	1.570	...	...
Dividend Payout %	51.41	...	107.41	194.06	93.45	...	...
Income Statement							
Total Revenue	13,278,000	13,807,000	13,070,000	12,997,000	11,707,000	7,296,000	6,641,000
EBITDA	...	...	...	...	...	1,987,000	1,940,000
Depn & Amortn	890,000	833,000	660,000	538,000	493,000	724,000	681,000
Income Before Taxes	...	...	...	...	...	1,251,000	1,038,000
Income Taxes	157,000	293,000	139,000	(299,000)	350,000	155,000	119,000
Net Income	2,070,000	(1,390,000)	909,000	844,000	1,307,000	4,004,000	1,120,000
Average Shares	828,185	833,459	836,447	832,942	775,179	644,430	646,026
Balance Sheet							
Current Assets	4,151,000	3,914,000	3,659,000	3,663,000	3,686,000	9,678,000	3,265,000
Total Assets	32,572,000	32,476,000	35,531,000	34,573,000	34,589,000	22,831,000	20,132,000
Current Liabilities	4,995,000	4,604,000	5,011,000	4,712,000	4,645,000	3,239,000	3,739,000
Long-Term Obligations	6,223,000	7,160,000	6,873,000	6,821,000	6,783,000	4,264,000	3,681,000
Total Liabilities	15,427,000	16,071,000	16,209,000	15,306,000	16,173,000	9,260,000	9,651,000
Stockholders' Equity	17,145,000	16,405,000	19,322,000	19,267,000	18,416,000	13,571,000	10,481,000
Shares Outstanding	826,902	827,867	833,396	829,758	827,275	638,682	640,437
Statistical Record							
Return on Assets %	6.35	N.M.	2.59	2.44	...	18.64	5.66
Return on Equity %	12.31	N.M.	4.71	4.48	...	33.29	10.96
EBITDA Margin %	...	...	...	...	...	27.23	29.21
Net Margin %	15.59	N.M.	6.95	6.49	11.16	54.88	16.86
Asset Turnover	0.41	0.41	0.37	0.38	...	0.34	0.34
Current Ratio	0.83	0.85	0.73	0.78	0.79	2.99	0.87
Debt to Equity	0.36	0.44	0.36	0.35	0.37	0.31	0.35
Price Range	30.02-26.85	41.49-26.21	39.90-33.60	37.95-28.25	40.51-25.86	51.25-37.11	49.18-39.69
P/E Ratio	12.06-10.78	...	36.94-31.11	37.57-27.97	24.11-15.39	8.27-5.99	28.43-22.94
Average Yield %	4.49	3.65	3.10	5.84	4.65	...	...

Address: 3 Times Square, New York, NY 10036 **Telephone:** 646-223-4000	**Web Site:** www.thomsonreuters.com **Officers:** Thomas H. Glocer - Chief Executive Officer Robert D. Daleo - Executive Vice President, Chief Financial Officer	**Auditors:** PricewaterhouseCoopers LLP **Investor Contact:** 646-223-5288 **Transfer Agents:** Computershare Trust Company of Canada, Toronto, Montreal, Calgary, Vancouver, Canada

THOR INDUSTRIES, INC.

Exchange	Symbol	Price	52Wk Range	Yield	P/E
NYS	THO	$36.79 (3/28/2013)	44.25-26.90	1.96	14.37

*7 Year Price Score 96.01   *NYSE Composite Index=100   *12 Month Price Score 101.68

TRADING VOLUME (thousand shares)

Interim Earnings (Per Share)

Qtr.	Oct	Jan	Apr	Jul
2009-10	0.42	0.22	0.66	0.77
2010-11	0.44	0.10	0.72	0.66
2011-12	0.41	0.25	0.78	0.83
2012-13	0.58	0.37	...	...

Interim Dividends (Per Share)

Amt	Decl	Ex	Rec	Pay
0.18Q	09/10/2012	09/20/2012	09/24/2012	10/05/2012
0.18Q	12/11/2012	12/19/2012	12/21/2012	12/28/2012
1.50Sp	12/11/2012	12/19/2012	12/21/2012	12/28/2012
0.18Q	03/22/2013	04/05/2013	04/09/2013	04/19/2013

Indicated Div: $0.72

Valuation Analysis   Institutional Holding

Forecast EPS	$2.87	No of Institutions
	(04/05/2013)	300
Market Cap	$2.0 Billion	Shares
Book Value	$803.9 Million	48,417,436
Price/Book	2.43	% Held
Price/Sales	0.57	86.25

Business Summary: Autos- Manufacturing (MIC: 1.8.1 SIC: 3716 NAIC: 336213)

Thor Industries manufactures and sells a range of recreation vehicles and small and mid-size buses in the U.S. and Canada. Co. has three reportable segments: towable recreation vehicles; motorized recreation vehicles; and buses. The principal types of recreation vehicles that Co.'s recreation vehicles segments produce include travel trailers, fifth wheels, park models, and Class A, Class C and Class B motorhomes. The buses segment manufactures and sells small and mid-size bus products which consist of units used by mass transit, airport shuttles, nursing and retirement homes, church organizations and other commercial and tourist uses.

Recent Developments: For the quarter ended Jan 31 2013, net income increased 45.4% to US$19.9 million from US$13.7 million in the year-earlier quarter. Revenues were US$741.6 million, up 24.2% from US$597.0 million the year before. Direct operating expenses rose 24.3% to US$668.2 million from US$537.6 million in the comparable period the year before. Indirect operating expenses increased 25.5% to US$49.0 million from US$39.0 million in the equivalent prior-year period.

Prospects: Our evaluation of Thor Industries Inc. as of Apr. 7, 2013 is the result of our systematic analysis on three basic characteristics: earnings strength, relative valuation, and recent stock price movement. The company has managed to produce a neutral trend in earnings per share over the past 5 quarters. However, while recent estimates for the company have been lowered by analysts, THO has posted results that fell short of analysts expectations. Based on operating earnings yield, the company is undervalued when compared to all of the companies in our coverage universe. Share price changes over the past year indicates that THO will perform very well over the near term.

Financial Data
(US$ in Thousands)

	6 Mos	3 Mos	07/31/2012	07/31/2011	07/31/2010	07/31/2009	07/31/2008	07/31/2007
Earnings Per Share	2.56	2.44	2.26	1.92	2.07	0.31	1.66	2.41
Cash Flow Per Share	1.59	2.10	2.20	2.08	1.90	0.88	2.19	4.18
Tang Book Value Per Share	8.33	8.32	9.29	8.36	9.44	9.79	9.50	10.49
Dividends Per Share	2.160	0.630	0.600	0.400	0.780	0.280	2.280	1.280
Dividend Payout %	84.38	25.82	26.55	20.83	37.68	90.32	137.35	53.11
Income Statement								
Total Revenue	1,617,212	875,612	3,084,660	2,755,508	2,276,557	1,521,896	2,640,680	2,856,308
EBITDA	84,249	53,124	202,464	172,938	179,502	31,873	159,232	200,163
Depn & Amortn	12,454	6,212	24,978	24,009	13,229	13,483	17,021	13,905
Income Before Taxes	73,142	47,611	180,691	152,627	171,393	23,395	152,407	196,860
Income Taxes	22,258	16,623	58,952	46,354	61,329	6,252	59,701	62,129
Net Income	50,884	30,988	121,739	106,273	110,064	17,143	92,706	134,731
Average Shares	53,116	53,035	53,899	55,373	53,119	55,476	55,731	55,923
Balance Sheet								
Current Assets	657,532	707,197	684,886	623,767	601,770	604,018	527,920	705,528
Total Assets	1,208,994	1,267,553	1,243,054	1,198,070	964,073	951,124	996,562	1,059,297
Current Liabilities	324,321	311,841	311,090	278,598	256,764	184,474	248,416	277,199
Total Liabilities	405,082	393,937	392,227	361,796	306,795	246,091	296,866	292,966
Stockholders' Equity	803,912	873,616	850,827	836,274	657,278	705,033	699,696	766,331
Shares Outstanding	53,041	61,821	52,920	55,840	51,461	55,440	55,439	55,780
Statistical Record								
Return on Assets %	11.62	10.64	9.95	9.83	11.49	1.76	8.99	13.01
Return on Equity %	17.25	15.30	14.39	14.23	16.16	2.44	12.61	18.21
EBITDA Margin %	5.21	6.07	6.56	6.28	7.88	2.09	6.03	7.01
Net Margin %	3.15	3.54	3.95	3.86	4.83	1.13	3.51	4.72
Asset Turnover	2.92	2.68	2.52	2.55	2.38	1.56	2.56	2.76
Current Ratio	2.03	2.27	2.20	2.24	2.34	3.27	2.13	2.55
Price Range	44.25-26.90	38.87-22.49	34.47-18.00	37.71-23.24	36.39-23.51	31.63-9.71	52.00-19.62	47.52-38.90
P/E Ratio	17.29-10.51	15.93-9.22	15.25-7.96	19.64-12.10	17.58-11.36	102.03-31.32	31.33-11.82	19.72-16.14
Average Yield %	6.39	2.08	2.21	1.29	2.60	1.58	6.67	2.99

Address: 419 West Pike Street, Jackson Center, OH 45334-0629 **Telephone:** 937-596-6849	**Web Site:** www.thorindustries.com **Officers:** Peter B. Orthwein - Chairman, President, Chief Executive Officer Robert W. Martin - President, Chief Operating Officer, Division Officer	**Auditors:** Deloitte & Touche LLP **Transfer Agents:** Computershare Investor Services

3M CO

*7 Year Price Score 102.08 *NYSE Composite Index=100 *12 Month Price Score 103.10

Interim Earnings (Per Share)

Qtr.	Mar	Jun	Sep	Dec
2008	1.38	1.33	1.41	0.78
2009	0.74	1.12	1.35	1.31
2010	1.29	1.54	1.53	1.27
2011	1.49	1.60	1.52	1.35
2012	1.59	1.66	1.65	1.41

Interim Dividends (Per Share)

Amt	Decl	Ex	Rec	Pay
0.59Q	05/08/2012	05/16/2012	05/18/2012	06/12/2012
0.59Q	08/14/2012	08/22/2012	08/24/2012	09/12/2012
0.59Q	11/12/2012	11/20/2012	11/23/2012	12/12/2012
0.635Q	02/05/2013	02/13/2013	02/15/2013	03/12/2013

Indicated Div: $2.54 (Div. Reinv. Plan)

Valuation Analysis / **Institutional Holding**

Forecast EPS	$6.83 (04/05/2013)	No of Institutions	1724
Market Cap	$73.0 Billion	Shares	520,663,456
Book Value	$17.6 Billion	% Held	66.97
Price/Book	4.16		
Price/Sales	2.44		

Business Summary: Medical Instruments & Equipment (MIC: 4.3.1 SIC: 3841 NAIC: 339112)

3M is a technology company. Co.'s segments are: Industrial and Transportation, providing tapes, and filtration products among others; Health Care, providing medical and surgical supplies, and skin health and infection prevention products among others; Consumer and Office, providing office supply, and stationery products among others; Safety, Security and Protection Services, providing personal protection, and electronic surveillance products among others; Display and Graphics, providing optical film applications for LCD electronic displays, and mobile interactive applications among others; and Electro and Communications, providing telecommunications and electrical products among others.

Recent Developments: For the year ended Dec 31 2012, net income increased 3.5% to US$4.51 billion from US$4.36 billion in the prior year. Revenues were US$29.90 billion, up 1.0% from US$29.61 billion the year before. Operating income was US$6.48 billion versus US$6.18 billion in the prior year, an increase of 4.9%. Direct operating expenses was unchanged at US$15.69 billion versus the comparable period the year before. Indirect operating expenses were unchanged at US$7.74 billion versus the equivalent prior-year period.

Prospects: Our evaluation of 3M Co as of Apr. 7, 2013 is the result of our systematic analysis on three basic characteristics: earnings strength, relative valuation, and recent stock price movement. The company has managed to produce a neutral trend in earnings per share over the past 5 quarters. However, while recent estimates for the company have been lowered by analysts, MMM has posted results that were in line with analysts expectations. Based on operating earnings yield, the company is undervalued when compared to all of the companies in our coverage universe. Share price changes over the past year indicates that MMM will perform in line with the market over the near term.

Financial Data
(US$ in Millions)

	12/31/2012	12/31/2011	12/31/2010	12/31/2009	12/31/2008	12/31/2007	12/31/2006	12/31/2005
Earnings Per Share	6.32	5.96	5.63	4.52	4.89	5.60	5.06	4.12
Cash Flow Per Share	7.62	7.46	7.25	7.05	6.47	5.95	5.14	5.57
Tang Book Value Per Share	12.03	9.29	9.86	7.87	3.93	8.96	7.04	8.14
Dividends Per Share	2.360	2.200	2.100	2.040	2.000	1.920	1.840	1.680
Dividend Payout %	37.34	36.91	37.30	45.13	40.90	34.29	36.36	40.78
Income Statement								
Total Revenue	29,904	29,611	26,662	23,123	25,269	24,462	22,923	21,167
EBITDA	7,771	7,414	7,038	5,971	6,371	7,265	6,775	5,995
Depn & Amortn	1,288	1,236	1,120	1,157	1,153	1,072	1,079	986
Income Before Taxes	6,351	6,031	5,755	4,632	5,108	6,115	5,625	4,983
Income Taxes	1,840	1,674	1,592	1,388	1,588	1,964	1,723	1,694
Net Income	4,444	4,283	4,085	3,193	3,460	4,096	3,851	3,199
Average Shares	703	719	725	706	707	732	761	776
Balance Sheet								
Current Assets	13,630	12,240	12,215	10,795	9,598	9,838	8,946	7,115
Total Assets	33,876	31,616	30,156	27,250	25,547	24,694	21,294	20,513
Current Liabilities	6,200	5,441	6,089	4,897	5,839	5,362	7,323	5,238
Long-Term Obligations	4,987	4,563	4,277	5,204	5,224	4,088	1,112	1,368
Total Liabilities	16,301	16,196	14,493	14,486	15,668	12,947	11,335	10,413
Stockholders' Equity	17,575	15,420	15,663	12,764	9,879	11,747	9,959	10,100
Shares Outstanding	'687	694	711	710	693	709	734	754
Statistical Record								
Return on Assets %	13.53	13.87	14.23	12.10	13.74	17.81	18.42	15.52
Return on Equity %	26.86	27.56	28.74	28.20	31.91	37.74	38.40	31.24
EBITDA Margin %	25.99	25.04	26.40	25.82	25.21	29.70	29.56	28.32
Net Margin %	14.86	14.46	15.32	13.81	13.69	16.74	16.80	15.11
Asset Turnover	0.91	0.96	0.93	0.88	1.00	1.06	1.10	1.03
Current Ratio	2.20	2.25	2.01	2.20	1.64	1.83	1.22	1.36
Debt to Equity	0.28	0.30	0.27	0.41	0.53	0.35	0.11	0.14
Price Range	95.37-82.51	97.97-70.93	90.90-74.74	84.13-41.83	84.32-53.50	95.85-73.01	88.13-68.11	86.80-70.07
P/E Ratio	15.09-13.06	16.44-11.90	16.15-13.28	18.61-9.25	17.24-10.94	17.12-13.04	17.42-13.46	21.07-17.01
Average Yield %	2.65	2.54	2.51	3.19	2.79	2.29	2.39	2.16

Address: 3M Center, St. Paul, MN 55144	Web Site: www.3M.com	Auditors: PricewaterhouseCoopers LLP
Telephone: 651-733-1110	Officers: Inge G. Thulin - President, Chief Executive	Investor Contact: 651-737-8503
Fax: 651-733-9973	Officer, Executive Vice President, Chief Operating Officer Joaquin Delgado - Executive Vice President	Transfer Agents: Wells Fargo Shareowner Services, St. Paul, MN

TIDEWATER INC.

Exchange	Symbol	Price	52Wk Range	Yield	P/E
NYS	TDW	$50.50 (3/28/2013)	55.93-42.98	1.98	18.36

*7 Year Price Score 83.91   *NYSE Composite Index=100   *12 Month Price Score 92.59

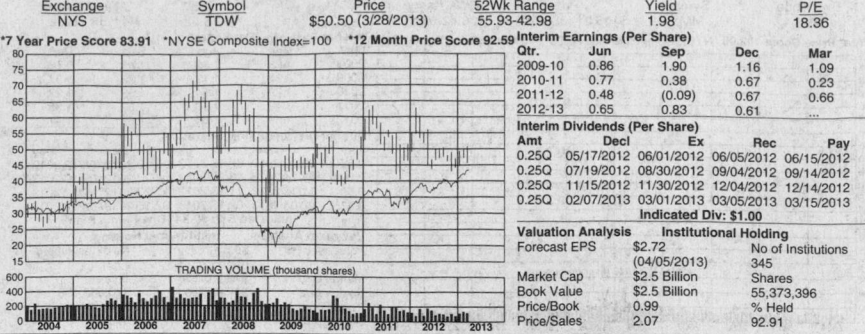

Interim Earnings (Per Share)

Qtr.	Jun	Sep	Dec	Mar
2009-10	0.86	1.90	1.16	1.09
2010-11	0.77	0.38	0.67	0.23
2011-12	0.48	(0.09)	0.67	0.66
2012-13	0.65	0.83	0.61	...

Interim Dividends (Per Share)

Amt	Decl	Ex	Rec	Pay
0.25Q	05/17/2012	06/01/2012	06/05/2012	06/15/2012
0.25Q	07/19/2012	08/30/2012	09/04/2012	09/14/2012
0.25Q	11/15/2012	11/30/2012	12/04/2012	12/14/2012
0.25Q	02/07/2013	03/01/2013	03/05/2013	03/15/2013

Indicated Div: $1.00

Valuation Analysis

		Institutional Holding	
Forecast EPS	$2.72 (04/05/2013)	No of Institutions	345
Market Cap	$2.5 Billion	Shares	55,373,396
Book Value	$2.5 Billion	% Held	92.91
Price/Book	0.99		
Price/Sales	2.07		

Business Summary: Equipment & Services (MIC: 9.1.3 SIC: 4424 NAIC: 213112)

Tidewater is engaged in providing offshore vessel services in support of offshore exploration, field development and production, including towing of, and anchor handling for, mobile offshore drilling units; transporting supplies and personnel necessary to sustain drilling, workover and production activities; offshore construction, remotely operated vehicle operations, and seismic support; and a variety of services such as pipe and cable laying. In addition, through its Quality Shipyards, L.L.C. subsidiary, Co. operates shipyards in Houma, LA that performs repair work and new construction work for third-party customers, as well as the construction, repair and modification of its vessels.

Recent Developments: For the quarter ended Dec 31 2012, net income decreased 12.1% to US$29.9 million from US$34.1 million in the year-earlier quarter. Revenues were US$309.5 million, up 13.7% from US$272.1 million the year before. Operating income was US$41.0 million versus US$41.2 million in the prior-year quarter, a decrease of 0.5%. Direct operating expenses rose 17.3% to US$185.1 million from US$157.8 million in the comparable period the year before. Indirect operating expenses increased 14.1% to US$83.4 million from US$73.1 million in the equivalent prior-year period.

Prospects: Our evaluation of Tidewater Inc. as of Apr. 7, 2013 is the result of our systematic analysis on three basic characteristics: earnings strength, relative valuation, and recent stock price movement. The company has generated a negative trend in earnings per share over the past 5 quarters. However, while recent estimates for the company have been mixed, TDW has posted better than expected results. Based on operating earnings yield, the company is about fairly valued when compared to all of the companies in our coverage universe. Share price changes over the past year indicates that TDW will perform very poorly over the near term.

Financial Data

(US$ in Thousands)	9 Mos	6 Mos	3 Mos	03/31/2012	03/31/2011	03/31/2010	03/31/2009	03/31/2008
Earnings Per Share	2.75	2.81	1.89	1.70	2.05	5.02	7.89	6.39
Cash Flow Per Share	5.03	5.70	5.28	4.34	5.16	6.38	10.25	9.00
Tang Book Value Per Share	45.11	44.61	43.92	43.48	42.12	41.20	37.06	30.61
Dividends Per Share	1.000	1.000	1.000	1.000	1.000	1.000	1.000	0.600
Dividend Payout %	36.36	35.59	52.91	58.82	48.78	19.92	12.67	9.39
Income Statement								
Total Revenue	915,832	606,366	294,448	1,067,007	1,055,388	1,168,634	1,390,835	1,270,171
EBITDA	255,500	177,293	83,520	255,219	282,214	374,624	594,395	521,971
Depn & Amortn	109,012	71,831	35,784	138,356	140,600	130,200	126,231	120,837
Income Before Taxes	127,353	92,574	40,868	97,995	135,910	249,627	474,537	411,099
Income Taxes	31,553	24,082	10,375	23,625	42,479	8,258	84,617	76,806
Net Income	104,159	74,212	32,856	87,411	105,616	259,476	406,898	348,763
Average Shares	49,384	49,625	50,367	51,429	51,487	51,689	51,546	54,606
Balance Sheet								
Current Assets	489,984	541,781	639,563	694,100	579,147	585,627	634,451	630,595
Total Assets	4,055,664	4,022,088	4,042,264	4,061,618	3,748,116	3,293,357	3,073,804	2,751,780
Current Liabilities	263,924	263,441	321,156	238,929	183,589	204,712	203,350	198,904
Long-Term Obligations	930,000	890,000	890,000	950,000	700,000	275,000	300,000	300,000
Total Liabilities	1,529,353	1,501,811	1,556,187	1,535,261	1,234,172	829,327	829,126	821,696
Stockholders' Equity	2,526,311	2,520,277	2,486,077	2,526,357	2,513,944	2,464,030	2,244,678	1,930,084
Shares Outstanding	49,397	49,823	49,820	51,250	51,876	51,830	51,696	52,318
Statistical Record								
Return on Assets %	3.47	3.59	2.45	2.23	3.00	8.15	13.97	12.88
Return on Equity %	5.48	5.64	3.82	3.46	4.24	11.02	19.49	18.23
EBITDA Margin %	27.90	29.24	28.36	23.92	26.74	32.06	42.74	41.09
Net Margin %	11.37	12.24	11.16	8.19	10.01	22.20	29.26	27.46
Asset Turnover	0.30	0.29	0.28	0.27	0.30	0.37	0.48	0.47
Current Ratio	1.86	2.06	1.99	2.91	3.15	2.86	3.12	3.17
Debt to Equity	0.37	0.35	0.36	0.38	0.28	0.11	0.13	0.16
Price Range	62.72-42.98	62.72-40.53	62.72-40.53	62.72-40.53	63.50-38.33	51.37-37.13	70.18-31.44	79.29-46.91
P/E Ratio	22.81-15.63	22.32-14.42	33.19-21.44	36.89-23.84	30.98-18.70	10.23-7.40	8.89-3.98	12.41-7.34
Average Yield %	2.03	2.01	1.97	1.91	2.07	2.20	2.01	0.99

Address: 601 Poydras Street, Suite 1900, New Orleans, LA 70130 **Telephone:** 504-568-1010	**Web Site:** www.tdw.com **Officers:** Jeffrey M. Platt - President, Chief Executive Officer, Executive Vice President, Chief Operating Officer Quinn P. Fanning - Executive Vice President, Chief Financial Officer	**Auditors:** Deloitte & Touche LLP **Investor Contact:** 713-470-5300 **Transfer Agents:** Computershare Trust Company, N.A., Providence, RI

TIFFANY & CO.

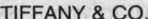

Exchange	Symbol	Price	52Wk Range	Yield	P/E	Div Achiever
NYS	TIF	$69.54 (3/28/2013)	70.88-50.29	1.84	21.40	10 Years

*7 Year Price Score 113.91 *NYSE Composite Index=100 ***12 Month Price Score 100.39**

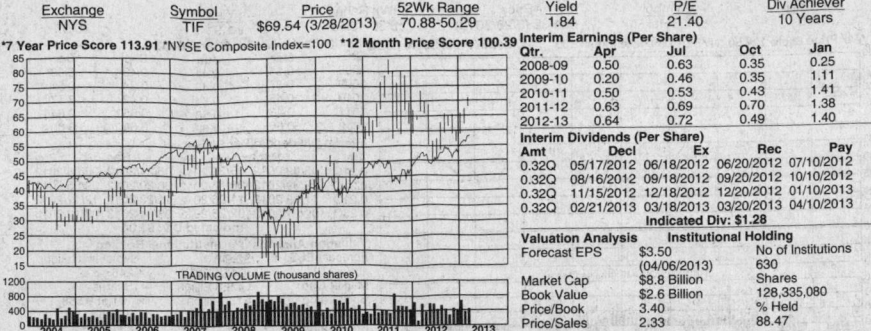

Interim Earnings (Per Share)

Qtr.	Apr	Jul	Oct	Jan
2008-09	0.50	0.63	0.35	0.25
2009-10	0.20	0.46	0.35	1.11
2010-11	0.50	0.53	0.43	1.41
2011-12	0.63	0.69	0.70	1.38
2012-13	0.64	0.72	0.49	1.40

Interim Dividends (Per Share)

Amt	Decl	Ex	Rec	Pay
0.32Q	05/17/2012	06/18/2012	06/20/2012	07/10/2012
0.32Q	08/16/2012	09/18/2012	09/20/2012	10/10/2012
0.32Q	11/15/2012	12/18/2012	12/20/2012	01/10/2013
0.32Q	02/21/2013	03/18/2013	03/20/2013	04/10/2013

Indicated Div: $1.28

Valuation Analysis — **Institutional Holding**

Forecast EPS	$3.50 (04/06/2013)	No of Institutions 630
Market Cap	$8.8 Billion	Shares 128,335,080
Book Value	$2.6 Billion	% Held 88.47
Price/Book	3.40	
Price/Sales	2.33	

Business Summary: Retail - Specialty (MIC: 2.1.3 SIC: 5944 NAIC: 448310)

Tiffany & Co. is a holding company. Through its subsidiaries, Co. is engaged in selling jewelry and other items that it manufactures or has made by others to its specifications. In addition, Co. sells timepieces, sterling silverware, china, crystal, stationery, fragrances and accessories. Through Tiffany and Company and other subsidiaries, Co. is engaged in product design, manufacturing and retailing activities. Co. has five reportable segments: Americas, Asia-Pacific, Japan, Europe, and Other. As of Jan 31 2012, Co. operated 247 TIFFANY & CO. stores.

Recent Developments: For the year ended Jan 31 2013, income from continuing operations decreased 5.2% to US$416.2 million from US$439.2 million a year earlier. Net income decreased 5.2% to US$416.2 million from US$439.2 million in the prior year. Revenues were US$3.79 billion, up 4.2% from US$3.64 billion the year before. Operating income was US$697.2 million versus US$708.4 million in the prior year, a decrease of 1.6%. Direct operating expenses rose 9.3% to US$1.63 billion from US$1.49 billion in the comparable period the year before. Indirect operating expenses increased 1.6% to US$1.47 billion from US$1.44 billion in the equivalent prior-year period.

Prospects: Our evaluation of Tiffany & Co. as of Apr. 7, 2013 is the result of our systematic analysis on three basic characteristics: earnings strength, relative valuation, and recent stock price movement. The company has produced a positive trend in earnings per share over the past 5 quarters and while recent estimates for the company have been raised by analysts, TIF has posted better than expected results. Based on operating earnings yield, the company is about fairly valued when compared to all of the companies in our coverage universe. Share price changes over the past year indicates that TIF will perform poorly over the near term.

Financial Data

(US$ in Thousands)	01/31/2013	01/31/2012	01/31/2011	01/31/2010	01/31/2009	01/31/2008	01/31/2007	01/31/2006
Earnings Per Share	3.25	3.40	2.87	2.11	1.74	2.20	1.80	1.75
Cash Flow Per Share	2.58	1.65	2.36	5.53	1.07	2.90	1.69	1.84
Tang Book Value Per Share	20.47	18.54	17.15	14.91	12.83	12.92	13.28	12.85
Dividends Per Share	1.250	1.120	0.950	0.680	0.660	0.520	0.380	0.300
Dividend Payout %	38.46	32.94	33.10	32.23	37.93	23.64	21.11	17.14
Income Statement								
Total Revenue	3,794,249	3,642,937	3,085,290	2,709,704	2,859,997	2,938,771	2,648,321	2,395,153
EBITDA	861,663	862,634	751,172	582,720	512,397	676,388	550,944	503,498
Depn & Amortn	159,018	149,109	149,403	137,705	137,331	129,462	120,427	112,462
Income Before Taxes	643,576	664,951	547,434	389,974	346,075	522,202	404,435	367,974
Income Taxes	227,419	225,761	179,031	124,298	126,053	190,883	150,508	113,319
Net Income	416,157	439,190	368,403	264,823	220,022	303,772	253,927	254,655
Average Shares	127,934	129,083	128,406	125,383	126,410	138,140	140,841	145,578
Balance Sheet								
Current Assets	3,151,589	2,889,675	2,684,545	2,445,666	2,048,734	1,843,567	1,706,644	1,698,843
Total Assets	4,630,850	4,158,992	3,735,669	3,488,360	3,102,283	2,922,156	2,845,510	2,777,272
Current Liabilities	586,592	626,677	479,913	600,273	601,922	584,861	452,671	364,610
Long-Term Obligations	765,238	538,352	588,494	519,592	425,412	343,465	406,383	426,548
Total Liabilities	2,032,118	1,810,087	1,558,194	1,605,121	1,513,912	1,284,789	1,040,615	946,359
Stockholders' Equity	2,598,732	2,348,905	2,177,475	1,883,239	1,588,371	1,637,367	1,804,895	1,830,913
Shares Outstanding	126,934	126,676	126,969	126,326	123,844	126,753	135,875	142,509
Statistical Record								
Return on Assets %	9.44	11.13	10.20	8.04	7.28	10.53	9.03	9.36
Return on Equity %	16.78	19.41	18.14	15.26	13.60	17.65	13.97	14.42
EBITDA Margin %	22.71	23.68	24.35	21.50	17.92	23.02	20.80	21.02
Net Margin %	10.97	12.06	11.94	9.77	7.69	10.34	9.59	10.63
Asset Turnover	0.86	0.92	0.85	0.82	0.95	1.02	0.94	0.88
Current Ratio	5.37	4.61	5.59	4.07	3.40	3.15	3.77	4.66
Debt to Equity	0.29	0.23	0.27	0.28	0.27	0.21	0.23	0.23
Price Range	73.27-50.29	83.82-56.27	65.44-36.29	46.89-16.94	49.03-17.71	56.83-34.04	40.28-29.93	43.28-29.30
P/E Ratio	22.54-15.47	24.65-16.55	22.80-12.64	22.22-8.03	28.18-10.18	25.83-15.47	22.38-16.63	24.73-16.74
Average Yield %	2.04	1.63	1.96	2.12	1.85	1.09	1.08	0.85

Address: 727 Fifth Avenue, New York, NY 10022	Web Site: www.tiffany.com	Auditors: PricewaterhouseCoopers LLP
Telephone: 212-755-8000	Officers: Michael J. Kowalski - Chairman, Chief Executive Officer Frederic Cumenal - Executive Vice President	Investor Contact: 212-230-5301
Fax: 212-605-4465		Transfer Agents: Computershare, Jersey City, NJ

TIM HORTONS, INC.

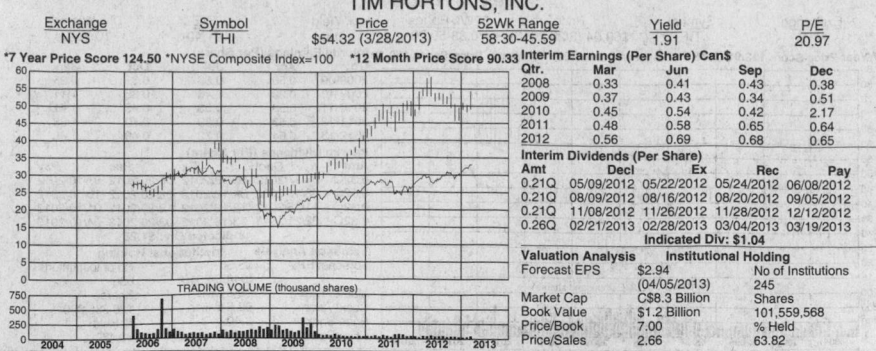

Exchange	Symbol	Price	52Wk Range	Yield	P/E
NYS	THI	$54.32 (3/28/2013)	58.30-45.59	1.91	20.97

*7 Year Price Score 124.50 *NYSE Composite Index=100   *12 Month Price Score 90.33

Interim Earnings (Per Share) Can$

Qtr.	Mar	Jun	Sep	Dec
2008	0.33	0.41	0.43	0.38
2009	0.37	0.43	0.34	0.51
2010	0.45	0.54	0.42	2.17
2011	0.48	0.58	0.65	0.64
2012	0.56	0.69	0.68	0.65

Interim Dividends (Per Share)

Amt	Decl	Ex	Rec	Pay
0.21Q	05/09/2012	05/22/2012	05/24/2012	06/08/2012
0.21Q	08/09/2012	08/16/2012	08/20/2012	09/05/2012
0.21Q	11/08/2012	11/26/2012	11/28/2012	12/12/2012
0.26Q	02/21/2013	02/28/2013	03/04/2013	03/19/2013

Indicated Div: $1.04

Valuation Analysis / **Institutional Holding**

Forecast EPS	$2.94 (04/05/2013)	No of Institutions 245
Market Cap	C$8.3 Billion	Shares
Book Value	$1.2 Billion	101,559,568
Price/Book	7.00	% Held
Price/Sales	2.66	63.82

Business Summary: Hotels, Restaurants & Travel (MIC: 2.2.1 SIC: 5812 NAIC: 722410)

Tim Hortons is engaged in the quick service restaurant chain business. Co. directly owns and operates (without restaurant owners) a small number of company restaurants in Canada and the U.S. Co. also has warehouse and distribution operations that supply paper and dry goods to the majority of its Canadian restaurants, and supply frozen baked goods and some refrigerated products to most of its Ontario restaurants and Quebec restaurants. As of Jan 1 2012, the number of Tim Hortons restaurants, both standard and non-standard locations across Canada, the U.S. and the Gulf Cooperation Council, totaled 4,014. At Jan 1 2012, all but 18 of the Tim Hortons restaurants were franchise-operated.

Recent Developments: For the year ended Dec 30 2012, net income increased 5.7% to C$407.8 million from C$385.7 million in the prior year. Revenues were C$3.12 billion, up 9.4% from C$2.85 billion the year before. Operating income was C$594.5 million versus C$569.5 million in the prior year, an increase of 4.4%. Direct operating expenses rose 10.4% to C$1.96 billion from C$1.77 billion in the comparable period the year before. Indirect operating expenses increased 11.2% to C$566.6 million from C$509.4 million in the equivalent prior-year period.

Prospects: Our evaluation of Tim Hortons Inc. as of Apr. 7, 2013 is the result of our systematic analysis on three basic characteristics: earnings strength, relative valuation, and recent stock price movement. The company has managed to produce a neutral trend in earnings per share over the past 5 quarters. However, while recent estimates for the company have been mixed, THI has posted results that fell short of analysts expectations. Based on operating earnings yield, the company is about fairly valued when compared to all of the companies in our coverage universe. Share price changes over the past year indicates that THI will perform very poorly over the near term.

Financial Data
(Can$ in Thousands)

	12/30/2012	01/01/2012	01/02/2011	01/03/2010	12/28/2008	12/30/2007	12/31/2006	01/01/2006
Earnings Per Share	2.59	2.35	3.58	1.64	1.55	1.43	1.40	1.19
Cash Flow Per Share	3.61	2.42	3.03	2.27	1.95	2.10	1.41	2.37
Tang Book Value Per Share	7.73	7.29	8.40	6.57	6.28	5.37	5.31	0.22
Dividends Per Share	0.840	0.680	0.520	0.100	0.360	0.280	0.140	...
Dividend Payout %	32.43	28.94	14.53	6.10	23.23	19.58	10.00	...
Income Statement								
Total Revenue	3,120,504	2,852,966	2,536,495	2,242,138	2,043,693	1,895,850	1,659,549	1,482,027
EBITDA	711,999	662,737	975,974	560,895	497,562	470,244	416,675	330,288
Depn & Amortn	132,167	107,616	118,385	101,447	91,278	83,595	72,695	71,999
Income Before Taxes	549,419	529,248	833,409	440,178	386,652	369,942	325,522	243,772
Income Taxes	156,346	157,854	200,940	178,263	139,256	138,851	101,162	84,439
Net Income	402,885	382,812	623,959	296,367	284,678	269,551	259,596	191,091
Average Shares	155,676	162,597	174,215	180,609	183,492	188,759	185,401	159,952
Balance Sheet								
Current Assets	609,328	620,966	1,009,121	491,806	465,034	402,818	386,894	344,072
Total Assets	2,284,179	2,203,950	2,481,516	1,996,653	1,992,627	1,797,131	1,744,987	1,596,863
Current Liabilities	463,372	476,650	491,496	339,242	366,060	327,298	275,189	1,419,793
Long-Term Obligations	510,703	447,289	427,411	403,566	398,487	394,831	393,701	87,970
Total Liabilities	1,096,941	1,051,402	1,044,715	827,609	852,223	795,048	726,583	1,557,485
Stockholders' Equity	1,187,238	1,152,548	1,436,801	1,169,044	1,140,404	1,002,083	1,018,404	39,378
Shares Outstanding	153,087	157,537	170,386	177,040	181,190	186,131	191,106	159,952
Statistical Record								
Return on Assets %	18.00	16.39	27.94	14.62	15.06	15.26	15.58	11.43
Return on Equity %	34.53	29.65	48.02	25.25	26.65	26.76	49.22	36.12
EBITDA Margin %	22.82	23.23	38.48	25.02	24.35	24.80	25.11	22.29
Net Margin %	12.91	13.42	24.60	13.22	13.93	14.22	15.64	12.89
Asset Turnover	1.39	1.22	1.14	1.11	1.08	1.07	1.00	0.89
Current Ratio	1.31	1.30	2.05	1.45	1.27	1.23	1.41	0.24
Debt to Equity	0.43	0.39	0.30	0.35	0.35	0.39	0.39	2.23
Price Range	58.30-45.59	51.37-40.84	41.36-28.64	30.51-22.40	37.34-20.57	39.73-28.78	30.88-23.94	...
P/E Ratio	22.51-17.60	21.86-17.38	11.55-8.00	18.60-13.66	24.09-13.27	27.78-20.13	22.06-17.10	...
Average Yield %	1.63	1.46	1.51	0.37	1.18	0.84	0.52	...

Address: 874 Sinclair Road, Oakville, L6K 2Y1 Telephone: 905-845-6511	Web Site: www.timhortons.com Officers: Paul D. House - Executive Chairman, President, Chief Executive Officer John M. Hemeon - Executive Vice President	Auditors: PricewaterhouseCoopers LLP Investor Contact: 905-339-6186 Transfer Agents: Computershare Trust Company of Canada, Toronto, Ontario, Canada

TIME WARNER CABLE INC

Exchange	Symbol	Price	52Wk Range	Yield	P/E
NYS	TWC	$96.06 (3/28/2013)	100.83-73.99	2.71	13.92

*7 Year Price Score N/A *NYSE Composite Index=100 *12 Month Price Score 93.61

Interim Earnings (Per Share)

Qtr.	Mar	Jun	Sep	Dec
2008	0.75	0.84	0.93	(25.08)
2009	0.48	0.89	0.76	0.91
2010	0.60	0.95	1.00	1.09
2011	0.93	1.24	1.08	1.73
2012	1.20	1.43	2.60	1.68

Interim Dividends (Per Share)

Amt	Decl	Ex	Rec	Pay
0.56Q	05/17/2012	05/29/2012	05/31/2012	06/15/2012
0.56Q	07/26/2012	08/29/2012	08/31/2012	09/17/2012
0.56Q	10/25/2012	11/28/2012	11/30/2012	12/17/2012
0.65Q	01/31/2013	02/26/2013	02/28/2013	03/15/2013

Indicated Div: $2.60

Valuation Analysis / Institutional Holding

Forecast EPS	$6.51 (04/06/2013)	No of Institutions	756
Market Cap	$28.6 Billion	Shares	274,952,256
Book Value	$7.3 Billion	% Held	N/A
Price/Book	3.93		
Price/Sales	1.34		

Business Summary: Radio & Television (MIC: 2.3.1 SIC: 4841 NAIC: 515210)

Time Warner Cable is a provider of video, data and voice services, with cable systems located mainly in five geographic areas: New York State, the Carolinas, the Midwest, Southern California and Texas. Co. provides data and voice services to residential and business services customers over its broadband cable systems. Co.'s business services also include networking and transport services (including cell tower backhaul services) and managed and outsourced information technology applications and cloud services. At Dec 31 2012, Co. served about 15.2 million customers who subscribed to one or more of its three primary services, totaling approximately 28.9 million primary service units.

Recent Developments: For the year ended Dec 31 2012, net income increased 29.5% to US$2.16 billion from US$1.67 billion in the prior year. Revenues were US$21.39 billion, up 8.7% from US$19.68 billion the year before. Operating income was US$4.45 billion versus US$4.07 billion in the prior year, an increase of 9.2%. Direct operating expenses rose 8.8% to US$9.94 billion from US$9.14 billion in the comparable period the year before. Indirect operating expenses increased 8.2% to US$7.00 billion from US$6.47 billion in the equivalent prior-year period.

Prospects: Our evaluation of Time Warner Cable Inc. as of Apr. 7, 2013 is the result of our systematic analysis on three basic characteristics: earnings strength, relative valuation, and recent stock price movement. The company has managed to produce a neutral trend in earnings per share over the past 5 quarters and while recent estimates for the company have been raised by analysts, TWC has posted better than expected results. Based on operating earnings yield, the company is undervalued when compared to all of the companies in our coverage universe. Share price changes over the past year indicates that TWC will perform poorly over the near term.

Financial Data
(US$ in Millions)

	12/31/2012	12/31/2011	12/31/2010	12/31/2009	12/31/2008	12/31/2007	12/31/2006	12/31/2005
Earnings Per Share	6.90	4.97	3.64	3.05	(22.56)	3.45	6.00	3.75
Cash Flow Per Share	17.90	17.25	14.73	14.84	16.23	14.01	10.89	7.62
Dividends Per Share	2.240	1.920	1.600	30.810	...	...	...	...
Dividend Payout %	32.46	38.63	43.96	1,010.16	...	...	...	...
Income Statement								
Total Revenue	21,386	19,675	18,868	17,868	17,200	15,955	11,767	8,812
EBITDA	4,725	4,277	3,885	3,405	(9,323)	5,615	4,064	3,252
Depn & Amortn	237	209	185	174	2,826	2,704	1,883	1,465
Income Before Taxes	2,882	2,550	2,306	1,912	(13,072)	2,017	1,535	1,323
Income Taxes	1,177	795	883	820	(4,706)	740	620	153
Net Income	2,155	1,665	1,308	1,070	(7,344)	1,123	1,976	1,253
Average Shares	312	335	359	350	325	325	330	333
Balance Sheet								
Current Assets	4,877	6,398	4,340	2,102	6,659	1,163	910	487
Total Assets	49,809	48,276	45,822	43,694	47,889	56,600	55,743	43,677
Current Liabilities	5,325	5,370	3,086	2,958	2,873	2,536	2,490	1,696
Long-Term Obligations	25,171	24,320	23,121	22,331	17,727	13,577	14,428	4,463
Total Liabilities	42,530	40,746	36,612	35,009	30,725	31,894	32,179	22,346
Stockholders' Equity	7,279	7,530	9,210	8,685	17,164	24,706	23,564	21,331
Shares Outstanding	297	315	348	352	325	325	325	319
Statistical Record								
Return on Assets %	4.38	3.54	2.92	2.34	N.M.	2.00	3.98	...
Return on Equity %	29.02	19.89	14.62	8.28	N.M.	4.65	8.80	...
EBITDA Margin %	22.09	21.74	20.59	19.06	N.M.	35.19	34.54	36.90
Net Margin %	10.08	8.46	6.93	5.99	N.M.	7.04	16.79	14.22
Asset Turnover	0.43	0.42	0.42	0.39	0.33	0.28	0.24	...
Current Ratio	0.92	1.19	1.41	0.71	2.32	0.46	0.37	0.29
Debt to Equity	3.46	3.23	2.51	2.57	1.03	0.55	0.61	0.21
Price Range	100.31-64.03	79.99-57.41	66.11-41.33	67.95-20.37	94.56-49.98	125.55-72.09	...	...
P/E Ratio	14.54-9.28	16.09-11.55	18.16-11.35	22.28-6.68	...	36.39-20.90	...	...
Average Yield %	2.65	2.78	2.97	78.92	...	...	...	...

Address: 60 Columbus Circle, New York, NY 10023 Telephone: 212-364-8200	Web Site: www.timewarnercable.com Officers: Glenn A. Britt - Chairman, Chief Executive Officer Robert D. Marcus - President, Chief Operating Officer, Acting Chief Financial Officer	Auditors: Ernst & Young LLP Investor Contact: 877-446-3689 Transfer Agents: Computershare Shareowner Services, Providence, RI

TIME WARNER INC

Exchange	Symbol	Price	52Wk Range	Yield	P/E
NYS	TWX	$57.62 (3/28/2013)	57.62-33.76	N/A	18.65

*7 Year Price Score 113.72 *NYSE Composite Index=100 *12 Month Price Score 112.76

Interim Earnings (Per Share)

Qtr.	Mar	Jun	Sep	Dec
2008	0.63	0.66	0.90	(13.41)
2009	0.55	0.43	0.55	0.54
2010	0.62	0.49	0.46	0.68
2011	0.59	0.59	0.78	0.76
2012	0.59	0.44	0.86	1.20

Interim Dividends (Per Share)

Amt	Decl	Ex	Rec	Pay
0.188Q	07/31/2008	08/27/2008	08/31/2008	09/15/2008
0.188Q	10/30/2008	11/25/2008	11/30/2008	12/15/2008
0.188Q	01/29/2009	02/25/2009	02/28/2009	03/15/2009
1-for-3	,	... 03/27/2009	...	...

Valuation Analysis

		Institutional Holding	
Forecast EPS	$3.68 (04/05/2013)	No of Institutions	968
Market Cap	$53.7 Billion	Shares	1,001,545,408
Book Value	$29.9 Billion	% Held	N/A
Price/Book	1.80		
Price/Sales	1.87		

Business Summary: Entertainment (MIC: 2.3.2 SIC: 7812 NAIC: 512110)

Time Warner is a media and entertainment company. Co. classifies its businesses into three reporting segments: Networks, consisting principally of domestic and international cable television networks, pay and basic tier television services and digital media properties, which primarily consist of brand-aligned websites; Film and TV Entertainment, which produces and distributes feature films, television, videogames and other programming, distributes home video product, and licenses rights to its feature films, television programming and characters; and Publishing, consisting principally of magazine publishing and related websites as well as book publishing and marketing businesses.

Recent Developments: For the year ended Dec 31 2012, net income increased 4.6% to US$3.02 billion from US$2.88 billion in the prior year. Revenues were US$28.73 billion, down 0.8% from US$28.97 billion the year before. Operating income was US$5.92 billion versus US$5.81 billion in the prior year, an increase of 1.9%. Direct operating expenses declined 2.3% to US$15.93 billion from US$16.31 billion in the comparable period the year before. Indirect operating expenses increased 0.3% to US$6.88 billion from US$6.86 billion in the equivalent prior-year period.

Prospects: Our evaluation of Time Warner Inc. as of Apr. 7, 2013 is the result of our systematic analysis on three basic characteristics: earnings strength, relative valuation, and recent stock price movement. The company has produced a positive trend in earnings per share over the past 5 quarters and while recent estimates for the company have remained steady, TWX has posted better than expected results. Based on operating earnings yield, the company is undervalued when compared to all of the companies in our coverage universe. Share price changes over the past year indicates that TWX will perform well over the near term.

Financial Data
(US$ in Thousands)

	12/31/2012	12/31/2011	12/31/2010	12/31/2009	12/31/2008	12/31/2007	12/31/2006	12/31/2005
Earnings Per Share	3.09	2.71	2.25	2.07	(11.22)	3.51	4.65	1.86
Cash Flow Per Share	3.60	3.30	2.94	2.86	8.63	6.84	6.17	3.20
Dividends Per Share	1.040	0.940	0.850	0.563	0.750	0.705	0.630	0.300
Dividend Payout %	33.66	34.69	37.78	27.17	...	20.09	13.55	16.13
Income Statement								
Total Revenue	28,729,000	28,974,000	26,888,000	25,785,000	46,984,000	46,482,000	44,224,000	43,652,000
EBITDA	6,089,000	5,885,000	5,355,000	4,820,000	(15,623,000)	9,782,000	11,962,000	8,860,000
Depn & Amortn	248,000	269,000	264,000	319,000	784,000	674,000	3,579,000	3,277,000
Income Before Taxes	4,588,000	4,406,000	3,913,000	3,346,000	(18,657,000)	6,809,000	6,708,000	4,317,000
Income Taxes	1,526,000	1,484,000	1,348,000	1,194,000	(3,247,000)	2,336,000	1,337,000	1,187,000
Net Income	3,019,000	2,886,000	2,578,000	2,468,000	(13,402,000)	4,387,000	6,552,000	2,905,000
Average Shares	976,300	1,064,500	1,145,300	1,195,100	1,194,200	1,254,100	1,408,266	1,570,000
Balance Sheet								
Current Assets	13,288,000	13,432,000	13,138,000	13,007,000	16,602,000	12,451,000	10,851,000	13,463,000
Total Assets	68,304,000	67,801,000	66,524,000	65,730,000	113,896,000	133,830,000	131,669,000	122,475,000
Current Liabilities	9,829,000	8,922,000	8,643,000	8,765,000	13,976,000	12,193,000	12,780,000	12,588,000
Long-Term Obligations	19,122,000	19,501,000	16,523,000	15,357,000	37,616,000	37,004,000	34,933,000	20,238,000
Total Liabilities	38,427,000	37,844,000	33,584,000	32,347,000	71,608,000	75,294,000	71,280,000	59,760,000
Stockholders' Equity	29,877,000	29,957,000	32,940,000	33,383,000	42,288,000	58,536,000	60,389,000	62,715,000
Shares Outstanding	932,000	974,000	1,099,000	1,157,000	1,196,000	1,197,666	1,294,133	1,528,400
Statistical Record								
Return on Assets %	4.42	4.30	3.90	2.75	N.M.	3.30	5.16	2.36
Return on Equity %	10.06	9.18	7.77	6.52	N.M.	7.38	10.64	4.70
EBITDA Margin %	21.19	20.31	19.92	18.69	N.M.	21.04	27.05	20.30
Net Margin %	10.51	9.96	9.59	9.57	N.M.	9.44	14.82	6.65
Asset Turnover	0.42	0.43	0.41	0.29	0.38	0.35	0.35	0.36
Current Ratio	1.35	1.51	1.52	1.48	1.19	1.02	0.85	1.07
Debt to Equity	0.64	0.65	0.50	0.46	0.89	0.63	0.58	0.32
Price Range	48.26-33.76	38.20-27.74	33.88-26.01	30.58-14.57	34.47-14.59	47.40-33.63	45.87-32.55	40.15-33.54
P/E Ratio	15.62-10.93	14.10-10.24	15.06-11.92	14.77-7.04	...	13.50-9.58	9.86-7.00	21.59-18.03
Average Yield %	2.59	2.74	2.76	2.36	2.63	1.73	1.71	0.82

Address: One Time Warner Center, New York, NY 10019-8016 **Telephone:** 212-484-8000 **Fax:** 212-489-6183	**Web Site:** www.timewarner.com **Officers:** Jeffrey L. Bewkes - Chairman, Chief Executive Officer Paul T. Cappuccio - Executive Vice President, General Counsel	**Auditors:** Ernst & Young LLP **Investor Contact:** 212-484-8000 **Transfer Agents:** Computershare Trust Company, N.A., Providence, RI

TIMKEN CO. (THE)

Exchange	Symbol	Price	52Wk Range	Yield	P/E
NYS	TKR	$56.58 (3/28/2013)	58.15-35.21	1.63	11.16

*7 Year Price Score 119.69 *NYSE Composite Index=100 ***12 Month Price Score 109.90**

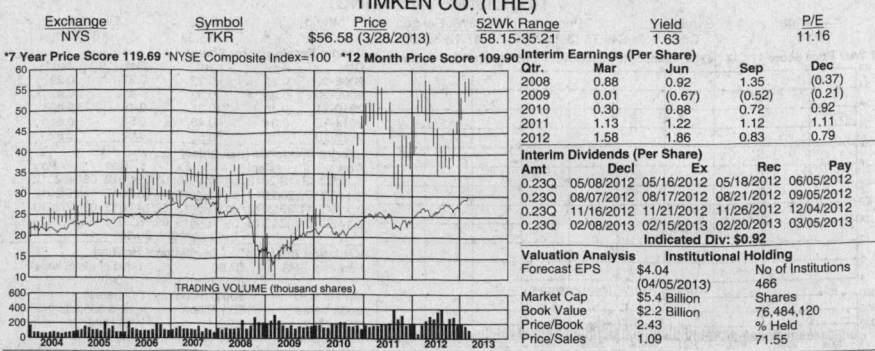

Interim Earnings (Per Share)

Qtr.	Mar	Jun	Sep	Dec
2008	0.88	0.92	1.35	(0.37)
2009	0.01	(0.67)	(0.52)	(0.21)
2010	0.30	0.88	0.72	0.92
2011	1.13	1.22	1.12	1.11
2012	1.58	1.86	0.83	0.79

Interim Dividends (Per Share)

Amt	Decl	Ex	Rec	Pay
0.23Q	05/08/2012	05/16/2012	05/18/2012	06/05/2012
0.23Q	08/07/2012	08/17/2012	08/21/2012	09/05/2012
0.23Q	11/16/2012	11/21/2012	11/26/2012	12/04/2012
0.23Q	02/08/2013	02/15/2013	02/20/2013	03/05/2013

Indicated Div: $0.92

Valuation Analysis / Institutional Holding

Forecast EPS	$4.04 (04/05/2013)	No of Institutions	466
Market Cap	$5.4 Billion	Shares	76,484,120
Book Value	$2.2 Billion	% Held	71.55
Price/Book	2.43		
Price/Sales	1.09		

Business Summary: Industrial Machinery & Equipment (MIC: 7.2.1 SIC: 3562 NAIC: 332991)

Timken develops, manufactures, markets and sells products for friction management and power transmission, alloy steels and steel components. Co. has four segments: Mobile Industries provides bearings, mechanical power transmission components, drive- and roller-chains, augers and related products and services; Process Industries provides bearings, mechanical power transmission components, industrial chains, and related products; Aerospace and Defense provides bearings, helicopter transmission systems, rotor head assemblies, turbine engine components, gears and other flight components; and Steel, which produces over 450 grades of carbon and alloy steel that are sold as ingots, bars and tubes.

Recent Developments: For the year ended Dec 31 2012, net income increased 8.6% to US$495.9 million from US$456.6 million in the prior year. Revenues were US$4.99 billion, down 3.5% from US$5.17 billion the year before. Operating income was US$692.9 million versus US$729.1 million in the prior year, a decrease of 5.0%. Direct operating expenses declined 4.7% to US$3.62 billion from US$3.80 billion in the comparable period the year before. Indirect operating expenses increased 5.1% to US$673.4 million from US$640.6 million in the equivalent prior-year period.

Prospects: Our evaluation of Timken Co. as of Apr. 7, 2013 is the result of our systematic analysis on three basic characteristics: earnings strength, relative valuation, and recent stock price movement. The company has generated a negative trend in earnings per share over the past 5 quarters. However, while recent estimates for the company have been mixed, TKR has posted better than expected results. Based on operating earnings yield, the company is undervalued when compared to all of the companies in our coverage universe. Share price changes over the past year indicates that TKR will perform in line with the market over the near term.

Financial Data

(US$ in Thousands)	12/31/2012	12/31/2011	12/31/2010	12/31/2009	12/31/2008	12/31/2007	12/31/2006	12/31/2005
Earnings Per Share	5.07	4.59	2.81	(1.39)	2.78	2.30	2.36	2.81
Cash Flow Per Share	6.46	2.17	3.24	6.11	5.94	3.56	3.61	3.48
Tang Book Value Per Share	17.40	14.94	16.07	12.64	12.81	15.95	12.43	11.92
Dividends Per Share	0.920	0.780	0.530	0.450	0.700	0.660	0.620	0.600
Dividend Payout %	18.15	16.99	18.86	...	25.18	28.70	26.27	21.35
Income Statement								
Total Revenue	4,987,000	5,170,200	4,055,500	3,141,627	5,663,660	5,236,020	4,973,365	5,168,434
EBITDA	973,200	906,500	619,600	134,460	680,473	524,120	484,912	656,753
Depn & Amortn	179,000	178,500	179,600	188,711	215,914	206,224	185,896	218,059
Income Before Taxes	766,000	696,800	405,500	(94,230)	425,596	282,257	254,234	390,546
Income Taxes	270,100	240,200	136,000	(28,193)	157,926	62,868	77,795	130,265
Net Income	495,500	454,300	274,800	(133,961)	267,670	220,054	222,527	260,281
Average Shares	97,602	98,655	97,516	96,135	96,272	95,612	94,294	92,537
Balance Sheet								
Current Assets	2,174,100	2,292,300	2,399,200	2,022,560	2,033,465	2,045,251	1,900,280	1,983,309
Total Assets	4,244,700	4,352,100	4,180,400	4,006,893	4,536,050	4,379,237	4,031,533	3,993,734
Current Liabilities	667,900	844,600	719,900	540,433	798,313	904,422	835,569	1,074,475
Long-Term Obligations	455,100	478,800	481,700	469,287	515,250	580,587	547,390	561,747
Total Liabilities	2,012,500	2,323,800	2,255,400	2,429,309	2,895,753	2,418,568	2,555,353	2,496,667
Stockholders' Equity	2,232,200	2,028,300	1,925,000	1,577,584	1,640,297	1,960,669	1,476,180	1,497,067
Shares Outstanding	95,898	97,666	97,803	96,854	96,546	95,808	94,164	93,005
Statistical Record								
Return on Assets %	11.50	10.65	6.71	N.M.	5.99	5.23	5.55	6.56
Return on Equity %	23.20	22.98	15.69	N.M.	14.83	12.81	14.97	18.81
EBITDA Margin %	19.51	17.53	15.28	4.28	12.01	10.01	9.75	12.71
Net Margin %	9.94	8.79	6.78	N.M.	4.73	4.20	4.47	5.04
Asset Turnover	1.16	1.21	0.99	0.74	1.27	1.25	1.24	1.30
Current Ratio	3.26	2.71	3.33	3.74	2.55	2.26	2.27	1.85
Debt to Equity	0.20	0.24	0.25	0.30	0.31	0.30	0.37	0.38
Price Range	57.72-35.21	56.39-30.89	49.17-22.41	25.61-10.04	37.64-11.11	38.02-27.63	36.18-26.77	32.63-22.90
P/E Ratio	11.38-6.94	12.29-6.73	17.50-7.98	...	13.54-4.00	16.53-12.01	15.33-11.34	11.61-8.15
Average Yield %	2.04	1.73	1.58	2.35	2.49	2.02	1.96	2.21

Address: 1835 Dueber Ave., S.W., Canton, OH 44706
Telephone: 330-438-3000
Fax: 330-471-3452

Web Site: www.timken.com
Officers: Ward J. Timken - Chairman James W. Griffith - President, Chief Executive Officer

Auditors: Ernst & Young LLP
Investor Contact: 330-471-7446
Transfer Agents: Wells Fargo Shareowner Services, Saint Paul, MN

TJX COMPANIES, INC.

Exchange	Symbol	Price	52Wk Range	Yield	P/E	Div Achiever
NYS	TJX	$46.75 (3/28/2013)	47.12-38.67	1.24	18.33	16 Years

*7 Year Price Score 173.14 *NYSE Composite Index=100 *12 Month Price Score 95.97

Interim Earnings (Per Share)

Qtr.	Apr	Jul	Oct	Jan
2008-09	0.22	0.23	0.27	0.29
2009-10	0.25	0.30	0.41	0.47
2010-11	0.40	0.37	0.46	0.42
2011-12	0.34	0.45	0.53	0.61
2012-13	0.12	0.56	0.62	0.82

Interim Dividends (Per Share)

Amt	Decl	Ex	Rec	Pay
0.115Q	06/13/2012	08/07/2012	08/09/2012	08/30/2012
0.115Q	09/20/2012	11/06/2012	11/08/2012	11/29/2012
0.115Q	11/29/2012	02/12/2013	02/14/2013	03/07/2013
0.145Q	04/02/2013	05/14/2013	05/16/2013	06/06/2013

Indicated Div: $0.58

Valuation Analysis | **Institutional Holding**

Forecast EPS	$2.80	No of Institutions
	(04/06/2013)	1009
Market Cap	$33.8 Billion	Shares
Book Value	$3.7 Billion	693,335,232
Price/Book	9.23	% Held
Price/Sales	1.31	86.77

Business Summary: Retail - Apparel and Accessories (MIC: 2.1.5 SIC: 5651 NAIC: 448140)

TJX Companies is an apparel and home fashions retailer. Co. has four segments: in the U.S., Marmaxx (which operates T.J. Maxx and Marshalls) and HomeGoods; TJX Canada (which operates Winners, HomeSense and Marshalls); and TJX Europe (which operates T.K. Maxx and HomeSense). Through its stores, Co. sells family apparel (including footwear and accessories), home fashions (including home basics, accent furniture, lamps, rugs, wall decor, decorative accessories and giftware) and other merchandise. As of Jan 28 2012, Co. operates 2,241 T.J. Maxx, Marshalls and HomeGoods stores in the U.S., 308 Winners, HomeSense and Marshalls stores in Canada, and 356 T.K. Maxx and HomeSense stores in Europe.

Recent Developments: For the year ended Feb 2 2013, income from continuing operations increased 27.4% to US$1.91 billion from US$1.50 billion a year earlier. Net income increased 27.4% to US$1.91 billion from US$1.50 billion in the prior year. Revenues were US$25.88 billion, up 11.6% from US$23.19 billion the year before. Direct operating expenses rose 9.9% to US$18.52 billion from US$16.85 billion in the comparable period the year before. Indirect operating expenses increased 9.0% to US$4.28 billion from US$3.93 billion in the equivalent prior-year period.

Prospects: Our evaluation of TJX Companies Inc. as of Apr. 7, 2013 is the result of our systematic analysis on three basic characteristics: earnings strength, relative valuation, and recent stock price movement. The company has managed to produce a neutral trend in earnings per share over the past 5 quarters and while recent estimates for the company have remained steady, TJX has posted better than expected results. Based on operating earnings yield, the company is about fairly valued when compared to all of the companies in our coverage universe. Share price changes over the past year indicates that TJX will perform poorly over the near term.

Financial Data

(US$ in Thousands)	02/02/2013	01/28/2012	01/29/2011	01/30/2010	01/31/2009	01/26/2008	01/27/2007	01/28/2006
Earnings Per Share	2.55	1.93	1.65	1.42	1.00	0.83	0.78	0.70
Cash Flow Per Share	4.08	2.52	2.48	2.73	1.36	1.54	1.32	1.24
Tang Book Value Per Share	4.63	4.06	3.75	3.31	2.37	2.28	2.32	1.85
Dividends Per Share	0.440	0.360	0.285	0.235	0.210	0.170	0.135	0.113
Dividend Payout %	17.25	18.65	17.27	16.55	21.00	20.48	17.42	15.96
Income Statement								
Total Revenue	25,878,372	23,191,455	21,942,193	20,288,444	18,999,505	18,647,126	17,404,637	16,057,935
EBITDA	3,108,226	2,449,262	2,205,429	1,993,271	1,467,431	1,243,291	1,264,614	1,444,434
Depn & Amortn	1,700	2,200	2,200	2,200	2,200	2,200	2,200	405,475
Income Before Taxes	3,077,351	2,411,414	2,164,092	1,951,562	1,450,940	1,242,689	1,246,848	1,009,327
Income Taxes	1,170,664	915,324	824,562	737,990	536,054	470,939	470,092	318,904
Net Income	1,906,687	1,496,090	1,343,141	1,213,572	880,617	771,750	738,039	690,423
Average Shares	747,555	773,772	812,826	855,238	884,510	936,092	960,090	983,000
Balance Sheet								
Current Assets	5,711,543	5,132,632	5,099,527	4,803,856	3,626,129	3,992,294	3,748,813	3,140,127
Total Assets	9,511,855	8,281,605	7,971,763	7,463,977	6,178,242	6,599,934	6,085,700	5,496,305
Current Liabilities	3,760,596	3,063,423	3,133,121	2,894,986	2,767,891	2,760,993	2,382,980	2,251,851
Long-Term Obligations	774,552	784,623	787,517	790,169	383,782	853,460	808,027	807,150
Total Liabilities	5,845,918	5,072,315	4,871,864	4,574,701	4,043,685	4,468,689	3,795,579	3,603,651
Stockholders' Equity	3,665,937	3,209,290	3,099,899	2,889,276	2,134,557	2,131,245	2,290,121	1,892,654
Shares Outstanding	723,902	746,702	779,314	818,772	825,643	855,899	907,299	921,934
Statistical Record								
Return on Assets %	21.08	18.46	17.45	17.84	13.56	12.20	12.78	13.10
Return on Equity %	54.57	47.56	44.98	48.45	40.62	35.01	35.39	39.05
EBITDA Margin %	12.01	10.56	10.05	9.82	7.72	6.67	7.27	9.00
Net Margin %	7.37	6.45	6.12	5.98	4.63	4.14	4.24	4.30
Asset Turnover	2.86	2.86	2.85	2.98	2.93	2.95	3.01	3.05
Current Ratio	1.52	1.68	1.63	1.66	1.31	1.45	1.57	1.39
Debt to Equity	0.21	0.24	0.25	0.27	0.18	0.40	0.35	0.43
Price Range	46.64-33.73	33.98-23.57	24.31-18.76	20.11-9.73	18.50-9.21	15.94-13.00	15.02-11.12	12.95-10.13
P/E Ratio	18.29-13.23	17.61-12.21	14.73-11.37	14.16-6.86	18.50-9.21	19.20-15.66	19.26-14.25	18.49-14.47
Average Yield %	1.04	1.30	1.30	1.44	1.43	1.19	1.03	0.97

Address: 770 Cochituate Road, Framingham, MA 01701 **Telephone:** 508-390-1000 **Fax:** 508-390-2091	**Web Site:** www.tjx.com **Officers:** Bernard Cammarata - Chairman Ernie L. Herrman - President	**Auditors:** PricewaterhouseCoopers LLP **Investor Contact:** 508-390-2323 **Transfer Agents:** Computershare, Pittsburgh, PA

TOLL BROTHERS INC.

Exchange	Symbol	Price	52Wk Range	Yield	P/E
NYS	TOL	$34.24 (3/28/2013)	37.98-21.81	N/A	11.81

*7 Year Price Score 118.92 *NYSE Composite Index=100 *12 Month Price Score 103.66

TRADING VOLUME (thousand shares)

Interim Earnings (Per Share)

Qtr.	Jan	Apr	Jul	Oct
2009-10	(0.25)	(0.24)	0.16	0.31
2010-11	0.02	(0.12)	0.25	0.09
2011-12	(0.02)	0.10	0.36	2.41
2012-13	0.03	...	...	...

Interim Dividends (Per Share)

No Dividends Paid

Valuation Analysis

		Institutional Holding	
Forecast EPS	$0.71	No of Institutions	
	(04/05/2013)	466	
Market Cap	$5.8 Billion	Shares	
Book Value	$3.1 Billion	145,393,488	
Price/Book	1.85	% Held	
Price/Sales	2.92	80.68	

Business Summary: Builders (MIC: 2.2.5 SIC: 1531 NAIC: 236117)

Toll Brothers designs, builds, markets and arranges financing for detached and attached homes in residential communities. Co. is also involved, directly and through joint ventures, in projects where it is building or converting existing rental apartment buildings into homes. Co. is also developing, through joint ventures, a condominium/hotel project and a for-rent apartment complex. Co. operates its own land development, architectural, engineering, mortgage, title, landscaping, security monitoring, lumber distribution, house component assembly, and manufacturing operations. Co. also develops, owns and operates golf courses and country clubs associated with several of its communities.

Recent Developments: For the quarter ended Jan 31 2013, net income amounted to US$4.4 million versus a net loss of US$2.8 million in the year-earlier quarter. Revenues were US$424.6 million, up 31.9% from US$322.0 million the year before. Operating income was US$617,000 versus a loss of US$19.3 million in the prior-year quarter. Direct operating expenses rose 27.4% to US$345.9 million from US$271.6 million in the comparable period the year before. Indirect operating expenses increased 12.1% to US$78.0 million from US$69.6 million in the equivalent prior-year period.

Prospects: Our evaluation of Toll Brothers Inc. as of Apr. 7, 2013 is the result of our systematic analysis on three basic characteristics: earnings strength, relative valuation, and recent stock price movement. The company has generated a negative trend in earnings per share over the past 5 quarters. However, while recent estimates for the company have been mixed, TOL has posted results that fell short of analysts' expectations. Based on operating earnings yield, the company is overvalued when compared to all of the companies in our coverage universe. Share price changes over the past year indicates that TOL will perform very well over the near term.

Financial Data
(US$ in Thousands)

	3 Mos	10/31/2012	10/31/2011	10/31/2010	10/31/2009	10/31/2008	10/31/2007	10/31/2006
Earnings Per Share	2.90	2.86	0.24	(0.02)	(4.68)	(1.88)	0.22	4.17
Cash Flow Per Share	(1.85)	(1.01)	0.32	(0.88)	1.75	5.19	2.13	(0.68)
Tang Book Value Per Share	18.53	18.51	15.61	15.36	15.26	20.19	22.47	22.20
Income Statement								
Total Revenue	424,601	1,882,781	1,475,881	1,494,771	1,755,310	3,158,213	4,646,979	6,123,453
EBITDA	10,293	86,015	(26,929)	(132,692)	(506,928)	(372,199)	27,140	1,057,905
Depn & Amortn	6,525	22,586	23,142	20,044	23,925	28,333	31,240	32,314
Income Before Taxes	5,243	89,350	(28,172)	(140,657)	(488,947)	(280,394)	111,033	1,078,255
Income Taxes	3,894	(374,204)	(69,161)	(113,813)	259,360	(168,977)	35,029	439,403
Net Income	4,432	487,146	39,795	(3,374)	(755,825)	(297,810)	35,651	687,213
Average Shares	171,903	170,154	168,381	165,666	161,549	158,730	164,166	164,852
Balance Sheet								
Current Assets	4,982,379	5,384,411	4,576,395	4,681,148	5,254,300	6,166,673	6,689,414	6,898,337
Total Assets	6,118,251	6,181,044	5,055,246	5,171,555	5,634,444	6,586,836	7,220,316	7,583,541
Current Liabilities	911,780	800,229	807,758	901,574	982,573	1,211,277	1,419,221	1,812,106
Long-Term Obligations	2,065,361	2,252,944	1,654,937	1,710,968	2,135,389	2,137,906	2,265,850	2,347,806
Total Liabilities	2,983,329	3,059,344	2,468,893	2,616,102	3,121,245	3,349,183	3,693,082	4,167,615
Stockholders' Equity	3,134,922	3,121,700	2,586,353	2,555,453	2,513,199	3,237,653	3,527,234	3,415,926
Shares Outstanding	169,158	168,637	165,729	166,408	164,725	160,369	157,008	153,899
Statistical Record								
Return on Assets %	8.91	8.65	0.78	N.M.	N.M.	N.M.	0.48	9.87
Return on Equity %	17.25	17.02	1.55	N.M.	N.M.	N.M.	1.03	22.24
EBITDA Margin %	2.42	4.57	N.M.	N.M.	N.M.	N.M.	0.58	17.28
Net Margin %	1.04	25.87	2.70	N.M.	N.M.	N.M.	0.77	11.22
Asset Turnover	0.36	0.33	0.29	0.28	0.29	0.46	0.63	0.88
Current Ratio	5.46	6.73	5.67	5.19	5.35	5.09	4.71	3.81
Debt to Equity	0.66	0.72	0.64	0.67	0.85	0.66	0.64	0.69
Price Range	37.98-21.81	36.43-17.05	21.90-13.75	23.15-16.02	23.42-14.26	26.84-16.04	35.35-19.57	39.90-22.67
P/E Ratio	13.10-7.52	12.74-5.96	91.25-57.29	...	...	...	160.68-88.95	9.57-5.44

Address: 250 Gibraltar Road, Horsham, PA 19044	Web Site: www.tollbrothers.com	Auditors: Ernst & Young LLP
Telephone: 215-938-8000	Officers: Robert I. Toll - Executive Chairman Bruce E. Toll - Vice-Chairman	Investor Contact: 215-938-8312
Fax: 215-938-8023		Transfer Agents: American Stock Transfer & Trust Company, New York, NY

TOOTSIE ROLL INDUSTRIES INC

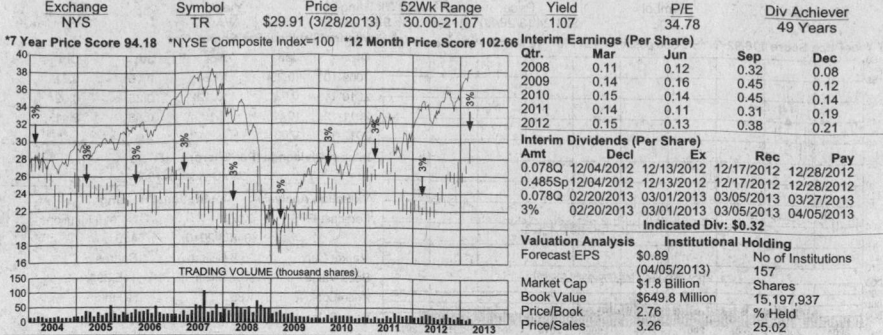

Exchange	Symbol	Price	52Wk Range	Yield	P/E	Div Achiever
NYS	TR	$29.91 (3/28/2013)	30.00-21.07	1.07	34.78	49 Years

*7 Year Price Score 94.18 *NYSE Composite Index=100 *12 Month Price Score 102.66

Interim Earnings (Per Share)

Qtr.	Mar	Jun	Sep	Dec
2008	0.11	0.12	0.32	0.08
2009	0.14	0.16	0.45	0.12
2010	0.15	0.14	0.45	0.14
2011	0.14	0.11	0.31	0.19
2012	0.15	0.13	0.38	0.21

Interim Dividends (Per Share)

Amt	Decl	Ex	Rec	Pay
0.078Q	12/04/2012	12/13/2012	12/17/2012	12/28/2012
0.485Sp	12/04/2012	12/13/2012	12/17/2012	12/28/2012
0.078Q	02/20/2013	03/01/2013	03/05/2013	03/27/2013
3%	02/20/2013	03/01/2013	03/05/2013	04/05/2013

Indicated Div: $0.32

Valuation Analysis

		Institutional Holding	
Forecast EPS	$0.89 (04/05/2013)	No of Institutions	157
Market Cap	$1.8 Billion	Shares	15,197,937
Book Value	$649.8 Million	% Held	25.02
Price/Book	2.76		
Price/Sales	3.26		

Business Summary: Food (MIC: 1.2.1 SIC: 2064 NAIC: 311340)

Tootsie Roll Industries and its consolidated subsidiaries are engaged in the manufacture and sale of confectionery products. This is the only industry segment in which Co. operates. The majority of Co.'s products are sold under the registered trademarks TOOTSIE ROLL, TOOTSIE ROLL POPS, CHILD'S PLAY, CARAMEL APPLE POPS, CHARMS, BLOW-POP, BLUE RAZZ, CHARMS MINI POPS, CELLA'S, MASON DOTS, MASON CROWS, JUNIOR MINTS, CHARLESTON CHEW, SUGAR DADDY, SUGAR BABIES, ANDES, FLUFFY STUFF, DUBBLE BUBBLE, RAZZLES, CRY BABY and NIK-L-NIP. Co.'s principal markets are in the U.S., Canada and Mexico.

Recent Developments: For the year ended Dec 31 2012, net income increased 18.4% to US$52.0 million from US$43.9 million in the prior year. Revenues were US$549.9 million, up 3.3% from US$532.5 million the year before. Operating income was US$69.5 million versus US$58.0 million in the prior year, an increase of 19.9%. Direct operating expenses rose 0.1% to US$366.5 million from US$366.3 million in the comparable period the year before. Indirect operating expenses increased 5.1% to US$113.8 million from US$108.3 million in the equivalent prior-year period.

Prospects: Our evaluation of Tootsie Roll Industries Inc. as of Apr. 7, 2013 is the result of our systematic analysis on three basic characteristics: earnings strength, relative valuation, and recent stock price movement. The company has managed to produce a neutral trend in earnings per share over the past 5 quarters. Because the company lacks sufficient analyst estimate data, we place greater weight on the historical EPS trend as the measure of earnings strength. Based on operating earnings yield, the company is overvalued when compared to all of the companies in our coverage universe. Share price changes over the past year indicates that TR will perform in line with the market over the near term.

Financial Data

(US$ in Thousands)	12/31/2012	12/31/2011	12/31/2010	12/31/2009	12/31/2008	12/31/2007	12/31/2006	12/31/2005
Earnings Per Share	0.86	0.74	0.89	0.87	0.62	0.81	1.02	1.21
Cash Flow Per Share	1.68	0.85	1.37	1.23	0.92	1.41	0.86	1.29
Tang Book Value Per Share	6.70	7.06	7.02	6.65	6.02	5.98	5.73	5.58
Dividends Per Share	0.794	0.299	0.291	0.282	0.274	0.266	0.258	0.227
Dividend Payout %	91.87	40.58	32.81	32.47	44.06	32.81	25.28	18.85
Income Statement								
Total Revenue	549,870	532,505	521,448	499,331	496,016	497,717	495,990	487,739
EBITDA	93,707	79,175	91,631	85,478	70,349	87,884	107,721	127,326
Depn & Amortn	19,925	19,229	18,279	17,862	17,036	15,859	15,816	14,687
Income Before Taxes	75,014	60,912	74,089	68,812	56,386	76,985	93,794	112,734
Income Taxes	22,160	16,974	20,375	10,704	17,132	25,542	28,796	36,425
Net Income	52,004	43,938	53,714	53,475	38,777	51,625	65,919	77,227
Average Shares	60,504	59,628	60,468	61,271	62,079	63,736	64,711	63,931
Balance Sheet								
Current Assets	197,241	212,201	237,591	211,878	187,979	199,726	190,917	246,596
Total Assets	846,737	857,856	860,383	838,247	812,092	812,725	791,639	813,696
Current Liabilities	60,765	58,355	58,505	56,066	59,252	57,972	62,211	113,656
Long-Term Obligations	7,500	7,500	7,500	7,500	7,500	7,500	7,500	7,500
Total Liabilities	196,922	191,921	191,429	185,762	177,322	174,495	160,958	196,291
Stockholders' Equity	649,815	665,935	668,954	652,485	634,770	638,230	630,681	617,405
Shares Outstanding	59,949	59,155	59,892	60,814	61,846	62,870	64,111	63,517
Statistical Record								
Return on Assets %	6.08	5.11	6.32	6.48	4.76	6.44	8.21	9.50
Return on Equity %	7.88	6.58	8.13	8.31	6.08	8.14	10.56	13.01
EBITDA Margin %	17.04	14.87	17.57	17.12	14.18	17.66	21.72	26.11
Net Margin %	9.46	8.25	10.30	10.71	7.82	10.37	13.29	15.83
Asset Turnover	0.64	0.62	0.61	0.61	0.61	0.62	0.62	0.60
Current Ratio	3.25	3.64	4.06	3.78	3.17	3.45	3.07	2.17
Debt to Equity	0.01	0.01	0.01	0.01	0.01	0.01	0.01	0.01
Price Range	27.77-21.07	28.09-21.54	27.31-21.36	24.93-17.05	27.04-18.50	26.58-19.72	27.04-21.42	26.54-22.84
P/E Ratio	32.29-24.50	37.96-29.11	30.68-24.00	28.66-19.60	43.62-29.84	32.81-24.35	26.51-21.00	21.93-18.87
Average Yield %	3.35	1.19	1.22	1.34	1.25	1.14	1.08	0.94

Address: 7401 South Cicero Avenue, Chicago, IL 60629	Web Site: www.tootsie.com	Auditors: PricewaterhouseCoopers LLP
Telephone: 773-838-3400	Officers: Melvin J. Gordon - Chairman, Chief Executive Officer Ellen R. Gordon - President, Chief Operating Officer	Investor Contact: 866-814-2690
Fax: 773-838-3534		Transfer Agents: American Stock Transfer and Trust Company, Brooklyn, NY

TORCHMARK CORP.

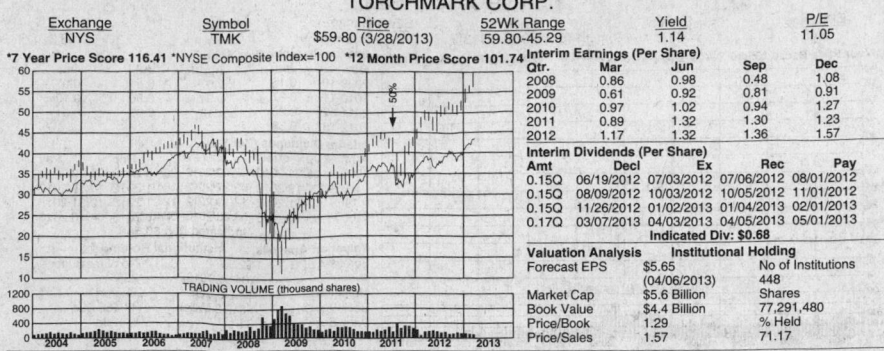

Exchange	Symbol	Price	52Wk Range	Yield	P/E
NYS	TMK	$59.80 (3/28/2013)	59.80-45.29	1.14	11.05

*7 Year Price Score 116.41 *NYSE Composite Index=100 *12 Month Price Score 101.74

Interim Earnings (Per Share)

Qtr.	Mar	Jun	Sep	Dec
2008	0.86	0.98	0.48	1.08
2009	0.61	0.92	0.81	0.91
2010	0.97	1.02	0.94	1.27
2011	0.89	1.32	1.30	1.23
2012	1.17	1.32	1.36	1.57

Interim Dividends (Per Share)

Amt	Decl	Ex	Rec	Pay
0.15Q	06/19/2012	07/03/2012	07/06/2012	08/01/2012
0.15Q	08/09/2012	10/03/2012	10/05/2012	11/01/2012
0.15Q	11/26/2012	01/02/2013	01/04/2013	02/01/2013
0.17Q	03/07/2013	04/03/2013	04/05/2013	05/01/2013

Indicated Div: $0.68

Valuation Analysis

		Institutional Holding
Forecast EPS	$5.65	No of Institutions
	(04/06/2013)	448
Market Cap	$5.6 Billion	Shares
Book Value	$4.4 Billion	77,291,480
Price/Book	1.29	% Held
Price/Sales	1.57	71.17

TRADING VOLUME (thousand shares)

Business Summary: Life & Health (MIC: 5.2.2 SIC: 6311 NAIC: 524113)

Torchmark is an insurance holding company. Through its subsidiaries, Co. provides a range of life and health insurance products and annuities. Co. manages its operations by segments, which are the insurance product lines of life, health, and annuities, and the investment segment that supports the product lines which mainly consist of investment-grade securities. Co.'s life insurance products include whole life insurance as well as term life insurance; while its health products include Medicare Supplement, Medicare Part D, cancer, accident, long-term care, and limited-benefit hospital and surgical coverages; and its annuities products include fixed-benefit contracts.

Recent Developments: For the year ended Dec 31 2012, net income increased 6.5% to US$529.3 million from US$497.2 million in the prior year. Revenues were US$3.59 billion, up 6.3% from US$3.38 billion the year before. Net premiums earned were US$2.86 billion versus US$2.66 billion in the prior year, an increase of 7.5%. Net investment income rose 0.1% to US$693.6 million from US$693.0 million a year ago.

Prospects: Our evaluation of Torchmark Corp. as of Apr. 7, 2013 is the result of our systematic analysis on three basic characteristics: earnings strength, relative valuation, and recent stock price movement. The company has managed to produce a neutral trend in earnings per share over the past 5 quarters and while recent estimates for the company have remained steady, TMK has posted better than expected results. Based on operating earnings yield, the company is undervalued when compared to all of the companies in our coverage universe. Share price changes over the past year indicates that TMK will perform in line with the market over the near term.

Financial Data

(US$ in Thousands)	12/31/2012	12/31/2011	12/31/2010	12/31/2009	12/31/2008	12/31/2007	12/31/2006	12/31/2005
Earnings Per Share	5.41	4.72	4.20	3.25	3.41	3.67	3.42	3.12
Cash Flow Per Share	9.73	7.94	8.43	7.84	5.52	6.01	5.79	5.46
Tang Book Value Per Share	41.60	38.10	30.45	23.94	14.16	20.98	20.93	19.66
Dividends Per Share	0.570	0.443	0.407	0.280	0.460	0.347	0.320	0.293
Dividend Payout %	10.54	9.39	9.68	8.61	13.50	9.45	9.36	9.40
Income Statement								
Premium Income	2,856,462	2,656,318	2,651,758	2,687,199	2,758,256	2,827,231	2,784,713	2,508,074
Total Revenue	3,589,516	3,377,401	3,367,632	3,222,397	3,326,918	3,486,697	3,421,178	3,125,910
Benefits & Claims	1,955,682	1,793,276	1,793,044	1,812,800	1,872,915	1,902,428	1,863,531	1,661,186
Income Before Taxes	765,993	755,666	778,567	605,193	661,257	796,805	773,570	731,521
Income Taxes	236,669	237,326	256,274	200,240	208,998	269,270	254,939	236,131
Net Income	529,324	517,885	517,064	404,953	452,259	527,535	518,631	495,390
Average Shares	97,898	109,815	123,123	124,550	132,774	143,768	151,668	158,627
Balance Sheet								
Total Assets	18,776,910	17,156,391	16,159,762	16,023,759	13,529,050	15,241,428	14,980,355	14,768,903
Total Liabilities	14,415,124	12,927,483	12,143,521	12,624,868	11,306,143	11,916,801	11,521,162	11,336,135
Stockholders' Equity	4,361,786	4,228,908	4,016,241	3,398,891	2,222,907	3,324,627	3,459,193	3,432,768
Shares Outstanding	94,235	100,579	118,864	124,261	127,061	138,263	147,171	155,353
Statistical Record								
Return on Assets %	2.94	3.11	3.21	2.74	3.14	3.49	3.49	3.41
Return on Equity %	12.29	12.56	13.95	14.41	16.26	15.55	15.05	14.46
Loss Ratio %	68.47	67.51	67.62	67.46	67.90	67.29	66.92	66.23
Net Margin %	14.75	15.33	15.35	12.57	13.59	15.13	15.16	15.85
Price Range	52.97-43.36	45.23-33.18	41.33-29.30	31.18-11.37	43.51-18.45	46.88-39.19	42.82-36.17	38.09-33.61
P/E Ratio	9.79-8.01	9.58-7.03	9.84-6.98	9.59-3.50	12.76-5.41	12.77-10.68	12.52-10.58	12.21-10.77
Average Yield %	1.15	1.08	1.16	1.14	1.24	0.81	0.80	0.83

Address: 3700 South Stonebridge Drive, McKinney, TX 75070
Telephone: 972-569-4000

Web Site: www.torchmarkcorp.com
Officers: Mark S. McAndrew - Chairman, Chief Executive Officer Gary L. Coleman - Co-Chief Executive Officer, Executive Vice President, Chief Financial Officer

Auditors: Deloitte & Touche LLP
Investor Contact: 972-569-3627
Transfer Agents: Wells Fargo Shareowner Services, St. Paul, M

TORO CO. (THE)

Exchange	Symbol	Price	52Wk Range	Yield	P/E
NYS	TTC	$46.04 (3/28/2013)	48.31-32.88	1.22	19.68

*7 Year Price Score 135.86 *NYSE Composite Index=100 ***12 Month Price Score 104.52**

TRADING VOLUME (thousand shares)

Interim Earnings (Per Share)

Qtr.	Jan	Apr	Jul	Oct
2009-10	0.16	0.67	0.51	0.07
2010-11	0.27	0.94	0.56	0.10
2011-12	0.33	1.13	0.67	0.01
2012-13	0.53	...	...	...

Interim Dividends (Per Share)

Amt	Decl	Ex	Rec	Pay
100%	05/24/2012	07/02/2012	06/15/2012	06/29/2012
0.11Q	09/18/2012	09/27/2012	10/01/2012	10/15/2012
0.14Q	12/11/2012	12/19/2012	12/21/2012	12/31/2012
0.14Q	03/14/2013	03/26/2013	03/28/2013	04/15/2013

Indicated Div: $0.56

Valuation Analysis

		Institutional Holding	
Forecast EPS	$2.50 (04/05/2013)	No of Institutions	295
Market Cap	$2.7 Billion	Shares	47,480,504
Book Value	$312.8 Million	% Held	72.23
Price/Book	8.51		
Price/Sales	1.35		

Business Summary: Construction Services (MIC: 7.5.4 SIC: 3524 NAIC: 333112)

Toro designs, manufactures, and markets turf maintenance equipment and services, turf irrigation systems, landscaping equipment and lighting, agricultural micro-irrigation systems, rental and construction equipment, and residential yard and snow removal products. Co. has three segments: Professional, which designs turf, landscape, construction, and agricultural products and markets them through distributors and dealers; Residential, which markets products to homeowners, such as walk power mower products, riding products, home solutions products, and gas snow removal products, among others; and Distribution, which consists of Co.-owned domestic distributorships and corporate activities.

Recent Developments: For the quarter ended Feb 1 2013, net income increased 57.6% to US$31.4 million from US$19.9 million in the year-earlier quarter. Revenues were US$444.7 million, up 4.9% from US$423.8 million the year before. Operating income was US$46.2 million versus US$34.0 million in the prior-year quarter, an increase of 35.8%. Direct operating expenses rose 0.6% to US$278.8 million from US$277.2 million in the comparable period the year before. Indirect operating expenses increased 6.2% to US$119.6 million from US$112.6 million in the equivalent prior-year period.

Prospects: Our evaluation of Toro Co. as of Apr. 7, 2013 is the result of our systematic analysis on three basic characteristics: earnings strength, relative valuation, and recent stock price movement. The company has managed to produce a neutral trend in earnings per share over the past 5 quarters. However, while recent estimates for the company have been lowered by analysts, TTC has posted better than expected results. Based on operating earnings yield, the company is about fairly valued when compared to all of the companies in our coverage universe. Share price changes over the past year indicates that TTC will perform well over the near term.

Financial Data
(US$ in Thousands)

	3 Mos	10/31/2012	10/31/2011	10/31/2010	10/31/2009	10/31/2008	10/31/2007	10/31/2006
Earnings Per Share	2.34	2.14	1.85	1.40	0.86	1.55	1.70	1.46
Cash Flow Per Share	3.05	3.12	1.82	2.93	3.51	2.85	2.26	2.22
Tang Book Value Per Share	3.29	3.23	2.35	2.65	3.08	3.66	3.55	3.78
Dividends Per Share	0.470	0.440	0.400	0.360	0.300	0.300	0.240	0.180
Dividend Payout %	20.09	20.56	21.62	25.81	34.68	19.35	14.12	12.37
Income Statement								
Total Revenue	444,661	1,958,690	1,883,953	1,690,378	1,523,447	1,878,184	1,876,904	1,835,991
EBITDA	61,164	253,226	228,581	196,834	154,635	245,724	270,414	251,771
Depn & Amortn	13,517	46,840	43,539	42,108	42,031	46,099	40,529	41,219
Income Before Taxes	43,398	190,266	169,144	138,669	95,924	182,148	213,588	194,313
Income Taxes	12,002	66,721	57,168	48,031	32,951	61,638	70,791	63,609
Net Income	31,396	129,541	117,658	93,237	62,837	119,651	142,436	129,145
Average Shares	59,628	60,618	63,594	66,874	72,480	77,158	83,728	88,688
Balance Sheet								
Current Assets	665,886	612,134	532,882	584,973	582,138	643,948	664,928	657,093
Total Assets	984,143	935,199	870,663	885,622	872,682	932,260	950,837	921,983
Current Liabilities	427,493	378,122	359,080	368,283	316,801	324,451	341,470	345,539
Long-Term Obligations	223,498	223,482	225,178	223,578	225,046	227,515	227,598	175,000
Total Liabilities	671,300	622,797	603,896	609,812	557,470	567,585	580,399	529,954
Stockholders' Equity	312,843	312,402	266,767	275,810	315,212	364,675	370,438	392,029
Shares Outstanding	57,854	58,266	59,206	62,789	66,738	70,969	75,901	80,711
Statistical Record								
Return on Assets %	14.68	14.31	13.40	10.61	6.96	12.67	15.21	14.05
Return on Equity %	46.88	44.61	43.37	31.55	18.48	32.46	37.36	33.03
EBITDA Margin %	13.76	12.93	12.13	11.64	10.15	13.08	14.41	13.71
Net Margin %	7.06	6.61	6.25	5.52	4.12	6.37	7.59	7.03
Asset Turnover	2.06	2.16	2.15	1.92	1.69	1.99	2.00	2.00
Current Ratio	1.56	1.62	1.48	1.59	1.84	1.98	1.95	1.90
Debt to Equity	0.71	0.72	0.84	0.81	0.71	0.62	0.61	0.45
Price Range	45.07-30.27	42.22-26.02	33.95-22.82	29.14-18.50	20.85-10.21	29.48-14.19	31.11-21.30	26.18-18.25
P/E Ratio	19.26-12.94	19.73-12.16	18.35-12.33	20.81-13.22	24.24-11.87	19.02-9.15	18.30-12.53	17.93-12.50
Average Yield %	1.23	1.26	1.36	1.47	1.90	1.41	0.90	0.81

Address: 8111 Lyndale Avenue South, Bloomington, MN 55420-1196 **Telephone:** 952-888-8801	**Web Site:** www.toro.com **Officers:** Michael J. Hoffman - Chairman, President, Chief Executive Officer Thomas J. Larson - Vice President, Treasurer	**Auditors:** KPMG LLP **Transfer Agents:** Wells Fargo Shareowner Services, St. Paul, MN

TOTAL SYSTEM SERVICES, INC.

Exchange	Symbol	Price	52Wk Range	Yield	P/E
NYS	TSS	$24.78 (3/28/2013)	24.78-21.23	1.61	19.21

*7 Year Price Score 100.21 *NYSE Composite Index=100 *12 Month Price Score 94.01

Interim Earnings (Per Share)

Qtr.	Mar	Jun	Sep	Dec
2008	0.29	0.32	0.33	0.34
2009	0.24	0.27	0.28	0.30
2010	0.26	0.25	0.23	0.25
2011	0.25	0.28	0.30	0.32
2012	0.30	0.35	0.32	0.32

Interim Dividends (Per Share)

Amt	Decl	Ex	Rec	Pay
0.10Q	05/29/2012	06/19/2012	06/21/2012	07/02/2012
0.10Q	09/04/2012	09/18/2012	09/20/2012	10/01/2012
0.10Q	12/03/2012	12/13/2012	12/17/2012	12/26/2012
0.10Q	02/25/2013	03/19/2013	03/21/2013	04/01/2013

Indicated Div: $0.40

Valuation Analysis | **Institutional Holding**

Forecast EPS	$1.45	No of Institutions
	(04/05/2013)	419
Market Cap	$4.6 Billion	Shares
Book Value	$1.4 Billion	141,832,320
Price/Book	3.25	% Held
Price/Sales	2.48	66.82

Business Summary: Business Services (MIC: 7.5.2 SIC: 7389 NAIC: 561499)

Total System Services provides payment processing and other services to card-issuing and merchant acquiring institutions in the U.S. and internationally through online accounting and electronic payment processing systems. Co. operates through its three operating segments: North America Services, which includes electronic payment processing services and other services provided from within the North America region; International Services, which includes electronic payment processing and other services provided from outside the North America region; and Merchant Services, which includes electronic processing and other services provided to merchant acquiring institutions.

Recent Developments: For the year ended Dec 31 2012, income from continuing operations increased 12.2% to US$249.9 million from US$222.7 million a year earlier. Net income increased 12.2% to US$249.9 million from US$222.7 million in the prior year. Revenues were US$1.87 billion, up 3.4% from US$1.81 billion the year before. Operating income was US$357.7 million versus US$322.5 million in the prior year, an increase of 10.9%. Direct operating expenses was unchanged at US$1.26 billion versus the comparable period the year before. Indirect operating expenses increased 9.8% to US$251.0 million from US$228.5 million in the equivalent prior-year period.

Prospects: Our evaluation of Total System Services Inc. as of Apr. 7, 2013 is the result of our systematic analysis on three basic characteristics: earnings strength, relative valuation, and recent stock price movement. The company has managed to produce a neutral trend in earnings per share over the past 5 quarters and while recent estimates for the company have remained steady, TSS has posted results that fell short of analysts expectations. Based on operating earnings yield, the company is about fairly valued when compared to all of the companies in our coverage universe. Share price changes over the past year indicates that TSS will perform poorly over the near term.

Financial Data
(US$ in Thousands)

	12/31/2012	12/31/2011	12/31/2010	12/31/2009	12/31/2008	12/31/2007	12/31/2006	12/31/2005
Earnings Per Share	1.29	1.15	0.99	1.09	1.27	1.20	1.26	0.99
Cash Flow Per Share	2.43	2.28	1.99	2.16	1.80	1.70	1.96	1.21
Tang Book Value Per Share	2.08	2.57	2.18	3.39	2.38	1.67	3.45	2.30
Dividends Per Share	0.400	0.310	0.280	0.280	0.280	3.311	0.270	0.220
Dividend Payout %	31.01	26.96	28.28	25.69	22.05	275.91	21.43	22.22
Income Statement								
Total Revenue	1,870,972	1,808,966	1,717,577	1,688,062	1,938,608	1,805,836	1,787,171	1,602,931
EBITDA	525,762	485,876	471,077	495,217	537,244	506,367	543,208	437,503
Depn & Amortn	170,908	169,325	163,265	156,625	159,844	152,468	184,894	151,214
Income Before Taxes	354,854	316,551	307,812	338,592	377,400	377,691	371,854	291,927
Income Taxes	115,102	102,597	106,088	121,238	131,795	143,668	126,182	103,286
Net Income	244,280	220,559	193,947	215,213	250,100	237,443	249,163	194,520
Average Shares	188,665	191,239	195,378	195,623	196,705	197,165	197,077	197,345
Balance Sheet								
Current Assets	574,726	650,181	721,813	810,896	625,101	586,578	744,716	512,289
Total Assets	2,023,838	1,858,392	1,952,261	1,710,954	1,550,252	1,479,020	1,634,241	1,410,897
Current Liabilities	230,519	380,576	227,270	220,779	248,711	273,795	295,787	277,012
Long-Term Obligations	192,014	63,593	225,276	205,123	209,870	256,593	3,625	3,555
Total Liabilities	598,628	557,103	711,137	535,153	559,304	634,547	416,881	398,125
Stockholders' Equity	1,425,210	1,301,289	1,241,124	1,175,801	990,948	844,473	1,217,360	1,012,772
Shares Outstanding	187,031	189,031	194,528	197,180	196,703	197,965	196,912	197,283
Statistical Record								
Return on Assets %	12.55	11.58	10.59	13.20	16.47	15.25	16.36	14.45
Return on Equity %	17.87	17.35	16.05	19.87	27.18	23.03	22.35	20.72
EBITDA Margin %	28.10	26.86	27.43	29.34	27.71	28.04	30.39	27.29
Net Margin %	13.06	12.19	11.29	12.75	12.90	13.15	13.94	12.14
Asset Turnover	0.96	0.95	0.94	1.04	1.28	1.16	1.17	1.19
Current Ratio	2.49	1.71	3.18	3.67	2.51	2.14	2.52	1.85
Debt to Equity	0.13	0.05	0.18	0.17	0.21	0.30	N.M.	N.M.
Price Range	24.39-19.40	20.41-15.38	17.27-13.60	17.59-11.40	28.00-10.95	34.33-25.50	26.54-18.07	25.38-18.91
P/E Ratio	18.91-15.04	17.75-13.37	17.44-13.74	16.14-10.46	22.05-8.62	28.61-21.25	21.06-14.34	25.64-19.10
Average Yield %	1.76	1.70	1.85	1.91	1.39	11.14	1.26	0.94

Address: One TSYS Way, Post Office Box 1755, Columbus, GA 31902	Web Site: www.tsys.com	Auditors: KPMG LLP
Telephone: 706-649-2310	Officers: Philip W. Tomlinson - Chairman, Chief Executive Officer M. Troy Woods - President, Chief Operating Officer	Investor Contact: 706-644-6081
Fax: 706-649-2456		Transfer Agents: American Stock & Transfer & Trust Company, Brooklyn, NY

TOWERS WATSON & CO.

Exchange	Symbol	Price	52Wk Range	Yield	P/E
NYS	TW	$69.32 (3/28/2013)	69.32-50.01	0.66	18.10

*7 Year Price Score 103.71 *NYSE Composite Index=100 *12 Month Price Score 102.92

Interim Earnings (Per Share)

Qtr.	Sep	Dec	Mar	Jun
2010-11	0.45	0.65	0.94	0.59
2011-12	0.82	0.92	0.95	0.91
2012-13	0.82	1.15	...	...

Interim Dividends (Per Share)

Amt	Decl	Ex	Rec	Pay
0.10Q	05/15/2012	06/27/2012	06/29/2012	07/16/2012
0.115Q	08/17/2012	09/26/2012	09/28/2012	10/15/2012
0.115Q	11/16/2012	12/13/2012	12/17/2012	12/26/2012
0.345Q	12/05/2012	12/13/2012	12/17/2012	12/26/2012

Indicated Div: $0.46

Valuation Analysis

		Institutional Holding	
Forecast EPS	$5.38 (04/05/2013)	No of Institutions	260
Market Cap	$4.9 Billion	Shares	50,999,760
Book Value	$2.5 Billion	% Held	63.35
Price/Book	1.94		
Price/Sales	1.40		

TRADING VOLUME (thousand shares)

Business Summary: Business Services (MIC: 7.5.2 SIC: 8742 NAIC: 541612)

Towers Watson is a services holding company. Through its subsidiaries, Co. is engaged in four segments: Benefits, which includes retirement, health and group benefits, technology and administration solutions, and international consulting group lines of business; Risk and Financial Services, which includes Co.'s risk consulting and software, reinsurance and insurance brokerage, and investment consulting and solutions lines of business; Talent and Reward, which includes the executive compensation, rewards, talent and communication, as well as data, surveys and technology lines of business; and Exchange Solution, which includes its Extend Health line of business.

Recent Developments: For the quarter ended Dec 31 2012, net income increased 23.2% to US$80.6 million from US$65.4 million in the year-earlier quarter. Revenues were US$946.2 million, up 7.6% from US$879.7 million the year before. Operating income was US$117.6 million versus US$99.1 million in the prior-year quarter, an increase of 18.6%. Indirect operating expenses increased 6.2% to US$828.7 million from US$780.6 million in the equivalent prior-year period.

Prospects: Our evaluation of Towers Watson & Co. as of Apr. 7, 2013 is the result of our systematic analysis on three basic characteristics: earnings strength, relative valuation, and recent stock price movement. The company has generated a negative trend in earnings per share over the past 5 quarters and while recent estimates for the company have remained steady, TW has posted better than expected results. Based on operating earnings yield, the company is undervalued when compared to all of the companies in our coverage universe. Share price changes over the past year indicates that TW will perform very poorly over the near term.

Financial Data

(US$ in Thousands)	6 Mos	3 Mos	06/30/2012	06/30/2011	06/30/2010
Earnings Per Share	3.83	3.60	3.59	2.62	2.03
Cash Flow Per Share	5.49	4.07	4.36	7.31	...
Dividends Per Share	0.775	0.415	0.400	0.300	0.150
Dividend Payout %	20.23	11.53	11.14	11.45	7.39
Income Statement					
Total Revenue	1,780,494	834,249	3,417,736	3,259,451	2,387,829
EBITDA	301,708	135,787	524,585	463,226	242,949
Depn & Amortn	89,272	43,608	113,319	130,714	67,200
Income Before Taxes	207,381	89,918	405,970	325,560	171,191
Income Taxes	68,932	32,076	145,756	129,916	50,907
Net Income	141,017	58,727	260,213	194,437	120,597
Average Shares	71,847	71,993	72,542	74,139	59,372
Balance Sheet					
Current Assets	1,673,179	1,661,263	1,759,397	1,650,551	1,445,301
Total Assets	5,337,200	5,318,426	5,356,978	5,098,950	4,573,450
Current Liabilities	962,945	885,063	1,102,982	1,178,477	965,613
Long-Term Obligations	512,500	583,150	458,000	...	...
Total Liabilities	2,792,905	2,806,670	2,924,458	2,507,423	2,617,843
Stockholders' Equity	2,544,295	2,511,756	2,432,520	2,591,527	1,955,607
Shares Outstanding	71,037	71,429	71,702	73,601	74,203
Statistical Record					
Return on Assets %	5.38	5.12	4.96	4.02	...
Return on Equity %	10.71	10.27	10.33	8.55	...
EBITDA Margin %	16.95	16.28	15.35	14.21	10.17
Net Margin %	7.92	7.04	7.61	5.97	5.05
Asset Turnover	0.69	0.68	0.65	0.67	...
Current Ratio	1.74	1.88	1.60	1.40	1.50
Debt to Equity	0.20	0.23	0.19	...	...
Price Range	66.85-50.01	66.85-51.68	66.85-52.26	65.71-38.35	51.48-35.42
P/E Ratio	17.45-13.06	18.57-14.36	18.62-14.56	25.08-14.64	25.36-17.45
Average Yield %	1.32	0.68	0.65	0.57	0.34

Address: 875 Third Avenue, New York, NY 10022 **Telephone:** 212-725-7550	**Web Site:** www.towerswatson.com **Officers:** John J. Haley - Chairman, Chief Executive Officer, President Roger F. Millay - Vice President, Chief Financial Officer	**Auditors:** Deloitte & Touche LLP **Investor Contact:** 703-258-8000 **Transfer Agents:** American Stock Transfer & Trust Company, LLC

TRAVELERS COMPANIES INC (THE)

Exchange	Symbol	Price	52Wk Range	Yield	P/E
NYS	TRV	$84.19 (3/28/2013)	84.19-57.75	2.19	13.36

*7 Year Price Score 116.26 *NYSE Composite Index=100 *12 Month Price Score 107.66

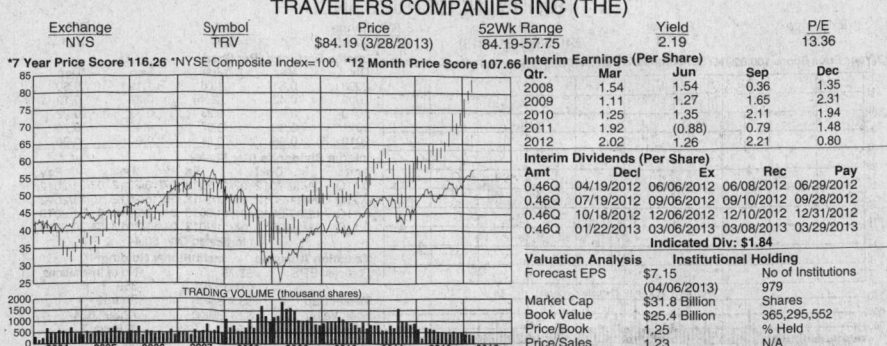

Interim Earnings (Per Share)

Qtr.	Mar	Jun	Sep	Dec
2008	1.54	1.54	0.36	1.35
2009	1.11	1.27	1.65	2.31
2010	1.25	1.35	2.11	1.94
2011	1.92	(0.88)	0.79	1.48
2012	2.02	1.26	2.21	0.80

Interim Dividends (Per Share)

Amt	Decl	Ex	Rec	Pay
0.46Q	04/19/2012	06/06/2012	06/08/2012	06/29/2012
0.46Q	07/19/2012	09/06/2012	09/10/2012	09/28/2012
0.46Q	10/18/2012	12/06/2012	12/10/2012	12/31/2012
0.46Q	01/22/2013	03/06/2013	03/08/2013	03/29/2013

Indicated Div: $1.84

Valuation Analysis — **Institutional Holding**

Forecast EPS	$7.15	No of Institutions
	(04/2013)	979
Market Cap	$31.8 Billion	Shares
Book Value	$25.4 Billion	365,295,552
Price/Book	1.25	% Held
Price/Sales	1.23	N/A

Business Summary: General Insurance (MIC: 5.2.1 SIC: 6331 NAIC: 524126)

Travelers Companies is a holding company. Through its subsidiaries, Co. provides insurance products and services. Co. has three segments: Business Insurance, which provides property and casualty insurance and insurance-related services; Financial, Professional & International Insurance, which includes surety and financial liability coverages that mainly use credit-based underwriting processes, as well as property and casualty products that are marketed on a domestic basis in the U.K., Canada and the Republic of Ireland, and on an international basis as a corporate member of Lloyd's; and Personal Insurance, which writes property and casualty insurance covering individuals' personal risks.

Recent Developments: For the year ended Dec 31 2012, net income increased 73.4% to US$2.47 billion from US$1.43 billion in the prior year. Revenues were US$25.74 billion, up 1.2% from US$25.45 billion the year before. Net premiums earned were US$22.36 billion versus US$22.09 billion in the prior year, an increase of 1.2%. Net investment income rose 0.3% to US$2.89 billion from US$2.88 billion a year ago.

Prospects: Our evaluation of The Travelers Companies Inc. as of Apr. 7, 2013 is the result of our systematic analysis on three basic characteristics: earnings strength, relative valuation, and recent stock price movement. The company has suffered a very negative trend in earnings per share over the past 5 quarters and while recent estimates for the company have been raised by analysts, TRV has posted better than expected results. Based on operating earnings yield, the company is undervalued when compared to all of the companies in our coverage universe. Share price changes over the past year indicates that TRV will perform well over the near term.

Financial Data
(US$ in Thousands)

	12/31/2012	12/31/2011	12/31/2010	12/31/2009	12/31/2008	12/31/2007	12/31/2006	12/31/2005
Earnings Per Share	6.30	3.36	6.62	6.33	4.82	6.86	5.91	2.33
Cash Flow Per Share	8.34	5.22	6.41	7.51	5.25	8.10	6.95	5.34
Tang Book Value Per Share	57.39	52.65	49.56	44.94	36.19	35.56	30.67	25.66
Dividends Per Share	1.790	1.590	1.410	1.230	1.190	1.130	1.010	0.910
Dividend Payout %	28.41	47.32	21.30	19.43	24.69	16.47	17.09	39.06
Income Statement								
Premium Income	22,357,000	22,090,000	21,432,000	21,418,000	21,579,000	21,470,000	20,760,000	20,341,000
Total Revenue	25,740,000	25,446,000	25,112,000	24,680,000	24,477,000	26,017,000	25,090,000	24,365,000
Benefits & Claims	14,676,000	16,276,000	13,210,000	12,408,000	12,993,000	12,397,000	12,244,000	14,927,000
Income Before Taxes	3,166,000	1,352,000	4,306,000	4,711,000	3,716,000	6,216,000	5,725,000	2,671,000
Income Taxes	693,000	(74,000)	1,090,000	1,089,000	792,000	1,615,000	1,517,000	610,000
Net Income	2,473,000	1,426,000	3,216,000	3,622,000	2,924,000	4,601,000	4,208,000	1,622,000
Average Shares	389,800	420,500	482,500	568,600	607,300	672,300	716,700	712,800
Balance Sheet								
Total Assets	104,938,000	104,602,000	105,181,000	109,560,000	109,751,000	115,224,000	113,761,000	113,187,000
Total Liabilities	79,533,000	80,125,000	79,706,000	82,145,000	84,432,000	88,608,000	88,626,000	90,884,000
Stockholders' Equity	25,405,000	24,477,000	25,475,000	27,415,000	25,319,000	26,616,000	25,135,000	22,303,000
Shares Outstanding	377,400	392,800	434,600	520,300	585,100	627,800	678,300	693,400
Statistical Record								
Return on Assets %	2.35	1.36	3.00	3.30	2.59	4.02	3.71	1.44
Return on Equity %	9.89	5.71	12.16	13.74	11.23	17.78	17.74	7.46
Loss Ratio %	65.64	73.68	61.64	57.93	60.21	57.74	58.98	73.38
Net Margin %	9.61	5.60	12.81	14.68	11.95	17.68	16.77	6.66
Price Range	74.33-56.87	64.05-46.80	57.44-47.94	54.31-33.52	53.80-30.50	56.76-48.38	54.23-40.75	46.70-33.71
P/E Ratio	11.80-9.03	19.06-13.93	8.68-7.24	8.58-5.30	11.16-6.33	8.27-7.05	9.18-6.90	20.04-14.47
Average Yield %	2.84	2.81	2.72	2.78	2.63	2.15	2.22	2.24

Address: 485 Lexington Avenue, New York, NY 10017 Telephone: 917-778-6000	Web Site: www.travelers.com Officers: Jay Steven Fishman - Chairman, Chief Executive Officer, President Jay Steven Benet - Vice-Chairman, Chief Financial Officer	Auditors: KPMG LLP Investor Contact: 917-778-9844 Transfer Agents: Wells Fargo Shareowner Services, Mendota Heights, MN

TRINITY INDUSTRIES, INC.

Exchange	Symbol	Price	52Wk Range	Yield	P/E
NYS	TRN	$45.33 (3/28/2013)	45.39-21.85	0.97	14.21

*7 Year Price Score 100.02 *NYSE Composite Index=100 ***12 Month Price Score 122.74**

Interim Earnings (Per Share)

Qtr.	Mar	Jun	Sep	Dec
2008	0.81	1.06	1.12	0.60
2009	0.43	(2.75)	0.29	0.19
2010	0.02	0.23	0.37	0.22
2011	0.30	0.37	0.40	0.70
2012	0.66	0.84	0.80	0.90

Interim Dividends (Per Share)

Amt	Decl	Ex	Rec	Pay
0.11Q	04/30/2012	07/11/2012	07/13/2012	07/31/2012
0.11Q	09/11/2012	10/11/2012	10/15/2012	10/31/2012
0.11Q	12/07/2012	01/11/2013	01/15/2013	01/31/2013
0.11Q	03/12/2013	04/11/2013	04/15/2013	04/30/2013

Indicated Div: $0.44

Valuation Analysis — **Institutional Holding**

Forecast EPS	$3.75 (04/05/2013)	No of Institutions	359
Market Cap	$3.7 Billion	Shares	72,397,624
Book Value	$2.1 Billion	% Held	80.08
Price/Book	1.80		
Price/Sales	0.97		

TRADING VOLUME (thousand shares)

Business Summary: Construction Services (MIC: 7.5.4 SIC: 3743 NAIC: 336510)

Trinity Industries is a diversified industrial company that owns a variety of businesses which provide products and services to the industrial, energy, transportation, and construction sectors. Co. manufactures and sells a variety of products including: railcars and railcar parts in addition to leasing railcars to its customers through its integrated business model, which includes a captive leasing business, Trinity Industries Leasing Company (TILC"); inland barges; structural wind towers; highway products; aggregates; containers; and parts and steel components.

Recent Developments: For the year ended Dec 31 2012, income from continuing operations increased 71.6% to US$251.9 million from US$146.8 million a year earlier. Net income increased 74.1% to US$253.7 million from US$145.7 million in the prior year. Revenues were US$3.81 billion, up 29.7% from US$2.94 billion the year before. Operating income was US$574.8 million versus US$426.8 million in the prior year, an increase of 34.7%. Direct operating expenses rose 29.4% to US$3.05 billion from US$2.36 billion in the comparable period the year before. Indirect operating expenses increased 20.5% to US$185.6 million from US$154.0 million in the equivalent prior-year period.

Prospects: Our evaluation of Trinity Industries Inc. as of Apr. 7, 2013 is the result of our systematic analysis on three basic characteristics: earnings strength, relative valuation, and recent stock price movement. The company has generated a negative trend in earnings per share over the past 5 quarters and while recent estimates for the company have been raised by analysts, TRN has posted better than expected results. Based on operating earnings yield, the company is undervalued when compared to all of the companies in our coverage universe. Share price changes over the past year indicates that TRN will perform well over the near term.

Financial Data
(US$ in Thousands)

	12/31/2012	12/31/2011	12/31/2010	12/31/2009	12/31/2008	12/31/2007	12/31/2006	12/31/2005
Earnings Per Share	3.19	1.77	0.85	(1.81)	3.59	3.65	2.90	1.13
Cash Flow Per Share	6.80	1.35	2.13	8.63	5.33	4.38	1.70	2.40
Tang Book Value Per Share	22.19	20.05	19.64	20.52	16.72	15.03	11.75	9.98
Dividends Per Share	0.400	0.340	0.320	0.320	0.300	0.250	0.213	0.167
Dividend Payout %	12.54	19.21	37.65	...	8.36	6.85	7.36	14.79
Income Statement								
Total Revenue	3,811,900	3,075,100	2,189,100	2,575,200	3,882,800	3,832,800	3,218,900	2,902,000
EBITDA	772,800	614,200	486,800	135,400	698,400	646,100	485,400	271,400
Depn & Amortn	193,700	192,900	189,600	160,800	140,300	118,900	87,600	88,900
Income Before Taxes	385,900	237,500	116,500	(146,900)	462,800	463,200	348,500	143,600
Income Taxes	134,000	91,800	40,900	(9,400)	175,500	169,400	133,000	57,300
Net Income	255,200	142,200	67,400	(137,700)	285,800	293,100	230,100	86,300
Average Shares	77,500	77,800	77,000	76,400	79,700	80,400	79,300	76,650
Balance Sheet								
Current Assets	1,630,700	1,286,900	1,082,700	1,084,300	1,123,600	1,172,800	1,092,900	845,200
Total Assets	6,669,900	6,121,000	5,760,000	4,656,400	4,915,800	4,043,200	3,425,600	2,586,500
Current Liabilities	771,300	628,700	508,400	451,300	699,400	684,300	655,800	629,900
Long-Term Obligations	3,055,000	2,974,900	2,907,700	1,845,100	1,905,900	1,374,200	1,198,900	689,000
Total Liabilities	4,616,900	4,257,200	3,995,200	2,850,100	3,084,600	2,316,500	2,022,100	1,413,400
Stockholders' Equity	2,053,000	1,863,800	1,764,800	1,806,300	1,831,200	1,726,700	1,403,500	1,173,100
Shares Outstanding	81,700	81,700	79,800	79,200	79,400	81,400	80,000	74,100
Statistical Record								
Return on Assets %	3.98	2.39	1.29	N.M.	6.36	7.85	7.65	3.60
Return on Equity %	13.00	7.84	3.77	N.M.	16.02	18.73	17.86	7.69
EBITDA Margin %	20.27	19.97	22.24	5.26	17.99	16.86	15.08	9.35
Net Margin %	6.69	4.62	3.08	N.M.	7.36	7.65	7.15	2.97
Asset Turnover	0.59	0.52	0.42	0.54	0.86	1.03	1.07	1.21
Current Ratio	2.11	2.05	2.13	2.40	1.61	1.71	1.67	1.34
Debt to Equity	1.49	1.60	1.65	1.02	1.04	0.80	0.85	0.59
Price Range	36.05-21.85	37.76-19.94	26.68-15.22	19.45-6.47	40.85-10.14	47.94-24.32	47.49-29.30	29.83-15.49
P/E Ratio	11.30-6.85	21.33-11.27	31.39-17.91	...	11.38-2.82	13.13-6.66	16.38-10.10	26.40-13.71
Average Yield %	1.34	1.14	1.54	2.18	1.08	0.65	0.59	0.74

Address: 2525 Stemmons Freeway, Dallas, TX 75207-2401	Web Site: www.trin.net	Auditors: Ernst & Young LLP
Telephone: 214-631-4420	Officers: Timothy R. Wallace - Chairman, President, Chief Executive Officer William A. McWhirter - Senior Vice President, Chief Financial Officer, Group President	Investor Contact: 214-631-4420
Fax: 214-589-8501		Transfer Agents: American Stock Transfer & Trust Company

TRW AUTOMOTIVE HOLDINGS CORP

Exchange	Symbol	Price	52Wk Range	Yield	P/E
NYS	TRW	$55.00 (3/28/2013)	61.42-33.40	N/A	7.02

*7 Year Price Score 132.73 *NYSE Composite Index=100 *12 Month Price Score 113.37

Interim Earnings (Per Share)

Qtr.	Mar	Jun	Sep	Dec
2008	0.92	1.24	(0.53)	(9.34)
2009	(1.30)	(0.11)	0.50	1.33
2010	1.61	1.78	1.54	1.56
2011	2.13	2.21	1.22	3.25
2012	1.59	1.71	1.28	3.25

Interim Dividends (Per Share)

No Dividends Paid

Valuation Analysis		Institutional Holding	
Forecast EPS	$6.33	No of Institutions	
	(04/05/2013)	395	
Market Cap	$6.6 Billion	Shares	
Book Value	$3.6 Billion	118,184,656	
Price/Book	1.83	% Held	
Price/Sales	0.40	92.06	

Business Summary: Auto Parts (MIC: 1.8.2 SIC: 3714 NAIC: 336340)

TRW Automotive Holdings is a holding company. Co. supplies automotive systems, modules and components to automotive original equipment manufacturers and related aftermarkets. Through its subsidiaries, Co. designs, manufactures and sells active and passive safety related products. Active safety related products principally refer to vehicle dynamic controls (primarily braking and steering), and passive safety related products principally refer to occupant restraints (primarily airbags and seat belts) and safety electronics (electronic control units and crash and occupant weight sensors). Co. has four segments: Chassis Systems, Occupant Safety Systems, Electronics and Automotive Components.

Recent Developments: For the year ended Dec 31 2012, net income decreased 12.9% to US$1.04 billion from US$1.20 billion in the prior year. Revenues were US$16.44 billion, up 1.2% from US$16.24 billion the year before. Operating income was US$1.09 billion versus US$1.26 billion in the prior year, a decrease of 13.9%. Direct operating expenses rose 1.9% to US$14.66 billion from US$14.38 billion in the comparable period the year before. Indirect operating expenses increased 17.3% to US$704.0 million from US$600.0 million in the equivalent prior-year period.

Prospects: Our evaluation of TRW Automotive Holdings Corp. as of Apr. 7, 2013 is the result of our systematic analysis on three basic characteristics; earnings strength, relative valuation, and recent stock price movement. The company has managed to produce a neutral trend in earnings per share over the past 5 quarters. However, while recent estimates for the company have been lowered by analysts, TRW has posted better than expected results. Based on operating earnings yield, the company is undervalued when compared to all of the companies in our coverage universe. Share price changes over the past year indicates that TRW will perform very well over the near term.

Financial Data

(US$ in Thousands)	12/31/2012	12/31/2011	12/31/2010	12/31/2009	12/31/2008	12/31/2007	12/31/2006	12/31/2005
Earnings Per Share	7.83	8.82	6.49	0.51	(7.71)	0.88	1.71	1.99
Cash Flow Per Share	7.79	9.07	8.78	4.22	7.63	7.38	6.49	5.07
Tang Book Value Per Share	12.81	7.18	N.M.	N.M.	N.M.	2.38	N.M.	N.M.
Income Statement								
Total Revenue	16,444,000	16,244,000	14,383,000	11,614,000	14,995,000	14,702,000	13,144,000	12,643,000
EBITDA	1,488,000	1,674,000	1,638,000	806,000	106,000	1,021,000	1,093,000	1,052,000
Depn & Amortn	409,000	447,000	469,000	495,000	576,000	557,000	517,000	509,000
Income Before Taxes	968,000	1,109,000	1,007,000	125,000	(652,000)	236,000	329,000	315,000
Income Taxes	(33,000)	(47,000)	166,000	67,000	126,000	155,000	166,000	124,000
Net Income	1,008,000	1,157,000	834,000	55,000	(779,000)	90,000	176,000	204,000
Average Shares	129,700	133,000	131,300	108,700	101,100	102,800	103,100	102,300
Balance Sheet								
Current Assets	4,728,000	4,627,000	4,140,000	3,592,000	3,239,000	4,326,000	3,676,000	3,599,000
Total Assets	10,857,000	10,262,000	9,288,000	8,732,000	9,272,000	12,290,000	11,133,000	10,230,000
Current Liabilities	3,881,000	3,840,000	3,519,000	3,308,000	3,164,000	3,715,000	3,675,000	3,590,000
Long-Term Obligations	1,369,000	1,428,000	1,803,000	2,325,000	2,803,000	3,150,000	2,862,000	3,101,000
Total Liabilities	7,279,000	7,322,000	7,225,000	7,572,000	8,141,000	9,098,000	8,736,000	9,022,000
Stockholders' Equity	3,578,000	2,940,000	2,063,000	1,160,000	1,131,000	3,192,000	2,397,000	1,208,000
Shares Outstanding	119,372	123,751	122,465	117,894	101,172	100,629	98,204	99,245
Statistical Record								
Return on Assets %	9.52	11.84	9.26	0.61	N.M.	0.77	1.65	2.01
Return on Equity %	30.85	46.25	51.75	4.80	N.M.	3.22	9.76	17.64
EBITDA Margin %	9.05	10.31	11.39	6.94	0.71	6.94	8.32	8.32
Net Margin %	6.13	7.12	5.80	0.47	N.M.	0.61	1.34	1.61
Asset Turnover	1.55	1.66	1.60	1.29	1.39	1.26	1.23	1.24
Current Ratio	1.22	1.20	1.18	1.09	1.02	1.16	1.00	1.00
Debt to Equity	0.38	0.49	0.87	2.00	2.48	0.99	1.19	2.57
Price Range	53.61-33.32	62.48-28.89	53.43-21.41	25.43-1.52	29.20-2.26	41.90-20.90	28.34-22.18	29.58-17.81
P/E Ratio	6.85-4.26	7.08-3.28	8.23-3.30	49.86-2.98	...	47.61-23.75	16.57-12.97	14.86-8.95

Address: 12001 Tech Center Drive, Livonia, MI 48150	Web Site: www.trw.com	Auditors: Ernst & Young LLP
Telephone: 734-855-2600	Officers: John C. Plant - Chairman, President, Chief Executive Officer Joseph S. Cantie - Executive Vice President, Chief Financial Officer	Investor Contact: 800-219-7411 Transfer Agents: Computershare Trust Company, N. A.

TRANSDIGM GROUP INC

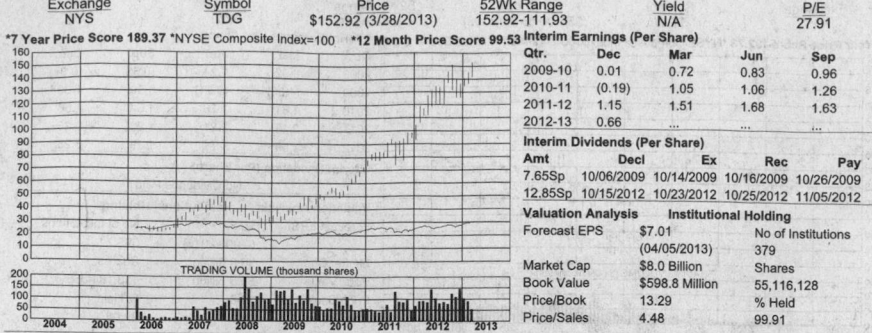

Exchange	Symbol	Price	52Wk Range	Yield	P/E
NYS	TDG	$152.92 (3/28/2013)	152.92-111.93	N/A	27.91

*7 Year Price Score 189.37 *NYSE Composite Index=100 *12 Month Price Score 99.53

Interim Earnings (Per Share)

Qtr.	Dec	Mar	Jun	Sep
2009-10	0.01	0.72	0.83	0.96
2010-11	(0.19)	1.05	1.06	1.26
2011-12	1.15	1.51	1.68	1.63
2012-13	0.66	...	...	...

Interim Dividends (Per Share)

Amt	Decl	Ex	Rec	Pay
7.65Sp	10/06/2009	10/14/2009	10/16/2009	10/26/2009
12.85Sp	10/15/2012	10/23/2012	10/25/2012	11/05/2012

Valuation Analysis — **Institutional Holding**

Forecast EPS	$7.01	No of Institutions
	(04/05/2013)	379
Market Cap	$8.0 Billion	Shares
Book Value	$598.8 Million	55,116,128
Price/Book	13.29	% Held
Price/Sales	4.48	99.91

Business Summary: Aerospace (MIC: 7.1.1 SIC: 3728 NAIC: 336412)

Transdigm Group is a holding company. Through its subsidiaries, Co. designs, produces and supplies aerospace components (and certain systems/subsystems) with aftermarket content. Some of Co.'s main products include mechanical/electro-mechanical actuators and controls, ignition systems and engine technology, pumps and valves, power conditioning devices, alternate current/direct current electric motors and generators, NiCad batteries and chargers, engineered latching and locking devices, rods and locking devices, connectors and elastomers, cockpit security components and systems, cockpit displays, aircraft audio systems, and lavatory components, seatbelts and safety restraints, among others.

Recent Developments: For the quarter ended Dec 29 2012, net income increased 13.9% to US$74.2 million from US$65.1 million in the year-earlier quarter. Revenues were US$430.4 million, up 22.1% from US$352.5 million the year before. Operating income was US$172.8 million versus US$145.3 million in the prior-year quarter, an increase of 19.0%. Direct operating expenses rose 25.5% to US$191.9 million from US$152.9 million in the comparable period the year before. Indirect operating expenses increased 21.0% to US$65.7 million from US$54.3 million in the equivalent prior-year period.

Prospects: Our evaluation of Transdigm Group Inc. as of Apr. 7, 2013 is the result of our systematic analysis on three basic characteristics: earnings strength, relative valuation, and recent stock price movement. The company has generated a negative trend in earnings per share over the past 5 quarters and while recent estimates for the company have been raised by analysts, TDG has posted better than expected results. Based on operating earnings yield, the company is about fairly valued when compared to all of the companies in our coverage universe. Share price changes over the past year indicates that TDG will perform well over the near term.

Financial Data
(US$ in Thousands)

	3 Mos	09/30/2012	09/30/2011	09/30/2010	09/30/2009	09/30/2008	09/30/2007	09/30/2006
Earnings Per Share	5.48	5.97	3.17	2.52	3.23	2.65	1.83	0.53
Cash Flow Per Share	8.16	7.66	4.89	3.73	4.07	3.95	2.46	0.07
Dividends Per Share	12.850	...	...	7.650	...	...	...	...
Dividend Payout %	234.49	...	...	303.57	...	...	...	...
Income Statement								
Total Revenue	430,418	1,700,208	1,206,021	827,654	761,552	713,711	592,798	435,164
EBITDA	194,094	768,002	475,141	393,234	362,921	324,533	257,790	134,278
Depn & Amortn	21,248	68,227	60,460	30,165	27,521	25,254	23,952	16,111
Income Before Taxes	109,970	487,869	229,425	250,835	251,002	206,602	142,071	41,435
Income Taxes	35,800	162,900	77,200	87,390	88,100	73,476	53,426	16,318
Net Income	74,170	324,969	172,134	163,445	162,902	133,126	88,645	25,117
Average Shares	54,453	53,882	53,333	52,923	50,459	50,220	48,542	47,481
Balance Sheet								
Current Assets	1,155,396	1,050,531	870,292	583,508	494,754	423,434	365,599	234,181
Total Assets	5,549,616	5,459,617	4,513,636	2,677,818	2,454,440	2,255,821	2,061,053	1,416,712
Current Liabilities	233,703	233,915	206,859	113,012	99,752	88,502	67,219	43,439
Long-Term Obligations	4,297,125	3,598,625	3,122,875	1,771,646	1,356,761	1,357,230	1,357,854	925,000
Total Liabilities	4,950,769	4,240,783	3,702,687	2,084,839	1,635,278	1,601,921	1,573,502	1,053,671
Stockholders' Equity	598,847	1,218,834	810,949	592,979	819,162	653,900	487,551	363,041
Shares Outstanding	52,037	51,651	50,335	49,434	48,953	48,600	47,041	44,664
Statistical Record								
Return on Assets %	6.62	6.50	4.79	6.37	6.92	6.15	5.10	1.77
Return on Equity %	44.96	31.93	24.52	23.15	22.12	23.26	20.84	7.22
EBITDA Margin %	45.09	45.17	39.40	47.51	47.66	45.47	43.49	30.86
Net Margin %	17.23	19.11	14.27	19.75	21.39	18.65	14.95	5.77
Asset Turnover	0.35	0.34	0.34	0.32	0.32	0.33	0.34	0.31
Current Ratio	4.94	4.49	4.21	5.16	4.96	4.78	5.44	5.39
Debt to Equity	7.18	2.95	3.85	2.99	1.66	2.08	2.79	2.55
Price Range	150.90-93.13	145.61-77.38	93.94-61.00	63.56-39.19	49.81-24.24	50.19-31.81	47.00-23.39	26.50-22.17
P/E Ratio	27.54-16.99	24.39-12.96	29.63-19.24	25.22-15.55	15.42-7.50	18.94-12.00	25.68-12.78	50.00-41.83
Average Yield %	10.23	...	...	14.92	...	...	...	...

Address: 1301 East 9th Street, Suite 3000, Cleveland, OH 44114
Telephone: 216-706-2960

Web Site: www.transdigm.com
Officers: W. Nicholas Howley - Chairman, Chief Executive Officer Raymond F. Laubenthal - President, Chief Operating Officer

Auditors: Ernst & Young LLP
Investor Contact: 216-706-2945
Transfer Agents: Computershare Trust Company, Providence, RI

TUPPERWARE BRANDS CORP

Exchange	Symbol	Price	52Wk Range	Yield	P/E
NYS	TUP	$81.74 (3/28/2013)	81.74-51.16	3.03	23.90

*7 Year Price Score 133.89 *NYSE Composite Index=100 *12 Month Price Score 115.88

TRADING VOLUME (thousand shares)

Interim Earnings (Per Share)

Qtr.	Mar	Jun	Sep	Dec
2008	0.51	0.56	0.44	1.05
2009	0.41	0.52	0.50	1.31
2010	0.73	0.90	0.62	1.27
2011	0.88	1.03	0.17	1.45
2012	1.02	0.22	0.85	1.33

Interim Dividends (Per Share)

Amt	Decl	Ex	Rec	Pay
0.36Q	05/22/2012	06/18/2012	06/20/2012	07/06/2012
0.36Q	08/20/2012	09/17/2012	09/19/2012	10/05/2012
0.36Q	11/08/2012	12/17/2012	12/19/2012	12/31/2012
0.62Q	01/29/2013	03/18/2013	03/20/2013	04/05/2013
		Indicated Div: $2.48		

Valuation Analysis / Institutional Holding

Valuation Analysis		Institutional Holding	
Forecast EPS	$5.71 (04/05/2013)	No of Institutions	457
Market Cap	$4.4 Billion	Shares	51,510,624
Book Value	$479.1 Million	% Held	80.71
Price/Book	9.22		
Price/Sales	1.71		

Business Summary: Plastics (MIC: 8.4.2 SIC: 3089 NAIC: 326199)

Tupperware Brands is a direct seller of products across multiple brands and categories. Co.'s product brands and categories include preparation, storage and serving applications for the kitchen and home through the Tupperware® brand and beauty and personal care products through its Armand Dupree®, Avroy Shlain®, BeautiControl®, Fuller®, NaturCare®, Nutrimetics® and Nuvo® brands. As of Dec 31 2011, Co. operated its business under five reporting segments (Europe, Asia Pacific, Tupperware North America, Beauty North America, and South America) in three geographic regions: Europe (Europe, Africa and the Middle East), Asia Pacific and the Americas.

Recent Developments: For the year ended Dec 29 2012, net income decreased 11.6% to US$193.0 million from US$218.3 million in the prior year. Revenues were US$2.58 billion, down 0.0% from US$2.59 billion the year before. Operating income was US$306.5 million versus US$342.3 million in the prior year, a decrease of 10.5%. Direct operating expenses declined 0.7% to US$856.4 million from US$862.5 million in the comparable period the year before. Indirect operating expenses increased 2.9% to US$1.42 billion from US$1.38 billion in the equivalent prior-year period.

Prospects: Our evaluation of Tupperware Corp. as of Apr. 7, 2013 is the result of our systematic analysis on three basic characteristics: earnings strength, relative valuation, and recent stock price movement. The company has managed to produce a neutral trend in earnings per share over the past 5 quarters and while recent estimates for the company have remained steady, TUP has posted better than expected results. Based on operating earnings yield, the company is undervalued when compared to all of the companies in our coverage universe. Share price changes over the past year indicates that TUP will perform in line with the market over the near term.

Financial Data

(US$ in Thousands)	12/29/2012	12/31/2011	12/25/2010	12/26/2009	12/27/2008	12/29/2007	12/30/2006	12/31/2005
Earnings Per Share	3.42	3.55	3.53	2.75	2.56	1.87	1.54	1.41
Cash Flow Per Share	5.42	4.50	4.80	4.03	2.13	2.92	2.88	2.77
Tang Book Value Per Share	2.64	1.68	5.19	2.93	0.14	N.M.	N.M.	N.M.
Dividends Per Share	1.440	1.200	1.050	0.910	0.880	0.880	0.880	0.880
Dividend Payout %	42.11	33.80	29.75	33.09	34.38	47.06	57.14	62.41
Income Statement								
Total Revenue	2,583,800	2,585,000	2,300,400	2,127,500	2,161,800	1,981,400	1,743,700	1,279,300
EBITDA	352,800	388,000	372,300	312,400	290,400	240,500	198,600	159,900
Depn & Amortn	47,600	46,900	45,800	46,600	51,600	49,900	47,800	49,100
Income Before Taxes	272,800	295,300	299,700	237,100	201,900	141,400	103,800	65,700
Income Taxes	79,800	77,000	74,100	62,000	40,500	24,500	9,600	(20,500)
Net Income	193,000	218,300	225,600	175,100	161,400	116,900	94,200	85,400
Average Shares	56,400	61,400	63,800	63,400	63,100	62,614	61,171	60,617
Balance Sheet								
Current Assets	766,500	769,400	849,200	696,800	703,800	699,500	586,600	672,700
Total Assets	1,821,800	1,844,200	2,015,800	1,795,300	1,815,600	1,868,700	1,712,100	1,740,200
Current Liabilities	694,500	675,400	500,400	460,500	451,500	450,300	381,600	454,700
Long-Term Obligations	414,400	415,200	426,800	426,200	567,400	589,800	680,500	750,500
Total Liabilities	1,342,700	1,343,400	1,226,000	1,157,600	1,341,600	1,346,000	1,311,600	1,404,700
Stockholders' Equity	479,100	500,800	789,800	637,700	474,000	522,700	400,500	335,500
Shares Outstanding	54,059	56,507	62,706	63,054	62,300	61,521	60,561	60,431
Statistical Record								
Return on Assets %	10.56	11.13	11.87	9.73	8.79	6.55	5.47	6.17
Return on Equity %	39.50	33.28	31.69	31.59	32.48	25.39	25.67	26.83
EBITDA Margin %	13.65	15.01	16.18	14.68	13.43	12.14	11.39	12.50
Net Margin %	7.47	8.44	9.81	8.23	7.47	5.90	5.40	6.68
Asset Turnover	1.41	1.32	1.21	1.18	1.18	1.11	1.01	0.92
Current Ratio	1.10	1.14	1.70	1.51	1.56	1.55	1.54	1.48
Debt to Equity	0.86	0.83	0.54	0.67	1.20	1.13	1.70	2.24
Price Range	66.56-51.16	71.45-45.63	53.92-37.45	49.15-11.40	44.94-15.91	36.10-22.30	23.41-17.73	24.37-19.70
P/E Ratio	19.46-14.96	20.13-12.85	15.27-10.61	17.87-4.15	17.55-6.21	19.30-11.93	15.20-11.11	17.28-13.97
Average Yield %	2.47	2.05	2.34	3.00	2.73	3.05	4.30	4.02

Address: 14901 South Orange Blossom Trail, Orlando, FL 32837 Telephone: 407-826-5050	Web Site: www.tupperwarebrands.com Officers: E. V. Goings - Chairman, Chief Executive Officer Simon C. Hemus - President, Chief Operating Officer	Auditors: PricewaterhouseCoopers LLP Investor Contact: 407-826-4475 Transfer Agents: Wells Fargo Shareowner Services, St. Paul, MN

TUTOR PERINI CORP

Exchange	Symbol	Price	52Wk Range	Yield	P/E
NYS	TPC	$19.30 (3/28/2013)	19.30-9.92	N/A	N/A

*7 Year Price Score 48.24 *NYSE Composite Index=100 *12 Month Price Score 122.05

Interim Earnings (Per Share)

Qtr.	Mar	Jun	Sep	Dec
2008	0.91	1.03	1.01	(5.15)
2009	0.80	0.79	0.54	0.66
2010	0.42	0.66	0.65	0.40
2011	0.14	0.41	0.74	0.50
2012	(0.03)	(7.35)	0.88	0.88

Interim Dividends (Per Share)

Amt	Decl	Ex	Rec	Pay
1.00Sp	10/25/2010	11/02/2010	11/04/2010	11/12/2010

Valuation Analysis

	Institutional Holding	
Forecast EPS	$1.95	No of Institutions
	(04/05/2013)	24
Market Cap	$917.8 Million	Shares
Book Value	$1.1 Billion	446,616
Price/Book	0.80	% Held
Price/Sales	0.22	N/A

TRADING VOLUME (thousand shares)

Business Summary: Construction Services (MIC: 7.5.4 SIC: 1542 NAIC: 236220)

Tutor Perini is a construction company providing general contracting, construction management and design-build services to private clients and public agencies. Co. has four segments: Civil, which focuses on public works construction and the repair, replacement and reconstruction of infrastructure; Building, which provides services to various building markets for private and public works clients; Specialty Contractors, which focuses on plumbing, heating, ventilation, and air conditioning, electrical, mechanical, and pneumatically placed concrete for civil, building and management services construction projects; and Management Services, which provides construction and design-build services.

Recent Developments: For the year ended Dec 31 2012, net loss amounted to US$265.4 million versus net income of US$86.1 million in the prior year. Revenues were US$4.11 billion, up 10.6% from US$3.72 billion the year before. Operating loss was US$221.8 million versus an income of US$168.4 million in the prior year. Direct operating expenses rose 11.3% to US$3.70 billion from US$3.32 billion in the comparable period the year before. Indirect operating expenses increased 180.6% to US$636.9 million from US$227.0 million in the equivalent prior-year period.

Prospects: Our evaluation of Tutor Perini Corp. as of Apr. 7, 2013 is the result of our systematic analysis on three basic characteristics: earnings strength, relative valuation, and recent stock price movement. The company has enjoyed a very positive trend in earnings per share over the past 5 quarters. However, while recent estimates for the company have been lowered by analysts, TPC has posted results that fell short of analysts expectations. Based on operating earnings yield, the company is undervalued when compared to all of the companies in our coverage universe. Share price changes over the past year indicates that TPC will perform poorly over the near term.

Financial Data

(US$ in Thousands)	12/31/2012	12/31/2011	12/31/2010	12/31/2009	12/31/2008	12/31/2007	12/31/2006	12/31/2005
Earnings Per Share	(5.59)	1.80	2.13	2.79	(2.19)	3.54	1.54	0.20
Cash Flow Per Share	(1.43)	(0.65)	0.55	(0.54)	3.67	10.50	4.44	1.19
Tang Book Value Per Share	9.39	6.53	11.86	11.36	8.80	12.52	7.99	5.78
Dividends Per Share	...	...	1.000	...	...	...	...	...
Dividend Payout %	...	...	46.95	...	...	...	...	...
Income Statement								
Total Revenue	4,111,471	3,716,317	3,199,210	5,151,966	5,660,286	4,628,358	3,042,839	1,733,477
EBITDA	(185,927)	202,226	186,954	229,267	(16,240)	151,756	76,686	13,346
Depn & Amortn	40,583	32,193	21,380	21,292	12,345	9,225	7,549	5,462
Income Before Taxes	(267,842)	137,047	159,468	205,140	(19,850)	154,395	69,689	6,921
Income Taxes	(2,442)	50,899	55,968	68,079	55,290	57,281	28,153	2,872
Net Income	(265,400)	86,148	103,500	137,061	(75,140)	97,114	41,536	4,049
Average Shares	47,470	47,890	48,649	49,084	34,272	27,419	26,758	26,150
Balance Sheet								
Current Assets	1,981,847	1,950,034	1,561,042	1,614,554	1,910,300	1,526,082	1,078,253	805,890
Total Assets	3,296,410	3,613,127	2,779,220	2,820,654	3,073,078	1,654,115	1,195,992	915,256
Current Liabilities	1,234,270	1,393,234	968,114	1,311,436	1,685,251	1,232,561	884,301	652,555
Long-Term Obligations	669,380	612,548	374,350	84,771	61,580	13,358	34,135	39,969
Total Liabilities	2,152,546	2,213,300	1,466,226	1,532,228	1,934,852	1,285,781	952,133	732,081
Stockholders' Equity	1,143,864	1,399,827	1,312,994	1,288,426	1,138,226	368,334	243,859	183,175
Shares Outstanding	47,556	47,329	47,089	48,538	48,319	26,986	26,554	26,037
Statistical Record								
Return on Assets %	N.M.	2.70	3.70	4.65	N.M.	6.81	3.93	0.52
Return on Equity %	N.M.	6.35	7.96	11.30	N.M.	31.73	19.45	2.27
EBITDA Margin %	N.M.	5.44	5.84	4.45	N.M.	3.28	2.52	0.77
Net Margin %	N.M.	2.32	3.24	2.66	N.M.	2.10	1.37	0.23
Asset Turnover	1.19	1.16	1.14	1.75	2.39	3.25	2.88	2.21
Current Ratio	1.61	1.40	1.61	1.23	1.13	1.24	1.22	1.23
Debt to Equity	0.59	0.44	0.29	0.07	0.05	0.04	0.14	0.22
Price Range	16.76-9.92	26.66-10.57	25.26-15.88	25.50-10.77	42.05-12.49	73.89-28.50	32.98-20.05	26.50-12.22
P/E Ratio	...	14.81-5.87	11.86-7.46	9.14-3.86	...	20.87-8.05	21.42-13.02	132.50-61.10
Average Yield %	...	...	4.86	...	...	...	...	...

Address: 15901 Olden Street, Sylmar, CA 91342-1093	**Web Site:** www.tutorperini.com	**Auditors:** Deloitte & Touche LLP
Telephone: 818-362-8391	**Officers:** Ronald N. Tutor - Chairman, Chief Executive Officer Michael R. Klein - Vice-Chairman	**Investor Contact:** 818-362-8391
		Transfer Agents: Computershare Investor Services, Canton, MA

TYCO INTERNATIONAL LTD. (SWITZERLAND)

Exchange	Symbol	Price	52Wk Range	Yield	P/E
NYS	TYC	$32.00 (3/28/2013)	32.34-24.83	2.22	49.23

*7 Year Price Score 118.89 *NYSE Composite Index=100 *12 Month Price Score 102.67

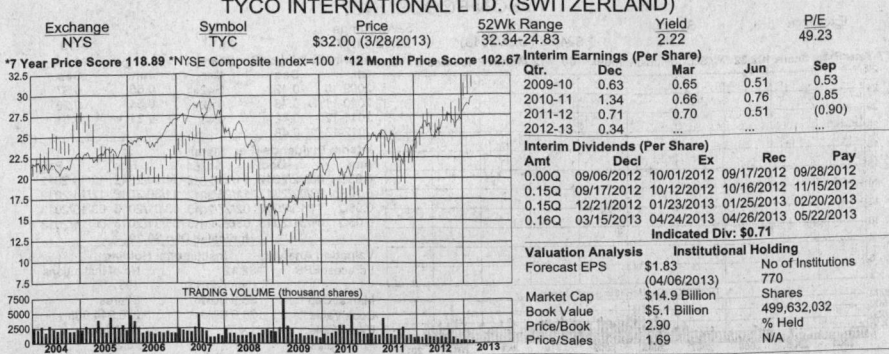

Interim Earnings (Per Share)

Qtr.	Dec	Mar	Jun	Sep
2009-10	0.63	0.65	0.51	0.53
2010-11	1.34	0.66	0.76	0.85
2011-12	0.71	0.70	0.51	(0.90)
2012-13	0.34	...	...	...

Interim Dividends (Per Share)

Amt	Decl	Ex	Rec	Pay
0.00Q	09/06/2012	10/01/2012	09/17/2012	09/28/2012
0.15Q	09/17/2012	10/12/2012	10/16/2012	11/15/2012
0.15Q	12/21/2012	01/23/2013	01/25/2013	02/20/2013
0.16Q	03/15/2013	04/24/2013	04/26/2013	05/22/2013

Indicated Div: $0.71

Valuation Analysis

Forecast EPS	$1.83
	(04/06/2013)
Market Cap	$14.9 Billion
Book Value	$5.1 Billion
Price/Book	2.90
Price/Sales	1.69

Institutional Holding

No of Institutions	770
Shares	499,632,032
% Held	N/A

Business Summary: Business Services (MIC: 7.5.2 SIC: 7382 NAIC: 334417)

Tyco International is a provider of security products and services, fire detection and suppression products and services and life safety products. Co.'s portfolio of products and services, sold under brands such as Tyco, SimplexGrinnell, Sensormatic, Wormald, Ansul, Simplex, Grinnell, Scott and ADT (in jurisdictions outside of North America) serve security, fire detection and suppression and life safety needs across commercial, industrial, retail, institutional and governmental markets, as well as non-U.S. residential and small business markets. Co. operates three segments: North America Systems Installation & Services; Rest of World Systems Installation & Services; and Global Products.

Recent Developments: For the quarter ended Dec 28 2012, income from continuing operations increased 64.3% to US$161.0 million from US$98.0 million in the year-earlier quarter. Net income decreased 48.8% to US$165.0 million from US$322.0 million in the year-earlier quarter. Revenues were US$2.60 billion, up 4.9% from US$2.48 billion the year before. Operating income was US$235.0 million versus US$186.0 million in the prior-year quarter, an increase of 26.3%. Direct operating expenses rose 5.6% to US$1.67 billion from US$1.58 billion in the comparable period the year before. Indirect operating expenses decreased 2.2% to US$697.0 million from US$713.0 million in the equivalent prior-year period.

Prospects: Our evaluation of Tyco International Ltd. as of Apr. 7, 2013 is the result of our systematic analysis on three basic characteristics: earnings strength, relative valuation, and recent stock price movement. The company has managed to produce a neutral trend in earnings per share over the past 5 quarters. However, while recent estimates for the company have been mixed, TYC has posted better than expected results. Based on operating earnings yield, the company is overvalued when compared to all of the companies in our coverage universe. Share price changes over the past year indicates that TYC will perform well over the near term.

Financial Data

(US$ in Thousands)	3 Mos	09/28/2012	09/30/2011	09/24/2010	09/25/2009	09/26/2008	09/28/2007	09/29/2006
Earnings Per Share	0.65	1.02	3.62	2.32	(3.80)	3.19	(3.52)	7.20
Cash Flow Per Share	4.74	5.60	5.04	5.49	5.13	(1.84)	11.88	11.11
Tang Book Value Per Share	N.M.	N.M.	1.19	2.17	3.14	2.81	2.49	10.91
Dividends Per Share	0.900	0.900	0.979	0.852	0.840	0.650	1.600	1.600
Dividend Payout %	138.46	88.24	26.72	36.73	...	20.38	...	22.22
Income Statement								
Total Revenue	2,600,000	10,403,000	17,355,000	17,016,000	17,237,000	20,199,000	18,781,000	40,960,000
EBITDA	331,000	658,000	3,433,000	2,747,000	(336,000)	2,930,000	(812,000)	7,544,000
Depn & Amortn	105,000	427,000	1,330,000	1,224,000	1,158,000	1,213,000	1,158,000	2,081,000
Income Before Taxes	206,000	41,000	1,893,000	1,270,000	(1,751,000)	1,431,000	(2,181,000)	4,884,000
Income Taxes	39,000	348,000	326,000	138,000	78,000	335,000	334,000	799,000
Net Income	163,000	472,000	1,733,000	1,132,000	(1,798,000)	1,553,000	(1,742,000)	3,713,000
Average Shares	473,000	463,000	479,000	488,000	473,000	488,000	495,000	521,000
Balance Sheet								
Current Assets	4,081,000	4,334,000	6,433,000	7,353,000	7,967,000	8,541,000	12,345,000	18,785,000
Total Assets	12,125,000	12,365,000	26,777,000	27,128,000	25,553,000	28,804,000	32,815,000	63,722,000
Current Liabilities	2,735,000	3,097,000	4,330,000	5,268,000	4,716,000	5,657,000	9,101,000	11,066,000
Long-Term Obligations	1,481,000	1,481,000	4,146,000	3,652,000	4,029,000	3,709,000	4,076,000	9,365,000
Total Liabilities	6,999,000	7,371,000	12,595,000	13,044,000	12,612,000	13,310,000	17,191,000	28,303,000
Stockholders' Equity	5,126,000	4,994,000	14,182,000	14,084,000	12,941,000	15,494,000	15,624,000	35,419,000
Shares Outstanding	465,340	462,188	464,624	488,405	479,346	477,667	496,301	498,030
Statistical Record								
Return on Assets %	1.56	2.42	6.33	4.31	N.M.	5.05	N.M.	5.89
Return on Equity %	3.11	4.94	12.06	8.40	N.M.	10.01	N.M.	10.97
EBITDA Margin %	12.73	6.33	19.78	16.14	N.M.	14.51	N.M.	18.42
Net Margin %	6.27	4.54	9.99	6.65	N.M.	7.69	N.M.	9.06
Asset Turnover	0.46	0.53	0.63	0.65	0.64	0.66	0.39	0.65
Current Ratio	1.49	1.40	1.49	1.40	1.69	1.51	1.36	1.70
Debt to Equity	0.29	0.30	0.29	0.26	0.31	0.24	0.26	0.26
Price Range	29.48-22.88	28.47-19.29	25.71-17.88	19.92-16.37	17.87-7.69	23.29-16.57	26.45-19.94	23.92-19.11
P/E Ratio	45.35-35.19	27.91-18.91	7.10-4.94	8.59-7.06	...	7.30-5.19	...	3.32-2.65
Average Yield %	3.44	3.57	2.18	2.31	6.79	3.15	6.74	7.71

Address: Freier Platz 10, Schaffhausen, CH-8200 **Telephone:** 526-330-244	**Web Site:** www.tyco.com **Officers:** Edward D. Breen - Chairman, Chief Executive Officer George R. Oliver - Chief Executive Officer, Division Officer	**Auditors:** Deloitte & Touche LLP **Transfer Agents:** Computershare, Jersey City, NJ

TYSON FOODS, INC.

Exchange	Symbol	Price	52Wk Range	Yield	P/E
NYS	TSN	$24.82 (3/28/2013)	24.82-14.17	0.81	15.13

*7 Year Price Score 102.32 *NYSE Composite Index=100 *12 Month Price Score 115.43

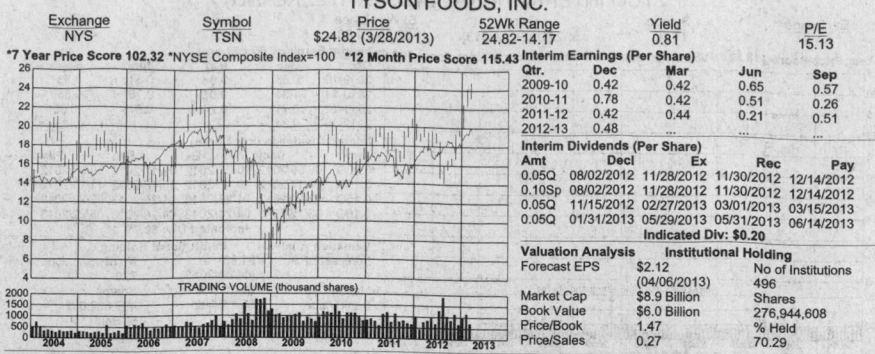

Interim Earnings (Per Share)

Qtr.	Dec	Mar	Jun	Sep
2009-10	0.42	0.42	0.65	0.57
2010-11	0.78	0.42	0.51	0.26
2011-12	0.42	0.44	0.21	0.51
2012-13	0.48	...	...	...

Interim Dividends (Per Share)

Amt	Decl	Ex	Rec	Pay
0.05Q	08/02/2012	11/28/2012	11/30/2012	12/14/2012
0.10Sp	08/02/2012	11/28/2012	11/30/2012	12/14/2012
0.05Q	11/15/2012	02/27/2013	03/01/2013	03/15/2013
0.05Q	01/31/2013	05/29/2013	05/31/2013	06/14/2013

Indicated Div: $0.20

Valuation Analysis

		Institutional Holding	
Forecast EPS	$2.12 (04/06/2013)	No of Institutions	496
Market Cap	$8.9 Billion	Shares	276,944,608
Book Value	$6.0 Billion	% Held	70.29
Price/Book	1.47		
Price/Sales	0.27		

Business Summary: Food (MIC: 1.2.1 SIC: 2015 NAIC: 311615)

Tyson Foods produces, distributes and markets chicken, beef, pork, prepared foods and related allied products. Co. operates an integrated poultry production process, consisting of breeding stock, contract growers, feed production, processing, further-processing, marketing and transportation of chicken and related allied products, including animal and pet food ingredients. Co. also processes live fed cattle and hogs and fabricate dressed beef and pork carcasses into primal and sub-primal meat cuts, case ready beef and pork and fully-cooked meats. In addition, Co. provides allied products such as hides and variety meats, as well as a range of frozen and refrigerated food products.

Recent Developments: For the quarter ended Dec 29 2012, net income increased 7.7% to US$168.0 million from US$156.0 million in the year-earlier quarter. Revenues were US$8.40 billion, up 0.9% from US$8.33 billion the year before. Operating income was US$300.0 million versus US$278.0 million in the prior-year quarter, an increase of 7.9%. Direct operating expenses rose 0.4% to US$7.87 billion from US$7.84 billion in the comparable period the year before. Indirect operating expenses increased 10.2% to US$237.0 million from US$215.0 million in the equivalent prior-year period.

Prospects: Our evaluation of Tyson Foods Inc. as of Apr. 7, 2013 is the result of our systematic analysis on three basic characteristics: earnings strength, relative valuation, and recent stock price movement. The company has produced a positive trend in earnings per share over the past 5 quarters and while recent estimates for the company have been raised by analysts, TSN has posted better than expected results. Based on operating earnings yield, the company is undervalued when compared to all of the companies in our coverage universe. Share price changes over the past year indicates that TSN will perform in line with the market over the near term.

Financial Data

(US$ in Thousands)	3 Mos	09/29/2012	10/01/2011	10/02/2010	10/03/2009	09/27/2008	09/29/2007	09/30/2006
Earnings Per Share	1.64	1.58	1.97	2.06	(1.44)	0.24	0.75	(0.58)
Cash Flow Per Share	2.93	3.28	2.81	3.85	2.71	0.82	1.95	0.83
Tang Book Value Per Share	11.25	11.12	9.77	8.24	5.98	6.30	5.96	5.05
Dividends Per Share	0.270	0.160	0.160	0.160	0.160	0.160	0.160	0.160
Dividend Payout %	16.46	10.13	8.12	7.77	...	66.67	21.33	...
Income Statement								
Total Revenue	8,402,000	33,278,000	32,266,000	28,430,000	26,704,000	26,862,000	26,900,000	25,559,000
EBITDA	430,000	1,714,000	1,738,000	1,952,000	212,000	828,000	1,116,000	426,000
Depn & Amortn	130,000	443,000	433,000	416,000	445,000	468,000	482,000	481,000
Income Before Taxes	264,000	927,000	1,074,000	1,203,000	(526,000)	154,000	410,000	(293,000)
Income Taxes	96,000	351,000	341,000	438,000	14,000	68,000	142,000	(102,000)
Net Income	173,000	583,000	750,000	780,000	(537,000)	86,000	268,000	(196,000)
Average Shares	362,000	370,000	380,000	379,000	372,000	356,000	355,000	345,000
Balance Sheet								
Current Assets	5,387,000	5,403,000	4,780,000	4,618,000	4,375,000	4,361,000	3,596,000	4,187,000
Total Assets	11,874,000	11,896,000	11,071,000	10,752,000	10,595,000	10,850,000	10,227,000	11,121,000
Current Liabilities	2,846,000	2,830,000	2,374,000	2,545,000	1,993,000	2,103,000	2,115,000	2,846,000
Long-Term Obligations	1,907,000	1,917,000	2,112,000	2,135,000	3,333,000	2,888,000	2,642,000	2,987,000
Total Liabilities	5,840,000	5,884,000	5,414,000	5,586,000	6,243,000	5,836,000	5,496,000	6,681,000
Stockholders' Equity	6,034,000	6,012,000	5,657,000	5,166,000	4,352,000	5,014,000	4,731,000	4,440,000
Shares Outstanding	357,000	359,000	370,000	377,000	376,000	377,000	356,000	355,000
Statistical Record								
Return on Assets %	5.19	5.09	6.89	7.33	N.M.	0.82	2.52	N.M.
Return on Equity %	10.16	10.02	13.90	16.44	N.M.	1.77	5.86	N.M.
EBITDA Margin %	5.12	5.15	5.39	6.87	0.79	3.08	4.15	1.67
Net Margin %	2.06	1.75	2.32	2.74	N.M.	0.32	1.00	N.M.
Asset Turnover	2.89	2.91	2.97	2.67	2.45	2.56	2.53	2.37
Current Ratio	1.89	1.91	2.01	1.81	2.20	2.07	1.70	1.47
Debt to Equity	0.32	0.32	0.37	0.41	0.77	0.58	0.56	0.67
Price Range	20.86-14.17	20.91-14.17	19.92-14.84	20.40-12.02	13.88-4.40	19.44-12.14	24.08-14.20	18.70-12.92
P/E Ratio	12.72-8.64	13.23-8.97	10.11-7.53	9.90-5.83	...	81.00-50.58	32.11-18.93	...
Average Yield %	1.51	0.87	0.91	1.00	1.55	1.02	0.84	1.04

Address: 2200 Don Tyson Parkway, Springdale, AR 72762-6999 Telephone: 479-290-4000 Fax: 479-290-7984	Web Site: www.tyson.com Officers: John Tyson - Chairman Donald J. Smith - President, Chief Executive Officer	Auditors: PricewaterhouseCoopers LLP Investor Contact: 479-290-3918 Transfer Agents: Computershare Trust Company, N.A., Providence, RI

UDR INC

	Exchange	Symbol	Price	52Wk Range	Yield	P/E
	NYS	UDR	$24.19 (3/28/2013)	27.06-22.51	3.70	28.46

*7 Year Price Score 97.61 *NYSE Composite Index=100 *12 Month Price Score 89.18

Interim Earnings (Per Share)

Qtr.	Mar	Jun	Sep	Dec
2008	5.48	(0.02)	(0.06)	(0.58)
2009	(0.10)	(0.10)	(0.27)	(0.16)
2010	(0.17)	(0.18)	(0.16)	(0.17)
2011	(0.17)	0.06	(0.07)	0.22
2012	0.37	0.62	(0.04)	(0.07)

Interim Dividends (Per Share)

Amt	Decl	Ex	Rec	Pay
0.22Q	06/18/2012	07/06/2012	07/10/2012	07/31/2012
0.22Q	09/19/2012	10/05/2012	10/10/2012	10/31/2012
0.22Q	12/12/2012	01/08/2013	01/10/2013	01/31/2013
0.235Q	03/19/2013	04/05/2013	04/09/2013	04/30/2013

Indicated Div: $0.90

Valuation Analysis		Institutional Holding	
Forecast EPS	$0.00	No of Institutions	
	(04/05/2013)	374	
Market Cap	$6.1 Billion	Shares	
Book Value	$3.2 Billion	244,709,360	
Price/Book	1.88	% Held	
Price/Sales	8.30	N/A	

Business Summary: REITs (MIC: 5.3.1 SIC: 6798 NAIC: 525930)

UDR is a real estate investment trust that owns, operates, acquires, renovates, develops, redevelops, and manages multifamily apartment communities in certain markets throughout the U.S. As of Dec 31 2011, Co.'s consolidated apartment portfolio included 163 communities located in 22 markets, with a total of 47,343 completed apartment homes, which are held through its operating partnerships, including United Dominion Realty, L.P., its subsidiaries and consolidated joint ventures. Co. also has an ownership interest in 39 communities containing 10,496 completed apartment homes through unconsolidated joint ventures. Co. reports in two segments: Same Communities and Non-Mature/Other Communities.

Recent Developments: For the year ended Dec 31 2012, loss from continuing operations was US$43.0 million compared with a loss of US$123.2 million a year earlier. Net income increased 970.2% to US$220.3 million from US$20.6 million in the prior year. Revenues were US$729.4 million, up 13.9% from US$640.4 million the year before. Revenues from property income rose 14.6% to US$713.9 million from US$623.0 million in the corresponding earlier year.

Prospects: Our evaluation of UDR Inc. as of Apr. 7, 2013 is the result of our systematic analysis on three basic characteristics: earnings strength, relative valuation, and recent stock price movement. The company has enjoyed a very positive trend in earnings per share over the past 5 quarters. Because the company lacks sufficient analyst estimate data, we place greater weight on the historical EPS trend as the measure of earnings strength. Based on operating earnings yield, the company is overvalued when compared to all of the companies in our coverage universe. Share price changes over the past year indicates that UDR will perform poorly over the near term.

Financial Data

(US$ in Thousands)	12/31/2012	12/31/2011	12/31/2010	12/31/2009	12/31/2008	12/31/2007	12/31/2006	12/31/2005
Earnings Per Share	0.85	0.05	(0.68)	(0.64)	4.95	1.53	0.85	1.02
Cash Flow Per Share	1.32	1.21	1.29	1.54	1.27	1.87	1.72	1.82
Tang Book Value Per Share	12.67	11.03	8.73	8.76	9.50	6.28	6.47	6.91
Dividends Per Share	0.875	0.770	0.725	0.665	2.610	1.303	1.238	1.192
Dividend Payout %	102.94	1,540.00	...	...	52.73	85.13	145.59	116.91
Income Statement								
Total Revenue	729,363	708,685	646,596	617,173	590,598	500,194	698,058	701,217
EBITDA	463,437	591,975	525,466	516,137	376,350	348,956	405,256	387,103
Depn & Amortn	367,404	393,862	332,187	303,393	271,636	274,875	252,997	206,005
Income Before Taxes	(43,036)	46,969	47,217	71,364	(53,988)	(100,596)	(30,026)	18,590
Net Income	212,177	20,023	(102,899)	(87,532)	706,929	221,349	128,605	155,166
Average Shares	238,851	201,294	165,857	149,090	140,982	134,016	133,732	137,013
Balance Sheet								
Current Assets	35,676	37,137	28,799	52,514	20,466	9,514	7,745	20,126
Total Assets	6,888,509	6,721,354	5,529,540	5,132,617	5,144,295	4,801,121	4,675,875	4,541,593
Current Liabilities	261,926	247,725	232,949	208,288	220,992	188,058	186,967	178,479
Long-Term Obligations	3,409,333	3,918,370	3,567,504	3,426,589	3,274,047	3,502,676	3,338,785	3,159,777
Total Liabilities	3,672,175	4,170,829	3,804,140	3,638,418	3,573,618	3,781,728	3,620,620	3,433,869
Stockholders' Equity	3,216,334	2,550,525	1,725,400	1,494,199	1,570,677	1,019,393	1,055,255	1,107,724
Shares Outstanding	250,139	219,650	182,496	155,465	148,781	133,317	135,029	134,012
Statistical Record								
Return on Assets %	3.11	0.33	N.M.	N.M.	14.18	4.67	2.79	3.50
Return on Equity %	7.34	0.94	N.M.	N.M.	54.44	21.34	11.89	13.47
EBITDA Margin %	63.54	83.53	81.27	83.63	63.72	69.76	58.05	55.20
Net Margin %	29.09	2.83	N.M.	N.M.	119.70	44.25	18.42	22.13
Asset Turnover	0.11	0.12	0.12	0.12	0.12	0.11	0.15	0.16
Current Ratio	0.14	0.15	0.12	0.25	0.09	0.05	0.04	0.11
Debt to Equity	1.06	1.54	2.07	2.29	2.08	3.44	3.16	2.85
Price Range	27.06-22.51	27.14-20.77	24.05-14.70	16.98-7.10	28.00-10.81	33.95-19.64	33.66-23.93	25.85-20.64
P/E Ratio	31.84-26.48	542.80-415.40	...	...	5.66-2.18	22.19-12.84	39.60-28.15	25.34-20.24
Average Yield %	3.47	3.17	3.65	5.58	11.91	4.82	4.33	5.21

Address: 1745 Shea Center Drive, Suite 200, Highlands Ranch, CO 80129 Telephone: 720-283-6120	Web Site: www.udrt.com Officers: Robert C. Larson - Chairman James D. Klingbeil - Vice-Chairman	Auditors: Ernst & Young LLP Investor Contact: 720-348-7762 Transfer Agents: Wells Fargo Shareowner Services, South St. Paul, MN

UGI CORP.

Exchange	Symbol	Price	52Wk Range	Yield	P/E	Div Achiever
NYS	UGI	$38.39 (3/28/2013)	38.39-26.40	2.81	20.31	25 Years

*7 Year Price Score 102.57 *NYSE Composite Index=100 ***12 Month Price Score 105.43**

Interim Earnings (Per Share)

Qtr.	Dec	Mar	Jun	Sep
2009-10	0.90	1.43	0.03	0.01
2010-11	1.01	1.32	(0.06)	(0.20)
2011-12	0.77	1.18	(0.06)	(0.13)
2012-13	0.90	...	...	...

Interim Dividends (Per Share)

Amt	Decl	Ex	Rec	Pay
0.27Q	04/24/2012	06/13/2012	06/15/2012	07/01/2012
0.27Q	07/31/2012	09/12/2012	09/14/2012	10/01/2012
0.27Q	11/16/2012	12/12/2012	12/14/2012	01/01/2013
0.27Q	01/24/2013	03/13/2013	03/15/2013	04/01/2013

Indicated Div: $1.08 (Div. Reinv. Plan)

Valuation Analysis / Institutional Holding

Forecast EPS	$2.44	No of Institutions	361
	(04/05/2013)		
Market Cap	$4.3 Billion	Shares	95,602,728
Book Value	$2.3 Billion	% Held	74.82
Price/Book	1.86		
Price/Sales	0.63		

Business Summary: Gas Utilities (MIC: 3.3.1 SIC: 4932 NAIC: 221210)

UGI is a holding company. Through its subsidiaries, Co. provides energy products and related services. Co. is a distributor of propane and butane (which are liquefied petroleum gases); a provider of natural gas and electric service through regulated local distribution utilities; a generator of electricity; a marketer of energy commodities; an owner and manager of midstream assets; and a provider of heating, ventilation, air conditioning, refrigeration and electrical contracting services. Co.'s subsidiaries and affiliates operate in six segments: AmeriGas Propane, International Propane - Antargaz, International Propane - Flaga and Other, Energy Services, Electric Generation, and Gas Utility.

Recent Developments: For the quarter ended Dec 31 2012, net income increased 55.0% to US$170.7 million from US$110.1 million in the year-earlier quarter. Revenues were US$2.02 billion, up 19.8% from US$1.69 billion the year before. Operating income was US$296.1 million versus US$188.3 million in the prior-year quarter, an increase of 57.2%. Direct operating expenses rose 10.6% to US$1.22 billion from US$1.10 billion in the comparable period the year before. Indirect operating expenses increased 27.5% to US$508.3 million from US$398.7 million in the equivalent prior-year period.

Prospects: Our evaluation of UGI Corp. as of Apr. 7, 2013 is the result of our systematic analysis on three basic characteristics: earnings strength, relative valuation, and recent stock price movement. The company has enjoyed a very positive trend in earnings per share over the past 5 quarters. However, while recent estimates for the company have been mixed, UGI has posted results that fell short of analysts expectations. Based on operating earnings yield, the company is undervalued when compared to all of the companies in our coverage universe. Share price changes over the past year indicates that UGI will perform in line with the market over the near term.

Financial Data

(US$ in Thousands)	3 Mos	09/30/2012	09/30/2011	09/30/2010	09/30/2009	09/30/2008	09/30/2007	09/30/2006
Earnings Per Share	1.89	1.76	2.06	2.36	2.36	1.99	1.89	1.65
Cash Flow Per Share	6.73	6.27	4.97	5.46	6.13	4.31	4.29	2.65
Tang Book Value Per Share	N.M.	N.M.	2.39	1.01	N.M.	N.M.	N.M.	N.M.
Dividends Per Share	1.070	1.060	1.020	0.900	0.785	0.755	0.723	0.690
Dividend Payout %	56.61	60.23	49.51	38.14	33.26	37.94	38.23	41.82
Income Statement								
Total Revenue	2,023,200	6,519,200	6,091,300	5,591,400	5,737,800	6,648,200	5,476,900	5,221,000
EBITDA	372,200	769,800	776,800	843,900	860,500	756,200	737,300	580,800
Depn & Amortn	71,800	264,200	201,200	187,600	180,200	182,600	167,500	147,400
Income Before Taxes	240,100	286,500	439,900	525,400	544,200	442,700	441,700	325,600
Income Taxes	69,400	99,600	130,800	167,600	159,100	134,500	126,700	98,500
Net Income	102,600	199,400	232,900	261,000	258,500	215,500	204,300	176,200
Average Shares	114,490	113,432	112,944	110,511	109,339	108,521	107,941	106,727
Balance Sheet								
Current Assets	1,919,700	1,504,500	1,306,100	1,220,100	1,185,100	1,338,600	1,173,600	1,040,600
Total Assets	10,167,500	9,709,700	6,663,300	6,374,300	6,042,600	5,685,000	5,502,700	5,080,500
Current Liabilities	1,783,200	1,487,000	1,077,900	1,674,700	1,097,300	1,184,200	1,057,500	1,026,600
Long-Term Obligations	3,358,400	3,347,600	2,110,300	1,432,200	2,038,600	1,987,300	2,038,800	1,965,000
Total Liabilities	7,832,500	7,476,600	4,685,600	4,549,800	4,451,200	4,267,300	4,180,800	3,980,900
Stockholders' Equity	2,335,000	2,233,100	1,977,700	1,824,500	1,591,400	1,417,700	1,321,900	1,099,600
Shares Outstanding	113,177	112,620	111,836	110,373	108,746	107,860	106,646	105,454
Statistical Record								
Return on Assets %	2.48	2.43	3.57	4.20	4.41	3.84	3.86	3.65
Return on Equity %	9.93	9.45	12.25	15.28	17.18	15.69	16.87	16.80
EBITDA Margin %	18.40	11.81	12.75	15.09	15.00	11.37	13.46	11.12
Net Margin %	5.07	3.06	3.82	4.67	4.51	3.24	3.73	3.37
Asset Turnover	0.79	0.79	0.93	0.90	0.98	1.19	1.04	1.08
Current Ratio	1.08	1.01	1.21	0.73	1.08	1.13	1.11	1.01
Debt to Equity	1.44	1.50	1.07	0.78	1.28	1.40	1.54	1.79
Price Range	33.36-26.40	31.75-24.89	33.30-25.93	28.79-23.36	27.23-19.93	28.71-24.67	29.30-23.78	28.15-20.46
P/E Ratio	17.65-13.97	18.04-14.14	16.17-12.59	12.20-9.90	11.54-8.44	14.43-12.40	15.50-12.58	17.06-12.40
Average Yield %	3.58	3.67	3.30	3.48	3.23	2.86	2.70	2.99

Address: 460 North Gulph Road, King of Prussia, PA 19406
Telephone: 610-337-1000

Web Site: www.ugicorp.com
Officers: John L. Walsh - President, Chief Executive Officer, Chief Operating Officer Davinder S. Athwal - Vice President, Chief Risk Officer

Auditors: PricewaterhouseCoopers LLP
Investor Contact: 610-337-1000ext.32
Transfer Agents: ComputerShare Investor Services, Providence, RI

ULTRA PETROLEUM CORP.

Exchange	Symbol	Price	52Wk Range	Yield	P/E
NYS	UPL	$20.10 (3/28/2013)	24.07-16.00	N/A	N/A

*7 Year Price Score 39.00   *NYSE Composite Index=100   *12 Month Price Score 80.29

TRADING VOLUME (thousand shares)

Interim Earnings (Per Share)

Qtr.	Mar	Jun	Sep	Dec
2008	0.64	0.73	0.95	0.43
2009	(3.39)	(0.17)	(0.06)	0.63
2010	1.31	0.40	1.05	0.24
2011	0.44	0.67	0.97	0.86
2012	0.55	(7.76)	(3.94)	(3.08)

Interim Dividends (Per Share)

No Dividends Paid

Valuation Analysis

		Institutional Holding	
Forecast EPS	$1.24	No of Institutions	
	(04/06/2013)	420	
Market Cap	$3.1 Billion	Shares	
Book Value	N/A	134,932,224	
Price/Book	N/A	% Held	
Price/Sales	3.80	84.56	

Business Summary: Production & Extraction (MIC: 9.1.1 SIC: 1311 NAIC: 211111)

Ultra Petroleum is an independent oil and gas company engaged in the development, production, operation, exploration and acquisition of oil and natural gas properties. Co.'s operations are primarily located in the Green River Basin of southwest Wyoming and the north-central Pennsylvania area of the Appalachian Basin. Co. also has acreage in eastern Colorado's Denver Julesburg Basin. As of Dec 31 2011, Co. had total proved reserves of 4.97 trillion cubic feet of natural gas equivalent. As of Dec 31 2011, proved undeveloped reserves represent 58.9% of Co.'s total proved reserves.

Recent Developments: For the year ended Dec 31 2012, net loss amounted to US$2.18 billion versus net income of US$453.2 million in the prior year. Revenues were US$810.0 million, down 26.5% from US$1.10 billion the year before. Operating loss was US$2.85 billion versus an income of US$459.8 million in the prior year. Indirect operating expenses increased 469.3% to US$3.66 billion from US$642.0 million in the equivalent prior-year period.

Prospects: Our evaluation of Ultra Petroleum Corp. as of Apr. 7, 2013 is the result of our systematic analysis on three basic characteristics: earnings strength, relative valuation, and recent stock price movement. The company has produced a positive trend in earnings per share over the past 5 quarters and while recent estimates for the company have been raised by analysts, UPL has posted results that fell short of analysts expectations. Based on operating earnings yield, the company is undervalued when compared to all of the companies in our coverage universe. Share price changes over the past year indicates that UPL will perform very poorly over the near term.

Financial Data

(US$ in Thousands)	12/31/2012	12/31/2011	12/31/2010	12/31/2009	12/31/2008	12/31/2007	12/31/2006
Earnings Per Share	(14.24)	2.94	3.01	(2.98)	2.65	1.66	1.43
Cash Flow Per Share	4.27	6.76	5.41	3.92	5.51	2.83	2.83
Tang Book Value Per Share	...	10.45	7.47	4.27	7.21	5.62	4.14
Income Statement							
Total Revenue	809,974	1,101,796	979,386	666,762	1,084,400	566,638	508,659
EBITDA	(2,399,946)	1,120,422	1,013,902	(457,196)	860,435	439,093	403,027
Depn & Amortn	388,985	346,394	241,796	201,826	184,795	135,470	79,675
Income Before Taxes	(2,877,111)	710,872	723,074	(696,189)	654,364	285,863	319,443
Income Taxes	(700,213)	257,670	258,615	(245,136)	240,504	105,621	122,741
Net Income	(2,176,898)	453,202	464,459	(451,053)	414,275	263,036	231,195
Average Shares	152,845	154,336	154,253	151,367	156,531	158,616	161,615
Balance Sheet							
Current Assets	125,848	419,920	361,049	153,741	198,218	168,453	241,260
Total Assets	2,007,345	4,869,705	3,595,615	2,060,005	2,558,162	1,776,200	1,258,299
Current Liabilities	514,092	670,979	418,016	291,191	347,573	239,925	186,224
Long-Term Obligations	1,837,000	1,903,000	1,560,000	795,000	570,000	290,000	165,000
Total Liabilities	2,585,212	3,275,996	2,456,639	1,411,808	1,467,376	922,621	629,294
Stockholders' Equity	(577,867)	1,593,709	1,138,976	648,197	1,090,786	853,579	629,005
Shares Outstanding	152,929	152,476	152,567	151,759	151,232	152,003	151,795
Statistical Record							
Return on Assets %	N.M.	10.71	16.42	N.M.	19.06	17.34	...
Return on Equity %	N.M.	33.17	51.98	N.M.	42.50	35.48	...
EBITDA Margin %	N.M.	101.69	103.52	N.M.	79.35	77.49	79.23
Net Margin %	N.M.	41.13	47.42	N.M.	38.20	46.42	45.45
Asset Turnover	0.23	0.26	0.35	0.29	0.50	0.37	...
Current Ratio	0.24	0.63	0.86	0.53	0.57	0.70	1.30
Debt to Equity	...	1.19	1.37	1.23	0.52	0.34	0.26
Price Range	30.45-17.88	50.79-25.70	53.28-38.33	56.31-31.12	99.69-31.18	71.94-45.10	69.60-44.00
P/E Ratio	...	17.28-8.74	17.70-12.73	...	37.62-11.77	43.34-27.17	48.67-30.77

Address: 400 North Sam Houston Parkway E., Suite 1200, Houston, TX 77060	**Web Site:** www.ultrapetroleum.com	**Auditors:** Ernst & Young LLP
Telephone: 281-876-0120	**Officers:** Michael D. Watford - Chairman, President, Chief Executive Officer William R. Picquet - Vice President	**Investor Contact:** 281-582-6602
Fax: 281-876-2831		**Transfer Agents:** Computershare Investor Services L.L.C., Denver, CO

UNDER ARMOUR INC

Exchange	Symbol	Price	52Wk Range	Yield	P/E
NYS	UA	$51.20 (3/28/2013)	60.03-44.50	N/A	42.31

*7 Year Price Score 172.00   *NYSE Composite Index=100   *12 Month Price Score 88.63

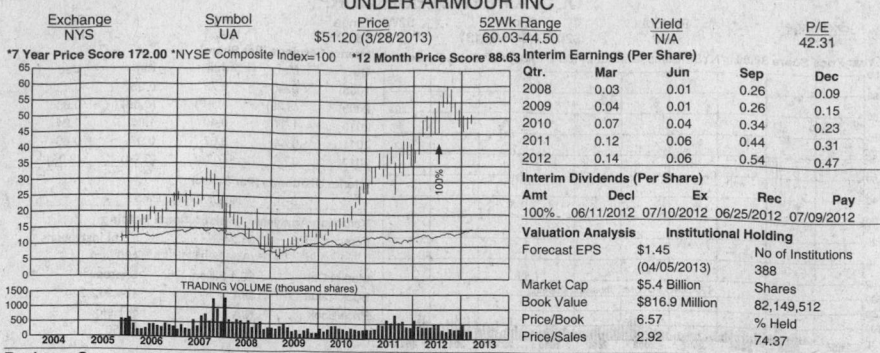

Interim Earnings (Per Share)

Qtr.	Mar	Jun	Sep	Dec
2008	0.03	0.01	0.26	0.09
2009	0.04	0.01	0.26	0.15
2010	0.07	0.04	0.34	0.23
2011	0.12	0.06	0.44	0.31
2012	0.14	0.06	0.54	0.47

Interim Dividends (Per Share)

Amt	Decl	Ex	Rec	Pay
100%.	06/11/2012	07/10/2012	06/25/2012	07/09/2012

Valuation Analysis   Institutional Holding

Forecast EPS	$1.45	No of Institutions	
	(04/05/2013)	388	
Market Cap	$5.4 Billion	Shares	
Book Value	$816.9 Million	82,149,512	
Price/Book	6.57	% Held	
Price/Sales	2.92	74.37	

Business Summary: Apparel, Footwear & Accessories (MIC: 1.4.2 SIC: 5136 NAIC: 448110)

Under Armour is engaged in the development, marketing and distribution of branded performance apparel, footwear and accessories for men, women and youth. Co.'s registered trademarks include UNDER ARMOUR®, HEATGEAR®, COLDGEAR®, ALLSEASONGEAR® and the Under Armour UA Logo. Co.'s apparel offers a variety of styles and fits intended to enhance comfort and mobility, regulate body temperature and improve performance regardless of weather conditions. Co.'s footwear offerings include football, baseball, lacrosse, softball and soccer cleats, slides, performance training footwear, running footwear, basketball footwear and hunting boots. Co.'s accessories include the sale of headwear, bags and gloves.

Recent Developments: For the year ended Dec 31 2012, net income increased 32.9% to US$128.8 million from US$96.9 million in the prior year. Revenues were US$1.83 billion, up 24.6% from US$1.47 billion the year before. Operating income was US$208.7 million versus US$162.8 million in the prior year, an increase of 28.2%. Direct operating expenses rose 25.8% to US$955.6 million from US$759.8 million in the comparable period the year before. Indirect operating expenses increased 21.9% to US$670.6 million from US$550.1 million in the equivalent prior-year period.

Prospects: Our evaluation of Under Armour Inc. as of Apr. 7, 2013 is the result of our systematic analysis on three basic characteristics: earnings strength, relative valuation, and recent stock price movement. The company has generated a negative trend in earnings per share over the past 5 quarters and while recent estimates for the company have been mixed, UA has posted better than expected results. Based on operating earnings yield, the company is overvalued when compared to all of the companies in our coverage universe. Share price changes over the past year indicates that UA will perform poorly over the near term.

Financial Data
(US$ in Thousands)

	12/31/2012	12/31/2011	12/31/2010	12/31/2009	12/31/2008	12/31/2007	12/31/2006	12/31/2005
Earnings Per Share	1.21	0.93	0.67	0.46	0.39	0.53	0.40	0.18
Cash Flow Per Share	1.91	0.15	0.49	1.19	0.71	(0.15)	0.11	0.21
Tang Book Value Per Share	7.76	6.10	4.82	3.92	3.30	2.81	2.16	1.62
Income Statement								
Total Revenue	1,834,921	1,472,684	1,063,927	856,411	725,244	606,561	430,689	281,053
EBITDA	248,422	193,403	139,877	110,062	90,350	101,194	68,108	42,113
Depn & Amortn	39,800	32,700	28,700	25,300	19,600	12,900	9,021	6,224
Income Before Taxes	203,439	156,862	108,919	82,418	69,900	89,043	59,087	32,974
Income Taxes	74,661	59,943	40,442	35,633	31,671	36,485	20,108	13,255
Net Income	128,778	96,919	68,477	46,785	38,229	52,558	38,979	19,719
Average Shares	106,380	105,052	102,564	101,300	99,780	99,918	99,174	79,372
Balance Sheet								
Current Assets	903,598	689,663	555,850	448,000	396,423	322,245	244,952	181,790
Total Assets	1,157,083	919,210	675,378	545,588	487,555	390,613	289,368	203,687
Current Liabilities	252,228	183,607	149,147	120,162	133,110	95,699	71,563	47,672
Long-Term Obligations	52,757	70,842	9,077	10,948	13,158	9,756	2,815	4,583
Total Liabilities	340,161	282,778	178,412	145,591	156,458	110,128	74,980	52,857
Stockholders' Equity	816,922	636,432	496,966	399,997	331,097	280,485	214,388	150,830
Shares Outstanding	104,761	103,492	102,320	100,495	98,617	97,379	95,611	92,846
Statistical Record								
Return on Assets %	12.37	12.16	11.22	9.06	8.68	15.46	15.81	12.53
Return on Equity %	17.67	17.10	15.27	12.80	12.47	21.24	21.35	22.06
EBITDA Margin %	13.54	13.13	13.15	12.85	12.46	16.68	15.81	14.98
Net Margin %	7.02	6.58	6.44	5.46	5.27	8.66	9.05	7.02
Asset Turnover	1.76	1.85	1.74	1.66	1.65	1.78	1.75	1.79
Current Ratio	3.58	3.76	3.73	3.73	2.98	3.37	3.42	3.81
Debt to Equity	0.06	0.11	0.02	0.03	0.04	0.03	0.01	0.03
Price Range	60.03-36.09	43.00-26.39	30.00-11.97	16.55-6.17	22.87-8.78	33.55-21.16	25.68-13.28	19.93-10.68
P/E Ratio	49.61-29.83	46.24-28.38	44.78-17.87	35.97-13.40	58.64-22.50	63.30-39.93	64.19-33.19	110.72-59.31

Address: 1020 Hull Street, Baltimore, MD 21230
Telephone: 410-454-6428

Web Site: www.underarmour.com
Officers: Kevin A. Plank - Chairman, President, Chief Executive Officer William J. Kraus - Senior Vice President

Auditors: PricewaterhouseCoopers LLP
Transfer Agents: American Stock Transfer & Trust Company, New York, NY

UNION PACIFIC CORP

Exchange	Symbol	Price	52Wk Range	Yield	P/E
NYS	UNP	$142.41 (3/28/2013)	142.41-104.98	1.94	17.22

*7 Year Price Score 142.38 *NYSE Composite Index=100 *12 Month Price Score 102.85

Interim Earnings (Per Share)

Qtr.	Mar	Jun	Sep	Dec
2008	0.85	1.02	1.38	1.30
2009	0.72	0.92	1.02	1.08
2010	1.01	1.40	1.56	1.55
2011	1.29	1.59	1.85	1.98
2012	1.79	2.10	2.19	2.19

Interim Dividends (Per Share)

Amt	Decl	Ex	Rec	Pay
0.60Q	05/10/2012	05/29/2012	05/31/2012	07/02/2012
0.60Q	07/26/2012	08/29/2012	08/31/2012	10/01/2012
0.69Q	11/15/2012	11/28/2012	11/30/2012	01/02/2013
0.69Q	02/07/2012	02/26/2013	02/28/2013	04/01/2013

Indicated Div: $2.76

Valuation Analysis

		Institutional Holding	
Forecast EPS	$9.44	No of Institutions	
	(04/06/2013)	1333	
Market Cap	$66.9 Billion	Shares	
Book Value	$19.9 Billion	405,232,768	
Price/Book	3.36	% Held	
Price/Sales	3.19	79.85	

Business Summary: Rail (MIC: 7.4.3 SIC: 4011 NAIC: 482111)

Union Pacific, through its operating subsidiary, Union Pacific Railroad Co., is a railroad operator. As of Dec 31 2012, Co.'s network included 31,868 route miles, linking Pacific Coast and Gulf Coast ports with the Midwest and eastern U.S. gateways and providing several corridors to key Mexican gateways. Co. serves the western two-thirds of the country and maintains coordinated schedules with other rail carriers for the handling of freight to and from the Atlantic Coast, the Pacific Coast, the Southeast, the Southwest, Canada, and Mexico. Co. transports freight or other materials from its agricultural, automotive, chemicals, coal, industrial products, and intermodal commodity groups.

Recent Developments: For the year ended Dec 31 2012, net income increased 19.8% to US$3.94 billion from US$3.29 billion in the prior year. Revenues were US$20.93 billion, up 7.0% from US$19.56 billion the year before. Operating income was US$6.75 billion versus US$5.72 billion in the prior year, an increase of 17.8%. Direct operating expenses rose 2.9% to US$6.95 billion from US$6.75 billion in the comparable period the year before. Indirect operating expenses increased 2.2% to US$7.23 billion from US$7.08 billion in the equivalent prior-year period.

Prospects: Our evaluation of Union Pacific Corp. as of Apr. 7, 2013 is the result of our systematic analysis on three basic characteristics: earnings strength, relative valuation, and recent stock price movement. The company has managed to produce a neutral trend in earnings per share over the past 5 quarters. However, while recent estimates for the company have been mixed, UNP has posted better than expected results. Based on operating earnings yield, the company is undervalued when compared to all of the companies in our coverage universe. Share price changes over the past year indicates that UNP will perform well over the near term.

Financial Data
(US$ in Thousands)	12/31/2012	12/31/2011	12/31/2010	12/31/2009	12/31/2008	12/31/2007	12/31/2006	12/31/2005
Earnings Per Share	8.27	6.72	5.53	3.75	4.54	3.46	2.96	1.93
Cash Flow Per Share	12.99	12.09	8.24	6.43	7.95	6.16	5.35	4.93
Tang Book Value Per Share	42.34	38.71	36.14	33.54	30.70	29.87	28.34	25.70
Dividends Per Share	2.490	1.930	1.310	1.080	0.980	0.745	0.600	0.600
Dividend Payout %	30.11	28.72	23.69	28.80	21.59	21.56	20.30	31.17
Income Statement								
Total Revenue	20,926,000	19,557,000	16,965,000	14,143,000	17,970,000	16,283,000	15,578,000	13,578,000
EBITDA	8,610,000	7,450,000	6,518,000	5,026,000	5,533,000	4,762,000	4,210,000	3,098,000
Depn & Amortn	1,760,000	1,617,000	1,487,000	1,444,000	1,387,000	1,321,000	1,237,000	1,175,000
Income Before Taxes	6,318,000	5,264,000	4,433,000	2,987,000	3,656,000	3,009,000	2,525,000	1,436,000
Income Taxes	2,375,000	1,972,000	1,653,000	1,089,000	1,318,000	1,154,000	919,000	410,000
Net Income	3,943,000	3,292,000	2,780,000	1,898,000	2,338,000	1,855,000	1,606,000	1,026,000
Average Shares	476,500	489,800	502,900	505,800	515,000	536,800	544,000	533,000
Balance Sheet								
Current Assets	3,614,000	3,727,000	3,432,000	3,680,000	2,813,000	2,594,000	2,411,000	2,325,000
Total Assets	47,153,000	45,096,000	43,088,000	42,410,000	39,722,000	38,033,000	36,515,000	35,620,000
Current Liabilities	3,119,000	3,317,000	2,952,000	2,682,000	2,880,000	3,041,000	3,539,000	3,384,000
Long-Term Obligations	8,801,000	8,697,000	9,003,000	9,636,000	8,607,000	7,543,000	6,000,000	6,760,000
Total Liabilities	27,276,000	26,518,000	25,325,000	25,469,000	24,275,000	22,448,000	21,203,000	21,913,000
Stockholders' Equity	19,877,000	18,578,000	17,763,000	16,941,000	15,447,000	15,585,000	15,312,000	13,707,000
Shares Outstanding	469,465	479,929	491,565	505,039	503,225	521,739	540,344	533,269
Statistical Record								
Return on Assets %	8.53	7.47	6.50	4.62	6.00	4.98	4.45	2.92
Return on Equity %	20.45	18.12	16.02	11.72	15.03	12.01	11.07	7.78
EBITDA Margin %	41.14	38.09	38.42	35.54	30.79	29.25	27.03	22.82
Net Margin %	18.84	16.83	16.39	13.42	13.01	11.39	10.31	7.56
Asset Turnover	0.45	0.44	0.40	0.34	0.46	0.44	0.43	0.39
Current Ratio	1.16	1.12	1.16	1.37	0.98	0.85	0.68	0.69
Debt to Equity	0.44	0.47	0.51	0.57	0.56	0.48	0.39	0.49
Price Range	128.43-104.98	106.76-79.83	94.55-60.50	66.23-33.62	83.90-42.81	67.63-45.06	48.60-39.29	40.50-29.31
P/E Ratio	15.53-12.69	15.89-11.88	17.10-10.94	17.66-8.97	18.48-9.43	19.55-13.02	16.42-13.27	20.98-15.18
Average Yield %	2.13	1.99	1.71	2.03	1.48	1.31	1.35	1.77

Address: 1400 Douglas Street, Omaha, NE 68179	**Web Site:** www.up.com	**Auditors:** Deloitte & Touche LLP
	Officers: James R. Young - Chairman, President, Chief Executive Officer John J. Koraleski - Acting President, Acting Chief Executive Officer	**Investor Contact:** 187-754-77261
Telephone: 402-544-5000		**Transfer Agents:** Computershare Investor Services, LLC, Providence, RI

UNISYS CORP.

Exchange	Symbol	Price	52Wk Range	Yield	P/E
NYS	UIS	$22.75 (3/28/2013)	24.43-14.50	N/A	8.01

*7 Year Price Score 47.39   *NYSE Composite Index=100   *12 Month Price Score 112.01

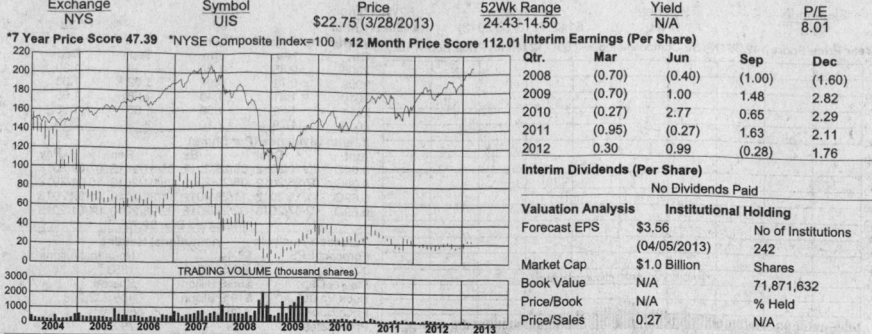

Interim Earnings (Per Share)

Qtr.	Mar	Jun	Sep	Dec
2008	(0.70)	(0.40)	(1.00)	(1.60)
2009	(0.70)	1.00	1.48	2.82
2010	(0.27)	2.77	0.65	2.29
2011	(0.95)	(0.27)	1.63	2.11
2012	0.30	0.99	(0.28)	1.76

Interim Dividends (Per Share)

No Dividends Paid

Valuation Analysis		Institutional Holding	
Forecast EPS	$3.56 (04/05/2013)	No of Institutions	242
Market Cap	$1.0 Billion	Shares	71,871,632
Book Value	N/A	% Held	N/A
Price/Book	N/A		
Price/Sales	0.27		

Business Summary: IT Services (MIC: 6.3.1 SIC: 7373 NAIC: 541512)

Unisys is an information technology (IT) company. Co. provides a portfolio of IT services, software, and technology for its clients. As of Dec 31 2011, Co. operated in two business segments, Services and Technology. In the Services segment, Co. provides services including outsourcing, systems integration and consulting, infrastructure services and core maintenance. In the Technology segment, Co. designs and develops servers and related products including the ClearPath family of servers and the ES7000 family of Intel-based servers, as well as operating system software and middleware. Co. serves commercial organizations and government agencies throughout the world.

Recent Developments: For the year ended Dec 31 2012, income from continuing operations increased 11.0% to US$156.8 million from US$141.2 million a year earlier. Net income increased 11.0% to US$156.8 million from US$141.2 million in the prior year. Revenues were US$3.71 billion, down 3.8% from US$3.85 billion the year before. Operating income was US$319.2 million versus US$324.6 million in the prior year, a decrease of 1.7%. Direct operating expenses declined 4.7% to US$2.73 billion from US$2.87 billion in the comparable period the year before. Indirect operating expenses decreased 1.2% to US$654.3 million from US$662.4 million in the equivalent prior-year period.

Prospects: Our evaluation of Unisys Corp. as of Apr. 7, 2013 is the result of our systematic analysis on three basic characteristics: earnings strength, relative valuation, and recent stock price movement. The company has generated a negative trend in earnings per share over the past 5 quarters. However, while recent estimates for the company have been mixed, UIS has posted better than expected results. Based on operating earnings yield, the company is undervalued when compared to all of the companies in our coverage universe. Share price changes over the past year indicates that UIS will perform well over the near term.

Financial Data
(US$ in Thousands)

	12/31/2012	12/31/2011	12/31/2010	12/31/2009	12/31/2008	12/31/2007	12/31/2006	12/31/2005
Earnings Per Share	2.84	2.71	5.45	4.75	(3.60)	(2.30)	(8.10)	(50.90)
Cash Flow Per Share	5.94	7.35	7.91	10.11	7.06	4.95	0.83	8.29
Income Statement								
Total Revenue	3,706,400	3,853,800	4,019,600	4,597,700	5,233,200	5,652,500	5,757,200	5,758,700
EBITDA	518,200	529,600	638,200	786,900	575,800	581,900	347,700	18,500
Depn & Amortn	236,600	260,500	313,500	457,100	567,700	502,100	521,400	124,700
Income Before Taxes	254,100	206,000	222,900	234,600	(77,000)	3,500	(250,900)	(170,900)
Income Taxes	97,300	64,800	58,500	41,600	53,100	82,600	27,800	1,561,000
Net Income	129,400	120,500	236,100	189,300	(130,100)	(79,100)	(278,700)	(1,731,900)
Average Shares	51,216	49,478	43,333	39,834	35,977	34,966	34,374	34,021
Balance Sheet								
Current Assets	1,512,400	1,603,400	1,875,400	1,703,400	1,638,400	2,212,200	2,238,500	2,153,300
Total Assets	2,420,400	2,612,200	3,020,900	2,956,900	2,824,100	4,137,100	4,037,900	4,028,900
Current Liabilities	1,030,300	1,116,100	1,336,700	1,394,800	1,426,400	1,896,000	1,931,700	1,814,800
Long-Term Obligations	210,000	358,800	823,200	845,900	1,059,100	1,058,300	1,049,100	1,049,000
Total Liabilities	4,020,600	3,930,300	3,958,200	4,225,200	4,278,400	3,770,500	4,102,100	4,061,500
Stockholders' Equity	(1,600,200)	(1,318,100)	(937,300)	(1,268,300)	(1,454,300)	366,600	(64,200)	(32,600)
Shares Outstanding	43,980	43,442	42,648	42,286	36,988	35,340	34,525	34,196
Statistical Record								
Return on Assets %	5.13	4.28	7.90	6.55	N.M.	N.M.	N.M.	N.M.
EBITDA Margin %	13.98	13.74	15.88	17.12	11.00	10.29	6.04	0.32
Net Margin %	3.49	3.13	5.87	4.12	N.M.	N.M.	N.M.	N.M.
Asset Turnover	1.47	1.37	1.34	1.59	1.50	1.38	1.43	1.19
Current Ratio	1.47	1.44	1.40	1.22	1.15	1.17	1.16	1.19
Debt to Equity	...	...	...	...	...	2.89	...	...
Price Range	22.71-14.50	41.02-14.28	39.96-17.10	39.87-3.30	50.60-3.80	96.00-44.70	78.40-47.70	101.80-45.00
P/E Ratio	8.00-5.11	15.14-5.27	7.33-3.14	8.39-0.69	...	...	...	...

Address: 801 Lakeview Drive, Suite 100, Blue Bell, PA 19422
Telephone: 215-986-4011

Web Site: www.unisys.com
Officers: J. Edward Coleman - Chairman, Chief Executive Officer Ronald S. Frankenfield - Senior Vice President, Division Officer

Auditors: KPMG LLP
Investor Contact: 215-986-6999
Transfer Agents: Computershare, Providence, R.I.

UNIT CORP.

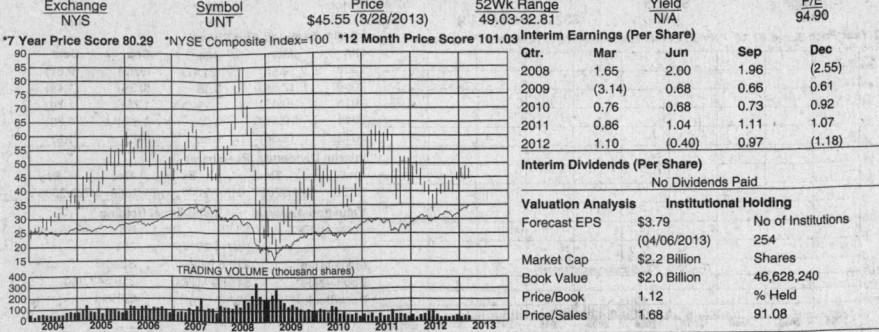

Exchange	Symbol	Price	52Wk Range	Yield	P/E
NYS	UNT	$45.55 (3/28/2013)	49.03-32.81	N/A	94.90

*7 Year Price Score 80.29   *NYSE Composite Index=100   *12 Month Price Score 101.03

Interim Earnings (Per Share)

Qtr.	Mar	Jun	Sep	Dec
2008	1.65	2.00	1.96	(2.55)
2009	(3.14)	0.68	0.66	0.61
2010	0.76	0.68	0.73	0.92
2011	0.86	1.04	1.11	1.07
2012	1.10	(0.40)	0.97	(1.18)

Interim Dividends (Per Share)

No Dividends Paid

Valuation Analysis

Valuation Analysis		Institutional Holding	
Forecast EPS	$3.79	No of Institutions	
	(04/06/2013)	254	
Market Cap	$2.2 Billion	Shares	
Book Value	$2.0 Billion	46,628,240	
Price/Book	1.12	% Held	
Price/Sales	1.68	91.08	

Business Summary: Production & Extraction (MIC: 9.1.1 SIC: 1311 NAIC: 213111)

Unit is a contract drilling company. In addition to its drilling operations, Co. has operations in the exploration and production and mid-stream areas. Co. operates three principal business segments: Contract Drilling, which contracts to drill onshore oil and natural gas wells for others and for its own account; Oil and Natural Gas, which explores, develops, acquires and produces oil and natural gas properties for its own account; and Mid-Stream, which buys, sells, gathers, processes and treats natural gas. As of Dec 31 2011, Co.'s total proved reserves of natural gas, oil, and natural gas liquid were 442.1 million cubic feet, 20.3 million barrels, and 22.1 million barrels, respectively.

Recent Developments: For the year ended Dec 31 2012, net income decreased 88.2% to US$23.2 million from US$195.9 million in the prior year. Revenues were US$1.32 billion, up 8.9% from US$1.21 billion the year before. Operating income was US$54.7 million versus US$322.3 million in the prior year, a decrease of 83.0%. Indirect operating expenses increased 42.4% to US$1.26 billion from US$885.2 million in the equivalent prior-year period.

Prospects: Our evaluation of Unit Corp. as of Apr. 7, 2013 is the result of our systematic analysis on three basic characteristics: earnings strength, relative valuation, and recent stock price movement. The company has generated a negative trend in earnings per share over the past 5 quarters. However, while recent estimates for the company have been mixed, UNT has posted better than expected results. Based on operating earnings yield, the company is undervalued when compared to all of the companies in our coverage universe. Share price changes over the past year indicates that UNT will perform well over the near term.

Financial Data
(US$ in Thousands)

	12/31/2012	12/31/2011	12/31/2010	12/31/2009	12/31/2008	12/31/2007	12/31/2006	12/31/2005
Earnings Per Share	0.48	4.08	3.09	(1.18)	3.06	5.71	6.72	4.60
Cash Flow Per Share	14.38	12.77	8.25	10.44	14.77	12.46	10.96	6.92
Tang Book Value Per Share	39.33	39.09	34.33	31.50	33.03	28.88	23.41	17.27
Income Statement								
Total Revenue	1,315,123	1,208,371	881,845	709,898	1,358,093	1,158,754	1,162,385	885,608
EBITDA	134,546	402,836	307,191	(41,861)	296,724	476,577	545,488	380,986
Depn & Amortn	81,007	79,667	69,970	45,326	69,841	56,804	51,959	42,876
Income Before Taxes	39,402	319,002	237,221	(87,726)	225,579	413,411	488,256	334,673
Income Taxes	16,226	123,135	90,737	(32,226)	81,954	147,153	176,079	122,231
Net Income	23,176	195,867	146,484	(55,500)	143,625	266,258	312,177	212,442
Average Shares	48,154	47,951	47,454	46,990	46,909	46,653	46,451	46,189
Balance Sheet								
Current Assets	195,644	228,465	188,180	128,095	286,585	197,015	232,940	223,685
Total Assets	3,761,120	3,256,720	2,669,240	2,228,399	2,581,866	2,199,819	1,874,096	1,456,195
Current Liabilities	207,139	212,750	147,128	105,147	196,399	156,404	160,942	172,512
Long-Term Obligations	716,359	300,000	163,000	30,000	199,500	120,600	174,300	145,000
Total Liabilities	1,786,819	1,309,703	958,623	662,589	948,767	765,002	716,060	619,233
Stockholders' Equity	1,974,301	1,947,017	1,710,617	1,565,810	1,633,099	1,434,817	1,158,036	836,962
Shares Outstanding	48,581	48,151	47,910	47,530	47,255	47,035	46,283	46,178
Statistical Record								
Return on Assets %	0.66	6.61	5.98	N.M.	5.99	13.07	18.75	17.14
Return on Equity %	1.18	10.71	8.94	N.M.	9.34	20.54	31.30	29.40
EBITDA Margin %	10.23	33.34	34.84	N.M.	21.85	41.13	46.93	43.02
Net Margin %	1.76	16.21	16.61	N.M.	10.58	22.98	26.86	23.99
Asset Turnover	0.37	0.41	0.36	0.30	0.57	0.57	0.70	0.71
Current Ratio	0.94	1.07	1.28	1.22	1.46	1.26	1.45	1.30
Debt to Equity	0.36	0.15	0.10	0.02	0.12	0.08	0.15	0.17
Price Range	50.56-32.81	63.43-34.88	49.91-33.82	46.94-17.83	85.41-21.75	64.99-43.93	63.46-42.50	59.21-34.10
P/E Ratio	105.33-68.35	15.55-8.55	16.15-10.94	...	27.91-7.11	11.38-7.69	9.44-6.32	12.87-7.41

Address: 7130 South Lewis, Suite 1000, Tulsa, OK 74136 **Telephone:** 918-493-7700	**Web Site:** www.unitcorp.com **Officers:** John G. Nikkel - Chairman Larry D. Pinkston - President, Chief Executive Officer, Chief Operating Officer	**Auditors:** PricewaterhouseCoopers LLP **Investor Contact:** 918-493-7700 **Transfer Agents:** American Stock Transfer & Trust Co., New York, NY

UNITED CONTINENTAL HOLDINGS INC

Exchange	Symbol	Price	52Wk Range	Yield	P/E
NYS	UAL	$32.01 (3/28/2013)	32.50-17.78	N/A	N/A

*7 Year Price Score 87.46   *NYSE Composite Index=100   *12 Month Price Score 112.88

Interim Earnings (Per Share)

Qtr.	Mar	Jun	Sep	Dec
2008	(4.45)	(21.47)	(6.13)	(9.87)
2009	(2.64)	0.19	(0.39)	(1.49)
2010	(0.49)	1.29	1.75	(1.70)
2011	(0.65)	1.39	1.69	(0.33)
2012	(1.36)	0.89	0.02	(1.87)

Interim Dividends (Per Share)

Amt	Decl	Ex	Rec	Pay
2.15U	12/07/2007	01/07/2008	01/09/2008	01/23/2008

Valuation Analysis

Forecast EPS	$3.75 (04/11/2013)
Market Cap	$10.6 Billion
Book Value	$481.0 Million
Price/Book	22.13
Price/Sales	0.29

Institutional Holding

No of Institutions	391
Shares	359,543,040
% Held	N/A

Business Summary: Airlines/Air Freight (MIC: 7.4.4 SIC: 4512 NAIC: 481111)

United Continental Holdings is a holding company. Through its subsidiaries, United Air Lines, Inc. (United) and Continental Airlines, Inc. (Continental), Co. is engaged in the transportation of people and cargo through their mainline operations, which utilize jet aircraft, and its regional operations. As of Dec 31 2012, Co., through United and Continental and their regional carriers, operated more than 5,500 flights a day to more than 375 U.S. domestic and international destinations from its hubs. As of the same date, United and Continental operated 629 and 624 aircraft, respectively.

Recent Developments: For the year ended Dec 31 2012, net loss amounted to US$723.0 million versus net income of US$840.0 million in the prior year. Revenues were US$37.15 billion, up 0.1% from US$37.11 billion the year before. Operating income was US$39.0 million versus US$1.82 billion in the prior year, a decrease of 97.9%. Direct operating expenses rose 3.8% to US$21.81 billion from US$21.01 billion in the comparable period the year before. Indirect operating expenses increased 7.1% to US$15.30 billion from US$14.28 billion in the equivalent prior-year period.

Prospects: Our evaluation of United Continental Holdings Inc. as of Apr. 7, 2013 is the result of our systematic analysis on three basic characteristics: earnings strength, relative valuation, and recent stock price movement. The company has suffered a very negative trend in earnings per share over the past 5 quarters and while recent estimates for the company have been raised by analysts, UAL has posted better than expected results. Based on operating earnings yield, the company is about fairly valued when compared to all of the companies in our coverage universe. Share price changes over the past year indicates that UAL will perform well over the near term.

Financial Data

(US$ in Thousands)	12/31/2012	12/31/2011	12/31/2010	12/31/2009	12/31/2008	12/31/2007	12/31/2006	01/31/2006
Earnings Per Share	(2.18)	2.26	1.08	(4.32)	(42.21)	2.79	0.14	196.61
Cash Flow Per Share	2.82	7.32	9.21	6.41	(9.74)	18.18	12.13	13.98
Dividends Per Share	...	...	...	...	2.150	...	...	...
Income Statement								
Total Revenue	37,152,000	37,110,000	23,229,000	16,335,000	20,194,000	20,143,000	17,882,000	1,458,000
EBITDA	132,000	1,875,000	2,133,000	875,000	(4,007,000)	1,957,000	682,000	22,883,000
Depn & Amortn	81,000	133,000	1,115,000	999,000	981,000	877,000	169,000	1,000
Income Before Taxes	(724,000)	845,000	250,000	(672,000)	(5,379,000)	695,000	43,000	22,846,000
Income Taxes	(1,000)	5,000	...	(17,000)	(25,000)	297,000	21,000	...
Net Income	(723,000)	840,000	253,000	(651,000)	(5,348,000)	403,000	25,000	22,851,000
Average Shares	331,000	383,000	253,000	150,700	126,800	153,700	116,200	116,200
Balance Sheet								
Current Assets	10,049,000	10,997,000	12,045,000	5,105,000	4,861,000	6,095,000	6,273,000	...
Total Assets	37,628,000	37,988,000	39,598,000	18,684,000	19,461,000	24,220,000	25,369,000	...
Current Liabilities	12,818,000	11,394,000	12,645,000	6,473,000	7,281,000	7,979,000	7,945,000	...
Long-Term Obligations	11,232,000	11,424,000	12,470,000	7,572,000	7,199,000	7,521,000	8,803,000	...
Total Liabilities	37,147,000	36,182,000	37,871,000	21,495,000	21,926,000	21,802,000	23,221,000	...
Stockholders' Equity	481,000	1,806,000	1,727,000	(2,811,000)	(2,465,000)	2,418,000	2,148,000	...
Shares Outstanding	332,472	330,906	327,922	167,610	140,037	116,921	112,280	116,220
Statistical Record								
Return on Assets %	N.M.	2.17	0.87	N.M.	N.M.	1.63	0.11	...
Return on Equity %	N.M.	47.55	...	...	...	17.65	...	...
EBITDA Margin %	0.36	5.05	9.18	5.36	N.M.	9.72	3.81	1,569.48
Net Margin %	N.M.	2.26	1.09	N.M.	N.M.	2.00	0.14	1,567.28
Asset Turnover	0.98	0.96	0.80	0.86	0.92	0.81	0.80	...
Current Ratio	0.78	0.97	0.95	0.79	0.67	0.76	0.79	...
Debt to Equity	23.35	6.33	7.22	...	...	3.11	4.10	...
Price Range	25.17-17.48	27.48-15.53	29.53-12.23	13.09-3.17	41.14-3.13	51.49-33.20	45.24-22.33	43.50-41.98
P/E Ratio	...	12.16-6.87	27.34-11.32	...	...	18.46-11.90	323.14-159.50	0.22-0.21
Average Yield %	...	...	...	...	13.38	...	...	...

Address: 77 W. Wacker Drive, Chicago, IL 60601 **Telephone:** 312-997-8000 **Fax:** 847-700-2214	**Web Site:** www.unitedcontinentalholdings.com **Officers:** Jeffery A. Smisek - Chairman, President, Chief Executive Officer James E. Compton - Vice-Chairman, Executive Vice President, Chief Revenue Officer	**Auditors:** Ernst & Young LLP **Investor Contact:** 312-997-8610 **Transfer Agents:** ComputerShare Investor Services, Chicago, IL

UNITED PARCEL SERVICE INC

Exchange	Symbol	Price	52Wk Range	Yield	P/E
NYS	UPS	$85.90 (3/28/2013)	85.90-70.02	2.89	103.49

*7 Year Price Score 99.53   *NYSE Composite Index=100   *12 Month Price Score 99.99

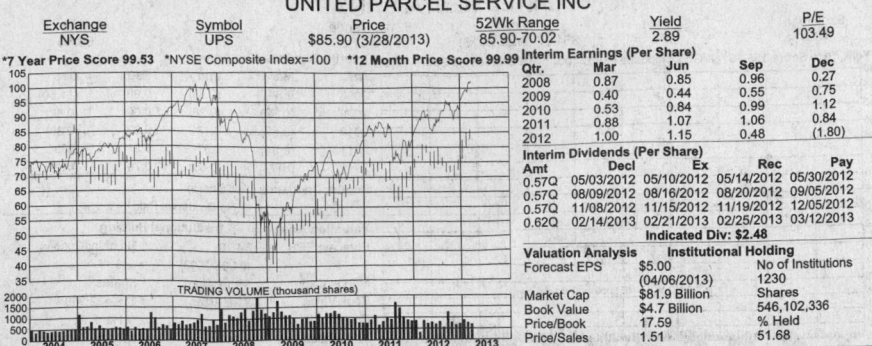

Interim Earnings (Per Share)

Qtr.	Mar	Jun	Sep	Dec
2008	0.87	0.85	0.96	0.27
2009	0.40	0.44	0.55	0.75
2010	0.53	0.84	0.99	1.12
2011	0.88	1.07	1.06	0.84
2012	1.00	1.15	0.48	(1.80)

Interim Dividends (Per Share)

Amt	Decl	Ex	Rec	Pay
0.57Q	05/03/2012	05/10/2012	05/14/2012	05/30/2012
0.57Q	08/09/2012	08/16/2012	08/20/2012	09/05/2012
0.57Q	11/08/2012	11/15/2012	11/19/2012	12/05/2012
0.62Q	02/14/2013	02/21/2013	02/25/2013	03/12/2013
Indicated Div: $2.48				

Valuation Analysis / Institutional Holding

Valuation Analysis		Institutional Holding	
Forecast EPS	$5.00 (04/06/2013)	No of Institutions	1230
Market Cap	$81.9 Billion	Shares	546,102,336
Book Value	$4.7 Billion	% Held	51.68
Price/Book	17.59		
Price/Sales	1.51		

Business Summary: Airlines/Air Freight (MIC: 7.4.4 SIC: 4215 NAIC: 492110)

United Parcel Service is engaged in the field of transportation services, primarily domestic and international letter and package delivery. Through its Supply Chain & Freight subsidiaries, Co. is also a provider of transportation, logistics, and financial services. Co.'s global small package operations provide delivery services for express letters, documents, small packages and palletized freight via air and ground services. As of Dec 31 2012, Co. provided domestic delivery services within 56 countries and export services to more than 220 countries and territories around the world. Co. has three reportable segments: U.S. Domestic Package, International Package and Supply Chain & Freight.

Recent Developments: For the year ended Dec 31 2012, net income decreased 78.8% to US$807.0 million from US$3.80 billion in the prior year. Revenues were US$54.13 billion, up 1.9% from US$53.11 billion the year before. Operating income was US$1.34 billion versus US$6.08 billion in the prior year, a decrease of 77.9%. Direct operating expenses rose 0.9% to US$12.67 billion from US$12.56 billion in the comparable period the year before. Indirect operating expenses increased 16.4% to US$40.11 billion from US$34.46 billion in the equivalent prior-year period.

Prospects: Our evaluation of United Parcel Service Inc. as of Apr. 7, 2013 is the result of our systematic analysis on three basic characteristics: earnings strength, relative valuation, and recent stock price movement. The company has produced a positive trend in earnings per share over the past 5 quarters. However, while recent estimates for the company have been lowered by analysts, UPS has posted results that fell short of analysts expectations. Based on operating earnings yield, the company is about fairly valued when compared to all of the companies in our coverage universe. Share price changes over the past year indicates that UPS will perform poorly over the near term.

Financial Data
(US$ in Millions)

	12/31/2012	12/31/2011	12/31/2010	12/31/2009	12/31/2008	12/31/2007	12/31/2006	12/31/2005
Earnings Per Share	0.83	3.84	3.48	2.14	2.94	0.36	3.86	3.47
Cash Flow Per Share	7.50	7.21	3.86	5.30	8.27	1.06	5.15	5.20
Tang Book Value Per Share	1.97	4.52	5.35	4.97	4.29	8.62	11.46	12.44
Dividends Per Share	2.280	2.080	1.880	1.800	1.800	1.680	1.520	1.320
Dividend Payout %	274.70	54.17	54.02	84.11	61.22	466.67	39.38	38.04
Income Statement								
Total Revenue	54,127	53,105	49,545	45,297	51,486	49,692	47,547	42,581
EBITDA	3,225	7,906	7,669	5,558	7,271	913	6,976	6,502
Depn & Amortn	1,858	1,782	1,792	1,747	1,814	236	255	255
Income Before Taxes	974	5,776	5,523	3,366	5,015	431	6,510	6,075
Income Taxes	167	1,972	2,035	1,214	2,012	49	2,308	2,205
Net Income	807	3,804	3,488	2,152	3,003	382	4,202	3,870
Average Shares	969	991	1,003	1,004	1,022	1,063	1,089	1,116
Balance Sheet								
Current Assets	15,591	12,284	11,569	9,275	8,845	11,760	9,377	11,003
Total Assets	38,863	34,701	33,597	31,883	31,879	39,042	33,210	35,222
Current Liabilities	8,390	6,514	5,902	6,239	7,817	9,840	6,719	6,793
Long-Term Obligations	11,089	11,095	10,491	8,668	7,797	7,506	3,133	3,159
Total Liabilities	34,210	27,666	25,618	24,253	25,099	26,859	17,728	18,338
Stockholders' Equity	4,653	7,035	7,979	7,630	6,780	12,183	15,482	16,884
Shares Outstanding	953	963	991	994	998	1,041	1,070	1,097
Statistical Record								
Return on Assets %	2.19	11.14	10.65	6.75	8.45	1.06	12.28	11.34
Return on Equity %	13.77	50.67	44.69	29.87	31.59	2.76	25.97	23.27
EBITDA Margin %	5.96	14.89	15.48	12.27	14.12	1.84	14.67	15.27
Net Margin %	1.49	7.16	7.04	4.75	5.83	0.77	8.84	9.09
Asset Turnover	1.47	1.56	1.51	1.42	1.45	1.38	1.39	1.25
Current Ratio	1.86	1.89	1.96	1.49	1.13	1.20	1.40	1.62
Debt to Equity	2.38	1.58	1.31	1.14	1.15	0.62	0.20	0.19
Price Range	81.11-70.02	76.47-61.70	73.76-56.15	59.29-38.30	74.73-44.68	78.37-69.26	83.35-65.92	85.46-66.86
P/E Ratio	97.72-84.36	19.91-16.07	21.20-16.14	27.71-17.90	25.42-15.20	217.69-192.39	21.59-17.08	24.63-19.27
Average Yield %	3.02	2.94	2.91	3.45	2.79	2.29	1.99	1.80

Address: 55 Glenlake Parkway, N.E., Atlanta, GA 30328 **Telephone:** 404-828-6000 **Fax:** 404-828-6562	**Web Site:** www.ups.com **Officers:** D. Scott Davis - Chairman, Chief Executive Officer Kurt P. Kuehn - Senior Vice President, Chief Financial Officer	**Auditors:** Deloitte & Touche LLP **Investor Contact:** 404-828-6977 **Transfer Agents:** Computershare Shareowner Services, Jersey City, NJ

UNITED RENTALS, INC.

Exchange	Symbol	Price	52Wk Range	Yield	P/E
NYS	URI	$54.97 (3/28/2013)	55.90-27.23	N/A	69.58

*7 Year Price Score 155.76 *NYSE Composite Index=100 *12 Month Price Score 120.47

TRADING VOLUME (thousand shares)

Interim Earnings (Per Share)

Qtr.	Mar	Jun	Sep	Dec
2008	0.34	(2.33)	0.98	(11.50)
2009	(0.32)	(0.28)	0.00	(0.42)
2010	(0.67)	0.18	0.33	(0.35)
2011	(0.34)	0.37	0.91	0.39
2012	0.17	(0.63)	0.70	0.42

Interim Dividends (Per Share)

No Dividends Paid

Valuation Analysis | Institutional Holding

Forecast EPS	$4.70	No of Institutions
	(04/06/2013)	448
Market Cap	$5.1 Billion	Shares
Book Value	$1.6 Billion	116,432,208
Price/Book	3.25	% Held
Price/Sales	1.24	108.34

Business Summary: Construction Services (MIC: 7.5.4 SIC: 7359 NAIC: 532412)

United Rentals is an equipment rental company. Co. provides approximately 3,300 classes of equipment for rent to customers that include construction and industrial companies, manufacturers, utilities, municipalities, homeowners, and government entities. Co. has two reportable segments which are general rentals and trench safety, power and heating, ventilating and air conditioning. Co.'s principal products and services are equipment rental, sales of rental equipment, sales of new equipment, contractor supplies sales, and service and other. As of Dec 31 2012, Co.'s fleet of rental equipment included approximately 400,000 units.

Recent Developments: For the year ended Dec 31 2012, income from continuing operations decreased 25.7% to US$75.0 million from US$101.0 million a year earlier. Net income decreased 25.7% to US$75.0 million from US$101.0 million in the prior year. Revenues were US$4.12 billion, up 57.7% from US$2.61 billion the year before. Operating income was US$591.0 million versus US$396.0 million in the prior year, an increase of 49.2%. Direct operating expenses rose 47.7% to US$2.53 billion from US$1.71 billion in the comparable period the year before. Indirect operating expenses increased 98.4% to US$996.0 million from US$502.0 million in the equivalent prior-year period.

Prospects: Our evaluation of United Rentals Inc. as of Apr. 7, 2013 is the result of our systematic analysis on three basic characteristics: earnings strength, relative valuation, and recent stock price movement. The company has produced a positive trend in earnings per share over the past 5 quarters. However, while recent estimates for the company have been lowered by analysts, URI has posted better than expected results. Based on operating earnings yield, the company is undervalued when compared to all of the companies in our coverage universe. Share price changes over the past year indicates that URI will perform very well over the near term.

Financial Data

(US$ in Thousands)	12/31/2012	12/31/2011	12/31/2010	12/31/2009	12/31/2008	12/31/2007	12/31/2006	12/31/2005
Earnings Per Share	0.79	1.38	(0.44)	(1.02)	(12.62)	3.25	2.06	1.80
Cash Flow Per Share	8.67	9.78	7.48	7.29	10.19	8.64	8.88	6.78
Tang Book Value Per Share	N.M.	N.M.	...	...	...	7.11	2.00	N.M.
Income Statement								
Total Revenue	4,117,000	2,611,000	2,237,000	2,358,000	3,267,000	3,731,000	3,640,000	3,563,000
EBITDA	1,303,000	822,000	589,000	532,000	(175,000)	1,208,000	1,034,000	894,000
Depn & Amortn	699,000	423,000	389,000	417,000	455,000	434,000	408,000	385,000
Income Before Taxes	88,000	164,000	(63,000)	(107,000)	(813,000)	578,000	405,000	310,000
Income Taxes	13,000	63,000	(41,000)	(47,000)	(109,000)	215,000	156,000	123,000
Net Income	75,000	101,000	(26,000)	(62,000)	(704,000)	362,000	224,000	187,000
Average Shares	94,848	73,349	60,455	60,100	74,734	113,722	113,793	110,036
Balance Sheet								
Current Assets	1,343,000	723,000	725,000	705,000	703,000	1,120,000	1,005,000	1,216,000
Total Assets	11,026,000	4,143,000	3,693,000	3,859,000	4,191,000	5,842,000	5,366,000	5,274,000
Current Liabilities	1,351,000	864,000	569,000	461,000	427,000	520,000	599,000	631,000
Long-Term Obligations	6,734,000	2,647,000	2,700,000	2,950,000	3,332,000	2,701,000	2,665,000	3,152,000
Total Liabilities	9,452,000	4,040,000	3,713,000	3,878,000	4,220,000	3,824,000	3,828,000	4,045,000
Stockholders' Equity	1,574,000	103,000	(20,000)	(19,000)	(29,000)	2,018,000	1,538,000	1,229,000
Shares Outstanding	92,984	62,877	60,621	60,163	59,890	86,329	81,178	77,302
Statistical Record								
Return on Assets %	0.99	2.58	N.M.	N.M.	N.M.	6.46	4.21	3.68
Return on Equity %	8.92	243.37	...	...	N.M.	20.36	16.19	16.59
EBITDA Margin %	31.65	31.48	26.33	22.56	N.M.	32.38	28.41	25.09
Net Margin %	1.82	3.87	N.M.	N.M.	N.M.	9.70	6.15	5.25
Asset Turnover	0.54	0.67	0.59	0.59	0.65	0.67	0.68	0.70
Current Ratio	0.99	0.84	1.27	1.53	1.65	2.15	1.68	1.93
Debt to Equity	4.28	25.70	...	...	...	1.34	1.73	2.56
Price Range	46.82-27.23	34.09-13.11	23.51-7.02	11.03-3.03	22.09-4.40	34.70-17.91	37.57-20.30	24.42-16.22
P/E Ratio	59.27-34.47	24.70-9.50	...	...	...	10.68-5.51	18.24-9.85	13.57-9.01

Address: Five Greenwich Office Park, Greenwich, CT 06831 **Telephone:** 203-622-3131 **Fax:** 203-622-6080	Web Site: www.ur.com **Officers:** Jenne K. Britell - Chairman Michael J. Kneeland - President, Chief Executive Officer	**Auditors:** Ernst & Young LLP **Investor Contact:** 203-618-7318 **Transfer Agents:** American Stock Transfer & Trust Company, New York, NY

UNITED STATES STEEL CORP.

Exchange	Symbol	Price	52Wk Range	Yield	P/E
NYS	X	$19.50 (3/28/2013)	30.26-17.89	1.03	N/A

*7 Year Price Score 33.04 *NYSE Composite Index=100 ***12 Month Price Score 87.94**

TRADING VOLUME (thousand shares)

Interim Earnings (Per Share)

Qtr.	Mar	Jun	Sep	Dec
2008	1.98	5.65	7.79	2.53
2009	(3.78)	(2.92)	(2.11)	(1.80)
2010	(1.10)	(0.17)	(0.35)	(1.74)
2011	(0.60)	1.33	0.15	(1.39)
2012	(1.52)	0.62	0.28	(0.35)

Interim Dividends (Per Share)

Amt	Decl	Ex	Rec	Pay
0.05Q	04/24/2012	05/07/2012	05/09/2012	06/09/2012
0.05Q	07/31/2012	08/08/2012	08/10/2012	09/10/2012
0.05Q	10/30/2012	11/09/2012	11/14/2012	12/10/2012
0.05Q	01/29/2013	02/08/2013	02/12/2013	03/08/2013

Indicated Div: $0.20

Valuation Analysis		Institutional Holding	
Forecast EPS	$1.02	No of Institutions	
	(04/05/2013)	488	
Market Cap	$2.8 Billion	Shares	
Book Value	$3.5 Billion	104,220,584	
Price/Book	0.81	% Held	
Price/Sales	0.15	65.81	

Business Summary: Non-Precious Metals (MIC: 8.2.2 SIC: 3325 NAIC: 331513)

United States Steel is a steel producer of flat-rolled and tubular products. Co. has three segments: Flat-rolled Products, which includes its North American steel mills and equity investees involved in the production of slabs, rounds, strip mill plates, sheets and tin mill products, and iron ore and coke production facilities in the U.S. and Canada; U. S. Steel Europe, which includes U. S. Steel Kosice, Co.'s steel mill and coke production facilities in Slovakia; and Tubular Products, which includes tubular production facilities in the U.S. and equity investees in the U.S. and Brazil that produces and sells seamless and electric resistance welded steel casing and tubing.

Recent Developments: For the year ended Dec 31 2012, net loss amounted to US$125.0 million versus a net loss of US$53.0 million in the prior year. Revenues were US$19.33 billion, down 2.8% from US$19.88 billion the year before. Operating income was US$247.0 million versus US$265.0 million in the prior year, a decrease of 6.8%. Direct operating expenses declined 3.8% to US$17.63 billion from US$18.33 billion in the comparable period the year before. Indirect operating expenses increased 12.2% to US$1.45 billion from US$1.29 billion in the equivalent prior-year period.

Prospects: Our evaluation of United States Steel Corp. as of Apr. 7, 2013 is the result of our systematic analysis on three basic characteristics: earnings strength, relative valuation, and recent stock price movement. The company has managed to produce a neutral trend in earnings per share over the past 5 quarters. However, while recent estimates for the company have been lowered by analysts, X has posted better than expected results. Based on operating earnings yield, the company is overvalued when compared to all of the companies in our coverage universe. Share price changes over the past year indicates that X will perform very well over the near term.

Financial Data

(US$ in Millions)	12/31/2012	12/31/2011	12/31/2010	12/31/2009	12/31/2008	12/31/2007	12/31/2006	12/31/2005
Earnings Per Share	(0.86)	(0.37)	(3.36)	(10.42)	17.96	7.40	11.18	7.00
Cash Flow Per Share	7.85	1.17	(2.64)	(0.45)	14.12	14.78	14.67	10.73
Tang Book Value Per Share	9.72	10.10	12.64	18.63	25.85	28.81	36.82	26.00
Dividends Per Share	0.200	0.200	0.200	0.450	1.100	0.800	0.600	0.380
Dividend Payout %	...	...	...	...	6.12	10.81	5.37	5.43
Income Statement								
Total Revenue	19,328	19,884	17,374	11,048	23,754	16,873	15,715	14,039
EBITDA	730	807	441	(1,006)	3,674	1,661	2,156	1,687
Depn & Amortn	661	681	658	661	605	506	441	366
Income Before Taxes	(138)	(58)	(403)	(1,816)	2,914	1,082	1,666	1,282
Income Taxes	131	80	97	(439)	853	218	324	365
Net Income	(124)	(53)	(482)	(1,401)	2,112	879	1,374	910
Average Shares	144	143	143	134	117	118	122	129
Balance Sheet								
Current Assets	5,374	5,774	5,304	5,015	5,732	4,959	5,196	4,831
Total Assets	15,217	16,073	15,350	15,422	16,087	15,632	10,586	9,822
Current Liabilities	2,990	3,649	3,147	2,474	2,778	3,003	2,702	2,749
Long-Term Obligations	3,936	3,828	3,517	3,345	3,064	3,147	943	1,363
Total Liabilities	11,740	12,573	11,499	10,746	11,192	10,101	6,221	6,498
Stockholders' Equity	3,477	3,500	3,851	4,676	4,895	5,531	4,365	3,324
Shares Outstanding	144	144	143	143	116	117	118	108
Statistical Record								
Return on Assets %	N.M.	N.M.	N.M.	N.M.	13.28	6.71	13.47	8.76
Return on Equity %	N.M.	N.M.	N.M.	N.M.	40.40	17.76	35.74	24.95
EBITDA Margin %	3.78	4.06	2.54	N.M.	15.47	9.84	13.72	12.02
Net Margin %	N.M.	N.M.	N.M.	N.M.	8.89	5.21	8.74	6.48
Asset Turnover	1.23	1.27	1.13	0.70	1.49	1.29	1.54	1.35
Current Ratio	1.80	1.58	1.69	2.03	2.06	1.65	1.92	1.76
Debt to Equity	1.13	1.09	0.91	0.72	0.63	0.57	0.22	0.41
Price Range	32.25-17.89	63.64-20.19	69.71-37.66	56.86-16.88	191.96-20.97	125.05-69.72	78.75-49.44	63.12-34.10
P/E Ratio	...	...	...	...	10.69-1.17	16.90-9.42	7.04-4.42	9.02-4.87
Average Yield %	0.85	0.50	0.40	1.25	0.99	0.81	0.95	0.85

Address: 600 Grant Street, Pittsburgh, PA 15219-2800	**Web Site:** www.ussteel.com	**Auditors:** PricewaterhouseCoopers LLP
Telephone: 412-433-1121	**Officers:** John P. Surma - Chairman, President, Chief Executive Officer Gretchen R. Haggerty - Executive	**Investor Contact:** 412-433-1184
Fax: 412-433-4818	Vice President, Chief Financial Officer	**Transfer Agents:** Wells Fargo Bank Shareowner Services, St. Paul, MN

UNITEDHEALTH GROUP INC

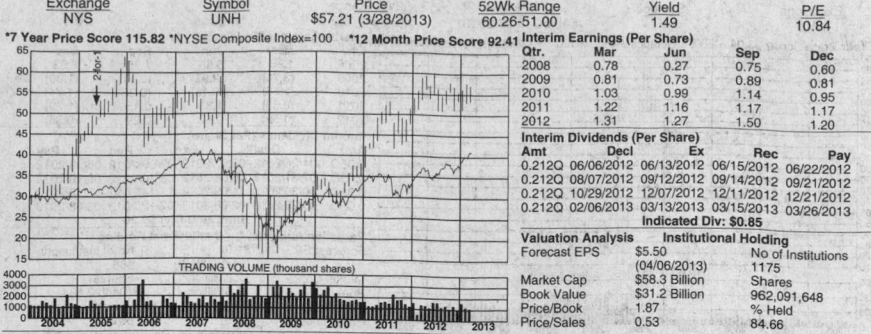

Exchange	Symbol	Price	52Wk Range	Yield	P/E
NYS	UNH	$57.21 (3/28/2013)	60.26-51.00	1.49	10.84

*7 Year Price Score 115.82 *NYSE Composite Index=100 *12 Month Price Score 92.41

Interim Earnings (Per Share)

Qtr.	Mar	Jun	Sep	Dec
2008	0.78	0.27	0.75	0.60
2009	0.81	0.73	0.89	0.81
2010	1.03	0.99	1.14	0.95
2011	1.22	1.16	1.17	1.17
2012	1.31	1.27	1.50	1.20

Interim Dividends (Per Share)

Amt	Decl	Ex	Rec	Pay
0.212Q	06/06/2012	06/13/2012	06/15/2012	06/22/2012
0.212Q	08/07/2012	09/12/2012	09/14/2012	09/21/2012
0.212Q	10/29/2012	12/07/2012	12/11/2012	12/21/2012
0.212Q	02/06/2013	03/13/2013	03/15/2013	03/26/2013

Indicated Div: $0.85

Valuation Analysis

		Institutional Holding	
Forecast EPS	$5.50 (04/06/2013)	No of Institutions	1175
Market Cap	$58.3 Billion	Shares	962,091,648
Book Value	$31.2 Billion	% Held	84.66
Price/Book	1.87		
Price/Sales	0.53		

Business Summary: Life & Health (MIC: 5.2.2 SIC: 6324 NAIC: 524114)

UnitedHealth Group is a health and well-being company. Co. provides a range of products and services through two platforms: UnitedHealthcare, which provides health care coverage and benefits services; and Optum, which provides information and technology-enabled health services. Co.'s two business platforms have four reportable segments: UnitedHealthcare, which includes UnitedHealthcare Employer & Individual, UnitedHealthcare Medicare & Retirement, UnitedHealthcare Community & State and UnitedHealthcare International; OptumHealth; OptumInsight; and OptumRx.

Recent Developments: For the year ended Dec 31 2012, net income increased 7.5% to US$5.53 billion from US$5.14 billion in the prior year. Revenues were US$110.62 billion, up 8.6% from US$101.86 billion the year before. Net premiums earned were US$99.73 billion versus US$91.98 billion in the prior year, an increase of 8.4%.

Prospects: Our evaluation of UnitedHealth Group Inc. as of Apr. 7, 2013 is the result of our systematic analysis on three basic characteristics: earnings strength, relative valuation, and recent stock price movement. The company has generated a negative trend in earnings per share over the past 5 quarters and while recent estimates for the company have remained steady, UNH has posted better than expected results. Based on operating earnings yield, the company is undervalued when compared to all of the companies in our coverage universe. Share price changes over the past year indicates that UNH will perform very poorly over the near term.

Financial Data
(US$ in Thousands)

	12/31/2012	12/31/2011	12/31/2010	12/31/2009	12/31/2008	12/31/2007	12/31/2006	12/31/2005
Earnings Per Share	5.28	4.73	4.10	3.24	2.40	3.42	2.97	2.48
Cash Flow Per Share	6.95	6.51	5.60	4.82	3.48	4.48	4.86	3.42
Tang Book Value Per Share	N.M.	1.46	0.16	0.43	N.M.	1.17	1.55	N.M.
Dividends Per Share	0.800	0.613	0.405	0.030	0.030	0.030	0.030	0.015
Dividend Payout %	15.15	12.95	9.88	0.93	1.25	0.88	1.01	0.60
Income Statement								
Premium Income	99,728,000	91,983,000	85,405,000	79,315,000	73,608,000	68,781,000	65,666,000	41,058,000
Total Revenue	110,618,000	101,862,000	94,155,000	87,138,000	81,186,000	75,431,000	71,542,000	45,365,000
Benefits & Claims	80,226,000	74,332,000	68,841,000	65,289,000	60,359,000	55,435,000	53,308,000	32,725,000
Income Before Taxes	8,622,000	7,959,000	7,383,000	5,808,000	4,624,000	7,305,000	6,528,000	5,132,000
Income Taxes	3,096,000	2,817,000	2,749,000	1,986,000	1,647,000	2,651,000	2,369,000	1,832,000
Net Income	5,526,000	5,142,000	4,634,000	3,822,000	2,977,000	4,654,000	4,159,000	3,300,000
Average Shares	1,046,000	1,087,000	1,131,000	1,179,000	1,241,000	1,361,000	1,402,000	1,330,000
Balance Sheet								
Total Assets	80,885,000	67,889,000	63,063,000	59,045,000	55,815,000	50,899,000	48,320,000	41,374,000
Total Liabilities	49,707,000	39,597,000	37,238,000	35,439,000	35,035,000	30,836,000	27,510,000	23,641,000
Stockholders' Equity	31,178,000	28,292,000	25,825,000	23,606,000	20,780,000	20,063,000	20,810,000	17,733,000
Shares Outstanding	1,019,000	1,039,000	1,086,000	1,147,000	1,201,000	1,253,000	1,345,000	1,358,000
Statistical Record								
Return on Assets %	7.41	7.85	7.59	6.66	5.56	9.38	9.27	9.53
Return on Equity %	18.53	19.00	18.75	17.22	14.54	22.77	21.58	23.20
Loss Ratio %	80.44	80.81	80.61	82.32	82.00	80.60	81.18	79.70
Net Margin %	5.00	5.05	4.92	4.39	3.67	6.17	5.81	7.27
Price Range	60.26-50.35	53.13-36.11	38.05-27.85	32.32-16.35	58.20-16.30	58.99-46.33	62.90-42.09	63.79-42.87
P/E Ratio	11.41-9.54	11.23-7.63	9.28-6.79	9.98-5.05	24.25-6.79	17.25-13.55	21.18-14.17	25.72-17.28
Average Yield %	1.45	1.32	1.23	0.11	0.09	0.06	0.06	0.03

Address: UnitedHealth Group Center, 9900 Bren Road East, Minnetonka, MN 55343
Telephone: 952-936-1300

Web Site: www.unitedhealthgroup.com
Officers: Stephen J. Hemsley - President, Chief Executive Officer, Senior Executive Vice President, Chief Operating Officer David S. Wichmann - Executive Vice President, Chief Financial Officer, Division Officer

Auditors: Deloitte & Touche LLP
Investor Contact: 800-328-5979
Transfer Agents: Wells Fargo Shareowner Services, St. Paul, MN

UNITED STATES CELLULAR CORP

Exchange	Symbol	Price	52Wk Range	Yield	P/E
NYS	USM	$36.00 (3/28/2013)	41.30-33.76	N/A	27.48

*7 Year Price Score 65.14 *NYSE Composite Index=100 *12 Month Price Score 90.25

Interim Earnings (Per Share)

Qtr.	Mar	Jun	Sep	Dec
2008	0.80	0.83	1.02	(2.27)
2009	0.97	0.96	0.41	0.15
2010	0.55	0.47	0.43	0.08
2011	0.40	0.87	0.73	0.03
2012	0.73	0.62	0.42	(0.46)

Interim Dividends (Per Share)

No Dividends Paid

Valuation Analysis | **Institutional Holding**

Forecast EPS	$0.25	No of Institutions
	(04/05/2013)	150
Market Cap	$3.0 Billion	Shares
Book Value	$3.7 Billion	12,719,173
Price/Book	0.81	% Held
Price/Sales	0.68	14.67

Business Summary: Services (MIC: 6.1.2 SIC: 4812 NAIC: 517212)

United States Cellular is a wireless telecommunications service provider that owns, operates and invests in wireless systems throughout the U.S. At Dec 31 2011, Co. provided services to 5.9 million customers in five geographic market areas in 26 states. Co. provides its customers a range of national bundled plans with voice, messaging and data pricing. In addition, Co. provides prepaid service plans that include voice minutes, messaging and data in a variety of ways. Co. also provides a range of wireless devices such as handsets, modems and tablets for use by its customers. Co. has established service facilities certain markets to ensure service and repair of the wireless devices it sells.

Recent Developments: For the year ended Dec 31 2012, net income decreased 29.0% to US$141.1 million from US$198.7 million in the prior year. Revenues were US$4.45 billion, up 2.5% from US$4.34 billion the year before. Operating income was US$156.7 million versus US$280.8 million in the prior year, a decrease of 44.2%. Direct operating expenses rose 9.4% to US$1.88 billion from US$1.72 billion in the comparable period the year before. Indirect operating expenses increased 3.0% to US$2.41 billion from US$2.34 billion in the equivalent prior-year period.

Prospects: Our evaluation of United States Cellular Corp. as of Apr. 7, 2013 is the result of our systematic analysis on three basic characteristics: earnings strength, relative valuation, and recent stock price movement. The company has suffered a very negative trend in earnings per share over the past 5 quarters. However, while recent estimates for the company have been lowered by analysts, USM has posted results that fell short of analysts expectations. Based on operating earnings yield, the company is overvalued when compared to all of the companies in our coverage universe. Share price changes over the past year indicates that USM will perform poorly over the near term.

Financial Data
(US$ in Thousands)

	12/31/2012	12/31/2011	12/31/2010	12/31/2009	12/31/2008	12/31/2007	12/31/2006	12/31/2005
Earnings Per Share	1.31	2.05	1.53	2.48	0.38	3.56	2.04	1.54
Cash Flow Per Share	10.60	11.64	10.15	10.14	10.52	9.84	7.94	7.40
Tang Book Value Per Share	22.04	19.56	17.92	16.99	14.55	13.78	11.25	9.96
Income Statement								
Total Revenue	4,452,084	4,343,346	4,177,681	4,214,611	4,243,185	3,946,264	3,473,155	3,035,887
EBITDA	751,138	856,575	757,046	882,749	595,707	1,071,188	813,756	773,087
Depn & Amortn	597,700	565,100	561,600	554,900	550,100	543,100	516,600	465,400
Income Before Taxes	114,689	229,256	137,699	255,079	(25,853)	456,468	220,019	234,260
Income Taxes	63,977	114,078	79,609	114,103	8,055	216,711	120,604	88,404
Net Income	111,006	175,041	132,324	216,008	32,990	314,734	179,490	134,748
Average Shares	85,067	85,335	86,518	87,168	87,754	88,481	88,109	87,464
Balance Sheet								
Current Assets	1,196,476	1,292,843	1,109,624	1,005,588	815,047	833,753	854,918	543,650
Total Assets	6,587,450	6,327,976	5,933,610	5,745,217	5,566,042	5,611,874	5,680,616	5,434,028
Current Liabilities	754,999	722,280	665,995	644,565	601,883	604,243	856,710	654,260
Long-Term Obligations	878,858	880,320	867,941	867,522	996,636	1,002,293	1,001,839	1,161,241
Total Liabilities	2,853,595	2,708,015	2,453,027	2,340,921	2,359,400	2,415,718	2,687,337	2,683,288
Stockholders' Equity	3,733,855	3,619,961	3,480,583	3,404,296	3,206,642	3,196,156	2,993,279	2,750,740
Shares Outstanding	84,168	84,557	85,547	86,540	87,279	87,596	87,721	87,088
Statistical Record								
Return on Assets %	1.71	2.86	2.27	3.82	0.59	5.57	3.23	2.54
Return on Equity %	3.01	4.93	3.84	6.53	1.03	10.17	6.25	5.05
EBITDA Margin %	16.87	19.72	18.12	20.94	14.04	27.14	23.43	25.46
Net Margin %	2.49	4.03	3.17	5.13	0.78	7.98	5.17	4.44
Asset Turnover	0.69	0.71	0.72	0.75	0.76	0.70	0.62	0.57
Current Ratio	1.58	1.79	1.67	1.56	1.35	1.38	1.00	0.83
Debt to Equity	0.24	0.24	0.25	0.25	0.31	0.31	0.33	0.42
Price Range	47.61-33.76	51.99-36.07	50.05-34.75	47.08-30.34	84.75-28.60	104.23-68.50	69.83-49.80	56.12-43.20
P/E Ratio	36.34-25.77	25.36-17.60	32.71-22.71	18.98-12.23	223.03-75.26	29.28-19.24	34.23-24.41	36.44-28.05

Address: 8410 West Bryn Mawr, Chicago, IL 60631	Web Site: www.uscellular.com	Auditors: PricewaterhouseCoopers LLP
Telephone: 773-399-8900	Officers: LeRoy T. Carlson - Chairman Mary N. Dillon - President, Chief Executive Officer	Investor Contact: 312-592-5379
		Transfer Agents: ComputerShare Investor Services, Chicago, IL

U.S. BANCORP (DE)

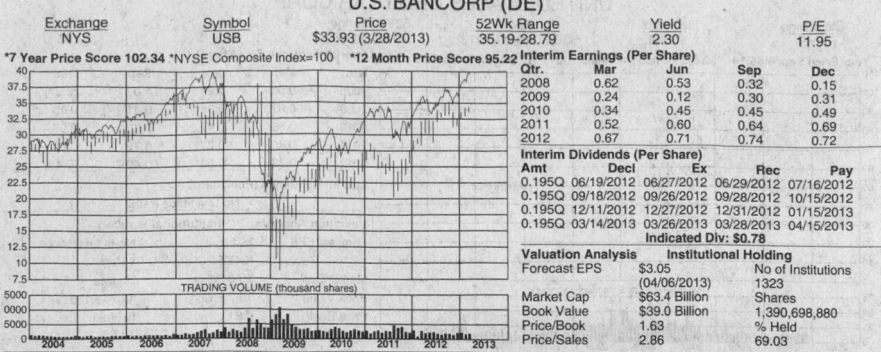

Exchange	Symbol	Price	52Wk Range	Yield	P/E
NYS	USB	$33.93 (3/28/2013)	35.19-28.79	2.30	11.95

*7 Year Price Score 102.34 *NYSE Composite Index=100   *12 Month Price Score 95.22

Interim Earnings (Per Share)

Qtr.	Mar	Jun	Sep	Dec
2008	0.62	0.53	0.32	0.15
2009	0.24	0.12	0.30	0.31
2010	0.34	0.45	0.45	0.49
2011	0.52	0.60	0.64	0.69
2012	0.67	0.71	0.74	0.72

Interim Dividends (Per Share)

Amt	Decl	Ex	Rec	Pay
0.195Q	06/19/2012	06/27/2012	06/29/2012	07/16/2012
0.195Q	09/18/2012	09/26/2012	09/28/2012	10/15/2012
0.195Q	12/11/2012	12/27/2012	12/31/2012	01/15/2013
0.195Q	03/14/2013	03/26/2013	03/28/2013	04/15/2013

Indicated Div: $0.78

Valuation Analysis / Institutional Holding

Forecast EPS	$3.05	No of Institutions	1323
	(04/06/2013)		
Market Cap	$63.4 Billion	Shares	1,390,698,880
Book Value	$39.0 Billion	% Held	69.03
Price/Book	1.63		
Price/Sales	2.86		

Business Summary: Banking (MIC: 5.1.1 SIC: 6021 NAIC: 522110)

U.S. Bancorp is a financial services holding company. Through its subsidiaries, Co. provides a range of financial services, including lending and depository services, cash management, capital markets, and trust and investment management services. Co. also engages in credit card services, merchant and automatic teller machine processing, mortgage banking, insurance, brokerage and leasing. Lending services include credit products as well as leasing, financing and import/export trade, asset-backed lending and agricultural finance. Depository services include savings accounts and time certificate contracts. At Dec 31 2012, Co. had total assets of $353.86 billion and deposits of $249.18 billion.

Recent Developments: For the year ended Dec 31 2012, net income increased 14.7% to US$5.49 billion from US$4.79 billion in the prior year. Net interest income increased 6.1% to US$10.75 billion from US$10.12 billion in the prior year. Provision for loan losses was US$1.88 billion versus US$2.34 billion in the prior year, a decrease of 19.7%. Non-interest income rose 6.4% to US$9.32 billion from US$8.76 billion, while non-interest expense advanced 5.5% to US$10.46 billion.

Prospects: Our evaluation of U.S. Bancorp as of Apr. 7, 2013 is the result of our systematic analysis on three basic characteristics: earnings strength, relative valuation, and recent stock price movement. The company has managed to produce a neutral trend in earnings per share over the past 5 quarters. However, while recent estimates for the company have been lowered by analysts, USB has posted better than expected results. Based on operating earnings yield, the company is undervalued when compared to all of the companies in our coverage universe. Share price changes over the past year indicates that USB will perform in line with the market over the near term.

Financial Data
(US$ in Thousands)

	12/31/2012	12/31/2011	12/31/2010	12/31/2009	12/31/2008	12/31/2007	12/31/2006	12/31/2005
Earnings Per Share	2.84	2.46	1.73	0.97	1.61	2.43	2.61	2.42
Cash Flow Per Share	4.21	5.13	2.74	4.11	3.04	1.50	3.05	1.86
Tang Book Value Per Share	11.97	10.32	8.03	6.30	3.97	5.41	5.34	5.62
Dividends Per Share	0.780	0.500	0.200	0.200	1.700	1.625	1.390	1.230
Dividend Payout %	27.46	20.33	11.56	20.62	105.59	66.87	53.26	50.83
Income Statement								
Interest Income	12,883,000	12,639,000	12,158,000	11,538,000	12,418,000	13,136,000	12,263,000	10,551,000
Interest Expense	2,138,000	2,516,000	2,579,000	3,020,000	4,686,000	6,447,000	5,522,000	3,496,000
Net Interest Income	10,745,000	10,123,000	9,579,000	8,518,000	7,732,000	6,689,000	6,741,000	7,055,000
Provision for Losses	1,882,000	2,343,000	4,356,000	5,557,000	3,096,000	792,000	544,000	666,000
Non-Interest Income	9,319,000	8,760,000	8,360,000	7,952,000	6,811,000	7,172,000	6,846,000	6,045,000
Non-Interest Expense	10,456,000	9,911,000	9,383,000	8,281,000	7,414,000	6,862,000	6,180,000	5,863,000
Income Before Taxes	7,726,000	6,629,000	4,200,000	2,632,000	4,033,000	6,207,000	6,863,000	6,571,000
Income Taxes	2,236,000	1,841,000	935,000	395,000	1,087,000	1,883,000	2,112,000	2,082,000
Net Income	5,647,000	4,872,000	3,317,000	2,205,000	2,946,000	4,324,000	4,751,000	4,489,000
Average Shares	1,896,000	1,923,000	1,921,000	1,859,000	1,757,000	1,758,000	1,804,000	1,857,000
Balance Sheet								
Net Loans & Leases	226,881,000	212,238,000	200,122,000	195,101,000	184,925,000	156,588,000	144,831,000	137,451,000
Total Assets	353,855,000	340,122,000	307,786,000	281,176,000	265,912,000	237,615,000	219,232,000	209,465,000
Total Deposits	249,183,000	230,885,000	204,252,000	183,242,000	159,350,000	131,445,000	124,882,000	124,709,000
Total Liabilities	314,857,000	306,144,000	278,267,000	255,213,000	239,612,000	216,569,000	198,035,000	189,379,000
Stockholders' Equity	38,998,000	33,978,000	29,519,000	25,963,000	26,300,000	21,046,000	21,197,000	20,086,000
Shares Outstanding	1,869,431	1,909,821	1,920,903	1,912,938	1,755,032	1,727,856	1,764,714	1,814,954
Statistical Record								
Return on Assets %	1.62	1.50	1.13	0.81	1.17	1.89	2.22	2.22
Return on Equity %	15.43	15.35	11.96	8.44	12.41	20.47	23.02	22.66
Net Interest Margin %	83.40	80.09	78.79	73.83	62.26	50.92	54.97	66.87
Efficiency Ratio %	47.09	46.32	45.73	42.49	38.56	33.79	32.34	35.33
Loans to Deposits	0.91	0.92	0.98	1.06	1.16	1.19	1.16	1.10
Price Range	35.19-27.57	28.70-20.31	28.26-20.71	25.35-8.82	37.99-22.12	36.68-29.26	36.69-29.03	31.32-27.16
P/E Ratio	12.39-9.71	11.67-8.26	16.34-11.97	26.13-9.09	23.60-13.74	15.09-12.04	14.06-11.12	12.94-11.22
Average Yield %	2.45	1.97	0.82	1.03	5.51	4.85	4.35	4.17

Address: 800 Nicollet Mall, Minneapolis, MN 55402	Web Site: www.usbank.com	Auditors: Ernst & Young LLP
Telephone: 651-466-3000	Officers: Richard K. Davis - Chairman, President, Chief Executive Officer, Chief Operating Officer Andrew Cecere - Vice-Chairman, Chief Financial Officer	Investor Contact: 612-303-0783 Transfer Agents: Computershare Investor Services

UNITED TECHNOLOGIES CORP.

Exchange	Symbol	Price	52Wk Range	Yield	P/E	Div Achiever
NYS	UTX	$93.43 (3/28/2013)	93.59-70.88	2.29	16.51	19 Years

*7 Year Price Score 101.98 *NYSE Composite Index=100 *12 Month Price Score 103.49

Interim Earnings (Per Share)

Qtr.	Mar	Jun	Sep	Dec
2008	1.03	1.32	1.33	1.22
2009	0.78	1.05	1.14	1.15
2010	0.93	1.20	1.30	1.31
2011	1.11	1.45	1.47	1.47
2012	0.36	1.47	1.56	2.27

Interim Dividends (Per Share)

Amt	Decl	Ex	Rec	Pay
0.48Q	04/11/2012	05/16/2012	05/18/2012	06/10/2012
0.535Q	06/13/2012	08/15/2012	08/17/2012	09/10/2012
0.535Q	10/10/2012	11/14/2012	11/16/2012	12/10/2012
0.535Q	02/04/2013	02/13/2013	02/15/2013	03/10/2013

Indicated Div: $2.14 (Div. Reinv. Plan)

Valuation Analysis — **Institutional Holding**

Forecast EPS	$6.11	No of Institutions
	(04/06/2013)	1616
Market Cap	$85.8 Billion	Shares
Book Value	$25.9 Billion	850,071,424
Price/Book	3.31	% Held
Price/Sales	1.49	83.54

Business Summary: Aerospace (MIC: 7.1.1 SIC: 3724 NAIC: 336412)

United Technologies provides technology products and services to the building systems and aerospace industries worldwide. Co.'s operations are classified into five principal segments: Otis, UTC Climate, Controls & Security, Pratt & Whitney, UTC Aerospace Systems, and Sikorsky. Co.'s principal products and services include elevators, escalators, heating, ventilating, air conditioning and refrigeration systems, commercial, military, business jet and general aviation aircraft engines, aerospace products and aftermarket services, military and commercial helicopters, helicopter and aircraft aftermarket parts and services.

Recent Developments: For the year ended Dec 31 2012, income from continuing operations decreased 0.3% to US$5.20 billion from US$5.22 billion a year earlier. Net income increased 2.2% to US$5.49 billion from US$5.37 billion in the prior year. Revenues were US$57.71 billion, up 3.5% from US$55.75 billion the year before. Operating income was US$7.68 billion versus US$7.85 billion in the prior year, a decrease of 2.1%. Direct operating expenses rose 4.4% to US$42.15 billion from US$40.37 billion in the comparable period the year before. Indirect operating expenses increased 4.4% to US$7.87 billion from US$7.54 billion in the equivalent prior-year period.

Prospects: Our evaluation of United Technologies Corp. as of Apr. 7, 2013 is the result of our systematic analysis on three basic characteristics: earnings strength, relative valuation, and recent stock price movement. The company has managed to produce a neutral trend in earnings per share over the past 5 quarters and while recent estimates for the company have been raised by analysts, UTX has posted better than expected results. Based on operating earnings yield, the company is undervalued when compared to all of the companies in our coverage universe. Share price changes over the past year indicates that UTX will perform in line with the market over the near term.

Financial Data
(US$ in Millions)

	12/31/2012	12/31/2011	12/31/2010	12/31/2009	12/31/2008	12/31/2007	12/31/2006	12/31/2005
Earnings Per Share	5.66	5.49	4.74	4.12	4.90	4.27	3.71	3.03
Cash Flow Per Share	7.36	7.39	6.51	5.83	6.55	5.53	4.90	4.37
Tang Book Value Per Share	N.M.	0.02	N.M.	0.25	N.M.	1.50	N.M.	0.91
Dividends Per Share	2.030	1.865	1.700	1.540	1.345	1.170	1.015	0.880
Dividend Payout %	35.87	33.97	35.86	37.38	27.45	27.40	27.36	29.04
Income Statement								
Total Revenue	57,708	58,190	54,326	52,920	58,681	54,759	47,829	42,725
EBITDA	8,604	8,989	8,086	7,317	8,490	7,820	6,822	5,891
Depn & Amortn	920	890	900	852	865	770	724	709
Income Before Taxes	6,911	7,605	6,538	5,760	6,936	6,384	5,492	4,684
Income Taxes	1,711	2,231	1,827	1,581	1,883	1,836	1,494	1,253
Net Income	5,130	4,979	4,373	3,829	4,689	4,224	3,732	3,069
Average Shares	906	906	922	928	956	988	1,005	1,014
Balance Sheet								
Current Assets	29,610	25,758	23,510	23,194	24,099	22,071	18,844	17,206
Total Assets	89,409	61,452	58,493	55,762	56,469	54,575	47,141	45,925
Current Liabilities	23,786	18,616	17,732	17,913	19,434	17,469	15,208	15,345
Long-Term Obligations	21,597	9,501	10,010	8,257	9,337	8,015	7,037	5,935
Total Liabilities	63,495	39,572	37,108	35,696	40,552	33,220	29,844	28,934
Stockholders' Equity	25,914	21,880	21,385	20,066	15,917	21,355	17,297	16,991
Shares Outstanding	918	907	921	936	943	983	955	1,013
Statistical Record								
Return on Assets %	6.78	8.30	7.65	6.82	8.42	8.31	8.02	7.14
Return on Equity %	21.41	23.02	21.10	21.28	25.09	21.86	21.77	19.80
EBITDA Margin %	14.91	15.45	14.88	13.83	14.47	14.28	14.26	13.79
Net Margin %	8.89	8.56	8.05	7.24	7.99	7.71	7.80	7.18
Asset Turnover	0.76	0.97	0.95	0.94	1.05	1.08	1.03	0.99
Current Ratio	1.24	1.38	1.33	1.29	1.24	1.26	1.24	1.12
Debt to Equity	0.83	0.43	0.47	0.41	0.59	0.38	0.41	0.35
Price Range	86.89-70.88	91.39-67.44	79.52-63.22	70.49-37.56	76.54-43.22	82.07-62.47	66.79-54.47	58.03-48.77
P/E Ratio	15.35-12.52	16.65-12.28	16.78-13.34	17.11-9.12	15.62-8.82	19.22-14.63	18.00-14.68	19.15-16.10
Average Yield %	2.59	2.33	2.38	2.79	2.10	1.63	1.65	1.70

Address: One Financial Plaza, Hartford, CT 06103	Web Site: www.utc.com	Auditors: PricewaterhouseCoopers LLP
Telephone: 860-728-7000	Officers: Louis R. Chenevert - Chairman, President, Chief Executive Officer Gregory J. Hayes - Senior Vice President, Chief Financial Officer	Transfer Agents: Computershare Trust Company, N.A., Canton, MA
Fax: 860-728-7028		

US AIRWAYS GROUP INC

Exchange	Symbol	Price	52Wk Range	Yield	P/E
NYS	LCC	$16.97 (3/28/2013)	17.23-7.47	N/A	5.17

*7 Year Price Score 67.20 *NYSE Composite Index=100 *12 Month Price Score 109.90

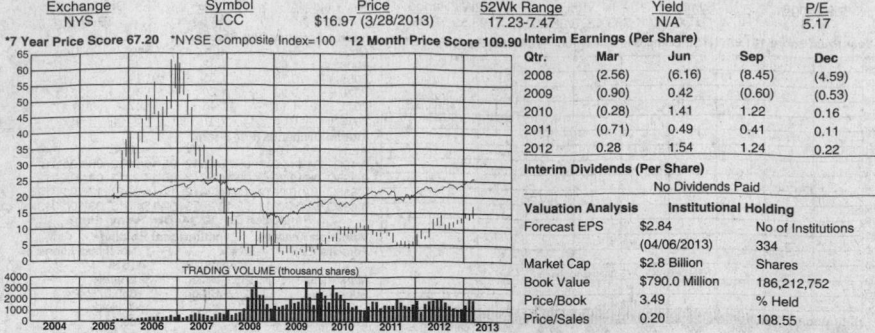

Interim Earnings (Per Share)

Qtr.	Mar	Jun	Sep	Dec
2008	(2.56)	(6.16)	(8.45)	(4.59)
2009	(0.90)	0.42	(0.60)	(0.53)
2010	(0.28)	1.41	1.22	0.16
2011	(0.71)	0.49	0.41	0.11
2012	0.28	1.54	1.24	0.22

Interim Dividends (Per Share)

No Dividends Paid

Valuation Analysis   **Institutional Holding**

Forecast EPS	$2.84	No of Institutions
	(04/06/2013)	334
Market Cap	$2.8 Billion	Shares
Book Value	$790.0 Million	186,212,752
Price/Book	3.49	% Held
Price/Sales	0.20	108.55

Business Summary: Airlines/Air Freight (MIC: 7.4.4 SIC: 4512 NAIC: 481111)

US Airways Group is a holding company whose primary business activity is the operation of a network air carrier through its wholly owned subsidiaries US Airways, Inc., Piedmont Airlines, Inc., PSA Airlines, Inc., Material Services Company, Inc. and Airways Assurance Limited. As of Dec. 31 2012 Co. provided scheduled passenger service to 198 communities in the U.S., Canada, Mexico, Europe, the Middle East, the Caribbean, and Central and South America. As of the same date, Co. operated 340 mainline jets and was supported by its regional airline subsidiaries and affiliates operating as US Airways Express under capacity purchase agreements, which operated 238 regional jets and 44 turboprops.

Recent Developments: For the year ended Dec 31 2012, net income increased 797.2% to US$637.0 million from US$71.0 million in the prior year. Revenues were US$13.83 billion, up 5.9% from US$13.06 billion the year before. Operating income was US$856.0 million versus US$426.0 million in the prior year, an increase of 100.9%. Direct operating expenses rose 0.5% to US$5.03 billion from US$5.01 billion in the comparable period the year before. Indirect operating expenses increased 4.2% to US$7.94 billion from US$7.62 billion in the equivalent prior-year period.

Prospects: Our evaluation of US Airways Group Inc. as of Apr. 7, 2013 is the result of our systematic analysis on three basic characteristics: earnings strength, relative valuation, and recent stock price movement. The company has suffered a very negative trend in earnings per share over the past 5 quarters. However, while recent estimates for the company have been lowered by analysts, LCC has posted better than expected results. Based on operating earnings yield, the company is undervalued when compared to all of the companies in our coverage universe. Share price changes over the past year indicates that LCC will perform very well over the near term.

Financial Data
(US$ in Thousands)

	12/31/2012	12/31/2011	12/31/2010	12/31/2009	12/31/2008	12/31/2007	12/31/2006	12/31/2005
Earnings Per Share	3.28	0.44	2.61	(1.54)	(22.06)	4.52	3.33	(17.06)
Cash Flow Per Share	6.25	2.91	4.98	0.44	(9.76)	4.83	7.15	1.46
Tang Book Value Per Share	1.54	N.M.	N.M.	...	...	2.87	N.M.	N.M.
Income Statement								
Total Revenue	13,831,000	13,055,000	11,908,000	10,458,000	12,118,000	11,700,000	11,557,000	5,077,000
EBITDA	1,260,000	672,000	1,085,000	292,000	(1,823,000)	721,000	727,000	(86,000)
Depn & Amortn	282,000	259,000	267,000	255,000	217,000	186,000	181,000	132,000
Income Before Taxes	637,000	90,000	502,000	(243,000)	(2,210,000)	434,000	404,000	(335,000)
Income Taxes	...	19,000	...	(38,000)	...	7,000	101,000	...
Net Income	637,000	71,000	502,000	(205,000)	(2,210,000)	427,000	304,000	(537,000)
Average Shares	203,978	163,743	201,131	133,000	100,168	95,603	93,821	31,487
Balance Sheet								
Current Assets	3,582,000	3,049,000	2,909,000	2,331,000	2,418,000	3,347,000	3,354,000	2,559,000
Total Assets	9,396,000	8,335,000	7,819,000	7,454,000	7,214,000	8,040,000	7,576,000	6,964,000
Current Liabilities	3,303,000	3,160,000	2,840,000	2,789,000	3,044,000	2,551,000	2,712,000	2,659,000
Long-Term Obligations	4,376,000	4,130,000	4,003,000	4,024,000	3,634,000	3,031,000	2,907,000	2,749,000
Total Liabilities	8,606,000	8,185,000	7,735,000	7,809,000	7,719,000	6,601,000	6,606,000	6,544,000
Stockholders' Equity	790,000	150,000	84,000	(355,000)	(505,000)	1,439,000	970,000	420,000
Shares Outstanding	162,502	162,116	161,874	161,102	114,113	91,865	91,283	81,664
Statistical Record								
Return on Assets %	7.17	0.88	6.57	N.M.	N.M.	5.47	4.18	N.M.
Return on Equity %	135.16	60.68	...	...	N.M.	35.45	43.74	N.M.
EBITDA Margin %	9.11	5.15	9.11	2.79	N.M.	6.16	6.29	N.M.
Net Margin %	4.61	0.54	4.22	N.M.	N.M.	3.65	2.63	N.M.
Asset Turnover	1.56	1.62	1.56	1.43	1.58	1.50	1.59	1.20
Current Ratio	1.08	0.96	1.02	0.84	0.79	1.31	1.24	0.96
Debt to Equity	5.54	27.53	47.65	...	...	2.11	3.00	6.55
Price Range	14.45-5.03	11.47-4.00	12.07-4.77	9.57-1.97	15.40-1.76	61.96-14.71	62.95-28.89	37.73-19.30
P/E Ratio	4.41-1.53	26.07-9.09	4.62-1.83	...	...	13.71-3.25	18.90-8.68	...

Address: 111 West Rio Salado Parkway, Tempe, AZ 85281 **Telephone:** 480-693-0800	**Web Site:** www.usairways.com **Officers:** W. Douglas Parker - Chairman, Chief Executive Officer J. Scott Kirby - President	**Auditors:** KPMG LLP **Investor Contact:** 480-.69-3.1227 **Transfer Agents:** American Stock Transfer & Trust Co., Brooklyn, NY

UNIVERSAL CORP.

Exchange	Symbol	Price	52Wk Range	Yield	P/E	Div Achiever
NYS	UVV	$56.04 (3/28/2013)	58.36-44.03	3.57	12.03	42 Years

*7 Year Price Score 96.66 *NYSE Composite Index=100 *12 Month Price Score 104.67

TRADING VOLUME (thousand shares)

Interim Earnings (Per Share)

Qtr.	Jun	Sep	Dec	Mar
2009-10	1.47	1.77	1.54	0.90
2010-11	0.87	1.78	1.82	0.96
2011-12	0.52	(0.51)	2.06	0.91
2012-13	0.81	1.68	1.26	...

Interim Dividends (Per Share)

Amt	Decl	Ex	Rec	Pay
0.49Q	05/22/2012	07/05/2012	07/09/2012	08/13/2012
0.49Q	08/07/2012	10/04/2012	10/09/2012	11/12/2012
0.50Q	11/06/2012	01/10/2013	01/14/2013	02/11/2013
0.50Q	02/05/2013	04/04/2013	04/08/2013	05/13/2013

Indicated Div: $2.00 (Div. Reinv. Plan)

Valuation Analysis / **Institutional Holding**

Forecast EPS	$4.40 (04/05/2013)	No of Institutions	231
Market Cap	$1.3 Billion	Shares	26,409,338
Book Value	$1.2 Billion	% Held	94.03
Price/Book	1.05		
Price/Sales	0.53		

Business Summary: Tobacco Products (MIC: 1.3.1 SIC: 5159 NAIC: 424590)

Universal is a holding company that operates through directly and indirectly owned subsidiaries. Co. operates in over 30 countries on five continents. Co.'s principle business involves the procuring and processing of flue-cured and burley leaf tobacco for manufacturers of consumer tobacco products. Co. does not manufacture cigarettes or other consumer tobacco products. Co.'s reportable segments for its flue-cured and burley tobacco operations are North America and Other Regions. Co. also has a third reportable segment, Other Tobacco Operations, which comprises of its dark tobacco business, its oriental tobacco joint venture, and certain tobacco-related services.

Recent Developments: For the quarter ended Dec 31 2012, net income decreased 35.5% to US$39.7 million from US$61.6 million in the year-earlier quarter. Revenues were US$680.0 million, up 1.1% from US$672.4 million the year before. Operating income was US$64.5 million versus US$93.1 million in the prior-year quarter, a decrease of 30.7%. Direct operating expenses rose 5.6% to US$554.6 million from US$525.3 million in the comparable period the year before. Indirect operating expenses increased 12.8% to US$60.9 million from US$54.0 million in the equivalent prior-year period.

Prospects: Our evaluation of Universal Corp. as of Apr. 7, 2013 is the result of our systematic analysis on three basic characteristics: earnings strength, relative valuation, and recent stock price movement. The company has generated a negative trend in earnings per share over the past 5 quarters. Because the company lacks sufficient analyst estimate data, we place greater weight on the historical EPS trend as the measure of earnings strength. Based on operating earnings yield, the company is undervalued when compared to all of the companies in our coverage universe. Share price changes over the past year indicates that UVV will perform well over the near term.

Financial Data

(US$ in Thousands)	9 Mos	6 Mos	3 Mos	03/31/2012	03/31/2011	03/31/2010	03/31/2009	03/31/2008
Earnings Per Share	4.66	5.46	3.27	3.25	5.42	5.68	4.57	3.70
Cash Flow Per Share	14.59	11.42	12.32	8.58	2.27	6.56	3.87	3.31
Tang Book Value Per Share	40.12	38.94	37.22	37.46	37.57	33.05	28.42	29.30
Dividends Per Share	1.960	1.950	1.940	1.930	1.890	1.850	1.810	1.770
Dividend Payout %	42.06	35.71	59.33	59.38	34.87	32.57	39.61	47.84
Income Statement								
Total Revenue	1,816,607	1,136,578	461,391	2,446,877	2,571,527	2,491,738	2,554,659	2,145,822
EBITDA	216,123	140,416	54,064	222,462	298,254	298,497	250,693	232,896
Depn & Amortn	33,696	22,502	11,237	42,158	43,654	41,288	40,761	41,383
Income Before Taxes	165,059	106,033	36,814	158,783	234,265	234,252	176,606	166,783
Income Taxes	50,633	32,563	12,950	61,159	78,349	86,283	64,588	63,799
Net Income	106,648	71,106	23,125	92,057	156,565	168,397	131,739	119,156
Average Shares	28,517	28,501	28,391	28,339	28,888	29,662	25,570	32,186
Balance Sheet								
Current Assets	1,741,566	1,723,481	1,797,151	1,690,629	1,578,234	1,693,076	1,503,919	1,417,060
Total Assets	2,300,725	2,285,199	2,354,502	2,266,919	2,227,867	2,371,040	2,138,176	2,134,112
Current Liabilities	567,442	377,918	491,608	392,708	512,351	614,999	549,875	402,326
Long-Term Obligations	185,000	387,500	390,000	392,500	320,193	414,764	331,808	402,942
Total Liabilities	1,052,748	1,061,547	1,172,818	1,083,468	1,042,261	1,248,470	1,108,703	1,018,481
Stockholders' Equity	1,247,977	1,223,652	1,181,684	1,183,451	1,185,606	1,122,570	1,029,473	1,115,631
Shares Outstanding	23,324	23,408	23,356	23,257	23,240	24,325	24,999	27,162
Statistical Record								
Return on Assets %	5.79	6.77	4.18	4.08	6.81	7.47	6.17	5.33
Return on Equity %	10.86	13.07	8.38	7.75	13.57	15.65	12.28	11.07
EBITDA Margin %	11.90	12.35	11.72	9.09	11.60	11.98	9.81	10.85
Net Margin %	5.87	6.26	5.01	3.76	6.09	6.76	5.16	5.55
Asset Turnover	1.08	1.07	1.02	1.09	1.12	1.11	1.20	0.96
Current Ratio	3.07	4.56	3.66	4.31	3.08	2.75	2.74	3.52
Debt to Equity	0.15	0.32	0.33	0.33	0.27	0.37	0.32	0.36
Price Range	52.25-44.03	51.10-35.78	48.11-35.11	48.11-35.11	55.92-35.44	55.19-29.27	65.53-25.82	67.08-44.48
P/E Ratio	11.21-9.45	9.36-6.55	14.71-10.74	14.80-10.80	10.32-6.54	9.72-5.15	14.34-5.65	18.13-12.02
Average Yield %	4.15	4.29	4.52	4.61	4.48	4.43	4.11	3.19

Address: 9201 Forest Hill Avenue, Richmond, VA 23235 **Telephone:** 804-359-9311	**Web Site:** www.universalcorp.com **Officers:** George C. Freeman - Chairman, President, Chief Executive Officer W. Keith Brewer - Executive Vice President, Chief Operating Officer	**Auditors:** Ernst & Young LLP **Investor Contact:** 804-359-9311 **Transfer Agents:** Wells Fargo Bank, N.A., St. Paul, MN

UNIVERSAL HEALTH REALTY INCOME TRUST

Exchange	Symbol	Price	52Wk Range	Yield	P/E	Div Achiever
NYS	UHT	$57.71 (3/28/2013)	58.03-37.85	4.30	37.47	25 Years

*7 Year Price Score 113.13 *NYSE Composite Index=100 *12 Month Price Score 111.26

Interim Earnings (Per Share)

Qtr.	Mar	Jun	Sep	Dec
2008	0.35	0.35	0.35	(0.07)
2009	0.39	0.40	0.38	0.38
2010	0.37	0.35	0.27	0.33
2011	0.33	0.29	0.26	4.95
2012	0.75	0.19	0.24	0.36

Interim Dividends (Per Share)

Amt	Decl	Ex	Rec	Pay
0.615Q	06/07/2012	06/14/2012	06/18/2012	06/29/2012
0.615Q	09/06/2012	09/13/2012	09/17/2012	09/28/2012
0.62Q	12/07/2012	12/13/2012	12/17/2012	12/31/2012
0.62Q	03/07/2013	03/14/2013	03/18/2013	03/29/2013

Indicated Div: $2.48 (Div. Reinv. Plan)

Valuation Analysis

		Institutional Holding	
Forecast EPS	$1.31 (04/05/2013)	No of Institutions	158
Market Cap	$732.3 Million	Shares	6,363,257
Book Value	$177.7 Million	% Held	47.15
Price/Book	4.12		
Price/Sales	13.57		

TRADING VOLUME (thousand shares)

Business Summary: REITs (MIC: 5.3.1 SIC: 6798 NAIC: 525930)

Universal Health Realty Income Trust is real estate investment trust. Co. invests in health care and human service related facilities including acute care hospitals, behavioral healthcare facilities, rehabilitation hospitals, sub-acute facilities, surgery centers, childcare centers and medical office buildings (MOBs). As of Feb 29 2012, Co. had 54 real estate investments or commitments located in fifteen states in the U.S. consisting of: seven hospital facilities including three acute care, one behavioral healthcare, one rehabilitation and two sub-acute; 43 MOBs (including 14 owned by various unconsolidated limited liability companies), and; four preschool and childcare centers.

Recent Developments: For the year ended Dec 31 2012, net income decreased 73.6% to US$19.5 million from US$73.8 million in the prior year. Revenues were US$54.0 million, up 82.9% from US$29.5 million the year before.

Prospects: Our evaluation of Universal Health Realty Income Trust as of Apr. 7, 2013 is the result of our systematic analysis on three basic characteristics: earnings strength, relative valuation, and recent stock price movement. The company has enjoyed a very positive trend in earnings per share over the past 5 quarters. Because the company lacks sufficient analyst estimate data, we place greater weight on the historical EPS trend as the measure of earnings strength. Based on operating earnings yield, the company is overvalued when compared to all of the companies in our coverage universe. Share price changes over the past year indicates that UHT will perform very well over the near term.

Financial Data
(US$ in Thousands)

	12/31/2012	12/31/2011	12/31/2010	12/31/2009	12/31/2008	12/31/2007	12/31/2006	12/31/2005
Earnings Per Share	1.54	5.83	1.33	1.56	0.98	1.87	2.92	2.15
Cash Flow Per Share	2.42	1.69	1.88	2.10	1.84	1.93	2.10	2.15
Tang Book Value Per Share	11.93	12.69	11.49	11.66	12.21	13.54	13.92	13.20
Dividends Per Share	2.460	2.425	2.415	2.380	2.340	2.300	2.260	2.175
Dividend Payout %	159.74	41.60	181.58	152.56	238.78	122.99	77.40	101.16
Income Statement								
Total Revenue	53,950	29,494	28,878	31,914	29,184	27,960	32,509	33,338
EBITDA	41,322	15,377	20,578	23,687	18,235	20,981	22,580	23,947
Depn & Amortn	19,559	7,306	6,286	6,399	5,904	5,209	5,757	5,825
Income Before Taxes	13,995	5,669	12,353	14,840	9,940	14,023	14,540	14,824
Net Income	19,477	73,794	16,310	18,576	11,653	22,191	34,697	25,423
Average Shares	12,669	12,649	12,262	11,897	11,882	11,875	11,866	11,841
Balance Sheet								
Current Assets	7,872	15,687	3,863	6,057	3,545	2,837	2,637	13,166
Total Assets	383,038	370,929	216,135	228,825	221,056	199,749	194,139	196,889
Current Liabilities	539	473	113	142	190	125	84	357
Long-Term Obligations	197,936	174,836	67,563	84,267	71,692	36,617	26,337	35,548
Total Liabilities	205,367	182,068	70,722	87,863	76,128	39,444	29,942	41,439
Stockholders' Equity	177,671	188,861	145,413	140,962	144,928	160,305	164,197	155,450
Shares Outstanding	12,688	12,666	12,653	12,089	11,865	11,841	11,791	11,777
Statistical Record								
Return on Assets %	5.15	25.14	7.33	8.26	5.52	11.27	17.75	12.66
Return on Equity %	10.60	44.15	11.39	13.00	7.61	13.68	21.71	16.43
EBITDA Margin %	76.59	52.14	71.26	74.22	62.48	75.04	69.46	71.83
Net Margin %	36.10	250.20	56.48	58.21	39.93	79.37	106.73	76.26
Asset Turnover	0.14	0.10	0.13	0.14	0.14	0.14	0.17	0.17
Current Ratio	14.60	33.16	34.19	42.65	18.66	22.70	31.39	36.88
Debt to Equity	1.11	0.93	0.46	0.60	0.49	0.23	0.16	0.23
Price Range	50.61-37.77	43.38-32.21	38.40-30.79	35.28-25.11	39.14-23.27	42.05-29.23	40.24-29.72	40.80-27.47
P/E Ratio	32.86-24.53	7.44-5.52	28.87-23.15	22.62-16.10	39.94-23.74	22.49-15.63	13.78-10.18	18.98-12.78
Average Yield %	5.76	6.33	7.08	7.51	6.97	6.48	6.50	6.56

Address: Universal Corporate Center, 367 South Gulph Road, P.O. Box 61558, King of Prussia, PA 19406-0958 Telephone: 610-265-0688 Fax: 610-768-3336	Web Site: www.uhrit.com Officers: Alan B. Miller - Chairman, President, Chief Executive Officer Charles F. Boyle - Vice President, Chief Financial Officer	Auditors: KPMG LLP Transfer Agents: EquiServe Trust Company, N.A., Providence, RI

UNIVERSAL HEALTH SERVICES, INC.

Exchange	Symbol	Price	52Wk Range	Yield	P/E
NYS	UHS	$63.87 (3/28/2013)	64.38-37.30	0.31	14.10

*7 Year Price Score 119.62 *NYSE Composite Index=100 ***12 Month Price Score 118.09**

Interim Earnings (Per Share)

Qtr.	Mar	Jun	Sep	Dec
2008	0.60	0.54	0.36	0.47
2009	0.69	0.82	0.52	0.62
2010	0.73	0.67	0.57	0.38
2011	1.15	1.04	0.86	0.98
2012	1.31	1.10	0.73	1.38

Interim Dividends (Per Share)

Amt	Decl	Ex	Rec	Pay
0.05Q	07/18/2012	08/30/2012	09/04/2012	09/18/2012
0.05Q	11/21/2012	11/29/2012	12/03/2012	12/17/2012
0.40Sp	12/06/2012	12/13/2012	12/17/2012	12/28/2012
0.05Q	01/16/2013	02/27/2013	03/01/2013	03/15/2013

Indicated Div: $0.20

Valuation Analysis

Forecast EPS	$4.45 (04/05/2013)
Market Cap	$6.2 Billion
Book Value	$2.7 Billion
Price/Book	2.30
Price/Sales	0.90

Institutional Holding

No of Institutions	374
Shares	100,570,976
% Held	88.63

TRADING VOLUME (thousand shares)

Business Summary: Hospitals & Health Care Facilities (MIC: 4.2.1 SIC: 8062 NAIC: 622110)

Universal Health Services owns and operates acute care hospitals, behavioral health centers, surgical hospitals, ambulatory surgery centers and radiation oncology centers. As of Feb 24 2012, Co. owned and/or operated 25 acute care hospitals and 198 behavioral health centers located in 36 states, Washington, D.C., Puerto Rico and the U.S. Virgin Islands. As part of its ambulatory treatment centers division, Co. manages and/or owns outright or in partnerships with physicians, six surgical hospitals and surgery and radiation oncology centers located in four states and Puerto Rico. Co. has two segments: acute care hospital services and behavioral health care services.

Recent Developments: For the year ended Dec 31 2012, net income increased 9.0% to US$489.0 million from US$448.9 million in the prior year. Revenues were US$6.96 billion, up 3.0% from US$6.76 billion the year before. Operating income was US$942.6 million versus US$897.1 million in the prior year, an increase of 5.1%. Indirect operating expenses increased 2.7% to US$6.02 billion from US$5.86 billion in the equivalent prior-year period.

Prospects: Our evaluation of Universal Health Services Inc. as of Apr. 7, 2013 is the result of our systematic analysis on three basic characteristics: earnings strength, relative valuation, and recent stock price movement. The company has produced a positive trend in earnings per share over the past 5 quarters and while recent estimates for the company have been raised by analysts, UHS has posted better than expected results. Based on operating earnings yield, the company is undervalued when compared to all of the companies in our coverage universe. Share price changes over the past year indicates that UHS will perform in line with the market over the near term.

Financial Data
(US$ in Thousands)

	12/31/2012	12/31/2011	12/31/2010	12/31/2009	12/31/2008	12/31/2007	12/31/2006	12/31/2005
Earnings Per Share	4.53	4.04	2.34	2.64	1.97	1.59	2.28	2.00
Cash Flow Per Share	8.40	7.39	5.18	5.45	4.56	3.26	1.55	3.82
Tang Book Value Per Share	N.M.	N.M.	N.M.	10.51	8.20	7.29	6.33	4.81
Dividends Per Share	0.600	0.200	0.200	0.170	0.160	0.160	0.160	0.160
Dividend Payout %	13.25	4.95	8.55	6.44	8.14	10.06	7.02	8.00
Income Statement								
Total Revenue	6,961,400	7,500,198	5,568,185	5,202,379	5,022,417	4,751,005	4,191,300	3,935,480
EBITDA	1,213,081	1,165,628	708,497	705,132	586,319	532,256	637,968	369,422
Depn & Amortn	270,500	268,500	202,800	184,600	176,100	162,200	146,700	138,700
Income Before Taxes	763,663	696,336	428,097	474,722	357,012	318,430	458,710	197,789
Income Taxes	274,616	247,466	152,302	170,475	123,378	104,550	152,878	62,301
Net Income	443,446	398,167	230,183	260,373	199,377	170,387	259,458	240,845
Average Shares	97,711	98,537	97,973	98,275	101,552	107,138	115,816	125,294
Balance Sheet								
Current Assets	1,407,496	1,364,905	1,331,116	796,197	789,417	774,847	728,506	608,298
Total Assets	8,200,843	7,665,245	7,527,936	3,964,463	3,742,462	3,608,657	3,277,042	2,858,709
Current Liabilities	894,058	836,933	826,299	582,817	561,125	487,711	502,451	524,170
Long-Term Obligations	3,727,431	3,651,428	3,912,102	956,429	990,661	1,008,786	821,363	637,654
Total Liabilities	5,487,498	5,368,893	5,549,164	2,213,392	2,198,612	2,091,458	1,874,578	1,653,611
Stockholders' Equity	2,713,345	2,296,352	1,978,772	1,751,071	1,543,850	1,517,199	1,402,464	1,205,098
Shares Outstanding	97,591	96,609	97,450	96,914	98,888	105,127	107,747	107,942
Statistical Record								
Return on Assets %	5.57	5.24	4.01	6.76	5.41	4.95	8.46	8.19
Return on Equity %	17.66	18.63	12.34	15.80	12.99	11.67	19.90	19.86
EBITDA Margin %	17.43	15.54	12.72	13.55	11.67	11.20	15.22	9.39
Net Margin %	6.37	5.31	4.13	5.00	3.97	3.59	6.19	6.12
Asset Turnover	0.88	0.99	0.97	1.35	1.36	1.38	1.37	1.34
Current Ratio	1.57	1.63	1.61	1.37	1.41	1.59	1.45	1.16
Debt to Equity	1.37	1.59	1.98	0.55	0.64	0.66	0.59	0.53
Price Range	49.46-36.82	56.41-31.91	43.74-28.75	33.17-15.39	32.54-16.22	31.50-24.23	30.04-22.64	31.60-21.21
P/E Ratio	10.92-8.13	13.96-7.90	18.69-12.29	12.57-5.83	16.52-8.23	19.81-15.24	13.17-9.93	15.80-10.61
Average Yield %	1.43	0.45	0.54	0.67	0.60	0.57	0.61	0.62

Address: Universal Corporate Center, 367 South Gulph Road, King of Prussia, PA 19406-0958 **Telephone:** 610-768-3300	**Web Site:** www.uhsinc.com **Officers:** Alan B. Miller - Chairman, Chief Executive Officer, Division Officer Marc D. Miller - President	**Auditors:** PricewaterhouseCoopers LLP **Investor Contact:** 610-768-3300 **Transfer Agents:** Computershare, Jersey City, NJ

UNUM GROUP

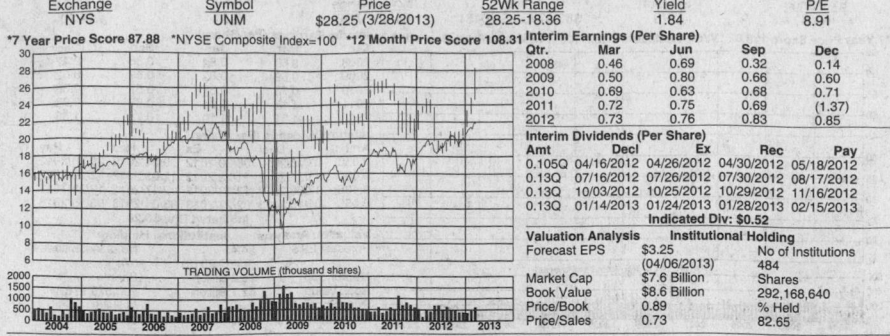

Exchange	Symbol	Price	52Wk Range	Yield	P/E
NYS	UNM	$28.25 (3/28/2013)	28.25-18.36	1.84	8.91

*7 Year Price Score 87.88 *NYSE Composite Index=100 *12 Month Price Score 108.31

Interim Earnings (Per Share)

Qtr.	Mar	Jun	Sep	Dec
2008	0.46	0.69	0.32	0.14
2009	0.50	0.80	0.66	0.60
2010	0.69	0.63	0.68	0.71
2011	0.72	0.75	0.69	(1.37)
2012	0.73	0.76	0.83	0.85

Interim Dividends (Per Share)

Amt	Decl	Ex	Rec	Pay
0.105Q	04/16/2012	04/26/2012	04/30/2012	05/18/2012
0.13Q	07/16/2012	07/26/2012	07/30/2012	08/17/2012
0.13Q	10/03/2012	10/25/2012	10/29/2012	11/16/2012
0.13Q	01/14/2013	01/24/2013	01/28/2013	02/15/2013

Indicated Div: $0.52

Valuation Analysis

		Institutional Holding	
Forecast EPS	$3.25 (04/06/2013)	No of Institutions	484
Market Cap	$7.6 Billion	Shares	292,168,640
Book Value	$8.6 Billion	% Held	82.65
Price/Book	0.89		
Price/Sales	0.73		

Business Summary: Life & Health (MIC: 5.2.2 SIC: 6321 NAIC: 524114)

Unum Group is an insurance holding company. Through its subsidiaries, Co. provides disability insurance products and other insurance products. As of Dec 31 2012, Co. had three primary business segments: Unum U.S., which includes group disability insurance, group life and accidental death and dismemberment products, and supplemental and voluntary lines of business; Unum U.K., which includes group disability, group life, and supplemental and voluntary lines of business; and Colonial Life, which includes insurance for accident, sickness, and disability products, life products, and cancer and critical illness products issued primarily by Colonial Life & Accident Insurance Company.

Recent Developments: For the year ended Dec 31 2012, net income increased 214.7% to US$894.4 million from US$284.2 million in the prior year. Revenues were US$10.52 billion, up 2.3% from US$10.28 billion the year before. Net premiums earned were US$7.72 billion versus US$7.51 billion in the prior year, an increase of 2.7%. Net investment income was unchanged at US$2.52 billion versus a year ago.

Prospects: Our evaluation of UNUM Group as of Apr. 7, 2013 is the result of our systematic analysis on three basic characteristics: earnings strength, relative valuation, and recent stock price movement. The company has enjoyed a very positive trend in earnings per share over the past 5 quarters and while recent estimates for the company have remained steady, UNM has posted better than expected results. Based on operating earnings yield, the company is undervalued when compared to all of the companies in our coverage universe. Share price changes over the past year indicates that UNM will perform poorly over the near term.

Financial Data
(US$ in Thousands)

	12/31/2012	12/31/2011	12/31/2010	12/31/2009	12/31/2008	12/31/2007	12/31/2006	12/31/2005
Earnings Per Share	3.17	0.78	2.71	2.57	1.62	1.91	1.23	1.64
Cash Flow Per Share	4.89	3.95	3.67	3.73	3.88	4.96	4.41	5.08
Tang Book Value Per Share	31.13	28.61	27.62	25.01	18.72	21.71	21.93	23.75
Dividends Per Share	0.470	0.395	0.350	0.315	0.300	0.300	0.300	0.300
Dividend Payout %	14.83	50.64	12.92	12.26	18.52	15.71	24.39	18.29
Income Statement								
Premium Income	7,716,100	7,514,200	7,431,400	7,475,500	7,783,300	7,901,100	7,948,200	7,815,600
Total Revenue	10,515,400	10,278,000	10,193,200	10,091,000	9,982,300	10,519,900	10,535,300	10,437,200
Income Before Taxes	1,249,500	257,200	1,331,300	1,292,300	824,000	997,200	465,400	709,600
Income Taxes	355,100	21,800	445,200	439,700	270,800	324,800	61,800	196,000
Net Income	894,400	235,400	886,100	852,600	553,200	679,300	411,000	513,600
Average Shares	281,756	303,571	327,221	332,136	341,560	355,776	334,361	312,512
Balance Sheet								
Total Assets	62,236,100	60,179,000	57,307,700	54,477,000	49,417,400	52,432,700	52,823,300	51,866,800
Total Liabilities	53,623,500	51,602,000	48,363,300	45,976,900	43,019,500	44,392,800	45,104,500	44,502,900
Stockholders' Equity	8,612,600	8,577,000	8,944,400	8,500,100	6,397,900	8,039,900	7,718,800	7,363,900
Shares Outstanding	270,205	292,715	316,573	331,809	331,120	360,893	342,627	298,557
Statistical Record								
Return on Assets %	1.46	0.40	1.59	1.64	1.08	1.29	0.79	1.00
Return on Equity %	10.38	2.69	10.16	11.45	7.64	8.62	5.45	7.04
Net Margin %	8.51	2.29	8.69	8.45	5.54	6.46	3.90	4.92
Price Range	24.68-18.36	26.90-19.91	26.41-18.73	22.89-7.99	26.14-9.48	27.57-19.93	24.05-16.23	22.76-15.98
P/E Ratio	7.79-5.79	34.49-25.53	9.75-6.91	8.91-3.11	16.14-5.85	14.43-10.43	19.55-13.20	13.88-9.74
Average Yield %	2.24	1.63	1.56	1.82	1.40	1.24	1.53	1.59

Address: 1 Fountain Square, Chattanooga, TN 37402 **Telephone:** 423-294-1011	**Web Site:** www.unum.com **Officers:** William J. Ryan - Chairman Thomas R. Watjen - President, Chief Executive Officer	**Auditors:** Ernst & Young LLP **Investor Contact:** 423-294-8996 **Transfer Agents:** Computershare Trust Company, N.A, Providence, RI

URS CORP

Exchange	Symbol	Price	52Wk Range	Yield	P/E
NYS	URS	$47.41 (3/28/2013)	47.41-32.60	1.77	11.37

*7 Year Price Score 80.24   *NYSE Composite Index=100   ***12 Month Price Score 103.79**

Interim Earnings (Per Share)

Qtr.	Mar	Jun	Sep	Dec
2008	0.60	0.72	0.79	0.55
2009	0.92	1.16	0.79	0.42
2010	1.17	0.76	0.87	0.75
2011	0.79	0.86	(8.05)	0.33
2012	1.07	0.72	1.43	0.95

Interim Dividends (Per Share)

Amt	Decl	Ex	Rec	Pay
0.20Q	05/04/2012	06/13/2012	06/15/2012	07/06/2012
0.20Q	08/03/2012	09/12/2012	09/14/2012	10/05/2012
0.20Q	11/02/2012	12/12/2012	12/14/2012	01/04/2013
0.21Q	02/25/2013	03/13/2013	03/15/2013	04/05/2013

Indicated Div: $0.84

Valuation Analysis   **Institutional Holding**

Forecast EPS	$4.50	No of Institutions
	(04/05/2013)	393
Market Cap	$3.6 Billion	Shares
Book Value	$3.6 Billion	78,430,592
Price/Book	1.01	% Held
Price/Sales	0.33	88.41

Business Summary: Construction Services (MIC: 7.5.4 SIC: 8711 NAIC: 541330)

URS provides engineering, construction and technical services, which include a range of program management, planning, design, engineering, construction and construction management, operations and maintenance, and decommissioning and closure services to public agencies and private sector clients. Co. also is a U.S. federal government contractor in the areas of systems engineering and technical assistance, operations and maintenance, and information technology services. Co. provides its services through four segments: Infrastructure and Environment, Federal Services, Energy and Construction, and Oil and Gas. Co.'s market sectors are federal, infrastructure, oil and gas, power and industrial.

Recent Developments: For the year ended Dec 28 2012, net income amounted to US$425.8 million versus a net loss of US$337.3 million in the prior year. Revenues were US$10.97 billion, up 15.0% from US$9.55 billion the year before. Operating income was US$685.9 million versus a loss of US$223.4 million in the prior year. Direct operating expenses rose 14.5% to US$10.29 billion from US$8.99 billion in the comparable period the year before. Indirect operating income amounted to US$7.9 million compared with an expense of US$779.6 million in the equivalent prior-year period.

Prospects: Our evaluation of URS Corp. as of Apr. 7, 2013 is the result of our systematic analysis on three basic characteristics: earnings strength, relative valuation, and recent stock price movement. The company has generated a negative trend in earnings per share over the past 5 quarters and while recent estimates for the company have remained steady, URS has posted better than expected results. Based on operating earnings yield, the company is undervalued when compared to all of the companies in our coverage universe. Share price changes over the past year indicates that URS will perform poorly over the near term.

Financial Data
(US$ in Thousands)

	12/28/2012	12/30/2011	12/31/2010	01/01/2010	01/02/2009	12/28/2007	12/29/2006	12/30/2005
Earnings Per Share	4.17	(6.03)	3.54	3.29	2.66	2.35	2.19	1.72
Cash Flow Per Share	5.81	6.55	6.53	8.03	4.13	5.66	3.26	4.30
Tang Book Value Per Share	N.M.	1.07	2.56	3.69	N.M.	N.M.	9.83	7.00
Dividends Per Share	0.800	...	...	...	...	...	...	...
Dividend Payout %	19.18	...	...	...	...	...	...	...
Income Statement								
Total Revenue	10,972,500	9,545,000	9,177,051	9,249,088	10,086,289	5,383,007	4,240,150	3,917,565
EBITDA	680,000	(212,900)	607,567	555,658	541,496	283,134	255,189	210,422
Depn & Amortn	101,200	142,700	133,472	139,723	142,640	51,866	36,400	36,000
Income Before Taxes	508,100	(377,700)	443,547	367,542	308,093	203,538	199,049	142,835
Income Taxes	189,900	91,800	154,884	177,556	172,813	97,254	84,793	60,360
Net Income	310,600	(465,800)	287,889	269,120	219,791	132,243	113,012	82,475
Average Shares	74,500	77,300	81,291	81,842	82,494	56,275	51,652	47,826
Balance Sheet								
Current Assets	3,517,200	3,088,900	3,009,026	2,880,820	2,640,481	2,588,378	1,374,153	1,273,060
Total Assets	8,786,500	6,862,600	7,351,355	6,904,416	7,001,152	6,929,965	2,581,029	2,469,448
Current Liabilities	2,001,000	1,734,900	1,645,085	1,529,514	1,587,355	1,681,603	785,985	698,621
Long-Term Obligations	1,992,500	737,000	641,300	689,725	1,091,528	1,288,817	163,910	315,762
Total Liabilities	5,165,400	3,485,400	3,234,181	2,998,602	3,376,521	3,451,395	1,074,342	1,124,944
Stockholders' Equity	3,621,100	3,377,200	4,117,174	3,905,814	3,624,631	3,478,570	1,506,687	1,344,504
Shares Outstanding	76,800	76,700	81,855	84,019	83,952	83,303	52,257	50,380
Statistical Record								
Return on Assets %	3.98	N.M.	4.05	3.88	3.10	2.79	4.49	3.47
Return on Equity %	8.90	N.M.	7.20	7.17	6.09	5.32	7.95	6.82
EBITDA Margin %	6.20	N.M.	6.62	6.01	5.37	5.26	6.02	5.37
Net Margin %	2.83	N.M.	3.14	2.91	2.18	2.46	2.67	2.11
Asset Turnover	1.41	1.35	1.29	1.33	1.42	1.14	1.68	1.65
Current Ratio	1.76	1.78	1.83	1.88	1.66	1.54	1.75	1.82
Debt to Equity	0.55	0.22	0.16	0.18	0.30	0.37	0.11	0.23
Price Range	46.75-32.60	47.41-28.46	52.82-35.28	52.45-28.00	54.80-20.78	62.40-40.83	48.87-36.79	43.29-27.21
P/E Ratio	11.21-7.82	...	14.92-9.97	15.94-8.51	20.60-7.81	26.55-17.37	22.32-16.80	25.17-15.82
Average Yield %	2.10	...	...	...	...	...	...	...

Address: 600 Montgomery Street, 26th Floor, San Francisco, CA 94111-2728 **Telephone:** 415-774-2700	**Web Site:** www.urs.com **Officers:** Martin M. Koffel - Chairman, President, Chief Executive Officer Hugh Blackwood - Senior Vice President	**Auditors:** PricewaterhouseCoopers LLP **Investor Contact:** 877-877-8970 **Transfer Agents:** BNY Mellon Shareowner Services, Pittsburgh, PA

URSTADT BIDDLE PROPERTIES INC

Exchange	Symbol	Price	52Wk Range	Yield	P/E	Div Achiever
NYS	UBA	$21.76 (3/28/2013)	21.78-17.45	4.60	80.59	14 Years

*7 Year Price Score 100.45 *NYSE Composite Index=100 *12 Month Price Score 99.38

Interim Earnings (Per Share)

Qtr.	Jan	Apr	Jul	Oct
2009-10	0.11	0.10	0.16	0.14
2010-11	0.23	0.12	0.14	0.12
2011-12	0.12	0.11	0.14	0.04
2012-13	(0.02)	...	...	...

Interim Dividends (Per Share)

Amt	Decl	Ex	Rec	Pay
0.248Q	06/05/2012	07/03/2012	07/06/2012	07/20/2012
0.248Q	09/06/2012	10/03/2012	10/05/2012	10/19/2012
0.25Q	12/12/2012	01/02/2013	01/04/2013	01/18/2013
0.25Q	03/21/2013	04/03/2013	04/05/2013	04/19/2013

Indicated Div: $1.00

Valuation Analysis

	Institutional Holding	
Forecast EPS	$0.47	No of Institutions
	(04/06/2013)	33
Market Cap	$708.4 Million	Shares
Book Value	$477.4 Million	772,983
Price/Book	1.48	% Held
Price/Sales	7.64	2.77

TRADING VOLUME (thousand shares)

Business Summary: REITs (MIC: 5.3.1 SIC: 6798 NAIC: 525930)

Urstadt Biddle Properties is a real estate investment trust engaged in the acquisition, ownership and management of commercial real estate. Co.'s sole business is the ownership of real estate investments, which consist principally of investments in income-producing properties, with primary emphasis on properties in the northeastern part of the U.S. with a concentration in Fairfield County, CT, Westchester and Putnam Counties, NY and Bergen County, NJ. At Oct 31 2012, Co. owned or had equity interests in 54 properties comprised of neighborhood and community shopping centers, office buildings, office/retail mixed use and industrial facilities located in seven states throughout the U.S.

Recent Developments: For the quarter ended Jan 31 2013, net income increased 1.2% to US$7.2 million from US$7.1 million in the year-earlier quarter. Revenues were US$24.1 million, up 6.4% from US$22.7 million the year before. Revenues from property income rose 5.9% to US$23.4 million from US$22.1 million in the corresponding quarter a year earlier.

Prospects: Our evaluation of Urstadt Biddle Properties Inc. as of Apr. 7, 2013 is the result of our systematic analysis on three basic characteristics: earnings strength, relative valuation, and recent stock price movement. The company has generated a negative trend in earnings per share over the past 5 quarters. Because the company lacks sufficient analyst estimate data, we place greater weight on the historical EPS trend as the measure of earnings strength. Based on operating earnings yield, the company is overvalued when compared to all of the companies in our coverage universe. Share price changes over the past year indicates that UBA will perform in line with the market over the near term.

Financial Data

(US$ in Thousands)	3 Mos	10/31/2012	10/31/2011	10/31/2010	10/31/2009	10/31/2008	10/31/2007	10/31/2006
Earnings Per Share	0.27	0.41	0.60	0.52	0.54	0.58	1.25	0.57
Cash Flow Per Share	1.70	1.86	1.68	1.78	1.71	1.78	1.95	1.42
Tang Book Value Per Share	8.81	9.09	11.41	11.69	11.66	12.03	10.74	10.29
Dividends Per Share	0.993	0.990	0.980	0.970	0.960	0.950	0.920	0.900
Dividend Payout %	367.59	241.46	163.33	186.54	177.78	163.79	73.60	157.89
Income Statement								
Total Revenue	24,136	91,295	91,011	85,149	82,572	80,856	81,880	73,249
EBITDA	13,963	63,161	61,340	57,725	56,756	56,921	61,600	54,277
Depn & Amortn	4,155	16,721	15,292	15,066	15,366	14,374	13,482	13,243
Income Before Taxes	8,320	37,292	38,183	35,074	34,695	35,535	40,345	32,747
Net Income	7,014	28,260	31,643	27,542	27,743	28,525	44,388	25,032
Average Shares	30,663	29,168	28,665	26,118	25,418	25,759	25,987	25,872
Balance Sheet								
Current Assets	78,738	164,614	29,043	37,972	31,808	20,862	23,135	22,576
Total Assets	651,971	724,243	576,264	557,053	504,539	506,117	471,770	451,350
Current Liabilities	5,010	1,632	893	1,397	771	606	3,970	1,785
Long-Term Obligations	142,502	154,836	159,985	129,802	116,417	110,054	108,482	104,341
Total Liabilities	174,540	239,725	177,843	153,399	134,755	129,617	124,820	118,147
Stockholders' Equity	477,431	484,518	398,421	403,654	369,784	376,500	346,950	333,203
Shares Outstanding	32,556	32,315	29,563	29,281	26,463	26,198	26,610	26,440
Statistical Record								
Return on Assets %	4.57	4.33	5.58	5.19	5.49	5.82	9.62	5.47
Return on Equity %	6.47	6.38	7.89	7.12	7.43	7.86	13.05	7.46
EBITDA Margin %	57.85	69.18	67.40	67.79	68.74	70.40	75.23	74.10
Net Margin %	29.06	30.95	34.77	32.35	33.60	35.28	54.21	34.17
Asset Turnover	0.15	0.14	0.16	0.16	0.16	0.16	0.18	0.16
Current Ratio	15.72	100.87	32.52	27.18	41.26	34.43	5.83	12.65
Debt to Equity	0.30	0.32	0.40	0.32	0.31	0.29	0.31	0.31
Price Range	20.78-17.45	20.78-15.61	20.05-15.31	19.55-13.72	16.94-10.08	19.28-12.79	19.62-14.97	19.44-15.58
P/E Ratio	76.96-64.63	50.68-38.07	33.42-25.52	37.60-26.38	31.37-18.67	33.24-22.05	15.70-11.98	34.11-27.33
Average Yield %	5.15	5.25	5.35	5.84	6.56	5.84	5.17	5.28

Address: 321 Railroad Avenue, Greenwich, CT 06830 **Telephone:** 203-863-8200 **Fax:** 203-861-6755	Web Site: www.ubproperties.com Officers: Charles J. Urstadt - Chairman, Chief Executive Officer Robert R. Douglass - Vice-Chairman	Auditors: PKF O' Conner Davies **Transfer Agents:** BNY Mellon Shareowner Services, Jersey City, N

USG CORP

Exchange	Symbol	Price	52Wk Range	Yield	P/E
NYS	USG	$26.44 (3/28/2013)	30.44-13.55	N/A	N/A

*7 Year Price Score 74.54 *NYSE Composite Index=100 *12 Month Price Score 115.51

Interim Earnings (Per Share)

Qtr.	Mar	Jun	Sep	Dec
2008	(0.45)	(0.40)	(0.40)	(3.41)
2009	(0.42)	(0.53)	(0.96)	(6.02)
2010	(1.10)	(0.74)	(1.00)	(1.18)
2011	(1.01)	(0.69)	(1.09)	(0.96)
2012	(0.26)	(0.53)	(0.28)	(0.12)

Interim Dividends (Per Share)

No Dividends Paid

Valuation Analysis

		Institutional Holding	
Forecast EPS	$0.63	No of Institutions	
	(04/05/2013)	295	
Market Cap	$2.9 Billion	Shares	
Book Value	$6.0 Million	84,359,008	
Price/Book	475.26	% Held	
Price/Sales	0.88	77.42	

TRADING VOLUME (thousand shares)

Business Summary: Construction Materials (MIC: 8.5.1 SIC: 3275 NAIC: 327420)

USG, through its subsidiaries, is a manufacturer and distributor of building materials. Co. produces a range of products for use in new residential, new nonresidential, and residential and nonresidential repair and remodel construction as well as products used in certain industrial processes. Co. operates three reportable segments: North American Gypsum, which manufactures and markets gypsum and related products in the U.S., Canada and Mexico; Building Products Distribution, which consists of L&W Supply Corporation, a distributor of gypsum wallboard and other building materials in the U.S.; and Worldwide Ceilings, which manufactures and markets interior systems products worldwide.

Recent Developments: For the year ended Dec 31 2012, loss from continuing operations was US$182.0 million compared with a loss of US$396.0 million a year earlier. Net loss amounted to US$125.0 million versus a net loss of US$390.0 million in the prior year. Revenues were US$3.22 billion, up 10.8% from US$2.91 billion the year before. Operating income was US$73.0 million versus a loss of US$206.0 million in the prior year. Direct operating expenses rose 2.8% to US$2.83 billion from US$2.75 billion in the comparable period the year before. Indirect operating expenses decreased 11.5% to US$322.0 million from US$364.0 million in the equivalent prior-year period.

Prospects: Our evaluation of USG Corp. as of Apr. 7, 2013 is the result of our systematic analysis on three basic characteristics: earnings strength, relative valuation, and recent stock price movement. The company has generated a negative trend in earnings per share over the past 5 quarters and while recent estimates for the company have been mixed, USG has posted results that fell short of analysts' expectations. Based on operating earnings yield, the company is overvalued when compared to all of the companies in our coverage universe. Share price changes over the past year indicates that USG will perform very well over the near term.

Financial Data

(US$ in Thousands)	12/31/2012	12/31/2011	12/31/2010	12/31/2009	12/31/2008	12/31/2007	12/31/2006	12/31/2005
Earnings Per Share	(1.19)	(3.76)	(4.03)	(7.93)	(4.67)	0.78	4.33	(32.92)
Cash Flow Per Share	0.64	(1.87)	(0.94)	1.40	(1.66)	13.46	(55.70)	11.60
Tang Book Value Per Share	0.06	1.48	6.02	9.37	15.51	19.86	15.36	...
Income Statement								
Total Revenue	3,224,000	3,024,000	2,939,000	3,235,000	4,608,000	5,202,000	5,810,000	5,139,000
EBITDA	168,000	(51,000)	(83,000)	27,000	(320,000)	345,000	1,126,000	(2,229,000)
Depn & Amortn	136,000	144,000	178,000	203,000	182,000	176,000	138,000	125,000
Income Before Taxes	(170,000)	(400,000)	(439,000)	(337,000)	(581,000)	86,000	476,000	(2,349,000)
Income Taxes	12,000	(10,000)	(34,000)	450,000	(118,000)	10,000	188,000	(924,000)
Net Income	(126,000)	(390,000)	(405,000)	(787,000)	(463,000)	76,000	288,000	(1,436,000)
Average Shares	106,382	103,902	100,472	99,238	99,100	97,303	66,563	43,622
Balance Sheet								
Current Assets	1,327,000	1,226,000	1,437,000	1,431,000	1,494,000	1,251,000	2,707,000	2,179,000
Total Assets	3,723,000	3,719,000	4,087,000	4,097,000	4,719,000	4,621,000	5,365,000	6,142,000
Current Liabilities	551,000	525,000	529,000	492,000	756,000	567,000	1,764,000	600,000
Long-Term Obligations	2,305,000	2,297,000	2,301,000	1,955,000	1,642,000	1,238,000	1,439,000	...
Total Liabilities	3,717,000	3,563,000	3,468,000	3,167,000	3,169,000	2,428,000	3,831,000	6,444,000
Stockholders' Equity	6,000	156,000	619,000	930,000	1,550,000	2,193,000	1,534,000	(302,000)
Shares Outstanding	107,850	105,329	102,876	99,300	99,179	99,051	89,865	44,637
Statistical Record								
Return on Assets %	N.M.	N.M.	N.M.	N.M.	N.M.	1.52	5.01	N.M.
Return on Equity %	N.M.	N.M.	N.M.	N.M.	N.M.	4.08	46.75	N.M.
EBITDA Margin %	5.21	N.M.	N.M.	0.83	N.M.	6.63	19.38	N.M.
Net Margin %	N.M.	N.M.	N.M.	N.M.	N.M.	1.46	4.96	N.M.
Asset Turnover	0.86	0.77	0.72	0.73	0.98	1.04	1.01	0.99
Current Ratio	2.41	2.34	2.72	2.91	1.98	2.21	1.53	3.63
Debt to Equity	384.17	14.72	3.72	2.10	1.06	0.56	0.94	...
Price Range	28.43-10.56	19.40-6.13	24.97-11.48	19.64-4.21	40.25-5.66	58.03-34.96	115.76-44.69	69.31-27.72
P/E Ratio	...	...	...	...	...	74.40-44.82	26.73-10.32	...

Address: 550 West Adams Street, Chicago, IL 60661-3676 **Telephone:** 312-436-4000	**Web Site:** www.usg.com **Officers:** James S. Metcalf - Chairman, President, Chief Executive Officer Stanley L. Ferguson - Executive Vice President, General Counsel	**Auditors:** Deloitte & Touche LLP **Investor Contact:** 312-436-6098 **Transfer Agents:** Computershare Trust Company, Providence, RI

VALASSIS COMMUNICATIONS, INC.

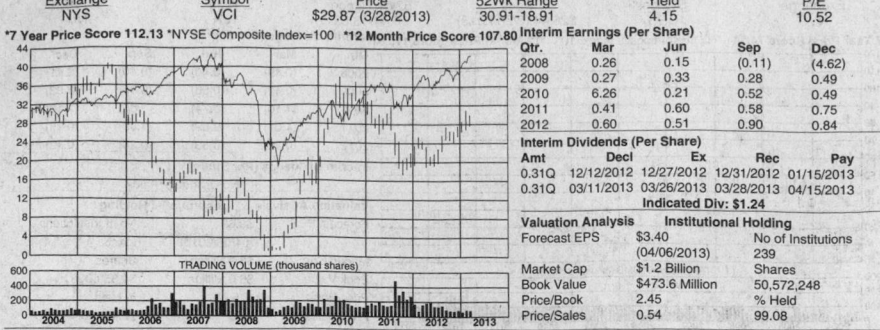

Exchange	Symbol	Price	52Wk Range	Yield	P/E
NYS	VCI	$29.87 (3/28/2013)	30.91-18.91	4.15	10.52

*7 Year Price Score 112.13 *NYSE Composite Index=100 *12 Month Price Score 107.80

Interim Earnings (Per Share)

Qtr.	Mar	Jun	Sep	Dec
2008	0.26	0.15	(0.11)	(4.62)
2009	0.27	0.33	0.28	0.49
2010	6.26	0.21	0.52	0.49
2011	0.41	0.60	0.58	0.75
2012	0.60	0.51	0.90	0.84

Interim Dividends (Per Share)

Amt	Decl	Ex	Rec	Pay
0.31Q	12/12/2012	12/27/2012	12/31/2012	01/15/2013
0.31Q	03/11/2013	03/26/2013	03/28/2013	04/15/2013

Indicated Div: $1.24

Valuation Analysis

		Institutional Holding	
Forecast EPS	$3.40	No of Institutions	
	(04/06/2013)	239	
Market Cap	$1.2 Billion	Shares	
Book Value	$473.6 Million	50,572,248	
Price/Book	2.45	% Held	
Price/Sales	0.54	99.08	

Business Summary: Publishing (MIC: 2.3.3 SIC: 7331 NAIC: 541860)

Valassis Communications is a media and marketing services company. Co.'s reportable segments are: Shared Mail, which combines the individual print advertisements of clients into a single shared mail package delivered through the United States Postal Service; Neighborhood Targeted, which includes newspaper inserts, polybag advertising and sampling, and Run of Press; and Free-standing Inserts, which include booklets containing promotions distributed through newspapers and shared mail. Co.'s other lines of business, International, Digital Media and Services, includes NCH Marketing Services, Inc., Valassis Canada, Inc., Promotion Watch, Inc., direct mail, analytics, digital and in-store.

Recent Developments: For the year ended Dec 31 2012, net income increased 4.9% to US$119.0 million from US$113.4 million in the prior year. Revenues were US$2.16 billion, down 3.3% from US$2.24 billion the year before. Operating income was US$213.3 million versus US$224.0 million in the prior year, a decrease of 4.8%. Direct operating expenses declined 3.6% to US$1.61 billion from US$1.67 billion in the comparable period the year before. Indirect operating expenses decreased 0.9% to US$338.6 million from US$341.7 million in the equivalent prior-year period.

Prospects: Our evaluation of Valassis Communications Inc. as of Apr. 7, 2013 is the result of our systematic analysis on three basic characteristics: earnings strength, relative valuation, and recent stock price movement. The company has suffered a very negative trend in earnings per share over the past 5 quarters. However, while recent estimates for the company have been lowered by analysts, VCI has posted results that fell short of analysts expectations. Based on operating earnings yield, the company is undervalued when compared to all of the companies in our coverage universe. Share price changes over the past year indicates that VCI will perform very well over the near term.

Financial Data
(US$ in Thousands)

	12/31/2012	12/31/2011	12/31/2010	12/31/2009	12/31/2008	12/31/2007	12/31/2006	12/31/2005
Earnings Per Share	2.84	2.33	7.42	1.36	(4.32)	1.21	1.07	1.90
Cash Flow Per Share	3.63	4.29	9.43	4.10	2.00	3.29	1.04	2.35
Tang Book Value Per Share	N.M.	N.M.	N.M.	N.M.	N.M.	N.M.	0.71	N.M.
Dividends Per Share	0.310	...	...	...	...	...	...	...
Dividend Payout %	10.92	...	...	...	...	...	...	...
Income Statement								
Total Revenue	2,162,084	2,235,959	2,333,512	2,244,248	2,381,907	2,242,171	1,043,491	1,131,043
EBITDA	257,427	263,168	745,706	265,286	(50,479)	230,934	123,261	173,126
Depn & Amortn	44,100	48,100	48,800	67,848	69,368	62,492	14,974	15,974
Income Before Taxes	184,866	179,744	632,655	110,943	(212,513)	88,860	83,538	146,225
Income Taxes	65,881	66,314	247,250	44,175	(5,022)	30,858	32,256	50,829
Net Income	118,985	113,430	385,405	66,768	(207,491)	58,002	51,282	95,396
Average Shares	41,947	48,777	51,957	49,270	47,977	47,885	47,780	50,183
Balance Sheet								
Current Assets	601,452	629,066	786,531	648,778	703,101	710,252	542,492	450,916
Total Assets	1,589,035	1,644,447	1,845,658	1,744,022	1,853,181	2,190,453	801,426	697,683
Current Liabilities	450,882	487,762	489,273	512,805	575,608	541,396	362,220	323,451
Long-Term Obligations	565,061	587,560	699,169	1,004,875	1,111,712	1,279,640	259,931	259,896
Total Liabilities	1,115,472	1,194,913	1,316,774	1,646,161	1,847,767	1,970,562	633,852	594,158
Stockholders' Equity	473,563	449,534	528,884	97,861	5,414	219,891	167,574	103,525
Shares Outstanding	38,766	42,347	50,361	48,762	48,053	47,935	47,783	47,629
Statistical Record								
Return on Assets %	7.34	6.50	21.47	3.71	N.M.	3.88	6.84	13.29
Return on Equity %	25.71	23.19	122.99	129.30	N.M.	29.94	37.83	78.18
EBITDA Margin %	11.91	11.77	31.96	11.82	N.M.	10.30	11.81	15.31
Net Margin %	5.50	5.07	16.52	2.98	N.M.	2.59	4.91	8.43
Asset Turnover	1.33	1.28	1.30	1.25	1.17	1.50	1.39	1.58
Current Ratio	1.33	1.29	1.61	1.27	1.22	1.31	1.50	1.39
Debt to Equity	1.19	1.31	1.32	10.27	205.34	5.82	1.55	2.51
Price Range	27.52-18.91	33.08-17.29	38.01-18.26	20.71-1.14	16.55-1.11	19.70-7.88	30.67-14.28	40.57-28.89
P/E Ratio	9.69-6.66	14.20-7.42	5.12-2.46	15.23-0.84	...	16.28-6.51	28.66-13.35	21.35-15.21
Average Yield %	1.33	...	...	...	...	...	...	...

Address: 19975 Victor Parkway, Livonia, MI 48152	Web Site: www.valassis.com	Auditors: Deloitte & Touche LLP
Telephone: 734-591-3000	Officers: Alan F. Schultz - Chairman, President, Chief Executive Officer James D. Parkinson - Executive Vice President, Chief Technology Officer	Investor Contact: 734-591-7375 Transfer Agents: Computershare, Providence, RI

VALERO ENERGY CORP.

Exchange	Symbol	Price	52Wk Range	Yield	P/E
NYS	VLO	$45.49 (3/28/2013)	48.51-20.37	1.76	12.13

*7 Year Price Score 78.63   ***NYSE Composite Index=100**   ***12 Month Price Score 133.03**

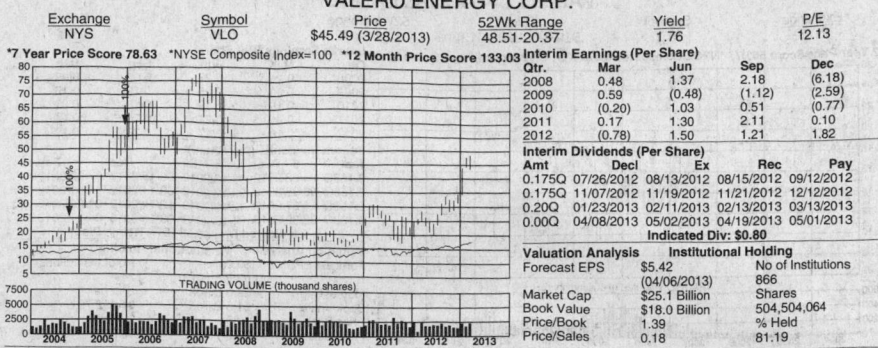

Interim Earnings (Per Share)

Qtr.	Mar	Jun	Sep	Dec
2008	0.48	1.37	2.18	(6.18)
2009	0.59	(0.48)	(1.12)	(2.59)
2010	(0.20)	1.03	0.51	(0.77)
2011	0.17	1.30	2.11	0.10
2012	(0.78)	1.50	1.21	1.82

Interim Dividends (Per Share)

Amt	Decl	Ex	Rec	Pay
0.175Q	07/26/2012	08/13/2012	08/15/2012	09/12/2012
0.175Q	11/07/2012	11/19/2012	11/21/2012	12/12/2012
0.20Q	01/23/2013	02/11/2013	02/13/2013	03/13/2013
0.00Q	04/08/2013	05/02/2013	04/19/2013	05/01/2013

Indicated Div: $0.80

Valuation Analysis   **Institutional Holding**

Forecast EPS	$5.42 (04/06/2013)	No of Institutions 866
Market Cap	$25.1 Billion	Shares
Book Value	$18.0 Billion	504,504,064
Price/Book	1.39	% Held
Price/Sales	0.18	81.19

Business Summary: Refining & Marketing (MIC: 9.1.2 SIC: 2911 NAIC: 324110)

Valero Energy is a petroleum refining and marketing company. Co. markets its refined products through a bulk and rack marketing network and sells refined products through a network of retail and wholesale branded outlets in the the U.S., Canada, the U.K., Aruba, and Ireland. Co. has three reportable business segments: refining, which consists of refining operations; wholesale marketing, product supply and distribution, and transportation operations; ethanol, which includes sales of internally produced ethanol and distillers grains; and retail, which includes Co.-operated convenience stores in the U.S. and Canada, filling stations, cardlock facilities, and heating oil operations in Canada.

Recent Developments: For the year ended Dec 31 2012, income from continuing operations decreased 0.8% to US$2.08 billion from US$2.10 billion a year earlier. Net income decreased 0.4% to US$2.08 billion from US$2.09 billion in the prior year. Revenues were US$139.25 billion, up 10.5% from US$125.99 billion the year before. Operating income was US$4.01 billion versus US$3.68 billion in the prior year, an increase of 9.0%. Direct operating expenses rose 9.9% to US$130.94 billion from US$119.13 billion in the comparable period the year before. Indirect operating expenses increased 35.3% to US$4.30 billion from US$3.18 billion in the equivalent prior-year period.

Prospects: Our evaluation of Valero Energy Corp. as of Apr. 7, 2013 is the result of our systematic analysis on three basic characteristics: earnings strength, relative valuation, and recent stock price movement. The company has produced a positive trend in earnings per share over the past 5 quarters and while recent estimates for the company have been mixed, VLO has posted better than expected results. Based on operating earnings yield, the company is undervalued when compared to all of the companies in our coverage universe. Share price changes over the past year indicates that VLO will perform very well over the near term.

Financial Data

(US$ in Thousands)	12/31/2012	12/31/2011	12/31/2010	12/31/2009	12/31/2008	12/31/2007	12/31/2006	12/31/2005
Earnings Per Share	3.75	3.68	0.57	(3.67)	(2.16)	8.88	8.64	6.10
Cash Flow Per Share	9.56	7.17	5.41	3.37	5.69	9.31	10.33	10.56
Tang Book Value Per Share	32.28	29.09	26.04	25.67	29.83	26.38	23.34	15.80
Dividends Per Share	0.650	0.300	0.200	0.600	0.570	0.480	0.300	0.190
Dividend Payout %	17.33	8.15	35.09	...	...	5.41	3.47	3.11
Income Statement								
Total Revenue	139,250,000	125,987,000	82,233,000	68,144,000	119,114,000	95,327,000	91,833,000	82,162,000
EBITDA	5,119,000	4,823,000	2,967,000	932,000	1,666,000	8,001,000	9,173,000	6,106,000
Depn & Amortn	1,100,000	1,100,000	985,000	973,000	990,000	916,000	812,000	594,000
Income Before Taxes	3,706,000	3,322,000	1,498,000	(449,000)	336,000	6,726,000	8,151,000	5,246,000
Income Taxes	1,626,000	1,226,000	575,000	(97,000)	1,467,000	2,161,000	2,726,000	1,697,000
Net Income	2,083,000	2,090,000	324,000	(1,982,000)	(1,131,000)	5,234,000	5,463,000	3,590,000
Average Shares	556,000	569,000	568,000	541,000	524,000	579,000	632,000	588,000
Balance Sheet								
Current Assets	16,460,000	15,972,000	13,518,000	10,923,000	9,450,000	14,792,000	10,760,000	8,276,000
Total Assets	44,477,000	42,783,000	37,621,000	35,629,000	34,417,000	42,722,000	37,753,000	32,728,000
Current Liabilities	11,929,000	12,708,000	8,784,000	7,798,000	6,209,000	11,914,000	8,822,000	7,305,000
Long-Term Obligations	6,463,000	6,732,000	7,515,000	7,195,000	6,302,000	6,521,000	4,722,000	5,208,000
Total Liabilities	26,445,000	26,360,000	22,596,000	20,904,000	18,797,000	24,215,000	19,148,000	17,678,000
Stockholders' Equity	18,032,000	16,423,000	15,025,000	14,725,000	15,620,000	18,507,000	18,605,000	15,050,000
Shares Outstanding	552,095	556,812	568,388	564,702	516,211	536,659	603,763	617,422
Statistical Record								
Return on Assets %	4.76	5.20	0.88	N.M.	N.M.	13.01	15.50	13.78
Return on Equity %	12.06	13.29	2.18	N.M.	N.M.	28.21	32.46	31.43
EBITDA Margin %	3.68	3.83	3.61	1.37	1.40	8.39	9.99	7.43
Net Margin %	1.50	1.66	0.39	N.M.	N.M.	5.49	5.95	4.37
Asset Turnover	3.18	3.13	2.25	1.95	3.08	2.37	2.61	3.15
Current Ratio	1.38	1.26	1.54	1.40	1.52	1.24	1.22	1.13
Debt to Equity	0.36	0.41	0.50	0.49	0.40	0.35	0.25	0.35
Price Range	34.38-19.61	30.73-17.17	23.35-15.65	25.85-15.57	70.03-14.05	77.71-48.21	69.10-48.15	58.06-21.08
P/E Ratio	9.17-5.23	8.35-4.67	40.96-27.46	...	...	8.75-5.43	8.00-5.57	9.52-3.46
Average Yield %	2.41	1.22	1.07	3.12	1.45	0.72	0.52	0.46

Address: One Valero Way, San Antonio, TX 78249 **Telephone:** 210-345-2000 **Fax:** 210-246-2646	**Web Site:** www.valero.com **Officers:** William R. Klesse - Chairman, President, Chief Executive Officer Joseph W. Gorder - President, Executive Vice President, Chief Commercial Officer, Chief Operating Officer	**Auditors:** KPMG LLP **Investor Contact:** 800-531-7911 **Transfer Agents:** Computershare Trust Company, N.A., Chicago, IL

VALLEY NATIONAL BANCORP

Exchange	Symbol	Price	52Wk Range	Yield	P/E
NYS	VLY	$10.24 (3/28/2013)	12.44-8.72	6.35	14.03

*7 Year Price Score 66.07 *NYSE Composite Index=100 *12 Month Price Score 90.69

Interim Earnings (Per Share)

Qtr.	Mar	Jun	Sep	Dec
2008	0.21	0.27	0.02	0.09
2009	0.20	0.05	0.16	0.16
2010	0.15	0.19	0.18	0.21
2011	0.21	0.21	0.20	0.14
2012	0.18	0.17	0.20	0.19

Interim Dividends (Per Share)

Amt	Decl	Ex	Rec	Pay
0.163Q	05/23/2012	06/13/2012	06/15/2012	07/02/2012
0.163Q	08/28/2012	09/12/2012	09/14/2012	10/01/2012
0.163Q	11/27/2012	12/12/2012	12/14/2012	01/02/2013
0.163Q	02/20/2013	03/13/2013	03/15/2013	04/01/2013

Indicated Div: $0.65 (Div. Reinv. Plan)

Valuation Analysis

		Institutional Holding	
Forecast EPS	$0.69 (04/05/2013)	No of Institutions	244
Market Cap	$2.0 Billion	Shares	84,492,792
Book Value	$1.5 Billion	% Held	48.23
Price/Book	1.35		
Price/Sales	2.57		

Business Summary: Banking (MIC: 5.1.1 SIC: 6021 NAIC: 522110)

Valley National Bancorp is a bank holding company. Co. operates through its principal subsidiary, Valley National Bank (the Bank). The Bank provides a range of commercial, retail and wealth management financial services products, and a range of banking services including automated teller machines, telephone and internet banking, overdraft facilities, drive-in and night deposit services, and safe deposit facilities. The Bank also provides certain international banking services including standby letters of credit, documentary letters of credit and related products, and certain ancillary services. At Dec 31 2011, Co. had total assets of $14.24 billion and total deposits of $9.67 billion.

Recent Developments: For the year ended Dec 31 2012, net income increased 8.4% to US$143.6 million from US$132.5 million in the prior year. Net interest income increased 3.2% to US$489.9 million from US$474.8 million in the prior year. Provision for loan losses was US$25.6 million versus US$53.3 million in the prior year, a decrease of 52.1%. Non-interest income rose 7.7% to US$120.9 million from US$112.3 million, while non-interest expense advanced 10.7% to US$374.9 million.

Prospects: Our evaluation of Valley National Bancorp as of Apr. 7, 2013 is the result of our systematic analysis on three basic characteristics: earnings strength, relative valuation, and recent stock price movement. The company has managed to produce a neutral trend in earnings per share over the past 5 quarters. However, while recent estimates for the company have been mixed, VLY has posted results that fell short of analysts expectations. Based on operating earnings yield, the company is undervalued when compared to all of the companies in our coverage universe. Share price changes over the past year indicates that VLY will perform poorly over the near term.

Financial Data
(US$ in Thousands)

	12/31/2012	12/31/2011	12/31/2010	12/31/2009	12/31/2008	12/31/2007	12/31/2006	12/31/2005
Earnings Per Share	0.73	0.75	0.73	0.58	0.58	1.00	1.04	1.06
Cash Flow Per Share	1.63	1.07	1.57	0.63	5.90	6.39	1.48	0.76
Tang Book Value Per Share	5.26	5.19	5.35	5.26	4.58	4.87	4.78	4.56
Dividends Per Share	0.652	0.656	0.654	0.657	0.658	0.654	0.638	0.621
Dividend Payout %	89.29	87.20	89.01	113.50	114.28	65.73	61.03	58.67
Income Statement								
Interest Income	671,193	673,824	676,812	712,184	729,694	725,007	707,371	625,084
Interest Expense	181,312	199,013	214,060	262,870	308,895	343,322	316,250	226,659
Net Interest Income	489,881	474,811	462,752	449,314	420,799	381,685	391,121	398,425
Provision for Losses	25,552	53,335	49,456	47,992	28,282	11,875	9,270	4,340
Non-Interest Income	120,946	112,297	91,327	72,251	3,256	86,280	72,064	73,708
Non-Interest Expense	374,900	336,588	317,682	306,028	285,248	251,164	250,340	237,566
Income Before Taxes	210,375	197,185	186,941	167,545	110,525	204,926	203,575	230,227
Income Taxes	66,748	63,532	55,771	51,484	16,934	51,698	39,884	66,778
Net Income	143,627	133,653	131,170	116,061	93,591	153,228	163,691	163,449
Average Shares	197,354	178,426	177,577	167,223	158,632	153,940	156,814	153,868
Balance Sheet								
Net Loans & Leases	11,012,829	9,691,008	9,300,049	9,293,573	10,054,988	8,426,541	8,261,641	8,058,766
Total Assets	16,012,646	14,244,507	14,143,826	14,284,153	14,718,129	12,748,959	12,395,027	12,436,102
Total Deposits	11,264,018	9,673,102	9,363,614	9,547,285	9,232,923	8,091,004	8,487,651	8,570,001
Total Liabilities	14,510,269	12,978,259	12,848,621	13,031,299	13,354,520	11,799,899	11,445,437	11,504,192
Stockholders' Equity	1,502,377	1,266,248	1,295,205	1,252,854	1,363,609	949,060	949,590	931,910
Shares Outstanding	198,438	178,683	178,010	177,102	164,122	152,964	154,589	156,647
Statistical Record								
Return on Assets %	0.95	0.94	0.92	0.80	0.68	1.22	1.32	1.41
Return on Equity %	10.35	10.44	10.30	8.87	8.07	16.14	17.40	19.94
Net Interest Margin %	72.99	70.47	68.37	63.09	57.67	52.65	55.29	63.74
Efficiency Ratio %	47.33	42.82	41.36	39.01	38.92	30.96	32.12	34.00
Loans to Deposits	0.98	1.00	0.99	0.97	1.09	1.04	0.97	0.94
Price Range	12.59-8.72	13.52-9.42	14.47-11.27	16.66-7.24	19.74-11.88	19.73-13.89	20.15-16.46	18.83-15.66
P/E Ratio	17.25-11.95	18.03-12.56	19.82-15.43	28.72-12.48	34.04-20.48	19.73-13.89	19.37-15.83	17.76-14.77
Average Yield %	6.07	5.50	5.19	6.06	4.36	3.69	3.43	3.63

Address: 1455 Valley Road, Wayne, NJ 07470 **Telephone:** 973-305-8800	**Web Site:** www.valleynationalbank.com **Officers:** Gerald H. Lipkin - Chairman, President, Chief Executive Officer Alan D. Eskow - Senior Executive Vice President, Chief Financial Officer, Corporate Secretary	**Auditors:** KPMG LLP **Investor Contact:** 973-305-8800 **Transfer Agents:** American Stock Transfer & Trust Co., New York, NY

VALMONT INDUSTRIES, INC.

Exchange	Symbol	Price	52Wk Range	Yield	P/E	Div Achiever
NYS	VMI	$157.27 (3/28/2013)	164.50-108.21	0.57	17.97	11 Years

*7 Year Price Score 138.78 *NYSE Composite Index=100 *12 Month Price Score 108.15

Interim Earnings (Per Share)

Qtr.	Mar	Jun	Sep	Dec
2008	1.13	1.41	1.40	1.09
2009	1.37	1.69	1.53	1.14
2010	0.62	0.65	0.98	1.32
2011	0.97	1.72	1.59	4.32
2012	1.96	2.24	2.12	2.43

Interim Dividends (Per Share)

Amt	Decl	Ex	Rec	Pay
0.225Q	04/24/2012	06/27/2012	06/29/2012	07/16/2012
0.225Q	09/10/2012	09/26/2012	09/28/2012	10/15/2012
0.225Q	12/04/2012	12/26/2012	12/28/2012	01/15/2013
0.225Q	03/11/2013	03/27/2013	04/01/2013	04/15/2013

Indicated Div: $0.90 (Div. Reinv. Plan)

Valuation Analysis | **Institutional Holding**

Forecast EPS	$10.37 (04/05/2013)	No of Institutions	321
Market Cap	$4.2 Billion	Shares	27,840,672
Book Value	$1.3 Billion	% Held	72.94
Price/Book	3.11		
Price/Sales	1.38		

TRADING VOLUME (thousand shares)

Business Summary: Industrial Machinery & Equipment (MIC: 7.2.1 SIC: 3499 NAIC: 332323)

Valmont Industries is a global producer of fabricated metal products. Co. is a producer of steel and aluminum pole, tower and other structures in its Engineered Infrastructure Products segment, steel and concrete pole structures in its Utilities Support Structures segment and is a producer of mechanized irrigation systems in its Irrigation segment. Co. also provides metal coating services, including galvanizing, painting and anodizing in its Coatings segment. Customers and end-users of Co.'s products include state and federal governments, contractors, utility and telecommunications companies, manufacturers of commercial lighting fixtures and farms.

Recent Developments: For the year ended Dec 29 2012, net income increased 0.7% to US$238.9 million from US$237.2 million in the prior year. Revenues were US$3.03 billion, up 13.8% from US$2.66 billion the year before. Operating income was US$382.3 million versus US$263.3 million in the prior year, an increase of 45.2%. Direct operating expenses rose 11.7% to US$2.23 billion from US$1.99 billion in the comparable period the year before. Indirect operating expenses increased 4.1% to US$420.2 million from US$403.5 million in the equivalent prior-year period.

Prospects: Our evaluation of Valmont Industries Inc. as of Apr. 7, 2013 is the result of our systematic analysis on three basic characteristics: earnings strength, relative valuation, and recent stock price movement. The company has managed to produce a neutral trend in earnings per share over the past 5 quarters. However, while recent estimates for the company have been mixed, VMI has posted better than expected results. Based on operating earnings yield, the company is undervalued when compared to all of the companies in our coverage universe. Share price changes over the past year indicates that VMI will perform very well over the near term.

Financial Data

(US$ in Thousands)	12/29/2012	12/31/2011	12/25/2010	12/26/2009	12/27/2008	12/29/2007	12/30/2006	12/31/2005
Earnings Per Share	8.75	8.60	3.57	5.73	5.04	3.63	2.38	1.54
Cash Flow Per Share	7.47	5.59	5.85	13.51	2.04	4.33	2.35	5.42
Tang Book Value Per Share	31.75	25.08	15.75	19.45	13.16	12.96	9.23	6.54
Dividends Per Share	0.855	0.705	0.480	0.580	0.495	0.410	0.370	0.335
Dividend Payout %	9.77	8.20	13.45	10.12	9.82	11.29	15.55	21.75
Income Statement								
Total Revenue	3,029,541	2,661,480	1,975,505	1,786,601	1,907,278	1,499,834	1,281,281	1,108,100
EBITDA	452,861	335,227	238,752	285,082	261,060	190,261	148,000	121,868
Depn & Amortn	70,218	74,560	59,663	44,748	39,597	35,176	36,541	39,807
Income Before Taxes	359,290	233,757	152,982	226,084	205,519	140,169	96,319	64,373
Income Taxes	126,502	4,590	55,008	72,894	70,213	44,020	30,820	24,348
Net Income	234,072	228,308	94,379	150,562	132,397	94,713	61,544	39,079
Average Shares	26,764	26,550	26,422	26,289	26,273	26,122	25,863	25,367
Balance Sheet								
Current Assets	1,425,940	1,252,943	1,094,226	715,422	755,799	621,597	494,658	408,312
Total Assets	2,568,551	2,306,076	2,090,743	1,302,169	1,326,288	1,052,613	892,310	802,042
Current Liabilities	412,433	408,070	346,914	256,817	280,584	271,036	216,922	179,151
Long-Term Obligations	472,593	474,415	468,596	160,251	337,128	200,738	202,784	218,757
Total Liabilities	1,218,639	1,159,114	1,174,851	515,908	702,157	542,000	491,029	473,367
Stockholders' Equity	1,349,912	1,146,962	915,892	786,261	624,131	510,613	401,281	328,675
Shares Outstanding	26,674	26,481	26,374	26,297	26,168	25,945	25,633	24,764
Statistical Record								
Return on Assets %	9.63	10.22	5.58	11.49	11.16	9.77	7.28	4.69
Return on Equity %	18.80	21.78	11.12	21.41	23.40	20.83	16.91♦	12.34
EBITDA Margin %	14.95	12.60	12.09	15.96	13.69	12.69	11.55	11.00
Net Margin %	7.73	8.58	4.78	8.43	6.94	6.31	4.80	3.53
Asset Turnover	1.25	1.19	1.17	1.36	1.61	1.55	1.52	1.33
Current Ratio	3.46	3.07	3.15	2.79	2.69	2.29	2.28	2.28
Debt to Equity	0.35	0.41	0.51	0.20	0.54	0.39	0.51	0.67
Price Range	141.13-92.07	110.26-74.27	87.74-67.03	88.50-38.45	119.45-38.22	98.78-51.85	60.45-33.97	35.20-21.37
P/E Ratio	16.13-10.52	12.82-8.64	24.58-18.78	15.45-6.71	23.70-7.58	27.21-14.28	25.40-14.27	22.86-13.88
Average Yield %	0.70	0.76	0.62	0.85	0.57	0.56	0.77	1.24

Address: One Valmont Plaza, Omaha, NE 68154-5215	Web Site: www.valmont.com	Auditors: Deloitte & Touche LLP
Telephone: 402-963-1000	Officers: Mogens C. Bay - Chairman, Chief Executive Officer Todd G. Atkinson - Executive Vice President	Investor Contact: 402-963-1000
		Transfer Agents: Wells Fargo Shareowner Services, South St. Paul, MN

VALSPAR CORP.

Exchange	Symbol	Price	52Wk Range	Yield	P/E	Div Achiever
NYS	VAL	$62.25 (3/28/2013)	68.32-45.52	1.48	20.02	34 Years

*7 Year Price Score 155.38 *NYSE Composite Index=100 *12 Month Price Score 103.58

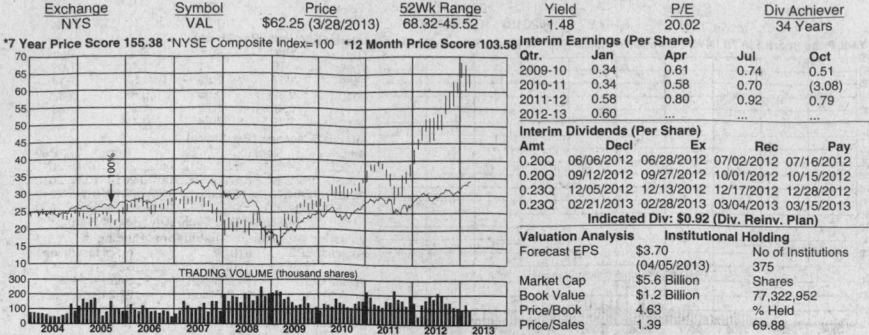

Interim Earnings (Per Share)

Qtr.	Jan	Apr	Jul	Oct
2009-10	0.34	0.61	0.74	0.51
2010-11	0.34	0.58	0.70	(3.08)
2011-12	0.58	0.80	0.92	0.79
2012-13	0.60	...	...	...

Interim Dividends (Per Share)

Amt	Decl	Ex	Rec	Pay
0.20Q	06/06/2012	06/28/2012	07/02/2012	07/16/2012
0.20Q	09/12/2012	09/27/2012	10/01/2012	10/15/2012
0.23Q	12/05/2012	12/13/2012	12/17/2012	12/28/2012
0.23Q	02/21/2013	02/28/2013	03/04/2013	03/15/2013

Indicated Div: $0.92 (Div. Reinv. Plan)

Valuation Analysis

Institutional Holding	
Forecast EPS	$3.70 (04/05/2013)	No of Institutions 375
Market Cap	$5.6 Billion	Shares 77,322,952
Book Value	$1.2 Billion	% Held 69.88
Price/Book	4.63	
Price/Sales	1.39	

Business Summary: Specialty Chemicals (MIC: 8.3.2 SIC: 2851 NAIC: 325510)

Valspar is a paint and coatings supplier. Co. has two reportable segments: Coatings, which provides coatings for metal, wood and plastic, as well as interior and exterior coatings used in metal packaging containers, principally food containers and beverage cans; and Paints, which provides consumer paint products including interior and exterior paints, stains, primers, varnishes, floor paints and specialty products, such as enamels, aerosols and faux varnishes, as well as automotive paint products including refinish paints and aerosol spray paints. Co. also provides polymers and colorants, and sells furniture protection plans and furniture care and repair products under the Guardsman brand.

Recent Developments: For the quarter ended Jan 25 2013, net income decreased 1.3% to US$55.0 million from US$55.8 million in the year-earlier quarter. Revenues were US$875.2 million, down 1.2% from US$885.6 million the year before. Operating income was US$93.5 million versus US$90.7 million in the prior-year quarter, an increase of 3.1%. Direct operating expenses declined 1.9% to US$580.9 million from US$592.3 million in the comparable period the year before. Indirect operating expenses decreased 0.9% to US$200.8 million from US$202.6 million in the equivalent prior-year period.

Prospects: Our evaluation of Valspar Corp. as of Apr. 7, 2013 is the result of our systematic analysis on three basic characteristics: earnings strength, relative valuation, and recent stock price movement. The company has generated a negative trend in earnings per share over the past 5 quarters and while recent estimates for the company have been mixed, VAL has posted results that fell short of analysts expectations. Based on operating earnings yield, the company is about fairly valued when compared to all of the companies in our coverage universe. Share price changes over the past year indicates that VAL will perform very well over the near term.

Financial Data
(US$ in Thousands)

	3 Mos	10/26/2012	10/28/2011	10/29/2010	10/30/2009	10/31/2008	10/26/2007	10/27/2006
Earnings Per Share	3.11	3.10	(1.47)	2.20	1.49	1.38	1.50	1.71
Cash Flow Per Share	4.19	3.83	3.10	2.71	3.38	2.61	1.89	2.82
Dividends Per Share	0.830	0.800	0.720	0.640	0.600	0.560	0.520	0.440
Dividend Payout %	26.69	25.81	...	29.09	40.27	40.58	34.67	25.73
Income Statement								
Total Revenue	875,242	4,020,851	3,952,954	3,226,687	2,879,042	3,482,378	3,249,287	2,978,062
EBITDA	113,150	571,979	48,466	451,503	364,009	359,336	387,301	367,388
Depn & Amortn	20,569	87,151	90,109	74,039	75,287	72,894	65,868	63,750
Income Before Taxes	76,708	417,224	(103,154)	319,197	238,328	228,697	259,771	257,432
Income Taxes	21,679	124,727	35,447	97,141	78,175	77,931	87,656	82,180
Net Income	55,029	292,497	(138,601)	222,056	160,153	150,766	172,115	175,252
Average Shares	92,397	94,380	94,309	100,866	100,921	100,326	102,617	102,726
Balance Sheet								
Current Assets	1,413,257	1,449,177	1,325,137	1,284,922	1,062,466	1,047,020	1,029,642	967,123
Total Assets	3,630,667	3,626,836	3,500,151	3,867,936	3,511,024	3,520,042	3,452,281	3,188,253
Current Liabilities	1,041,153	1,026,772	1,259,933	884,851	711,479	880,343	1,029,147	1,195,683
Long-Term Obligations	1,012,563	1,012,578	679,805	943,216	873,095	763,129	648,988	350,267
Total Liabilities	2,425,835	2,403,313	2,287,601	2,237,571	2,006,517	2,033,597	2,034,142	1,929,467
Stockholders' Equity	1,204,832	1,223,523	1,212,550	1,630,365	1,504,507	1,486,445	1,418,139	1,258,786
Shares Outstanding	89,541	90,165	93,554	98,027	99,482	99,992	100,634	101,904
Statistical Record								
Return on Assets %	8.07	8.23	N.M.	6.04	4.57	4.25	5.20	5.91
Return on Equity %	24.13	24.08	N.M.	14.21	10.74	10.21	12.89	15.15
EBITDA Margin %	12.93	14.23	1.23	13.99	12.64	10.32	11.92	12.34
Net Margin %	6.29	7.27	N.M.	6.88	5.56	4.33	5.30	5.88
Asset Turnover	1.11	1.13	1.08	0.88	0.82	0.98	0.98	1.00
Current Ratio	1.36	1.41	1.05	1.45	1.49	1.19	1.00	0.81
Debt to Equity	0.84	0.83	0.56	0.58	0.58	0.51	0.46	0.28
Price Range	68.32-42.10	59.75-33.53	40.18-27.59	32.91-25.25	28.35-14.57	26.04-16.96	29.22-24.57	29.42-21.75
P/E Ratio	21.97-13.54	19.27-10.82	...	14.96-11.48	19.03-9.78	18.87-12.29	19.48-16.38	17.20-12.72
Average Yield %	1.55	1.68	2.05	2.16	2.75	2.59	1.88	1.68

Address: 901 3rd Avenue South, Minneapolis, MN 55402 Telephone: 612-851-7000	Web Site: www.valsparglobal.com Officers: Gary E. Hendrickson - Chairman, President, Chief Executive Officer Rolf Engh - Executive Vice President, Secretary, General Counsel	Auditors: Ernst & Young LLP Investor Contact: 612-851-7358 Transfer Agents: Mellon Investor Services LLC

VANGUARD HEALTH SYSTEMS, INC.

Exchange	Symbol	Price	52Wk Range	Yield	P/E
NYS	VHS	$14.87 (3/28/2013)	17.45-7.35	N/A	13.52

*7 Year Price Score N/A *NYSE Composite Index=100 *12 Month Price Score 128.09

Interim Earnings (Per Share)

Qtr.	Sep	Dec	Mar	Jun
2009-10	0.08	(0.46)	(0.73)	0.06
2010-11	0.02	0.11	0.06	(0.21)
2011-12	(0.26)	0.15	0.55	0.24
2012-13	0.17	0.14	...	...

Interim Dividends (Per Share)

No Dividends Paid

Valuation Analysis		Institutional Holding	
Forecast EPS	$0.80 (04/05/2013)	No of Institutions	104
Market Cap	$1.2 Billion	Shares	
Book Value	$324.8 Million		66,674,120
Price/Book	3.55	% Held	
Price/Sales	0.19		N/A

TRADING VOLUME (thousand shares)

Business Summary: Hospitals & Health Care Facilities (MIC: 4.2.1 SIC: 6324 NAIC: 621999)

Vanguard Health Systems is a healthcare delivery networks operator. As of June 30 2012, Co. operated 28 hospitals with 7,064 beds in San Antonio, Harlingen and Brownsville, TX; metropolitan Detroit, MI; metropolitan Phoenix, AZ; metropolitan Chicago, IL; and Massachusetts. Co.'s hospitals provide various medical and surgical services, including emergency services, cardiology, orthopedics and neurology. Co. also provides outpatient and ancillary services, including outpatient surgery, physical therapy, and laboratory services. As of June 30 2012, Co. owned four health plans: Phoenix Health Plan, Abrazo Advantage Health Plan, Chicago Health Systems, and Valley Baptist Insurance Company.

Recent Developments: For the quarter ended Dec 31 2012, income from continuing operations decreased 28.0% to US$12.1 million from US$16.8 million in the year-earlier quarter. Net income decreased 26.7% to US$12.1 million from US$16.5 million in the year-earlier quarter. Revenues were US$1.51 billion, up 2.6% from US$1.48 billion the year before.

Prospects: Our evaluation of Vanguard Health Systems, Inc. as of Apr. 7, 2013 is the result of our systematic analysis on three basic characteristics: earnings strength, relative valuation, and recent stock price movement. The company has generated a negative trend in earnings per share over the past 5 quarters. However, while recent estimates for the company have been mixed, VHS has posted results that fell short of analysts expectations. Based on operating earnings yield, the company is about fairly valued when compared to all of the companies in our coverage universe. Share price changes over the past year indicates that VHS will perform very well over the near term.

Financial Data
(US$ in Thousands)

	6 Mos	3 Mos	06/30/2012	06/30/2011	06/30/2010	06/30/2009	06/30/2008
Earnings Per Share	1.10	1.11	0.71	(0.24)	(1.10)	0.63	(0.01)
Cash Flow Per Share	2.51	1.92	1.51	6.10	7.06	7.01	...
Income Statement							
Total Revenue	2,983,800	1,470,700	5,949,000	4,895,900	3,376,900	3,185,400	2,775,600
EBITDA	143,900	72,700	526,600	368,800	192,700	285,700	253,800
Depn & Amortn	4,400	2,200	265,200	189,700	135,600	125,200	126,100
Income Before Taxes	39,000	19,700	78,600	7,900	(58,400)	48,900	5,600
Income Taxes	12,100	4,900	22,200	9,300	(13,800)	16,800	2,200
Net Income	26,100	13,900	57,300	(10,900)	(49,200)	28,600	(700)
Average Shares	79,625	78,813	78,873	45,329	44,650	45,201	44,661
Balance Sheet							
Current Assets	1,394,600	1,407,900	1,583,000	1,747,600	721,000	731,700	...
Total Assets	4,638,400	4,591,400	4,788,100	4,568,400	2,729,600	2,731,100	...
Current Liabilities	901,400	826,600	988,700	1,396,000	616,000	480,100	...
Long-Term Obligations	2,690,600	2,692,100	2,695,400	2,325,800	1,743,800	1,543,600	...
Total Liabilities	4,313,600	4,280,600	4,439,900	4,333,400	2,483,100	2,143,300	...
Stockholders' Equity	324,800	310,800	348,200	235,000	246,500	587,800	...
Shares Outstanding	77,492	77,366	75,474	71,482	44,634	44,661	44,661
Statistical Record							
Return on Assets %	2.01	2.04	1.22	N.M.	N.M.	...	...
Return on Equity %	28.81	30.24	19.60	N.M.	N.M.	...	...
EBITDA Margin %	4.82	4.94	8.85	7.53	5.71	8.97	9.14
Net Margin %	0.87	0.95	0.96	N.M.	N.M.	0.90	N.M.
Asset Turnover	1.35	1.36	1.27	1.34	1.24	...	...
Current Ratio	1.55	1.70	1.60	1.25	1.17	1.52	...
Debt to Equity	8.28	8.66	7.74	9.90	7.07	2.63	...
Price Range	12.60-7.35	12.37-7.35	18.00-7.35	18.05-17.17	...	...	...
P/E Ratio	11.45-6.68	11.14-6.62	25.35-10.35	...	...	...	...

Address: 20 Burton Hills Boulevard, Suite 100, Nashville, TN 37215 **Telephone:** 615-665-6000	**Web Site:** www.vanguardhealth.com **Officers:** Charles N. Martin - Chairman, President, Chief Executive Officer Keith B. Pitts - Vice-Chairman	**Auditors:** Ernst & Young LLP **Investor Contact:** 615-.66-5.6000 **Transfer Agents:** American Stock Transfer & Trust Company, LLC, Brooklyn, NY

VARIAN MEDICAL SYSTEMS, INC.

Exchange	Symbol	Price	52Wk Range	Yield	P/E
NYS	VAR	$72.00 (3/28/2013)	75.25-53.73	N/A	18.80

*7 Year Price Score 108.34 *NYSE Composite Index=100 *12 Month Price Score 101.17

Interim Earnings (Per Share)

Qtr.	Dec	Mar	Jun	Sep
2009-10	0.63	0.73	0.69	0.86
2010-11	0.80	0.86	0.83	0.87
2011-12	0.79	0.94	0.96	1.07
2012-13	0.86	...	...	...

Interim Dividends (Per Share)

No Dividends Paid

Valuation Analysis		Institutional Holding	
Forecast EPS	$4.13	No of Institutions	
	(04/05/2013)	645	
Market Cap	$7.9 Billion	Shares	
Book Value	$1.6 Billion	116,753,688	
Price/Book	4.99	% Held	
Price/Sales	2.75	91.26	

Business Summary: Medical Instruments & Equipment (MIC: 4.3.1 SIC: 3845 NAIC: 334510)

Varian Medical Systems operates in two segments: Oncology Systems and X-ray Products. The Oncology Systems segment designs, manufactures, sells and services hardware and software products for treating cancer with radiotherapy, stereotactic radiotherapy, stereotactic body radiotherapy (SBRT), stereotactic radiosurgery (SRS) and brachytherapy. The X-ray Products segment provider of advanced hardware and software products for treatment of cancer with conventional radiation therapy, intensity-modulated radiation therapy, image-guided radiation therapy, volumetric modulated arc therapy, stereotactic radiotherapy, SRS, SBRT and brachytherapy.

Recent Developments: For the quarter ended Dec 28 2012, net income increased 5.6% to US$95.3 million from US$90.2 million in the year-earlier quarter. Revenues were US$678.4 million, up 8.5% from US$625.3 million the year before. Operating income was US$137.5 million versus US$128.9 million in the prior-year quarter, an increase of 6.6%. Direct operating expenses rose 8.6% to US$387.3 million from US$356.6 million in the comparable period the year before. Indirect operating expenses increased 9.8% to US$153.6 million from US$139.8 million in the equivalent prior-year period.

Prospects: Our evaluation of Varian Medical Systems Inc. as of Apr. 7, 2013 is the result of our systematic analysis on three basic characteristics: earnings strength, relative valuation, and recent stock price movement. The company has managed to produce a neutral trend in earnings per share over the past 5 quarters and while recent estimates for the company have been mixed, VAR has posted results that fell short of analysts expectations. Based on operating earnings yield, the company is about fairly valued when compared to all of the companies in our coverage universe. Share price changes over the past year indicates that VAR will perform well over the near term.

Financial Data

(US$ in Thousands)	3 Mos	09/28/2012	09/30/2011	10/01/2010	10/02/2009	09/26/2008	09/28/2007	09/29/2006
Earnings Per Share	3.83	3.76	3.36	2.91	2.55	2.19	1.83	1.81
Cash Flow Per Share	4.68	4.44	4.06	3.79	2.41	2.99	2.36	1.54
Tang Book Value Per Share	12.38	11.77	9.18	9.04	8.79	6.51	4.92	5.21
Income Statement								
Total Revenue	678,398	2,807,015	2,596,666	2,356,585	2,214,060	2,069,730	1,776,624	1,597,820
EBITDA	154,446	655,056	641,042	582,495	518,755	456,113	367,371	338,932
Depn & Amortn	16,956	60,982	52,591	48,293	44,609	36,709	32,206	29,576
Income Before Taxes	138,163	595,924	588,710	532,925	474,643	426,023	342,539	318,682
Income Taxes	42,880	168,875	180,084	165,444	143,167	130,767	103,083	75,120
Net Income	95,283	427,049	398,933	360,422	319,022	279,484	239,456	245,091
Average Shares	111,144	113,473	118,735	124,025	124,995	127,604	130,622	135,439
Balance Sheet								
Current Assets	2,228,313	2,170,515	1,854,617	1,681,344	1,672,451	1,394,401	1,160,229	1,156,049
Total Assets	2,938,564	2,878,726	2,498,761	2,323,952	2,308,248	1,975,512	1,684,375	1,511,751
Current Liabilities	1,231,772	1,236,531	1,125,912	903,541	842,320	781,677	781,687	643,956
Long-Term Obligations	6,250	6,250	6,250	17,869	23,394	32,399	40,386	49,356
Total Liabilities	1,361,676	1,368,950	1,254,870	1,048,585	996,465	948,327	862,920	714,498
Stockholders' Equity	1,576,888	1,509,776	1,243,891	1,275,367	1,311,783	1,027,185	821,455	797,253
Shares Outstanding	109,322	109,407	112,344	118,007	125,281	125,590	125,215	129,721
Statistical Record								
Return on Assets %	15.66	15.93	16.59	15.60	14.65	15.31	15.03	17.37
Return on Equity %	29.43	31.10	31.76	27.94	26.84	30.32	29.67	33.75
EBITDA Margin %	22.77	23.34	24.69	24.72	23.43	22.04	20.68	21.21
Net Margin %	14.05	15.21	15.36	15.29	14.41	13.50	13.48	15.34
Asset Turnover	1.04	1.05	1.08	1.02	1.02	1.13	1.11	1.13
Current Ratio	1.81	1.76	1.65	1.86	1.99	1.78	1.48	1.80
Debt to Equity	N.M.	N.M.	0.01	0.01	0.02	0.03	0.05	0.06
Price Range	72.35-53.73	71.70-50.10	71.96-49.63	60.80-39.14	61.18-27.45	64.97-40.53	54.86-37.82	60.63-36.79
P/E Ratio	18.89-14.03	19.07-13.32	21.42-14.77	20.89-13.45	23.99-10.76	29.67-18.51	29.98-20.67	33.50-20.33

Address: 3100 Hansen Way, Palo Alto, CA 94304-1030	Web Site:	Auditors: PricewaterhouseCoopers LLP
Telephone: 650-493-4000	Officers: Richard M. Levy - Chairman Timothy E. Guertin - Vice-Chairman, President, Chief Executive Officer	Investor Contact: 650-424-5782 Transfer Agents: Computershare Trust Company, N.A., Providence, RI

VECTOR GROUP LTD

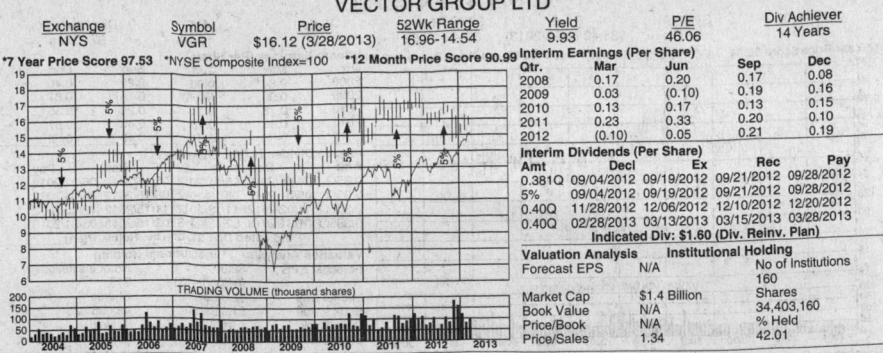

Exchange	Symbol	Price	52Wk Range	Yield	P/E	Div Achiever
NYS	VGR	$16.12 (3/28/2013)	16.96-14.54	9.93	46.06	14 Years

*7 Year Price Score 97.53   *NYSE Composite Index=100   *12 Month Price Score 90.99

Interim Earnings (Per Share)

Qtr.	Mar	Jun	Sep	Dec
2008	0.17	0.20	0.17	0.08
2009	0.03	(0.10)	0.19	0.16
2010	0.13	0.17	0.13	0.15
2011	0.23	0.33	0.20	0.10
2012	(0.10)	0.05	0.21	0.19

Interim Dividends (Per Share)

Amt	Decl	Ex	Rec	Pay
0.381Q	09/04/2012	09/19/2012	09/21/2012	09/28/2012
5%	09/04/2012	09/19/2012	09/21/2012	09/28/2012
0.40Q	11/28/2012	12/06/2012	12/10/2012	12/20/2012
0.40Q	02/28/2013	03/13/2013	03/15/2013	03/28/2013

Indicated Div: $1.60 (Div. Reinv. Plan)

Valuation Analysis   **Institutional Holding**

Forecast EPS	N/A	No of Institutions
		160
Market Cap	$1.4 Billion	Shares
Book Value	N/A	34,403,160
Price/Book	N/A	% Held
Price/Sales	1.34	42.01

Business Summary: Tobacco Products (MIC: 1.3.1 SIC: 2111 NAIC: 312221)

Vector Group is a holding company. Co. operates two business segments. The Tobacco segment consists of the manufacture and sale of cigarettes. Co.'s subsidiary, Liggett Group LLC (Liggett) produces cigarettes in approximately 118 combinations of length, style and packaging. Liggett's brand portfolio includes: PYRAMID; GRAND PRIX; LIGGETT SELECT; EVE; and USA and several Partner Brands and private label brands. The Real Estate segment includes Co.'s investments in consolidated and non-consolidated real estate businesses. Co.'s subsidiary, New Valley LLC is engaged in the real estate business.

Recent Developments: For the year ended Dec 31 2012, net income decreased 59.2% to US$30.6 million from US$75.0 million in the prior year. Revenues were US$1.08 billion, down 4.3% from US$1.13 billion the year before. Operating income was US$154.9 million versus US$143.3 million in the prior year, an increase of 8.1%. Direct operating expenses declined 7.8% to US$823.5 million from US$892.9 million in the comparable period the year before. Indirect operating expenses increased 9.2% to US$106.2 million from US$97.2 million in the equivalent prior-year period.

Prospects: Our evaluation of Vector Group Ltd. as of Apr. 7, 2013 is the result of our systematic analysis on three basic characteristics: earnings strength, relative valuation, and recent stock price movement. The company has generated a negative trend in earnings per share over the past 5 quarters. Because the company lacks sufficient analyst estimate data, we place greater weight on the historical EPS trend as the measure of earnings strength. Based on operating earnings yield, the company is overvalued when compared to all of the companies in our coverage universe. Share price changes over the past year indicates that VGR will perform poorly over the near term.

Financial Data
(US$ in Thousands)

	12/31/2012	12/31/2011	12/31/2010	12/31/2009	12/31/2008	12/31/2007	12/31/2006	12/31/2005
Earnings Per Share	0.35	0.89	0.64	0.29	0.66	0.89	0.53	0.75
Cash Flow Per Share	0.99	0.44	0.82	0.07	1.16	1.44	0.63	1.10
Dividends Per Share	1.543	1.469	1.399	1.333	1.269	1.209	1.151	1.096
Dividend Payout %	440.82	165.90	217.30	453.79	192.88	136.55	217.31	145.56
Income Statement								
Total Revenue	1,084,546	1,133,380	1,063,289	801,494	565,186	555,430	506,252	478,427
EBITDA	145,924	215,363	156,493	91,720	136,701	156,427	98,058	110,994
Depn & Amortn	10,608	10,607	10,790	10,398	10,057	10,202	9,888	11,349
Income Before Taxes	25,214	104,050	61,607	13,324	70,173	110,360	59,394	73,275
Income Taxes	23,095	48,137	31,486	3,731	34,068	52,800	25,768	40,352
Net Income	30,622	75,020	54,084	24,806	60,504	73,803	42,712	49,082
Average Shares	84,692	82,820	82,349	80,547	86,452	78,209	74,620	65,279
Balance Sheet								
Current Assets	639,056	509,741	526,763	389,208	355,283	395,626	303,156	319,099
Total Assets	1,086,731	927,768	949,595	735,542	717,712	785,289	637,462	603,130
Current Liabilities	195,159	315,198	226,872	149,008	296,159	109,337	168,786	128,100
Long-Term Obligations	586,946	493,356	506,052	334,920	210,301	277,178	103,304	243,590
Total Liabilities	1,165,983	1,016,798	995,829	740,224	684,107	684,437	542,485	569,727
Stockholders' Equity	(79,252)	(89,030)	(46,234)	(4,682)	33,605	100,852	94,977	33,403
Shares Outstanding	89,898	83,414	82,620	82,495	80,240	77,037	76,427	70,143
Statistical Record								
Return on Assets %	3.03	7.99	6.42	3.41	8.03	10.37	6.89	8.62
Return on Equity %	...	...	...	171.53	89.75	75.37	66.54	...
EBITDA Margin %	13.45	19.00	14.72	11.44	24.19	28.16	19.37	23.20
Net Margin %	2.82	6.62	5.09	3.09	10.71	13.29	8.44	10.26
Asset Turnover	1.07	1.21	1.26	1.10	0.75	0.78	0.82	0.84
Current Ratio	3.27	1.62	2.32	2.61	1.20	3.62	1.80	2.49
Debt to Equity	...	...	...	...	6.26	2.75	1.09	7.29
Price Range	17.66-14.54	17.47-14.40	17.96-11.82	13.74-9.27	15.72-10.93	18.44-12.97	13.70-11.26	14.66-10.18
P/E Ratio	50.45-41.54	19.63-16.18	28.06-18.46	47.38-31.97	23.81-16.55	20.72-14.57	25.85-21.24	19.55-13.57
Average Yield %	9.42	9.05	9.39	11.10	9.30	7.77	9.17	8.91

Address: 100 S.E. Second Street, Miami, FL 33131 Telephone: 305-579-8000	Web Site: www.vectorgroupltd.com Officers: Bennett S. LeBow - Chairman Howard M. Lorber - President, Chief Executive Officer	Auditors: PricewaterhouseCoopers LLP Investor Contact: 212-687-8080 Transfer Agents: American Stock Transfer & Trust Company, New York, NY

VECTREN CORP

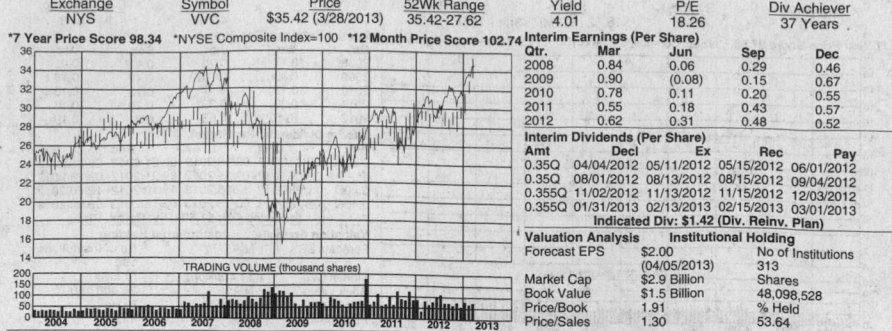

Exchange	Symbol	Price	52Wk Range	Yield	P/E	Div Achiever
NYS	VVC	$35.42 (3/28/2013)	35.42-27.62	4.01	18.26	37 Years

*7 Year Price Score 98.34   *NYSE Composite Index=100   *12 Month Price Score 102.74

Interim Earnings (Per Share)

Qtr.	Mar	Jun	Sep	Dec
2008	0.84	0.06	0.29	0.46
2009	0.90	(0.08)	0.15	0.67
2010	0.78	0.11	0.20	0.55
2011	0.55	0.18	0.43	0.57
2012	0.62	0.31	0.48	0.52

Interim Dividends (Per Share)

Amt	Decl	Ex	Rec	Pay
0.35Q	04/04/2012	05/11/2012	05/15/2012	06/01/2012
0.35Q	08/01/2012	08/13/2012	08/15/2012	09/04/2012
0.355Q	11/02/2012	11/13/2012	11/15/2012	12/03/2012
0.355Q	01/31/2013	02/13/2013	02/15/2013	03/01/2013

Indicated Div: $1.42 (Div. Reinv. Plan)

Valuation Analysis / **Institutional Holding**

Forecast EPS	$2.00 (04/05/2013)	No of Institutions 313
Market Cap	$2.9 Billion	Shares
Book Value	$1.5 Billion	48,098,528
Price/Book	1.91	% Held
Price/Sales	1.30	53.64

TRADING VOLUME (thousand shares)

Business Summary: Electric Utilities (MIC: 3.1.1 SIC: 4932 NAIC: 221210)

Vectren is an energy holding company. Co. segregates its operations into three groups: the utility group, the nonutility group, and other businesses. Co.'s utility group is engaged in gas utility services operating segment and an electric utility services operating segment. Co.'s nonutility activities comprised of: infrastructure services, energy services, coal mining, and energy marketing. Other businesses include a range of wholly owned operations and investments that have invested in energy-related opportunities and services, real estate, and leases, among other investments.

Recent Developments: For the year ended Dec 31 2012, net income increased 12.3% to US$159.0 million from US$141.6 million in the prior year. Revenues were US$2.23 billion, down 4.0% from US$2.33 billion the year before. Operating income was US$352.5 million versus US$370.0 million in the prior year, a decrease of 4.7%. Direct operating expenses declined 21.2% to US$788.4 million from US$1.00 billion in the comparable period the year before. Indirect operating expenses increased 14.4% to US$1.09 billion from US$954.1 million in the equivalent prior-year period.

Prospects: Our evaluation of Vectren Corp. as of Apr. 7, 2013 is the result of our systematic analysis on three basic characteristics: earnings strength, relative valuation, and recent stock price movement. The company has generated a negative trend in earnings per share over the past 5 quarters. However, while recent estimates for the company have been mixed, VVC has posted better than expected results. Based on operating earnings yield, the company is about fairly valued when compared to all of the companies in our coverage universe. Share price changes over the past year indicates that VVC will perform poorly over the near term.

Financial Data

(US$ in Thousands)	12/31/2012	12/31/2011	12/31/2010	12/31/2009	12/31/2008	12/31/2007	12/31/2006	12/31/2005
Earnings Per Share	1.94	1.73	1.64	1.64	1.63	1.87	1.43	1.80
Cash Flow Per Share	4.71	5.10	4.74	5.57	5.39	3.93	4.10	3.55
Tang Book Value Per Share	15.37	14.69	14.65	14.24	13.72	13.05	12.30	12.32
Dividends Per Share	1.405	1.385	1.365	1.345	1.310	1.270	1.230	1.190
Dividend Payout %	72.42	80.06	83.23	82.01	80.37	67.91	86.01	66.11
Income Statement								
Total Revenue	2,232,800	2,325,200	2,129,500	2,088,900	2,484,700	2,281,900	2,041,600	2,028,000
EBITDA	607,900	604,800	545,500	497,000	455,500	479,200	386,100	373,700
Depn & Amortn	254,600	244,300	229,100	211,900	192,300	184,800	172,300	158,200
Income Before Taxes	264,800	260,000	217,000	193,800	167,700	196,300	122,200	135,400
Income Taxes	82,500	86,400	74,700	64,100	76,100	76,000	30,300	44,100
Net Income	159,000	141,600	133,700	133,100	129,000	143,100	108,800	136,800
Average Shares	82,100	81,800	81,300	81,000	78,900	76,600	76,200	76,100
Balance Sheet								
Current Assets	678,400	610,000	645,200	581,900	775,600	699,600	715,900	725,200
Total Assets	5,089,100	4,878,900	4,764,200	4,671,800	4,632,900	4,296,400	4,091,600	3,868,100
Current Liabilities	794,300	693,500	820,700	747,700	1,120,300	1,027,400	961,400	839,500
Long-Term Obligations	1,553,400	1,559,600	1,435,200	1,540,500	1,247,900	1,245,400	1,208,000	1,198,000
Total Liabilities	3,563,000	3,413,400	3,325,300	3,274,600	3,281,300	3,062,700	2,917,400	2,724,800
Stockholders' Equity	1,526,100	1,465,500	1,438,900	1,397,200	1,351,600	1,233,700	1,174,200	1,143,300
Shares Outstanding	82,200	81,900	81,700	81,100	81,000	76,300	76,100	76,000
Statistical Record								
Return on Assets %	3.18	2.94	2.83	2.86	2.88	3.41	2.73	3.67
Return on Equity %	10.60	9.75	9.43	9.68	9.95	11.89	9.39	12.22
EBITDA Margin %	27.23	26.01	25.62	23.79	18.33	21.00	18.91	18.43
Net Margin %	7.12	6.09	6.28	6.37	5.19	6.27	5.33	6.75
Asset Turnover	0.45	0.48	0.45	0.45	0.56	0.54	0.51	0.54
Current Ratio	0.85	0.88	0.79	0.78	0.69	0.68	0.74	0.86
Debt to Equity	1.02	1.06	1.00	1.10	0.92	1.01	1.03	1.05
Price Range	30.27-27.62	30.54-23.90	27.74-22.41	26.72-18.27	32.10-21.60	30.41-24.96	29.25-25.61	29.32-25.39
P/E Ratio	15.60-14.24	17.65-13.82	16.91-13.66	16.29-11.14	19.69-13.25	16.26-13.35	20.45-17.91	16.29-14.11
Average Yield %	4.83	5.06	5.52	5.83	4.80	4.52	4.52	4.35

Address: One Vectren Square, Evansville, IN 47708	Web Site: www.vectren.com	Auditors: Deloitte & Touche LLP
Telephone: 812-491-4000	Officers: Carl L. Chapman - President, Chief Executive Officer Jerome A. Benkert - Executive Vice President, Chief Financial Officer	Investor Contact: 812-491-4080
Fax: 812-491-4149		Transfer Agents: Wells Fargo Shareowner Services, St. Paul, MN

VENTAS, INC.

Exchange	Symbol	Price	52Wk Range	Yield	P/E
NYS	VTR	$73.20 (3/28/2013)	73.20-54.06	3.66	59.51

*7 Year Price Score 122.59 *NYSE Composite Index=100 ***12 Month Price Score 101.12**

TRADING VOLUME (thousand shares)

Interim Earnings (Per Share)

Qtr.	Mar	Jun	Sep	Dec
2008	0.23	0.51	0.46	0.41
2009	0.52	0.57	0.32	0.34
2010	0.34	0.37	0.37	0.49
2011	0.30	0.11	0.35	0.77
2012	0.31	0.25	0.38	0.29

Interim Dividends (Per Share)

Amt	Decl	Ex	Rec	Pay
0.62Q	05/17/2012	06/06/2012	06/08/2012	06/29/2012
0.62Q	08/30/2012	09/07/2012	09/11/2012	09/28/2012
0.62Q	12/06/2012	12/13/2012	12/17/2012	12/28/2012
0.67Q	02/15/2013	03/06/2013	03/08/2013	03/28/2013
		Indicated Div: $2.68		

Valuation Analysis

Forecast EPS	$1.42
	(04/06/2013)
Market Cap	$21.4 Billion
Book Value	$9.2 Billion
Price/Book	2.32
Price/Sales	8.60

Institutional Holding

No of Institutions	521
Shares	309,097,728
% Held	98.94

Business Summary: REITs (MIC: 5.3.1 SIC: 6798 NAIC: 525930)

Ventas is a real estate investment trust. Co. acquires and owns seniors housing and healthcare properties and leases its properties to unaffiliated tenants or operate them through independent third-party managers. Through its Lillibridge Healthcare Services, Inc. subsidiary and its interest in PMB Real Estate Services LLC, Co. provides medical office building management, leasing, marketing, facility development and advisory services to hospitals and health systems. Co. also makes secured and unsecured loans and other investments relating to seniors housing and healthcare operators or properties. As of Dec 31 2012, Co. owned 1,442 properties in 46 states, the District of Columbia and Canada.

Recent Developments: For the year ended Dec 31 2012, income from continuing operations decreased 15.8% to US$304.5 million from US$361.9 million a year earlier. Net income decreased 0.4% to US$361.8 million from US$363.3 million in the prior year. Revenues were US$2.49 billion, up 42.5% from US$1.74 billion the year before. Revenues from property income rose 43.1% to US$2.44 billion from US$1.71 billion in the corresponding earlier year.

Prospects: Our evaluation of Ventas Inc. as of Apr. 7, 2013 is the result of our systematic analysis on three basic characteristics: earnings strength, relative valuation, and recent stock price movement. The company has produced a positive trend in earnings per share over the past 5 quarters. However, while recent estimates for the company have been lowered by analysts, VTR has posted results that fell short of analysts expectations. Based on operating earnings yield, the company is overvalued when compared to all of the companies in our coverage universe. Share price changes over the past year indicates that VTR will perform in line with the market over the near term.

Financial Data

(US$ in Thousands)	12/31/2012	12/31/2011	12/31/2010	12/31/2009	12/31/2008	12/31/2007	12/31/2006	12/31/2005
Earnings Per Share	1.23	1.58	1.56	1.74	1.62	2.25	1.25	1.36
Cash Flow Per Share	3.39	3.38	2.86	2.77	2.60	3.26	2.29	2.35
Tang Book Value Per Share	29.73	30.87	15.18	15.74	14.99	13.64	6.69	6.45
Dividends Per Share	2.480	2.300	2.140	2.050	2.050	1.900	1.580	1.440
Dividend Payout %	201.63	145.57	137.18	117.82	126.54	84.44	126.40	105.88
Income Statement								
Total Revenue	2,485,299	1,764,991	1,016,867	936,094	929,766	771,791	428,349	332,988
EBITDA	1,263,073	1,001,734	615,598	575,333	575,188	552,251	393,018	319,005
Depn & Amortn	707,714	434,382	208,274	200,938	226,719	227,682	120,494	88,002
Income Before Taxes	261,958	330,545	228,461	195,892	145,285	120,351	131,430	125,422
Income Taxes	(6,282)	(31,131)	5,201	(1,719)	(15,885)	(28,042)	...	...
Net Income	361,775	363,261	249,729	269,360	226,288	282,318	131,430	130,583
Average Shares	294,488	230,790	157,657	152,758	139,912	123,012	104,731	95,775
Balance Sheet								
Current Assets	67,908	45,807	21,812	107,397	176,812	28,334	1,246	1,641
Total Assets	18,980,000	17,271,910	5,758,021	5,616,245	5,769,984	5,716,628	3,253,800	2,639,118
Current Liabilities	1,302,436	1,384,013	467,782	457,769	447,628	491,956	206,677	126,721
Long-Term Obligations	8,413,646	6,429,116	2,900,044	2,670,101	3,147,694	3,360,499	2,329,053	1,802,564
Total Liabilities	9,786,317	7,894,116	3,371,295	3,150,734	3,621,516	3,892,974	2,543,924	1,971,799
Stockholders' Equity	9,193,683	9,377,794	2,386,726	2,465,511	2,148,468	1,823,654	709,876	667,319
Shares Outstanding	291,866	288,809	157,265	156,612	143,287	133,651	106,137	103,523
Statistical Record								
Return on Assets %	1.99	3.15	4.39	4.73	3.93	6.29	4.46	6.93
Return on Equity %	3.89	6.18	10.29	11.68	11.36	22.29	19.09	31.56
EBITDA Margin %	50.82	56.76	60.54	61.46	61.86	71.55	91.75	95.80
Net Margin %	14.56	20.58	24.56	28.77	24.34	36.58	30.68	39.22
Asset Turnover	0.14	0.15	0.18	0.16	0.16	0.17	0.15	0.18
Current Ratio	0.05	0.03	0.05	0.23	0.39	0.06	0.01	0.01
Debt to Equity	0.92	0.69	1.22	1.08	1.47	1.84	3.28	2.70
Price Range	67.33-53.68	57.19-43.96	55.43-40.95	44.71-20.32	51.26-18.37	47.70-31.51	42.32-30.12	32.67-24.67
P/E Ratio	54.74-43.64	36.20-27.82	35.53-26.25	25.70-11.68	31.64-11.34	21.20-14.00	33.86-24.10	24.02-18.14
Average Yield %	4.07	4.34	4.39	6.23	4.97	4.61	4.49	4.97

Address: 353 N. Clark Street, Suite 3300, Chicago, IL 60654 Telephone: 877-483-6827	Web Site: www.ventasreit.com Officers: Debra A. Cafaro - Chairman, Chief Executive Officer Raymond J. Lewis - President	Auditors: Ernst & Young LLP Investor Contact: 312-660-3848 Transfer Agents: Wells Fargo Shareowner Services, St. Paul, MN

VERIFONE SYSTEMS INC.

Exchange	Symbol	Price	52Wk Range	Yield	P/E
NYS	PAY	$20.68 (3/28/2013)	54.45-18.24	N/A	28.33

*7 Year Price Score 105.61 *NYSE Composite Index=100 *12 Month Price Score 65.02

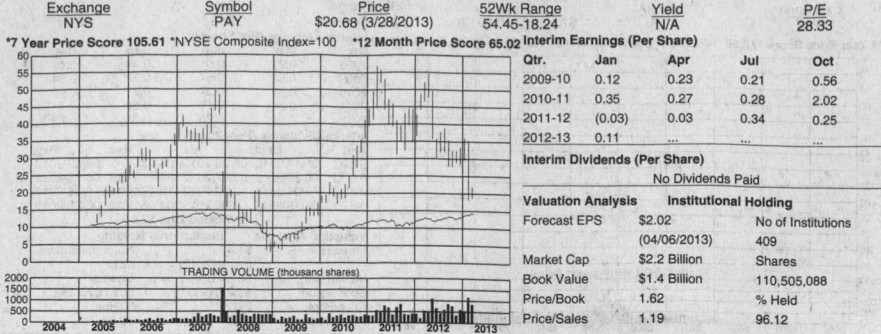

Interim Earnings (Per Share)

Qtr.	Jan	Apr	Jul	Oct
2009-10	0.12	0.23	0.21	0.56
2010-11	0.35	0.27	0.28	2.02
2011-12	(0.03)	0.03	0.34	0.25
2012-13	0.11	...	...	...

Interim Dividends (Per Share)

No Dividends Paid

Valuation Analysis		Institutional Holding	
Forecast EPS	$2.02 (04/06/2013)	No of Institutions	409
Market Cap	$2.2 Billion	Shares	
Book Value	$1.4 Billion		110,505,088
Price/Book	1.62	% Held	
Price/Sales	1.19		96.12

Business Summary: Internet & Software (MIC: 6.3.2 SIC: 3578 NAIC: 333313)

VeriFone Systems is a holding company. Through its subsidiaries, Co. is a provider of payment applications that enable electronic payment transactions and services at the point of sale (POS). Co.'s payment applications consist of POS electronic payment devices that run its proprietary and third-party operating systems, security, encryption, application, and certified payment software as well as other applications. In addition, Co. provides payment system consulting, on-site and telephone-based installation and training, repair, and replacement of impaired system applications. Co. also provides technical support for its installed payment systems, consulting and project management services.

Recent Developments: For the quarter ended Jan 31 2013, net income amounted to US$11.7 million versus a net loss of US$2.8 million in the year-earlier quarter. Revenues were US$428.7 million, up 2.2% from US$419.5 million the year before. Operating income was US$21.7 million versus US$21.9 million in the prior-year quarter, a decrease of 0.8%. Direct operating expenses declined 2.3% to US$256.8 million from US$262.9 million in the comparable period the year before. Indirect operating expenses increased 11.5% to US$150.2 million from US$134.7 million in the equivalent prior-year period.

Prospects: Our evaluation of Verifone Systems Inc. as of Apr. 7, 2013 is the result of our systematic analysis on three basic characteristics: earnings strength, relative valuation, and recent stock price movement. The company has generated a negative trend in earnings per share over the past 5 quarters. However, while recent estimates for the company have been lowered by analysts, PAY has posted better than expected results. Based on operating earnings yield, the company is undervalued when compared to all of the companies in our coverage universe. Share price changes over the past year indicates that PAY will perform very poorly over the near term.

Financial Data

(US$ in Thousands)	3 Mos	10/31/2012	10/31/2011	10/31/2010	10/31/2009	10/31/2008	10/31/2007	10/31/2006
Earnings Per Share	0.73	0.59	2.92	1.13	(1.63)	(5.05)	(0.41)	0.86
Cash Flow Per Share	2.22	2.03	1.89	1.83	2.40	(0.10)	1.09	0.25
Tang Book Value Per Share	N.M.	N.M.	3.49	N.M.	N.M.	N.M.	N.M.	0.43
Income Statement								
Total Revenue	428,747	1,865,971	1,303,866	1,001,537	844,714	921,931	902,892	581,070
EBITDA	62,671	256,479	149,176	134,035	(58,348)	(269,052)	81,286	113,474
Depn & Amortn	36,996	129,695	31,829	28,724	59,278	59,954	60,688	11,559
Income Before Taxes	14,173	68,353	90,992	78,245	(128,590)	(351,438)	(9,298)	91,670
Income Taxes	2,463	2,050	(191,412)	(20,582)	9,246	73,884	24,718	32,159
Net Income	11,838	65,033	282,404	98,827	(137,836)	(425,322)	(34,016)	59,511
Average Shares	110,558	110,315	96,616	87,785	84,473	84,220	82,194	68,894
Balance Sheet								
Current Assets	1,158,745	1,135,443	1,160,448	761,091	622,782	562,850	603,582	319,244
Total Assets	3,534,066	3,490,607	2,313,561	1,075,326	918,910	1,079,752	1,547,309	452,945
Current Liabilities	547,358	570,390	703,280	259,806	245,653	266,534	306,767	152,668
Long-Term Obligations	1,238,966	1,252,701	211,756	468,231	504,165	543,357	547,766	190,904
Total Liabilities	2,150,404	2,182,812	1,119,368	869,301	886,861	937,598	966,387	354,204
Stockholders' Equity	1,383,662	1,307,795	1,194,193	206,025	32,049	142,154	580,922	98,741
Shares Outstanding	108,265	107,930	105,697	86,832	84,544	84,443	84,060	68,148
Statistical Record								
Return on Assets %	2.20	2.23	16.67	9.91	N.M.	N.M.	N.M.	15.21
Return on Equity %	6.15	5.18	40.34	83.02	N.M.	N.M.	N.M.	95.01
EBITDA Margin %	14.62	13.75	11.44	13.38	N.M.	N.M.	9.00	19.53
Net Margin %	2.76	3.49	21.66	9.87	N.M.	N.M.	N.M.	10.24
Asset Turnover	0.52	0.64	0.77	1.00	0.85	0.70	0.90	1.49
Current Ratio	2.12	1.99	1.65	2.93	2.54	2.11	1.97	2.09
Debt to Equity	0.90	0.96	0.18	2.27	15.73	3.82	0.94	1.93
Price Range	54.45-27.85	54.45-27.85	56.84-31.12	33.83-13.26	15.89-3.22	49.43-8.61	49.56-29.21	32.94-21.62
P/E Ratio	74.59-38.15	92.29-47.20	19.47-10.66	29.94-11.73	...	...	...	38.30-25.14

Address: 2099 Gateway Place, Suite 600, San Jose, CA 95110 **Telephone:** 408-232-7800	**Web Site:** www.verifone.com **Officers:** Leslie G. Denend - Interim Chairman Richard A. McGinn - Chairman, Interim Chief Executive Officer	**Auditors:** Ernst & Young LLP **Transfer Agents:** Computershare, Canton, MA

VERIZON COMMUNICATIONS INC

Exchange	Symbol	Price	52Wk Range	Yield	P/E
NYS	VZ	$49.15 (3/28/2013)	49.48-36.80	4.19	158.55

*7 Year Price Score 111.95 *NYSE Composite Index=100   ***12 Month Price Score 98.46**

Interim Earnings (Per Share)

Qtr.	Mar	Jun	Sep	Dec
2008	0.57	0.66	0.59	0.44
2009	0.58	0.52	0.41	(0.22)
2010	0.14	(0.07)	0.31	0.51
2011	0.51	0.57	0.49	(0.71)
2012	0.59	0.64	0.56	(1.48)

Interim Dividends (Per Share)

Amt	Decl	Ex	Rec	Pay
0.50Q	06/07/2012	07/06/2012	07/10/2012	08/01/2012
0.515Q	09/06/2012	10/05/2012	10/10/2012	11/01/2012
0.515Q	12/06/2012	01/08/2013	01/10/2013	02/01/2013
0.515Q	03/08/2013	04/08/2013	04/10/2013	05/01/2013

Indicated Div: $2.06

Valuation Analysis

		Institutional Holding	
Forecast EPS	$2.75 (04/06/2013)	No of Institutions	1814
Market Cap	$145.9 Billion	Shares	1,727,315,328
Book Value	$33.2 Billion	% Held	55.45
Price/Book	4.40		
Price/Sales	1.26		

Business Summary: Services (MIC: 6.1.2 SIC: 4813 NAIC: 517110)

Verizon Communications is a holding company. Through its subsidiaries, Co. is a provider of communications, information and entertainment products and services to consumers, businesses and governmental agencies. Co. has two primary reportable segments, Verizon Wireless and Wireline. Verizon Wireless' communications products and services include wireless voice and data services and equipment sales, which are provided to consumer, business and government customers across the U.S. Wireline's voice, data and video communications products and services include voice, broadband Internet access and video, data center and cloud services, and security and managed network services.

Recent Developments: For the year ended Dec 31 2012, net income increased 3.5% to US$10.56 billion from US$10.20 billion in the prior year. Revenues were US$115.85 billion, up 4.5% from US$110.88 billion the year before. Operating income was US$13.16 billion versus US$12.88 billion in the prior year, an increase of 2.2%. Direct operating expenses rose 0.9% to US$46.28 billion from US$45.88 billion in the comparable period the year before. Indirect operating expenses increased 8.2% to US$56.41 billion from US$52.12 billion in the equivalent prior-year period.

Prospects: Our evaluation of Verizon Communications Inc. as of Apr. 7, 2013 is the result of our systematic analysis on three basic characteristics: earnings strength, relative valuation, and recent stock price movement. The company has generated a negative trend in earnings per share over the past 5 quarters. However, while recent estimates for the company have been mixed, VZ has posted results that fell short of analysts expectations. Based on operating earnings yield, the company is about fairly valued when compared to all of the companies in our coverage universe. Share price changes over the past year indicates that VZ will perform in line with the market over the near term.

Financial Data
(US$ in Thousands)

	12/31/2012	12/31/2011	12/31/2010	12/31/2009	12/31/2008	12/31/2007	12/31/2006	12/31/2005
Earnings Per Share	0.31	0.85	0.90	1.29	2.26	1.90	2.12	2.65
Cash Flow Per Share	11.01	10.51	11.79	11.11	9.32	8.88	8.28	7.96
Dividends Per Share	2.015	1.962	1.913	1.855	1.750	1.645	1.620	1.600
Dividend Payout %	650.00	230.88	212.50	143.80	77.43	86.58	76.42	60.38
Income Statement								
Total Revenue	115,846,000	110,875,000	106,565,000	107,808,000	97,354,000	93,469,000	88,144,000	75,112,000
EBITDA	27,007,000	27,789,000	29,200,000	28,604,000	29,986,000	28,657,000	26,689,000	27,450,000
Depn & Amortn	14,920,000	14,991,000	14,593,000	14,562,000	13,182,000	13,036,000	13,122,000	12,519,000
Income Before Taxes	9,573,000	10,039,000	12,176,000	11,015,000	15,347,000	13,960,000	11,419,000	12,871,000
Income Taxes	(660,000)	285,000	2,467,000	1,210,000	3,331,000	3,982,000	2,674,000	3,210,000
Net Income	875,000	2,404,000	2,549,000	3,651,000	6,428,000	5,521,000	6,197,000	7,397,000
Average Shares	2,862,000	2,839,000	2,833,000	2,841,000	2,850,000	2,902,000	2,938,000	2,817,000
Balance Sheet								
Current Assets	21,235,000	30,939,000	22,348,000	22,608,000	26,075,000	18,698,000	22,538,000	16,448,000
Total Assets	225,222,000	230,461,000	220,005,000	227,251,000	202,352,000	186,959,000	188,804,000	168,130,000
Current Liabilities	26,956,000	30,761,000	30,597,000	29,136,000	25,906,000	24,741,000	32,280,000	25,063,000
Long-Term Obligations	47,618,000	50,303,000	45,252,000	55,051,000	46,959,000	28,203,000	28,646,000	31,869,000
Total Liabilities	192,065,000	194,491,000	181,436,000	185,645,000	160,646,000	136,378,000	140,269,000	128,450,000
Stockholders' Equity	33,157,000	35,970,000	38,569,000	41,606,000	41,706,000	50,581,000	48,535,000	39,680,000
Shares Outstanding	2,967,610	2,834,016	2,827,023	2,835,668	2,840,520	2,876,824	2,967,596	2,763,409
Statistical Record								
Return on Assets %	0.38	1.07	1.14	1.70	3.29	2.94	3.47	4.43
Return on Equity %	2.52	6.45	6.36	8.76	13.89	11.14	14.05	19.15
EBITDA Margin %	23.31	25.06	27.40	26.53	30.80	30.66	30.28	36.55
Net Margin %	0.76	2.17	2.39	3.39	6.60	5.91	7.03	9.85
Asset Turnover	0.51	0.49	0.48	0.50	0.50	0.50	0.49	0.45
Current Ratio	0.79	1.01	0.73	0.78	1.01	0.76	0.70	0.66
Debt to Equity	1.44	1.40	1.17	1.32	1.13	0.56	0.59	0.80
Price Range	47.26-36.80	40.12-33.12	35.78-25.16	32.36-24.46	40.62-23.43	42.84-33.18	34.79-27.21	36.28-26.15
P/E Ratio	152.45-118.71	47.20-38.96	39.76-27.95	25.09-18.96	17.98-10.37	22.55-17.46	16.41-12.83	13.69-9.87
Average Yield %	4.80	5.36	6.49	6.52	5.37	4.29	5.29	5.27

Address: 140 West Street, New York, NY 10007	Web Site: www.verizon.com	Auditors: Ernst & Young LLP
Telephone: 212-395-1000	Officers: Lowell C. McAdam - Chairman, President, Chief Executive Officer, Chief Operating Officer, Division Officer John G. Stratton - Executive Vice President, Chief Marketing Officer, Chief Operating Officer	Transfer Agents: EquiServe Trust Company, N.A., Providence, RI

VF CORP.

Exchange	Symbol	Price	52Wk Range	Yield	P/E	Div Achiever
NYS	VFC	$167.75 (3/28/2013)	168.86-131.41	2.07	17.29	40 Years

*7 Year Price Score 146.10 *NYSE Composite Index=100   *12 Month Price Score 96.77

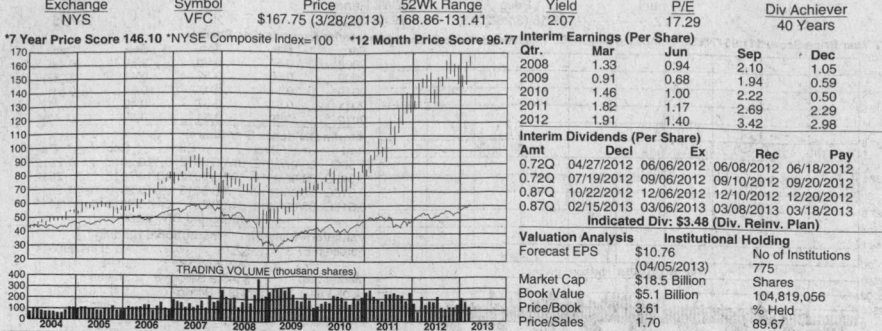

Interim Earnings (Per Share)

Qtr.	Mar	Jun	Sep	Dec
2008	1.33	0.94	2.10	1.05
2009	0.91	0.68	1.94	0.59
2010	1.46	1.00	2.22	0.50
2011	1.82	1.17	2.69	2.29
2012	1.91	1.40	3.42	2.98

Interim Dividends (Per Share)

Amt	Decl	Ex	Rec	Pay
0.72Q	04/27/2012	06/06/2012	06/08/2012	06/18/2012
0.72Q	07/19/2012	09/06/2012	09/10/2012	09/20/2012
0.87Q	10/22/2012	12/06/2012	12/10/2012	12/20/2012
0.87Q	02/15/2013	03/06/2013	03/08/2013	03/18/2013

Indicated Div: $3.48 (Div. Reinv. Plan)

Valuation Analysis   **Institutional Holding**

Forecast EPS	$10.76 (04/05/2013)	No of Institutions 775
Market Cap	$18.5 Billion	Shares
Book Value	$5.1 Billion	104,819,056
Price/Book	3.61	% Held
Price/Sales	1.70	89.67

Business Summary: Apparel, Footwear & Accessories (MIC: 1.4.2 SIC: 2329 NAIC: 315228)

VF is an apparel and footwear company. Co. designs and manufactures or sources from independent contractors a variety of products for consumers, including jeanswear, outerwear, footwear, packs, luggage, sportswear, and occupational and performance apparel. Products are marketed mainly under Co.-owned brand names. These products are marketed to consumers shopping in specialty stores, department stores, national chains and mass merchants. Co.'s businesses are grouped by product categories, and by brands within those categories. These groupings of businesses are called coalitions, and Co.'s five coalitions are Outdoor & Action Sports, Jeanswear, Imagewear, Sportswear and Contemporary Brands.

Recent Developments: For the year ended Dec 29 2012, net income increased 22.0% to US$1.09 billion from US$890.4 million in the prior year. Revenues were US$10.88 billion, up 15.0% from US$9.46 billion the year before. Operating income was US$1.47 billion versus US$1.24 billion in the prior year, an increase of 17.7%. Direct operating expenses rose 13.4% to US$5.82 billion from US$5.13 billion in the comparable period the year before. Indirect operating expenses increased 16.6% to US$3.60 billion from US$3.09 billion in the equivalent prior-year period.

Prospects: Our evaluation of VF Corp. as of Apr. 7, 2013 is the result of our systematic analysis on three basic characteristics: earnings strength, relative valuation, and recent stock price movement. The company has managed to produce a neutral trend in earnings per share over the past 5 quarters and while recent estimates for the company have been raised by analysts, VFC has posted better than expected results. Based on operating earnings yield, the company is undervalued when compared to all of the companies in our coverage universe. Share price changes over the past year indicates that VFC will perform poorly over the near term.

Financial Data

(US$ in Thousands)	12/29/2012	12/31/2011	12/31/2010	01/02/2010	01/03/2009	12/29/2007	12/30/2006	12/31/2005
Earnings Per Share	9.70	7.98	5.18	4.13	5.42	5.22	4.72	4.44
Cash Flow Per Share	11.64	9.89	9.26	8.84	6.11	7.45	4.45	5.06
Tang Book Value Per Share	0.85	N.M.	10.75	7.90	7.54	7.38	12.62	7.98
Dividends Per Share	3.030	2.610	2.430	2.370	2.330	2.230	1.940	1.100
Dividend Payout %	31.24	32.71	46.91	57.38	42.99	42.72	41.10	24.77
Income Statement								
Total Revenue	10,879,855	9,459,232	7,702,589	7,220,286	7,642,600	7,219,359	6,215,794	6,502,377
EBITDA	1,709,025	1,406,454	981,824	892,052	1,080,378	1,090,028	936,880	949,470
Depn & Amortn	196,898	168,911	156,210	153,707	144,486	121,646	108,377	116,233
Income Before Taxes	1,421,875	1,164,743	750,212	654,673	847,957	905,570	777,238	770,813
Income Taxes	335,737	274,350	176,700	196,215	245,209	292,324	242,187	252,278
Net Income	1,085,999	888,089	571,362	461,271	602,748	591,621	533,516	506,702
Average Shares	111,904	111,288	110,328	111,605	111,255	113,348	113,040	114,192
Balance Sheet								
Current Assets	3,449,583	3,187,944	2,826,060	2,629,356	2,653,010	2,645,129	2,578,010	2,365,376
Total Assets	9,633,021	9,313,126	6,457,556	6,470,657	6,433,868	6,446,685	5,465,693	5,171,071
Current Liabilities	1,732,212	1,666,032	1,109,475	1,092,583	1,012,182	1,134,387	1,014,848	1,152,143
Long-Term Obligations	1,429,166	1,831,781	935,882	938,494	1,141,546	1,144,810	635,359	647,728
Total Liabilities	4,507,396	4,787,135	2,596,337	2,655,506	2,877,976	2,869,856	2,200,521	2,339,532
Stockholders' Equity	5,125,625	4,525,991	3,861,219	3,815,151	3,555,892	3,576,829	3,265,172	2,831,539
Shares Outstanding	110,204	110,556	107,938	110,285	109,847	109,797	112,184	110,107
Statistical Record								
Return on Assets %	11.50	11.26	8.89	7.17	9.21	9.96	10.06	9.99
Return on Equity %	22.57	21.18	14.97	12.55	16.63	17.34	17.55	18.92
EBITDA Margin %	15.71	14.87	12.75	12.35	14.14	15.10	15.07	14.60
Net Margin %	9.98	9.39	7.42	6.39	7.89	8.19	8.58	7.79
Asset Turnover	1.15	1.20	1.20	1.12	1.17	1.22	1.17	1.28
Current Ratio	1.99	1.91	2.55	2.41	2.62	2.33	2.54	2.05
Debt to Equity	0.28	0.40	0.24	0.25	0.32	0.32	0.19	0.23
Price Range	168.86-129.67	141.04-81.34	89.32-69.91	78.49-47.65	84.34-39.88	95.65-68.90	82.60-53.66	61.52-50.85
P/E Ratio	17.41-13.37	17.67-10.19	17.24-13.50	19.00-11.54	15.56-7.36	18.32-13.20	17.50-11.37	13.86-11.45
Average Yield %	2.05	2.38	3.06	3.73	3.32	2.68	2.92	1.93

Address: 105 Corporate Center Boulevard, Greensboro, NC 27408
Telephone: 336-424-6000

Web Site: www.vfc.com
Officers: Eric C. Wiseman - Chairman, President, Chief Executive Officer Robert K. Shearer - Senior Vice President, Chief Financial Officer

Auditors: PricewaterhouseCoopers LLP
Transfer Agents: Computershare Trust Company, N.A, Providence, RI

VISA INC

Exchange	Symbol	Price	52Wk Range	Yield	P/E
NYS	V	$169.84 (3/28/2013)	169.84-112.25	0.78	47.84

*7 Year Price Score N/A   *NYSE Composite Index=100   *12 Month Price Score 107.08

Interim Earnings (Per Share)

Qtr.	Dec	Mar	Jun	Sep
2009-10	1.02	0.96	0.97	1.05
2010-11	1.23	1.23	1.43	1.27
2011-12	1.49	1.91	(2.74)	2.45
2012-13	1.93	...	...	...

Interim Dividends (Per Share)

Amt	Decl	Ex	Rec	Pay
0.22Q	04/26/2012	05/16/2012	05/18/2012	06/05/2012
0.22Q	07/19/2012	08/15/2012	08/17/2012	09/04/2012
0.33Q	10/24/2012	11/14/2012	11/16/2012	12/04/2012
0.33Q	01/30/2013	02/13/2013	02/15/2013	03/05/2013

Indicated Div: $1.32

Valuation Analysis

Forecast EPS	$7.36 (04/06/2013)
Market Cap	$136.6 Billion
Book Value	$27.6 Billion
Price/Book	4.95
Price/Sales	12.74

Institutional Holding

No of Institutions	1159
Shares	461,171,008
% Held	N/A

Business Summary: Business Services (MIC: 7.5.2 SIC: 7389 NAIC: 561499)

Visa is a payments technology company. Co.'s business primarily consists of the following: owning, managing and promoting payment brands, including Visa, Visa Electron, PLUS and Interlink; providing branded payments product platforms, which its clients, primarily financial institutions, use to develop and provide credit, debit, prepaid and cash access programs, as well as digital, mobile and eCommerce platforms for their customers; providing transaction processing and services to its clients through VisaNet, Visa Debit Processing Services, Visa Processing Services, CyberSource, PlaySpan and Fundamo; and promoting and enforcing a set of operating regulations adhered to by its clients.

Recent Developments: For the quarter ended Dec 31 2012, net income increased 25.9% to US$1.29 billion from US$1.03 billion in the year-earlier quarter. Revenues were US$2.85 billion, up 11.7% from US$2.55 billion the year before. Operating income was US$1.80 billion versus US$1.62 billion in the prior-year quarter, an increase of 11.2%. Indirect operating expenses increased 12.6% to US$1.05 billion from US$929.0 million in the equivalent prior-year period.

Prospects: Our evaluation of Visa Inc. as of Apr. 7, 2013 is the result of our systematic analysis on three basic characteristics: earnings strength, relative valuation, and recent stock price movement. The company has managed to produce a neutral trend in earnings per share over the past 5 quarters. However, while recent estimates for the company have been mixed, V has posted better than expected results. Based on operating earnings yield, the company is about fairly valued when compared to all of the companies in our coverage universe. Share price changes over the past year indicates that V will perform well over the near term.

Financial Data

(US$ in Thousands)	3 Mos	09/30/2012	09/30/2011	09/30/2010	09/30/2009	09/30/2008	10/01/2007
Earnings Per Share	3.55	3.16	5.16	4.01	3.10	0.96	...
Cash Flow Per Share	1.69	6.17	4.70	3.21	0.66	0.62	...
Tang Book Value Per Share	5.60	5.58	4.10	2.50	2.48	1.23	N.M.
Dividends Per Share	0.990	0.880	0.600	0.500	0.420	0.105	...
Dividend Payout %	27.89	27.85	11.63	12.47	13.55	10.94	...
Income Statement							
Total Revenue	2,846,000	10,421,000	9,188,000	8,065,000	6,911,000	6,263,000	...
EBITDA	2,354,000	2,426,000	5,897,000	4,956,000	4,228,000	1,436,000	...
Depn & Amortn	553,000	265,000	225,000	265,000	226,000	237,000	...
Income Before Taxes	1,801,000	2,207,000	5,656,000	4,615,000	4,000,000	1,335,000	...
Income Taxes	508,000	65,000	2,010,000	1,674,000	1,648,000	532,000	...
Net Income	1,293,000	2,144,000	3,650,000	2,966,000	2,353,000	804,000	...
Average Shares	669,000	678,000	707,000	739,000	758,000	769,195	...
Balance Sheet							
Current Assets	7,387,000	11,786,000	9,190,000	8,734,000	9,241,000	11,174,000	4,700,656
Total Assets	35,859,000	40,013,000	34,760,000	33,408,000	32,281,000	34,981,000	27,069,266
Current Liabilities	3,747,000	7,954,000	3,451,000	3,498,000	4,442,000	7,165,000	4,785,822
Long-Term Obligations	...	...	...	32,000	44,000	55,000	39,954
Total Liabilities	8,271,000	12,383,000	8,323,000	8,397,000	9,088,000	12,704,000	10,783,664
Stockholders' Equity	27,588,000	27,630,000	26,437,000	25,011,000	23,193,000	22,277,000	16,285,602
Shares Outstanding	804,000	811,000	812,000	835,000	846,000	959,868	775,080
Statistical Record							
Return on Assets %	6.72	5.72	10.71	9.03	7.00	2.59	...
Return on Equity %	8.77	7.91	14.19	12.31	10.35	4.17	...
EBITDA Margin %	82.71	23.28	64.18	61.45	61.18	22.93	...
Net Margin %	45.43	20.57	39.73	36.78	34.05	12.84	...
Asset Turnover	0.30	0.28	0.27	0.25	0.21	0.20	...
Current Ratio	1.97	1.48	2.66	2.50	2.08	1.56	0.98
Price Range	152.46-99.11	135.00-84.26	92.84-66.90	96.59-65.48	74.41-42.42	88.50-56.50	...
P/E Ratio	42.95-27.92	42.72-26.66	17.99-12.97	24.09-16.33	24.00-13.68	92.19-58.85	...
Average Yield %	0.78	0.78	0.77	0.62	0.71	0.14	...

Address: P.O. Box 8999, San Francisco, CA 94128-8999 Telephone: 415-932-2100	Web Site: www.corporate.visa.com Officers: Joseph W. Saunders - Chairman, Chief Executive Officer Charles W. Scharf - Chief Executive Officer	Auditors: KPMG LLP Investor Contact: 650-432-7644 Transfer Agents: Wells Fargo Shareowner Services, St. Paul, MN

VISHAY INTERTECHNOLOGY, INC.

Exchange	Symbol	Price	52Wk Range	Yield	P/E
NYS	VSH	$13.61 (3/28/2013)	13.95-8.18	N/A	17.23

*7 Year Price Score 90.90   ***NYSE Composite Index=100**   ***12 Month Price Score 113.30**

Interim Earnings (Per Share)

Qtr.	Mar	Jun	Sep	Dec
2008	(0.13)	(3.98)	(1.68)	(3.50)
2009	(0.16)	(0.32)	0.01	0.15
2010	0.24	0.40	0.47	0.79
2011	0.43	0.48	0.31	0.20
2012	0.21	0.29	0.15	0.14

Interim Dividends (Per Share)

No Dividends Paid

Valuation Analysis   **Institutional Holding**

Forecast EPS	$0.78	No of Institutions
	(04/05/2013)	311
Market Cap	$1.9 Billion	Shares
Book Value	$1.6 Billion	161,612,432
Price/Book	1.20	% Held
Price/Sales	0.87	100.53

Business Summary: Electrical Equipment (MIC: 7.3.1 SIC: 3679 NAIC: 334419)

Vishay Intertechnology is a manufacturer and supplier of semiconductors and passive components. Semiconductors include MOSFETs, diodes, and optoelectronic components. Passive components include resistive products, capacitors, and inductors. Co.'s semiconductor components are used for various functions, including power control, power conversion, power management, signal switching, signal routing, signal amplification, two-way data transfer, and circuit isolation. Co.'s passive components are used to restrict current flow, suppress voltage increases, store and discharge energy, control alternating current and voltage, filter out electrical signals, and perform other functions.

Recent Developments: For the year ended Dec 31 2012, net income decreased 48.5% to US$123.5 million from US$240.0 million in the prior year. Revenues were US$2.23 billion, down 14.0% from US$2.59 billion the year before. Operating income was US$189.2 million versus US$346.6 million in the prior year, a decrease of 45.4%. Direct operating expenses declined 9.1% to US$1.70 billion from US$1.87 billion in the comparable period the year before. Indirect operating expenses decreased 9.6% to US$337.5 million from US$373.4 million in the equivalent prior-year period.

Prospects: Our evaluation of Vishay Intertechnology Inc. as of Apr. 7, 2013 is the result of our systematic analysis on three basic characteristics: earnings strength, relative valuation, and recent stock price movement. The company has enjoyed a positive trend in earnings per share over the past 5 quarters and while recent estimates for the company have remained steady, VSH has posted better than expected results. Based on operating earnings yield, the company is about fairly valued when compared to all of the companies in our coverage universe. Share price changes over the past year indicates that VSH will perform in line with the market over the near term.

Financial Data
(US$ in Thousands)

	12/31/2012	12/31/2011	12/31/2010	12/31/2009	12/31/2008	12/31/2007	12/31/2006	12/31/2005
Earnings Per Share	0.79	1.42	1.89	(0.31)	(9.29)	0.69	0.73	0.34
Cash Flow Per Share	1.92	2.35	2.97	1.56	1.43	1.91	1.90	1.14
Tang Book Value Per Share	10.15	9.48	8.35	7.30	7.33	7.98	7.85	6.77
Income Statement								
Total Revenue	2,230,097	2,594,029	2,725,092	2,042,033	2,822,211	2,833,266	2,581,477	2,296,521
EBITDA	338,816	505,029	583,405	172,698	(1,460,216)	411,461	382,916	271,921
Depn & Amortn	153,801	165,022	169,724	206,009	199,847	196,564	181,552	174,439
Income Before Taxes	170,037	331,116	405,533	(39,715)	(1,671,685)	205,664	191,550	77,772
Income Taxes	46,506	91,119	45,240	16,800	11,187	64,133	50,836	11,737
Net Income	122,738	238,821	359,106	(57,188)	(1,731,416)	130,764	139,736	62,274
Average Shares	155,844	168,514	190,227	186,605	186,403	198,226	210,316	189,321
Balance Sheet								
Current Assets	1,791,263	1,830,676	1,794,504	1,407,543	1,328,534	1,742,801	1,727,247	1,606,632
Total Assets	3,016,277	2,993,730	2,966,093	2,719,546	2,815,960	4,995,235	4,691,896	4,527,591
Current Liabilities	412,170	439,788	527,161	407,501	462,129	596,928	534,414	470,166
Long-Term Obligations	392,931	399,054	431,682	320,052	333,631	607,237	608,434	751,553
Total Liabilities	1,392,949	1,390,724	1,474,362	1,203,100	1,271,102	1,638,460	1,611,083	1,671,739
Stockholders' Equity	1,623,328	1,603,006	1,491,731	1,516,446	1,544,858	3,356,775	3,080,813	2,855,852
Shares Outstanding	143,272	157,188	164,964	186,636	186,553	186,342	184,463	184,141
Statistical Record								
Return on Assets %	4.07	8.01	12.63	N.M.	N.M.	2.70	3.03	1.36
Return on Equity %	7.59	15.43	23.88	N.M.	N.M.	4.06	4.71	2.21
EBITDA Margin %	15.19	19.47	21.41	8.46	N.M.	14.52	14.83	11.84
Net Margin %	5.50	9.21	13.18	N.M.	N.M.	4.62	5.41	2.71
Asset Turnover	0.74	0.87	0.96	0.74	0.72	0.58	0.56	0.50
Current Ratio	4.35	4.16	3.40	3.45	2.87	2.92	3.23	3.42
Debt to Equity	0.24	0.25	0.29	0.21	0.22	0.18	0.20	0.26
Price Range	12.74-8.18	19.08-8.09	15.39-6.59	7.72-1.97	10.18-2.92	16.20-10.01	15.52-11.32	13.39-9.41
P/E Ratio	16.13-10.35	13.44-5.70	8.14-3.49	...	...	23.48-14.51	21.27-15.50	39.39-27.67

Address: 63 Lancaster Avenue, Malvern, PA 19355-2143 **Telephone:** 610-644-1300 **Fax:** 610-296-0657	**Web Site:** www.vishay.com **Officers:** Marc Zandman - Executive Chairman, Chief Business Development Officer Gerald Paul - President, Chief Executive Officer, Chief Technical Officer	**Auditors:** Ernst & Young LLP **Investor Contact:** 610-644-1300 **Transfer Agents:** American Stock Transfer & Trust Co., New York, NY

VMWARE, INC.

*7 Year Price Score N/A   *NYSE Composite Index=100   *12 Month Price Score 77.98

Interim Earnings (Per Share)

Qtr.	Mar	Jun	Sep	Dec
2008	0.11	0.13	0.21	0.28
2009	0.18	0.08	0.09	0.14
2010	0.19	0.18	0.20	0.28
2011	0.29	0.51	0.41	0.47
2012	0.44	0.44	0.36	0.48

Interim Dividends (Per Share)

No Dividends Paid

Valuation Analysis   **Institutional Holding**

Forecast EPS	$3.23	No of Institutions
	(04/05/2013)	489
Market Cap	$33.8 Billion	Shares
Book Value	$5.7 Billion	94,114,048
Price/Book	5.89	% Held
Price/Sales	7.34	N.M.

Business Summary: Internet & Software (MIC: 6.3.2 SIC: 7372 NAIC: 511210)

VMWARE is a provider of virtualization and virtualization-based cloud infrastructure applications. Co.'s applications enable organizations to aggregate multiple servers, storage infrastructure and networks together into shared pools of capacity. Co. has three main product groups: cloud infrastructure and management, which include the products VMware vCenter Server, VMware vCloud Director, VMware vCenter Site Recovery Manager, VMware vCenter Operations, and VMware vShield; cloud application platform, which include the VMware vFabric family of products; and end-user computing, which include the products VMware View, VMware ThinApp, VMware Zimbra, VMware Workstation and VMware Fusion.

Recent Developments: For the year ended Dec 31 2012, net income increased 3.0% to US$745.7 million from US$723.9 million in the prior year. Revenues were US$4.61 billion, up 22.2% from US$3.77 billion the year before. Operating income was US$871.9 million versus US$735.2 million in the prior year, an increase of 18.6%. Direct operating expenses rose 16.0% to US$721.3 million from US$622.0 million in the comparable period the year before. Indirect operating expenses increased 25.0% to US$3.01 billion from US$2.41 billion in the equivalent prior-year period.

Prospects: Our evaluation of VMware Inc. as of Apr. 7, 2013 is the result of our systematic analysis on three basic characteristics: earnings strength, relative valuation, and recent stock price movement. The company has produced a positive trend in earnings per share over the past 5 quarters and while recent estimates for the company have been raised by analysts, VMW has posted better than expected results. Based on operating earnings yield, the company is overvalued when compared to all of the companies in our coverage universe. Share price changes over the past year indicates that VMW will perform very poorly over the near term.

Financial Data

(US$ in Thousands)	12/31/2012	12/31/2011	12/31/2010	12/31/2009	12/31/2008	12/31/2007	12/31/2006	12/31/2005
Earnings Per Share	1.72	1.68	0.84	0.49	0.73	0.61	0.26	0.20
Cash Flow Per Share	4.44	4.81	2.87	2.50	2.07	1.58	0.84	0.72
Tang Book Value Per Share	5.04	6.15	4.87	3.81	3.18	1.75	...	N.M.
Income Statement								
Total Revenue	4,605,047	3,767,096	2,857,343	2,023,937	1,881,027	1,325,811	703,904	387,074
EBITDA	1,028,668	924,619	534,644	332,707	427,101	300,135	141,247	102,540
Depn & Amortn	130,900	126,300	114,200	102,300	89,500	41,900	18,700	7,200
Income Before Taxes	893,114	794,413	416,375	223,449	319,285	240,478	122,547	95,340
Income Taxes	147,412	70,477	58,936	26,351	29,152	22,341	36,832	28,565
Net Income	745,702	723,936	357,439	197,098	290,133	218,137	85,890	66,775
Average Shares	433,974	431,750	423,446	399,776	397,185	359,189	332,500	332,500
Balance Sheet								
Current Assets	6,120,039	5,677,772	4,297,655	3,182,480	2,390,088	1,603,334	422,431	161,974
Total Assets	10,596,392	8,680,808	6,797,319	5,066,984	3,839,205	2,695,700	1,145,950	799,803
Current Liabilities	2,960,234	2,401,506	1,789,152	1,294,042	879,750	670,012	477,749	296,172
Long-Term Obligations	450,000	450,000	450,000	450,000	450,000	450,000	800,000	
Total Liabilities	4,856,411	3,910,526	2,988,876	2,324,033	1,769,138	1,355,083	1,376,762	345,974
Stockholders' Equity	5,739,981	4,770,282	3,808,443	2,742,951	2,070,067	1,340,617	(230,812)	453,829
Shares Outstanding	428,688	423,610	416,701	402,785	390,448	382,924	332,500	332,500
Statistical Record								
Return on Assets %	7.72	9.35	6.03	4.43	8.86	11.36	8.83	...
Return on Equity %	14.15	16.88	10.91	8.19	16.97	39.31	77.03	...
EBITDA Margin %	22.34	24.54	18.71	16.44	22.71	22.64	20.07	26.49
Net Margin %	16.19	19.22	12.51	9.74	15.42	16.45	12.20	17.25
Asset Turnover	0.48	0.49	0.48	0.45	0.57	0.69	0.72	...
Current Ratio	2.07	2.36	2.40	2.46	2.72	2.39	0.88	0.55
Debt to Equity	0.08	0.09	0.12	0.16	0.22	0.34	...	...
Price Range	114.62-80.29	107.75-74.81	91.02-41.58	45.57-19.89	84.99-17.88	124.83-51.00	...	...
P/E Ratio	66.64-46.68	64.14-44.53	108.36-49.50	93.00-40.59	116.42-24.49	204.64-83.61	...	...

Address: 3401 Hillview Avenue, Palo Alto, CA 94304 **Telephone:** 650-427-5000	**Web Site:** www.vmware.com **Officers:** Joseph M. Tucci - Chairman Carl M. Eschenbach - Co-President, Interim Chief Financial Officer, Chief Operating Officer	**Auditors:** PricewaterhouseCoopers LLP **Investor Contact:** 650-427-2892 **Transfer Agents:** American Stock Transfer & Trust Company

VORNADO REALTY TRUST

Exchange	Symbol	Price	52Wk Range	Yield	P/E
NYS	VNO	$83.64 (3/28/2013)	88.07-73.23	3.49	28.45

*7 Year Price Score 85.38   *NYSE Composite Index=100   *12 Month Price Score 93.09

Interim Earnings (Per Share)

Qtr.	Mar	Jun	Sep	Dec
2008	2.47	0.79	0.20	(1.34)
2009	0.79	(0.30)	0.69	(0.88)
2010	1.09	0.31	0.52	2.06
2011	2.12	0.49	0.22	0.37
2012	1.25	0.11	1.24	0.33

Interim Dividends (Per Share)

Amt	Decl	Ex	Rec	Pay
0.69Q	07/31/2012	08/08/2012	08/10/2012	08/21/2012
0.69Q	10/30/2012	11/07/2012	11/09/2012	11/19/2012
1.00U	11/30/2012	12/06/2012	12/10/2012	12/21/2012
0.73Q	01/17/2013	01/24/2013	01/28/2013	02/19/2013

Indicated Div: $2.92

Valuation Analysis

		Institutional Holding	
Forecast EPS	$2.32 (04/06/2013)	No of Institutions	513
Market Cap	$15.6 Billion	Shares	181,667,072
Book Value	$6.9 Billion	% Held	91.93
Price/Book	2.28		
Price/Sales	5.65		

Business Summary: REITs (MIC: 5.3.1 SIC: 6798 NAIC: 525930)

Vornado Realty Trust is a real estate investment trust. As of Dec 31 2010, through its 93.5%-owned Vornado Realty L.P., Co. owned and operated office, retail and showroom properties, including office and retail properties in the New York City metropolitan area and in the Washington, DC / Northern Virginia area. In addition, as of such date, Co. had a 32.7% interest in Toys "R" Us, Inc.; a 32.4% interest in Alexander's, Inc., which owned seven properties New York; as well as interests in other real estate and related investments. Co. operates in five business segments: New York Office Properties, Washington, DC Office Properties, Retail Properties, Merchandise Mart Properties and Toys "R" Us.

Recent Developments: For the year ended Dec 31 2012, income from continuing operations decreased 29.4% to US$408.6 million from US$578.9 million a year earlier. Net income decreased 6.1% to US$694.5 million from US$740.0 million in the prior year. Revenues were US$2.77 billion, up 1.2% from US$2.73 billion the year before. Revenues from property income rose 1.5% to US$2.62 billion from US$2.58 billion in the corresponding earlier year.

Prospects: Our evaluation of Vornado Realty Trust as of Apr. 7, 2013 is the result of our systematic analysis on three basic characteristics: earnings strength, relative valuation, and recent stock price movement. The company has generated a negative trend in earnings per share over the past 5 quarters. Because the company lacks sufficient analyst estimate data, we place greater weight on the historical EPS trend as the measure of earnings strength. Based on operating earnings yield, the company is overvalued when compared to all of the companies in our coverage universe. Share price changes over the past year indicates that VNO will perform poorly over the near term.

Financial Data
(US$ in Thousands)

	12/31/2012	12/31/2011	12/31/2010	12/31/2009	12/31/2008	12/31/2007	12/31/2006	12/31/2005
Earnings Per Share	2.94	3.23	3.24	0.28	2.14	3.23	3.35	3.50
Cash Flow Per Share	4.43	3.81	4.23	3.69	5.30	4.59	5.80	5.70
Tang Book Value Per Share	28.06	29.65	28.23	27.46	27.79	30.65	33.21	29.98
Dividends Per Share	3.760	2.760	2.600	3.200	3.650	3.450	3.790	3.900
Dividend Payout %	127.89	85.45	80.25	1,142.86	170.56	106.81	113.13	111.43
Income Statement								
Total Revenue	2,766,457	2,915,665	2,779,727	2,742,578	2,697,051	3,270,629	2,712,095	2,547,628
EBITDA	900,561	1,486,619	1,663,495	1,262,077	1,302,951	1,367,977	1,311,941	1,180,260
Depn & Amortn	503,529	517,946	490,110	486,572	481,162	462,635	389,348	332,978
Income Before Taxes	(70,331)	476,098	657,128	24,892	232,749	499,287	707,006	673,756
Income Taxes	8,132	24,827	22,476	20,737	(204,537)	10,530	...	...
Net Income	617,260	662,302	647,883	106,169	395,043	568,906	560,140	539,604
Average Shares	186,530	186,021	184,159	173,503	158,119	158,558	150,411	141,012
Balance Sheet								
Current Assets	1,737,481	1,617,740	1,814,873	1,407,406	2,438,629	2,127,603	2,921,303	1,001,620
Total Assets	21,965,975	20,446,487	20,517,471	20,185,472	21,418,210	22,478,935	17,954,281	13,637,163
Current Liabilities	484,746	423,512	438,479	475,242	515,607	557,605	531,977	476,523
Long-Term Obligations	11,296,190	10,562,002	10,893,639	10,939,615	12,649,086	12,951,812	9,554,798	6,254,883
Total Liabilities	15,115,040	13,618,171	14,201,761	13,942,703	15,753,725	16,360,536	11,803,511	8,373,653
Stockholders' Equity	6,850,935	6,828,316	6,315,710	6,242,769	5,664,485	6,118,399	6,150,770	5,263,510
Shares Outstanding	186,734	185,080	183,661	181,214	155,285	153,076	151,093	141,153
Statistical Record								
Return on Assets %	2.90	3.23	3.18	0.51	1.79	2.81	3.55	4.28
Return on Equity %	9.00	10.08	10.32	1.78	6.69	9.27	9.81	11.63
EBITDA Margin %	32.55	50.99	59.84	46.02	48.31	41.83	48.37	46.33
Net Margin %	22.31	22.72	23.31	3.87	14.65	17.39	20.65	21.18
Asset Turnover	0.13	0.14	0.14	0.13	0.12	0.16	0.17	0.20
Current Ratio	3.58	3.82	4.14	2.96	4.73	3.82	5.49	2.10
Debt to Equity	1.65	1.55	1.72	1.75	2.23	2.12	1.55	1.19
Price Range	88.07-73.23	98.60-69.97	91.08-62.49	72.50-28.59	105.74-41.64	135.75-84.52	129.49-85.62	88.64-68.70
P/E Ratio	29.96-24.91	30.53-21.66	28.11-19.29	258.93-103.39	49.41-19.46	42.03-26.17	38.65-25.56	25.33-19.63
Average Yield %	4.62	3.23	3.31	6.10	4.35	3.08	3.72	4.92

Address: 888 Seventh Avenue, New York, NY 10019	Web Site: www.vno.com	Auditors: Deloitte & Touche LLP
Telephone: 212-894-7000	Officers: Steven Roth - Chairman, Chief Executive Officer Michelle Felman - Executive Vice President	Investor Contact: 201-587-1000 Transfer Agents: American Stock Transfer & Trust Co., New York, NY

VULCAN MATERIALS CO (HOLDING COMPANY)

Exchange	Symbol	Price	52Wk Range	Yield	P/E
NYS	VMC	$51.70 (3/28/2013)	58.74-32.57	0.08	N/A

*7 Year Price Score 68.21   ***NYSE Composite Index=100**   ***12 Month Price Score 106.39**

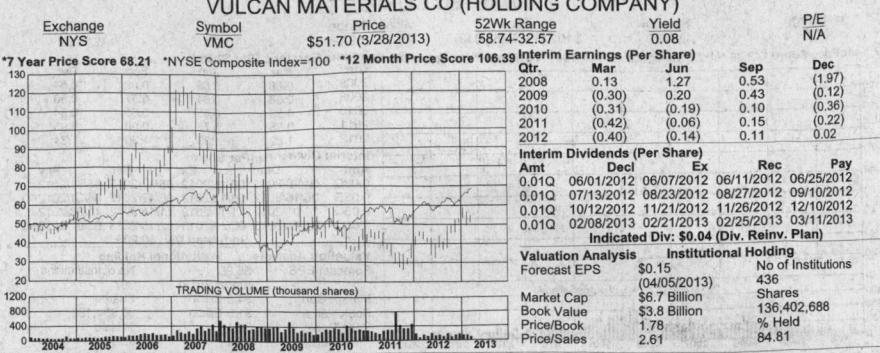

Interim Earnings (Per Share)

Qtr.	Mar	Jun	Sep	Dec
2008	0.13	1.27	0.53	(1.97)
2009	(0.30)	0.20	0.43	(0.12)
2010	(0.31)	(0.19)	0.10	(0.36)
2011	(0.42)	(0.06)	0.15	(0.22)
2012	(0.40)	(0.14)	0.11	0.02

Interim Dividends (Per Share)

Amt	Decl	Ex	Rec	Pay
0.01Q	06/01/2012	06/07/2012	06/11/2012	06/25/2012
0.01Q	07/13/2012	08/23/2012	08/27/2012	09/10/2012
0.01Q	10/12/2012	11/21/2012	11/26/2012	12/10/2012
0.01Q	02/08/2013	02/21/2013	02/25/2013	03/11/2013

Indicated Div: $0.04 (Div. Reinv. Plan)

Valuation Analysis

		Institutional Holding	
Forecast EPS	$0.15 (04/05/2013)	No of Institutions	436
Market Cap	$6.7 Billion	Shares	136,402,688
Book Value	$3.8 Billion	% Held	84.81
Price/Book	1.78		
Price/Sales	2.61		

Business Summary: Mining (MIC: 8.2.4 SIC: 1429 NAIC: 212319)

Vulcan Materials is a producer of construction aggregates, primarily crushed stone, sand and gravel, as well as asphalt mix and ready-mixed concrete, and cement. Co. has four reporting segments. Co.'s aggregates segment produces and sells aggregates (crushed stone, sand and gravel, sand, and other aggregates) and related products. Co.'s concrete segment produces and sells ready-mixed concrete in California, Florida, Georgia, Maryland, Texas, Virginia and the District of Columbia. Co.'s asphalt mix segment produces and sells asphalt mix in Arizona, California, and Texas. Co.'s cement segment produces Portland and masonry cement in both bulk form and bags.

Recent Developments: For the year ended Dec 31 2012, loss from continuing operations was US$53.9 million compared with a loss of US$75.3 million a year earlier. Net loss amounted to US$52.6 million versus a net loss of US$70.8 million in the prior year. Revenues were US$2.57 billion, up 0.1% from US$2.56 billion the year before. Operating income was US$84.8 million versus US$63.4 million in the prior year, an increase of 33.6%. Direct operating expenses declined 2.1% to US$2.23 billion from US$2.28 billion in the comparable period the year before. Indirect operating expenses increased 13.1% to US$249.2 million from US$220.4 million in the equivalent prior-year period.

Prospects: Our evaluation of Vulcan Materials Co. as of Apr. 7, 2013 is the result of our systematic analysis on three basic characteristics: earnings strength, relative valuation, and recent stock price movement. The company has suffered a very negative trend in earnings per share over the past 5 quarters. However, while recent estimates for the company have been lowered by analysts, VMC has posted results that fell short of analysts expectations. Based on operating earnings yield, the company is overvalued when compared to all of the companies in our coverage universe. Share price changes over the past year indicates that VMC will perform very well over the near term.

Financial Data

(US$ in Thousands)	12/31/2012	12/31/2011	12/31/2010	12/31/2009	12/31/2008	12/31/2007	12/31/2006	12/31/2005
Earnings Per Share	(0.41)	(0.55)	(0.75)	0.25	(0.04)	4.54	4.69	3.73
Cash Flow Per Share	1.83	1.31	1.58	3.81	3.95	7.30	5.94	4.63
Tang Book Value Per Share	N.M.	0.06	1.37	2.19	N.M.	N.M.	14.60	15.05
Dividends Per Share	0.040	0.760	1.000	1.480	1.960	1.840	1.480	1.160
Dividend Payout %	...	...	...	592.00	...	40.53	31.56	31.10
Income Statement								
Total Revenue	2,567,310	2,564,550	2,558,862	2,690,490	3,651,438	3,327,787	3,342,475	2,895,327
EBITDA	392,654	391,518	337,994	515,289	609,922	963,010	931,146	709,319
Depn & Amortn	301,146	328,072	349,460	361,530	365,177	253,764	207,540	208,563
Income Before Taxes	(120,418)	(153,738)	(192,206)	(19,221)	75,058	667,653	703,461	480,237
Income Taxes	(66,492)	(78,483)	(89,663)	(37,869)	76,724	204,416	225,963	136,402
Net Income	(52,593)	(70,778)	(96,490)	30,314	(4,115)	450,910	467,534	388,757
Average Shares	129,745	129,381	128,050	119,430	109,774	99,403	99,777	104,085
Balance Sheet								
Current Assets	984,972	863,100	772,106	743,289	893,890	1,157,229	731,379	1,164,722
Total Assets	8,126,599	8,229,314	8,337,891	8,532,950	8,914,169	8,936,370	3,424,225	3,588,884
Current Liabilities	436,411	406,253	565,672	856,695	1,663,066	2,528,187	493,687	579,014
Long-Term Obligations	2,526,401	2,680,677	2,427,516	2,116,120	2,153,588	1,529,828	322,064	323,392
Total Liabilities	4,365,537	4,437,697	4,372,911	4,480,928	5,391,433	5,176,770	1,423,114	1,462,343
Stockholders' Equity	3,761,062	3,791,617	3,964,980	4,052,022	3,522,736	3,759,600	2,001,111	2,126,541
Shares Outstanding	129,721	129,245	128,570	125,912	110,270	108,234	94,606	100,326
Statistical Record								
Return on Assets %	N.M.	N.M.	N.M.	0.35	N.M.	7.30	13.33	10.72
Return on Equity %	N.M.	N.M.	N.M.	0.80	N.M.	15.65	22.65	18.78
EBITDA Margin %	15.29	15.27	13.21	19.15	16.70	28.94	27.86	24.50
Net Margin %	N.M.	N.M.	N.M.	1.13	N.M.	13.55	13.99	13.43
Asset Turnover	0.31	0.31	0.30	0.31	0.41	0.54	0.95	0.80
Current Ratio	2.26	2.12	1.36	0.87	0.54	0.46	1.48	2.01
Debt to Equity	0.67	0.71	0.61	0.52	0.61	0.41	0.16	0.15
Price Range	53.25-32.57	46.98-26.19	58.89-35.70	69.95-34.55	83.00-40.56	123.67-77.43	93.49-66.97	75.79-52.44
P/E Ratio	...	...	...	279.80-138.20	...	27.24-17.06	19.93-14.28	20.32-14.06
Average Yield %	0.09	2.02	2.24	3.07	2.94	1.83	1.85	1.84

Address: 1200 Urban Center Drive, Birmingham, AL 35242	**Web Site:** www.vulcanmaterials.com	**Auditors:** Deloitte & Touche LLP
Telephone: 205-298-3000	**Officers:** Donald M. James - Chairman, Chief Executive Officer Daniel F. Sansone - Executive Vice President, Senior Vice President, Chief Financial Officer	**Investor Contact:** 205-298-3220
Fax: 205-298-2963		**Transfer Agents:** BNY Mellon Shareowner Services, Pittsburg, PA

WABTEC CORP.

Exchange	Symbol	Price	52Wk Range	Yield	P/E
NYS	WAB	$102.11 (3/28/2013)	102.11-69.04	0.20	19.67

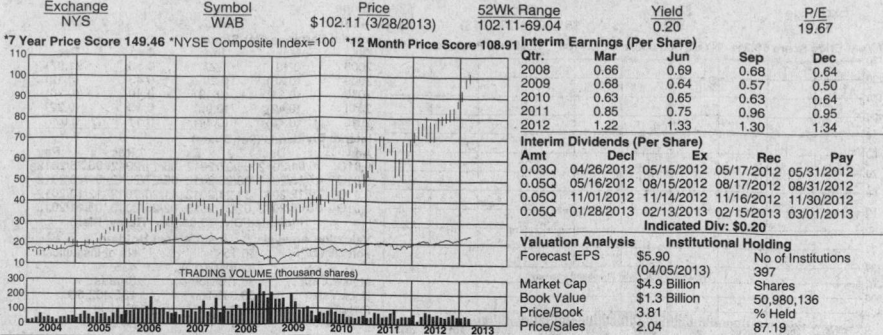

*7 Year Price Score 149.46 *NYSE Composite Index=100 ***12 Month Price Score 108.91**

Interim Earnings (Per Share)

Qtr.	Mar	Jun	Sep	Dec
2008	0.66	0.69	0.68	0.64
2009	0.68	0.64	0.57	0.50
2010	0.63	0.65	0.63	0.64
2011	0.85	0.75	0.96	0.95
2012	1.22	1.33	1.30	1.34

Interim Dividends (Per Share)

Amt	Decl	Ex	Rec	Pay
0.03Q	04/26/2012	05/15/2012	05/17/2012	05/31/2012
0.05Q	05/16/2012	08/15/2012	08/17/2012	08/31/2012
0.05Q	11/01/2012	11/14/2012	11/16/2012	11/30/2012
0.05Q	01/28/2013	02/13/2013	02/15/2013	03/01/2013

Indicated Div: $0.20

Valuation Analysis / **Institutional Holding**

Forecast EPS	$5.90 (04/05/2013)	No of Institutions	397
Market Cap	$4.9 Billion	Shares	50,980,136
Book Value	$1.3 Billion	% Held	87.19
Price/Book	3.81		
Price/Sales	2.04		

Business Summary: Construction Services (MIC: 7.5.4 SIC: 3743 NAIC: 336510)

Wabtec is a provider of technology-based equipment and services for the rail industry. Co. provides its products and services through two principal business segments: the Freight Segment, which primarily manufactures and services components for locomotive and freight cars , supplies railway electronics, positive train control equipment, signal design and engineering services, builds switcher locomotives, rebuilds freight locomotives and provides heat exchangers and cooling systems for rail and other industrial markets; and the Transit Segment, which primarily manufactures and services components for passenger transit vehicles, builds new commuter locomotives and refurbishes subway cars.

Recent Developments: For the year ended Dec 31 2012, net income increased 47.9% to US$251.7 million from US$170.1 million in the prior year. Revenues were US$2.39 billion, up 21.5% from US$1.97 billion the year before. Operating income was US$392.3 million versus US$270.7 million in the prior year, an increase of 44.9%. Direct operating expenses rose 21.4% to US$1.70 billion from US$1.40 billion in the comparable period the year before. Indirect operating expenses increased 0.9% to US$302.3 million from US$299.7 million in the equivalent prior-year period.

Prospects: Our evaluation of Wabtec Corp. as of Apr. 7, 2013 is the result of our systematic analysis on three basic characteristics: earnings strength, relative valuation, and recent stock price movement. The company has managed to produce a neutral trend in earnings per share over the past 5 quarters and while recent estimates for the company have been mixed, WAB has posted better than expected results. Based on operating earnings yield, the company is about fairly valued when compared to all of the companies in our coverage universe. Share price changes over the past year indicates that WAB will perform well over the near term.

Financial Data

(US$ in Thousands)	12/31/2012	12/31/2011	12/31/2010	12/31/2009	12/31/2008	12/31/2007	12/31/2006	12/31/2005
Earnings Per Share	5.19	3.51	2.56	2.39	2.67	2.23	1.73	1.17
Cash Flow Per Share	4.96	5.20	3.70	3.38	3.30	2.94	3.13	1.79
Tang Book Value Per Share	6.34	4.18	2.86	2.23	1.86	6.69	5.23	4.62
Dividends Per Share	0.160	0.080	0.040	0.040	0.040	0.040	0.040	0.040
Dividend Payout %	3.08	2.28	1.56	1.67	1.50	1.79	2.31	3.42
Income Statement								
Total Revenue	2,391,122	1,967,637	1,507,012	1,401,616	1,574,749	1,360,088	1,087,620	1,034,024
EBITDA	420,509	300,221	231,150	205,733	242,508	205,091	153,343	123,002
Depn & Amortn	28,900	29,900	28,400	25,700	29,700	29,000	25,200	24,800
Income Before Taxes	377,358	255,314	186,827	163,359	204,300	172,454	126,557	89,516
Income Taxes	125,626	85,165	63,728	48,304	73,746	63,067	40,063	31,831
Net Income	251,732	170,149	123,099	115,055	130,551	109,570	84,804	55,776
Average Shares	48,371	48,329	48,005	47,977	48,847	49,141	49,108	47,595
Balance Sheet								
Current Assets	1,092,938	1,055,782	801,953	689,509	725,349	665,767	547,191	482,926
Total Assets	2,351,542	2,158,953	1,803,081	1,585,835	1,507,520	1,158,702	972,842	836,357
Current Liabilities	553,059	541,385	348,374	305,348	388,051	295,235	243,791	241,479
Long-Term Obligations	317,853	395,805	382,007	359,039	356,699	150,177	150,000	150,000
Total Liabilities	1,074,712	1,113,764	903,310	808,928	862,149	541,434	502,953	457,150
Stockholders' Equity	1,276,830	1,045,189	899,771	776,907	645,371	617,268	469,889	379,207
Shares Outstanding	47,703	47,946	47,954	47,688	47,907	48,698	48,250	48,002
Statistical Record								
Return on Assets %	11.13	8.59	7.26	7.44	9.77	10.28	9.37	7.20
Return on Equity %	21.62	17.50	14.68	16.18	20.62	20.16	19.98	16.13
EBITDA Margin %	17.59	15.26	15.34	14.68	15.40	15.08	14.10	11.90
Net Margin %	10.53	8.65	8.17	8.21	8.29	8.06	7.80	5.39
Asset Turnover	1.06	0.99	0.89	0.91	1.18	1.28	1.20	1.33
Current Ratio	1.98	1.95	2.30	2.26	1.87	2.26	2.24	2.00
Debt to Equity	0.25	0.38	0.42	0.46	0.55	0.24	0.32	0.40
Price Range	88.69-68.79	71.56-50.15	53.24-36.89	42.40-23.36	59.69-29.98	41.30-28.65	39.73-25.26	28.11-16.75
P/E Ratio	17.09-13.25	20.39-14.29	20.80-14.41	17.74-9.77	22.36-11.23	18.52-12.85	22.97-14.60	24.03-14.32
Average Yield %	0.21	0.13	0.09	0.11	0.09	0.11	0.13	0.18

Address: 1001 Air Brake Avenue, Wilmerding, PA 15148 Telephone: 412-825-1000	Web Site: www.wabtec.com Officers: William E. Kassling - Chairman Emilio A. Fernandez - Vice-Chairman	Auditors: Ernst & Young LLP Transfer Agents: Computershare, Pittsburgh, PA

WADDELL & REED FINANCIAL, INC.

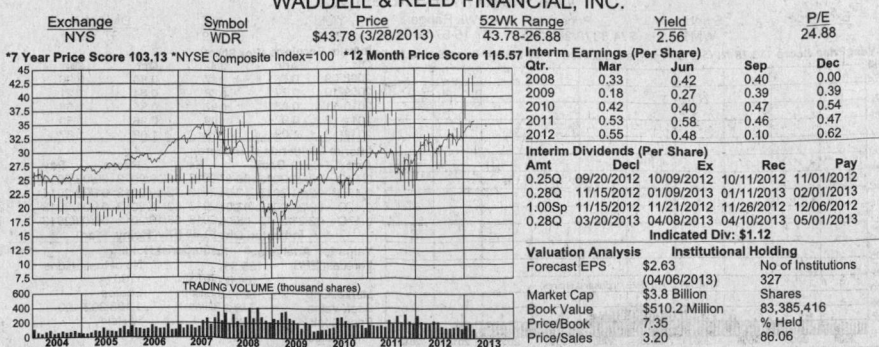

Exchange	Symbol	Price	52Wk Range	Yield	P/E
NYS	WDR	$43.78 (3/28/2013)	43.78-26.88	2.56	24.88

*7 Year Price Score 103.13 *NYSE Composite Index=100 *12 Month Price Score 115.57

Interim Earnings (Per Share)

Qtr.	Mar	Jun	Sep	Dec
2008	0.33	0.42	0.40	0.00
2009	0.18	0.27	0.39	0.39
2010	0.42	0.40	0.47	0.54
2011	0.53	0.58	0.46	0.47
2012	0.55	0.48	0.10	0.62

Interim Dividends (Per Share)

Amt	Decl	Ex	Rec	Pay
0.25Q	09/20/2012	10/09/2012	10/11/2012	11/01/2012
0.28Q	11/15/2012	01/09/2013	01/11/2013	02/01/2013
1.00Sp	11/15/2012	11/21/2012	11/26/2012	12/06/2012
0.28Q	03/20/2013	04/08/2013	04/10/2013	05/01/2013

Indicated Div: $1.12

Valuation Analysis

		Institutional Holding	
Forecast EPS	$2.63 (04/06/2013)	No of Institutions	327
Market Cap	$3.8 Billion	Shares	83,385,416
Book Value	$510.2 Million	% Held	86.06
Price/Book	7.35		
Price/Sales	3.20		

Business Summary: Finance Intermediaries & Services (MIC: 5.5.1 SIC: 6211 NAIC: 523120)

Waddell & Reed Financial is a holding company. Co. provides investment management, investment product underwriting and distribution, and shareholder services administration to mutual funds and institutional and separately managed accounts.Co. provides investment advisory and management services pursuant to investment management agreements with each fund within the Advisors Funds family, the Ivy Funds family, the Ivy Funds VIP family, and InvestEd. Co. also acts as an investment adviser for institutional and other private investors and provides subadvisory services to other investment companies. As of Dec 31 2012, Co. had $96.37 billion in assets under management.

Recent Developments: For the year ended Dec 31 2012, income from continuing operations increased 11.8% to US$192.5 million from US$172.2 million a year earlier. Net income decreased 14.0% to US$151.0 million from US$175.5 million in the prior year. Revenues were US$1.17 billion, up 4.6% from US$1.12 billion the year before. Operating income was US$302.5 million versus US$286.2 million in the prior year, an increase of 5.7%. Direct operating expenses rose 5.3% to US$590.0 million from US$560.2 million in the comparable period the year before. Indirect operating expenses increased 1.9% to US$281.3 million from US$276.1 million in the equivalent prior-year period.

Prospects: Our evaluation of Waddell & Reed Financial Inc. as of Apr. 7, 2013 is the result of our systematic analysis on three basic characteristics: earnings strength, relative valuation, and recent stock price movement. The company has produced a positive trend in earnings per share over the past 5 quarters and while recent estimates for the company have been raised by analysts, WDR has posted better than expected results. Based on operating earnings yield, the company is about fairly valued when compared to all of the companies in our coverage universe. Share price changes over the past year indicates that WDR will perform well over the near term.

Financial Data
(US$ in Thousands)

	12/31/2012	12/31/2011	12/31/2010	12/31/2009	12/31/2008	12/31/2007	12/31/2006	12/31/2005
Earnings Per Share	1.76	2.05	1.83	1.23	1.15	1.52	0.55	0.73
Cash Flow Per Share	2.72	3.30	1.64	1.82	1.51	1.59	1.22	1.29
Tang Book Value Per Share	4.06	3.53	2.75	1.72	1.17	1.77	0.19	N.M.
Dividends Per Share	1.750	0.850	0.770	0.760	0.740	0.660	0.600	0.600
Dividend Payout %	99.43	41.46	42.08	61.79	64.35	43.42	109.09	82.19
Income Statement								
Total Revenue	1,173,805	1,195,177	1,044,885	839,089	919,120	837,554	718,655	622,080
EBITDA	325,514	309,341	273,207	188,551	181,707	223,484	113,127	120,528
Depn & Amortn	13,200	15,200	14,000	13,700	13,200	12,400	11,700	10,300
Income Before Taxes	301,003	282,728	246,484	162,156	156,420	199,160	89,200	95,950
Income Taxes	108,475	107,269	89,525	56,651	60,257	73,663	43,088	35,829
Net Income	150,952	175,459	156,959	105,505	96,163	125,497	46,112	60,121
Average Shares	85,728	85,793	85,647	85,544	83,969	82,824	83,212	82,045
Balance Sheet								
Current Assets	804,893	699,611	605,050	618,716	430,835	547,948	352,003	299,722
Total Assets	1,152,843	1,082,196	976,931	983,382	775,360	893,750	662,714	632,271
Current Liabilities	365,333	288,898	281,942	360,757	204,708	272,602	189,551	156,784
Long-Term Obligations	190,000	190,000	189,799	199,984	199,969	199,955	199,942	198,230
Total Liabilities	642,603	558,553	519,770	614,327	455,235	512,132	418,014	384,897
Stockholders' Equity	510,240	523,643	457,161	369,055	320,125	381,618	244,700	247,374
Shares Outstanding	85,679	85,564	85,751	85,807	84,877	86,630	84,660	83,804
Statistical Record								
Return on Assets %	13.47	17.04	16.01	12.00	11.49	16.13	7.12	9.60
Return on Equity %	29.12	35.78	37.99	30.62	27.33	40.07	18.74	25.79
EBITDA Margin %	27.73	25.88	26.15	22.47	19.77	26.68	15.74	19.38
Net Margin %	12.86	14.68	15.02	12.57	10.46	14.98	6.42	9.66
Asset Turnover	1.05	1.16	1.07	0.95	1.10	1.08	1.11	0.99
Current Ratio	2.20	2.42	2.15	1.72	2.10	2.01	1.86	1.91
Debt to Equity	0.37	0.36	0.42	0.54	0.62	0.52	0.82	0.80
Price Range	35.49-25.00	42.16-23.39	39.05-21.83	31.00-11.84	37.50-9.15	37.34-22.24	27.67-19.40	23.90-16.79
P/E Ratio	20.16-14.20	20.57-11.41	21.34-11.93	25.20-9.63	32.61-7.96	24.57-14.63	50.31-35.27	32.74-23.00
Average Yield %	5.68	2.52	2.57	3.19	3.17	2.44	2.60	3.02

Address: 6300 Lamar Avenue, Overland Park, KS 66202 Telephone: 913-236-2000	Web Site: www.waddell.com Officers: Alan W. Kosloff - Chairman Michael L. Avery - President, Chief Investment Officer	Auditors: KPMG LLP Investor Contact: 913-236-1880 Transfer Agents: Computershare, Kansas City, MO

WAL-MART STORES, INC.

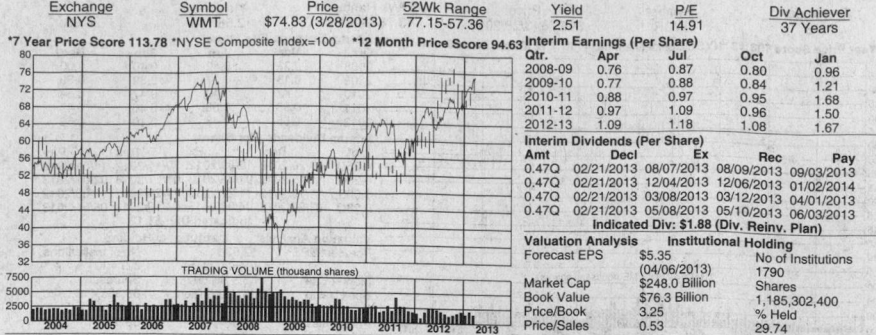

Exchange	Symbol	Price	52Wk Range	Yield	P/E	Div Achiever
NYS	WMT	$74.83 (3/28/2013)	77.15-57.36	2.51	14.91	37 Years

*7 Year Price Score 113.78 *NYSE Composite Index=100   *12 Month Price Score 94.63

Interim Earnings (Per Share)

Qtr.	Apr	Jul	Oct	Jan
2008-09	0.76	0.87	0.80	0.96
2009-10	0.77	0.88	0.84	1.21
2010-11	0.88	0.97	0.95	1.68
2011-12	0.97	1.09	0.96	1.50
2012-13	1.09	1.18	1.08	1.67

Interim Dividends (Per Share)

Amt	Decl	Ex	Rec	Pay
0.47Q	02/21/2013	08/07/2013	08/09/2013	09/03/2013
0.47Q	02/21/2013	12/04/2013	12/06/2013	01/02/2014
0.47Q	02/21/2013	03/08/2013	03/12/2013	04/01/2013
0.47Q	02/21/2013	05/08/2013	05/10/2013	06/03/2013

Indicated Div: $1.88 (Div. Reinv. Plan)

Valuation Analysis

		Institutional Holding	
Forecast EPS	$5.35 (04/06/2013)	No of Institutions	1790
Market Cap	$248.0 Billion	Shares	1,185,302,400
Book Value	$76.3 Billion	% Held	29.74
Price/Book	3.25		
Price/Sales	0.53		

Business Summary: Retail - General Merchandise/Department Stores (MIC: 2.1.1 SIC: 5331 NAIC: 452990)

Wal-Mart Stores operates retail stores in various formats. Co.'s operations comprise of three business segments: Walmart U.S., which operates retail stores in various formats in all 50 states in the U.S. and Puerto Rico, as well as its online retail operations, walmart.com; Walmart International, which consists of retail operations in 26 countries and includes several formats of retail stores, restaurants, wholesale clubs, including Sam's Clubs, and various retail websites that operate outside the U.S.; and Sam's Club, which consists of membership warehouse clubs operated in 47 states in the U.S. and Puerto Rico, as well as the segment's online retail operations, samsclub.com.

Recent Developments: For the year ended Jan 31 2013, income from continuing operations increased 7.9% to US$17.76 billion from US$16.45 billion a year earlier. Net income increased 8.4% to US$17.76 billion from US$16.39 billion in the prior year. Revenues were US$469.16 billion, up 5.0% from US$446.95 billion the year before. Operating income was US$27.80 billion versus US$26.56 billion in the prior year, an increase of 4.7%. Direct operating expenses rose 5.2% to US$352.49 billion from US$335.13 billion in the comparable period the year before. Indirect operating expenses increased 4.2% to US$88.87 billion from US$85.27 billion in the equivalent prior-year period.

Prospects: Our evaluation of Wal-Mart Stores Inc. as of Apr. 7, 2013 is the result of our systematic analysis on three basic characteristics: earnings strength, relative valuation, and recent stock price movement. The company has managed to produce a neutral trend in earnings per share over the past 5 quarters and while recent estimates for the company have been raised by analysts, WMT has posted better than expected results. Based on operating earnings yield, the company is undervalued when compared to all of the companies in our coverage universe. Share price changes over the past year indicates that WMT will perform in line with the market over the near term.

Financial Data

(US$ in Thousands)	01/31/2013	01/31/2012	01/31/2011	01/31/2010	01/31/2009	01/31/2008	01/31/2007	01/31/2006
Earnings Per Share	5.02	4.52	4.47	3.70	3.39	3.13	2.71	2.68
Cash Flow Per Share	7.56	7.01	6.47	6.79	5.86	5.01	4.84	4.22
Tang Book Value Per Share	16.85	14.82	14.73	14.43	12.75	12.22	11.57	9.84
Dividends Per Share	1.590	1.460	1.210	1.090	0.950	0.880	0.670	0.600
Dividend Payout %	31.67	32.30	27.07	29.46	28.02	28.12	24.72	22.39
Income Statement								
Total Revenue	469,162,000	446,950,000	421,849,000	408,214,000	405,607,000	378,799,000	348,650,000	315,654,000
EBITDA	36,201,000	34,658,000	33,142,000	31,150,000	29,498,000	28,296,000	25,997,000	23,230,000
Depn & Amortn	8,400,000	8,100,000	7,600,000	7,200,000	6,700,000	6,300,000	5,500,000	4,700,000
Income Before Taxes	25,737,000	24,398,000	23,538,000	22,066,000	20,898,000	20,198,000	18,968,000	17,358,000
Income Taxes	7,981,000	7,944,000	7,579,000	7,139,000	7,145,000	6,908,000	6,365,000	5,803,000
Net Income	16,999,000	15,699,000	16,389,000	14,335,000	13,400,000	12,731,000	11,284,000	11,231,000
Average Shares	3,389,000	3,474,000	3,670,000	3,877,000	3,951,000	4,072,000	4,168,000	4,188,000
Balance Sheet								
Current Assets	59,940,000	54,975,000	51,893,000	48,331,000	48,949,000	47,585,000	46,588,000	43,824,000
Total Assets	203,105,000	193,406,000	180,663,000	170,706,000	163,429,000	163,514,000	151,193,000	138,187,000
Current Liabilities	71,818,000	62,300,000	58,484,000	55,561,000	55,390,000	58,454,000	51,754,000	48,826,000
Long-Term Obligations	41,417,000	47,079,000	43,842,000	36,401,000	34,549,000	33,402,000	30,735,000	30,171,000
Total Liabilities	126,762,000	122,091,000	112,121,000	99,957,000	98,144,000	98,906,000	89,620,000	85,016,000
Stockholders' Equity	76,343,000	71,315,000	68,542,000	70,749,000	65,285,000	64,608,000	61,573,000	53,171,000
Shares Outstanding	3,314,000	3,418,000	3,516,000	3,786,000	3,925,000	3,973,000	4,131,000	4,165,000
Statistical Record								
Return on Assets %	8.55	8.39	9.33	8.58	8.17	8.09	7.80	8.69
Return on Equity %	22.96	22.45	23.53	21.08	20.58	20.18	19.67	21.90
EBITDA Margin %	7.72	7.75	7.86	7.63	7.27	7.47	7.46	7.36
Net Margin %	3.62	3.51	3.89	3.51	3.30	3.36	3.24	3.56
Asset Turnover	2.36	2.39	2.40	2.44	2.47	2.41	2.41	2.44
Current Ratio	0.83	0.88	0.89	0.87	0.88	0.81	0.90	0.90
Debt to Equity	0.54	0.66	0.64	0.51	0.53	0.52	0.50	0.57
Price Range	77.15-57.36	61.47-48.41	57.57-48.00	55.01-46.42	63.17-47.86	51.21-42.27	51.75-43.02	53.51-42.49
P/E Ratio	15.37-11.43	13.60-10.71	12.88-10.74	14.87-12.55	18.63-14.12	16.36-13.50	19.10-15.87	19.97-15.85
Average Yield %	2.33	2.67	2.28	2.15	1.72	1.87	1.43	1.25

Address: 702 S.W. 8th Street, Bentonville, AR 72716 Telephone: 479-273-4000	Web Site: Officers: S. Robson Walton - Chairman Eduardo Castro-Wright - Vice-Chairman, Division Officer	Auditors: Ernst & Young LLP Investor Contact: 479-273-6463 Transfer Agents: Computershare Trust Company, N.A., Providence, RI

WALGREEN CO.

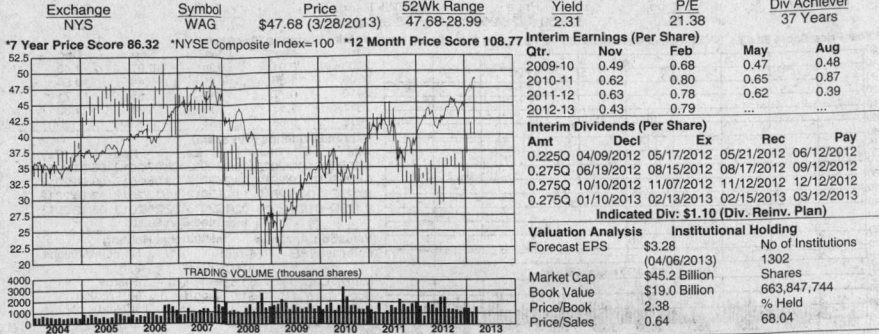

Exchange	Symbol	Price	52Wk Range	Yield	P/E	Div Achiever
NYS	WAG	$47.68 (3/28/2013)	47.68-28.99	2.31	21.38	37 Years

*7 Year Price Score 86.32 ***NYSE Composite Index=100** ***12 Month Price Score 108.77**

Interim Earnings (Per Share)

Qtr.	Nov	Feb	May	Aug
2009-10	0.49	0.68	0.47	0.48
2010-11	0.62	0.80	0.65	0.87
2011-12	0.63	0.78	0.62	0.39
2012-13	0.43	0.79	...	...

Interim Dividends (Per Share)

Amt	Decl	Ex	Rec	Pay
0.225Q	04/09/2012	05/17/2012	05/21/2012	06/12/2012
0.275Q	06/19/2012	08/15/2012	08/17/2012	09/12/2012
0.275Q	10/10/2012	11/07/2012	11/12/2012	12/12/2012
0.275Q	01/10/2013	02/13/2013	02/15/2013	03/12/2013

Indicated Div: $1.10 (Div. Reinv. Plan)

Valuation Analysis

		Institutional Holding	
Forecast EPS	$3.28	No of Institutions	
	(04/06/2013)	1302	
Market Cap	$45.2 Billion	Shares	
Book Value	$19.0 Billion	663,847,744	
Price/Book	2.38	% Held	
Price/Sales	0.64	68.04	

Business Summary: Retail - Food & Beverage, Drug & Tobacco (MIC: 2.1.2 SIC: 5912 NAIC: 446110)

Walgreen is a retail drugstore chain that sells prescription and non-prescription drugs and general merchandise. General merchandise includes household items, convenience and fresh foods, personal care, beauty care, photofinishing and candy. Co. provides pharmacy, health and wellness services such as retail, pharmacy, infusion and respiratory services, mail service, convenient care clinics and worksite clinics. Co. also provides services through its Take Care Health Systems, Inc. subsidiary, which manages its Take Care Clinics at select drugstores. As of Aug 31 2012, Co. operated 8,385 locations in 50 states, the District of Columbia, Guam and Puerto Rico, excluding 360 Take Care clinics.

Recent Developments: For the quarter ended Feb 28 2013, net income increased 10.7% to US$756.0 million from US$683.0 million in the year-earlier quarter. Revenues were US$18.65 billion, unchanged from the year before. Operating income was US$1.22 billion versus US$1.11 billion in the prior-year quarter, an increase of 10.0%. Direct operating expenses declined 1.7% to US$13.04 billion from US$13.26 billion in the comparable period the year before. Indirect operating expenses increased 2.5% to US$4.39 billion from US$4.28 billion in the equivalent prior-year period.

Prospects: Our evaluation of Walgreen Co. as of Apr. 7, 2013 is the result of our systematic analysis on three basic characteristics: earnings strength, relative valuation, and recent stock price movement. The company has enjoyed a very positive trend in earnings per share over the past 5 quarters and while recent estimates for the company have been mixed, WAG has posted better than expected results. Based on operating earnings yield, the company is undervalued when compared to all of the companies in our coverage universe. Share price changes over the past year indicates that WAG will perform very poorly over the near term.

Financial Data

(US$ in Thousands)	6 Mos	3 Mos	08/31/2012	08/31/2011	08/31/2010	08/31/2009	08/31/2008	08/31/2007
Earnings Per Share	2.23	2.22	2.42	2.94	2.12	2.02	2.17	2.03
Cash Flow Per Share	4.67	4.47	5.05	3.98	3.81	4.15	3.06	2.36
Tang Book Value Per Share	17.51	16.90	15.67	13.06	12.14	13.06	11.56	10.13
Dividends Per Share	1.050	1.000	0.950	0.750	0.588	0.475	0.398	0.328
Dividend Payout %	47.09	45.05	39.26	25.51	27.71	23.51	18.32	16.13
Income Statement								
Total Revenue	35,963,000	17,316,000	71,633,000	72,184,000	67,420,000	63,335,000	59,034,000	53,762,000
EBITDA	2,281,000	920,000	4,305,000	5,174,000	4,262,000	3,287,000	3,477,000	3,180,000
Depn & Amortn	450,000	219,000	841,000	809,000	804,000	40,000	36,000	29,300
Income Before Taxes	1,771,000	664,000	3,376,000	4,294,000	3,373,000	3,164,000	3,430,000	3,189,100
Income Taxes	691,000	255,000	1,249,000	1,580,000	1,282,000	1,158,000	1,273,000	1,147,800
Net Income	1,169,000	413,000	2,127,000	2,714,000	2,091,000	2,006,000	2,157,000	2,041,300
Average Shares	953,400	951,200	880,100	924,500	987,900	991,330	995,543	1,006,340
Balance Sheet								
Current Assets	12,432,000	12,162,000	10,760,000	12,322,000	11,922,000	12,049,000	10,433,000	9,510,500
Total Assets	35,564,000	35,259,000	33,462,000	27,454,000	26,275,000	25,142,000	22,410,000	19,313,600
Current Liabilities	9,025,000	9,320,000	8,722,000	8,083,000	7,433,000	6,769,000	6,644,000	6,744,300
Long-Term Obligations	5,058,000	5,069,000	4,073,000	2,396,000	2,389,000	2,336,000	1,337,000	...
Total Liabilities	16,591,000	16,880,000	15,226,000	12,607,000	11,875,000	10,766,000	9,541,000	8,209,300
Stockholders' Equity	18,973,000	18,379,000	18,236,000	14,847,000	14,400,000	14,376,000	12,869,000	11,104,300
Shares Outstanding	947,485	945,104	944,055	889,294	938,605	988,561	989,176	991,141
Statistical Record								
Return on Assets %	6.62	6.34	6.96	10.10	8.13	8.44	10.31	11.20
Return on Equity %	12.19	12.02	12.82	18.56	14.53	14.73	17.95	19.24
EBITDA Margin %	6.34	5.31	6.01	7.17	6.32	5.19	5.89	5.91
Net Margin %	3.25	2.39	2.97	3.76	3.10	3.17	3.65	3.80
Asset Turnover	2.28	2.26	2.35	2.69	2.62	2.66	2.82	2.95
Current Ratio	1.38	1.30	1.23	1.52	1.60	1.78	1.57	1.41
Debt to Equity	0.27	0.28	0.22	0.16	0.17	0.16	0.10	...
Price Range	41.95-28.99	36.95-28.99	37.30-28.99	45.18-26.88	40.37-26.36	36.67-21.40	47.93-31.39	51.48-40.10
P/E Ratio	18.81-13.00	16.64-13.06	15.41-11.98	15.37-9.14	19.04-12.43	18.15-10.59	22.09-14.47	25.36-19.75
Average Yield %	3.00	2.97	2.84	1.93	1.71	1.70	1.07	0.73

Address: 108 Wilmot Road, Deerfield, IL 60015	**Web Site:** www.walgreens.com	**Auditors:** Deloitte & Touche LLP
Telephone: 847-315-2500	**Officers:** James A. Skinner - Chairman Gregory D. Wasson - President, Chief Executive Officer	**Investor Contact:** 847-315-2385
Fax: 847-914-2804		**Transfer Agents:** Wells Fargo Bank, N.A., South St. Paul, MN

WALTER ENERGY, INC.

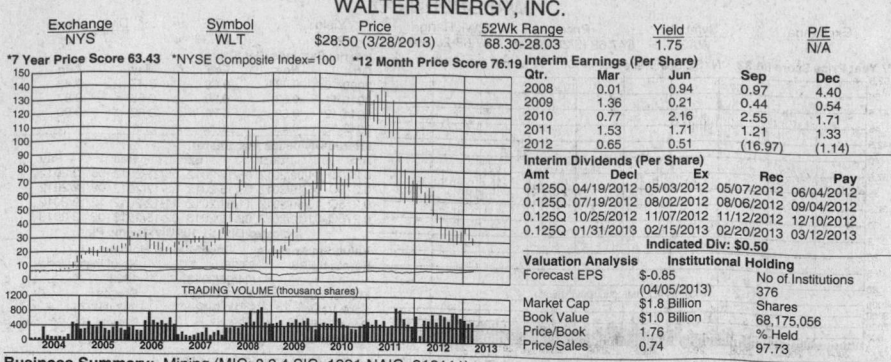

Exchange	Symbol	Price	52Wk Range	Yield	P/E
NYS	WLT	$28.50 (3/28/2013)	68.30-28.03	1.75	N/A

*7 Year Price Score 63.43   *NYSE Composite Index=100   *12 Month Price Score 76.19

Interim Earnings (Per Share)

Qtr.	Mar	Jun	Sep	Dec
2008	0.01	0.94	0.97	4.40
2009	1.36	0.21	0.44	0.54
2010	0.77	2.16	2.55	1.71
2011	1.53	1.71	1.21	1.33
2012	0.65	0.51	(16.97)	(1.14)

Interim Dividends (Per Share)

Amt	Decl	Ex	Rec	Pay
0.125Q	04/19/2012	05/03/2012	05/07/2012	06/04/2012
0.125Q	07/19/2012	08/02/2012	08/06/2012	09/04/2012
0.125Q	10/25/2012	11/07/2012	11/12/2012	12/10/2012
0.125Q	01/31/2013	02/15/2013	02/20/2013	03/12/2013

Indicated Div: $0.50

Valuation Analysis

		Institutional Holding	
Forecast EPS	$-0.85 (04/05/2013)	No of Institutions	376
Market Cap	$1.8 Billion	Shares	68,175,056
Book Value	$1.0 Billion	% Held	
Price/Book	1.76	97.73	
Price/Sales	0.74		

Business Summary: Mining (MIC: 8.2.4 SIC: 1221 NAIC: 212111)

Walter Energy is a holding company. Co. is a producer and exporter of metallurgical coal for the steel industry and also produces thermal coal and industrial coal, anthracite, metallurgical coke, coal bed methane gas and other related products. Co. has two business segments, U.S. Operations segment, which includes the operations of its underground mines, surface mines, coke plant and natural gas operations located in Alabama, and its underground and surface mining operations located in West Virginia; and Canadian and U.K. Operations segment, which includes the operations of surface mines in Northeast British Columbia (Canada) and underground and surface mines in South Wales (U.K.).

Recent Developments: For the year ended Dec 31 2012, loss from continuing operations was US$1.07 billion compared with income of US$363.6 million a year earlier. Net loss amounted to US$1.06 billion versus net income of US$363.6 million in the prior year. Revenues were US$2.40 billion, down 6.7% from US$2.57 billion the year before. Operating loss was US$1.01 billion versus an income of US$573.4 million in the prior year. Direct operating expenses rose 15.1% to US$1.80 billion from US$1.56 billion in the comparable period the year before. Indirect operating expenses increased 270.0% to US$1.62 billion from US$436.8 million in the equivalent prior-year period.

Prospects: Our evaluation of Walter Energy, Inc. as of Apr. 7, 2013 is the result of our systematic analysis on three basic characteristics: earnings strength, relative valuation, and recent stock price movement. The company has generated a negative trend in earnings per share over the past 5 quarters. Because the company lacks sufficient analyst estimate data, we place greater weight on the historical EPS trend as the measure of earnings strength. Based on operating earnings yield, the company is overvalued when compared to all of the companies in our coverage universe. Share price changes over the past year indicates that WLT will perform very well over the near term.

Financial Data

(US$ in Thousands)	12/31/2012	12/31/2011	12/31/2010	12/31/2009	12/31/2008	12/31/2007	12/31/2006	12/31/2005
Earnings Per Share	(16.96)	5.76	7.18	2.55	6.35	2.13	3.87	0.18
Cash Flow Per Share	5.26	11.73	10.80	5.35	6.57	2.69	4.11	7.44
Tang Book Value Per Share	16.16	15.97	11.20	4.87	11.64	2.00	N.M.	N.M.
Dividends Per Share	0.500	0.500	0.475	0.400	0.300	0.200	0.160	0.160
Dividend Payout %	...	8.68	6.62	15.69	4.72	9.39	4.13	88.89
Income Statement								
Total Revenue	2,399,895	2,571,358	1,587,730	966,827	1,487,070	1,241,372	1,309,856	2,054,140
EBITDA	(687,369)	842,872	692,764	275,556	498,705	352,621	410,584	284,471
Depn & Amortn	338,838	266,663	98,702	73,386	61,050	49,227	41,422	78,728
Income Before Taxes	(1,164,759)	479,995	577,596	183,994	292,336	165,457	212,405	27,886
Income Taxes	(99,204)	130,819	188,171	42,144	(75,798)	51,229	67,821	20,142
Net Income	(1,060,375)	349,176	385,797	137,158	346,580	111,999	198,369	7,046
Average Shares	62,536	60,611	53,700	53,819	54,585	52,490	52,078	39,404
Balance Sheet								
Current Assets	815,816	841,060	635,539	472,698	2,279,783	2,165,238	2,224,769	2,889,619
Total Assets	5,768,420	6,812,203	1,657,765	1,259,356	3,067,993	2,767,281	2,684,115	5,373,012
Current Liabilities	554,254	485,497	193,847	138,672	175,376	169,084	176,311	623,304
Long-Term Obligations	2,397,372	2,269,020	154,570	163,147	1,598,206	1,932,078	1,986,197	3,899,782
Total Liabilities	4,757,849	4,690,108	1,062,699	999,961	2,437,724	2,652,568	2,682,207	5,084,396
Stockholders' Equity	1,010,571	2,122,095	595,066	259,395	630,269	114,713	1,908	288,616
Shares Outstanding	62,521	62,444	53,136	53,256	54,143	51,991	51,958	39,046
Statistical Record								
Return on Assets %	N.M.	8.25	26.45	6.34	11.85	4.11	4.92	0.17
Return on Equity %	N.M.	25.70	90.30	30.83	92.79	192.07	136.56	2.57
EBITDA Margin %	N.M.	32.78	43.63	28.50	33.54	28.41	31.35	13.85
Net Margin %	N.M.	13.58	24.30	14.19	23.31	9.02	15.14	0.34
Asset Turnover	0.38	0.61	1.09	0.45	0.51	0.46	0.33	0.50
Current Ratio	1.47	1.73	3.28	3.41	13.00	12.81	12.62	4.64
Debt to Equity	2.37	1.07	0.26	0.63	2.54	16.84	1,040.98	13.51
Price Range	76.21-28.29	141.17-56.90	129.84-59.23	79.14-15.62	109.77-12.20	38.50-21.62	35.79-20.31	26.59-15.39
P/E Ratio	...	24.51-9.88	18.08-8.25	31.04-6.13	17.29-1.92	18.08-10.15	9.25-5.25	147.75-85.53
Average Yield %	1.08	0.51	0.57	0.94	0.50	0.74	0.58	0.75

Address: 3000 Riverchase Galleria, Suite 1700, Birmingham, AL 35244 Telephone: 205-745-2000	Web Site: www.walterenergy.com Officers: Michael T. Tokarz - Chairman Walter J. Scheller - Chief Executive Officer	Auditors: Ernst & Young, LLP Investor Contact: 205-745-2627 Transfer Agents: American Stock Transfer & Trust Company, LLC, New York, NY

WASHINGTON POST CO.

Exchange	Symbol	Price	52Wk Range	Yield	P/E
NYS	WPO	$447.00 (3/28/2013)	455.58-327.75	2.19	25.70

*7 Year Price Score 63.02   *NYSE Composite Index=100   *12 Month Price Score 103.10

TRADING VOLUME (thousand shares)

Interim Earnings (Per Share)

Qtr.	Mar	Jun	Sep	Dec
2008	4.08	(0.31)	1.08	2.01
2009	(2.04)	1.30	1.81	8.70
2010	4.91	10.00	6.84	9.29
2011	1.87	5.74	(0.82)	7.89
2012	4.07	6.84	12.64	(6.00)

Interim Dividends (Per Share)

Amt	Decl	Ex	Rec	Pay
2.45Q	02/23/2012	04/19/2012	04/23/2012	05/04/2012
2.45Q	06/07/2012	07/19/2012	07/23/2012	08/03/2012
2.45Q	09/13/2012	10/18/2012	10/22/2012	11/02/2012
9.80A	12/07/2012	12/13/2012	12/17/2012	12/27/2012

Indicated Div: $9.80

Valuation Analysis

		Institutional Holding	
Forecast EPS	$23.56	No of Institutions	
	(04/05/2013)	319	
Market Cap	$3.3 Billion	Shares	
Book Value	$2.6 Billion	6,074,273	
Price/Book	1.28	% Held	
Price/Sales	0.83	72.99	

Business Summary: Publishing (MIC: 2.3.3 SIC: 8299 NAIC: 611699)

Washington Post is an education and media company. Through its Kaplan, Inc. subsidiary, Co. provides educational services for individuals, schools and businesses domestically and outside the U.S. Kaplan has four segments: Kaplan Higher Education, Kaplan Test Preparation, Kaplan International and Kaplan Ventures. Co. is also engaged in media operations, which consist of the ownership and operation of cable television systems; newspaper publishing (principally The Washington Post); and television broadcasting, through the ownership and operation of VHF television broadcast stations serving the Detroit, Houston, Miami, San Antonio, Orlando and Jacksonville television markets.

Recent Developments: For the year ended Dec 31 2012, income from continuing operations decreased 66.3% to US$49.0 million from US$145.6 million a year earlier. Net income increased 12.8% to US$132.2 million from US$117.2 million in the prior year. Revenues were US$4.02 billion, down 2.7% from US$4.13 billion the year before. Operating income was US$144.5 million versus US$325.9 million in the prior year, a decrease of 55.6%. Direct operating expenses declined 1.3% to US$1.88 billion from US$1.90 billion in the comparable period the year before. Indirect operating expenses increased 4.8% to US$1.99 billion from US$1.99 billion in the equivalent prior-year period.

Prospects: Our evaluation of Washington Post Co. as of Apr. 7, 2013 is the result of our systematic analysis on three basic characteristics: earnings strength, relative valuation, and recent stock price movement. The company has enjoyed a very positive trend in earnings per share over the past 5 quarters. Because the company lacks sufficient analyst estimate data, we place greater weight on the historical EPS trend as the measure of earnings strength. Based on operating earnings yield, the company is undervalued when compared to all of the companies in our coverage universe. Share price changes over the past year indicates that WPO will perform poorly over the near term.

Financial Data

(US$ in Thousands)	12/31/2012	12/31/2011	01/02/2011	01/03/2010	12/28/2008	12/30/2007	12/31/2006	01/01/2006
Earnings Per Share	17.39	14.70	31.04	9.78	6.87	30.19	33.68	32.59
Cash Flow Per Share	64.66	50.53	78.43	68.84	57.10	61.40	62.33	54.64
Tang Book Value Per Share	93.42	80.74	104.65	98.88	91.15	145.38	144.91	104.94
Dividends Per Share	19.600	9.400	9.000	8.600	8.600	8.200	7.800	7.400
Dividend Payout %	112.71	63.95	28.99	87.93	125.18	27.16	23.16	22.71
Income Statement								
Total Revenue	4,017,653	4,214,833	4,723,573	4,569,731	4,461,580	4,180,406	3,904,927	3,553,887
EBITDA	429,119	524,491	830,475	529,731	460,076	726,650	745,594	721,915
Depn & Amortn	290,044	283,733	274,991	322,542	288,131	238,810	212,338	198,021
Income Before Taxes	106,524	211,679	527,557	178,221	152,959	475,132	518,344	500,525
Income Taxes	71,600	96,300	216,600	57,600	79,400	192,500	189,600	185,300
Net Income	132,113	117,150	278,114	92,774	65,722	288,607	324,459	314,344
Average Shares	7,404	7,905	8,931	9,392	9,430	9,528	9,605	9,615
Balance Sheet								
Current Assets	1,453,762	1,245,625	1,361,898	1,388,064	1,351,540	994,970	934,825	818,326
Total Assets	5,105,069	5,016,986	5,158,543	5,186,206	5,158,434	6,004,509	5,381,372	4,584,773
Current Liabilities	1,126,286	995,556	1,008,277	989,583	1,094,248	1,013,473	803,200	694,721
Long-Term Obligations	453,384	452,229	396,650	396,236	400,003	400,519	401,571	403,635
Total Liabilities	2,507,945	2,403,795	2,332,477	2,235,130	2,289,068	2,531,524	2,209,738	1,934,083
Stockholders' Equity	2,597,124	2,613,191	2,825,890	2,951,076	2,869,366	3,472,985	3,171,634	2,650,690
Shares Outstanding	7,427	7,591	8,193	9,266	9,365	9,516	9,536	9,601
Statistical Record								
Return on Assets %	2.60	2.32	5.39	1.76	1.18	5.08	6.53	7.08
Return on Equity %	5.06	4.33	9.65	3.14	2.08	8.71	11.18	12.42
EBITDA Margin %	10.68	12.44	17.58	11.59	10.31	17.38	19.09	20.31
Net Margin %	3.29	2.78	5.89	2.03	1.47	6.90	8.31	8.85
Asset Turnover	0.79	0.83	0.92	0.87	0.80	0.74	0.79	0.80
Current Ratio	1.29	1.25	1.35	1.40	1.24	0.98	1.16	1.18
Debt to Equity	0.17	0.17	0.14	0.13	0.14	0.12	0.13	0.15
Price Range	400.00-327.75	451.17-313.00	541.38-315.65	492.36-307.50	808.00-322.41	857.92-742.45	813.02-710.65	963.50-717.00
P/E Ratio	23.00-18.85	30.69-21.29	17.44-10.17	50.34-31.44	117.61-46.93	28.42-24.59	24.14-21.10	29.56-22.00
Average Yield %	5.39	2.39	2.11	2.12	1.45	1.05	1.03	0.88

Address: 1150 15th Street N.W., Washington, DC 20071	**Web Site:** www.washpostco.com	**Auditors:** PricewaterhouseCoopers LLP
Telephone: 202-334-6000	**Officers:** Donald E. Graham - Chairman, Chief Executive Officer Veronica Dillon - Senior Vice President, Secretary, General Counsel	**Investor Contact:** 781-575-2723
Fax: 202-334-1031		**Transfer Agents:** ComputerShare Investor Services, Providence, RI

WASHINGTON REAL ESTATE INVESTMENT TRUST

Exchange	Symbol	Price	52Wk Range	Yield	P/E
NYS	WRE	$27.84 (3/28/2013)	30.25-24.36	4.31	79.54

*7 Year Price Score 79.05   *NYSE Composite Index=100   *12 Month Price Score 93.23

Interim Earnings (Per Share)

Qtr.	Mar	Jun	Sep	Dec
2008	(0.03)	0.44	0.12	0.14
2009	0.20	0.23	0.16	0.11
2010	0.09	0.24	0.10	0.17
2011	0.07	0.10	0.95	0.46
2012	0.08	0.09	0.14	0.04

Interim Dividends (Per Share)

Amt	Decl	Ex	Rec	Pay
0.434Q	04/25/2012	06/13/2012	06/15/2012	06/29/2012
0.30Q	07/26/2012	09/12/2012	09/14/2012	09/28/2012
0.30Q	10/25/2012	12/12/2012	12/14/2012	12/31/2012
0.30Q	02/13/2013	03/13/2013	03/15/2013	03/29/2013

Indicated Div: $1.20 (Div. Reinv. Plan)

Valuation Analysis

		Institutional Holding	
Forecast EPS	$0.34	No of Institutions	279
	(04/05/2013)		
Market Cap	$1.8 Billion	Shares	51,362,280
Book Value	$792.1 Million	% Held	74.32
Price/Book	2.34		
Price/Sales	6.06		

TRADING VOLUME (thousand shares)

Business Summary: REITs (MIC: 5.3.1 SIC: 6798 NAIC: 525930)

Washington Real Estate Investment Trust is a self-administered, self-managed, equity real estate investment trust. Co.'s business consists of the ownership and operation of real property in the Washington metro region. As of Dec 31 2011, Co. had four reportable segments: office, medical office, retail, and multifamily properties. In addition, at Dec 31 2011, Co. owned a portfolio of 71 properties, totaling approximately 8.6 million square feet of commercial space and 2,540 residential units, and land held for development. These 71 properties consisted of 26 office properties, 18 medical office properties, 16 retail centers and 11 multifamily properties.

Recent Developments: For the year ended Dec 31 2012, income from continuing operations was US$17.1 million compared with a loss of US$2.9 million a year earlier. Net income decreased 77.5% to US$23.7 million from US$105.4 million in the prior year. Revenues were US$305.0 million, up 7.3% from US$284.2 million the year before.

Prospects: Our evaluation of Washington Real Estate Investment Trust as of Apr. 7, 2013 is the result of our systematic analysis on three basic characteristics: earnings strength, relative valuation, and recent stock price movement. The company has produced a positive trend in earnings per share over the past 5 quarters. Because the company lacks sufficient analyst estimate data, we place greater weight on the historical EPS trend as the measure of earnings strength. Based on operating earnings yield, the company is overvalued when compared to all of the companies in our coverage universe. Share price changes over the past year indicates that WRE will perform poorly over the near term.

Financial Data
(US$ in Thousands)

	12/31/2012	12/31/2011	12/31/2010	12/31/2009	12/31/2008	12/31/2007	12/31/2006	12/31/2005
Earnings Per Share	0.35	1.58	0.60	0.71	0.67	1.34	0.88	1.84
Cash Flow Per Share	1.97	1.79	1.80	1.81	1.97	2.52	1.98	2.08
Tang Book Value Per Share	11.92	12.96	13.01	12.46	11.95	10.42	9.81	9.03
Dividends Per Share	1.468	1.735	1.731	1.730	1.720	1.680	1.640	1.600
Dividend Payout %	419.29	109.81	288.54	243.66	256.72	125.37	186.36	86.96
Income Statement								
Total Revenue	304,983	289,527	297,977	306,929	282,312	255,655	219,662	190,046
EBITDA	158,620	136,545	158,020	176,822	154,323	150,345	134,107	119,986
Depn & Amortn	76,824	71,200	76,500	75,800	69,200	56,300	47,600	41,800
Income Before Taxes	17,099	(1,128)	13,131	26,021	15,214	32,139	38,661	40,443
Net Income	23,708	104,884	37,426	40,745	32,841	61,881	38,661	77,638
Average Shares	66,376	65,982	62,264	56,968	49,373	46,115	43,874	42,203
Balance Sheet								
Current Assets	90,982	86,017	155,495	80,898	76,136	64,113	45,504	31,960
Total Assets	2,124,376	2,120,758	2,167,881	2,045,225	2,111,391	1,898,326	1,531,265	1,141,285
Current Liabilities	26,250	121,601	122,135	149,150	86,442	212,856	76,976	36,965
Long-Term Obligations	1,249,160	1,085,180	1,133,758	1,094,363	1,324,186	1,131,607	965,328	689,617
Total Liabilities	1,332,319	1,261,714	1,310,801	1,299,970	1,484,998	1,411,782	1,089,334	760,980
Stockholders' Equity	792,057	859,044	857,080	745,255	626,393	486,544	441,931	380,305
Shares Outstanding	66,437	66,265	65,870	59,811	52,434	46,682	45,042	42,139
Statistical Record								
Return on Assets %	1.11	4.89	1.78	1.96	1.63	3.61	2.89	7.21
Return on Equity %	2.86	12.22	4.67	5.94	5.89	13.33	9.40	20.81
EBITDA Margin %	52.01	47.16	53.03	57.61	54.66	58.81	61.05	63.14
Net Margin %	7.77	36.23	12.56	13.28	11.63	24.20	17.60	40.85
Asset Turnover	0.14	0.14	0.14	0.15	0.14	0.15	0.16	0.18
Current Ratio	3.47	0.71	1.27	0.54	0.88	0.30	0.59	0.86
Debt to Equity	1.58	1.26	1.32	1.47	2.11	2.33	2.18	1.81
Price Range	30.99-24.36	34.53-25.51	34.05-25.09	30.02-15.60	37.61-20.33	43.20-29.65	43.30-31.26	33.87-28.15
P/E Ratio	88.54-69.60	21.85-16.15	56.75-41.82	42.28-21.97	56.13-30.34	32.24-22.13	49.20-35.52	18.41-15.30
Average Yield %	5.28	5.75	5.78	7.21	5.43	4.72	4.39	5.24

Address: 6110 Executive Boulevard, Suite 800, Rockville, MD 20852
Telephone: 301-984-9400
Fax: 301-984-9610

Web Site: www.writ.com
Officers: John P. McDaniel - Chairman George F. McKenzie - President, Chief Executive Officer

Auditors: Ernst & Young LLP
Investor Contact: 301-984-9400
Transfer Agents: Computershare Trust Company, N.A., Providence, RI

WASTE CONNECTIONS, INC.

Exchange	Symbol	Price	52Wk Range	Yield	P/E
NYS	WCN	$35.98 (3/28/2013)	36.41-28.91	1.11	27.47

*7 Year Price Score 117.66 *NYSE Composite Index=100 *12 Month Price Score 100.16

TRADING VOLUME (thousand shares)

Interim Earnings (Per Share)

Qtr.	Mar	Jun	Sep	Dec
2008	0.23	0.26	0.27	0.23
2009	0.18	0.25	0.29	0.19
2010	0.23	0.26	0.35	0.32
2011	0.32	0.39	0.41	0.33
2012	0.27	0.34	0.40	0.29

Interim Dividends (Per Share)

Amt	Decl	Ex	Rec	Pay
0.09Q	04/25/2012	05/07/2012	05/09/2012	05/23/2012
0.09Q	07/23/2012	08/02/2012	08/06/2012	08/20/2012
0.10Q	10/22/2012	11/01/2012	11/05/2012	11/19/2012
0.10Q	01/15/2013	02/01/2013	02/05/2013	02/19/2013

Indicated Div: $0.40

Valuation Analysis

		Institutional Holding	
Forecast EPS	$1.76	No of Institutions	
	(04/05/2013)	299	
Market Cap	$4.4 Billion	Shares	
Book Value	$1.9 Billion	120,603,920	
Price/Book	2.36	% Held	
Price/Sales	2.66	92.49	

Business Summary: Sanitation Services (MIC: 7.5.3 SIC: 4953 NAIC: 562219)

Waste Connections is a solid waste services company that provides solid waste collection, transfer, disposal and recycling services to commercial, industrial and residential customers. Co. also provides intermodal services for the rail haul movement of cargo and solid waste containers in the Pacific Northwest through a network of seven intermodal facilities. Co. also treats and disposes of non-hazardous waste that is generated in the exploration and production of oil and natural gas primarily at a facility in Southwest Louisiana. As of Dec 31 2011, Co. served over 2.0 million residential, commercial and industrial customers from a network of operations in 29 states.

Recent Developments: For the year ended Dec 31 2012, net income decreased 3.9% to US$159.7 million from US$166.2 million in the prior year. Revenues were US$1.66 billion, up 10.4% from US$1.51 billion the year before. Operating income was US$316.1 million versus US$317.1 million in the prior year, a decrease of 0.3%. Direct operating expenses rose 11.5% to US$956.4 million from US$857.6 million in the comparable period the year before. Indirect operating expenses increased 17.7% to US$389.1 million from US$330.7 million in the equivalent prior-year period.

Prospects: Our evaluation of Waste Connections Inc. as of Apr. 7, 2013 is the result of our systematic analysis on three basic characteristics: earnings strength, relative valuation, and recent stock price movement. The company has enjoyed a very positive trend in earnings per share over the past 5 quarters. However, while recent estimates for the company have been lowered by analysts, WCN has posted results that fell short of analysts expectations. Based on operating earnings yield, the company is about fairly valued when compared to all of the companies in our coverage universe. Share price changes over the past year indicates that WCN will perform in line with the market over the near term.

Financial Data

(US$ in Thousands)	12/31/2012	12/31/2011	12/31/2010	12/31/2009	12/31/2008	12/31/2007	12/31/2006	12/31/2005
Earnings Per Share	1.31	1.45	1.16	0.91	0.99	0.95	0.73	0.77
Cash Flow Per Share	3.43	3.44	2.84	2.55	2.57	2.14	2.00	1.90
Tang Book Value Per Share	N.M.	N.M.	0.50	0.79	0.93	N.M.	N.M.	N.M.
Dividends Per Share	0.370	0.315	0.075	...	...	...	...	...
Dividend Payout %	28.24	21.72	6.47	...	...	...	...	...
Income Statement								
Total Revenue	1,661,618	1,505,366	1,319,757	1,191,393	1,049,603	958,541	824,354	721,899
EBITDA	395,353	380,400	320,486	353,882	309,152	292,926	242,492	233,537
Depn & Amortn	77,986	63,281	55,466	130,758	97,429	85,628	74,865	65,038
Income Before Taxes	265,103	273,129	225,476	175,376	176,196	173,868	138,657	145,010
Income Taxes	105,443	106,958	89,334	64,565	58,400	59,917	48,329	48,066
Net Income	159,093	165,239	135,104	109,825	105,556	99,081	77,423	83,943
Average Shares	121,824	113,583	116,894	120,506	107,129	104,992	105,613	108,475
Balance Sheet								
Current Assets	362,486	249,258	215,561	199,854	429,211	170,865	160,233	124,376
Total Assets	5,076,026	3,328,005	2,915,984	2,820,448	2,600,640	1,981,958	1,773,891	1,676,307
Current Liabilities	417,572	284,102	253,537	244,913	215,464	195,714	149,865	150,001
Long-Term Obligations	2,204,967	1,172,758	909,978	867,554	830,758	719,518	637,308	586,104
Total Liabilities	3,197,869	1,933,095	1,549,835	1,466,643	1,345,913	1,206,813	1,037,409	958,107
Stockholders' Equity	1,878,157	1,394,910	1,366,149	1,353,805	1,254,727	775,145	736,482	718,200
Shares Outstanding	123,019	110,907	113,950	117,898	119,763	100,578	102,399	103,090
Statistical Record								
Return on Assets %	3.78	5.29	4.71	4.05	4.59	5.28	4.49	5.30
Return on Equity %	9.69	11.97	9.93	8.42	10.37	13.11	10.64	11.78
EBITDA Margin %	23.79	25.27	24.28	29.70	29.45	30.56	29.42	32.35
Net Margin %	9.57	10.98	10.24	9.22	10.06	10.34	9.39	11.63
Asset Turnover	0.39	0.48	0.46	0.44	0.44	0.51	0.48	0.46
Current Ratio	0.87	0.88	0.85	0.82	1.99	0.87	1.07	0.83
Debt to Equity	1.17	0.84	0.67	0.64	0.66	0.93	0.87	0.82
Price Range	33.88-28.91	35.49-27.11	27.67-20.64	22.57-13.95	25.73-17.81	22.69-18.32	18.61-15.11	16.92-13.85
P/E Ratio	25.86-22.07	24.48-18.70	23.85-17.79	24.81-15.33	25.99-17.99	23.88-19.28	25.49-20.70	21.98-17.99
Average Yield %	1.18	1.01	0.31	...	...	...	...	...

Address: Waterway Plaza Two, 10001 Woodloch Forest Drive, Suite 400, The Woodlands, TX 77380 **Telephone:** 832-442-2200	**Web Site:** www.wasteconnections.com **Officers:** Ronald J. Mittelstaedt - Chairman, Chief Executive Officer Steven F. Bouck - President	**Auditors:** PricewaterhouseCoopers LLP **Investor Contact:** 832-442-2200 **Transfer Agents:** Wells Fargo Shareowner Services, South Saint Paul, MN

WASTE MANAGEMENT, INC. (DE)

Exchange	Symbol	Price	52Wk Range	Yield	P/E
NYS	WM	$39.21 (3/28/2013)	39.21-30.96	3.72	22.28

*7 Year Price Score 88.83   *NYSE Composite Index=100   *12 Month Price Score 100.53

Interim Earnings (Per Share)

Qtr.	Mar	Jun	Sep	Dec
2008	0.48	0.64	0.63	0.44
2009	0.31	0.50	0.56	0.64
2010	0.37	0.51	0.51	0.59
2011	0.39	0.50	0.58	0.58
2012	0.37	0.45	0.46	0.48

Interim Dividends (Per Share)

Amt	Decl	Ex	Rec	Pay
0.355Q	05/10/2012	06/06/2012	06/08/2012	06/22/2012
0.355Q	08/24/2012	09/05/2012	09/07/2012	09/21/2012
0.355Q	11/06/2012	11/26/2012	11/28/2012	12/14/2012
0.365Q	02/25/2013	03/07/2013	03/11/2013	03/22/2013

Indicated Div: $1.46

Valuation Analysis

Forecast EPS	$2.18 (04/05/2013)
Market Cap	$18.2 Billion
Book Value	$6.4 Billion
Price/Book	2.86
Price/Sales	1.33

Institutional Holding

No of Institutions	826
Shares	407,866,176
% Held	78.53

Business Summary: Sanitation Services (MIC: 7.5.3 SIC: 4953 NAIC: 562211)

Waste Management is a holding company. Through its subsidiaries, Co. is engaged in providing waste management services in North America, including collection, transfer, recycling and resource recovery, and disposal services for residential, commercial, industrial and municipal customers. Co. is also a developer, operator and owner of waste-to-energy and landfill gas-to-energy facilities in the U.S. Co. also provides other services, including recycling brokerage services, in-plant services, and disposal services for oilfield drilling and operations, among others. At Dec 31 2012, Co. owned or operated 264 solid waste landfills, and also operated five hazardous waste landfills in the U.S.

Recent Developments: For the year ended Dec 31 2012, net income decreased 14.8% to US$860.0 million from the prior year. Revenues were US$13.65 billion, up 2.0% from US$13.38 billion the year before. Operating income was US$1.85 billion versus US$2.03 billion in the prior year, a decrease of 8.7%. Direct operating expenses rose 4.0% to US$8.88 billion from US$8.54 billion in the comparable period the year before. Indirect operating expenses increased 3.9% to US$2.92 billion from US$2.81 billion in the equivalent prior-year period.

Prospects: Our evaluation of Waste Management Inc. as of Apr. 7, 2013 is the result of our systematic analysis on three basic characteristics: earnings strength, relative valuation, and recent stock price movement. The company has produced a positive trend in earnings per share over the past 5 quarters and while recent estimates for the company have been mixed, WM has posted results that fell short of analysts expectations. Based on operating earnings yield, the company is about fairly valued when compared to all of the companies in our coverage universe. Share price changes over the past year indicates that WM will perform poorly over the near term.

Financial Data

(US$ in Thousands)	12/31/2012	12/31/2011	12/31/2010	12/31/2009	12/31/2008	12/31/2007	12/31/2006	12/31/2005
Earnings Per Share	1.76	2.04	1.98	2.01	2.19	2.23	2.10	2.09
Cash Flow Per Share	4.94	5.26	4.74	4.81	5.22	4.71	4.70	4.26
Tang Book Value Per Share	N.M.	N.M.	0.50	0.85	0.57	0.52	1.52	1.10
Dividends Per Share	1.420	1.360	1.260	1.160	1.080	0.960	0.880	0.800
Dividend Payout %	80.68	66.67	63.64	57.71	49.32	43.05	41.90	38.28
Income Statement								
Total Revenue	13,649,000	13,378,000	12,515,000	11,791,000	13,388,000	13,310,000	13,363,000	13,074,000
EBITDA	3,061,000	3,202,000	3,274,000	3,025,000	3,451,000	3,494,000	3,338,000	3,042,000
Depn & Amortn	1,228,000	1,178,000	1,153,000	1,137,000	1,214,000	1,236,000	1,308,000	1,330,000
Income Before Taxes	1,349,000	1,551,000	1,652,000	1,475,000	1,801,000	1,784,000	1,554,000	1,247,000
Income Taxes	443,000	511,000	629,000	413,000	669,000	540,000	325,000	(90,000)
Net Income	817,000	961,000	953,000	994,000	1,087,000	1,163,000	1,149,000	1,182,000
Average Shares	464,400	471,400	482,200	493,600	495,400	521,800	546,100	565,100
Balance Sheet								
Current Assets	2,423,000	2,379,000	2,482,000	3,010,000	2,335,000	2,480,000	3,182,000	3,451,000
Total Assets	23,097,000	22,569,000	21,476,000	21,154,000	20,227,000	20,175,000	20,600,000	21,135,000
Current Liabilities	3,036,000	3,068,000	2,485,000	2,901,000	3,036,000	2,598,000	3,268,000	3,257,000
Long-Term Obligations	9,173,000	9,125,000	8,674,000	8,124,000	7,491,000	8,008,000	7,495,000	8,165,000
Total Liabilities	16,743,000	16,499,000	15,216,000	14,869,000	14,325,000	14,383,000	14,378,000	15,014,000
Stockholders' Equity	6,354,000	6,070,000	6,260,000	6,285,000	5,902,000	5,792,000	6,222,000	6,121,000
Shares Outstanding	464,220	460,532	475,046	486,120	490,735	500,118	533,683	552,253
Statistical Record								
Return on Assets %	3.57	4.36	4.47	4.80	5.37	5.70	5.51	5.62
Return on Equity %	13.12	15.59	15.19	16.31	18.54	19.36	18.62	19.55
EBITDA Margin %	22.43	23.93	26.16	25.66	25.78	26.25	24.98	23.27
Net Margin %	5.99	7.18	7.61	8.43	8.12	8.74	8.60	9.04
Asset Turnover	0.60	0.61	0.59	0.57	0.66	0.65	0.64	0.62
Current Ratio	0.80	0.78	1.00	1.04	0.77	0.95	0.97	1.06
Debt to Equity	1.44	1.50	1.39	1.29	1.27	1.38	1.20	1.33
Price Range	36.08-30.96	39.61-28.17	36.99-31.29	34.10-22.23	39.10-25.76	40.30-32.67	38.52-30.27	31.01-27.04
P/E Ratio	20.50-17.59	19.42-13.81	18.68-15.80	16.97-11.06	17.85-11.76	18.07-14.65	18.34-14.41	14.84-12.94
Average Yield %	4.22	3.89	3.69	3.96	3.21	2.62	2.49	2.76

Address: 1001 Fannin Street, Suite 4000, Houston, TX 77002 Telephone: 713-512-6200 Fax: 713-512-6299	Web Site: www.wm.com Officers: David P. Steiner - President, Chief Executive Officer James C. Fish - Executive Vice President, Chief Financial Officer	Auditors: Ernst & Young LLP Investor Contact: 713-265-1656 Transfer Agents: Computershare Shareowner Services

WATERS CORP.

Exchange	Symbol	Price	52Wk Range	Yield	P/E
NYS	WAT	$93.91 (3/28/2013)	94.96-74.66	N/A	18.09

*7 Year Price Score 113.74   *NYSE Composite Index=100   *12 Month Price Score 101.27

Interim Earnings (Per Share)

Qtr.	Mar	Jun	Sep	Dec
2008	0.67	0.82	0.71	1.00
2009	0.75	0.72	0.79	1.08
2010	0.79	0.90	1.02	1.35
2011	1.01	1.07	1.10	1.51
2012	0.98	1.10	1.12	2.00

Interim Dividends (Per Share)

No Dividends Paid

Valuation Analysis / Institutional Holding

Valuation Analysis		Institutional Holding	
Forecast EPS	$5.35 (04/06/2013)	No of Institutions	531
Market Cap	$8.1 Billion	Shares	86,270,672
Book Value	$1.5 Billion	% Held	88.30
Price/Book	5.53		
Price/Sales	4.40		

Business Summary: Biotechnology (MIC: 4.1.2 SIC: 3826 NAIC: 334516)

Waters is a holding company, engaged an analytical instrument manufacturer. As of Dec 31 2011, Co. had two operating segments: Waters Division, which designs, manufactures, sells and services high performance liquid chromatography, ultra performance liquid chromatography and mass spectrometry technology systems and support products, including chromatography columns, other consumable products and post-warranty service plans; and TA Division, which designs, manufactures, sells and services thermal analysis, rheometry and calorimetry instruments. Co. also develops and supplies software-based products that interface with its instruments as well as other manufacturers' instruments.

Recent Developments: For the year ended Dec 31 2012, net income increased 6.6% to US$461.4 million from US$433.0 million in the prior year. Revenues were US$1.84 billion, down 0.4% from US$1.85 billion the year before. Operating income was US$511.5 million versus US$528.6 million in the prior year, a decrease of 3.2%. Direct operating expenses rose 1.0% to US$737.6 million from US$730.5 million in the comparable period the year before. Indirect operating expenses increased 0.4% to US$594.5 million from US$592.1 million in the equivalent prior-year period.

Prospects: Our evaluation of Waters Corp. as of Apr. 7, 2013 is the result of our systematic analysis on three basic characteristics: earnings strength, relative valuation, and recent stock price movement. The company has managed to produce a neutral trend in earnings per share over the past 5 quarters and while recent estimates for the company have remained steady, WAT has posted better than expected results. Based on operating earnings yield, the company is about fairly valued when compared to all of the companies in our coverage universe. Share price changes over the past year indicates that WAT will perform in line with the market over the near term.

Financial Data
(US$ in Thousands)

	12/31/2012	12/31/2011	12/31/2010	12/31/2009	12/31/2008	12/31/2007	12/31/2006	12/31/2005
Earnings Per Share	5.19	4.69	4.06	3.34	3.21	2.62	2.13	1.74
Cash Flow Per Share	5.10	5.48	4.96	4.37	4.20	3.69	2.57	2.61
Tang Book Value Per Share	10.77	8.29	6.49	3.97	2.48	1.70	N.M.	N.M.
Income Statement								
Total Revenue	1,843,641	1,851,184	1,643,371	1,498,700	1,575,124	1,473,048	1,280,229	1,158,236
EBITDA	580,321	594,987	512,490	451,874	455,025	402,196	335,463	323,737
Depn & Amortn	68,831	66,387	62,558	57,272	65,271	53,317	46,159	43,685
Income Before Taxes	487,625	509,252	437,863	386,652	372,192	323,192	262,959	274,563
Income Taxes	26,182	76,284	56,100	63,339	49,713	55,120	40,759	72,588
Net Income	461,443	432,968	381,763	323,313	322,479	268,072	222,200	201,975
Average Shares	88,979	92,325	94,057	96,862	100,555	102,505	104,240	115,945
Balance Sheet								
Current Assets	2,257,726	1,942,104	1,586,641	1,172,376	956,302	1,237,062	999,680	912,992
Total Assets	3,168,150	2,723,234	2,327,670	1,907,931	1,622,898	1,881,055	1,617,313	1,428,931
Current Liabilities	504,242	601,863	385,850	394,568	289,506	658,434	685,834	603,891
Long-Term Obligations	1,045,000	700,000	700,000	500,000	500,000	500,000	500,000	500,000
Total Liabilities	1,700,793	1,496,656	1,258,873	1,058,982	961,893	1,294,979	1,254,930	1,145,299
Stockholders' Equity	1,467,357	1,226,578	1,068,797	848,949	661,005	586,076	362,383	283,632
Shares Outstanding	86,390	88,996	91,848	94,118	97,891	100,975	101,371	105,336
Statistical Record								
Return on Assets %	15.62	17.14	18.03	18.31	18.36	15.33	14.59	13.98
Return on Equity %	34.16	37.73	39.81	42.82	51.58	56.53	68.79	41.98
EBITDA Margin %	31.48	32.14	31.19	30.15	28.89	27.30	26.20	27.95
Net Margin %	25.03	23.39	23.23	21.57	20.47	18.20	17.36	17.44
Asset Turnover	0.62	0.73	0.78	0.85	0.90	0.84	0.84	0.80
Current Ratio	4.48	3.23	4.11	2.97	3.30	1.88	1.46	1.51
Debt to Equity	0.71	0.57	0.65	0.59	0.76	0.85	1.38	1.76
Price Range	94.03-73.71	99.56-71.61	80.47-56.18	62.58-30.75	80.77-34.77	80.07-48.67	51.38-37.26	51.11-34.43
P/E Ratio	18.12-14.20	21.23-15.27	19.82-13.84	18.74-9.21	25.16-10.83	30.56-18.58	24.12-17.49	29.37-19.79

Address: 34 Maple Street, Milford, MA 01757
Telephone: 508-478-2000
Fax: 508-872-1990

Web Site: www.waters.com
Officers: Douglas A. Berthiaume - Chairman, Chief Executive Officer Arthur G. Caputo - Executive Vice President, Division Officer

Auditors: PricewaterhouseCoopers LLP
Investor Contact: 508-482-2349
Transfer Agents: BNY Mellon Shareowner Services, Jersey City, NJ

WATSCO INC.

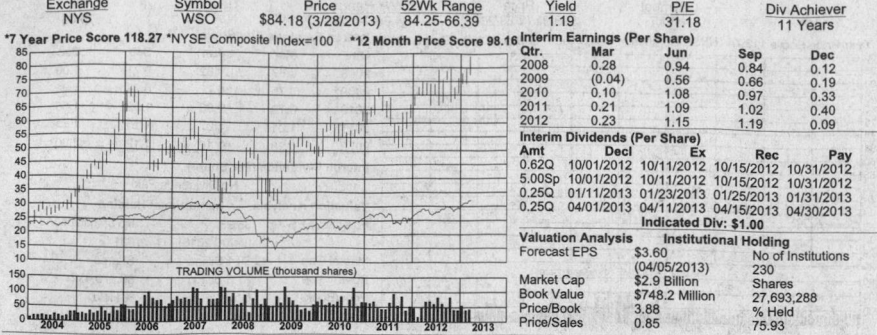

Exchange	Symbol	Price	52Wk Range	Yield	P/E	Div Achiever
NYS	WSO	$84.18 (3/28/2013)	84.25-66.39	1.19	31.18	11 Years

*7 Year Price Score 118.27 *NYSE Composite Index=100 *12 Month Price Score 98.16

Interim Earnings (Per Share)

Qtr.	Mar	Jun	Sep	Dec
2008	0.28	0.94	0.84	0.12
2009	(0.04)	0.56	0.66	0.19
2010	0.10	1.08	0.97	0.33
2011	0.21	1.09	1.02	0.40
2012	0.23	1.15	1.19	0.09

Interim Dividends (Per Share)

Amt	Decl	Ex	Rec	Pay
0.62Q	10/01/2012	10/11/2012	10/15/2012	10/31/2012
5.00Sp	10/01/2012	10/11/2012	10/15/2012	10/31/2012
0.25Q	01/11/2013	01/23/2013	01/25/2013	01/31/2013
0.25Q	04/01/2013	04/11/2013	04/15/2013	04/30/2013

Indicated Div: $1.00

Valuation Analysis / **Institutional Holding**

Forecast EPS	$3.60 (04/05/2013)	No of Institutions	230
Market Cap	$2.9 Billion	Shares	27,693,288
Book Value	$748.2 Million	% Held	75.93
Price/Book	3.88		
Price/Sales	0.85		

TRADING VOLUME (thousand shares)

Business Summary: Industrial Machinery & Equipment (MIC: 7.2.1 SIC: 5075 NAIC: 423730)

Watsco distributes air conditioning, heating and refrigeration equipment and related parts and supplies. Co. operates in 38 states, Mexico and Puerto Rico, and exports to Latin America and the Caribbean. The products Co. distribute consist of: equipment, including residential central air conditioners, gas, electric and oil furnaces, commercial air conditioning and heating equipment and systems and other equipment; parts, including replacement compressors, evaporator coils, motors and other component parts; and supplies, including thermostats, insulation material, refrigerants, ductwork, grills, registers, sheet metal, tools, copper tubing, concrete pads, tape, adhesives and other supplies.

Recent Developments: For the year ended Dec 31 2012, net income increased 14.4% to US$157.6 million from US$137.7 million in the prior year. Revenues were US$3.43 billion, up 15.2% from US$2.98 billion the year before. Operating income was US$224.9 million versus US$199.1 million in the prior year, an increase of 13.0%. Direct operating expenses rose 16.4% to US$2.62 billion from US$2.25 billion in the comparable period the year before. Indirect operating expenses increased 11.4% to US$589.5 million from US$529.2 million in the equivalent prior-year period.

Prospects: Our evaluation of Watsco Inc. as of Apr. 7, 2013 is the result of our systematic analysis on three basic characteristics: earnings strength, relative valuation, and recent stock price movement. The company has managed to produce a neutral trend in earnings per share over the past 5 quarters and while recent estimates for the company have been raised by analysts, WSO has posted results that fell short of analysts expectations. Based on expected earnings yield, the company is about fairly valued when compared to all of the companies in our coverage universe. Share price changes over the past year indicates that WSO will perform in line with the market over the near term.

Financial Data

(US$ in Thousands)	12/31/2012	12/31/2011	12/31/2010	12/31/2009	12/31/2008	12/31/2007	12/31/2006	12/31/2005
Earnings Per Share	2.70	2.74	2.49	1.40	2.18	2.36	2.96	2.52
Cash Flow Per Share	5.46	2.00	5.02	3.10	4.28	4.11	2.62	1.37
Tang Book Value Per Share	3.81	12.36	12.45	11.71	12.39	11.90	12.76	10.45
Dividends Per Share	7.480	2.230	2.040	1.890	1.750	1.310	0.950	0.620
Dividend Payout %	277.04	81.39	81.93	135.00	80.28	55.51	32.09	24.60
Income Statement								
Total Revenue	3,431,712	2,977,759	2,844,595	2,001,815	1,700,237	1,758,022	1,800,759	1,682,724
EBITDA	235,894	208,414	176,343	89,593	105,679	117,574	141,511	125,175
Depn & Amortn	10,986	9,364	10,771	8,533	7,071	6,420	5,908	8,717
Income Before Taxes	220,243	194,592	162,082	78,329	96,590	107,982	131,783	113,116
Income Taxes	62,642	56,850	50,360	26,756	36,221	40,493	49,419	43,097
Net Income	103,334	90,450	80,760	43,314	60,369	65,577	82,364	70,019
Average Shares	31,744	30,753	30,578	28,521	27,736	27,823	27,829	27,769
Balance Sheet								
Current Assets	1,015,451	828,177	838,004	755,298	456,703	487,228	517,808	493,991
Total Assets	1,682,055	1,268,148	1,237,227	1,160,613	716,061	748,169	711,371	678,731
Current Liabilities	282,358	223,039	266,005	223,926	107,824	129,364	156,191	179,298
Long-Term Obligations	316,196	...	10,016	13,429	20,783	55,042	30,118	40,189
Total Liabilities	933,841	465,358	472,766	422,587	145,401	198,212	194,985	228,081
Stockholders' Equity	748,214	802,790	764,461	738,026	570,660	549,957	516,386	450,650
Shares Outstanding	34,521	33,005	32,449	32,138	28,325	27,969	27,832	27,462
Statistical Record								
Return on Assets %	6.99	7.22	6.74	4.62	8.22	8.99	11.85	10.88
Return on Equity %	13.29	11.54	10.75	6.62	10.74	12.30	17.03	16.41
EBITDA Margin %	6.87	7.00	6.20	4.48	6.22	6.69	7.86	7.44
Net Margin %	3.01	3.04	2.84	2.16	3.55	3.73	4.57	4.16
Asset Turnover	2.32	2.38	2.37	2.13	2.32	2.41	2.59	2.61
Current Ratio	3.60	3.71	3.15	3.37	4.24	3.77	3.32	2.76
Debt to Equity	0.42	...	0.01	0.02	0.04	0.10	0.06	0.09
Price Range	80.12-66.22	72.76-51.10	64.55-47.86	56.82-30.97	58.49-30.62	63.50-35.54	72.25-42.20	66.90-34.03
P/E Ratio	29.67-24.53	26.55-18.65	25.92-19.22	40.59-22.12	26.83-14.05	26.91-15.06	24.41-14.26	26.55-13.50
Average Yield %	10.29	3.54	3.60	4.10	4.19	2.67	1.68	1.34

Address: 2665 South Bayshore Drive, Suite 901, Miami, FL 33133
Telephone: 305-714-4100

Web Site: www.watsco.com
Officers: Albert H. Nahmad - Chairman, President
Barry S. Logan - Senior Vice President, Secretary

Auditors: KPMG LLP
Investor Contact: 305-714-4100
Transfer Agents: American Stock Transfer & Trust Company, New York, NY

WEBSTER FINANCIAL CORP (WATERBURY, CONN)

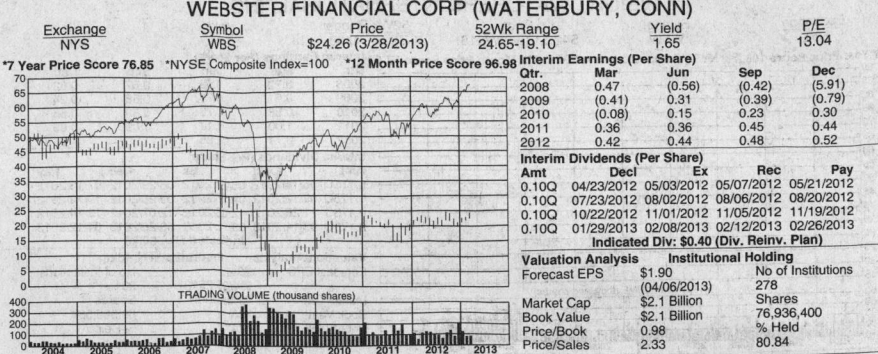

Exchange	Symbol	Price	52Wk Range	Yield	P/E
NYS	WBS	$24.26 (3/28/2013)	24.65-19.10	1.65	13.04

*7 Year Price Score 76.85 *NYSE Composite Index=100 *12 Month Price Score 96.98

Interim Earnings (Per Share)

Qtr.	Mar	Jun	Sep	Dec
2008	0.47	(0.56)	(0.42)	(5.91)
2009	(0.41)	0.31	(0.39)	(0.79)
2010	(0.08)	0.15	0.23	0.30
2011	0.36	0.36	0.45	0.44
2012	0.42	0.44	0.48	0.52

Interim Dividends (Per Share)

Amt	Decl	Ex	Rec	Pay
0.10Q	04/23/2012	05/03/2012	05/07/2012	05/21/2012
0.10Q	07/23/2012	08/02/2012	08/06/2012	08/20/2012
0.10Q	10/22/2012	11/01/2012	11/05/2012	11/19/2012
0.10Q	01/29/2013	02/08/2013	02/12/2013	02/26/2013
	Indicated Div: $0.40 (Div. Reinv. Plan)			

Valuation Analysis

		Institutional Holding	
Forecast EPS	$1.90	No of Institutions	
	(04/06/2013)	278	
Market Cap	$2.1 Billion	Shares	
Book Value	$2.1 Billion	76,936,400	
Price/Book	0.98	% Held	
Price/Sales	2.33	80.84	

Business Summary: Banking (MIC: 5.1.1 SIC: 6021 NAIC: 522110)

Webster Financial is a bank and financial holding company. Co., through Webster Bank, National Association and various subsidiaries, provides business and consumer banking, mortgage lending, financial planning, trust and investment services to individuals, families and businesses primarily throughout southern New England and into Westchester County, NY through its 168 banking offices, 473 automated teller machines, mobile banking and its Internet website, www.websteronline.com. Co. has four business segments: Commercial Banking, Retail Banking, Consumer Finance and Other. As of Dec 31 2011, Co. had total assets of $18.71 billion and total deposits of $13.66 billion.

Recent Developments: For the year ended Dec 31 2012, income from continuing operations increased 16.3% to US$173.7 million from US$149.4 million a year earlier. Net income increased 14.7% to US$173.7 million from US$151.4 million in the prior year. Net interest income increased 2.7% to US$578.9 million from US$563.8 million in the prior year. Provision for loan losses was US$21.5 million versus US$22.5 million in the prior year, a decrease of 4.4%. Non-interest income rose 8.9% to US$192.8 million from US$177.0 million, while non-interest expense declined 1.8% to US$501.8 million.

Prospects: Our evaluation of Webster Financial Corp. (CT) as of Apr. 7, 2013 is the result of our systematic analysis on three basic characteristics: earnings strength, relative valuation, and recent stock price movement. The company has managed to produce a neutral trend in earnings per share over the past 5 quarters. However, while recent estimates for the company have been mixed, WBS has posted better than expected results. Based on operating earnings yield, the company is undervalued when compared to all of the companies in our coverage universe. Share price changes over the past year indicates that WBS will perform poorly over the near term.

Financial Data

(US$ in Thousands)	12/31/2012	12/31/2011	12/31/2010	12/31/2009	12/31/2008	12/31/2007	12/31/2006	12/31/2005
Earnings Per Share	1.86	1.61	0.60	(2.14)	(6.42)	1.76	2.47	3.43
Cash Flow Per Share	2.94	3.06	4.31	1.87	9.30	5.61	2.95	1.08
Tang Book Value Per Share	16.50	14.58	13.74	12.45	13.30	18.64	18.82	17.86
Dividends Per Share	0.350	0.160	0.040	0.040	1.200	1.170	1.060	0.980
Dividend Payout %	18.82	9.94	6.67	...	...	66.48	42.91	28.57
Income Statement								
Interest Income	693,502	699,723	706,186	745,342	869,273	995,595	1,014,738	871,847
Interest Expense	114,594	135,955	171,376	250,704	363,482	487,403	506,188	354,506
Net Interest Income	578,908	563,768	534,810	494,638	505,791	508,192	508,550	517,341
Provision for Losses	21,500	22,500	115,000	303,000	186,300	67,750	11,000	9,500
Non-Interest Income	192,758	177,042	206,856	187,108	(28,052)	202,312	170,471	220,885
Non-Interest Expense	501,804	510,976	538,974	507,394	676,036	483,970	474,948	455,570
Income Before Taxes	248,362	207,334	87,692	(128,648)	(384,597)	158,784	193,073	273,156
Income Taxes	74,665	57,951	13,468	(52,736)	(65,840)	48,088	59,283	87,301
Net Income	173,697	151,379	74,315	(75,632)	(321,830)	96,773	133,790	185,855
Average Shares	91,649	91,688	82,172	63,916	52,020	54,996	54,065	54,236
Balance Sheet								
Net Loans & Leases	11,959,200	11,049,308	10,755,198	10,708,053	11,976,786	12,509,425	13,130,570	12,406,719
Total Assets	20,146,765	18,714,340	18,038,068	17,739,197	17,583,537	17,201,960	17,097,471	17,836,562
Total Deposits	14,530,835	13,656,025	13,608,785	13,632,127	11,884,890	12,354,158	12,458,396	11,631,145
Total Liabilities	18,053,235	16,868,566	16,264,646	15,790,804	15,699,841	15,455,751	15,211,031	16,179,759
Stockholders' Equity	2,093,530	1,845,774	1,773,422	1,948,393	1,883,696	1,746,209	1,886,440	1,656,803
Shares Outstanding	84,963	87,215	86,858	77,896	52,883	52,475	56,388	53,661
Statistical Record								
Return on Assets %	0.89	0.82	0.42	N.M.	N.M.	0.56	0.77	1.07
Return on Equity %	8.79	8.37	3.99	N.M.	N.M.	5.33	7.55	11.58
Net Interest Margin %	83.48	80.57	75.73	66.36	58.19	51.04	50.12	59.34
Efficiency Ratio %	56.62	58.28	59.03	54.42	80.36	40.40	40.07	41.69
Loans to Deposits	0.82	0.81	0.79	0.79	1.01	1.01	1.05	1.07
Price Range	24.65-19.10	23.65-14.60	21.67-11.87	14.12-2.97	34.50-11.59	51.13-30.93	49.38-45.36	50.64-43.67
P/E Ratio	13.25-10.27	14.69-9.07	36.12-19.78	...	...	29.05-17.57	19.99-18.36	14.76-12.73
Average Yield %	1.62	0.80	0.23	0.44	5.25	2.72	2.23	2.11

Address: 145 Bank Street (Webster Plaza), Waterbury, CT 06702 **Telephone:** 203-578-2202	**Web Site:** www.websteronline.com **Officers:** James C. Smith - Chairman, President, Chief Executive Officer Gerald P. Plush - Vice-Chairman, President, Chief Financial Officer, Chief Operating Officer, Chief Risk Officer	**Auditors:** Ernst & Young LLP **Transfer Agents:** Computershare, Pittsburgh, PA

WEIGHT WATCHERS INTERNATIONAL, INC.

Exchange	Symbol	Price	52Wk Range	Yield	P/E
NYS	WTW	$42.11 (3/28/2013)	78.61-40.33	1.66	9.96

*7 Year Price Score 106.09 *NYSE Composite Index=100   *12 Month Price Score 77.03

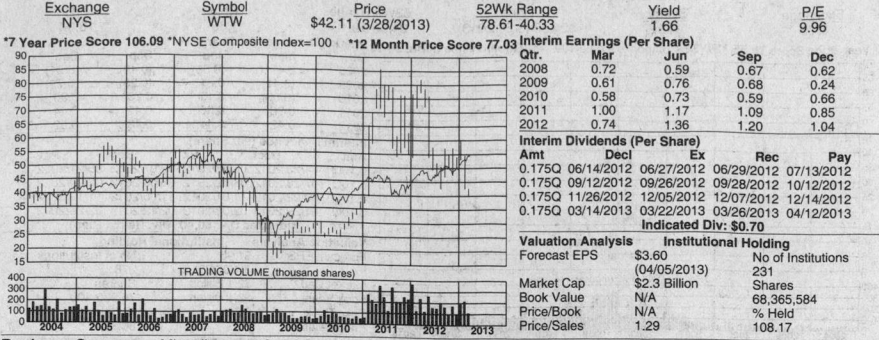

Interim Earnings (Per Share)

Qtr.	Mar	Jun	Sep	Dec
2008	0.72	0.59	0.67	0.62
2009	0.61	0.76	0.68	0.24
2010	0.58	0.73	0.59	0.66
2011	1.00	1.17	1.09	0.85
2012	0.74	1.36	1.20	1.04

Interim Dividends (Per Share)

Amt	Decl	Ex	Rec	Pay
0.175Q	06/14/2012	06/27/2012	06/29/2012	07/13/2012
0.175Q	09/12/2012	09/26/2012	09/28/2012	10/12/2012
0.175Q	11/26/2012	12/05/2012	12/07/2012	12/14/2012
0.175Q	03/14/2013	03/22/2013	03/26/2013	04/12/2013

Indicated Div: $0.70

Valuation Analysis / **Institutional Holding**

Forecast EPS	$3.60 (04/05/2013)	No of Institutions	231
Market Cap	$2.3 Billion	Shares	68,365,584
Book Value	N/A	% Held	108.17
Price/Book	N/A		
Price/Sales	1.29		

Business Summary: Miscellaneous Consumer Services (MIC: 2.2.3 SIC: 7299 NAIC: 812191)

Weight Watchers International is a consumer company and a provider of weight management services, operating through a network of Co.-owned and franchise operations. Co. sells a range of products, including bars, snacks, cookbooks, food and restaurant guides, Weight Watchers magazines and PointsPlus calculators. Through WeightWatchers.com, Co. provides Internet subscription weight management products to consumers and maintains a presence on the Internet for the Weight Watchers brand. At Dec 31 2011, Co. provided two Internet subscription products in 11 countries, including the U.S., the U.K., Germany and Australia. Co. has two segments: Weight Watchers International and WeightWatchers.com.

Recent Developments: For the year ended Dec 29 2012, net income decreased 15.4% to US$257.4 million from US$304.3 million in the prior year. Revenues were US$1.83 billion, up 0.4% from US$1.82 billion the year before. Operating income versus US$510.8 million versus US$546.3 million in the prior year, a decrease of 6.5%. Direct operating expenses declined 3.6% to US$744.0 million from US$772.0 million in the comparable period the year before. Indirect operating expenses increased 14.2% to US$572.0 million from US$500.8 million in the equivalent prior-year period.

Prospects: Our evaluation of Weight Watchers International Inc. as of Apr. 7, 2013 is the result of our systematic analysis on three basic characteristics: earnings strength, relative valuation, and recent stock price movement. The company has generated a negative trend in earnings per share over the past 5 quarters and while recent estimates for the company have been raised by analysts, WTW has posted better than expected results. Based on operating earnings yield, the company is undervalued when compared to all of the companies in our coverage universe. Share price changes over the past year indicates that WTW will perform poorly over the near term.

Financial Data
(US$ in Thousands)

	12/29/2012	12/31/2011	01/01/2011	01/02/2010	01/03/2009	12/29/2007	12/31/2006	12/31/2005
Earnings Per Share	4.23	4.11	2.56	2.30	2.60	2.48	2.11	1.67
Cash Flow Per Share	5.81	5.49	3.73	3.46	3.03	3.97	2.69	2.90
Dividends Per Share	0.700	0.700	0.700	0.700	0.700	0.700	0.700	...
Dividend Payout %	16.55	17.03	27.34	30.43	26.92	28.23	33.18	...
Income Statement								
Total Revenue	1,826,812	1,819,156	1,452,037	1,398,913	1,535,812	1,467,167	1,233,325	1,151,251
EBITDA	526,342	557,392	403,500	371,089	440,368	446,466	388,500	308,092
Depn & Amortn	18,844	14,450	14,118	14,211	13,352	10,698	8,326	7,808
Income Before Taxes	416,961	483,092	313,178	290,156	334,349	326,491	330,642	279,315
Income Taxes	159,535	178,748	120,656	115,585	132,002	125,311	120,817	104,913
Net Income	257,426	304,867	194,235	177,344	204,331	201,180	209,825	174,402
Average Shares	60,923	74,131	75,880	77,117	78,495	81,107	99,426	104,203
Balance Sheet								
Current Assets	217,967	214,526	190,442	199,951	225,041	186,336	154,746	127,710
Total Assets	1,218,607	1,121,628	1,091,987	1,087,509	1,106,752	1,046,221	1,002,392	835,491
Current Liabilities	447,855	494,207	539,135	536,055	495,124	358,431	236,532	165,888
Long-Term Obligations	2,291,669	926,868	1,167,561	1,238,000	1,485,000	1,602,500	830,237	741,425
Total Liabilities	2,884,066	1,531,394	1,786,753	1,824,021	1,994,268	1,972,551	1,070,759	916,142
Stockholders' Equity	(1,665,459)	(409,766)	(694,766)	(736,512)	(887,516)	(926,330)	(68,367)	(80,651)
Shares Outstanding	55,754	73,599	73,370	77,041	76,921	79,410	111,988	111,988
Statistical Record								
Return on Assets %	22.06	27.62	17.87	16.21	18.67	19.75	22.83	21.18
Return on Equity %	...	...	...	...	...	...	...	302.07
EBITDA Margin %	28.81	30.64	27.79	26.53	28.67	30.43	31.50	26.76
Net Margin %	14.09	16.76	13.38	12.68	13.30	13.71	17.01	15.15
Asset Turnover	1.57	1.65	1.34	1.28	1.40	1.44	1.34	1.40
Current Ratio	0.49	0.43	0.35	0.37	0.45	0.52	0.65	0.77
Price Range	82.00-42.66	85.76-37.08	37.57-24.39	29.98-16.70	49.40-22.26	57.75-44.95	53.87-38.24	58.03-40.58
P/E Ratio	19.39-10.09	20.87-9.02	14.68-9.53	13.03-7.26	19.00-8.56	23.29-18.13	25.53-18.12	34.75-24.30
Average Yield %	1.18	1.09	2.38	2.80	1.80	1.38	1.52	...

Address: 11 Madison Avenue, 17th Floor, New York, NY 10010 Telephone: 212-589-2700	Web Site: www.weightwatchersinternational.com Officers: Raymond Debbane - Chairman James R. Chambers - President, Chief Operating Officer, Division Officer, Region Officer	Auditors: PricewaterhouseCoopers LLP Investor Contact: 212-986-6667 Transfer Agents: Computershare, Canton, MA

WEINGARTEN REALTY INVESTORS

Exchange	Symbol	Price	52Wk Range	Yield	P/E
NYS	WRI	$31.55 (3/28/2013)	31.55-24.36	3.87	35.06

*7 Year Price Score 85.40 ***NYSE Composite Index=100** ***12 Month Price Score 102.04**

Interim Earnings (Per Share)

Qtr.	Mar	Jun	Sep	Dec
2008	0.34	0.79	0.34	(0.12)
2009	0.38	0.35	(0.08)	0.64
2010	0.08	(0.05)	0.07	(0.02)
2011	0.06	(0.06)	(0.35)	0.18
2012	0.10	0.19	0.26	0.36

Interim Dividends (Per Share)

Amt	Decl	Ex	Rec	Pay
0.29Q	05/08/2012	06/05/2012	06/07/2012	06/15/2012
0.29Q	08/07/2012	09/04/2012	09/06/2012	09/14/2012
0.29Q	10/26/2012	12/04/2012	12/06/2012	12/14/2012
0.305Q	02/14/2013	03/05/2013	03/07/2013	03/15/2013

Indicated Div: $1.22 (Div. Reinv. Plan)

Valuation Analysis / Institutional Holding

Forecast EPS	$0.55	No of Institutions
	(04/05/2013)	349
Market Cap	$3.8 Billion	Shares
Book Value	$1.6 Billion	113,003,672
Price/Book	2.43	% Held
Price/Sales	7.61	87.24

Business Summary: REITs (MIC: 5.3.1 SIC: 6798 NAIC: 525930)

Weingarten Realty Investors is a real estate investment trust. Co.'s primary business is leasing space to tenants in the shopping and industrial centers it owns or leases. Co. also provides property management services for both joint ventures in which it is partners and for other outside owners for which it charges fees. As of Dec 31 2012, Co. owned or operated under long-term leases, either directly or through its interest in real estate joint ventures or partnerships, a total of 292 developed income-producing properties and two properties under various stages of construction and development.

Recent Developments: For the year ended Dec 31 2012, income from continuing operations was US$72.2 million compared with a loss of US$6.5 million a year earlier. Net income increased 810.6% to US$152.4 million from US$16.7 million in the prior year. Revenues were US$503.5 million, up 5.3% from US$478.4 million the year before. Revenues from property income rose 5.8% to US$491.4 million from US$464.2 million in the corresponding earlier year.

Prospects: Our evaluation of Weingarten Realty Investors as of Apr. 7, 2013 is the result of our systematic analysis on three basic characteristics: earnings strength, relative valuation, and recent stock price movement. The company has generated a negative trend in earnings per share over the past 5 quarters. Because the company lacks sufficient analyst estimate data, we place greater weight on the historical EPS trend as the measure of earnings strength. Based on operating earnings yield, the company is overvalued when compared to all of the companies in our coverage universe. Share price changes over the past year indicates that WRI will perform poorly over the near term.

Financial Data
(US$ in Thousands)

	12/31/2012	12/31/2011	12/31/2010	12/31/2009	12/31/2008	12/31/2007	12/31/2006	12/31/2005
Earnings Per Share	0.90	(0.17)	0.09	1.23	1.36	2.44	3.27	2.31
Cash Flow Per Share	1.88	1.78	1.79	2.23	2.60	2.61	2.77	2.25
Tang Book Value Per Share	12.98	13.70	14.94	15.83	16.40	17.29	13.13	12.87
Dividends Per Share	1.160	1.100	1.040	1.275	2.100	1.980	1.860	1.760
Dividend Payout %	128.89	...	1,155.56	103.66	154.41	81.15	56.88	76.19
Income Statement								
Total Revenue	503,538	541,561	554,667	572,108	614,968	599,054	561,380	544,045
EBITDA	330,839	300,921	330,572	391,626	368,145	420,695	414,641	408,448
Depn & Amortn	147,251	162,505	156,124	157,971	157,894	134,676	131,992	128,573
Income Before Taxes	73,824	1,721	35,479	91,875	66,110	145,676	144,751	149,114
Income Taxes	79	395	240	6,338	(10,148)	4,073	1,366	...
Net Income	146,640	15,621	46,206	171,102	151,681	238,017	305,010	219,653
Average Shares	121,705	120,331	120,780	110,178	84,917	88,893	91,779	93,166
Balance Sheet								
Current Assets	99,144	100,172	119,718	249,956	162,819	160,384	149,896	103,595
Total Assets	4,184,784	4,588,226	4,807,855	4,890,385	5,114,699	4,993,343	4,375,540	3,737,741
Current Liabilities	119,699	124,888	126,767	137,727	179,432	155,137	132,821	102,143
Long-Term Obligations	2,204,030	2,531,837	2,589,448	2,531,847	3,171,537	3,165,059	2,900,952	2,299,855
Total Liabilities	2,607,654	2,932,846	3,007,866	2,989,095	3,686,461	3,521,520	3,249,759	2,587,455
Stockholders' Equity	1,577,130	1,655,380	1,799,989	1,901,290	1,428,238	1,471,823	1,125,781	1,150,286
Shares Outstanding	121,505	120,844	120,492	120,098	87,102	85,146	85,765	89,403
Statistical Record								
Return on Assets %	3.33	0.33	0.95	3.42	2.99	5.08	7.52	6.09
Return on Equity %	9.05	0.90	2.50	10.28	10.43	18.33	26.80	19.56
EBITDA Margin %	65.70	55.57	59.60	68.45	59.86	70.23	73.86	75.08
Net Margin %	29.12	2.88	8.33	29.91	24.66	39.73	54.33	40.37
Asset Turnover	0.11	0.12	0.11	0.11	0.12	0.13	0.14	0.15
Current Ratio	0.83	0.80	0.94	1.81	0.91	1.03	1.13	1.01
Debt to Equity	1.40	1.53	1.44	1.33	2.22	2.15	2.58	2.00
Price Range	28.85-21.56	26.80-19.35	25.92-18.16	22.29-8.41	40.00-10.10	52.16-31.44	47.83-37.10	40.50-33.49
P/E Ratio	32.06-23.96	...	288.00-201.78	18.12-6.84	29.41-7.43	21.38-12.89	14.63-11.35	17.53-14.50
Average Yield %	4.41	4.63	4.79	7.80	7.08	4.60	4.50	4.73

Address: 2600 Citadel Plaza Drive, P.O. Box 924133, Houston, TX 77292-4133 **Telephone:** 713-866-6000	**Web Site:** www.weingarten.com **Officers:** Stanford Alexander - Chairman Andrew M. Alexander - President, Chief Executive Officer	**Auditors:** Doloitte & Touche LLP **Investor Contact:** 800-298-9974 **Transfer Agents:** Computershare

WELLCARE HEALTH PLANS INC

Exchange	Symbol	Price	52Wk Range	Yield	P/E
NYS	WCG	$57.96 (3/28/2013)	74.24-45.78	N/A	13.51

*7 Year Price Score 107.32 *NYSE Composite Index=100 *12 Month Price Score 93.45

Interim Earnings (Per Share)

Qtr.	Mar	Jun	Sep	Dec
2008	0.03	0.26	(0.44)	(0.75)
2009	(0.89)	0.88	0.68	0.27
2010	0.15	(3.05)	1.00	0.62
2011	0.50	1.61	2.03	1.96
2012	1.18	1.06	0.87	1.18

Interim Dividends (Per Share)

No Dividends Paid

Valuation Analysis | Institutional Holding

Forecast EPS	$4.83	No of Institutions
	(04/06/2013)	343
Market Cap	$2.5 Billion	Shares
Book Value	$1.3 Billion	47,053,840
Price/Book	1.89	% Held
Price/Sales	0.34	95.60

Business Summary: Hospitals & Health Care Facilities (MIC: 4.2.1 SIC: 6324 NAIC: 524114)

WellCare Health Plans provides managed care services to government-sponsored health care programs. Through its subsidiaries, as of Dec. 31, 2012, Co. operated its Medicaid health plans in Florida, Georgia, Hawaii, Illinois, Kentucky, New York and Ohio, and its Medicare Advantage (MA) coordinated care plans (CCPs) in California, Connecticut, Florida, Georgia, Hawaii, Illinois, Louisiana, Missouri, New Jersey, New York, Ohio and Texas. Co. also operates a stand-alone Medicare prescription drug plan (PDP) in 49 states and the District of Columbia.

Recent Developments: For the year ended Dec 31 2012, net income decreased 30.1% to US$184.7 million from US$264.2 million in the prior year. Revenues were US$7.41 billion, up 21.3% from US$6.11 billion the year before. Net premiums earned were US$7.40 billion versus US$6.10 billion in the prior year, an increase of 21.4%.

Prospects: Our evaluation of WellCare Health Plans Inc. as of Apr. 7, 2013 is the result of our systematic analysis on three basic characteristics: earnings strength, relative valuation, and recent stock price movement. The company has managed to produce a neutral trend in earnings per share over the past 5 quarters and while recent estimates for the company have been mixed, WCG has posted better than expected results. Based on operating earnings yield, the company is undervalued when compared to all of the companies in our coverage universe. Share price changes over the past year indicates that WCG will perform very poorly over the near term.

Financial Data
(US$ in Thousands)

	12/31/2012	12/31/2011	12/31/2010	12/31/2009	12/31/2008	12/31/2007	12/31/2006	12/31/2005
Earnings Per Share	4.29	6.10	(1.26)	0.95	(0.89)	5.16	3.43	1.32
Cash Flow Per Share	(0.71)	3.78	5.27	1.38	7.14	6.82	13.03	2.16
Tang Book Value Per Share	24.21	23.24	16.68	17.87	16.10	14.37	8.67	4.13
Income Statement								
Total Revenue	7,409,032	6,106,868	5,440,225	6,878,164	6,521,907	5,390,792	3,762,926	1,879,539
EBITDA	329,804	449,906	(50,207)	121,235	(21,859)	408,191	250,857	103,166
Depn & Amortn	29,243	24,922	22,413	21,804	19,531	16,188	10,072	4,431
Income Before Taxes	296,439	418,474	(72,849)	93,020	(53,170)	377,968	226,698	85,173
Income Taxes	111,711	154,228	(19,449)	53,149	(16,337)	161,732	87,511	33,245
Net Income	184,728	264,246	(53,400)	39,871	(36,833)	216,236	139,187	51,928
Average Shares	43,826	43,328	42,365	42,150	41,396	41,940	40,621	39,293
Balance Sheet								
Current Assets	2,100,710	2,119,894	1,815,171	1,717,465	1,704,570	1,690,942	1,338,414	605,457
Total Assets	2,675,516	2,488,111	2,247,293	2,118,447	2,203,461	2,082,731	1,663,965	887,489
Current Liabilities	1,113,426	1,123,140	1,185,701	1,180,070	1,364,556	1,201,996	904,107	340,042
Long-Term Obligations	120,000	135,000	...	...	...	...	154,021	155,461
Total Liabilities	1,352,352	1,371,265	1,415,247	1,237,547	1,397,632	1,274,840	1,100,910	517,365
Stockholders' Equity	1,323,164	1,116,846	832,046	880,900	805,829	807,891	563,055	370,124
Shares Outstanding	43,212	42,848	42,541	42,361	42,261	41,912	40,900	39,428
Statistical Record								
Return on Assets %	7.14	11.16	N.M.	1.85	N.M.	11.54	10.91	6.16
Return on Equity %	15.10	27.12	N.M.	4.73	N.M.	31.55	29.83	15.30
EBITDA Margin %	4.45	7.37	N.M.	1.76	N.M.	7.57	6.67	5.49
Net Margin %	2.49	4.33	N.M.	0.58	N.M.	4.01	3.70	2.76
Asset Turnover	2.86	2.58	2.49	3.18	3.03	2.88	2.95	2.23
Current Ratio	1.89	1.89	1.53	1.46	1.25	1.41	1.48	1.78
Debt to Equity	0.09	0.12	...	...	...	...	0.27	0.42
Price Range	74.24-45.90	58.45-29.90	37.18-22.92	38.63-6.23	56.43-7.01	122.27-22.04	70.72-37.27	43.36-27.80
P/E Ratio	17.31-10.70	9.58-4.90	...	40.66-6.56	...	23.70-4.27	20.62-10.87	32.85-21.06

Address: 8725 Henderson Road, Renaissance One, Tampa, FL 33634 Telephone: 813-290-6200	Web Site: www.wellcare.com Officers: Heath G. Schiesser - President, Chief Executive Officer Jonathan P. Rich - Senior Vice President, Chief Compliance Officer	Auditors: Deloitte & Touche LLP Investor Contact: 813-206-3916 Transfer Agents: Computershare Trust Company, N.A., Providence, RI

WELLPOINT INC

Exchange	Symbol	Price	52Wk Range	Yield	P/E
NYS	WLP	$66.23 (3/28/2013)	72.95-52.93	2.26	8.10

*7 Year Price Score 87.57   *NYSE Composite Index=100   *12 Month Price Score 94.59

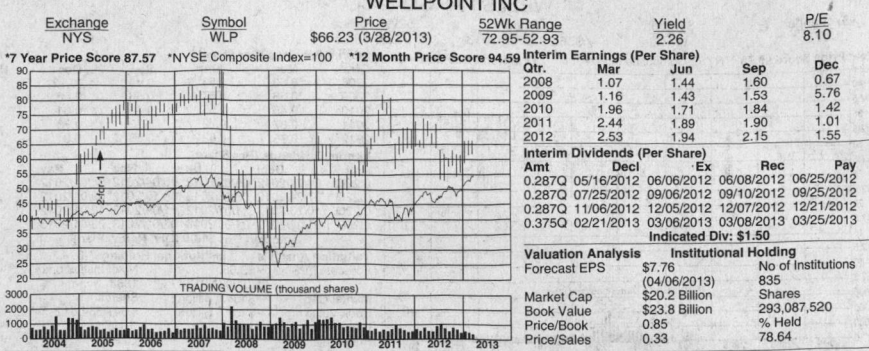

Interim Earnings (Per Share)

Qtr.	Mar	Jun	Sep	Dec
2008	1.07	1.44	1.60	0.67
2009	1.16	1.43	1.53	5.76
2010	1.96	1.71	1.84	1.42
2011	2.44	1.89	1.90	1.01
2012	2.53	1.94	2.15	1.55

Interim Dividends (Per Share)

Amt	Decl	Ex	Rec	Pay
0.287Q	05/16/2012	06/06/2012	06/08/2012	06/25/2012
0.287Q	07/25/2012	09/06/2012	09/10/2012	09/25/2012
0.287Q	11/06/2012	12/05/2012	12/07/2012	12/21/2012
0.375Q	02/21/2013	03/06/2013	03/08/2013	03/25/2013

Indicated Div: $1.50

Valuation Analysis

Forecast EPS	$7.76
	(04/06/2013)
Market Cap	$20.2 Billion
Book Value	$23.8 Billion
Price/Book	0.85
Price/Sales	0.33

Institutional Holding

No of Institutions	835
Shares	293,087,520
% Held	78.64

Business Summary: Life & Health (MIC: 5.2.2 SIC: 6324 NAIC: 524114)

WellPoint is a holding company. Through its subsidiaries, Co. provides a range of network-based managed care plans to the large and small employer, individual, Medicaid and senior markets. Co.'s managed care plans include: preferred provider organizations; health maintenance organizations; point-of-service plans; indemnity plans and other hybrid plans, including consumer-driven health plans; and hospital only and limited benefit products. Co. manages its operations through three reportable segments: Commercial, Consumer, and Other. Co. served 34.3 million medical members through its affiliated health plans and a total of 65.3 million individuals through all subsidiaries as of Dec 31 2011.

Recent Developments: For the year ended Dec 31 2012, net income increased 0.3% to US$2.66 billion from US$2.65 billion in the prior year. Revenues were US$61.71 billion, up 1.6% from US$60.71 billion the year before. Net premiums earned were US$56.50 billion versus US$55.97 billion in the prior year, an increase of 0.9%. Net investment income fell 2.5% to US$686.1 million from US$703.7 million a year ago.

Prospects: Our evaluation of WellPoint Inc. as of Apr. 7, 2013 is the result of our systematic analysis on three basic characteristics: earnings strength, relative valuation, and recent stock price movement. The company has managed to produce a neutral trend in earnings per share over the past 5 quarters. However, while recent estimates for the company have been mixed, WLP has posted better than expected results. Based on operating earnings yield, the company is undervalued when compared to all of the companies in our coverage universe. Share price changes over the past year indicates that WLP will perform very poorly over the near term.

Financial Data

(US$ in Thousands)	12/31/2012	12/31/2011	12/31/2010	12/31/2009	12/31/2008	12/31/2007	12/31/2006	12/31/2005
Earnings Per Share	8.18	7.25	6.94	9.88	4.76	5.56	4.82	3.94
Cash Flow Per Share	8.51	9.37	3.45	6.38	4.86	7.32	6.44	5.33
Tang Book Value Per Share	N.M.	4.41	6.75	7.42	N.M.	0.60	2.92	2.78
Dividends Per Share	1.150	1.000	...	...	...	...	...	...
Dividend Payout %	14.06	13.79	...	...	...	...	...	...
Income Statement								
Premium Income	56,496,700	55,969,600	53,973,600	56,382,000	57,101,000	55,865,000	51,971,900	41,216,700
Total Revenue	61,711,700	60,710,700	58,801,800	65,028,100	61,251,100	61,134,300	56,953,000	45,136,000
Benefits & Claims	48,213,600	47,647,500	44,926,900	46,571,100	47,742,400	46,036,100	42,218,800	33,219,900
Income Before Taxes	3,865,500	3,957,900	4,353,800	7,403,000	3,122,400	5,257,900	4,914,400	3,890,300
Income Taxes	1,210,000	1,311,200	1,466,700	2,657,100	631,700	1,912,500	1,819,500	1,426,500
Net Income	2,655,500	2,646,700	2,887,100	4,745,900	2,490,700	3,345,400	3,094,900	2,463,800
Average Shares	324,800	365,100	415,800	480,500	523,000	602,000	642,100	625,800
Balance Sheet								
Total Assets	58,955,400	52,018,800	50,166,900	52,125,400	48,403,200	52,060,000	51,759,800	51,405,200
Total Liabilities	35,152,700	28,730,600	26,354,300	27,262,100	26,971,500	29,069,600	27,184,000	26,412,100
Stockholders' Equity	23,802,700	23,288,200	23,812,600	24,863,300	21,431,700	22,990,400	24,575,800	24,993,100
Shares Outstanding	304,715	339,372	377,736	449,789	503,230	556,212	615,500	660,424
Statistical Record								
Return on Assets %	4.77	5.18	5.64	9.44	4.94	6.44	6.00	5.41
Return on Equity %	11.25	11.24	11.86	20.50	11.18	14.07	12.49	11.09
Loss Ratio %	85.34	85.13	83.24	82.60	83.61	82.41	81.23	80.60
Net Margin %	4.30	4.36	4.91	7.30	4.07	5.47	5.43	5.46
Price Range	73.80-52.93	81.78-56.86	68.06-47.43	60.36-30.10	89.28-29.44	89.72-74.45	79.77-67.50	80.00-55.50
P/E Ratio	9.02-6.47	11.28-7.84	9.81-6.83	6.11-3.05	18.76-6.18	16.14-13.39	16.55-14.00	20.30-14.09
Average Yield %	1.81	1.46	...	...	...	...	...	...

Address: 120 Monument Circle, Indianapolis, IN 46204-4903
Telephone: 317-488-6000

Web Site: www.wellpoint.com
Officers: John Cannon - Interim President, Interim Chief Executive Officer, Executive Vice President, Chief Public Affairs Officer, Secretary, General Counsel Joseph R. Swedish - Chief Executive Officer

Auditors: Ernst & Young LLP
Investor Contact: 212-476-1473
Transfer Agents: EquiServe Trust Company, N.A., Providence, RI

WELLS FARGO & CO.

Exchange	Symbol	Price	52Wk Range	Yield	P/E
NYS	WFC	$36.99 (3/28/2013)	38.20-30.05	2.70	11.01

*7 Year Price Score 99.78 *NYSE Composite Index=100 *12 Month Price Score 97.38

Interim Earnings (Per Share)

Qtr.	Mar	Jun	Sep	Dec
2008	0.60	0.53	0.49	(0.92)
2009	0.56	0.57	0.56	0.06
2010	0.45	0.55	0.60	0.61
2011	0.67	0.70	0.72	0.73
2012	0.75	0.82	0.88	0.91

Interim Dividends (Per Share)

Amt	Decl	Ex	Rec	Pay
0.22Q	04/24/2012	05/02/2012	05/04/2012	06/01/2012
0.22Q	07/24/2012	08/08/2012	08/10/2012	09/01/2012
0.22Q	10/23/2012	11/07/2012	11/09/2012	12/01/2012
0.25Q	01/22/2013	01/30/2013	02/01/2013	03/01/2013

Indicated Div: $1.00 (Div. Reinv. Plan)

Valuation Analysis / **Institutional Holding**

Forecast EPS	$3.65 (04/06/2013)	No of Institutions 1886
Market Cap	$194.8 Billion	Shares 4,347,584,512
Book Value	$157.6 Billion	% Held 75.91
Price/Book	1.24	
Price/Sales	2.13	

Business Summary: Banking (MIC: 5.1.1 SIC: 6021 NAIC: 522110)

Wells Fargo is a financial holding company and a bank holding company. Through its subsidiaries, Co. operates in three segments: Community Banking, which provides a line of financial products and services including investment, insurance and trust services for consumers and businesses; Wholesale Banking, which provides commercial loans and lines of credit, letters of credit, asset-based lending, equipment leasing, international trade facilities, and trade financing; and Wealth, Brokerage and Retirement, which provides financial planning, private banking, credit, investment management and trust. At Dec 31 2012, Co. had total assets of $1.42 trillion and total deposits of $1.00 trillion.

Recent Developments: For the year ended Dec 31 2012, net income increased 19.5% to US$19.37 billion from US$16.21 billion in the prior year. Net interest income increased 1.1% to US$43.23 billion from US$42.76 billion in the prior year. Provision for loan losses was US$7.22 billion versus US$7.90 billion in the prior year, a decrease of 8.6%. Non-interest income rose 12.2% to US$42.86 billion from US$38.19 billion, while non-interest expense advanced 2.0% to US$50.40 billion.

Prospects: Our evaluation of Wells Fargo & Co. as of Apr. 7, 2013 is the result of our systematic analysis on three basic characteristics: earnings strength, relative valuation, and recent stock price movement. The company has managed to produce a neutral trend in earnings per share over the past 5 quarters and while recent estimates for the company have remained steady, WFC has posted better than expected results. Based on operating earnings yield, the company is undervalued when compared to all of the companies in our coverage universe. Share price changes over the past year indicates that WFC will perform poorly over the near term.

Financial Data

(US$ in Thousands)	12/31/2012	12/31/2011	12/31/2010	12/31/2009	12/31/2008	12/31/2007	12/31/2006	12/31/2005
Earnings Per Share	3.36	2.82	2.21	1.75	0.70	2.38	2.49	2.25
Cash Flow Per Share	11.04	2.59	3.59	6.30	(1.43)	2.71	9.53	(2.77)
Tang Book Value Per Share	18.81	15.34	12.60	9.35	3.18	4.98	4.70	4.93
Dividends Per Share	0.880	0.480	0.200	0.490	1.300	1.180	1.080	1.000
Dividend Payout %	26.19	17.02	9.05	28.00	185.71	49.58	43.37	44.44
Income Statement								
Interest Income	48,391,000	49,412,000	52,796,000	56,274,000	34,898,000	35,177,000	32,239,000	25,962,000
Interest Expense	5,161,000	6,649,000	8,039,000	9,950,000	9,755,000	14,203,000	12,288,000	7,458,000
Net Interest Income	43,230,000	42,763,000	44,757,000	46,324,000	25,143,000	20,974,000	19,951,000	18,504,000
Provision for Losses	7,217,000	7,899,000	15,753,000	21,668,000	15,979,000	4,939,000	2,204,000	2,383,000
Non-Interest Income	42,856,000	38,185,000	40,453,000	42,362,000	16,754,000	18,416,000	15,740,000	14,445,000
Non-Interest Expense	50,398,000	49,393,000	50,456,000	49,020,000	22,661,000	22,824,000	20,742,000	19,018,000
Income Before Taxes	28,471,000	23,656,000	19,001,000	17,998,000	3,257,000	11,627,000	12,745,000	11,548,000
Income Taxes	9,103,000	7,445,000	6,338,000	5,331,000	602,000	3,570,000	4,263,000	3,877,000
Net Income	18,897,000	15,869,000	12,362,000	12,275,000	2,655,000	8,057,000	8,482,000	7,671,000
Average Shares	5,351,499	5,323,399	5,263,099	4,562,699	3,391,300	3,382,800	3,410,100	3,411,000
Balance Sheet								
Net Loans & Leases	782,624,000	751,597,000	735,535,000	763,987,000	850,045,000	377,836,000	316,073,000	307,578,000
Total Assets	1,422,968,000	1,313,867,000	1,258,128,000	1,243,646,000	1,309,639,000	575,442,000	481,996,000	481,741,000
Total Deposits	1,002,835,000	920,070,000	847,942,000	824,018,000	781,402,000	344,460,000	310,243,000	314,450,000
Total Liabilities	1,265,414,000	1,173,626,000	1,131,720,000	1,131,860,000	1,210,555,000	527,814,000	436,120,000	441,081,000
Stockholders' Equity	157,554,000	140,241,000	126,408,000	111,786,000	99,084,000	47,628,000	45,876,000	40,660,000
Shares Outstanding	5,266,313	5,262,611	5,262,282	5,178,624	4,228,631	3,297,102	3,377,150	3,355,166
Statistical Record								
Return on Assets %	1.38	1.23	0.99	0.96	0.28	1.52	1.76	1.69
Return on Equity %	12.66	11.90	10.38	11.64	3.61	17.23	19.60	19.54
Net Interest Margin %	89.33	86.54	84.77	82.32	72.05	59.62	61.88	71.27
Efficiency Ratio %	55.23	56.39	54.11	49.70	43.87	42.59	43.23	47.07
Loans to Deposits	0.78	0.82	0.87	0.93	1.09	1.10	1.02	0.98
Price Range	36.13-28.43	34.10-22.88	33.88-23.25	31.38-8.12	39.80-20.51	37.47-29.49	36.81-30.52	32.17-28.89
P/E Ratio	10.75-8.46	12.09-8.11	15.33-10.52	17.93-4.64	56.86-29.30	15.74-12.39	14.78-12.26	14.30-12.84
Average Yield %	2.68	1.71	0.71	2.09	4.43	3.44	3.17	3.30

Address: 420 Montgomery Street, San Francisco, CA 94163	Web Site: www.wellsfargo.com	Auditors: KPMG LLP
Telephone: 866-249-3302	Officers: John G. Stumpf - Chairman, President, Chief Executive Officer Patricia R. Callahan - Executive Vice President, Senior Executive Vice President, Chief Administrative Officer	Investor Contact: 415-371-2921 Transfer Agents: Wells Fargo Shareowners Services, St. Paul, MN

WESCO INTERNATIONAL, INC.

Exchange	Symbol	Price	52Wk Range	Yield	P/E
NYS	WCC	$72.61 (3/28/2013)	77.49-52.31	N/A	18.38

*7 Year Price Score 119.66 *NYSE Composite Index=100 *12 Month Price Score 107.32

Interim Earnings (Per Share)

Qtr.	Mar	Jun	Sep	Dec
2008	1.02	1.38	1.53	0.99
2009	0.55	0.62	0.79	0.51
2010	0.44	0.60	0.74	0.71
2011	0.74	1.00	1.11	1.12
2012	1.03	1.15	1.25	0.52

Interim Dividends (Per Share)

No Dividends Paid

Valuation Analysis　**Institutional Holding**

Forecast EPS	$5.75	No of Institutions
	(04/05/2013)	322
Market Cap	$3.2 Billion	Shares
Book Value	$1.6 Billion	56,510,028
Price/Book	2.06	% Held
Price/Sales	0.49	107.78

TRADING VOLUME (thousand shares)

Business Summary: Electrical Equipment (MIC: 7.3.1 SIC: 5063 NAIC: 444190)

WESCO International is a provider of electrical, industrial, and communications maintenance, repair and operating and original equipment manufacturers products, construction materials, and supply chain management and logistics services. Co.'s key product categories include electrical and industrial supplies, wire, cable and conduit, data and broadband communications, power distribution equipment, lighting and lighting control systems, control and automation, and motors. Co. also provides a portfolio of services, including supply chain management, logistics and transportation procurement, warehousing and inventory management, as well as kitting, assembly of products and system installation.

Recent Developments: For the year ended Dec 31 2012, net income increased 2.8% to US$201.8 million from US$196.2 million in the prior year. Revenues were US$6.58 billion, up 7.4% from US$6.13 billion the year before. Operating income was US$332.9 million versus US$333.0 million in the prior year, a decrease of 0.0%. Direct operating expenses rose 7.3% to US$5.25 billion from US$4.89 billion in the comparable period the year before. Indirect operating expenses increased 10.5% to US$998.6 million from US$903.6 million in the equivalent prior-year period.

Prospects: Our evaluation of Wesco International Inc. as of Apr. 7, 2013 is the result of our systematic analysis on three basic characteristics: earnings strength, relative valuation, and recent stock price movement. The company has generated a negative trend in earnings per share over the past 5 quarters and while recent estimates for the company have been mixed, WCC has posted results that fell short of analysts expectations. Based on operating earnings yield, the company is undervalued when compared to all of the companies in our coverage universe. Share price changes over the past year indicates that WCC will perform well over the near term.

Financial Data

(US$ in Thousands)	12/31/2012	12/31/2011	12/31/2010	12/31/2009	12/31/2008	12/31/2007	12/31/2006	12/31/2005
Earnings Per Share	3.95	3.96	2.50	2.46	4.91	4.99	4.14	2.10
Cash Flow Per Share	6.58	3.88	2.99	6.90	6.59	5.74	4.25	6.27
Tang Book Value Per Share	N.M.	4.17	0.06	1.22	N.M.	N.M.	N.M.	N.M.
Income Statement								
Total Revenue	6,579,301	6,125,718	5,063,862	4,623,954	6,110,840	6,003,452	5,320,603	4,421,103
EBITDA	343,801	345,479	226,904	204,605	369,719	413,224	357,888	199,667
Depn & Amortn	14,400	12,500	11,700	13,700	14,700	19,000	15,700	18,600
Income Before Taxes	281,639	279,376	157,641	137,151	304,943	331,028	317,566	150,884
Income Taxes	79,880	83,136	42,164	32,063	92,252	90,397	100,246	47,358
Net Income	201,777	196,251	115,477	105,088	212,691	240,631	217,320	103,526
Average Shares	51,133	49,623	46,112	42,671	43,305	48,250	52,463	49,238
Balance Sheet								
Current Assets	2,101,837	1,737,420	1,513,686	1,331,004	1,557,663	1,680,499	1,618,012	908,863
Total Assets	4,629,629	3,078,452	2,826,774	2,494,193	2,720,977	2,859,887	2,823,983	1,651,159
Current Liabilities	1,007,995	845,846	708,233	680,834	1,006,009	1,291,925	1,153,672	719,886
Long-Term Obligations	1,695,413	642,922	725,893	597,869	841,928	811,311	743,887	352,232
Total Liabilities	3,075,832	1,732,454	1,678,180	1,497,904	1,988,981	2,251,411	2,060,756	1,159,709
Stockholders' Equity	1,553,797	1,345,998	1,148,594	996,289	731,996	608,476	763,227	491,450
Shares Outstanding	44,061	43,424	43,009	42,416	42,239	43,144	49,545	47,711
Statistical Record								
Return on Assets %	5.22	6.65	4.34	4.03	7.60	8.47	9.71	6.88
Return on Equity %	13.88	15.73	10.77	12.16	31.65	35.09	34.64	24.50
EBITDA Margin %	5.23	5.64	4.48	4.42	6.05	6.88	6.73	4.52
Net Margin %	3.07	3.20	2.28	2.27	3.48	4.01	4.08	2.34
Asset Turnover	1.70	2.07	1.90	1.77	2.18	2.11	2.38	2.94
Current Ratio	2.09	2.05	2.14	1.95	1.55	1.30	1.40	1.26
Debt to Equity	1.09	0.48	0.63	0.60	1.15	1.33	0.97	0.72
Price Range	67.60-52.31	63.79-32.09	53.21-27.01	30.14-13.42	46.11-11.89	69.35-38.25	79.85-43.49	43.76-23.47
P/E Ratio	17.11-13.24	16.11-8.10	21.28-10.80	12.25-5.46	9.39-2.42	13.90-7.67	19.29-10.50	20.84-11.18

| **Address:** 225 West Station Square Drive, Suite 700, Pittsburgh, PA 15219 **Telephone:** 412-454-2200 | **Web Site:** www.wesco.com **Officers:** John J. Engel - Chairman, President, Chief Executive Officer Stephen A. Van Oss - Senior Vice President, Chief Operating Officer, Chief Administrative Officer, Interim Chief Financial Officer | **Auditors:** PricewaterhouseCoopers LLP **Transfer Agents:** Computershare, Pittsburgh, PA |

WEST PHARMACEUTICAL SERVICES, INC.

Exchange	Symbol	Price	52Wk Range	Yield	P/E	Div Achiever
NYS	WST	$64.94 (3/28/2013)	64.94-39.65	1.17	28.23	20 Years

*7 Year Price Score 109.55 *NYSE Composite Index=100 *12 Month Price Score 107.96

Interim Earnings (Per Share)

Qtr.	Mar	Jun	Sep	Dec
2008	0.76	0.82	0.40	0.52
2009	0.46	0.57	0.50	0.59
2010	0.57	0.62	0.51	0.19
2011	0.56	0.57	0.49	0.54
2012	0.81	0.45	0.43	0.60

Interim Dividends (Per Share)

Amt	Decl	Ex	Rec	Pay
0.18Q	05/01/2012	07/16/2012	07/18/2012	08/01/2012
0.19Q	10/01/2012	10/22/2012	10/24/2012	11/07/2012
0.19Q	12/27/2012	01/18/2013	01/23/2013	02/06/2013
0.19Q	03/15/2013	04/15/2013	04/17/2013	05/01/2013

Indicated Div: $0.76 (Div. Reinv. Plan)

Valuation Analysis

Institutional Holding	
Forecast EPS	$3.10 (04/05/2013)	No of Institutions 231
Market Cap	$2.2 Billion	Shares 37,409,260
Book Value	$728.9 Million	% Held
Price/Book	3.06	89.35
Price/Sales	1.76	

Business Summary: Medical Instruments & Equipment (MIC: 4.3.1 SIC: 3069 NAIC: 326299)

West Pharmaceutical Services is a manufacturer of components and systems for the packaging and delivery of injectable drugs as well as delivery system components for the pharmaceutical, healthcare and consumer products industries. Co.'s products include stoppers and seals for vials, prefillable syringe components and systems, components for intravenous and blood collection systems, safety and administration systems, and contract design and manufacturing services. Co.'s customers include producers and distributors of pharmaceuticals, biologics, medical devices and personal care products. Co. operates through two segments: Pharmaceutical Packaging Systems and Pharmaceutical Delivery Systems.

Recent Developments: For the year ended Dec 31 2012, net income increased 6.9% to US$80.7 million from US$75.5 million in the prior year. Revenues were US$1.27 billion, up 6.2% from US$1.19 billion the year before. Operating income was US$135.1 million versus US$109.6 million in the prior year, an increase of 23.3%. Direct operating expenses rose 3.0% to US$878.7 million from US$853.0 million in the comparable period the year before. Indirect operating expenses increased 10.0% to US$252.6 million from US$229.7 million in the equivalent prior-year period.

Prospects: Our evaluation of West Pharmaceutical Services Inc. as of Apr. 7, 2013 is the result of our systematic analysis on three basic characteristics: earnings strength, relative valuation, and recent stock price movement. The company has generated a negative trend in earnings per share over the past 5 quarters and while recent estimates for the company have remained steady, WST has posted better than expected results. Based on operating earnings yield, the company is about fairly valued when compared to all of the companies in our coverage universe. Share price changes over the past year indicates that WST will perform well over the near term.

Financial Data

(US$ in Thousands)	12/31/2012	12/31/2011	12/31/2010	12/31/2009	12/31/2008	12/31/2007	12/31/2006	12/31/2005
Earnings Per Share	2.30	2.16	1.89	2.12	2.50	2.05	2.00	1.40
Cash Flow Per Share	5.50	3.88	4.15	4.20	4.12	3.95	4.33	2.75
Tang Book Value Per Share	16.50	14.58	13.76	12.40	10.15	9.97	7.46	5.49
Dividends Per Share	0.730	0.690	0.650	0.610	0.570	0.530	0.490	0.450
Dividend Payout %	31.74	31.94	34.39	28.77	22.80	25.85	24.50	32.14
Income Statement								
Total Revenue	1,266,400	1,192,300	1,104,700	1,055,700	1,051,100	1,020,100	913,300	699,700
EBITDA	196,300	180,700	159,500	161,400	180,200	146,500	143,200	114,800
Depn & Amortn	72,800	71,100	68,800	63,900	56,100	51,600	48,100	42,600
Income Before Taxes	108,600	92,700	74,500	83,100	109,500	86,400	84,500	60,200
Income Taxes	32,700	23,500	13,600	13,500	23,700	17,200	24,600	17,300
Net Income	80,700	75,500	65,300	72,600	86,000	70,700	67,100	45,600
Average Shares	35,900	37,000	36,700	36,300	36,200	36,200	33,600	32,525
Balance Sheet								
Current Assets	557,300	472,000	436,600	397,200	366,200	412,300	281,700	237,200
Total Assets	1,564,000	1,399,100	1,294,300	1,271,000	1,168,700	1,185,600	918,200	823,600
Current Liabilities	261,800	243,200	169,700	171,100	159,100	182,900	156,900	124,800
Long-Term Obligations	378,800	299,300	358,100	379,100	382,100	394,600	235,800	280,700
Total Liabilities	835,100	744,200	668,600	691,900	681,600	700,300	503,700	490,100
Stockholders' Equity	728,900	654,900	625,700	579,100	487,100	485,300	414,500	333,500
Shares Outstanding	34,300	33,700	33,300	33,000	32,700	32,200	32,900	31,772
Statistical Record								
Return on Assets %	5.43	5.61	5.09	5.95	7.29	6.72	7.70	6.15
Return on Equity %	11.63	11.79	10.84	13.62	17.64	15.71	17.94	14.37
EBITDA Margin %	15.50	15.16	14.44	15.29	17.14	14.36	15.68	16.41
Net Margin %	6.37	6.33	5.91	6.88	8.18	6.93	7.35	6.52
Asset Turnover	0.85	0.89	0.86	0.87	0.89	0.97	1.05	0.94
Current Ratio	2.13	1.94	2.57	2.32	2.30	2.25	1.80	1.90
Debt to Equity	0.52	0.46	0.57	0.65	0.78	0.81	0.57	0.84
Price Range	55.73-37.79	47.44-35.63	44.57-33.04	41.52-28.12	51.66-31.13	52.14-36.12	52.13-25.30	29.83-23.10
P/E Ratio	24.23-16.43	21.96-16.50	23.58-17.48	19.58-13.26	20.66-12.45	25.43-17.62	26.07-12.65	21.31-16.50
Average Yield %	1.53	1.67	1.71	1.69	1.33	1.13	1.30	1.70

Address: 530 Herman O. West Drive,, Exton, PA 19341-0645 Telephone: 610-594-2900 Fax: 610-594-3000	Web Site: www.westpharma.com Officers: Donald E. Morel - Chairman, Chief Executive Officer Daniel J. Malone - Vice President, Controller	Auditors: PricewaterhouseCoopers LLP Investor Contact: 610-594-3345 Transfer Agents: Broadbridge Corporate Issuer Solutions, Philadelphia PA

WESTAR ENERGY INC

Exchange	Symbol	Price	52Wk Range	Yield	P/E
NYS	WR	$33.18 (3/28/2013)	33.18-26.90	4.10	15.43

*7 Year Price Score 107.07 *NYSE Composite Index=100 *12 Month Price Score 98.43

Interim Earnings (Per Share)

Qtr.	Mar	Jun	Sep	Dec
2008	0.62	0.06	0.81	0.20
2009	0.40	0.35	0.73	0.10
2010	0.27	0.47	1.01	0.04
2011	0.27	0.38	1.14	0.14
2012	0.21	0.48	1.09	0.36

Interim Dividends (Per Share)

Amt	Decl	Ex	Rec	Pay
0.33Q	05/16/2012	06/06/2012	06/08/2012	07/02/2012
0.33Q	08/28/2012	09/05/2012	09/07/2012	10/01/2012
0.33Q	11/21/2012	12/05/2012	12/07/2012	01/02/2013
0.34Q	02/28/2013	03/07/2013	03/11/2013	04/01/2013

Indicated Div: $1.36

Valuation Analysis / **Institutional Holding**

Forecast EPS	$2.09	No of Institutions
	(04/06/2013)	342
Market Cap	$4.2 Billion	Shares
Book Value	$2.9 Billion	87,422,872
Price/Book	1.45	% Held
Price/Sales	1.86	60.21

Business Summary: Electric Utilities (MIC: 3.1.1 SIC: 4931 NAIC: 221122)

Westar Energy is an electric utility. As of Dec 31 2012, Co. provided electric generation, transmission and distribution services to approximately 690,000 customers in Kansas. Co. provides these services in central and northeastern Kansas, including the cities of Topeka, Lawrence, Manhattan, Salina and Hutchinson. Kansas Gas and Electric Company, Co.'s wholly owned subsidiary, provides these services in south-central and southeastern Kansas, including the city of Wichita. Co. also supplies electric energy at wholesale to municipalities and electric cooperatives in Kansas. In addition, Co. has contracts for the sale, purchase or exchange of wholesale electricity with other utilities.

Recent Developments: For the year ended Dec 31 2012, net income increased 19.6% to US$282.5 million from US$236.2 million in the prior year. Revenues were US$2.26 billion, up 4.2% from US$2.17 billion the year before. Operating income was US$562.1 million versus US$512.4 million in the prior year, an increase of 9.7%. Direct operating expenses rose 1.2% to US$1.20 billion from US$1.19 billion in the comparable period the year before. Indirect operating expenses increased 5.6% to US$496.5 million from US$470.0 million in the equivalent prior-year period.

Prospects: Our evaluation of Westar Energy Inc. as of Apr. 7, 2013 is the result of our systematic analysis on three basic characteristics: earnings strength, relative valuation, and recent stock price movement. The company has produced a positive trend in earnings per share over the past 5 quarters and while recent estimates for the company have been raised by analysts, WR has posted better than expected results. Based on operating earnings yield, the company is undervalued when compared to all of the companies in our coverage universe. Share price changes over the past year indicates that WR will perform poorly over the near term.

Financial Data

(US$ in Thousands)	12/31/2012	12/31/2011	12/31/2010	12/31/2009	12/31/2008	12/31/2007	12/31/2006	12/31/2005
Earnings Per Share	2.15	1.93	1.80	1.58	1.70	1.83	1.87	1.54
Cash Flow Per Share	4.72	3.96	5.44	4.37	2.64	2.72	2.93	4.07
Tang Book Value Per Share	22.89	22.03	21.28	20.62	20.22	19.19	17.69	16.31
Dividends Per Share	1.320	1.280	1.240	1.200	1.160	1.080	1.000	0.920
Dividend Payout %	61.40	66.32	68.89	75.95	68.24	59.02	53.48	59.74
Income Statement								
Total Revenue	2,261,470	2,170,991	2,056,171	1,858,231	1,838,996	1,726,834	1,605,743	1,583,278
EBITDA	832,735	774,584	717,797	586,140	469,326	506,076	480,171	434,607
Depn & Amortn	247,800	262,600	249,200	228,600	180,800	170,000	159,900	130,146
Income Before Taxes	408,598	339,524	293,656	200,180	182,076	232,193	221,621	195,381
Income Taxes	126,136	103,344	85,032	58,850	3,936	63,839	56,312	60,513
Net Income	275,146	230,239	203,896	175,075	178,140	168,354	165,309	135,610
Average Shares	126,898	118,290	112,014	109,648	104,407	91,260	88,099	87,409
Balance Sheet								
Current Assets	643,075	633,585	601,609	629,482	743,131	667,679	536,720	475,620
Total Assets	9,265,231	8,682,851	8,079,638	7,525,483	7,443,259	6,395,430	5,455,175	5,210,069
Current Liabilities	846,141	827,287	782,846	682,478	872,409	744,763	663,176	550,067
Long-Term Obligations	3,042,014	2,740,392	2,776,547	2,600,034	2,310,447	2,013,635	1,563,265	1,562,990
Total Liabilities	6,369,091	5,892,204	5,671,870	5,255,255	5,232,257	4,541,726	3,887,609	3,772,630
Stockholders' Equity	2,896,140	2,790,647	2,407,768	2,270,228	2,211,002	1,853,704	1,567,566	1,437,439
Shares Outstanding	126,503	125,698	112,128	109,072	108,311	95,463	87,394	86,835
Statistical Record								
Return on Assets %	3.06	2.75	2.61	2.34	2.57	2.84	3.10	2.63
Return on Equity %	9.65	8.86	8.72	7.81	8.74	9.84	11.00	9.53
EBITDA Margin %	36.82	35.68	34.91	31.54	25.52	29.31	29.90	27.45
Net Margin %	12.17	10.61	9.92	9.42	9.69	9.75	10.29	8.57
Asset Turnover	0.25	0.26	0.26	0.25	0.27	0.29	0.30	0.31
Current Ratio	0.76	0.77	0.77	0.92	0.85	0.90	0.81	0.86
Debt to Equity	1.05	0.98	1.15	1.15	1.04	1.09	1.00	1.09
Price Range	30.97-26.90	28.96-22.76	25.55-20.80	22.18-14.95	25.94-17.06	28.40-23.02	27.12-20.16	24.75-21.15
P/E Ratio	14.40-12.51	15.01-11.79	14.19-11.56	14.04-9.46	15.26-10.04	15.52-12.58	14.50-10.78	16.07-13.73
Average Yield %	4.57	4.85	5.32	6.26	5.23	4.16	4.38	4.00

Address: 818 South Kansas Avenue, Topeka, KS 66612 **Telephone:** 785-575-6300 **Fax:** 785-575-6596	**Web Site:** www.westarenergy.com **Officers:** Charles Q. Chandler - Chairman Mark A. Ruelle - President, Chief Executive Officer, Chief Financial Officer	**Auditors:** Deloitte & Touche LLP **Investor Contact:** 785-575-8227 **Transfer Agents:** Westar Energy Inc.

WABCO HOLDINGS INC

Exchange	Symbol	Price	52Wk Range	Yield	P/E
NYS	WBC	$70.59 (3/28/2013)	71.90-48.09	N/A	15.28

*7 Year Price Score N/A   ***NYSE Composite Index=100**   ***12 Month Price Score 106.20**

Interim Earnings (Per Share)

Qtr.	Mar	Jun	Sep	Dec
2008	0.91	1.00	0.97	0.35
2009	(0.57)	(0.27)	0.52	0.60
2010	0.47	(5.68)	0.66	1.02
2011	1.66	1.26	1.22	1.06
2012	1.34	1.15	1.19	0.93

Interim Dividends (Per Share)

Dividend Payment Suspended

Valuation Analysis   **Institutional Holding**

Forecast EPS	$4.71	No of Institutions
	(04/05/2013)	291
Market Cap	$4.4 Billion	Shares
Book Value	$676.4 Million	62,273,752
Price/Book	6.55	% Held
Price/Sales	1.79	92.05

TRADING VOLUME (thousand shares)

Business Summary: Construction Services (MIC: 7.5.4 SIC: 3711 NAIC: 336111)

WABCO Holdings develops, manufactures and sells braking, stability, suspension and transmission control systems for commercial vehicles. Co.'s products include pneumatic anti-lock braking systems, electronic braking systems, automated manual transmission systems, air disk brakes, and a range of mechanical products such as actuators, air compressors and air control valves. Co. supplies electronic suspension controls and vacuum pumps to the car and sport utility vehicles markets in Europe, North America and Asia. Co. also sells replacement parts, diagnostic tools, training, remanufacturing and other services to commercial vehicle aftermarket distributors, repair shops and fleet operators.

Recent Developments: For the year ended Dec 31 2012, net income decreased 15.1% to US$312.5 million from US$368.2 million in the prior year. Revenues were US$2.48 billion, down 11.3% from US$2.79 billion the year before. Operating income was US$324.5 million versus US$369.9 million in the prior year, a decrease of 12.3%. Direct operating expenses declined 12.5% to US$1.74 billion from US$1.99 billion in the comparable period the year before. Indirect operating expenses decreased 5.1% to US$415.7 million from US$438.1 million in the equivalent prior-year period.

Prospects: Our evaluation of WABCO Holdings Inc. as of Apr. 7, 2013 is the result of our systematic analysis on three basic characteristics: earnings strength, relative valuation, and recent stock price movement. The company has managed to produce a neutral trend in earnings per share over the past 5 quarters and while recent estimates for the company have been raised by analysts, WBC has posted better than expected results. Based on operating earnings yield, the company is undervalued when compared to all of the companies in our coverage universe. Share price changes over the past year indicates that WBC will perform well over the near term.

Financial Data
(US$ in Thousands)

	12/31/2012	12/31/2011	12/31/2010	12/31/2009	12/31/2008	12/31/2007	12/31/2006	12/31/2005
Earnings Per Share	4.62	5.19	(3.50)	0.29	3.24	1.81	...	...
Cash Flow Per Share	5.59	4.98	(2.94)	2.29	4.97	(0.00)	...	...
Tang Book Value Per Share	4.23	2.90	N.M.	3.07	3.41	2.94	...	...
Dividends Per Share	...	...	...	0.070	0.280	0.140	...	...
Dividend Payout %				24.14	8.64	7.73		
Income Statement								
Total Revenue	2,477,400	2,794,100	2,175,700	1,491,500	2,588,000	2,415,900	2,015,200	1,831,000
EBITDA	396,400	468,300	(101,700)	99,200	333,900	327,400	298,000	284,400
Depn & Amortn	76,900	78,200	83,300	89,600	94,200	92,300	81,800	76,500
Income Before Taxes	318,000	388,400	(187,200)	10,100	243,400	230,600	204,900	210,000
Income Taxes	23,600	36,700	36,900	(10,700)	38,200	111,300	87,900	87,400
Net Income	302,000	357,000	(226,100)	18,800	213,300	125,400	137,800	145,300
Average Shares	65,323	68,829	64,562	65,030	65,871	69,270	...	...
Balance Sheet								
Current Assets	792,600	750,700	657,700	815,700	948,000	887,400	426,800	...
Total Assets	1,747,100	1,623,200	1,524,900	1,715,600	1,776,000	1,794,200	1,276,900	...
Current Liabilities	445,700	451,600	500,500	355,200	428,400	484,300	476,300	...
Long-Term Obligations	...	52,000	96,800	154,400	173,600	116,000	57,300	...
Total Liabilities	1,070,600	1,036,000	1,112,600	1,075,500	1,174,500	1,186,600	961,700	...
Stockholders' Equity	676,400	587,200	412,300	640,100	601,500	607,600	315,200	...
Shares Outstanding	62,747	64,765	66,458	64,077	63,964	66,528	...	...
Statistical Record								
Return on Assets %	17.87	22.68	N.M.	1.08	11.92	8.17	...	...
Return on Equity %	47.67	71.44	N.M.	3.03	35.19	27.18	...	...
EBITDA Margin %	16.00	16.76	N.M.	6.65	12.90	13.55	14.79	15.53
Net Margin %	12.19	12.78	N.M.	1.26	8.24	5.19	6.84	7.94
Asset Turnover	1.47	1.78	1.34	0.85	1.45	1.57	...	...
Current Ratio	1.78	1.66	1.31	2.30	2.21	1.83	0.90	...
Debt to Equity	...	0.09	0.23	0.24	0.29	0.19	0.18	...
Price Range	65.19-44.66	74.30-35.47	60.93-25.06	25.94-8.18	54.80-11.74	56.55-43.59	...	...
P/E Ratio	14.11-9.67	14.32-6.83	...	89.45-28.21	16.91-3.62	31.24-24.08	...	...
Average Yield %	...	...	...	0.38	0.73	0.29	...	...

Address: Chaussee de Wavre, 1789, Brussels, 1160 **Telephone:** 266-398-00 **Fax:** 267-543-42	**Web Site:** www.wabco-auto.com **Officers:** Jacques Esculier - Chairman, Chief Executive Officer Ulrich Michel - Senior Vice President, Chief Financial Officer	**Auditors:** Ernst & Young Bedrijfsrevisor **Investor Contact:** 732-369-7477

WESTERN REFINING INC

Exchange	Symbol	Price	52Wk Range	Yield	P/E
NYS	WNR	$35.41 (3/28/2013)	38.82-17.51	1.36	9.54

*7 Year Price Score 126.11 *NYSE Composite Index=100 *12 Month Price Score 125.42

Interim Earnings (Per Share)

Qtr.	Mar	Jun	Sep	Dec
2008	(0.60)	0.12	1.61	(0.19)
2009	0.86	(4.20)	(0.05)	(1.14)
2010	(0.35)	0.16	0.08	(0.08)
2011	0.13	0.94	0.81	(0.56)
2012	(0.60)	2.19	0.07	1.87

Interim Dividends (Per Share)

Amt	Decl	Ex	Rec	Pay
1.00Sp	11/06/2012	11/15/2012	11/19/2012	12/07/2012
1.50Sp	12/10/2012	12/19/2012	12/21/2012	12/28/2012
0.12Q	01/15/2013	01/28/2013	01/30/2013	02/14/2013
0.12Q	04/08/2013	04/19/2013	04/23/2013	05/08/2013

Indicated Div: $0.48

Valuation Analysis

Forecast EPS	$4.40 (04/06/2013)
Market Cap	$3.1 Billion
Book Value	$909.1 Million
Price/Book	3.39
Price/Sales	0.32

Institutional Holding

No of Institutions	288
Shares	76,098,624
% Held	80.38

Business Summary: Refining & Marketing (MIC: 9.1.2 SIC: 2911 NAIC: 324110)

Western Refining is a holding company. Through its subsidiaries, Co. is engaged as an independent crude oil refiner and marketer of refined products and also operates service stations and convenience stores. Co. has three segments: refining, which makes various grades of gasoline, diesel fuel, jet fuel, and other products from crude oil, other feedstocks, and blending components; wholesale, which includes lubricant and bulk petroleum distribution plants, unmanned fleet fueling operations, a bulk lubricant terminal facility, and a fleet of crude oil and refined product trucks and lubricant delivery trucks; and retail, which operates service stations that include convenience stores or kiosks.

Recent Developments: For the year ended Dec 31 2012, net income increased 200.7% to US$398.9 million from US$132.7 million in the prior year. Revenues were US$9.50 billion, up 4.8% from US$9.07 billion the year before. Operating income was US$711.9 million versus US$383.8 million in the prior year, an increase of 85.5%. Direct operating expenses rose 6.8% to US$8.54 billion from US$8.00 billion in the comparable period the year before. Indirect operating expenses decreased 63.3% to US$253.8 million from US$691.3 million in the equivalent prior-year period.

Prospects: Our evaluation of Western Refining Inc. as of Apr. 7, 2013 is the result of our systematic analysis on three basic characteristics: earnings strength, relative valuation, and recent stock price movement. The company has generated a negative trend in earnings per share over the past 5 quarters and while recent estimates for the company have been raised by analysts, WNR has posted better than expected results. Based on operating earnings yield, the company is undervalued when compared to all of the companies in our coverage universe. Share price changes over the past year indicates that WNR will perform very well over the near term.

Financial Data

(US$ in Thousands)	12/31/2012	12/31/2011	12/31/2010	12/31/2009	12/31/2008	12/31/2007	12/31/2006	12/31/2005
Earnings Per Share	3.71	1.34	(0.19)	(4.43)	0.95	3.53	3.11	...
Cash Flow Per Share	10.24	5.71	1.52	1.78	4.21	1.69	3.75	...
Tang Book Value Per Share	9.98	8.68	6.97	7.12	6.43	5.70	7.79	...
Dividends Per Share	2.740	...	...	...	0.060	0.220	0.160	...
Dividend Payout %	73.85	...	...	...	6.32	6.23	5.14	...
Income Statement								
Total Revenue	9,503,134	9,071,037	7,965,053	6,807,368	10,725,581	7,305,032	4,199,474	...
EBITDA	795,200	476,845	243,321	(125,561)	294,882	435,506	323,124	(51)
Depn & Amortn	90,600	131,300	130,600	137,700	105,300	58,100	14,124	...
Income Before Taxes	617,087	202,528	(43,126)	(391,204)	84,421	340,503	317,153	(51)
Income Taxes	218,202	69,861	(26,077)	(40,583)	20,224	101,892	112,373	(18)
Net Income	398,885	132,667	(17,049)	(350,621)	64,197	238,611	204,780	(33)
Average Shares	111,822	109,792	88,204	79,163	67,756	67,597	65,774	...
Balance Sheet								
Current Assets	1,292,403	1,210,655	825,703	944,158	815,247	1,437,152	620,693	37
Total Assets	2,480,407	2,570,344	2,628,146	2,824,654	3,076,792	3,559,716	908,523	37
Current Liabilities	733,190	665,674	552,953	632,904	500,726	815,790	343,985	68
Long-Term Obligations	499,657	800,395	1,006,531	1,053,664	1,327,500	1,570,500	...	...
Total Liabilities	1,571,337	1,750,516	1,952,553	2,136,202	2,265,303	2,803,231	386,922	68
Stockholders' Equity	909,070	819,828	675,593	688,452	811,489	756,485	521,601	(31)
Shares Outstanding	86,938	89,303	88,327	87,990	67,780	67,538	66,896	100.00
Statistical Record								
Return on Assets %	15.75	5.10	N.M.	N.M.	1.93	10.68	45.08	...
Return on Equity %	46.02	17.74	N.M.	N.M.	8.17	37.34	78.52	...
EBITDA Margin %	8.37	5.26	3.05	N.M.	2.75	5.96	7.69	...
Net Margin %	4.20	1.46	N.M.	N.M.	0.60	3.27	4.88	...
Asset Turnover	3.75	3.49	2.92	2.31	3.22	3.27	9.24	...
Current Ratio	1.76	1.82	1.49	1.49	1.63	1.76	1.80	0.55
Debt to Equity	0.55	0.98	1.49	1.53	1.64	2.08	...	...
Price Range	31.04-13.98	21.44-10.23	10.62-4.11	15.43-4.49	24.83-4.73	65.16-24.01	28.89-14.55	...
P/E Ratio	8.37-3.77	16.00-7.63	...	...	26.14-4.98	18.46-6.80	9.29-4.68	...
Average Yield %	12.15	...	...	...	0.51	0.55	0.74	...

Address: 123 W. Mills Ave., Suite 200, El Paso, TX 79901 **Telephone:** 915-534-1400	**Web Site:** www.wnr.com **Officers:** Paul L. Foster - Executive Chairman Jeff A. Stevens - President, Chief Executive Officer	**Auditors:** Deloitte & Touche LLP **Investor Contact:** 602-286-1530 **Transfer Agents:** American Stock Transfer & Trust Company

WESTERN UNION CO.

Exchange	Symbol	Price	52Wk Range	Yield	P/E
NYS	WU	$15.04 (3/28/2013)	19.11-11.95	3.32	8.90

*7 Year Price Score N/A ***NYSE Composite Index=100** ***12 Month Price Score 84.74**

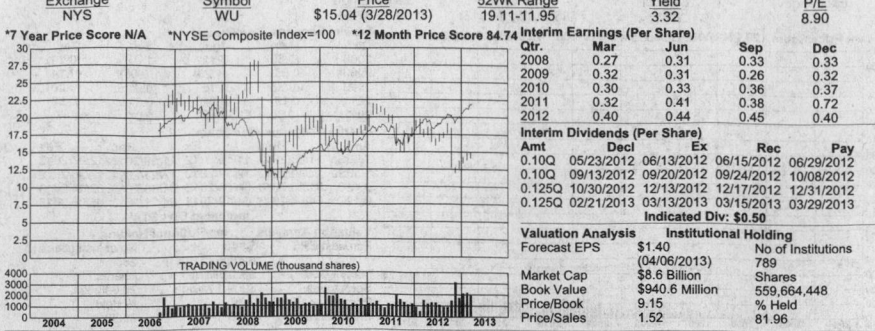

Interim Earnings (Per Share)

Qtr.	Mar	Jun	Sep	Dec
2008	0.27	0.31	0.33	0.33
2009	0.32	0.31	0.26	0.32
2010	0.30	0.33	0.36	0.37
2011	0.32	0.41	0.38	0.72
2012	0.40	0.44	0.45	0.40

Interim Dividends (Per Share)

Amt	Decl	Ex	Rec	Pay
0.10Q	05/23/2012	06/13/2012	06/15/2012	06/29/2012
0.10Q	09/13/2012	09/20/2012	09/24/2012	10/08/2012
0.125Q	10/30/2012	12/13/2012	12/17/2012	12/31/2012
0.125Q	02/21/2013	03/13/2013	03/15/2013	03/29/2013

Indicated Div: $0.50

Valuation Analysis

		Institutional Holding	
Forecast EPS	$1.40 (04/06/2013)	No of Institutions	789
Market Cap	$8.6 Billion	Shares	559,664,448
Book Value	$940.6 Million	% Held	81.96
Price/Book	9.15		
Price/Sales	1.52		

Business Summary: Business Services (MIC: 7.5.2 SIC: 7389 NAIC: 522320)

Western Union is a holding company. Through its subsidiaries, Co. is a provider of money transfer and payment services. Co. operates two segments: consumer-to-consumer, which provides money transfer services through a global network of third-party agents using Co.'s multi-currency, real-time money transfer processing systems; and global business payments, which processes payments from consumers or businesses to other businesses, allowing consumers to make payments to various organizations including utilities, auto finance companies, mortgage servicers, and government agencies. Co.'s other businesses include its money orders, which are sold in the U. S. and Canada, and its prepaid services.

Recent Developments: For the year ended Dec 31 2012, net income decreased 12.0% to US$1.03 billion from US$1.17 billion in the prior year. Revenues were US$5.66 billion, up 3.2% from US$5.49 billion the year before. Operating income was US$1.33 billion versus US$1.39 billion in the prior year, a decrease of 4.0%. Direct operating expenses rose 3.0% to US$3.19 billion from US$3.10 billion in the comparable period the year before. Indirect operating expenses increased 13.6% to US$1.14 billion from US$1.00 billion in the equivalent prior-year period.

Prospects: Our evaluation of Western Union Co as of Apr. 7, 2013 is the result of our systematic analysis on three basic characteristics: earnings strength, relative valuation, and recent stock price movement. The company has generated a negative trend in earnings per share over the past 5 quarters and while recent estimates for the company have remained steady, WU has posted better than expected results. Based on operating earnings yield, the company is undervalued when compared to all of the companies in our coverage universe. Share price changes over the past year indicates that WU will perform very poorly over the near term.

Financial Data

(US$ in Thousands)	12/31/2012	12/31/2011	12/31/2010	12/31/2009	12/31/2008	12/31/2007	12/31/2006	12/31/2005
Earnings Per Share	1.69	1.84	1.36	1.21	1.24	1.11	1.19	...
Cash Flow Per Share	1.95	1.86	1.49	1.74	1.71	1.45	1.45	...
Tang Book Value Per Share	N.M.	N.M.	N.M.	N.M.	...	N.M.	...	N.M.
Dividends Per Share	0.425	0.310	0.250	0.060	0.040	0.040	0.010	...
Dividend Payout %	25.15	16.85	18.38	4.96	3.23	3.60	0.84	...
Income Statement								
Total Revenue	5,664,800	5,491,400	5,192,700	5,083,600	5,282,000	4,900,200	4,470,200	3,987,900
EBITDA	1,404,600	1,512,300	1,373,800	1,335,900	1,426,400	1,381,100	1,387,600	1,351,800
Depn & Amortn	61,700	61,000	61,500	55,900	61,700	49,100	34,800	32,000
Income Before Taxes	1,168,800	1,274,600	1,145,200	1,131,500	1,238,700	1,222,400	1,335,100	1,344,100
Income Taxes	142,900	109,200	235,300	282,700	319,700	365,100	421,100	416,700
Net Income	1,025,900	1,165,400	909,900	848,800	919,000	857,300	914,000	927,400
Average Shares	607,400	634,200	668,900	701,000	738,200	772,900	768,600	...
Balance Sheet								
Current Assets	1,849,000	1,443,800	2,245,400	1,774,400	1,663,400	1,857,900	1,518,200	1,488,300
Total Assets	9,465,700	9,069,900	7,929,200	7,353,400	5,578,300	5,784,200	5,321,100	4,606,400
Current Liabilities	1,157,100	1,557,700	1,900,500	1,334,500	1,679,700	1,805,800	1,240,500	573,800
Long-Term Obligations	4,029,200	3,286,200	2,593,600	3,048,500	2,560,600	2,499,800	2,995,900	163,500
Total Liabilities	8,525,100	8,175,100	7,346,500	6,999,900	5,586,400	5,733,500	5,635,900	1,794,600
Stockholders' Equity	940,600	894,800	582,700	353,500	(8,100)	50,700	(314,800)	2,811,800
Shares Outstanding	572,100	619,400	654,000	686,500	709,600	749,800	771,100	100.00
Statistical Record								
Return on Assets %	11.04	13.71	11.91	13.13	16.13	15.44	18.41	23.37
Return on Equity %	111.48	157.75	194.38	491.49	4,302.77	...	73.21	39.08
EBITDA Margin %	24.80	27.54	26.46	26.28	27.00	28.18	31.04	33.90
Net Margin %	18.11	21.22	17.52	16.70	17.40	17.50	20.45	23.26
Asset Turnover	0.61	0.65	0.68	0.79	0.93	0.88	0.90	1.00
Current Ratio	1.60	0.93	1.18	1.33	0.99	1.03	1.22	2.59
Debt to Equity	4.28	3.67	4.45	8.62	...	49.31	...	0.06
Price Range	19.73-11.95	21.99-14.89	21.13-14.90	20.56-10.43	28.35-10.87	24.72-18.36	24.12-17.35	...
P/E Ratio	11.67-7.07	11.95-8.09	14.80-10.96	16.99-8.62	22.86-8.77	22.27-16.54	20.27-14.58	...
Average Yield %	2.52	1.64	1.46	0.36	0.19	0.19	0.05	...

Address: 12500 East Belford Avenue, Englewood, CO 80112	Web Site: www.westernunion.com	Auditors: Ernst & Young LLP
Telephone: 866-405-5012	Officers: Hikmet Ersek - President, Chief Executive Officer Rajesh K. Agrawal - Executive Vice President	Transfer Agents: Wells Fargo Bank, National Association, South St. Paul, MN

WESTLAKE CHEMICAL CORP

Exchange	Symbol	Price	52Wk Range	Yield	P/E
NYS	WLK	$93.50 (3/28/2013)	97.21-48.68	0.80	16.26

*7 Year Price Score 178.35 *NYSE Composite Index=100 ***12 Month Price Score 116.87**

TRADING VOLUME (thousand shares)

Interim Earnings (Per Share)

Qtr.	Mar	Jun	Sep	Dec
2008	0.08	0.72	0.42	(1.68)
2009	(0.09)	0.26	0.45	0.19
2010	0.27	0.86	0.95	1.27
2011	1.25	1.21	1.01	0.39
2012	1.31	1.72	1.30	1.42

Interim Dividends (Per Share)

Amt	Decl	Ex	Rec	Pay
0.188Q	08/20/2012	08/28/2012	08/30/2012	09/12/2012
3.75Sp	11/19/2012	11/27/2012	11/29/2012	12/12/2012
0.188Q	11/19/2012	11/27/2012	11/29/2012	12/12/2012
0.188Q	02/15/2013	02/27/2013	03/01/2013	03/15/2013

Indicated Div: $0.75

Valuation Analysis | **Institutional Holding**

Forecast EPS $6.20	No of Institutions
(04/05/2013)	215
Market Cap $6.3 Billion	Shares
Book Value $1.9 Billion	23,942,516
Price/Book 3.34	% Held
Price/Sales 1.75	35.04

Business Summary: Specialty Chemicals (MIC: 8.3.2 SIC: 2869 NAIC: 325211)

Westlake Chemical is a manufacturer and marketer of basic chemicals, vinyls, polymers and fabricated building products. Co.'s products include chemicals, which are used in consumer and industrial markets, including residential and commercial construction. Co. operates in two business segments: Olefins and Vinyls. The Olefins segment manufactures and markets ethylene, polyethylene, styrene monomer and various ethylene co-products. The Vinyls segment manufactures and markets polyvinyl chloride (PVC), vinyl chloride monomer, chlorine, caustic soda and ethylene. Co. also manufactures and sells products fabricated from PVC that it produces, including pipe, window and door profiles and fence.

Recent Developments: For the year ended Dec 31 2012, net income increased 48.9% to US$385.6 million from US$259.0 million in the prior year. Revenues were US$3.57 billion, down 1.3% from US$3.62 billion the year before. Operating income was US$615.4 million versus US$446.8 million in the prior year, an increase of 37.7%. Direct operating expenses declined 7.4% to US$2.83 billion from US$3.06 billion in the comparable period the year before. Indirect operating expenses increased 8.4% to US$121.6 million from US$112.2 million in the equivalent prior-year period.

Prospects: Our evaluation of Westlake Chemical Corp. as of Apr. 7, 2013 is the result of our systematic analysis on three basic characteristics: earnings strength, relative valuation, and recent stock price movement. The company has generated a negative trend in earnings per share over the past 5 quarters and while recent estimates for the company have been raised by analysts, WLK has posted better than expected results. Based on operating earnings yield, the company is undervalued when compared to all of the companies in our coverage universe. Share price changes over the past year indicates that WLK will perform very well over the near term.

Financial Data

(US$ in Thousands)	12/31/2012	12/31/2011	12/31/2010	12/31/2009	12/31/2008	12/31/2007	12/31/2006	12/31/2005
Earnings Per Share	5.75	3.87	3.34	0.80	(0.45)	1.76	2.98	3.48
Cash Flow Per Share	9.39	5.50	4.28	3.57	2.84	0.95	3.64	4.90
Tang Book Value Per Share	27.26	25.66	21.93	18.62	17.94	18.66	16.83	15.00
Dividends Per Share	4.273	0.275	0.242	0.220	0.205	0.180	0.135	0.098
Dividend Payout %	74.30	7.09	7.25	27.50	...	10.23	4.53	2.80
Income Statement								
Total Revenue	3,571,041	3,619,848	3,171,787	2,325,723	3,692,353	3,192,178	2,484,366	2,441,105
EBITDA	743,688	556,937	484,857	208,843	63,891	257,112	362,107	433,764
Depn & Amortn	120,924	110,268	105,744	100,333	93,137	85,421	74,879	69,130
Income Before Taxes	583,725	398,542	340,748	74,935	(58,643)	156,161	280,783	345,234
Income Taxes	199,614	142,466	121,567	25,758	(28,479)	44,228	87,990	118,511
Net Income	385,555	258,966	221,393	52,995	(29,543)	114,729	194,559	226,817
Average Shares	66,641	66,300	66,342	66,012	65,316	65,324	65,254	65,251
Balance Sheet								
Current Assets	1,751,413	1,756,156	1,475,960	988,378	798,989	1,092,185	849,787	902,863
Total Assets	3,412,196	3,266,821	2,954,144	2,446,356	2,286,989	2,569,335	2,082,098	1,827,189
Current Liabilities	398,510	364,595	323,578	286,566	212,288	441,262	321,912	305,849
Long-Term Obligations	763,761	764,563	764,482	515,400	510,319	511,414	260,156	265,689
Total Liabilities	1,539,940	1,510,509	1,449,074	1,161,374	1,047,929	1,282,665	908,557	833,083
Stockholders' Equity	1,872,256	1,756,312	1,505,070	1,284,982	1,239,060	1,286,670	1,173,541	994,106
Shares Outstanding	66,902	66,532	66,256	65,979	65,658	65,487	65,268	65,121
Statistical Record								
Return on Assets %	11.51	8.33	8.20	2.24	N.M.	4.93	9.95	13.27
Return on Equity %	21.19	15.88	15.87	4.20	N.M.	9.33	17.95	25.72
EBITDA Margin %	20.83	15.39	15.29	8.98	1.73	8.05	14.58	17.77
Net Margin %	10.80	7.15	6.98	2.28	N.M.	3.59	7.83	9.29
Asset Turnover	1.07	1.16	1.17	0.98	1.52	1.37	1.27	1.43
Current Ratio	4.39	4.82	4.56	3.45	3.76	2.48	2.64	2.95
Debt to Equity	0.41	0.44	0.51	0.40	0.41	0.40	0.22	0.27
Price Range	80.09-40.86	66.18-32.31	43.59-17.56	28.18-10.40	21.94-12.45	37.11-18.50	36.75-26.38	37.03-22.29
P/E Ratio	13.93-7.11	17.10-8.35	13.05-5.26	35.23-13.00	...	21.09-10.51	12.33-8.85	10.64-6.41
Average Yield %	6.67	0.59	0.89	1.05	1.21	0.67	0.43	0.33

Address: 2801 Post Oak Boulevard, Suite 600, Houston, TX 77056 **Telephone:** 713-960-9111	**Web Site:** www.westlake.com **Officers:** James Chao - Chairman Albert Chao - President, Chief Executive Officer	**Auditors:** PricewaterhouseCoopers LLP **Investor Contact:** 713-585-2643 **Transfer Agents:** American Stock Transfer & Trust Company, Brooklyn, N

823

WESTWOOD HOLDINGS GROUP, INC.

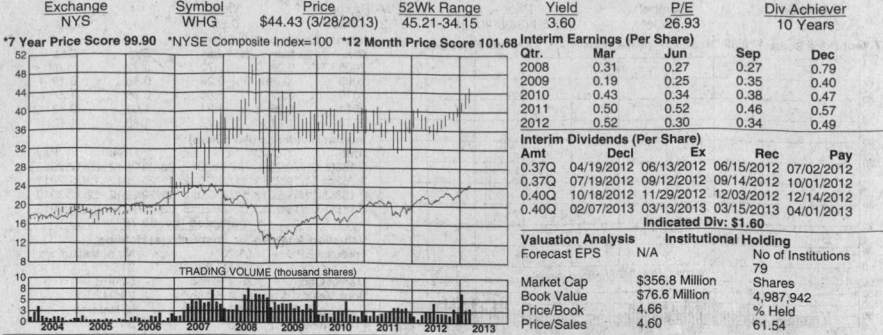

Exchange	Symbol	Price	52Wk Range	Yield	P/E	Div Achiever
NYS	WHG	$44.43 (3/28/2013)	45.21-34.15	3.60	26.93	10 Years

*7 Year Price Score 99.90   *NYSE Composite Index=100   *12 Month Price Score 101.68

Interim Earnings (Per Share)

Qtr.	Mar	Jun	Sep	Dec
2008	0.31	0.27	0.27	0.79
2009	0.19	0.25	0.35	0.40
2010	0.43	0.34	0.38	0.47
2011	0.50	0.52	0.46	0.57
2012	0.52	0.30	0.34	0.49

Interim Dividends (Per Share)

Amt	Decl	Ex	Rec	Pay
0.37Q	04/19/2012	06/13/2012	06/15/2012	07/02/2012
0.37Q	07/19/2012	09/12/2012	09/14/2012	10/01/2012
0.40Q	10/18/2012	11/29/2012	12/03/2012	12/14/2012
0.40Q	02/07/2013	03/13/2013	03/15/2013	04/01/2013

Indicated Div: $1.60

Valuation Analysis

Forecast EPS: N/A

Market Cap	$356.8 Million
Book Value	$76.6 Million
Price/Book	4.66
Price/Sales	4.60

Institutional Holding

No of Institutions: 79

Shares: 4,987,942

% Held: 61.54

TRADING VOLUME (thousand shares)

Business Summary: Wealth Management (MIC: 5.5.2 SIC: 6282 NAIC: 523930)

Westwood Holdings Group is a holding company. Through its subsidiary, Westwood Management Corp. (Westwood Management), Co. provides investment advisory services to corporate retirement plans, public retirement plans, endowments and foundations, a family of mutual funds called the Westwood Funds®, other mutual funds, individuals and clients of Co.'s other subsidiary, Westwood Trust. Westwood Trust provides trust and custodial services and participation in self-sponsored common trust funds to institutions and individuals. As of Dec 31 2011, Westwood Management and Westwood Trust collectively managed assets valued at approximately $13.10 billion.

Recent Developments: For the year ended Dec 31 2012, net income decreased 17.7% to US$12.1 million from US$14.7 million in the prior year. Revenues were US$77.5 million, up 12.5% from US$68.9 million the year before. Indirect operating expenses increased 25.5% to US$57.5 million from US$45.8 million in the equivalent prior-year period.

Prospects: Our evaluation of Westwood Holdings Group Inc. as of Apr. 7, 2013 is the result of our systematic analysis on three basic characteristics: earnings strength, relative valuation, and recent stock price movement. The company has enjoyed a very positive trend in earnings per share over the past 5 quarters. Because the company lacks sufficient analyst estimate data, we place greater weight on the historical EPS trend as the measure of earnings strength. Based on operating earnings yield, the company is about fairly valued when compared to all of the companies in our coverage universe. Share price changes over the past year indicates that WHG will perform well over the near term.

Financial Data
(US$ in Thousands)

	12/31/2012	12/31/2011	12/31/2010	12/31/2009	12/31/2008	12/31/2007	12/31/2006	12/31/2005
Earnings Per Share	1.65	2.04	1.58	1.18	1.63	1.28	0.79	0.66
Cash Flow Per Share	1.92	2.66	2.77	1.67	(1.03)	2.00	1.29	1.15
Tang Book Value Per Share	7.61	7.12	5.79	5.91	5.24	3.97	3.08	3.22
Dividends Per Share	1.510	1.420	1.650	1.230	1.200	1.150	1.330	1.090
Dividend Payout %	91.52	69.61	104.43	104.24	73.62	89.84	168.35	165.15
Income Statement								
Total Revenue	77,495	68,909	55,313	42,553	46,456	36,292	27,364	21,940
EBITDA	20,847	23,871	18,150	12,572	16,767	17,751	12,020	8,429
Depn & Amortn	821	762	429	254	232	5,544	4,766	2,386
Income Before Taxes	20,026	23,109	17,721	12,318	16,535	12,207	7,254	6,043
Income Taxes	7,936	8,423	6,441	4,423	5,992	4,263	2,785	2,407
Net Income	12,090	14,686	11,280	7,895	10,543	7,944	4,508	3,636
Average Shares	7,338	7,208	6,795	6,664	6,451	6,199	5,690	5,540
Balance Sheet								
Current Assets	77,370	72,482	55,882	54,343	46,769	35,466	24,953	22,637
Total Assets	96,615	90,597	72,628	59,886	50,847	39,024	28,722	27,310
Current Liabilities	18,826	17,523	11,744	11,361	11,612	9,090	5,274	4,935
Total Liabilities	20,064	19,840	11,951	12,668	12,053	9,678	5,987	5,751
Stockholders' Equity	76,551	70,757	60,677	47,218	38,794	29,346	22,735	21,559
Shares Outstanding	8,031	7,707	7,645	7,151	6,958	6,807	6,638	5,986
Statistical Record								
Return on Assets %	12.88	17.99	17.02	14.26	23.40	23.45	16.09	13.57
Return on Equity %	16.37	22.35	20.91	18.36	30.86	30.51	20.35	16.82
EBITDA Margin %	26.90	34.64	32.81	29.54	36.09	48.91	43.93	38.42
Net Margin %	15.60	21.31	20.39	18.55	22.69	21.89	16.47	16.57
Asset Turnover	0.83	0.84	0.83	0.77	1.03	1.07	0.98	0.82
Current Ratio	4.11	4.14	4.76	4.78	4.03	3.90	4.73	4.59
Price Range	40.92-34.15	40.91-31.11	40.62-28.98	44.19-24.90	51.65-23.82	39.80-22.50	26.02-18.05	19.88-16.00
P/E Ratio	24.80-20.70	20.05-15.25	25.71-18.34	37.45-21.10	31.69-14.61	31.09-17.58	32.94-22.85	30.12-24.24
Average Yield %	3.98	3.87	4.52	3.31	3.12	3.90	6.72	5.91

Address: 200 Crescent Court, Suite 1200, Dallas, TX 75201 **Telephone:** 214-756-6900	**Web Site:** www.westwoodgroup.com **Officers:** Susan M. Byrne - Chairman, Chief Investment Officer Brian O. Casey - President, Chief Executive Officer, Secretary	**Auditors:** Grant Thornton LLP **Investor Contact:** 214-756-6900 **Transfer Agents:** American Stock Transfer & Trust Company, New York, NY

WEX INC

Exchange	Symbol	Price	52Wk Range	Yield	P/E
NYS	WXS	$78.50 (3/28/2013)	79.91-53.29	N/A	31.65

*7 Year Price Score 156.54 *NYSE Composite Index=100 ***12 Month Price Score 102.64**

Interim Earnings (Per Share)

Qtr.	Mar	Jun	Sep	Dec
2008	0.36	(0.63)	1.82	1.65
2009	0.28	2.36	0.60	0.30
2010	0.48	0.77	0.53	0.48
2011	0.31	1.04	1.23	0.84
2012	0.59	0.78	0.37	0.74

Interim Dividends (Per Share)

No Dividends Paid

Valuation Analysis / Institutional Holding

Valuation Analysis		Institutional Holding	
Forecast EPS	$4.43	No of Institutions	
	(04/05/2013)	266	
Market Cap	$3.1 Billion	Shares	
Book Value	$817.9 Million	44,215,564	
Price/Book	3.73	% Held	
Price/Sales	4.90	N/A	

Business Summary: Miscellaneous Consumer Services (MIC: 2.2.3 SIC: 7389 NAIC: 561499)

Wex is a provider of business payment processing and information management products and services to businesses in North America, Asia Pacific and Europe. Co. is organized under two segments: Fleet Payment Solutions, which provides customers with fleet vehicle payment processing services designed for the needs of commercial and government fleets; and Other Payment Solutions, which provides customers with payment processing services for their corporate purchasing and transaction monitoring needs through Co.'s corporate purchase card, its prepaid and gift card products and services in Australia and through its payroll prepaid card product and services in the U.S.

Recent Developments: For the year ended Dec 31 2012, net income decreased 27.6% to US$96.7 million from US$133.6 million in the prior year. Revenues were US$623.2 million, up 12.7% from US$553.1 million the year before. Operating income was US$221.6 million versus US$233.3 million in the prior year, a decrease of 5.0%. Indirect operating expenses increased 25.6% to US$401.5 million from US$319.8 million in the equivalent prior-year period.

Prospects: Our evaluation of Wex Inc. as of Apr. 7, 2013 is the result of our systematic analysis on three basic characteristics: earnings strength, relative valuation, and recent stock price movement. The company has produced a positive trend in earnings per share over the past 5 quarters and while recent estimates for the company have remained steady, WXS has posted better than expected results. Based on operating earnings yield, the company is about fairly valued when compared to all of the companies in our coverage universe. Share price changes over the past year indicates that WXS will perform well over the near term.

Financial Data

(US$ in Thousands)	12/31/2012	12/31/2011	12/31/2010	12/31/2009	12/31/2008	12/31/2007	12/31/2006	12/31/2005
Earnings Per Share	2.48	3.43	2.25	3.55	3.22	1.27	1.81	0.46
Cash Flow Per Share	1.84	1.32	(0.27)	(0.87)	8.70	(2.30)	1.50	(1.02)
Tang Book Value Per Share	N.M.	1.29	N.M.	2.39	N.M.	N.M.	N.M.	N.M.
Income Statement								
Total Revenue	623,151	553,076	390,406	318,224	393,582	336,128	291,247	241,333
EBITDA	260,025	259,427	181,956	261,077	251,346	198,312	151,972	53,492
Depn & Amortn	48,852	45,369	31,504	22,559	20,588	1,089	12,081	11,100
Income Before Taxes	206,183	208,605	145,082	225,244	195,765	163,137	116,476	27,873
Income Taxes	109,474	74,983	57,453	85,585	68,125	111,560	41,867	9,220
Net Income	96,922	133,622	87,629	139,639	127,640	51,577	74,609	18,653
Average Shares	39,092	38,998	39,052	39,364	39,787	40,751	41,553	40,735
Balance Sheet								
Current Assets	1,753,476	1,357,871	1,178,527	889,608	942,539	1,116,612	837,225	700,426
Total Assets	3,106,684	2,278,060	2,097,951	1,499,662	1,611,855	1,785,076	1,551,015	1,420,421
Current Liabilities	1,537,266	1,164,518	1,013,910	810,778	824,144	1,005,763	784,075	653,856
Long-Term Obligations	621,000	295,300	407,300	128,000	170,600	199,400	149,760	220,508
Total Liabilities	2,288,753	1,568,745	1,538,944	1,058,346	1,317,193	1,580,817	1,367,888	1,345,682
Stockholders' Equity	817,931	709,315	559,007	441,316	294,662	204,259	183,127	74,739
Shares Outstanding	38,908	38,765	38,437	38,196	38,244	39,625	40,430	40,210
Statistical Record								
Return on Assets %	3.59	6.11	4.87	8.98	7.49	3.09	5.02	1.67
Return on Equity %	12.66	21.07	17.52	37.95	51.03	26.63	57.87	10.39
EBITDA Margin %	41.73	46.91	46.61	82.04	63.86	59.00	52.18	22.17
Net Margin %	15.55	24.16	22.45	43.89	32.43	15.34	25.62	7.73
Asset Turnover	0.23	0.25	0.22	0.20	0.23	0.20	0.20	0.22
Current Ratio	1.14	1.17	1.16	1.10	1.14	1.11	1.07	1.07
Debt to Equity	0.76	0.42	0.73	0.29	0.58	0.98	0.82	2.95
Price Range	75.37-53.29	57.05-36.36	46.39-27.98	32.60-11.20	35.49-8.59	40.82-27.57	32.19-23.20	24.36-15.51
P/E Ratio	30.39-21.49	16.63-10.60	20.62-12.44	9.18-3.15	11.02-2.67	32.14-21.71	17.78-12.82	52.96-33.72

Address: 97 Darling Avenue, South Portland, ME 04106 Telephone: 207-773-8171	Web Site: www.wrightexpress.com Officers: Michael E. Dubyak - President, Chief Executive Officer Robert C. Cornett - Senior Vice President, Chief People Officer	Auditors: Deloitte & Touche LLP Investor Contact: 800-230-1633 Transfer Agents: Wilmer Cutler Pickering Hale and Dorr LLP

WEYERHAEUSER CO.

Exchange	Symbol	Price	52Wk Range	Yield	P/E
NYS	WY	$31.38 (3/28/2013)	31.50-18.69	2.17	44.20

*7 Year Price Score 53.91 *NYSE Composite Index=100 *12 Month Price Score 108.87

Interim Earnings (Per Share)

Qtr.	Mar	Jun	Sep	Dec
2008	(0.70)	(0.45)	1.33	(5.74)
2009	(1.25)	(0.50)	0.00	(0.83)
2010	(0.10)	0.07	3.50	(0.49)
2011	0.18	0.02	0.29	0.12
2012	0.08	0.16	0.22	0.26

Interim Dividends (Per Share)

Amt	Decl	Ex	Rec	Pay
0.15Q	04/12/2012	05/09/2012	05/11/2012	06/01/2012
0.15Q	08/09/2012	08/28/2012	08/30/2012	09/14/2012
0.17Q	10/11/2012	11/07/2012	11/09/2012	11/30/2012
0.17Q	02/14/2013	02/27/2013	03/01/2013	03/15/2013

Indicated Div: $0.68

Valuation Analysis

		Institutional Holding	
Forecast EPS	$1.06 (04/05/2013)	No of Institutions	702
Market Cap	$17.0 Billion	Shares	473,067,776
Book Value	$4.1 Billion	% Held	80.47
Price/Book	4.18		
Price/Sales	2.41		

Business Summary: REITs (MIC: 5.3.1 SIC: 6798 NAIC: 525930)

Weyerhaeuser is a real estate investment trust. Co.'s segments are: Timberlands, which include logs, timber, minerals, oil and gas and international wood products; Wood Products, which include softwood lumber, engineered lumber, structural panels and building materials distribution; Cellulose Fibers, which include pulp, liquid packaging board and an equity interest in a newsprint joint venture; and Real Estate, which includes real estate development and single-family home building operations. As of Dec 31 2012, Co.'s Timberlands business segment managed 6.3 million acres of private commercial forestland worldwide and had licenses on 13.9 million acres of forestland located Canada.

Recent Developments: For the year ended Dec 31 2012, income from continuing operations increased 20.4% to US$384.0 million from US$319.0 million a year earlier. Net income increased 16.0% to US$384.0 million from US$331.0 million in the prior year. Revenues were US$7.06 billion, up 13.6% from US$6.22 billion the year before. Operating income was US$735.0 million versus US$594.0 million in the prior year, an increase of 23.7%. Direct operating expenses rose 13.5% to US$5.81 billion from US$5.12 billion in the comparable period the year before. Indirect operating expenses increased 2.4% to US$514.0 million from US$502.0 million in the equivalent prior-year period.

Prospects: Our evaluation of Weyerhaeuser Co. as of Apr. 7, 2013 is the result of our systematic analysis on three basic characteristics: earnings strength, relative valuation, and recent stock price movement. The company has enjoyed a very positive trend in earnings per share over the past 5 quarters and while recent estimates for the company have been raised by analysts, WY has posted better than expected results. Based on operating earnings yield, the company is overvalued when compared to all of the companies in our coverage universe. Share price changes over the past year indicates that WY will perform well over the near term.

Financial Data
(US$ in Thousands)

	12/31/2012	12/31/2011	12/31/2010	12/31/2009	12/31/2008	12/30/2007	12/31/2006	12/25/2005
Earnings Per Share	0.71	0.61	3.99	(2.58)	(5.57)	3.59	1.84	2.98
Cash Flow Per Share	1.07	0.54	2.33	(0.77)	(6.28)	2.89	6.46	7.17
Tang Book Value Per Share	7.43	7.87	8.53	18.94	22.58	27.35	28.91	27.81
Dividends Per Share	0.620	0.600	26.663	0.600	2.400	2.400	2.200	1.900
Dividend Payout %	87.32	98.36	668.26	...	...	66.85	119.57	63.76
Income Statement								
Total Revenue	7,059,000	6,216,000	6,552,000	5,528,000	8,018,000	16,308,000	21,896,000	22,629,000
EBITDA	1,191,000	1,074,000	968,000	88,000	(1,756,000)	1,347,000	2,492,000	2,785,000
Depn & Amortn	456,000	480,000	503,000	508,000	541,000	859,000	1,200,000	1,200,000
Income Before Taxes	439,000	257,000	96,000	(854,000)	(2,743,000)	32,000	761,000	855,000
Income Taxes	55,000	(62,000)	(1,187,000)	(274,000)	(888,000)	8,000	471,000	324,000
Net Income	385,000	331,000	1,281,000	(545,000)	(1,176,000)	790,000	453,000	733,000
Average Shares	542,310	539,879	321,096	211,342	211,258	220,277	245,707	245,559
Balance Sheet								
Current Assets	2,140,000	2,068,000	2,590,000	3,674,000	4,139,000	3,035,000	4,141,000	5,162,000
Total Assets	12,592,000	12,598,000	13,429,000	15,250,000	16,735,000	23,806,000	26,862,000	28,229,000
Current Liabilities	1,230,000	941,000	1,074,000	955,000	1,812,000	2,607,000	3,129,000	3,255,000
Long-Term Obligations	3,951,000	4,466,000	5,060,000	5,683,000	5,609,000	6,834,000	7,675,000	8,262,000
Total Liabilities	8,522,000	8,335,000	8,817,000	11,206,000	11,921,000	15,825,000	17,777,000	18,429,000
Stockholders' Equity	4,070,000	4,263,000	4,612,000	4,044,000	4,814,000	7,981,000	9,085,000	9,800,000
Shares Outstanding	542,392	536,425	535,975	211,358	211,289	211,146	238,008	245,183
Statistical Record								
Return on Assets %	3.05	2.54	8.93	N.M.	N.M.	3.13	1.62	2.53
Return on Equity %	9.22	7.46	29.60	N.M.	N.M.	9.28	4.72	7.71
EBITDA Margin %	16.87	17.28	14.77	1.59	N.M.	8.26	11.38	12.31
Net Margin %	5.45	5.32	19.55	N.M.	N.M.	4.84	2.07	3.24
Asset Turnover	0.56	0.48	0.46	0.35	0.39	0.65	0.78	0.78
Current Ratio	1.74	2.20	2.41	3.85	2.28	1.16	1.32	1.59
Debt to Equity	0.97	1.05	1.10	1.41	1.17	0.86	0.84	0.84
Price Range	28.52-18.69	25.20-15.25	53.30-15.23	44.15-19.36	73.74-28.94	86.20-62.97	75.09-55.35	71.52-61.12
P/E Ratio	40.17-26.32	41.31-25.00	13.36-3.82	...	...	24.01-17.54	40.81-30.08	24.00-20.51
Average Yield %	2.67	2.98	86.30	1.78	4.43	3.18	3.37	2.89

Address: 33663 Weyerhaeuser Way South, Federal Way, WA 98063-9777	Web Site: www.weyerhaeuser.com	Auditors: KPMG LLP
Telephone: 253-924-2345	Officers: Charles R. Williamson - Chairman Daniel S. Fulton - President, Chief Executive Officer	Transfer Agents: BNY Mellon Shareowner Services, Jersey City, NJ

WGL HOLDINGS, INC.

Exchange	Symbol	Price	52Wk Range	Yield	P/E	Div Achiever
NYS	WGL	$44.10 (3/28/2013)	44.17-36.85	3.81	16.09	36 Years

*7 Year Price Score 101.04 *NYSE Composite Index=100 *12 Month Price Score 97.71

Interim Earnings (Per Share)

Qtr.	Dec	Mar	Jun	Sep
2009-10	0.94	1.56	0.19	(0.53)
2010-11	1.28	1.55	0.06	(0.60)
2011-12	0.98	1.44	0.14	0.15
2012-13	1.01	...	...	...

Interim Dividends (Per Share)

Amt	Decl	Ex	Rec	Pay
0.40Q	06/27/2012	07/06/2012	07/10/2012	08/01/2012
0.40Q	09/26/2012	10/05/2012	10/10/2012	11/01/2012
0.40Q	12/14/2012	01/08/2013	01/10/2013	02/01/2013
0.42Q	02/06/2013	04/08/2013	04/10/2013	05/01/2013

Indicated Div: $1.68 (Div. Reinv. Plan)

Valuation Analysis | **Institutional Holding**

Forecast EPS	$2.45 (04/05/2013)	No of Institutions	278
Market Cap	$2.3 Billion	Shares	39,228,896
Book Value	$1.3 Billion	% Held	61.60
Price/Book	1.71		
Price/Sales	0.96		

Business Summary: Gas Utilities (MIC: 3.3.1 SIC: 4924 NAIC: 221210)

WGL Holdings is a holding company. Through its subsidiaries, Co. operates in four segments, including: Regulated Utility, which delivers natural gas to retail customers and operates and owns full and partial interests in underground natural gas storage facilities; Retail Energy-Marketing, which sells natural gas and/or electricity directly to residential, commercial and industrial customers; Commercial Energy Systems, which provides commercial energy efficiency and sustainability solutions to governmental and commercial clients; and Wholesale Energy Solutions, which acquires, manages and optimizes natural gas storage and transportation assets.

Recent Developments: For the quarter ended Dec 31 2012, net income increased 3.8% to US$52.7 million from US$50.8 million in the year-earlier quarter. Revenues were US$686.7 million, down 5.6% from US$727.8 million the year before. Operating income was US$94.7 million versus US$93.9 million in the prior-year quarter, an increase of 0.9%. Direct operating expenses declined 7.4% to US$552.9 million from US$597.0 million in the comparable period the year before. Indirect operating expenses increased 6.2% to US$39.1 million from US$36.8 million in the equivalent prior-year period.

Prospects: Our evaluation of WGL Holdings Inc. as of Apr. 7, 2013 is the result of our systematic analysis on three basic characteristics: earnings strength, relative valuation, and recent stock price movement. The company has generated a negative trend in earnings per share over the past 5 quarters. However, while recent estimates for the company have been mixed, WGL has posted better than expected results. Based on operating earnings yield, the company is about fairly valued when compared to all of the companies in our coverage universe. Share price changes over the past year indicates that WGL will perform poorly over the near term.

Financial Data

(US$ in Thousands)	3 Mos	09/30/2012	09/30/2011	09/30/2010	09/30/2009	09/30/2008	09/30/2007	09/30/2006
Earnings Per Share	2.74	2.71	2.28	2.16	2.39	2.33	2.19	1.79
Cash Flow Per Share	5.40	4.21	5.78	5.76	6.13	1.25	4.34	1.76
Tang Book Value Per Share	25.76	24.60	23.41	22.63	21.89	20.99	19.89	18.86
Dividends Per Share	1.587	1.575	1.530	1.490	1.445	1.395	1.360	1.340
Dividend Payout %	57.94	58.12	67.11	68.98	60.46	59.87	62.10	74.86
Income Statement								
Total Revenue	686,736	2,425,310	2,751,501	2,708,876	2,706,856	2,628,194	2,646,008	2,637,883
EBITDA	95,528	504,621	493,870	446,089	456,096	433,953	420,184	396,445
Depn & Amortn	238	98,251	101,383	98,464	99,492	98,598	93,256	95,947
Income Before Taxes	86,097	369,942	351,941	307,558	311,701	288,558	278,060	252,194
Income Taxes	33,379	228,804	233,571	196,353	191,328	172,035	170,160	157,500
Net Income	52,718	141,138	118,370	111,205	120,373	116,523	107,900	87,578
Average Shares	51,688	51,589	51,295	50,765	50,382	49,912	49,377	48,905
Balance Sheet								
Current Assets	1,010,974	832,761	724,733	717,265	683,514	742,349	573,725	562,022
Total Assets	4,340,937	4,110,947	3,809,034	3,643,894	3,349,890	3,243,543	3,046,361	2,791,406
Current Liabilities	970,212	757,015	576,740	544,051	634,616	748,479	557,056	560,842
Long-Term Obligations	553,694	589,202	587,213	592,875	561,830	603,738	616,419	576,139
Total Liabilities	3,009,850	2,813,218	2,578,146	2,462,326	2,224,019	2,167,806	2,037,421	1,841,426
Stockholders' Equity	1,331,087	1,297,729	1,230,888	1,181,568	1,125,871	1,075,737	1,008,940	949,980
Shares Outstanding	51,668	51,611	51,365	50,974	50,143	49,916	49,316	48,878
Statistical Record								
Return on Assets %	3.37	3.55	3.18	3.18	3.65	3.69	3.70	3.25
Return on Equity %	11.03	11.13	9.81	9.64	10.94	11.15	11.02	9.36
EBITDA Margin %	13.91	20.81	17.95	16.47	16.85	16.51	15.88	15.03
Net Margin %	7.68	5.82	4.30	4.11	4.45	4.43	4.08	3.32
Asset Turnover	0.56	0.61	0.74	0.77	0.82	0.83	0.91	0.98
Current Ratio	1.04	1.10	1.26	1.32	1.08	0.99	1.03	1.00
Debt to Equity	0.42	0.45	0.48	0.50	0.50	0.56	0.61	0.61
Price Range	44.31-36.85	44.70-37.34	41.60-35.06	37.78-31.27	36.29-24.84	36.01-30.76	35.46-29.94	32.31-27.38
P/E Ratio	16.17-13.45	16.49-13.78	18.25-15.38	17.49-14.48	15.18-10.39	15.45-13.20	16.19-13.67	18.05-15.30
Average Yield %	3.96	3.86	4.01	4.35	4.55	4.18	4.17	4.47

Address: 101 Constitution Ave., N.W., Washington, DC 20080 Telephone: 703-750-2000	Web Site: www.wglholdings.com Officers: Terry D. McCallister - Chairman, Chief Executive Officer Adrian P. Chapman - President, Chief Operating Officer	Auditors: Deloitte & Touche LLP Investor Contact: 202-624-6129 Transfer Agents: BNY Mellon Shareowner Services, Pittsburgh, PA

WHIRLPOOL CORP

Exchange	Symbol	Price	52Wk Range	Yield	P/E
NYS	WHR	$118.46 (3/28/2013)	119.29-54.86	1.69	23.41

*7 Year Price Score 98.51   *NYSE Composite Index=100   *12 Month Price Score 121.44

Interim Earnings (Per Share)

Qtr.	Mar	Jun	Sep	Dec
2008	1.22	1.53	2.15	0.61
2009	0.91	1.04	1.15	1.24
2010	2.13	2.64	1.02	2.18
2011	2.17	(2.10)	2.27	2.62
2012	1.17	1.43	0.94	1.53

Interim Dividends (Per Share)

Amt	Decl	Ex	Rec	Pay
0.50Q	04/17/2012	05/16/2012	05/18/2012	06/15/2012
0.50Q	08/21/2012	08/29/2012	08/31/2012	09/15/2012
0.50Q	10/16/2012	11/14/2012	11/16/2012	12/15/2012
0.50Q	02/19/2013	02/27/2013	03/01/2013	03/15/2013
		Indicated Div: $2.00		

Valuation Analysis

		Institutional Holding	
Forecast EPS	$9.63 (04/05/2013)	No of Institutions	567
Market Cap	$9.3 Billion	Shares	83,628,216
Book Value	$4.3 Billion	% Held	96.04
Price/Book	2.18		
Price/Sales	0.51		

Business Summary: Household Appliances, Electronics & Goods (MIC: 1.5.1 SIC: 3639 NAIC: 335228)

Whirlpool is a manufacturer and marketer of home appliances. Co.'s principal products are laundry appliances, refrigerators and freezers, cooking appliances, dishwashers, mixers and other portable household appliances. Co. also produces hermetic compressors for refrigeration systems. Co. manufactures products in 11 countries and markets and markets products in nearly every country around the world under brand names such as Whirlpool, Maytag, KitchenAid, Jenn-Air, Amana, Bauknecht, Brastemp and Consul. Co.'s geographic segments consist of North America; Latin America; Europe, Middle East and Africa; and Asia.

Recent Developments: For the year ended Dec 31 2012, net income increased 4.2% to US$425.0 million from US$408.0 million in the prior year. Revenues were US$18.14 billion, down 2.8% from US$18.67 billion the year before. Operating income was US$869.0 million versus US$792.0 million in the prior year, an increase of 9.7%. Direct operating expenses declined 5.2% to US$15.25 billion from US$16.09 billion in the comparable period the year before. Indirect operating expenses increased 13.4% to US$2.02 billion from US$1.79 billion in the equivalent prior-year period.

Prospects: Our evaluation of Whirlpool Corp. as of Apr. 7, 2013 is the result of our systematic analysis on three basic characteristics: earnings strength, relative valuation, and recent stock price movement. The company has enjoyed a very positive trend in earnings per share over the past 5 quarters and while recent estimates for the company have been raised by analysts, WHR has posted better than expected results. Based on operating earnings yield, the company is undervalued when compared to all of the companies in our coverage universe. Share price changes over the past year indicates that WHR will perform very well over the near term.

Financial Data

(US$ in Thousands)	12/31/2012	12/31/2011	12/31/2010	12/31/2009	12/31/2008	12/31/2007	12/31/2006	12/31/2005
Earnings Per Share	5.06	4.99	7.97	4.34	5.50	8.01	5.67	6.19
Cash Flow Per Share	8.89	6.90	14.15	20.78	4.34	11.81	11.72	13.13
Tang Book Value Per Share	10.34	9.12	9.29	1.85	N.M.	3.91	N.M.	21.49
Dividends Per Share	2.000	1.930	1.720	1.720	1.720	1.720	1.720	1.720
Dividend Payout %	39.53	38.68	21.58	39.63	31.27	21.47	30.34	27.79
Income Statement								
Total Revenue	18,143,000	18,666,000	18,366,000	17,099,000	18,907,000	19,408,000	18,080,000	14,317,000
EBITDA	1,420,000	1,350,000	1,563,000	1,213,000	1,146,000	1,663,000	1,373,000	1,233,000
Depn & Amortn	551,000	558,000	555,000	525,000	597,000	593,000	550,000	441,000
Income Before Taxes	558,000	(28,000)	586,000	294,000	246,000	804,000	619,000	597,000
Income Taxes	133,000	(436,000)	(64,000)	(61,000)	(201,000)	117,000	126,000	171,000
Net Income	401,000	390,000	619,000	328,000	418,000	640,000	433,000	422,000
Average Shares	79,300	78,100	77,600	75,600	76,000	79,900	76,500	68,300
Balance Sheet								
Current Assets	6,827,000	6,422,000	7,315,000	7,025,000	6,044,000	6,555,000	6,476,000	4,710,000
Total Assets	15,396,000	15,181,000	15,584,000	15,094,000	13,532,000	14,009,000	13,878,000	8,248,000
Current Liabilities	6,510,000	6,297,000	6,149,000	5,941,000	5,563,000	5,893,000	6,002,000	4,301,000
Long-Term Obligations	1,944,000	2,129,000	2,195,000	2,502,000	2,002,000	1,668,000	1,798,000	745,000
Total Liabilities	11,136,000	11,000,000	11,358,000	11,430,000	10,526,000	10,098,000	10,595,000	6,503,000
Stockholders' Equity	4,260,000	4,181,000	4,226,000	3,664,000	3,006,000	3,911,000	3,283,000	1,745,000
Shares Outstanding	78,407	76,451	76,000	75,000	73,000	76,000	78,000	68,000
Statistical Record								
Return on Assets %	2.62	2.54	4.04	2.29	3.03	4.59	3.91	5.14
Return on Equity %	9.48	9.28	15.69	9.84	12.05	17.79	17.22	25.19
EBITDA Margin %	7.83	7.23	8.51	7.09	6.06	8.57	7.59	8.61
Net Margin %	2.21	2.09	3.37	1.92	2.21	3.30	2.39	2.95
Asset Turnover	1.18	1.21	1.20	1.19	1.37	1.39	1.63	1.74
Current Ratio	1.05	1.02	1.19	1.18	1.09	1.11	1.08	1.10
Debt to Equity	0.46	0.51	0.52	0.68	0.67	0.43	0.55	0.43
Price Range	102.73-48.51	91.28-45.37	112.42-71.62	83.65-19.39	93.90-30.92	116.85-73.86	95.95-75.00	85.65-61.13
P/E Ratio	20.30-9.59	18.29-9.09	14.11-8.99	19.27-4.47	17.07-5.62	14.59-9.22	16.92-13.23	13.84-9.88
Average Yield %	2.69	2.75	1.99	3.30	2.43	1.83	2.02	2.38

Address: 2000 North M-63, Benton Harbor, MI 49022-2692 Telephone: 269-923-5000	Web Site: www.whirlpoolcorp.com Officers: Jeff M. Fettig - Chairman, Chief Executive Officer Bracken P. Darrell - Executive Vice President, Region Officer	Auditors: Ernst & Young LLP Investor Contact: 269-923-2641 Transfer Agents: Computershare Trust Company, N.A, Providence, RI

WHITE MOUNTAINS INSURANCE GROUP, LTD.

Exchange	Symbol	Price	52Wk Range	Yield	P/E
NYS	WTM	$567.12 (3/28/2013)	579.31-495.05	0.18	18.59

*7 Year Price Score 109.01 *NYSE Composite Index=100 *12 Month Price Score 97.89

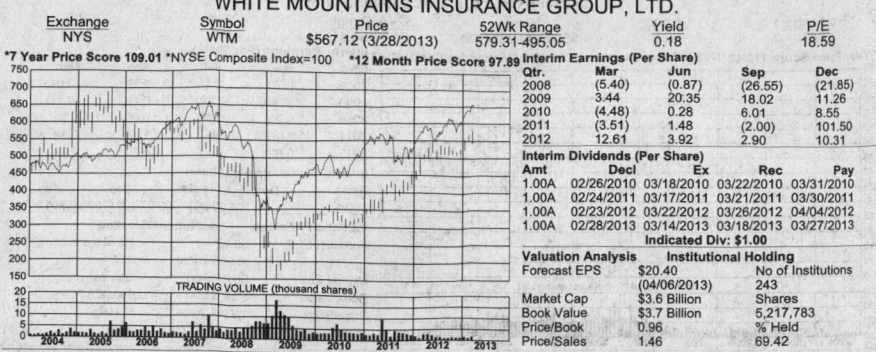

Interim Earnings (Per Share)

Qtr.	Mar	Jun	Sep	Dec
2008	(5.40)	(0.87)	(26.55)	(21.85)
2009	3.44	20.35	18.02	11.26
2010	(4.48)	0.28	6.01	8.55
2011	(3.51)	1.48	(2.00)	101.50
2012	12.61	3.92	2.90	10.31

Interim Dividends (Per Share)

Amt	Decl	Ex	Rec	Pay
1.00A	02/26/2010	03/18/2010	03/22/2010	03/31/2010
1.00A	02/24/2011	03/17/2011	03/21/2011	03/30/2011
1.00A	02/23/2012	03/22/2012	03/26/2012	04/04/2012
1.00A	02/28/2013	03/14/2013	03/18/2013	03/27/2013

Indicated Div: $1.00

Valuation Analysis / **Institutional Holding**

Forecast EPS	$20.40	No of Institutions
	(04/06/2013)	243
Market Cap	$3.6 Billion	Shares
Book Value	$3.7 Billion	5,217,783
Price/Book	0.96	% Held
Price/Sales	1.46	69.42

Business Summary: General Insurance (MIC: 5.2.1 SIC: 6331 NAIC: 524126)

White Mountains Insurance Group is a holding company. Through its property and casualty insurance and reinsurance subsidiaries, Co. operates three segments: OneBeacon, which owns a family of U.S. based property and casualty insurance companies; Sirius Group, which provides insurance and reinsurance products for property, accident and health, aviation and space, trade credit, marine, casualty, agriculture and certain other exposures on a worldwide basis; and Other Operations, which includes, among others, its investment management subsidiary, White Mountains Advisors LLC, and its variable annuity reinsurance business, White Mountains Life Reinsurance (Bermuda) Ltd.

Recent Developments: For the year ended Dec 31 2012, income from continuing operations increased 33.9% to US$278.5 million from US$208.0 million a year earlier. Net income decreased 76.1% to US$193.4 million from US$809.4 million in the prior year. Revenues were US$2.44 billion, up 12.1% from US$2.17 billion the year before. Net premiums earned were US$2.06 billion versus US$1.92 billion in the prior year, an increase of 7.2%.

Prospects: Our evaluation of White Mountains Insurance Group Ltd. as of Apr. 7, 2013 is the result of our systematic analysis on three basic characteristics: earnings strength, relative valuation, and recent stock price movement. The company has suffered a very negative trend in earnings per share over the past 5 quarters and while recent estimates for the company have remained steady, WTM has posted better than expected results. Based on operating earnings yield, the company is undervalued when compared to all of the companies in our coverage universe. Share price changes over the past year indicates that WTM will perform in line with the market over the near term.

Financial Data
(US$ in Thousands)

	12/31/2012	12/31/2011	12/31/2010	12/31/2009	12/31/2008	12/31/2007	12/31/2006	12/31/2005
Earnings Per Share	30.50	97.44	10.12	53.10	(54.54)	37.89	62.32	26.56
Cash Flow Per Share	(33.57)	(14.66)	6.63	(5.33)	8.73	33.01	8.87	(26.48)
Tang Book Value Per Share	593.20	539.43	445.76	412.79	329.08	446.62	413.19	355.61
Dividends Per Share	1.000	1.000	1.000	1.000	4.000	8.000	8.000	8.000
Dividend Payout %	3.28	1.03	9.88	1.88	...	21.11	12.84	30.12
Income Statement								
Premium Income	2,063,600	1,927,800	3,162,400	3,600,400	3,710,000	3,783,700	3,712,700	3,798,600
Total Revenue	2,435,700	2,178,100	3,571,100	4,448,100	2,955,700	4,733,800	4,794,200	4,631,900
Benefits & Claims	1,193,900	1,206,900	2,068,000	2,119,100	2,506,400	2,406,400	2,452,700	2,858,200
Income Before Taxes	262,800	61,600	150,500	764,000	(1,140,100)	681,500	729,800	293,000
Income Taxes	(15,700)	(122,700)	20,900	208,800	(498,700)	210,500	98,900	36,500
Net Income	207,400	767,900	86,500	470,000	(555,300)	407,400	673,200	290,100
Average Shares	6,708	7,811	8,549	8,764	10,183	10,751	10,803	10,794
Balance Sheet								
Total Assets	12,895,400	14,064,000	14,534,100	15,443,200	15,895,800	19,105,600	19,443,700	19,418,100
Total Liabilities	9,163,600	9,976,300	10,881,100	11,785,800	12,997,000	14,392,200	14,988,400	15,584,900
Stockholders' Equity	3,731,800	4,087,700	3,653,000	3,657,400	2,898,800	4,713,400	4,455,300	3,833,200
Shares Outstanding	6,290	7,577	8,194	8,860	8,808	10,553	10,782	10,779
Statistical Record								
Return on Assets %	1.53	5.37	0.58	3.00	N.M.	2.11	3.46	1.51
Return on Equity %	5.29	19.84	2.37	14.34	N.M.	8.89	16.24	7.52
Loss Ratio %	57.86	62.61	65.39	58.86	67.56	63.60	66.06	75.24
Net Margin %	8.52	35.26	2.42	10.57	(18.79)	8.61	14.04	6.26
Price Range	547.67-439.94	453.46-335.60	362.90-297.22	338.08-150.00	514.05-211.75	606.40-500.00	602.25-450.30	702.50-555.63
P/E Ratio	17.96-14.42	4.65-3.44	35.86-29.37	6.37-2.82	...	16.00-13.20	9.66-7.23	26.45-20.92
Average Yield %	0.20	0.25	0.30	0.39	0.95	1.44	1.54	1.28

Address: 14 Wesley Street, Hamilton, HM 12
Telephone: 441-278-3160

Web Site: www.whitemountains.com
Officers: Raymond Barrette - Chairman, Chief Executive Officer David T. Foy - Executive Vice President, Chief Financial Officer

Auditors: PricewaterhouseCoopers LLP
Investor Contact: 203-458-2380
Transfer Agents: Computershare Trust Company, N.A., Canton, MA, United States

WHITING PETROLEUM CORP

Exchange	Symbol	Price	52Wk Range	Yield	P/E
NYS	WLL	$50.84 (3/28/2013)	57.67-36.41	N/A	14.61

*7 Year Price Score 112.42 *NYSE Composite Index=100   *12 Month Price Score 98.43

TRADING VOLUME (thousand shares)

Interim Earnings (Per Share)

Qtr.	Mar	Jun	Sep	Dec
2008	0.73	0.95	1.33	(0.04)
2009	(0.46)	(0.92)	0.29	(0.11)
2010	0.73	1.06	0.06	0.55
2011	0.16	1.71	1.74	0.52
2012	0.83	1.27	0.70	0.69

Interim Dividends (Per Share)

Amt	Decl	Ex	Rec	Pay
100%	...	02/23/2011	02/07/2011	02/22/2011

Valuation Analysis

		Institutional Holding	
Forecast EPS	$3.79	No of Institutions	
	(04/06/2013)	477	
Market Cap	$6.0 Billion	Shares	
Book Value	$3.4 Billion	108,428,760	
Price/Book	1.74	% Held	
Price/Sales	2.75	86.80	

Business Summary: Production & Extraction (MIC: 9.1.1 SIC: 1311 NAIC: 211111)

Whiting Petroleum is an independent oil and gas company engaged in the acquisition, development, exploitation, production and exploration activities primarily in the Rocky Mountains, Permian Basin, Mid-Continent, Michigan and Gulf Coast regions of the U.S. Co. sells its oil and gas production to end users, marketers and other purchasers that have access to nearby pipeline facilities. In areas with no access to pipelines, oil is trucked to storage facilities. As of Dec 31 2011, Co. had estimated total proved reserves of 345.2 million barrels of oil equivalent, with 297.8 million barrels of oil or other liquid hydrocarbons and 284.98 billion cubic feet of natural gas.

Recent Developments: For the year ended Dec 31 2012, net income decreased 15.8% to US$414.1 million from US$491.6 million in the prior year. Revenues were US$2.17 billion, up 14.4% from US$1.90 billion the year before. Indirect operating expenses increased 35.0% to US$1.51 billion from US$1.12 billion in the equivalent prior-year period.

Prospects: Our evaluation of Whiting Petroleum Corp. as of Apr. 7, 2013 is the result of our systematic analysis on three basic characteristics: earnings strength, relative valuation, and recent stock price movement. The company has produced a positive trend in earnings per share over the past 5 quarters. However, while recent estimates for the company have been mixed, WLL has posted better than expected results. Based on operating earnings yield, the company is undervalued when compared to all of the companies in our coverage universe. Share price changes over the past year indicates that WLL will perform poorly over the near term.

Financial Data
(US$ in Thousands)

	12/31/2012	12/31/2011	12/31/2010	12/31/2009	12/31/2008	12/31/2007	12/31/2006	12/31/2005
Earnings Per Share	3.48	4.14	2.55	(1.18)	2.97	1.65	2.13	1.94
Cash Flow Per Share	11.88	10.16	9.38	4.35	8.99	4.99	5.60	5.27
Tang Book Value Per Share	29.29	25.74	21.62	22.32	21.24	17.55	16.06	13.54
Income Statement								
Total Revenue	2,173,452	1,899,622	1,516,099	979,360	1,222,119	818,718	778,827	540,448
EBITDA	740,893	845,523	602,812	(95,080)	477,337	282,789	309,436	239,600
Depn & Amortn	3,672	2,688	2,291	3,147	3,439	3,123	2,675	1,457
Income Before Taxes	662,011	780,319	541,443	(162,835)	408,820	207,162	233,272	196,098
Income Taxes	247,912	288,691	204,790	(55,953)	156,677	76,562	76,908	74,176
Net Income	414,189	491,687	336,653	(106,882)	252,143	130,600	156,364	121,922
Average Shares	119,028	118,668	107,846	100,088	84,894	79,290	73,652	62,898
Balance Sheet								
Current Assets	384,412	298,703	233,543	176,025	217,074	162,167	121,712	134,474
Total Assets	7,272,419	6,045,609	4,648,777	4,029,542	4,029,081	2,952,011	2,585,403	2,235,196
Current Liabilities	636,979	567,034	459,205	282,732	351,168	254,664	143,042	168,514
Long-Term Obligations	1,800,000	1,380,000	800,000	779,585	1,239,751	868,248	995,396	875,098
Total Liabilities	3,827,431	3,024,752	2,117,462	1,759,457	2,220,290	1,461,185	1,398,733	1,237,334
Stockholders' Equity	3,444,988	3,020,857	2,531,315	2,270,085	1,808,791	1,490,826	1,186,670	997,862
Shares Outstanding	117,631	117,380	117,098	101,690	85,164	84,960	73,895	73,683
Statistical Record								
Return on Assets %	6.20	9.20	7.76	N.M.	7.20	4.72	6.49	7.33
Return on Equity %	12.78	17.71	14.02	N.M.	15.24	9.76	14.32	15.14
EBITDA Margin %	34.09	44.51	39.76	N.M.	39.06	34.54	39.73	44.33
Net Margin %	19.06	25.88	22.21	N.M.	20.63	15.95	20.08	22.56
Asset Turnover	0.33	0.36	0.35	0.24	0.35	0.30	0.32	0.32
Current Ratio	0.60	0.53	0.51	0.62	0.62	0.64	0.85	0.80
Debt to Equity	0.52	0.46	0.32	0.34	0.69	0.58	0.84	0.88
Price Range	62.47-36.41	74.50-30.66	59.10-32.70	37.34-9.87	55.34-13.13	28.90-17.98	24.86-16.98	22.83-14.29
P/E Ratio	17.95-10.46	18.00-7.41	23.18-12.82	...	18.63-4.42	17.51-10.90	11.67-7.97	11.77-7.37

Address: 1700 Broadway, Suite 2300, Denver, CO 80290-2300 Telephone: 303-837-1661	Web Site: www.whiting.com Officers: James J. Volker - Chairman, Chief Executive Officer James T. Brown - President, Vice President, Chief Operating Officer	Auditors: Deloitte & Touche LLP Investor Contact: 303-390-4051

WILEY (JOHN) & SONS INC.

Exchange	Symbol	Price	52Wk Range	Yield	P/E	Div Achiever
NYS	JW A	$38.96 (3/28/2013)	51.32-36.09	2.46	12.82	18 Years

*7 Year Price Score 94.20 ***NYSE Composite Index=100** ***12 Month Price Score 80.27**

Interim Earnings (Per Share)

Qtr.	Jul	Oct	Jan	Apr
2009-10	0.45	0.78	0.71	0.46
2010-11	0.72	0.88	0.74	0.46
2011-12	0.82	0.83	1.03	0.78
2012-13	0.60	0.71	0.95	...

Interim Dividends (Per Share)

Amt	Decl	Ex	Rec	Pay
0.24Q	06/21/2012	07/02/2012	07/05/2012	07/19/2012
0.24Q	09/19/2012	09/27/2012	10/01/2012	10/16/2012
0.24Q	11/30/2012	12/10/2012	12/12/2012	12/28/2012
0.24Q	03/13/2013	03/22/2013	03/26/2013	04/12/2013

Indicated Div: $0.96

Valuation Analysis / Institutional Holding

Forecast EPS	$3.02 (04/05/2013)	No of Institutions 316
Market Cap	$2.3 Billion	Shares 49,757,600
Book Value	$1.1 Billion	% Held 73.97
Price/Book	2.11	
Price/Sales	1.31	

Business Summary: Publishing (MIC: 2.3.3 SIC: 2731 NAIC: 511130)

John Wiley & Sons provides content and content-enabled digital services to customers worldwide. Co. has three core businesses which include Scientific, Technical, Medical and Scholarly (STMS); Professional/Trade; and Global Education. Core businesses produce STMS journals, reference works, books, database services, and advertising; subscription products, certification and training services and online applications; and educational content and services. Education content and services includes integrated online teaching and learning resources for undergraduate and graduate students, educators, and lifelong learners worldwide and secondary school students in Australia.

Recent Developments: For the quarter ended Jan 31 2013, net income decreased 9.2% to US$57.1 million from US$62.9 million in the year-earlier quarter. Revenues were US$472.4 million, up 4.7% from US$451.1 million the year before. Operating income was US$83.6 million versus US$78.5 million in the prior-year quarter, an increase of 6.6%. Direct operating expenses declined 0.2% to US$141.8 million from US$142.1 million in the comparable period the year before. Indirect operating expenses increased 7.2% to US$247.0 million from US$230.5 million in the equivalent prior-year period.

Prospects: Our evaluation of Wiley (John) & Sons Inc. as of Apr. 7, 2013 is the result of our systematic analysis on three basic characteristics: earnings strength, relative valuation, and recent stock price movement. The company has managed to produce a neutral trend in earnings per share over the past 5 quarters. However, while recent estimates for the company have been mixed, JW.A has posted better than expected results. Based on operating earnings yield, the company is undervalued when compared to all of the companies in our coverage universe. Share price changes over the past year indicates that JW.A will perform very poorly over the near term.

Financial Data
(US$ in Thousands)

	9 Mos	6 Mos	3 Mos	04/30/2012	04/30/2011	04/30/2010	04/30/2009	04/30/2008
Earnings Per Share	3.04	3.12	3.24	3.47	2.80	2.41	2.15	2.49
Cash Flow Per Share	4.63	5.39	5.66	6.29	6.24	7.16	5.84	4.82
Dividends Per Share	0.920	0.880	0.840	0.800	0.640	0.560	0.520	0.440
Dividend Payout %	30.26	28.21	25.93	23.05	22.86	23.24	24.19	17.67
Income Statement								
Total Revenue	1,314,924	842,489	410,734	1,782,742	1,742,551	1,699,062	1,611,390	1,673,734
EBITDA	294,538	172,981	76,113	365,305	327,045	307,148	278,697	295,300
Depn & Amortn	110,575	71,497	36,098	87,147	81,085	75,439	71,978	72,310
Income Before Taxes	175,975	96,981	37,719	272,095	231,060	200,209	164,475	161,528
Income Taxes	39,701	17,807	1,602	59,349	59,171	56,666	36,217	13,992
Net Income	136,274	79,174	36,117	212,746	171,889	143,543	128,258	147,536
Average Shares	60,254	60,633	60,433	61,272	61,359	59,679	59,610	59,323
Balance Sheet								
Current Assets	663,521	439,793	490,057	574,600	527,490	485,714	439,569	447,580
Total Assets	2,880,884	2,631,684	2,415,558	2,532,946	2,430,141	2,316,202	2,223,708	2,588,814
Current Liabilities	620,727	411,670	498,949	640,930	756,365	674,372	596,967	691,161
Long-Term Obligations	734,800	701,900	514,000	475,000	330,500	559,000	754,900	797,318
Total Liabilities	1,784,393	1,543,217	1,400,997	1,515,378	1,452,252	1,593,766	1,710,192	1,899,696
Stockholders' Equity	1,096,491	1,088,467	1,014,561	1,017,568	977,889	722,436	513,516	689,118
Shares Outstanding	59,291	60,151	60,050	59,515	60,709	60,017	58,380	58,626
Statistical Record								
Return on Assets %	6.89	7.77	8.32	8.55	7.24	6.32	5.33	5.75
Return on Equity %	17.41	18.15	19.48	21.26	20.22	23.23	21.33	24.15
EBITDA Margin %	22.40	20.53	18.53	20.49	18.77	18.08	17.30	17.64
Net Margin %	10.36	9.40	8.79	11.93	9.86	8.45	7.96	8.81
Asset Turnover	0.66	0.71	0.74	0.72	0.73	0.75	0.67	0.65
Current Ratio	1.07	1.07	0.98	0.90	0.70	0.72	0.74	0.65
Debt to Equity	0.67	0.64	0.51	0.47	0.34	0.77	1.47	1.16
Price Range	51.32-36.53	51.32-36.53	50.80-42.35	53.00-42.35	52.64-35.59	43.95-29.77	49.76-26.21	49.35-35.98
P/E Ratio	16.88-12.02	16.45-13.74	15.68-13.07	15.27-12.20	18.80-12.71	18.24-12.35	23.14-12.19	19.82-14.45
Average Yield %	2.04	1.89	1.81	1.68	1.48	1.51	1.36	1.04

Address: 111 River Street, Hoboken, NJ 07030 Telephone: 201-748-6000	Web Site: www.wiley.com Officers: William J. Pesce - President, Chief Executive Officer Ellis E. Cousens - Executive Vice President, Chief Financial & Operations Officer	Auditors: KPMG LLP Investor Contact: 201-748-6874 Transfer Agents: Registrar and Transfer Company, Cranford, NJ

WILLIAMS COS INC (THE)

Exchange	Symbol	Price	52Wk Range	Yield	P/E
NYS	WMB	$37.46 (3/28/2013)	37.46-27.36	3.62	27.34

*7 Year Price Score 127.83 *NYSE Composite Index=100 ***12 Month Price Score 98.84**

Interim Earnings (Per Share)

Qtr.	Mar	Jun	Sep	Dec
2008	0.84	0.73	0.62	0.21
2009	(0.30)	0.24	0.24	0.30
2010	(0.33)	0.31	(2.16)	0.29
2011	0.54	0.38	0.46	(0.74)
2012	0.70	0.21	0.25	0.22

Interim Dividends (Per Share)

Amt	Decl	Ex	Rec	Pay
0.30Q	05/17/2012	06/06/2012	06/08/2012	06/25/2012
0.313Q	07/19/2012	08/22/2012	08/24/2012	09/10/2012
0.325Q	10/15/2012	12/05/2012	12/07/2012	12/24/2012
0.339Q	01/17/2013	03/06/2013	03/08/2013	03/25/2013

Indicated Div: $1.36

Valuation Analysis

Forecast EPS	$0.98 (04/06/2013)
Market Cap	$25.5 Billion
Book Value	$4.8 Billion
Price/Book	5.37
Price/Sales	3.41

Institutional Holding

No of Institutions	831
Shares	594,775,168
% Held	92.15

Business Summary: Equipment & Services (MIC: 9.1.3 SIC: 4922 NAIC: 486210)

Williams Companies is an energy infrastructure company focused on connecting North America's hydrocarbon resource plays to markets for natural gas, natural gas liquids (NGLs), and olefins. Co.'s operations are located principally in the U.S., but span from the deepwater Gulf of Mexico to the Canadian oil sands. Co.'s interstate gas pipeline, domestic midstream, and domestic olefins production interests are held through its investment in Williams Partners L.P., an energy master limited partnership. Substantially all Co.'s operations are conducted through its subsidiaries. Co.'s business segments are: Williams Partners; Williams NGL & Petchem Services; and Access Midstream Partners.

Recent Developments: For the year ended Dec 31 2012, net income increased 61.1% to US$1.07 billion from US$661.0 million in the prior year. Revenues were US$7.49 billion, down 5.6% from US$7.93 billion the year before. Operating income was US$1.61 billion versus US$1.87 billion in the prior year, a decrease of 13.7%. Direct operating expenses declined 8.1% to US$4.52 billion from US$4.92 billion in the comparable period the year before. Indirect operating expenses increased 18.6% to US$1.35 billion from US$1.14 billion in the equivalent prior-year period.

Prospects: Our evaluation of Williams Cos Inc. as of Apr. 7, 2013 is the result of our systematic analysis on three basic characteristics: earnings strength, relative valuation, and recent stock price movement. The company has generated a negative trend in earnings per share over the past 5 quarters. However, while recent estimates for the company have been lowered by analysts, WMB has posted results that fell short of analysts expectations. Based on operating earnings yield, the company is overvalued when compared to all of the companies in our coverage universe. Share price changes over the past year indicates that WMB will perform poorly over the near term.

Financial Data

(US$ in Thousands)	12/31/2012	12/31/2011	12/31/2010	12/31/2009	12/31/2008	12/31/2007	12/31/2006	12/31/2005
Earnings Per Share	1.37	0.63	(1.88)	0.49	2.40	1.63	0.51	0.53
Cash Flow Per Share	2.95	5.84	4.54	4.42	5.76	3.75	3.18	2.54
Tang Book Value Per Share	3.52	3.03	12.44	12.75	12.85	9.15	8.48	7.70
Dividends Per Share	1.196	0.775	0.485	0.440	0.430	0.390	0.345	0.250
Dividend Payout %	87.32	123.02	...	89.80	17.92	23.93	67.65	47.17
Income Statement								
Total Revenue	7,486,000	7,930,000	9,616,000	8,255,000	12,352,000	10,558,000	11,812,900	12,583,600
EBITDA	2,399,000	2,271,000	969,000	2,885,000	3,921,000	2,956,000	1,909,700	1,825,500
Depn & Amortn	712,000	658,000	1,500,000	1,500,000	1,300,000	1,100,000	865,100	739,000
Income Before Taxes	1,178,000	1,047,000	(1,109,000)	807,000	2,084,000	1,324,000	480,200	491,400
Income Taxes	360,000	124,000	(30,000)	359,000	713,000	524,000	206,300	213,900
Net Income	859,000	376,000	(1,097,000)	285,000	1,418,000	990,000	308,500	313,600
Average Shares	625,486	598,175	584,552	589,385	592,719	609,866	608,627	605,847
Balance Sheet								
Current Assets	1,924,000	1,894,000	2,530,000	3,793,000	4,411,000	5,538,000	6,322,000	9,697,300
Total Assets	24,327,000	16,502,000	24,972,000	25,280,000	26,006,000	25,061,000	25,402,400	29,442,600
Current Liabilities	1,549,000	1,675,000	2,574,000	2,477,000	3,519,000	4,431,000	4,693,600	8,450,200
Long-Term Obligations	10,735,000	8,369,000	8,600,000	8,259,000	7,683,000	7,757,000	7,622,000	7,590,500
Total Liabilities	19,575,000	14,709,000	17,684,000	16,833,000	17,566,000	18,686,000	19,329,200	24,015,100
Stockholders' Equity	4,752,000	1,793,000	7,288,000	8,447,000	8,440,000	6,375,000	6,073,200	5,427,500
Shares Outstanding	681,000	591,000	585,000	583,000	578,000	586,000	597,100	573,400
Statistical Record								
Return on Assets %	4.20	1.81	N.M.	1.11	5.54	3.92	1.12	1.17
Return on Equity %	26.18	8.28	N.M.	3.38	19.09	15.91	5.36	6.04
EBITDA Margin %	32.05	28.64	10.08	34.95	31.74	28.00	16.17	14.51
Net Margin %	11.47	4.74	N.M.	3.45	11.48	9.38	2.61	2.49
Asset Turnover	0.37	0.38	0.38	0.32	0.48	0.42	0.43	0.47
Current Ratio	1.24	1.13	0.98	1.53	1.25	1.25	1.35	1.15
Debt to Equity	2.26	4.67	1.18	0.98	0.91	1.22	1.26	1.40
Price Range	36.77-26.82	27.09-19.07	20.21-14.43	17.45-8.03	32.92-9.91	30.34-20.68	22.82-15.92	20.74-12.69
P/E Ratio	26.84-19.58	42.99-30.27	...	35.61-16.38	13.72-4.13	18.62-12.68	44.75-31.21	39.13-23.56
Average Yield %	3.81	3.26	2.79	3.33	1.79	1.53	1.80	1.53

Address: One Williams Center, Tulsa, OK 74172	**Web Site:** www.williams.com	**Auditors:** Ernst & Young LLP
Telephone: 918-573-2000	**Officers:** Alan S. Armstrong - President, Chief Executive Officer Donald R. Chappel - Senior Vice President, Chief Financial Officer	**Transfer Agents:** Computershare Trust Company, N.A., Providence, RI

WILLIAMS-SONOMA, INC.

Exchange	Symbol	Price	52Wk Range	Yield	P/E
NYS	WSM	$51.52 (3/28/2013)	51.52-33.06	2.41	20.28

*7 Year Price Score 124.49 ***NYSE Composite Index=100** ***12 Month Price Score 103.62**

Interim Earnings (Per Share)

Qtr.	Apr	Jul	Oct	Jan
2008-09	0.10	0.17	(0.10)	0.11
2009-10	(0.18)	0.00	0.07	0.82
2010-11	0.18	0.28	0.34	1.04
2011-12	0.29	0.37	0.41	1.15
2012-13	0.30	0.43	0.49	1.33

Interim Dividends (Per Share)

Amt	Decl	Ex	Rec	Pay
0.22Q	06/22/2012	07/25/2012	07/27/2012	08/24/2012
0.22Q	10/01/2012	10/24/2012	10/26/2012	11/23/2012
0.22Q	12/21/2012	01/23/2013	01/25/2013	02/25/2013
0.31Q	03/19/2013	04/24/2013	04/26/2013	05/24/2013

Indicated Div: $1.24

Valuation Analysis / Institutional Holding

Valuation Analysis		Institutional Holding	
Forecast EPS	$2.75 (04/06/2013)	No of Institutions	386
Market Cap	$5.0 Billion	Shares	98,417,032
Book Value	$1.3 Billion	% Held	87.67
Price/Book	3.85		
Price/Sales	1.25		

Business Summary: Retail - Furniture & Home Furnishings (MIC: 2.1.6 SIC: 5023 NAIC: 442210)

Williams-Sonoma is a retailer of products for the home. Co. has two segments: direct-to-customer, which sells Co.'s products through its six e-commerce websites (williams-sonoma.com, potterybarn.com, potterybarnkids.com, pbteen.com, westelm.com and rejuvenation.com) and seven direct-mail catalogs (Williams-Sonoma, Pottery Barn, Pottery Barn Kids, Pottery Barn Bed and Bath, PBteen, West Elm and Rejuvenation); and retail, which sells similar products through Co.'s five retail store concepts (Williams-Sonoma, Pottery Barn, Pottery Barn Kids, West Elm and Rejuvenation). As of Jan 29 2012, Co. operated 576 stores in 44 states, Washington, DC, Canada and Puerto Rico.

Recent Developments: For the year ended Feb 3 2013, net income increased 8.4% to US$256.7 million from US$236.9 million in the prior year. Revenues were US$4.04 billion, up 8.7% from US$3.72 billion the year before. Operating income was US$409.2 million versus US$381.7 million in the prior year, an increase of 7.2%. Direct operating expenses rose 8.4% to US$2.45 billion from US$2.26 billion in the comparable period the year before. Indirect operating expenses increased 9.8% to US$1.18 billion from US$1.08 billion in the equivalent prior-year period.

Prospects: Our evaluation of Williams-Sonoma Inc. as of Apr. 7, 2013 is the result of our systematic analysis on three basic characteristics: earnings strength, relative valuation, and recent stock price movement. The company has managed to produce a neutral trend in earnings per share over the past 5 quarters. However, while recent estimates for the company have been lowered by analysts, WSM has posted better than expected results. Based on operating earnings yield, the company is about fairly valued when compared to all of the companies in our coverage universe. Share price changes over the past year indicates that WSM will perform poorly over the near term.

Financial Data

(US$ in Thousands)	02/03/2013	01/29/2012	01/30/2011	01/31/2010	02/01/2009	02/03/2008	01/28/2007	01/29/2006
Earnings Per Share	2.54	2.22	1.83	0.72	0.28	1.76	1.79	1.81
Cash Flow Per Share	3.61	2.80	3.34	4.65	2.19	2.21	2.72	3.02
Tang Book Value Per Share	13.39	12.50	12.00	11.33	10.86	11.07	10.48	9.80
Dividends Per Share	0.880	0.730	0.580	0.480	0.480	0.460	0.400	...
Dividend Payout %	34.65	32.88	31.69	66.67	171.43	26.14	22.35	...
Income Statement								
Total Revenue	4,042,870	3,720,895	3,504,158	3,102,704	3,361,472	3,944,934	3,727,513	3,538,947
EBITDA	516,922	484,738	430,929	236,439	158,970	424,699	433,849	443,380
Depn & Amortn	107,759	103,006	107,515	114,997	116,817	111,301	106,348	98,290
Income Before Taxes	409,956	381,830	323,060	120,289	41,953	316,340	337,186	348,798
Income Taxes	153,226	144,899	122,833	42,847	11,929	120,583	128,318	133,932
Net Income	256,730	236,931	200,227	77,442	30,024	195,757	208,868	214,866
Average Shares	101,051	106,582	109,522	107,373	106,880	111,447	116,773	118,427
Balance Sheet								
Current Assets	1,316,772	1,276,366	1,347,594	1,180,193	940,673	1,049,775	1,100,963	1,083,164
Total Assets	2,187,679	2,060,838	2,131,762	2,079,169	1,935,464	2,093,854	2,048,331	1,981,620
Current Liabilities	657,127	571,799	611,716	563,482	460,737	611,534	627,734	590,392
Long-Term Obligations	3,753	5,478	7,130	8,672	10,259	11,238	12,822	14,490
Total Liabilities	878,541	805,576	872,899	867,574	787,480	928,131	896,900	856,302
Stockholders' Equity	1,309,138	1,255,262	1,258,863	1,211,595	1,147,984	1,165,723	1,151,431	1,125,318
Shares Outstanding	97,734	100,451	104,888	106,962	105,664	105,349	109,868	114,779
Statistical Record								
Return on Assets %	11.89	11.33	9.54	3.87	1.49	9.30	10.39	11.56
Return on Equity %	19.70	18.90	16.25	6.58	2.60	16.62	18.40	20.69
EBITDA Margin %	12.79	13.03	12.30	7.62	4.73	10.77	11.64	12.53
Net Margin %	6.35	6.37	5.71	2.50	0.89	4.96	5.60	6.07
Asset Turnover	1.87	1.78	1.67	1.55	1.67	1.87	1.85	1.90
Current Ratio	2.00	2.23	2.20	2.09	2.04	1.72	1.75	1.83
Debt to Equity	N.M.	N.M.	0.01	0.01	0.01	0.01	0.01	0.01
Price Range	47.93-33.06	45.24-28.81	36.09-18.93	23.23-7.55	27.72-4.72	36.52-20.01	44.33-28.57	45.09-33.49
P/E Ratio	18.87-13.02	20.38-12.98	19.72-10.34	32.26-10.49	99.00-16.86	20.75-11.37	24.77-15.96	24.91-18.50
Average Yield %	2.19	1.98	2.00	3.09	2.70	1.46	1.12	...

Address: 3250 Van Ness Avenue, San Francisco, CA 94109 **Telephone:** 415-421-7900 **Fax:** 415-434-0881	**Web Site:** www.williams-sonomainc.com **Officers:** Adrian D.P. Bellamy - Chairman Laura J. Alber - President, Chief Executive Officer	**Auditors:** Deloitte & Touche LLP **Transfer Agents:** Wells Fargo Shareowner Services, St. Paul, MN

WISCONSIN ENERGY CORP.

Exchange	Symbol	Price	52Wk Range	Yield	P/E
NYS	WEC	$42.89 (3/28/2013)	42.89-34.59	3.17	18.25

*7 Year Price Score 126.74 *NYSE Composite Index=100 ***12 Month Price Score 98.51**

Interim Earnings (Per Share)

Qtr.	Mar	Jun	Sep	Dec
2008	0.52	0.25	0.33	0.42
2009	0.60	0.27	0.25	0.50
2010	0.55	0.38	0.47	0.54
2011	0.72	0.46	0.55	0.50
2012	0.74	0.51	0.67	0.43

Interim Dividends (Per Share)

Amt	Decl	Ex	Rec	Pay
0.30Q	04/19/2012	05/10/2012	05/14/2012	06/01/2012
0.30Q	07/19/2012	08/10/2012	08/14/2012	09/01/2012
0.30Q	10/18/2012	11/09/2012	11/14/2012	12/01/2012
0.34Q	01/17/2013	02/12/2013	02/14/2013	03/01/2013

Indicated Div: $1.36

Valuation Analysis / Institutional Holding

Valuation Analysis		Institutional Holding	
Forecast EPS	$2.42 (04/06/2013)	No of Institutions	583
Market Cap	$9.8 Billion	Shares	155,571,152
Book Value	$4.2 Billion	% Held	63.99
Price/Book	2.36		
Price/Sales	2.31		

Business Summary: Electric Utilities (MIC: 3.1.1 SIC: 4931 NAIC: 221121)

Wisconsin Energy is a holding company. Co.'s main subsidiaries are Wisconsin Electric Power Company (Wisconsin Electric), Wisconsin Gas LLC (Wisconsin Gas) and W.E. Power, LLC (We Power). Co.'s Wispark LLC and Bostco LLC subsidiaries are engaged in developing and investing in real estate. Co. conducts its operations in two segments: a utility energy segment and a non-utility energy segment. Co.'s utility energy segment consists of Wisconsin Electric and Wisconsin Gas, operating together under the trade name of We Energies. Co.'s non-utility energy segment consists primarily of We Power, which designs, constructs, owns and leases the new generating capacity in its Power The Future strategy.

Recent Developments: For the year ended Dec 31 2012, income from continuing operations increased 6.5% to US$546.3 million from US$512.8 million a year earlier. Net income increased 3.8% to US$546.3 million from US$526.2 million in the prior year. Revenues were US$4.25 billion, down 5.3% from US$4.49 billion the year before. Operating income was US$1.00 billion versus US$887.3 million in the prior year, an increase of 12.7%. Direct operating expenses declined 12.5% to US$2.76 billion from US$3.16 billion in the comparable period the year before. Indirect operating expenses increased 9.4% to US$485.6 million from US$443.9 million in the equivalent prior-year period.

Prospects: Our evaluation of Wisconsin Energy Corp. as of Apr. 7, 2013 is the result of our systematic analysis on three basic characteristics: earnings strength, relative valuation, and recent stock price movement. The company has generated a negative trend in earnings per share over the past 5 quarters. However, while recent estimates for the company have been mixed, WEC has posted better than expected results. Based on operating earnings yield, the company is about fairly valued when compared to all of the companies in our coverage universe. Share price changes over the past year indicates that WEC will perform in line with the market over the near term.

Financial Data
(US$ in Thousands)

	12/31/2012	12/31/2011	12/31/2010	12/31/2009	12/31/2008	12/31/2007	12/31/2006	12/31/2005
Earnings Per Share	2.35	2.24	1.93	1.62	1.52	1.42	1.34	1.30
Cash Flow Per Share	5.09	4.27	3.47	2.69	3.14	2.28	3.12	2.47
Tang Book Value Per Share	16.12	15.28	14.37	13.37	12.38	11.36	10.46	9.57
Dividends Per Share	1.200	1.040	0.800	0.675	0.540	0.500	0.460	0.440
Dividend Payout %	51.06	46.43	41.45	41.67	35.53	35.34	34.46	33.72
Income Statement								
Total Revenue	4,246,400	4,486,400	4,202,500	4,127,900	4,431,000	4,237,800	3,996,400	3,815,500
EBITDA	1,406,800	1,286,400	969,600	810,800	521,800	1,038,600	987,100	964,600
Depn & Amortn	371,700	336,400	119,000	118,700	(155,800)	361,200	365,500	373,000
Income Before Taxes	786,900	714,200	644,200	535,400	523,900	509,800	448,900	418,200
Income Taxes	306,300	263,900	249,900	217,300	217,100	216,400	175,000	149,200
Net Income	546,300	526,200	456,500	382,400	359,100	335,600	316,400	308,700
Average Shares	232,800	235,400	236,800	235,800	236,400	237,000	236,800	236,800
Balance Sheet								
Current Assets	1,313,900	1,426,200	1,331,100	1,461,700	1,693,100	1,849,700	1,228,000	1,377,000
Total Assets	14,285,000	13,862,100	13,059,800	12,697,900	12,617,800	11,720,300	11,130,200	10,462,000
Current Liabilities	1,443,300	1,364,500	1,721,100	1,881,900	1,734,800	2,502,800	1,888,000	1,646,800
Long-Term Obligations	4,453,800	4,614,300	3,932,000	3,875,800	4,074,700	3,172,500	3,073,400	3,031,000
Total Liabilities	10,119,500	9,868,400	9,227,300	9,100,600	9,250,500	8,590,700	8,210,800	7,751,500
Stockholders' Equity	4,165,500	3,993,700	3,832,500	3,597,300	3,367,300	3,129,600	2,919,400	2,710,500
Shares Outstanding	229,039	230,486	233,771	233,816	233,835	233,886	233,938	233,961
Statistical Record								
Return on Assets %	3.87	3.91	3.54	3.02	2.94	2.94	2.93	3.08
Return on Equity %	13.35	13.45	12.29	10.98	11.02	11.10	11.24	11.80
EBITDA Margin %	33.13	28.67	23.07	19.64	11.78	24.51	24.70	25.28
Net Margin %	12.87	11.73	10.86	9.26	8.10	7.92	7.92	8.09
Asset Turnover	0.30	0.33	0.33	0.33	0.36	0.37	0.37	0.38
Current Ratio	0.91	1.05	0.77	0.78	0.98	0.74	0.65	0.84
Debt to Equity	1.07	1.16	1.03	1.08	1.21	1.01	1.05	1.12
Price Range	41.28-33.92	35.29-27.94	30.25-23.83	25.21-18.27	24.52-18.80	25.00-20.91	24.29-19.20	20.20-16.73
P/E Ratio	17.57-14.43	15.75-12.47	15.67-12.35	15.56-11.28	16.13-12.37	17.61-14.73	18.12-14.33	15.54-12.87
Average Yield %	3.23	3.35	2.98	3.16	2.41	2.14	2.19	2.38

Address: 231 West Michigan Street, Milwaukee, WI 53201 Telephone: 414-221-2345 Fax: 414-221-2172	Web Site: www.wisconsinenergy.com Officers: Gale E. Klappa - Chairman, President, Chief Executive Officer James Patrick Keyes - Chief Executive Officer, Chief Financial Officer	Auditors: Deloitte & Touche LLP Investor Contact: 414-221-2592 Transfer Agents: Computershare Shareowner Services LLC, Pittsburgh, PA

WMS INDUSTRIES INC.

Exchange	Symbol	Price	52Wk Range	Yield	P/E
NYS	WMS	$25.21 (3/28/2013)	25.21-14.65	N/A	24.01

*7 Year Price Score 59.67   ***NYSE Composite Index=100**   ***12 Month Price Score 116.12**

Interim Earnings (Per Share)

Qtr.	Sep	Dec	Mar	Jun
2009-10	0.34	0.44	0.55	0.56
2010-11	0.33	0.46	0.41	0.18
2011-12	0.07	0.29	0.40	0.40
2012-13	0.17	0.08	...	...

Interim Dividends (Per Share)

No Dividends Paid

Valuation Analysis

		Institutional Holding	
Forecast EPS	$0.94	No of Institutions	
	(04/05/2013)	249	
Market Cap	$1.4 Billion	Shares	
Book Value	$898.3 Million	61,385,732	
Price/Book	1.53	% Held	
Price/Sales	2.00	100.31	

TRADING VOLUME (thousand shares)

Business Summary: Sporting & Recreational (MIC: 2.2.4 SIC: 3999 NAIC: 339999)

WMS Industries is engaged in designing, manufacturing and distributing games, video and mechanical reel-spinning gaming machines and video lottery terminals (VLTs). Co. sells to casinos and other gaming machine operators new and used gaming machines and VLTs, conversion kits (including game, hardware or operating system conversions) and parts. Co. also licenses its game content and intellectual property to third parties for distribution, leases gaming machines and VLTs to casinos and other gaming machine operators, operates an online gaming site, provides social games on Facebook®; and provides games on third-party online gaming platforms that are interoperable with its game server.

Recent Developments: For the quarter ended Dec 31 2012, net income decreased 73.3% to US$4.3 million from US$16.1 million in the year-earlier quarter. Revenues were US$157.5 million, down 2.9% from US$162.2 million the year before. Operating income was US$7.0 million versus US$21.0 million in the prior-year quarter, a decrease of 66.7%. Direct operating expenses declined 9.8% to US$56.9 million from US$63.1 million in the comparable period the year before. Indirect operating expenses increased 19.8% to US$93.6 million from US$78.1 million in the equivalent prior-year period.

Prospects: Our evaluation of WMS Industries Inc. as of Apr. 7, 2013 is the result of our systematic analysis on three basic characteristics: earnings strength, relative valuation, and recent stock price movement. The company has generated a negative trend in earnings per share over the past 5 quarters. However, while recent estimates for the company have been lowered by analysts, WMS has posted results that fell short of analysts expectations. Based on operating earnings yield, the company is about fairly valued when compared to all of the companies in our coverage universe. Share price changes over the past year indicates that WMS will perform very poorly over the near term.

Financial Data

(US$ in Thousands)	6 Mos	3 Mos	06/30/2012	06/30/2011	06/30/2010	06/30/2009	06/30/2008	06/30/2007
Earnings Per Share	1.05	1.26	1.15	1.37	1.88	1.59	1.15	0.86
Cash Flow Per Share	2.98	3.02	2.82	2.72	2.33	3.64	3.70	2.46
Tang Book Value Per Share	13.24	13.04	12.74	12.36	12.50	10.00	8.06	6.73
Income Statement								
Total Revenue	316,600	159,100	689,700	783,300	765,100	706,400	650,100	539,800
EBITDA	84,700	44,600	165,200	181,500	235,100	205,000	176,300	137,100
Depn & Amortn	65,100	32,000	77,800	71,100	67,200	68,400	71,900	62,900
Income Before Taxes	24,200	14,300	99,100	123,600	170,500	140,400	105,600	71,700
Income Taxes	10,600	5,000	35,000	42,600	57,600	48,200	38,100	22,800
Net Income	13,600	9,300	64,100	81,000	112,900	92,200	67,500	48,900
Average Shares	54,600	54,700	55,800	59,000	60,400	59,100	60,600	59,600
Balance Sheet								
Current Assets	474,000	454,300	452,300	497,500	555,000	450,000	413,300	342,200
Total Assets	1,146,700	1,151,700	1,154,100	1,046,300	1,007,000	856,000	772,700	655,700
Current Liabilities	115,600	130,300	170,800	152,400	140,800	115,700	116,600	86,700
Long-Term Obligations	85,000	85,000	60,000	...	...	115,000	115,000	115,000
Total Liabilities	248,400	263,000	276,800	190,400	173,100	264,600	261,900	222,100
Stockholders' Equity	898,300	888,700	877,300	855,900	833,900	591,400	510,800	433,600
Shares Outstanding	54,600	54,600	54,800	56,800	58,800	49,200	50,200	50,000
Statistical Record								
Return on Assets %	5.28	6.45	5.81	7.89	12.12	11.32	9.43	8.27
Return on Equity %	6.64	8.09	7.38	9.59	15.84	16.73	14.26	12.88
EBITDA Margin %	26.75	28.03	23.95	23.17	30.73	29.02	27.12	25.40
Net Margin %	4.30	5.85	9.29	10.34	14.76	13.05	10.38	9.06
Asset Turnover	0.63	0.64	0.63	0.76	0.82	0.87	0.91	0.91
Current Ratio	4.10	3.49	2.65	3.26	3.94	3.89	3.54	3.95
Debt to Equity	0.09	0.10	0.07	...	...	0.19	0.23	0.27
Price Range	24.58-14.65	24.58-14.99	30.72-16.53	48.75-28.09	51.52-29.51	35.84-15.67	40.78-24.61	28.87-16.49
P/E Ratio	23.41-13.95	19.51-11.90	26.71-14.37	35.58-20.50	27.40-15.70	22.54-9.86	35.46-21.40	33.57-19.17

Address: 800 South Northpoint Blvd., Waukegan, IL 60085
Telephone: 847-785-3000

Web Site: www.wms.com
Officers: Brian R. Gamache - Chairman, Chief Executive Officer Orrin J. Edidin - President

Auditors: Ernst & Young LLP
Investor Contact: 847-785-3167
Transfer Agents: American Stock Transfer & Trust Company, LLC, Brooklyn, NY

WORLD FUEL SERVICES CORP.

Exchange	Symbol	Price	52Wk Range	Yield	P/E
NYS	INT	$39.72 (3/28/2013)	45.11-34.00	0.38	15.05

*7 Year Price Score 130.14 *NYSE Composite Index=100   *12 Month Price Score 94.94

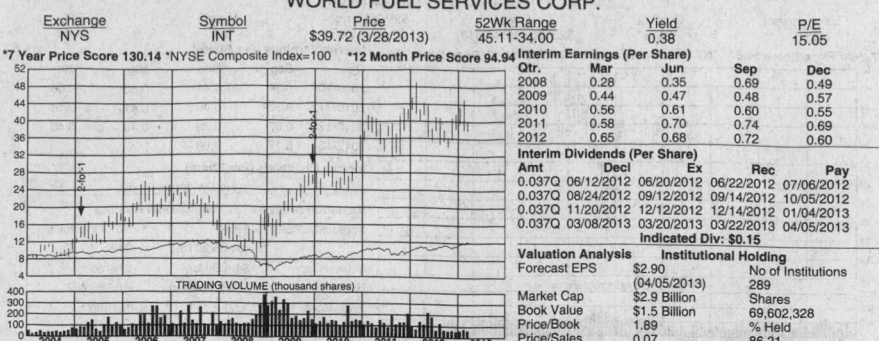

Interim Earnings (Per Share)

Qtr.	Mar	Jun	Sep	Dec
2008	0.28	0.35	0.69	0.49
2009	0.44	0.47	0.48	0.57
2010	0.56	0.61	0.60	0.55
2011	0.58	0.70	0.74	0.69
2012	0.65	0.68	0.72	0.60

Interim Dividends (Per Share)

Amt	Decl	Ex	Rec	Pay
0.037Q	06/12/2012	06/20/2012	06/22/2012	07/06/2012
0.037Q	08/24/2012	09/12/2012	09/14/2012	10/05/2012
0.037Q	11/20/2012	12/12/2012	12/14/2012	01/04/2013
0.037Q	03/08/2013	03/20/2013	03/22/2013	04/05/2013

Indicated Div: $0.15

Valuation Analysis | **Institutional Holding**

Forecast EPS $2.90 (04/05/2013)	No of Institutions 289
Market Cap $2.9 Billion	Shares
Book Value $1.5 Billion	69,602,328
Price/Book 1.89	% Held
Price/Sales 0.07	86.21

Business Summary: Refining & Marketing (MIC: 9.1.2 SIC: 5172 NAIC: 424720)

World Fuel Services is a fuel logistics company. Co. has three segments: aviation, which provides fuel and related services to commercial airlines, second and third-tier airlines, regional and low cost carriers, military fleets and to the U.S. and foreign governments; marine, which provides fuel and related services to marine customers, including international container and tanker fleets, commercial cruise lines, and to the U.S. and foreign governments; and land, which provides fuel and related services to petroleum distributors operating in the land transportation market, retail petroleum operators, and industrial, commercial and government customers.

Recent Developments: For the year ended Dec 31 2012, net income increased 1.1% to US$201.4 million from US$199.2 million in the prior year. Revenues were US$38.95 billion, up 12.5% from US$34.62 billion the year before. Operating income was unchanged at US$257.0 million versus the prior year. Direct operating expenses rose 12.6% to US$38.27 billion from US$33.99 billion in the comparable period the year before. Indirect operating expenses increased 10.2% to US$416.4 million from US$378.0 million in the equivalent prior-year period.

Prospects: Our evaluation of World Fuel Services Corp. as of Apr. 7, 2013 is the result of our systematic analysis on three basic characteristics: earnings strength, relative valuation, and recent stock price movement. The company has managed to produce a neutral trend in earnings per share over the past 5 quarters and while recent estimates for the company have remained steady, INT has posted results that fell short of analysts expectations. Based on operating earnings yield, the company is undervalued when compared to all of the companies in our coverage universe. Share price changes over the past year indicates that INT will perform in line with the market over the near term.

Financial Data

(US$ in Thousands)	12/31/2012	12/31/2011	12/31/2010	12/31/2009	12/31/2008	12/31/2007	12/31/2006	12/31/2005
Earnings Per Share	2.64	2.71	2.31	1.96	1.81	1.12	1.11	0.79
Cash Flow Per Share	2.04	(2.02)	(0.57)	1.32	6.84	(1.39)	1.24	(0.08)
Tang Book Value Per Share	12.12	12.35	10.37	8.53	7.28	7.09	6.61	5.58
Dividends Per Share	0.150	0.150	0.150	0.150	0.075	0.075	0.075	0.075
Dividend Payout %	5.68	5.54	6.49	7.65	4.14	6.73	6.79	9.55
Income Statement								
Total Revenue	38,945,338	34,622,854	19,131,147	11,295,177	18,509,403	13,729,555	10,785,136	8,733,947
EBITDA	277,292	269,528	201,381	170,528	159,900	90,376	82,912	60,299
Depn & Amortn	18,600	15,500	19,106	16,956	13,870	6,901	4,866	3,826
Income Before Taxes	239,595	238,203	177,530	149,909	137,575	86,586	81,399	55,828
Income Taxes	38,244	39,001	31,027	32,346	32,370	21,235	17,353	15,475
Net Income	189,345	194,029	146,865	117,139	105,039	64,773	63,948	39,609
Average Shares	71,817	71,510	63,441	59,901	58,058	58,124	57,846	50,428
Balance Sheet								
Current Assets	3,281,377	3,122,227	2,067,867	1,463,978	1,172,150	1,665,308	1,196,091	948,310
Total Assets	4,107,751	3,697,246	2,566,450	1,741,228	1,404,626	1,798,046	1,277,400	1,014,001
Current Liabilities	2,149,298	2,026,142	1,358,484	947,742	751,046	1,231,111	826,761	635,556
Long-Term Obligations	354,253	269,348	24,566	9,925	9,537	45,191	20,062	20,006
Total Liabilities	2,590,577	2,364,285	1,439,242	1,008,207	796,739	1,314,169	851,431	660,654
Stockholders' Equity	1,517,174	1,332,961	1,127,208	733,021	607,887	483,877	425,969	353,347
Shares Outstanding	72,147	71,154	69,602	59,385	58,590	57,158	56,976	54,740
Statistical Record								
Return on Assets %	4.84	6.20	6.82	7.45	6.54	4.21	5.58	4.59
Return on Equity %	13.25	15.77	15.79	17.47	19.19	14.24	16.41	14.62
EBITDA Margin %	0.71	0.78	1.05	1.51	0.86	0.66	0.77	0.69
Net Margin %	0.49	0.56	0.77	1.04	0.57	0.47	0.59	0.45
Asset Turnover	9.95	11.06	8.88	7.18	11.53	8.93	9.41	10.12
Current Ratio	1.53	1.54	1.52	1.54	1.56	1.35	1.45	1.49
Debt to Equity	0.23	0.20	0.02	0.01	0.02	0.09	0.05	0.06
Price Range	48.94-34.00	42.87-31.65	36.70-22.68	27.58-13.07	19.23-7.80	24.11-14.46	25.93-15.15	18.52-11.34
P/E Ratio	18.54-12.88	15.82-11.68	15.89-9.82	14.07-6.67	10.62-4.31	21.53-12.91	23.36-13.65	23.45-14.35
Average Yield %	0.38	0.40	0.55	0.72	0.57	0.37	0.36	0.52

Address: 9800 Northwest 41st Street, Suite 400, Miami, FL 33178 **Telephone:** 305-428-8000 **Fax:** 305-392-5621	**Web Site:** www.wfscorp.com **Officers:** Paul H. Stebbins - Chairman, Chief Executive Officer Michael J. Kasbar - President, Chief Operating Officer	**Auditors:** PricewaterhouseCoopers LLP **Investor Contact:** 305-428-8000 **Transfer Agents:** Wells Fargo Shareowner Services, St. Paul, MN

WORTHINGTON INDUSTRIES, INC.

Exchange	Symbol	Price	52Wk Range	Yield	P/E
NYS	WOR	$30.98 (3/28/2013)	31.36-15.88	3.36	14.02

*7 Year Price Score 112.93 *NYSE Composite Index=100 ***12 Month Price Score 116.28**

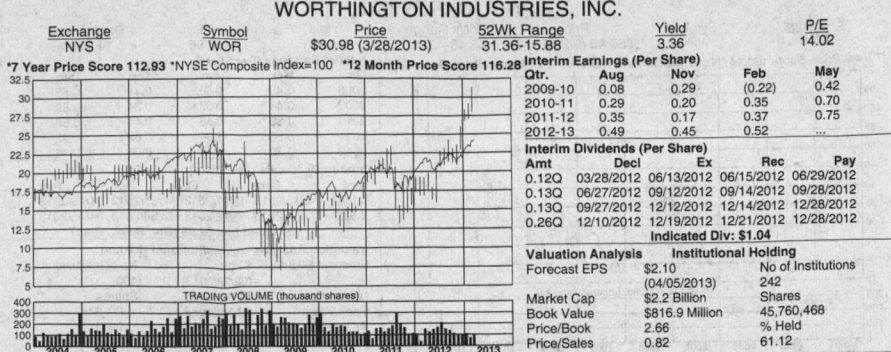

Interim Earnings (Per Share)

Qtr.	Aug	Nov	Feb	May
2009-10	0.08	0.29	(0.22)	0.42
2010-11	0.29	0.20	0.35	0.70
2011-12	0.35	0.17	0.37	0.75
2012-13	0.49	0.45	0.52	

Interim Dividends (Per Share)

Amt	Decl	Ex	Rec	Pay
0.12Q	03/28/2012	06/13/2012	06/15/2012	06/29/2012
0.13Q	06/27/2012	09/12/2012	09/14/2012	09/28/2012
0.13Q	09/27/2012	12/12/2012	12/14/2012	12/28/2012
0.26Q	12/10/2012	12/19/2012	12/21/2012	12/28/2012

Indicated Div: $1.04

Valuation Analysis

		Institutional Holding	
Forecast EPS	$2.10 (04/05/2013)	No of Institutions	242
Market Cap	$2.2 Billion	Shares	
Book Value	$816.9 Million		45,760,468
Price/Book	2.66	% Held	61.12
Price/Sales	0.82		

Business Summary: Non-Precious Metals (MIC: 8.2.2 SIC: 3312 NAIC: 331111)

Worthington Industries is a metals processing company, focused on steel processing and manufactured metal products. Co.'s manufactured metal products include: pressure cylinder products such as propane, oxygen and helium tanks, hand torches, refrigerant and industrial cylinders, camping cylinders, scuba tanks, compressed natural gas cylinders and helium balloon kits; engineered cabs and operator stations and cab components; framing systems; steel pallets and racks; and, through joint ventures, suspension grid systems for concealed and lay-in panel ceilings; laser welded blanks; light gauge steel framing for commercial and residential construction; and automotive service stampings.

Recent Developments: For the quarter ended Feb 28 2013, net income increased 31.5% to US$37.3 million from US$28.4 million in the year-earlier quarter. Revenues were US$619.5 million, up 1.4% from US$611.3 million the year before. Operating income was US$33.4 million versus US$18.1 million in the prior-year quarter, an increase of 84.8%. Direct operating expenses declined 1.0% to US$522.5 million from US$527.9 million in the comparable period the year before. Indirect operating expenses decreased 2.5% to US$63.6 million from US$65.3 million in the equivalent prior-year period.

Prospects: Our evaluation of Worthington Industries Inc. as of Apr. 7, 2013 is the result of our systematic analysis on three basic characteristics: earnings strength, relative valuation, and recent stock price movement. The company has generated a negative trend in earnings per share over the past 5 quarters and while recent estimates for the company have been raised by analysts, WOR has posted better than expected results. Based on operating earnings yield, the company is undervalued when compared to all of the companies in our coverage universe. Share price changes over the past year indicates that WOR will perform very well over the near term.

Financial Data

(US$ in Thousands)	9 Mos	6 Mos	3 Mos	05/31/2012	05/31/2011	05/31/2010	05/31/2009	05/31/2008
Earnings Per Share	2.21	2.06	1.78	1.65	1.53	0.57	(1.37)	1.31
Cash Flow Per Share	3.33	4.11	3.80	2.49	0.96	1.40	3.22	2.22
Tang Book Value Per Share	7.48	6.97	7.07	6.48	8.04	7.67	7.36	8.85
Dividends Per Share	0.760	0.490	0.480	0.460	0.400	0.400	0.680	0.680
Dividend Payout %	34.39	23.79	26.97	27.88	26.14	70.18	...	51.91
Income Statement								
Total Revenue	1,908,184	1,288,657	666,035	2,534,701	2,442,624	1,943,034	2,631,267	3,067,161
EBITDA	144,846	93,796	48,570	154,573	182,718	83,619	(113,645)	160,840
Depn & Amortn	48,136	31,088	14,987	50,644	57,765	60,529	60,178	61,154
Income Before Taxes	78,955	51,115	28,324	84,432	106,197	13,556	(194,557)	78,234
Income Taxes	47,721	31,492	16,102	51,904	58,496	26,650	(37,754)	38,616
Net Income	102,919	65,788	33,962	115,595	115,066	45,241	(108,214)	107,077
Average Shares	71,914	70,411	69,571	70,252	75,409	79,143	78,903	81,898
Balance Sheet								
Current Assets	863,580	795,114	846,185	914,234	891,635	782,285	598,935	1,104,970
Total Assets	1,885,182	1,820,835	1,805,506	1,877,797	1,667,249	1,520,347	1,363,829	1,988,031
Current Liabilities	380,709	362,824	392,724	658,263	525,002	379,802	372,080	664,895
Long-Term Obligations	406,523	406,811	407,097	257,462	250,254	250,238	100,400	245,000
Total Liabilities	1,068,307	1,044,689	1,064,401	1,180,623	977,339	808,934	657,760	1,102,654
Stockholders' Equity	816,875	776,146	741,105	697,174	689,910	711,413	706,069	885,377
Shares Outstanding	70,168	69,060	68,679	67,906	71,683	79,217	78,997	79,308
Statistical Record								
Return on Assets %	8.28	8.38	7.18	6.50	7.22	3.14	N.M.	5.62
Return on Equity %	20.56	19.97	17.41	16.62	16.42	6.38	N.M.	11.73
EBITDA Margin %	7.59	7.28	7.29	6.10	7.48	4.30	N.M.	5.24
Net Margin %	5.39	5.11	5.10	4.56	4.71	2.33	N.M.	3.49
Asset Turnover	1.42	1.55	1.51	1.43	1.53	1.35	1.57	1.61
Current Ratio	2.27	2.19	2.15	1.39	1.70	2.06	1.61	1.66
Debt to Equity	0.50	0.52	0.55	0.37	0.36	0.35	0.14	0.28
Price Range	29.10-15.88	24.27-15.58	23.16-13.21	23.45-13.21	21.83-12.05	17.67-11.05	24.11-7.15	25.86-14.58
P/E Ratio	13.17-7.19	11.78-7.56	13.01-7.42	14.21-8.01	14.27-7.88	31.00-19.39	...	19.74-11.13
Average Yield %	3.51	2.50	2.68	2.59	2.34	2.81	4.94	3.41

Address: 200 Old Wilson Bridge Road, Columbus, OH 43085 **Telephone:** 614-438-3210 **Fax:** 614-438-3256	**Web Site:** www.worthingtonindustries.com **Officers:** John P. McConnell - Chairman, Chief Executive Officer Mark A. Russell - President, Chief Operating Officer	**Auditors:** KPMG LLP **Investor Contact:** 614-438-3077 **Transfer Agents:** Wells Fargo Shareowner Services, St. Paul, MN

W.P. CAREY INC

Exchange	Symbol	Price	52Wk Range	Yield	P/E	Div Achiever
NYS	WPC	$67.40 (3/28/2013)	68.45-42.36	4.39	52.66	14 Years

*7 Year Price Score 133.14 *NYSE Composite Index=100 ***12 Month Price Score 111.96**

Interim Earnings (Per Share)

Qtr.	Mar	Jun	Sep	Dec
2008	0.43	0.50	0.48	0.55
2009	0.44	0.37	0.34	0.59
2010	0.36	0.59	0.41	0.50
2011	0.58	1.94	0.62	0.23
2012	0.30	0.77	0.06	0.16

Interim Dividends (Per Share)

Amt	Decl	Ex	Rec	Pay
0.66Q	12/13/2012	12/27/2012	12/31/2012	01/15/2013
0.82Q	03/14/2013	03/26/2013	03/28/2013	04/15/2013

Indicated Div: $2.96 (Div. Reinv. Plan)

Valuation Analysis   **Institutional Holding**

Forecast EPS	$2.03	No of Institutions
	(02/28/2013)	100
Market Cap	$4.6 Billion	Shares
Book Value	$2.0 Billion	1,471,315
Price/Book	2.28	% Held
Price/Sales	12.34	0.60

Business Summary: REITs (MIC: 5.3.1 SIC: 6798 NAIC: 525930)

W.P. Carey provides long-term financing via sale-leaseback and build-to-suit transactions for companies and manages a global investment portfolio. Co. has two key segments: investment management, which structures and negotiates investments and debt placement transactions for the Corporate Property Associates® real estate investment trusts and Co.'s Carey Watermark Investors Incorporated business, and manages their portfolios of real estate investments; and real estate ownership, which owns and invests in commercial properties in the U.S. and the European Union that are then leased to companies. At Dec 31 2011, Co. owned and managed over 980 properties domestically and globally.

Recent Developments: For the year ended Dec 31 2012, income from continuing operations decreased 47.8% to US$79.4 million from US$152.0 million a year earlier. Net income decreased 54.9% to US$62.8 million from US$139.1 million in the prior year. Revenues were US$374.0 million, up 14.1% from US$327.8 million the year before. Revenues from property income rose 80.4% to US$135.0 million from US$74.9 million in the corresponding earlier year.

Prospects: Our evaluation of W.P.Carey Inc. as of Apr. 7, 2013 is the result of our systematic analysis on three basic characteristics: earnings strength, relative valuation, and recent stock price movement. The company has enjoyed a very positive trend in earnings per share over the past 5 quarters. Because the company lacks sufficient analyst estimate data, we place greater weight on the historical EPS trend as the measure of earnings strength. Based on operating earnings yield, the company is overvalued when compared to all of the companies in our coverage universe. Share price changes over the past year indicates that WPC will perform poorly over the near term.

Financial Data

(US$ in Thousands)	12/31/2012	12/31/2011	12/31/2010	12/31/2009	12/31/2008	12/31/2007	12/31/2006	12/31/2005
Earnings Per Share	1.28	3.42	1.86	1.74	1.96	2.05	2.22	1.25
Cash Flow Per Share	1.70	2.01	2.19	1.91	1.61	1.25	3.18	1.40
Tang Book Value Per Share	14.03	14.01	13.62	13.79	14.01	13.63	13.71	13.34
Dividends Per Share	0.660	2.190	2.030	2.000	1.960	1.880	1.820	1.790
Dividend Payout %	51.56	64.04	109.14	114.94	100.00	91.71	81.98	143.20
Income Statement								
Total Revenue	373,995	336,409	273,910	235,876	243,873	263,129	273,258	174,117
EBITDA	121,448	170,632	113,818	107,754	127,357	147,487	168,162	82,548
Depn & Amortn	48,509	23,325	24,443	24,476	27,197	27,321	27,207	11,939
Income Before Taxes	23,762	127,388	74,409	69,803	83,755	106,128	126,249	57,333
Income Taxes	6,783	37,228	25,822	22,793	23,521	51,739	45,491	19,390
Net Income	62,132	139,079	73,972	69,023	78,047	79,252	86,303	48,604
Average Shares	48,078	40,098	40,007	39,712	40,221	39,868	39,093	39,020
Balance Sheet								
Current Assets	159,906	67,666	103,486	54,448	69,873	100,466	110,992	95,947
Total Assets	4,609,042	1,462,623	1,172,326	1,093,336	1,111,136	1,153,284	1,093,010	983,262
Current Liabilities	335,791	149,152	102,324	126,906	119,902	166,193	120,740	50,020
Long-Term Obligations	1,968,397	589,369	396,982	326,330	326,874	316,751	278,653	246,113
Total Liabilities	2,581,896	780,042	547,313	467,703	463,000	519,013	461,025	375,794
Stockholders' Equity	2,027,146	682,581	625,013	625,633	648,136	634,271	631,985	607,468
Shares Outstanding	68,485	39,729	39,454	39,204	39,589	39,216	38,262	37,706
Statistical Record								
Return on Assets %	2.04	10.56	6.53	6.26	6.87	7.06	8.31	4.87
Return on Equity %	4.57	21.27	11.83	10.84	12.14	12.52	13.93	7.93
EBITDA Margin %	32.47	50.72	41.55	45.68	52.22	56.05	61.54	47.41
Net Margin %	16.61	41.34	27.01	29.26	32.00	30.12	31.58	27.91
Asset Turnover	0.12	0.26	0.24	0.21	0.21	0.23	0.26	0.17
Current Ratio	0.48	0.45	1.01	0.43	0.58	0.60	0.92	1.92
Debt to Equity	0.97	0.86	0.64	0.52	0.50	0.50	0.44	0.41
Price Range	54.70-41.65	44.34-29.85	31.96-25.00	30.27-17.00	34.00-18.45	36.43-29.62	30.82-24.20	35.52-23.95
P/E Ratio	42.73-32.54	12.96-8.73	17.18-13.44	17.40-9.77	17.35-9.41	17.77-14.45	13.88-10.90	28.42-19.16
Average Yield %	1.41	5.91	7.02	7.91	6.93	5.77	6.70	6.21

Address: 50 Rockefeller Plaza, New York, NY 10020	Web Site: www.wpcarey.com	Auditors: PricewaterhouseCoopers LLP
Telephone: 212-492-1100	Officers: Polk Carey - Chairman Trevor P. Bond - President, Chief Executive Officer	Investor Contact: 180-097-22739 Transfer Agents: Computershare, Pittsburgh, PA

WPX ENERGY, INC.

Exchange	Symbol	Price	52Wk Range	Yield	P/E
NYS	WPX	$16.02 (3/28/2013)	18.61-13.37	N/A	N/A

*7 Year Price Score N/A   *NYSE Composite Index=100   *12 Month Price Score 89.22

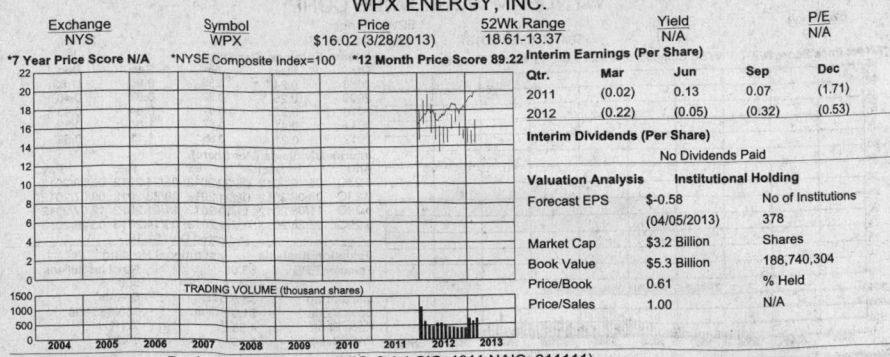

Interim Earnings (Per Share)

Qtr.	Mar	Jun	Sep	Dec
2011	(0.02)	0.13	0.07	(1.71)
2012	(0.22)	(0.05)	(0.32)	(0.53)

Interim Dividends (Per Share)

No Dividends Paid

Valuation Analysis

		Institutional Holding	
Forecast EPS	$-0.58	No of Institutions	
	(04/05/2013)	378	
Market Cap	$3.2 Billion	Shares	
Book Value	$5.3 Billion	188,740,304	
Price/Book	0.61	% Held	
Price/Sales	1.00	N/A	

Business Summary: Production & Extraction (MIC: 9.1.1 SIC: 1311 NAIC: 211111)

WPX Energy is an independent natural gas and oil exploration and production company engaged in the exploitation and development of long-life unconventional properties. Co. is focused on profitably exploiting its significant natural gas reserves base and related natural gas liquids in the Piceance Basin of the Rocky Mountain region, and on developing and growing its positions in the Bakken Shale oil play in North Dakota and the Marcellus Shale natural gas play in Pennsylvania. Co.'s other areas of domestic operations include the Powder River Basin in Wyoming and the San Juan Basin in the southwestern United States.

Recent Developments: For the year ended Dec 31 2012, loss from continuing operations was US$233.0 million compared with a loss of US$150.0 million a year earlier. Net loss amounted to US$211.0 million versus a net loss of US$292.0 million in the prior year. Revenues were US$3.19 billion, down 17.9% from US$3.88 billion the year before. Operating loss was US$280.0 million versus a loss of US$142.0 million in the prior year. Indirect operating expenses decreased 13.8% to US$3.47 billion from US$4.02.0 billion in the equivalent prior-year period.

Prospects: Our evaluation of WPX Energy Inc. as of Apr. 7, 2013 is the result of our systematic analysis on three basic characteristics: earnings strength, relative valuation, and recent stock price movement. The company has produced a positive trend in earnings per share over the past 5 quarters. Because the company lacks sufficient analyst estimate data, we place greater weight on the historical EPS trend as the measure of earnings strength. Based on operating earnings yield, the company is overvalued when compared to all of the companies in our coverage universe. Share price changes over the past year indicates that WPX will perform very poorly over the near term.

Financial Data
(US$ in Millions)

	12/31/2012	12/31/2011	12/31/2010	12/31/2009
Earnings Per Share	(1.12)	(1.53)	(6.55)	0.68
Cash Flow Per Share	3.98	6.12	5.36	...
Tang Book Value Per Share	26.43	28.82	...	...
Income Statement				
Total Revenue	3,189	3,988	4,034	3,681
EBITDA	721	623	(454)	1,201
Depn & Amortn	1,001	956	882	894
Income Before Taxes	(374)	(441)	(1,444)	225
Income Taxes	(111)	(145)	(149)	96
Net Income	(223)	(302)	(1,291)	134
Average Shares	198	197	197	197
Balance Sheet				
Current Assets	772	1,674	958	...
Total Assets	9,456	10,432	9,846	...
Current Liabilities	726	1,156	3,167	...
Long-Term Obligations	1,508	1,503	...	...
Total Liabilities	4,188	4,754	5,434	...
Stockholders' Equity	5,268	5,678	4,412	...
Shares Outstanding	199	197	...	...
Statistical Record				
EBITDA Margin %	22.61	15.62	N.M.	32.63
Net Margin %	N.M.	N.M.	N.M.	3.64
Asset Turnover	0.32	0.39	...	...
Current Ratio	1.06	1.45	0.30	...
Debt to Equity	0.29	0.26	...	...
Price Range	19.67-13.37	...	...	...

Address: One Williams Center, Tulsa, OK 74172-0172
Telephone: 855-979-2012

Web Site: www.wpxenergy.com
Officers: William G. Lowrie - Chairman Ralph A. Hill - President, Chief Executive Officer

Auditors: Ernst & Young LLP
Investor Contact: 539-573-9360
Transfer Agents: Computershare Trust Company, N.A., Canton, MA

WYNDHAM WORLDWIDE CORP

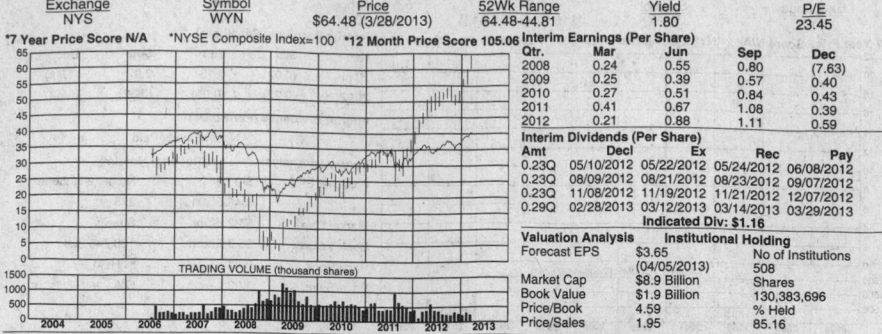

Exchange	Symbol	Price	52Wk Range	Yield	P/E
NYS	WYN	$64.48 (3/28/2013)	64.48-44.81	1.80	23.45

*7 Year Price Score N/A   *NYSE Composite Index=100   *12 Month Price Score 105.06

Interim Earnings (Per Share)

Qtr.	Mar	Jun	Sep	Dec
2008	0.24	0.55	0.80	(7.63)
2009	0.25	0.39	0.57	0.40
2010	0.27	0.51	0.84	0.43
2011	0.41	0.67	1.08	0.39
2012	0.21	0.88	1.11	0.59

Interim Dividends (Per Share)

Amt	Decl	Ex	Rec	Pay
0.23Q	05/10/2012	05/22/2012	05/24/2012	06/08/2012
0.23Q	08/09/2012	08/21/2012	08/23/2012	09/07/2012
0.23Q	11/08/2012	11/19/2012	11/21/2012	12/07/2012
0.29Q	02/28/2013	03/12/2013	03/14/2013	03/29/2013

Indicated Div: $1.16

Valuation Analysis		Institutional Holding	
Forecast EPS	$3.65 (04/05/2013)	No of Institutions	508
Market Cap	$8.9 Billion	Shares	130,383,696
Book Value	$1.9 Billion	% Held	85.16
Price/Book	4.59		
Price/Sales	1.95		

Business Summary: Hotels, Restaurants & Travel (MIC: 2.2.1 SIC: 7011 NAIC: 721110)

Wyndham Worldwide is a hospitality company. Co. provides hospitality services and products through its portfolio of brands. Co.'s operations are grouped into three segments: Lodging, which franchises hotels, and provides hotel management services; Vacation Exchange and Rentals, which provides vacation exchange services and products to owners of intervals of vacation ownership interests (VOIs) and markets vacation rental properties primarily on behalf of independent owners; and Vacation Ownership, which develops, markets and sells VOIs to individual consumers, provides consumer financing in connection with the sale of VOIs and provides property management services at resorts.

Recent Developments: For the year ended Dec 31 2012, net income decreased 4.3% to US$399.0 million from US$417.0 million in the prior year. Revenues were US$4.53 billion, up 6.6% from US$4.25 billion the year before. Operating income was US$852.0 million versus US$767.0 million in the prior year, an increase of 11.1%. Direct operating expenses rose 3.4% to US$2.09 billion from US$2.03 billion in the comparable period the year before. Indirect operating expenses increased 8.7% to US$1.59 billion from US$1.46 billion in the equivalent prior-year period.

Prospects: Our evaluation of Wyndham Worldwide Corp. as of Apr. 7, 2013 is the result of our systematic analysis on three basic characteristics: earnings strength, relative valuation, and recent stock price movement. The company has managed to produce a neutral trend in earnings per share over the past 5 quarters. However, while recent estimates for the company have been mixed, WYN has posted better than expected results. Based on operating earnings yield, the company is about fairly valued when compared to all of the companies in our coverage universe. Share price changes over the past year indicates that WYN will perform well over the near term.

Financial Data
(US$ in Millions)

	12/31/2012	12/31/2011	12/31/2010	12/31/2009	12/31/2008	12/31/2007	12/31/2006	12/31/2005
Earnings Per Share	2.75	2.51	2.05	1.61	(6.05)	2.20	1.44	...
Cash Flow Per Share	7.00	6.19	3.57	3.85	0.61	0.06	0.83	...
Tang Book Value Per Share	N.M.	N.M.	1.53	1.41	N.M.	N.M.	N.M.	...
Dividends Per Share	0.920	0.600	0.480	0.160	0.160	0.080	...	...
Dividend Payout %	33.45	23.90	23.41	9.94	...	3.64	...	...
Income Statement								
Total Revenue	4,534	4,254	3,851	3,750	4,281	4,360	3,842	3,470
EBITDA	783	924	870	750	(665)	856	690	714
Depn & Amortn	31	146	145	150	154	139	113	99
Income Before Taxes	628	650	563	493	(887)	655	542	621
Income Taxes	229	233	184	200	187	252	190	193
Net Income	400	417	379	293	(1,074)	403	287	428
Average Shares	145	166	185	182	178	183	199	...
Balance Sheet								
Current Assets	1,866	1,730	1,752	1,740	1,914	2,056	2,052	2,569
Total Assets	9,463	9,023	9,416	9,352	9,573	10,459	9,520	9,164
Current Liabilities	1,931	1,563	1,575	1,885	2,169	2,180	1,977	1,295
Long-Term Obligations	4,018	3,773	3,510	3,138	3,331	3,195	2,607	1,687
Total Liabilities	7,533	6,791	6,499	6,664	7,231	6,943	5,961	4,134
Stockholders' Equity	1,930	2,232	2,917	2,688	2,342	3,516	3,559	5,030
Shares Outstanding	137	147	173	178	177	177	190	...
Statistical Record								
Return on Assets %	4.32	4.52	4.04	3.10	N.M.	4.03	3.07	4.89
Return on Equity %	19.17	16.20	13.52	11.65	N.M.	11.39	6.68	8.82
EBITDA Margin %	17.27	21.72	22.59	20.00	N.M.	19.63	17.96	20.58
Net Margin %	8.82	9.80	9.84	7.81	N.M.	9.24	7.47	12.33
Asset Turnover	0.49	0.46	0.41	0.40	0.43	0.44	0.41	0.40
Current Ratio	0.97	1.11	1.11	0.92	0.88	0.94	1.04	1.98
Debt to Equity	2.08	1.69	1.20	1.17	1.42	0.91	0.73	0.34
Price Range	55.04-36.87	38.09-25.38	31.08-20.12	21.20-2.92	24.94-2.98	38.69-23.56	34.41-26.07	...
P/E Ratio	20.01-13.41	15.18-10.11	15.16-9.81	13.17-1.81	...	17.59-10.71	23.90-18.10	...
Average Yield %	1.87	1.87	1.89	1.31	0.94	0.24	...	...

Address: 22 Sylvan Way, Parsippany, NJ 07054	**Web Site:** www.wyndhamworldwide.com	**Auditors:** Deloitte & Touche LLP
Telephone: 973-753-6000	**Officers:** Stephen P. Holmes - Chairman, Chief Executive Officer Thomas F. Anderson - Executive	**Investor Contact:** 973-753-5500
Fax: 973-496-8906	Vice President, Chief Real Estate Development Officer	**Transfer Agents:** Wells Fargo Shareowner Services, Saint Paul, MN

XCEL ENERGY, INC.

Exchange	Symbol	Price	52Wk Range	Yield	P/E
NYS	XEL	$29.70 (3/28/2013)	29.70-26.00	3.64	16.05

*7 Year Price Score 109.41 *NYSE Composite Index=100 *12 Month Price Score 94.79

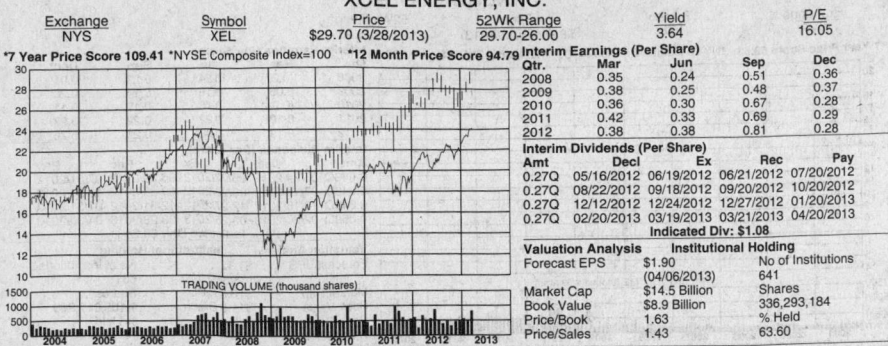

Interim Earnings (Per Share)

Qtr.	Mar	Jun	Sep	Dec
2008	0.35	0.24	0.51	0.36
2009	0.38	0.25	0.48	0.37
2010	0.36	0.30	0.67	0.28
2011	0.42	0.33	0.69	0.29
2012	0.38	0.38	0.81	0.28

Interim Dividends (Per Share)

Amt	Decl	Ex	Rec	Pay
0.27Q	05/16/2012	06/19/2012	06/21/2012	07/20/2012
0.27Q	08/22/2012	09/18/2012	09/20/2012	10/20/2012
0.27Q	12/12/2012	12/24/2012	12/27/2012	01/20/2013
0.27Q	02/20/2013	03/19/2013	03/21/2013	04/20/2013

Indicated Div: $1.08

Valuation Analysis & **Institutional Holding**

Forecast EPS	$1.90	No of Institutions
	(04/06/2013)	641
Market Cap	$14.5 Billion	Shares
Book Value	$8.9 Billion	336,293,184
Price/Book	1.63	% Held
Price/Sales	1.43	63.60

Business Summary: Electric Utilities (MIC: 3.1.1 SIC: 4931 NAIC: 221121)

Xcel Energy is a holding company. Co.'s subsidiaries engaged primarily in the utility business. Co. has four wholly owned utility subsidiaries that serves electric and natural gas customers in eight states. These utility subsidiaries are Northern States Power Company (NSP)-Minnesota, NSP-Wisconsin, Public Service Company of Colorado and Southwestern Public Service Co., and serve customers in portions of Colorado, Michigan, Minnesota, New Mexico, North Dakota, South Dakota, Texas and Wisconsin. Co.'s nonregulated subsidiary is Eloigne Company, which invests in rental housing projects that qualify for low-income housing tax credits.

Recent Developments: For the year ended Dec 31 2012, income from continuing operations increased 7.6% to US$905.2 million from US$841.4 million a year earlier. Net income increased 7.6% to US$905.2 million from US$841.2 million in the prior year. Revenues were US$10.13 billion, down 4.9% from US$10.65 billion the year before. Operating income was US$1.82 billion versus US$1.78 billion in the prior year, an increase of 2.3%. Direct operating expenses declined 8.4% to US$6.71 billion from US$7.33 billion in the comparable period the year before. Indirect operating expenses increased 3.1% to US$1.60 billion from US$1.55 billion in the equivalent prior-year period.

Prospects: Our evaluation of Xcel Energy Inc. as of Apr. 7, 2013 is the result of our systematic analysis on three basic characteristics: earnings strength, relative valuation, and recent stock price movement. The company has managed to produce a neutral trend in earnings per share over the past 5 quarters and while recent estimates for the company have been mixed, XEL has posted better than expected results. Based on operating earnings yield, the company is undervalued when compared to all of the companies in our coverage universe. Share price changes over the past year indicates that XEL will perform poorly over the near term.

Financial Data

(US$ in Thousands)	12/31/2012	12/31/2011	12/31/2010	12/31/2009	12/31/2008	12/31/2007	12/31/2006	12/31/2005
Earnings Per Share	1.85	1.72	1.62	1.48	1.46	1.35	1.36	1.23
Cash Flow Per Share	4.10	4.96	4.10	4.20	3.83	3.78	4.74	2.94
Tang Book Value Per Share	18.19	17.44	16.76	15.92	15.35	14.70	14.28	13.37
Dividends Per Share	1.070	1.033	1.002	0.973	0.943	0.912	0.882	0.853
Dividend Payout %	57.84	60.03	61.88	65.71	64.55	67.59	64.89	69.31
Income Statement								
Total Revenue	10,128,223	10,654,770	10,310,947	9,644,303	11,203,156	10,034,170	9,840,304	9,625,477
EBITDA	2,928,372	2,844,818	2,689,143	2,477,794	2,404,765	2,293,295	2,101,487	1,938,590
Depn & Amortn	1,047,001	1,013,377	992,902	938,693	940,397	900,670	894,854	815,784
Income Before Taxes	1,325,431	1,279,163	1,158,643	1,032,174	980,240	866,325	743,281	670,066
Income Taxes	450,203	468,316	436,635	371,314	338,686	294,484	181,411	173,539
Net Income	905,229	841,172	755,834	680,887	645,554	577,348	571,754	512,972
Average Shares	488,434	485,615	463,391	457,139	441,813	433,131	429,605	425,671
Balance Sheet								
Current Assets	2,625,139	2,982,564	2,732,643	2,763,411	3,015,529	2,807,193	2,634,186	3,141,861
Total Assets	31,140,686	29,497,267	27,387,690	25,488,428	24,958,495	23,184,727	21,958,346	21,648,316
Current Liabilities	2,937,073	3,588,639	2,536,533	3,015,257	3,046,245	3,641,124	2,865,281	3,672,826
Long-Term Obligations	10,143,905	8,848,513	9,263,144	7,888,628	7,731,688	6,342,160	6,449,638	5,897,789
Total Liabilities	22,266,609	21,015,069	19,199,191	18,100,203	17,889,774	16,778,745	16,036,544	16,148,081
Stockholders' Equity	8,874,077	8,482,198	8,188,499	7,388,225	7,068,721	6,405,982	5,921,802	5,500,235
Shares Outstanding	487,959	486,493	482,333	457,509	453,791	428,782	407,296	403,387
Statistical Record								
Return on Assets %	2.98	2.96	2.86	2.70	2.67	2.56	2.62	2.45
Return on Equity %	10.40	10.09	9.70	9.42	9.56	9.37	10.01	9.49
EBITDA Margin %	28.91	26.70	26.08	25.69	21.47	22.85	21.36	20.14
Net Margin %	8.94	7.89	7.33	7.06	5.76	5.75	5.81	5.33
Asset Turnover	0.33	0.37	0.39	0.38	0.46	0.44	0.45	0.46
Current Ratio	0.89	0.83	1.08	0.92	0.99	0.77	0.92	0.86
Debt to Equity	1.14	1.04	1.13	1.07	1.09	0.99	1.09	1.07
Price Range	29.58-26.00	27.71-21.82	24.33-20.04	21.77-16.19	22.75-16.29	24.99-19.80	23.47-17.89	19.90-16.57
P/E Ratio	15.99-14.05	16.11-12.69	15.02-12.37	14.71-10.94	15.58-11.16	18.51-14.67	17.26-13.15	16.18-13.47
Average Yield %	3.90	4.21	4.55	5.15	4.72	4.06	4.42	4.62

Address: 414 Nicollet Mall, Minneapolis, MN 55401 **Telephone:** 612-330-5500	**Web Site:** www.xcelenergy.com **Officers:** Benjamin G.S. Fowke - Chairman, President, Chief Executive Officer Teresa S. Madden - Senior Vice President, Chief Financial Officer, Principal Financial Officer, Vice President, Controller	**Auditors:** Deloitte & Touche LLP **Investor Contact:** 612-215-4535 **Transfer Agents:** Wells Fargo Shareowner Services, South St. Paul, MN

XEROX CORP

Exchange	Symbol	Price	52Wk Range	Yield	P/E
NYS	XRX	$8.60 (3/28/2013)	8.76-6.23	2.67	9.77

*7 Year Price Score 59.63 *NYSE Composite Index=100 ***12 Month Price Score 102.16**

TRADING VOLUME (thousand shares)

Interim Earnings (Per Share)

Qtr.	Mar	Jun	Sep	Dec
2008	(0.27)	0.24	0.29	0.01
2009	0.05	0.16	0.14	0.20
2010	(0.04)	0.16	0.17	0.11
2011	0.19	0.22	0.22	0.27
2012	0.19	0.22	0.21	0.26

Interim Dividends (Per Share)

Amt	Decl	Ex	Rec	Pay
0.043Q	05/24/2012	06/27/2012	06/29/2012	07/31/2012
0.043Q	07/17/2012	09/26/2012	09/28/2012	10/31/2012
0.043Q	10/16/2012	12/27/2012	12/31/2012	01/31/2013
0.058Q	02/20/2013	03/26/2013	03/28/2013	04/30/2013

Indicated Div: $0.23

Valuation Analysis

		Institutional Holding	
Forecast EPS	$1.12 (04/06/2013)	No of Institutions	631
Market Cap	$10.5 Billion	Shares	1,165,011,968
Book Value	$11.9 Billion	% Held	76.31
Price/Book	0.89		
Price/Sales	0.47		

Business Summary: Peripherals (MIC: 6.2.2 SIC: 3577 NAIC: 333315)

Xerox is a provider of business process and document management. Co. is a Business Process Outsourcing (BPO) company engaged in managing transaction processes. Co. designs, develops and delivers Information Technology applications that utilize its data centers, help desks and managed storage facilities. Co.'s document technology products and applications support the work processes of its customers and provide them a printing and communications infrastructure. Co. operates in two segments: Services, which comprises three service offerings: BPO, Information Technology Outsourcing and document outsourcing; and Technology, comprising three product groups: entry, mid-range and high-end.

Recent Developments: For the year ended Dec 31 2012, net income decreased 7.9% to US$1.22 billion from US$1.33 billion in the prior year. Revenues were US$22.39 billion, down 1.0% from US$22.63 billion the year before. Direct operating expenses rose 1.3% to US$15.16 billion from US$14.97 billion in the comparable period the year before. Indirect operating expenses decreased 3.6% to US$5.88 billion from US$6.10 billion in the equivalent prior-year period.

Prospects: Our evaluation of Xerox Corp. as of Apr. 7, 2013 is the result of our systematic analysis on three basic characteristics: earnings strength, relative valuation, and recent stock price movement. The company has managed to produce a neutral trend in earnings per share over the past 5 quarters and while recent estimates for the company have remained steady, XRX has posted better than expected results. Based on operating earnings yield, the company is undervalued when compared to all of the companies in our coverage universe. Share price changes over the past year indicates that XRX will perform very poorly over the near term.

Financial Data

(US$ in Thousands)	12/31/2012	12/31/2011	12/31/2010	12/31/2009	12/31/2008	12/31/2007	12/31/2006	12/31/2005
Earnings Per Share	0.88	0.90	0.43	0.55	0.26	1.19	1.22	0.94
Cash Flow Per Share	1.98	1.41	2.06	2.54	1.06	2.00	1.71	1.48
Tang Book Value Per Share	0.02	0.28	0.24	3.49	2.83	4.93	5.04	4.68
Dividends Per Share	0.170	0.170	0.170	0.170	0.170	0.043	...	...
Dividend Payout %	19.32	18.89	39.53	30.91	65.38	3.57	...	...
Income Statement								
Total Revenue	22,390,000	22,626,000	21,633,000	15,179,000	17,608,000	17,228,000	15,895,000	15,701,000
EBITDA	2,822,000	2,828,000	2,396,000	1,773,000	1,031,000	2,569,000	1,857,000	1,791,000
Depn & Amortn	1,059,000	806,000	1,008,000	640,000	613,000	577,000	552,000	527,000
Income Before Taxes	1,348,000	1,565,000	815,000	627,000	(114,000)	1,468,000	830,000	845,000
Income Taxes	277,000	386,000	256,000	152,000	(231,000)	400,000	(288,000)	(5,000)
Net Income	1,195,000	1,295,000	606,000	485,000	230,000	1,135,000	1,210,000	978,000
Average Shares	1,329,184	1,443,774	1,350,728	879,520	895,542	952,941	996,522	1,045,353
Balance Sheet								
Current Assets	8,273,000	7,912,000	8,639,000	9,731,000	8,150,000	8,540,000	8,754,000	8,736,000
Total Assets	30,015,000	30,116,000	30,600,000	24,032,000	22,447,000	23,543,000	21,709,000	21,953,000
Current Liabilities	5,910,000	6,381,000	6,417,000	4,461,000	5,450,000	4,077,000	4,698,000	4,346,000
Long-Term Obligations	7,447,000	7,088,000	7,237,000	8,276,000	6,774,000	6,939,000	5,660,000	6,139,000
Total Liabilities	18,145,000	17,891,000	18,245,000	16,982,000	16,209,000	14,955,000	14,629,000	14,745,000
Stockholders' Equity	11,870,000	12,225,000	12,355,000	7,050,000	6,238,000	8,588,000	7,080,000	7,208,000
Shares Outstanding	1,223,772	1,337,341	1,397,578	869,381	864,777	917,177	946,205	931,189
Statistical Record								
Return on Assets %	3.96	4.27	2.22	2.09	1.00	5.02	5.54	4.18
Return on Equity %	9.89	10.54	6.25	7.30	3.09	14.49	16.94	13.64
EBITDA Margin %	12.60	12.50	11.08	11.68	5.86	14.91	11.68	11.41
Net Margin %	5.34	5.72	2.80	3.20	1.31	6.59	7.61	6.23
Asset Turnover	0.74	0.75	0.79	0.65	0.76	0.76	0.73	0.67
Current Ratio	1.40	1.24	1.35	2.18	1.50	2.09	1.86	2.01
Debt to Equity	0.63	0.58	0.59	1.17	1.09	0.81	0.80	0.85
Price Range	8.76-6.23	11.71-6.72	12.01-7.91	9.57-4.17	16.19-5.25	19.90-15.79	17.22-13.28	17.01-12.41
P/E Ratio	9.95-7.08	13.01-7.47	27.93-18.40	17.40-7.58	62.27-20.19	16.72-13.27	14.11-10.89	18.10-13.20
Average Yield %	2.28	1.81	1.71	2.37	1.36	0.24	...	...

Address: P.O. Box 4505, 45 Glover Avenue, Norwalk, CT 06856-4505 **Telephone:** 203-968-3000	**Web Site:** www.xerox.com **Officers:** Ursula M. Burns - Chairman, President, Chief Executive Officer James A. Firestone - Executive Vice President, Division Officer	**Auditors:** PricewaterhouseCoopers LLP **Transfer Agents:** Computershare Trust Company, N.A., Providence, RI

XL GROUP PLC

Exchange	Symbol	Price	52Wk Range	Yield	P/E
NYS	XL	$30.30 (3/28/2013)	30.40-19.60	1.85	14.43

*7 Year Price Score 65.02   *NYSE Composite Index=100   *12 Month Price Score 111.09

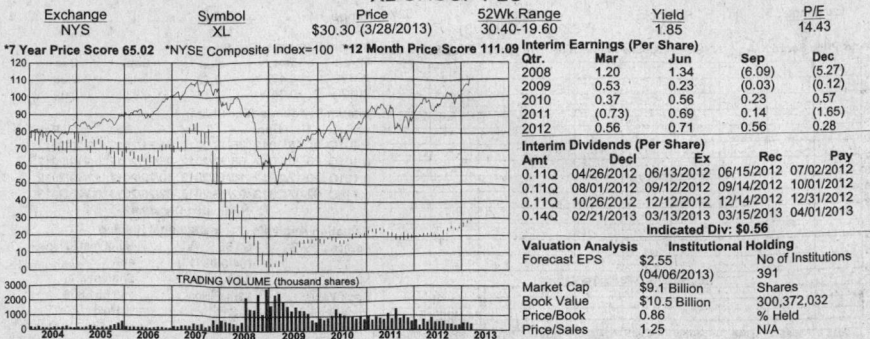

Interim Earnings (Per Share)

Qtr.	Mar	Jun	Sep	Dec
2008	1.20	1.34	(6.09)	(5.27)
2009	0.53	0.23	(0.03)	(0.12)
2010	0.37	0.56	0.23	0.57
2011	(0.73)	0.69	0.14	(1.65)
2012	0.56	0.71	0.56	0.28

Interim Dividends (Per Share)

Amt	Decl	Ex	Rec	Pay
0.11Q	04/26/2012	06/13/2012	06/15/2012	07/02/2012
0.11Q	08/01/2012	09/12/2012	09/14/2012	10/01/2012
0.11Q	10/26/2012	12/12/2012	12/14/2012	12/31/2012
0.14Q	02/21/2013	03/13/2013	03/15/2013	04/01/2013

Indicated Div: $0.56

Valuation Analysis

Forecast EPS	$2.55 (04/06/2013)
Market Cap	$9.1 Billion
Book Value	$10.5 Billion
Price/Book	0.86
Price/Sales	1.25

Institutional Holding

No of Institutions	391
Shares	300,372,032
% Held	N/A

Business Summary: General Insurance (MIC: 5.2.1 SIC: 6351 NAIC: 524126)

XL Group is an insurance and reinsurance holding company. Through its subsidiaries, Co. is engaged in providing property, casualty and products to industrial, commercial and other firms, insurance companies and other enterprises. Co. is organized into three operating segments: Insurance, which includes the business units of International Property and Casualty, North America Property and Casualty, Global Professional and Global Specialty Lines; Reinsurance, which provides casualty, property risk, property catastrophe, marine, aviation, treaty and other reinsurance; and Life Operations, which covers various geographic markets with an emphasis on the U.K., U.S., Ireland and Continental Europe.

Recent Developments: For the year ended Dec 31 2012, net income amounted to US$730.4 million versus a net loss of US$403.9 million in the prior year. Revenues were US$7.23 billion, up 8.0% from US$6.70 billion the year before. Net premiums earned were US$6.09 billion versus US$5.69 billion in the prior year, an increase of 7.0%. Net investment income fell 11.0% to US$1.01 billion from US$1.14 billion a year ago.

Prospects: Our evaluation of XL Group plc as of Apr. 7, 2013 is the result of our systematic analysis on three basic characteristics: earnings strength, relative valuation, and recent stock price movement. The company has produced a positive trend in earnings per share over the past 5 quarters and while recent estimates for the company have been raised by analysts, XL has posted better than expected results. Based on operating earnings yield, the company is undervalued when compared to all of the companies in our coverage universe. Share price changes over the past year indicates that XL will perform in line with the market over the near term.

Financial Data
(US$ in Thousands)

	12/31/2012	12/31/2011	12/31/2010	12/31/2009	12/31/2008	12/31/2007	12/31/2006	12/31/2006
Earnings Per Share	2.10	(1.52)	1.73	0.61	(11.02)	1.15	9.60	...
Cash Flow Per Share	3.43	1.05	1.77	(0.13)	(1.78)	12.55	13.64	...
Tang Book Value Per Share	33.82	28.57	31.11	25.63	17.42	45.57	45.93	...
Dividends Per Share	...	...	0.400	0.400	1.140	1.520	1.520	...
Dividend Payout %	...	...	23.12	65.57	...	132.17	15.83	...
Income Statement								
Premium Income	6,090,441	5,690,130	5,414,061	5,706,840	6,640,102	7,205,356	7,569,518	...
Total Revenue	7,230,480	6,696,803	6,398,582	6,193,647	7,148,119	9,135,722	9,833,195	...
Benefits & Claims	3,765,482	4,078,391	3,211,800	3,168,837	3,962,898	3,841,003	4,201,194	...
Income Before Taxes	708,606	(420,962)	684,746	134,714	(872,989)	1,593,587	1,895,758	...
Income Taxes	34,028	59,707	162,737	120,307	222,578	233,922	219,645	...
Net Income	651,134	(403,883)	643,377	74,991	(2,553,813)	275,889	1,762,767	...
Average Shares	310,282	312,896	337,709	340,966	238,862	179,693	179,450	...
Balance Sheet								
Total Assets	45,387,779	44,626,077	45,023,351	45,579,675	45,682,005	57,762,264	59,308,870	...
Total Liabilities	34,877,707	35,201,139	34,340,698	35,966,890	39,066,772	47,814,122	49,177,704	...
Stockholders' Equity	10,510,072	9,424,938	10,682,653	9,612,785	6,615,233	9,948,142	10,131,166	...
Shares Outstanding	298,681	315,645	316,396	342,118	330,812	177,910	180,983	...
Statistical Record								
Return on Assets %	1.44	N.M.	1.42	0.16	N.M.	0.47	...	...
Return on Equity %	6.51	N.M.	6.34	0.92	N.M.	2.75	...	...
Loss Ratio %	61.83	71.67	59.32	55.53	59.68	53.31	55.50	...
Net Margin %	9.01	(6.03)	10.05	1.21	(35.73)	3.02	17.93	...
Price Range	25.76-19.60	25.19-18.17	22.22-15.97	18.95-2.67	51.48-2.68	85.03-49.23	...	72.55-60.25
P/E Ratio	12.27-9.33	...	12.84-9.23	31.07-4.38	...	73.94-42.81	...	7.56-6.28
Average Yield %	...	...	2.09	3.46	4.70	2.08	...	2.27

Address: No. 1 Hatch Street Upper, 4th Floor, Dublin, 2 **Telephone:** 140-520-33	**Web Site:** www.xlgroup.com **Officers:** Gregory Hendrick - Executive Vice President Michael S. McGavick - Chief Executive Officer	**Auditors:** PricewaterhouseCoopers LLP **Investor Contact:** 203-964-3470

XYLEM INC.

Exchange	Symbol	Price	52Wk Range	Yield	P/E
NYS	XYL	$27.56 (3/28/2013)	29.34-23.16	1.51	17.33

*7 Year Price Score N/A   ***NYSE Composite Index=100**   ***12 Month Price Score 99.51**

Interim Earnings (Per Share)

Qtr.	Mar	Jun	Sep	Dec
2011	0.42	0.39	0.42	0.28
2012	0.34	0.48	0.38	0.39

Interim Dividends (Per Share)

Amt	Decl	Ex	Rec	Pay
0.101Q	05/10/2012	05/17/2012	05/21/2012	06/20/2012
0.101Q	08/20/2012	08/23/2012	08/27/2012	09/19/2012
0.101Q	10/12/2012	10/18/2012	10/22/2012	12/19/2012
0.116Q	02/07/2013	02/15/2013	02/20/2013	03/20/2013

Indicated Div: $0.42

Valuation Analysis / Institutional Holding

Valuation Analysis		Institutional Holding	
Forecast EPS	$1.86 (04/06/2013)	No of Institutions	457
Market Cap	$5.1 Billion	Shares	160,651,808
Book Value	$2.1 Billion	% Held	N/A
Price/Book	2.47		
Price/Sales	1.35		

TRADING VOLUME (thousand shares)

Business Summary: Industrial Machinery & Equipment (MIC: 7.2.1 SIC: 3561 NAIC: 333911)

Xylem is an equipment and service provider for water and wastewater applications with a portfolio of products and services addressing the cycle of water, from collection, distribution and use to the return of water to the environment. Co. operates in two segments, Water Infrastructure and Applied Water. The Water Infrastructure segment focuses on the transportation, treatment and testing of water, providing a range of products such as water and wastewater pumps, treatment and testing equipment, and controls and systems. The Applied Water segment provides pumps, valves, heat exchangers, controls and dispensing equipment for the residential, commercial, industrial and agricultural markets.

Recent Developments: For the year ended Dec 31 2012, net income increased 6.5% to US$297.0 million from US$279.0 million in the prior year. Revenues were US$3.79 billion, down 0.3% from US$3.80 billion the year before. Operating income was US$443.0 million versus US$395.0 million in the prior year, an increase of 12.2%. Direct operating expenses declined 2.3% to US$2.29 billion from US$2.34 billion in the comparable period the year before. Indirect operating expenses decreased 0.7% to US$1.06 billion from US$1.07 billion in the equivalent prior-year period.

Prospects: Our evaluation of Xylem Inc. as of Apr. 7, 2013 is the result of our systematic analysis on three basic characteristics: earnings strength, relative valuation, and recent stock price movement. The company has managed to produce a neutral trend in earnings per share over the past 5 quarters. However, while recent estimates for the company have been mixed, XYL has posted better than expected results. Based on operating earnings yield, the company is undervalued when compared to all of the companies in our coverage universe. Share price changes over the past year indicates that XYL will perform in line with the market over the near term.

Financial Data
(US$ in Millions)

	12/31/2012	12/31/2011	12/31/2010	12/31/2009	12/31/2008
Earnings Per Share	1.59	1.50	...	...	...
Cash Flow Per Share	2.13	...	...	...	...
Dividends Per Share	0.405	0.101	...	...	...
Dividend Payout %	25.46	6.75	...	...	...
Income Statement					
Total Revenue	3,791	3,803	3,202	2,849	3,291
EBITDA	533	490	480	347	374
Depn & Amortn	94	93	92	70	62
Income Before Taxes	388	383	388	277	312
Income Taxes	91	104	59	14	88
Net Income	297	279	329	263	224
Average Shares	186	185	...	...	...
Balance Sheet					
Current Assets	1,874	1,642	1,336	1,088	...
Total Assets	4,679	4,393	3,735	2,535	...
Current Liabilities	781	817	649	571	...
Long-Term Obligations	1,199	1,201	...	...	...
Total Liabilities	2,605	2,566	1,016	848	...
Stockholders' Equity	2,074	1,827	2,719	1,687	...
Shares Outstanding	185	184	...	...	...
Statistical Record					
Return on Assets %	6.53	...	10.49	...	...
Return on Equity %	15.19	...	14.93	...	...
EBITDA Margin %	14.06	12.88	14.99	12.18	11.36
Net Margin %	7.83	7.34	10.27	9.23	6.81
Asset Turnover	0.83	...	1.02	...	...
Current Ratio	2.40	2.01	2.06	1.91	...
Debt to Equity	0.58	0.66	...	...	...
Price Range	28.73-23.16	27.31-23.06	...	...	...
P/E Ratio	18.07-14.57	18.21-15.37	...	...	...
Average Yield %	1.58	0.41	...	...	...

Address: 1133 Westchester Avenue, Suite N200, White Plains, NY 10604 **Telephone:** 914-323-5700	**Web Site:** www.xyleminc.com **Officers:** Markos I. Tambakeras - Chairman Steven R. Loranger - Chairman Emeritus	**Auditors:** Deloitte & Touche LLP **Investor Contact:** 914-323-5930 **Transfer Agents:** Computershare Trust Company, N.A., Pittsburgh, PA

YUM! BRANDS, INC.

Exchange	Symbol	Price	52Wk Range	Yield	P/E
NYS	YUM	$71.94 (3/28/2013)	74.47-61.95	1.86	21.28

*7 Year Price Score 139.70 *NYSE Composite Index=100 *12 Month Price Score 90.75

Interim Earnings (Per Share)

Qtr.	Mar	Jun	Aug	Dec
2008	0.50	0.45	0.58	0.43
2009	0.46	0.63	0.69	0.45
2010	0.50	0.59	0.74	0.56
2011	0.54	0.65	0.80	0.75
2012	0.96	0.69	1.00	0.73

Interim Dividends (Per Share)

Amt	Decl	Ex	Rec	Pay
0.285Q	05/17/2012	07/11/2012	07/13/2012	08/03/2012
0.335Q	09/20/2012	10/10/2012	10/12/2012	11/02/2012
0.335Q	11/16/2012	01/09/2013	01/11/2013	02/01/2013
0.335Q	03/22/2013	04/10/2013	04/12/2013	05/03/2013

Indicated Div: $1.34

Valuation Analysis

Forecast EPS	$3.13
	(04/06/2013)
Market Cap	$32.4 Billion
Book Value	$2.2 Billion
Price/Book	15.06
Price/Sales	2.38

Institutional Holding

No of Institutions	1028
Shares	368,357,184
% Held	72.48

Business Summary: Food (MIC: 1.2.1 SIC: 5812 NAIC: 722211)

Yum! Brands is a service restaurant company. Through the three concepts of KFC, Pizza Hut and Taco Bell, Co. develops, operates, franchises and licenses a worldwide system of restaurants which prepare, package and sell a menu of food items. Co.'s business consists of six operating segments: YUM Restaurants China, which includes mainland China; YUM Restaurants International, which includes the remainder of Co.'s international operations; the U.S., which consists of Taco Bell U.S., KFC U.S., and Pizza Hut U.S.; and YUM Restaurants India, which includes India, Bangladesh, Mauritius, Nepal and Sri Lanka. As of Dec 29 2012, Co. had about 39,000 units in more than 125 countries and territories.

Recent Developments: For the year ended Dec 29 2012, net income increased 20.4% to US$1.61 billion from US$1.34 billion in the prior year. Revenues were US$13.63 billion, up 8.0% from US$12.63 billion the year before. Operating income was US$2.29 billion versus US$1.82 billion in the prior year, an increase of 26.4%. Direct operating expenses rose 7.8% to US$9.85 billion from US$9.14 billion in the comparable period the year before. Indirect operating expenses decreased 11.0% to US$1.49 billion from US$1.67 billion in the equivalent prior-year period.

Prospects: Our evaluation of Yum! Brands Inc. as of Apr. 7, 2013 is the result of our systematic analysis on three basic characteristics: earnings strength, relative valuation, and recent stock price movement. The company has generated a negative trend in earnings per share over the past 5 quarters and while recent estimates for the company have been raised by analysts, YUM has posted better than expected results. Based on operating earnings yield, the company is about fairly valued when compared to all of the companies in our coverage universe. Share price changes over the past year indicates that YUM will perform poorly over the near term.

Financial Data
(US$ in Millions)

	12/29/2012	12/31/2011	12/25/2010	12/26/2009	12/27/2008	12/29/2007	12/30/2006	12/31/2005
Earnings Per Share	3.38	2.74	2.38	2.22	1.96	1.68	1.46	1.27
Cash Flow Per Share	4.99	4.55	4.16	2.99	3.21	3.01	2.39	2.13
Tang Book Value Per Share	0.95	1.83	0.94	N.M.	...	0.27	0.81	1.04
Dividends Per Share	1.190	1.035	0.880	0.780	0.680	0.525	0.265	0.215
Dividend Payout %	35.21	37.77	36.97	35.14	34.69	31.25	18.15	16.86
Income Statement								
Total Revenue	13,633	12,626	11,343	10,836	11,279	10,416	9,561	9,349
EBITDA	2,876	2,367	2,292	2,107	2,018	1,820	1,677	1,612
Depn & Amortn	629	599	565	553	542	514	466	459
Income Before Taxes	2,098	1,612	1,552	1,360	1,250	1,140	1,057	1,026
Income Taxes	537	324	416	313	316	282	284	264
Net Income	1,597	1,319	1,158	1,071	964	909	824	762
Average Shares	473	481	486	483	491	541	564	596
Balance Sheet								
Current Assets	1,909	2,321	2,313	1,208	951	1,481	901	837
Total Assets	9,011	8,834	8,316	7,148	6,527	7,242	6,353	5,698
Current Liabilities	2,188	2,450	2,448	1,653	1,722	2,062	1,724	1,605
Long-Term Obligations	2,932	2,997	2,915	3,207	3,564	2,924	2,045	1,649
Total Liabilities	6,798	7,011	6,740	6,123	6,635	6,103	4,916	4,249
Stockholders' Equity	2,154	1,823	1,576	1,025	(108)	1,139	1,437	1,449
Shares Outstanding	451	460	469	469	459	499	530	556
Statistical Record								
Return on Assets %	17.95	15.13	15.02	15.71	14.04	13.41	13.71	13.16
Return on Equity %	80.53	76.36	89.29	234.23	187.52	70.77	57.26	49.26
EBITDA Margin %	21.10	18.75	20.21	19.44	17.89	17.47	17.54	17.24
Net Margin %	11.71	10.45	10.21	9.88	8.55	8.73	8.62	8.15
Asset Turnover	1.53	1.45	1.47	1.59	1.64	1.54	1.59	1.61
Current Ratio	0.87	0.95	0.94	0.73	0.55	0.72	0.52	0.52
Debt to Equity	1.36	1.64	1.85	3.13	...	2.57	1.42	1.14
Price Range	74.47-58.57	59.58-46.40	51.90-32.72	36.64-23.47	41.34-22.25	40.27-27.69	31.73-22.47	26.66-22.56
P/E Ratio	22.03-17.33	21.74-16.93	21.81-13.75	16.50-10.57	21.09-11.35	23.97-16.48	21.74-15.39	20.99-17.76
Average Yield %	1.77	1.96	2.09	2.38	1.96	1.59	1.02	0.87

Address: 1441 Gardiner Lane, Louisville, KY 40213 **Telephone:** 502-874-8300 **Fax:** 502-874-8790	**Web Site:** www.yum.com **Officers:** David C. Novak - Chairman, President, Chief Executive Officer Jing-Shyh Sam Su - Vice-Chairman, Division Officer	**Auditors:** KPMG LLP **Transfer Agents:** American Stock Transfer & Trust Company

ZIMMER HOLDINGS, INC.

Exchange	Symbol	Price	52Wk Range	Yield	P/E
NYS	ZMH	$75.22 (3/28/2013)	76.34-57.95	1.06	17.53

*7 Year Price Score 93.89 *NYSE Composite Index=100 ***12 Month Price Score 103.96**

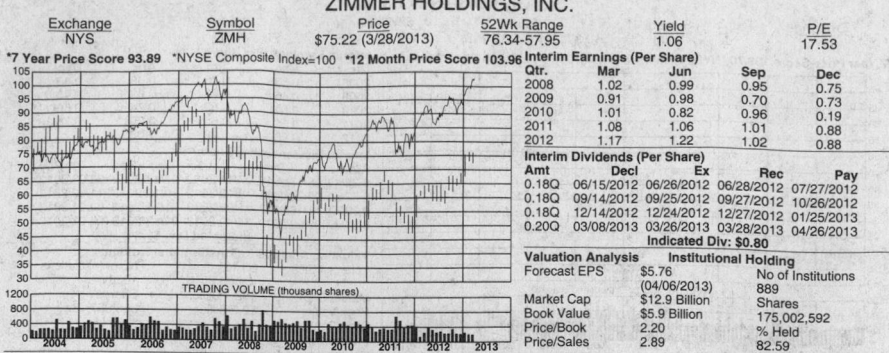

Interim Earnings (Per Share)

Qtr.	Mar	Jun	Sep	Dec
2008	1.02	0.99	0.95	0.75
2009	0.91	0.98	0.70	0.73
2010	1.01	0.82	0.96	0.19
2011	1.08	1.06	1.01	0.88
2012	1.17	1.22	1.02	0.88

Interim Dividends (Per Share)

Amt	Decl	Ex	Rec	Pay
0.18Q	06/15/2012	06/26/2012	06/28/2012	07/27/2012
0.18Q	09/14/2012	09/25/2012	09/27/2012	10/26/2012
0.18Q	12/14/2012	12/24/2012	12/27/2012	01/25/2013
0.20Q	03/08/2013	03/26/2013	03/28/2013	04/26/2013

Indicated Div: $0.80

Valuation Analysis

		Institutional Holding	
Forecast EPS	$5.76 (04/06/2013)	No of Institutions	889
Market Cap	$12.9 Billion	Shares	175,002,592
Book Value	$5.9 Billion	% Held	82.59
Price/Book	2.20		
Price/Sales	2.89		

Business Summary: Medical Instruments & Equipment (MIC: 4.3.1 SIC: 3842 NAIC: 339113)

Zimmer Holdings is engaged in the design, development, manufacture and marketing of: orthopaedic reconstructive devices to restore function lost due to disease or trauma in joints such as knees, hips, shoulders and elbows; dental reconstructive implants to restore function and aesthetics in patients who have lost teeth due to trauma or disease; spinal devices used in the treatment of degenerative diseases, deformities and trauma in the spine; trauma products used to reattach or stabilize damaged bone and tissue; and related surgical products to aid in orthopaedic surgical procedures and post-operation rehabilitation. Co. has three reportable segments, the Americas, Europe and Asia Pacific.

Recent Developments: For the year ended Dec 31 2012, net income decreased 0.9% to US$752.9 million from US$760.0 million in the prior year. Revenues were US$4.47 billion, up 0.4% from US$4.45 billion the year before. Operating income was US$1.05 billion versus US$1.02 billion in the prior year, an increase of 2.3%. Direct operating expenses rose 0.3% to US$1.13 billion from US$1.12 billion in the comparable period the year before. Indirect operating expenses decreased 0.3% to US$2.30 billion from US$2.31 billion in the equivalent prior-year period.

Prospects: Our evaluation of Zimmer Holdings Inc. as of Apr. 7, 2013 is the result of our systematic analysis on three basic characteristics: earnings strength, relative valuation, and recent stock price movement. The company has managed to produce a neutral trend in earnings per share over the past 5 quarters and while recent estimates for the company have remained steady, ZMH has posted better than expected results. Based on operating earnings yield, the company is undervalued when compared to all of the companies in our coverage universe. Share price changes over the past year indicates that ZMH will perform well over the near term.

Financial Data

(US$ in Thousands)	12/31/2012	12/31/2011	12/31/2010	12/31/2009	12/31/2008	12/31/2007	12/31/2006	12/31/2005
Earnings Per Share	4.29	4.03	2.97	3.32	3.72	3.26	3.40	2.93
Cash Flow Per Share	6.57	6.27	5.97	5.20	4.55	4.60	4.28	3.55
Tang Book Value Per Share	14.85	11.70	12.08	9.78	8.96	8.95	7.14	6.04
Dividends Per Share	0.720	...	...	...	...	...	...	...
Dividend Payout %	16.78	...	...	...	...	...	...	...
Income Statement								
Total Revenue	4,471,700	4,451,800	4,220,200	4,095,400	4,121,100	3,897,500	3,495,400	3,286,100
EBITDA	1,313,400	1,290,200	1,164,600	1,263,000	1,305,800	1,310,200	1,320,200	1,199,000
Depn & Amortn	266,000	266,100	247,900	244,200	215,800	182,600	155,000	144,000
Income Before Taxes	990,100	978,900	860,200	998,200	1,121,800	1,131,600	1,169,000	1,040,700
Income Taxes	237,200	218,900	263,300	280,800	272,300	357,900	334,000	307,300
Net Income	755,000	760,800	596,600	717,400	848,600	773,200	834,500	732,500
Average Shares	176,000	188,700	201,100	215,800	228,300	237,500	245,400	249,800
Balance Sheet								
Current Assets	3,708,700	3,276,600	3,009,700	2,738,000	2,178,600	2,082,700	1,746,200	1,575,600
Total Assets	9,012,400	8,515,300	7,999,900	7,785,500	7,239,000	6,633,700	5,974,400	5,721,900
Current Liabilities	866,000	867,100	702,500	690,700	771,100	748,600	628,200	606,900
Long-Term Obligations	1,720,800	1,576,000	1,142,100	1,127,600	460,100	104,300	99,600	81,600
Total Liabilities	3,151,500	3,008,100	2,228,600	2,146,800	1,588,700	1,184,100	1,053,900	1,039,100
Stockholders' Equity	5,860,900	5,507,200	5,771,300	5,638,700	5,650,300	5,449,600	4,920,500	4,682,800
Shares Outstanding	171,600	178,000	195,600	204,200	223,600	232,900	236,800	247,740
Statistical Record								
Return on Assets %	8.59	9.21	7.56	9.55	12.20	12.27	14.27	12.83
Return on Equity %	13.25	13.49	10.46	12.71	15.25	14.91	17.38	16.98
EBITDA Margin %	29.37	28.98	27.60	30.84	31.69	33.62	37.77	36.49
Net Margin %	16.88	17.09	14.14	17.52	20.59	19.84	23.87	22.29
Asset Turnover	0.51	0.54	0.53	0.55	0.59	0.62	0.60	0.58
Current Ratio	4.28	3.78	4.28	3.96	2.83	2.78	2.78	2.60
Debt to Equity	0.29	0.29	0.20	0.20	0.08	0.02	0.02	0.02
Price Range	68.80-53.21	69.69-47.42	63.71-46.97	60.34-32.13	79.63-34.93	91.87-63.48	78.66-53.05	87.40-61.50
P/E Ratio	16.04-12.40	17.29-11.77	21.45-15.81	18.17-9.68	21.41-9.39	28.18-19.47	23.14-15.60	29.83-20.99
Average Yield %	1.15	...	...	...	...	...	...	...

Address: 345 East Main Street, Warsaw, IN 46580 **Telephone:** 574-267-6131	**Web Site:** www.zimmer.com **Officers:** David C. Dvorak - President, Chief Executive Officer James T. Crines - Executive Vice President, Chief Financial Officer	**Auditors:** PricewaterhouseCoopers LLP **Investor Contact:** 574-267-6131 **Transfer Agents:** American Stock Transfer & Trust Company LLC

CONDENSED

STATISTICAL

TABULATION

The tab section consists of statistical highlights for all U.S. companies listed on the New York Stock Exchange.

Statistics for companies whose fiscal year ends prior to June 30 are listed under the prior calendar year. Statistics for companies whose fiscal year ends June 30 or after are listed under the current calendar year. Dividends and price ranges are on a calendar year basis.

Because of editorial constraints a column for fourth quarter results was not included. At fiscal year-end, full fiscal year per share earnings are listed and quarterly figures are eliminated. Quarterly per share earnings are inserted as the company reports in the current fiscal year.

NOTE: Figures listed under "Earnings Per Share" for investment companies are net asset value per share.

For abbreviations, see the blue section of the Handbook.

SYMBOL	COMPANY	NATURE OF BUSINESS	FISCAL YEAR-END	TOTAL REV. $MILL	NET INCOME $MILL	TOTAL ASSETS $MILL	NET STK EQUITY $MILL	NO OF INST	INST. HOLDINGS (SHARES)
DDD	3D Systems Corp. (DE)	Computer Hardware & Equipment	12/31/12	353.6	38.9	677.4	480.3	263	42278946
MMM	3M Co	Medical Instruments & Equipment	12/31/12	29904.0	4444.0	33876.0	17575.0	1724	520663449
SVN	7 Days Group Holdings Ltd	Hotels, Restaurants & Travel	12/31/11	2003.4	128.9	2810.2	1526.3	62	13674938
AHC	A.H. Belo Corp	Publishing	12/31/12	440.0	0.5	291.9	102.0	81	14207709
AIR	AAR Corp	Aerospace	5/31/12	2065.0	67.7	2195.7	864.6	204	37360426
AAN	Aaron's, Inc.	Retail - Furniture & Home Furnishing	12/31/12	2222.6	173.0	1812.9	1136.1	276	73831253
ABB	ABB Ltd	Electrical Equipment	12/31/12	39336.0	2704.0	49070.0	16906.0	451	119549489
ABT	Abbott Laboratories	Medical Instruments & Equipment	12/31/12	39873.9	5962.9	67234.9	26721.0	1912	1101276717
ABBV	AbbVie Inc.	Pharmaceuticals	12/31/12	18380.0	5275.0	27008.0	3363.0		
ABBV	AbbVie Inc.	Pharmaceuticals	12/31/12	18380.0	5275.0	27008.0	3363.0		
ANF	Abercrombie & Fitch Co.	Retail - Apparel and Accessories	2/2/13	4510.8	237.0	2987.4	1818.3	451	88251277
ETF	Aberdeen Emerging Markets Smalle	Holding and other Investment Office	10/31/11	5.9	3.4	165.4	165.1	29	2749516
ABM	ABM Industries, Inc.	Sanitation Services	10/31/12	4300.3	62.6	1869.3	850.4	176	47158493
AKR	Acadia Realty Trust	REITs	12/31/12	134.4	39.7	1908.4	622.8	163	59359446
ACN	Accenture plc	IT Services	8/31/12	29778.0	2553.5	16665.4	4145.8		
ACMP	Access Midstream Partners LP	Equipment & Services	12/31/12	608.4	178.5	6561.1		123	51931203
ACCO	Acco Brands Corp	Office Equipment & Furniture	12/31/12	1758.5	115.4	2507.7	639.2	251	112619467
ACCO	Acco Brands Corp	Office Equipment & Furniture	12/31/12	1758.5	115.4	2507.7	639.2	251	112619467
AH	Accretive Health, Inc.	Services	12/31/11	826.3	29.2	364.2	238.1	121	50584897
ACW	Accuride Corp	Construction Services	12/31/12	929.8	-178.0	677.8	64.9	119	42661477
ACE	ACE, Ltd.	General Insurance	12/31/12	17936.0	2706.0	92545.0	27531.0	672	309746800
ATV	Acorn International Inc	Retail - Specialty	12/31/11	362.1	5.1	245.7	196.4	7	482941
ACT	Actavis, Inc	Pharmaceuticals	12/31/12	5914.9	97.3	14103.5	3833.8	623	116486255
ACTV	Active Network Inc	Internet & Software	12/31/12	418.9	-43.0	542.5	332.4	124	38242869
ATU	Actuant Corp.	Industrial Machinery & Equipment	8/31/12	1605.3	87.3	2007.1	1051.8	281	71656898
AYI	Acuity Brands Inc (Holding Compan	Electrical Equipment	8/31/12	1933.7	116.3	1736.9	834.0	282	42562448
ADX	Adams Express Co.	Holding and other Investment Office	12/31/12	24.9	17.5	1178.5	1156.0	89	20842391
AGRO	Adecoagro SA	Agricultural Crop Production	12/31/11	645.4	56.0	1700.7	1079.9	60	63049359
PVD	Administradora de Fondos de Pensi	Wealth Management	12/31/11	149778.4	78854.9	390348.6	304780.5	55	1866881
ADT	ADT Corp	Business Services	9/28/12	3228.0	394.0	9260.0	5157.0	8	4371984
ADT	ADT Corp	Business Services	9/28/12	3228.0	394.0	9260.0	5157.0	8	4371984
AAP	Advance Auto Parts Inc	Retail - Automotive	12/29/12	6205.0	387.7	4613.8	1210.7	486	73475239
AMD	Advanced Micro Devices, Inc.	Semiconductors	12/29/12	5422.0	-1183.0	4000.0	538.0	395	312912863
ASX	Advanced Semiconductor Engineeri	Semiconductors	12/31/11	185347.2	13978.9	223878.1	102282.5	108	97035187
ATE	Advantest Corp.	Semiconductors	3/31/12	141048.0	-2195.0	219226.0	131552.0	27	768400
LCM	Advent / Claymore Enhanced Growt	Holding and other Investment Office	10/31/12	8.8	5.5	200.5	144.2	29	1971376
AVK	Advent Claymore Convertible Secur	Holding and other Investment Office	12/31/12	32.1	25.1	678.4	667.5	60	4111371
AGC	Advent Claymore Convertible Secur	Holding and other Investment Office	10/30/12	18.2	12.8	408.0	401.5	47	6286222
ACM	Aecom Technology Corp (DE)	Construction Services	9/30/12	8218.2	-58.6	5664.6	2169.5	285	70198015
ANW	Aegean Marine Petroleum Network	Shipping	12/31/11	6965.6	10.2	1472.4	478.1	91	20931752
AEG	AEGON N.V.	Life & Health	12/31/12	43503.0	1531.0	366066.0	29648.0	170	154909010
AEI	AEI	Production & Extraction	12/31/09	8185.0	297.0	10225.0	2832.0		
AER	Aercap Holdings NV	Aerospace	12/31/12	972.5	163.7	8581.4	2122.0	136	76168369
ARX	Aeroflex Holding Corp.	Semiconductors	6/30/12	673.0	-53.6	1189.8	326.8	64	51047600
ARO	Aeropostale Inc	Retail - Apparel and Accessories	2/2/13	2386.2	34.9	740.8	410.4	323	79913909
AES	AES Corp.	Electric Utilities	12/31/12	18141.0	-912.0	41830.0	4647.0	520	601440334
AET	Aetna Inc.	Life & Health	12/31/12	36595.9	1657.9	41494.5	10405.8	763	354013487
AMG	Affiliated Managers Group Inc.	Wealth Management	12/31/12	1805.5	411.4	6187.1	2084.2	479	55940248
AFL	AFLAC Inc.	Life & Health	12/31/12	25364.0	2866.0	131094.0	15978.0	949	309349313
MITT	AG Mortgage Investment Trust Inc	REITs	12/31/12	96.4	134.9	4855.6	794.6	109	14112958
AGCO	AGCO Corp.	Construction Services	12/31/12	9962.2	516.4	7721.8	3464.7	472	94330113
A	Agilent Technologies, Inc.	Biotechnology	10/31/12	6858.0	1153.0	10536.0	5182.0	706	324827231
ATG PR	AGL Capital Trust II	Gas Utilities							
GAS	AGL Resources Inc.	Gas Utilities	12/31/12	3922.0	271.0	14141.0	3413.0	424	79798508
AEM	Agnico-Eagle Mines Ltd	Precious Metals	12/31/11	1821.8	-568.9	5034.3	3203.0	335	106869386
ADC	Agree Realty Corp.	REITs	12/31/12	35.8	18.0	370.1	195.3	128	6859163
GRO	Agria Corp	Agricultural Crop Production	6/30/12	6918.8	-16.0	5219.8	1449.0	17	8933633
AGU	Agrium, Inc.	Agricultural Chemicals	12/31/11	15470.0	1371.0	13140.0	6424.0	447	98399958
RRE	Aim Select Real Estate Income Fun	Holding and other Investment Office	8/31/07	13.6	10.6	236.8	224.5	1	520
AL	Air Lease Corp	Miscellaneous Transportation Servic	12/31/12	655.7	131.9	7353.6	2332.6	137	75821365
APD	Air Products & Chemicals, Inc.	Specialty Chemicals	9/30/12	9611.7	1167.3	16941.8	6477.2	858	213634433
AYR	Aircastle Ltd.	Construction Services	12/31/12	686.6	32.9	5812.2	1415.6	179	60517077
ARG	Airgas Inc.	Industrial Machinery & Equipment	3/31/12	4746.3	313.4	5320.6	1750.3	469	71076109
AKS	AK Steel Holding Corp.	Non-Precious Metals	12/31/12	5933.7	-1027.3	3903.1	-505.3	279	86903471
ALP PRN	Alabama Power Co.	Electric Utilities	12/31/12	5520.0	743.0	18712.0	6083.0		
ALG	Alamo Group, Inc.	Construction Services	12/31/12	628.4	28.9	404.3	310.3	106	7949189
AGI	Alamos Gold Inc	Precious Metals	12/31/12	329.4	118.0	753.9	660.5	5	4319377
ALK	Alaska Air Group, Inc.	Airlines/Air Freight	12/31/12	4657.0	316.0	5505.0	1421.0	308	69320852
AIN	Albany International Corp	Industrial Machinery & Equipment	12/31/12	760.9	31.0	1156.7	493.5	152	30493098
ALB	Albemarle Corp.	Specialty Chemicals	12/31/12	2745.4	311.5	3437.3	1833.6	432	75489713
ALU	Alcatel-Lucent	Services	12/31/12	14446.0	-1374.0	21365.0	1946.0	343	206904493
AA	Alcoa, Inc.	Non-Precious Metals	12/31/12	23700.0	191.0	40179.0	13199.0	773	655272746
ALR	Alere Inc.	Medical Instruments & Equipment	12/31/12	2818.8	-78.2	7067.9	2180.4	256	74886769
ALEX	Alexander & Baldwin Inc.	Property, Real Estate & Developmen	12/31/12	296.7	20.5	1437.3	914.4		
ALEX	Alexander & Baldwin Inc.	Property, Real Estate & Developmen	12/31/12	296.7	20.5	1437.3	914.4		
ALX	Alexander's, Inc.	REITs	12/31/12	191.3	674.4	1481.8	332.2	120	1878814
ARE	Alexandria Real Estate Equities, Inc	REITs	12/31/12	586.1	105.5	7150.1	3441.9	318	69355494
Y	Alleghany Corp.	General Insurance	12/31/12	4753.2	702.2	22808.0	6403.8	330	15961912
ATI	Allegheny Technologies, Inc	Non-Precious Metals	12/31/12	5031.5	158.4	6247.8	2479.6	464	91765486
AGN	Allergan, Inc	Pharmaceuticals	12/31/12	5806.1	1098.8	9179.3	5837.1	853	310020431

T2

EARNINGS PER SHARE QUARTERLY 1st	2nd	3rd	ANNUAL 2012	2011	2010	P/E RATIO		DIVIDENDS PER SHARE 2012	2011	2010	AV. YLD %	DIV. DECLARED AMOUNT	PAYABLE	PRICE RANGE 2012	
-	-	0.16	0.47	0.47	0.28	99.0 -	0.0	-	-	-	-	-	-	46.5 -	0.0
-	-	1.65	6.32	5.96	5.63	16.8 -	0.0	2.36	2.20	2.10	2.6	0.6350Y	81/16/21	106.4 -	0.0
-	-	0.43	-	0.85	0.78	-		-	-	-	-	-	-	13.4 -	0.0
-	-	0.06	0.01	-0.51	-5.92	584.0 -	0.0	0.48	0.18	-	10.3	0.060Y	6/7/13	5.8 -	0.0
-	-	0.46	1.65	1.73	1.16	12.2 -	0.0	0.30	0.07	-	1.9	0.0750Y	2/12/13	20.1 -	0.0
-	-	0.38	2.25	1.43	1.44	14.2 -	0.0	0.62	0.05	0.05	2.2	0.0170Y	81/16/21	32.0 -	0.0
-	-	0.33	1.18	1.38	1.12	19.6 -	0.0	0.69	0.67	0.47	3.6	-	-	23.2 -	0.0
-	-	1.21	3.72	3.01	2.96	9.5 -	0.0	2.01	1.88	1.72	6.4	0.140Y	81/16/21	35.3 -	0.0
-	-	-	3.35	-	-	10.6 -	9.9	-	-	-	-	0.40Y	5/15/13	35.4 -	33.0
-	-	-	3.35	-	-	12.2 -	10.1	-	-	-	-	0.40Y	5/15/13	40.8 -	33.7
-	-	0.87	1.43	1.67	0.00	37.3 -	0.0	0.70	0.70	0.70	1.7	0.20Y	81/16/21	53.3 -	0.0
-	-	-	-	0.41	0.57	-		-	0.53	0.39	-	0.12220	1/11/13	22.4 -	0.0
0.24	-	-	1.14	1.27	1.23	21.3 -	0.0	0.58	0.56	0.54	2.8	0.150Y	81/16/21	24.3 -	0.0
-	-	0.16	0.85	1.26	0.74	32.9 -	0.0	0.72	0.72	0.72	2.9	0.210Z	4/15/13	28.0 -	0.0
-	1.65	-	3.84	3.40	2.66	20.4 -	0.0	1.35	0.90	1.13	2.1	0.810	81/16/21	78.3 -	0.0
-	-	0.32	1.11	1.37	0.78	37.1 -	0.0	1.65	1.43	0.22	5.2	0.450	2/13/13	41.2 -	0.0
-	-	0.48	1.20	0.98	0.22	9.1 -	0.0	-	-	-	-	-	-	10.9 -	0.0
-	-	0.48	1.20	0.98	0.22	10.7 -	0.0	-	-	-	-	-	-	12.9 -	0.0
-	-	0.03	-	0.29	0.13	-		-	-	-	-	-	-	20.3 -	0.0
-	-	-0.37	-3.76	-0.36	-8.07	-		-	-	-	-	-	-	8.8 -	0.0
-	-	1.86	7.89	4.65	9.11	11.3 -	0.0	2.06	1.38	1.30	2.7	0.490	81/16/21	89.1 -	0.0
-	-	-0.04	-	0.06	-0.07	-		-	-	0.67	-	-	-	4.4 -	0.0
-	-	0.60	0.76	2.06	1.48	121.2 -	0.0	-	-	-	-	-	-	92.1 -	0.0
-	-	-0.10	-0.73	-0.75	-7.83	-		-	-	-	-	-	-	17.0 -	0.0
-	0.38	-	1.17	1.50	0.35	27.2 -	0.0	0.04	0.04	0.04	0.1	0.040Y	10/16/12	31.8 -	0.0
-	0.57	-	2.72	2.42	1.80	26.8 -	0.0	0.52	0.52	0.52	0.8	0.130Y	81/16/21	72.9 -	0.0
-	-	-	0.19	0.16	0.15	61.8 -	0.0	0.67	0.65	0.51	6.2	0.050	6/3/13	11.7 -	0.0
-	-	-0.02	-	0.48	-0.54	-		-	-	-	-	-	-	10.8 -	0.0
-	-	-	-	-	-	-		-	0.01	0.01	-	-	-	111.7 -	0.0
0.44	-	-	1.67	1.59	1.01	22.8 -	0.0	-	-	-	-	0.1250Y	5/15/13	38.1 -	0.0
0.44	-	-	1.67	1.59	1.01	29.8 -	0.0	-	-	-	-	0.1250Y	5/15/13	49.7 -	0.0
-	-	1.21	5.22	5.11	3.95	17.7 -	0.0	0.24	0.24	0.24	0.3	0.060Y	81/16/21	92.4 -	0.0
-	-	-0.21	-1.60	0.66	0.64	-		-	-	-	-	0.005F	81/16/21	8.2 -	0.0
-	-	0.45	-	1.78	2.40	-		-	-	-	-	-	-	4.6 -	0.0
-	6.32	-	-12.67	18.03	-64.09	-		0.00	0.00	0.00	0.0	-	-	17.2 -	0.0
-	-	-	0.41	0.42	0.40	24.5 -	0.0	0.89	1.06	1.06	9.4	0.210	2/28/13	10.0 -	0.0
-	-	-	1.06	1.37	1.29	16.3 -	0.0	1.13	1.58	1.13	7.0	0.09390	4/30/13	17.3 -	0.0
-	-	-	0.40	0.44	0.55	18.0 -	0.0	0.62	0.80	0.80	9.4	0.0470	4/30/13	7.2 -	0.0
0.36	-	-	-0.52	2.33	2.05	-		-	-	-	-	-	-	33.0 -	0.0
-	-	-	-	0.22	0.40	-		-	-	0.04	-	0.010	3/27/13	7.8 -	0.0
-	-	0.17	0.67	-0.06	0.83	10.2 -	0.0	0.29	-	-	5.4	0.45310Z	6/17/13	6.8 -	0.0
-	0.61	-	-	-	-	-		-	-	-	-	-	-	16.3 -	0.0
-	-	0.45	1.24	1.17	1.81	13.2 -	0.0	-	-	-	-	-	-	11.5 -	0.0
-	0.01	-	-0.63	-0.45	-0.19	-		-	-	-	-	-	-	23.1 -	0.0
-	-	0.31	0.85	2.49	2.27	27.1 -	0.0	-	-	-	-	-	-	13.3 -	0.0
-	-	-2.10	-1.21	0.07	0.01	-		0.04	-	-	0.3	0.040Y	81/16/21	51.5 -	0.0
-	-	1.47	4.81	5.22	4.18	10.7 -	0.0	0.70	0.45	0.04	1.6	0.20Y	81/16/21	155.2 -	0.0
-	-	1.04	3.28	3.11	2.81	47.3 -	0.0	-	-	-	-	0.32810Z	4/15/13	54.7 -	0.0
-	-	2.16	6.11	4.18	4.95	9.0 -	0.0	1.34	1.23	1.14	2.8	0.350Y	4/26/13	26.7 -	0.0
-	-	3.10	7.18	3.20	-	3.7 -	0.0	2.97	1.10	-	13.0	0.80Z	81/16/21	55.1 -	0.0
-	-	0.96	5.30	5.95	2.29	10.4 -	0.0	-	-	-	-	0.10Y	81/16/21	45.3 -	0.0
0.51	-	-	3.27	2.85	1.94	13.9 -	0.0	0.30	-	-	0.8	0.120Y	81/16/21	42.3 -	0.0
-	-	0.08	2.31	2.12	3.00	18.3 -	0.0	1.74	1.90	1.76	4.4	0.470Y	81/16/21	57.3 -	0.0
-	-	0.62	-	-3.36	2.00	-		-	0.64	0.18	-	0.220	3/15/13	30.1 -	0.0
-	-	0.35	1.62	0.99	1.64	18.6 -	0.0	1.60	1.60	2.04	6.4	0.410Z	4/9/13	1.2 -	0.0
-	-	-	-0.14	0.23	-0.50	-		-	-	-	-	-	-	115.4 -	0.0
-	-	0.80	-	8.68	4.51	-		-	0.28	0.11	-	0.50	7/10/13		
-	-	-	-	-	-	-		-	-	-	-	0.0937C	2/28/07		
-	-	0.36	1.28	0.59	-1.32	22.9 -	0.0	-	-	-	-	0.025GY	81/16/21	29.4 -	0.0
1.31	-	-	5.44	5.63	4.74	17.0 -	0.0	2.50	2.23	1.92	3.0	0.710Y	81/16/21	92.7 -	0.0
-	-	-0.65	0.46	1.64	0.83	30.8 -	0.0	0.61	0.50	0.40	5.0	0.1650Y	3/15/13	14.2 -	0.0
-	-	1.05	4.00	2.93	2.34	25.9 -	0.0	1.25	1.01	0.76	1.4	0.40Y	81/16/21	103.5 -	0.0
-	-	-0.55	-9.06	-1.41	-1.17	-		0.10	0.20	0.20	1.9	0.050Y	81/16/21	7.7 -	0.0
-	-	-	-	-	-	-		1.41	1.41	1.41	5.5	0.40630Y	7/1/13	26.4 -	0.0
-	-	0.71	2.40	2.68	1.79	16.8 -	0.0	0.24	0.24	0.24	0.7	0.070Y	5/1/13	40.4 -	0.0
-	-	0.21	0.98	0.51	0.55	20.6 -	13.5	0.20	0.12	0.07	1.2	0.10	4/30/13	20.2 -	13.2
-	-	2.27	4.40	3.33	3.42	14.5 -	0.0	-	-	-	-	0.025	81/16/21	64.0 -	0.0
-	-	0.30	0.97	1.11	1.21	30.8 -	0.0	0.55	0.51	0.48	2.5	0.140Y	4/5/13	29.9 -	0.0
-	-	1.10	3.47	4.77	3.51	19.1 -	0.0	0.80	0.67	0.56	1.3	0.240Y	81/16/21	66.2 -	0.0
-	-	-0.06	-0.61	0.42	-0.15	-		-	-	-	-	-	-	2.3 -	0.0
-	-	-0.13	0.18	0.55	0.24	56.5 -	0.0	0.12	0.12	0.12	1.4	0.93750Y	81/16/21	10.2 -	0.0
-	-	-0.11	-1.23	-1.58	-12.33	-		-	-	-	-	3.0Y	4/15/13	25.9 -	0.0
-	-	0.31	0.48	0.56	-	76.1 -	0.0	-	-	-	-	-	-	36.5 -	0.0
-	-	0.31	0.48	0.56	-	58.1 -	0.0	-	-	-	-	-	-	27.9 -	0.0
-	-	3.69	132.04	15.55	13.01	3.5 -	0.0	137.00	12.00	7.50	34.6	2.750Z	2/19/13	461.3 -	0.0
-	-	0.17	1.09	1.73	2.19	70.3 -	0.0	2.09	1.86	1.50	2.9	0.40310Z	81/16/21	76.7 -	0.0
-	-	7.41	45.48	16.20	21.85	8.7 -	0.0	-	-	-	-	3.80360Y	6/15/09	395.9 -	0.0
-	-	0.32	1.43	1.97	0.72	30.7 -	0.0	0.72	0.72	0.72	2.3	0.180Y	81/16/21	43.9 -	0.0
-	-	0.82	3.58	3.01	0.00	31.3 -	0.0	0.20	0.20	0.20	0.2	0.050Y	81/16/21	111.9 -	0.0

SYMBOL	COMPANY	NATURE OF BUSINESS	FISCAL YEAR-END	TOTAL REV. $MILL	NET INCOME $MILL	TOTAL ASSETS $MILL	NET STK EQUITY $MILL	NO OF INST	INST. HOLDINGS (SHARES)
ALE	Allete Inc.	Electric Utilities	12/31/12	961.2	97.1	3253.4	1201.0	210	26160244
AKP	Alliance California Municipal Income	Holding and other Investment Office	10/31/12	9.0	7.2	219.8	201.3	18	555053
ADS	Alliance Data Systems Corp.	Business Services	12/31/12	3641.4	422.3	12000.1	528.5	493	72709789
AYN	Alliance New York Municipal Incom	Holding and other Investment Office	10/31/12	4.9	3.8	123.6	113.3	21	407348
AOI	Alliance One International Inc	Tobacco Products	3/31/12	2150.8	29.5	1949.8	327.5	153	85794276
AWF	AllianceBernstein Global High Inco	Holding and other Investment Office	3/31/12	117.4	105.0	1418.1	1267.2	92	7445212
AB	AllianceBernstein Holding L P	Wealth Management	12/31/12	-	51.1	1566.5		203	36304325
ACG	AllianceBernstein Income Fund Inc	Holding and other Investment Office	12/31/12	111.7	97.3	3456.2	2159.4	147	48292916
AFB	AllianceBernstein National Municipa	Holding and other Investment Office	10/31/12	32.1	27.4	756.4	680.0	38	2339462
LNT	Alliant Energy Corp.	Electric Utilities	12/31/12	3094.5	335.7	10785.5	3194.9	419	68401890
ATK	Alliant Techsystems Inc.	Defense	3/31/12	4613.4	262.6	4541.7	1226.8	320	33810638
NCV	AllianzGI Convertible & Income Fun	Holding and other Investment Office	2/29/12	88.3	79.9	1024.2	1010.4	50	8132082
NCZ	AllianzGI Convertible & Income Fun	Holding and other Investment Office	2/29/12	67.0	60.6	777.9	767.1	52	6758796
NIE	AllianzGI Equity & Convertible Inco	Holding and other Investment Office	1/31/12	12.7	8.0	439.5	430.1	39	3302647
NGZ	AllianzGI Global Equity & Convertibl	Holding and other Investment Office	8/31/12	3.5	2.2	104.6	104.3	24	1277601
NAI	AllianzGI International & Premium S	Holding and other Investment Office	2/29/12	5.4	3.8	117.3	117.1	32	1169211
NFJ	AllianzGI NFJ Dividend Interest & P	Holding and other Investment Office	1/31/12	65.9	49.0	1757.2	1706.8	83	15452175
AWH	Allied World Assurance Company H	General Insurance	12/31/12	2222.5	493.0	12029.9	3326.3	261	34752000
ALSN	Allison Transmission Holdings Inc	Auto Parts	12/31/12	2141.8	514.2	4866.0	1356.9	106	190578657
ALL	Allstate Corp.	General Insurance	12/31/12	33315.0	2306.0	126947.0	20580.0	904	418243946
ALLY PRB	Ally Financial Inc	Credit & Lending	12/31/12	10497.0	1106.0	182347.0	19898.0	12	1205610
BSI	Alon Holdings Blue Square Israel Lt	Retail - Food & Beverage, Drug & To	12/31/11	12482.6	59.5	9094.2	1180.7	8	53807
ALJ	Alon USA Energy Inc	Refining & Marketing	12/31/12	8017.7	90.6	2223.6	584.7	151	19485496
ALDW	Alon USA Partners LP	Refining & Marketing	12/31/12	3476.8	37.1	763.4			
ANR	Alpha Natural Resources Inc	Mining	12/31/12	6974.9	-2437.1	13089.8	4967.8	33	9443582
AGD	Alpine Global Dynamic Dividend Fu	Holding and other Investment Office	10/31/12	19.5	17.7	133.3	129.2	24	503698
AWP	Alpine Global Premier Properties Fu	Holding and other Investment Office	10/31/12	38.4	29.3	666.9	666.3	75	12905116
AOD	Alpine Total Dynamic Dividend Fun	Holding and other Investment Office	10/31/12	164.7	151.2	1104.0	1019.1	88	11490790
MO	Altria Group Inc	Tobacco Products	12/31/12	24618.0	4180.0	35329.0	3168.0	1399	1348291037
ACH	Aluminum Corp of China Ltd.	Non-Precious Metals	12/31/11	145874.4	238.0	157134.2	51826.0	78	3775875
AMBO	Ambow Education Holding Ltd.	Publishing	12/31/11	1669.2	21.2	4720.6	2711.6	20	6309541
ACO	AMCOL International Corp.	Mining	12/31/11	942.4	59.1	842.7	396.0	137	24376349
DOX	Amdocs Ltd.	IT Services	9/30/12	3246.9	391.4	4645.2	3033.2	316	178272164
AEE	Ameren Corp.	Electric Utilities	12/31/12	6828.0	-974.0	21835.0	6616.0	525	168658869
AMRC	Ameresco Inc.	Construction Services	12/31/12	631.2	18.4	675.5	261.8	89	9623177
AMX	America Movil, S.A.B. de C.V.	Services	12/31/11	665301.5	82853.5	945616.9	285640.2	560	606044617
AAT	American Assets Trust, Inc.	Property, Real Estate & Developmen	12/31/12	235.5	51.6	1827.6	638.4	150	33462194
AXL	American Axle & Manufacturing Hol	Auto Parts	12/31/12	2930.9	367.7	2866.0	-120.8	217	69940943
ACC	American Campus Communities Inc	REITs	12/31/12	491.3	56.6	5119.0	2648.4	335	110903992
AEO	American Eagle Outfitters, Inc.	Retail - Apparel and Accessories	2/2/13	3475.8	232.1	1756.1	1221.2	466	186086970
AEP	American Electric Power Company,	Electric Utilities	12/31/12	14945.0	1259.0	54367.0	15237.0	813	324940482
AEL	American Equity Investment Life Ho	Life & Health	12/31/12	1588.6	57.8	35133.5	1720.2	219	79558019
AXP	American Express Co.	Credit & Lending	12/31/12	33808.0	4482.0	153140.0	18886.0	1440	1000979811
AFG	American Financial Group, Inc. (Hol	General Insurance	12/31/12	5062.0	488.0	39171.0	4578.0	302	65564169
AM	American Greetings Corp.	Printing	2/29/12	1695.1	57.2	1549.5	727.5	210	35569512
MRF	American Income Fund Inc	Holding and other Investment Office	8/31/12	6.6	5.6	109.7	80.4	24	1535229
AIG	American International Group Inc	General Insurance	12/31/12	65656.0	3438.0	548633.0	98002.0	1151	1345265360
AMID	American Midstream Partners LP	Miscellaneous Transportation Servic	12/31/11	244.7	-11.7	199.6		25	2222662
XAA	American Municipal Income Portfoli	Holding and other Investment Office	8/31/12	6.8	5.6	134.7	134.3	19	325166
ARL	American Realty Investors, Inc.	Property, Real Estate & Developmen	12/31/12	119.5	-5.6	1135.3	50.5	13	82054
ASI	American Safety Insurance Holding	General Insurance	12/31/12	297.1	11.8	1373.1	337.3	31	1908346
SLA	American Select Portfolio, Inc.	Holding and other Investment Office	8/31/12	10.9	8.5	180.3	127.8	37	3083252
AWR	American States Water Co.	Water Utilities	12/31/12	466.9	54.1	1280.9	454.6	219	13391708
ASP	American Strategic Income Portfolio	Holding and other Investment Office	8/31/12	4.6	3.6	76.9	55.1	23	1112046
BSP	American Strategic Income Portfolio	Holding and other Investment Office	8/31/12	12.9	9.8	230.4	163.3	37	5317668
CSP	American Strategic Income Portfolio	Holding and other Investment Office	8/31/12	13.9	10.2	248.5	175.1	48	5456338
AMT	American Tower Corp (New)	Services	12/31/12	2876.0	637.3	14089.1	3573.1	809	405614747
AVD	American Vanguard Corp.	Agricultural Chemicals	12/31/12	366.2	36.9	399.9	225.1	184	24438434
AWK	American Water Works Co, Inc.	Water Utilities	12/31/12	2876.9	358.1	14719.0	4445.0	450	156261972
APU	AmeriGas Partners, L.P.	Gas Utilities	9/30/12	2921.6	11.0	4517.3		188	9340688
AMP	Ameriprise Financial Inc	Wealth Management	12/31/12	10217.0	1029.0	134729.0	9092.0	649	202791599
ABC	AmerisourceBergen Corp.	Pharmaceuticals	9/30/12	79489.6	719.0	15444.1	2456.7	627	234322728
AME	AMETEK, Inc.	Electrical Equipment	12/31/12	3334.2	459.1	5190.1	2535.2	492	219701192
AHS	AMN Healthcare Services, Inc.	Diagnostic & Health Related Service	12/31/12	954.0	17.1	517.4	182.1	166	38443373
AP	Ampco-Pittsburgh Corp.	Industrial Machinery & Equipment	12/31/12	292.9	8.4	533.2	192.1	80	6856947
APH	Amphenol Corp.	Electrical Equipment	12/31/12	4292.1	555.3	5215.5	2430.0	557	178451816
AMRE	AmREIT, Inc	REITs	12/31/12	41.3	4.5	397.4	165.7		
AXR	AMREP Corp.	Business Services	4/30/12	85.4	-1.1	203.0	74.6	29	997036
APC	Anadarko Petroleum Corp	Production & Extraction	12/31/12	13411.0	2391.0	52589.0	20629.0	1088	505238664
AU	AngloGold Ashanti Ltd	Precious Metals	12/31/11	47849.0	11282.0	86858.0	40432.0	271	178652872
BUD	Anheuser-Busch Inbev SA	Beverages	12/31/12	39758.0	7243.0	122621.0	41142.0	392	83071005
AXE	Anixter International Inc	Electrical Equipment	12/28/12	6253.1	124.8	3089.6	969.9	252	35312027
ANN	ANN INC	Retail - Apparel and Accessories	2/2/13	2375.5	102.6	942.2	385.1	333	54730864
NLY	Annaly Capital Management Inc	REITs	12/31/12	2674.5	1735.9	133452.3	15924.4	763	476983802
BNNY	Annie's Inc	Food	3/31/12	141.3	9.6	72.4	46.9	118	12968642
ANH	Anworth Mortgage Asset Corp.	REITs	12/31/12	201.7	100.2	9285.1	1087.7	212	86063821
AOL	AOL Inc.	Internet & Software	12/31/12	2191.7	1048.4	2797.3	2138.1	351	79823831
AON	Aon Plc	Brokers & Intermediaries	12/31/12	11514.0	993.0	30486.0	7762.0	514	259023629
APA	Apache Corp.	Production & Extraction	12/31/12	17078.0	2001.0	60737.0	31331.0	1304	355698602
AIV	Apartment Investment & Manageme	REITs	12/31/12	1033.2	132.5	6401.4	915.4	349	152925884

T4

1st	2nd	3rd	2012	2011	2010	P/E RATIO		2012	2011	2010	AV. YLD %	AMOUNT	PAYABLE	PRICE RANGE 2012	
-	-	0.78	2.58	2.65	2.19	19.0 -	0.0	1.84	1.78	1.76	4.4	0.4750Y	3/1/13	49.0 -	0.0
-	-	-	0.85	0.98	1.02	20.1 -	0.0	0.91	0.91	0.91	5.9	0.0627M	4/19/13	17.1 -	0.0
-	-	1.84	6.58	5.45	3.48	24.6 -	0.0							161.9 -	0.0
-	-	-	0.79	0.95	1.01	20.4 -	0.0	0.85	0.85	0.85	5.6	0.0514M	4/19/13	16.1 -	0.0
-	-	0.20	0.30	-0.81	0.78	13.6 -	0.0					0.030Y	9/23/05	4.1 -	0.0
-	-	-	1.23	1.30	1.19	14.0 -	0.0	1.52	1.20	1.14	9.7	0.10	4/19/13	17.2 -	0.0
-	-0.23	0.51	-0.90	1.32		45.2 -	0.0	0.95	1.44	1.51	5.9	0.40	3/14/13	23.0 -	0.0
-	-	-	0.40	0.44	0.47	21.8 -	0.0	1.01	0.57	0.49	12.1	0.040	4/19/13	8.7 -	0.0
-	-	-	0.95	1.04	1.07	17.7 -	0.0	0.93	0.93	0.93	6.0	0.0729M	4/19/13	16.8 -	0.0
-	-	1.36	2.89	2.74	2.60	17.4 -	0.0	1.80	1.70	1.58	4.0	0.470Y	81/16/21	50.2 -	0.0
-	-	1.93	7.93	9.32	8.33	9.1 -	0.0	0.80	0.20		1.4	0.260Y	81/16/21	72.4 -	0.0
-	-	-	1.07	1.20	1.07	9.0 -	0.0	1.13	1.25	1.08	12.5	0.090	5/1/13	9.7 -	0.0
-	-	-	0.97	1.09	0.98	9.2 -	0.0	1.02	1.16	1.14	12.3	0.0850	5/1/13	8.9 -	0.0
-	-	-	0.36	0.40	0.40	50.6 -	0.0	1.12	1.12	1.12	6.5	0.280	3/28/13	18.2 -	0.0
								1.20	1.20	1.20	9.0	0.30	3/28/13	14.7 -	0.0
-	-	-	0.38	0.26	0.31	29.1 -	0.0	1.60	1.72	1.84	15.7	0.2750	3/28/13	11.1 -	0.0
-	-	-	0.52	0.64	0.61	34.3 -	0.0	1.80	0.90	0.60	10.9	0.450	3/28/13	17.9 -	0.0
-	-	6.00	13.30	6.92	13.32	7.0 -	0.0	1.88	0.75	1.05	2.4	0.3750	81/16/21	92.7 -	0.0
-	-	0.17	2.76	0.56	0.16	9.1 -	0.0	0.18			0.9	0.120Y	81/16/21	25.0 -	0.0
-	-	1.48	4.68	1.51	1.71	10.5 -	0.0	0.88	0.84	0.80	2.3	0.250Y	81/16/21	49.1 -	0.0
-	-	137.00	296.00	-691.00	-	0.1 -	0.0	2.13	1.36		8.7	17.50Y	2/15/13	27.1 -	0.0
-	-0.27		0.79	0.96					0.06	0.85				3.9 -	0.0
-	0.69	1.24	0.69	-2.27		17.0 -	0.0	0.16	0.16	0.16	1.2	0.040Y	3/15/13	21.1 -	0.0
-	-	-	0.59			48.9 -	31.0	0.57			2.4	0.57G	3/1/13	28.9 -	18.3
-	-0.21	-11.06	-3.76	0.79										16.8 -	0.0
-	-	-	0.70	0.69	0.88	8.7 -	0.0	0.72	0.86	1.18	13.3	0.030	4/30/13	6.1 -	0.0
-	-	-	0.16	0.34	0.37	52.4 -	0.0	0.60	0.77	0.65	8.6	0.050	4/30/13	8.4 -	0.0
-	-	-	0.68	0.66	0.76	7.0 -	0.0	0.66	0.67	1.19	15.6	0.0270	4/30/13	4.8 -	0.0
-	-	0.32	2.06	1.64	1.87	17.6 -	0.0	1.70	1.58	1.46	5.1	0.440Y	81/16/21	36.2 -	0.0
-	-	-	-	0.02	0.06				0.01					13.3 -	0.0
-0.55	-	-	-	0.15	0.63									8.0 -	0.0
-	0.58	-		1.84	0.96				0.72	0.72		0.20Y	4/9/13	35.8 -	0.0
0.61	-	-	2.31	1.86	1.69	15.8 -	0.0					0.130	81/16/21	36.6 -	0.0
-	-	1.54	-4.01	2.15	0.58			1.60	1.55	1.54	4.9	0.40Y	81/16/21	-35.0 -	0.0
-	-	0.15	0.40	0.78	0.69	34.6 -	0.0							13.8 -	0.0
-	-	0.40	-	1.05	1.15				0.02	0.02				28.3 -	0.0
-	-	0.08	0.90	0.08		36.3 -	0.0	0.84	0.80		3.2	0.210Z	3/29/13	32.6 -	0.0
-	-	-0.11	4.87	1.89	1.55	2.8 -	0.0					0.020Y	12/29/08	13.7 -	0.0
-	-	-	0.65	0.80	0.26	73.7 -	0.0	1.35	1.35	1.35	3.0	0.33750Z	81/16/21	47.9 -	0.0
-	-	0.39	0.77	0.66	0.81	30.9 -	0.0	0.44	0.93	0.40	2.2	0.110Y	81/16/21	23.8 -	0.0
-	-	1.00	2.60	4.02	2.53	18.7 -	0.0	1.88	1.85	1.71	4.4	0.470Y	81/16/21	48.6 -	0.0
-	-	-0.13	0.89	1.37	0.68	16.8 -	0.0	0.15	0.12	0.10	1.3	0.150Y	12/17/12	15.0 -	0.0
-	-	1.09	3.89	4.12	3.35	17.3 -	0.0	0.78	0.72	0.72	1.3	0.20Y	81/16/21	67.5 -	0.0
-	-	2.39	5.09	3.33	4.33	9.3 -	0.0	0.97	0.66	0.57	2.5	0.1950Y	81/16/21	47.4 -	0.0
-	-	-0.03	1.42	2.11	2.03	12.2 -	0.0	0.60	0.56	0.48	3.9	0.150Z	81/16/21	17.4 -	0.0
-	-	-	0.59	0.63	0.71	14.9 -	0.0	0.61	0.67	0.75	7.5	0.04750	4/17/13	8.8 -	0.0
-	-	1.13	2.04	9.44	11.60	19.4 -	0.0					0.220Y	81/16/21	39.6 -	0.0
-	-	-0.46	-	-1.64	-1.67				0.27			0.43250	2/14/13	22.8 -	0.0
-	-	-	0.98	0.98	0.99	19.2 -	0.0	0.93	0.95	0.98	5.8	0.08M	4/17/13	18.8 -	0.0
-	-	-	-0.70	-0.19	-8.48									4.1 -	0.0
-	-	0.60	1.14	1.01	2.87	22.5 -	0.0					0.120	1/6/03	25.7 -	0.0
-	-	-	0.80	0.79	0.78	14.2 -	0.0	0.84	1.23	1.27	7.8	0.060	4/17/13	11.4 -	0.0
-	-	0.97	2.82	2.43	1.77	20.4 -	0.0	1.27	1.10	1.04	2.9	0.3550Y	81/16/21	57.6 -	0.0
-	-	0.84	0.79	0.85		14.7 -	0.0	0.90	1.24	1.19	7.7	0.060	4/17/13	12.3 -	0.0
-	-	-	0.61	0.59	0.64	15.1 -	0.0	0.62	1.13	1.16	7.1	0.050	4/17/13	9.2 -	0.0
-	-	-	0.48	0.46	0.43	16.0 -	0.0	0.50	1.07	1.05	6.9	0.03750	4/17/13	7.7 -	0.0
-	-	0.58	1.60	0.99	0.92	49.9 -	0.0	0.90	0.35		1.3	0.260Y	81/16/21	79.9 -	0.0
-	-	0.28	1.28	0.79	0.40	28.7 -	0.0	0.22	0.08	0.03	0.7	0.070Y	4/19/13	36.7 -	0.0
-	-	0.86	2.01	1.75	1.53	20.6 -	0.0	1.21	0.90	0.86	3.3	0.250Y	81/16/21	41.4 -	0.0
0.93	-	-	-0.11	2.30	2.80			3.10	2.89	2.75	7.5	0.80	2/19/13	45.0 -	0.0
-	-	0.79	4.62	4.37	4.18	16.2 -	0.0	1.43	0.87	0.71	2.5	0.450Y	81/16/21	74.9 -	0.0
0.71	-	-	2.80	2.54	2.22	18.4 -	0.0	0.52	0.43	0.32	1.3	0.210Y	81/16/21	51.5 -	0.0
-	-	0.47	1.88	1.58	1.17	23.1 -	0.0	0.22	0.16	0.12	0.6	0.060Y	81/16/21	43.4 -	0.0
-	-	0.12	0.37	-0.57	-1.49	42.8 -	0.0							15.8 -	0.0
-	-	0.15	0.80	2.05	1.50	26.1 -	0.0	0.72	0.72	0.72	4.0	0.180Y	4/30/13	20.9 -	0.0
-	-	0.90	3.39	3.05	2.82	22.0 -	0.0	0.42	0.06	0.06	0.7	0.1050Y	81/16/21	74.7 -	0.0
-	-	0.07	0.32	0.36	0.52	60.8 -	0.0	0.60	0.80	0.90	3.7	0.20Z	3/29/13	19.5 -	0.0
-	-	0.00	-0.19	-1.26	-1.58							1.7	8/24/07	15.1 -	0.0
-	-	0.24	4.74	-5.32	1.52	18.8 -	0.0	0.36	0.36	0.36	0.5	0.090Y	81/16/21	88.9 -	0.0
-	-	0.43	-	25.33	1.71									37.7 -	0.0
-	-	1.15	4.45	3.63	2.50	22.4 -	0.0	1.56	1.18	0.49	1.9			99.5 -	0.0
-	-	0.61	3.69	5.36	3.05	19.8 -	0.0	4.50		3.25	7.3	4.57	81/16/21	73.1 -	0.0
-	-	0.84	1.64	1.24	-0.32	24.0 -	0.0							39.3 -	0.0
-	-	0.22	1.71	0.37	2.04	10.4 -	0.0	1.97	1.97	1.97	12.4	0.450Z	81/16/21	17.8 -	0.0
-	-	0.08	0.26	0.50	0.20	186.7 -	0.0		0.80	0.22				48.5 -	0.0
-	-	0.15	0.67	0.90	0.87	10.5 -	0.0	0.69	0.94	0.97	10.8	0.150Z	4/29/13	7.0 -	0.0
-	-	0.22	11.21	0.12	-7.34	3.9 -	0.0	5.15			16.4	5.15GDY	81/16/21	43.7 -	0.0
-	-	0.62	2.99	2.87	2.37	20.7 -	0.0	0.62	0.60	0.60	1.2	0.15750	2/15/13	61.8 -	0.0
-	-	0.41	4.92	11.47	8.46	20.5 -	0.0	0.66	0.60	0.60	0.8	0.20Y	81/16/21	101.0 -	0.0
-	-	0.17	0.61	-0.86	-1.08	50.6 -	0.0	0.76	0.48	0.30	2.8	0.240Z	81/16/21	30.9 -	0.0

SYMBOL	COMPANY	NATURE OF BUSINESS	FISCAL YEAR-END	TOTAL REV. $MILL	NET INCOME $MILL	TOTAL ASSETS $MILL	NET STK EQUITY $MILL	NO OF INST	INST. HOLDINGS (SHARES)
ARI	Apollo Commercial Real Estate Fina	REITs	12/31/12	57.1	40.2	788.4	546.9	126	15707605
APO	Apollo Global Management LLC	Finance Intermediaries & Services	12/31/12	2860.0	311.0	20636.9	2666.8	78	56391645
AMTG	Apollo Residential Mortgage, Inc.	REITs	12/31/12	94.4	172.8	4487.9	716.8	98	10542336
AFT	Apollo Senior Floating Rate Fund In	Holding and other Investment Office	12/31/12	30.6	21.5	480.6	321.5	19	1854984
AIF	Apollo Tactical Income Fund Inc	Holding and other Investment Office	1/16/13			0.4	0.1		
AIT	Applied Industrial Technologies, Inc.	Industrial Machinery & Equipment	6/30/12	2375.4	108.8	962.2	672.1	218	40672380
ATR	AptarGroup Inc.	Plastics	12/31/12	2331.0	162.6	2324.4	1379.9	323	76433799
WTR	Aqua America Inc	Water Utilities	12/31/12	757.8	196.6	4858.5	1385.7	364	72479301
ARSD	Arabian American Development Co.	Refining & Marketing	12/31/12	222.9	11.4	121.5	83.0	45	4712978
RMK	ARAMARK Corp.	Hotels, Restaurants & Travel	9/30/11	13082.4	100.1	10509.6	1445.2	21	7237914
ARB	Arbitron Inc.	Advertising	12/31/12	449.9	56.9	269.1	153.4	208	29064225
ABR	Arbor Realty Trust Inc	REITs	12/31/12	111.5	21.5	1701.9	229.3	78	8804521
ARC	ARC Document Solutions, Inc.	Office Equipment & Furniture	12/31/12	406.1	-32.0	415.8	103.9	106	31906358
MT	ArcelorMittal SA	Non-Precious Metals	12/31/12	84213.0	-3726.0	114573.0	51723.0	2	55542
ACI	Arch Coal, Inc.	Mining	12/31/12	4159.0	-684.0	10006.8	2854.6	404	165959989
ADM	Archer Daniels Midland Co.	Food	12/31/12	46729.0	692.0	45136.0	18920.0	796	588594170
ARCO	Arcos Dorados Holdings Inc	Hotels, Restaurants & Travel	12/31/11	3657.6	115.5	1875.4	678.6	155	97057406
ACRE	Ares Commercial Real Estate Corp	REITs	12/31/12	9.3	0.9	387.9	165.4	60	4549089
ARDC	Ares Dynamic Credit Allocation Fun	Finance Intermediaries & Services	10/17/12			0.7	0.1		
AI	Arlington Asset Investment Corp	Credit & Lending	12/31/12	53.4	191.8	2074.2	465.2	129	18320135
ARR	ARMOUR Residential REIT Inc.	REITs	12/31/12	247.7	222.3	20878.9	2307.8	171	89664489
AWI	Armstrong World Industry Inc	Metal Products	12/31/12	2618.9	131.3	2854.3	719.1	166	42431874
ARW	Arrow Electronics, Inc.	Electrical Equipment	12/31/12	20405.1	506.3	10785.7	3983.2	380	117723156
ART	Artio Global Investors Inc	Wealth Management	12/31/12	124.3	-47.5	216.6	141.0	99	31851958
APAM	Artisan Partners Asset Management	Wealth Management			-0.0	0.0	-0.1		
ASA	ASA Gold and Precious Metals Ltd	Holding and other Investment Office	11/30/11	5.9	2.0	632.7	626.1	60	7634286
ABG	Asbury Automotive Group, Inc	Retail - Automotive	12/31/12	4640.3	82.2	1661.4	402.8	172	33488375
AHT	Ashford Hospitality Trust Inc	REITs	12/31/12	922.6	-53.8	3464.7	831.9	192	68000897
ASH	Ashland Inc	Specialty Chemicals	9/30/12	8206.0	26.0	12524.0	4029.0	448	73422788
APB	Asia Pacific Fund, Inc. (The)	Holding and other Investment Office	3/31/12	2.2	-0.5	130.8	120.7	46	5169187
GRR	Asia Tigers Fund, Inc. (The)	Holding and other Investment Office	10/31/12	1.4	0.3	55.1	54.6	26	600046
GRR	Asia Tigers Fund, Inc. (The)	Holding and other Investment Office	10/31/12	1.4	0.3	55.1	54.6	26	600046
AHL	Aspen Insurance Holdings Ltd	General Insurance	12/31/12	2329.4	280.4	10310.6	3488.2	300	76657642
ALC	Assisted Living Concepts Inc	Hospitals & Health Care Facilities	12/31/12	228.4	-26.1	515.8	277.6	101	18278251
AEC	Associated Estates Realty Corp.	REITs	12/31/12	174.9	30.6	1172.5	403.4	175	46075652
AIZ	Assurant Inc	Life & Health	12/31/12	8508.3	483.7	28946.6	5185.4	409	81327549
AGO	Assured Guaranty Ltd	General Insurance	12/31/12	973.0	110.0	17242.0	4994.0	255	186145481
AF	Astoria Financial Corp.	Credit & Lending	12/31/12	673.7	53.1	16496.6	1294.0	208	76378028
AZN	AstraZeneca Plc	Pharmaceuticals	12/31/12	27973.0	6297.0	53534.0	23737.0	402	104878714
T	AT&T Inc	Services	12/31/12	127434.0	7264.0	272315.0	92362.0	1959	3320531074
AT	Atlantic Power Corp	Electric Utilities	12/31/12	440.4	-112.8	4002.7	950.9		
ATLS	Atlas Energy L P	Equipment & Services	12/31/12	1521.4	-16.9	4597.2		94	39714339
APL	Atlas Pipeline Partners LP	Gas Utilities	12/31/12	1246.0	68.1	3065.6		163	29355663
ARP	Atlas Resource Partners, L.P.	Production & Extraction	12/31/12	267.6	-51.9	1499.0		68	28707143
ATO	Atmos Energy Corp.	Gas Utilities	9/30/12	3438.5	216.7	7495.7	2359.2	363	61869959
ATW	Atwood Oceanics, Inc.	Equipment & Services	9/30/12	787.4	272.2	2943.8	1939.4	377	58825214
AUO	AU Optronics Corp.	Electrical Equipment	12/31/12	378470.0	-55907.0	539802.5	163235.5	128	71417515
AUQ	AuRico Gold Inc	Precious Metals	12/31/12	163.6	33.2	2897.2	2297.8	195	201887230
ALV	Autoliv Inc.	Auto Parts	12/31/12	8266.7	483.1	6570.3	3758.6	334	37303545
AN	AutoNation, Inc.	Retail - Automotive	12/31/12	15668.8	316.4	7203.0	1688.5	304	86573155
AZO	AutoZone, Inc.	Retail - Automotive	8/25/12	8603.9	930.4	6265.6	-1548.0	601	35478004
AVB	AvalonBay Communities, Inc.	REITs	12/31/12	1038.7	423.9	11160.1	6837.2	519	126439086
ACP	Avenue Income Credit Strategies F	Finance Intermediaries & Services	10/31/12	17.1	13.3	249.3	181.0	17	1632406
AVY	Avery Dennison Corp.	Office Equipment & Furniture	12/29/12	6035.6	215.4	5105.3	1580.9	459	104645435
AVG	AVG Technologies N.V.	IT Services	12/31/11	272.4	100.4	311.6	-322.3		
AVA	Avista Corp.	Electric Utilities	12/31/12	1547.0	78.2	4313.2	1259.5	238	44102206
AV	Aviva Plc	General Insurance	12/31/12	43095.0	-3218.0	315689.0	9786.0		
AVT	Avnet Inc	Electrical Equipment	6/30/12	25707.5	567.0	10167.9	3905.7	453	152374844
AVP	Avon Products, Inc.	Household & Personal Products	12/31/12	10717.1	-42.5	7382.5	1217.1	595	421397948
AVX	AVX Corp.	Electrical Equipment	3/31/12	1545.3	152.8	2468.0	2120.8	145	45712595
AXLL	Axiall Corp	Specialty Chemicals	12/31/12	3325.8	120.6	1801.3	603.5	239	41919540
AXLL	Axiall Corp	Specialty Chemicals	12/31/12	3325.8	120.6	1801.3	603.5	239	41919540
AXS	Axis Capital Holdings Ltd	General Insurance	12/31/12	3926.6	547.2	18852.3	5779.8	327	105897151
AZZ	AZZ Inc	Business Services	2/29/12	469.1	40.7	606.8	287.6	192	19335247
BGS	B&G Foods Inc	Food	12/29/12	633.8	59.3	1192.0	361.2	232	32858267
BWC	Babcock & Wilcox Co. (The)	Electric Utilities	12/31/12	3291.4	227.7	2840.4	986.4		
MCI	Babson Capital Corporate Investors	Holding and other Investment Office	12/31/12	30.3	24.5	299.4	257.4	40	1065777
MPV	Babson Capital Participating Investo	Holding and other Investment Office	12/31/12	13.5	11.0	147.6	127.9	22	509646
BMI	Badger Meter, Inc.	Electronic Instruments & Related Pro	12/31/12	319.7	28.0	290.5	171.2	164	11516016
BHI	Baker Hughes Inc.	Equipment & Services	12/31/12	21361.0	1311.0	26689.0	17069.0	818	392706563
BLL	Ball Corp	Metal Products	12/31/12	8735.7	403.5	7507.1	1114.6	482	124611865
BYI	Bally Technologies Inc	Internet & Software	6/30/12	879.8	101.1	970.5	196.1	279	45313199
BALT	Baltic Trading Ltd	Shipping	12/31/12	27.3	-17.3	364.4	260.7	49	5818210
BBVA	Banco Bilbao Vizcaya Argentaria S	Banking	12/31/11	36470.0	3004.0	597688.0	38165.0	182	39263615
BBD	Banco Bradesco S.A.	Banking	12/31/11	96750.9	10958.1	722086.9	59139.0		
BCH	Banco de Chile	Banking	12/31/11	1785644.0	428805.0	21740947.0	1739173.0	78	1464900
BLX	Banco Latinoamericano de Comerci	Banking	12/31/11		83.2	6360.0	759.3	52	7097069
BMA	Banco Macro S.A.	Banking	12/31/11		1176.1	41442.1	4719.6	73	8250121
BNC E04	Banco Nacional de Comercio Exteri	Banking	12/31/11	7764.0	681.0	195316.0	9024.0		
BSBR	Banco Santander Brasil SA	Banking	12/31/12	61713.7	5448.7	421085.0	81316.9	170	560255808

T6

1st	2nd	3rd	2012	2011	2010	P/E RATIO		Div 2012	Div 2011	Div 2010	AV. YLD %	AMOUNT	PAYABLE	PR 2012	
-	-	0.52	1.64	1.35	0.87	11.1 -	0.0	1.60	1.60	1.50	9.6	0.53910Z	4/15/13	18.1 -	0.0
-	-	0.55	2.06	-4.18	0.83	11.7 -	0.0	1.35	0.66	0.21	8.6	0.987	2/28/13	24.0 -	0.0
-	-	2.91	8.36	0.43	-	2.8 -	0.0	3.40	0.30	-	16.5	0.50Z	4/30/13	23.4 -	0.0
-	-	-	1.39	1.00	-	14.6 -	0.0	1.39	0.90	-	7.4	0.1050	4/30/13	20.3 -	0.0
														20.0 -	20.0
-	0.64	-	2.54	2.24	1.54	18.0 -	0.0	0.80	0.70	0.60	2.0	0.230Y	2/28/13	45.6 -	0.0
-	-	0.62	2.38	2.65	2.48	24.1 -	0.0	0.88	0.80	0.66	1.7	0.250Y	81/16/21	57.4 -	0.0
-	-	0.36	1.40	1.03	0.90	22.5 -	0.0	0.67	0.63	0.59	2.6	0.1750Y	81/16/21	31.4 -	0.0
-	-	0.14	0.46	0.35	0.11	23.6 -	0.0							10.9 -	0.0
0.47												0.070 Y	12/7/06		
-	-	0.59	2.11	1.93	1.64	22.3 -	0.0	0.40	0.40	0.40	1.0	0.10Y	4/1/13	47.1 -	0.0
-	-	0.07	0.79	-1.61	4.39	10.6 -	0.0	0.28	-	-	4.6	0.120Z	3/12/13	8.4 -	0.0
-	-	-0.44	-0.70	-2.93	-0.61									5.9 -	0.0
-	-	-0.46	-2.41	1.19	1.72			0.48	0.64	0.64	3.1	0.3708GHZ	4/15/13	19.2 -	0.0
-	-	0.22	-3.24	0.74	0.97			0.20	0.43	0.39	2.9	0.030Y	81/16/21	10.6 -	0.0
0.28	-	-	1.05	3.13	3.00	32.1 -	0.0	0.70	0.62	0.58	2.4	0.190Y	81/16/21	33.7 -	0.0
-	-	0.16	-	0.54	0.44							0.05970	1/3/14	19.0 -	0.0
-	-	-0.06	0.03	-8.56		600.0 -	0.0	0.37	-	-	2.2	0.250Z	4/18/13	18.0 -	0.0
-	-	-	-	-								0.1170	6/28/13	20.2 -	19.1
-	-	0.31	18.73	1.96	3.38	1.4 -	0.0	3.50	3.38	1.90	15.3	0.8750Y	4/30/13	26.9 -	0.0
-	-	0.20	0.98	-0.15	1.12	7.9 -	0.0	1.20	1.41	1.52	17.1	0.16410Z	6/27/13	7.8 -	0.0
-	-	1.05	2.19	1.90	0.19	26.0 -	0.0	8.55	-	13.74	17.7	8.557	81/16/21	57.0 -	0.0
-	-	0.94	4.56	5.17	4.01	9.3 -	0.0					0.025	81/16/21	42.6 -	0.0
-	-	-0.87	-0.80	0.99	1.58			0.12	0.24	0.24	4.2	0.020Y	11/20/12	4.8 -	0.0
														39.5 -	36.7
-	-	-	0.11	-0.01								0.030	5/29/13	25.9 -	0.0
-	-	0.66	2.61	2.08	1.14	14.6 -	0.0					0.2250Y	81/16/21	38.0 -	0.0
-	-	-0.35	-1.30	-0.73	-1.43			0.44	0.40	-	4.7	0.56250Z	4/15/13	12.6 -	0.0
1.26	-	-	0.33	5.17	4.18	261.7 -	0.0	0.80	0.65	0.45	1.1	0.2250Y	81/16/21	86.4 -	0.0
-	-	-	-0.05	-0.06	-0.06							5.057C	1/12/09	11.2 -	0.0
-	-	-	0.08	-	-0.01	0.0 -	0.0	3.16	3.17	0.52	1.$	2.6348C	1/31/13	15.2 -	0.0
-	-	-	0.08	-	-0.01	186.5 -	0.0	3.16	3.17	0.52	24.2	2.6348C	1/31/13	14.9 -	0.0
-	-	1.45	3.38	-1.82	3.62	11.4 -	0.0	-	0.60	0.60	1.8	0.45310	81/16/21	38.6 -	0.0
-	-	-0.18	-1.14	1.05	0.70			0.20	0.30	-	1.8	0.10Y	6/15/12	19.2 -	0.0
-	-	0.04	0.66	0.13	-0.38	28.3 -	0.0	0.71	0.68	0.68	4.5	0.190Z	5/1/13	18.6 -	0.0
-	-	1.52	5.67	5.58	2.50	7.9 -	0.0	0.81	0.70	0.63	2.2	0.210Y	81/16/21	45.0 -	0.0
-	-	0.73	0.57	4.18	2.90	36.8 -	0.0	0.36	0.18	0.18	2.5	0.10	81/16/21	20.9 -	0.0
-	-	0.14	0.55	0.70	0.78	19.9 -	0.0	0.25	0.52	0.52	2.6	0.040Y	81/16/21	10.9 -	0.0
-	-	1.21	4.98	7.30	5.57	10.1 -	0.0	2.85	2.70	2.41	6.2			50.1 -	0.0
-	-	0.63	1.25	0.66	3.35	30.7 -	0.0	1.76	1.72	1.68	5.0	0.450Y	81/16/21	38.3 -	0.0
-	-	-0.06	-0.97	-0.50	-0.06			1.15	1.12	1.06	9.1	0.03330	5/31/13	15.2 -	0.0
-	-	-0.22	-1.02	0.88	1.01			1.01	0.64	0.05	2.9	0.30	2/19/13	44.3 -	0.0
-	-	-0.17	0.95	5.22	5.07	38.0 -	0.0	2.24	1.78	0.35	6.8	0.580	2/14/13	36.1 -	0.0
-	-	-0.32	-1.59	-	-			0.95	-	-	3.9	0.480	2/14/13	28.8 -	0.0
0.88	-	-	2.37	2.27	2.20	18.0 -	0.0	1.38	1.36	1.34	3.9	0.350Y	81/16/21	42.7 -	0.0
1.10	-	-	4.14	4.15	3.95	13.4 -	0.0							55.4 -	0.0
-	-	-	-6.19	-6.94	0.70									5.0 -	0.0
-	-	0.07	0.12	0.82	-0.97	77.4 -	0.0					0.04G	4/18/13	9.3 -	0.0
-	-	1.23	5.08	6.65	6.39	13.7 -	0.0	1.89	1.73	0.65	3.1	0.50Y	81/16/21	69.6 -	0.0
-	-	0.66	2.52	1.91	1.43	19.3 -	0.0							48.6 -	0.0
-	4.78	-	23.48	19.47	14.97	16.9 -	0.0							397.1 -	0.0
-	-	0.89	4.32	4.87	2.07	35.0 -	0.0	3.88	3.57	3.57	2.8	1.070Z	81/16/21	151.0 -	0.0
-	-	1.51	1.01	-		13.1 -	0.0	1.46	0.91	-	8.3	0.120	4/30/13	19.8 -	0.0
-	-	0.57	2.08	1.78	2.97	21.0 -	0.0	1.08	1.00	0.80	3.3	0.270Y	81/16/21	43.6 -	0.0
-	-	-	1.69	0.99										16.1 -	0.0
-	-	0.10	1.32	1.72	1.65	21.1 -	0.0	1.16	1.10	1.00	4.5	0.3050Y	81/16/21	27.9 -	0.0
-	-	-	-1.13	0.06	0.50			1.31	1.33	1.12	12.7	0.51560	6/1/13	12.6 -	0.0
-	0.99	-	3.79	4.34	2.68	9.7 -	0.0					0.0750	81/16/21	36.9 -	0.0
-	-	0.07	-0.10	1.18	1.39			0.75	0.92	0.88	4.4	0.060Y	81/16/21	23.5 -	0.0
-	-	0.12	0.90	1.43	0.84	14.8 -	0.0	0.26	0.19	0.16	2.4	0.0750Y	81/16/21	13.4 -	0.0
-	-	1.12	3.45	1.66	1.22	16.5 -	15.6	0.24	-	-	0.4	0.080Y	4/10/13	56.9 -	53.6
-	-	1.12	3.45	1.66	1.22	18.7 -	0.0	0.24	-	-	0.6	0.080Y	4/10/13	64.7 -	0.0
-	-	1.82	4.00	0.07	6.02	10.5 -	0.0	0.97	0.93	0.86	2.7	0.42970	4/15/13	41.8 -	0.0
-	-	0.60	1.61	1.39	1.51	30.0 -	0.0	0.50	0.50	0.13	1.4	0.140Y	5/3/13	48.3 -	0.0
-	-	0.35	1.20	1.04	0.67	27.1 -	0.0	1.10	0.86	0.68	4.0	0.290Y	4/30/13	32.5 -	0.0
-	-	0.34	1.91	1.43	1.30	14.9 -	0.0	0.08	-	-	0.3	0.080Y	81/16/21	28.4 -	0.0
-	-	-	1.28	1.29	1.14	13.5 -	0.0	1.30	1.35	1.08	8.0	0.17	1/11/13	17.3 -	0.0
-	-	-	1.08	1.14	1.02	14.8 -	0.0	1.08	1.23	1.00	7.4	0.270	1/11/13	16.0 -	0.0
-	-	0.62	1.95	1.27	1.91	27.6 -	0.0	0.66	0.60	0.52	1.6	0.170Y	81/16/21	53.8 -	0.0
-	-	0.63	2.97	3.97	2.06	16.9 -	0.0	0.60	0.60	0.60	1.4	0.150Y	81/16/21	50.1 -	0.0
-	-	0.73	2.55	2.63	2.55	18.7 -	0.0	0.40	0.28	0.20	0.9	0.130Y	81/16/21	47.6 -	0.0
-	0.80	-	2.28	1.81	2.38	23.0 -	0.0							52.5 -	0.0
-	-	-0.22	-0.78	-0.02	0.46			0.24	0.45	0.32	6.9	0.010Z	3/14/13	4.8 -	0.0
-	-	-	-	0.64	1.14			-	0.85	1.07				10.5 -	0.0
-	-	-	-	-	-									17.4 -	0.0
-	-	-	-	2.49	2.29			-	0.35	0.25				102.0 -	0.0
-	-	-	-	4.92	4.42			-	0.01	0.01		0.30	2/8/13	19.1 -	0.0
-	-	-	-	-	-										
-	-	3.51	13.07	18.55	17.67	0.7 -	0.0	0.15	0.26	0.27	2.0			9.3 -	0.0

SYMBOL	COMPANY	NATURE OF BUSINESS	FISCAL YEAR-END	TOTAL REV. $MILL	NET INCOME $MILL	TOTAL ASSETS $MILL	NET STK EQUITY $MILL	NO OF INST	INST. HOLDINGS (SHARES)
BSAC	Banco Santander Chile	Banking	12/31/11	1930725.0	401733.0	24668993.0	2060717.0	154	89035574
SAN	Banco Santander SA	Banking	12/31/11	84159.0	5351.0	1251526.0	76414.0	270	81318505
CIB	BanColombia, S.A.	Banking	12/31/11		1663894.0	85463020.0	8993360.0	167	36920567
BXS PRA	Bancorpsouth Capital Trust I	Banking						1	8900
BXS	BancorpSouth Inc.	Banking	12/31/12	766.6	84.3	13397.2	1449.1	217	59851470
BAC	Bank of America Corp.	Banking	12/31/12	100078.0	4188.0	2209974.0	236956.0	1670	6557843068
BOH	Bank of Hawaii Corp	Banking	12/31/12	620.8	166.1	13728.4	1021.7	304	39502201
IRE	Bank of Ireland (Ireland)	Banking	12/31/11	8014.0	45.0	154880.0	10202.0	61	6276218
BMO	Bank of Montreal	Banking	10/31/12	20967.0	4115.0	525449.0	28655.0	395	295518519
BK	Bank of New York Mellon Corp	Banking	12/31/12	15653.0	2445.0	358990.0	36431.0	896	974939762
BNS	Bank of Nova Scotia Halifax	Banking	10/31/12	27114.0	6023.0	668044.0	39636.0	321	600150961
RATE	Bankrate Inc (DE)	Internet & Software	12/31/12	457.2	29.3	1160.1	828.2		
BKU	BankUnited Inc.	Banking	12/31/12	810.1	211.3	12576.0	1806.7	141	103413109
BCS	Barclays PLC	Banking	12/31/12	34625.0	-1041.0	1490321.0	53586.0	258	81511698
BCR	Bard (C.R.), Inc.	Medical Instruments & Equipment	12/31/12	2958.1	530.1	4151.3	1925.7	617	80674686
BKS	Barnes & Noble Inc	Retail - Specialty	4/28/12	7129.2	-68.9	3765.2	747.7	235	39439320
B	Barnes Group Inc.	Industrial Machinery & Equipment	12/31/12	1230.0	95.2	1868.6	800.1	223	50967303
BBG	Barrett (Bill) Corp	Production & Extraction	12/31/12	700.2	0.6	2869.4	1182.8	235	62787225
ABX	Barrick Gold Corp.	Precious Metals	12/31/12	14547.0	-665.0	47282.0	21845.0	714	610804872
BAS	Basic Energy Services Inc	Equipment & Services	12/31/12	1374.9	20.9	1595.9	374.2	186	41595143
BAX	Baxter International Inc.	Medical Instruments & Equipment	12/31/12	14190.0	2326.0	20390.0	6938.0	1149	530517648
BTE	Baytex Energy Corp	Production & Extraction	12/31/11	1096.6	217.4	2461.8	1206.7		
BBT	BB&T Corp.	Banking	12/31/12	10737.0	2028.0	183872.0	21158.0	796	405279149
BFR	BBVA Banco Frances S.A. (Argenti	Banking	12/31/11		1005.6	39005.6	3868.3	47	3710082
BBX	BBX Capital Corp	Banking	12/31/12	28.3	235.8	470.7	240.3	26	3966314
BCE	BCE Inc.	Services	12/31/12	19975.0	2624.0	40968.0	13875.0	478	378661215
BEAM	Beam Inc	Beverages	12/31/12	2465.9	382.4	8636.9	4612.1	641	137837593
BZH	Beazer Homes USA, Inc.	Builders	9/30/12	1005.7	-145.3	1982.2	262.2	199	31856402
BDX	Becton, Dickinson and Co.	Medical Instruments & Equipment	9/30/12	7708.4	1169.9	11360.9	4135.9	1012	180213124
BDC	Belden Inc	Electrical Equipment	12/31/12	1840.7	194.5	2584.6	811.9	232	55014609
T 28A	BellSouth Telecommunications, Inc.	Services	12/31/99	17478.0	2770.0	25295.0	8805.0		
BLC	Belo Corp.	Radio & Television	12/31/12	714.7	100.2	1499.6	300.2	244	97508890
BMS	Bemis Co Inc	Containers & Packaging	12/31/12	5139.2	173.8	4185.7	1640.9	424	96458221
BHE	Benchmark Electronics, Inc.	Electrical Equipment	12/31/12	2468.2	56.6	1501.5	1139.5	199	57956568
WRB	Berkley (W. R.) Corp.	General Insurance	12/31/12	5823.6	510.6	20155.9	4306.2	412	124942034
BRK B	Berkshire Hathaway Inc.	General Insurance	12/31/12	162463.0	14824.0	427452.0	187647.0	1563	741194454
BHLB	Berkshire Hills Bancorp, Inc.	Credit & Lending	12/31/12	230.0	33.2	5296.8	667.3	145	18640740
BRY	Berry Petroleum Co	Production & Extraction	12/31/12	978.6	171.5	3325.4	1014.8	218	48481297
BERY	Berry Plastics Group Inc	Plastics	9/29/12	4766.0	2.0	5106.0	-455.0		
BBY	Best Buy Inc	Retail - Appliances and Electronics	2/2/13	45085.0	-441.0	16787.0	3061.0	657	243683428
BHP	BHP Billiton Ltd.	Non-Precious Metals	6/30/12	72226.0	15417.0	129273.0	65870.0	644	83954030
BBL	BHP Billiton Plc	Non-Precious Metals	6/30/12	72226.0	15417.0	129273.0	65870.0	187	17891612
BIG	Big Lots, Inc.	Retail - General Merchandise/Depart	2/2/13	5400.1	177.1	1753.6	758.1	376	70694488
BH	Biglari Holdings Inc.	Retail - Food & Beverage, Drug & To	9/26/12	740.2	21.6	773.8	349.1	141	2428912
BIO	Bio-Rad Laboratories, Inc.	Biotechnology	12/31/12	2069.2	163.8	3436.8	2010.7	242	18276200
BMR	Biomed Realty Trust Inc	REITs	12/31/12	518.2	11.8	4834.5	2476.9	295	165689514
BITA	Bitauto Holdings Ltd	Internet & Software	12/31/11	670.0	87.2	1301.3	885.9	20	8348261
BKH	Black Hills Corporation	Electric Utilities	12/31/12	1173.9	81.5	3729.5	1232.5	244	31946414
BKH 39	Black Hills Power Inc.	Electric Utilities	12/31/12	243.3	27.1	872.9	319.5		
BBN	Blackrock Build America Bond Trust	Holding and other Investment Office	7/31/12	102.2	88.2	1954.2	1367.8	44	5535105
BJZ	Blackrock California Municipal 2018	Holding and other Investment Office	12/31/12	5.5	4.6	157.4	157.3	15	262793
BFZ	BlackRock California Municipal Inco	Holding and other Investment Office	7/31/12	37.5	30.4	870.0	519.6	27	1364220
BHK	Blackrock Core Bond Trust	Holding and other Investment Office	8/31/12	27.5	23.9	634.1	411.1	49	4199569
CYE	BlackRock Corporate High Yield Fu	Holding and other Investment Office	2/29/12	27.4	23.6	384.4	277.2	49	3993185
COY	BlackRock Corporate High Yield Fu	Holding and other Investment Office	2/29/12	24.3	21.4	340.6	254.2	41	1916744
HYV	BlackRock Corporate High Yield Fu	Holding and other Investment Office	8/31/12	41.0	35.4	599.5	416.7	54	5502715
HYT	BlackRock Corporate High Yield Fu	Holding and other Investment Office	8/31/12	42.9	36.7	625.1	436.0	43	5379615
BTZ	BlackRock Credit Allocation Income	Holding and other Investment Office	10/31/12	57.5	48.6	1190.3	796.8	93	28315094
DSU	BlackRock Debt Strategies Fund Inc	Holding and other Investment Office	2/29/12	41.5	35.4	622.2	445.8	56	16863577
BHL	Blackrock Defined Opportunity Cred	Holding and other Investment Office	8/31/12	10.1	7.7	189.0	127.5	21	1194230
BQR	Blackrock Ecosolutions Investment	Holding and other Investment Office	10/31/12	2.7	1.1	117.9	114.9	24	1115995
BGR	Blackrock Energy & Resources Trus	Holding and other Investment Office	10/31/12	13.5	3.9	794.1	772.5	75	6389962
CII	BlackRock Enhanced Capital & Inco	Holding and other Investment Office	10/31/12	20.5	14.6	629.4	622.7	67	8434091
BDJ	BlackRock Enhanced Equity Divide	Holding and other Investment Office	10/31/12	37.5	26.0	1515.6	1490.1	103	29515059
EGF	BlackRock Enhanced Government	Holding and other Investment Office	9/30/12	9.9	7.3	269.1	159.5	26	3295988
EF	BlackRock Europe Fund Inc	Holding and other Investment Office	12/31/05	2.9	1.3	121.6	120.5		
FRA	BlackRock Floating Rate Income Str	Holding and other Investment Office	8/31/12	22.4	17.9	407.9	277.0	67	8610287
BGT	BlackRock Floating Rate Income Tr	Holding and other Investment Office	8/31/12	28.3	22.9	538.8	343.3	49	3620982
BFO	BlackRock Florida Municipal 2020 T	Holding and other Investment Office	7/31/12	5.7	4.8	133.5	132.2	15	309383
BOE	BlackRock Global Opportunities Eq	Holding and other Investment Office	10/31/12	25.6	14.1	1063.4	1041.2	80	10360057
BME	BlackRock Health Sciences Trust	Holding and other Investment Office	10/31/12	3.0	0.6	227.4	218.4	33	2673532
HIS	Blackrock High Income Shares	Holding and other Investment Office	8/31/12	12.8	11.0	167.4	123.7	37	4067821
BHY	Blackrock High Yield Trust	Holding and other Investment Office	8/31/12	4.3	3.4	66.6	46.9	25	520109
BNA	BlackRock Income Opportunity Trus	Holding and other Investment Office	8/31/12	26.6	23.1	636.6	408.1	54	5464533
BKT	Blackrock Income Trust Inc. (The)	Holding and other Investment Office	8/31/12	29.7	24.8	1073.1	507.9	73	17894416
BGY	BlackRock International Growth & In	Holding and other Investment Office	10/31/12	27.9	17.9	930.2	910.5	80	18417630
BKN	BlackRock Investment Quality Muni	Holding and other Investment Office	4/30/12	19.8	16.8	435.1	263.4	33	1130392
BLW	BlackRock Limited Duration Income	Holding and other Investment Office	8/31/12	55.1	48.5	956.7	642.4	52	5642535
BTA	BlackRock Long-Term Municipal Ad	Holding and other Investment Office	4/30/12	12.2	10.1	265.4	163.2	33	2022719
BIT	Blackrock Multi-Sector Income Trust	Holding and other Investment Office	12/31/12		-0.0	0.1	0.1		

EARNINGS PER SHARE — QUARTERLY			EARNINGS PER SHARE — ANNUAL			P/E RATIO		DIVIDENDS PER SHARE			AV. YLD %	DIV. DECLARED		PRICE RANGE 2012	
1st	2nd	3rd	2012	2011	2010			2012	2011	2010		AMOUNT	PAYABLE		
-	-	0.27	-	2.13	2.53			-	0.00	0.00		-		33.7 -	0.0
-	-	0.01	-	0.60	0.94			-	0.61	0.60		-		8.8 -	0.0
-	-	-	-	-	-			-	-	-		-		70.5 -	0.0
-	-	-	-	-	-							0.50940Z	7/1/13	26.7 -	0.0
-	-	0.25	0.90	0.45	0.27	18.2 -	0.0	0.04	0.14	0.88	0.3	0.010Y	81/16/21	16.4 -	0.0
-	-	0.00	0.25	0.01	-0.37	51.1 -	0.0	0.04	0.04	0.04	0.4	1.750Y	81/16/21	12.8 -	0.0
-	-	0.92	3.67	3.39	3.80	13.8 -	0.0	1.80	1.80	1.80	3.9	0.450Y	81/16/21	50.8 -	0.0
-	-	-	-	-0.01	-0.22			-	-	-		-		9.5 -	0.0
1.53	-	-	6.15	4.84	4.75	10.5 -	0.0	2.82	2.80	3.50	4.8	0.24370	5/27/13	64.5 -	0.0
-	-	0.61	2.03	2.03	2.05	14.3 -	0.0	0.52	0.48	0.36	2.2	0.330Y	81/16/21	29.0 -	0.0
1.25	-	-	5.22	4.62	3.91	11.8 -	0.0	2.19	2.05	1.96	4.0	0.23130	4/26/13	61.4 -	0.0
-	-	0.03	0.29	-0.14	-0.70	85.9 -	0.0	-	-	-		-		24.9 -	0.0
-	-	0.48	2.05	0.62	1.99	13.9 -	0.0	0.72	0.56	-	2.9	0.210Y	81/16/21	28.6 -	0.0
-	-	-	-0.09	0.24	0.28			0.60	0.58	0.42	4.1	-		20.6 -	0.0
-	-	1.50	6.16	3.69	5.32	17.5 -	0.0	0.78	0.74	0.70	0.8	0.20Y	81/16/21	107.8 -	0.0
-	-	-0.18	-1.41	-1.31	0.63			-	0.75	1.00		0.250Y	81/16/21	20.8 -	0.0
-	-	0.34	1.72	1.16	0.95	16.9 -	0.0	0.40	0.34	0.32	1.7	0.10Y	3/11/13	29.1 -	0.0
-	-	-1.11	0.01	0.65	1.75	2658.0 -	0.0	-	-	-		-		26.6 -	0.0
-	-	0.62	-0.66	4.48	3.59			0.75	0.51	0.44	2.1	0.20	3/15/13	44.2 -	0.0
-	-	0.16	0.51	1.14	-1.10	35.3 -	0.0	-	-	-		-		18.0 -	0.0
-	-	1.06	4.18	3.88	2.39	17.4 -	0.0	1.57	1.26	1.18	2.6	0.450Y	81/16/21	72.6 -	0.0
-	-	0.22	-	1.83	1.54			-	2.42	-		0.220	4/15/13	54.0 -	0.0
-	-	0.66	2.70	1.83	1.16	12.6 -	0.0	0.76	0.64	0.60	2.5	0.230Y	81/16/21	34.0 -	0.0
-	-	-	-	-	-			-	-	-		-		6.1 -	0.0
-	-	-	-	-	-			-	-	-		-		8.3 -	0.0
-	-	17.59	15.00	-2.04	-12.90	0.6 -	0.0	-	-	-		-		47.5 -	0.0
-	-	0.74	3.39	2.88	2.74	14.0 -	0.0	2.22	2.04	1.78	5.2	0.06251	4/12/13	63.5 -	0.0
-	-	0.47	2.38	5.78	3.16	26.7 -	0.0	0.82	0.76	0.76	1.4	0.2250Y	81/16/21	19.9 -	0.0
-0.84	-	-	-7.87	-13.85	-2.85			-	-	-		0.45310	5/15/13	95.6 -	0.0
3.13	-	-	5.59	5.62	5.49	17.1 -	0.0	1.80	1.64	1.48	2.3	0.4950Y	81/16/21	53.2 -	0.0
-	-	-0.87	4.23	2.38	2.27	12.6 -	0.0	0.20	0.20	0.20	0.5	0.050Y	4/2/13		
-	-	0.24	0.95	0.55	0.83	10.3 -	0.0	0.54	0.10	-	7.3	0.080Y	5/31/13	9.8 -	0.0
-	-	0.45	1.66	1.73	1.85	24.3 -	0.0	1.00	0.96	0.92	3.0	0.260Y	81/16/21	40.4 -	0.0
-	-	0.34	1.00	0.87	1.29	18.3 -	0.0	-	-	-		-		18.3 -	0.0
-	-	0.71	3.56	2.71	2.90	12.5 -	0.0	1.35	0.31	0.27	3.5	0.090Y	81/16/21	44.4 -	0.0
-	-	-2373.00	8977.00	6215.00	7928.00	0.0 -	0.0	-	-	-		-		104.2 -	0.0
-	-	0.46	1.49	0.98	0.99	17.3 -	0.0	0.69	0.65	0.64	3.0	0.180Y	2/28/13	25.7 -	0.0
-	-	0.33	3.09	-4.21	1.52	15.7 -	0.0	0.32	0.31	0.30	0.8	0.080Y	3/29/13	48.6 -	0.0
-0.09	-	-	0.02	-3.55	-1.34	988.5 -	0.0	-	-	-		-		19.8 -	0.0
-	-	-0.03	-3.36	3.08	3.10			0.62	0.58	0.56	3.5	0.170Y	81/16/21	23.6 -	0.0
-	-	-	2.88	4.27	2.28	27.9 -	0.0	2.20	1.82	1.66	3.1	-		80.5 -	0.0
-	-	-	2.88	4.27	2.28	25.0 -	0.0	2.20	1.82	1.66	3.6	-		72.1 -	0.0
-	-	-0.10	2.99	2.83	2.42	15.3 -	0.0	-	-	-		-		45.9 -	0.0
3.42	-	-	16.15	25.86	19.99	25.9 -	0.0	-	-	-		-		418.5 -	0.0
-	-	1.48	5.72	6.26	6.59	22.0 -	0.0	-	-	-		-		126.0 -	0.0
-	-	0.02	-0.03	0.19	0.19			0.88	0.80	0.63	4.6	0.2350Z	4/15/13	22.1 -	0.0
-	-	-	-	2.06	-38.29			-	-	-		-		10.2 -	0.0
-	-	0.78	1.85	1.24	1.76	23.8 -	0.0	1.48	1.46	1.44	4.2	0.380Y	81/16/21	44.1 -	0.0
-	-	-	1.20	-	-			1.54	1.18	-	6.8	0.13180	4/30/13	24.0 -	0.0
-	-	-	0.71	-	-	23.8 -	0.0	0.76	-	-	4.8	0.0513M	5/1/13	16.9 -	0.0
-	-	-	0.95	0.98	1.00	18.4 -	0.0	0.92	0.91	0.91	5.6	0.0777M	5/1/10	17.5 -	0.0
-	-	-	0.88	0.83	0.87	18.4 -	0.0	0.82	0.88	1.00	5.5	0.0730	4/30/13	16.2 -	0.0
-	-	-	0.63	0.65	0.64	13.0 -	0.0	0.63	0.61	0.68	8.1	0.05250	4/30/13	8.2 -	0.0
-	-	-	0.62	0.65	0.65	13.4 -	0.0	0.61	0.61	0.73	7.9	0.0510	4/30/13	8.3 -	0.0
-	-	-	1.08	1.09	1.06	12.6 -	0.0	1.07	1.06	1.02	8.3	0.090	4/30/13	13.6 -	0.0
-	-	-	1.04	1.06	1.05	12.8 -	0.0	1.04	1.00	1.02	8.2	0.08750	4/30/13	13.3 -	0.0
-	-	-	0.94	0.88	0.85	15.3 -	0.0	0.94	0.85	1.10	6.9	0.07850	4/30/13	14.4 -	0.0
-	-	-	0.33	0.33	0.39	13.9 -	0.0	0.32	0.34	0.40	7.5	0.0270	4/30/13	4.6 -	0.0
-	-	-	0.85	0.86	0.85	18.2 -	0.0	0.80	0.79	0.70	5.8	0.06850	4/30/13	15.5 -	0.0
-	-	-	0.08	0.10	0.05	126.0 -	0.0	0.88	1.07	1.20	10.0	0.17920	3/28/13	10.1 -	0.0
-	-	-	0.13	0.06	0.26	204.5 -	0.0	1.77	1.62	1.62	7.3	0.4050	3/28/13	26.6 -	0.0
-	-	-	0.33	0.35	0.31	41.1 -	0.0	1.38	1.69	1.94	10.7	0.30	3/28/13	13.6 -	0.0
-	-	-	0.18	0.16	0.17	43.9 -	0.0	0.68	0.83	0.98	9.2	0.140	3/28/13	7.9 -	0.0
-	-	-	0.67	0.70	0.64	23.9 -	0.0	0.83	0.92	0.98	5.4	0.0650	4/30/13	16.0 -	0.0
-	-	-	-	-	-			-	-	-		3.60	10/13/06		
-	-	-	0.97	0.96	0.90	17.2 -	0.0	0.92	0.92	0.96	6.1	0.0770	4/30/13	16.7 -	0.0
-	-	-	0.97	1.00	0.97	16.7 -	0.0	1.10	1.09	0.83	7.4	0.07750	4/30/13	16.2 -	0.0
-	-	-	0.85	0.92	0.95	19.2 -	0.0	0.70	0.67	0.67	4.5	0.097	7/31/13	16.3 -	0.0
-	-	-	0.20	0.17	0.19	77.2 -	0.0	1.96	2.27	2.27	14.5	0.31160	2/28/13	15.4 -	0.0
-	-	-	0.08	-0.01	0.02	399.0 -	0.0	2.50	2.24	1.54	8.8	0.38440	3/28/13	31.9 -	0.0
-	-	-	0.20	0.20	0.20	12.5 -	0.0	0.20	0.21	0.17	8.6	0.01520	4/30/13	2.5 -	0.0
-	-	-	0.53	0.51	0.51	15.9 -	0.0	0.53	0.52	0.52	6.9	0.04450	4/30/13	8.4 -	0.0
-	-	-	0.67	0.63	0.59	17.9 -	0.0	0.65	0.65	0.79	5.8	0.0570	4/30/13	12.0 -	0.0
-	-	-	0.39	0.35	0.20	19.8 -	0.0	0.47	0.34	0.29	6.3	0.04050	4/30/13	7.7 -	0.0
-	-	-	0.16	0.14	0.14	49.6 -	0.0	0.95	1.36	1.59	12.9	0.16790	3/28/13	7.9 -	0.0
-	-	-	0.98	1.04	1.07	17.8 -	0.0	1.01	1.01	0.95	6.1	0.08M	5/1/13	17.4 -	0.0
-	-	-	1.31	1.34	1.12	14.6 -	0.0	1.33	1.24	0.90	7.4	0.10950	4/30/13	19.2 -	0.0
-	-	-	0.75	0.76	0.75	18.0 -	0.0	0.77	0.73	0.69	6.0	0.062M	5/1/13	13.5 -	0.0
-	-	-	-	-	-			-	-	-		0.1167G	4/30/13	20.1 -	20.0

SYMBOL	COMPANY	NATURE OF BUSINESS	FISCAL YEAR-END	TOTAL REV. $MILL	NET INCOME $MILL	TOTAL ASSETS $MILL	NET STK EQUITY $MILL	NO OF INST	INST. HOLDINGS (SHARES)
MUI	BlackRock Muni Intermediate Durati	Holding and other Investment Office	4/30/12	43.8	32.8	1002.9	617.4	46	3032467
MNE	BlackRock Muni New York Intermed	Holding and other Investment Office	7/31/12	4.3	3.1	104.6	67.2	12	218154
MUA	BlackRock MuniAssets Fund, Inc.	Holding and other Investment Office	4/30/12	30.8	27.3	554.2	481.6	43	1399231
BPK	Blackrock Municipal 2018 Term Tru	Holding and other Investment Office	12/31/12	16.0	13.9	393.6	389.6	29	975042
BKK	BlackRock Municipal 2020 Term Tr	Holding and other Investment Office	4/30/12	23.8	20.7	514.8	504.9	36	1662481
BIE	BlackRock Municipal Bond Investm	Holding and other Investment Office	8/31/12	4.2	3.1	93.7	56.3	11	121702
BBK	Blackrock Municipal Bond Trust	Holding and other Investment Office	8/31/12	13.3	10.5	286.4	176.2	26	506212
BAF	BlackRock Municipal Income Invest	Holding and other Investment Office	8/31/12	9.3	7.2	224.1	144.6	19	366872
BBF	BlackRock Municipal Income Invest	Holding and other Investment Office	7/31/12	7.7	5.8	178.8	106.6	19	504740
BYM	BlackRock Municipal Income Qualit	Holding and other Investment Office	8/31/12	30.3	24.5	670.0	424.8	42	1317600
BFK	BlackRock Municipal Income Trust	Holding and other Investment Office	4/30/12	51.1	42.4	1086.9	648.5	48	1705730
BTT	Blackrock Municipal Target Term Tr	Holding and other Investment Office	7/12/12	-	-0.0	0.1	0.1	19	1478113
MEN	BlackRock MuniEnhanced Fund Inc	Holding and other Investment Office	4/30/12	26.0	20.3	574.5	357.0	38	3007461
MUC	BlackRock MuniHoldings California	Holding and other Investment Office	7/31/12	47.5	38.7	1140.2	671.1	37	1989063
MUH	BlackRock MuniHoldings Fund II Inc	Holding and other Investment Office	4/30/12	13.8	11.5	291.9	182.6	24	1125076
MHD	BlackRock MuniHoldings Fund Inc	Holding and other Investment Office	4/30/12	18.8	15.7	397.7	244.0	26	951827
MFL	BlackRock MuniHoldings Investmen	Holding and other Investment Office	8/31/12	42.9	32.6	1012.6	602.8	43	3261500
MUJ	BlackRock MuniHoldings New Jerse	Holding and other Investment Office	7/31/12	23.5	17.6	556.4	351.8	23	881505
MHN	BlackRock MuniHoldings New York	Holding and other Investment Office	8/31/12	36.3	27.6	810.7	485.5	28	1132027
MUE	BlackRock MuniHoldings Quality Fu	Holding and other Investment Office	7/31/12	23.9	19.3	576.1	341.1	30	1754420
MUS	BlackRock MuniHoldings Quality Fu	Holding and other Investment Office	4/30/12	14.0	11.5	322.1	189.6	23	2265072
MVT	BlackRock MuniVest Fund II Inc	Holding and other Investment Office	4/30/12	27.5	23.2	572.8	330.9	42	650036
MYC	BlackRock MuniYield California.Fun	Holding and other Investment Office	7/31/12	25.5	20.0	599.8	361.3	28	1789961
MCA	BlackRock MuniYield California Qua	Holding and other Investment Office	7/31/12	39.6	31.0	954.3	570.6	27	2509813
MYD	BlackRock MuniYield Fund Inc	Holding and other Investment Office	4/30/12	55.6	45.5	1157.6	703.3	38	2154640
MYF	BlackRock MuniYield Investment Fu	Holding and other Investment Office	7/31/12	16.0	12.6	375.7	221.8	26	2097690
MFT	BlackRock MuniYield Investment Q	Holding and other Investment Office	7/31/12	9.3	7.3	232.1	133.2	21	768151
MYM	BlackRock MuniYield Michigan Qual	Holding and other Investment Office	7/31/12	12.7	9.7	291.3	183.1	20	448849
MIY	BlackRock MuniYield Michigan Qual	Holding and other Investment Office	7/31/12	20.8	15.9	475.9	294.8	24	559651
MJI	BlackRock MuniYield New Jersey Q	Holding and other Investment Office	7/31/12	9.6	7.3	224.6	144.9	15	523612
MYN	BlackRock MuniYield New York Qu	Holding and other Investment Office	7/31/12	42.0	32.6	966.1	594.8	40	1437140
MYJ	BlackRock MuniYield NJ Fund Inc	Holding and other Investment Office	7/31/12	15.9	12.3	371.0	240.8	16	752659
MPA	BlackRock MuniYield Pennsylvania	Holding and other Investment Office	7/31/12	12.8	9.8	312.7	190.6	28	544323
MQT	BlackRock MuniYield Quality Fund I	Holding and other Investment Office	4/30/12	22.9	19.1	507.6	317.3	35	2256939
MYI	BlackRock MuniYield Quality Fund I	Holding and other Investment Office	7/31/12	73.8	58.6	1654.1	1036.0	59	4145671
MQY	BlackRock MuniYield Quality Fund I	Holding and other Investment Office	4/30/12	35.8	29.1	790.0	495.3	46	2270585
BNJ	Blackrock New Jersey Municipal Inc	Holding and other Investment Office	7/31/12	9.0	7.3	194.0	123.5	19	549870
BLH	Blackrock New York Municipal 2018	Holding and other Investment Office	12/31/12	2.9	2.4	88.4	88.3	9	118195
BQH	Blackrock New York Municipal Bond	Holding and other Investment Office	8/31/12	3.4	2.4	77.8	46.2	10	87957
BSE	BlackRock New York Municipal Inco	Holding and other Investment Office	8/31/12	7.0	5.2	164.0	100.9	13	338566
BNY	Blackrock New York Municipal Inco	Holding and other Investment Office	7/31/12	14.7	11.9	330.6	200.0	19	224601
BCF	Blackrock Real Asset Equity Trust	Holding and other Investment Office	10/31/12	14.5	7.1	641.2	630.8	70	11305466
BCX	Blackrock Resources & Commoditie	Holding and other Investment Office	10/31/12	15.9	8.3	731.6	718.0	31	4843040
ARK	BlackRock Senior High Income Fun	Holding and other Investment Office	2/29/12	21.1	18.2	320.7	235.3	50	8325757
BHD	Blackrock Strategic Bond Trust	Holding and other Investment Office	8/31/12	8.4	7.0	132.7	101.7	27	1020981
BSD	Blackrock Strategic Municipal Trust	Holding and other Investment Office	4/30/12	8.0	6.5	175.0	105.3	26	445389
BUI	Blackrock Utility & Infrastructure Tru	Holding and other Investment Office	10/12/11	-	-0.0	0.1	0.1	24	1503483
BLK	BlackRock, Inc.	Finance Intermediaries & Services	12/31/12	9337.0	2458.0	200451.0	25403.0	774	143304680
BGX	Blackstone / GSO Long-Short Credi	Holding and other Investment Office	12/31/12	19.9	15.5	301.7	241.0	19	2422522
BSL	Blackstone / GSO Senior Floating R	Holding and other Investment Office	12/31/12	28.8	20.7	468.1	341.6	26	2130956
BGB	Blackstone / GSO Strategic Credit F	Holding and other Investment Office	8/22/12	-	-	1.0	0.1	21	1647210
BX	Blackstone Group LP	Wealth Management	12/31/12	4019.4	218.6	28931.6	-	313	295093937
HRB	Block (H & R), Inc.	Miscellaneous Consumer Services	4/30/12	2893.8	265.9	4649.6	1325.9	540	257191889
BLT	Blount International, Inc.	Industrial Machinery & Equipment	12/31/12	927.7	39.6	905.3	111.5	146	61679082
BLU	Blue Chip Value Fund, Inc.	Holding and other Investment Office	12/31/10	2.0	0.5	109.9	109.1	2	720
BXC	BlueLinx Holdings Inc	Construction Services	12/29/12	1907.8	-23.0	544.7	-20.6	61	55694504
BTH	Blyth, Inc.	Miscellaneous Consumer Goods	12/31/12	1179.5	44.0	434.9	205.1	172	13933514
BWP	Boardwalk Pipeline Partners LP	Equipment & Services	12/31/12	1185.0	306.0	7862.5	3801.3	263	153661266
BA	Boeing Co. (The)	Aerospace	12/31/12	81698.0	3900.0	88896.0	5867.0	1259	596240442
BZ	Boise, Inc.	Containers & Packaging	12/31/12	2555.4	52.1	2208.4	748.2	185	96715303
BCEI	Bonanza Creek Energy, Inc.	Production & Extraction	12/31/12	231.2	46.5	1002.5	578.5	116	38666218
BAH	Booz Allen Hamilton Holding Corp.	IT Services	3/31/12	5859.2	240.0	3314.8	1185.2	134	214411435
BWA	Borg Warner Inc	Auto Parts	12/31/12	7183.2	500.9	6400.8	3082.6	539	119660913
SAM	Boston Beer Co., Inc	Beverages	12/29/12	580.2	59.5	359.5	245.1	199	11070647
BXP	Boston Properties, Inc.	REITs	12/31/12	1876.3	289.6	15462.3	5207.9	534	167627115
BSX	Boston Scientific Corp.	Medical Instruments & Equipment	12/31/12	7249.0	-4068.0	17154.0	6870.0	608	1190758290
BIF	Boulder Growth & Income Fund Inc.	Holding and other Investment Office	11/30/12	9.0	2.6	243.1	242.6	34	6544517
BTF	Boulder Total Return Fund Inc	Holding and other Investment Office	11/30/12	5.4	0.5	350.6	350.1	38	2817971
TEU	Box Ships Inc	Shipping	12/31/12	65.9	13.2	445.1	220.8	34	4100137
BYD	Boyd Gaming Corp.	Hotels, Restaurants & Travel	12/31/12	2487.4	-908.9	6332.2	303.8	203	54742401
BP	BP p.l.c.	Production & Extraction	12/31/12	381589.0	11582.0	300193.0	118414.0	1050	443069087
BPT	BP Prudhoe Bay Royalty Trust	Oil Royalty Traders	12/31/12	200.0	198.9	1.0	0.8	192	2992380
BPZ	BPZ Resources, Inc.	Production & Extraction	12/31/12	123.0	-39.1	527.4	186.3	135	65410399
BRC	Brady Corp.	Electrical Equipment	7/31/12	1324.3	-17.9	1607.7	1009.4	199	46158006
BDN	Brandywine Realty Trust	REITs	12/31/12	559.8	6.6	4506.7	1752.3	299	154885346
LND	Brasilagro Cia Brasileira De Proprie	Agricultural Crop Production	6/30/07	0.7	21.5	674.5	574.8	-	-
BAK	Braskem S A	Refining & Marketing	12/31/12	35513.4	-731.1	41163.6	8576.0	77	21375963
BRE	BRE Properties, Inc.	REITs	12/31/12	390.1	137.1	3499.0	1686.5	304	76130642
BRFS	BRF- Brasil Foods S.A.	Food	12/31/12	28517.4	813.2	30772.3	14538.6	156	84223776
BPI	Bridgepoint Education, Inc.	Educational Services	12/31/12	968.2	128.0	755.3	496.1	-	-

T10

EARNINGS PER SHARE						P/E RATIO		DIVIDENDS PER SHARE			AV. YLD %	DIV. DECLARED		PRICE RANGE	
QUARTERLY			ANNUAL											2012	
1st	2nd	3rd	2012	2011	2010			2012	2011	2010	%	AMOUNT	PAYABLE		
-	-	-	0.86	0.95	1.02	20.7 -	0.0	0.86	0.84	0.78	5.1	0.0715M	5/1/13	17.8 -	0.0
-	-	-	0.74	0.87	0.88	22.3 -	0.0	0.74	0.73	0.67	4.8	0.0625M	5/1/13	16.5 -	0.0
-	-	-	0.76	0.73	0.80	19.2 -	0.0	0.75	0.76	0.82	5.5	0.0625M	5/1/13	14.6 -	0.0
-	-	-	0.87	1.04	1.07	20.0 -	0.0	0.94	0.94	0.94	5.6	0.061M	5/1/13	17.4 -	0.0
-	-	-	1.02	1.06	1.10	16.9 -	0.0	0.75	0.75	0.75	4.5	0.165M7	4/30/13	17.2 -	0.0
-	-	-	0.92	1.03	1.02	19.4 -	0.0	0.97	0.96	0.92	5.8	0.076M	5/1/13	17.9 -	0.0
-	-	-	1.01	1.14	1.14	18.5 -	0.0	1.06	1.05	1.02	6.1	0.0785M	5/1/13	18.7 -	0.0
-	-	-	0.83	0.91	0.96	21.0 -	0.0	0.89	0.89	0.85	5.5	0.0685M	5/1/13	17.5 -	0.0
-	-	-	0.86	0.97	0.92	19.4 -	0.0	0.90	0.90	0.90	5.7	0.0724M	5/1/13	16.7 -	0.0
-	-	-	0.93	0.97	0.96	18.8 -	0.0	0.93	0.92	0.85	5.7	0.078M	5/1/13	17.4 -	0.0
-	-	-	0.95	1.01	1.03	17.6 -	0.0	0.96	0.95	0.93	6.1	0.0801M	5/1/13	16.7 -	0.0
-	-	-	-	-	-	-		-	-	-	-	0.099M	5/1/13	25.4 -	0.0
-	-	-	0.69	0.73	0.75	19.4 -	0.0	0.69	0.68	0.63	5.6	0.058M	5/1/13	13.4 -	0.0
-	-	-	0.95	0.97	0.92	18.5 -	0.0	0.93	0.90	0.79	5.7	0.079M	5/1/13	17.6 -	0.0
-	-	-	1.03	1.03	1.02	17.8 -	0.0	0.98	1.04	0.90	5.7	0.083M	5/1/13	18.4 -	0.0
-	-	-	1.12	1.14	1.13	17.8 -	0.0	1.09	1.18	1.02	5.9	0.0915M	5/1/13	19.9 -	0.0
-	-	-	0.86	0.95	0.96	20.0 -	0.0	0.92	0.91	0.85	5.8	0.0765M	5/1/13	17.2 -	0.0
-	-	-	0.83	0.93	1.00	20.8 -	0.0	0.89	0.89	0.86	5.5	0.074M	5/1/13	17.3 -	0.0
-	-	-	0.89	0.97	1.04	19.1 -	0.0	0.95	0.96	0.87	6.0	0.0765M	5/1/13	17.0 -	0.0
-	-	-	0.86	0.89	0.92	18.8 -	0.0	0.88	0.88	0.85	5.8	0.0705M	5/1/13	16.2 -	0.0
-	-	-	0.89	0.91	0.94	19.1 -	0.0	0.89	0.89	0.81	5.8	0.074M	5/1/13	17.0 -	0.0
-	-	-	1.12	1.14	1.18	16.5 -	0.0	1.07	1.05	0.99	6.1	0.091M	5/1/13	18.4 -	0.0
-	-	-	0.74	0.95	0.94	24.0 -	0.0	0.95	0.93	0.83	5.7	0.079M	5/1/13	17.8 -	0.0
-	-	-	0.90	0.91	0.87	19.0 -	0.0	0.89	0.87	0.76	5.5	0.076M	5/1/13	17.1 -	0.0
-	-	-	0.99	1.04	1.04	17.5 -	0.0	0.99	0.98	0.84	6.1	0.0835M	5/1/13	17.3 -	0.0
-	-	-	0.93	0.97	0.96	19.4 -	0.0	0.94	0.92	0.81	5.7	0.079M	5/1/13	18.1 -	0.0
-	-	-	0.87	0.91	0.92	19.3 -	0.0	0.85	0.85	0.82	5.5	0.071M	5/1/13	16.8 -	0.0
-	-	-	0.80	0.86	0.91	19.7 -	0.0	0.87	0.86	0.82	6.0	0.069M	5/1/13	15.7 -	0.0
-	-	-	0.87	0.93	0.98	19.6 -	0.0	0.93	0.92	0.88	5.9	0.0765M	5/1/13	17.0 -	0.0
-	-	-	0.82	0.91	0.98	21.2 -	0.0	0.89	0.86	0.94	5.5	0.072M	5/1/13	17.4 -	0.0
-	-	-	0.83	0.87	0.90	19.6 -	0.0	0.85	0.85	0.70	5.7	0.071M	5/1/13	16.3 -	0.0
-	-	-	0.86	0.92	1.00	21.0 -	0.0	0.89	0.87	0.85	5.3	0.074M	5/1/13	18.0 -	0.0
-	-	-	0.85	0.92	0.92	20.0 -	0.0	0.91	0.92	0.81	5.7	0.074M	5/1/13	17.0 -	0.0
-	-	-	0.85	0.86	0.88	18.7 -	0.0	0.82	0.81	0.73	5.7	0.0695M	5/1/13	15.9 -	0.0
-	-	-	0.87	0.89	0.89	19.0 -	0.0	0.87	0.86	0.77	5.7	0.072M	5/1/13	16.5 -	0.0
-	-	-	0.85	0.99	0.99	21.6 -	0.0	0.93	0.92	0.82	5.5	0.08M	5/1/13	18.4 -	0.0
-	-	-	0.95	0.98	1.02	19.5 -	0.0	0.95	0.95	0.93	5.5	0.0751M	5/1/13	18.5 -	0.0
-	-	-	0.65	1.00	1.03	26.4 -	0.0	0.83	0.98	1.06	5.1	0.0453M	5/1/13	17.1 -	0.0
-	-	-	0.87	1.04	1.07	19.8 -	0.0	0.96	0.99	1.04	5.9	0.0665M	5/1/13	17.3 -	0.0
-	-	-	0.81	0.90	0.91	21.2 -	0.0	0.86	0.86	0.82	5.4	0.0675M	5/1/13	17.1 -	0.0
-	-	-	0.93	1.01	1.04	18.4 -	0.0	0.99	0.99	0.99	6.0	0.069M	5/1/13	17.1 -	0.0
-	-	-	0.12	0.11	0.17	101.7 -	0.0	1.04	1.09	1.09	9.9	0.22150	3/28/13	12.2 -	0.0
-	-	-	0.18	0.03		85.0 -	0.0	1.40	0.70		10.3	0.290	3/28/13	15.3 -	0.0
-	-	-	0.32	0.32	0.36	14.3 -	0.0	0.33	0.33	0.30	7.7	0.0250	4/30/13	4.6 -	0.0
-	-	-	0.99	1.06	1.01	16.2 -	0.0	1.08	1.11	0.91	7.3	0.08450	4/30/13	16.0 -	0.0
-	-	-	0.89	0.94	0.96	18.3 -	0.0	0.89	0.88	0.84	5.9	0.074M	5/1/13	16.3 -	0.0
-	-	-	-	-	-	-		-	-	-	-	0.36250	2/28/13	19.8 -	0.0
-	-	3.65	13.79	12.37	10.55	18.8 -	0.0	6.00	5.50	4.00	3.1	1.680Y	81/16/21	258.7 -	0.0
-	-	-	1.22	0.86		16.1 -	0.0	1.30	1.08		6.9	0.1080	5/31/13	19.7 -	0.0
-	-	-	1.36	1.34	0.62	16.0 -	0.0	1.42	1.38	0.66	7.1	0.110	5/31/13	21.7 -	0.0
-	-	-	-	-	-	-		-	-	-	-	0.1170	5/31/13	20.1 -	0.0
-	-	0.24	0.41	-0.35	-1.02	51.0 -	0.0	0.52	0.62	0.60	3.5	0.420Z	2/10/10	20.0 -	0.0
-	-	-0.07	0.89	1.31	1.43	33.1 -	0.0	0.70	0.60	0.60	3.8	0.20Y	81/16/21	29.4 -	0.0
-	-	0.23	0.79	1.01	0.97	22.0 -	0.0	-	-	-	-	-		17.4 -	0.0
-	-	-	-	-	0.02	-		-	-	0.02	-	0.0159A	3/22/11	-	
-	-	0.05	-0.38	-0.89	-1.73	-		-	-	-	-	0.1250Y	12/28/07	3.4 -	0.0
-	-	0.04	0.58	0.97	0.99	78.6 -	0.0	0.17	0.85	0.60	0.6	0.10Y	4/15/13	45.6 -	0.0
-	-	0.26	1.37	1.09	1.47	21.4 -	0.0	2.13	2.10	2.03	7.9	0.53250	2/28/13	29.3 -	0.0
-	-	1.35	5.11	5.34	4.45	17.0 -	0.0	1.76	1.68	1.68	2.4	0.4850Y	81/16/21	86.6 -	0.0
-	-	0.04	0.52	0.70	0.75	17.4 -	0.0	1.20	0.40	0.40	15.3	0.727Y	12/12/12	9.1 -	0.0
-	-	0.09	1.17	0.43	-0.01	35.5 -	0.0	-	-	-	-	-		41.5 -	0.0
-	-	0.68	1.70	0.66	0.22	11.2 -	0.0	0.09			0.6	0.090	81/16/21	19.1 -	0.0
-	-	0.85	4.17	4.45	3.07	20.5 -	0.0	-	-	0.00	-	0.120Y	81/16/21	85.5 -	0.0
-	-	1.53	4.39	4.81	3.52	37.2 -	0.0	-	-	-	-	-		163.5 -	0.0
-	-	0.38	1.92	1.86	1.14	60.5 -	0.0	2.30	2.05	2.00	2.2	0.650Z	81/16/21	116.1 -	0.0
-	-	-0.48	-2.89	0.29	-0.70	-		-	-	-	-	-		7.8 -	0.0
-	-	-	0.10	0.05	0.04	73.3 -	0.0	0.11	0.10		1.7	0.15C	1/11/13	7.3 -	0.0
-	-	-	0.04	0.08	0.07	522.5 -	0.0	-	-	-	-	0.2730	10/31/08	20.9 -	0.0
-	-	0.16	0.54	0.83	-38.22	17.2 -	0.0	-	-	-	-	0.220	3/28/13	9.3 -	0.0
-	-	-0.18	-10.37	-0.04	0.12	-		-	-	-	-	0.150Y	81/16/21	8.7 -	0.0
-	-	0.28	0.60	1.34	-0.20	75.6 -	0.0	1.98	1.68	0.84	4.8	-		45.3 -	0.0
-	-	-	-	-	-	-		9.29	9.40	9.99	9.7	2.41480	4/20/13	128.4 -	0.0
-	-	-0.15	-0.34	-0.29	-0.52	-		-	-	-	-	-		4.5 -	0.0
-	-0.17	-	-0.35	2.04	1.55	-		0.74	0.72	0.70	2.4	0.190Y	81/16/21	36.3 -	0.0
-	-	0.10	-0.06	-0.10	-0.19	-		0.60	0.60	0.60	4.9	0.43130Z	81/16/21	14.9 -	0.0
-	-	-	-	-	-	-		-	-	-	-	-		5.3 -	0.0
-	-	-	-1.30	-0.66	2.65	-		0.30	0.64	0.01	2.2	-		16.8 -	0.0
-	-	0.17	1.74	0.93	0.67	30.6 -	0.0	1.54	1.50	1.50	3.1	0.42190Z	81/16/21	53.3 -	0.0
-	-	0.10	0.94	1.57	0.92	24.6 -	0.0	0.02	0.19	0.08	0.1	-		23.1 -	0.0
-	-	0.56	2.29	3.02	2.14	11.1 -	0.0	-	-	-	-	-		25.4 -	0.0

SYMBOL	COMPANY	NATURE OF BUSINESS	FISCAL YEAR-END	TOTAL REV. $MILL	NET INCOME $MILL	TOTAL ASSETS $MILL	NET STK EQUITY $MILL	NO OF INST	INST. HOLDINGS (SHARES)
BGG	Briggs & Stratton Corp.	Industrial Machinery & Equipment	7/1/12	2066.5	29.0	1608.2	632.0	219	50115523
BFAM	Bright Horizons Family Solutions, In	Services	12/31/12	1070.9	8.2	1913.6	608.3	-	-
EAT	Brinker International, Inc.	Hotels, Restaurants & Travel	6/27/12	2820.7	151.2	1436.1	309.9	376	85508886
BCO	Brinks Co (The)	Business Services	12/31/12	3842.1	88.9	2553.9	501.8	270	52964385
BMY	Bristol-Myers Squibb Co.	Pharmaceuticals	12/31/12	17621.0	1960.0	35897.0	13623.0	1541	1194670402
BRS	Bristow Group Inc	Miscellaneous Transportation Servic	3/31/12	1341.8	63.5	2740.4	1513.1	210	40440339
BR	Broadridge Financial Solutions Inc	Finance Intermediaries & Services	6/30/12	2303.5	123.6	1987.6	850.5	378	115523732
BKD	Brookdale Senior Living Inc	Hospitals & Health Care Facilities	12/31/12	2770.1	-65.6	4666.0	1002.7	242	121298439
BAM	Brookfield Asset Management Inc	Property, Real Estate & Developmen	12/31/12	18697.0	1380.0	108644.0	21061.0	359	348930699
BOXC	Brookfield Canada Office Properties	REITs	12/31/12	515.1	147.7	5163.6	838.1	25	3822686
INF	Brookfield Global Listed Infrastructu	Holding and other Investment Office	12/31/12	8.7	5.0	219.2	165.9	16	1233572
BIP	Brookfield Infrastructure Partners L.	Electric Utilities	12/31/11	1636.0	187.0	13269.0	4206.0	158	81544422
BOI	Brookfield Mortgage Opportunity Inc	Holding and other Investment Office	1/30/13	-	-	0.2	0.1	-	-
BPO	Brookfield Office Properties Inc	Property, Real Estate & Developmen	12/31/12	2282.0	1287.0	27479.0	11431.0	237	478010145
BRP	Brookfield Residential Properties In	Builders	12/31/11	1008.1	7.3	2578.8	969.3	78	100396282
HTR	Brookfield Total Return Fund Inc	Holding and other Investment Office	11/30/12	25.8	21.8	486.1	343.3	41	2183704
BRO	Brown & Brown, Inc.	Brokers & Intermediaries	12/31/12	1200.0	184.0	3128.1	1807.3	301	119007680
BWS	Brown Shoe Co., Inc.	Retail - Apparel and Accessories	2/2/13	2598.1	27.5	1171.3	425.1	209	41295640
BF B	Brown-Forman Corp.	Beverages	4/30/12	2723.0	513.0	3477.0	2069.0	96	48095472
BRT	BRT Realty Trust	REITs	9/30/12	19.6	4.4	386.0	133.4	35	3368628
BC	Brunswick Corp.	Leisure Equipment	12/31/12	3717.6	50.0	2424.2	77.7	301	96871541
BT	BT Group Plc	Services	3/31/12	18897.0	2002.0	23948.0	1297.0	155	13584275
BPL	Buckeye Partners, L.P.	Equipment & Services	12/31/12	4357.2	226.4	5981.0	-	329	44892750
BKI	Buckeye Technologies Inc.	Paper & Forest Products	6/30/12	894.9	90.0	837.4	603.0	241	38263098
BKE	Buckle, Inc. (The)	Retail - Apparel and Accessories	2/2/13	1124.0	164.3	478.0	289.6	230	30964752
BBW	Build-A-Bear Workshop Inc	Retail - Specialty	12/29/12	380.9	-49.3	192.1	83.1	96	9942552
BG	Bunge Ltd.	Food	12/31/12	60991.0	64.0	27280.0	10862.0	478	105398712
BKW	Burger King Worldwide Inc	Miscellaneous Consumer Services	12/31/12	1966.3	117.7	5564.0	1175.0	74	79690883
CJES	C&J Energy Services Inc.	Production & Extraction	12/31/12	1111.5	182.3	1012.8	599.9	183	46697717
CAB	Cabelas Inc	Retail - Specialty	12/29/12	3112.7	173.5	5748.2	1376.0	307	50500302
CVC	Cablevision Systems Corp.	Radio & Television	12/31/12	6705.5	233.5	7246.2	-5639.2	426	212794105
CBT	Cabot Corp.	Specialty Chemicals	9/30/12	3300.0	388.0	4399.0	1813.0	296	61594333
COG	Cabot Oil & Gas Corp.	Production & Extraction	12/31/12	1204.5	131.7	4616.3	2131.4	499	212829491
CACI	CACI International Inc.	IT Services	6/30/12	3774.5	167.5	2392.9	1162.0	272	29177932
CAE	CAE Inc.	Aerospace	3/31/12	1821.2	180.3	3183.7	1021.9	120	141605066
CAP	CAI International Inc	Shipping	12/31/12	173.9	63.5	1387.9	346.8	110	15760859
DVR	Cal Dive International Inc	Equipment & Services	12/31/12	464.8	-65.0	630.7	271.6	157	94937802
CCC	Calgon Carbon Corp.	Specialty Chemicals	12/31/12	562.3	23.3	577.8	351.3	216	55151191
CWT	California Water Service Group (DE	Water Utilities	12/31/12	560.0	48.8	1995.9	473.7	183	22138125
CALX	Calix Inc	Manufacturing	12/31/12	330.2	-28.3	377.9	269.1	113	26906873
ELY	Callaway Golf Co. (DE)	Leisure Equipment	12/31/12	834.1	-122.9	637.6	319.0	202	68943421
CPE	Callon Petroleum Co. (DE)	Production & Extraction	12/31/12	110.7	2.7	378.2	206.0	129	32836411
CPN	Calpine Corp	Electric Utilities	12/31/12	5478.0	199.0	16549.0	3994.0	344	422490922
CBM	Cambrex Corp	Pharmaceuticals	12/31/12	276.5	62.3	394.5	163.3	180	32524320
CPT	Camden Property Trust	REITs	12/31/12	744.3	293.9	5385.2	2563.1	362	87933633
CCJ	Cameco Corp.	Mining	12/31/12	2321.5	266.1	8215.0	4943.7	349	242953100
CIS	Camelot Information Systems Inc	IT Services	12/31/11	227.1	-40.8	315.4	231.7	35	19673023
CAM	Cameron International Corp	Equipment & Services	12/31/12	8502.1	750.5	11158.2	5566.1	641	259789477
CPB	Campbell Soup Co.	Food	7/29/12	7707.0	774.0	6530.0	898.0	625	163599423
CCG	Campus Crest Communities, Inc.	REITs	12/31/12	137.4	10.6	696.3	340.5	143	36112806
CM	Canadian Imperial Bank of Commer	Banking	10/31/12	17130.0	3331.0	393385.0	16866.0	241	212405520
CNI	Canadian National Railway Co.	Rail	12/31/12	9920.0	2680.0	26659.0	11018.0	565	272257961
CNQ	Canadian Natural Resources Ltd.	Production & Extraction	12/31/12	14589.0	1892.0	48980.0	24283.0	474	672090759
CP	Canadian Pacific Railway Ltd.	Rail	12/31/12	5695.0	484.0	14727.0	5097.0	379	140126027
CAJ	Canon, Inc.	Leisure Equipment	12/31/12	3479788.0	224564.0	3955503.0	2598026.0	246	24538084
CMN	Cantel Medical Corp	Medical Instruments & Equipment	7/31/12	386.5	31.3	434.8	275.9	170	22041815
COF	Capital One Financial Corp	Credit & Lending	12/31/12	23771.0	3517.0	312918.0	40499.0	871	559026339
CSU	Capital Senior Living Corp.	Hospitals & Health Care Facilities	12/31/12	310.5	-3.1	636.9	168.6	124	32216463
CT	Capital Trust, Inc. (MD)	REITs	12/31/12	34.9	181.0	322.3	73.4	53	6059179
CSE	CapitalSource Inc	Banking	12/31/12	526.1	490.6	8549.0	1625.2	243	190973684
LSE	CapLease Inc	REITs	12/31/12	162.0	-1.7	1750.4	477.3	154	65638902
CMO	Capstead Mortgage Corp.	REITs	12/31/12	-	163.6	14469.3	1497.1	235	54572846
CRR	Carbo Ceramics Inc.	Equipment & Services	12/31/12	645.5	105.9	808.9	713.1	286	26395891
CAH	Cardinal Health, Inc.	Pharmaceuticals	6/30/12	107552.0	1069.0	24260.0	6244.0	688	319278758
CFN	CareFusion Corp	Medical Instruments & Equipment	6/30/12	3598.0	293.0	8488.0	5231.0	437	208837491
CSL	Carlisle Companies Inc.	Rubber Products	12/31/12	3629.4	270.2	3457.3	1788.1	300	56460710
KMX	Carmax Inc.	Retail - Automotive	2/29/12	10003.6	413.8	8331.5	2673.1	457	250485793
CCL	Carnival Corp.	Hotels, Restaurants & Travel	11/30/12	15382.0	1298.0	39161.0	23929.0	623	437182051
CUK	Carnival Plc	Hotels, Restaurants & Travel	11/30/12	15382.0	1298.0	39161.0	23929.0	84	2770531
CRS	Carpenter Technology Corp.	Non-Precious Metals	6/30/12	2028.7	121.2	2627.8	1103.8	305	45644208
CSV	Carriage Services, Inc.	Miscellaneous Consumer Services	12/31/12	204.1	11.4	738.1	135.0	90	10492825
CRI	Carter's Inc	Apparel, Footwear & Accessories	12/29/12	2381.7	161.2	1630.1	985.5	318	64965050
CSH	Cash America International, Inc.	Credit & Lending	12/31/12	1800.4	107.5	1818.3	991.9	257	37209864
CSFS	Cash Store Financial Services Inc	Credit & Lending	9/30/12	187.4	-43.1	200.7	39.0	-	-
CAS	Castle (A.M.) & Co.	Non-Precious Metals	12/31/12	1270.4	-9.7	788.8	337.3	118	21979539
CAT 08A	Caterpillar Financial Services Corp	Credit & Lending	12/31/12	2693.0	432.0	34742.0	3617.0	-	-
CAT	Caterpillar Inc.	Construction Services	12/31/12	65875.0	5681.0	89356.0	17532.0	1478	458040048
CATO	Cato Corp.	Retail - Apparel and Accessories	2/2/13	944.0	61.7	532.6	345.2	180	25764878
CBZ	CBIZ Inc	Business Services	12/31/12	766.1	31.1	970.2	295.2	129	45443653
CBL	CBL & Associates Properties, Inc.	REITs	12/31/12	1034.6	131.6	7089.7	1328.7	320	176153684

T12

EARNINGS PER SHARE — QUARTERLY			ANNUAL			P/E RATIO		DIVIDENDS PER SHARE			AV. YLD %	DIV. DECLARED		PRICE RANGE 2012	
1st	2nd	3rd	2012	2011	2010			2012	2011	2010		AMOUNT	PAYABLE		
-	-0.02	-	0.57	0.48	0.73	44.5 -	0.0	0.44	0.44	0.44	2.3	0.120Y	4/1/13	25.4 -	0.0
-	-	-	-12.62	-11.32	-12.64									35.5 -	27.5
-	0.50	-	1.87	1.53	1.34	20.1 -	0.0	0.64	0.56	0.47	2.0	0.20Y	81/16/21	37.6 -	0.0
-	-	0.28	1.83	1.55	1.18	16.7 -	0.0	0.40	0.40	0.40	1.6	0.10Y	81/16/21	30.6 -	0.0
-	-	-0.43	1.16	2.16	1.79	35.5 -	0.0	1.36	1.32	0.96	4.0	0.350Y	81/16/21	41.2 -	0.0
-	-	1.00	1.76	3.60	3.10	38.1 -	0.0	0.60	-	-	1.2	0.20Y	3/15/13	67.0 -	0.0
-	0.13	-	0.97	1.32	1.37	25.6 -	0.0	0.64	0.60	0.56	2.8	0.180Y	81/16/21	24.8 -	0.0
-	-	-0.10	-0.54	-0.56	-0.41							0.250Y	81/16/21	29.6 -	0.0
-	-	0.48	1.97	2.89	2.33	20.2 -	0.0	0.55	0.52	0.52	1.6	0.06250	4/12/13	39.8 -	0.0
-	-	-	-	-	-			1.11	1.08	0.64	4.9	0.09750	5/15/13	30.5 -	0.0
-	-	-	0.65	0.18	-	34.1 -	0.0	1.40	0.35	-	7.1	0.11670	4/26/13	22.1 -	0.0
-	-	-	-	1.13	4.25			-	1.32	1.10		0.430	3/29/13	41.3 -	0.0
-	-	-	-	-	-									20.0 -	0.0
-	-	0.66	2.25	2.92	2.73	8.2 -	0.0	-	-	0.56		0.28750	3/29/13	18.5 -	0.0
-	-	0.15	-	0.07	-							-		24.8 -	0.0
-	-	-	2.24	1.68	2.12	11.5 -	0.0	0.57	-	-	2.3	0.190	4/26/13	25.8 -	0.0
-	-	0.34	1.26	1.13	1.12	25.4 -	0.0	0.34	0.33	0.31	1.3	0.090Y	81/16/21	32.0 -	0.0
-	-	0.56	0.56	0.85	0.22	34.8 -	0.0	0.28	0.28	0.28	1.9	0.070Y	4/1/13	19.5 -	0.0
-	-	0.73	2.37	2.60	2.01	30.1 -	0.0	0.89	1.49	0.78	1.4	0.2550Y	81/16/21	71.4 -	0.0
-0.09	-	-	0.32	0.45	-0.58	26.6 -	0.0	-	-	-		1.157Y	10/30/13	8.5 -	0.0
-	-	0.02	0.54	0.78	-1.25	68.9 -	0.0	0.05	0.05	0.05	0.2	0.050Y	81/16/21	37.2 -	0.0
-	-	-	0.24	0.19	0.13	178.2 -	0.0	1.87	1.64	0.81	5.2	-		42.8 -	0.0
-	-	0.87	2.32	1.20	1.65	26.4 -	0.0	4.15	4.03	3.83	8.1	1.03750	81/16/21	61.2 -	0.0
-	0.33	-	2.24	3.05	2.90	15.2 -	0.0	0.27	0.18	-	0.9	0.090Y	3/15/13	34.0 -	0.0
-	-	0.88	3.20	2.86	2.73	16.0 -	0.0	3.05	3.30	2.60	7.0	0.20Y	4/26/13	51.2 -	0.0
-	-	-0.26	-3.02	-0.98	0.01									5.5 -	0.0
-	-	1.92	0.19	6.07	15.06	420.6 -	0.0	-	-	0.90		1.21880Z	81/16/21	79.9 -	0.0
-	-	0.02	0.33	880.37	157.00	60.5 -	0.0	0.04	3931.21	0.06	0.3	0.060Y	5/15/13	19.9 -	0.0
-	-	0.91	3.37	3.19	0.67	7.4 -	0.0	-	-	-		-		25.0 -	0.0
-	-	0.60	2.42	2.00	1.62	25.5 -	0.0	-	-	-		-		61.8 -	0.0
-	-	-0.01	0.87	1.02	1.20	21.3 -	0.0	0.60	0.57	0.47	4.2	0.150Y	81/16/21	18.5 -	0.0
0.31	-	-	5.99	3.57	2.35	7.5 -	0.0	0.76	0.72	0.72	2.0	0.20Y	81/16/21	44.7 -	0.0
-	-	0.17	0.62	0.58	0.49	110.1 -	0.0	0.08	0.06	0.06	0.2	0.020Y	81/16/21	68.3 -	0.0
-	1.69	-	5.96	4.61	3.47	10.5 -	0.0	-	-	-		-		62.9 -	0.0
-	-	0.15	0.70	0.62	0.56	15.7 -	0.0	0.16	0.15	0.12	1.6	0.050	3/28/13	11.0 -	0.0
-	-	0.84	3.18	2.55	1.56	9.4 -	0.0	-	-	-		-		29.7 -	0.0
-	-	-0.17	-0.70	-0.73	-3.47							-		3.9 -	0.0
-	-	-0.08	0.41	0.69	0.61	45.2 -	0.0	-	-	-		0.030Y	9/1/05	18.5 -	0.0
-	-	0.71	1.17	0.90	0.91	18.0 -	0.0	0.63	0.61	0.59	3.4	0.160Y	81/16/21	21.1 -	0.0
-	-	-0.15	-0.59	-1.15	-0.65							-		9.3 -	0.0
-	-	-1.33	-1.96	-2.82	-0.46			0.04	0.04	0.04	0.7	1.8750Y	3/15/13	7.2 -	0.0
-	-	-0.03	0.07	2.70	0.28	91.9 -	0.0	-	-	-		0.53130 Y	4/15/05	6.4 -	0.0
-	-	0.94	0.42	-0.39	0.06	49.0 -	0.0	-	-	-		-		20.6 -	0.0
-	-	0.06	2.06	0.37	0.33	6.8 -	0.0	-	-	-		14.7	5/3/07	14.0 -	0.0
-	-	0.35	3.30	0.66	0.33	21.7 -	0.0	2.24	1.96	1.80	3.3	0.630Z	81/16/21	71.6 -	0.0
-	-	0.21	0.67	1.14	1.31	34.9 -	0.0	0.40	0.40	0.28	1.9	0.10	4/15/13	23.4 -	0.0
-	-	-0.18	-	-0.23	0.11							-		3.9 -	0.0
-	-	0.90	3.02	2.09	2.27	22.1 -	0.0	-	-	-		-		66.7 -	0.0
-	0.60	-	2.41	2.42	2.42	18.8 -	0.0	1.16	1.15	1.08	3.3	0.290Y	81/16/21	45.4 -	0.0
-	-	0.20	0.19	0.12	-0.05	73.7 -	0.0	0.64	0.64	0.13	5.6	0.50Z	4/15/13	14.0 -	0.0
1.91	-	-	7.85	6.71	5.87	10.8 -	0.0	3.64	3.51	3.48	4.7	0.40630	4/29/13	84.7 -	0.0
-	-	1.52	6.12	5.41	4.48	17.3 -	0.0	1.50	1.30	1.08	1.7	0.430	3/28/13	105.6	0.0
-	-	0.33	1.72	2.40	1.63	20.4 -	0.0	0.42	0.36	0.30	1.4	0.1250	4/1/13	35.2 -	0.0
-	-	1.30	2.79	3.34	3.85	47.5 -	0.0	1.35	1.17	1.06	1.5	0.350	4/29/13	132.5 -	0.0
-	-	43.15	191.34	204.48	199.70	0.3 -	0.0	0.02	0.02	0.01	0.1	-		48.3 -	0.0
-	0.38	-	1.15	0.79	0.79	28.5 -	0.0	0.09	0.08	0.07	0.3	0.0550Y	12/12/12	32.8 -	0.0
-	-	2.01	6.16	6.80	6.01	10.2 -	0.0	0.20	0.20	0.20	0.4	0.3750Y	81/16/21	62.9 -	0.0
-	-	-0.03	-0.11	0.11	0.16							-		27.2 -	0.0
-	-	0.28	7.31	10.78	-8.28	0.5 -	0.0	2.00	-	-	66.7	2.7	12/20/12	4.0 -	0.0
-	-	0.14	2.13	-0.17	-0.34	4.6 -	0.0	0.54	0.04	0.04	7.3	0.010Y	81/16/21	9.8 -	0.0
-	-	-0.02	-0.17	-0.13	-0.33			0.28	0.26	0.25	5.7	0.4028GHZ	4/15/13	6.4 -	0.0
-	-	0.35	1.50	1.75	1.52	9.7 -	0.0	1.49	1.76	1.51	11.4	0.310Z	4/19/13	14.6 -	0.0
-	-	1.04	4.59	5.62	3.40	22.7 -	0.0	1.02	0.88	0.76	1.3	0.270Y	81/16/21	104.4 -	0.0
-	0.88	-	3.06	2.72	1.77	15.4 -	0.0	0.88	0.80	0.72	2.1	0.2750Y	81/16/21	47.1 -	0.0
-	0.48	-	1.30	1.08	0.87	26.9 -	0.0	-	-	-		-		35.0 -	0.0
-	-	1.08	4.22	2.86	2.34	16.6 -	0.0	0.76	0.70	0.66	1.4	0.20Y	81/16/21	69.9 -	0.0
-	-	0.41	1.79	1.67	1.26	23.3 -	0.0	-	-	-		-		41.7 -	0.0
0.05	-	-	1.67	2.42	2.47	23.5 -	0.0	1.00	1.00	0.40	2.8	0.250Y	81/16/21	39.3 -	0.0
0.05	-	-	1.67	2.42	2.47	24.7 -	0.0	1.00	1.00	0.40	2.8	-		41.3 -	0.0
-	0.62	-	2.53	1.59	0.04	22.5 -	0.0	0.72	0.72	0.72	1.5	0.180Y	81/16/21	56.8 -	0.0
-	-	0.03	0.63	0.38	0.45	33.7 -	0.0	0.10	0.07	-	0.9	0.0250Y	3/1/13	21.3 -	0.0
-	-	0.99	2.69	1.94	2.46	22.6 -	0.0	-	-	-		-		60.8 -	0.0
-	-	0.37	3.42	4.25	3.67	15.6 -	0.0	0.14	0.14	0.14	0.3	0.0350Y	2/20/13	53.3 -	0.0
-0.09	-	-	-2.47	0.51	1.51			0.36	0.46	0.40	7.5	0.060	9/7/12	6.3 -	0.0
-	-	0.13	-0.42	-0.08	-0.25			-	-	-		0.060Y	4/2/09	18.5 -	0.0
-	-	2.54	8.48	7.40	4.15	12.9 -	0.0	2.48	1.80	1.72	2.8	0.520Y	81/16/21	109.2 -	0.0
-	-	0.16	2.21	1.96	1.55	14.4 -	0.0	0.88	0.72	0.66	3.1	0.050Y	3/25/13	31.8 -	0.0
-	-	0.11	0.63	0.56	0.42	10.5 -	0.0	-	-	-		-		6.6 -	0.0
-	-	-0.02	0.54	0.62	0.21	44.1 -	0.0	0.88	0.84	0.80	4.3	0.41410Z	4/1/13	23.8 -	0.0

SYMBOL	COMPANY	NATURE OF BUSINESS	FISCAL YEAR-END	TOTAL REV. $MILL	NET INCOME $MILL	TOTAL ASSETS $MILL	NET STK EQUITY $MILL	NO OF INST	INST. HOLDINGS (SHARES)
IGR	CBRE Clarion Global Real Estate In	Holding and other Investment Office	12/31/12	48.9	38.6	1127.8	1105.0	97	17761306
CBG	CBRE Group Inc	Property, Real Estate & Developmen	12/31/12	6514.1	315.6	7809.5	1539.2	431	338020352
CBS	CBS Corp	Radio & Television	12/31/12	14089.0	1574.0	26466.0	10213.0	745	554623452
CDI	CDI Corp.	Business Services	12/31/12	1105.0	19.1	400.7	279.0	107	12043691
CCWE 05	CE Casecnan Water & Energy Inc.	Electric Utilities	12/31/09	146.9	93.3	385.8	339.0		
CEC	CEC Entertainment, Inc.	Hotels, Restaurants & Travel	12/30/12	803.5	43.6	801.8	143.3	174	19420280
FUN	Cedar Fair, L.P.	Sporting & Recreational	12/31/12	1068.5	101.2	2027.6		170	34890460
CDR	Cedar Realty Trust, Inc.	REITs	12/31/12	140.6	29.7	1369.9	513.7	153	57091321
CGI	Celadon Group, Inc.	Trucking	6/30/12	599.0	25.5	520.7	194.8	150	23075207
CE	Celanese Corp (DE)	Specialty Chemicals	12/31/12	6418.0	605.0	9000.0	1730.0	400	169516031
CLS	Celestica, Inc.	Electrical Equipment	12/31/11	7213.0	195.1	2969.6	1463.8	145	127480833
CLS	Celestica, Inc.	Electrical Equipment	12/31/11	7213.0	195.1	2969.6	1463.8	145	127480833
CEL	Cellcom Israel Ltd	Services	12/31/12	5938.0	530.0	8787.0	498.0	71	12106919
CPAC	Cementos Pacasmayo S.A.A.	Construction Materials						25	5587007
CX	Cemex S.A.B. de C.V.	Construction Materials	12/31/11	188938.0	-19127.0	548299.0	191017.0	302	503883578
CNCO	Cencosud SA	Retail - General Merchandise/Depart	12/31/11	7569195.6	285915.3	7504552.4	2874438.3		
CVE	Cenovus Energy Inc.	Production & Extraction	12/31/12	16842.0	993.0	24216.0	9806.0	387	441226410
CNC	Centene Corp	Hospitals & Health Care Facilities	12/31/12	8667.6	1.9	2741.7	953.1	307	58008593
CNP 18	CenterPoint Energy Resources Cor	Electric Utilities	12/31/12	4901.0	137.0	11190.0	4233.0		
CNP	CenterPoint Energy, Inc	Electric Utilities	12/31/12	7452.0	417.0	22871.0	4301.0	546	337668427
EBR	Centrais Eletricas Brasileiras S.A.-E	Electric Utilities	12/31/11	29532.7	3732.6	163142.4	76843.5	122	59234671
CEE	Central Europe and Russia Fund In	Holding and other Investment Office	10/31/12	15.7	10.0	511.9	477.4	43	7970638
CEE	Central Europe and Russia Fund In	Holding and other Investment Office	10/31/12	15.7	10.0	511.9	477.4	43	7970638
CPF	Central Pacific Financial Corp	Banking	12/31/12	184.2	47.4	4370.4	504.8	116	46176391
CTL	CenturyLink, Inc.	Services	12/31/12	18376.0	777.0	54020.0	19289.0	868	454886041
CVO	Cenveo Inc	Printing	12/31/12	1.8	-0.1	1.2	-0.5	127	47811616
CF	CF Industries Holdings Inc	Agricultural Chemicals	12/31/12	6104.0	1848.7	10166.9	5902.2	677	63195990
CGG	CGG Veritas	Equipment & Services	12/31/11	2270.0	-19.0	5555.9	2938.9	66	3001849
GIB	CGI Group, Inc.	IT Services	9/30/12	4772.5	131.5	10453.4	3422.3	173	211984520
CHG	CH Energy Group, Inc.	Electric Utilities	12/31/12	924.7	39.8	1784.9	518.3	155	9254263
CRL	Charles River Laboratories Internati	Biotechnology	12/29/12	1129.5	97.3	1586.3	600.8	315	55604242
CLDT	Chatham Lodging Trust	REITs	12/31/12	100.5	-1.5	457.2	205.0	92	11777159
CKP	Checkpoint Systems Inc	Electronic Instruments & Related Pro	12/30/12	690.8	-145.9	859.8	376.9	161	40289648
CHE	Chemed Corp	Diagnostic & Health Related Service	12/31/12	1430.0	89.3	859.6	453.3	242	22095420
CHMT	Chemtura Corp	Specialty Chemicals	12/31/12	2629.0	101.0	3030.0	1061.0	254	104240143
CHK	Chesapeake Energy Corp.	Production & Extraction	12/31/12	12316.0	-769.0	41611.0	15569.0	771	562657340
CHKR	Chesapeake Granite Wash Trust	Production & Extraction	12/31/12	127.3	116.5	429.6	421.5		
CHSP	Chesapeake Lodging Trust	REITs	12/31/12	278.3	27.2	1232.8	766.8	146	39645042
CPK	Chesapeake Utilities Corp.	Gas Utilities	12/31/12	392.5	28.9	733.7	256.6	145	4978286
CVX	Chevron Corporation	Refining & Marketing	12/31/12	241909.0	26179.0	232982.0	136524.0	2106	1381181985
CBI	Chicago Bridge & Iron Co., N.V. (Ne	Construction Services	12/31/12	5485.2	301.7	4329.7	1367.8	487	97885930
CHS	Chico's FAS Inc	Retail - Apparel and Accessories	2/2/13	2581.1	180.2	1580.6	1093.2	407	157125584
CIM	Chimera Investment Corp	Finance Intermediaries & Services	12/31/11	337.3	137.3	7747.1	3047.6	310	538247327
CO	China Cord Blood Corp	Diagnostic & Health Related Service	3/31/12	380.5	132.0	1824.1	1202.7		
STV	China Digital TV Holding Co Ltd	Radio & Television	12/31/11	99.1	41.0	321.3	206.4	38	15401445
DL	China Distance Education Holdings	Educational Services	9/30/12	52.1	8.2	90.0	64.6		
CEA	China Eastern Airlines Corp., Ltd.	Airlines/Air Freight	12/31/11	82403.1	4575.7	114738.9	20125.9	30	402176
CHN	China Fund, Inc. (The)	Holding and other Investment Office	10/31/12	13.2	5.8	450.3	396.1	71	4520157
CGA	China Green Agriculture Inc	Agricultural Chemicals	6/30/12	217.5	42.0	288.0	242.3	35	1760906
CHC	China Hydroelectric Corp	Electric Utilities	12/31/11	57.5	-45.4	814.9	394.4	21	9055312
LFC	China Life Insurance Co Ltd	Life & Health	12/31/11	373112.0	18331.0	1583907.0	191530.0	133	9469758
MY	China Ming Yang Wind Power Grou	Industrial Machinery & Equipment	12/31/11	5515.8	293.0	10447.4	3781.5	25	11265392
CHL	China Mobile Limited	Services	12/31/11	527999.0	125870.0	952558.0	649064.0	397	72909361
NPD	China Nepstar Chain Drugstore Ltd	Retail - Food & Beverage, Drug & To	12/31/11	2491.3	35.9	1942.2	1354.3	32	28026000
BORN	China New Borun Corp	Beverages	12/31/11	2685.2	313.0	1972.8	1329.4	14	629597
SNP	China Petroleum & Chemical Corp.	Production & Extraction	12/31/12	2786045.0	63879.0	1266693.0	510914.0	183	7256538
ZNH	China Southern Airlines Co Ltd	Airlines/Air Freight	12/31/11	90395.0	5110.0	129412.0	32175.0	44	802322
CHA	China Telecom Corp Ltd	Services	12/31/11	245041.0	16502.0	419115.0	256090.0	89	4680226
CHU	China Unicom (Hong Kong) Ltd	Services	12/31/11	209167.0	4227.0	456233.0	205898.0	131	36917921
XNY	China Xiniya Fashion Ltd.	Apparel, Footwear & Accessories	12/31/12	1383.7	175.5	1648.3	1403.0	14	4981155
CYD	China Yuchai International Ltd.	Auto Parts	12/31/11	15444.4	818.5	19151.0	5542.2	63	7268340
ZX	China Zenix Auto International Ltd.	Auto Parts	12/31/11	4093.9	452.2	4218.4	1935.6	11	9800114
CMG	Chipotle Mexican Grill Inc	Hotels, Restaurants & Travel	12/31/12	2731.2	278.0	1668.7	1245.9	519	33062129
CQB	Chiquita Brands International, Inc.	Food	12/31/12	3078.3	-405.0	1697.8	370.4	183	42433032
CHH	Choice Hotels International, Inc.	Hotels, Restaurants & Travel	12/31/12	691.5	120.7	510.8	-548.9	145	26216180
CBK	Christopher & Banks Corp.	Retail - Apparel and Accessories	2/2/13	430.3	-16.1	135.9	75.5	142	29761501
CB	Chubb Corp.	General Insurance	12/31/12	13595.0	1545.0	52184.0	15827.0	958	250656079
CHT	Chunghwa Telecom Co Ltd	Services	12/31/11	217493.0	48095.0	442920.0	373043.0	156	40702660
CHD	Church & Dwight Co., Inc.	Household & Personal Products	12/31/12	2921.9	349.8	4098.1	2060.9	610	129641045
CBR	CIBER, Inc.	IT Services	12/31/12	884.4	-14.6	580.6	358.6	152	61308432
CI	Cigna Corp	Life & Health	12/31/12	29119.0	1623.0	53734.0	9769.0	678	273864645
XEC	Cimarex Energy Co	Production & Extraction	12/31/12	1623.9	353.8	6305.2	3474.7	412	91443821
CBB	Cincinnati Bell Inc	Services	12/31/12	1473.9	11.2	2872.4	-698.2	243	188379374
CNK	Cinemark Holdings Inc	Entertainment	12/31/12	2473.5	168.9	3863.2	1084.1	307	102552467
CIR	Circor International Inc	Industrial Machinery & Equipment	12/31/12	845.6	30.8	710.0	418.2	156	17245691
CIT	CIT Group, Inc.	Banking	12/31/12	4006.8	-588.6	44012.0	8334.8	487	217210268
C	Citigroup Inc	Banking	12/31/12	90708.0	7541.0	1864660.0	189049.0	1416	2349743275
CIA	Citizens, Inc. (Austin, TX)	Life & Health	12/31/12	202.8	4.5	1174.9	263.1	65	9417185
CYN	City National Corp. (Beverly Hills, C	Banking	12/31/12	1244.2	208.0	28618.5	2505.3	288	46283507
CLC	Clarcor Inc.	Industrial Machinery & Equipment	11/30/12	1121.8	123.0	1205.5	900.8	274	53022454

T14

| EARNINGS PER SHARE | | | | | | P/E RATIO | | DIVIDENDS PER SHARE | | | AV. YLD % | DIV. DECLARED | | PRICE RANGE | |
| QUARTERLY | | | ANNUAL | | | | | | | | | | | 2012 | |
1st	2nd	3rd	2012	2011	2010			2012	2011	2010		AMOUNT	PAYABLE		
			0.33	0.34	0.36	29.6 -	0.0	0.58	0.54	0.54	6.7	0.0450	4/30/13	9.8 -	0.0
		0.12	0.97	0.74	0.63	26.1 -	0.0					0.120Y	81/16/21	25.4 -	0.0
		0.60	2.39	1.92	1.04	19.6 -	0.0	0.44	0.35	0.20	1.2	0.130Y	12/26/12	47.0 -	0.0
		0.27	0.97	0.77	-0.57	19.0 -	0.0	0.65	0.52	0.52	3.9			18.5 -	0.0
		0.45	2.47	2.88	2.55	15.7 -	0.0	0.90	0.82		2.7	0.240	4/18/13	38.7 -	0.0
		2.51	1.81	1.29	-0.57	22.0 -	0.0	1.60	1.00	0.25	4.9	0.6250	3/25/13	39.8 -	0.0
		-0.07	0.13	-1.79	-0.81	47.1 -	0.0	2.22	2.22	2.22	42.4	0.45310Z	5/20/13	6.1 -	0.0
	0.32		1.12	0.65	0.21	19.4 -	0.0	0.06			0.4	0.020Y	4/16/13	21.8 -	0.0
		0.73	3.79	3.82	2.38	13.3 -	0.0	0.27	0.22	0.18	0.6	0.0750Y	81/16/21	50.3 -	0.0
		0.21		0.89	0.44									0.0 -	0.0
		0.21		0.89	0.44									9.7 -	0.0
		1.25	5.33	8.28	12.98	2.3 -	0.0					1.310	7/26/12	12.5 -	0.0
														14.9 -	0.0
														12.4 -	0.0
				125.00	129.60									19.1 -	0.0
		0.38	1.31	1.95	1.43	28.1 -	0.0	0.88	0.80	0.80	2.7	0.2420	3/28/13	36.8 -	0.0
		0.07	0.03	2.12	1.88	1693.3 -	0.0							50.8 -	0.0
		0.02	0.97	3.17	1.07	24.7 -	0.0	0.81	0.79	0.78	4.0	0.20750Y	81/16/21	24.0 -	0.0
		2.69		2.60	1.71				0.29	3.15				9.5 -	0.0
		0.75	0.47	0.30		0.0 -	0.0	2.49	0.26	0.65	1.$	0.3529C	1/28/13	0.0 -	0.0
		0.75	0.47	0.30		48.0 -	0.0	2.49	0.26	0.65	7.7	0.3529C	1/28/13	36.0 -	0.0
		0.26	1.13	3.31	-171.13	14.3 -	0.0					2.0Y	12/19/08	16.2 -	0.0
		0.43	1.25	1.07	3.13	34.4 -	0.0	2.90	2.90	2.90	7.4	0.540Y	81/16/21	43.0 -	0.0
		0.06	-1.26	-0.14	-2.99									3.5 -	0.0
		6.35	28.59	21.98	5.34	8.1 -	0.0	1.60	1.00	0.40	0.8	0.40Y	81/16/21	230.5 -	0.0
		0.23		-0.13	-0.36							1.2961E	12/27/05	34.8 -	0.0
0.07			0.48	1.64	1.24	59.0 -	0.0							28.3 -	0.0
		0.60	2.58	2.93	2.41	26.1 -	0.0	2.22	2.17	2.16	3.4	0.5550Y	5/1/13	67.2 -	0.0
		0.46	2.01	2.14	-5.38	22.8 -	0.0							45.8 -	0.0
		0.10	-0.12	-0.69	-0.20			0.78	0.70	0.35	5.5	0.070Z	5/31/13	17.6 -	0.0
		-0.13	-3.56	-1.64	0.68							0.005F	4/8/97	13.9 -	0.0
		1.07	4.62	4.10	3.55	17.3 -	0.0	0.68	0.60	0.52	1.0	0.180Y	3/22/13	80.0 -	0.0
		0.09	1.02	1.19	-2.63	24.0 -	0.0					0.050Y	9/2/08	24.5 -	0.0
		-3.19	-1.46	2.32	2.51			0.35	0.25	0.30	1.9	14.3750Y	81/16/21	23.3 -	0.0
		0.61						2.63	0.58		13.3	0.670	3/1/13	26.6 -	0.0
		0.21	0.66	0.30	-0.07	35.5 -	0.0	0.88	0.80	0.40	4.6	0.48440Z	4/15/13	23.4 -	0.0
		0.33	2.99	2.87	2.73	16.8 -	0.0	1.44	1.37	1.30	3.2	0.3650Y	4/5/13	50.3 -	0.0
		2.69	13.32	13.44	9.48	9.1 -	0.0	3.51	3.09	2.84	3.2	0.90Y	81/16/21	121.2 -	0.0
		0.82	3.07	2.55	2.04	20.2 -	0.0	0.20	0.20		0.5	0.050Y	81/16/21	62.1 -	0.0
		0.25	0.82	0.64	0.39	24.0 -	0.0	0.20	0.16		1.2	0.0550Y	81/16/21	19.6 -	0.0
		0.06		0.13	0.65				0.51	0.69		0.090Z	81/16/21	3.3 -	0.0
	0.34		1.79	1.31	0.78	1.8 -	0.0							3.2 -	0.0
		-0.19		0.69	0.57				0.54	1.98		1.37	2/1/13	4.3 -	0.0
		0.01	0.06	-0.03	-0.01	89.2 -	0.0	0.46			13.3	0.487	12/17/12	5.3 -	0.0
				0.41	0.44									23.7 -	0.0
		0.28	0.27		0.21	86.3 -	0.0	3.00	2.27	0.26	13.7	2.9044C	12/28/12	24.2 -	0.0
	0.30		1.56	1.27	0.91	2.9 -	0.0							4.5 -	0.0
		-0.01		-0.29	-0.08									2.8 -	0.0
				0.65	1.19				0.12	0.20				52.6 -	0.0
		0.03		2.35	6.61									2.4 -	0.0
				6.20	5.00				0.29	0.24				59.5 -	0.0
		0.01		0.17	0.08				0.04	0.04				3.2 -	0.0
				12.17	11.07									3.2 -	0.0
		0.71	0.81	0.82		172.8 -	0.0	0.67	0.49	0.36	0.7			122.7 -	0.0
				0.52	0.70									30.0 -	0.0
									0.15	0.14				63.5 -	0.0
									0.02	0.03				17.8 -	0.0
				0.18	0.16									1.9 -	0.0
		0.25	0.76	1.09	1.24	2.4 -	0.0							18.4 -	0.0
				21.96	29.98							0.47	7/9/12	4.1 -	0.0
		0.27		2.38	2.05									440.4 -	0.0
		2.27	8.75	6.76	5.64	50.3 -	0.0							9.0 -	0.0
		-1.45	-8.79	1.23	1.25							0.10	7/14/06	44.2 -	0.0
		0.76	2.07	1.85	1.80	21.4 -	0.0	11.15	0.74	0.74	31.1	0.1850Y	81/16/21	6.6 -	0.0
		0.10	-2.00	-0.63	0.00			0.18	0.24	0.24	5.2	0.060Y	10/20/11	87.5 -	0.0
		1.98	5.69	5.76	6.76	15.4 -	0.0	1.64	1.56	1.48	2.2	0.440Y	81/16/21	32.9 -	0.0
		1.31		6.03	4.89									64.6 -	0.0
		0.66	2.45	2.12	1.88	26.4 -	0.0	0.96	0.68	0.31	1.8	0.280Y	81/16/21	5.0 -	0.0
		-0.13	-0.20	-0.94	-1.11									62.6 -	0.0
		1.61	5.61	4.84	4.89	11.2 -	0.0	0.04	0.04	0.04	0.1	0.040Y	81/16/21	78.2 -	0.0
		0.97	4.07	6.15	6.70	19.2 -	0.0	0.46	0.38	0.30	0.8	0.140Y	81/16/21	5.8 -	0.0
		0.01	0.00	0.04	0.09							0.84380Y	4/1/13	29.5 -	0.0
		0.41	1.47	1.14	1.29	20.1 -	0.0	0.84	0.84	0.75	3.4	0.210Y	81/16/21	43.8 -	0.0
		0.11	1.76	2.10	0.73	24.9 -	0.0	0.15	0.15	0.15	0.4	0.03750Y	3/29/13	44.7 -	0.0
		-1.52	-2.95	0.13	2.58							1.29730Y	6/15/09	47.6 -	0.0
		0.15	2.44	3.63	3.50	19.5 -	0.0	0.04	0.03	0.00	0.1	0.53130Y	81/16/21	11.5 -	0.0
		0.06	0.09	0.17	0.32	127.3 -	0.0					0.05640	3/20/79	59.6 -	0.0
		1.10	3.83	3.21	2.36	15.6 -	0.0	1.50	0.80	0.40	2.9	0.257Y	81/16/21	53.6 -	0.0
0.47			2.42	2.42	1.88	22.2 -	0.0	0.50	0.44	0.40	1.0	0.1350Y	81/16/21		

SYMBOL	COMPANY	NATURE OF BUSINESS	FISCAL YEAR-END	TOTAL REV. $MILL	NET INCOME $MILL	TOTAL ASSETS $MILL	NET STK EQUITY $MILL	NO OF INST	INST. HOLDINGS (SHARES)
CLH	Clean Harbors, Inc	Sanitation Services	12/31/12	2187.9	129.7	3825.8	1432.1	322	57047166
CCO	Clear Channel Outdoor Holdings Inc	Advertising	12/31/12	2946.9	-183.1	7105.8	198.2	133	45047562
CEM	ClearBridge Energy MLP Fund Inc	Holding and other Investment Office	11/30/12	6.3	-13.8	2292.7	1535.3	60	8082207
EMO	ClearBridge Energy MLP Opportunit	Holding and other Investment Office	11/30/12	2.0	-5.1	861.0	613.0	23	3287943
CTR	ClearBridge Energy MLP Total Retu	Holding and other Investment Office	4/30/12	-	-	0.7	0.1	18	1487264
CLW	Clearwater Paper Corp	Paper & Forest Products	12/31/12	1874.3	64.1	1633.5	540.9	159	19445107
CNL	Cleco Corp.	Electric Utilities	12/31/12	993.7	163.6	4147.3	1499.2	282	48020682
CNL 15	Cleco Power LLC	Electric Utilities	12/31/12	993.1	146.8	3871.7	1319.9		
CLF	Cliffs Natural Resources, Inc.	Non-Precious Metals	12/31/12	5872.7	-899.4	13574.9	4632.7	596	129069027
CLX	Clorox Co.	Household & Personal Products	6/30/12	5468.0	541.0	4355.0	-135.0	765	104144653
CLD	Cloud Peak Energy Inc	Mining	12/31/12	1516.8	173.7	2351.3	931.0		
CMS	CMS Energy Corp	Electric Utilities	12/31/12	6253.0	382.0	17131.0	3194.0	471	242887260
CNA	CNA Financial Corp.	General Insurance	12/31/12	9547.0	628.0	58522.0	12314.0	184	270900407
CNH	CNH Global N.V.	Industrial Machinery & Equipment	12/31/12	20447.0	1142.0	35426.0	8572.0	196	25746626
CNO	CNO Financial Group Inc	Life & Health	12/31/12	4342.7	221.0	34131.4	5049.3	262	262969604
CEO	Cnooc Ltd.	Production & Extraction	12/31/11	240944.0	70255.0	384264.0	262856.0	304	9645820
COH	Coach, Inc.	Apparel, Footwear & Accessories	6/30/12	4763.2	1038.9	3104.3	1992.9	953	278982342
CIE	Cobalt International Energy Inc.	Production & Extraction	12/31/12	-	-283.0	4011.5	2689.2	265	563047278
KO	Coca-Cola Co (The)	Beverages	12/31/12	48017.0	9019.0	86174.0	32790.0	1920	2841236513
KO	Coca-Cola Co (The)	Beverages	12/31/12	48017.0	9019.0	86174.0	32790.0	1920	2841236513
CCE	Coca-Cola Enterprises Inc	Beverages	12/31/12	8062.0	677.0	9510.0	2693.0	416	236109373
KOF	Coca-Cola FEMSA, S.A.B. de C.V.	Beverages	12/31/12	147739.0	13333.0	166103.0	101649.0	164	17716543
CCH	Coca-Cola Hellenic Bottling Co SA	Beverages	12/31/12	7044.7	190.4	7250.1	2988.7	52	14393164
CDE	Coeur d'Alene Mines Corp (Idaho)	Precious Metals	12/31/12	895.5	48.7	3221.4	2198.3	274	72769341
FOF	Cohen & Steers Closed-End Opport	Holding and other Investment Office	12/31/12	20.9	17.1	376.5	375.1	50	4867748
DVM	Cohen & Steers Dividend Majors Fu	Holding and other Investment Office	12/31/12	4.3	2.5	188.4	187.6	26	1768317
INB	Cohen & Steers Global Income Buil	Holding and other Investment Office	12/31/12	10.8	5.9	333.9	260.9	33	1924880
CNS	Cohen & Steers Inc	Wealth Management	12/31/12	-	66.1	337.3	216.6	142	21573983
UTF	Cohen & Steers Infrastructure Fund,	Holding and other Investment Office	12/31/12	105.8	71.9	2575.1	1769.4	109	14161950
LDP	Cohen & Steers Limited Duration Pr	Holding and other Investment Office	12/31/12	21.0	16.8	1053.9	734.5	16	735215
MIE	Cohen & Steers MLP Income & Ene	Finance Intermediaries & Services	2/8/13	-	-	0.1			
RQI	Cohen & Steers Quality Income Re	Holding and other Investment Office	12/31/12	52.0	31.0	1668.2	1200.8	100	11525621
RNP	Cohen & Steers Reit & Preferred In	Holding and other Investment Office	12/31/12	59.4	45.8	1236.7	883.1	79	5962414
PSF	Cohen & Steers Select Preferred & I	Holding and other Investment Office	12/31/12	30.1	24.9	459.0	325.7	25	1269194
RFI	Cohen & Steers Total Return Realty	Holding and other Investment Office	12/31/12	3.7	2.5	125.0	124.1	37	1355343
CFX	Colfax Corp	Industrial Machinery & Equipment	12/31/12	3913.9	-64.4	6129.7	1912.4		
CL	Colgate-Palmolive Co.	Household & Personal Products	12/31/12	17085.0	2472.0	13394.0	2189.0	1417	378676919
CLP	Colonial Properties Trust (AL)	REITs	12/31/12	393.5	8.2	3286.2	1149.3	220	85665696
CLNY	Colony Financial Inc.	REITs	12/31/12	107.2	62.0	1435.6	1223.3	182	45911851
STK	Columbia Seligman Premium Techn	Holding and other Investment Office	12/31/12	1.8	-1.2	236.5	234.6	22	1004744
CCZ	Comcast Holdings Corp	Radio & Television	12/31/04	8586.0	986.0	41942.0	19912.0	2	297000
CMA	Comerica, Inc.	Banking	12/31/12	2681.0	521.0	65359.0	6942.0	518	176544325
FIX	Comfort Systems USA, Inc.	Construction Services	12/31/12	1331.2	13.5	580.8	270.4	133	43699940
CMC	Commercial Metals Co.	Non-Precious Metals	8/31/12	7828.4	207.5	3441.2	1246.4	280	88990294
CWH	CommonWealth REIT	REITs	12/31/12	1013.1	-79.8	8189.6	3105.4	257	66531633
CBU	Community Bank System, Inc.	Banking	12/31/12	380.6	77.1	7496.8	902.8	174	26067309
CYH	Community Health Systems, Inc.	Hospitals & Health Care Facilities	12/31/12	13029.0	265.6	16606.3	2731.2	348	93736225
CBD	Companhia Brasileira de Distribuica	Retail - General Merchandise/Depart	12/31/11	46594.5	718.2	33769.0	7625.3		
ABV	Companhia de Bebidas das Americ	Beverages	12/31/12	27126.7	8641.0	46139.4	25611.3	378	239794168
SBS	Companhia de Saneamento Basico	Water Utilities	12/31/11	9941.6	1223.4	25215.0	10545.9	239	26687453
CIG	Companhia Energetica de Minas G	Electric Utilities	12/31/11	15814.0	2415.0	37358.0	11745.0	261	119716371
ELP	Companhia Paranaense De Energia	Electric Utilities	12/31/12	7776.2	1157.7	19121.7	12069.5	137	36518428
SID	Companhia Siderurgica Nacional	Non-Precious Metals	12/31/11	16519.6	3706.0	46869.7	7985.8		
CCU	Compania Cervecerias Unidas S.A.	Beverages	12/31/11	969550.7	122751.6	1298491.4	568975.9	114	16002305
BVN	Compania de Minas Buenaventura	Precious Metals	12/31/12	1556.6	858.9	3953.5	3178.3	222	112636472
CODI	Compass Diversified Holdings	Business Services	12/31/12	884.7	-3.9	955.2	414.6	111	15135861
CMP	Compass Minerals International Inc	Mining	12/31/12	941.9	88.9	1300.6	503.5	281	41051551
CSC	Computer Sciences Corp.	IT Services	3/30/12	15877.0	-4242.0	11189.0	2779.0	469	147029674
CRK	Comstock Resources, Inc.	Production & Extraction	12/31/12	456.2	-100.1	2567.1	933.5	240	61470016
CNW	Con-Way Inc	Trucking	12/31/12	5580.2	104.5	3141.5	838.4	261	53464010
CAG	ConAgra Foods, Inc.	Food	5/27/12	13262.6	467.9	11441.9	4439.5	749	337543878
CXO	Concho Resources Inc	Production & Extraction	12/31/12	1819.8	431.7	8589.4	3466.2	385	101244690
CCM	Concord Medical Services Holdings	Diagnostic & Health Related Service	12/31/11	450.1	-211.4	2393.4	1934.5	24	35229793
COP	ConocoPhillips	Production & Extraction	12/31/12	62004.0	8428.0	117144.0	47987.0	1767	928010678
COP	ConocoPhillips	Production & Extraction	12/31/12	62004.0	8428.0	117144.0	47987.0	1767	928010678
CNX	CONSOL Energy Inc	Mining	12/31/12	5430.3	388.5	12670.9	3953.8	457	243643297
ED PRA	Consolidated Edison Co. of New Yo	Electric Utilities	12/31/12	10187.0	1017.0	36885.0	10552.0		
ED	Consolidated Edison, Inc.	Electric Utilities	12/31/12	12188.0	1141.0	41209.0	11869.0	790	140026962
CGX	Consolidated Graphics, Inc.	Printing	3/31/12	1045.2	14.1	681.9	273.7	158	8413819
STZ	Constellation Brands Inc	Beverages	2/29/12	2654.3	445.0	7109.9	2676.0	491	161451533
CMS PRB	Consumers Energy Co.	Electric Utilities	12/31/12	6013.0	439.0	16275.0	4582.0		
CLR	Continental Resources Inc.	Production & Extraction	12/31/12	2572.5	739.4	9140.0	3163.7	352	41953170
CVG	Convergys Corp.	Miscellaneous Consumer Services	12/31/12	2005.0	100.6	2037.9	1371.9	281	109784277
COO	Cooper Companies, Inc. (The)	Medical Instruments & Equipment	10/31/12	1445.1	248.3	2941.4	2192.8	344	52490060
CTB	Cooper Tire & Rubber Co.	Auto Parts	12/31/12	4200.8	220.4	2801.2	757.6	308	63951609
CPA	Copa Holdings S.A.	Airlines/Air Freight	12/31/11	1830.9	310.4	3065.8	1389.5	270	32265686
CLB	Core Laboratories N.V. (Netherland	Equipment & Services	12/31/12	981.1	216.1	636.5	182.2	383	42211333
CLGX	CoreLogic Inc.	Business Services	12/31/12	1567.6	112.3	3029.8	1169.3	326	90917874
CORR	Corenergy Infrastructure Trust Inc	Holding and other Investment Office	11/30/12		12.3	111.4	98.9	36	7186856
COR	CoreSite Realty Corp.	REITs	12/31/12	206.9	5.0	845.3	338.2	149	21631104

EARNINGS PER SHARE QUARTERLY			ANNUAL			P/E RATIO		DIVIDENDS PER SHARE			AV. YLD %	DIV. DECLARED		PRICE RANGE 2012	
1st	2nd	3rd	2012	2011	2010			2012	2011	2010		AMOUNT	PAYABLE		
-	-	0.23	2.40	2.39	2.46	28.5 -	0.0	-	-	-	-	-	-	68.5 -	0.0
-	0.05	-0.54	0.11	-0.26		-		6.08	-	-	93.3	6.0832G7Y	81/16/21	8.2 -	0.0
-	-	-0.21	-0.30	0.00		-		1.47	1.43	0.70	6.2	0.380	2/22/13	26.8 -	0.0
-	-	-0.17	-0.09			-		1.34	0.66		6.5	0.340	2/22/13	23.5 -	0.0
												0.330	2/22/13	22.4 -	0.0
														52.9 -	0.0
-	-	0.80	2.72	1.66	3.12	19.4 -	0.0							47.0 -	0.0
-	-	1.05	2.70	3.22	4.20	17.4 -	0.0	1.30	1.12	0.97	3.1	0.33750Y	81/16/21	52.9 -	0.0
-	-	0.60	-6.32	11.48	7.49			2.15	0.84	0.51	5.2	0.150Y	81/16/21	71.2 -	0.0
-	0.93	-	4.09	4.02	4.24	21.6 -	0.0	2.40	2.20	2.00	3.2	0.640Y	81/16/21	88.5 -	0.0
-	-	1.39	2.85	3.13	0.98	7.5 -	0.0							21.5 -	0.0
-	-	0.55	1.42	1.58	1.28	19.7 -	0.0	0.96	0.84	0.66	4.0	0.2550Y	81/16/21	27.9 -	0.0
-	-	0.82	2.33	2.28	2.28	14.0 -	0.0	0.60	0.40		2.1	0.20Y	81/16/21	32.7 -	0.0
-	-	1.34	4.68	3.91	1.89	10.6 -	0.0					0.50	6/3/02	49.5 -	0.0
-	-	-0.02	0.83	1.31	0.99	14.0 -	0.0	0.06			0.7	0.020Y	3/25/13	11.6 -	0.0
				1.57	1.21				0.90	0.70				226.6 -	0.0
-	1.23	-	3.53	2.92	2.33	22.2 -	0.0	0.97	0.68	0.38	1.7	0.30Y	81/16/21	78.5 -	0.0
-	-	-0.10	-0.70	-0.35	-0.39									31.4 -	0.0
-	-	0.50	1.97	1.85	2.53	20.8 -	0.0	1.02	0.94	0.88	2.8	0.280Y	81/16/21	40.9 -	0.0
-	-	0.50	1.97	1.85	2.53	20.7 -	0.0	1.02	0.94	0.88	2.7	0.280Y	81/16/21	40.7 -	0.0
-	-	0.89	2.25	2.29	1.83	16.5 -	0.0	0.64	0.51	0.12	2.1	0.20Y	81/16/21	37.2 -	0.0
								0.14	0.18	-	0.1			168.6 -	0.0
-	-	0.40	0.52	0.74	1.16	56.4 -	0.0	0.52	1.03	0.41	2.5			29.4 -	0.0
-	-	-0.18	0.54	1.04	-1.05	59.0 -	0.0					0.3720	12/15/99	31.9 -	0.0
-	-	-	0.62	0.81	0.78	21.9 -	0.0	1.04	1.04	0.98	8.2	0.260	3/28/13	13.6 -	0.0
-	-	-	0.20	0.90	0.71	77.0 -	0.0	0.92	0.92	0.71	6.5	0.230	3/28/13	15.4 -	0.0
-	-	-	0.26	0.33	0.31	43.5 -	0.0	1.12	1.12	1.12	10.7	0.280	3/28/13	11.3 -	0.0
-	-	0.23	1.49	1.23	1.07	25.3 -	0.0	2.22	1.60	2.40	6.9	0.20Y	4/12/13	37.7 -	0.0
-	-	-	0.80	0.91	1.18	25.9 -	0.0	1.44	1.44	1.20	8.0	0.360	3/28/13	20.7 -	0.0
-	-	-	0.59			46.7 -	0.0	0.68	-	-	2.7	0.1560	4/30/13	27.6 -	0.0
														20.3 -	20.0
-	-	-	0.28	0.65	0.41	41.4 -	0.0	0.72	0.72	0.55	6.9	0.180	3/28/13	11.6 -	0.0
-	-	-	0.95	1.21	1.02	19.9 -	0.0	1.20	1.20	1.00	7.1	0.30	3/28/13	18.9 -	0.0
-	-	-	2.08	2.03	0.08	13.8 -	0.0	2.30	1.89	0.17	8.7	0.1720	4/30/13	28.7 -	0.0
-	-	-	0.27	0.24	0.29	57.4 -	0.0	1.41	0.88	1.44	10.2	0.220	3/28/13	15.5 -	0.0
-	-	0.04	-0.92	0.10	0.37									48.6 -	0.0
-	-	1.36	5.15	4.94	4.31	22.9 -	0.0	2.44	2.27	2.03	2.3	0.680Y	81/16/21	118.0 -	0.0
-	-	-0.08	0.09	0.04	-0.67	257.8 -	0.0	0.72	0.60	0.60	3.3	0.210Z	2/11/13	23.2 -	0.0
-	-	0.30	1.32	1.46	1.18	17.8 -	0.0	1.44	1.31	0.97	7.5	0.53130Z	4/15/13	23.5 -	0.0
-	-	-0.08	-0.07	-0.11				1.85	1.85	1.85	11.7	0.46250	2/27/13	18.9 -	0.0
												0.39460Z	4/15/13	43.3 -	0.0
-	-	0.61	2.67	2.09	0.88	13.8 -	0.0	0.55	0.40	0.25	1.8	0.170Y	81/16/21	36.8 -	0.0
-	-	0.15	0.36	-0.99	0.39	39.4 -	0.0	0.20	0.20	0.20	1.8	0.050Y	3/22/13	14.2 -	0.0
-	0.04	-	1.78	-1.13	-1.81	9.8 -	0.0	0.48	0.48	0.48	3.4	0.120Y	81/16/21	17.4 -	0.0
-	-	0.00	-1.81	0.81	1.26			1.75	2.00	1.00	10.2	0.45310Z	81/16/21	25.3 -	0.0
-	-	0.46	1.93	2.01	1.89	15.5 -	0.0	1.06	1.00	0.94	3.8	0.270Y	81/16/21	29.9 -	0.0
-	-	0.49	2.96	2.23	3.01	16.0 -	0.0	0.25	-		0.8	0.25G7	81/16/21	47.4 -	0.0
-	-	-	-	-	2.65			-	0.25	0.19				55.3 -	0.0
-	-	0.77	-	2.65	2.33			-	0.62	0.56				47.1 -	0.0
-	-	-	-	5.37	7.16			-	-	0.66				48.6 -	0.0
-	0.82	-	-	2.83	2.73			-	0.80	0.76				20.9 -	0.0
-	-	-	-	-	4.04			-	0.52	0.16				25.3 -	0.0
-	-	-	-	2.54	1.73			-	0.47	0.33				9.6 -	0.0
-	-	54.60	-	385.40	347.56			-	0.00	0.00				33.8 -	0.0
-	-	0.73	-	3.77	2.85			-	0.54	0.44		0.02250	4/21/97	42.3 -	0.0
-	-	0.07	-0.08	1.37	-1.19			1.44	1.42	1.36	10.0	0.360	4/30/13	16.2 -	0.0
-	-	0.28	2.65	4.45	4.51	30.4 -	0.0	1.98	1.80	1.56	2.7	0.5450Y	81/16/21	80.7 -	0.0
-	-	3.27	-27.37	4.73	5.28			0.80	0.70		2.4	0.20Y	81/16/21	50.5 -	0.0
-	-	-0.56	-2.16	-0.73	-0.43									20.4 -	0.0
-	-	0.45	1.85	1.57	0.07	20.6 -	0.0	0.40	0.40	0.40	1.3	0.10Y	81/16/21	38.1 -	0.0
-	-	0.29	1.12	1.88	1.62	32.0 -	0.0	0.95	0.89	0.79	3.4	0.250Y	81/16/21	35.8 -	0.0
-	-	0.06	4.15	5.28	2.18	26.1 -	0.0							108.2 -	0.0
-	-	-		-1.51	0.89			-	-	0.03				5.0 -	0.0
-	-	1.46	6.72	8.97	7.62	8.6 -	8.0	2.64	2.64	2.15	4.8	0.660Y	81/16/21	57.5 -	53.8
-	-	1.46	6.72	8.97	7.62	9.2 -	0.0	2.64	2.64	2.15	4.7	0.660Y	81/16/21	61.7 -	0.0
-	-	-0.05	1.70	2.76	1.60	21.5 -	0.0	0.63	0.42	0.40	2.0	0.1250Y	81/16/21	36.6 -	0.0
								2.50	5.00	5.00	3.4	1.16250Y	5/1/12	106.3 -	0.0
-	-	1.49	3.86	3.57	3.47	16.8 -	0.0	2.42	2.40	2.38	4.1	0.6150Y	81/16/21	64.9 -	0.0
-	-	1.68	1.32	3.57	1.23	34.3 -	0.0							45.2 -	0.0
-	-	0.58	2.13	2.62	0.45	22.4 -	0.0					0.35940 Y	9/1/06	47.6 -	0.0
								4.16	4.16	4.16	5.9	1.1250Y	4/1/13	99.4 -	0.0
-	-	0.24	4.07	2.41	0.99	22.8 -	0.0							92.7 -	0.0
-	-	0.24	0.86	2.72	-0.43	20.0 -	0.0	0.15			1.0	0.060Y	81/16/21	17.2 -	0.0
1.50	-	-	5.05	3.63	2.43	21.4 -	0.0	0.06	0.06	0.06	0.1	0.030Y	81/16/21	108.2 -	0.0
-	-	1.17	3.49	4.02	2.24	8.0 -	0.0	0.42	0.42	0.42	2.0	0.1050Y	3/29/13	28.1 -	0.0
-	-	2.52	-	6.98	5.48			-	1.64	1.09		2.250	12/27/12	119.6 -	0.0
-	-	1.14	4.54	3.82	3.00	31.3 -	0.0	1.12	1.00	0.89	0.9	0.320	2/22/13	141.9 -	0.0
-	-	0.37	1.09	-0.68	-0.60	26.4 -	0.0							28.8 -	0.0
-	-	0.54	1.34	0.32	0.00	7.0 -	0.0	0.44	0.41	0.43	5.4	0.1250	3/19/13	9.4 -	0.0
-	-	0.06	0.22	-0.24	-0.17	159.8 -	0.0	0.81	0.57	-	3.0	0.62GHZ	4/15/13	35.1 -	0.0

T17

SYMBOL	COMPANY	NATURE OF BUSINESS	FISCAL YEAR-END	TOTAL REV. $MILL	NET INCOME $MILL	TOTAL ASSETS $MILL	NET STK EQUITY $MILL	NO OF INST	INST. HOLDINGS (SHARES)
GLW	Corning, Inc.	Electrical Equipment	12/31/12	8012.0	1728.0	29375.0	21486.0	1091	1171612005
BCA	Corpbanca	Banking	12/31/11	628699.0	117318.0	8888684.0	739793.0	39	2517782
CEB	Corporate Executive Board Co.	Business Services	12/31/12	622.7	37.1	1322.2	115.5	244	34898298
OFC	Corporate Office Properties Trust	REITs	12/31/12	528.0	21.0	3653.8	1365.4	257	87256439
CXW	Corrections Corporation of America	REITs	12/31/12	1759.9	156.8	2974.7	1521.6	313	98947937
CZZ	Cosan Ltd	Food	3/31/12	24096.9	1181.3	22168.1	5577.3	151	90279008
CMRE	Costamare Inc.	Shipping	12/31/12	386.2	81.1	2311.3	520.5	54	12376678
COT	Cott Corp.	Beverages	12/29/12	2250.6	47.8	1565.9	611.8	142	66406813
CCSC	Country Style Cooking Restaurant	Hotels, Restaurants & Travel	12/31/11	1019.6	-6.9	920.8	777.9		
CUZ	Cousins Properties Inc.	REITs	12/31/12	148.3	45.7	1124.2	620.3	207	87907545
CVD	Covance Inc.	Biotechnology	12/31/12	2365.8	94.7	2288.3	1307.2	389	58358018
CVA	Covanta Holding Corp	Electric Utilities	12/31/12	1644.0	114.0	4526.0	1048.0	277	116351460
CVH	Coventry Health Care Inc.	Life & Health	12/31/12	14113.4	487.1	8751.0	4722.9	413	123011971
COV	Covidien Plc	Medical Instruments & Equipment	9/28/12	11852.0	1905.0	22257.0	10565.0	845	436149621
CPL	CPFL Energia SA	Electric Utilities	12/31/11	12764.0	1530.4	27413.1	7067.2	173	17664232
CR	Crane Co.	Industrial Machinery & Equipment	12/31/12	2579.1	217.0	2889.9	918.4	275	43111275
CRD A	Crawford & Co.	Brokers & Intermediaries	12/31/12	1266.1	48.9	844.8	136.2	36	11029630
BAP	CrediCorp Ltd.	Banking	12/31/11	3288.7	709.3	30732.8	3395.8	253	40346447
CS	Credit Suisse Group	Banking	12/31/12	23966.0	1483.0	924187.0	35632.0	219	33830533
CMLP	Crestwood Midstream Partners LP	Equipment & Services	12/31/12	214.0	31.7	1233.4		61	35191974
CXS	CreXus Investment Corp	REITs	12/31/12	89.9	71.0	974.0	907.9	155	52943716
CRH	CRH Plc	Construction Materials	12/31/12	18659.0	552.0	21168.0	10537.0	101	27462443
CRT	Cross Timbers Royalty Trust	Production & Extraction	12/31/12	15.3	14.9	13.8	12.5	70	847880
CCI	Crown Castle International Corp	Services	12/31/12	2432.7	188.6	16088.7	2938.7	516	291390006
CCK	Crown Holdings Inc	Metal Products	12/31/12	8470.0	557.0	7490.0	-162.0	414	144612889
CRY	CryoLife, Inc.	Medical Instruments & Equipment	12/31/12	131.7	7.9	157.2	128.1	122	16946433
CSS	CSS Industries, Inc.	Printing	3/31/12	384.7	15.7	286.6	243.2	96	8385625
CSX	CSX Corp.	Rail	12/28/12	11756.0	1859.0	30571.0	8988.0	940	701543742
CTS	CTS Corp.	Electrical Equipment	12/31/12	576.9	20.3	561.2	267.8	125	31111266
CUBE	CubeSmart	REITs	12/31/12	283.1	1.8	2150.3	989.8	209	136266547
CUB	Cubic Corp	Electronic Instruments & Related Pro	9/30/12	1381.5	91.9	1026.3	670.4	175	15242390
CFR	Cullen/Frost Bankers, Inc.	Banking	12/31/12	920.4	238.0	23124.1	2417.5	345	55296075
CFI	Culp Inc.	Textiles	4/29/12	254.4	13.3	144.7	89.0	66	7002241
CMI	Cummins, Inc.	Auto Parts	12/31/12	17334.0	1645.0	12548.0	6603.0	928	169911036
CW	Curtiss-Wright Corp.	Industrial Machinery & Equipment	12/31/12	2097.7	113.8	3114.6	1312.6	215	42461701
SRV	Cushing MLP Total Return Fund	Holding and other Investment Office	11/30/12	5.1	-5.3	257.5	220.0	52	5439170
SZC	Cushing Renaissance Fund	Holding and other Investment Office	8/15/12			0.2	0.1	15	472607
SRF	Cushing Royalty & Income Fund	Holding and other Investment Office	9/26/11			0.2	0.1	16	312432
CSI	Cutwater Select Income Fund	Holding and other Investment Office	3/31/12	13.2	11.6	218.5	218.3	35	1051047
CVI	CVR Energy Inc	Refining & Marketing	12/31/12	8567.3	378.6	3610.9	1525.2	182	91437861
UAN	CVR Partners LP	Agricultural Crop Production	12/31/12	302.3	112.2	623.0		80	3421126
CVRR	CVR Refining, LP	Refining & Marketing	12/31/12	8281.7	595.3	2258.5			
CVS	CVS Caremark Corporation	Retail - Food & Beverage, Drug & To	12/31/12	123133.0	3877.0	65912.0	37704.0	1420	1124817942
CYS	CYS Investments, Inc.	REITs	12/31/12	293.3	372.8	21057.5	2402.7	232	105555193
CYT	Cytec Industries, Inc.	Specialty Chemicals	12/31/12	1708.1	188.0	3922.1	1799.0	317	44145889
DAN	Dana Holding Corp	Auto Parts	12/31/12	7224.0	300.0	5144.0	1843.0	326	156489176
DHR	Danaher Corp.	Industrial Machinery & Equipment	12/31/12	18260.4	2392.2	32941.0	19016.5	1020	563632846
DAC	Danaos Corp	Shipping	12/31/12	589.0	-105.2	4212.0	440.3	29	7396776
DQ	DAQO New Energy Corp	Semiconductors	12/31/11	255.8	33.3	878.5	311.2	11	263731
DRI	Darden Restaurants, Inc.	Hotels, Restaurants & Travel	5/27/12	7998.7	475.5	5944.2	1842.0	674	120103937
DAR	Darling International Inc.	Food	12/29/12	1701.4	130.8	1552.4	1062.4	319	119321082
DVA	DaVita HealthCare Partners Inc	Diagnostic & Health Related Service	12/31/12	8186.3	536.0	16018.6	3763.1	535	98654426
DPM	DCP Midstream Partners LP	Equipment & Services	12/31/12	1720.7	168.0	2972.0		136	34040391
DCT	DCT Industrial Trust Inc	REITs	12/31/12	260.8	-15.1	3057.2	1329.1	209	307998114
DDR	DDR Corp.	REITs	12/31/12	800.4	-25.8	8055.8	3342.1	294	284518727
DF	Dean Foods Co.	Food	12/31/12	11462.3	158.6	5687.1	357.2	414	175090936
DE	Deere & Co.	Construction Services	10/31/12	36157.1	3064.7	56265.8	6842.1	1172	278051738
DEX	Delaware Enhanced Global Dividen	Holding and other Investment Office	11/30/12	12.8	8.8	273.4	190.6	32	2339596
DDF	Delaware Investments Dividend & I	Holding and other Investment Office	11/30/12	5.4	4.1	116.3	81.7	25	517078
DKL	Delek Logistics Partners LP	Equipment & Services	12/31/12	1022.6	34.1	245.8	104.5		
DK	Delek US Holdings Inc	Refining & Marketing	12/31/12	8726.7	272.8	2623.7	899.3	192	26417864
DLPH	Delphi Automotive Plc	Auto Parts	12/31/12	15519.0	1077.0	10176.0	2345.0	315	327275304
DAL	Delta Air Lines, Inc. (DE)	Airlines/Air Freight	12/31/12	36670.0	1009.0	44550.0	-2131.0	516	719406085
DEL	Deltic Timber Corp.	Paper & Forest Products	12/31/12	140.9	9.2	353.2	232.2	130	10709002
DLX	Deluxe Corp.	Printing	12/31/12	1514.9	170.5	1412.4	432.9	305	47424938
DMD	Demand Media Inc	Internet & Software	12/31/12	380.6	6.2	638.0	472.2		
DWRE	Demandware Inc	Internet & Software	12/31/12	79.5	-8.1	139.3	94.6	105	20605331
DNY	Denali Fund Inc (The)	Holding and other Investment Office	12/31/12	2.2	0.4	105.2	105.0	14	500191
DNR	Denbury Resources, Inc. (DE)	Production & Extraction	12/31/12	2456.5	525.4	11139.3	5114.9	508	380198116
HXM	Desarrolladora Homex SA De CV	Builders	12/31/11	21853.3	1304.4	41372.3	13488.0	103	20272259
DB	Deutsche Bank AG	Banking	12/31/11	50661.0	4132.0	2164103.0	53390.0	208	133057649
DVN	Devon Energy Corp.	Production & Extraction	12/31/12	9502.0	-206.0	43326.0	21278.0	1137	353785909
DV	DeVRY Inc.	Educational Services	6/30/12	2089.8	141.6	1838.6	1356.4	292	63368892
DEXO	Dex One Corp	Publishing	12/31/12	1300.0	62.4	2835.4	40.6	100	56070086
DHT	DHT Holdings, Inc.	Equipment & Services	12/31/12	100.1	-40.3	504.6	206.4	53	3701553
DEO	Diageo Plc	Beverages	6/30/12	10762.0	1942.0	22350.0	5588.0	662	93855271
DO	Diamond Offshore Drilling, Inc.	Equipment & Services	12/31/12	2986.5	720.5	7235.3	4576.4	546	143148177
DRH	DiamondRock Hospitality Co.	REITs	12/31/12	749.6	-16.6	2944.0	1695.1	243	226895589
DSX	Diana Shipping Inc	Shipping	12/31/12					137	36516405
DHX	Dice Holdings Inc	Internet & Software	12/31/12	195.4	38.1	354.2	190.6	161	60320113

T18

EARNINGS PER SHARE QUARTERLY 1st	2nd	3rd	ANNUAL 2012	2011	2010	P/E RATIO		DIVIDENDS PER SHARE 2012	2011	2010	AV. YLD %	DIV. DECLARED AMOUNT	PAYABLE	PRICE RANGE 2012	
-	-	0.35	1.15	1.77	2.25	12.6 -	0.0	0.32	0.23	0.20	2.6	0.090Y	81/16/21	14.4 -	0.0
-	-	-	-	0.50	0.23	-		-	0.01	0.00	-	-	-	22.2 -	0.0
-	-	-0.01	1.10	1.53	1.17	53.5 -	0.0	0.70	0.60	0.44	1.5	0.2250Y	81/16/21	58.8 -	0.0
-	-	-0.39	-0.03	-1.94	0.43	-		1.10	1.65	1.61	4.6	0.46090Z	81/16/21	27.4 -	0.0
-	-	0.42	1.56	1.54	1.39	25.0 -	0.0	0.60	-	-	1.8	6.637Z	81/16/21	39.1 -	0.0
-0.09	-	-	4.40	1.74	1.23	4.8 -	0.0	-	-	-	-	0.28590	9/11/12	21.3 -	0.0
-	-	-	1.20	1.45	1.65	13.8 -	0.0	-	-	-	-	0.270	5/8/13	16.5 -	0.0
-	-	0.15	0.50	0.40	0.63	20.5 -	0.0	0.06	-	-	0.7	0.060	4/5/13	10.3 -	0.0
-	-	0.30	-	-0.07	0.71	-		-	-	-	-	-	-	9.8 -	0.0
-	-	0.09	0.32	-1.36	-0.27	33.9 -	0.0	0.18	0.18	0.36	2.2	0.48440Z	5/15/13	10.8 -	0.0
-	-	-	-	-	-	-		-	-	-	-	-	-	74.3 -	0.0
-	-	0.69	1.68	2.16	1.06	44.2 -	0.0	-	-	-	-	-	-	20.1 -	0.0
-	-	0.19	0.86	1.54	0.40	23.4 -	0.0	0.60	0.30	1.50	3.4	0.1650Y	81/16/21	47.1 -	0.0
-	-	0.78	3.52	3.70	2.97	13.4 -	0.0	0.50	-	-	1.3	0.1250Y	81/16/21	67.8 -	0.0
1.03	-	-	3.92	3.76	3.24	17.3 -	0.0	-	-	-	-	0.20	81/16/21	31.0 -	0.0
-	-	-	-	1.59	1.60	-		-	0.91	0.96	-	-	-	56.8 -	0.0
-	-	0.99	3.72	0.44	2.59	15.3 -	0.0	1.08	0.98	0.86	2.5	0.280Y	81/16/21	5.9 -	0.0
-	-	0.33	1.78	1.68	0.53	3.3 -	0.0	0.16	0.08	-	3.7	0.030Y	3/22/13	166.1 -	0.0
-	-	-	-	8.90	7.17	-		-	-	-	-	2.60	5/10/13	30.3 -	0.0
-	-	0.16	0.90	1.36	3.89	33.6 -	0.0	0.90	1.71	1.63	3.9	-	-	29.1 -	0.0
-	-	0.15	0.37	1.00	1.03	78.6 -	0.0	2.00	1.81	1.62	8.1	0.510	2/12/13	13.4 -	0.0
-	-	0.30	0.93	1.73	0.66	14.4 -	0.0	1.18	1.13	0.58	10.5	0.250Z	4/25/13	23.1 -	0.0
-	-	-	0.76	0.83	0.61	30.3 -	0.0	1.03	1.24	1.09	5.4	-	-	41.6 -	0.0
-	-	0.54	2.48	2.99	2.79	16.8 -	0.0	2.48	2.99	2.79	7.6	0.13070	4/12/13	75.1 -	0.0
-	-	0.14	0.64	0.52	-1.16	117.4 -	0.0	-	-	-	-	0.78130Y	2/15/12	41.6 -	0.0
-	-	2.20	3.75	1.83	2.00	11.1 -	0.0	-	-	-	-	-	-	7.1 -	0.0
-	-	0.06	0.28	0.26	0.14	25.4 -	0.0	0.05	-	-	0.9	0.0250Y	3/21/13	26.0 -	0.0
-	-	1.22	1.61	0.58	-2.46	16.1 -	0.0	0.60	0.60	0.60	2.9	0.150Y	3/15/13	24.6 -	0.0
-	-	0.44	1.79	1.67	1.35	13.8 -	0.0	0.54	0.45	0.33	2.5	0.140Y	81/16/21	11.3 -	0.0
-	-	0.17	0.59	0.60	0.63	19.1 -	0.0	0.14	0.13	0.12	1.4	0.0350Y	5/3/13	15.9 -	0.0
-	-	0.00	-0.03	-0.02	-0.08	-		0.43	0.28	0.10	3.3	0.48440Z	4/15/13	52.0 -	0.0
0.47	-	-	3.44	3.17	2.64	15.1 -	0.0	0.24	0.28	0.18	0.5	0.120Y	3/11/13	62.5 -	0.0
-	-	0.95	3.86	3.54	3.44	16.2 -	0.0	1.90	1.83	1.78	3.3	0.480Y	81/16/21	18.1 -	0.0
-	0.67	-	1.03	1.22	1.01	17.5 -	0.0	-	-	-	-	0.030	4/15/13	121.7 -	0.0
-	-	1.86	8.67	9.55	5.28	14.0 -	0.0	1.80	1.33	-	1.8	0.50Y	81/16/21	37.4 -	0.0
-	-	0.24	2.40	2.77	2.30	15.6 -	0.0	0.35	0.32	0.32	1.1	0.090Y	4/11/13	10.0 -	0.0
-	-	-	-0.34	0.68	1.07	-		0.90	0.68	0.90	10.6	0.2250	3/20/13	25.1 -	0.0
-	-	-	-	-	-	-		-	-	-	-	0.410	3/20/13	24.6 -	0.0
-	-	-	-	-	-	-		-	-	-	-	0.50	3/20/13	20.8 -	0.0
-	-	1.08	1.14	1.19		19.2 -	0.0	1.15	1.15	1.15	5.8	0.2650	5/1/13	61.4 -	0.0
-	-	2.41	4.33	3.94	0.16	14.2 -	0.0	-	-	-	-	5.5G7	81/16/21	29.4 -	0.0
-	-	0.43	1.53	1.48		19.2 -	0.0	2.21	0.98	-	8.7	0.1920	2/14/13	35.4 -	24.8
-	-	-	-	-	-	-		-	-	-	-	-	-	55.3 -	0.0
-	-	0.79	3.03	2.57	2.49	18.3 -	0.0	0.65	0.50	0.35	1.4	0.2250Y	81/16/21	14.9 -	0.0
-	-	1.46	2.64	3.66	0.73	5.6 -	0.0	2.37	2.25	2.35	17.9	0.48440Z	4/15/13	78.4 -	0.0
-	-	1.13	4.02	4.24	3.46	19.5 -	0.0	0.50	0.50	0.05	0.8	0.1250Y	81/16/21	18.1 -	0.0
-	-	0.26	1.40	1.02	-0.16	13.0 -	0.0	0.20	-	-	1.4	1.0Y	81/16/21	62.6 -	0.0
-	-	0.77	3.36	3.11	2.64	18.6 -	0.0	0.10	0.09	0.08	0.2	0.0250Y	81/16/21	4.5 -	0.0
-	-	-0.06	-0.96	0.12	-1.36	-		-	-	-	-	0.4650	11/19/08	14.8 -	0.0
-	-	-	-	0.19	0.46	-		-	-	-	-	-	-	57.2 -	0.0
-	-	1.02	3.57	3.39	2.84	16.0 -	0.0	1.72	1.28	1.00	3.4	0.50Y	81/16/21	18.7 -	0.0
-	-	0.31	1.11	1.47	0.53	16.9 -	0.0	-	-	-	-	-	-	123.3 -	0.0
-	-	1.50	5.47	4.96	3.94	22.6 -	0.0	-	-	-	-	-	-	46.9 -	0.0
-	-	-0.16	2.29	1.72	0.88	20.6 -	0.0	2.66	2.52	2.42	6.2	0.690	2/14/13	7.5 -	0.0
-	-	0.03	-0.06	-0.11	-0.18	-		0.28	0.28	0.28	4.4	0.070Z	4/17/13	17.7 -	0.0
-	-	0.04	-0.21	-0.28	-1.03	-		0.48	0.22	0.08	3.1	0.1350Z	81/16/21	18.9 -	0.0
-	-	0.20	0.85	-8.59	0.50	22.3 -	0.0	-	-	-	-	15.7	81/16/21	95.0 -	0.0
1.65	-	-	7.63	6.63	4.35	12.5 -	0.0	1.79	1.52	1.16	2.2	0.510Y	81/16/21	12.8 -	0.0
-	-	-	0.56	0.59	0.57	22.9 -	0.0	1.15	1.23	1.23	9.9	0.0750	4/26/13	9.0 -	0.0
-	-	-	0.44	0.43	-	20.5 -	0.0	0.68	0.69	0.09	8.4	0.05250	4/26/13	31.2 -	21.2
-	-	-	0.34	-	-	91.7 -	62.5	-	-	-	-	0.224G	2/14/13	40.5 -	0.0
-	-	1.67	4.57	2.78	-1.47	8.9 -	0.0	0.50	0.33	0.15	2.0	0.17Y	4/16/13	44.5 -	0.0
-	-	0.84	3.33	2.72	-	13.4 -	0.0	-	-	-	-	0.17G	3/27/13	17.1 -	0.0
-	-	1.23	1.19	1.01	0.70	14.3 -	0.0	-	-	-	-	0.0250 Y	6/1/03	73.2 -	0.0
-	-	0.25	0.73	0.21	0.99	100.3 -	0.0	0.30	0.30	0.30	0.5	0.10Y	3/15/13	42.2 -	0.0
-	-	0.81	3.32	2.80	2.96	12.7 -	0.0	1.00	1.00	1.00	3.4	0.250Y	81/16/21	11.8 -	0.0
-	-	0.04	0.07	-0.27	-2.86	169.0 -	0.0	-	-	-	-	-	-	33.9 -	0.0
-	-	-0.12	-0.39	-1.75	-2.44	-		-	-	-	-	-	-	18.7 -	0.0
-	-	-	0.10	0.09	0.07	186.8 -	0.0	0.22	0.72	0.20	1.6	0.20	1/11/13	19.5 -	0.0
-	-	0.22	1.35	1.43	0.72	14.4 -	0.0	-	-	-	-	-	-	18.5 -	0.0
-	-	-	-	3.90	4.52	-		-	-	-	-	-	-	52.7 -	0.0
-	-	0.78	-	4.30	2.92	-		-	-	-	-	-	-	72.3 -	0.0
-	-	-1.80	-0.52	11.25	10.31	-		0.80	0.67	0.64	1.4	0.220Y	81/16/21	34.5 -	0.0
-	0.78	-	2.09	4.68	3.87	16.5 -	0.0	0.30	0.24	0.20	1.1	0.170Y	81/16/21	2.5 -	0.0
-	-	-0.25	1.23	-10.35	-18.46	2.0 -	0.0	-	-	-	-	0.01F	5/30/06	11.8 -	0.0
-	-	-6.27	-	-7.68	1.56	-		-	-	3.60	-	0.020	2/19/13	125.8 -	0.0
-	-	-	0.77	0.76	0.65	163.4 -	0.0	4.21	3.93	3.72	3.8	-	-	76.5 -	0.0
-	-	1.28	5.18	6.92	6.87	14.8 -	0.0	3.50	3.50	5.25	5.3	0.757Y	81/16/21	10.8 -	0.0
-	-	-0.24	-0.09	-0.05	-0.06	-		0.32	0.32	0.33	3.4	0.0850Z	4/12/13	10.7 -	0.0
-	-	-	-	-	-	-		-	-	-	-	0.950	12/11/08	11.0 -	0.0
-	-	0.17	0.59	0.49	0.28	18.6 -	0.0	-	-	-	-	-	-		

SYMBOL	COMPANY	NATURE OF BUSINESS	FISCAL YEAR-END	TOTAL REV. $MILL	NET INCOME $MILL	TOTAL ASSETS $MILL	NET STK EQUITY $MILL	NO OF INST	INST. HOLDINGS (SHARES)
DKS	Dick's Sporting Goods, Inc	Retail - Specialty	2/2/13	5836.1	290.7	2887.8	1587.3	428	111298489
DBD	Diebold, Inc.	Computer Hardware & Equipment	12/31/12	2991.7	78.5	2593.0	810.0	333	71166477
DLR	Digital Realty Trust, Inc.	REITs	12/31/12	1279.1	210.3	8819.2	3468.3	497	144606484
DGI	DigitalGlobe Inc	Services	12/31/12	421.4	39.0	1577.5	539.4	167	50133786
DDS	Dillard's Inc.	Retail - General Merchandise/Depart	2/2/13	6751.6	336.0	4048.7	1970.2	287	44326005
DIN	DineEquity Inc	Hotels, Restaurants & Travel	12/31/12	849.9	127.7	2415.4	308.8	160	20112574
DFS	Discover Financial Services	Credit & Lending	11/30/12	8984.0	2345.0	75283.0	9778.0	726	457611623
DIS	Disney (Walt) Co. (The)	Entertainment	9/29/12	42278.0	5682.0	74898.0	39759.0	1603	1304878141
DNI	Dividend & Income Fund	Holding and other Investment Office	12/31/12	5.8	3.4	115.6	94.0	23	274383
DNP	DNP Select Income Fund Inc	Holding and other Investment Office	12/31/12	140.6	103.7	3243.3	2219.5	186	14893269
DM	Dolan Company (The)	Business Services	12/31/12	254.3	-101.8	449.5	212.8	126	25467865
DLB	Dolby Laboratories Inc	Manufacturing	9/28/12	926.3	264.3	1960.8	1720.3	306	46071208
DOLE	Dole Food Co., Inc.	Food	12/29/12	4246.7	-144.5	4229.8	686.1	164	58061229
DG	Dollar General Corp	Retail - General Merchandise/Depart	2/1/13	16022.1	952.7	10367.7	4985.3	546	368411037
DDC	Dominion Diamond Corp	Precious Metals	1/31/12	702.0	25.5	1630.9	791.1	132	61243286
DOM	Dominion Resources Black Warrior	Production & Extraction	12/31/12	5.3	4.2	11.1	11.0	24	335282
D	Dominion Resources Inc	Electric Utilities	12/31/12	13093.0	302.0	46838.0	10825.0	1001	355218443
DPZ	Dominos Pizza Inc.	Hotels, Restaurants & Travel	12/30/12	1678.4	112.4	478.2	-1335.5	227	54760333
UFS	Domtar Corp	Paper & Forest Products	12/31/12	5482.0	172.0	6123.0	2877.0		
DCI	Donaldson Co. Inc.	Industrial Machinery & Equipment	7/31/12	2493.2	264.3	1730.1	910.0	388	126104018
DRL	Doral Financial Corp.	Credit & Lending	12/31/12	454.3	-3.3	8478.2	835.7	113	78644390
DBL	Doubleline Opportunistic Credit Fun	Holding and other Investment Office	11/9/11	-	-	0.7	0.1	29	1843029
PLOW	Douglas Dynamics, Inc.	Industrial Machinery & Equipment	12/31/12	140.0	6.0	338.4	153.7	92	21149124
DEI	Douglas Emmett Inc	REITs	12/31/12	579.0	22.9	6103.8	1979.7	243	150358618
DOV	Dover Corp	Industrial Machinery & Equipment	12/31/12	8104.3	811.1	10443.9	4919.2	724	172899652
DDE	Dover Downs Gaming & Entertainm	Hotels, Restaurants & Travel	12/31/12	225.9	4.8	205.3	113.5	48	10407662
DVD	Dover Motorsports, Inc.	Sporting & Recreational	12/31/12	46.7	4.6	95.8	48.1	44	10080384
DPO	Dow 30 Enhanced Premuim & Inco	Holding and other Investment Office	12/31/12	8.4	5.2	317.2	314.8	45	2783329
DPD	Dow 30 Premium & Dividend Incom	Holding and other Investment Office	12/31/12	4.8	3.0	174.4	172.3	29	815277
DOW	Dow Chemical Co.	Plastics	12/31/12	56786.0	1182.0	69605.0	20877.0	1007	876655941
DPS	Dr Pepper Snapple Group Inc	Beverages	12/31/12	5995.0	629.0	8928.0	2280.0	498	212684447
RDY	Dr. Reddy's Laboratories Ltd.	Pharmaceuticals	3/31/12	96737.0	14262.0	119477.0	57444.0	167	22823397
DRD	DRDGold Ltd	Precious Metals	6/30/12	3004.3	308.7	2492.3	1497.2	45	2896782
DRC	Dresser-Rand Group Inc	Equipment & Services	12/31/12	2736.4	179.0	3333.0	1091.2	316	81570370
DW	Drew Industries, Inc.	Auto Parts	12/31/12	901.1	37.3	373.9	284.2	149	22413201
DHF	Dreyfus High Yield Strategies Fund	Holding and other Investment Office	3/31/12	35.1	29.8	408.3	281.9	44	5240371
DSM	Dreyfus Strategic Municipal Bond F	Holding and other Investment Office	11/30/12	31.2	26.7	659.2	595.2	48	2288486
LEO	Dreyfus Strategic Municipals, Inc.	Holding and other Investment Office	9/30/12	42.1	35.8	867.0	787.7	56	2371400
DRQ	Dril-Quip, Inc.	Equipment & Services	12/31/12	733.0	119.2	1231.4	1066.4	276	44540267
DST	DST Systems Inc. (DE)	IT Services	12/31/12	2576.6	324.0	3392.5	1079.7	330	32436658
DSW	DSW Inc	Retail - Apparel and Accessories	2/2/13	2257.8	146.4	1262.1	858.6	241	38114595
DTE	DTE Energy Co.	Electric Utilities	12/31/12	8791.0	610.0	26339.0	7373.0	537	108922601
DTF	DTF Tax-Free Income, Inc.	Holding and other Investment Office	10/31/12	9.4	7.7	215.2	213.1	29	600440
DD	Du Pont (E.I.) de Nemours & Co	Diversified Chemicals	12/31/12	35310.0	2788.0	49736.0	10088.0	1454	660588590
DCO	Ducommun Inc.	Aerospace	12/31/12	747.0	16.4	785.1	222.7	99	7435245
DUF	Duff & Phelps Corp	Finance Intermediaries & Services	12/31/12	484.7	22.3	715.9	390.2	133	32981796
DPG	Duff & Phelps Global Utility Income	Holding and other Investment Office	10/31/12	48.7	36.4	999.1	738.1	33	2740760
DUC	Duff & Phelps Utility & Corporate Bo	Holding and other Investment Office	12/31/12	19.4	13.5	518.0	375.1	53	1748989
DUK	Duke Energy Corp	Electric Utilities	12/31/12	19624.0	1768.0	113856.0	40956.0	1211	441258285
DRE	Duke Realty Corp.	REITs	12/31/12	1109.4	-75.9	7560.1	2591.4	411	275359783
DNB	Dun & Bradstreet Corp (DE)	Business Services	12/31/12	1663.0	295.5	1991.8	-1017.4	437	48229734
DFT	DuPont Fabros Technology Inc	REITs	12/31/12	332.4	53.0	2530.9	1720.3		
LBF	DWS Global High Income Fund	Holding and other Investment Office	10/31/12	5.8	4.2	102.0	69.5	37	2215481
DHG	DWS High Income Opportunities Fu	Holding and other Investment Office	9/30/12	26.4	21.0	400.7	270.1	37	4032905
KHI	DWS High Income Trust	Holding and other Investment Office	11/30/12	15.7	12.9	233.3	162.5	31	1512550
KMM	DWS Multi Market Income Trust	Holding and other Investment Office	11/30/12	23.8	19.7	364.5	251.5	35	2191857
KTF	DWS Municipal Income Trust	Holding and other Investment Office	12/31/12	41.0	34.8	905.2	587.8	59	4259671
KST	DWS Strategic Income Trust	Holding and other Investment Office	11/30/12	6.3	5.1	99.4	67.2	23	620074
KSM	DWS Strategic Municipal Income Tr	Holding and other Investment Office	11/30/12	12.5	10.5	242.2	169.9	20	221263
DY	Dycom Industries, Inc.	Construction Services	7/28/12	1201.1	39.4	772.2	392.9	192	30214683
DX	Dynex Capital, Inc.	REITs	12/31/12	113.5	74.0	4280.2	616.7	130	27124956
DANG	E-Commerce China Dangdang Inc.	Internet & Software	12/31/12	5193.8	-443.9	3583.1	739.5		
EJ	E-House China Holdings, Ltd	Property, Real Estate & Developmen	12/31/11	401.6	-270.4	1143.7	633.4	69	44308257
EXP	Eagle Materials Inc	Construction Materials	3/31/12	495.0	18.7	985.1	472.5	291	45890967
NGT	Eastern American Natural Gas Trus	Production & Extraction	12/31/12	5.0	2.7	7.6	7.2	23	271586
EGP	EastGroup Properties, Inc.	REITs	12/31/12	186.2	32.4	1354.1	486.3	214	29345547
EMN	Eastman Chemical Co.	Plastics	12/31/12	8102.0	437.0	11619.0	2943.0	597	140499536
ETN	Eaton Corp plc	Electrical Equipment	12/31/12	16311.0	1217.0	35848.0	15086.0		
EV	Eaton Vance Corp	Wealth Management	10/31/12	1209.0	203.5	1979.5	612.1	378	97957754
EOI	Eaton Vance Enhanced Equity Inco	Holding and other Investment Office	9/30/12	9.6	3.9	513.0	503.8	66	8742708
EOS	Eaton Vance Enhanced Equity Inco	Holding and other Investment Office		8.8	2.2	579.6	572.0	74	7604160
EFT	Eaton Vance Floating Rate Income	Holding and other Investment Office	5/31/12	49.5	38.8	941.2	662.0	67	6614694
ETX	Eaton Vance Municipal Income Ter	Holding and other Investment Office	2/7/13	-	-	0.4	0.1		
EVN	Eaton Vance Municipal Income Trus	Holding and other Investment Office	11/30/12	26.2	20.6	554.3	424.9	32	586065
EOT	Eaton Vance National Municipal Op	Holding and other Investment Office	3/31/12	20.8	18.0	377.2	331.2	23	1359187
ETJ	Eaton Vance Risk-Managed Diversif	Holding and other Investment Office	12/31/12	19.1	9.5	845.4	839.7	89	22756906
EFR	Eaton Vance Senior Floating Rate T	Holding and other Investment Office	10/31/12	46.4	37.1	859.2	659.8	73	5190035
EVF	Eaton Vance Senior Income Trust	Holding and other Investment Office	6/30/12	21.8	16.0	424.8	373.2	53	10740902
EVG	Eaton Vance Short Duration Diversif	Holding and other Investment Office	10/31/12	23.2	16.4	480.3	337.4	58	3814598
EVT	Eaton Vance Tax Advantaged Divid	Holding and other Investment Office	8/31/12	108.8	87.5	1801.6	1332.6	87	9426299

1st	2nd	3rd	2012	2011	2010	P/E RATIO		2012	2011	2010	AV. YLD %	AMOUNT	PAYABLE	PRICE RANGE 2012	
-	-	0.40	2.10	1.50	1.15	25.7 -	0.0	0.50			1.0	0.1250Y	81/16/21	53.9 -	0.0
-	-	0.27	1.23	2.24	-0.31	33.1 -	0.0	1.14	1.12	1.08	3.5	0.28750Y	81/16/21	40.7 -	0.0
-	-	0.37	1.48	1.32	0.68	54.3 -	0.0	2.92	2.72	2.02	4.2	0.41410Z	81/16/21	80.3 -	0.0
-	-	0.18	0.84	-0.61	0.09	35.3 -	0.0	-						29.7 -	0.0
-	-	1.01	8.52	2.67	0.93	10.5 -	0.0	0.19	0.16	0.16	0.3	0.050Y	81/16/21	89.0 -	0.0
-	-	3.14	6.63	3.89	-1.74	11.4 -	0.0	-				0.750Y	3/29/13	75.8 -	0.0
-	-	1.21	4.46	4.06	1.22	10.1 -	0.0	0.40	0.20	0.08	1.1	0.140Y	81/16/21	45.0 -	0.0
0.77	-	-	3.13	2.52	2.03	18.5 -	0.0	0.60	0.40	0.35	1.2	0.750Y	81/16/21	57.8 -	0.0
-	-	-	0.56	0.08	0.80	27.4 -	0.0	0.41	-		2.9	0.4080	3/28/13	15.4 -	0.0
-	-	-	0.48	0.45	0.54	24.2 -	0.0	0.78	0.78	0.78	7.6	0.0650	6/10/13	11.6 -	0.0
-	-	-3.41	-3.36	0.65	1.07	-		-				0.3542GHZ	4/1/13	9.4 -	0.0
0.50	-	-	2.46	2.75	2.46	18.3 -	0.0	-				4.G7Y	81/16/21	45.1 -	0.0
-	-	-0.17	-1.64	0.44	-0.39	-		-				-		14.4 -	0.0
-	-	0.62	2.22	1.82	1.04	25.0 -	0.0	-	-	0.75		-		55.6 -	0.0
-	-	0.04	0.30	0.27	-0.99	57.7 -	0.0	-	-			0.050	1/29/09	17.3 -	0.0
-	-	0.10	0.54	0.94	1.17	18.0 -	0.0	0.54	0.94	1.16	9.6	0.16060	3/11/13	9.7 -	0.0
-	-	0.36	0.53	2.45	4.76	109.8 -	0.0	2.11	1.97	1.83	4.0	0.56250Y	81/16/21	58.2 -	0.0
-	-	0.44	1.91	1.71	1.45	26.9 -	0.0	3.00	-	-	7.8	0.20	3/29/13	51.4 -	0.0
-	-	1.84	4.76	9.08	14.00	20.9 -	0.0	1.70	1.30	0.75	2.1	0.450	81/16/21	99.3 -	0.0
-	0.34	-	1.73	1.44	1.05	22.0 -	0.0	0.32	0.27	0.23	0.9	0.10Y	81/16/21	38.0 -	0.0
-	-	-0.27	-0.10	-0.16	-2.96	-		-	-			2.96880Y	3/16/09	1.9 -	0.0
-	-	-	-	-	-	-		-	-			0.1670	4/30/13	27.6 -	0.0
-	-	0.10	0.26	0.85	0.09	60.2 -	0.0	0.82	1.18	0.38	6.0	0.20750Y	3/29/13	15.7 -	0.0
-	-	0.04	0.16	0.01	-0.22	158.3 -	0.0	0.63	0.49	0.40	2.7	0.180Z	81/16/21	25.3 -	0.0
-	-	1.31	4.41	4.74	3.70	16.9 -	0.0	1.33	1.18	1.07	2.2	0.350Y	81/16/21	74.5 -	0.0
-	-	0.04	0.15	0.17	0.21	20.2 -	0.0	0.11	0.12	0.12	4.4	0.020Y	12/10/12	3.0 -	0.0
-	-	0.12	0.12	-0.25	-0.23	16.7 -	0.0	0.04	-	-	2.7	0.04GY	12/10/12	2.0 -	0.0
-	-	-	0.19	0.17	0.15	62.1 -	0.0	0.87	0.96	1.02	8.0	0.2180	4/1/13	11.8 -	0.0
-	-	-	0.25	0.23	0.22	58.7 -	0.0	1.06	1.16	1.24	7.8	0.2660	4/1/13	14.7 -	0.0
-	-	0.42	0.70	2.05	1.72	51.5 -	0.0	1.21	0.90	0.60	3.9	0.320Y	81/16/21	36.1 -	0.0
-	-	0.84	2.96	2.74	2.17	15.9 -	0.0	1.36	1.21	0.90	3.1	0.380Y	81/16/21	47.0 -	0.0
-	0.50	-	83.81	64.95	6.30	0.4 -	0.0	0.02	0.00	0.00	0.1			36.6 -	0.0
-	-	0.13	0.80	-0.75	0.55	10.5 -	0.0	0.01	0.01	0.01	0.1			8.4 -	0.0
-	-	0.54	2.35	1.53	1.80	26.9 -	0.0	-						63.2 -	0.0
-	-	0.43	1.64	1.34	1.26	23.6 -	0.0	2.00	-	1.50	6.5	2.7Y	12/20/12	38.7 -	0.0
-	-	-	0.41	0.47	0.44	11.5 -	0.0	0.50	0.52	0.39	11.5	0.0350	4/26/13	4.7 -	0.0
-	-	-	0.55	0.57	0.59	18.0 -	0.0	0.57	0.57	0.54	6.1	0.0475M	4/30/13	9.9 -	0.0
-	-	-	0.58	0.60	0.62	17.5 -	0.0	0.59	0.59	0.57	6.2	0.049M	4/30/13	10.2 -	0.0
-	-	0.73	2.94	2.36	2.55	29.9 -	0.0	-						88.0 -	0.0
-	-	1.87	7.08	3.95	6.73	10.1 -	0.0	0.80	0.70	0.60	1.4	0.30Y	81/16/21	71.3 -	0.0
-	-	1.10	4.54	2.40	1.23	15.5 -	0.0	2.30	-		3.7	0.180Y	81/16/21	70.5 -	0.0
-	-	1.31	3.55	4.18	3.74	19.3 -	0.0	2.42	2.32	2.18	4.0	0.620Y	81/16/21	68.3 -	0.0
-	-	-	0.90	0.92	0.95	21.1 -	0.0	0.90	0.90	0.77	5.2	0.07M	5/31/13	19.0 -	0.0
-	-	0.01	2.95	3.68	3.28	18.2 -	0.0	1.70	1.64	1.64	3.5	0.430Y	81/16/21	53.8 -	0.0
-	-	0.48	1.55	-4.52	1.87	12.8 -	0.0	-	0.07	0.30		0.0750Y	3/4/11	19.8 -	0.0
-	-	0.15	0.62	-0.63	0.60	26.1 -	0.0	0.36	0.32	0.23	2.5	0.090Y	3/19/13	16.2 -	0.0
-	-	-	0.96	0.27	-	20.2 -	0.0	1.40	0.35	-	7.7	0.350	3/28/13	19.4 -	0.0
-	-	-	-	0.53	0.66	-		0.84	0.84	0.84	6.8	0.070	5/31/13	12.7 -	0.0
-	-	0.85	3.07	3.84	3.00	23.6 -		1.53	2.97	2.91	2.3	0.7650Y	81/16/21	72.6 -	0.0
-	-	-0.11	-0.48	0.11	-0.07	-		0.68	0.68	0.68	4.7	0.41250Z	81/16/21	17.1 -	0.0
-	-	1.76	6.43	5.28	4.98	13.3 -	0.0	1.52	1.44	1.40	2.0	0.40Y	81/16/21	85.5 -	0.0
-	-	0.11	0.41	0.71	0.51	70.6 -	0.0	0.62	0.48	0.44	2.5	0.47660Z	4/15/13	28.9 -	0.0
-	-	-	0.59	0.50	0.55	15.6 -	0.0	0.51	0.55	0.51	5.9	0.0450	4/30/13	9.2 -	0.0
-	-	-	1.25	1.25	1.03	13.1 -	0.0	-	-			0.0950	4/30/13	16.4 -	0.0
-	-	-	0.80	0.90	1.00	13.8 -	0.0	0.89	1.13	0.87	8.6	0.06350	4/30/13	11.0 -	0.0
-	-	-	0.81	0.87	0.90	14.2 -	0.0	0.92	0.91	0.85	8.5	0.0770	4/30/13	11.5 -	0.0
-	-	-	0.89	0.93	0.94	17.4 -	0.0	0.85	0.84	0.84	5.8	0.07M	4/30/13	15.5 -	0.0
-	-	-	1.08	1.14	1.18	14.7 -	0.0	1.19	1.34	1.15	8.2	0.0950	4/30/13	15.9 -	0.0
-	-	-	0.95	1.01	1.00	17.0 -	0.0	0.93	0.98	0.93	6.2	0.077M	4/30/13	16.1 -	0.0
-	0.04	-	1.14	0.45	0.15	20.9 -	0.0	-	-			0.0228G	7/15/81	23.8 -	0.0
-	-	0.34	1.35	1.03	1.41	8.2 -	0.0	1.15	1.09	0.98	11.5	0.53130	4/15/13	11.0 -	0.0
-	-	-0.25	-1.11	-0.58	0.02	-		-	-			-		10.7 -	0.0
-	-	-0.18	-	-3.39	0.44	-		-	0.23	0.23		-		7.5 -	0.0
-	-	0.37	0.42	0.34	0.66	170.4 -	0.0	0.30	0.40	0.40	0.6	0.10Y	81/16/21	71.6 -	0.0
-	-	0.13	0.45	0.89	0.97	49.8 -	0.0	0.57	0.92	1.00	2.7	0.36310	12/15/98	22.4 -	0.0
-	-	0.23	1.13	0.83	0.68	51.9 -	0.0	2.10	2.08	2.08	4.0	0.530Z	3/28/13	58.6 -	0.0
-	-	0.99	2.93	4.86	2.96	25.5 -	0.0	1.08	0.99	0.90	1.9	0.30Y	81/16/21	74.8 -	0.0
-	-	1.02	3.46	3.93	2.73	18.3 -	0.0	1.52	1.36	0.54	3.1	0.42G	81/16/21	63.4 -	0.0
0.38	-	-	1.72	1.75	1.40	24.3 -	0.0	0.77	0.73	0.66	2.6	0.20Y	81/16/21	41.8 -	0.0
-	-	-	0.10	0.07	0.09	117.1 -	0.0	1.06	1.15	1.46	9.8	0.08640	4/30/13	11.7 -	0.0
-	-	-	0.04	0.03	0.07	283.8 -	0.0	1.06	1.11	1.41	9.9	0.08750	4/30/13	11.4 -	0.0
-	-	-	-	0.99	1.01	-		1.02	1.02	0.94	6.2	0.0840	4/30/13	17.8 -	0.0
-	-	-	-	-	-	-		-						20.0 -	20.0
-	-	-	0.91	0.99	1.04	15.9 -	0.0	0.96	0.99	0.94	6.9	0.0783M	4/17/13	14.5 -	0.0
-	-	-	1.17	-	1.01	21.3 -	0.0	1.16	1.37	1.01	5.2	0.0858M	4/30/13	24.9 -	0.0
-	-	-	0.13	0.08	0.11	85.1 -	0.0	1.16	1.28	1.80	11.1	0.0930	4/30/13	11.1 -	0.0
-	-	-	1.10	1.01	1.02	15.8 -	0.0	1.05	1.06	1.11	6.5	0.0860	4/30/13	17.4 -	0.0
-	-	-	0.44	0.42	0.40	18.0 -	0.0	0.44	0.44	0.36	6.0	0.0360	4/18/13	7.9 -	0.0
-	-	-	0.87	0.82	1.05	20.5 -	0.0	1.08	1.16	1.08	6.3	0.090	4/30/13	17.8 -	0.0
-	-	-	1.20	1.35	1.33	15.8 -	0.0	1.29	1.29	1.29	7.6	0.10750	4/30/13	19.0 -	0.0

SYMBOL	COMPANY	NATURE OF BUSINESS	FISCAL YEAR-END	TOTAL REV. $MILL	NET INCOME $MILL	TOTAL ASSETS $MILL	NET STK EQUITY $MILL	NO OF INST	INST. HOLDINGS (SHARES)
ETW	Eaton Vance Tax Managed Global	Holding and other Investment Office	12/31/12	38.5	23.9	1334.8	1317.3	97	29332111
ETG	Eaton Vance Tax-Advantage Global	Holding and other Investment Office	10/31/12	108.4	89.2	1571.6	1129.4	71	9010939
EXD	Eaton Vance Tax-Advantaged Bond	Holding and other Investment Office	12/31/12	3.1	0.4	200.7	193.1	19	2624598
ETO	Eaton Vance Tax-Advantaged Glob	Holding and other Investment Office	10/31/12	25.9	20.4	446.6	325.5	47	2455592
ETB	Eaton Vance Tax-Managed Buy-Wri	Holding and other Investment Office	12/31/12	9.3	5.1	370.2	367.3	48	4879400
ETV	Eaton Vance Tax-Managed Buy-Wri	Holding and other Investment Office	12/31/12	18.2	8.3	883.2	876.2	80	14495734
ETY	Eaton Vance Tax-Managed Diversifi	Holding and other Investment Office	10/31/12	38.7	21.0	1658.2	1654.3	105	29921562
EXG	Eaton Vance Tax-Managed Global	Holding and other Investment Office	10/31/12	91.4	58.9	3109.7	3100.3	145	52256464
ECT	ECA Marcellus Trust I	Oil Royalty Traders	12/31/12	36.4	35.6	276.0	267.0	40	1421521
ECT	ECA Marcellus Trust I	Oil Royalty Traders	12/31/12	36.4	35.6	276.0	267.0	40	1421521
ECL	Ecolab, Inc.	Specialty Chemicals	12/31/12	11838.7	703.6	17572.3	6077.0	789	247530097
EC	Ecopetrol SA	Refining & Marketing	12/31/11	65752268.0	5452334.0	92277386.0	54688855.0	190	35948248
EDG	Edgen Group Inc	Production & Extraction	12/31/12	2059.0	-21.4	961.1	103.9	65	11369118
EIX	Edison International	Electric Utilities	12/31/12	11862.0	-183.0	44394.0	9432.0	560	269943552
EDR	Education Realty Trust Inc	REITs	12/31/12	145.0	8.4	1324.7	757.7	195	124007613
EW	Edwards Lifesciences Corp	Medical Instruments & Equipment	12/31/12	1899.6	293.2	2221.5	1479.3	526	110453612
EE	El Paso Electric Company	Electric Utilities	12/31/12	852.9	90.8	2669.0	825.0	211	43522657
EPB	El Paso Pipeline Partners LP	Equipment & Services	12/31/12	1515.0	579.0	6581.0	10.0	244	94210371
ELN	Elan Corp Plc	Biotechnology	12/31/12	0.2	-137.4	1640.2	618.2	291	328279310
EGO	Eldorado Gold Corp	Precious Metals	12/31/12	1147.5	305.3	7928.1	5929.2	261	362311373
ELLI	Ellie Mae Inc	Internet & Software	12/31/12	101.8	19.5	185.6	166.9	163	22834924
EFC	Ellington Financial LLC	Property, Real Estate & Developmen	12/31/12	63.9	24.2	2152.1	506.4		
AKO B	Embotelladora Andina S.A.	Beverages	12/31/12	982864.4	97024.4	741959.3	421969.9	21	994812
ERJ	Embraer SA	Aerospace	12/31/12	6177.9	347.8	9490.4	3258.3	215	93659401
EMC	EMC Corp. (MA)	Computer Hardware & Equipment	12/31/12	21713.9	2732.6	38068.7	22357.1	1553	1886504713
EME	EMCOR Group, Inc.	Construction Services	12/31/12	6346.7	146.6	3107.1	1346.1	292	74890675
EBS	Emergent BioSolutions Inc	Biotechnology	12/31/12	281.9	23.5	564.2	441.4	157	24748333
ESC	Emeritus Corp.	Hospitals & Health Care Facilities	12/31/12	1568.1	-84.8	4660.8	211.4	135	30142086
EMR	Emerson Electric Co.	Electrical Equipment	9/30/12	24412.0	1968.0	23818.0	10295.0	1434	569202730
EDE	Empire District Electric Co.	Electric Utilities	12/31/12	557.1	55.7	2126.4	717.8	152	21497808
EIG	Employers Holdings Inc	General Insurance	12/31/12	579.2	106.9	3511.3	539.4	124	26634341
EDN	Empresa Distribuidora y Comerciali	Electric Utilities	12/31/11	3565.0	-435.4	5744.4	1314.5	12	1125365
EOC	Empresa Nacional de Electricidad S	Electric Utilities	12/31/12	2369386.4	234335.3	6488689.9	2541242.4	122	9219113
ICA	Empresas ICA S.A. de C.V.	Construction Services	12/31/11	42768.8	1480.3	98888.1	16807.9	52	10173285
ELX	Emulex Corporation	Peripherals	7/1/12	501.8	-11.1	713.0	575.1	233	87334601
EEQ	Enbridge Energy Management LLC	Equipment & Services	12/31/12		31.8	747.3	603.2	134	24299475
EEP	Enbridge Energy Partners, L.P.	Equipment & Services	12/31/12	6706.1	493.1	12796.8		366	106466455
ENB	Enbridge Inc	Equipment & Services	12/31/12	25306.0	715.0	47172.0	10500.0	326	501505257
ECA	EnCana Corp	Production & Extraction	12/31/12	5160.0	-2794.0	18700.0	5295.0	520	468238553
END	Endeavour International Corp	Production & Extraction	12/31/12	219.1	-126.2	1442.5	143.1	126	37471482
EXK	Endeavour Silver Corp	Precious Metals	12/31/12	208.1	42.1	477.5	340.2	104	32017961
ENH	Endurance Specialty Holdings Ltd	General Insurance	12/31/12	2256.3	162.5	8795.0	2710.6	242	48937095
NDRO	Enduro Royalty Trust	Production & Extraction	12/31/12	59.1	58.1	637.8	637.8	35	57375885
EGN	Energen Corp.	Production & Extraction	12/31/12	1617.2	253.6	6175.9	2676.7	364	65595057
ENR	Energizer Holdings, Inc.	Household & Personal Products	9/30/12	4567.2	408.9	6731.2	2069.5	470	57658850
ETE	Energy Transfer Equity L P	Equipment & Services	12/31/12	16964.0	304.0	48904.0	73.0	321	143904353
ETP	Energy Transfer Partners L P	Equipment & Services	12/31/12	15702.0	1569.0	43230.0		494	88302074
ETP	Energy Transfer Partners L P	Equipment & Services	12/31/12	15702.0	1569.0	43230.0		494	88302074
ES	EnergySolutions Inc	Sanitation Services	12/31/12	1807.5	4.0	2655.5	300.4	151	56142598
ERF	Enerplus Corp	Production & Extraction	12/31/12	1188.7	-155.7	5412.2	3049.6		
ENI	Enersis S.A.	Electric Utilities	12/31/12	6577667.3	377350.5	13317833.6	3893798.6	183	69458481
ENS	Enersys	Electrical Equipment	3/31/12	2283.4	144.0	1919.3	1032.2	304	51678443
EGL	Engility Holdings Inc.	Services	12/31/12	1655.3	-350.4	1027.5	375.4		
EGL	Engility Holdings Inc.	Services	12/31/12	1655.3	-350.4	1027.5	375.4		
E	ENI S.p.A.	Production & Extraction	12/31/11	110522.0	6860.0	142945.0	55472.0	220	30213044
EBF	Ennis Inc	Printing	2/29/12	517.0	31.4	532.0	359.9	135	25749264
NPO	EnPro Industries Inc	Industrial Machinery & Equipment	12/31/12	1184.2	41.0	1370.9	547.1	185	22466234
ESV	Ensco plc	Production & Extraction	12/31/12	4300.7	1169.7	18565.3	11846.4	598	214279004
ETM	Entercom Communications Corp	Radio & Television	12/31/12	388.9	11.3	915.6	264.7	96	21770038
EAB	Entergy Arkansas, Inc.	Electric Utilities	12/31/12	2127.0	152.4	7819.4	1696.0		
ETR	Entergy Corp.	Electric Utilities	12/31/12	10302.1	868.4	43202.5	9477.6	631	156762694
ELB	Entergy Louisiana LLC	Electric Utilities	12/31/12	2149.4	281.1	9074.1	3070.5	2	67207
EMZ	Entergy Mississippi, Inc	Electric Utilities	12/31/12	1120.4	46.8	3354.0	930.0	2	52925
ENJ	Entergy New Orleans Inc.	Electric Utilities	12/31/12	569.7	17.1	881.8	215.3		
EDT	Entergy Texas Inc	Electric Utilities	12/31/12	1581.5	42.0	4025.8	854.1	2	15000
EPD	Enterprise Products Partners L.P.	Equipment & Services	12/31/12	42583.1	2428.0	35934.4		757	249975595
EVC	Entravision Communications Corp.	Radio & Television	12/31/12	223.3	13.6	438.1	5.4	83	42936140
ENV	Envestnet Inc	Internet & Software	12/31/11	123.2	7.6	137.7	115.6	64	18797560
ENZ	Enzo Biochem, Inc.	Biotechnology	7/31/12	103.1	-39.3	69.1	49.1	97	14508176
EOG	EOG Resources, Inc.	Production & Extraction	12/31/12	11682.6	570.3	27336.6	13284.8	798	270730385
EPAM	Epam Systems, Inc.	Internet & Software	12/31/12	433.8	54.5	350.8	286.3	71	32807344
EPL	EPL Oil & Gas Inc	Production & Extraction	12/31/12	423.6	58.8	1705.6	546.0	32	5011281
EPR	EPR Properties	REITs	12/31/12	321.8	121.6	2946.7	1459.5	264	51191593
EQT	EQT Corp.	Production & Extraction	12/31/12	1641.6	183.4	8849.9	3603.8	530	131369394
EQM	EQT Midstream Partners LP	Gas Utilities	12/31/12	136.9	55.3	707.6		70	13471267
EQU	Equal Energy Ltd.	Production & Extraction	12/31/12	64.4	61.8	226.2	161.3		
EFX	Equifax, Inc.	Business Services	12/31/12	2160.5	272.1	4511.1	1933.2	513	136682351
ELS	Equity Lifestyle Properties Inc	REITs	12/31/12	709.9	74.5	3398.2	859.2	235	38620163
EQY	Equity One, Inc.	REITs	12/31/12	325.6	-3.5	3502.7	1396.7	219	65797461
EQR	Equity Residential	REITs	12/31/12	2123.7	881.2	17201.0	7289.8	599	337574533

T22

| EARNINGS PER SHARE | | | | | | P/E RATIO | | DIVIDENDS PER SHARE | | | AV. YLD % | DIV. DECLARED | | PRICE RANGE | |
| QUARTERLY | | | ANNUAL | | | | | PER SHARE | | | | | | 2012 | |
1st	2nd	3rd	2012	2011	2010			2012	2011	2010		AMOUNT	PAYABLE		
-	-	-	0.22	0.20	0.16	52.0 -	0.0	1.17	1.21	1.47	10.8	0.09730	4/30/13	11.4 -	0.0
-	-	-	1.17	1.33	1.24	13.7 -	0.0	1.23	1.23	1.23	8.8	0.10250	4/30/13	16.0 -	0.0
-	-	-	0.04	0.06	0.02	458.8 -	0.0	1.70	1.70	0.85	9.6	0.4250	3/28/13	18.4 -	0.0
-	-	-	1.41	1.43	1.48	16.5 -	0.0	1.40	1.40	1.40	7.1	0.1350	4/30/13	23.3 -	0.0
-	-	-	0.21	0.19	0.19	72.7 -	0.0	1.30	1.30	1.80	9.3	0.1080	4/30/13	15.3 -	0.0
-	-	-	0.13	0.09	0.09	102.8 -	0.0	1.33	1.33	1.53	10.5	0.11080	4/30/13	13.4 -	0.0
-	-	-	0.14	0.12	0.14	73.6 -	0.0	1.09	1.27	1.68	11.5	0.08430	4/30/13	10.3 -	0.0
-	-	-	0.19	0.19	0.20	50.1 -	0.0	1.06	1.24	1.62	12.1	0.08130	4/30/13	9.5 -	0.0
-	-	624.00	2.48	2.38	1.19	8.9 -	0.0	2.39	2.29	0.69	13.0	0.6820	2/28/13	22.1 -	0.0
-	-	624.00	2.48	2.38	1.19	6.4 -	0.0	2.39	2.29	0.69	21.8	0.6820	2/28/13	15.8 -	0.0
-	-	0.80	2.35	1.91	2.23	34.1 -	0.0	0.83	0.72	0.64	1.2	0.230Y	81/16/21	80.2 -	0.0
-	-	-	-	-	-			-	-	-		-		67.5 -	0.0
-	0.21	-1.21	-	-	-			-	-	-		-		9.5 -	0.0
-	0.58	-0.56	-0.11	3.82				1.31	1.28	1.26	2.9	0.33750Y	81/16/21	51.2 -	0.0
-	-	0.08	-0.15	-0.73		147.4 -	0.0	0.34	0.24	0.20	3.1	0.10Z	2/15/13	11.8 -	0.0
-	0.58	2.48	1.98	1.83		44.3 -	0.0	-	-	-		-		109.8 -	0.0
-	1.29	2.26	2.48	2.31		15.5 -	0.0	0.97	0.66	-	3.0	0.250Y	3/29/13	35.0 -	0.0
-	0.55	2.15	2.03	1.90		20.4 -	0.0	2.14	1.87	1.55	5.9	0.610	2/14/13	43.9 -	0.0
-	-0.38	-0.23	0.94	-0.56				-	-	-		1.157	4/12/01	15.0 -	0.0
-	0.11	0.44	0.58	0.40		36.3 -	0.0	0.15	0.11	0.05	1.2	0.070	2/14/13	16.0 -	0.0
-	0.25	0.76	0.18	0.05		38.1 -	0.0	-	-	-		-		28.9 -	0.0
-	0.04	1.35	2.71	1.91		19.8 -	0.0	2.50	2.51	0.80	11.2	0.757	3/15/13	26.8 -	0.0
-	16.95	-	255.23	272.53				-	0.00	0.00		-		41.9 -	0.0
-	0.09	0.48	0.15	0.46		74.3 -	0.0	0.35	0.52	0.72	1.2	-		35.7 -	0.0
-	0.28	1.23	1.10	0.88		24.3 -	0.0	-	-	-		-		29.9 -	0.0
-	0.59	2.16	1.91	-1.31		19.6 -	0.0	0.51	0.05	-	1.6	0.060Y	81/16/21	42.4 -	0.0
-	0.18	0.65	0.64	1.59		26.0 -	0.0	-	-	-		-		16.9 -	0.0
-	-0.36	-1.90	-1.63	-1.42				-	-	-		-		30.6 -	0.0
0.62	-	2.67	3.27	2.84		21.9 -	0.0	1.60	1.38	1.34	3.2	0.410Y	81/16/21	58.6 -	0.0
-	0.60	1.32	1.31	1.17		17.0 -	0.4	1.00	0.64	1.28	4.8	0.250Y	3/15/13	22.4 -	0.0
-	0.26	3.37	1.29	1.51		7.0 -	0.0	0.24	0.24	0.24	1.3	0.060Y	3/27/13	23.4 -	0.0
-	-	-	-	-				-	-	-		-		3.8 -	0.0
-	-	28.57	54.49	65.05		1.9 -	0.0	0.00	0.00	0.00	0.0	-		55.4 -	0.0
-	-	-	2.34	0.97				-	-	-		-		13.5 -	0.0
0.06	-	-0.13	-0.97	0.29				-	-	-		-		10.4 -	0.0
-	0.38	0.80	1.24	-0.69		40.8 -	0.0	-	-	-		-		32.6 -	0.0
-	0.60	1.27	1.99	-1.09		24.7 -	0.0	2.15	2.09	2.02	7.4	0.54350	81/16/21	31.4 -	0.0
-	0.24	0.78	1.30	1.29		60.6 -	0.0	1.13	0.98	0.85	2.8	0.2356GH	3/1/13	47.3 -	0.0
-	-1.69	-3.79	0.17	1.55				0.80	0.80	0.80	3.9	0.20	3/28/13	24.0 -	0.0
-	-0.73	-3.01	-3.70	1.95				-	-	-		-		12.8 -	0.0
-	0.00	0.42	0.22	-0.31		25.3 -	0.0	-	-	-		-		10.6 -	0.0
-	0.74	3.00	-2.95	6.38		15.9 -	0.0	1.24	4.08	2.94	3.1	0.320	81/16/21	47.8 -	0.0
-	0.43	-	-	-				1.75	0.46	-	9.9	0.05660Z	4/12/13	21.7 -	0.0
-	0.03	3.51	3.59	4.04		15.8 -	0.0	0.56	0.54	0.52	1.2	0.1450Y	81/16/21	55.5 -	0.0
2.07	-	6.22	3.72	5.72		16.0 -	0.0	0.40	-	-	0.5	0.40Y	81/16/21	99.7 -	0.0
-	0.13	1.13	1.38	0.86		51.8 -	0.0	2.50	2.35	2.16	5.6	0.6350	81/16/21	58.5 -	0.0
-	-0.33	4.42	1.10	1.19		10.1 -	9.3	3.58	3.58	3.58	8.3	0.89380	2/14/13	44.6 -	41.3
-	-0.33	4.42	1.10	1.19		11.5 -	0.0	3.58	3.58	3.58	8.0	0.89380	2/14/13	51.0 -	0.0
-	0.11	0.04	-2.21	-0.25		120.5 -	0.0	-	-	0.07		0.0250Y	9/10/10	4.8 -	0.0
-	-0.32	-0.80	0.16	-1.02				1.62	1.98	-	11.1	0.090Y	4/19/13	22.7 -	0.0
-	-	11.56	11.50	14.89		1.8 -	0.0	0.00	0.00	0.00	0.0	-		20.8 -	0.0
-	0.80	2.93	2.27	1.28		15.6 -	0.0	-	-	-		-		45.6 -	0.0
-	-25.80	-21.52	-	-				-	-	-		-		20.8 -	17.5
-	-25.80	-21.52	-	-				-	-	-		-		24.2 -	0.0
-	0.69	-	1.89	1.74				-	2.84	2.38		-		52.1 -	0.0
-	0.24	1.21	1.72	1.36		14.0 -	0.0	0.62	0.62	0.62	4.1	0.35HY	12/28/12	16.9 -	0.0
-	0.53	1.90	2.06	7.51		26.9 -	0.0	-	-	-		-		51.2 -	0.0
-	1.48	5.04	3.08	4.06		13.0 -	0.0	1.50	1.40	1.08	2.7	-		65.5 -	0.0
-	0.22	0.30	1.81	1.23		27.1 -	0.0	-	-	-		0.10Y	9/26/08	8.1 -	0.0
-	-	-	-	-				-	-	-		0.40310Y	4/1/13	25.5 -	24.8
-	1.89	4.76	7.55	6.66		15.3 -	0.0	3.32	3.32	3.24	5.0	0.830Y	81/16/21	73.1 -	0.0
-	-	-	-	-				0.65	-	-	2.4	1.73750Z	3/15/13	28.9 -	0.0
-	-	-	-	-				1.50	0.82	-	5.4	0.39060Y	5/1/13	29.4 -	0.0
-	-	-	-	-				-	-	-		1.390Y	4/1/13	25.2 -	24.8
-	-	-	-	-				1.97	1.97	1.97	6.9	0.49220Z	6/3/13	30.6 -	0.0
-	0.66	2.71	2.38	1.15		22.2 -	0.0	2.53	2.40	2.29	4.8	0.670	81/16/21	60.3 -	0.0
-	0.08	0.16	-0.10	-0.21		21.5 -	0.0	0.12	0.06	-	7.8	0.127Y	12/28/12	3.4 -	0.0
-	0.02	-	0.23	-0.05				-	-	-		-		17.5 -	0.0
-	-0.14	-	-1.01	-0.34	-0.59			-	-	-		-		3.1 -	0.0
-	1.31	2.11	4.10	0.63		63.6 -	0.0	0.67	0.64	0.61	0.6	0.18750Y	81/16/21	134.1 -	0.0
-	0.30	1.17	0.63	0.79		20.2 -	0.0	-	-	-		-		23.7 -	0.0
-	-0.06	1.50	0.66	-0.21		18.9 -	0.0	-	-	-		-		28.4 -	0.0
-	0.60	1.98	1.80	1.86		26.3 -	0.0	3.00	2.80	2.60	6.6	0.41410Z	4/15/13	52.0 -	0.0
-	0.21	1.22	3.19	1.57		55.9 -	0.0	0.88	0.88	0.88	1.6	0.030Y	81/16/21	68.2 -	0.0
-	-	0.90	-	-		44.7 -	0.0	0.35	-	-	1.1	0.350	2/14/13	40.3 -	0.0
-	0.35	1.58	-0.44	-1.73		2.6 -	0.0	-	-	-		0.05G	3/31/13	4.0 -	0.0
-	0.64	2.22	1.88	2.11		26.9 -	0.0	0.72	0.64	0.28	1.4	0.220Y	81/16/21	59.7 -	0.0
-	0.39	1.32	0.64	1.25		58.2 -	0.0	1.75	1.50	1.20	2.5	0.42190	81/16/21	76.8 -	0.0
-	0.07	-0.04	0.29	0.27				0.88	0.88	0.88	4.1	0.220Z	81/16/21	24.1 -	0.0
-	0.72	2.70	2.95	0.95		24.2 -	0.0	1.78	1.58	1.47	3.0	1.03620Z	81/16/21	65.5 -	0.0

SYMBOL	COMPANY	NATURE OF BUSINESS	FISCAL YEAR-END	TOTAL REV. $MILL	NET INCOME $MILL	TOTAL ASSETS $MILL	NET STK EQUITY $MILL	NO OF INST	INST. HOLDINGS (SHARES)
EQS	Equus Total Return, Inc.	Holding and other Investment Office	12/31/12	0.5	-2.7	33.3	32.9	16	1064510
ERA	ERA Group Inc	Equipment & Services	12/31/12	272.9	7.8	937.6	419.3	-	-
ERA	ERA Group Inc	Equipment & Services	12/31/12	272.9	7.8	937.6	419.3	-	-
ESE	ESCO Technologies, Inc.	Industrial Machinery & Equipment	9/30/12	688.4	46.9	1033.8	631.3	185	25862742
ESS	Essex Property Trust, Inc.	REITs	12/31/12	543.4	125.3	4847.2	1769.2	336	40373743
ESL	Esterline Technologies Corp	Electronic Instruments & Related Pro	10/26/12	1992.3	112.5	3227.1	1610.5	259	32257082
DEG	Etablissements Delhaize Freres et	Retail - Food & Beverage, Drug & To	12/31/11	21119.0	475.0	12242.0	5416.0	82	3606704
ETH	Ethan Allen Interiors, Inc.	Furniture	6/30/12	729.4	49.7	644.8	321.7	174	31138340
EEA	European Equity Fund Inc (The)	Holding and other Investment Office	12/31/12	2.5	1.2	79.2	77.5	32	4648767
EEA	European Equity Fund Inc (The)	Holding and other Investment Office	12/31/12	2.5	1.2	79.2	77.5	32	4648767
EVER	EverBank Financial Corp	Banking	12/31/12	1025.3	74.0	18242.9	1451.2	123	73802798
EVR	Evercore Partners Inc	Finance Intermediaries & Services	12/31/12	642.4	28.9	1145.2	428.5	142	29368948
RE	Everest Re Group Ltd	General Insurance	12/31/12	4922.8	829.0	19777.9	6733.5	394	50905105
ET	ExactTarget Inc	IT Services	12/31/12	292.3	-21.0	387.1	281.6	124	47671228
EXAM	ExamWorks Group Inc	Diagnostic & Health Related Service	12/31/12	521.2	-14.9	740.5	244.1	89	21743318
EXM	Excel Maritime Carriers Ltd.	Shipping	12/31/11	356.9	-211.6	2721.9	1549.0	62	4966773
EXL	Excel Trust Inc.	REITs	12/31/12	87.1	1.9	1079.3	594.0	102	39455183
XCO	Exco Resources Inc.	Production & Extraction	12/31/12	546.6	-1393.3	2323.7	149.4	271	202295063
XLS	Exelis Inc.	Manufacturing	12/31/12	5522.0	330.0	5212.0	1016.0	320	157611909
EXC	Exelon Corp.	Electric Utilities	12/31/12	23489.0	1171.0	78554.0	21518.0	1052	564718950
EXC 17A	Exelon Generation Co LLC	Electric Utilities	12/31/12	14437.0	562.0	40681.0	12557.0	1	0
EXPR	Express, Inc.	Retail - Apparel and Accessories	2/2/13	2148.1	139.3	1019.2	371.2	234	82250117
EXH	Exterran Holdings Inc	Equipment & Services	12/31/12	2803.6	-39.5	4254.8	1478.6	187	57680642
EXR	Extra Space Storage Inc	REITs	12/31/12	409.4	127.7	3223.5	1491.8	280	111297827
XOM	Exxon Mobil Corp.	Refining & Marketing	12/31/12	482295.0	44880.0	333795.0	165863.0	2313	2567675991
FNB	F.N.B. Corp.	Banking	12/31/12	563.4	110.4	12024.0	1402.1	223	90064049
FN	Fabrinet	Manufacturing	6/29/12	564.7	-56.5	461.4	250.7	91	29605307
FDS	FactSet Research Systems Inc.	Internet & Software	8/31/12	805.8	188.8	694.1	552.3	364	49783288
FICO	Fair Isaac Corp	Internet & Software	9/30/12	676.4	92.0	1158.6	474.4	273	38235261
FCS	Fairchild Semiconductor Internation	Semiconductors	12/30/12	1405.9	24.6	1883.9	1370.0	271	141565980
FDO	Family Dollar Stores, Inc.	Retail - General Merchandise/Depart	8/25/12	9331.0	422.2	3373.1	1297.6	553	127294940
FFG	FBL Financial Group, Inc.	Life & Health	12/31/12	655.5	79.9	8417.7	1212.2	102	7436264
AGM	Federal Agricultural Mortgage Corp.	Credit & Lending	12/31/12	268.4	46.8	12622.2	351.1	97	7285073
FRT	Federal Realty Investment Trust (M	REITs	12/31/12	608.0	151.9	3898.6	1286.8	397	64814227
FSS	Federal Signal Corp.	Industrial Machinery & Equipment	12/31/12	803.2	-27.5	613.2	146.9	162	53419759
FTT	Federated Enhanced Treasury Inco	Holding and other Investment Office	11/30/12	3.0	1.4	148.1	147.7	26	2901381
FII	Federated Investors Inc (PA)	Wealth Management	12/31/12	945.7	188.1	1090.1	495.4	396	96760815
FPT	Federated Premier Intermediate Mu	Holding and other Investment Office	11/30/12	6.7	5.2	171.9	121.5	24	655811
FMN	Federated Premier Municipal Incom	Holding and other Investment Office	11/30/12	7.2	5.8	156.3	117.5	10	174440
FDX	FedEx Corp	Airlines/Air Freight	5/31/12	42680.0	2032.0	29903.0	14727.0	1002	259909456
ADY	Feihe International Inc	Food	12/31/12	267.9	21.2	476.3	201.8	47	4869743
FCH	FelCor Lodging Trust, Inc.	REITs	12/31/12	909.5	-128.0	2202.4	394.7	208	104483226
FGP	Ferrellgas Partners, L.P.	Gas Utilities	7/31/12	2339.1	-11.0	1397.3	-	107	4085748
FOE	Ferro Corp.	Specialty Chemicals	12/31/12	1768.6	-374.3	1079.1	193.5	188	78165942
FBR	Fibria Celulose SA	Paper & Forest Products	12/31/11	5854.3	-872.6	27853.5	14510.9	111	58097119
FNF	Fidelity National Financial Inc	General Insurance	12/31/12	7201.7	606.5	9902.6	4268.0	426	202947653
FIS	Fidelity National Information Service	Business Services	12/31/12	5807.6	461.2	13549.7	6640.9	540	266144789
FMO	Fiduciary / Claymore MLP Opportun	Holding and other Investment Office	11/30/12	0.2	-6.0	943.6	570.1	56	4701607
FNP	Fifth & Pacific Companies, Inc.	Apparel, Footwear & Accessories	12/29/12	1505.1	-74.5	902.5	-126.9	269	127508284
FAC	First Acceptance Corp	General Insurance	12/31/12	228.1	-9.0	262.3	72.8	39	6582858
FAF	First American Financial Corp	General Insurance	12/31/12	4541.8	301.0	6050.8	2348.1	268	89399937
FBP	First Bancorp	Banking	12/31/12	687.2	29.8	13099.7	1485.0	143	151925978
FCF	First Commonwealth Financial Corp	Banking	12/31/12	284.5	42.0	5995.4	746.0	150	63428030
FHN	First Horizon National Corp	Banking	12/31/12	1470.3	-27.8	25520.1	2214.0	373	215342247
FR	First Industrial Realty Trust, Inc.	REITs	12/31/12	327.3	-1.3	2608.8	1103.4	236	98401452
AG	First Majestic Silver Corp	Precious Metals	12/31/12	247.2	88.9	813.0	593.5	118	49511949
FMD	First Marblehead Corp	Credit & Lending	6/30/12	40.7	1102.2	457.8	227.0	115	49051315
FPO	First Potomac Realty Trust	REITs	12/31/12	193.3	-7.4	1717.7	658.8	187	52134261
FRC	First Republic Bank (San Francisco,	Banking	12/31/11	1300.9	352.1	27791.8	2517.8	303	134411331
FEO	First Trust / Aberdeen Emerging Op	Holding and other Investment Office	12/31/12	6.9	4.8	132.5	126.1	24	2105455
FAM	First Trust / Aberdeen Global Oppor	Holding and other Investment Office	12/31/12	27.1	20.6	419.6	319.6	38	3747956
FAV	First Trust Active Dividend Income	Holding and other Investment Office	11/30/12	5.3	4.2	76.7	71.3	32	977043
FIF	First Trust Energy Infrastructure Fu	Holding and other Investment Office	11/30/12	12.0	4.8	543.0	399.1	22	1757539
FFA	First Trust Enhanced Equity Income	Holding and other Investment Office	12/31/12	8.3	5.1	265.9	265.0	37	3747721
FSD	First Trust High Income Long / Shor	Holding and other Investment Office	10/31/12	63.2	50.9	867.3	686.7	43	4867412
FEI	First Trust MLP & Energy Income F	Finance Intermediaries & Services	10/11/12			0.1	0.1	-	-
FMY	First Trust Mortgage Income Fund	Holding and other Investment Office	10/31/12	7.1	5.3	105.6	75.4	26	1268372
FCT	First Trust Senior Floating Rate Inco	Holding and other Investment Office	5/31/12	29.9	23.1	570.1	367.2	50	6091920
FGB	First Trust Specialty Finance and Fi	Holding and other Investment Office	11/30/12	10.4	8.5	138.8	112.1	21	1632450
FHY	First Trust Strategic High Income Fu	Holding and other Investment Office	11/30/12	16.2	12.8	199.0	144.2	38	1680280
FE	FirstEnergy Corp.	Electric Utilities	12/31/12	15303.0	770.0	50406.0	13084.0	653	309457422
OAKS	Five Oaks Investment Corp	REITs	12/31/12	6.0	4.8	97.0	32.3	-	-
FVE	Five Star Quality Care Inc	Hospitals & Health Care Facilities	12/31/12	1350.9	24.9	571.4	306.8	147	34529238
FBC	Flagstar Bancorp, Inc.	Credit & Lending	12/31/12	1502.2	68.4	14082.0	1159.4	141	49225562
PFD	Flaherty & Crumrine Preferred Inco	Holding and other Investment Office	11/30/12	16.3	13.6	225.5	147.5	36	462682
PFO	Flaherty & Crumrine Preferred Inco	Holding and other Investment Office	11/30/12	14.9	12.4	209.0	136.6	27	1105856
FFC	Flaherty & Crumrine Preferred Secu	Holding and other Investment Office	11/30/12	86.9	74.4	1251.2	821.3	71	4802810
FLC	Flaherty & Crumrine Total Return F	Holding and other Investment Office	11/30/12	20.4	16.8	310.4	199.4	29	1496184
FLT	FleetCor Technologies Inc	Business Services	12/31/12	707.5	216.2	2721.9	913.8	189	68806489
FLTX	Fleetmatics Group Plc	IT Services	12/31/12	127.5	5.4	210.6	121.0	-	-

| EARNINGS PER SHARE | | | | | | P/E RATIO | | DIVIDENDS PER SHARE | | | AV. YLD | DIV. DECLARED | | PRICE RANGE | |
| QUARTERLY | | | ANNUAL | | | | | PER SHARE | | | % | | | 2012 | |
1st	2nd	3rd	2012	2011	2010			2012	2011	2010		AMOUNT	PAYABLE		
		-0.50	-0.45	-0.09		-		-				0.1580	9/29/08	2.5 -	0.0
			-0.03	0.18	3639.00	-		-						20.4 -	18.1
			-0.03	0.18	3639.00	-		-						23.8 -	19.5
0.01			1.73	1.95	1.68	24.5 -	0.0	0.32	0.32	0.24	0.9	0.080Y	1/18/13	42.4 -	0.0
		0.45	3.41	1.24	1.14	47.0 -	0.0	4.40	4.16	4.13	2.9	0.44530Z	81/16/21	160.3 -	0.0
0.80			3.60	4.27	4.66	21.5 -	0.0	-				0.09	81/16/21	77.4 -	0.0
		1.87		4.68	5.68	-		-	2.71	1.81		-		54.8 -	0.0
	0.34		1.71	1.01	-1.53	19.4 -	0.0	0.28	0.20	0.20	1.1	0.090Y	4/25/13	33.1 -	0.0
			0.12	0.11	0.07	0.0 -	0.0	0.15	0.01	0.06	1.$	0.1520	1/28/13	0.0 -	0.0
			0.12	0.11	0.07	63.5 -	0.0	0.15	0.01	0.06	2.2	0.1520	1/28/13	7.6 -	0.0
		0.19	0.60	0.54	1.94	28.3 -	0.0	0.04	-		0.3	0.42190Y	4/5/13	17.0 -	0.0
		0.17	0.89	0.23	0.39	49.8 -	0.0	0.82	0.74	0.63	2.9	0.220Y	3/8/13	44.3 -	0.0
		4.82	15.79	-1.49	10.70	8.3 -	0.0	1.92	1.92	1.92	1.8	0.480	81/16/21	130.6 -	0.0
		-0.01	-0.39	-4.05	-1.52	-		-				-		27.0 -	0.0
		-0.14	-0.44	-0.25	-0.33	-		-				-		17.6 -	0.0
	-0.37		-	-2.51	3.10	-		-				0.40	12/5/08	2.0 -	0.0
		-0.07	-0.26	-0.15	-0.24	-		0.65	0.60	0.20	5.4	0.50780Z	4/15/13	13.8 -	0.0
		-1.62	-6.50	0.10	3.11	-		0.16	0.16	0.14	2.2	0.050Y	81/16/21	8.9 -	0.0
		0.47	1.76	1.75	3.14	6.9 -	0.0	0.41	0.10	-	3.8	0.10330	4/1/13	12.2 -	0.0
		0.35	1.42	3.75	3.87	27.8 -	0.0	2.10	2.10	2.10	6.1	0.5250Y	81/16/21	39.5 -	0.0
		0.20	1.58	1.48		15.9 -	0.0	-	0.56			0.567	12/23/10	25.1 -	0.0
		1.74	-0.62	-5.44	-1.64	-		-				-		27.3 -	0.0
		0.37	1.14	0.54	0.30	35.4 -	0.0	0.85	0.56	0.40	2.5	0.250Z	81/16/21	40.4 -	0.0
		2.09	9.70	8.42	6.22	9.6 -	0.0	2.18	1.85	1.74	2.5	0.570Y	81/16/21	93.5 -	0.0
		0.22	0.79	0.70	0.65	15.6 -	0.0	0.48	0.48	0.48	4.3	0.120Y	3/15/13	12.3 -	0.0
	0.48		-1.64	1.87	1.41	-		-		1.00		-		18.1 -	0.0
	1.00		4.12	3.61	3.13	26.3 -	0.0	1.16	1.00	0.86	1.2	0.310Y	81/16/21	108.5 -	0.0
0.65			2.64	1.79	1.42	18.1 -	0.0	0.08	0.08	0.08	0.2	0.020Y	81/16/21	47.9 -	0.0
		0.19	0.19	1.12	1.20	82.1 -	0.0	-				-		15.6 -	0.0
	1.21		3.58	3.12	2.62	20.5 -	0.0	0.78	0.67	0.58	1.2	0.260Y	81/16/21	73.3 -	0.0
		0.76	2.87	1.00	3.92	13.6 -	0.0	0.40	0.29	0.25	1.3	0.110Y	3/29/13	39.0 -	0.0
		1.49	3.98	1.28	2.08	9.5 -	0.0	0.40	0.20	0.20	1.4	0.3672GY	4/17/13	37.7 -	0.0
		0.60	2.35	2.28	1.98	46.8 -	0.0	2.84	2.72	2.66	2.7	0.730Z	81/16/21	110.0 -	0.0
		-0.24	-0.44	-0.23	-3.05	-		0.00	-	0.24	0.0	0.060Y	1/4/11	8.4 -	0.0
			0.15	0.21	0.15	99.7 -	0.0	0.88	1.02	1.08	6.2	0.0510	4/30/13	15.0 -	0.0
		0.54	1.79	1.45	1.73	14.1 -	0.0	2.47	0.96	2.22	11.6	0.240Y	81/16/21	25.2 -	0.0
			0.74	0.83	0.86	21.9 -	0.0	0.78	0.81	0.87	5.1	0.0605M	5/1/13	16.2 -	0.0
			0.94	1.02	1.05	18.7 -	0.0	1.00	1.02	1.05	6.1	0.0755M	5/1/13	17.6 -	0.0
		1.13	6.41	4.57	3.76	17.0 -	0.0	0.52	0.48	0.44	0.6	0.140Y	81/16/21	109.1 -	0.0
		0.38	1.05	0.00	-0.48	8.3 -	0.0	-				-		8.7 -	0.0
		-0.23	-1.35	-1.44	-3.25	-		-				0.50Z	4/30/13	6.0 -	0.0
	0.70		-0.14	-0.60	0.47	-		2.00	2.00	2.00	10.9	0.50	3/15/13	21.8 -	0.0
		-3.66	-4.34	0.36	0.06	-		-				0.010Y	3/10/09	6.9 -	0.0
			-1.87	1.28		-		-	0.21			-		13.1 -	0.0
		1.03	2.68	1.66	1.61	9.8 -	0.0	0.58	0.48	0.69	2.7	0.160Y	81/16/21	26.1 -	0.0
		0.29	1.55	1.53	1.15	25.6 -	0.0	0.80	0.20	0.20	2.4	0.220Y	81/16/21	39.6 -	0.0
			-0.41	-0.41	-0.36	-		1.50	1.39	1.34	6.6	0.3960	2/28/13	25.3 -	0.0
		-0.17	-0.68	-1.35	-2.67	-		-				0.05630Y	12/15/08	19.2 -	0.0
		0.08	-0.22	-0.62	0.14	-		-				0.0067	6/28/02	1.6 -	0.0
		0.95	2.77	0.73	1.20	0.2 -	0.0	0.00	0.24	0.40	1.7	0.120Y	3/15/13	25.6 -	0.0
		0.09	0.14	2.18	-10.79	45.0 -	0.0	-				1.050	6/30/09	6.3 -	0.0
		0.09	0.40	0.15	0.25	19.3 -	0.0	0.18	0.12	0.06	2.7	0.050Y	2/22/13	7.7 -	0.0
		0.10	-0.11	0.50	-0.25	-		0.04	0.04	-	0.4	0.050Y	81/16/21	11.3 -	0.0
		0.04	-0.24	-0.34	-3.53	-		0.00	0.00	0.00	0.0	0.45310Z	4/1/13	17.1 -	0.0
		0.21	0.79	0.96	0.36	30.0 -	0.0	-				-		23.7 -	0.0
	-0.12		9.96	-2.20	-1.46	0.1 -	0.0	-				0.120Y	12/21/07	1.3 -	0.0
		0.08	-0.40	-0.35	-0.33	-		0.80	0.80	0.80	6.4	0.48440Z	2/15/13	14.8 -	0.0
		0.72	-	2.65	1.12	-		-				0.120Y	5/15/13	38.6 -	0.0
			0.90	0.98	0.97	26.3 -	0.0	1.40	1.40	1.40	6.6	0.350	3/28/13	23.7 -	0.0
			1.18	1.22	1.28	15.8 -	0.0	1.56	1.56	1.56	8.8	0.130	4/15/13	18.6 -	0.0
			0.51	0.84	1.15	17.1 -	0.0	0.72	1.02	1.42	9.1	0.150	4/30/13	8.7 -	0.0
			0.27	0.05		88.3 -	0.0	1.30	-		6.0	0.110	4/15/13	23.8 -	0.0
			0.26	0.22	0.24	51.0 -	0.0	0.90	0.90	0.88	7.5	0.2250	3/28/13	13.3 -	0.0
			1.41	1.48	0.08	13.5 -	0.0	1.60	1.47	-	8.8	0.11550	4/15/13	19.1 -	0.0
						-		-				0.10830	4/15/13	21.1 -	20.0
			1.28	1.69	2.06	16.1 -	0.0	2.03	2.03	1.65	10.8	0.10	4/15/13	20.6 -	0.0
			0.91	0.73	0.47	18.4 -	0.0	0.87	0.70	0.42	5.7	0.08750	4/15/13	16.8 -	0.0
			0.59	0.66	0.56	15.2 -	0.0	0.65	0.63	0.60	8.3	0.1650	2/28/13	9.0 -	0.0
			1.52	0.59	1.86	11.8 -	0.0	1.55	0.12	-	9.1	0.120	4/15/13	17.9 -	0.0
		1.01	1.84	2.21	2.57	27.6 -	0.0	2.20	2.20	2.20	5.0	0.550Y	81/16/21	50.9 -	0.0
			2.88			5.1 -	5.0	0.64			4.4	0.160Z	6/27/13	14.6 -	14.5
		0.33	0.52	1.45	0.64	12.9 -	0.0	-				-		6.7 -	0.0
		1.36	0.87	-3.60	-24.40	23.3 -	0.0	-				0.50Y	12/31/07	20.3 -	0.0
			1.25	1.14	1.07	12.5 -	0.0	1.16	1.12	0.96	7.9	0.090	4/30/13	15.6 -	0.0
			1.02	0.89	0.89	12.3 -	0.0	0.95	0.92	0.78	8.1	0.0730	4/30/13	12.6 -	0.0
			1.72	1.67	1.57	12.0 -	0.0	1.70	1.62	1.43	8.8	0.1360	4/30/13	20.7 -	0.0
			1.71	1.69	1.60	12.6 -	0.0	1.73	1.68	1.48	8.6	0.1360	4/30/13	21.6 -	0.0
		0.69	2.52	1.76	1.34	30.4 -	0.0	-				-		76.7 -	0.0
			0.50	0.08	-0.77	54.4 -	0.0	-				-		27.2 -	0.0

SYMBOL	COMPANY	NATURE OF BUSINESS	FISCAL YEAR-END	TOTAL REV. $MILL	NET INCOME $MILL	TOTAL ASSETS $MILL	NET STK EQUITY $MILL	NO OF INST	INST. HOLDINGS (SHARES)
FTK	Flotek Industries Inc	Specialty Chemicals	12/31/12	312.8	49.8	219.9	154.7	148	35074055
FLO	Flowers Foods, Inc.	Food	12/29/12	3046.5	136.1	1995.8	858.6	297	92628809
FLS	Flowserve Corp.	Industrial Machinery & Equipment	12/31/12	4751.3	448.3	4811.0	1890.2	587	48280908
FLR	Fluor Corp.	Construction Services	12/31/12	27577.1	456.3	8276.0	3341.3	692	145727431
FLY	Fly Leasing Ltd.	Airlines/Air Freight	12/31/12	432.7	47.7	2968.7	532.0	68	16500607
FMC	FMC Corp.	Diversified Chemicals	12/31/12	3748.3	416.2	4373.9	1480.3	492	128091152
FTI	FMC Technologies, Inc.	Equipment & Services	12/31/12	6151.4	430.0	5902.9	1836.9	488	237488200
FMX	Fomento Economico Mexicano, S.A	Beverages	12/31/11	203044.0	15133.0	274704.0	133580.0	326	114852549
FL	Foot Locker, Inc.	Retail - Apparel and Accessories	2/2/13	6182.0	397.0	3367.0	2377.0	484	156229581
F	Ford Motor Co. (DE)	Autos- Manufacturing	12/31/12	134252.0	5665.0	190554.0	15947.0	1106	2444247936
F 12A	Ford Motor Credit Company LLC	Credit & Lending	12/31/12	2778.0	1214.0	105744.0	9653.0	1	2
FCE A	Forest City Enterprises, Inc.	Property, Real Estate & Development	1/31/13	1134.7	36.4	10612.4	1476.9	5	90170
FRX	Forest Laboratories, Inc.	Pharmaceuticals	3/31/12	4586.0	979.1	7491.8	5676.8	577	271242728
FST	Forest Oil Corp.	Production & Extraction	12/31/12	605.7	-1288.9	2201.9	-42.8	285	139691567
FOR	Forestar Group Inc	Property, Real Estate & Development	12/31/12	172.6	12.9	918.4	529.5	156	31864290
FDI	Fort Dearborn Income Securities Inc	Holding and other Investment Office	9/30/12	6.9	5.9	160.6	156.8	27	750533
FRF	Fortegra Financial Corp	Brokers & Intermediaries	12/31/12	291.6	15.2	728.0	140.4	46	18002904
FIG	Fortress Investment Group LLC	Wealth Management	12/31/12	891.8	78.3	2161.5	626.5	120	150958564
FSM	Fortuna Silver Mines Inc	Precious Metals	12/31/12	161.0	31.5	316.3	264.5		
FBHS	Fortune Brands Home & Security, In	Household Appliances, Electronics &	12/31/12	3591.1	118.7	3873.7	2381.1	341	142117529
FET	Forum Energy Technologies Inc	Equipment & Services	12/31/12	1414.9	151.5	1893.0	1161.5	105	40872112
FTE	France Telecom S.A.	Services	12/31/12	43253.0	820.0	89980.0	24306.0	217	58902697
FNV	Franco-Nevada Corp	Precious Metals	12/31/11	411.2	-6.8	2901.0	2834.2		
FC	Franklin Covey Co.	Business Services	8/31/12	170.5	7.8	164.1	90.6	64	6287889
BEN	Franklin Resources, Inc.	Wealth Management	9/30/12	7101.0	1931.4	14751.5	9201.3	728	119694028
FT	Franklin Universal Trust	Holding and other Investment Office	8/31/12	15.6	11.2	314.4	187.7	33	1850897
FCX	Freeport-McMoRan Copper & Gold	Non-Precious Metals	12/31/12	18010.0	3980.0	35440.0	17543.0	1307	719646690
FSL	Freescale Semiconductor Ltd	Semiconductors	12/31/12	3945.0	-102.0	3171.0	-4531.0	119	657609952
FMS	Fresenius Medical Care AG & Co K	Diagnostic & Health Related Service	12/31/12	13800.3	1186.8	22326.0	8942.5	217	23499921
FDP	Fresh Del Monte Produce Inc.	Food	12/28/12	3421.2	143.2	2533.4	1795.7	177	39303230
FRO	Frontline Ltd	Shipping	12/31/12	684.9	-82.8	1688.2	-119.7	130	11042594
FCN	FTI Consulting Inc.	Business Services	12/31/12	1576.9	-37.0	2275.5	1068.2	229	44440742
FUL	Fuller (H.B.) Company	Specialty Chemicals	12/1/12	1886.2	125.6	1786.3	778.3	219	54025593
FRM	Furmanite Corp	Construction Services	12/31/12	326.5	0.8	231.6	119.1	102	22583068
FBN	Furniture Brands International Inc.	Furniture	12/29/12	1072.3	-47.3	618.4	54.8	85	30422955
FIO	Fusion-io Inc.	Computer Hardware & Equipment	6/30/12	359.3	-5.6	541.0	460.9	245	94244128
FF	FutureFuel Corp	Specialty Chemicals	12/31/12	351.8	34.3	355.2	260.3	88	15373512
FXCM	FXCM Inc	Brokers & Intermediaries	12/31/12	417.3	9.0	2065.2	181.6	94	26496968
GCV	Gabelli Convertible and Income Sec	Holding and other Investment Office	12/31/12	2.9	1.4	101.5	101.1	17	2561664
GDV	Gabelli Dividend & Income Trust	Holding and other Investment Office	12/31/12	60.3	39.2	2007.8	1998.1	103	18927133
GAB	Gabelli Equity Trust Inc.	Holding and other Investment Office	12/31/12	30.9	15.7	1389.1	1385.0	72	5762640
GRX	Gabelli Healthcare & Wellness Trust	Holding and other Investment Office	12/31/12	2.7	0.6	141.5	137.2	40	1779216
GGT	Gabelli Multimedia Trust Inc.	Holding and other Investment Office	12/31/12	4.5	2.4	184.0	182.9	32	3865988
GUT	Gabelli Utility Trust	Holding and other Investment Office	12/31/12	7.9	5.0	278.3	277.1	46	2405939
GFA	Gafisa S.A.	Builders	12/31/12	3953.3	-76.4	9071.0	2544.5		
GCAP	GAIN Capital Holdings Inc	Finance Intermediaries & Services	12/31/12	151.4	2.6	629.9	163.7	60	6677658
AJG	Gallagher (Arthur J.) & Co.	Brokers & Intermediaries	12/31/12	2520.3	195.0	5352.3	1658.6	390	111278556
GBL	GAMCO Investors Inc	Finance Intermediaries & Services	12/31/12	344.3	75.5	690.7	367.6	84	3416379
GNT	Gamco Natural Resrouces, Gold & I	Holding and other Investment Office	12/31/11	4.2	0.3	316.7	310.8	23	2464239
GME	GameStop Corp	Retail - Appliances and Electronics	2/2/13	8886.7	-269.7	4133.6	2286.3	497	173425259
GCI	Gannett Co Inc	Publishing	12/30/12	5353.2	424.3	6379.9	2350.6	558	233258122
GDI	Gardner Denver, Inc.	Industrial Machinery & Equipment	12/31/12	2355.5	263.3	2490.2	1451.6	380	51852105
IT	Gartner, Inc.	IT Services	12/31/12	1615.8	165.9	1621.3	306.7	302	135999815
GLOG	GasLog Ltd	Miscellaneous Transportation Servic	12/31/12	68.5	4.2	908.8	603.2		
GMT	GATX Corp.	Rail	12/31/12	1243.2	137.3	6055.4	1244.2	266	51162540
GZT	Gazit-Global Ltd.	Property, Real Estate & Developmen	12/31/11	6496.0	626.0	66732.0	7136.0	19	2957564
GDL	GDL Fund	Holding and other Investment Office	12/31/12	3.8	-9.7	435.0	279.0	51	8790887
GEGI 26	GE Global Insurance Holdings Corp	Brokers & Intermediaries	12/31/03	11621.0	656.0	52542.0	7943.0		
GNK	Genco Shipping & Trading Ltd	Shipping	12/31/12	226.5	-144.9	2843.4	1066.3	124	21690468
GY	GenCorp Inc.	Defense	11/30/12	994.9	-2.6	919.3	-388.8	183	70872047
GNRC	Generac Holdings Inc	Electrical Equipment	12/31/12	1176.3	93.2	1603.8	463.6	168	36566170
GAM	General American Investors Co., In	Holding and other Investment Office	12/31/12	22.7	7.0	1173.3	1145.5	74	9974350
BGC	General Cable Corp. (DE)	Electrical Equipment	12/31/12	6014.3	9.8	4919.9	1353.3	308	56441232
GD	General Dynamics Corp.	Aerospace	12/31/12	31513.0	-332.0	34309.0	11390.0	932	329151838
GE	General Electric Co	Electrical Equipment	12/31/12	147359.0	13641.0	685328.0	123026.0	2213	6234354616
GGP	General Growth Properties Inc	REITs	12/31/12	2511.8	-481.2	27282.4	7621.7		
GIS	General Mills, Inc.	Food	5/27/12	16657.9	1567.3	21096.8	6421.7	1145	478603720
GM	General Motors Co.	Autos- Manufacturing	12/31/12	152256.0	6188.0	149422.0	36244.0	639	592096377
GSI	General Steel Holdings Inc	Non-Precious Metals	12/31/11	3563.9	-177.2	3054.1	-107.3	22	822889
GCO	Genesco Inc.	Retail - Apparel and Accessories	2/2/13	2604.8	110.5	1333.8	808.6	279	25850361
GWR	Genesee & Wyoming Inc.	Rail	12/31/12	874.9	52.4	5226.1	1894.5	303	53428136
GEL	Genesis Energy L.P.	Equipment & Services	12/31/12	4070.1	96.3	2109.7		143	48258370
GNE	Genie Energy Ltd.	Production & Extraction	12/31/12	229.5	-3.3	150.3	122.5	80	6996144
G	Genpact Ltd	Business Services	12/31/12	1902.0	178.2	2605.9	1168.4	177	130207034
GPC	Genuine Parts Co.	Retail - General Merchandise/Depart	12/31/12	13013.9	648.0	6807.1	2997.9	713	127932265
GNW	Genworth Financial, Inc. (Holding C	General Insurance	12/31/12	10023.0	323.0	113312.0	16537.0	489	419133892
GEO	GEO Group, Inc.	Business Services	12/31/12	1479.1	134.8	2839.2	1046.8	229	69175558
GAT	Georgia Power Co.	Electric Utilities	12/31/12	7998.0	1185.0	28803.0	9539.0		
GGB	Gerdau S.A.	Non-Precious Metals	12/31/12	37981.7	1425.6	53093.2	27245.6	190	222303368
GTY	Getty Realty Corp.	REITs	12/31/12	102.2	12.4	640.6	372.7	158	20169019

T26

| EARNINGS PER SHARE | | | | | | P/E RATIO | DIVIDENDS PER SHARE | | | AV. YLD % | DIV. DECLARED | | PRICE RANGE 2012 |
| QUARTERLY | | | ANNUAL | | | | | | | | | | |
1st	2nd	3rd	2012	2011	2010		2012	2011	2010		AMOUNT	PAYABLE	
		0.19	0.97	0.56	-1.94	16.9 - 0.0							16.4 - 0.0
		0.22	0.98	0.90	0.99	33.6 - 0.0	0.63	0.58	0.52	2.8	0.160Y	81/16/21	32.9 - 0.0
		2.07	8.51	7.64	6.88	19.9 - 0.0	1.44	1.28	1.16	1.1	0.420Y	81/16/21	169.1 - 0.0
		0.86	2.71	3.40	1.98	24.5 - 0.0	0.64	0.50	0.50	1.1	0.160Y	81/16/21	66.3 - 0.0
		-1.15	1.80	0.03	1.86	9.0 - 0.0	0.80	0.80	0.80	6.2			16.2 - 0.0
		0.65	3.00	2.55	1.18	20.9 - 0.0	0.41	0.30	0.25	0.7	0.1350Y	81/16/21	62.6 - 0.0
		0.41	1.78	1.64	1.53	30.6 - 0.0							54.4 - 0.0
				0.94	0.04								114.9 - 0.0
		0.69	1.80	1.07	0.30	20.7 - 0.0	0.66	0.60	0.60	2.0	0.20Y	81/16/21	37.3 - 0.0
		0.41	1.42	4.94	1.90	10.1 - 0.0	0.20	0.05		1.8	0.10Y	81/16/21	14.3 - 0.0
		-0.11	-0.61	0.30	-0.22						0.080Z	81/16/21	17.8 - 0.0
		-0.58	3.57	3.59	2.25	10.7 - 0.0					0.0001F	81/16/21	38.1 - 0.0
		-3.97	-11.21	1.19	2.00						0.18750	2/1/97	13.3 - 0.0
		-0.02	0.36	0.20	0.14	63.4 - 0.0							22.8 - 0.0
		0.67	0.75	0.81		25.8 - 0.0	1.43	1.35	1.19	8.7	0.1750	3/28/13	17.3 - 0.0
		0.20	0.74	0.68	0.94	13.0 - 0.0							9.6 - 0.0
		-0.04	0.27	-2.36	-1.83	25.6 - 0.0	0.20			4.6	0.060	3/15/13	6.9 - 0.0
		0.06	0.25	0.16	0.14	22.8 - 13.5							5.7 - 3.4
		0.24	0.71	-0.25	7223.00	53.1 - 0.0		3.54					37.7 - 0.0
		0.44	1.74	1.38	0.44	16.7 - 0.0							29.0 - 0.0
		0.31	1.46	1.82		48.2 - 0.0	2.18	2.83	2.14	18.0			14.9 - 0.0
		0.35		-0.05	0.64			0.39	0.29		0.060	6/27/13	60.9 - 0.0
0.15			0.43	0.27	-0.04	33.8 - 0.0							14.5 - 0.0
2.42			8.95	8.62	6.33	16.9 - 0.0	3.08	1.00	4.09	2.5	0.290Y	81/16/21	150.8 - 0.0
			0.45	0.45	0.47	16.8 - 0.0	0.46	0.46	0.46	6.4	0.0380	4/15/13	7.5 - 0.0
		0.86	3.19	4.78	4.57	13.4 - 0.0	1.19	1.50	0.95	3.4	0.31250Y	81/16/21	42.6 - 0.0
		-0.10	-0.41	-1.82	-5.35								16.0 - 0.0
		0.88	3.87	3.51	3.24	10.1 - 0.0	0.63	0.65	0.54	1.8			38.9 - 0.0
		0.40	2.46	1.56	1.02	11.3 - 0.0	0.40	0.30		1.6	0.1250	5/31/13	27.7 - 0.0
		-0.63	-1.06	-6.80	2.07			0.22	2.00		0.020	9/26/11	7.4 - 0.0
		0.55	-0.92	2.39	1.51								38.1 - 0.0
0.41			2.48	1.79	1.43	17.1 - 0.0	0.33	0.29	0.28	1.0	0.10Y	81/16/21	42.3 - 0.0
		-0.03	0.02	0.64	0.26	334.5 - 0.0					0.020	7/1/86	6.7 - 0.0
		-0.33	-0.86	-0.80	-0.76						0.040Y	8/29/08	1.7 - 0.0
	0.02		-0.06	0.06	-2.95								32.0 - 0.0
		0.30	0.83	0.84	0.62	16.8 - 0.0	1.60	0.40	0.80	14.2	0.110Y	12/16/13	14.0 - 0.0
		0.17	0.37	0.77	0.01	38.5 - 0.0	0.24	0.24		2.2	0.060Y	4/1/13	14.3 - 0.0
			0.10	0.10	0.15	61.5 - 0.0	0.48	0.48	0.47	8.7	0.3750	3/26/13	6.2 - 0.0
			0.47	0.38	0.34	40.3 - 0.0	0.96	0.90	0.76	5.8	0.3750	3/26/13	19.0 - 0.0
			0.09	0.07	0.05	72.9 - 0.0	0.56	0.57	0.51	9.9	0.31250	3/26/13	6.6 - 0.0
			0.05	0.01	-0.05	199.0 - 0.0	1.11			12.6	0.360	3/26/13	9.9 - 0.0
			0.13	-0.04	-0.07	69.1 - 0.0	0.80	0.87	0.60	10.6	0.3750	3/26/13	9.0 - 0.0
			0.15	0.15	0.15	56.8 - 0.0	0.60	0.60	0.72	8.1	0.35160	3/26/13	8.5 - 0.0
		0.01	-0.29	-2.19	1.00			0.14	0.07				5.1 - 0.0
		0.08	0.07	0.40	1.00	76.6 - 0.0	0.20	0.05		4.3	0.050Y	3/21/13	5.4 - 0.0
		0.50	1.59	1.28	1.66	26.0 - 0.0	1.36	1.32	1.28	3.8	0.350Y	81/16/21	41.3 - 0.0
		0.72	2.86	2.61	2.52	20.2 - 0.0	2.88	1.15	1.82	5.9	0.050Y	3/26/13	57.6 - 0.0
			0.02						1.26		0.020	6/21/13	16.1 - 0.0
		-5.08	2.41	2.65	2.25	11.6 - 0.0					0.2750Y	81/16/21	28.0 - 0.0
		0.56	1.79	1.89	2.43	12.3 - 0.0	0.80	0.24	0.16	4.8	0.20Y	81/16/21	22.1 - 0.0
		1.30	5.28	5.33	3.28	14.4 - 0.0	0.20	0.20	0.20	0.3	0.050Y	81/16/21	76.0 - 0.0
		0.33	1.73	1.39	0.96	31.5 - 0.0							54.4 - 0.0
			0.07	0.36	0.25	190.0 - 0.0		0.22	0.44		0.110	3/25/13	13.3 - 0.0
		1.13	2.88	2.35	1.72	18.0 - 0.0	1.20	1.16	1.12	2.8	0.310Y	81/16/21	52.0 - 0.0
		1.06		3.75	5.57						0.120	4/22/13	13.8 - 0.0
			-0.46	-0.55	-0.56		1.28	1.28	1.28	10.9	0.320	3/21/13	12.4 - 0.0
		-0.90	-3.47	0.72	4.07						1.0Y	11/28/08	6.3 - 0.0
-0.24				-0.04	0.05	0.12					0.030Y	5/28/04	13.6 - 0.0
		0.37	1.35	4.79	-1.65	30.0 - 0.0	6.00			21.2	6.G7Y	6/29/12	40.5 - 0.0
			0.24	0.18	0.19	130.3 - 0.0	2.00	0.50	0.43	7.0	0.37190Y	6/24/13	31.3 - 0.0
		-0.41	0.08	1.57	1.31	457.9 - 0.0					0.050	81/16/21	36.6 - 0.0
		1.70	-0.94	6.87	6.81		2.51	1.83	1.64	3.8	0.560Y	81/16/21	74.1 - 0.0
		0.33	1.29	1.23	1.06	18.4 - 0.0	0.70	0.61	0.46	3.3	0.190Y	81/16/21	23.8 - 0.0
		-0.23	-0.52	-0.37	-0.27		0.42	0.40	0.38	2.2	0.120Z	81/16/21	21.0 - 0.0
		0.60	2.35	2.70	2.24	21.0 - 0.0	1.22	1.12	0.96	3.0	0.380Y	81/16/21	49.3 - 0.0
		0.89	2.92	4.58	2.89	10.5 - 0.0					0.59380Y	6/3/13	30.6 - 0.0
		-0.25		-3.24	-0.14								1.4 - 0.0
		1.70	3.43	2.24	1.30	23.0 - 0.0					0.3750Y	4/30/13	78.8 - 0.0
		-0.47	1.02	2.79	1.94	92.3 - 0.0					1.250	7/1/13	94.1 - 0.0
		0.39	1.23	0.75	0.49	39.3 - 0.0	1.82	1.65	1.49	5.3	0.49750	5/15/13	48.4 - 0.0
		-0.13	-0.17	0.04			0.13	0.05		1.8	0.15940	5/15/13	9.5 - 0.0
		0.11	0.78	0.81	0.63	23.9 - 0.0	2.24			13.5	2.24G7	81/16/21	18.7 - 0.0
		1.11	4.14	3.58	3.00	18.8 - 0.0	1.98	1.80	1.64	3.1	0.53750Y	81/16/21	78.0 - 0.0
		0.07	0.65	0.25	0.29	16.2 - 0.0							10.5 - 0.0
		0.25	2.20	1.23	1.13	17.1 - 0.0	6.08			22.7	0.50Z	3/1/13	37.6 - 0.0
							2.05	2.05	2.05	7.0	0.38280Y	7/1/13	32.3 - 0.0
		0.23	0.84	1.22	1.50	12.4 - 0.0	0.07	0.11	0.16	0.8			10.4 - 0.0
		-0.10	0.37	0.37	1.85	59.2 - 0.0	0.38	1.46	1.91	2.1	0.20Z	4/11/13	21.9 - 0.0

SYMBOL	COMPANY	NATURE OF BUSINESS	FISCAL YEAR-END	TOTAL REV. $MILL	NET INCOME $MILL	TOTAL ASSETS $MILL	NET STK EQUITY $MILL	NO OF INST	INST. HOLDINGS (SHARES)
GFIG	GFI Group Inc	Finance Intermediaries & Services	12/31/12	924.6	-10.0	1180.1	425.1	120	55698359
GA	Giant Interactive Group Inc	Internet & Software	12/31/11	1792.2	880.0	3551.2	2495.6	109	41625434
GIL	Gildan Activewear Inc	Apparel, Footwear & Accessories	9/30/12	1948.3	148.5	1896.4	1426.3	218	92641273
GSK	GlaxoSmithKline Plc	Pharmaceuticals	12/31/12	26431.0	4565.0	41475.0	5810.0	774	323897410
GRT	Glimcher Realty Trust	REITs	12/31/12	326.0	-2.1	2329.4	699.6	192	138859079
GCA	Global Cash Access Holdings Inc	Credit & Lending	12/31/12	584.5	25.7	553.9	198.8	185	69711173
GGS	Global Geophysical Services Inc	Equipment & Services	12/31/12	339.0	-13.3	552.9	107.5	79	12175623
GHI	Global High Income Fund Inc	Holding and other Investment Office	10/31/12	20.9	17.1	296.0	290.4	34	1692086
GLP	Global Partners LP	Equipment & Services	12/31/12	17626.0	46.7	2329.8		45	11083321
GPN	Global Payments, Inc.	Business Services	5/31/12	2203.8	188.2	2688.1	1172.2	368	80485214
GSL	Global Ship Lease, Inc.	Shipping	12/31/11	156.3	9.1	939.5	334.2		
GMED	Globus Med Inc	Medical Instruments & Equipment	12/31/12	386.0	73.8	447.1	386.5		
GOM	GMAC LLC	Credit & Lending	12/31/09	17668.0	-10298.0	172306.0	20839.0		
GNC	GNC Holdings Inc	Retail - Food & Beverage, Drug & To	12/31/12	2430.0	240.2	2552.0	882.0	290	106394077
GOL	Gol Linhas Aereas Inteligentes SA	Airlines/Air Freight	12/31/11	7539.3	-751.5	10655.1	2205.9	84	46016869
GFI	Gold Fields Ltd.	Precious Metals	12/31/11	41876.8	7026.7	84282.0	46886.9	253	262016757
GG	Goldcorp Inc	Precious Metals	12/31/12	5435.0	1749.0	31212.0	22716.0	556	430703327
GS	Goldman Sachs Group, Inc.	Finance Intermediaries & Services	12/31/12	41664.0	7475.0	938555.0	75716.0	1216	339953098
GDP	Goodrich Petroleum Corp. (Holding	Production & Extraction	12/31/12	180.8	-84.2	768.4	60.2	171	34885001
GOV	Government Properties Income Tru	REITs	12/31/12	211.1	50.0	1562.1	1027.5	190	29135673
GPX	GP Strategies Corp.	Business Services	12/31/12	401.6	22.7	244.4	167.3	116	16714612
GRA	Grace (W.R.) Co. (DE)	Specialty Chemicals	12/31/12	3155.5	94.1	5090.2	308.4	285	63750218
GGG	Graco Inc.	Industrial Machinery & Equipment	12/28/12	1012.5	149.1	1321.7	454.1	325	57930143
GTI	Graftech International Ltd.	Electrical Equipment	12/31/12	1248.3	117.6	2297.9	1349.9	237	125762483
GWW	Grainger (W.W.) Inc.	Electrical Equipment	12/31/12	8950.0	689.9	5014.6	3023.9	687	55403288
GKK	Gramercy Property Trust Inc	REITs	12/31/12	36.8	-171.5	2168.8	-252.7	108	17980838
GVA	Granite Construction Inc.	Construction Services	12/31/12	2083.0	45.3	1729.5	830.0	228	36167715
GRP U	Granite Real Estate Investment Tru	REITs	12/31/12	181.1	71.3	1218.2	877.0		
GPK	Graphic Packaging Holding Co	Containers & Packaging	12/31/12	4337.1	122.6	4620.8	974.0	183	368279535
GTN	Gray Television Inc	Radio & Television	12/31/12	404.8	28.1	1249.8	143.9	86	33299404
GNI	Great Northern Iron Ore Properties	Patent Owners & Lessors	12/31/12	24.2	20.1	19.1	9.4	40	128334
GXP	Great Plains Energy, Inc.	Electric Utilities	12/31/12	2309.9	199.9	9647.3	3379.0	348	114713896
GB	GreatBatch Inc	Medical Instruments & Equipment	12/28/12	646.2	-4.8	889.9	480.9	170	24446665
GCH	Greater China Fund, Inc. (The)	Holding and other Investment Office	12/31/12	7.3	1.2	327.8	325.5	49	14497771
GDOT	Green Dot Corp	Credit & Lending	12/31/12	546.3	47.2	725.7	327.8	142	25776513
GBX	Greenbrier Companies Inc (The)	Construction Services	8/31/12	1807.7	58.7	1384.5	431.8	179	21363730
GHL	Greenhill & Co Inc	Finance Intermediaries & Services	12/31/12	285.1	42.1	387.0	302.2	205	32197495
GWAY	Greenway Medical Technologies, In	Business Services	6/30/12	124.0	2.9	133.1	98.8	84	17305679
GEF	Greif Inc	Containers & Packaging	10/31/12	4269.5	126.1	3856.9	1200.8	249	23509394
GFF	Griffon Corp.	Metal Products	9/30/12	1861.1	17.0	1806.2	654.2	156	50489083
GPI	Group 1 Automotive, Inc.	Retail - Automotive	12/31/12	7476.1	100.2	3023.0	892.8	218	31197965
GMK	Gruma S.A.B. de C.V.	Food	12/31/11	57644.7	545.1	44542.6	13431.2	28	931557
PAC	Grupo Aeroportuario del Pacifico, S.	Airlines/Air Freight	12/31/11	4938.7	1484.4	29391.8	26342.7	86	6472850
ASR	Grupo Aeroportuario del Sureste SA	Airlines/Air Freight	12/31/11	4573.3	1592.4	18803.3	15487.8	103	13164948
BSMX	Grupo Financiero Santander Mexico	Banking	12/31/11	61.2	18.7	739.2	88.5		
BSMX	Grupo Financiero Santander Mexico	Banking							
TV	Grupo Televisa, S.A.	Radio & Television	12/31/11	62581.5	6889.6	155061.4	51659.8	248	278828144
GSE	GSE Holding, Inc.	Plastics	12/31/12	476.6	1.1	336.1	102.7	57	8156474
GSH	Guangshen Railway Co., Ltd.	Rail	12/31/11	14690.8	1804.1	32207.3	25334.6	47	2594646
GES	GUESS ?, Inc.	Retail - Apparel and Accessories	2/2/13	2658.6	178.7	1713.5	1087.0	309	67217435
GBAB	Guggenheim Build America Bonds	Holding and other Investment Office	5/31/12	32.9	27.7	538.2	409.0	20	1981901
GPM	Guggenheim Enhanced Equity Inco	Holding and other Investment Office	12/31/12	1.1	-2.0	234.7	170.3	34	3041904
GGE	Guggenheim Enhanced Equity Strat	Holding and other Investment Office	10/31/12	1.1	-0.7	137.1	96.5	30	936778
GEQ	Guggenheim Equal Weight Enhanc	Holding and other Investment Office	6/30/12	2.9	0.8	209.3	168.4	13	584250
GOF	Guggenheim Strategic Opportunitie	Holding and other Investment Office	5/31/12	22.5	17.7	297.7	207.3	26	1109822
GWRE	Guidewire Software Inc	Internet & Software	7/31/12	232.1	15.2	284.2	184.0	143	44161710
GUA	Gulf Power Company	Electric Utilities	12/31/12	1439.8	132.1	4177.4	1278.7		
GLF	GulfMark Offshore, Inc.	Equipment & Services	12/31/12	389.2	19.3	1745.7	1027.9	171	24805205
HQH	H&Q HealthCare Investors	Holding and other Investment Office	9/30/12	5.0	-1.3	511.0	510.4	69	6538321
HQL	H&Q Life Sciences Investors	Holding and other Investment Office	9/30/12	2.1	-1.3	227.5	227.1	46	4154380
HAE	Haemonetics Corp.	Medical Instruments & Equipment	3/31/12	727.8	66.9	911.1	732.6	257	56841007
HK	Halcon Resources Corp	Production & Extraction	12/31/12	247.9	-53.9	5041.0	2093.2	234	117208775
HAL	Halliburton Company	Equipment & Services	12/31/12	28503.0	2635.0	27410.0	15765.0	1121	795322756
HPS	Hancock John Preferred Income Fd	Holding and other Investment Office	7/31/12	57.0	47.3	896.9	598.6	44	4194037
HPF	Hancock John Preferred Income Fu	Holding and other Investment Office	7/31/12	44.7	37.1	700.5	466.2	49	1406849
HTD	Hancock John Tax-Advantaged Divi	Holding and other Investment Office	10/31/12	57.0	45.2	1168.7	773.1	62	5350465
HBI	Hanesbrands Inc	Apparel, Footwear & Accessories	12/29/12	4525.7	164.7	3631.7	886.9	375	101128266
HGR	Hanger Inc	Hospitals & Health Care Facilities	12/31/12	985.5	63.7	1237.3	503.1	189	33089739
THG	Hanover Insurance Group Inc	General Insurance	12/31/12	4590.7	55.9	13484.9	2595.4	269	46115129
HRG	Harbinger Group Inc	Household & Personal Products	9/30/12	4480.7	89.6	25200.5	1496.8	100	141383562
HOG	Harley-Davidson Inc	Autos- Manufacturing	12/31/12	5580.5	623.9	9170.8	2557.6	578	201803182
HAR	Harman International Industries, Inc	Household Appliances, Electronics &	6/30/12	4364.1	329.5	3169.5	1529.6	387	70749760
HMY	Harmony Gold Mining Co. Ltd.	Precious Metals	6/30/12	1953.0	341.0	5263.0	4152.0	140	126334215
HRS	Harris Corp.	Defense	6/29/12	5451.3	30.6	5592.8	1938.9	614	129400801
HBC PR	Harris Preferred Capital Corp.	REITs	12/31/12	21.1	18.6	576.0	575.4	3	52300
HTSI	Harris Teeter Supermarkets, Inc.	Retail - Food & Beverage, Drug & To	10/2/12	4535.4	82.5	1952.5	1037.6	215	50503465
HSC	Harsco Corp.	Industrial Machinery & Equipment	12/31/12	3046.0	-254.6	2976.0	811.8	311	65654575
HHS	Harte-Hanks, Inc.	Advertising	12/31/12	767.7	-83.4	706.2	328.2	165	41070480
HIG	Hartford Financial Services Group I	General Insurance	12/31/12	26412.0	-38.0	298513.0	22447.0	712	474215801
HNR	Harvest Natural Resources Inc	Production & Extraction	12/31/11	-	53.9	513.0	363.8	137	33339650

| EARNINGS PER SHARE | | | | | | P/E RATIO | | DIVIDENDS PER SHARE | | | AV. YLD | DIV. DECLARED | | PRICE RANGE | |
| QUARTERLY | | | ANNUAL | | | | | | | | % | | | 2012 | |
1st	2nd	3rd	2012	2011	2010			2012	2011	2010		AMOUNT	PAYABLE		
-	-	-0.08	-0.09	-0.03	0.20	-		0.25	0.20	0.45	8.0	0.050Y	12/27/12	3.8 -	0.0
-	-	1.28	-	3.79	3.47	-		-	0.49	0.02	-			6.5 -	0.0
0.29	-	-	1.22	1.91	1.63	33.2 -	0.0	0.30	0.23	-	0.9	0.090	3/18/13	40.5 -	0.0
-	-	0.23	0.92	1.03	0.32	51.6 -	0.0	3.92	3.58	3.11	8.7			47.5 -	0.0
-	-	-0.07	-0.23	-0.05	-0.22	-		0.40	0.40	0.40	3.8	0.46880Z	4/15/13	11.7 -	0.0
-	-	0.10	0.38	0.14	0.26	22.7 -	0.0	-	-	-	-			8.6 -	0.0
-	-	0.16	-0.36	0.15	-1.44	-		-	-	-	-			10.4 -	0.0
-	-	-	0.79	0.63	0.77	17.1 -	0.0	0.99	1.40	1.06	7.8	0.07850	4/30/13	13.5 -	0.0
-	-	0.24	1.71	0.87	1.59	22.1 -	0.0	2.06	2.00	1.96	7.9	0.570	81/16/21	37.8 -	0.0
-	-	0.75	2.37	2.60	2.48	21.5 -	0.0	0.08	0.08	0.08	0.2	0.020Y	81/16/21	51.0 -	0.0
-	-	0.18	-	0.19	-0.08	-		-	-	-	-	0.230	3/5/09	4.6 -	0.0
-	-	0.18	0.80	0.67	0.59	23.4 -	0.0	-	-	-	-			18.8 -	0.0
-	-	-	-	-	-	-		-	-	-	-	0.45620Z	6/10/13	25.5 -	0.0
-	-	0.60	2.29	1.24	0.85	18.5 -	0.0	0.44	-	-	1.2	0.150Y	3/29/13	42.4 -	0.0
-	-	-1.14	-	-2.78	0.80	-		-	0.06	0.22	-			7.6 -	0.0
-	-	1.94	-	9.62	-0.11	-		-	0.03	0.02	-			14.0 -	0.0
-	-	-	1.95	2.18	2.13	24.1 -	0.0	0.54	0.41	0.21	1.4	0.050	4/26/13	46.9 -	0.0
-	-	2.85	14.13	4.51	13.18	11.2 -	0.0	1.77	1.40	1.40	1.5	0.37190Y	5/10/13	158.7 -	0.0
-	-	0.30	-2.48	-1.05	-7.47	-		-	-	-	-	0.67190Y	3/15/13	19.5 -	0.0
-	-	0.25	1.03	1.06	0.81	26.3 -	0.0	1.69	1.67	1.22	7.3	0.430Z	5/24/13	27.1 -	0.0
-	-	0.32	1.18	0.94	0.68	20.4 -	0.0	-	-	-	-	0.025	2/1/89	24.0 -	0.0
-	-	0.99	1.23	3.57	2.78	63.8 -	0.0	-	-	-	-			78.5 -	0.0
-	-	0.60	2.42	2.32	1.69	24.6 -	0.0	0.90	0.84	0.80	1.8	0.250Y	81/16/21	59.5 -	0.0
-	-	0.22	0.84	1.05	1.42	14.5 -	0.0	-	-	-	-			12.2 -	0.0
-	-	2.15	9.52	9.07	6.93	24.3 -	0.0	3.06	2.52	2.08	1.5	0.80Y	81/16/21	231.8 -	0.0
-	-	-0.09	-3.44	6.48	-19.40	-		-	-	-	-	0.50780Z	10/15/08	5.2 -	0.0
-	-	0.94	1.15	1.31	-1.56	32.6 -	0.0	0.52	0.52	0.52	1.8	0.130Y	81/16/21	37.5 -	0.0
-	-	0.40	1.52	3.24	-1.13	26.3 -	0.0	-	-	-	-	0.1750	4/15/13	39.9 -	0.0
-	-	0.10	0.31	0.73	0.03	24.5 -	0.0	-	-	-	-			7.6 -	0.0
-	-	0.26	0.42	0.03	0.16	11.3 -	0.0	-	-	-	-	0.030Y	10/15/08	4.8 -	0.0
-	-	2.84	13.38	15.37	11.65	7.2 -	0.0	14.00	15.00	14.85	19.0	2.250	4/30/13	96.3 -	0.0
-	-	0.95	1.35	1.25	1.53	17.2 -	0.0	0.85	0.83	0.83	4.0	1.1250Y	81/16/21	23.2 -	0.0
-	-	-0.32	-0.20	1.40	1.40	-		-	-	-	-			30.4 -	0.0
-	-	-	0.05	0.08	0.04	267.8 -	0.0	0.05	0.21	0.01	0.4	0.05070	12/28/12	13.4 -	0.0
-	-	0.48	1.07	1.19	0.98	25.1 -	0.0	-	-	-	-			26.9 -	0.0
-	0.45	-	1.91	0.24	0.21	11.9 -	0.0	-	-	0.00	-	0.040Y	2/16/09	22.7 -	0.0
-	-	0.28	1.38	1.44	1.12	44.8 -	0.0	1.80	1.80	1.80	3.9	0.450Y	81/16/21	61.8 -	0.0
-0.03	-	-	0.11	-1.90	-0.48	176.7 -	0.0	-	-	-	-			19.4 -	0.0
0.43	-	-	2.17	3.01	3.58	26.0 -	0.0	1.68	1.68	1.60	3.7	0.630Y	81/16/21	56.5 -	0.0
0.01	-	-	0.30	-0.13	0.16	40.7 -	0.0	0.08	-	-	0.8	0.0250Y	3/27/13	12.2 -	0.0
-	-	1.32	4.19	3.47	2.16	16.5 -	0.0	0.59	0.48	0.10	1.0	0.150Y	81/16/21	69.3 -	0.0
-	-	-	-	-	-	-		-	-	-	-			18.6 -	0.0
-	-	-	-	2.76	2.69	-		-	-	-	-			63.3 -	0.0
-	-	1.36	-	-	-	-		-	-	-	-			137.4 -	0.0
-	-	-	-	-	-	-		-	-	-	-			17.8 -	0.0
-	-	-	-	-	-	-		-	-	-	-			17.8 -	0.0
-	-	-	-	-	-	-		-	-	-	-			29.2 -	0.0
-	-	0.26	0.06	0.08	-1.55	223.3 -	0.0	-	-	-	-			13.4 -	0.0
-	-	-	-	0.25	0.21	-		-	0.09	0.07	-			26.4 -	0.0
-	-	0.43	2.86	3.11	2.61	11.7 -	0.0	0.80	2.68	0.45	3.0	0.20Y	81/16/21	33.5 -	0.0
-	-	-	1.59	0.68	-	15.3 -	0.0	1.49	0.58	-	6.5	0.13920	4/30/13	24.3 -	0.0
-	-	-	-0.11	0.01	0.01	-		0.96	0.96	0.96	10.7	0.240	3/28/13	9.6 -	0.0
-	-	-	-0.15	0.23	0.49	-		1.25	0.71	0.56	7.2	0.4850	2/28/13	18.9 -	0.0
-	-	-	0.09	-	-	221.6 -	0.0	0.88	-	-	4.7	0.43750	4/30/13	19.9 -	0.0
-	-	-	1.08	1.94	1.76	21.6 -	0.0	1.85	1.88	1.85	8.6	0.16940	4/30/13	23.4 -	0.0
-	0.09	-	0.25	0.76	0.30	155.0 -	0.0	-	-	-	-			38.8 -	0.0
-	-	-	-	-	-	-		1.44	0.77	-	5.1	1.61250Y	7/1/13	30.9 -	0.0
-	-	0.49	0.73	1.91	-1.36	67.2 -	0.0	1.00	-	-	2.8	0.250Y	3/28/13	49.1 -	0.0
-	-	-	-0.05	-0.16	-0.07	-		1.32	1.26	0.37	7.5	0.370	3/28/13	20.0 -	0.0
-	-	-	-0.09	-0.19	-0.09	-		1.49	1.01	0.29	10.0	0.30	3/28/13	17.4 -	0.0
-	-	0.19	1.29	1.56	1.12	34.4 -	0.0	-	-	-	-			44.4 -	0.0
-	-	-0.11	-0.91	-0.05	0.09	-		-	-	-	-			11.0 -	0.0
-	-	0.65	2.84	3.08	2.01	15.3 -	0.0	0.36	0.36	0.36	1.1	0.1250Y	81/16/21	43.3 -	0.0
-	-	-	1.50	1.48	1.49	13.5 -	0.0	1.39	1.35	1.35	7.2	0.12220	4/30/13	20.3 -	0.0
-	-	-	1.75	1.71	1.70	13.5 -	0.0	1.68	1.54	1.49	7.5	0.140	4/30/13	23.7 -	0.0
-	-	-	1.20	1.20	1.10	16.7 -	0.0	1.18	1.12	1.09	6.4	0.09850	4/30/13	20.0 -	0.0
-	-	1.10	1.64	2.69	2.16	27.8 -	0.0	-	-	-	-	0.2GY	81/16/21	45.6 -	0.0
-	-	0.50	1.83	1.61	0.65	17.4 -	0.0	-	-	-	-			31.8 -	0.0
-	-	0.89	1.23	0.81	3.34	40.4 -	0.0	1.23	1.13	1.00	3.2	0.330Y	81/16/21	49.7 -	0.0
0.03	-	-	0.15	0.04	-1.16	70.7 -	0.0	-	-	-	-			10.6 -	0.0
-	-	0.59	2.72	2.55	0.62	20.4 -	0.0	0.62	0.47	0.40	1.3	0.210Y	81/16/21	55.4 -	0.0
-	0.68	-	4.57	1.90	2.25	11.0 -	0.0	0.30	0.05	0.00	0.7	0.150Y	81/16/21	50.3 -	0.0
1.21	-	-	0.79	1.44	-0.46	14.0 -	0.0	0.13	0.01	0.01	1.5			11.0 -	0.0
-	0.43	-	0.26	4.60	4.28	199.9 -	0.0	1.22	1.00	0.88	2.7	0.370Y	81/16/21	52.0 -	0.0
-	-	117.00	113.00	574.00	293.00	0.2 -	0.0	1.84	1.84	1.84	7.2	0.46090Z	4/1/13	26.2 -	0.0
0.46	-	-	1.68	1.87	2.31	26.2 -	0.0	0.55	0.52	0.48	1.4	0.150Y	81/16/21	44.0 -	0.0
-	-	0.33	-3.16	-0.14	0.08	-		0.82	0.82	0.82	3.8	0.2050Y	81/16/21	25.8 -	0.0
-	-	0.14	-1.33	0.70	0.84	-		0.42	0.32	0.30	5.8	0.0850Y	12/28/12	9.7 -	0.0
-	-	0.83	-0.18	1.30	2.49	-		0.40	0.40	0.20	2.0	0.45310Y	81/16/21	26.5 -	0.0
-	-	0.15	-	1.37	0.43	-		-	-	-	-			10.3 -	0.0

SYMBOL	COMPANY	NATURE OF BUSINESS	FISCAL YEAR-END	TOTAL REV. $MILL	NET INCOME $MILL	TOTAL ASSETS $MILL	NET STK EQUITY $MILL	NO OF INST	INST. HOLDINGS (SHARES)
HTS	Hatteras Financial Corp	REITs	12/31/12	506.3	349.2	26404.1	3072.9	279	61954847
HVT	Haverty Furniture Cos., Inc.	Retail - Furniture & Home Furnishing	12/31/12	670.1	14.9	402.1	259.4	127	16341729
HE	Hawaiian Electric Industries, Inc.	Electric Utilities	12/31/12	3375.0	140.5	10149.1	1628.2	281	34843918
HCA	HCA Holdings Inc	Hospitals & Health Care Facilities	12/31/12	33013.0	1605.0	28075.0	-9660.0	418	354938438
HCC	HCC Insurance Holdings, Inc.	General Insurance	12/31/12	2525.8	391.2	10267.8	3542.6	371	112517281
HCP	HCP, Inc.	REITs	12/31/12	1900.7	832.5	19915.6	10551.2	709	449891636
HDB	HDFC Bank Ltd	Banking	3/31/12	325300.5	51670.9	3379095.0	299246.8	269	120415538
HW	Headwaters Inc	Refining & Marketing	9/30/12	632.8	-62.2	680.9	-3.1	210	60246060
HCN	Health Care REIT Inc.	REITs	12/31/12	1822.1	294.8	19549.1	10294.8	641	232293403
HMA	Health Management Associates, Inc	Hospitals & Health Care Facilities	12/31/12	5878.2	164.3	6400.8	1216.4	331	255751918
HNT	Health Net, Inc.	Hospitals & Health Care Facilities	12/31/12	11289.1	122.1	3934.4	1557.0	312	85826084
HR	Healthcare Realty Trust, Inc.	REITs	12/31/12	316.3	5.5	2540.0	1120.9	256	89301871
HTA	Healthcare Trust Of America Inc	REITs	12/31/12	299.6	-24.4	2414.1	1254.3	106	15620593
HTA	Healthcare Trust Of America Inc	REITs	12/31/12	299.6	-24.4	2414.1	1254.3	106	15620593
HLS	HealthSouth Corp.	Hospitals & Health Care Facilities	12/31/12	2134.9	185.0	2423.8	633.8	262	101609255
HPY	Heartland Payment Systems Inc	Business Services	12/31/12	2013.4	65.9	813.4	209.8	228	39952175
HEK	Heckmann Corp	Equipment & Services	12/31/12	352.0	2.5	1644.3	847.8	6	740400
HL	Hecla Mining Co.	Precious Metals	12/31/12	321.1	15.0	1378.3	1138.0	269	162828265
HEI	Heico Corp.	Aerospace	10/31/12	897.3	85.1	1192.8	616.7	161	16456078
HNZ	Heinz (H.J.) Co.	Food	4/29/12	11649.1	923.2	11983.3	2758.6	1074	231731249
HAV	Helios Advantage Income Fund, Inc	Holding and other Investment Office	3/31/12	6.4	5.0	82.1	58.3	27	450123
HIH	Helios High Income Fund, Inc.	Holding and other Investment Office	3/31/12	6.4	5.0	58.6	41.1	21	316621
HHY	Helios High Yield Fund	Holding and other Investment Office	6/30/12	7.7	6.2	99.3	67.5	14	183016
HMH	Helios Multi-Sector High Income Fu	Holding and other Investment Office	3/31/12	5.1	3.9	66.4	46.5	27	559156
HSA	Helios Strategic Income Fund, Inc.	Holding and other Investment Office	3/31/12	3.8	2.8	55.3	39.2	31	1492904
HLX	Helix Energy Solutions Group Inc	Equipment & Services	12/31/12	846.1	-46.3	3386.6	1393.4	335	96550486
HP	Helmerich & Payne, Inc.	Production & Extraction	9/30/12	3151.8	581.0	5721.1	3835.0	599	111326694
HLF	Herbalife Ltd.	Household & Personal Products	12/31/12	4072.3	477.2	1703.9	420.8	421	122549978
HTGC	Hercules Technology Growth Capita	Holding and other Investment Office	12/31/12	87.6	48.1	1123.6	516.0	147	33831311
HT	Hersha Hospitality Trust	REITs	12/31/12	358.2	22.2	1707.7	829.8	203	178006214
HSY	Hershey Company (The)	Food	12/31/12	6644.3	660.9	4754.8	1036.7	719	129602286
HTZ	Hertz Global Holdings Inc	Hotels, Restaurants & Travel	12/31/12	9020.8	243.1	23286.0	2507.3	389	563943761
HES	Hess Corp	Production & Extraction	12/31/12	38373.0	2025.0	43441.0	21090.0	739	274827071
HPQ	Hewlett-Packard Co	Computer Hardware & Equipment	10/31/12	120357.0	-12650.0	108768.0	22436.0	1321	1742748287
HXL	Hexcel Corp.	Plastics	12/31/12	1578.2	164.3	1603.1	994.1	314	106485089
HF	HFF Inc	Credit & Lending	12/31/12	285.0	43.9	589.2	121.0	121	30223596
HGG	hhgregg Inc	Retail - Appliances and Electronics	3/31/12	2493.4	81.4	642.8	359.5	117	17651614
HCLP	Hi-Crush Partners LP	Mining	12/31/12	28.9	18.5	102.2	-	-	-
ONE	Higher One Holdings Inc.	Business Services	12/31/12	197.7	36.9	190.9	57.7	108	27989860
HIW	Highwoods Properties, Inc.	REITs	12/31/12	516.1	84.2	3350.4	1160.1	279	91326824
HIW 06	Highwoods Realty Ltd Partnership	Property, Real Estate & Developmen	12/31/12	516.1	84.3	3349.5	141.3	-	-
HIL	Hill International Inc	Business Services	12/31/12	480.8	-28.2	421.7	127.5	57	19393211
HRC	Hill-Rom Holdings, Inc.	Medical Instruments & Equipment	9/30/12	1634.3	120.8	1627.6	812.6	26	4647947
HI	Hillenbrand Inc	Miscellaneous Consumer Services	9/30/12	983.2	104.8	1087.5	506.3	202	46897286
HSH	Hillshire Brands Co	Food	6/30/12	4094.0	845.0	2450.0	235.0	479	203515962
HSH	Hillshire Brands Co	Food	6/30/12	4094.0	845.0	2450.0	235.0	479	203515962
HTH	Hilltop Holdings, Inc.	General Insurance	12/31/12	263.3	-5.6	7286.9	1144.5	140	37786225
HNI	HNI Corp	Office Equipment & Furniture	12/29/12	2004.0	49.0	1079.6	420.4	168	41747873
HEP	Holly Energy Partners LP	Equipment & Services	12/31/12	292.6	91.1	1394.1	-	95	13950074
HFC	HollyFrontier Corp.	Refining & Marketing	12/31/12	20090.7	1727.2	10329.0	6053.0	508	175948449
HD	Home Depot Inc	Retail - Hardware & Home Improvem	2/3/13	74754.0	4535.0	41084.0	17777.0	1552	1201349043
HME	Home Properties Inc	REITs	12/31/12	644.3	163.6	4451.5	1321.0	318	49027622
HCI	Homeowners Choice Inc	General Insurance	12/31/12	163.1	30.2	338.3	121.3	1	113706
HMC	Honda Motor Co., Ltd.(Honda Giken	Autos- Manufacturing	3/31/12	7948095.0	211482.0	11780759.0	4402614.0	263	31660657
HON	Honeywell International, Inc.	Auto Parts	12/31/12	37665.0	2926.0	41853.0	13125.0	1203	695870228
HMN	Horace Mann Educators Corp.	General Insurance	12/31/12	1010.8	103.9	8167.7	1245.8	200	42643514
HRL	Hormel Foods Corp.	Food	10/28/12	8230.7	500.0	4564.0	2819.5	421	89075032
HOS	Hornbeck Offshore Services Inc	Equipment & Services	12/31/12	512.7	37.0	2631.7	1165.8	247	34911960
DHI	Horton (D.R.) Inc.	Builders	9/30/12	4354.0	956.3	7248.2	3592.1	535	310349074
HSP	Hospira Inc	Pharmaceuticals	12/31/12	4092.1	44.2	6088.6	3041.7	531	167401486
HPT	Hospitality Properties Trust	REITs	12/31/12	1297.0	151.9	5635.1	2733.8	379	105856154
HST	Host Hotels & Resorts Inc	REITs	12/31/12	5286.0	61.0	12994.0	6825.0	477	798506894
HOV	Hovnanian Enterprises, Inc.	Builders	10/31/12	1485.4	-66.2	1684.3	-485.6	204	72828122
HHC	Howard Hughes Corp	Property, Real Estate & Developmen	12/31/12	376.9	-127.5	3503.0	2305.2	190	32028019
HSBC PR	HSBC Finance Corp	Credit & Lending	12/31/12	1304.0	-845.0	46778.0	6105.0	-	-
HBC	HSBC Holdings Plc	Banking	12/31/12	108851.0	14027.0	2692538.0	175242.0	467	118859352
HBA PRF	HSBC USA, Inc.	Credit & Lending	12/31/12	5128.0	-1045.0	196567.0	17836.0	2	13293
HNP	Huaneng Power International, Inc.	Electric Utilities	12/31/11	133420.8	1180.5	257415.9	50882.9	104	3099606
HUB B	Hubbell Inc.	Electrical Equipment	12/31/12	3044.4	299.7	2947.0	1661.2	56	5513436
HBM	HudBay Minerals Inc	Non-Precious Metals	12/31/11	890.8	-153.9	2448.8	1813.2	92	96770017
HPP	Hudson Pacific Properties Inc	REITs	12/31/12	166.2	-17.2	1559.7	852.7	117	48205770
HVB	Hudson Valley Holding Corp.	Banking	12/31/12	143.9	29.2	2891.2	291.0	64	6665423
HGT	Hugoton Royalty Trust (TX)	Oil Royalty Traders	12/31/12	25.1	23.3	113.0	109.9	140	7858111
HUM	Humana Inc.	Life & Health	12/31/12	39126.0	1222.0	19979.0	8847.0	626	160658515
HII	Huntington Ingalls Industries, Inc.	Defense	12/31/12	6708.0	146.0	6392.0	667.0	282	42936002
HUN	Huntsman Corp	Specialty Chemicals	12/31/12	11187.0	363.0	8884.0	1773.0	378	172333451
H	Hyatt Hotels Corp	Hotels, Restaurants & Travel	12/31/12	3949.0	88.0	7640.0	4821.0	197	48842347
HDY	Hyperdynamics Corp.	Production & Extraction	6/30/12	-	-149.3	102.8	76.1	73	42887242
HY	Hyster-Yale Materials Handling, Inc.	Autos- Manufacturing	12/31/12	2469.1	98.0	1064.4	341.3	110	8343538
HY	Hyster-Yale Materials Handling, Inc.	Autos- Manufacturing	12/31/12	2469.1	98.0	1064.4	341.3	110	8343538

EARNINGS PER SHARE						P/E RATIO		DIVIDENDS PER SHARE			AV. YLD	DIV. DECLARED		PRICE RANGE	
QUARTERLY			ANNUAL								%			2012	
1st	2nd	3rd	2012	2011	2010			2012	2011	2010		AMOUNT	PAYABLE		
-	-	0.83	3.67	3.97	4.30	8.1 -	0.0	3.30	3.90	4.40	11.9	0.47660Z	81/16/21	29.7 -	0.0
-	-	0.15	0.67	0.70	0.38	30.9 -	0.0	1.12	0.12	0.10	7.8	0.040Y	3/19/13	20.7 -	0.0
-	-	0.49	1.42	1.44	1.21	20.6 -	0.0	1.24	1.24	1.24	4.7	0.310Y	81/16/21	29.2 -	0.0
-	-	0.78	3.49	4.97	2.76	11.6 -	0.0	6.50	-	9.43	21.2	2.7Y	81/16/21	40.6 -	0.0
-	-	1.05	3.83	2.30	2.99	11.0 -	0.0	0.64	0.60	0.56	1.8	0.1650Y	81/16/21	42.0 -	0.0
-	-	0.45	1.90	1.29	1.00	26.2 -	0.0	2.00	1.92	1.86	4.5	0.5250Z	81/16/21	49.9 -	0.0
-	-	-	21.91	16.81	13.37	2.0 -	0.0	-	-	-				42.9 -	0.0
-0.09	-	-	-1.02	-3.80	-0.83			-	-	-				11.1 -	0.0
-	-	0.16	0.98	0.90	0.83	69.3 -	0.0	2.96	2.84	2.74	5.0	0.7650Z	81/16/21	67.9 -	0.0
-	-	0.16	0.64	0.70	0.60	20.2 -	0.0	-	-	-		10.7	81/16/21	12.9 -	0.0
-	-	0.22	1.47	0.80	2.06	27.6 -	0.0							40.5 -	0.0
-	-	0.08	0.07	0.00	0.13	405.6 -	0.0	1.20	1.20	1.20	5.0	0.30Z	3/1/13	28.4 -	0.0
-	-	-0.01	-0.11	0.02	-0.05			0.34	-	-	1.$	0.14370	4/4/13	0.0 -	0.0
-	-	-0.01	-0.11	0.02	-0.05			0.34	-	-	3.3	0.14370	4/4/13	12.0 -	0.0
-	-	0.44	1.69	1.96	8.28	15.6 -	0.0					16.250Y	4/15/13	26.4 -	0.0
-	-	0.48	1.64	1.09	0.88	20.4 -	0.0	0.24	0.16	0.04	0.8	0.070Y	3/15/13	33.5 -	0.0
-	-	-0.06	0.02	-0.20	-0.14	245.5 -	0.0	-	-	-				4.9 -	0.0
-	-	0.00	0.05	0.51	0.13	136.8 -	0.0	0.06	0.02	-	1.2	0.8750Y	4/1/13	6.8 -	0.0
0.37	-	-	1.60	1.37	1.04	29.4 -	0.0	0.11	0.09	0.07	0.3	2.147Y	12/31/12	47.1 -	0.0
-	-	0.83	2.85	3.06	2.71	25.5 -	0.0	1.92	1.80	1.68	3.3	0.5150Y	81/16/21	72.7 -	0.0
-	-	-	0.76	0.74	0.70	12.4 -	0.0	0.72	0.72	0.42	8.0	0.06250	4/26/13	9.4 -	0.0
-	-	-	0.73	-	0.72	12.5 -	0.0	0.72	0.72	0.42	8.3	0.060	4/26/13	9.1 -	0.0
-	-	-	0.91	-	0.67	12.1 -	0.0	0.94	0.95	0.56	9.1	0.0750	4/26/13	11.0 -	0.0
-	-	-	0.52	0.49	0.50	12.4 -	0.0	0.48	0.48	0.28	7.9	0.04250	4/26/13	6.5 -	0.0
-	-	-	0.47	0.48	0.51	14.2 -	0.0	0.42	0.47	0.28	6.7	0.040	4/26/13	6.7 -	0.0
-	-	0.14	-0.44	1.22	-1.22			-	-	-				25.4 -	0.0
1.48	-	-	5.34	3.99	1.45	12.7 -	0.0	0.28	0.25	0.21		0.150Y	81/16/21	67.9 -	0.0
-	-	1.04	4.05	3.30	2.34	17.9 -	0.0	1.20	0.73	0.45	2.5	0.30	81/16/21	72.7 -	0.0
-	-	0.23	0.96	0.91	0.80	13.4 -	0.0	0.95	0.88	0.80	8.5	0.250Y	3/19/13	12.8 -	0.0
-	-	0.01	0.04	-0.21	-0.16	154.8 -	0.0	0.24	0.23	0.20	4.7	0.1862GHZ	4/15/13	6.2 -	0.0
-	-	0.77	2.89	2.74	2.21	30.3 -	0.0	1.56	1.38	1.28	2.2	0.380Y	81/16/21	87.5 -	0.0
-	-	0.55	0.54	0.40	-0.12	41.2 -	0.0	-	-	-				22.3 -	0.0
-	-	1.64	5.95	5.01	6.47	12.2 -	0.0	0.40	0.40	0.40	0.7	0.10Y	81/16/21	72.5 -	0.0
0.63	-	-	-6.41	3.32	3.69			0.50	0.40	0.32	2.7	0.1320Y	81/16/21	25.3 -	0.0
-	-	0.39	1.61	1.35	0.77	18.8 -	0.0	-	-	-				30.2 -	0.0
-	-	0.27	1.18	1.11	0.40	16.9 -	0.0	1.52	-	-	10.1	1.52G7Y	12/20/12	19.9 -	0.0
-	-	0.51	2.14	1.19	1.03	5.5 -	0.0	-	-	-				11.8 -	0.0
-	-	0.33	0.68	-	-	33.4 -	0.0	0.24	-	-	1.3	0.4750	2/15/13	22.7 -	0.0
-	-	0.13	0.65	0.54	0.44	25.3 -	0.0	-	-	-				16.4 -	0.0
-	-	0.43	1.02	0.54	0.86	38.8 -	0.0	1.70	1.70	1.70	5.0	21.56250Z	81/16/21	39.6 -	0.0
-	-	0.44	1.02	0.54	0.87			1.70	1.70	1.70					
-	-	0.03	-0.73	-0.16	0.36			1.70	1.70	1.70				4.5 -	0.0
0.39	-	-	1.94	2.09	1.97	18.2 -	0.0	0.49	0.43	0.41	1.6	0.1250Y	81/16/21	35.2 -	0.0
0.23	-	-	1.68	1.71	1.49	15.0 -	0.0	0.77	0.76	0.75	3.7	0.1950Y	81/16/21	25.3 -	0.0
-	0.53	-	7.13	10.30	3.65	4.1 -	3.5	1.15	2.30	2.20	4.2	0.1250Y	81/16/21	29.0 -	25.3
-	0.53	-	7.13	10.30	3.65	15.7 -	0.0	1.15	2.30	2.20	2.4	0.1250Y	81/16/21	111.6 -	0.0
-	-	-0.07	-0.10	-0.12	-0.24			-	-	-		0.51560Y	7/30/10	14.4 -	0.0
-	-	0.53	1.07	1.01	0.59	33.2 -	0.0	0.95	0.92	0.86	3.4	0.240Y	81/16/21	35.5 -	0.0
-	-	0.34	1.29	1.34	1.06	34.4 -	0.0	1.81	1.72	1.64	5.5	0.470	2/14/13	44.4 -	0.0
-	-	2.94	8.38	6.42	0.97	7.0 -	0.0	1.30	1.34	0.30	7.7	0.30Y	81/16/21	58.4 -	0.0
-	-	0.63	2.47	2.01	1.57	28.9 -	0.0	1.04	0.01	0.90	1.8	0.390Y	81/16/21	71.4 -	0.0
-	-	0.71	2.69	0.89	0.54	24.6 -	0.0	2.64	2.48	2.32	4.3	0.70Z	81/16/21	66.2 -	0.0
-	-	0.27	3.02	1.34	0.81	9.0 -	0.0	0.88	0.53	0.30	4.5	0.2250Y	6/21/13	27.3 -	0.0
-	45.63	-	117.34	295.67	147.91	0.3 -	0.0	0.01	0.01	0.00	0.0	-		40.0 -	0.0
-	-	1.20	3.69	2.61	2.59	20.5 -	0.0	1.53	1.37	1.21	2.5	0.410Y	81/16/21	75.5 -	0.0
-	-	0.78	2.51	1.70	1.97	8.8 -	0.0	0.55	0.46	0.35	2.9	0.1950Y	81/16/21	22.0 -	0.0
0.48	-	-	1.86	1.74	1.46	22.2 -	0.0	0.60	0.51	0.42	1.9	0.170Y	81/16/21	41.3 -	0.0
-	-	0.20	1.03	-0.09	1.34	45.3 -	0.0	-	-	-				46.6 -	0.0
0.20	-	-	2.77	0.23	0.77	9.2 -	0.0	0.15	0.15	0.15	0.8	0.15HY	81/16/21	25.4 -	0.0
-	-	0.01	0.27	-0.06	2.11	139.3 -	0.0	-	-	-				37.6 -	0.0
-	-	0.24	0.84	1.30	-0.07	32.9 -	0.0	1.82	1.80	1.80	7.4	0.470Z	81/16/21	27.6 -	0.0
-	-	-0.05	0.08	-0.02	-0.21	221.6 -	0.0	0.30	0.14	0.04	1.9	0.10Z	81/16/21	17.7 -	0.0
-0.08	-	-	-0.52	-2.85	0.03			-	-	-		0.47660Z	10/15/07	7.0 -	0.0
-	-	-1.30	-3.36	1.17	-1.84			-	-	-				84.0 -	0.0
-	-	-	-	-	-			1.59	1.59	1.59	6.4	0.39750Y	3/15/13	25.7 -	0.0
-	-	0.13	0.74	0.91	0.72	77.2 -	0.0	2.05	1.95	1.70	4.3	0.50	6/17/13	57.1 -	0.0
-	-	-	-	-	-			0.89	0.89	0.88	4.1	0.40630Y	4/1/13	23.1 -	0.0
-	-	-	-	0.08	0.28			-	0.17	0.16				44.0 -	0.0
-	-	1.45	5.00	4.42	3.59	19.5 -	0.0	1.68	1.52	1.44	2.0	0.450Y	81/16/21	97.7 -	0.0
-	-	-0.03	-	-0.92	0.48			-	0.20	0.10		0.10	3/28/13	12.0 -	0.0
-	-	-0.07	-0.41	-0.35	-			0.50	0.50	0.19	2.7	0.52340Z	4/1/13	23.1 -	0.0
-	-	0.16	1.49	-0.11	0.26	12.5 -	0.0	0.72	0.64	0.59	4.4	0.060Y	2/22/13	18.6 -	0.0
-	-	0.05	0.58	1.39	1.55	24.8 -	0.0	0.58	1.39	1.55	7.1	0.06130Z	4/12/13	14.4 -	0.0
-	-	2.62	7.47	8.46	6.47	12.3 -	0.0	1.03	0.75	-	1.4	0.260Y	81/16/21	91.8 -	0.0
-	-	0.26	2.91	-1.93	-	18.6 -	0.0	0.10	-	-	0.2	0.10Y	3/15/13	54.1 -	0.0
-	-	0.48	1.51	1.02	0.11	12.9 -	0.0	0.40	0.40	0.40	2.6	0.1250Y	81/16/21	19.4 -	0.0
-	-	0.14	0.53	0.67	0.32	82.7 -	0.0	-	-	-				43.8 -	0.0
-0.03	-	-	-0.93	-0.09	-0.09			-	-	-				1.3 -	0.0
-	-	1.48	5.83	4.91	1.94	9.8 -	0.0	2.25	-	-	4.8	0.250Y	3/15/13	57.2 -	0.0
-	-	1.48	5.83	4.91	1.94	7.3 -	7.3	2.25	-	-	5.3	0.250Y	3/15/13	42.7 -	42.7

SYMBOL	COMPANY	NATURE OF BUSINESS	FISCAL YEAR-END	TOTAL REV. $MILL	NET INCOME $MILL	TOTAL ASSETS $MILL	NET STK EQUITY $MILL	NO OF INST	INST. HOLDINGS (SHARES)
IAG	IAMGold Corp	Precious Metals	12/31/11	1673.2	806.7	4349.7	3474.5	234	228315302
IBN	ICICI Bank Ltd (India)	Banking	3/31/12	663635.8	76429.4	6041914.1	612765.0	318	158210310
IDA	Idacorp, Inc.	Electric Utilities	12/31/12	1080.7	168.8	5319.5	1758.8	229	42975495
IEX	IDEX Corporation	Industrial Machinery & Equipment	12/31/12	1954.3	37.6	2785.4	1465.0	341	86218768
IDT	IDT Corp.	Services	7/31/12	1506.8	38.6	451.1	102.2	110	9805823
CTC	IFM Investments Ltd.	Property, Real Estate & Developmen	12/31/11	604.6	-336.5	725.1	406.0	11	4523702
IHS	IHS Inc	Business Services	11/30/12	1529.9	158.2	3549.2	1584.4	320	65273191
ITW	Illinois Tool Works, Inc.	Industrial Machinery & Equipment	12/31/12	17924.0	2870.0	19309.0	10561.0	1049	422775640
IMN	Imation Corp.	Electrical Equipment	12/31/12	1099.6	-340.7	793.5	400.4	155	30159254
IMAX	IMAX Corp.	Entertainment	12/31/12	284.3	41.3	421.9	253.1	170	54584311
IFT	Imperial Holdings Inc	Finance Intermediaries & Services	12/31/12	19.1	-44.6	160.3	126.6	48	12328557
IMPV	Imperva Inc.	Internet & Software	12/31/12	104.2	-7.4	154.0	85.3	121	16792602
IHC	Independence Holding Co.	Life & Health	12/31/12	428.1	19.7	1262.3	285.7	52	4581676
IFN	India Fund, Inc. (The)	Holding and other Investment Office	12/31/12	15.5	4.6	967.7	877.1	134	10296826
IFN	India Fund, Inc. (The)	Holding and other Investment Office	12/31/12	15.5	4.6	967.7	877.1	134	10296826
IBA	Industrias Bachoco S.A.B. de C.V.	Food	12/31/11	27735.0	157.0	23169.9	16208.9	-	-
NRGY	Inergy L.P.	Equipment & Services	9/30/12	2006.8	554.9	2207.6		179	60324257
NRGM	Inergy Midstream L.P.	Production & Extraction	9/30/12	189.8	65.7	1027.9		38	24487537
BLOX	Infoblox Inc	Internet & Software	7/31/12	169.2	-8.2	243.0	142.1	114	29623410
INFY	Infosys Ltd.	IT Services	3/31/12	6994.0	1716.0	7537.0	6576.0	295	84671911
IAE	ING Asia Pacific High Dividend Equi	Holding and other Investment Office	2/29/12	7.9	4.9	209.0	207.4	33	1825442
IHD	ING Emerging Markets High Divide	Holding and other Investment Office	2/29/12	8.5	4.7	322.0	319.6	16	2156035
IGA	ING Global Advantage & Premium	Holding and other Investment Office	2/29/12	6.3	4.0	238.9	232.2	31	4279780
IGD	ING Global Equity Dividend & Premi	Holding and other Investment Office	2/29/12	46.3	34.9	997.2	976.7	74	6916022
ING	ING Groep N.V.	Life & Health	12/31/12	89881.0	3259.0	1162128.0	51761.0	222	52224700
IDE	ING Infrastructure Industrials & Mat	Holding and other Investment Office	2/29/12	9.8	5.0	397.2	394.3	26	2434830
IID	ING International High Dividend Eq	Holding and other Investment Office	2/29/12	3.6	2.5	85.5	82.2	17	252181
PPR	ING Prime Rate Trust	Holding and other Investment Office	2/29/12	70.3	51.6	1282.6	851.3	99	28584906
IRR	ING Risk Managed Natural Resourc	Holding and other Investment Office	2/29/12	5.2	1.4	305.6	298.7	48	3913324
IR	Ingersoll-Rand Plc	Industrial Machinery & Equipment	12/31/12	14034.9	1018.6	18492.9	7147.8	-	-
IM	Ingram Micro Inc.	Computer Hardware & Equipment	12/29/12	37827.3	305.9	11480.4	3611.3	292	171883735
INGR	Ingredion Inc	Food	12/31/12	6532.0	428.0	5592.0	2437.0	444	76408917
IRC	Inland Real Estate Corp	REITs	12/31/12	159.8	17.8	1243.4	409.6	190	69810743
IPHI	Inphi Corp	Semiconductors	12/31/12	91.2	-20.7	170.1	153.0	95	21750263
NSP	Insperity Inc	Business Services	12/31/12	2158.8	40.4	750.2	240.9	168	22688119
TEG	Integrys Energy Group Inc	Electric Utilities	12/31/12	4212.4	284.3	10327.4	3076.9	437	42653910
IHG	InterContinental Hotels Group Plc	Hotels, Restaurants & Travel	12/31/12	1835.0	545.0	3263.0	308.0	135	15035079
ICE	IntercontinentalExchange Inc	Finance Intermediaries & Services	12/31/12	1363.0	551.6	37214.8	3643.4	530	75214227
IN	Intermec Inc	Peripherals	12/31/12	790.1	-282.5	556.3	126.6	176	57695352
IBM	International Business Machines Co	IT Services	12/31/12	104507.0	16604.0	119213.0	18860.0	2139	771339331
IFF	International Flavors & Fragrances I	Specialty Chemicals	12/31/12	2821.4	254.1	3249.6	1248.8	418	80526784
IGT	International Game Technology	Hotels, Restaurants & Travel	9/30/12	2150.7	245.9	4285.1	1197.8	468	251094245
AIG 09	International Lease Finance Corp.	Business Services	12/31/12	4504.2	410.3	39810.4	7942.9	-	-
IP	International Paper Co.	Paper & Forest Products	12/31/12	27833.0	794.0	32153.0	6304.0	722	431285200
IRF	International Rectifier Corp.	Semiconductors	6/24/12	1050.6	-55.0	1531.8	1276.3	223	79129840
ISH	International Shipholding Corp.	Shipping	12/31/12	243.5	22.0	637.7	262.3	74	3549266
IOC	InterOil Corp.	Production & Extraction	12/31/12	1320.6	1.6	1299.8	776.1	139	35837792
IPG	Interpublic Group of Companies Inc.	Advertising	12/31/12	6956.2	446.7	13493.9	2420.6	485	454366451
IPL PRD	Interstate Power & Light Co	Electric Utilities	12/31/12	1650.3	150.2	5457.0	1664.3	2	322313
INXN	InterXion Holding NV	IT Services	12/31/11	244.3	25.6	744.3	330.6	131	34571340
IL	IntraLinks Holdings Inc	IT Services	12/31/12	216.7	-17.4	489.8	322.1	113	49041500
IPI	Intrepid Potash Inc	Agricultural Chemicals	12/31/12	451.3	87.4	994.6	905.7	230	55039782
IVC	Invacare Corp	Medical Instruments & Equipment	12/31/12	1455.5	1.8	1262.3	621.0	178	32480369
INVN	InvenSense, Inc.	Semiconductors	4/1/12	153.0	36.9	193.3	176.9	-	-
VBF	Invesco Bond Fund	Holding and other Investment Office	2/29/12	11.5	10.2	241.4	234.2	29	1417671
VCV	Invesco California Value Municipal I	Holding and other Investment Office	2/29/12	23.6	20.0	510.5	409.0	37	2943391
VTA	Invesco Dynamic Credit Opportuniti	Holding and other Investment Office	2/29/12	82.6	62.2	1294.8	916.2	64	10291423
VLT	Invesco High Income Trust II	Holding and other Investment Office	2/29/12	6.6	5.2	86.4	61.8	26	592537
IVZ	Invesco Ltd	Wealth Management	12/31/12	4177.0	677.1	17492.4	8316.8	471	408372309
IVR	Invesco Mortgage Capital Inc.	REITs	12/31/12	566.8	339.9	18914.8	2558.1	205	58331386
OIA	Invesco Municipal Income Opportun	Holding and other Investment Office	2/29/12	9.1	8.1	148.9	140.1	-	-
VMO	Invesco Municipal Opportunity Trust	Holding and other Investment Office	2/29/12	38.3	32.1	832.2	667.3	66	2423751
VKQ	Invesco Municipal Trust	Holding and other Investment Office	2/29/12	41.6	35.1	904.6	734.9	54	2368327
VPV	Invesco Pennsylvania Value Munici	Holding and other Investment Office	2/29/12	26.1	22.2	568.9	486.9	39	1133585
IQI	Invesco Quality Municipal Income T	Holding and other Investment Office	2/29/12	23.1	19.8	524.2	443.1	-	-
VVR	Invesco Senior Income Trust	Holding and other Investment Office	2/29/12	72.6	55.2	1358.7	1079.7	103	27634470
VGM	Invesco Trust for Investment Grade	Holding and other Investment Office	2/29/12	62.3	52.3	1345.6	1078.8	67	2261350
VTN	Invesco Trust For Investment Grade	Holding and other Investment Office	2/29/12	17.8	14.8	389.0	314.7	29	615963
IIM	Invesco Value Municipal Income Tr	Holding and other Investment Office	2/29/12	21.5	18.3	498.8	408.1	-	-
ITG	Investment Technology Group Inc.	Finance Intermediaries & Services	12/31/12	504.4	-247.9	2196.8	409.8	190	40290324
IRET	Investors Real Estate Trust	REITs	4/30/12	241.8	8.2	1714.4	433.0	159	37311990
IO	ION Geophysical Corp	Equipment & Services	12/31/12	526.3	63.3	820.6	500.6	206	120714152
IRM	Iron Mountain Inc	Business Services	12/31/12	3005.3	171.7	6358.3	1150.0	431	180422546
IRS	IRSA Inversiones y Representacion	Property, Real Estate & Developmen	6/30/12	1567.3	280.1	6600.6	2335.3	46	8390806
ISS	iSoftStone Holdings Ltd.	IT Services	12/31/11	283.4	18.8	378.1	293.2	33	23871927
SFI	iStar Financial Inc	REITs	12/31/12	400.5	-239.9	6150.8	1238.9	208	70863096
ITUB	Itau Unibanco Holding S.A.	Banking	12/31/11	147550.0	13837.0	818136.0	73941.0	367	691881088
ITC	ITC Holdings Corp	Electric Utilities	12/31/12	830.5	187.9	5564.8	1414.9	320	56457101
ITT	ITT Corporation	Industrial Machinery & Equipment	12/31/12	2227.8	125.4	3386.1	703.2	453	103503969
ESI	ITT Educational Services, Inc.	Educational Services	12/31/12	1287.2	140.5	672.2	127.0	254	29202981

| EARNINGS PER SHARE | | | | | | P/E RATIO | | DIVIDENDS PER SHARE | | | AV. YLD | DIV. DECLARED | | PRICE RANGE | |
| QUARTERLY | | | ANNUAL | | | | | PER SHARE | | | % | | | 2012 | |
1st	2nd	3rd	2012	2011	2010			2012	2011	2010		AMOUNT	PAYABLE		
-	-	0.21	-	2.14	0.70	-						0.1250	1/7/13	16.4 -	0.0
-	16.91	-	66.06	53.25	41.72	0.7 -	0.0							47.8 -	0.0
-	-	1.84	3.37	3.36	2.95	14.3 -	0.0	1.37	1.20	1.20	3.2	0.380Y	81/16/21	48.3 -	0.0
-	-	0.60	0.45	2.32	1.90	119.2 -	0.0	0.77	0.66	0.57	1.8	0.230Y	81/16/21	53.6 -	0.0
-	0.13	-	1.75	1.19	0.94	6.9 -	0.0	0.66	0.67	-	6.8	0.6DY	11/13/12	12.1 -	0.0
-	-	0.00	-	-0.50	-0.25	-		-							
0.37	-	-	2.37	2.06	2.18	50.1 -	0.0	-						118.6 -	0.0
-	-	1.12	6.06	4.19	3.03	10.8 -	0.0	1.48	1.40	1.30	2.5	0.380Y	81/16/21	65.4 -	0.0
-	-	-0.17	-9.09	-1.24	-4.19			-				0.080Y	12/29/08	6.3 -	0.0
-	-	0.22	0.61	0.23	1.51	44.9 -	0.0							27.4 -	0.0
-	-	-1.48	-2.10	-2.03	-3.51	-		-						4.5 -	0.0
-	-	-0.08	-0.32	-1.34	-2.46	-								41.9 -	0.0
-	-	0.22	1.09	0.74	1.29	9.8 -	0.0	0.09	0.05	0.05	0.9	0.0350Y	12/21/12	10.6 -	0.0
-	-		0.11	-0.02	-0.02	0.0 -	0.0	2.37	1.20	3.87	1.$	2.2246C	1/31/13	0.0 -	0.0
-	-		0.11	-0.02	-0.02	218.0 -	0.0	2.37	1.20	3.87	11.2	2.2246C	1/31/13	24.0 -	0.0
														33.9 -	0.0
0.01	-	-	4.22	0.15	-0.37	5.2 -	0.0	2.16	2.82	2.76	11.4	0.290	81/16/21	21.9 -	0.0
0.06	-	-	0.58			42.7 -	0.0	0.79	-		3.5	0.390	2/14/13	24.8 -	0.0
-	-0.07	-	-0.40	-0.54	0.01									23.9 -	0.0
-	0.75	-	3.00	2.62	2.30	19.2 -	0.0	0.75	1.22	0.50	1.6			57.6 -	0.0
-	-	-	0.38	0.33	0.32	45.1 -	0.0	1.67	1.73	1.94	10.8	0.3550	4/15/13	17.1 -	0.0
-	-	-	0.24			66.0 -	0.0	1.20			8.3	0.360	4/15/13	15.9 -	0.0
-	-	-	0.22	0.20	0.21	63.0 -	0.0	1.32	1.38	1.77	11.5	0.280	4/15/13	13.9 -	0.0
-	-	-	0.36	0.35	0.38	26.4 -	0.0	1.19	1.30	1.78	13.3	0.0840	4/15/13	9.5 -	0.0
-	-	-	0.69	0.85	0.62	15.1 -	0.0	0.00	0.00	0.00	0.0	0.53130Z	6/15/13	10.4 -	0.0
-	-	-	0.25	0.19	0.00	75.2 -	0.0	1.80	1.80		10.5	0.4050	4/15/13	18.8 -	0.0
-	-	-	0.30	0.26	0.25	35.3 -	0.0	1.09	1.20	1.81	11.3	0.0770	4/15/13	10.6 -	0.0
-	-	-	0.35	0.30	0.28	19.4 -	0.0	0.32	0.32	0.32	5.3	0.0380	4/22/13	6.8 -	0.0
-	-	-	0.06	0.12	0.13	202.5 -	0.0	1.42	1.47	1.66	12.9	0.280	4/15/13	12.2 -	0.0
-	-	1.03	3.28	1.01	1.89	17.2 -	0.0	0.69	0.59	0.28	1.5	0.210	81/16/21	56.5 -	0.0
-	-	0.35	1.99	1.53	1.94	10.1 -	0.0	-						20.1 -	0.0
-	-	1.45	5.47	5.32	2.20	13.2 -	0.0	0.92	0.66	0.56	1.6	0.380Y	81/16/21	72.3 -	0.0
-	-	-0.01	0.11	-0.09		91.7 -	0.0	0.57	0.57	0.57	6.7	0.16930Z	5/15/13	10.1 -	0.0
-	-	-0.04	-0.73	0.07	0.61									14.6 -	0.0
-	-	0.45	1.56	1.16	0.86	21.9 -	0.0	1.66	0.60	0.52	6.0	0.170Y	3/22/13	34.2 -	0.0
-	-	0.83	3.55	2.87	2.83	17.3 -	0.0	2.72	2.72	2.72	5.0	0.680Y	81/16/21	61.3 -	0.0
-	-	0.59	1.86	1.60	0.95	16.5 -	0.0	-						30.6 -	0.0
-	-	1.79	7.52	6.90	5.35	21.7 -	0.0	-						163.1 -	0.0
-	-	0.12	-4.68	-0.51	-0.09									9.9 -	0.0
-	-	3.33	14.37	13.06	11.52	15.0 -	0.0	3.30	2.90	2.50	1.7	0.850Y	81/16/21	215.8 -	0.0
-	-	0.20	3.09	3.26	3.26	24.9 -	0.0	1.30	1.16	1.04	2.1	0.340Y	81/16/21	76.9 -	0.0
0.24	-	-	0.85	0.94	0.62	20.4 -	0.0	0.24	0.24	0.24	1.7	0.080Y	81/16/21	17.3 -	0.0
												0.025	7/11/90		
-	-	0.54	1.80	3.07	1.48	26.1 -	0.0	1.09	0.97	0.40	3.0	0.30Y	81/16/21	47.0 -	0.0
-	-0.47	-	-0.79	2.33	1.13							0.0533	81/16/21	22.6 -	0.0
-	-	0.25	3.04	4.40	2.12	7.7 -	0.0	1.13	1.50	1.63	6.2	0.250Y	3/4/13	23.4 -	0.0
-	-	0.11	0.03	0.36	-1.00	3041.3 -	0.0	-						91.2 -	0.0
-	-	0.15	0.94	0.99	0.47	14.2 -	0.0	0.24	0.24	-	2.1	0.0750Y	81/16/21	13.4 -	0.0
								2.09	2.09	2.09	8.3	0.52340Y	3/15/13	25.2 -	24.9
-	-	0.12	-	0.39	0.31									26.3 -	0.0
-	-	-0.02	-0.32	-0.02	-0.58			-						0.8 -	0.0
-	-	0.44	1.16	1.45	0.60	21.7 -	0.0	0.75			3.5	0.75G7	81/16/21	25.1 -	0.0
-	-	0.09	0.08	-0.13	0.78	286.3 -	0.0	0.04	0.06	0.04	0.3	0.01140Y	4/12/13	17.2 -	0.0
-	-	0.19	0.37	0.08	0.17	51.2 -	0.0	-						18.9 -	0.0
-	-	-	0.90	0.62	1.04	25.0 -	0.0	1.37	1.00	1.02	6.5	0.07550	4/30/13	22.5 -	0.0
-	-	-	0.91	0.32	0.98	16.0 -	0.0	-				0.066M	4/30/13	14.6 -	0.0
-	-	-	0.84	0.43	0.80	16.2 -	0.0	0.88	1.03	1.06	7.1	0.0750	4/30/13	13.6 -	0.0
-	-	-	1.37	0.24	1.61	13.9 -	0.0	1.39	1.53	1.55	8.0	0.1160	4/30/13	19.0 -	0.0
-	-	0.38	1.49	1.57	1.01	19.6 -	0.0	0.64	0.48	0.43	2.6	0.17250	81/16/21	29.1 -	0.0
-	-	0.65	2.89	3.27	3.78	7.7 -	0.0	2.60	3.42	3.49	13.2	0.48440Z	4/25/13	22.3 -	0.0
-	-	-	0.41	0.32	0.44	19.5 -	0.0	0.42	0.42	0.42	5.7	0.035M	4/30/13	8.0 -	0.0
-	-	-	0.95	0.34	1.06	16.7 -	0.0	1.03	1.03	1.03	6.9	0.08M	4/30/13	15.9 -	0.0
-	-	-	0.90	0.32	1.00	17.5 -	0.0	0.96	0.96	0.96	6.5	0.0762M	4/30/13	15.8 -	0.0
-	-	-	0.93	0.32	1.00	18.2 -	0.0	-				0.075M	4/30/13	16.9 -	0.0
-	-	-	0.84	0.27	0.93	17.8 -	0.0	0.87	0.85	0.85	6.2	0.0688M	4/30/13	15.0 -	0.0
-	-	-	0.31	0.17	0.29	18.5 -	0.0	-				0.03050	4/30/13	5.7 -	0.0
-	-	-	0.97	0.34	1.08	16.8 -	0.0	1.06	1.06	1.05	6.8	0.083M	4/30/13	16.3 -	0.0
-	-	-	0.97	0.35	1.03	17.8 -	0.0	1.01	1.01	1.00	6.2	0.084M	4/30/13	17.3 -	0.0
-	-	-	0.89	0.27	0.93	19.3 -	0.0	0.89	0.87	0.87	5.4	0.075M	4/30/13	17.2 -	0.0
-	-	0.01	-6.45	-4.42	0.55			-				0.03330	3/15/99	12.5 -	0.0
-	-	0.03	0.07	0.22	0.03	142.9 -	0.0	0.56	0.69	0.68	6.8	0.49690Z	4/1/13	10.0 -	0.0
-	-	0.09	0.39	0.15	-0.27	19.9 -	0.0	-						7.8 -	0.0
-	-	0.31	0.98	2.02	-0.27	38.5 -	0.0	5.12	0.94	0.38	15.7	0.270Y	81/16/21	37.7 -	0.0
0.07	-	-	0.48	0.49	0.58	20.1 -	0.0	-						9.7 -	0.0
-	0.01	-	0.03	-0.05										9.1 -	0.0
-	-	-0.86	-3.26	-0.70	0.39								0.46880Z	3/15/13	10.9 -	0.0
-	0.73	-	3.05	2.57				-	0.38	0.25				19.4 -	0.0
-	-	0.98	3.60	3.31	2.84	24.8 -	0.0	1.46	1.38	1.31	1.9	0.37750Y	81/16/21	89.3 -	0.0
-	-	0.78	1.33	-1.40	8.60	21.9 -	0.0	0.36	0.09	2.00	1.6	0.091GY	81/16/21	29.2 -	0.0
-	-	1.83	5.85	11.13	11.17	11.8 -	0.0	-						68.8 -	0.0

SYMBOL	COMPANY	NATURE OF BUSINESS	FISCAL YEAR-END	TOTAL REV. $MILL	NET INCOME $MILL	TOTAL ASSETS $MILL	NET STK EQUITY $MILL	NO OF INST	INST. HOLDINGS (SHARES)
JBL	Jabil Circuit, Inc.	Electrical Equipment	8/31/12	17151.9	394.7	7803.1	2105.1	467	180802429
JEC	Jacobs Engineering Group, Inc.	Construction Services	9/28/12	10893.8	379.0	6839.4	3722.5	582	127237336
JAG	Jaguar Mining Inc	Precious Metals	12/31/12	172.4	-84.5	503.9	153.8	78	18488697
JHX	James Hardie Industries Plc	Construction Materials	3/31/12	1237.5	604.3	2310.0	126.4	23	872842
JNS	Janus Capital Group Inc	Wealth Management	12/31/12	850.0	102.3	2660.4	1417.9	299	210668731
JEQ	Japan Equity Fund, Inc. (The)	Holding and other Investment Office	10/31/12	2.0	0.7	81.6	81.3	40	7228838
JOF	Japan Smaller Capitalization Fund I	Holding and other Investment Office	2/29/12	4.5	1.5	251.7	250.7	66	10464693
JAH	Jarden Corp.	Leisure Equipment	12/31/12	6696.1	243.9	7710.6	1759.6	374	77476107
JMI	Javelin Mortgage Investment Corp	REITs	12/31/12	8.4	6.1	1286.5	148.0		
JFC	JF China Region Fund Inc	Holding and other Investment Office	12/31/12	2.4	0.5	106.3	99.7	28	4477437
JKS	JinkoSolar Holding Co., Ltd.	Semiconductors	12/31/11	7385.0	273.3	9176.4	2895.2	35	1745528
JMP	JMP Group Inc	Finance Intermediaries & Services	12/31/12	143.1	2.8	709.9	126.9	66	10095621
JBT	John Bean Technologies Corp	Industrial Machinery & Equipment	12/31/12	917.3	36.2	678.0	105.6	160	26814837
BTO	John Hancock Bank and Thrift Opp	Holding and other Investment Office	10/31/12	7.7	3.1	350.9	350.5	57	3029385
HEQ	John Hancock Hedged Equity & Inc	Holding and other Investment Office	12/31/12	1.2	0.7	244.9	240.8	21	1350694
JHS	John Hancock Income Securities Tr	Holding and other Investment Office	10/31/12	14.7	12.0	277.8	185.8	25	1360169
HTY	John Hancock Investment Trust	Holding and other Investment Office	8/31/92	3.9	2.6	119.5	119.5		
JHI	John Hancock Investors Trust	Holding and other Investment Office	10/31/12	18.7	16.1	263.8	176.4	39	477244
HPI	John Hancock Preferred Income Fu	Holding and other Investment Office	7/31/12	54.5	45.1	859.1	571.7	57	1543473
PDT	John Hancock Premium Dividend F	Holding and other Investment Office	10/31/12	57.3	44.6	1100.7	728.2	70	3955937
JNJ	Johnson & Johnson	Pharmaceuticals	12/30/12	67224.0	10853.0	121347.0	64826.0	2319	2080929393
JCI	Johnson Controls Inc	Auto Parts	9/30/12	41955.0	1226.0	30884.0	11555.0	881	559264339
JNY	Jones Group Inc	Apparel, Footwear & Accessories	12/31/12	3798.1	-56.1	2595.5	1005.4	240	85529178
JLL	Jones Lang LaSalle Inc	Property, Real Estate & Developmen	12/31/12	3932.8	208.0	4351.5	1951.2	321	41735280
JRN	Journal Communications Inc	Publishing	12/30/12	400.0	33.3	625.8	205.5	134	44682785
JOY	Joy Global Inc	Industrial Machinery & Equipment	10/26/12	5660.9	762.0	6142.5	2577.2	600	101484991
JPM	JPMorgan Chase & Co.	Banking	12/31/12	108184.0	21284.0	2359141.0	204069.0	2051	3048403337
JNPR	Juniper Networks Inc	Peripherals	12/31/12	4365.4	186.5	9832.1	6999.0	503	509454337
JE	Just Energy Group Inc.	Electric Utilities	3/31/12	2785.3	-126.6	1543.0	-500.8		
LRN	K12 Inc	Educational Services	6/30/12	708.4	17.5	648.8	473.5	121	39748814
KAI	Kadant Inc	Industrial Machinery & Equipment	12/29/12	331.8	31.6	358.9	248.6	140	13444895
KAMN	Kaman Corp.	Industrial Machinery & Equipment	12/31/12	1592.6	55.0	1097.0	420.2	163	26292402
KSU	Kansas City Southern	Rail	12/31/12	2238.6	377.3	6395.9	3096.6	492	110049854
KSU 15	Kansas City Southern Railway Com	Rail	12/31/00	572.2	380.5	1944.5	643.4		
KS	KapStone Paper & Packaging Corp	Paper & Forest Products	12/31/12	1216.6	62.5	1131.2	517.9	183	40190639
KAR	KAR Auction Services Inc.	Retail - Automotive	12/31/12	1963.4	92.0	4922.3	1443.7		
KDN	Kaydon Corp.	Industrial Machinery & Equipment	12/31/12	475.2	0.5	615.2	330.8	195	35038366
KED	Kayne Anderson Energy Developm	Holding and other Investment Office	11/30/12	32.6	0.8	347.1	247.0	54	3707743
KYE	Kayne Anderson Energy Total Retur	Holding and other Investment Office	11/30/12	39.2	-1.5	1347.4	901.8	89	5875435
KMF	Kayne Anderson Midstream / Energ	Holding and other Investment Office	11/30/12	27.2	3.6	920.5	635.2	33	3427561
KYN	Kayne Anderson MLP Investment C	Holding and other Investment Office	11/30/12	32.7	-58.6	4497.8	2520.8	181	23406131
KB	KB Financial Group, Inc.	Banking	12/31/11	77826841.0	2373690.0	277600817.0	22917975.0	146	36278230
KBH	KB HOME	Builders	11/30/12	1560.1	-59.0	2561.7	376.8	276	73845801
KBR	KBR Inc	Construction Services	12/31/12	7921.0	144.0	5767.0	2542.0	402	153846564
K	Kellogg Co	Food	12/29/12	14197.0	961.0	15184.0	2419.0	809	484997707
KEM	KEMET Corp.	Electrical Equipment	3/31/12	984.8	6.7	975.6	359.0	140	37526960
KMPR	Kemper Corp. (DE)	General Insurance	12/31/12	2462.3	103.4	8009.1	2161.7	185	27598304
KMT	Kennametal Inc.	Industrial Machinery & Equipment	6/30/12	2736.2	307.2	3034.2	1643.8	352	83777302
KW	Kennedy-Wilson Holdings Inc	Property, Real Estate & Developmen	12/31/12	64.1	4.3	1283.8	509.6	4	2975087
KEG	Key Energy Services, Inc.	Equipment & Services	12/31/12	1960.1	7.6	2761.6	1253.8	256	156651423
KEY	KeyCorp	Banking	12/31/12	4672.0	858.0	89236.0	10271.0	689	791297434
KID	Kid Brands, Inc.	Furniture	12/31/11	252.6	-38.6	192.8	89.8	65	9823174
KRC	Kilroy Realty Corp	REITs	12/31/12	404.9	270.9	4616.1	2189.6	274	88014972
KMB	Kimberly-Clark Corp.	Household & Personal Products	12/31/12	21063.0	1750.0	19873.0	5534.0	1299	302704357
KIM	Kimco Realty Corp.	REITs	12/31/12	922.3	266.1	9740.8	4765.2	449	424401070
KMP	Kinder Morgan Energy Partners, L.	Equipment & Services	12/31/12	8642.0	1339.0	32094.0		741	65816548
KMI	Kinder Morgan Inc.	Equipment & Services	12/31/12	9973.0	315.0	68185.0	13865.0		
KMR	Kinder Morgan Management, LLC	Equipment & Services	12/31/12		-20.0	3476.0	3464.0	423	70751909
KND	Kindred Healthcare Inc	Hospitals & Health Care Facilities	12/31/12	6181.3	-40.4	4237.9	1256.2	198	55678587
KFS	Kingsway Financial Services Inc.	General Insurance	12/31/12	150.4	-52.1	372.8	65.1	6	42066
KGC	Kinross Gold Corp.	Precious Metals	12/31/12	4311.4	-2504.9	14882.4	9850.2	380	595909833
KEX	Kirby Corp.	Shipping	12/31/12	2112.7	209.4	3653.1	1695.0	304	57936641
KRG	Kite Realty Group Trust	REITs	12/31/12	101.1	-4.3	1288.7	473.1	176	80570576
KKR	KKR & Co L P (DE)	Finance Intermediaries & Services	12/31/12	568.4	560.8	44426.4		180	207545041
KFN	KKR Financial Holdings LLC	Finance Intermediaries & Services	12/31/12	696.8	348.2	8358.9	1839.1	195	112276280
KMG	KMG Chemicals, Inc.	Specialty Chemicals	7/31/12	272.7	13.8	167.7	106.8	80	7561965
KCG	Knight Capital Group Inc	Finance Intermediaries & Services	12/31/12	736.1	-347.1	9778.4	1482.5	203	163862997
KNX	Knight Transportation Inc.	Trucking	12/31/12	936.0	64.1	782.5	490.2	183	66337014
KNL	Knoll Inc	Office Equipment & Furniture	12/31/12	887.5	50.0	695.1	188.1	136	52352657
KNOP	KNOT Offshore Partners LP	Shipping							
KOG	Kodiak Oil & Gas Corp	Production & Extraction	12/31/12	408.7	131.6	2373.6	1035.9	277	207790095
KSS	Kohl's Corp.	Retail - General Merchandise/Depart	2/2/13	19279.0	986.0	13905.0	6048.0	779	226603216
KNM	Konami Corp	Internet & Software	3/31/12	265758.0	23012.0	328006.0	215458.0	26	223335
PHG	Koninklijke Philips Electronics N.V.	Household Appliances, Electronics &	12/31/12	24788.0	226.0	29079.0	11140.0	248	61703275
KOP	Koppers Holdings Inc	Paper & Forest Products	12/31/12	1555.0	65.6	780.0	150.6	202	21290506
KEP	Korea Electric Power Corp	Electric Utilities	12/31/11	43532302.0	-3370464.0	136467850.0	53270296.0	130	107610721
KEF	Korea Equity Fund, Inc.	Holding and other Investment Office	10/31/12	1.0	-0.9	105.2	103.6	29	6320300
KF	Korea Fund, Inc. (The)	Holding and other Investment Office	6/30/12	3.7	-1.3	405.1	387.6	50	4543643
KFY	Korn/Ferry International (DE)	Business Services	4/30/12	826.8	54.3	1014.7	629.5	179	47672643
KOS	Kosmos Energy Ltd	Production & Extraction	12/31/12	672.2	-67.0	2366.1	1028.9	95	317724475

T34

| EARNINGS PER SHARE | | | | | | P/E RATIO | | DIVIDENDS PER SHARE | | | AV. YLD % | DIV. DECLARED | | PRICE RANGE | |
| QUARTERLY | | | ANNUAL | | | | | | | | | | | 2012 | |
1st	2nd	3rd	2012	2011	2010			2012	2011	2010		AMOUNT	PAYABLE		
-	0.43	-	1.87	1.73	0.78	13.6 -	0.0	0.32	0.28	0.28	1.6	0.080Y	81/16/21	25.4 -	0.0
0.76	-	-	2.94	2.60	1.96	19.1 -	0.0	-	-		-	0.00710	81/16/21	56.2 -	0.0
-	-	-0.26	-1.00	-0.78	0.26			-	-		-			4.8 -	0.0
-	0.03	-	1.38	-0.80	-0.20	38.6 -	0.0	0.04	-		0.1			53.3 -	0.0
-	-	0.14	0.55	0.78	0.88	17.9 -	0.0	0.29	0.15	0.04	3.5	0.060Y	81/16/21	9.8 -	0.0
-	-	-	0.05	0.04	0.03	125.2 -	0.0	0.05	0.06	0.04	0.9	0.06460	1/11/13	6.3 -	0.0
-	-	-	0.06	0.03	0.02	143.7 -	0.0	0.04	0.08	0.05	0.5	0.0810	12/6/12	8.6 -	0.0
-	-	0.67	2.07	1.54	0.79	21.1 -	0.0	-	0.23	0.22	-	0.05750Y	81/16/21	43.7 -	0.0
-	-	-1.20	1.88	-		10.6 -	0.0	0.46	-		2.4	0.230Z	6/27/13	20.0 -	0.0
-	-	-	0.08	0.14	0.05	187.0 -	0.0	0.10	0.10	0.02	0.8	0.1046	12/14/12	15.0 -	0.0
-	-	-0.62	-	-1.23	10.92			-	-		-			9.7 -	0.0
-	-	-0.07	0.12	-0.11	0.40	63.7 -	0.0	0.14	0.11	0.06	2.3	0.0350Y	4/5/13	7.6 -	0.0
-	-	0.20	1.23	1.04	1.28	17.2 -	0.0	0.28	0.28	0.28	1.7	0.070Y	3/25/13	21.2 -	0.0
-	-	-	0.17	0.08	0.07	123.1 -	0.0	0.94	0.91	0.73	5.4	0.29610	3/28/13	20.9 -	0.0
-	-	-	0.05	0.02		335.8 -	0.0	1.30	0.36		8.2	0.3230	3/28/13	16.8 -	0.0
-	-	-	1.03	1.08	1.19	17.0 -	0.0	1.10	1.13	1.16	6.8	0.22980	3/28/13	17.5 -	0.0
-	-	-	-	-				-	-		-	0.320	3/28/13	13.7 -	0.0
-	-	-	1.88	1.93	2.15	13.2 -	0.0	1.94	1.97	2.07	8.4	0.42080	3/28/13	24.9 -	0.0
-	-	-	1.74	1.72	1.70	13.9 -	0.0	1.68	1.54	1.49	7.4	0.140	4/30/13	24.1 -	0.0
-	-	-	0.89	0.88		17.2 -	0.0	0.91	0.91	0.87	6.5	0.07550	4/30/13	15.3 -	0.0
-	-	1.05	3.86	3.49	4.78	21.1 -	0.0	2.40	2.25	2.11	3.5	0.610Y	81/16/21	81.5 -	0.0
0.52	-	-	1.78	2.36	2.19	19.7 -	0.0	0.72	0.64	0.52	2.5	0.190Y	81/16/21	35.1 -	0.0
-	-	0.22	-0.72	0.61	0.62			0.20	0.20	0.20	1.8	0.050Y	3/15/13	13.9 -	0.0
-	-	1.10	4.63	3.70	3.48	21.7 -	0.0	0.40	0.30	0.20	0.5	0.20Y	81/16/21	100.7 -	0.0
-	-	0.14	0.61	0.37	0.59	11.1 -	0.0	0.35	0.57	0.57	6.6	0.020Y	3/6/09	6.8 -	0.0
1.33	-	-	7.13	5.72	4.40	10.8 -	0.0	0.70	0.70	0.70	1.2	0.1750Y	81/16/21	76.8 -	0.0
-	-	1.40	5.20	4.48	3.98	9.8 -	0.0	1.15	0.80	0.20	2.8	0.30Y	81/16/21	51.0 -	0.0
-	-	0.03	0.35	0.79	1.15	64.9 -	0.0	-	-		-			22.7 -	0.0
-	-	0.28	-0.92	2.40	1.79			1.24	0.31		11.9	0.070	4/30/13	14.1 -	0.0
-	0.24	-	0.45	0.37	0.71	58.5 -	0.0	-	-		-			26.3 -	0.0
-	-	0.74	2.73	2.74	1.48	10.2 -	0.0	-	-		-	0.125GY	5/9/13	27.9 -	0.0
-	-	0.56	2.07	1.93	1.47	18.5 -	0.0	0.64	0.60	0.56	1.9	0.160Y	4/2/13	38.4 -	0.0
-	-	0.82	3.43	3.00	1.67	32.3 -	0.0	0.78	-		1.0	0.250Y	81/16/21	110.9 -	0.0
-	-	0.15	-	-				-	-		-			-	
-	-	0.38	1.31	2.61	1.38	21.3 -	0.0	2.00	-		9.8	2.G7Y	12/20/12	27.9 -	0.0
-	-	0.14	0.66	0.52	0.51	33.6 -	0.0	0.19	-		1.0	0.190Y	81/16/21	22.2 -	0.0
-	-	-0.99	0.02	1.52	1.67	1297.0 -	0.0	11.30	0.78	0.74	49.2	0.20Y	3/28/13	25.9 -	0.0
-	-	-	0.08	0.25	-0.18	347.1 -	0.0	1.62	1.37	1.20	6.4	0.4350	4/26/13	27.8 -	0.0
-	-	-	-0.04	-0.08	0.16			1.92	1.92	1.92	7.2	0.480	4/12/13	29.8 -	0.0
-	-	-	0.17	0.29	-0.02	197.6 -	0.0	1.71	1.20		6.0	0.450	4/26/13	33.6 -	0.0
-	-	-	-0.71	-0.69	-0.44			2.09	1.98	1.92	6.7	0.0681G	5/1/13	35.5 -	0.0
-	-1059.00		-6445.00	427.00				-	0.00	0.00	-			38.2 -	0.0
-0.16	-	-	-0.76	-2.32	-0.90	--		0.14	0.25	0.25	1.1	0.0250Y	81/16/21	22.1 -	0.0
-	-	-0.55	0.97	3.16	2.07	36.6 -	0.0	0.20	0.20	0.20	0.7	0.080Y	81/16/21	35.5 -	0.0
-	-	0.82	2.67	3.38	3.30	24.2 -	0.0	1.74	1.67	1.56	3.3	0.440Y	81/16/21	64.6 -	0.0
-	-	-0.32	0.13	1.22	-2.58	74.1 -	0.0	-	-		-			9.6 -	0.0
-	-	0.95	1.74	1.38	2.98	19.4 -	0.0	0.96	0.96	0.88	3.1	0.240Y	81/16/21	33.8 -	0.0
-	0.52	-	3.77	2.76	0.57	12.2 -	0.0	0.54	0.48	0.48	1.4	0.160Y	81/16/21	46.2 -	0.0
-	-	-0.11	-0.07	-0.05	-0.03			0.20	0.12		1.4	0.070Z	4/2/13	17.1 -	0.0
-	-	-0.25	0.05	0.69	0.57	314.6 -	0.0	-	-		-			15.7 -	0.0
-	-	0.23	0.89	0.87	0.44	11.4 -	0.0	0.18	0.10	0.04	2.1	1.93750Y	81/16/21	10 2-	0.0
-	-	-2.27	-	-1.78	1.59			-	-		-	0.10Y	4/21/05	2.6 -	0.0
-	-	-0.04	2.56	0.87	0.07	21.1 -	0.0	1.40	1.40	1.40	2.9	0.39840Z	81/16/21	54.0 -	0.0
-	-	1.31	4.42	3.99	4.45	22.2 -	0.0	2.96	2.80	2.64	3.5	0.810Y	81/16/21	98.0 -	0.0
-	-	0.07	0.42	0.27	0.22	53.3 -	0.0	0.78	0.73	0.66	4.0	0.5GHZ	81/16/21	22.4 -	0.0
-	-	-0.06	-0.22	0.25	1.40			4.85	4.58	4.32	5.9	1.290	81/16/21	89.8 -	0.0
-	-	0.19	0.35	0.74		113.9 -	0.0	1.34	0.74		3.8	0.370Z	81/16/21	39.9 -	0.0
-	-	-0.03	-0.19	0.14	0.84			-	-		-			87.8 -	0.0
-	-	0.14	-0.78	-1.16	1.43			-	-		-			12.5 -	0.0
-	-	-1.52	-4.05	-0.52	-3.10			-	-		-	0.080	6/30/09	4.5 -	0.0
-	-	0.20	-2.20	-1.83	0.92			0.16	0.11	0.10	1.8	0.080	3/28/13	11.1 -	0.0
-	-	0.95	3.73	3.33	2.15	20.7 -	0.0	-	-		-	0.05	81/16/21	77.0 -	0.0
-	-	-0.05	-0.18	-0.01	-0.14			0.24	0.24	0.24	4.5	0.060Z	4/12/13	6.8 -	0.0
-	-	0.49	2.21	0.01	1.62	8.9 -	0.0	0.84	0.71	0.23	5.7	0.70	3/5/13	19.7 -	0.0
-	-	0.61	1.87	1.75	2.33	6.2 -	0.0	0.86	0.67	0.43	8.8	0.4507GHZ	4/15/13	11.7 -	0.0
-	0.14	-	1.20	0.85	1.34	17.3 -	0.0	0.11	0.09	0.08	0.6	0.030Y	3/22/13	20.8 -	0.0
-	-	-6.30	-6.05	1.21	0.97			-	-		-			13.5 -	0.0
-	-	0.21	0.80	0.74	0.70	22.3 -	0.0	0.74	0.24	0.98	4.8	0.060Y	3/29/13	17.8 -	0.0
-	-	0.26	1.06	1.24	0.61	17.4 -	0.0	0.44	0.36	0.12	3.0	0.120Y	3/28/13	18.4 -	0.0
-	-	0.01	0.49	0.02	-0.02	20.2 -	0.0	-	-		-			9.9 -	0.0
-	-	0.91	4.30	3.65	3.23	12.8 -	0.0	1.00	-		2.1	0.350Y	81/16/21	55.1 -	0.0
-	30.59	-	166.23	96.48	99.76	0.2 -	0.0	0.01	0.01	0.01	0.0			29.7 -	0.0
-	-	0.18	0.24	-1.36	1.53	132.2 -	0.0	1.05	1.35	1.07	4.4			31.7 -	0.0
-	-	0.77	3.13	1.77	2.13	14.5 -	0.0	0.96	0.88	0.88	2.6	0.250Y	4/8/13	45.3 -	0.0
-	-	-1508.00	-5411.00	-193.00				-	-		-	0.08821	4/20/97	16.4 -	0.0
-	-	-	-0.10	-0.16	-0.07			-	-		-	1.053C	1/4/13	10.0 -	0.0
-	-	-	-0.14	0.01	0.02			5.45	0.30		14.2	0.95B	1/20/12	42.3 -	0.0
-	-	0.20	1.15	1.27	0.12	16.7 -	0.0	-	-		-			19.3 -	0.0
-	-	-0.10	-0.18	0.06				-	-		-			13.6 -	0.0

SYMBOL	COMPANY	NATURE OF BUSINESS	FISCAL YEAR-END	TOTAL REV. $MILL	NET INCOME $MILL	TOTAL ASSETS $MILL	NET STK EQUITY $MILL	NO OF INST	INST. HOLDINGS (SHARES)
KRA	Kraton Performance Polymers Inc	Plastics	12/31/12	1423.1	-16.2	1229.2	492.2	170	31273276
KKD	Krispy Kreme Doughnuts Inc	Hotels, Restaurants & Travel	1/29/12	403.2	166.3	334.9	249.1	189	44853205
KR	Kroger Co.	Retail - Food & Beverage, Drug & To	2/2/13	96751.0	1497.0	24652.0	4207.0	696	504413018
KRO	Kronos Worldwide Inc	Specialty Chemicals	12/31/12	1976.3	218.5	2027.0	1062.1	167	22218886
KT	KT Corp (Korea)	Services	12/31/11	21990051.0	1446551.0	32085409.0	11704236.0	171	144668704
KUB	Kubota Corp. (Japan)	Construction Services	3/31/12	1008019.0	61552.0	1487669.0	653283.0	103	6423519
KYO	Kyocera Corp	Electrical Equipment	3/31/12	1190870.0	79357.0	1994103.0	1469505.0	88	867577
LTD	L Brands, Inc	Retail - Apparel and Accessories	2/2/13	10459.0	753.0	6019.0	-1015.0	532	232927661
LLL	L-3 Communications Holdings, Inc.	Aerospace	12/31/12	13146.0	810.0	13826.0	5463.0	625	87520937
LZB	La-Z-Boy Inc.	Furniture	4/28/12	1231.7	88.0	685.7	441.9	175	46022137
LH	Laboratory Corp. of America Holdin	Diagnostic & Health Related Service	12/31/12	5671.4	583.1	6795.0	2717.4	677	105068712
LG	Laclede Group Inc	Gas Utilities	9/30/12	1125.5	62.6	1880.3	601.6	193	12490882
LDR	Landauer, Inc.	Diagnostic & Health Related Service	9/30/12	152.4	19.3	302.1	79.7	168	8621999
LKB 04	Landesbank Baden-Wurttemberg	Banking	12/31/11	47976.0	88.0	373059.0	9502.0		
LPI	Laredo Petroleum Holdings Inc	Production & Extraction	12/31/12	588.1	61.7	2338.3	831.7	112	130547731
LVS	Las Vegas Sands Corp	Hotels, Restaurants & Travel	12/31/12	11131.1	1524.1	22163.7	7061.8	595	327799997
LHO	LaSalle Hotel Properties	REITs	12/31/12	867.1	71.3	3256.6	1853.1	290	100581313
LFL	LATAM Airlines Group SA	Airlines/Air Freight	12/31/11	5585.4	320.2	7648.7	1445.3	106	19961706
LDF	Latin American Discovery Fund, Inc.	Holding and other Investment Office	12/31/12	2.9	1.0	121.1	118.0	35	2846175
LDF	Latin American Discovery Fund, Inc.	Holding and other Investment Office	12/31/12	2.9	1.0	121.1	118.0	35	2846175
EL	Lauder (Estee) Cos., Inc. (The)	Household & Personal Products	6/30/12	9713.6	856.9	6593.0	2733.2	591	232160678
LGI	Lazard Global Total Return & Incom	Holding and other Investment Office	12/31/12	6.5	4.0	182.6	167.3	34	2900464
LAZ	Lazard Ltd	Finance Intermediaries & Services	12/31/12	1994.0	84.3	2986.9	569.7	258	102226818
LOR	Lazard World Dividend & Income Fu	Holding and other Investment Office	12/31/12	5.6	3.8	111.0	99.4	28	1888652
LDK	LDK Solar Co., Ltd.	Semiconductors	12/31/11	2157.8	-620.9	6853.9	609.9	76	12157503
LF	Leapfrog Enterprises Inc	Leisure Equipment	12/31/12	581.3	86.5	428.9	329.9	228	52957392
LEA	Lear Corp.	Auto Parts	12/31/12	14567.0	1282.8	8194.1	3487.1	379	111754856
LEE	Lee Enterprises, Inc.	Publishing	9/30/12	710.5	-16.7	1061.1	-114.6	76	21114557
BWG	Legg Mason BW Global Income Op	Holding and other Investment Office	11/18/11	-	-	0.7	0.1	16	1239733
LM	Legg Mason, Inc.	Wealth Management	3/31/12	2662.6	220.8	8555.7	5677.3	450	137906475
LEG	Leggett & Platt, Inc.	Furniture	12/31/12	3720.8	248.2	3254.9	1434.5	442	117054558
LGP	Lehigh Gas Partners LP	Gas Utilities	12/31/12	311.7	-1.4	315.8			
LEH 06	Lehman Brothers, Inc.	Finance Intermediaries & Services	11/30/07	12124.0	740.0	196219.0	3152.0		
LPS	Lender Processing Services Inc	Business Services	12/31/12	1997.7	70.4	2445.8	542.9	320	78732034
LEN	Lennar Corp.	Builders	11/30/12	4104.7	679.1	10362.2	3414.8	538	194061938
LII	Lennox International Inc	Metal Products	12/31/12	2949.4	90.0	1691.9	496.8	257	37358842
LAS	Lentuo International Inc	Retail - Automotive	12/31/11	3036.2	67.9	2570.9	804.4	8	495861
LUK	Leucadia National Corp.	Paper & Forest Products	12/31/12	9193.7	854.5	9349.1	6767.3	488	171003726
LVLT	Level 3 Communications, Inc.	Services	12/31/12	6376.0	-422.0	13307.0	1171.0	333	360100161
LXP	Lexington Realty Trust	REITs	12/31/12	344.9	180.3	3418.2	1306.7	266	147930631
LXK	Lexmark International, Inc.	Peripherals	12/31/12	3797.6	106.3	3523.4	1281.2	388	89401578
LPL	LG Display Co Ltd	Electrical Equipment	12/31/11	24291289.0	-771223.0	25162931.0	10115732.0	130	28453003
USA	Liberty All-Star Equity Fund	Holding and other Investment Office	12/31/12	17.4	7.0	1005.1	991.1	78	45299908
ASG	Liberty All-Star Growth Fund Inc.	Holding and other Investment Office	12/31/12	1.0	-0.7	105.3	104.2	37	1730693
LRY	Liberty Property Trust	REITs	12/31/12	685.6	137.4	5178.0	2091.0	398	126539577
LTM	Life-Time Fitness Inc	Sporting & Recreational	12/31/12	1126.9	111.5	2072.2	1072.9	248	52975588
LOCK	Lifelock Inc	IT Services	12/31/12	276.4	23.5	339.6	220.0		
LLY	Lilly (Eli) & Co.	Pharmaceuticals	12/31/12	22603.4	4088.6	34398.9	14765.2	1300	898374649
TVL	LIN TV Corp	Radio & Television	12/31/12	553.5	-7.0	1241.4	-91.6	134	22430209
LNC	Lincoln National Corp.	Life & Health	12/31/12	11532.0	1313.0	218869.0	14973.0	615	260245588
LNN	Lindsay Corp	Construction Services	8/31/12	551.3	43.3	415.5	310.8	245	16216706
LNKD	LinkedIn Corp	Internet & Software	12/31/12	972.3	21.6	1382.3	908.4	386	81888416
LGF	Lions Gate Entertainment Corp.	Entertainment	3/31/12	1587.6	-39.1	2788.0	89.8	192	141604891
LAD	Lithia Motors, Inc.	Retail - Automotive	12/31/12	3316.5	80.4	1492.7	428.1	199	25923649
LYV	Live Nation Entertainment, Inc.	Entertainment	12/31/12	5819.0	-163.2	5290.8	1355.4	234	141308732
LYG	Lloyds Banking Group Plc	Banking	12/31/12	54804.0	-1427.0	924552.0	43999.0	145	55808061
SCD	LMP Capital & Income Fund Inc	Holding and other Investment Office	11/30/12	17.9	13.7	337.0	259.5	27	2190082
SCD	LMP Capital & Income Fund Inc	Holding and other Investment Office	11/30/12	17.9	13.7	337.0	259.5	27	2190082
TLI	LMP Corporate Loan Fund Inc	Holding and other Investment Office	9/30/12	10.8	8.4	223.6	161.9	30	4173254
RIT	LMP Real Estate Income Fund Inc	Holding and other Investment Office	12/31/12	7.4	5.2	178.2	139.1	32	1713644
LMT	Lockheed Martin Corp.	Defense	12/31/12	47182.0	2745.0	38657.0	39.0	946	314856080
L	Loews Corp.	General Insurance	12/31/12	14552.0	568.0	80021.0	19459.0	547	275542404
LPR	Lone Pine Resources Inc	Production & Extraction	12/31/12	161.8	-274.5	622.8	215.0	101	47941461
LO	Lorillard, Inc.	Tobacco Products	12/31/12	6623.0	1099.0	3396.0	-1777.0	580	139148851
LPX	Louisiana-Pacific Corp.	Paper & Forest Products	12/31/12	1715.8	28.8	2331.0	1033.8	313	142496810
LOW	Lowe's Companies Inc	Retail - Hardware & Home Improvem	2/1/13	50521.0	1959.0	32666.0	13857.0	1216	932868500
LRE	LRR Energy, L.P.	Production & Extraction	12/31/12	105.5	-0.0	502.5		42	7043574
LXU	LSB Industries, Inc.	Specialty Chemicals	12/31/12	759.0	58.6	576.6	354.5	192	18204197
LTC	LTC Properties, Inc.	REITs	12/31/12	94.0	51.3	789.6	463.1	219	24906952
LUB	Luby's, Inc.	Hotels, Restaurants & Travel	8/29/12	350.1	6.9	231.0	172.7	82	13558932
LL	Lumber Liquidators Holdings Inc	Retail - Hardware & Home Improvem	12/31/12	813.3	47.1	347.4	234.5	184	30303618
LXFR	Luxfer Holdings Plc	Metal Products	12/31/12	511.6	42.4	390.5	148.8		
LUX	Luxottica Group S.P.A.	Medical Instruments & Equipment	12/31/11	6222.5	452.3	8644.2	3612.9	145	13694719
LDL	Lydall, Inc.	Industrial Machinery & Equipment	12/31/12	378.9	16.8	251.9	174.5	135	15195286
LYB	LyondellBasell Industries NV	Diversified Chemicals	12/31/12	45352.0	2848.0	24220.0	11139.0	478	425820684
MTB	M & T Bank Corp	Banking	12/31/12	4609.0	1029.5	83008.8	10202.6	567	108873523
MTB PRA	M & T Capital Trust IV	Banking						15	370442
MDC	M.D.C. Holdings, Inc.	Builders	12/31/12	1203.0	62.7	1945.4	880.9	262	48480390
MHO	M/I Homes Inc.	Builders	12/31/12	761.9	13.3	831.3	335.4	148	22976777
TUC	Mac-Gray Corp.	Miscellaneous Consumer Services	12/31/12	322.1	4.3	401.4	117.3	65	10700296

T36

EARNINGS PER SHARE — QUARTERLY			— ANNUAL —			P/E RATIO	DIVIDENDS PER SHARE			AV. YLD	DIV. DECLARED		PRICE RANGE
1st	2nd	3rd	2012	2011	2010		2012	2011	2010	%	AMOUNT	PAYABLE	2012
-	-	-0.48	-0.50	2.81	3.07	-							28.2 - 0.0
-	-	0.07	2.33	0.11	0.00	6.5 - 0.0							15.1 - 0.0
-	-	0.60	1.01	1.74	0.11	32.8 - 0.0	0.43	0.39	0.36	1.7	0.150Y	81/16/21	33.1 - 0.0
-	-	0.30	1.89	2.77	1.29	13.0 - 0.0	0.60	1.08	0.13	3.5	0.150Y	3/21/13	24.5 - 0.0
-	-1472.00			-5946.00	5328.00			0.00	0.00				18.2 - 0.0
-	14.17	-	48.75	43.11	33.28	1.5 - 0.0	0.01	0.01	0.01	0.0			72.2 - 0.0
-	102.49	-	432.58	667.23	218.47	0.2 - 0.0	0.02	0.02	0.01	0.0			97.8 - 0.0
-	-	0.25	2.70	2.42	1.37	19.3 - 0.0	3.80	4.60	0.60	8.1	0.30Y	81/16/21	52.1 - 0.0
-	-	1.97	8.30	9.03	8.25	9.8 - 0.0	2.00	1.80	1.60	2.8	0.550Y	81/16/21	81.2 - 0.0
-	-	0.32	1.64	0.45	0.62	11.7 - 0.0					0.040Y	3/8/13	19.1 - 0.0
-	-	1.53	5.99	5.11	5.29	15.9 - 0.0					0.0826L	6/30/00	95.3 - 0.0
1.14	-	-	2.79	2.86	2.43	15.6 - 0.0	1.66	1.62	1.58	4.1	0.4250Y	4/2/13	43.5 - 0.0
0.52	-	-	2.03	2.58	2.52	32.4 - 0.0	2.20	2.20	2.15	3.9	0.550Y	4/3/13	65.7 - 0.0
-	-	-0.06	0.48	0.98		55.5 - 0.0							26.6 - 0.0
-	-	0.42	1.85	1.56	0.51	33.0 - 0.0	3.75			7.9	0.350Z	81/16/21	61.0 - 0.0
-	-	0.31	0.52	0.16	-0.36	57.9 - 0.0	0.71	0.44	0.24	2.7	0.1815GHZ	4/15/13	30.1 - 0.0
-	-	-	-	0.94	1.24			0.37	0.29				29.4 - 0.0
-	-	0.14	0.33	0.10		0.0 - 0.0	0.44	0.88	0.61	1.$	0.2799C	1/4/13	0.0 - 0.0
-	-	0.14	0.33	0.10		118.6 - 0.0	0.44	0.88	0.61	3.0	0.2799C	1/4/13	16.6 - 0.0
-	1.13	-	2.16	1.74	1.19	30.5 - 0.0	0.53	0.38	0.28	0.9	0.180Y	81/16/21	65.9 - 0.0
-	-	0.41	0.44	0.39		40.2 - 0.0	1.18	1.05	1.08	7.9	0.09070	4/23/13	16.5 - 0.0
-	-	0.26	0.65	1.36	1.36	57.9 - 0.0	1.16	0.60	0.50	4.0	0.27	81/16/21	37.6 - 0.0
-	-	0.55	0.63	0.62		25.7 - 0.0	0.80	0.90	0.85	6.6	0.07820	4/23/13	14.1 - 0.0
-	-	-	-4.90	2.27									3.9 - 0.0
-	-	0.60	1.24	0.30	0.08	9.8 - 0.0							12.1 - 0.0
-	-	1.23	12.85	5.08	4.05	4.4 - 0.0	0.56	0.50		1.3	0.170Y	81/16/21	56.5 - 0.0
0.28	-	-	-0.34	-3.27	1.03						0.190Y	10/1/08	1.8 - 0.0
											0.120	5/31/13	21.0 - 0.0
-	-	-3.45	1.54	1.63	1.32	20.9 - 0.0	0.32	0.20	0.12	1.2	0.110Y	81/16/21	32.1 - 0.0
-	-	0.45	1.70	1.04	1.15	19.9 - 0.0	1.14	1.10	1.06	4.5	0.290Y	81/16/21	33.8 - 0.0
-	-	-	-0.09								0.2948G	2/15/13	23.9 - 0.0
-	-	0.69	0.83	1.13	3.23	36.9 - 0.0	0.40	0.40	0.40	1.6	0.10Y	81/16/21	30.6 - 0.0
0.26	-	-	3.11	0.48	0.51	14.0 - 0.0	0.16	0.16	0.16	0.5	0.040Y	81/16/21	43.4 - 0.0
-	-	0.57	1.75	1.65	2.08	37.3 - 0.0	0.76	0.72	0.60	1.5	0.20Y	81/16/21	65.3 - 0.0
-	-	-0.11	-	1.15	3.77								3.8 - 0.0
-	-	0.43	3.44	0.10	7.85	8.2 - 0.0	0.25	0.25	0.25	1.1	0.06250Y	81/16/21	28.2 - 0.0
-	-	-0.76	-1.96	-5.51	-5.55								26.7 - 0.0
-	-	0.96	0.93	-0.68	-0.44	13.0 - 0.0	0.55	0.47	0.41	5.7	0.81250Z	8/15/13	12.1 - 0.0
-	-	0.00	1.53	4.12	4.28	21.7 - 0.0	1.15	0.25		4.8	0.30Y	81/16/21	33.2 - 0.0
-	443.00	-		-2155.00	3152.00			0.00	0.00				16.8 - 0.0
-	-	-	0.04	0.02	0.06	129.8 - 0.0	0.32	0.34	0.31	6.8	0.080	3/11/13	5.2 - 0.0
-	-	-	-0.03	-0.05	-0.04		0.27	0.27	0.25	6.6	0.070	3/11/13	4.5 - 0.0
-	-	0.24	1.17	1.59	1.12	34.3 - 0.0	1.90	1.90	1.90	5.2	0.4750Z	81/16/21	40.2 - 0.0
-	-	0.77	2.66	2.26	2.00	19.7 - 0.0							52.3 - 0.0
-	-	-0.16	0.09	-1.24	-1.74	134.0 - 0.0							12.1 - 0.0
-	-	1.18	3.66	3.90	4.58	15.5 - 0.0	1.96	1.96	1.96	4.2	0.490Y	81/16/21	56.8 - 0.0
-	-	0.36	-0.13	0.85	0.66								12.6 - 0.0
-	-	1.41	4.56	0.92	2.54	7.3 - 0.0	0.32	0.20	0.04	1.3	0.120Y	81/16/21	33.5 - 0.0
1.50	-	-	3.38	2.90	1.98	28.0 - 0.0	0.39	0.34	0.33	0.5	0.1150Y	81/10/21	94.6 - 0.0
-	-	0.02	0.19	0.11	0.07	955.2 - 0.0							181.5 - 0.0
-	-	0.27	-0.30	-0.41	-0.17								23.9 - 0.0
-	-	0.90	3.07	2.21	0.52	15.5 - 0.0	0.47	0.26	0.15	1.4	0.10Y	12/28/12	47.5 - 0.0
-	-	0.31	-0.87	-0.46	-1.39								12.6 - 0.0
-	-	-	-0.02	-0.01	-0.01		0.10			4.0	0.48440	7/15/13	3.6 - 0.0
-	-	0.75	0.86	0.54		0.0 - 0.0	1.12	0.73	0.54	1.$	0.280	3/22/13	0.0 - 0.0
-	-	0.75	0.86	0.54		20.8 - 0.0	1.12	0.73	0.54	8.1	0.280	3/22/13	15.6 - 0.0
-	-	0.85	0.80	0.59		16.4 - 0.0	0.79	0.67	0.53	6.2	0.07250	4/26/13	13.9 - 0.0
-	-	0.45	0.45	0.36		29.2 - 0.0	0.72	0.72	0.72	6.5	0.060	6/28/13	13.1 - 0.0
-	-	2.21	8.36	7.81	7.94	11.5 - 0.0	4.15	3.25	2.64	4.6	1.150Y	81/16/21	96.5 - 0.0
-	-	0.45	1.43	2.63	3.07	31.2 - 0.0	0.25	0.25	0.25	0.6	0.06250Y	81/16/21	44.6 - 0.0
-	-	-1.46	-3.23	0.44	1222.00								6.6 - 0.0
-	-	0.72	2.81	2.66	2.26	16.6 - 0.0	2.07	1.73	1.42	5.1	0.550Y	81/16/21	46.5 - 0.0
-	-	0.22	0.20	-1.36	-0.30	110.9 - 0.0					0.150Y	81/16/21	22.2 - 0.0
-	-	0.35	1.43	1.42	1.21	27.8 - 0.0	0.53	0.42	0.35	1.7	0.160Y	81/16/21	39.8 - 0.0
-	-	-0.69	0.00	0.54			1.66			9.5	0.480	2/14/13	20.6 - 0.0
-	-	0.28	2.49	3.58	1.32	18.0 - 0.0					10.0Y	4/1/10	44.7 - 0.0
-	-	0.38	1.57	1.36	1.21	25.9 - 0.0	1.79	1.68	1.58	5.2	0.1550Z	6/28/13	40.7 - 0.0
0.01	-	-	0.24	0.10	-0.10	35.6 - 0.0					0.10	9/25/00	8.6 - 0.0
-	-	0.46	1.68	0.93	0.93	41.8 - 0.0							70.2 - 0.0
-	-	-	3.95	2.70	1.69	4.0 - 0.0							15.9 - 0.0
-	-	-	-	0.98	0.87			0.64	0.39				51.8 - 0.0
-	-	0.23	0.99	0.82	0.16	16.2 - 0.0					0.0194	9/15/82	16.1 - 0.0
-	-	1.46	4.92	3.74	2.78	13.3 - 0.0	4.20	5.05		8.4	0.40	3/18/13	65.4 - 0.0
-	-	2.17	7.54	6.35	5.69	14.0 - 0.0	2.80	2.80	2.80	3.0	0.70Y	81/16/21	105.8 - 0.0
-	-	-									0.53130Z	6/17/13	26.5 - 0.0
-	-	0.41	1.28	-2.12	-1.40	32.6 - 0.0	2.00	1.00	1.00	5.9	1.HY	81/16/21	41.8 - 0.0
-	-	0.42	0.67	-1.81	-1.42	42.5 - 0.0					0.60940Y	6/16/08	28.5 - 0.0
-	-	0.10	0.29	0.22	0.18	53.1 - 0.0	0.24	0.22	0.20	1.8	0.08750Y	4/1/13	15.4 - 0.0

SYMBOL	COMPANY	NATURE OF BUSINESS	FISCAL YEAR-END	TOTAL REV. $MILL	NET INCOME $MILL	TOTAL ASSETS $MILL	NET STK EQUITY $MILL	NO OF INST	INST. HOLDINGS (SHARES)
MAC	Macerich Co. (The)	REITs	12/31/12	881.3	337.4	9311.2	3077.5	383	153766732
CLI	Mack Cali Realty Corp	REITs	12/31/12	704.7	46.3	4526.0	1767.0	316	97200019
MGU	Macquarie Global Infrastructure Tot	Holding and other Investment Office	11/30/12	23.1	14.7	412.4	296.2	58	5492909
MGU	Macquarie Global Infrastructure Tot	Holding and other Investment Office	11/30/12	23.1	14.7	412.4	296.2	58	5492909
MIC	Macquarie Infrastructure Co LLC	Aerospace	12/31/12	-	13.3	2223.7	655.0	175	37054022
MFD	Macquarie/First Trust Global Infrastr	Holding and other Investment Office	11/30/12	12.8	9.8	189.6	135.7	35	1777168
M	Macys Inc	Retail - General Merchandise/Depart	2/2/13	27686.0	1335.0	20991.0	6051.0	742	370222624
MCN	Madison Covered Call & Equity Stra	Holding and other Investment Office	12/31/12	2.1	-0.2	174.7	166.3	38	2738719
MSP	Madison Strategic Sector Premium	Holding and other Investment Office	12/31/12	0.9	0.2	78.5	74.4	24	773585
MMP	Magellan Midstream Partners LP	Equipment & Services	12/31/12	1772.1	435.7	4420.1	-	433	129206769
MGA	Magna International Inc.	Auto Parts	12/31/12	30837.0	1433.0	17109.0	9429.0	298	159771536
MX	MagnaChip Semiconductor Corp	Semiconductors	12/31/12	819.6	193.3	790.0	310.3	102	33388554
MHR	Magnum Hunter Resources Corp (D	Production & Extraction	12/31/11	129.2	-76.7	1168.4	588.5	182	97014244
MFB	Maidenform Brands Inc	Retail - General Merchandise/Depart	12/29/12	600.3	33.5	436.0	254.3	149	26936146
MAIN	Main Street Capital Corp	Holding and other Investment Office	12/31/12	90.5	59.3	1036.2	643.0	131	9214765
MMD	MainStay DefinedTerm Municipal Hi	Holding and other Investment Office	5/11/12	-	-	1.0	0.1	-	-
MZF	Managed Duration Investment Grad	Holding and other Investment Office	7/31/12	8.7	7.4	176.9	174.1	26	1189408
HYF	Managed High Yield Plus Fund Inc	Holding and other Investment Office	5/31/12	14.2	12.3	166.4	131.2	52	4552549
MANU	Manchester United Plc	Sporting & Recreational	6/30/12	320.3	23.0	947.1	237.1	-	-
MTW	Manitowoc Co., Inc.	Construction Services	12/31/12	3927.0	101.7	4057.3	600.3	306	100586576
MN	Manning & Napier Inc.	Wealth Management	12/31/12	339.1	2.5	218.2	164.9	81	13069220
MAN	ManpowerGroup	Business Services	12/31/12	20678.0	197.6	7012.6	2500.8	364	87623657
MFC	Manulife Financial Corp.	Life & Health	12/31/12	26000.0	1736.0	486056.0	25595.0	367	876083803
MRO	Marathon Oil Corp.	Production & Extraction	12/31/12	16221.0	1582.0	35306.0	18283.0	956	634055255
MPC	Marathon Petroleum Corp.	Refining & Marketing	12/31/12	82492.0	3389.0	27223.0	11694.0	728	278851594
MCS	Marcus Corp. (The)	Hotels, Restaurants & Travel	5/31/12	413.9	22.7	733.0	343.8	134	15641635
MRIN	Marin Software Inc.	IT Services	12/31/12	59.6	-26.5	57.2	33.0	-	-
MPX	Marine Products Corp.	Leisure Equipment	12/31/12	148.9	7.0	97.3	77.7	55	7580042
HZO	MarineMax, Inc.	Retail - Specialty	9/30/12	524.5	1.1	365.1	200.9	127	24297785
MKL	Markel Corp (Holding Co)	General Insurance	12/31/12	3000.1	253.4	12556.6	3888.7	309	8348835
MWE	Markwest Energy Partners L.P.	Equipment & Services	12/31/12	1451.8	220.4	6835.7	-	275	76756538
MAR	Marriott International, Inc.	Hotels, Restaurants & Travel	12/28/12	11814.0	571.0	6342.0	-1285.0	539	187609034
VAC	Marriott Vacations Worldwide Corp.	Hotels, Restaurants & Travel	12/28/12	1648.0	16.0	2604.0	1151.0	222	25466529
MMC	Marsh & McLennan Companies Inc.	Brokers & Intermediaries	12/31/12	11924.0	1176.0	16288.0	6542.0	648	501994207
MSO	Martha Stewart Living Omnimedia, I	Publishing	12/31/12	197.6	-56.1	154.3	95.5	120	11956398
MLM	Martin Marietta Materials, Inc.	Construction Materials	12/31/12	2037.7	84.5	3160.9	1410.5	370	51947901
MAS	Masco Corp.	Metal Products	12/31/12	7745.0	-114.0	6875.0	322.0	487	362519447
MTZ	MasTec Inc. (FL)	Construction Services	12/31/12	3726.8	107.4	2407.9	857.2	280	68663449
MA	MasterCard Inc	Business Services	12/31/12	7391.0	2759.0	12462.0	6917.0	1007	101615456
MTDR	Matador Resources Co	Production & Extraction	12/31/12	165.2	-33.3	632.0	379.1	68	23705587
MTRN	Materion Corp	Metal Products	12/31/12	1273.1	24.7	814.9	415.0	166	19621720
MATX	Matson Inc	Shipping	12/31/12	1560.0	45.9	1174.3	279.9	239	38056754
MATX	Matson Inc	Shipping	12/31/12	1560.0	45.9	1174.3	279.9	239	38056754
MLP	Maui Land & Pineapple Co., Inc.	Property, Real Estate & Developmen	12/31/12	16.2	-4.6	61.5	-34.4	31	2792764
MXT	Maxcom Telecomunicaciones SA d	Services	12/31/12	2375.9	-536.5	5758.9	2459.1	-	-
MMS	MAXIMUS Inc.	Business Services	9/30/12	1050.1	76.1	695.3	451.1	247	36732283
MXL	MaxLinear Inc	Semiconductors	12/31/12	97.7	-13.3	110.6	80.2	90	18205620
MBI	MBIA Inc.	General Insurance	12/31/12	2435.0	1234.0	21724.0	3173.0	336	186793950
MNI	McClatchy Co. (The)	Publishing	12/30/12	1230.7	-0.1	3005.1	42.5	138	55411142
MKC	McCormick & Co., Inc.	Food	11/30/12	4014.2	407.8	4165.4	1682.9	652	114803124
MDR	McDermott International, Inc. (Pana	Industrial Machinery & Equipment	12/31/12	3641.6	206.7	3333.6	1887.3	398	226665664
MCD	McDonald's Corp	Hotels, Restaurants & Travel	12/31/12	27567.0	5464.8	35386.5	15293.6	1810	714888616
MUX	McEwen Mining Inc.	Precious Metals	12/31/12	26.8	-66.7	1150.9	889.6	139	103887699
MHP	McGraw-Hill Cos., Inc. (The)	Publishing	12/31/12	4450.0	437.0	7052.0	767.0	730	270559399
MCK	McKesson Corp.	Pharmaceuticals	3/31/12	122734.0	1403.0	33093.0	6831.0	894	221851811
MMR	McMoran Exploration Co	Production & Extraction	12/31/12	376.9	-104.3	2677.1	1603.2	256	104352522
MDU	MDU Resources Group Inc.	Mining	12/31/12	4075.4	-0.8	6682.5	2648.2	395	111317211
MJN	Mead Johnson Nutrition Co	Food	12/31/12	3901.3	604.5	3258.2	18.7	568	189380671
MIG	Meadowbrook Insurance Group Inc	General Insurance	12/31/12	996.8	11.7	2473.3	558.3	198	42254822
MWV	MeadWestvaco Corp.	Containers & Packaging	12/31/12	5459.0	205.0	8908.0	3360.0	436	162613372
MTL	Mechel OAO	Non-Precious Metals						160	53098557
MEG	Media General, Inc.	Publishing	12/31/12	359.7	-193.4	773.4	-176.2	78	24388257
MPW	Medical Properties Trust Inc	REITs	12/31/12	201.4	89.9	2178.9	1049.8	268	103814006
MED	Medifast Inc	Household & Personal Products	12/31/12	356.7	15.9	130.3	90.8	162	11138548
MCC	Medley Capital Corp	Holding and other Investment Office	9/30/12	44.5	23.5	415.8	289.3	103	14810639
MD	Mednax, Inc.	Diagnostic & Health Related Service	12/31/12	1816.6	240.9	2750.3	2035.4	333	59858778
MDT	Medtronic, Inc.	Medical Instruments & Equipment	*4/27/12	16184.0	3617.0	33083.0	17113.0	1308	885287799
WFR	MEMC Electronic Materials, Inc.	Semiconductors	12/31/12	2529.9	-150.6	4701.6	575.3	337	204305792
MW	Men's Wearhouse, Inc. (The)	Retail - Apparel and Accessories	2/2/13	2488.3	131.7	1496.3	1096.3	267	54946500
MRK	Merck & Co., Inc	Pharmaceuticals	12/31/12	47267.0	6168.0	106132.0	53020.0	1822	2322805928
MCY	Mercury General Corp.	General Insurance	12/31/12	2783.4	116.9	4189.7	1842.5	231	25629942
MDP	Meredith Corp.	Publishing	6/30/12	1376.7	104.4	2016.3	797.4	255	48401426
MTH	Meritage Homes Corp	Builders	12/31/12	1193.7	105.2	1575.6	694.2	215	38624871
MTOR	Meritor Inc	Construction Services	9/30/12	4418.0	52.0	2501.0	-1023.0	208	80909334
MTR	Mesa Royalty Trust	Oil Royalty Traders	12/31/12	3.8	3.6	6.3	5.5	22	93844
MSB	Mesabi Trust	Non-Precious Metals	1/31/12	34.2	33.2	11.2	1.0	75	2121609
MPR	Met-Pro Corp.	Industrial Machinery & Equipment	1/31/13	109.9	8.0	116.3	88.7	79	8404746
MEI	Methode Electronics, Inc.	Electrical Equipment	4/28/12	465.1	8.4	403.6	255.0	141	37226797
MET	MetLife Inc	Life & Health	12/31/12	68150.0	1324.0	836781.0	64574.0	1036	857430167
PCS	MetroPCS Communications Inc	Services	12/31/12	5101.3	394.2	10189.4	3358.9	408	312752439

T38

EARNINGS PER SHARE — QUARTERLY			EARNINGS PER SHARE — ANNUAL			P/E RATIO		DIVIDENDS PER SHARE			AV. YLD	DIV. DECLARED		PRICE RANGE 2012	
1st	2nd	3rd	2012	2011	2010	ratio		2012	2011	2010	%	AMOUNT	PAYABLE		
-	-	0.33	2.51	1.18	0.19	25.6 -	0.0	2.23	2.05	2.10	3.8	0.580Z	81/16/21	64.4 -	0.0
-	-	0.16	0.47	0.81	0.67	62.4 -	0.0	1.80	1.80	1.80	6.6	0.450Z	81/16/21	29.3 -	0.0
-	-	-	0.97	0.76	0.54	0.0 -	0.0	0.96	0.72	1.04	1.$	0.320	3/20/13	0.0 -	0.0
-	-	-	0.97	0.76	0.54	21.9 -	0.0	0.96	0.72	1.04	5.1	0.320	3/20/13	21.2 -	0.0
-	-	-0.04	0.29	0.59	1.99	186.3 -	0.0	2.40	0.60	-	5.8	0.68750Z	12/28/12	54.0 -	0.0
-	-	-	1.15	1.43	0.55	14.3 -	0.0	1.40	1.40	0.68	9.1	0.350	2/28/13	16.4 -	0.0
-	-	0.36	2.92	1.98	0.83	14.6 -	0.0	0.35	0.20	0.20	0.9	0.20Y	81/16/21	42.7 -	0.0
-	-	-	-0.01	-0.03	-0.05	-		0.72	0.72	0.72	9.2	0.180	3/29/13	8.3 -	0.0
-	-	-	0.03	0.00	-0.03	402.3 -	0.0	1.04	1.04	1.04	9.2	0.260	3/29/13	12.1 -	0.0
-	-	0.22	1.92	1.83	1.43	27.8 -	0.0	1.78	1.56	1.45	4.3	0.50	81/16/21	53.4 -	0.0
-	-	1.66	6.09	4.20	4.18	9.8 -	0.0	1.10	1.00	0.42	2.4	0.320	3/27/13	59.7 -	0.0
-	-	1.30	5.16	0.55	1.89	3.4 -								17.5 -	0.0
-	-	-0.25	-	-0.80	-0.25							0.16670Y	4/1/13	6.7 -	0.0
-	-	0.46	1.43	1.42	1.94	16.6 -	0.0							23.8 -	0.0
-	-	0.49	2.01	1.69	1.16	17.1 -	0.0	1.73	1.70	1.50	6.2	0.3786GHZ	7/1/13	34.4 -	0.0
-	-	-	-	-	-							0.0958M	4/30/13	21.2 -	0.0
-	-	-	1.09	1.12	1.06	15.3 -	0.0	0.99	0.99	0.97	6.3	0.07750	4/30/13	16.7 -	0.0
-	-	-	0.20	0.23	0.24	11.4 -	0.0	0.21	0.24	0.22	9.7	0.0150	4/30/13	2.3 -	0.0
0.13	-	-	0.15	12.78	-48.24	125.5 -								18.8 -	0.0
-	-	0.17	0.76	-0.08	-0.56	28.0 -	0.0	0.08	0.08	0.08	0.6	0.080Y	81/16/21	21.3 -	0.0
-	-	0.12	0.18	-	-	93.2 -	0.0	0.48			3.6	0.160	5/1/13	16.8 -	0.0
-	-	0.79	2.47	3.04	-3.26	23.2 -	0.0	0.86	0.80	0.74	2.1	0.430Y	81/16/21	57.3 -	0.0
-	-	-0.14	0.88	0.02	-0.99	17.8 -	0.0	0.52	0.52	0.52	4.1	0.2877GH	3/19/13	15.7 -	0.0
-	-	0.63	2.23	4.13	3.61	16.0 -	0.0	0.68	0.80	0.99	2.3	0.170Y	81/16/21	35.7 -	0.0
-	-	3.59	9.89	6.67	-	9.2 -	0.0	1.20	0.45	-	2.2	0.350Y	81/16/21	91.1 -	0.0
-	-	-0.05	0.78	0.46	0.54	18.3 -	0.0	0.34	0.34	0.34	2.7	0.1545HY	12/28/12	14.3 -	0.0
-	-	-	-6.00	-4.29	-3.27									17.0 -	15.9
-	-	0.06	0.19	0.18	0.11	38.7 -	0.0	0.63			10.7	0.030Y	3/8/13	7.4 -	0.0
-0.18	-	-	0.05	-0.52	0.11	278.0 -	0.0							13.9 -	0.0
-	-	5.32	25.89	14.60	27.27	19.7 -	0.0							508.9 -	0.0
-	-	-0.13	1.69	0.75	-0.01	36.2 -	0.0	3.16	2.75	2.56	5.9	0.820	2/14/13	61.1 -	0.0
-	-	0.44	1.72	0.55	1.21	24.6 -	0.0	0.49	0.39	0.21	1.3	0.130Y	81/16/21	42.2 -	0.0
-	-	0.17	0.44	-5.29	2.00	106.5 -	0.0							46.9 -	0.0
-	-	0.44	2.13	1.79	1.55	17.8 -	0.0	0.90	0.86	0.81	2.6	0.230Y	81/16/21	38.0 -	0.0
-	-	-0.76	-0.83	-0.28	-0.18				0.25			0.257Y	12/30/11	3.8 -	0.0
-	-	1.36	1.83	1.78	2.10	57.3 -	0.0	1.60	1.60	1.60	1.9	0.40Y	81/16/21	104.9 -	0.0
-	-	0.04	-0.33	-1.66	-3.00			0.30	0.30	0.30	2.0	0.0750Y	81/16/21	20.9 -	0.0
-	-	0.34	1.31	1.23	1.05	23.5 -	0.0							30.8 -	0.0
-	-	6.17	21.94	14.85	14.05	24.7 -	0.0	1.05	0.60	0.60	0.2	0.60Y	81/16/21	541.1 -	0.0
-	-	-0.17	-0.62	-0.25	0.15									11.6 -	0.0
-	-	0.39	1.19	1.93	2.25	24.7 -	0.0	0.23			1.0	0.0750Y	3/6/13	29.4 -	0.0
-	-	0.45	1.08	0.81	2.22	24.5 -	0.0	0.30	1.26	1.26	2.2	0.150Y	3/7/13	26.5 -	0.0
-	-	0.45	1.08	0.81	2.22	26.0 -	0.0	0.30	1.26	1.26	1.2	0.150Y	3/7/13	28.1 -	0.0
-	-	-0.09	-0.25	0.27	1.99							0.1250	3/31/00	4.5 -	0.0
-	-	0.06	-	-0.68	-1.47									3.0 -	0.0
0.61	-	-	2.19	2.28	1.96	36.5 -	0.0	0.36	0.30	0.24	0.6	0.090Y	2/28/13	80.0 -	0.0
-	-	0.01	-0.40	-0.68	0.30									7.2 -	0.0
-	-	0.04	6.33	-6.69	0.26	2.1 -	0.0					0.340Y	81/16/21	13.0 -	0.0
-	-	0.06	-	0.63	0.43							0.090Y	4/1/09	3.4 -	0.0
0.57	-	-	3.04	2.79	2.75	24.2 -	0.0	1.24	1.12	1.04	2.0	0.340Y	81/16/21	73.5 -	0.0
-	-	0.21	0.87	0.59	0.85	15.5 -	0.0					0.01670	81/16/21	13.5	0.0
-	-	1.43	5.36	5.27	4.58	18.6 -	0.0	2.87	2.63	2.26	3.1	0.770Y	81/16/21	99.7 -	0.0
-	-	-0.01	-0.26	0.45	-0.27									4.9 -	0.0
-	-	1.10	1.53	3.00	2.65	38.1 -	0.0	3.52	1.00	0.94	7.1	0.280Y	81/16/21	58.3 -	0.0
-	-	1.24	5.59	4.57	4.62	19.9 -	0.0	0.80	0.72	0.48	0.9	0.20Y	81/16/21	111.2 -	0.0
-	-	-0.40	-0.90	-0.37	-2.08							14.3750Y	2/15/13	16.4 -	0.0
-	-	-0.16	-0.01	1.12	1.27			0.68	0.66	0.64	3.1	1.2750Y	81/16/21	25.0 -	0.0
-	-	0.69	2.95	2.47	2.20	30.0 -	0.0	1.20	1.04	0.90	1.6	0.340Y	01/16/21	88.6 -	0.0
-	-	-0.53	0.23	0.83	1.10	41.9 -	0.0	0.17	0.17	0.13	2.3	0.020Y	4/4/13	9.6 -	0.0
-	-	0.20	1.16	1.42	0.62	32.8 -	0.0	1.00	1.00	0.94	3.3	0.250Y	81/16/21	38.0 -	0.0
														9.5 -	0.0
-	-	-1.34	-8.15	-3.31	-1.01							0.120Y	12/15/08	5.9 -	0.0
-	-	0.23	0.67	0.23	0.22	23.9 -	0.0	0.80	0.80	0.80	7.2	0.20Z	4/11/13	16.0 -	0.0
-	-	0.52	1.16	1.31	1.35	27.8 -	0.0							32.3 -	0.0
0.39	-	-	1.31	0.56	-	12.3 -	0.0	1.20	0.37	-	9.0	0.44530Z	7/1/13	16.1 -	0.0
-	-	1.32	4.85	4.47	4.26	18.5 -	0.0							89.6 -	0.0
-	-	0.97	3.41	2.86	2.79	13.8 -	0.0	0.97	0.90	0.82	2.4	0.260Y	81/16/21	47.2 -	0.0
-	-	0.16	-0.66	-6.68	0.15									5.7 -	0.0
-	-	0.95	2.30	1.27	0.86	17.1 -	0.0	0.48	0.36	0.28	1.5	0.180Y	6/28/13	39.2 -	0.0
-	-	0.56	2.00	2.02	0.28	24.0 -	0.0	1.69	1.56	1.52	4.0	0.430Y	81/16/21	48.0 -	0.0
-	-	1.21	2.13	3.49	2.78	21.4 -	0.0	2.44	2.41	2.37	6.1	0.61250Y	81/16/21	45.6 -	0.0
-	0.79	-	2.31	2.78	2.28	19.1 -	0.0	1.40	0.97	0.91	4.2	0.40750Y	81/16/21	44.2 -	0.0
-	-	0.19	3.00	-0.65	0.22	16.0 -	0.0							48.1 -	0.0
-0.22	-	-	0.54	0.59	0.14	15.2 -	0.0					0.10Y	81/16/21	8.2 -	0.0
-	-	0.37	1.93	2.96	3.50	20.6 -	0.0	1.93	2.96	3.50	7.3	0.17480Z	4/30/13	39.7 -	0.0
-	-	0.89	2.53	2.47	0.95	12.6 -	0.0	2.53	2.48	1.15	9.8	0.080	5/20/13	31.8 -	0.0
-	-	0.19	0.48	0.42	0.30	22.9 -	0.0	0.27	0.25	0.24	2.9	0.07250Y	6/14/13	11.0 -	0.0
-	-	0.09	0.22	0.52	0.37	61.9 -	0.0	0.28	0.28	0.28	2.9	0.070Y	4/26/13	13.6 -	0.0
-	-	-0.92	1.12	6.29	3.00	35.9 -	0.0	0.74	0.74	0.74	2.2	0.1850Y	81/16/21	40.2 -	0.0
-	-	0.52	1.07	0.82	0.54	12.7 -	0.0							13.6 -	0.0

SYMBOL	COMPANY	NATURE OF BUSINESS	FISCAL YEAR-END	TOTAL REV. $MILL	NET INCOME $MILL	TOTAL ASSETS $MILL	NET STK EQUITY $MILL	NO OF INST	INST. HOLDINGS (SHARES)
MTD	Mettler-Toledo International, Inc.	Biotechnology	12/31/12	2341.5	290.8	2117.4	827.2	347	34145250
MXF	Mexico Fund, Inc.	Holding and other Investment Office	10/31/12	6.8	1.5	383.6	383.0	36	1580857
MFA	MFA Financial, Inc.	REITs	12/31/12	498.0	306.8	13517.5	3311.0	334	293315203
MIL	MFC Industrial Ltd.	Non-Precious Metals	-	-	-	-	-	18	1360787
MCR	MFS Charter Income Trust	Holding and other Investment Office	11/30/12	39.4	33.9	685.8	570.7	62	16760792
MGF	MFS Government Markets Income	Holding and other Investment Office	11/30/12	9.4	7.6	255.3	223.9	50	4488767
CXE	MFS High Income Municipal Trust	Holding and other Investment Office	11/30/12	14.2	11.4	276.9	182.1	30	479499
CMU	MFS High Yield Municipal Trust	Holding and other Investment Office	11/30/12	11.2	9.1	219.7	146.2	30	321169
CMK	MFS Intermarket Income Trust I	Holding and other Investment Office	11/30/12	5.9	4.7	120.1	103.7	32	2892743
CIF	MFS Intermediate High Income Fun	Holding and other Investment Office	11/30/12	6.5	5.4	88.3	65.7	21	378047
MIN	MFS Intermediate Income Trust	Holding and other Investment Office	10/31/12	29.5	24.3	736.1	735.1	86	15479087
CXH	MFS Investment Grade Municipal Tr	Holding and other Investment Office	11/30/12	8.8	7.1	186.0	127.8	32	963705
MMT	MFS Multimarket Income Trust	Holding and other Investment Office	10/31/12	43.3	36.9	721.7	600.0	86	17625116
MFM	MFS Municipal Income Trust	Holding and other Investment Office	10/31/12	23.6	19.5	441.2	315.3	47	697641
MFV	MFS Special Value Trust	Holding and other Investment Office	10/31/12	3.4	2.7	47.9	47.6	11	142487
MTG	MGIC Investment Corp. (WI)	Credit & Lending	12/31/12	1504.3	-485.9	7216.2	1196.8	254	182026382
MGM	MGM Resorts International	Hotels, Restaurants & Travel	12/31/12	9160.8	-1767.7	26284.7	4365.5	399	341756212
KORS	Michael Kors Holdings Ltd.	Retail - Apparel and Accessories	3/31/12	1302.3	147.4	674.4	456.2	332	148753638
MAA	Mid-America Apartment Communiti	REITs	12/31/12	497.2	105.2	2751.1	918.8	304	41880732
MPO	Midstates Petroleum Co Inc	Production & Extraction	12/31/12	247.7	-156.6	1684.0	643.6	90	50757479
MM	Millennial Media Inc	Advertising	12/31/12	177.7	-5.4	208.4	163.8	110	77464740
MILL	Miller Energy Resources, Inc.	Production & Extraction	4/30/12	35.4	-18.7	536.4	299.8	74	11319918
MLR	Miller Industries Inc. (TN)	Construction Services	12/31/12	342.7	9.1	202.4	157.5	96	9268423
MR	Mindray Medical International Ltd	Medical Instruments & Equipment	12/31/11	880.7	166.6	1459.0	1142.5	185	82533120
MSA	Mine Safety Appliances Co	Office Equipment & Furniture	12/31/12	1179.9	90.6	1111.7	463.0	203	23625616
MTX	Minerals Technologies, Inc.	Specialty Chemicals	12/31/12	1005.6	74.1	1211.2	790.4	225	38254229
MP PRD	Mississippi Power Co.	Electric Utilities	12/31/12	1036.0	149.8	5451.6	1830.2	1	0
MG	Mistras Group, Inc.	Business Services	5/31/12	436.9	21.4	329.8	193.0	106	17857520
MTU	Mitsubishi UFJ Financial Group Inc	Banking	3/31/12	3799343.0	416231.0	215202514.0	8583158.0	244	157652574
MFG	Mizuho Financial Group Inc	Banking	3/31/12	-	656389.0	66361633.0	4470766.0	97	41953931
MBT	Mobile Telesystems OJSC	Services	12/31/11	12318.7	1443.9	15318.2	3482.1	264	309177837
MODN	Model N, Inc	IT Services	9/30/12	84.3	-5.7	40.6	-10.5	-	-
MOD	Modine Manufacturing Co	Auto Parts	3/31/12	1577.2	38.5	893.5	324.9	141	40761134
MHK	Mohawk Industries, Inc.	Furniture	12/31/12	5788.0	250.3	6303.7	3719.6	368	64410544
MOH	Molina Healthcare Inc	Hospitals & Health Care Facilities	12/31/12	6028.8	9.8	1944.8	782.3	209	32088173
TAP	Molson Coors Brewing Co.	Beverages	12/29/12	3916.5	443.0	16212.2	7966.9	556	136995833
MCP	Molycorp Inc. (DE)	Metal Products	12/31/12	528.9	-449.6	2994.7	1237.1	262	64752645
MGI	MoneyGram International Inc	Business Services	12/31/12	1341.2	-49.3	5150.6	-161.4	136	60140719
MNR	Monmouth Real Estate Investment	REITs	9/30/12	53.7	18.7	574.5	315.7	128	18832220
MON	Monsanto Co.	Agricultural Chemicals	8/31/12	13504.0	2045.0	20224.0	11833.0	1200	494520522
MWW	Monster Worldwide Inc	Business Services	12/31/12	890.4	-258.7	1684.9	880.0	314	122056025
MTS	Montgomery Street Income Securiti	Holding and other Investment Office	12/31/12	7.6	6.2	229.7	190.6	36	4476261
MRH	Montpelier Re Holdings Ltd.	General Insurance	12/31/12	757.2	227.6	3810.1	1629.4	203	51140328
MCO	Moody's Corp.	Business Services	12/31/12	2730.3	690.0	3960.9	385.2	547	238974010
MOG A	Moog, Inc.	Industrial Machinery & Equipment	9/29/12	2469.5	152.5	3105.9	1304.8	196	39723438
MS	Morgan Stanley	Finance Intermediaries & Services	12/31/12	32036.0	68.0	780960.0	62109.0	914	1679205679
APF	Morgan Stanley Asia-Pacific Fund, I	Holding and other Investment Office	12/31/12	6.5	2.6	324.8	319.8	67	11438937
APF	Morgan Stanley Asia-Pacific Fund, I	Holding and other Investment Office	12/31/12	6.5	2.6	324.8	319.8	67	11438937
CAF	Morgan Stanley China A Share Fun	Holding and other Investment Office	12/31/12	8.6	-0.4	513.0	508.7	70	6621348
RNE	Morgan Stanley Eastern Europe Fu	Holding and other Investment Office	12/31/12	2.4	0.8	67.5	66.3	26	1910830
RNE	Morgan Stanley Eastern Europe Fu	Holding and other Investment Office	12/31/12	2.4	0.8	67.5	66.3	26	1910830
MSD	Morgan Stanley Emerging Markets	Holding and other Investment Office	12/31/12	17.0	13.7	348.4	309.6	47	5164079
EDD	Morgan Stanley Emerging Markets	Holding and other Investment Office	10/31/12	122.2	95.3	1685.6	1283.1	82	9659324
MSF	Morgan Stanley Emerging Markets	Holding and other Investment Office	12/31/12	5.3	1.4	258.6	250.9	42	5187524
MSF	Morgan Stanley Emerging Markets	Holding and other Investment Office	12/31/12	5.3	1.4	258.6	250.9	42	5187524
ICB	Morgan Stanley Funds - Income Se	Holding and other Investment Office	9/30/12	8.1	7.0	178.8	176.5	28	1124887
IIF	Morgan Stanley India Investment Fu	Holding and other Investment Office	12/31/12	5.0	-0.2	387.7	387.1	64	5852431
IIF	Morgan Stanley India Investment Fu	Holding and other Investment Office	12/31/12	5.0	-0.2	387.7	387.1	64	5852431
ICB	Morgan Stanley Trusts	Holding and other Investment Office	10/31/02	5.5	4.8	103.9	103.8	-	-
MOS	Mosaic Co (The)	Agricultural Chemicals	5/31/12	11107.8	1930.2	16690.4	11983.1	751	258334899
MSI	Motorola Solutions Inc.	Manufacturing	12/31/12	8698.0	881.0	12679.0	3265.0	699	383487370
MOV	Movado Group, Inc.	Miscellaneous Consumer Goods	1/31/13	505.5	57.1	526.4	423.7	203	20278411
MPG	MPG Office Trust Inc	REITs	12/31/12	231.2	384.3	1466.9	-511.9	112	38984540
MPLX	MPLX LP	Equipment & Services	12/31/12	461.9	130.8	1301.3			
MRC	MRC Global Inc	Industrial Machinery & Equipment	12/31/12	5570.9	118.0	3369.7	1185.9	112	103722018
MSM	MSC Industrial Direct Co., Inc.	Industrial Machinery & Equipment	9/1/12	2355.9	259.0	1444.9	1187.1	312	51483711
MSCI	MSCI Inc	Publishing	12/31/12	950.1	184.2	3019.6	1425.2	257	124588324
MLI	Mueller Industries, Inc.	Industrial Machinery & Equipment	12/29/12	2189.9	82.4	1104.2	506.9	221	31241817
MWA	Mueller Water Products Inc	Industrial Machinery & Equipment	9/30/12	1023.9	-108.4	1240.9	231.2	223	129333122
MUR	Murphy Oil Corp	Refining & Marketing	12/31/12	28626.0	970.9	17522.6	8942.0	605	173236907
MVO	MV Oil Trust	Production & Extraction	12/31/12	41.5	40.8	30.1	30.1	53	743424
MVC	MVC Capital Inc	Holding and other Investment Office	10/31/12	29.9	21.1	456.4	386.0	124	16478875
MFO R	MVR, Inc.	Holding and other Investment Office							
MYE	Myers Industries Inc.	Plastics	12/31/12	791.2	30.0	484.9	230.0	157	31597498
NBR	Nabors Industries Ltd.	Production & Extraction	12/31/12	6751.4	164.0	12656.0	6014.1	548	256757122
NC	NACCO Industries Inc.	Household Appliances, Electronics &	12/31/12	873.4	108.7	776.3	281.4	174	4734018
NTE	Nam Tai Electronics, Inc.	Peripherals	12/31/12	1147.9	66.9	636.0	362.8	85	11093138
NBG	National Bank Of Greece S A	Banking							79	8411006
NFP	National Financial Partners Corp	Brokers & Intermediaries	12/31/12	1061.7	29.9	899.9	412.0	193	45949430
NFG	National Fuel Gas Co. (NJ)	Gas Utilities	9/30/12	1626.9	220.1	5935.1	1960.1	412	51177786

EARNINGS PER SHARE						P/E RATIO		DIVIDENDS PER SHARE			AV. YLD	DIV. DECLARED		PRICE RANGE	
QUARTERLY			ANNUAL			2012		2012	2011	2010	%	AMOUNT	PAYABLE	2012	
1st	2nd	3rd	2012	2011	2010										
-	-	2.28	9.14	8.21	6.80	24.2 -	0.0					-		221.6 -	0.0
-	-	-	0.12	0.24	0.17	315.2 -	0.0	2.61	3.04	2.35	9.6	0.77030	4/24/13	37.8 -	0.0
-	-	0.21	0.83	0.90	0.93	11.6 -	0.0	0.88	1.00	0.89	10.8	0.220Z	4/30/13	9.6 -	0.0
-	-	-	-	-	-							0.060	4/22/13	10.3 -	0.0
-	-	-	0.62	0.66	0.68	17.1 -	0.0	0.65	0.75	0.70	6.5	0.0520	4/30/13	10.6 -	0.0
-	-	-	0.23	0.26	0.30	32.2 -	0.0	0.51	0.51	0.52	7.4	0.04030	4/30/13	7.4 -	0.0
-	-	-	0.36	0.39	0.42	16.8 -	0.0	0.37	0.39	0.39	6.6	0.027M	4/30/13	6.0 -	0.0
-	-	-	0.32	0.35	0.37	17.0 -	0.0	0.33	0.36	0.35	6.5	0.024M	4/30/13	5.5 -	0.0
-	-	-	0.43	0.43	0.47	21.5 -	0.0	0.49	0.48	0.49	5.7	0.037M	4/30/13	9.3 -	0.0
-	-	-	0.26	0.27	0.29	12.7 -	0.0	0.29	0.31	0.27	9.2	0.0210	4/30/13	3.3 -	0.0
-	-	-	0.21	0.22	0.26	32.1 -	0.0	0.53	0.56	0.58	8.2	0.04310	4/30/13	6.8 -	0.0
-	-	-	0.61	0.67	0.68	18.9 -	0.0	0.63	0.65	0.65	5.9	0.046M	4/30/13	11.5 -	0.0
-	-	-	0.47	0.50	0.52	15.8 -	0.0	0.51	0.54	0.54	7.1	0.0390	4/30/13	7.4 -	0.0
-	-	:	0.47	0.52	0.53	17.6 -	0.0	0.49	0.50	0.50	6.4	0.037M	4/30/13	8.3 -	0.0
-	-	-	0.39	0.40	0.44	20.1 -	0.0	0.67	0.72	0.69	9.3	0.05860	4/30/13	7.8 -	0.0
-	-1.22	-	-2.42	-2.06								0.0250Y	9/2/08	13.9 -	0.0
-	-	-0.37	-3.62	5.62	-3.19							0.05G	81/16/21	64.8 -	0.0
-	0.49	-	0.78	0.40	0.22	83.1 -	0.0							70.7 -	0.0
-	-	0.74	2.56	1.31	0.56	27.6 -	0.0	2.64	2.51	2.46	4.0	0.6950Z	81/16/21	16.4 -	0.0
-	-	-0.27	-2.61	-											
-	-	-0.02	-0.11	-0.32	-0.56									22.6 -	0.0
-	-	-0.14	-0.48	-0.12	8.29							0.67190Y	3/1/13	5.5 -	0.0
-	-	0.26	0.82	1.92	0.96	21.3 -	0.0	0.52	0.48	0.10	3.3	0.140Y	3/25/13	17.4 -	0.0
-	-	-	0.30	-	1.41	1.32			0.26	0.16				40.4 -	0.0
-	-	0.51	2.42	1.87	1.05	20.8 -	0.0	1.38	1.03	0.99	3.4	0.280Y	81/16/21	50.4 -	0.0
-	-	0.53	2.09	1.87	1.79	20.6 -	0.0	0.13	0.10	0.10	0.4	0.050Y	81/16/21	43.0 -	0.0
-	-	-	-	-	-			1.31	1.31	1.31	6.8	1.31250Y	4/1/13	27.6 -	0.0
-	-	0.09	0.74	0.61	0.43	36.4 -	0.0							26.9 -	0.0
-	-	-	28.09	31.08	67.87	0.2 -	0.0	0.00	0.00	0.00	0.0			6.1 -	0.0
-	-	-	26.78	19.22	61.64	0.2 -	0.0	0.00	0.00	0.00	0.0			4.7 -	0.0
-	-	0.32	-	0.73	0.72			1.05	1.00					21.6 -	0.0
-0.16	-	-	-0.73	-										20.1 -	18.4
-	-	-0.19	0.82	0.13	-0.75	11.5 -	0.0					0.10Y	81/16/21	9.5 -	0.0
-	-	1.01	3.61	2.52	2.65	31.7 -	0.0							114.6 -	0.0
-	-	0.07	0.21	0.45	1.32	167.0 -	0.0							35.1 -	0.0
-	-	1.09	2.44	3.63	3.78	20.2 -	0.0	1.28	1.24	1.08	3.0	0.320Y	81/16/21	49.3 -	0.0
-	-	-0.19	-4.31	1.27	-0.79							1.3750Y	3/1/13	34.8 -	0.0
-	-	-0.77	-0.69	-9.03	-8.80							0.050Y	81/16/21	18.1 -	0.0
0.09	-	0.47	0.44	0.37		25.3 -	0.0	0.60	0.60	0.60	5.6	0.49220Z	6/17/13	11.9 -	0.0
-	2.74	3.79	2.96	2.01		27.9 -	0.0	1.20	1.12	1.06	1.4	0.3750Y	81/16/21	105.6 -	0.0
-	-	-1.75	-2.27	0.43	-0.27									9.8 -	0.0
-	-	-	0.60	0.74	0.72	28.9 -	0.0	0.85	0.71	0.73	5.1	0.290	12/31/12	17.3 -	0.0
-	-	1.25	3.67	-2.01	2.97	7.1 -	0.0	0.43	0.41	0.37	1.9	0.55470	4/15/13	26.2 -	0.0
-	-	0.81	3.05	2.49	2.15	18.1 -	0.0	0.64	0.54	0.42	1.5	0.20Y	81/16/21	55.4 -	0.0
0.75	-	-	3.33	2.95	2.36	14.2 -	0.0					0.01480	10/5/88	47.4 -	0.0
-	-	-0.55	-0.02	1.23	2.63			0.20	0.20	0.20	1.2	0.050Y	81/16/21	24.3 -	0.0
-	-	-	0.13	0.13	0.13	0.0 -	0.0	0.10	1.12	0.28	1.$	0.10110	1/4/13	0.0 -	0.0
-	-	-	0.13	0.13	0.13	125.0 -	0.0	0.10	1.12	0.28	0.7	0.10110	1/4/13	16.3 -	0.0
-	-	-	-0.02	-0.30	-0.21			2.04	0.37	1.72	9.8	0.3886B	4/13/12	27.4 -	0.0
-	-	-	0.21	0.06	-0.07	0.0 -	0.0	0.04	-	-	1.$	0.04470	8/15/12	0.0 -	0.0
-	-	-	0.21	0.06	-0.07	86.0 -	0.0	0.04	-	-	0.3	0.04470	8/15/12	19.1	0.0
-	-	-	0.58	0.61	0.74	21.6 -	0.0	0.63	0.66	0.07	5.4	0.140	4/15/13	12.5 -	0.0
-	-	-	1.32	1.52	1.40	13.4 -	0.0	1.15	1.20	1.20	7.0	0.250	4/15/13	17.6 -	0.0
-	-	-	0.09	0.13	0.03	0.0 -	0.0	0.08	-	0.08	1.$	0.08210	1/4/13	0.0 -	0.0
-	-	-	0.09	0.13	0.03	180.0 -	0.0	0.08	-	0.08	0.5	0.08210	1/4/13	16.2 -	0.0
-	-	-	0.78	0.86	0.95	24.8 -	0.0	0.83	0.91	1.05	4.5	0.05750	4/26/13	19.4 -	0.0
-	-	-	-0.01	-0.06	-0.03			-	1.18	2.47		0.1842B	7/15/11	19.1 -	0.0
-	-	-	-0.01	-0.06	-0.03			-	1.18	2.47		0.1842B	7/15/11	19.1 -	0.0
												0.05750	4/26/13	19.4 -	0.0
-	-	0.81	4.42	5.62	1.85	14.3 -	0.0	0.28	0.20	1.50	0.5	0.250Y	81/16/21	63.2 -	0.0
-	-	0.72	2.96	3.41	1.87	21.6 -	0.0	0.96	0.44	-	1.8	0.260Y	81/16/21	64.0 -	0.0
-	-	1.34	1.27	-1.81	-2.23	30.4 -	0.0	0.12	-	-	0.4	0.050Y	4/16/13	38.6 -	0.0
-	-	1.57	6.77	1.47	-3.92	0.6 -	0.0	0.18	-	-		0.47660Z	10/31/08	3.8 -	0.0
-	-	-	0.17	-	-	223.1 -	0.0	0.18	-	-	0.6	0.1769GH	2/14/13	37.9 -	0.0
-	-	0.54	1.22	0.34	-0.61	27.0 -	0.0							32.9 -	0.0
1.00	-	-	4.09	3.43	2.37	21.5 -	0.0	1.00	1.88	0.82	1.4	0.30Y	81/16/21	87.8 -	0.0
-	-	0.39	1.48	1.41	0.11	25.5 -	0.0							37.7 -	0.0
-	-	0.41	2.31	2.26	2.28	23.8 -	0.0	0.42	0.40	0.40	0.9	0.1250Y	3/15/13	55.1 -	0.0
0.04	-	-	-0.69	-0.25	-0.29			0.07	0.07	0.07	1.5	0.01750Y	2/20/13	6.2 -	0.0
-	-	1.16	4.99	4.49	4.13	12.8 -	0.0	3.67	1.10	1.05	6.6	0.31250Y	81/16/21	63.8 -	0.0
-	-	0.95	3.55	3.45	2.75	12.2 -	0.0	3.55	3.45	2.75	11.1	0.870Z	4/25/13	43.2 -	0.0
0.04	-	-	0.88	-0.10	0.23	15.1 -	0.0	0.50	0.48	0.48	4.0	0.1350	4/30/13	13.3 -	0.0
-	-	0.17	0.88	0.71	-1.21	20.3 -	0.0	0.32	0.28	0.26	2.1	0.090Y	81/16/21	17.9 -	0.0
-	-	0.26	0.56	0.83	0.33	32.1 -	0.0					0.04G	81/16/21	18.0 -	0.0
-	-	4.52	20.82	19.28	9.53	3.2 -	0.0	5.38	2.12	2.09	11.4	0.250Y	81/16/21	66.3 -	0.0
-	-	0.54	1.48	0.01	0.33	10.8 -	0.0	0.36	0.22	0.05	3.6	0.150	10/31/13	15.9 -	0.0
-	-	-0.58	-	-	0.46									3.2 -	0.0
-	-	0.00	0.71	0.84	0.96	32.1 -	0.0					0.210Y	10/7/08	22.8 -	0.0
0.81	-	-	2.63	3.09	2.73	23.3 -	0.0	1.44	1.40	1.36	2.8	0.3650Y	81/16/21	61.4 -	0.0

SYMBOL	COMPANY	NATURE OF BUSINESS	FISCAL YEAR-END	TOTAL REV. $MILL	NET INCOME $MILL	TOTAL ASSETS $MILL	NET STK EQUITY $MILL	NO OF INST	INST. HOLDINGS (SHARES)
NGG	National Grid plc	Electric Utilities	3/31/12	13832.0	2036.0	47335.0	9239.0	337	41342533
NHI	National Health Investors, Inc.	REITs	12/31/12	97.0	90.9	706.0	457.2	187	14781352
NOV	National Oilwell Varco Inc	Equipment & Services	12/31/12	20041.0	2491.0	31484.0	20239.0	1114	394929771
NPK	National Presto Industries, Inc.	Metal Products	12/31/12	472.5	38.9	353.9	290.6	138	3815826
NNN	National Retail Properties Inc	REITs	12/31/12	331.8	142.0	3988.0	2296.3	325	106132700
NRU	National Rural Utilities Cooperative	Credit & Lending	5/31/12	674.6	-144.7	19951.3	483.2		-
NW PRC	National Westminster Bank Plc	Banking	12/31/11	9752.0	-3852.0	367552.0	16135.0		-
NBM	Nations Balanced Target Maturity F	Holding and other Investment Office	3/31/04	3.6	3.0	50.0	49.9		-
NSM	Nationstar Mortgage Holdings Inc	Credit & Lending	12/31/12	984.3	205.3	7126.1	757.7	167	89638300
NGS	Natural Gas Services Group Inc	Equipment & Services	12/31/12	93.7	12.7	232.8	175.8	109	11260177
NGVC	Natural Grocers By Vitamin Cottage	Retail - Food & Beverage, Drug & To	9/30/12	336.4	6.6	125.7	72.9	86	7832683
NRP	Natural Resources Partners L.P.	Mining	12/31/12	379.1	213.4	1764.7		155	19379519
NTZ	Natuzzi S.p.A.	Furniture	12/31/11	486.4	-19.6	511.0	310.5	22	12701169
NLS	Nautilus Inc	Leisure Equipment	12/31/12	193.9	16.9	94.3	43.3	89	17873879
NCI	Navigant Consulting, Inc.	Business Services	12/31/12	844.6	46.2	954.4	559.7	186	52114099
NNA	Navios Maritime Acquisition Corp	Equipment & Services	12/31/12	151.1	-3.8	1370.6	231.3	25	5752085
NM	Navios Maritime Holdings Inc	Shipping	12/31/11	728.0	40.8	2913.8	1059.1	88	30850567
NMM	Navios Maritime Partners LP	Shipping	12/31/12	205.4	95.9	955.0		83	16825564
NAV	Navistar International Corp.	Autos- Manufacturing	10/31/12	12948.0	-3010.0	9102.0	-3305.0	241	95494382
NCS	NCI Building Systems, Inc.	Metal Products	10/28/12	1154.0	4.9	751.5	249.4	139	15949733
NCR	NCR Corp.	Computer Hardware & Equipment	12/31/12	5730.0	146.0	6371.0	1247.0	417	161373789
NP	Neenah Paper Inc	Paper & Forest Products	12/31/12	808.8	44.3	610.7	197.8	172	17861553
NNI	Nelnet Inc	Credit & Lending	12/31/12	998.1	178.4	26607.9	1165.2	150	22481637
NPTN	NeoPhotonics Corp	Semiconductors	12/31/12	245.4	-17.5	295.6	202.8	58	8434667
N	Netsuite Inc	Internet & Software	12/31/12	308.8	-35.2	369.8	158.8	212	31137074
NSR	NeuStar, Inc.	Services	12/31/12	831.4	156.1	1526.7	646.6	331	74873355
HYB	New America High Income Fund, In	Holding and other Investment Office	12/31/12	25.2	21.7	336.8	244.6	42	9261604
GF	New Germany Fund, Inc.	Holding and other Investment Office	12/31/12	7.1	3.9	297.8	280.7	42	9669361
GF	New Germany Fund, Inc.	Holding and other Investment Office	12/31/12	7.1	3.9	297.8	280.7	42	9669361
IRL	New Ireland Fund, Inc. (The)	Holding and other Investment Office	10/31/12	1.2	-0.2	49.7	49.5	28	666415
IRL	New Ireland Fund, Inc. (The)	Holding and other Investment Office	10/31/12	1.2	-0.2	49.7	49.5	28	666415
NJR	New Jersey Resources Corp	Gas Utilities	9/30/12	2248.9	92.9	2770.0	813.9	225	29370103
NMFC	New Mountain Finance Corp	Wealth Management	12/31/12	37.5	19.8	345.3	341.9	95	13995089
EDU	New Oriental Education & Technolo	Educational Services	5/31/12	771.7	132.7	1128.8	690.4	131	108962209
NSLP	New Source Energy Partners LP	Production & Extraction							-
NWY	New York & Company Inc	Retail - Apparel and Accessories	1/28/12	956.5	-38.9	297.4	100.1	99	26548211
NYCB	New York Community Bancorp Inc.	Credit & Lending	12/31/12	2088.5	501.1	44145.1	5656.3	474	255723626
NYT	New York Times Co.	Publishing	12/30/12	1990.1	133.2	2806.3	632.5	259	144081593
NCT	Newcastle Investment Corp	REITs	12/31/12	330.5	434.1	3945.3	1073.1	203	76535071
NWL	Newell Rubbermaid, Inc.	Plastics	12/31/12	5902.7	401.3	6222.0	1996.7	542	287290632
NFX	Newfield Exploration Co.	Production & Extraction	12/31/12	2567.0	-1184.0	7912.0	2780.0	472	136699698
NEU	NewMarket Corp	Specialty Chemicals	12/31/12	2223.3	239.6	1257.5	402.2	309	8423222
NEM	Newmont Mining Corp. (Holding Co.	Precious Metals	12/31/12	9868.0	1809.0	29650.0	13773.0	966	412572936
NR	Newpark Resources, Inc.	Equipment & Services	12/31/12	1038.0	60.0	994.5	513.6	180	97447242
NHF	NexPoint Credit Strategies Fund	Holding and other Investment Office	12/31/12	41.7	27.4	746.5	476.3	49	16682477
NEE PRJ	NextEra Energy Capital Holdings In	Electric Utilities							-
NEE	NextEra Energy Inc	Electric Utilities	12/31/12	14256.0	1911.0	64439.0	16068.0	1101	314698230
NGL	NGL Energy Partners LP	Production & Extraction	3/31/12	1310.5	7.9	749.1		26	5047279
NJ	Nidec Corp	Electrical Equipment	3/31/12	682320.0	40731.0	800401.0	370182.0	95	3030624
NLSN	Nielsen Holdings NV	Business Services	12/31/12	5612.0	273.0	14585.0	4930.0	198	358858874
NKE	NIKE, Inc	Apparel, Footwear & Accessories	5/31/12	24128.0	2223.0	15465.0	10381.0	1096	607359925
NTT	Nippon Telegraph & Telephone Cor	Services	3/31/12	10507362.0	467701.0	19389699.0	7882587.0	186	29007765
NKA	Niska Gas Storage Partners LLC	Equipment & Services	3/31/12	268.6	-165.8	1803.4	690.4	47	54744005
NI	NiSource Inc. (Holding Co.)	Electric Utilities	12/31/12	5061.2	416.1	21844.7	5554.3	510	270178041
NL	NL Industries, Inc.	Office Equipment & Furniture	12/31/12	83.2	74.5	680.8	374.8	54	3655964
NED	Noah Education Holdings Ltd	Educational Services	6/30/12	163.0	-53.6	877.0	715.0	11	628170
NOAH	Noah Holdings Ltd	Wealth Management	12/31/11	72.2	24.0	180.9	161.0	25	6094966
NE	Noble Corp (Switzerland)	Equipment & Services	12/31/12	3547.0	522.3	14607.8	7723.2		-
NBL	Noble Energy, Inc.	Production & Extraction	12/31/12	4223.0	1027.0	17554.0	8258.0	640	180200313
NOK	Nokia Corp.	Manufacturing	12/31/12	30176.0	-3106.0	29949.0	8061.0	532	520890447
NMR	Nomura Holdings Inc	Finance Intermediaries & Services	3/31/12	737550.0	11583.0	35697312.0	2107241.0	94	15723252
NOR	Noranda Aluminum Holding Corp	Metal Products	12/31/12	1394.9	49.5	1357.7	146.3	96	66076569
NAT	Nordic American Tankers Ltd	Equipment & Services	12/31/12	130.7	-73.2	1085.6	809.4	147	14754138
NDZ	Nordion Inc.	Biotechnology	10/31/12	244.8	-28.9	428.6	194.8	98	98119659
JWN	Nordstrom, Inc.	Retail - General Merchandise/Depart	2/2/13	12148.0	735.0	8089.0	1913.0	670	133743722
NSC	Norfolk Southern Corp.	Rail	12/31/12	11040.0	1749.0	30342.0	9760.0	1133	224829222
NTL	Nortel Inversora S.A.	Services	12/31/12	18553.0	1273.0	15390.0	4022.0		-
NOA	North American Energy Partners Inc	Equipment & Services	3/31/12	1006.5	-21.2	750.0	127.8	57	24054840
NRT	North European Oil Royalty Trust	Oil Royalty Traders	10/31/12	23.7	22.6	4.8	0.1	59	1263384
NU	Northeast Utilities	Electric Utilities	12/31/12	6273.8	525.9	28302.8	9237.0	536	218245576
NTI	Northern Tier Energy LP	Refining & Marketing	12/31/12	4653.9	197.6	1136.8		56	83627283
NOC	Northrop Grumman Corp	Defense	12/31/12	25218.0	1978.0	26543.0	9514.0	719	260694274
NRF	Northstar Realty Finance Corp	REITs	12/31/12	504.7	-273.1	5513.8	1301.9	209	97377337
NWN	Northwest Natural Gas Co.	Gas Utilities	12/31/12	730.6	59.9	2818.8	733.0	198	18176235
NWE	Northwestern Corp.	Electric Utilities	12/31/12	1070.3	98.4	3485.5	934.0	233	37173946
NVS	Novartis AG Basel	Pharmaceuticals	12/31/12	57561.0	9505.0	124216.0	69093.0	946	264838474
NVO	Novo-Nordisk A/S (Denmark)	Pharmaceuticals	12/31/12	66346.0	17097.0	64698.0	37448.0	477	45113610
NQ	NQ Mobile Inc	IT Services	12/31/11	40.7	10.3	160.5	148.2	59	9317718
NRG	NRG Energy Inc	Electric Utilities	12/31/12	8422.0	559.0	35128.0	10264.0	477	341327629
DCM	NTT DOCOMO, Inc.	Services	3/31/12	4240003.0	463912.0	6948082.0	5062527.0	138	21310363

T42

EARNINGS PER SHARE						P/E RATIO		DIVIDENDS PER SHARE			AV. YLD %	DIV. DECLARED		PRICE RANGE 2012	
QUARTERLY			ANNUAL												
1st	2nd	3rd	2012	2011	2010			2012	2011	2010	%	AMOUNT	PAYABLE		
-	-	-	0.57	0.64	0.56	101.8 -	0.0	-	-	0.37	-	-	-	58.0 -	0.0
-	-	0.52	3.26	2.92	2.50	20.5 -	0.0	2.64	2.71	2.36	4.8	0.6950Z	81/16/21	66.9 -	0.0
-	-	1.43	5.83	4.70	3.98	14.6 -	0.0	0.49	0.45	0.41	0.7	0.130Y	81/16/21	84.8 -	0.0
-	-	1.36	5.64	6.98	9.26	14.5 -	0.0	12.50	8.25	8.15	17.2	5.56Y	12/28/12	82.0 -	0.0
-	-	0.30	1.11	0.96	0.80	32.6 -	0.0	1.56	1.53	1.51	5.1	0.3950Z	81/16/21	36.2 -	0.0
-	-	-	-	-	-	-	-	1.49	1.49	1.49	5.9	0.37190Z	5/15/13	26.0 -	0.0
-	-	-	-	-	-	-	-	-	3.12	2.97	-	-	-	25.8 -	0.0
-	-	-	-	-	-	-	-	-	-	-	-	0.110	9/29/03	-	
-	-	0.61	2.40	-	-	17.5 -	0.0	-	-	-	-	-	-	42.0 -	0.0
-	-	0.21	1.03	0.80	0.58	18.7 -	0.0	-	-	-	-	-	-	19.3 -	0.0
0.10	-	-	0.30	5.60	7.04	82.5 -	0.0	-	-	-	-	-	-	24.8 -	0.0
-	-	0.48	1.97	0.50	1.54	12.7 -	0.0	2.20	2.17	2.16	10.2	0.550	2/14/13	24.9 -	0.0
-	-	-	-	-0.36	-0.20	-	-	-	-	-	-	-	-	3.1 -	0.0
-	-	0.03	0.55	0.05	-0.74	13.7 -	0.0	-	-	-	-	0.10Y	9/10/07	7.5 -	0.0
-	-	0.22	0.90	0.80	0.48	16.1 -	0.0	-	-	-	-	-	-	14.5 -	0.0
-	-	-0.03	-0.08	-0.08	-0.43	-	-	-	-	-	-	0.050	4/4/13	3.4 -	0.0
-	-	0.04	-	0.37	1.24	-	-	-	-	-	-	0.060	3/27/13	4.6 -	0.0
-	-	-	1.61	1.33	1.51	10.4 -	0.0	-	-	-	-	0.44250	2/14/13	16.7 -	0.0
-1.53	-	-	-43.56	22.64	3.05	-	-	-	-	-	-	-	-	40.6 -	0.0
-0.19	-	-	-3.81	-2.58	-17.07	-	-	-	-	-	-	-	-	17.7 -	0.0
-	-	0.35	0.89	0.33	0.83	32.8 -	0.0	-	-	-	-	-	-	29.2 -	0.0
-	-	0.55	2.68	1.81	10.21	12.0 -	0.0	0.48	0.44	0.40	1.7	0.150Y	3/4/13	32.2 -	0.0
-	-	0.77	3.74	4.23	3.81	9.2 -	0.0	1.40	0.37	0.70	5.3	0.10Y	3/15/13	34.6 -	0.0
-	-	0.02	-0.62	-1.42	-	-	-	-	-	-	-	-	-	6.0 -	0.0
-	-	-0.11	-0.50	-0.48	-0.43	-	-	-	-	-	-	-	-	80.1 -	0.0
-	-	0.68	2.30	2.16	1.40	20.5 -	0.0	-	-	-	-	-	-	47.1 -	0.0
-	-	-	0.93	1.03	1.06	12.5 -	0.0	0.96	1.04	1.02	9.0	0.0650	4/30/13	11.6 -	0.0
-	-	-	0.23	0.24	0.08	0.0 -	0.0	0.63	0.59	0.12	1.$	0.63340	1/28/13	11.0 -	0.0
-	-	-	0.23	0.24	0.08	75.9 -	0.0	0.63	0.59	0.12	4.2	0.63340	1/28/13	17.5 -	0.0
-	-	-	-0.04	0.01	0.05	-	-	0.02	0.06	-	1.$	0.020	12/30/11	10.5 -	0.0
-	-	-	-0.04	0.01	0.05	-	-	0.02	0.06	-	0.2	0.020	12/30/11	10.5 -	0.0
1.44	-	-	2.23	2.44	2.82	21.0 -	0.0	1.54	1.44	1.36	3.6	0.40Y	81/16/21	46.9 -	0.0
-	-	-	1.33	0.78	-	11.7 -	0.0	1.71	0.86	-	11.9	0.340Y	3/28/13	15.5 -	0.0
-	-	0.14	0.85	0.65	0.50	33.9 -	0.0	-	-	-	-	-	-	28.8 -	0.0
-	-	-	-	-	-	-	-	-	-	-	-	-	-	20.3 -	19.5
-	-	-0.06	-0.64	-1.29	-0.23	-	-	-	-	-	-	-	-	4.6 -	0.0
-	-	0.29	1.13	1.09	1.24	13.2 -	0.0	1.00	1.00	1.00	7.6	0.250Y	81/16/21	14.9 -	0.0
-	-	0.02	0.87	-0.27	0.71	12.5 -	0.0	-	-	0.00	-	0.060Y	81/16/21	10.9 -	0.0
-	-	1.63	2.94	3.09	10.96	3.9 -	0.0	0.84	0.40	-	10.3	0.52340Z	4/30/13	11.6 -	0.0
-	-	0.37	1.37	0.42	0.96	19.1 -	0.0	0.43	0.29	0.20	2.1	0.150Y	81/16/21	26.1 -	0.0
-	-	-0.24	-8.80	3.99	3.91	-	-	-	-	-	-	-	-	36.2 -	0.0
-	-	4.83	17.85	15.09	12.09	16.1 -	0.0	28.00	2.39	1.56	11.7	0.90Y	4/1/13	288.2 -	0.0
-	-	0.74	3.63	0.73	4.55	15.8 -	0.0	1.40	1.00	0.50	3.0	0.4250Y	81/16/21	57.2 -	0.0
-	-	0.20	0.62	0.80	0.46	15.5 -	0.0	-	-	-	-	-	-	9.6 -	0.0
-	-	-	0.43	0.47	0.59	18.0 -	0.0	0.42	0.53	0.63	6.4	0.0420	4/30/13	7.7 -	0.0
-	-	-	-	-	-	-	-	-	-	-	-	0.3021GHZ	4/15/13	24.8 -	24.3
-	-	0.98	4.56	4.59	4.74	17.0 -	0.0	2.40	2.20	2.00	3.5	0.660Y	81/16/21	77.7 -	0.0
-	-	0.75	0.32	1.16	-	84.1 -	0.0	0.85	-	-	3.6	0.46250	2/14/13	26.9 -	0.0
-	94.37	-	-276.89	362.80	373.04	0.1 -	0.0	0.00	0.00	0.00	0.0	-	-	23.1 -	0.0
-	-	0.29	0.75	0.24	0.46	47.8 -	0.0	-	-	-	-	0.16G	81/16/21	35.8 -	0.0
-	-	0.95	2.37	2.19	1.93	25.1 -	0.0	0.85	0.58	0.52	1.7	0.210Y	81/16/21	59.6 -	0.0
-	111.84	-	366.67	385.16	372.01	0.1 -	0.0	0.01	0.01	0.01	0.0	-	-	24.6 -	0.0
-	-	0.15	-2.39	0.31	-	-	-	1.40	0.87	-	11.8	0.350	2/15/13	13.7 -	0.0
-	-	0.06	1.39	1.03	1.04	21.1 -	0.0	0.94	0.92	0.92	3.7	0.240Y	81/16/21	29.3 -	0.0
-	-	0.57	1.53	1.68	1.40	9.8 -	0.0	0.50	0.50	0.50	4.1	0.1250Y	3/26/13	15.0 -	0.0
0.01	-	-	-1.47	-11.16	0.14	-	-	-	-	-	-	-	-	2.4 -	0.0
-	-	0.07	-	0.84	0.46	-	-	-	-	-	-	-	-	8.7 -	0.0
-	-	0.45	2.05	1.46	3.02	20.2 -	0.0	-	-	0.88	-	0.130Y	81/16/21	41.4 -	0.0
-	-	1.23	5.71	2.54	4.10	20.4 -	0.0	0.91	0.80	0.72	1.0	0.250Y	81/16/21	116.5 -	0.0
-	-	-0.26	-0.84	-0.31	0.50	-	-	0.33	0.85	0.62	10.4	-	-	5.5 -	0.0
-	0.74	-	3.14	7.86	21.59	2.0 -	0.0	0.00	0.00	0.00	0.0	-	-	6.3 -	0.0
-	-	0.05	0.72	2.06	1.27	15.1 -	0.0	1.41	1.03	-	20.9	0.040Y	3/27/13	10.9 -	0.0
-	-	-0.44	-1.39	-1.53	-0.02	-	-	1.20	1.15	1.70	11.0	0.160	2/13/13	15.7 -	0.0
-	-	-	-0.47	0.26	-2.60	-	-	0.30	0.30	-	3.8	0.10	7/3/12	10.7 -	0.0
-	-	0.71	3.14	2.75	2.01	18.5 -	0.0	0.92	0.76	0.64	1.7	0.30Y	81/16/21	58.2 -	0.0
-	-	1.24	5.37	5.45	4.00	14.4 -	0.0	1.94	1.66	1.40	2.8	0.50Y	81/16/21	77.1 -	0.0
-	-	32.08	-	121.91	85.71	-	-	-	-	-	-	2.10	10/15/98	20.6 -	0.0
-	-	0.13	-0.58	-0.96	0.77	-	-	-	-	-	-	-	-	4.9 -	0.0
0.60	-	-	2.46	2.63	2.04	13.7 -	0.0	2.59	2.55	1.86	9.4	0.590Z	2/27/13	33.7 -	0.0
-	-	0.66	1.89	2.22	2.19	23.0 -	0.0	1.32	1.10	1.02	3.4	0.36750Y	81/16/21	43.5 -	0.0
-	-	0.46	-	-	-	-	-	1.48	-	-	6.4	1.270	2/28/13	32.7 -	0.0
-	-	1.82	7.81	7.52	6.82	9.1 -	0.0	2.15	1.97	1.84	3.3	0.550Y	81/16/21	71.1 -	0.0
-	-	-1.11	-2.31	-2.94	-5.17	-	-	0.61	0.42	0.40	9.5	0.180Z	3/1/13	9.7 -	0.0
-	-	-0.39	2.22	2.39	2.73	22.7 -	0.0	1.79	1.75	1.68	3.9	0.4550Y	81/16/21	50.5 -	0.0
-	-	-0.10	2.66	2.53	2.14	15.0 -	0.0	1.48	1.44	1.36	4.1	0.380Y	3/31/13	39.9 -	0.0
-	-	1.00	3.89	3.78	4.26	18.3 -	0.0	2.48	2.36	1.95	4.1	-	-	71.3 -	0.0
-	-	10.33	-	29.99	24.60	-	-	-	0.26	0.18	-	-	-	194.3 -	0.0
-	-	0.00	-	0.04	-0.34	-	-	-	-	-	-	-	-	12.1 -	0.0
-	-	-0.01	2.35	0.78	1.84	11.3 -	0.0	0.18	-	-	0.9	0.090Y	81/16/21	26.5 -	0.0
-2932.05	-	1187.34	1797.07	1863.62		0.0 -	0.0	5400.00	5200.00	5000.00	34421.0	-	-	17.4 -	0.0

SYMBOL	COMPANY	NATURE OF BUSINESS	FISCAL YEAR-END	TOTAL REV. $MILL	NET INCOME $MILL	TOTAL ASSETS $MILL	NET STK EQUITY $MILL	NO OF INST	INST. HOLDINGS (SHARES)
NUS	NU Skin Enterprises, Inc.	Household & Personal Products	12/31/12	2169.7	221.6	1152.9	590.6	341	56094502
NUE	Nucor Corp.	Non-Precious Metals	12/31/12	19429.3	504.6	14152.1	7641.6	752	292726905
NS	NuStar Energy L.P.	Refining & Marketing	12/31/12	5955.7	-226.6	5613.1	-	277	30937420
NSH	NuStar GP Holdings LLC	Equipment & Services	12/31/12	-4.6	2.1	517.7	412.8	115	28937722
NUW	Nuveen AMT-Free Municipal Value	Holding and other Investment Office	10/31/12	12.4	10.9	232.1	231.1	18	302946
NBB	Nuveen Build America Bond Fund	Holding and other Investment Office	3/31/12	41.8	36.1	666.6	566.0	39	2478356
NBD	Nuveen Build America Bond Opport	Holding and other Investment Office	3/31/12	12.0	10.5	170.6	162.6	-	-
NKX	Nuveen California AMT-Free Munici	Holding and other Investment Office	2/29/12	6.5	4.9	126.2	86.7	36	1355798
NAC	Nuveen California Dividend Advanta	Holding and other Investment Office	2/29/12	26.8	22.0	520.7	349.2	27	1335872
NQC	Nuveen California Investment Qualit	Holding and other Investment Office	2/29/12	16.3	12.9	320.3	207.8	25	753353
NCO	Nuveen California Municipal Market	Holding and other Investment Office	2/29/12	9.8	7.8	185.0	127.1	22	638202
NCA	Nuveen California Municipal Value	Holding and other Investment Office	2/29/12	13.6	12.0	261.2	254.6	33	1181863
NCP	Nuveen California Performance Plu	Holding and other Investment Office	2/29/12	15.2	12.3	290.7	199.6	23	664695
NUC	Nuveen California Quality Income M	Holding and other Investment Office	2/29/12	28.3	22.8	540.8	351.4	30	844587
NVC	Nuveen California Select Quality Mu	Holding and other Investment Office	2/29/12	28.6	23.2	544.9	363.8	31	1031697
NXC	Nuveen California Select Tax-Free I	Holding and other Investment Office	3/31/12	4.7	4.4	96.4	94.4	21	339969
NTC	Nuveen Connecticut Premium Inco	Holding and other Investment Office	5/31/12	5.6	3.1	127.3	82.3	27	408462
JCE	Nuveen Core Equity Alpha Fund	Holding and other Investment Office	12/31/12	5.2	2.7	237.0	236.4	30	1612742
JQC	Nuveen Credit Strategies Income F	Holding and other Investment Office	12/31/12	131.5	106.9	1993.2	1345.7	105	23607864
JGT	Nuveen Diversified Currency Opport	Holding and other Investment Office	12/31/12	16.8	10.5	711.3	705.1	76	11493090
JDD	Nuveen Diversified Dividend and In	Holding and other Investment Office	12/31/12	13.8	9.1	360.5	247.8	43	3120213
NAD	Nuveen Dividend Advantage Munici	Holding and other Investment Office	10/31/12	45.9	33.7	942.2	630.5	69	4134487
JMF	Nuveen Energy MLP Total Return F	Holding and other Investment Office	11/30/12	0.0	1.3	1005.7	696.4	43	4797606
NEV	Nuveen Enhanced Municipal Value	Holding and other Investment Office	10/31/12	22.7	19.5	326.3	305.3	25	1931845
JPG	Nuveen Equity Premium & Growth	Holding and other Investment Office	12/31/12	6.3	4.1	237.5	232.0	35	2736087
JLA	Nuveen Equity Premium Advantage	Holding and other Investment Office	12/31/12	7.1	3.6	351.7	342.2	44	4797526
JPZ	Nuveen Equity Premium Income Fu	Holding and other Investment Office	12/31/12	14.0	9.4	519.2	505.0	61	4413552
JSN	Nuveen Equity Premium Opportunit	Holding and other Investment Office	12/31/12	20.7	12.9	891.2	866.4	59	9162851
JFR	Nuveen Floating Rate Income Fund	Holding and other Investment Office	7/31/12	58.5	49.0	840.4	572.1	81	10394726
JRO	Nuveen Floating Rate Income Oppo	Holding and other Investment Office	7/31/12	40.6	34.7	547.3	369.9	66	5858283
JGG	Nuveen Global Income Opportunitie	Holding and other Investment Office	12/31/12	3.8	2.1	208.5	144.3	31	1632720
JGV	Nuveen Global Value Opportunities	Holding and other Investment Office	12/31/12	11.9	8.2	322.0	306.6	37	5412357
NID	Nuveen Intermediate Duration Muni	Finance Intermediaries & Services	11/6/12	-	-	0.5	0.1	-	-
NIQ	Nuveen Intermediate Duration Quali	Holding and other Investment Office	1/10/13	-	-	0.5	0.1	-	-
NQM	Nuveen Investment Quality Municip	Holding and other Investment Office	10/31/12	43.0	33.5	890.4	596.7	51	2354690
NMY	Nuveen Maryland Premium Income	Holding and other Investment Office	5/31/12	12.0	7.3	256.1	167.2	36	937435
NMT	Nuveen Massachusetts Premium In	Holding and other Investment Office	5/31/12	5.3	3.2	113.3	73.8	15	137383
NUM	Nuveen Michigan Quality Income M	Holding and other Investment Office	2/29/12	13.0	10.3	278.0	184.3	20	235747
JLS	Nuveen Mortgage Opportunity Term	Holding and other Investment Office	12/31/12	25.8	20.2	484.8	422.1	28	1669781
JMT	Nuveen Mortgage Opportunity Term	Holding and other Investment Office	12/31/12	25.8	20.2	147.3	130.9	24	613765
NMA	Nuveen Municipal Advantage Fund,	Holding and other Investment Office	10/31/12	49.2	37.7	1036.2	688.8	65	2726644
NMD	Nuveen Municipal High Income Opp	Holding and other Investment Office	10/31/12	19.2	16.0	280.1	242.6	23	865168
NMI	Nuveen Municipal Income Fund, Inc	Holding and other Investment Office	10/31/12	5.5	4.7	100.1	96.3	20	258546
NMO	Nuveen Municipal Market Opportuni	Holding and other Investment Office	10/31/12	50.1	38.0	1093.7	699.4	65	4016706
NIO	Nuveen Municipal Opportunity Fund	Holding and other Investment Office	10/31/12	103.2	80.8	2321.1	1526.8	102	6404875
NUV	Nuveen Municipal Value Fund, Inc.	Holding and other Investment Office	10/31/12	105.3	93.7	2130.6	2105.3	140	13419370
NUJ PRC	Nuveen New Jersey Dividend Adva	Holding and other Investment Office	4/30/12	5.1	3.5	104.5	68.9	9	280404
NQJ	Nuveen New Jersey Investment Qu	ETFs	4/30/12	21.8	17.0	459.0	313.1	28	1097869
NNJ	Nuveen New Jersey Premium Inco	Holding and other Investment Office	4/30/12	13.3	10.3	280.7	191.0	24	602598
NAN	Nuveen New York Dividend Advant	Holding and other Investment Office	9/30/12	10.2	6.8	223.5	149.4	18	541266
NNY	Nuveen New York Municipal Value	Holding and other Investment Office	9/30/12	7.4	6.4	161.8	158.0	22	718363
NNP	Nuveen New York Performance Plu	Holding and other Investment Office	9/30/12	16.9	12.9	378.3	253.4	21	876238
NXN	Nuveen New York Select Tax-Free I	Holding and other Investment Office	3/31/12	2.9	2.6	58.4	57.2	8	155120
NNC	Nuveen North Carolina Premium Inc	Holding and other Investment Office	5/31/12	6.7	3.6	157.9	97.5	32	382889
NUO	Nuveen Ohio Quality Income Munici	Holding and other Investment Office	2/29/12	12.0	9.6	242.4	167.7	23	465830
NXM PRC	Nuveen Pennsylvania Dividend Adv	Holding and other Investment Office	4/30/12	3.7	2.5	78.8	51.3	12	116581
NVY PRC	Nuveen Pennsylvania Dividend Adv	Holding and other Investment Office	4/30/12	4.3	2.9	86.6	56.6	16	128936
NQP	Nuveen Pennsylvania Investment Q	ETFs	4/30/12	18.5	14.5	402.2	253.9	42	639651
NPY	Nuveen Pennsylvania Premium Inc	Holding and other Investment Office	4/30/12	16.6	13.0	350.3	236.0	38	617669
NPP	Nuveen Performance Plus Municipa	Holding and other Investment Office	10/31/12	70.9	55.0	1455.0	1000.8	78	5669522
JPI	Nuveen Preferred & Income Term F	Holding and other Investment Office	7/31/12	0.0	-0.0	533.9	476.3	22	641717
JPC	Nuveen Preferred Income Opportun	Holding and other Investment Office	12/31/12	90.1	73.4	1392.5	997.5	87	13824548
NPF	Nuveen Premier Municipal Income	Holding and other Investment Office	10/31/12	21.9	16.4	488.0	311.3	44	2026215
NIF	Nuveen Premier Municipal Opportu	Holding and other Investment Office	10/31/12	21.3	16.5	468.8	313.7	40	1179979
NPM	Nuveen Premium Income Municipal	Holding and other Investment Office	10/31/12	80.5	61.9	1711.5	1130.6	72	4734284
NPT	Nuveen Premium Income Municipal	Holding and other Investment Office	10/31/12	46.4	35.8	954.8	628.4	56	4941904
NPI	Nuveen Premium Income Municipal	Holding and other Investment Office	10/31/12	70.2	54.0	1482.5	987.7	61	4818026
NPX	Nuveen Premium Income Municipal	Holding and other Investment Office	FISCAL	37.5	28.6	826.5	557.6	54	3269076
NQU	Nuveen Quality Income Municipal F	Holding and other Investment Office	10/31/12	62.3	47.0	1329.1	878.1	85	6503244
NQI	Nuveen Quality Municipal Fund, Inc.	Holding and other Investment Office	10/31/12	41.7	32.3	899.5	595.7	57	1613431
JTP	Nuveen Quality Preferred Income F	Holding and other Investment Office	7/31/12	52.1	42.6	781.0	557.0	81	7207930
JPS	Nuveen Quality Preferred Income F	Holding and other Investment Office	7/31/12	101.7	83.3	1538.3	1097.4	100	11868353
JHP	Nuveen Quality Preferred Income F	Holding and other Investment Office	7/31/12	19.3	15.7	292.4	208.7	44	2956816
JRI	Nuveen Real Asset Income & Growt	Holding and other Investment Office	3/9/12	-	-	0.5	0.1	22	720515
NIM	Nuveen Select Maturities Municipal	Holding and other Investment Office	3/31/12	5.8	5.0	130.9	129.9	36	930378
NQS	Nuveen Select Quality Municipal Fu	Holding and other Investment Office	10/31/12	39.5	30.1	822.8	557.6	50	946831
NXQ	Nuveen Select Tax Free Income Po	Holding and other Investment Office	3/31/12	12.6	11.7	247.9	245.8	42	856443
NXP	Nuveen Select Tax-Free Income Po	Holding and other Investment Office	3/31/12	12.8	12.0	241.8	240.7	36	612910
NXR	Nuveen Select Tax-Free Income Po	Holding and other Investment Office	3/31/12	9.7	9.0	188.9	188.0	27	535336
NSL	Nuveen Senior Income Fund	Holding and other Investment Office	7/31/12	22.5	18.5	344.0	231.9	46	5861554

T44

\	EARNINGS PER SHARE						P/E RATIO		DIVIDENDS PER SHARE			AV. YLD %	DIV. DECLARED		PRICE RANGE 2012	
1st	2nd	3rd	2012	2011	2010			2012	2011	2010		AMOUNT	PAYABLE		
-	-	0.87	3.52	2.38	2.11	17.0 -	0.0	0.80	0.59	0.50	1.8	0.30Y	81/16/21	59.9 -	0.0
-	0.35	1.58	2.45	0.42		30.5 -	0.0	1.46	1.45	1.44	3.6	0.36750Y	81/16/21	48.2 -	0.0
-	-0.09	-3.61	2.78	3.19		-		4.38	4.34	4.27	8.7	1.0950	81/16/21	59.5 -	0.0
-	0.45	0.05	1.64	1.70		693.0 -	0.0	2.08	1.95	1.83	6.8	0.5450	2/19/13	34.6 -	0.0
-	-	0.84	0.93	0.91		22.9 -	0.0	0.82	0.92	0.91	4.6	0.067M	5/1/13	19.3 -	0.0
-	-	1.36	1.19	-		16.1 -	0.0	1.40	1.17	-	6.7	0.11350	5/1/13	21.9 -	0.0
-	-	1.45	0.47	-		15.4 -	0.0	1.49	0.38	-	6.9	0.11050	5/1/13	22.4 -	0.0
-	-	0.83	0.81	0.85		19.6 -	0.0	0.83	0.80	1.36	5.5	0.07M	5/1/13	16.3 -	0.0
-	-	-	0.98	1.01				0.91	0.89	0.81	5.9	0.0246M	5/1/13	16.6 -	0.0
-	-	0.95	1.01	1.04		18.1 -	0.0	0.96	0.91	0.83	6.0	0.077M	5/1/13	17.2 -	0.0
-	-	0.95	0.95	1.03		18.3 -	0.0	0.95	0.93	0.84	5.8	0.08M	5/1/13	17.4 -	0.0
-	-	0.48	0.47	0.47		22.5 -	0.0	0.46	0.46	0.46	4.5	0.039M	5/1/13	10.8 -	0.0
-	-	0.95	1.00	1.02		17.7 -	0.0	0.95	0.90	0.80	6.0	0.079M	5/1/13	16.8 -	0.0
-	-	1.03	1.04	1.10		17.6 -	0.0	1.02	0.97	0.89	6.0	0.085M	5/1/13	18.1 -	0.0
-	-	1.00	1.02	1.02		17.6 -	0.0	1.00	0.97	0.88	6.0	0.083M	5/1/13	17.6 -	0.0
-	-	0.70	0.68	0.67		23.1 -	0.0	0.68	0.67	0.67	4.4	0.057M	5/1/13	16.2 -	0.0
-	-	0.58	0.67	0.80		25.3 -	0.0	0.75	0.71	0.69	5.3	0.0221M	5/1/13	14.7 -	0.0
-	-	0.17	0.10	0.10		92.5 -	0.0	1.08	1.08	1.10	7.8	0.270	4/1/13	15.7 -	0.0
-	-	0.78	0.55	0.53		13.4 -	0.0	0.80	0.79	0.70	8.4	0.06920	5/1/13	10.5 -	0.0
-	-	0.24	0.12	0.36		56.0 -	0.0	1.21	1.30	1.42	9.4	0.29750	4/1/13	13.4 -	0.0
-	-	0.45	0.44	0.36		29.3 -	0.0	1.00	1.00	0.94	8.4	0.250	4/1/13	13.2 -	0.0
-	-	0.86	0.92	1.00		18.9 -	0.0	0.96	0.91	0.91	6.2	0.0225M	5/1/13	16.3 -	0.0
-	-	0.05	-0.24	-		409.2 -	0.0	1.26	0.95	-	6.9	0.3160	5/15/13	20.5 -	0.0
-	-	1.01	1.01	-		16.8 -	0.0	0.96	0.93	0.91	6.0	0.08M	5/1/13	17.0 -	0.0
-	-	0.25	0.24	0.24		55.9 -	0.0	1.12	1.12	1.12	8.5	0.280	4/1/13	14.0 -	0.0
-	-	0.14	0.12	0.11		91.2 -	0.0	1.14	1.22	1.30	9.4	0.2840	4/1/13	12.8 -	0.0
-	-	0.24	0.23	0.27		54.0 -	0.0	1.08	1.16	1.25	8.9	0.2710	4/1/13	13.0 -	0.0
-	-	0.19	0.18	0.18		67.4 -	0.0	1.12	1.20	1.30	9.2	0.2790	4/1/13	12.8 -	0.0
-	-	0.57	1.07	0.82		23.9 -	0.0	0.96	0.69	0.58	7.9	0.0760	5/1/13	13.7 -	0.0
-	-	1.13	1.12	1.01		12.1 -	0.0	1.01	0.79	0.71	8.2	0.080	5/1/13	13.7 -	0.0
-	-	0.23	0.17	0.14		64.7 -	0.0	1.20	1.30	1.56	8.3	0.2950	4/1/13	14.9 -	0.0
-	-	0.42	0.46	0.36		39.0 -	0.0	1.27	1.37	1.20	8.7	0.290	4/1/13	16.4 -	0.0
-	-	-				-		-			-	0.0550	5/1/13	15.1 -	13.9
-	-	-				-		-			-	0.048GM	5/1/13	15.0 -	14.6
-	-	0.93	1.00	1.04		18.9 -	0.0	1.01	0.97	0.91	6.2	0.08M	5/1/13	17.6 -	0.0
-	-	0.68	0.80	0.84		23.9 -	0.0	0.77	0.76	0.73	5.0	0.0217M	5/1/13	16.3 -	0.0
-	-	0.67	0.75	0.87		23.8 -	0.0	0.82	0.82	0.77	5.5	0.0229M	5/1/13	15.9 -	0.0
-	-	0.89	0.94	0.93		18.5 -	0.0	0.86	0.83	0.73	5.5	0.0192M	5/1/13	16.5 -	0.0
-	-	1.27	1.91	1.81		23.7 -	0.0	2.07	2.07	1.96	7.8	0.17250	5/1/13	30.1 -	0.0
-	-	1.19	1.90	1.19		25.2 -	0.0	2.07	2.03	1.34	7.8	0.17250	5/1/13	29.9 -	0.0
-	-	0.86	0.93	1.01		18.7 -	0.0	1.11	0.99	1.04	7.3	0.067M	5/1/13	16.1 -	0.0
-	-	0.88	0.87	0.91		15.9 -	0.0	0.79	0.87	0.96	6.1	0.0655M	5/1/13	13.9 -	0.0
-	-	0.57	0.58	0.58		22.6 -	0.0	0.57	0.57	0.57	4.7	0.0475M	5/1/13	12.9 -	0.0
-	-	0.83	0.88	0.99		18.5 -	0.0	0.88	0.97	0.96	6.0	0.0645M	5/1/13	15.3 -	0.0
-	-	0.84	0.88	0.97		19.0 -	0.0	0.88	0.87	0.84	5.8	0.073M	5/1/13	16.0 -	0.0
-	-	0.46	0.48	0.49		23.1 -	0.0	0.53	0.49	0.47	5.2	0.037M	5/1/13	10.6 -	0.0
-	-	0.77	0.85	0.94		13.1 -	0.0	0.87	0.89	0.81	16.8	0.0167M	5/1/13	10.1 -	0.0
-	-	0.83	0.85	0.92		19.6 -	0.0	0.84	0.85	0.76	5.4	0.067M	5/1/13	16.3 -	0.0
-	-	0.85	0.86	0.90		20.8 -	0.0	0.86	0.83	0.76	5.2	0.071M	5/1/13	17.7 -	0.0
-	-	0.73	0.76	0.84		22.4 -	0.0	0.79	0.82	0.83	5.2	0.0208M	5/1/13	16.3 -	0.0
-	-	0.42	0.43	0.42		25.7 -	0.0	0.42	0.43	0.45	4.1	0.033M	5/1/13	10.8 -	0.0
-	-	0.86	0.88	0.91		20.5 -	0.0	0.88	0.89	0.85	5.0	0.0U/1M	5/1/13	17.6 -	0.0
-	-	0.66	0.64	0.62		24.1 -	0.0	0.64	0.61	0.61	4.3	0.0525M	5/1/13	15.9 -	0.0
-	-	0.57	0.69	0.81		28.2 -	0.0	0.71	0.74	0.71	4.6	0.0217M	5/1/13	16.1 -	0.0
-	-	0.99	1.01	1.01		20.3 -	0.0	0.93	0.90	0.80	5.1	0.0188GH	5/1/13	20.1 -	0.0
-	-	0.74	0.85	0.96		13.7 -	0.0	0.93	0.92	0.83	21.4	0.0175M	5/1/13	10.2 -	0.0
-	-	0.79	0.89	0.97		12.8 -	0.0	0.96	0.94	0.88	28.9	0.0179M	5/1/13	10.1 -	0.0
-	-	0.90	0.93	0.96		18.6 -	0.0	0.93	0.90	0.80	5.9	0.07M	5/1/13	16.7 -	0.0
-	-	0.83	0.85	0.91		19.0 -	0.0	0.84	0.84	0.77	5.6	0.07M	5/1/13	15.8 -	0.0
-	-	0.92	0.97	1.03		18.9 -	0.0	0.96	1.04	0.93	5.9	0.077M	5/1/13	17.4 -	0.0
-	-	-				-		-			-	0.1690	5/1/13	25.9 -	0.0
-	-	0.76	0.51	0.50		13.6 -	0.0	0.76	0.75	0.68	8.0	0.06330	5/1/13	10.3 -	0.0
-	-	0.83	0.94	0.98		19.0 -	0.0	0.92	0.89	0.85	6.1	0.07M	5/1/13	15.8 -	0.0
-	-	0.85	0.88	0.96		19.2 -	0.0	0.91	0.89	0.87	5.8	0.072M	5/1/13	16.3 -	0.0
-	-	0.88	0.95	1.01		18.3 -	0.0	0.94	0.92	0.88	6.1	0.072M	5/1/13	16.1 -	0.0
-	-	0.83	0.82	0.87		18.1 -	0.0	0.85	0.85	0.83	6.0	0.068M	5/1/13	15.0 -	0.0
-	-	0.84	0.90	0.99		18.9 -	0.0	0.92	0.92	0.88	6.1	0.072M	5/1/13	15.9 -	0.0
-	-	0.77	0.77	0.78		20.1 -	0.0	0.74	0.74	0.74	5.1	0.062M	5/1/13	15.5 -	0.0
-	-	0.86	0.93	1.04		19.1 -	0.0	0.97	0.95	0.92	6.2	0.0655M	5/1/13	16.4 -	0.0
-	-	0.84	0.87	0.95		19.0 -	0.0	0.90	0.87	0.85	6.0	0.073M	5/1/13	16.0 -	0.0
-	-	0.66	0.35	0.65		14.0 -	0.0	0.60	0.60	0.58	7.0	0.050	5/1/13	9.2 -	0.0
-	-	0.69	0.37	0.69		14.0 -	0.0	0.66	0.66	0.65	7.2	0.0550	5/1/13	9.7 -	0.0
-	-	0.66	0.36	0.65		14.3 -	0.0	0.62	0.62	0.62	7.0	0.0520	5/1/13	9.4 -	0.0
-	-	-				-		-			-	0.36750	5/1/13	20.3 -	0.0
-	-	0.40	0.43	0.44		28.3 -	0.0	0.41	0.42	0.42	3.8	0.0295M	5/1/13	11.3 -	0.0
-	-	0.87	1.03	1.12		19.2 -	0.0	1.08	1.12	1.01	6.9	0.065M	5/1/13	16.7 -	0.0
-	-	0.66	0.64	0.68		23.1 -	0.0	0.64	0.67	0.67	4.5	0.0525M	5/1/13	15.3 -	0.0
-	-	0.73	0.71	0.73		22.2 -	0.0	0.72	0.71	0.72	4.7	0.0525M	5/1/13	16.2 -	0.0
-	-	0.69	0.66	0.67		23.2 -	0.0	0.70	0.64	0.64	4.7	0.0525M	5/1/13	16.0 -	0.0
-	-	0.57	0.64	0.37		14.6 -	0.0	0.54	0.49	0.46	7.3	0.04550	5/1/13	8.3 -	0.0

SYMBOL	COMPANY	NATURE OF BUSINESS	FISCAL YEAR-END	TOTAL REV. $MILL	NET INCOME $MILL	TOTAL ASSETS $MILL	NET STK EQUITY $MILL	NO OF INST	INST. HOLDINGS (SHARES)
JSD	Nuveen Short Duration Credit Oppo	Holding and other Investment Office	7/31/12	18.9	15.6	292.0	195.2	14	1819431
JTD	Nuveen Tax-Advantaged Dividend	Holding and other Investment Office	12/31/12	11.9	7.4	317.8	219.7	29	2281343
JTA	Nuveen Tax-Advantaged Total Retu	Holding and other Investment Office	12/31/11	7.9	5.0	223.7	151.9	37	1648164
NTX	Nuveen Texas Quality Income Muni	Holding and other Investment Office	2/29/12	10.7	7.2	227.9	148.2	16	337585
NPV	Nuveen Virginia Premium Income M	Holding and other Investment Office	5/31/12	9.9	6.1	209.9	141.1	22	410583
NVE	NV Energy, Inc.	Electric Utilities	12/31/12	2979.2	321.9	11984.1	3557.4	32	13343843
NVR	NVR Inc.	Builders	12/31/12	3193.2	180.6	2604.8	1480.5	291	4799555
NYX	NYSE Euronext	Finance Intermediaries & Services	12/31/12	3749.0	348.0	12556.0	6345.0	545	198350896
OAK	Oaktree Capital Group LLC	Wealth Management	12/31/12	145.0	107.8	43870.0	306.4	105	24667974
OAS	Oasis Petroleum Inc.	Production & Extraction	12/31/12	686.7	153.4	2528.8	795.0	254	85923716
OXY	Occidental Petroleum Corp	Production & Extraction	12/31/12	24253.0	4598.0	64210.0	40016.0	1250	691031800
OII	Oceaneering International, Inc.	Equipment & Services	12/31/12	2782.6	289.0	2768.1	1815.5	444	103173906
OZM	Och-Ziff Capital Management Grou	Wealth Management	12/31/12	1211.4	-315.8	3535.1	-250.5	131	78282062
OCN	Ocwen Financial Corp.	Credit & Lending	12/31/12		180.9	5671.9	1764.8	324	115454978
ODP	Office Depot, Inc.	Retail - Specialty	12/29/12	10695.7	-77.1	4010.8	1047.8	288	224871984
OMX	OfficeMax Inc (DE)	Retail - Specialty	12/29/12	6920.4	416.8	3784.3	1034.4	250	82664166
OGE	OGE Energy Corp.	Electric Utilities	12/31/12	3671.2	355.0	9922.2	2767.2	389	63937247
OIBR	Oi S. A.	Services	12/31/11	9245.3	1005.7	31664.0	10588.8	144	158227965
OIS	Oil States International, Inc.	Equipment & Services	12/31/12	4413.1	448.6	4440.0	2464.4	399	57377918
ODC	Oil-Dri Corp. of America	Household & Personal Products	7/31/12	240.7	6.1	174.3	85.3	62	3904098
OILT	Oiltanking Partners LP	Miscellaneous Transportation Servic	12/31/12	135.5	62.6	469.2		45	11576569
ONB	Old National Bancorp (Evansville, I	Banking	12/31/12	534.5	91.7	9543.6	1194.6	207	70294438
ORI	Old Republic International Corp.	General Insurance	12/31/12	4970.1	-68.6	16226.8	3596.2	342	219368089
OLN	Olin Corp.	Diversified Chemicals	12/31/12	2184.7	149.6	2777.7	998.4	286	71752238
OMG	OM Group, Inc.	Specialty Chemicals	12/31/12	1637.8	-38.9	2499.4	1206.7	203	31042820
OHI	Omega Healthcare Investors, Inc.	REITs	12/31/12	350.5	120.7	2982.0	1011.3	323	103426200
OME	Omega Protein Corp.	Food	12/31/12	235.6	4.1	295.3	205.6	111	14695845
OCR	Omnicare Inc.	Diagnostic & Health Related Service	12/31/12	6160.4	194.9	6989.3	3505.7	411	143634762
OMC	Omnicom Group, Inc.	Advertising	12/31/12	14219.4	998.3	22151.9	3460.8	728	284657776
OMN	Omnova Solutions, Inc.	Specialty Chemicals	11/30/12	1125.5	27.6	873.7	130.2	140	40659479
ASGN	On Assignment, Inc.	Business Services	12/31/12	1239.7	42.7	1098.0	532.7	200	48576862
OLP	One Liberty Properties, Inc.	REITs	12/31/12	44.8	32.3	481.2	237.1	104	5376829
OB	OneBeacon Insurance Group Ltd	General Insurance	12/31/12	1240.8	-19.2	5401.5	1014.5	105	19801667
OKE	Oneok Inc.	Gas Utilities	12/31/12	12632.6	360.6	15855.3	2129.6	569	146832541
OKS	ONEOK Partners LP	Equipment & Services	12/31/12	10182.2	888.0	10959.2		353	59401741
OPK	Opko Health Inc	Pharmaceuticals	12/31/12	47.0	-29.0	289.8	203.8	140	50540944
OPY	Oppenheimer Holdings Inc	Finance Intermediaries & Services	12/31/12	952.6	-3.6	2678.0	500.7	71	5923611
ORB	Orbital Sciences Corp.	Manufacturing	12/31/12	1436.8	61.0	1211.5	713.5	203	54703578
OWW	Orbitz Worldwide Inc	Hotels, Restaurants & Travel	12/31/12	778.8	-301.7	834.3	-142.7	99	95316631
OEH	Orient Express Hotels Ltd.	Hotels, Restaurants & Travel	12/31/12	546.9	-7.1	1892.0	936.0	162	83941136
OFG	Oriental Financial Group, Inc.	Banking	12/31/12	284.8	24.6	9193.4	863.6	153	45521846
ORN	Orion Marine Group Inc	Construction Services	12/31/12	292.0	-11.9	317.3	225.2	127	28163200
IX	Orix Corp. (Japan)	Credit & Lending	3/31/12	972884.0	86150.0	8354874.0	1396137.0	91	2835614
ORA	Ormat Technologies Inc	Electric Utilities	12/31/12	514.4	-206.4	2094.1	695.1	130	10215422
OSK	Oshkosh Corp	Construction Services	9/30/12	8180.9	230.8	4947.8	1853.5	349	79078833
OMI	Owens & Minor, Inc.	Pharmaceuticals	12/31/12	8908.1	109.0	2207.7	972.5	291	71303477
OC	Owens Corning	Construction Materials	12/31/12	5172.0	-19.0	7568.0	3538.0	287	128906156
OI	Owens-Illinois, Inc.	Containers & Packaging	12/31/12	7000.0	184.0	8598.0	881.0	417	159033529
OXM	Oxford Industries, Inc.	Apparel, Footwear & Accessories	2/2/13	855.5	31.3	556.1	229.8	184	15240875
OXF	Oxford Resource Partners LP	Mining	12/31/12	373.5	-26.8	220.9		27	1574808
TLK	P.T. Telekomunikasi Indonesia (Per	Services	12/31/12	77127.0	12864.0	110211.0	46700.0	174	52268834
PNG	PAA Natural Gas Storage L P	Equipment & Services	12/31/12	387.7	73.3	1869.1			
T 34D	Pacific Bell	Services	12/31/98	9406.0	1077.0	15093.0	3260.0	-	
ROYT	Pacific Coast Oil Trust	Production & Extraction	12/31/12	41.3	40.8	271.2	271.2	32	26875617
PACD	Pacific Drilling S.A.	Production & Extraction	12/31/12	638.0	34.0	4893.9	2315.2	76	40908811
PKG	Packaging Corp of America	Containers & Packaging	12/31/12	2843.9	163.8	2453.8	969.5	345	107642968
PLL	Pall Corp.	Industrial Machinery & Equipment	7/31/12	2671.7	319.3	3347.9	1510.0	528	112454308
PANW	Palo Alto Networks, Inc	IT Services	7/31/12	255.1	0.7	407.8	229.1	145	45523990
PAM	Pampa Energia SA	Electric Utilities	12/31/11	6774.5	-931.1	11449.3	2358.8		
PC	Panasonic Corp	Household Appliances, Electronics &	3/31/12	7846216.0	-772172.0	6601055.0	1929786.0	112	60459491
P	Pandora Media Inc	Radio & Television	1/31/13	427.1	-38.1	218.8	99.0	188	170419082
PHX	Panhandle Oil & Gas Inc	Production & Extraction	9/30/12	48.5	7.4	135.2	83.9	67	3487503
PAR	Par Technology Corp.	Electronic Instruments & Related Pro	12/31/12	245.2	-0.3	123.8	72.8	44	3556492
PRGN	Paragon Shipping Inc	Shipping	12/31/12	50.3	-17.6	420.0	215.5	47	720245
PKE	Park Electrochemical Corp.	Electrical Equipment	2/26/12	193.3	23.4	366.0	343.2	124	18931297
PKD	Parker Drilling Co.	Production & Extraction	12/31/12	678.0	37.3	1255.7	591.4	201	94245511
PH	Parker Hannifin Corp.	Industrial Machinery & Equipment	6/30/12	13145.9	1155.5	11170.3	4896.5	705	127762877
PKY	Parkway Properties Inc.	REITs	12/31/12	226.5	-39.4	1906.6	694.0	178	52887879
PRE	PartnerRe Ltd.	Life & Health	12/31/12	5562.6	1134.5	22980.4	6933.5	384	51824997
PBF	PBF Energy Inc	Refining & Marketing	12/31/12	20138.7	2.0	4253.7	419.8		
PCM	PCM Fund Inc	Holding and other Investment Office	12/31/12	15.3	12.2	230.8	130.5	35	2136923
BTU	Peabody Energy Corp	Mining	12/31/12	8077.5	-585.7	15809.0	4904.9	698	234773837
PSO	Pearson Plc	Publishing	12/31/12	5059.0	326.0	11348.0	5686.0	132	30708167
PEB	Pebblebrook Hotel Trust	REITs	12/31/12	380.7	26.1	1846.2	1313.0	174	63371327
PBA	Pembina Pipeline Corp	Equipment & Services	12/31/12	3458.9	224.8	8276.5	4270.3	193	76235807
PGH	Pengrowth Energy Corp	Production & Extraction	12/31/12	1233.4	12.7	7469.9	4190.3	237	141417942
PVA	Penn Virginia Corp.	Production & Extraction	12/31/12	317.1	-104.6	1843.0	895.1	199	58698378
PWE	Penn West Petroleum Ltd	Production & Extraction	12/31/11	2951.0	638.0	15584.0	9067.0	317	175445486
JCP	Penney (J.C.) Co.,Inc. (Holding Co.)	Retail - General Merchandise/Depart	2/2/13	12985.0	-985.0	9781.0	3171.0	531	278792652
PEI	Pennsylvania Real Estate Investme	REITs	12/31/12	427.2	-40.8	2877.6	674.6	208	43279811

T46

EARNINGS PER SHARE — QUARTERLY			EARNINGS PER SHARE — ANNUAL			P/E RATIO		DIVIDENDS PER SHARE			AV. YLD	DIV. DECLARED		PRICE RANGE 2012	
1st	2nd	3rd	2012	2011	2010			2012	2011	2010	%	AMOUNT	PAYABLE		
-	-	-	1.56	0.05	-	13.9 -	0.0	1.40	0.11	-	7.0	0.1320	5/1/13	21.7 -	0.0
-	-	-	0.51	0.50	0.50	30.7 -	0.0	1.04	1.04	1.04	7.4	0.2750	4/1/13	15.7 -	0.0
-	-	-	-	0.36	0.27			-	0.90	0.94		0.230	4/1/13	11.9 -	0.0
-	-	-	0.75	0.48	0.94	23.0 -	0.0	0.88	0.85	0.83	5.4	0.0192M	5/1/13	17.3 -	0.0
-	-	-	0.68	0.77	0.88	25.8 -	0.0	0.83	0.80	0.81	5.1	0.0233M	5/1/13	17.5 -	0.0
-	-	0.94	1.35	0.69	0.96	15.0 -	0.0	0.64	0.49	0.45	3.6	0.190Y	81/16/21	20.2 -	0.0
-	-	10.33	35.12	23.01	33.42	30.8 -	0.0	-	-	-				1080.1 -	0.0
-	-	0.44	1.39	2.36	2.21	27.8 -	0.0	1.20	1.20	1.20	4.3	0.30Y	81/16/21	38.6 -	0.0
-	-	0.84	3.83	-4.23	-2.18	13.8 -	0.0	1.89	2.34	2.17	4.5	1.050	3/1/13	53.0 -	0.0
-	-	0.20	1.66	0.86	-0.61	23.7 -	0.0	-	-	-				39.3 -	0.0
-	-	1.69	5.67	8.32	5.56	17.2 -	0.0	2.16	1.84	1.47	2.6	0.640Y	81/16/21	97.5 -	0.0
-	-	0.78	2.66	2.16	1.83	25.0 -	0.0	0.69	0.45	-	1.3	0.180Y	81/16/21	66.5 -	0.0
-	-	-0.89	-2.21	-4.07	-3.35			0.40	1.07	0.88	4.6	0.750	2/26/13	10.7 -	0.0
-	-	0.37	1.31	0.71	0.36	31.7 -	0.0	-	-	-				41.5 -	0.0
-	-	-0.25	-0.39	0.22	-0.01			-	-	-				5.0 -	0.0
-	-	4.92	4.74	0.38	0.79	2.7 -	0.0	0.04	-	-	0.5	0.020Y	81/16/21	13.0 -	0.0
-	-	1.87	3.58	3.45	2.99	19.5 -	0.0	1.57	1.50	1.45	2.8	0.41750Y	81/16/21	70.0 -	0.0
-	-	-	1.71	3.34				-	0.25	0.05				6.1 -	0.0
-	-	1.87	8.10	5.86	3.19	10.7 -	0.0	-	-	-				86.7 -	0.0
-	0.31	-	0.85	1.26	1.30	33.9 -	0.0	0.68	0.64	0.60	2.9	0.27HY	81/16/21	28.8 -	0.0
-	-	0.38	1.57	0.60		33.6 -	0.0	1.43	0.27	-	4.0	0.390	2/14/13	52.8 -	0.0
-	-	0.20	0.95	0.76	0.44	14.9 -	0.0	0.36	0.28	0.28	2.9	0.10Y	3/15/13	14.2 -	0.0
-	-	-0.06	-0.27	-0.55	0.13			0.71	0.70	0.69	7.0	0.180Y	81/16/21	12.7 -	0.0
-	-	0.35	1.85	2.99	0.81	13.6 -	0.0	0.80	0.80	0.80	3.7	0.20Y	81/16/21	25.2 -	0.0
-	-	0.17	-1.22	1.21	2.73			-	-	-		0.140	8/30/02	28.1 -	0.0
-	-	0.27	1.12	0.46	0.52	27.1 -	0.0	1.69	1.55	1.37	7.1	0.450Z	81/16/21	30.4 -	0.0
-	-	0.01	0.20	1.71	0.97	53.8 -	0.0	-	-	-				10.8 -	0.0
-	-	0.55	1.73	0.76	-0.91	23.5 -	0.0	0.42	0.15	0.11	1.2	0.140Y	81/16/21	40.7 -	0.0
-	-	0.74	3.61	3.33	2.70	16.6 -	0.0	1.20	1.00	0.80	2.4	0.40Y	81/16/21	60.0 -	0.0
-	-	-	0.60	-0.06	2.40	14.7 -	0.0	-	-	-		0.050	5/31/01	8.8 -	0.0
-	-	-0.33	0.89	0.64	-0.27	28.8 -	0.0	-	-	-				25.7 -	0.0
-	-	1.23	2.16	0.96	0.81	10.5 -	0.0	1.34	1.32	1.23	6.8	0.350Z	4/3/13	22.7 -	0.0
-	-	-0.65	-0.21	0.58	1.25			0.84	1.84	3.34	6.3	0.210	3/29/13	15.4 -	0.0
-	-	0.31	1.71	1.68	1.55	28.9 -	0.0	1.27	1.08	0.91	2.9	0.360Y	81/16/21	49.4 -	0.0
-	-	0.78	3.04	3.35	1.75	20.0 -	0.0	2.59	2.33	2.23	4.6	0.710	2/14/13	61.0 -	0.0
-	-	-0.03	-0.11	-0.01	-0.08			-	-	-				7.8 -	0.0
-	-	0.16	-0.27	0.74	2.76			0.44	0.44	0.44	2.7	0.110	2/22/13	20.9 -	0.0
-	-	0.33	1.02	1.13	0.81	16.5 -	0.0	-	-	-				16.9 -	0.0
-	-	0.14	-2.86	-0.36	-0.58			-	-	-				5.9 -	0.0
-	-	0.17	-0.07	-0.86	-0.68			-	-	-		0.0250	11/4/08	12.5 -	0.0
-	-	0.35	0.35	0.67	-0.50	45.4 -	0.0	0.24	0.21	0.17	2.0	0.14580	7/1/13	15.9 -	0.0
-	-	-0.06	-0.44	-0.49	0.81			-	-	-				10.3 -	0.0
-	-195.67	-	670.34	527.75	315.91	0.1 -	0.0	0.01	0.00	0.00	0.0			64.5 -	0.0
-	-	-0.01	-4.54	-0.95	0.82			0.08	0.13	0.27	0.4	0.040Y	81/16/21	22.0 -	0.0
0.51	-	-	2.51	2.99	8.69	16.9 -	0.0	-	-	-		0.10Y	81/16/21	42.5 -	0.0
-	-	0.39	1.72	1.81	1.75	18.9 -	0.0	0.88	0.80	0.71	3.0	0.240Y	81/16/21	32.6 -	0.0
-	-	0.37	-0.16	2.23	7.37			-	-	-				43.4 -	0.0
-	-	0.54	1.11	-3.11	-0.28	24.9 -	0.0	-	-	-		0.59380 Y	2/15/08	27.7 -	0.0
-	-	0.18	1.78	4.75	0.90	33.1 -	0.0	0.52	0.44	0.36	1.1	0.180Y	5/3/13	58.8 -	0.0
-	-	-0.16	-1.27	-0.62	-0.45			1.51	1.75	0.35	22.3	0.20	11/14/12	11.3 -	0.0
-	-	-	669.92	553.70	580.95	0.1 -	0.0	0.00	0.00	0.00	0.0			45.1	0.0
-	-	0.24	0.99	0.85	0.54	21.9 -	0.0	1.43	1.00	0.55	7.5	0.35750	5/15/13	21.7 -	0.0
-	-	0.45	1.06	-	-	18.9 -	0.0	1.20	-	-	6.6	0.13660Z	4/15/13	20.0 -	0.0
-	-	-0.01	0.16	-0.01	0.25	66.5 -	0.0	-	-	-				10.6 -	0.0
-	-	0.41	1.68	1.57	2.00	26.7 -	0.0	1.00	0.80	0.60	3.0	0.31250Y	81/16/21	44.9 -	0.0
-	0.67	-	2.71	2.67	2.03	25.5 -	0.0	0.77	0.67	0.61	1.3	0.250Y	81/16/21	69.0 -	0.0
-	-0.04	-	0.00	-0.88	-1.78			-	-	-				71.8 -	0.0
-	-	-	-	-	-			-	-	-				8.6 -	0.0
-	-301.93	-	-333.96	35.75	-49.97			0.00	0.00	0.00	0.0			9.3 -	0.0
-	-	0.01	-0.19	-1.03	-3.84			-	-	-				14.3 -	0.0
0.26	-	-	0.88	1.01	1.36	37.5 -	0.0	0.28	0.28	0.28	1.0	0.070Y	3/8/13	33.0 -	0.0
-	-	0.09	-0.02	-1.04	0.21			-	-	-				5.5 -	0.0
-	-	-3.08	-2.84	-47.60	4.40			-	0.50	2.00		0.50Y	3/24/11	8.2 -	0.0
-	-	0.23	1.13	1.58	1.23	27.5 -	0.0	0.40	1.40	0.36	1.6	0.10Y	5/3/13	31.1 -	0.0
-	-	0.09	0.31	-0.43	-0.13	19.9 -	0.0	-	-	-		0.01	2/17/87	6.2 -	0.0
-	1.19	-	7.45	6.37	3.40	13.1 -	0.0	1.54	1.25	1.01	1.8	0.430Y	81/16/21	98.0 -	0.0
-	-	-0.02	-1.62	-6.37	-0.42			0.38	0.30	0.30	2.9	0.50Z	4/15/13	18.6 -	0.0
-	-	7.53	16.87	-8.40	10.46	5.6 -	0.0	2.48	-	2.05	3.2	0.45310	3/1/13	93.8 -	0.0
-	-	-	0.08	-		524.8 -	328.1	-	-	-		0.3GY	3/15/13	42.0 -	26.3
-	-	-	1.06	1.13	1.12	12.4 -	0.0	1.12	1.06	1.25	9.5	0.080	5/1/13	13.2 -	0.0
-	-	0.16	-2.19	3.52	2.85			0.34	0.34	0.29	1.4	0.0850Y	81/16/21	31.6 -	0.0
-	-	-	0.41	1.19	1.62	49.6 -	0.0	1.10	1.05	0.83	5.8			20.4 -	0.0
-	-	0.13	0.14	0.08	-0.23	184.3 -	0.0	0.48	0.48	0.12	2.1	0.1219GHZ	4/15/13	25.8 -	0.0
-	-	0.11	0.87	0.99	1.07	36.9 -	0.0	1.61	1.56	0.39	5.7	0.1350	5/15/13	32.1 -	0.0
-	-	-0.05	0.03	0.25	0.49	316.7 -	0.0	0.66	0.84	-	10.6	0.040Y	5/15/13	9.5 -	0.0
-	-	-0.71	-2.22	-2.90	-0.19			0.11	0.23	0.23	2.1	1.50Y	4/15/13	7.5 -	0.0
-	-	-0.14	-	1.36	0.50			-	1.08	-		0.270	4/15/13	19.7 -	0.0
-	-	-0.56	-0.70	1.63	1.08			0.80	0.80	0.80	3.4	0.20Y	81/16/21	36.7 -	0.0
-	-	-0.27	-0.89	-1.66	-1.04			0.63	0.60	0.60	3.9	0.46090Z	3/15/13	19.7 -	0.0

SYMBOL	COMPANY	NATURE OF BUSINESS	FISCAL YEAR-END	TOTAL REV. $MILL	NET INCOME $MILL	TOTAL ASSETS $MILL	NET STK EQUITY $MILL	NO OF INST	INST. HOLDINGS (SHARES)
PMT	Pennymac Mortgage Investment Tr	REITs	12/31/12	335.2	138.2	2559.7	1201.3		
PAG	Penske Automotive Group Inc	Retail - Automotive	12/31/12	13163.5	185.5	5379.0	1304.2	198	100611868
PNR	Pentair Ltd	Industrial Machinery & Equipment	12/31/12	4416.1	-107.2	11795.3	6366.9	543	172055528
PNR	Pentair Ltd	Industrial Machinery & Equipment	12/31/12	4416.1	-107.2	11795.3	6366.9	543	172055528
PBY	Pep Boys-Manny, Moe & Jack	Retail - Automotive	1/28/12	2063.6	28.9	1633.8	504.3	221	61331269
POM	Pepco Holdings Inc.	Electric Utilities	12/31/12	5081.0	285.0	15776.0	4446.0	474	151566086
PEP	PepsiCo Inc.	Beverages	12/29/12	65492.0	6178.0	74638.0	22294.0	1964	1187206580
PKI	PerkinElmer, Inc.	Biotechnology	12/30/12	2115.2	69.9	3901.8	1939.8	399	122765386
PBT	Permian Basin Royalty Trust	Oil Royalty Traders	12/31/12	55.1	54.0	3.4	0.8	115	7331049
PZE	Petrobras Argentina SA	Production & Extraction	12/31/11	14278.0	704.0	22170.0	10371.0		
PTR	PetroChina Co Ltd	Production & Extraction	12/31/11	2003843.0	132961.0	1917586.0	1002745.0	244	8317961
PBR	Petroleo Brasileiro S.A.	Production & Extraction	12/31/11	145915.0	20121.0	319410.0	175838.0	571	558809788
PEO	Petroleum & Resources Corp.	Holding and other Investment Office	12/31/12	17.2	12.4	740.2	733.0	65	5547397
PDH	PetroLogistics LP	Specialty Chemicals	12/31/12	750.7	-56.7	798.1		49	37886583
PQ	PetroQuest Energy Inc	Production & Extraction	12/31/12	141.6	-132.1	433.4	87.6	171	48944344
PFE	Pfizer Inc	Pharmaceuticals	12/31/12	58986.0	14570.0	185798.0	81260.0	2083	5737206417
PCG	PG&E Corp. (Holding Co.)	Electric Utilities	12/31/12	15040.0	830.0	52449.0	13074.0	594	339783785
GLT	PH Glatfelter Co	Paper & Forest Products	12/31/12	1584.8	59.4	1243.0	539.7	205	43842779
PMC	PharMerica Corp	Pharmaceuticals	12/31/12	1832.6	22.9	885.7	442.6	192	31057657
PHH	PHH Corp	Credit & Lending	12/31/12	2743.0	34.0	9603.0	1526.0	272	82516364
PM	Philip Morris International Inc	Tobacco Products	12/31/12	77393.0	8800.0	37670.0	-3476.0	1558	1199731401
PHI	Philippine Long Distance Telephone	Services	12/31/12	163484.0	35454.0	410468.0	149060.0	148	29826355
PSX	Phillips 66	Refining & Marketing	12/31/12	182922.0	4124.0	48073.0	20775.0	1007	431909694
PSX	Phillips 66	Refining & Marketing	12/31/12	182922.0	4124.0	48073.0	20775.0	1007	431909694
PGC PR	Phillips Gas Co.	Production & Extraction	12/31/96	1723.6	128.2	1293.1	619.1		
PNX	Phoenix Companies, Inc. (The)	Life & Health	12/31/11	1849.7	8.1	21439.9	1126.2	115	21844514
FENG	Phoenix New Media Ltd	Radio & Television	12/31/11	950.6	102.5	1564.5	1306.8	25	9337890
PNY	Piedmont Natural Gas Co., Inc.	Gas Utilities	10/31/12	1122.8	119.8	3769.9	1027.0	277	40360508
PDM	Piedmont Office Realty Trust Inc	REITs	12/31/12	536.4	93.2	4254.9	2638.9	208	103074429
PIR	Pier 1 Imports Inc.	Retail - Furniture & Home Furnishing	2/25/12	1533.6	168.9	823.4	493.6	263	93851511
PIKE	Pike Electric Corp	Construction Services	6/30/12	685.2	10.9	538.1	276.9	122	19772344
PCQ	Pimco California Municipal Income	Holding and other Investment Office	4/30/12	23.2	20.0	441.6	403.9	27	877706
PCK	Pimco California Municipal Income	Holding and other Investment Office	5/31/12	26.0	22.4	479.5	435.6	27	719623
PZC	Pimco California Municipal Income	Holding and other Investment Office	9/30/12	20.7	17.8	385.1	349.6	26	930391
PTY	PIMCO Corporate & Income Opport	Holding and other Investment Office	11/30/12	125.6	114.3	1567.8	1530.1	98	6107537
PCN	PIMCO Corporate & Income Strateg	Holding and other Investment Office	10/31/11	71.8	64.5	818.1	684.0		
PCI	PIMCO Dynamic Credit Income Fun	Holding and other Investment Office	12/7/12			0.1			
PDI	PIMCO Dynamic Income Fund	Holding and other Investment Office	4/16/12			0.1		46	3952468
PGP	PIMCO Global StocksPLUS & Inco	Holding and other Investment Office	3/31/12	19.9	16.4	257.3	129.0	35	406033
PHK	Pimco High Income Fund	Holding and other Investment Office	3/31/12	128.1	116.6	1370.5	1252.5	94	8623084
PKO	PIMCO Income Opportunity Fund	Holding and other Investment Office	10/31/12	46.9	38.4	693.1	412.0	46	2478228
PFL	PIMCO Income Strategy Fund	Holding and other Investment Office	7/31/12	33.5	28.6	443.7	362.3	56	3453762
PFN	PIMCO Income Strategy Fund II	Holding and other Investment Office	7/31/12	68.2	60.0	841.1	758.7	74	9521994
PMF	Pimco Municipal Income Fund	Holding and other Investment Office	4/30/12	29.2	25.3	534.8	516.7	37	796264
PML	Pimco Municipal Income Fund II	Holding and other Investment Office	5/31/12	61.3	53.4	1143.6	1089.2	64	4572331
PMX	Pimco Municipal Income Fund III	Holding and other Investment Office	9/30/12	31.1	26.9	581.2	546.1	36	1315361
PNI	Pimco New York Municipal Fund II	Holding and other Investment Office	5/31/12	10.8	9.1	217.7	202.7	19	190381
PNF	Pimco New York Municipal Income	Holding and other Investment Office	4/30/12	6.8	5.7	145.2	134.1	21	506762
PYN	Pimco New York Municipal Income	Holding and other Investment Office	9/30/12	5.2	4.4	95.7	86.3	8	53146
RCS	PIMCO Strategic Governme	Holding and other Investment Office	1/31/12	59.7	54.1	2037.1	357.7	55	2105406
PNK	Pinnacle Entertainment Inc	Hotels, Restaurants & Travel	12/31/12	1197.1	-31.8	2109.0	447.1	182	58387738
PF	Pinnacle Foods Inc.	Food	12/30/12	2478.5	52.5	4400.0	888.7		
PNW	Pinnacle West Capital Corp.	Electric Utilities	12/31/12	3301.8	381.5	13379.6	3972.8	453	86892810
PES	Pioneer Energy Services Corp	Production & Extraction	12/31/12	919.4	30.0	1339.8	547.7	182	54858392
PHD	Pioneer Floating Rate Trust	Holding and other Investment Office	11/30/12	34.2	29.3	519.6	505.2	41	6134307
PHT	Pioneer High Income Trust	Holding and other Investment Office	3/31/12	51.7	47.7	536.7	530.5	45	2225802
MAV	Pioneer Municipal High Income Adv	Holding and other Investment Office	3/31/12	29.0	25.1	458.1	449.6	37	1195416
MHI	Pioneer Municipal High Income Tru	Holding and other Investment Office	4/30/12	26.3	23.0	419.1	418.6	47	936684
PXD	Pioneer Natural Resources Co	Production & Extraction	12/31/12	3228.3	192.3	13069.0	5689.4	590	137225787
PSE	Pioneer Southwest Energy Partners	Production & Extraction	12/31/12	208.3	107.6	430.9		8	8798534
PJC	Piper Jaffray Companies	Finance Intermediaries & Services	12/31/12	489.0	41.3	2087.7	733.3	185	13858242
PBI	Pitney Bowes Inc	Office Equipment & Furniture	12/31/12	4904.0	445.2	7859.9	110.6	582	211349258
PBI 08	Pitney-Bowes Credit Corp	Credit & Lending	12/31/01	587.8	160.1	5721.0	1476.4		
PAA	Plains All American Pipeline, L.P.	Equipment & Services	12/31/12	37797.0	1094.0	19235.0		508	180943188
PXP	Plains Exploration & Production Co.	Production & Extraction	12/31/12	2565.3	306.4	17298.3	3516.5	480	121760198
PLT	Plantronics, Inc.	Manufacturing	3/31/12	713.4	109.0	672.5	527.2	232	49661392
PTP	Platinum Underwriters Holdings, Ltd	General Insurance	12/31/12	751.9	327.2	4333.3	1894.5	201	40850128
PCL	Plum Creek Timber Co., Inc.	REITs	12/31/12	1339.0	203.0	4384.0	1223.0	724	123454966
PNC	PNC Financial Services Group (The	Banking	12/31/12	16606.0	3001.0	305107.0	39003.0	1027	455186108
PNM	PNM Resources Inc	Electric Utilities	12/31/12	1342.4	120.1	5372.6	1619.7	256	80606488
PII	Polaris Industries Inc.	Autos- Manufacturing	12/31/12	3209.8	312.3	1486.5	690.5	453	53327280
POL	PolyOne Corp.	Specialty Chemicals	12/31/12	2992.6	71.8	2128.0	629.1	221	89753293
PPO	Polypore International Inc	Electrical Equipment	12/29/12	717.4	71.0	1586.1	579.1	224	62042764
POR	Portland General Electric Co.	Electric Utilities	12/31/12	1805.0	141.0	5670.0	1728.0	313	83297420
PT	Portugal Telecom, SGPS, S.A.	Services	12/31/11	6146.8	339.1	22943.8	2828.1	98	12873254
PKX	POSCO (South Korea)	Non-Precious Metals	12/31/1	88938725.1	3648136.0	78408837.8	38356349.8	212	28646533
POST	Post Holdings Inc	Food	9/30/12	958.9	49.9	2732.3	1231.5	211	28329654
PPS	Post Properties, Inc.	REITs	12/31/12	334.9	83.9	2363.4	1126.9	262	57982590
POT	Potash Corp. of Saskatchewan Inc.	Agricultural Chemicals	12/31/12	7927.0	2079.0	18206.0	9912.0	707	534625006
PPG	PPG Industries, Inc.	Construction Materials	12/31/12	15200.0	941.0	15878.0	4063.0	830	131376199

T48

| EARNINGS PER SHARE | | | | | | P/E RATIO | DIVIDENDS PER SHARE | | | AV. YLD % | DIV. DECLARED | | PRICE RANGE 2012 |
| QUARTERLY | | | ANNUAL | | | | | | | | AMOUNT | PAYABLE | |
1st	2nd	3rd	2012	2011	2010		2012	2011	2010	%			
-	-	0.81	3.14	2.41	1.44	9.1 - 0.0	2.22	1.84	0.77	9.8	0.570Z	3/1/13	28.7 - 0.0
-	-	0.45	2.05	1.94	1.18	16.5 - 0.0	0.46	0.24	-	1.7	0.140Y	81/16/21	33.7 - 0.0
-	-	0.30	-0.84	0.34	1.99		0.88	0.72	0.76	2.0	0.230	5/10/13	44.3 - 41.9
-	-	0.30	-0.84	0.34	1.99		0.88	0.72	0.76	2.0	0.230	5/10/13	53.5 - 0.0
-	-	-0.13	0.54	0.69	0.44	27.7 - 0.0	0.12	0.12	0.12	1.1	0.030Y	1/23/12	14.9 - 0.0
-	-	0.49	1.25	1.14	0.14	17.1 - 0.0	1.08	1.08	1.08	5.6	0.270Y	81/16/21	21.4 - 0.0
-	-	1.21	3.92	4.03	3.91	20.2 - 0.0	2.13	2.02	1.89	3.0	0.53750Y	81/16/21	79.1 - 0.0
-	-	0.26	0.61	0.07	3.25	58.8 - 0.0	0.28	0.28	0.28	1.0	0.070Y	81/16/21	35.9 - 0.0
-	-	0.19	1.16	1.36	1.38	19.8 - 0.0	1.16	1.36	1.38	7.3	0.0580	4/12/13	23.0 - 0.0
													6.5 - 0.0
-	-	0.14	-	0.73	0.76		-	0.74	0.56		-		151.0 - 0.0
-	-	-		1.54	1.94		-	0.93	0.99				26.6 - 0.0
-	-	0.48	0.41	0.35		55.8 - 0.0	1.60	1.97	1.27	6.4	0.10	6/3/13	26.8 - 0.0
-	-	0.00	0.39	-		43.6 - 0.0	0.47	-	-	3.5	0.280	2/26/13	17.0 - 0.0
-	-	-0.62	-2.20	0.08	0.66						0.85940Y	7/16/12	7.0 - 0.0
-	-	0.43	1.94	1.27	1.02	14.9 - 0.0	0.88	0.80	0.72	3.6	0.240Y	81/16/21	28.9 - 0.0
-	-	0.84	1.92	2.10	2.82	24.2 - 0.0	1.82	1.82	1.82	4.2	0.4550Y	81/16/21	46.5 - 0.0
-	-	0.46	1.36	0.93	1.17	17.2 - 0.0	0.36	0.36	0.36	2.1	0.10Y	5/1/13	23.4 - 0.0
-	-	0.20	0.77	0.79	0.64	19.8 - 0.0							15.3 - 0.0
-	-	-0.74	0.56	-2.26	0.86	42.2 - 0.0							23.6 - 0.0
-	-	1.32	5.17	4.85	3.92	18.1 - 0.0	3.24	2.82	2.44	3.7	0.850Y	81/16/21	93.7 - 0.0
-	-	42.58	163.86	163.10	212.85	0.4 - 0.0	0.09	0.12	0.11	0.1	0.8	10/14/94	73.4 - 0.0
-	-	2.51	6.48	-	-	5.7 - 5.2	0.45	-	-	1.3	0.31250Y	81/16/21	37.0 - 34.0
-	-	2.51	6.48	-	-	10.8 - 0.0	0.45	-	-	1.0	0.31250Y	81/16/21	70.0 - 0.0
											0.58250	11/15/97	
-	-2.20	-	-	1.40	-2.20						0.46560Z	7/15/13	49.2 - 0.0
-	-	-		-1.30	-0.51								7.8 - 0.0
1.18	-	-	1.66	1.57	1.96	20.2 - 0.0	1.19	1.15	1.11	3.8	0.310Y	81/16/21	33.6 - 0.0
-	-	0.06	0.55	1.30	0.70	36.3 - 0.0	0.80	1.26	1.26	4.5	0.20Z	81/16/21	20.0 - 0.0
-	-	0.22	1.48	0.85	0.86	15.8 - 0.0					0.050Y	81/16/21	23.4 - 0.0
-	0.67	-	0.31	0.04	-0.41	48.6 - 0.0					1.G7	12/21/12	15.1 - 0.0
-	-	-	1.08	1.12	1.21	15.5 - 0.0	0.92	0.92	0.92	5.9	0.077M	5/1/13	16.7 - 0.0
-	-	-	0.71	0.91	0.76	15.7 - 0.0	0.75	0.75	0.77	7.1	0.0625M	5/1/13	11.1 - 0.0
-	-	-	0.81	0.77	0.76	14.6 - 0.0	0.72	0.72	0.72	6.4	0.06M	5/1/13	11.8 - 0.0
-	-	-	1.68	1.88	1.80	13.1 - 0.0	2.17	2.07	1.96	11.0	0.130	5/1/13	22.1 - 0.0
-	-	-	1.72	1.61			-	1.68	1.87		0.11250	5/1/13	19.1 - 0.0
											0.15630	5/1/13	25.9 - 24.6
											0.1770	5/1/13	31.1 - 0.0
-	-	-	1.61	1.75	1.24	13.9 - 0.0	2.20	2.20	2.20	10.7	0.18340	5/1/13	22.4 - 0.0
-	-	-	0.96	1.13	1.13	14.9 - 0.0	1.46	1.46	1.46	11.5	0.12190	5/1/13	14.3 - 0.0
-	-	-	2.61	3.24	3.11	12.1 - 0.0	3.06	3.38	2.12	10.7	0.190	5/1/13	31.6 - 0.0
-	-	-	1.16	1.24	1.38	11.7 - 0.0	1.11	1.21	2.06	8.9	0.090	5/1/13	13.6 - 0.0
-	-	-	1.16	1.03	1.38	10.1 - 0.0	0.82	0.97	1.64	7.5	0.080	5/1/13	11.7 - 0.0
-	-	-	1.01	1.07	1.18	16.6 - 0.0	0.97	0.97	0.97	6.1	0.0813M	5/1/13	16.7 - 0.0
-	-	-	0.88	0.91	0.88	15.7 - 0.0	0.78	0.78	0.78	6.0	0.065M	5/1/13	13.8 - 0.0
-	-	-	0.83	0.87	0.86	16.2 - 0.0	0.84	0.84	0.84	6.7	0.07M	5/1/13	13.4 - 0.0
-	-	-	0.85	0.88	0.98	16.2 - 0.0	0.80	0.80	0.80	6.2	0.0663M	5/1/13	13.8 - 0.0
-	-	-	0.74	0.80	0.88	18.0 - 0.0	0.68	0.68	0.68	5.5	0.057M	5/1/13	13.3 - 0.0
-	-	-	0.77	0.69	0.66	14.3 - 0.0	0.63	0.63	0.63	6.1	0.0525M	5/1/13	11.0 - 0.0
-	-	-	1.36	1.27	1.13	9.2 - 0.0	1.39	1.42	1.34	12.0	0.080	5/1/13	12.6 - 0.0
-	-0.01	-0.52	-0.04	-0.38							0.048G	3/31/92	16.7 - 0.0
-	-	-	0.61	-0.58	0.30	36.4 - 36.4							22.2 - 22.2
-	-	2.21	3.45	3.09	3.27	16.0 - 0.0	2.12	2.10	2.10	4.1	0.5450Y	81/16/21	57.9 - 0.0
-	-	0.04	0.48	0.19	-0.62	20.6 - 0.0							9.9 - 0.0
-	-	-	1.19	1.28	1.17	12.0 - 0.0	1.01	0.94	0.88	7.6	0.0750	4/30/13	14.3 - 0.0
-	-	-	1.70	1.68	1.65	11.1 - 0.0	1.65	1.65	1.65	9.6	0.13750	4/30/13	18.8 - 0.0
-	-	-	1.08	1.18	1.18	15.1 - 0.0	1.31	1.06	0.96	8.4	0.095M	4/30/13	16.3 - 0.0
-	-	-	1.03	1.12	1.17	16.3 - 0.0	1.10	1.06	0.97	7.0	0.095M	4/30/13	16.8 - 0.0
-	-	0.15	1.50	6.88	5.08	88.3 - 0.0	0.08	0.08	0.08	0.1	0.040Y	81/16/21	132.4 - 0.0
-	-	0.15	3.00	3.68	3.19	9.5 - 0.0	2.07	2.03	2.00	8.2	0.520	2/11/13	28.5 - 0.0
													42.0 - 0.0
-	-	1.11	2.26	-6.51	1.23	18.6 - 0.0							17.8 - 0.0
-	-	0.38	2.21	3.05	1.41	8.0 - 0.0	1.50	1.48	1.46	11.0	0.3750Y	81/16/21	56.5 - 0.0
-	-	0.27	2.40	2.44	1.20	23.5 - 0.0	2.11	1.95	1.88	4.7	0.5750	81/16/21	48.3 - 0.0
-	-	-0.41	2.32	1.44	0.73	20.8 - 0.0							45.6 - 0.0
-	-	0.66	2.41	2.21	1.16	18.9 - 0.0	0.20	0.20	0.20	0.6	0.10Y	81/16/21	55.9 - 0.0
-	-	2.54	9.60	-6.04	4.78	5.8 - 0.0	0.32	0.32	0.32	0.7	0.080	3/29/13	52.2 - 0.0
-	-	0.36	1.25	1.19	1.31	41.8 - 0.0	1.68	1.68	1.68	3.9	0.420	81/16/21	67.3 - 0.0
-	-	1.64	5.30	5.64	5.74	12.7 - 0.0					0.33590Y	81/16/21	23.3 - 0.0
-	-	0.72	1.31	1.96	-0.49	17.8 - 0.0	0.56	0.50	0.50	2.7	0.1650Y	81/16/21	93.2 - 0.0
-	-	1.33	4.40	3.20	2.14	21.2 - 0.0	1.48	0.90	0.80	1.8	0.420Y	81/16/21	25.3 - 0.0
-	-	0.27	0.80	1.83	1.69	31.6 - 0.0	0.20	0.16		1.1	0.060Y	4/5/13	47.5 - 0.0
-	-	0.30	1.50	2.23	1.39	31.7 - 0.0							30.3 - 0.0
-	-	0.50	1.87	1.95	1.66	16.2 - 0.0	1.08	1.05	1.03	4.0	0.270Y	4/15/13	5.9 - 0.0
-	-	0.07	-	0.39	6.06			3.06	2.06				86.7 - 0.0
-	-9461.00	47224.06	3927.00					0.00	0.00				42.9 - 0.0
0.23	-	-	1.45	-	-	29.6 - 0.0							52.3 - 0.0
-	-	0.39	1.48	0.38	-0.30	35.4 - 0.0	0.97	0.84	0.80	2.0	1.06250Z	4/1/13	46.8 - 0.0
-	-	-		0.56	0.24	0.13				1.4	0.280	5/2/13	140.7 - 138.0
-	-	2.18	6.06	6.87	4.63	23.2 - 22.8	2.34	2.26	2.18	1.7	0.590Y	81/16/21	

SYMBOL	COMPANY	NATURE OF BUSINESS	FISCAL YEAR-END	TOTAL REV. $MILL	NET INCOME $MILL	TOTAL ASSETS $MILL	NET STK EQUITY $MILL	NO OF INST	INST. HOLDINGS (SHARES)
PPG	PPG Industries, Inc.	Construction Materials	12/31/12	15200.0	941.0	15878.0	4063.0	830	131376199
PPL	PPL Corp	Electric Utilities	12/31/12	12286.0	1526.0	43634.0	10480.0	751	420569038
PLS	PPL Energy Supply, LLC	Electric Utilities	12/31/12	5500.0	474.0	12375.0	3830.0	-	
PX	Praxair, Inc.	Specialty Chemicals	12/31/12	11224.0	1692.0	18090.0	6064.0	1047	284265343
PCP	Precision Castparts Corp.	Non-Precious Metals	4/1/12	7214.6	1224.1	10558.8	8360.7	714	154076722
PDS	Precision Drilling Corp.	Production & Extraction	12/31/11	1951.0	193.5	4427.9	2132.6	219	177121322
PGI	Premiere Global Services Inc	Business Services	12/31/12	505.3	27.6	545.8	252.2	151	48711771
PBH	Prestige Brands Holdings Inc	Household & Personal Products	3/31/12	441.1	37.2	1758.3	402.7	206	53791546
PVG	Pretium Resources Inc	Precious Metals			-15.2	647.5	621.3	-	
PRI	Primerica Inc.	Life & Health	12/31/12	1190.7	173.8	10337.9	1275.4	141	51180294
PPP	Primero Mining Corp	Precious Metals	12/31/11	156.5	67.8	624.7	503.3	-	
PTGI	Primus Telecommunications Group,	Services	12/31/12	260.6	27.9	301.2	68.5	2	39552
PFG	Principal Financial Group, Inc.	Life & Health	12/31/12	9215.1	805.9	161926.5	9813.6	425	203272958
PRA	ProAssurance Corp.	General Insurance	12/31/12	715.9	275.5	4876.6	2270.6	300	48784925
PG	Procter & Gamble Co.	Household & Personal Products	6/30/12	83680.0	10756.0	132244.0	63439.0	2125	1808405879
PGR	Progressive Corp. (OH)	General Insurance	12/31/12	17083.9	902.3	22694.7	6007.0	509	518623259
BIN	Progressive Waste Solutions Ltd.	Sanitation Services	12/31/12	1840.1	-196.1	3077.6	1293.1	126	82634740
PLD	Prologis Inc	REITs	12/31/12	2006.0	-39.7	27310.1	13069.0	59	10123665
PRIS	Promotora de Informaciones S.A.	Radio & Television	12/31/12	2664.7	-255.0	7662.0	2185.7	35	4178853
PRO	Pros Holdings Inc	Internet & Software	12/31/12	117.8	5.0	146.5	88.7	122	25921613
PB	Prosperity Bancshares Inc.	Banking	12/31/12	495.4	167.9	14583.6	2089.4	252	46350512
PL	Protective Life Corp.	Life & Health	12/31/12	3623.0	302.5	57384.7	4615.2	333	85988131
PLFA 08	Protective Life Insurance Co	General Insurance	12/31/12	3456.1	308.5	57157.6	5687.2	-	
PRLB	Proto Labs Inc	Manufacturing	12/31/12	126.0	24.0	172.7	156.7	105	14055770
PFS	Provident Financial Services Inc	Credit & Lending	12/31/12	305.9	67.3	7283.7	981.2	151	38867924
PBNY	Provident New York Bancorp	Credit & Lending	9/30/12	147.2	19.9	4023.0	491.1	101	26233324
PRU	Prudential Financial, Inc.	Life & Health	12/31/12	84815.0	469.0	709298.0	38575.0	792	312399468
GHY	Prudential Global Short Duration Hi	Finance Intermediaries & Services	10/1/12	-	-	0.8	0.1	-	
PUK	Prudential Plc	Life & Health	12/31/11	36506.0	1490.0	273580.0	9117.0	145	20375722
ISD	Prudential Short Duration High Yield	Holding and other Investment Office	5/31/12	2.7	2.1	756.8	571.9	21	1123568
PSB PRV	PS Business Parks, Inc	REITs	12/31/12	347.2	89.1	2151.8	1445.7	219	19612711
PEG 31	PSEG Power LLC	Electric Utilities	12/31/12	4865.0	647.0	11032.0	5439.0	-	
IIT	PT Indosat Tbk	Services	12/31/1	20389326.0	1009080.0	53760438.0	19003466.0	25	3486002
PEG	Public Service Enterprise Group Inc	Electric Utilities	12/31/12	9781.0	1275.0	31725.0	10780.0	677	328372952
PSA	Public Storage	REITs	12/31/12	1826.7	939.3	8793.4	8093.8	602	141543527
PULS	Pulse Electronics Corp	Electrical Equipment	12/28/12	373.2	-32.0	188.6	-55.6	109	56784577
PHM	PulteGroup, Inc.	Builders	12/31/12	4820.0	206.1	6734.4	2189.6	519	325195505
PBYI	Puma Biotechnology, Inc.	Biotechnology	12/31/12	-	-74.4	151.7	128.9	-	
PCF	Putnam High Income Securities Fun	Holding and other Investment Office	8/31/12	9.6	8.3	142.3	141.0	41	4480136
PMM	Putnam Managed Municipal Income	Holding and other Investment Office	10/31/12	31.7	27.7	604.1	590.2	53	2751857
PIM	Putnam Master Intermediate Incom	Holding and other Investment Office	9/30/12	20.9	17.5	513.2	356.3	75	11363115
PMO	Putnam Municipal Opportunities Tru	Holding and other Investment Office	4/30/12	39.6	34.4	780.5	735.0	58	4490078
PPT	Putnam Premier Income Trust	Holding and other Investment Office	7/31/12	46.1	39.0	1114.0	818.1	110	24007772
PVH	PVH Corp	Apparel, Footwear & Accessories	2/3/13	6043.0	433.8	7781.5	3252.6	447	76462942
PVR	PVR Partners LP	Equipment & Services	12/31/12	1007.8	-70.6	2998.7	-	204	51171244
PZN	Pzena Investment Management Inc	Wealth Management	12/31/12	76.3	3.8	64.7	14.6	59	7112945
QEP	QEP Resources Inc	Production & Extraction	12/31/12	2349.8	128.3	9108.5	3266.0	439	150884973
QIHU	Qihoo 360 Technology Co, Ltd.	Internet & Software	12/31/11	167.9	15.6	424.0	370.9	132	44946251
QRE	QR Energy LP	Production & Extraction	12/31/12	372.0	79.8	1686.5	-	68	7650461
QUAD	Quad/Graphics, Inc.	Printing	12/31/12	4094.0	87.4	4098.9	1235.4	110	26433112
KWR	Quaker Chemical Corp.	Specialty Chemicals	12/31/12	708.2	47.4	536.6	281.1	161	11401843
NX	Quanex Building Products Corp	Metal Products	10/31/12	829.0	-16.5	589.5	421.8	118	37634684
PWR	Quanta Services, Inc.	Construction Services	12/31/12	5920.3	306.6	5140.8	3766.5	497	205865793
QTM	Quantum Corp.	Computer Hardware & Equipment	3/31/12	652.4	-8.8	395.3	-46.7	154	214561575
DGX	Quest Diagnostics, Inc.	Diagnostic & Health Related Service	12/31/12	7382.6	555.7	9283.9	4163.0	592	166230052
STR	Questar Corp.	Gas Utilities	12/31/12	1098.9	212.0	3757.1	1035.6	448	141327370
KWK	Quicksilver Resources, Inc.	Production & Extraction	12/31/12	709.0	-2352.6	1381.8	-1132.8	223	133122857
ZQK	Quiksilver, Inc.	Apparel, Footwear & Accessories	10/31/12	2013.2	-10.8	1718.2	583.3	188	108426482
CTU	Qwest Corp	Services	12/31/12	8848.0	849.0	23945.0	9974.0	-	
RAX	Rackspace Hosting Inc	Internet & Software	12/31/12	1309.2	105.4	1295.6	843.6	334	112334616
RDN	Radian Group, Inc.	Credit & Lending	12/31/12	825.4	-451.5	5903.2	736.3	198	111734225
RSH	RadioShack Corp.	Retail - Appliances and Electronics	12/31/12	4257.8	-139.4	2299.1	598.7	268	77932238
RAS	RAIT Financial Trust	REITs	12/31/12	200.8	-168.3	2924.0	886.2	143	35285390
RL	Ralph Lauren Corp	Apparel, Footwear & Accessories	3/31/12	6859.5	681.0	5416.4	3652.5	481	70391635
RPT	Ramco-Gershenson Properties Trus	REITs	12/31/12	128.7	7.2	1165.3	529.8	181	49392973
RRC	Range Resources Corp	Production & Extraction	12/31/12	1457.7	13.0	6728.7	2357.4	544	178748995
RJF	Raymond James Financial, Inc.	Finance Intermediaries & Services	9/30/12	3897.9	295.9	21160.3	3268.9	369	105364636
RYN	Rayonier Inc.	REITs	12/31/12	1571.0	278.7	3123.0	1438.0	523	116239558
RTN	Raytheon Co.	Defense	12/31/12	24414.0	1888.0	26686.0	8026.0	877	286411822
RLD	RealD Inc.	Electronic Instruments & Related Pro	3/23/12	246.6	37.0	302.2	197.2	101	44924111
RLGY	Realogy Holdings Corp	Property, Real Estate & Developmen	12/31/12	4672.0	-543.0	7445.0	1516.0	-	
O	Realty Income Corp.	REITs	12/31/12	475.5	159.2	5443.4	2412.8	391	71663315
RHT	Red Hat Inc	Internet & Software	2/29/12	1133.1	146.6	2491.1	1398.8	475	196517273
RLH	Red Lions Hotels Corp	Hotels, Restaurants & Travel	12/31/12	150.7	-14.7	260.9	152.9	71	15322554
RWT	Redwood Trust Inc.	REITs	12/31/12	-	131.8	4444.1	1140.2	245	80985233
ENL	Reed Elsevier N.V.	Publishing	12/31/12	654.0	658.0	1460.0	1402.0	87	8190934
RUK	Reed Elsevier Plc	Publishing	12/31/12	-	552.0	1207.0	1206.0	93	4262756
RGC	Regal Entertainment Group	Entertainment	12/27/12	2824.2	144.8	2209.5	-696.8	294	84888561
RBC	Regal-Beloit Corp.	Electrical Equipment	12/29/12	3166.9	195.6	3569.1	1953.4	297	45395516
REG	Regency Centers Corp.	REITs	12/31/12	496.9	25.9	3853.5	1730.8	318	102907526

Stock data table — columns: EARNINGS PER SHARE (QUARTERLY: 1st, 2nd, 3rd; ANNUAL: 2012, 2011, 2010); P/E RATIO (2012); DIVIDENDS PER SHARE (2012, 2011, 2010); AV. YLD %; DIV. DECLARED (AMOUNT, PAYABLE); PRICE RANGE (2012).

1st	2nd	3rd	Ann 2012	2011	2010	P/E 2012		Div 2012	2011	2010	Av Yld %	Amount	Payable	Price 2012	
-	-	2.18	6.06	6.87	4.63	23.8 -	0.0	2.34	2.26	2.18	2.0	0.590Y	81/16/21	144.2 -	0.0
-	-	0.61	2.60	2.70	2.17	12.0 -	0.0	1.44	1.40	1.40	5.0	1.18750Z	81/16/21	31.3 -	0.0
-	-	-	-	-	-			-	0.88	1.75					
-	-	1.43	5.61	5.45	3.84	20.8 -	0.0	2.20	2.00	1.80	2.0	0.60Y	81/16/21	116.5 -	0.0
-	-	2.30	8.41	7.04	6.49	23.2 -	0.0	0.12	0.12	0.12	0.1	0.030Y	81/16/21	195.2 -	0.0
-	-	0.14	-	0.67	0.22							0.050	3/15/13	10.0 -	0.0
-	-	0.12	0.57	0.43	0.08	19.9 -	0.0	-	-	-				11.4 -	0.0
-	-	0.24	0.73	0.58	0.64	35.3 -	0.0	-	-	-				25.8 -	0.0
-	-	-0.03	-0.17	-0.20	-1.25			-	-	-				16.9 -	0.0
-	-	0.72	2.71	2.36	3.40	12.4 -	0.0	0.24	0.10	0.02	0.8	0.110Y	3/8/13	33.6 -	0.0
-	-	0.12	-	0.73	-0.93			-	-	-				7.8 -	0.0
-	-	-1.81	2.02	-2.98	-1.96	8.7 -	0.0	4.00	-	-	28.5	0.57	12/28/12	17.6 -	0.0
-	-	0.60	2.57	2.15	2.06	13.4 -	0.0	0.78	0.70	0.55	2.8	0.40740Y	81/16/21	34.4 -	0.0
-	-	0.97	4.46	4.66	3.60	10.7 -	0.0	3.50	0.50	-	7.9	0.250Y	4/11/13	47.9 -	0.0
-	1.39	-	3.66	3.93	4.11	21.2 -	0.0	2.14	1.97	1.80	3.1	0.60150Y	81/16/21	77.6 -	0.0
-	-	0.46	1.48	1.59	1.61	17.1 -	0.0	1.41	0.40	1.16	6.5	0.28450Y	81/16/21	25.4 -	0.0
-	-	0.28	-	-1.63	0.76			-	0.50	0.49		0.140	4/15/13	22.9 -	0.0
-	-	-0.10	-0.18	-0.51	0.06			1.12	1.12	1.12	3.2	0.42810Z	81/16/21	40.9 -	0.0
-	-	-	-	-	-			-	0.08	-				3.1 -	0.0
-	-	0.05	0.17	0.23	-0.07	164.5 -	0.0	-	-	-				28.0 -	0.0
-	-	0.82	3.23	3.01	2.73	14.7 -	0.0	0.80	0.72	0.64	1.9	0.2150Y	81/16/21	47.5 -	0.0
-	-	0.73	3.66	3.92	2.97	9.8 -	0.0	0.70	0.62	0.54	2.4	0.180Y	81/16/21	35.9 -	0.0
-	-	0.26	0.98	0.67	0.34	53.9 -	0.0							52.8 -	0.0
-	-	0.28	1.18	1.01	0.88	13.7 -	0.0	0.71	0.47	0.44	4.8	0.130Y	2/28/13	16.1 -	0.0
0.16	-	-	0.52	0.31	0.54	18.6 -	0.0	0.24	0.24	0.24	2.8	0.060Y	2/14/13	9.7 -	0.0
-	-	-1.41	0.94	7.22	5.75	68.6 -	0.0	1.60	1.45	1.15	3.0	0.40Y	81/16/21	64.5 -	0.0
-	-	-	-	-	-			-	-	-		0.1250	5/31/13	20.1 -	18.6
-	-	-	-	0.59	0.57			-	1.29	0.93		0.42190Z	6/24/13	35.0 -	0.0
-	-	0.07	-	-	-	299.3 -	0.0	-	-	-		0.12250	5/31/13	20.9 -	0.0
-	-	0.21	0.81	2.12	1.58	30.7 -	30.4	1.76	1.76	1.76	7.1	0.35940Z	3/28/13	24.9 -	24.6
-	-	-	-	185.70	151.76			-	0.00	0.00				36.5 -	0.0
-	-	0.68	2.51	2.96	3.08	13.7 -	0.0	1.42	1.37	1.37	4.5	0.360Y	81/16/21	34.3 -	0.0
-	-	1.18	3.90	3.29	2.35	40.4 -	0.0	4.40	3.65	3.05	3.1	0.2744GHZ	3/28/13	157.4 -	0.0
-	-	-0.21	-0.69	-1.30	-0.94			-	0.10	0.07		0.0250Y	10/21/11	2.5 -	0.0
-	-	0.30	0.54	-0.55	-2.90	40.1 -	0.0	-	-	-		0.040Y	81/16/21	21.7 -	0.0
-	-	-1.29	-3.42	-1.32	-0.00			-	-	-				33.4 -	0.0
-	-	-	0.49	0.50	0.51	17.4 -	0.0	0.53	0.53	0.53	6.5	0.0390Z	6/3/13	8.5 -	0.0
-	-	-	0.48	0.51	0.52	18.0 -	0.0	0.47	0.53	0.52	5.8	0.0389M	6/3/13	8.6 -	0.0
-	-	-	0.27	0.35	0.58	19.6 -	0.0	0.34	0.46	1.08	6.6	0.0260Z	6/3/13	5.3 -	0.0
-	-	-	0.80	0.79	0.81	17.4 -	0.0	0.80	0.80	0.78	6.1	0.0559M	6/3/13	13.9 -	0.0
-	-	-	0.27	0.45	0.61	21.9 -	0.0	0.40	0.68	0.84	7.3	0.0260Z	6/3/13	5.9 -	0.0
-	-	2.24	4.36	0.80	3.08	28.7 -	0.0	0.15	0.15	0.15	0.2	0.03750Y	81/16/21	125.1 -	0.0
-	-	0.16	-1.43	1.45	0.83			2.10	1.94	1.88	8.6	0.550	2/14/13	27.3 -	0.0
-	-	0.09	0.32	0.32	0.34	22.5 -	0.0	0.28	0.12	0.24	5.3	0.160Y	3/7/13	7.2 -	0.0
-	-	-0.02	0.72	1.50	1.84	46.1 -	0.0	0.08	0.08	0.04	0.3	0.020Y	81/16/21	33.2 -	0.0
-	-	0.07	-	0.09	0.05			-	-	-				34.8 -	0.0
-	-	-1.25	0.19	0.10	-0.21	113.0 -	0.0	1.93	1.28	-	10.8	0.48750	2/15/13	21.5 -	0.0
-	-	0.84	1.78	-1.00	-6.67	13.7 -	0.0	3.00	0.60	-	17.4	0.30Y	3/29/13	24.4 -	0.0
-	-	0.80	3.63	3.47	2.77	17.3 -	0.0	0.97	0.95	0.93	2.0	0.2450Y	4/30/13	62.8 -	0.0
-0.22	-	-	-0.45	0.24	0.61			0.16	0.16	0.14	0.0	0.040Y	3/29/13	22.2 -	0.0
-	-	0.45	1.44	0.62	0.72	20.8 -	0.0	-	-	-				29.9 -	0.0
-	-	-0.04	-0.04	0.02	0.02			-	-	-				2.7 -	0.0
-	-	1.01	3.46	2.92	4.05	18.7 -	0.0	0.68	0.40	0.40	1.2	0.30Y	81/16/21	64.7 -	0.0
-	-	0.19	1.19	1.16	1.91	20.4 -	0.0	0.67	0.62	0.54	3.3	0.170Y	81/16/21	24.3 -	0.0
-	-	-3.83	-13.83	0.52	2.45			-	-	-				5.8 -	0.0
-0.19	-	-	-0.07	-0.13	-0.07			-	-	-				6.8 -	0.0
-	-	-	-	-	-			1.31	-	-	5.0	0.46880Z	6/17/13	27.1 -	0.0
-	-	0.19	0.75	0.55	0.35	105.7 -	0.0	-	-	-				79.2 -	0.0
-	-	0.11	-3.41	2.26	-15.74			0.01	0.01	0.01	0.2	0.00250Y	3/6/13	10.7 -	0.0
-	-	-0.47	-1.39	0.70	1.68			0.25	0.50	0.25	7.6	0.1250Y	81/16/21	6.3 -	0.0
-	-	-0.37	-3.75	-1.33	3.33			0.31	0.12	-	5.7	0.120Z	4/30/13	8.1 -	0.0
-	-	2.31	7.13	5.75	4.73	25.0 -	0.0	0.80	0.50	0.30	0.5	0.40Y	81/16/21	178.1 -	0.0
-	-	0.03	-	-0.84	-0.57			0.66	0.65	0.65	5.0	0.90630Z	4/1/13	16.8 -	0.0
-	-	-0.34	0.08	0.36	-1.53	1030.8 -	0.0	0.16	0.16	0.16	0.2	0.040Y	81/16/21	82.5 -	0.0
0.61	-	-	2.20	2.19	1.83	21.9 -	0.0	0.52	0.52	0.44	1.4	0.140Y	81/16/21	48.1 -	0.0
-	-	0.62	2.17	2.20	1.79	27.5 -	0.0	1.68	1.23	0.82	3.4	0.440Z	81/16/21	59.7 -	0.0
-	-	1.50	5.65	5.28	4.88	10.5 -	0.0	2.00	2.10	1.13	3.6	0.550Y	81/16/21	59.3 -	0.0
-	-	-0.08	0.65	-0.29	-2.09	23.3 -	0.0	-	-	-				15.1 -	0.0
-	-	-4.24	-14.41	-55.00	-12.25			-	-	-				49.8 -	0.0
-	-	0.20	0.86	1.05	1.01	54.2 -	0.0	1.78	1.74	1.72	4.3	0.1380Z	81/16/21	46.6 -	0.0
-	-	0.18	0.75	0.55	0.45	82.6 -	0.0	-	-	-				62.0 -	0.0
-	-	-0.05	-0.76	-0.38	-0.47			-	-	-				8.7 -	0.0
-	-	0.48	1.59	0.31	1.36	14.8 -	0.0	1.00	1.00	1.00	6.6	0.280Y	3/29/13	23.6 -	0.0
-	-	-	0.89	0.59	0.51	38.4 -	0.0	1.27	1.45	1.14	4.8			34.2 -	0.0
-	-	-	0.45	0.32	0.27	105.6 -	0.0	2.21	2.21	1.84	5.9			47.5 -	0.0
-	-	0.15	0.93	0.26	0.50	17.9 -	0.0	1.84	0.84	2.12	12.9	0.210Y	81/16/21	16.7 -	0.0
-	-	1.29	4.64	3.79	3.84	18.2 -	0.0	0.75	0.71	0.67	1.1	0.190Y	81/16/21	84.7 -	0.0
-	-	0.13	-0.08	0.35	-0.10			1.85	1.85	1.85	3.9	0.46250Z	81/16/21	53.4 -	0.0

SYMBOL	COMPANY	NATURE OF BUSINESS	FISCAL YEAR-END	TOTAL REV. $MILL	NET INCOME $MILL	TOTAL ASSETS $MILL	NET STK EQUITY $MILL	NO OF INST	INST. HOLDINGS (SHARES)
RGP	Regency Energy Partners LP	Equipment & Services	12/31/12	1339.0	46.0	6157.0	73.0	178	105839751
RM	Regional Management Corp	Credit & Lending	12/31/12	136.0	25.4	435.0	130.6	51	4950251
RF	Regions Financial Corp	Banking	12/31/12	6003.0	1120.0	121347.0	15499.0	680	1069650832
RGS	Regis Corp.	Miscellaneous Consumer Services	6/30/12	2273.8	-114.1	1571.8	889.2	199	69512795
RGA	Reinsurance Group of America, Inc.	Life & Health	12/31/12	9840.9	631.9	40360.4	6910.2	31	783941
RS	Reliance Steel & Aluminum Co.	Non-Precious Metals	12/31/12	8442.3	403.5	5857.7	3558.4	328	64224090
RNR	RenaissanceRe Holdings Ltd.	General Insurance	12/31/12	1405.9	600.9	7928.6	3503.1	308	48946397
SOL	Renesola Ltd.	Semiconductors	12/31/11	985.3	0.3	1949.0	601.0		
RENN	Renren Inc	Internet & Software	12/31/11	118.0	41.3	1278.0	1210.2	79	10477757
RNF	Rentech Nitrogen Partners L.P.	Agricultural Chemicals	12/31/12	261.6	107.0	376.6		79	5344979
RSG	Republic Services, Inc.	Sanitation Services	12/31/12	8118.3	571.8	19616.9	7703.3	583	322893321
RMD	ResMed Inc.	Medical Instruments & Equipment	6/30/12	1368.5	254.8	2137.9	1607.6	404	81227531
REN	Resolute Energy Corp	Production & Extraction	12/31/12	258.3	18.0	1364.1	532.2	110	55999057
RFP	Resolute Forest Products Inc	Paper & Forest Products	12/31/12	4503.0	-2.0	6324.0	3093.0	173	103766684
RSO	Resource Capital Corp	REITs	12/31/12	166.5	64.4	2478.3	613.3	137	37781133
RH	Restoration Hardware Holdings, Inc.	Furniture	1/28/12	-	-	0.0	0.0		
RPAI	Retail Properties of America, Inc	REITs	12/31/12	567.0	-0.4	5237.4	2374.3		
REV	Revlon Inc	Household & Personal Products	12/31/12	1426.1	51.1	1236.6	-649.3	105	13033108
REX	REX American Resources Corp	Refining & Marketing	1/31/12	410.0	28.3	408.0	252.5	83	4710443
RXN	Rexnord Corp (New)	Industrial Machinery & Equipment	3/31/12	1969.6	29.9	3290.9	-79.9	83	95477067
RAI	Reynolds American Inc	Tobacco Products	12/31/12	8304.0	1272.0	16557.0	5257.0	604	283167309
RNO	Rhino Resource Partners LP	Mining	12/31/12	352.0	40.2	559.5			
RIOM	Rio Alto Mining, Ltd.	Precious Metals	12/31/12	316.5	100.4	353.5	227.6		
RIO	Rio Tinto Plc	Mining	12/31/12	50967.0	-14.0	117573.0	46865.0	414	94729721
RBA	Ritchie Bros. Auctioneers, Inc.	Business Services	12/31/12	438.0	79.5	1132.5	656.5	189	92640347
RAD	Rite Aid Corp.	Retail - Food & Beverage, Drug & To	3/3/12	26121.2	-368.6	7364.3	-2586.8	266	405586365
RLI	RLI Corp.	General Insurance	12/31/12	660.8	103.3	2644.6	796.4	195	20695076
RLJ	RLJ Lodging Trust	REITs	12/31/12	854.2	41.3	3346.4	1789.8	156	99963799
RRTS	Roadrunner Transportation System	Miscellaneous Transportation Servic	12/31/12	1073.4	37.5	700.8	392.1	99	34285336
RHI	Robert Half International Inc.	Business Services	12/31/12	4111.2	209.9	1381.3	842.0	440	139033596
RGE	Rochester Gas & Electric Corp	Electric Utilities	12/31/11	950.4	61.0	2692.0	645.5		
RKT	Rock-Tenn Co.	Containers & Packaging	9/30/12	9207.6	249.1	10687.1	3405.7	368	71515950
ROK	Rockwell Automation, Inc.	Electrical Equipment	9/30/12	6259.4	737.0	5636.5	1851.7	645	113045100
COL	Rockwell Collins, Inc.	Aerospace	9/30/12	4726.0	609.0	5314.0	1259.0	533	121505589
ROC	Rockwood Holdings Inc	Specialty Chemicals	12/31/12	3506.9	383.5	5973.7	1669.1	322	84161919
RCI 14A	Rogers Cable Inc.	Radio & Television	12/31/06	3201.0	177.0	5245.0	419.0		
RCI	Rogers Communications Inc.	Services	12/31/12	12486.0	1700.0	19618.0	3768.0	300	260493167
ROG	Rogers Corp.	Plastics	12/31/12	498.8	68.7	760.0	434.2	151	16186212
ROL	Rollins, Inc.	Business Services	12/31/12	1270.9	111.3	692.5	355.0	217	55285865
ROP	Roper Industries, Inc	Electrical Equipment	12/31/12	2993.5	483.4	7071.1	3687.7	575	102759780
RRMS	Rose Rock Midstream L P	Production & Extraction	12/31/12	620.4	24.0	544.7	308.3	41	4851332
RST	Rosetta Stone, Inc.	Internet & Software	12/31/12	273.2	-35.8	275.9	144.6	87	10541357
RNDY	Roundy's Inc	Retail - Food & Beverage, Drug & To	12/29/12	3890.5	-69.2	1380.1	193.3	101	14762473
RSE	Rouse Properties, Inc.	Property, Real Estate & Developmen	12/31/12	234.0	-68.7	1905.1	532.8	126	48947485
RDC	Rowan Companies Plc	Production & Extraction	12/31/12	1392.6	180.6	7699.5	4531.7	395	104950383
RY	Royal Bank of Canada	Banking	10/31/12	38126.0	7442.0	825100.0	44267.0	387	664014578
RBS	Royal Bank of Scotland Group Plc	Banking	12/31/12	25903.0	-5956.0	1312295.0	68130.0	79	12411574
RCL	Royal Caribbean Cruises Ltd.	Hotels, Restaurants & Travel	12/31/12	7688.0	18.3	19827.9	8308.7	361	97198247
RDS A	Royal Dutch Shell Plc	Production & Extraction	12/31/12	481700.0	26592.0	360325.0	188494.0	878	271490373
RMT	Royce Micro-Cap Trust, Inc.	Holding and other Investment Office	12/31/12	8.2	4.4	363.9	318.5	57	6826541
RVT	Royce Value Trust, Inc.	Holding and other Investment Office	12/31/12	23.5	16.2	1233.5	1082.4	122	20414146
RES	RPC, Inc.	Equipment & Services	12/31/12	1945.0	274.4	1367.2	899.2	206	59319279
RPM	RPM International Inc (DE)	Specialty Chemicals	5/31/12	3777.4	215.9	3560.0	1183.7	396	97569095
RTI	RTI International Metals, Inc.	Non-Precious Metals	12/31/12	738.6	23.5	1259.7	745.6	187	35248882
RT	Ruby Tuesday, Inc.	Hotels, Restaurants & Travel	6/5/12	1325.8	-0.2	1173.5	576.2	192	57471204
RKUS	Ruckus Wireless Inc	Services	12/31/12	214.7	31.7	243.8	170.2		
R	Ryder System, Inc.	Trucking	12/31/12	6257.0	210.0	8319.0	1467.5	365	55313231
RYL	Ryland Group, Inc.	Builders	12/31/12	1308.5	40.4	1933.9	503.9	281	56598364
RHP	Ryman Hospitality Properties Inc	REITs	12/31/12	986.6	-26.6	2543.1	853.6	218	64522980
SBR	Sabine Royalty Trust	Production & Extraction	12/31/12	54.7	52.3	5.3	4.1	89	1512977
SB	Safe Bulkers Inc	Shipping	12/31/12	184.3	96.1	1082.2	425.9	66	7427946
SFE	Safeguard Scientifics, Inc.	Venture Capital	12/31/12	-	-39.4	374.1	314.0	134	23415491
SWY	Safeway Inc.	Retail - Food & Beverage, Drug & To	12/29/12	44206.5	596.5	14657.0	2927.9	547	335467974
SAI	SAIC Inc	IT Services	1/31/13	11173.0	525.0	5875.0	2618.0	387	203713977
SKS	Saks, Inc.	Retail - General Merchandise/Depart	2/2/13	3147.6	62.9	2090.2	1149.8	255	96182900
CRM	Salesforce.Com Inc	Internet & Software	1/31/13	3050.2	-270.4	5529.0	2371.2	595	158136486
SMM	Salient Midstream & MLP Fund	Holding and other Investment Office	4/16/12	-	-	0.2	0.1	9	372222
SMF	Salient MLP & Energy Infrastructure	Holding and other Investment Office	11/30/12	3.8	0.2	215.2	145.0		
SBH	Sally Beauty Holdings Inc	Retail - Specialty	9/30/12	3523.6	233.1	2065.8	-115.1	342	177414467
SJT	San Juan Basin Royalty Trust	Production & Extraction	12/31/12	35.1	33.5	13.6	12.2	156	11777745
SN	Sanchez Energy Corp.	Production & Extraction	12/31/12	43.2	-16.3	426.6	366.7	92	16927827
SD	Sandridge Energy, Inc.	Production & Extraction	12/31/12	2731.0	141.6	9790.7	2368.9	344	418390556
SDT	SandRidge Mississippian Trust I	Production & Extraction	12/31/12	90.0	84.6	260.9	260.9	55	3177410
SDR	SandRidge Mississippian Trust II	Production & Extraction	12/31/12	74.5	68.4	438.0	438.0	55	7548354
PER	SandRidge Permian Trust	Production & Extraction	12/31/12	133.3	122.4	491.4			
SNY	Sanofi	Pharmaceuticals	12/31/12	35957.0	4967.0	100407.0	57338.0	545	218157173
SAN PRB	Santander Finance Preferred SA Un	Finance Intermediaries & Services	12/31/11		1.3	3844.4	3.0		
SOV PRC	Santander Holdings USA Inc.	Banking	12/31/12	3687.5	561.2	85790.2	13242.0	56	8731682
SAP	SAP AG	Internet & Software	12/31/12	16223.0	2823.0	26835.0	14163.0	389	53144592
SPP	Sappi Ltd. (South Africa)	Paper & Forest Products	9/30/12	6347.0	104.0	6168.0	1525.0	28	5903431

T52

EPS 1st	EPS 2nd	EPS 3rd	EPS 2012	EPS 2011	EPS 2010	P/E RATIO		DIV 2012	DIV 2011	DIV 2010	AV. YLD %	DIV AMOUNT	PAYABLE	PRICE RANGE 2012	
-	-	-0.04	0.13	0.32	-0.10	196.6 -	0.0	1.84	1.79	1.78	8.0	0.460	2/14/13	25.6 -	0.0
-	-	0.55	2.12	2.21	1.70	9.7 -	0.0							20.5 -	0.0
-	-	0.21	0.71	-0.34	-0.62	11.8 -	0.0	0.04	0.04	0.04	0.6	0.39840Y	81/16/21	8.4 -	0.0
-	-0.22	-	-2.00	-0.16	0.75			0.24	0.20	0.16	1.4	0.060Y	81/16/21	19.5 -	0.0
-	-	1.95	8.52	8.09	7.69	7.1 -	0.0	0.84	0.60	0.48	1.5	0.240Y	81/16/21	60.9 -	0.0
-	-	1.30	5.33	4.58	2.61	13.5 -	0.0	0.80	0.48	0.40	1.4	0.30Y	81/16/21	72.0 -	0.0
-	-	3.62	11.23	-1.84	12.31	8.2 -	0.0	1.08	1.04	1.00	1.4	0.280	81/16/21	92.0 -	0.0
-	-	-0.46	-	0.00	0.97									2.8 -	0.0
-	-	-0.01	-	0.05	-0.31									7.3 -	0.0
-	-	0.75	2.78	0.30		17.4 -	0.0	3.08	-	-	9.0	0.750	2/14/13	48.4 -	0.0
-	-	0.42	1.55	1.56	1.32	21.3 -	0.0	0.91	0.84	0.78	3.2	0.2350Y	81/16/21	33.0 -	0.0
-	0.53	-	1.71	1.44	1.23	28.3 -	0.0					0.170Y	81/16/21	48.4 -	0.0
-	-	-0.04	0.30	0.47	0.12	38.5 -	0.0							11.5 -	0.0
-	-	0.32	-0.02	0.42	27.63									17.4 -	0.0
-	-	0.20	0.71	0.53	0.41	9.7 -	0.0	0.80	1.00	1.00	13.8	0.51560Z	4/30/13	6.9 -	0.0
-	-	16850.00	-	-	-									39.6 -	31.5
-	-	-0.07	-	-0.38	-0.50			0.66	0.63	0.49	5.8	0.4861GHZ	4/1/13	15.1 -	0.0
-	-	-0.29	0.98	1.02	6.26	23.8 -	0.0					0.16380Y	4/8/13	23.3 -	0.0
-	-	0.05	3.08	0.52	0.91	10.3 -	0.0							31.8 -	0.0
-	-	0.09	0.42	-0.77	1.27	52.6 -	0.0							22.1 -	0.0
-	-	0.74	2.24	2.40	1.91	20.8 -	0.0	2.33	2.15	1.84	5.4	0.590Y	81/16/21	46.7 -	0.0
-	-	0.31	1.42	1.43	0.22	13.3 -	0.0	1.85	1.81	-	12.5	0.4450	2/14/13	18.9 -	0.0
-	-	0.06	0.57	0.00	-0.16	10.3 -	0.0							5.9 -	0.0
-	-	-	-1.62	3.01	7.26			1.66	1.17	0.88	3.3			59.9 -	0.0
-	-	0.08	0.74	0.72	0.62	31.9 -	0.0	0.47	0.44	0.41	2.3	0.12250	3/8/13	23.6 -	0.0
-	-	0.07	-0.43	-0.64	-0.59							0.1150	81/16/21	1.9 -	0.0
-	-	1.19	4.79	6.09	6.00	15.1 -	0.0	6.26	6.19	8.15	9.3	0.320Y	81/16/21	72.3 -	0.0
-	-	0.14	0.38	0.12	-	59.9 -	0.0	0.70	0.38	-	3.7	0.2050Z	4/15/13	22.8 -	0.0
-	-	0.31	1.16	0.82	0.11	20.4 -	0.0							23.6 -	0.0
-	-	0.41	1.50	1.04	0.44	25.0 -	0.0	0.60	0.56	0.52	2.0	0.160Y	81/16/21	37.5 -	0.0
-	-	-	-	-	-							1.650 Y	3/1/04		
1.18	-	-	3.45	2.77	5.70	26.9 -	0.0	0.80	0.80	0.60	1.2	0.2250Y	81/16/21	92.8 -	0.0
1.14	-	-	5.13	4.80	3.22	17.8 -	0.0	1.75	1.48	1.22	2.3	0.520Y	81/16/21	91.5 -	0.0
0.94	-	-	4.15	4.06	3.52	15.4 -	0.0	1.08	0.96	0.96	2.0	0.30Y	81/16/21	63.8 -	0.0
-	-	0.77	4.80	5.15	3.07	13.6 -	0.0	1.05	-	-	2.1	0.40Y	81/16/21	65.4 -	0.0
-	-	0.90	3.26	2.86	2.59	15.9 -	0.0	1.58	1.42	1.28	3.8	0.4350	4/2/13	51.9 -	0.0
-	-	3.46	4.04	2.21	2.16	12.8 -	0.0	-	-	-	-	0.0075	2/12/92	51.7 -	0.0
-	-	0.22	0.76	0.69	0.61	33.6 -	0.0	0.44	0.28	0.24	1.9	0.090Y	81/16/21	25.6 -	0.0
-	-	1.17	4.86	4.34	3.34	26.2 -	0.0	0.71	0.44	0.38	0.7	0.1650Y	81/16/21	127.3 -	0.0
-	-	0.38	1.40	0.06	-	28.3 -	0.0	1.21	-	-	4.2	0.40250	2/14/13	39.6 -	0.0
-	-	-1.58	-1.70	-0.96	0.63									15.4 -	0.0
-	-	0.18	-1.61	1.58	1.01			0.58	-	2.90	7.6	0.120Y	3/18/13	12.4 -	0.0
-	-	-0.27	-1.49	-0.76	-			0.14	-	-	0.9	0.070Z	1/30/13	18.5 -	0.0
-	-	0.22	1.46	5.83	2.36	25.6 -	0.0							37.3 -	0.0
1.36	-	-	4.93	4.19	3.46	13.1 -	0.0	2.28	2.08	2.00	4.0	0.38120	5/24/13	64.5 -	0.0
-	-	-0.13	-0.54	-0.18	-0.05			-	-	-	-	0.53130	3/31/99	11.8 -	0.0
-	-	1.68	0.08	2.77	2.51	480.3 -	0.0	-	-	-	-	0.120	81/16/21	38.4 -	0.0
-	-	1.14	4.24	4.98	3.28	17.3 -	0.0	3.42	3.36	3.36	5.0	-	-	73.2 -	0.0
-	-	-	0.15	0.04	0.08	71.6 -	0.0	0.51	0.39	0.08	5.5	0.130	3/25/13	10.7 -	0.0
-	-	0.23	0.10	0.24		65.5 -	0.0	0.80	0.78	0.03	6.0	0.190	3/25/13	15.1 -	0.0
-	-	0.30	1.27	1.35	-0.67	13.6 -	0.0	0.52	0.21	-	4.2	0.10Y	81/16/21	17.2 -	0.0
-	-	-0.33	1.65	1.45	1.39	10.5 -	0.0	0.85	0.83	0.81	3.0	0.2250Y	81/16/21	32.2 -	0.0
-	-	0.19	0.77	0.22	0.11	42.0 -	0.0	-	-	-	-	-	-	32.3 -	0.0
-	-0.24	-	0.00	0.72	0.73							0.250Y	81/16/21	9.1 -	0.0
-	-	0.24	0.02	-0.30		107.8 -	51.0	-	-	-	-	-	-	25.9 -	12.3
-	-	1.47	4.09	3.28	2.25	15.0 -	0.0	1.20	1.12	1.04	2.6	0.310Y	81/16/21	61.4 -	0.0
-	-	0.22	0.84	-1.14	-1.93	50.2 -	0.0	0.12	0.12	0.12	0.4	0.030Y	4/30/13	42.2 -	0.0
-	-	-0.57	-0.56	0.20	-1.89			6.84	-	-	18.0	0.50	4/12/13	46.4 -	0.0
-	-	0.82	3.59	4.02	3.70	17.3 -	0.0	3.70	3.97	3.70	7.4	0.44060Z	4/29/13	62.1 -	0.0
-	-	0.27	1.27	1.29	1.73	5.5 -	0.0	0.50	-	0.60	9.5	0.050	3/8/13	6.9 -	0.0
-	-	-0.42	-1.88	4.74	1.26			-	-	-	-	0.02670	12/31/79	17.6 -	0.0
-	-	0.66	2.40	1.49	1.55	11.0 -	0.0	0.67	0.56	0.46	3.7	0.1750Y	81/16/21	26.4 -	0.0
-	-	0.33	0.18	1.63	1.24	75.3 -	0.0	-	-	-	-	1.7Y	81/16/21	13.6 -	0.0
-	-	0.14	0.45	0.30	-0.40	26.6 -	0.0	-	-	-	-	4.7	81/16/21	12.0 -	0.0
-	-	-1.55	-0.09	0.47	0.63									186.4 -	0.0
-	-	-	-	-	-							0.3350	2/28/13	22.8 -	0.0
-	-	-	0.03	0.13		949.7 -	0.0	1.74	0.81	-	6.8	0.4550	2/28/13	28.5 -	0.0
0.32	-	-	1.24	1.14	0.78	24.0 -	0.0							29.7 -	0.0
-	-	0.10	0.72	1.44	1.68	26.5 -	0.0	0.72	1.44	1.68	4.8	0.02670	3/14/13	19.1 -	0.0
-	-	0.04	-0.56	0.09										24.8 -	0.0
-	-	-0.39	0.19	0.13	0.52	42.8 -	0.0	-	-	-	-	3.0Y	1/15/13	8.1 -	0.0
-	-	0.73	-	-				2.99	1.88	-	13.3	0.65070Z	3/1/13	32.9 -	0.0
-	-	-	-	-				1.36	-	-	7.4	0.53260Z	3/1/13	23.7 -	0.0
-	-	0.61	2.33	0.74		10.2 -	0.0	2.33	-	-	12.2	0.6030Z	3/1/13	23.7 -	0.0
-	-	-	3.74	4.29	4.18	13.7 -	0.0	2.65	2.50	2.40	6.3			51.1 -	0.0
-	-	-	-	-	-			-	2.40	2.31		0.40630	4/30/13	21.1 -	0.0
-	-	-	-	-	-			1.83	1.83	1.83	10.8	0.45620Y	5/15/13	25.9 -	0.0
-	-	0.52	2.37	2.89	1.52	35.7 -	0.0	1.30	0.85	0.51	1.9			84.6 -	0.0
-	-	-0.20	0.20	-0.45	0.13	18.8 -	0.0							3.8 -	0.0

SYMBOL	COMPANY	NATURE OF BUSINESS	FISCAL YEAR-END	TOTAL REV. $MILL	NET INCOME $MILL	TOTAL ASSETS $MILL	NET STK EQUITY $MILL	NO OF INST	INST. HOLDINGS (SHARES)
SAR	Saratoga Investment Corp	Holding and other Investment Office	2/29/12	13.5	5.7	125.5	97.4	18	5740590
SSL	Sasol Ltd.	Production & Extraction	6/30/12	169446.0	23583.0	203753.0	125234.0	200	28945285
BFS PRC	Saul Centers, Inc.	REITs	12/31/12	190.1	33.4	1207.3	267.7	141	8591936
SCG	SCANA Corp	Electric Utilities	12/31/12	4176.0	420.0	14616.0	4154.0	487	72592462
SGK	Schawk, Inc.	Business Services	12/31/12	460.7	-23.4	458.8	250.8	85	11178403
SLB	Schlumberger Ltd.	Equipment & Services	12/31/12	42321.0	5490.0	61547.0	34751.0	1714	1069657859
SCHW	Schwab (Charles) Corp.	Finance Intermediaries & Services	12/31/12	4883.0	883.0	133637.0	9589.0	723	1039555031
SWM	Schweitzer-Mauduit International, In	Paper & Forest Products	12/31/12	788.1	79.8	886.7	511.8	229	29804865
STNG	Scorpio Tankers Inc.	Shipping	12/31/12	115.4	-26.5	573.3	414.8	88	50570453
SMG	Scotts Miracle-Gro Co (The)	Agricultural Chemicals	9/30/12	2826.1	106.5	2074.4	601.9	276	47027516
SSP	Scripps (E.W.) Co.	Publishing	12/31/12	903.5	40.2	1030.8	537.7	184	32858220
SNI	Scripps Networks Interactive Inc	Radio & Television	12/31/12	2307.2	681.5	4138.8	1820.9	433	97936181
SA	Seabridge Gold Inc	Precious Metals	12/31/11		-20.1	228.7	217.4	79	18945604
CKH	SEACOR Holdings Inc	Equipment & Services	12/31/12	1581.2	61.2	3700.8	1713.7	215	20068132
BOX	SeaCube Container Leasing Ltd	Industrial Machinery & Equipment	12/31/12	198.9	46.4	1728.9	255.8	84	16254529
SDRL	Seadrill Ltd	Production & Extraction	12/31/11	4192.0	1401.0	18304.0	5977.0	370	94277906
SDLP	Seadrill Partners LLC	Production & Extraction							
SEE	Sealed Air Corp.	Containers & Packaging	12/31/12	7648.1	-1410.3	9437.2	1443.8	455	187372367
SSW	Seaspan Corp	Shipping	12/31/12	660.8	121.3	5650.9	1218.6	120	14054951
SIR	Select Income Real Estate Investm	REITs	12/31/12	122.8	65.9	1430.7	900.2	113	14926723
SEM	Select Medical Holdings Corp	Hospitals & Health Care Facilities	12/31/12	2949.0	148.2	2761.4	717.0	144	49809779
SEMG	SemGroup Corp	Equipment & Services	12/31/12	1237.5	22.1	1748.2	892.4	173	42266370
SMI	Semiconductor Manufacturing Inter	Semiconductors	12/31/11	1319.5	-246.8	3773.9	2244.8	40	18551524
SRE	Sempra Energy	Electric Utilities	12/31/12	9647.0	920.0	36499.0	10282.0	596	188605473
SNH	Senior Housing Properties Trust	REITs	12/31/12	644.8	135.9	4748.0	2646.6	348	154746415
ST	Sensata Technologies Holding NV	Electrical Equipment	12/31/12	1913.9	177.5	3648.4	1222.3	158	189944526
SXT	Sensient Technologies Corp.	Specialty Chemicals	12/31/12	1459.1	123.9	1776.6	1153.9	249	53086321
SQNS	Sequans Communications S A	Semiconductors	12/31/12	22.3	-33.0	68.4	55.5	16	1519157
SCI	Service Corp. International	Miscellaneous Consumer Services	12/31/12	2410.5	152.5	9683.6	1343.0	289	181690236
NOW	ServiceNow Inc	IT Services	12/31/12	243.7	-37.3	478.1	243.4	126	101569583
SJR	Shaw Communications Inc	Radio & Television	8/31/12	4998.0	728.0	12722.0	3754.0	185	223653108
TFC	Shelton Greater China Fund	Holding and other Investment Office	12/31/11		-1.4	50.0	49.8	6	638563
SHW	Sherwin-Williams Co.	Specialty Chemicals	12/31/12	9534.5	631.0	6234.7	1791.8	648	88282045
SHG	Shinhan Financial Group Co. Ltd.	Banking	12/31/11	7658433.0	3100011.0	88117481.0	24396501.0	103	16196584
SFL	Ship Finance International Ltd	Equipment & Services	12/31/11	295.1	131.2	2896.1	857.1	172	25096634
SSTK	Shutterstock Inc	Internet & Software	12/31/12	169.6	47.5	147.1	76.9		
SBGL	Sibanye Gold Ltd	Mining							
SBGL	Sibanye Gold Ltd	Mining							
SI	Siemens AG (Germany)	Electrical Equipment	9/30/12	78296.0	4458.0	108282.0	30733.0	384	17781639
SIG	Signet Jewelers Ltd	Retail - Specialty	2/2/13	3983.4	359.9	3715.8	2329.9	266	86845996
SBY	Silver Bay Realty Trust Corp	REITs	12/31/12	3.6	-5.5	677.3	659.9		
SSNI	Silver Spring Networks Inc	Computer Hardware & Equipment	12/31/12	196.7	-89.7	417.7	-228.8		
SLW	Silver Wheaton Corp	Precious Metals	12/31/12	849.6	586.0	3189.3	3107.1	381	157520695
SVM	Silvercorp Metals Inc	Precious Metals	3/31/12	238.0	73.8	575.4	433.8	113	53838602
SCR	Simcere Pharmaceutical Group	Pharmaceuticals	12/31/11	2040.5	178.4	3734.1	2056.2	33	2397588
SPG	Simon Property Group, Inc.	REITs	12/31/12	4880.1	1719.6	32586.6	6088.6	765	327686931
SSD	Simpson Manufacturing Co., Inc. (D	Metal Products	12/31/12	657.2	41.9	890.3	789.6	185	49084722
SMS	Sims Metal Management Ltd	Non-Precious Metals	6/30/12	9042.3	-521.4	3620.0	2394.4		
SGF	Singapore Fund, Inc.	Holding and other Investment Office	10/31/12	4.3	2.3	114.6	114.2	34	2970498
SHI	Sinopec Shanghai Petrochemical C	Refining & Marketing	12/31/11	89509.7	956.1	30718.9	17925.6	37	290470
SIX	Six Flags Entertainment Corp	Sporting & Recreational	12/31/12	1070.3	354.0	3056.4	892.2	236	65035137
SJW	SJW Corp.	Water Utilities	12/31/12	261.5	22.3	1087.5	274.6	92	9395795
SKM	SK Telecom Co., Ltd. (South Korea	Internet & Software	12/31/11	15988277.6	1612889.1	24366036.4	11661880.9	227	160864626
SKX	Skechers U S A, Inc.	Apparel, Footwear & Accessories	12/31/12	1567.4	9.5	1340.2	876.0	216	40091085
SKH	Skilled Healthcare Group Inc	Hospitals & Health Care Facilities	12/31/12	872.6	21.6	682.6	99.8	115	13834523
SKY	Skyline Corp.	Builders	5/31/12	182.8	-19.4	78.9	56.2	57	4349363
SLG	SL Green Realty Corp.	REITs	12/31/12	1400.3	196.4	14387.8	6469.4	373	101800074
SM	SM Energy Co.	Production & Extraction	12/31/12	1505.1	-54.2	4199.5	1414.5	342	66055696
SNN	Smith & Nephew Plc	Medical Instruments & Equipment	12/31/12	4137.0	729.0	5642.0	3884.0	142	7991381
AOS	Smith (A.O.) Corp	Metal Products	12/31/12	1939.3	158.7	2265.2	1194.1	297	39285850
SFD	Smithfield Foods, Inc.	Food	4/29/12	13094.3	361.3	7422.2	3387.3	365	130306112
SJM	Smucker (J.M.) Co.	Food	4/30/12	5525.8	459.7	9115.2	5163.4	689	83758666
SNA	Snap-On, Inc.	Industrial Machinery & Equipment	12/29/12	3099.2	306.1	3902.3	1802.1	439	52757537
SNH PRZ	SNH Capital Trust I	REITs							
SQM	Sociedad Quimica y Minera de Chil	Agricultural Chemicals	12/31/11	2145.3	545.8	3871.6	1812.8	260	42074855
SWI	Solarwinds Inc	Internet & Software	12/31/12	269.0	81.3	517.4	382.8	293	65018896
SLH	Solera Holdings Inc	Internet & Software	6/30/12	790.2	107.0	2151.8	677.2	232	74447943
SAH	Sonic Automotive, Inc.	Retail - Automotive	12/31/12	8365.5	89.1	2776.7	526.5	197	39828619
SON	Sonoco Products Co.	Containers & Packaging	12/31/12	4786.1	196.0	4176.1	1489.0	370	74403658
SNE	Sony Corp	Household Appliances, Electronics &	3/31/12	6493212.0	-456660.0	13295667.0	2028891.0	177	50328574
BID	Sotheby's	Miscellaneous Consumer Services	12/31/12	768.5	108.3	2575.1	992.8	275	74560434
SFUN	SouFun Holdings Ltd	Internet & Software	12/31/12	430.3	151.8	801.2	186.9	52	27259115
SOR	Source Capital, Inc.	Holding and other Investment Office	12/31/12	7.4	2.8	512.7	511.2	65	943263
SJI	South Jersey Industries, Inc.	Gas Utilities	12/31/12	706.3	91.6	2631.4	736.2	200	20776184
SXE	Southcross Energy Partners LP	Gas Utilities	9/30/12			0.0			
SO	Southern Company (The)	Electric Utilities	12/31/12	16537.0	2415.0	63149.0	19379.0	1134	421662309
SCCO	Southern Copper Corp	Non-Precious Metals	12/31/12	6669.3	1934.6	10383.7	4765.1	465	100443732
LUV	Southwest Airlines Co	Airlines/Air Freight	12/31/12	17088.0	421.0	18596.0	6992.0	607	617101820
SWX	Southwest Gas Corporation	Gas Utilities	12/31/12	1927.8	133.3	4488.1	1310.2	230	37341983
SWN	Southwestern Energy Company	Production & Extraction	12/31/12	2715.0	-707.1	6737.5	3035.9	634	353693471

T54

EARNINGS PER SHARE						P/E RATIO		DIVIDENDS PER SHARE			AV. YLD %	DIV. DECLARED		PRICE RANGE	
QUARTERLY			ANNUAL											2012	
1st	2nd	3rd	2012	2011	2010			2012	2011	2010		AMOUNT	PAYABLE		
-	-	1.66	2.15	5.40	12.0 -	0.0		3.00	4.40	-	19.1	4.257	12/31/12	20.0 -	0.0
-	-	38.95	32.85	26.54	1.3 -	0.0		0.25	0.23	0.16	0.6	-		49.7 -	0.0
-	-	0.21	0.93	0.61	1.18	28.2 -	27.7	1.44	1.44	1.44	5.5	0.360Z	4/30/13	26.2 -	25.8
-	-	0.91	3.15	2.97	2.98	16.2 -	0.0	1.98	1.94	1.90	4.2	0.50750Y	81/16/21	51.2 -	0.0
-	-	-0.09	-0.90	0.79	1.25			0.32	0.32	0.20	2.6	0.080Y	3/29/13	14.4 -	0.0
-	-	1.07	4.10	3.67	3.38	19.9 -	0.0	1.10	1.00	0.84	1.5	0.31250Y	81/16/21	81.6 -	0.0
-	-	0.19	0.69	0.70	0.38	26.2 -	0.0	0.24	0.24	0.24	1.7	0.3750	81/16/21	18.1 -	0.0
-	-	0.87	2.51	2.73	1.76	16.9 -	0.0	0.45	0.30	0.30	1.3	0.30Y	3/21/13	42.3 -	0.0
-	-	-0.30	-0.64	-2.88	-0.18			-	-	-		-		8.9 -	0.0
-1.10	-	-	1.71	2.54	3.02	32.2 -	0.0	1.23	1.05	0.63	2.8	0.3250Y	81/16/21	55.0 -	0.0
-	-	0.21	0.69	-0.27	2.03	17.4 -	0.0	-	-	0.00		0.15GY	9/10/08	12.0 -	0.0
-	-	0.78	4.44	2.49	2.45	14.7 -	0.0	0.48	0.38	0.30	0.8	0.150Y	81/16/21	65.4 -	0.0
-	-	-0.12	-	-0.48	0.09			-	-	-		-		20.0 -	0.0
-	-	0.78	2.95	1.91	11.25	25.4 -	0.0	5.00	-	15.00	7.3	5.7Y	81/16/21	75.0 -	0.0
-	-	0.56	2.29	1.96	1.75	10.1 -	0.0	1.13	0.92	0.38	6.0	0.30	12/14/12	23.1 -	0.0
-	-	0.40	-	2.96	2.73			-	3.06	2.73		1.70	12/21/12	41.6 -	0.0
-	-	-	-	-	-			-	-	-		0.2906G	2/14/13	29.6 -	0.0
-	-	-6.38	-7.31	0.80	1.44			0.52	0.52	0.50	3.0	0.130Y	81/16/21	24.3 -	0.0
-	-	0.01	0.81	-2.04	-1.70	24.9 -	0.0	0.94	-	-	5.5	0.250	2/27/13	20.2 -	0.0
-	-	0.50	2.43	-	-	11.5 -	0.0	0.91	-	-	3.7	0.440Z	5/20/13	28.0 -	0.0
-	-	0.17	1.05	0.71	0.48	13.1 -	0.0	1.50	-	-	15.2	1.5G7Y	12/12/12	13.7 -	0.0
-	-	-0.07	0.52	-0.60	-3.20	99.5 -	0.0	-	-	-		-		51.7 -	0.0
-	-	0.00	-	-0.01	0.00			-	-	-		-		3.4 -	0.0
-	-	1.09	3.48	5.62	2.98	23.0 -	0.0	2.40	1.92	1.56	3.5	0.630Y	81/16/21	80.2 -	0.0
-	-	0.15	0.80	1.01	0.91	33.5 -	0.0	1.53	1.49	1.45	6.8	0.390Z	81/16/21	26.8 -	0.0
-	-	0.23	0.98	0.04	0.75	35.4 -	0.0	-	-	-		-		34.7 -	0.0
-	-	0.66	2.49	2.41	2.17	15.8 -	0.0	0.87	0.84	0.79	2.4	0.220Y	81/16/21	39.4 -	0.0
-	-	-0.17	-0.95	-0.01	-0.11			-	-	-		-		2.7 -	0.0
-	-	0.19	0.70	0.61	0.50	23.9 -	0.0	0.28	0.19	0.16	2.1	0.060Y	81/16/21	16.7 -	0.0
-	-	-0.11	-0.51	-0.33	-1.31			-	-	-		-		40.4 -	0.0
0.49	-	-	1.61	1.03	1.23	15.6 -	0.0	0.94	0.90	0.86	4.4	0.28130	7/2/13	25.2 -	0.0
-	-	-	-	-	-0.04			-	-	-		0.370	1/26/01	7.0 -	0.0
-	-	2.24	6.02	4.14	4.21	28.6 -	0.0	1.56	1.46	1.44	1.1	0.50Y	81/16/21	172.1 -	0.0
-	-	974.00	-5832.00	5076.00				-	0.00	0.00		-		39.5 -	0.0
-	-	0.44	-	1.62	2.09			-	-	1.34		0.390	12/28/12	17.7 -	0.0
-	-	0.31	1.79	-	-	25.1 -	0.0	-	-	-		-		45.0 -	0.0
-	-	-	-	-	-			-	-	-		-		7.5 -	5.7
-	-	-	-	-	-			-	-	-		-		6.3 -	5.3
1.40	-	-	5.04	6.96	4.44	22.3 -	0.0	3.67	3.64	2.30	3.8	-		112.5 -	0.0
-	-	0.43	3.73	2.32	1.91	18.0 -	0.0	0.20	-	-	0.4	0.150	81/16/21	67.0 -	0.0
-	-	-	-0.04	-	-			-	-	-		0.01GZ	4/12/13	22.0 -	18.2
-	-	-	-24.45	-26.07	-46.00			-	-	-		-		22.0 -	17.1
-	-	0.34	1.65	1.55	0.44	24.9 -	0.0	0.35	0.18	-	1.1	0.140	4/12/13	41.1 -	0.0
-	-	0.03	0.43	0.40	0.24	16.3 -	0.0	0.09	0.08	0.07	1.6	0.0250	4/22/13	7.0 -	0.0
-	-	0.21	-	1.61	1.55			-	-	-		-		9.3 -	0.0
-	-	0.84	4.72	3.48	2.10	34.6 -	0.0	4.10	3.50	2.60	2.7	1.04690Z	81/16/21	163.5 -	0.0
-	-	0.27	0.87	1.04	0.58	38.9 -	0.0	0.75	0.47	0.40	2.5	0.125LY	12/28/12	33.9 -	0.0
-	-	-	-2.53	0.93	0.65			0.41	0.32	0.15	3.9	-		15.5 -	0.0
-	-	-	0.27	0.16	0.15	53.1 -	0.0	0.64	1.85	0.26	4.8	0.230	4/12/13	14.3 -	0.0
-	-	-	-	0.13	0.39			-	0.21	0.06		-		48.1 -	0.0
-	-	4.46	6.38	-0.41	0.91	11.4 -	0.0	2.70	0.18	0.03	4.7	0.90Y	3/11/13	72.5 -	0.0
-	-	0.53	1.18	1.11	1.30	23.8 -	0.0	0.71	0.69	0.68	2.9	0.18250Y	81/10/21	25.1 -	0.0
-	-	-2566.00	22223.00	4942.00				-	0.00	0.00		-		18.7 -	0.0
-	-	0.22	0.19	-1.39	2.78	117.1 -	0.0	-	-	-		-		22.3 -	0.0
-	-	0.16	0.57	-5.47	-0.03	14.1 -	0.0	-	-	-		-		8.0 -	0.0
-	-	-0.64	-2.31	-3.17	-3.46			0.18	0.72	0.72	3.8	0.090Y	10/3/11	7.8 -	0.0
-	-	0.09	1.74	7.33	3.45	49.6 -	0.0	1.08	0.55	0.40	1.4	0.40630Z	81/16/21	86.3 -	0.0
-	-	-0.58	-0.83	3.19	3.04			0.10	0.10	0.10	0.2	0.050Y	81/16/21	71.0 -	0.0
-	-	0.15	0.81	0.65	0.69	71.6		1.00	0.79	0.72	1.9	-		58.0 -	0.0
-	-	0.79	3.41	6.57	2.42	21.9 -	0.0	0.72	0.60	0.54	1.3	0.20Y	81/16/21	74.7 -	0.0
-	-	0.58	2.21	3.12	-0.65	12.1 -	0.0	-	-	-		-		26.9 -	0.0
-	-	1.42	4.06	4.05	4.15	24.4 -	0.0	1.88	1.64	1.40	2.2	0.520Y	81/16/21	99.2 -	0.0
-	-	1.26	5.20	4.71	3.19	15.9 -	0.0	1.40	1.30	1.22	2.0	0.380Y	81/16/21	82.7 -	0.0
-	-	0.63	-	2.07	1.45			-	0.76	0.51		-		65.1 -	0.0
-	-	0.29	1.07	0.84	0.61	56.9 -	0.0	-	-	-		-		60.9 -	0.0
-	0.28	-	1.51	2.22	1.20	38.6 -	0.0	0.40	0.30	0.25	0.8	0.1250Y	81/16/21	58.3 -	0.0
-	-	0.18	1.53	1.29	1.49	16.4 -	0.0	0.10	0.10	0.03	0.5	0.0250Y	81/16/21	25.1 -	0.0
-	-	0.57	1.91	2.13	1.96	18.3 -	0.0	1.19	1.15	1.11	3.8	0.30Y	81/16/21	35.0 -	0.0
-	-15.41	-	-455.03	-258.66	-40.66			0.00	0.00	0.00		-		20.8 -	0.0
-	-	-0.48	1.57	2.46	2.34	25.6 -	0.0	0.52	0.23	0.20	1.6	0.2HY	81/16/21	40.2 -	0.0
-	-	0.61	1.85	1.24	0.79	15.4 -	0.0	0.98	1.96	-	5.1	-		28.5 -	0.0
-	-	0.32	0.22	0.48		188.0 -	0.0	3.47	3.00	2.40	6.7	0.750Y	3/15/13	60.1 -	0.0
-	-	0.07	2.97	2.97	2.22	18.8 -	0.0	1.65	1.50	1.36	3.2	0.44250Y	81/16/21	55.8 -	0.0
-	-	-10.09	-	-	-			-	-	-		0.24GH	2/14/13	26.3 -	20.3
-	-	1.11	2.67	2.55	2.36	18.1 -	0.0	1.94	1.87	1.80	4.3	0.490Y	81/16/21	48.4 -	0.0
-	-	0.26	2.28	2.76	1.83	18.4 -	0.0	3.71	2.46	1.68	10.8	0.240	81/16/21	42.0 -	0.0
-	-	0.02	0.56	0.23	0.61	24.1 -	0.0	0.03	0.02	0.02	0.3	0.010Y	81/16/21	13.5 -	0.0
-	-	-0.09	2.86	2.43	2.27	16.7 -	0.0	1.15	1.04	0.99	2.7	0.330Y	6/3/13	47.8 -	0.0
-	-	-0.42	-2.03	1.82	1.73			-	-	-		0.00750	81/16/21	38.9 -	0.0

SYMBOL	COMPANY	NATURE OF BUSINESS	FISCAL YEAR-END	TOTAL REV. $MILL	NET INCOME $MILL	TOTAL ASSETS $MILL	NET STK EQUITY $MILL	NO OF INST	INST. HOLDINGS (SHARES)
SSS	Sovran Self Storage, Inc.	REITs	12/31/12	236.0	55.1	1484.4	728.7	241	29535886
CODE	Spansion Inc	Semiconductors	12/30/12	915.9	24.9	1172.2	561.8	135	54532080
SPA	Sparton Corp.	Electrical Equipment	6/30/12	223.6	9.5	144.6	82.5	67	5588029
SPE	Special Opportunities Fund, Inc.	Holding and other Investment Office	12/31/12	4.9	2.8	162.2	154.7	29	3378779
SE	Spectra Energy Corp	Equipment & Services	12/31/12	5075.0	940.0	30587.0	8972.0	816	485328204
SEP	Spectra Energy Partners LP	Equipment & Services	12/31/12	236.8	193.5	2805.7	-	128	35298226
SPB	Spectrum Brands Holdings Inc	Household & Personal Products	9/30/12	3252.4	48.6	3751.6	989.1		
TRK	Speedway Motorsports, Inc.	Sporting & Recreational	12/31/12	490.2	42.1	1877.1	857.9	102	12235029
SPR	Spirit AeroSystems Holdings Inc	Aerospace	12/31/12	5397.7	34.8	5415.3	1996.4	290	123594759
SRC	Spirit Realty Capital Inc	REITs	12/31/12	282.7	-76.2	3247.7	1253.4	9	1280994
S	Sprint Nextel Corp	Services	12/31/12	35345.0	-4326.0	51570.0	7087.0	725	2751681700
SPW	SPX Corp.	Industrial Machinery & Equipment	12/31/12	5100.2	259.2	7130.1	2268.7	376	43825934
JOE	St. Joe Co. (The)	Property, Real Estate & Developmen	12/31/12	139.4	6.0	645.5	552.0	222	99427183
STJ	St. Jude Medical, Inc.	Medical Instruments & Equipment	12/29/12	5503.0	752.0	9271.0	4094.0	702	284202415
STAG	STAG Industrial Inc.	REITs	12/31/12	85.5	-6.5	1005.1	427.6	142	31184998
SSI	Stage Stores Inc.	Retail - Apparel and Accessories	2/2/13	1645.8	38.2	794.9	464.9	217	34700699
SFG	Stancorp Financial Group Inc	Life & Health	12/31/12	2898.4	138.5	19791.3	2169.0	239	39097239
SMP	Standard Motor Products, Inc.	Auto Parts	12/31/12	948.9	41.4	576.6	307.6	162	15699507
SPF	Standard Pacific Corp.	Builders	12/31/12	1258.3	531.4	3113.1	1255.8	245	140016851
SR	Standard Register Co.	Printing	12/30/12	602.0	-9.1	259.9	-126.9	49	9537566
SXI	Standex International Corp.	Industrial Machinery & Equipment	6/30/12	634.6	30.9	479.8	242.9	163	11506864
SWK	Stanley Black & Decker, Inc.	Industrial Machinery & Equipment	12/29/12	10190.5	883.8	15844.0	6667.1	626	149683532
STN	Stantec Inc	Business Services	12/31/12	1556.4	120.9	1468.6	727.1	1	6402
SGU	Star Gas Partners L.P.	Gas Utilities	9/30/12	1497.6	26.0	639.3	-	47	9455866
SCX	Starrett (L.S.) Co.	Industrial Machinery & Equipment	6/30/12	260.1	0.9	252.2	127.8	43	3108216
SRT	Startek, Inc.	Business Services	12/31/12	198.1	-10.5	93.1	66.3	49	6456854
HOT	Starwood Hotels & Resorts Worldwi	Hotels, Restaurants & Travel	12/31/12	6321.0	562.0	8861.0	3137.0	589	203604021
STWD	Starwood Property Trust Inc.	REITs	12/31/12	307.0	201.2	4324.4	2719.3	269	113794061
STT	State Street Corp.	Banking	12/31/12	10125.0	2061.0	222582.0	20869.0	942	423643580
STO	Statoil ASA	Refining & Marketing	12/31/12	723400.0	68900.0	784400.0	319200.0	317	66407229
SCS	Steelcase, Inc.	Office Equipment & Furniture	2/24/12	2749.5	56.7	1701.0	708.6	230	76128056
LVB	Steinway Musical Instruments Inc.	Leisure Equipment	12/31/12	353.7	13.5	425.7	241.8	77	8495527
SCM	Stellus Capital Investment Corp	Finance Intermediaries & Services	12/31/12	3.7	1.3	262.5	173.8		
SCL	Stepan Co.	Specialty Chemicals	12/31/12	1803.7	79.4	985.5	479.0	165	13273699
STE	Steris Corp.	Medical Instruments & Equipment	3/31/12	1406.8	136.1	1405.7	821.4	298	61955158
STL	Sterling Bancorp (N.Y.)	Banking	12/31/12	145.7	20.0	2750.8	228.1	132	23901985
SLT	Sterlite Industries (India) Ltd.	Non-Precious Metals	3/31/12	412063.0	38998.0	842889.0	445477.0	137	63828803
STC	Stewart Information Services Corp.	General Insurance	12/31/12	1910.4	109.2	1291.2	568.8	186	22316127
SF	Stifel Financial Corp.	Finance Intermediaries & Services	12/31/12	1646.0	138.6	6966.1	1494.7	232	45771999
SWC	Stillwater Mining Co.	Precious Metals	12/31/12	800.2	55.0	1890.8	1080.8	239	104793015
STM	STMicroelectronics N.V.	Semiconductors	12/31/12	8493.0	-1158.0	10434.0	6225.0	134	33058168
SGY	Stone Energy Corp.	Production & Extraction	12/31/12	951.5	149.4	2776.4	872.1	267	48789129
EDF	Stone Harbor Emerging Markets Inc	Holding and other Investment Office	11/30/12	41.0	34.4	523.3	370.9		
STON	StoneMor Partners L P	Miscellaneous Consumer Services	12/31/12	242.6	-3.0	1343.7		67	2005139
SRI	Stoneridge Inc.	Auto Parts	12/31/12	938.5	5.4	592.7	149.8	104	21619376
STRI	STR Holdings Inc.	Semiconductors	12/31/12	95.3	-207.3	147.2	127.4	99	38435096
SGL	Strategic Global Income Fund, Inc.	Holding and other Investment Office	11/30/12	10.5	8.1	258.6	213.6	40	2311436
BEE	Strategic Hotels & Resorts, Inc.	REITs	12/31/12	808.3	-55.3	2406.4	707.3	219	162100859
SYK	Stryker Corp.	Medical Instruments & Equipment	12/31/12	8657.0	1298.0	13206.0	8597.0	1047	276936161
RGR	Sturm, Ruger & Co., Inc.	Leisure Equipment	12/31/12	491.8	70.6	174.5	95.0	229	18941932
SPH	Suburban Propane Partners L.P.	Gas Utilities	9/29/12	1063.5	1.9	2884.4	-	218	17350543
SPH	Suburban Propane Partners L.P.	Gas Utilities	9/29/12	1063.5	1.9	2884.4	-	218	17350543
SMFG	Sumitomo Mitsui Financial Group In	Banking	3/31/12	3973072.0	518536.0	143040672.0	5210400.0		
INN	Summit Hotel Properties Inc	REITs	12/31/12	189.5	-1.1	810.8	436.8	122	42352766
SMLP	Summit Midstream Partners LP	Production & Extraction	12/31/12	165.5	41.7	1063.5		32	14217878
SUI	Sun Communities, Inc.	REITs	12/31/12	339.6	8.0	1754.1	192.5	185	25068225
SLF	Sun Life Financial Inc	Life & Health	12/31/12	17559.0	4602.0	225782.0	16751.0	252	256881623
FGF	SunAmerica Focused Alpha Growth	Holding and other Investment Office	12/31/11	2.4	-1.4	266.4	266.0	5	974520
FGI	SunAmerica Focused Alpha Large-	Holding and other Investment Office	12/31/11	2.0	-0.1	120.3	120.0	5	607196
SXC	SunCoke Energy Inc	Mining	12/31/12	1914.1	98.8	2011.0	539.1	216	60911889
SXCP	SunCoke Energy Partners LP	Metal Products	12/31/12	-0.0	-0.0	0.0	-0.0		
SU	Suncor Energy Inc.	Refining & Marketing	12/31/12	38616.0	2783.0	76449.0	39223.0	675	871407487
SXL	Sunoco Logistics Partners L.P.	Equipment & Services	12/31/12	3194.0	139.0	10361.0	-	226	48506365
SHO	Sunstone Hotel Investors Inc	REITs	12/31/12	829.1	49.6	3136.7	1563.9	226	144333342
STP	Suntech Power Holdings Co Ltd	Semiconductors	12/31/11	3146.6	-1018.6	4537.3	946.4	145	31875405
STI 15	SunTrust Bank, Middle Georgia, N.	Banking							
STI	SunTrust Banks, Inc.	Banking	12/31/12	11240.0	1958.0	173442.0	20985.0	717	483450466
SPN	Superior Energy Services, Inc.	Equipment & Services	12/31/12	4568.1	365.9	7802.9	4231.1	418	151090999
SUP	Superior Industries International, Inc	Auto Parts	12/31/12	821.5	30.9	599.6	466.9	155	20237555
SVU	Supervalu Inc.	Retail - Food & Beverage, Drug & To	2/25/12	36100.0	-1040.0	12053.0	21.0	381	209652233
SUSS	Susser Holdings Corp	Retail - Food & Beverage, Drug & To	12/30/12	5818.1	46.7	1571.4	389.5	182	18152615
SUSP	Susser Petroleum Partners LP	Services	12/31/12	4277.3	17.6	355.8	78.3	39	6456629
SLD	Sutherland Asset Management Cor	REITs							
SFY	Swift Energy Company	Production & Extraction	12/31/12	557.3	20.9	2444.1	1036.9	230	48682722
SWFT	Swift Transportation Co	Trucking	12/31/12	3493.2	114.6	2632.2	229.9	163	84954636
SWZ	Swiss Helvetia Fund, Inc. (The)	Holding and other Investment Office	12/31/12	10.4	5.0	402.9	402.3	66	14226500
SWS	SWS Group, Inc.	Finance Intermediaries & Services	6/29/12	289.7	-4.7	3546.8	355.7	137	24004899
SYA	Symetra Financial Corp	Life & Health	12/31/12	2101.2	205.4	29460.9	3630.1	169	114976176
SMA	Symmetry Medical Inc.	Medical Instruments & Equipment	12/31/12	410.5	9.1	605.3	314.7	142	39216883
SYT	Syngenta AG	Agricultural Chemicals	12/31/12	14202.0	1872.0	19401.0	8745.0	310	20971591

EARNINGS PER SHARE						P/E RATIO		DIVIDENDS PER SHARE			AV. YLD %	DIV. DECLARED		PRICE RANGE 2012	
QUARTERLY			ANNUAL												
1st	2nd	3rd	2012	2011	2010			2012	2011	2010	%	AMOUNT	PAYABLE	2012	
		0.63	1.87	1.10	1.48	35.8 -	0.0	1.80	1.80	1.80	3.1	0.480Z	4/26/13	67.0 -	0.0
	0.08	0.41	-0.91	-1.60		34.4 -	0.0							14.1 -	0.0
	0.43		0.93	0.73	0.75	16.7 -	0.0					0.09070	10/5/05	15.5 -	0.0
			0.34	0.22	0.04	49.6 -	0.0	0.95	0.54	0.03	6.2	0.35650	3/28/13	16.9 -	0.0
		0.27	1.44	1.81	1.61	21.9 -	0.0	1.15	1.06	1.00	4.0	0.3050Y	81/16/21	31.6 -	0.0
		0.40	1.69	1.63	1.70	23.6 -	0.0	1.93	1.85	1.70	6.0	0.4950	2/14/13	40.0 -	0.0
-0.26			0.91	-1.47	-5.28	62.2 -	0.0	1.00			2.4	0.250Y	3/12/13	56.6 -	0.0
		0.26	1.02	-0.16	1.06	18.7 -	0.0	0.60	0.40	0.40	3.6	0.150Y	3/15/13	19.1 -	0.0
		-0.94	0.24	1.35	1.55	107.7 -	0.0							25.9 -	0.0
		-1.70	-1.85	-2.47	-3.35			0.33			1.9	0.31250Z	4/16/13	20.2 -	0.0
		-0.26	-1.44	-0.96	-1.16							0.0250Y	81/16/21	6.2 -	0.0
		1.16	5.18	3.54	4.08	15.8 -	0.0	1.00	1.00	1.00	1.4	0.250Y	81/16/21	82.0 -	0.0
		0.17	0.07	-3.58	-0.39	348.3 -	0.0					0.160Y	81/16/21	24.4 -	0.0
		0.56	2.39	2.52	2.75	18.4 -	0.0	0.92	0.84		2.4	0.250Y	81/16/21	43.9 -	0.0
		-0.18	-0.51	-0.44				1.07	0.73		6.4	0.56250Z	4/1/13	22.1 -	0.0
		-0.28	0.92	0.99	0.75	29.2 -	0.0	0.33	0.25	0.20	1.6	0.10Y	3/20/13	26.8 -	0.0
		1.01	3.12	3.09	4.02	13.7 -	0.0	0.93	0.89	0.86	2.6	0.930Y	3/1/13	42.8 -	0.0
		0.74	1.79	2.70	0.97	15.7 -	0.0	0.36	0.28	0.20	2.0	0.110Y	3/1/13	28.1 -	0.0
		0.05	1.44	-0.05	-0.05	6.3 -	0.0					0.040Y	8/23/07	9.1 -	0.0
		-0.09	-0.31	-3.02	0.09			0.05	0.20	0.20	7.1	0.050Y	3/9/12	1.3 -	0.0
	0.86		2.42	2.77	2.26	23.7 -	0.0	0.27	0.23	0.20	0.6	0.080Y	2/25/13	57.3 -	0.0
		0.69	5.30	3.97	1.32	15.4 -	0.0	1.80	1.64	1.34	2.5	0.490Y	81/16/21	81.6 -	0.0
		0.74	2.64	0.28	2.06	17.0 -	0.0	0.60			1.7	0.1650	4/18/13	44.8 -	0.0
0.15			0.40	0.35	0.38	12.3 -	0.0	0.31	0.30	0.28	7.4	0.07750	2/5/13	4.9 -	0.0
	0.07		0.13	1.02	-0.45	102.8 -	0.0	0.40	0.32	0.30	3.5	0.10Y	4/1/13	13.4 -	0.0
		-0.08	-0.69	-1.75	-1.30							0.250Y	11/27/06	5.9 -	0.0
		0.87	2.86	2.51	2.51	22.3 -	0.0	1.25	0.50	0.30	2.2	1.250Y	81/16/21	63.7 -	0.0
		0.43	1.76	1.38	1.14	16.2 -	0.0	1.86	1.74	1.20	8.1	0.440Z	4/15/13	28.5 -	0.0
		1.36	4.20	3.79	3.09	14.4 -	0.0	0.96	0.72	0.04	2.1	0.260Y	81/16/21	60.5 -	0.0
		4.51	21.60	24.70	11.94	1.3 -	0.0	0.18	0.21	0.14	0.7			27.5 -	0.0
		0.18	0.43	0.15	-0.10	35.8 -	0.0	0.24	0.16	0.20	2.3	0.10Y	81/16/21	15.4 -	0.0
		0.33	1.08	0.13	0.68	24.0 -	0.0					3.7	3/9/07	26.0 -	0.0
			0.11			152.1 -	131.9	0.18			1.2	0.340	3/28/13	16.7 -	14.5
		0.89	3.49	6.42	5.90	18.4 -	0.0	0.58	0.53	0.49	1.2	0.160Y	81/16/21	64.3 -	0.0
		0.82	2.31	0.85	2.16	18.0 -	0.0	0.66	0.56	2.44	1.9	0.190Y	81/16/21	41.6 -	0.0
		0.17	0.65	0.51	0.18	16.3 -	0.0	0.36	0.36	0.36	3.7	0.090Y	3/31/13	10.6 -	0.0
			11.60	13.87	12.03	0.8 -	0.0	0.00	0.00	0.00	0.0			9.0 -	0.0
		1.45	4.61	0.12	-0.69	6.4 -	0.0	0.10	0.05	0.05	0.5	0.10Y	12/28/13	29.7 -	0.0
		0.60	2.20	1.33	0.03	17.8 -	0.0					0.4255GHZ	4/15/13	39.3 -	0.0
		0.11	0.46	1.30	0.51	31.8 -	0.0							14.6 -	0.0
		-0.54	-1.31	0.72	0.94			0.34	0.31	0.20	5.4			9.1 -	0.0
		0.48	3.03	3.97	1.99	9.6 -	0.0							29.1 -	0.0
			2.20	1.99		12.0 -	0.0	2.16	1.80		8.9	0.180	4/25/13	26.5 -	0.0
		0.05	-0.15	-0.50	-0.10			2.35	2.33	2.23	9.7	0.590	2/14/13	28.1 -	0.0
		0.02	0.20	2.00	0.44	50.5 -	0.0							10.1 -	0.0
		0.02	-5.02	-0.03	1.17									5.0 -	0.0
			0.44	0.46	0.51	25.8 -	0.0	0.97	1.77	0.88	9.0	0.05730	4/30/13	11.4 -	0.0
		-0.05	-0.40	-0.13	-2.13							0.53130Z	4/1/13	8.5 -	0.0
		0.92	3.39	3.45	3.19	19.7 -	0.0	0.90	0.75	0.63	1.6	0.2650Y	81/16/21	66.8 -	0.0
		0.88	3.60	2.09	1.46	16.6 -	0.0	5.79	0.43	0.33	12.2	0.4040Y	3/22/13	59.8 -	0.0
1.04			0.05	3.22	3.24	765.4 -	0.0	3.41	3.41	3.35	124.7	0.8750	81/16/21	38.3 -	0.0
1.04			0.05	3.22	3.24	907.0 -	0.0	3.41	3.41	3.35	8.4	0.8750	81/16/21	45.4 -	0.0
	-157.42		-373.99	336.78	244.18	0.0 -	0.0							8.7 -	0.0
		0.01	-0.17	-0.12				0.45	0.28		5.2	0.432GHZ	2/28/13	10.5 -	0.0
			0.35			79.3 -	0.0					0.41GH	2/14/13	27.7 -	0.0
		-0.02	0.18	-0.05	-0.15	274.1 -	0.0	2.52	3.15	2.52	5.8	0.44310Z	4/15/13	49.3 -	0.0
		0.64	2.59	-0.52	2.39	11.6 -	0.0	1.44	1.44	1.44	5.8	0.26560	3/28/13	30.0 -	0.0
				-0.10	0.01				0.48	0.20		0.330	12/29/11		
				-0.01	0.06				0.73	0.20		0.580	12/29/11		
		0.45	1.40	0.07	1.99	12.5 -	0.0							17.5 -	0.0
														20.9 -	18.3
		1.01	1.79	2.67	2.43	19.7 -	0.0	0.50	0.43	0.40	1.6	0.130	3/25/13	35.3 -	0.0
		1.09	1.10	2.54	3.11	61.6 -	0.0	1.84	1.61	1.50	3.9	0.5450	81/16/21	67.8 -	0.0
		0.23	0.14	0.45	0.18	87.9 -	0.0					0.50Z	4/15/13	12.3 -	0.0
-0.74				-5.64	1.30									3.0 -	0.0
		1.98	3.59	0.94	-0.18	8.4 -	0.0	0.20	0.12	0.04	0.8	0.3468GY	81/16/21	30.3 -	0.0
		0.59	2.42	1.76	1.03	11.3 -	0.0							27.3 -	0.0
		0.55	1.13	2.46	1.93	19.4 -	0.0	1.28	0.48	0.64	7.1	0.64HY	12/28/12	21.9 -	0.0
		0.08	-4.91	-7.13	1.85			0.26	0.35	0.61	7.3	0.08750Y	81/16/21	6.6 -	0.0
		0.32	2.19	2.68	0.05	23.4 -	0.0							51.2 -	0.0
		0.03	0.42			78.2 -	0.0	0.03			0.1	0.43750	3/1/13	32.8 -	0.0
														30.4 -	0.0
		0.07	0.48	2.27	1.18	63.4 -	0.0							15.0 -	0.0
		0.20	0.82	0.65	-1.98	18.3 -	0.0								
		0.16	0.17	0.09		77.6 -	0.0	0.07	1.98	0.49	0.6	0.0530	12/28/12	12.4 -	0.0
	0.09		-0.14	-0.71	-0.10				0.12	0.36		0.010Y	7/1/11	6.8 -	0.0
		0.40	1.49	1.45	1.48	9.4 -	0.0	0.28	0.23	0.15	2.3	0.080Y	3/29/13	14.0 -	0.0
		0.10	0.25	0.08	0.39	45.8 -	0.0							11.4 -	0.0
			20.32	17.31	14.99	4.3 -	0.0	1.73	1.58	1.09	2.3			87.5 -	0.0

SYMBOL	COMPANY	NATURE OF BUSINESS	FISCAL YEAR-END	TOTAL REV. $MILL	NET INCOME $MILL	TOTAL ASSETS $MILL	NET STK EQUITY $MILL	NO OF INST	INST. HOLDINGS (SHARES)
SNX	Synnex Corp	IT Services	11/30/12	10285.5	151.4	2963.3	1319.0	221	30978775
SNV	Synovus Financial Corp.	Banking	12/31/12	1313.4	830.2	26760.0	3569.4	353	631355521
SYY	Sysco Corp.	Retail - Food & Beverage, Drug & To	6/30/12	42380.9	1121.6	12095.0	4685.0	1118	551086955
SYX	Systemax, Inc.	Retail - Appliances and Electronics	12/31/12	3544.6	-8.3	962.3	446.3	95	10119330
TAHO	Tahoe Resources Inc.	Precious Metals	12/31/12	-	-93.5	852.9	831.3	-	-
TWN	Taiwan Fund, Inc. (The)	Holding and other Investment Office	8/31/12	5.0	0.4	155.2	154.6	35	5296300
TSM	Taiwan Semiconductor Manufacturi	Semiconductors	12/31/12	506248.6	166158.8	955034.6	723197.7	541	1091564322
XRS	TAL Education Group	Educational Services	2/29/12	177.5	24.3	294.7	190.1	29	16896271
TAL	Tal International Group Inc	Miscellaneous Transportation Servic	12/31/12	589.2	130.1	3701.2	616.0	180	25223075
TLM	Talisman Energy, Inc.	Production & Extraction	12/31/12	7312.0	132.0	21858.0	9910.0	323	676154135
SKT	Tanger Factory Outlet Centers, Inc.	REITs	12/31/12	357.0	53.2	1672.4	482.6	293	89120313
TAOM	Taomee Holdings Ltd.	Entertainment	12/31/11	45.4	19.5	134.5	103.2	6	111385
TRGP	Targa Resources Corp	Equipment & Services	12/31/12	5885.7	38.1	5105.0	144.1	168	33584658
NGLS	Targa Resources Partners LP	Equipment & Services	12/31/12	5883.6	174.6	5025.7	-	194	53758095
TGT	Target Corp	Retail - General Merchandise/Depart	2/2/13	73301.0	2999.0	48163.0	16558.0	1327	585250859
TARO	Taro Pharmaceutical Industries Ltd.	Pharmaceuticals	3/31/12	145.1	47.3	856.4	619.0	29	2190882
TCL	Tata Communications Ltd	Services	3/31/12	139885.0	3312.0	246981.0	37546.0	1	0
TTM	Tata Motors Ltd	Autos- Manufacturing	3/31/12	1664852.9	115659.1	1429212.6	328412.6	268	71599514
TCO	Taubman Centers, Inc.	REITs	12/31/12	748.0	106.2	3268.5	-255.6	330	69635436
TMHC	Taylor Morrison Home Corp	Builders	12/31/12	-	-	0.1	0.0	-	-
TCP	TC PipeLines, LP	Equipment & Services	12/31/12	194.0	137.0	1998.0	-	154	24700634
TCB	TCF Financial Corp.	Banking	12/31/12	1375.0	-212.9	18225.9	1863.4	279	159612682
TSI	TCW Strategic Income Fund Inc	Holding and other Investment Office	12/31/12	23.7	20.5	290.0	266.8	57	6363165
AMTD	TD Ameritrade Holding Corp	Finance Intermediaries & Services	9/30/12	2647.0	586.0	19513.0	4425.0	370	223736117
TEL	TE Connectivity Ltd	Electrical Equipment	9/28/12	13282.0	1112.0	19306.0	7971.0	524	387013055
TMH	Team Health Holdings Inc	Business Services	12/31/12	2069.0	63.8	1199.4	116.9	185	69316976
TISI	Team, Inc.	Miscellaneous Consumer Services	5/31/12	623.7	32.9	403.8	239.9	145	21166952
TCK	Teck Resources Ltd	Mining	12/31/12	10343.0	811.0	34617.0	17801.0	336	330836875
TE	TECO Energy Inc.	Electric Utilities	12/31/12	2996.6	212.7	7356.5	2291.8	456	141108374
TK	Teekay Corp	Equipment & Services	12/31/11	1953.8	-368.9	11131.4	1429.7	160	30896764
TGP	Teekay LNG Partners LP	Equipment & Services	12/31/11	380.0	97.4	3582.2	-	155	30585666
TOO	Teekay Offshore Partners L.P.	Equipment & Services	12/31/11	949.1	-96.9	3144.7	-	110	41977912
TNK	Teekay Tankers Ltd	Equipment & Services	12/31/11	121.0	-9.1	881.9	489.4	110	26449601
TRC	Tejon Ranch Co.	Property, Real Estate & Developmen	12/31/12	47.1	4.3	327.9	268.6	111	14762413
TEO	Telecom Argentina SA	Services	12/31/11	18525.0	2422.0	14825.0	7786.0	89	13969699
TI	Telecom Italia SPA	Radio & Television	12/31/11	30825.0	-4726.0	83859.0	22791.0	121	46449035
TDY	Teledyne Technologies, Inc.	Electronic Instruments & Related Pro	12/30/12	2127.3	164.1	2406.4	1147.8	239	34893548
TFX	Teleflex Incorporated	Medical Instruments & Equipment	12/31/12	1551.0	-190.1	3739.5	1778.9	344	41290489
VIV	Telefonica Brasil SA	Services	12/31/12	33931.4	4453.6	70254.7	44751.6	203	83014016
TEF	Telefonica, S.A.	Services	12/31/12	62356.0	3928.0	129773.0	20461.0	323	82067900
TMX	Telefonos de Mexico SAB de CV	Services	12/31/11	112066.1	14581.7	160761.0	49113.4	53	6080085
TDS	Telephone & Data Systems, Inc.	Services	12/31/12	5345.3	81.9	8623.9	4012.4	299	87450554
TU	TELUS Corp.	Services	12/31/12	10852.0	1318.0	20445.0	7686.0	219	104877878
TDF	Templeton Dragon Fund, Inc.	Holding and other Investment Office	12/31/12	35.6	20.9	1190.7	1174.2	97	18571874
EMF	Templeton Emerging Markets Fund	Holding and other Investment Office	8/31/12	10.1	5.1	350.8	348.0	62	3864566
TEI	Templeton Emerging Markets Inco	Holding and other Investment Office	8/31/12	59.8	51.3	764.1	759.0	82	6895529
GIM	Templeton Global Income Fund (DE	Holding and other Investment Office	8/31/12	64.1	55.1	1249.0	1209.3	138	22442777
TRF	Templeton Russia and East Europe	Holding and other Investment Office	3/31/12	2.0	0.2	102.4	102.2	35	1041113
TPX	Tempur-Pedic International Inc	Furniture	12/31/12	1402.9	106.8	1313.0	22.3	317	67019352
TS	Tenaris SA	Equipment & Services	12/31/11	9972.5	1331.2	14863.6	10506.2	241	141305184
THC	Tenet Healthcare Corp.	Hospitals & Health Care Facilities	12/31/12	9119.0	133.0	9044.0	1143.0	383	170518667
TNC	Tennant Co.	Industrial Machinery & Equipment	12/31/12	739.0	41.6	420.8	235.1	165	15932416
TEN	Tenneco Inc	Auto Parts	12/31/12	7363.0	275.0	3608.0	246.0	267	58099485
TVE	Tennessee Valley Authority	Electric Utilities	9/30/12	11220.0	60.0	47334.0	5326.0	-	-
TDC	Teradata Corp (DE)	IT Services	12/31/12	2665.0	419.0	3066.0	1779.0	615	151750231
TER	Teradyne, Inc.	Semiconductors	12/31/12	1656.8	217.0	2429.3	1778.4	426	218113144
TEX	Terex Corp.	Industrial Machinery & Equipment	12/31/12	7348.4	105.8	6746.2	2007.7	418	112972109
TX	Ternium S A	Non-Precious Metals	12/31/11	9157.2	513.5	10746.6	5756.4	114	38997251
TNH	Terra Nitrogen Co., L.P.	Agricultural Chemicals	12/31/12	780.1	560.8	298.6	-	117	1675937
TRNO	Terreno Realty Corp	REITs	12/31/12	31.2	4.1	445.3	255.3	82	12885483
TSO	Tesoro Corporation	Refining & Marketing	12/31/12	32974.0	743.0	10702.0	4251.0	489	143107682
TLLP	Tesoro Logistics LP	Production & Extraction	12/31/12	156.8	55.5	363.2	8.9	71	16442873
TTI	TETRA Technologies, Inc.	Equipment & Services	12/31/12	880.8	18.8	1261.8	551.1	203	80604072
TEVA	Teva Pharmaceutical Industries Ltd	Pharmaceuticals	12/31/12	20317.0	1963.0	50609.0	22768.0	1122	458975038
TXI	Texas Industries Inc.	Construction Materials	5/31/12	647.0	7.5	1576.9	696.3	180	27150364
TPL	Texas Pacific Land Trust	Property, Real Estate & Developmen	12/31/12	32.6	19.6	21.2	15.6	55	4812568
TGH	Textainer Group Holdings Ltd	Shipping	12/31/12	487.1	206.9	3476.1	1007.5	152	15655618
TXT 04	Textron Financial Corp	Credit & Lending	1/1/11	207.0	-230.0	4570.0	501.0	-	-
TXT	Textron Inc.	Aerospace	12/29/12	12237.0	589.0	13033.0	2991.0	509	229972605
TTF	Thai Fund, Inc. (The)	Holding and other Investment Office	12/31/12	8.8	4.8	352.1	343.5	42	9077054
GPS	The Gap, Inc.	Retail - Apparel and Accessories	2/2/13	15651.0	1135.0	7470.0	2894.0	608	302148426
TGX	Theragenics Corp.	Medical Instruments & Equipment	12/31/12	82.6	2.1	105.7	76.9	50	17352993
TMO	Thermo Fisher Scientific Inc	Biotechnology	12/31/12	12509.9	1177.9	27444.6	15464.7	993	357882502
THR	Thermon Group Holdings Inc	Electrical Equipment	3/31/12	270.5	12.0	425.6	192.5	125	27717256
TC	Thompson Creek Metals Co., Inc.	Non-Precious Metals	12/31/12	401.4	-546.3	3410.2	1401.9	155	76649815
TRI	Thomson Reuters Corp	Publishing	12/31/12	13278.0	2070.0	32572.0	17145.0	305	261135728
THO	Thor Industries, Inc.	Autos- Manufacturing	7/31/12	3084.7	121.7	1243.1	850.8	300	48417435
TDW	Tidewater Inc.	Equipment & Services	3/31/12	1067.0	87.4	4061.6	2526.4	345	55373397
TIF	Tiffany & Co.	Retail - Specialty	1/31/13	3794.2	416.2	4630.8	2598.7	630	128335078
TLYS	Tillys, Inc.	Retail - Apparel and Accessories	2/2/13	467.3	23.9	205.4	117.3	97	8743048

T58

QUARTERLY 1st	2nd	3rd	ANNUAL 2012	2011	2010	P/E RATIO	·	DIV 2012	2011	2010	AV. YLD %	DIV AMOUNT	PAYABLE	PRICE RANGE 2012	·
0.88	-	-	3.99	4.08	3.58	10.2 -	0.0	-	-	-	-	-	-	40.9 -	0.0
-	-	0.02	0.85	-0.15	-1.24	3.4 -	0.0	0.04	0.04	0.04	1.8	0.010Y	81/16/21	2.9 -	0.0
-	0.38	-	1.90	1.96	1.99	18.5 -	0.0	0.80	1.03	0.99	2.6	0.280Y	81/16/21	35.2 -	0.0
-	-	0.38	-0.22	1.47	1.13			0.25	-	-	2.1	0.257	12/21/12	17.7 -	0.0
-	-	-0.15	-0.65	-0.48	-0.12			-	-	-	-	-	-	22.8 -	0.0
-	-	-	0.02	0.14	0.16	844.5 -	0.0	0.56	0.08	0.07	3.6	0.5605C	1/9/12	16.9 -	0.0
-	-	-	6.41	5.18	6.23	3.0 -	0.0	0.01	0.01	0.01	0.1	-	-	19.1 -	0.0
0.03	-	-	0.16	0.18	0.11	74.4 -	0.0	-	-	-	-	-	-	11.9 -	0.0
-	-	0.93	3.87	3.34	1.88	12.0 -	0.0	2.35	1.99	1.30	6.4	0.640	3/28/13	46.4 -	0.0
-	-	-0.71	0.01	0.38	0.93	1500.0 -	0.0	0.27	0.27	0.24	2.2	0.26250	4/1/13	15.0 -	0.0
-	-	0.16	0.57	0.52	0.32	64.0 -	0.0	0.83	0.79	0.77	2.5	0.2250Z	81/16/21	36.5 -	0.0
-	-	0.00	-	0.03	0.04			-	-	-	-	-	-	5.7 -	0.0
-	-	0.21	0.91	0.74	-30.94	74.7 -	0.0	1.52	0.93	-	3.0	0.45750Y	81/16/21	68.0 -	0.0
-	-	0.08	1.20	1.98	0.92	38.4 -	0.0	2.53	2.26	2.10	6.4	0.680	2/14/13	46.0 -	0.0
-	-	0.96	4.28	4.00	3.30	16.1 -	0.0	1.10	0.84	0.66	1.8	0.360Y	81/16/21	69.0 -	0.0
1.41	-	-	1.06	4.11	1.53	56.0 -	0.0	-	-	-	-	-	-	59.3 -	0.0
-	-9.62	-	11.62	-28.40	-13.46	0.8 -	0.0	0.00	-	0.00	0.0	-	-	9.8 -	0.0
-	-	10.24	36.00	4.90	2.88	0.9 -	0.0	0.01	0.01	0.00	0.0	-	-	30.7 -	0.0
-	-	0.35	-1.37	3.03	0.86	60.1 -	0.0	1.85	1.76	1.87	2.4	0.50Z	81/16/21	82.3 -	0.0
-	-	0.64	2.51	3.02	2.91	19.3 -	0.0	3.10	3.04	2.94	7.1	0.780	81/16/21	48.5 -	0.0
-	-	0.06	-1.37	0.71	1.05			0.20	0.20	0.20	1.7	0.050Y	81/16/21	15.0 -	0.0
-	-	-	0.43	0.54	0.90	13.8 -	0.0	0.55	0.89	0.62	10.0	0.0980	4/12/13	5.9 -	0.0
0.27	-	-	1.06	1.11	1.00	20.2 -	0.0	0.24	0.20	-	1.4	0.090Y	81/16/21	21.4 -	0.0
0.65	-	-	2.59	2.81	2.41	16.4 -	0.0	0.78	0.68	0.64	2.2	0.210Y	81/16/21	42.5 -	0.0
-	-	0.30	0.93	0.98	0.21	39.8 -	0.0	-	-	-	-	-	-	37.0 -	0.0
-	-	-0.03	1.59	1.32	0.63	29.2 -	0.0	-	-	-	-	0.010	3/1/93	46.5 -	0.0
-	-	0.31	1.38	4.50	3.14	27.8 -	0.0	0.85	0.70	0.50	2.6	0.450	1/2/13	38.4 -	0.0
-	-	0.20	0.99	1.27	1.11	18.6 -	0.0	0.88	0.85	0.81	5.1	0.220Y	81/16/21	18.4 -	0.0
-	-	-0.29	-	-5.25	-3.67			-	1.26	1.26	-	0.31620	81/16/21	36.7 -	0.0
-	-	-	1.33	1.46				-	-	-	-	0.6750	2/14/13	42.4 -	0.0
-	-	-	-1.74	1.22				-	1.98	1.88	-	0.51250	2/14/13	30.2 -	0.0
-	-	-0.12	-	-0.15	0.37			-	0.83	1.28	-	0.030	3/11/13	6.2 -	0.0
-	-	0.20	0.22	0.80	0.22	140.4 -	0.0	-	-	-	-	0.0250	12/10/99	30.9 -	0.0
-	-	0.63	-	-				-	-	-	-	-	-	17.6 -	0.0
-	-	-	-	-0.24	0.16			-	1.25	0.81	-	-	-	12.0 -	0.0
-	-	1.14	4.39	6.84	3.27	17.9 -	0.0	-	-	-	-	-	-	78.5 -	0.0
-	-	0.52	-4.65	7.92	4.99			1.36	1.36	1.36	2.0	0.340Y	81/16/21	84.5 -	0.0
-	-	-	3.72	4.40	4.45	8.4 -	0.0	0.72	1.91	1.32	3.0	-	-	31.2 -	0.0
-	-	-	0.87	1.18	2.21	18.9 -	0.0	1.32	3.04	2.31	10.0	-	-	16.5 -	0.0
-	-	-	1.62	1.70				-	-	-	-	-	-	26.2 -	0.0
-	-	0.27	0.75	1.83	1.36	34.9 -	0.0	0.49	0.47	0.45	2.1	0.36720Z	81/16/21	71.5 -	0.0
-	-	1.07	4.03	3.74	3.27	17.7 -	0.0	2.44	2.21	2.00	4.0	0.640	4/1/13	21.0 -	0.0
-	-	-	0.55	0.49	0.34	54.6 -	0.0	1.47	2.24	1.77	5.5	0.1151C	12/31/12	18.1 -	0.0
-	-	-	0.28	0.22	0.15	74.9 -	0.0	0.33	0.15	0.14	1.8	0.1732C	12/31/12	9.8 -	0.0
-	-	-	1.08	1.17	1.12	16.8 -	0.0	1.40	1.24	1.12	8.4	0.250	4/12/13	18.1 -	0.0
-	-	-	0.41	0.54	0.56	24.0 -	0.0	1.16	0.96	0.52	12.3	0.0350Z	4/30/13	9.8 -	0.0
-	-	-	0.04	-0.11	-0.08	417.8 -	0.0	-	0.11	-	-	0.008B	12/31/12	16.7 -	0.0
-	-	-0.03	1.70	3.18	2.16	51.3 -	0.0	-	-	-	-	0.080Y	81/16/21	87.3 -	0.0
-	-	0.37	-	1.13	0.95			-	0.68	0.68	-	-	-	44.5 -	0.0
-	-	0.37	1.30	0.48	8.16	36.6 -	0.0	-	-	-	-	0.0267F	81/16/21	47.6 -	0.0
-	-	0.46	2.18	1.69	1.80	22.9 -	0.0	0.69	0.68	0.59	1.6	0.180Y	81/16/21	49.8 -	0.0
-	-	2.05	4.50	2.55	0.63	8.8 -	0.0	-	-	-	-	0.050	81/16/21	39.5 -	0.0
-	-	-	-	-				1.18	1.18	1.18	4.5	0.24720Z	8/1/13	27.2 -	0.0
-	-	0.60	2.44	2.05	1.77	33.0 -	0.0	-	-	-	-	-	-	80.6 -	0.0
-	-	0.39	0.94	1.65	1.73	18.8 -	0.0	-	-	-	-	-	-	17.6 -	0.0
-	-	0.27	0.93	0.41	3.30	39.4 -	0.0	-	-	-	-	0.03	81/16/21	36.7 -	0.0
-	-	0.01	-	0.26	0.31			-	0.75	0.50	-	-	-	24.7 -	0.0
-	-	4.00	17.06	15.33	8.01	17.2 -	0.0	16.86	13.91	5.01	7.6	3.630	2/28/13	292.6 -	0.0
-	-	-0.01	0.19	-0.41	-0.59	94.9 -	0.0	0.56	0.30	-	3.7	0.48440Z	4/1/13	18.0 -	0.0
-	-	1.92	5.25	3.81	-0.21	11.2 -	0.0	0.27	0.00	0.00	0.7	0.20Y	81/16/21	59.0 -	0.0
-	-	0.54	1.89	1.11		29.3 -	0.0	1.61	0.59	-	3.9	0.47250	2/14/13	55.4 -	0.0
-	-	0.10	0.20	0.05	-0.58	52.4 -	0.0	-	-	-	-	-	-	10.5 -	0.0
-	-	-0.09	2.25	3.09	3.67	20.4 -	0.0	0.80	0.78	0.67	2.0	0.0033	81/16/21	45.9 -	0.0
-	-	-0.21	0.27	-2.33	-1.40	247.2 -	0.0	0.07	0.30	0.30	0.2	0.0750Y	8/31/11	66.8 -	0.0
-	-	0.48	2.20	2.21	1.17	32.0 -	0.0	0.48	0.21	0.20	0.9	0.250Y	12/21/12	70.5 -	0.0
-	-	0.99	3.96	3.80	2.43	10.9 -	0.0	1.63	1.28	0.99	4.7	0.450	3/5/13	43.1 -	0.0
-	-	-	-	-				-	-	-	-	-	-		
-	-	0.51	2.00	0.79	0.28	15.6 -	0.0	0.08	0.08	0.08	0.3	0.020Y	81/16/21	31.2 -	0.0
-	-	-	0.32	0.25	0.34	75.5 -	0.0	0.55	0.54	0.55	3.0	0.16560	1/31/13	24.1 -	0.0
-	-	0.63	1.56	1.88	1.58	23.9 -	0.0	0.45	0.40	0.34	1.4	0.150Y	81/16/21	37.3 -	0.0
-	-	0.02	0.07	0.09	0.06	29.7 -	0.0	-	-	-	-	-	-	2.1 -	0.0
-	-	0.79	3.21	3.46	2.53	24.2 -	0.0	0.54	-	-	0.9	0.150Y	81/16/21	77.7 -	0.0
-	-	0.24	0.40	-0.60	-0.44	65.0 -	0.0	-	-	182.18	-	-	-	26.0 -	0.0
-	-	-0.29	-3.24	1.73	0.75			-	-	-	-	0.40630	5/15/13	6.9 -	0.0
-	-	0.56	2.49	-1.67	1.08	13.4 -	0.0	1.28	1.24	1.16	4.4	0.3250	81/16/21	33.3 -	0.0
-	0.37	-	2.26	1.92	2.07	19.6 -	0.0	0.60	0.40	0.78	1.7	0.180Y	81/16/21	44.3 -	0.0
-	-	0.61	1.70	2.05	5.02	32.9 -	0.0	1.00	1.00	1.00	2.1	0.250Y	81/16/21	55.9 -	0.0
-	-	0.49	3.40	2.87	2.11	20.8 -	0.0	1.12	0.95	0.68	1.8	0.320Y	81/16/21	70.9 -	0.0
-	-	0.33	1.68	1.21	1.04	11.4 -	0.0	-	-	-	-	-	-	19.2 -	0.0

SYMBOL	COMPANY	NATURE OF BUSINESS	FISCAL YEAR-END	TOTAL REV. $MILL	NET INCOME $MILL	TOTAL ASSETS $MILL	NET STK EQUITY $MILL	NO OF INST	INST. HOLDINGS (SHARES)
THI	Tim Hortons, Inc.	Hotels, Restaurants & Travel	12/30/12	3120.5	402.9	2284.2	1187.2	245	101559565
TSU	TIM Participacoes S.A.	Services	12/31/11	17086.0	1281.2	23438.2	12956.7	158	67987634
TWC	Time Warner Cable Inc	Radio & Television	12/31/12	21386.0	2155.0	49809.0	7279.0	756	274952248
TWX	Time Warner Inc	Entertainment	12/31/12	28729.0	3019.0	68304.0	29877.0	968	1001545379
TKR	Timken Co. (The)	Industrial Machinery & Equipment	12/31/12	4987.0	495.5	4244.7	2232.2	466	76484121
TWI	Titan International, Inc. (IL)	Construction Services	12/31/12	1820.7	95.6	1693.1	594.5	249	60411761
TJX	TJX Companies, Inc.	Retail - Apparel and Accessories	2/2/13	25878.4	1906.7	9511.9	3665.9	1009	693335248
TMS	TMS International Corp	Metal Products	12/31/12	2526.2	26.1	1009.8	305.3	98	13248850
TOL	Toll Brothers Inc.	Builders	10/31/12	1882.8	487.1	6181.0	3121.7	466	145393485
TR	Tootsie Roll Industries Inc	Food	12/31/12	549.9	52.0	846.7	649.8	157	15197937
TMK	Torchmark Corp.	Life & Health	12/31/12	3589.5	529.3	18776.9	4361.8	448	77291483
TTC	Toro Co. (The)	Construction Services	10/31/12	1958.7	129.5	935.2	312.4	295	47480506
TD	Toronto Dominion Bank	Banking	10/31/12	30568.0	6171.0	811106.0	47523.0	453	509065855
TYY	Tortoise Energy Capital Corp	Holding and other Investment Office	11/30/12	3.7	-11.4	889.9	540.5	76	4935444
NDP	Tortoise Energy Independence Fun	Holding and other Investment Office	5/3/12	-	-	0.1	0.1	20	587143
TYG	Tortoise Energy Infrastructure Corp	Holding and other Investment Office	11/30/12	8.0	-17.9	1729.3	1020.4	151	12412072
NTG	Tortoise MLP Fund, Inc.	Holding and other Investment Office	11/30/12	0.5	-18.5	1633.8	1140.6	-	
TYN	Tortoise North American Energy Co	Holding and other Investment Office	11/30/12	0.8	-1.4	226.0	160.7	32	973176
TTP	Tortoise Pipeline & Energy Fund Inc	Holding and other Investment Office	11/30/11	0.2	-0.2	309.3	244.3	18	1168698
TPZ	Tortoise Power & Energy Infrastruct	Holding and other Investment Office	11/30/12	8.2	5.0	224.1	186.0	32	1074375
TOT	Total S.A.	Production & Extraction	12/31/12	182299.0	10694.0	171829.0	72912.0	588	155132040
TSS	Total System Services, Inc.	Business Services	12/31/12	1871.0	244.3	2023.8	1425.2	419	141832320
TOWR	Tower International Inc	Auto Parts	12/31/12	2084.9	18.0	1238.1	63.2	53	18504627
TW	Towers Watson & Co.	Business Services	6/30/12	3417.7	260.2	5357.0	2432.5	260	50999759
TM	Toyota Motor Corp	Autos- Manufacturing	3/31/12	18583653.0	283559.0	30650965.0	10550261.0	344	26250325
TM 10	Toyota Motor Credit Corp.	Credit & Lending	3/31/12	8146.0	1486.0	88913.0	7662.0	-	
TAC	TransAlta Corp.	Electric Utilities	12/31/12	2262.0	-583.0	9451.0	3010.0	127	118369669
TAI	Transamerica Income Shares, Inc.	Holding and other Investment Office	3/31/12	9.8	8.7	160.2	140.5	18	515022
TRP	TransCanada Corp	Equipment & Services	12/31/12	8007.0	1354.0	48333.0	16911.0	343	357978834
TCI	Transcontinental Realty Investors, I	Property, Real Estate & Developmen	12/31/12	116.1	-8.3	1045.3	116.3	14	56162
TDG	Transdigm Group Inc	Aerospace	9/30/12	1700.2	325.0	5459.6	1218.8	379	55116130
TLP	Transmontaigne Partners L.P.	Equipment & Services	12/31/12	156.2	38.6	569.8	-0.5	66	7599152
RIG	Transocean Ltd.	Production & Extraction	12/31/12	9196.0	-219.0	34255.0	15745.0	-	
TGS	Transportadora de Gas del Sur S.A.	Gas Utilities	12/31/11	1853.9	230.7	5024.2	1953.5	-	
TA	TravelCenters of America LLC	Retail - Automotive	12/31/12	7995.7	32.2	1018.3	353.4	98	8809535
TRV	Travelers Companies Inc (The)	General Insurance	12/31/12	25740.0	2473.0	104938.0	25405.0	979	365295564
TRR	TRC Companies, Inc.	Sanitation Services	6/30/12	302.7	33.6	275.1	68.3	62	15260659
TG	Tredegar Corp.	Non-Precious Metals	12/31/12	900.3	28.3	783.2	372.3	147	19943903
THS	TreeHouse Foods Inc	Food	12/31/12	2182.1	88.4	2525.9	1179.3	248	37918965
TREX	Trex Co., Inc.	Metal Products	12/31/12	307.4	2.7	168.6	94.0	179	17702815
TPH	Tri Pointe Homes Inc	Builders	12/31/12	78.5	2.5	217.5	149.2	-	
TY	Tri-Continental Corp.	Holding and other Investment Office	12/31/12	46.3	40.1	1225.8	1220.9	76	12198735
TCAP	Triangle Capital Corp	Holding and other Investment Office	12/31/12	90.4	57.7	794.5	417.3	124	7816433
TSL	Trina Solar Ltd	Semiconductors	12/31/12	1296.7	-266.6	2864.9	881.6	123	48228946
TRN	Trinity Industries, Inc.	Construction Services	12/31/12	3811.9	255.2	6669.9	2053.0	359	72397621
GTS	Triple-S Management Corp	Hospitals & Health Care Facilities	12/31/12	2422.0	54.0	2059.3	761.9	103	16669196
TGI	Triumph Group Inc.	Aerospace	3/31/12	3407.9	280.9	4554.8	1793.4	370	64352801
TROX	Tronox Ltd	Specialty Chemicals	12/31/12	1832.0	1133.0	5511.0	2649.0	-	
TBI	TrueBlue Inc	Business Services	12/28/12	1389.5	33.6	601.7	333.7	162	39847016
TRLA	Trulia, Inc	IT Services	12/31/12	68.1	-10.9	119.0	86.5	56	8388061
TRW	TRW Automotive Holdings Corp	Auto Parts	12/31/12	16444.0	1008.0	10857.0	3578.0	395	118184660
TYW	TS&W / Claymore Tax Advantaged	Holding and other Investment Office	12/31/11	13.6	9.9	288.2	287.2	5	130935
TNP	Tsakos Energy Navigation Ltd.	Equipment & Services		-	-	-	-	77	14597371
TUMI	Tumi Holdings Inc	Apparel, Footwear & Accessories	12/31/12	398.6	36.8	469.2	311.1	111	37606452
TUP	Tupperware Brands Corp	Plastics	12/29/12	2583.8	193.0	1821.8	479.1	457	51510626
TKC	Turkcell Iletisim Hizmetleri AS	Services	12/31/12	5865.8	1158.8	10483.2	7238.9	140	63221323
TKF	Turkish Investment Fund, Inc. (The)	Holding and other Investment Office	10/31/12	2.7	1.5	112.8	112.7	39	1292048
TKF	Turkish Investment Fund, Inc. (The)	Holding and other Investment Office	10/31/12	2.7	1.5	112.8	112.7	39	1292048
TRQ	Turquoise Hill Resources Ltd.	Non-Precious Metals	12/31/11	179.0	-570.4	6136.8	4722.8	203	354996771
TPC	Tutor Perini Corp	Construction Services	12/31/12	4111.5	-265.4	3296.4	1143.9	24	446616
TWO	Two Harbors Investment Corp	REITs	12/31/12	296.0	291.9	16813.9	3450.6	285	182260589
TYC	Tyco International Ltd. (Switzerland)	Business Services	9/28/12	10403.0	472.0	12365.0	4994.0	770	499632017
TYL	Tyler Technologies, Inc.	Internet & Software	12/31/12	363.3	33.0	338.3	145.3	213	32705676
TSN	Tyson Foods, Inc.	Food	9/29/12	33278.0	583.0	11896.0	6012.0	496	276944621
USB	U.S. Bancorp (DE)	Banking	12/31/12	22202.0	5647.0	353855.0	38998.0	1323	1390698938
USPH	U.S. Physical Therapy, Inc.	Hospitals & Health Care Facilities	12/31/12	252.1	17.9	171.7	117.3	132	10689983
UBS	UBS AG (Switzerland)	Banking	12/31/12	35535.0	-2511.0	1259232.0	45896.0	265	643312109
UDR	UDR Inc	REITs	12/31/12	729.4	212.2	6888.5	3216.3	374	244709358
UGI	UGI Corp.	Gas Utilities	9/30/12	6519.2	199.4	9709.7	2233.1	361	95602731
UIL	UIL Holding Corp	Electric Utilities	12/31/12	1486.5	103.7	4960.1	1116.9	211	31745001
UPL	Ultra Petroleum Corp.	Production & Extraction	12/31/12	810.0	-2176.9	2007.3	-577.9	420	134932232
UGP	Ultrapar Participacoes S.A.	Equipment & Services	12/31/11	48661.3	848.8	13742.7	5551.1	122	27429077
UMH	UMH Properties Inc	REITs	12/31/12	46.8	6.5	300.3	175.0	89	5227014
UA	Under Armour Inc	Apparel, Footwear & Accessories	12/31/12	1834.9	128.8	1157.1	816.9	388	82149509
UFI	Unifi, Inc.	Textiles	6/24/12	705.1	11.5	482.2	289.5	107	12627399
UNF	Unifirst Corp.	Business Services	8/25/12	1256.3	95.0	1240.5	896.9	194	16771505
UN	Unilever N.V.	Miscellaneous Consumer Goods	12/31/12	51324.0	4480.0	46166.0	15159.0	519	201223727
UL	Unilever Plc	Food	12/31/12	51324.0	4480.0	46166.0	15159.0	452	126347126
UNP	Union Pacific Corp	Rail	12/31/12	20926.0	3943.0	47153.0	19877.0	1333	405232752
UIS	Unisys Corp.	IT Services	12/31/12	3706.4	129.4	2420.4	-1600.2	242	71871628

1st	2nd	3rd	2012	2011	2010	P/E RATIO		2012	2011	2010	AV. YLD %	AMOUNT	PAYABLE	PRICE RANGE 2012	
-	-	0.68	2.59	2.35	3.58	22.5 -	0.0	0.84	0.68	0.52	1.6	0.260	81/16/21	58.3 -	0.0
-	-	-	-	0.57	2.63			-	-	-		-	-	33.0 -	0.0
-	-	2.60	6.90	4.97	3.64	14.6 -	0.0	2.24	1.92	1.60	2.5	0.650Y	81/16/21	100.8 -	0.0
-	-	0.86	3.09	2.71	2.25	18.6 -	0.0	1.04	0.94	0.85	2.4	0.18750 Y	81/16/21	57.6 -	0.0
-	-	0.83	5.07	4.59	2.81	11.5 -	0.0	0.92	0.78	0.53	2.0	0.230Y	81/16/21	58.1 -	0.0
-	-	0.39	1.83	1.18	0.01	15.9 -	0.0	0.02	0.02	0.02	0.1	0.0050Y	4/15/13	29.2 -	0.0
-	-	0.62	1.93	1.65	1.42	24.4 -	0.0	0.36	0.28	0.23	0.8	0.1450Y	81/16/21	47.1 -	0.0
-	-	0.25	0.66	0.59	-3.17	21.9 -	0.0	-	-	-		-	-	14.4 -	0.0
0.03	-	-	2.86	0.24	-0.02	13.3 -	0.0	-	-	-		-	-	38.0 -	0.0
-	-	0.38	0.86	0.74	0.89	34.9 -	0.0	0.79	0.30	0.29	3.2	0.07770Y	81/16/21	30.0 -	0.0
-	-	1.36	5.41	4.72	4.20	11.1 -	0.0	0.57	0.44	0.41	1.1	0.170Y	81/16/21	59.8 -	0.0
0.53	-	-	2.14	1.85	1.40	22.6 -	0.0	0.44	0.40	0.36	1.1	0.140Y	81/16/21	48.3 -	0.0
1.86	-	-	6.76	6.43	5.10	12.6 -	0.0	2.89	2.61	2.44	3.6	0.30310	4/30/13	85.4 -	0.0
-	-	-	-0.58	-0.75	-0.60			1.66	1.62	1.60	5.9	0.03290	5/1/13	33.0 -	0.0
-	-	-	-	-	-			-	-	-		0.43750	3/1/13	25.9 -	0.0
-	-	-	-0.64	-0.77	-0.66			-	-	-		0.03650	5/1/13	50.1 -	0.0
-	-	-	-0.40	-0.34	-0.04			1.66	1.64	0.36	6.5	0.41630	3/1/13	28.1 -	0.0
-	-	-	-0.23	-0.12	-0.09			1.55	1.51	1.48	6.0	0.3950	3/1/13	30.0 -	0.0
-	-	-	-	-0.02	-			-	-	-		0.40750	3/1/13	27.9 -	0.0
-	-	0.72	0.72	0.72	0.73	38.0 -	0.0	1.50	1.50	1.50	5.9	0.1250	5/31/13	27.3 -	0.0
-	1.35	-	4.72	5.44	4.71	11.6 -	0.0	-	-	-		-	-	54.9 -	0.0
-	-	0.32	1.29	1.15	0.99	19.2 -	0.0	0.40	0.31	0.28	1.7	0.10Y	81/16/21	24.8 -	0.0
-	-0.24	-	0.88	0.40	-3.43	16.3 -	0.0	-	-	-		-	-	14.3 -	0.0
-	1.15	-	3.59	2.62	2.03	19.3 -	0.0	0.40	0.30	0.15	0.7	0.345HY	81/16/21	69.3 -	0.0
-	81.44	-	90.20	130.16	66.79	1.2 -	0.0	0.02	0.01	0.01	0.0	-	-	105.9 -	0.0
-	-	-	-	-	-			-	-	-		-	-		
-	-3.51	-	-2.61	1.31	1.16			1.16	1.16	1.16	7.3	0.31250	3/31/13	18.8 -	0.0
-	-	-	1.37	1.47	1.50	19.2 -	0.0	1.49	1.68	1.54	6.4	0.0750	4/15/13	26.3 -	0.0
-	-	0.52	1.84	2.17	1.78	27.2 -	0.0	1.76	1.68	1.60	3.9	0.2750	4/30/13	50.1 -	0.0
-	-	-0.07	-1.12	-5.67	-8.42			-	-	-		0.180	9/29/00	6.4 -	0.0
0.66	-	-	5.97	3.17	2.52	25.6 -	0.0	-	-	7.65		12.857Y	81/16/21	152.9 -	0.0
-	-	0.59	2.31	2.91	1.68	22.0 -	0.0	2.54	2.46	2.39	6.9	0.640	2/7/13	50.7 -	0.0
-	-	-1.06	-0.62	-17.79	2.99			-	-	-		0.790	3/21/12	59.3 -	0.0
-	-	-	-	-	-			-	-	-		-	-	2.8 -	0.0
-	-	0.66	1.12	0.98	-3.78	8.6 -	0.0	-	-	-		0.51560Z	7/15/13	9.7 -	0.0
-	-	2.21	6.30	3.36	6.62	13.4 -	0.0	1.79	1.59	1.41	2.6	0.460Y	81/16/21	84.2 -	0.0
-	0.14	-	1.16	-0.69	-1.17	7.2 -	0.0	-	-	-		-	-	8.3 -	0.0
-	-	0.23	0.88	0.77	0.83	34.9 -	0.0	0.96	0.18	0.16	5.2	0.070Y	4/1/13	30.7 -	0.0
-	-	0.58	2.38	2.56	2.51	27.4 -	0.0	-	-	-		-	-	65.2 -	0.0
-	-	-0.86	0.16	-0.75	-0.66	321.4 -	0.0	-	-	-		-	-	51.4 -	0.0
-	-	-	-	-	-			-	-	-		-	-	20.5 -	18.0
-	-	-	0.63	0.33	0.30	27.9 -	0.0	0.60	0.28	0.25	3.7	0.190	3/26/13	17.6 -	0.0
-	-	0.58	2.16	2.06	1.58	14.0 -	0.0	2.02	1.77	1.65	8.3	0.540	3/27/13	30.3 -	0.0
-	-	-0.02	-0.08	-0.01	0.08			-	-	-		-	-	7.8 -	0.0
-	-	0.80	3.19	1.77	0.85	14.2 -	0.0	0.40	0.34	0.32	1.3	0.110Y	81/16/21	45.4 -	0.0
-	-	0.41	1.90	2.01	2.28	12.2 -	0.0	-	-	-		-	-	23.1 -	0.0
-	-	1.43	5.41	3.15	2.04	14.7 -	0.0	0.14	0.08	0.08	0.2	0.040Y	3/15/13	79.3 -	0.0
-	-	-0.14	11.10	3.09	0.03	2.6 -	0.0	-	-	-		0.250	3/20/13	29.1 -	0.0
-	-	0.36	0.84	0.73	0.46	25.3 -	0.0	-	-	-		-	-	21.3 -	0.0
-	-	-0.19	-0.87	-0.92	-0.64			-	-	-		-	-	35.4 -	0.0
-	-	1.28	7.83	8.82	6.49	7.8 -	0.0	-	-	-		-	-	61.4 -	0.0
-	-	-	-	0.64	0.71			-	0.80	0.76		0.20	12/30/11	-	
-	-	-	-	-	-			-	-	-		0.050	12/20/12	8.7 -	0.0
-	-	0.15	0.58	0.33	0.00	45.8 -	0.0	-	-	-		-	-	26.6 -	0.0
-	-	0.85	3.42	3.55	3.53	23.9 -	0.0	1.44	1.20	1.05	2.3	0.620Y	81/16/21	81.7 -	0.0
-	-	0.14	0.53	0.34	0.53	33.5 -	0.0	-	-	0.59		-	-	17.8 -	0.0
-	-	-	0.21	0.30	0.20	0.0 -	0.0	0.30	0.20	0.13	1.$	0.22760	1/4/13	0.0 -	0.0
-	-	-	0.21	0.30	0.20	89.4 -	0.0	0.30	0.20	0.13	2.0	0.22760	1/4/13	18.8	
-	-0.35	-	-	-0.83	-0.42			-	-	-		-	-	15.8 -	0.0
-	-	0.88	-5.59	1.80	2.13			-	-	1.00		1.7Y	81/16/21	19.3 -	0.0
-	-	0.10	1.20	1.29	1.60	10.8 -	0.0	1.71	1.60	1.48	16.1	0.320Z	4/24/13	13.0 -	0.0
0.34	-	-	1.02	3.62	2.32	31.7 -	0.0	0.90	-	-	3.2	0.160	81/16/21	32.3 -	0.0
-	-	0.33	1.00	0.83	0.71	61.3 -	0.0	-	-	-		-	-	61.3 -	0.0
0.48	-	-	1.58	1.97	2.06	15.7 -	0.0	0.16	0.16	0.16	0.9	0.0450Y	81/16/21	24.8 -	0.0
-	-	0.74	2.84	2.46	1.73	12.4 -	0.0	0.78	0.50	0.20	2.4	0.3750Y	81/16/21	35.2 -	0.0
-	-	0.34	1.51	1.75	1.32	18.5 -	0.0	0.76	0.32	-	3.0	0.10Z	3/29/13	28.0 -	0.0
-	-	-0.58	-0.67	1.08	1.96			-	-	-		0.150	5/10/13	17.6 -	0.0
-	-	-0.04	0.85	0.05	-0.68	31.8 -	0.0	0.88	0.77	0.72	3.5	0.32020Z	81/16/21	27.1 -	0.0
0.90	-	-	1.76	2.06	2.36	21.8 -	0.0	1.06	1.02	0.90	3.4	0.270Y	81/16/21	38.4 -	0.0
-	-	0.31	2.02	1.95	1.52	19.6 -	0.0	1.73	1.73	1.73	4.8	0.4320Y	4/1/13	39.7 -	0.0
-	-	-3.94	-14.24	2.94	3.01			-	-	-		-	-	24.1 -	0.0
-	-	0.54	-	1.58	1.43			-	0.35	0.20		-	-	26.6 -	0.0
-	-	0.08	0.40	0.25	0.52	30.4 -	0.0	0.72	0.72	0.72	6.7	0.51560Z	6/17/13	12.2 -	0.0
-	-	0.54	1.21	0.93	0.67	49.6 -	0.0	-	-	-		-	-	60.0 -	0.0
-	0.12	-	0.56	1.22	0.51	34.6 -	0.0	-	-	-		0.140	5/8/98	19.4 -	0.0
-	1.33	-	4.76	3.85	3.90	19.0 -	0.0	0.15	0.15	0.15	0.2	0.030Y	7/2/13	90.5 -	0.0
-	-	-	1.54	1.46	1.46	26.7 -	0.0	1.57	1.74	1.49	4.4	-	-	41.2 -	0.0
-	-	-	1.54	1.46	1.46	27.4 -	0.0	1.57	1.74	1.49	4.3	-	-	42.2 -	0.0
-	-	2.19	8.27	6.72	5.53	17.2 -	0.0	2.49	1.93	1.31	2.0	0.690Y	81/16/21	142.4 -	0.0
-	-	-0.28	2.84	2.71	5.45	8.6 -	0.0	-	-	-		1.56250Y	3/1/13	24.4 -	0.0

SYMBOL	COMPANY	NATURE OF BUSINESS	FISCAL YEAR-END	TOTAL REV. $MILL	NET INCOME $MILL	TOTAL ASSETS $MILL	NET STK EQUITY $MILL	NO OF INST	INST. HOLDINGS (SHARES)
UNT	Unit Corp.	Production & Extraction	12/31/12	1315.1	23.2	3761.1	1974.3	254	46628240
UAL	United Continental Holdings Inc	Airlines/Air Freight	12/31/12	37152.0	-723.0	37628.0	481.0	391	359543030
UMC	United Microelectronics Corp.	Semiconductors	12/31/11	116702.7	8466.9	279831.7	212125.0	134	234493818
UPS	United Parcel Service Inc	Airlines/Air Freight	12/31/12	54127.0	807.0	38863.0	4653.0	1230	546102348
URI	United Rentals, Inc.	Construction Services	12/31/12	4117.0	75.0	11026.0	1574.0	448	116432205
USM	United States Cellular Corp	Services	12/31/12	4452.1	111.0	6587.4	3733.9	150	12719173
X	United States Steel Corp.	Non-Precious Metals	12/31/12	19328.0	-124.0	15217.0	3477.0	488	104220585
UTX	United Technologies Corp.	Aerospace	12/31/12	57708.0	5130.0	89409.0	25914.0	1616	850071414
UNH	UnitedHealth Group Inc	Life & Health	12/31/12	110618.0	5526.0	80885.0	31178.0	1175	962091666
UTL	UNITIL Corp	Electric Utilities	12/31/12	353.1	18.2	886.6	260.6	121	6728359
UAM	Universal American Corp.	Life & Health	12/31/12	2177.5	53.0	2531.3	1012.5	120	71267985
UVV	Universal Corp.	Tobacco Products	3/31/12	2446.9	92.1	2266.9	1183.5	231	26409338
UHT	Universal Health Realty Income Tru	REITs	12/31/12	53.9	19.5	383.0	177.7	158	6363257
UHS	Universal Health Services, Inc.	Hospitals & Health Care Facilities	12/31/12	6961.4	443.4	8200.8	2713.3	374	100570972
UTI	Universal Technical Institute, Inc.	Educational Services	9/30/12	413.6	9.0	268.2	146.1	127	23830709
UNS	UNS Energy Corp	Electric Utilities	12/31/12	1461.8	90.9	4140.4	1065.5	222	37898884
UNM	Unum Group	Life & Health	12/31/12	10515.4	894.4	62236.1	8612.6	484	292168655
URS	URS Corp	Construction Services	12/28/12	10972.5	310.6	8786.5	3621.1	393	78430593
UBA	Urstadt Biddle Properties Inc	REITs	10/31/12	91.3	28.3	724.2	484.5	33	772983
LCC	US Airways Group Inc	Airlines/Air Freight	12/31/12	13831.0	637.0	9396.0	790.0	334	186212754
SLCA	US Silica Holdings, Inc.	Mining	12/31/12	441.9	79.2	686.8	231.7	110	50614042
USNA	USANA Health Sciences Inc	Household & Personal Products	12/29/12	648.7	66.4	267.4	185.6	176	9267828
USB PRI	USB Capital X	Banking						1	15070
USU	USEC, Inc.	Mining	12/31/12	1918.1	-1200.6	2266.4	-472.9	120	56644356
USG	USG Corp	Construction Materials	12/31/12	3224.0	-126.0	3723.0	6.0	295	84359006
EGY	VAALCO Energy, Inc.	Production & Extraction	12/31/12	195.3	0.6	268.0	212.5	180	55749478
MTN	Vail Resorts Inc.	Sporting & Recreational	7/31/12	1024.4	16.5	1927.6	802.3	194	42510524
VCI	Valassis Communications, Inc.	Publishing	12/31/12	2162.1	119.0	1589.0	473.6	239	50572246
RIO 34	Vale Overseas Ltd	Finance Intermediaries & Services	12/31/05	84.1	0.0	1289.4	-0.0		
VALE	Vale S. A.	Non-Precious Metals	12/31/12	47694.0	5511.0	131478.0	74241.0	542	459853531
VRX	Valeant Pharmaceuticals Internation	Pharmaceuticals	12/31/12	3546.6	-116.0	17950.4	3717.4	349	253514976
VLO	Valero Energy Corp.	Refining & Marketing	12/31/12	139250.0	2083.0	44477.0	18032.0	866	504504076
VHI	Valhi, Inc.	Specialty Chemicals	12/31/12	2157.9	159.8	3170.5	733.6	64	2780275
VR	Validus Holdings Ltd	General Insurance	12/31/12	2060.9	408.4	10020.3	4020.8	265	111166543
VLY	Valley National Bancorp	Banking	12/31/12	792.1	143.6	16012.6	1502.4	244	84492793
VMI	Valmont Industries, Inc.	Industrial Machinery & Equipment	12/29/12	3029.5	234.1	2568.6	1349.9	321	27840673
VAL	Valspar Corp.	Specialty Chemicals	10/26/12	4020.9	292.5	3626.8	1223.5	375	77322955
VHS	Vanguard Health Systems, Inc.	Hospitals & Health Care Facilities	6/30/12	5949.0	57.3	4788.1	348.2	104	66674122
VNR	Vanguard Natural Resource LLC	Production & Extraction	12/31/12	347.2	-168.8	2200.1	797.5	141	8951235
VAR	Varian Medical Systems, Inc.	Medical Instruments & Equipment	9/28/12	2807.0	427.0	2878.7	1509.8	645	116753691
VGR	Vector Group Ltd	Tobacco Products	12/31/12	1084.5	30.6	1086.7	-79.3	160	34403159
VVC	Vectren Corp	Electric Utilities	12/31/12	2232.8	159.0	5089.1	1526.1	313	48098528
VVC 13	Vectren Utility Holdings Inc.	Electric Utilities	12/31/11	1457.0	122.9	3974.5	1346.6		
VTR	Ventas, Inc.	REITs	12/31/12	2485.3	361.8	18980.0	9193.7	521	309097729
VE	Veolia Environnement	Sanitation Services	12/31/12	29438.5	393.8	44612.1	7152.1	143	9601885
PAY	VeriFone Systems Inc.	Internet & Software	10/31/12	1866.0	65.0	3490.6	1307.8	409	110505087
VZ	Verizon Communications Inc	Services	12/31/12	115846.0	875.0	225222.0	33157.0	1814	1727315353
VET	Vermilion Energy Inc.	Production & Extraction	12/31/12	1031.0	190.6	3076.3	1418.6		
VRS	Verso Paper Corp	Paper & Forest Products	12/31/12	1474.6	-173.8	1208.9	-321.7	47	74802614
VFC	VF Corp.	Apparel, Footwear & Accessories	12/29/12	10879.9	1086.0	9633.0	5125.6	775	104819060
VVI	Viad Corp.	Business Services	12/31/12	1025.2	5.9	650.6	388.1	150	19389428
VIP	VimpelCom Ltd.	Services	12/31/12	23061.0	2145.0	55360.0	14869.0	117	83399849
VCO	Vina Concha y Toro S.A. (Chile)	Beverages	12/31/11	422735.4	50482.4	774130.3	398211.6	36	354364
VIPS	Vipshop Holdings Ltd	Retail - Apparel and Accessories	12/31/11	227.1	-107.3	167.4	18.3	21	1631482
VEL PRE	Virginia Electric & Power Co.	Electric Utilities	12/31/12	7226.0	1050.0	24811.0	9490.0		
VGI	Virtus Global Multi-Sector Income F	Holding and other Investment Office	1/9/12			0.1	0.1	15	1173770
DCA	Virtus Total Return Fund	Holding and other Investment Office	12/31/12	7.5	5.2	165.3	121.7	28	6840650
V	Visa Inc	Business Services	9/30/12	10421.0	2144.0	40013.0	27630.0	1159	461171016
VSH	Vishay Intertechnology, Inc.	Electrical Equipment	12/31/12	2230.1	122.7	3016.3	1623.3	311	161612427
VPG	Vishay Precision Group Inc.	Electronic Instruments & Related Pro	12/31/12	217.6	11.7	263.2	196.6	105	11539913
VC	Visteon Corp.	Auto Parts	12/31/12	6857.0	100.0	5156.0	1385.0	262	59848674
VSI	Vitamin Shoppe Inc	Retail - Specialty	12/29/12	950.9	60.8	586.3	447.4	214	35351572
VMW	VMWARE, Inc.	Internet & Software	12/31/12	4605.0	745.7	10596.4	5740.0	489	94114045
VOC	VOC Energy Trust	Oil Royalty Traders	12/31/12	38.1	37.2	122.3	122.3	41	3225410
VCRA	Vocera Communications, Inc.	Computer Hardware & Equipment	12/31/12	101.0	2.9	167.3	123.1	107	20462563
VG	Vonage Holdings Corp	Services	12/31/12	849.1	36.6	547.4	321.4	170	145235656
VNOD	Vornado Realty L.P.	REITs	12/31/12	2766.5	662.5	21966.0	944.2	10	155730
VNO	Vornado Realty Trust	REITs	12/31/12	2766.5	617.3	21966.0	6850.9	513	181667068
VMC	Vulcan Materials Co (Holding Comp	Mining	12/31/12	2567.3	-52.6	8126.6	3761.1	436	136402696
WTI	W & T Offshore Inc	Production & Extraction	12/31/12	874.5	72.0	2349.0	541.2	167	46017156
WPC	W.P. Carey Inc	REITs	12/31/12	374.0	62.1	4609.0	2027.1	100	1471315
WNC	Wabash National Corp.	Autos- Manufacturing	12/31/12	1461.9	105.6	902.6	268.7	191	71794259
WBC	WABCO Holdings Inc	Construction Services	12/31/12	2477.4	302.0	1747.0	676.4	291	62273750
WAB	Wabtec Corp.	Construction Services	12/31/12	2391.1	251.7	2351.5	1276.8	397	50980135
WNA PR	Wachovia Preferred Funding Corp	REITs	12/31/12	870.7	581.9	14068.8	13296.9	9	222150
WDR	Waddell & Reed Financial, Inc.	Finance Intermediaries & Services	12/31/12	1173.8	151.0	1152.8	510.2	327	83385419
WAGE	WageWorks Inc	Business Services	12/31/12	177.3	10.5	518.8	156.4	95	19339201
WMT	Wal-Mart Stores, Inc.	Retail - General Merchandise/Depart	1/31/13	469162.0	16999.0	203105.0	76343.0	1790	1185302368
WAG	Walgreen Co.	Retail - Food & Beverage, Drug & To	8/31/12	71633.0	2127.0	33462.0	18236.0	1302	663847722
WD	Walker & Dunlop Inc	Business Services	12/31/12	256.8	33.8	1688.6	353.2	86	28302094

EARNINGS PER SHARE QUARTERLY			ANNUAL			P/E RATIO		DIVIDENDS PER SHARE			AV. YLD %	DIV. DECLARED		PRICE RANGE 2012	
1st	2nd	3rd	2012	2011	2010			2012	2011	2010		AMOUNT	PAYABLE		
-	-	0.97	0.48	4.08	3.09	102.1 -	0.0	-				-		49.0 -	0.0
-	-	0.02	-2.18	2.26	1.08	-						2.15G7Y	81/16/21	32.5 -	0.0
-	-	-	-	0.81	1.87									2.7 -	0.0
-	-	0.48	0.83	3.84	3.48	103.5 -	0.0	2.28	2.08	1.88	3.0	0.620Y	81/16/21	85.9 -	0.0
-	-	0.70	0.79	1.38	-0.44	70.8 -	0.0							55.9 -	0.0
-	-	0.42	1.31	2.05	1.53	31.5 -	0.0					0.43440Z	6/17/13	41.3 -	0.0
-	-	0.28	-0.86	-0.37	-3.36			0.20	0.20	0.20	0.9	0.050Y	81/16/21	30.3 -	0.0
-	-	1.56	5.66	5.49	4.74	16.5 -	0.0	2.03	1.87	1.70	2.5	0.5350Y	81/16/21	93.6 -	0.0
-	-	1.50	5.28	4.73	4.10	11.4 -	0.0	0.80	0.61	0.41	1.5	0.21250Y	81/16/21	60.3 -	0.0
-	-	0.03	1.43	1.50	0.88	19.7 -	0.0	1.38	1.38	1.38	5.2	0.3450Y	5/15/13	28.1 -	0.0
-	-	0.16	0.61	-0.53	2.38	17.8 -	0.0	1.00	-	2.00	10.8	1.G7	11/19/12	10.9 -	0.0
-	-	1.26	3.25	5.42	5.68	18.0 -	0.0	1.93	1.89	1.85	3.9	16.8750Y	81/16/21	58.4 -	0.0
-	-	0.24	1.54	5.83	1.33	37.7 -	0.0	2.46	2.42	2.42	5.3	0.620Z	81/16/21	58.0 -	0.0
-	-	0.73	4.53	4.04	2.34	14.2 -	0.0	0.60	0.20	0.20	1.3	0.050Y	81/16/21	64.4 -	0.0
0.14	-	-	0.36	1.10	1.18	38.9 -	0.0	0.30	-	1.50	2.5	0.10Y	3/29/13	14.0 -	0.0
-	-	1.21	2.20	2.75	2.82	22.2 -	0.0	1.72	1.68	1.56	4.2	0.4350Y	3/25/13	48.9 -	0.0
-	-	0.83	3.17	0.78	2.71	8.9 -	0.0	0.47	0.40	0.35	2.2	0.130Y	81/16/21	28.3 -	0.0
-	-	1.43	4.17	-6.03	3.54	11.4 -	0.0	0.80	-	-	2.1	0.210Y	81/16/21	47.4 -	0.0
-0.02	-	-	0.41	0.60	0.52	53.1 -	0.0	0.99	0.98	0.97	5.1	0.44530Z	81/16/21	21.8 -	0.0
-	-	1.24	3.28	0.44	2.61	5.3 -	0.0	-	-	-		-		17.2 -	0.0
-	-	0.36	1.50	0.61	0.23	17.7 -	0.0	0.50	-	-	3.2	0.5G7Y	12/28/12	26.5 -	0.0
-	-	1.18	4.45	3.26	2.86	11.1 -	0.0	-	-	-		-		49.3 -	0.0
-	-	0.04	-9.84	-4.48	0.05			-	-	-		0.13750Y	12/15/05	1.2 -	0.0
-	-	-0.28	-1.19	-3.76	-4.03							0.0250	81/16/21	30.4 -	0.0
-	-	0.00	0.01	0.59	0.65	1011.0 -	0.0					0.001F	8/1/09	10.1 -	0.0
-	1.65	-	0.45	0.94	0.83	140.9 -	0.0	0.68	0.15	0.15	1.3	0.20750Z	4/9/13	63.4 -	0.0
-	-	0.90	2.84	2.33	7.42	10.9 -	0.0	0.31	-	-	1.3	0.310Y	81/16/21	30.9 -	0.0
-	-	0.32	1.07	4.33	3.23	22.4 -	0.0	0.99	1.56	0.45	5.2	-		23.9 -	0.0
-	-	0.02	-0.38	0.49	-1.06			-	-	1.28		1.7	12/22/10	76.3 -	0.0
-	-	1.21	3.75	3.68	0.57	12.9 -	0.0	0.65	0.30	0.20	2.1	0.20Y	81/16/21	48.5 -	0.0
-	-	0.07	0.47	0.64	-0.14	38.3 -	0.0	0.19	0.16	0.13	1.4	0.050Y	3/28/13	18.0 -	0.0
-	-	2.11	3.99	0.14	3.34	9.4 -	0.0	1.00	1.00	0.88	3.0	0.30	3/29/13	37.6 -	0.0
-	-	0.20	0.73	0.75	0.73	17.0 -	0.0	0.65	0.66	0.65	6.4	0.16250Y	81/16/21	12.4 -	0.0
-	-	2.12	8.75	8.60	3.57	18.8 -	0.0	0.85	0.70	0.48	0.6	0.2250Y	81/16/21	164.5 -	0.0
0.60	-	-	3.10	-1.47	2.20	22.0 -	0.0	0.80	0.72	0.64	1.4	0.230Y	81/16/21	68.3 -	0.0
-	0.14	-	0.71	-0.24	-1.10	24.6 -	0.0	-	-	-		-		17.4 -	0.0
-	-	-1.29	-3.11	1.95	1.00			2.79	2.28	2.15	10.1	0.20250Z	4/12/13	30.0 -	0.0
0.86	-	-	3.76	3.36	2.91	20.0 -	0.0	-	-	-		0.0250		75.3 -	0.0
-	-	0.21	0.35	0.89	0.64	48.5 -	0.0	1.54	1.47	1.40	9.6	0.40Y	81/16/21	17.0 -	0.0
-	-	0.48	1.94	1.73	1.64	18.3 -	0.0	1.41	1.39	1.37	4.7	0.3550Y	81/16/21	35.4 -	0.0
-	-,	0.38	1.23	1.58	1.56	59.5 -	0.0	2.48	2.30	2.14	3.9	0.670Z	81/16/21	73.2 -	0.0
-	-	-	0.78	-0.99	1.21	21.3 -	0.0	1.12	2.47	1.84	9.5	-		16.6 -	0.0
0.11	-	-	0.59	2.92	1.13	92.3 -	0.0	-	-	-		-		54.5 -	0.0
-	-	0.56	0.31	0.85	0.90	159.6 -	0.0	2.02	1.96	1.91	4.6	0.5150Y	81/16/21	49.5 -	0.0
-	-	0.31	1.92	1.55	0.53	27.8 -	21.2	2.28	2.28	0.76	4.7	0.20	5/15/13	53.3 -	40.7
-	-	-1.98	-3.29	-2.61	-2.50			-	-	-		0.030Y	11/25/08	2.0 -	0.0
-	-	3.42	9.70	7.98	5.18	17.4 -	0.0	3.03	2.61	2.43	2.0	0.870Y	81/16/21	168.9 -	0.0
-	-	0.99	0.29	0.45	0.02	97.2 -	0.0	0.28	0.16	0.16	1.3	0.10Y	4/1/13	2R 2 -	0.0
-	-	0.33	1.32	0.36	1.50	9.5 -	0.0	0.66	0.63	0.46	6.4	-		12.6 -	0.0
-	-	-	-	-	-				0.00	0.00		-		47.0 -	0.0
-	-	-	-	-	-							-		31.1 -	0.0
-	-	-	-	-	-			5.00	5.00	5.00	9.9	1.7450Y	3/20/13	114.6 -	0.0
-	-	-	-	-	-							0.1170	6/18/12	20.1 -	0.0
-	-	-	0.19	0.18	0.23	21.8 -	0.0	0.23	0.15	0.19	6.0	0.050	4/18/13	4.2 -	0.0
1.93	-	-	3.16	5.16	4.01	53.7 -	0.0	0.88	0.60	0.50	0.6	0.330Y	81/16/21	169.8 -	0.0
-	-	0.15	0.79	1.42	1.89	17.7 -	0.0	-	-	-		-		13.9 -	0.0
-	-	0.14	0.84	0.78	0.85	17.9 -	0.0	-	-	-		-		15.0 -	0.0
-	-	0.28	1.88	1.54	1.66	32.6 -	0.0	-	-			0.060Y	12/1/04	61.3 -	0.0
-	-	0.54	2.02	1.52	1.03	32.1 -	0.0	-	-			-		64.8 -	0.0
-	-	0.36	1.72	1.68	0.84	66.6 -	0.0					-		114.6 -	0.0
-	-	0.60	-	-				2.19	1.42	-	13.1	0.260	2/14/13	23.4 -	0.0
-	-	0.07	0.08	-0.74	0.00	394.0 -	0.0	-	-			-		31.5 -	0.0
-	-	0.06	0.16	1.69	-0.40	18.1 -	0.0	-	-			-		2.9 -	0.0
-	-	1.24	2.93	3.23	3.23	9.7 -	0.0	1.97	1.97	1.97	7.1	0.49220Z	7/1/13	28.5 -	0.0
-	-	1.24	2.94	3.23	3.24	30.0 -	0.0	3.76	2.76	2.60	4.6	0.730Z	81/16/21	88.1 -	0.0
-	-	0.11	-0.41	-0.55	-0.75			0.04	0.76	1.00	0.1	0.010Y	81/16/21	58.7 -	0.0
-	-	-0.02	0.95	2.29	1.58	22.7 -	0.0	1.11	0.79	0.80	6.5	0.080Y	3/29/13	21.6 -	0.0
-	-	0.06	1.28	3.42	1.86	53.5 -	0.0	0.66	2.19	2.03	1.3	0.820Z	81/16/21	68.5 -	0.0
-	-	0.27	1.53	0.22	-3.36	7.1 -	0.0	-	-			0.0450Z	10/10/08	10.9 -	0.0
-	-	1.19	4.62	5.19	-3.50	15.6 -	0.0	-	-			0.070Y	81/16/21	71.9 -	0.0
-	-	1.30	5.19	3.51	2.56	19.7 -	0.0	0.16	0.08	0.04	0.2	0.050Y	81/16/21	102.1 -	0.0
-	-	0.91	3.89	6.12	5.84	7.2 -	0.0	1.81	1.81	1.81	6.7	0.45310Z	4/1/13	27.9 -	0.0
-	-	0.10	1.76	2.05	1.83	24.9 -	0.0	1.75	0.85	0.77	5.3	0.280Y	81/16/21	43.8 -	0.0
-	-	0.08	0.33	1.43	-15.70	78.5 -	0.0	-	-			-		25.9 -	0.0
-	-	1.08	4.52	4.47	3.70	17.1 -	0.0	1.46	1.21	1.09	2.1	0.470Y	81/16/21	77.2 -	0.0
-	0.79	-	2.42	2.94	2.12	19.7 -	0.0	0.95	0.75	0.59	2.7	0.2750Y	81/16/21	47.7 -	0.0
-	-	0.28	1.31	1.60	0.55	16.6 -	0.0	-	-			-		21.7 -	0.0

T63

SYMBOL	COMPANY	NATURE OF BUSINESS	FISCAL YEAR-END	TOTAL REV. $MILL	NET INCOME $MILL	TOTAL ASSETS $MILL	NET STK EQUITY $MILL	NO OF INST	INST. HOLDINGS (SHARES)
WLT	Walter Energy, Inc.	Mining	12/31/12	2399.9	-1060.4	5768.4	1010.6	376	68175053
WAC	Walter Investment Management Cor	Credit & Lending	12/31/12	667.0	-22.1	10978.2	894.9	1	87220
WPO	Washington Post Co.	Publishing	12/31/12	4017.7	132.1	5105.1	2597.1	319	6074273
WRE	Washington Real Estate Investment	REITs	12/31/12	305.0	23.7	2124.4	792.1	279	51362281
WCN	Waste Connections, Inc.	Sanitation Services	12/31/12	1661.6	159.1	5076.0	1878.2	299	120603922
WM	Waste Management, Inc. (DE)	Sanitation Services	12/31/12	13649.0	817.0	23097.0	6354.0	826	407866186
WAT	Waters Corp.	Biotechnology	12/31/12	1843.6	461.4	3168.1	1467.4	531	86270669
WSO	Watsco Inc.	Industrial Machinery & Equipment	12/31/12	3431.7	103.3	1682.1	748.2	230	27693288
WTS	Watts Water Technologies Inc	Industrial Machinery & Equipment	12/31/12	1445.6	68.4	1709.0	939.5	216	29096202
WPP	Wausau Paper Corp	Paper & Forest Products	12/31/12	822.2	0.7	700.7	205.5	148	41627335
WFT	Weatherford International, Ltd.	Equipment & Services	12/31/12	15215.0	-778.0	22795.0	8786.0	-	
WBS	Webster Financial Corp (Waterbury,	Banking	12/31/12	886.3	173.7	20146.8	2093.5	278	76936401
WTW	Weight Watchers International, Inc.	Miscellaneous Consumer Services	12/29/12	1826.8	257.4	1218.6	-1665.5	231	68365580
WRI	Weingarten Realty Investors	REITs	12/31/12	503.5	146.6	4184.8	1577.1	349	113003670
WMK	Weis Markets, Inc.	Retail - Food & Beverage, Drug & To	12/29/12	2701.4	82.5	1090.4	795.7	130	10272046
WCG	WellCare Health Plans Inc	Hospitals & Health Care Facilities	12/31/12	7409.0	184.7	2675.5	1323.2	343	47053838
WLP	WellPoint Inc	Life & Health	12/31/12	61711.7	2655.5	58955.4	23802.7	835	293087531
WFC	Wells Fargo & Co.	Banking	12/31/12	91247.0	18897.0	1422968.0	157554.0	1886	4347584728
EOD	Wells Fargo Advantage Global Divid	Holding and other Investment Office	10/31/12	49.4	44.9	428.8	405.5	47	4737440
WSF	Wells Fargo Capital IV	Banking							
WAIR	Wesco Aircraft Holdings Inc.	Aerospace	9/30/12	776.2	92.2	1537.4	753.4	85	133167916
WCC	Wesco International, Inc.	Electrical Equipment	12/31/12	6579.3	201.8	4629.6	1553.8	322	56510027
WST	West Pharmaceutical Services, Inc.	Medical Instruments & Equipment	12/31/12	1266.4	80.7	1564.0	728.9	231	37409261
WR	Westar Energy Inc	Electric Utilities	12/31/12	2261.5	275.1	9265.2	2896.1	342	87422873
WAL	Western Alliance Bancorporation	Banking	12/31/12	363.0	72.8	7622.6	759.6	152	63087780
ESD	Western Asset Emerging Markets D	Holding and other Investment Office	12/31/12	45.1	37.6	692.9	689.5	54	5437418
EMD	Western Asset Emerging Markets In	Holding and other Investment Office	5/31/12	30.1	24.8	424.0	423.3	16	1551861
GDO	Western Asset Global Credit Define	Holding and other Investment Office	10/31/12	24.2	20.3	365.9	316.1	29	2281725
EHI	Western Asset Global High Income	Holding and other Investment Office	5/31/12	42.5	36.6	517.3	395.1	44	6498287
GDF	Western Asset Global Partners Inco	Holding and other Investment Office	8/31/12	19.4	16.7	243.6	188.1	34	1884985
HIX	Western Asset High Income Fund II	Holding and other Investment Office	4/30/12	92.5	81.3	1021.4	756.4	73	5631399
HIF	Western Asset High Income Fund In	Holding and other Investment Office	12/31/12	4.4	3.8	51.3	50.9	22	832905
HIO	Western Asset High Income Opport	Holding and other Investment Office	9/30/12	41.2	37.2	484.3	472.9	62	8115643
HYI	Western Asset High Yield Defined	Holding and other Investment Office	8/31/12	40.4	36.8	418.8	416.7	-	
PAI	Western Asset Income Fund	Holding and other Investment Office	12/31/12	7.9	6.9	142.4	142.3	24	1391545
IMF	Western Asset Inflation Manageme	Holding and other Investment Office	12/31/12	3.6	2.5	142.6	142.3	28	4246691
IGI	Western Asset Investment Grade D	Holding and other Investment Office	11/30/12	13.5	11.7	244.1	243.5	19	1038229
MHY	Western Asset Managed High Inco	Holding and other Investment Office	2/29/12	25.2	22.7	287.2	279.1	55	5226413
MMU	Western Asset Managed Municipals	Holding and other Investment Office	5/31/12	41.0	36.0	850.6	845.0	50	4401050
WMC	Western Asset Mortgage Capital Co	REITs	12/31/12	53.3	57.3	5365.0	523.2	-	
DMO	Western Asset Mortgage Defined O	Holding and other Investment Office	12/31/12	21.9	17.5	288.3	248.4	14	555361
MHF	Western Asset Municipal High Inco	Holding and other Investment Office	10/31/12	9.9	8.7	177.7	176.8	29	1646207
MNP	Western Asset Municipal Partners F	Holding and other Investment Office	11/30/12	10.7	8.8	256.1	253.1	26	1094122
MTT	Western Asset Municipal Term Trus	Holding and other Investment Office	11/30/12	14.8	12.9	284.3	283.1	23	663486
WEA	Western Asset Premier Bond Fund	Holding and other Investment Office	12/31/12	15.8	13.8	249.2	248.2	29	879168
GFY	Western Asset Variable Rate Strate	Holding and other Investment Office	9/30/12	7.4	6.0	132.6	122.9	27	1960297
SBW	Western Asset Worldwide Income F	Holding and other Investment Office	12/31/12	14.2	11.4	211.9	210.8	26	1557754
WIW	Western Asset/Claymore Inflation-Li	Holding and other Investment Office	12/31/12	23.4	17.2	914.9	913.2	72	26821417
WIA	Western Asset/Claymore Inflation-Li	Holding and other Investment Office	12/31/12	10.5	7.6	430.4	429.6	50	13980472
WGP	Western Gas Equity Partners LP	Production & Extraction	12/31/12	849.4	34.0	3477.0		-	
WES	Western Gas Partners LP	Equipment & Services	12/31/12	849.4	107.0	3476.1		-	
WNR	Western Refining Inc	Refining & Marketing	12/31/12	9503.1	398.9	2804.9	909.1	288	76098621
WU	Western Union Co.	Business Services	12/31/12	5664.8	1025.9	9465.7	940.6	789	559664474
WLK	Westlake Chemical Corp	Specialty Chemicals	12/31/12	3571.0	385.6	3412.2	1872.3	215	23942517
WBK	Westpac Banking Corp	Banking	9/30/12	42354.0	5970.0	674965.0	44249.0	167	3265153
WHG	Westwood Holdings Group, Inc.	Wealth Management	12/31/12	77.5	12.1	96.6	76.6	79	4987942
WXS	Wex Inc	Miscellaneous Consumer Services	12/31/12	623.2	96.9	3106.7	817.9	266	44215563
WY	Weyerhaeuser Co.	REITs	12/31/12	7059.0	385.0	12592.0	4070.0	702	473067786
WGL	WGL Holdings, Inc.	Gas Utilities	9/30/12	2425.3	141.1	4110.9	1297.7	278	39228895
WHR	Whirlpool Corp	Household Appliances, Electronics &	12/31/12	18143.0	401.0	15396.0	4260.0	567	83628217
WTM	White Mountains Insurance Group,	General Insurance	12/31/12	2435.7	207.4	12895.4	3731.8	243	5217783
WSR	Whitestone REIT	REITs	12/31/12	46.6	0.0	385.4	166.0	87	5988793
WWAV	Whitewave Foods Co.	Retail - Food & Beverage, Drug & To	12/31/12	2289.4	113.7	2168.0	785.0	-	
WLL	Whiting Petroleum Corp	Production & Extraction	12/31/12	2173.5	414.2	7272.4	3445.0	477	108428758
WHX	Whiting USA Trust I	Oil Royalty Traders	12/31/12	37.9	-36.7	31.3	31.1	35	917138
WHZ	Whiting USA Trust II	Production & Extraction	12/31/12	49.0	48.0	171.5	171.4	40	3613012
JW A	Wiley (John) & Sons Inc.	Publishing	4/30/12	1782.7	212.7	2532.9	1017.6	316	49757601
WG	Willbros Group Inc (DE)	Equipment & Services	12/31/12	2004.2	-30.2	978.2	205.7	-	
WMB	Williams Cos Inc (The)	Equipment & Services	12/31/12	7486.0	859.0	24327.0	4752.0	831	594775136
WPZ	Williams Partners L.P.	Equipment & Services	12/31/12	7320.0	1232.0	19709.0	10372.0	296	72891627
WSM	Williams-Sonoma, Inc.	Retail - Furniture & Home Furnishing	2/3/13	4042.9	256.7	2187.7	1309.1	386	98417029
WSH	Willis Group Holdings Plc	Brokers & Intermediaries	12/31/12	3480.0	-446.0	15112.0	1699.0	321	160640557
WGO	Winnebago Industries, Inc.	Autos- Manufacturing	8/25/12	581.7	45.0	286.1	144.7	172	25926279
FUR	Winthrop Realty Trust	REITs	12/31/12	72.5	24.6	923.2	454.5	134	22408631
WIT	Wipro Ltd	IT Services	3/31/12	371971.0	55730.0	436001.0	285314.0	101	41940856
WEC	Wisconsin Energy Corp.	Electric Utilities	12/31/12	4246.4	546.3	14285.0	4165.5	583	155571150
WMS	WMS Industries Inc.	Sporting & Recreational	6/30/12	689.7	64.1	1154.1	877.3	249	61385733
WNS	WNS (Holdings) Ltd	IT Services	3/31/12	474.1	12.5	525.0	284.1	51	43242775
WWW	Wolverine World Wide, Inc.	Apparel, Footwear & Accessories	12/29/12	1640.8	80.7	2614.4	642.4	281	56438136
WF	Woori Finance Holdings Co., Ltd	Banking	12/31/11	8231347.0	2136828.0	12791649.0	17523998.0	45	4185662

EARNINGS PER SHARE — QUARTERLY 1st	2nd	3rd	ANNUAL 2012	2011	2010	P/E RATIO		DIVIDENDS PER SHARE 2012	2011	2010	AV. YLD %	DIV. DECLARED AMOUNT	PAYABLE	PRICE RANGE 2012	
-	-	-16.97	-16.96	5.76	7.18	-		0.50	0.50	0.47	1.3	0.1250Y	81/16/21	68.3 -	0.0
-	-	0.21	-0.73	-2.51	1.38	-		-	0.22	2.00	-	0.22427Z	11/15/11	49.6 -	0.0
-	-	12.64	17.39	14.70	31.04	26.2 -	0.0	19.60	9.40	9.00	5.3	9.8HY	81/16/21	455.6 -	0.0
-	-	0.14	0.35	1.58	0.60	86.4 -	0.0	1.47	1.74	1.73	5.4	0.30Z	81/16/21	30.3 -	0.0
-	-	0.40	1.31	1.45	1.16	27.8 -	0.0	0.37	0.32	0.07	1.2	0.10Y	81/16/21	36.4 -	0.0
-	-	0.46	1.76	2.04	1.98	22.3 -	0.0	1.42	1.36	1.26	4.2	0.3650Y	81/16/21	39.2 -	0.0
-	-	1.12	5.19	4.69	4.06	18.3 -	0.0	-	-	-	-	-		95.0 -	0.0
-	-	1.19	2.70	2.74	2.49	31.2 -	0.0	7.48	2.23	2.04	10.1	0.250Y	81/16/21	84.3 -	0.0
-	-	0.53	1.90	1.78	1.57	26.1 -	0.0	0.44	0.44	0.44	1.1	0.110Y	3/15/13	49.6 -	0.0
-	-	-0.11	0.01	-0.44	0.75	1094.0 -	0.0	0.12	0.12	0.03	1.3	0.030Y	2/15/13	10.9 -	0.0
-	-	0.09	-1.02	0.34	-0.15	-		-	-	-	-	-		15.3 -	0.0
-	-	0.48	1.86	1.61	0.60	13.3 -	0.0	0.35	0.16	0.04	1.6	0.4489GH	81/16/21	24.6 -	0.0
-	-	1.20	4.23	4.11	2.56	18.6 -	0.0	0.70	0.70	0.70	1.3	0.1750Y	81/16/21	78.6 -	0.0
-	-	0.26	0.90	-0.17	0.09	35.1 -	0.0	1.16	1.10	1.04	4.2	0.40630Z	81/16/21	45.8 -	0.0
-	-	0.64	3.07	2.81	2.54	14.9 -	0.0	1.20	2.17	1.16	2.9	0.30Y	3/5/13	45.8 -	0.0
-	-	0.87	4.29	6.10	-1.26	17.3 -	0.0	-	-	-	-	-		74.2 -	0.0
-	-	2.15	8.18	7.25	6.94	8.9 -	0.0	1.15	1.00	-	1.8	0.3750Y	81/16/21	73.0 -	0.0
-	-	0.88	3.36	2.82	2.21	11.4 -	0.0	0.88	0.48	0.20	2.6	0.250Y	81/16/21	38.2 -	0.0
-	-	-	0.91	1.00	0.99	9.8 -	0.0	1.12	1.12	1.12	14.0	0.210	4/1/13	8.9 -	0.0
0.19	-	-	0.96	0.81	0.81	17.4 -	0.0	-	-	-	-	-		16.7 -	0.0
-	-	1.25	3.95	3.96	2.50	19.6 -	0.0	-	-	-	-	-		77.5 -	0.0
-	-	0.43	2.30	2.16	1.89	28.2 -	0.0	0.73	0.69	0.65	1.4	0.190Y	81/16/21	64.9 -	0.0
-	-	1.09	2.15	1.93	1.80	15.4 -	0.0	1.32	1.28	1.24	4.5	0.340Y	81/16/21	33.2 -	0.0
-	-	0.18	0.83	0.19	-0.23	17.4 -	0.0	-	-	-	-	-		14.5 -	0.0
-	-	-	1.22	1.28	1.39	18.6 -	0.0	1.42	1.33	1.37	6.7	0.120	5/31/13	22.7 -	0.0
-	-	-	0.87	0.99	0.84	19.1 -	0.0	0.94	0.92	1.00	6.2	0.2550	3/22/13	16.6 -	0.0
-	-	-	1.33	1.39	1.21	15.9 -	0.0	1.52	1.55	1.30	7.7	0.120	5/31/13	21.2 -	0.0
-	-	-	1.19	1.19	1.06	12.0 -	0.0	1.16	1.12	1.03	8.6	0.09630	5/31/13	14.2 -	0.0
-	-	-	1.07	1.10	1.21	13.0 -	0.0	1.14	1.14	1.14	8.9	0.09250	5/31/13	13.9 -	0.0
-	-	-	0.96	1.00	1.07	11.2 -	0.0	1.00	1.04	1.14	10.0	0.07750	5/31/13	10.7 -	0.0
-	-	-	0.72	0.73	0.81	13.9 -	0.0	0.73	0.85	0.90	7.6	0.05920	5/31/13	10.0 -	0.0
-	-	-	0.49	0.50	0.56	13.9 -	0.0	0.51	0.53	0.61	7.9	0.0390	5/31/13	6.8 -	0.0
-	-	-	1.63	1.33	-	12.2 -	0.0	1.76	1.32	-	9.3	0.1350	5/31/13	19.9 -	0.0
-	-	-	0.73	0.77	0.79	22.2 -	0.0	0.72	0.75	0.79	4.9	0.05750	5/31/13	16.2 -	0.0
-	-	-	0.35	0.67	0.39	54.8 -	0.0	0.55	0.82	0.60	3.0	0.050	4/26/13	19.2 -	0.0
-	-	-	1.09	1.15	1.17	22.2 -	0.0	1.40	1.29	1.25	6.1	0.10	5/31/13	24.2 -	0.0
-	-	-	0.48	0.52	0.61	14.0 -	0.0	0.53	0.59	0.59	8.4	0.03850	5/31/13	6.7 -	0.0
-	-	-	-	0.87	0.88	-		0.78	0.78	0.72	5.3	0.065M	5/31/13	16.2 -	0.0
0.41	-	-	3.63	-		6.7 -	0.0	2.35	-	-	11.3	0.950	4/30/13	24.4 -	0.0
-	-	-	1.68	2.21	1.77	16.2 -	0.0	2.88	1.92	1.12	11.8	0.150	5/31/13	27.3 -	0.0
-	-	-	0.40	0.42	0.43	22.6 -	0.0	0.41	0.44	0.44	5.0	0.031M	5/31/13	9.0 -	0.0
-	-	-	0.91	0.91	0.95	20.0 -	0.0	0.85	0.83	0.80	5.0	0.07M	5/31/13	18.2 -	0.0
-	-	-	1.08	1.08	1.10	23.2 -	0.0	1.01	1.01	1.12	4.3	0.0840	5/31/13	25.1 -	0.0
-	-	-	1.16	1.32	1.47	14.5 -	0.0	1.31	1.49	1.45	8.2	0.10	5/31/13	16.9 -	0.0
-	-	-	0.90	0.86	-	21.7 -	0.0	0.80	0.69	0.67	4.5	0.07250	5/31/13	19.5 -	0.0
-	-	-	0.87	0.91	0.94	18.9 -	0.0	0.98	0.90	0.93	6.5	0.0840	5/31/13	16.5 -	0.0
-	-	-	0.28	0.51	0.36	48.2 -	0.0	0.37	0.53	0.48	2.8	0.03350	4/30/13	13.5 -	0.0
-	-	-	0.26	0.52	0.33	52.1 -	0.0	0.35	0.50	0.45	2.7	0.0320	4/30/13	13.6 -	0.0
-	-	-	0.01	-		3491.0 -	2746.0	-	-	-	-	0.0359GH	2/21/13	34.9 -	27.5
-	-	0.33	0.84	1.64	1.64	70.7 -	0.0	1.88	1.60	1.39	3.9	0.520	2/12/13	59.4 -	0.0
-	-	0.07	3.71	1.34	-0.19	10.5 -	0.0	2.74	-	-	10.5	0.120Y	81/16/21	38.8 -	0.0
-	-	0.45	1.69	1.84	1.36	11.3 -	0.0	0.42	0.31	0.25	2.7	0.1250Y	81/16/21	19.1 -	0.0
-	-	1.30	5.75	3.87	3.34	16.9 -	0.0	4.27	0.27	0.24	6.0	0.18750Y	81/16/21	97.2 -	0.0
-	-	-	1.91	2.24	2.07	84.8 -	0.0	8.25	8.03	4.85	6.5	-		162.0 -	0.0
-	-	0.34	1.65	2.04	1.58	27.4 -	0.0	1.51	1.42	1.65	3.9	0.40Y	81/16/21	45.2 -	0.0
-	-	0.37	2.48	3.43	2.25	32.2 -	0.0	-	-	-	-	-		79.9 -	0.0
-	-	0.22	0.71	0.61	3.99	44.4 -	0.0	0.62	0.60	26.66	2.4	0.20Z	81/16/21	31.5 -	0.0
1.01	-	-	2.71	2.28	2.16	16.3 -	0.0	1.58	1.53	1.49	4.0	0.420Y	81/16/21	44.2 -	0.0
-	-	0.94	5.06	4.99	7.97	23.6 -	0.0	2.00	1.93	1.72	2.4	0.50Y	81/16/21	119.3 -	0.0
-	-	2.90	30.50	97.44	10.12	19.0 -	0.0	1.00	1.00	1.00	0.2	1.0	81/16/21	579.3 -	0.0
-	-	0.01	0.00	0.12	0.27	-		1.14	1.14	0.48	8.4	0.0950Z	6/10/13	-	
-	-	-	0.74	0.72	0.53	23.8 -	0.0	-	-	-	-	1.56250Y	6/17/13	17.6 -	0.0
-	-	0.70	3.48	4.14	2.55	16.6 -	0.0	-	-	-	-	-		57.7 -	0.0
-	-	0.69	2.65	2.95	2.70	7.0 -	0.0	2.65	2.95	2.70	26.2	0.57760Z	3/1/13	18.5 -	0.0
-	-	0.89	-			-		2.61	-	-	14.1	0.65080Z	3/1/13	23.9 -	0.0
-	-	0.95	3.47	2.80	2.41	14.8 -	0.0	0.80	0.64	0.56	1.8	0.240Y	81/16/21	51.3 -	0.0
-	-	0.01	-0.63	-6.19	-0.86	-		-	-	-	-	-		9.8 -	0.0
-	-	0.25	1.37	0.63	-1.88	27.3 -	0.0	1.20	0.78	0.48	3.7	0.33880Y	81/16/21	37.5 -	0.0
-	-	0.38	1.89	3.69	2.66	30.8 -	0.0	3.14	2.90	2.65	6.1	0.82750	2/8/13	58.2 -	0.0
-	-	0.49	2.22	1.83	0.72	23.2 -	0.0	0.73	0.58	0.48	1.8	0.310Y	81/16/21	51.5 -	0.0
-	-	0.15	-2.58	1.15	2.66	-		1.08	1.04	1.04	3.0	0.280	4/15/13	39.5 -	0.0
-	0.22	-	1.54	0.41	0.35	14.5 -	0.0	-	-	-	-	0.120Y	10/6/08	22.3 -	0.0
-	0.37	0.46	0.32	0.72		27.7 -	0.0	0.65	0.65	0.65	5.7	0.57810Z	4/1/13	12.7 -	0.0
-	6.55	-	22.69	21.61	18.75	0.5 -	0.0	0.00	0.00	0.00	0.0	-		11.0 -	0.0
-	0.67	-	2.35	2.24	1.93	18.3 -	0.0	1.20	1.04	0.80	3.1	0.340Y	81/16/21	42.9 -	0.0
-	0.08	-	1.15	1.37	1.88	21.9 -	0.0	-	-	-	-	0.05	81/16/21	25.2 -	0.0
-	0.08	-	0.27	0.21	0.08	55.4 -	0.0	-	-	-	-	-		15.0 -	0.0
-	-	0.68	1.63	2.48	2.11	29.3 -	0.0	0.48	0.48	0.44	1.1	0.120Y	5/1/13	47.8 -	0.0
-	-	616.00	-2649.00	1599.00		-		-	0.00	0.00	-	-		36.3 -	0.0

SYMBOL	COMPANY	NATURE OF BUSINESS	FISCAL YEAR-END	TOTAL REV. $MILL	NET INCOME $MILL	TOTAL ASSETS $MILL	NET STK EQUITY $MILL	NO OF INST	INST. HOLDINGS (SHARES)
WDAY	Workday Inc	IT Services	1/31/13	273.7	-119.2	959.1	592.3	-	-
INT	World Fuel Services Corp.	Refining & Marketing	12/31/12	38945.3	189.3	4107.8	1517.2	289	69602327
WWE	World Wrestling Entertainment Inc	Entertainment	12/31/12	484.0	31.4	381.4	294.7	141	21427547
WOR	Worthington Industries, Inc.	Non-Precious Metals	5/31/12	2534.7	115.6	1877.8	697.2	242	45760468
WPX	WPX Energy, Inc.	Production & Extraction	12/31/12	3189.0	-223.0	9456.0	5268.0	378	188740309
WH	WSP Holdings Ltd	Equipment & Services	12/31/11	686.1	-68.5	1571.1	233.9	13	1626981
WX	Wuxi Pharmatech Cayman Inc	Biotechnology	12/31/11	407.2	81.0	663.9	505.7	124	54457104
WYN	Wyndham Worldwide Corp	Hotels, Restaurants & Travel	12/31/12	4534.0	400.0	9463.0	1930.0	508	130383697
XEL	Xcel Energy, Inc.	Electric Utilities	12/31/12	10128.2	905.2	31140.7	8874.1	641	336293168
XRM	Xerium Technologies Inc	Industrial Machinery & Equipment	12/31/11	538.7	-18.0	618.8	-29.1	62	6489016
XRX	Xerox Corp	Peripherals	12/31/12	22390.0	1195.0	30015.0	11870.0	631	1165012017
XIN	Xinyuan Real Estate Co Ltd	Property, Real Estate & Developmen	12/31/11	687.5	102.3	1390.6	634.6	51	23692119
XL	XL Group Plc	General Insurance	12/31/12	7230.5	651.1	45387.8	10510.1	391	300372036
XOXO	XO Group Inc	Internet & Software	12/31/12	129.1	8.7	183.4	144.5	149	21849635
XPO	XPO Logistics, Inc.	Airlines/Air Freight	12/31/12	278.6	-20.3	413.2	245.1	89	13424352
XUE	Xueda Education Group	Educational Services	12/31/12	293.2	2.0	316.3	127.9	26	15532052
XYL	Xylem Inc.	Industrial Machinery & Equipment	12/31/12	3791.0	297.0	4679.0	2074.0	457	160651806
AUY	Yamana Gold, Inc.	Precious Metals	12/31/12	2336.8	442.1	11800.2	7815.1	424	406610548
YZC	Yanzhou Coal Mining Co., Ltd.	Mining	12/31/11	47065.8	8928.1	97151.6	42634.5	93	10315265
YELP	Yelp Inc	Internet & Software	12/31/12	137.6	-19.1	187.7	165.7	110	27805240
YGE	Yingli Green Energy Holding Co., Lt	Semiconductors	12/31/11	14678.0	-3208.9	27483.4	5161.2	105	22460525
YOKU	Youku Tudou Inc	Internet & Software	12/31/11	897.6	-172.1	4675.6	4205.2	117	92236753
YPF	YPF SA	Refining & Marketing	12/31/11	56697.0	5296.0	55399.0	18735.0	98	62643165
YUM	Yum! Brands, Inc.	Food	12/29/12	13633.0	1597.0	9011.0	2154.0	1028	368357169
ZFC	ZAIS Financial Corp	REITs	12/31/12	9.4	20.3	201.6	45.0	-	-
ZLC	Zale Corp.	Retail - Specialty	7/31/12	1866.9	-27.3	1171.0	178.9	144	28671865
ZEP	Zep Inc	Specialty Chemicals	8/31/12	653.5	21.9	435.3	167.9	127	19027175
ZMH	Zimmer Holdings, Inc.	Medical Instruments & Equipment	12/31/12	4471.7	755.0	9012.4	5860.9	889	175002600
ZTS	Zoetis Inc	Pharmaceuticals	12/31/12	4336.0	436.0	6262.0	4026.0	-	-
ZA	Zuoan Fashion Ltd	Apparel, Footwear & Accessories	12/31/11	1230.9	255.7	1182.8	1012.8	5	766035
ZF	Zweig Fund, Inc. (The)	Holding and other Investment Office	12/31/12	6.0	2.3	323.9	309.1	46	3490775
ZTR	Zweig Total Return Fund, Inc. (The)	Holding and other Investment Office	12/31/12	14.8	9.9	510.9	492.2	59	11316777

1st	2nd	3rd	2012	2011	2010	P/E		2012	2011	2010	AV. YLD %	AMOUNT	PAYABLE	2012	
-	-	-0.67	-2.71	-0.20	-2.22	-		-	-	-	-	-		64.5 -	0.0
-	-	0.72	2.64	2.71	2.31	17.1 -	0.0	0.15	0.15	0.15	0.4	0.03750Y	81/16/21	45.1 -	0.0
-	-	0.05	0.42	0.33	0.71	21.3 -	0.0	0.48	0.72	1.44	5.9	0.120Y	3/25/13	8.9 -	0.0
-	-	0.52	1.65	1.53	0.57	19.0 -	0.0	0.46	0.40	0.40	2.0	0.260Y	81/16/21	31.4 -	0.0
-	-	-0.32	-1.12	-1.53	-6.55	-		-	-	-	-	-		18.6 -	0.0
-	-	-0.11	-	-0.34	-0.58	-		-	-	-	-	-		3.1 -	0.0
-	-	0.30	-	0.13	0.15	-		-	-	-	-	-		17.9 -	0.0
-	-	1.11	2.75	2.51	2.05	23.4 -	0.0	0.92	0.60	0.48	1.7	0.290Y	81/16/21	64.5 -	0.0
-	-	0.81	1.85	1.72	1.62	16.1 -	0.0	1.07	1.03	1.00	3.9	0.270Y	81/16/21	29.7 -	0.0
-	-	-0.24	-1.18	0.54	-7.29	-		-	-	-	-	0.11250Y	12/17/07	6.7 -	0.0
-	-	0.21	0.88	0.90	0.43	10.0 -	0.0	0.17	0.17	0.17	2.3	0.05750Y	81/16/21	8.8 -	0.0
-	-	0.22	-	0.68	0.33	-		-	0.09	-	-	-		5.9 -	0.0
-	-	0.56	2.10	-1.52	1.73	14.5 -	0.0	-	-	-	-	0.140	81/16/21	30.4 -	0.0
-	-	0.08	0.35	0.20	0.11	28.6 -	0.0	-	-	-	-	-		10.0 -	0.0
-	-	-0.22	-1.49	-5.41	0.60	-		-	-	-	-	-		19.0 -	0.0
-	-	-	0.01	0.03	0.09	405.0 -	0.0	0.48	-	-	15.4	-		4.0 -	0.0
-	-	0.38	1.59	1.50	-	18.5 -	0.0	0.40	0.10	-	1.5	0.11640Y	81/16/21	29.3 -	0.0
-	-	0.08	0.59	0.74	0.61	34.6 -	0.0	0.24	0.16	0.09	1.5	0.0650	4/11/13	20.4 -	0.0
-	-	-0.02	-	-	-	-		-	0.12	0.05	-	-		22.2 -	0.0
-	-	-0.03	-0.35	-1.10	-0.71	-		-	-	-	-	-		28.8 -	0.0
-	-	-6.13	-	-20.46	8.86	-		-	-	-	-	-		3.8 -	0.0
-	-	-0.04	-	-0.09	-0.44	-		-	-	-	-	-		25.5 -	0.0
-	-	1.92	-	-	-	-		-	-	-	-	-		24.0 -	0.0
-	-	1.00	3.38	2.74	2.38	22.0 -	0.0	1.19	1.03	0.88	1.8	0.3350Y	81/16/21	74.5 -	0.0
-	-	-	7.13	-1.70		2.9 -	2.8	-	-	-	-	-		20.8 -	19.6
1.02	-	-0.85	-3.50	-2.92		-		-	-	-	-	-		7.5 -	0.0
0.12	-	0.98	0.78	0.61		16.2 -	0.0	0.16	0.16	0.16	1.1	0.040Y	5/1/13	15.9 -	0.0
-	-	1.02	4.29	4.03	2.97	17.8 -	0.0	0.72	-	-	1.1	0.20Y	81/6/21	76.3 -	0.0
-	-	-	0.87	-		39.8 -	35.6	-	-	-	-	0.065GY	6/6/13	34.6 -	31.0
-	-	0.83	-	2.37	2.29	-		-	-	-	-	-		4.2 -	0.0
-	-	-	0.10	0.04	0.04	130.0 -	0.0	0.42	-	-	3.4	0.2230	4/18/13	13.0 -	0.0
-	-	-	0.28	0.24	0.20	46.5 -	0.0	0.50	-	-	4.0	0.0850	4/18/13	13.0 -	0.0